オールカラー・6か国語
大図典

THE NEW VISUAL DICTIONARY

●日本語 ●英語 ●ドイツ語 ●フランス語 ●スペイン語 ●イタリア語●

MULTILINGUAL

著

社会言語学者
ジャン=クロード・コルベイユ

応用言語学者
アリアーヌ・アルシャンボ

編

小学館外国語辞典編集部

小学館

謝辞
The New Visual Dictionary を準備するにあたり、最新の技術資料をご提供くださいました下記の個人、機関、協会、企業に深甚の謝意を表する次第です。

Arcand, Denis (réalisateur); Association Internationale de Signalisation Maritime; Association canadienne des paiements (Charlie Clarke); Association des banquiers canadiens (Lise Provost); Automobiles Citroën; Automobiles Peugeot; Banque du Canada (Lyse Brousseau); Banque Royale du Canada (Raymond Chouinard, Francine Morel, Carole Trottier); Barrett Xplore inc.; Bazarin, Christine;Bibliothèque du Parlement canadien (Service de renseignements); Bibliothèque nationale du Québec (Jean-François Palomino); Bluechip Kennels (Olga Gagne); Bombardier Aéronautique; Bridgestone-Firestone; Brother (Canada); Canadien National; Casavant Frères ltée; C.O.J.O. ATHENES 2004 (Bureau des Médias Internationaux); Centre Eaton de Montréal; Centre national du Costume (Recherche et de Diffusion); Cetacean Society International (William R. Rossiter); Chagnon, Daniel (architecte D.E.S. – M.E.Q.); Cohen et Rubin Architectes (Maggy Cohen); Commission Scolaire de Montréal (École St-Henri); Compagnie de la Baie d'Hudson (Nunzia Iavarone, Ron Oyama); Corporation d'hébergement du Québec (Céline Drolet); École nationale de théâtre du Canada (Bibliothèque); Élevage Le Grand Saphir (Stéphane Ayotte); Énergie atomique du Canada ltée; Eurocopter; Famous Players; Fédération bancaire française (Védi Hékiman); Fontaine, PierreHenry (biologiste); Future Shop; Garaga; Groupe Jean Coutu; Hôpital du Sacré-Cœur de Montréal; Hôtel Inter-Continental; Hydro-Québec; I.P.I.Q. (Serge Bouchard); IGA Barcelo; International Entomological Society (Dr. Michael Geisthardt); Irisbus; Jérôme, Danielle (O.D.); La Poste (Colette Gouts); Le Groupe Canam Manac inc.; Lévesque, Georges (urgentologue); Lévesque, Robert (chef machiniste); Manutan; Marriot Spring Hill suites; MATRA S.A.; Métro inc.; ministère canadien de la Défense nationale (Affaires publiques); ministère de la Défense, République Française; ministère de la Justice du Québec (Service de la gestion immobilière – Carol Sirois); ministère de l'Éducation du Québec (Direction de l'équipement scolaire-Daniel Chagnon); Muse Productions (Annick Barbery); National Aeronautics and Space Administration; National Oceanic and Atmospheric Administration; Nikon Canada inc.; Normand, Denis (consultant en télécommunications); Office de la langue française du Québec (Chantal Robinson); Paul Demers & Fils inc.; Phillips (France); Pratt & Whitney Canada inc.; Prévost Car inc.; Radio Shack Canada ltée; Réno-Dépôt inc.; Robitaille, Jean-François (Département de biologie, Université Laurentienne); Rocking T Ranch and Poultry Farm (Pete and Justine Theer); RONA inc.; Sears Canada inc.; Secrétariat d'État du Canada : Bureau de la traduction ; Service correctionnel du Canada; Société d'Entomologie Africaine (Alain Drumont); Société des musées québécois (Michel Perron); Société Radio-Canada; Sony du Canada ltée; Sûreté du Québec; Théâtre du Nouveau Monde; Transports Canada (Julie Poirier); Urgences-Santé (Éric Berry); Ville de Longueuil (Direction de la Police); Ville de Montréal (Service de la prévention des incendies); Vimont Lexus Toyota; Volvo Bus Corporation; Yamaha Motor Canada Ltd.

The New Visual Dictionary は QA International の編集、制作による。
329, rue de la Commune Ouest, 3ᵉ étage
Montréal (Québec) Canada
H2Y 2E1

Tel.: 514.499.3000
Fax: 514.499.3010

©QA International 2004. All rights reserved

Printed and bound in Singapore.
www.qa-international.com
ISBN 4-09-505081-0

オールカラー・6か国語　大図典

2004年　7月10日　初版第1刷発行
2004年11月20日　初版第2刷発行

著　者　ジャン＝クロード・コルベイユ
　　　　アリアーヌ・アルシャンボ
編　集　小学館外国語辞典編集部
発行者　大澤　昇
発行所　〒101-8001　東京都千代田区一ツ橋2-3-1
　　　　株式会社　小学館
　　　　電話　編集　東京（03）3230-5169
　　　　　　　制作　東京（03）3230-5333
　　　　　　　販売　東京（03）5281-3555
　　　　　　　振替　　　　00180-1-200
印刷所（カバー）　凸版印刷株式会社

©SHOGAKUKAN 2004
Printed and bound in Singapore
ISBN 4-09-505081-0

●本書の一部あるいは全部を無断で複製・転載することは、法律で認められた場合を除き、著作者および出版者の権利の侵害となります。あらかじめ小社あて許諾を求めてください。
● Ⓡ＜日本複写権センター委託出版物＞
本書の一部あるいは全部を無断で複写（コピー）することは、著作権法上での例外を除き、禁じられています。本書からの複写を希望される場合は、日本複写権センター（電話03-3401-2382）にご連絡ください。
●造本には十分注意しておりますが、万一、落丁・乱丁などの不良品がありましたら、「小学館制作局」あてにお送りください。送料小社負担にてお取り替えいたします。

Japanese translation right was arranged with QA International through Tuttle-Mori Agency, Inc., Tokyo

QA International のスタッフ

編集
- 発行者：Jacques Fortin
- 著者：Jean-Claude Corbeil et Ariane Archambault
- 編集局長：François Fortin
- 編集長：Serge D'Amico
- グラフィックデザイナー：Anne Tremblay

制作
- Mac Thien Nguyen Hoang
- Guylaine Houle

専門用語検討
- Jean Beaumont
- Catherine Briand
- Nathalie Guillo

イラスト
- Art Direction: Jocelyn Gardner
- Jean-Yves Ahern
- Rielle Lévesque
- Alain Lemire
- Mélanie Boivin
- Yan Bohler
- Claude Thivierge
- Pascal Bilodeau
- Michel Rouleau
- Anouk Noël
- Carl Pelletier

レイアウト
- Pascal Goyette
- Janou-Ève LeGuerrier
- Véronique Boisvert
- Josée Gagnon
- Karine Raymond
- Geneviève Théroux Béliveau

文献調査
- Gilles Vézina
- Kathleen Wynd
- Stéphane Batigne
- Sylvain Robichaud
- Jessie Daigle

データ管理
- Programmer：Daniel Beaulieu
- Nathalie Fréchette

校正
- Marie-Nicole Cimon

プリプレス
- Sophie Pellerin
- Tony O'Riley

協力

Québec Amérique は下記の皆様のご尽力に感謝申し上げます。

Jean-Louis Martin, Marc Lalumière, Jacques Perrault, Stéphane Roy, Alice Comtois, Michel Blais, Christiane Beauregard, Mamadou Togola, Annie Maurice, Charles Campeau, Mivil Deschênes, Jonathan Jacques, Martin Lortie, Raymond Martin, Frédérick Simard, Yan Tremblay, Mathieu Blouin, Sébastien Dallaire, Hoang Khanh Le, Martin Desrosiers, Nicolas Oroc, François Escalmel, Danièle Lemay, Pierre Savoie, Benoît Bourdeau, Marie-Andrée Lemieux, Caroline Soucy, Yves Chabot, Anne-Marie Ouellette, Anne-Marie Villeneuve, Anne-Marie Brault, Nancy Lepage, Daniel Provost, François Vézina.

・・

日本語版のスタッフ

編集協力

株式会社ジャレックス

飯田邦生　井口英一　板倉俊　岩瀬直子　日下部利人　古作登
佐々木啓策（牧製本印刷株式会社）　佐藤宏　株式会社ステクトル
大亀哲郎　中井真吾　能登瞬　藤田一郎　藤野隆一
東海達夫（マコー技研株式会社）　村石利夫　吉田恭子
吉田慶子

DTP組版

株式会社ジャレックス

装丁

有限会社バンブー・アイランド

制作

太田真由美

資材

市村浩一

販売

滝沢利幸　栗原弘

宣伝

下河原哲夫

編集

頴川栄治

『大図典』The New Visual Dictionaryについて

『大図典』は、6,000点以上のイラストと結び付いた一般語・専門語により、明確で、興味深い、広範な知識を読者に提供しています。

編集方針

『大図典』は、工業化された現代社会に生き、きわめて多岐にわたる分野の膨大な専門語を知り、かつ使わなければならない人にとって、物質的な環境を目録化したものと言うことができます。

本辞典は広く一般読者を対象とし、個人的な関心あるいは仕事上の必要性から、厳密で正確な用語を追究しているすべての人のニーズに合わせて編集しています。例えば、未知の用語を探したり、意味を確認したり、翻訳したり、発表したり、母国語や外国語を教えたり、学習補助教材に使ったり、用途は実にさまざまです。

本辞典は、そのような読者を念頭に、私たちの日常を形成するいろいろな専門分野から、現代社会を浮き彫りにするのに必要な専門用語を集め、1冊の本にまとめたものです。

構成

『大図典』は、章索引（テーマ・リスト）と目次を含む前付け、各テーマを詳しく扱う本文、日本語・英語・ドイツ語・フランス語・スペイン語・イタリア語による6か国語索引の3部構成となっています。そして情報を、テーマ、サブテーマ、見出し、小見出し、イラスト、用語といった順に、より抽象的なものからより具体的なものへと提示しています。

本辞典の内容は、「天文学」から「スポーツとゲーム」まで17のテーマに分かれ、さらに多角的なテーマは合計94のサブテーマに細分化されています。例えば「地球」のテーマは「地理」「地質」「気象」「環境」に分類されるといった具合です。

合計658ある見出しは、訳付けされた主要各部から成る本体のイラストを一つの見出しにまとめたり（例：「氷河」「窓」）、同一の概念範疇に属してはいても、固有の名称と用語を持ち、相互に異なる諸要素を併せ持つ複数のイラストを一つの見出しにまとめたり（例：「大陸の配置」「家電製品」）、異なった機能を果たしています。

また時として、同一の範疇に属する主要な構成要素を、用語を詳細に分析することなく、それぞれの名称と共に、同じ副見出しのもとにまとめた場合もあります。（例：「肘掛け椅子」における「肘掛け椅子の例」）

イラストは、物、過程、あるいは現象を、それらを構成する細部に至るまで、写実的かつ精密に描いていますから、提示した各用語の視覚的な定義として役に立つはずです。

用　語

『大図典』中の用語は、読者が必要とするはずの専門レベルを念頭に置き、信頼度の高い資料を吟味して、入念に選びました。

資料を検討してみると、同一概念を表すのに異なった用語が使われていることが時折あります。この場合は、信頼のおける専門家たちの間で最も頻繁に使われている用語を採用しました。

本辞典の索引に収録している用語は約20,800語ですが（日本語は複数訳語を収録した関係でもっと多い）、各国語共に35,000以上の概念を含んでいることになります。

索引では、日本語はあいうえお順に、ほかの5か国語ではアルファベット順に用語が並べられています。

引き方

『大図典』には多くの活用法があります。

・前付けの最終ページにある、爪見出しの付いた章索引から引く。

・各テーマ冒頭の中扉ページにある、ページ番号を示した、内容が一目で分かる全見出しリスト（テーマが細分化されている場合はサブテーマまで表示しています）から引く。

・巻末索引に収録している用語から本文イラストの対応箇所に当たる。イラストを細かく見ると、その正確さが確認できます。

・本辞典の独創的な特長は、読者が名称に関して漠然とした観念しか持っていない場合でも、イラストから用語を見つけることができるところにあります。その他の辞書を引くためには前もって用語を知らなければならず、用語を知らなくても引けるのは『大図典』だけと言えるでしょう。

日本語訳について

・ひときわ目立つように太字で示しています。用語の前後の（　）の中に細字で示しているものは補足説明です。

・ほかの5か国語と異なり、日本語では複数の用語を／で区切って可能な限り挙げています。

・難読語には、続けて（　）の中に読み方を細字で示しています。

・動植物用語に関しては、最初にカタカナ表記を示し、続けて（　）の中に対応する漢字を細字で示している場合があります。

・カタカナ表記は、英単語の区切りに対応し・で区切って示しています。

・本辞典では「ヴ」の表記は用いず、「バ、ビ、ブ、ベ、ボ」で統一しています。

・カタカナ表記における最後の音引き（ー）に関しては、『大図典』における表記統一上、原則として付けています。必要に応じて音引きを省いて使い分けてください。

・（　）の中の太字は用語の中で省略することができます。

・［　］の中の太字は前の語の一部と交換することができます。

見出し
日本語で大きく強調して表示し、初出のページのみ真下に5か国語で表示しています。

爪

すべてのテーマを色で区別しています。最初に本辞典を引く場合は、前付けの最終ページにある章索引の色と同じ色の爪を小口で探せば、引きたいテーマのページにすぐに飛ぶことができます。

サブテーマ
ほとんどのテーマはサブテーマに細分化されています。日本語版では6か国語で表示しています。

イラスト
用語と結び付いて視覚的に定義しています。

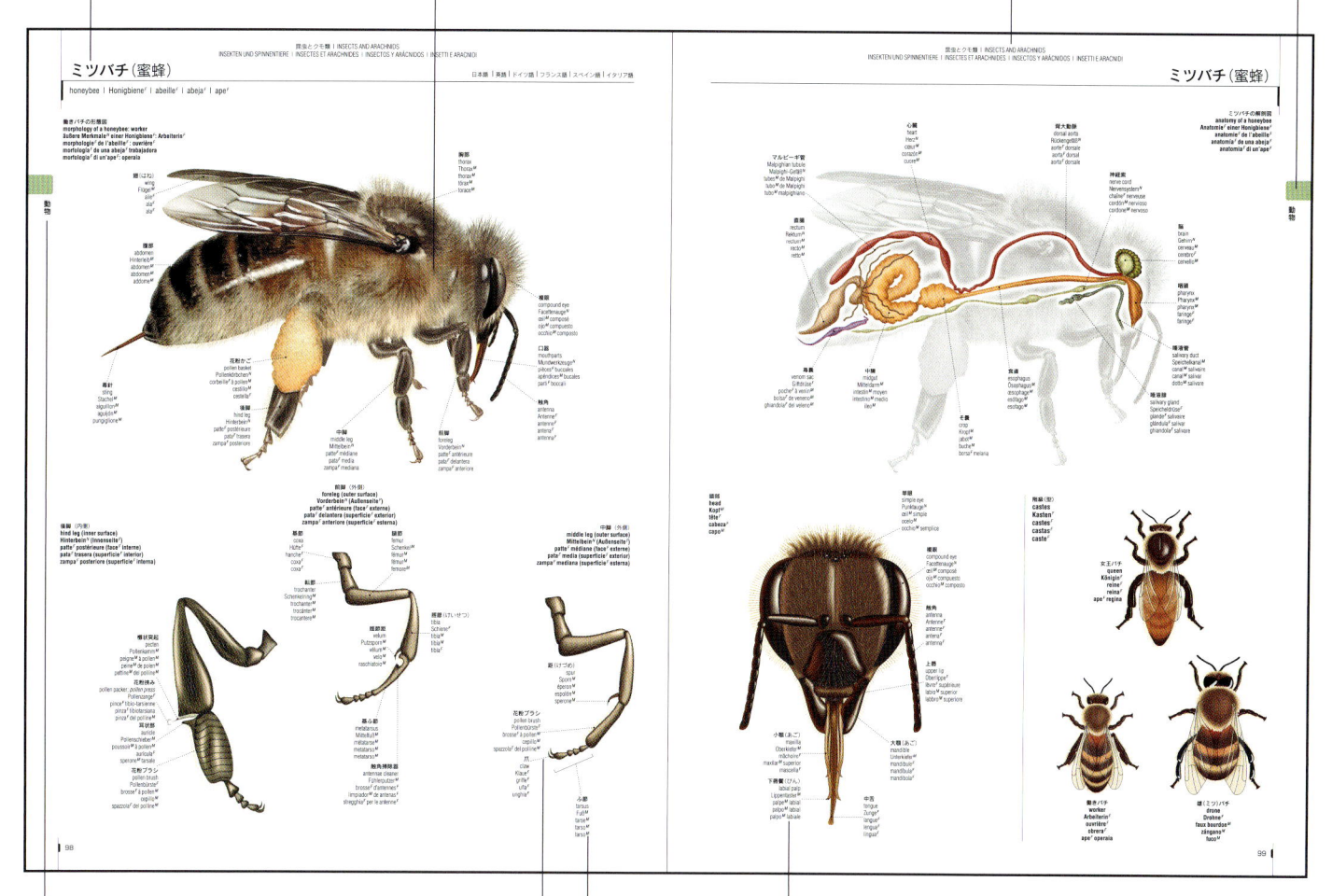

テーマ
日本語で表示しています。

用語
6か国語で表示しています。すべての用語がページ数と共に巻末索引に収録されています。

引き出し線
指しているイラスト部分と用語を結び付けています。

性の表示
M：男性　F：女性　N：中性（ドイツ語のみ）

用語を構成するすべての名詞に性を示していますが、それが複数形であってもその表示はしていません。複数の語から成る名詞全体の性は、最初に示された名詞の性に一致します。また、職務が男女に共通している場合は、本辞典で描かれている人物にそろえて男（男性名詞）、（女）女性名詞のどちらかで示しています。

目　次

天文学　2

天体 4
太陽系, 惑星と衛星, 太陽, 月, 隕石, 彗星, 星, 銀河

天体観測 10
プラネタリウム, 南半球の星座, 北半球の星座, 天球座標, 屈折(式)望遠鏡, 反射(式)望遠鏡, 電波望遠鏡, ハッブル宇宙望遠鏡, 天文台

宇宙航行学 18
宇宙探査機, 宇宙服, 国際宇宙ステーション, スペース・シャトル, 打ち上げロケット

地球　26

地理 28
大陸の配置, 地図作成法, 遠隔計測[探査]/隔測/リモート・センシング

地質 42
地殻断面図, 地球の構造, 地殻[構造]プレート, 地震, 火山, 山, 氷河, 洞穴, 地滑り, 水流, 湖, 波, 海洋底, 海溝と海嶺, 海岸の地形, 砂漠

気象 53
大気圏断面図, 季節, 気象予報, 天気図, 観測地天気記号記入様式, 国際式天気図記号, 気象観測所/測候所, 気象観測機器, 気象衛星, 世界の気候, 雲, 竜巻, 熱帯性低気圧, 降水

環境 66
植生と生物圏, 食物連鎖, 水の循環, 温室効果, 大気汚染, 土壌汚染, 水質汚染, 酸性雨, ごみ[廃棄物]の分別

植物　72
植物細胞, 地衣類, 蘚類, 藻類, キノコ(茸), シダ, 植物, 葉, 花, 果実, 穀類, ブドウ(葡萄), 樹木, 針葉樹

動物　90

生命の進化 92
種の起源と進化

単純な生物と棘皮(きょくひ)動物 94
動物細胞, 単細胞動物, 海綿動物, 棘皮(きょくひ)動物

昆虫とクモ類 96
チョウ(蝶), ミツバチ(蜜蜂), 昆虫の例, クモ類, クモ

軟体動物 104
カタツムリ(蝸牛), 巻き貝, 二枚貝, タコ(蛸)

甲殻類 107
ロブスター

魚類 108
軟骨魚, 硬骨魚

両生類 110
カエル(蛙), 両生類の例

爬虫類 112
ヘビ(蛇), カメ(亀), 爬虫類の例

鳥類 115
鳥, 鳥の例

食虫哺乳動物 121
モグラ(土竜), 食虫哺乳動物の例

齧歯(げっし)類とウサギ目の動物 122
齧歯類(動物), 齧歯類動物の例, 齧歯類とウサギ目の動物の顎(あご), ウサギ目の動物の例

有蹄哺乳動物 124
ウマ(馬), 蹄(ひづめ)の例, 有蹄哺乳動物の例

肉食哺乳動物 130
イヌ(犬), イヌの品種, ネコ(猫), ネコの品種, 肉食哺乳動物の例

海棲哺乳動物 136
イルカ(海豚), 海棲哺乳動物の例

霊長類 138
ゴリラ, 霊長類の動物の例

飛行哺乳動物 140
コウモリ(蝙蝠), コウモリの例

有袋哺乳動物 142
カンガルー, 有袋動物の例

人間　144

人体 146
男／男性, 女／女性

解剖学 150
筋肉, 骨格, 歯, 血液循環, 呼吸系, 消化器系, 泌尿器系, 神経系, 男性生殖器, 女性生殖器, 乳房

感覚器官 172
触覚, 聴覚, 嗅覚(きゅうかく)と味覚, 視覚

食べ物と台所　178

食べ物 180
スーパーマーケット, 農場, キノコ(茸), 海草, 野菜, 豆果, 果物, 香辛料, 調味料, ハーブ, 穀類, 穀物[シリアル]食品, コーヒー・茶, チョコレート, 砂糖, 油脂類, 乳製品, 臓物, 猟鳥[猟獣]肉, 鳥肉, 卵, 食肉, 調整食品, 軟体動物, 甲殻類, 軟骨魚, 硬骨魚

台所 222	工芸 452
包装, 台所, ガラス器, 食器, 銀器, 台所用品, 調理器具, 家電製品, その他の家電製品, コーヒー・メーカー	裁縫, 編み機, 編み物, ボビン・レース, 刺繍 (ししゅう), 紡織, 陶芸

家屋　242

敷地 244	**情報伝達とオフィス・オートメーション　466**
家屋の外観, プール	
家屋の構成要素 247	情報伝達 468
外ドア, 錠 (前), 窓	世界の言語, 筆記用具, 新聞, 活版印刷／タイポグラフィー, 区別的発音符／区分表示符, その他の符号, 句読点／句読記号符, 郵便網 [ネットワーク], 写真, 衛星中継, 通信衛星, 衛星通信, ダイナミック・マイク, ラジオ：スタジオとコントロール・ルーム, テレビ, 音声再生装置, ステレオ・コンボ, ポータブル音響装置, 無線通信, 電話
家屋の構造 250	
主な部屋, 枠組み, 屋根のトラス, 基礎, 寄せ木張り, 敷物, 階段, 階段の段	
暖房 256	
薪 (まき) 燃料, 強制送風システム, 強制送水システム, 熱ポンプ, 補助暖房	オフィス・オートメーション 509
空気調節 261	オフィス／事務所, オフィス家具, パーソナル・コンピューター／パソコン, 入力装置, 出力装置, 補助 [無停電] 電源装置 (UPS), データ記憶装置, 通信装置, ネットワークの例, コンピューター・ネットワーク, インターネット, インターネットの利用, ラップトップ (型) コンピューター, 電子ブック, ポケット・コンピューター, 文房具
空調装置	
配管 262	
配管システム, 汚水排水ポンプ, 浄化槽, 浴室／バスルーム, 便器, 湯沸かし装置／ボイラー, 蛇口, 継ぎ手, 分岐管の例	**交通と機械　536**
電気 272	道路交通 538
配電盤, ネットワーク接続, 電力メーター, 接続装置, 照明具	道路網, 固定橋, 可動橋, 道路トンネル, 道路標識, ガソリン・スタンド, 自動車, ブレーキ, タイヤ, ラジエーター／放熱器, 点火プラグ, バッテリー／蓄電池, 電気自動車, ハイブリッド (自動) 車, エンジンの種類, トレーラー・ハウス, バス, トラック運送, オートバイ, 四輪駆動の全地形型車両, 自転車
家具調度 276	
肘掛け椅子, 背もたれ椅子, 椅子, テーブル, 収納家具, ベッド, 幼児用家具, 窓付属品, 照明具, 家電製品, 家事用品	
	鉄道輸送 582
	旅客駅, 鉄道駅, 客車の種類, 高速列車, ディーゼル電気機関車, 貨車, 操車場, 鉄道線路, 踏切, 地下鉄, 路面 [市街] 電車

日曜大工・園芸　296

日曜大工 298	海上交通 596
基礎建材, 被覆剤, 断熱材, 木材, 木工：釘を打つ道具, 木工：ねじを締める道具, 木工：木材を切る道具, 木工：穴を空ける道具, 木工：成形する道具, 木工：つかむ [締める] 道具, 木工：測定して印を付ける道具, 木工：その他の道具, 配管工具, 石工用の工具, 電設工具, はんだ付け・溶接工具, 塗装, はしごと脚立 (きゃたつ)	港, 運河の閘門 (こうもん), 昔の船, 伝統的な船, 帆の例, 帆装の例, 4本マスト・バーク (型帆船), ボートと船の例, 錨, 救命用具, 航海計器, 海路標識, 海上浮標式
	航空交通 618
	空港, 大型 [長距離] ジェット機, 操縦室／フライト・デッキ, ターボファン・エンジン, 飛行機の例, 尾翼形状の例, 主翼形状の例, 飛行機に作用する力, 飛行機の動き, ヘリコプター, ヘリコプターの例
園芸 322	
庭, いろいろな器具, 種蒔 (ま) き・植え付け用具, 小型園芸用具, 土をほぐす用具, 水撒 (ま) き用具, 剪定 (せんてい) 用具, 芝の手入れ	搬送 632
	搬送装置, クレーン, コンテナ
	重機器 636
	ブルドーザー, ホイール・ローダー, スクレーパー, 油圧式ショベル, グレーダー／地均 (なら) し機, ダンプ・トラック, トラクター, 農業機械

衣服　334

昔の衣装, 伝統的衣装, 帽子, 靴, 手袋, 繊維製品取り扱い表示 [マーク], 男性用衣類, セーター, 女性用衣類, ベビー服, 子供服, スポーツウエア	**エネルギー　644**
	地熱・化石エネルギー 646
	地熱発電, 熱エネルギー, 炭鉱, 石油

装身具類と日用品　372

装身具類 374	水力電気 657
宝飾品, ネイル・ケア, 化粧用品, ボディー・ケア, 整髪	水力発電所, 発電装置, ダムの例, 電気の発生過程, 送電, 潮汐 [潮力] 発電所
日用品 383	核エネルギー 665
髭 (ひげ) 剃り, 歯磨き, コンタクト・レンズ, 眼鏡, 革製品, ハンドバッグ, 旅行用鞄, 喫煙具, 傘とステッキ	核エネルギー発電, 燃料取り扱いの流れ, 燃料集合体, 原子炉, 原子力発電所, 炭酸ガス炉, 重水炉, 加圧水型炉, 沸騰水型炉
	太陽エネルギー 672
	太陽電池, 平板型太陽 (熱) 集熱器, 太陽電池の仕組み, 太陽炉, 太陽エネルギー発電, ソーラー・ハウス

芸術と建築　392

美術 394	風力エネルギー 676
美術館, 絵画と線画, 木彫	風車, 風力タービンと発電
建築 402	**科学　678**
ピラミッド, ギリシャ劇場, ギリシャ神殿, 建築様式, 古代ローマの住宅, 古代ローマの円形闘技場, 城, ボーバン式要塞, 大聖堂, 仏塔, アステカ神殿, 建築の要素, エスカレーター, エレベーター, 伝統的な家屋, 都市の住宅	化学 680
	物質, 化学元素, 化学記号, 実験器具
グラフィック・アート 420	物理：力学 686
印刷, 凸版印刷方式, 凹版印刷方式, 平版印刷方式, 製本	歯車装置, 定滑車と動滑車の組み合わせ, てこ
舞台芸術 427	物理：電気学と磁気学 687
映画館, 映画のセット, 劇場	磁気, 並列電気回路, 発電機, 乾電池, 電子工学／エレクトロニクス
音楽 432	物理：光学 690
伝統 [民族] 楽器, 楽譜記号, 演奏用付属品, 交響 [管弦] 楽団, 楽器編成の例, 弦楽器, 鍵盤楽器, 管楽器, 打楽器, 電子楽器	電磁スペクトル, 波, 色の合成, 視覚, レンズ, パルス・ルビー・レーザー, プリズム双眼鏡, 眼鏡照準器／(光学式) 照準眼鏡, ルーペと顕微鏡

目次

計測機器 695
　温度測定, 時間測定, 重量測定, 長さ測定, 距離測定, 厚み測定, 角度測定

科学記号 702
　国際単位系, 生物学, 数学, 幾何学, 幾何学的な形

社会　706

都市 708
　都市圏, 中心街, 道の断面図, オフィス・ビル, ショッピング・センター, デパート, コンベンション・センター, レストラン, セルフ・サービス式レストラン, ホテル, 一般的な案内標識

司法 726
　刑務所, 裁判所

経済と金融 728
　通貨省略記号の例, 通貨と支払い形態, 銀行

教育 732
　図書館, 学校

宗教 736
　宗教年表, 教会, シナゴーグ, モスク

政治 739
　紋章, 旗

兵器 748
　石器時代の武器, ローマ時代の武器, 鎧（兜）（よろいかぶと）／甲冑（かっちゅう）, 弓と石弓, 刀剣, 火打ち石銃, 17世紀の大砲と臼砲（きゅうほう）, 短機関銃, ピストル, 回転式（連発）拳銃／リボルバー, 自動小銃, 軽機関銃, 現代の榴弾砲, 現代の迫撃砲, 手榴弾, バズーカ砲, 無反動ライフル, 対人地雷, 戦車, ミサイル, 戦闘機, 航空母艦／空母, フリゲート艦, 原子力潜水艦

安全 764
　火災予防, 犯罪防止, 耳の保護具, 目の保護具, 頭部の保護具, 呼吸器系の保護具, 足の保護具, 安全標識

健康 775
　救急車, 救急処置の用具, 救急箱, 体温計, 血圧計, 病院, 歩行補助具, 車椅子, 薬の様々な形態

親族 784
　家族関係

スポーツとゲーム　786

スポーツ施設 788
　スポーツ総合競技場, 得点掲示板／スコアボード, 試合／競技会

陸上競技 790
　競技場／アリーナ, 跳躍／ジャンプ, 投てき

球技 794
　野球, ソフトボール, クリケット, （フィールド）ホッケー, サッカー, ラグビー, アメリカン・フットボール, カナディアン・フットボール, ネットボール, バスケットボール, バレーボール, ハンドボール

ラケット・スポーツ 815
　卓球, バドミントン, ラケットボール, スカッシュ, テニス

体操競技 823
　新体操, トランポリン, 体操

水上・水中スポーツと海上スポーツ 827
　水球, 飛び込み, 水泳, セーリング, ウインドサーフィン, カヌー・カヤック：激流, ローイング[漕ぐこと]とスカーリング[幅寄せ], カヌー・カヤック：静水競漕, 水上スキー, サーフィン, スキューバ・ダイビング

格闘技 842
　ボクシング, レスリング, 柔道, 空手, カンフー, 柔術, 合気道, 剣道, 相撲, フェンシング

筋力スポーツ 850
　ウエイトリフティング, トレーニング用器具

乗馬スポーツ 852
　障害飛越（ひえつ）競技, 乗馬, 馬場馬術, 競馬：競馬場, 競馬：繋駕速歩（けいがはやあし）競走, ポロ

正確さを競うスポーツ 859
　アーチェリー, クレー射撃, ライフル射撃, ピストル射撃, ビリヤード／撞球（どうきゅう）／玉突き, ローン・ボウリング／ローン・ボウルズ, ペタンク, ボウリング, ゴルフ

自転車競技 870
　ロード・レース, マウンテン・バイキング, トラック・レース, バイシクル・モトクロス

モーター・スポーツ 872
　カー[自動車]レース, オートバイ・レース, 水上オートバイ／ジェット・スキー, スノーモービル

ウインター・スポーツ 877
　カーリング, アイス・ホッケー, フィギュア・スケート, スピード・スケート, ボブスレー, リュージュ, スケルトン, コース, スキー場, スノーボーディング, アルペン・スキー, フリースタイル・スキー, ジャンプ, スピード・スキー, クロス・カントリー・スキー, バイアスロン, スノーシュー／かんじき

ローラー・スポーツ 894
　スケートボーディング, イン・ライン・スケーティング

空中スポーツ 896
　スカイ・ダイビング, パラグライディング, ハング・グライディング, グライダー, 気球乗り

マウンテン・スポーツ 900
　登山／岩登り

アウトドア・レジャー 902
　キャンプ, ロープワーク／結び, 釣り, ハンティング／狩猟

ゲーム 914
　さいころ[ダイス]とドミノ牌（はい）, トランプ／カード, ボード・ゲーム, ジグソー・パズル, 麻雀, ビデオ・ゲーム, ダーツ, ルーレット・テーブル, スロット・マシン, サッカー・テーブル

章索引

- **2** 天文学
- **26** 地球
- **72** 植物
- **90** 動物
- **144** 人間
- **178** 食べ物と台所
- **242** 家屋
- **296** 日曜大工・園芸
- **334** 衣服
- **372** 装身具類と日用品
- **392** 芸術と建築
- **466** 情報伝達とオフィス・オートメーション
- **536** 交通と機械
- **644** エネルギー
- **678** 科学
- **706** 社会
- **786** スポーツとゲーム
- **921** 索引

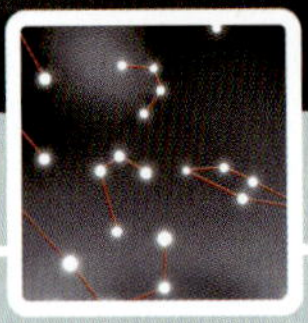
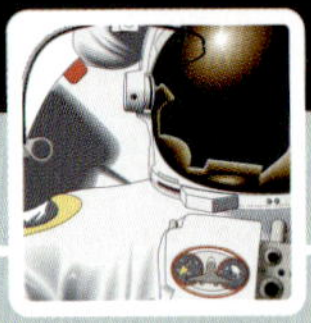
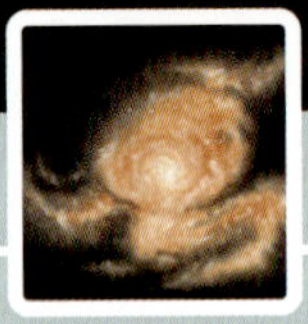

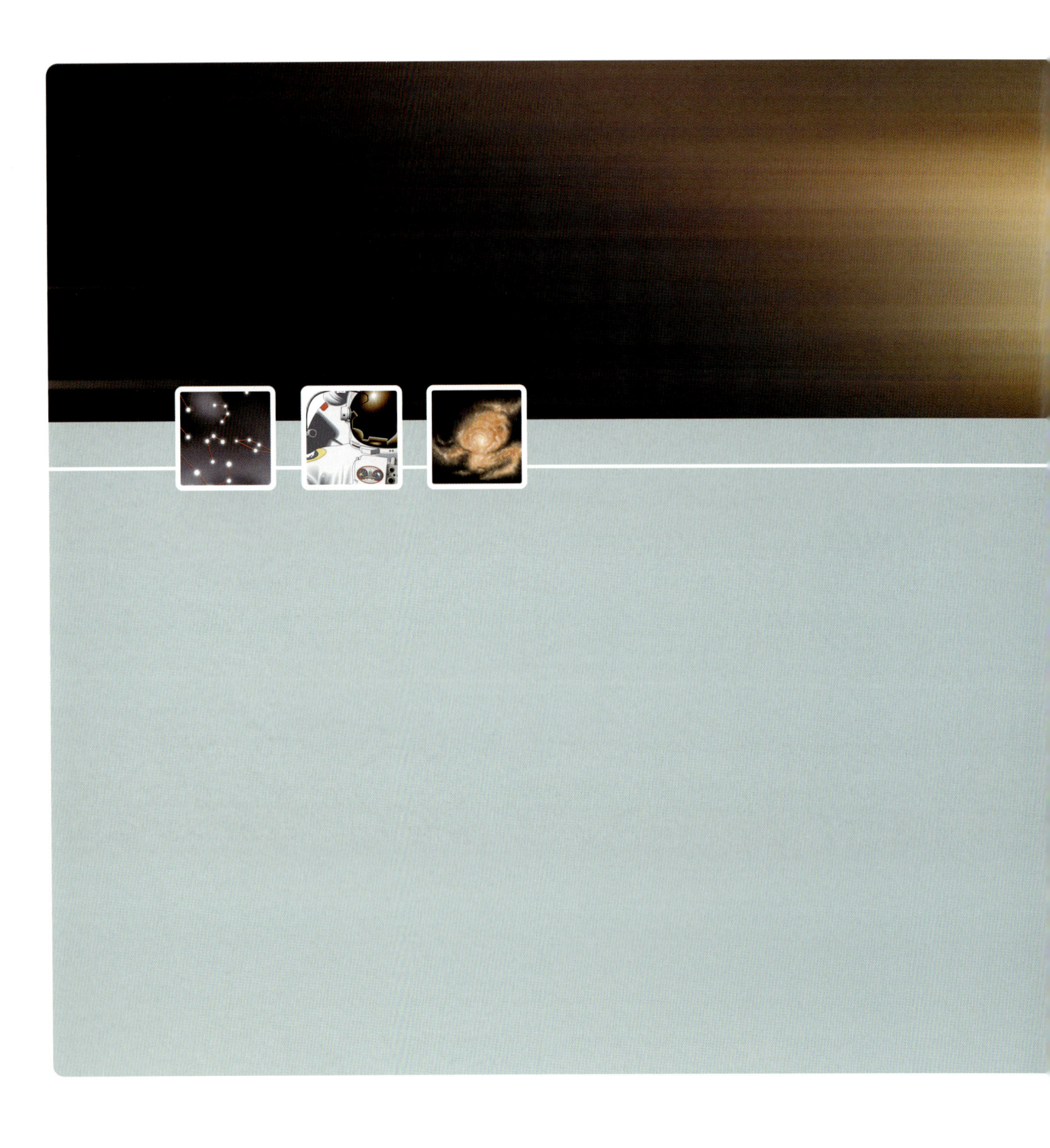

天文学

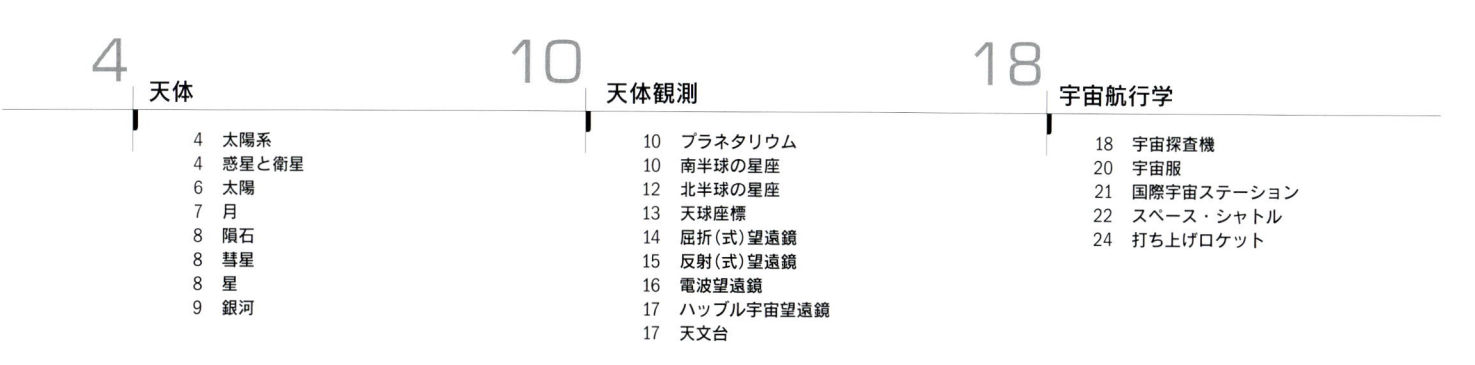

ASTRONOMY | ASTRONOMIE | ASTRONOMIE | ASTRONOMÍA | ASTRONOMIA

4 天体

- 4 太陽系
- 4 惑星と衛星
- 6 太陽
- 7 月
- 8 隕石
- 8 彗星
- 8 星
- 9 銀河

10 天体観測

- 10 プラネタリウム
- 10 南半球の星座
- 12 北半球の星座
- 13 天球座標
- 14 屈折(式)望遠鏡
- 15 反射(式)望遠鏡
- 16 電波望遠鏡
- 17 ハッブル宇宙望遠鏡
- 17 天文台

18 宇宙航行学

- 18 宇宙探査機
- 20 宇宙服
- 21 国際宇宙ステーション
- 22 スペース・シャトル
- 24 打ち上げロケット

天体 | CELESTIAL BODIES
HIMMELSKÖRPER | CORPS CÉLESTES | CUERPOS CELESTES | CORPI CELESTI

太陽系

日本語 | 英語 | ドイツ語 | フランス語 | スペイン語 | イタリア語

solar system | Sonnensystem[N] | système[M] solaire | sistema[M] solar | sistema[M] solare

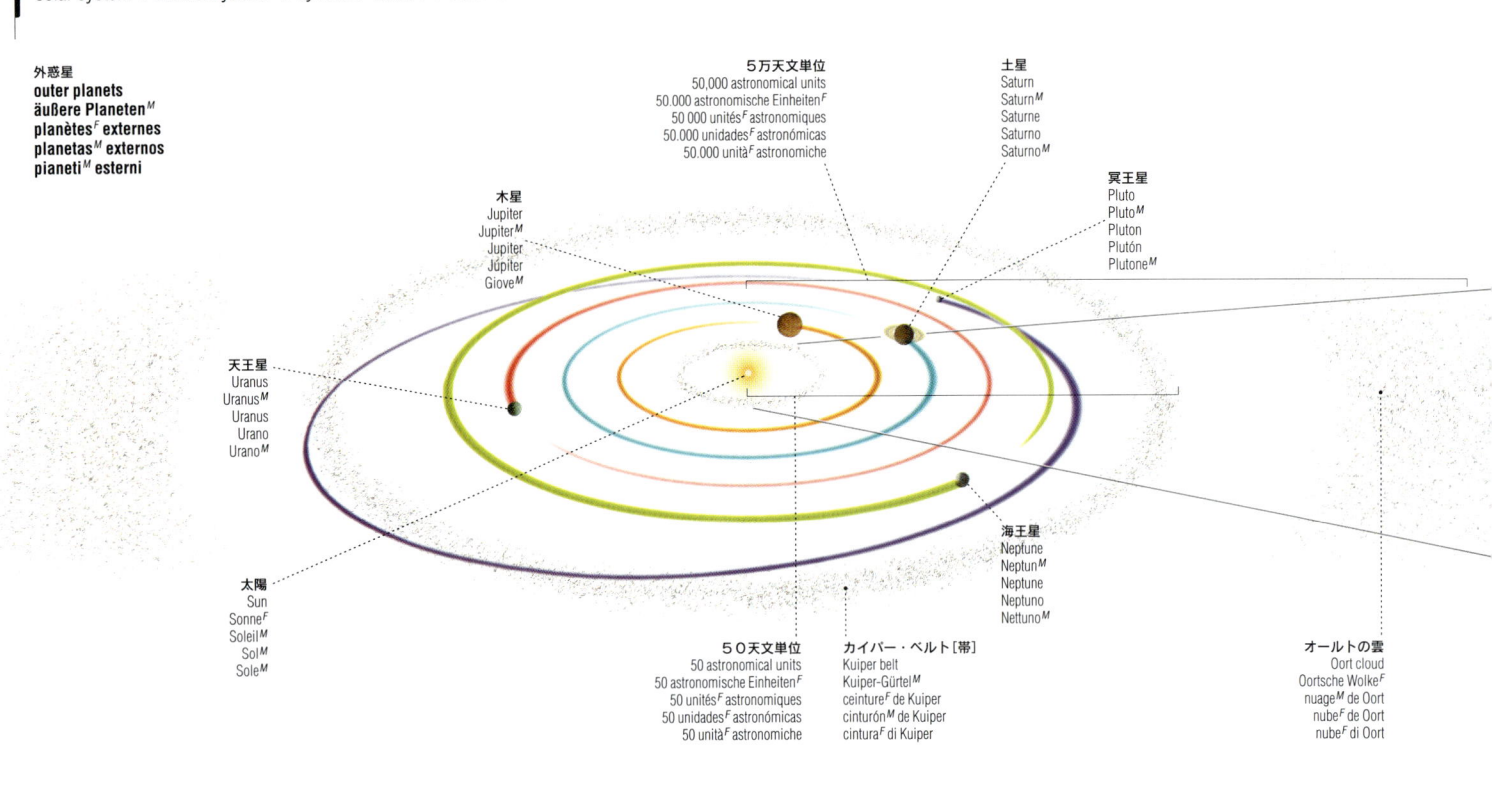

外惑星
outer planets
äußere Planeten[M]
planètes[F] externes
planetas[M] externos
pianeti[M] esterni

5万天文単位
50,000 astronomical units
50.000 astronomische Einheiten[F]
50.000 unités[F] astronomiques
50.000 unidades[F] astronómicas
50.000 unità[F] astronomiche

土星
Saturn
Saturn[M]
Saturne
Saturno
Saturno[M]

木星
Jupiter
Jupiter[M]
Jupiter
Júpiter
Giove[M]

冥王星
Pluto
Pluto[M]
Pluton
Plutón
Plutone[M]

天王星
Uranus
Uranus[M]
Uranus
Urano
Urano[M]

海王星
Neptune
Neptun[M]
Neptune
Neptuno
Nettuno[M]

太陽
Sun
Sonne[F]
Soleil[M]
Sol[M]
Sole[M]

50天文単位
50 astronomical units
50 astronomische Einheiten[F]
50 unités[F] astronomiques
50 unidades[F] astronómicas
50 unità[F] astronomiche

カイパー・ベルト[帯]
Kuiper belt
Kuiper-Gürtel[M]
ceinture[F] de Kuiper
cinturón[M] de Kuiper
cintura[F] di Kuiper

オールトの雲
Oort cloud
Oortsche Wolke[F]
nuage[M] de Oort
nube[F] de Oort
nube[F] di Oort

惑星と衛星

planets and moons | Planeten[M] und Monde[M] | planètes[F] et satellites[M] | planetas[M] y satélites[M] | pianeti[M] e satelliti[M]

デイモス
Deimos
Deimos[M]
Deimos
Deimos
Deimos[M]

フォボス
Phobos
Phobos[M]
Phobos
Fobos
Fobos[M]

月
Moon
Mond[M]
Lune[F]
Luna[F]
Luna[F]

金星
Venus
Venus[F]
Vénus
Venus
Venere[M]

水星
Mercury
Merkur[M]
Mercure
Mercurio
Mercurio[M]

地球
Earth
Erde[F]
Terre[F]
Tierra[F]
Terra[F]

火星
Mars
Mars[M]
Mars
Marte
Marte[M]

木星
Jupiter
Jupiter[M]
Jupiter
Júpiter
Giove[M]

イオ
Io
Io[F]
Io
Io
Io[M]

カリスト
Callisto
Callisto[F]
Callisto
Calixto
Callisto[M]

エウロパ
Europa
Europa[F]
Europe
Europa
Europa[F]

ガニメデ
Ganymede
Ganymed[M]
Ganymède
Ganimedes
Ganimede[M]

太陽
Sun
Sonne[F]
Soleil[M]
Sol[M]
Sole[M]

天体 | CELESTIAL BODIES
HIMMELSKÖRPER | CORPS CÉLESTES | CUERPOS CELESTES | CORPI CELESTI

太陽系

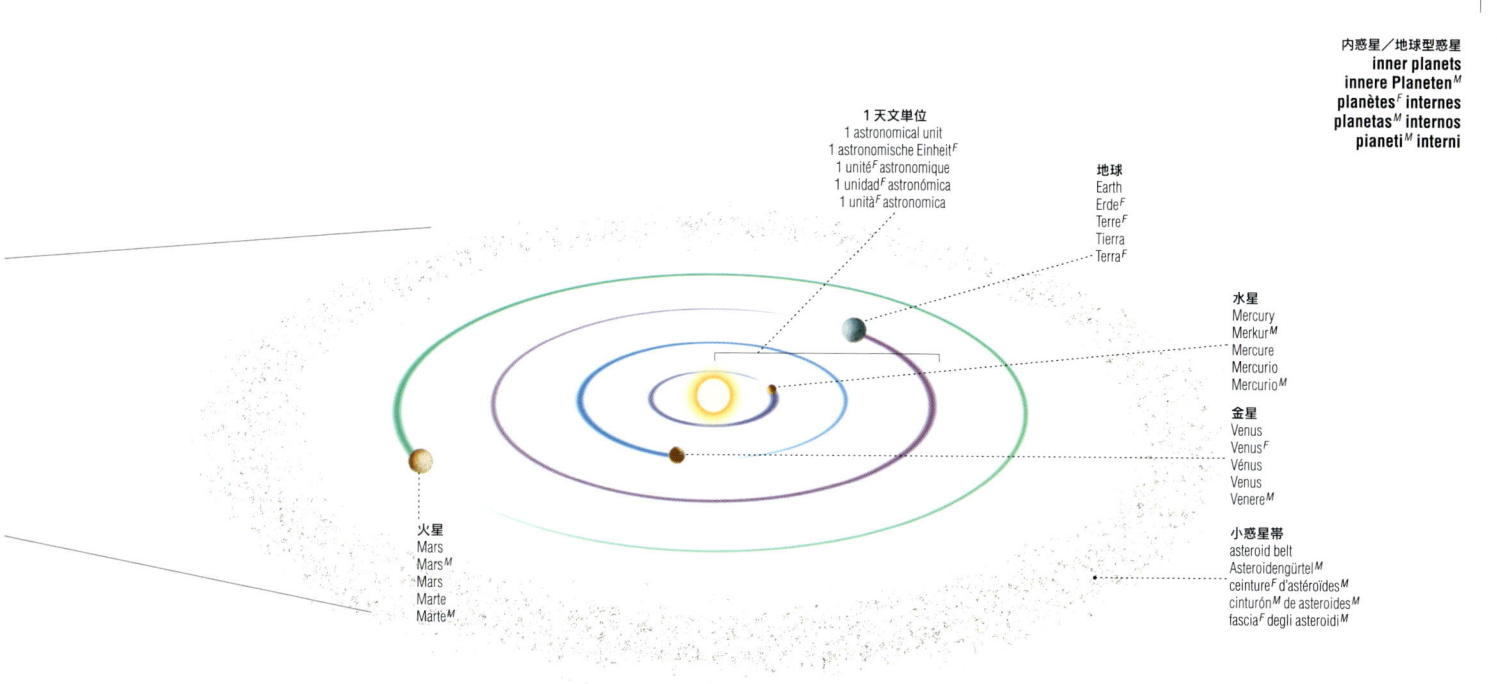

天文学

内惑星／地球型惑星
inner planets
innere Planetenᴹ
planètesᶠ internes
planetasᴹ internos
pianetiᴹ interni

1 天文単位
1 astronomical unit
1 astronomische Einheitᶠ
1 unitéᶠ astronomique
1 unidadᶠ astronómica
1 unitàᶠ astronomica

地球
Earth
Erdeᶠ
Terreᶠ
Tierra
Terraᶠ

水星
Mercury
Merkurᴹ
Mercure
Mercurio
Mercurioᴹ

金星
Venus
Venusᶠ
Vénus
Venus
Venereᴹ

小惑星帯
asteroid belt
Asteroidengürtelᴹ
ceintureᶠ d'astéroïdesᴹ
cinturónᴹ de asteroidesᴹ
fasciaᶠ degli asteroidiᴹ

火星
Mars
Marsᴹ
Mars
Marte
Marteᴹ

惑星と衛星

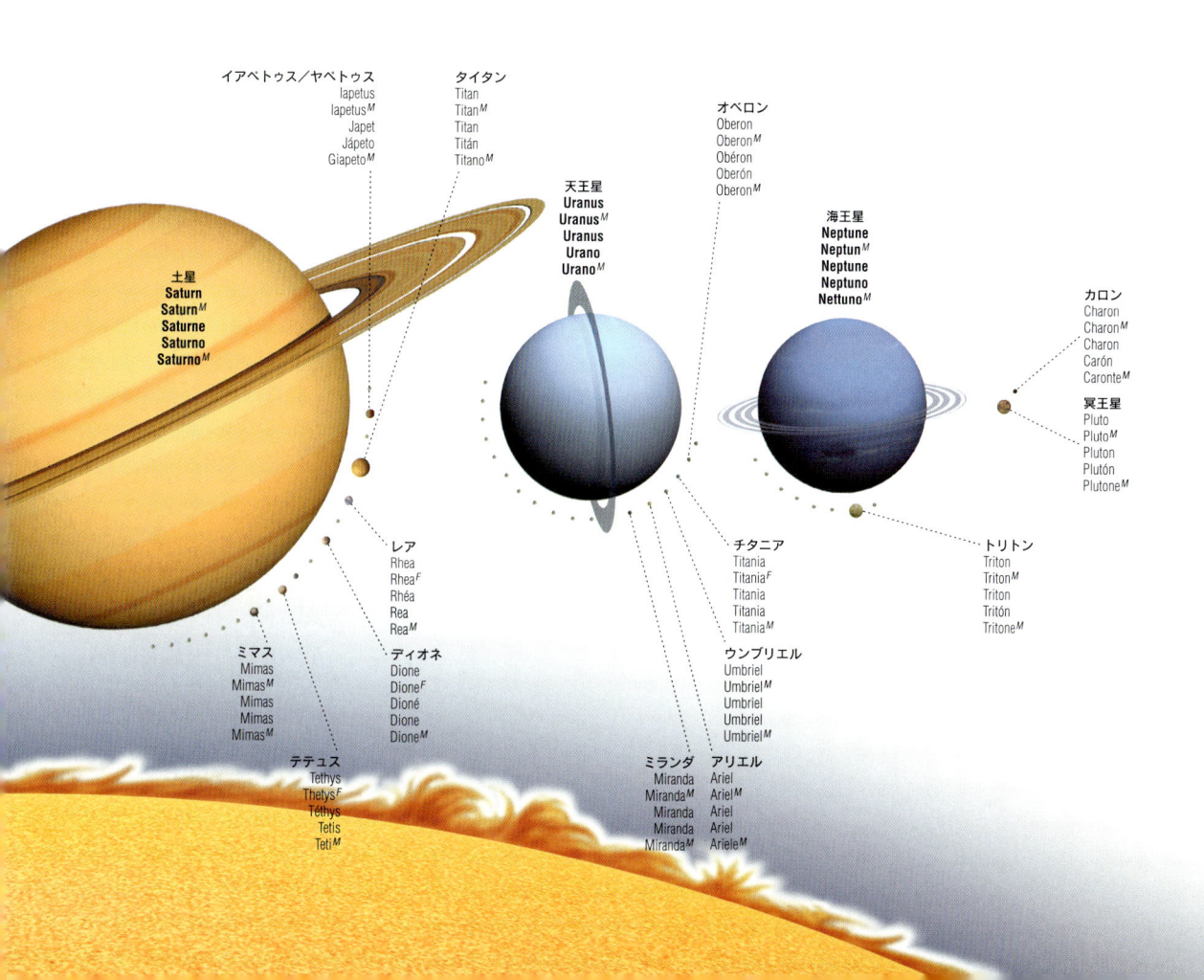

イアペトゥス／ヤペトゥス
Iapetus
Iapetusᴹ
Japet
Jápeto
Giapetoᴹ

タイタン
Titan
Titanᴹ
Titan
Titán
Titanoᴹ

オベロン
Oberon
Oberon
Obéron
Oberón
Oberonᴹ

天王星
Uranus
Uranusᴹ
Uranus
Urano
Uranoᴹ

海王星
Neptune
Neptunᴹ
Neptune
Neptuno
Nettunoᴹ

カロン
Charon
Charonᴹ
Charon
Carón
Caronteᴹ

土星
Saturn
Saturnᴹ
Saturne
Saturno
Saturnoᴹ

冥王星
Pluto
Plutoᴹ
Pluton
Plutón
Plutoneᴹ

レア
Rhea
Rheaᶠ
Rhéa
Rea
Reaᴹ

チタニア
Titania
Titaniaᶠ
Titania
Titania
Titaniaᴹ

トリトン
Triton
Tritonᴹ
Triton
Tritón
Tritoneᴹ

ミマス
Mimas
Mimasᴹ
Mimas
Mimas
Mimasᴹ

ディオネ
Dione
Dioneᶠ
Dioné
Dione
Dioneᴹ

ウンブリエル
Umbriel
Umbrielᴹ
Umbriel
Umbriel
Umbrielᴹ

テテュス
Tethys
Thetysᶠ
Téthys
Tetis
Tetiᴹ

ミランダ
Miranda
Mirandaᴹ
Miranda
Miranda
Mirandaᴹ

アリエル
Ariel
Arielᴹ
Ariel
Ariel
Arieleᴹ

天体 | CELESTIAL BODIES
HIMMELSKÖRPER | CORPS CÉLESTES | CUERPOS CELESTES | CORPI CELESTI

太陽
Sun | Sonne^F | Soleil^M | Sol^M | Sole^M

日本語 | 英語 | ドイツ語 | フランス語 | スペイン語 | イタリア語

天文学

太陽の構造
structure of the Sun
Aufbau^M der Sonne^F
structure^F du Soleil^M
estructura^F del Sol^M
struttura^F del Sole^M

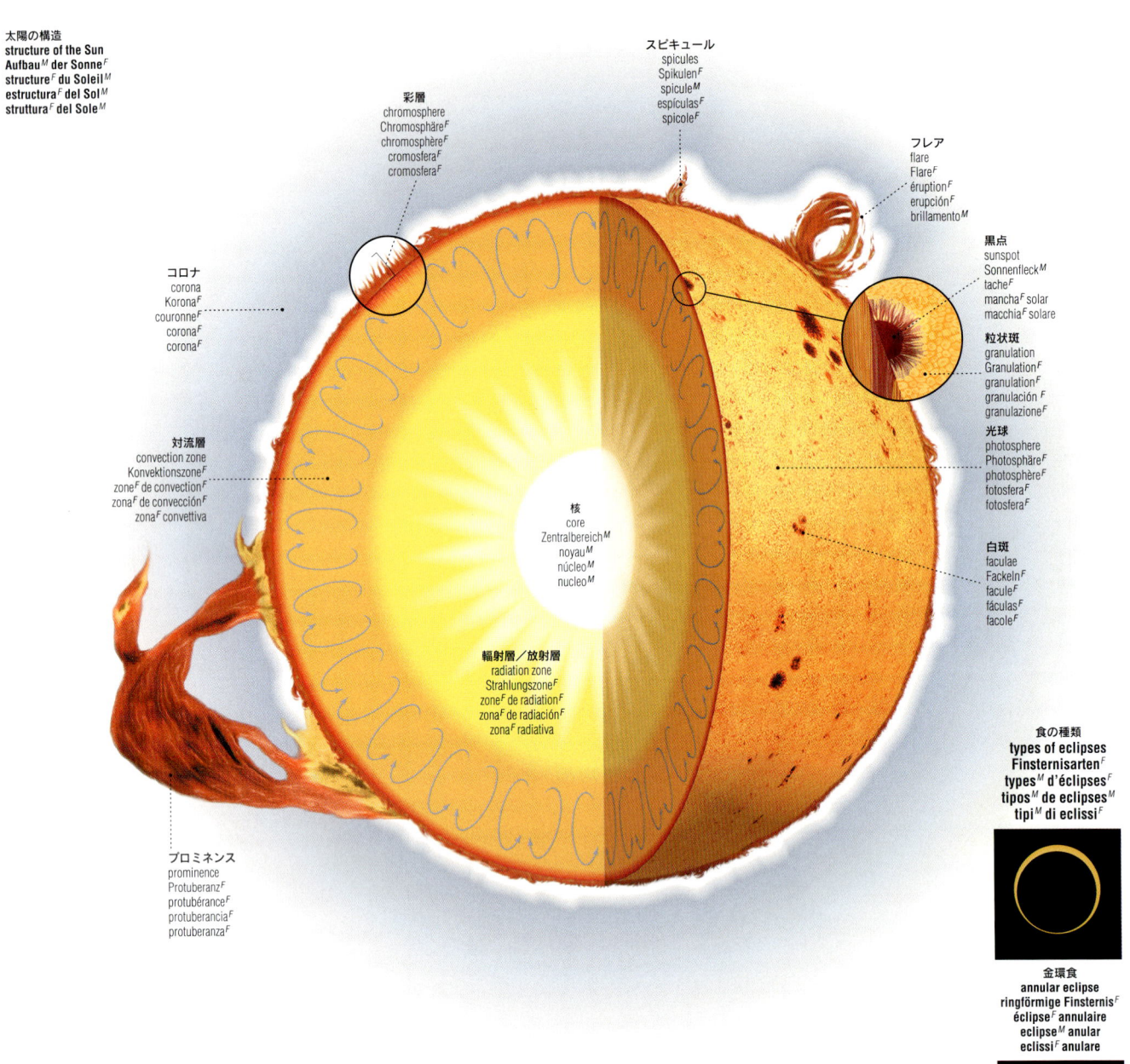

彩層
chromosphere
Chromosphäre^F
chromosphère^F
cromosfera^F
cromosfera^F

スピキュール
spicules
Spikulen^F
spicule^M
espículas^F
spicole^F

フレア
flare
Flare^F
éruption^F
erupción^F
brillamento^M

黒点
sunspot
Sonnenfleck^M
tache^F
mancha^F solar
macchia^F solare

コロナ
corona
Korona^F
couronne^F
corona^F
corona^F

粒状斑
granulation
Granulation^F
granulation^F
granulación^F
granulazione^F

対流層
convection zone
Konvektionszone^F
zone^F de convection^F
zona^F de convección^F
zona^F convettiva

光球
photosphere
Photosphäre^F
photosphère^F
fotosfera^F
fotosfera^F

核
core
Zentralbereich^M
noyau^M
núcleo^M
nucleo^M

白斑
faculae
Fackeln^F
facule^F
fáculas^F
facole^F

輻射層／放射層
radiation zone
Strahlungszone^F
zone^F de radiation^F
zona^F de radiación^F
zona^F radiativa

プロミネンス
prominence
Protuberanz^F
protubérance^F
protuberancia^F
protuberanza^F

食の種類
types of eclipses
Finsternisarten^F
types^M d'éclipses^F
tipos^M de eclipses^M
tipi^M di eclissi^F

金環食
annular eclipse
ringförmige Finsternis^F
éclipse^F annulaire
eclipse^M anular
eclissi^F anulare

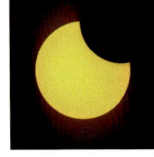

日食
solar eclipse
Sonnenfinsternis^F
éclipse^F de Soleil^M
eclipse^M solar
eclissi^F di Sole^M

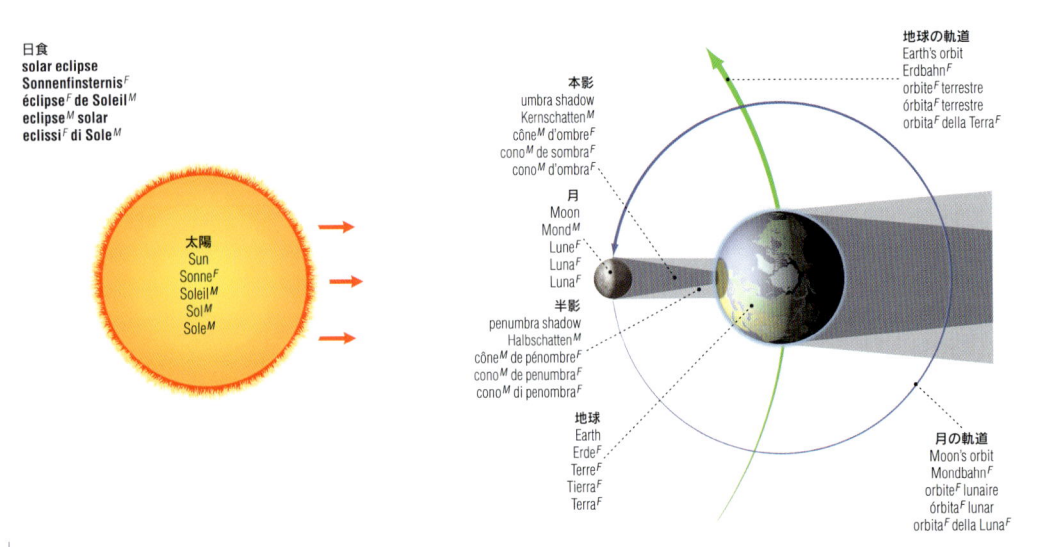

地球の軌道
Earth's orbit
Erdbahn^F
orbite^F terrestre
órbita^F terrestre
orbita^F della Terra^F

本影
umbra shadow
Kernschatten^M
cône^M d'ombre^F
cono^M de sombra^F
cono^M d'ombra^F

月
Moon
Mond^M
Lune^F
Luna^F
Luna^F

部分食
partial eclipse
partielle Finsternis^F
éclipse^F partielle
eclipse^M parcial
eclissi^F parziale

太陽
Sun
Sonne^F
Soleil^M
Sol^M
Sole^M

半影
penumbra shadow
Halbschatten^M
cône^M de pénombre^F
cono^M de penumbra^F
cono^M di penombra^F

地球
Earth
Erde^F
Terre^F
Tierra^F
Terra^F

月の軌道
Moon's orbit
Mondbahn^F
orbite^F lunaire
órbita^F lunar
orbita^F della Luna^F

皆既食
total eclipse
totale Finsternis^F
éclipse^F totale
eclipse^M total
eclissi^F totale

6

天体 | CELESTIAL BODIES
HIMMELSKÖRPER | CORPS CÉLESTES | CUERPOS CELESTES | CORPI CELESTI

月

Moon | Mond^M | Lune^F | Luna^F | Luna^F

天文学

食の種類
types of eclipses
Finsternisarten^F
types^M d'éclipses^F
tipos^M de eclipses^M
tipi^M di eclissi^F

部分食
partial eclipse
partielle Finsternis^F
éclipse^F partielle
eclipse^M parcial
eclissi^F parziale

皆既食
total eclipse
totale Finsternis^F
éclipse^F totale
eclipse^M total
eclissi^F totale

月の地形
lunar features
Oberflächenformationen^F des Mondes
relief^M lunaire
superficie^F lunar
caratteristiche^F della Luna^F

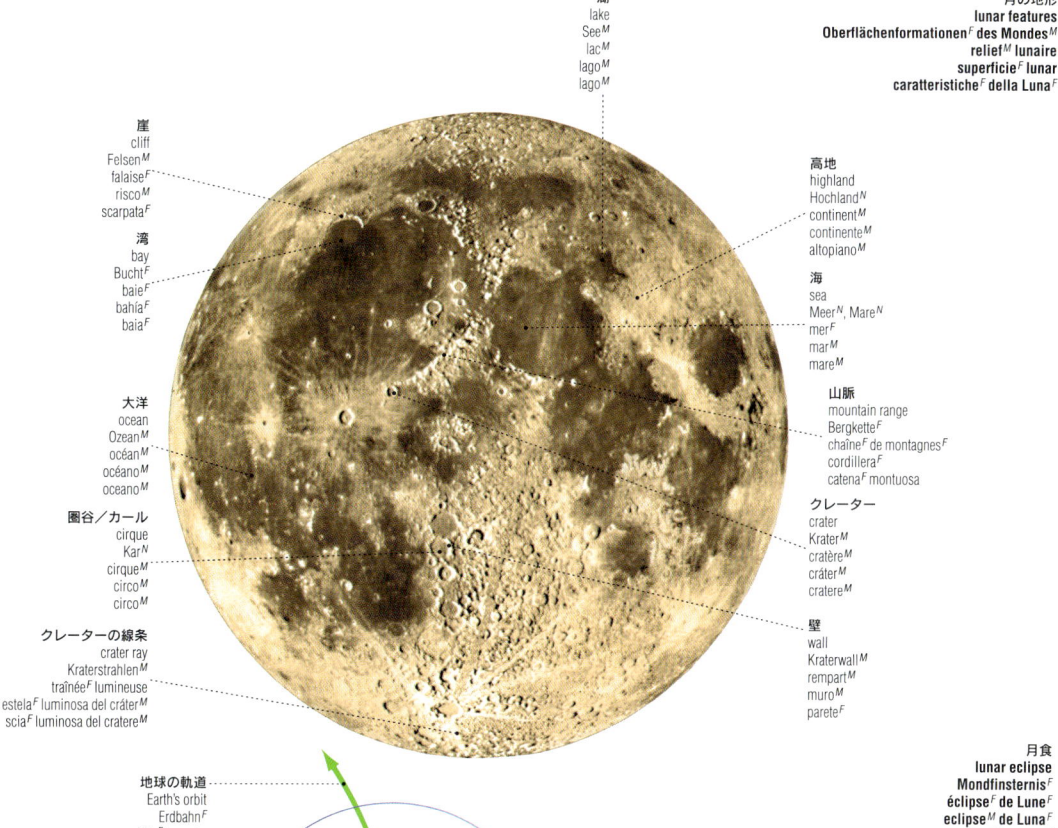

湖 — lake / See^M / lac^M / lago^M / lago^M

崖 — cliff / Felsen^M / falaise^F / risco^M / scarpata^F

湾 — bay / Bucht^F / baie^F / bahía^F / baia^F

高地 — highland / Hochland^N / continent^M / continente^M / altopiano^M

海 — sea / Meer^N, Mare^N / mer^F / mar^M / mare^M

大洋 — ocean / Ozean^M / océan^M / océano^M / oceano^M

山脈 — mountain range / Bergkette^F / chaîne^F de montagnes^F / cordillera^F / catena^F montuosa

圏谷／カール — cirque / Kar^N / cirque^M / circo^M / circo^M

クレーター — crater / Krater^M / cratère^M / cráter^M / cratere^M

クレーターの線条 — crater ray / Kraterstrahlen^M / traînée^F lumineuse / estela^F luminosa del cráter^M / scia^F luminosa del cratere^M

壁 — wall / Kraterwall^M / rempart^M / muro^M / parete^F

月食
lunar eclipse
Mondfinsternis^F
éclipse^F de Lune^F
eclipse^M de Luna^F
eclissi^F di Luna^F

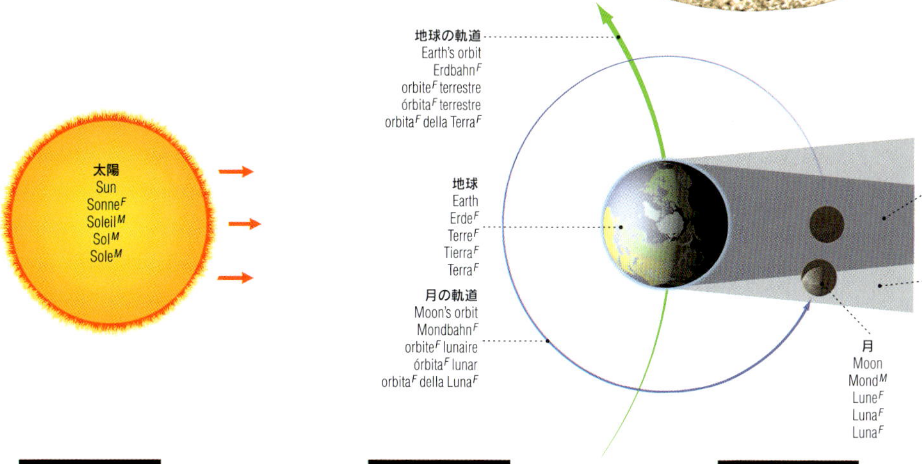

地球の軌道 — Earth's orbit / Erdbahn^F / orbite^F terrestre / órbita^F terrestre / orbita^F della Terra^F

太陽 — Sun / Sonne^F / Soleil^M / Sol^M / Sole^M

地球 — Earth / Erde^F / Terre^F / Tierra^F / Terra^F

本影 — umbra shadow / Kernschatten^M / cône^M d'ombre^F / cono^M de sombra^F / cono^M d'ombra^F

半影 — penumbra shadow / Halbschatten^M / cône^M de pénombre^F / cono^M de penumbra^F / cono^M di penombra^F

月の軌道 — Moon's orbit / Mondbahn^F / orbite^F lunaire / órbita^F lunar / orbita^F della Luna^F

月 — Moon / Mond^M / Lune^F / Luna^F / Luna^F

月相（月の満ち欠け）
phases of the Moon
Mondphasen^F
phases^F de la Lune^F
fases^F de la Luna^F
fasi^F della Luna^F

新月
new moon
Neumond^M
nouvelle Lune^F
Luna^F nueva
Luna^F nuova

三日月
new crescent
Mondsichel^F (zunehmender Mond^M)
premier croissant^M
creciente^F
Luna^F crescente

上弦の月
first quarter
Halbmond^M (erstes Viertel^N)
premier quartier^M
cuarto^M creciente
primo quarto^M

満ちていく月
waxing gibbous
zunehmender Mond^M
gibbeuse^F croissante
quinto^M octante
Luna^F gibbosa crescente

満月
full moon
Vollmond^M
pleine Lune^F
Luna^F llena
Luna^F piena

欠けていく月
waning gibbous
abnehmender Mond^M
gibbeuse^F décroissante
tercer^M octante
Luna^F gibbosa calante

下弦の月
last quarter
Halbmond^M (letztes Viertel^N)
dernier quartier^M
cuarto^M menguante
ultimo quarto^M

二十四夜の月
old crescent
Mondsichel^F (abnehmender Mond^M)
dernier croissant^M
Luna^F menguante
Luna^F calante

7

天体 | CELESTIAL BODIES
HIMMELSKÖRPER | CORPS CÉLESTES | CUERPOS CELESTES | CORPI CELESTI

隕石

meteorite | Meteorit^M | météorite^F | meteorito^M | meteorite^F/M

日本語 | 英語 | ドイツ語 | フランス語 | スペイン語 | イタリア語

隕鉄
iron meteorite
Eisenmeteorit^M
météorite^F ferreuse
meteorito^M ferroso
meteorite^F/M ferrosa

石鉄隕石
stony-iron meteorite
Steineisenmeteorit^M
météorite^F métallo-rocheuse
meteorito^M pétreo-ferroso
meteorite^F/M ferro-rocciosa

石質隕石
stony meteorites
Steinmeteoriten^M
météorites^F rocheuses
meteoritos^M pétreos
meteoriti^F/M rocciose

球粒[球顆]隕石／コンドライト
chondrite
Chondrit^M
chondrite^F
condrito^M
condrite^F

無球粒[球顆]隕石／エイコンドライト
achondrite
Achondrit^M
achondrite^F
acondrito^M
acondrite^F

彗星

comet | Komet^M | comète^F | cometa^M | cometa^F

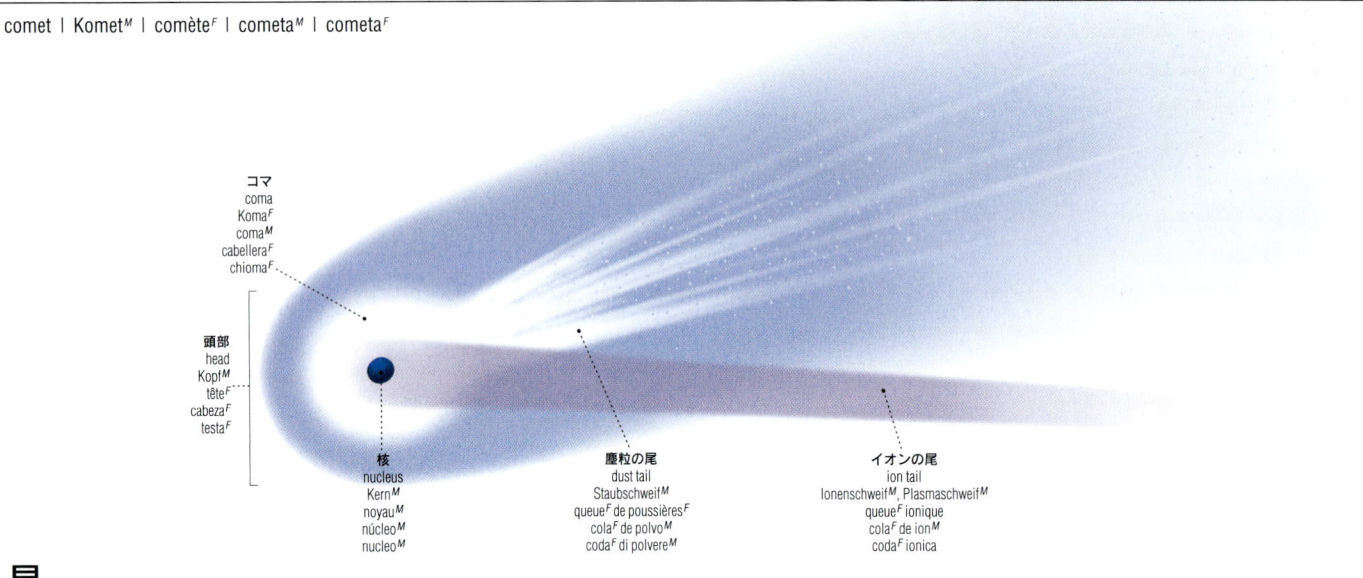

コマ
coma
Koma^F
coma^M
cabellera^F
chioma^F

頭部
head
Kopf^M
tête^F
cabeza^F
testa^F

核
nucleus
Kern^M
noyau^M
núcleo^M
nucleo^M

塵粒の尾
dust tail
Staubschweif^M
queue^F de poussières
cola^F de polvo^M
coda^F di polvere^M

イオンの尾
ion tail
Ionenschweif^M, Plasmaschweif^M
queue^F ionique
cola^F de ion^M
coda^F ionica

星

star | Stern^M | étoile^F | estrella^F | stella^F

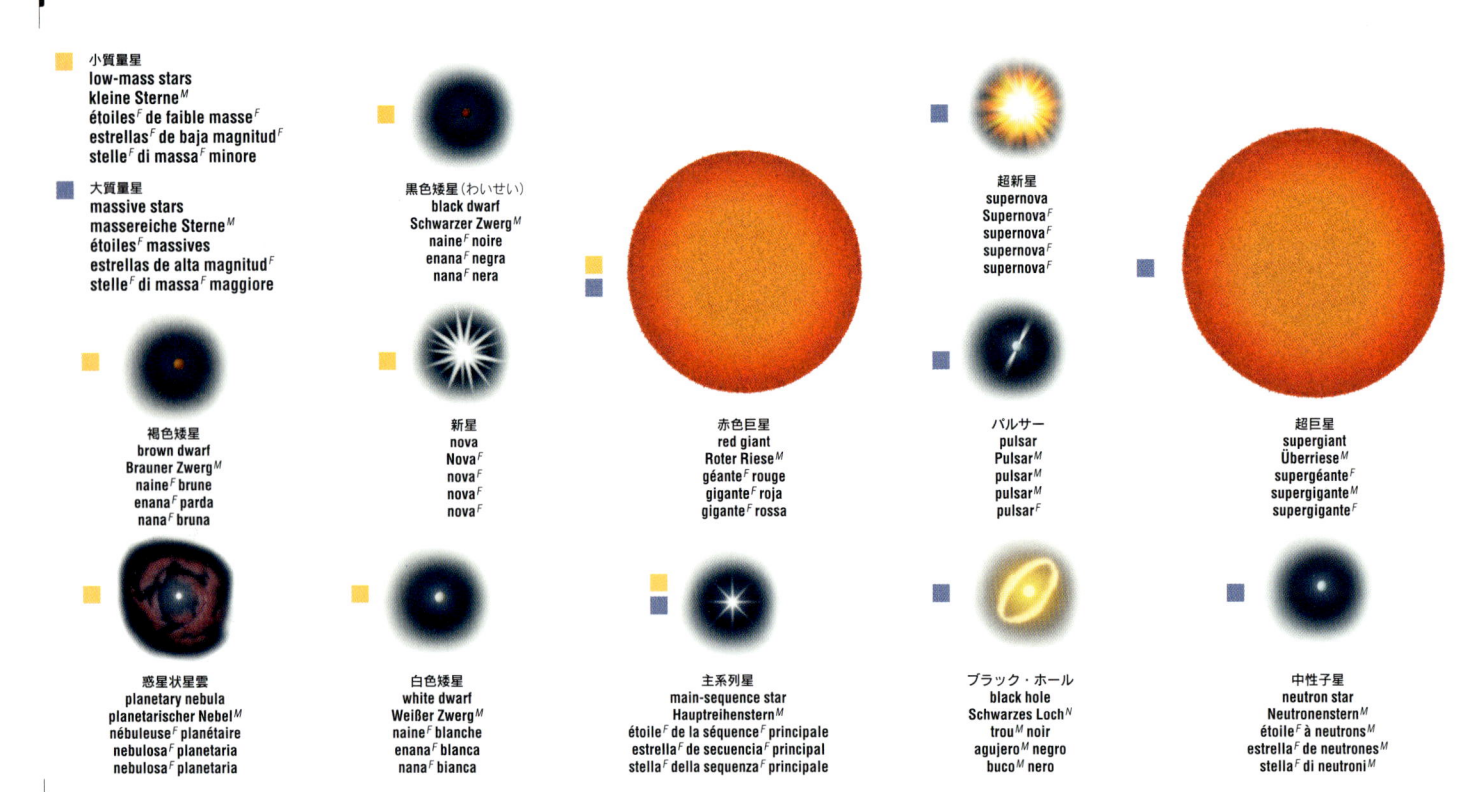

■ 小質量星
low-mass stars
kleine Sterne^M
étoiles^F de faible masse^F
estrellas^F de baja magnitud^F
stelle^F di massa^F minore

■ 大質量星
massive stars
massereiche Sterne^M
étoiles^F massives
estrellas de alta magnitud^F
stelle^F di massa^F maggiore

褐色矮星
brown dwarf
Brauner Zwerg^M
naine^F brune
enana^F parda
nana^F bruna

黒色矮星（わいせい）
black dwarf
Schwarzer Zwerg^M
naine^F noire
enana^F negra
nana^F nera

新星
nova
Nova^F
nova^F
nova^F
nova^F

赤色巨星
red giant
Roter Riese^M
géante^F rouge
gigante^F roja
gigante^F rossa

超新星
supernova
Supernova^F
supernova^F
supernova^F
supernova^F

パルサー
pulsar
Pulsar^M
pulsar^M
pulsar^M
pulsar^F

超巨星
supergiant
Überriese^M
supergéante^F
supergigante^M
supergigante^F

惑星状星雲
planetary nebula
planetarischer Nebel^M
nébuleuse^F planétaire
nebulosa^F planetaria
nebulosa^F planetaria

白色矮星
white dwarf
Weißer Zwerg^M
naine^F blanche
enana^F blanca
nana^F bianca

主系列星
main-sequence star
Hauptreihenstern^M
étoile^F de la séquence^F principale
estrella^F de secuencia^F principal
stella^F della sequenza^F principale

ブラック・ホール
black hole
Schwarzes Loch^N
trou^M noir
agujero^M negro
buco^M nero

中性子星
neutron star
Neutronenstern^M
étoile^F à neutrons^M
estrella^F de neutrones^M
stella^F di neutroni^M

8

天体 | CELESTIAL BODIES
HIMMELSKÖRPER | CORPS CÉLESTES | CUERPOS CELESTES | CORPI CELESTI

銀河

galaxy | Galaxie^F | galaxie^F | galaxia^F | galassia^F

天文学

ハッブル分類
Hubble's classification
Hubblesche Klassifikation^F
classification^F de Hubble
clasificación^F de Hubble
classificazione^F di Hubble

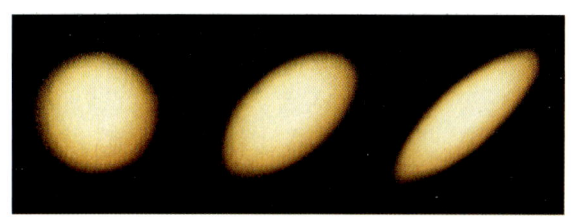

銀河／天の川
Milky Way
Milchstraße^F
Voie^F lactée
Vía^F Láctea
Via^F Lattea

楕円銀河
elliptical galaxy
elliptische Galaxie^F
galaxie^F elliptique
galaxia^F elíptica
galassia^F ellittica

銀河／天の川（上から見た姿）
Milky Way (seen from above)
Milchstraße^F (Ansicht^F von oben)
Voie^F lactée (vue^F de dessus^M)
Vía^F Láctea (vista^F desde arriba)
Via^F Lattea (vista^F dall'alto)

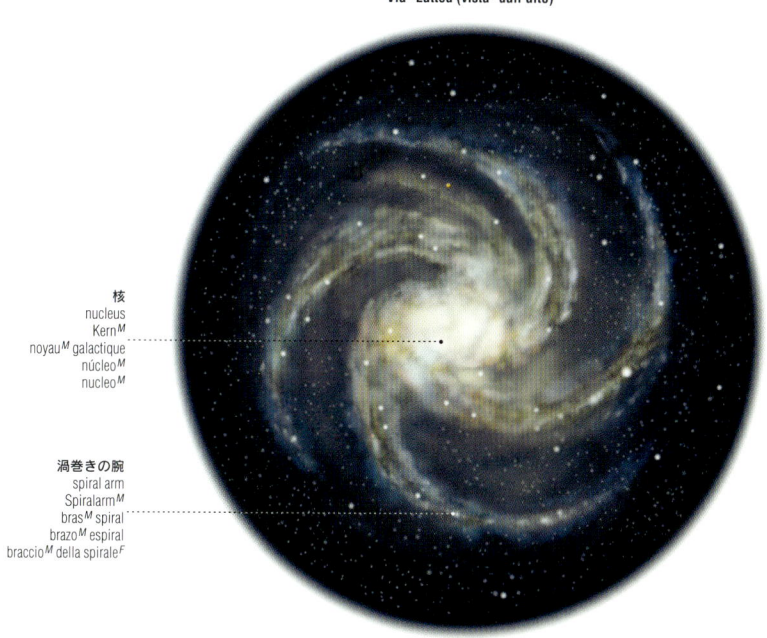

レンズ状銀河
lenticular galaxy
linsenförmige Galaxie^F
galaxie^F lenticulaire
galaxia^F lenticular
galassia^F lenticolare

核
nucleus
Kern^M
noyau^M galactique
núcleo^M
nucleo^M

渦巻きの腕
spiral arm
Spiralarm^M
bras^M spiral
brazo^M espiral
braccio^M della spirale^F

通常の渦巻き銀河
normal spiral galaxy
normale Spiralgalaxie^F
galaxie^F spirale normale
galaxia^F espiral normal
galassia^F a spirale^F normale

銀河／天の川（横から見た姿）
Milky Way (side view)
Milchstraße^F (Seitenansicht^F)
Voie^F lactée (vue^F de profil^F)
Vía^F Láctea (vista^F lateral)
Via^F Lattea (vista^F laterale)

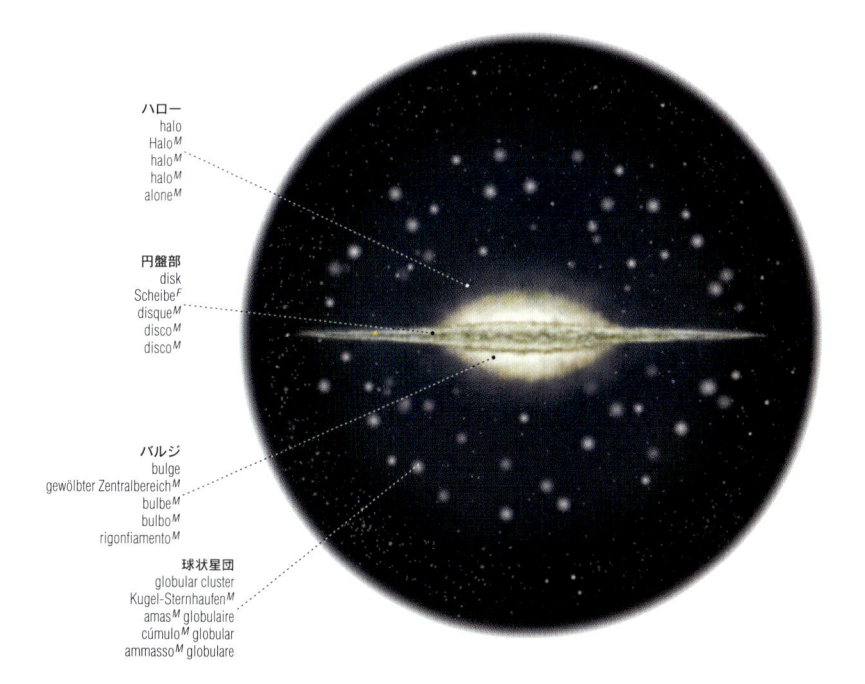

ハロー
halo
Halo^M
halo^M
halo^M
alone^M

円盤部
disk
Scheibe^F
disque^M
disco^M
disco^M

棒渦巻き銀河
barred spiral galaxy
Balkenspiralgalaxie^F
galaxie^F spirale barrée
galaxia^F espiral barrada
galassia^F a spirale^F barrata

バルジ
bulge
gewölbter Zentralbereich^M
bulbe^M
bulbo^M
rigonfiamento^M

球状星団
globular cluster
Kugel-Sternhaufen^M
amas^M globulaire
cúmulo^M globular
ammasso^M globulare

不規則銀河 I 型
type I irregular galaxy
irreguläre Galaxie^F Typ^M I
galaxie^F irrégulière de type^M I
galaxia^F irregular de tipo^M I
galassia^F irregolare di tipo^M I

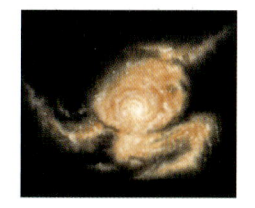

不規則銀河 II 型
type II irregular galaxy
irreguläre Galaxie^F Typ^M II
galaxie^F irrégulière de type^M II
galaxia^F irregular de tipo^M II
galassia^F irregolare di tipo^M II

9

天体観測 | ASTRONOMICAL OBSERVATION
BEOBACHTUNG DES WELTRAUMS | OBSERVATION ASTRONOMIQUE | OBSERVACIÓN ASTRONÓMICA | OSSERVAZIONE ASTRONOMICA

プラネタリウム

日本語 | 英語 | ドイツ語 | フランス語 | スペイン語 | イタリア語

planetarium | Planetarium[N] | planétarium[M] | planetario[M] | planetario[M]

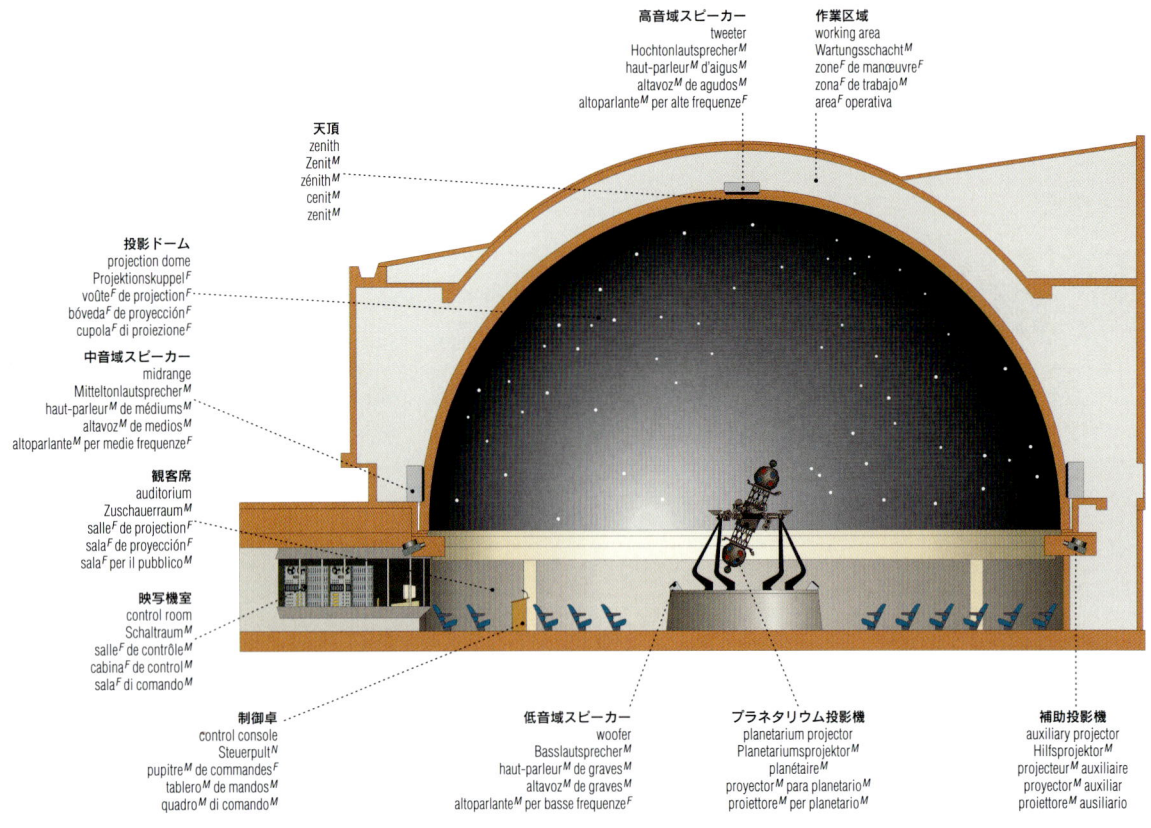

天文学

高音域スピーカー
tweeter
Hochtonlautsprecher[M]
haut-parleur[M] d'aigus[M]
altavoz[M] de agudos[M]
altoparlante[M] per alte frequenze[F]

作業区域
working area
Wartungsschacht[M]
zone[F] de manœuvre[F]
zona[F] de trabajo[M]
area[F] operativa

天頂
zenith
Zenit[M]
zénith[M]
cenit[M]
zenit[M]

投影ドーム
projection dome
Projektionskuppel[F]
voûte[F] de projection[F]
bóveda[F] de proyección[F]
cupola[F] di proiezione[F]

中音域スピーカー
midrange
Mitteltonlautsprecher[M]
haut-parleur[M] de médiums[M]
altavoz[M] de medios[M]
altoparlante[F] per medie frequenze[F]

観客席
auditorium
Zuschauerraum[M]
salle[F] de projection[F]
sala[F] de proyección[F]
sala[F] per il pubblico[M]

映写機室
control room
Schaltraum[M]
salle[F] de contrôle[F]
cabina[F] de control[M]
sala[F] di comando[M]

制御卓
control console
Steuerpult[N]
pupitre[M] de commandes[F]
tablero[M] de mandos[M]
quadro[M] di comando[M]

低音域スピーカー
woofer
Basslautsprecher[M]
haut-parleur[M] de graves[M]
altavoz[M] de graves[M]
altoparlante[M] per basse frequenze[F]

プラネタリウム投影機
planetarium projector
Planetariumsprojektor[M]
planétaire[M]
proyector[M] para planetario[M]
proiettore[M] per planetario[M]

補助投影機
auxiliary projector
Hilfsprojektor[M]
projecteur[M] auxiliaire
proyector[M] auxiliar
proiettore[M] ausiliario

南半球の星座

constellations of the southern hemisphere | Sternbilder[N] der südlichen Halbkugel[F] | constellations[F] de l'hémisphère[M] austral | constelaciones[F] del hemisferio[M] austral | costellazioni[F] dell'emisfero[M] meridionale

1 くじら（鯨）座
Whale
Walfisch[M]
Baleine[F]
Ballena[F]
Balena[F]

2 みずがめ（水瓶）座
Water Bearer
Wassermann[M]
Verseau[M]
Acuario[M]
Acquario[M]

3 わし（鷲）座
Eagle
Adler[M]
Aigle[M]
Águila[F]
Aquila[F]

4 やぎ（山羊）座
Sea Goat
Steinbock[M]
Capricorne[M]
Capricornio[M]
Capricorno[M]

5 けんびきょう（顕微鏡）座
Microscope
Mikroskop[N]
Microscope[M]
Microscopio[M]
Microscopio[M]

6 みなみのうお（南の魚）座
Southern Fish
Südlicher Fisch[M]
Poisson[M] austral
Pez[M] Austral
Pesce[M] Australe

7 つる（鶴）座
Crane
Kranich[M]
Grue[F]
Grulla[M]
Gru[F]

8 ちょうこくぐ（彫刻具）座
Sculptor's Tools
Bildhauer[M]
Atelier[M] du Sculpteur[M]
Taller[M] de Escultor[M]
Strumenti[M] dello Scultore[M]

9 エリダヌス座
River
Eridanus[M]
Éridan[M]
Erídano[M]
Eridano[M]

10 ろ（炉）座
Furnace
Ofen[M]
Fourneau[M]
Horno[M]
Fornace[F]

11 とけい（時計）座
Clock
Pendeluhr[F]
Horloge[F]
Reloj[M]
Orologio[M]

12 ほうおう（鳳凰）座
Phoenix
Phönix[M]
Phénix[M]
Fénix[M]
Fenice[F]

13 きょしちょう（巨嘴鳥）座
Toucan
Tukan[M]
Toucan[M]
Tucán[M]
Tucano[M]

14 くじゃく（孔雀）座
Peacock
Pfau[M]
Paon[M]
Pavo[M]
Pavone[M]

15 インディアン座
Indian
Inder[M]
Indien[M]
Indio[M]
Indiano[M]

16 ほうえんきょう（望遠鏡）座
Telescope
Fernrohr[N]
Télescope[M]
Telescopio[M]
Telescopio[M]

17 みなみのかんむり（南の冠）座
Southern Crown
Südliche Krone[F]
Couronne[F] australe
Corona[F] Austral
Corona[F] Australe

18 いて（射手）座
Archer
Schütze[M]
Sagittaire[M]
Sagitario[M]
Sagittario[M]

19 たて（盾）座
Shield
Schild[N]
Écu[M]
Escudo[M]
Scudo[M]

20 さそり（蠍）座
Scorpion
Skorpion[M]
Scorpion[M]
Escorpión[M]
Scorpione[M]

21 じょうぎ（定規）座
Carpenter's Square
Winkelmaß[N]
Règle[F]
Regla[F]
Squadra[F]

22 さいだん（祭壇）座
Altar
Altar[M]
Autel[M]
Altar[M]
Altare[M]

23 みなみのさんかく（南の三角）座
Southern Triangle
Südliches Dreieck[N]
Triangle[M] austral
Triángulo[M] Austral
Triangolo[M] Australe

24 ふうちょう（風鳥）座
Bird of Paradise
Paradiesvogel[M]
Oiseau[M] de Paradis[M]
Ave[F] del Paraíso[M]
Uccello[M] del Paradiso[M]

25 はちぶんぎ（八分儀）座
Octant
Oktant[M]
Octant[M]
Octante[M]
Ottante[M]

26 みずへび（水蛇）座
Sea Serpent
Kleine Wasserschlange[F]
Hydre[F] mâle
Hidra[F] macho
Idra[F] Maschio

27 テーブルさん（テーブル山）座
Table Mountain
Tafelberg[M]
Table[F]
Mesa[F]
Mensa[F]

28 レチクル座
Net
Netz[N]
Réticule[M]
Retículo[M]
Reticolo[M]

天体観測 | ASTRONOMICAL OBSERVATION
BEOBACHTUNG DES WELTRAUMS | OBSERVATION ASTRONOMIQUE | OBSERVACIÓN ASTRONÓMICA | OSSERVAZIONE ASTRONOMICA

南半球の星座

天文学

29 かじき(旗魚)座
Swordfish
Schwertfisch[M]
Dorade[F]
Dorado[M]
Dorado[M]

30 がか(画架)座
Painter's Easel
Malerstaffelei[F]
Chevalet[M] du Peintre[M]
Caballete[M] del pintor[M]
Cavalletto[M] del Pittore[M]

31 はと(鳩)座
Dove
Taube[F]
Colombe[F]
Paloma[F]
Colomba[F]

32 ちょうこくぐ(彫刻具)座
Chisel
Grabstichel[M]
Burin[M]
Buril[M]
Bulino[M]

33 うさぎ(兎)座
Hare
Hase[M]
Lièvre[M]
Liebre[M]
Lepre[F]

34 オリオン座
Hunter
Orion[M]
Orion
Orión[M]
Orione[M]

35 おおいぬ(大犬)座
Big Dog
Großer Hund[M]
Grand Chien[M]
Can[M] Mayor
Cane[M] Maggiore

36 いっかくじゅう(一角獣)座
Unicorn
Einhorn[N]
Licorne[F]
Unicornio[M]
Unicorno[M]

37 とも(艫)座
Ship's Stern
Achterschiff[N]
Poupe[F]
Popa[F]
Poppa[F]

38 コンパス座
Compass
Zirkel[M]
Boussole[F]
Brújula[F]
Bussola[F]

39 ほ(帆)座
Ship's Sails
Schiffssegel[N]
Voiles[F]
Vela[F]
Vela[F]

40 りゅうこつ(竜骨)座
Ship's Keel
Schiffskiel[M]
Carène[F]
Carena[F]
Carena[F]

41 とびうお(飛魚)座
Flying Fish
Fliegender Fisch[M]
Poisson[M] volant
Pez[M] Volador
Pesce[M] Volante

42 カメレオン座
Chameleon
Chamäleon[N]
Caméléon[M]
Camaleón[M]
Camaleonte[M]

43 はえ(蝿)座
Fly
Fliege[F]
Mouche[F]
Mosca[F]
Mosca[F]

44 コンパス座
Pair of Compasses
Kompass[M]
Compas[M]
Compás[M]
Compasso[M]

45 みなみじゅうじ(南十字)座
Southern Cross
Kreuz[N] des Südens[M]
Croix[F] du Sud[M]
Cruz[F] del Sur
Croce[F] del Sud[M]

46 ケンタウルス座
Centaur
Zentaurus[M]
Centaure[M]
Centauro[M]
Centauro[M]

47 おおかみ(狼)座
Wolf
Wolf[M]
Loup[M]
Lobo[M]
Lupo[M]

48 へびつかい(蛇遣い)座
Serpent Bearer
Schlangenträger[M]
Ophiuchus
Ofiuco[M]
Ofiuco[M]

49 へび(蛇)座
Serpent
Schlange[F]
Serpent[M]
Serpiente[M]
Serpente[M]

50 てんびん(天秤)座
Scales
Waage[F]
Balance[F]
Libra[F]
Bilancia[F]

51 おとめ(乙女)座
Virgin
Jungfrau[F]
Vierge[F]
Virgo[F]
Vergine[F]

52 からす(烏)座
Crow
Rabe[M]
Corbeau[M]
Cuervo[M]
Corvo[M]

53 コップ座
Cup
Becher[M]
Coupe[F]
Copa[F]
Cratere[M]

54 ろくぶんぎ(六分儀)座
Sextant
Sextant[M]
Sextant[M]
Sextante[M]
Sestante[M]

55 うみへび(海蛇)座
Water Monster
Südliche Wasserschlange[F]
Hydre[F] femelle
Hidra[F] Hembra
Idra[F] Femmina

56 ポンプ座
Air Pump
Luftpumpe[F]
Machine[F] pneumatique
Máquina[F] Pneumática
Macchina[F] Pneumatica

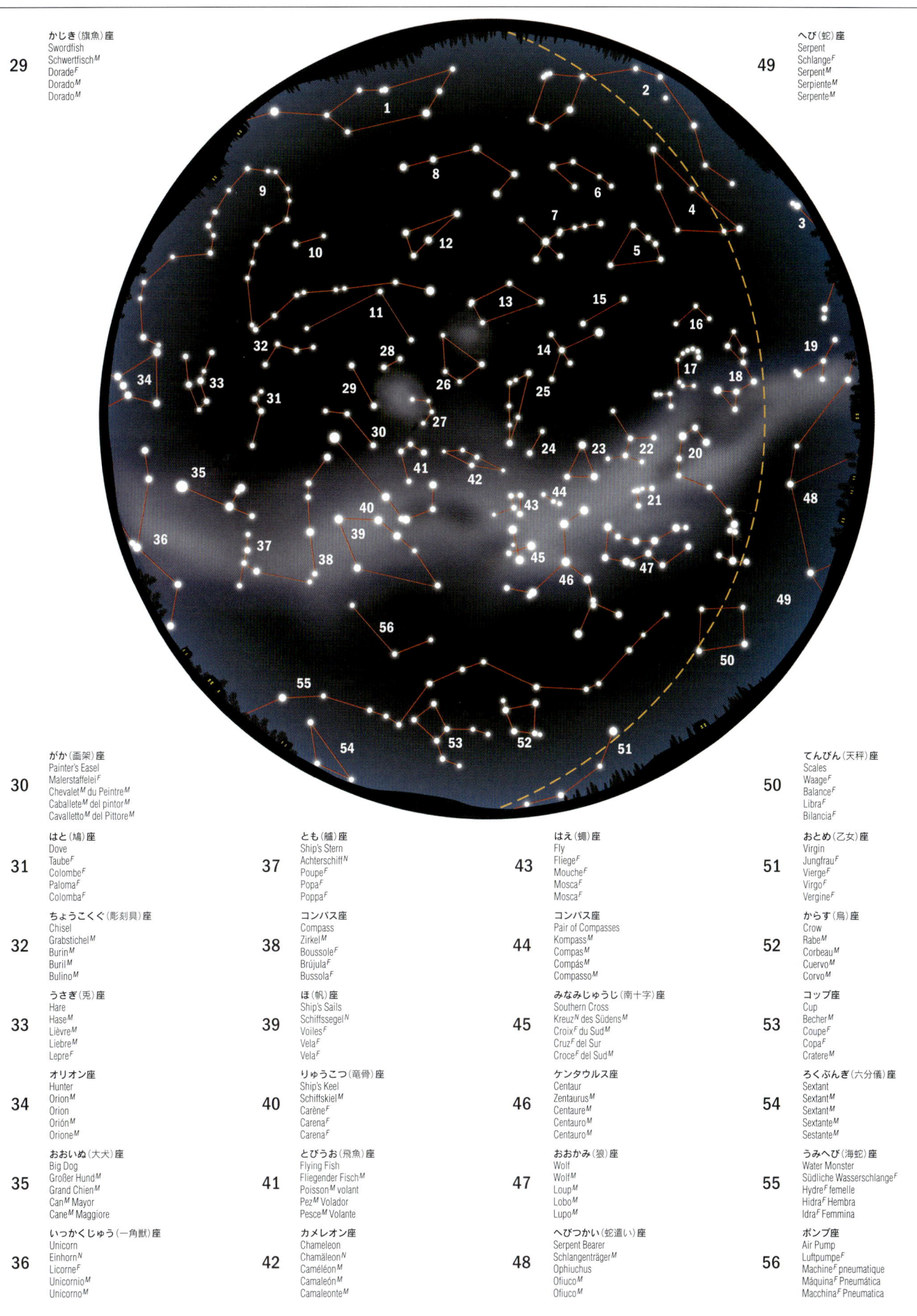

北半球の星座

constellations of the northern hemisphere | Sternbilder[N] der nördlichen Halbkugel[F] | constellations[F] de l'hémisphère[M] boréal | constelaciones[F] del hemisferio[M] boreal | costellazioni[F] dell'emisfero[M] settentrionale

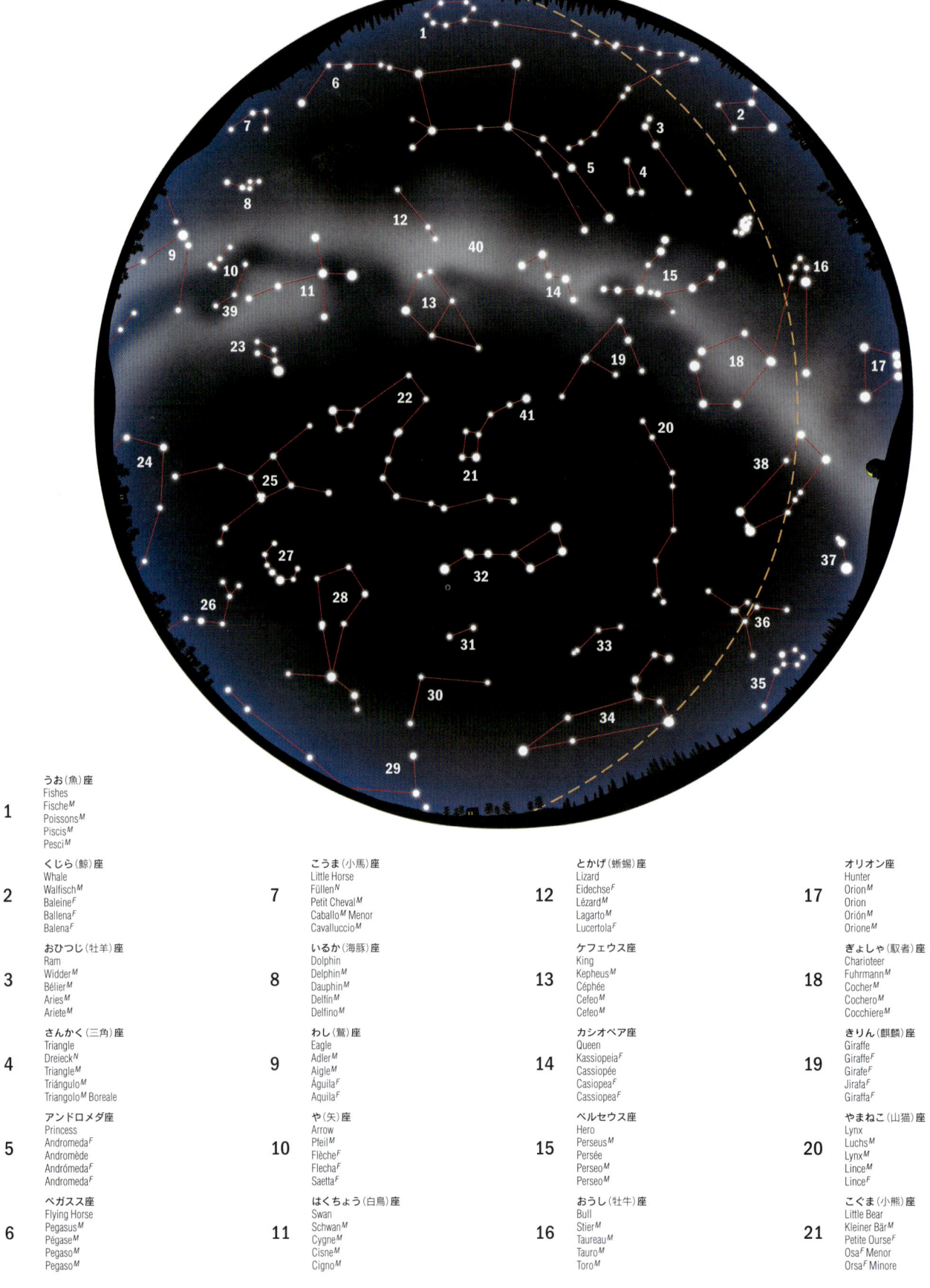

天体観測 | ASTRONOMICAL OBSERVATION
BEOBACHTUNG DES WELTRAUMS | OBSERVATION ASTRONOMIQUE | OBSERVACIÓN ASTRONÓMICA | OSSERVAZIONE ASTRONOMICA

1. うお(魚)座 / Fishes / Fische[F] / Poissons[M] / Piscis[M] / Pesci[M]
2. くじら(鯨)座 / Whale / Walfisch[M] / Baleine[F] / Ballena[F] / Balena[F]
3. おひつじ(牡羊)座 / Ram / Widder[M] / Bélier[M] / Aries[M] / Ariete[M]
4. さんかく(三角)座 / Triangle / Dreieck[N] / Triangle[M] / Triángulo[M] / Triangolo[M] Boreale
5. アンドロメダ座 / Princess / Andromeda[F] / Andromède / Andrómeda[F] / Andromeda[F]
6. ペガスス座 / Flying Horse / Pegasus[M] / Pégase[M] / Pegaso[M] / Pegaso[M]
7. こうま(小馬)座 / Little Horse / Füllen[N] / Petit Cheval[M] / Caballo[M] Menor / Cavalluccio[M]
8. いるか(海豚)座 / Dolphin / Delphin[M] / Dauphin[M] / Delfín[M] / Delfino[M]
9. わし(鷲)座 / Eagle / Adler[M] / Aigle[M] / Águila[F] / Aquila[F]
10. や(矢)座 / Arrow / Pfeil[M] / Flèche[F] / Flecha[F] / Saetta[F]
11. はくちょう(白鳥)座 / Swan / Schwan[M] / Cygne[M] / Cisne[M] / Cigno[M]
12. とかげ(蜥蜴)座 / Lizard / Eidechse[F] / Lézard[M] / Lagarto[M] / Lucertola[F]
13. ケフェウス座 / King / Kepheus[M] / Céphée / Cefeo[M] / Cefeo[M]
14. カシオペア座 / Queen / Kassiopeia[F] / Cassiopée / Casiopea[F] / Cassiopea[F]
15. ペルセウス座 / Hero / Perseus[M] / Persée / Perseo[M] / Perseo[M]
16. おうし(牡牛)座 / Bull / Stier[M] / Taureau[M] / Tauro[M] / Toro[M]
17. オリオン座 / Hunter / Orion[F] / Orion / Orión[M] / Orione[M]
18. ぎょしゃ(馭者)座 / Charioteer / Fuhrmann[M] / Cocher[M] / Cochero[M] / Cocchiere[M]
19. きりん(麒麟)座 / Giraffe / Giraffe[F] / Girafe[F] / Jirafa[F] / Giraffa[F]
20. やまねこ(山猫)座 / Lynx / Luchs[M] / Lynx[M] / Lince[M] / Lince[M]
21. こぐま(小熊)座 / Little Bear / Kleiner Bär[M] / Petite Ourse[F] / Osa[F] Menor / Orsa[F] Minore

天体観測 | ASTRONOMICAL OBSERVATION
BEOBACHTUNG DES WELTRAUMS | OBSERVATION ASTRONOMIQUE | OBSERVACIÓN ASTRONÓMICA | OSSERVAZIONE ASTRONOMICA

北半球の星座

22 りゅう(竜)座 / Dragon / Drache^M / Dragon^M / Dragón^M / Dragone^M

23 こと(琴)座 / Lyre / Leier^F / Lyre^F / Lira^F / Lira^F

24 へびつかい(蛇遣い)座 / Serpent Bearer / Schlangenträger^M / Ophiuchus / Ofiuco^M / Ofiuco^M

25 ヘラクレス座 / Strong Man / Herkules^M / Hercule / Hércules^M / Ercole^M

26 へび(蛇)座 / Serpent / Schlange^F / Serpent^M / Serpiente^F / Serpente^M

27 きたのかんむり(北の冠)座 / Northern Crown / Nördliche Krone^F / Couronne^F boréale / Corona^F Boreal / Corona^F Boreale

28 うしかい(牛飼い)座 / Herdsman / Bärenhüter^M / Bouvier^M / Boyero^M / Boote^M

29 おとめ(乙女)座 / Virgin / Jungfrau^F / Vierge^F / Virgo^M / Vergine^F

30 かみのけ(髪の毛)座 / Berenice's Hair / Haar^N der Berenike^F / Chevelure^F de Bérénice / Cabellera^F de Berenice / Chioma^F di Berenice

31 りょうけん(猟犬)座 / Hunting Dogs / Jagdhunde^M / Chiens^M de Chasse^F / Lebreles^M / Levrieri^M

32 おおぐま(大熊)座 / Great Bear / Großer Bär^M / Grande Ourse^F / Osa^F Mayor / Orsa^F Maggiore

33 こじし(小獅子)座 / Little Lion / Kleiner Löwe^M / Petit Lion^M / León^M Menor / Leoncino^M

34 しし(獅子)座 / Lion / Löwe^M / Lion^M / León^M / Leone^M

35 うみへび(海蛇)座 / Water Monster / Nördliche Wasserschlange^F / Hydre^F femelle / Hidra^F Hembra / Idra^F Femmina

36 かに(蟹)座 / Crab / Krebs^M / Cancer / Cáncer^M / Cancro^M

37 こいぬ(小犬)座 / Little Dog / Kleiner Hund^M / Petit Chien^M / Can^M Menor / Cane^M Minore

38 ふたご(双子)座 / Twins / Zwillinge^M / Gémeaux^M / Géminis^F / Gemelli^M

39 こぎつね(小狐)座 / Fox / Füchslein^M / Petit Renard^M / Zorra^F / Volpetta^F

40 ぎんが(銀河) / Milky Way / Milchstraße^F / Voie^F Lactée / Vía^F Láctea / Via^F Lattea

41 ほっきょくせい(北極星) / North Star / Polarstern^M / Étoile^F polaire / Estrella^F Polar / Stella^F Polare

天球座標

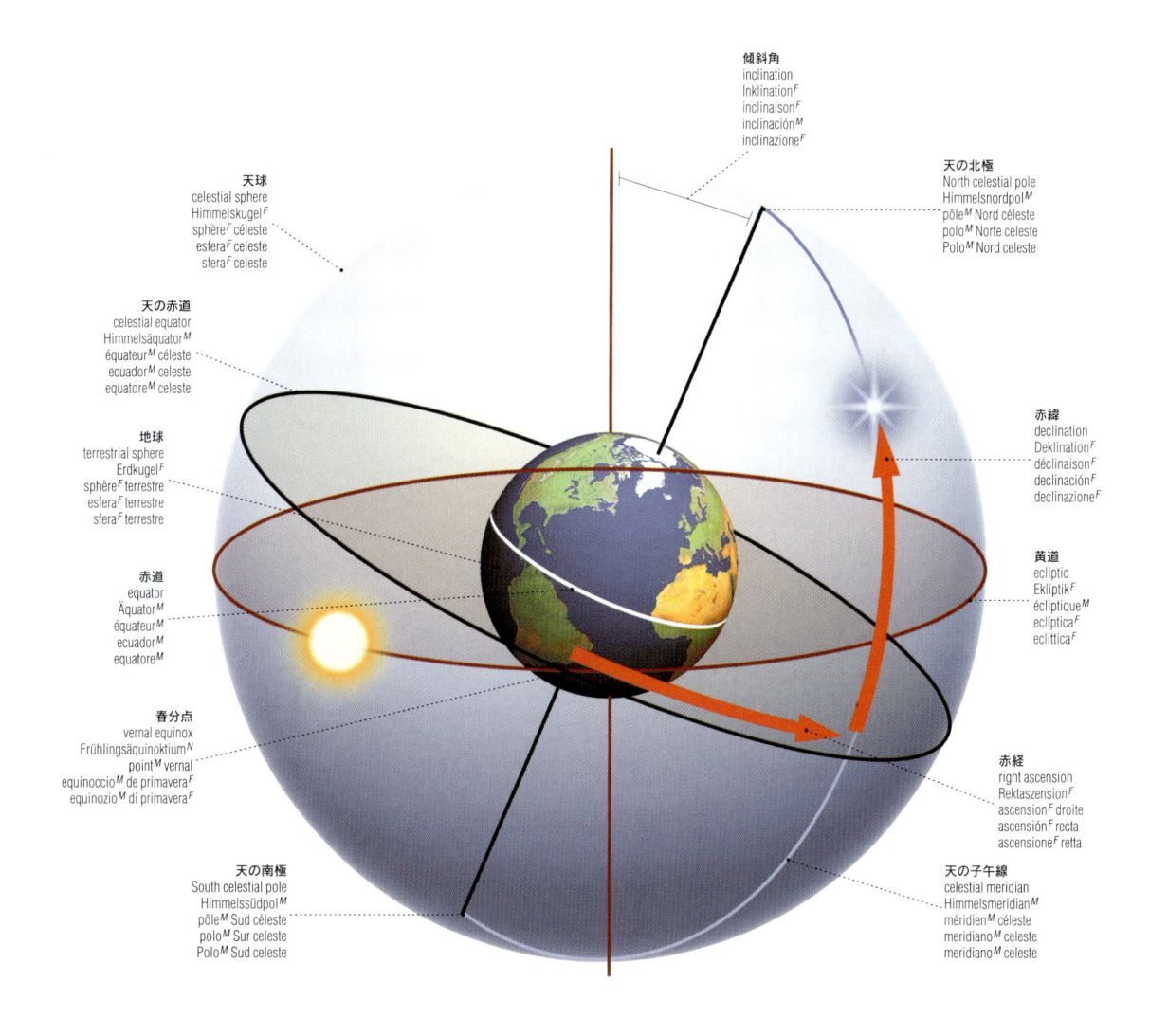

celestial coordinate system | Koordinatensystem^N der Himmelskugel^F | coordonnées^F célestes | sistema^M de coordenadas^F astronómicas | sistema^M di coordinate^F celesti

- 傾斜角 / inclination / Inklination^F / inclinaison^F / inclinación^M / inclinazione^F
- 天の北極 / North celestial pole / Himmelsnordpol^M / pôle^M Nord céleste / polo^M Norte celeste / Polo^M Nord celeste
- 天球 / celestial sphere / Himmelskugel^F / sphère^F céleste / esfera^F celeste / sfera^F celeste
- 天の赤道 / celestial equator / Himmelsäquator^M / équateur^M céleste / ecuador^M celeste / equatore^M celeste
- 地球 / terrestrial sphere / Erdkugel^F / sphère^F terrestre / esfera^F terrestre / sfera^F terrestre
- 赤緯 / declination / Deklination^F / déclinaison^F / declinación^F / declinazione^F
- 赤道 / equator / Äquator^M / équateur^M / ecuador^M / equatore^M
- 黄道 / ecliptic / Ekliptik^F / écliptique^M / eclíptica^F / eclittica^F
- 春分点 / vernal equinox / Frühlingsäquinoktium^N / point^M vernal / equinoccio^M de primavera / equinozio^M di primavera
- 赤経 / right ascension / Rektaszension^F / ascension^F droite / ascensión^F recta / ascensione^F retta
- 天の南極 / South celestial pole / Himmelssüdpol^M / pôle^M Sud céleste / polo^M Sur celeste / Polo^M Sud celeste
- 天の子午線 / celestial meridian / Himmelsmeridian^M / méridien^M céleste / meridiano^M celeste / meridiano^M celeste

天体観測 | ASTRONOMICAL OBSERVATION
BEOBACHTUNG DES WELTRAUMS | OBSERVATION ASTRONOMIQUE | OBSERVACIÓN ASTRONÓMICA | OSSERVAZIONE ASTRONOMICA

屈折（式）望遠鏡

日本語 | 英語 | ドイツ語 | フランス語 | スペイン語 | イタリア語

refracting telescope | Linsenfernrohr(N) | lunette(F) astronomique | telescopio(M) refractor | cannocchiale(M)

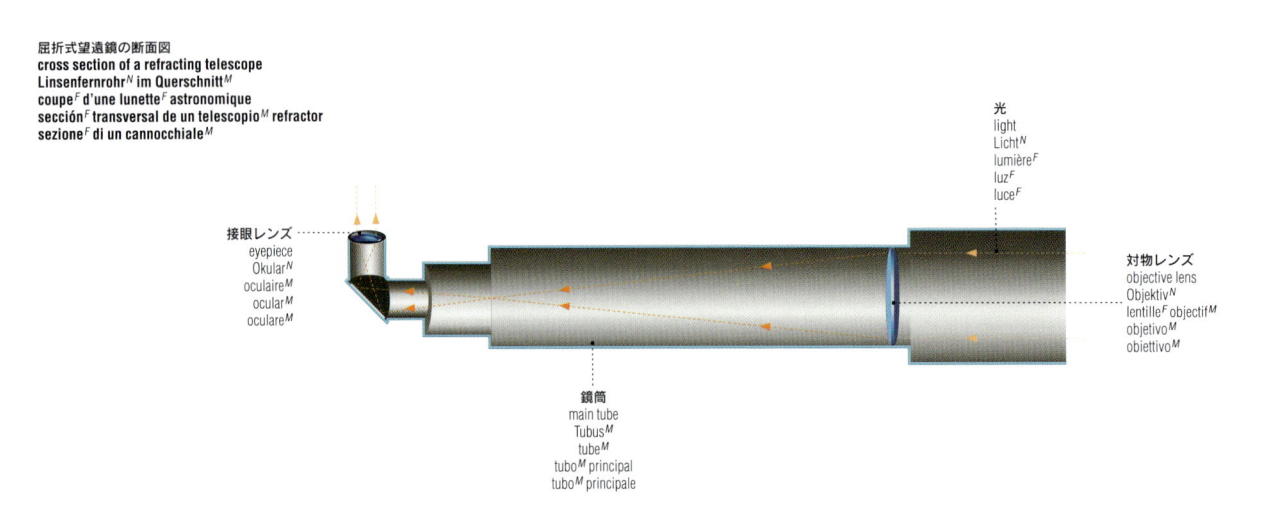

天文学

ファインダー
finderscope
Suchfernrohr(N)
chercheur(M)
anteojo(M) buscador
cannocchiale(M) cercatore

鏡筒バンド
cradle
Wiege(F)
bride(F) de fixation(F)
abrazadera(F)
giogo(M) di supporto(M)

鏡筒
main tube
Tubus(M)
tube(M)
tubo(M) principal
tubo(M) principale

フード
dew shield
Sonnenblende(F)
pare-soleil(M)
parasol(M)
paraluce(M)

接眼レンズ／アイピース
eyepiece
Okular(N)
oculaire(M)
ocular(M)
oculare(M)

接眼レンズ・アダプター
eyepiece holder
Okularhalterung(F)
tube(M) porte-oculaire(M)
portaocular(M)
portaoculare(M)

天頂プリズム
star diagonal
Zenitprisma(N)
oculaire(M) coudé
ocular(M) acodado
prisma(M) astronomico

ピント調節ハンドル
focusing knob
Scharfeinstellung(F)
bouton(M) de mise(F) au point(M)
botón(M) de enfoque(M)
manopola(F) della messa(F) a fuoco(M)

赤緯目盛り環
declination setting scale
Einstellung(F) der Deklinationsachse(F)
cercle(M) de déclinaison(F)
círculo(M) graduado de declinación(F)
cerchio(M) graduato della declinazione(F)

赤緯クランプ
azimuth clamp
Azimutfeststeller(M)
vis(F) de blocage(M) (azimut(M))
palanca(F) de bloqueo(M) del acimut(M)
leva(F) di bloccaggio(M) dell'asse(M) orizzontale

極軸クランプ
altitude clamp
Höhenfeststeller(M)
vis(F) de blocage(M) (latitude(F))
palanca(F) de bloqueo(M) de la altura(F)
leva(F) di bloccaggio(M) dell'altezza(F)

赤緯微動ハンドル
azimuth fine adjustment
Azimutfeineinstellung(F)
réglage(M) micrométrique (azimut(M))
ajuste(M) fino del acimut(M)
regolazione(F) micrometrica dell'asse(M) orizzontale

赤経目盛り環
right ascension setting scale
Einstellung(F) der Rektaszensionsachse(F)
cercle(M) d'ascension(F) droite
anillo(M) graduado(M) de ascensión(F) recta
cerchio(M) graduato dell'ascensione(F) retta

極軸微動ハンドル
altitude fine adjustment
Höhenfeineinstellung(F)
réglage(M) micrométrique (latitude(F))
ajuste(M) fino de la altura(F)
regolazione(F) micrometrica dell'altezza(F)

バランス・ウェイト
counterweight
Gegengewicht(N)
contrepoids(M)
contrapeso(M)
contrappeso(M)

フォーク
fork
Gabel(F)
fourche(F)
horquilla(F)
forcella(F)

三角板／載物台
tripod accessories shelf
Stativablage(F)
plateau(M) pour accessoires(M)
repisa(F) para accesorios(M)
mensola(F) portaccessori

三脚
tripod
Stativ(N)
trépied(M)
trípode(M)
treppiede(M)

屈折式望遠鏡の断面図
cross section of a refracting telescope
Linsenfernrohr(N) im Querschnitt(M)
coupe(F) d'une lunette(F) astronomique
sección(F) transversal de un telescopio(M) refractor
sezione(F) di un cannocchiale(M)

接眼レンズ
eyepiece
Okular(N)
oculaire(M)
ocular(M)
oculare(M)

光
light
Licht(N)
lumière(F)
luz(F)
luce(F)

対物レンズ
objective lens
Objektiv(N)
lentille(F) objectif(M)
objetivo(M)
obiettivo(M)

鏡筒
main tube
Tubus(M)
tube(M)
tubo(M) principal
tubo(M) principale

天体観測 | ASTRONOMICAL OBSERVATION
BEOBACHTUNG DES WELTRAUMS | OBSERVATION ASTRONOMIQUE | OBSERVACIÓN ASTRONÓMICA | OSSERVAZIONE ASTRONOMICA

反射(式)望遠鏡

reflecting telescope | Spiegelteleskop[N] | télescope[M] | telescopio[M] reflector | telescopio[M]

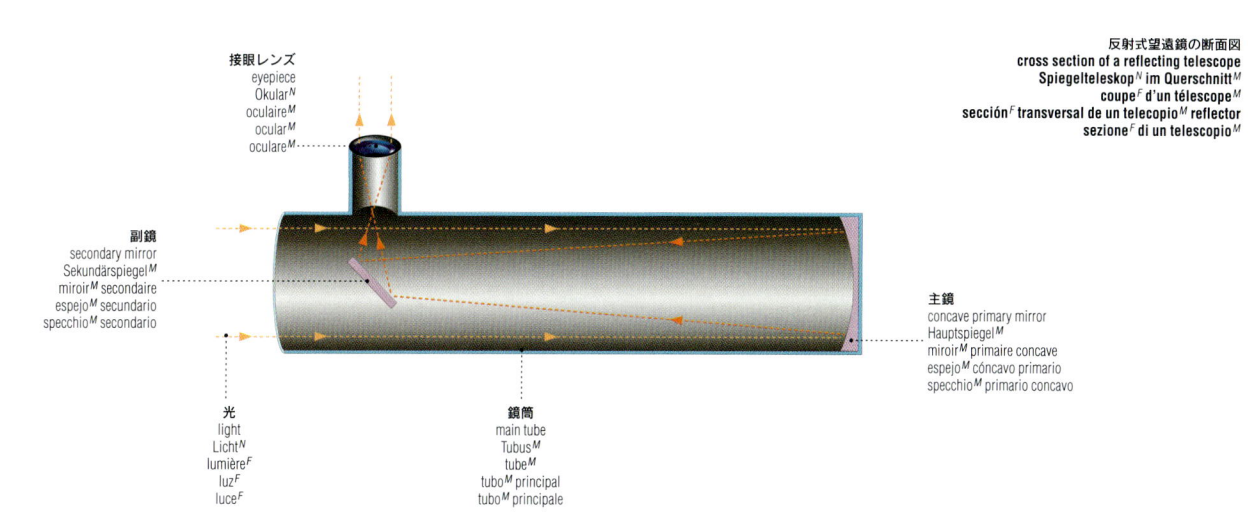

天文学

ファインダー
finderscope
Suchfernrohr[N]
chercheur[M]
anteojo[M] buscador
cannocchiale[M] cercatore

接眼レンズ／アイピース
eyepiece
Okular[N]
oculaire[M]
ocular[M]
oculare[M]

鏡筒バンド
cradle
Wiege[F]
bride[F] de fixation[F]
abrazadera[F]
giogo[M] di supporto[M]

ファインダー支持脚
support
Halterung[F]
support[M] de fixation[F]
soporte[M]
supporto[M]

鏡筒
main tube
Tubus[M]
tube[M]
tubo[M] principal
tubo[M] principale

ピント調節ハンドル
focusing knob
Scharfeinstellung[F]
bouton[M] de mise[F] au point[M]
botón[M] de enfoque[M]
manopola[F] della messa[F] a fuoco[M]

赤経目盛り環
right ascension setting scale
Einstellung der Rektaszensionsachse[F]
cercle[M] d'ascension[F] droite
anillo[M] graduado de ascensión[F] recta
cerchio[M] graduato dell'ascensione[F] retta

赤緯目盛り環
declination setting scale
Einstellung[F] der Deklinationsachse[F]
cercle[M] de déclinaison[F]
anillo[M] graduado de declinación[F]
cerchio[M] graduato della declinazione[F]

赤緯微動ハンドル
azimuth fine adjustment
Azimutfeineinstellung[F]
réglage[M] micrométrique (azimut[M])
ajuste[M] fino del acimut[M]
regolazione[F] micrometrica dell'asse[M] orizzontale

赤緯クランプ
azimuth clamp
Azimutfeststeller[M]
vis[F] de blocage[M] (azimut[M])
palanca[F] de bloqueo[M] del acimut[M]
leva[F] di bloccaggio[M] dell'asse orizzontale

極軸微動ハンドル
altitude fine adjustment
Höhenfeineinstellung[F]
réglage[M] micrométrique (latitude[F])
ajuste[M] fino de la altura[F]
regolazione[F] micrometrica dell'altezza[F]

極軸クランプ
altitude clamp
Höhenfeststeller[M]
vis[F] de blocage[M] (latitude[F])
palanca[F] de bloqueo[M] de la altura[F]
leva[F] di bloccaggio[M] dell'altezza[F]

反射式望遠鏡の断面図
cross section of a reflecting telescope
Spiegelteleskop[N] im Querschnitt[M]
coupe[F] d'un télescope[M]
sección[F] transversal de un telecopio[M] reflector
sezione[F] di un telescopio[M]

接眼レンズ
eyepiece
Okular[N]
oculaire[M]
ocular[M]
oculare[M]

副鏡
secondary mirror
Sekundärspiegel[M]
miroir[M] secondaire
espejo[M] secundario
specchio[M] secondario

主鏡
concave primary mirror
Hauptspiegel[M]
miroir[M] primaire concave
espejo[M] cóncavo primario
specchio[M] primario concavo

光
light
Licht[N]
lumière[F]
luz[F]
luce[F]

鏡筒
main tube
Tubus[M]
tube[M]
tubo[M] principal
tubo[M] principale

15

天体観測 | ASTRONOMICAL OBSERVATION
BEOBACHTUNG DES WELTRAUMS | OBSERVATION ASTRONOMIQUE | OBSERVACIÓN ASTRONÓMICA | OSSERVAZIONE ASTRONOMICA

電波望遠鏡

radio telescope | Radioteleskop[N] | radiotélescope[M] | radiotelescopio[M] | radiotelescopio[M]

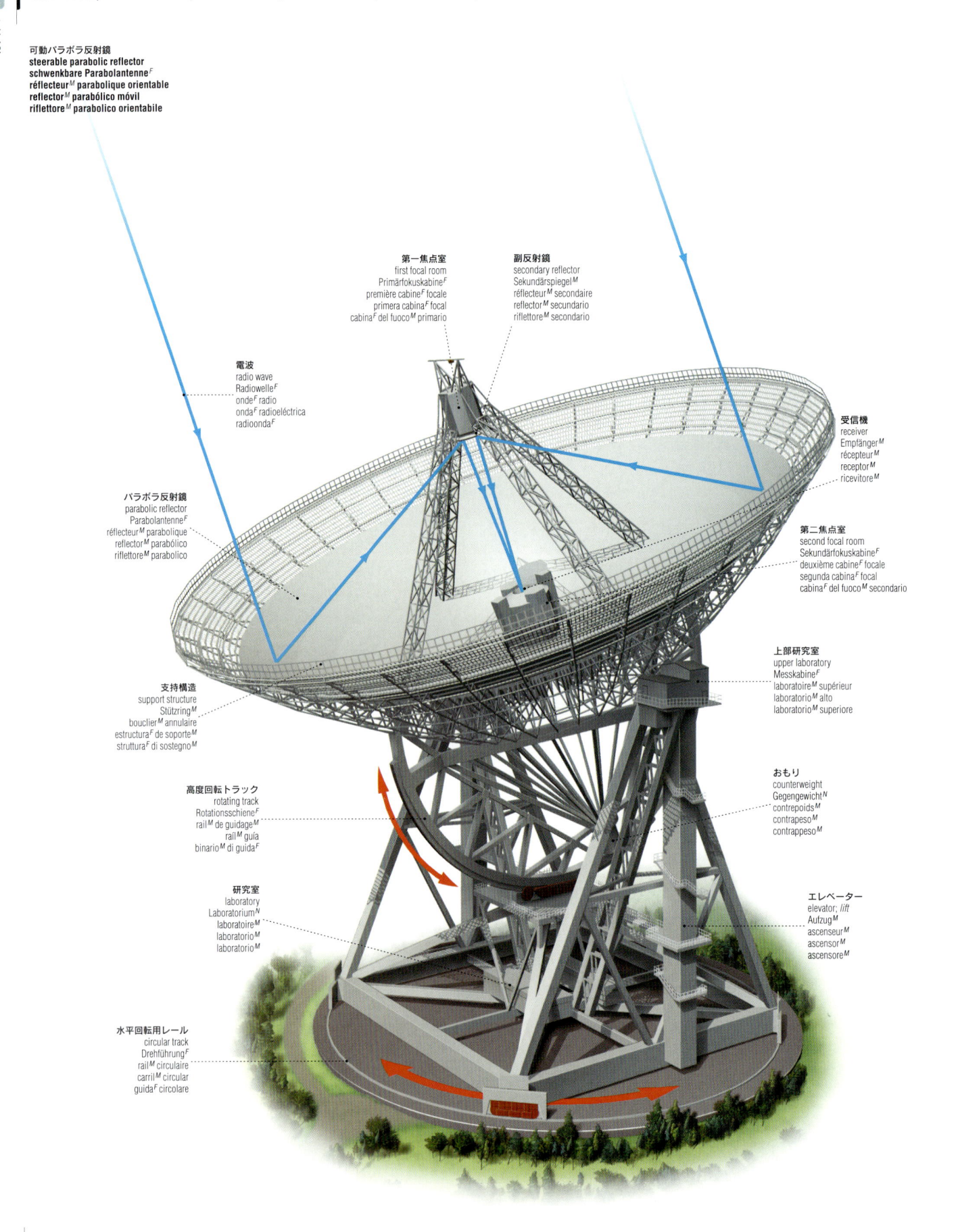

可動パラボラ反射鏡
steerable parabolic reflector
schwenkbare Parabolantenne[F]
réflecteur[M] parabolique orientable
reflector[M] parabólico móvil
riflettore[M] parabolico orientabile

第一焦点室
first focal room
Primärfokuskabine[F]
première cabine[F] focale
primera cabina[F] focal
cabina[F] del fuoco[M] primario

副反射鏡
secondary reflector
Sekundärspiegel[M]
réflecteur[M] secondaire
reflector[M] secundario
riflettore[M] secondario

電波
radio wave
Radiowelle[F]
onde[F] radio
onda[F] radioeléctrica
radioonda[F]

受信機
receiver
Empfänger[M]
récepteur[M]
receptor[M]
ricevitore[M]

パラボラ反射鏡
parabolic reflector
Parabolantenne[F]
réflecteur[M] parabolique
reflector[M] parabólico
riflettore[M] parabolico

第二焦点室
second focal room
Sekundärfokuskabine[F]
deuxième cabine[F] focale
segunda cabina[F] focal
cabina[F] del fuoco[M] secondario

上部研究室
upper laboratory
Messkabine[F]
laboratoire[M] supérieur
laboratorio[M] alto
laboratorio[M] superiore

支持構造
support structure
Stützring[M]
bouclier[M] annulaire
estructura[F] de soporte[M]
struttura[F] di sostegno[M]

高度回転トラック
rotating track
Rotationsschiene[F]
rail[M] de guidage[M]
rail[M] guía
binario[M] di guida[F]

おもり
counterweight
Gegengewicht[N]
contrepoids[M]
contrapeso[M]
contrappeso[M]

研究室
laboratory
Laboratorium[N]
laboratoire[M]
laboratorio[M]
laboratorio[M]

エレベーター
elevator; lift
Aufzug[M]
ascenseur[M]
ascensor[M]
ascensore[M]

水平回転用レール
circular track
Drehführung[F]
rail[M] circulaire
carril[M] circular
guida[F] circolare

16

天体観測 | ASTRONOMICAL OBSERVATION
BEOBACHTUNG DES WELTRAUMS | OBSERVATION ASTRONOMIQUE | OBSERVACIÓN ASTRONÓMICA | OSSERVAZIONE ASTRONOMICA

ハッブル宇宙望遠鏡

Hubble space telescope | Hubble-Weltraumteleskop[N] | télescope[M] spatial Hubble | telescopio[M] espacial Hubble | telescopio[M] spaziale Hubble

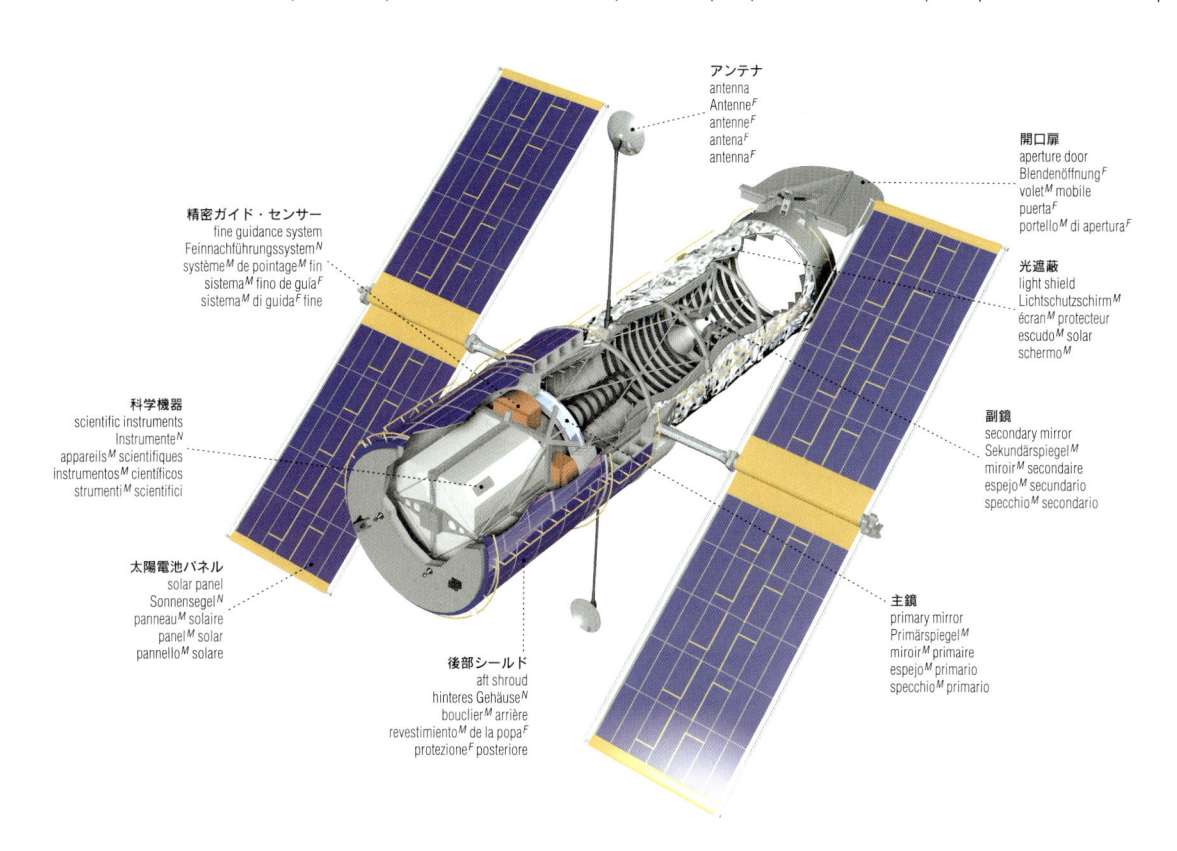

天文学

アンテナ
antenna
Antenne[F]
antenne[F]
antena[F]
antenna[F]

開口扉
aperture door
Blendenöffnung[F]
volet[M] mobile
puerta[F]
portello[M] di apertura[F]

精密ガイド・センサー
fine guidance system
Feinnachführungssystem[N]
système[M] de pointage[M] fin
sistema[M] fino de guía[F]
sistema[M] di guida[F] fine

光遮蔽
light shield
Lichtschutzschirm[M]
écran[M] protecteur
escudo[M] solar
schermo[M]

科学機器
scientific instruments
Instrumente[N]
appareils[M] scientifiques
instrumentos[M] científicos
strumenti[M] scientifici

副鏡
secondary mirror
Sekundärspiegel[M]
miroir[M] secondaire
espejo[M] secundario
specchio[M] secondario

太陽電池パネル
solar panel
Sonnensegel[N]
panneau[M] solaire
panel[M] solar
pannello[M] solare

主鏡
primary mirror
Primärspiegel[M]
miroir[M] primaire
espejo[M] primario
specchio[M] primario

後部シールド
aft shroud
hinteres Gehäuse[N]
bouclier[M] arrière
revestimiento[M] de la popa[F]
protezione[F] posteriore

天文台

astronomical observatory | Sternwarte[F] | observatoire[M] astronomique | observatorio[M] astronómico | osservatorio[M] astronomico

天文台の断面図
cross section of an astronomical observatory
Querschnitt[M] durch eine Sternwarte[F]
coupe[F] d'un observatoire[M] astronomique
sección[F] transversal de un observatorio[M] astronómico
sezione[F] trasversale di un osservatorio[M] astronomico

副鏡
secondary mirror
Sekundärspiegel[M]
miroir[M] secondaire
espejo[M] secundario
specchio[M] secondario

光
light
Licht[N]
lumière[F]
luz[M]
luce[F]

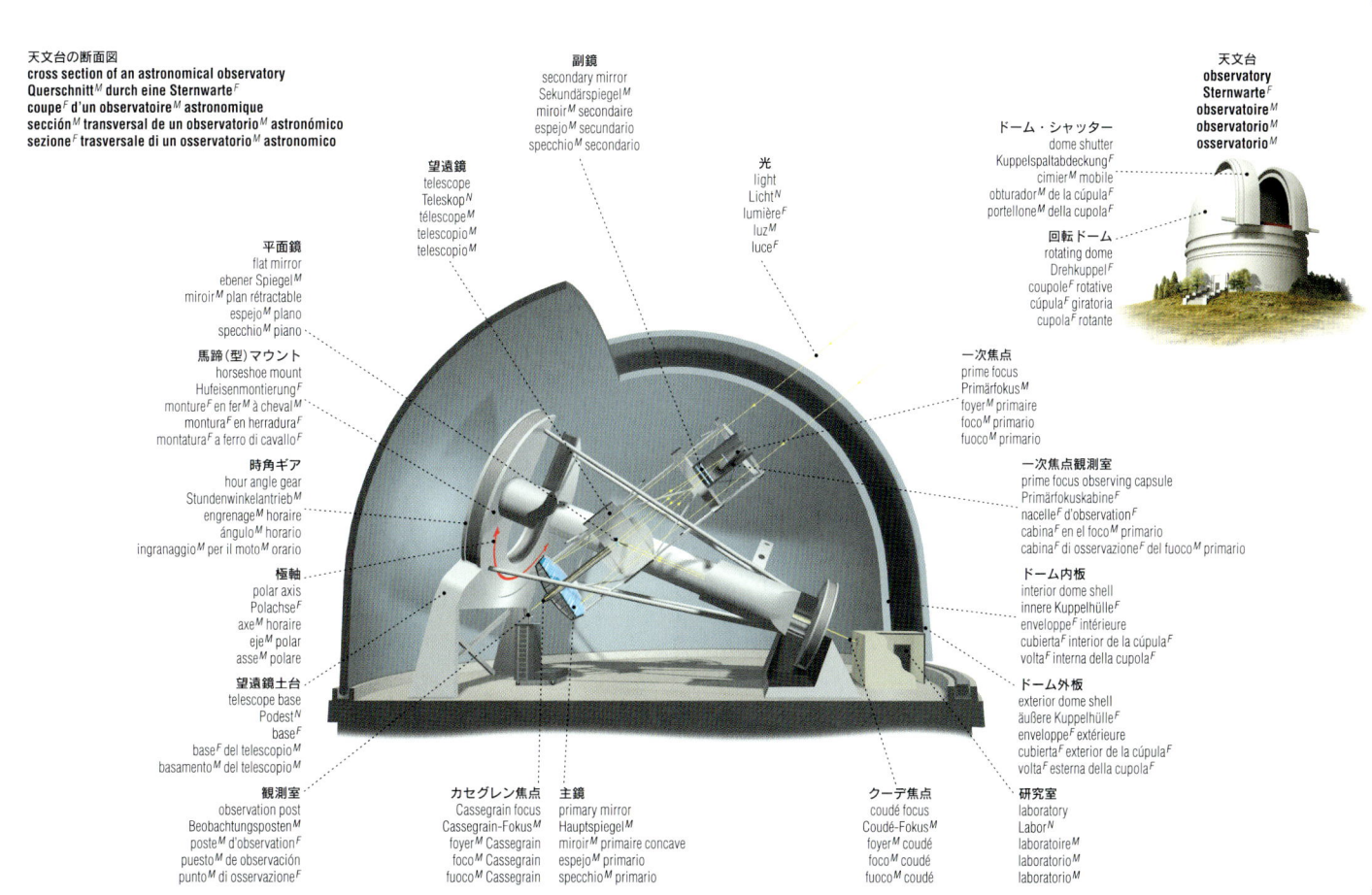

天文台
observatory
Sternwarte[F]
observatoire[M]
observatorio[M]
osservatorio[M]

ドーム・シャッター
dome shutter
Kuppelspaltabdeckung[F]
cimier[M] mobile
obturador[M] de la cúpula[F]
portellone[M] della cupola[F]

望遠鏡
telescope
Teleskop[N]
télescope[M]
telescopio[M]
telescopio[M]

回転ドーム
rotating dome
Drehkuppel[F]
coupole[F] rotative
cúpula[F] giratoria
cupola[F] rotante

平面鏡
flat mirror
ebener Spiegel[M]
miroir[M] plan rétractable
espejo[M] plano
specchio[M] piano

一次焦点
prime focus
Primärfokus[M]
foyer[M] primaire
foco[M] primario
fuoco[M] primario

馬蹄(型)マウント
horseshoe mount
Hufeisenmontierung[F]
monture[F] en fer[M] à cheval[M]
montura[F] en herradura[F]
montatura[F] a ferro di cavallo[F]

一次焦点観測室
prime focus observing capsule
Primärfokuskabine[F]
nacelle[F] d'observation[F]
cabina[F] en el foco[M] primario
cabina[F] di osservazione[F] del fuoco[M] primario

時角ギア
hour angle gear
Stundenwinkelantrieb[M]
engrenage[M] horaire
ángulo[M] horario
ingranaggio[M] per il moto[M] orario

ドーム内板
interior dome shell
innere Kuppelhülle[F]
enveloppe[F] intérieure
cubierta[F] interior de la cúpula[F]
volta[F] interna della cupola[F]

極軸
polar axis
Polachse[F]
axe[M] horaire
eje[M] polar
asse[M] polare

ドーム外板
exterior dome shell
äußere Kuppelhülle[F]
enveloppe[F] extérieure
cubierta[F] exterior de la cúpula[F]
volta[F] esterna della cupola[F]

望遠鏡土台
telescope base
Podest[N]
base[F]
base[F] del telescopio[M]
basamento[M] del telescopio[M]

観測室
observation post
Beobachtungsposten[M]
poste[M] d'observation[F]
puesto[M] de observación[F]
punto[M] di osservazione[F]

カセグレン焦点
Cassegrain focus
Cassegrain-Fokus[M]
foyer[M] Cassegrain
foco[M] Cassegrain
fuoco[M] Cassegrain

主鏡
primary mirror
Hauptspiegel[M]
miroir[M] primaire concave
espejo[M] primario
specchio[M] primario

クーデ焦点
coudé focus
Coudé-Fokus[M]
foyer[M] coudé
foco[M] coudé
fuoco[M] coudé

研究室
laboratory
Labor[N]
laboratoire[M]
laboratorio[M]
laboratorio[M]

宇宙航行学 | ASTRONAUTICS
RAUMFAHRT | ASTRONAUTIQUE | ASTRONÁUTICA | ASTRONAUTICA

宇宙探査機

space probe | Raumsonde^F | sonde^F spatiale | sonda^F espacial | sonda^F spaziale

天文学

日本語 | 英語 | ドイツ語 | フランス語 | スペイン語 | イタリア語

軌道船／オービター（バイキング）
orbiter (Viking)
Orbiter^M (Viking)
orbiteur^M (Viking)
módulo^M orbital (Viking)
modulo^M orbitante (Viking)

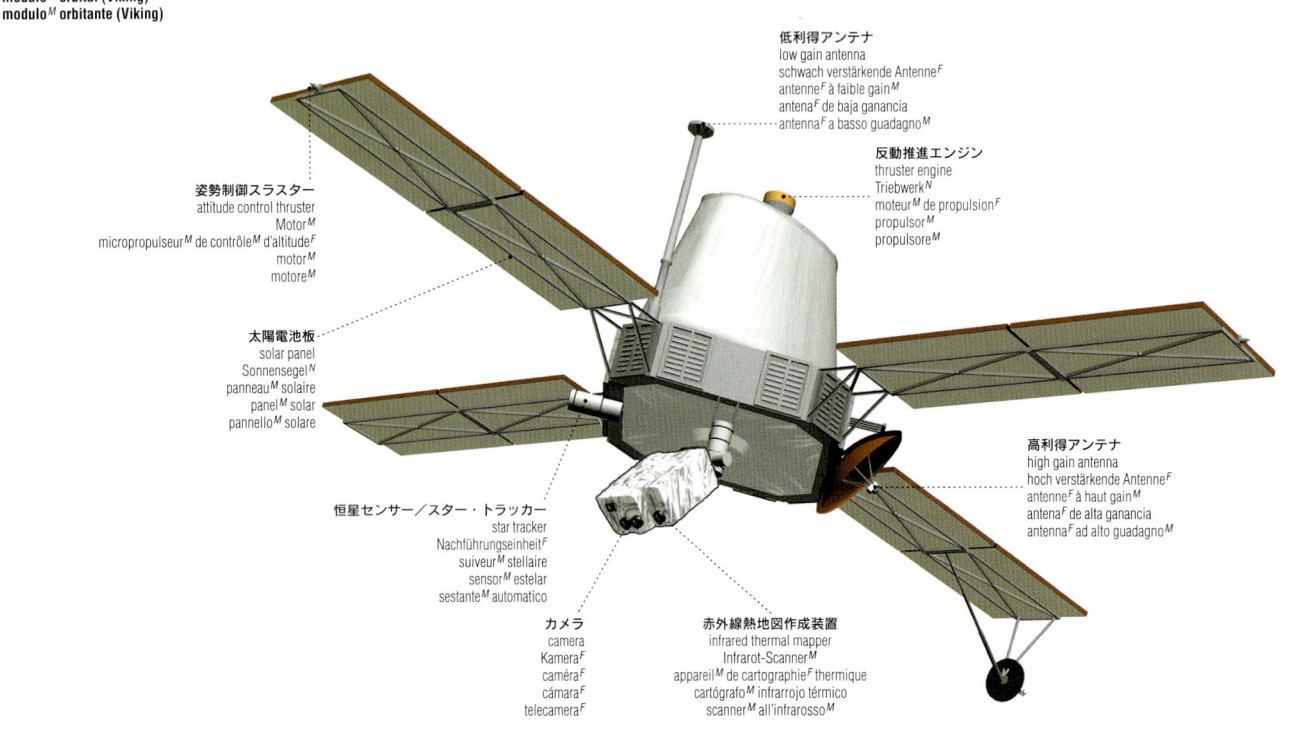

低利得アンテナ
low gain antenna
schwach verstärkende Antenne^F
antenne^F à faible gain^M
antena^F de baja ganancia
antenna^F a basso guadagno^M

反動推進エンジン
thruster engine
Triebwerk^N
moteur^M de propulsion^F
propulsor^M
propulsore^M

姿勢制御スラスター
attitude control thruster
Motor^M
micropropulseur^M de contrôle^M d'altitude^F
motor^M
motore^M

太陽電池板
solar panel
Sonnensegel^N
panneau^M solaire
panel^M solar
pannello^M solare

恒星センサー／スター・トラッカー
star tracker
Nachführungseinheit^F
suiveur^M stellaire
sensor^M estelar
sestante^M automatico

高利得アンテナ
high gain antenna
hoch verstärkende Antenne^F
antenne^F à haut gain^M
antena^F de alta ganancia
antenna^F ad alto guadagno^M

カメラ
camera
Kamera^F
caméra^F
cámara^F
telecamera^F

赤外線熱地図作成装置
infrared thermal mapper
Infrarot-Scanner^M
appareil^M de cartographie^F thermique
cartógrafo^M infrarrojo térmico
scanner^M all'infrarosso^M

着陸船（バイキング）
lander (Viking)
Landemodul^N (Viking)
atterrisseur^M (Viking)
módulo^M de aterrizaje^M (Viking)
modulo^M di atterraggio^M (Viking)

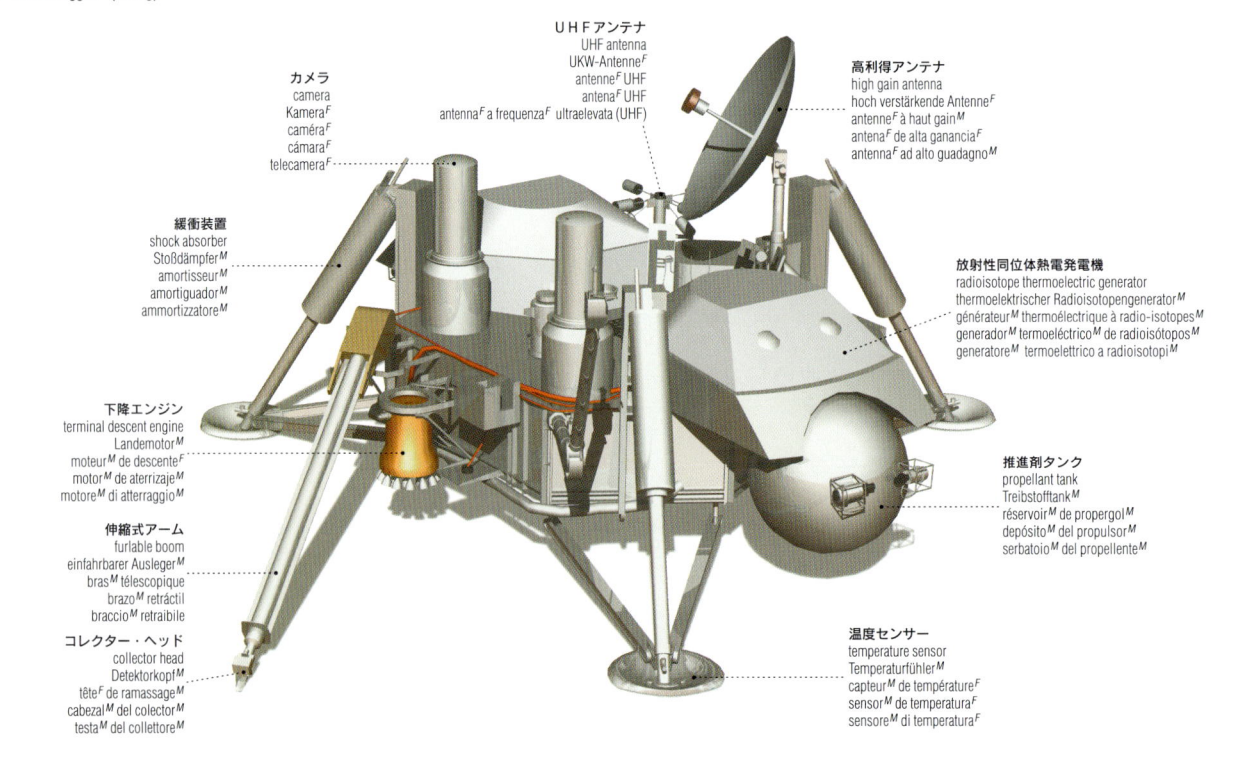

UHFアンテナ
UHF antenna
UKW-Antenne^F
antenne^F UHF
antena^F UHF
antenna^F a frequenza^F ultraelevata (UHF)

高利得アンテナ
high gain antenna
hoch verstärkende Antenne^F
antenne^F à haut gain^M
antena^F de alta ganancia^F
antenna^F ad alto guadagno^M

カメラ
camera
Kamera^F
caméra^F
cámara^F
telecamera^F

緩衝装置
shock absorber
Stoßdämpfer^M
amortisseur^M
amortiguador^M
ammortizzatore^M

放射性同位体熱電発電機
radioisotope thermoelectric generator
thermoelektrischer Radioisotopengenerator^M
générateur^M thermoélectrique à radio-isotopes^M
generador^M termoeléctrico de radioisótopos^M
generatore^M termoelettrico a radioisotopi^M

下降エンジン
terminal descent engine
Landemotor^M
moteur^M de descente^F
motor^M de aterrizaje^M
motore^M di atterraggio^M

推進剤タンク
propellant tank
Treibstofftank^M
réservoir^M de propergol^M
depósito^M del propulsor^M
serbatoio^M del propellente^M

伸縮式アーム
furlable boom
einfahrbarer Ausleger^M
bras^M télescopique
brazo^M retráctil
braccio^M retraibile

コレクター・ヘッド
collector head
Detektorkopf^M
tête^F de ramassage^M
cabezal^M del colector^M
testa^M del collettore^M

温度センサー
temperature sensor
Temperaturfühler^M
capteur^M de température^F
sensor^M de temperatura^F
sensore^M di temperatura^F

宇宙航行学 | ASTRONAUTICS
RAUMFAHRT | ASTRONAUTIQUE | ASTRONÁUTICA | ASTRONAUTICA

宇宙探査機

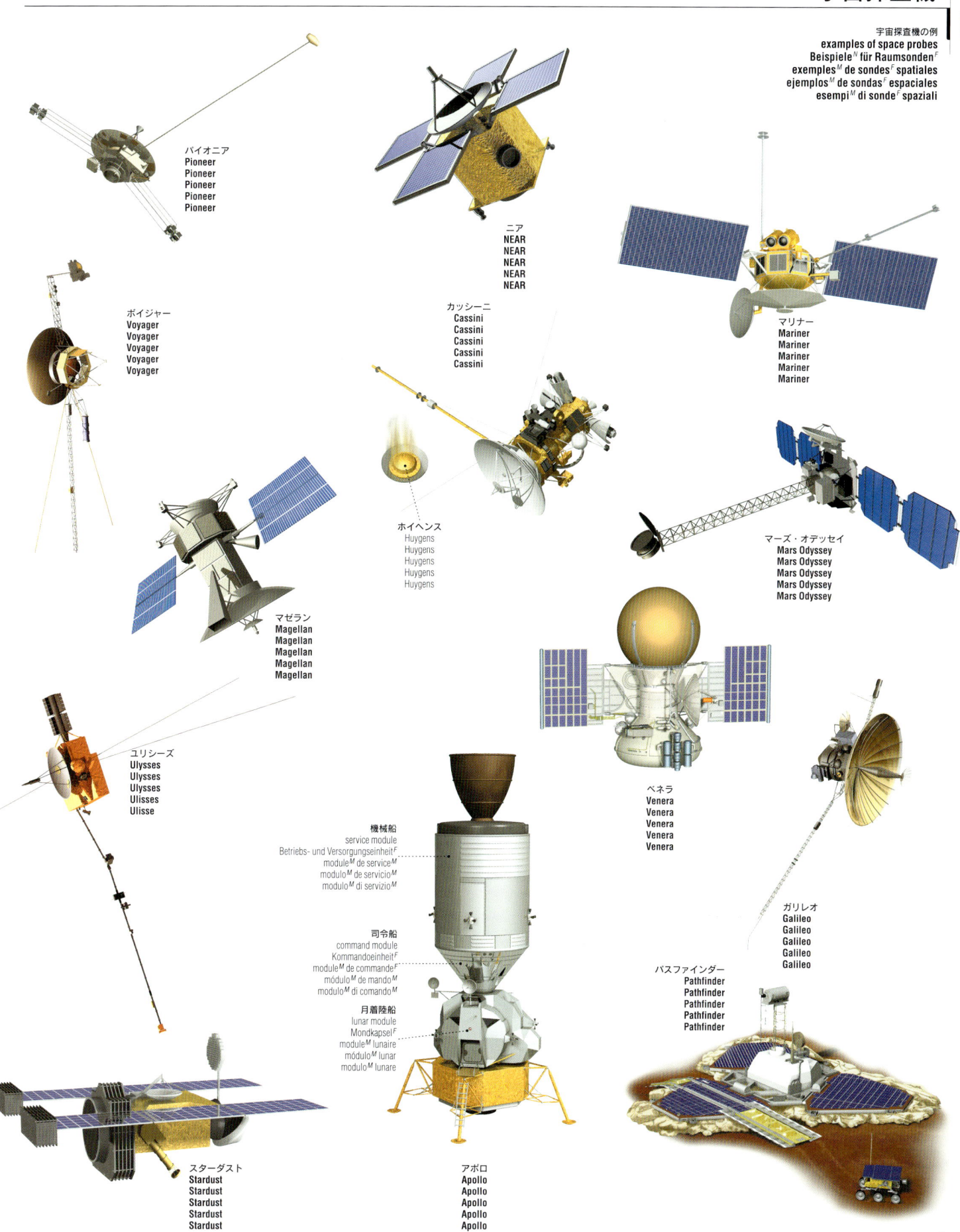

宇宙探査機の例
examples of space probes
Beispiele^N für Raumsonden^F
exemples^M de sondes^F spatiales
ejemplos^M de sondas^F espaciales
esempi^M di sonde^F spaziali

天文学

パイオニア
Pioneer
Pioneer
Pioneer
Pioneer
Pioneer

ニア
NEAR
NEAR
NEAR
NEAR
NEAR

ボイジャー
Voyager
Voyager
Voyager
Voyager
Voyager

カッシーニ
Cassini
Cassini
Cassini
Cassini
Cassini

マリナー
Mariner
Mariner
Mariner
Mariner
Mariner

ホイヘンス
Huygens
Huygens
Huygens
Huygens
Huygens

マーズ・オデッセイ
Mars Odyssey
Mars Odyssey
Mars Odyssey
Mars Odyssey
Mars Odyssey

マゼラン
Magellan
Magellan
Magellan
Magellan
Magellan

ベネラ
Venera
Venera
Venera
Venera
Venera

ユリシーズ
Ulysses
Ulysses
Ulysses
Ulisses
Ulisse

機械船
service module
Betriebs- und Versorgungseinheit^F
module^M de service^M
modulo^M de servicio^M
modulo^M di servizio^M

司令船
command module
Kommandoeinheit^F
module^M de commande^F
módulo^M de mando^M
modulo^M di comando^M

月着陸船
lunar module
Mondkapsel^F
module^M lunaire
módulo^M lunar
modulo^M lunare

ガリレオ
Galileo
Galileo
Galileo
Galileo
Galileo

パスファインダー
Pathfinder
Pathfinder
Pathfinder
Pathfinder
Pathfinder

スターダスト
Stardust
Stardust
Stardust
Stardust
Stardust

アポロ
Apollo
Apollo
Apollo
Apollo
Apollo

19

宇宙航行学 | ASTRONAUTICS
RAUMFAHRT | ASTRONAUTIQUE | ASTRONÁUTICA | ASTRONAUTICA

宇宙服

spacesuit | Raumanzug^M | scaphandre^M spatial | traje^M espacial | tuta^F spaziale

天文学

日本語 | 英語 | ドイツ語 | フランス語 | スペイン語 | イタリア語

35mm静止カメラ
35 mm still camera
35mm-Fotoapparat^M
appareil^M photographique 35 mm
cámara^F rígida de 35 mm
fotocamera^F 35 mm

ヘルメット接続リング
helmet ring
Ringverschluss^M
collier^M de serrage^M du casque^M
anillo^M de unión^M del casco^M
collare^M di chiusura^F del casco^M

コンピューター画面明度調節装置
computer screen intensity controls
Helligkeitsregelung^F des Computerbildschirms^M
réglage^M de l'écran^M de l'ordinateur^M
controles^M de intensidad^F de la pantalla^F del ordenador^M
regolazione^F della luminosità^F dello schermo^M del computer^M

交信音量調節装置
communications volume controls
Lautstärkeregler^M des Funkübertragungssystems^N
réglage^M du volume^M des communications^F
controles^M de volumen^M de comunicaciones^F
regolazione^F del livello^M sonoro delle comunicazioni^F

手袋
glove
Handschuh^M
gant^M
guante^M
guanto^M

命綱
safety tether
Sicherheitsriemen^M
attache^F de sécurité^F
correa^F de seguridad^F
attacco^M di sicurezza^F

推進装置
thruster
Schubdüse^F
propulseur^M
propulsor^M
propulsore^M

生命維持装置
life support system
Lebenserhaltungssystem^N
équipement^M de survie^F
sistema^M de soporte^M vital
sistema^M di sopravvivenza^F

バイザー
solar shield
Sonnenschutzschicht^F
visière^F antisolaire
protector^M solar
visiera^F antisolare

ヘルメット
helmet
Helm^M
casque^M
casco^M
casco^M

カラー・テレビ・カメラ
color television camera; colour television camera
Farbfernsehkamera^F
caméra^F de télévision^F couleur
cámara^F de televisión^F en color^M
telecamera^F a colori^M

手順チェックリスト
procedure checklist
Checkliste^F
aide-mémoire^M des procédures^F
lista^F de procedimientos^M
lista^F di controllo^M delle procedure^F

工具綱
tool tether
Werkzeughalter^M
attache^F pour outils^M
correa^F para herramientas^F
attacco^M per attrezzi^M

リーディング・ミラー
reading mirror
Spiegel^M
miroir^M de lecture^F
espejo^M de lectura^F
specchio^M di lettura^F

生命維持装置制御ユニット
life support system controls
Steuerung^F des Lebenserhaltungssystems^N
contrôles^M de l'équipement^M de survie^F
controles^M del sistema^M de soporte^M vital
regolazione^F del sistema^M di sopravvivenza^F

体温調節装置
body temperature control unit
Körpertemperaturregelung^F
contrôle^M de la température^F du corps^M
unidad^F de control^M de la temperatura^F del cuerpo^M
regolazione^F della temperatura^F corporea

酸素圧制御装置
oxygen pressure actuator
Sauerstoffdruck-Stelleinrichtung^F
réglage^M de la pression^F d'oxygène^M
accionador^M de presión^F del oxígeno^M
regolazione^F della pressione^F dell'ossigeno^M

有人移動ユニット
manned maneuvering unit; manned manœuvring unit
bemannte Manövriereinheit^F
véhicule^M spatial autonome
unidad^F para maniobras^F en el espacio^M
unità^F individuale di propulsione^F e manovra^F

下部トルソ
protection layer
Schutzschicht^F
revêtement^M de sécurité^F
capa^F protectora
strato^M protettivo

宇宙航行学 | ASTRONAUTICS
RAUMFAHRT | ASTRONAUTIQUE | ASTRONÁUTICA | ASTRONAUTICA

国際宇宙ステーション

international space station | internationale Raumstation^F | station^F spatiale internationale | estación^F espacial internacional | stazione^F spaziale internazionale

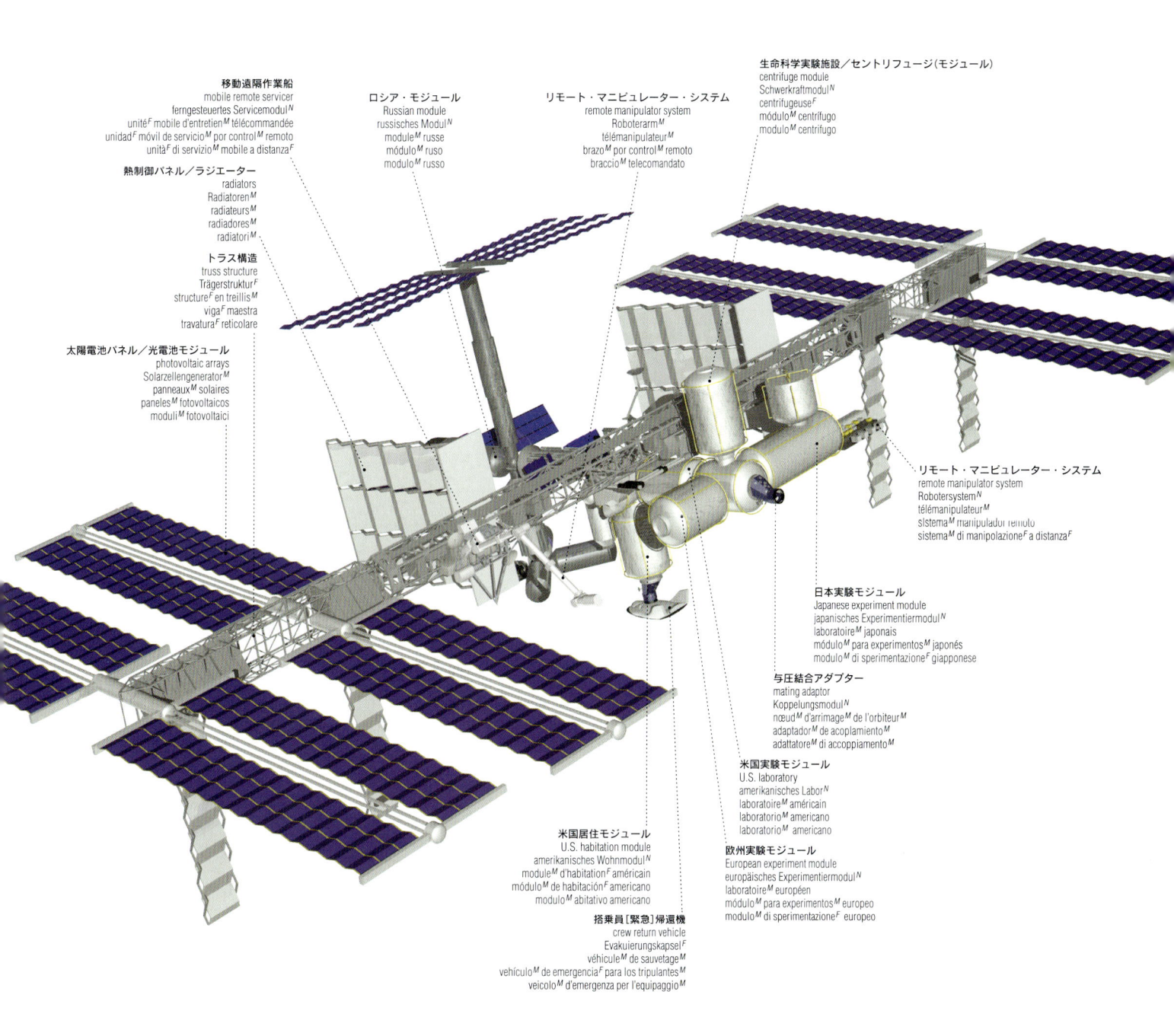

移動遠隔作業船
mobile remote servicer
ferngesteuertes Servicemodul^N
unité^F mobile d'entretien^M télécommandée
unidad^F móvil de servicio^M por control^M remoto
unità^F di servizio^M mobile a distanza^F

熱制御パネル／ラジエーター
radiators
Radiatoren^M
radiateurs^M
radiadores^M
radiatori^M

トラス構造
truss structure
Trägerstruktur^F
structure^F en treillis^M
viga^F maestra
travatura^F reticolare

太陽電池パネル／光電池モジュール
photovoltaic arrays
Solarzellengenerator^M
panneaux^M solaires
paneles^M fotovoltaicos
moduli^M fotovoltaici

ロシア・モジュール
Russian module
russisches Modul^N
module^M russe
módulo^M ruso
modulo^M russo

リモート・マニピュレーター・システム
remote manipulator system
Roboterarm^M
télémanipulateur^M
brazo^M por control^M remoto
braccio^M telecomandato

生命科学実験施設／セントリフュージ(モジュール)
centrifuge module
Schwerkraftmodul^N
centrifugeuse^F
módulo^M centrífugo
modulo^M centrifugo

リモート・マニピュレーター・システム
remote manipulator system
Robotersystem^N
télémanipulateur^M
sistema^M manipulador remoto
sistema^M di manipolazione^F a distanza^F

日本実験モジュール
Japanese experiment module
japanisches Experimentiermodul^N
laboratoire^M japonais
módulo^M para experimentos^M japonés
modulo^M di sperimentazione^F giapponese

与圧結合アダプター
mating adaptor
Koppelungsmodul^N
nœud^M d'arrimage^M de l'orbiteur^M
adaptador^M de acoplamiento^M
adattatore^M di accoppiamento^M

米国実験モジュール
U.S. laboratory
amerikanisches Labor^N
laboratoire^M américain
laboratorio^M americano
laboratorio^M americano

欧州実験モジュール
European experiment module
europäisches Experimentiermodul^N
laboratoire^M européen
módulo^M para experimentos^M europeo
modulo^M di sperimentazione^F europeo

米国居住モジュール
U.S. habitation module
amerikanisches Wohnmodul^N
module^M d'habitation^F américain
módulo^M de habitación^F americano
modulo^M abitativo americano

搭乗員[緊急]帰還機
crew return vehicle
Evakuierungskapsel^F
véhicule^M de sauvetage^M
vehículo^M de emergencia^F para los tripulantes^M
veicolo^M d'emergenza per l'equipaggio^M

天文学

宇宙航行学 | ASTRONAUTICS
RAUMFAHRT | ASTRONAUTIQUE | ASTRONÁUTICA | ASTRONAUTICA

スペース・シャトル

space shuttle | Raumfähre^F | navette^F spatiale | transbordador^M espacial | navetta^F spaziale

日本語 | 英語 | ドイツ語 | フランス語 | スペイン語 | イタリア語

天文学

発射時のスペース・シャトル
space shuttle at takeoff
Raumfähre^F beim Start^M
navette^F spatiale au décollage^M
transbordador^M espacial en posición^F de lanzamiento^M
navetta^F spaziale al decollo^M

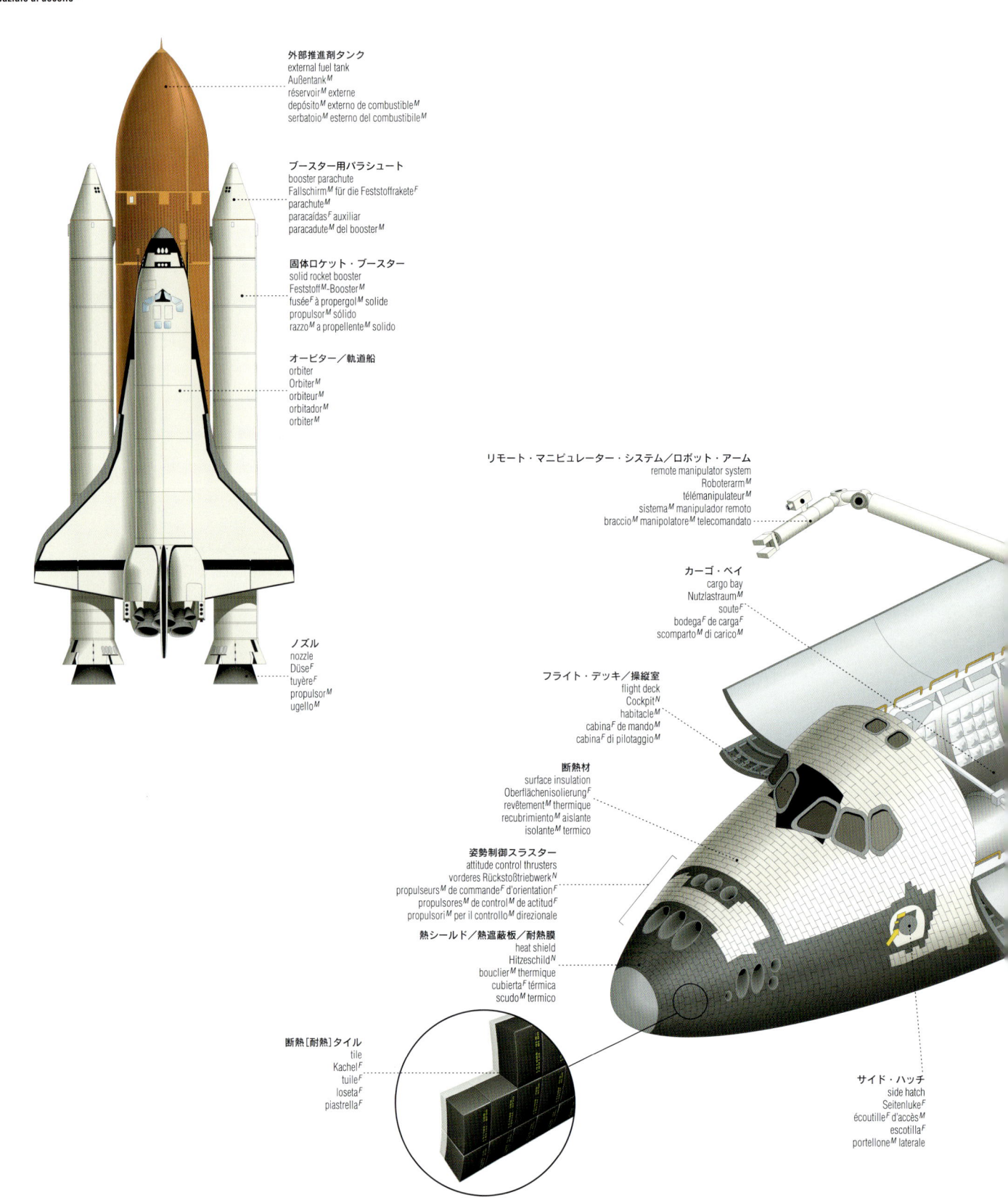

外部推進剤タンク
external fuel tank
Außentank^M
réservoir^M externe
depósito^M externo de combustible^M
serbatoio^M esterno del combustibile^M

ブースター用パラシュート
booster parachute
Fallschirm^M für die Feststoffrakete^F
parachute^M
paracaídas^F auxiliar
paracadute^M del booster^M

固体ロケット・ブースター
solid rocket booster
Feststoff^M-Booster^M
fusée^F à propergol^M solide
propulsor^M sólido
razzo^M a propellente^M solido

オービター／軌道船
orbiter
Orbiter^M
orbiteur^M
orbitador^M
orbiter^M

リモート・マニピュレーター・システム／ロボット・アーム
remote manipulator system
Roboterarm^M
télémanipulateur^M
sistema^M manipulador remoto
braccio^M manipolatore^M telecomandato

カーゴ・ベイ
cargo bay
Nutzlastraum^M
soute^F
bodega^F de carga^F
scomparto^M di carico^M

ノズル
nozzle
Düse^F
tuyère^F
propulsor^M
ugello^M

フライト・デッキ／操縦室
flight deck
Cockpit^N
habitacle^N
cabina^F de mando^M
cabina^F di pilotaggio^M

断熱材
surface insulation
Oberflächenisolierung^F
revêtement^M thermique
recubrimiento^M aislante
isolante^M termico

姿勢制御スラスター
attitude control thrusters
vorderes Rückstoßtriebwerk^N
propulseurs^M de commande^F d'orientation^F
propulsores^M de control^M de actitud^F
propulsori^M per il controllo^M direzionale

熱シールド／熱遮蔽板／耐熱膜
heat shield
Hitzeschild^N
bouclier^M thermique
cubierta^F térmica
scudo^M termico

断熱［耐熱］タイル
tile
Kachel^F
tuile^F
loseta^F
piastrella^F

サイド・ハッチ
side hatch
Seitenluke^F
écoutille^F d'accès^M
escotilla^F
portellone^M laterale

22

宇宙航行学 | ASTRONAUTICS
RAUMFAHRT | ASTRONAUTIQUE | ASTRONÁUTICA | ASTRONAUTICA

スペース・シャトル

天文学

オービター／軌道船
orbiter
Orbiter[M]
orbiteur[M]
orbitador[M]
orbiter[M]

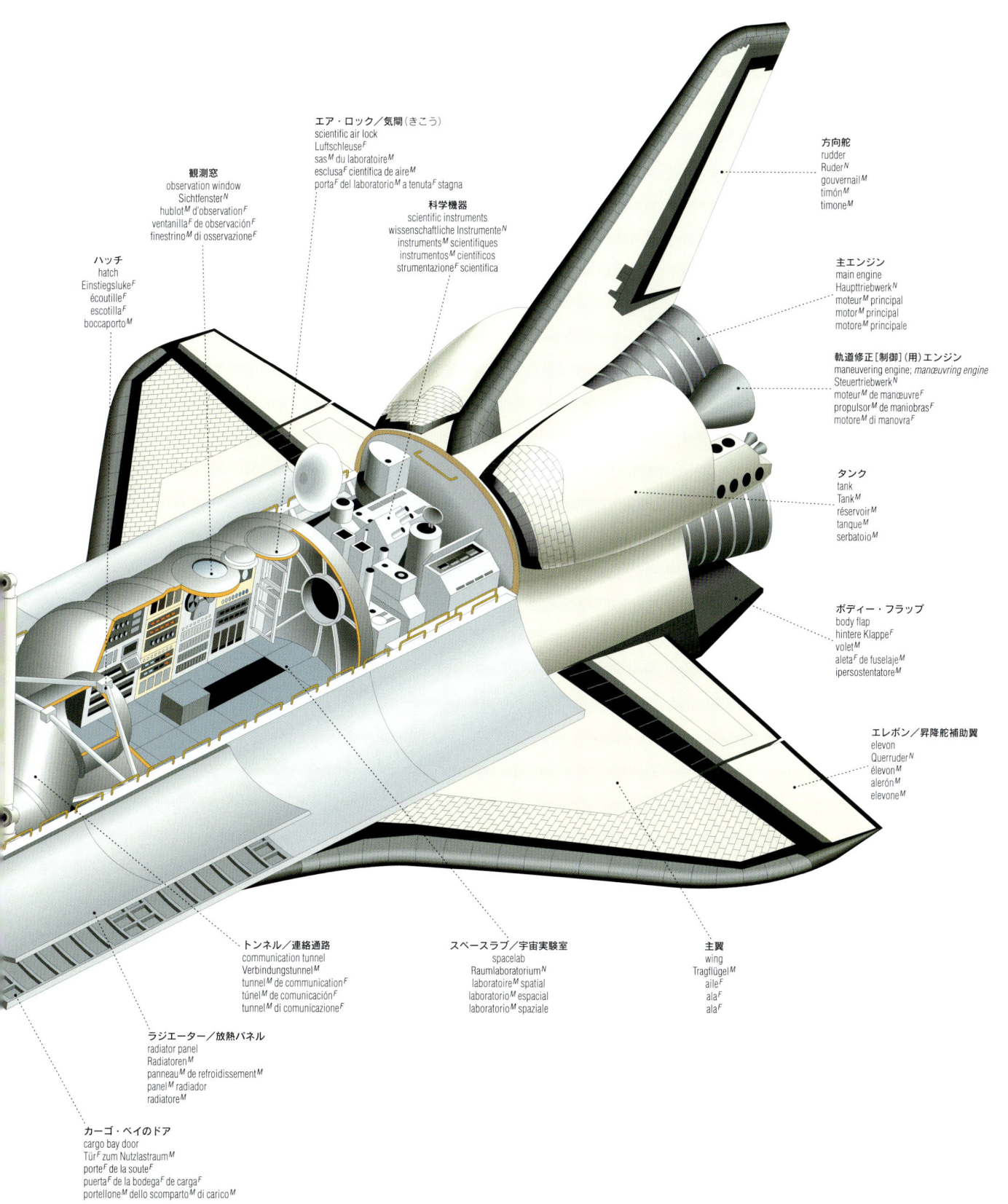

観測窓
observation window
Sichtfenster[N]
hublot[M] d'observation
ventanilla[F] de observación
finestrino[M] di osservazione

エア・ロック／気間（きこう）
scientific air lock
Luftschleuse[F]
sas[M] du laboratoire[M]
esclusa[F] científica de aire[M]
porta[F] del laboratorio[M] a tenuta[F] stagna

科学機器
scientific instruments
wissenschaftliche Instrumente[N]
instruments[M] scientifiques
instrumentos[M] científicos
strumentazione[F] scientifica

方向舵
rudder
Ruder[N]
gouvernail[M]
timón[M]
timone[M]

主エンジン
main engine
Haupttriebwerk[N]
moteur[M] principal
motor[M] principal
motore[M] principale

軌道修正[制御]（用）エンジン
maneuvering engine; manœuvring engine
Steuertriebwerk[N]
moteur[M] de manœuvre
propulsor[M] de maniobras[F]
motore[M] di manovra[F]

ハッチ
hatch
Einstiegsluke[F]
écoutille[F]
escotilla[F]
boccaporto[M]

タンク
tank
Tank[M]
réservoir[M]
tanque[M]
serbatoio[M]

ボディー・フラップ
body flap
hintere Klappe[F]
volet[M]
aleta[F] de fuselaje[M]
ipersostentatore[M]

エレボン／昇降舵補助翼
elevon
Querruder[N]
élevon[M]
alerón[M]
elevone[M]

トンネル／連絡通路
communication tunnel
Verbindungstunnel[M]
tunnel[M] de communication[F]
túnel[M] de comunicación[F]
tunnel[M] di comunicazione[F]

スペースラブ／宇宙実験室
spacelab
Raumlaboratorium[N]
laboratoire[M] spatial
laboratorio[M] espacial
laboratorio[M] spaziale

主翼
wing
Tragflügel[M]
aile[F]
ala[F]
ala[F]

ラジエーター／放熱パネル
radiator panel
Radiatoren[M]
panneau[M] de refroidissement[M]
panel[M] radiador[M]
radiatore[M]

カーゴ・ベイのドア
cargo bay door
Tür[F] zum Nutzlastraum[M]
porte[F] de la soute[F]
puerta[F] de la bodega[F] de carga[F]
portellone[M] dello scomparto[M] di carico[M]

23

宇宙航行学 | ASTRONAUTICS
RAUMFAHRT | ASTRONAUTIQUE | ASTRONÁUTICA | ASTRONAUTICA

打ち上げロケット

日本語 | 英語 | ドイツ語 | フランス語 | スペイン語 | イタリア語

space launcher | TrägerraketeF | lanceurM spatial | coheteM espacial | razzoM spaziale

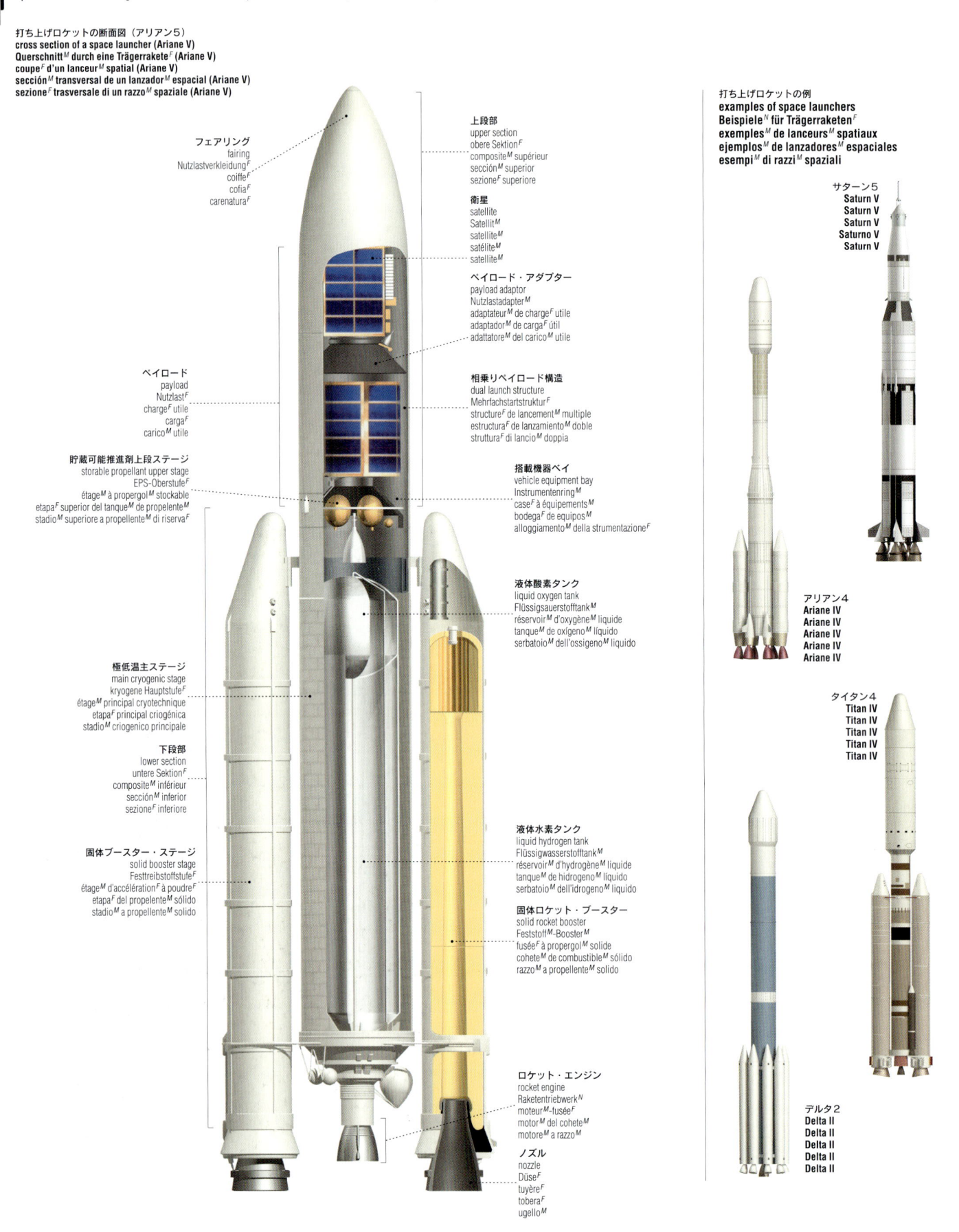

打ち上げロケットの断面図（アリアン5）
cross section of a space launcher (Ariane V)
QuerschnittM durch eine TrägerraketeF (Ariane V)
coupeF d'un lanceurM spatial (Ariane V)
secciónF transversal de un lanzadorM espacial (Ariane V)
sezioneF trasversale di un razzoM spaziale (Ariane V)

フェアリング
fairing
NutzlastverkleidungF
coiffeF
cofiaF
carenaturaF

上段部
upper section
obere SektionF
compositeM supérieur
secciónM superior
sezioneF superiore

衛星
satellite
SatellitM
satelliteM
satéliteM
satelliteM

ペイロード・アダプター
payload adaptor
NutzlastadapterM
adaptateurM de chargeF utile
adaptadorM de cargaF útil
adattatoreM del caricoM utile

ペイロード
payload
NutzlastF
chargeF utile
cargaF
caricoM utile

相乗りペイロード構造
dual launch structure
MehrfachstartstrukturF
structureF de lancementM multiple
estructuraF de lanzamientoM doble
strutturaF di lancioM doppia

貯蔵可能推進剤上段ステージ
storable propellant upper stage
EPS-OberstufeF
étageM à propergolM stockable
etapaF superior del tanqueM de propelenteM
stadioM superiore a propellenteM di riservaF

搭載機器ベイ
vehicle equipment bay
InstrumentenringM
caseF à équipementsM
bodegaF de equiposM
alloggiamentoM della strumentazioneF

液体酸素タンク
liquid oxygen tank
FlüssigsauerstofftankM
réservoirM d'oxygèneM liquide
tanqueM de oxígenoM líquido
serbatoioM dell'ossigenoM liquido

極低温主ステージ
main cryogenic stage
kryogene HauptstufeF
étageM principal cryotechnique
etapaF principal criogénica
stadioM criogenico principale

下段部
lower section
untere SektionF
compositeM inférieur
secciónM inferior
sezioneF inferiore

液体水素タンク
liquid hydrogen tank
FlüssigwasserstofftankM
réservoirM d'hydrogèneM liquide
tanqueM de hidrogenoM líquido
serbatoioM dell'idrogenoM liquido

固体ブースター・ステージ
solid booster stage
FesttreibstoffstufeF
étageM d'accélérationF à poudreF
etapaF del propelenteM sólido
stadioM a propellenteM solido

固体ロケット・ブースター
solid rocket booster
FeststoffM-BoosterM
fuséeF à propergolM solide
coheteM de combustibleM sólido
razzoM a propellenteM solido

ロケット・エンジン
rocket engine
RaketentriebwerkN
moteurM-fuséeF
motorM del coheteM
motoreM a razzoM

ノズル
nozzle
DüseF
tuyèreF
toberaF
ugelloM

打ち上げロケットの例
examples of space launchers
BeispieleN für TrägerraketenF
exemplesM de lanceursM spatiaux
ejemplosM de lanzadoresM espaciales
esempiM di razziM spaziali

サターン5
Saturn V
Saturn V
Saturn V
Saturno V
Saturn V

アリアン4
Ariane IV
Ariane IV
Ariane IV
Ariane IV
Ariane IV

タイタン4
Titan IV
Titan IV
Titan IV
Titan IV
Titan IV

デルタ2
Delta II
Delta II
Delta II
Delta II
Delta II

宇宙航行学 | ASTRONAUTICS
RAUMFAHRT | ASTRONAUTIQUE | ASTRONÁUTICA | ASTRONAUTICA

打ち上げロケット

打ち上げロケットの断面図（サターン5）
cross section of a space launcher (Saturn V)
Querschnitt^M durch eine Trägerrakete^F (Saturn V)
coupe^F d'un lanceur^M spatial (Saturn V)
sección^M transversal de un lanzador^M espacial (Saturn V)
sezione^F trasversale di un razzo^M spaziale (Saturn V)

天文学

緊急脱出システム
launch escape system
Rettungsturm^M für die Startphase^F
tour^F de sauvetage^M
torre^F de escape^M
sistema^M di uscita^F d'emergenza^F

司令船
command module
Kommandokapsel^F
module^M de commande^F
módulo^M de mando^M
modulo^M di comando^M

機械船
service module
Versorgungskapsel^F
module^M de service^M
módulo^M de servicio^M
modulo^M di servizio^M

月着陸船
lunar module
Mondlandeeinheit^F
module^M lunaire
módulo^M lunar
modulo^M lunare

計器ユニット
instrument unit
Instrumenteneinheit^F
bloc^M d'équipement^M
unidad^F de instrumentos^M
equipaggiamento^M di guida^F

ヘリウム気蓄器
helium sphere
Heliumsphäre^F
sphère^F d'hélium^M
esfera^F de helio^M
serbatoio^M dell'elio^M

J2エンジン
J-2 engine
J-2-Triebwerk^N
moteur^M J-2
propulsor J-2^M
motore^M J-2

液体水素タンク
liquid hydrogen tank
Flüssigwasserstofftank^M
réservoir^M d'hydrogène^M liquide
tanque^M de hidrógeno^M líquido
serbatoio^M dell'idrogeno^M liquido

液体酸素タンク
liquid oxygen tank
Flüssigsauerstofftank^M
réservoir^M d'oxygène^M liquide
tanque^M de oxígeno^M líquido
serbatoio^M dell'ossigeno^M liquido

液体酸素タンク隔壁
liquid oxygen tank baffle
Schlingerwand^F
déflecteur^M de réservoir^M d'oxygène^M liquide
deflector^M del tanque^M de oxígeno^M liquido
diaframma^M del serbatoio^M dell'ossigeno^M liquido

燃料[ケロシン]タンク
kerosene tank
Kerosintank^M
réservoir^M de kérosène^M
tanque^M de keroseno^M
serbatoio^M del kerosene^M

燃料移送パイプ
fuel transfer pipe
Kraftstoffschlauch^M
conduite^F de transfert^M de carburant^M
tubería^F de conducción^F de carburante^M
tubo^M di trasferimento^M del carburante^M

安定板
stabilizing fin
Stabilisierungsflosse^F
empennage^M de stabilisation^F
estabilizador^M
pinna^F stabilizzatrice

ノズル
nozzle
Düse^F
tuyère^F
propulsor^M
ugello^M

F1エンジン
F-1 engine
F-1-Triebwerk^N
moteur^M F-1
propulsor F-1^M
motore^M F-1

ペイロード
payload
Nutzlast^F
charge^F utile
carga^F útil
carico^M utile

第3段
third stage
dritte Stufe^F
troisième étage^M
tercera etapa^F
terzo stadio^M

第2段
second stage
zweite Stufe^F
deuxième étage^M
segunda etapa^F
secondo stadio^M

第1段
first stage
erste Stufe^F
premier étage^M
primera etapa^F
primo stadio^M

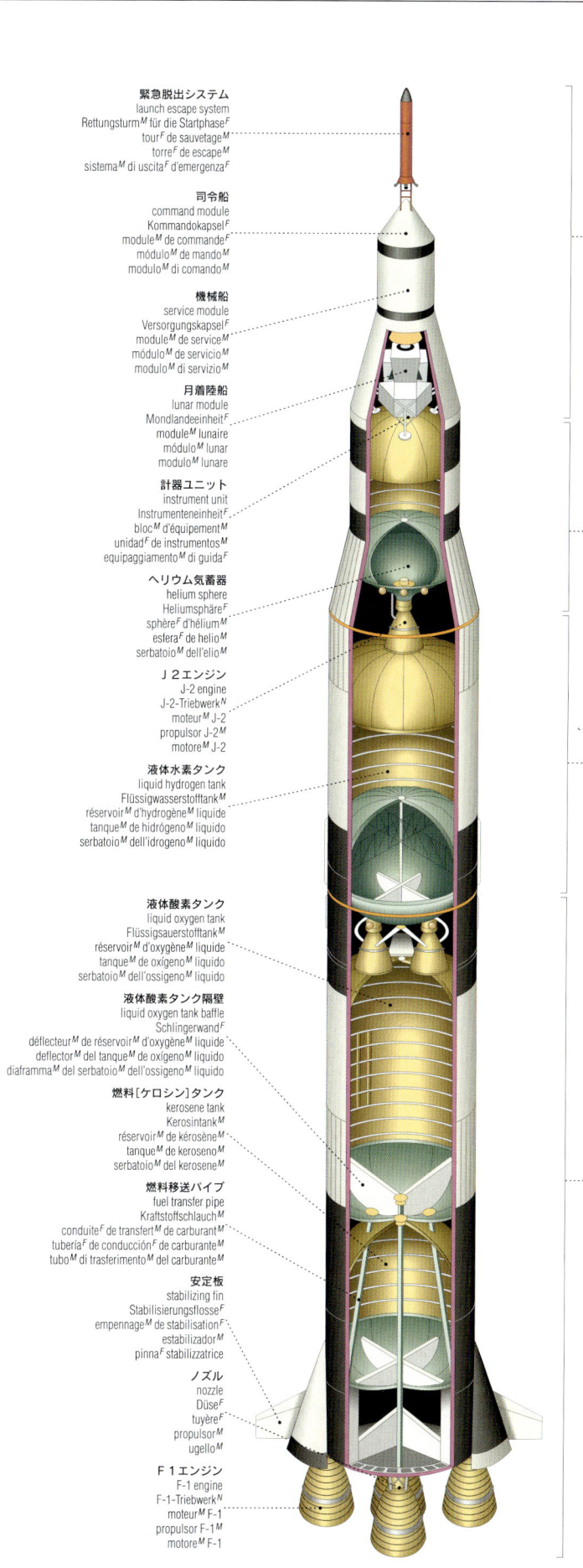

25

28
地理

28 大陸の配置
35 地図作成法
40 遠隔計測［探査］／隔測／リモート・センシング

地 球

EARTH | ERDE | TERRE | TIERRA | TERRA

42 地質

- 42 地殻断面図
- 42 地球の構造
- 43 地殻[構造]プレート
- 43 地震
- 44 火山
- 45 山
- 46 氷河
- 47 洞穴
- 47 地滑り
- 48 水流
- 48 湖
- 49 波
- 49 海洋底
- 50 海溝と海嶺
- 51 海岸の地形
- 52 砂漠

53 気象

- 53 大気圏断面図
- 54 季節
- 54 気象予報
- 55 天気図
- 55 観測地天気記号記入様式
- 56 国際式天気図記号
- 58 気象観測所／測候所
- 58 気象観測機器
- 60 気象衛星
- 61 世界の気候
- 62 雲
- 63 竜巻
- 63 熱帯性低気圧
- 64 降水

66 環境

- 66 植生と生物圏
- 67 食物連鎖
- 67 水の循環
- 68 温室効果
- 69 大気汚染
- 69 土壌汚染
- 70 水質汚染
- 70 酸性雨
- 71 ごみ[廃棄物]の分別

地理 | GEOGRAPHY
GEOGRAPHIE | GÉOGRAPHIE | GEOGRAFÍA | GEOGRAFIA

大陸の配置

configuration of the continents | Lage^F der Kontinente^M | configuration^F des continents^M | configuración^F de los continentes^M | carta^F dei continenti^M

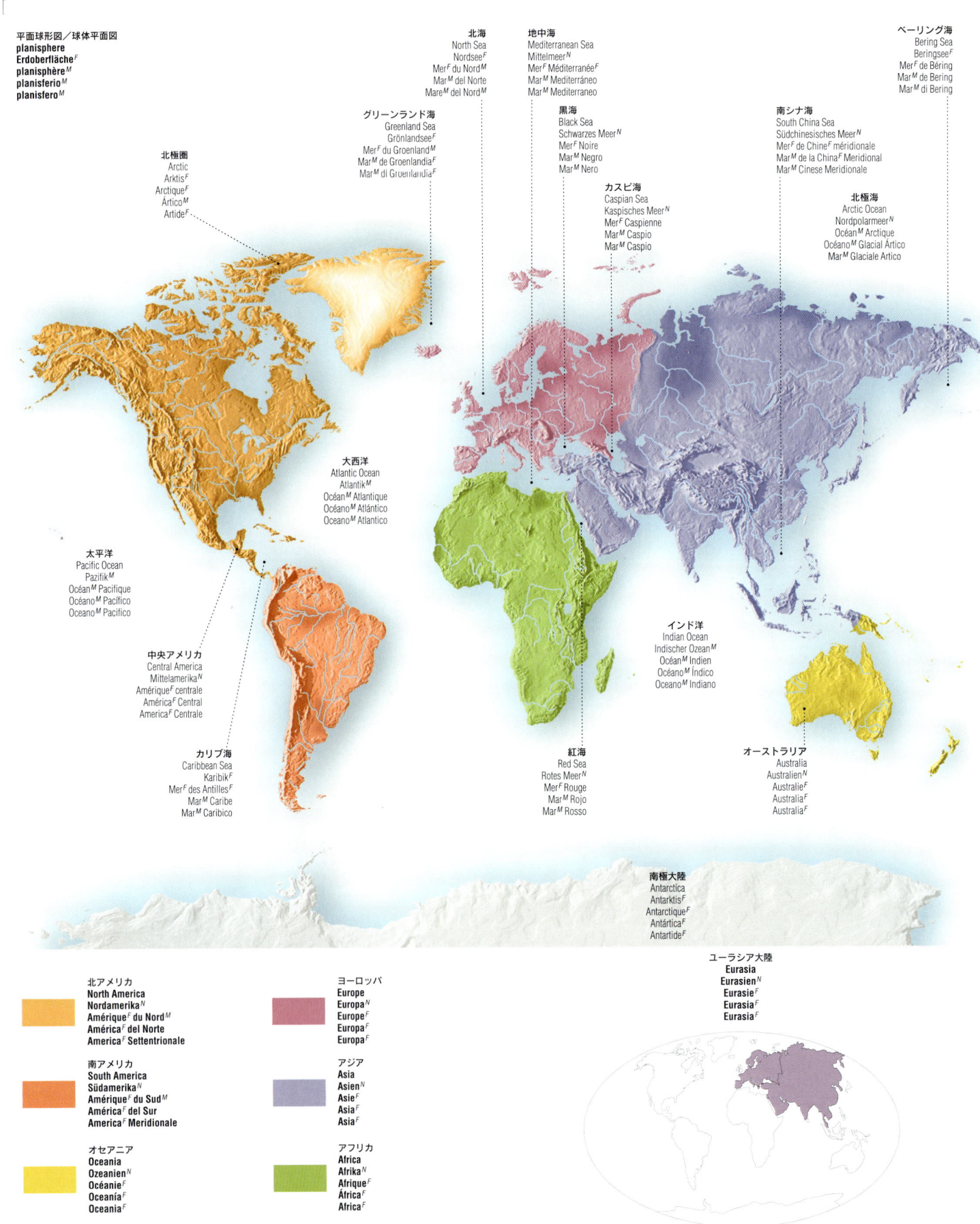

日本語 | 英語 | ドイツ語 | フランス語 | スペイン語 | イタリア語

地球

平面球形図／球体平面図
planisphere
Erdoberfläche^F
planisphère^M
planisferio^M
planisfero^M

北極圏
Arctic
Arktis^F
Arctique^F
Ártico^M
Artide^F

グリーンランド海
Greenland Sea
Grönlandsee^F
Mer^F du Groenland^M
Mar^F de Groenlandia^F
Mar^M di Groenlandia^F

北海
North Sea
Nordsee^F
Mer^F du Nord^M
Mar^M del Norte
Mare^M del Nord^M

地中海
Mediterranean Sea
Mittelmeer^N
Mer^F Méditerranée^F
Mar^M Mediterráneo
Mar^M Mediterraneo

黒海
Black Sea
Schwarzes Meer^N
Mer^F Noire
Mar^M Negro
Mar^M Nero

カスピ海
Caspian Sea
Kaspisches Meer^N
Mer^F Caspienne
Mar^M Caspio
Mar^M Caspio

ベーリング海
Bering Sea
Beringsee^F
Mer^F de Béring
Mar^M de Bering
Mar^M di Bering

南シナ海
South China Sea
Südchinesisches Meer^N
Mer^F de Chine^F méridionale
Mar^M de la China^F Meridional
Mar^M Cinese Meridionale

北極海
Arctic Ocean
Nordpolarmeer^N
Océan^M Arctique
Océano^M Glacial Ártico
Mar^M Glaciale Artico

大西洋
Atlantic Ocean
Atlantik^M
Océan^M Atlantique
Océano^M Atlántico
Oceano^M Atlantico

太平洋
Pacific Ocean
Pazifik^M
Océan^M Pacifique
Océano^M Pacífico
Oceano^M Pacifico

中央アメリカ
Central America
Mittelamerika^N
Amérique^F centrale
América^F Central
America^F Centrale

カリブ海
Caribbean Sea
Karibik^F
Mer^F des Antilles^F
Mar^M Caribe
Mar^M Caribico

紅海
Red Sea
Rotes Meer^N
Mer^F Rouge
Mar^M Rojo
Mar^M Rosso

インド洋
Indian Ocean
Indischer Ozean^M
Océan^M Indien
Océano^M Índico
Oceano^M Indiano

オーストラリア
Australia
Australien^N
Australie^F
Australia^F
Australia^F

南極大陸
Antarctica
Antarktis^F
Antarctique^F
Antártica^F
Antartide^F

北アメリカ
North America
Nordamerika^N
Amérique^F du Nord^M
América^F del Norte
America^F Settentrionale

南アメリカ
South America
Südamerika^N
Amérique^F du Sud^M
América^F del Sur
America^F Meridionale

オセアニア
Oceania
Ozeanien^N
Océanie^F
Oceanía^F
Oceania^F

ヨーロッパ
Europe
Europa^N
Europe^F
Europa^F
Europa^F

アジア
Asia
Asien^N
Asie^F
Asia^F
Asia^F

アフリカ
Africa
Afrika^N
Afrique^F
África^F
Africa^F

ユーラシア大陸
Eurasia
Eurasien^N
Eurasie^F
Eurasia^F
Eurasia^F

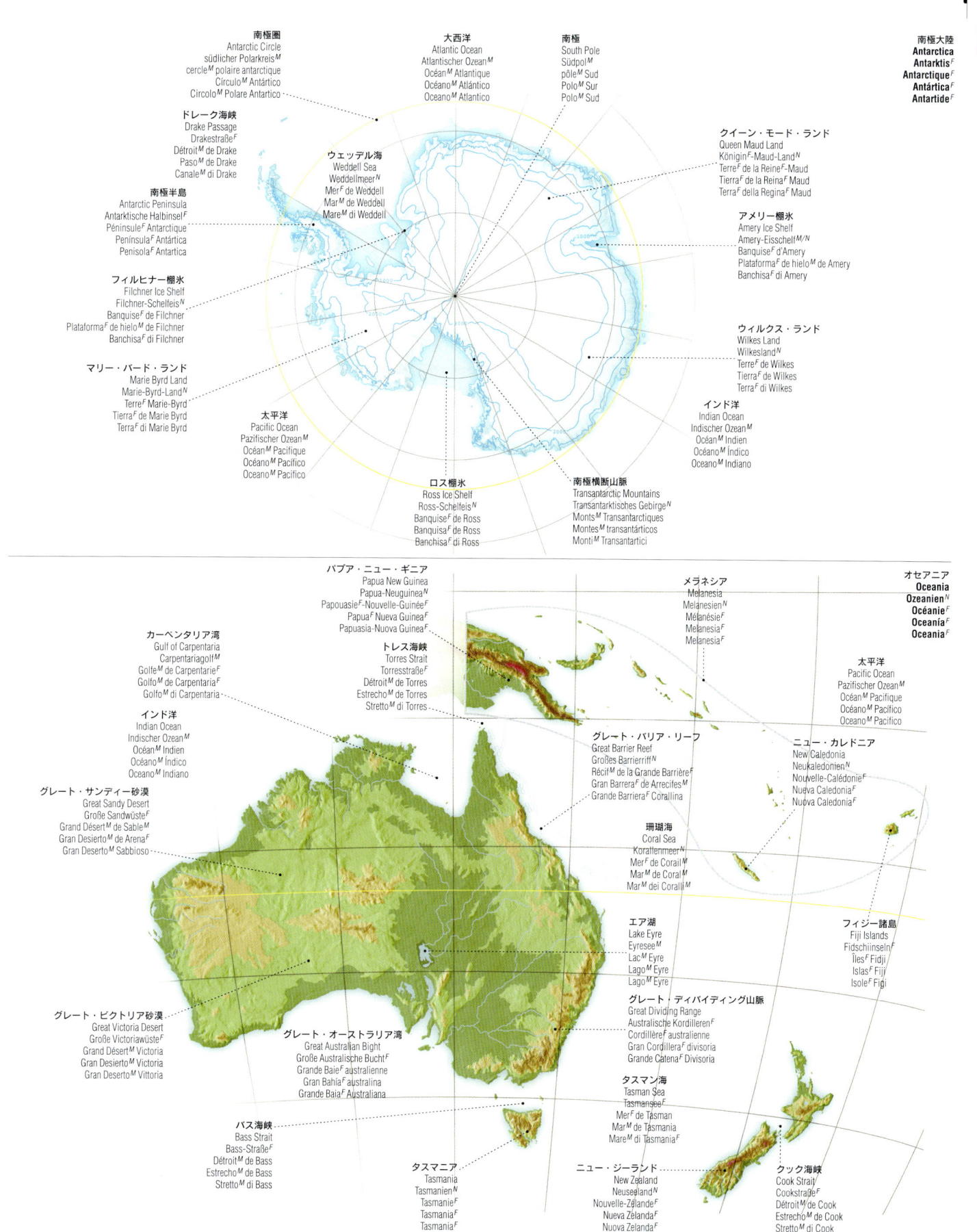

地理 | GEOGRAPHY
GEOGRAPHIE | GÉOGRAPHIE | GEOGRAFÍA | GEOGRAFIA

大陸の配置

南極圏
Antarctic Circle
südlicher Polarkreis^M
cercle^M polaire antarctique
Círculo^M Antártico
Circolo^M Polare Antartico

大西洋
Atlantic Ocean
Atlantischer Ozean^M
Océan^M Atlantique
Océano^M Atlántico
Oceano^M Atlantico

南極
South Pole
Südpol^M
pôle^M Sud
Polo^M Sur
Polo^M Sud

南極大陸
Antarctica
Antarktis
Antarctique
Antártica^F
Antartide^F

地球

ドレーク海峡
Drake Passage
Drakestraße^F
Détroit^M de Drake
Paso^M de Drake
Canale^M di Drake

ウェッデル海
Weddell Sea
Weddellmeer^N
Mer^F de Weddell
Mar^M de Weddell
Mare^M di Weddell

クイーン・モード・ランド
Queen Maud Land
Königin^F-Maud-Land^N
Terre^F de la Reine^F-Maud
Tierra^F de la Reina^F Maud
Terra^F della Regina^F Maud

南極半島
Antarctic Peninsula
Antarktische Halbinsel^F
Péninsule^F Antarctique
Península^F Antártica
Penisola^F Antartica

アメリー棚氷
Amery Ice Shelf
Amery-Eisschelf$^{M/N}$
Banquise^F d'Amery
Plataforma^F de hielo^M de Amery
Banchisa^F di Amery

フィルヒナー棚氷
Filchner Ice Shelf
Filchner-Schelfeis^N
Banquise^F de Filchner
Plataforma^F de hielo^M de Filchner
Banchisa^F di Filchner

ウィルクス・ランド
Wilkes Land
Wilkesland^N
Terre^F de Wilkes
Tierra^F de Wilkes
Terra^F di Wilkes

マリー・バード・ランド
Marie Byrd Land
Marie-Byrd-Land^N
Terre^F Marie-Byrd
Tierra^F de Marie Byrd
Terra^F di Marie Byrd

太平洋
Pacific Ocean
Pazifischer Ozean^M
Océan^M Pacifique
Océano^M Pacífico
Oceano^M Pacifico

インド洋
Indian Ocean
Indischer Ozean^M
Océan^M Indien
Océano^M Índico
Oceano^M Indiano

ロス棚氷
Ross Ice Shelf
Ross-Schelfeis^N
Banquise^F de Ross
Banquisa^F de Ross
Banchisa^F di Ross

南極横断山脈
Transantarctic Mountains
Transantarktisches Gebirge^N
Monts^M Transantarctiques
Montes^M transantárticos
Monti^M Transantartici

パプア・ニュー・ギニア
Papua New Guinea
Papua-Neuguinea^N
Papouasie^F-Nouvelle-Guinée^F
Papúa^F Nueva Guinea^F
Papuasia-Nuova Guinea^F

メラネシア
Melanesia
Melanesien^N
Mélanésie^F
Melanesia^F
Melanesia^F

オセアニア
Oceania
Ozeanien^N
Océanie^F
Oceanía^F
Oceania

カーペンタリア湾
Gulf of Carpentaria
Carpentariagolf^M
Golfe^M de Carpentarie^F
Golfo^M de Carpentaria^F
Golfo^M di Carpentaria^F

トレス海峡
Torres Strait
Torresstraße^F
Détroit^M de Torres
Estrecho^M de Torres
Stretto^M di Torres

太平洋
Pacific Ocean
Pazifischer Ozean^M
Océan^M Pacifique
Océano^M Pacífico
Oceano^M Pacifico

インド洋
Indian Ocean
Indischer Ozean^M
Océan^M Indien
Océano^M Índico
Oceano^M Indiano

グレート・バリア・リーフ
Great Barrier Reef
Großes Barrierriff^N
Récif^M de la Grande Barrière^F
Gran Barrera^F de Arrecifes^M
Grande Barriera^F Corallina

ニュー・カレドニア
New Caledonia
Neukaledonien^N
Nouvelle-Calédonie^F
Nueva Caledonia^F
Nuova Caledonia^F

グレート・サンディー砂漠
Great Sandy Desert
Große Sandwüste^F
Grand Désert^M de Sable^M
Gran Desierto^M de Arena^F
Gran Deserto^M Sabbioso

珊瑚海
Coral Sea
Korallenmeer^N
Mer^F de Corail^M
Mar^M de Coral^M
Mar^M dei Coralli^M

エア湖
Lake Eyre
Eyresee^M
Lac^M Eyre
Lago^M Eyre
Lago^M Eyre

フィジー諸島
Fiji Islands
Fidschiinseln^F
Îles^F Fidji
Islas^F Fiji
Isole^F Figi

グレート・ビクトリア砂漠
Great Victoria Desert
Große Victoriawüste^F
Grand Désert^M Victoria
Gran Desierto^M Victoria
Gran Deserto^M Vittoria

グレート・オーストラリア湾
Great Australian Bight
Große Australische Bucht^F
Grande Baie^F australienne
Gran Bahía^F australiana
Grande Baia^F Australiana

グレート・ディバイディング山脈
Great Dividing Range
Australische Kordilleren^F
Cordillère^F australienne
Gran Cordillera^F divisoria
Grande Catena^F Divisoria

タスマン海
Tasman Sea
Tasmansee^F
Mer^F de Tasman
Mar^M de Tasmania
Mare^M di Tasmania

バス海峡
Bass Strait
Bass-Straße^F
Détroit^M de Bass
Estrecho^M de Bass
Stretto^M di Bass

タスマニア
Tasmania
Tasmanien^N
Tasmanie^F
Tasmania^F
Tasmania^F

ニュー・ジーランド
New Zealand
Neuseeland^N
Nouvelle-Zélande^F
Nueva Zelanda^F
Nuova Zelanda^F

クック海峡
Cook Strait
Cookstraße^F
Détroit^M de Cook
Estrecho^M de Cook
Stretto^M di Cook

地理 | GEOGRAPHY
GEOGRAPHIE | GÉOGRAPHIE | GEOGRAFÍA | GEOGRAFIA

大陸の配置

日本語 | 英語 | ドイツ語 | フランス語 | スペイン語 | イタリア語

北アメリカ
North America
Nordamerika[N]
Amérique[F] du Nord[M]
América[F] del Norte
America[F] Settentrionale

ボーフォート海
Beaufort Sea
Beaufortsee[F]
Mer[F] de Beaufort
Mar[M] de Beaufort
Mar[M] di Beaufort

マッケンジー川
Mackenzie River
Mackenzie[M]
Mackenzie[M]
Río[M] Mackenzie
Fiume[M] Mackenzie

ハドソン湾
Hudson Bay
Hudson Bay[F]
Baie[F] d'Hudson
Bahía[F] de Hudson
Baia[F] di Hudson

バッフィン島
Baffin Island
Baffinland[N]
Terre[F] de Baffin
Bahía[F] de Baffin
Isola[F] di Baffin

ベーリング海峡
Bering Strait
Beringstraße[F]
Détroit[M] de Béring
Estrecho[M] de Bering
Stretto[M] di Bering

グリーンランド
Greenland
Grönland[N]
Groenland[M]
Groenlandia[F]
Groenlandia[F]

五大湖
Great Lakes
Große Seen[M]
Grands Lacs[M]
Grandes Lagos[M]
Grandi Laghi[M]

ニューファンドランド島
Newfoundland Island
Neufundland[N]
Île[F] de Terre-Neuve
Isla[F] de Terranova
Isola[F] di Terranova

アラスカ湾
Gulf of Alaska
Golf[M] von Alaska[N]
Golfe[M] d'Alaska
Golfo[M] de Alaska[F]
Golfo[M] dell'Alaska[F]

アリューシャン列島
Aleutian Islands
Aleuten
Îles[F] Aléoutiennes
Islas[F] Aleutianas
Isole[F] Aleutine

ロッキー山脈
Rocky Mountains
Rocky Mountains
Montagnes[F] Rocheuses
Montañas[F] Rocosas
Montagne[F] Rocciose

セント・ローレンス川
Saint Lawrence River
Sankt-Lorenz-Strom[M]
Saint-Laurent[M]
Río[M] San Lorenzo
Fiume[M] San Lorenzo

グランド・キャニオン
Grand Canyon
Grand Canyon[M]
Grand Canyon[M]
Gran Cañón[M]
Grand Canyon[M]

アパラチア山脈
Appalachian Mountains
Appalachen
Appalaches[F]
Montes[M] Apalaches[M]
Monti[M] Appalachi

ミシシッピ川
Mississippi River
Mississippi[M]
Mississippi[M]
Río[M] Mississippi
Fiume[M] Mississippi

カリフォルニア湾
Gulf of California
Golf[M] von Kalifornien[N]
Golfe[M] de Californie[F]
Golfo[M] de California[F]
Golfo[M] di California[F]

メキシコ湾
Gulf of Mexico
Golf[M] von Mexiko[N]
Golfe[M] du Mexique[M]
Golfo[M] de México[M]
Golfo[M] del Messico[M]

ユカタン半島
Yucatan Peninsula
Yucatan[N]-Halbinsel[F]
Péninsule[F] du Yucatan[M]
Península[F] del Yucatán[M]
Penisola[F] dello Yucatan

西インド諸島
West Indies
Westindien[N]
Antilles[F]
Antillas[F]
Indie[F] Occidentali

カリブ海
Caribbean Sea
Karibik[F]
Mer[F] des Antilles[F]
Mar[M] de Caribe
Mar[M] Caribico

中央アメリカ
Central America
Mittelamerika[N]
Amérique[F] centrale
América[F] Central
America[F] Centrale

パナマ地峡
Isthmus of Panama
Landenge[F] von Panama[N]
Isthme[M] de Panama[M]
Istmo[M] de Panamá[M]
Istmo[M] di Panama

地理 | GEOGRAPHY
GEOGRAPHIE | GÉOGRAPHIE | GEOGRAFÍA | GEOGRAFIA

大陸の配置

南アメリカ
South America
Südamerika[N]
Amérique[F] du Sud[M]
América[F] del Sur
America[F] Meridionale

地球

オリノコ川
Orinoco River
Orinoko[M]
Orénoque[M]
Río[M] Orinoco
Fiume[M] Orinoco

アマゾン川
Amazon River
Amazonas[M]
Amazone[F]
Río[M] Amazonas
Rio[M] delle Amazzoni[F]

パナマ湾
Gulf of Panama
Golf[M] von Panama[N]
Golfe[M] de Panama
Golfo[M] de Panamá[M]
Golfo[M] di Panama

赤道
Equator
Äquator[M]
équateur[M]
ecuador[M]
Equatore[M]

アンデス山脈
Andes Cordillera
Anden
Cordillère[F] des Andes[F]
Cordillera[F] de los Andes[M]
Cordigliera[F] delle Ande[F]

チチカカ湖
Lake Titicaca
Titicacasee[M]
Lac[M] Titicaca
Lago[M] Titicaca
Lago[M] Titicaca

アタカマ砂漠
Atacama Desert
Atacama-Wüste[F]
Désert[M] d'Atacama
Desierto[M] de Atacama
Deserto[M] di Atacama

パラナ川
Paraná River
Paraná[M]
Paraná[M]
Río[M] Paraná
Fiume[M] Paranà

パタゴニア
Patagonia
Patagonien[N]
Patagonie[F]
Patagonia[F]
Patagonia[F]

フォークランド諸島
Falkland Islands
Falkland-Inseln[F]
Îles[F] Falkland
Islas[F] Malvinas
Isole[F] Falkland

フエゴ島
Tierra del Fuego
Feuerland[N]
Terre[F] de Feu[M]
Tierra[F] del Fuego[M]
Terra[F] del Fuoco[M]

ホーン岬
Cape Horn
Kap[N] Horn
Cap[M] Horn
Cabo[M] de Hornos
Capo[M] Horn

ドレーク海峡
Drake Passage
Drakestraße[F]
Détroit[M] de Drake
Paso[M] de Drake
Canale[M] di Drake

31

地理 | GEOGRAPHY
GEOGRAPHIE | GÉOGRAPHIE | GEOGRAFÍA | GEOGRAFIA

大陸の配置

日本語 | 英語 | ドイツ語 | フランス語 | スペイン語 | イタリア語

地球

ヨーロッパ
Europe
Europa[N]
Europe[F]
Europa[F]
Europa[F]

ラドガ湖
Lake Ladoga
Ladogasee[M]
Lac[M] Ladoga
Lago[M] Ladoga
Lago[M] Ladoga

バレンツ海
Barents Sea
Barentssee[F]
Mer[F] de Barents
Mar[M] de Barents
Mar[M] di Barents

ウラル山脈
Ural Mountains
Ural[M]
Monts[M] Oural[M]
Montes[M] Urales[M]
Monti[M] Urali

ボスニア湾
Gulf of Bothnia
Bottnischer Meerbusen[M]
Golfe[M] de Botnie
Golfo[M] de Botnia[F]
Golfo[M] di Botnia

コラ半島
Kola Peninsula
Kola-Halbinsel[F]
Péninsule[F] de Kola
Península[F] de Kola
Penisola[F] di Kola

ボルガ川
Volga River
Wolga[F]
Volga[F]
Río[M] Volga
Fiume[M] Volga

ノルウェー海
Norwegian Sea
Nordmeer[N]
Mer[F] de Norvège[F]
Mar[M] de Noruega[F]
Mar[M] di Norvegia[F]

ドニエプル川
Dnieper River
Dnjepr[M]
Dniepr[M]
Río[M] Diniéper
Fiume[M] Dnepr

アイスランド
Iceland
Island[N]
Islande[F]
Islandia[F]
Islanda[F]

北海
North Sea
Nordsee[F]
Mer[F] du Nord
Mar[M] del Norte
Mare[M] del Nord[M]

スカンジナビア半島
Scandinavian Peninsula
Skandinavische Halbinsel[F]
Péninsule[F] Scandinave
Península[F] Escandinava
Penisola[F] Scandinava

バルト海
Baltic Sea
Ostsee[F]
Mer[F] Baltique[F]
Mar[M] Báltico
Mar[M] Baltico

アイリッシュ海
Irish Sea
Irische See[F]
Mer[F] d'Irlande[F]
Mar[M] de Irlanda[F]
Mar[M] d'Irlanda[F]

大西洋
Atlantic Ocean
Atlantischer Ozean[M]
Océan[M] Atlantique
Océano[M] Atlántico
Oceano[M] Atlantico

イギリス海峡
English Channel
Ärmelkanal[M]
Manche[F]
Canal[M] de la Mancha[F]
Canale[M] della Manica[F]

ビスワ川／ビストゥラ川
Vistula River
Weichsel[F]
Vistule[F]
Río[M] Vístula
Fiume[M] Vistola

アルプス山脈
Alps
Alpen
Alpes[F]
Alpes[M]
Alpi[F]

黒海
Black Sea
Schwarzes Meer[N]
Mer[F] Noire
Mar[M] Negro
Mar[M] Nero

イベリア半島
Iberian Peninsula
Iberische Halbinsel[F]
Péninsule[F] Ibérique
Península[F] Ibérica
Penisola[F] Iberica

ジブラルタル海峡
Strait of Gibraltar
Straße[F] von Gibraltar[N]
Détroit[M] de Gibraltar
Estrecho[M] de Gibraltar
Stretto[M] di Gibilterra

ピレネー山脈
Pyrenees
Pyrenäen
Pyrénées[F]
Pirineos[M]
Pirenei[M]

ドナウ川
Danube River
Donau[F]
Danube[M]
Río[M] Danubio
Fiume[M] Danubio

バルカン半島
Balkan Peninsula
Balkanhalbinsel[F]
Péninsule[F] des Balkans[M]
Península[F] de los Balcanes[M]
Penisola[F] Balcanica

カルパート山脈／カルパティア山脈
Carpathian Mountains
Karpaten
Carpates[F]
Montes[M] Cárpatos[M]
Monti[M] Carpazi

地中海
Mediterranean Sea
Mittelmeer[N]
Mer[F] Méditerranée[F]
Mar[M] Mediterráneo
Mar[M] Mediterraneo

アドリア海
Adriatic Sea
Adria[F]
Mer[F] Adriatique
Mar[M] Adriático
Mar[M] Adriatico

エーゲ海
Aegean Sea
Ägäis[F]
Mer[F] Égée
Mar[M] Egeo
Mare[M] Egeo

地理 | GEOGRAPHY
GEOGRAPHIE | GÉOGRAPHIE | GEOGRAFÍA | GEOGRAFIA

大陸の配置

アジア
Asia
Asien[N]
Asie[F]
Asia[F]
Asia[F]

地球

アラル海
Aral Sea
Aralsee[M]
Mer[F] d'Aral
Mar[M] de Aral
Lago[M] di Aral

バイカル湖
Lake Baikal
Baikalsee[M]
Lac[M] Baïkal
Lago[M] Baikal
Lago[M] Baikal

ゴビ砂漠
Gobi Desert
Wüste Gobi[F]
Désert[M] de Gobi[M]
Desierto de Gobi
Deserto[M] dei Gobi

カムチャツカ半島
Kamchatka Peninsula
Kamtschatka[N]-Halbinsel[F]
Péninsule[F] du Kamtchatka[M]
Península[F] de Kamchatka
Penisola[F] di Camciatca

カスピ海
Caspian Sea
Kaspisches Meer[N]
Mer[F] Caspienne
Mar[M] Caspio
Mar[M] Caspio

日本海
Sea of Japan
Japanisches Meer[N]
Mer[F] du Japon[M]
Mar[M] de Japón[M]
Mar[M] del Giappone[M]

黒海
Black Sea
Schwarzes Meer[N]
Mer[F] Noire
Mar[M] Negro
Mar[M] Nero

太平洋
Pacific Ocean
Pazifischer Ozean[M]
Océan[M] Pacifique
Océano[M] Pacífico
Oceano[M] Pacifico

紅海
Red Sea
Rotes Meer[N]
Mer[F] Rouge
Mar[M] Rojo
Mar[M] Rosso

日本
Japan
Japan[N]
Japon[M]
Japón[M]
Giappone[M]

朝鮮半島
Korean Peninsula
Korea[N]
Péninsule[F] de Corée[F]
Península[F] de Corea[F]
Penisola[F] Coreana

東シナ海
East China Sea
Ostchinesisches Meer[N]
Mer[F] de Chine[F] orientale
Mar[M] de la China[F] Oriental
Mar[M] Cinese Orientale

フィリピン諸島
Philippines
Philippinen
Philippines[F]
Filipinas[F]
Filippine[F]

アデン湾
Gulf of Aden
Golf[M] von Aden[N]
Golfe[M] d'Aden
Golfo[M] de Adén
Golfo[M] di Aden

ヒマラヤ山脈
Himalayas
Himalaja[M]
Himalaya
Himalaya[M]
Himalaya[M]

アラビア半島
Arabian Peninsula
Arabische Halbinsel[F]
Péninsule[F] d'Arabie[F]
Península[F] de Arabia[F]
Penisola[F] Arabica

オマーン湾
Gulf of Oman
Golf[M] von Oman[N]
Golfe[M] d'Oman[M]
Golfo[M] de Omán
Golfo[M] di Oman

南シナ海
South China Sea
Südchinesisches Meer[N]
Mer[F] de Chine[F] méridionale
Mar[M] de la China[F] Meridional
Mar[M] Cinese Meridionale

ペルシア湾
Persian Gulf
Persischer Golf[M]
Golfe[M] Persique
Golfo[M] Pérsico
Golfo[M] Persico

アラビア海
Arabian Sea
Arabisches Meer[N]
Mer[F] d'Oman[M]
Mar[M] Arábigo
Mare[M] Arabico

インドネシア
Indonesia
Indonesien[N]
Indonésie[F]
Indonesia[F]
Indonesia[F]

インド洋
Indian Ocean
Indischer Ozean[M]
Océan[M] Indien
Océano[M] Índico
Oceano[M] Indiano

ベンガル湾
Bay of Bengal
Golf[M] von Bengalen[N]
Golfe[M] du Bengale[M]
Bahía[F] de Bengala
Golfo[M] del Bengala[M]

地理 | GEOGRAPHY
GEOGRAPHIE | GÉOGRAPHIE | GEOGRAFÍA | GEOGRAFIA

大陸の配置

日本語 | 英語 | ドイツ語 | フランス語 | スペイン語 | イタリア語

地球

アフリカ
Africa
Afrika[N]
Afrique[F]
África[F]
Africa[F]

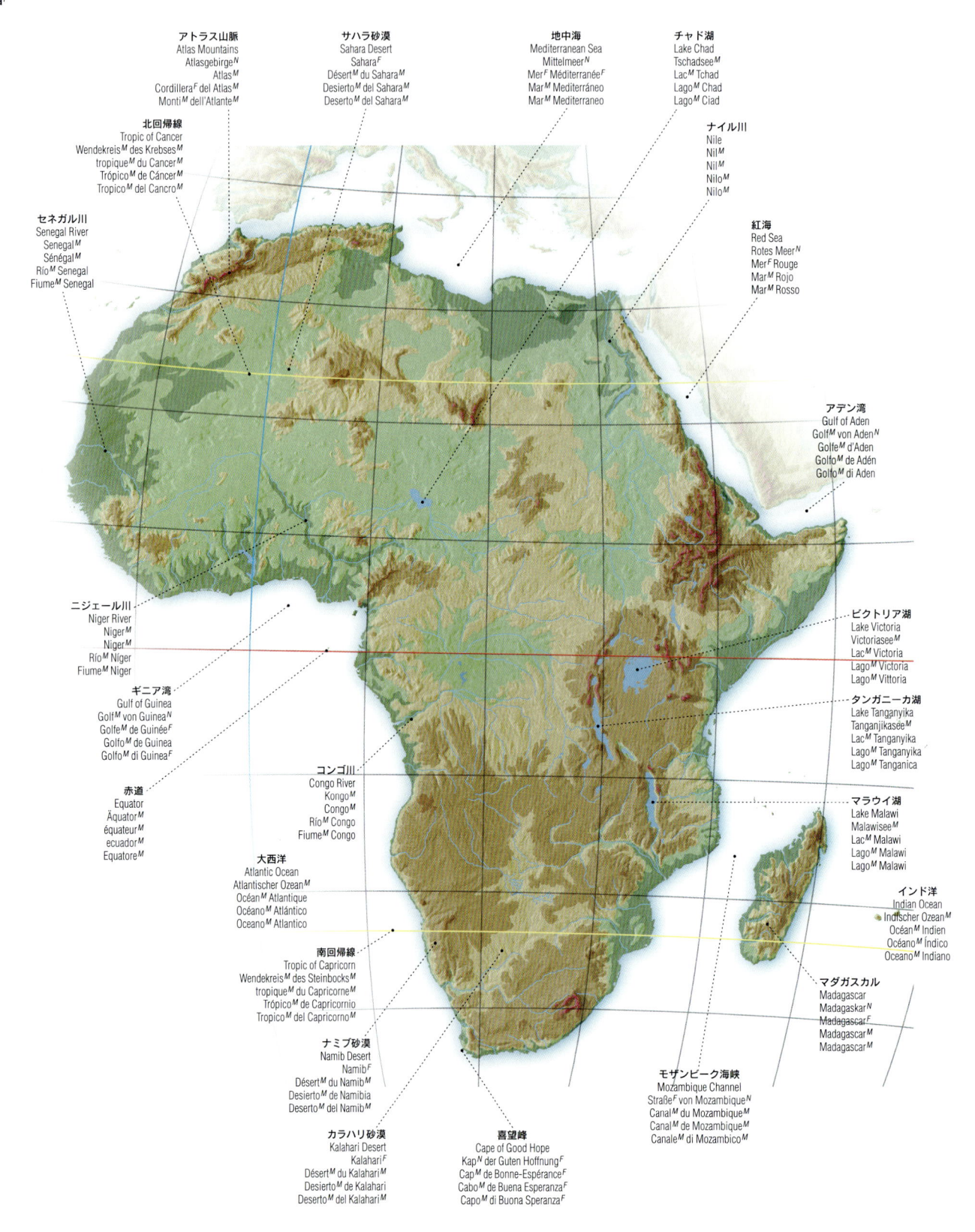

アトラス山脈
Atlas Mountains
Atlasgebirge[N]
Atlas[M]
Cordillera[F] del Atlas[M]
Monti[M] dell'Atlante[M]

サハラ砂漠
Sahara Desert
Sahara[F]
Désert[M] du Sahara[M]
Desierto[M] del Sahara[M]
Deserto[M] del Sahara[M]

地中海
Mediterranean Sea
Mittelmeer[N]
Mer[F] Méditerranée[F]
Mar[M] Mediterráneo
Mar[M] Mediterraneo

チャド湖
Lake Chad
Tschadsee[M]
Lac[M] Tchad
Lago[M] Chad
Lago[M] Ciad

北回帰線
Tropic of Cancer
Wendekreis[M] des Krebses[M]
tropique[M] du Cancer[M]
Trópico[M] de Cáncer[M]
Tropico[M] del Cancro[M]

ナイル川
Nile
Nil[M]
Nil[M]
Nilo[M]
Nilo[M]

セネガル川
Senegal River
Senegal[M]
Sénégal[M]
Río[M] Senegal
Fiume[M] Senegal

紅海
Red Sea
Rotes Meer[N]
Mer[F] Rouge
Mar[M] Rojo
Mar[M] Rosso

アデン湾
Gulf of Aden
Golf[M] von Aden[N]
Golfe[M] d'Aden
Golfo[M] de Adén
Golfo[M] di Aden

ニジェール川
Niger River
Niger[M]
Niger[M]
Río[M] Níger
Fiume[M] Niger

ビクトリア湖
Lake Victoria
Victoriasee[M]
Lac[M] Victoria
Lago[M] Victoria
Lago[M] Vittoria

ギニア湾
Gulf of Guinea
Golf[M] von Guinea[N]
Golfe[M] de Guinée[F]
Golfo[M] de Guinea
Golfo[M] di Guinea

タンガニーカ湖
Lake Tanganyika
Tanganjikasee[M]
Lac[M] Tanganyika
Lago[M] Tanganyika
Lago[M] Tanganica

赤道
Equator
Äquator[M]
équateur[M]
ecuador[M]
Equatore[M]

コンゴ川
Congo River
Kongo[M]
Congo[M]
Río[M] Congo
Fiume[M] Congo

マラウイ湖
Lake Malawi
Malawisee[M]
Lac[M] Malawi
Lago[M] Malawi
Lago[M] Malawi

大西洋
Atlantic Ocean
Atlantischer Ozean[M]
Océan[M] Atlantique
Océano[M] Atlántico
Oceano[M] Atlantico

インド洋
Indian Ocean
Indischer Ozean[M]
Océan[M] Indien
Océano[M] Índico
Oceano[M] Indiano

南回帰線
Tropic of Capricorn
Wendekreis[M] des Steinbocks[M]
tropique[M] du Capricorne[M]
Trópico[M] de Capricornio
Tropico[M] del Capricorno[M]

マダガスカル
Madagascar
Madagaskar
Madagascar[N]
Madagascar[M]
Madagascar[M]

ナミブ砂漠
Namib Desert
Namib[F]
Désert[M] du Namib[M]
Desierto[M] de Namibia
Deserto[M] del Namib[M]

モザンビーク海峡
Mozambique Channel
Straße[F] von Mozambique[N]
Canal[M] du Mozambique[M]
Canal[M] de Mozambique[M]
Canale[M] di Mozambico[M]

カラハリ砂漠
Kalahari Desert
Kalahari[F]
Désert[M] du Kalahari[M]
Desierto[M] de Kalahari
Deserto[M] del Kalahari[M]

喜望峰
Cape of Good Hope
Kap[N] der Guten Hoffnung[F]
Cap[M] de Bonne-Espérance[F]
Cabo[M] de Buena Esperanza[F]
Capo[M] di Buona Speranza[F]

地理 | GEOGRAPHY
GEOGRAPHIE | GÉOGRAPHIE | GEOGRAFÍA | GEOGRAFIA

地図作成法

cartography | Kartographie^F | cartographie^F | cartografía^F | cartografia^F

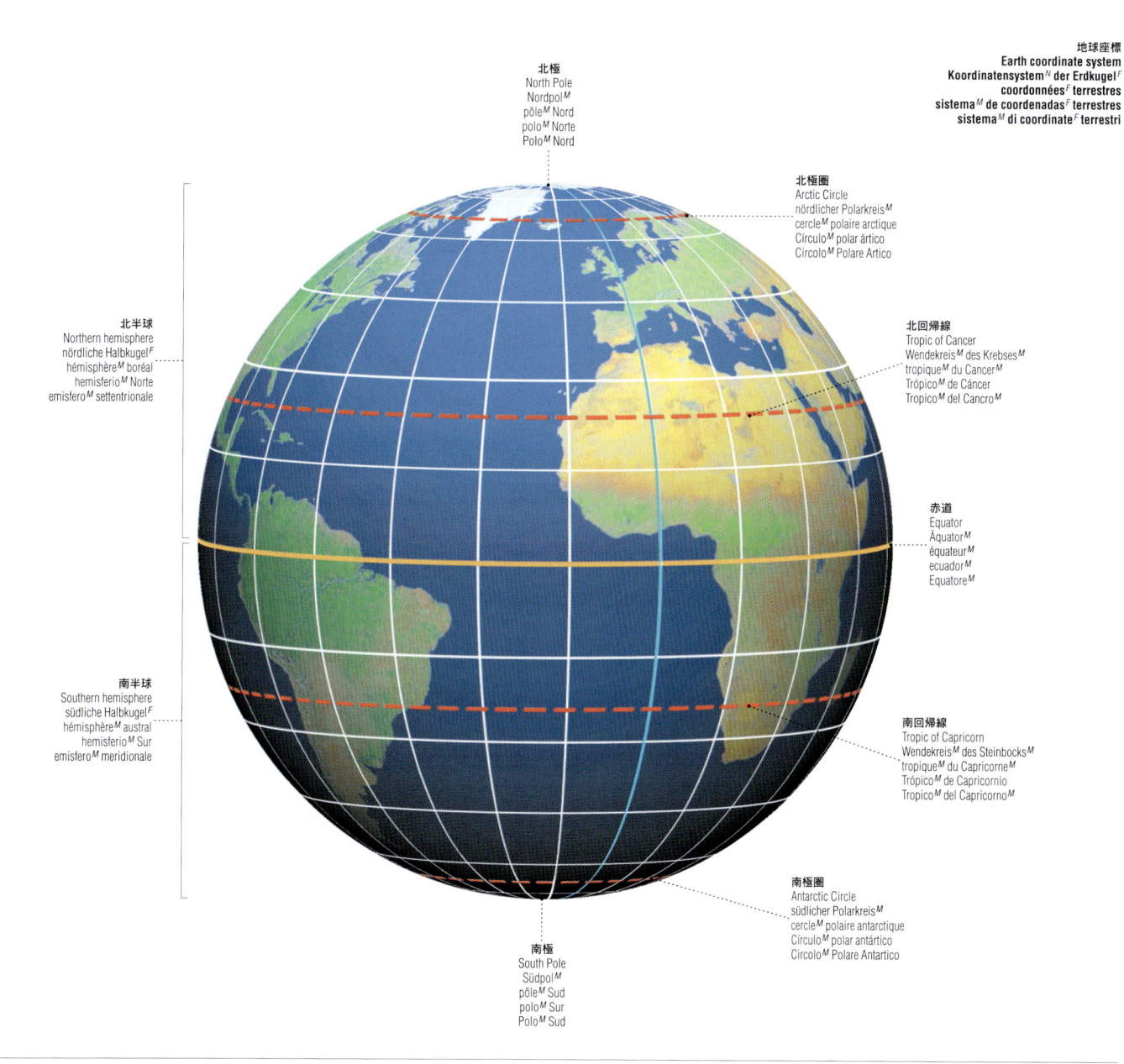

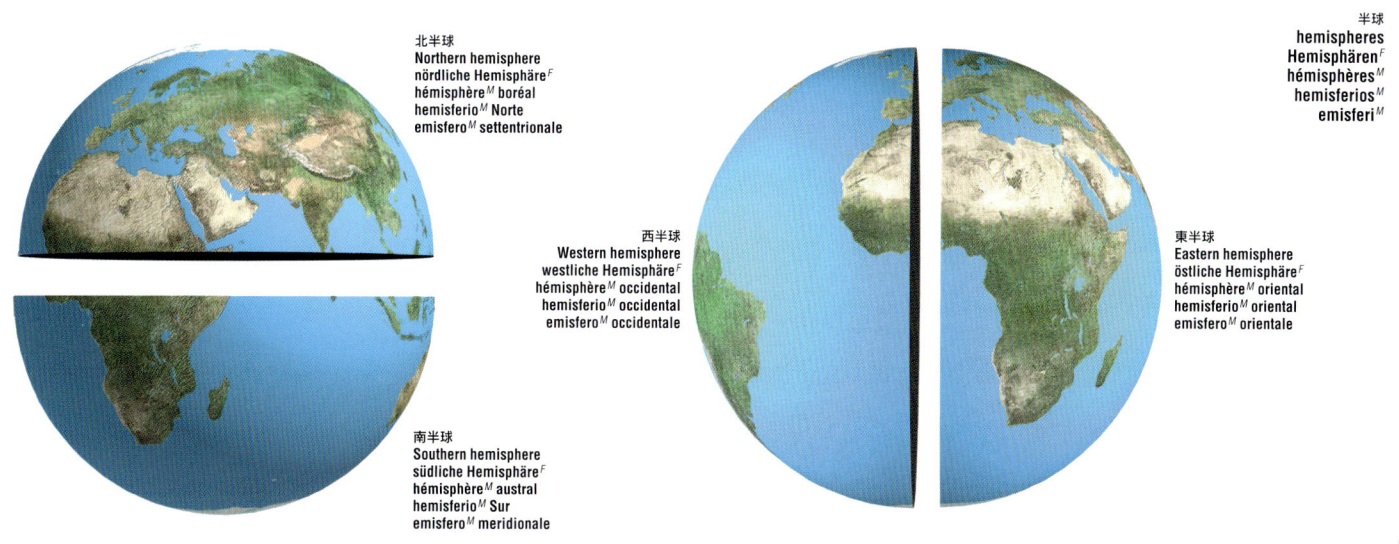

地球

地球座標
Earth coordinate system
Koordinatensystem^N der Erdkugel^F
coordonnées^F terrestres
sistema^M de coordenadas^F terrestres
sistema^M di coordinate^F terrestri

北極
North Pole
Nordpol^M
pôle^M Nord
polo^M Norte
Polo^M Nord

北極圏
Arctic Circle
nördlicher Polarkreis^M
cercle^M polaire arctique
Círculo^M polar ártico
Circolo^M Polare Artico

北半球
Northern hemisphere
nördliche Halbkugel^F
hémisphère^M boréal
hemisferio^M Norte
emisfero^M settentrionale

北回帰線
Tropic of Cancer
Wendekreis^M des Krebses^M
tropique^M du Cancer^M
Trópico^M de Cáncer
Tropico^M del Cancro^M

赤道
Equator
Äquator^M
équateur^M
ecuador^M
Equatore^M

南半球
Southern hemisphere
südliche Halbkugel^F
hémisphère^M austral
hemisferio^M Sur
emisfero^M meridionale

南回帰線
Tropic of Capricorn
Wendekreis^M des Steinbocks^M
tropique^M du Capricorne^M
Trópico^M de Capricornio
Tropico^M del Capricorno^M

南極圏
Antarctic Circle
südlicher Polarkreis^M
cercle^M polaire antarctique
Círculo^M polar antártico
Circolo^M Polare Antartico

南極
South Pole
Südpol^M
pôle^M Sud
polo^M Sur
Polo^M Sud

北半球
Northern hemisphere
nördliche Hemisphäre^F
hémisphère^M boréal
hemisferio^M Norte
emisfero^M settentrionale

西半球
Western hemisphere
westliche Hemisphäre^F
hémisphère^M occidental
hemisferio^M occidental
emisfero^M occidentale

南半球
Southern hemisphere
südliche Hemisphäre^F
hémisphère^M austral
hemisferio^M Sur
emisfero^M meridionale

半球
hemispheres
Hemisphären^F
hémisphères^M
hemisferios^M
emisferi^M

東半球
Eastern hemisphere
östliche Hemisphäre^F
hémisphère^M oriental
hemisferio^M oriental
emisfero^M orientale

35

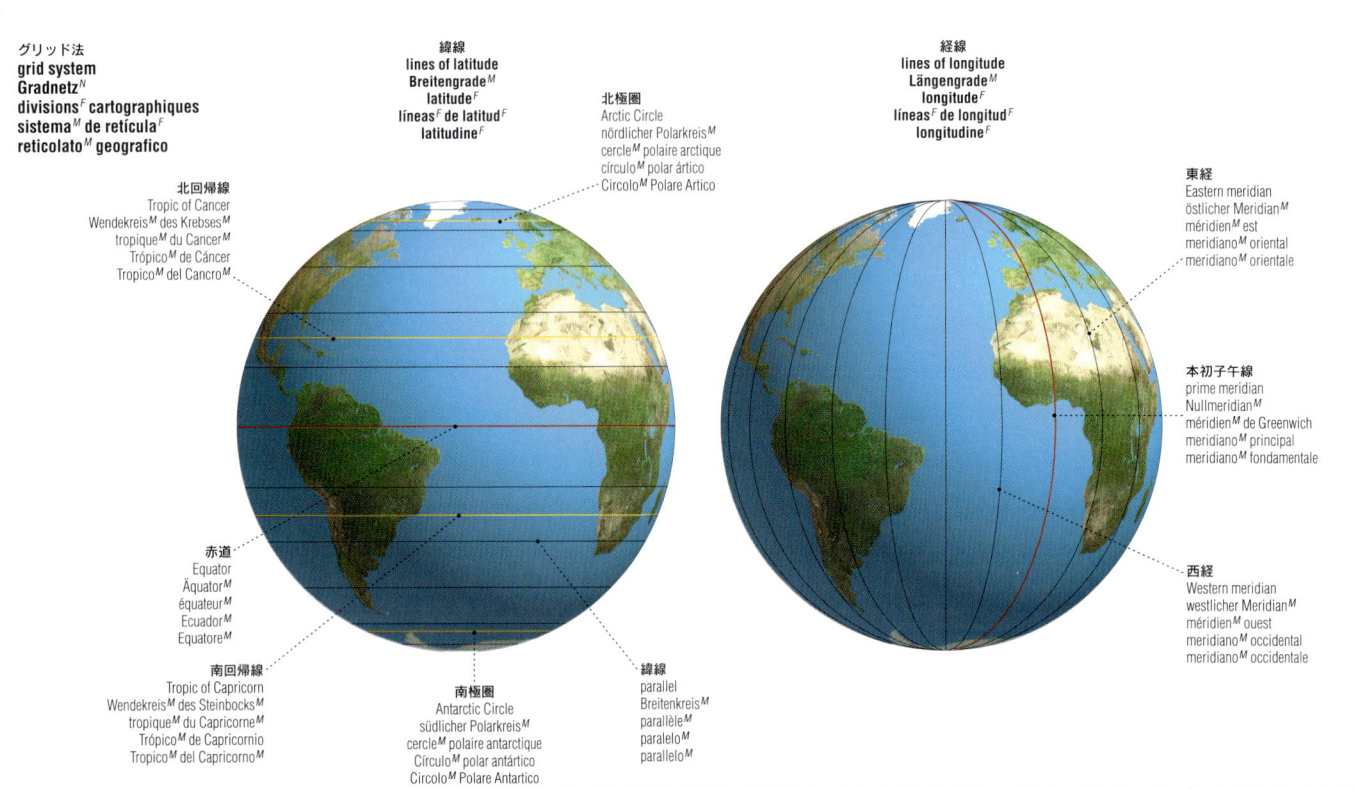

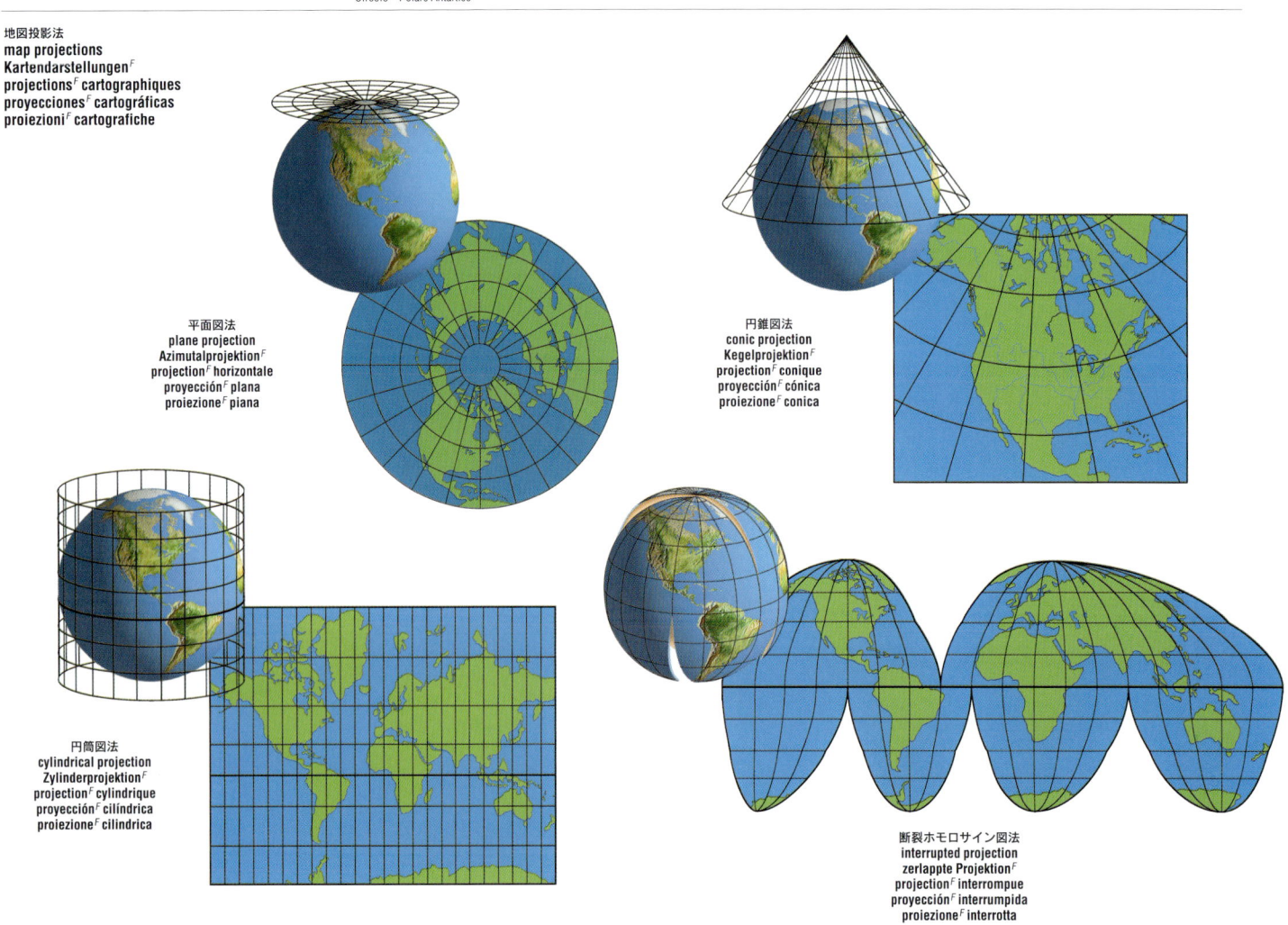

地理 | GEOGRAPHY
GEOGRAPHIE | GÉOGRAPHIE | GEOGRAFÍA | GEOGRAFIA

地図作成法

日本語 | 英語 | ドイツ語 | フランス語 | スペイン語 | イタリア語

グリッド法
grid system
Gradnetz^N
divisions^F cartographiques
sistema^M de retícula^F
reticolato^M geografico

緯線
lines of latitude
Breitengrade^M
latitude^F
líneas^F de latitud^F
latitudine^F

北極圏
Arctic Circle
nördlicher Polarkreis^M
cercle^M polaire arctique
círculo^M polar ártico
Circolo^M Polare Artico

経線
lines of longitude
Längengrade^M
longitude^F
líneas^F de longitud^F
longitudine^F

東経
Eastern meridian
östlicher Meridian^M
méridien^M est
meridiano^M oriental
meridiano^M orientale

北回帰線
Tropic of Cancer
Wendekreis^M des Krebses^M
tropique^M du Cancer^M
Trópico^M de Cáncer
Tropico^M del Cancro^M

本初子午線
prime meridian
Nullmeridian^M
méridien^M de Greenwich
meridiano^M principal
meridiano^M fondamentale

赤道
Equator
Äquator^M
équateur^M
Ecuador^M
Equatore^M

西経
Western meridian
westlicher Meridian^M
méridien^M ouest
meridiano^M occidental
meridiano^M occidentale

南回帰線
Tropic of Capricorn
Wendekreis^M des Steinbocks^M
tropique^M du Capricorne^M
Trópico^M de Capricornio
Tropico^M del Capricorno^M

南極圏
Antarctic Circle
südlicher Polarkreis^M
cercle^M polaire antarctique
Círculo^M polar antártico
Circolo^M Polare Antartico

緯線
parallel
Breitenkreis^M
parallèle^M
paralelo^M
parallelo^M

地図投影法
map projections
Kartendarstellungen^F
projections^F cartographiques
proyecciones^F cartográficas
proiezioni^F cartografiche

平面図法
plane projection
Azimutalprojektion^F
projection^F horizontale
proyección^F plana
proiezione^F piana

円錐図法
conic projection
Kegelprojektion^F
projection^F conique
proyección^F cónica
proiezione^F conica

円筒図法
cylindrical projection
Zylinderprojektion^F
projection^F cylindrique
proyección^F cilíndrica
proiezione^F cilindrica

断裂ホモロサイン図法
interrupted projection
zerlappte Projektion^F
projection^F interrompue
proyección^F interrumpida
proiezione^F interrotta

地理 | GEOGRAPHY
GEOGRAPHIE | GÉOGRAPHIE | GEOGRAFÍA | GEOGRAFIA

地図作成法

コンパス・カード／羅牌（らはい）
compass card
Windrose^F
rose^F des vents^M
rosa^F de los vientos^M
rosa^F dei venti^M

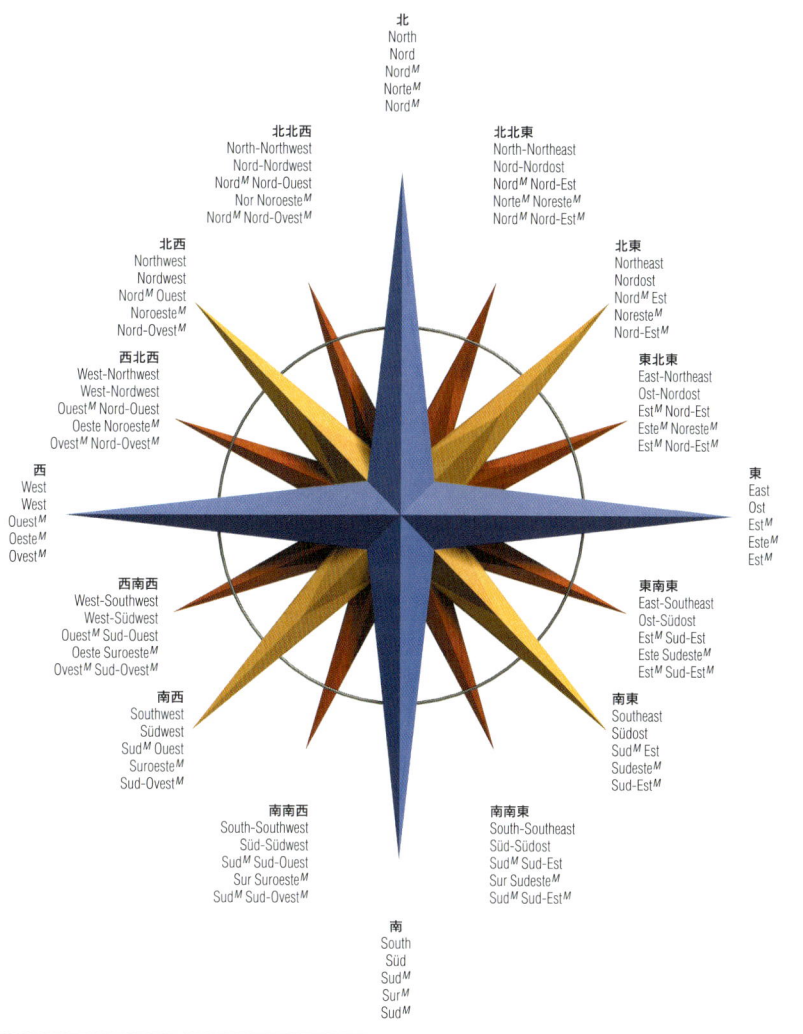

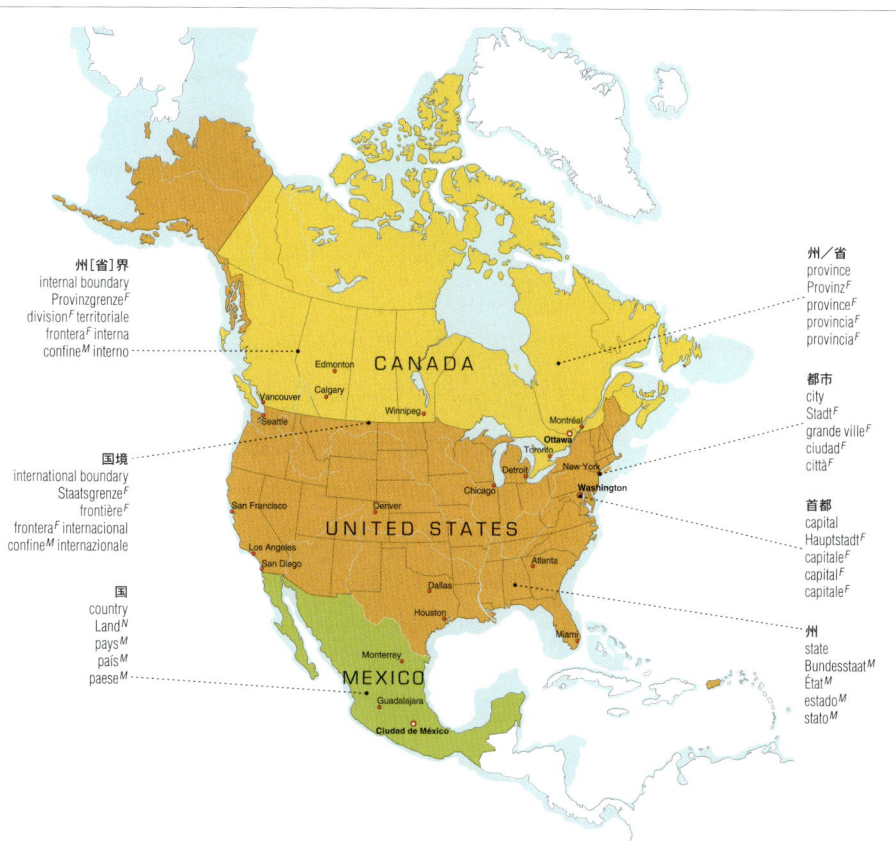

北
North
Nord
Nord^M
Norte^M
Nord^M

北北西
North-Northwest
Nord-Nordwest
Nord^M Nord-Ouest
Nor Noroeste^M
Nord^M Nord-Ovest^M

北北東
North-Northeast
Nord-Nordost
Nord^M Nord-Est
Norte^M Noreste^M
Nord^M Nord-Est^M

北西
Northwest
Nordwest
Nord^M Ouest
Noroeste^M
Nord-Ovest^M

北東
Northeast
Nordost
Nord^M Est
Noreste^M
Nord-Est^M

西北西
West-Northwest
West-Nordwest
Ouest^M Nord-Ouest
Oeste Noroeste^M
Ovest^M Nord-Ovest^M

東北東
East-Northeast
Ost-Nordost
Est^M Nord-Est
Este^M Noreste^M
Est^M Nord-Est^M

西
West
West
Ouest^M
Oeste^M
Ovest^M

東
East
Ost
Est^M
Este^M
Est^M

西南西
West-Southwest
West-Südwest
Ouest^M Sud-Ouest
Oeste Suroeste^M
Ovest^M Sud-Ovest^M

東南東
East-Southeast
Ost-Südost
Est^M Sud-Est
Este Sudeste^M
Est^M Sud-Est^M

南西
Southwest
Südwest
Sud^M Ouest
Suroeste^M
Sud-Ovest^M

南東
Southeast
Südost
Sud^M Est
Sudeste^M
Sud-Est^M

南南西
South-Southwest
Süd-Südwest
Sud^M Sud-Ouest
Sur Suroeste^M
Sud^M Sud-Ovest^M

南南東
South-Southeast
Süd-Südost
Sud^M Sud-Est
Sur Sudeste^M
Sud^M Sud-Est^M

南
South
Süd
Sud^M
Sur^M
Sud^M

行政区画図
political map
politische Karte^F
carte^F politique
mapa^M político
carta^F politica

州[省]界
internal boundary
Provinzgrenze^F
division^F territoriale
frontera^F interna
confine^M interno

州／省
province
Provinz^F
province^F
provincia^F
provincia^F

都市
city
Stadt^F
grande ville^F
ciudad^F
città^F

国境
international boundary
Staatsgrenze^F
frontière^F
frontera^F internacional
confine^M internazionale

首都
capital
Hauptstadt^F
capitale^F
capital^F
capitale^F

国
country
Land^N
pays^M
país^M
paese^M

州
state
Bundesstaat^M
État
estado^M
stato^M

地理 | GEOGRAPHY
GEOGRAPHIE | GÉOGRAPHIE | GEOGRAFÍA | GEOGRAFIA

地図作成法

日本語 | 英語 | ドイツ語 | フランス語 | スペイン語 | イタリア語

地勢図
physical map
physische Karte^F
carte^F physique
mapa^M físico
carta^F física

山脈
mountain range
Gebirgskette^F
chaîne^F de montagnes^F
cordillera^F
catena^F montuosa

湾
bay
Bucht^F
baie^F
bahía^F
baia^F

海
sea
Meer^N
mer^F
mar^M
mare^M

海峡
strait
Meerenge^F
détroit^M
estrecho^M
stretto^M

島
island
Insel^F
île^F
isla^F
isola^F

大洋
ocean
Ozean^M
océan^M
océano^M
oceano^M

大草原／プレーリー
prairie
Prärie^F
prairie^F
llanura^F
prateria^F

山地
mountain mass
Gebirgsmassiv^N
massif^M montagneux
macizo^M
massiccio montuoso^M

河口
river estuary
Flussmündung^F
estuaire^M
estuario^M
estuario^M

湖
lake
See^M
lac^M
lago^M
lago^M

川
river
Fluss^M
rivière^F
río^M
fiume^M

群島／列島
archipelago
Archipel^M
archipel^M
archipiélago^M
arcipelago^M

高原
plateau
Plateau^N, Hochebene^F
plateau^M
meseta^F
altopiano^M

半島
peninsula
Halbinsel^F
péninsule^F
península^F
penisola^F

湾
gulf
Golf^M
golfe^M
golfo^M
golfo^M

岬
cape
Kap^N
cap^M
cabo^M
capo^M

平野
plain
Ebene^F
plaine^F
planicie^F
pianura^F

大河
river
Fluss^M
fleuve^M
río^M
fiume^M

地峡
isthmus
Landenge^F
isthme^M
istmo^M
istmo^M

地理 | GEOGRAPHY
GEOGRAPHIE | GÉOGRAPHIE | GEOGRAFÍA | GEOGRAFIA

地図作成法

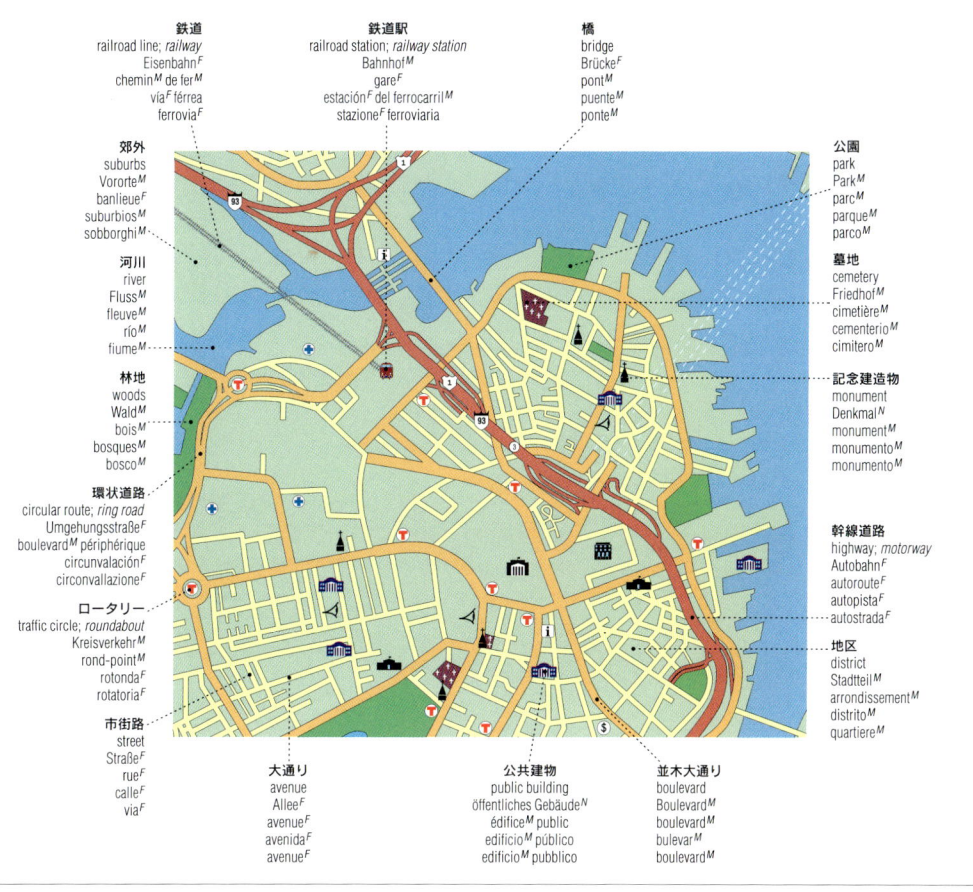

鉄道
railroad line; railway
Eisenbahn^F
chemin^M de fer^M
vía^F férrea
ferrovia^F

鉄道駅
railroad station; railway station
Bahnhof^M
gare^F
estación^F del ferrocarril^M
stazione^F ferroviaria

橋
bridge
Brücke^F
pont^M
puente^M
ponte^M

市街図
urban map
Stadtplan^M
plan^M urbain
mapa^M urbano
pianta^F di città^F

地球

郊外
suburbs
Vororte^M
banlieue^F
suburbios^M
sobborghi^M

公園
park
Park^M
parc^M
parque^M
parco^M

河川
river
Fluss^M
fleuve^M
río^M
fiume^M

墓地
cemetery
Friedhof^M
cimetière^M
cementerio^M
cimitero^M

林地
woods
Wald^M
bois^M
bosques^M
bosco^M

記念建造物
monument
Denkmal^N
monument^M
monumento^M
monumento^M

環状道路
circular route; ring road
Umgehungsstraße^F
boulevard^M périphérique
circunvalación^F
circonvallazione^F

幹線道路
highway; motorway
Autobahn^F
autoroute^F
autopista^F
autostrada^F

ロータリー
traffic circle; roundabout
Kreisverkehr^M
rond-point^M
rotonda^F
rotatoria^F

地区
district
Stadtteil^M
arrondissement^M
distrito^M
quartiere^M

市街路
street
Straße^F
rue^F
calle^F
vía^F

大通り
avenue
Allee^F
avenue^F
avenida^F
avenue^F

公共建物
public building
öffentliches Gebäude^N
édifice^M public
edificio^M público
edificio^M pubblico

並木大通り
boulevard
Boulevard^M
boulevard^M
bulevar^M
boulevard^M

道路地図
road map
Straßenkarte^F
carte^F routière
mapa^M de carreteras^F
carta^F stradale

幹線道路番号
highway number; motorway number
Autobahnnummer^F
numéro^M d'autoroute^F
número^M de la autopista^F
numero^M di autostrada^F

道路
road
Straße^F
route^F
carretera^F
strada^F

幹線道路
highway; motorway
Autobahn^F
autoroute^F
autopista^F
autostrada^F

道路番号
road number
Straßennummer^F
numéro^M de route^F
número^M de la carretera^F
numero^M di strada^F

レスト・エリア
rest area
Rastplatz^M
aire^F de repos^M
área^F de descanso^M
area^F di sosta^F

空港
airport
Flughafen^M
aéroport^M
aeropuerto^M
aeroporto^M

サービス・エリア
service area
Raststätte^F
aire^F de service^M
área^F de servicio^M
area^F di servizio^M

国立公園
national park
Nationalpark^M
parc^M national
parque^M nacional
parco^M nazionale

環状道路
belt highway
Umgehungsstraße^F
autoroute^F de ceinture^F
carretera^F de circunvalación^F
tangenziale^F

景観道路
scenic route
landschaftlich schöne Strecke^F
parcours^M pittoresque
ruta^F pintoresca
strada^F panoramica

二級道路
secondary road
Nebenstraße^F
route^F secondaire
carretera^F secundaria
strada^F secondaria

名所
point of interest
Sehenswürdigkeit^F
curiosité^F
punto^M de interés^M
punto^M di interesse^M

39

地理 | GEOGRAPHY
GEOGRAPHIE | GÉOGRAPHIE | GEOGRAFÍA | GEOGRAFIA

遠隔計測［探査］／隔測／リモート・センシング

remote sensing | Fernerkundung^F | télédétection^F | teledetección^M | telerilevamento^M

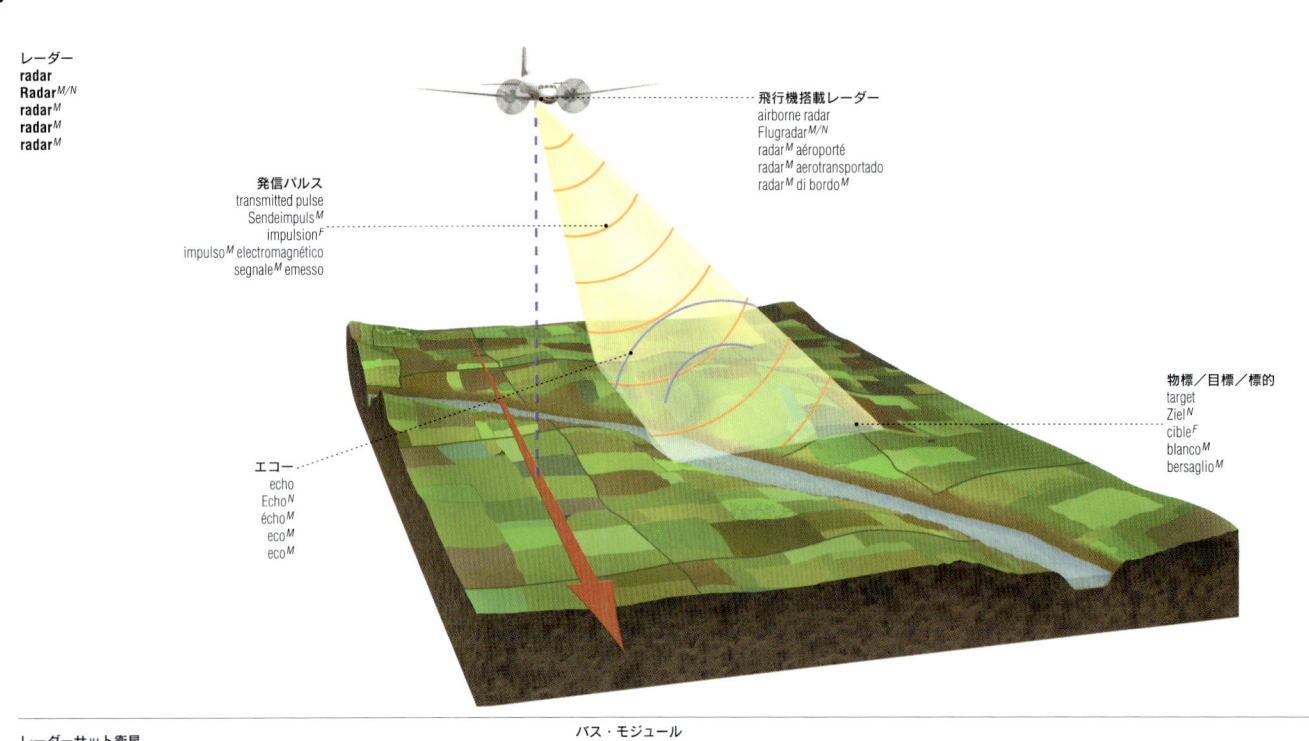

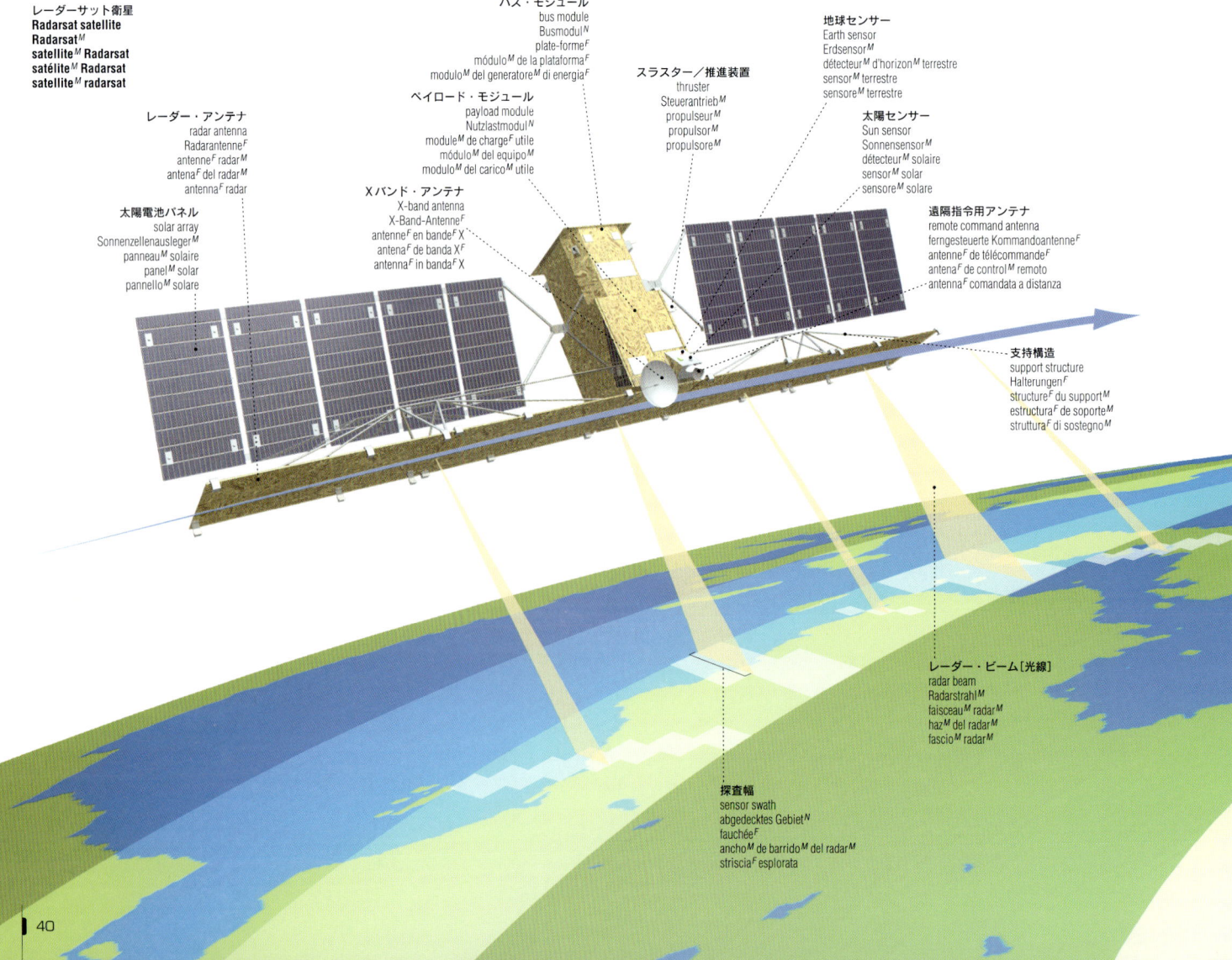

日本語 | 英語 | ドイツ語 | フランス語 | スペイン語 | イタリア語

地球

レーダー
radar
Radar^(M/N)
radar^M
radar^M
radar^M

飛行機搭載レーダー
airborne radar
Flugradar^(M/N)
radar aéroporté
radar^M aerotransportado
radar^M di bordo^M

発信パルス
transmitted pulse
Sendeimpuls^M
impulsion^F
impulso^M electromagnético
segnale^M emesso

物標／目標／標的
target
Ziel^N
cible^F
blanco^M
bersaglio^M

エコー
echo
Echo^N
écho^M
eco^M
eco^M

レーダーサット衛星
Radarsat satellite
Radarsat^M
satellite^M Radarsat
satélite^M Radarsat
satellite^M radarsat

バス・モジュール
bus module
Busmodul^N
plate-forme^F
módulo^M de la plataforma^F
modulo^M del generatore^M di energia^F

地球センサー
Earth sensor
Erdsensor^M
détecteur^M d'horizon^M terrestre
sensor^M terrestre
sensore^M terrestre

レーダー・アンテナ
radar antenna
Radarantenne^F
antenne^F radar
antena^F del radar^M
antenna^F radar

ペイロード・モジュール
payload module
Nutzlastmodul^N
module^M de charge^F utile
módulo^M del equipo^M
modulo^M del carico^M utile

スラスター／推進装置
thruster
Steuerantrieb^M
propulseur^M
propulsor^M
propulsore^M

太陽センサー
Sun sensor
Sonnensensor^M
détecteur^M solaire
sensor^M solar
sensore^M solare

太陽電池パネル
solar array
Sonnenzellenausleger^M
panneau^F solaire
panel^M solar
pannello^M solare

Xバンド・アンテナ
X-band antenna
X-Band-Antenne^F
antenne^F en bande^F X
antena^F de banda X^F
antenna^F in banda^F X

遠隔指令用アンテナ
remote command antenna
ferngesteuerte Kommandoantenne^F
antenne^F de télécommande^F
antena^F de control^M remoto
antenna^F comandata a distanza

支持構造
support structure
Halterungen^F
structure^F du support^M
estructura^F de soporte^M
struttura^F di sostegno^M

レーダー・ビーム［光線］
radar beam
Radarstrahl^M
faisceau^M radar
haz^M del radar^M
fascio^M radar

探査幅
sensor swath
abgedecktes Gebiet^N
fauchée^F
ancho^M de barrido^M del radar^M
striscia^F esplorata

40

地理 | GEOGRAPHY
GEOGRAPHIE | GÉOGRAPHIE | GEOGRAFÍA | GEOGRAFIA

遠隔計測［探査］／隔測／リモート・センシング

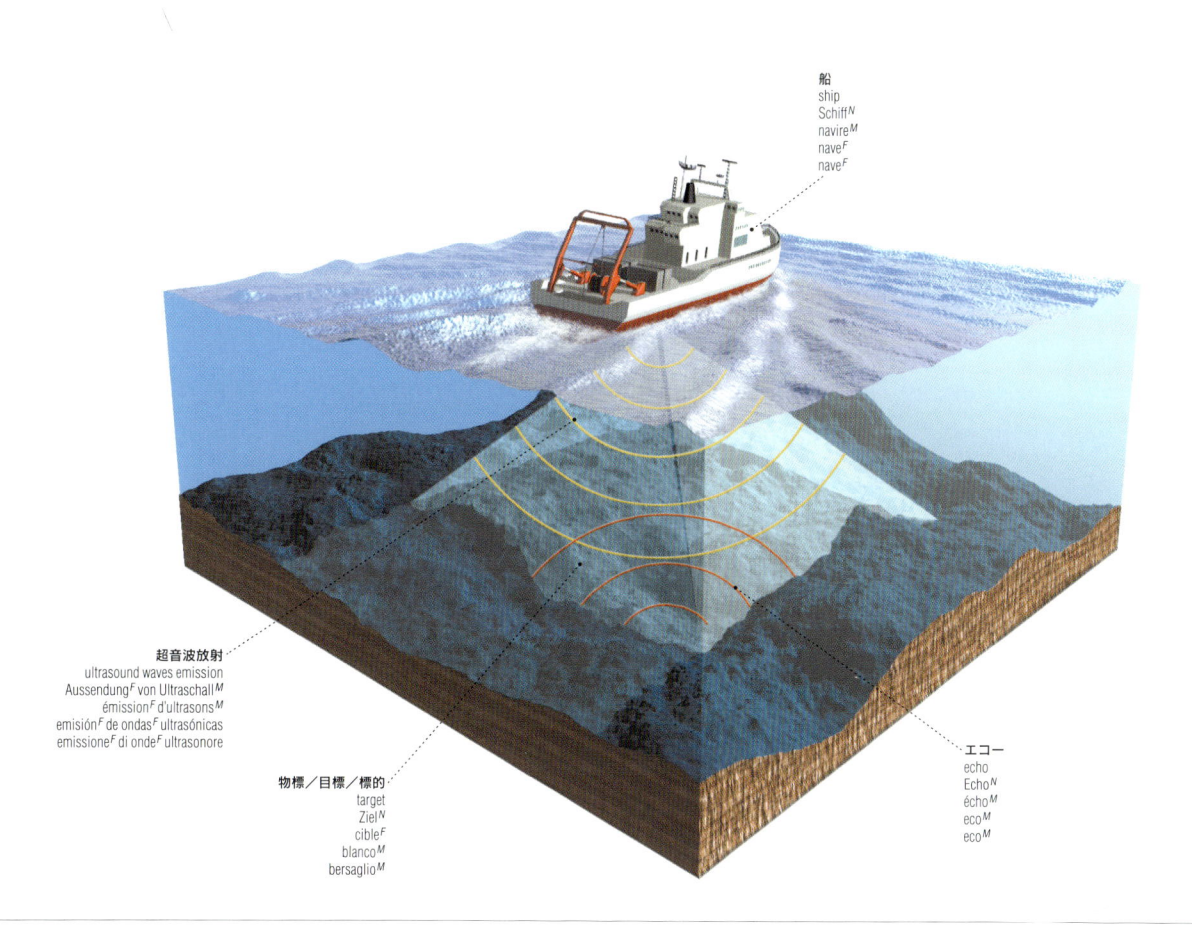

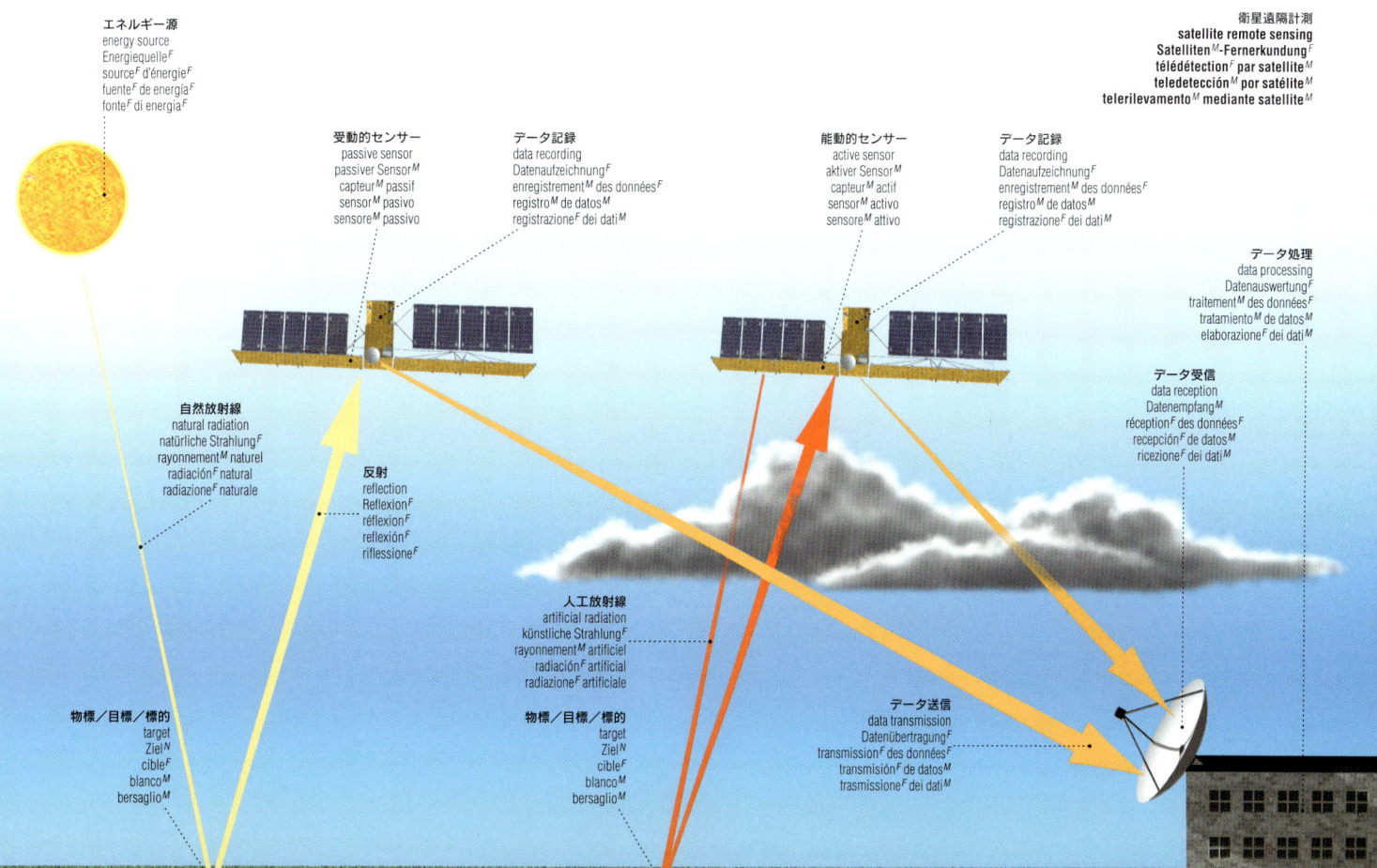

ソナー
sonar
Sonar[N]
sonar[N]
sonar[M]
sonar[M]

船
ship
Schiff[N]
navire[M]
nave[F]
nave[F]

超音波放射
ultrasound waves emission
Aussendung[F] von Ultraschall[M]
émission[F] d'ultrasons[M]
emisión[F] de ondas[F] ultrasónicas
emissione[F] di onde[F] ultrasonore

物標／目標／標的
target
Ziel[N]
cible[F]
blanco[M]
bersaglio[M]

エコー
echo
Echo[N]
écho[M]
eco[M]
eco[M]

エネルギー源
energy source
Energiequelle[F]
source[F] d'énergie[F]
fuente[F] de energía[F]
fonte[F] di energia[F]

受動的センサー
passive sensor
passiver Sensor[M]
capteur[M] passif
sensor[M] pasivo
sensore[M] passivo

データ記録
data recording
Datenaufzeichnung[F]
enregistrement[M] des données[F]
registro[M] de datos[M]
registrazione[F] dei dati[M]

能動的センサー
active sensor
aktiver Sensor[M]
capteur[M] actif
sensor[M] activo
sensore[M] attivo

データ記録
data recording
Datenaufzeichnung[F]
enregistrement[M] des données[F]
registro[M] de datos[M]
registrazione[F] dei dati[M]

衛星遠隔計測
satellite remote sensing
Satelliten[M]-Fernerkundung[F]
télédétection[F] par satellite[M]
teledetección[M] por satélite[M]
telerilevamento[M] mediante satellite[M]

データ処理
data processing
Datenauswertung[F]
traitement[M] des données[F]
tratamiento[M] de datos[M]
elaborazione[F] dei dati[M]

データ受信
data reception
Datenempfang[M]
réception[F] des données[F]
recepción[F] de datos[M]
ricezione[F] dei dati[M]

自然放射線
natural radiation
natürliche Strahlung[F]
rayonnement[M] naturel
radiación[F] natural
radiazione[F] naturale

反射
reflection
Reflexion[F]
réflexion[F]
reflexión[F]
riflessione[F]

人工放射線
artificial radiation
künstliche Strahlung[F]
rayonnement[M] artificiel
radiación[F] artificial
radiazione[F] artificiale

物標／目標／標的
target
Ziel[N]
cible[F]
blanco[M]
bersaglio[M]

物標／目標／標的
target
Ziel[N]
cible[F]
blanco[M]
bersaglio[M]

データ送信
data transmission
Datenübertragung[F]
transmission[F] des données[F]
transmisión[F] de datos[M]
trasmissione[F] dei dati[M]

地球

地質 | GEOLOGY
GEOLOGIE | GÉOLOGIE | GEOLOGÍA | GEOLOGIA

地殻断面図

日本語 | 英語 | ドイツ語 | フランス語 | スペイン語 | イタリア語

section of the Earth's crust | Erdkruste^F im Querschnitt^M | coupe^F de la croûte^F terrestre | corte^M de la corteza^F terrestre | sezione^F della crosta^F terrestre

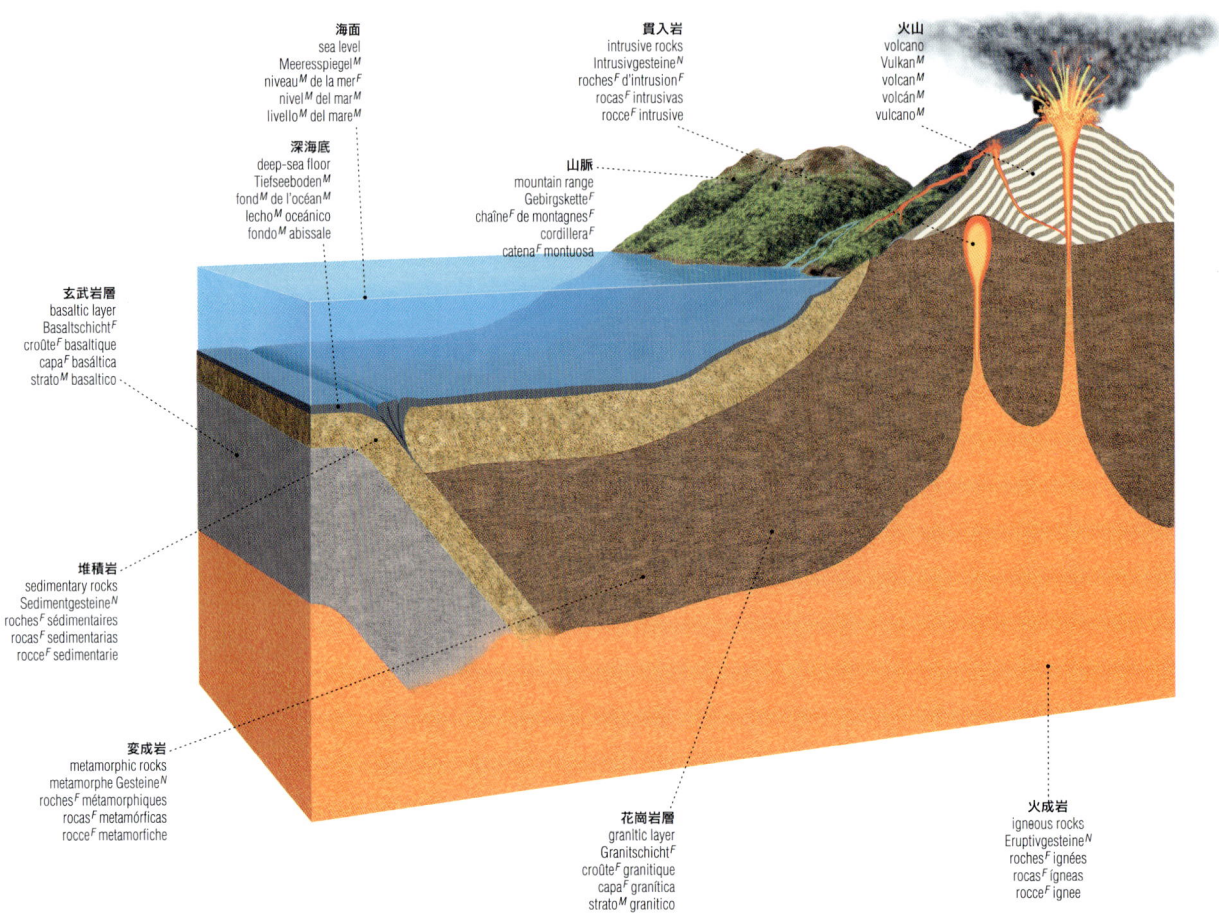

海面
sea level
Meeresspiegel^M
niveau^M de la mer^F
nivel^M del mar^M
livello^M del mare^M

貫入岩
intrusive rocks
Intrusivgesteine^N
roches^F d'intrusion^F
rocas^F intrusivas
rocce^F intrusive

火山
volcano
Vulkan^M
volcan
volcán
vulcano^M

深海底
deep-sea floor
Tiefseeboden^M
fond^M de l'océan^M
lecho^M oceánico
fondo^M abissale

山脈
mountain range
Gebirgskette^F
chaîne^F de montagnes^F
cordillera^F
catena^F montuosa

玄武岩層
basaltic layer
Basaltschicht^F
croûte^F basaltique
capa^F basáltica
strato^M basaltico

堆積岩
sedimentary rocks
Sedimentgesteine^N
roches^F sédimentaires
rocas^F sedimentarias
rocce^F sedimentarie

変成岩
metamorphic rocks
metamorphe Gesteine^N
roches^F métamorphiques
rocas^F metamórficas
rocce^F metamorfiche

花崗岩層
granitic layer
Granitschicht^F
croûte^F granitique
capa^F granítica
strato^M granitico

火成岩
igneous rocks
Eruptivgesteine^N
roches^F ignées
rocas^F ígneas
rocce^F ignee

地球の構造

structure of the Earth | Erdaufbau^M | structure^F de la Terre^F | estructura^F de la Tierra^F | struttura^F della Terra^F

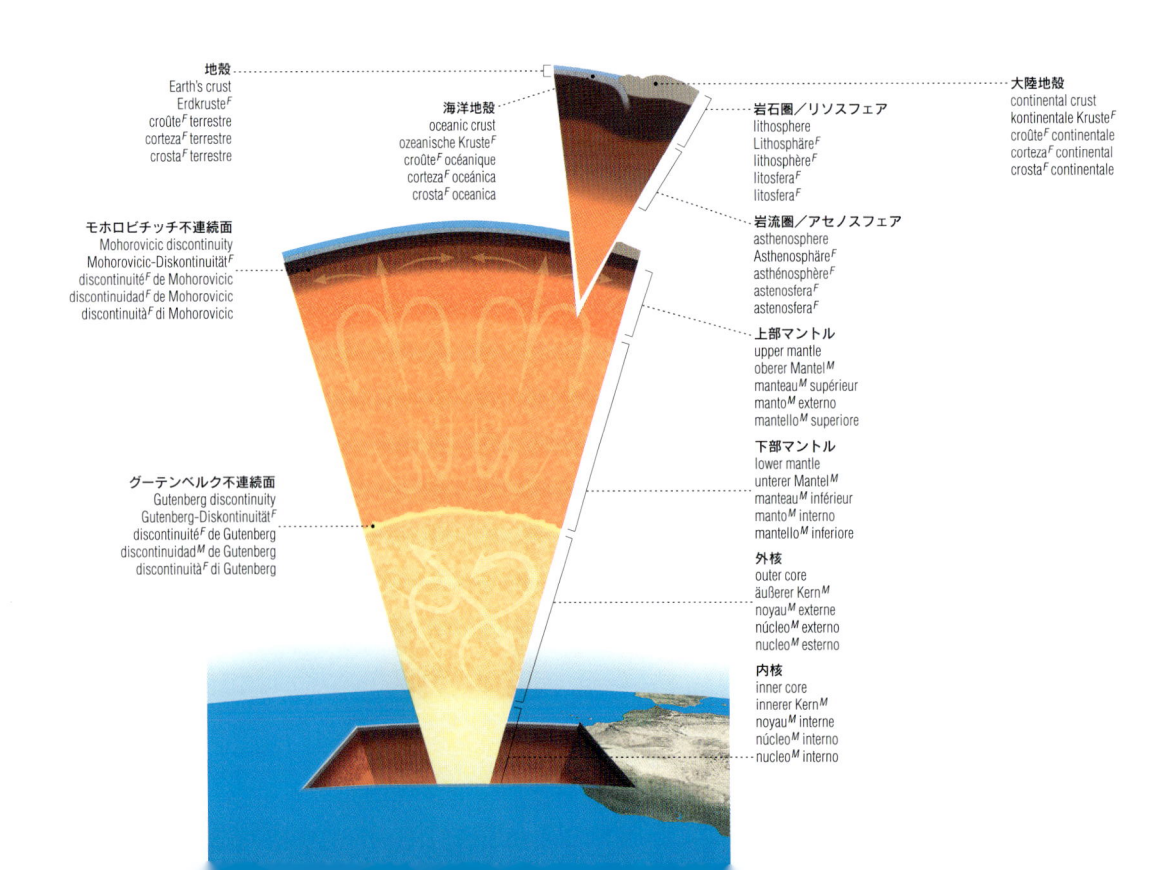

地殻
Earth's crust
Erdkruste^F
croûte^F terrestre
corteza^F terrestre
crosta^F terrestre

海洋地殻
oceanic crust
ozeanische Kruste^F
croûte^F océanique
corteza^F oceánica
crosta^F oceanica

岩石圏／リソスフェア
lithosphere
Lithosphäre^F
lithosphère^F
litosfera^F
litosfera^F

大陸地殻
continental crust
kontinentale Kruste^F
croûte^F continentale
corteza^F continental
crosta^F continentale

モホロビチッチ不連続面
Mohorovicic discontinuity
Mohorovicic-Diskontinuität^F
discontinuité^F de Mohorovicic
discontinuidad^F de Mohorovicic
discontinuità^F di Mohorovicic

岩流圏／アセノスフェア
asthenosphere
Asthenosphäre^F
asthénosphère^F
astenosfera^F
astenosfera^F

上部マントル
upper mantle
oberer Mantel^M
manteau^M supérieur
manto^M externo
mantello^M superiore

下部マントル
lower mantle
unterer Mantel^M
manteau^M inférieur
manto^M interno
mantello^M inferiore

グーテンベルク不連続面
Gutenberg discontinuity
Gutenberg-Diskontinuität^F
discontinuité^F de Gutenberg
discontinuidad^M de Gutenberg
discontinuità^F di Gutenberg

外核
outer core
äußerer Kern^M
noyau^M externe
núcleo^M externo
nucleo^M esterno

内核
inner core
innerer Kern^M
noyau^M interne
núcleo^M interno
nucleo^M interno

地質 | GEOLOGY
GEOLOGIE | GÉOLOGIE | GEOLOGÍA | GEOLOGIA

地殻[構造]プレート

tectonic plates | tektonische Platten^F | plaques^F tectoniques | placas^F tectónicas | placche^F tettoniche

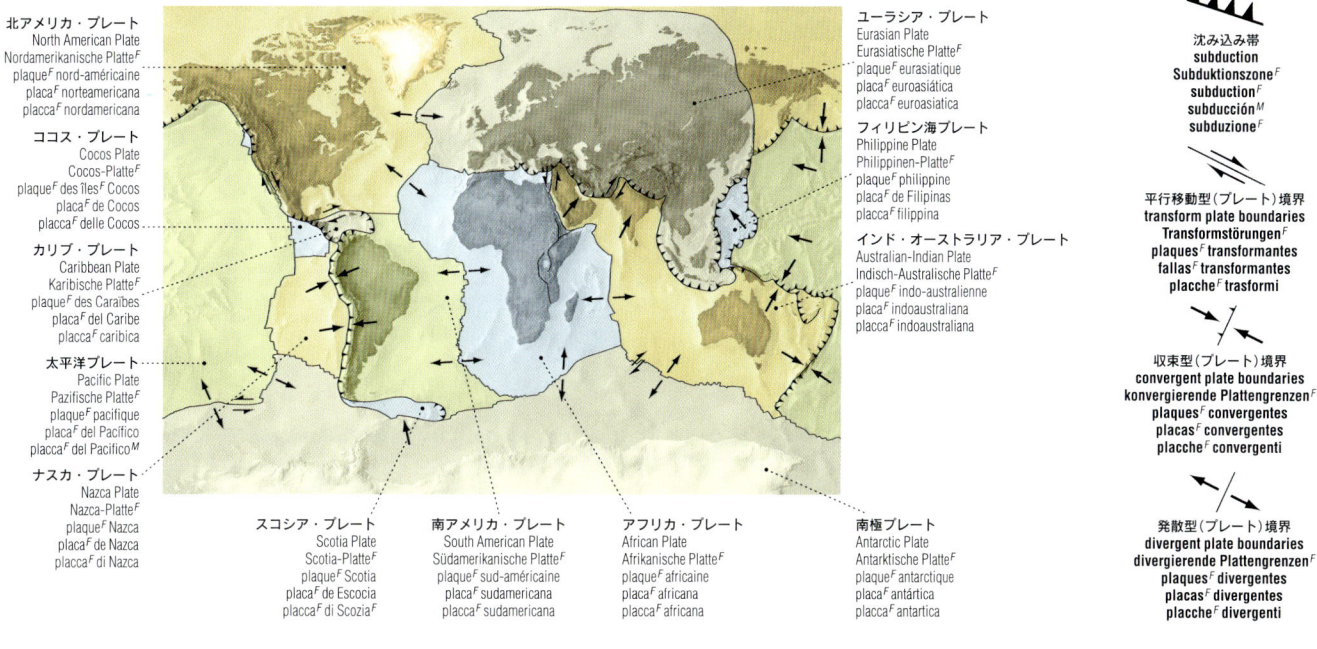

地球

北アメリカ・プレート
North American Plate
Nordamerikanische Platte^F
plaque^F nord-américaine
placa^F norteamericana
placca^F nordamericana

ココス・プレート
Cocos Plate
Cocos-Platte^F
plaque^F des îles^F Cocos
placa^F de Cocos
placca^F delle Cocos

カリブ・プレート
Caribbean Plate
Karibische Platte^F
plaque^F des Caraïbes
placa^F del Caribe
placca^F caribica

太平洋プレート
Pacific Plate
Pazifische Platte^F
plaque^F pacifique
placa^F del Pacífico
placca^F del Pacifico^M

ナスカ・プレート
Nazca Plate
Nazca-Platte^F
plaque^F Nazca
placa^F de Nazca
placca^F di Nazca

スコシア・プレート
Scotia Plate
Scotia-Platte^F
plaque^F Scotia
placa^F de Escocia
placca^F di Scozia^F

南アメリカ・プレート
South American Plate
Südamerikanische Platte^F
plaque^F sud-américaine
placa^F sudamericana
placca^F sudamericana

アフリカ・プレート
African Plate
Afrikanische Platte^F
plaque^F africaine
placa^F africana
placca^F africana

ユーラシア・プレート
Eurasian Plate
Eurasiatische Platte^F
plaque^F eurasiatique
placa^F euroasiática
placca^F euroasiatica

フィリピン海プレート
Philippine Plate
Philippinen-Platte^F
plaque^F philippine
placa^F de Filipinas
placca^F filippina

インド・オーストラリア・プレート
Australian-Indian Plate
Indisch-Australische Platte^F
plaque^F indo-australienne
placa^F indoaustraliana
placca^F indoaustraliana

南極プレート
Antarctic Plate
Antarktische Platte^F
plaque^F antarctique
placa^F antártica
placca^F antartica

沈み込み帯
subduction
Subduktionszone^F
subduction^F
subducción^M
subduzione^F

平行移動型(プレート)境界
transform plate boundaries
Transformstörungen^F
plaques^F transformantes
fallas^F transformantes
placche^F trasformi

収束型(プレート)境界
convergent plate boundaries
konvergierende Plattengrenzen^F
plaques^F convergentes
placas^F convergentes
placche^F convergenti

発散型(プレート)境界
divergent plate boundaries
divergierende Plattengrenzen^F
plaques^F divergentes
placas^F divergentes
placche^F divergenti

地震

earthquake | Erdbeben^N | séisme^M | terremoto^M | terremoto^M

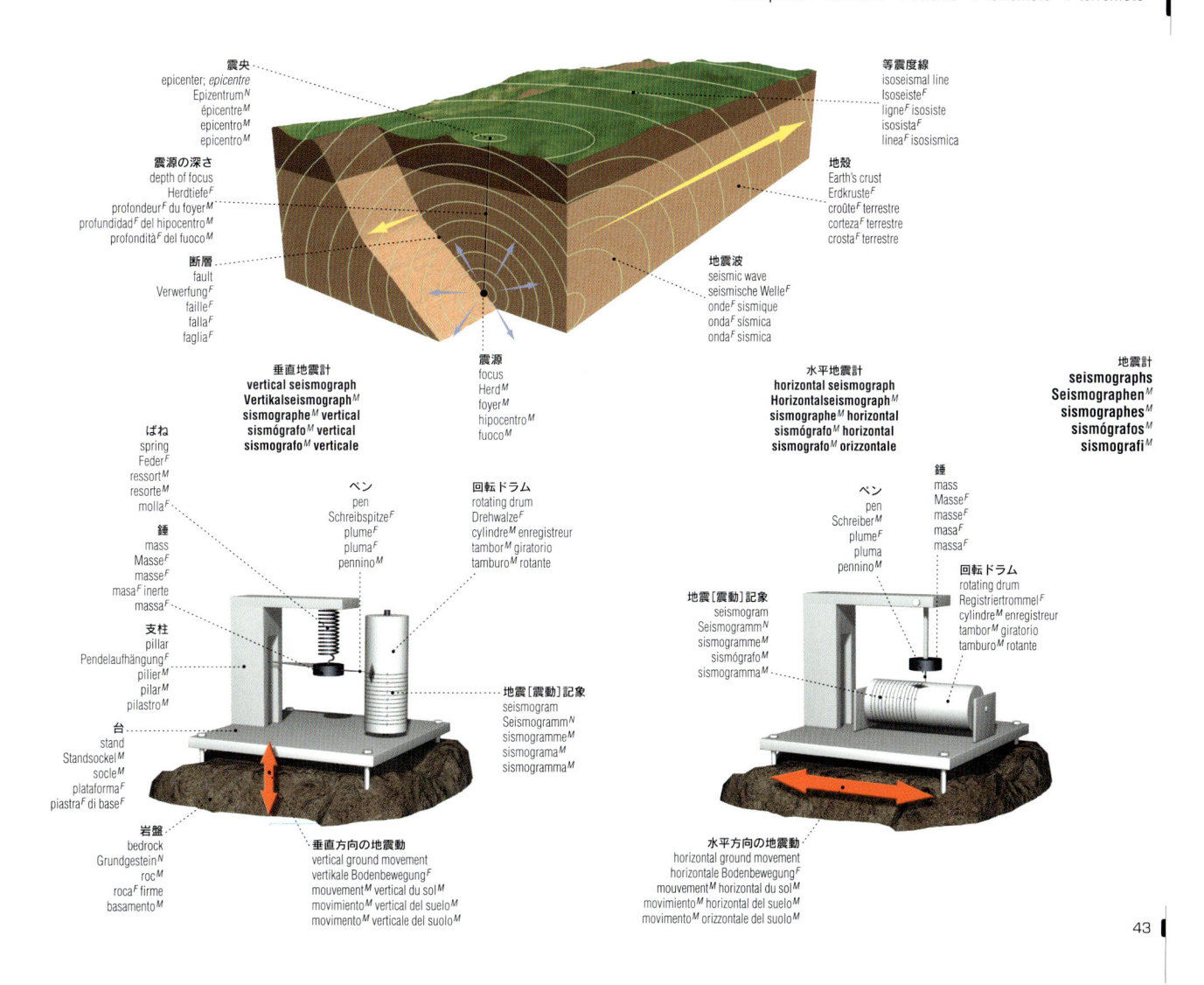

震央
epicenter; *epicentre*
Epizentrum^N
épicentre^M
epicentro^M
epicentro^M

震源の深さ
depth of focus
Herdtiefe^F
profondeur^F du foyer^M
profundidad^F del hipocentro^M
profondità^F del fuoco^M

断層
fault
Verwerfung^F
faille^F
falla^F
faglia^F

垂直地震計
vertical seismograph
Vertikalseismograph^M
sismographe^M vertical
sismógrafo^M vertical
sismografo^M verticale

ばね
spring
Feder^F
ressort^M
resorte^M
molla^F

錘
mass
Masse^F
masse^F inerte
massa^F

支柱
pillar
Pendelaufhängung^F
pilier^M
pilar^M
pilastro^M

台
stand
Standsockel^M
socle^M
plataforma^F
piastra^F di base^F

岩盤
bedrock
Grundgestein^N
roc^M
roca^F firme
basamento^M

震源
focus
Herd^M
foyer^M
hipocentro^M
fuoco^M

ペン
pen
Schreibspitze^F
plume^F
pluma^F
pennino^M

回転ドラム
rotating drum
Drehwalze^F
cylindre^M enregistreur
tambor^M giratorio
tamburo^M rotante

地震[震動]記象
seismogram
Seismogramm^N
sismogramme^M
sismógrafo^M
sismograma^M
sismogramma^M

垂直方向の地震動
vertical ground movement
vertikale Bodenbewegung^F
mouvement^M vertical du sol^M
movimiento^M vertical del suelo^M
movimento^M verticale del suolo^M

等震度線
isoseismal line
Isoseiste^F
ligne^F isosiste
isosista^F
linea^F isosismica

地殻
Earth's crust
Erdkruste^F
croûte^F terrestre
corteza^F terrestre
crosta^F terrestre

地震波
seismic wave
seismische Welle^F
onde^F sismique
onda^F sísmica
onda^F sismica

水平地震計
horizontal seismograph
Horizontalseismograph^M
sismographe^M horizontal
sismógrafo^M horizontal
sismografo^M orizzontale

ペン
pen
Schreiber^M
plume^F
pluma
pennino^M

地震[震動]記象
seismogram
Seismogramme
sismogramme
sismógrafo^M
sismogramma^M

回転ドラム
rotating drum
Registriertrommel^F
cylindre^M enregistreur
tambor^M giratorio
tamburo^M rotante

水平方向の地震動
horizontal ground movement
horizontale Bodenbewegung^F
mouvement^M horizontal du sol^M
movimiento^M horizontal del suelo^M
movimento^M orizzontale del suolo^M

地震計
seismographs
Seismographen^M
sismographes^M
sismógrafos^M
sismografi^M

錘
mass
Masse^F
masse^F
masa^F
massa^F

43

地質 | GEOLOGY
GÉOLOGIE | GÉOLOGIE | GEOLOGÍA | GEOLOGIA

火山

volcano | Vulkan^M | volcan^M | volcán^M | vulcano^M

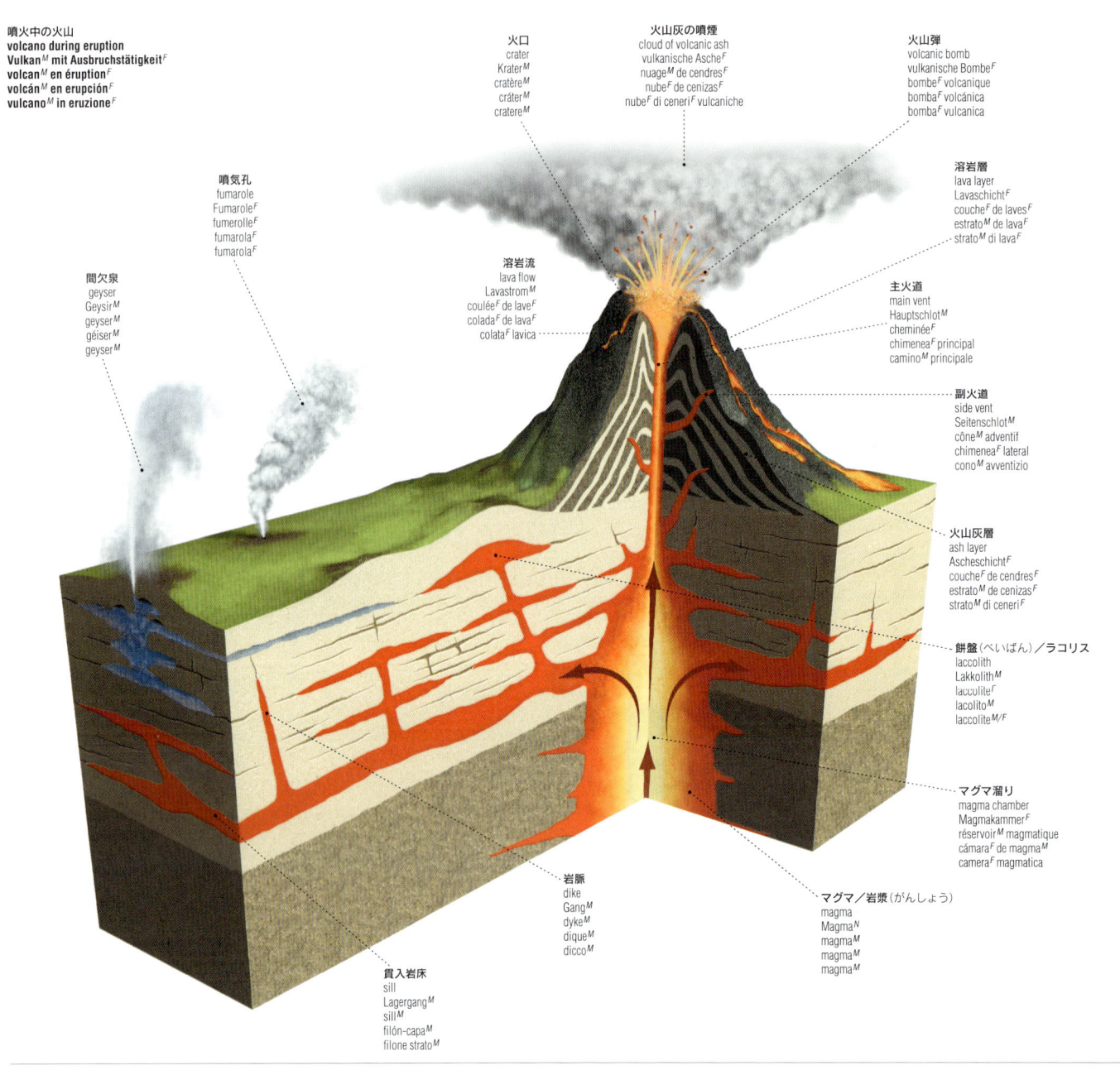

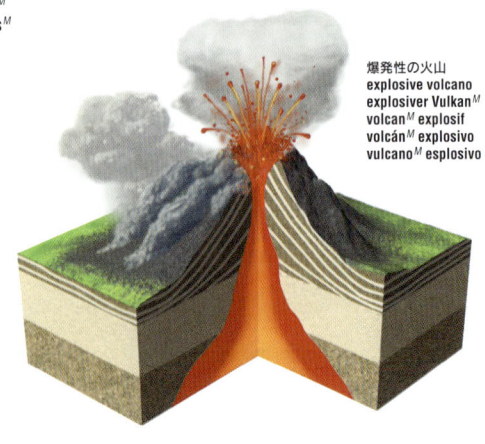

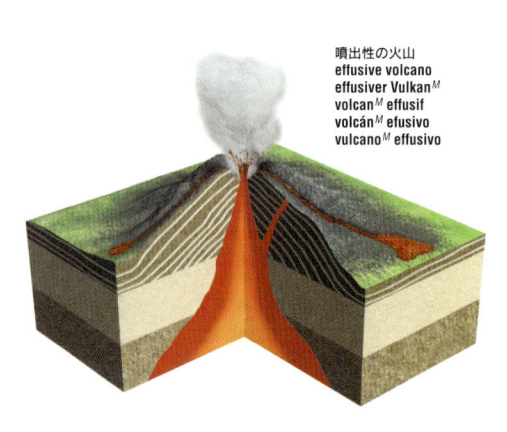

日本語 | 英語 | ドイツ語 | フランス語 | スペイン語 | イタリア語

地球

噴火中の火山
volcano during eruption
Vulkan^M mit Ausbruchstätigkeit^F
volcan^M en éruption^F
volcán^M en erupción^F
vulcano^M in eruzione^F

噴気孔
fumarole
Fumarole
fumerolle^F
fumarola^F
fumarola^F

間欠泉
geyser
Geysir^M
geyser^M
géiser^M
geyser^M

火口
crater
Krater^M
cratère^M
cráter^M
cratere^M

火山灰の噴煙
cloud of volcanic ash
vulkanische Asche^F
nuage^M de cendres^F
nube^F de cenizas^F
nube^F di ceneri^F vulcaniche

溶岩流
lava flow
Lavastrom^M
coulée^F de lave^F
colada^F de lava^F
colata^F lavica

火山弾
volcanic bomb
vulkanische Bombe^F
bombe^F volcanique
bomba^F volcánica
bomba^F vulcanica

溶岩層
lava layer
Lavaschicht^F
couche^F de laves^F
estrato^M de lava^F
strato^M di lava^F

主火道
main vent
Hauptschlot^M
cheminée^F
chimenea^F principal
camino^M principale

副火道
side vent
Seitenschlot^M
cône^M adventif
chimenea^F lateral
cono^M avventizio

火山灰層
ash layer
Ascheschicht^F
couche^F de cendres^F
estrato^M de cenizas^F
strato^M di ceneri^F

餅盤（べいばん）／ラコリス
laccolith
Lakkolith^M
laccolite^F
lacolito^M
laccolite^M/F

マグマ溜り
magma chamber
Magmakammer^F
réservoir^M magmatique
cámara^F de magma^M
camera^F magmatica

岩脈
dike
Gang^M
dyke^M
dique^M
dicco^M

マグマ／岩漿（がんしょう）
magma
Magma^N
magma^M
magma^M
magma^M

貫入岩床
sill
Lagergang^M
sill^M
filón-capa^M
filone strato^M

火山の例
examples of volcanoes
Vulkantypen^M
exemples^M de volcans^M
ejemplos^M de volcanes^M
esempi^M di vulcani^M

爆発性の火山
explosive volcano
explosiver Vulkan^M
volcan^M explosif
volcán^M explosivo
vulcano^M esplosivo

噴出性の火山
effusive volcano
effusiver Vulkan^M
volcan^M effusif
volcán^M efusivo
vulcano^M effusivo

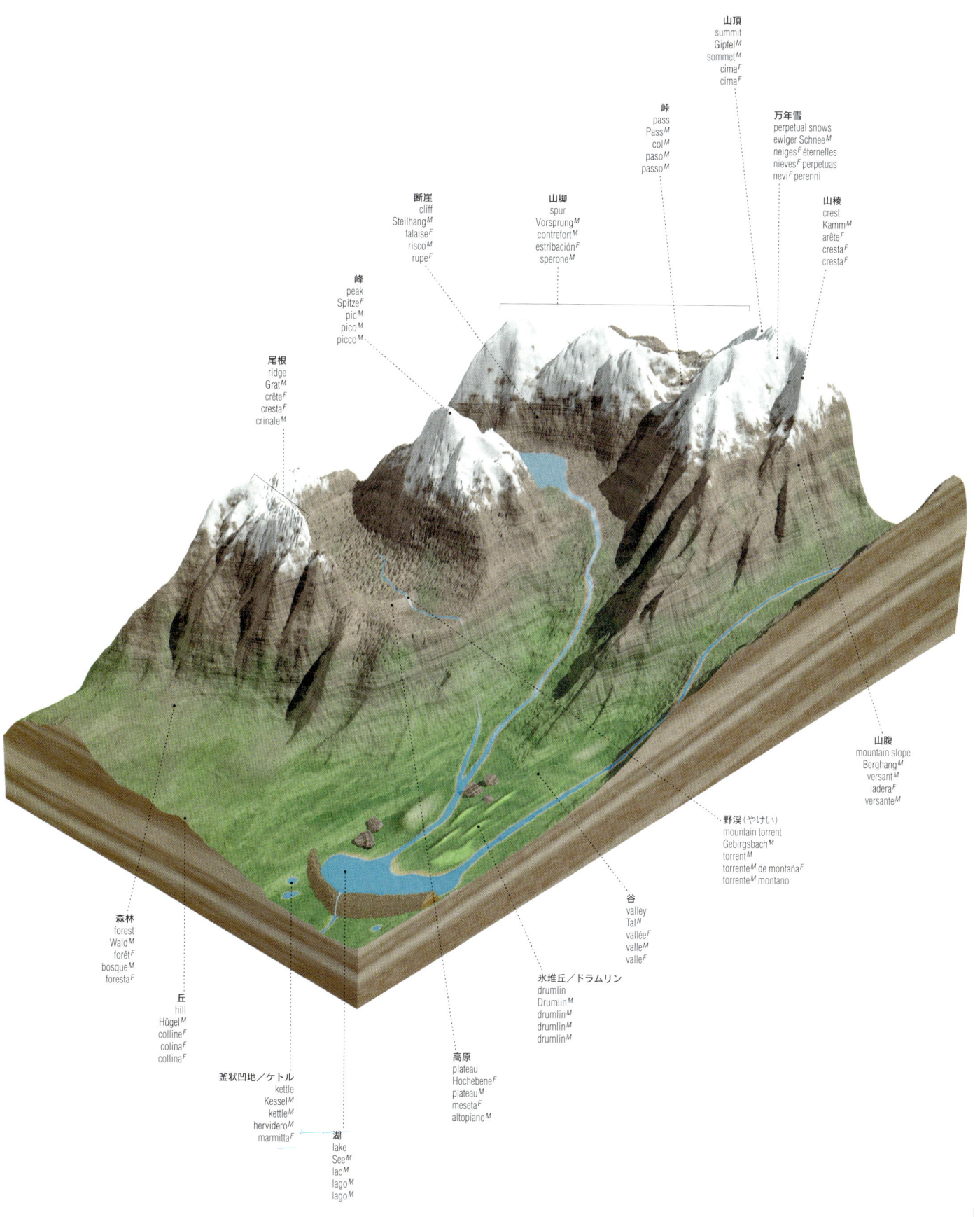

地質 | GEOLOGY
GEOLOGIE | GÉOLOGIE | GEOLOGÍA | GEOLOGIA

山

mountain | Berg^M | montagne^F | montaña^F | montagna^F

山頂
summit
Gipfel^M
sommet^M
cima^F
cima^F

峠
pass
Pass^M
col^M
paso^M
passo^M

万年雪
perpetual snows
ewiger Schnee^M
neiges^F éternelles
nieves^F perpetuas
nevi^F perenni

断崖
cliff
Steilhang^M
falaise^F
risco^M
rupe^F

山脚
spur
Vorsprung^M
contrefort^M
estribación^F
sperone^M

山稜
crest
Kamm^M
arête^F
cresta^F
cresta^F

峰
peak
Spitze^F
pic^M
pico^M
picco^M

尾根
ridge
Grat^M
crête^F
cresta^F
crinale^M

山腹
mountain slope
Berghang^M
versant^M
ladera^F
versante^M

野渓（やけい）
mountain torrent
Gebirgsbach^M
torrent^M
torrente^M de montaña^F
torrente^M montano

森林
forest
Wald^M
forêt^F
bosque^M
foresta^F

谷
valley
Tal^N
vallée^F
valle^M
valle^F

氷堆丘／ドラムリン
drumlin
Drumlin^M
drumlin^M
drumlin^M
drumlin^M

丘
hill
Hügel^M
colline^F
colina^F
collina^F

高原
plateau
Hochebene^F
plateau^M
meseta^F
altopiano^M

釜状凹地／ケトル
kettle
Kessel^M
kettle^M
hervidero^M
marmitta^F

湖
lake
See^M
lac^M
lago^M
lago^M

地球

45

地質 | GEOLOGY
GEOLOGIE | GÉOLOGIE | GEOLOGÍA | GEOLOGIA

氷河

日本語 | 英語 | ドイツ語 | フランス語 | スペイン語 | イタリア語

glacier | Gletscher^M | glacier^M | glaciar^M | ghiacciaio^M

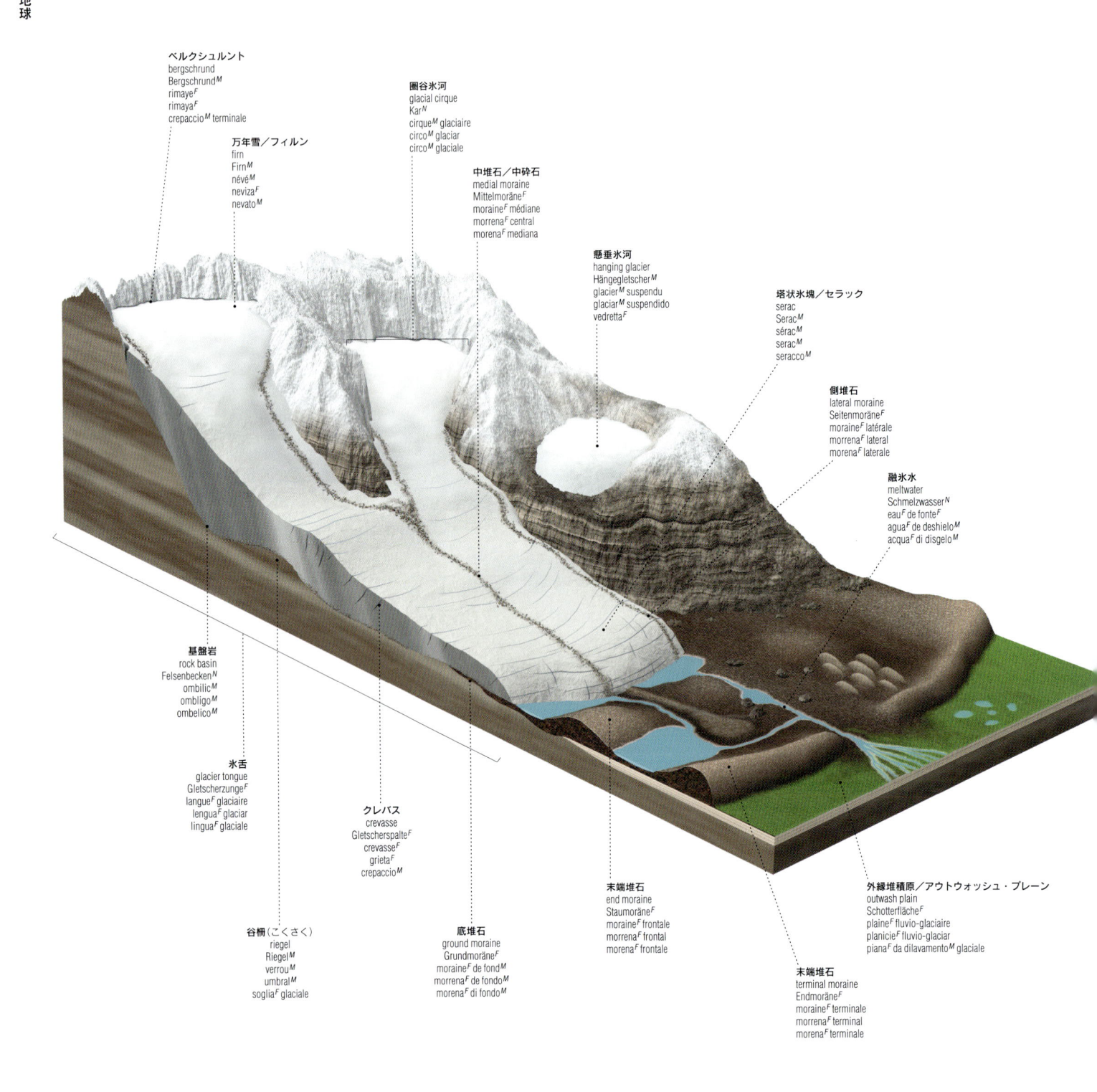

地球

ベルクシュルント
bergschrund
Bergschrund^M
rimaye^F
rimaya^F
crepaccio^M terminale

万年雪／フィルン
firn
Firn^M
névé^M
neviza^F
nevato^M

圏谷氷河
glacial cirque
Kar^N
cirque^M glaciaire
circo^M glaciar
circo^M glaciale

中堆石／中碓石
medial moraine
Mittelmoräne^F
moraine^F médiane
morrena^F central
morena^F mediana

懸垂氷河
hanging glacier
Hängegletscher^M
glacier^M suspendu
glaciar^M suspendido
vedretta^F

塔状氷塊／セラック
serac
Serac^M
sérac^M
serac^M
seracco^M

側堆石
lateral moraine
Seitenmoräne^F
moraine^F latérale
morrena^F lateral
morena^F laterale

融氷水
meltwater
Schmelzwasser^N
eau^F de fonte^F
agua^F de deshielo^M
acqua^F di disgelo^M

基盤岩
rock basin
Felsenbecken^N
ombilic^M
ombligo^M
ombelico^M

氷舌
glacier tongue
Gletscherzunge^F
langue^F glaciaire
lengua^F glaciar
lingua^F glaciale

クレバス
crevasse
Gletscherspalte^F
crevasse^F
grieta^F
crepaccio^M

谷柵（こくさく）
riegel
Riegel^M
verrou^M
umbral^M
soglia^F glaciale

底堆石
ground moraine
Grundmoräne^F
moraine^F de fond^M
morrena^F de fondo^M
morena^F di fondo^M

末端堆石
end moraine
Staumoräne^F
moraine^F frontale
morrena^F frontal
morena^F frontale

外縁堆積原／アウトウォッシュ・プレーン
outwash plain
Schotterfläche^F
plaine^F fluvio-glaciaire
planicie^F fluvio-glaciar
piana^F da dilavamento^M glaciale

末端堆石
terminal moraine
Endmoräne^F
moraine^F terminale
morrena^F terminal
morena^F terminale

地質 | GEOLOGY
GEOLOGIE | GÉOLOGIE | GEOLOGÍA | GEOLOGIA

洞穴
cave | Höhle^F | grotte^F | gruta^F | grotta^F

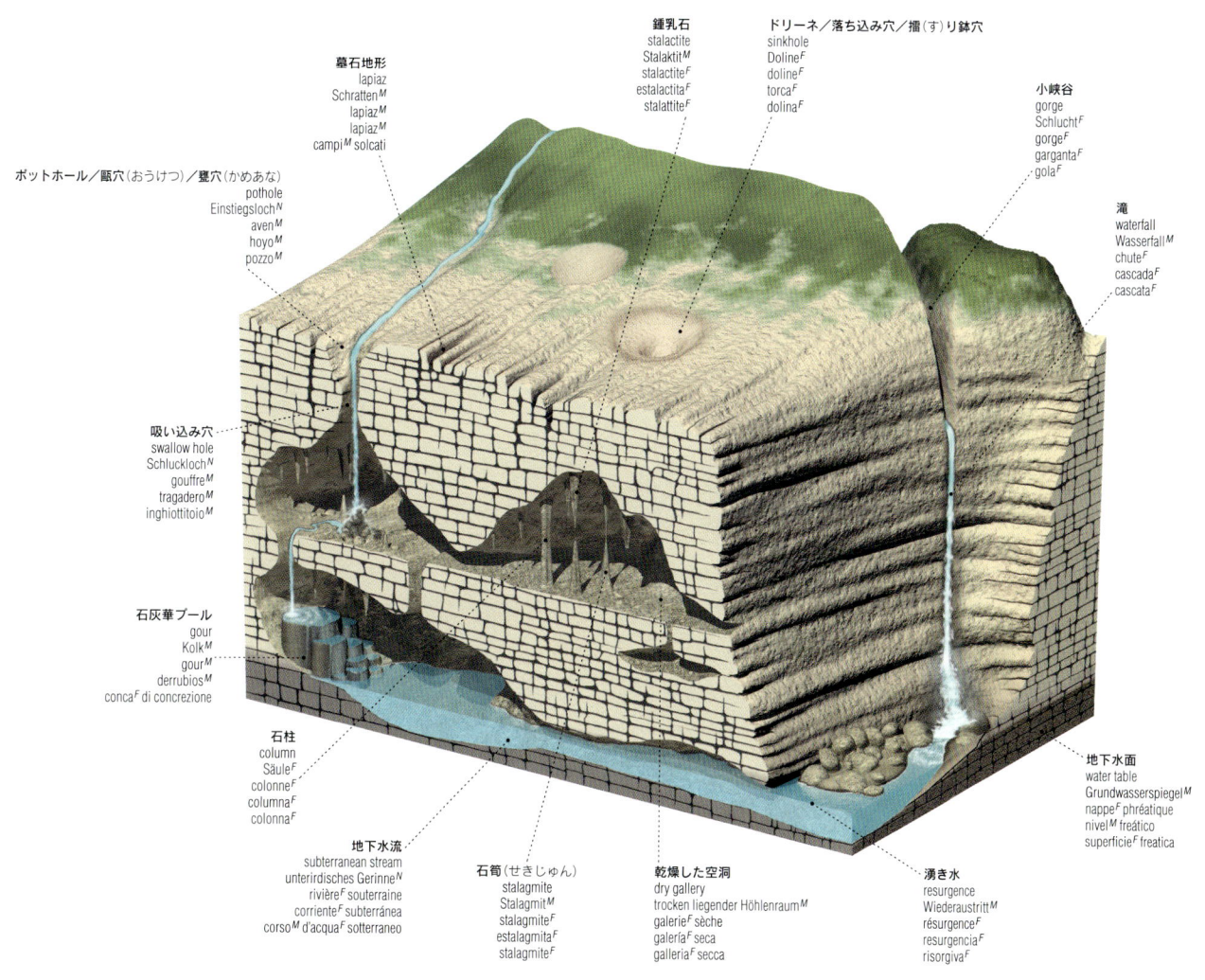

墓石地形
lapiaz
Schratten^M
lapiaz^M
lapiaz^M
campi^M solcati

鍾乳石
stalactite
Stalaktit^M
stalactite^F
estalactita^F
stalattite^F

ドリーネ／落ち込み穴／擂(す)り鉢穴
sinkhole
Doline^F
doline^F
torca^F
dolina^F

小峡谷
gorge
Schlucht^F
gorge^F
garganta^F
gola^F

ポットホール／甌穴（おうけつ）／甕穴（かめあな）
pothole
Einstiegsloch^N
aven^M
hoyo^M
pozzo^M

滝
waterfall
Wasserfall^M
chute^F
cascada^F
cascata^F

吸い込み穴
swallow hole
Schluckloch^N
gouffre^M
tragadero^M
inghiottitoio^M

石灰華プール
gour
Kolk^M
gour^M
derrubios^M
conca^F di concrezione

石柱
column
Säule^F
colonne^F
columna^F
colonna^F

地下水面
water table
Grundwasserspiegel^M
nappe^F phréatique
nivel^M freático
superficie^F freatica

地下水流
subterranean stream
unterirdisches Gerinne^N
rivière^F souterraine
corriente^F subterránea
corso^M d'acqua^F sotterraneo

石筍（せきじゅん）
stalagmite
Stalagmit^M
stalagmite^F
estalagmita^F
stalagmite^F

乾燥した空洞
dry gallery
trocken liegender Höhlenraum^M
galerie^F sèche
galería^F seca
galleria^F secca

湧き水
resurgence
Wiederaustritt^M
résurgence^F
resurgencia^F
risorgiva^F

地滑り
landslides | Bodenbewegungen^F | mouvements^M de terrain^M | desprendimientos^M de tierras^F | movimenti del terreno^M

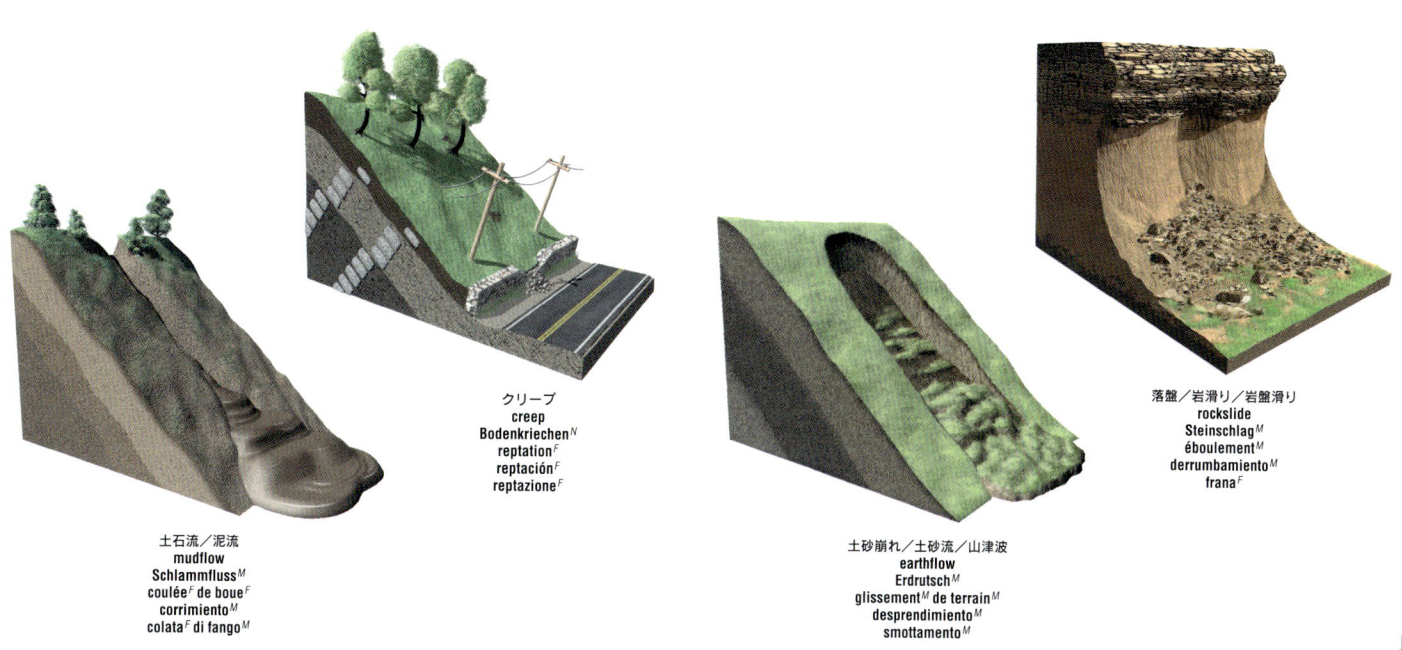

土石流／泥流
mudflow
Schlammfluss^M
coulée^F de boue^F
corrimiento^M
colata^F di fango^M

クリープ
creep
Bodenkriechen^N
reptation^F
reptación^F
reptazione^F

土砂崩れ／土砂流／山津波
earthflow
Erdrutsch^M
glissement^M de terrain^M
desprendimiento^M
smottamento^M

落盤／岩滑り／岩盤滑り
rockslide
Steinschlag^M
éboulement^M
derrumbamiento^M
frana^F

地質 | GEOLOGY
GEOLOGIE | GÉOLOGIE | GEOLOGÍA | GEOLOGIA

水流

watercourse | Flusslandschaft^F | cours^M d'eau^F | corriente^F de agua^F | corso^M d'acqua^F

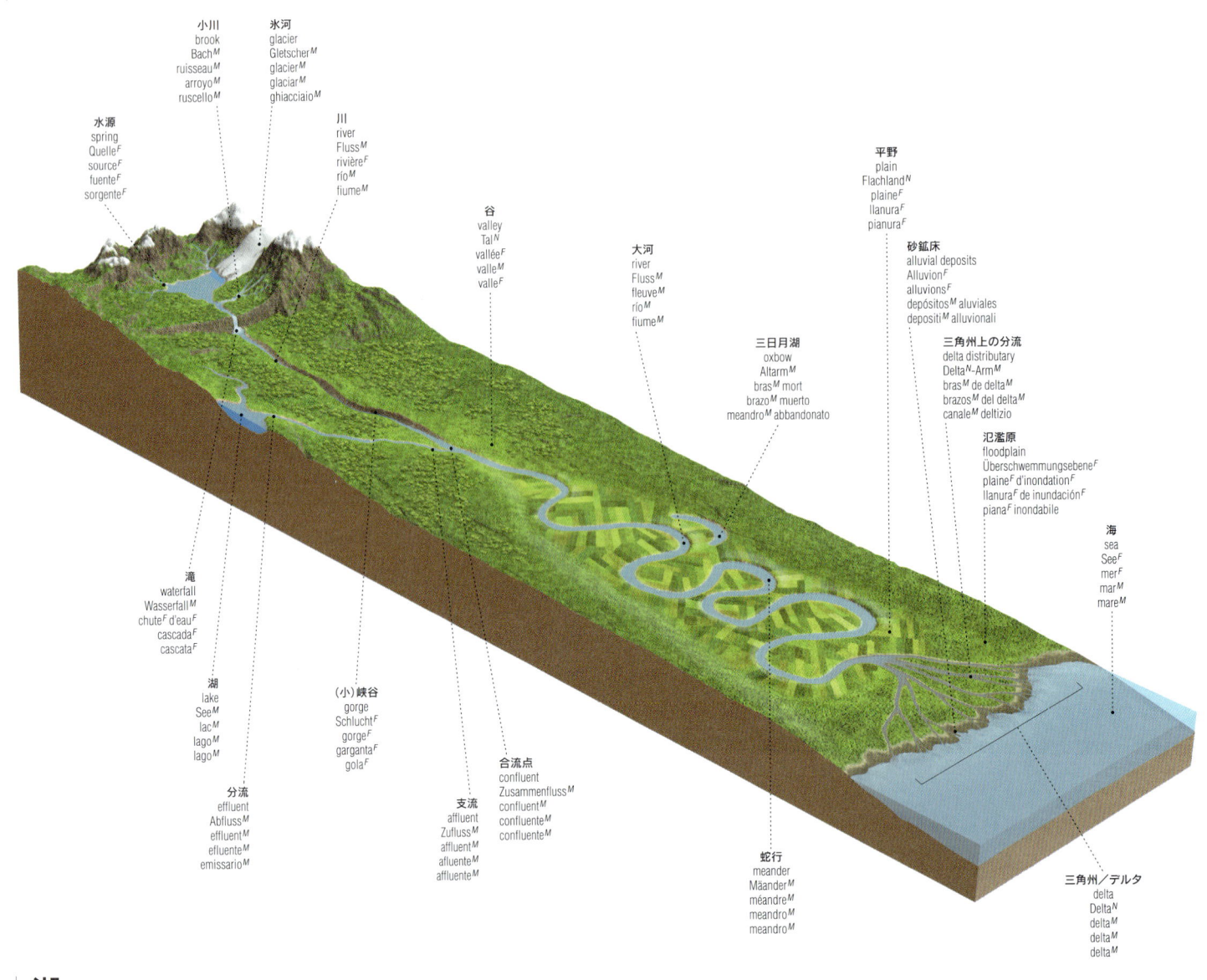

日本語 | 英語 | ドイツ語 | フランス語 | スペイン語 | イタリア語

地球

小川
brook
Bach^M
ruisseau^M
arroyo^M
ruscello^M

氷河
glacier
Gletscher^M
glacier^M
glaciar^M
ghiacciaio^M

水源
spring
Quelle^F
source^F
fuente^F
sorgente^F

川
river
Fluss^M
rivière^F
río^M
fiume^M

谷
valley
Tal^N
vallée^F
valle^M
valle^F

大河
river
Fluss^M
fleuve^M
río^M
fiume^M

平野
plain
Flachland^N
plaine^F
llanura^F
pianura^F

砂鉱床
alluvial deposits
Alluvion^F
alluvions^F
depósitos^M aluviales
depositi^M alluvionali

三日月湖
oxbow
Altarm^M
bras^M mort
brazo^M muerto
meandro^M abbandonato

三角州上の分流
delta distributary
Delta^N-Arm^M
bras^M de delta^M
brazos^M del delta^M
canale^M deltizio

氾濫原
floodplain
Überschwemmungsebene^F
plaine^F d'inondation^F
llanura^F de inundación^F
piana^F inondabile

海
sea
See^F
mer^F
mar^M
mare^M

滝
waterfall
Wasserfall^M
chute^F d'eau^F
cascada^F
cascata^F

湖
lake
See^M
lac^M
lago^M
lago^M

(小)峡谷
gorge
Schlucht^F
gorge^F
garganta^F
gola^F

合流点
confluent
Zusammenfluss^M
confluent^M
confluente^M
confluente^M

分流
effluent
Abfluss^M
effluent^M
efluente^M
emissario^M

支流
affluent
Zufluss^M
affluent^M
afluente^M
affluente^M

蛇行
meander
Mäander^M
méandre^M
meandro^M
meandro^M

三角州／デルタ
delta
Delta^N
delta^M
delta^M
delta^M

湖

lakes | Seen^M | lacs^M | lagos^M | laghi^M

氷河湖
glacial lake
Gletschersee^M
lac^M d'origine^F glaciaire
lago^M glaciar
lago^M glaciale

火口湖
volcanic lake
vulkanischer See^M
lac^M d'origine^F volcanique
lago^M volcánico
lago^M vulcanico

構造湖
tectonic lake
tektonischer See^M
lac^M d'origine^F tectonique
lago^M tectónico
lago^M tettonico

三日月湖
oxbow lake
Altarm^M
lac^M en croissant^M
lago^M de brazo^M muerto
lago^M di meandro^M abbandonato

オアシス
oasis
Oase^F
oasis^F
oasis^M
oasi^F

人工湖
artificial lake
künstlicher See^M
lac^M artificiel
embalse^M
lago^M artificiale

地質 | GEOLOGY
GEOLOGIE | GÉOLOGIE | GEOLOGÍA | GEOLOGIA

波
wave | Welle^F | vague^F | ola^F | onda^F

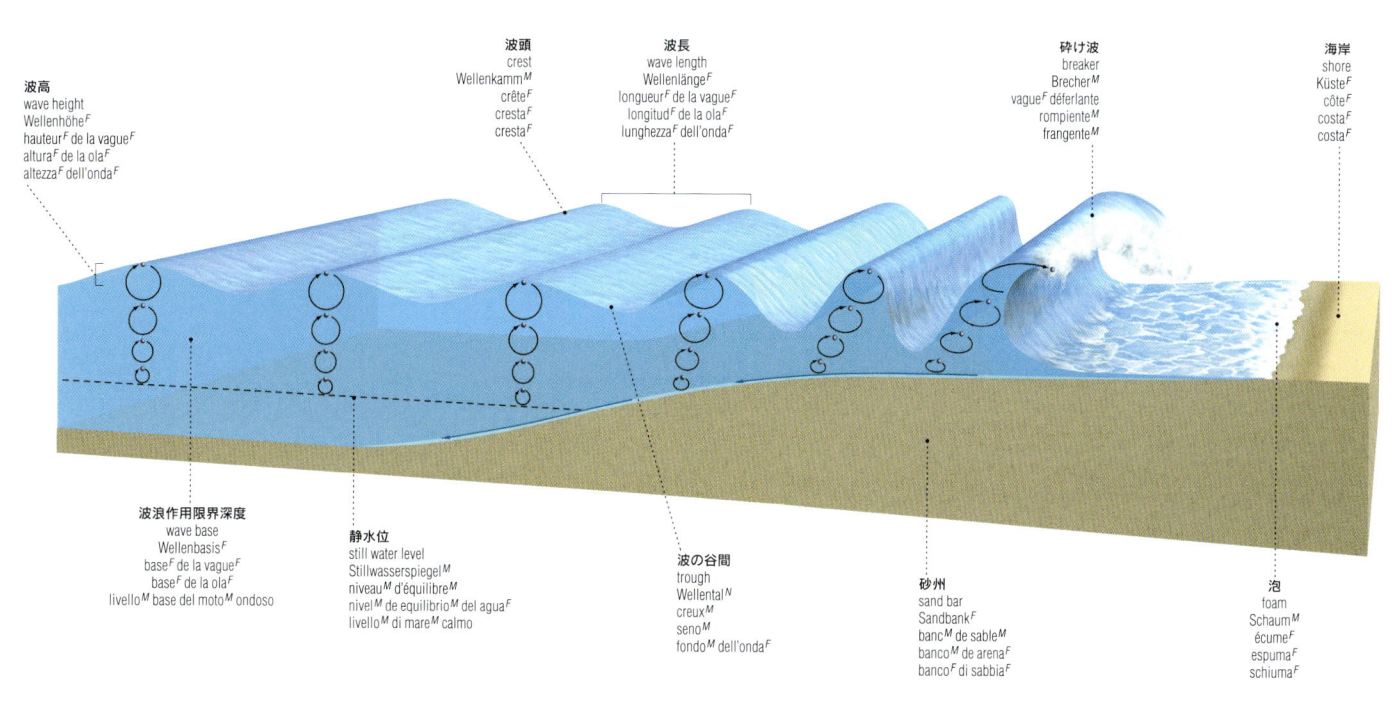

地球

波高
wave height
Wellenhöhe^F
hauteur^F de la vague^F
altura^F de la ola^F
altezza^F dell'onda^F

波頭
crest
Wellenkamm^M
crête^F
cresta^F
cresta^F

波長
wave length
Wellenlänge^F
longueur^F de la vague^F
longitud^F de la ola^F
lunghezza^F dell'onda^F

砕け波
breaker
Brecher^M
vague^F déferlante
rompiente^F
frangente^M

海岸
shore
Küste^F
côte^F
costa^F
costa^F

波浪作用限界深度
wave base
Wellenbasis^F
base^F de la vague^F
base^F de la ola^F
livello^M base del moto^M ondoso

静水位
still water level
Stillwasserspiegel^M
niveau^M d'équilibre^M
nivel^M de equilibrio^M del agua^F
livello^M di mare^M calmo

波の谷間
trough
Wellental^N
creux^M
seno^M
fondo^M dell'onda^F

砂州
sand bar
Sandbank^F
banc^M de sable^M
banco^M de arena^F
banco^F di sabbia^F

泡
foam
Schaum^M
écume^F
espuma^F
schiuma^F

海洋底
ocean floor | Meeresboden^M | fond^M de l'océan^M | fondo^M oceánico | fondale^M oceanico

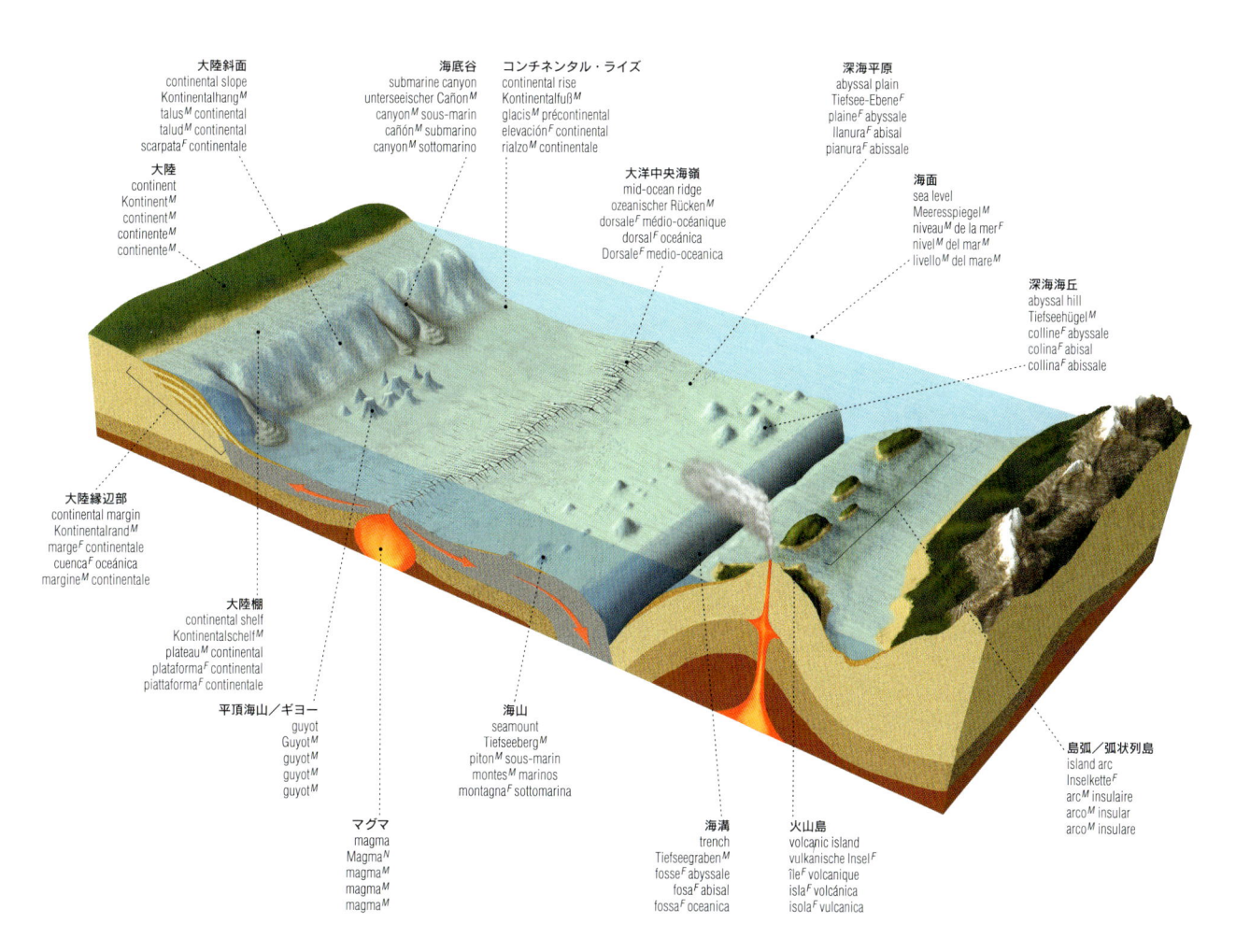

大陸斜面
continental slope
Kontinentalhang^M
talus^M continental
talud^M continental
scarpata^F continentale

海底谷
submarine canyon
unterseeischer Cañon^M
canyon^M sous-marin
cañón^M submarino
canyon^M sottomarino

コンチネンタル・ライズ
continental rise
Kontinentalfuß^M
glacis^M précontinental
elevación^F continental
rialzo^M continentale

深海平原
abyssal plain
Tiefsee-Ebene^F
plaine^F abyssale
llanura^F abisal
pianura^F abissale

大陸
continent
Kontinent^M
continent^M
continente^M
continente^M

大洋中央海嶺
mid-ocean ridge
ozeanischer Rücken^M
dorsale^F médio-océanique
dorsal^F oceánica
Dorsale^F medio-oceanica

海面
sea level
Meeresspiegel^M
niveau^M de la mer^F
nivel^M del mar^M
livello^M del mare^M

深海海丘
abyssal hill
Tiefseehügel^M
colline^F abyssale
colina^F abisal
collina^F abissale

大陸縁辺部
continental margin
Kontinentalrand^M
marge^F continentale
cuenca^F oceánica
margine^M continentale

大陸棚
continental shelf
Kontinentalschelf^M
plateau^M continental
plataforma^F continental
piattaforma^F continentale

平頂海山／ギヨー
guyot
Guyot^M
guyot^M
guyot^M
guyot^M

マグマ
magma
Magma^N
magma^M
magma^M
magma^M

海山
seamount
Tiefseeberg^M
piton^M sous-marin
montes^M marinos
montagna^F sottomarina

海溝
trench
Tiefseegraben^M
fosse^F abyssale
fosa^F abisal
fossa^F oceanica

火山島
volcanic island
vulkanische Insel^F
île^F volcanique
isla^F volcánica
isola^F vulcanica

島弧／弧状列島
island arc
Inselkette^F
arc^M insulaire
arco^M insular
arco^M insulare

49

地質 | GEOLOGY
GEOLOGIE | GÉOLOGIE | GEOLOGÍA | GEOLOGIA

海溝と海嶺

日本語 | 英語 | ドイツ語 | フランス語 | スペイン語 | イタリア語

ocean trenches and ridges | ozeanische Rücken^M und Gräben^M | fosses^F et dorsales^F océaniques | fosas^F y dorsales^F oceánicas | fosse^F e dorsali^F oceaniche

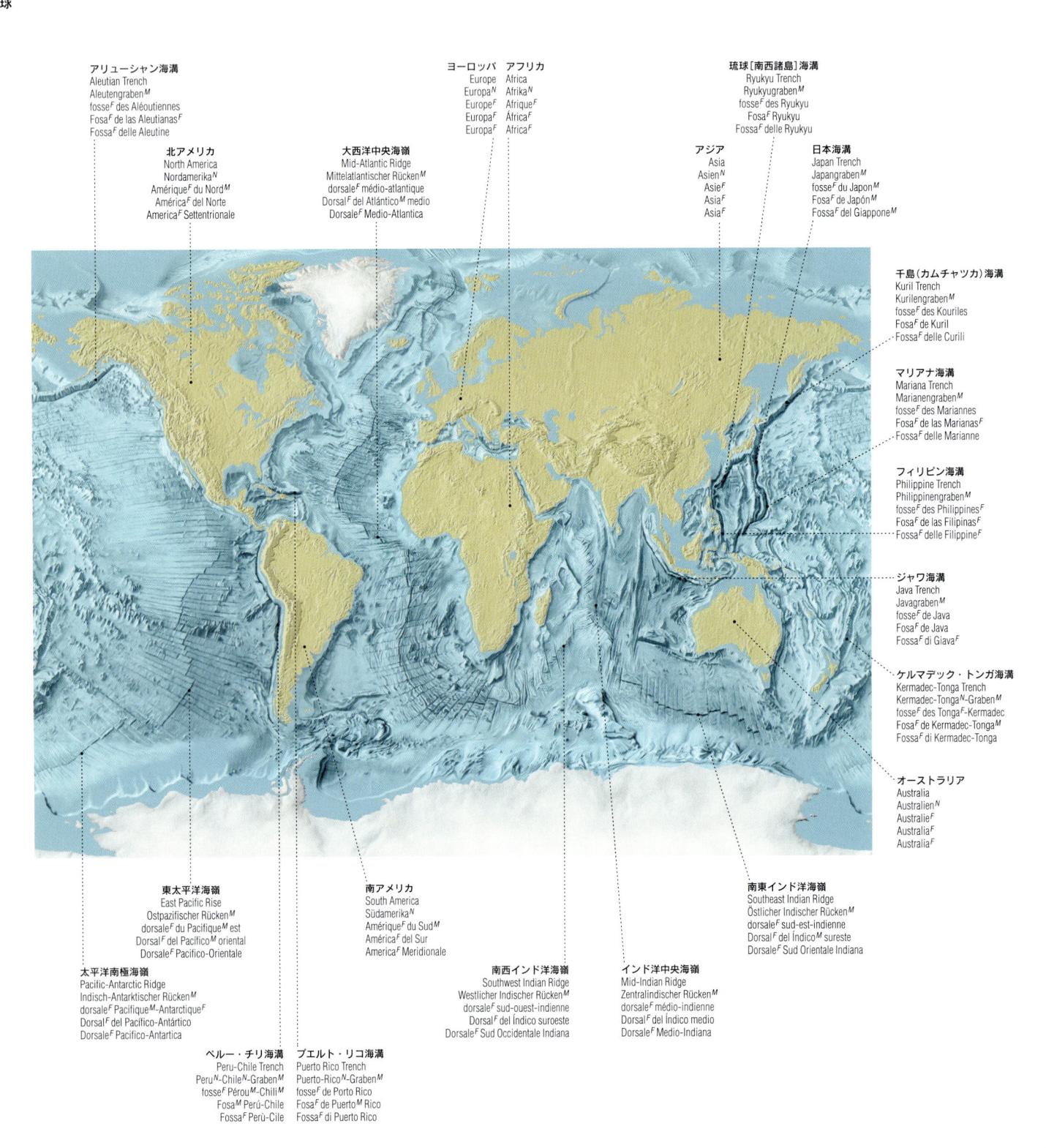

地球

アリューシャン海溝
Aleutian Trench
Aleutengraben^M
fosse^F des Aléoutiennes
Fosa^F de las Aleutianas^F
Fossa^F delle Aleutine

北アメリカ
North America
Nordamerika^N
Amérique^F du Nord^M
América^F del Norte
America^F Settentrionale

ヨーロッパ
Europe
Europa^N
Europe^F
Europa^F
Europa^F

アフリカ
Africa
Afrika^N
Afrique^F
África^F
Africa^F

大西洋中央海嶺
Mid-Atlantic Ridge
Mittelatlantischer Rücken^M
dorsale^F médio-atlantique
Dorsal^F del Atlántico^M medio
Dorsale^F Medio-Atlantica

アジア
Asia
Asien^N
Asie^F
Asia^F
Asia^F

琉球[南西諸島]海溝
Ryukyu Trench
Ryukyugraben^M
fosse^F des Ryukyu
Fosa^F Ryukyu
Fossa^F delle Ryukyu

日本海溝
Japan Trench
Japangraben^M
fosse^F du Japon^M
Fosa^F de Japón^M
Fossa^F del Giappone^M

千島（カムチャツカ）海溝
Kuril Trench
Kurilengraben^M
fosse^F des Kouriles
Fosa^F de Kuril
Fossa^F delle Curili

マリアナ海溝
Mariana Trench
Marianengraben^M
fosse^F des Mariannes
Fosa^F de las Marianas^F
Fossa^F delle Marianne

フィリピン海溝
Philippine Trench
Philippinengraben^M
fosse^F des Philippines^F
Fosa^F de las Filipinas^F
Fossa^F delle Filippine

ジャワ海溝
Java Trench
Javagraben^M
fosse^F de Java
Fosa^F de Java
Fossa^F di Giava

ケルマデック・トンガ海溝
Kermadec-Tonga Trench
Kermadec-Tonga^N-Graben^M
fosse^F des Tonga^F-Kermadec
Fosa^F de Kermadec-Tonga^M
Fossa^F di Kermadec-Tonga

オーストラリア
Australia
Australien^N
Australie^F
Australia^F
Australia^F

東太平洋海嶺
East Pacific Rise
Ostpazifischer Rücken^M
dorsale^F du Pacifique^M est
Dorsal^F del Pacífico^M oriental
Dorsale^F Pacifico-Orientale

南アメリカ
South America
Südamerika^N
Amérique^F du Sud^M
América^F del Sur
America^F Meridionale

南東インド洋海嶺
Southeast Indian Ridge
Östlicher Indischer Rücken^M
dorsale^F sud-est-indienne
Dorsal^F del Índico^M sureste
Dorsale^F Sud Orientale Indiana

太平洋南極海嶺
Pacific-Antarctic Ridge
Indisch-Antarktischer Rücken^M
dorsale^F Pacifique^M-Antarctique^F
Dorsal^F del Pacífico-Antártico
Dorsale^F Pacifico-Antartica

南西インド洋海嶺
Southwest Indian Ridge
Westlicher Indischer Rücken^M
dorsale^F sud-ouest-indienne
Dorsal^F del Índico suroeste
Dorsale^F Sud Occidentale Indiana

インド洋中央海嶺
Mid-Indian Ridge
Zentralindischer Rücken^M
dorsale^F médio-indienne
Dorsal^F del Índico medio
Dorsale^F Medio-Indiana

ペルー・チリ海溝
Peru-Chile Trench
Peru^N-Chile^N-Graben^M
fosse^F Pérou^M-Chili^M
Fosa^M Perú-Chile
Fossa^F Perù-Cile

プエルト・リコ海溝
Puerto Rico Trench
Puerto-Rico^N-Graben^M
fosse^F de Porto Rico
Fosa^F de Puerto^M Rico
Fossa^F di Puerto Rico

地質 | GEOLOGY
GEOLOGIE | GÉOLOGIE | GEOLOGÍA | GEOLOGIA

海岸の地形

common coastal features | typische Küstenformen[F] | configuration[F] du littoral[M] | configuración[F] del litoral[M] | caratteristiche[F] della costa[F]

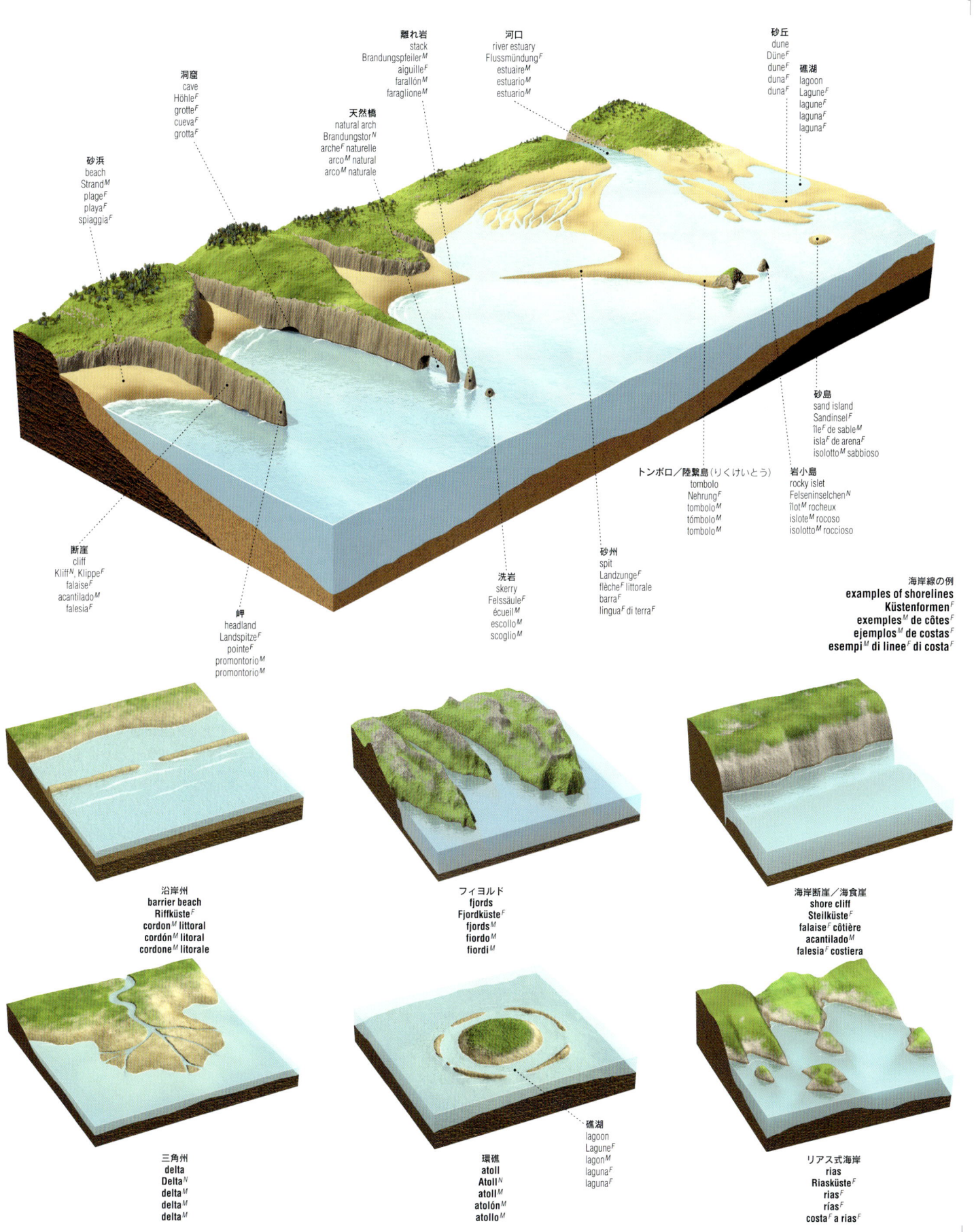

地球

離れ岩
stack
Brandungspfeiler[M]
aiguille[F]
farallón[M]
faraglione[M]

河口
river estuary
Flussmündung[F]
estuaire[M]
estuario[M]
estuario[M]

砂丘
dune
Düne[F]
dune[F]
duna[F]
duna[F]

礁湖
lagoon
Lagune[F]
lagune[F]
laguna[F]
laguna[F]

洞窟
cave
Höhle[F]
grotte[F]
cueva[F]
grotta[F]

天然橋
natural arch
Brandungstor[N]
arche[F] naturelle
arco[M] natural
arco[M] naturale

砂浜
beach
Strand[M]
plage[F]
playa[F]
spiaggia[F]

砂島
sand island
Sandinsel[F]
île[F] de sable[M]
isla[F] de arena[F]
isolotto[M] sabbioso

岩小島
rocky islet
Felseninselchen[N]
îlot[M] rocheux
islote[M] rocoso
isolotto[M] roccioso

トンボロ／陸繋島（りくけいとう）
tombolo
Nehrung[F]
tombolo[M]
tómbolo[M]
tombolo[M]

砂州
spit
Landzunge[F]
flèche[F] littorale
barra[F]
lingua[F] di terra[F]

洗岩
skerry
Felssäule[F]
écueil[M]
escollo[M]
scoglio[M]

岬
headland
Landspitze[F]
pointe[F]
promontorio[M]
promontorio[M]

断崖
cliff
Kliff[N], Klippe[F]
falaise[F]
acantilado[M]
falesia[F]

海岸線の例
examples of shorelines
Küstenformen[F]
exemples[M] de côtes[F]
ejemplos[M] de costas[F]
esempi[M] di linee[F] di costa[F]

沿岸州
barrier beach
Riffküste[F]
cordon[M] littoral
cordón[M] litoral
cordone[M] litorale

フィヨルド
fjords
Fjordküste[F]
fjords[M]
fiordo[M]
fiordi[M]

海岸断崖／海食崖
shore cliff
Steilküste[F]
falaise[F] côtière
acantilado[M]
falesia[F] costiera

三角州
delta
Delta[N]
delta[M]
delta[M]
delta[M]

環礁
atoll
Atoll[N]
atoll[M]
atolón[M]
atollo[M]

礁湖
lagoon
Lagune[F]
lagon[M]
laguna[F]
laguna[F]

リアス式海岸
rias
Riasküste[F]
rias[F]
rías[F]
costa[F] a rias[F]

51

地質 | GEOLOGY
GEOLOGIE | GÉOLOGIE | GEOLOGÍA | GEOLOGIA

砂漠

desert | Wüste^F | désert^M | desierto^M | deserto^M

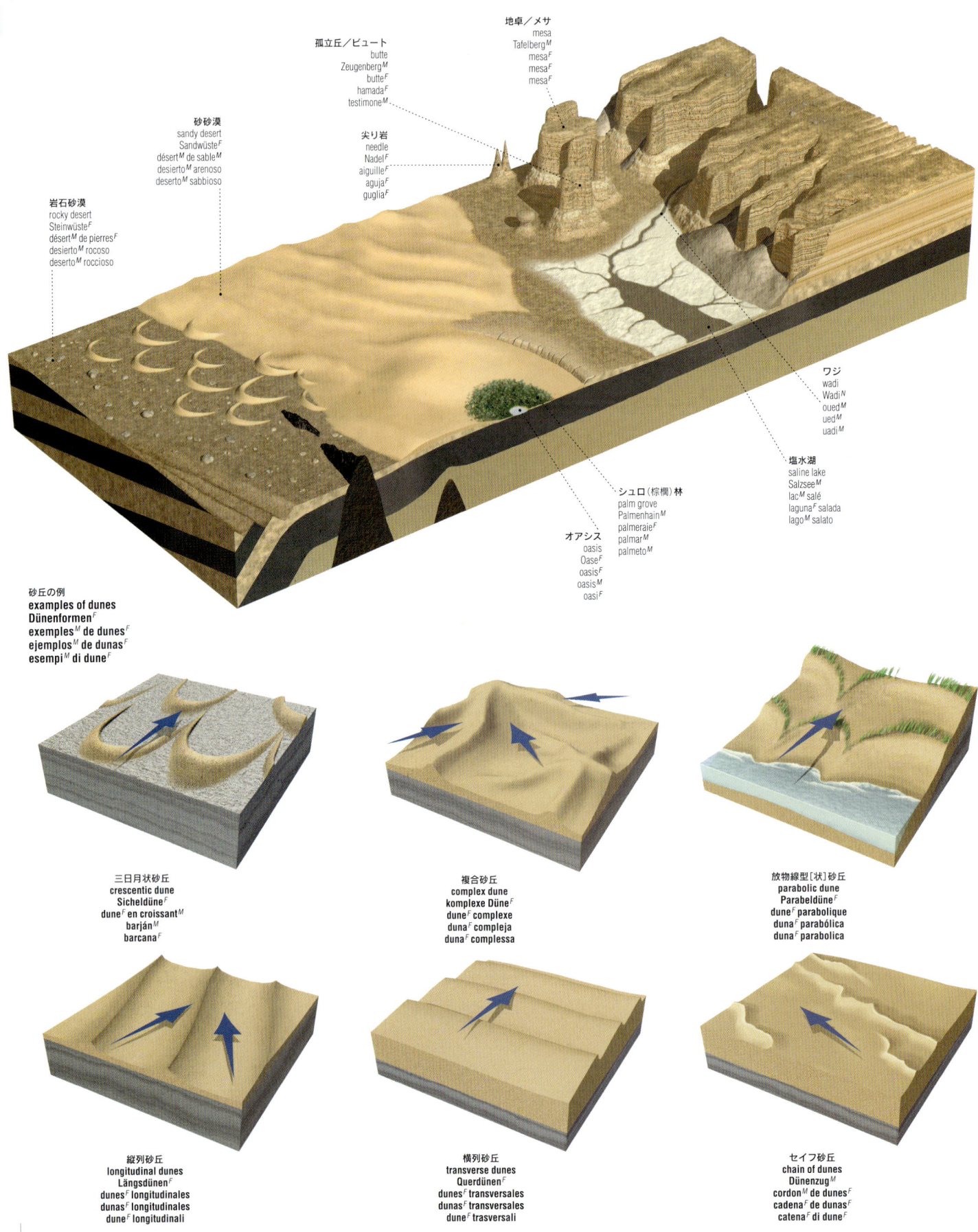

日本語 | 英語 | ドイツ語 | フランス語 | スペイン語 | イタリア語

地球

地卓／メサ
mesa
Tafelberg^M
mesa^F
mesa^F
mesa^F

孤立丘／ビュート
butte
Zeugenberg^M
butte^F
hamada^F
testimone^M

砂砂漠
sandy desert
Sandwüste^F
désert^M de sable^M
desierto^M arenoso
deserto^M sabbioso

尖り岩
needle
Nadel^F
aiguille^F
aguja^F
guglia^F

岩石砂漠
rocky desert
Steinwüste^F
désert^M de pierres^F
desierto^M rocoso
deserto^M roccioso

ワジ
wadi
Wadi^N
oued^M
ued^M
uadi^M

塩水湖
saline lake
Salzsee^M
lac^M salé
laguna^F salada
lago^M salato

シュロ（棕櫚）林
palm grove
Palmenhain^M
palmeraie^F
palmar^M
palmeto^M

オアシス
oasis
Oase^F
oasis^F
oasis^M
oasi^F

砂丘の例
examples of dunes
Dünenformen^F
exemples^M de dunes^F
ejemplos^M de dunas^F
esempi^M di dune^F

三日月状砂丘
crescentic dune
Sicheldüne^F
dune^F en croissant^M
barján^M
barcana^F

複合砂丘
complex dune
komplexe Düne^F
dune^F complexe
duna^F compleja
duna^F complessa

放物線型[状]砂丘
parabolic dune
Parabeldüne^F
dune^F parabolique
duna^F parabólica
duna^F parabolica

縦列砂丘
longitudinal dunes
Längsdünen^F
dunes^F longitudinales
dunas^F longitudinales
dune^F longitudinali

横列砂丘
transverse dunes
Querdünen^F
dunes^F transversales
dunas^F transversales
dune^F trasversali

セイフ砂丘
chain of dunes
Dünenzug^M
cordon^M de dunes^F
cadena^F de dunas^F
catena^F di dune^F

気象 | METEOROLOGY
METEOROLOGIE | MÉTÉOROLOGIE | METEOROLOGÍA | METEOROLOGIA

大気圏断面図

profile of the Earth's atmosphere | Erdatmosphäre^F im Querschnitt^M | coupe^F de l'atmosphère^F terrestre | corte^M de la atmósfera^F terrestre | profilo^M dell'atmosfera^F terrestre

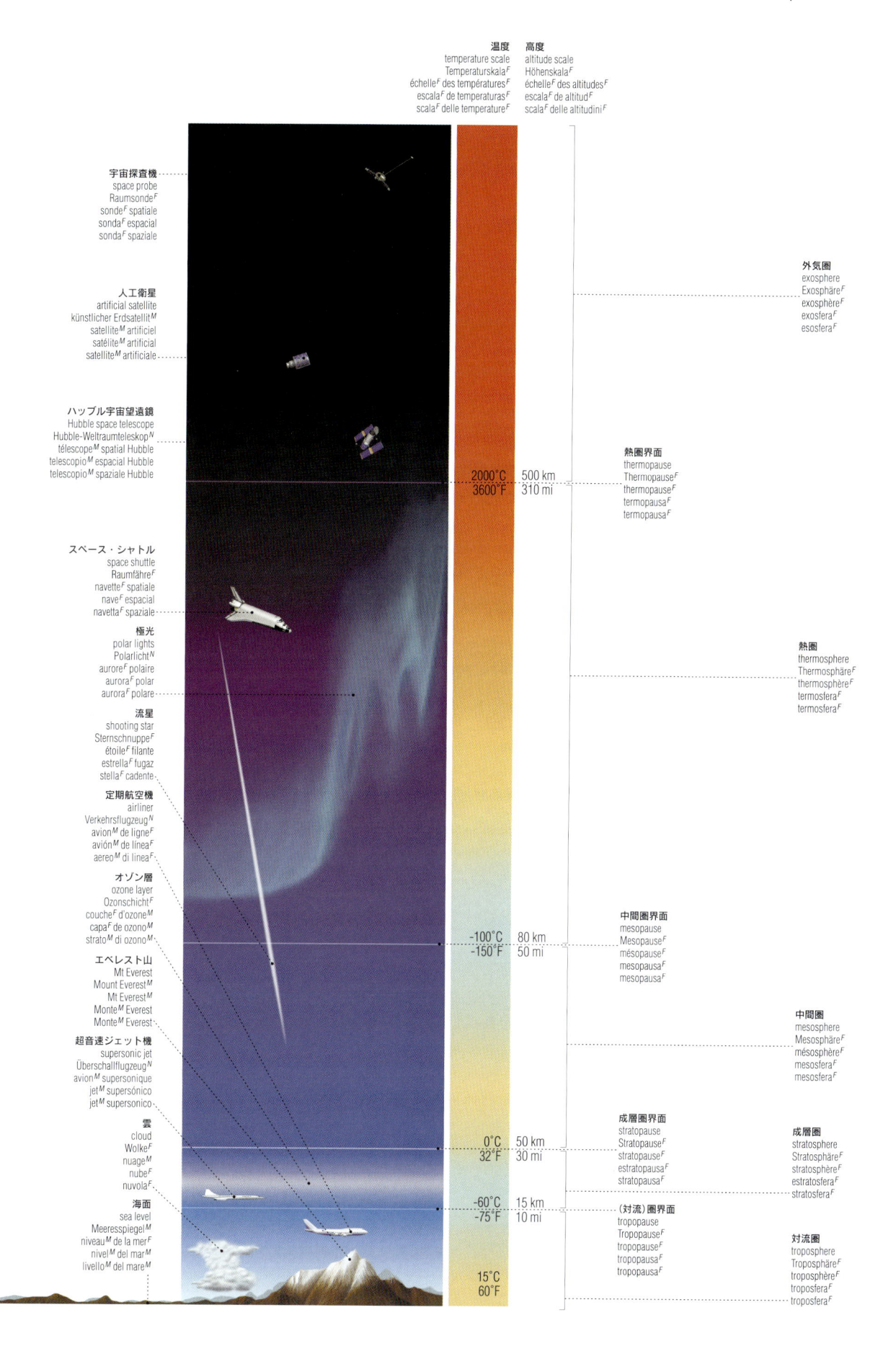

地球

温度　高度
temperature scale　altitude scale
Temperaturskala^F　Höhenskala^F
échelle^F des températures^F　échelle^F des altitudes^F
escala^F de temperaturas^F　escala^F de altitud^F
scala^F delle temperature^F　scala^F delle altitudini^F

宇宙探査機
space probe
Raumsonde^F
sonde^F spatiale
sonda^F espacial
sonda^F spaziale

人工衛星
artificial satellite
künstlicher Erdsatellit^M
satellite^M artificiel
satélite^M artificial
satellite^M artificiale

ハッブル宇宙望遠鏡
Hubble space telescope
Hubble-Weltraumteleskop^N
télescope^M spatial Hubble
telescopio^M espacial Hubble
telescopio^M spaziale Hubble

2000°C　500 km
3600°F　310 mi

熱圏界面
thermopause
Thermopause^F
thermopause^F
termopausa^F
termopausa^F

スペース・シャトル
space shuttle
Raumfähre^F
navette^F spatiale
nave^F espacial
navetta^F spaziale

極光
polar lights
Polarlicht^N
aurore^F polaire
aurora^F polar
aurora^F polare

熱圏
thermosphere
Thermosphäre^F
thermosphère^F
termosfera^F
termosfera^F

流星
shooting star
Sternschnuppe^F
étoile^F filante
estrella^F fugaz
stella^F cadente

定期航空機
airliner
Verkehrsflugzeug^N
avion^M de ligne^F
avión^M de línea^F
aereo^M di linea^F

オゾン層
ozone layer
Ozonschicht^F
couche^F d'ozone^M
capa^F de ozono^M
strato^M di ozono^M

-100°C　80 km
-150°F　50 mi

中間圏界面
mesopause
Mesopause^F
mésopause^F
mesopausa^F
mesopausa^F

エベレスト山
Mt Everest
Mount Everest^M
Mt Everest^M
Monte^M Everest
Monte^M Everest

中間圏
mesosphere
Mesosphäre^F
mésosphère^F
mesosfera^F
mesosfera^F

超音速ジェット機
supersonic jet
Überschallflugzeug^N
avion^M supersonique
jet^M supersónico
jet^M supersonico

雲
cloud
Wolke^F
nuage^M
nube^F
nuvola^F

0°C　50 km
32°F　30 mi

成層圏界面
stratopause
Stratopause^F
stratopause^F
estratopausa^F
stratopausa^F

成層圏
stratosphere
Stratosphäre^F
stratosphère^F
estratosfera^F
stratosfera^F

海面
sea level
Meeresspiegel^M
niveau^M de la mer^F
nivel^M del mar^M
livello^M del mare^M

-60°C　15 km
-75°F　10 mi

(対流)圏界面
tropopause
Tropopause^F
tropopause^F
tropopausa^F
tropopausa^F

15°C
60°F

対流圏
troposphere
Troposphäre^F
troposphère^F
troposfera^F
troposfera^F

53

気象 | METEOROLOGY
METEOROLOGIE | MÉTÉOROLOGIE | METEOROLOGÍA | METEOROLOGIA

季節

seasons of the year | Jahreszeiten^F | cycle^M des saisons^F | estaciones^F del año^M | stagioni^F dell'anno^M

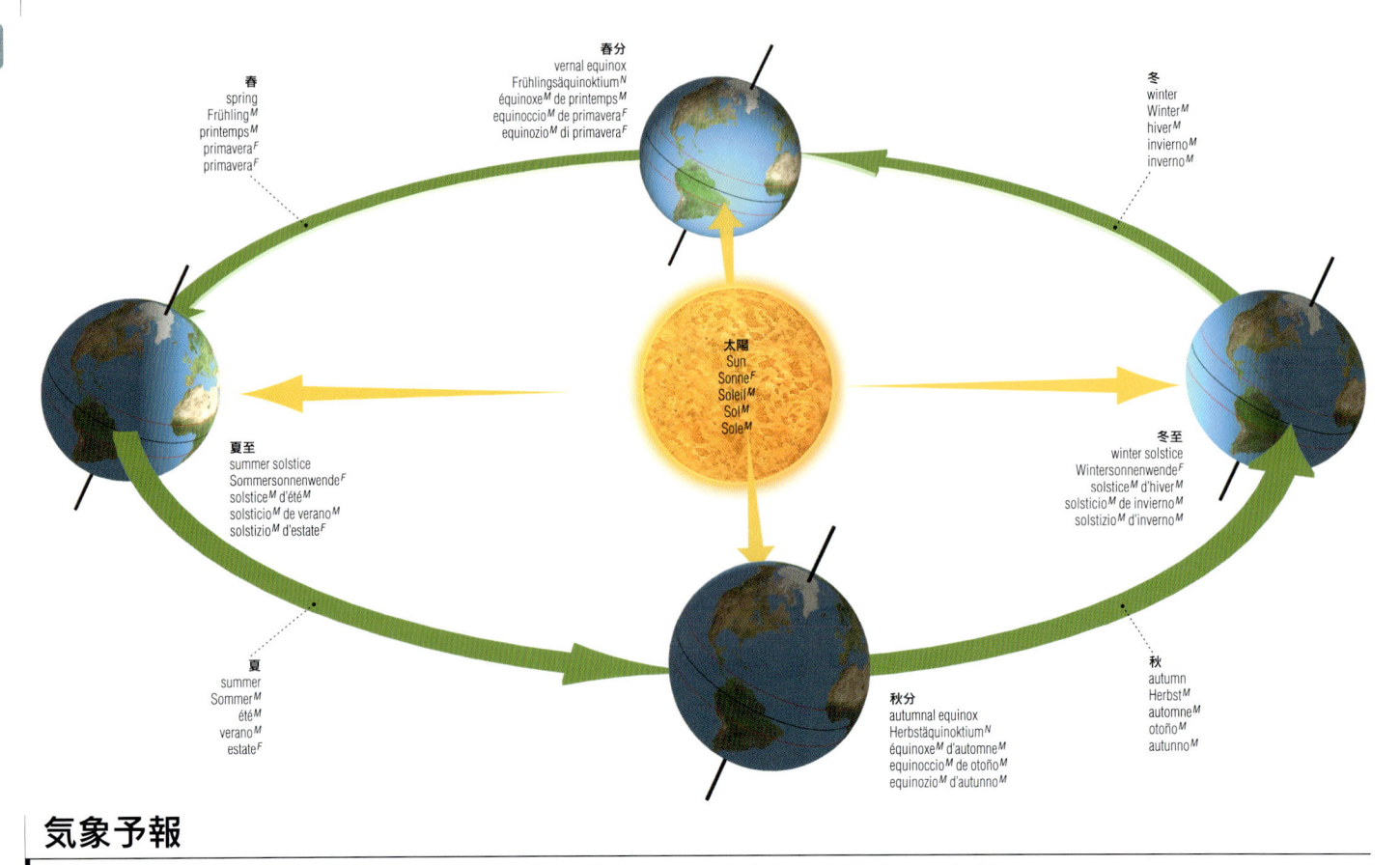

春分
vernal equinox
Frühlingsäquinoktium^N
équinoxe^M de printemps^M
equinoccio^M de primavera^F
equinozio^M di primavera^F

春
spring
Frühling^M
printemps^M
primavera^F
primavera^F

冬
winter
Winter^M
hiver^M
invierno^M
inverno^M

太陽
Sun
Sonne^F
Soleil^M
Sol^M
Sole^M

夏至
summer solstice
Sommersonnenwende^F
solstice^M d'été^M
solsticio^M de verano^M
solstizio^M d'estate^F

冬至
winter solstice
Wintersonnenwende^F
solstice^M d'hiver^M
solsticio^M de invierno^M
solstizio^M d'inverno^M

夏
summer
Sommer^M
été^M
verano^M
estate^F

秋分
autumnal equinox
Herbstäquinoktium^N
équinoxe^M d'automne^M
equinoccio^M de otoño^M
equinozio^M d'autunno^M

秋
autumn
Herbst^M
automne^M
otoño^M
autunno^M

気象予報

meteorological forecast | Wettervorhersage^F | prévision^F météorologique | previsión^F meteorológica | previsioni^F meteorologiche

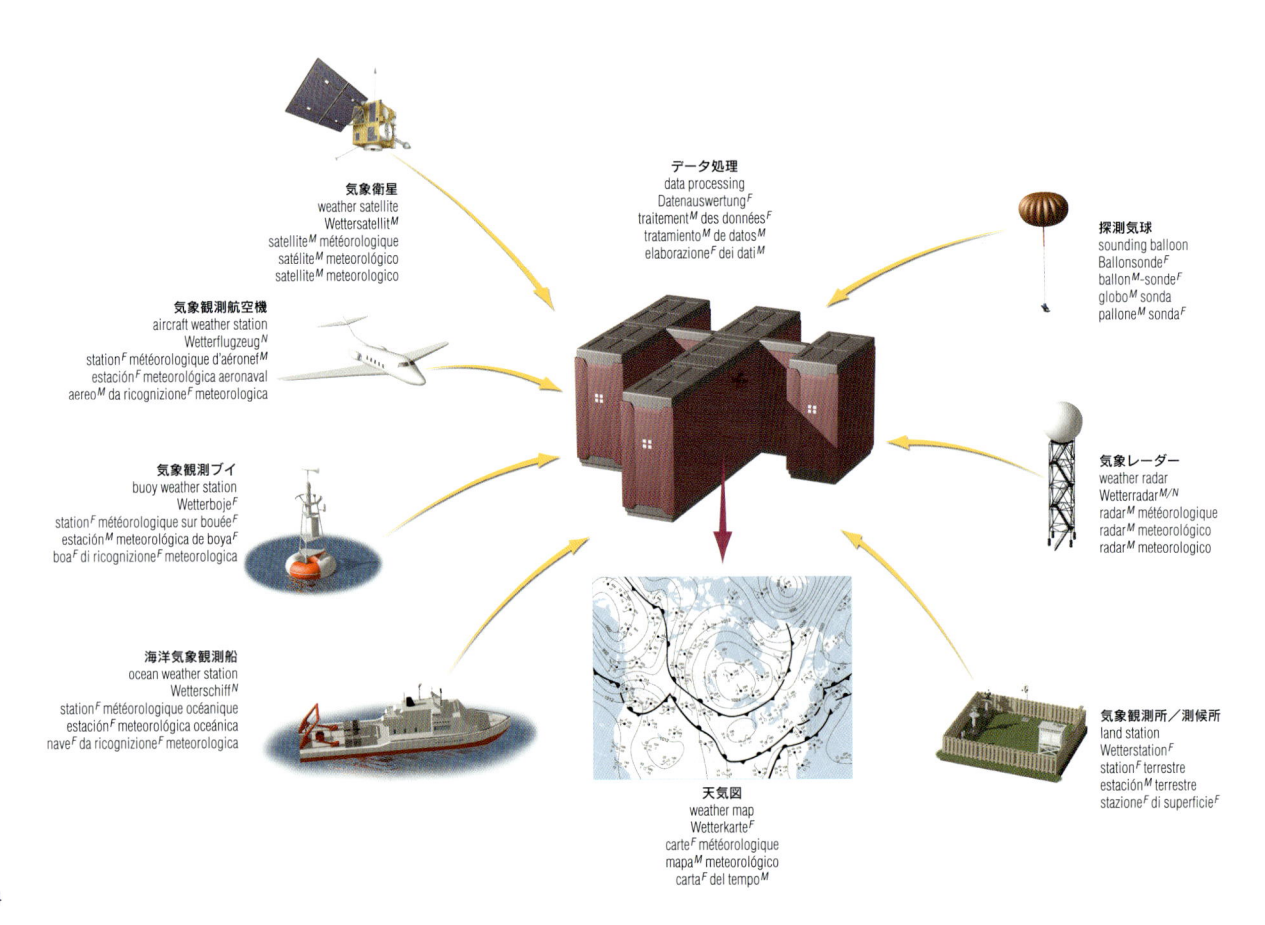

気象衛星
weather satellite
Wettersatellit^M
satellite^M météorologique
satélite^M meteorológico
satellite^M meteorologico

データ処理
data processing
Datenauswertung^F
traitement^M des données^F
tratamiento^M de datos^M
elaborazione^F dei dati^M

探測気球
sounding balloon
Ballonsonde^F
ballon^M-sonde^F
globo^M sonda
pallone^M sonda^F

気象観測航空機
aircraft weather station
Wetterflugzeug^N
station^F météorologique d'aéronef^M
estación^F meteorológica aeronaval
aereo^M da ricognizione^F meteorologica

気象レーダー
weather radar
Wetterradar$^{M/N}$
radar^M météorologique
radar^M meteorológico
radar^M meteorologico

気象観測ブイ
buoy weather station
Wetterboje^F
station^F météorologique sur bouée^F
estación^F meteorológica de boya^F
boa^F di ricognizione^F meteorologica

海洋気象観測船
ocean weather station
Wetterschiff^N
station^F météorologique océanique
estación^F meteorológica oceánica
nave^F da ricognizione^F meteorologica

天気図
weather map
Wetterkarte^F
carte^F météorologique
mapa^M meteorológico
carta^F del tempo^M

気象観測所／測候所
land station
Wetterstation^F
station^F terrestre
estación^M terrestre
stazione^F di superficie^F

気象 | METEOROLOGY
METEOROLOGIE | MÉTÉOROLOGIE | METEOROLOGÍA | METEOROLOGIA

天気図

weather map | Wetterkarte^F | carte^F météorologique | mapa^M meteorológico | carta^F del tempo^M

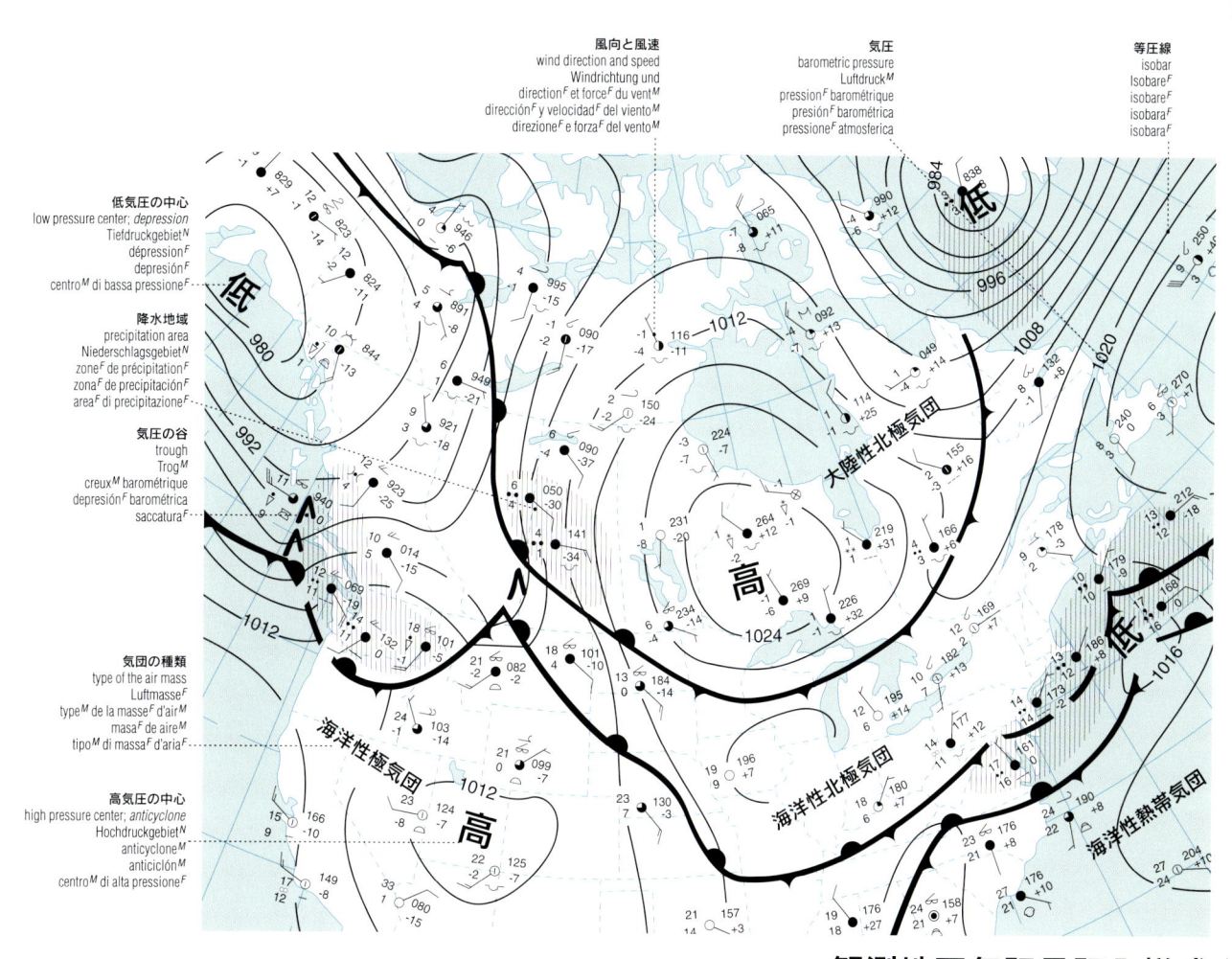

風向と風速
wind direction and speed
Windrichtung und
direction^F et force^F du vent^M
dirección^F y velocidad^F del viento^M
direzione^F e forza^F del vento^M

気圧
barometric pressure
Luftdruck^M
pression^F barométrique
presión^F barométrica
pressione^F atmosferica

等圧線
isobar
Isobare^F
isobare^F
isobara^F
isobara^F

低気圧の中心
low pressure center; depression
Tiefdruckgebiet^N
dépression^F
depresión^F
centro^M di bassa pressione^F

降水地域
precipitation area
Niederschlagsgebiet^N
zone^F de précipitation^F
zona^F de precipitación^F
area^F di precipitazione^F

気圧の谷
trough
Trog^M
creux^M barométrique
depresión^F barométrica
saccatura^F

気団の種類
type of the air mass
Luftmasse^F
type^M de la masse^F d'air^M
masa^F de aire^M
tipo^M di massa^F d'aria^F

高気圧の中心
high pressure center; anticyclone
Hochdruckgebiet^N
anticyclone^M
anticiclón^M
centro^M di alta pressione^F

地球

観測地天気記号記入様式

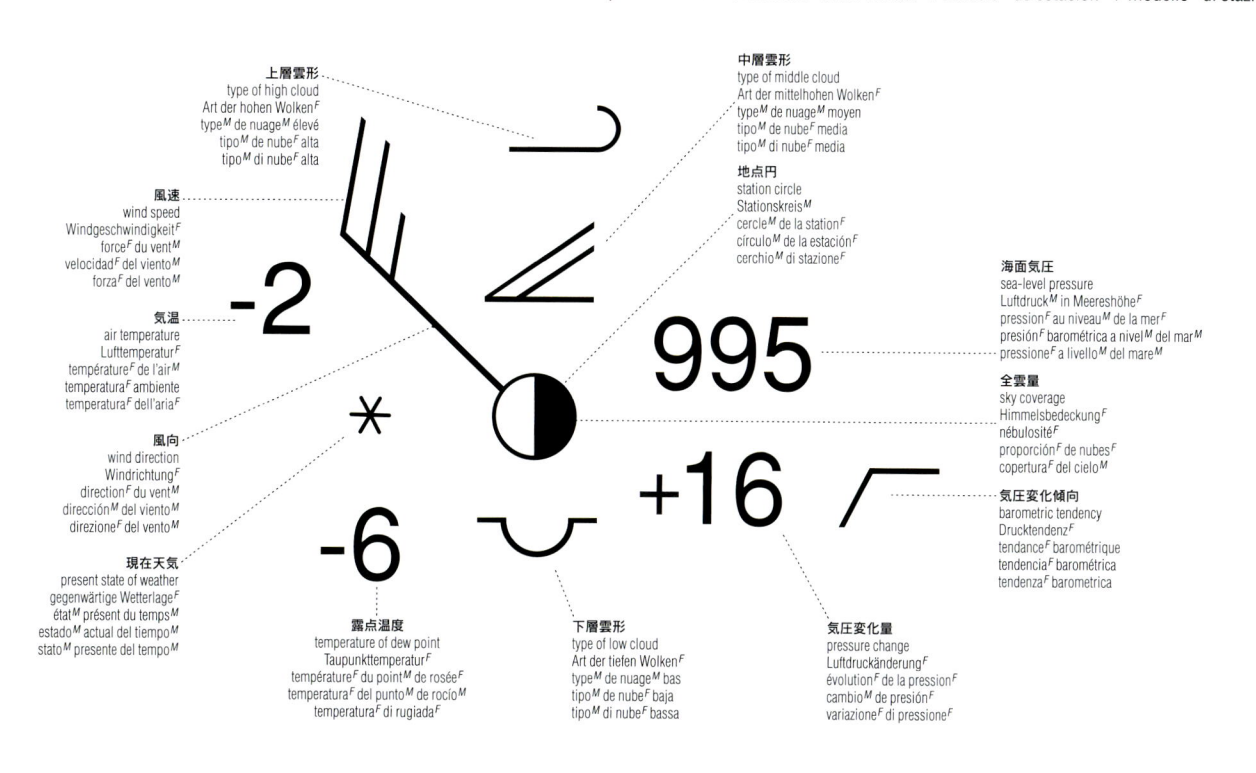

station model | Stationsmodell^N | disposition^F des informations^F d'une station^F | modelo^M de estación^F | modello^M di stazione^F

上層雲形
type of high cloud
Art der hohen Wolken^F
type^M de nuage^M élevé
tipo^M de nube^F alta
tipo^M di nube^F alta

中層雲形
type of middle cloud
Art der mittelhohen Wolken^F
type^M de nuage^M moyen
tipo^M de nube^F media
tipo^M di nube^F media

地点円
station circle
Stationskreis^M
cercle^M de la station^F
círculo^M de la estación^F
cerchio^M di stazione^F

風速
wind speed
Windgeschwindigkeit^F
force^F du vent^M
velocidad^F del viento^M
forza^F del vento^M

気温
air temperature
Lufttemperatur^F
température^F de l'air^M
temperatura^F ambiente
temperatura^F dell'aria^F

海面気圧
sea-level pressure
Luftdruck^M in Meereshöhe^F
pression^F au niveau^M de la mer^F
presión^F barométrica a nivel^M del mar^M
pressione^F a livello^M del mare^M

全雲量
sky coverage
Himmelsbedeckung^F
nébulosité^F
proporción^F de nubes^F
copertura^F del cielo^M

風向
wind direction
Windrichtung^F
direction^F du vent^M
dirección^F del viento^M
direzione^F del vento^M

気圧変化傾向
barometric tendency
Drucktendenz^F
tendance^F barométrique
tendencia^F barométrica
tendenza^F barometrica

現在天気
present state of weather
gegenwärtige Wetterlage^F
état^M présent du temps^M
estado^M actual del tiempo^M
stato^M presente del tempo^M

露点温度
temperature of dew point
Taupunkttemperatur^F
température^F du point^M de rosée^F
temperatura^F del punto^M de rocío^M
temperatura^F di rugiada^F

下層雲形
type of low cloud
Art der tiefen Wolken^F
type^M de nuage^M bas
tipo^M de nube^F baja
tipo^M di nube^F bassa

気圧変化量
pressure change
Luftdruckänderung^F
évolution^F de la pression^F
cambio^M de presión^F
variazione^F di pressione^F

気象 | METEOROLOGY
METEOROLOGIE | MÉTÉOROLOGIE | METEOROLOGÍA | METEOROLOGIA

国際式天気図記号

日本語 | 英語 | ドイツ語 | フランス語 | スペイン語 | イタリア語

international weather symbols | internationale Wettersymbole^N | symboles^M météorologiques internationaux | símbolos^M meteorológicos internacionales | simboli^M meteorologici internazionali

地球

風
wind
Wind^M
vent^M
viento^M
vento^M

静穏
calm
Windstille^F
air^M calme
sosegado^M
calma^F

風向軸
shaft
Pfeil^M
hampe^F
brisa^F leve
segmento^M orientato

長矢羽根
barb
ganzer Querstrich^M
barbule^F
viento^M moderado
barbetta^F

矢羽根
wind arrow
Windstärkefähnchen^N
flèche^F du vent
flecha^F indicadora de la dirección^F del viento^M
freccia^F del vento^M

短矢羽根
half barb
halber Querstrich^M
demi-barbule^F
viento^M suave
mezza barbetta^F

旗
pennant
Fähnchen^N
fanion^M
tempestad^F
banderuola^F

前線
fronts
Fronten^F
fronts^M
frentes^M
fronti^M

地上の寒冷前線
surface cold front
Kaltfront^F am Boden^M
front^M froid en surface^F
frente^M frío de superficie^F
fronte freddo al suolo^M

地上の温暖前線
surface warm front
Warmfront^F am Boden^M
front^M chaud en surface^F
frente^M cálido de superficie^F
fronte caldo al suolo^M

閉塞前線
occluded front
Okklusion^F
front^M occlus
frente^M ocluido
fronte^M occluso al suolo^M

上空の寒冷前線
upper cold front
Höhenkaltfront^F
front^M froid en altitude^F
frente^M frío en las alturas^F
fronte^M freddo in quota^F

上空の温暖前線
upper warm front
Höhenwarmfront^F
front^M chaud en altitude^F
frente^M cálido en las alturas^F
fronte^M caldo in quota^F

停滞前線
stationary front
stationäre Front^F
front^M stationnaire
frente^M estacionario
fronte^M stazionario

全雲量
sky coverage; cloud amount
Bedeckungsgrad^M
nébulosité^F
nubosidad^F
nuvolosità^F

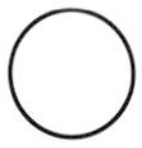

雲量0雲なし
cloudless sky
wolkenloser Himmel^M
ciel^M sans nuages^M
cielo^M despejado
cielo^M sereno

雲量2～3
slightly covered sky
heiterer Himmel^M
ciel^M peu nuageux
cielo^M ligeramente nuboso
cielo^M poco nuvoloso

雲量7～8
very cloudy sky
stark bewölkter Himmel^M
ciel^M très nuageux
cielo^M muy nuboso
cielo^M molto nuvoloso

雲量1以下
clear sky
klarer Himmel^M
ciel^M clair
cielo^M sereno
cielo^M límpido

雲量5
cloudy sky
bewölkter Himmel^M
ciel^M nuageux
cielo^M medio nuboso
cielo^M nuvoloso

雲量10隙間なし
overcast sky
bedeckter Himmel^M
ciel^M couvert
cielo^M completamente nuboso
cielo^M coperto

天空不明
obscured sky
nicht angebbar (da nicht erkennbar)
ciel^M complètement obscurci
cielo^M no observable
cielo^M invisibile

雲
clouds
Wolken^F
nuages^M
nubes^M
nuvole^F

高層雲
altostratus
Altostratus^M
alto-stratus^M
altostrato^M
altostrato^M

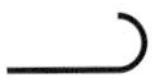

巻雲
cirrus
Zirrus^M
cirrus^M
cirro^M
cirro^M

層雲
stratus
Stratus^M
stratus^M
estrato^M
strato^M

乱層雲
nimbostratus
Nimbostratus^M
nimbo-stratus^M
nimbostrato^M
nembostrato^M

巻層雲
cirrostratus
Zirrostratus^M
cirro-stratus^M
cirrostrato^M
cirrostrato^M

積乱雲
cumulonimbus
Kumulonimbus^M
cumulo-nimbus^M
cumulonimbo^M
cumulonembo^M

高積雲
altocumulus
Altokumulus^M
alto-cumulus^M
altocúmulo^M
altocumulo^M

巻積雲
cirrocumulus
Zirrokumulus^M
cirro-cumulus^M
cirrocúmulo^M
cirrocumulo^M

積雲
cumulus
Kumulus^M
cumulus^M
cúmulo^M
cumulo^M

層積雲
stratocumulus
Stratokumulus^M
strato-cumulus^M
estratocúmulo^M
stratocumulo^M

気象 | METEOROLOGY
METEOROLOGIE | MÉTÉOROLOGIE | METEOROLOGÍA | METEOROLOGIA

国際式天気図記号

現在天気
present weather; *present weather*
Niederschläge^M
météores^M
fenómenos^M atmosféricos
meteore^F

砂塵（さじん）嵐
sandstorm or dust storm
Sand- oder Staubsturm^M
tempête^F de sable^M ou de poussière^F
tormenta^F de polvo^M y arena^F
tempesta^F di sabbia^F o di polvere^F

雷電
thunderstorm
Gewitter^N
orage^M
tormenta^F
temporale^M

強い雷電
heavy thunderstorm
starkes Gewitter^N
orage^M fort
tormenta^F eléctrica
temporale^M forte

電光
lightning
Blitz^M
éclair^M
relámpago^M
fulmine^M

熱帯暴風
tropical storm
tropischer Sturm^M
tempête^F tropicale
tormenta^F tropical
tempesta^F tropicale

ハリケーン
hurricane
Orkan^M
ouragan^M
huracán^M
uragano^M

竜巻き
tornado
Tornado^M
tornade^F
tornado^M
tornado^M

弱い断続性の雨
light intermittent rain
zeitweise leichter Regen^M
pluie^F intermittente faible
lluvia^F ligera intermitente
pioggia^F leggera intermittente

弱い断続性の霧雨
light intermittent drizzle
zeitweise leichter Sprühregen^M
bruine^F intermittente faible
llovizna^F ligera intermitente
pioviggine^F leggera intermittente

弱い断続性の雪
light intermittent snow
zeitweise leichter Schneefall^M
neige^F intermittente faible
nieve^F ligera intermitente
neve^F leggera intermittente

並の断続性の雨
moderate intermittent rain
zeitweise mäßiger Regen^M
pluie^F intermittente modérée
lluvia^F moderada intermitente
pioggia^F moderata intermittente

並の断続性の霧雨
moderate intermittent drizzle
zeitweise mäßiger Sprühregen^M
bruine^F intermittente modérée
llovizna^F moderada intermitente
pioviggine^F moderata intermittente

並の断続性の雪
moderate intermittent snow
zeitweise mäßiger Schneefall^M
neige^F intermittente modérée
nieve^F moderada intermitente
neve^F moderata intermittente

強い断続性の雨
heavy intermittent rain
zeitweise starker Regen^M
pluie^F intermittente forte
lluvia^F intensa intermitente
pioggia^F forte intermittente

強い断続性の霧雨
thick intermittent drizzle
zeitweise dichter Sprühregen^M
bruine^F intermittente forte
llovizna^F fuerte intermitente
pioviggine^F spessa intermittente

強い断続性の雪
heavy intermittent snow
zeitweise starker Schneefall^M
neige^F intermittente forte
nieve^F fuerte intermitente
neve^F forte intermittente

弱い連続性の雨
light continuous rain
anhaltend leichter Regen^M
pluie^F continue faible
lluvia^F ligera continua
pioggia^F leggera continua

弱い連続性の霧雨
light continuous drizzle
anhaltend leichter Sprühregen^M
bruine^F continue faible
llovizna^F ligera continua
pioviggine^F leggera continua

弱い連続性の雪
light continuous snow
anhaltend leichter Schneefall^M
neige^F continue faible
nieve^F ligera continua
neve^F leggera continua

並の連続性の雨
moderate continuous rain
anhaltend mäßiger Regen^M
pluie^F continue modérée
lluvia^F moderada continua
pioggia^F moderata continua

並の連続性の霧雨
moderate continuous drizzle
anhaltend mäßiger Sprühregen^M
bruine^F continue modérée
llovizna^F moderada continua
pioviggine^F moderata continua

並の連続性の雪
moderate continuous snow
anhaltend mäßiger Schneefall^M
neige^F continue modérée
nieve^F moderada continua
neve^F moderata continua

強い連続性の雨
heavy continuous rain
anhaltend starker Regen^M
pluie^F continue forte
lluvia^F fuerte continua
pioggia^F forte continua

強い連続性の霧雨
thick continuous drizzle
anhaltend dichter Sprühregen^M
bruine^F continue forte
llovizna^F fuerte continua
pioviggine^F spessa continua

強い連続性の雪
heavy continuous snow
anhaltend starker Schneefall^M
neige^F continue forte
nieve^F fuerte continua
neve^F forte continua

凍雨
sleet
Schneeregen^M
grésil^M
aguanieve^F
nevischio^M

靄（もや）
mist
Dunst^M
brume^F
neblina^F
bruma^F umida

弱い驟雪（しゅうせつ）
snow shower
Schneeschauer^M
averse^F de neige
chubasco^M de nieve^F
rovesci^M di neve^F

目の高さ以下の弱か並の地吹雪
drifting snow low
Schneefegen^N
chasse-neige^F basse
viento^M fuerte invernal alto
scaccianeve^M basso

霧
fog
Nebel^M
brouillard^M
niebla^F
nebbia^F

弱い驟雨（しゅうう）
rain shower
Regenschauer^M
averse^F de pluie^F
chubasco^M
rovesci^M di pioggia^F

目の高さ以上の弱か並の地吹雪
drifting snow high
Schneetreiben^N
chasse-neige^F haute
viento^M fuerte invernal bajo
scaccianeve^M alto

煙霧
haze
Dunst^M
brume^F sèche
neblina^F
foschia^F

弱い驟雨性の雹（ひょう）
hail shower
Hagelschauer^M
averse^F de grêle
granizada^F
rovesci^M di grandine^F

着氷性の雨
freezing rain
Eisregen^M
pluie^F verglaçante
lluvia^F helada
pioggia^F congelantesi

煙
smoke
Rauch^M
fumée^F
humo^M
fumo^M

スコール
squall
Bö^F
grain^M
chaparrón$^{M\ F}$
groppo^M

地球

57

気象 | METEOROLOGY
METEOROLOGIE | MÉTÉOROLOGIE | METEOROLOGÍA | METEOROLOGIA

気象観測所／測候所

日本語 | 英語 | ドイツ語 | フランス語 | スペイン語 | イタリア語

meteorological station | Wetterstation^F | station^F météorologique | estación^F meteorológica | stazione^F meteorologica

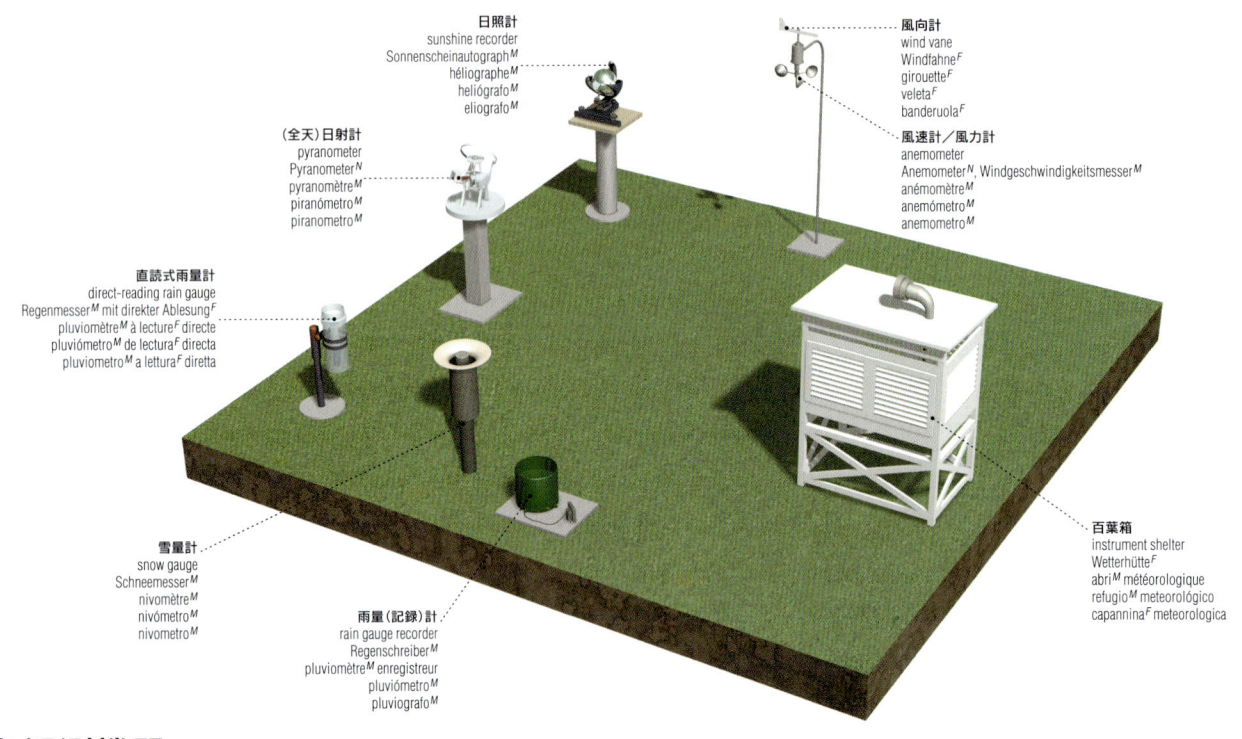

地球

日照計
sunshine recorder
Sonnenscheinautograph^M
héliographe^M
heliógrafo^M
eliografo^M

風向計
wind vane
Windfahne^F
girouette^F
veleta^F
banderuola^F

（全天）日射計
pyranometer
Pyranometer^N
pyranomètre^M
piranómetro^M
piranometro^M

風速計／風力計
anemometer
Anemometer^N, Windgeschwindigkeitsmesser^M
anémomètre^M
anemómetro^M
anemometro^M

直読式雨量計
direct-reading rain gauge
Regenmesser^M mit direkter Ablesung^F
pluviomètre^M à lecture^F directe
pluviómetro^M de lectura^F directa
pluviometro^M a lettura^F diretta

百葉箱
instrument shelter
Wetterhütte^F
abri^M météorologique
refugio^M meteorológico
capannina^F meteorologica

雪量計
snow gauge
Schneemesser^M
nivomètre^M
nivómetro^M
nivometro^M

雨量（記録）計
rain gauge recorder
Regenschreiber^M
pluviomètre^M enregistreur
pluviómetro^M
pluviografo^M

気象観測機器

meteorological measuring instruments | meteorologische Messinstrumente^N | instruments^M de mesure^F météorologique | instrumentos^M de medición^F meteorológica | strumenti^M di misurazione^F meteorologica

日照時間を観測する器具
measure of sunshine
Messung^F der Sonneneinstrahlung^F
mesure^F de l'ensoleillement^M
medición^F de la insolación^F
misurazione^F della luce^F solare

日照計
sunshine recorder
Sonnenscheinautograph^M
héliographe^M
heliógrafo^M
eliografo^M

ガラス球
glass sphere
Glaskugel^F
sphère^F de verre^M
esfera^F de vidrio^M
sfera^F di vetro^M

ガラス球支持台
sphere support
Kugelhalterung^F
support^M de sphère^F
soporte^M de la esfera^F
supporto^M della sfera^F

下部ガラス球締め金
lower sphere clamp
untere Klemmschraube^F
bague^F inférieure de blocage^F de la sphère^F
abrazadera^F inferior
morsetto^M inferiore della sfera^F

記録紙受け台
card support
Halterung^F für die Registrierkarten^F
porte-cartes^M
caja^F
supporto^M della lastra^F

日射量を測定する器具
measure of sky radiation
Messung^F der Himmelsstrahlung^F
mesure^F du rayonnement^M du ciel^M
medida^F de radiación^F del cielo^M
misurazione^F delle radiazioni^F solari

全天日射計
pyranometer
Pyranometer^N
pyranomètre^M
piranómetro^M
piranometro^M

下部支持ねじ
lower support screw
untere Halterungsschraube^F
vis^F de support^M inférieure
tornillo^M de soporte^M inferior
vite^F del supporto^M inferiore

シャドー・バンド
shadow band
Schattenring^M
bande^F pare-soleil^M
banda^F parasol
anello^M di schermo^M

センサー
sensor
Sensor^M
capteur^M
sensor^M
sensore^M

方位微調整ナット
check nut
Kontrollmutter^F
écrou^M de contrôle^M
tuerca^F de seguridad^F
controdado^M

日照記録紙
sunshine card
Registrierstreifen^M
carte^F d'insolation^F
banda^F fotosensible
lastra^F di insolazione^F

データ・ロガー
data logger
Messwertsammler^M
enregistreur^M de données^F
registrador^M de datos^M
registratore^M di dati^M

水平調節ねじ
leveling screw; levelling screw
Nivellierschraube^F
vis^F de nivellement^M
tornillo^M nivelador
vite^F di livello^M

台座板
base plate
Grundplatte^F
base^F
placa^F base^F
piastra^F di base^F

固定ナット
lock nut
Gegenmutter^F
écrou^M à cabestan^M
tuerca^F de fijación^F
controdado^M

台座
sub-base
Sockel^M
socle^M
base^M
base^F inferiore

気象 | METEOROLOGY
METEOROLOGIE | MÉTÉOROLOGIE | METEOROLOGÍA | METEOROLOGIA

気象観測機器

直読式雨量計
direct-reading rain gauge
selbst schreibender Regenmesser^M
pluviomètre^M à lecture^F directe
pluviómetro^M de lectura^F directa
pluviometro^M a lettura^F diretta

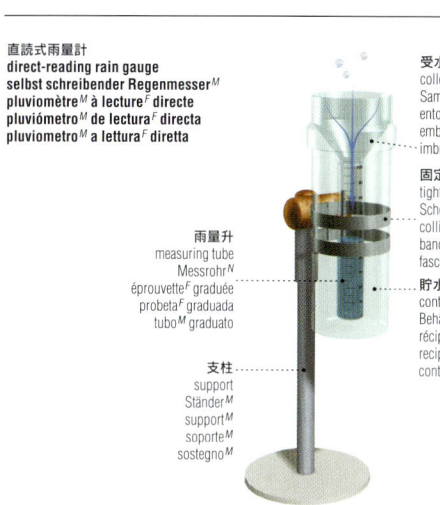

受水漏斗
collecting funnel
Sammeltrichter^M
entonnoir^M collecteur
embudo^M colector
imbuto^M collettore

雨量記録計
rain gauge recorder
Niederschlagsschreiber^M
pluviomètre^M enregistreur
pluviómetro^M
pluviografo^M

雨量を測定する器具
measure of rainfall
Messung^F der Regenmenge^F
mesure^F de la pluviosité^F
medición^F de la lluvia^F
misurazione^F delle precipitazioni^F

固定バンド
tightening band
Schelle^F
collier^M de serrage^M
banda^F de tensión^F
fascetta^F di fissaggio^M

雨量升
measuring tube
Messrohr^N
éprouvette^F graduée
probeta^F graduada
tubo^M graduato

貯水器
container
Behälter^M
récipient^M
recipiente^M de vertido^M
contenitore^M

受水器
collecting vessel
Auffanggefäß^N
récipient^M collecteur
recipiente^M de acumulación^F
recipiente^M di raccolta^F

支柱
support
Ständer^M
support^M
soporte^M
sostegno^M

記録装置
recording unit
Aufzeichnungsgerät^N
appareil^M enregistreur
unidad^F de registro^M
registratore^M

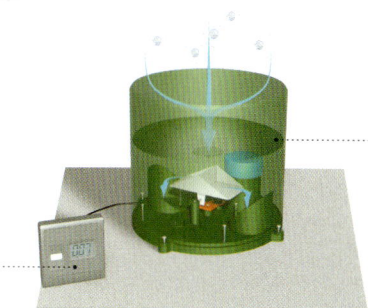

高層大気の探測
upper-air sounding
Messung^F in der oberen Atmosphäre^F
sondage^M en altitude^F
sondeo^M en altitud^F
scandagliamento^M ad alta quota^F

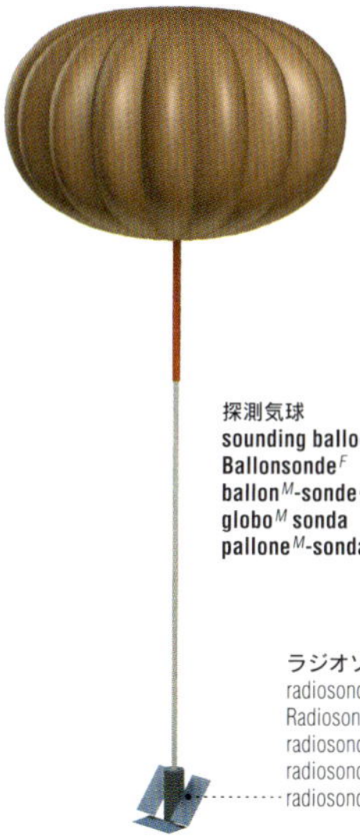

気圧を測定する器具
measure of air pressure
Messung^F des Luftdrucks^M
mesure^F de la pression^F
medición^F de la presión^F del aire^M
misurazione^F della pressione^F dell'aria^F

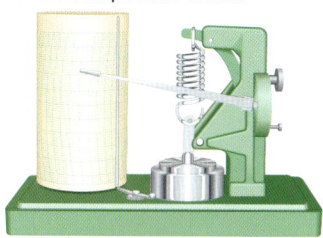

降雪量を測定する器具
measure of snowfall
Messung^F des Schneefalls^M
mesure^F de la chute^F de neige^F
medición^F de nevadas^F
misurazione^F delle precipitazioni^F nevose

探測気球
sounding balloon
Ballonsonde^F
ballon^M-sonde^F
globo^M sonda
pallone^M-sonda^F

自記気圧計
barograph
Barograph^M
baromètre^M enregistreur
barógrafo^M
barografo^M

水銀気圧計
mercury barometer
Quecksilberbarometer^N
baromètre^M à mercure^M
barómetro^M de mercurio^M
barometro^M a mercurio^M

雪量計
snow gauge
Schneemesser^M
nivomètre^F
nivómetro^M
nivometro^M

ラジオゾンデ
radiosonde
Radiosonde^F
radiosonde^F
radiosonda^F
radiosonda^F

湿度を測定する器具
measure of humidity
Messung^F der Luftfeuchtigkeit^F
mesure^F de l'humidité^F
medición^F de la humedad^F
misurazione^F dell'umidità^F

温度を測定する器具
measure of temperature
Messung^F der Temperatur^F
mesure^F de la température^F
medición^F de la temperatura^F
misurazione^F della temperatura^F

最低温度計
minimum thermometer
Minimumthermometer^N
thermomètre^M à minima
termómetro^M de mínima
termometro^M a minima

風向を測定する器具
measure of wind direction
Messung^F der Windrichtung^F
mesure^F de la direction^F du vent^M
medición^F de la dirección^F del viento^M
misurazione^F della direzione^F del vento^M

風向計
wind vane
Windfahne^F
girouette^F
veleta^F
banderuola^F

自記湿度計
hygrograph
Hygrograph^M
hygromètre^M enregistreur
higrógrafo^M
igrografo^M

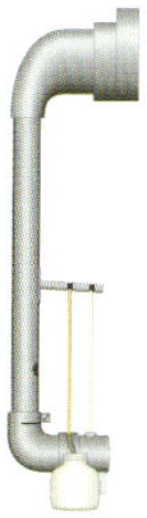

乾湿計
psychrometer
Psychrometer^N
psychromètre^M
psicrómetro^M
psicrometro^M

最高温度計
maximum thermometer
Maximumthermometer^N
thermomètre^M à maxima
termómetro^M de máxima
termometro^M a massima

雲底高度を測定する器具
measure of cloud ceiling
Messung^F der Wolkenhöhe^F
mesure^F de la hauteur^F des nuages^M
medición^F de la altura^F de las nubes^F
misurazione^F dell'altezza^F delle nubi^F

風力を測定する器具
measure of wind strength
Messung^F der Windstärke^F
mesure^F de la vitesse^F du vent^M
medición^F de la fuerza^F del viento^M
misurazione^F della forza^F del vento^M

風速計／風力計
anemometer
Anemometer^N
anémomètre^M
anemómetro^M
anemometro^M

指方規
alidade
Alhidade^F
alidade^F
alidada^F
alidada^F

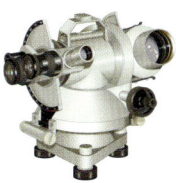

経緯儀
theodolite
Theodolit^M
théodolite^F
teodolito^M
teodolite^M

雲照灯
ceiling projector
Wolkenhöhenmesser^M
projecteur^M de plafond^M
proyector^M de altura^F máxima
proiettore^M per determinare l'altezza^F delle nubi^F

地球

59

気象 | METEOROLOGY
METEOROLOGIE | MÉTÉOROLOGIE | METEOROLOGÍA | METEOROLOGIA

気象衛星

weather satellites | Wettersatellit[M] | satellites[M] météorologiques | satélite[M] meteorológico | satelliti[M] meteorologici

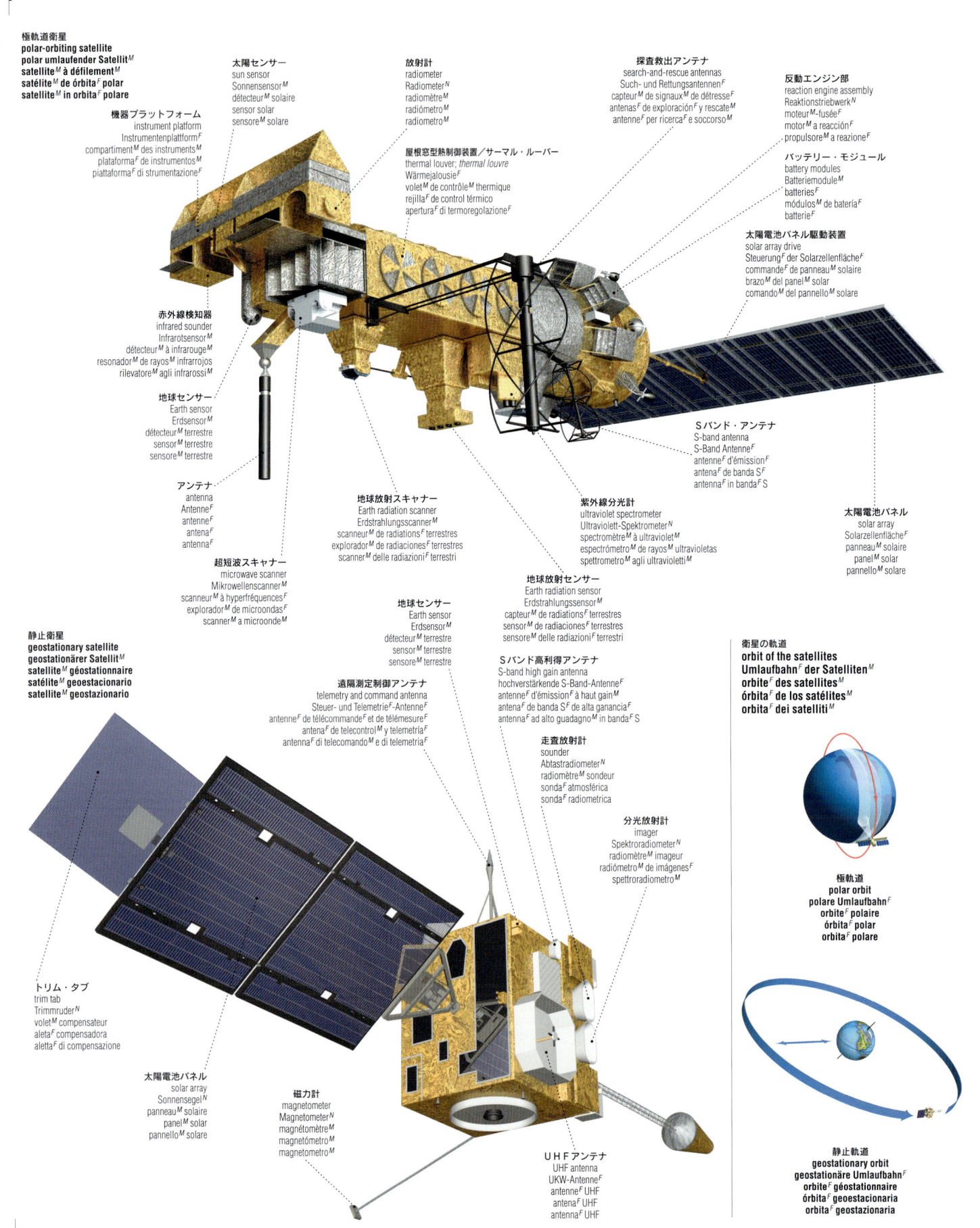

極軌道衛星
polar-orbiting satellite
polar umlaufender Satellit[M]
satellite[M] à défilement[M]
satélite[M] de órbita[F] polar
satellite[M] in orbita[F] polare

太陽センサー
sun sensor
Sonnensensor[M]
détecteur[M] solaire
sensor solar
sensore[M] solare

放射計
radiometer
Radiometer[N]
radiomètre[M]
radiómetro[M]
radiometro[M]

探査救出アンテナ
search-and-rescue antennas
Such- und Rettungsantennen[F]
capteur de signaux[M] de détresse[F]
antenas[F] de exploración[F] y rescate[M]
antenne[F] per ricerca[F] e soccorso[M]

反動エンジン部
reaction engine assembly
Reaktionstriebwerk[N]
moteur[M]-fusée[F]
motor[M] a reacción[F]
propulsore[M] a reazione[F]

機器プラットフォーム
instrument platform
Instrumentenplattform[F]
compartiment[M] des instruments[M]
plataforma[F] de instrumentos[M]
piattaforma[F] di strumentazione[F]

屋根窓型熱制御装置／サーマル・ルーバー
thermal louver; thermal louvre
Wärmejalousie[F]
volet[M] de contrôle[M] thermique
rejilla[F] de control térmico
apertura[F] di termoregolazione[F]

バッテリー・モジュール
battery modules
Batteriemodule[M]
batteries[F]
módulos[M] de batería[F]
batterie[F]

太陽電池パネル駆動装置
solar array drive
Steuerung[F] der Solarzellenfläche[F]
commande[F] de panneau[M] solaire
brazo[M] del panel[M] solar
comando[M] del pannello[M] solare

赤外線検知器
infrared sounder
Infrarotsensor[M]
détecteur[M] à infrarouge[M]
resonador[M] de rayos[M] infrarrojos
rilevatore[M] agli infrarossi[M]

地球センサー
Earth sensor
Erdsensor[M]
détecteur[M] terrestre
sensor[M] terrestre
sensore[M] terrestre

アンテナ
antenna
Antenne[F]
antenne[F]
antena[F]
antenna[F]

地球放射スキャナー
Earth radiation scanner
Erdstrahlungsscanner[M]
scanner[M] de radiations[F] terrestres
explorador[M] de radiaciones[F] terrestres
scanner[M] delle radiazioni[F] terrestri

紫外線分光計
ultraviolet spectrometer
Ultraviolett-Spektrometer[N]
spectromètre[M] à ultraviolet[M]
espectrómetro[M] de rayos[M] ultravioletas
spettrometro[M] agli ultravioletti[M]

Sバンド・アンテナ
S-band antenna
S-Band Antenne[F]
antenne[F] d'émission[F]
antena[F] de banda S[F]
antenna[F] in banda[F] S

太陽電池パネル
solar array
Solarzellenfläche[F]
panneau[M] solaire
panel[M] solar
pannello[M] solare

超短波スキャナー
microwave scanner
Mikrowellenscanner[M]
scanneur[M] à hyperfréquences[F]
explorador[M] de microondas[F]
scanner[M] a microonde[F]

地球センサー
Earth sensor
Erdsensor[M]
détecteur[M] terrestre
sensor[M] terrestre
sensore[M] terrestre

地球放射センサー
Earth radiation sensor
Erdstrahlungssensor[M]
capteur[M] de radiations[F] terrestres
sensor[M] de radiaciones[F] terrestres
sensore[M] delle radiazioni[F] terrestri

静止衛星
geostationary satellite
geostationärer Satellit[M]
satellite[M] géostationnaire
satélite[M] geoestacionario
satellite[M] geostazionario

遠隔測定制御アンテナ
telemetry and command antenna
Steuer- und Telemetrie[F]-Antenne[F]
antenne[F] de télécommande[F] et de télémesure[F]
antenna[F] de telecontrol[M] y telemetría[F]
antenna[F] di telecomando[M] e di telemetria[F]

Sバンド高利得アンテナ
S-band high gain antenna
hochverstärkende S-Band-Antenne[F]
antenne[F] d'émission[F] à haut gain[M]
antena[F] de banda S[F] de alta ganancia[F]
antenna[F] ad alto guadagno[M] in banda[F] S

衛星の軌道
orbit of the satellites
Umlaufbahn[F] der Satelliten[M]
orbite[F] des satellites[M]
órbita[F] de los satélites[M]
orbita[F] dei satelliti[M]

走査放射計
sounder
Abtastradiometer[N]
radiomètre[M] sondeur
sonda[F] atmosférica
sonda[F] radiometrica

分光放射計
imager
Spektroradiometer[N]
radiomètre[M] imageur
radiómetro[M] de imágenes[F]
spettroradiometro[M]

極軌道
polar orbit
polare Umlaufbahn[F]
orbite[F] polaire
órbita[F] polar
orbita[F] polare

トリム・タブ
trim tab
Trimmruder[N]
volet[M] compensateur
aleta[F] compensadora
aletta[F] di compensazione

太陽電池パネル
solar array
Sonnensegel[N]
panneau[M] solaire
panel[M] solar
pannello[M] solare

磁力計
magnetometer
Magnetometer[N]
magnétomètre[M]
magnetómetro[M]
magnetometro[M]

UHFアンテナ
UHF antenna
UKW-Antenne[F]
antenne[F] UHF
antena[F] UHF
antenna[F] UHF

静止軌道
geostationary orbit
geostationäre Umlaufbahn[F]
orbite[F] géostationnaire
órbita[F] geoestacionaria
orbita[F] geostazionaria

気象 | METEOROLOGY
METEOROLOGIE | MÉTÉOROLOGIE | METEOROLOGÍA | METEOROLOGIA

世界の気候

climates of the world | Klimate[N] der Welt[F] | climats[M] du monde[M] | climas[M] del mundo[M] | climi[M] del mondo[M]

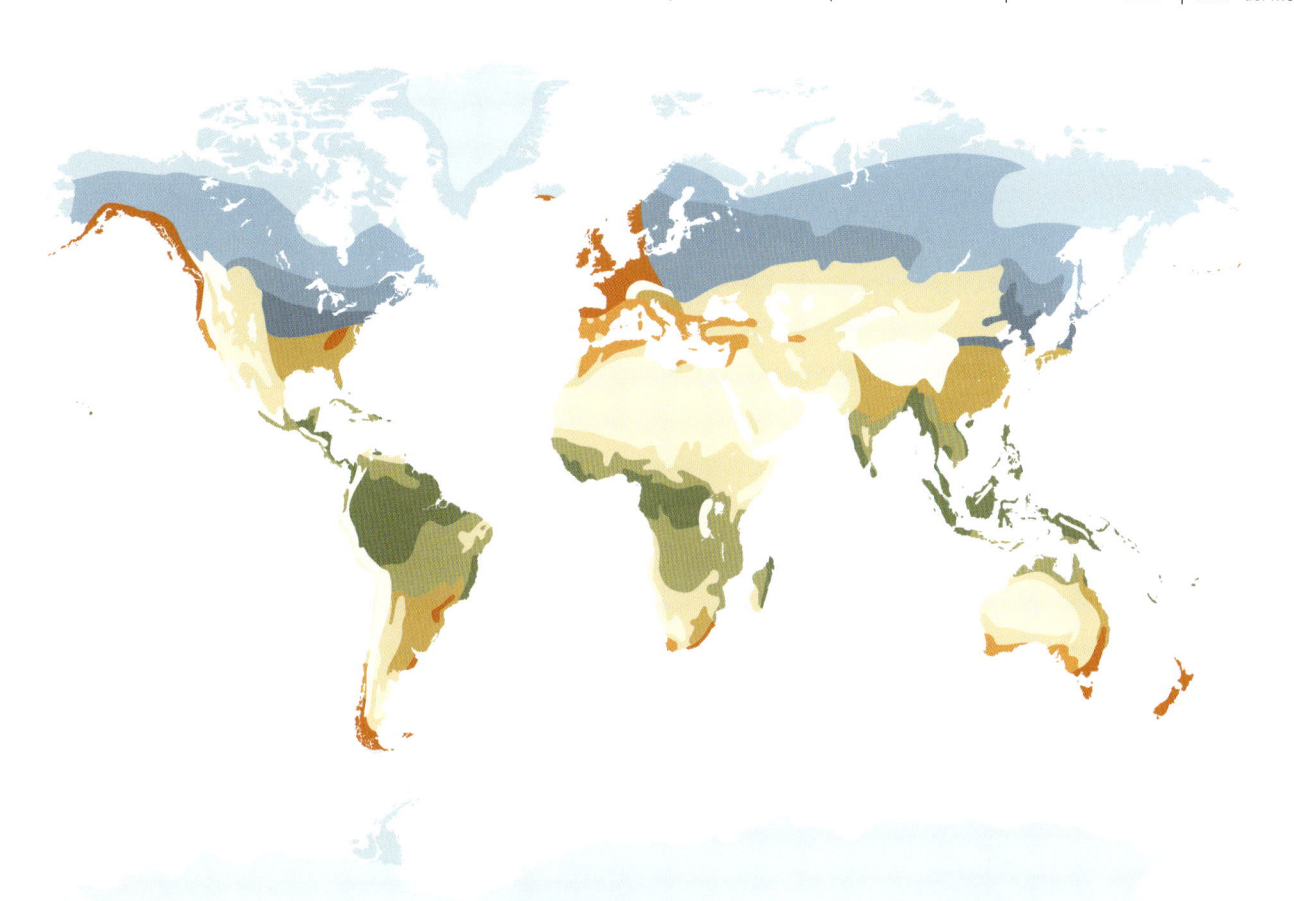

地球

熱帯気候
tropical climates
tropische Klimate[N]
climats[M] **tropicaux**
climas[M] **tropicales**
climi[M] **tropicali**

  熱帯雨林気候
  tropical rain forest
  tropischer Regenwald[M]
  tropical humide
  tropical[M] lluvioso
  tropicale della foresta[F] pluviale

  熱帯サバ(ン)ナ気候
  tropical wet-and-dry (savanna)
  tropisch feucht und trocken (Savanne[F])
  tropical humide et sec (savane[F])
  tropical[M] húmedo y seco (sabana[F])
  tropicale umido e secco (savana[F])

乾燥気候
dry climates
Trockenklimate[N]
climats[M] **arides**
climas[M] **áridos**
climi[M] **aridi**

  ステップ[草原]気候
  steppe
  Steppe[F]
  steppe[F]
  estepario
  steppico[M]

  砂漠気候
  desert
  Wüste[F]
  désert[M]
  desértico
  desertico[M]

亜寒帯気候／冷帯気候／冷温帯気候
cold temperate climates
kaltgemäßigte Klimate[N]
climats[M] **tempérés froids**
climas[M] **templados fríos**
climi[M] **temperati freddi**

  湿潤大陸性気候（夏季高温）
  humid continental - hot summer
  feucht-kontinental - heißer Sommer[M]
  continental humide, à été[M] chaud
  continental[M] húmedo - verano[M] tórrido
  continentale umido - estate[F] torrida

  湿潤大陸性気候（夏季温暖）
  humid continental - warm summer
  feucht-kontinental - warmer Sommer[M]
  continental humide, à été[M] frais
  continental[M] húmedo - verano[M] fresco
  continentale umido - estate[F] calda

  亜北極気候
  subarctic
  subarktisch
  subarctique
  subártico[M]
  subartico

亜熱帯気候／温帯気候
warm temperate climates
warmgemäßigte Klimate[N]
climats[M] **tempérés chauds**
climas[M] **templados cálidos**
climi[M] **temperati caldi**

  亜熱帯多雨気候
  humid subtropical
  feuchte Subtropen
  subtropical humide
  subtropical húmedo
  subtropicale umido

  地中海性亜熱帯気候
  Mediterranean subtropical
  mediterrane Subtropen
  méditerranéen
  subtropical mediterráneo
  subtropicale mediterraneo

  海洋性気候
  marine
  maritim
  océanique
  marítimo
  marino

寒帯気候／極気候
polar climates
Polarklimate[N]
climats[M] **polaires**
climas[M] **polares**
climi[M] **polari**

  ツンドラ気候
  polar tundra
  Polartundra[F]
  toundra[F]
  tundra[F]
  della tundra[F] polare

  氷雪気候
  polar ice cap
  Eiskappe[F]
  calotte[F] glaciaire
  hielos[M] perpetuos
  della calotta[F] polare

高原気候
highland climates
Hochlandklimate[N]
climats[F] **de montagne**
climas[F] **de alta montaña**
climi[M] **di montagna**

  高山気候
  highland
  Hochgebirge[N]
  climats[M] de montagne
  climas[M] de montaña[F]
  di montagna[F]

61

気象 | METEOROLOGY
METEOROLOGIE | MÉTÉOROLOGIE | METEOROLOGÍA | METEOROLOGIA

雲

日本語 | 英語 | ドイツ語 | フランス語 | スペイン語 | イタリア語

clouds | Wolken^F | nuages^M | nubes^F | nuvole^F

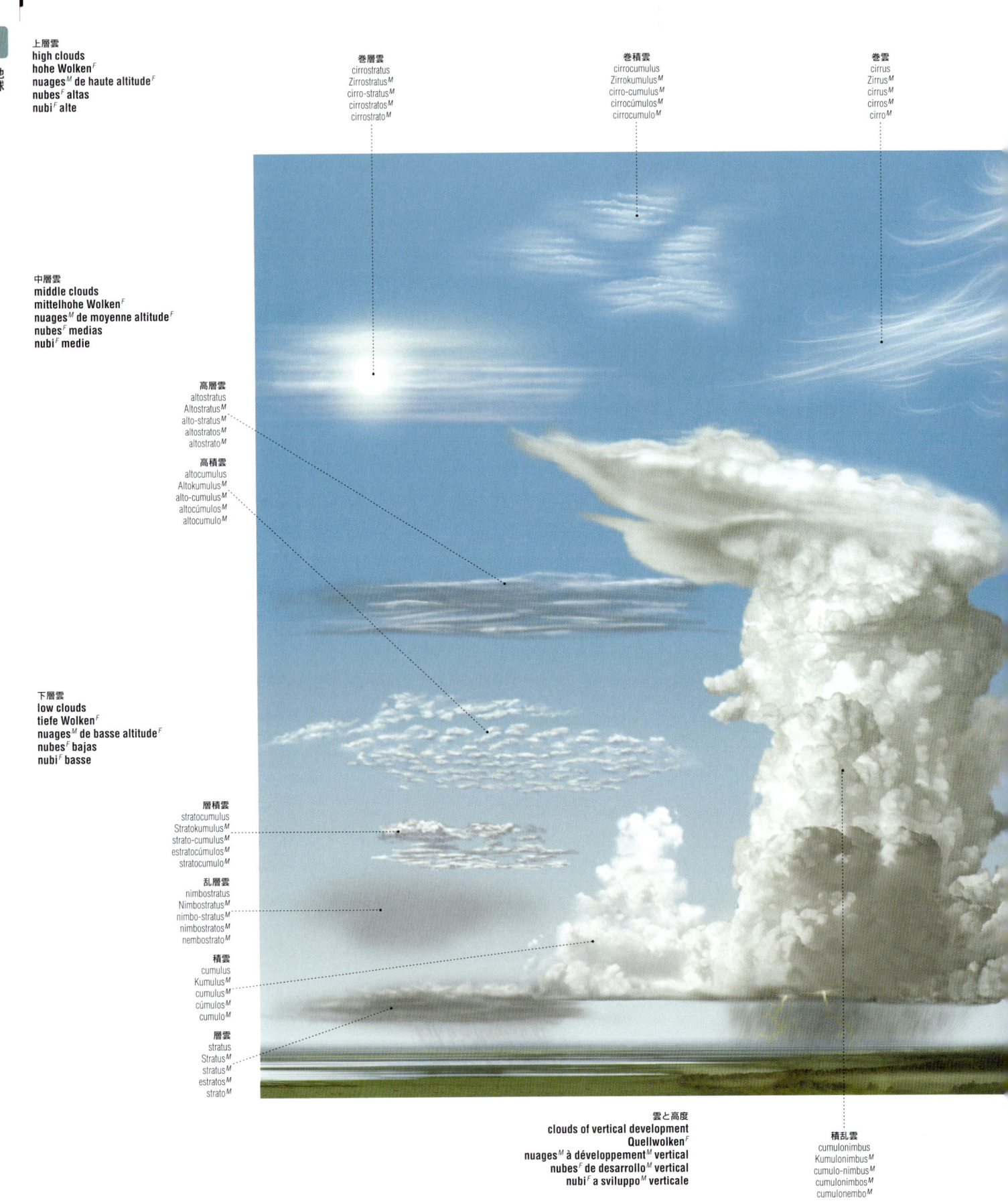

地球

上層雲
high clouds
hohe Wolken^F
nuages^M de haute altitude^F
nubes^F altas
nubi^F alte

巻層雲
cirrostratus
Zirrostratus^M
cirro-stratus^M
cirrostratos^M
cirrostrato^M

巻積雲
cirrocumulus
Zirrokumulus^M
cirro-cumulus^M
cirrocúmulos^M
cirrocumulo^M

巻雲
cirrus
Zirrus^M
cirrus^M
cirros^M
cirro^M

中層雲
middle clouds
mittelhohe Wolken^F
nuages^M de moyenne altitude^F
nubes^F medias
nubi^F medie

高層雲
altostratus
Altostratus^M
alto-stratus^M
altostratos^M
altostrato^M

高積雲
altocumulus
Altokumulus^M
alto-cumulus^M
altocúmulos^M
altocumulo^M

下層雲
low clouds
tiefe Wolken^F
nuages^M de basse altitude^F
nubes^F bajas
nubi^F basse

層積雲
stratocumulus
Stratokumulus^M
strato-cumulus^M
estratocúmulos^M
stratocumulo^M

乱層雲
nimbostratus
Nimbostratus^M
nimbo-stratus^M
nimbostratos^M
nembostrato^M

積雲
cumulus
Kumulus^M
cumulus^M
cúmulos^M
cumulo^M

層雲
stratus
Stratus^M
stratus^M
estratos^M
strato^M

雲と高度
clouds of vertical development
Quellwolken^F
nuages^M à développement^M vertical
nubes^F de desarrollo^M vertical
nubi^F a sviluppo^M verticale

積乱雲
cumulonimbus
Kumulonimbus^M
cumulo-nimbus^M
cumulonimbos^M
cumulonembo^M

気象 | METEOROLOGY
METEOROLOGIE | MÉTÉOROLOGIE | METEOROLOGÍA | METEOROLOGIA

竜巻

tornado and waterspout | Tornado^M und Wasserhose^F | tornade^F et trombe^F marine | tornado^M y tromba^F marina | tornado^M e tromba^F marina

壁雲
wall cloud
Gewitterwolken^F
mur^M de nuages^M
muro^M de nubes^F
parete^F di nuvole^F

漏斗雲
funnel cloud
Wolkentrichter^M
nuage^M en entonnoir^M
nube^F en forma^F de embudo^M
nube^F a proboscide^F

破片
debris
aufgewirbelter Staub^M
buisson^M
detritos^M
detriti^M

水上竜巻
waterspout
Wasserhose^F
trombe^F marine
tromba^F marina
tromba^F marina

トルネード
tornado
Tornado^M
tornade^F
tornado^M
tornado^M

熱帯性低気圧

tropical cyclone | tropischer Wirbelsturm^M | cyclone^M tropical | ciclón^M tropical | ciclone^M tropicale

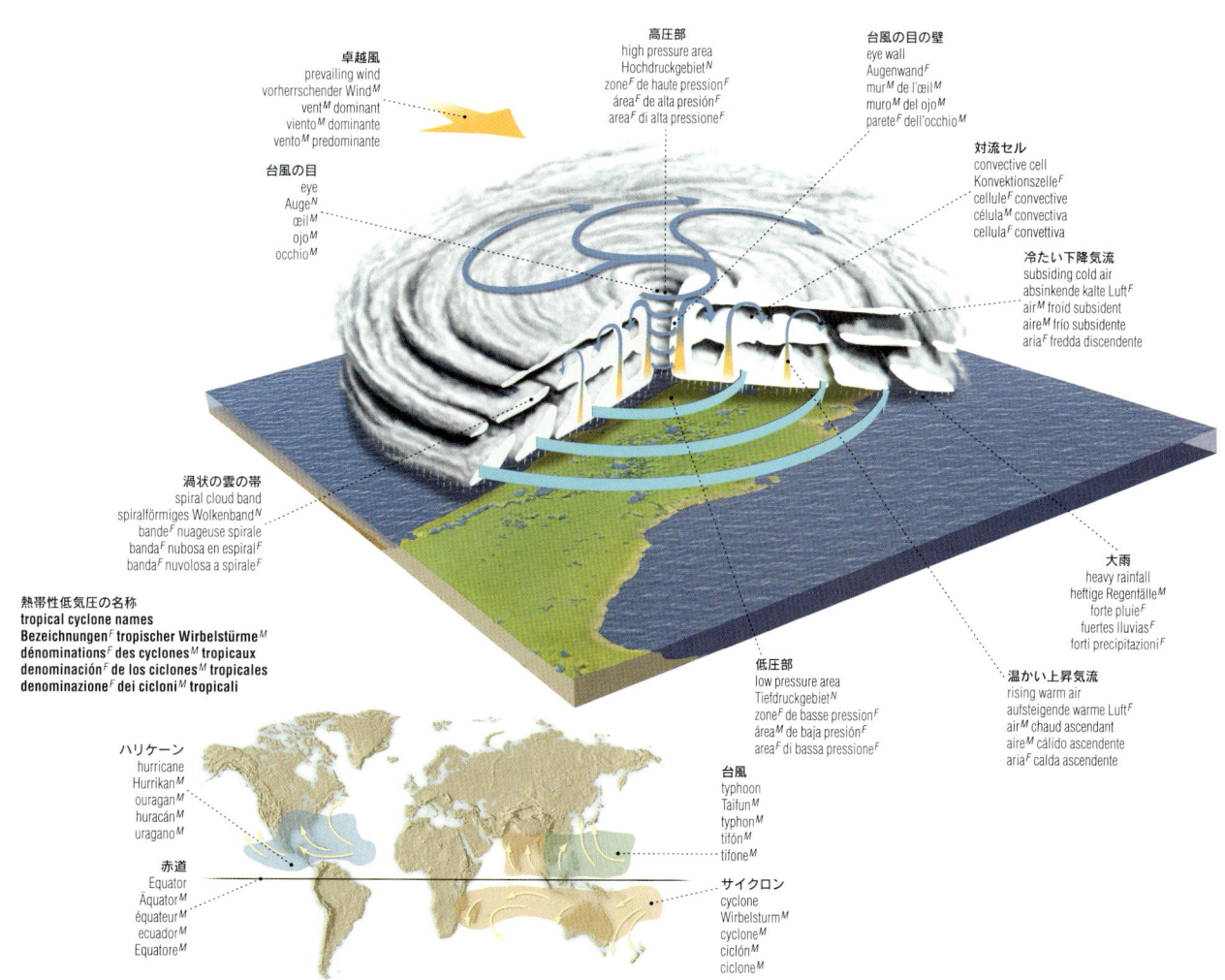

卓越風
prevailing wind
vorherrschender Wind^M
vent^M dominant
viento^M dominante
vento^M predominante

高圧部
high pressure area
Hochdruckgebiet^N
zone^F de haute pression^F
área^M de alta presión^F
area^F di alta pressione^F

台風の目の壁
eye wall
Augenwand^F
mur^M de l'œil^M
muro^M del ojo^M
parete^F dell'occhio^M

台風の目
eye
Auge^N
œil^M
ojo^M
occhio^M

対流セル
convective cell
Konvektionszelle^F
cellule^F convective
célula^M convectiva
cellula^F convettiva

冷たい下降気流
subsiding cold air
absinkende kalte Luft^F
air^M froid subsident
aire^M frío subsidente
aria^F fredda discendente

渦状の雲の帯
spiral cloud band
spiralförmiges Wolkenband^N
bande^F nuageuse spirale
banda^F nubosa en espiral^F
banda^F nuvolosa a spirale^F

熱帯性低気圧の名称
tropical cyclone names
Bezeichnungen^F tropischer Wirbelstürme^M
dénominations^F des cyclones^M tropicaux
denominación^F de los ciclones^M tropicales
denominazione^F dei cicloni^M tropicali

低圧部
low pressure area
Tiefdruckgebiet^N
zone^F de basse pression^F
área^M de baja presión^F
area^F di bassa pressione^F

大雨
heavy rainfall
heftige Regenfälle^M
forte pluie^F
fuertes lluvias^F
forti precipitazioni^F

温かい上昇気流
rising warm air
aufsteigende warme Luft^F
air^M chaud ascendant
aire^M cálido ascendente
aria^F calda ascendente

ハリケーン
hurricane
Hurrikan^M
ouragan^M
huracán^M
uragano^M

赤道
Equator
Äquator^M
équateur^M
ecuador^M
Equatore^M

台風
typhoon
Taifun^M
typhon^M
tifón^M
tifone^M

サイクロン
cyclone
Wirbelsturm^M
cyclone^M
ciclón^M
ciclone^M

63

気象 | METEOROLOGY
METEOROLOGIE | MÉTÉOROLOGIE | METEOROLOGÍA | METEOROLOGIA

降水

日本語 | 英語 | ドイツ語 | フランス語 | スペイン語 | イタリア語

précipitations | Niederschläge^M | précipitations^F | precipitaciones^F | precipitazioni^F

地球

雨の形態
rain forms
Regenarten^F
formes^F de pluie^F
formas^F de lluvia^F
tipologie^F di pioggia^F

霧雨
drizzle
Sprühregen^M
bruine^F
llovizna^F
pioviggine^F

小雨
light rain
leichter Regen^M
pluie^F faible
lluvia^F ligera
pioggia^F leggera

並雨
moderate rain
mäßiger Regen^M
pluie^F modérée
lluvia^F moderada
pioggia^F moderata

大雨
heavy rain
starker Regen^M
pluie^F forte
lluvia^F intensa
pioggia^F forte

冬季の降水
winter precipitations
Winterniederschläge^M
précipitations^F hivernales
precipitaciones^F invernales
precipitazioni^F invernali

温かい空気
warm air
warme Luft^F
air^M chaud
aire^M caliente
aria^F calda

冷たい空気
cold air
kalte Luft^F
air^M froid
aire^M frío
aria^F fredda

雨
rain
Regen^M
pluie^F
lluvia^F
pioggia^F

着氷性の雨／氷晶雨
freezing rain
gefrierender Regen^M
pluie^F verglaçante
lluvia^F helada
pioggia^F congelantesi

霙（みぞれ）／氷霰（あられ）
sleet
Schneeregen^M
grésil^M
aguanieve^M
nevischio^M

雪
snow
Schnee^M
neige^F
nieve^M
neve^F

雪の結晶
snow crystals
Schneekristalle^M
cristaux^M de neige^F
cristales^M de nieve^F
cristalli^M di neve^F

針状結晶
needle
Nadel^F
aiguille^F
aguja^F
ago^M

鼓状結晶
capped column
bedeckte Säule^F
colonne^F avec capuchon^M
columna^F con capuchón^M
colonna^F con lamelle terminali

雹（ひょう）／霰
hail
Hagel^M
grêlon^M
granizo^M
grandine^F

霙／氷霰
sleet
Eiskörnchen^N
grésil^M
cellisca^F
nevischio^M

雪霰
snow pellet
Reif- und Frostgraupel^F
neige^F roulée
copo^M de nieve^F
pallottoline^F di neve^F

柱状結晶
column
Säule^F
colonne^F
columna^F
colonna^F

板状結晶
plate crystal
Plättchen^N
plaquette^F
placa^F de hielo^M
cristallo^M lamellare

立体樹状結晶
spatial dendrite
räumlicher Dendrit^M
dendrite^F spatiale
dendrita^F espacial
cristallo^M dendritico spaziale

不規則結晶
irregular crystal
irreguläres Aggregat^N
cristaux^M irréguliers
cristales^M irregulares
cristallo^M irregolare

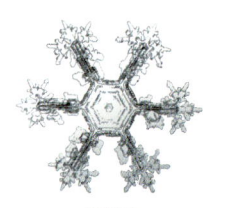

星状結晶
stellar crystal
Stern^M
étoile^F
estrella^F
cristallo^M stellare

気象 | METEOROLOGY
METEOROLOGIE | MÉTÉOROLOGIE | METEOROLOGÍA | METEOROLOGIA

降水

地球

荒天
stormy sky
stürmischer Himmel^M
ciel^M d'orage^M
cielo^M turbulento
cielo^M tempestoso

雲
cloud
Wolke^F
nuage^M
nube^M
nube^F

稲光／稲妻
lightning
Blitz^M
éclair^M
rayo^M
fulmine^M

虹
rainbow
Regenbogen^M
arc-en-ciel^M
arco^M iris
arcobaleno^M

雨
rain
Regen^M
pluie^F
lluvia^F
pioggia^F

露
dew
Tau^M
rosée^F
rocío^M
rugiada^F

霧(もや)
mist
Dunst^M
brume^F
neblina^F
foschia^F

霧
fog
Nebel^M
brouillard^M
niebla^F
nebbia^F

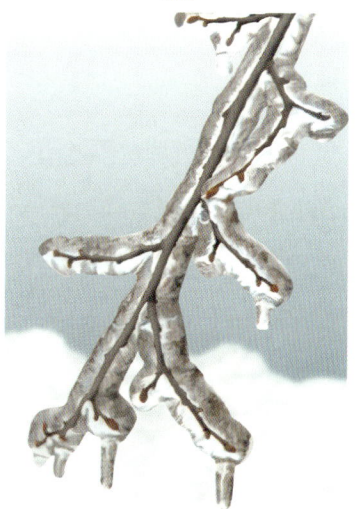

霜
rime
Reif^M
givre^M
escarcha^F
brina^F

霧氷
frost; *glazed frost*
Raureif^M
verglas^M
hielo^M
vetrone^M

65

環境 | ENVIRONMENT
UMWELT | ENVIRONNEMENT | AMBIENTE | AMBIENTE

植生と生物圏

vegetation and biosphere | Vegetation^F und Biosphäre^F | végétation^F et biosphère^F | vegetación^F y biosfera^F | vegetazione^F e biosfera^F

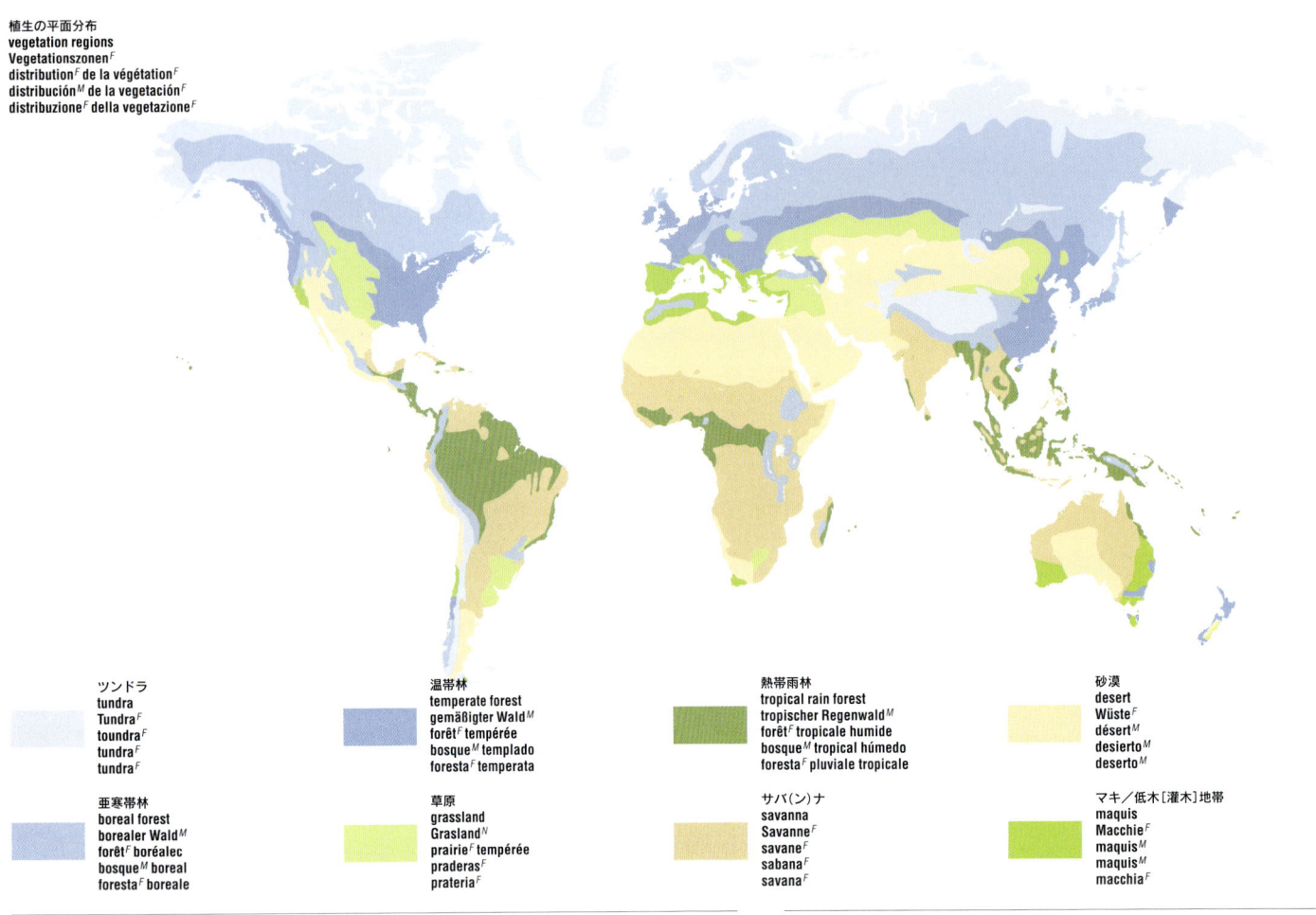

植生の平面分布
vegetation regions
Vegetationszonen^F
distribution^F de la végétation^F
distribución^M de la vegetación^F
distribuzione^F della vegetazione^F

ツンドラ
tundra
Tundra^F
toundra^F
tundra^F
tundra^F

亜寒帯林
boreal forest
borealer Wald^M
forêt^F boréalec
bosque^M boreal
foresta^F boreale

温帯林
temperate forest
gemäßigter Wald^M
forêt^F tempérée
bosque^M templado
foresta^F temperata

草原
grassland
Grasland^N
prairie^F tempérée
praderas^F
prateria^F

熱帯雨林
tropical rain forest
tropischer Regenwald^M
forêt^F tropicale humide
bosque^M tropical húmedo
foresta^F pluviale tropicale

サバ(ン)ナ
savanna
Savanne^F
savane^F
sabana^F
savana^F

砂漠
desert
Wüste^F
désert^M
desierto^M
deserto^M

マキ／低木[灌木]地帯
maquis
Macchie^F
maquis^M
maquis^M
macchia^F

植生の垂直分布
elevation zones and vegetation
Vegetationsbild^N nach Höhenlagen^F
paysage^M végétal selon l'altitude^F
altitud^F y vegetación^F
altitudine^F e vegetazione^F

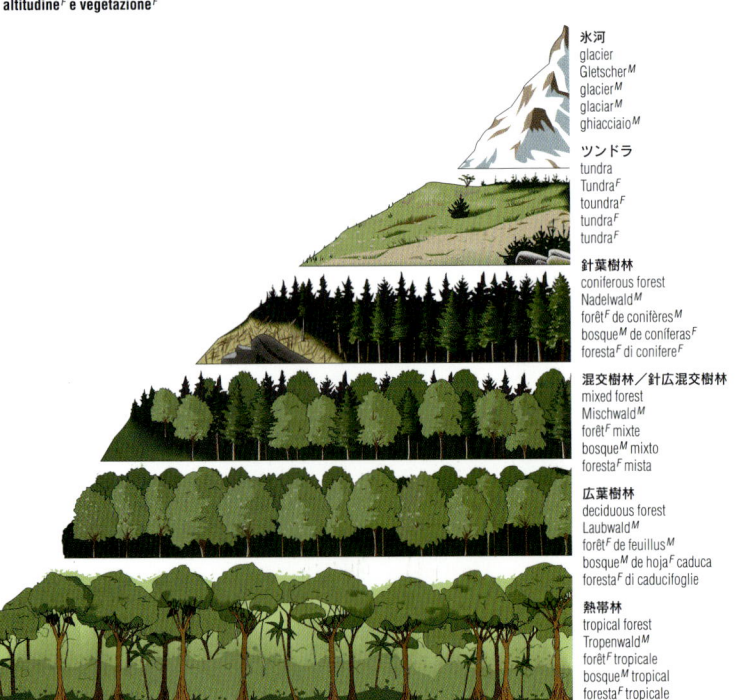

氷河
glacier
Gletscher^M
glacier^M
glaciar^M
ghiacciaio^M

ツンドラ
tundra
Tundra^F
toundra^F
tundra^F
tundra^F

針葉樹林
coniferous forest
Nadelwald^M
forêt^F de conifères^M
bosque^M de coníferas^F
foresta^F di conifere^F

混交樹林／針広混交樹林
mixed forest
Mischwald^M
forêt^F mixte
bosque^M mixto
foresta^F mista

広葉樹林
deciduous forest
Laubwald^M
forêt^F de feuillus^M
bosque^M de hoja^F caduca
foresta^F di caducifoglie

熱帯林
tropical forest
Tropenwald^M
forêt^F tropicale
bosque^M tropical
foresta^F tropicale

生物圏の構造
structure of the biosphere
Aufbau^M der Biosphäre^F
structure^F de la biosphère^F
estructura^F de la biosfera^F
struttura^F della biosfera^F

大気圏
atmosphere
Atmosphäre^F
atmosphère^F
atmósfera^F
atmosfera^F

岩圏
lithosphere
Lithosphäre^F
lithosphère^F
litosfera^F
litosfera^F

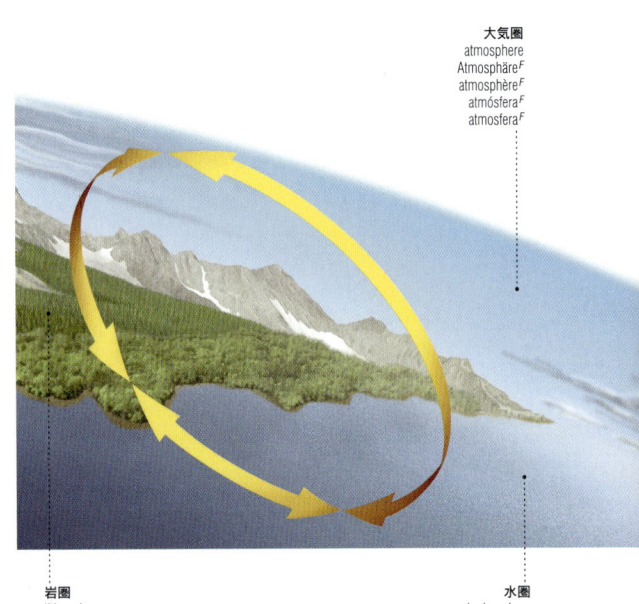

水圏
hydrosphere
Hydrosphäre^F
hydrosphère^F
hidrosfera^F
idrosfera^F

環境 | ENVIRONMENT
UMWELT | ENVIRONNEMENT | AMBIENTE | AMBIENTE

食物連鎖

food chain | Nahrungskette^F | chaîne^F alimentaire | cadena^F alimentaria | catena^F alimentare

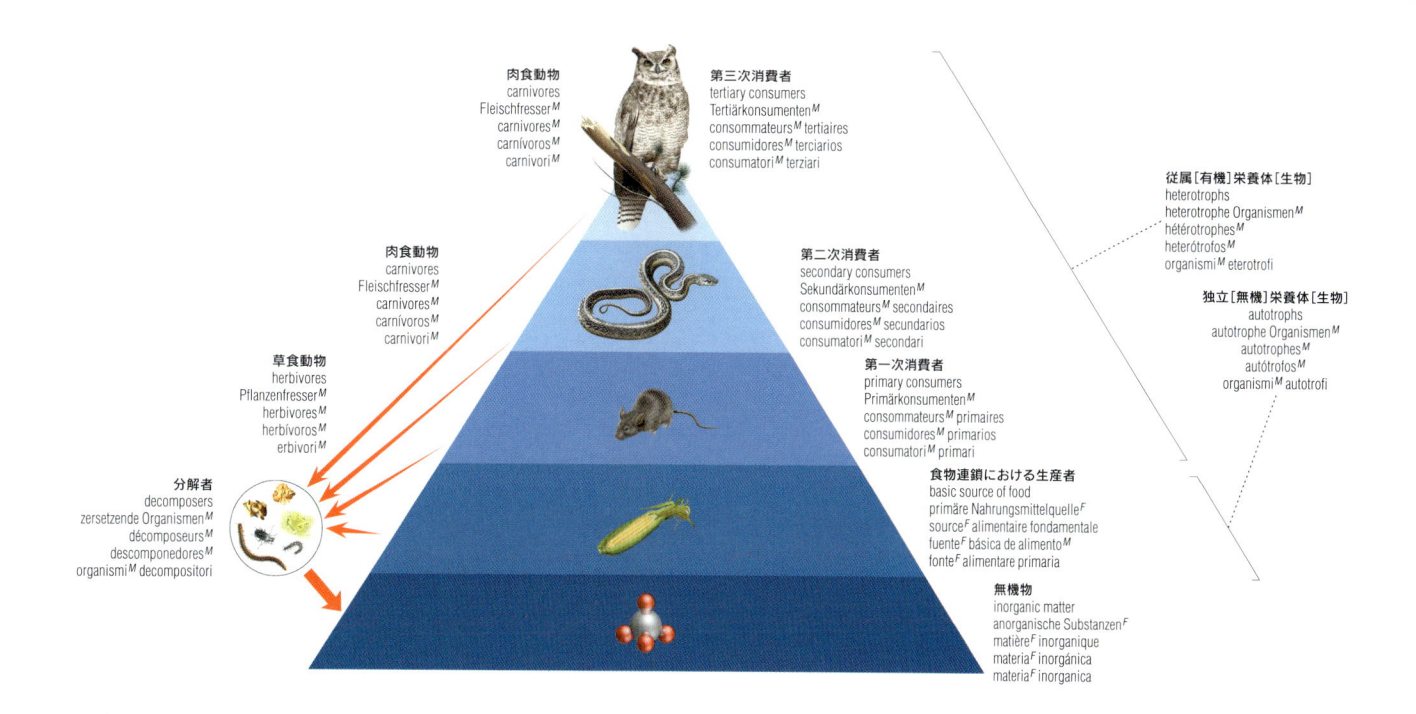

肉食動物
carnivores
Fleischfresser^M
carnivores^M
carnívoros^M
carnivori^M

第三次消費者
tertiary consumers
Tertiärkonsumenten^M
consommateurs^M tertiaires
consumidores^M terciarios
consumatori^M terziari

従属[有機]栄養体[生物]
heterotrophs
heterotrophe Organismen^M
hétérotrophes
heterótrofos
organismi^M eterotrofi

肉食動物
carnivores
Fleischfresser^M
carnivores^M
carnívoros^M
carnivori^M

第二次消費者
secondary consumers
Sekundärkonsumenten^M
consommateurs^M secondaires
consumidores^M secundarios
consumatori^M secondari

独立[無機]栄養体[生物]
autotrophs
autotrophe Organismen^M
autotrophes^M
autótrofos^M
organismi^M autotrofi

草食動物
herbivores
Pflanzenfresser^M
herbivores^M
herbívoros^M
erbivori^M

第一次消費者
primary consumers
Primärkonsumenten^M
consommateurs^M primaires
consumidores^M primarios
consumatori^M primari

分解者
decomposers
zersetzende Organismen^M
décomposeurs^M
descomponedores^M
organismi^M decompositori

食物連鎖における生産者
basic source of food
primäre Nahrungsmittelquelle^F
source^F alimentaire fondamentale
fuente^F básica de alimento
fonte^F alimentare primaria

無機物
inorganic matter
anorganische Substanzen^F
matière^F inorganique
materia^F inorgánica
materia^F inorganica

水の循環

hydrologic cycle | Wasserkreislauf^M | cycle^M de l'eau^F | ciclo^M hidrológico | ciclo^M idrologico

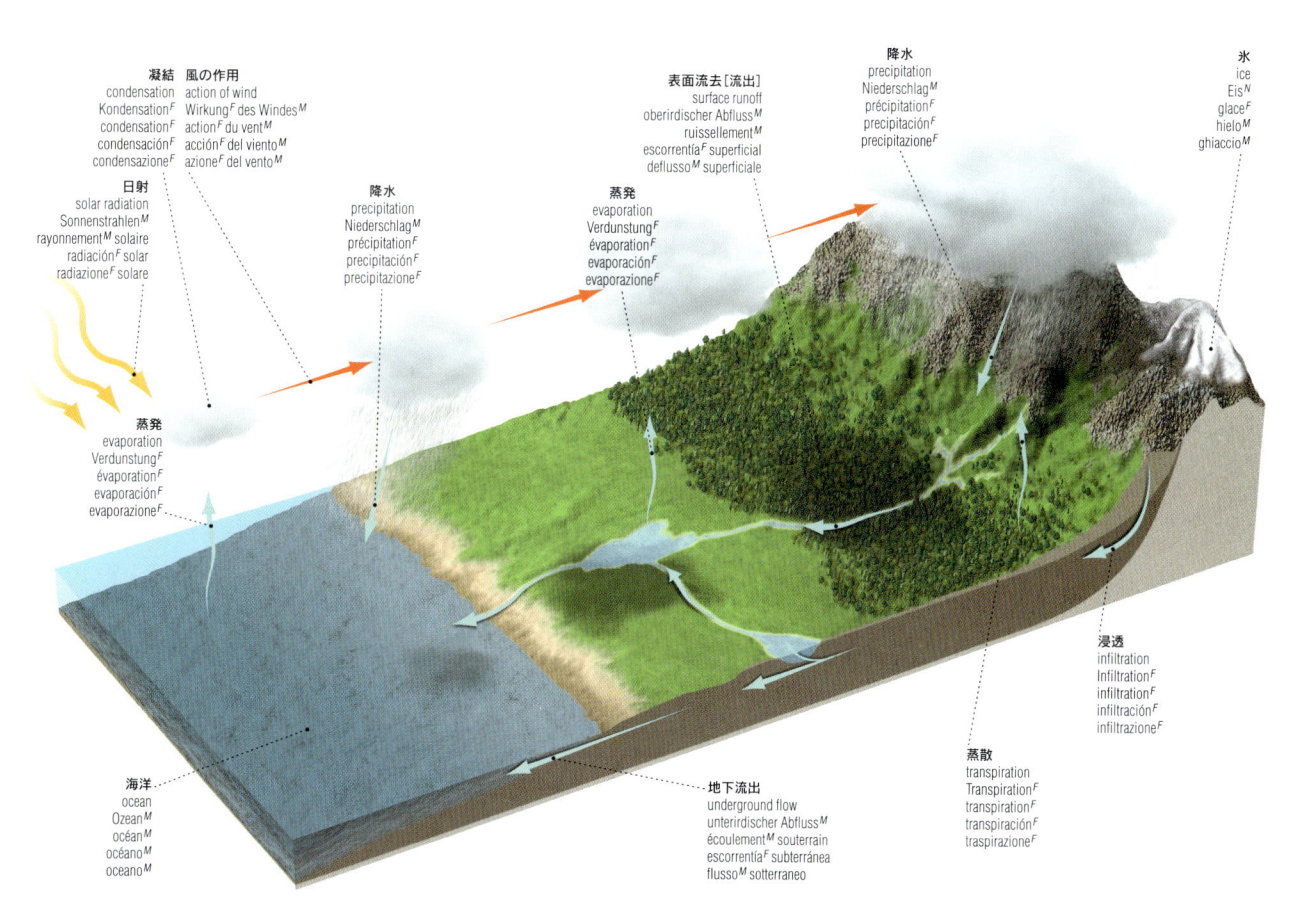

凝結
condensation
Kondensation^F
condensation^F
condensación^F
condensazione^F

風の作用
action of wind
Wirkung^F des Windes^M
action^F du vent^M
acción^F del viento^M
azione^F del vento^M

表面流去[流出]
surface runoff
oberirdischer Abfluss^M
ruissellement^M
escorrentía^F superficial
deflusso^M superficiale

降水
precipitation
Niederschlag^M
précipitation^F
precipitación^F
precipitazione^F

氷
ice
Eis^N
glace^F
hielo^M
ghiaccio^M

日射
solar radiation
Sonnenstrahlen^M
rayonnement^M solaire
radiación^F solar
radiazione^F solare

降水
precipitation
Niederschlag^M
précipitation^F
precipitación^F
precipitazione^F

蒸発
evaporation
Verdunstung^F
évaporation^F
evaporación^F
evaporazione^F

蒸発
evaporation
Verdunstung^F
évaporation^F
evaporación^F
evaporazione^F

浸透
infiltration
Infiltration^F
infiltration^F
infiltración^F
infiltrazione^F

蒸散
transpiration
Transpiration^F
transpiration^F
transpiración^F
traspirazione^F

海洋
ocean
Ozean^M
océan^M
océano^M
oceano^M

地下流出
underground flow
unterirdischer Abfluss^M
écoulement^M souterrain
escorrentía^F subterránea
flusso^M sotterraneo

環境 | ENVIRONMENT
UMWELT | ENVIRONNEMENT | AMBIENTE | AMBIENTE

温室効果
greenhouse effect | Treibhauseffekt^M | effet^M de serre^F | efecto^M invernadero | effetto^M serra^F

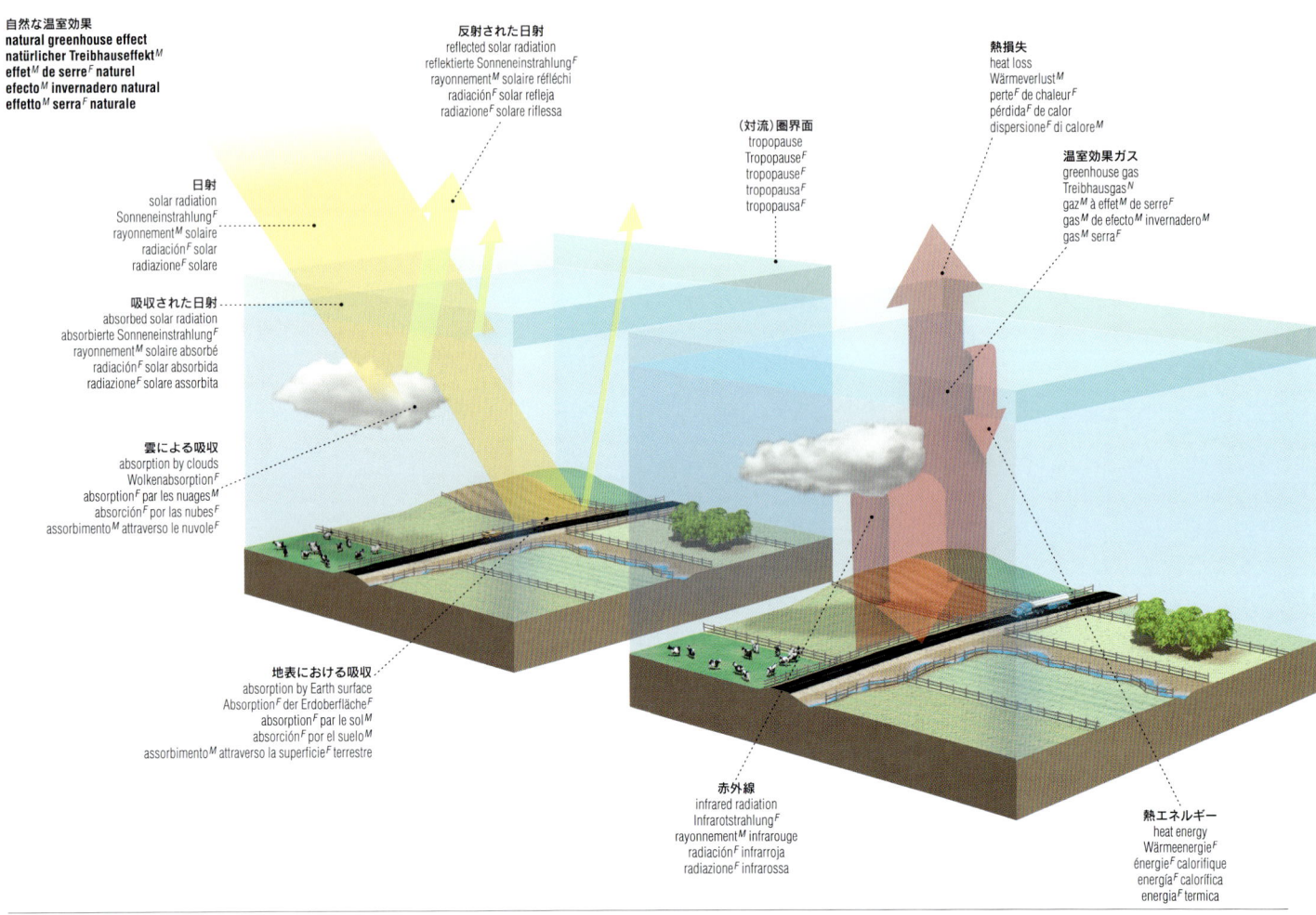

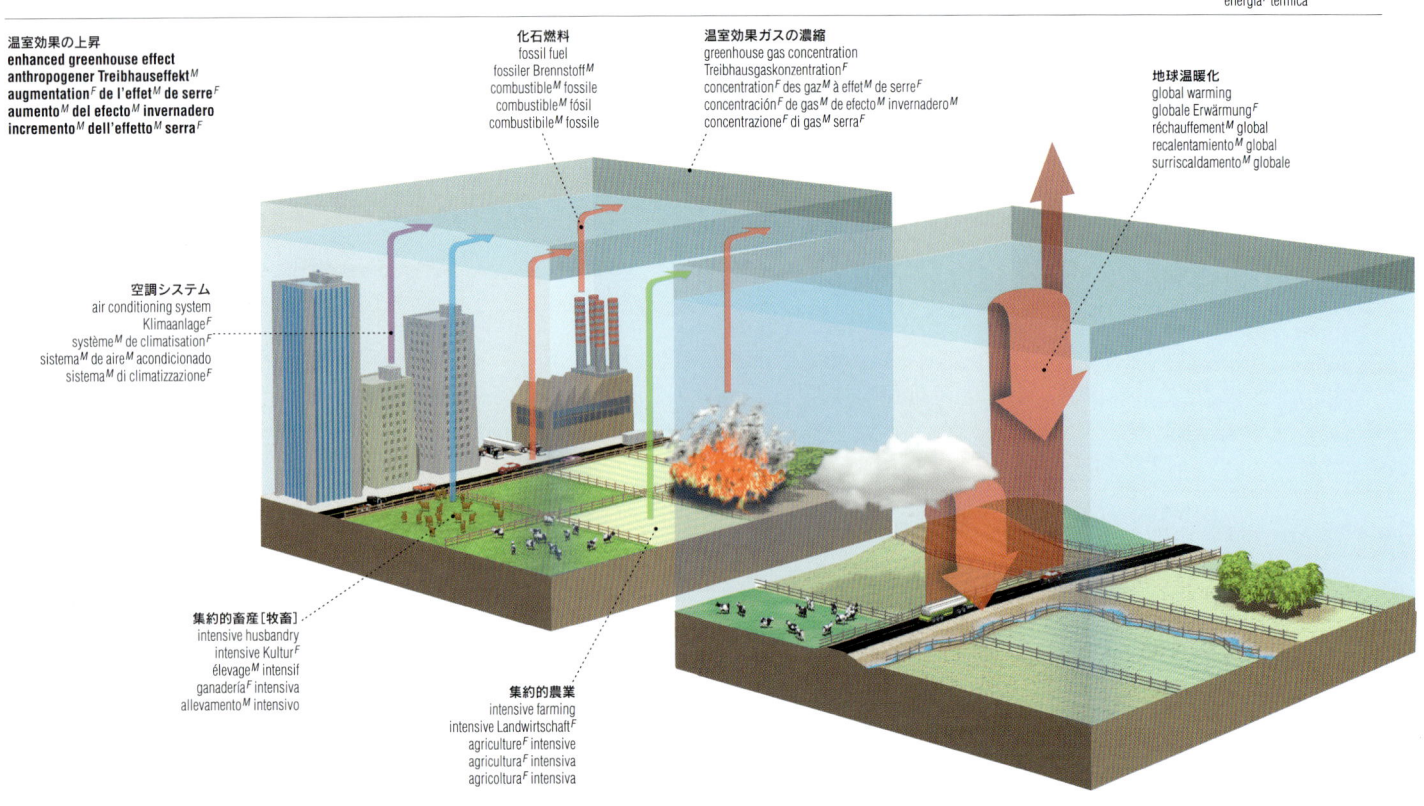

日本語 | 英語 | ドイツ語 | フランス語 | スペイン語 | イタリア語

地球

自然な温室効果
natural greenhouse effect
natürlicher Treibhauseffekt^M
effet^M de serre^F naturel
efecto^M invernadero natural
effetto^M serra^F naturale

反射された日射
reflected solar radiation
reflektierte Sonneneinstrahlung^F
rayonnement^M solaire réfléchi
radiación^F solar refleja
radiazione^F solare riflessa

熱損失
heat loss
Wärmeverlust^M
perte^F de chaleur
pérdida^F de calor
dispersione^F di calore^M

日射
solar radiation
Sonneneinstrahlung^F
rayonnement^M solaire
radiación^F solar
radiazione^F solare

(対流)圏界面
tropopause
Tropopause^F
tropopause^F
tropopausa^F
tropopausa^F

温室効果ガス
greenhouse gas
Treibhausgas^N
gaz^M à effet^M de serre^F
gas^M de efecto^M invernadero^M
gas^M serra^F

吸収された日射
absorbed solar radiation
absorbierte Sonneneinstrahlung^F
rayonnement^M solaire absorbé
radiación^F solar absorbida
radiazione^F solare assorbita

雲による吸収
absorption by clouds
Wolkenabsorption^F
absorption^F par les nuages^M
absorción^F por las nubes^F
assorbimento^M attraverso le nuvole^F

地表における吸収
absorption by Earth surface
Absorption^F der Erdoberfläche^F
absorption^F par le sol^M
absorción^F por el suelo^M
assorbimento^M attraverso la superficie^F terrestre

赤外線
infrared radiation
Infrarotstrahlung^F
rayonnement^M infrarouge
radiación^F infrarroja
radiazione^F infrarossa

熱エネルギー
heat energy
Wärmeenergie^F
énergie^F calorifique
energía^F calorífica
energia^F termica

温室効果の上昇
enhanced greenhouse effect
anthropogener Treibhauseffekt^M
augmentation^F de l'effet^M de serre^F
aumento^M del efecto^M invernadero
incremento^M dell'effetto^M serra^F

化石燃料
fossil fuel
fossiler Brennstoff^M
combustible^M fossile
combustible^M fósil
combustibile^M fossile

温室効果ガスの濃縮
greenhouse gas concentration
Treibhausgaskonzentration^F
concentration^F des gaz^M à effet^M de serre^F
concentración^F de gas^M de efecto^M invernadero^M
concentrazione^F di gas^M serra^F

地球温暖化
global warming
globale Erwärmung^F
réchauffement^M global
recalentamiento^M global
surriscaldamento^M globale

空調システム
air conditioning system
Klimaanlage^F
système^M de climatisation^F
sistema^M de aire^M acondicionado
sistema^M di climatizzazione^F

集約的畜産[牧畜]
intensive husbandry
intensive Kultur^F
élevage^M intensif
ganadería^F intensiva
allevamento^M intensivo

集約的農業
intensive farming
intensive Landwirtschaft^F
agriculture^F intensive
agricultura^F intensiva
agricoltura^F intensiva

68

環境 | ENVIRONMENT
UMWELT | ENVIRONNEMENT | AMBIENTE | AMBIENTE

大気汚染

air pollution | Luftverschmutzung^F | pollution^F de l'air^M | contaminación^F del aire^M | inquinamento^M dell'aria^F

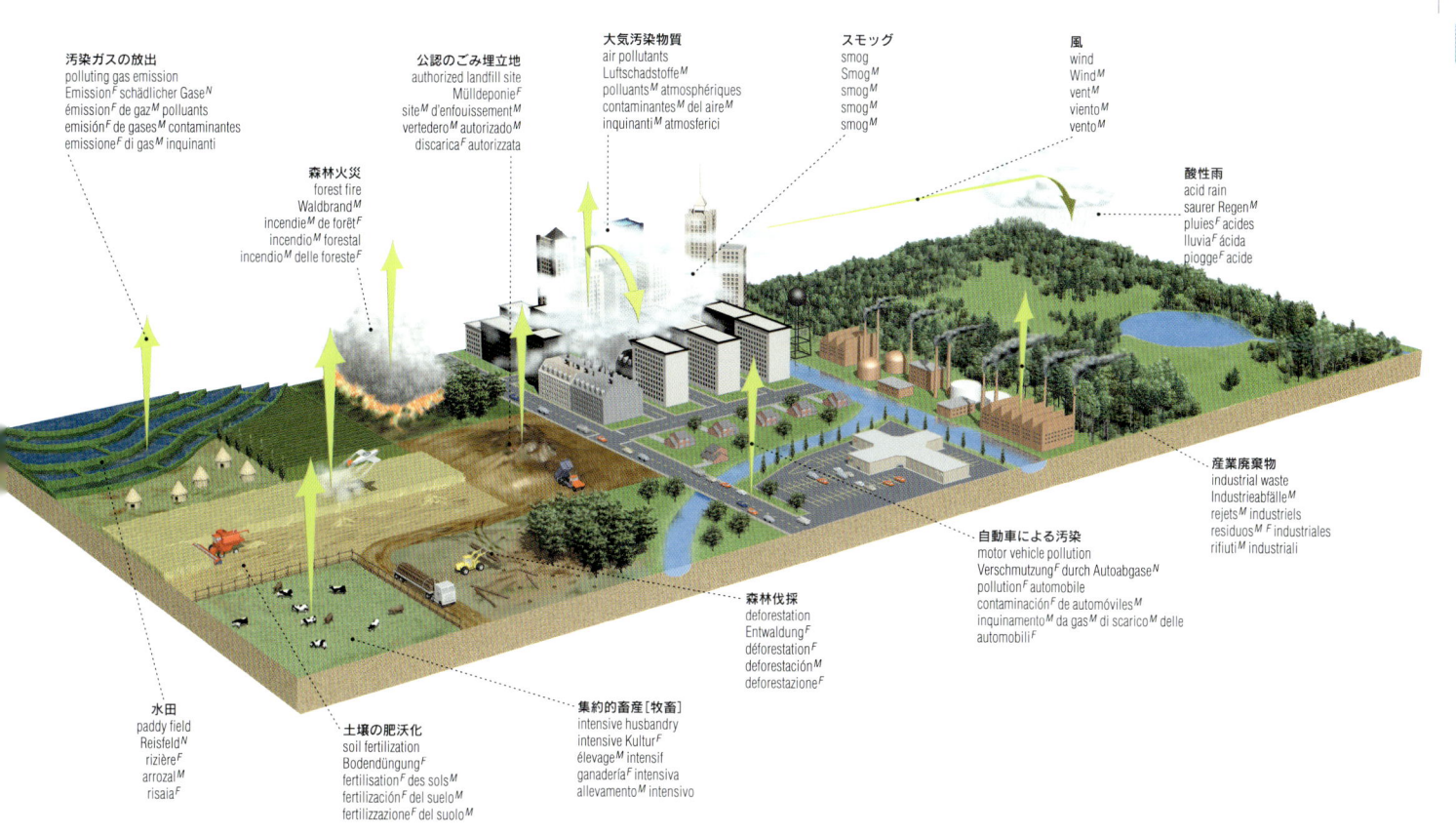

地球

汚染ガスの放出
polluting gas emission
Emission^F schädlicher Gase^N
émission^F de gaz^M polluants
emisión^F de gases^M contaminantes
emissione^F di gas^M inquinanti

森林火災
forest fire
Waldbrand^M
incendie^M de forêt^F
incendio^M forestal
incendio^M delle foreste^F

公認のごみ埋立地
authorized landfill site
Mülldeponie^F
site^M d'enfouissement^M
vertedero^M autorizado
discarica^F autorizzata

大気汚染物質
air pollutants
Luftschadstoffe^M
polluants^M atmosphériques
contaminantes^M del aire^M
inquinanti^M atmosferici

スモッグ
smog
Smog^M
smog^M
smog^M
smog^M

風
wind
Wind^M
vent^M
viento^M
vento^M

酸性雨
acid rain
saurer Regen^M
pluies^F acides
lluvia^F ácida
piogge^F acide

産業廃棄物
industrial waste
Industrieabfälle^M
rejets^M industriels
residuos^{M F} industriales
rifiuti^M industriali

自動車による汚染
motor vehicle pollution
Verschmutzung^F durch Autoabgase^N
pollution^F automobile
contaminación^F de automóviles^M
inquinamento^M da gas^M di scarico^M delle automobili^F

森林伐採
deforestation
Entwaldung^F
déforestation^F
deforestación^M
deforestazione^F

水田
paddy field
Reisfeld^N
rizière^F
arrozal^M
risaia^F

土壌の肥沃化
soil fertilization
Bodendüngung^F
fertilisation^F des sols^M
fertilización^F del suelo^M
fertilizzazione^F del suolo^M

集約的畜産［牧畜］
intensive husbandry
intensive Kultur^F
élevage^M intensif
ganadería^F intensiva
allevamento^M intensivo

土壌汚染

land pollution | Bodenverschmutzung^F | pollution^F du sol^M | contaminación^F del suelo^M | inquinamento^M del suolo^M

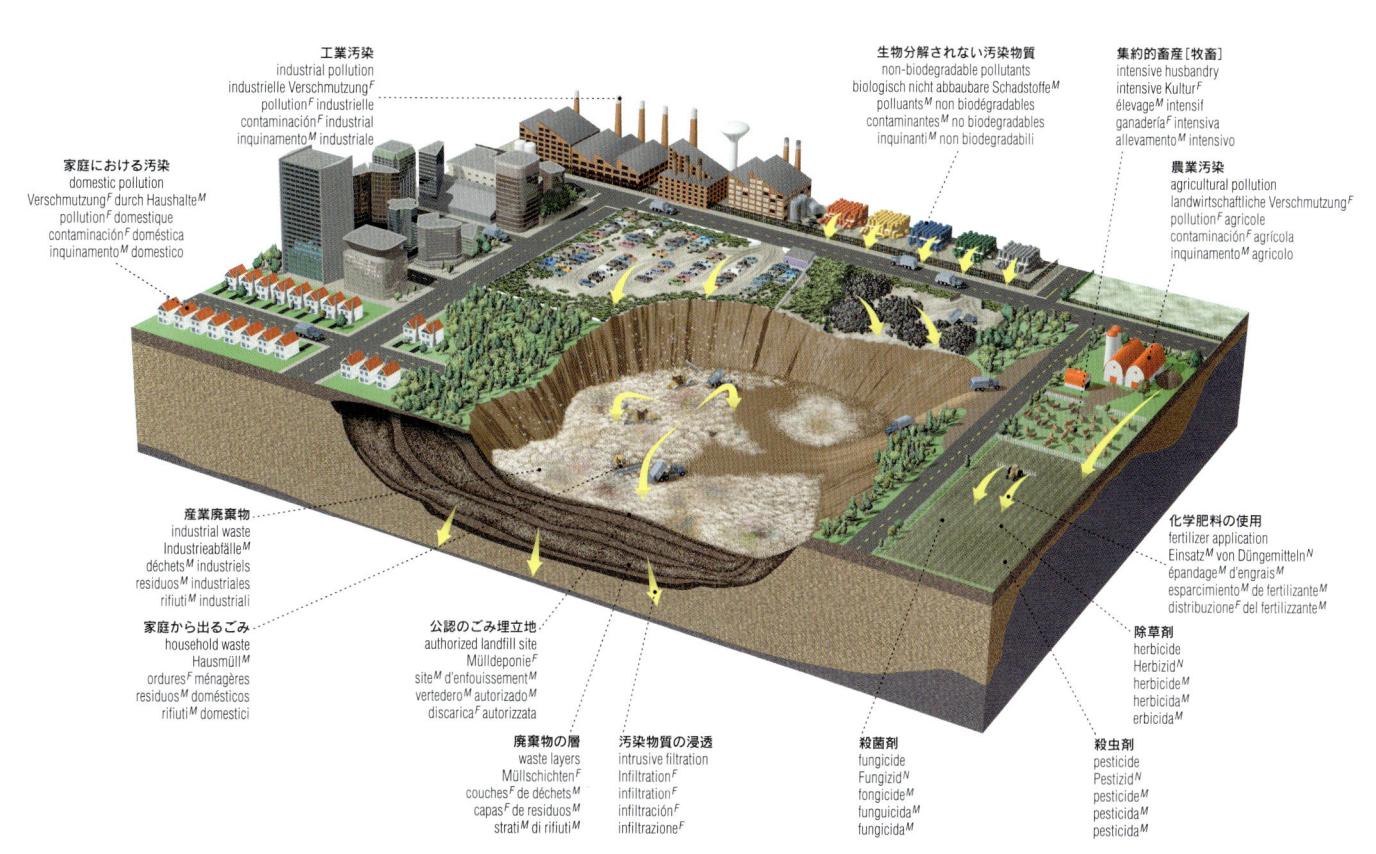

工業汚染
industrial pollution
industrielle Verschmutzung^F
pollution^F industrielle
contaminación^F industrial
inquinamento^M industriale

生物分解されない汚染物質
non-biodegradable pollutants
biologisch nicht abbaubare Schadstoffe^M
polluants^M non biodégradables
contaminantes^M no biodegradables
inquinanti^M non biodegradabili

集約的畜産［牧畜］
intensive husbandry
intensive Kultur^F
élevage^M intensif
ganadería^F intensiva
allevamento^M intensivo

家庭における汚染
domestic pollution
Verschmutzung^F durch Haushalte^M
pollution^F domestique
contaminación^F doméstica
inquinamento^M domestico

農業汚染
agricultural pollution
landwirtschaftliche Verschmutzung^F
pollution^F agricole
contaminación^F agrícola
inquinamento^M agricolo

産業廃棄物
industrial waste
Industrieabfälle^M
déchets^M industriels
residuos^M industriales
rifiuti^M industriali

家庭から出るごみ
household waste
Hausmüll^M
ordures^F ménagères
residuos^M domésticos
rifiuti^M domestici

公認のごみ埋立地
authorized landfill site
Mülldeponie^F
site^M d'enfouissement^M
vertedero^M autorizado
discarica^F autorizzata

廃棄物の層
waste layers
Müllschichten^F
couches^F de déchets^M
capas^F de residuos^M
strati^M di rifiuti^M

汚染物質の浸透
intrusive filtration
Infiltration^F
infiltration^F
infiltración^F
infiltrazione^F

殺菌剤
fungicide
Fungizid^N
fongicide^M
fungicida^M
fungicida^M

殺虫剤
pesticide
Pestizid^N
pesticide^M
pesticida^M
pesticida^M

化学肥料の使用
fertilizer application
Einsatz^M von Düngemitteln^N
épandage^M d'engrais^M
esparcimiento^M de fertilizante^M
distribuzione^F del fertilizzante^M

除草剤
herbicide
Herbizid^N
herbicide^M
herbicida^M
erbicida^M

69

環境 | ENVIRONMENT
UMWELT | ENVIRONNEMENT | AMBIENTE | AMBIENTE

水質汚染

water pollution | Wasserverschmutzung^F | pollution^F de l'eau^F | contaminación^F del agua^F | inquinamento^M dell'acqua^F

産業廃棄物
industrial waste
Industrieabfälle^M
rejets^M industriels
residuos^M industriales
rifiuti^M industriali

集約的農業
intensive farming
intensive Landwirtschaft^F
agriculture^F intensive
agricultura^F intensiva
agricoltura^F intensiva

放射性廃棄物
nuclear waste
radioaktiver Abfall^M
déchets^M nucléaires
residuos^M nucleares
rifiuti^M nucleari

石油汚染
oil pollution
Ölverschmutzung^F
pollution^F par le pétrole^M
contaminación^F de petróleo^M
inquinamento^M petrolifero

廃水
waste water
Abwasser^N
eaux^F usées
aguas^M residuales
acque^F reflue

家庭から出るごみ
household waste
Hausmüll^M
ordures^F ménagères
residuos^M domésticos
rifiuti^M domestici

地下水面
water table
Grundwasserspiegel^M
nappe^F phréatique
manto^M freático
falda^F freatica

汚水処理槽
septic tank
Faulbecken^N
fosse^F septique
fosa^F séptica
fossa^F settica

殺虫剤
pesticide
Pestizid^N
pesticide^M
pesticida^M
pesticida^M

石油流出
oil spill
Ölausfluss^M
déversement^M d'hydrocarbures^M
vertido^M de hidrocarburos^M
fuoriuscita^F di idrocarburi^M

畜糞
animal dung
Dung^M
déjections^F animales
excrementos^M de animales^M
concime^M organico

酸性雨

acid rain | saurer Regen^M | pluies^F acides | lluvia^F ácida | piogge^F acide

硝酸の放出
nitric acid emission
Emission^F von Salpetersäure^F
émission^F d'acide^M nitrique
emisión^F de ácido^M nítrico
emissione^F di acido^M nitrico

窒素酸化物の放出
nitrogen oxide emission
Emission^F von Stickoxiden^N
émission^F d'oxyde^M d'azote^M
emisión^F de óxido^M de nitrógeno^M
emissione^F di ossido^M d'azoto^M

大気
atmosphere
Atmosphäre^F
atmosphère^F
atmósfera^F
atmosfera^F

風
wind
Wind^M
vent^M
viento^M
vento^M

酸性雨
acid rain
saurer Regen^M
pluies^F acides
lluvia^F ácida
piogge^F acide

雲の水分
cloudwater
Wolkenwasser^N
eau^F des nuages^M
agua^F de nubes^M
umidità^F contenuta nelle nuvole^F

硫酸の放出
sulfuric acid emission
Emission^F von Schwefelsäure^F
émission^F d'acide^M sulfurique
emisión^M de ácido^M sulfúrico
emissione^F di acido^M solforico

酸性雪
acid snow
saurer Schnee^M
neiges^F acides
nieve^F ácida
neve^F acida

亜硫酸ガスの放出
sulfur dioxide emission
Emission^F von Schwefeldioxid^N
émission^F de dioxyde^M de soufre^M
emisión^M de dióxido^M de sulfuro^M
emissione^F di anidride^F solforosa

化石燃料
fossil fuel
fossiler Brennstoff^M
combustible^M fossile
combustible^M fósil
combustibile^M fossile

水流
watercourse
Wasserlauf^M
cours^M d'eau^F
corriente^F de agua^F
corso^M d'acqua^F

溶脱
leaching
Auswaschung^F
lessivage^M du sol^M
lixiviación^F
lisciviazione^F

土壌
soil
Boden^M
sol^M
suelo^M
suolo^M

地下水面
water table
Grundwasserspiegel^M
nappe^F phréatique
manto^M freático
falda^F freatica

湖の酸性化
lake acidification
Seenversauerung^F
acidification^F des lacs^M
acidificación^F de los lagos^M
acidificazione^F dei laghi^M

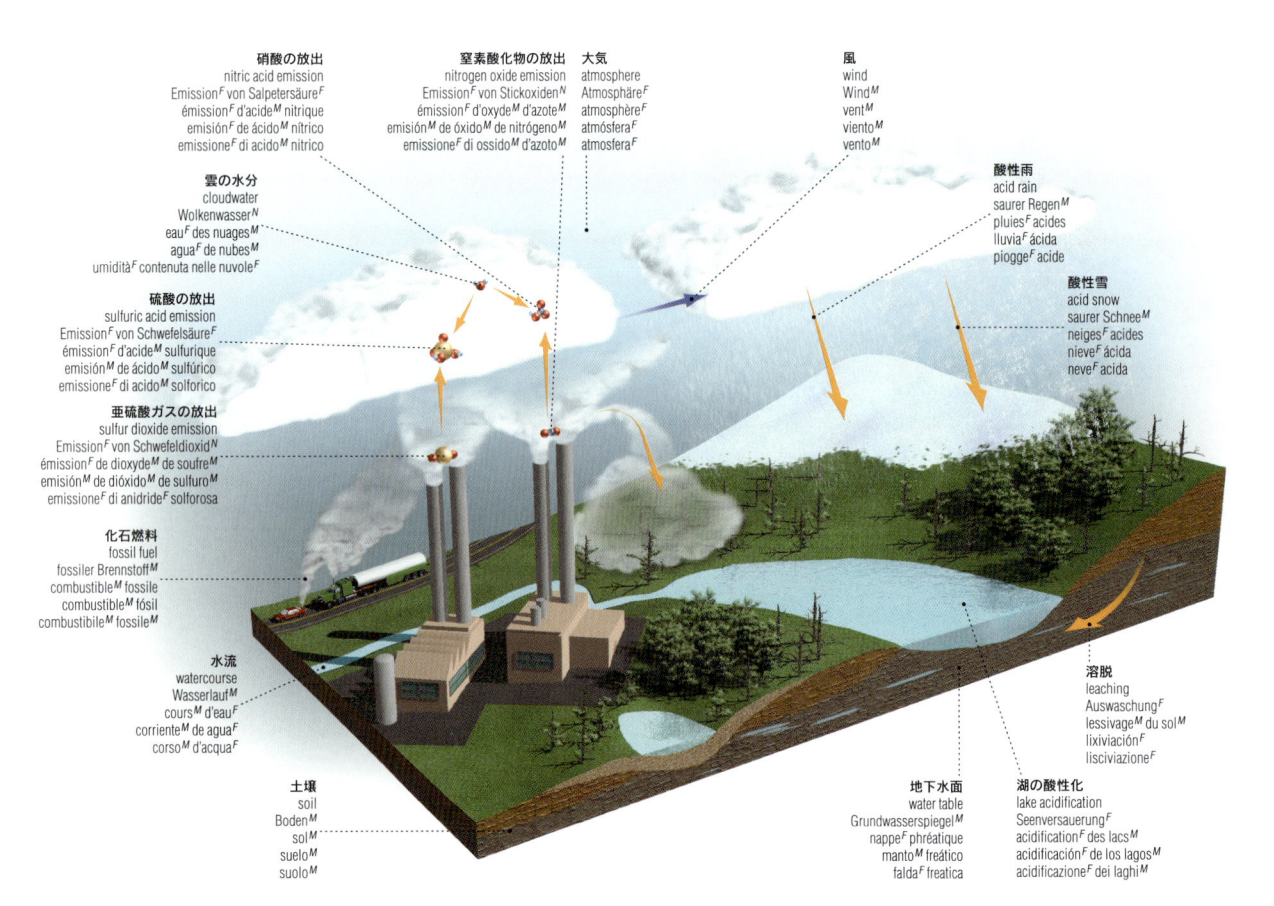

環境 | ENVIRONMENT
UMWELT | ENVIRONNEMENT | AMBIENTE | AMBIENTE

ごみ[廃棄物]の分別

selective sorting of waste | Mülltrennung^F | tri^M sélectif des déchets^M | separación^F selectiva de residuos^M | smistamento^M selettivo dei rifiuti^M

地球

粉砕機
crusher
Zerkleinerer^M
broyeur^M
trituradora^F
frantumatrice^F

紙・ボール紙の分別
paper/paperboard sorting
Sortierung^N von Papier^N/Pappe^F
tri^M du papier^M/carton^M
selección^F de papel^M/cartón^M
smistamento^M della carta^F/del cartone^M

分別工場
sorting plant
Sortieranlage^F
centre^M de tri^M
planta^F de separación^F selectiva
impianto^M di smistamento

ガラスの分別
glass sorting
Sortierung^N von Glas^N
tri^M du verre^M
selección^F de vidrio^M
smistamento^M del vetro^M

再利用できないごみ
non-reusable residue waste
nicht wieder verwertbarer Restmüll^M
résidus^M non recyclables
residuos^M no reciclables
rifiuti^M non riciclabili

埋め立て
burial
Endlagerung^F
enfouissement^M
enterramiento^M
interramento^M

手作業による分別
manual sorting
Nachsortierung^F von Hand^F
tri^M manuel
selección^F manual
smistamento^M manuale

プラスチックの分別
plastics sorting
Sortierung^F von Kunststoff^M
tri^M du plastique^M
clasificación^F de plásticos^M
smistamento^M della plastica^F

焼却
incineration
Verbrennen^N
incinération^F
incineración^F
incenerimento^M

ベルト・コンベヤー
conveyor belt
Förderband^N
bande^F transporteuse
cinta^F transportadora
nastro^M trasportatore

種類別収集
separate collection
getrennte Sammlung^F
collecte^F sélective
recogida^F diferenciada
raccolta^F differenziata

紙・ボール紙の分離
paper/paperboard separation
Sortierung^F von Papier^N/Pappe^F
séparation^F papier^M/carton^M
separación^M papel^M/cartón^M
separazione^F della carta^F/del cartone^M

梱包(こんぽう)
baling
Verpackung^F
mise^F en balles^F
embalaje^M
imballaggio^M

金属の分別
metal sorting
Sortierung^F von Metall^N
tri^M des métaux^M
selección^F de metal^M
smistamento^M dei materiali^M metallici

磁石による分離
magnetic separation
magnetische Trennung^F
séparation^F magnétique
separación^F magnética
separazione^M magnetica

圧縮
compacting
Verdichtung^F
compactage^M
compresión^F
compattazione^F

光線による分別
optical sorting
optische Sortierung^F
tri^M optique
selección^F óptica
smistamento^M ottico

リサイクリング
recycling
Recycling^N
recyclage^M
reciclado^M
riciclaggio^M

細断
shredding
Zerkleinerung^F
déchiquetage^M
desmenuzamiento^M
sminuzzamento^M

リサイクル容器
recycling containers
Wertstoff^M-Sammelbehälter^M
conteneurs^M de collecte^F sélective
contenedores^M de reciclaje^M
contenitori^M per la raccolta^F differenziata

紙のリサイクル容器
paper recycling container
Altpapier^N-Sammelbehälter^M
conteneur^M à papier^M
contenedor^M de reciclado^M de papel^M
bidone^M carrellato per il riciclaggio^M della carta^F

ガラスのリサイクル容器
glass recycling container
Altglas^N-Sammelbehälter^M
conteneur^M à verre^M
contenedor^M de reciclado^M de vidrio^M
bidone^M carrellato per il riciclaggio^M del vetro^M

アルミニウムのリサイクル容器
aluminum recycling container
Altaluminium^N-Sammelbehälter^M
conteneur^M à boîtes^F métalliques
contenedor^M de reciclado^M de aluminio^M
bidone^M carrellato per il riciclaggio^M dell'alluminio^M

紙の収集箱
paper collection unit
Altpapier^N-Container^M
colonne^F de collecte^F du papier^M
contenedor^M de recogida^F de papel^M
campana^F per la raccolta^F della carta^F

ガラスの収集箱
glass collection unit
Altglas^N-Container^M
colonne^F de collecte^F du verre^M
contenedor^M de recogida^F de vidrio^M
campana^F per la raccolta^F del vetro^M

リサイクル用の大箱
recycling bin
Bioabfallbehälter^M
bac^M de recyclage^M
cubo^M de basura^F reciclable
contenitore^M per il riciclaggio^M

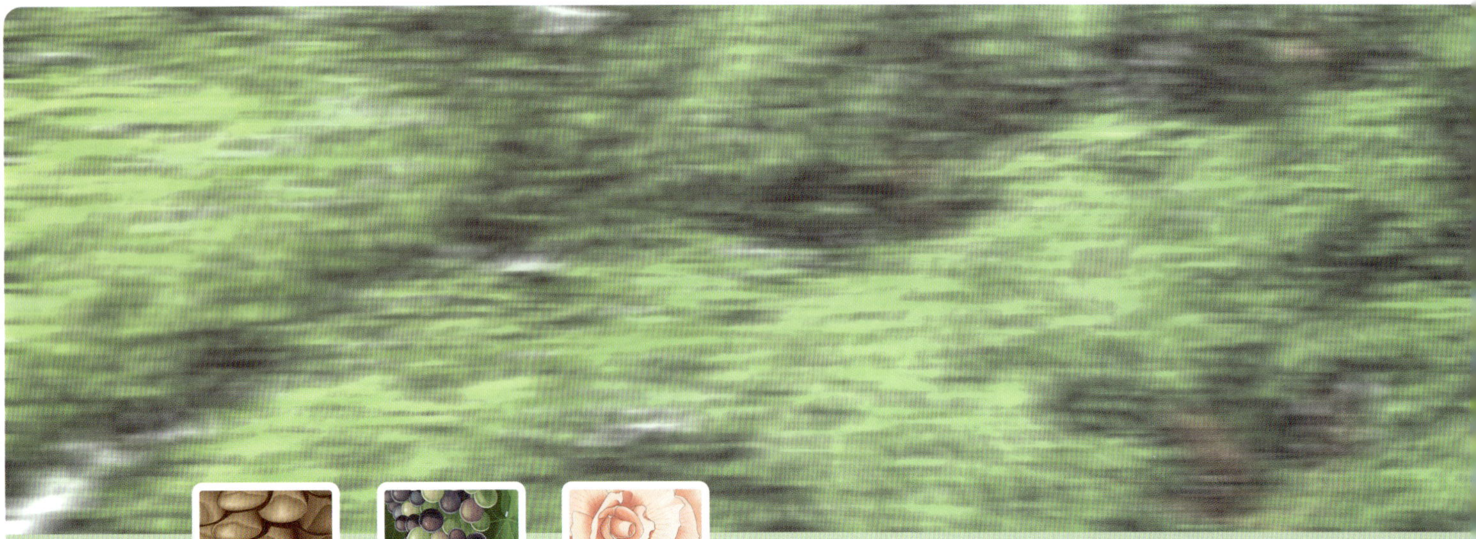
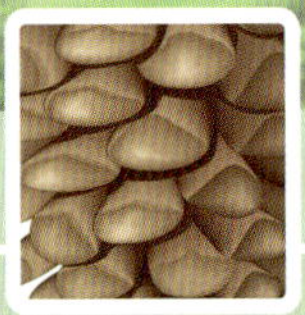
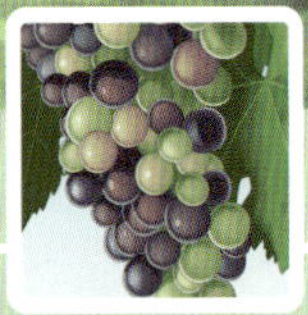
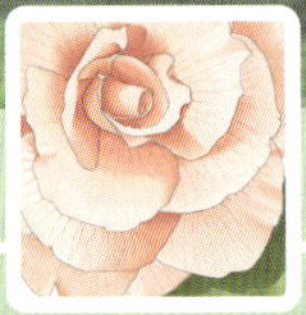

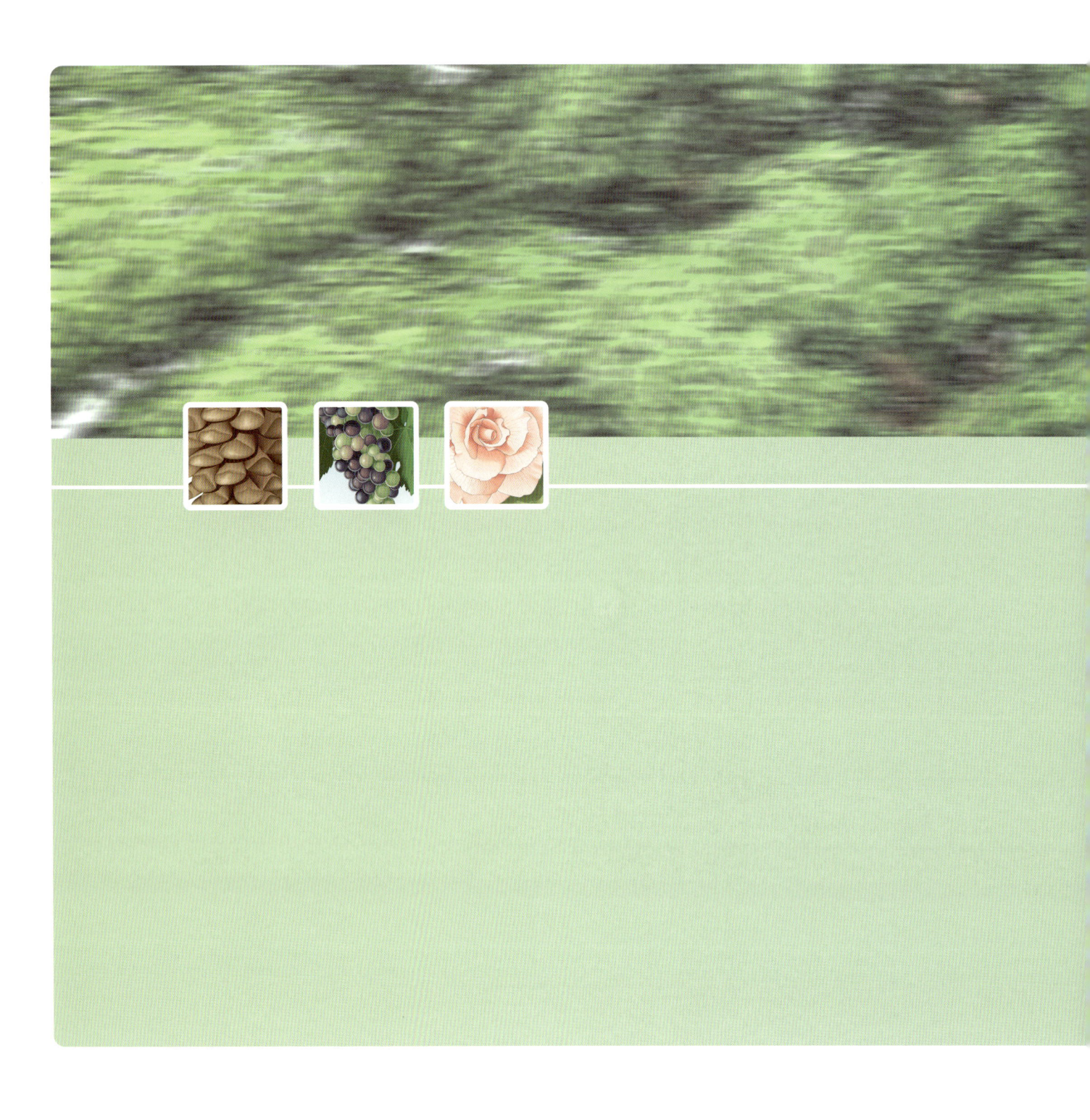

植 物

VEGETABLE KINGDOM I PFLANZENREICH I RÈGNE VÉGÉTAL I REINO VEGETAL I REGNO VEGETALE

74

74	植物細胞
74	地衣類
75	蘚類
75	藻類
76	キノコ（茸）
76	シダ
77	植物
79	葉
80	花
81	果実
85	穀類
86	ブドウ（葡萄）
87	樹木
89	針葉樹

植物細胞

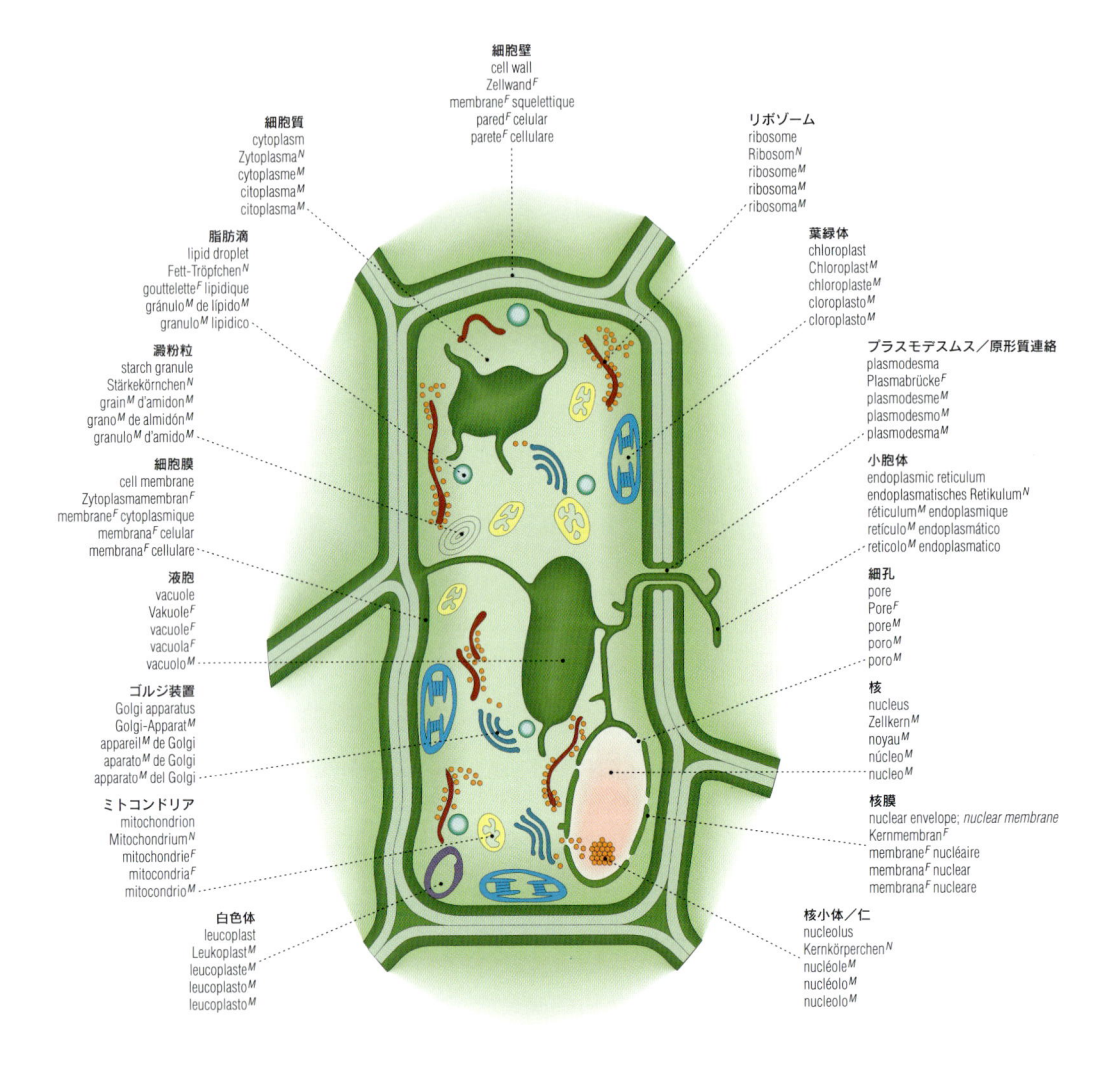

plant cell | Pflanzenzelle^F | cellule^F végétale | célula^F vegetal | cellula^F vegetale

細胞壁
cell wall
Zellwand^F
membrane^F squelettique
pared^F celular
parete^F cellulare

細胞質
cytoplasm
Zytoplasma^N
cytoplasme^M
citoplasma^M
citoplasma^M

リボゾーム
ribosome
Ribosom^N
ribosome^M
ribosoma^M
ribosoma^M

脂肪滴
lipid droplet
Fett-Tröpfchen^N
gouttelette^F lipidique
gránulo^M de lípido^M
granulo^M lipidico

葉緑体
chloroplast
Chloroplast^M
chloroplaste^M
cloroplasto^M
cloroplasto^M

澱粉粒
starch granule
Stärkekörnchen^N
grain^M d'amidon
grano^M de almidón^M
granulo^M d'amido

プラスモデスムス／原形質連絡
plasmodesma
Plasmabrücke^F
plasmodesme^M
plasmodesmo^M
plasmodesma

細胞膜
cell membrane
Zytoplasmamembran^F
membrane^F cytoplasmique
membrana^F celular
membrana^F cellulare

小胞体
endoplasmic reticulum
endoplasmatisches Retikulum^N
réticulum^M endoplasmique
retículo^M endoplasmático
reticolo^M endoplasmatico

液胞
vacuole
Vakuole^F
vacuole^F
vacuola^F
vacuolo^M

細孔
pore
Pore^F
pore^M
poro^M
poro^M

ゴルジ装置
Golgi apparatus
Golgi-Apparat^M
appareil^M de Golgi
aparato^M de Golgi
apparato^M del Golgi

核
nucleus
Zellkern^M
noyau^M
núcleo^M
nucleo^M

ミトコンドリア
mitochondrion
Mitochondrium^N
mitochondrie^F
mitocondria^F
mitocondrio^M

核膜
nuclear envelope; nuclear membrane
Kernmembran^F
membrane^F nucléaire
membrana^F nuclear
membrana^F nucleare

白色体
leucoplast
Leukoplast^M
leucoplaste^M
leucoplasto^M
leucoplasto^M

核小体／仁
nucleolus
Kernkörperchen^N
nucléole^M
nucléolo^M
nucleolo^M

地衣類

lichen | Flechte^F | lichen^M | liquen | lichene^M

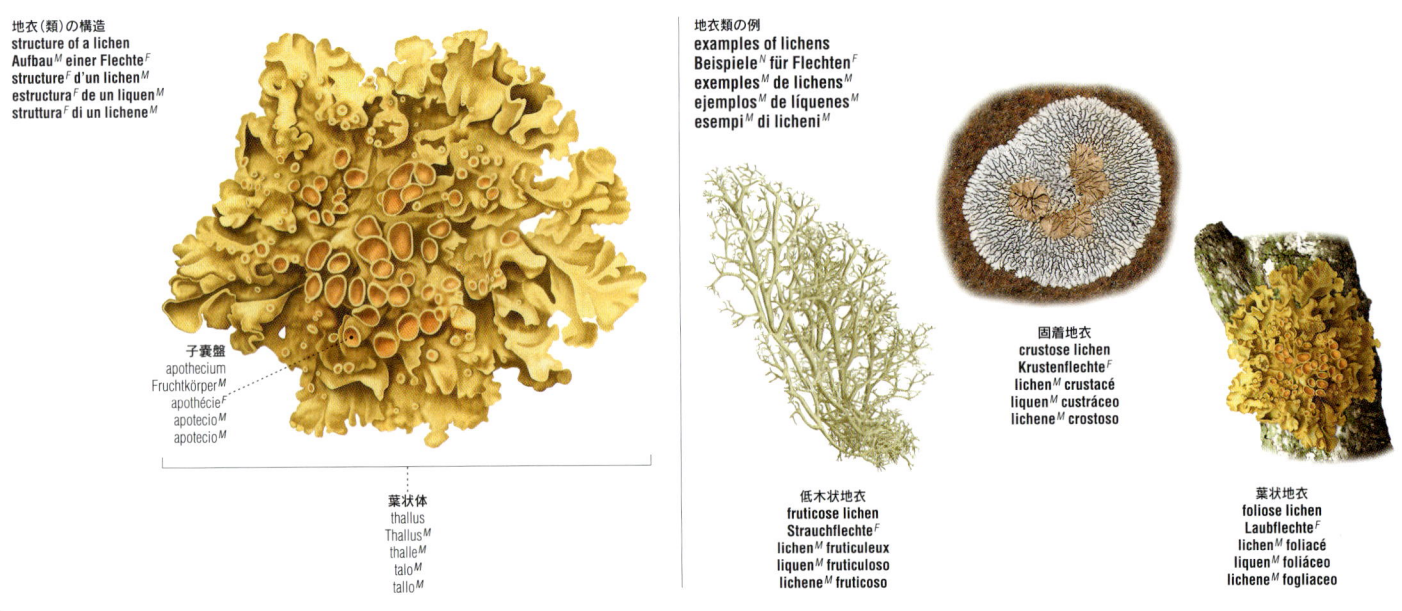

地衣（類）の構造
structure of a lichen
Aufbau^M einer Flechte^F
structure^F d'un lichen^M
estructura^F de un liquen^M
struttura^F di un lichene^M

地衣類の例
examples of lichens
Beispiele^N für Flechten^F
exemples^M de lichens^M
ejemplos^M de líquenes^M
esempi^M di licheni^M

子嚢盤
apothecium
Fruchtkörper^M
apothécie^F
apotecio^M
apotecio^M

固着地衣
crustose lichen
Krustenflechte^F
lichen^M crustacé
liquen^M custráceo
lichene^M crostoso

葉状体
thallus
Thallus^M
thalle^M
talo^M
tallo^M

低木状地衣
fruticose lichen
Strauchflechte^F
lichen^M fruticuleux
liquen^M fruticuloso
lichene^M fruticoso

葉状地衣
foliose lichen
Laubflechte^F
lichen^M foliacé
liquen^M foliáceo
lichene^M fogliaceo

蘚類

moss | Moos[N] | mousse[F] | musgo[M] | muschio[M]

蘚類の構造
structure of a moss
Aufbau[M] eines Mooses[N]
structure[F] d'une mousse[F]
estructura[F] de un musgo[M]
struttura[F] di un muschio[M]

さく
capsule
Kapsel[F]
capsule[F]
cápsula[F]
capsula[F]

さく軸
stalk
Stiel[M]
pédicelle[M]
pedúnculo[M]
stelo[M]

葉
leaf
Blättchen[N]
feuille[F]
hoja[F]
foglia[F]

茎
stem
Stämmchen[N]
tige[F]
tallo[M]
gambo[M]

仮根
rhizoid
Rhizoid[N]
rhizoïde[M]
rizoide[M]
rizoide[M]

とげのあるミズゴケ（水苔）
prickly sphagnum
sparriges Torfmoos[N]
sphaigne[F] squarreuse
esfagno[M]
sfagno[M] pungente

蘚類の例
examples of mosses
Beispiele[N] für Moose[N]
exemples[M] de mousses[F]
ejemplos[M] de musgos[M]
esempi[M] di muschi[M]

一般的なスギゴケ（杉苔）
common hair cap moss
gemeines Widertonmoos[N]
polytric[M] commun
polítrico[M]
politrico[M] comune

藻類

alga | Alge[F] | algue[F] | alga[F] | alga[F]

藻（類）の構造
structure of an alga
Aufbau[M] einer Alge[F]
structure[F] d'une algue[F]
estructura[F] de un alga[F]
struttura[F] di un'alga[F]

生殖器床
receptacle
Rezeptakel[N]
réceptacle[M]
receptáculo[M]
ricettacolo[M]

葉状体
thallus
Thallus[M]
thalle[M]
talo[M]
tallo[M]

藻体
lamina
Spreite[F]
fronde[F]
lámina[F]
lamina[F]

固着部
hapteron
Haftorgan[N]
haptère[F]
hapterio[M]
aptero[M]

紅藻
red alga
Rotalge[F]
algue[F] rouge
alga[F] roja
alga[F] rossa

気嚢
aerocyst
Blase[F]
aérocyste[F]
aerocisto[M]
aerociste[F]

中肋
midrib
Mittelrippe[F]
nervure[F] médiane
nervio[M] central
nervatura[F] centrale

examples of algae
藻類の例
Beispiele[N] für Algen[F]
exemples[M] d'algues[F]
ejemplos[M] de algas[F]
esempi[M] di alghe[F]

緑藻
green alga
Grünalge[F]
algue[F] verte
alga[F] verde
alga[F] verde

褐藻
brown alga
Braunalge[F]
algue[F] brune
alga[F] parda
alga[F] bruna

キノコ（茸）

mushroom | Pilz^M | champignon^M | hongo^M | fungo^M

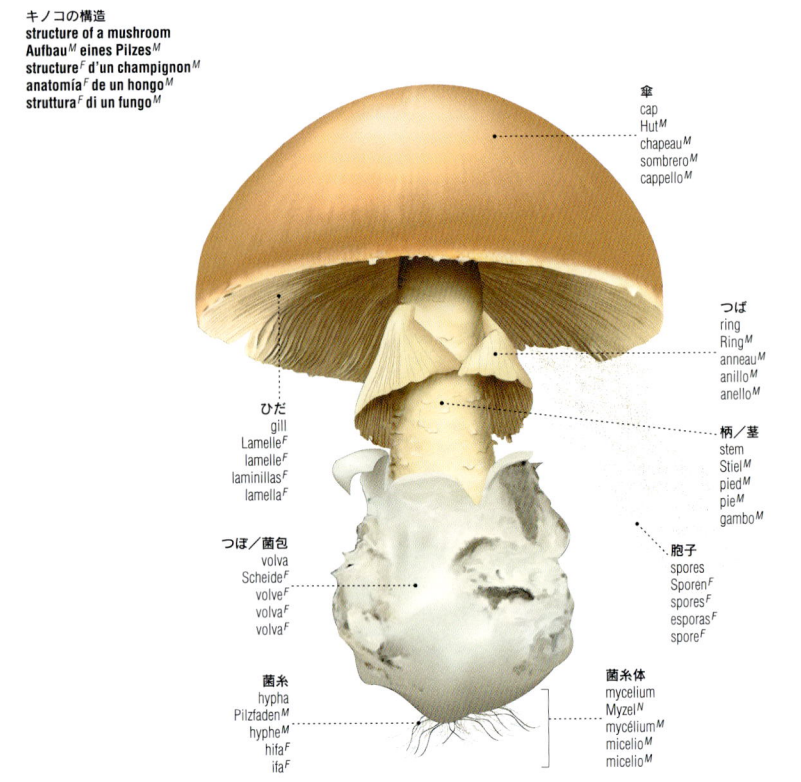

日本語 | 英語 | ドイツ語 | フランス語 | スペイン語 | イタリア語

キノコの構造
structure of a mushroom
Aufbau^M eines Pilzes^M
structure^F d'un champignon^M
anatomía^F de un hongo^M
struttura^F di un fungo^M

傘
cap
Hut^M
chapeau^M
sombrero^M
cappello^M

つば
ring
Ring^M
anneau^M
anillo^M
anello^M

ひだ
gill
Lamelle^F
lamelle^F
laminillas^F
lamella^F

柄／茎
stem
Stiel^M
pied^M
pie^M
gambo^M

つぼ／菌包
volva
Scheide^F
volve^F
volva^F
volva^F

胞子
spores
Sporen^F
spores^F
esporas^F
spore^F

菌糸
hypha
Pilzfaden^M
hyphe^M
hifa^F
ifa^F

菌糸体
mycelium
Myzel^N
mycélium^M
micelio^M
micelio^M

猛毒キノコ
deadly poisonous mushroom
tödlich giftiger Pilz^M
champignon^M mortel
hongo^M mortal
fungo^M velenoso e mortale

シロタマゴテングタケ（白玉子天狗茸）
destroying angel
Knollenblätterpilz^M
amanite^F vireuse
amanita^F virosa
amanita^F virosa

毒キノコ
poisonous mushroom
Giftpilz^M
champignon^M vénéneux
hongo^M venenoso
fungo^M velenoso

ベニテングタケ（紅天狗茸）
fly agaric
Fliegenpilz^M
fausse oronge^F
falsa oronja^F
amanita^F muscaria

シダ

fern | Farn^M | fougère^F | helecho | felce^F

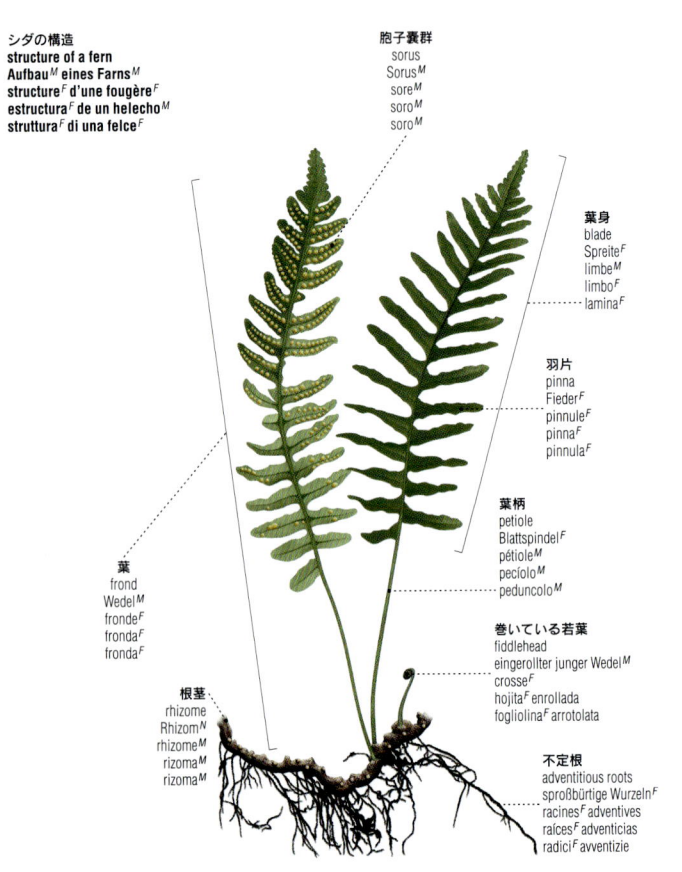

シダの構造
structure of a fern
Aufbau^M eines Farns^M
structure^F d'une fougère^F
estructura^F de un helecho^M
struttura^F di una felce^F

胞子嚢群
sorus
Sorus^M
sore^M
soro^M
soro^M

葉身
blade
Spreite^F
limbe^M
limbo^F
lamina^F

羽片
pinna
Fieder^F
pinnule^F
pinna^F
pinnula^F

葉柄
petiole
Blattspindel^F
pétiole^M
pecíolo^M
peduncolo^M

葉
frond
Wedel^M
fronde^F
fronda^F
fronda^F

巻いている若葉
fiddlehead
eingerollter junger Wedel^M
crosse^F
hojita^F enrollada
fogliolina^F arrotolata

根茎
rhizome
Rhizom^N
rhizome^M
rizoma^M
rizoma^M

不定根
adventitious roots
sproßbürtige Wurzeln^F
racines^F adventives
raíces^F adventicias
radici^F avventizie

シダの例
examples of ferns
Beispiele^N für Farne^M
exemples^M de fougères^F
ejemplos^M de helechos^M
esempi^M di felci^F

木生シダ
tree fern
Baumfarn^M
fougère^F arborescente
helecho^M arbóreo
felce^F arborea

幹
trunk
Stamm^M
tronc^M
tronco^M
tronco^M

オオエゾデンダ（大蝦夷でんだ）
common polypody
gemeiner Tüpfelfarn^M
polypode^M commun
polipodio^M común
polipodio^M comune

シマオオタニワタリ（島大谷渡り）
bird's nest fern
Nestfarn^M
fougère^F nid d'oiseau^M
helecho^M nido de pájaro^M
lingua^F di cervo

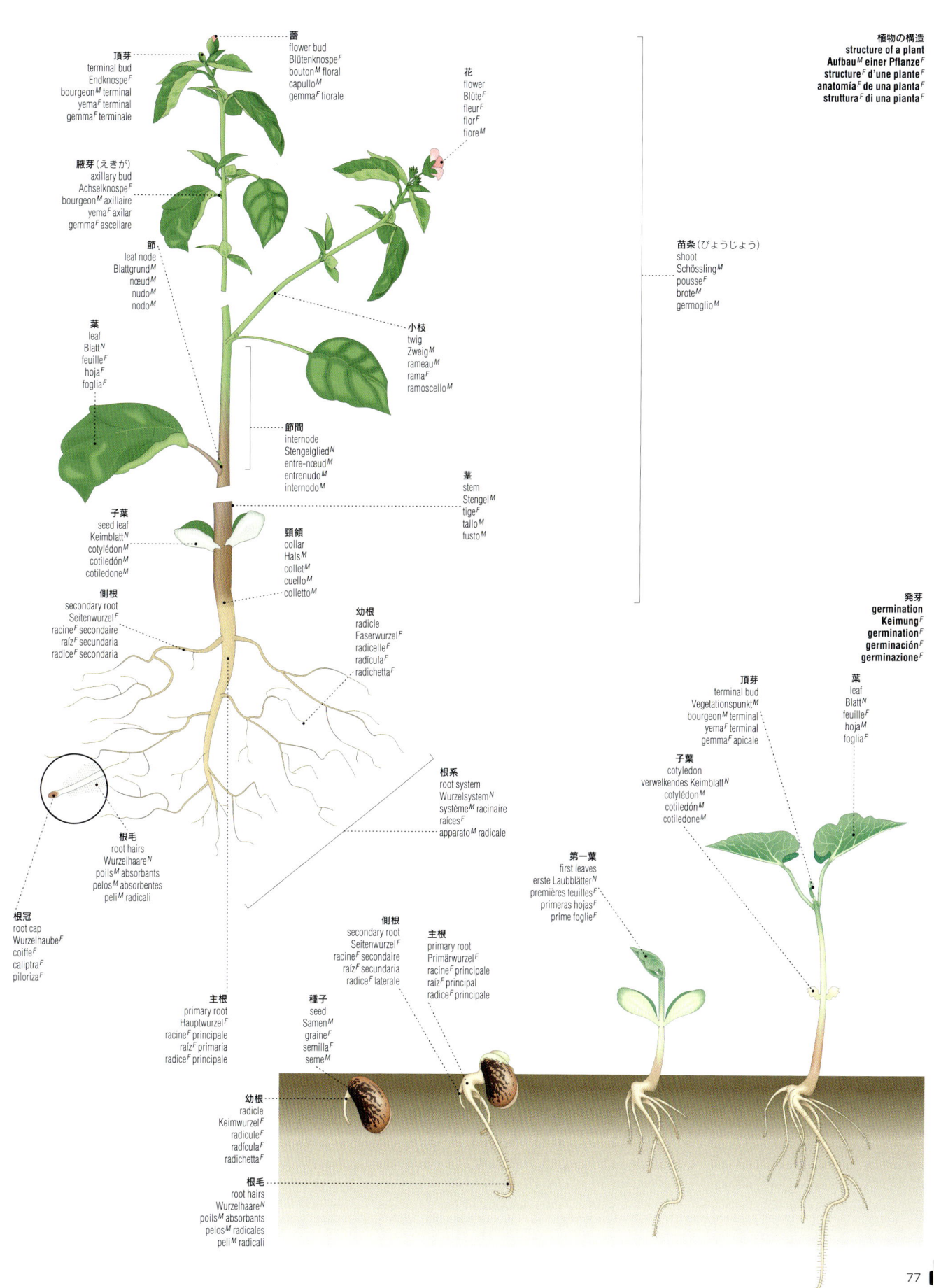

植物

plant | Pflanze^F | plante^F | planta^F | pianta^F

植物の構造
structure of a plant
Aufbau^M einer Pflanze^F
structure^F d'une plante^F
anatomía^F de una planta^F
struttura^F di una pianta^F

蕾
flower bud
Blütenknospe^F
bouton^M floral
capullo^M
gemma^F fiorale

頂芽
terminal bud
Endknospe^F
bourgeon^M terminal
yema^F terminal
gemma^F terminale

花
flower
Blüte^F
fleur^F
flor^F
fiore^M

腋芽（えきが）
axillary bud
Achselknospe^F
bourgeon^M axillaire
yema^F axilar
gemma^F ascellare

苗条（びょうじょう）
shoot
Schössling^M
pousse^F
brote^M
germoglio^M

節
leaf node
Blattgrund^M
nœud^M
nudo^M
nodo^M

小枝
twig
Zweig^M
rameau^M
rama^F
ramoscello^M

葉
leaf
Blatt^N
feuille^F
hoja^F
foglia^F

節間
internode
Stengelglied^N
entre-nœud^M
entrenudo^M
internodo^M

茎
stem
Stengel^M
tige^F
tallo^M
fusto^M

子葉
seed leaf
Keimblatt^N
cotylédon^M
cotiledón^M
cotiledone^M

頸領
collar
Hals^M
collet^M
cuello^M
colletto^M

側根
secondary root
Seitenwurzel^F
racine^F secondaire
raíz^F secundaria
radice^F secondaria

幼根
radicle
Faserwurzel^F
radicelle^F
radícula^F
radichetta^F

発芽
germination
Keimung^F
germination^F
germinación^F
germinazione^F

頂芽
terminal bud
Vegetationspunkt^M
bourgeon^M terminal
yema^F terminal
gemma^F apicale

葉
leaf
Blatt^N
feuille^F
hoja^M
foglia^F

根系
root system
Wurzelsystem^N
système^M racinaire
raíces^F
apparato^M radicale

子葉
cotyledon
verwelkendes Keimblatt^N
cotylédon^M
cotiledón^M
cotiledone^M

根毛
root hairs
Wurzelhaare^N
poils^M absorbants
pelos^M absorbentes
peli^M radicali

第一葉
first leaves
erste Laubblätter^N
premières feuilles^F
primeras hojas^F
prime foglie^F

根冠
root cap
Wurzelhaube^F
coiffe^F
caliptra^F
piloriza^F

側根
secondary root
Seitenwurzel^F
racine^F secondaire
raíz^F secundaria
radice^F laterale

主根
primary root
Primärwurzel^F
racine^F principale
raíz^F principal
radice^F principale

主根
primary root
Hauptwurzel^F
racine^F principale
raíz^F primaria
radice^F principale

種子
seed
Samen^M
graine^F
semilla^F
seme^M

幼根
radicle
Keimwurzel^F
radicule^F
radícula^F
radichetta^F

根毛
root hairs
Wurzelhaare^N
poils^M absorbants
pelos^M radicales
peli^M radicali

植物

| 日本語 | 英語 | ドイツ語 | フランス語 | スペイン語 | イタリア語 |

光合成
photosynthesis
Photosynthese^F
photosynthèse^F
fotosíntesis^F
fotosintesi^F

太陽エネルギー — solar energy / Sonnenenergie^F / énergie^F solaire / energía^F solar / energia^F solare

葉 — leaf / Blatt^N / feuille^F / hoja^F / foglia^F

酸素の放出 — release of oxygen / Abgabe^F von Sauerstoff^M / rejet^M d'oxygène^M / producción^F de oxígeno^M / produzione^F di ossigeno^M

茎 — stem / Stiel^M / tige^F / tallo^M / stelo^M

グルコース — glucose / Glukose^F / glucose^M / glucosa^F / glucosio^M

二酸化炭素の吸収 — carbon dioxide absorption / Aufnahme^F von Kohlendioxid^N / absorption^F de dioxyde^M de carbone^M / absorción^F de dióxido^M de carbono^M / assorbimento^M di anidride^F carbonica

水と鉱物塩の吸収 — absorption of water and mineral salts / Aufnahme^F von Wasser^N und Mineralstoffen^M / absorption^F d'eau^F et de sels^M minéraux / absorción^F de agua^M y sales^F minerales / assorbimento^M di acqua^F e sali^M minerali

土壌断面
soil profile
Bodenprofil^N
profil^M du sol^M
perfil^M del suelo^M
profilo^M del suolo^M

腐植土／腐葉土 — plant litter / Auflagehumus^M / litière^F / humus^M / humus^M

表土 — topsoil / Oberboden^M / couche^F arable / capa^F superficial del suelo^M / strato^M superficiale del suolo^M

下層土 — subsoil / Unterboden^M / sous-sol^M / subsuelo^M / sottosuolo^M

岩盤 — bedrock / Muttergestein^N / roche^F mère^F / roca^F madre / roccia^F in posto^M

球根の断面図
section of a bulb
Zwiebel^F im Querschnitt^M
coupe^F d'un bulbe^M
corte de un bulbo^M
sezione^F di un bulbo^M

鱗片葉 — scale leaf / Laubblatt^N / tunique^F / hoja^F / tunica^F

芽 — bud / Knospe^F / bourgeon^M / yema^F / gemma^F

多汁葉 — fleshy leaf / Schuppenblatt^N / écaille^F / hoja^F flexible / foglia^F carnosa

珠芽 — bulbil / Brutzwiebel^F / caïeu^M / bulbillo^M / bulbillo^M

地下茎 — underground stem / Blütenstandstiel^M / tige^F / tallo^M del bulbo^M / fusto^M del bulbo^M

基部 — base / Spross^M / plateau^M / base^F del bulbo^M / base^F del bulbo^M

根 — root / Wurzel^F / racine^F / raíz^F / radice^F

葉

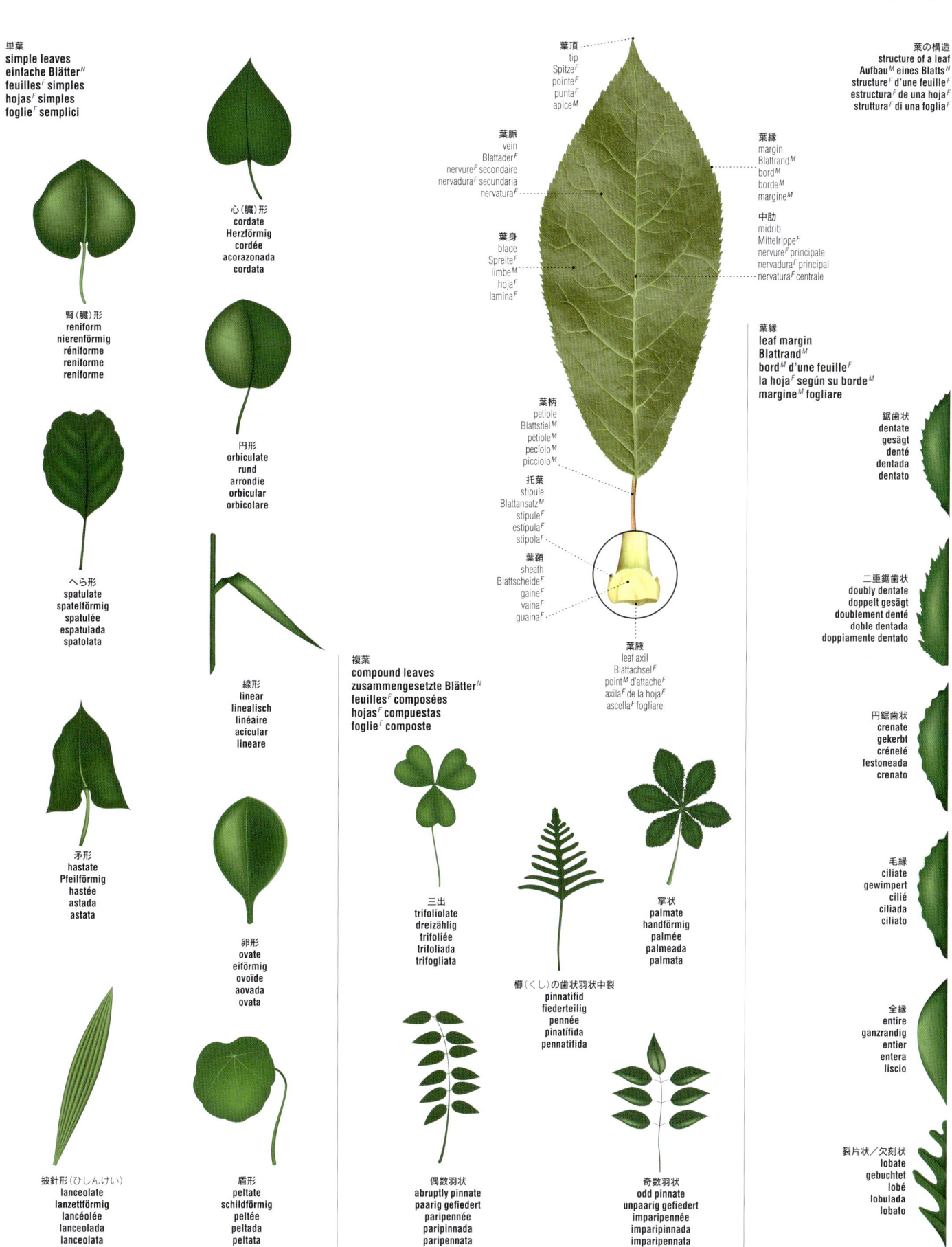

leaf | Blatt[N] | feuille[F] | hoja[F] | foglia[F]

単葉
simple leaves
einfache Blätter[N]
feuilles[F] simples
hojas[F] simples
foglie[F] semplici

心(臓)形
cordate
Herzförmig
cordée
acorazonada
cordata

腎(臓)形
reniform
nierenförmig
réniforme
reniforme
reniforme

円形
orbiculate
rund
arrondie
orbicular
orbicolare

へら形
spatulate
spatelförmig
spatulée
espatulada
spatolata

線形
linear
linealisch
linéaire
acicular
lineare

矛形
hastate
Pfeilförmig
hastée
astada
astata

卵形
ovate
eiförmig
ovoïde
aovada
ovata

披針形(ひしんけい)
lanceolate
lanzettförmig
lancéolée
lanceolada
lanceolata

盾形
peltate
schildförmig
peltée
peltada
peltata

葉の構造
structure of a leaf
Aufbau[M] eines Blatts[N]
structure[F] d'une feuille[F]
estructura[F] de una hoja[F]
struttura[F] di una foglia[F]

葉頂
tip
Spitze[F]
pointe[F]
punta[F]
apice[M]

葉脈
vein
Blattader[F]
nervure[F] secondaire
nervadura[F] secundaria
nervatura[F]

葉身
blade
Spreite[F]
limbe[M]
hoja[F]
lamina[F]

葉柄
petiole
Blattstiel[M]
pétiole[M]
pecíolo[M]
picciolo[M]

托葉
stipule
Blattansatz[M]
stipule[F]
estípula[F]
stipola[F]

葉鞘
sheath
Blattscheide[F]
gaine[F]
vaina[F]
guaina[F]

葉縁
margin
Blattrand[M]
bord[M]
borde[M]
margine[M]

中肋
midrib
Mittelrippe[F]
nervure[F] principale
nervadura[F] principal
nervatura[F] centrale

葉腋
leaf axil
Blattachsel[F]
point[M] d'attache[F]
axila[F] de la hoja[F]
ascella[F] fogliare

複葉
compound leaves
zusammengesetzte Blätter[N]
feuilles[F] composées
hojas[F] compuestas
foglie[F] composte

三出
trifoliolate
dreizählig
trifoliée
trifoliada
trifogliata

櫛(くし)の歯状羽状中裂
pinnatifid
fiederteilig
pennée
pinatífida
pennatifida

偶数羽状
abruptly pinnate
paarig gefiedert
paripennée
paripinnada
paripennata

掌状
palmate
handförmig
palmée
palmeada
palmata

奇数羽状
odd pinnate
unpaarig gefiedert
imparipennée
imparipinnada
imparipennata

葉縁
leaf margin
Blattrand[M]
bord[M] d'une feuille[F]
la hoja[F] según su borde[M]
margine[M] fogliare

鋸歯状
dentate
gesägt
denté
dentada
dentato

二重鋸歯状
doubly dentate
doppelt gesägt
doublement denté
doble dentada
doppiamente dentato

円鋸歯状
crenate
gekerbt
crénelé
festoneada
crenato

毛縁
ciliate
gewimpert
cilié
ciliada
ciliato

全縁
entire
ganzrandig
entier
entera
liscio

裂片状／欠刻状
lobate
gebuchtet
lobé
lobulada
lobato

植物

79

花

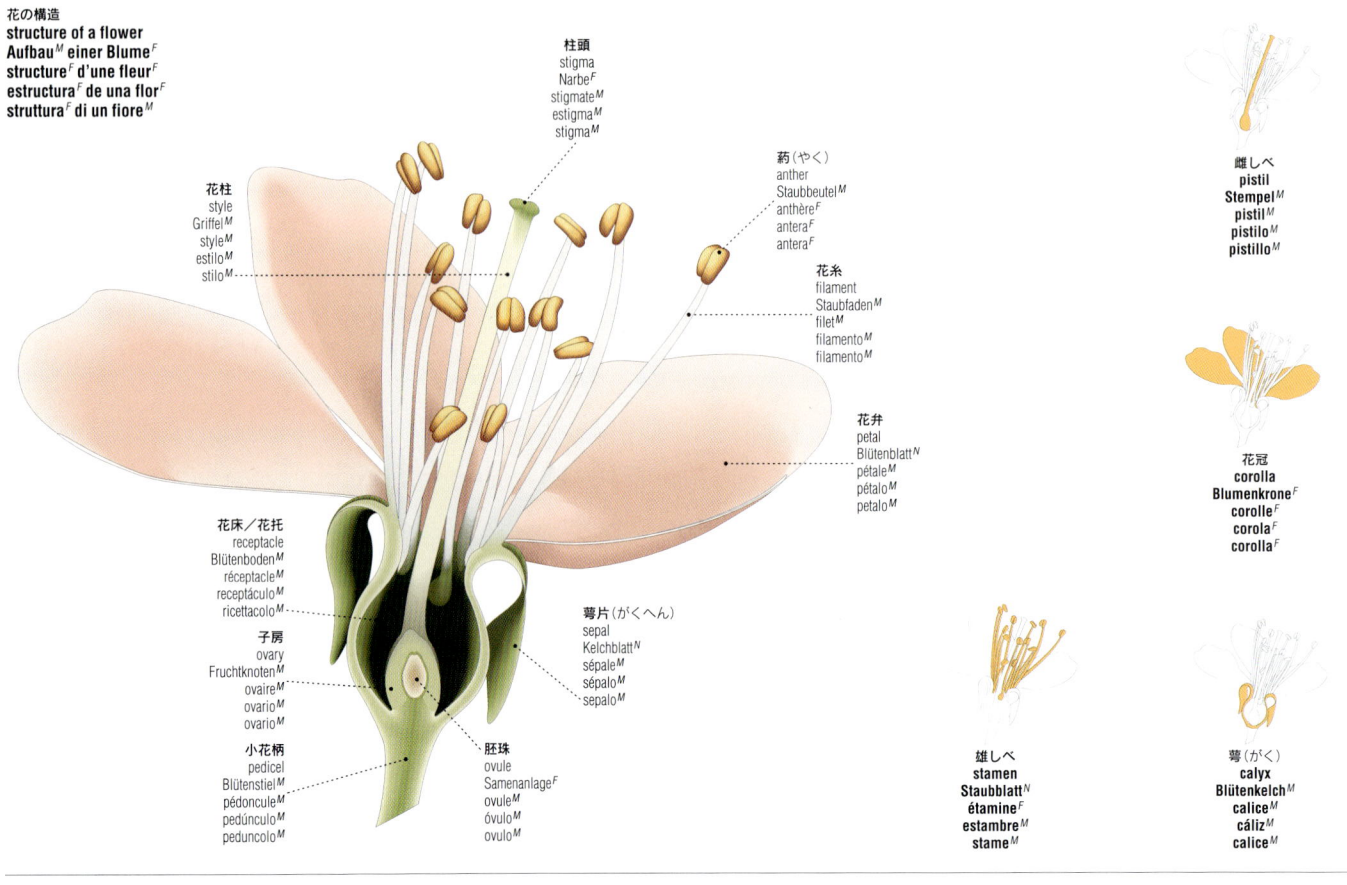

flower | Blüte^F | fleur^F | flor^F | fiore^M

日本語 | 英語 | ドイツ語 | フランス語 | スペイン語 | イタリア語

植物

花の構造
structure of a flower
Aufbau^M einer Blume^F
structure^F d'une fleur^F
estructura^F de una flor^F
struttura^F di un fiore^M

柱頭
stigma
Narbe^F
stigmate^M
estigma^M
stigma^M

花柱
style
Griffel^M
style^M
estilo^M
stilo^M

葯（やく）
anther
Staubbeutel^M
anthère^F
antera^F
antera^F

花糸
filament
Staubfaden^M
filet^M
filamento^M
filamento^M

花弁
petal
Blütenblatt^N
pétale^M
pétalo^M
petalo^M

花床／花托
receptacle
Blütenboden^M
réceptacle^M
receptáculo^M
ricettacolo^M

子房
ovary
Fruchtknoten^M
ovaire^M
ovario^M
ovario^M

萼片（がくへん）
sepal
Kelchblatt^N
sépale^M
sépalo^M
sepalo^M

小花柄
pedicel
Blütenstiel^M
pédoncule^M
pedúnculo^M
peduncolo^M

胚珠
ovule
Samenanlage^F
ovule^M
óvulo^M
ovulo^M

雌しべ
pistil
Stempel^M
pistil^M
pistilo^M
pistillo^M

花冠
corolla
Blumenkrone^F
corolle^F
corola^F
corolla^F

雄しべ
stamen
Staubblatt^N
étamine^F
estambre^M
stame^M

萼（がく）
calyx
Blütenkelch^M
calice^M
cáliz^M
calice^M

花の例
examples of flowers
Beispiele^N für Blumen^F
exemples^M de fleurs^F
ejemplos^M de flores^F
esempi^M di fiori^M

ラン（蘭）
orchid
Orchidee^F
orchidée^F
orquídea^F
orchidea^F

ラッパズイセン（らっぱ水仙）
daffodil
Narzisse^F
jonquille^F
narciso^M
trombone^M

ケシ（芥子）
poppy
Mohn^M
coquelicot^M
amapola^F
papavero^M

チューリップ
tulip
Tulpe^F
tulipe^F
tulipán^M
tulipano^M

スズラン（鈴蘭）
lily of the valley
Maiglöckchen^N
muguet^M
muguete^M
mughetto^M

カーネーション
carnation
Nelke^F
œillet^M
clavel^M
garofano^M

バラ
rose
Rose^F
rose^F
rosa^F
rosa^F

ベゴニア
begonia
Begonie^F
bégonia^M
begonia^F
begonia^F

ユリ（百合）
lily
Lilie^F
lis^M
azucena^F
giglio^M

スミレ（菫）
violet
Veilchen^N
violette^F
violeta^F
viola^F

クロッカス
crocus
Krokus^M
crocus^M
croco^M
croco^M

ヒマワリ（向日葵）
sunflower
Sonnenblume^F
tournesol^M
girasol^M
girasole^M

80

花

花序の種類
types of inflorescences
Arten F von Blütenständen M
modes M d'inflorescence F
variedades F de inflorescencias F
tipi M di infiorescenze

植物

総状花序
raceme
geschlossene Traube F
grappe F
racimo M
racemo M

単出集散花序
uniparous cyme
eingliedrige Trugdolde F
cyme F unipare
cima F unípara
cima F unipara

散形花序
umbel
Dolde F
ombelle F
umbela F
ombrella F

頭状花序
capitulum
Körbchen N
capitule M
cabezuela F
capolino M

穂状(すいじょう)花序
spike
Ähre F
épi M
espiga F
spiga F

二出集散花序
biparous cyme
zweigliedrige Trugdolde F
cyme F bipare
cima F bípara
cima F bipara

散房花序
corymb
Doldentraube F
corymbe M
corimbo M
corimbo M

肉穂(にくすい)花序
spadix
Kolben M
spadice M
espádice M
spadice M

果実

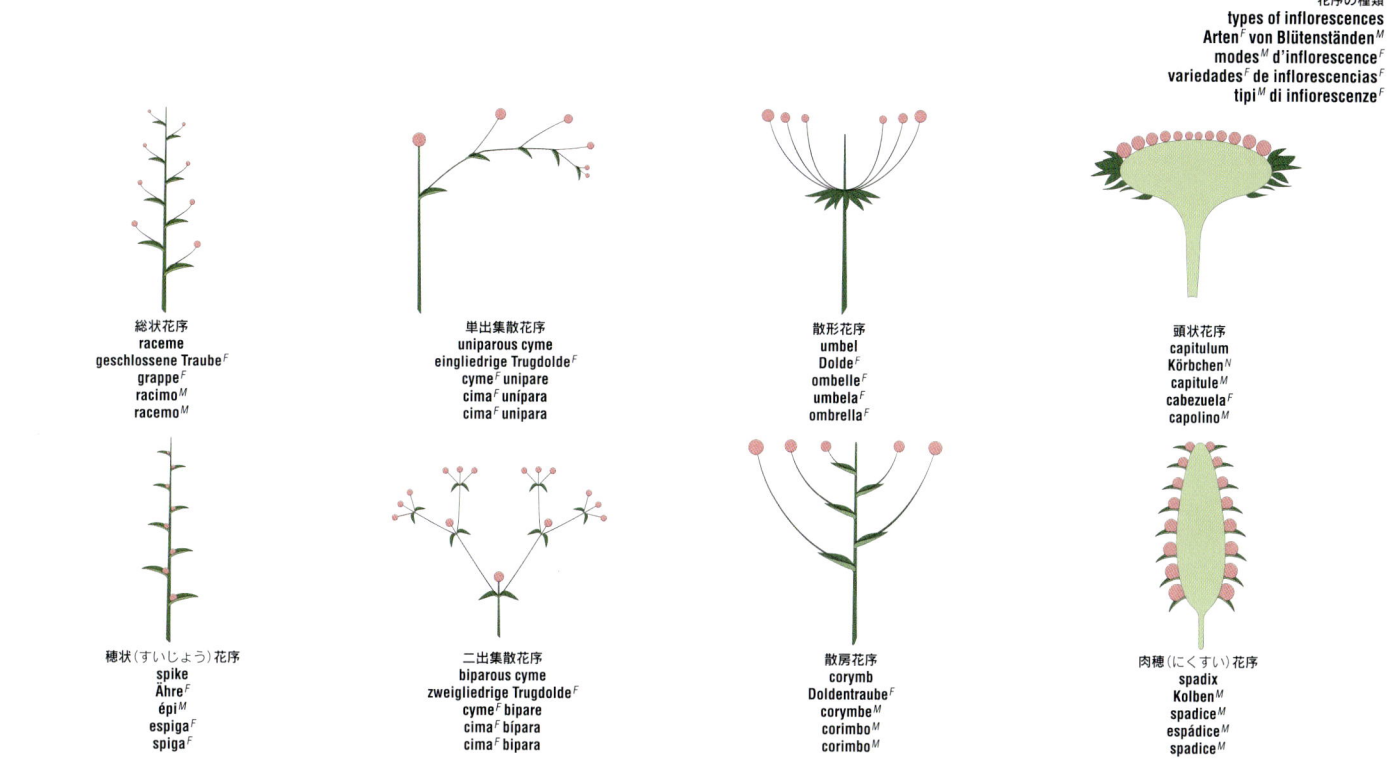

fruits | Früchte F | fruits M | frutos M | frutti M

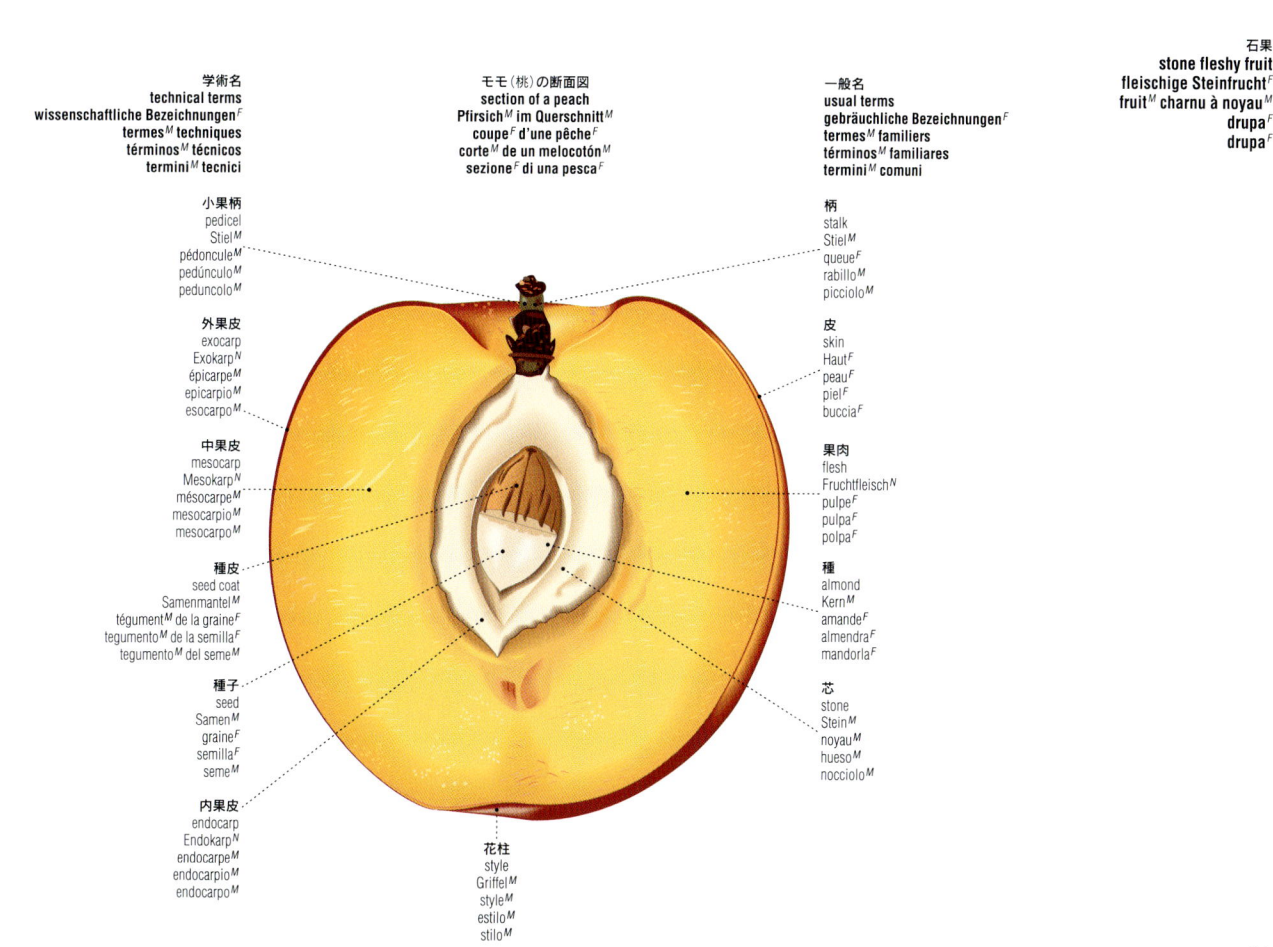

学術名
technical terms
wissenschaftliche Bezeichnungen F
termes M techniques
términos M técnicos
termini M tecnici

モモ(桃)の断面図
section of a peach
Pfirsich M im Querschnitt M
coupe F d'une pêche F
corte M de un melocotón M
sezione F di una pesca F

一般名
usual terms
gebräuchliche Bezeichnungen F
termes M familiers
términos M familiares
termini M comuni

石果
stone fleshy fruit
fleischige Steinfrucht F
fruit M charnu à noyau M
drupa F
drupa F

小果柄
pedicel
Stiel M
pédoncule M
pedúnculo M
pedunculo M

外果皮
exocarp
Exokarp N
épicarpe F
epicarpio M
esocarpo M

中果皮
mesocarp
Mesokarp N
mésocarpe M
mesocarpio M
mesocarpo M

種皮
seed coat
Samenmantel M
tégument M de la graine F
tegumento M de la semilla F
tegumento M del seme M

種子
seed
Samen M
graine F
semilla F
seme M

内果皮
endocarp
Endokarp N
endocarpe M
endocarpio M
endocarpo M

柄
stalk
Stiel M
queue F
rabillo M
picciolo M

皮
skin
Haut F
peau F
piel F
buccia F

果肉
flesh
Fruchtfleisch N
pulpe F
pulpa F
polpa F

種
almond
Kern M
amande F
almendra F
mandorla F

芯
stone
Stein M
noyau M
hueso M
nocciolo M

花柱
style
Griffel M
style M
estilo M
stilo M

81

果実

日本語 | 英語 | ドイツ語 | フランス語 | スペイン語 | イタリア語

ナシ(梨)状果
pome fleshy fruit
fleischige Apfelfrucht^F
fruit^M **charnu à pépins**^{M}
pomo carnoso
frutto^M **carnoso: mela**

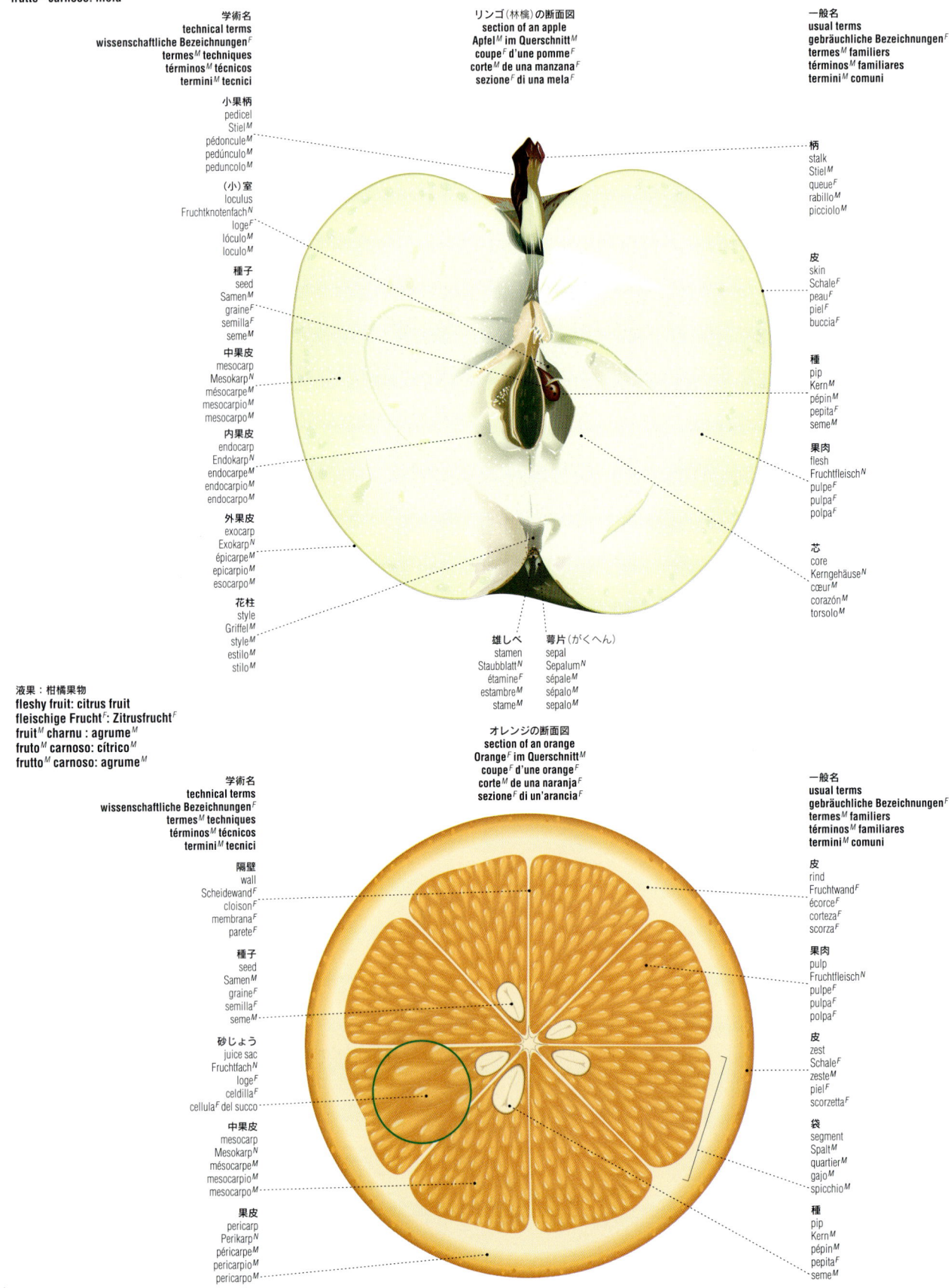

学術名
technical terms
wissenschaftliche Bezeichnungen^F
termes^M techniques
términos^M técnicos
termini^M tecnici

リンゴ(林檎)の断面図
section of an apple
Apfel^M im Querschnitt^M
coupe^F d'une pomme^F
corte^F de una manzana^F
sezione^F di una mela^F

一般名
usual terms
gebräuchliche Bezeichnungen^F
termes^M familiers
términos^M familiares
termini^M comuni

小果柄
pedicel
Stiel^M
pédoncule^M
pedúnculo^M
peduncolo^M

柄
stalk
Stiel^M
queue^F
rabillo^M
picciolo^M

(小)室
loculus
Fruchtknotenfach^N
loge^F
lóculo^M
loculo^M

皮
skin
Schale^F
peau^F
piel^F
buccia^F

種子
seed
Samen^M
graine^F
semilla^F
seme^M

種
pip
Kern^M
pépin^M
pepita^F
seme^M

中果皮
mesocarp
Mesokarp^N
mésocarpe^F
mesocarpio^M
mesocarpo^M

果肉
flesh
Fruchtfleisch^N
pulpe^F
pulpa^F
polpa^F

内果皮
endocarp
Endokarp^N
endocarpe^F
endocarpio^M
endocarpo^M

芯
core
Kerngehäuse^N
cœur^M
corazón^M
torsolo^M

外果皮
exocarp
Exokarp^N
épicarpe^F
epicarpio^M
esocarpo^M

花柱
style
Griffel^M
style^M
estilo^M
stilo^M

雄しべ
stamen
Staubblatt^N
étamine^F
estambre^M
stame^M

萼片(がくへん)
sepal
Sepalum^N
sépale^F
sépalo^M
sepalo^M

液果:柑橘果物
fleshy fruit: citrus fruit
fleischige Frucht^F**: Zitrusfrucht**^{F}
fruit^M **charnu : agrume**^{M}
fruto^M **carnoso: cítrico**^{M}
frutto^M **carnoso: agrume**^{M}

学術名
technical terms
wissenschaftliche Bezeichnungen^F
termes^M techniques
términos^M técnicos
termini^M tecnici

オレンジの断面図
section of an orange
Orange^F im Querschnitt^M
coupe^F d'une orange^F
corte^F de una naranja^F
sezione^F di un'arancia^F

一般名
usual terms
gebräuchliche Bezeichnungen^F
termes^M familiers
términos^M familiares
termini^M comuni

隔壁
wall
Scheidewand^F
cloison^F
membrana^F
parete^F

皮
rind
Fruchtwand^F
écorce^F
corteza^F
scorza^F

種子
seed
Samen^M
graine^F
semilla^F
seme^M

果肉
pulp
Fruchtfleisch^N
pulpe^F
pulpa^F
polpa^F

砂じょう
juice sac
Fruchtfach^N
loge^F
celdilla^F
cellula^F del succo

皮
zest
Schale^F
zeste^M
piel^F
scorzetta^F

中果皮
mesocarp
Mesokarp^N
mésocarpe^F
mesocarpio^M
mesocarpo^M

袋
segment
Spalt^M
quartier^M
gajo^M
spicchio^M

果皮
pericarp
Perikarp^N
péricarpe^F
pericarpio^M
pericarpo^M

種
pip
Kern^M
pépin^M
pepita^F
seme^M

果実

液果：イチゴ（苺）の仲間
fleshy fruit: berry fruit
fleischige Frucht^F: Beere^F
fruit^M charnu : baie^F
fruto^F carnoso: baya^F
frutto^M carnoso: bacca^F

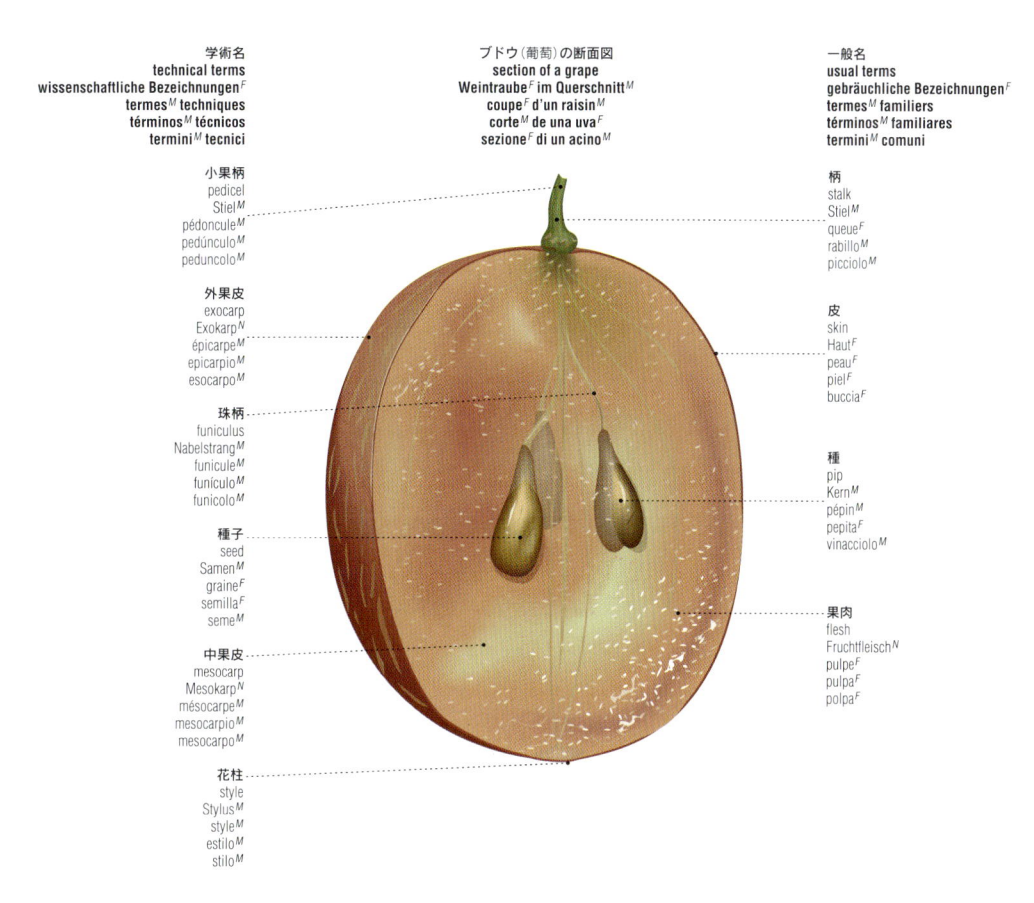

植物

学術名 / technical terms
wissenschaftliche Bezeichnungen^F
termes^M techniques
términos^M técnicos
termini^M tecnici

ブドウ（葡萄）の断面図 / section of a grape
Weintraube^F im Querschnitt^M
coupe^F d'un raisin^M
corte^M de una uva^F
sezione^F di un acino^M

一般名 / usual terms
gebräuchliche Bezeichnungen^F
termes^M familiers
términos^M familiares
termini^M comuni

小果柄 / pedicel / Stiel^M / pédoncule^M / pedúnculo^M / peduncolo^M

外果皮 / exocarp / Exokarp^N / épicarpe^M / epicarpio^M / esocarpo^M

珠柄 / funiculus / Nabelstrang^M / funicule^M / funículo^M / funicolo^M

種子 / seed / Samen^M / graine^F / semilla^F / seme^M

中果皮 / mesocarp / Mesokarp^N / mésocarpe^M / mesocarpio^M / mesocarpo^M

花柱 / style / Stylus^M / style^M / estilo^M / stilo^M

柄 / stalk / Stiel^M / queue^F / rabillo^M / picciolo^M

皮 / skin / Haut^F / peau^F / piel^F / buccia^F

種 / pip / Kern^M / pépin^M / pepita^F / vinacciolo^M

果肉 / flesh / Fruchtfleisch^N / pulpe^F / pulpa^F / polpa^F

イチゴ（苺）の断面図 / section of a strawberry
Erdbeere^F im Querschnitt^M
coupe^F d'une fraise^F
corte^M de una fresa^F
sezione^F di una fragola^F

小果柄 / pedicel / Stiel^M / pédoncule^M / pedúnculo^M / peduncolo^M

萼状総苞（がくじょうそうほう） / epicalyx / Außenkelch^M / calicule^M / calículo^M / calicetto^M

萼（がく） / calyx / Kelch^M / calice^M / cáliz^M / calice^M

痩果（そうか） / achene / Samen^M / akène^M / aquenio^M / achenio^M

果肉 / flesh / Fruchtfleisch^N / pulpe^F / pulpa^F / polpa^F

花床 / receptacle / Blütenboden^M / réceptacle^M / receptáculo^M / ricettacolo^M

ラズベリーの断面図 / section of a raspberry
Himbeere^F im Querschnitt^M
coupe^F d'une framboise^F
corte^M de una frambuesa^F
sezione^F di un lampone^M

小果柄 / pedicel / Stiel^M / pédoncule^M / pedúnculo^M / peduncolo^M

萼片（がくへん） / sepal / Kelchblatt^N / sépale^M / sépalo^M / sepalo^M

種子 / seed / Samen^M / graine^F / semilla^F / seme^M

花床 / receptacle / Blütenboden^M / réceptacle^M / receptáculo^M / ricettacolo^M

小核果 / drupelet / Steinfrüchtchen^N / drupéole^F / drupéola^F / drupeola^F

果実

|日本語|英語|ドイツ語|フランス語|スペイン語|イタリア語|

乾果
dry fruits
Trockenfrüchte^F
fruits^M secs
frutos^M secos
frutti^M secchi

殻皮
husk
Hülle^F
brou^M
cáscara^F
mallo^M

ハシバミ（榛）の実の断面図
section of a hazelnut
Längsschnitt^M durch eine Haselnuss^F
coupe^F d'une noisette^F
corte^M de una avellana^F
sezione^F di una nocciola^F

殻斗（かくと）
cupule
Fruchtbecher^M
cupule^F
cúpula^F
cupola^F

苞葉（ほうよう）
bract
Deckblatt^N
bractée^F
bráctea^F
brattea^F

種子
seed
Samen^M
graine^F
semilla^F
seme^M

果皮
pericarp
Fruchtwand^F
péricarpe^M
pericarpio^M
pericarpo^M

瘦果（そうか）
achene
Schließfrucht^F
akène^F
aquenio^M
achenio^M

柱頭
stigma
Narbe^F
stigmate^M
estigma^M
stigma^M

クルミ（胡桃）の断面図
section of a walnut
Längsschnitt^M durch eine Walnuss^F
coupe^F d'une noix^F
corte^M de una nuez^F
sezione^F di una noce^F

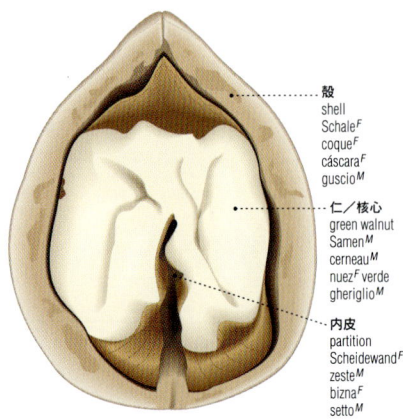

殻
shell
Schale^F
coque^F
cáscara^F
guscio^M

仁／核心
green walnut
Samen^M
cerneau^M
nuez^M verde
gheriglio^M

内皮
partition
Scheidewand^F
zeste^M
bizna^F
setto^M

袋果（たいか）の断面図：トウシキミ（唐樒）
section of a follicle: star anise
Balg^M im Querschnitt^M: Sternanis^M
coupe^F d'un follicule^M : anis^M étoilé
corte^M de un folículo^M: anís^M estrellado
sezione^F di un follicolo^M: anice^M stellato

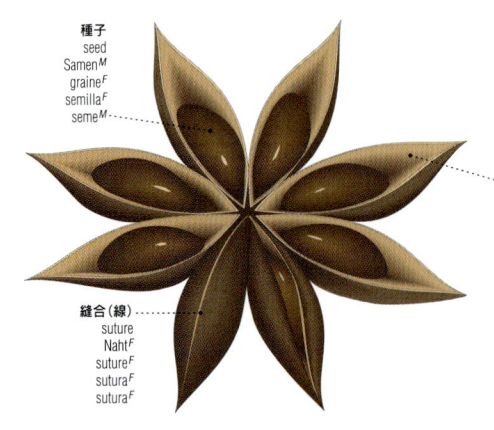

種子
seed
Samen^M
graine^F
semilla^F
seme^M

袋果
follicle
Fruchtkapsel^F
follicule^M
folículo^M
follicolo^M

縫合（線）
suture
Naht^F
suture^F
sutura^F
sutura^F

豆果（とうか）の断面図：エンドウ
section of a legume: pea
Hülsenfrucht^F im Querschnitt^M: Erbse^F
coupe^F d'une gousse^F : pois^M
corte^M de una legumbre^F : guisante^M
sezione^F di un legume^M : pisello^M

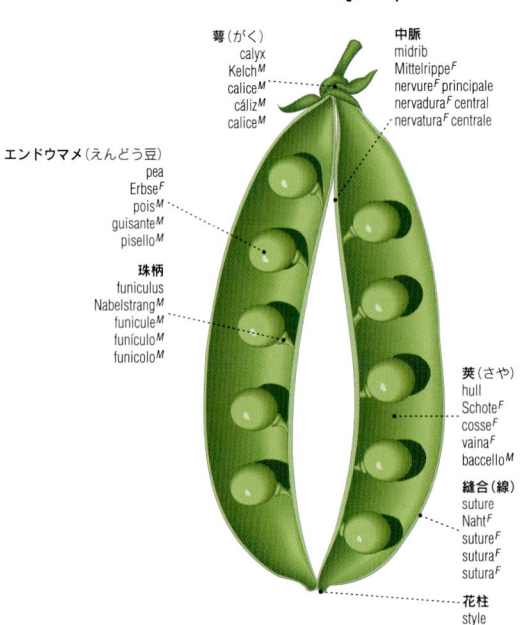

萼（がく）
calyx
Kelch^M
calice^M
cáliz^M
calice^M

エンドウマメ（えんどう豆）
pea
Erbse^F
pois^M
guisante^M
pisello^M

珠柄
funiculus
Nabelstrang^M
funicule^M
funículo^M
funicolo^M

中脈
midrib
Mittelrippe^F
nervure^F principale
nervadura^F central
nervatura^F centrale

莢（さや）
hull
Schote^F
cosse^F
vaina^F
baccello^M

縫合（線）
suture
Naht^F
suture^F
sutura^F
sutura^F

花柱
style
Griffel^M
style^M
estilo^M
stilo^M

長角果の断面図：カラシ（芥子）
section of a silique: mustard
Schote^F im Querschnitt^M: Senf^M
coupe^F d'une silique^F : moutarde^F
corte^M de una silicua^F: mostaza^F
sezione^F di una siliqua^F: senape^F nera

花柱
style
Griffel^M
style^M
estilo^M
stilo^M

種子
seed
Samen^M
graine^F
semilla^F
seme^M

隔壁／隔膜
septum
Scheidewand^F
membrane^F médiane
septum^M
replo^M

さく片
valve
Fruchtblatt^N
valve^F
ventalla^F
valva^F

さく果の断面図：ケシ（芥子）
section of a capsule: poppy
Fruchtkapsel^F im Querschnitt^M: Mohn^M
coupe^F d'une capsule^F : pavot^M
corte^M de una cápsula^F: amapola^F
sezione^F di una capsula^F: papavero^M

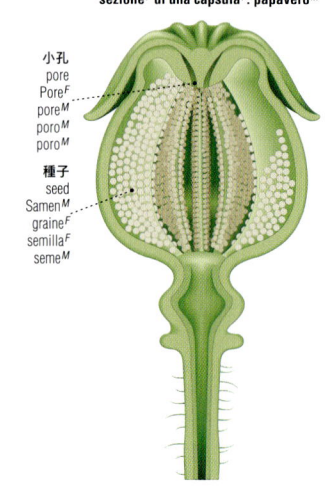

小孔
pore
Pore^F
pore^M
poro^M
poro^M

種子
seed
Samen^M
graine^F
semilla^F
seme^M

穀類

cereals | Getreide(N) | céréales(F) | cereales(M) | cereali(M)

小麦の断面図
section of a grain of wheat
Längsschnitt(M) durch ein Weizenkorn(N)
coupe(F) d'un grain(M) de blé(M)
corte(M) de un grano(M) de trigo(M)
sezione(F) di un chicco(M) di grano(M)

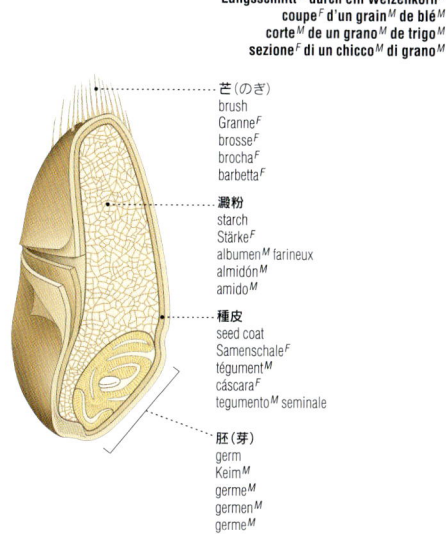

芒(のぎ)
brush
Granne(F)
brosse(F)
brocha(F)
barbetta(F)

澱粉
starch
Stärke(F)
albumen(M) farineux
almidón(M)
amido(M)

種皮
seed coat
Samenschale(F)
tégument(M)
cáscara(F)
tegumento(M) seminale

胚(芽)
germ
Keim(M)
germe(M)
germen(M)
germe(M)

ソバ(蕎麦)
buckwheat
Buchweizen(M)
sarrasin(M)
trigo(M) sarraceno
grano(M) saraceno

ソバ:総状花序
buckwheat: raceme
Buchweizen(M): Doldenrispe(F)
sarrasin(M): grappe(F)
trigo(M) sarraceno: racimo(M)
grano(M) saraceno: racemo(M)

小麦
wheat
Weizen(M)
blé(M)
trigo(M)
grano(M)

小麦:穂状(すいじょう)花序
wheat: spike
Weizen(M): Ähre(F)
blé(M): épi(M)
trigo(M): espiga(F)
grano(M): spiga(F)

大麦
barley
Gerste(F)
orge(F)
cebada(F)
orzo(M)

大麦:穂状(すいじょう)花序
barley: spike
Gerste(F): Ähre(F)
orge(F): épi(M)
cebada(F): espiga(F)
orzo(M): spiga(F)

米
rice
Reis(M)
riz(M)
arroz(M)
riso(M)

米:穂状花序
rice: spike
Reis(M): Rispe(F)
riz(M): épi(M)
arroz(M): espiga(F)
riso(M): spiga(F)

オート麦／カラス(烏)麦
oats
Hafer(M)
avoine(F)
avena(F)
avena(F)

オート麦:円錐花序
oats: panicle
Hafer(M): Ährchen(N)
avoine(F): panicule(F)
avena(F): panícula(F)
avena(F): pannocchia(F)

モロコシ
sorghum
Mohrenhirse(F)
sorgho(M)
sorgo(M)
sorgo(M)

モロコシ:円錐花序
sorghum: panicle
Mohrenhirse(F): Rispe(F)
sorgho(M): panicule(F)
sorgo(M): panícula(F)
sorgo(M): pannocchia(F)

ライ麦
rye
Roggen(M)
seigle(M)
centeno(M)
segale(F)

ライ麦:穂状花序
rye: spike
Roggen(M): Ähre(F)
seigle(M): épi(M)
centeno(M): espiga(F)
segale(F): spiga(F)

毛
silk
Bart(M)
barbe(F)
pelo(M) de maíz(M)
barba(F)

穂軸(すいじく)
cob
Kolben(M)
épi(M)
mazorca(M)
pannocchia(F)

殻
husk
Hülse(F)
feuille(F)
hoja(F)
cartoccio(M)

穀粒
kernel
Kern(M)
grain(M)
grano(M)
cariosside(F)

アワ(粟)
millet
Hirse(F)
millet(M)
mijo(M)
miglio(M)

アワ:穂状(すいじょう)花序
millet: spike
Hirse(F): Ährenrispe(F)
millet(M): épi(M)
mijo(M): espiga(F)
miglio(M): spiga(F)

トウモロコシ
corn; sweetcorn
Mais(M)
maïs(M)
maíz(M)
mais(M)

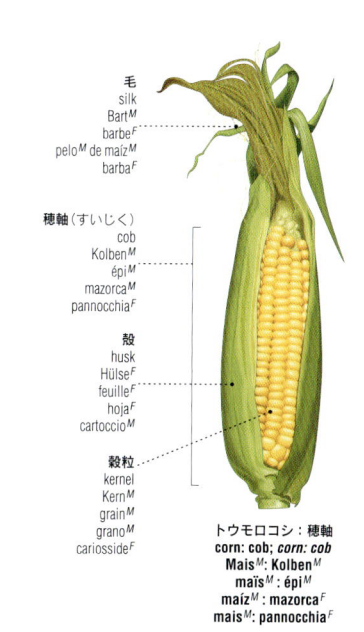

トウモロコシ:穂軸
corn: cob; corn: cob
Mais(M): Kolben(M)
maïs(M): épi(M)
maíz(M): mazorca(F)
mais(M): pannocchia(F)

植物

ブドウ（葡萄）

grape | Rebe^F | vigne^F | uva^F | vite^F

日本語｜英語｜ドイツ語｜フランス語｜スペイン語｜イタリア語

植物

ブドウの房
bunch of grapes
Traubenhenkel^M
grappe^F de raisins^M
racimo^M de uvas^F
grappolo^M d'uva^F

分枝
branch
Fruchtholz^N
rameau^M
ramificación^F
ramo^M

小果柄
pedicel
Blütenstiel^M
pédoncule^M
pedúnculo^M
peduncolo^M

巻きひげ
tendril
Weinranke^F
vrille^F
zarcillo^M
viticcio^M

主花柄
main stalk
Hauptstiel^M
axe^M principal
tallo^M principal
rachide^F

ブドウ
grape
Weintraube^F
raisin^M
vid^F
acino^M

ブドウの株
vine stock
Rebstock^M
cep^M de vigne^F
cepa^F de vid^F
albero^M della vite^F

結果枝（し）
fruit branch
Fruchtholz^N
branche^F à fruits^M
rama^F con fruto^M
ramo^M con frutti^M

若枝
vine shoot
Trieb^M
sarment^M
sarmiento^M
tralcio^M

徒長枝（し）
sucker
Trieb^M
gourmand^M
serpollo^M
femminella^F

幹
trunk
Stamm^M
tronc^M
tronco^M
tronco^M

ブドウの葉
grape leaf; *vine leaf*
Weinblatt^N
feuille^F de vigne^F
hoja^F de la vid^F
pampino^M

頂裂片
terminal lobe
Endlappen^M
lobe^M terminal
lóbulo^M terminal
lobo^M terminale

上側裂片
upper lateral lobe
oberer seitlicher Lappen^M
lobe^M latéral supérieur
lóbulo^M lateral superior
lobo^M laterale superiore

上側湾欠
upper lateral sinus
oberer seitlicher Einschnitt^M
sinus^M latéral supérieur
seno^M lateral superior
seno^M laterale superiore

下側裂片
lower lateral lobe
unterer seitlicher Lappen^M
lobe^M latéral inférieur
lóbulo^M lateral inferior
lobo^M laterale inferiore

下側湾欠
lower lateral sinus
unterer seitlicher Einschnitt^M
sinus^M latéral inférieur
seno^M lateral inferior
seno^M laterale inferiore

葉柄湾欠
petiolar sinus
Blattstieleinschnitt^M
sinus^M pétiolaire
seno^M del pecíolo^M
seno^M peziolato

根系
root system
Wurzelsystem^N
système^M racinaire
raíces^F
apparato^M radicale

生長過程
maturing steps
Stufen^F der Reife^F
étapes^F de maturation^F
etapas^F de la maduración^F
stadi^M di maturazione^F

開花
flowering
Blüte^F
floraison^F
floración^F
fioritura^F

結実
fruition
Fruchtbildung^F
nouaison^F
fructificación^F
fruttificazione^F

成熟
ripening
Reifeprozess^M
véraison^F
envero^M
maturazione^F

完熟
ripeness
Vollreife^F
maturité^F
madurez^F
maturità^F

樹木

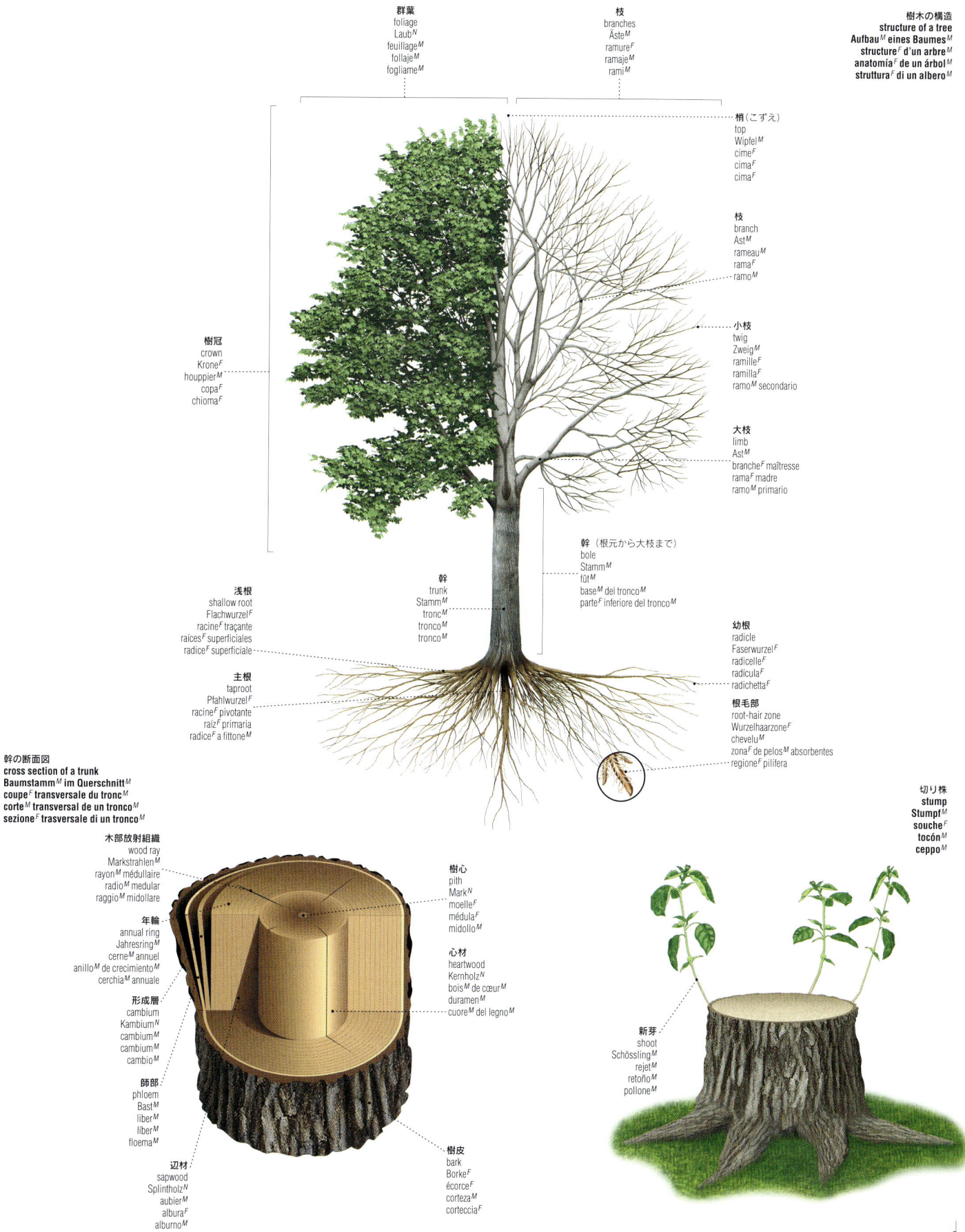

tree | Baum[M] | arbre[M] | árbol[M] | albero[M]

樹木の構造
structure of a tree
Aufbau[M] eines Baumes[M]
structure[F] d'un arbre[M]
anatomía[F] de un árbol[M]
struttura[F] di un albero[M]

植物

群葉
foliage
Laub[N]
feuillage[M]
follaje[M]
fogliame[M]

枝
branches
Äste[M]
ramure[F]
ramaje[M]
rami[M]

梢（こずえ）
top
Wipfel[M]
cime[F]
cima[F]
cima[F]

枝
branch
Ast[M]
rameau[M]
rama[F]
ramo[M]

小枝
twig
Zweig[M]
ramille[F]
ramilla[F]
ramo[M] secondario

大枝
limb
Ast[M]
branche[F] maîtresse
rama[F] madre
ramo[M] primario

樹冠
crown
Krone[F]
houppier[M]
copa[F]
chioma[F]

幹（根元から大枝まで）
bole
Stamm[M]
fût[M]
base[M] del tronco[M]
parte[F] inferiore del tronco[M]

浅根
shallow root
Flachwurzel[F]
racine[F] traçante
raíces[F] superficiales
radice[F] superficiale

幹
trunk
Stamm[M]
tronc[M]
tronco[M]
tronco[M]

幼根
radicle
Faserwurzel[F]
radicelle[F]
radícula[F]
radichetta[F]

主根
taproot
Pfahlwurzel[F]
racine[F] pivotante
raíz[F] primaria
radice[F] a fittone

根毛部
root-hair zone
Wurzelhaarzone[F]
chevelu[M]
zona[F] de pelos[M] absorbentes
regione[F] pilifera

幹の断面図
cross section of a trunk
Baumstamm[M] im Querschnitt[M]
coupe[F] transversale du tronc[M]
corte[M] transversal de un tronco[M]
sezione[F] trasversale di un tronco[M]

切り株
stump
Stumpf[M]
souche[F]
tocón[M]
ceppo[M]

木部放射組織
wood ray
Markstrahlen[M]
rayon[M] médullaire
radio[M] medular
raggio[M] midollare

樹心
pith
Mark[N]
moelle[F]
médula[F]
midollo[M]

年輪
annual ring
Jahresring[M]
cerne[M] annuel
anillo[M] de crecimiento[M]
cerchia[M] annuale

心材
heartwood
Kernholz[N]
bois[M] de cœur[M]
duramen[M]
cuore[M] del legno[M]

形成層
cambium
Kambium[N]
cambium[M]
cambium[M]
cambio[M]

師部
phloem
Bast[M]
liber[M]
liber[M]
floema[M]

新芽
shoot
Schössling[M]
rejet[M]
retoño[M]
pollone[M]

樹皮
bark
Borke[F]
écorce[F]
corteza[F]
corteccia[F]

辺材
sapwood
Splintholz[N]
aubier[M]
albura[F]
alburno[M]

87

樹木

日本語 | 英語 | ドイツ語 | フランス語 | スペイン語 | イタリア語

広葉樹の例
examples of broadleaved trees
Beispiele[N] für Laubhölzer[N]
exemples[M] d'arbres[M] feuillus
ejemplos[M] de latifolios[M]
esempi[M] di latifoglie[F]

オーク
oak
Eiche[F]
chêne[M]
roble[M]
quercia[F]

カバノキ（樺の木）
birch
Birke[F]
bouleau[M]
abedul[M]
betulla[F]

シダレヤナギ（枝垂れ柳）
weeping willow
Trauerweide[F]
saule[M] pleureur
sauce[M] llorón
salice[M] piangente

ポプラ
poplar
Pappel[F]
peuplier[M]
álamo[M]
pioppo[M]

ヤシ（椰子）
palm tree
Palme[F]
palmier[M]
palmera[F]
palma[F]

カエデ（楓）
maple
Ahorn[M]
érable[M]
arce[M]
acero[M]

ブナノキ（ぶなの木）
beech
Buche[F]
hêtre[M]
haya[F]
faggio[M]

クルミノキ（胡桃の木）
walnut
Walnuss[F]
noyer[M]
nogal[M]
noce[M]

針葉樹

conifer | Nadelbaum^M | conifère^M | conífera^F | conifera^F

枝
branch
Ast^M
rameau^M
rama^F
ramo^M

雄花
male cone
männliche Blütenstände^M
cône^M mâle
cono^M masculino
cono^M maschile

雌花
female cone
weibliche Blütenstände^M
cône^M femelle
cono^M femenino
cono^M femminile

球果
cone
Zapfen^M
cône^M
piña^F
cono^M

マツ(松)の実
pine seed
Pinienkern^M
pignon^M
piñón^M
pinolo^M

葉の例
examples of leaves
Beispiele^N für Nadelblätter^N
exemples^M de feuilles^F
ejemplos^M de hojas^F
esempi^M di foglie^F

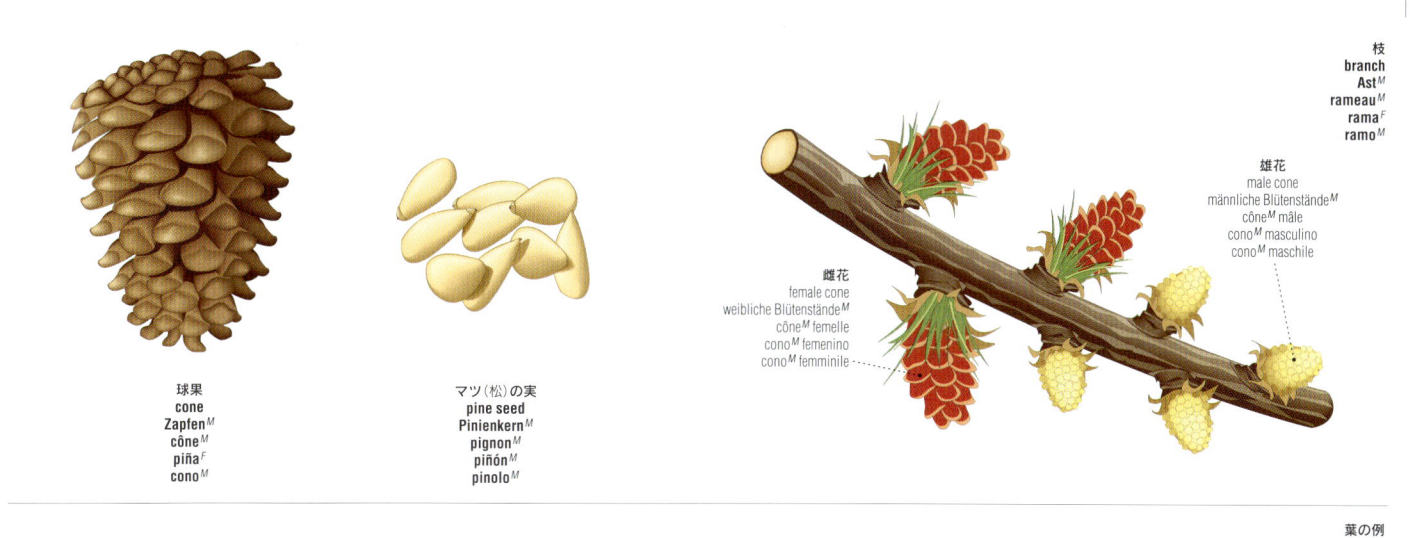

モミ(樅)の針葉
fir needles
Tannennadeln^F
aiguilles^F de sapin^M
agujas^F del abeto^M
aghi^M d'abete^M

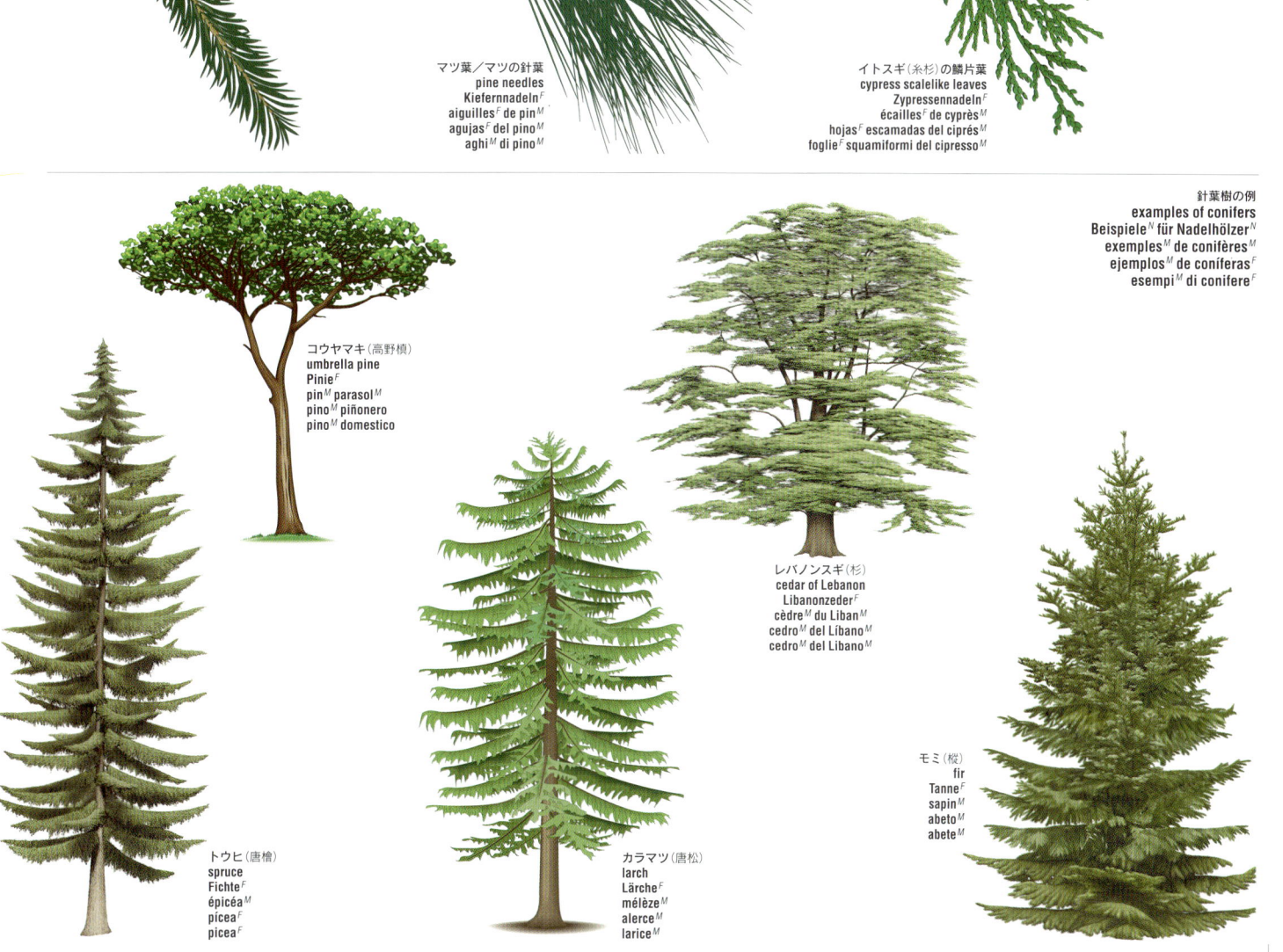

マツ葉／マツの針葉
pine needles
Kiefernnadeln^F
aiguilles^F de pin^M
agujas^F del pino^M
aghi^M di pino^M

イトスギ(糸杉)の鱗片葉
cypress scalelike leaves
Zypressennadeln^F
écailles^F de cyprès^M
hojas^F escamadas del ciprés^M
foglie^F squamiformi del cipresso^M

針葉樹の例
examples of conifers
Beispiele^N für Nadelhölzer^N
exemples^M de conifères^M
ejemplos^M de coníferas^F
esempi^M di conifere^F

コウヤマキ(高野槙)
umbrella pine
Pinie^F
pin^M parasol^M
pino^M piñonero
pino^M domestico

レバノンスギ(杉)
cedar of Lebanon
Libanonzeder^F
cèdre^M du Liban^M
cedro^M del Líbano^M
cedro^M del Libano^M

トウヒ(唐檜)
spruce
Fichte^F
épicéa^M
pícea^F
picea^F

カラマツ(唐松)
larch
Lärche^F
mélèze^M
alerce^M
larice^M

モミ(樅)
fir
Tanne^F
sapin^M
abeto^M
abete^M

植物

89

92 生命の進化
- 92 種の起源と進化

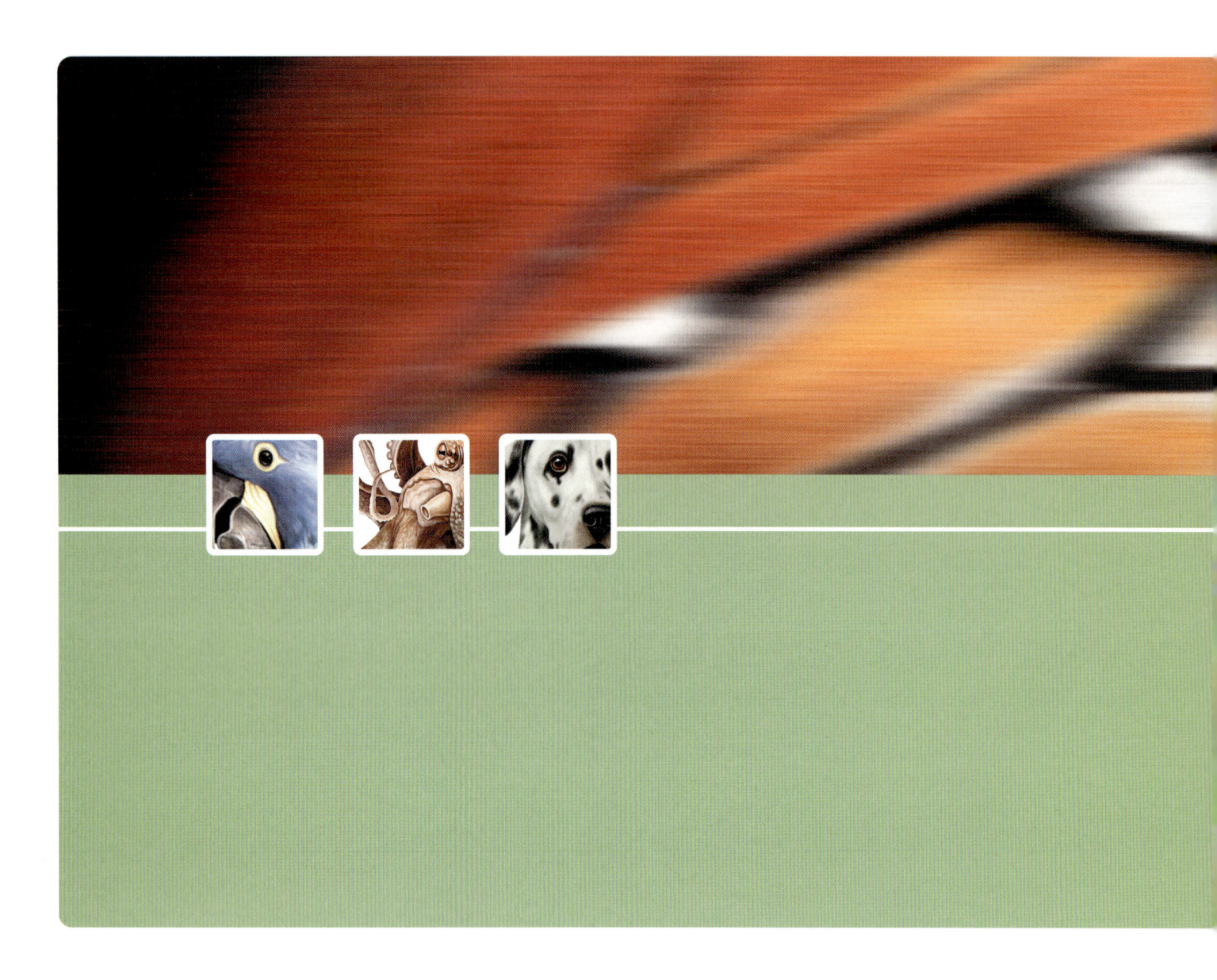

94 単純な生物と棘皮(きょくひ)動物
- 94 動物細胞
- 94 単細胞動物
- 95 海綿動物
- 95 棘皮動物

96 昆虫とクモ類
- 96 チョウ(蝶)
- 98 ミツバチ(蜜蜂)
- 101 昆虫の例
- 102 クモ類
- 103 クモ

104 軟体動物
- 104 カタツムリ(蝸牛)
- 105 巻き貝
- 105 二枚貝
- 106 タコ(蛸)

107 甲殻類
- 107 ロブスター

108 魚類
- 108 軟骨魚
- 108 硬骨魚

110 両生類
- 110 カエル(蛙)
- 111 両生類の例

112 爬虫類
- 112 ヘビ(蛇)
- 113 カメ(亀)
- 114 爬虫類の例

115 鳥類
- 115 鳥
- 118 鳥の例

動物

ANIMAL KINGDOM | TIERREICH | RÈGNE ANIMAL | REINO ANIMAL | REGNO ANIMALE

121 食虫哺乳動物
- 121 モグラ（土竜）
- 121 食虫哺乳動物の例

122 齧歯（げっし）類とウサギ目の動物
- 122 齧歯類（動物）
- 123 齧歯類動物の例
- 123 齧歯類とウサギ目の動物の顎（あご）
- 123 ウサギ目の動物の例

124 有蹄哺乳動物
- 124 ウマ（馬）
- 127 蹄（ひづめ）の例
- 128 有蹄哺乳動物の例

130 肉食哺乳動物
- 130 イヌ（犬）
- 130 イヌの品種
- 132 ネコ（猫）
- 132 ネコの品種
- 134 肉食哺乳動物の例

136 海棲哺乳動物
- 136 イルカ（海豚）
- 137 海棲哺乳動物の例

138 霊長類
- 138 ゴリラ
- 139 霊長類の動物の例

140 飛行哺乳動物
- 140 コウモリ（蝙蝠）
- 141 コウモリの例

142 有袋哺乳動物
- 142 カンガルー
- 143 有袋動物の例

生命の進化 | EVOLUTION OF LIFE
ENTWICKLUNG DES LEBENS | ÉVOLUTION DE LA VIE | EVOLUCIÓN DE LA VIDA | EVOLUZIONE DELLA VITA

種の起源と進化

origin and evolution of species | Entstehung^F und Entwicklung^F der Arten^F | origine^F et évolution^F des espèces^F | origen^M y evolución^F de las especies^F | origine^F ed evoluzione^F delle specie^F

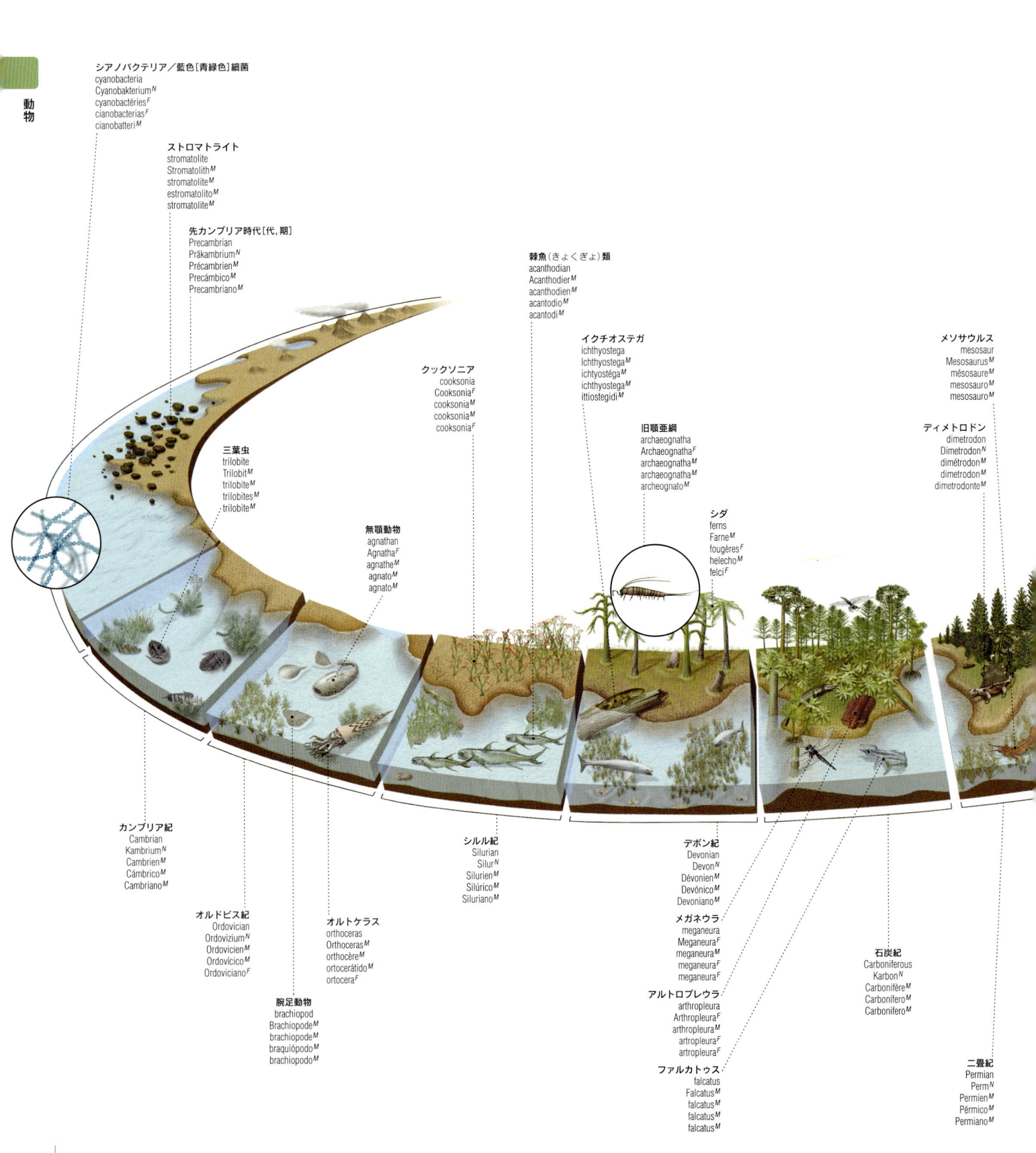

日本語 | 英語 | ドイツ語 | フランス語 | スペイン語 | イタリア語

動物

シアノバクテリア／藍色[青緑色]細菌
cyanobacteria
Cyanobakterium^N
cyanobactéries^F
cianobacterias^F
cianobatteri^M

ストロマトライト
stromatolite
Stromatolith^M
stromatolite^F
estromatolito^M
stromatolite^M

先カンブリア時代[代, 期]
Precambrian
Präkambrium^N
Précambrien^M
Precámbico^M
Precambriano^M

棘魚(きょくぎょ)類
acanthodian
Acanthodier^M
acanthodien^M
acantodio^M
acantodi^M

イクチオステガ
ichthyostega
Ichthyostega^F
ichtyostéga^M
ichthyostega^F
ittiostegidi^M

メソサウルス
mesosaur
Mesosaurus^M
mésosaure^M
mesosauro^M
mesosauro^M

クックソニア
cooksonia
Cooksonia^F
cooksonia^F
cooksonia^M
cooksonia^F

旧顎亜綱
archaeognatha
Archaeognatha^F
archaeognatha^F
archaeognatha^F
archeognato^M

ディメトロドン
dimetrodon
Dimetrodon^N
dimétrodon^M
dimetrodon^M
dimetrodonte^M

三葉虫
trilobite
Trilobit^M
trilobite^M
trilobites^M
trilobite^M

シダ
ferns
Farne^M
fougères^F
helecho^M
felci^F

無顎動物
agnathan
Agnatha^F
agnathe^M
agnato^M
agnato^M

カンブリア紀
Cambrian
Kambrium^N
Cambrien^M
Cámbrico^M
Cambriano^M

シルル紀
Silurian
Silur^N
Silurien^M
Silúrico^M
Siluriano^M

デボン紀
Devonian
Devon^N
Dévonien^M
Devónico^M
Devoniano^M

オルドビス紀
Ordovician
Ordovizium^N
Ordovicien^M
Ordovícico^M
Ordoviciano^F

オルトケラス
orthoceras
Orthoceras^M
orthocère^M
ortocerátido^M
ortocera^F

メガネウラ
meganeura
Meganeura^F
méganeura^M
meganeura^F
meganeura^F

石炭紀
Carboniferous
Karbon^N
Carbonifère^M
Carbonífero^M
Carbonifero^M

腕足動物
brachiopod
Brachiopode^M
brachiopode^M
braquiópodo^M
brachiopodo^M

アルトロプレウラ
arthropleura
Arthropleura^F
arthropleura^F
artropleura^M
artropleura^F

二畳紀
Permian
Perm^N
Permien^M
Pérmico^M
Permiano^M

ファルカトゥス
falcatus
Falcatus^M
falcatus^M
falcatus^M
falcatus^M

92

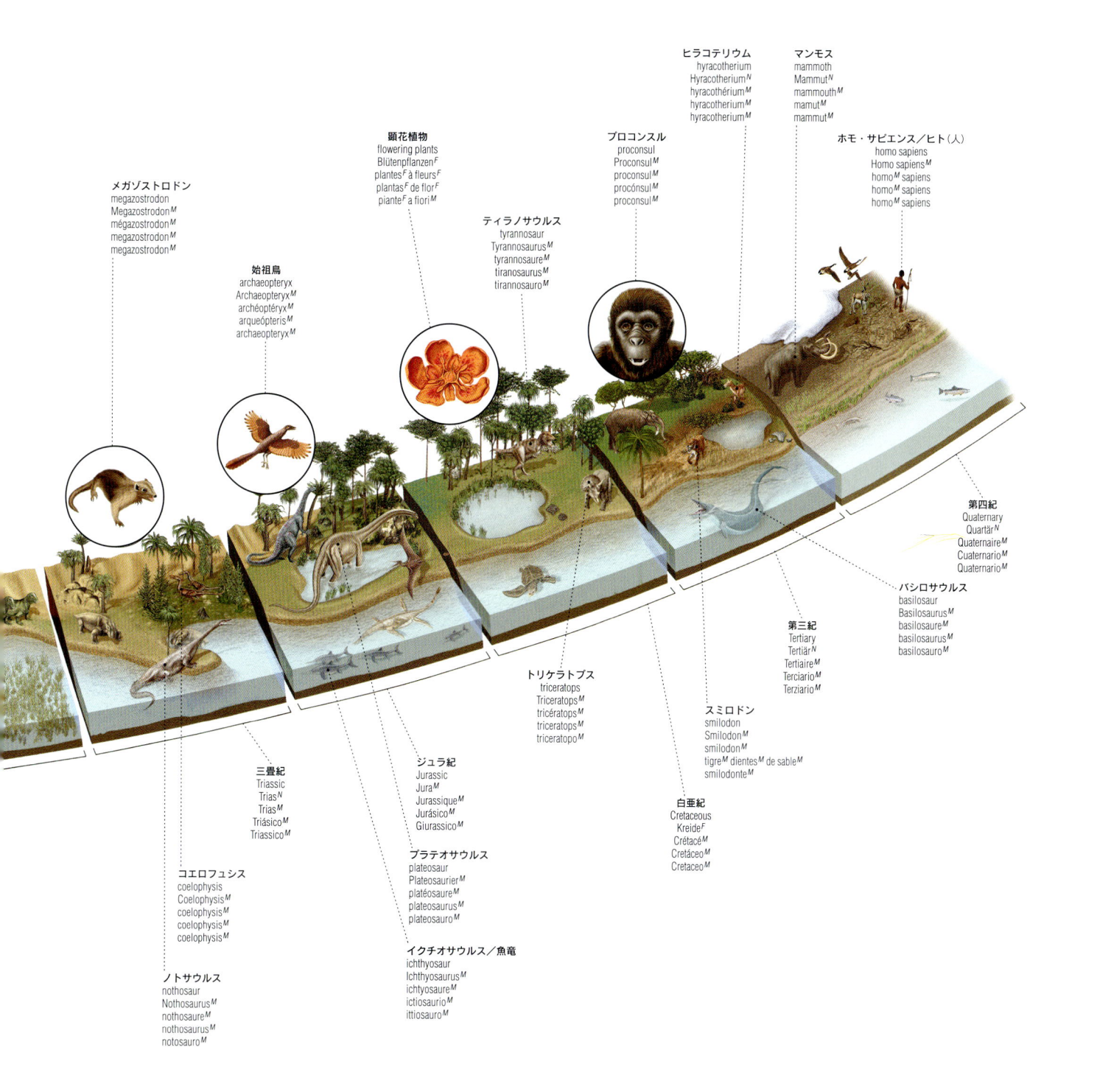

生命の進化 | EVOLUTION OF LIFE
ENTWICKLUNG DES LEBENS | ÉVOLUTION DE LA VIE | EVOLUCIÓN DE LA VIDA | EVOLUZIONE DELLA VITA

種の起源と進化

動物

ヒラコテリウム
hyracotherium
Hyracotherium[N]
hyracothérium[M]
hyracotherium[M]
hyracotherium[M]

マンモス
mammoth
Mammut[N]
mammouth[M]
mamut[M]
mammut[M]

顕花植物
flowering plants
Blütenpflanzen[F]
plantes[F] à fleurs[F]
plantas[F] de flor[F]
piante[F] a fiori[M]

プロコンスル
proconsul
Proconsul[M]
proconsul[M]
procónsul[M]
proconsul[M]

ホモ・サピエンス／ヒト（人）
homo sapiens
Homo sapiens[M]
homo[M] sapiens
homo[M] sapiens
homo[M] sapiens

メガゾストロドン
megazostrodon
Megazostrodon[M]
mégazostrodon[M]
megazostrodon[M]
megazostrodon[M]

始祖鳥
archaeopteryx
Archaeopteryx[M]
archéoptéryx[M]
arqueópteris[M]
archaeopteryx[M]

ティラノサウルス
tyrannosaur
Tyrannosaurus[M]
tyrannosaure[M]
tiranosaurus[M]
tirannosauro[M]

第四紀
Quaternary
Quartär[N]
Quaternaire[M]
Cuaternario[M]
Quaternario[M]

バシロサウルス
basilosaur
Basilosaurus[M]
basilosaure[M]
basilosaurus[M]
basilosauro[M]

第三紀
Tertiary
Tertiär[N]
Tertiaire[M]
Terciario[M]
Terziario[M]

トリケラトプス
triceratops
Triceratops[M]
tricératops[M]
triceratops[M]
triceratopo[M]

スミロドン
smilodon
Smilodon[M]
smilodon[M]
tigre[M] dientes[M] de sable[M]
smilodonte[M]

白亜紀
Cretaceous
Kreide[F]
Crétacé[M]
Cretácео[M]
Cretaceo[M]

三畳紀
Triassic
Trias[N]
Trias[M]
Triásico[M]
Triassico[M]

ジュラ紀
Jurassic
Jura[M]
Jurassique[M]
Jurásico[M]
Giurassico[M]

コエロフュシス
coelophysis
Coelophysis[M]
coelophysis[M]
coelophysis[M]
coelophysis[M]

プラテオサウルス
plateosaur
Plateosaurier[M]
plateosaure[M]
plateosaurus[M]
plateosauro[M]

ノトサウルス
nothosaur
Nothosaurus[M]
nothosaure[M]
notiosaurus[M]
notosauro[M]

イクチオサウルス／魚竜
ichthyosaur
Ichthyosaurus[M]
ichtyosaure[M]
ictiosaurio[M]
ittiosauro[M]

93

単純な生物と棘皮(きょくひ)動物 | SIMPLE ORGANISMS AND ECHINODERMS
EINFACHE ORGANISMEN UND ECHINODERMEN | ORGANISMES SIMPLES ET ÉCHINODERMES | ORGANISMOS SIMPLES Y EQUINODERMOS | ORGANISMI SEMPLICI E ECHINODERMI

動物細胞

animal cell | tierische Zelle F | cellule F animale | célula F animal | cellula F animale

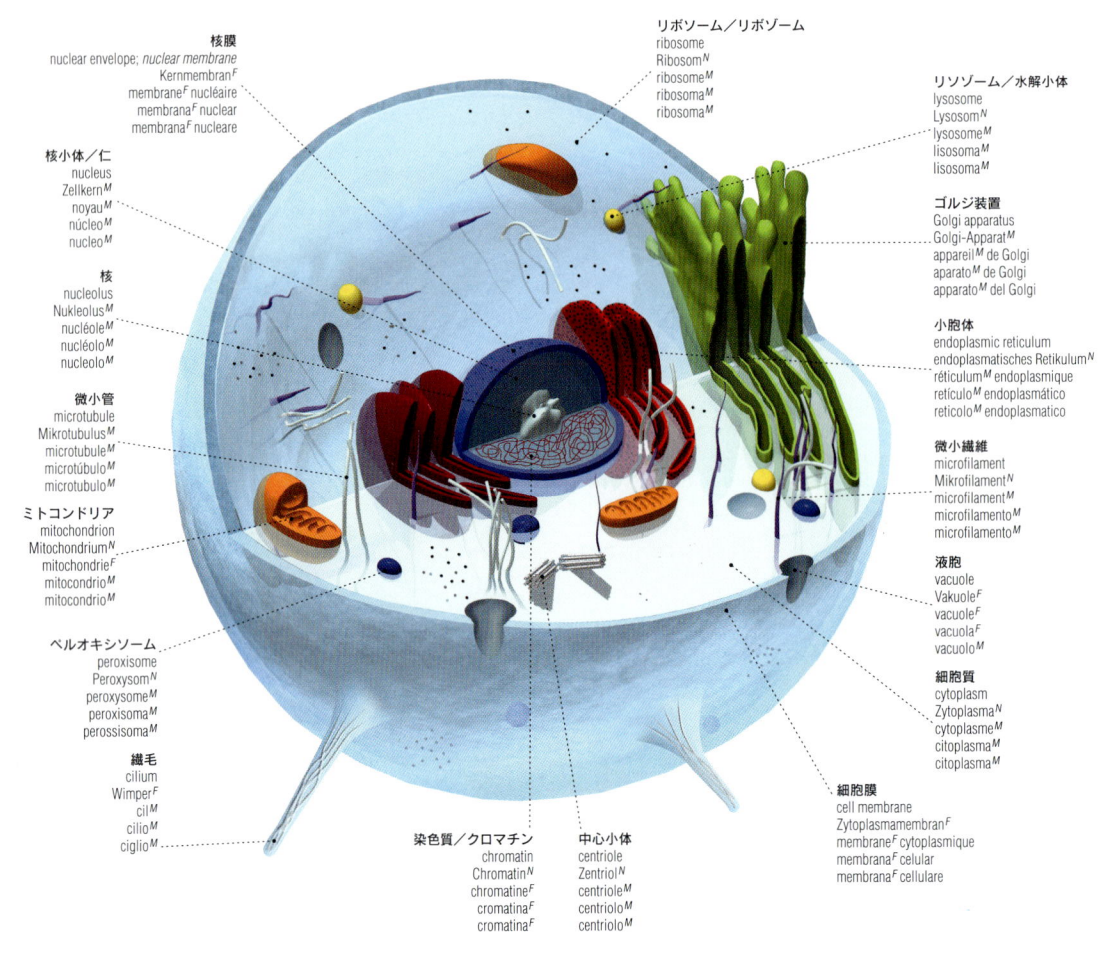

核膜
nuclear envelope; nuclear membrane
Kernmembran
membrane F nucléaire
membrana F nuclear
membrana F nucleare

リボソーム／リボゾーム
ribosome
Ribosom N
ribosome M
ribosoma M
ribosoma M

リソソーム／水解小体
lysosome
Lysosom N
lysosome M
lisosoma M
lisosoma M

核小体／仁
nucleus
Zellkern M
noyau M
núcleo M
nucleo M

ゴルジ装置
Golgi apparatus
Golgi-Apparat M
appareil M de Golgi
aparato M de Golgi
apparato M del Golgi

核
nucleolus
Nukleolus M
nucléole M
nucléolo M
nucleolo M

小胞体
endoplasmic reticulum
endoplasmatisches Retikulum N
réticulum M endoplasmique
retículo M endoplasmático
reticolo M endoplasmatico

微小管
microtubule
Mikrotubulus M
microtubule M
microtúbulo M
microtubulo M

微小繊維
microfilament
Mikrofilament N
microfilament M
microfilamento M
microfilamento M

ミトコンドリア
mitochondrion
Mitochondrium N
mitochondrie F
mitocondrio M
mitocondrio M

液胞
vacuole
Vakuole F
vacuole F
vacuola F
vacuolo M

ペルオキシソーム
peroxisome
Peroxysom N
peroxysome M
peroxisoma M
perossisoma M

細胞質
cytoplasm
Zytoplasma N
cytoplasme M
citoplasma M
citoplasma M

繊毛
cilium
Wimper F
cil M
cilio M
ciglio M

細胞膜
cell membrane
Zytoplasmamembran F
membrane F cytoplasmique
membrana F celular
membrana F cellulare

染色質／クロマチン
chromatin
Chromatin N
chromatine F
cromatina F
cromatina F

中心小体
centriole
Zentriol N
centriole M
centriolo M
centriolo M

単細胞動物

unicellulars | Einzeller M | unicellulaires M | unicelulares M | unicellulari M

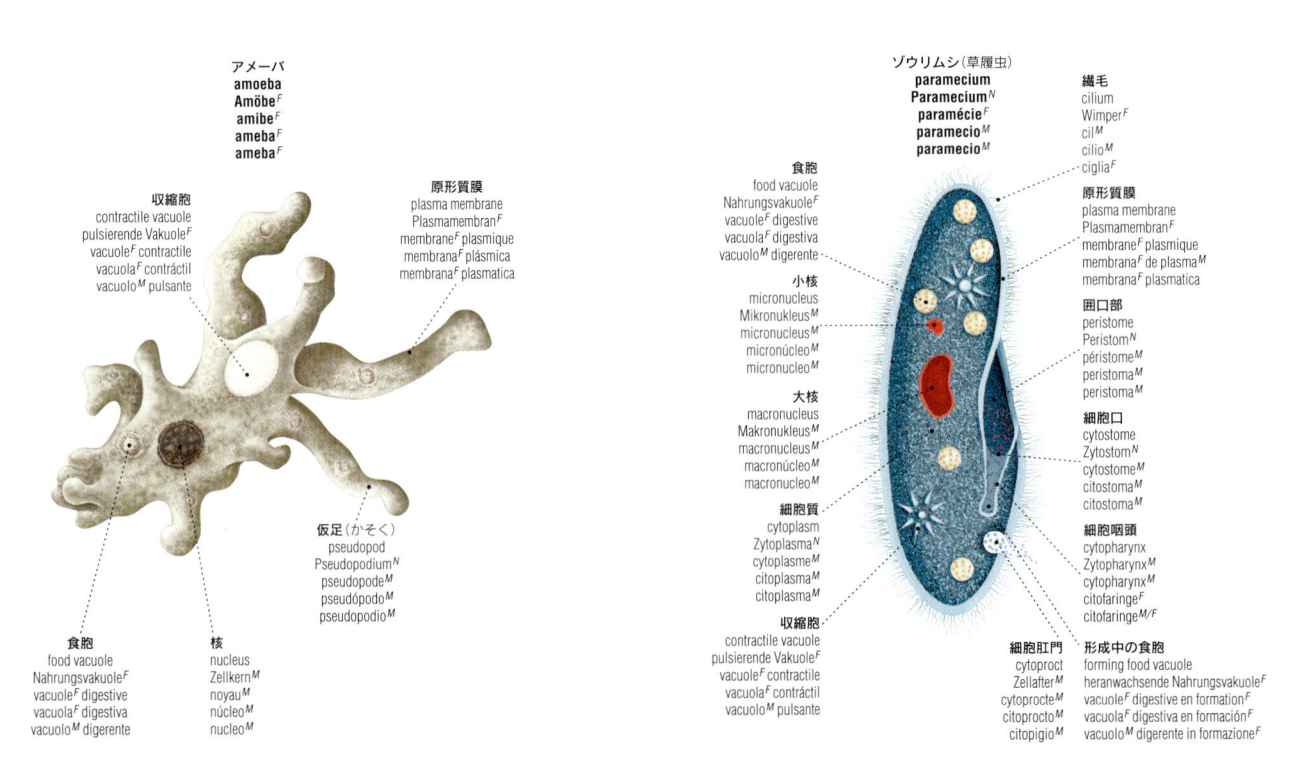

アメーバ
amoeba
Amöbe F
amibe F
ameba F
ameba F

ゾウリムシ(草履虫)
paramecium
Paramecium N
paramécie F
paramecio M
paramecio M

繊毛
cilium
Wimper F
cil M
cilio M
ciglia F

収縮胞
contractile vacuole
pulsierende Vakuole F
vacuole F contractile
vacuola F contráctil
vacuolo M pulsante

原形質膜
plasma membrane
Plasmamembran F
membrane F plasmique
membrana F plásmica
membrana F plasmatica

食胞
food vacuole
Nahrungsvakuole F
vacuole F digestive
vacuola F digestiva
vacuolo M digerente

原形質膜
plasma membrane
Plasmamembran F
membrane F plasmique
membrana F de plasma
membrana F plasmatica

小核
micronucleus
Mikronukleus M
micronucleus M
micronúcleo M
micronucleo M

囲口部
peristome
Peristom N
péristome M
peristoma M
peristoma M

大核
macronucleus
Makronukleus M
macronucleus M
macronúcleo M
macronucleo M

細胞口
cytostome
Zytostom N
cytostome M
citostoma M
citostoma M

細胞質
cytoplasm
Zytoplasma N
cytoplasme M
citoplasma M
citoplasma M

細胞咽頭
cytopharynx
Zytopharynx N
cytopharynx M
citofaringe F
citofaringe M/F

食胞
food vacuole
Nahrungsvakuole F
vacuola F digestive
vacuola F digestiva
vacuolo M digerente

核
nucleus
Zellkern M
noyau M
núcleo M
nucleo M

仮足(かそく)
pseudopod
Pseudopodium N
pseudopode M
pseudópodo M
pseudopodio M

収縮胞
contractile vacuole
pulsierende Vakuole F
vacuole F contractile
vacuola F contráctil
vacuolo M pulsante

細胞肛門
cytoproct
Zellafter M
cytoprocte M
citoprocto M
citopigio M

形成中の食胞
forming food vacuole
heranwachsende Nahrungsvakuole F
vacuole F digestive en formation F
vacuola F digestiva en formación F
vacuolo M digerente in formazione F

単純な生物と棘皮動物 | SIMPLE ORGANISMS AND ECHINODERMS
EINFACHE ORGANISMEN UND ECHINODERMEN | ORGANISMES SIMPLES ET ÉCHINODERMES | ORGANISMOS SIMPLES Y EQUINODERMOS | ORGANISMI SEMPLICI E ECHINODERMI

海綿動物

sponge | Schwamm[M] | éponge[F] | esponja[F] | spugna[F]

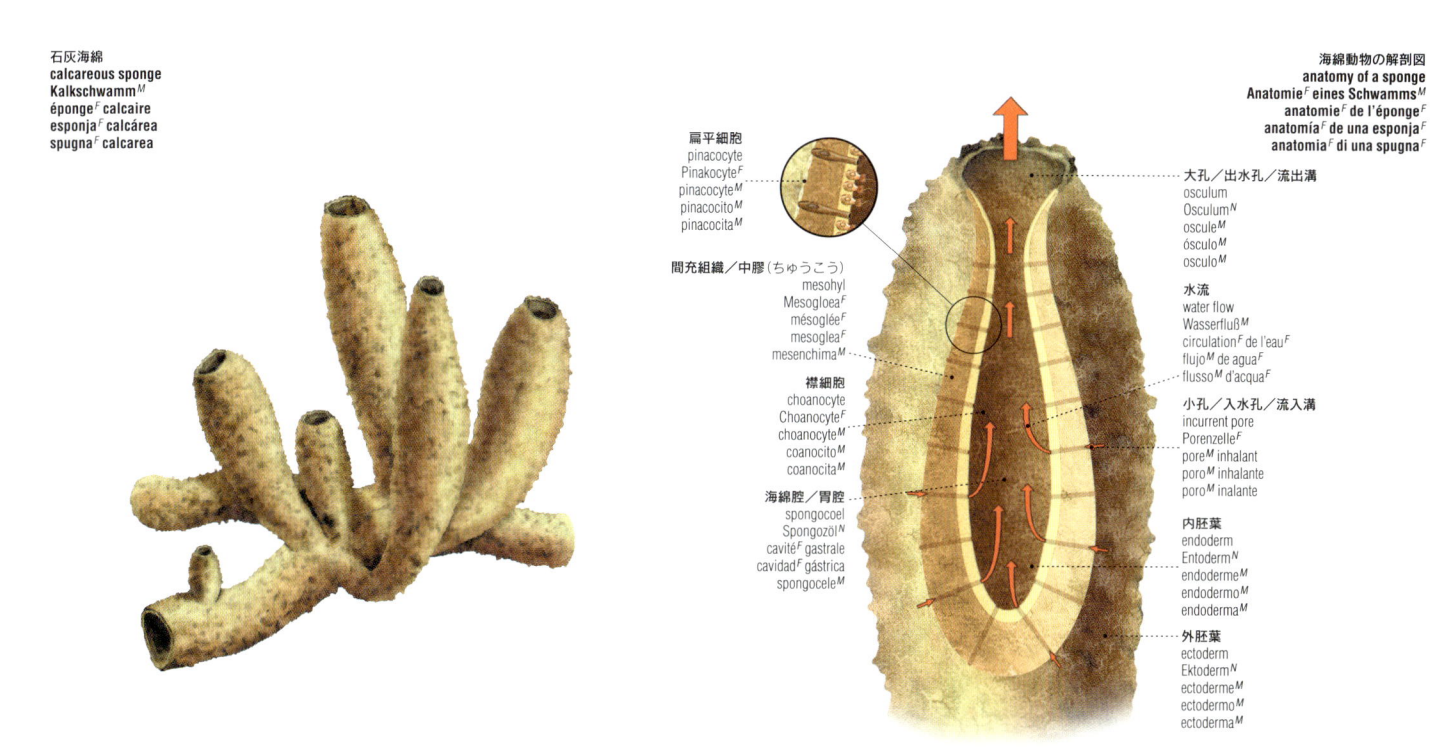

石灰海綿
calcareous sponge
Kalkschwamm[M]
éponge[F] calcaire
esponja[F] calcárea
spugna[F] calcarea

海綿動物の解剖図
anatomy of a sponge
Anatomie[F] eines Schwamms[M]
anatomie[F] de l'éponge[F]
anatomía[F] de una esponja[F]
anatomia[F] di una spugna[F]

扁平細胞
pinacocyte
Pinakocyte[F]
pinacocyte[M]
pinacocito[M]
pinacocita[M]

間充組織／中膠（ちゅうこう）
mesohyl
Mesogloea[F]
mésoglée[F]
mesoglea[F]
mesenchima[M]

襟細胞
choanocyte
Choanocyte[M]
choanocyte[M]
coanocito[M]
coanocita[M]

海綿腔／胃腔
spongocoel
Spongozöl[N]
cavité[F] gastrale
cavidad[F] gástrica
spongocele[M]

大孔／出水孔／流出溝
osculum
Osculum[N]
oscule[M]
ósculo[M]
osculo[M]

水流
water flow
Wasserfluß[M]
circulation[F] de l'eau[F]
flujo[M] de agua[F]
flusso[M] d'acqua[F]

小孔／入水孔／流入溝
incurrent pore
Porenzelle[F]
pore[M] inhalant
poro[M] inhalante
poro[M] inalante

内胚葉
endoderm
Entoderm[N]
endoderme[M]
endodermo[M]
endoderma[M]

外胚葉
ectoderm
Ektoderm[N]
ectoderme[M]
ectodermo[M]
ectoderma[M]

動物

棘皮（きょくひ）動物

echinoderms | Echinodermen[M] | échinodermes[M] | equinodermos[M] | echinodermi[M]

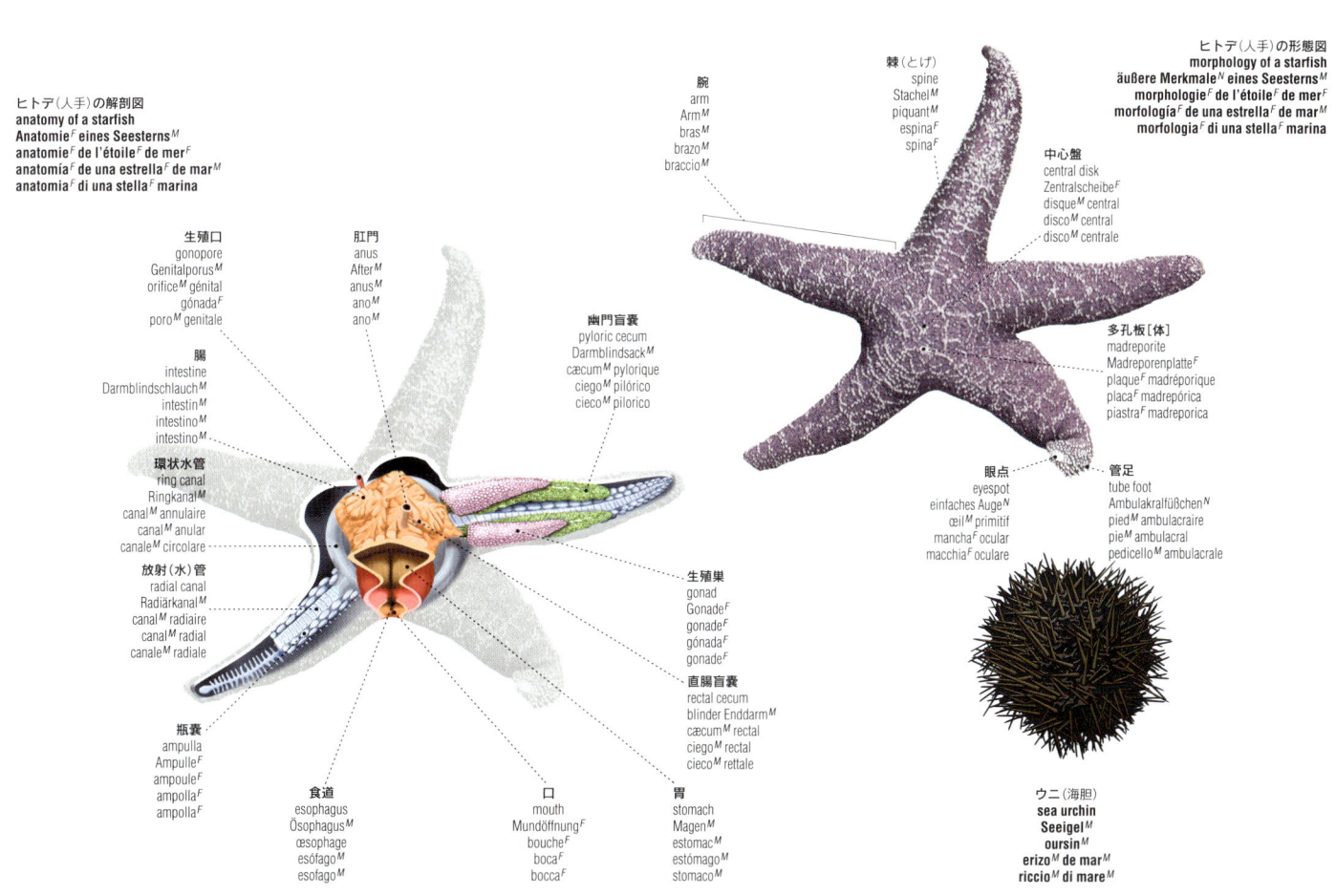

ヒトデ（人手）の解剖図
anatomy of a starfish
Anatomie[F] eines Seesterns[M]
anatomie[F] de l'étoile[F] de mer[F]
anatomía[F] de una estrella[F] de mar[M]
anatomia[F] di una stella[F] marina

生殖口
gonopore
Genitalporus[M]
orifice[M] génital
gónada[F]
poro[M] genitale

腸
intestine
Darmblindschlauch[M]
intestin[M]
intestino[M]
intestino[M]

環状水管
ring canal
Ringkanal[M]
canal[M] annulaire
canal[M] anular
canale[M] circolare

放射(水)管
radial canal
Radiärkanal[M]
canal[M] radiaire
canal[M] radial
canale[M] radiale

瓶嚢
ampulla
Ampulle[F]
ampoule[F]
ampolla[F]
ampolla[F]

肛門
anus
After[M]
anus[M]
ano[M]
ano[M]

幽門盲嚢
pyloric cecum
Darmblindsack[M]
cæcum[M] pylorique
ciego[M] pilórico
cieco[M] pilorico

生殖巣
gonad
Gonade[F]
gonade[F]
gónada[F]
gonade[F]

直腸盲嚢
rectal cecum
blinder Enddarm[M]
cæcum[M] rectal
ciego[M] rectal
cieco[M] rettale

食道
esophagus
Ösophagus[M]
œsophage[M]
esófago[M]
esofago[M]

口
mouth
Mundöffnung[F]
bouche[F]
boca[F]
bocca[F]

胃
stomach
Magen[M]
estomac[M]
estómago[M]
stomaco[M]

腕
arm
Arm[M]
bras[M]
brazo[M]
braccio[M]

棘（とげ）
spine
Stachel[M]
piquant[M]
espina[F]
spina[F]

ヒトデ（人手）の形態図
morphology of a starfish
äußere Merkmale[N] eines Seesterns[M]
morphologie[F] de l'étoile[F] de mer[F]
morfología[F] de una estrella[F] de mar[M]
morfologia[F] di una stella[F] marina

中心盤
central disk
Zentralscheibe[F]
disque[M] central
disco[M] central
disco[M] centrale

多孔板［体］
madreporite
Madreporenplatte[F]
plaque[F] madréporique
placa[F] madrepórica
piastra[F] madreporica

眼点
eyespot
einfaches Auge[N]
œil[M] primitif
mancha[F] ocular
macchia[F] oculare

管足
tube foot
Ambulakralfüßchen[N]
pied[M] ambulacraire
pie[M] ambulacral
pedicello[M] ambulacrale

ウニ（海胆）
sea urchin
Seeigel[M]
oursin[M]
erizo[M] de mar[M]
riccio[M] di mare[M]

95

昆虫とクモ類 | INSECTS AND ARACHNIDS
INSEKTEN UND SPINNENTIERE | INSECTES ET ARACHNIDES | INSECTOS Y ARÁCNIDOS | INSETTI E ARACNIDI

チョウ（蝶）

butterfly | Schmetterling[M] | papillon[M] | mariposa[F] | farfalla[F]

日本語 | 英語 | ドイツ語 | フランス語 | スペイン語 | イタリア語

チョウの形態図
morphology of a butterfly
äußere Merkmale[N] eines Schmetterlings[M]
morphologie[F] du papillon[M]
morfología[F] de una mariposa[F]
morfologia[F] di una farfalla[F]

翅室（ししつ）
cell
Zelle[F]
cellule[F]
celda[F]
cella[F]

前翅（ぜんし）
forewing
Vorderflügel[M]
aile[F] antérieure
ala[F] delantera
ala[F] anteriore

翅脈（しみゃく）
wing vein
Flügelader[F]
nervure[F]
nervio[M]
nervatura[F] alare

後翅（こうし）
hind wing
Hinterflügel[M]
aile[F] postérieure
ala[F] trasera
ala[F] posteriore

頭部
head
Kopf[M]
tête[F]
cabeza[F]
capo[M]

複眼
compound eye
Facettenauge[N]
œil[M] composé
ojo[M] compuesto
occhio[M] composto

下唇鬚（びん）
labial palp
Lippentaster[M]
palpe[M] labial
palpo[M] labial
palpo[M] labiale

触角
antenna
Antenne[F]
antenne[F]
antena[F]
antenna[F]

口吻
proboscis
Rüssel[M]
trompe[F]
probóscide[M]
proboscide[F]

胸部
thorax
Thorax[M]
thorax[M]
tórax[M]
torace[M]

前脚
foreleg
Vorderbein[N]
patte[F] antérieure
pata[F] delantera
zampa[F] anteriore

中脚
middle leg
Mittelbein[N]
patte[F] médiane
pata[F] media
zampa[F] mediana

後脚
hind leg
Hinterbein[N]
patte[F] postérieure
pata[F] trasera
zampa[F] posteriore

腹部
abdomen
Hinterleib[M]
abdomen[M]
abdomen[M]
addome[M]

気門
spiracle
Stigma[N]
stigmate[M]
estigma[M]
stigma[M]

後脚
hind leg
Hinterbein[N]
patte[F] postérieure
pata[F] trasera
zampa[F] posteriore

基節
coxa
Hüfte[F]
hanche[F]
coxa[F]
coxa[F]

転節
trochanter
Schenkelring[M]
trochanter[M]
trocánter[M]
trocantere[M]

腿節（たいせつ）
femur
Schenkel[M]
fémur[M]
fémur[M]
femore[M]

脛節（けいせつ）
tibia
Schiene[F]
tibia[M]
tibia[F]
tibia[F]

ふ節
tarsus
Fuß[M]
tarse[M]
tarso[M]
tarso[M]

爪
claw
Klaue[F]
griffe[F]
pinza[F]
unghia[F]

動物

96

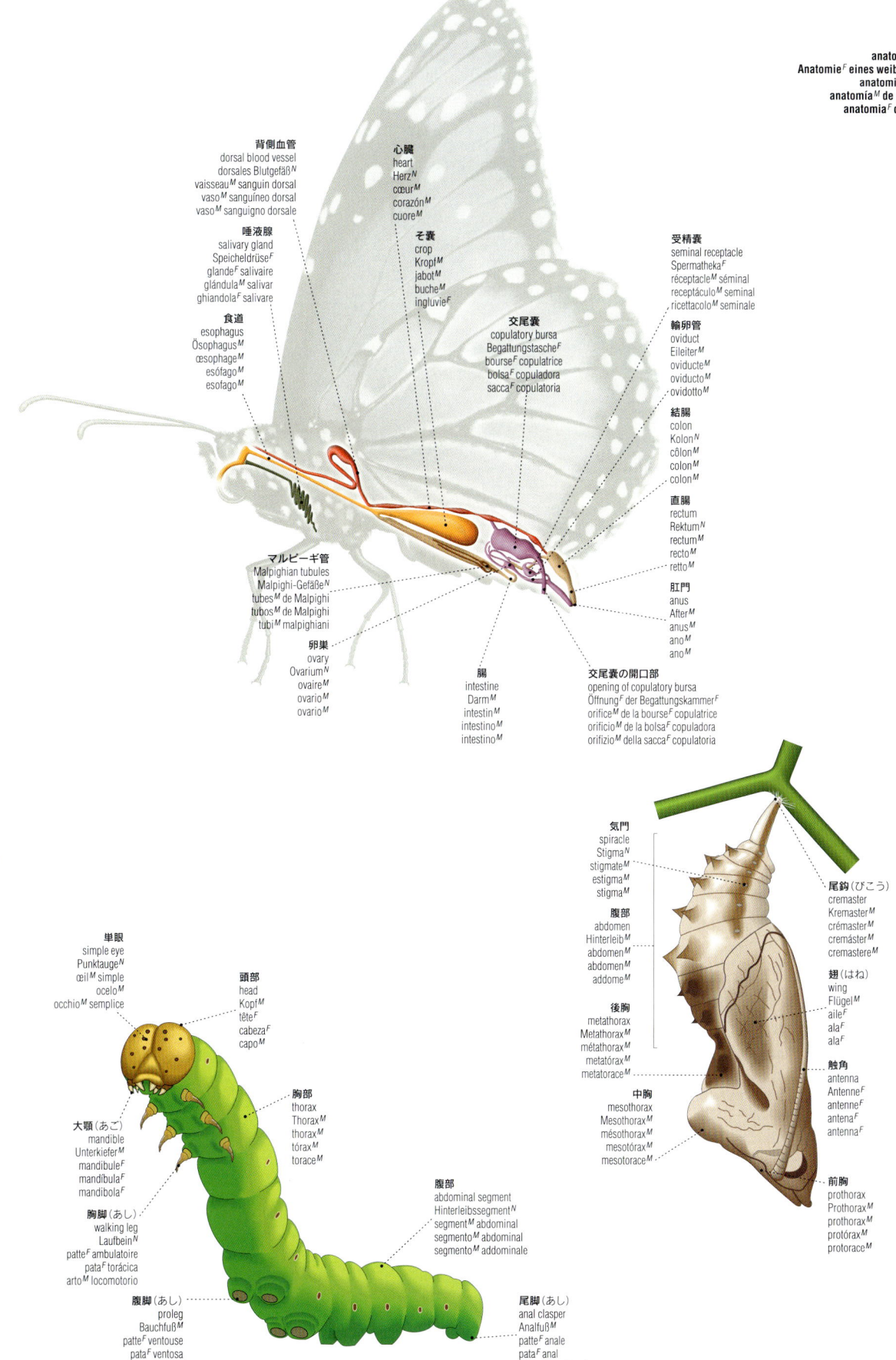

昆虫とクモ類 | INSECTS AND ARACHNIDS
INSEKTEN UND SPINNENTIERE | INSECTES ET ARACHNIDES | INSECTOS Y ARÁCNIDOS | INSETTI E ARACNIDI

チョウ（蝶）

雌のチョウの解剖図
anatomy of a female butterfly
Anatomie^F eines weiblichen Schmetterlings^M
anatomie^F du papillon^M femelle
anatomía^F de una mariposa^F hembra^F
anatomia^F di una farfalla^F femmina

動物

背側血管
dorsal blood vessel
dorsales Blutgefäß^N
vaisseau^M sanguin dorsal
vaso^M sanguíneo dorsal
vaso^M sanguigno dorsale

心臓
heart
Herz^N
cœur^M
corazón^M
cuore^M

唾液腺
salivary gland
Speicheldrüse^F
glande^F salivaire
glándula^M salivar
ghiandola^F salivare

そ嚢
crop
Kropf^M
jabot^M
buche^M
ingluvie^F

受精嚢
seminal receptacle
Spermatheka^F
réceptacle^M séminal
receptáculo^M seminal
ricettacolo^M seminale

食道
esophagus
Ösophagus^M
œsophage^M
esófago^M
esofago^M

交尾嚢
copulatory bursa
Begattungstasche^F
bourse^F copulatrice
bolsa^F copuladora
sacca^F copulatoria

輸卵管
oviduct
Eileiter^M
oviducte^M
oviducto^M
ovidotto^M

結腸
colon
Kolon^N
côlon^M
colon^M
colon^M

直腸
rectum
Rektum^N
rectum^M
recto^M
retto^M

マルピーギ管
Malpighian tubules
Malpighi-Gefäße^N
tubes^M de Malpighi
tubos^M de Malpighi
tubi^M malpighiani

肛門
anus
After^M
anus^M
ano^M
ano^M

卵巣
ovary
Ovarium^N
ovaire^M
ovario^M
ovario^M

腸
intestine
Darm^M
intestin^M
intestino^M
intestino^M

交尾嚢の開口部
opening of copulatory bursa
Öffnung^F der Begattungskammer^F
orifice^M de la bourse^F copulatrice
orificio^M de la bolsa^F copuladora
orifizio^M della sacca^F copulatoria

蛹（さなぎ）
chrysalis
Puppe^F
chrysalide^F
crisálida^F
crisalide^F

幼虫
caterpillar
Raupe^F
chenille^F
oruga^F
bruco^M

気門
spiracle
Stigma^N
stigmate^M
estigma^M
stigma^M

尾鈎（びこう）
cremaster
Kremaster^M
crémaster^M
cremáster^M
cremastere^M

単眼
simple eye
Punktauge^N
œil^M simple
ocelo^M
occhio^M semplice

頭部
head
Kopf^M
tête^F
cabeza^F
capo^M

腹部
abdomen
Hinterleib^M
abdomen^M
abdomen^M
addome^M

翅（はね）
wing
Flügel^M
aile^F
ala^F
ala^F

後胸
metathorax
Metathorax^M
métathorax^M
metatórax^M
metatorace^M

触角
antenna
Antenne^F
antenne^F
antena^F
antenna^F

大顎（あご）
mandible
Unterkiefer^M
mandibule^F
mandíbula^F
mandibola^F

胸部
thorax
Thorax^M
thorax^M
tórax^M
torace^M

中胸
mesothorax
Mesothorax^M
mésothorax^M
mesotórax^M
mesotorace^M

前胸
prothorax
Prothorax^M
prothorax^M
protórax^M
protorace^M

胸脚（あし）
walking leg
Laufbein^N
patte^F ambulatoire
pata^F torácica
arto^M locomotorio

腹部
abdominal segment
Hinterleibssegment^N
segment^M abdominal
segmento^M abdominal
segmento^M addominale

腹脚（あし）
proleg
Bauchfuß^M
patte^F ventouse
pata^F ventosa
falsa zampa^F

尾脚（あし）
anal clasper
Analfuß^M
patte^F anale
pata^F anal
falsa zampa^F anale

97

昆虫とクモ類 | INSECTS AND ARACHNIDS
INSEKTEN UND SPINNENTIERE | INSECTES ET ARACHNIDES | INSECTOS Y ARÁCNIDOS | INSETTI E ARACNIDI

ミツバチ（蜜蜂）

日本語 | 英語 | ドイツ語 | フランス語 | スペイン語 | イタリア語

honeybee | Honigbiene[F] | abeille[F] | abeja[F] | ape[F]

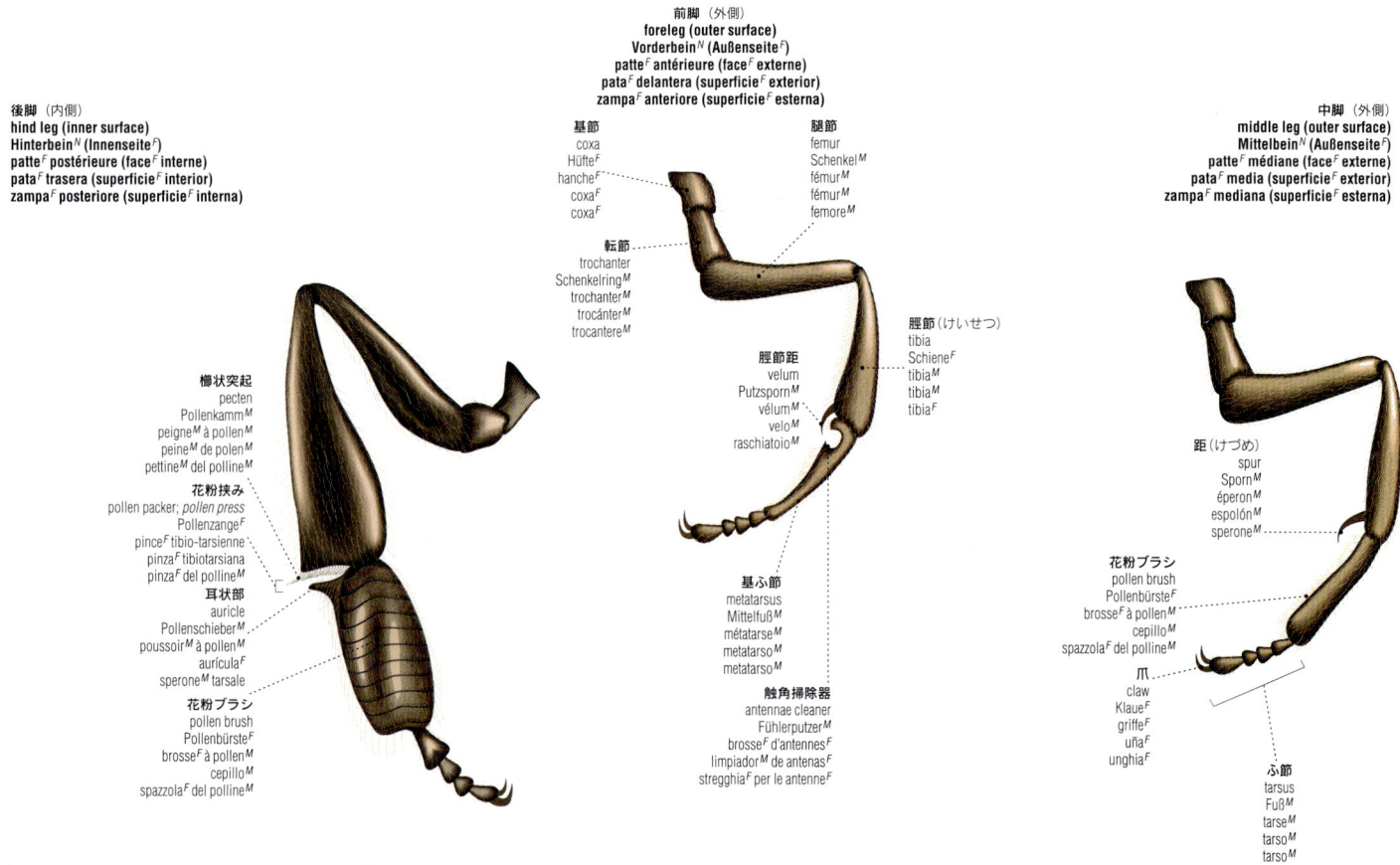

働きバチの形態図
morphology of a honeybee: worker
äußere Merkmale[N] einer Honigbiene[F]: Arbeiterin[F]
morphologie[F] de l'abeille[F] : ouvrière[F]
morfología[F] de una abeja[F] trabajadora
morfologia[F] di un'ape[F]: operaia

翅（はね）
wing
Flügel[M]
aile[F]
ala[F]
ala[F]

胸部
thorax
Thorax[M]
thorax[M]
tórax[M]
torace[M]

腹部
abdomen
Hinterleib[M]
abdomen[M]
abdomen[M]
addome[M]

複眼
compound eye
Facettenauge[N]
œil[M] composé
ojo[M] compuesto
occhio[M] composto

口器
mouthparts
Mundwerkzeuge[N]
pièces[F] buccales
apéndices[M] bucales
parti[F] boccali

毒針
sting
Stachel[M]
aiguillon[M]
aguijón[M]
pungiglione[M]

花粉かご
pollen basket
Pollenkörbchen[N]
corbeille[F] à pollen[M]
cestillo[M]
cestella[F]

触角
antenna
Antenne[F]
antenne[F]
antena[F]
antenna[F]

後脚
hind leg
Hinterbein[N]
patte[F] postérieure
pata[F] trasera
zampa[F] posteriore

中脚
middle leg
Mittelbein[N]
patte[F] médiane
pata[F] media
zampa[F] mediana

前脚
foreleg
Vorderbein[N]
patte[F] antérieure
pata[F] delantera
zampa[F] anteriore

前脚（外側）
foreleg (outer surface)
Vorderbein[N] (Außenseite[F])
patte[F] antérieure (face[F] externe)
pata[F] delantera (superficie[F] exterior)
zampa[F] anteriore (superficie[F] esterna)

後脚（内側）
hind leg (inner surface)
Hinterbein[N] (Innenseite[F])
patte[F] postérieure (face[F] interne)
pata[F] trasera (superficie[F] interior)
zampa[F] posteriore (superficie[F] interna)

中脚（外側）
middle leg (outer surface)
Mittelbein[N] (Außenseite[F])
patte[F] médiane (face[F] externe)
pata[F] media (superficie[F] exterior)
zampa[F] mediana (superficie[F] esterna)

基節
coxa
Hüfte[F]
hanche[F]
coxa[F]
coxa[F]

腿節
femur
Schenkel[M]
fémur[M]
fémur[M]
femore[M]

転節
trochanter
Schenkelring[M]
trochanter[M]
trocánter[M]
trocantere[M]

脛節距
velum
Putzsporn[M]
vélum[M]
velo[M]
raschiatoio[M]

脛節（けいせつ）
tibia
Schiene[F]
tibia[M]
tibia[M]
tibia[F]

距（けづめ）
spur
Sporn[M]
éperon[M]
espolón[M]
sperone[M]

櫛状突起
pecten
Pollenkamm[M]
peigne[M] à pollen[M]
peine[M] de polen[M]
pettine[M] del polline[M]

花粉挟み
pollen packer; pollen press
Pollenzange[F]
pince[F] tibio-tarsienne
pinza[F] tibiotarsiana
pinza[F] del polline[M]

耳状部
auricle
Pollenschieber[M]
poussoir[M] à pollen[M]
aurícula[F]
sperone[M] tarsale

花粉ブラシ
pollen brush
Pollenbürste[F]
brosse[F] à pollen[M]
cepillo[M]
spazzola[F] del polline[M]

基ふ節
metatarsus
Mittelfuß[M]
métatarse[M]
metatarso[M]
metatarso[M]

触角掃除器
antennae cleaner
Fühlerputzer[M]
peigne[M] d'antennes[F]
limpiador[M] de antenas[F]
streggia[F] per le antenne[F]

花粉ブラシ
pollen brush
Pollenbürste[F]
brosse[F] à pollen[M]
cepillo[M]
spazzola[F] del polline[M]

爪
claw
Klaue[F]
griffe[F]
uña[F]
unghia[F]

ふ節
tarsus
Fuß[M]
tarse[M]
tarso[M]
tarso[M]

98

昆虫とクモ類 | INSECTS AND ARACHNIDS
INSEKTEN UND SPINNENTIERE | INSECTES ET ARACHNIDES | INSECTOS Y ARÁCNIDOS | INSETTI E ARACNIDI

ミツバチ（蜜蜂）

ミツバチの解剖図
anatomy of a honeybee
Anatomie^F einer Honigbiene
anatomie^F de l'abeille^F
anatomía^F de una abeja^F
anatomia^F di un'ape^F

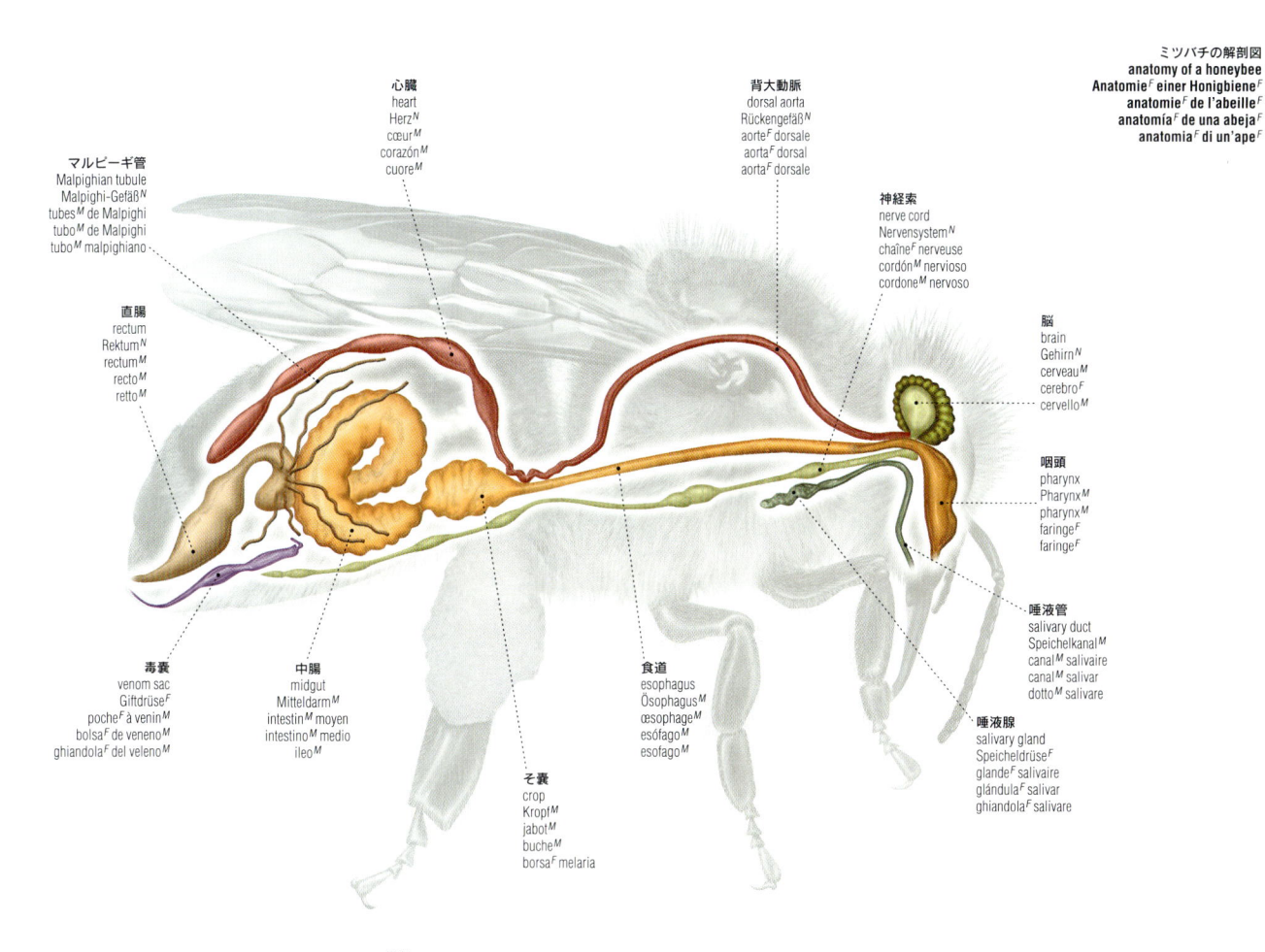

動物

マルピーギ管
Malpighian tubule
Malpighi-Gefäß^N
tubes^M de Malpighi
tubo de Malpighi
tubo^M malpighiano

心臓
heart
Herz^N
cœur^M
corazón^M
cuore^M

背大動脈
dorsal aorta
Rückengefäß^N
aorte^F dorsale
aorta^F dorsal
aorta^F dorsale

神経索
nerve cord
Nervensystem^N
chaîne^F nerveuse
cordón^M nervioso
cordone^M nervoso

脳
brain
Gehirn^N
cerveau^M
cerebro^F
cervello^M

直腸
rectum
Rektum^N
rectum^M
recto^M
retto^M

咽頭
pharynx
Pharynx^M
pharynx^M
faringe^F
faringe^F

唾液管
salivary duct
Speichelkanal^M
canal^M salivaire
canal^M salivar
dotto^M salivare

毒嚢
venom sac
Giftdrüse^F
poche^F à venin^M
bolsa^F de veneno^M
ghiandola^F del veleno^M

中腸
midgut
Mitteldarm^M
intestin^M moyen
intestino^M medio
ileo^M

食道
esophagus
Ösophagus^M
œsophage^M
esófago^M
esofago^M

唾液腺
salivary gland
Speicheldrüse^F
glande^F salivaire
glándula^F salivar
ghiandola^F salivare

そ嚢
crop
Kropf^M
jabot^M
buche^M
borsa^F melaria

頭部
head
Kopf^M
tête^F
cabeza^F
capo^M

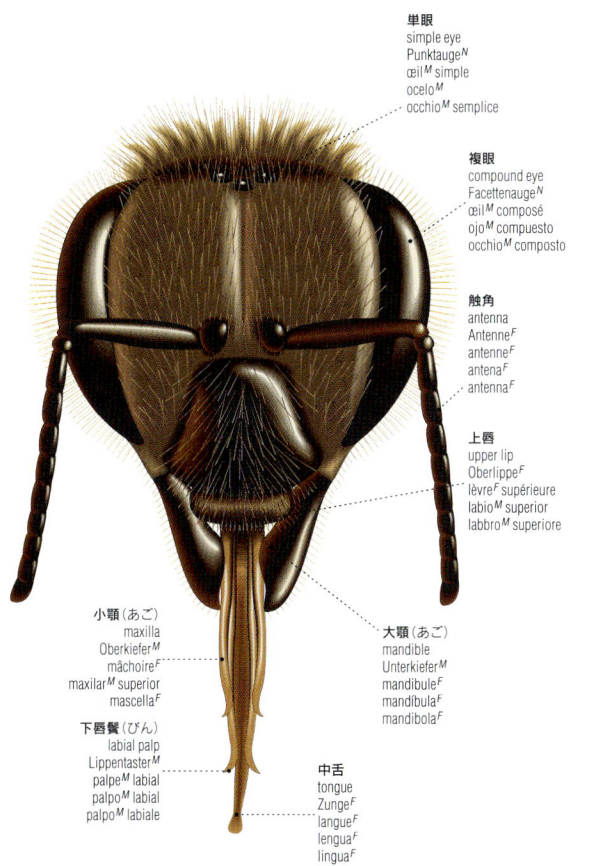

単眼
simple eye
Punktauge^N
œil^M simple
ocelo^M
occhio^M semplice

階級（型）
castes
Kasten^F
castes^F
castas^F
caste^F

複眼
compound eye
Facettenauge^N
œil^M composé
ojo^M compuesto
occhio^M composto

女王バチ
queen
Königin^F
reine^F
reina^F
ape^F regina

触角
antenna
Antenne^F
antenne^F
antena^F
antenna^F

上唇
upper lip
Oberlippe^F
lèvre^F supérieure
labio^M superior
labbro^M superiore

小顎（あご）
maxilla
Oberkiefer^M
mâchoire^F
maxilar^M superior
mascella^F

大顎（あご）
mandible
Unterkiefer^M
mandibule^F
mandíbula^F
mandibola^F

下唇鬚（びん）
labial palp
Lippentaster^M
palpe^M labial
palpo^M labial
palpo^M labiale

中舌
tongue
Zunge^F
langue^F
lengua^F
lingua^F

働きバチ
worker
Arbeiterin^F
ouvrière^F
obrera^F
ape^F operaia

雄（ミツ）バチ
drone
Drohne^F
faux bourdon^M
zángano^M
fuco^M

99

昆虫とクモ類 | INSECTS AND ARACHNIDS
INSEKTEN UND SPINNENTIERE | INSECTES ET ARACHNIDES | INSECTOS Y ARÁCNIDOS | INSETTI E ARACNIDI

ミツバチ（蜜蜂）

日本語 | 英語 | ドイツ語 | フランス語 | スペイン語 | イタリア語

ミツバチの巣箱
hive
Bienenstock^M
ruche^F
colmena^F
arnia^F

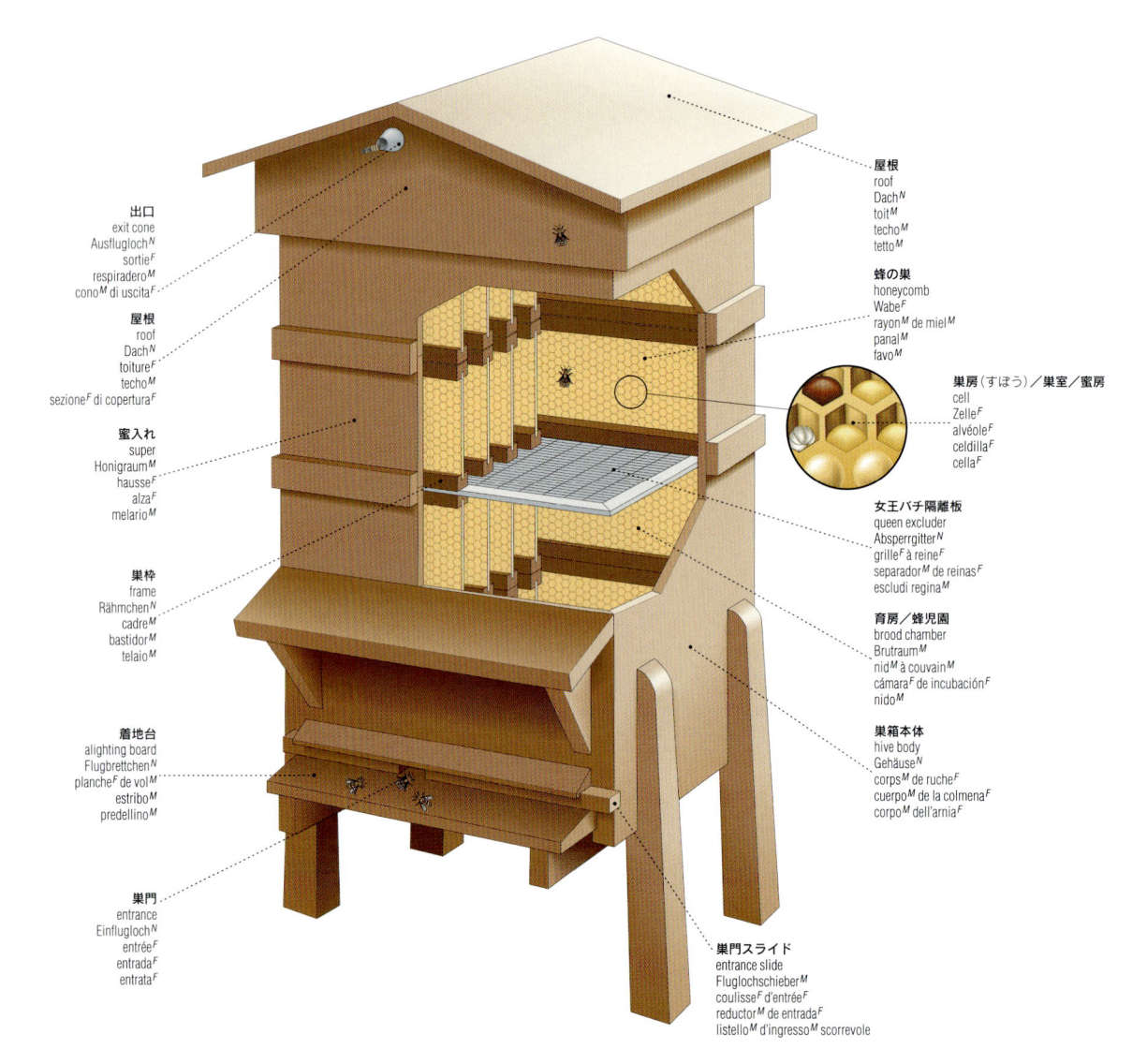

出口
exit cone
Ausflugloch^N
sortie^F
respiradero^M
cono^M di uscita^F

屋根
roof
Dach^N
toiture^F
techo^M
sezione^F di copertura^F

蜜入れ
super
Honigraum^M
hausse^F
alza^F
melario^M

巣枠
frame
Rähmchen^N
cadre^M
bastidor^M
telaio^M

着地台
alighting board
Flugbrettchen^N
planche^F de vol^M
estribo^M
predellino^M

巣門
entrance
Einflugloch^N
entrée^F
entrada^F
entrata^F

屋根
roof
Dach^N
toit^M
techo^M
tetto^M

蜂の巣
honeycomb
Wabe^F
rayon^M de miel^M
panal^M
favo^M

巣房（すぼう）／巣室／蜜房
cell
Zelle^F
alvéole^F
celdilla^F
cella^F

女王バチ隔離板
queen excluder
Absperrgitter^N
grille^F à reine^F
separador^M de reinas^F
escludi regina^M

育房／蜂児圏
brood chamber
Brutraum^M
nid^M à couvain^M
cámara^F de incubación^F
nido^M

巣箱本体
hive body
Gehäuse^N
corps^M de ruche^F
cuerpo^M de la colmena^F
corpo^M dell'arnia^F

巣門スライド
entrance slide
Fluglochschieber^M
coulisse^F d'entrée^F
reductor^M de entrada^F
listello^M d'ingresso^M scorrevole

ミツバチの巣の断面
honeycomb section
Wabenausschnitt^M
coupe^F d'un rayon^M de miel^M
corte^M de un panal^M
sezione^F del favo^M

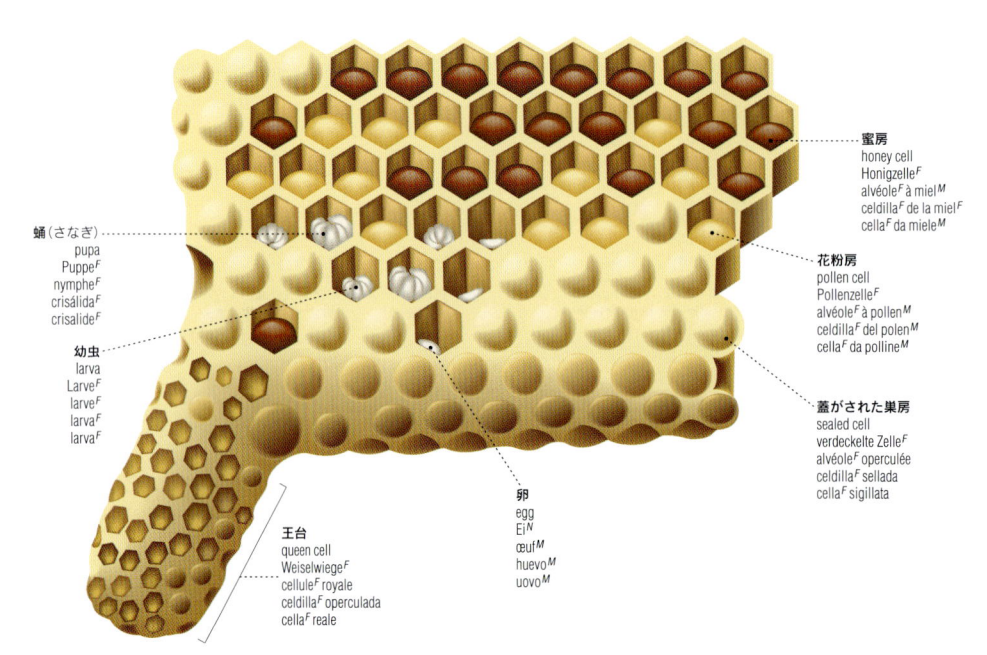

蛹（さなぎ）
pupa
Puppe^F
nymphe^F
crisálida^F
crisalide^F

幼虫
larva
Larve^F
larve^F
larva^F
larva^F

蜜房
honey cell
Honigzelle^F
alvéole^F à miel^M
celdilla^F de la miel^F
cella^F da miele^M

花粉房
pollen cell
Pollenzelle^F
alvéole^F à pollen^M
celdilla^F del polen^M
cella^F da polline^M

蓋がされた巣房
sealed cell
verdeckelte Zelle^F
alvéole^F operculée
celdilla^F sellada
cella^F sigillata

卵
egg
Ei^N
œuf^M
huevo^M
uovo^M

王台
queen cell
Weiselwiege^F
cellule^F royale
celdilla^F operculada
cella^F reale

昆虫とクモ類 | INSECTS AND ARACHNIDS
INSEKTEN UND SPINNENTIERE | INSECTES ET ARACHNIDES | INSECTOS Y ARÁCNIDOS | INSETTI E ARACNIDI

昆虫の例

examples of insects | Beispiele^N für Insekten^N | exemples^M d'insectes^M | ejemplos^M de insectos^M | esempi^M di insetti^M

動物

ノミ(蚤)
flea
Floh^M
puce^F
pulga
pulce^F

シラミ(虱)
louse
Laus^F
pou^M
piojo^M
pidocchio^M

カ(蚊)
mosquito
Moskito^M
moustique^M
mosquito^M
zanzara^F

ツェツェバエ(蠅)
tsetse fly
Tsetsefliege^F
mouche^F tsé-tsé
mosca^F tsetsé
mosca^F tse-tse

シロアリ(白蟻)
termite
Termite^F
termite^M
termita^F
termite^F

キクイムシ(木食い虫)
furniture beetle
Bockkäfer^M
petite vrillette^F
carcoma
tarlo^M

アリ(蟻)
ant
Ameise^F
fourmi^F
hormiga^F
formica^F

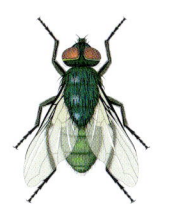

ハエ(蠅)
fly
Fliege^F
mouche^F
mosca^F
mosca^F

テントウムシ(天道虫)
ladybird beetle; *ladybird*
Marienkäfer^M
coccinelle^F
mariquita^F
coccinella^F

カメムシ(亀虫)
shield bug
Schildwanze^F
punaise^F rayée
chinche^F de campo^M
cimice^F rigata

シデムシ(埋葬虫)
sexton beetle
Totengräber^M
nécrophore^M
escarabajo^M necrófaro
necroforo^M

スズメバチ(雀蜂)
yellowjacket
Wespe^F
guêpe^F
avispa^F
vespa^F

モンスズメバチ(紋雀蜂)
hornet
Hornisse^F
frelon^M
avispón^M
calabrone^M

アブ(虻)
horsefly
Bremse^F
taon^M
tábano^M
tafano^M

マルハナバチ(丸[円]花蜂)
bumblebee
Hummel^F
bourdon^M
abejorro^M
bombo^M

トウヨウゴキブリ(東洋ごきぶり)
oriental cockroach
orientalische Schabe^F
blatte^F orientale
cucaracha^F oriental
blatta^F orientale

オオシモフリエダシャク(大霜降枝尺)
peppered moth
Birkenspanner^M
phalène^F du bouleau^M
polilla^F de abedul^M
falena^F della betulla^F

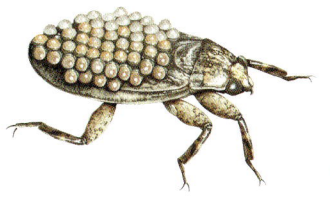

タガメ(田亀)
giant water bug
Riesenwasserwanze^F
punaise^F d'eau^F géante
chinche^F acuática gigante
cimice^F acquatica gigante

コフキコガネ(粉吹金亀子)
cockchafer
Maikäfer^M
hanneton^M
escarabajo^M
maggiolino^M

オオカバマダラ(大樺斑)
monarch butterfly
Monarchfalter^M
monarque^F
mariposa^F monarca^M
monarca^F

バッタ(飛蝗)
great green bush-cricket
Laubheuschrecke^F
grande sauterelle^F verte
saltamontes^M verde
cavalletta^F verde

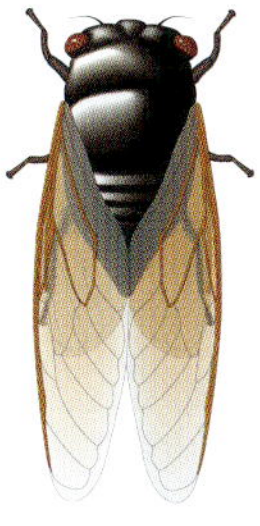

セミ(蟬)
cicada
Zikade^F
cigale^F
cigarra^F
cicala^F

昆虫とクモ類 | INSECTS AND ARACHNIDS
INSEKTEN UND SPINNENTIERE | INSECTES ET ARACHNIDES | INSECTOS Y ARÁCNIDOS | INSETTI E ARACNIDI

昆虫の例

日本語 | 英語 | ドイツ語 | フランス語 | スペイン語 | イタリア語

ヨナグニサン(与那国蚕)
atlas moth
Atlasspinner^M
atlas^M
oruga^F de polilla^F
Vanessa atalanta^F

アメンボ(水馬)
water strider
Wasserläufer^M
patineur^M d'eau^F
opilión^M
opilione^M

バッタ／イナゴ(蝗)
bow-winged grasshopper
Nachtigall^F-Grashüpfer^M
criquet^M mélodieux
grillo^M campestre
cavalletta^F

カマキリ(蟷螂)
mantid
Gottesanbeterin^F
mante^F religieuse
mantis^F religiosa
mantide^F religiosa

トンボ(蜻蛉)
dragonfly
Libelle^F
libellule^F
libélula^F
libellula^F

クモ類

examples of arachnids | Beispiele^N für Spinnentiere^N | exemples^M d'arachnides^M | ejemplos^M de arácnidos^M | esempi^M di aracnidi^M

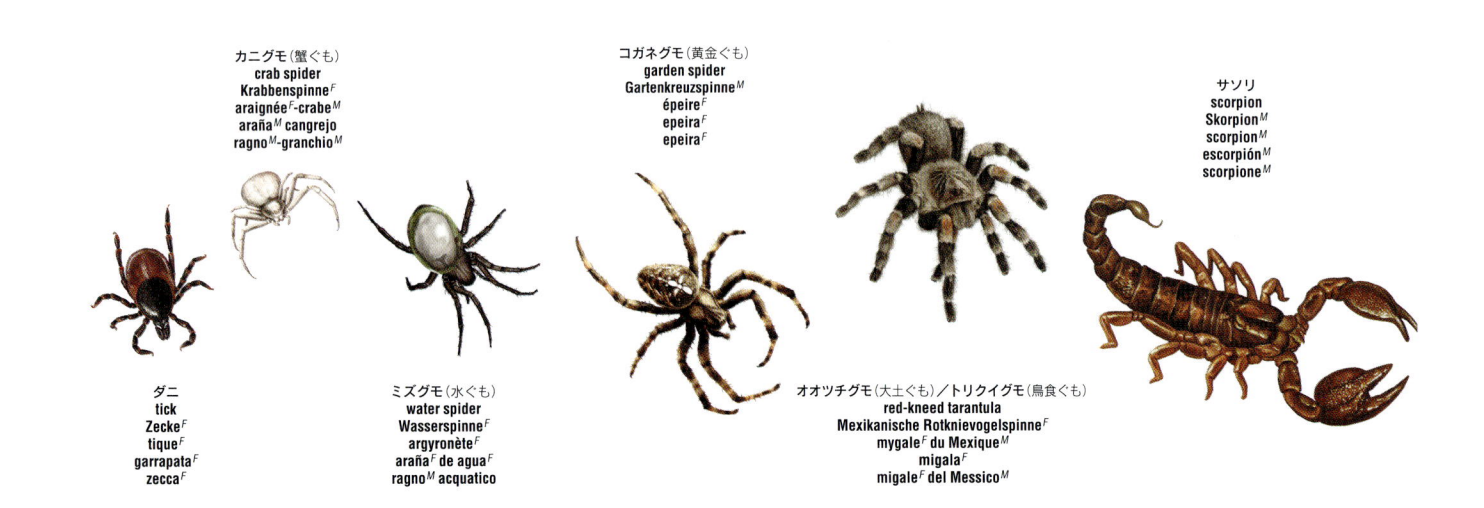

カニグモ(蟹ぐも)
crab spider
Krabbenspinne^F
araignée^F-crabe^M
araña^M cangrejo
ragno^M-granchio^M

コガネグモ(黄金ぐも)
garden spider
Gartenkreuzspinne^F
épeire^F
epeira^F
epeira^F

サソリ
scorpion
Skorpion^M
scorpion^M
escorpión^M
scorpione^M

ダニ
tick
Zecke^F
tique^F
garrapata^F
zecca^F

ミズグモ(水ぐも)
water spider
Wasserspinne^F
argyronète^F
araña^F de agua^F
ragno^M acquatico

オオツチグモ(大土ぐも)／トリクイグモ(鳥食ぐも)
red-kneed tarantula
Mexikanische Rotknievogelspinne^F
mygale^F du Mexique^M
migala^F
migale^F del Messico^M

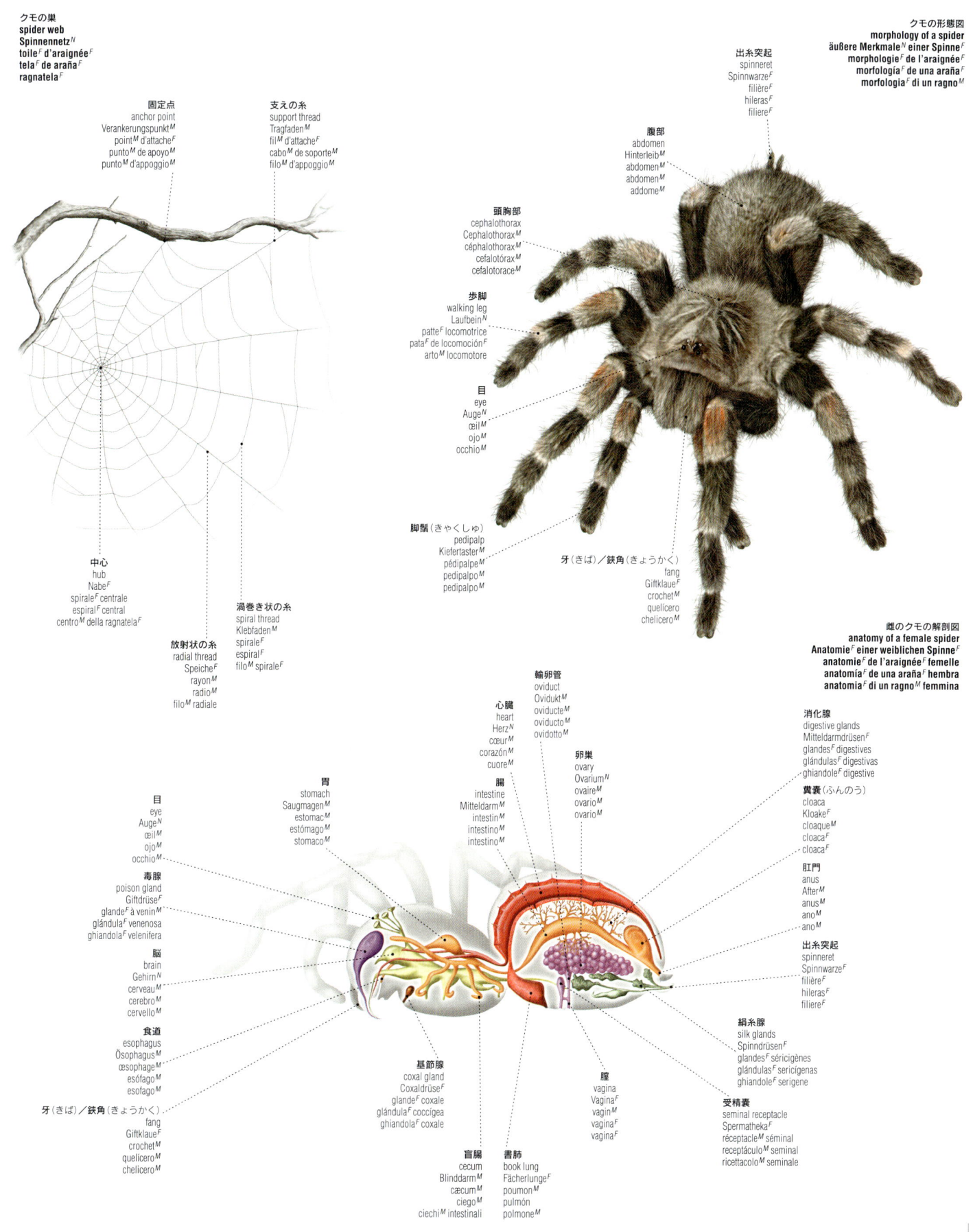

昆虫とクモ類 | INSECTS AND ARACHNIDS
INSEKTEN UND SPINNENTIERE | INSECTES ET ARACHNIDES | INSECTOS Y ARÁCNIDOS | INSETTI E ARACNIDI

クモ

spider | Spinne[F] | araignée[F] | araña[F] | ragno[M]

クモの巣
spider web
Spinnennetz[N]
toile[F] d'araignée[F]
tela[F] de araña[F]
ragnatela[F]

固定点
anchor point
Verankerungspunkt[M]
point[M] d'attache[F]
punto[M] de apoyo[M]
punto[M] d'appoggio[M]

支えの糸
support thread
Tragfaden[M]
fil[M] d'attache[F]
cabo[M] de soporte[M]
filo[M] d'appoggio[M]

中心
hub
Nabe[F]
spirale[F] centrale
espiral[F] central
centro[M] della ragnatela[F]

放射状の糸
radial thread
Speiche[F]
rayon[M]
radio[M]
filo[M] radiale

渦巻き状の糸
spiral thread
Klebfaden[M]
spirale[F]
espiral[F]
filo[M] spirale[F]

クモの形態図
morphology of a spider
äußere Merkmale[N] einer Spinne[F]
morphologie[F] de l'araignée[F]
morfología[F] de una araña[F]
morfologia[F] di un ragno[M]

出糸突起
spinneret
Spinnwarze[F]
filière[F]
hileras[F]
filiere[F]

腹部
abdomen
Hinterleib[M]
abdomen[M]
abdomen[M]
addome[M]

頭胸部
cephalothorax
Cephalothorax[M]
céphalothorax[M]
cefalotórax[M]
cefalotorace[M]

歩脚
walking leg
Laufbein[N]
patte[F] locomotrice
pata[F] de locomoción[F]
arto[M] locomotore

目
eye
Auge[N]
œil[M]
ojo[M]
occhio[M]

脚鬚（きゃくしゅ）
pedipalp
Kiefertaster[M]
pédipalpe[M]
pedipalpo[M]
pedipalpo[M]

牙（きば）／鋏角（きょうかく）
fang
Giftklaue[F]
crochet[M]
quelícero[M]
chelicero[M]

雌のクモの解剖図
anatomy of a female spider
Anatomie[F] einer weiblichen Spinne[F]
anatomie[F] de l'araignée[F] femelle
anatomía[F] de una araña[F] hembra
anatomia[F] di un ragno[M] femmina

目
eye
Auge[N]
œil[M]
ojo[M]
occhio[M]

毒腺
poison gland
Giftdrüse[F]
glande[F] à venin[M]
glándula[F] venenosa
ghiandola[F] velenifera

脳
brain
Gehirn[N]
cerveau[M]
cerebro[M]
cervello[M]

食道
esophagus
Ösophagus[M]
œsophage[M]
esófago[M]
esofago[M]

牙（きば）／鋏角（きょうかく）
fang
Giftklaue[F]
crochet[M]
quelícero[M]
chelicero[M]

胃
stomach
Saugmagen[M]
estomac[M]
estómago[M]
stomaco[M]

心臓
heart
Herz[N]
cœur[M]
corazón[M]
cuore[M]

腸
intestine
Mitteldarm[M]
intestin[M]
intestino[M]
intestino[M]

基節腺
coxal gland
Coxaldrüse[F]
glande[F] coxale
glándula[F] coccígea
ghiandola[F] coxale

盲腸
cecum
Blinddarm[M]
cæcum[M]
ciego[M]
ciechi[M] intestinali

輸卵管
oviduct
Ovidukt[M]
oviducte[M]
oviducto[M]
ovidotto[M]

卵巣
ovary
Ovarium[N]
ovaire[M]
ovario[M]
ovario[M]

膣
vagina
Vagina[F]
vagin[M]
vagina[F]
vagina[F]

書肺
book lung
Fächerlunge[F]
poumon[M]
pulmón[M]
polmone[M]

消化腺
digestive glands
Mitteldarmdrüsen[F]
glandes[F] digestives
glándulas[F] digestivas
ghiandole[F] digestive

糞嚢（ふんのう）
cloaca
Kloake[F]
cloaque[M]
cloaca[F]
cloaca[F]

肛門
anus
After[M]
anus[M]
ano[M]
ano[M]

出糸突起
spinneret
Spinnwarze[F]
filière[F]
hileras[F]
filiere[F]

絹糸腺
silk glands
Spinndrüsen[F]
glandes[F] séricigènes
glándulas[F] sericígenas
ghiandole[F] serigene

受精嚢
seminal receptacle
Spermatheka[F]
réceptacle[M] séminal
receptáculo[M] seminal
ricettacolo[M] seminale

動物

軟体動物 | MOLLUSKS
WEICHTIERE | MOLLUSQUES | MOLUSCOS | MOLLUSCHI

カタツムリ（蝸牛）

snail | Schnecke[F] | escargot[M] | caracol[M] | chiocciola[F]

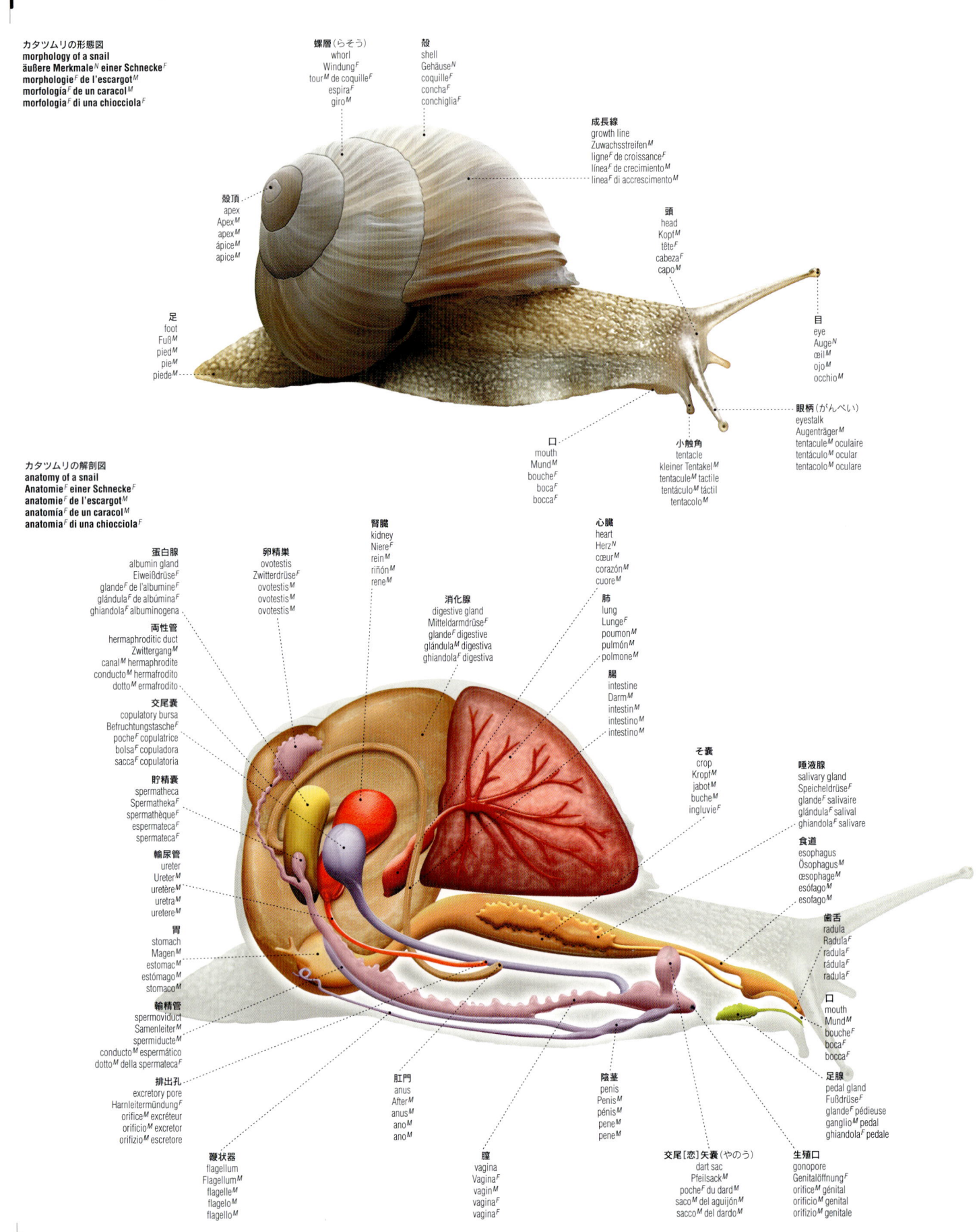

日本語 | 英語 | ドイツ語 | フランス語 | スペイン語 | イタリア語

カタツムリの形態図
morphology of a snail
äußere Merkmale[N] einer Schnecke[F]
morphologie[F] de l'escargot[M]
morfología[F] de un caracol[M]
morfologia[F] di una chiocciola[F]

螺層（らそう）
whorl
Windung[F]
tour[M] de coquille[F]
espira[F]
giro[M]

殻
shell
Gehäuse[N]
coquille[F]
concha[F]
conchiglia[F]

成長線
growth line
Zuwachsstreifen[M]
ligne[F] de croissance[F]
línea[F] de crecimiento[M]
linea[F] di accrescimento[M]

殻頂
apex
Apex[M]
apex[M]
ápice[M]
apice[M]

頭
head
Kopf[M]
tête[F]
cabeza[F]
capo[M]

足
foot
Fuß[M]
pied[M]
pie[M]
piede[M]

目
eye
Auge[N]
œil[M]
ojo[M]
occhio[M]

眼柄（がんぺい）
eyestalk
Augenträger[M]
tentacule[M] oculaire
tentáculo[M] ocular
tentacolo[M] oculare

口
mouth
Mund[M]
bouche[F]
boca[F]
bocca[F]

小触角
tentacle
kleiner Tentakel[M]
tentacule[M] tactile
tentáculo[M] táctil
tentacolo[M]

カタツムリの解剖図
anatomy of a snail
Anatomie[F] einer Schnecke[F]
anatomie[F] de l'escargot[M]
anatomía[F] de un caracol[M]
anatomia[F] di una chiocciola[F]

蛋白腺
albumin gland
Eiweißdrüse[F]
glande[F] de l'albumine[F]
glándula[F] de albúmina[F]
ghiandola[F] albuminogena

卵精巣
ovotestis
Zwitterdrüse[F]
ovotestis[M]
ovotestis[M]
ovotestis[M]

腎臓
kidney
Niere[F]
rein[M]
riñón[M]
rene[M]

消化腺
digestive gland
Mitteldarmdrüse[F]
glande[F] digestive
glándula[M] digestiva
ghiandola[F] digestiva

心臓
heart
Herz[N]
cœur[M]
corazón[M]
cuore[M]

肺
lung
Lunge[F]
poumon[M]
pulmón[M]
polmone[M]

両性管
hermaphroditic duct
Zwittergang[M]
canal[M] hermaphrodite
conducto[M] hermafrodito
dotto[M] ermafrodito

腸
intestine
Darm[M]
intestin[M]
intestino[M]
intestino[M]

交尾嚢
copulatory bursa
Befruchtungstasche[F]
poche[F] copulatrice
bolsa[F] copuladora
sacca[F] copulatoria

そ嚢
crop
Kropf[M]
jabot[M]
buche[M]
ingluvie[F]

唾液腺
salivary gland
Speicheldrüse[F]
glande[F] salivaire
glándula[F] salival
ghiandola[F] salivare

貯精嚢
spermatheca
Spermatheka[F]
spermathèque[F]
espermateca[F]
spermateca[F]

食道
esophagus
Ösophagus[M]
œsophage[M]
esófago[M]
esofago[M]

輸尿管
ureter
Ureter[M]
uretère[M]
uretra[F]
uretere[M]

胃
stomach
Magen[M]
estomac[M]
estómago[M]
stomaco[M]

歯舌
radula
Radula[F]
radula[F]
rádula[F]
radula[F]

輸精管
spermoviduct
Samenleiter[M]
spermiducte[M]
conducto[M] espermático
dotto[M] della spermateca[F]

口
mouth
Mund[M]
bouche[F]
boca[F]
bocca[F]

排出孔
excretory pore
Harnleitermündung[F]
orifice[M] excréteur
orificio[M] excretor
orifizio[M] escretore

肛門
anus
After[M]
anus[M]
ano[M]
ano[M]

陰茎
penis
Penis[M]
pénis[M]
pene[M]
pene[M]

足腺
pedal gland
Fußdrüse[F]
glande[F] pédieuse
ganglio[M] pedal
ghiandola[F] pedale

鞭状器
flagellum
Flagellum[M]
flagellum[M]
flagelo[M]
flagello[M]

膣
vagina
Vagina[F]
vagin[M]
vagina[F]
vagina[F]

交尾[恋]矢嚢（やのう）
dart sac
Pfeilsack[M]
poche[F] du dard
saco[M] del aguijón[M]
sacco[M] del dardo[M]

生殖口
gonopore
Genitalöffnung[F]
orifice[M] génital
orificio[M] genital
orifizio[M] genitale

軟体動物 | MOLLUSKS
WEICHTIERE | MOLLUSQUES | MOLUSCOS | MOLLUSCHI

巻き貝

univalve shell | einschalige Muschel^F | coquillage^M univalve | concha^F univalva | conchiglia^F univalve

巻き貝の形態図
morphology of a univalve shell
äußere Merkmale^N einer einschaligen Muschel^F
morphologie^F du coquillage^M univalve
morfología de una concha^F univalva
morfologia^F di una conchiglia^F univalve

- 殻頂 / apex / Apex^M / apex^M / ápice^M / apice^M
- 胎殻／原殻 / nuclear whorl / Embryonalgewinde^N / tour^M embryonnaire / espiral^F embrionaria / giro^M embrionale
- 殻軸 / columella / Spindel^F / columelle^F / columela^F / columella^F
- 次体層 / whorl / Windung^F / tour^M de spire / espiral^F / giro^M della spira
- 縦張肋（じゅうちょうろく）/ axial rib / Axialrippe^F / côte^F axiale / costilla^F axial / costa^F assiale
- 縫合 / suture / Naht^F / ligne^F de suture / sutura^F / sutura^F
- 螺肋（らろく）/ spiral rib / Spiralskulptur^F / côte^F spiralée / costilla^F espiral / costa^F spirale
- 殻口 / aperture / Mündung^F / ouverture^F / apertura^F terminal / apertura^F
- 外唇 / outer lip / Außenlippe^F / bord^M externe / labio^M externo / labbro^M esterno
- 軸ひだ / columella fold / Spindelfalte^F / pli^M de la columelle / pliegue^M de la columela / piega^F della columella
- 内唇 / inner lip / Innenlippe^F / bord^M interne / labio^M interno / labbro^M interno
- 水管溝 / siphonal canal / Siphonalkanal^M / canal^M siphonal / canal^M del sifón / canale^M del sifone

動物

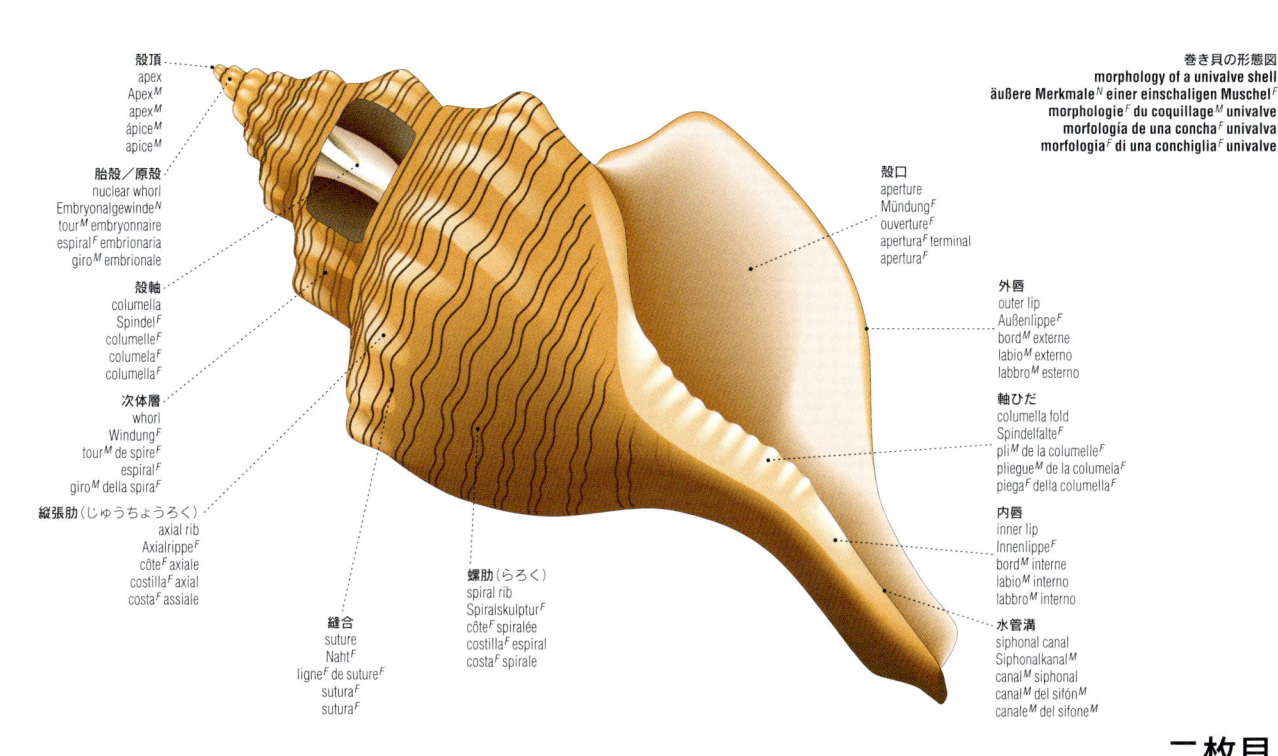

二枚貝

bivalve shell | zweischalige Muschel^F | coquillage^M bivalve | concha^F bibalva | conchiglia^F bivalve

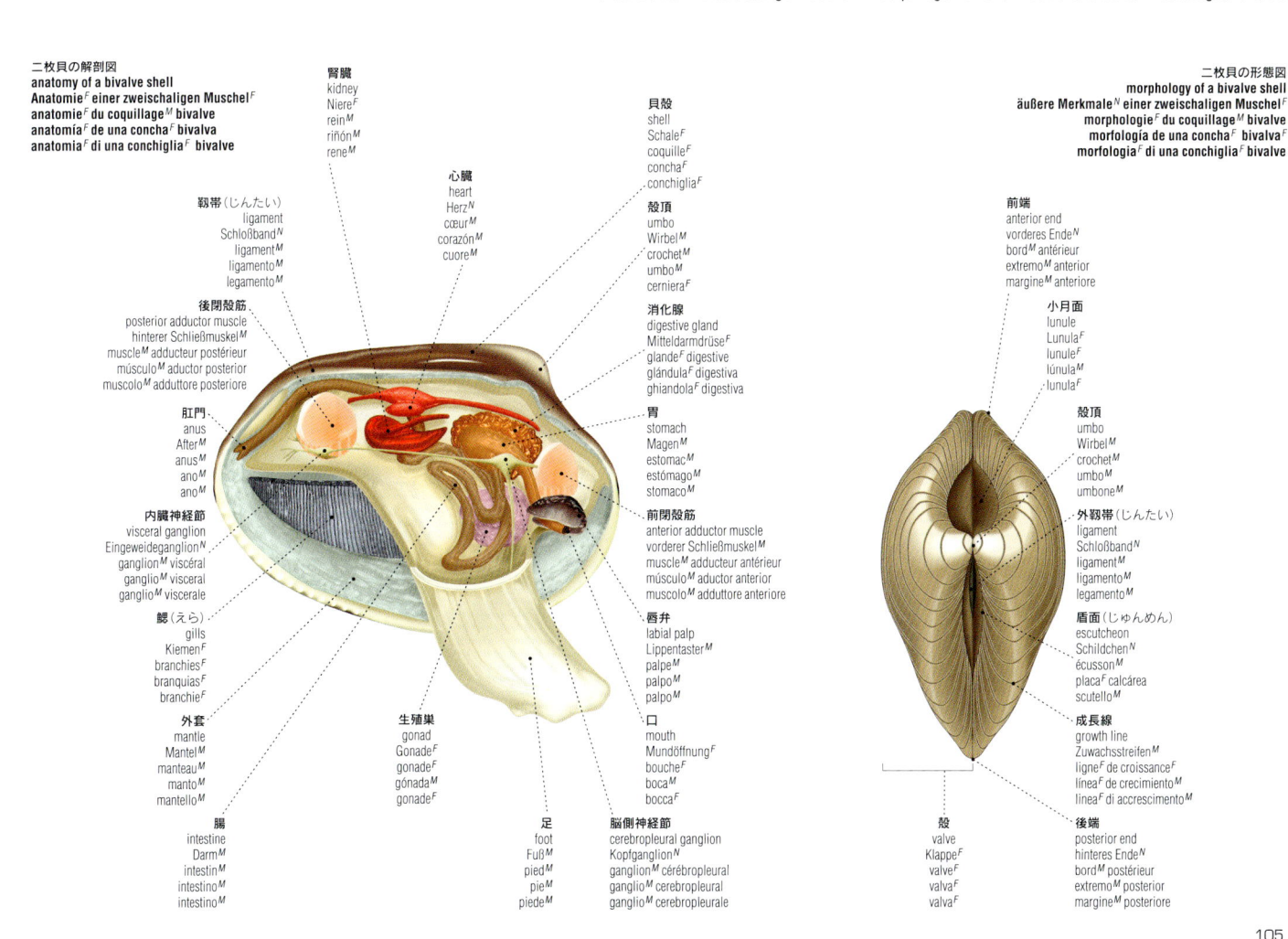

二枚貝の解剖図
anatomy of a bivalve shell
Anatomie^F einer zweischaligen Muschel^F
anatomie^F du coquillage^M bivalve
anatomía^F de una concha^F bivalva
anatomia^F di una conchiglia^F bivalve

- 靱帯（じんたい）/ ligament / Schloßband^N / ligament^M / ligamento^M / legamento^M
- 後閉殻筋 / posterior adductor muscle / hinterer Schließmuskel^M / muscle^M adducteur postérieur / músculo^M aductor posterior / muscolo^M adduttore posteriore
- 肛門 / anus / After^M / anus^M / ano^M / ano^M
- 内臓神経節 / visceral ganglion / Eingeweideganglion^N / ganglion^M viscéral / ganglio^M visceral / ganglio^M viscerale
- 鰓（えら）/ gills / Kiemen^F / branchies^F / branquias^F / branchie^F
- 外套 / mantle / Mantel^M / manteau^M / manto^M / mantello^M
- 腸 / intestine / Darm^M / intestin^M / intestino^M / intestino^M
- 腎臓 / kidney / Niere^F / rein^M / riñón^M / rene^M
- 心臓 / heart / Herz^N / cœur^M / corazón^M / cuore^M
- 消化腺 / digestive gland / Mitteldarmdrüse^F / glande^F digestive / glándula^F digestiva / ghiandola^F digestiva
- 胃 / stomach / Magen^M / estomac^M / estómago^M / stomaco^M
- 前閉殻筋 / anterior adductor muscle / vorderer Schließmuskel^M / muscle^M adducteur antérieur / músculo^M aductor anterior / muscolo^M adduttore anteriore
- 唇弁 / labial palp / Lippentaster^M / palpe^M / palpo^M / palpo^M
- 生殖巣 / gonad / Gonade^F / gonade^F / gónada^F / gonade^F
- 足 / foot / Fuß^M / pied^M / pie^M / piede^M
- 脳側神経節 / cerebropleural ganglion / Kopfganglion^N / ganglion^M cérébropleural / ganglio^M cerebropleural / ganglio^M cerebropleurale
- 口 / mouth / Mundöffnung^F / bouche^F / boca^F / bocca^F
- 貝殻 / shell / Schale^F / coquille^F / concha^F / conchiglia^F
- 殻頂 / umbo / Wirbel^M / crochet^M / umbo^M / cerniera^F
- 殻 / valve / Klappe^F / valve^F / valva^F / valva^F

二枚貝の形態図
morphology of a bivalve shell
äußere Merkmale^N einer zweischaligen Muschel^F
morphologie^F du coquillage^M bivalve
morfología de una concha^F bivalva^F
morfologia^F di una conchiglia^F bivalve

- 前端 / anterior end / vorderes Ende^N / bord^M antérieur / extremo^M anterior / margine^M anteriore
- 小月面 / lunule / Lunula^F / lunule^F / lúnula^M / lunula^F
- 殻頂 / umbo / Wirbel^M / crochet^M / umbo^M / umbone^M
- 外靱帯（じんたい）/ ligament / Schloßband^N / ligament^M / ligamento^M / legamento^M
- 盾面（じゅんめん）/ escutcheon / Schildchen^N / écusson^M / placa^F calcárea / scutello^M
- 成長線 / growth line / Zuwachsstreifen^M / ligne^F de croissance / línea^F de crecimiento / linea^F di accrescimento
- 後端 / posterior end / hinteres Ende^N / bord^M postérieur / extremo^M posterior / margine^M posteriore

105

軟体動物 | MOLLUSKS
WEICHTIERE | MOLLUSQUES | MOLUSCOS | MOLLUSCHI

タコ（蛸）

octopus | Tintenfisch^M | pieuvre^F | pulpo^M | polpo^M

日本語 | 英語 | ドイツ語 | フランス語 | スペイン語 | イタリア語

タコの形態図
morphology of an octopus
äußere Merkmale^N eines Tintenfischs^M
morphologie^F de la pieuvre^F
morfología^F de un pulpo^M
morfologia^F di un polpo^M

水管
siphon
Trichter^M
entonnoir^M
sifón^M
sifone^M

目
eye
Auge^N
œil^M
ojo^M
occhio^M

触腕
tentacle
Tentakel^M
tentacule^M
tentáculo^M
tentacolo^M

外套
mantle
Mantel^M
manteau^M
manto^M
mantello^M

吸盤
sucker
Saugnapf^M
ventouse^F
ventosa^F
ventosa^F

タコの解剖図
anatomy of an octopus
Anatomie^F eines Tintenfischs^M
anatomie^F de la pieuvre^F
anatomía^F de un pulpo^M
anatomia^F di un polpo^M

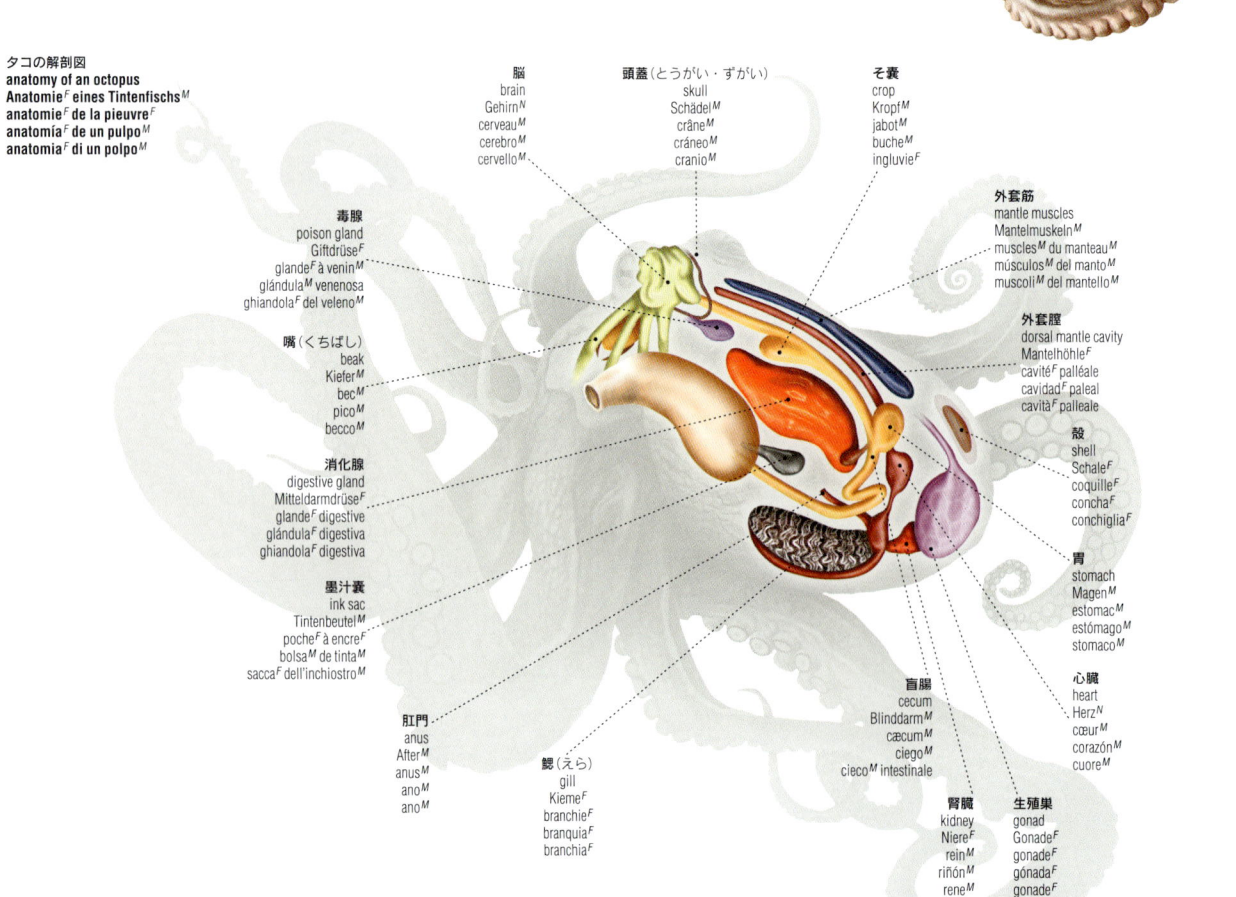

脳
brain
Gehirn^N
cerveau^M
cerebro^M
cervello^M

頭蓋（とうがい・ずがい）
skull
Schädel^M
crâne^M
cráneo^M
cranio^M

そ嚢
crop
Kropf^M
jabot^M
buche^F
ingluvie^F

毒腺
poison gland
Giftdrüse^F
glande^F à venin^M
glándula^F venenosa
ghiandola^F del veleno^M

外套筋
mantle muscles
Mantelmuskeln^M
muscles^M du manteau^M
músculos^M del manto^M
muscoli^M del mantello^M

嘴（くちばし）
beak
Kiefer^M
bec^M
pico^M
becco^M

外套腔
dorsal mantle cavity
Mantelhöhle^F
cavité^F palléale
cavidad^F paleal
cavità^F palleale

消化腺
digestive gland
Mitteldarmdrüse^F
glande^F digestive
glándula^F digestiva
ghiandola^F digestiva

殻
shell
Schale^F
coquille^F
concha^F
conchiglia^F

墨汁嚢
ink sac
Tintenbeutel^M
poche^F à encre^F
bolsa^F de tinta^M
sacca^F dell'inchiostro^M

胃
stomach
Magen^M
estomac^M
estómago^M
stomaco^M

肛門
anus
After^M
anus^M
ano^M
ano^M

盲腸
cecum
Blinddarm^M
cæcum^M
ciego^M
cieco^M intestinale

心臓
heart
Herz^N
cœur^M
corazón^M
cuore^M

鰓（えら）
gill
Kieme^F
branchie^F
branquia^F
branchia^F

腎臓
kidney
Niere^F
rein^M
riñón^M
rene^M

生殖巣
gonad
Gonade^F
gonade^F
gónada^F
gonade^F

甲殻類 | CRUSTACEANS
KREBSE | CRUSTACÉS | CRUSTÁCEOS | CROSTACEI

ロブスター

lobster | Hummer^M | homard^M | bogavante^M | astice^M

ロブスターの形態図
morphology of a lobster
äußere Merkmale^N eines Hummers^M
morphologie^F du homard^M
morfología de un bogavante^M
morfologia^F di un astice^M

胸脚
thoracic legs
Brustbeine^N
pattes^F thoraciques
apéndices^M torácicos
arti^M toracici

腹部
abdomen
Hinterleib^N
abdomen^M
abdomen^M
addome^M

尾
tail
Schwanz^M
nageoire^F caudale
cola^F
coda^F

頭胸部
cephalothorax
Kopfbruststück^N
céphalothorax^M
cefalotórax^M
cefalotorace^M

小触角／第一触角
antennule
Antennula^F
antennule^F
anténula^F
antennula^F

目
eye
Auge^N
œil^M
ojo^M
occhio^M

尾節
telson
Telson^N
telson^M
telson^M
telson^M

尾脚
uropod
Schwanzfächer^M
uropode^M
urópodo^M
uropodio^M

大触角／第二触角
antenna
Antenne^F
antenne^F
antena^F
antenna^F

はさみ
claw
Schere^F
pince^F
pinza^F
chela^F

頭胸甲
carapace
Carapax^M
carapace^F
caparazón^M
carapace^M

爪
claw
Klaue^F
griffe^F
pinza^F
unghia^F

動物

ロブスターの解剖図
anatomy of a lobster
Anatomie^F eines Hummers^M
anatomie^F du homard^M
anatomía^F de un bogavante^M
anatomia^F di un astice^M

脳
brain
Gehirn^N
cerveau^M
cerebro^M
cervello^M

緑腺
green gland
Nephridium^N
néphridie^F
nefridio^M
nefridio^M

口
mouth
Mund^M
bouche^F
boca^F
bocca^F

消化腺
digestive gland
Mitteldarmdrüse^F
glande^F digestive
glándula^F digestiva
ghiandola^F digestiva

前胃
cardiac stomach
Magenmund^M
estomac^M cardiaque
estómago^M cardíaco
stomaco^M cardiaco

胸骨動脈
sternal artery
Sternalarterie^F
artère^F sternale
arteria^F esternal
arteria^F sternale

後胃
pyloric stomach
Magenpförtner^M
estomac^M pylorique
estómago^M pilórico
stomaco^M pilorico

心臓
heart
Herz^N
cœur^M
corazón^M
cuore^M

腹動脈
ventral abdominal artery
Baucharterie^F
artère^F abdominale ventrale
arteria^F ventral
arteria^F ventrale

精巣
testis
Hoden^M
testicules^M
testículos^M
testicoli^M

腹背動脈
dorsal abdominal artery
Abdomenarterie^F
artère^F abdominale dorsale
arteria^F dorsoabdominal
arteria^F addominale dorsale

腸
intestine
Darm^M
intestin^M
intestino^M
intestino^M

腹神経索
ventral nerve cord
ventraler Nervenstrang^M
chaîne^F nerveuse ventrale
cordón^F nervioso ventral
cordone^M nervoso ventrale

肛門
anus
After^M
anus^M
ano^M
ano^M

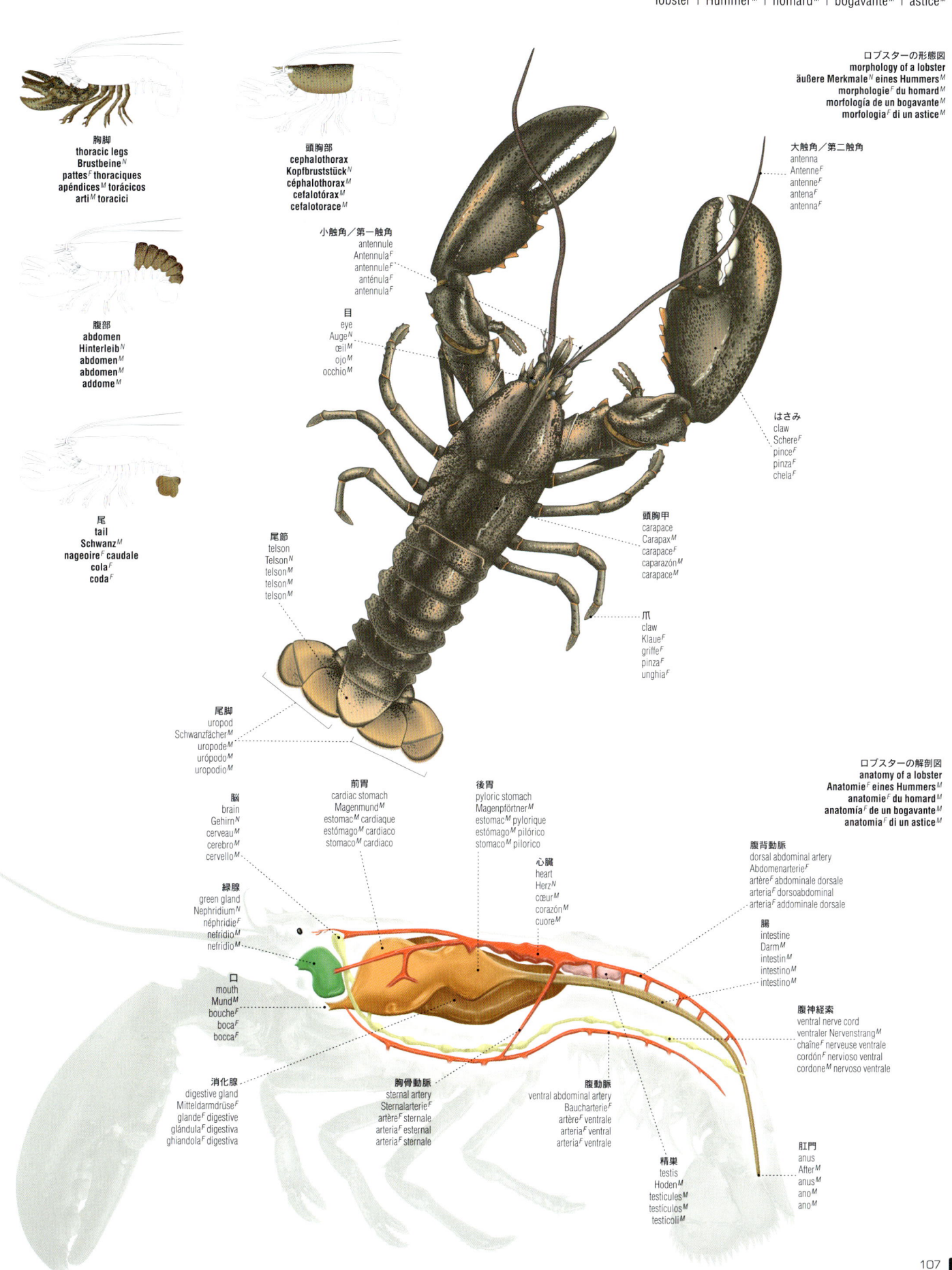

107

魚類 | FISHES
FISCHE | POISSONS | PECES | PESCI

軟骨魚

日本語 | 英語 | ドイツ語 | フランス語 | スペイン語 | イタリア語

cartilaginous fish | Knorpelfisch^M | poisson^M cartilagineux | pez^M cartilaginoso | pesce^M cartilagineo

サメ(鮫)の形態図
morphology of a shark
äußere Merkmale^N eines Hais^M
morphologie^F du requin^M
morfología^F de un tiburón^M
morfologia^F di uno squalo^M

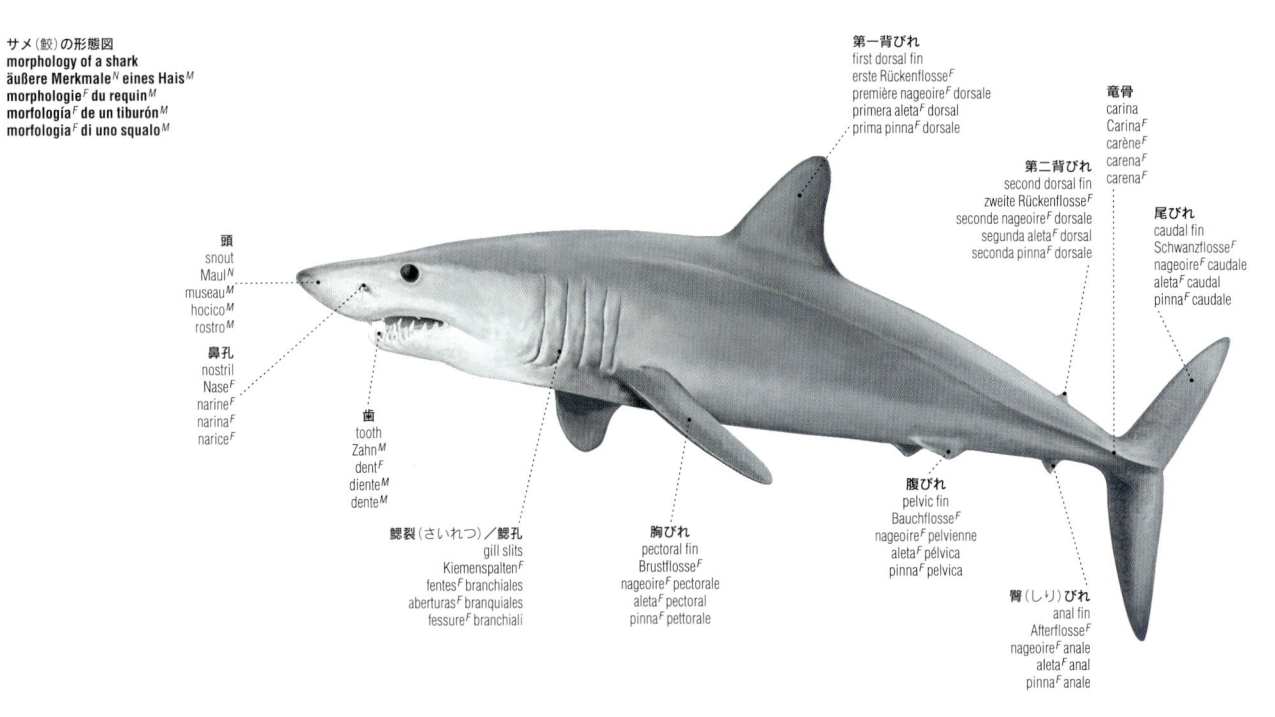

頭
snout
Maul^N
museau^M
hocico^M
rostro^M

鼻孔
nostril
Nase^F
narine^F
narina^F
narice^F

歯
tooth
Zahn^M
dent^F
diente^M
dente^M

鰓裂(さいれつ)／鰓孔
gill slits
Kiemenspalten^F
fentes^F branchiales
aberturas^F branquiales
fessure^F branchiali

胸びれ
pectoral fin
Brustflosse^F
nageoire^F pectorale
aleta^F pectoral
pinna^F pettorale

第一背びれ
first dorsal fin
erste Rückenflosse^F
première nageoire^F dorsale
primera aleta^F dorsal
prima pinna^F dorsale

第二背びれ
second dorsal fin
zweite Rückenflosse^F
seconde nageoire^F dorsale
segunda aleta^F dorsal
seconda pinna^F dorsale

腹びれ
pelvic fin
Bauchflosse^F
nageoire^F pelvienne
aleta^F pélvica
pinna^F pelvica

臀(しり)びれ
anal fin
Afterflosse^F
nageoire^F anale
aleta^F anal
pinna^F anale

竜骨
carina
Carina^F
carène^F
carena^F
carena^F

尾びれ
caudal fin
Schwanzflosse^F
nageoire^F caudale
aleta^F caudal
pinna^F caudale

硬骨魚

bony fish | Knochenfisch^M | poisson^M osseux | pez^M óseo | pesce^M osseo

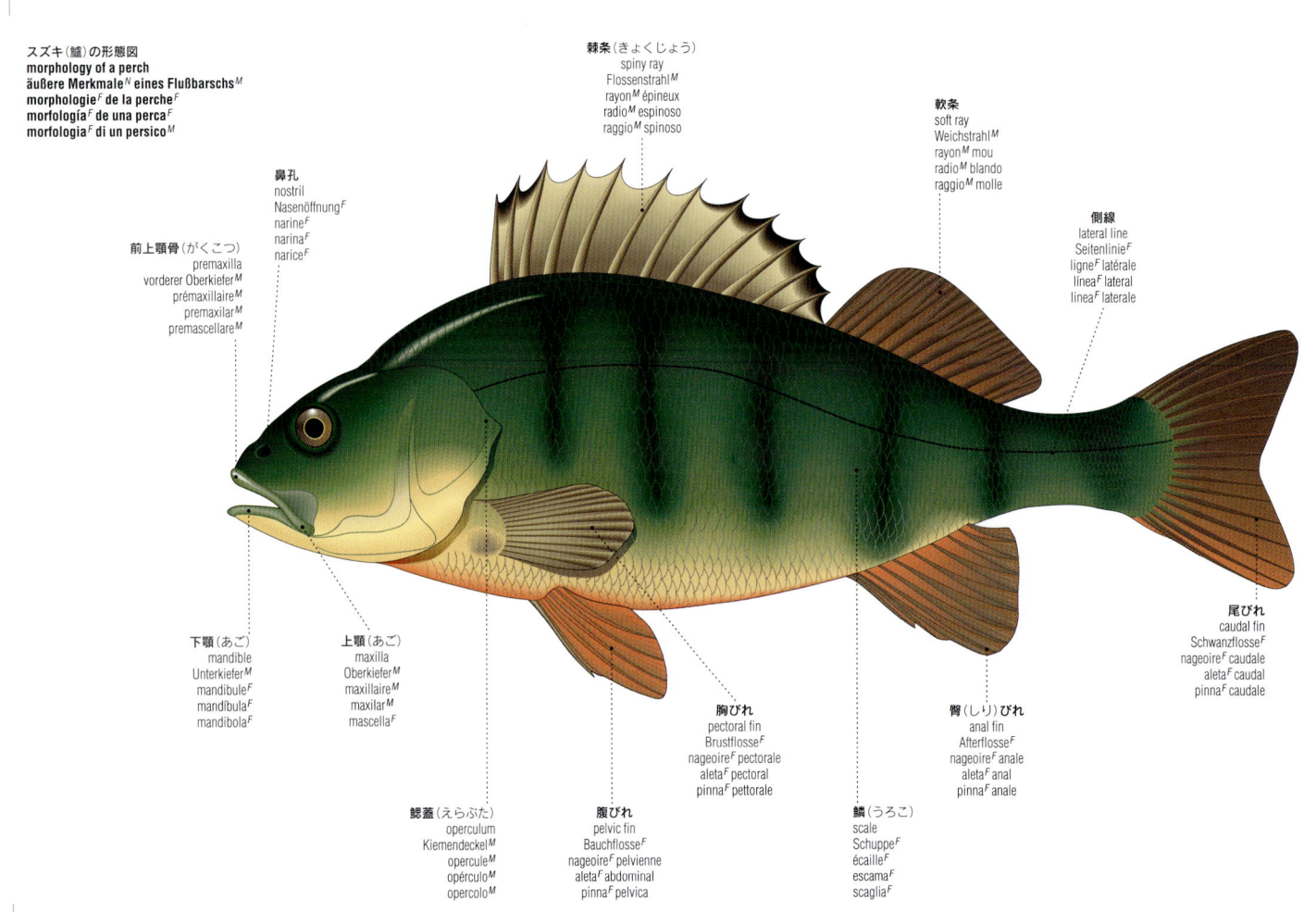

スズキ(鱸)の形態図
morphology of a perch
äußere Merkmale^N eines Flußbarschs^M
morphologie^F de la perche^F
morfología^F de una perca^F
morfologia^F di un persico^M

前上顎骨(がくこつ)
premaxilla
vorderer Oberkiefer^M
prémaxillaire^M
premaxilar^M
premascellare^M

鼻孔
nostril
Nasenöffnung^F
narine^F
narina^F
narice^F

棘条(きょくじょう)
spiny ray
Flossenstrahl^M
rayon^M épineux
radio^M espinoso
raggio^M spinoso

軟条
soft ray
Weichstrahl^M
rayon^M mou
radio^M blando
raggio^M molle

側線
lateral line
Seitenlinie^F
ligne^F latérale
línea^F lateral
linea^F laterale

下顎(あご)
mandible
Unterkiefer^M
mandibule^F
mandíbula^F
mandibola^F

上顎(あご)
maxilla
Oberkiefer^M
maxillaire^M
maxilar^M
mascella^F

鰓蓋(えらぶた)
operculum
Kiemendeckel^M
opercule^M
opérculo^M
opercolo^M

腹びれ
pelvic fin
Bauchflosse^F
nageoire^F pelvienne
aleta^F abdominal
pinna^F pelvica

胸びれ
pectoral fin
Brustflosse^F
nageoire^F pectorale
aleta^F pectoral
pinna^F pettorale

臀(しり)びれ
anal fin
Afterflosse^F
nageoire^F anale
aleta^F anal
pinna^F anale

鱗(うろこ)
scale
Schuppe^F
écaille^F
escama^F
scaglia^F

尾びれ
caudal fin
Schwanzflosse^F
nageoire^F caudale
aleta^F caudal
pinna^F caudale

魚類 | FISHES
FISCHE | POISSONS | PECES | PESCI

硬骨魚

スズキの解剖図
anatomy of a perch
Anatomie^F eines Flußbarschs^M
anatomie^F de la perche^F
anatomía^M de una perca^F
anatomia^F di un persico^M

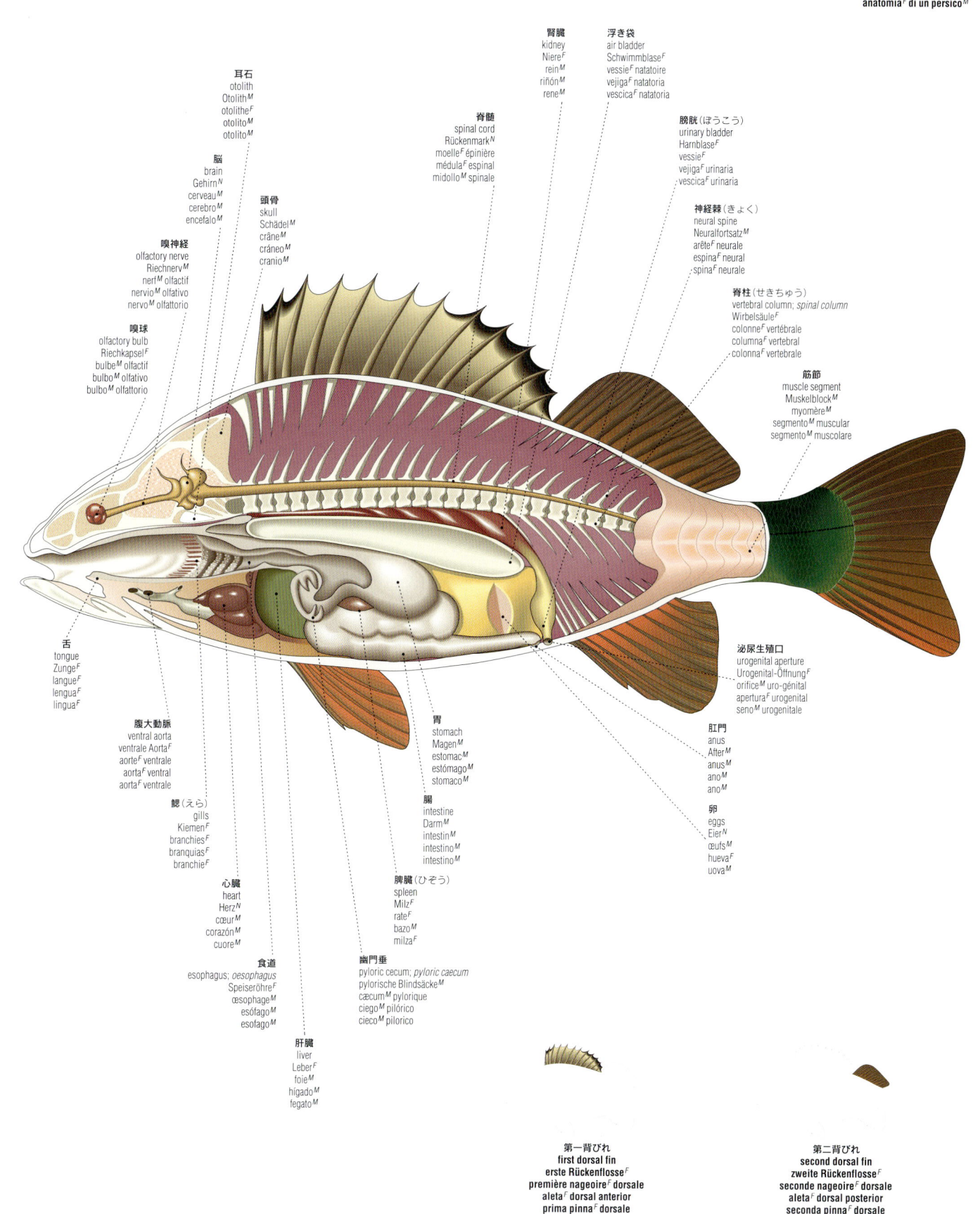

動物

腎臓
kidney
Niere^F
rein^M
riñón^M
rene^M

浮き袋
air bladder
Schwimmblase^F
vessie^F natatoire
vejiga^F natatoria
vescica^F natatoria

耳石
otolith
Otolith^M
otolithe^F
otolito^M
otolito^M

脊髄
spinal cord
Rückenmark^N
moelle^F épinière
médula^F espinal
midollo^M spinale

膀胱（ぼうこう）
urinary bladder
Harnblase^F
vessie^F
vejiga^F urinaria
vescica^F urinaria

脳
brain
Gehirn^N
cerveau^M
cerebro^M
encefalo^M

頭骨
skull
Schädel^M
crâne^M
cráneo^M
cranio^M

神経棘（きょく）
neural spine
Neuralfortsatz^M
arête^F neurale
espina^F neural
spina^F neurale

嗅神経
olfactory nerve
Riechnerv^M
nerf^M olfactif
nervio^M olfativo
nervo^M olfattorio

脊柱（せきちゅう）
vertebral column; *spinal column*
Wirbelsäule^F
colonne^F vertébrale
columna^F vertebral
colonna^F vertebrale

嗅球
olfactory bulb
Riechkapsel^F
bulbe^M olfactif
bulbo^M olfativo
bulbo^M olfattorio

筋節
muscle segment
Muskelblock^M
myomère^F
segmento^M muscular
segmento^M muscolare

舌
tongue
Zunge^F
langue^F
lengua^F
lingua^F

泌尿生殖口
urogenital aperture
Urogenital-Öffnung^F
orifice^M uro-génital
apertura^F urogenital
seno^M urogenitale

腹大動脈
ventral aorta
ventrale Aorta^F
aorte^F ventrale
aorta^F ventral
aorta^F ventrale

胃
stomach
Magen^M
estomac^M
estómago^M
stomaco^M

肛門
anus
After^M
anus^M
ano^M
ano^M

鰓（えら）
gills
Kiemen^F
branchies^F
branquias^F
branchie^F

腸
intestine
Darm^M
intestin^M
intestino^M
intestino^M

卵
eggs
Eier^N
œufs^M
hueva^F
uova^M

心臓
heart
Herz^N
cœur^M
corazón^M
cuore^M

脾臓（ひぞう）
spleen
Milz^F
rate^F
bazo^M
milza^F

食道
esophagus; *oesophagus*
Speiseröhre^F
œsophage^M
esófago^M
esofago^M

幽門垂
pyloric cecum; *pyloric caecum*
pylorische Blindsäcke^M
cæcum^M pylorique
ciego^M pilórico
cieco^M pilorico

肝臓
liver
Leber^F
foie^M
hígado^M
fegato^M

第一背びれ
first dorsal fin
erste Rückenflosse^F
première nageoire^F dorsale
aleta^F dorsal anterior
prima pinna^F dorsale

第二背びれ
second dorsal fin
zweite Rückenflosse^F
seconde nageoire^F dorsale
aleta^F dorsal posterior
seconda pinna^F dorsale

109

両生類 | AMPHIBIANS
AMPHIBIEN | AMPHIBIENS | ANFIBIOS | ANFIBI

カエル（蛙）

frog | Frosch[M] | grenouille[F] | rana[F] | rana[F]

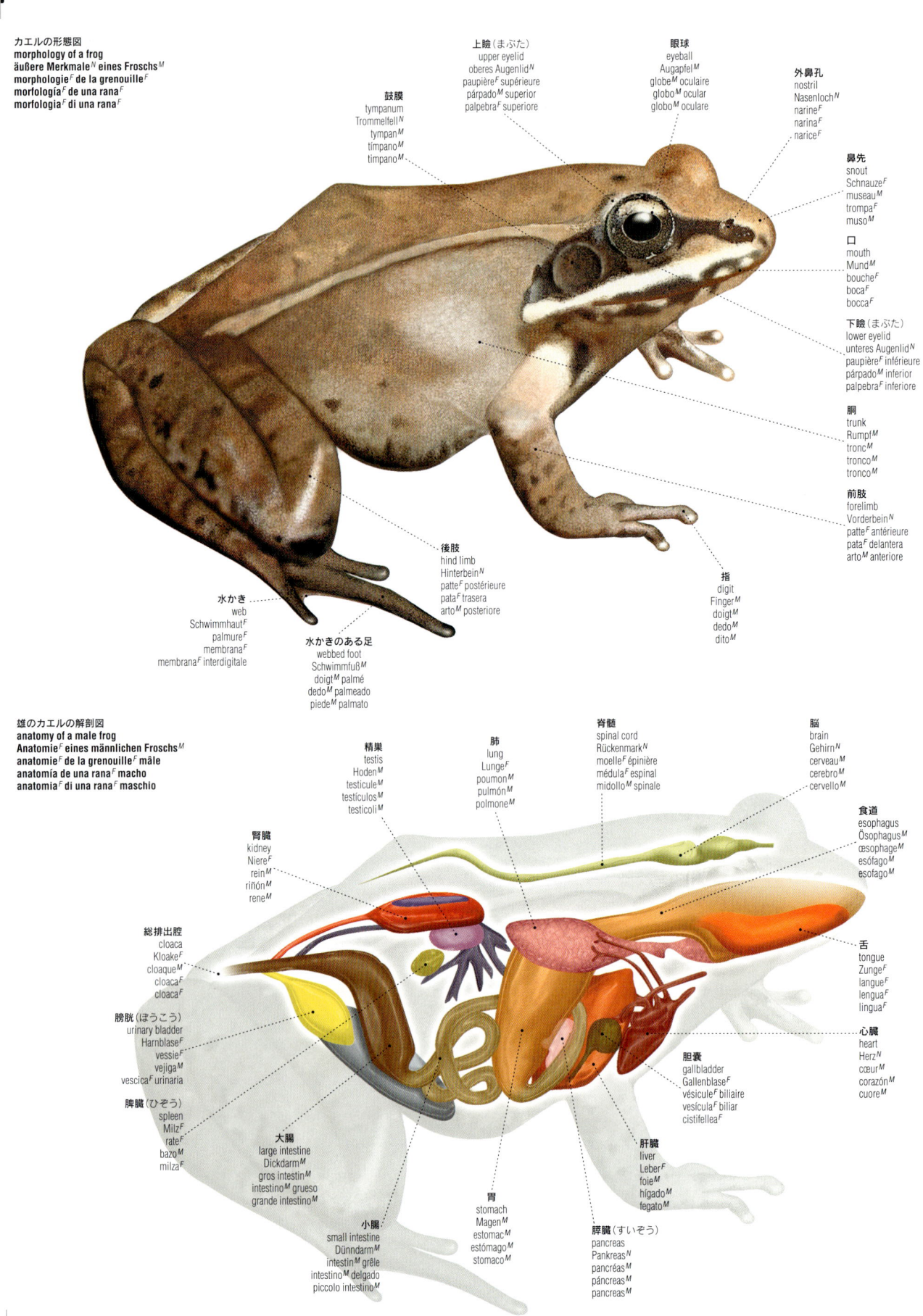

日本語 | 英語 | ドイツ語 | フランス語 | スペイン語 | イタリア語

動物

カエルの形態図
morphology of a frog
äußere Merkmale[N] eines Froschs[M]
morphologie[F] de la grenouille[F]
morfología[F] de una rana[F]
morfologia[F] di una rana[F]

鼓膜
tympanum
Trommelfell[N]
tympan[M]
tímpano[M]
timpano[M]

上瞼（まぶた）
upper eyelid
oberes Augenlid[N]
paupière[F] supérieure
párpado[M] superior
palpebra[F] superiore

眼球
eyeball
Augapfel[M]
globe[M] oculaire
globo[M] ocular
globo[M] oculare

外鼻孔
nostril
Nasenloch[N]
narine[F]
narina[F]
narice[F]

鼻先
snout
Schnauze[F]
museau[M]
trompa[F]
muso[M]

口
mouth
Mund[M]
bouche[F]
boca[F]
bocca[F]

下瞼（まぶた）
lower eyelid
unteres Augenlid[N]
paupière[F] inférieure
párpado[M] inferior
palpebra[F] inferiore

胴
trunk
Rumpf[M]
tronc[M]
tronco[M]
tronco[M]

前肢
forelimb
Vorderbein[N]
patte[F] antérieure
pata[F] delantera
arto[M] anteriore

指
digit
Finger[M]
doigt[M]
dedo[M]
dito[M]

後肢
hind limb
Hinterbein[N]
patte[F] postérieure
pata[F] trasera
arto[M] posteriore

水かき
web
Schwimmhaut[F]
palmure[F]
membrana[F]
membrana[F] interdigitale

水かきのある足
webbed foot
Schwimmfuß[M]
doigt[M] palmé
dedo[M] palmeado
piede[M] palmato

雄のカエルの解剖図
anatomy of a male frog
Anatomie[F] eines männlichen Froschs[M]
anatomie[F] de la grenouille[F] mâle
anatomía[F] de una rana[F] macho
anatomia[F] di una rana[F] maschio

精巣
testis
Hoden[M]
testicule[F]
testículos[M]
testicoli[M]

肺
lung
Lunge[F]
poumon[M]
pulmón[M]
polmone[M]

脊髄
spinal cord
Rückenmark[N]
moelle[F] épinière
médula[F] espinal
midollo[M] spinale

脳
brain
Gehirn[N]
cerveau[M]
cerebro[M]
cervello[M]

腎臓
kidney
Niere[F]
rein[M]
riñón[M]
rene[M]

食道
esophagus
Ösophagus[M]
œsophage[M]
esófago[M]
esofago[M]

総排出腔
cloaca
Kloake[F]
cloaque[M]
cloaca[F]
cloaca[F]

舌
tongue
Zunge[F]
langue[F]
lengua[F]
lingua[F]

膀胱（ぼうこう）
urinary bladder
Harnblase[F]
vessie[F]
vejiga[F]
vescica[F] urinaria

胆嚢
gallbladder
Gallenblase[F]
vésicule[F] biliaire
vesícula[F] biliar
cistifellea[F]

脾臓（ひぞう）
spleen
Milz[F]
rate[F]
bazo[M]
milza[F]

大腸
large intestine
Dickdarm[M]
gros intestin[M]
intestino[M] grueso
grande intestino[M]

肝臓
liver
Leber[F]
foie[M]
hígado[M]
fegato[M]

小腸
small intestine
Dünndarm[M]
intestin[M] grêle
intestino[M] delgado
piccolo intestino[M]

胃
stomach
Magen[M]
estomac[M]
estómago[M]
stomaco[M]

膵臓（すいぞう）
pancreas
Pankreas[N]
pancréas[M]
páncreas[M]
pancreas[M]

心臓
heart
Herz[N]
cœur[M]
corazón[M]
cuore[M]

110

両生類 | AMPHIBIANS
AMPHIBIEN | AMPHIBIENS | ANFIBIOS | ANFIBI

カエル（蛙）

カエルの骨格図
skeleton of a frog
Skelett^N eines Froschs^M
squelette^M de la grenouille^F
esqueleto^M de una rana^F
scheletro^M di una rana^F

腸骨 — ilium / Ilium^N / ilium^M / ilion^M / ileo^M

仙椎 — sacral vertebra / Sakralwirbel^M / vertèbre^F sacrée / vértebra^F sacra / vertebra^F sacrale

肩甲骨 — scapula / Schulterblatt^N / omoplate^F / omóplato^M / scapola^F

烏口骨（うこうこつ） — coracoid / Korakoid^N / coracoïde^F / coracoides^M / coracoide^M

尾端骨 — urostyle / Urostyl^N / urostyle^M / urostilo^M / urostilo^M

椎骨（ついこつ） — vertebrae / Wirbel^M / vertèbres^F / vértebras^F / vertebre^F

環椎 — atlas / Atlas^M / atlas^M / atlas^M / atlante^M

前頭頭頂骨 — frontoparietal / Frontoparietale^N / fronto-pariétal^M / frontoparietal^F / frontoparietale^M

座骨 — ischium / Ischium^N / ischion^M / isquion^M / ischio^M

上顎骨（じょうがくこつ） — maxilla / Oberkiefer^M / maxillaire^M / maxilar^M / mascella^F

大腿骨 — femur / Oberschenkel^M / fémur^M / fémur^M / femore^M

下顎骨（かがくこつ） — mandible / Unterkiefer^M / mandibule^F / mandíbula^F / mandibola^F

脛腓骨（けいひこつ） — tibiofibula / Tibia^F und Fibula^F / tibia^M et péroné^M / tibia^F y peroné^F / tibiofibula^F

鎖骨 — clavicle / Klavikula^F / clavicule^F / clavícula^F / clavicola^F

ふ骨／足根骨 — tarsus / Tarsus^M / tarse^M / tarso^M / tarso^M

上腕骨 — humerus / Oberarmknochen^M / humérus^M / húmero^M / omero^M

指骨 — phalanges / Phalangen^F / phalanges^F / falanges^M / falangi^F

蹠骨（しょこつ）／中足骨 — metatarsus / Metatarsus^M / métatarse^M / metatarso^M / metatarso^M

趾骨（しこつ） — phalanges / Phalangen^F / phalanges^F / falanges^M / falangi^F

胸骨 — sternum / Sternum^N / sternum^M / esternón^M / sterno^M

橈尺骨（とうしゃくこつ） — radio-ulna / Radius^M-Ulna^F / radius^M et cubitus^M / radio^M y cúbito^M / radio^M-ulna^F

掌骨／中手骨 — metacarpus / Metacarpus^M / métacarpe^M / metacarpo^M / metacarpo^M

カエルの一生 — life cycle of the frog / Lebenszyklus^M des Frosches^M / métamorphose^F de la grenouille^F / metamórfosis^F de la rana^F / ciclo^M biologico della rana^F

卵 — eggs / Eier^N / œufs^M / huevos^M / uova^M

オタマジャクシ — tadpole / Kaulquappe^F / têtard^M / renacuajo^M / girino^M

外鰓（がいさい） — external gills / äußere Kiemen^F / branchies^F externes / branquias^F externas / branchie^F esterne

後肢 — hind limb / Hinterbein^N / patte^F postérieure / extremidad^F posterior / zampa^F posteriore

鰓蓋（えらぶた） — operculum / Kiemendeckel^M / opercule^M / opérculo^M / opercolo^M

前肢 — forelimb / Vorderbein^N / patte^F antérieure / extremidad^F delantera / zampa^F anteriore

---

両生類の例

examples of amphibians | Beispiele^N für Amphibien^F | exemples^M d'amphibiens^M | ejemplos^M de anfibios^M | esempi^M di anfibi^M

サンショウウオ（山椒魚） — salamander / Salamander^M / salamandre^F / salamandra^F / salamandra^F

アメリカアカガエル（赤蛙） — wood frog / Waldfrosch^M / grenouille^F des bois / rana^F de bosque^M / rana^F dei boschi^M

一般的なカエル — common frog / Wasserfrosch^M / grenouille^F rousse / rana^F bermeja / rana^F comune

アマガエル（雨蛙） — tree frog / Laubfrosch^M / rainette^F / rana^F arborícola / raganella^F

イモリ（井守） — newt / Molch^M / triton^M / tritón^M / tritone^M

一般的なヒキガエル（蟇蛙） — common toad / gemeine Erdkröte^F / crapaud^M commun / sapo^M común / rospo^M comune

ヒョウガエル（豹蛙） — Northern leopard frog / Leopardfrosch^M / grenouille^F léopard / rana^F leopardo / rana^F leopardo

吸盤 — adhesive disk; adhesive disc / Haftscheibe^F / ventouse^F / ventosa^F / disco^M adesivo

動物

爬虫類 | REPTILES
REPTILIEN | REPTILES | REPTILES | RETTILI

ヘビ（蛇）

snake | Schlange^F | serpent^M | serpiente^F | serpente^M

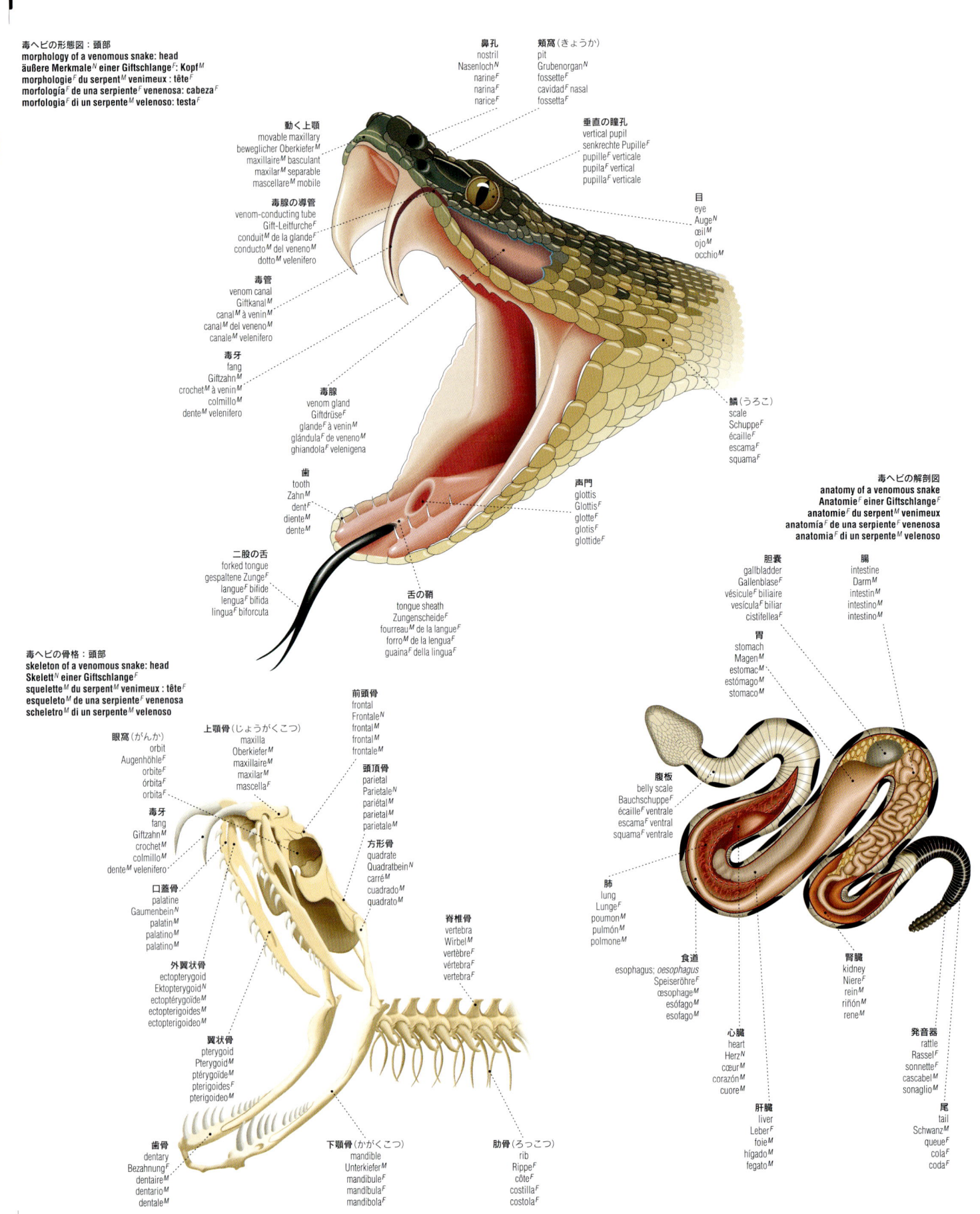

日本語 | 英語 | ドイツ語 | フランス語 | スペイン語 | イタリア語

毒ヘビの形態図：頭部
morphology of a venomous snake: head
äußere Merkmale^N einer Giftschlange^F: Kopf^M
morphologie^F du serpent^M venimeux : tête^F
morfología^F de una serpiente^F venenosa: cabeza^F
morfologia^F di un serpente^M velenoso: testa^F

鼻孔
nostril
Nasenloch^N
narine^F
narina^F
narice^F

頬窩（きょうか）
pit
Grubenorgan^N
fossette^F
cavidad^F nasal
fossetta^F

動く上顎
movable maxillary
beweglicher Oberkiefer^M
maxillaire^M basculant
maxilar^M separable
mascellare^M mobile

垂直の瞳孔
vertical pupil
senkrechte Pupille^F
pupille^F verticale
pupila^F vertical
pupilla^F verticale

毒腺の導管
venom-conducting tube
Gift-Leitfurche^F
conduit^M de la glande^F
conducto^M del veneno^M
dotto^M velenifero

目
eye
Auge^N
œil^M
ojo^M
occhio^M

毒管
venom canal
Giftkanal^M
canal^M à venin^M
canal^M del veneno^M
canale^M velenifero

毒牙
fang
Giftzahn^M
crochet^M à venin^M
colmillo^M
dente^M velenifero

毒腺
venom gland
Giftdrüse^F
glande^F à venin^M
glándula^F de veneno^M
ghiandola^F velenigena

鱗（うろこ）
scale
Schuppe^F
écaille^F
escama^F
squama^F

歯
tooth
Zahn^M
dent^F
diente^M
dente^M

声門
glottis
Glottis^F
glotte^F
glotis^F
glottide^F

毒ヘビの解剖図
anatomy of a venomous snake
Anatomie^F einer Giftschlange^F
anatomie^F du serpent^M venimeux
anatomía^F de una serpiente^F venenosa
anatomia^F di un serpente^M velenoso

二股の舌
forked tongue
gespaltene Zunge^F
langue^F bifide
lengua^F bífida
lingua^F biforcuta

舌の鞘
tongue sheath
Zungenscheide^F
fourreau^M de la langue^F
forro^M de la lengua^F
guaina^F della lingua^F

胆嚢
gallbladder
Gallenblase^F
vésicule^F biliaire
vesícula^F biliar
cistifellea^F

腸
intestine
Darm^M
intestin^M
intestino^M
intestino^M

毒ヘビの骨格：頭部
skeleton of a venomous snake: head
Skelett^N einer Giftschlange^F
squelette^M du serpent^M venimeux : tête^F
esqueleto^M de una serpiente^F venenosa
scheletro^M di un serpente^M velenoso

胃
stomach
Magen^M
estomac^M
estómago^M
stomaco^M

眼窩（がんか）
orbit
Augenhöhle^F
orbite^F
órbita^F
orbita^F

上顎骨（じょうがくこつ）
maxilla
Oberkiefer^M
maxillaire^M
maxilar^M
mascella^F

前頭骨
frontal
Frontale^N
frontal^M
frontal^M
frontale^M

腹板
belly scale
Bauchschuppe^F
écaille^F ventrale
escama^F ventral
squama^F ventrale

毒牙
fang
Giftzahn^M
crochet^M
colmillo^M
dente^M velenifero

頭頂骨
parietal
Parietale^N
pariétal^M
parietal^M
parietale^M

口蓋骨
palatine
Gaumenbein^N
palatin^M
palatino^M
palatino^M

方形骨
quadrate
Quadratbein^N
carré^M
cuadrado^M
quadrato^M

肺
lung
Lunge^F
poumon^M
pulmón^M
polmone^M

脊椎骨
vertebra
Wirbel^M
vertèbre^F
vértebra^F
vertebra^F

食道
esophagus; oesophagus
Speiseröhre^F
œsophage^M
esófago^M
esofago^M

腎臓
kidney
Niere^F
rein^M
riñón^M
rene^M

外翼状骨
ectopterygoid
Ektopterygoid
ectoptérygoïde^M
ectopterigoides^M
ectopterigoideo^M

翼状骨
pterygoid
Pterygoid^M
ptérygoïde^M
pterigoides^M
pterigoideo^M

心臓
heart
Herz^N
cœur^M
corazón^M
cuore^M

発音器
rattle
Rassel^F
sonnette^F
cascabel^M
sonaglio^M

肝臓
liver
Leber^F
foie^M
hígado^M
fegato^M

尾
tail
Schwanz^M
queue^F
cola^F
coda^F

歯骨
dentary
Bezahnung^F
dentaire^F
dentario^M
dentale^M

下顎骨（かがくこつ）
mandible
Unterkiefer^M
mandibule^F
mandíbula^F
mandibola^F

肋骨（ろっこつ）
rib
Rippe^F
côte^F
costilla^F
costola^F

爬虫類 | REPTILES
REPTILIEN | REPTILES | REPTILES | RETTILI

カメ（亀）

turtle | Schildkröte^F | tortue^F | tortuga^F | tartaruga^F

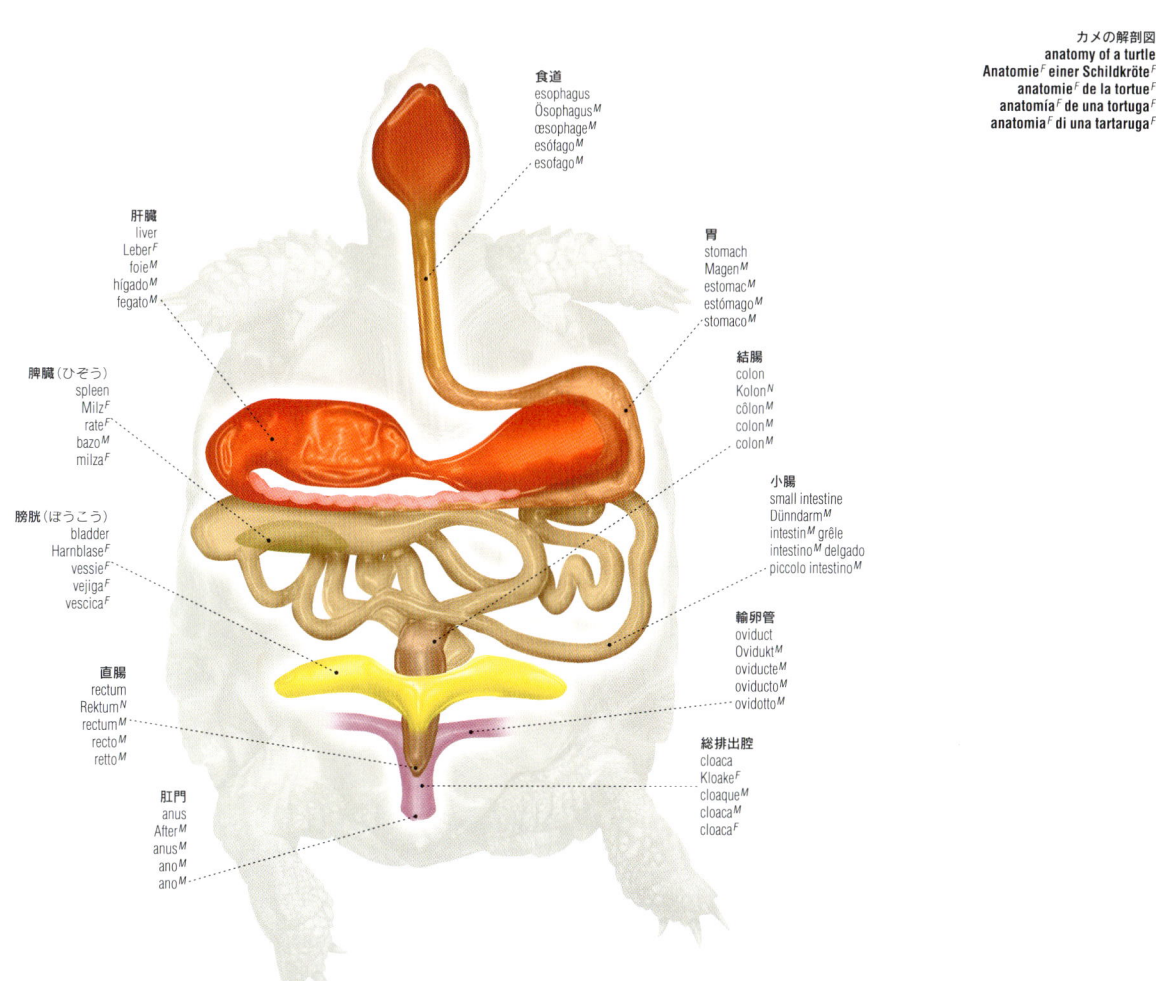

カメの形態図
morphology of a turtle
äußere Merkmale^N einer Schildkröte^F
morphologie^F de la tortue^F
morfología^F de una tortuga^F
morfologia^F di una tartaruga^F

椎甲板（ついこうばん）
vertebral shield
Vertebralschild^M
plaque^F vertébrale
placa^F vertebral
piastra^F neurale

肋甲板（ろっこうばん）
costal shield
Costalschild^M
plaque^F costale
placa^F costal
piastra^F costale

背甲
carapace
Rückenpanzer^M
dossière^F
espaldar^M
carapace^M

臀甲板（でんこうばん）
pygal shield
Pygalschild^M
plaque^F supra-caudale
placa^F supracaudal
piastra^F sopracaudale

瞼（まぶた）
eyelid
Augenlid^N
paupière^F
párpado^M
palpebra^F

目
eye
Auge^N
œil^M
ojo^M
occhio^M

尾
tail
Schwanz^M
queue^F
cola^F
coda^F

脚
leg
Bein^N
patte^F
pata^F
zampa^F

縁甲板（えんこうばん）
marginal shield
Marginalschild^M
plaque^F marginale
placa^F marginal
piastra^F marginale

角質の口
horny beak
Hornschnabel^M
bec^M corné
labio^M córneo
becco^M corneo

首
neck
Hals^M
cou^M
cuello^M
collo^M

鱗（うろこ）
scale
Schuppe^F
écaille^F
escama^F
squama^F

腹甲
plastron
Bauchpanzer^M
plastron^M
plastrón^M
piastrone^M

爪
claw
Kralle^F
griffe^F
uña^F
unghia^F

動物

カメの解剖図
anatomy of a turtle
Anatomie^F einer Schildkröte^F
anatomie^F de la tortue^F
anatomía^F de una tortuga^F
anatomia^F di una tartaruga^F

食道
esophagus
Ösophagus^M
œsophage^M
esófago^M
esofago^M

肝臓
liver
Leber^F
foie^M
hígado^M
fegato^M

胃
stomach
Magen^M
estomac^M
estómago^M
stomaco^M

脾臓（ひぞう）
spleen
Milz^F
rate^F
bazo^M
milza^F

結腸
colon
Kolon^N
côlon^M
colon^M
colon^M

膀胱（ぼうこう）
bladder
Harnblase^F
vessie^F
vejiga^F
vescica^F

小腸
small intestine
Dünndarm^M
intestin^M grêle
intestino^M delgado
piccolo intestino^M

直腸
rectum
Rektum^N
rectum^M
recto^M
retto^M

輸卵管
oviduct
Ovidukt^M
oviducte^M
oviducto^M
oviducto^M

総排出腔
cloaca
Kloake^F
cloaque^M
cloaca^M
cloaca^F

肛門
anus
After^M
anus^M
ano^M
ano^M

113

爬虫類 | REPTILES
REPTILIEN | REPTILES | REPTILES | RETTILI

爬虫類の例

examples of reptiles | Beispiele^N für Reptilien^N | exemples^M de reptiles^M | ejemplos^M de reptiles^M | esempi^M di rettili^M

日本語 | 英語 | ドイツ語 | フランス語 | スペイン語 | イタリア語

クサリヘビ (鎖蛇)
viper
Viper^F
vipère^F
víbora^F
vipera^F

ガーターヘビ (蛇)
garter snake
Ringelnatter^F
couleuvre^F rayée
serpiente^F de jarretera^F
serpente^M giarrettiera^F

カメレオン
chameleon
Chamäleon^N
caméléon^M
camaleón^M
camaleonte^M

トカゲ
lizard
Eidechse^F
lézard^M
lagarto^M
lucertola^F

ガラガラヘビ
rattlesnake
Klapperschlange^F
serpent^M à sonnette^F
serpiente^M de cascabel^M
serpente^M a sonagli^M

コブラ
cobra
Kobra^F
cobra^M
cobra^F
cobra^M

サンゴヘビ (珊瑚蛇)
coral snake
Korallennatter^F
serpent^M corail^M
serpiente^F coral
serpente^M corallo^M

ニシキヘビ (錦蛇)
python
Python^M
python^M
pitón^M
pitone^M

オオトカゲ (大とかげ)
monitor lizard
Waran^M
varan^M
varano^M
varano^M

イグアナ
iguana
Leguan^M
iguane^M
iguana^F
iguana^F

ボア
boa
Boa^F
boa^M
boa^F
boa^M

アリゲーター
alligator
Alligator^M
alligator^M
aligátor^M
alligatore^M

クロコダイル
crocodile
Krokodil^N
crocodile^M
cocodrilo^M
coccodrillo^M

カイマン
caiman
Kaiman^M
caïman^M
caimán^M
caimano^M

鳥類 | BIRDS
VÖGEL | OISEAUX | AVES | UCCELLI

鳥
bird | Vogel^M | oiseau^M | ave^F | uccello^M

鳥の形態図
morphology of a bird
äußere Merkmale^N eines Vogels^M
morphologie^F de l'oiseau^M
morfología^F de un pájaro^M
morfologia^F di un uccello^M

背 back / Rücken^M / dos^M / lomo^M / dorso^M

頭(くび) nape / Nacken^M / nuque^F / cerviz^F / nuca^F

嘴(くちばし) bill / Schnabel^M / bec^M / pico^M / becco^M

腰 rump / Bürzel^M / croupion^M / obispillo^M / codrione^M

翼 wing / Flügel^M / aile^F / ala^F / ala^F

腮(えら)／顎(あご) chin / Kinn^N / menton^M / mentón^M / mento^M

尾羽 tail feather / Schwanzfeder^F / rectrice^F / plumas^F timoneras / penna^F timoniera

咽 throat / Kehle^F / gorge^F / garganta^F / gola^F

上尾筒 upper tail covert / Oberschwanzdecken^F / tectrice^F sus-caudale / cobertera^F superior de la cola^F / penna^F copritrice superiore della coda^F

雨覆い(あまおおい) wing covert / Deckfeder^F / tectrice^F sus-alaire / coberteras^F / penna^F copritrice

胸 breast / Brust^F / poitrine^F / pechuga^F / petto^M

下尾筒 under tail covert / Unterschwanzdecken^F / tectrice^F sous-caudale / cobertera^F inferior de la cola^F / penna^F copritrice inferiore della coda^F

脇腹 flank / Flanke^F / flanc^M / flanco^M / fianco^M

腹 abdomen / Bauch^M / abdomen^M / abdomen^M / addome^M

腿 thigh / Schenkel^M / tibia^M / muslo^M / tibia^F

ふ蹠(しょ) tarsus / Lauf^M / tarse^M / tarso^M / tarso^M

第二趾(し)／内趾 inner toe / zweite Zehe^F / doigt^M interne / dedo^M interno / dito^M interno

第一趾(し)／後趾 hind toe / Hinterzehe^F / doigt^M postérieur / dedo^M posterior / dito^M posteriore

大羽 contour feather / Konturfeder^F / penne^F / pluma^F / penna^F del contorno^M

第四趾(し)／外趾 outer toe / vierte Zehe^F / doigt^M externe / dedo^M externo / dito^M esterno

第三趾(し)／中趾 middle toe / dritte Zehe^F / doigt^M médian / dedo^M medio / dito^M medio

鉤爪 claw / Kralle^F / griffe^F / uña^F / unghia^F

頭部 head / Kopf^M / tête^F / cabeza^F / capo^M

羽軸 rachis / Schaft^M / rachis^M / raquis^M / rachide^F

羽枝 barb / Ast^M / barbe^F / barba^F / barba^F

羽弁 vane / Fahne^F / vexille^M / barbilla^F / vessillo^M

前頭 forehead / Stirn^F / front^M / frente^F / fronte^F

鼻孔 nostril / Nasenloch^N / narine^F / narina^F / narice^F

頭頂 crown / Scheitel^M / calotte^F / penacho^M / vertice^F

上嘴(じょうし) upper mandible / Oberschnabel^M / maxillaire^M supérieur / mandíbula^F superior / mandibola^F superiore

後羽 afterfeather / Afterfeder^F / duvet^M / plumón^M / iporachide^F

上臍(じょうさい) superior umbilicus / oberer Nabel^M / ombilic^M supérieur / ombligo^M superior / ombelico^M superiore

眉斑(びはん) eyebrow stripe / Augenstreif^M / raie^F sourcilière / lista^F superciliar / fascia^F sopraccigliare

耳羽／耳毛 auriculars / Ohrdecken^F / région^F auriculaire / auriculares^M / regione^F auricolare

下嘴(かし) lower mandible / Unterschnabel^M / mandibule^F / mandíbula^F inferior / mandibola^F inferiore

羽柄 calamus / Spule^F / calamus^M / cálamo^M / calamo^M

頬 malar region / Bartregion^F / région^F malaire / región^F malar / regione^F malare

目先 lore / Zügel^M / lorum^M / puente^M / redine^F

囲眼羽／アイ・リング eye ring / Augenring^M / anneau^M oculaire / anillo^M ocular / anello^M oculare

下臍(かさい) inferior umbilicus / unterer Nabel^M / ombilic^M inférieur / ombligo^M inferior / ombelico^M inferiore

初列雨覆い(あまおおい)(羽) primary covert / große Handdecken^F / tectrice^F primaire / coberteras^F primarias / copritrice^F primaria

小翼(羽(う)) alula / Daumenfittich^M / alule^F / álula^F / alula^F

中雨覆い(羽) middle covert / mittlere Armdecken^F / moyenne sus-alaire^F / coberteras^F medias / copritrice^F secondaria mediana

小雨覆い(羽) lesser covert / kleine Armdecken^F / petite sus-alaire^F / coberteras^F menores / piccola copritrice^F secondaria

翼 wing / Flügel^M / aile^F / ala^F / ala^F

初列風切り(かざきり)(羽) primaries / Handschwingen^F / rémige^F primaire / remeras^F primarias / remigante^F primaria

初列中雨覆い(羽) middle primary covert / mittlere Handdecken^F / moyenne tectrice^F primaire / coberteras^F primarias medias / copritrice^F primaria media

肩羽 scapular / Schulterfeder^F / scapulaire^F / escapulares^M / scapolare^F

大雨覆い(羽) greater covert / große Armdecken^F / grande sus-alaire^F / coberteras^F mayores / grande copritrice^F secondaria

次[二]列風切り(羽) secondaries / Armschwingen^F / rémige^F secondaire / remeras^F secundarias / remigante^F secondaria

三列風切り(羽) tertial / Schirmfeder^F / rémige^F tertiaire / remeras^F terciarias / remigante^F terziaria

動物

115

鳥類 | BIRDS
VÖGEL | OISEAUX | AVES | UCCELLI

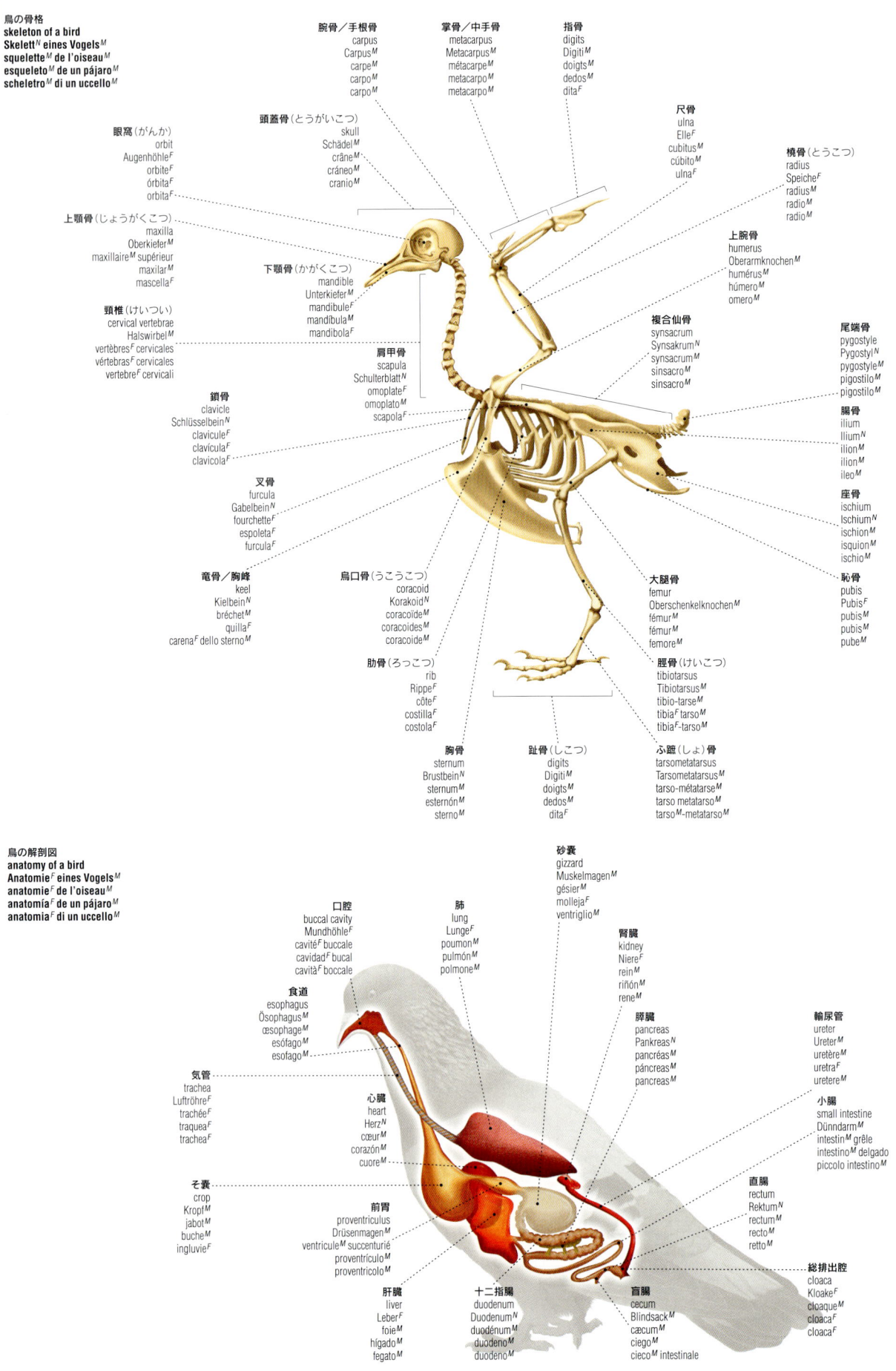

鳥

日本語 | 英語 | ドイツ語 | フランス語 | スペイン語 | イタリア語

動物

鳥の骨格
skeleton of a bird
Skelett^N eines Vogels^M
squelette^M de l'oiseau^M
esqueleto^M de un pájaro^M
scheletro^M di un uccello^M

腕骨／手根骨
carpus
Carpus^M
carpe^M
carpo^M
carpo^M

掌骨／中手骨
metacarpus
Metacarpus^M
métacarpe^M
metacarpo^M
metacarpo^M

指骨
digits
Digiti^M
doigts^M
dedos^M
dita^F

尺骨
ulna
Elle^F
cubitus^M
cúbito^M
ulna^F

橈骨（とうこつ）
radius
Speiche^F
radius^M
radio^M
radio^M

眼窩（がんか）
orbit
Augenhöhle^F
orbite^F
órbita^F
orbita^F

頭蓋骨（とうがいこつ）
skull
Schädel^M
crâne^M
cráneo^M
cranio^M

上腕骨
humerus
Oberarmknochen^M
humérus^M
húmero^M
omero^M

上顎骨（じょうがくこつ）
maxilla
Oberkiefer^M
maxillaire^M supérieur
maxilar^M
mascella^F

下顎骨（かがくこつ）
mandible
Unterkiefer^M
mandibule^F
mandíbula^F
mandibola^F

複合仙骨
synsacrum
Synsakrum^N
synsacrum^M
sinsacro^M
sinsacro^M

尾端骨
pygostyle
Pygostyl^N
pygostyle^M
pigostilo^M
pigostilo^M

頸椎（けいつい）
cervical vertebrae
Halswirbel^M
vertèbres^F cervicales
vértebras^F cervicales
vertebre^F cervicali

肩甲骨
scapula
Schulterblatt^N
omoplate^F
omoplato^M
scapola^F

腸骨
ilium
Ilium^N
ilion^M
ilion^M
ileo^M

鎖骨
clavicle
Schlüsselbein^N
clavicule^F
clavícula^F
clavicola^F

座骨
ischium
Ischium^N
ischion^M
isquion^M
ischio^M

叉骨
furcula
Gabelbein^N
fourchette^F
espoleta^F
furcula^F

恥骨
pubis
Pubis^F
pubis^M
pubis^M
pube^M

竜骨／胸峰
keel
Kielbein^N
bréchet^M
quilla^F
carena^F dello sterno^M

烏口骨（うこうこつ）
coracoid
Korakoid^N
coracoïde^M
coracoides^M
coracoide^M

大腿骨
femur
Oberschenkelknochen^M
fémur^M
fémur^M
femore^M

肋骨（ろっこつ）
rib
Rippe^F
côte^F
costilla^F
costola^F

脛骨（けいこつ）
tibiotarsus
Tibiotarsus^M
tibio-tarse^M
tibia^F tarso^M
tibia^F-tarso^M

胸骨
sternum
Brustbein^N
sternum^M
esternón^M
sterno^M

趾骨（しこつ）
digits
Digiti^M
doigts^M
dedos^M
dita^F

ふ蹠（しょ）骨
tarsometatarsus
Tarsometatarsus^M
tarso-métatarse^M
tarso metatarso^M
tarso^M-metatarso^M

鳥の解剖図
anatomy of a bird
Anatomie^F eines Vogels^M
anatomie^F de l'oiseau^M
anatomía^F de un pájaro^M
anatomia^F di un uccello^M

砂嚢
gizzard
Muskelmagen^M
gésier^M
molleja^F
ventriglio^M

口腔
buccal cavity
Mundhöhle^F
cavité^F buccale
cavidad^F bucal
cavità^F boccale

肺
lung
Lunge^F
poumon^M
pulmón^M
polmone^M

腎臓
kidney
Niere^F
rein^M
riñón^M
rene^M

食道
esophagus
Ösophagus^M
œsophage^M
esófago^M
esofago^M

膵臓
pancreas
Pankreas^N
pancréas^M
páncreas^M
pancreas^M

輸尿管
ureter
Ureter^M
uretère^M
uretra^F
uretere^M

気管
trachea
Luftröhre^F
trachée^F
tráquea^F
trachea^F

心臓
heart
Herz^N
cœur^M
corazón^M
cuore^M

小腸
small intestine
Dünndarm^M
intestin^M grêle
intestino^M delgado
piccolo intestino^M

そ嚢
crop
Kropf^M
jabot^M
buche^M
ingluvie^F

前胃
proventriculus
Drüsenmagen^M
ventricule^M succenturié
proventrículo^M
proventricolo^M

直腸
rectum
Rektum^N
rectum^M
recto^M
retto^M

肝臓
liver
Leber^F
foie^M
hígado^M
fegato^M

十二指腸
duodenum
Duodenum^N
duodénum^M
duodeno^M
duodeno^M

盲腸
cecum
Blindsack^M
cæcum^M
ciego^M
cieco^M intestinale

総排出腔
cloaca
Kloake^F
cloaque^M
cloaca^F
cloaca^F

鳥類 | BIRDS
VÖGEL | OISEAUX | AVES | UCCELLI

卵 / egg / Ei(N) / œuf(M) / huevo(M) / uovo(M)

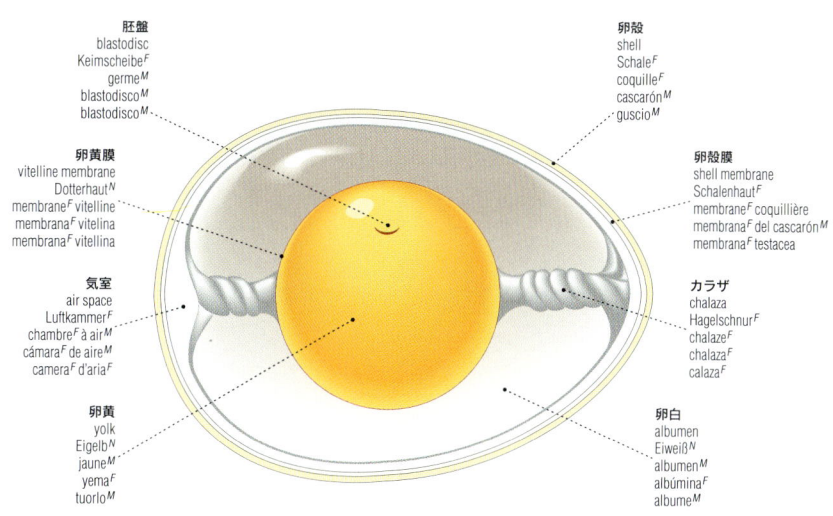

- 胚盤 / blastodisc / Keimscheibe(F) / germe(M) / blastodisco(M) / blastodisco(M)
- 卵黄膜 / vitelline membrane / Dotterhaut(N) / membrane(F) vitelline / membrana(F) vitelina / membrana(F) vitellina
- 気室 / air space / Luftkammer(F) / chambre(F) à air(M) / cámara(F) de aire(M) / camera(F) d'aria(F)
- 卵黄 / yolk / Eigelb(N) / jaune(M) / yema(F) / tuorlo(M)
- 卵殻 / shell / Schale(F) / coquille(F) / cascarón(M) / guscio(M)
- 卵殻膜 / shell membrane / Schalenhaut(F) / membrane(F) coquillière / membrana(F) del cascarón(M) / membrana(F) testacea
- カラザ / chalaza / Hagelschnur(F) / chalaze(F) / chalaza(F) / calaza(F)
- 卵白 / albumen / Eiweiß(N) / albumen(M) / albúmina(F) / albume(M)

嘴(くちばし)の例 / examples of bills / Beispiele(N) für Vogelschnäbel(M) / exemples(M) de becs(M) / ejemplos(M) de picos(M) / esempi(M) di becchi(M)

- 水鳥 / aquatic bird / Wasservogel(M) / oiseau(M) aquatique / ave(F) acuática / uccello(M) acquatico
- 穀食鳥 / granivorous bird / Körnerfresser(M) / oiseau(M) granivore / ave(F) granívora / uccello(M) granivoro
- 猛禽(もうきん) / bird of prey / Raubvogel(M) / oiseau(M) de proie(F) / ave(F) de rapiña(F) / uccello(M) predatore
- 食虫性の鳥 / insectivorous bird / Insektenfresser(M) / oiseau(M) insectivore / ave(F) insectívora / uccello(M) insettivoro
- 渉禽(しょうきん)/渉水鳥 / wading bird / Watvogel(M) / oiseau(M) échassier / ave(F) zancuda / uccello(M) trampoliere

足の例 / examples of feet / Beispiele(N) für Vogelfüße(M) / exemples(M) de pattes(F) / ejemplos(M) de patas(F) / esempi(M) di zampe(F)

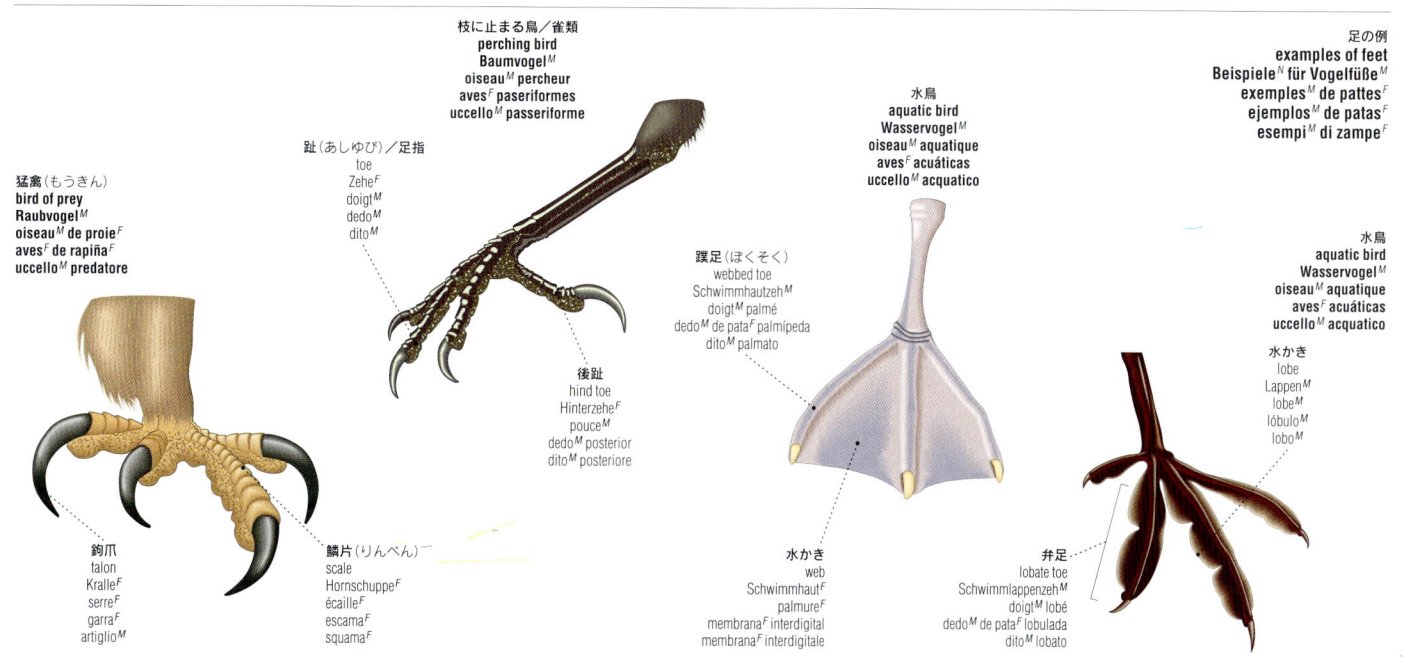

- 枝に止まる鳥／雀類 / perching bird / Baumvogel(M) / oiseau(M) percheur / aves(F) paseriformes / uccello(M) passeriforme
  - 趾(あしゆび)／足指 / toe / Zehe(F) / doigt(M) / dedo(M) / dito(M)
  - 後趾 / hind toe / Hinterzehe(F) / pouce(M) / dedo(M) posterior / dito(M) posteriore
  - 鱗片(りんぺん) / scale / Hornschuppe(F) / écaille(F) / escama(F) / squama(F)
- 猛禽(もうきん) / bird of prey / Raubvogel(M) / oiseau(M) de proie / aves(F) de rapiña(F) / uccello(M) predatore
  - 鉤爪 / talon / Kralle(F) / serre(F) / garra(F) / artiglio(M)
- 水鳥 / aquatic bird / Wasservogel(M) / oiseau(M) aquatique / aves(F) acuáticas / uccello(M) acquatico
  - 蹼足(ぼくそく) / webbed toe / Schwimmhautzeh(M) / doigt(M) palmé / dedo(M) de pata(F) palmípeda / dito(M) palmato
  - 水かき / web / Schwimmhaut(F) / palmure(F) / membrana(F) interdigital / membrana(F) interdigitale
- 水鳥 / aquatic bird / Wasservogel(M) / oiseau(M) aquatique / aves(F) acuáticas / uccello(M) acquatico
  - 水かき / lobe / Lappen(M) / lobe(M) / lóbulo(M) / lobo(M)
  - 弁足 / lobate toe / Schwimmlappenzeh(M) / doigt(M) lobé / dedo(M) de pata(F) lobulada / dito(M) lobato

117

鳥類 | BIRDS
VÖGEL | OISEAUX | AVES | UCCELLI

鳥の例

examples of birds | unterschiedliche Vogeltypen[M] | exemples[M] d'oiseaux | ejemplos[M] de pájaros[M] | esempi[M] di uccelli[M]

日本語 | 英語 | ドイツ語 | フランス語 | スペイン語 | イタリア語

動物

ハチドリ（蜂鳥）
hummingbird
Kolibri[M]
colibri[M]
colibri[M]
colibri[M]

コマドリ（駒鳥）／ロビン
European robin
Rotkehlchen[N]
rouge-gorge[M]
petirrojo[M]
pettirosso[M]

アトリ（花鶏）／フィンチ
finch
Fink[M]
pinson[M]
pinzón[M]
fringuello[M]

ゴシキヒワ（五色ひわ）
goldfinch
Stieglitz[M]
chardonneret[M]
jilguero[M]
cardellino[M]

ウソ
bullfinch
Gimpel[M]
bouvreuil[M]
pardillo[M]
ciuffolotto[M]

スズメ（雀）
sparrow
Sperling[M]
moineau[M]
gorrión[M]
passerotto[M]

ナイチンゲール
nightingale
Nachtigall[F]
rossignol[M]
ruiseñor[M]
usignolo[M]

ツバメ（燕）
swallow
Schwalbe[F]
hirondelle[F]
golondrina[F]
rondine[F]

カワセミ（川蝉）
kingfisher
Eisvogel[M]
martin-pêcheur[M]
martín[M] pescador
martin pescatore[M]

カササギ（鵲）
magpie
Elster[F]
pie[F]
urraca[M]
gazza[F]

ショウジョウコウカンチョウ（猩々紅冠鳥）
cardinal
Kardinal[M]
cardinal[M]
cardenal[M]
cardinale[M]

カケス（懸巣）
jay
Eichelhäher[M]
geai[M]
arrendajo[M]
ghiandaia[F]

ムクドリ（椋鳥）
starling
Star[M]
étourneau[M]
estornino[M]
stornello[M]

アマツバメ（雨燕）
swift
Mauersegler[M]
martinet[M]
vencejo[M]
rondone[M]

アメリカキンメフクロウ（金目梟）
northern saw-whet owl
Sägekauz[M]
petite nyctale[F]
lechuza[F] norteña
civetta[F] acadica

ヨーロッパヤマウズラ（山鶉）
partridge
Rebhuhn[N]
perdrix[F]
perdiz[F]
pernice[F]

タゲリ（田鳧）
lapwing
Kiebitz[M]
vanneau[M]
avefría[F]
pavoncella[F]

ミヤコドリ（都鳥）
oystercatcher
Austernfischer[M]
huîtrier[M] pie[F]
ostrero[M]
beccaccia[F] di mare[M]

キツツキ（啄木鳥）
woodpecker
Specht[M]
pic[M]
pájaro[M] carpintero
picchio[M]

カラス（烏）
raven
Rabe[M]
corbeau[M]
cuervo[M]
corvo[M]

コンゴウインコ（金剛いんこ）
macaw
Ara[M]
ara[M]
guacamayo[M]
macao[M]

オウム（鸚鵡）
cockatoo
Kakadu[M]
cacatoès[M]
cacatúa[F]
cacatua[F]

アジサシ（鯵刺）
tern
Seeschwalbe[F]
sterne[F]
golondrina[F] de mar
rondine[F] di mare[M]

118

鳥類 | BIRDS
VÖGEL | OISEAUX | AVES | UCCELLI

鳥の例

動物

アホウドリ（信天翁）
albatross
Albatros^M
albatros^M
albatros^M
albatros^M

オオハシ（巨嘴鳥）
toucan
Tukan^M
toucan^M
tucán^M
tucano^M

タカ（鷹）
falcon
Falke^M
faucon^M
halcón^M
falco^M

アメリカワシミミズク（鷲木菟）
great horned owl
Uhu^M
grand duc^M d'Amérique^F
búho^M real
gufo^M reale

サギ（鷺）
heron
Reiher^M
héron^M
garza^F
airone^M

コンドル
condor
Kondor^M
condor^M
cóndor^M
condor^M

ワシ（鷲）
eagle
Adler^M
aigle^M
águila^F
aquila^F

ペンギン
penguin
Pinguin^M
manchot^M
pingüino^M
pinguino^M

ペリカン
pelican
Pelikan^M
pélican^M
pelícano^M
pellicano^M

コウノトリ（鸛）
stork
Storch^M
cigogne^F
cigüeña^F
cicogna^F

ハゲワシ（禿鷲）
vulture
Geier^M
vautour^M
buitre^M
avvoltoio^M

ダチョウ（駝鳥）
ostrich
Strauß^M
autruche^F
avestruz^F
struzzo^M

クジャク（孔雀）
peacock
Pfau^M
paon^M
pavo^M real
pavone^M

フラミンゴ
flamingo
Flamingo^M
flamant^M
flamenco^M
fenicottero^M

119

鳥類 | BIRDS
VÖGEL | OISEAUX | AVES | UCCELLI

鳥の例

日本語 | 英語 | ドイツ語 | フランス語 | スペイン語 | イタリア語

動物

ヒヨコ（雛）
chick
Küken[N]
poussin[M]
polluelo[M]
pulcino[M]

ウズラ（鶉）
quail
Wachtel[F]
caille[F]
codorniz[F]
quaglia[F]

ハト（鳩）
pigeon
Taube[F]
pigeon[M]
paloma[F]
piccione[M]

カモ（鴨）
duck
Ente[F]
canard[M]
pato[M]
anatra[F]

雌鳥
hen
Huhn[N]
poule[F]
gallina[F]
gallina[F]

雄鶏
rooster
Hahn[M]
coq[M]
gallo[M]
gallo[M]

キジ（雉）
pheasant
Fasan[M]
faisan[M]
faisán[M]
fagiano[M]

ホロホロチョウ（珠鶏）
guinea fowl
Perlhuhn[N]
pintade[F]
pintada[F]
faraona[F]

ガチョウ（鵞鳥）
goose
Gans[F]
oie[F]
oca[F]
oca[F]

シチメンチョウ（七面鳥）
turkey
Truthahn[M]
dindon[M]
pavo[M]
tacchino[M]

120

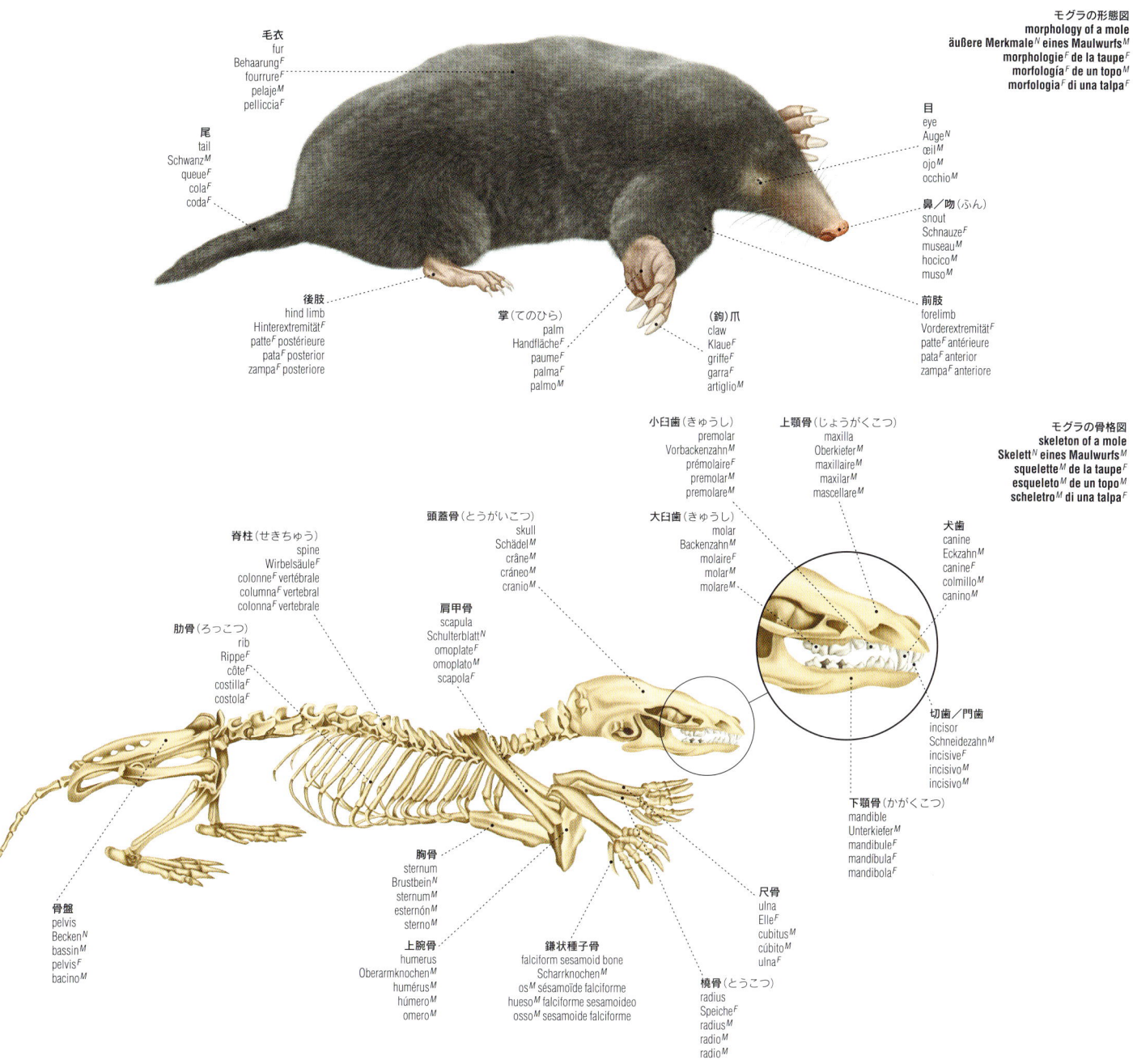

食虫哺乳動物 | INSECTIVOROUS MAMMALS
INSEKTENFRESSER | MAMMIFÈRES INSECTIVORES | MAMÍFEROS INSECTÍVOROS | MAMMIFERI INSETTIVORI

モグラ（土竜）

mole | Maulwurf^M | taupe^F | topo^M | talpa^F

モグラの形態図
morphology of a mole
äußere Merkmale^N eines Maulwurfs^M
morphologie^F de la taupe^F
morfología^F de un topo^M
morfologia^F di una talpa^F

- 毛衣 / fur / Behaarung^F / fourrure^F / pelaje^M / pelliccia^F
- 尾 / tail / Schwanz^M / queue^F / cola^F / coda^F
- 目 / eye / Auge^N / œil^M / ojo^M / occhio^M
- 鼻／吻（ふん）/ snout / Schnauze^F / museau^M / hocico^M / muso^M
- 後肢 / hind limb / Hinterextremität^F / patte^F postérieure / pata^F posterior / zampa^F posteriore
- 掌（てのひら）/ palm / Handfläche^F / paume^F / palma^F / palmo^M
- （鉤）爪 / claw / Klaue^F / griffe^F / garra^F / artiglio^M
- 前肢 / forelimb / Vorderextremität^F / patte^F antérieure / pata^F anterior / zampa^F anteriore

モグラの骨格図
skeleton of a mole
Skelett^N eines Maulwurfs^M
squelette^M de la taupe^F
esqueleto^M de un topo^M
scheletro^M di una talpa^F

- 小臼歯（きゅうし）/ premolar / Vorbackenzahn^M / prémolaire^F / premolar^M / premolare^M
- 上顎骨（じょうがくこつ）/ maxilla / Oberkiefer^M / maxillaire^M / maxilar^M / mascellare^M
- 頭蓋骨（とうがいこつ）/ skull / Schädel^M / crâne^M / cráneo^M / cranio^M
- 大臼歯（きゅうし）/ molar / Backenzahn^M / molaire^F / molar^M / molare^M
- 犬歯 / canine / Eckzahn^M / canine^F / colmillo^M / canino^M
- 脊柱（せきちゅう）/ spine / Wirbelsäule^F / colonne^F vertébrale / columna^F vertebral / colonna^F vertebrale
- 肩甲骨 / scapula / Schulterblatt^N / omoplate^F / omóplato^M / scapola^F
- 肋骨（ろっこつ）/ rib / Rippe^F / côte^F / costilla^F / costola^F
- 切歯／門歯 / incisor / Schneidezahn^M / incisive^F / incisivo^M / incisivo^M
- 下顎骨（かがくこつ）/ mandible / Unterkiefer^M / mandibule^F / mandíbula^F / mandibola^F
- 骨盤 / pelvis / Becken^N / bassin^M / pelvis^F / bacino^M
- 胸骨 / sternum / Brustbein^N / sternum^M / esternón^M / sterno^M
- 上腕骨 / humerus / Oberarmknochen^M / humérus^M / húmero^M / omero^M
- 鎌状種子骨 / falciform sesamoid bone / Scharrknochen^M / os^M sésamoïde falciforme / hueso^M falciforme sesamoideo / osso^M sesamoide falciforme
- 尺骨 / ulna / Elle^F / cubitus^M / cúbito^M / ulna^F
- 橈骨（とうこつ）/ radius / Speiche^F / radius^M / radio^M / radio^M

食虫哺乳動物の例

examples of insectivorous mammals | Beispiele^N für Insektenfresser^M | exemples^M de mammifères^M insectivores | ejemplos^M de mamíferos^M insectívoros | esempi^M di mammiferi^M insettivori

モグラ（土竜）
mole
Maulwurf^M
taupe^F
topo^M
talpa^F

ハリネズミ（針鼠）
hedgehog
Igel^M
hérisson^M
erizo^M
riccio^M

トガリネズミ（尖鼠）
shrew
Spitzmaus^F
musaraigne^F
musaraña^F
toporagno^M

齧歯類とウサギ目の動物 | RODENTS AND LAGOMORPHS
NAGETIERE UND HASENTIERE | MAMMIFÈRES RONGEURS ET LAGOMORPHES | ROEDORES Y LAGOMORFOS | RODITORI E LAGOMORFI

齧歯（げっし）類（動物）

日本語 | 英語 | ドイツ語 | フランス語 | スペイン語 | イタリア語

rodent | Nagetier[N] | rongeur[M] | roedor[M] | roditore[M]

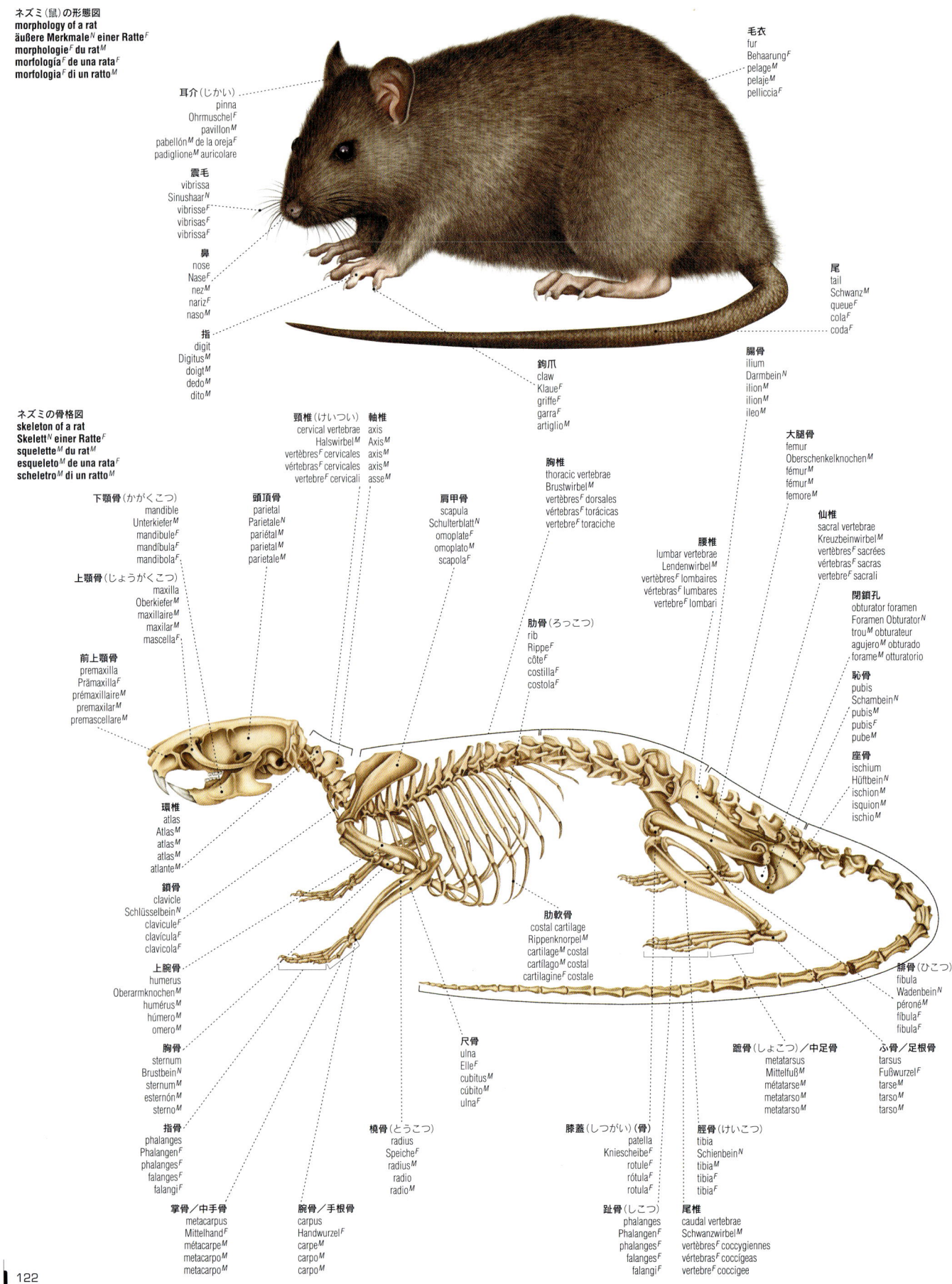

動物

ネズミ（鼠）の形態図
morphology of a rat
äußere Merkmale[N] einer Ratte[F]
morphologie[F] du rat[M]
morfología[F] de una rata[F]
morfologia[F] di un ratto[M]

耳介（じかい）
pinna
Ohrmuschel[F]
pavillon[M]
pabellón[M] de la oreja[F]
padiglione[M] auricolare

震毛
vibrissa
Sinushaar[N]
vibrisse[F]
vibrissa[F]
vibrissa[F]

鼻
nose
Nase[F]
nez[M]
nariz[F]
naso[M]

指
digit
Digitus[M]
doigt[M]
dedo[M]
dito[M]

鉤爪
claw
Klaue[F]
griffe[F]
garra[F]
artiglio[M]

毛衣
fur
Behaarung[F]
pelage[M]
pelaje[M]
pelliccia[F]

尾
tail
Schwanz[M]
queue[F]
cola[F]
coda[F]

ネズミの骨格図
skeleton of a rat
Skelett[N] einer Ratte[F]
squelette[M] du rat[M]
esqueleto[M] de una rata[F]
scheletro[M] di un ratto[M]

頸椎（けいつい）
cervical vertebrae
Halswirbel[M]
vertèbres[F] cervicales
vértebras[F] cervicales
vertebre[F] cervicali

軸椎
axis
Axis[M]
axis[M]
axis[M]
asse[M]

胸椎
thoracic vertebrae
Brustwirbel
vertèbres[F] dorsales
vértebras[F] torácicas
vertebre[F] toraciche

腰椎
lumbar vertebrae
Lendenwirbel[M]
vertèbres[F] lombaires
vértebras[F] lumbares
vertebre[F] lombari

腸骨
ilium
Darmbein[N]
ilion[M]
ilion[M]
ileo[M]

大腿骨
femur
Oberschenkelknochen[M]
fémur[M]
fémur[M]
femore[M]

仙椎
sacral vertebrae
Kreuzbeinwirbel[M]
vertèbres[F] sacrées
vértebras[F] sacras
vertebre[F] sacrali

下顎骨（かがくこつ）
mandible
Unterkiefer[M]
mandibule[F]
mandíbula[F]
mandibola[F]

頭頂骨
parietal
Parietale[N]
pariétal[M]
parietal[M]
parietale[M]

肩甲骨
scapula
Schulterblatt[N]
omoplate[F]
omoplato[M]
scapola[F]

閉鎖孔
obturator foramen
Foramen Obturator[N]
trou[M] obturateur
agujero[M] obturado
forame[M] otturatorio

上顎骨（じょうがくこつ）
maxilla
Oberkiefer[M]
maxillaire[M]
maxilar[M]
mascella[F]

肋骨（ろっこつ）
rib
Rippe[F]
côte[F]
costilla[F]
costola[F]

恥骨
pubis
Schambein[N]
pubis[M]
pubis[M]
pube[M]

前上顎骨
premaxilla
Prämaxilla[F]
prémaxillaire[M]
premaxilar[M]
premascellare[M]

座骨
ischium
Hüftbein[N]
ischion[M]
isquion[M]
ischio[M]

環椎
atlas
Atlas[M]
atlas[M]
atlas[M]
atlante[M]

鎖骨
clavicle
Schlüsselbein[N]
clavicule[F]
clavícula[F]
clavicola[F]

肋軟骨
costal cartilage
Rippenknorpel[M]
cartilage[M] costal
cartílago[M] costal
cartilagine[F] costale

上腕骨
humerus
Oberarmknochen[M]
humérus[M]
húmero[M]
omero[M]

腓骨（ひこつ）
fibula
Wadenbein[N]
péroné[M]
fíbula[F]
fibula[F]

胸骨
sternum
Brustbein[N]
sternum[M]
esternón[M]
sterno[M]

尺骨
ulna
Elle[F]
cubitus[M]
cúbito[M]
ulna[F]

蹠骨（しょこつ）／中足骨
metatarsus
Mittelfuß[M]
métatarse[M]
metatarso[M]
metatarso[M]

ふ骨／足根骨
tarsus
Fußwurzel[F]
tarse[M]
tarso[M]
tarso[M]

指骨
phalanges
Phalangen[F]
phalanges[F]
falanges[F]
falangi[F]

橈骨（とうこつ）
radius
Speiche[F]
radius[M]
radio[M]
radio[M]

膝蓋（しつがい）（骨）
patella
Kniescheibe[F]
rotule[F]
rótula[F]
rotula[F]

脛骨（けいこつ）
tibia
Schienbein[N]
tibia[M]
tibia[F]
tibia[F]

掌骨／中手骨
metacarpus
Mittelhand[F]
métacarpe[M]
metacarpo[M]
metacarpo[M]

腕骨／手根骨
carpus
Handwurzel[F]
carpe[M]
carpo[M]
carpo[M]

趾骨（しこつ）
phalanges
Phalangen[F]
phalanges[F]
falanges[F]
falangi[F]

尾椎
caudal vertebrae
Schwanzwirbel[M]
vertèbres[F] coccygiennes
vértebras[F] coccígeas
vertebre[F] coccigee

齧歯類とウサギ目の動物 | RODENTS AND LAGOMORPHS
NAGETIERE UND HASENTIERE | MAMMIFÈRES RONGEURS ET LAGOMORPHES | ROEDORES Y LAGOMORFOS | RODITORI E LAGOMORFI

齧歯(げっし)類動物の例

examples of rodents | Beispiele^N für Nagetiere^N | exemples^M de mammifères^M rongeurs^M | ejemplos^M de roedores^M | esempi^M di roditori^M

ノネズミ(野鼠)
field mouse
Feldmaus^F
mulot^M
ratón^M de campo^M
topo^M campagnolo

ネズミ(鼠)
rat
Ratte^F
rat^M
rata^F
ratto^M

シマリス(縞栗鼠)
chipmunk
Backenhörnchen^N
tamia^M
ardilla^M listada
tamia^M

テンジクネズミ(天竺鼠)／モルモット
guinea pig
Meerschweinchen^N
cobaye^N
cobaya^F
cavia^F

トビネズミ(跳鼠)
jerboa
Wüstenspringmaus^F
gerboise^F
jerbo^M
gerboa^M

マーモット
groundhog
Waldmurmeltier^N
marmotte^F
marmota^F
marmotta^F

ハムスター
hamster
Hamster^M
hamster^M
hámster^M
criceto^M

ヤマアラシ(山荒らし)
porcupine
Stachelschwein^N
porc-épic^M
puerco^M espín
porcospino^M

リス(栗鼠)
squirrel
Eichhörnchen^N
écureuil^M
ardilla^F
scoiattolo^M

ビーバー
beaver
Biber^M
castor^M
castor^M
castoro^M

齧歯(げっし)類とウサギ目の動物の顎(あご)

rodent's and lagomorph's jaws | Nagetierkiefer^M und Hasentierkiefer^M | mâchoires^F de rongeur et de lagomorphe^M | mandíbulas^F de roedores^M y lagomorfos^M | fauci^F di roditori^M e lagomorfi^M

齧歯類の顎
rodent's jaw: rat
Nagetierkiefer^M: Ratte^F
mâchoire^F de rongeur^M: rat^M
mandíbula^F de un roedor^M: rata^F
fauce^F di un roditore^M: ratto^M

大臼歯(きゅうし)
molar
Molar^M
molaire^F
molar^M
molare^M

小臼歯(きゅうし)
premolar
Prämolar^M
prémolaire^F
premolar^M
premolare^M

切歯／門歯
incisor
Schneidezahn^M
incisive^F
incisivo^M
incisivo^M

歯隙(しげき)
diastema
Laden^M
barre^F
diastema^F
diastema^M

ウサギ目の動物の顎: ウサギ(兎)
lagomorph's jaw: rabbit
Hasentierkiefer^M: Kaninchen^N
mâchoire^F de lagomorphe^M: lapin^M
mandíbula^F de un lagomorfo^M: conejo^M
fauce^F di un lagomorfo^M: coniglio^M

大臼歯(きゅうし)
molar
Backenzahn^M
molaire^F
molar^M
molare^M

小臼歯(きゅうし)
premolar
Vorbackenzahn^M
prémolaire^F
premolar^M
premolare^M

下顎骨(かがくこつ)
mandible
Unterkiefer^M
mandibule^F
mandíbula^F
mandibola^F

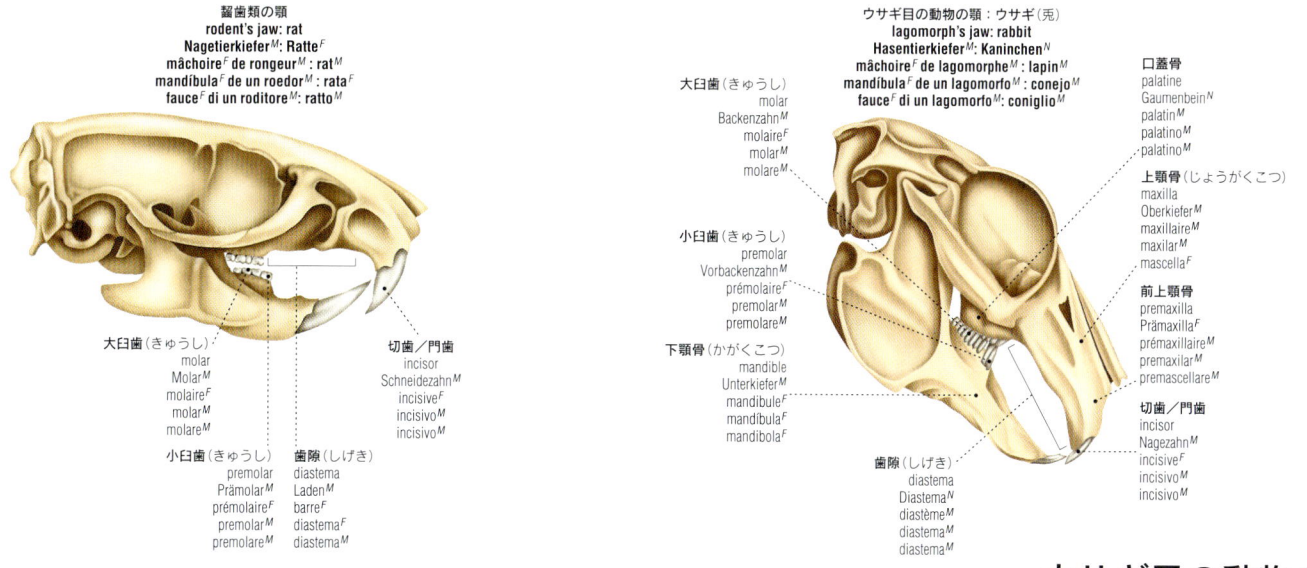

歯隙(しげき)
diastema
Diastema^N
diastème^M
diastema^M
diastema^M

口蓋骨
palatine
Gaumenbein^N
palatin^M
palatino^M
palatino^M

上顎骨(じょうがくこつ)
maxilla
Oberkiefer^M
maxillaire^M
maxilar^M
mascella^F

前上顎骨
premaxilla
Prämaxilla^F
prémaxillaire^M
premaxilar^M
premascellare^M

切歯／門歯
incisor
Nagezahn^M
incisive^F
incisivo^M
incisivo^M

ウサギ目の動物の例

examples of lagomorphs | Beispiele^N für Hasentiere^N | exemples^M de mammifères^M lagomorphes^M | ejemplos^M de lagomorfos^M | esempi^M di lagomorfi^M

ナキウサギ(啼兎)
pika
Pfeifhase^M
pika^M
pica^F
lepre^F fischiante

(アナ)ウサギ((穴)兎)
rabbit
Kaninchen^N
lapin^M
conejo^M
coniglio^M

ノウサギ(野兎)
hare
Hase^M
lièvre^M
liebre^F
lepre^F

有蹄哺乳動物 | UNGULATE MAMMALS
HUFTIERE | MAMMIFÈRES ONGULÉS | MAMÍFEROS UNGULADOS | MAMMIFERI UNGULATI

ウマ（馬）

日本語 | 英語 | ドイツ語 | フランス語 | スペイン語 | イタリア語

horse | Pferd[N] | cheval[M] | caballo[M] | cavallo[M]

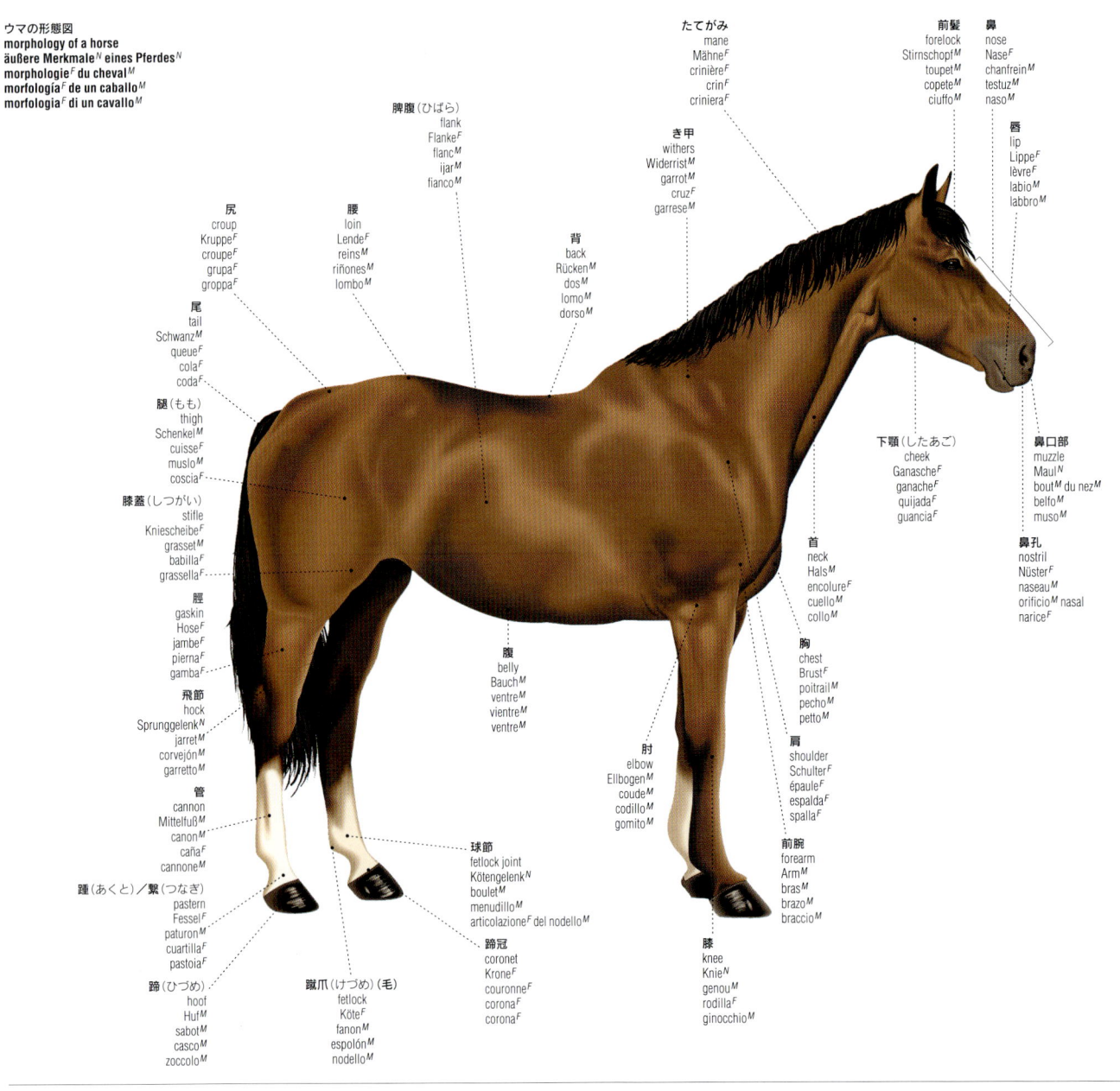

動物

ウマの形態図
morphology of a horse
äußere Merkmale[N] **eines Pferdes**[N]
morphologie[F] **du cheval**[M]
morfología[F] **de un caballo**[M]
morfologia[F] **di un cavallo**[M]

脾腹（ひばら）
flank
Flanke[F]
flanc[M]
ijar[M]
fianco[M]

たてがみ
mane
Mähne[F]
crinière[F]
crin[F]
criniera[F]

前髪
forelock
Stirnschopf[M]
toupet[M]
copete[M]
ciuffo[M]

鼻
nose
Nase[F]
chanfrein[M]
testuz[M]
naso[M]

尻
croup
Kruppe[F]
croupe[F]
grupa[F]
groppa[F]

腰
loin
Lende[F]
reins[M]
riñones[M]
lombo[M]

背
back
Rücken[M]
dos[M]
lomo[M]
dorso[M]

き甲
withers
Widerrist[M]
garrot[M]
cruz[F]
garrese[M]

唇
lip
Lippe[F]
lèvre[F]
labio[M]
labbro[M]

尾
tail
Schwanz[M]
queue[F]
cola[F]
coda[F]

腿（もも）
thigh
Schenkel[M]
cuisse[F]
muslo[M]
coscia[F]

下顎（したあご）
cheek
Ganasche[F]
ganache[F]
quijada[F]
guancia[F]

鼻口部
muzzle
Maul[N]
bout[M] du nez[M]
belfo[M]
muso[M]

膝蓋（しつがい）
stifle
Kniescheibe[F]
grasset[M]
babilla[F]
grassella[F]

鼻孔
nostril
Nüster[F]
naseau[M]
orificio[M] nasal
narice[F]

脛
gaskin
Hose[F]
jambe[F]
pierna[F]
gamba[F]

首
neck
Hals[M]
encolure[F]
cuello[M]
collo[M]

腹
belly
Bauch[M]
ventre[M]
vientre[M]
ventre[M]

胸
chest
Brust[F]
poitrail[M]
pecho[M]
petto[M]

飛節
hock
Sprunggelenk[N]
jarret[M]
corvejón[M]
garretto[M]

肘
elbow
Ellbogen[M]
coude[M]
codillo[M]
gomito[M]

肩
shoulder
Schulter[F]
épaule[F]
espalda[F]
spalla[F]

管
cannon
Mittelfuß[M]
canon[M]
caña[F]
cannone[M]

球節
fetlock joint
Kötengelenk[N]
boulet[M]
menudillo[M]
articolazione[F] del nodello[M]

前腕
forearm
Arm[M]
bras[M]
brazo[M]
braccio[M]

踵（あくと）／繋（つなぎ）
pastern
Fessel[F]
paturon[M]
cuartilla[F]
pastoia[F]

蹄冠
coronet
Krone[F]
couronne[F]
corona[F]
corona[F]

膝
knee
Knie[N]
genou[M]
rodilla[F]
ginocchio[M]

蹄（ひづめ）
hoof
Huf[M]
sabot[M]
casco[M]
zoccolo[M]

蹴爪（けづめ）（毛）
fetlock
Köte[F]
fanon[M]
espolón[M]
nodello[M]

足並み
gaits
Gangarten[F]
allures[F]
andaduras[F]
andature[F]

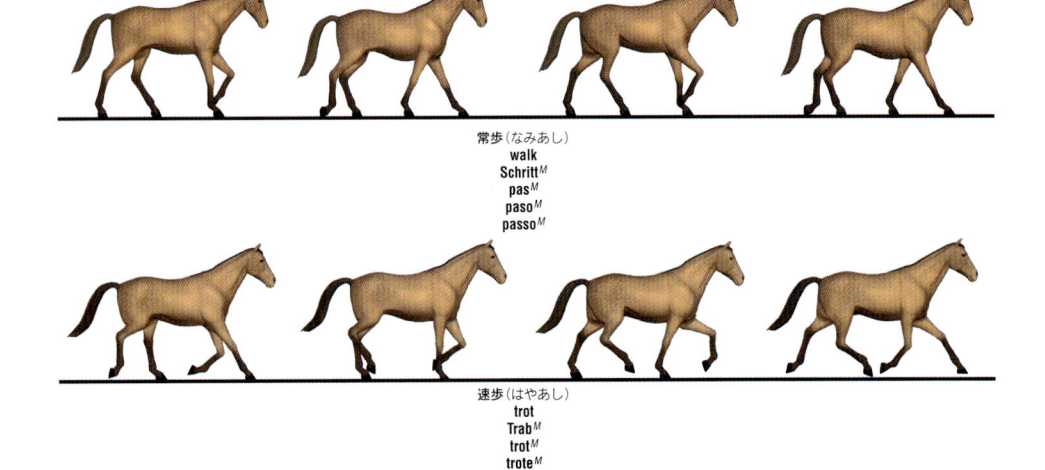

常歩（なみあし）
walk
Schritt[M]
pas[M]
paso[M]
passo[M]

速歩（はやあし）
trot
Trab[M]
trot[M]
trote[M]
trotto[M]

124

有蹄哺乳動物 | UNGULATE MAMMALS
HUFTIERE | MAMMIFÈRES ONGULÉS | MAMÍFEROS UNGULADOS | MAMMIFERI UNGULATI

ウマ（馬）

ウマの解剖図
anatomy of a horse
Anatomie^F eines Pferdes^N
anatomie^F du cheval^M
anatomía^F de un caballo^M
anatomia^F di un cavallo^M

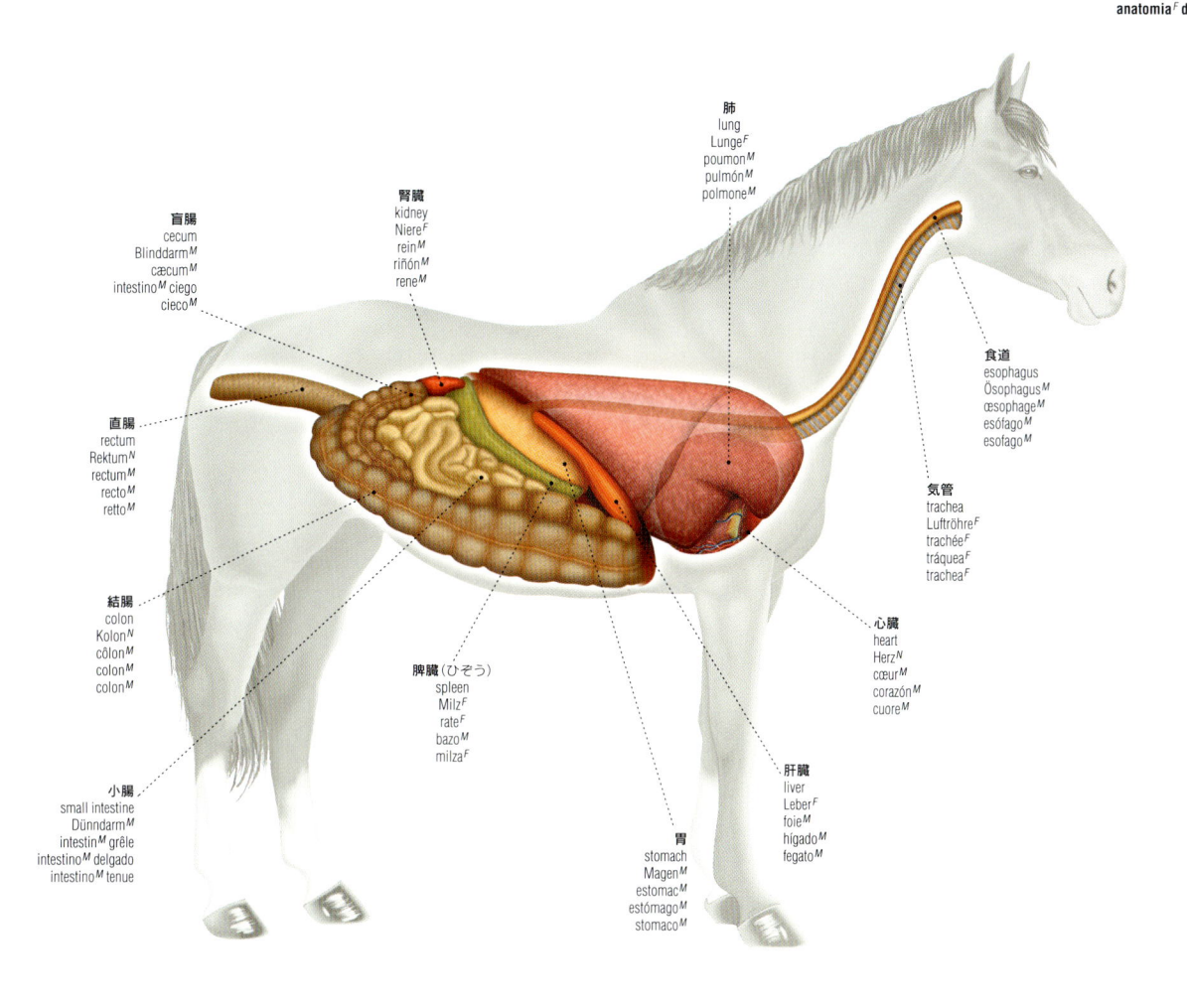

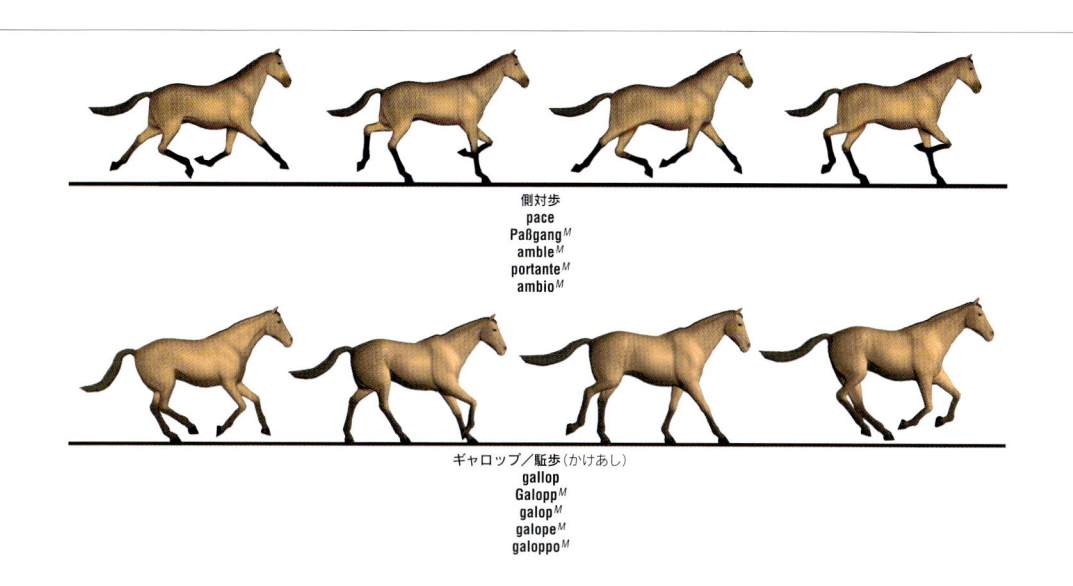

動物

肺
lung
Lunge^F
poumon^M
pulmón^M
polmone^M

腎臓
kidney
Niere^F
rein^M
riñón^M
rene^M

盲腸
cecum
Blinddarm^M
cæcum^M
intestino^M ciego
cieco^M

食道
esophagus
Ösophagus^M
œsophage^M
esófago^M
esofago^M

直腸
rectum
Rektum^N
rectum^M
recto^M
retto^M

気管
trachea
Luftröhre^F
trachée^F
tráquea^F
trachea^F

結腸
colon
Kolon^N
côlon^M
colon^M
colon^M

心臓
heart
Herz^N
cœur^M
corazón^M
cuore^M

脾臓（ひぞう）
spleen
Milz^F
rate^F
bazo^M
milza^F

肝臓
liver
Leber^F
foie^M
hígado^M
fegato^M

小腸
small intestine
Dünndarm^M
intestin^M grêle
intestino^M delgado
intestino^M tenue

胃
stomach
Magen^M
estomac^M
estómago^M
stomaco^M

側対歩
pace
Paßgang^M
amble^M
portante^M
ambio^M

ギャロップ／駈歩（かけあし）
gallop
Galopp^M
galop^M
galope^M
galoppo^M

有蹄哺乳動物 | UNGULATE MAMMALS
HUFTIERE | MAMMIFÈRES ONGULÉS | MAMÍFEROS UNGULADOS | MAMMIFERI UNGULATI

ウマ（馬）

日本語 | 英語 | ドイツ語 | フランス語 | スペイン語 | イタリア語

ウマの骨格図
skeleton of a horse
Skelett^N eines Pferdes^N
squelette^M du cheval^M
esqueleto^M de un caballo^M
scheletro^M di un cavallo^M

頭蓋骨（とうがいこつ）
skull
Schädel^M
crâne^M
cráneo^M
cranio^M

環椎
atlas
Atlas^M
atlas^M
atlas^M
atlante^M

肋骨（ろっこつ）
rib
Rippe^F
côte^F
costilla^F
costola^F

大腿骨
femur
Oberschenkel^M
fémur^M
fémur^M
femore^M

肩甲骨
scapula
Schulterblatt^N
omoplate^F
omoplato^M
scapola^F

骨盤
pelvis
Darmbein^N
bassin^M
pelvis^M
pelvi^F

腓骨（ひこつ）
fibula
Griffelbein^N
péroné^M
peroné^M
fibula^F

下顎骨（かがくこつ）
mandible
Unterkiefer^M
mandibule^F
mandíbula^F inferior
mandibola^F

上腕骨
humerus
Oberarmbein^N
humérus^M
húmero^M
omero^M

踵骨（しょうこつ）
calcaneus
Fersenbeinhöcker^M
calcanéum^M
calcáneo^M
calcagno^M

肘頭（ちゅうとう）
olecranon
Ellbogenhöcker^M
olécrane^M
olécrano^M
olecrano^M

胸骨
sternum
Brustbein^N
sternum^M
esternón^M
sterno^M

膝蓋（しつがい）（骨）
patella
Kniescheibe^F
rotule^F
rótula^F
patella^F

橈骨（とうこつ）
radius
Speiche^F
radius^M
radio^M
radio^M

尺骨
ulna
Elle^F
cubitus^M
cúbito^M
ulna^F

脛骨（けいこつ）
tibia
Unterschenkel^M
tibia^M
tibia^F
tibia^F

腕骨／手根骨
carpus
Vorderfußwurzel^F
carpe^M
carpo^M
carpo^M

基節骨／基趾骨（きしこつ）
proximal phalanx
Fesselbein^N
première phalange^F
primera falange^F
prima falange^F

掌骨／中手骨
metacarpus
Röhrbein^N
métacarpe^M
metacarpo^M
metacarpo^M

中節骨／中趾骨（ちゅうしこつ）
middle phalanx
Kronbein^N
deuxième phalange^F
falangina^F
seconda falange^F

基種子骨
proximal sesamoid
Sesambein^N
grand sésamoïde^M
sesamoideo^M mayor
sesamoide^M prossimale

末種子骨
distal sesamoid
Strahlbein^N
petit sésamoïde^M
sesamoideo^M menor
sesamoide^M distale

末節骨／末趾骨（まっしこつ）
distal phalanx
Hufbein^N
troisième phalange^F
falangeta^F
terza falange^F

跗骨／足根骨
tarsus
Fußwurzel^F
tarse^M
tarso^M
tarso^M

蹠骨（しょこつ）／中足骨
metatarsus
Mittelfußknochen^M
métatarse^M
metatarso^M
metatarso^M

頸椎
cervical vertebrae
Halswirbel^M
vertèbres^F cervicales
vértebras^F cervicales
vertebre^F cervicali

胸椎
thoracic vertebrae
Brustwirbel^M
vertèbres^F dorsales
vértebras^F torácicas
vertebre^F toraciche

腰椎
lumbar vertebrae
Lendenwirbel^M
vertèbres^F lombaires
vértebras^F lumbares
vertebre^F lombari

仙椎
sacral vertebrae
Kreuzbeinwirbel^M
vertèbres^F sacrées
vértebras^F sacras
vertebre^F sacrali

尾椎
caudal vertebrae
Schwanzwirbel^M
vertèbres^F coccygiennes
vértebras^F caudales
vertebre^F coccigee

有蹄哺乳動物 | UNGULATE MAMMALS
HUFTIERE | MAMMIFÈRES ONGULÉS | MAMÍFEROS UNGULADOS | MAMMIFERI UNGULATI

ウマ（馬）

蹄鉄の打ち付け面
plantar surface of the hoof
Unterseite^F des Hufs^M
face^F plantaire du sabot^M
superficie^F plantar del casco^M
superficie^F plantare dello zoccolo^M

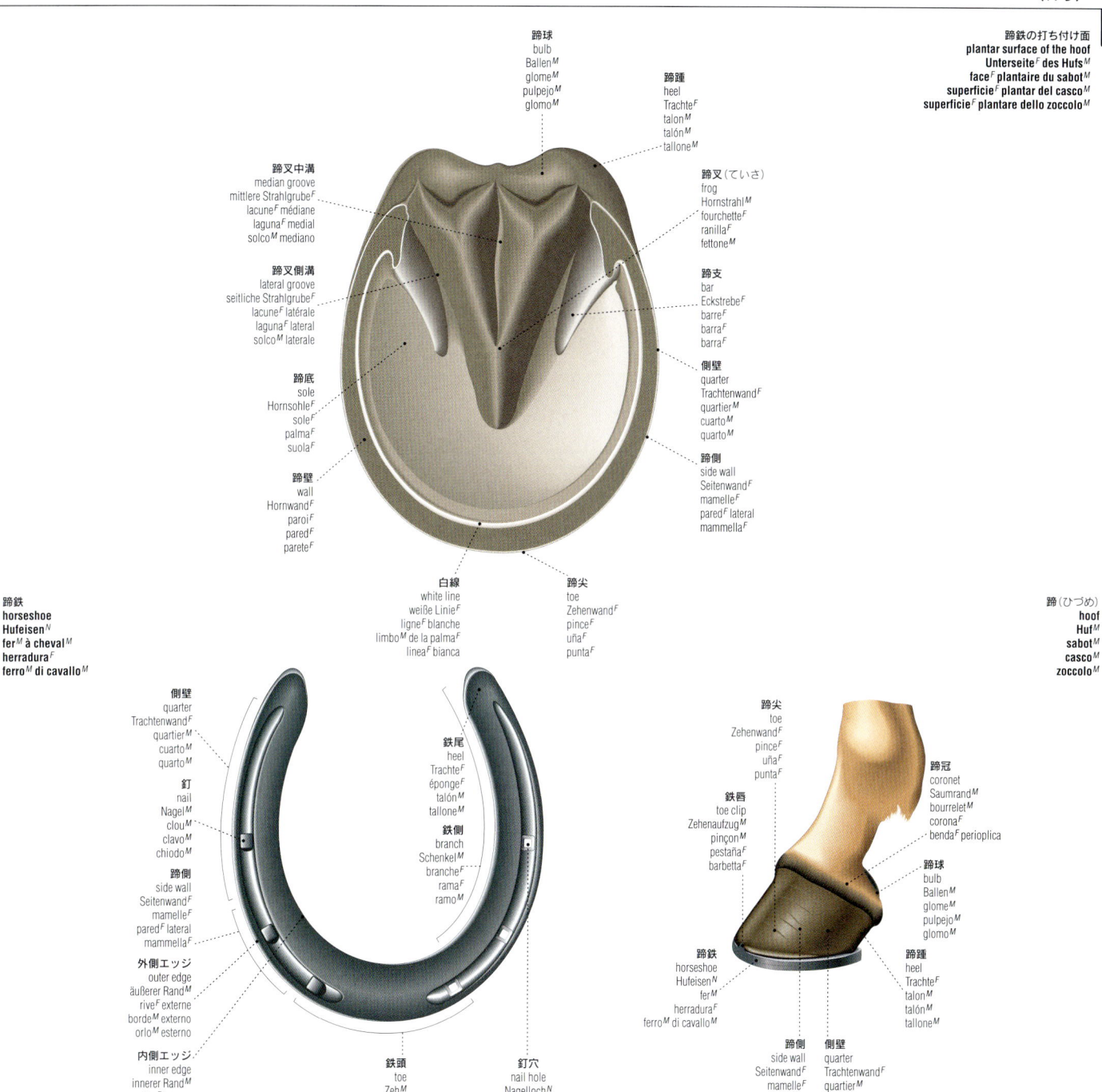

蹄球
bulb
Ballen^M
glome^M
pulpejo^M
glomo^M

蹄踵
heel
Trachte^F
talon^M
talón^M
tallone^M

蹄叉中溝
median groove
mittlere Strahlgrube^F
lacune^F médiane
laguna^F medial
solco^M mediano

蹄叉（ていさ）
frog
Hornstrahl^M
fourchette^F
ranilla^F
fettone^M

蹄叉側溝
lateral groove
seitliche Strahlgrube^F
lacune^F latérale
laguna^F lateral
solco^M laterale

蹄支
bar
Eckstrebe^F
barre^F
barra^F
barra^F

蹄底
sole
Hornsohle^F
sole^F
palma^F
suola^F

側壁
quarter
Trachtenwand^F
quartier^M
cuarto^M
quarto^M

蹄壁
wall
Hornwand^F
paroi^F
pared^F
parete^F

蹄鉄
horseshoe
Hufeisen^N
fer^M à cheval^M
herradura^F
ferro^M di cavallo^M

白線
white line
weiße Linie^F
ligne^F blanche
limbo^M de la palma^F
linea^F bianca

蹄尖
toe
Zehenwand^F
pince^F
uña^F
punta^F

蹄（ひづめ）
hoof
Huf^M
sabot^M
casco^M
zoccolo^M

側壁
quarter
Trachtenwand^F
quartier^M
cuarto^M
quarto^M

鉄尾
heel
Trachte^F
éponge^F
talón^M
tallone^M

釘
nail
Nagel^M
clou^M
clavo^M
chiodo^M

鉄側
branch
Schenkel^M
branche^F
rama^F
ramo^M

蹄側
side wall
Seitenwand^F
mamelle^F
pared^F lateral
mammella^F

外側エッジ
outer edge
äußerer Rand^M
rive^F externe
borde^M externo
orlo^M esterno

内側エッジ
inner edge
innerer Rand^M
rive^F interne
borde^M interno
orlo^M interno

鉄頭
toe
Zeh^M
pince^F
uña^F
punta^F

鉄唇
toe clip
Zehenaufzug^M
pinçon^M
pestaña^F
barbetta^F

釘穴
nail hole
Nagelloch^N
étampure^F
clavera^F
stampa^F

蹄尖
toe
Zehenwand^F
pince^F
uña^F
punta^F

蹄冠
coronet
Saumrand^M
bourrelet^M
corona^F
benda^F perioplica

蹄球
bulb
Ballen^M
glome^M
pulpejo^M
glomo^M

蹄踵
heel
Trachte^F
talon^M
talón^M
tallone^M

蹄鉄
horseshoe
Hufeisen^M
fer^M
herradura^F
ferro^M di cavallo^M

蹄側
side wall
Seitenwand^F
mamelle^F
pared^F lateral
mammella^F

側壁
quarter
Trachtenwand^F
quartier^M
cuarto^M
quarto^M

動物

蹄（ひづめ）の例

examples of hoofs | Beispiele^N für Hufe^M | exemples^M de sabots^M | ejemplos^M de pezuñas^F | esempi^M di zoccoli^M

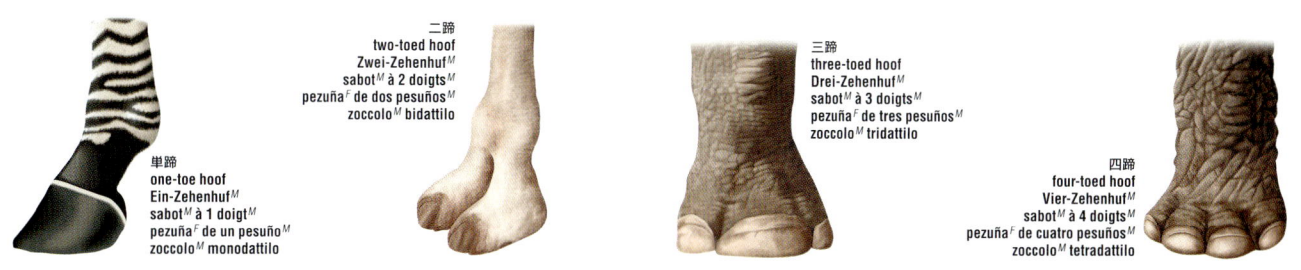

単蹄
one-toe hoof
Ein-Zehenhuf^M
sabot^M à 1 doigt^M
pezuña^F de un pesuño^M
zoccolo^M monodattilo

二蹄
two-toed hoof
Zwei-Zehenhuf^M
sabot^M à 2 doigts^M
pezuña^F de dos pesuños^M
zoccolo^M bidattilo

三蹄
three-toed hoof
Drei-Zehenhuf^M
sabot^M à 3 doigts^M
pezuña^F de tres pesuños^M
zoccolo^M tridattilo

四蹄
four-toed hoof
Vier-Zehenhuf^M
sabot^M à 4 doigts^M
pezuña^F de cuatro pesuños^M
zoccolo^M tetradattilo

有蹄哺乳動物 | UNGULATE MAMMALS
HUFTIERE | MAMMIFÈRES ONGULÉS | MAMÍFEROS UNGULADOS | MAMMIFERI UNGULATI

有蹄哺乳動物の例

日本語 | 英語 | ドイツ語 | フランス語 | スペイン語 | イタリア語

examples of ungulate mammals | Beispiele[N] für Huftiere | exemples[M] de mammifères[M] ongulés | ejemplos[M] de mamíferos[M] ungulados | esempi[M] di mammiferi[M] ungulati

ペッカリー
peccary
Nabelschwein[N]
pécari[M]
pécari[M]
pecari[M]

イノシシ（猪）
wild boar
Wildschwein[N]
sanglier[M]
jabalí[M]
cinghiale[M]

ブタ（豚）
pig
Schwein[N]
porc[M]
cerdo[M]
maiale[M]

ヤギ（山羊）
goat
Ziege[F]
chèvre[F]
cabra[F]
capra[F]

アンテロープ／レイヨウ（羚羊）
antelope
Antilope[F]
antilope[F]
antílope[M]
antilope[F]

ヒツジ（羊）
sheep
Schaf[N]
mouton[M]
oveja[F]
pecora[F]

子牛
calf
Kalb[N]
veau[M]
ternero[M]
vitello[M]

オジロジカ（尾白鹿）
white-tailed deer
Reh[N]
cerf[M] de Virginie
ciervo[M] de Virginia[F]
cervo[M] dalla coda[F] bianca

ムフロン
mouflon
Mufflon[M]
mouflon[M]
muflón[M]
muflone[M]

トナカイ
caribou; *reindeer*
Rentier[N]
renne[M]
reno[M]
renna[F]

ワピチ
wapiti; *Canadian elk*
Wapitihirsch[M]
cerf[M] du Canada
uapití[M]
wapiti[M]

オカピ
okapi
Okapi[N]
okapi[M]
okapi[M]
okapi[M]

ロバ（驢馬）
ass
Esel[M]
âne[M]
asno[M]
asino[M]

ラバ（騾馬）
mule
Maultier[N]
mulet[M]
mula[F]
mulo[M]

雌牛
cow
Kuh[F]
vache[F]
vaca[F]
mucca[F]

シマウマ（縞馬）／ゼブラ
zebra
Zebra[N]
zèbre[M]
cebra[F]
zebra[F]

ラマ
llama
Lama[N]
lama[M]
llama[F]
lama[M]

バイソン
bison
Bison[M]
bison[M]
bisonte[M]
bisonte[M]

スイギュウ（水牛）／バッファロー
buffalo
Büffel[M]
buffle[M]
búfalo[M]
bufalo[M]

128

有蹄哺乳動物 | UNGULATE MAMMALS
HUFTIERE | MAMMIFÈRES ONGULÉS | MAMÍFEROS UNGULADOS | MAMMIFERI UNGULATI

有蹄哺乳動物の例

雄牛
ox
Ochse^M
bœuf^M
buey^M
bue^M

ヤク
yak
Yak^M
yack^M
yak^M
yak^M

ウマ（馬）
horse
Pferd^N
cheval^M
caballo^M
cavallo^M

ヘラジカ（へら鹿）
moose; *elk*
Elch^M
élan^M
alce^M
alce^F

フタコブラクダ（双峰駱駝）
bactrian camel
Kamel^N
chameau^M
camello^M
cammello^M

ヒトコブラクダ（単峰駱駝）
dromedary camel
Dromedar^N
dromadaire^M
dromedario^M
dromedario^M

サイ（犀）
rhinoceros
Nashorn^N
rhinocéros^M
rinoceronte^M
rinoceronte^M

カバ（河馬）
hippopotamus
Nilpferd^N
hippopotame^M
hipopótamo^M
ippopotamo^M

キリン
giraffe
Giraffe^F
girafe^F
jirafa^F
giraffa^F

ゾウ（象）
elephant
Elefant^M
éléphant^M
elefante^M
elefante^M

129

肉食哺乳動物 | CARNIVOROUS MAMMALS
RAUBTIERE | MAMMIFÈRES CARNIVORES | MAMÍFEROS CARNÍVOROS | MAMMIFERI CARNIVORI

イヌ（犬）

日本語 | 英語 | ドイツ語 | フランス語 | スペイン語 | イタリア語

dog | Hund[M] | chien[M] | perro[M] | cane[M]

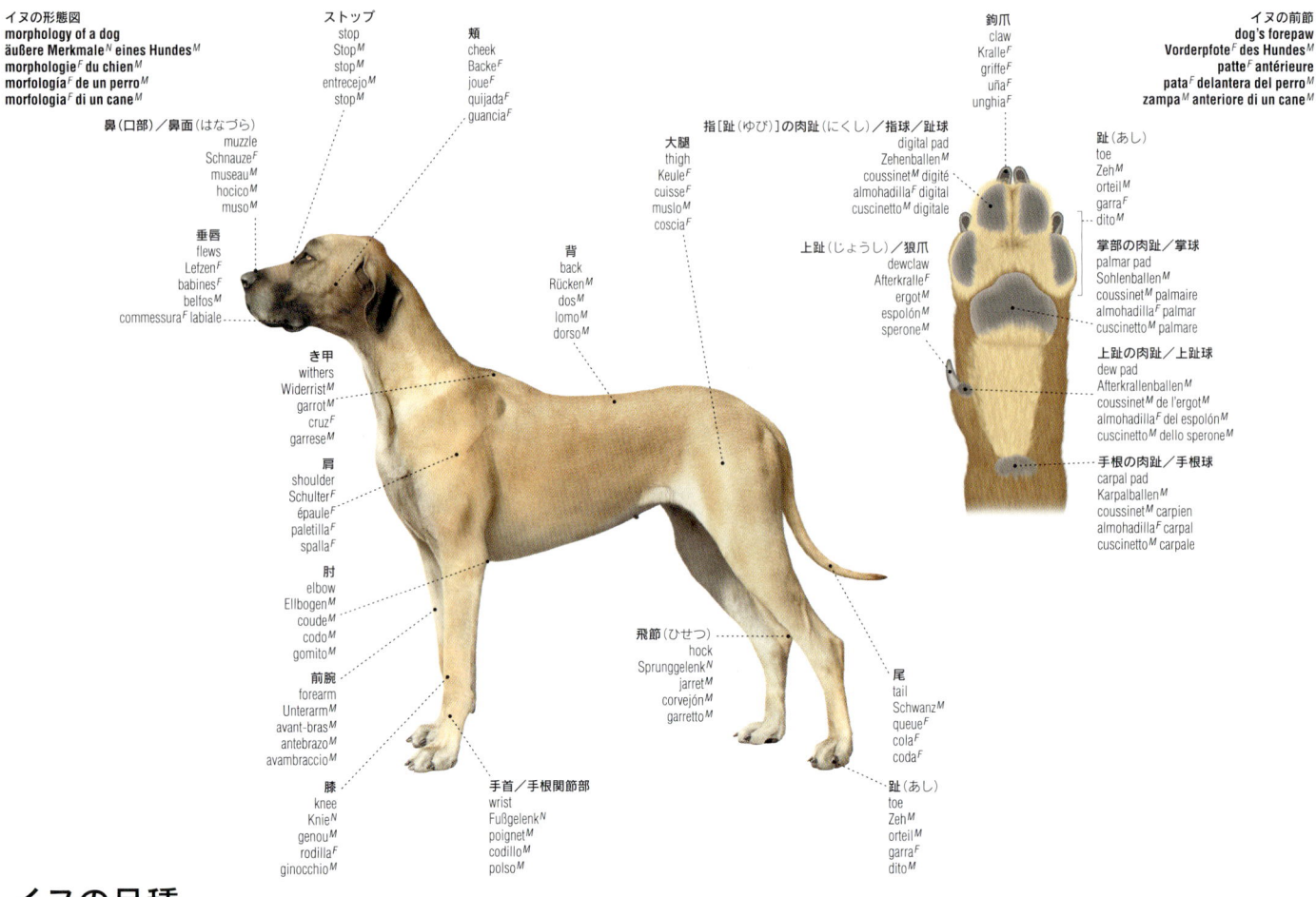

イヌの形態図
morphology of a dog
äußere Merkmale[N] eines Hundes[M]
morphologie[F] du chien[M]
morfología[F] de un perro[M]
morfologia[F] di un cane[M]

鼻（口部）／鼻面（はなづら）
muzzle
Schnauze[F]
museau[M]
hocico[M]
muso[M]

垂唇
flews
Lefzen[F]
babines[F]
belfos[M]
commessura[F] labiale

き甲
withers
Widerrist[M]
garrot[M]
cruz[F]
garrese[M]

肩
shoulder
Schulter[F]
épaule[F]
paletilla[F]
spalla[F]

肘
elbow
Ellbogen[M]
coude[M]
codo[M]
gomito[M]

前腕
forearm
Unterarm[M]
avant-bras[M]
antebrazo[M]
avambraccio[M]

膝
knee
Knie[N]
genou[M]
rodilla[F]
ginocchio[M]

ストップ
stop
Stop[M]
stop[M]
entrecejo[M]
stop[M]

頬
cheek
Backe[F]
joue[F]
quijada[F]
guancia[F]

大腿
thigh
Keule[F]
cuisse[F]
muslo[M]
coscia[F]

背
back
Rücken[M]
dos[M]
lomo[M]
dorso[M]

飛節（ひせつ）
hock
Sprunggelenk[N]
jarret[M]
corvejón[M]
garretto[M]

手首／手根関節部
wrist
Fußgelenk[N]
poignet[M]
codillo[M]
polso[M]

指［趾（ゆび）］の肉趾（にくし）／指球／趾球
digital pad
Zehenballen[M]
coussinet[M] digité
almohadilla[F] digital
cuscinetto[M] digitale

上趾（じょうし）／狼爪
dewclaw
Afterkralle[F]
ergot[M]
espolón[M]
sperone[M]

尾
tail
Schwanz[M]
queue[F]
cola[F]
coda[F]

趾（あし）
toe
Zeh[M]
orteil[M]
garra[F]
dito[M]

鉤爪
claw
Kralle[F]
griffe[F]
uña[F]
unghia[F]

イヌの前節
dog's forepaw
Vorderpfote[F] des Hundes[M]
patte[F] antérieure
pata[F] delantera del perro[M]
zampa[M] anteriore di un cane[M]

趾（あし）
toe
Zeh[M]
orteil[M]
garra[F]
dito[M]

掌部の肉趾／掌球
palmar pad
Sohlenballen[M]
coussinet[M] palmaire
almohadilla[F] palmar
cuscinetto[M] palmare

上趾の肉趾／上趾球
dew pad
Afterkrallenballen[M]
coussinet[M] de l'ergot[M]
almohadilla[F] del espolón[M]
cuscinetto[M] dello sperone[M]

手根の肉趾／手根球
carpal pad
Karpalballen[M]
coussinet[M] carpien
almohadilla[F] carpal
cuscinetto[M] carpale

イヌの品種

dog breeds | Hunderassen[F] | races[F] de chiens[M] | razas[F] de perros[M] | razze[F] canine

ブルドッグ
bulldog
Bulldogge[F]
bouledogue[M]
buldog[M]
bulldog[M]

シュナウツァー
schnauzer
Schnauzer[M]
schnauzer[M]
schnauzer[M]
schnauzer[M]

プードル
poodle
Pudel[M]
caniche[M]
caniche[M]
barbone[M]

チャウ・チャウ
chow chow
Chow-Chow[M]
chow-chow[M]
chow chow[M]
chow-chow[M]

コリー
collie
Collie[M]
colley[M]
collie[M]
collie[M]

ジャーマン［ドイツ］・シェパード
German shepherd
Deutscher Schäferhund[M]
berger[M] allemand
pastor[M] alemán
pastore[M] tedesco

肉食哺乳動物 | CARNIVOROUS MAMMALS
RAUBTIERE | MAMMIFÈRES CARNIVORES | MAMÍFEROS CARNÍVOROS | MAMMIFERI CARNIVORI

イヌ（犬）

イヌの骨格図
skeleton of a dog
Skelett^N eines Hunds^M
squelette^M du chien^M
esqueleto^M de un perro^M
scheletro^M di un cane^M

前頭骨
frontal bone
Stirnbein^N
frontal^M
hueso^M frontal^M
osso^M frontale

頭頂骨
parietal bone
Scheitelbein^N
pariétal^M
hueso^M parietal^M
osso^M parietale

眼窩（がんか）
orbit
Augenhöhle^F
orbite^F
órbita^F
orbita^F

上顎骨（じょうがくこつ）
maxilla
Oberkiefer^M
maxillaire^M supérieur
maxilar^F
mascella^F

橈骨（とうこつ）
radius
Speiche^F
radius^M
radio^M
radio^M

尺骨
ulna
Elle^F
cubitus^M
cúbito^M
ulna^F

掌骨／中手骨
metacarpus
Mittelhand^F
métacarpe^M
metacarpo^M
metacarpo^M

環椎
atlas
Atlas^M
atlas^M
atlas^M
atlante^M

後頭骨
occipital bone
Hinterhauptbein^N
occipital^M
hueso^M occipital^M
osso^M occipitale

肩甲骨
scapula
Schulterblatt^N
omoplate^F
omoplato^M
scapola^F

下顎骨（かがくこつ）
mandible
Unterkiefer^M
mandibule^F
mandíbula^F
mandibola^F

上腕骨
humerus
Oberarmknochen^M
humérus^M
húmero^M
omero^M

腕骨／手根骨
carpus
Handwurzel^F
carpe^M
carpo^M
carpo^M

頸椎
cervical vertebrae
Halswirbel^M
vertèbres^F cervicales
vértebras^F cervicales
vertebre^F cervicali

胸椎
thoracic vertebrae
Brustwirbel^M
vertèbres^F dorsales
vértebras^F torácicas
vertebre^F toraciche

膝蓋（しつがい）（骨）
patella
Kniescheibe^F
rotule^F
rótula^F
rotula^F

ふ骨／足根骨
tarsus
Fußwurzel^F
tarse^M
tarso^M
tarso^M

胸骨
sternum
Brustbein^N
sternum^M
esternón^M
sterno^M

肋骨（ろっこつ）
rib
Rippe^F
côte^F
costilla^F
costola^F

腰椎
lumbar vertebrae
Lendenwirbel^M
vertèbres^F lombaires
vértebras^F lumbares
vertebre^F lombari

仙椎
sacral vertebrae
Kreuzbeinwirbel^M
vertèbres^F sacrées
vértebras^F sacras
vertebre^F sacrali

大腿骨
femur
Oberschenkelknochen^M
fémur^M
fémur^M
femore^M

尾椎
caudal vertebrae
Schwanzwirbel^M
vertèbres^F coccygiennes
vértebras^F caudales
vertebre^F coccigee

腓骨（ひこつ）
fibula
Wadenbein^N
péroné^M
peroné^M
fibula^F

脛骨（けいこつ）
tibia
Schienbein^N
tibia^M
tibia^M
tibia^F

蹠骨（しょこつ）／中足骨
metatarsus
Mittelfuß^M
métatarse^M
metatarso^M
metatarso^M

趾骨（しこつ）
phalanges
Zehenglieder^N
phalanges^F
falanges^F
falangi^F

動物

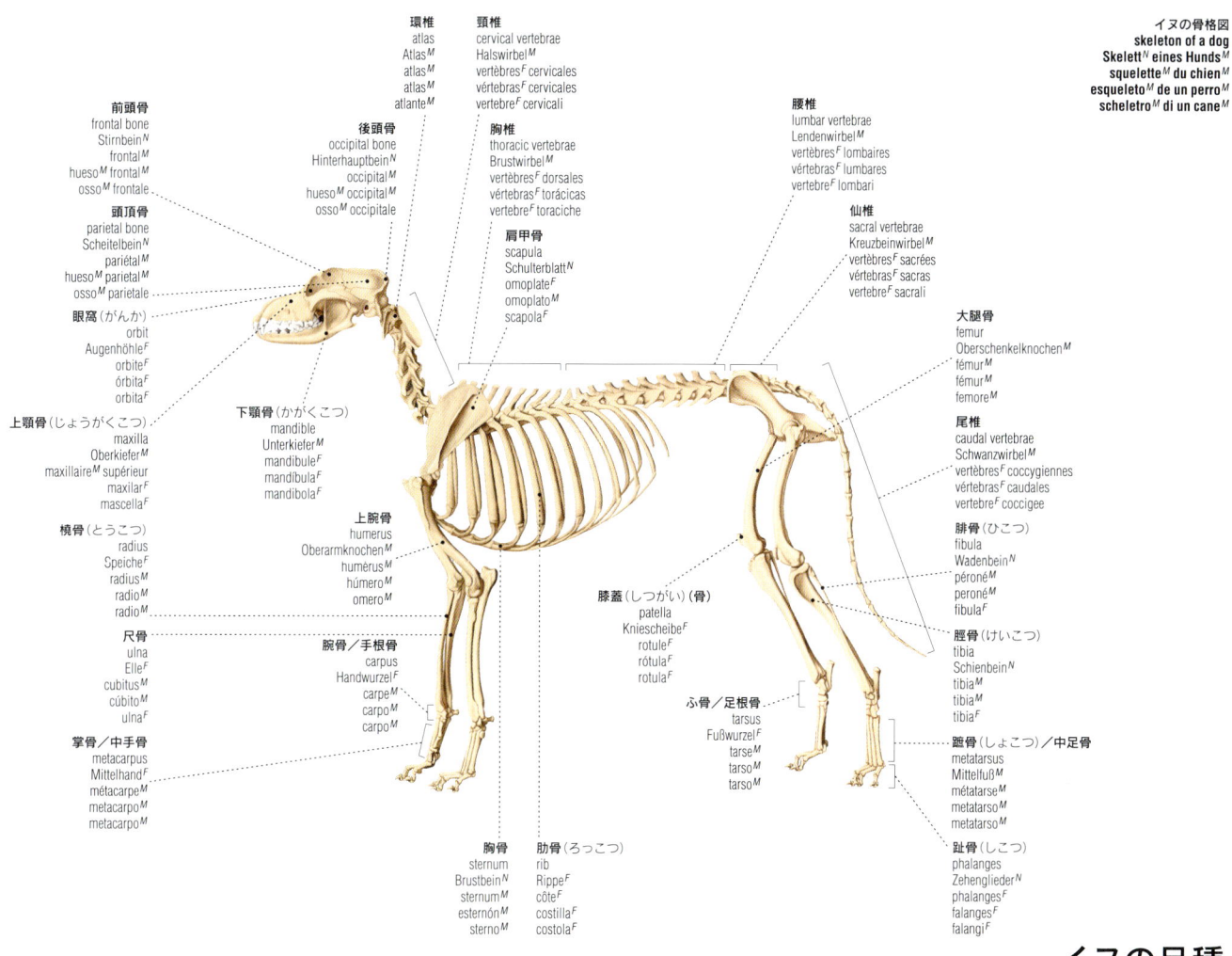

イヌの品種

ダルマシアン／ダルメシアン
dalmatian
Dalmatiner^M
dalmatien^M
dálmata^M
dalmata^M

セント・バーナード
Saint Bernard
Bernhardiner^M
saint-bernard^M
San Bernardo^M
sanbernardo^M

グレーハウンド
greyhound
Windhund^M
lévrier^M
lebrero^M
levriero^M

グレート・デーン
Great Dane
Dänische Dogge^F
danois^M
Gran Danés^M
alano^M

肉食哺乳動物 | CARNIVOROUS MAMMALS
RAUBTIERE | MAMMIFÈRES CARNIVORES | MAMÍFEROS CARNÍVOROS | MAMMIFERI CARNIVORI

ネコ（猫）

cat | Katze[F] | chat[M] | gato[M] doméstico | gatto[M]

日本語 | 英語 | ドイツ語 | フランス語 | スペイン語 | イタリア語

動物

ネコの頭部
cat's head
Kopf[M] der Katze[F]
tête[F]
cabeza[F]
testa[F] di gatto[M]

触毛
whiskers
Schnurrhaare[N]
sourcils[M]
bigotes[M]
vibrisse[F]

上瞼（まぶた）
upper eyelid
oberes Augenlid[N]
paupière[F] supérieure
párpado[M] superior
palpebra[F] superiore

下瞼（まぶた）
lower eyelid
unteres Augenlid[N]
paupière[F] inférieure
párpado[M] inferior
palpebra[F] inferiore

瞬膜
nictitating membrane
Nickhaut[F]
paupière[F] interne
párpado[M] interno
membrana[F] nittitante

触毛
whiskers
Schnurrhaare[N]
moustaches[F]
bigotes[M]
vibrisse[F]

唇
lip
Lippe[F]
lèvre[F]
labio[M]
labbro[M]

睫（まつげ）
eyelashes
Wimpern[F]
cils[M]
pestañas[F]
ciglia[F]

瞳孔
pupil
Pupille[F]
pupille[F]
pupila[F]
pupilla[F]

鼻鏡
nose leather
Nasenspiegel[M]
truffe[F]
ala[F] de la nariz[F]
rinario

鼻（口部）／鼻面（はなづら）
muzzle
Schnauze[F]
museau[M]
hocico[M]
muso[M]

ネコの品種

cat breeds | Katzenrassen[F] | races[F] de chats[M] | razas[F] de gatos[M] | razze[F] di gatti[M]

アメリカン・ショートヘア
American shorthair
Amerikanische Kurzhaarkatze[F]
américain[M] à poil[M] court
American[M] shorthair
gatto[M] americano a pelo[M] corto

ペルシャ・ネコ
Persian
Perserkatze[F]
persan[M]
persa[M]
persiano[M]

メイン・クーン
Maine coon
Maine Coon[F]
Maine coon[M]
Maine Coon[M]
gatto[M] del Maine

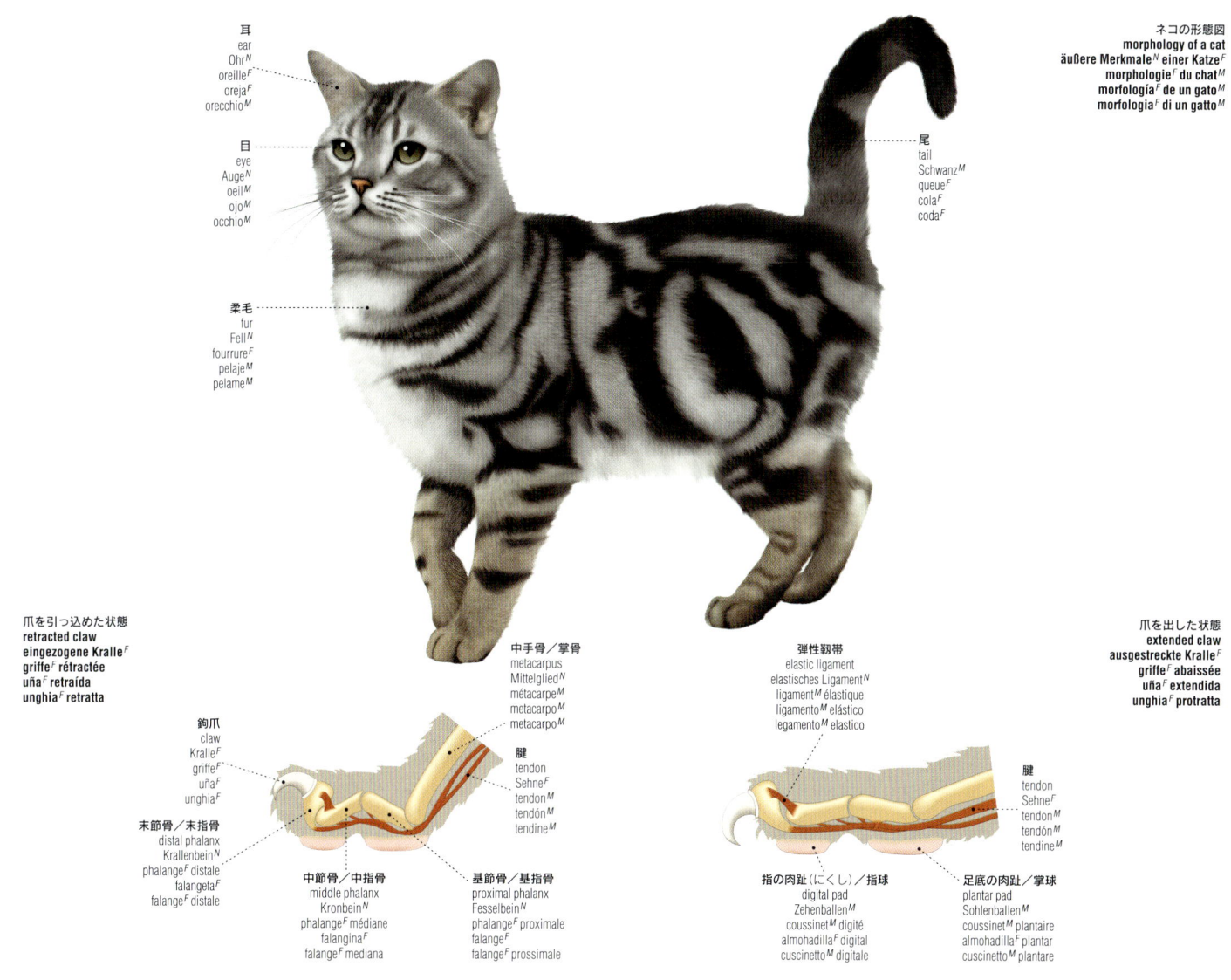

肉食哺乳動物 | CARNIVOROUS MAMMALS
RAUBTIERE | MAMMIFÈRES CARNIVORES | MAMÍFEROS CARNÍVOROS | MAMMIFERI CARNIVORI

ネコ（猫）

ネコの形態図
morphology of a cat
äußere Merkmale^N einer Katze^F
morphologie^F du chat^M
morfología^F de un gato^M
morfologia^F di un gatto^M

耳
ear
Ohr^N
oreille^F
oreja^F
orecchio^M

目
eye
Auge^N
oeil^M
ojo^M
occhio^M

尾
tail
Schwanz^M
queue^F
cola^F
coda^F

柔毛
fur
Fell^N
fourrure^F
pelaje^M
pelame^M

爪を引っ込めた状態
retracted claw
eingezogene Kralle^F
griffe^F rétractée
uña^F retraída
unghia^F retratta

爪を出した状態
extended claw
ausgestreckte Kralle^F
griffe^F abaissée
uña^F extendida
unghia^F protratta

中手骨／掌骨
metacarpus
Mittelglied^N
métacarpe^M
metacarpo^M
metacarpo^M

弾性靱帯
elastic ligament
elastisches Ligament^N
ligament^M élastique
ligamento^M elástico
legamento^M elastico

鉤爪
claw
Kralle^F
griffe^F
uña^F
unghia^F

腱
tendon
Sehne^F
tendon^M
tendón^M
tendine^M

腱
tendon
Sehne^F
tendon^M
tendón^M
tendine^M

末節骨／末指骨
distal phalanx
Krallenbein^N
phalange^F distale
falangeta^F
falange^F distale

中節骨／中指骨
middle phalanx
Kronbein^N
phalange^F médiane
falangina^F
falange^F mediana

基節骨／基指骨
proximal phalanx
Fesselbein^N
phalange^F proximale
falange^F
falange^F prossimale

指の肉趾（にくし）／指球
digital pad
Zehenballen^M
coussinet^M digité
almohadilla^F digital
cuscinetto^M digitale

足底の肉趾／掌球
plantar pad
Sohlenballen^M
coussinet^M plantaire
almohadilla^F plantar
cuscinetto^M plantare

ネコの品種

シャム・ネコ
Siamese
Siamkatze^F
siamois^M
siamés^M
siamese^M

アビシニアン
Abyssinian
Abessinierkatze^F
abyssin^M
abisinio^M
abissino^M

マンクス
Manx
Manxkatze^F
chat^M de l'île^F de Man
Manx^M
gatto^M dell'isola^F di Man

肉食哺乳動物 | CARNIVOROUS MAMMALS
RAUBTIERE | MAMMIFÈRES CARNIVORES | MAMÍFEROS CARNÍVOROS | MAMMIFERI CARNIVORI

肉食哺乳動物の例

examples of carnivorous mammals | Beispiele^N für Raubtiere^N | exemples^M de mammifères^M carnivores | ejemplos^M de mamíferos^M carnívoros | esempi^M di mammiferi^M carnivori

日本語 | 英語 | ドイツ語 | フランス語 | スペイン語 | イタリア語

ミンク
mink
Nerz^M
vison^M
visón^M
visone^M

ムナジロテン（胸白貂）
stone marten
Steinmarder^M
fouine^F
garduña^F
faina^F

テン（貂）
marten
Marder^M
martre^F
marta^F
martora^F

イタチ
weasel
Wiesel^N
belette^F
comadreja^F
donnola^F

キツネ（狐）
fox
Fuchs^M
renard^M
zorro^M
volpe^F

アライグマ（洗い熊）
raccoon
Waschbär^M
raton^M laveur
mapache^M
procione^M

フェネック
fennec
Wüstenfuchs^M
fennec^M
fenec^M
volpe^F del deserto^M

カワウソ（獺）
river otter
Seeotter^M
loutre^F de rivière^F
nutria^F de río^M
lontra^F comune

ハイイロ（灰色）マングース
mongoose
Mungo^M
mangouste^F
mangosta^F
mangusta^F

アナグマ（穴熊）
badger
Dachs^M
blaireau^M
tejón^M
tasso^M

スカンク
skunk
Stinktier^N
moufette^F
mofeta^M
moffetta^F

ハイエナ
hyena
Hyäne^F
hyène^F
hiena^F
iena^F

オオヤマネコ（大山猫）
lynx
Luchs^M
lynx^M
lince^M
lince^F

オオカミ（狼）
wolf
Wolf^M
loup^M
lobo^M
lupo^M

クーガー
cougar
Puma^M
puma^M
puma^M
puma^M

肉食哺乳動物 | CARNIVOROUS MAMMALS
RAUBTIERE | MAMMIFÈRES CARNIVORES | MAMÍFEROS CARNÍVOROS | MAMMIFERI CARNIVORI

肉食哺乳動物の例

動物

チーター
cheetah
Gepard^M
guépard^M
guepardo^M
ghepardo^M

ヒョウ(豹)
leopard
Leopard^M
léopard^M
leopardo^M
leopardo^M

ライオン
lion
Löwe^M
lion^M
león^M
leone^M

ジャガー
jaguar
Jaguar^M
jaguar^M
jaguar^M
giaguaro^M

トラ(虎)
tiger
Tiger^M
tigre^M
tigre^M
tigre^F

ホッキョクグマ(北極熊)
polar bear
Eisbär^M
ours^M polaire
oso^M polar
orso^M polare

アメリカクロクマ(黒熊)
black bear
Schwarzbär^M
ours^M noir
oso^M negro
orso^M bruno

135

海棲哺乳動物 | MARINE MAMMALS
MEERESSÄUGETIERE | MAMMIFÈRES MARINS | MAMÍFEROS ACUÁTICOS | MAMMIFERI MARINI

イルカ（海豚）

日本語 | 英語 | ドイツ語 | フランス語 | スペイン語 | イタリア語

dolphin | Delphin^M | dauphin^M | delfín^M | delfino^M

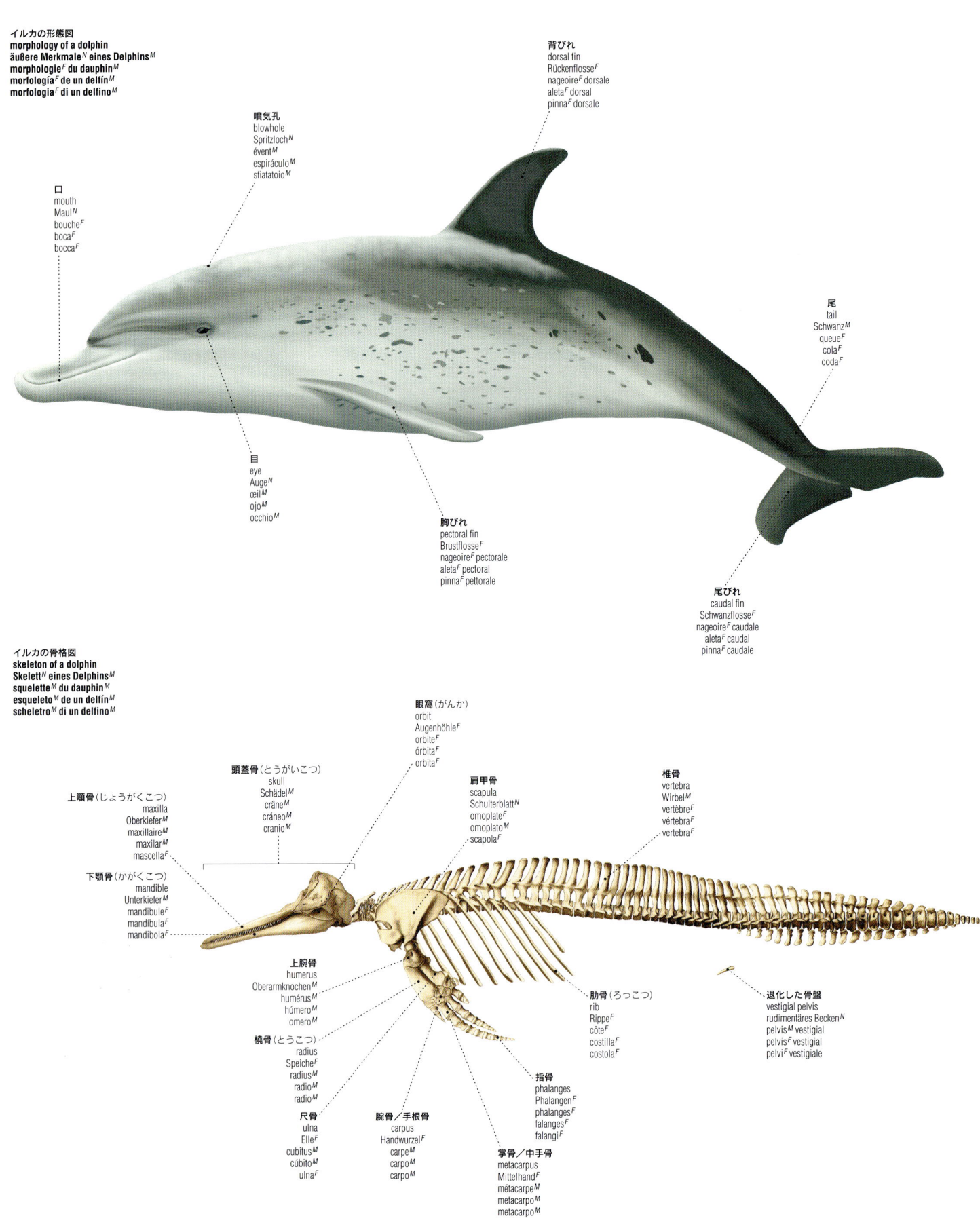

イルカの形態図
morphology of a dolphin
äußere Merkmale^N eines Delphins^M
morphologie^F du dauphin^M
morfología^F de un delfín^M
morfologia^F di un delfino^M

噴気孔
blowhole
Spritzloch^N
évent^M
espiráculo^M
sfiatatoio^M

背びれ
dorsal fin
Rückenflosse^F
nageoire^F dorsale
aleta^F dorsal
pinna^F dorsale

口
mouth
Maul^N
bouche^F
boca^F
bocca^F

尾
tail
Schwanz^M
queue^F
cola^F
coda^F

目
eye
Auge^N
œil^M
ojo^M
occhio^M

胸びれ
pectoral fin
Brustflosse^F
nageoire^F pectorale
aleta^F pectoral
pinna^F pettorale

尾びれ
caudal fin
Schwanzflosse^F
nageoire^F caudale
aleta^F caudal
pinna^F caudale

イルカの骨格図
skeleton of a dolphin
Skelett^N eines Delphins^M
squelette^M du dauphin^M
esqueleto^M de un delfín^M
scheletro^M di un delfino^M

眼窩（がんか）
orbit
Augenhöhle^F
orbite^F
órbita^F
orbita^F

頭蓋骨（とうがいこつ）
skull
Schädel^M
crâne^M
cráneo^M
cranio^M

肩甲骨
scapula
Schulterblatt^N
omoplate^F
omoplato^M
scapola^F

椎骨
vertebra
Wirbel^M
vertèbre^F
vértebra^F
vertebra^F

上顎骨（じょうがくこつ）
maxilla
Oberkiefer^M
maxillaire^M
maxilar^M
mascella^F

下顎骨（かがくこつ）
mandible
Unterkiefer^M
mandibule^F
mandíbula^F
mandibola^F

上腕骨
humerus
Oberarmknochen^M
humérus^M
húmero^M
omero^M

肋骨（ろっこつ）
rib
Rippe^F
côte^F
costilla^F
costola^F

退化した骨盤
vestigial pelvis
rudimentäres Becken^N
pelvis^M vestigial
pelvis^F vestigial
pelvi^F vestigiale

橈骨（とうこつ）
radius
Speiche^F
radius^M
radio^M
radio^M

指骨
phalanges
Phalangen^F
phalanges^F
falanges^F
falangi^F

尺骨
ulna
Elle^F
cubitus^M
cúbito^M
ulna^F

腕骨／手根骨
carpus
Handwurzel^F
carpe^M
carpo^M
carpo^M

掌骨／中手骨
metacarpus
Mittelhand^F
métacarpe^M
metacarpo^M
metacarpo^M

海棲哺乳動物 | MARINE MAMMALS
MEERESSÄUGETIERE | MAMMIFÈRES MARINS | MAMÍFEROS ACUÁTICOS | MAMMIFERI MARINI

海棲哺乳動物の例

examples of marine mammals | Beispiele^N für Meeressäugetiere^N | exemples^M de mammifères^M marins | ejemplos^M de mamíferos^M marinos | esempi^M di mammiferi^M marini

アザラシ（海豹）
seal
Seehund^M
phoque^M
foca^F
foca^F

アシカ（海驢）
sea lion
Seelöwe^M
otarie^F
otaria^F
leone^M marino

イルカ（海豚）
dolphin
Delphin^M
dauphin^M
delfín^M
delfino

ネズミイルカ（鼠海豚）
porpoise
Tümmler^M
marsouin^M
marsopa^F
focena^F

イッカク（一角）
narwhal
Narwal^M
narval^M
narval^M
narvalo^M

シロイルカ（白海豚）／シロクジラ（白鯨）
beluga whale
Weißwal^M
béluga^M
ballena^F blanca
balena^F bianca

シャチ（鯱）
killer whale
Schwertwal^M
orque^F
orca^F
orca^F

セイウチ（海象）
walrus
Walroß^N
morse^M
morsa^F
tricheco^M

ザトウクジラ（座頭鯨）
humpback whale
Buckelwal^M
rorqual^M
rorcual^M
balenottera^F

セミクジラ（背美鯨）
northern right whale
Wal^M
baleine^F
ballena^F
balena^F

マッコウクジラ（抹香鯨）
sperm whale
Pottwal^M
cachalot^M
cachalote^M
capodoglio^M

霊長類 | PRIMATE MAMMALS
PRIMATEN | MAMMIFÈRES PRIMATES | MAMÍFEROS PRIMATES | PRIMATI

ゴリラ

gorilla | Gorilla^M | gorille^M | gorila^M | gorilla^M

日本語 | 英語 | ドイツ語 | フランス語 | スペイン語 | イタリア語

ゴリラの骨格図
skeleton of a gorilla
Skelett^N eines Gorillas^M
squelette^M du gorille^M
esqueleto^M de un gorila^M
scheletro^M di un gorilla^M

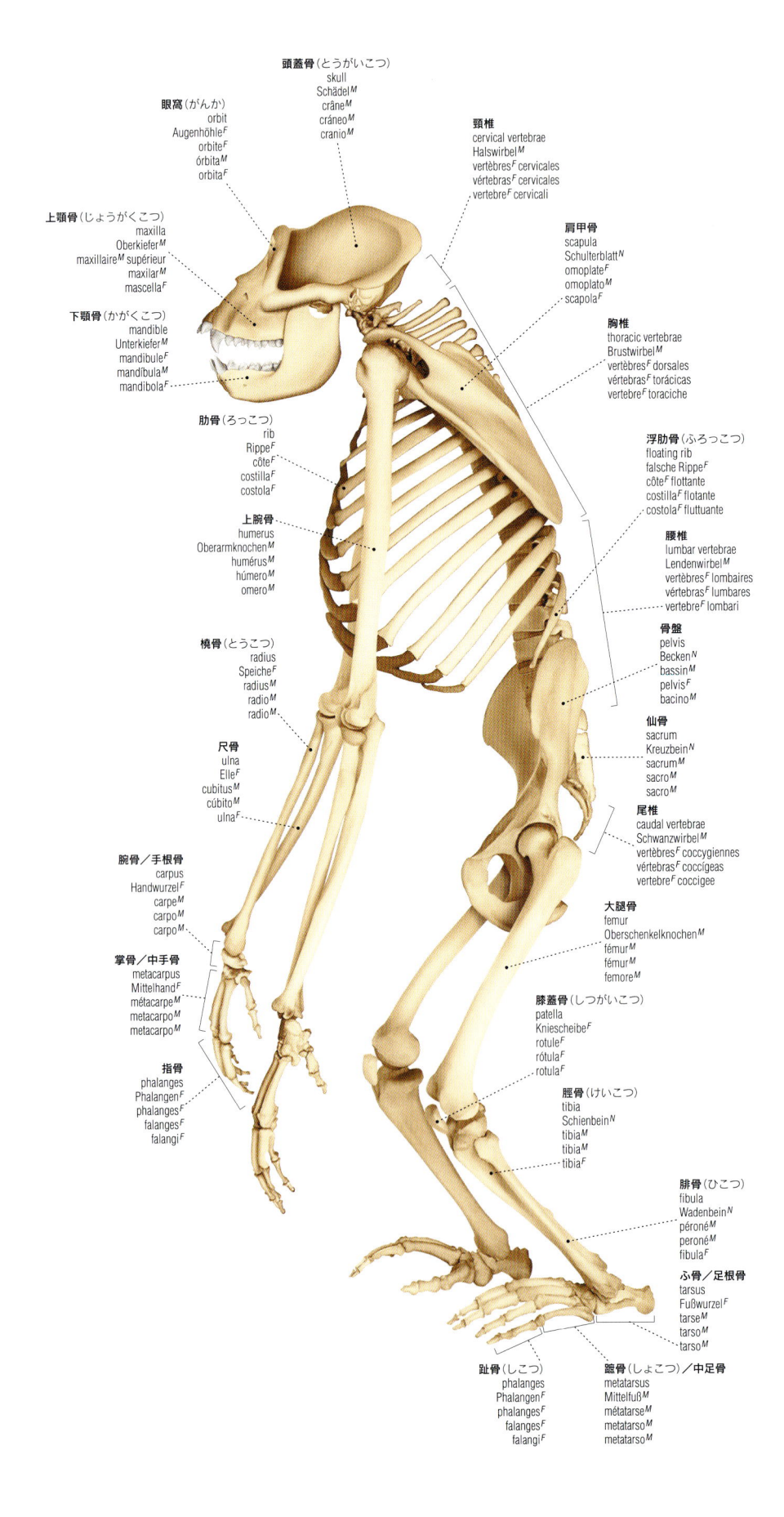

動物

眼窩(がんか)
orbit
Augenhöhle^F
orbite^F
órbita^M
orbita^F

頭蓋骨(とうがいこつ)
skull
Schädel^M
crâne^M
cráneo^M
cranio^M

頸椎
cervical vertebrae
Halswirbel
vertèbres^F cervicales
vértebras^F cervicales
vertebre^F cervicali

上顎骨(じょうがくこつ)
maxilla
Oberkiefer^M
maxillaire^M supérieur
maxilar^M
mascella^F

肩甲骨
scapula
Schulterblatt^N
omoplate^F
omoplato^M
scapola^F

下顎骨(かがくこつ)
mandible
Unterkiefer^M
mandibule^F
mandíbula^M
mandibola^F

胸椎
thoracic vertebrae
Brustwirbel^M
vertèbres^F dorsales
vértebras^F torácicas
vertebre^F toraciche

肋骨(ろっこつ)
rib
Rippe^F
côte^F
costilla^F
costola^F

浮肋骨(ふろっこつ)
floating rib
falsche Rippe^F
côte^F flottante
costilla^F flotante
costola^F fluttuante

上腕骨
humerus
Oberarmknochen^M
humérus^M
húmero^M
omero^M

腰椎
lumbar vertebrae
Lendenwirbel^M
vertèbres^F lombaires
vértebras^F lumbares
vertebre^F lombari

橈骨(とうこつ)
radius
Speiche^F
radius^M
radio^M
radio^M

骨盤
pelvis
Becken^N
bassin^M
pelvis^F
bacino^M

仙骨
sacrum
Kreuzbein^N
sacrum^M
sacro^M
sacro^M

尺骨
ulna
Elle^F
cubitus^M
cúbito^M
ulna^F

尾椎
caudal vertebrae
Schwanzwirbel^M
vertèbres^F coccygiennes
vértebras^F coccígeas
vertebre^F coccigee

腕骨／手根骨
carpus
Handwurzel^F
carpe^M
carpo^M
carpo^M

大腿骨
femur
Oberschenkelknochen^M
fémur^M
fémur^M
femore^M

掌骨／中手骨
metacarpus
Mittelhand^F
métacarpe^M
metacarpo^M
metacarpo^M

膝蓋骨(しつがいこつ)
patella
Kniescheibe^F
rotule^F
rótula^F
rotula^F

指骨
phalanges
Phalangen^F
phalanges^F
falanges^F
falangi^F

脛骨(けいこつ)
tibia
Schienbein^N
tibia^M
tibia^M
tibia^F

腓骨(ひこつ)
fibula
Wadenbein^N
péroné^M
peroné^M
fibula^F

ふ骨／足根骨
tarsus
Fußwurzel^F
tarse^M
tarso^M
tarso^M

趾骨(しこつ)
phalanges
Phalangen^F
phalanges^F
falanges^F
falangi^F

蹠骨(しょこつ)／中足骨
metatarsus
Mittelfuß^M
métatarse^M
metatarso^M
metatarso^M

霊長類 | PRIMATE MAMMALS
PRIMATEN | MAMMIFÈRES PRIMATES | MAMÍFEROS PRIMATES | PRIMATI

ゴリラ

ゴリラの形態図
morphology of a gorilla
äußere Merkmale^N eines Gorillas^M
morphologie^F du gorille^M
morfología^F de un gorila^F
morfologia^F di un gorilla^M

顔
face
Gesicht^N
face^F
cara^F
muso^M

毛(皮)
fur
Behaarung^F
pelage^M
pelaje^M
pelliccia^F

つかむのに適した指
prehensile digit
Greiffinger^M
doigt^M préhensile
dedos^M prensiles
dito^M prensile

ほかの指に対置できる親指
opposable thumb
opponierbarer Daumen^M
pouce^M opposable
pulgar^M oponible
pollice^M opponibile

腕
arm
Arm^M
bras^M
brazo^M
braccio^M

手
hand
Hand^F
main^F
mano^F
mano^M

脚
leg
Bein^N
jambe^F
pierna^F
gamba^F

足
foot
Fuß^M
pied^M
pie^M
piede^M

動物

霊長類の動物の例

examples of primates | Beispiele^N für Primaten^M | exemples^M de mammifères^M primates | ejemplos^M de primates^M | esempi^M di primati^M

タマリン
tamarin
Tamarin^M
tamarin^M
tamarino^M
tamarino^M

キヌザル(絹猿)／マーモセット
marmoset
Pinseläffchen^N
ouistiti^M
tití^M
uistiti^M

ヒヒ(狒狒)
baboon
Pavian^M
babouin^M
babuino^M
babbuino^M

マカク
macaque
Makak^M
macaque^M
macaco^M
macaco^M

オランウータン
orangutan
Orang-Utan^M
orang-outan^M
orangután^M
orangotango^M

チンパンジー
chimpanzee
Schimpanse^M
chimpanzé^M
chimpancé^M
scimpanzé^M

キツネザル(狐猿)
lemur
Lemure^M
lémurien^M
lémur^M
lemure^M

テナガザル(手長猿)
gibbon
Gibbon^M
gibbon^M
gibón^M
gibbone^M

飛行哺乳動物 | FLYING MAMMAL
FLEDERTIERE | MAMMIFÈRE VOLANT | MAMÍFEROS VOLADORES | MAMMIFERI VOLANTI

コウモリ（蝙蝠）

日本語 | 英語 | ドイツ語 | フランス語 | スペイン語 | イタリア語

bat | Fledermaus^F | chauve-souris^F | murciélago^M | pipistrello^M

コウモリの形態図
morphology of a bat
äußere Merkmale^N einer Fledermaus^F
morphologie^F de la chauve-souris^F
morfología^F de un murciélago^M
morfologia^F di un pipistrello^M

第二指
2nd metacarpal
2. Finger^M
2e mÈtacarpien^M
2º hueso^M metacarpiano
2° metacarpale^M

第三指
3rd metacarpal
3. Finger^M
3e mÈtacarpien^M
3er hueso^M metacarpiano
3° metacarpale^M

第四指
4th metacarpal
4. Finger^M
4e mÈtacarpien^M
4º hueso^M metacarpiano
4° metacarpale^M

第一指
thumb
Daumen^M
pouce^M
pulgar^M
pollice^M

肘
elbow
Ellbogen^M
coude^M
codo^M
gomito^M

手首
wrist
Handgelenk^N
poignet^M
muñeca^F
polso^M

鉤爪
claw
Klaue^F
griffe^F
uña^F
unghia^F

飛膜
wing membrane
Flughaut^F
membrane^F alaire
membrana^F del ala^F
membrana^F alare

血管
blood vessels
Blutgefäße^N
vaisseaux^M sanguins
vasos^M sanguíneos
vasi^M sanguigni

橈骨（とうこつ）
radius
Unterarm^M
radius^M
radio^M
radio^M

第五指
5th metacarpal
5. Finger^M
5e mÈtacarpien^M
5º hueso^M metacarpiano
5° metacarpale^M

耳
ear
Ohr^N
oreille^F
oreja^F
orecchio^M

脛骨（けいこつ）
tibia
Unterschenkel^M
tibia^M
tibia^F
tibia^F

足
foot
Fuß^M
pied^M
pie^M
piede^M

耳珠（じしゅ）
tragus
Ohrklappe^F
tragus^M
trago^M
trago^M

鼻葉
nose leaf
Nasenblatt^N
appendice^M nasal
apéndice^M nasal
foglia^F nasale

頭
head
Kopf^M
tête^F
cabeza^F
testa^F

蹴爪（けづめ）
calcar
Sporn^M
éperon^M calcanéen
calcáneo^M
calcare^M

股間膜
interfemoral membrane
Schwanzflughaut^F
membrane^F interfémorale
membrana^F interfemoral
membrana^F interfemorale

尾
tail
Schwanz^M
queue^F
cola^F
coda^F

翼
wings
Flügel^M
ailes^F
alas^F
ali^F

140

飛行哺乳動物 | FLYING MAMMAL
FLEDERTIERE | MAMMIFÈRE VOLANT | MAMÍFEROS VOLADORES | MAMMIFERI VOLANTI

コウモリ（蝙蝠）

コウモリの骨格図
skeleton of a bat
Skelett^N einer Fledermaus^F
squelette^M de la chauve-souris^F
esqueleto^M de un murciélago^M
scheletro^M di un pipistrello^M

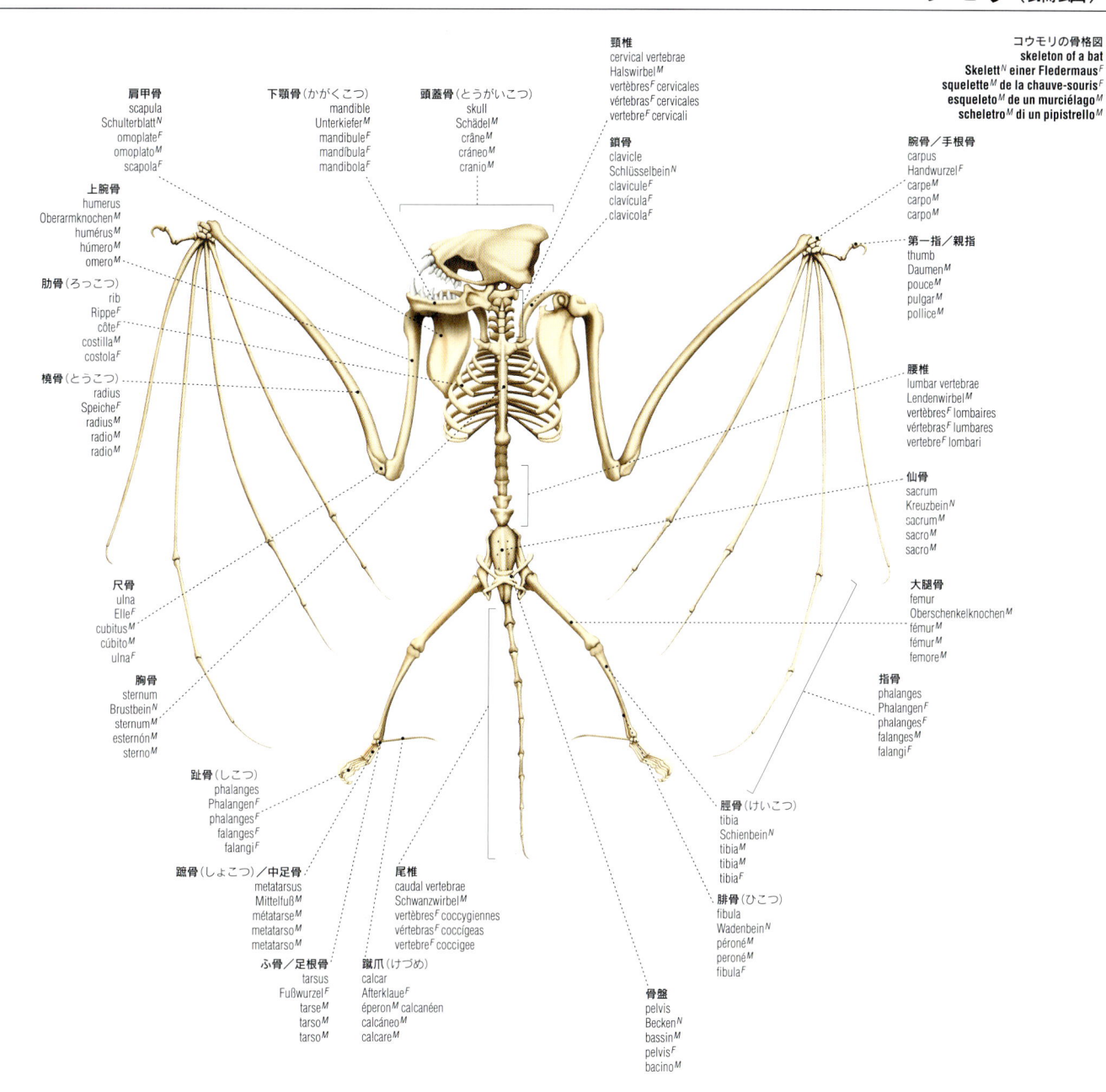

肩甲骨
scapula
Schulterblatt^N
omoplate^F
omoplato^M
scapola^F

下顎骨（かがくこつ）
mandible
Unterkiefer^M
mandibule^F
mandíbula^F
mandibola^F

頭蓋骨（とうがいこつ）
skull
Schädel^M
crâne^M
cráneo^M
cranio^M

頸椎
cervical vertebrae
Halswirbel^M
vertèbres^F cervicales
vértebras^F cervicales
vertebre^F cervicali

鎖骨
clavicle
Schlüsselbein^N
clavicule^F
clavícula^F
clavicola^F

腕骨／手根骨
carpus
Handwurzel^F
carpe^M
carpo^M
carpo^M

上腕骨
humerus
Oberarmknochen^M
humérus^M
húmero^M
omero^M

第一指／親指
thumb
Daumen^M
pouce^M
pulgar^M
pollice^M

肋骨（ろっこつ）
rib
Rippe^F
côte^F
costilla^F
costola^F

腰椎
lumbar vertebrae
Lendenwirbel^M
vertèbres^F lombaires
vértebras^F lumbares
vertebre^F lombari

橈骨（とうこつ）
radius
Speiche^F
radius^M
radio^M
radio^M

仙骨
sacrum
Kreuzbein^N
sacrum^M
sacro^M
sacro^M

尺骨
ulna
Elle^F
cubitus^M
cúbito^M
ulna^F

大腿骨
femur
Oberschenkelknochen^M
fémur^M
fémur^M
femore^M

胸骨
sternum
Brustbein^N
sternum^M
esternón^M
sterno^M

指骨
phalanges
Phalangen^F
phalanges^F
falanges^M
falangi^F

趾骨（しこつ）
phalanges
Phalangen^F
phalanges^F
falanges^F
falangi^F

脛骨（けいこつ）
tibia
Schienbein^N
tibia^M
tibia^M
tibia^F

蹠骨（しょこつ）／中足骨
metatarsus
Mittelfuß^M
métatarse^M
metatarso^M
metatarso^M

尾椎
caudal vertebrae
Schwanzwirbel^M
vertèbres^F coccygiennes
vértebras^F coccígeas
vertebre^F coccigee

腓骨（ひこつ）
fibula
Wadenbein^N
péroné^M
peroné^M
fibula^F

ふ骨／足根骨
tarsus
Fußwurzel^F
tarse^M
tarso^M
tarso^M

蹴爪（けづめ）
calcar
Afterklaue^F
éperon^M calcanéen
calcáneo^M
calcare^M

骨盤
pelvis
Becken^N
bassin^M
pelvis^F
bacino^M

コウモリの例

examples of bats | Beispiele^N für Fledertiere^N | exemples^M de chauves-souris^F | ejemplos^M de mamíferos^M voladores | esempi^M di mammiferi^M volanti

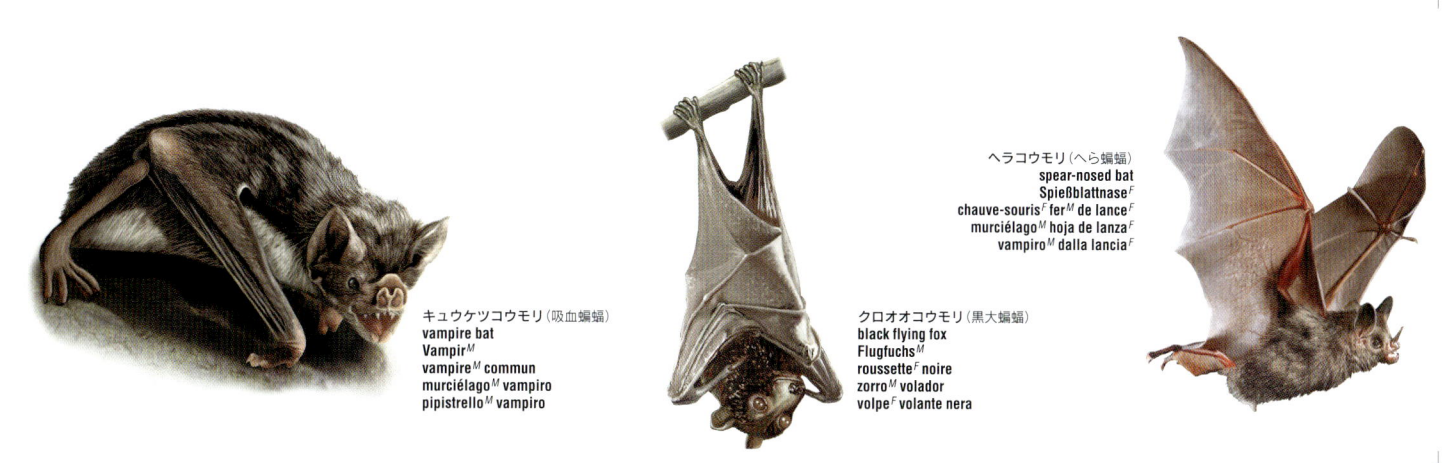

キュウケツコウモリ（吸血蝙蝠）
vampire bat
Vampir^M
vampire^M commun
murciélago^M vampiro
pipistrello^M vampiro

クロオオコウモリ（黒大蝙蝠）
black flying fox
Flugfuchs^M
roussette^F noire
zorro^M volador
volpe^F volante nera

ヘラコウモリ（へら蝙蝠）
spear-nosed bat
Spießblattnase^F
chauve-souris^F fer^M de lance^F
murciélago^M hoja de lanza^F
vampiro^M dalla lancia^F

有袋哺乳動物 | MARSUPIAL MAMMALS
BEUTELTIERE | MAMMIFÈRES MARSUPIAUX | MAMÍFEROS MARSUPIALES | MAMMIFERI MARSUPIALI

カンガルー

kangaroo | Känguru[N] | kangourou[M] | canguro[M] | canguro[M]

日本語 | 英語 | ドイツ語 | フランス語 | スペイン語 | イタリア語

カンガルーの骨格図
skeleton of a kangaroo
Skelett[N] eines Kängurus[N]
squelette[M] du kangourou[M]
esqueleto[M] de un canguro[M]
scheletro[M] di un canguro[M]

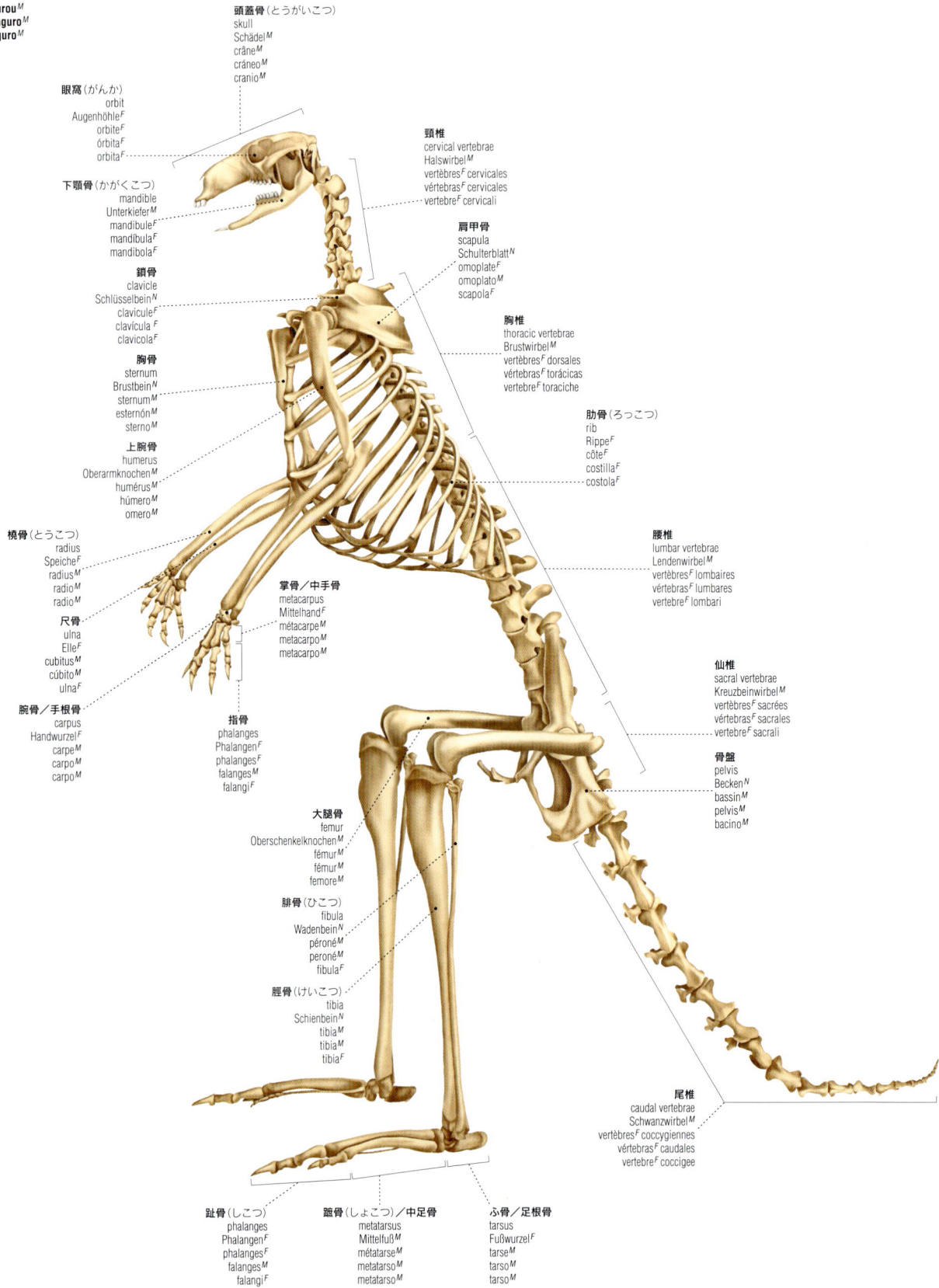

動物

頭蓋骨（とうがいこつ）
skull
Schädel[M]
crâne[M]
cráneo[M]
cranio[M]

眼窩（がんか）
orbit
Augenhöhle[F]
orbite[F]
órbita[F]
orbita[F]

下顎骨（かがくこつ）
mandible
Unterkiefer[M]
mandibule[F]
mandíbula[F]
mandibola[F]

頸椎
cervical vertebrae
Halswirbel[M]
vertèbres[F] cervicales
vértebras[F] cervicales
vertebre[F] cervicali

鎖骨
clavicle
Schlüsselbein[N]
clavicule[F]
clavícula[F]
clavicola[F]

肩甲骨
scapula
Schulterblatt[N]
omoplate[F]
omoplato[M]
scapola[F]

胸骨
sternum
Brustbein[N]
sternum[M]
esternón[M]
sterno[M]

胸椎
thoracic vertebrae
Brustwirbel[M]
vertèbres[F] dorsales
vértebras[F] torácicas
vertebre[F] toraciche

上腕骨
humerus
Oberarmknochen[M]
humérus[M]
húmero[M]
omero[M]

肋骨（ろっこつ）
rib
Rippe[F]
côte[F]
costilla[F]
costola[F]

橈骨（とうこつ）
radius
Speiche[F]
radius[M]
radio[M]
radio[M]

腰椎
lumbar vertebrae
Lendenwirbel[M]
vertèbres[F] lombaires
vértebras[F] lumbares
vertebre[F] lombari

尺骨
ulna
Elle[F]
cubitus[M]
cúbito[M]
ulna[F]

掌骨／中手骨
metacarpus
Mittelhand[F]
métacarpe[M]
metacarpo[M]
metacarpo[M]

仙椎
sacral vertebrae
Kreuzbeinwirbel[M]
vertèbres[F] sacrées
vértebras[F] sacrales
vertebre[F] sacrali

腕骨／手根骨
carpus
Handwurzel[F]
carpe[M]
carpo[M]
carpo[M]

指骨
phalanges
Phalangen[F]
phalanges[F]
falanges[M]
falangi[F]

骨盤
pelvis
Becken[N]
bassin[M]
pelvis[M]
bacino[M]

大腿骨
femur
Oberschenkelknochen[M]
fémur[M]
fémur[M]
femore[M]

腓骨（ひこつ）
fibula
Wadenbein[N]
péroné[M]
peroné[M]
fibula[F]

脛骨（けいこつ）
tibia
Schienbein[N]
tibia[M]
tibia[M]
tibia[F]

尾椎
caudal vertebrae
Schwanzwirbel[M]
vertèbres[F] coccygiennes
vértebras[F] caudales
vertebre[F] coccigee

趾骨（しこつ）
phalanges
Phalangen[F]
phalanges[F]
falanges[M]
falangi[F]

蹠骨（しょこつ）／中足骨
metatarsus
Mittelfuß[M]
métatarse[M]
metatarso[M]
metatarso[M]

跗骨／足根骨
tarsus
Fußwurzel[F]
tarse[M]
tarso[M]
tarso[M]

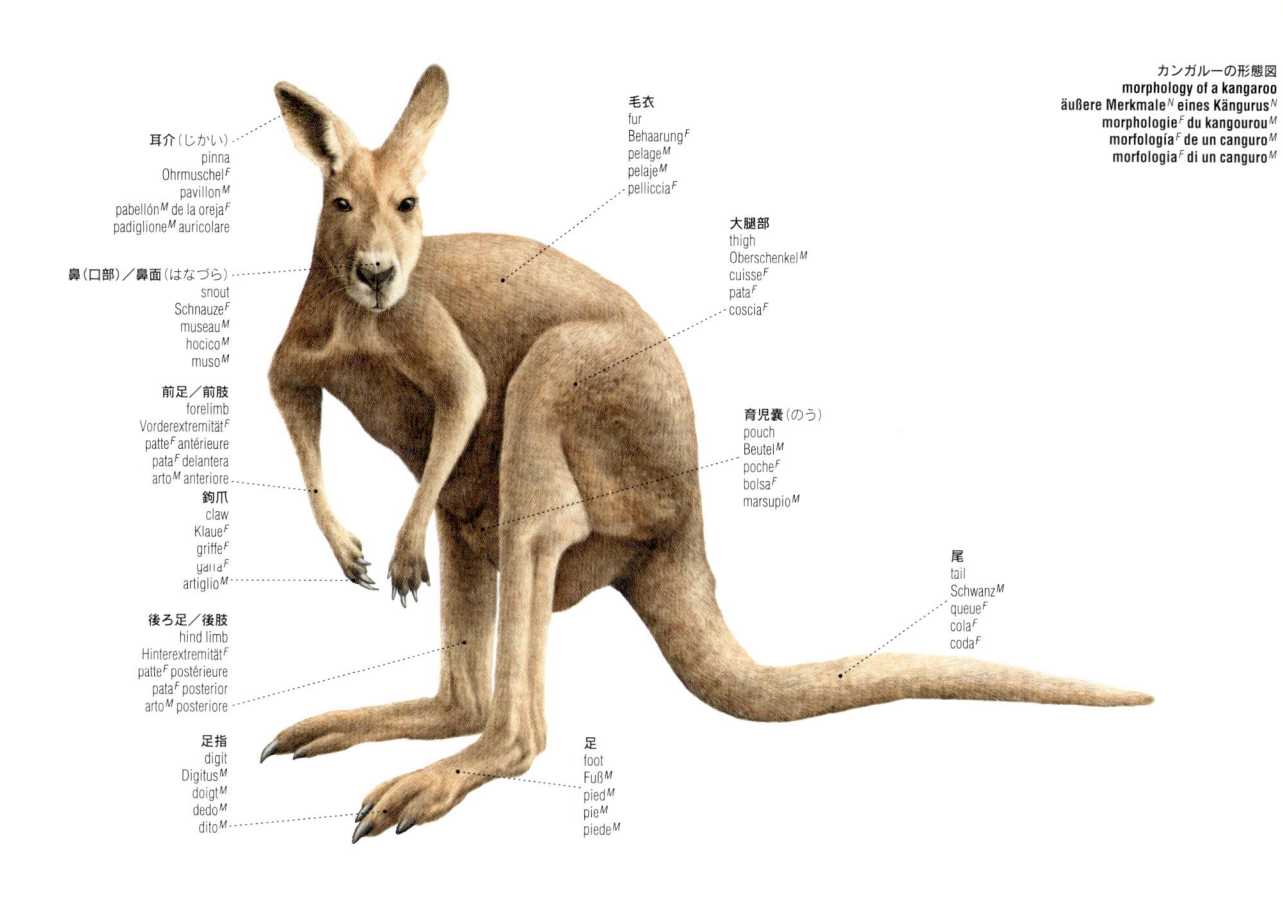

有袋哺乳動物 | MARSUPIAL MAMMALS
BEUTELTIERE | MAMMIFÈRES MARSUPIAUX | MAMÍFEROS MARSUPIALES | MAMMIFERI MARSUPIALI

カンガルー

カンガルーの形態図
morphology of a kangaroo
äußere Merkmale[N] eines Kängurus[N]
morphologie[F] du kangourou[M]
morfología[F] de un canguro[M]
morfologia[F] di un canguro[M]

動物

耳介（じかい）
pinna
Ohrmuschel[F]
pavillon[M]
pabellón[M] de la oreja[F]
padiglione[M] auricolare

鼻（口部）／鼻面（はなづら）
snout
Schnauze[F]
museau[M]
hocico[M]
muso[M]

前足／前肢
forelimb
Vorderextremität[F]
patte[F] antérieure
pata[F] delantera
arto[M] anteriore

鉤爪
claw
Klaue[F]
griffe[F]
garra[F]
artiglio[M]

後ろ足／後肢
hind limb
Hinterextremität[F]
patte[F] postérieure
pata[F] posterior
arto[M] posteriore

足指
digit
Digitus[M]
doigt[M]
dedo[M]
dito[M]

毛衣
fur
Behaarung[F]
pelage[M]
pelaje[M]
pelliccia[F]

大腿部
thigh
Oberschenkel[M]
cuisse[F]
pata[F]
coscia[F]

育児嚢（のう）
pouch
Beutel[M]
poche[F]
bolsa[F]
marsupio[M]

尾
tail
Schwanz[M]
queue[F]
cola[F]
coda[F]

足
foot
Fuß[M]
pied[M]
pie[M]
piede[M]

有袋動物の例

examples of marsupials | Beispiele[N] für Beuteltiere[N] | exemples[M] de marsupiaux[M] | ejemplos[M] de marsupiales[M] | esempi[M] di marsupiali[M]

タスマニア・デビル
Tasmanian devil
Tasmanischer Teufel[M]
diable[M] de Tasmanie[F]
diablo[M] de Tasmania[F]
diavolo[M] della Tasmania[F]

ワラビー
wallaby
Wallaby[N]
wallaby[M]
walaby[M]
wallaby[M]

キタ（北）オポッサム／フクロネズミ（袋鼠）
opossum
Opossum[N]
opossum[M]
oposum[M]
opossum[M]

コアラ
koala
Koala[M]
koala[M]
koala[F]
koala[M]

カンガルー
kangaroo
Känguru[N]
kangourou[M]
canguro[M]
canguro[M]

143

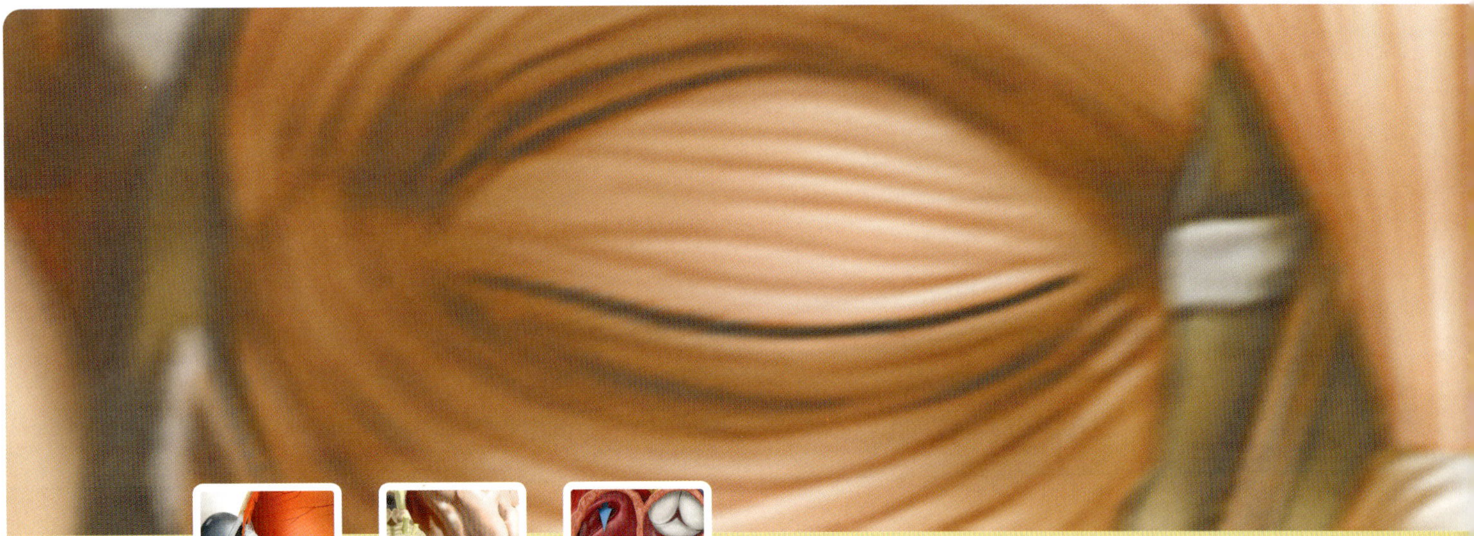

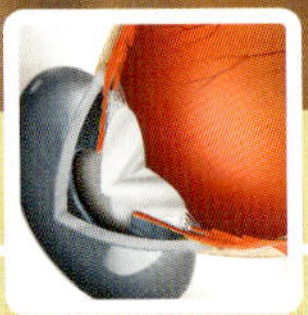

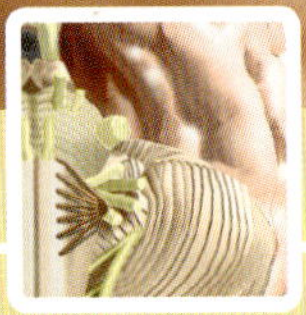

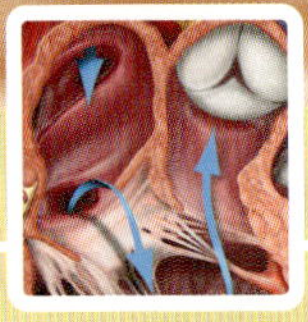

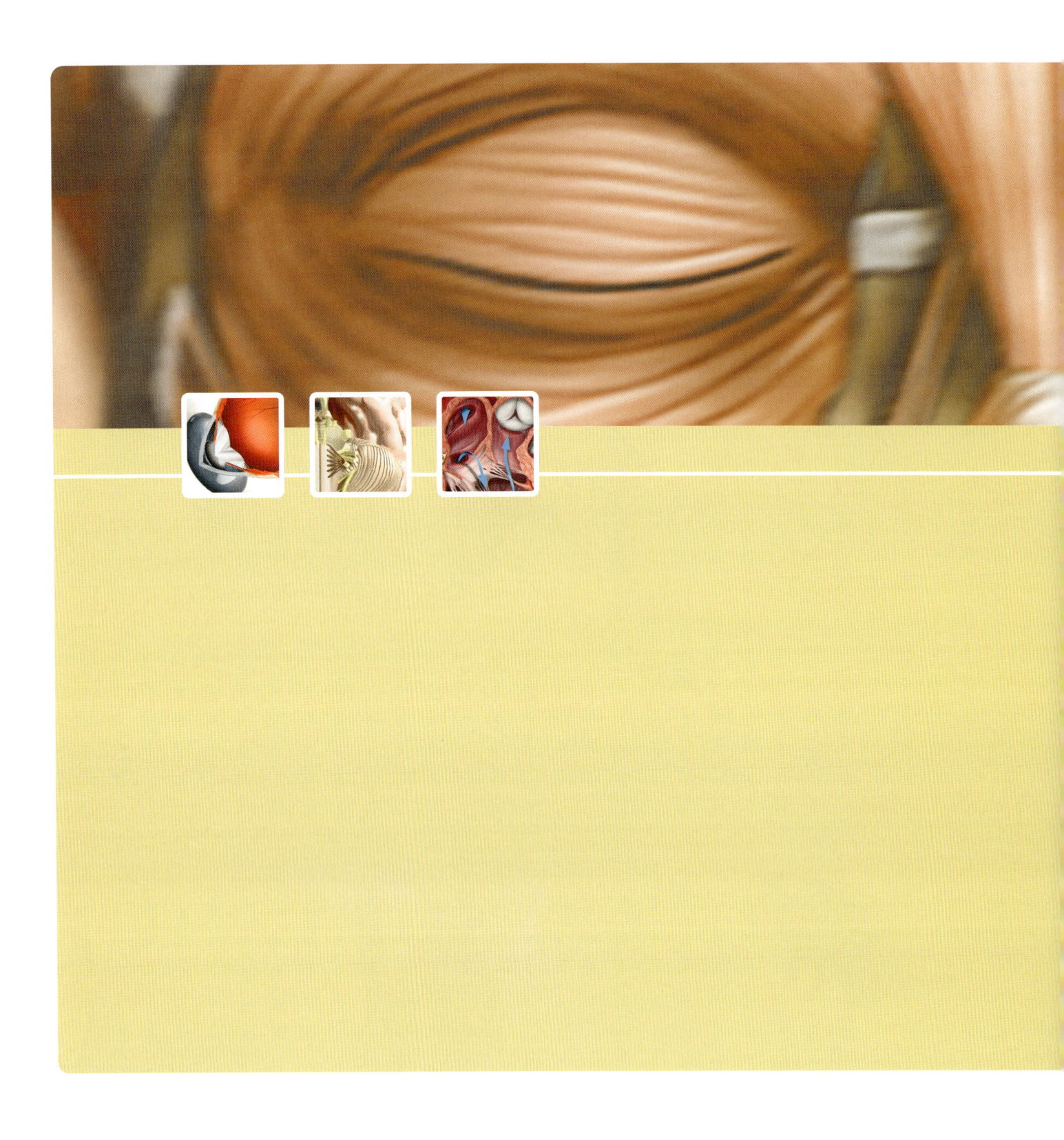

人間

HUMAN BEING | MENSCH | ÊTRE HUMAIN | SER HUMANO | ESSERE UMANO

146 人体

- 146 男／男性
- 148 女／女性

150 解剖学

- 150 筋肉
- 152 骨格
- 159 歯
- 160 血液循環
- 163 呼吸器系
- 164 消化器系
- 165 泌尿器系
- 166 神経系
- 169 男性生殖器
- 170 女性生殖器
- 171 乳房

172 感覚器官

- 172 触覚
- 173 聴覚
- 174 嗅覚（きゅうかく）と味覚
- 177 視覚

人体 | HUMAN BODY
MENSCHLICHER KÖRPER | CORPS HUMAIN | CUERPO HUMANO | CORPO UMANO

男／男性
man | Mann(M) | homme(M) | hombre(M) | uomo(M)

日本語 | 英語 | ドイツ語 | フランス語 | スペイン語 | イタリア語

前面図
anterior view
Vorderansicht(F)
face(F) antérieure
vista(F) anterior
vista(F) anteriore

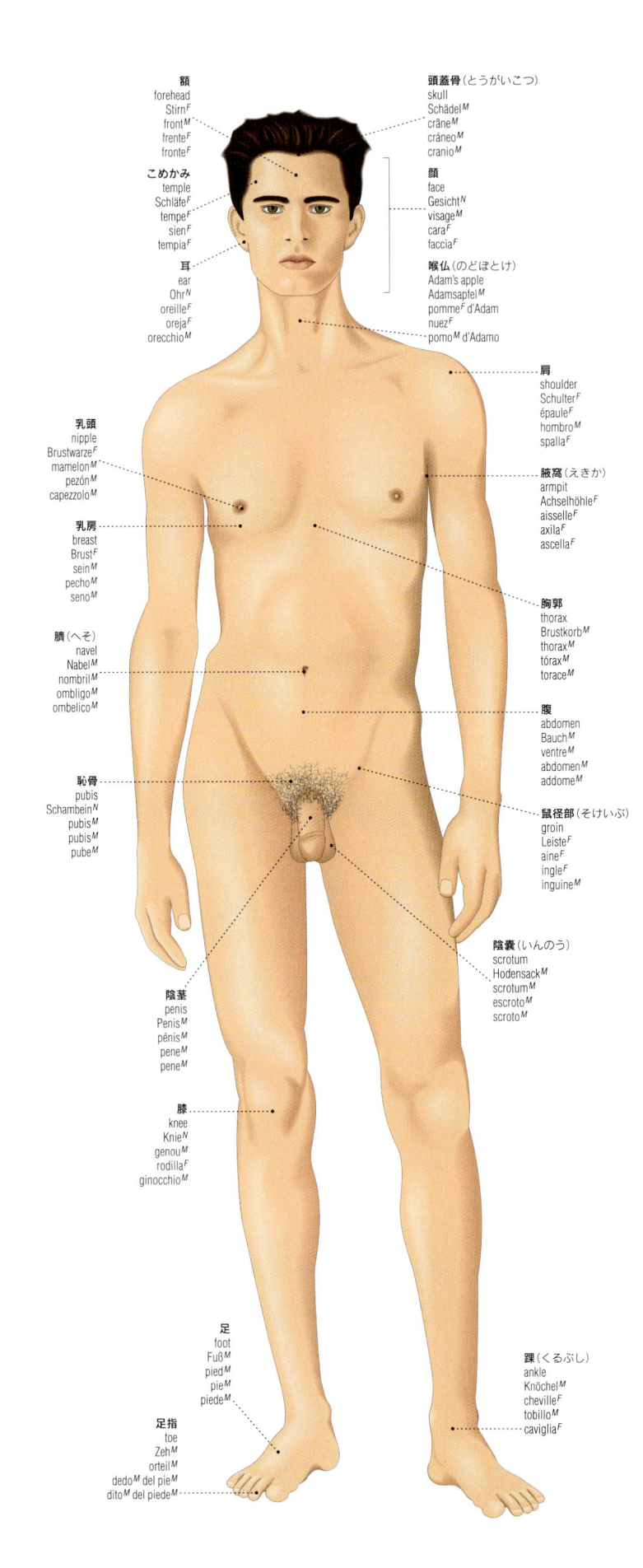

人間

- 額 / forehead / Stirn(F) / front(M) / frente(F) / fronte(F)
- こめかみ / temple / Schläfe(F) / tempe(F) / sien(F) / tempia(F)
- 耳 / ear / Ohr(N) / oreille(F) / oreja(F) / orecchio(M)
- 頭蓋骨（とうがいこつ） / skull / Schädel(M) / crâne(M) / cráneo(M) / cranio(M)
- 顔 / face / Gesicht(N) / visage(M) / cara(F) / faccia(F)
- 喉仏（のどぼとけ） / Adam's apple / Adamsapfel(M) / pomme(F) d'Adam / nuez(F) / pomo(M) d'Adamo
- 肩 / shoulder / Schulter(F) / épaule(F) / hombro(M) / spalla(F)
- 乳頭 / nipple / Brustwarze(F) / mamelon(M) / pezón(M) / capezzolo(M)
- 腋窩（えきか） / armpit / Achselhöhle(F) / aisselle(F) / axila(F) / ascella(F)
- 乳房 / breast / Brust(F) / sein(M) / pecho(M) / seno(M)
- 胸郭 / thorax / Brustkorb(M) / thorax(M) / tórax(M) / torace(M)
- 臍（へそ） / navel / Nabel(M) / nombril(M) / ombligo(M) / ombelico(M)
- 腹 / abdomen / Bauch(M) / ventre(M) / abdomen(M) / addome(M)
- 恥骨 / pubis / Schambein(N) / pubis(M) / pubis(M) / pube(M)
- 鼠径部（そけいぶ） / groin / Leiste(F) / aine(F) / ingle(F) / inguine(M)
- 陰嚢（いんのう） / scrotum / Hodensack(M) / scrotum(M) / escroto(M) / scroto(M)
- 陰茎 / penis / Penis(M) / pénis(M) / pene(M) / pene(M)
- 膝 / knee / Knie(N) / genou(M) / rodilla(F) / ginocchio(M)
- 足 / foot / Fuß(M) / pied(M) / pie(M) / piede(M)
- 踝（くるぶし） / ankle / Knöchel(M) / cheville(F) / tobillo(M) / caviglia(F)
- 足指 / toe / Zeh(M) / orteil(M) / dedo(M) del pie(M) / dito(M) del piede(M)

人体 | HUMAN BODY
MENSCHLICHER KÖRPER | CORPS HUMAIN | CUERPO HUMANO | CORPO UMANO

男／男性

背面図
posterior view
Rückenansicht^F
face^F postérieure
vista^F posterior
vista^F posteriore

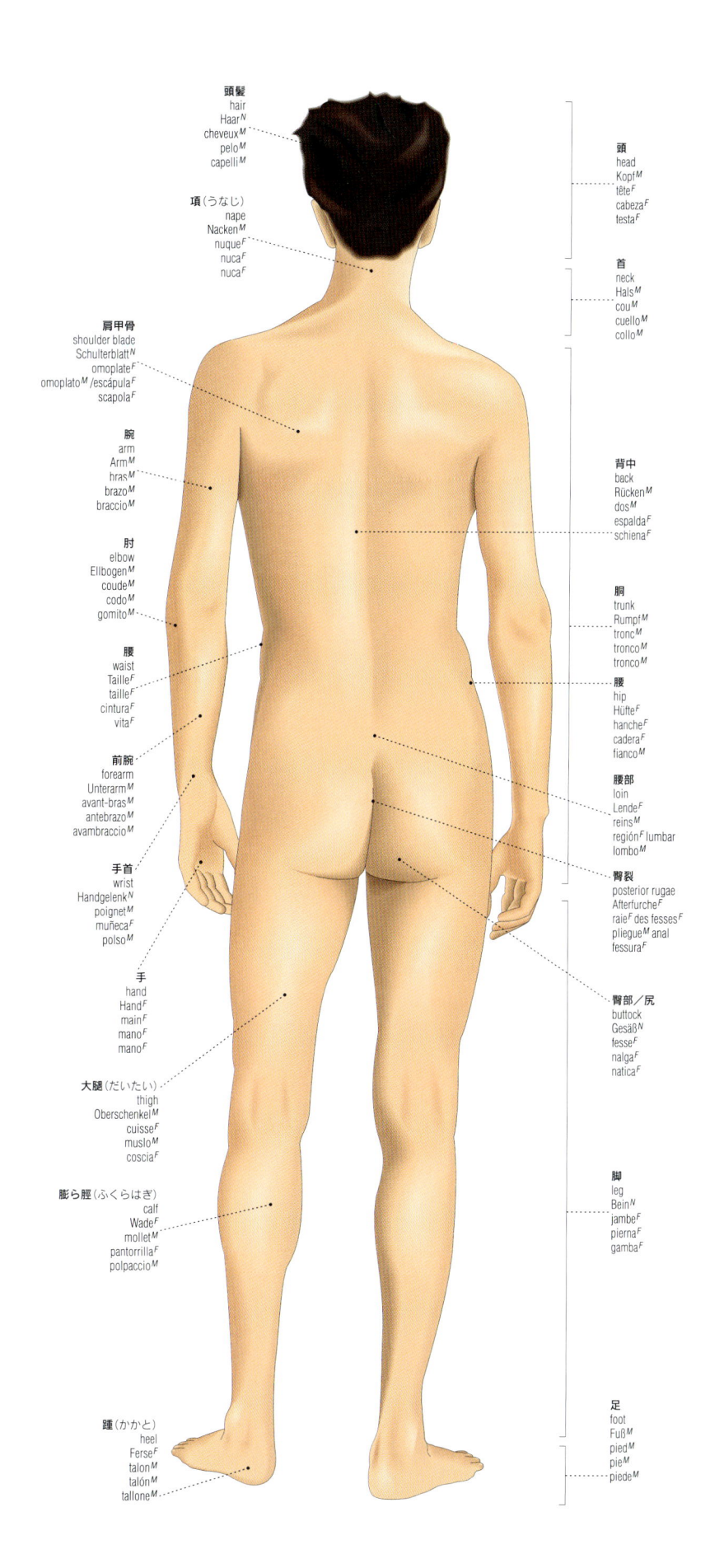

頭髪
hair
Haar^N
cheveux^M
pelo^M
capelli^M

項（うなじ）
nape
Nacken^M
nuque^F
nuca^F
nuca^F

肩甲骨
shoulder blade
Schulterblatt^N
omoplate^F
omoplato^M/escápula^F
scapola^F

腕
arm
Arm^M
bras^M
brazo^M
braccio^M

肘
elbow
Ellbogen^M
coude^M
codo^M
gomito^M

腰
waist
Taille^F
taille^F
cintura^F
vita^F

前腕
forearm
Unterarm^M
avant-bras^M
antebrazo^M
avambraccio^M

手首
wrist
Handgelenk^N
poignet^M
muñeca^F
polso^M

手
hand
Hand^F
main^F
mano^M
mano^F

大腿（だいたい）
thigh
Oberschenkel^M
cuisse^F
muslo^M
coscia^F

膨ら脛（ふくらはぎ）
calf
Wade^F
mollet^M
pantorrilla^F
polpaccio^M

踵（かかと）
heel
Ferse^F
talon^M
talón^M
tallone^M

頭
head
Kopf^M
tête^F
cabeza^F
testa^F

首
neck
Hals^M
cou^M
cuello^M
collo^M

背中
back
Rücken^M
dos^M
espalda^F
schiena^F

胴
trunk
Rumpf^M
tronc^M
tronco^M
tronco^M

腰
hip
Hüfte^F
hanche^F
cadera^F
fianco^M

腰部
loin
Lende^F
reins^M
región^F lumbar
lombo^M

臀裂
posterior rugae
Afterfurche^F
raie^F des fesses^F
pliegue^M anal
fessura^F

臀部／尻
buttock
Gesäß^N
fesse^F
nalga^F
natica^F

脚
leg
Bein^N
jambe^F
pierna^F
gamba^F

足
foot
Fuß^M
pied^M
pie^M
piede^M

人間

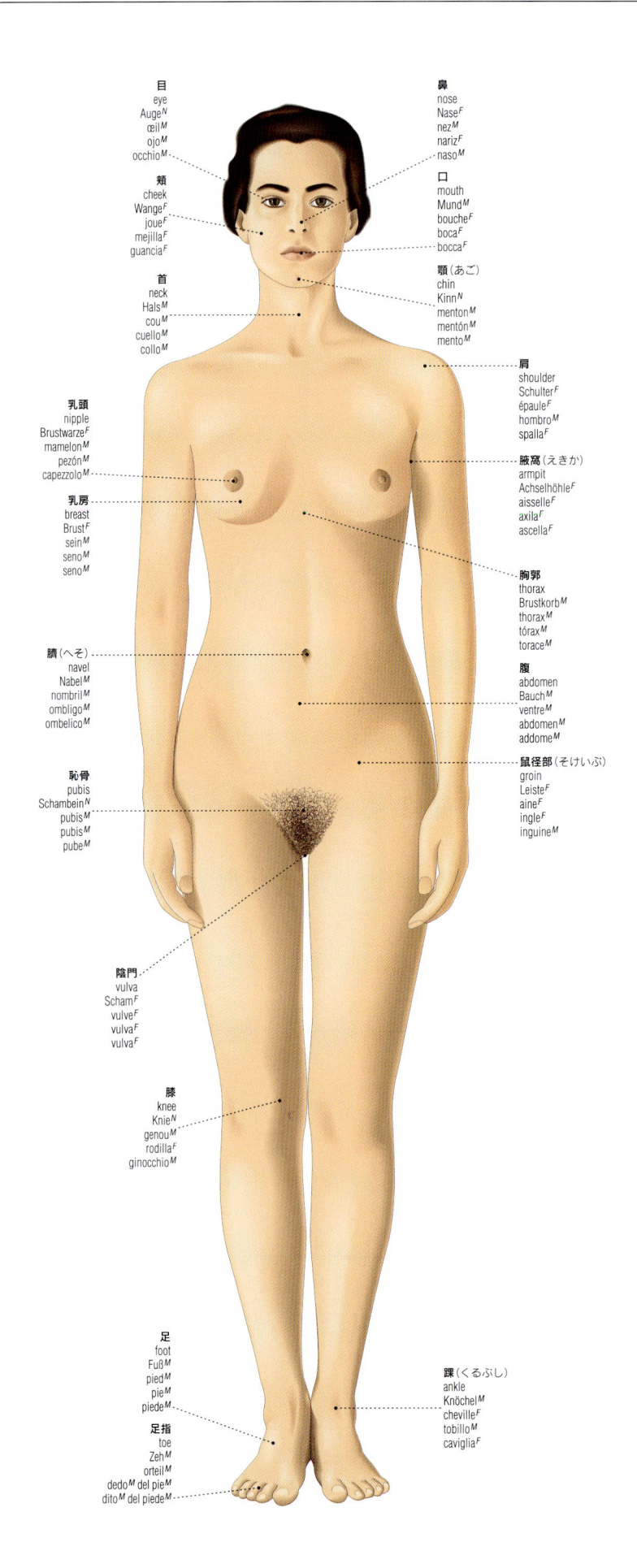

人体 | HUMAN BODY
MENSCHLICHER KÖRPER | CORPS HUMAIN | CUERPO HUMANO | CORPO UMANO

女／女性

woman | Frau^F | femme^F | mujer^F | donna^F

日本語 | 英語 | ドイツ語 | フランス語 | スペイン語 | イタリア語

前面図
anterior view
Vorderansicht^F
face^F antérieure
vista^F anterior
vista^F anteriore

人間

目
eye
Auge^N
œil^M
ojo^M
occhio^M

頬
cheek
Wange^F
joue^F
mejilla^F
guancia^F

首
neck
Hals^M
cou^M
cuello^M
collo^M

乳頭
nipple
Brustwarze^F
mamelon^M
pezón^M
capezzolo^M

乳房
breast
Brust^F
sein^M
seno^M
seno^M

臍（へそ）
navel
Nabel^M
nombril^M
ombligo^M
ombelico^M

恥骨
pubis
Schambein^N
pubis^M
pubis^M
pube^M

陰門
vulva
Scham^F
vulve^F
vulva^F
vulva^F

膝
knee
Knie^N
genou^M
rodilla^F
ginocchio^M

足
foot
Fuß^M
pied^M
pie^M
piede^M

足指
toe
Zeh^M
orteil^M
dedo^M del pie^M
dito^M del piede^M

鼻
nose
Nase^F
nez^M
nariz^F
naso^M

口
mouth
Mund^M
bouche^F
boca^F
bocca^F

顎（あご）
chin
Kinn^N
menton^M
mentón^M
mento^M

肩
shoulder
Schulter^F
épaule^F
hombro^M
spalla^F

腋窩（えきか）
armpit
Achselhöhle^F
aisselle^F
axila^F
ascella^F

胸郭
thorax
Brustkorb^M
thorax^M
tórax^M
torace^M

腹
abdomen
Bauch^M
ventre^M
abdomen^M
addome^M

鼠径部（そけいぶ）
groin
Leiste^F
aine^F
ingle^F
inguine^M

踝（くるぶし）
ankle
Knöchel^M
cheville^F
tobillo^M
caviglia^F

人体 | HUMAN BODY
MENSCHLICHER KÖRPER | CORPS HUMAIN | CUERPO HUMANO | CORPO UMANO

女／女性

背面図
posterior view
RückenansichtF
faceF postérieure
vistaF posterior
vistaF posteriore

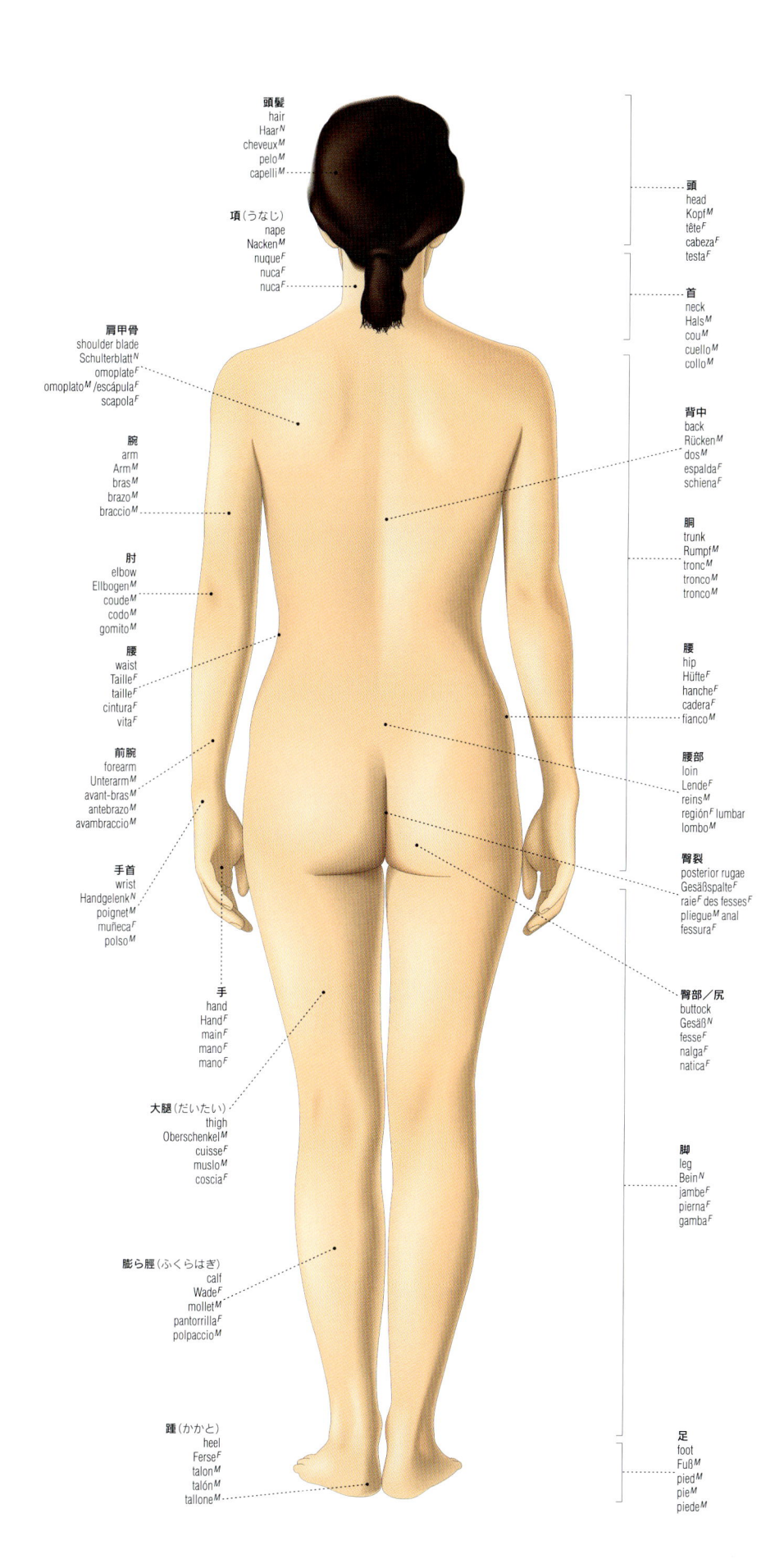

人間

頭髪
hair
HaarN
cheveuxM
peloM
capelliM

項（うなじ）
nape
NackenM
nuqueF
nucaF
nucaF

肩甲骨
shoulder blade
SchulterblattN
omoplateF
omoplatoM /escápulaF
scapolaF

腕
arm
ArmM
brasM
brazoM
braccioM

肘
elbow
EllbogenM
coudeM
codoM
gomitoM

腰
waist
TailleF
tailleF
cinturaF
vitaF

前腕
forearm
UnterarmM
avant-brasM
antebrazoM
avambraccioM

手首
wrist
HandgelenkN
poignetM
muñecaF
polsoM

手
hand
HandF
mainF
manoF
manoM

大腿（だいたい）
thigh
OberschenkelM
cuisseF
musloM
cosciaF

膨ら脛（ふくらはぎ）
calf
WadeF
molletM
pantorrillaF
polpaccioM

踵（かかと）
heel
FerseF
talonM
talónM
talloneM

頭
head
KopfM
têteF
cabezaF
testaF

首
neck
HalsM
couM
cuelloM
colloM

背中
back
RückenM
dosM
espaldaF
schienaF

胴
trunk
RumpfM
troncM
troncoM
troncoM

腰
hip
HüfteF
hancheF
caderaF
fiancoM

腰部
loin
LendeF
reinsM
regiónF lumbar
lomboM

臀裂
posterior rugae
GesäßspalteF
raieF des fessesF
pliegueM anal
fessuraF

臀部／尻
buttock
GesäßN
fesseF
nalgaF
naticaF

脚
leg
BeinN
jambeF
piernaF
gambaF

足
foot
FußM
piedM
pieM
piedeM

149

解剖学 | ANATOMY
ANATOMIE | ANATOMIE | ANATOMÍA | ANATOMIA

筋肉

muscles | Muskeln^M | muscles^M | músculos^M | muscoli^M

日本語 | 英語 | ドイツ語 | フランス語 | スペイン語 | イタリア語

前面図
anterior view
Vorderansicht^F
face^F antérieure
vista^F anterior
vista^F anteriore

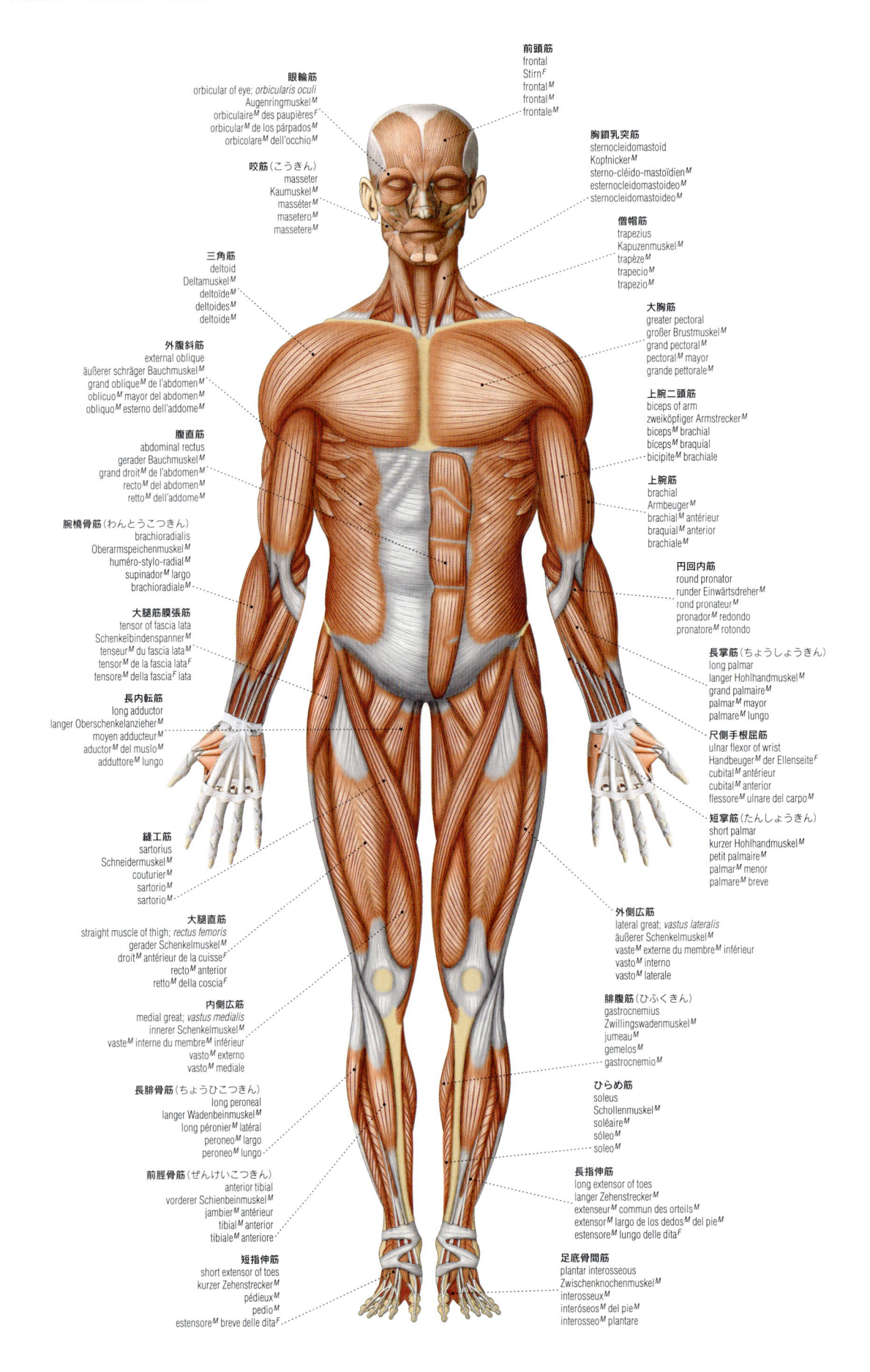

人間

眼輪筋
orbicular of eye; *orbicularis oculi*
Augenringmuskel^M
orbiculaire^M des paupières^F
orbicular^M de los párpados^M
orbicolare^M dell'occhio^M

咬筋（こうきん）
masseter
Kaumuskel^M
masséter^M
masetero^M
massetere^M

三角筋
deltoid
Deltamuskel^M
deltoïde^M
deltoides^M
deltoide^M

外腹斜筋
external oblique
äußerer schräger Bauchmuskel^M
grand oblique de l'abdomen^M
oblicuo^M mayor del abdomen^M
obliquo^M esterno dell'addome^M

腹直筋
abdominal rectus
gerader Bauchmuskel^M
grand droit de l'abdomen^M
recto^M del abdomen^M
retto^M dell'addome^M

腕橈骨筋（わんとうこつきん）
brachioradialis
Oberarmspeichenmuskel^M
huméro-stylo-radial^M
supinador^M largo
brachioradiale^M

大腿筋膜張筋
tensor of fascia lata
Schenkelbindenspanner^M
tenseur^M du fascia lata^M
tensor^M de la fascia lata^M
tensore^M della fascia^F lata

長内転筋
long adductor
langer Oberschenkelanzieher^M
moyen adducteur^M
aductor^M del muslo^M
adduttore^M lungo

縫工筋
sartorius
Schneidermuskel^M
couturier^M
sartorio^M
sartorio^M

大腿直筋
straight muscle of thigh; *rectus femoris*
gerader Schenkelmuskel^M
droit^M antérieur de la cuisse^F
recto^M anterior
retto^M della coscia^F

内側広筋
medial great; *vastus medialis*
innerer Schenkelmuskel^M
vaste^M interne du membre^M inférieur
vasto^M externo
vasto^M mediale

長腓骨筋（ちょうひこつきん）
long peroneal
langer Wadenbeinmuskel^M
long péronier^M latéral
peroneo^M largo
peroneo^M lungo

前脛骨筋（ぜんけいこつきん）
anterior tibial
vorderer Schienbeinmuskel^M
jambier^M antérieur
tibial^M anterior
tibiale^M anteriore

短指伸筋
short extensor of toes
kurzer Zehenstrecker^M
pédieux^M
pedio^M
estensore^M breve delle dita^F

前頭筋
frontal
Stirn^F
frontal^M
frontal^M
frontale^M

胸鎖乳突筋
sternocleidomastoid
Kopfnicker^M
sterno-cléido-mastoïdien^M
esternocleidomastoideo^M
sternocleidomastoideo^M

僧帽筋
trapezius
Kapuzenmuskel^M
trapèze^M
trapecio^M
trapezio^M

大胸筋
greater pectoral
großer Brustmuskel^M
grand pectoral^M
pectoral^M mayor
grande pettorale^M

上腕二頭筋
biceps of arm
zweiköpfiger Armstrecker^M
biceps^M brachial
bíceps^M braquial
bicipite^M brachiale

上腕筋
brachial
Armbeuger^M
brachial^M antérieur
braquial^M anterior
brachiale^M

円回内筋
round pronator
runder Einwärtsdreher^M
rond pronateur^M
pronador^M redondo
pronatore^M rotondo

長掌筋（ちょうしょうきん）
long palmar
langer Hohlhandmuskel^M
grand palmaire^M
palmar^M mayor
palmare^M lungo

尺側手根屈筋
ulnar flexor of wrist
Handbeuger^M der Ellenseite^F
cubital^M antérieur
cubital^M anterior
flessore^M ulnare del carpo^M

短掌筋（たんしょうきん）
short palmar
kurzer Hohlhandmuskel^M
petit palmaire^M
palmar^M menor
palmare^M breve

外側広筋
lateral great; *vastus lateralis*
äußerer Schenkelmuskel^M
vaste^M externe du membre^M inférieur
vasto^M interno
vasto^M laterale

腓腹筋（ひふくきん）
gastrocnemius
Zwillingswadenmuskel^M
jumeau^M
gemelos^M
gastrocnemio^M

ひらめ筋
soleus
Schollenmuskel^M
soléaire^M
sóleo^M
soleo^M

長指伸筋
long extensor of toes
langer Zehenstrecker^M
extenseur^M commun des orteils^M
extensor^M largo de los dedos^M del pie^M
estensore^M lungo delle dita^F

足底骨間筋
plantar interosseous
Zwischenknochenmuskel^M
interosseux^M
interóseos^M del pie^M
interosseo^M plantare

解剖学 | ANATOMY
ANATOMIE | ANATOMIE | ANATOMÍA | ANATOMIA

筋肉

背面図
posterior view
Rückansicht^F
face^F postérieure
vista^F posterior
vista^F posteriore

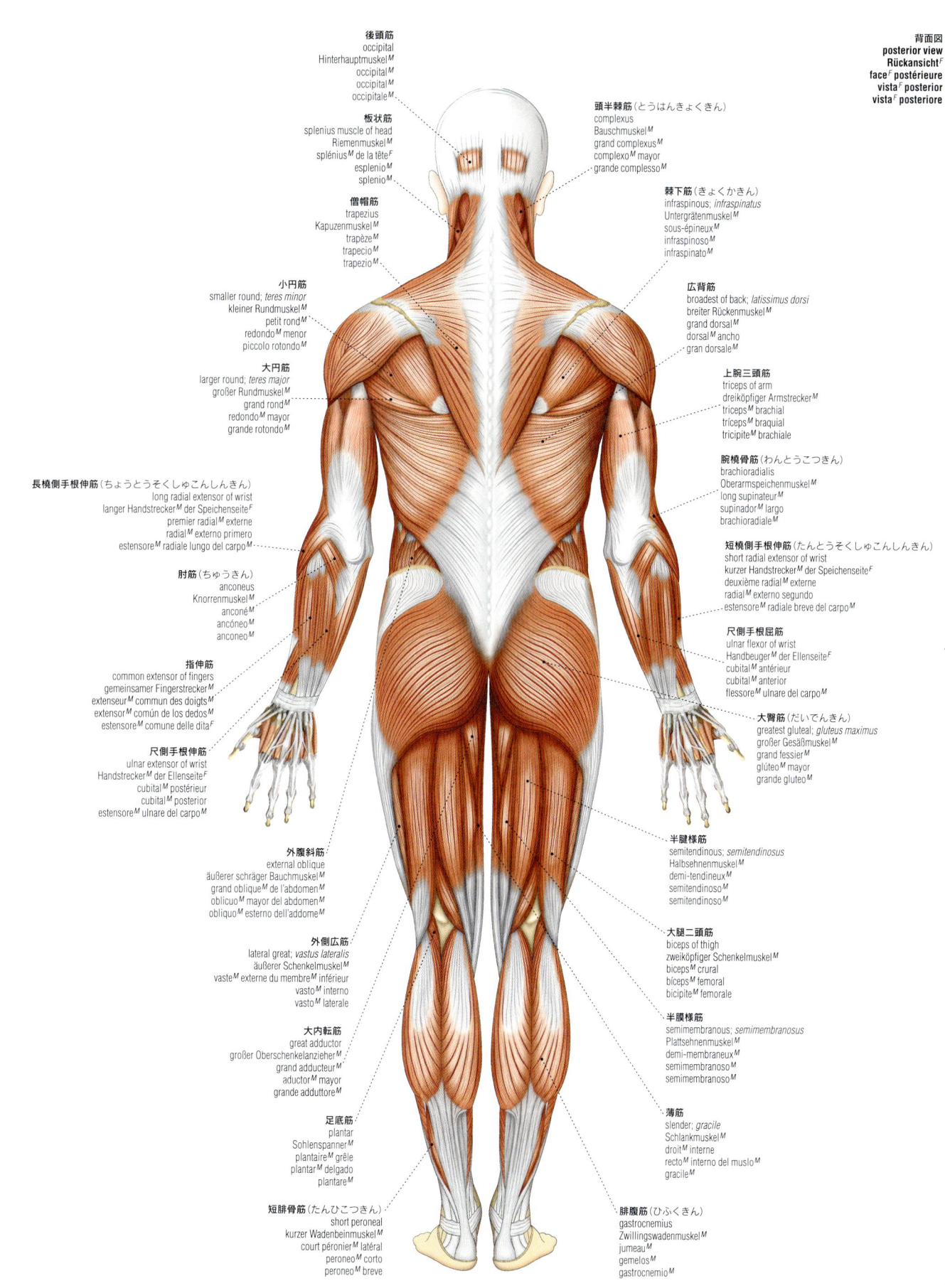

人間

後頭筋
occipital
Hinterhauptmuskel^M
occipital
occipital^M
occipitale^M

板状筋
splenius muscle of head
Riemenmuskel^M
splénius^M de la tête^F
esplenio^M
splenio^M

僧帽筋
trapezius
Kapuzenmuskel^M
trapèze^M
trapecio^M
trapezio^M

小円筋
smaller round; *teres minor*
kleiner Rundmuskel^M
petit rond^M
redondo^M menor
piccolo rotondo^M

大円筋
larger round; *teres major*
großer Rundmuskel^M
grand rond^M
redondo^M mayor
grande rotondo^M

長橈側手根伸筋（ちょうとうそくしゅこんしんきん）
long radial extensor of wrist
langer Handstrecker^M der Speichenseite^F
premier radial^M externe
radial^M externo primero
estensore^M radiale lungo del carpo^M

肘筋（ちゅうきん）
anconeus
Knorrenmuskel^M
ancóné^M
ancóneo^M
anconeo^M

指伸筋
common extensor of fingers
gemeinsamer Fingerstrecker^M
extenseur^M commun des doigts^M
extensor^M común de los dedos^M
estensore^M comune delle dita^F

尺側手根伸筋
ulnar extensor of wrist
Handstrecker^M der Ellenseite^F
cubital^M postérieur
cubital^M posterior
estensore^M ulnare del carpo^M

外腹斜筋
external oblique
äußerer schräger Bauchmuskel^M
grand oblique^M de l'abdomen^M
oblicuo^M mayor del abdomen^M
obliquo^M esterno dell'addome^M

外側広筋
lateral great; *vastus lateralis*
äußerer Schenkelmuskel^M
vaste^M externe du membre^M inférieur
vasto^M interno
vasto^M laterale

大内転筋
great adductor
großer Oberschenkelanzieher^M
grand adducteur^M
aductor^M mayor
grande adduttore^M

足底筋
plantar
Sohlenspanner^M
plantaire^M grêle
plantar^M delgado
plantare^M

短腓骨筋（たんひこつきん）
short peroneal
kurzer Wadenbeinmuskel^M
court péronier^M latéral
peroneo^M corto
peroneo^M breve

頭半棘筋（とうはんきょくきん）
complexus
Bauschmuskel^M
grand complexus^M
complexo^M mayor
grande complesso^M

棘下筋（きょくかきん）
infraspinous; *infraspinatus*
Untergrätenmuskel^M
sous-épineux^M
infraspinoso^M
infraspinato^M

広背筋
broadest of back; *latissimus dorsi*
breiter Rückenmuskel^M
grand dorsal^M
dorsal^M ancho
gran dorsale^M

上腕三頭筋
triceps of arm
dreiköpfiger Armstrecker^M
triceps^M brachial
tríceps^M braquial
tricipite^M brachiale

腕橈骨筋（わんとうこつきん）
brachioradialis
Oberarmspeichenmuskel^M
long supinateur^M
supinador^M largo
brachioradiale^M

短橈側手根伸筋（たんとうそくしゅこんしんきん）
short radial extensor of wrist
kurzer Handstrecker^M der Speichenseite^F
deuxième radial^M externe
radial^M externo segundo
estensore^M radiale breve del carpo^M

尺側手根屈筋
ulnar flexor of wrist
Handbeuger^M der Ellenseite^F
cubital^M antérieur
cubital^M anterior
flessore^M ulnare del carpo^M

大臀筋（だいでんきん）
greatest gluteal; *gluteus maximus*
großer Gesäßmuskel^M
grand fessier^M
glúteo^M mayor
grande gluteo^M

半腱様筋
semitendinous; *semitendinosus*
Halbsehnenmuskel^M
demi-tendineux^M
semitendinoso^M
semitendinoso^M

大腿二頭筋
biceps of thigh
zweiköpfiger Schenkelmuskel^M
biceps^M crural
bíceps^M femoral
bicipite^M femorale

半膜様筋
semimembranous; *semimembranosus*
Plattsehnenmuskel^M
demi-membraneux^M
semimembranoso^M
semimembranoso^M

薄筋
slender; *gracile*
Schlankmuskel^M
droit interne
recto^M interno del muslo^M
gracile^M

腓腹筋（ひふくきん）
gastrocnemius
Zwillingswadenmuskel^M
jumeau
gemelos^M
gastrocnemio^M

151

解剖学 | ANATOMY
ANATOMIE | ANATOMIE | ANATOMÍA | ANATOMIA

骨格

skeleton | Skelett[N] | squelette[M] | esqueleto[M] | scheletro[M]

日本語 | 英語 | ドイツ語 | フランス語 | スペイン語 | イタリア語

前面図
anterior view
Vorderansicht[F]
vue[F] **antérieure**
vista[F] **anterior**
vista[F] **anteriore**

人間

前頭骨
frontal bone
Stirnbein[N]
frontal[M]
hueso[M] frontal
osso[M] frontale

側頭骨
temporal bone
Schläfenbein[N]
temporal[M]
hueso[M] temporal
osso[M] temporale

頬骨（きょうこつ）
zygomatic bone
Jochbein[N]
malaire[M]
pómulo[M]
osso[M] zigomatico

上顎骨（じょうがくこつ）
maxilla
Oberkiefer[M]
maxillaire[M] supérieur
maxilar[M] superior
mascella[F]

鎖骨
clavicle
Schlüsselbein[N]
clavicule[F]
clavícula[F]
clavicola[F]

下顎骨（かがくこつ）
mandible
Unterkiefer[M]
maxillaire[M] inférieur
mandíbula[F]
mandibola[F]

肩甲骨
scapula
Schulterblatt[N]
omoplate[F]
escápula[F] /omóplato[M]
scapola[F]

肋骨（ろっこつ）
ribs
Rippen[F]
côtes[F]
costillas[F]
costole[F]

胸骨
sternum
Brustbein[N]
sternum[M]
esternón[M]
sterno[M]

上腕骨
humerus
Oberarmknochen[M]
humérus[M]
húmero[M]
omero[M]

浮動肋骨（ふどうろっこつ）
floating rib (2)
frei endende Rippe[F] (2)
côte[F] flottante (2)
costilla[F] flotante (2)
costole[F] fluttuanti (2)

尺骨
ulna
Elle[F]
cubitus[M]
cúbito[M]
ulna[F]

脊柱（せきちゅう）
vertebral column; *spinal column*
Wirbelsäule[F]
colonne[F] vertébrale
columna[F] vertebral
colonna[F] vertebrale

橈骨（とうこつ）
radius
Speiche[F]
radius[M]
radio[M]
radio[M]

腸骨
ilium
Darmbein[N]
os[M] iliaque
hueso[M] ilíaco
ileo[M]

仙骨
sacrum
Kreuzbein[N]
sacrum[M]
sacro[M]
sacro[M]

大腿骨
femur
Oberschenkelknochen[M]
fémur[M]
fémur[M]
femore[M]

尾骨
coccyx
Steißbein[N]
coccyx[M]
cóccix[M]
coccige[M]

膝蓋骨（しつがいこつ）
patella
Kniescheibe[F]
rotule[F]
rótula[F]
rotula[F]

脛骨（けいこつ）
tibia
Schienbein[N]
tibia[M]
tibia[F]
tibia[F]

腓骨（ひこつ）
fibula
Wadenbein[N]
péroné[M]
peroné[M] /fíbula[F]
perone[M]

解剖学 | ANATOMY
ANATOMIE | ANATOMIE | ANATOMÍA | ANATOMIA

骨格

背面図
posterior view
Rückansicht^F
vue^F postérieure
vista^F posterior
vista^F posteriore

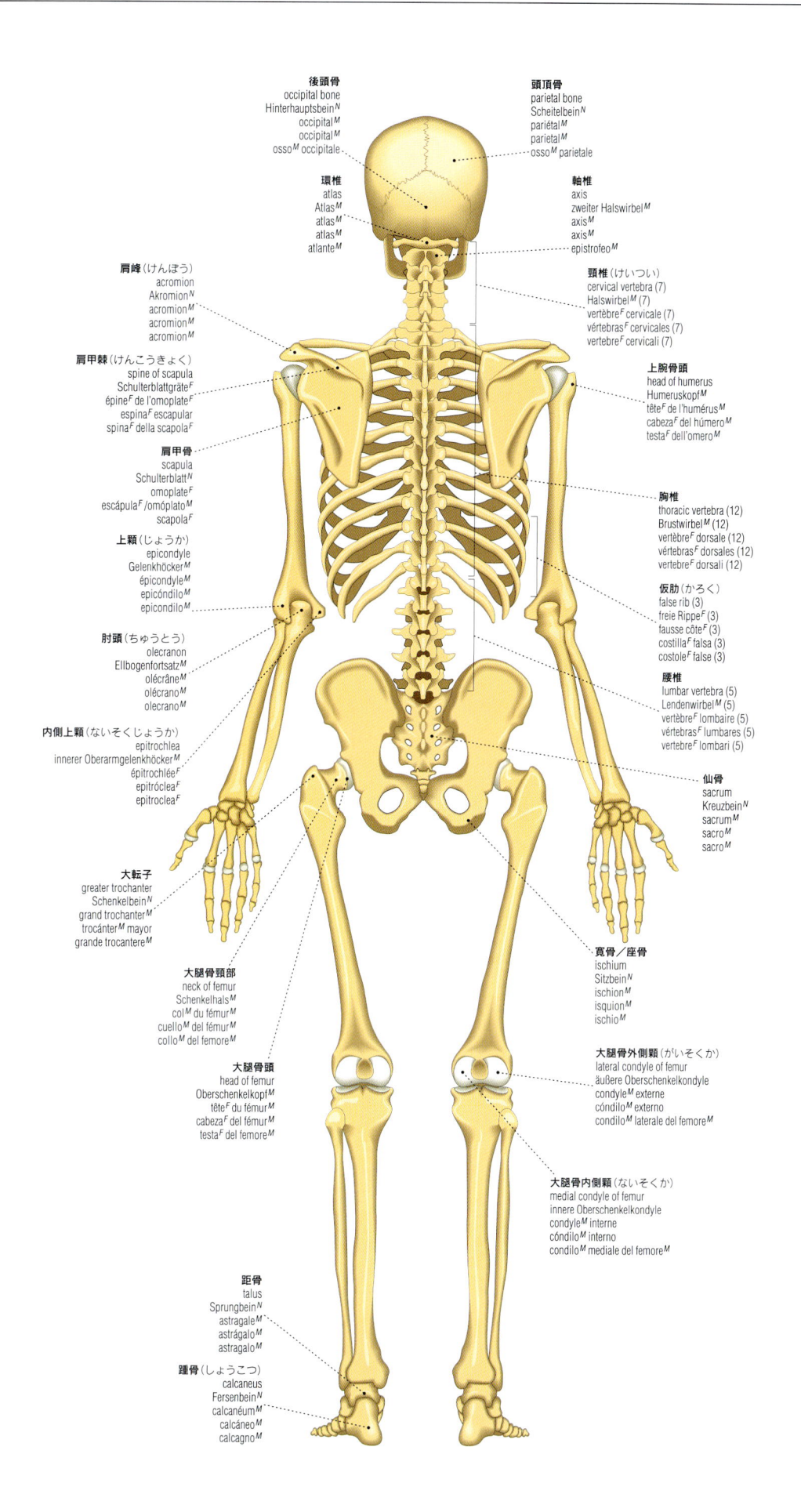

人間

後頭骨
occipital bone
Hinterhauptsbein^N
occipital^M
occipital^M
osso^M occipitale

頭頂骨
parietal bone
Scheitelbein^N
pariétal^M
parietal^M
osso^M parietale

環椎
atlas
Atlas^M
atlas^M
atlas^M
atlante^M

軸椎
axis
zweiter Halswirbel^M
axis^M
axis^M
epistrofeo^M

肩峰（けんぽう）
acromion
Akromion^N
acromion^M
acromion^M
acromion^M

頸椎（けいつい）
cervical vertebra (7)
Halswirbel^M (7)
vertèbre^F cervicale (7)
vértebras^F cervicales (7)
vertebre^F cervicali (7)

肩甲棘（けんこうきょく）
spine of scapula
Schulterblattgräte^F
épine^F de l'omoplate
espina^F escapular
spina^F della scapola

上腕骨頭
head of humerus
Humeruskopf^M
tête^F de l'humérus^M
cabeza^F del húmero^M
testa^F dell'omero^M

肩甲骨
scapula
Schulterblatt^N
omoplate^F
escápula^F/omóplato^M
scapola^F

胸椎
thoracic vertebra (12)
Brustwirbel^M (12)
vertèbre^F dorsale (12)
vértebras^F dorsales (12)
vertebre^F dorsali (12)

上顆（じょうか）
epicondyle
Gelenkhöcker^M
épicondyle^M
epicóndilo^M
epicondilo^M

仮肋（かろく）
false rib (3)
freie Rippe^F (3)
fausse côte^F (3)
costilla^F falsa (3)
costole^F false (3)

肘頭（ちゅうとう）
olecranon
Ellbogenfortsatz^M
olécrâne^M
olécrano^M
olecrano^M

腰椎
lumbar vertebra (5)
Lendenwirbel^M (5)
vertèbre^F lombaire (5)
vértebras^F lumbares (5)
vertebre^F lombari (5)

内側上顆（ないそくじょうか）
epitrochlea
innerer Oberarmgelenkhöcker^M
épitrochlée^F
epitróclea^F
epitroclea^F

仙骨
sacrum
Kreuzbein^N
sacrum^M
sacro^M
sacro^M

大転子
greater trochanter
Schenkelbein^N
grand trochanter^M
trocánter^M mayor
grande trocantere^M

寛骨／座骨
ischium
Sitzbein^N
ischion^M
isquion^M
ischio^M

大腿骨頸部
neck of femur
Schenkelhals^M
col^M du fémur^M
cuello^M del fémur^M
collo^M del femore^M

大腿骨外側顆（がいそくか）
lateral condyle of femur
äußere Oberschenkelkondyle
condyle^M externe
cóndilo^M externo
condilo^M laterale del femore^M

大腿骨頭
head of femur
Oberschenkelkopf^M
tête^F du fémur^M
cabeza^F del fémur^M
testa^F del femore^M

大腿骨内側顆（ないそくか）
medial condyle of femur
innere Oberschenkelkondyle
condyle^M interne
cóndilo^M interno
condilo^M mediale del femore^M

距骨
talus
Sprungbein^N
astragale^M
astrágalo^M
astragalo^M

踵骨（しょうこつ）
calcaneus
Fersenbein^N
calcanéum^M
calcáneo^M
calcagno^M

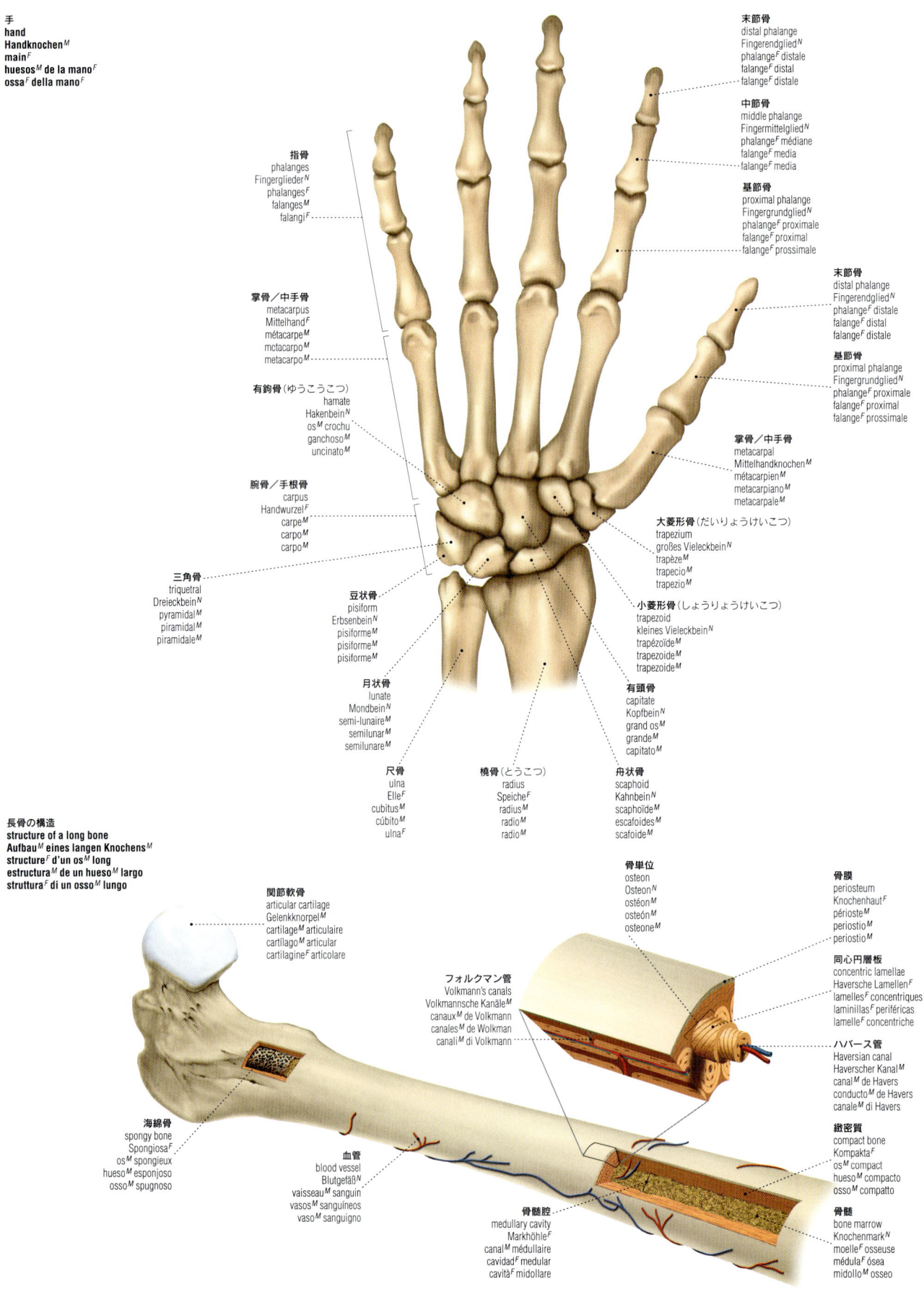

解剖学 | ANATOMY
ANATOMIE | ANATOMIE | ANATOMÍA | ANATOMIA

骨格

日本語 | 英語 | ドイツ語 | フランス語 | スペイン語 | イタリア語

人間

手
hand
Handknochen^M
main^F
huesos^M de la mano^F
ossa^F della mano^F

指骨
phalanges
Fingerglieder^N
phalanges^F
falanges^M
falangi^F

掌骨／中手骨
metacarpus
Mittelhand^F
métacarpe^M
mctacarpo^M
metacarpo^M

有鉤骨（ゆうこうこつ）
hamate
Hakenbein^N
os^M crochu
ganchoso^M
uncinato^M

腕骨／手根骨
carpus
Handwurzel^F
carpe^M
carpo^M
carpo^M

三角骨
triquetral
Dreieckbein^N
pyramidal^M
piramidal^M
piramidale^M

豆状骨
pisiform
Erbsenbein^N
pisiforme^M
pisiforme^M
pisiforme^M

月状骨
lunate
Mondbein^N
semi-lunaire^M
semilunar^M
semilunare^M

尺骨
ulna
Elle^F
cubitus^M
cúbito^M
ulna^F

橈骨（とうこつ）
radius
Speiche^F
radius^M
radio^M
radio^M

末節骨
distal phalange
Fingerendglied^N
phalange^F distale
falange^F distal
falange^F distale

中節骨
middle phalange
Fingermittelglied^N
phalange^F médiane
falange^F media
falange^F media

基節骨
proximal phalange
Fingergrundglied^N
phalange^F proximale
falange^F proximal
falange^F prossimale

末節骨
distal phalange
Fingerendglied^N
phalange^F distale
falange^F distal
falange^F distale

基節骨
proximal phalange
Fingergrundglied^N
phalange^F proximale
falange^F proximal
falange^F prossimale

掌骨／中手骨
metacarpal
Mittelhandknochen^M
métacarpien^M
metacarpiano^M
metacarpale^M

大菱形骨（だいりょうけいこつ）
trapezium
großes Vieleckbein^N
trapèze^M
trapecio^M
trapezio^M

小菱形骨（しょうりょうけいこつ）
trapezoid
kleines Vieleckbein^N
trapézoïde^M
trapezoide^M
trapezoide^M

有頭骨
capitate
Kopfbein^N
grand os^M
grande^M
capitato^M

舟状骨
scaphoid
Kahnbein^N
scaphoïde^M
escafoides^M
scafoide^M

長骨の構造
structure of a long bone
Aufbau^M eines langen Knochens^M
structure^F d'un os^M long
estructura^M de un hueso^M largo
struttura^F di un osso^M lungo

関節軟骨
articular cartilage
Gelenkknorpel^M
cartilage^M articulaire
cartílago^M articular
cartilagine^F articolare

海綿骨
spongy bone
Spongiosa^F
os^M spongieux
hueso^M esponjoso
osso^M spugnoso

フォルクマン管
Volkmann's canals
Volkmannsche Kanäle^F
canaux de Volkmann
canales^M de Wolkman
canali^M di Volkmann

血管
blood vessel
Blutgefäß^N
vaisseau^M sanguin
vasos^M sanguíneos
vaso^M sanguigno

骨髄腔
medullary cavity
Markhöhle^F
canal^M médullaire
cavidad^F medular
cavità^F midollare

骨単位
osteon
Osteon^N
ostéon^M
osteón^M
osteone^M

骨膜
periosteum
Knochenhaut^F
périoste^M
periostio^M
periostio^M

同心円層板
concentric lamellae
Haversche Lamellen^F
lamelles^F concentriques
laminillas^F periféricas
lamelle^F concentriche

ハバース管
Haversian canal
Haverscher Kanal^M
canal^M de Havers
conducto^M de Havers
canale^M di Havers

緻密質
compact bone
Kompakta^F
os^M compact
hueso^M compacto
osso^M compatto

骨髄
bone marrow
Knochenmark^N
moelle^F osseuse
médula^F ósea
midollo^M osseo

解剖学 | ANATOMY
ANATOMIE | ANATOMIE | ANATOMÍA | ANATOMIA

骨格

足
foot
Fußknochen^M
pied^M
huesos^M del pie
ossa^F del piede^M

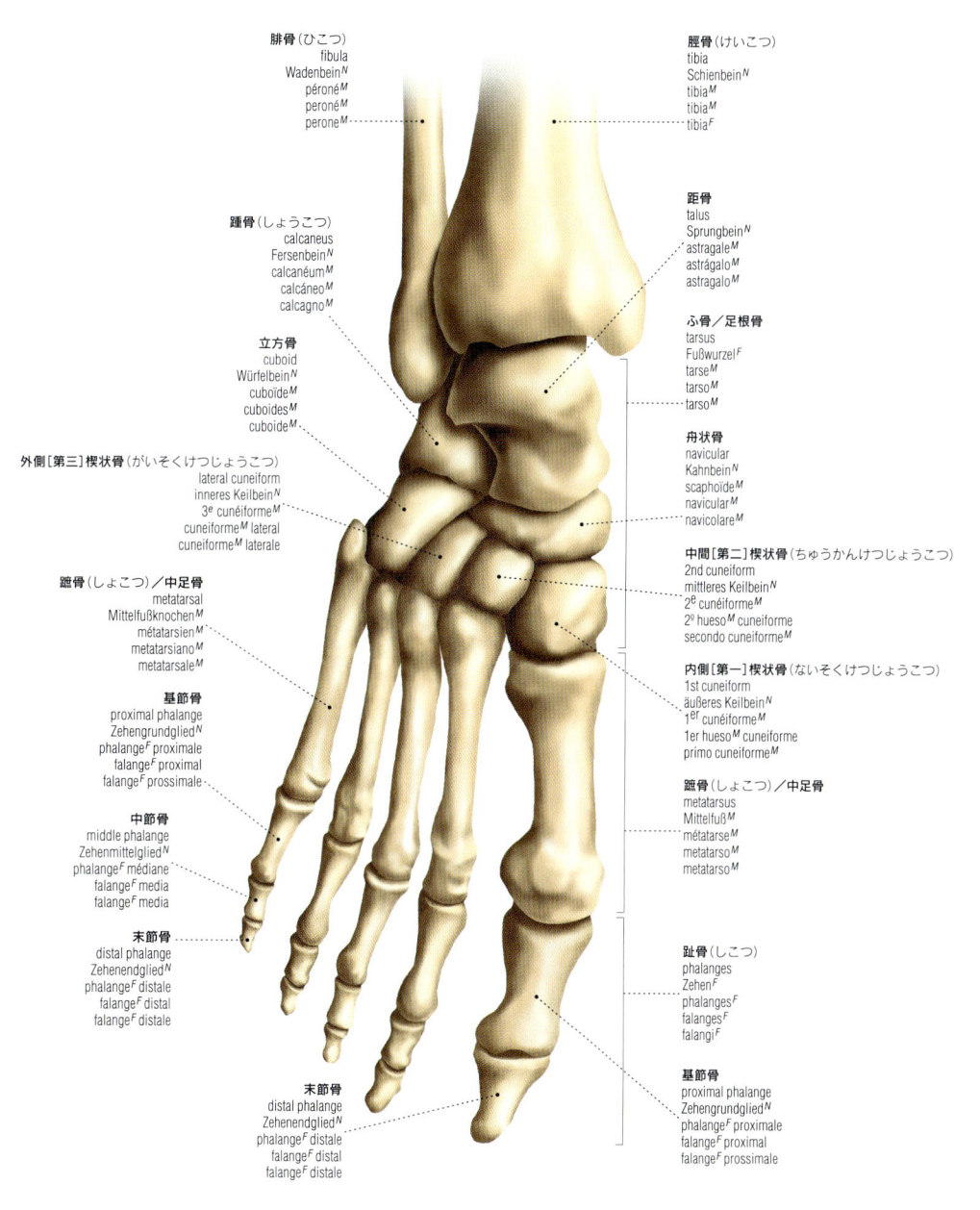

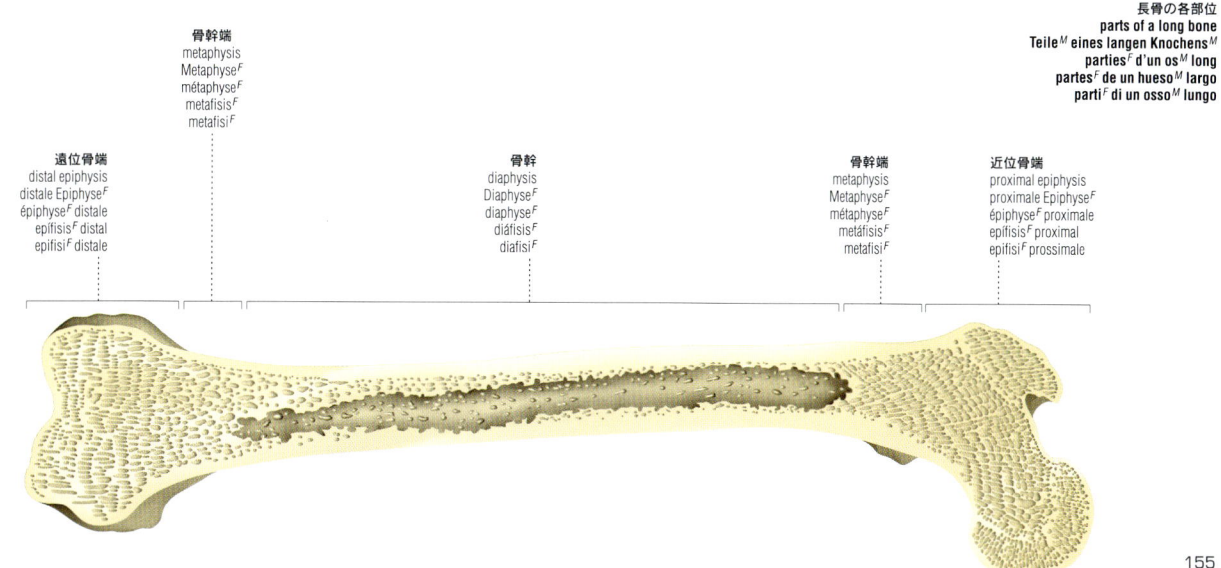

腓骨（ひこつ）
fibula
Wadenbein^N
péroné^M
peroné^M
perone^M

脛骨（けいこつ）
tibia
Schienbein^N
tibia^M
tibia^M
tibia^F

距骨
talus
Sprungbein^N
astragale^M
astrágalo^M
astragalo^M

踵骨（しょうこつ）
calcaneus
Fersenbein^N
calcanéum^M
calcáneo^M
calcagno^M

ふ骨／足根骨
tarsus
Fußwurzel^F
tarse^M
tarso^M
tarso^M

立方骨
cuboid
Würfelbein^N
cuboïde^M
cuboides^M
cuboide^M

舟状骨
navicular
Kahnbein^N
scaphoïde^M
navicular^M
navicolare^M

外側［第三］楔状骨（がいそくけつじょうこつ）
lateral cuneiform
inneres Keilbein^N
3e cunéiforme^M
cuneiforme^M lateral
cuneiforme^M laterale

中間［第二］楔状骨（ちゅうかんけつじょうこつ）
2nd cuneiform
mittleres Keilbein^N
2e cunéiforme^M
2º hueso^M cuneiforme
secondo cuneiforme^M

内側［第一］楔状骨（ないそくけつじょうこつ）
1st cuneiform
äußeres Keilbein^N
1er cunéiforme^M
1er hueso^M cuneiforme
primo cuneiforme^M

蹠骨（しょこつ）／中足骨
metatarsal
Mittelfußknochen^M
métatarsien^M
metatarsiano^M
metatarsale^M

蹠骨（しょこつ）／中足骨
metatarsus
Mittelfuß^M
métatarse^M
metatarso^M
metatarso^M

基節骨
proximal phalange
Zehengrundglied^N
phalange^F proximale
falange^F proximal
falange^F prossimale

中節骨
middle phalange
Zehenmittelglied^N
phalange^F médiane
falange^F media
falange^F media

末節骨
distal phalange
Zehenendglied^N
phalange^F distale
falange^F distal
falange^F distale

末節骨
distal phalange
Zehenendglied^N
phalange^F distale
falange^F distal
falange^F distale

趾骨（しこつ）
phalanges
Zehen^F
phalanges^F
falanges^F
falangi^F

基節骨
proximal phalange
Zehengrundglied^N
phalange^F proximale
falange^F proximal
falange^F prossimale

人間

長骨の各部位
parts of a long bone
Teile^M eines langen Knochens^M
parties^F d'un os^M long
partes^F de un hueso^M largo
parti^F di un osso^M lungo

骨幹端
metaphysis
Metaphyse^F
métaphyse^F
metáfisis^F
metafisi^F

遠位骨端
distal epiphysis
distale Epiphyse^F
épiphyse^F distale
epífisis^F distal
epifisi^F distale

骨幹
diaphysis
Diaphyse^F
diaphyse^F
diáfisis^F
diafisi^F

骨幹端
metaphysis
Metaphyse^F
métaphyse^F
metáfisi^F
metafisi^F

近位骨端
proximal epiphysis
proximale Epiphyse^F
épiphyse^F proximale
epífisis^F proximal
epifisi^F prossimale

155

解剖学 | ANATOMY
ANATOMIE | ANATOMIE | ANATOMÍA | ANATOMIA

骨格

日本語 | 英語 | ドイツ語 | フランス語 | スペイン語 | イタリア語

滑膜性の連結の種類
types of synovial joints
Arten^F von echten Gelenken^N
types^M d'articulations^F synoviales
tipos^M de articulaciones^F sinoviales
tipi^M di articolazioni^F sinoviali

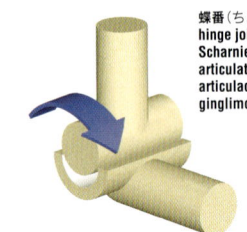

蝶番（ちょうつがい）関節
hinge joint
Scharniergelenk^N
articulation^F charnière^F
articulación^F en bisagra^F
ginglimo^M

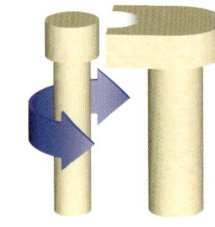

車軸関節
pivot joint
Drehgelenk^N
articulation^F pivot^M
articulación^F en pivote^M
articolazione^F a perno^M

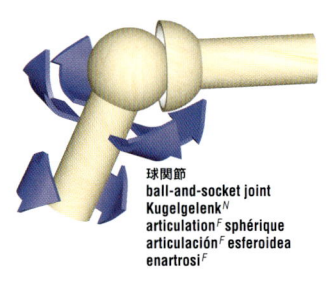

球関節
ball-and-socket joint
Kugelgelenk^N
articulation^F sphérique
articulación^F esferoidea
enartrosi^F

脚
leg
Bein^N
jambe^F
pierna
gamba^F

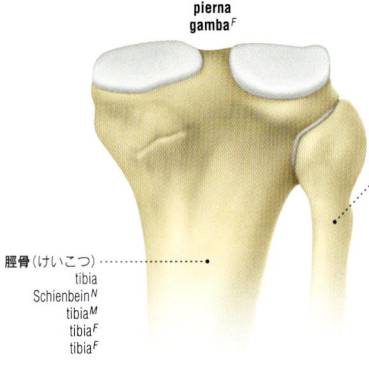

腓骨（ひこつ）
fibula
Wadenbein^N
péroné^M
peroné^M
perone^M

肩
shoulder
Schulter^F
épaule^F
hombro^M
spalla^F

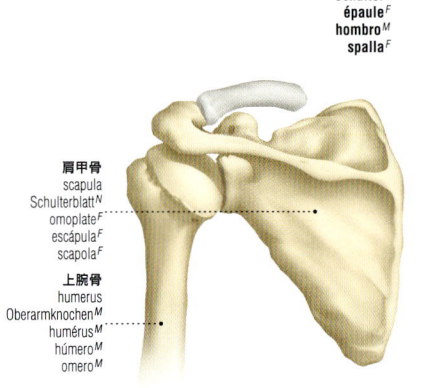

肘
elbow
Ellbogen^M
coude^M
codo^M
gomito^M

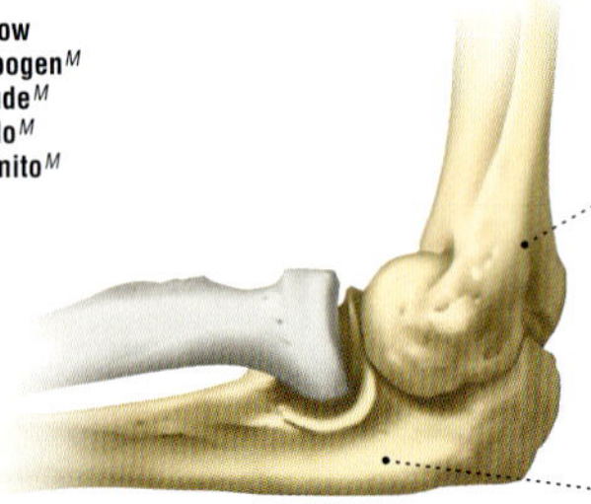

上腕骨
humerus
Oberarmknochen^M
humérus^M
húmero^M
omero^M

脛骨（けいこつ）
tibia
Schienbein^N
tibia
tibia^F
tibia^F

肩甲骨
scapula
Schulterblatt^N
omoplate^F
escápula^F
scapola^F

上腕骨
humerus
Oberarmknochen^M
humérus^M
húmero^M
omero^M

尺骨
ulna
Elle^F
cubitus^M
cúbito^M
ulna^F

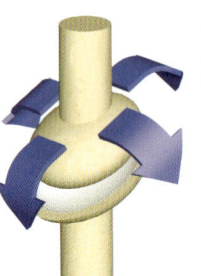

顆状（かじょう）関節
condyloid joint
Ellipsoidgelenk^N
articulation^F ellipsoïdale
articulación^F condilar
articolazione^F condiloidea

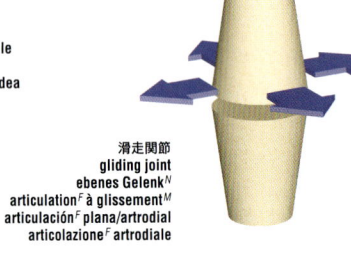

滑走関節
gliding joint
ebenes Gelenk^N
articulation^F à glissement^M
articulación^F plana/artrodial
articolazione^F artrodiale

鞍（あん）関節
saddle joint
Sattelgelenk^N
articulation^F en selle^F
articulación^F en silla^F de montar
articolazione^F a sella^F

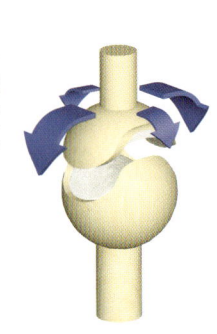

手首
wrist
Handgelenk^N
poignet^M
muñeca^F
polso^M

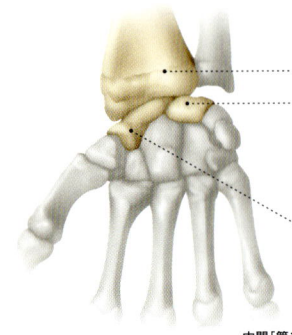

橈骨（とうこつ）
radius
Speiche^F
radius^M
radio^M
radio^M

月状骨
lunate
Mondbein^N
semi-lunaire^M
semilunar^M
semilunare^M

舟状骨
scaphoid
Kahnbein^N
scaphoïde^M
escafoides^M
scafoide^M

足首
tarsus
Fußwurzel^F
tarse^M
tarso^M
tarso^M

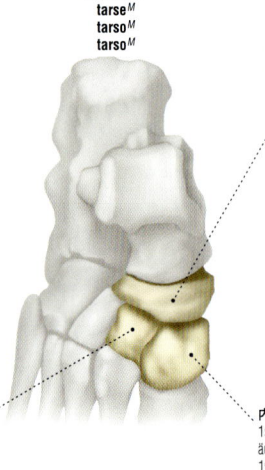

舟状骨
navicular
Kahnbein^N
scaphoïde^M
navicular^M
navicolare^M

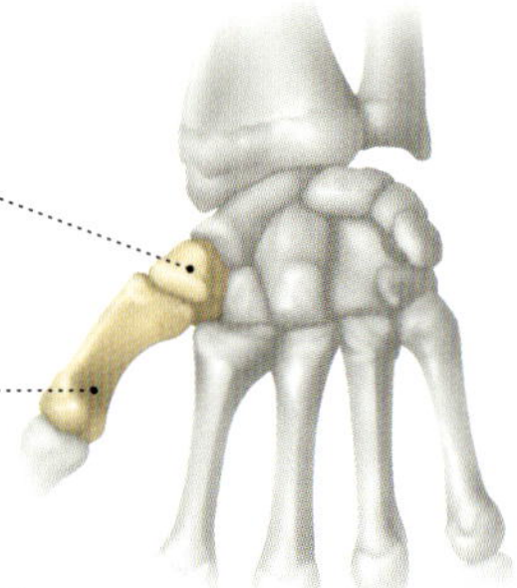

大菱形骨（だいりょうけいこつ）
trapezium
großes Vieleckbein^N
trapèze^M
trapecio^M
trapezio^M

親指
thumb
Daumen^M
pouce^M
pulgar^M
pollice^M

掌骨／中手骨
metacarpal
Mittelhandknochen^M
métacarpien^M
metacarpiano^M
metacarpale^M

中間[第二]楔状骨（ちゅうかんけつじょうこつ）
2nd cuneiform
mittleres Keilbein^N
2e cunéiforme^M
2º hueso^M cuneiforme
secondo cuneiforme^M

内側[第一]楔状骨（ないそくけつじょうこつ）
1st cuneiform
äußeres Keilbein^N
1er cunéiforme^M
1er hueso^M cuneiforme
primo cuneiforme^M

解剖学 | ANATOMY
ANATOMIE | ANATOMIE | ANATOMÍA | ANATOMIA

骨格

脊柱（せきちゅう）
vertebral column
Wirbelsäule^F
os^M de la colonne^F vertébrale
columna^F vertebral
colonna^F vertebrale

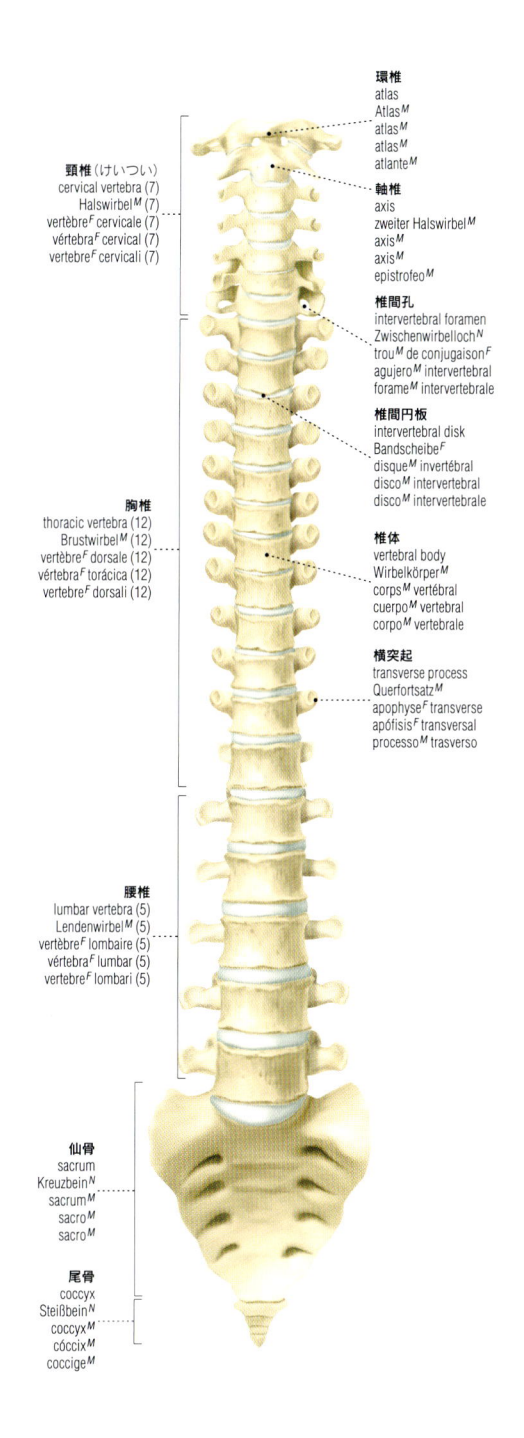

骨の種類
types of bones
Knochenarten^F
types^M d'os^M
tipos^M de huesos^M
tipi^M di ossa^F

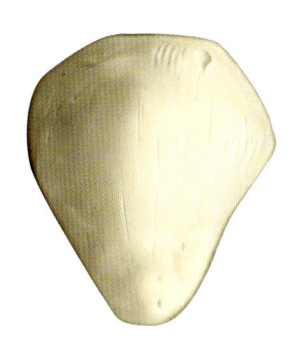

環椎
atlas
Atlas^M
atlas^M
atlas^M
atlante^M

頸椎（けいつい）
cervical vertebra (7)
Halswirbel^M (7)
vertèbre^F cervicale (7)
vértebra^F cervical (7)
vertebre^F cervicali (7)

軸椎
axis
zweiter Halswirbel^M
axis^M
axis^M
epistrofeo^M

椎間孔
intervertebral foramen
Zwischenwirbelloch^N
trou^M de conjugaison^F
agujero^M intervertebral
forame^M intervertebrale

椎間円板
intervertebral disk
Bandscheibe^F
disque^M invertébral
disco^M intervertebral
disco^M intervertebrale

胸椎
thoracic vertebra (12)
Brustwirbel^M (12)
vertèbre^F dorsale (12)
vértebra^F torácica (12)
vertebre^F dorsali (12)

椎体
vertebral body
Wirbelkörper^M
corps^M vertébral
cuerpo^M vertebral
corpo^M vertebrale

横突起
transverse process
Querfortsatz^M
apophyse^F transverse
apófisis^F transversal
processo^M trasverso

短骨
short bone
kurzer Knochen^M
os^M court
hueso^M corto
osso^M corto

長骨
long bone
langer Knochen^M
os^M long
hueso^M largo
osso^M lungo

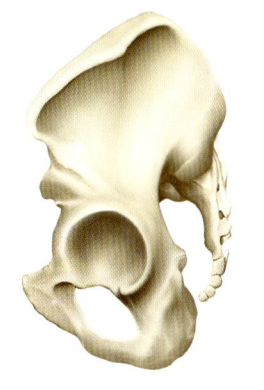

不規則骨
irregular bone
unregelmäßiger Knochen^M
os^M irrégulier
hueso^M irregular
osso^M irregolare

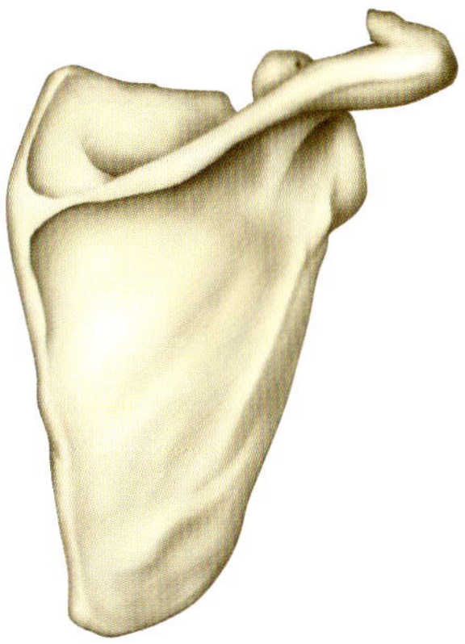

腰椎
lumbar vertebra (5)
Lendenwirbel^M (5)
vertèbre^F lombaire (5)
vértebra^F lumbar (5)
vertebre^F lombari (5)

仙骨
sacrum
Kreuzbein^N
sacrum^M
sacro^M
sacro^M

尾骨
coccyx
Steißbein^N
coccyx^M
cóccix^M
coccige^M

扁平骨
flat bone
platter Knochen^M
os^M plat
hueso^M plano
osso^M piatto

人間

解剖学 | ANATOMY
ANATOMIE | ANATOMIE | ANATOMÍA | ANATOMIA

骨格

日本語 | 英語 | ドイツ語 | フランス語 | スペイン語 | イタリア語

頭蓋（とうがい）の側面図
lateral view of skull
Seitenansicht^F eines Schädels^M
vue^F latérale du crâne^M
vista^F lateral del cráneo^M
vista^F laterale del cranio^M

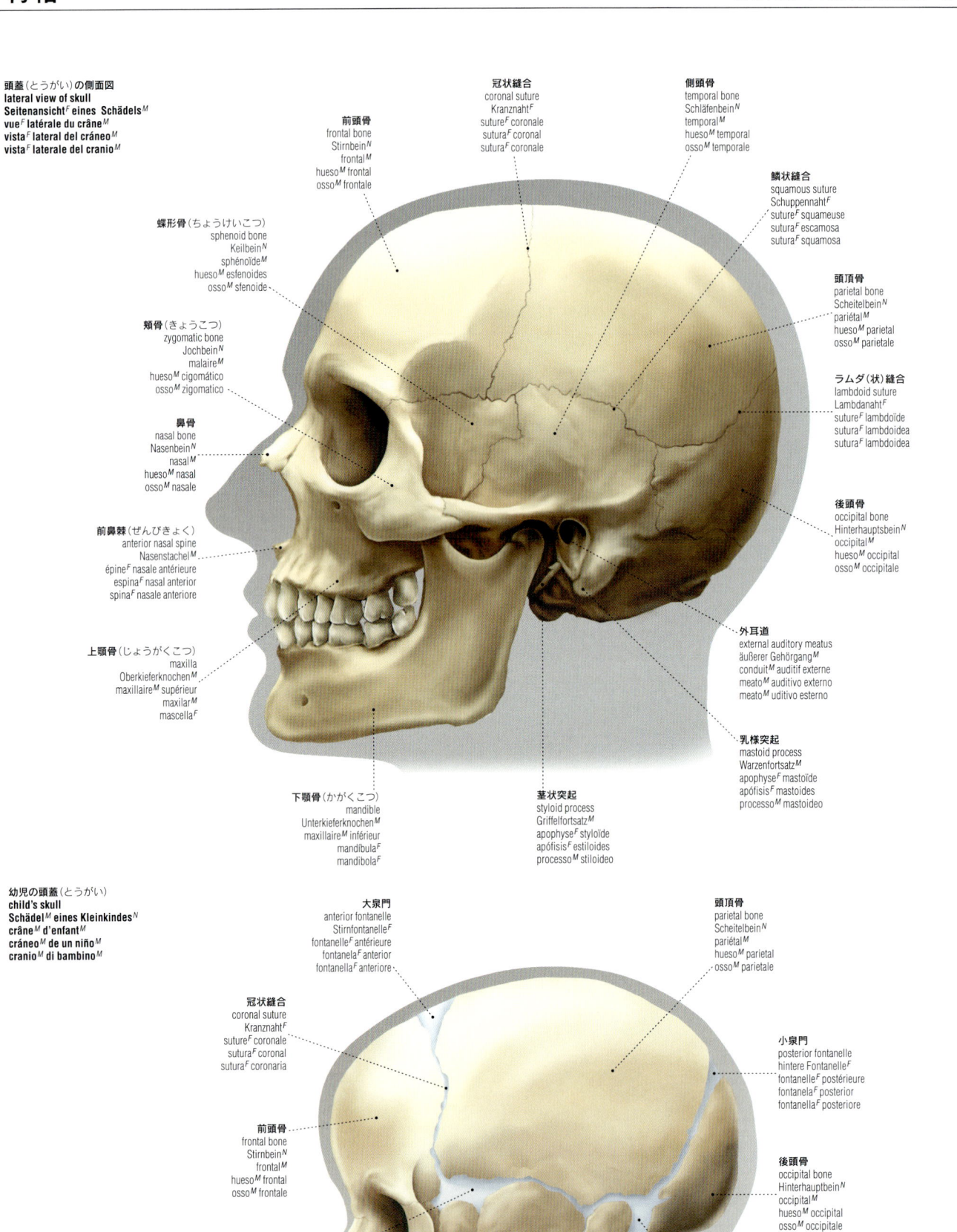

蝶形骨（ちょうけいこつ）
sphenoid bone
Keilbein^N
sphénoïde^M
hueso^M esfenoides
osso^M sfenoide

頬骨（きょうこつ）
zygomatic bone
Jochbein^N
malaire^M
hueso^M cigomático
osso^M zigomatico

鼻骨
nasal bone
Nasenbein^N
nasal^M
hueso^M nasal
osso^M nasale

前鼻棘（ぜんびきょく）
anterior nasal spine
Nasenstachel^M
épine^F nasale antérieure
espina^F nasal anterior
spina^F nasale anteriore

上顎骨（じょうがくこつ）
maxilla
Oberkieferknochen^M
maxillaire^M supérieur
maxilar^M
mascella^F

下顎骨（かがくこつ）
mandible
Unterkieferknochen^M
maxillaire^M inférieur
mandíbula^F
mandibola^F

冠状縫合
coronal suture
Kranznaht^F
suture^F coronale
sutura^F coronal
sutura^F coronale

前頭骨
frontal bone
Stirnbein^N
frontal^M
hueso^M frontal
osso^M frontale

茎状突起
styloid process
Griffelfortsatz^M
apophyse^F styloïde
apófisis^F estiloides
processo^M stiloideo

側頭骨
temporal bone
Schläfenbein^N
temporal^M
hueso^M temporal
osso^M temporale

鱗状縫合
squamous suture
Schuppennaht^F
suture^F squameuse
sutura^F escamosa
sutura^F squamosa

頭頂骨
parietal bone
Scheitelbein^N
pariétal^M
hueso^M parietal
osso^M parietale

ラムダ（状）縫合
lambdoid suture
Lambdanaht^F
suture^F lambdoïde
sutura^F lambdoidea
sutura^F lambdoidea

後頭骨
occipital bone
Hinterhauptbein^N
occipital^M
hueso^M occipital
osso^M occipitale

外耳道
external auditory meatus
äußerer Gehörgang^M
conduit^M auditif externe
meato^M auditivo externo
meato^M uditivo esterno

乳様突起
mastoid process
Warzenfortsatz^M
apophyse^F mastoïde
apófisis^F mastoides
processo^M mastoideo

幼児の頭蓋（とうがい）
child's skull
Schädel^M eines Kleinkindes^N
crâne^M d'enfant^M
cráneo^M de un niño^M
cranio^M di bambino^M

冠状縫合
coronal suture
Kranznaht^F
suture^F coronale
sutura^F coronal
sutura^F coronaria

前頭骨
frontal bone
Stirnbein^N
frontal^M
hueso^M frontal
osso^M frontale

前側頭泉門
sphenoidal fontanelle
vordere Seitenfontanelle^F
fontanelle^F sphénoïdale
fontanela^F esfenoidal
fontanella^F sfenoidale

大泉門
anterior fontanelle
Stirnfontanelle^F
fontanelle^F antérieure
fontanela^F anterior
fontanella^F anteriore

頭頂骨
parietal bone
Scheitelbein^N
pariétal^M
hueso^M parietal
osso^M parietale

小泉門
posterior fontanelle
hintere Fontanelle^F
fontanelle^F postérieure
fontanela^F posterior
fontanella^F posteriore

後頭骨
occipital bone
Hinterhauptbein^N
occipital^M
hueso^M occipital
osso^M occipitale

後側頭泉門
mastoid fontanelle
hintere Seitenfontanelle^F
fontanelle^F mastoïdienne
fontanela^F mastoidea
fontanella^F mastoidea

解剖学 | ANATOMY
ANATOMIE | ANATOMIE | ANATOMÍA | ANATOMIA

歯
teeth | Zähne(M) | dents(F) | dientes(M) | denti(M)

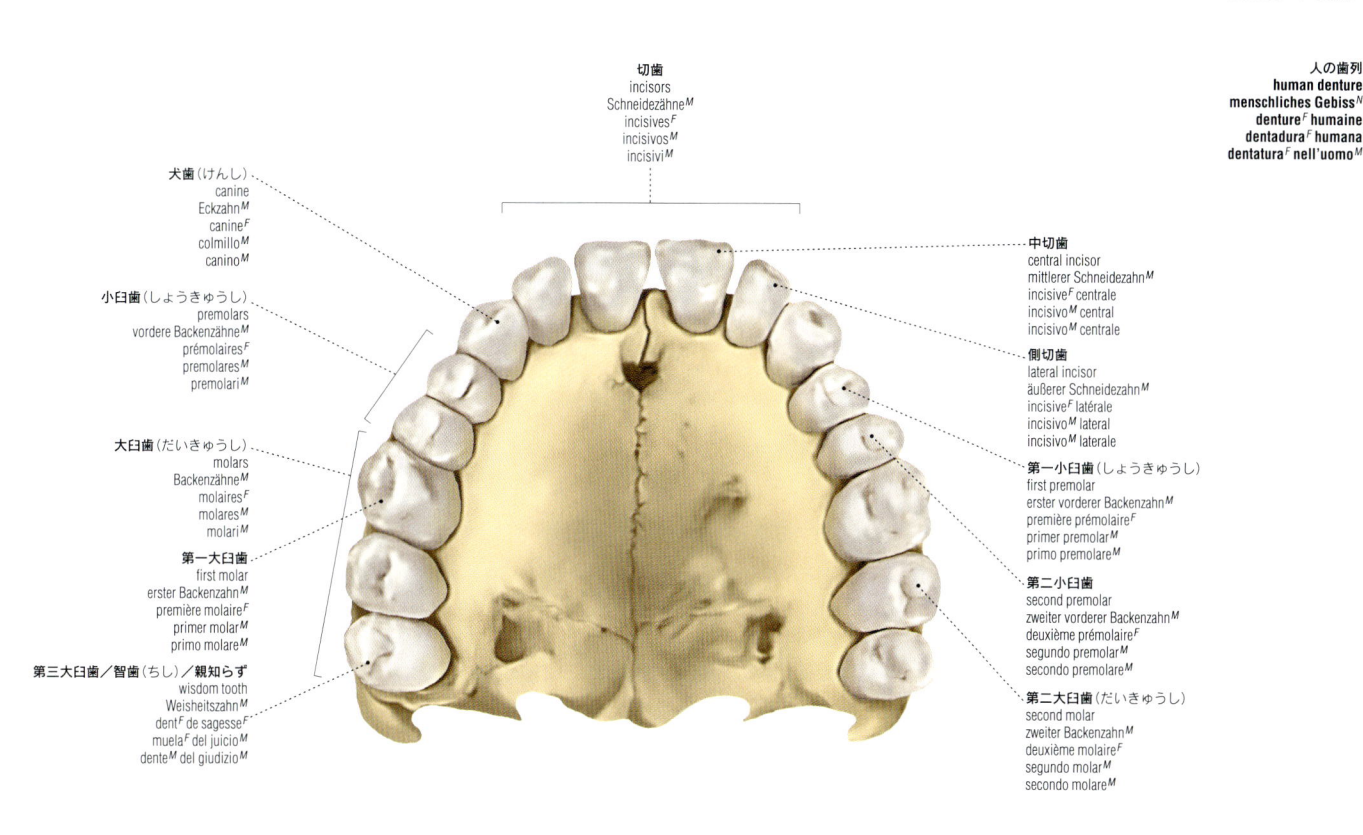

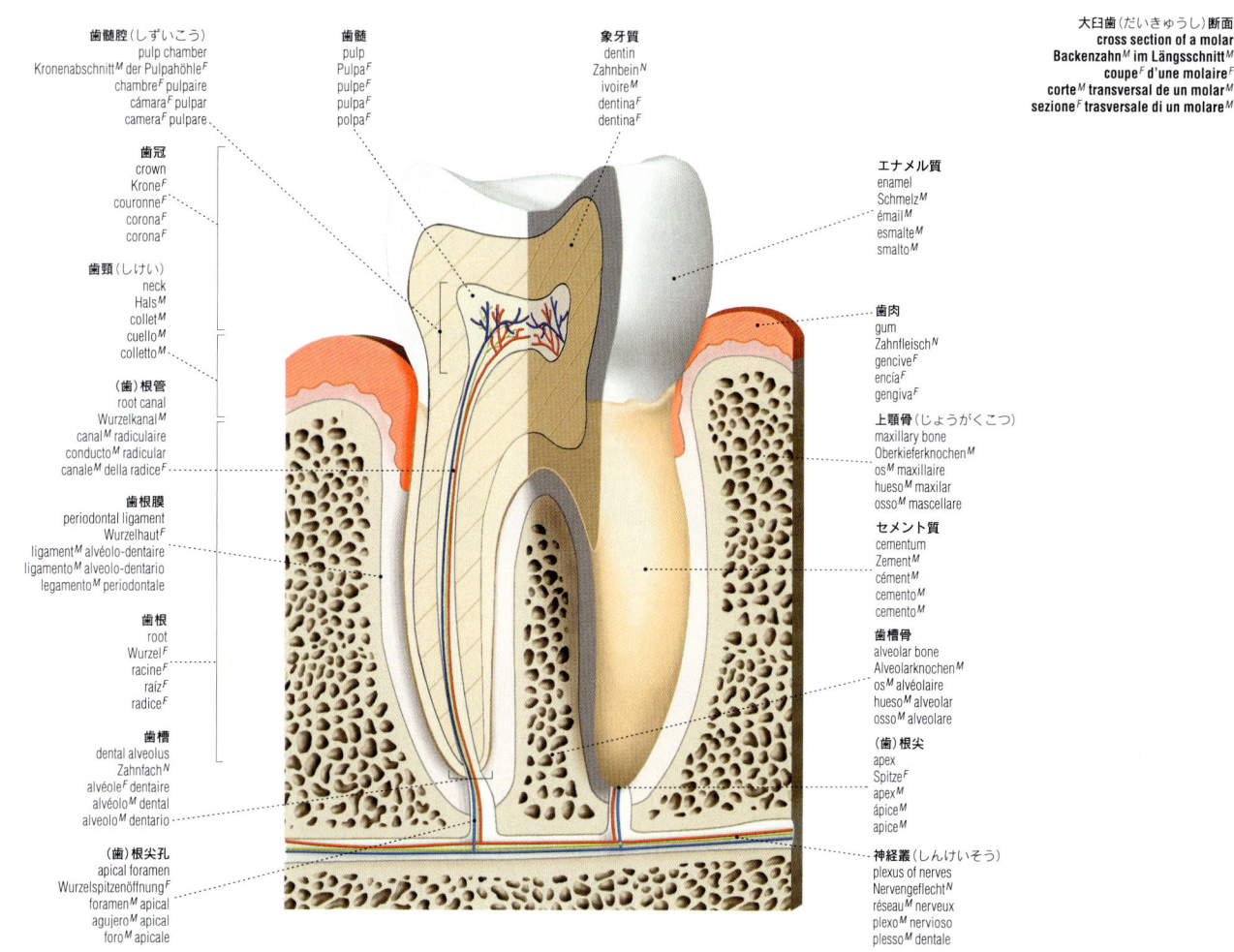

人の歯列
human denture
menschliches Gebiss(N)
denture(F) humaine
dentadura(F) humana
dentatura(F) nell'uomo

切歯
incisors
Schneidezähne(M)
incisives(F)
incisivos(M)
incisivi(M)

犬歯（けんし）
canine
Eckzahn(M)
canine(F)
colmillo(M)
canino(M)

小臼歯（しょうきゅうし）
premolars
vordere Backenzähne(M)
prémolaires(F)
premolares(M)
premolari(M)

大臼歯（だいきゅうし）
molars
Backenzähne(M)
molaires(F)
molares(M)
molari(M)

第一大臼歯
first molar
erster Backenzahn(M)
première molaire(F)
primer molar(M)
primo molare(M)

第三大臼歯／智歯（ちし）／親知らず
wisdom tooth
Weisheitszahn(M)
dent(F) de sagesse(F)
muela(F) del juicio(M)
dente(M) del giudizio(M)

中切歯
central incisor
mittlerer Schneidezahn(M)
incisive(F) centrale
incisivo(M) central
incisivo(M) centrale

側切歯
lateral incisor
äußerer Schneidezahn(M)
incisive(F) latérale
incisivo(M) lateral
incisivo(M) laterale

第一小臼歯（しょうきゅうし）
first premolar
erster vorderer Backenzahn(M)
première prémolaire(F)
primer premolar(M)
primo premolare(M)

第二小臼歯
second premolar
zweiter vorderer Backenzahn(M)
deuxième prémolaire(F)
segundo premolar(M)
secondo premolare(M)

第二大臼歯（だいきゅうし）
second molar
zweiter Backenzahn(M)
deuxième molaire(F)
segundo molar(M)
secondo molare(M)

大臼歯（だいきゅうし）断面
cross section of a molar
Backenzahn(M) im Längsschnitt(M)
coupe(F) d'une molaire(F)
corte(M) transversal de un molar(M)
sezione(F) trasversale di un molare(M)

歯髄腔（しずいこう）
pulp chamber
Kronenabschnitt(M) der Pulpahöhle(F)
chambre(F) pulpaire
cámara(F) pulpar
camera(F) pulpare

歯髄
pulp
Pulpa(F)
pulpe(F)
pulpa(F)
polpa(F)

象牙質
dentin
Zahnbein(N)
ivoire(M)
dentina(F)
dentina(F)

歯冠
crown
Krone(F)
couronne(F)
corona(F)
corona(F)

歯頸（しけい）
neck
Hals(M)
collet(M)
cuello(M)
colletto(M)

（歯）根管
root canal
Wurzelkanal(M)
canal(M) radiculaire
conducto(M) radicular
canale(M) della radice(F)

歯根膜
periodontal ligament
Wurzelhaut(F)
ligament(M) alvéolo-dentaire
ligamento(M) alveolo-dentario
legamento(M) periodontale

歯根
root
Wurzel(F)
racine(F)
raíz(F)
radice(F)

歯槽
dental alveolus
Zahnfach(N)
alvéole(F) dentaire
alvéolo(M) dental
alveolo(M) dentario

（歯）根尖孔
apical foramen
Wurzelspitzenöffnung(F)
foramen(M) apical
agujero(M) apical
foro(M) apicale

エナメル質
enamel
Schmelz(M)
émail(M)
esmalte(M)
smalto(M)

歯肉
gum
Zahnfleisch(N)
gencive(F)
encía(F)
gengiva(F)

上顎骨（じょうがくこつ）
maxillary bone
Oberkieferknochen(M)
os(M) maxillaire
hueso(M) maxilar
osso(M) mascellare

セメント質
cementum
Zement(M)
cément(M)
cemento(M)
cemento(M)

歯槽骨
alveolar bone
Alveolarknochen(M)
os(M) alvéolaire
hueso(M) alveolar
osso(M) alveolare

（歯）根尖
apex
Spitze(F)
apex(M)
ápice(M)
apice(M)

神経叢（しんけいそう）
plexus of nerves
Nervengeflecht(N)
réseau(M) nerveux
plexo(M) nervioso
plesso(M) dentale

人間

解剖学 | ANATOMY
ANATOMIE | ANATOMIE | ANATOMÍA | ANATOMIA

血液循環

blood circulation | Blutkreislauf^M | circulation^F sanguine | circulación^F sanguínea | circolazione^F del sangue^M

日本語 | 英語 | ドイツ語 | フランス語 | スペイン語 | イタリア語

主な静脈と動脈
principal veins and arteries
die wichtigsten Venen^F und Arterien^F
principales veines^F et artères^F
principales venas^F y arterias^F
principali vene^F e arterie^F

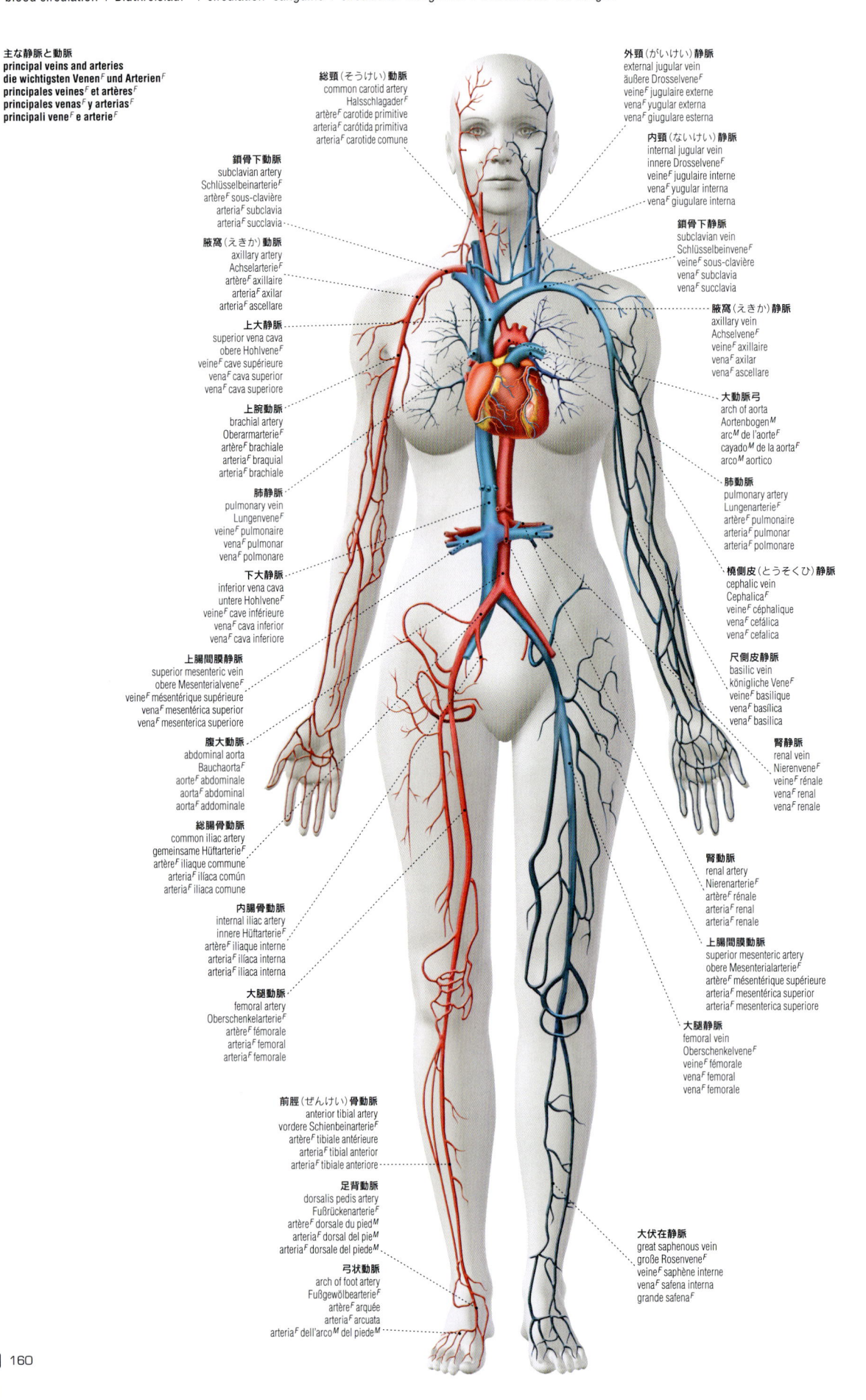

総頸（そうけい）動脈
common carotid artery
Halsschlagader^F
artère^F carotide primitive
arteria^F carótida primitiva
arteria^F carotide comune

鎖骨下動脈
subclavian artery
Schlüsselbeinarterie^F
artère^F sous-clavière
arteria^F subclavia
arteria^F succlavia

腋窩（えきか）動脈
axillary artery
Achselarterie^F
artère^F axillaire
arteria^F axilar
arteria^F ascellare

上大静脈
superior vena cava
obere Hohlvene^F
veine^F cave supérieure
vena^F cava superior
vena^F cava superiore

上腕動脈
brachial artery
Oberarmarterie^F
artère^F brachiale
arteria^F braquial
arteria^F brachiale

肺静脈
pulmonary vein
Lungenvene^F
veine^F pulmonaire
vena^F pulmonar
vena^F polmonare

下大静脈
inferior vena cava
untere Hohlvene^F
veine^F cave inférieure
vena^F cava inferior
vena^F cava inferiore

上腸間膜静脈
superior mesenteric vein
obere Mesenterialvene^F
veine^F mésentérique supérieure
vena^F mesentérica superior
vena^F mesenterica superiore

腹大動脈
abdominal aorta
Bauchaorta^F
aorte^F abdominale
aorta^F abdominal
aorta^F addominale

総腸骨動脈
common iliac artery
gemeinsame Hüftarterie^F
artère^F iliaque commune
arteria^F ilíaca común
arteria^F iliaca comune

内腸骨動脈
internal iliac artery
innere Hüftarterie^F
artère^F iliaque interne
arteria^F ilíaca interna
arteria^F iliaca interna

大腿動脈
femoral artery
Oberschenkelarterie^F
artère^F fémorale
arteria^F femoral
arteria^F femorale

前脛（ぜんけい）骨動脈
anterior tibial artery
vordere Schienbeinarterie^F
artère^F tibiale antérieure
arteria^F tibial anterior
arteria^F tibiale anteriore

足背動脈
dorsalis pedis artery
Fußrückenarterie^F
artère^F dorsale du pied^M
arteria^F dorsal del pie^M
arteria^F dorsale del piede^M

弓状動脈
arch of foot artery
Fußgewölbearterie^F
artère^F arquée
arteria^F arcuata
arteria^F dell'arco^M del piede^M

外頸（がいけい）静脈
external jugular vein
äußere Drosselvene^F
veine^F jugulaire externe
vena^F yugular externa
vena^F giugulare esterna

内頸（ないけい）静脈
internal jugular vein
innere Drosselvene^F
veine^F jugulaire interne
vena^F yugular interna
vena^F giugulare interna

鎖骨下静脈
subclavian vein
Schlüsselbeinvene^F
veine^F sous-clavière
vena^F subclavia
vena^F succlavia

腋窩（えきか）静脈
axillary vein
Achselvene^F
veine^F axillaire
vena^F axilar
vena^F ascellare

大動脈弓
arch of aorta
Aortenbogen^M
arc^M de l'aorte^F
cayado^M de la aorta^F
arco^M aortico

肺動脈
pulmonary artery
Lungenarterie^F
artère^F pulmonaire
arteria^F pulmonar
arteria^F polmonare

橈側皮（とうそくひ）静脈
cephalic vein
Cephalica^F
veine^F céphalique
vena^F cefálica
vena^F cefalica

尺側皮静脈
basilic vein
königliche Vene^F
veine^F basilique
vena^F basílica
vena^F basilica

腎静脈
renal vein
Nierenvene^F
veine^F rénale
vena^F renal
vena^F renale

腎動脈
renal artery
Nierenarterie^F
artère^F rénale
arteria^F renal
arteria^F renale

上腸間膜動脈
superior mesenteric artery
obere Mesenterialarterie^F
artère^F mésentérique supérieure
arteria^F mesentérica superior
arteria^F mesenterica superiore

大腿静脈
femoral vein
Oberschenkelvene^F
veine^F fémorale
vena^F femoral
vena^F femorale

大伏在静脈
great saphenous vein
große Rosenvene^F
veine^F saphène interne
vena^F safena interna
grande safena^F

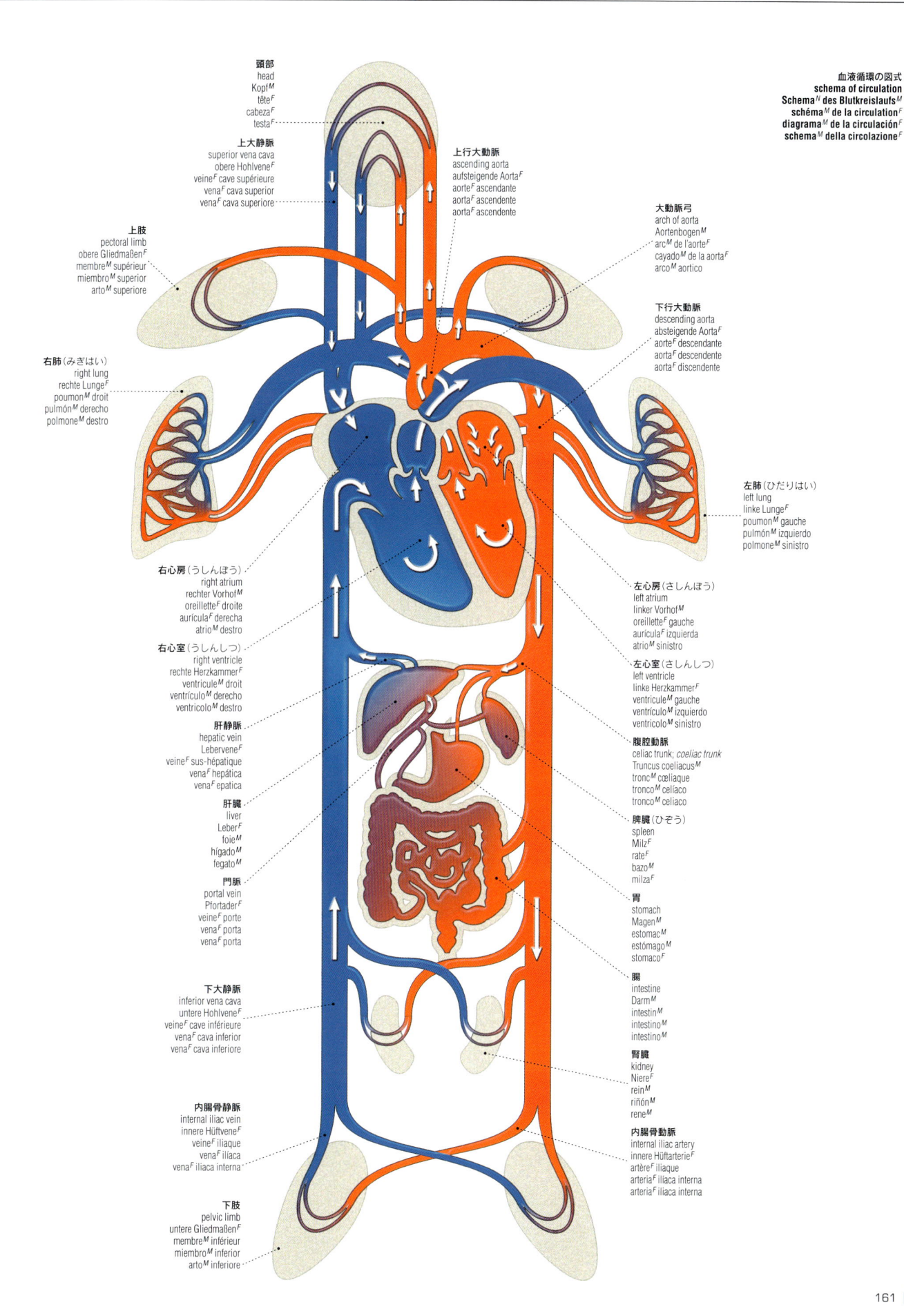

解剖学 | ANATOMY
ANATOMIE | ANATOMIE | ANATOMÍA | ANATOMIA

血液循環

血液循環の図式
schema of circulation
Schema^N des Blutkreislaufs^M
schéma^M de la circulation^F
diagrama^M de la circulación^F
schema^M della circolazione^F

人間

頭部
head
Kopf^M
tête^F
cabeza^F
testa^F

上大静脈
superior vena cava
obere Hohlvene^F
veine^F cave supérieure
vena^F cava superior
vena^F cava superiore

上行大動脈
ascending aorta
aufsteigende Aorta^F
aorte^F ascendante
aorta^F ascendente
aorta^F ascendente

上肢
pectoral limb
obere Gliedmaßen^F
membre^M supérieur
miembro^M superior
arto^M superiore

大動脈弓
arch of aorta
Aortenbogen^M
arc^M de l'aorte^F
cayado^M de la aorta^F
arco^M aortico

下行大動脈
descending aorta
absteigende Aorta^F
aorte^F descendante
aorta^F descendente
aorta^F discendente

右肺（みぎはい）
right lung
rechte Lunge^F
poumon^M droit
pulmón^M derecho
polmone^M destro

左肺（ひだりはい）
left lung
linke Lunge^F
poumon^M gauche
pulmón^M izquierdo
polmone^M sinistro

右心房（うしんぼう）
right atrium
rechter Vorhof^M
oreillette^F droite
aurícula^F derecha
atrio^M destro

左心房（さしんぼう）
left atrium
linker Vorhof^M
oreillette^F gauche
aurícula^F izquierda
atrio^M sinistro

右心室
right ventricle
rechte Herzkammer^F
ventricule^M droit
ventrículo^M derecho
ventricolo^M destro

左心室（さしんしつ）
left ventricle
linke Herzkammer^F
ventricule^M gauche
ventrículo^M izquierdo
ventricolo^M sinistro

肝静脈
hepatic vein
Lebervene^F
veine^F sus-hépatique
vena^F hepática
vena^F epatica

腹腔動脈
celiac trunk; coeliac trunk
Truncus coeliacus^M
tronc^M cœliaque
tronco^M celíaco
tronco^M celiaco

肝臓
liver
Leber^F
foie^M
hígado^M
fegato^M

脾臓（ひぞう）
spleen
Milz^F
rate^F
bazo^M
milza^F

門脈
portal vein
Pfortader^F
veine^F porte
vena^F porta
vena^F porta

胃
stomach
Magen^M
estomac^M
estómago^M
stomaco^F

下大静脈
inferior vena cava
untere Hohlvene^F
veine^F cave inférieure
vena^F cava inferior
vena^F cava inferiore

腸
intestine
Darm^M
intestin^M
intestino^M
intestino^M

腎臓
kidney
Niere^F
rein^M
riñón^M
rene^M

内腸骨静脈
internal iliac vein
innere Hüftvene^F
veine^F iliaque
vena^F ilíaca
vena^F iliaca interna

内腸骨動脈
internal iliac artery
innere Hüftarterie^F
artère^F iliaque
arteria^F ilíaca interna
arteria^F iliaca interna

下肢
pelvic limb
untere Gliedmaßen^F
membre^M inférieur
miembro^M inferior
arto^M inferiore

161

解剖学 | ANATOMY
ANATOMIE | ANATOMIE | ANATOMÍA | ANATOMIA

血液循環

日本語 | 英語 | ドイツ語 | フランス語 | スペイン語 | イタリア語

血液の組成
composition of the blood
Blutbestandteile^M
composition^F du sang^M
composición^F de la sangre^F
composizione^F del sangue^M

白血球
white blood cell
weißes Blutkörperchen^N, Leukozyt^M
globule^M blanc
glóbulo^F blanco
globulo^M bianco

血管
blood vessel
Blutgefäß^N
vaisseau^M sanguin
vaso^M sanguíneo
vaso^M sanguigno

赤血球
red blood cell
rotes Blutkörperchen^N, Erythrozyt^M
globule^M rouge
glóbulo^M rojo
globulo^M rosso

血小板
platelet
Blutplättchen^N, Thrombozyt^M
plaquette^F
plaqueta^F
piastrina^F

血漿（けっしょう）
plasma
Blutplasma^N
plasma^M
plasma^M
plasma^M

心臓
heart
Herz^N
cœur^M
corazón^M
cuore^M

酸素を含む血液
oxygenated blood
sauerstoffreiches Blut^N
sang^M oxygéné
sangre^F oxigenada
sangue^M ossigenato

酸素が取り除かれた血液
deoxygenated blood
sauerstoffarmes Blut^N
sang^M désoxygéné
sangre^F desoxigenada
sangue^M deossigenato

大動脈弓
arch of aorta
Aortenbogen^M
arc^M de l'aorte^F
cayado^M de la aorta^F
arco^M aortico

肺動脈幹
pulmonary trunk
Lungenarterienstamm^M
artère^F pulmonaire
arteria^F pulmonar
arteria^M polmonare

肺動脈弁
pulmonary valve
Pulmonalklappe^F
valvule^F pulmonaire
válvula^F pulmonar
valvola^F polmonare

上大静脈
superior vena cava
obere Hohlvene^F
veine^F cave supérieure
vena^F cava superior
vena^F cava superiore

左肺（ひだりはい）静脈
left pulmonary vein
linke Lungenvene^F
veine^F pulmonaire gauche
vena^F pulmonar izquierda
vena^F polmonare sinistra

右肺（みぎはい）静脈
right pulmonary vein
rechte Lungenvene^F
veine^F pulmonaire droite
vena^F pulmonar derecha
vena^F polmonare destra

左心房（さしんぼう）
left atrium
linker Vorhof^M
oreillette^F gauche
aurícula^F izquierda
atrio^M sinistro

大動脈弁
aortic valve
Aortenklappe^F
valvule^F aortique
válvula^F aórtica
valvola^F aortica

右心房（うしんぼう）
right atrium
rechter Vorhof^M
oreillette^F droite
aurícula^F derecha
atrio^M destro

僧帽弁
mitral valve
Mitralklappe^F
valvule^F mitrale
válvula^F mitral
valvola^F mitrale

三尖弁
tricuspid valve
Trikuspidalklappe^F
valvule^F tricuspide
válvula^F tricúspide
valvola^F tricuspide

左心室（さしんしつ）
left ventricle
linke Herzkammer^F
ventricule^M gauche
ventrículo^M izquierdo
ventricolo^M sinistro

心内膜
endocardium
Herzwandschicht^F
endocarde^M
endocardio^M
endocardio^M

乳頭筋
papillary muscle
Papillarmuskel^M
muscle^M papillaire
músculo^M papilar
muscolo^M papillare

下大静脈
inferior vena cava
untere Hohlvene^F
veine^F cave inférieure
vena^F cava inferior
vena^F cava inferiore

心室中隔
interventricular septum
Kammerseptum^N
septum^M interventriculaire
tabique^M interventricular
setto^M interventricolare

大動脈
aorta
Aorta^F
aorte^F
aorta^F
aorta^F

右心室（うしんしつ）
right ventricle
rechte Herzkammer^F
ventricule^M droit
ventrículo^M derecho
ventricolo^M destro

心筋層
myocardium
Herzmuskel^M
myocarde^M
miocardio^M
miocardio^M

解剖学 | ANATOMY
ANATOMIE | ANATOMIE | ANATOMÍA | ANATOMIA

呼吸器系

respiratory system | Luftwege^M | appareil^M respiratoire | aparato^M respiratorio | apparato^M respiratorio

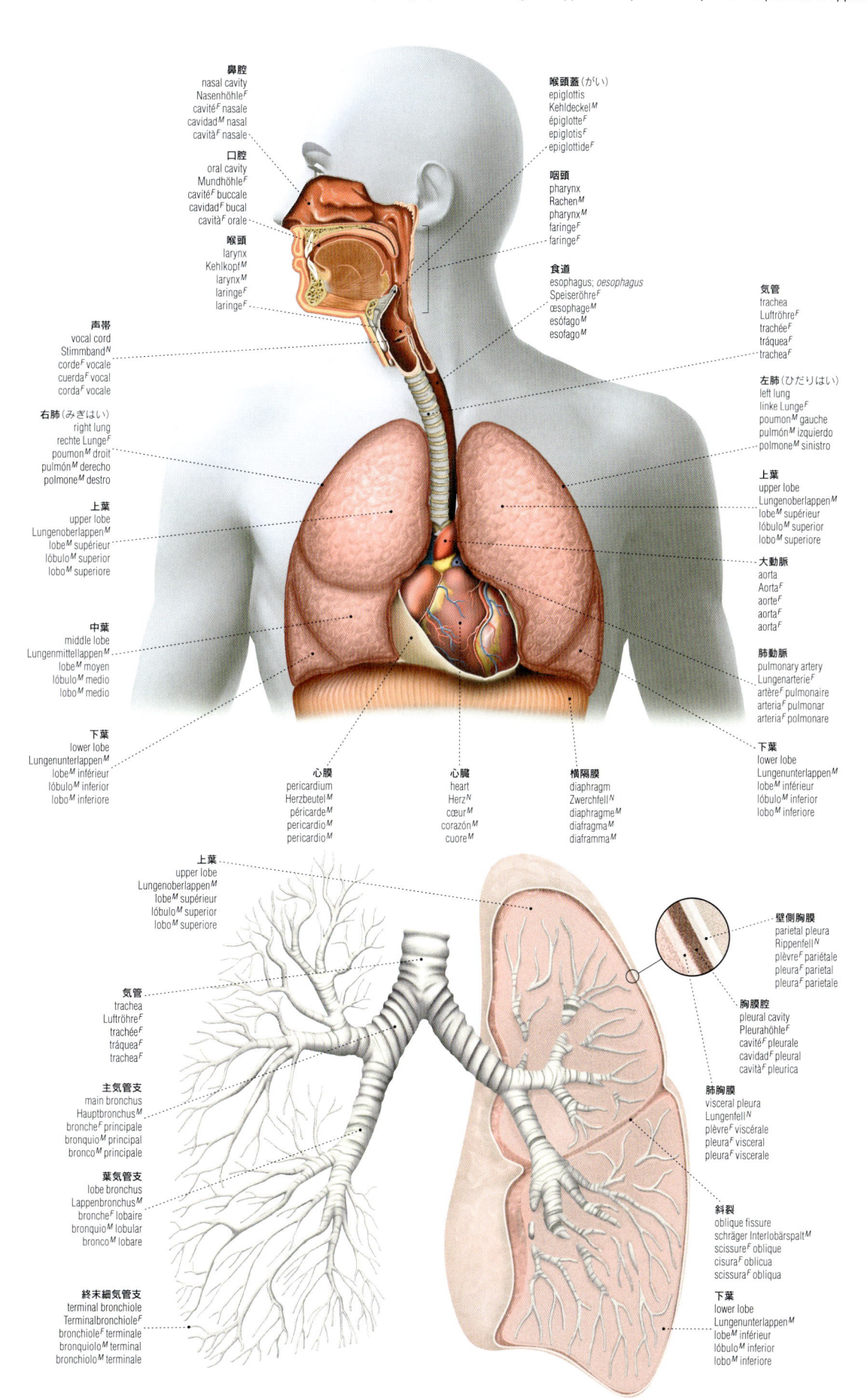

鼻腔 nasal cavity / Nasenhöhle^F / cavité^F nasale / cavidad^F nasal / cavità^F nasale

口腔 oral cavity / Mundhöhle^F / cavité^F buccale / cavidad^F bucal / cavità^F orale

喉頭 larynx / Kehlkopf^M / larynx^M / laringe^F / laringe^F

声帯 vocal cord / Stimmband^N / corde^F vocale / cuerda^F vocal / corda^F vocale

右肺（みぎはい） right lung / rechte Lunge^F / poumon^M droit / pulmón^M derecho / polmone^M destro

上葉 upper lobe / Lungenoberlappen^M / lobe^M supérieur / lóbulo^M superior / lobo^M superiore

中葉 middle lobe / Lungenmittellappen^M / lobe^M moyen / lóbulo^M medio / lobo^M medio

下葉 lower lobe / Lungenunterlappen^M / lobe^M inférieur / lóbulo^M inferior / lobo^M inferiore

喉頭蓋（がい） epiglottis / Kehldeckel^M / épiglotte^F / epiglotis^F / epiglottide^F

咽頭 pharynx / Rachen^M / pharynx^M / faringe^F / faringe^F

食道 esophagus; oesophagus / Speiseröhre^F / œsophage^M / esófago^M / esofago^M

気管 trachea / Luftröhre^F / trachée^F / tráquea^F / trachea^F

左肺（ひだりはい） left lung / linke Lunge^F / poumon^M gauche / pulmón^M izquierdo / polmone^M sinistro

上葉 upper lobe / Lungenoberlappen^M / lobe^M supérieur / lóbulo^M superior / lobo^M superiore

大動脈 aorta / Aorta^F / aorte^F / aorta^F / aorta^F

肺動脈 pulmonary artery / Lungenarterie / artère^F pulmonaire / arteria^F pulmonar / arteria^F polmonare

下葉 lower lobe / Lungenunterlappen^M / lobe^M inférieur / lóbulo^M inferior / lobo^M inferiore

心膜 pericardium / Herzbeutel^M / péricarde^M / pericardio^M / pericardio^M

心臓 heart / Herz^N / cœur^M / corazón^M / cuore^M

横隔膜 diaphragm / Zwerchfell^N / diaphragme^M / diafragma^M / diaframma^M

上葉 upper lobe / Lungenoberlappen^M / lobe^M supérieur / lóbulo^M superior / lobo^M superiore

気管 trachea / Luftröhre^F / trachée^F / tráquea^F / trachea^F

主気管支 main bronchus / Hauptbronchus^M / bronche^F principale / bronquio^M principal / bronco^M principale

葉気管支 lobe bronchus / Lappenbronchus^M / bronche^F lobaire / bronquio^M lobular / bronco^M lobare

終末細気管支 terminal bronchiole / Terminalbronchiole^F / bronchiole^F terminale / bronquiolo^M terminal / bronchiolo^M terminale

壁側胸膜 parietal pleura / Rippenfell^N / plèvre^F pariétale / pleura^F parietal / pleura^F parietale

胸膜腔 pleural cavity / Pleurahöhle^F / cavité^F pleurale / cavidad^F pleural / cavità^F pleurica

肺胸膜 visceral pleura / Lungenfell^N / plèvre^F viscérale / pleura^F visceral / pleura^F viscerale

斜裂 oblique fissure / schräger Interlobärspalt^M / scissure^F oblique / cisura^F oblicua / scissura^F obliqua

下葉 lower lobe / Lungenunterlappen^M / lobe^M inférieur / lóbulo^M inferior / lobo^M inferiore

人間

肺 lungs / Lungen^F / poumons^M / pulmones^M / polmoni^M

解剖学 | ANATOMY
ANATOMIE | ANATOMIE | ANATOMÍA | ANATOMIA

消化器系

日本語 | 英語 | ドイツ語 | フランス語 | スペイン語 | イタリア語

digestive system | VerdauungsapparatM | appareilM digestif | aparatoM digestivo | apparatoM digerente

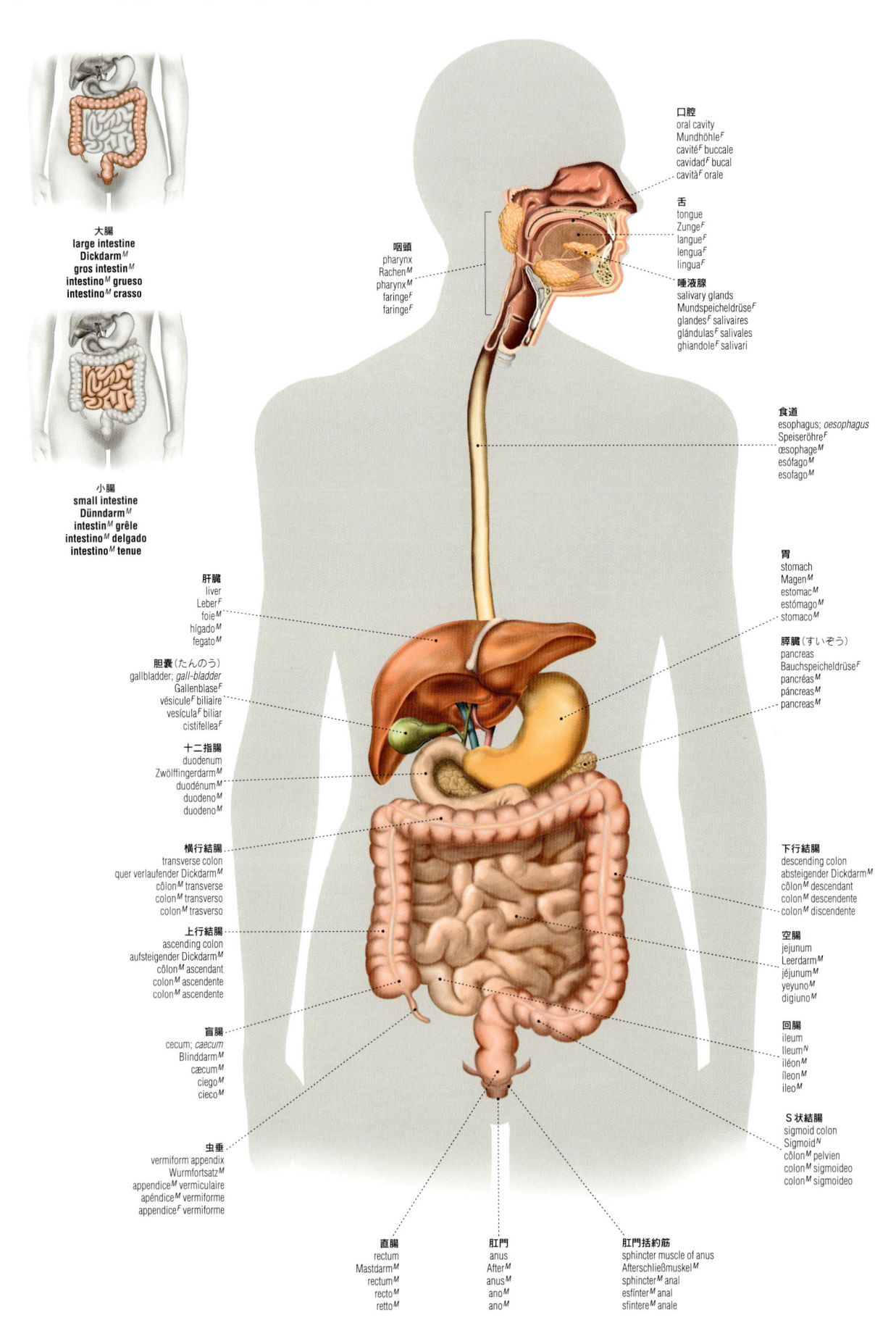

大腸
large intestine
DickdarmM
gros intestinM
intestinoM grueso
intestinoM crasso

小腸
small intestine
DünndarmM
intestinM grêle
intestinoM delgado
intestinoM tenue

口腔
oral cavity
MundhöhleF
cavitéF buccale
cavidadF bucal
cavitàF orale

舌
tongue
ZungeF
langueF
lenguaF
linguaF

咽頭
pharynx
RachenM
pharynxM
faringeF
faringeF

唾液腺
salivary glands
MundspeicheldrüseF
glandesF salivaires
glándulasF salivales
ghiandoleF salivari

食道
esophagus; *oesophagus*
SpeiseröhreF
œsophageM
esófagoM
esofagoM

胃
stomach
MagenM
estomacM
estómagoM
stomacoM

膵臓（すいぞう）
pancreas
BauchspeicheldrüseF
pancréasM
páncreasM
pancreasM

肝臓
liver
LeberF
foieM
hígadoM
fegatoM

胆嚢（たんのう）
gallbladder; *gall-bladder*
GallenblaseF
vésiculeF biliaire
vesículaF biliar
cistifelleaF

十二指腸
duodenum
ZwölffingerdarmM
duodénumM
duodenoM
duodenoM

横行結腸
transverse colon
quer verlaufender DickdarmM
côlonM transverse
colonM transverso
colonM trasverso

下行結腸
descending colon
absteigender DickdarmM
côlonM descendant
colonM descendente
colonM discendente

上行結腸
ascending colon
aufsteigender DickdarmM
côlonM ascendant
colonM ascendente
colonM ascendente

空腸
jejunum
LeerdarmM
jéjunumM
yeyunoM
digiunoM

盲腸
cecum; *caecum*
BlinddarmM
cæcumM
ciegoM
ciecoM

回腸
ileum
IleumN
iléonM
íleonM
ileoM

虫垂
vermiform appendix
WurmfortsatzM
appendiceM vermiculaire
apéndiceM vermiforme
appendiceM vermiforme

S状結腸
sigmoid colon
SigmoidN
côlonM pelvien
colonM sigmoideo
colonM sigmoideo

直腸
rectum
MastdarmM
rectumM
rectoM
rettoM

肛門
anus
AfterM
anusM
anoM
anoM

肛門括約筋
sphincter muscle of anus
AfterschließmuskelM
sphincterM anal
esfínterM anal
sfintereM anale

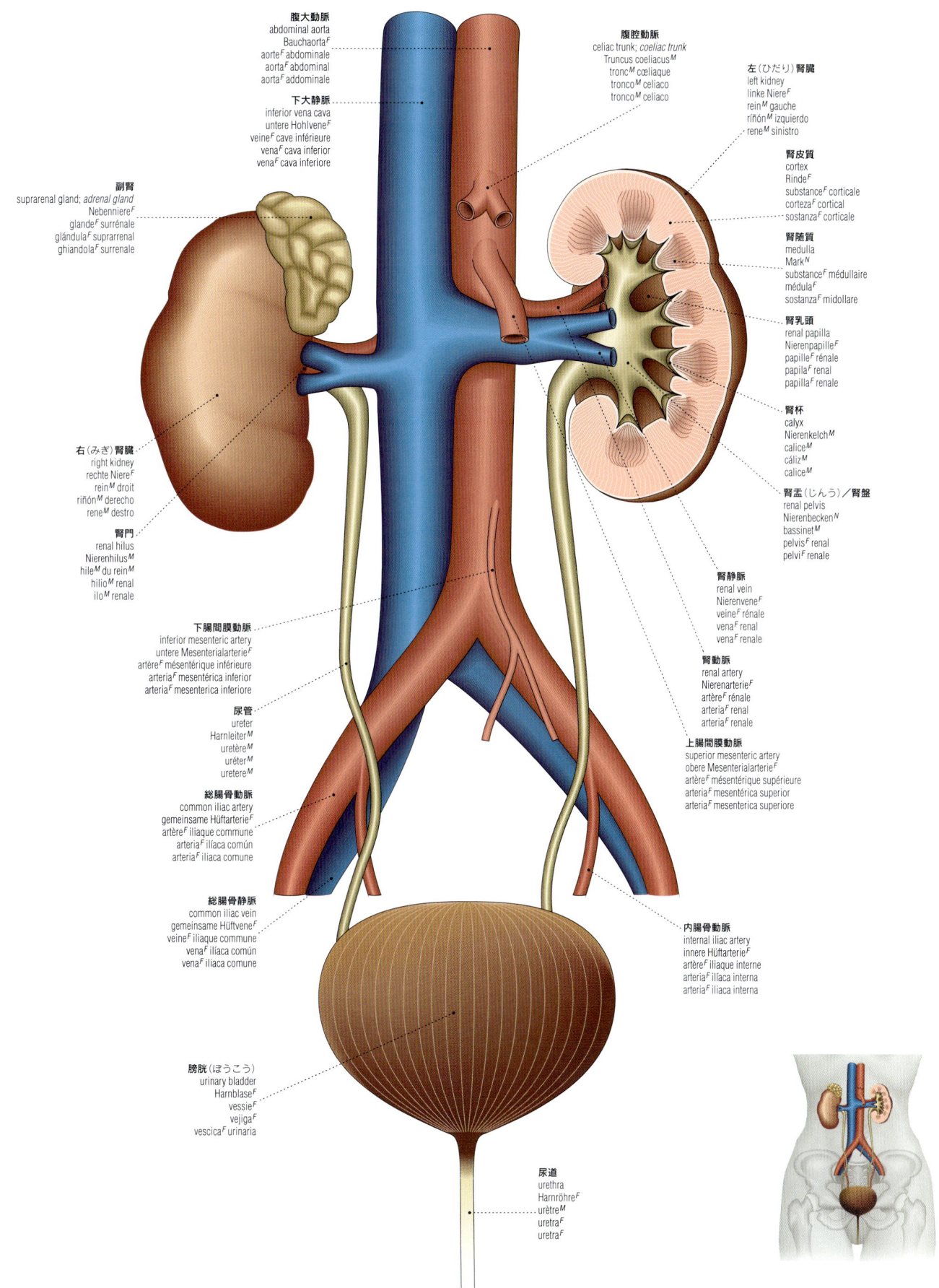

解剖学 | ANATOMY
ANATOMIE | ANATOMIE | ANATOMÍA | ANATOMIA

泌尿器系

urinary system | Harnapparat^M | appareil^M urinaire | aparato^M urinario | apparato^M urinario

腹大動脈
abdominal aorta
Bauchaorta^F
aorte^F abdominale
aorta^F abdominal
aorta^F addominale

腹腔動脈
celiac trunk; *coeliac trunk*
Truncus coeliacus^M
tronc^M cœliaque
tronco^M celiaco
tronco^M celiaco

左（ひだり）腎臓
left kidney
linke Niere^F
rein^M gauche
riñón^M izquierdo
rene^M sinistro

下大静脈
inferior vena cava
untere Hohlvene^F
veine^F cave inférieure
vena^F cava inferior
vena^F cava inferiore

腎皮質
cortex
Rinde^F
substance^F corticale
corteza^F cortical
sostanza^F corticale

副腎
suprarenal gland; *adrenal gland*
Nebenniere^F
glande^F surrénale
glándula^F suprarrenal
ghiandola^F surrenale

腎髄質
medulla
Mark^N
substance^F médullaire
médula^F
sostanza^F midollare

腎乳頭
renal papilla
Nierenpapille^F
papille^F rénale
papila^F renal
papilla^F renale

腎杯
calyx
Nierenkelch^M
calice^M
cáliz^M
calice^M

右（みぎ）腎臓
right kidney
rechte Niere^F
rein^M droit
riñón^M derecho
rene^M destro

腎門
renal hilus
Nierenhilus^M
hile^M du rein^M
hilio^M renal
ilo^M renale

腎盂（じんう）／腎盤
renal pelvis
Nierenbecken^N
bassinet^M
pelvis^F renal
pelvi^F renale

腎静脈
renal vein
Nierenvene^F
veine^F rénale
vena^F renal
vena^F renale

下腸間膜動脈
inferior mesenteric artery
untere Mesenterialarterie^F
artère^F mésentérique inférieure
arteria^F mesentérica inferior
arteria^F mesenterica inferiore

腎動脈
renal artery
Nierenarterie^F
artère^F rénale
arteria^F renal
arteria^F renale

尿管
ureter
Harnleiter^M
uretère^M
uréter^M
uretere^M

上腸間膜動脈
superior mesenteric artery
obere Mesenterialarterie^F
artère^F mésentérique supérieure
arteria^F mesentérica superior
arteria^F mesenterica superiore

総腸骨動脈
common iliac artery
gemeinsame Hüftarterie^F
artère^F iliaque commune
arteria^F ilíaca común
arteria^F iliaca comune

総腸骨静脈
common iliac vein
gemeinsame Hüftvene^F
veine^F iliaque commune
vena^F ilíaca común
vena^F iliaca comune

内腸骨動脈
internal iliac artery
innere Hüftarterie^F
artère^F iliaque interne
arteria^F ilíaca interna
arteria^F iliaca interna

膀胱（ぼうこう）
urinary bladder
Harnblase^F
vessie^F
vejiga^F
vescica^F urinaria

尿道
urethra
Harnröhre^F
urètre^M
uretra^F
uretra^F

165

解剖学 | ANATOMY
ANATOMIE | ANATOMIE | ANATOMÍA | ANATOMIA

神経系

日本語 | 英語 | ドイツ語 | フランス語 | スペイン語 | イタリア語

nervous system | Nervensystem[N] | système[M] nerveux | sistema[M] nervioso | sistema[M] nervoso

末梢神経系
peripheral nervous system
peripheres Nervensystem[N]
système[M] nerveux périphérique
sistema[M] nervioso periférico
sistema[M] nervoso periferico

腕神経叢（わんしんけいそう）
brachial plexus
Armgeflecht[N]
plexus[M] brachial
plexo[M] braquial
plesso[M] brachiale

正中神経
median nerve
Mittelarmnerv[M]
nerf[M] médian
nervio[M] mediano
nervo[M] mediano

尺骨神経
ulnar nerve
Ellennerv[M]
nerf[M] cubital
nervio[M] cubital
nervo[M] ulnare

閉鎖神経
obturator nerve
Hüftlochnerv[M]
nerf[M] obturateur
nervio[M] obturador
nervo[M] otturatorio

腸骨下腹神経
iliohypogastric nerve
Hüft-Becken-Nerv[M]
nerf[M] grand abdomino-génital
nervio[M] abdominogenital mayor
nervo[M] ileoipogastrico

腸骨鼠径（そけい）神経
ilioinguinal nerve
Hüft-Leisten-Nerv[M]
nerf[M] petit abdomino-génital
nervio[M] abdominogenital menor
nervo[M] ileoinguinale

外側大腿皮神経
lateral cutaneous nerve of thigh; *lateral cutaneous femoral nerve*
seitlicher Hautnerv[M] des Oberschenkels[M]
nerf[M] fémoro-cutané
nervio[M] femorocutáneo
nervo[M] cutaneo laterale della coscia[F]

大腿神経
femoral nerve
Oberschenkelnerv[M]
nerf[M] crural
nervio[M] crural
nervo[M] femorale

座骨神経
sciatic nerve
Ischiasnerv[M]
nerf[M] grand sciatique
nervio[M] ciático mayor
nervo[M] ischiatico

伏在神経
saphenous nerve
Rosennerv[M]
nerf[M] saphène interne
nervio[M] safeno interno
nervo[M] safeno interno

総腓骨（そうひこつ）神経
common peroneal nerve
gemeinsamer Wadenbeinnerv[M]
nerf[M] sciatique poplité externe
nervio[M] ciático poplíteo externo
nervo[M] peroniero comune

浅腓骨（せんひこつ）神経
superficial peroneal nerve
oberflächlicher Wadenbeinnerv[M]
nerf[M] musculo-cutané
nervio[M] musculocutáneo de la pierna[F]
nervo[M] peroniero superficiale

深腓骨（しんひこつ）神経
deep peroneal nerve
tiefer Wadenbeinnerv[M]
nerf[M] tibial antérieur
nervio[M] tibial anterior
nervo[M] peroniero profondo

脳神経
cranial nerves
Hirnnerven[M]
nerfs[M] crâniens
nervios[M] craneales
nervi[M] cranici

腋窩（えきか）神経
axillary nerve
Achselnerv[M]
nerf[M] circonflexe
nervio[M] circonflejo
nervo[M] ascellare

橈骨（とうこつ）神経
radial nerve
Speichennerv[M]
nerf[M] radial
nervio[M] radial
nervo[M] radiale

肋間（ろっかん）神経
intercostal nerve
Zwischenrippennerv[M]
nerf[M] intercostal
nervio[M] intercostal
nervo[M] intercostale

腰神経叢（ようしんけいそう）
lumbar plexus
Lendengeflecht[N]
plexus[M] lombaire
plexo[M] lumbar
plesso[M] lombare

仙骨神経叢（しんけいそう）
sacral plexus
Kreuzgeflecht[N]
plexus[M] sacré
plexo[M] sacro
plesso[M] sacrale

臀（でん）神経
gluteal nerve
Gesäßnerv[M]
nerf[M] fessier
nervio[M] glúteo
nervo[M] gluteo

指神経
digital nerve
Fingernerv[M]
nerf[M] digital
nervio[M] digital
nervo[M] digitale

後大腿皮神経
posterior cutaneous nerve of thigh; *minor sciatic nerve*
kleiner Ischiasnerv[M]
nerf[M] petit sciatique
nervio[M] ciático menor
nervo[M] cutaneo posteriore della coscia[F]

脛骨（けいこつ）神経
tibial nerve
Schienbeinnerv[M]
nerf[M] sciatique poplité interne
nervio[M] ciático poplíteo interno
nervo[M] tibiale

腓腹（ひふく）神経
sural nerve
Wadennerv[M]
nerf[M] saphène externe
nervio[M] safeno externo
nervo[M] safeno esterno

人間

解剖学 | ANATOMY
ANATOMIE | ANATOMIE | ANATOMÍA | ANATOMIA

神経系

中枢神経系
central nervous system
Zentralnervensystem^N
système^M nerveux central
sistema^M nervioso central
sistema^M nervoso centrale

大脳
cerebrum
Großhirn^N
cerveau^M
cerebro^M
cervello^M

小脳
cerebellum
Kleinhirn^N
cervelet^M
cerebelo^M
cervelletto^M

脳梁（のうりょう）
corpus callosum
Balken^M
corps^M calleux
cuerpo^M calloso
corpo^M calloso

脊柱（せきちゅう）
vertebral column; spinal column
Wirbelsäule^F
colonne^F vertébrale
columna^F vertebral
colonna^F vertebrale

大脳
cerebrum
Großhirn^N
cerveau^M
cerebro^M
cervello^M

脳弓体
body of fornix
Gewölbekörper^M
corps^M du fornix
cuerpo^M del fórnix^M
corpo^M del fornice^M

透明中隔
septum pellucidum
Septum^N pellucidum
septum^M lucidum
septum^M pellucidum
setto^M pellucido

視（神経）交叉
optic chiasm
Sehnervenkreuzung^F
chiasma^M optique
quiasma^M óptico
chiasma^M ottico

小脳
cerebellum
Kleinhirn^N
cervelet^M
cerebelo^M
cervelletto^M

（脳）下垂体
pituitary gland
Hirnanhangdrüse^F
hypophyse^F
hipófisis^F
ipofisi^F

松果体
pineal body
Zirbeldrüse^F
épiphyse^F
epífisis^F
epifisi^F

延髄
medulla oblongata
verlängertes Mark^N
bulbe^M rachidien
bulbo^M raquídeo
midollo^M allungato

脳橋
pons Varolii
Brücke^F
pont^M de Varole
puente^M de Varolio
ponte^M di Varolio

脊髄（せきずい）
spinal cord
Rückenmark^N
moelle^F épinière
médula^F espinal
midollo^M spinale

知覚神経根
sensitive root
hintere Nervenwurzel^F
racine^F sensitive
raíz^F sensitiva
radice^F sensoriale

灰白質（かいはくしつ）
gray matter
graue Substanz^F
substance^F grise
sustancia^F gris
sostanza^F grigia

脊髄の構造
structure of the spinal cord
Aufbau^M des Rückenmarks^N
structure^F de la moelle^F épinière
estructura^F de la médula^F espinal
struttura^F del midollo^M spinale

終糸の軟膜部
internal filum terminale
filum^N terminale
cul-de-sac^M dural
filum^M terminal interno
filum^M terminale interno

脊髄神経節
spinal ganglion
Spinalganglion^N
ganglion^M spinal
ganglio^M espinal
ganglio^M spinale

後角
posterior horn
Hinterhorn^N
corne^F postérieure
cuerno^M posterior
corno^M posteriore

白質
white matter
weiße Substanz^F
substance^F blanche
sustancia^F blanca
sostanza^F bianca

前角
anterior horn
Vorderhorn^N
corne^F antérieure
cuerno^M anterior
corno^M anteriore

硬膜
dura mater
harte Rückenmarkshaut^F
dure-mère^F
duramadre^F
dura madre^F

脊髄（せきずい）
spinal cord
Rückenmark^N
moelle^F épinière
médula^F espinal
midollo^M spinale

終糸
terminal filament
Endfaden^M
filum^M terminal
filum^M terminal
filum^M terminale esterno

運動根
motor root
vordere Nervenwurzel^F
racine^F motrice
raíz^F motora
radice^F motoria

蜘蛛膜（くももまく）
arachnoid
Arachnoidea^F
arachnoïde^F
aracnoides^M
aracnoide^F

硬膜
dura mater
harte Rückenmarkshaut^F
dure-mère^F
duramadre^F
dura madre^F

脊髄神経
spinal nerve
Rückenmarksnerv^M
nerf^M rachidien
nervio^M espinal
nervo^M spinale

交感神経節
sympathetic ganglion
sympathisches Ganglion^N
ganglion^M du tronc^M sympathique
ganglio^M simpático
ganglio^M simpatico

脳脊髄膜
meninges
Rückenmarkshaut^F
méninges^F
meninges^F
meningi^F

軟膜
pia mater
Pia Mater^F
pie-mère^F
piamadre^F
pia madre^F

人間

167

解剖学 | ANATOMY
ANATOMIE | ANATOMIE | ANATOMÍA | ANATOMIA

神経系

日本語 | 英語 | ドイツ語 | フランス語 | スペイン語 | イタリア語

ニューロン結合
chain of neurons
Neuronenkette^F
chaîne^F de neurones^M
cadena^F de neuronas^F
catena^F di neuroni^M

シナプス
synapse
Synapse^F
synapse^F
sinapsis^F
sinapsi^F

側枝
collateral
Kollaterale^F
collatérale^F
ramificación^F colateral
ramificazione^F collaterale

シュワン鞘
sheath of Schwann
Schwannsche Scheide^F
gaine^F de Schwann
célula^F de Schwann
guaina^F di Schwann

細胞体
cell body
Zellkörper^M
corps^M cellulaire
cuerpo^M celular
corpo^M cellulare

核小体
nucleus
Zellkern^M
noyau^M
núcleo^M
nucleo^M

樹状突起
dendrite
Dendrit^M
dendrite^F
dendrita^F
dendrite^F

終末分枝
terminal arborization
Endverzweigung^F
arborisation^F terminale
arborización^F terminal
arborizzazione^F terminale

ランビエ絞輪
node of Ranvier
Ranviersche Schnürringe^M
nœud^M de Ranvier
nódulo^M de Ranvier
nodo^M di Ranvier

髄鞘（ずいしょう）／ミエリン鞘
myelin sheath
Markscheide^F
gaine^F de myéline
vaina^F de mielina
guaina^F mielinica

軸索
axon
Axon^N
axone^M
axón^M
assone^M

軸索小丘
axon hillock
Ursprungskegel^M
collet^M de l'axone^M
cuerpos^M de Nissl
cono^M di emergenza

感覚のインパルス
sensory impulse
Nervenimpuls^M
influx^M nerveux
impulso^M nervioso
impulso^M sensoriale

知覚根
sensory root
hintere Nervenwurzel^F
racine^F sensitive
raíz^F sensitiva
radice^F sensoriale

プロトニューロン
protoneuron
peripher-sensorisches Neuron^N
protoneurone^F sensitif
protoneurona^F
protoneurone^F

脊髄神経節
spinal ganglion
Spinalganglion^N
ganglion^M spinal
ganglio^M espinal
ganglio^M spinale

運動終板
motor end plate
motorische Endplatte^F
plaque^F motrice
placa^F motora
placca^F motrice

皮膚
skin
Haut^F
peau^F
piel^F
cute^F

白質
white matter
weiße Substanz^F
substance^F blanche
sustancia^F blanca
sostanza^F bianca

脊髄（せきずい）神経
spinal nerve
Rückenmarksnerv^M
nerf^M rachidien
nervio^M raquídeo
nervo^M spinale

灰白質（かいはくしつ）
gray matter; *grey matter*
graue Substanz^F
substance^F grise
sustancia^F gris
sostanza^F grigia

運動ニューロン
motor neuron
motorisches Neuron^N
neurone^M moteur
neurona^F motora
neurone^M motorio

感覚受容器
sense receptor; *sensory receptor*
sensorischer Rezeptor^M
récepteur^M sensoriel
receptor^M sensorial
recettore^M sensoriale

脊髄
spinal cord
Rückenmark^N
moelle^F épinière
médula^F espinal
midollo^M spinale

シナプス
synapse
Synapse^F
synapse^F
sinapsis^F
sinapsi^F

運動根
motor root
vordere Nervenwurzel^F
racine^F motrice
raíz^F motora
radice^F motoria

筋線維
muscle fiber; *muscle fibre*
Muskelfaser^F
fibre^F musculaire
fibra^F muscular
fibra^F muscolare

感覚ニューロン
sensory neuron
sensibles Neuron^N
neurone^M sensoriel
neurona^F sensorial
neurone^M sensoriale

腰椎
lumbar vertebra
Lendenwirbel^M
vertèbre^F lombaire
vértebra^F lumbar
vertebra^F lombare

棘突起（きょくとっき）
spinous process
Dornfortsatz^M
apophyse^F épineuse
apófisis^F espinosa
processo^M spinoso

硬膜上腔[外腔]
epidural space
Epiduralraum^M
espace^M épidural
espacio^M epidural
spazio^M epidurale

硬膜
dura mater
harte Rückenmarkshaut^F
dure-mère^F
duramadre^F
dura madre^F

脳脊髄液
cerebrospinal fluid
Gehirn-Rückenmark-Flüssigkeit^N
liquide^M céphalo-rachidien
líquido^M cerebroespinal
liquido^M cefalorachidiano

脊髄（せきずい）
spinal cord
Rückenmark^N
moelle^F épinière
médula^F espinal
midollo^M spinale

後根
posterior root
hintere Nervenwurzel^F
racine^F postérieure
raíz^F posterior
radice^F posteriore

横突起
transverse process
Querfortsatz^M
apophyse^F transverse
apófisis^F trasversa
processo^M trasverso

交通枝
communicating ramus
Verbindungsast^M
rameau^M communicant
rama^F comunicante
ramo^M comunicante

前根
anterior root
vordere Nervenwurzel^F
racine^F antérieure
raíz^F anterior
radice^F anteriore

椎体
vertebral body
Wirbelkörper^M
corps^M vertébral
cuerpo^M vertebral
corpo^M vertebrale

脊髄神経
spinal nerve
Rückenmarksnerv^M
nerf^M rachidien
nervio^M raquídeo
nervo^M spinale

人間

168

解剖学 | ANATOMY
ANATOMIE | ANATOMIE | ANATOMÍA | ANATOMIA

男性生殖器

male reproductive organs | männliche Geschlechtsorgane^N | organes^M génitaux masculins | órganos^M genitales masculinos | organi^M genitali maschili

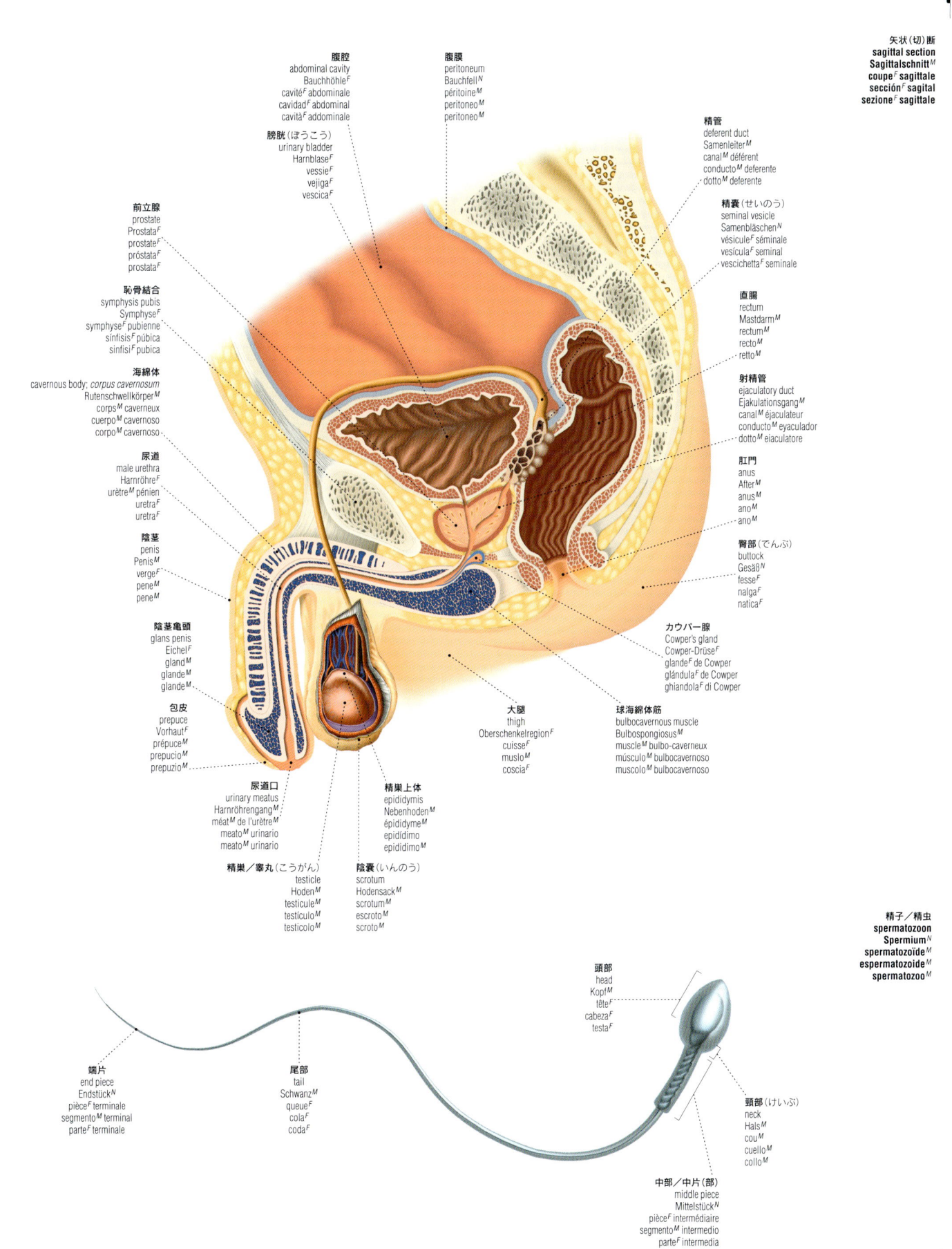

矢状(切)断
sagittal section
Sagittalschnitt^M
coupe^F sagittale
sección^F sagital
sezione^F sagittale

腹腔
abdominal cavity
Bauchhöhle^F
cavité^F abdominale
cavidad^F abdominal
cavità^F addominale

腹膜
peritoneum
Bauchfell^N
péritoine^M
peritoneo^M
peritoneo^M

精管
deferent duct
Samenleiter^M
canal^M déférent
conducto^M deferente
dotto^M deferente

膀胱（ぼうこう）
urinary bladder
Harnblase^F
vessie^F
vejiga^F
vescica^F

精嚢（せいのう）
seminal vesicle
Samenbläschen^N
vésicule^F séminale
vesícula^F seminal
vescichetta^F seminale

前立腺
prostate
Prostata^F
prostate^F
próstata^F
prostata^F

直腸
rectum
Mastdarm^M
rectum^M
recto^M
retto^M

恥骨結合
symphysis pubis
Symphyse^F
symphyse^F pubienne
sínfisis^F púbica
sinfisi^F pubica

射精管
ejaculatory duct
Ejakulationsgang^M
canal^M éjaculateur
conducto^M eyaculador
dotto^M eiaculatore

海綿体
cavernous body; *corpus cavernosum*
Rutenschwellkörper^M
corps^M caverneux
cuerpo^M cavernoso
corpo^M cavernoso

肛門
anus
After^M
anus^M
ano^M
ano^M

尿道
male urethra
Harnröhre^F
urètre^M pénien
uretra^F
uretra^F

臀部（でんぶ）
buttock
Gesäß^N
fesse^F
nalga^F
natica^F

陰茎
penis
Penis^M
verge^F
pene^M
pene^M

カウパー腺
Cowper's gland
Cowper-Drüse^F
glande^F de Cowper
glándula^F de Cowper
ghiandola^F di Cowper

陰茎亀頭
glans penis
Eichel^F
gland^M
glande^M
glande^M

球海綿体筋
bulbocavernous muscle
Bulbospongiosus^M
muscle^M bulbo-caverneux
músculo^M bulbocavernoso
muscolo^M bulbocavernoso

包皮
prepuce
Vorhaut^F
prépuce^M
prepucio^M
prepuzio^M

尿道口
urinary meatus
Harnröhrengang^M
méat^M de l'urètre^M
meato^M urinario
meato^M urinario

精巣上体
epididymis
Nebenhoden^M
épididyme^M
epidídimo^M
epididimo^M

精巣／睾丸（こうがん）
testicle
Hoden^M
testicule^M
testículo^M
testicolo^M

陰嚢（いんのう）
scrotum
Hodensack^M
scrotum^M
escroto^M
scroto^M

大腿
thigh
Oberschenkelregion^F
cuisse^F
muslo^M
coscia^F

人間

精子／精虫
spermatozoon
Spermium^N
spermatozoïde^M
espermatozoide^M
spermatozoo^M

頭部
head
Kopf^M
tête^F
cabeza^F
testa^F

端片
end piece
Endstück^N
pièce^F terminale
segmento^M terminal
parte^F terminale

尾部
tail
Schwanz^M
queue^F
cola^F
coda^F

頸部（けいぶ）
neck
Hals^M
cou^M
cuello^M
collo^M

中部／中片(部)
middle piece
Mittelstück^N
pièce^F intermédiaire
segmento^M intermedio
parte^F intermedia

169

解剖学 | ANATOMY
ANATOMIE | ANATOMIE | ANATOMÍA | ANATOMIA

女性生殖器

female reproductive organs | weibliche Geschlechtsorgane[N] | organes[M] génitaux féminins | órganos[M] genitales femeninos | organi[M] genitali femminili

矢状(切)断
sagittal section
Sagittalschnitt[M]
coupe[F] sagittale
sección[F] sagital
sezione[F] sagittale

腹腔
abdominal cavity
Bauchhöhle[F]
cavité[F] abdominale
cavidad[F] abdominal
cavità[F] addominale

腹膜
peritoneum
Bauchfell[N]
péritoine[M]
peritoneo[M]
peritoneo[M]

ファローピウス管／卵管
fallopian tube
Eileiter[M]
trompe[F] de Fallope
trompa[F] de Falopio
tuba[F] di Falloppio

卵巣
ovary
Eierstock[M]
ovaire[M]
ovario[M]
ovaia[F]

子宮
uterus
Gebärmutter[F]
utérus[M]
útero[M]
utero[M]

ダグラス窩(か)／直腸子宮窩
pouch of Douglas
Douglasscher Raum[M]
cul-de-sac[M] de Douglas
saco[M] de Douglas
tasca[F] di Douglas

膀胱子宮窩(か)
uterovesical pouch
vorderer Douglasscher Raum[M]
cul-de-sac[M] vésico-utérin
excavación[F] vesicouterina
tasca[F] vescicouterina

直腸
rectum
Mastdarm[M]
rectum[M]
recto[M]
retto[M]

膀胱(ぼうこう)
urinary bladder
Harnblase[F]
vessie[F]
vejiga[F]
vescica[F]

子宮頸部(けいぶ)
cervix of uterus
Gebärmutterhals[M]
col[M] de l'utérus[M]
cuello[M] del útero[M]
collo[M] dell'utero[M]

恥丘
mons pubis
Schamhügel[M]
mont[M] de Vénus
monte[M] de Venus
monte[M] di Venere

膣(ちつ)
vagina
Scheide[F]
vagin[M]
vagina[F]
vagina[F]

恥骨結合
symphysis pubis
Symphyse[F]
symphyse[F] pubienne
sínfisis[F] púbica
sinfisi[F] pubica

臀部(でんぶ)
buttock
Gesäß[N]
fesse[F]
nalga[F]
natica[F]

陰核／クリトリス
clitoris
Klitoris[F]
clitoris[M]
clítoris[M]
clitoride[F/M]

肛門
anus
After[M]
anus[M]
ano[M]
ano[M]

尿道
urethra
Harnröhre[F]
urètre[M]
uretra[F]
uretra[F]

小陰唇
labium minus
kleine Schamlippe[F]
petite lèvre[F]
labio[M] menor
piccolo labbro[M]

大陰唇
labium majus
große Schamlippe[F]
grande lèvre[F]
labio[M] mayor
grande labbro[M]

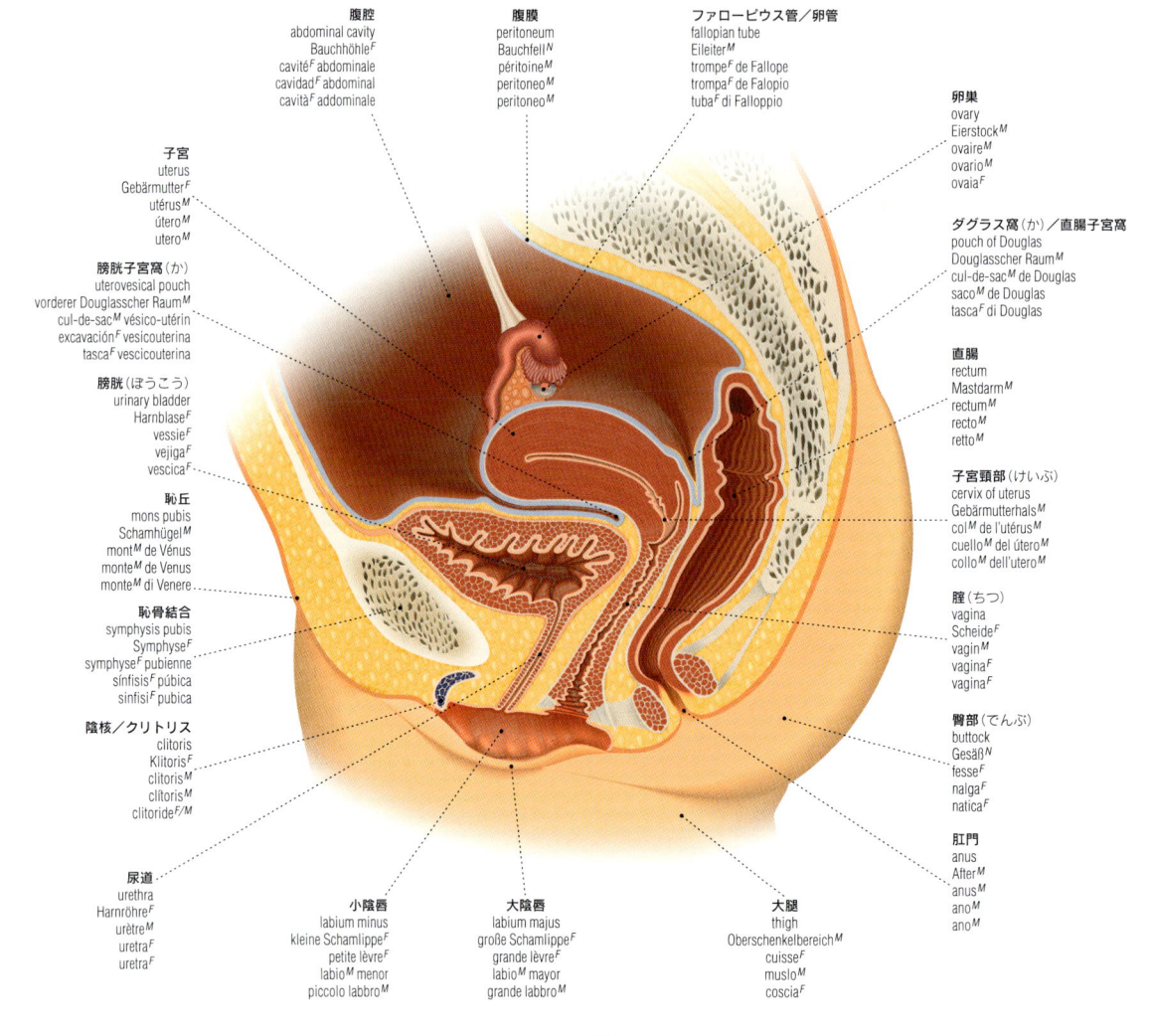

大腿
thigh
Oberschenkelbereich[M]
cuisse[F]
muslo[M]
coscia[F]

卵(子)
egg
Eizelle[F]
ovule[M]
óvulo[M]
ovulo[M]

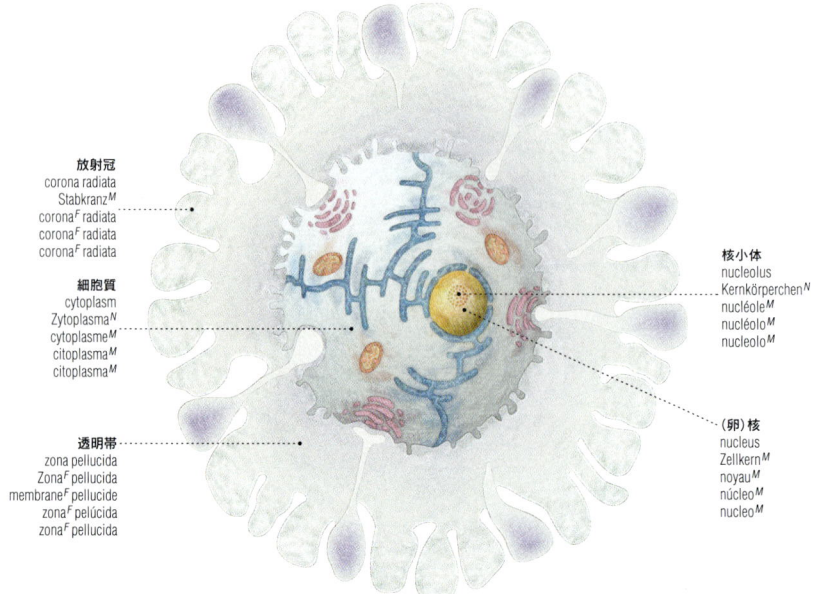

放射冠
corona radiata
Stabkranz[M]
corona[F] radiata
corona[F] radiata
corona[F] radiata

核小体
nucleolus
Kernkörperchen[N]
nucléole[M]
nucléolo[M]
nucleolo[M]

細胞質
cytoplasm
Zytoplasma[N]
cytoplasme[M]
citoplasma[M]
citoplasma[M]

(卵)核
nucleus
Zellkern[M]
noyau[M]
núcleo[M]
nucleo[M]

透明帯
zona pellucida
Zona pellucida
membrane[F] pellucide
zona[F] pelúcida
zona[F] pellucida

170

解剖学 | ANATOMY
ANATOMIE | ANATOMIE | ANATOMÍA | ANATOMIA

女性生殖器

背面図
posterior view
Rückansicht^F
vue^F postérieure
vista^F posterior
vista^F posteriore

卵管膨大部
ampulla of fallopian tube
Eileiterampulle^F
ampoule^F de la trompe^F utérine
ampolla^F de la trompa^F uterina
ampolla^F della tuba^F di Falloppio

卵管峡部
isthmus of fallopian tube
Eileiterenge^F
isthme^M de la trompe^F utérine
istmo^M de la trompa^F de Falopio
istmo^M della tuba^F di Falloppio

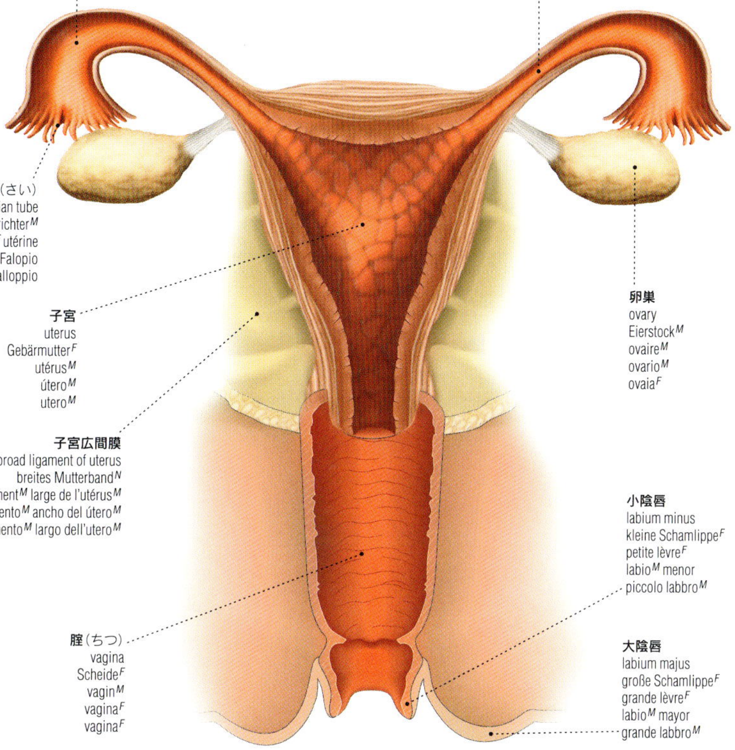

卵管采（さい）
infundibulum of fallopian tube
Eileitertrichter^M
pavillon^M de la trompe^F utérine
pabellón^M de la trompa^F de Falopio
infundibolo^M della tuba^F di Falloppio

子宮
uterus
Gebärmutter^F
utérus^M
útero^M
utero^M

子宮広間膜
broad ligament of uterus
breites Mutterband^N
ligament^M large de l'utérus^M
ligamento^M ancho del útero^M
legamento^M largo dell'utero^M

卵巣
ovary
Eierstock^M
ovaire^M
ovario^M
ovaia^F

小陰唇
labium minus
kleine Schamlippe^F
petite lèvre^F
labio^M menor
piccolo labbro^M

腟（ちつ）
vagina
Scheide^F
vagin^M
vagina^F
vagina^F

大陰唇
labium majus
große Schamlippe^F
grande lèvre^F
labio^M mayor
grande labbro^M

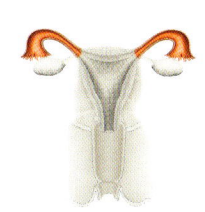

ファローピウス管／卵管
fallopian tubes
Eileiter^M
trompes^F de Fallope
trompa^F de Falopio
tube^F di Falloppio

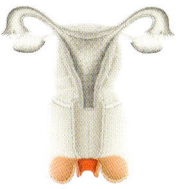

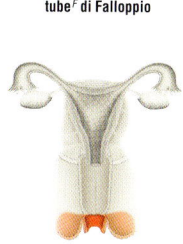

外陰部
vulva
Scham^F
vulve^F
vulva^F
vulva^F

人間

乳房

breast | Brust^F | sein^M | seno^M | seno^M

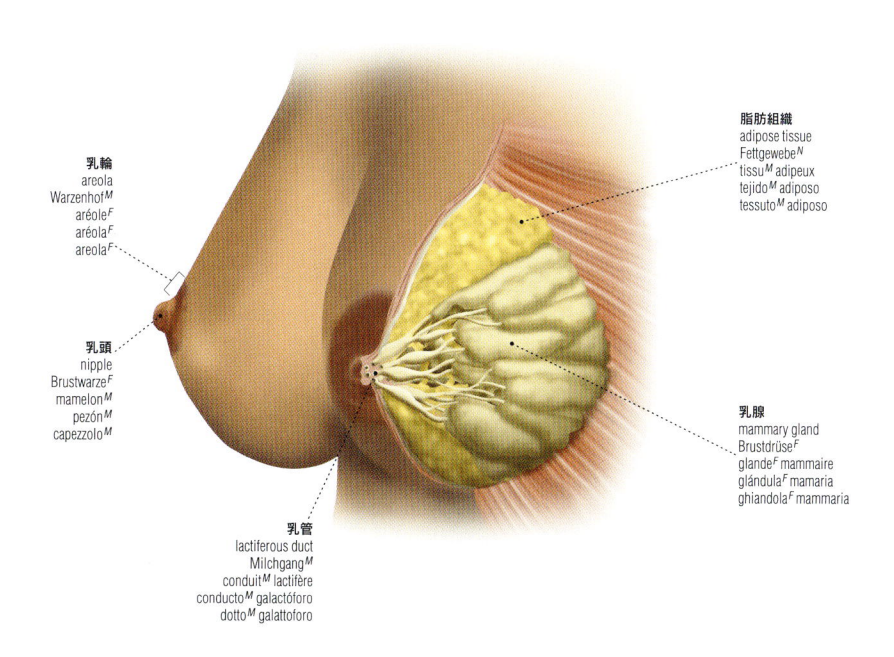

乳輪
areola
Warzenhof^M
aréole^F
aréola^F
areola^F

乳頭
nipple
Brustwarze^F
mamelon^M
pezón^M
capezzolo^M

脂肪組織
adipose tissue
Fettgewebe^N
tissu^M adipeux
tejido^M adiposo
tessuto^M adiposo

乳腺
mammary gland
Brustdrüse^F
glande^F mammaire
glándula^F mamaria
ghiandola^F mammaria

乳管
lactiferous duct
Milchgang^M
conduit^M lactifère
conducto^M galactóforo
dotto^M galattoforo

感覚器官 | SENSE ORGANS
SINNESORGANE | ORGANES DES SENS | ÓRGANOS SENSORIALES | ORGANI DI SENSO

触覚
touch | Tastsinn^M | toucher^M | tacto^M | tatto^M

日本語 | 英語 | ドイツ語 | フランス語 | スペイン語 | イタリア語

皮膚 / skin / Haut^F / peau^F / piel^F / cute^F

角質層 / stratum corneum / Hornschicht^F / couche^F cornée / estrato^M córneo / strato^M corneo

毛幹 / hair shaft / Haarschaft^M / tige^F du poil / tallo^M / scapo^M

毛 / hair / Haar^N / poil^M / pelo^M / pelo^M

マイスネル小体 / Meissner's corpuscle / Meissnersches Tast-Körperchen^N / corpuscule^M de Meissner / corpúsculo^M de Meissner / corpuscolo^M di Meissner

淡明層 / stratum lucidum / Glanzschicht^F / couche^F claire / estrato^M lúcido / strato^M lucido

汗孔 / pore / Pore^F / pore^M sudoripare / poro^M / poro^M sudoriparo

皮膚の表面 / skin surface / Hautoberfläche^F / surface^F de la peau^F / superficie^F de la piel^F / superficie^F della cute^F

顆粒層（かりゅうそう） / stratum granulosum / Körnerschicht^F / couche^F granuleuse / estrato^M granuloso / strato^M granulare

表皮 / epidermis / Oberhaut^F / épiderme^M / epidermis^F / epidermide^F

有棘層（ゆうきょくそう） / stratum spinosum / Stachelzellenschicht^F / couche^F de Malpighi / estrato^M de Malpighi / strato^M spinoso

結合組織 / connective tissue / Bindegewebe^N / tissu^M conjonctif / tejido^M conjuntivo / tessuto^M connettivo

基底層 / stratum basale / Basalschicht^F / couche^F basale / estrato^M basal / strato^M basale

真皮 / dermis / Lederhaut^F / derme^M / dermis^F / derma^M

神経終末 / nerve termination / Nervenendung^F / terminaison^F nerveuse / terminación^F nerviosa / terminazione^F nervosa

毛細血管 / capillary blood vessel / Kapillargefäß^N / vaisseau^M capillaire / vaso^M capilar / vaso^M capillare

立毛筋 / arrector pili muscle / Haaraufrichter^M / muscle^M arrecteur / músculo^M erector del pelo^M / muscolo^M erettore del pelo^M

脂肪組織 / adipose tissue / Fettgewebe^N / tissu^M adipeux / tejido^M adiposo / tessuto^M adiposo

皮脂腺 / sebaceous gland / Talgdrüse^F / glande^F sébacée / glándula^F sebácea / ghiandola^F sebacea

皮下組織 / subcutaneous tissue / Unterhautbindegewebe^N / hypoderme^M / tejido^M subcutáneo / tessuto^M sottocutaneo

ルフィニ小体 / Ruffini's corpuscle / Ruffinisches Körperchen^N / corpuscule^M de Ruffini / corpúsculo^M de Ruffini / corpuscolo^M di Ruffini

パチニ小体 / Pacinian corpuscle / Vater-Pacinisches Körperchen^N / corpuscule^M de Pacini / corpúsculo^M de Pacini / corpuscolo^M di Pacini

神経繊維 / nerve fiber; nerve fibre / Nervenfaser^F / fibre^F nerveuse / fibra^F nerviosa / fibra^F nervosa

汗管 / sudoriferous duct / Ausführungsgang^M der Schweißdrüse^F / canal^M sudoripare / conducto^M sudorífero / dotto^M sudoriparo

神経 / nerve / Nerv^M / nerf^M / nervio^M / nervo^M

血管 / blood vessel / Blutgefäß^N / vaisseau^M sanguin / vaso^M sanguíneo / vaso^M sanguigno

エクリン汗腺 / eccrine sweat gland / ekkrine Schweißdrüse^F / glande^F sudoripare eccrine / glándula^F sudorípara ecrina / ghiandola^F sudoripara eccrina

毛嚢（もうのう）／毛包 / hair follicle / Haarbalg^M / follicule^M / folículo^M piloso / follicolo^M pilifero

毛乳頭 / papilla / Papille^F / papille^F / papila^F / papilla^F

アポクリン汗腺 / apocrine sweat gland / apokrine Schweißdrüse^F / glande^F sudoripare apocrine / glándula^F sudorípara apocrina / ghiandola^F sudoripara apocrina

毛根 / hair bulb / Haarzwiebel^F / bulbe^M / bulbo^M piloso / bulbo^M del pelo^M

指 / finger / Finger^M / doigt^M / dedo^M / dito^M

真皮 / dermis / Lederhaut^F / derme^M / dermis^F / derma^M

爪母基（そうぼき） / nail matrix / Nagelbettepitel^N / matrice^F de l'ongle^M / matriz^F ungular / matrice^F ungueale

半月 / lunula / Nagelhalbmond^M / lunule^F / lúnula^F / lunula^F

表皮 / epidermis / Oberhaut^F / épiderme^M / epidermis^F / epidermide^F

爪板（そうばん） / body of nail / Nagelkörper^M / corps^M de l'ongle^M / cuerpo^M de la uña^F / corpo^M dell'unghia^F

中節骨 / middle phalanx / Fingermittelglied^N / phalange^F médiane / falangina^F / seconda falange^F

自由縁 / free margin / freier Nagelrand^M / bord^M libre / extremo^M libre / margine^M libero

末節骨 / distal phalanx / Fingerendglied^N / phalange^F distale / falangeta^F / terza falange^F

指頭髄 / digital pulp / Fingerbeere^F / pulpe^F / yema^F / polpastrello^M

爪根（そうこん） / root of nail / Nagelwurzel^F / racine^F de l'ongle^M / raíz^F de la uña^F / radice^F dell'unghia^F

爪床（そうしょう） / nail bed / Nagelbett^N / lit^M de l'ongle^M / lecho^M ungular / letto^M ungueale

感覚器官 | SENSE ORGANS
SINNESORGANE | ORGANES DES SENS | ÓRGANOS SENSORIALES | ORGANI DI SENSO

触覚

手
hand
Hand^F
main^F
mano^F
mano^F

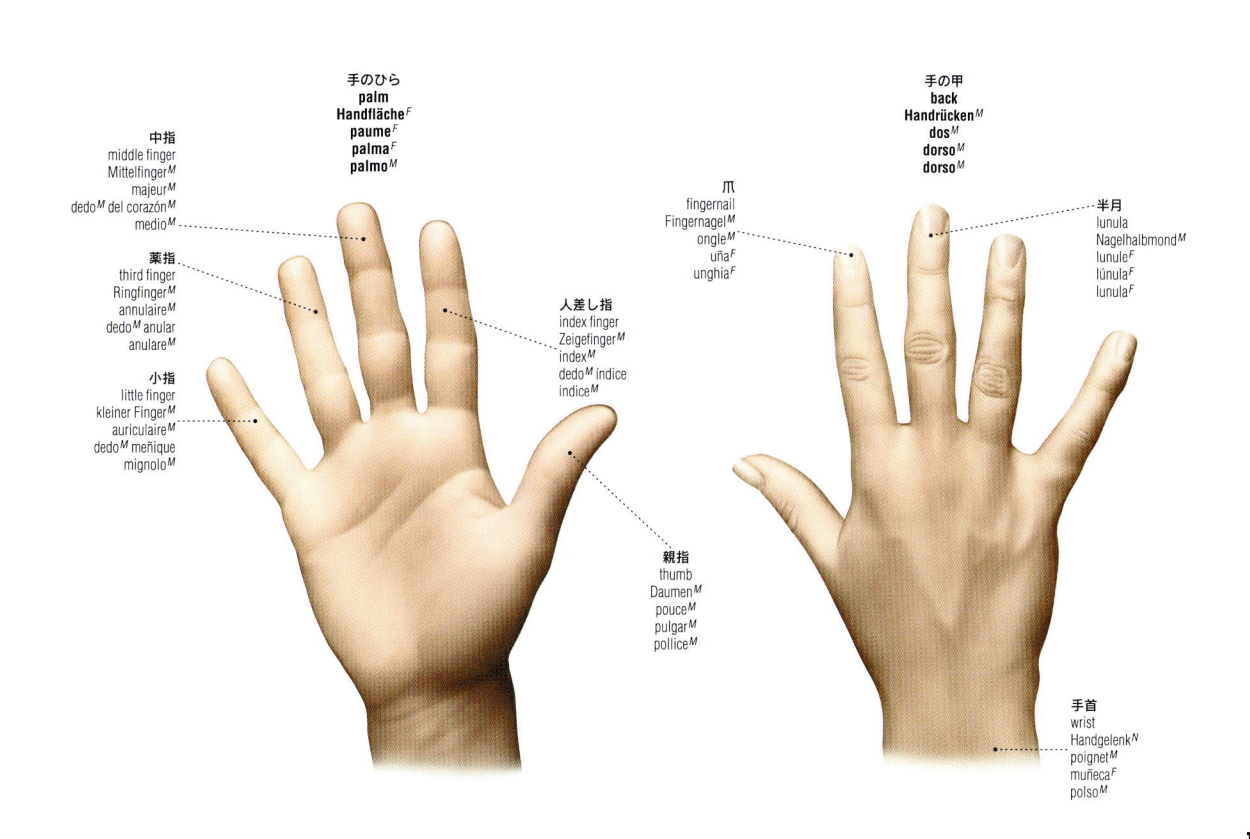

手のひら
palm
Handfläche^F
paume^F
palma^F
palmo^M

手の甲
back
Handrücken^M
dos^M
dorso^M
dorso^M

中指
middle finger
Mittelfinger^M
majeur^M
dedo^M del corazón^M
medio^M

爪
fingernail
Fingernagel^M
ongle^M
uña^F
unghia^F

半月
lunula
Nagelhalbmond^M
lunule^F
lúnula^F
lunula^F

薬指
third finger
Ringfinger^M
annulaire^M
dedo^M anular
anulare^M

人差し指
index finger
Zeigefinger^M
index^M
dedo^M índice
indice^M

小指
little finger
kleiner Finger^M
auriculaire^M
dedo^M meñique
mignolo^M

親指
thumb
Daumen^M
pouce^M
pulgar^M
pollice^M

手首
wrist
Handgelenk^N
poignet^M
muñeca^F
polso^M

人間

聴覚

hearing | Gehör^N | ouïe^F | oído^M | udito^M

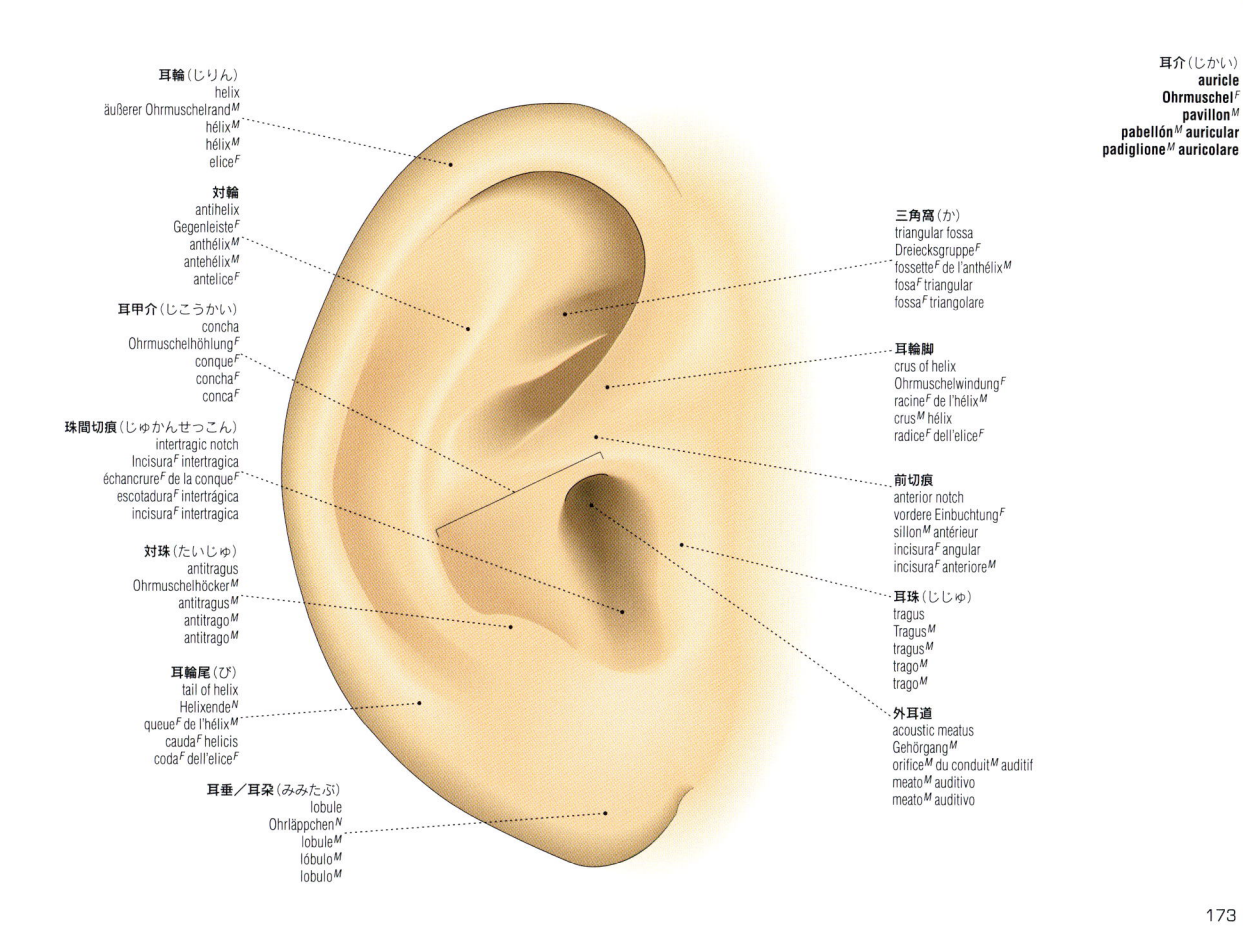

耳輪（じりん）
helix
äußerer Ohrmuschelrand^M
hélix^M
hélix^M
elice^F

耳介（じかい）
auricle
Ohrmuschel^F
pavillon^M
pabellón^M auricular
padiglione^M auricolare

対輪
antihelix
Gegenleiste^F
anthélix^M
antehélix^M
antelice^F

三角窩（か）
triangular fossa
Dreiecksgruppe^F
fossette^F de l'anthélix^M
fosa^F triangular
fossa^F triangolare

耳甲介（じこうかい）
concha
Ohrmuschelhöhlung^F
conque^F
concha^F
conca^F

耳輪脚
crus of helix
Ohrmuschelwindung^F
racine^F de l'hélix^M
crus^M hélix
radice^F dell'elice^F

珠間切痕（じゅかんせっこん）
intertragic notch
Incisura^F intertragica
échancrure^F de la conque^F
escotadura^F intertrágica
incisura^F intertragica

前切痕
anterior notch
vordere Einbuchtung^F
sillon^M antérieur
incisura^F angular
incisura^F anteriore

対珠（たいじゅ）
antitragus
Ohrmuschelhöcker^M
antitragus^M
antitrago^M
antitrago^M

耳珠（じじゅ）
tragus
Tragus^M
tragus^M
trago^M
trago^M

耳輪尾（び）
tail of helix
Helixende^N
queue^F de l'hélix^M
cauda^F helicis
coda^F dell'elice^F

外耳道
acoustic meatus
Gehörgang^M
orifice^M du conduit^M auditif
meato^M auditivo
meato^M auditivo

耳垂／耳朶（みみたぶ）
lobule
Ohrläppchen^N
lobule^M
lóbulo^M
lobulo^M

173

感覚器官 | SENSE ORGANS
SINNESORGANE | ORGANES DES SENS | ÓRGANOS SENSORIALES | ORGANI DI SENSO

聴覚

日本語 | 英語 | ドイツ語 | フランス語 | スペイン語 | イタリア語

耳の構造
structure of the ear
Aufbau^M des Ohres^N
structure^F de l'oreille^F
estructura^F del oído^M
struttura^F dell'orecchio^M

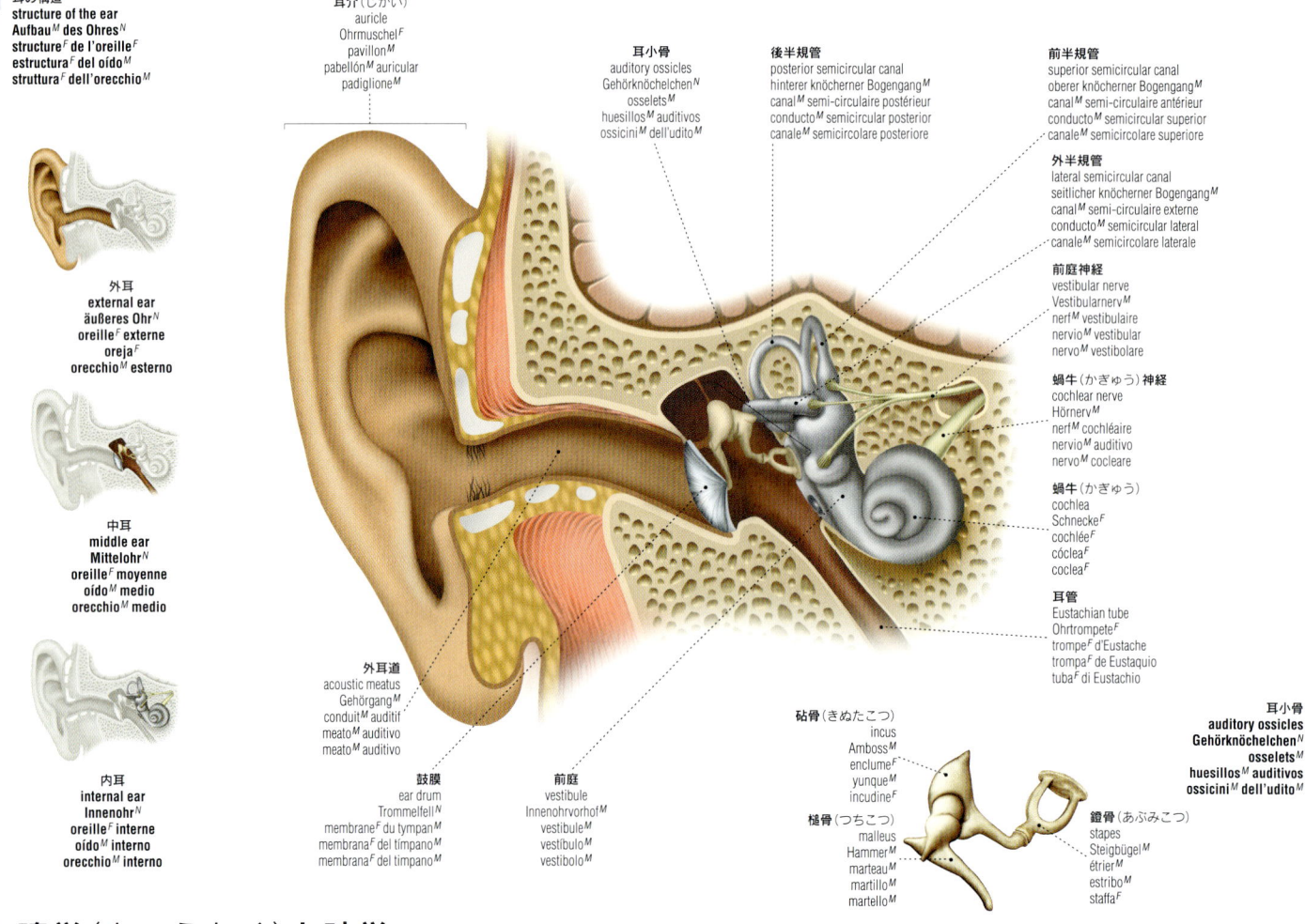

外耳
external ear
äußeres Ohr^N
oreille^F externe
oreja^F
orecchio^M esterno

中耳
middle ear
Mittelohr^N
oreille^F moyenne
oído^M medio
orecchio^M medio

内耳
internal ear
Innenohr^N
oreille^F interne
oído^M interno
orecchio^M interno

耳介（じかい）
auricle
Ohrmuschel^F
pavillon^M
pabellón^M auricular
padiglione^M

耳小骨
auditory ossicles
Gehörknöchelchen^N
osselets^M
huesillos^M auditivos
ossicini^M dell'udito

後半規管
posterior semicircular canal
hinterer knöcherner Bogengang^M
canal^M semi-circulaire postérieur
conducto^M semicircular posterior
canale^M semicircolare posteriore

前半規管
superior semicircular canal
oberer knöcherner Bogengang^M
canal^M semi-circulaire antérieur
conducto^M semicircular superior
canale^M semicircolare superiore

外半規管
lateral semicircular canal
seitlicher knöcherner Bogengang^M
canal^M semi-circulaire externe
conducto^M semicircular lateral
canale^M semicircolare laterale

前庭神経
vestibular nerve
Vestibularnerv^M
nerf^M vestibulaire
nervio^M vestibular
nervo^M vestibolare

蝸牛（かぎゅう）神経
cochlear nerve
Hörnerv^M
nerf^M cochléaire
nervio^M auditivo
nervo^M cocleare

蝸牛（かぎゅう）
cochlea
Schnecke^F
cochlée^F
cóclea^F
coclea^F

耳管
Eustachian tube
Ohrtrompete^F
trompe^F d'Eustache
trompa^F de Eustaquio
tuba^F di Eustachio

外耳道
acoustic meatus
Gehörgang^M
conduit^M auditif
meato^M auditivo
meato^M auditivo

鼓膜
ear drum
Trommelfell^N
membrane^F du tympan
membrana^F del tímpano
membrana^F del timpano^M

前庭
vestibule
Innenohrvorhof^M
vestibule^M
vestíbulo^M
vestibolo^M

砧骨（きぬたこつ）
incus
Amboss^M
enclume^F
yunque^M
incudine^F

槌骨（つちこつ）
malleus
Hammer^M
marteau^M
martillo^M
martello^M

耳小骨
auditory ossicles
Gehörknöchelchen^N
osselets^M
huesillos^M auditivos
ossicini^M dell'udito

鐙骨（あぶみこつ）
stapes
Steigbügel^M
étrier^M
estribo^M
staffa^F

嗅覚（きゅうかく）と味覚

smell and taste | Geruchs-^{M} und Geschmackssinn^M | odorat^M et goût^M | olfato^M y gusto^M | olfatto^M e gusto^M

口
mouth
Mund^M
bouche^F
boca^F
bocca^F

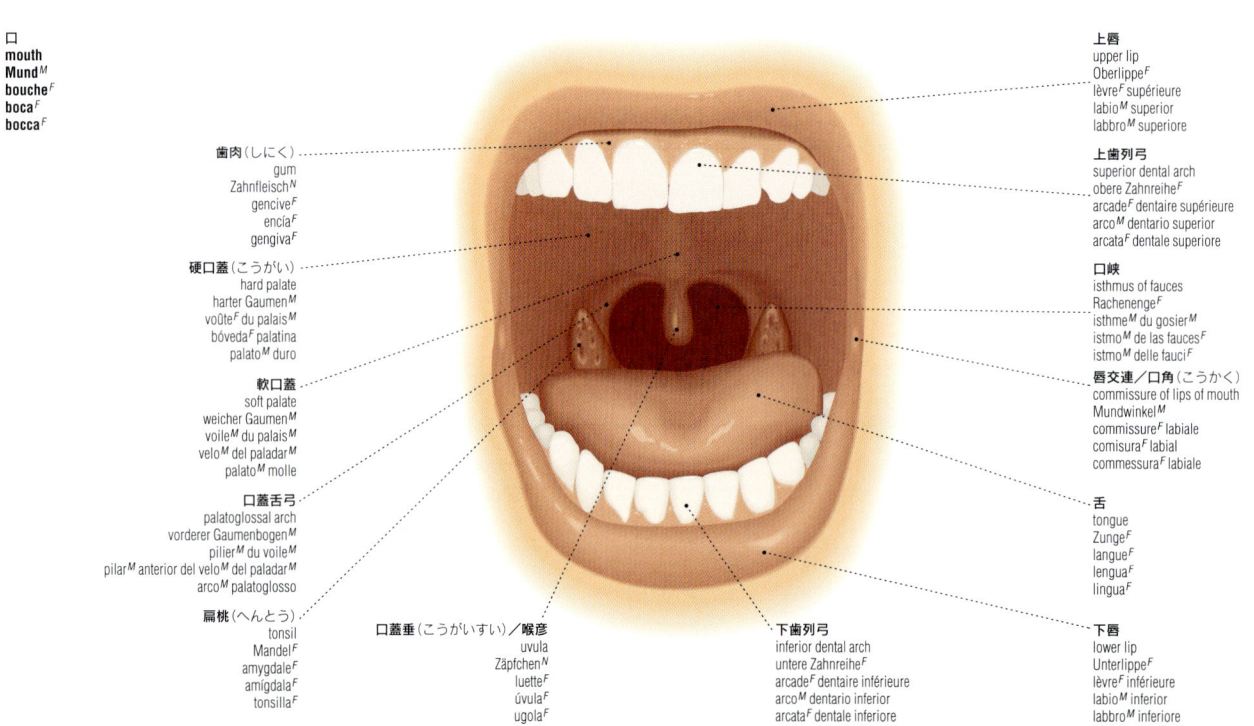

歯肉（しにく）
gum
Zahnfleisch^N
gencive^F
encía^F
gengiva^F

硬口蓋（こうがい）
hard palate
harter Gaumen^M
voûte^F du palais^M
bóveda^F palatina
palato^M duro

軟口蓋
soft palate
weicher Gaumen^M
voile^M du palais^M
velo^M del paladar^M
palato^M molle

口蓋舌弓
palatoglossal arch
vorderer Gaumenbogen^M
pilier^M du voile^M
pilar^M anterior del velo^M del paladar^M
arco^M palatoglosso

扁桃（へんとう）
tonsil
Mandel^F
amygdale^F
amígdala^F
tonsilla^F

口蓋垂（こうがいすい）／喉彦
uvula
Zäpfchen^N
luette^F
úvula^F
ugola^F

上唇
upper lip
Oberlippe^F
lèvre^F supérieure
labio^M superior
labbro^M superiore

上歯列弓
superior dental arch
obere Zahnreihe^F
arcade^F dentaire supérieure
arco^M dentario superior
arcata^F dentale superiore

口峡
isthmus of fauces
Rachenenge^F
isthme^M du gosier^M
istmo^M de las fauces^F
istmo^M delle fauci^F

唇交連／口角（こうかく）
commissure of lips of mouth
Mundwinkel^M
commissure^F labiale
comisura^F labial
commessura^F labiale

舌
tongue
Zunge^F
langue^F
lengua^F
lingua^F

下歯列弓
inferior dental arch
untere Zahnreihe^F
arcade^F dentaire inférieure
arco^M dentario inferior
arcata^F dentale inferiore

下唇
lower lip
Unterlippe^F
lèvre^F inférieure
labio^M inferior
labbro^M inferiore

感覚器官 | SENSE ORGANS
SINNESORGANE | ORGANES DES SENS | ÓRGANOS SENSORIALES | ORGANI DI SENSO

嗅覚と味覚

外鼻
external nose
äußere Nase^F
parties^F externes du nez^F
nariz^F
naso^M esterno

鼻根
root of nose; bridge of nose
Nasenwurzel^F
racine^F du nez^M
puente^M de la nariz^F
radice^F del naso^M

鼻背
dorsum of nose
Nasenrücken^M
dos^M du nez^M
dorso^M de la nariz^F
dorso^M del naso^M

鼻翼
ala
Nasenflügel^M
aile^F du nez^M
aleta^F de la nariz^F
ala^F

鼻尖
tip of nose
Nasenspitze^F
lobe^M du nez^M
lóbulo^M
punta^F del naso^M

鼻孔
naris
Nasenloch^N
narine^F
ventana^F de la nariz^F
narice^F

鼻中隔
septum
Scheidewand^F
cloison^F
tabique^M nasal
setto^M

人中 (じんちゅう)
philtrum
Oberlippenrinne^F
sillon^M naso-labial
surco^M nasolabial
filtro^M

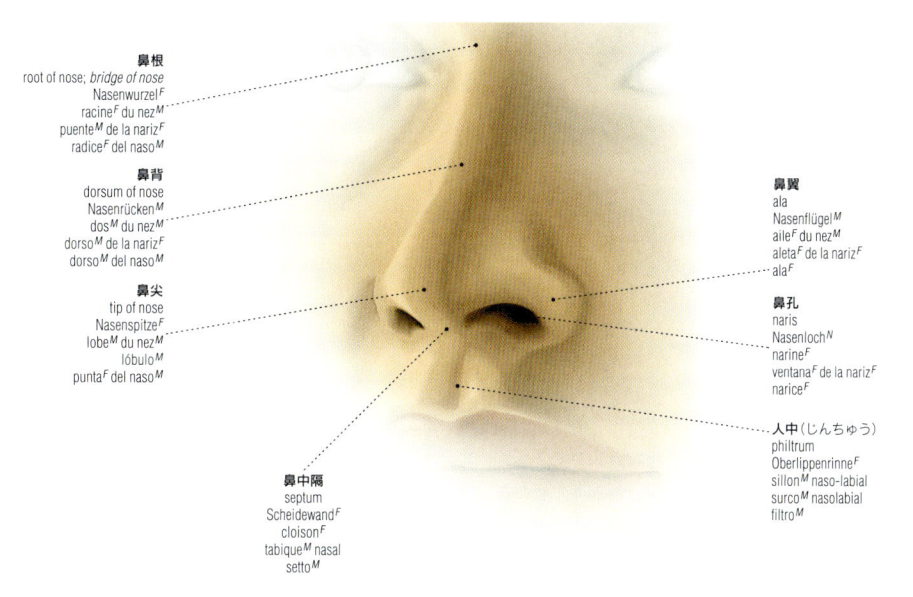

鼻腔
nasal fossae
Nasenhöhle^F
fosses^F nasales
fosas^F nasales
fosse^F nasali

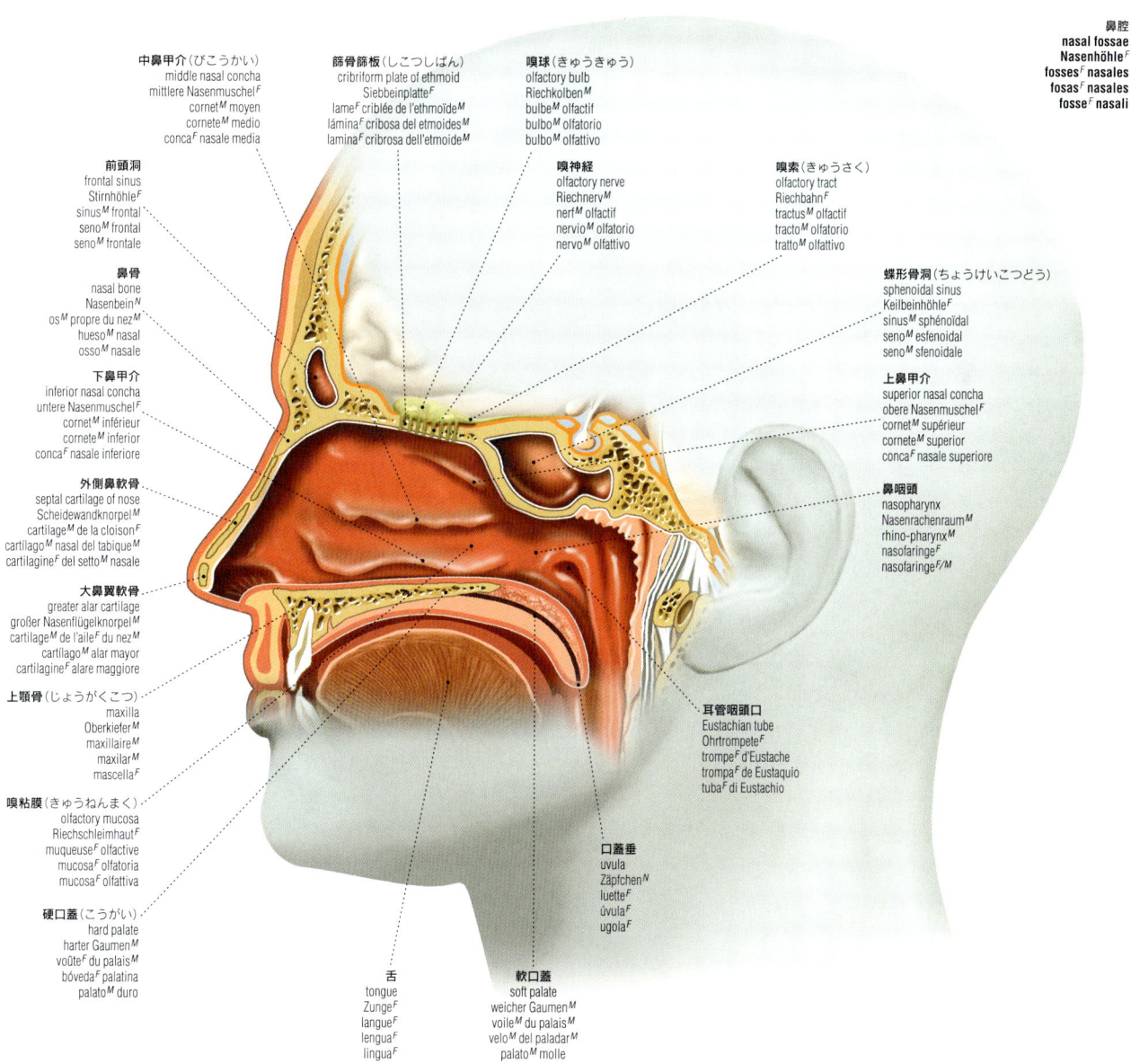

中鼻甲介 (びこうかい)
middle nasal concha
mittlere Nasenmuschel^F
cornet^M moyen
cornete^M medio
conca^F nasale media

篩骨篩板 (しこつしばん)
cribriform plate of ethmoid
Siebbeinplatte^F
lame^F criblée de l'ethmoïde^M
lámina^F cribosa del etmoides^M
lamina^F cribrosa dell'etmoide^M

嗅球 (きゅうきゅう)
olfactory bulb
Riechkolben^M
bulbe^M olfactif
bulbo^M olfatorio
bulbo^M olfattivo

前頭洞
frontal sinus
Stirnhöhle^F
sinus^M frontal
seno^M frontal
seno^M frontale

嗅神経
olfactory nerve
Riechnerv^M
nerf^M olfactif
nervio^M olfatorio
nervo^M olfattivo

嗅索 (きゅうさく)
olfactory tract
Riechbahn^F
tractus^M olfactif
tracto^M olfatorio
tratto^M olfattivo

鼻骨
nasal bone
Nasenbein^N
os^M propre du nez^M
hueso^M nasal
osso^M nasale

蝶形骨洞 (ちょうけいこつどう)
sphenoidal sinus
Keilbeinhöhle^F
sinus^M sphénoïdal
seno^M esfenoidal
seno^M sfenoidale

下鼻甲介
inferior nasal concha
untere Nasenmuschel^F
cornet^M inférieur
cornete^M inferior
conca^F nasale inferiore

上鼻甲介
superior nasal concha
obere Nasenmuschel^F
cornet^M supérieur
cornete^M superior
conca^F nasale superiore

外側鼻軟骨
septal cartilage of nose
Scheidewandknorpel^M
cartilage^M de la cloison^F
cartílago^M nasal del tabique^M
cartilagine^F del setto^M nasale

鼻咽頭
nasopharynx
Nasenrachenraum^M
rhino-pharynx^M
nasofaringe^F
nasofaringe^F/M

大鼻翼軟骨
greater alar cartilage
großer Nasenflügelknorpel^M
cartilage^M de l'aile^F du nez^M
cartílago^M alar mayor
cartilagine^F alare maggiore

上顎骨 (じょうがくこつ)
maxilla
Oberkiefer^M
maxillaire^M
maxilar^M
mascella^F

耳管咽頭口
Eustachian tube
Ohrtrompete^F
trompe^F d'Eustache
trompa^F de Eustaquio
tuba^F di Eustachio

嗅粘膜 (きゅうねんまく)
olfactory mucosa
Riechschleimhaut^F
muqueuse^F olfactive
mucosa^F olfatoria
mucosa^F olfattiva

口蓋垂
uvula
Zäpfchen^N
luette^F
úvula^F
ugola^F

硬口蓋 (こうこうがい)
hard palate
harter Gaumen^M
voûte^F du palais^M
bóveda^F palatina
palato^M duro

舌
tongue
Zunge^F
langue^F
lengua^F
lingua^F

軟口蓋
soft palate
weicher Gaumen^M
voile^M du palais^M
velo^M del paladar^M
palato^M molle

人間

感覚器官 | SENSE ORGANS
SINNESORGANE | ORGANES DES SENS | ÓRGANOS SENSORIALES | ORGANI DI SENSO

嗅覚（きゅうかく）と味覚

日本語 | 英語 | ドイツ語 | フランス語 | スペイン語 | イタリア語

人間

舌背（ぜっぱい）
dorsum of tongue
Zungenrücken^M
dos^M de la langue^F
lengua^F
dorso^M della lingua^F

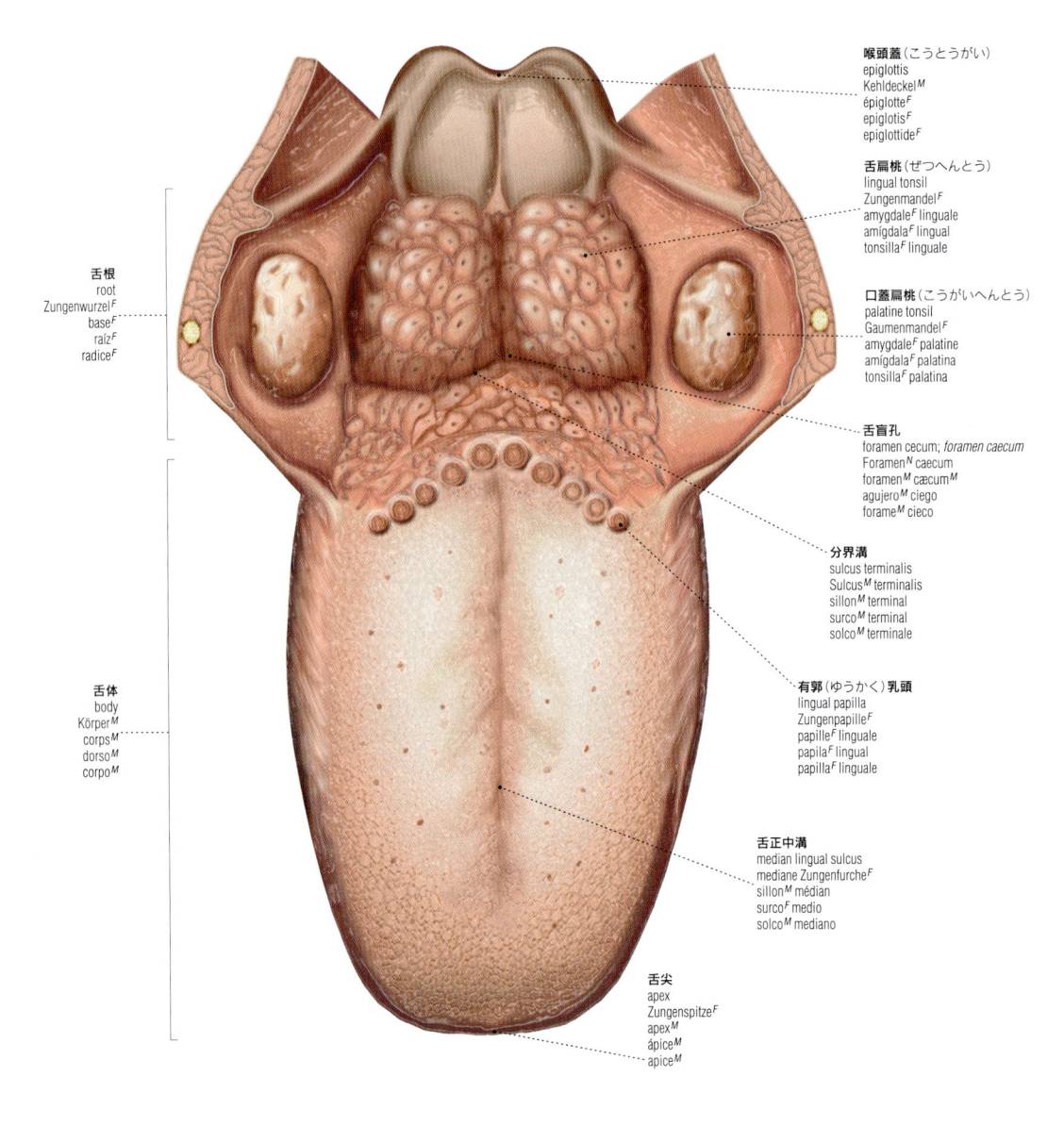

舌根
root
Zungenwurzel^F
base^F
raíz^F
radice^F

舌体
body
Körper^M
corps^M
dorso^M
corpo^M

味覚受容器
taste receptors
Geschmacksrezeptoren^M
récepteurs^M du goût^M
receptores^M gustativos
recettori^M gustativi

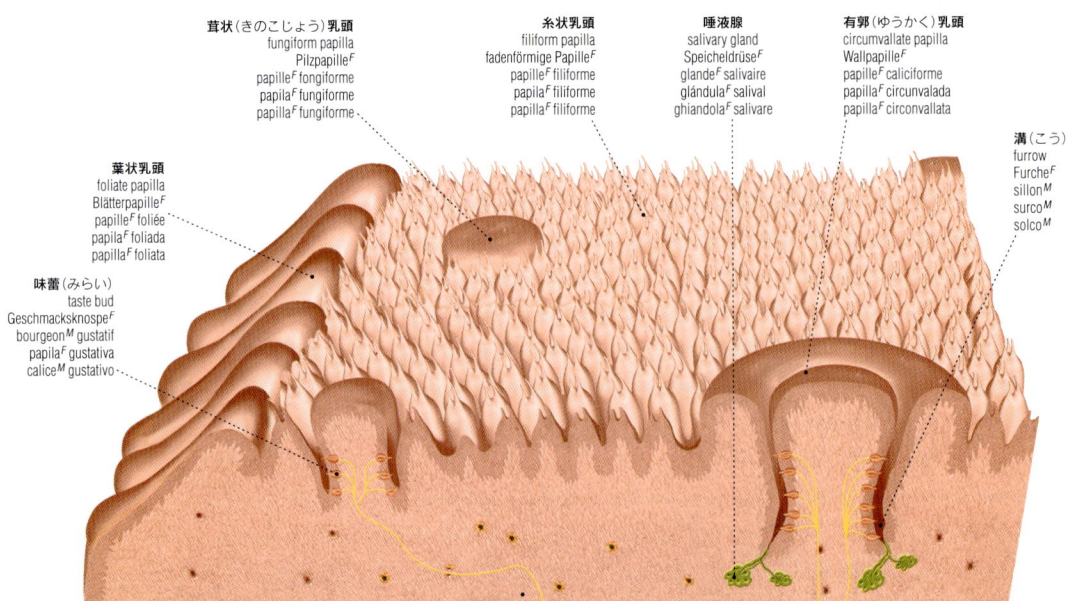

喉頭蓋（こうとうがい）
epiglottis
Kehldeckel^M
épiglotte^F
epiglotis^F
epiglottide^F

舌扁桃（ぜつへんとう）
lingual tonsil
Zungenmandel^F
amygdale^F linguale
amígdala^F lingual
tonsilla^F linguale

口蓋扁桃（こうがいへんとう）
palatine tonsil
Gaumenmandel^F
amygdale^F palatine
amígdala^F palatina
tonsilla^F palatina

舌盲孔
foramen cecum; *foramen caecum*
Foramen^N caecum
foramen^M cæcum^M
agujero^M ciego
forame^M cieco

分界溝
sulcus terminalis
Sulcus^M terminalis
sillon^M terminal
surco^M terminal
solco^M terminale

有郭（ゆうかく）乳頭
lingual papilla
Zungenpapille^F
papille^F linguale
papila^F lingual
papilla^F linguale

舌正中溝
median lingual sulcus
mediane Zungenfurche^F
sillon^F médian
surco^F medio
solco^M mediano

舌尖
apex
Zungenspitze^F
apex^M
ápice^M
apice^M

茸状（きのこじょう）乳頭
fungiform papilla
Pilzpapille^F
papille^F fongiforme
papila^F fungiforme
papilla^F fungiforme

葉状乳頭
foliate papilla
Blätterpapille^F
papille^F foliée
papila^F foliáda
papilla^F foliata

味蕾（みらい）
taste bud
Geschmacksknospe^F
bourgeon^M gustatif
papila^F gustativa
calice^M gustativo

糸状乳頭
filiform papilla
fadenförmige Papille^F
papille^F filiforme
papila^F filiforme
papilla^F filiforme

唾液腺
salivary gland
Speicheldrüse^F
glande^F salivaire
glándula^F salival
ghiandola^F salivare

有郭（ゆうかく）乳頭
circumvallate papilla
Wallpapille^F
papille^F caliciforme
papila^F circunvalada
papilla^F circonvallata

溝（こう）
furrow
Furche^F
sillon^M
surco^M
solco^M

176

感覚器官 | SENSE ORGANS
SINNESORGANE | ORGANES DES SENS | ÓRGANOS SENSORIALES | ORGANI DI SENSO

視覚

sight | Sehsinn^N | vue^F | vista^F | vista^F

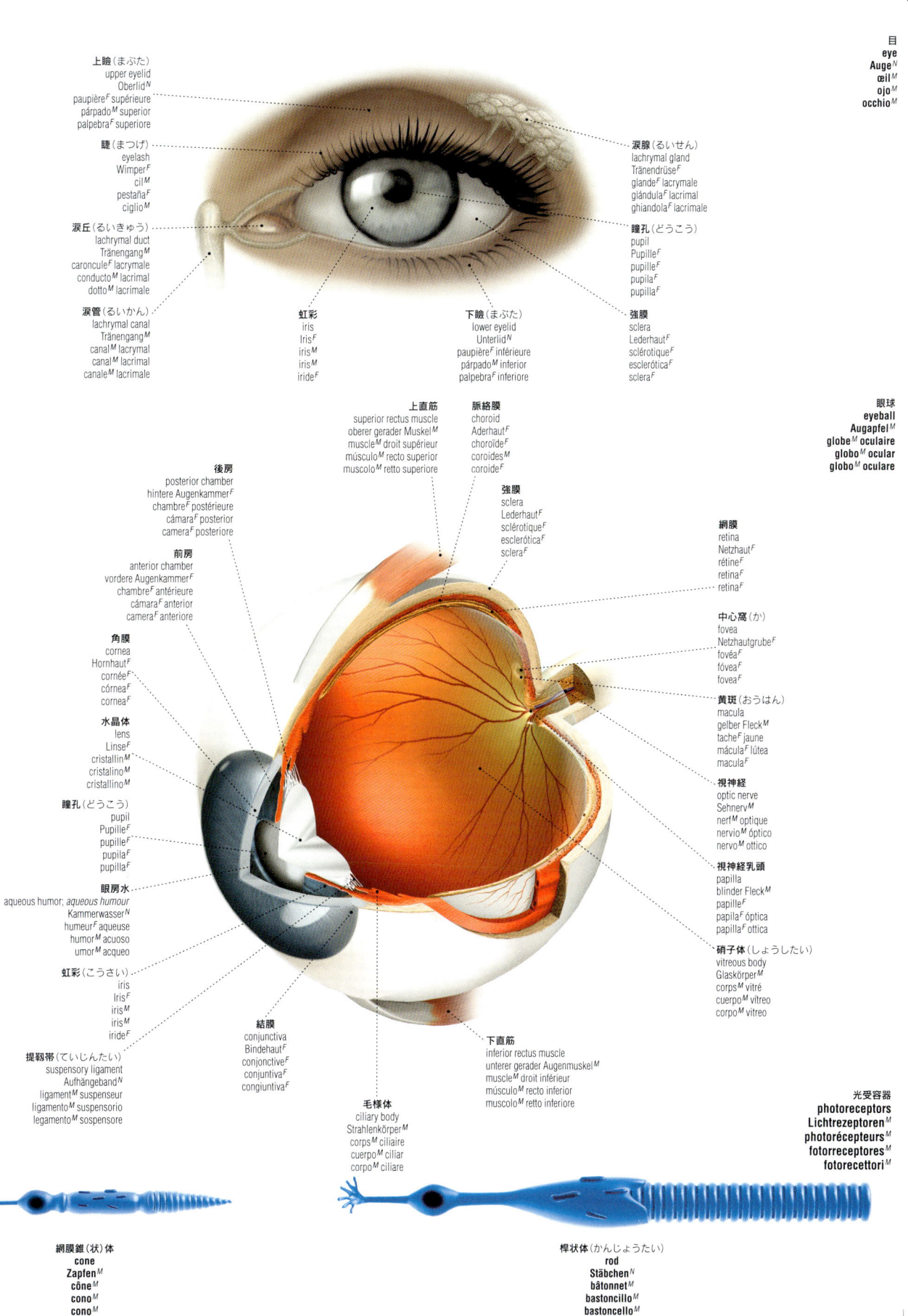

目
eye
Auge^N
œil^M
ojo^M
occhio^M

人間

上瞼（まぶた）
upper eyelid
Oberlid^N
paupière^F supérieure
párpado^M superior
palpebra^F superiore

睫（まつげ）
eyelash
Wimper^F
cil^M
pestaña^F
ciglio^M

涙腺（るいせん）
lachrymal gland
Tränendrüse^F
glande^F lacrymale
glándula^F lacrimal
ghiandola^F lacrimale

涙丘（るいきゅう）
lachrymal duct
Tränengang^M
caroncule^F lacrymale
conducto^M lacrimal
dotto^M lacrimale

瞳孔（どうこう）
pupil
Pupille^F
pupille^F
pupila^F
pupilla^F

涙管（るいかん）
lachrymal canal
Tränengang^M
canal^M lacrymal
canal^M lacrimal
canale^F lacrimale

虹彩
iris
Iris^F
iris^M
iris^M
iride^F

下瞼（まぶた）
lower eyelid
Unterlid^N
paupière^F inférieure
párpado^M inferior
palpebra^F inferiore

強膜
sclera
Lederhaut^F
sclérotique^F
esclerótica^F
sclera^F

眼球
eyeball
Augapfel^M
globe^M oculaire
globo^M ocular
globo^M oculare

上直筋
superior rectus muscle
oberer gerader Muskel^M
muscle^M droit supérieur
músculo^M recto superior
muscolo^M retto superiore

脈絡膜
choroid
Aderhaut^F
choroïde^F
coroides^F
coroide^F

後房
posterior chamber
hintere Augenkammer^F
chambre^F postérieure
cámara^F posterior
camera^F posteriore

強膜
sclera
Lederhaut^F
sclérotique^F
esclerótica^F
sclera^F

網膜
retina
Netzhaut^F
rétine^F
retina^F
retina^F

前房
anterior chamber
vordere Augenkammer^F
chambre^F antérieure
cámara^F anterior
camera^F anteriore

中心窩（か）
fovea
Netzhautgrube^F
fovéa^F
fóvea^F
fovea^F

角膜
cornea
Hornhaut^F
cornée^F
córnea^F
cornea^F

黄斑（おうはん）
macula
gelber Fleck^M
tache^F jaune
mácula^F lútea
macula^F

水晶体
lens
Linse^F
cristallin^M
cristalino^M
cristallino^M

視神経
optic nerve
Sehnerv^M
nerf^M optique
nervio^M óptico
nervo^M ottico

瞳孔（どうこう）
pupil
Pupille^F
pupille^F
pupila^F
pupilla^F

視神経乳頭
papilla
blinder Fleck^M
papille^F
papila^F óptica
papilla^F ottica

眼房水
aqueous humor; aqueous humour
Kammerwasser^N
humeur^F aqueuse
humor^M acuoso
umor^M acqueo

硝子体（しょうしたい）
vitreous body
Glaskörper^M
corps^M vitré
cuerpo^M vítreo
corpo^M vitreo

虹彩（こうさい）
iris
Iris^F
iris^M
iris^M
iride^F

結膜
conjunctiva
Bindehaut^F
conjonctive^F
conjuntiva^F
congiuntiva^F

下直筋
inferior rectus muscle
unterer gerader Augenmuskel^M
muscle^M droit inférieur
músculo^M recto inferior
muscolo^M retto inferiore

提靱帯（ていじんたい）
suspensory ligament
Aufhängeband^N
ligament^M suspenseur
ligamento^M suspensorio
legamento^M sospensore

毛様体
ciliary body
Strahlenkörper^M
corps^M ciliaire
cuerpo^M ciliar
corpo^M ciliare

光受容器
photoreceptors
Lichtrezeptoren^M
photorécepteurs^M
fotorreceptores^M
fotorecettori^M

網膜錐（状）体
cone
Zapfen^M
cône^M
cono^M
cono^M

桿状体（かんじょうたい）
rod
Stäbchen^N
bâtonnet^M
bastoncillo^M
bastoncello^M

177

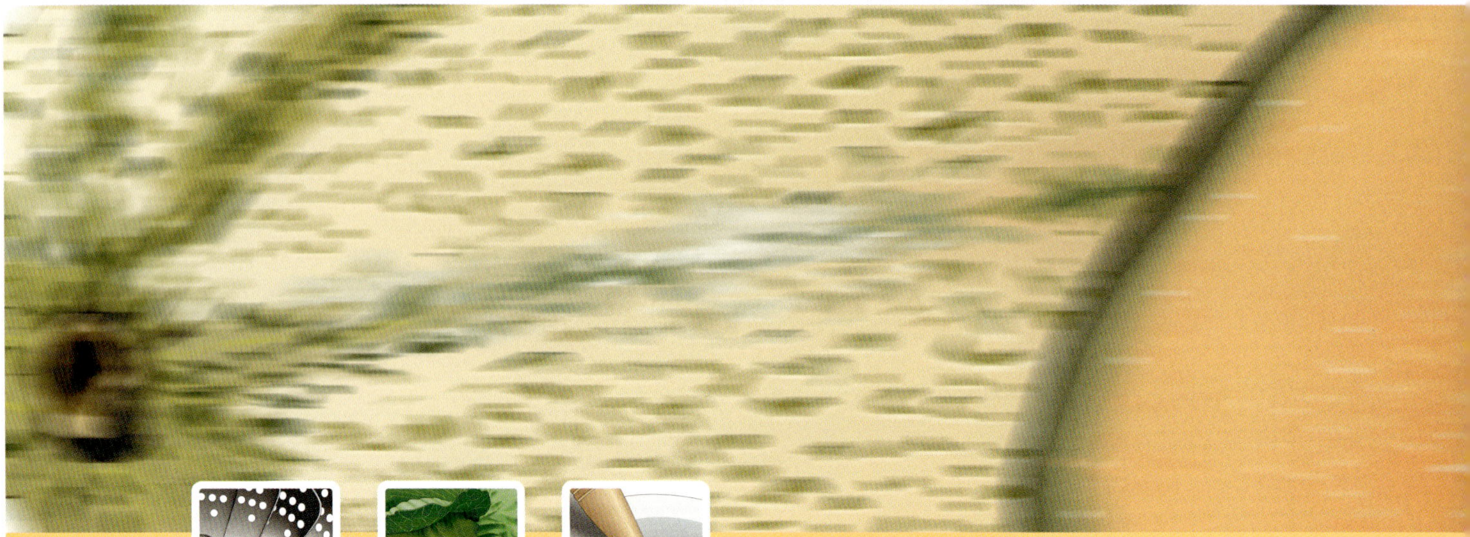
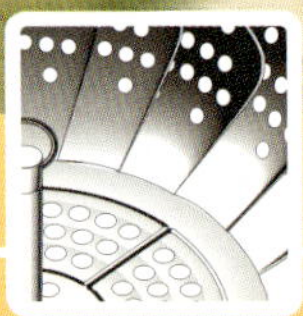
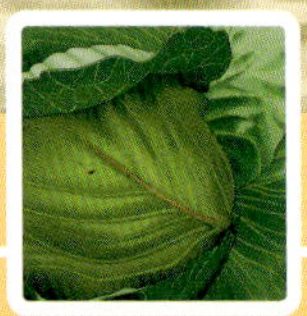
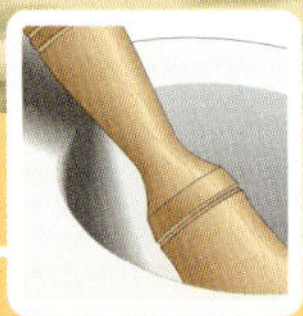

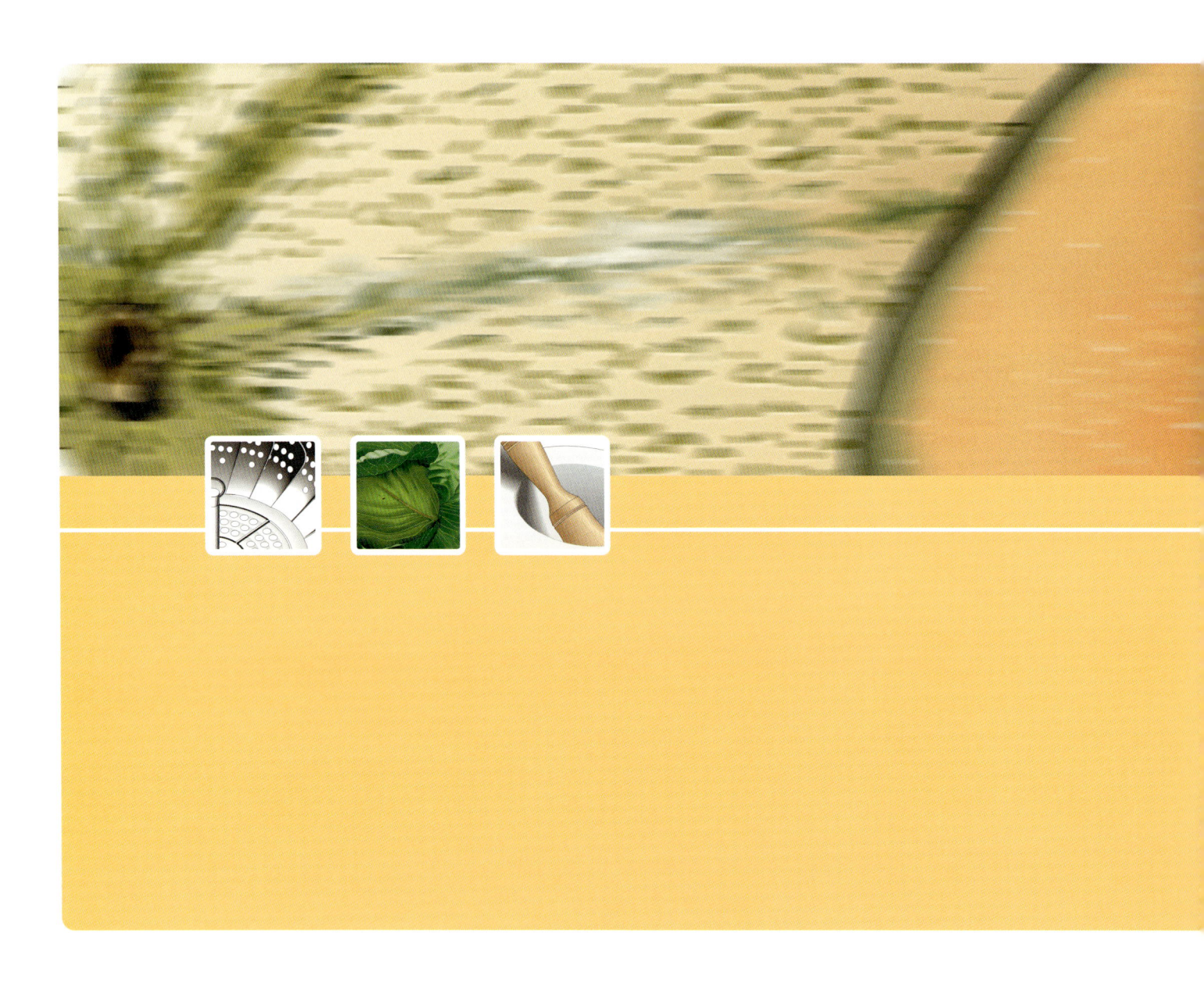

食べ物と台所

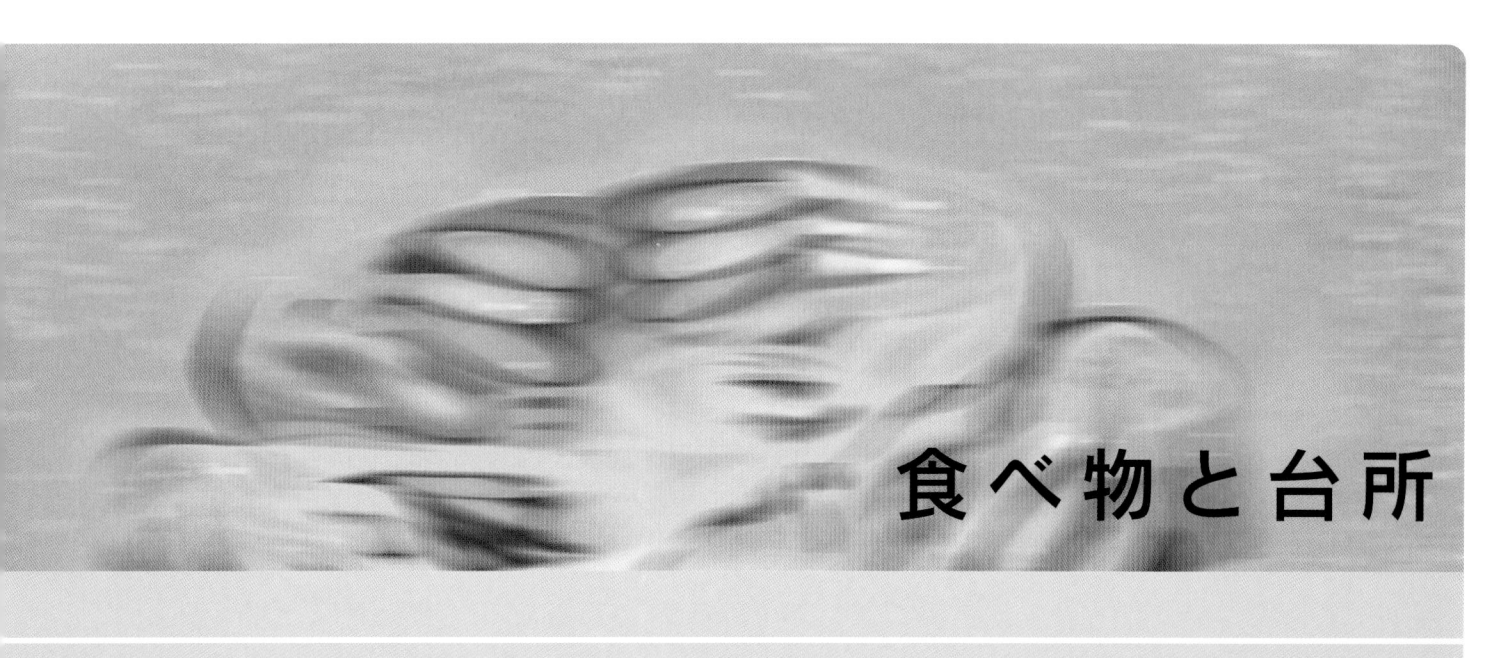

FOOD AND KITCHEN | NAHRUNGSMITTEL UND KÜCHE | ALIMENTATION ET CUISINE | PRODUCTOS ALIMENTARIOS Y DE COCINA | GENERI ALIMENTARI E CUCINA

180 食べ物

- 180 スーパーマーケット
- 182 農場
- 183 キノコ（茸）
- 183 海草
- 184 野菜
- 190 豆果
- 192 果物
- 198 香辛料
- 200 調味料
- 202 ハーブ
- 203 穀類
- 204 穀物[シリアル]食品
- 208 コーヒー・茶
- 208 チョコレート
- 209 砂糖
- 209 油脂類
- 210 乳製品
- 212 臓物
- 212 猟鳥[猟獣]肉
- 213 鳥肉
- 213 卵
- 214 食肉
- 216 調製食品
- 217 軟体動物
- 218 甲殻類
- 218 軟骨魚
- 219 硬骨魚

222 台所

- 222 包装
- 224 台所
- 225 ガラス器
- 226 食器
- 227 銀器
- 229 台所用品
- 234 調理器具
- 236 家電製品
- 240 その他の家電製品
- 241 コーヒー・メーカー

食べ物 | FOOD
NAHRUNGSMITTEL | ALIMENTATION | PRODUCTOS ALIMENTARIOS | GENERI ALIMENTARI

スーパーマーケット

supermarket | Supermarkt[M] | supermarché[M] | supermercado[M] | supermercato[M]

日本語 | 英語 | ドイツ語 | フランス語 | スペイン語 | イタリア語

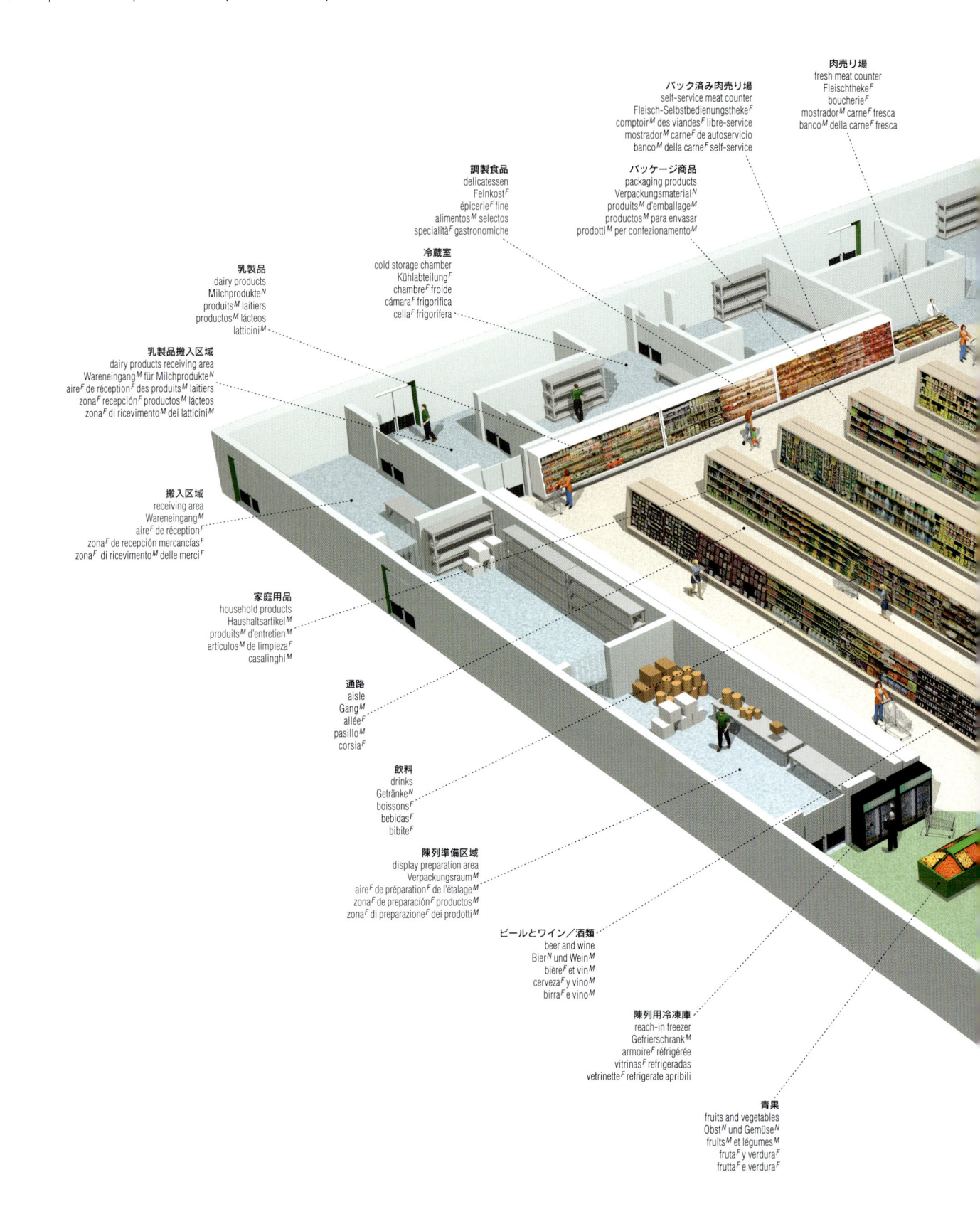

肉売り場
fresh meat counter
Fleischtheke[F]
boucherie[F]
mostrador[M] carne[F] fresca
banco[M] della carne[F] fresca

パック済み肉売り場
self-service meat counter
Fleisch-Selbstbedienungstheke[F]
comptoir[M] des viandes[F] libre-service
mostrador[M] carne[F] de autoservicio
banco[M] della carne[F] self-service

調製食品
delicatessen
Feinkost[F]
épicerie[F] fine
alimentos[M] selectos
specialità[F] gastronomiche

パッケージ商品
packaging products
Verpackungsmaterial[N]
produits[M] d'emballage
productos[M] para envasar
prodotti[M] per confezionamento

冷蔵室
cold storage chamber
Kühlabteilung[F]
chambre[F] froide
cámara[F] frigorífica
cella[F] frigorifera

乳製品
dairy products
Milchprodukte[N]
produits[M] laitiers
productos[M] lácteos
latticini[M]

乳製品搬入区域
dairy products receiving area
Wareneingang[M] für Milchprodukte[N]
aire[F] de réception[F] des produits[M] laitiers
zona[F] recepción[F] productos[M] lácteos
zona[F] di ricevimento[M] dei latticini[M]

搬入区域
receiving area
Wareneingang[M]
aire[F] de réception[F]
zona[F] de recepción mercancías[F]
zona[F] di ricevimento[M] delle merci[F]

家庭用品
household products
Haushaltsartikel[M]
produits[M] d'entretien[M]
artículos[M] de limpieza[F]
casalinghi[M]

通路
aisle
Gang[M]
allée[F]
pasillo[M]
corsia[F]

飲料
drinks
Getränke[N]
boissons[F]
bebidas[F]
bibite[F]

陳列準備区域
display preparation area
Verpackungsraum[M]
aire[F] de préparation[F] de l'étalage[M]
zona[F] de preparación[F] productos[M]
zona[F] di preparazione[F] dei prodotti[M]

ビールとワイン／酒類
beer and wine
Bier[N] und Wein[M]
bière[F] et vin[M]
cerveza[F] y vino[M]
birra[F] e vino[M]

陳列用冷凍庫
reach-in freezer
Gefrierschrank[M]
armoire[F] réfrigérée
vitrinas[F] refrigeradas
vetrinette[F] refrigerate apribili

青果
fruits and vegetables
Obst[N] und Gemüse[N]
fruits[M] et légumes[M]
fruta[F] y verdura[F]
frutta[F] e verdura[F]

食べ物と台所

180

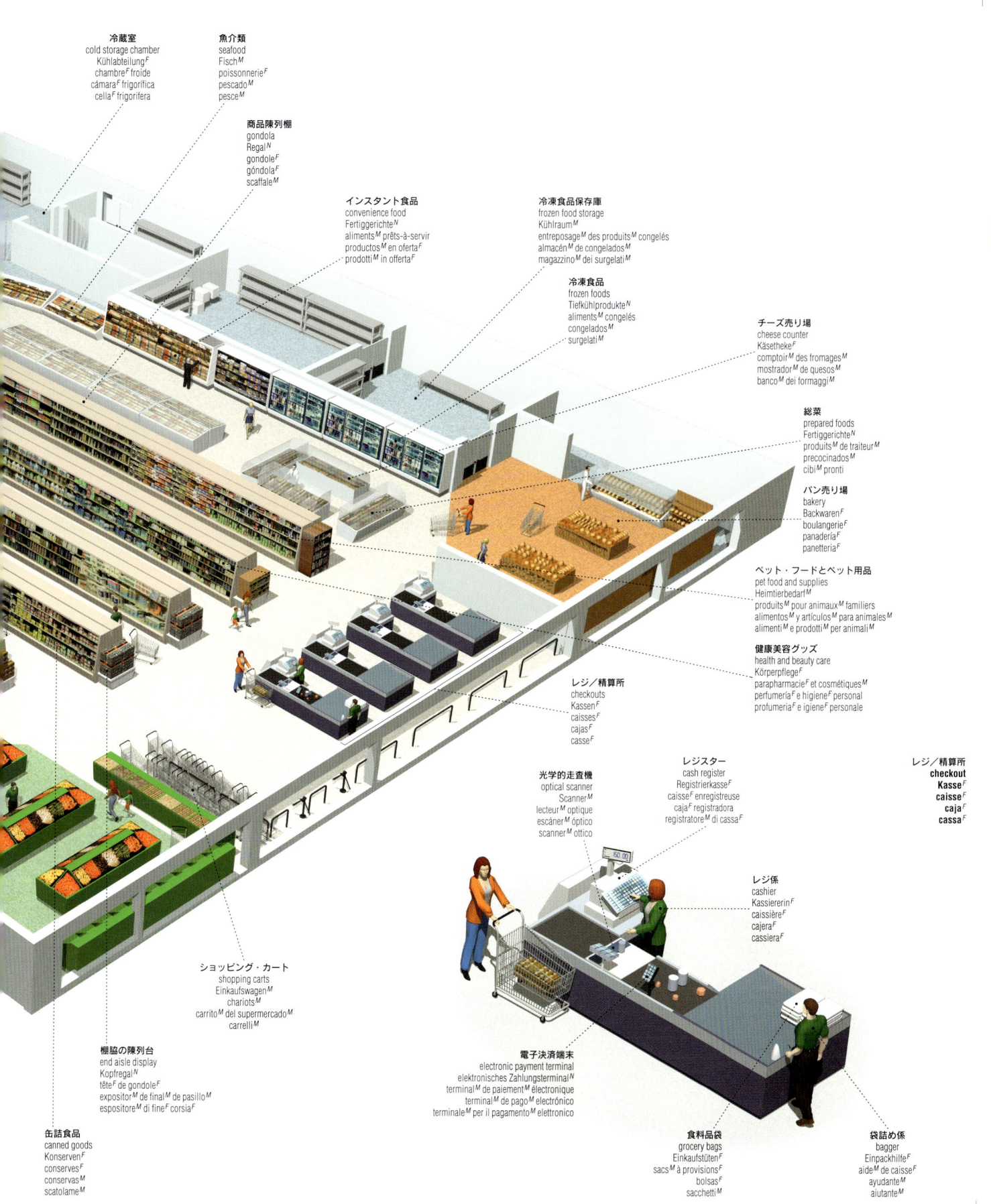

食べ物 | FOOD
NAHRUNGSMITTEL | ALIMENTATION | PRODUCTOS ALIMENTARIOS | GENERI ALIMENTARI

スーパーマーケット

食べ物と台所

冷蔵室
cold storage chamber
Kühlabteilung^F
chambre^F froide
cámara^F frigorífica
cella^F frigorifera

魚介類
seafood
Fisch^M
poissonnerie^F
pescado^M
pesce^M

商品陳列棚
gondola
Regal^N
gondole^F
góndola^F
scaffale^M

インスタント食品
convenience food
Fertiggerichte^N
aliments^M prêts-à-servir
productos^M en oferta
prodotti^M in offerta^F

冷凍食品保存庫
frozen food storage
Kühlraum^M
entreposage^M des produits congelés
almacén^M de congelados
magazzino^M dei surgelati

冷凍食品
frozen foods
Tiefkühlprodukte^N
aliments^M congelés
congelados^M
surgelati^M

チーズ売り場
cheese counter
Käsetheke^F
comptoir^M des fromages^M
mostrador^M de quesos^M
banco^M dei formaggi

総菜
prepared foods
Fertiggerichte^N
produits^M de traiteur^M
precocinados^M
cibi^M pronti

パン売り場
bakery
Backwaren^F
boulangerie^F
panadería^F
panetteria^F

ペット・フードとペット用品
pet food and supplies
Heimtierbedarf^M
produits^M pour animaux^M familiers
alimentos^M y artículos^M para animales^M
alimenti^M e prodotti^M per animali

健康美容グッズ
health and beauty care
Körperpflege^F
parapharmacie^F et cosmétiques^M
perfumería^F e higiene^F personal
profumeria^F e igiene^F personale

レジ／精算所
checkouts
Kassen^F
caisses^F
cajas^F
casse^F

光学的走査機
optical scanner
Scanner^M
lecteur^M optique
escáner^M óptico
scanner^M ottico

レジスター
cash register
Registrierkasse^F
caisse^F enregistreuse
caja^F registradora
registratore^M di cassa^F

レジ／精算所
checkout
Kasse
caisse^F
caja^F
cassa^F

レジ係
cashier
Kassiererin^F
caissière^F
cajera^F
cassiera^F

ショッピング・カート
shopping carts
Einkaufswagen^M
chariots^M
carrito^M del supermercado^M
carrelli^M

棚脇の陳列台
end aisle display
Kopfregal^N
tête^F de gondole^F
expositor^M de final^M de pasillo^M
espositore^M di fine^F corsia^F

電子決済端末
electronic payment terminal
elektronisches Zahlungsterminal^N
terminal^M de paiement^M électronique
terminal^M de pago^M electrónico
terminale^M per il pagamento^M elettronico

食料品袋
grocery bags
Einkaufstüten^F
sacs^M à provisions^F
bolsas^F
sacchetti^M

袋詰め係
bagger
Einpackhilfe^F
aide^M de caisse^F
ayudante^M
aiutante^M

缶詰食品
canned goods
Konserven^F
conserves^F
conservas^F
scatolame^M

181

食べ物 | FOOD
NAHRUNGSMITTEL | ALIMENTATION | PRODUCTOS ALIMENTARIOS | GENERI ALIMENTARI

農場
farmstead | Bauernhof^M | ferme^F | granja^F | fattoria^F

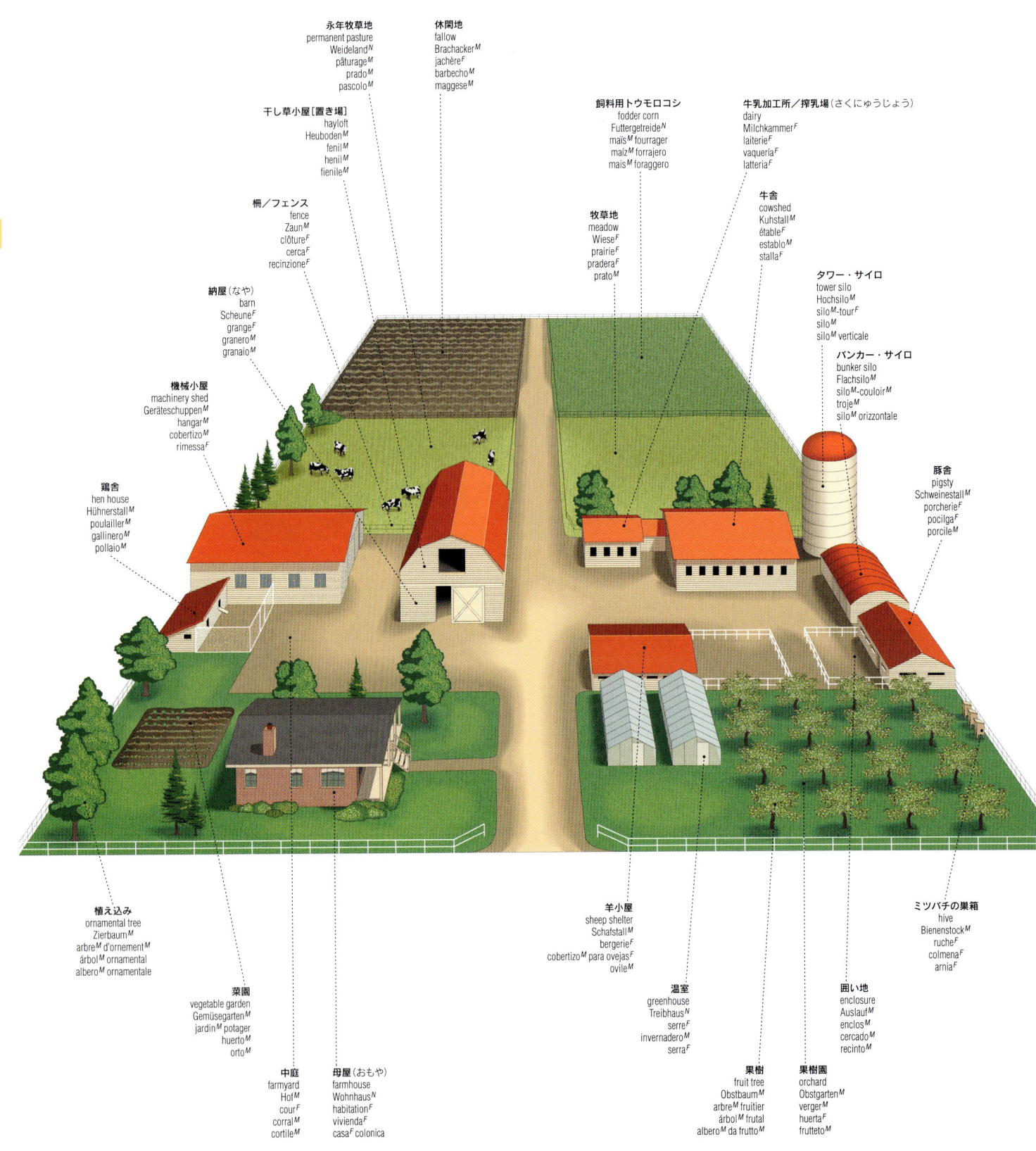

日本語 | 英語 | ドイツ語 | フランス語 | スペイン語 | イタリア語

食べ物と台所

永年牧草地
permanent pasture
Weideland^N
pâturage^M
prado^M
pascolo^M

休閑地
fallow
Brachacker^M
jachère^F
barbecho^M
maggese^M

干し草小屋［置き場］
hayloft
Heuboden^M
fenil^M
henil^M
fienile^M

飼料用トウモロコシ
fodder corn
Futtergetreide^N
maïs^M fourrager
maíz^M forrajero
mais^M foraggero

牛乳加工所／搾乳場（さくにゅうじょう）
dairy
Milchkammer^F
laiterie^F
vaquería^F
latteria^F

柵／フェンス
fence
Zaun^M
clôture^F
cerca^F
recinzione^F

牧草地
meadow
Wiese^F
prairie^F
pradera^F
prato^M

牛舎
cowshed
Kuhstall^M
étable^F
establo^M
stalla^F

納屋（なや）
barn
Scheune^F
grange^F
granero^M
granaio^M

タワー・サイロ
tower silo
Hochsilo^M
silo^M-tour^F
silo^M
silo^M verticale

機械小屋
machinery shed
Geräteschuppen^M
hangar^M
cobertizo^M
rimessa^F

バンカー・サイロ
bunker silo
Flachsilo^M
silo^M-couloir^M
troje^F
silo^M orizzontale

鶏舎
hen house
Hühnerstall^M
poulailler^M
gallinero^M
pollaio^M

豚舎
pigsty
Schweinestall^M
porcherie^F
pocilga^F
porcile^M

植え込み
ornamental tree
Zierbaum^M
arbre^M d'ornement
árbol^M ornamental
albero^M ornamentale

羊小屋
sheep shelter
Schafstall^M
bergerie^F
cobertizo^M para ovejas^F
ovile^M

ミツバチの巣箱
hive
Bienenstock^M
ruche^F
colmena^F
arnia^F

菜園
vegetable garden
Gemüsegarten^M
jardin^M potager
huerto^M
orto^M

温室
greenhouse
Treibhaus^N
serre^F
invernadero^M
serra^F

囲い地
enclosure
Auslauf^M
enclos^M
cercado^M
recinto^M

中庭
farmyard
Hof^M
cour^F
corral^M
cortile^M

母屋（おもや）
farmhouse
Wohnhaus^N
habitation^F
vivienda^F
casa^F colonica

果樹
fruit tree
Obstbaum^M
arbre^M fruitier
árbol^M frutal
albero^M da frutto

果樹園
orchard
Obstgarten^M
verger^M
huerta^F
frutteto^M

182

食べ物 | FOOD
NAHRUNGSMITTEL | ALIMENTATION | PRODUCTOS ALIMENTARIOS | GENERI ALIMENTARI

キノコ（茸）

mushrooms | Pilze^M | champignons^M | hongos^M | funghi^M

トリュフ
truffle
Trüffel^F
truffe^F
trufa^F
tartufo^M

キクラゲ（木耳）
wood ear
Holzohr^N
oreille-de-Judas^F
oreja^F de Judas
orecchio^M di Giuda

タマゴタケ（卵茸）
royal agaric
Kaiserling^M
oronge^F vraie
oronja^F
ovolo^M buono

アカモミタケ（赤樅茸）
delicious lactarius
echter Reizker^M
lactaire^M délicieux
mízcalo^M
agarico^M delizioso

エノキタケ（榎茸）
enoki mushroom
Enoki
collybie^F à pied^M velouté
seta^F enoki
collibia^F

ヒラタケ（平茸）
oyster mushroom
Austernseitling^M
pleurote^M en forme^F d'huître^F
orellana^F
gelone^M

ツクリタケ（作り茸）／マッシュルーム
cultivated mushroom
Zuchtchampignon^M
champignon^M de couche^F
champiñón^M
fungo^M coltivato

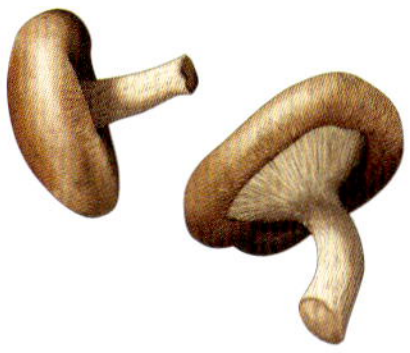

アイタケ（藍茸）
green russula
grasgrüner Täubling^M
russule^F verdoyante
rusula^F verde
verdone^M

アミガサタケ（編笠茸）
morel
Morchel^F
morille^F
morilla^F
spugnola^F

食用イグチタケ（猪口茸）
edible boletus
Steinpilz^M
cèpe^M
boleto^M comestible
porcino^M

シイタケ（椎茸）
shiitake mushroom
Schiitakepilz^M
shiitake^M
shiitake
shiitake^M

アンズタケ（杏茸）
chanterelle
Pfifferling^M
chanterelle^F commune
rebozuelo^M
cantarello^M

海草

seaweed | Meeresalgen^F | algues^F | algas^F | alga^F marina

アラメ（荒布）
arame
Arame^F
aramé^M
arame
arame^F

ワカメ（若布）
wakame
Wakame^F
wakamé^M
wakame
wakame^F

昆布
kombu
Kombu^F
kombu^M
kombu
kombu^F

スピルリナ
spirulina
Spirulina^F
spiruline^F
espirulina^F
spirulina^F

トチャカ
Irish moss
Irisch Moos^N
mousse^F d'Irlande^F
Irish moss
muschio^M d'Irlanda^M

ヒジキ（鹿尾菜）
hijiki
Hijiki^F
hijiki^M
hijiki
hijiki^F

アオサ
sea lettuce
Meersalat
laitue^F de mer^F
lechuga^F marina
lattuga^F marina

寒天
agar-agar
Agar-Agar$^{M/N}$
agar-agar^M
agar-agar
agar-agar^M

海苔
nori
Nori^N
nori^M
nori
nori

ダルス
dulse
Dulse^F
rhodyménie^M palmé
dulse
dulse^F

食べ物と台所

183

食べ物 | FOOD
NAHRUNGSMITTEL | ALIMENTATION | PRODUCTOS ALIMENTARIOS | GENERI ALIMENTARI

野菜

日本語 | 英語 | ドイツ語 | フランス語 | スペイン語 | イタリア語

vegetables | GemüseN | légumesM | hortalizasF | ortaggiM

食べ物と台所

根菜類
bulb vegetables
ZwiebelgemüseN
légumesM bulbesM
bulbosM
ortaggiM da bulboM

(エ)シャロット
shallot
SchalotteF
échaloteF
chaloteM
scalognoM

ヒシ(菱)
water chestnut
WassernussF
châtaigneF d'eauF
castañaF de agua
castagnaF d'acquaF

春タマネギ
green onion
FrühlingszwiebelF
oignonM vert
cebollaF verde
cipollaF verde

ネギ(葱)
scallion; *spring onion*
FrühlingszwiebelF
cibouleF
cebollaF verde
cipollaF d'invernoM

ニンニク(大蒜)
garlic
KnoblauchM
ailM
ajoM
aglioM

エゾネギ(蝦夷葱)
chive
SchnittlauchM
cibouletteF
cebollinoM
erbaF cipollina

リーキ／セイヨウニラネギ(西洋韮葱)
leek
LauchM
poireauM
puerroM
porroM

タマネギ(玉葱)
yellow onion
GemüsezwiebelF
oignonM jaune
cebollaF amarilla
cipollaF di SpagnaF

赤タマネギ
red onion
rote ZwiebelF
oignonM rouge
cebollaF roja
cipollaF rossa

白タマネギ
white onion
weiße ZwiebelF
oignonM blanc
cebollaF blanca
cipollaF bianca

小(こ)タマネギ／プチ・オニオン
pickling onion
PerlzwiebelF
oignonM à mariner
cebolletaM
cipollinaF

イモ(芋)類
tuber vegetables
KnollengemüseN
légumesM tuberculesM
tubérculosM
ortaggiM da tuberoM

キャッサバ／カッサバ
cassava
ManiokM
maniocM
mandiocaF
maniocaF

チョロギ(甘露子)
crosne
KnollenziestM
crosneM
crosneM
crosneM

タロイモ(芋)
taro
TaroM
taroM
taroM
taroM

クズイモ(葛芋)
jicama
JicamaM
jicamaF
jícamaF
jicamaF

ヤムイモ(芋)
yam
SüßkartoffelF
ignameF
batataF
patataF americana

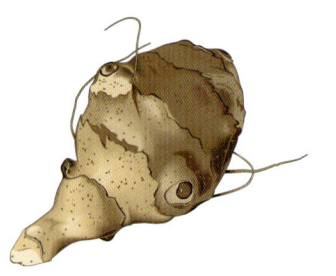

キクイモ(菊芋)
Jerusalem artichoke
TopinamburM/F
topinambourM
tupinamboM
topinamburM

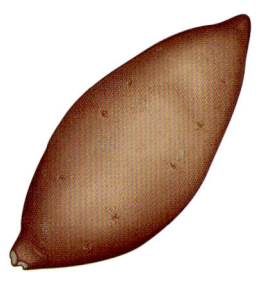

サツマイモ(薩摩芋)
sweet potato
SüßkartoffelF
patateF
batataF
patataF americana

ジャガイモ(芋)
potato
KartoffelF
pommeF de terreF
patataF
patataF

184

食べ物 | FOOD
NAHRUNGSMITTEL | ALIMENTATION | PRODUCTOS ALIMENTARIOS | GENERI ALIMENTARI

野菜

アスパラガス
asparagus
Spargel^M
asperge^F
espárrago^M
asparago^M

先
tip
Spitze^F
pointe^F
punta^F
punta^F

食用芽
spear
Stange^F
turion^M
turión^M
turione^M

束
bundle
Bund^N
botte^F
manojo^M
mazzo^M

フダンソウ (不断草)
Swiss chard
Mangold^M
bette^F à carde^F
acelga^F
bietola^F da coste^F

葉
leaf
Blatt^N
feuille^F
hoja^F
foglia^F

茎野菜類
stalk vegetables
Stengel- und Sprossengemüse^N
légumes^M tiges^F
hortalizas^F de tallos^M
ortaggi^M da fusto^M

コールラビ
kohlrabi
Kohlrabi^M
chou^M-rave^F
colinabo^M
cavolo^M rapa^F

ウイキョウ (茴香)
fennel
Fenchel^M
fenouil^M
hinojo^M
finocchio^M

葉肋 (ようろく)
rib
Rippe^F
carde^F
tallo^M
costa^F

茎
stalk
Stiel^M
tige^F
tallo^M
fusto^M

球根
bulb
Knolle^F
bulbe^M
bulbo^M
bulbo^M

竹の子
bamboo shoot
Bambussprosse^F
pousse^F de bambou^M
brote^M de bambú^M
germoglio^M di bambù^M

カルドン
cardoon
Kardone^F
cardon^M
cardo^M
cardo^M

セロリ
celery
Stangensellerie$^{M/F}$
céleri^M
apio^M
sedano^M

枝
branch
Stange^F
branche^F
tallo^M
costa^F

ゼンマイ
fiddlehead fern
Farnspitze^F
crosse^F de fougère^F
helecho^M canela
fronda^F arrotolata

葉柄の塊
head
Stielgrund^M
pied^M
base^F
cespo^M

ダイオウ (大黄)
rhubarb
Rhabarber^M
rhubarbe^F
ruibarbo^M
rabarbaro^M

食べ物と台所

食べ物 | FOOD
NAHRUNGSMITTEL | ALIMENTATION | PRODUCTOS ALIMENTARIOS | GENERI ALIMENTARI

野菜

日本語 | 英語 | ドイツ語 | フランス語 | スペイン語 | イタリア語

葉菜類
leaf vegetables
Blattgemüse^N
légumes^M feuilles^F
verduras^F de hojas^F
ortaggi^M da foglia^F

サラダナ（菜）
leaf lettuce
Friséesalat^M
laitue^F frisée
lechuga^F rizada
insalata^F riccia

チシャ（萵苣）
romaine lettuce; *cos lettuce*
Romagna-Salat^M
romaine^F
lechuga^F romana
lattuga^F romana

セルタス
celtuce
Spargelsalat^M
laitue^F asperge^F
lechuga^F de tallo^M
lattuga^F asparago^M

ハマナ（浜菜）
sea kale
Meerkohl^M
chou^M marin
col^F marina
cavolo^M marittimo

コラード
collards
Riesenkohl^M
chou^M cavalier^M
berza^F
gramigna^F crestata

キクヂシャ（菊萵苣）
escarole
Eskariol^M
scarole^F
escarola^F
scarola^F

バターヘッド・レタス
butterhead lettuce
Kopfsalat^M
laitue^F pommée
lechuga^F de cogollo^M
lattuga^F cappuccina

（アイスバーグ）レタス
iceberg lettuce
Eisbergsalat^M
laitue^F iceberg^M
lechuga^F iceber
lattuga^F iceberg

赤チコリ
radicchio
Radicchio^M
chicorée^F de Trévise
achicoria^F de Treviso
radicchio^M

ケール
ornamental kale
Zierkohl^M
chou^M laitue^F
col^M ornamental
cavolo^M ornamentale

ハゴロモカンラン（羽衣甘藍）
curled kale; *curly kale*
Grünkohl^M
chou^M frisé
col^F rizada
cavolo^M riccio

ブドウの葉
grape leaf; *vine leaf*
Weinblatt^N
feuille^F de vigne^F
hoja^F de parra^F
pampino^M

メ（芽）キャベツ
Brussels sprouts
Rosenkohl^M
choux^M de Bruxelles
coles^F de Bruselas
cavolini^M di Bruxelles

赤キャベツ
red cabbage
Rotkohl^M
chou^M pommé rouge
col^F lombarda
cavolo^M rosso

白キャベツ
white cabbage
Weißkohl^M
chou^M pommé blanc
repollo^M
cavolo^M bianco

サボイ・キャベツ
savoy cabbage
Wirsing^M
chou^M de Milan
col^F rizada de otoño^M
cavolo^M verzotto^M

キャベツ
green cabbage
Kohl^M
chou^M pommé vert
repollo^M verde
cavolo^M verza^F

白菜
pe-tsai
Chinakohl^M
pe-tsaï^M
col^F china
pe-tsai^M

チンゲンサイ（青梗菜）
pak-choi
Pak-Choi^M
pak-choï^M
pak-choi
pak-choi^M

食べ物 | FOOD
NAHRUNGSMITTEL | ALIMENTATION | PRODUCTOS ALIMENTARIOS | GENERI ALIMENTARI

野菜

スベリヒユ (滑ひゆ)
purslane
Portulak^M
pourpier^M
verdolaga^F
porcellana^F

イラクサ (刺草)
nettle
Nessel^F
ortie^F
ortiga^F
ortica^F

クレソン
watercress
Brunnenkresse^F
cresson^M de fontaine^F
berro^M
crescione^M

タンポポ (蒲公英)
dandelion
Löwenzahn^M
pissenlit^M
diente^M de león^M
dente^M di leone^M

コーン・サラダ
corn salad
Feldsalat^M
mâche^F
colleja^F
valerianella^F

キバナスズシロ (黄花すずしろ)
arugula
Rauke^F
roquette^F
ruqueta^F
rucola^F

ホウレンソウ
spinach
Spinat^M
épinard^M
espinaca^F
spinacio^M

コショウソウ (胡椒草)
garden cress
Gartenkresse^F
cresson^M alénois
berros^M de jardín
crescione^M d'orto^M

スイバ (酸葉)
garden sorrel
Garten-Sauerampfer^M
oseille^F
acedera^F
acetosa^F

エンダイブ
curled endive; *curly endive*
krause Endivie^F
chicorée^F frisée
escarola^F rizada
indivia^F riccia

チコリ
Belgian endive
Chicorée^{M/F}
endive^F
endivia^F
insalata^F belga

花菜類
inflorescent vegetables
Blütengemüse^N
légumes^M fleurs^F
inflorescencias^F
ortaggi^M da infiorescenza^F

カリフラワー
cauliflower
Blumenkohl^M
chou^M-fleur^F
coliflor^F
cavolfiore^M

ブロッコリ
broccoli
Broccoli^M
brocoli^M
brécol^M
broccolo^M

中国ブロッコリ
Gai-lohn
China-Broccoli^M
Gai lon^M
brécol^M chino
Gai-lohn^M

ブロッコリカブ (蕪)
broccoli rabe
Rübenspross^M
brocoli^M italien
nabiza^F
cime^F di rapa^F

アーティチョーク
artichoke
Artischocke^F
artichaut^M
alcachofa^F
carciofo^M

食べ物と台所

187

食べ物 | FOOD
NAHRUNGSMITTEL | ALIMENTATION | PRODUCTOS ALIMENTARIOS | GENERI ALIMENTARI

野菜

日本語 | 英語 | ドイツ語 | フランス語 | スペイン語 | イタリア語

果菜類
fruit vegetables
Fruchtgemüse[N]
légumes[M] fruits[M]
hortalizas[F] de fruto[M]
ortaggi[M] da frutto[M]

アボカド
avocado
Avocado[F]
avocat[M]
aguacate[M]
avocado[M]

トマト
tomato
Tomate[F]
tomate[F]
tomate[M]
pomodoro[M]

チェリー・トマト
currant tomato
Kirschtomate[F]
tomate[F] en grappe[F]
tomate[M] en rama[F]
pomodorini[M] a grappolo[M]

オオブドウホオズキ（大葡萄鬼灯）
tomatillo
Tomatillo[F]
tomatille[F]
tomatillo[M]
tomatillo[M]

オリーブ
olive
Olive[F]
olive[F]
aceituna[F]
oliva[F]

黄色のパプリカ
yellow sweet pepper
gelber Paprika[M]
poivron[M] jaune
pimiento[M] dulce amarillo
peperone[M] giallo

ピーマン
green sweet pepper
grüner Paprika[M]
poivron[M] vert
pimiento[M] dulce verde
peperone[M] verde

赤いパプリカ
red sweet pepper
roter Paprika[M]
poivron[M] rouge
pimiento[M] dulce rojo
peperone[M] rosso

トウガラシ（唐辛子）
hot pepper; *chilli*
Pfefferschote[F]
piment[M]
chile[M]
peperoncino[M]

オクラ
okra
Okraschote[F]
gombo[M]
gombo[M]
gombo[M]

ガーキン
gherkin
Einlegegurke[F]
cornichon[M]
pepinillo[M]
cetriolino[M]

キュウリ（胡瓜）
cucumber
Gurke[F]
concombre[M]
pepino[M]
cetriolo[M]

トウガン（冬瓜）
wax gourd
Wachskürbis[M]
melon[M] d'hiver[M] chinois
calabaza[F] de China
zucca[F] bianca

ナス（茄子）
eggplant; *aubergine*
Aubergine[F]
aubergine[F]
berenjena[F]
melanzana[F]

種なしキュウリ
seedless cucumber
kernlose Salatgurke[F]
concombre[M] sans pépins[M]
pepino[M] sin pepitas[F]
cetriolo[M] senza semi[M]

ペポカボチャ（南瓜）
summer squash; *marrow*
Gartenkürbis[M]
courge[F]
calabacín[M]
zucca[F] di Napoli

ズッキーニ
zucchini; *courgette*
Zucchini[F]
courgette[F]
calabacín[M]
zucchina[F]

ニガウリ（苦瓜）
bitter melon
Bittermelone[F]
margose[F]
pepino[M] amargo
melone[M] amaro

食べ物 | FOOD
NAHRUNGSMITTEL | ALIMENTATION | PRODUCTOS ALIMENTARIOS | GENERI ALIMENTARI

野菜

食べ物と台所

（スクワッシュ）パティパン
pattypan squash
Patisson^M
pâtisson^M
calabaza^F bonetera amarilla
zucca^F pasticcina

ヘチマカボチャ（糸瓜南瓜）
crookneck squash
Krummhalskürbis^M
courge^F à cou^M tors
calabaza de cuello^M retorcido
zucca^F torta^F

ナタウリ（鉈瓜）
straightneck squash
gelbe Zucchini^F
courge^F à cou^M droit
calabaza^F de cuello^M largo
zucca^F a collo^M allungato

ハヤトウリ（隼人瓜）
chayote
Chayote^F
chayote^F
chayote^M
chayote^F

カボチャ（南瓜）
pumpkin
Kürbis^M
citrouille^F
calabaza^F común
zucca^F

ソウメンカボチャ（素麺南瓜）
spaghetti squash
Spaghettikürbis^M
courge^F spaghetti^M
calabaza^F romana
zucca^F spaghetti^M

エイコーン・スクワッシュ
acorn squash
Eichelkürbis^M
courgeron^M
calabaza^F bonetera
zucchetta^F

セイヨウカボチャ（西洋南瓜）
autumn squash
Patisson-Kürbis^M
potiron^M
cidra^F cayote
melone^M invernale

根菜類
root vegetables
Wurzelgemüse^N
légumes^M racines^F
raíces^F
ortaggi^M da radice^F

バラモンジン（参）
salsify
Haferwurz^F
salsifis^M
salsifí^M
salsefica^F

ニンジン（人参）
carrot
Karotte^F
carotte^F
zanahoria^F
carota^F

クロダイコン（黒大根）
black radish
Schwarzrettich^M
radis^M noir
rábano^M negro
ravanello^M nero

ハツカダイコン（二十日大根）
radish
Radieschen^N
radis^M
rábano^M
ravanello^M

キクゴボウ（菊牛蒡）
black salsify
Schwarzwurzel^F
scorsonère^F
escorzonera^F
scorzonera^F

ワサビダイコン（山葵大根）
horseradish
Meerrettich^M
raifort^M
rábano^M blanco
barbaforte^M

パースニップ／アメリカボウフウ（防風）
parsnip
Pastinake^F
panais^M
chirivía^F
pastinaca^F

ダイコン（大根）
daikon
Rettich^M
radis^M oriental
rábano^M daikon
rafano^M giapponese

ゴボウ（牛蒡）
burdock
Klettenwurzel^F
bardane^F
bardana^F
bardana^F

ビート
beet; beetroot
rote Beete^F
betterave^F
remolacha^M
barbabietola^F

カブ（蕪）
turnip
Rübe^F
navet^M
nabo^M
rapa^F

セルリアク／コンヨウ（根用）セロリ
celeriac
Knollensellerie^F
céleri^M-rave^F
apio^M nabo
sedano^M rapa^F

カブカンラン（蕪甘藍）／スウェーデンカブ（蕪）
rutabaga; swede
Kohlrübe^F
rutabaga^M
nabo^M sueco
navone^M

サトイモ（里芋）／マランガ
malanga
japanischer Rettich^M
malanga^M
malanga^F
malanga^F

189

食べ物 | FOOD
NAHRUNGSMITTEL | ALIMENTATION | PRODUCTOS ALIMENTARIOS | GENERI ALIMENTARI

豆果

legumes | Hülsenfrüchte^F | légumineuses^F | legumbres^F | legumi^M

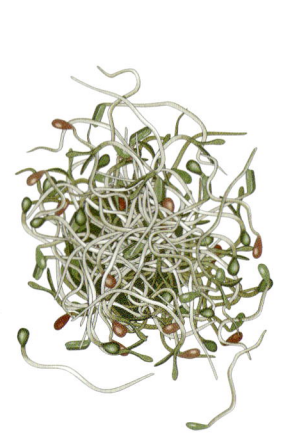

日本語 | 英語 | ドイツ語 | フランス語 | スペイン語 | イタリア語

ルピナス
lupine
Lupine^F
lupin^M
altramuz^M
lupino^M

ピーナッツ
peanut
Erdnuss^F
arachide^F
cacahuete^M
arachide^F

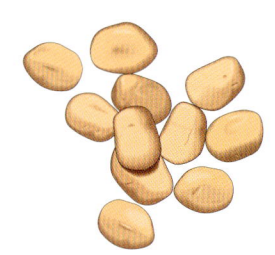

アルファルファ／ムラサキウマゴヤシ（紫馬肥）
alfalfa
blaue Luzerne^F
luzerne^F
alfalfa^F
erba^F medica

レンズマメ（豆）
lentils
Linsen^F
lentilles^F
lentejas^F
lenticchie^F

ソラマメ（空豆）
broad beans
dicke Bohnen^F
fèves^F
habas^F
fave^F

エンドウマメ（豌豆豆）
peas
Erbsen^F
pois^M
guisantes^M
piselli^M

インゲンマメ（隠元豆）
dolichos beans
Bohnen^F
doliques^M
dolichos^M
dolichi^M

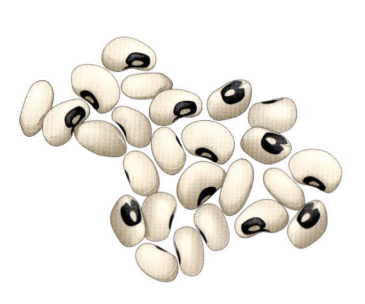

ヒヨコマメ（雛豆）
chick peas
Kichererbsen^F
pois^M chiches
garbanzos^M
ceci^M

鞘（さや）をむいたエンドウ
split peas
gespaltene Erbsen^F
pois^M cassés
guisantes partidos
piselli^M secchi spaccati

ササゲ（大角豆）／クロメマメ（黒目豆）
black-eyed pea
schwarzäugige Bohne^F
dolique^M à œil^M noir
judías^F de ojo
fagiolo^M dall'occhio^M nero

フジマメ（藤豆）
lablab bean
Helmbohne^F
dolique^M d'Égypte^F
judía^F de Egipto
fagiolo^M egiziano

グリン・ピース
green peas
grüne Erbsen^F
petits pois^M
guisantes^M
piselli^M

スイート・ピー
sweet peas; *mangetout*
Zuckererbsen^F
pois^M mange-tout^M
guisantes^M mollares
piselli^M mangiatutto

ジュウロクササゲ（十六大角豆）
yard-long bean
Spargelbohne^F
dolique^M asperge^F
judía^F china larga
fagiolo^M asparagio^M

食べ物 | FOOD
NAHRUNGSMITTEL | ALIMENTATION | PRODUCTOS ALIMENTARIOS | GENERI ALIMENTARI

豆果

インゲンマメ（隠元豆）
beans
Bohnen^F
haricots^M
judías^F
fagioli^M

サヤインゲン（莢隠元）
green bean
grüne Bohne^F
haricot^M vert
judías^F verdes
fagiolino^M

インゲン（隠元）
wax bean
Wachsbohne^F
haricot^M jaune
judía^F amarilla
fagiolino^M giallo

ローマン・ビーン
roman bean
römische Bohne^F
haricot^M romain
judía^F romana
fagiolo^M romano

アズキ（小豆）
adzuki bean
Asukibohne^F
haricot^M adzuki
judía^F adzuki
fagiolo^M adzuki

ベニバナインゲン（紅花隠元）
scarlet runner bean
Feuerbohne^F
haricot^M d'Espagne^F
judía^F pinta
fagiolo^M di Spagna^F

リョクトウ（緑豆）／ヤエナリ（八重生り）
mung bean
Mungobohne^F
haricot^M mungo
judía^F mungo
fagiolo^M mungo

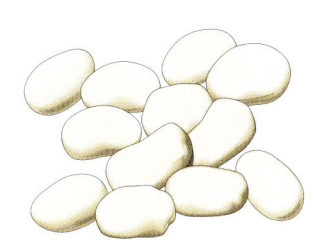

ライマメ（らい豆）
Lima bean
Limabohne^F
haricot^M de Lima
judía^F de Lima
fagiolo^M di Lima

ブチインゲン（斑隠元）
pinto bean
Pintobohne^F
haricot^M pinto
judía^F roja
fagiolo^M pinto

キントキマメ（金時豆）
red kidney bean
rote Kidneybohne^F
haricot^M rouge
judía^F roja
fagiolo^M borlotto

ケツルアズキ（毛蔓小豆）
black gram
schwarze Mungobohne^F
haricot^M mungo à grain^M noir
judía^F mungo negra
fagiolo^M mungo nero

ブラック・ビーン
black bean
schwarze Bohne^F
haricot^M noir
judía^F negra
fagiolo^M nero

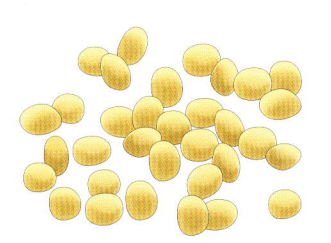

ダイズ（大豆）
soybeans
Sojabohnen^F
graine^F de soja^M
semillas^F de soja^F
semi^M di soia^F

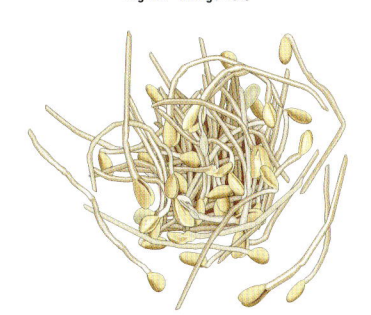

マメモヤシ（豆萌やし）
soybean sprouts
Sojasprossen^F
germes^M de soja^M
brotes^M de soja^F
germogli^M di soia^F

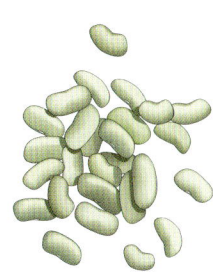

小形ライマメ（らい豆）
flageolet
Flageolet-Bohne^F
flageolet^M
frijol^M
fagiolo^M cannellino

食べ物と台所

191

食べ物 | FOOD
NAHRUNGSMITTEL | ALIMENTATION | PRODUCTOS ALIMENTARIOS | GENERI ALIMENTARI

果物

日本語 | 英語 | ドイツ語 | フランス語 | スペイン語 | イタリア語

fruits | Obst[N] | fruits[M] | frutas[F] | frutti[M]

液果
berries
Beeren[F]
baies[F]
bayas[F]
bacche[F]

スグリ（酸塊）
currant; *redcurrant*
Johannisbeere[F]
groseille[F] à grappes[F]
grosella[F]
ribes[M]

クロスグリ（黒酸塊）
black currant; *blackcurrant*
schwarze Johannisbeere[F]
cassis[M]
grosella[F] negra
ribes[M] nero

グズベリー
gooseberry
Stachelbeere[F]
groseille[F] à maquereau[M]
grosella[F] espinosa
uvaspina[F]

ブドウ（葡萄）
grape
Weintraube[F]
raisin[M]
uva[F]
uva[F]

ブルーベリー
blueberry
Heidelbeere[F]
bleuet[M]
arándano[M]
mirtillo[M]

コケモモ（苔桃）
bilberry
Heidelbeere[F]
myrtille[F]
arándano[M] negro
mirtillo[M]

アカコケモモ（赤苔桃）
red whortleberry
rote Heidelbeere[F]
airelle[F]
arándano[M] rojo
mirtillo[M] rosso

ホオズキ（鬼灯）
alkekengi
Physalis[F]
alkékenge[M]
alquequenje[M]
alchechengi[F]

ツルコケモモ（蔓苔桃）
cranberry
Preiselbeere[F]
canneberge[F]
arándano[M] agrio
mirtillo[M] palustre

ラズベリー
raspberry
Himbeere[F]
framboise[F]
frambuesa[F]
lampone[M]

クロイチゴ（黒苺）
blackberry
Brombeere[F]
mûre[F]
moras[F]
mora[F]

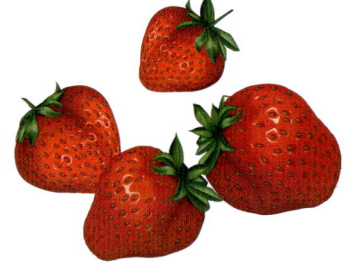

イチゴ（苺）
strawberry
Erdbeere[F]
fraise[F]
fresa[F]
fragola[F]

石果
stone fruits
Steinfrüchte[F]
fruits[M] à noyau[M]
drupas[F]
drupe[F]

プラム
plum
Pflaume[F]
prune[F]
ciruela[F]
prugna[F]

モモ（桃）
peach
Pfirsich[M]
pêche[F]
melocotón[M]
pesca[F]

ネクタリン
nectarine
Nektarine[F]
nectarine[F]
nectarina[F]
nettarina[F]

アンズ（杏）／アプリコット
apricot
Aprikose[F]
abricot[M]
albaricoque[M]
albicocca[F]

サクランボ（桜桃）
cherry
Kirsche[F]
cerise[F]
cereza[F]
ciliegia[F]

ナツメヤシ（棗椰子）
date
Dattel[F]
datte[F]
dátil[M]
dattero[M]

食べ物 | FOOD
NAHRUNGSMITTEL | ALIMENTATION | PRODUCTOS ALIMENTARIOS | GENERI ALIMENTARI

果物

乾果
dry fruits
Trockenfrüchte^F
fruits^M secs
frutas^F secas
frutti^M secchi

マカダミア・ナッツ
macadamia nut
Macadamianuss^F
noix^F de macadamia^M
nuez^F de macadamia^F
noce^F di macadamia^F

ギンナン(銀杏)
ginkgo nut
Ginkgonuss^F
noix^F de ginkgo^M
nuez^F de ginkgo
noce^F di ginco^M

ピスタチオ
pistachio nut
Pistazie^F
pistache^F
pistacho^M
pistacchio^M

マツ(松)の実
pine nut
Pinienkern^M
pignon^M
piñón^M
pinolo^M

コーラ・ナッツ
cola nut
Kolanuss^F
noix^F de cola^M
nuez^F de cola
noce^F di cola^F

ペカン・ナッツ
pecan nut
Pecannuss^F
noix^F de pacane^F
pacana^F
noce^F di pecan

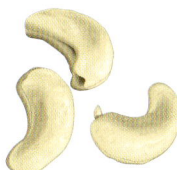

カシュー・ナッツ
cashew
Cashewkern^M
noix^F de cajou^M
anacardo^M
noce^F di acagiù^M

アーモンド
almond
Mandel^F
amande^F
almendra^F
mandorla^F

ハシバミ(榛)の実／ヘーゼルナッツ
hazelnut
Haselnuss^F
noisette^F
avellana^F
nocciola^F

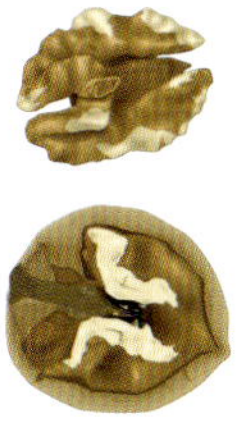

クルミ(胡桃)
walnut
Walnuss^F
noix^F
nuez^F
noce^F

ココナッツ
coconut
Kokosnuss^F
noix^F de coco^M
coco^M
noce^F di cocco^M

クリ(栗)
chestnut
Esskastanie^F
marron^M
castaña^M
castagna^F

ブナの実
beechnut
Buchecker^F
faîne^F
hayuco^M
faggiola^F

ブラジル・ナッツ
Brazil nut
Paranuss^F
noix^F du Brésil^M
nuez^F del Brasil^M
noce^F del Brasile^M

食べ物と台所

ナシ(梨)状果
pome fruits
Apfelfrüchte^F
fruits^M à pépins^M
frutas^F pomo
pomi^M

セイヨウナシ(西洋梨)
pear
Birne^F
poire^F
pera^F
pera^F

マルメロ
quince
Quitte^F
coing^M
membrillo^M
mela^F cotogna

リンゴ(林檎)
apple
Apfel^M
pomme^F
manzana^F
mela^F

スモモ(李)
Japanese plum
Mispel^F
nèfle^F du Japon^M
níspero^M
nespola^F del Giappone^M

193

食べ物 | FOOD
NAHRUNGSMITTEL | ALIMENTATION | PRODUCTOS ALIMENTARIOS | GENERI ALIMENTARI

果物

日本語 | 英語 | ドイツ語 | フランス語 | スペイン語 | イタリア語

柑橘(かんきつ)果物
citrus fruits
Zitrusfrüchte^F
agrumes^M
cítricos^M
agrumi^M

レモン
lemon
Zitrone^F
citron^M
limón^M
limone^M

キンカン(金柑)
kumquat
Kumquat^F
kumquat^M
naranja^F china
kumquat^M

ライム
lime
Limette^F
lime^F
lima^F
limetta^F

オレンジ
orange
Orange^F
orange^F
naranja^F
arancia^F

マンダリン
mandarin
Mandarine^F
mandarine^F
mandarina^F
mandarino^M

ベルガモット
bergamot
Bergamotte^F
bergamote^F
bergamota^M
bergamotto^M

グレープフルーツ
grapefruit
Grapefruit^F
pomelo^M
toronja^F
pompelmo^M

ザボン
pomelo
Pampelmuse^F
pamplemousse^M
pomelo^M
pomelo^M

シトロン
citron
Zitronatzitrone^F
cédrat^M
limón^M
cedro^M

食べ物と台所

194

食べ物 | FOOD
NAHRUNGSMITTEL | ALIMENTATION | PRODUCTOS ALIMENTARIOS | GENERI ALIMENTARI

果物

メロン類
melons
Melonen^F
melons^M
melones^M
meloni^M

カンタループ（メロン）
cantaloupe
Honigmelone^F
cantaloup^M
melón cantalupo
cantalupo^M

カサバ（メロン）
casaba melon
Casabamelone^F
melon^M Casaba
melón invernal
melone^M invernale

ハネジュー・メロン／甘露メロン
honeydew melon
Honigmelone^F
melon^M miel^M
melón de miel
melone^M mieloso

マスクメロン
muskmelon
Zuckermelone^F
melon^M brodé
melón escrito
melone^M retato

カナリア・メロン
canary melon
kanarische Melone^F
melon^M brésilien
melón amarillo
melone^M giallo canario

スイカ（西瓜）
watermelon
Wassermelone^F
pastèque^F
sandía^F
cocomero^M

オーゲン・メロン
Ogen melon
Ogenmelone^F
melon^M d'Ogen
melón de Ogen
melone^M Ogen

195

食べ物 | FOOD
NAHRUNGSMITTEL | ALIMENTATION | PRODUCTOS ALIMENTARIOS | GENERI ALIMENTARI

果物

日本語 | 英語 | ドイツ語 | フランス語 | スペイン語 | イタリア語

熱帯果物／トロピカル・フルーツ
tropical fruits
Südfrüchte^F
fruits^M tropicaux
frutas^F tropicales
frutti^M tropicali

食べ物と台所

プランテーン
plantain
Plantainbanane^F
banane^F plantain^M
plátano^M
banana^F plantain

バナナ
banana
Banane^F
banane^F
banana^F
banana^F

リュウガン（竜眼）
longan
Longanfrucht^F
longane^M
longan^M
longan^M

コダチ（木立）トマト
tamarillo
Baumtomate^F
tamarillo^M
tamarillo^M
tamarillo^M

パッション・フルーツ
passion fruit
Passionsfrucht^F
fruit^M de la Passion^F
fruta^F de la pasión^F
maracuja^F

キワノ／ツノ（角）メロン
horned melon
Kiwano^F
melon^M à cornes^F
kiwano^M
kiwano^M

マンゴスチン
mangosteen
Mangostane^F
mangoustan^M
mangostán^M
mangostano^M

キーウィ（フルーツ）
kiwi
Kiwi^F
kiwi^M
kiwi^M
kiwi^M

ザクロ（石榴）
pomegranate
Granatapfel^M
grenade^F
granada^F
melograno^M

チェリモヤ
cherimoya
Chirimoya^F
chérimole^F
chirimoya^F
cerimolia^F

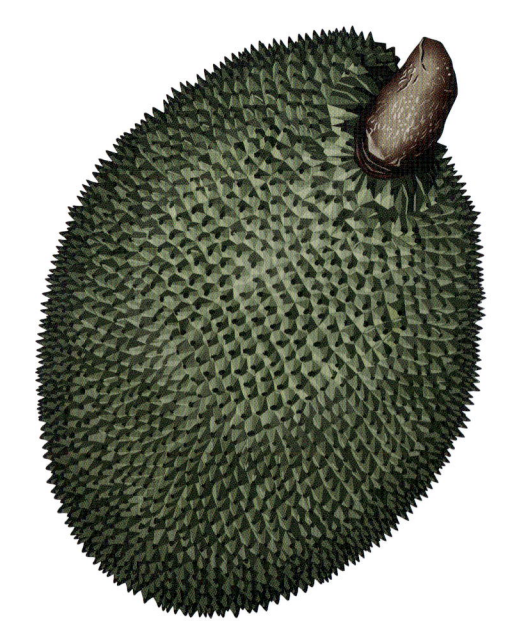

ジャックフルーツ
jackfruit
Jackfrucht^F
jaque^M
fruta^F de jack
frutto^M del jack

パイナップル
pineapple
Ananas^F
ananas^M
piña^F
ananas^M

食べ物 | FOOD
NAHRUNGSMITTEL | ALIMENTATION | PRODUCTOS ALIMENTARIOS | GENERI ALIMENTARI

果物

食べ物と台所

ジャボチカバ
jaboticaba
Jaboticaba^F
jaboticaba^M
jaboticaba^F
jaboticaba^F

ライチ
litchi
Litchi^F
litchi^M
lichi^M
litchi^M

イチジク(無花果)
fig
Feige^F
figue^F
higo^M
fico^M

ナツメ(棗)
jujube
chinesische Dattel^F
jujube^M
jojoba^F
giuggiola^F

サポジラ
sapodilla
Breiapfel^M
sapotille^F
zapote^M
sapotiglia^F

グアバ
guava
Guave^F
goyave^F
guayaba^F
guaiava^F

ランブータン
rambutan
Rambutan^F
ramboutan^M
rambután^M
rambutan^M

カキ(柿)
Japanese persimmon
Kaki^F
kaki^M
caqui^M
cachi^M

ウチワサボテン(団扇仙人掌)
prickly pear
Kaktusfeige^F
figue^F de Barbarie
higo^M chumbo
fico^M d'India^F

カランボーラ／ゴレンシ(五斂子)の実／ヨウトウ(羊桃)
carambola
Sternfrucht^F
carambole^F
carambola^F
carambola^F

ニホンナシ(日本梨)
Asian pear
asiatische Birne^F
pomme^F-poire^F
pera asiática
nashi^M

マンゴー
mango
Mango^F
mangue^F
mango^M
mango^M

ドリアン
durian
Durianfrucht^F
durian^M
durión^M
durian^M

パパイヤ
papaya
Papaya^F
papaye^F
papaya^F
papaia^F

ペピーノ
pepino
Birnenmelone^F
pepino^M
pepino^M dulce
pepino^M

フェイジョア
feijoa
Ananasguave^F
feijoa^M
feijoa^F
feijoa^F

197

香辛料

spices | Gewürze^N | épices^F | especias^F | spezie^F

ネズ(杜松)の実
juniper berry
Wacholderbeere^F
baie^F de genièvre^M
bayas^F de enebro^M
bacca^F di ginepro^M

丁子(ちょうじ)／クローブ
clove
Gewürznelke^F
clou^M de girofle^M
clavo^M
chiodo^M di garofano^M

オールスパイス
allspice
Jamaikapfeffer^M
piment^M de la Jamaïque^F
pimienta^F de Jamaica
pepe^M della Giamaica^F

シロガラシ(白辛子)
white mustard
weiße Senfkörner^N
moutarde^F blanche
mostaza^F blanca
senape^F bianca

クロガラシ(黒辛子)
black mustard
schwarze Senfkörner^N
moutarde^F noire
mostaza^F negra
senape^F nera

クロコショウ(黒胡椒)
black pepper
schwarzer Pfeffer^M
poivre^M noir
pimienta^F negra
pepe^M nero

シロコショウ(白胡椒)
white pepper
weißer Pfeffer^M
poivre^M blanc
pimienta^F blanca
pepe^M bianco

ピンク・ペッパー
pink pepper
rosa Pfeffer^M
poivre^M rose
pimienta^F rosa
pepe^M rosa

グリーン・ペッパー
green pepper
grüner Pfeffer^M
poivre^M vert
pimienta^F verde
pepe^M verde

ナツメグ
nutmeg
Muskatnuss^F
noix^F de muscade^F
nuez^M moscada
noce^F moscata

キャラウェー／カラム
caraway
Kümmel^M
carvi^M
alcaravea^F
carvi^M

カルダモン
cardamom
Kardamom^{M/N}
cardamome^F
cardamomo^M
cardamomo^M

シナモン／(肉)桂皮／セイロンニッケイ(肉桂)
cinnamon
Zimtstangen^M
cannelle^F
canela^F
cannella^F

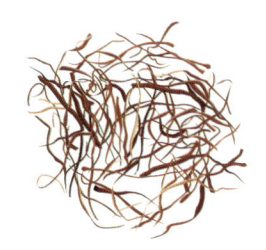

サフラン
saffron
Safran^M
safran^M
azafrán^M
zafferano^M

クミン／バキン(馬芹)
cumin
Kreuzkümmel^M
cumin^M
comino^M
cumino^M

カレー粉
curry
Curry^N
curry^M
curry^M
curry^M

ウコン／ターメリック
turmeric
Kurkuma^N
curcuma^F
cúrcuma^F
curcuma^F

コロハ(胡盧巴)
fenugreek
Bockshornkleesamen^M
fenugrec^M
fenogreco^M
fieno^M greco

食べ物 | FOOD
NAHRUNGSMITTEL | ALIMENTATION | PRODUCTOS ALIMENTARIOS | GENERI ALIMENTARI

香辛料

ハラペーニョ
jalapeño chile
Jalapeño-Chili^M
piment^M Jalapeño
chile^M jalapeño
peperoncino^M

アカトウガラシ(赤唐辛子)／レッド・ペッパー
bird's eye chile
Vogelaugenchili^M
piment^M oiseau^M
guindilla^F
peperoncino^M rosso

つぶしたチリ
crushed chiles
zerstoßene Chilis^M
piments^M broyés
guindilla^F triturada
peperoncino^M tritato

乾燥したチリ
dried chiles
getrocknete Chilis^M
piments^M séchés
guindilla^F seca
peperoncini^M secchi

カイエンヌ
cayenne chile
Cayennepfeffer^M
piment^M de Cayenne
pimienta^F de cayena^F
pepe^M di Cayenna

パプリカ
paprika
Paprika^M
paprika^M
pimentón^M
paprika^F

アジョワン
ajowan
Ajowan^N
ajowan^M
ajowán^M
ajowan^M

アギ(阿魏)
asafetida
Teufelsdreck^M
asa-fœtida^F
asafétida^M
assafetida^F

ガラム・マサラ
garam masala
Garam Masala^N
garam masala^M
garam masala^M
garam masala^M

ケージャン・スパイス
cajun spice seasoning
Cajun-Gewürzmischung^F
mélange^M d'épices^F cajun
condimento^M de especias^F cajún
condimento^M alle spezie^F cajun

マリネ・スパイス
marinade spices
Mariniergewürze^N
épices^F à marinade^F
especias^F para salmuera^F
spezie^F marinate

ウーシャンフェン(五香粉)
five spice powder
Fünf-Kräuter^N-Gewürz^N
cinq-épices^M chinois
cinco especias^F chinas
miscela^F di cinque spezie^F

チリ・パウダー
chili powder
Chilipulver^N
assaisonnement^M au chili^M
guindilla^F molida
peperoncino^M in polvere^F

ひいたコショウ(胡椒)
ground pepper
gemahlener Pfeffer^M
poivre^M moulu
pimienta^F molida
pepe^M macinato

ラス・エル・ハナウト
ras el hanout
Ras-El-Hanout^N
ras-el-hanout^M
ras el hanout^M
ras el hanout^M

スマック
sumac
Sumach^M
sumac^M
zumaque^M
sumac^M

ケシ(芥子)の実
poppy seeds
Mohnsamen^M
graines^F de pavot^M
semillas^F de adormidera^F
semi^M di papavero^M

ショウガ(生姜)
ginger
Ingwer
gingembre^M
jengibre^M
zenzero^M

食べ物 | FOOD
NAHRUNGSMITTEL | ALIMENTATION | PRODUCTOS ALIMENTARIOS | GENERI ALIMENTARI

調味料

日本語 | 英語 | ドイツ語 | フランス語 | スペイン語 | イタリア語

condiments | Würzen^F | condiments^M | condimentos^M | condimenti^M

食べ物と台所

タバスコ®
Tabasco™ sauce
Tabasco™-Soße^F
sauce^F Tabasco®
salsa^F Tabasco^M
salsa^F tabasco^M

ウースター・ソース
Worcestershire sauce
Worcestershire-Soße^F
sauce^F Worcestershire
salsa^F Worcertershire
salsa^F Worcestershire

タマリンド・ペースト
tamarind paste
Tamarindenmark^N
pâte^F de tamarin
salsa^F de tamarindo^M
pasta^F di tamarindo^M

バニラ・エキス
vanilla extract
Vanille-Extrakt^M
extrait^M de vanille^F
extracto^M de vainilla^F
estratto^M di vaniglia^F

トマト・ペースト
tomato paste
Tomatenmark^N
concentré^M de tomate^F
concentrado^M de tomate^M
concentrato^F di pomodoro^M

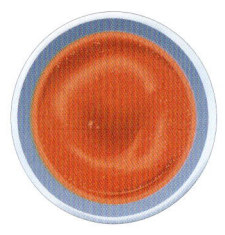

トマト・クーリ
tomato coulis
Passierte Tomaten^F
coulis^M de tomate^F
salsa^F de tomate^M
passata^F di pomodoro^M

ホムス
hummus
Hummus^M
hoummos^M
hummus^M
hummus^M

タヒニ
tahini
Tahinisoße^F
tahini^M
tajín^M
tahini^M

海鮮醬（しょう）
hoisin sauce
Hoisinsoße^F
sauce^F hoisin
salsa^F hoisin
salsa^F hoisin

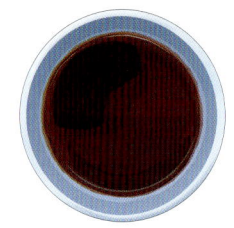

醬油（しょうゆ）
soy sauce
Sojasoße^F
sauce^F soja^M
salsa^F de soja^F
salsa^F di soia^F

粉末辛子／粉末マスタード
powdered mustard
Senfpulver^N
moutarde^F en poudre^F
mostaza^F en polvo^M
senape^F in polvere^F

粒辛子／粒マスタード
wholegrain mustard
Senfkörner^N
moutarde^F à l'ancienne^F
mostaza^F en grano
senape^F in granuli^M

ディジョン・マスタード
Dijon mustard
Dijon-Senf^M
moutarde^F de Dijon
mostaza^F de Dijon
senape^F di Digione

ジャーマン・マスタード
German mustard
deutscher Senf^M
moutarde^F allemande
mostaza^F alemana
senape^F tedesca

イングリッシュ・マスタード
English mustard
englischer Senf^M
moutarde^F anglaise
mostaza^F inglesa
senape^F inglese

アメリカン・マスタード
American mustard
amerikanischer Senf^M
moutarde^F américaine
mostaza^F americana
senape^F americana

食べ物 | FOOD
NAHRUNGSMITTEL | ALIMENTATION | PRODUCTOS ALIMENTARIOS | GENERI ALIMENTARI

調味料

食べ物と台所

プラム・ソース
plum sauce
Pflaumensoße^F
sauce^F aux prunes^F
salsa^F de ciruelas^F
salsa^F di prugne^F

マンゴー・チャツネ
mango chutney
Mangochutney^N
chutney^M à la mangue^F
chutney^M al mango^M
chutney^M al mango^M

ハリッサ
harissa
Harissasoße^F
harissa^F
harissa^F
harissa^F

サンバル・オレック
sambal oelek
Sambal Oelek^M
sambal oelek^M
sambal oelek^M
sambal oelek^M

ケチャップ
ketchup
Ketchup^M
ketchup^M
ketchup^M
ketchup^M

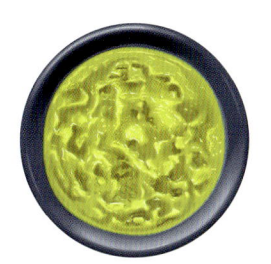

山葵（わさび）
wasabi
Wasabipaste^F
wasabi^M
wasabi^M
wasabi^M

食卓塩
table salt
Tafelsalz^N
sel^M fin
sal^F de mesa
sale^M fino

粗塩
coarse salt
grobes Salz^N
gros sel^M
sal^F gorda
sale^M grosso

海塩
sea salt
Meersalz^N
sel^M marin
sal^F marina
sale^M marino

アチェート・バルサミコ／バルサム・ビネガー
balsamic vinegar
Balsamessig^M
vinaigre^M balsamique
vinagre^M balsámico
aceto^M balsamico

米酢
rice vinegar
Reisessig^M
vinaigre^M de riz^M
vinagre^M de arroz^M
aceto^M di riso^M

りんご酢
apple cider vinegar
Apfelessig^M
vinaigre^M de cidre^M
vinagre^M de manzana^F
aceto^M di mele^F

モルト・ビネガー
malt vinegar
Malzessig^M
vinaigre^M de malt^M
vinagre^M de malta^F
aceto^M di malto^M

ワイン・ビネガー
wine vinegar
Weinessig^M
vinaigre^M de vin^M
vinagre^M de vino^M
aceto^M di vino^M

食べ物 | FOOD
NAHRUNGSMITTEL | ALIMENTATION | PRODUCTOS ALIMENTARIOS | GENERI ALIMENTARI

ハーブ

日本語 | 英語 | ドイツ語 | フランス語 | スペイン語 | イタリア語

herbs | Kräuter[N] | fines herbes[F] | hierbas[F] aromáticas | piante[F] aromatiche

ディル
dill
Dill[M]
aneth[M]
eneldo[M]
aneto[M]

アニス
anise
Anis[M]
anis[M]
anís[M]
anice[M]

ローレル／ゲッケイジュ (月桂樹)
sweet bay
Lorbeer[M]
laurier[M]
laurel[M]
alloro[M]

オレガノ
oregano
Origano[M]
origan[M]
orégano[M]
origano[M]

タラゴン
tarragon
Estragon[M]
estragon[M]
estragón[M]
dragoncello[M]

バジル
basil
Basilikum[N]
basilic[M]
albahaca[F]
basilico[M]

セージ
sage
Salbei[M]
sauge[F]
salvia[F]
salvia[F]

タイム
thyme
Thymian[M]
thym[M]
tomillo[M]
timo[M]

ミント
mint
Minze[F]
menthe[F]
hierbabuena[F]
menta[F]

パセリ
parsley
Petersilie[F]
persil[M]
perejil[M]
prezzemolo[M]

チャービル
chervil
Kerbel[M]
cerfeuil[M]
perifollo[M]
cerfoglio[M]

コリアンダー
coriander
Koriander[M]
coriandre[M]
cilantro[M]
coriandolo[M]

ローズマリー
rosemary
Rosmarin[M]
romarin[M]
romero[M]
rosmarino[M]

ヒソップ
hyssop
Ysop[M]
hysope[F]
hisopo[M]
issopo[M]

ルリヂシャ (瑠璃萵苣)
borage
Boretsch[M]
bourrache[F]
borraja[F]
borragine[F]

ラビッジ
lovage
Liebstöckel[M/N]
livèche[F]
alheña[F]
sedano[M] di monte

セボリー
savory
Bohnenkraut[N]
sarriette[F]
ajedrea[F]
santoreggia[F]

レモン・バーム
lemon balm
Zitronenmelisse[F]
mélisse[F]
melisa[F]
melissa[F]

食べ物と台所

202

食べ物 | FOOD
NAHRUNGSMITTEL | ALIMENTATION | PRODUCTOS ALIMENTARIOS | GENERI ALIMENTARI

穀類

cereal | Getreide^N | céréales^F | cereales^M | cereali^M

食べ物と台所

米
rice
Reis^M
riz^M
arroz^M
riso^M

マコモ（真菰）
wild rice
Wildreis^M
riz^M sauvage
arroz^M silvestre
riso^M nero selvatico

スペルトコムギ（小麦）
spelt wheat
Dinkel^M
épeautre^M
escanda^F común
farro^M

コムギ（小麦）
wheat
Weizen^M
blé^M
trigo^M
frumento^M

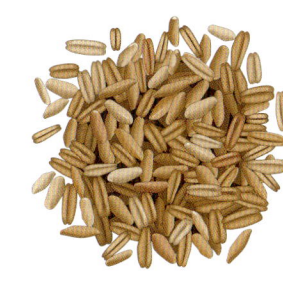

オートムギ（麦）
oats
Hafer^M
avoine^F
avena^F
avena^F

ライムギ（麦）
rye
Roggen^M
seigle^M
centeno^M
segale^F

アワ（粟）
millet
Hirse^F
millet^M
mijo^M
miglio^M

トウモロコシ（玉蜀黍）
corn
Mais^M
maïs^M
maíz^M
mais^M

オオムギ（大麦）
barley
Gerste^F
orge^M
cebada^F
orzo^M

ソバ（蕎麦）
buckwheat
Buchweizen^M
sarrasin^M
trigo^M sarraceno
grano^M saraceno

キノア
quinoa
Reismelde^F
quinoa^M
quinua^F
quinoa^M

アマランサス／アマランス
amaranth
Amarant^M
amarante^F
amaranto^M
amaranto^M

ライコムギ（小麦）
triticale
Triticale^M
triticale^M
triticale^M
triticale^M

203

食べ物 | FOOD
NAHRUNGSMITTEL | ALIMENTATION | PRODUCTOS ALIMENTARIOS | GENERI ALIMENTARI

穀物［シリアル］食品

日本語 | 英語 | ドイツ語 | フランス語 | スペイン語 | イタリア語

cereal products | Getreideprodukte^N | produits^M céréaliers | cereales^M | prodotti^M cerealicoli

穀粉
flour and semolina
Mehl^N und Grieß^M
farine^F et semoule^F
harina^F y sémola^F
farina^F e semolino^M

セモリーナ
semolina
Grieß^M
semoule^F
sémola^F
semolino^M

全粒小麦粉
whole-wheat flour
Vollkornmehl^N
farine^F de blé^M complet
harina^F integral
farina^F integrale

クスクス
couscous
Couscous^N
couscous^M
cuscús^M
cuscus^M

汎用の小麦粉
all-purpose flour
Haushaltsmehl^N
farine^F tout usage^M
harina^F común
farina^F semplice

無漂白の小麦粉
unbleached flour
ungebleichtes Mehl^N
farine^F non blanchie
harina^F sin blanquear
farina^F non trattata

オート麦粉
oat flour
Hafermehl^N
farine^F d'avoine^F
harina^F de avena^F
farina^F di avena^F

トウモロコシ粉
corn flour
Maismehl^N
farine^F de maïs^M
harina^F de maíz^M
farina^F di mais^M

パン
bread
Brot^N
pain^M
pan^M
pane^M

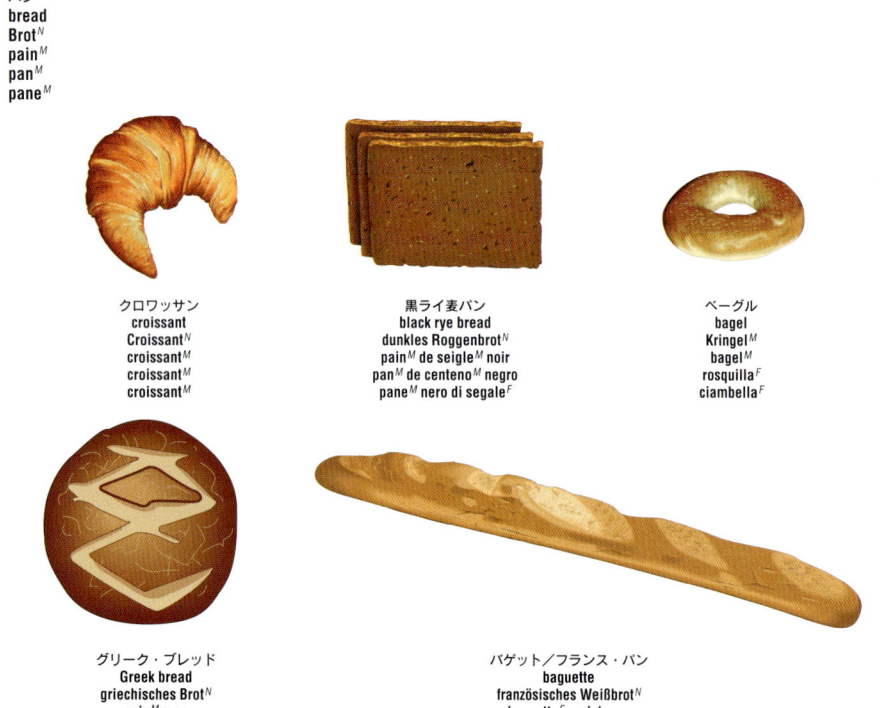

クロワッサン
croissant
Croissant^N
croissant^M
croissant^M
croissant^M

黒ライ麦パン
black rye bread
dunkles Roggenbrot^N
pain^M de seigle^M noir
pan^M de centeno^M negro
pane^M nero di segale^F

ベーグル
bagel
Kringel^M
bagel^M
rosquilla^F
ciambella^F

グリーク・ブレッド
Greek bread
griechisches Brot^N
pain^M grec
pan^M griego
pane^F greco

バゲット／フランス・パン
baguette
französisches Weißbrot^N
baguette^F parisienne
barra^F de pan^M
filone^M francese

エピ
ear loaf
Ährenbrot^N
baguette^F épi^M
pan^M espiga^F
spiga^F

フランス・パン／バゲット
French bread
Baguette^N
pain^M parisien
baguette^M
baguette^F

食べ物 | FOOD
NAHRUNGSMITTEL | ALIMENTATION | PRODUCTOS ALIMENTARIOS | GENERI ALIMENTARI

穀物［シリアル］食品

チャパティ
Indian chapati bread
indisches Fladenbrot^N
pain^M chapati indien
pan^M indio chapatí
pane^M chapati indiano

トルティーヤ／トルティージャ
tortilla
Tortilla^F
tortilla^F
tortilla^F
tortilla^F

ピタ
pita bread; *pitta bread*
Pittabrot^N
pain^M pita
pan^M de pita^F
pane^M pita

ナン
Indian naan bread
indisches Naanbrot^N
pain^M naan indien
pan^M indio naan
pane^M naan indiano

ライ麦クラッカー
cracked rye bread; *rye crispbread*
Roggenknäckebrot^N
cracker^M de seigle^M
galleta^F de centeno^M
galletta^F di segale^F

パフ・ペースト／フィロの生地
phyllo dough
Blätterteig^M
pâte^F phyllo
pasta^F de hojaldre^M
pasta^F sfoglia^F

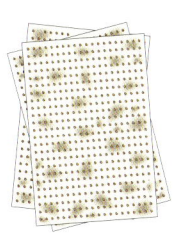

無酵母パン
unleavened bread
ungesäuertes Brot^N
pain^M azyme
pan^M ácimo
pane^M azzimo

デニッシュ・ライ麦パン
Danish rye bread
dänisches Roggenbrot^N
pain^M de seigle^M danois
pan^M danés de centeno^M
pane^M di segale^F danese

白パン
white bread
Weißbrot^N
pain^M blanc
pan^M blanco
pane^M bianco

雑穀パン
multigrain bread
Mehrkornbrot^N
pain^M multicéréales
pan^M multicereales
pane^M multicereali

スカンジナビア・クラッカー
Scandinavian cracked bread; *Scandinavian crispbread*
skandinavisches Knäckebrot^N
cracker^M scandinave
galleta^F escandinava
galletta^F scandinava

ツォプフ
Jewish hallah; *Jewish challah*
jüdisches Weißbrot^N
pain^M tchallah juif
pan^M judío hallah
pane^M ebraico

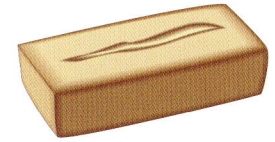

アメリカン・コーン・ブレッド
American corn bread
amerikanisches Maisbrot^N
pain^M de maïs^M américain
pan^M americano de maíz^M
pane^M di mais^M americano

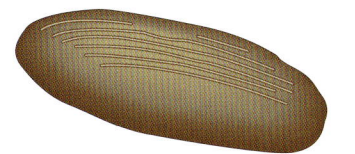

ジャーマン・ライ麦パン
German rye bread
deutsches Roggenbrot^N
pain^M de seigle^M allemand
pan^M alemán de centeno^M
pane^M di segale^F tedesco

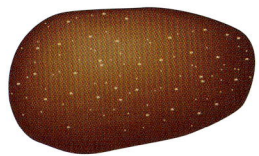

ロシア黒パン／ロシアン・プンパーニッケル
Russian pumpernickel
russischer Pumpernickel^M
pain^M noir russe
pan^M negro ruso
Pumpernickel^M russo

田舎パン
farmhouse bread
Bauernbrot^N
pain^M de campagne^F
pan^M campesino
pane^M casereccio

全粒粉パン
wholemeal bread
Vollkornbrot^N
pain^M complet
pan^M integral
pane^M integrale

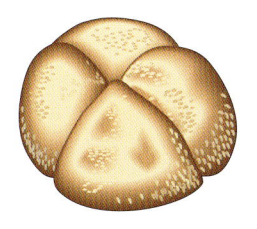

アイリッシュ・ブレッド
Irish bread
irisches Brot^N
pain^M irlandais
pan^M irlandés
pane^M irlandese

イギリス・パン
English loaf
englisches Weißbrot^N
pain^M de mie^F
pan^M de flor^F
pagnottella^F inglese

穀物［シリアル］食品

食べ物 | FOOD
NAHRUNGSMITTEL | ALIMENTATION | PRODUCTOS ALIMENTARIOS | GENERI ALIMENTARI

日本語 | 英語 | ドイツ語 | フランス語 | スペイン語 | イタリア語

パスタ
pasta
Teigwaren^F
pâtes^F **alimentaires**
pasta^F
pasta^F

リガトーニ
rigatoni
Rigatoni^M
rigatoni^M
rigatoni^M
rigatoni^M

ツイスト／エリケ
rotini
Rotini^M
rotini^M
sacacorchos^M
eliche^F

シェル／コンキリエ
conchiglie
Conchiglie^F
conchiglie^F
conchitas^F
conchiglie^F

カール／フジッリ
fusilli
Fusilli^M
fusilli^M
fusilli^M
fusilli^M

スパゲッティ
spaghetti
Spaghetti^M
spaghetti^M
espagueti^M
spaghetti^M

ディターリ
ditali
Ditali^M
ditali^M
dedalitos^M
ditali^M

ニョッキ
gnocchi
Gnocchi^M
gnocchi^M
ñoquis^M
gnocchi^M

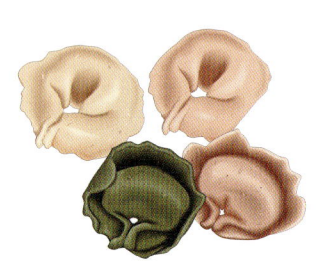

トルテッリーニ
tortellini
Tortellini^M
tortellini^M
tortellini^M
tortellini^M

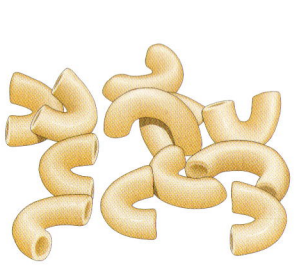

スパゲッティーニ
spaghettini
Spaghettini^M
spaghettini^M
fideos^M
spaghettini^M

エルボ
elbows
Hörnchennudeln^F
coudes^M
tiburones^M
gomiti^M

ペンネ
penne
Penne^F
penne^M
macarrones^M
penne^F

カネローニ
cannelloni
Cannelloni^M
cannelloni^M
canelones^M
cannelloni^M

ラザーニャ
lasagna
Lasagne^F
lasagne^F
lasañas^F
lasagne^F

ラビオリ
ravioli
Ravioli^M
ravioli^M
raviolis
ravioli^M

ホウレンソウのタリアテッレ
spinach tagliatelle
grüne Tagliatelle^F
tagliatelle^M **aux épinards**^{M}
tallarines^M **de espinacas**^{F}
tagliatelle^F **verdi**

フェットチーネ
fettucine
Fettuccine^F
fettucine^F
fetuchinas^F
fettuccine^F

食べ物 | FOOD
NAHRUNGSMITTEL | ALIMENTATION | PRODUCTOS ALIMENTARIOS | GENERI ALIMENTARI

穀物[シリアル]食品

アジアの麺類
Asian noodles
asiatische Teigwaren^F
nouilles^F asiatiques
fideos^M asiáticos
spaghetti^M asiatici

蕎麦(そば)
soba noodles
Sobanudeln^F
nouilles^F soba
fideos^M de soba^F
spaghetti^M soba

素麺(そうめん)
somen noodles
Somennudeln^F
nouilles^F somen
fideos^M de somen^M
spaghetti^M somen

うどん
udon noodles
Udonnudeln^F
nouilles^F udon
fideos^M de udon^M
spaghetti^M udon

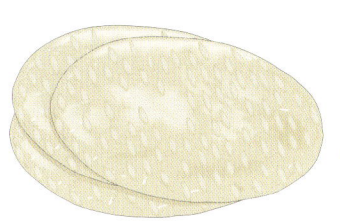

ライス・ペーパー
rice papers
Reispapier^N
galettes^F de riz^M
galletas^F de arroz^M
gallette^F di riso^M

米麺／フォー
rice noodles
Reisnudeln^F
nouilles^F de riz^M
fideos^M de arroz^M
spaghetti^M di riso^M

緑豆春雨(はるさめ)
bean thread cellophane noodles
Glasnudeln^F
nouilles^F de haricots^M mungo
fideos^M de judías$^{F\,F}$ mungo
spaghetti^M di fagioli^M mungo

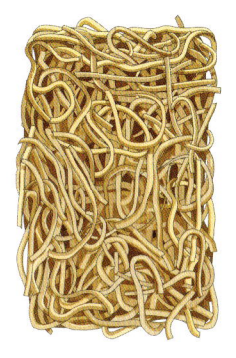

卵麺
egg noodles
asiatische Eiernudeln^F
nouilles^F aux œufs^M
fideos^M de huevo^M
spaghetti^M all'uovo^M

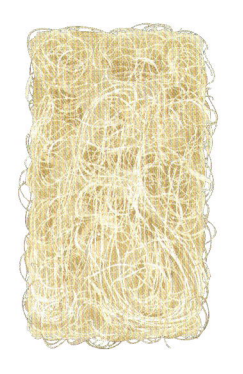

ビーフン
rice vermicelli
Reisfadennudeln^F
vermicelles^F de riz^M
vermicelli^M de arroz^M
vermicelli^M di riso^M

ワンタンの皮
won ton skins
Wan-tan-Teigblätter^N
pâtes^F won-ton
pasta^F won ton
pasta^F won ton

米
rice
Reis^M
riz^M
arroz^M
riso^M

白米
white rice
weißer Reis^M
riz^M blanc
arroz^M blanco
riso^M bianco

玄米
brown rice
Braunreis^M
riz^M complet
arroz^M integral
riso^M integrale

パーボイルド米
parboiled rice
Parboiled Reis^M
riz^M étuvé
arroz^M parboiled
riso^M parboiled

バスマティ米
basmati rice
Basmatireis^M
riz^M basmati
arroz^M basmati
riso^M basmati

207

食べ物 | FOOD
NAHRUNGSMITTEL | ALIMENTATION | PRODUCTOS ALIMENTARIOS | GENERI ALIMENTARI

日本語 | 英語 | ドイツ語 | フランス語 | スペイン語 | イタリア語

コーヒー・茶

coffee and infusions | KaffeeM und TeeM | caféM et infusionsF | caféM e infusionesF | caffèM e infusiM

コーヒー
coffee
KaffeeM
caféM
caféM
caffèM

生(き)コーヒー豆
green coffee beans
RohkaffeeF
grainsM de caféM verts
granosM verdes de caféM
chicchiM di caffèM verdi

焙煎(ばいせん)コーヒー豆
roasted coffee beans
geröstete KaffeebohnenF
grainsM de caféM torréfiés
granosM torrefactos de caféM
chicchiM di caffèM tostati

ハーブ・ティー
herbal teas
KräuterteesM
tisanesF
tisanasF
tisaneF

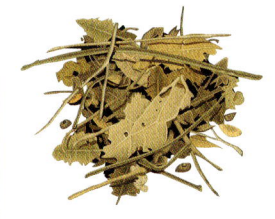

シナノキ(科木)
linden
LindeF
tilleulM
tilaF
tiglioM

カモミール
chamomile
KamilleF
camomilleF
manzanillaF
camomillaF

バーベナ
verbena
VerbeneF
verveineF
verbenaF
verbenaF

茶
tea
TeeM
théM
téM
tèM

緑茶
green tea
grüner TeeM
théM vert
téM verde
tèM verde

紅茶
black tea
schwarzer TeeM
théM noir
téM negro
tèM nero

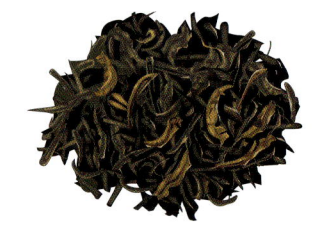

ウーロン茶
oolong tea
Oolong-TeeM
théM oolong
téM oolong
tèM oolong

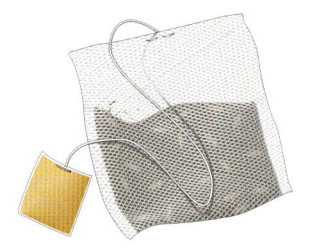

ティー・バッグ
tea bag
TeebeutelM
théM en sachetM
bolsitaF de téM
bustinaF di tèM

チョコレート

chocolate | SchokoladeF | chocolatM | chocolateM | cioccolatoM

ブラック[ビター]チョコレート
dark chocolate
BitterschokoladeF
chocolatM noir
chocolateM amargo
cioccolatoM fondente

ミルク・チョコレート
milk chocolate
MilchschokoladeF
chocolatM au laitM
chocolateM con lecheF
cioccolatoM al latteM

ココア
cocoa
KakaoM
cacaoM
cacaoM
cacaoM

ホワイト・チョコレート
white chocolate
weiße SchokoladeF
chocolatM blanc
chocolateM blanco
cioccolatoM bianco

食べ物 | FOOD
NAHRUNGSMITTEL | ALIMENTATION | PRODUCTOS ALIMENTARIOS | GENERI ALIMENTARI

砂糖

sugar | Zucker^M | sucre^M | azúcar^M | zucchero^M

グラニュー糖
granulated sugar
Kristallzucker^M
sucre^M granulé
azúcar^M granulado
zucchero^M in grani^M

粉糖
powdered sugar
Puderzucker^M
sucre^M glace^F
azúcar^M glas
zucchero^M a velo^M

赤砂糖
brown sugar
brauner Zucker^M
cassonade^F
azúcar^M moreno
zucchero^M di canna^F

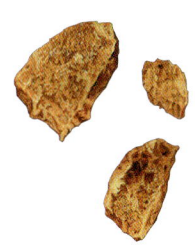

氷砂糖
rock candy
Kandiszucker^M
sucre^M candi
azúcar^M candi
zucchero^M candito

糖蜜
molasses
Melasse^F
mélasse^F
melazas^F
melassa^F

コーン・シロップ
corn syrup
Maissirup^M
sirop^M de maïs^M
jarabe^M de maíz^M
sciroppo^M di mais^M

メープル・シロップ
maple syrup
Ahornsirup^M
sirop^M d'érable^M
jarabe^M de arce^M
sciroppo^M d'acero^M

蜂蜜
honey
Honig^M
miel^M
miel^M
miele^M

食べ物と台所

油脂類

fats and oils | Fette^N und Öle^N | huiles^F et matières^F grasses | grasas^F y aceites^M | grassi^M e oli^M

トウモロコシ油
corn oil
Maisöl^N
huile^F de maïs^M
aceite^M de maíz^M
olio^M di mais^M

オリーブ油
olive oil
Olivenöl^N
huile^F d'olive^F
aceite^M de oliva^F
olio^M d'oliva^F

ヒマワリ油
sunflower-seed oil
Sonnenblumenöl^N
huile^F de tournesol^M
aceite^M de girasol^M
olio^M di semi^M di girasole^M

落花生油
peanut oil
Erdnussöl^N
huile^F d'arachide^F
aceite^M de cacahuete^M
olio^M di arachidi^F

ゴマ油
sesame oil
Sesamöl^N
huile^F de sésame^M
aceite^M de sésamo^M
olio^M di sesamo^M

ショートニング
shortening
Backfett^N
saindoux^M
manteca^F de cerdo^M
grasso^M alimentare

ラード
lard
Schweinespeck^M
lard^M
lardo^M
lardo^M

マーガリン
margarine
Margarine^F
margarine^F
margarina^F
margarina^F

식べ物 | FOOD
NAHRUNGSMITTEL | ALIMENTATION | PRODUCTOS ALIMENTARIOS | GENERI ALIMENTARI

乳製品

日本語 | 英語 | ドイツ語 | フランス語 | スペイン語 | イタリア語

dairy products | Milchprodukte[N] | produits[M] laitiers | productos[M] lácteos | prodotti[M] caseari

ヨーグルト
yogurt
Joghurt[M]
yaourt[M]
yogur[M]
yogurt[M]

ギー
ghee
Ghee[N]
ghee[M]
mantequilla[F] clarificada
ghi[M]

バター
butter
Butter[F]
beurre[M]
mantequilla[F]
burro[M]

クリーム
cream
Sahne[F]
crème[F]
nata[F]
panna[F]

ホイップ・クリーム
whipping cream
Schlagsahne[F]
crème[F] épaisse
nata[F] de montar
panna[F] da montare

サワー・クリーム
sour cream
saure Sahne[F]
crème[F] aigre
nata[F] agria
panna[F] acida

ミルク
milk
Milch[F]
lait[M]
leche[M]
latte[M]

ホモ牛乳
homogenized milk
homogenisierte Milch[F]
lait[M] homogénéisé
leche[M] homogeneizada
latte[M] omogeneizzato

ヤギ乳
goat's milk
Ziegenmilch[F]
lait[M] de chèvre
leche[M] de cabra
latte[M] di capra[F]

エバ・ミルク
evaporated milk
Kondensmilch[F]
lait[M] concentré
leche[F] evaporada
latte[M] evaporato

バターミルク
buttermilk
Buttermilch[F]
babeurre[M]
suero[M] de la leche[F]
latticello[M]

粉ミルク
powdered milk
Milchpulver[N]
lait[M] en poudre
leche[M] en polvo[M]
latte[M] in polvere[F]

生チーズ
fresh cheeses
Frischkäse[M]
fromages[M] frais
quesos[M] frescos
formaggi[M] freschi

ヤギ(山羊)チーズ
goat's-milk cheeses
Ziegenkäse[M]
fromages[M] de chèvre[F]
quesos[M] de cabra[F]
formaggi[M] di capra[F]

カテージ・チーズ
cottage cheese
Hüttenkäse[M]
cottage[M]
queso[M] cottage
cottage cheese[M]

モツァレラ(チーズ)
mozzarella
Mozzarella[M]
mozzarella[F]
mozzarella[F]
mozzarella[F]

シュブレ
Chèvre cheese
Ziegenfrischkäse[M]
chèvre[M] frais
queso[M] Chèvre
formaggio[M] fresco di capra[F]

リコッタ(チーズ)
ricotta
Ricotta[M]
ricotta[F]
ricotta[F]
ricotta[F]

クリーム・チーズ
cream cheese
Streichkäse[M]
fromage[M] à la crème[F]
queso[M] cremoso
formaggio[M] cremoso

クロタン・ド・シャビニョール
Crottin de Chavignol
Crottin de Chavignol[M]
crottin[M] de Chavignol
Crottin[M] de Chavignol
crottin[M] de chavignol

食べ物 | FOOD
NAHRUNGSMITTEL | ALIMENTATION | PRODUCTOS ALIMENTARIOS | GENERI ALIMENTARI

乳製品

プレス・チーズ
pressed cheeses
Hartkäse^M
fromages^M à pâte^F pressée
quesos^M prensados
formaggi^M a pasta^F dura

食べ物と台所

ヤールスバーグ
Jarlsberg
Jarlsberg^M
jarlsberg^M
Jarlsberg^M
jarlsberg^M

エメンタール
Emmenthal
Emmentaler^M
emmenthal^M
Emmenthal^M
emmental^M

ラクレット
Raclette
Raclette^M
raclette^F
Raclette^F
raclette^F

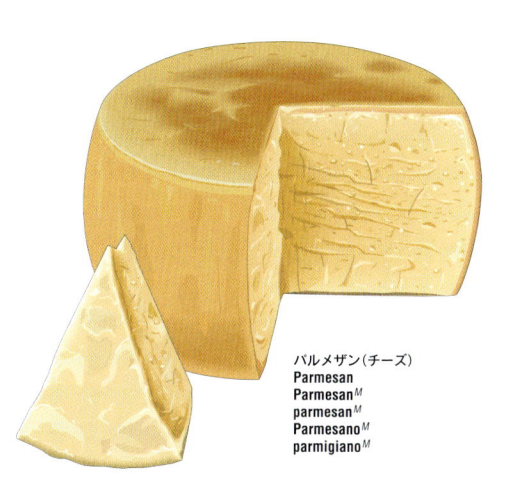

パルメザン（チーズ）
Parmesan
Parmesan^M
parmesan^M
Parmesano^M
parmigiano^M

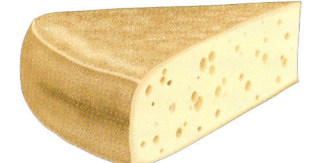

グリュイエール
Gruyère
Gruyèrekäse^M
gruyère^M
Gruyère^M
groviera^M

ロマーノ
Romano
Pecorino Romano^M
romano^M
Pecorino romano^M
pecorino^M romano

ブルー・チーズ
blue-veined cheeses
Edelpilzkäse^M
fromages^M à pâte^F persillée
quesos^M azules
formaggi^M erborinati

ロックフォール（チーズ）
Roquefort
Roquefort^M
roquefort^M
Roquefort^M
roquefort^M

スティルトン（チーズ）
Stilton
Stilton^M
stilton^M
Stilton^M
stilton^M

ゴルゴンゾラ（チーズ）
Gorgonzola
Gorgonzola^M
gorgonzola^M
Gorgonzola^M
gorgonzola^M

デニッシュ・ブルー
Danish Blue
Danish Blue^M
bleu^M danois
Azul danés^M
danish blue^M

ソフト・チーズ
soft cheeses
Weichkäse^M
fromages^M à pâte^F molle
quesos^M blandos
formaggi^M a pasta^F molle

ポンレベック
Pont-l'Évêque
Pont-l'Évêque^M
pont-l'évêque^M
Pont-l'Évêque^M
pont-l'évêque^M

クーロミエ
Coulommiers
Coulommiers^M
coulommiers^M
Coulommiers^M
coulommiers^M

カマンベール
Camembert
Camembert^M
camembert^M
Camembert^M
camembert^M

ブリー
Brie
Brie^M
brie^M
Brie^M
brie^M

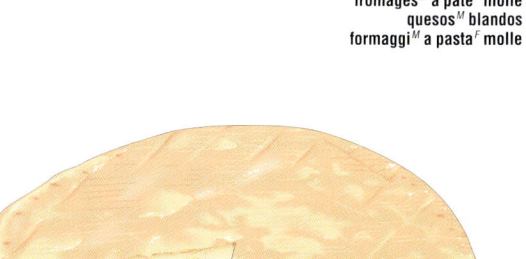

ムンステール
Munster
Munster^M
munster^M
Munster^M
munster^M

211

食べ物 | FOOD
NAHRUNGSMITTEL | ALIMENTATION | PRODUCTOS ALIMENTARIOS | GENERI ALIMENTARI

日本語 | 英語 | ドイツ語 | フランス語 | スペイン語 | イタリア語

臓物

variety meat | Innereien^F | abats^M | despojos^M | interiora^F

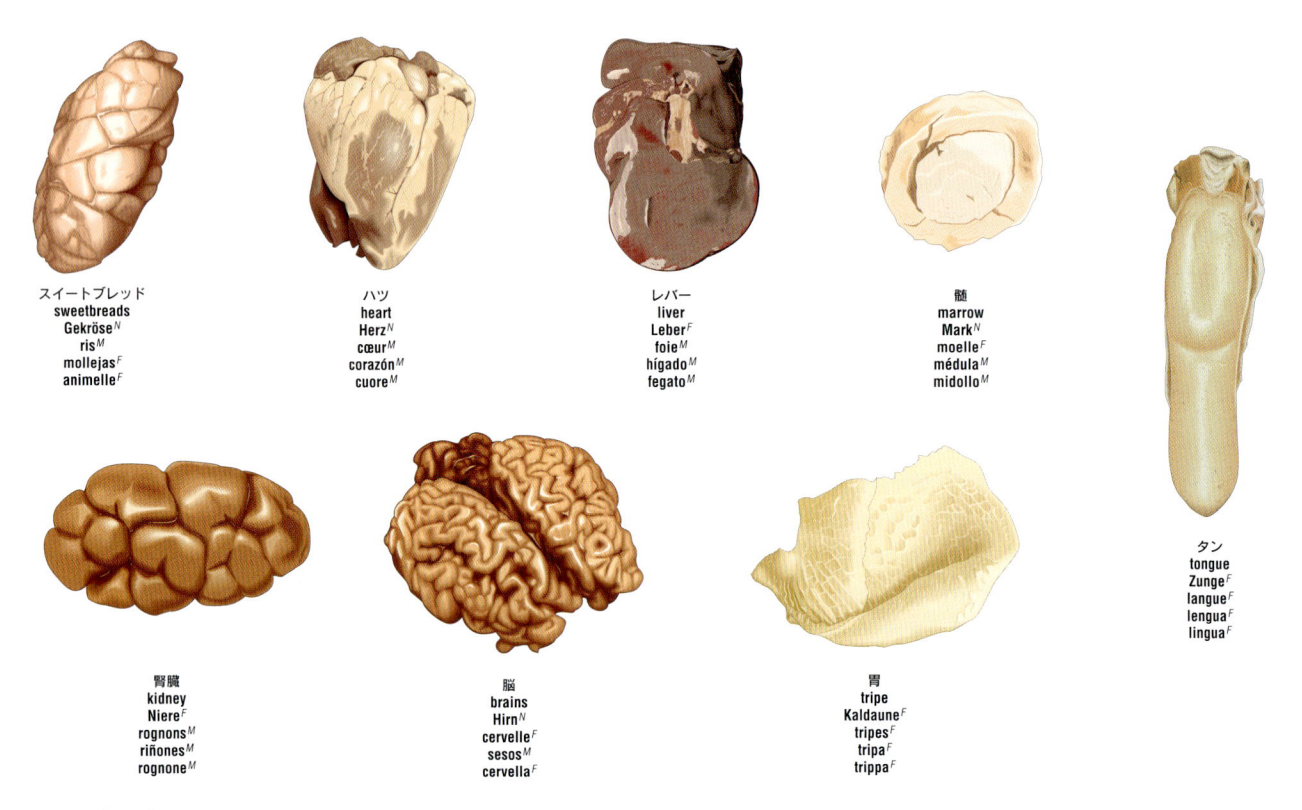

スイートブレッド
sweetbreads
Gekröse^N
ris^M
mollejas^F
animelle^F

ハツ
heart
Herz^N
cœur^M
corazón^M
cuore^M

レバー
liver
Leber^F
foie^M
hígado^M
fegato^M

髄
marrow
Mark^N
moelle^F
médula^F
midollo^M

タン
tongue
Zunge^F
langue^F
lengua^F
lingua^F

腎臓
kidney
Niere^F
rognons^M
riñones^M
rognone^M

脳
brains
Hirn^N
cervelle^F
sesos^M
cervella^F

胃
tripe
Kaldaune^F
tripes^F
tripa^F
trippa^F

猟鳥[猟獣]肉

game | Wild^N | gibier^M | caza^F | selvaggina^F

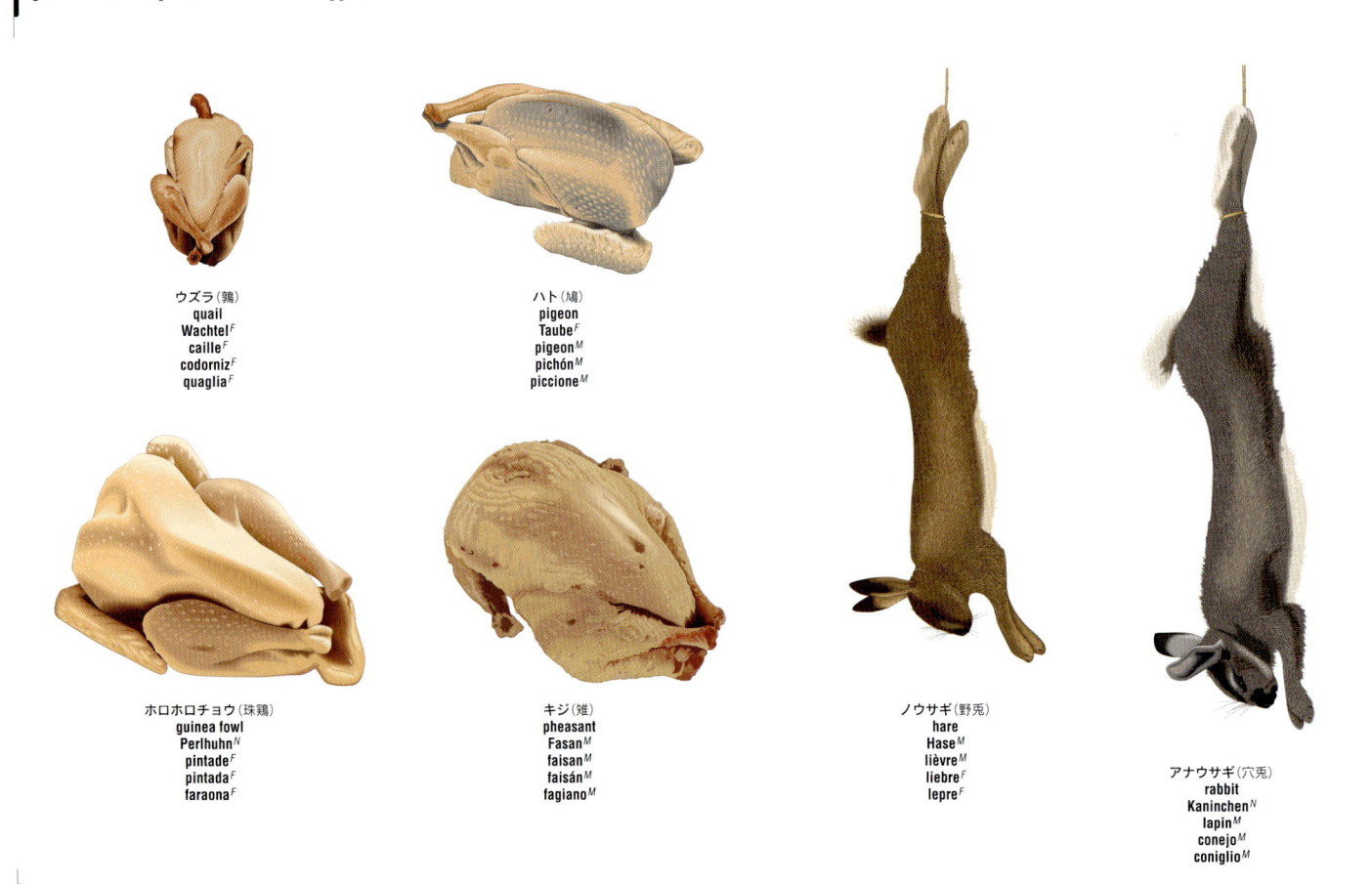

ウズラ(鶉)
quail
Wachtel^F
caille^F
codorniz^F
quaglia^F

ハト(鳩)
pigeon
Taube^F
pigeon^M
pichón^M
piccione^M

ホロホロチョウ(珠鶏)
guinea fowl
Perlhuhn^N
pintade^F
pintada^F
faraona^F

キジ(雉)
pheasant
Fasan^M
faisan^M
faisán^M
fagiano^M

ノウサギ(野兎)
hare
Hase^M
lièvre^M
liebre^F
lepre^F

アナウサギ(穴兎)
rabbit
Kaninchen^N
lapin^M
conejo^M
coniglio^M

食べ物 | FOOD
NAHRUNGSMITTEL | ALIMENTATION | PRODUCTOS ALIMENTARIOS | GENERI ALIMENTARI

鳥肉

poultry | Geflügel[N] | volaille[F] | aves[F] de corral[M] | volatili[M]

ニワトリ(鶏)
chicken
Huhn[N]
poulet[M]
pollo[F]
pollo[M]

カモ(鴨)
duck
Ente[F]
canard[M]
pato[M]
anatra[F]

去勢雄鶏(おんどり)／肥育鶏
capon
Kapaun[M]
chapon[M]
capón[M]
cappone[M]

シチメンチョウ(七面鳥)
turkey
Puter[M]
dinde[F]
pavo[M]
tacchino[M]

ガチョウ(鵞鳥)
goose
Gans[F]
oie[F]
oca[F]
oca[F]

卵

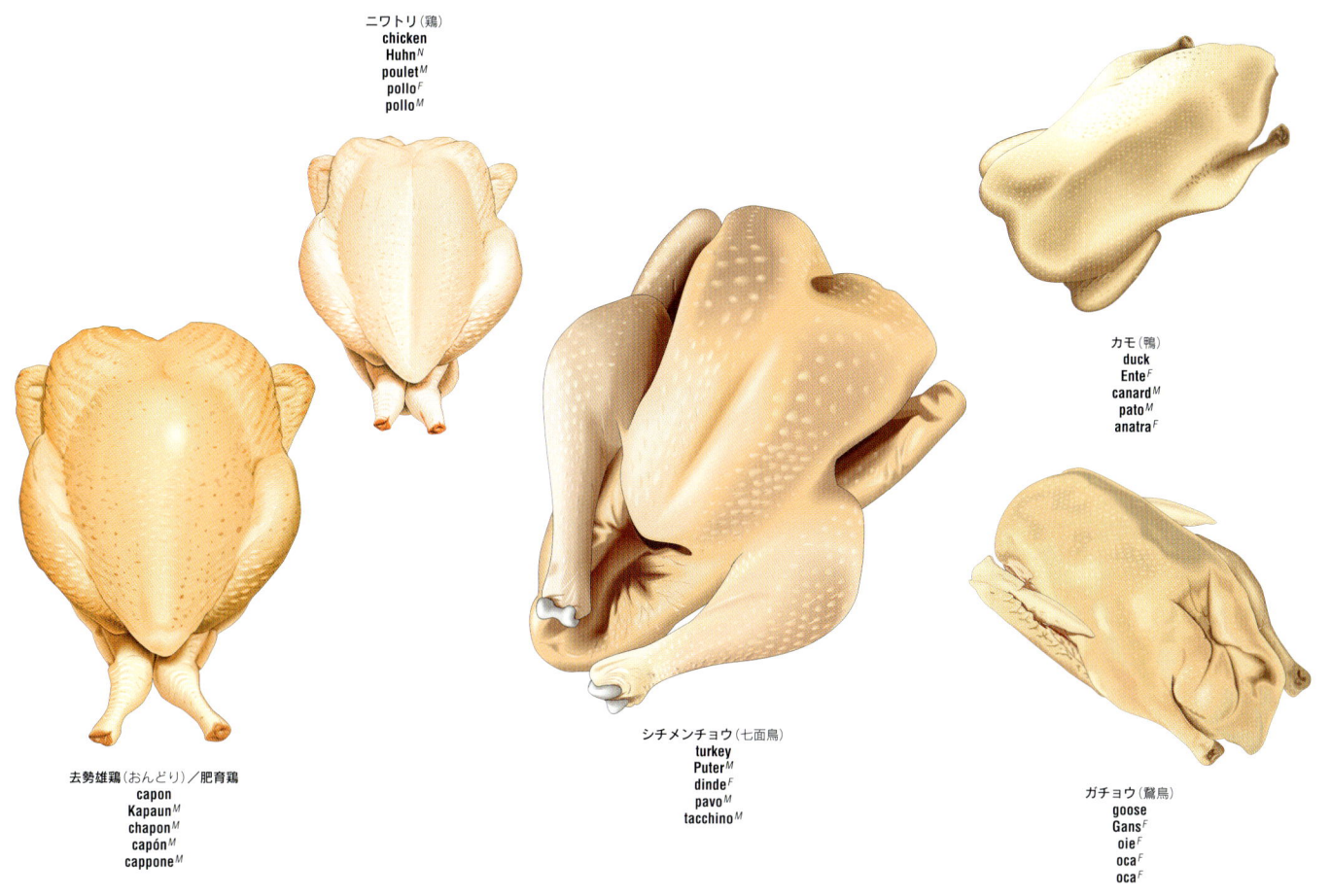

eggs | Eier[N] | œufs[M] | huevos[M] | uova[F]

ウズラ(鶉)の卵
quail egg
Wachtelei[N]
œuf[M] de caille[F]
huevo[F] de codorniz[F]
uovo[M] di quaglia[F]

キジ(雉)の卵
pheasant egg
Fasanenei[N]
œuf[M] de faisane[F]
huevo[M] de faisán[M]
uovo[M] di fagiano[M]

ガチョウ(鵞鳥)の卵
goose egg
Gänseei[N]
œuf[M] d'oie[F]
huevo[M] de oca[F]
uovo[M] di oca[F]

ダチョウ(駝鳥)の卵
ostrich egg
Straußenei[N]
œuf[M] d'autruche[F]
huevo[M] de avestruz[M]
uovo[M] di struzzo[M]

カモ(鴨)の卵
duck egg
Entenei[N]
œuf[M] de cane[F]
huevo[M] de pato[M]
uovo[M] di anatra[F]

鶏卵
hen egg
Hühnerei[N]
œuf[M] de poule[F]
huevo[M] de gallina[F]
uovo[M] di gallina[F]

食べ物と台所

食べ物 | FOOD
NAHRUNGSMITTEL | ALIMENTATION | PRODUCTOS ALIMENTARIOS | GENERI ALIMENTARI

食肉

meat | Fleisch[N] | viande[F] | carne[F] | carne[F]

日本語 | 英語 | ドイツ語 | フランス語 | スペイン語 | イタリア語

牛肉
cuts of beef
Rindfleisch[N]
découpes[F] de bœuf[M]
cortes[M] de vacuno[M]
tagli[M] di manzo[M]

ステーキ肉
steak
Steak[N]
bifteck[M]
bistec[M]
bistecca[F]

角切り肉
beef cubes
Rindfleischwürfel[M]
cubes[M] de bœuf[M]
carne[F] troceada de vacuno[F]
spezzatino[M]

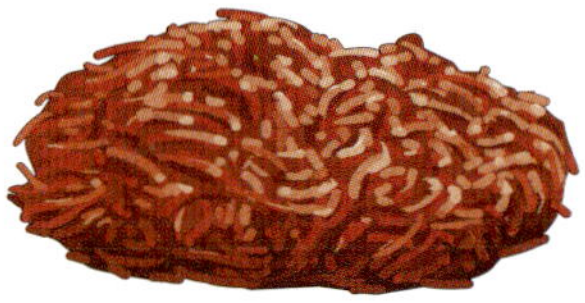

挽(ひ)き肉
ground beef
Rinderhackfleisch[N]
bœuf[M] haché
carne[F] picada
macinato[M]

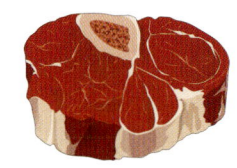

脛(すね)肉
shank
Hachse[F]
jarret[M]
morcillo[M]
ossobuco[M]

ヒレ肉／テンダーロイン・ロース(ト)
tenderloin roast
Rinderfilet[N]
filet[M] de bœuf[M]
lomo[M]
filetto[M]

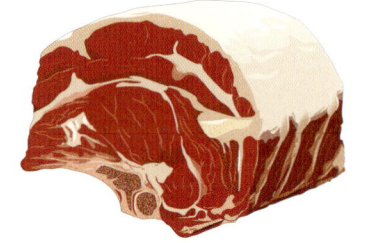

リブ・ロース(ト)
rib roast
hohe Rippe[F]
rôti[M] de côtes[F]
chuletón[M]
costate[F]

バック・リブ
back ribs
Querrippe[F]
côtes[F] levées de dos[M]
costillar[M]
costine[F]

子牛の肉
cuts of veal
Kalbfleisch[N]
découpes[F] de veau[M]
cortes[M] de ternera[F]
tagli[M] di vitello[M]

角切り肉
veal cubes
Kalbfleischwürfel[M]
cubes[M] de veau[M]
carne[F] troceada de ternera[F]
spezzatino[M]

挽(ひ)き肉
ground veal
Kalbshackfleisch[N]
veau[M] haché
carne[F] picada de vacuno[M]
macinato[M]

脛(すね)肉
shank
Hachse[F]
jarret[M]
paleta[F]
ossobuco[M]

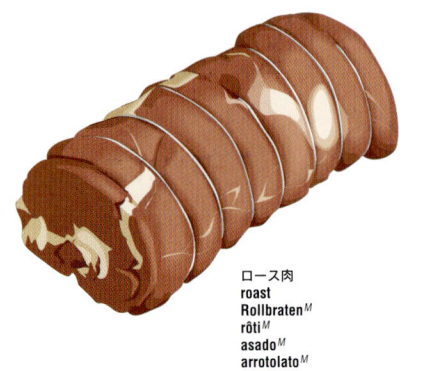

ロース肉
roast
Rollbraten[M]
rôti[M]
asado[M]
arrotolato[M]

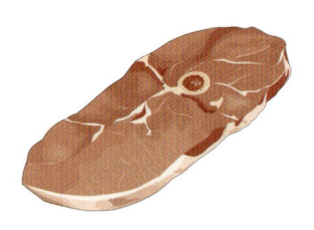

ステーキ肉
steak
Schnitzel[N]
bifteck[M]
bistec[M]
bistecca[F]

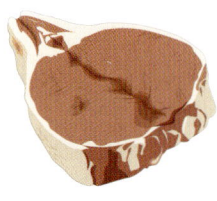

肋(あばら)肉／チョップ
chop
Kotelett[N]
côte[F]
chuleta[F]
braciola[F]

食べ物 | FOOD
NAHRUNGSMITTEL | ALIMENTATION | PRODUCTOS ALIMENTARIOS | GENERI ALIMENTARI

食肉

羊肉／ラム肉
cuts of lamb
Lammfleisch[N]
découpes[F] d'agneau[M]
cortes[M] de cordero[M]
tagli[M] di agnello[M]

肋(あばら)肉／チョップ
chop
Kotelett[N]
côte[F]
chuleta[F]
braciola[F]

挽(ひ)き肉
ground lamb
Lammhackfleisch[N]
agneau[M] haché
carne[F] picada de cordero[M]
macinato[M]

角切り肉
lamb cubes
Lammfleischwürfel[M]
cubes[M] d'agneau[M]
carne[F] troceada de cordero[M]
spezzatino[M]

ロース肉
roast
Braten[M]
rôti[M]
pierna[F] de cordero[M]
arrosto[M]

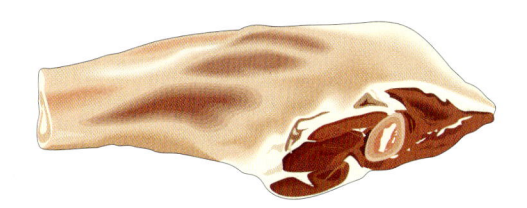

脛(すね)肉
shank
Hachse[F]
jarret[M]
paletilla[F]
stinco[M]

豚肉
cuts of pork
Schweinefleisch[N]
découpes[F] de porc[M]
cortes[M] de cerdo[M]
tagli[M] di maiale[M]

スペアリブ
spareribs
Spareribs/Schälrippchen[N]
travers[M]
costillar[M]
costolette[F]

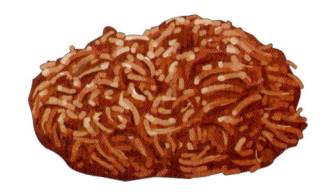

挽(ひ)き肉
ground pork
Schweinehackfleisch[N]
porc[M] haché
carne[F] picada de cerdo[M]
macinato[M]

足肉
hock
Eisbein[N]
jarret[M]
codillo[M]
piedino[M]

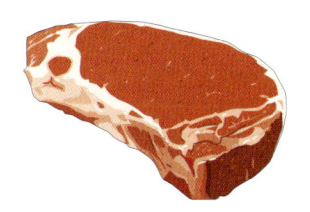

ロイン・チョップ
loin chop
Kotelett[N]
côtelette[F]
chuleta[F]
lonza[F]

スモーク・ハム
smoked ham
Räucherschinken[M]
jambon[M] fumé
jamón[M] ahumado
prosciutto[M] affumicato

ロース肉
roast
Braten[M]
rôti[M]
asado[M] de cerdo[M]
arrosto[M]

食べ物と台所

215

食べ物 | FOOD
NAHRUNGSMITTEL | ALIMENTATION | PRODUCTOS ALIMENTARIOS | GENERI ALIMENTARI

調製食品

日本語 | 英語 | ドイツ語 | フランス語 | スペイン語 | イタリア語

delicatessen | Spezialitäten^F | charcuterie^F | charcutería^F | gastronomia^F

食べ物と台所

リエット
rillettes
Rillettes^F
rillettes^F
chicharrones^F
ciccioli^M

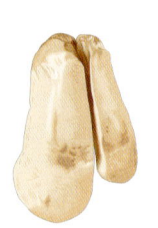

フォア・グラ
foie gras
Stopfleber^F
foie^M gras
foie gras
foie-gras^M

プロシウット
prosciutto
roher Schinken^M
prosciutto^M
jamón^M serrano
prosciutto^M

キールバーサ
kielbasa sausage
Kielbasa-Wurst^F
saucisson^M kielbasa
salchicha^F kielbasa
salsiccia^F kielbasa

モルタデッラ
mortadella
Mortadella
mortadelle^F
mortadela
mortadella^F

ブラッド・ソーセージ
blood sausage
Blutwurst^F
boudin^M
morcilla^F
sanguinaccio^M

チョリソ
chorizo
Chorizo-Wurst^F
chorizo^M
chorizo^M
chorizo^M

ペパローニ
pepperoni
Pepperoniwurst^F
pepperoni^M
pepperoni^M
salsiccia^F piccante

ジェノバ・サラミ
Genoa salami
grobe Salami^F
salami^M de Gênes
salami^M de Génova
salame^M di Genova

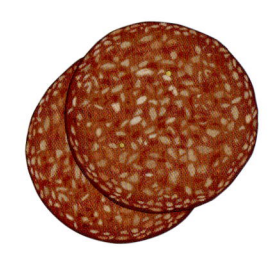

ジャーマン・サラミ
German salami
feine Salami^F
salami^M allemand
salami^M alemán
salame^M tedesco

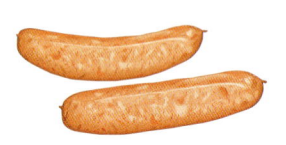

トゥールーズ・ソーセージ
Toulouse sausage
Toulouser Wurst^F
saucisse^F de Toulouse
salchicha^F de Toulouse
salame^M di Tolosa

メルゲーズ
merguez sausage
Merguez-Wurst^F
merguez^F
salchicha^F merguez
merguez^F

アンドゥイエット
andouillette
Kuttelwurst^F
andouillette^F
andouillete^F
salsiccia^F di trippa^F

チポラータ・ソーセージ
chipolata sausage
Bratwurst^F
chipolata^F
salchicha^F chipolata
salsiccia^F alle cipolle^F

フランクフルト・ソーセージ
frankfurter
Frankfurter Würstchen^N
saucisse^F de Francfort
salchicha^F de Frankfurt
salsiccia^F di Francoforte

パンチェッタ
pancetta
Bauchspeck^M
pancetta^F
panceta^M
pancetta^F

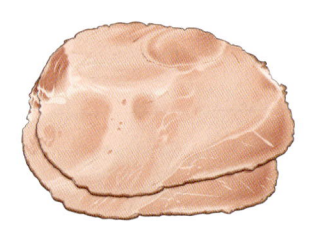

加熱ハム
cooked ham
gekochter Schinken^M
jambon^M cuit
jamón^M de York
prosciutto^M cotto

アメリカン・ベーコン
American bacon
amerikanischer Bacon^M
bacon^M américain
bacón^M americano
bacon^M americano

カナディアン・ベーコン
Canadian bacon
kanadischer Bacon^M
bacon^M canadien
bacón^M canadiense
bacon^M canadese

216

食べ物 | FOOD
NAHRUNGSMITTEL | ALIMENTATION | PRODUCTOS ALIMENTARIOS | GENERI ALIMENTARI

軟体動物

mollusks; *molluscs* | Mollusken[F] | mollusques[F] | moluscos[M] | molluschi[M]

タコ（蛸）
octopus
Krake[F]
pieuvre[F]
pulpo[M]
polpo[M]

コウイカ（甲烏賊）
cuttlefish
Tintenfisch[M]
seiche[F]
sepia[F]
seppia[F]

イカ（烏賊）
squid
Kalmar[M]
calmar[M]
calamar[M]
calamaro[M]

イタヤガイ（板屋貝）
scallop
Kammmuschel[F]
pétoncle[M]
venera[F]
pettine[M]

ホンビノスガイ（貝）
hard-shell clam
Kreuzmuster[N]-Teppichmuschel[F]
palourde[F]
almeja[F]
tartufo[M] di mare[M]

オオノガイ（大野貝）
soft shell clam
Klaffmuschel[F]
mye[F]
coquina[F]
vongola[F] molle

アワビ（鮑）
abalone
Meerohr[N]
ormeau[M]
oreja[F] de mar[M]
orecchia[F] di mare[M]

ホタテガイ（帆立貝）
great scallop
Jakobsmuschel[F]
coquille[F] Saint-Jacques
vieira[F]
capasanta[F]

エスカルゴ
snail
Schnecke[F]
escargot[M]
caracol[M] terrestre
chiocciola[F]

カサガイ（笠貝）
limpet
Napfschnecke[F]
patelle[F]
lapa[F]
patella[F]

ヨーロッパ・タマキビガイ（玉黍貝）
common periwinkle
Strandschnecke[F]
bigorneau[M]
bígaro
littorina[F]

ハマグリ（蛤）
clam
Venusmuschel[F]
praire[F]
almeja[F]
vongola[F]

ザルガイ（笊貝）
cockle
Herzmuschel[F]
coque[F]
berberecho[M]
cardio[M]

マテガイ（馬刀貝）
razor clam
Messermuschel[F]
couteau[M]
navaja[F]
cannolicchio[M]

カキ（牡蠣）
flat oyster
Auster[F]
huître[F] plate
ostra[F]
ostrica[F]

カキ（牡蠣）
cupped Pacific oyster
Auster[F]
huître[F] creuse du Pacifique[M]
ostra[F]
ostrica[F]

ムールガイ（貝）／イガイ（胎貝）
blue mussel
Miesmuschel[F]
moule[F]
mejillón[M]
mitilo[M]

エゾバイ（蝦夷貝）／ヨーロッパバイ（貝）
whelk
Wellhornschnecke[F]
buccin[M]
buccino[M]
buccino[M]

食べ物と台所

217

食べ物 | FOOD
NAHRUNGSMITTEL | ALIMENTATION | PRODUCTOS ALIMENTARIOS | GENERI ALIMENTARI

日本語 | 英語 | ドイツ語 | フランス語 | スペイン語 | イタリア語

甲殻類

crustaceans | Krebstiere[N] | crustacés[M] | crustáceo[M] | crostacei[M]

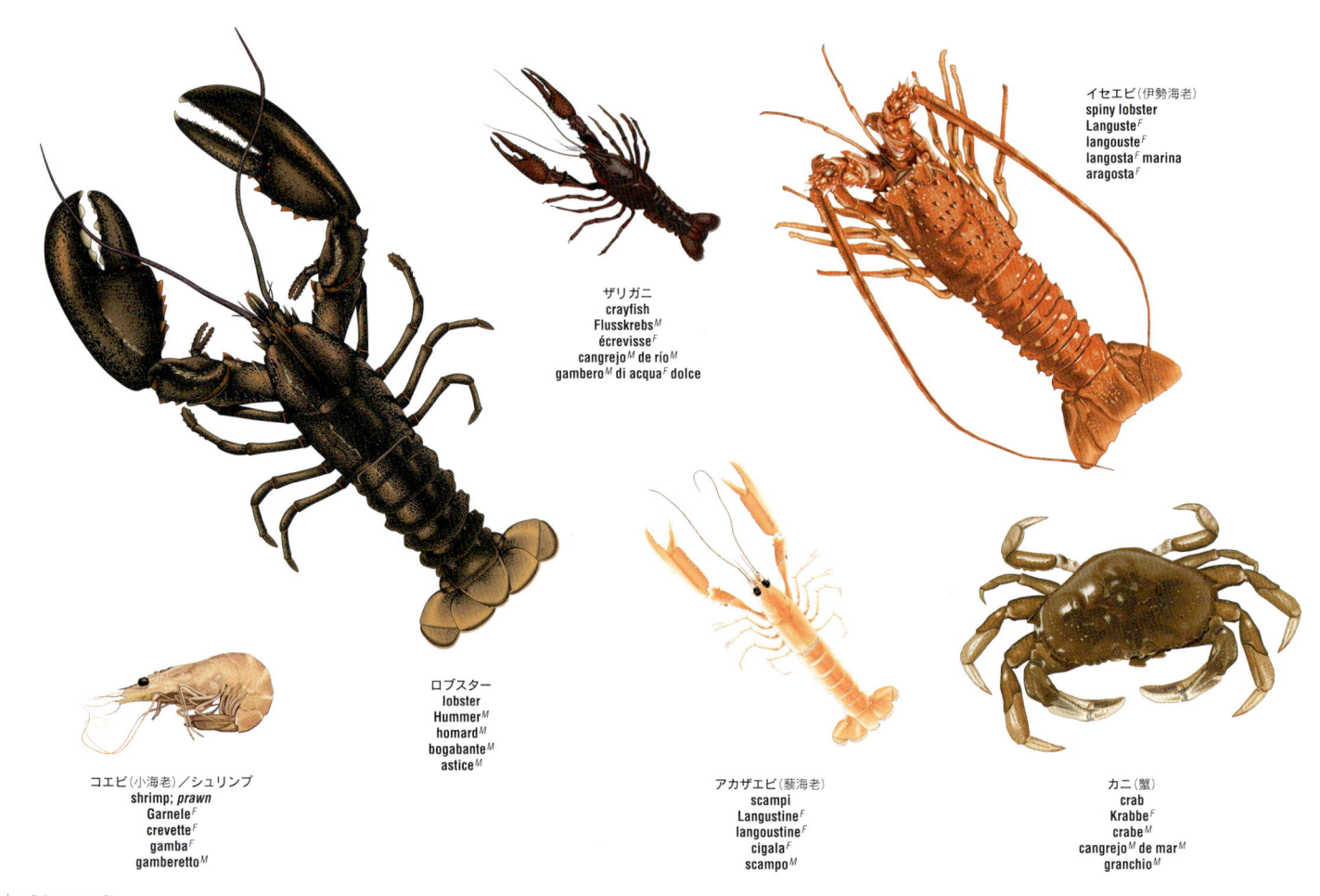

イセエビ（伊勢海老）
spiny lobster
Languste[F]
langouste[F]
langosta[F] marina
aragosta[F]

ザリガニ
crayfish
Flusskrebs[M]
écrevisse[F]
cangrejo[M] de río[M]
gambero[M] di acqua[F] dolce

ロブスター
lobster
Hummer[M]
homard[M]
bogabante[M]
astice[M]

コエビ（小海老）／シュリンプ
shrimp; prawn
Garnele[F]
crevette[F]
gamba[F]
gamberetto[M]

アカザエビ（藜海老）
scampi
Langustine[F]
langoustine[F]
cigala[F]
scampo[M]

カニ（蟹）
crab
Krabbe[F]
crabe[M]
cangrejo[M] de mar[M]
granchio[M]

軟骨魚

cartilaginous fishes | Knorpelfische[M] | poissons[M] cartilagineux | pescado[M] cartilaginoso | pesci[M] cartilaginei

トラザメ（虎鮫）
larger spotted dogfish
groß gefleckter Katzenhai[M]
grande roussette[F]
alitán[M]
gattuccio[M] stellato

ガンギエイ（雁木えい）
skate
Rochen[M]
raie[F]
raya[F]
razza[F]

ホシザメ（星鮫）
smooth hound
Hundshai[M]
émissole[F]
musola[F]
palombo[M] liscio

チョウザメ（蝶鮫）
sturgeon
Stör[M]
esturgeon[M]
esturión[M]
storione[M]

218

食べ物 | FOOD
NAHRUNGSMITTEL | ALIMENTATION | PRODUCTOS ALIMENTARIOS | GENERI ALIMENTARI

硬骨魚

bony fishes | Knochenfische^M | poissons^M osseux | pescado^M óseo | pesci^M ossei

アンチョビー／カタクチイワシ（片口鰯）
anchovy
Sardelle^F
anchois^M
anchoa^F
acciuga^F

イワシ（鰯）
sardine
Sardine^F
sardine^F
sardina^M
sardina^F

ニシン（鰊）
herring
Hering^M
hareng^M
arenque^M
aringa^F

キュウリウオ（胡瓜魚）
smelt
Stint^M
éperlan^M
eperlano^M
sperlano^M

タイ（鯛）
sea bream
Goldbrasse^F
dorade^F
dorada^F
orata^F

ヒメジ（非売知）
goatfish
rote Meerbarbe^F
rouget^M barbet^M
salmonete^M
triglia^F

タイセイヨウサバ（大西洋鯖）
mackerel
Makrele^F
maquereau^M
caballa^F
sgombro^M

ウナギ（鰻）
eel
Aal^M
anguille^F
anguila^F
anguilla^F

ホウボウ（魴ほう）
gurnard
Knurrhahn^M
grondin^M
rubio^M
pesce^M cappone^M

ヤツメウナギ（八つ目鰻）
lamprey
Meerneunauge^N
lamproie^F
lamprea^F
lampreda^F

メカジキ（目梶木）
swordfish
Schwertfisch^M
espadon^M
pez^M espada
pesce^M spada^F

食べ物 | FOOD
NAHRUNGSMITTEL | ALIMENTATION | PRODUCTOS ALIMENTARIOS | GENERI ALIMENTARI

硬骨魚

日本語 | 英語 | ドイツ語 | フランス語 | スペイン語 | イタリア語

バス
bass
Barsch^M
perche^F truitée
róbalo^M
persico^M trota^F

ボラ（鯔鯡）
mullet
Meeräsche^F
mulet^M
mújol^M
cefalo^M

コイ（鯉）
carp
Karpfen^M
carpe^F
carpa^F
carpa^F

パーチ
perch
Flussbarsch^M
perche^F
perca^F
persico^M

カワニシン（河鰊）
shad
Alse^F
alose^F
sábalo^M
alosa^F

カワカマス（河かます）
pike
Hecht^M
brochet^M
lucio^M
luccio^M

ホタルジャコ（蛍雑喉）
pike perch
Zander^M
sandre^M
lucioperca^M
lucioperca^M

アミキリ（網切）
bluefish
Blaufisch^M
tassergal^M
anjova^F
ballerino^M

スズキ（鱸）
sea bass
Seebarsch^M
bar^M commun
lubina^F
branzino^M

アンコウ（鮟鱇）
monkfish
Seeteufel^M
baudroie^F
rape^M
pesce^M rospo^M

マグロ（鮪）
tuna
Thunfisch^M
thon^M
atún^M
tonno^M

食べ物 | FOOD
NAHRUNGSMITTEL | ALIMENTATION | PRODUCTOS ALIMENTARIOS | GENERI ALIMENTARI

硬骨魚

メバル(目張)
redfish
Rotbarsch^M
sébaste^M
gallineta^F
salmone^M rosso

ホワイティング
whiting
Weißfisch^M
merlan^M
pescadilla^F
merlano^M

モンツキダラ(紋付鱈)
haddock
Schellfisch^M
églefin^M
abadejo^M
eglefino^M

タラ(鱈)
black pollock
Seelachs^M
lieu^M noir
merluza^F
merlano^M nero

タイセイヨウダラ(大西洋鱈)
Atlantic cod
atlantischer Kabeljau^M
morue^F de l'Atlantique^M
bacalao^M del Atlántico^M
merluzzo^M dell'Atlantico^M

マス(鱒)
trout
Forelle^F
truite^F
trucha^F
trota^F

タイヘイヨウサケ(太平洋鮭)
Pacific salmon
pazifischer Lachs^M
saumon^M du Pacifique^M
salmón^M del Pacífico^M
salmone^M del Pacifico^M

タイセイヨウサケ(大西洋鮭)
Atlantic salmon
atlantischer Lachs^M
saumon^M de l'Atlantique^M
salmón^M del Atlántico^M
salmone^M dell'Atlantico^M

カワマス(河鱒)
brook trout
Bachsaibling^M
omble^M de fontaine^F
salvelino^M
salmerino^M di fontana^F

マトウダイ(的鯛)
John dory
Heringskönig^M
saint-pierre^M
pez^M de San Pedro
pesce^M San Pietro

オヒョウ(大鮃)
halibut
Heilbutt^M
flétan^M
halibut^M
ippoglosso^M

ヒラメ(鮃)
turbot
Steinbutt^M
turbot^M
rodaballo^M
rombo^M

カレイ(鰈)
common plaice
Flunder^F
plie^F commune
platija^F
passera^F di mare^M

シタビラメ(舌鮃)
sole
Scholle^F
sole^F
lenguado^M
sogliola^F

食べ物と台所

221

台所 | KITCHEN
KÜCHE | CUISINE | COCINA | CUCINA

包装
packaging | Verpackungen^F | emballage^M | envases^M | confezioni^F

日本語 | 英語 | ドイツ語 | フランス語 | スペイン語 | イタリア語

食べ物と台所

パウチ袋
pouch
Beutel^M
sachet^M
bolsa^F
sacchetto^M

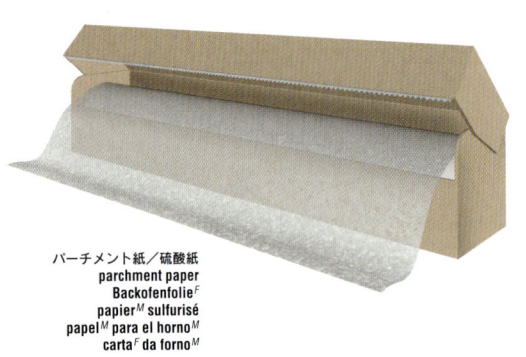

バーチメント紙／硫酸紙
parchment paper
Backofenfolie^F
papier^M sulfurisé
papel^M para el horno^M
carta^F da forno^M

アルミホイル
aluminum foil
Aluminiumfolie^F
papier^M aluminium
papel^M de aluminio^M
pellicola^F d'alluminio^M

ワックス・ペーパー
waxed paper
Wachspapier^N
papier^M paraffiné
papel^M encerado
carta^F cerata

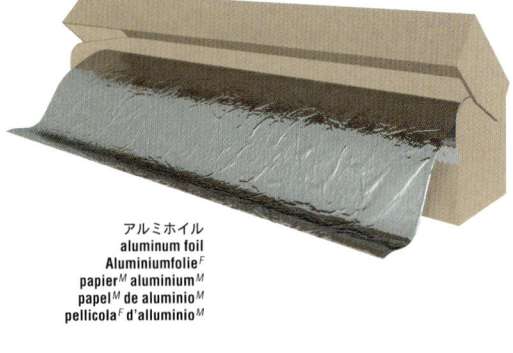

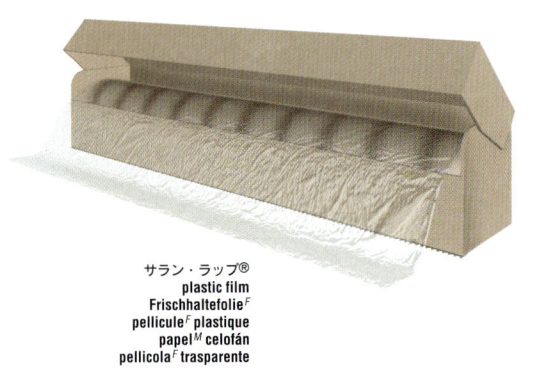

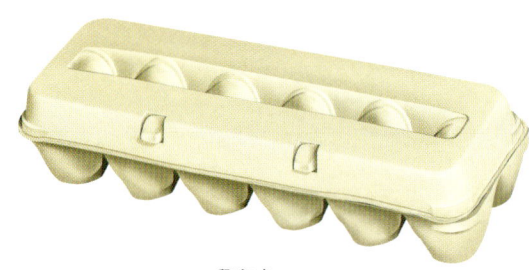

サラン・ラップ®
plastic film
Frischhaltefolie^F
pellicule^F plastique
papel^M celofán
pellicola^F trasparente

フリーザー・バッグ
freezer bag
Gefrierbeutel^M
sac^M de congélation^F
bolsa^F para congelador^M
sacchetto^M per freezer^M

卵パック
egg carton
Eierkarton^M
boîte^F à œufs^M
cajas^F de cartón^M para huevos^M
confezione^F in cartone^M per uova^F

ネット
mesh bag
Netz^N
sac^M-filet^M
bolsa^F de malla^F
rete^F per alimenti^M

キャニスター
canisters
Vorratsdosen^F
boîtes^F alimentaires
botes^M herméticos
barattoli^M

食品トレー
food tray
Schale^F
barquette^F
barqueta^F
vaschetta^F per alimenti^M

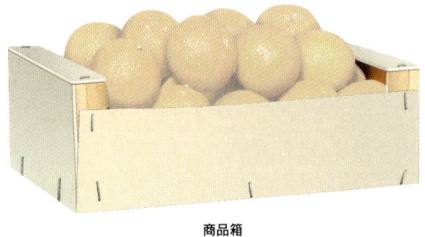

商品箱
small crate
Kiste^F
caissette^F
caja^F
cassetta^F

木箱
small open crate
Holzkiste^F
cageot^M
caja^F abierta
cassetta^F aperta

222

台所 | KITCHEN
KÜCHE | CUISINE | COCINA | CUCINA

包装

食べ物と台所

ねじ蓋（ふた）
screw cap
Schraubverschluss
capsule^F à vis
tapón^M de rosca^F
tappo^M a vite^F

プル・タブ
pull tab
Dosenöffner^M
onglet^M
tirador^M
anello^M a strappo^M

マルチパック
multipack
Multipack^N
pack^M
multipack^M
confezione^F multipla

ガラス瓶
glass bottle
Glasflasche^F
bouteille^F en verre^M
botella^F de vidrio^M
bottiglia^F di vetro^M

缶詰缶
food can
Konservendose^F
boîte^F de conserve^F
lata^F de conserva^F
latta^F per alimenti^M

飲料缶
beverage can
Getränkedose^F
cannette^F
lata^F
lattina^F

ヒート・シールしたフィルム
heat-sealed film
heißversiegelte Folie^F
opercule^M thermoscellé
película^F termosaldada
pellicola^F sigillata a caldo^M

ストロー
straw
Strohhalm^M
paille^F
pajita^F
cannuccia^F

フィルム包装
package
Packung^F
paquet^M
paquete^M
pacchetto^M

カップ
cup
Becher^M
pot^M
copa^F
vasetto^M

ブリック・パック
drink box
Trinkpackung^F
briquette^F
brick^M pequeño
brick^M

チューブ
tube
Tube^F
tube^M
tubo^M
tubetto^M

ゲーブルトップ
gabletop
Giebel^M
pignon^M
cierre^M en relieve^M
chiusura^F in rilievo^M

ミルク［クリーム］カップ
milk/cream cup
Milch-/Sahnebecher^M
godet^M de lait^M/crème^F
miniporción^F leche^F/nata^F
coppetta^F per latte^M/panna^F

バター・カップ
butter cup
Butterdose^F
godet^M de beurre^M
terrina^F para mantequilla^F
vaschetta^F per burro^M

ブリック・パック
brick carton
Getränkekarton^M
brique^F
brick^M
brick^M a tappo^M

チーズ箱
cheese box
Käseschachtel^F
boîte^F à fromage^M
caja^F para queso^M
scatola^F per formaggio^M

小型紙パック
small carton
Kleiner Getränkekarton^M
berlingot^M
cartón^M pequeño
cartone^M piccolo

紙パック
carton
Getränkekarton^M
carton^M
cartón^M
cartone^M

223

台所 | KITCHEN
KÜCHE | CUISINE | COCINA | CUCINA

台所

kitchen | Küche[F] | cuisine[F] | cocina[F] | cucina[F]

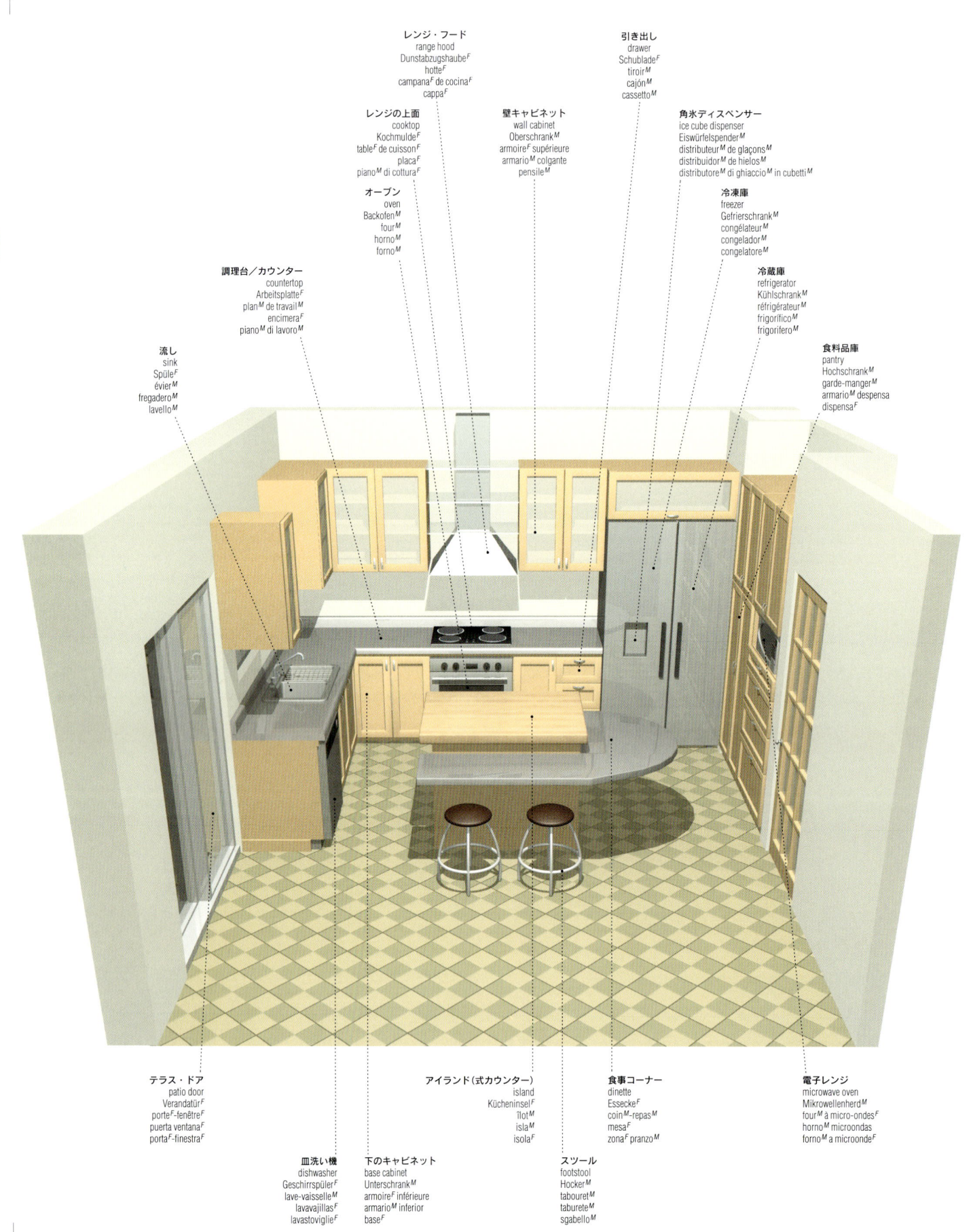

日本語 | 英語 | ドイツ語 | フランス語 | スペイン語 | イタリア語

食べ物と台所

レンジ・フード
range hood
Dunstabzugshaube[F]
hotte[F]
campana[F] de cocina[F]
cappa[F]

引き出し
drawer
Schublade[F]
tiroir[M]
cajón[M]
cassetto[M]

レンジの上面
cooktop
Kochmulde[F]
table[F] de cuisson[F]
placa[F]
piano[M] di cottura[F]

壁キャビネット
wall cabinet
Oberschrank[M]
armoire[F] supérieure
armario[M] colgante
pensile[M]

角氷ディスペンサー
ice cube dispenser
Eiswürfelspender[M]
distributeur[M] de glaçons[M]
distribuidor[M] de hielos[M]
distributore[M] di ghiaccio[M] in cubetti[M]

オーブン
oven
Backofen[M]
four[M]
horno[M]
forno[M]

冷凍庫
freezer
Gefrierschrank[M]
congélateur[M]
congelador[M]
congelatore[M]

調理台／カウンター
countertop
Arbeitsplatte[F]
plan[M] de travail[M]
encimera[F]
piano[M] di lavoro[M]

冷蔵庫
refrigerator
Kühlschrank[M]
réfrigérateur[M]
frigorífico[M]
frigorifero[M]

流し
sink
Spüle[F]
évier[M]
fregadero[M]
lavello[M]

食料品庫
pantry
Hochschrank[M]
garde-manger[M]
armario[M] despensa
dispensa[F]

テラス・ドア
patio door
Verandatür[F]
porte[F]-fenêtre[F]
puerta ventana[F]
porta[F]-finestra[F]

皿洗い機
dishwasher
Geschirrspüler[M]
lave-vaisselle[M]
lavavajillas[F]
lavastoviglie[F]

下のキャビネット
base cabinet
Unterschrank[M]
armoire[F] inférieure
armario[M] inferior
base[F]

アイランド(式カウンター)
island
Kücheninsel[F]
îlot[M]
isla[F]
isola[F]

食事コーナー
dinette
Essecke[F]
coin[M]-repas[M]
mesa[F]
zona[F] pranzo[M]

スツール
footstool
Hocker[M]
tabouret[M]
taburete[M]
sgabello[M]

電子レンジ
microwave oven
Mikrowellenherd[M]
four[M] à micro-ondes[M]
horno[M] microondas
forno[M] a microonde[F]

台所 | KITCHEN
KÜCHE | CUISINE | COCINA | CUCINA

ガラス器

glassware | Gläser[N] | verres[M] | cristalería[F] | cristalleria[F]

リキュール・グラス
liqueur glass
Likörglas[N]
verre[M] à liqueur[F]
copa[F] para licores[M]
bicchierino[M] da liquore[M]

ポート・グラス
port glass
Portweinglas[N]
verre[M] à porto[M]
copa[F] para oporto[M]
bicchiere[M] da porto[M]

スパークリング・ワイン・グラス
sparkling wine glass
Sektschale[F]
coupe[F] à mousseux[M]
copa[F] de champagne[M]
coppa[F] da spumante[M]

ブランデー・グラス
brandy snifter
Kognakschwenker[M]
verre[M] à cognac[M]
copa[F] para coñac[M]
bicchiere[M] da brandy[M]

アルザス・グラス
Alsace glass
Elsassglas[N]
verre[M] à vin[M] d'Alsace[F]
copa[F] para vino de Alsacia
bicchiere[M] da vino[M] alsaziano

バーガンディ・グラス
burgundy glass
Rotweinglas[N]
verre[M] à bourgogne[M]
copa[F] para vino de Borgoña
bicchiere[M] da Borgogna[M]

ボルドー・グラス
bordeaux glass
Bordeauxglas[N]
verre[M] à bordeaux[M]
copa[F] para vino de Burdeos
bicchiere[M] da Bordeaux[M]

白ワイン・グラス
white wine glass
Weißweinglas[N]
verre[M] à vin[M] blanc
copa[F] para vino[M] blanco
bicchiere[M] da vino[M] bianco

ウォーター・ゴブレット
water goblet
Wasserglas[N]
verre[M] à eau[F]
copa[F] de agua[F]
bicchiere[M] da acqua[F]

カクテル・グラス
cocktail glass
Cocktailglas[N]
verre[M] à cocktail[M]
copa[F] de cóctel[M]
calice[M] da cocktail[M]

ハイボール・グラス
highball glass; *tall tumbler*
Longdrinkglas[N]
verre[M] à gin[M]
vaso[M] largo
bicchiere[M] da bibita[F]

タンブラー・グラス
old-fashioned glass; *whisky tumbler*
Whiskyglas[M]
verre[M] à whisky[M]
vaso[M] corto
tumbler[M]

ビア・マグ
beer mug
Bierkrug[M]
chope[F] à bière[F]
jarra[M] de cerveza[F]
boccale[M] da birra[F]

シャンパン・グラス
champagne flute
Sektkelch[M]
flûte[F] à champagne[M]
copa[F] de flauta[F]
flûte[M]

小デカンタ
small decanter
kleine Karaffe[F]
carafon[M]
decantador[M]
caraffa[F]

デカンタ
decanter
Karaffe[F]
carafe[F]
garrafa[F]
bottiglia[F] da tavola[F]

食べ物と台所

台所 | KITCHEN
KÜCHE | CUISINE | COCINA | CUCINA

食器

dinnerware | Geschirr[N] | vaisselle[F] | vajilla[F] y servicio[M] de mesa[F] | vasellame[M] da tavola[F]

日本語 | 英語 | ドイツ語 | フランス語 | スペイン語 | イタリア語

食べ物と台所

デミタス
demitasse
Mokkatasse[F]
tasse[F] à café[M]
tacita[F] de café[M]
tazzina[F] da caffè[M]

カップ
cup
Tasse[F]
tasse[F] à thé[M]
taza[F]
tazza[F] da tè[M]

コーヒー・マグ
coffee mug
Becher[M]
chope[F] à café[M]
jarra[F] para café[M]
tazza[F] alta da caffè[M]

クリーム入れ／クリーマー
creamer; *cream jug*
Milchkännchen[N]
crémier[M]
jarrita[F] de leche[F]
bricco[M] del latte[M]

砂糖入れ／シュガー・ポット
sugar bowl
Zuckerdose[F]
sucrier[M]
azucarero[M]
zuccheriera[F]

塩入れ
salt shaker; *saltcellar*
Salzstreuer[M]
salière[F]
salero[M]
saliera[F]

胡椒（こしょう）入れ
pepper shaker; *pepperpot*
Pfefferstreuer[M]
poivrière[F]
pimentero[M]
pepaiola[F]

グレービー・ボート
gravy boat
Sauciere[F]
saucière[F]
salsera[F]
salsiera[F]

バター皿
butter dish
Butterdose[F]
beurrier[M]
mantequera[F]
burriera[F]

ラムカン皿
ramekin
Auflaufförmchen[N]
ramequin[M]
cuenco[M] de queso[M] blando
formina[F] da forno[M]

スープ皿
soup bowl
Suppenschale[F]
bol[M]
escudilla[F]
scodella[F]

縁付きスープ皿
rim soup bowl
Suppenteller[M]
assiette[F] creuse
plato[M] sopero
piatto[M] fondo

ディナー皿
dinner plate
flacher Teller[M]
assiette[F] plate
plato[M] llano
piatto[M] piano

サラダ皿
salad plate
Salatteller[M]
assiette[F] à salade[F]
plato[M] de postre[M]
piatto[M] frutta[F] / insalata[F]

パン皿
bread and butter plate
kleiner Teller[M]
assiette[F] à dessert[M]
platito[M] para el pan[M]
piattino[M] per pane[M] e burro[M]

ティーポット
teapot
Teekanne[F]
théière[F]
tetera[F]
teiera[F]

大皿
platter
Servierplatte[F]
plat[M] ovale
fuente[F] de servir
piatto[M] da portata[F]

野菜ボウル
vegetable bowl
Gemüseterrine[F]
légumier[M]
fuente[F] de verdura[F]
legumiera[F]

魚皿
fish platter
Fischplatte[F]
plat[M] à poisson[M]
fuente[F] para pescado[M]
piatto[M] per il pesce[M]

オードブル皿
hors d'oeuvre dish
Hors-d'Oeuvre-Schale[F]
ravier[M]
bandeja[F] para los entremeses[M]
antipastiera[F]

水差し
water pitcher; *water jug*
Wasserkrug[M]
pichet[M]
jarra[F] de agua[F]
caraffa[F]

サラダ・ボウル
salad bowl
Salatschüssel[F]
saladier[M]
ensaladera[F]
insalatiera[F]

サラダ盛り皿
salad dish
Salatschale[F]
bol[M] à salade[F]
bol[M] para ensalada[F]
coppetta[F] per l'insalata[F]

チューリン
soup tureen
Suppenterrine[F]
soupière[F]
sopera[F]
zuppiera[F]

226

台所 | KITCHEN
KÜCHE | CUISINE | COCINA | CUCINA

銀器

silverware | SilberbesteckN | couvertM | cuberteríaF | posateríaF

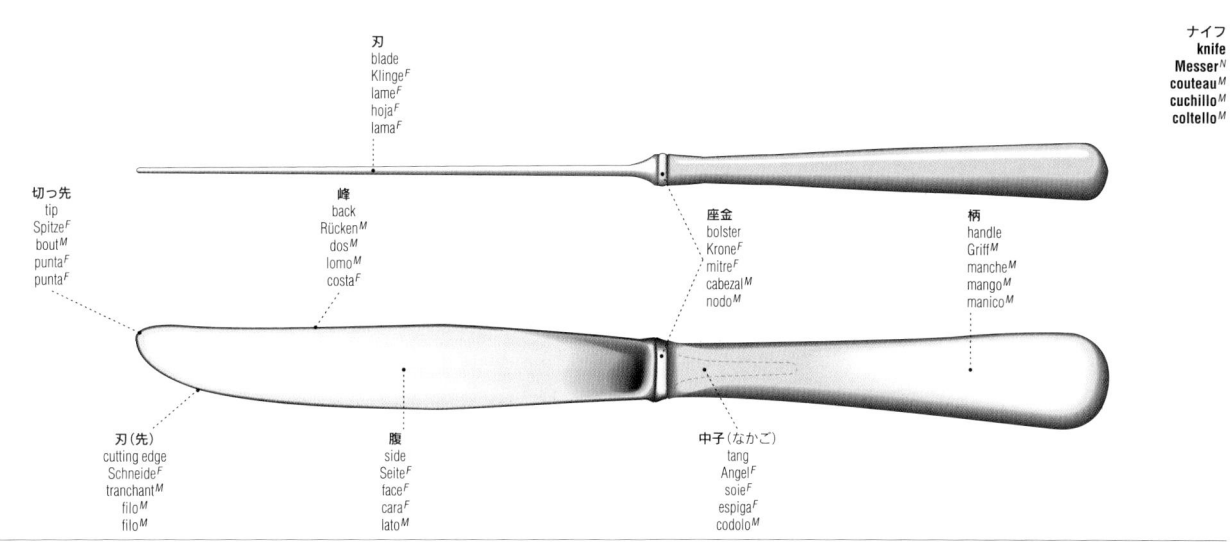

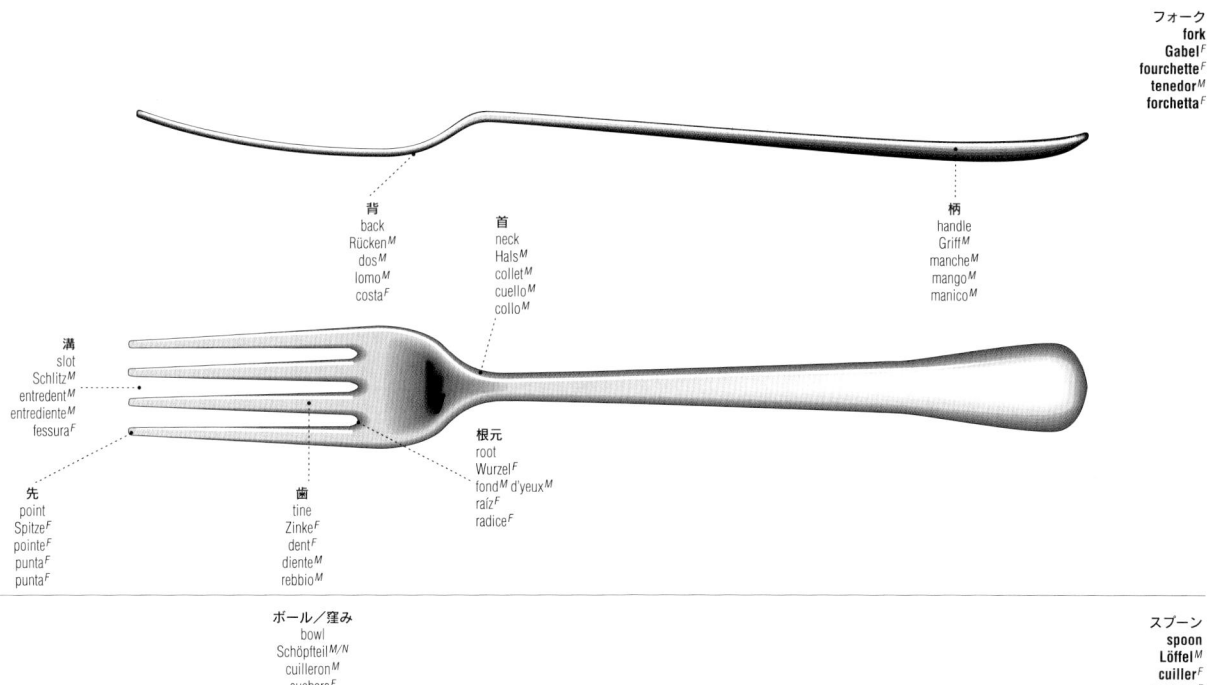

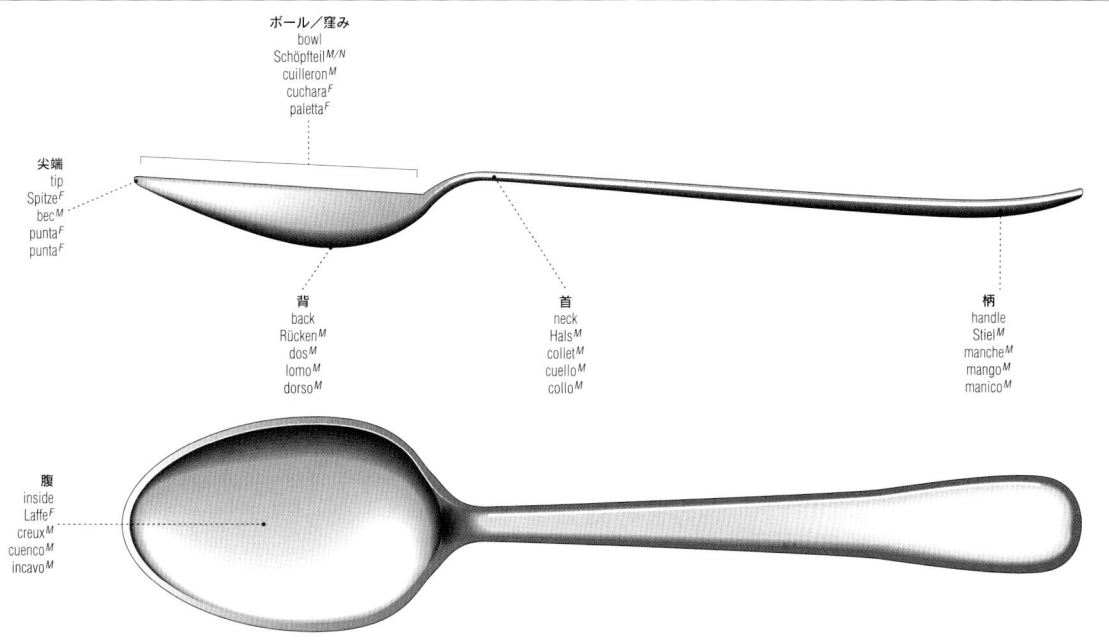

ナイフ
knife
MesserN
couteauM
cuchilloM
coltelloM

刃
blade
KlingeF
lameF
hojaF
lamaF

切っ先
tip
SpitzeF
boutM
puntaF
puntaF

峰
back
RückenM
dosM
lomoM
costaF

座金
bolster
KroneF
mitreF
cabezalM
nodoM

柄
handle
GriffM
mancheM
mangoM
manicoM

刃（先）
cutting edge
SchneideF
tranchantM
filoM
filoM

腹
side
SeiteF
faceF
caraF
latoM

中子（なかご）
tang
AngelF
soieF
espigaF
codoloM

フォーク
fork
GabelF
fourchetteF
tenedorM
forchettaF

背
back
RückenM
dosM
lomoM
costaF

首
neck
HalsM
colletM
cuelloM
colloM

柄
handle
GriffM
mancheM
mangoM
manicoM

溝
slot
SchlitzM
entredentM
entredienteM
fessuraF

根元
root
WurzelF
fondM d'yeuxM
raízF
radiceF

先
point
SpitzeF
pointeF
puntaF
puntaF

歯
tine
ZinkeF
dentF
dienteM
rebbioM

ボール／窪み
bowl
SchöpfteilM/N
cuilleronM
cucharaF
palettaF

スプーン
spoon
LöffelM
cuillerF
cucharaF
cucchiaioM

尖端
tip
SpitzeF
becM
puntaF
puntaF

背
back
RückenM
dosM
lomoM
dorsoM

首
neck
HalsM
colletM
cuelloM
colloM

柄
handle
StielM
mancheM
mangoM
manicoM

腹
inside
LaffeF
creuxM
cuencoM
incavoM

食べ物と台所

227

台所 | KITCHEN
KÜCHE | CUISINE | COCINA | CUCINA

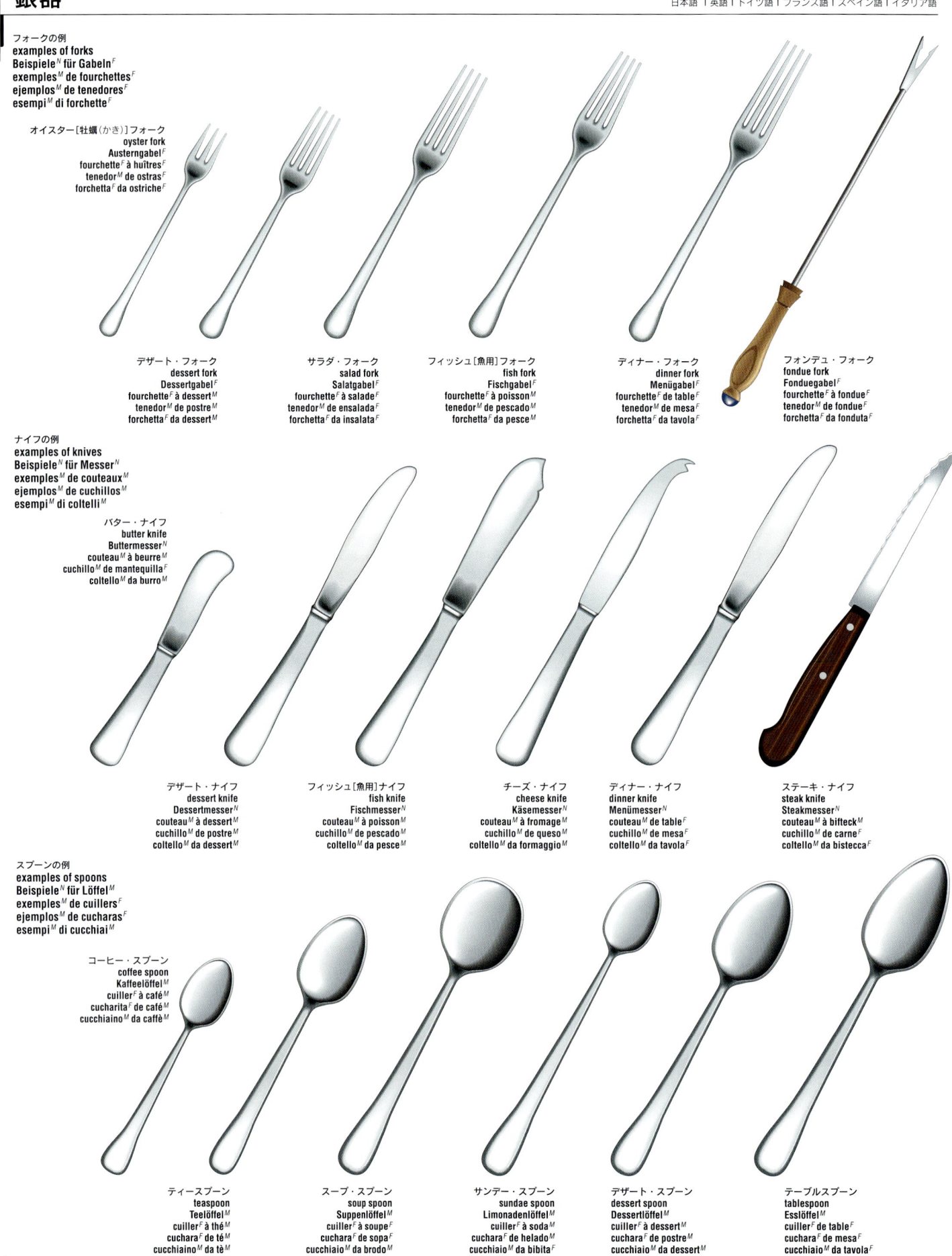

銀器

日本語 | 英語 | ドイツ語 | フランス語 | スペイン語 | イタリア語

フォークの例
examples of forks
Beispiele^N für Gabeln^F
exemples^M de fourchettes^F
ejemplos^M de tenedores^F
esempi^M di forchette^F

オイスター[牡蠣(かき)]フォーク
oyster fork
Austerngabel^F
fourchette^F à huîtres^F
tenedor^M de ostras^F
forchetta^F da ostriche^F

デザート・フォーク
dessert fork
Dessertgabel^F
fourchette^F à dessert^M
tenedor^M de postre^M
forchetta^F da dessert^M

サラダ・フォーク
salad fork
Salatgabel^F
fourchette^F à salade^F
tenedor^M de ensalada^F
forchetta^F da insalata^F

フィッシュ[魚用]フォーク
fish fork
Fischgabel^F
fourchette^F à poisson^M
tenedor^M de pescado^M
forchetta^F da pesce^M

ディナー・フォーク
dinner fork
Menügabel^F
fourchette^F de table^F
tenedor^M de mesa^F
forchetta^F da tavola^F

フォンデュ・フォーク
fondue fork
Fonduegabel^F
fourchette^F à fondue^F
tenedor^M de fondue^F
forchetta^F da fonduta^F

ナイフの例
examples of knives
Beispiele^N für Messer^N
exemples^M de couteaux^M
ejemplos^M de cuchillos^M
esempi^M di coltelli^M

バター・ナイフ
butter knife
Buttermesser^N
couteau^M à beurre^M
cuchillo^M de mantequilla^F
coltello^M da burro^M

デザート・ナイフ
dessert knife
Dessertmesser^N
couteau^M à dessert^M
cuchillo^M de postre^M
coltello^M da dessert^M

フィッシュ[魚用]ナイフ
fish knife
Fischmesser^N
couteau^M à poisson^M
cuchillo^M de pescado^M
coltello^M da pesce^M

チーズ・ナイフ
cheese knife
Käsemesser^N
couteau^M à fromage^M
cuchillo^M de queso^M
coltello^M da formaggio^M

ディナー・ナイフ
dinner knife
Menümesser^N
couteau^M de table^F
cuchillo^M de mesa^F
coltello^M da tavola^F

ステーキ・ナイフ
steak knife
Steakmesser^N
couteau^M à bifteck^M
cuchillo^M de carne^F
coltello^M da bistecca^F

スプーンの例
examples of spoons
Beispiele^N für Löffel^M
exemples^M de cuillers^F
ejemplos^M de cucharas^F
esempi^M di cucchiai^M

コーヒー・スプーン
coffee spoon
Kaffeelöffel^M
cuiller^F à café^M
cucharita^F de café^M
cucchiaino^M da caffè^M

ティースプーン
teaspoon
Teelöffel^M
cuiller^F à thé^M
cuchara^F de té^M
cucchiaino^M da tè^M

スープ・スプーン
soup spoon
Suppenlöffel^M
cuiller^F à soupe^F
cuchara^F de sopa^F
cucchiaio^M da brodo^M

サンデー・スプーン
sundae spoon
Limonadenlöffel^M
cuiller^F à soda^M
cuchara^F de helado^M
cucchiaio^M da bibita^F

デザート・スプーン
dessert spoon
Dessertlöffel^M
cuiller^F à dessert^M
cuchara^F de postre^M
cucchiaio^M da dessert^M

テーブルスプーン
tablespoon
Esslöffel^M
cuiller^F de table^F
cuchara^F de mesa^F
cucchiaio^M da tavola^F

台所 | KITCHEN
KÜCHE | CUISINE | COCINA | CUCINA

台所用品

kitchen utensils | Küchenutensilien[N] | ustensiles[M] de cuisine[F] | utensilios[M] de cocina[F] | utensili[M] da cucina[F]

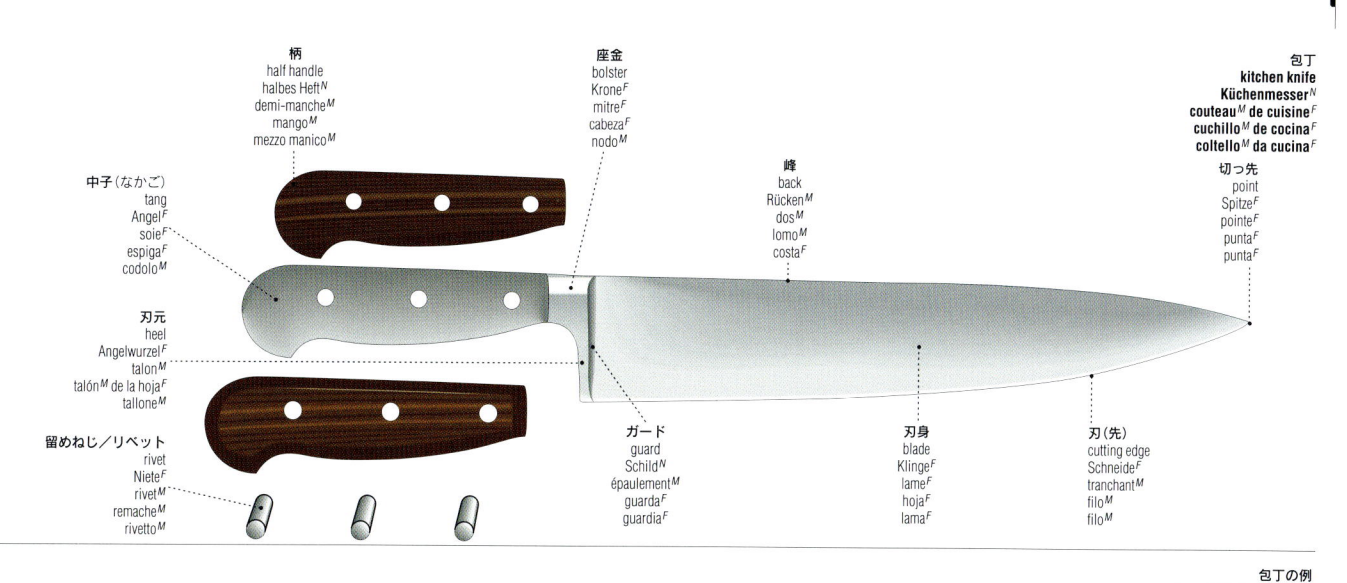

柄
half handle
halbes Heft[N]
demi-manche[M]
mango[M]
mezzo manico[M]

座金
bolster
Krone[F]
mitre[F]
cabeza[F]
nodo[M]

包丁
kitchen knife
Küchenmesser[N]
couteau[M] de cuisine[F]
cuchillo[M] de cocina[F]
coltello[M] da cucina[F]

中子（なかご）
tang
Angel[F]
soie[F]
espiga[F]
codolo[M]

峰
back
Rücken[M]
dos[M]
lomo[M]
costa[F]

切っ先
point
Spitze[F]
pointe[F]
punta[F]
punta[F]

刃元
heel
Angelwurzel[F]
talon[M]
talón[M] de la hoja[F]
tallone[M]

留めねじ／リベット
rivet
Niete[F]
rivet[M]
remache[M]
rivetto[M]

ガード
guard
Schild[N]
épaulement[M]
guarda[F]
guardia[F]

刃身
blade
Klinge[F]
lame[F]
hoja[F]
lama[F]

刃（先）
cutting edge
Schneide[F]
tranchant[M]
filo[M]
filo[M]

包丁の例
examples of kitchen knives
Beispiele[N] für Küchenmesser[N]
exemples[M] de couteaux[M] de cuisine[F]
ejemplos[M] de cuchillos[M] de cocina[F]
esempi[M] di coltelli[M] da cucina[F]

料理包丁
cook's knife
Kochmesser[N]
couteau[M] de chef[M]
cuchillo[M] de carnicero[M]
coltello[M] da cucina[F]

大包丁／骨切り包丁
cleaver
Küchenbeil[N]
couperet[M]
hacha[F] de cocinero[M]
mannaia[F]

パン切りナイフ［包丁］
bread knife
Brotmesser[N]
couteau[M] à pain[M]
cuchillo[M] de pan[M]
coltello[M] da pane[M]

ハム・ナイフ
ham knife
Schinkenmesser[N]
couteau[M] à jambon[M]
cuchillo[M] para jamón[M]
coltello[M] da prosciutto[M]

カービング・ナイフ／筋引き包丁
carving knife
Tranchiermesser[N]
couteau[M] à découper
cuchillo[M] de trinchar
trinciante[M]

身卸し包丁
filleting knife
Filiermesser[N]
couteau[M] à filets[M] de sole[F]
cuchillo[M] filetero
coltello[M] per affettare

果物ナイフ
paring knife
Schälmesser[N]
couteau[M] d'office[F]
cuchillo[M] de pelar
spelucchino[M]

カービング・フォーク
carving fork
Tranchiergabel[F]
fourchette[F] à découper
tenedor[M] de trinchar
forchettone[M]

棒やすり／やすり棒
sharpening steel
Wetzstahl[M]
fusil[M]
afilador[M]
acciaiolo[M]

ボーン・ナイフ
boning knife
Ausbeinmesser[N]
couteau[M] à désosser
cuchillo[M] para deshuesar
coltello[M] per disossare

砥石（といし）
sharpening stone
Wetzstein[M]
pierre[F] à affûter
piedra[F] de afilar
pietra[F] affilacoltelli

俎（まないた）
cutting board
Schneidbrett[N]
planche[F] à découper
tabla[F] de cortar
tagliere[M]

グレープフルーツ・ナイフ
grapefruit knife
Grapefruitmesser[N]
couteau[M] à pamplemousse[M]
cuchillo[M] para pomelos[M]
coltello[M] da pompelmo[M]

牡蠣（かき）ナイフ
oyster knife
Austernmesser[N]
couteau[M] à huîtres[F]
cuchillo[M] para ostras[F]
coltello[M] da ostriche[F]

ゼスター
zester
Zitronenschaber[M]
couteau[M] à zester
rallador[M]
sbuccialimoni[M]

皮むき器
peeler
Schäler[M]
éplucheur[M]
pelapatatas[M]
sbucciatore[M]

バター・カーラー
butter curler
Butterroller[M]
coquilleur[M] à beurre[M]
rizador[M] de mantequilla[F]
arricciaburro[M]

溝
groove
Saftrinne[F]
rainure[F]
ranura[F]
scanalatura[F]

台所 | KITCHEN
KÜCHE | CUISINE | COCINA | CUCINA

台所用品

日本語 | 英語 | ドイツ語 | フランス語 | スペイン語 | イタリア語

開ける
for opening
zum Öffnen[N]
pour ouvrir
utensilios[M] para abrir y descorchar
per aprire

缶切り
can opener; *tin opener*
Büchsenöffner[M]
ouvre-boîtes[M]
abrelatas[M]
apriscatole[M]

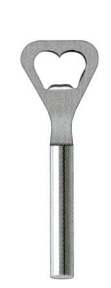

栓抜き
bottle opener
Flaschenöffner[M]
décapsuleur[M]
abrebotellas[M]
apribottiglie[M]

ソムリエ・ナイフ
wine waiter corkscrew
Kellnerbesteck[N]
tire-bouchon[M] de sommelier[M]
sacacorchos[M]
cavatappi[M] da cameriere[M]

レバー式コルク抜き
lever corkscrew
Hebel-Korkenzieher[M]
tire-bouchon[M] à levier[M]
sacacorchos[M] con brazos[M]
cavatappi[M] a leva[F]

つぶす・下ろす・搾る
for grinding and grating
zum Zerkleinern[N] und Zerreiben[N]
pour broyer et râper
para moler y rallar
per macinare e grattugiare

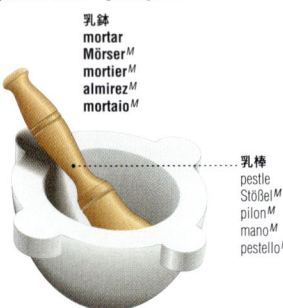

乳鉢
mortar
Mörser[M]
mortier[M]
almirez[M]
mortaio[M]

乳棒
pestle
Stößel[M]
pilon[M]
mano[M]
pestello[M]

肉挽(ひ)き器
meat grinder; *mincer*
Fleischwolf[M]
hachoir[M]
picadora[F] de carne[F]
tritacarne[M]

クルミ割り器
nutcracker
Nussknacker[M]
casse-noix[M]
cascanueces[M]
schiaccianoci[M]

ガーリック・プレス／にんにく搾り器
garlic press
Knoblauchpresse[F]
presse-ail[M]
triturador[M] de ajos[M]
spremiaglio[M]

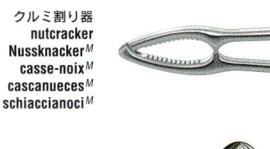

レモン搾り器
citrus juicer; *lemon squeezer*
Zitronenpresse[F]
presse-agrumes[M]
exprimidor[M]
spremiagrumi[M]

ナツメグ下ろし器
nutmeg grater
Muskatnussreibe[F]
râpe[F] à muscade[F]
rallador[M] de nuez[F] moscada
grattugia[F] per noce[F] moscata

チーズ下ろし器
grater
Reibe[F]
râpe[F]
rallador[M]
grattugia[F]

回転式チーズ下ろし器
rotary cheese grater
Käsereibe[F]
râpe[F] à fromage[M] cylindrique
rallador[M] cilíndrico de queso[M]
grattugiaformaggio[M]

プッシャー
pusher
Presshebel[M]
poussoir[M]
empujador[M]
pigiatore[M]

クランク
crank
Kurbel[F]
manivelle[F]
manivela[F]
levetta[F]

ドラム
drum
Trommel[F]
tambour[M]
tambor[M]
tamburo[M]

取っ手
handle
Griff[M]
poignée[F]
mango[M]
impugnatura[F]

パスタ・マシーン
pasta maker
Nudelmaschine[F]
machine[F] à faire les pâtes[F]
máquina[F] para hacer pasta[F] italiana
macchina[F] per fare la pasta[F]

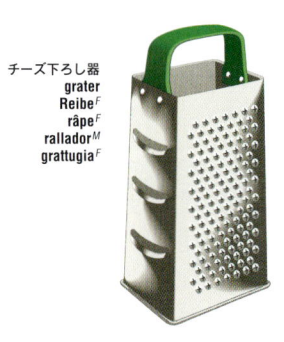

フード・ミル
food mill
Passiergerät[N]
moulin[M] à légumes[M]
pasaverduras[M]
passaverdure[M]

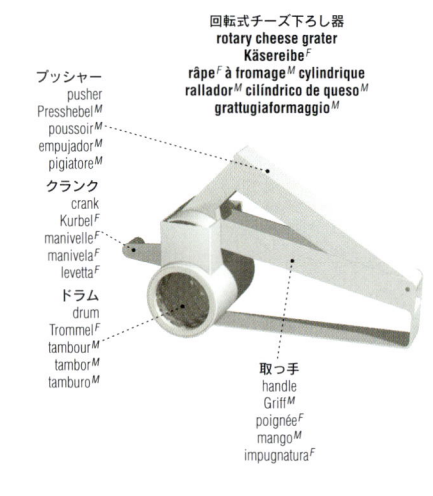

マンドリーヌ
mandoline
Küchenreibe[F]
mandoline[F]
mandolina[F]
affettaverdure[M]

230

台所 | KITCHEN
KÜCHE | CUISINE | COCINA | CUCINA

台所用品

計る
for measuring
zum Messen^N
pour mesurer
utensilios^M para medir
per misurare

計量スプーン
measuring spoons
Messlöffel^M
cuillers^F doseuses
cucharas^F dosificadoras
cucchiai^M dosatori

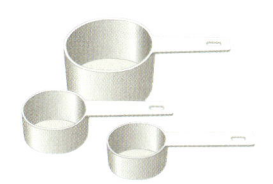

計量カップ
measuring cups
Messbecher^M
mesures^F
tazas^F medidoras
misurini^M

糖菓用温度計
candy thermometer
Einmachthermometer^N
thermomètre^M à sucre^M
termómetro^M de azúcar^M
termometro^M per zucchero^M

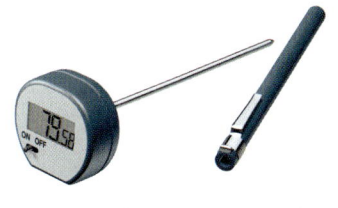

計量カップ
measuring cup
Maß^N
tasse^F à mesurer
jarra^F medidora
tazza^F graduata

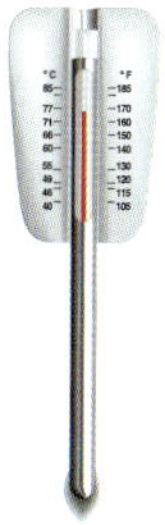

肉用温度計
meat thermometer
Fleischthermometer^N
thermomètre^M à viande^F
termómetro^M para carne^F
termometro^M per carne^F

オーブン用温度計
oven thermometer
Backofenthermometer^N
thermomètre^M de four^M
termómetro^M de horno^M
termometro^M del forno^M

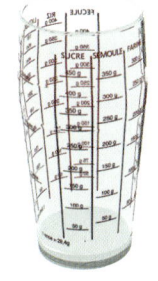

食品温度計
instant-read thermometer
digitales Bratenthermometer^N
thermomètre^M à mesure^F instantanée
termómetro^M de medida^F instantánea
termometro^M a lettura^F istantanea

食べ物と台所

計量ビーカー
measuring beaker
Messbecher^M
verre^M à mesurer
vaso^M medidor
recipiente^M graduato

キッチン・タイマー
kitchen timer
Küchenuhr^F
minuteur^M
minutero^M
contaminuti^M

エッグ・タイマー
egg timer
Eieruhr^F
sablier^M
reloj^M de arena^F
clessidra^F per uova^F alla coque

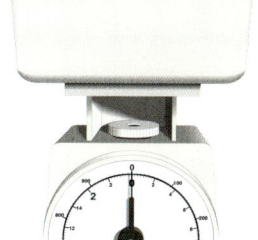

上皿秤
kitchen scale
Küchenwaage^F
balance^F de cuisine^F
báscula^F de cocina^F
bilancia^F da cucina^F

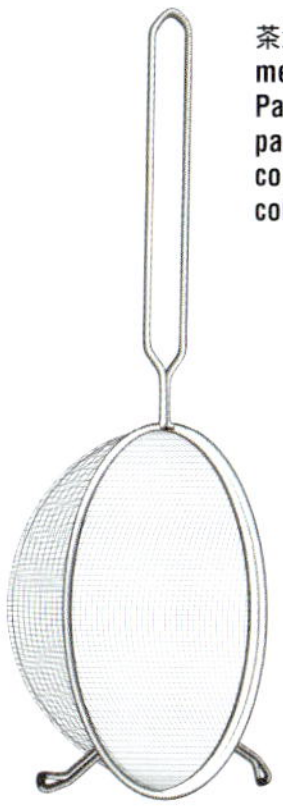

茶漉(こ)し
mesh strainer
Passiersieb^N
passoire^F fine
colador^M fino
colino^M

漉し布
muslin
Musselin^M
mousseline^F
muselina^F
mussolina^F

漉し器
chinois
Spitzsieb^N
chinois^M
chino^M
chinois^M

漉(こ)す・水気を切る
for straining and draining
zum Sieben^N und Abtropfen^N
pour passer et égoutter
coladores^M y escurridores^M
per scolare e filtrare

漏斗(じょうご)
funnel
Trichter^M
entonnoir^M
embudo^M
imbuto^M

水切り(用ざる)
colander
Seiher^M
passoire^F
escurridor^M
colapasta^M

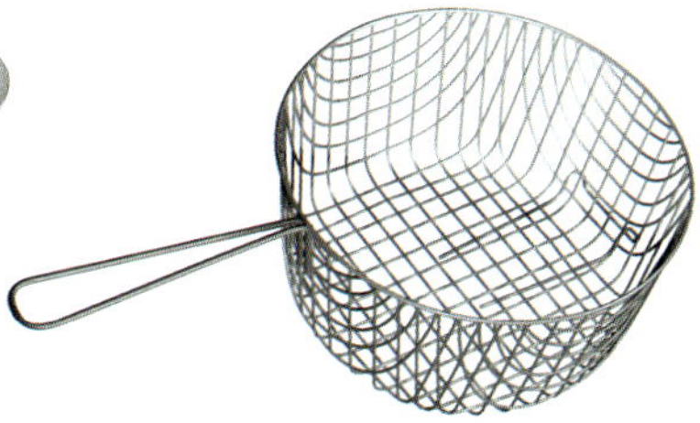

揚げ物用ざる
fry basket
Frittierkorb^M
panier^M à friture^F
cesta^F de freír
cestello^M per friggere

篩(ふるい)
sieve
Mehlsieb^N
tamis^M
tamiz^M
setaccio^M

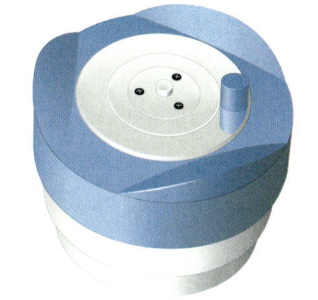

サラダ用水切り器
salad spinner
Salatschleuder^F
essoreuse^F à salade
secadora^F de ensalada
centrifuga^F scolainsalata

台所 | KITCHEN
KÜCHE | CUISINE | COCINA | CUCINA

台所用品

日本語 | 英語 | ドイツ語 | フランス語 | スペイン語 | イタリア語

製菓用具
baking utensils
Backgerät^N
pour la pâtisserie^F
utensilios^M para hornear
utensili^M per dolci^M

糖衣注入器
icing syringe
Garnierspritze^F
piston^M à décorer
jeringa^F de decoración^F
siringa^F per decorazioni

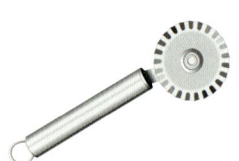

パイ・カッター
pastry cutting wheel
Kuchenrad^N
roulette^F de pâtissier^M
cortapastas^M
rotella^F tagliapasta

製菓用刷毛（はけ）
pastry brush
Kuchenpinsel^M
pinceau^M à pâtisserie^F
pincel^M de repostería^F
pennello^M per dolci^M

卵泡立て器
egg beater
Rad-Schneeschläger^M
batteur^M à œufs^M
batidor^M mecánico
frullino^M

泡立て器／ホイッパー
whisk
Schneebesen^M
fouet^F
batidor^M
frusta^F

絞り袋と口金
pastry bag and nozzles
Spritzbeutel^M mit Tüllen^F
poche^F à douilles^F
manga^F y boquillas^F
tasca^F e bocchette^F

粉篩（ふるい）
sifter
Mehlsieb^N
tamis^M à farine^F
tamiz^M
setaccio^M

クッキー型
cookie cutters; biscuit cutters
Ausstechformen^F
emporte-pièces^M
moldes^M de pastas^F
tagliabiscotti^M

粉振り器
dredger
Streuer^M
saupoudreuse^F
espolvoreador^M
spolverino^M

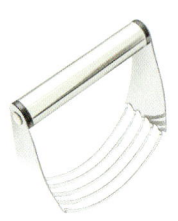

ブレンダー
pastry blender
Teigmischer^M
mélangeur^M à pâtisserie^F
mezclador^M de pastelería^F
miscelatore^M per dolci^M

ボウル
mixing bowls
Rührschüsseln^F
bols^M à mélanger
boles^M para batir
ciotole^F per mescolare

麺（めん）棒／伸（の）し棒
rolling pin
Nudelholz^N
rouleau^M à pâtisserie^F
rodillo^M
matterello^M

クッキー用天板（てんばん）
baking sheet; *baking sheet*
Backblech^N
plaque^F à pâtisserie^F
bandeja^F de pastelería^F
teglia^F da forno^M

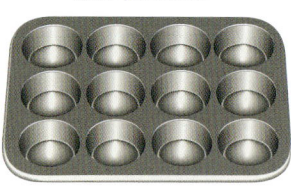

マフィン型
muffin pan; *bun tin*
Muffinform^F
moule^M à muffins^M
molde^M para magdalenas^F
stampini^M per dolci^M

スフレ型
soufflé dish
Souffléform^F
moule^M à soufflé^M
molde^M de soufflé^M
tegamino^M per sufflè^M

シャルロット型
charlotte mold
Charlottenform^F
moule^M à charlotte^F
molde^M de carlota^F
stampo^M per charlotte^F

底板取り外し式スポンジ型
removable-bottomed pan; *removable-bottomed tin*
Springform^F
moule^M à fond^M amovible
molde^M redondo con muelles^M
teglia^F con fondo^M staccabile

パイ型
pie pan; *pie tin*
flache Kuchenform^F
moule^M à tarte^F
molde^M para tartas^F
teglia^F per torta^F

タルト型
quiche plate; *quiche tin*
Quicheform^F
moule^M à quiche^F
molde^M acanalado
stampo^M per crostata^F

ケーキ型
cake pan; *cake tin*
Kuchenform^F
moule^M à gâteau^M
molde^M para bizcocho^M
tortiera^F

台所 | KITCHEN
KÜCHE | CUISINE | COCINA | CUCINA

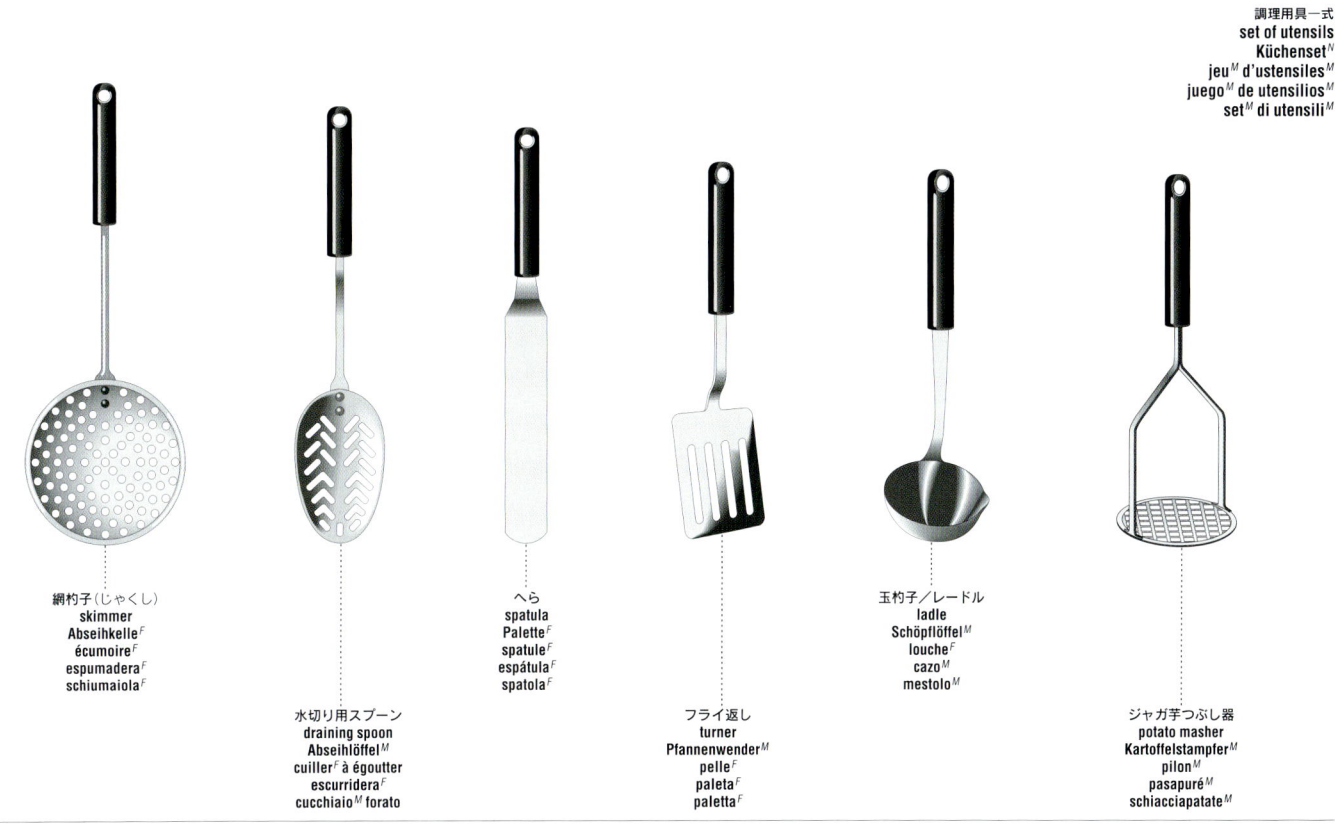

台所用品

調理用具一式
set of utensils
Küchenset[N]
jeu[M] d'ustensiles[M]
juego[M] de utensilios[M]
set[M] di utensili[M]

食べ物と台所

網杓子（じゃくし）
skimmer
Abseihkelle[F]
écumoire[F]
espumadera[F]
schiumaiola[F]

水切り用スプーン
draining spoon
Abseihlöffel[M]
cuiller[F] à égoutter
escurridera[F]
cucchiaio[M] forato

へら
spatula
Palette[F]
spatule[F]
espátula[F]
spatola[F]

フライ返し
turner
Pfannenwender[M]
pelle[F]
paleta[F]
paletta[F]

玉杓子／レードル
ladle
Schöpflöffel[M]
louche[F]
cazo[M]
mestolo[M]

ジャガ芋つぶし器
potato masher
Kartoffelstampfer[M]
pilon[M]
pasapuré[M]
schiacciapatate[M]

その他の用具
miscellaneous utensils
verschiedene Utensilien[N]
ustensiles[M] divers
utensilios[M] diversos
utensili[M] vari

種抜き器
stoner
Entsteiner[M]
dénoyauteur[M]
deshuesador[M]
snocciolatore[M]

脂身刺し込み針
larding needle
Spicknadel[F]
aiguille[F] à piquer
aguja[F] picadora
lardatoio[M]

芯抜き[取り]器
apple corer
Kerngehäuseausstecher[M]
vide-pomme[F]
descorazonador[M]
cavatorsoli[M]

エスカルゴ用トング
snail tongs
Schneckenzange[F]
pince[F] à escargots[M]
pinzas[F] para caracoles[M]
molle[F] per chiocciole[F]

エスカルゴ皿
snail dish
Schneckenpfännchen[N]
plat[M] à escargots[M]
plato[M] para caracoles[M]
tegamino[M] per chiocciole[F]

メロンくりぬき器
melon baller
Melonenlöffel[M]
cuiller[F] parisienne
vaciador[M]
scavamelone[M]

絡（から）げ針
trussing needle
Dressiernadel[F]
aiguille[F] à brider
aguja[F] de coser
ago[M] per legare

調理鋏（ばさみ）
kitchen shears
Küchenschere[F]
ciseaux[M] de cuisine
tijeras[F] de cocina
forbici[F] da cucina

アイスクリームすくい[スクープ]
ice cream scoop
Eisportionierer[M]
cuiller[F] à glace[F]
cuchara[F] para servir helado[M]
porzionatore[M] per gelato[M]

トング
tongs
Zange[F]
pince[F]
pinzas[F]
molle[F]

鳥用鋏
poultry shears
Geflügelschere[F]
cisaille[F] à volaille[F]
tijeras[F] para aves[F]
trinciapollo[M]

野菜ブラシ
vegetable brush
Gemüsebürste[F]
brosse[F] à légumes[M]
cepillo[M] para verduras[F]
spazzola[F] per verdura[F]

卵スライサー
egg slicer
Eierschneider[M]
coupe-œuf[M]
cortador[M] de huevos[M] duros
affettauova[M]

味見（用）スプーン
tasting spoon
Probierlöffel[M]
cuiller[F] à goûter
cuchara[F] de degustación[F]
cucchiaio[M] da assaggio[M]

茶漉（こ）し球
tea ball; *tea infuser*
Tee-Ei[N]
boule[F] à thé[M]
esfera[F] de té[M]
filtro[M] per il tè[M]

スパゲッティ用トング
spaghetti tongs
Spaghettizange[F]
pince[F] à spaghettis[M]
pinzas[F] para espagueti[M]
molle[F] per spaghetti[M]

スポイト
baster
Fettgießer[M]
poire[F] à jus[M]
engrasador[M]
peretta[F] per ingrassare

233

台所 | KITCHEN
KÜCHE | CUISINE | COCINA | CUCINA

調理器具

cooking utensils | Kochgeräte[N] | batterie[F] de cuisine[F] | utensilios[M] de cocina[F] | utensili[M] per cucinare

日本語 | 英語 | ドイツ語 | フランス語 | スペイン語 | イタリア語

中華鍋セット
wok set
Wok-Set[N]
wok[M]
wok[M]
servizio[M] da wok[M]

蓋（ふた）
lid
Deckel[M]
couvercle[M]
tapa[F]
coperchio[M]

ラック
rack
Gittereinsatz[M]
grille[F]
rejilla[F]
griglia[F]

中華鍋
wok
Wok[M]
wok[M]
wok[M]
wok[M]

火口（ほくち）
burner ring
Aufsatz[M]
collier[M]
quemador[M]
bruciatore[M] a corona[F]

タジン鍋
tajine
Tajine[F]
tajine[M]
tajina[F]
tajina[M]

フォンデュ・セット
fondue set
Fondue-Set[N]
service[M] à fondue[F]
servicio[M] para fondue[F]
servizio[M] da fonduta[F]

フォンデュ鍋
fondue pot
Fonduetopf[M]
caquelon[M]
cacerola[F] para fondue[F]
tegame[M] per fonduta[F]

魚用鍋
fish poacher; fish kettle
Fischkochtopf[M]
poissonnière[F]
besuguera[F]
pesciera[F]

ラック
rack
Gittereinsatz[M]
grille[F]
rejilla[F] desmontable
griglia[F]

スタンド
stand
Ständer[M]
support[M]
soporte[M]
base[F]

バーナー
burner
Brenner[M]
réchaud[M]
quemador[M]
fornellino[M]

蓋（ふた）
lid
Deckel[M]
couvercle[M]
tapa[F]
coperchio[M]

肉汁受け皿
dripping pan
Fettpfanne[F]
lèchefrite[F]
grasera[F]
leccarda[F]

テリーヌ
terrine
Terrine[F]
terrine[F]
terrina[F]
terrina[F]

ロースト鍋
roasting pans
Bräter[M]
plats[M] à rôtir
asadores[M]
teglie[F] da forno[M]

圧力鍋
pressure cooker
Schnellkochtopf[M]
autocuiseur[M]
olla[F] a presión[F]
pentola[F] a pressione[F]

圧力調節器
pressure regulator
Überdruckventil[N]
régulateur[M] de pression[F]
regulador[M] de presión[F]
regolatore[M] di pressione[F]

安全弁
safety valve
Sicherheitsventil[N]
soupape[F]
válvula[F] de seguridad[F]
valvola[F] di sicurezza[F]

台所 | KITCHEN
KÜCHE | CUISINE | COCINA | CUCINA

調理器具

浅型両手鍋
Dutch oven
flacher Bratentopf^M
faitout^M
cacerola^F refractaria
casseruola^F

深型両手鍋
stock pot
Suppentopf^M
marmite^F
olla^F
pentola^F

クスクス鍋
couscous kettle
Couscoustopf^M
couscoussier^M
olla^F para cuscús^M
pentola^F per cuscus^M

フライ・パン
frying pan
Bratpfanne^F
poêle^F à frire
sartén^F para freir
padella^F per friggere

蒸し器
steamer
Dampfkochtopf^M
cuit-vapeur^M
cazuela^F vaporera
pentola^F a vapore^M

落とし卵用鍋／エッグ・ポーチャー
egg poacher
Eipochierer^M
pocheuse^F
escalfador^M de huevos^M
tegame^M per uova^F in camicia^F

ソテー・パン
sauté pan
Schmorpfanne^F
sauteuse^F
sartén^F honda
padella^F per rosolare

小型ソースパン
small saucepan
Pfanne^F
poêlon^M
sartén^F pequeña
piccolo tegame^M

ディアブル
diable
Römertopf^M
diable^M
sartén^F doble
padella^F doppia

クレープ・パン
pancake pan
Crêpe-Pfanne^F
poêle^F à crêpes^F
sartén^F para crepes^F
padella^F per crêpe^F

蒸し器用かご
steamer basket
Dämpfeinsatz^M
panier^M cuit-vapeur^M
cesto^M de cocción^F al vapor^M
cestello^M per la cottura^F a vapore^M

二重鍋／湯煎（ゆせん）鍋
double boiler
Wasserbadtopf^M
bain-marie^M
cacerola^F para baño^M de María
pentola^F per cucinare a bagnomaria

ソースパン
saucepan
Stielkasserolle^F
casserole^F
cacerola^F
tegame^M

235

台所 | KITCHEN
KÜCHE | CUISINE | COCINA | CUCINA

家電製品

日本語 | 英語 | ドイツ語 | フランス語 | スペイン語 | イタリア語

domestic appliances | Haushaltsgeräte[N] | appareils[M] électroménagers | aparatos[M] electrodomésticos | elettrodomestici[M]

混ぜる
for mixing and blending
zum Mixen[N] und Kneten[N]
pour mélanger et battre
para mezclar y batir
per frullare e miscelare

ブレンダー／ミキサー
blender
Mixer[M]
mélangeur[M]
batidora[F] de vaso[F]
frullatore[M]

蓋（ふた）
cap
Deckelknopf[M]
bouchon[M]
tapa[F]
tappo[M]

容器／コンテナー
container
Behälter[M]
récipient[M]
vaso[M] mezclador
bicchiere[M]

切り刃
cutting blade
Schneidmesser[N]
couteau[M]
cuchilla[F]
coltello[M]

モーター内蔵部
motor unit
Motorblock[M]
bloc[M]-moteur[M]
motor[M]
blocco[M] motore[M]

（スピード調節）ボタン
push button
Drucktaste[F]
bouton[M]-poussoir[M]
botón[M] de velocidades[F]
interruttore[M]

ハンド・ブレンダー
hand blender
Stabmixer[M]
mélangeur[M] à main[F]
batidora[F] de pie[M]
frullatore[M] a immersione[F]

モーター内蔵部
motor unit
Motorblock[M]
bloc[M]-moteur[M]
motor[M]
blocco[M] motore[M]

攪拌（かくはん）器取り付け部
blending attachment
Messerschutz[M]
pied[M]-mélangeur[M]
cuchillas[F] para batir
coltello[M] miscelatore

攪拌（かくはん）器
beaters
Rührbesen[M]
fouets[M]
tipos[M] de varillas[F]
fruste[F]

四枚刃
four blade beater
Rührbesen[M]
fouet[M] quatre pales[F] de aspas[F]
frusta[F] a quattro bracci[M]

螺旋（らせん）状刃
spiral beater
Spiralkneter[M]
fouet[M] en spirale[F]
en espiral[F]
frusta[F] a spirale[F]

環状刃
wire beater
Drahtbesen[M]
fouet[M] à fil[M]
circular
frusta[F] ad anello[M]

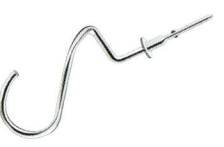

捏（こ）ね刃
dough hook
Knethaken[M]
crochet[M] pétrisseur
de gancho[M]
gancio[M] per l'impasto[M]

ハンド・ミキサー
hand mixer
Handrührgerät[N]
batteur[M] à main[F]
batidora[F] de mano[F]
frullatore[M] elettrico a mano[F]

攪拌器取り外しボタン
beater ejector
Auswurftaste[F]
éjecteur[M] de fouets[M]
eyector[M] de las varillas[F]
espulsore[M] degli accessori[M]

スピード調節つまみ
speed selector
Geschwindigkeitswähler[M]
sélecteur[M] de vitesse[F]
selector[M] de velocidad[F]
selettore[M] di velocità[F]

攪拌（かくはん）器
beater
Rührbesen[M]
fouet[M]
varilla[F] de batir
frusta[F]

取っ手
handle
Griff[M]
poignée[F]
asa[F]
impugnatura[F]

ヒール・レスト
heel rest
Heck[N]
talon[M] d'appui[M]
talón[M] de apoyo[M]
tallone[M] d'appoggio[M]

卓上ミキサー
table mixer
Tischrührgerät[N]
batteur[M] sur socle[M]
batidora[F] de mesa[F]
impastatrice[F]

攪拌器取り外しボタン
beater ejector
Auswurftaste[F]
éjecteur[M] de fouets[M]
eyector[M] de las varillas[F]
espulsore[M] degli accessori[M]

攪拌（かくはん）器
beater
Rührbesen[M]
fouet[M]
varilla[F] de batir
frusta[F]

上下動ヘッド
tilt-back head
Schwenkarm[M]
tête[F] basculante
cabeza[M] móvil
testa[F] ribaltabile

ボウル
mixing bowl
Rührschüssel[F]
bol[M]
bol[M] mezclador
ciotola[F]

ターンテーブル
turntable
Drehscheibe[F]
plateau[M] tournant
disco[M] giratorio
piattaforma[F] girevole

スピード調節つまみ
speed control
Geschwindigkeitsregelung[F]
commande[F] de vitesse[F]
selector[M] de velocidades[F]
regolatore[M] di velocità[F]

台／スタンド
stand
Ständer[M]
socle[M]
pie[M]
base[F]

236

台所 | KITCHEN
KÜCHE | CUISINE | COCINA | CUCINA

家電製品

フード・プロセッサー
food processor
Küchenmaschine^F
robot^M de cuisine^F
robot^M de cocina^F
robot^M da cucina^F

プッシャー
pusher
Stopfer^M
poussoir^M
empujador^M
pressatore^M

切る
for cutting
zum Schneiden^N
pour couper
para cortar
per tagliare

フィード・チューブ
feed tube
Einfüllschacht^M
entonnoir^M
tubo^M de entrada^F
bocchetta^F

ディスク・カッター
disks; *discs*
Scheiben^F
disques^M
disco^M
dischi^M

蓋（ふた）
lid
Deckel^M
couvercle^M
tapa^F
coperchio^M

刃
blade
Schneidmesser^N
couteau^M
cuchilla^F
lama^F

スピード調節つまみ
speed selector
Geschwindigkeitsregelung^F
sélecteur^M de vitesse^F
selector^M de velocidades^F
selettore^M di velocità^F

取っ手
handle
Griff^M
poignée^F
asa^F
impugnatura^F

容器
bowl
Schüssel^F
bol^M
bol^M
cestello^M

回転軸
spindle
Antriebswelle^F
arbre^M
eje^M
asse^M di trasmissione^F del motore^M

モーター内蔵部
motor unit
Motorblock^M
bloc^M-moteur^M
motor^M
blocco^M motore^M

搾る
for juicing
zum Auspressen^N
pour presser
para exprimir
per spremere

レモン搾り器
citrus juicer; *lemon squeezer*
Zitruspresse^F
presse-agrumes^M
exprimidor^M de cítricos^M
spremiagrumi^M elettrico

搾り器
reamer
Kegel^M
toupie^F
exprimidor^M
cono^M di spremitura^F

電気ナイフ
electric knife
Elektromesser^N
couteau^M électrique
cuchillo^M eléctrico
coltello^M elettrico

電気コード
power cord
Netzkabel^N
cordon^M d'alimentation^F
cordón^M de alimentación^F
cavo^M d'alimentazione^F

濾過（ろか）器
strainer
Sieb^N
passoire^F
colador^M
vaschetta^F filtrante

注ぎ口付き容器
bowl with serving spout
Behälter^M mit Gießer^M
bol^M verseur
recipiente^M con vertedor^M
vaschetta^F con beccuccio^M

刃
blade
Klinge^F
lame^F
cuchilla^F
lama^F

電源スイッチ
on-off switch
Ein- und Ausschalter^M
interrupteur^M
interruptor^M
interruttore^M

モーター内蔵部
motor unit
Motorblock^M
bloc^M-moteur^M
motor^M
blocco^M motore^M

食べ物と台所

台所 | KITCHEN
KÜCHE | CUISINE | COCINA | CUCINA

家電製品

日本語 | 英語 | ドイツ語 | フランス語 | スペイン語 | イタリア語

火を通す
for cooking
zum Kochen(N)
pour cuire
para cocinar
per cucinare

電子レンジ
microwave oven
Mikrowellengerät(N)
four(M) à micro-ondes(F)
horno(M) de microondas(F)
forno(M) a microonde(F)

扉
door
Tür(F)
porte(F)
puerta(F)
sportello(M)

温度センサー
sensor probe
Sensor(M)
sonde(F) thermique
sonda(F) térmica
termosonda(F)

センサー・プラグ
probe receptacle
Sensorhülse(F)
prise(F) de la sonde(F) thermique
enchufe(M) del termómetro(M)
innesto(M) della sonda(F)

覗き窓／オーブン窓
window
Sichtfenster(N)
hublot(M)
ventana(F)
finestra(F) di controllo(M)

タイマー／時計
clock timer
Zeitschalter(M)
horloge(F) programmatrice
reloj(M) programador
orologio(M) contaminuti(M)

掛け金
latch
Riegel(M)
loquet(M)
seguro(M)
chiusura(F) a scatto(M)

コントロール・パネル
control panel
Bedienblende(F)
tableau(M) de commande(F)
panel(M) de mandos(M)
quadro(M) di comando(M)

取っ手
handle
Griff(M)
poignée(F)
asa(F)
maniglia(F)

ワッフル焼き器
waffle iron
Waffeleisen(N)
gaufrier(M)-gril(M)
gofrera(F)
griglia(F) elettrica

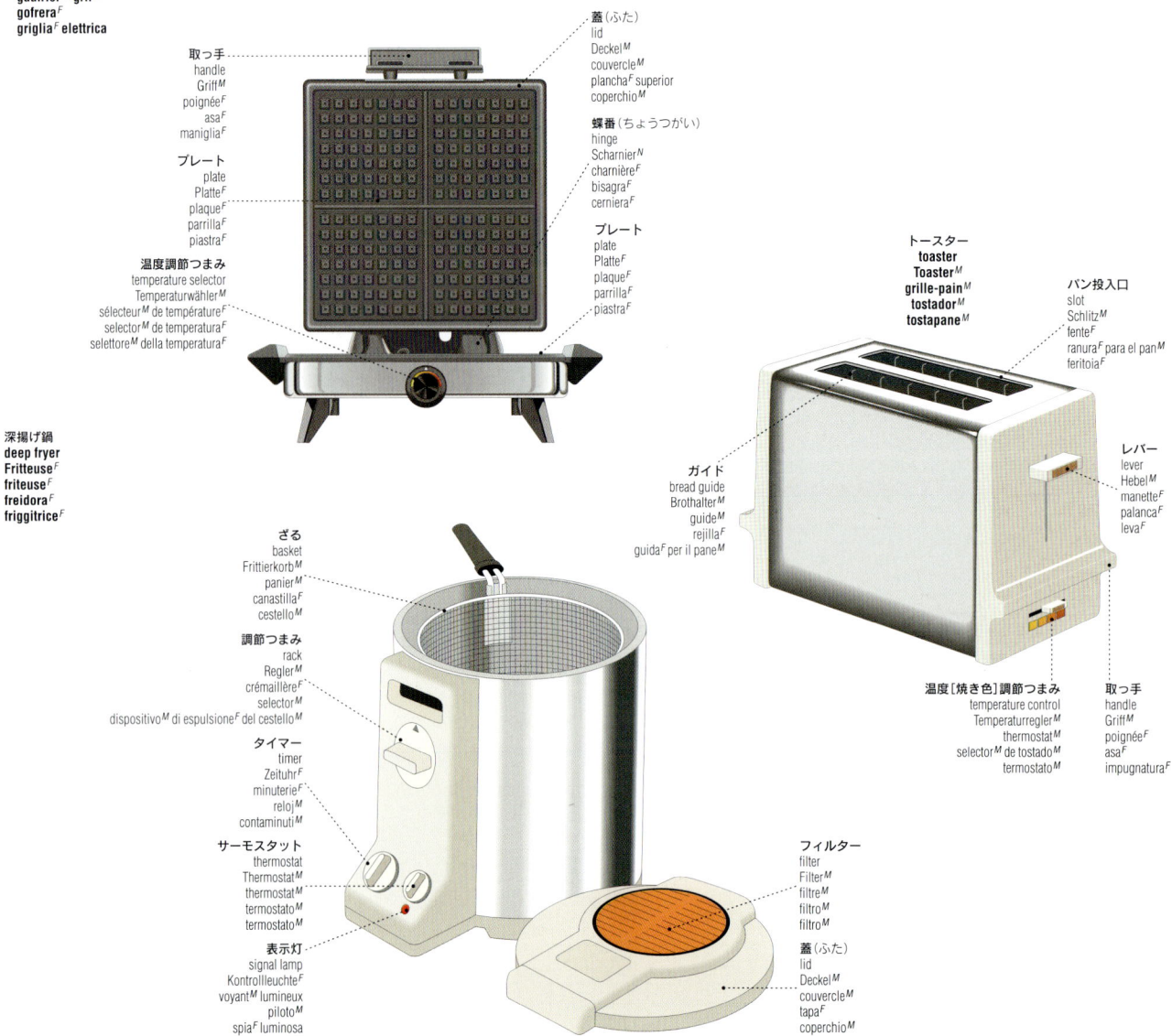

取っ手
handle
Griff(M)
poignée(F)
asa(F)
maniglia(F)

蓋（ふた）
lid
Deckel(M)
couvercle(M)
plancha(F) superior
coperchio(M)

プレート
plate
Platte(F)
plaque(F)
parrilla(F)
piastra(F)

蝶番（ちょうつがい）
hinge
Scharnier(N)
charnière(F)
bisagra(F)
cerniera(F)

プレート
plate
Platte(F)
plaque(F)
parrilla(F)
piastra(F)

温度調節つまみ
temperature selector
Temperaturwähler(M)
sélecteur(M) de température(F)
selector(M) de temperatura(F)
selettore(M) della temperatura(F)

トースター
toaster
Toaster(M)
grille-pain(M)
tostador(M)
tostapane(M)

パン投入口
slot
Schlitz(M)
fente(F)
ranura(F) para el pan(M)
feritoia(F)

レバー
lever
Hebel(M)
manette(F)
palanca(F)
leva(F)

深揚げ鍋
deep fryer
Fritteuse(F)
friteuse(F)
freidora(F)
friggitrice(F)

ざる
basket
Frittierkorb(M)
panier(M)
canastilla(F)
cestello(M)

調節つまみ
rack
Regler(M)
crémaillère(F)
selector(M)
dispositivo(M) di espulsione(F) del cestello(M)

ガイド
bread guide
Brothalter(M)
guide(M)
rejilla(F)
guida(F) per il pane(M)

タイマー
timer
Zeituhr(F)
minuterie(F)
reloj(M)
contaminuti(M)

サーモスタット
thermostat
Thermostat(M)
thermostat(M)
termostato(M)
termostato(M)

温度［焼き色］調節つまみ
temperature control
Temperaturregler(M)
thermostat(M)
selector(M) de tostado(M)
termostato(M)

取っ手
handle
Griff(M)
poignée(F)
asa(F)
impugnatura(F)

フィルター
filter
Filter(M)
filtre(M)
filtro(M)
filtro(M)

蓋（ふた）
lid
Deckel(M)
couvercle(M)
tapa(F)
coperchio(M)

表示灯
signal lamp
Kontrollleuchte(F)
voyant(M) lumineux
piloto(M)
spia(F) luminosa

食べ物と台所

238

台所 | KITCHEN
KÜCHE | CUISINE | COCINA | CUCINA

家電製品

ラクレット・グリル
raclette with grill
Raclette^F-Grill^M
raclette^F-grill^M
raclette-grill^M
griglia^F per raclette^F

電気蒸し器
electric steamer
elektrischer Schnellkocher^M
cuit-vapeur^M électrique
vaporera^F eléctrica
pentola^F a vapore^M elettrica

ポワロン／平鍋
dish
Pfännchen^N
poêlon^M
bandeja^F
piatto^M

グリル・プレート
cooking plate
Grillplatte^F
surface^F de cuisson^F
placa^F de cocción^F
piastra^F di cottura^F

台
base
Unterteil^M/N
socle^M
base^F
base^F

調理皿
cooking dishes
Einsätze^M
bols^M de cuisson^F
platos^M de cocción^F
piatti^M di cottura^F

水位表示器
water level indicator
Wasserstandsanzeiger^M
indicateur^M de niveau^M d'eau^F
indicador^M del nivel^M del agua^F
indicatore^M del livello^M d'acqua^F

表示灯
signal lamp
Kontrollleuchte^F
voyant^M lumineux
indicador^M luminoso
spia^F luminosa

タイマー
timer
Zeitschaltuhr^F
minuterie^F
minutero^M
contaminuti^M

絶縁取っ手
insulated handle
wärmeisolierter Griff^M
poignée^F isolante
asa^F aislante
maniglia^F isolata

屋内用電気グリル
indoor electric grill
Elektrischer Tischgrill^M
gril^M barbecue^M
parrilla^F eléctrica
griglia^F elettrica per interni^M

肉汁受け皿
drip pan
Fettpfanne^F
bac^M ramasse-jus^M
grasera^F
leccarda^F

調理面
cooking surface
Grillfläche^F
surface^F de cuisson^F
superficie^F de cocción^F
piano^M di cottura^F

温度調節サーモスタット
adjustable thermostat
regelbarer Thermostat^M
thermostat^M réglable
termostato^M regulable
termostato^M regolabile

パン焼き器
bread machine
Brotbackautomat^M
robot^M boulanger^M
amasadora^F
impastatrice^F

蓋（ふた）
lid
Deckel^M
couvercle^M
tapa^F
coperchio^M

コントロール・パネル
control panel
Bedienungsfeld^N
tableau^M de commande^F
panel^M de mandos^M
quadro^M di comando^M

覗き窓
window
Sichtfenster^N
hublot^M
ventana^F
finestra^F di controllo^M

パン型
loaf pan
Backform^F
moule^M à pain^M
molde^M de pan^M
stampo^M per pane^M

ホット・プレート
griddle
Grillplatte^F
gril^M électrique
plancha^F eléctrica
piastra^F elettrica

調理面
cooking surface
Kochfeld^N
surface^F de cuisson^F
plancha^F
piano^M di cottura^F

取っ手
handle
Griff^M
poignée^F
asa^F
maniglia^F

差し込み式温度調節つまみ
detachable control
abziehbarer Temperaturregler^M
commande^F amovible
enchufe^M y selector^M desmontables
regolatore^M staccabile

油受け
grease well
Fettauffangschale^F
collecteur^M de graisse^F
colector^M de grasa^F
bacinella^F raccogligrasso

239

台所 | KITCHEN
KÜCHE | CUISINE | COCINA | CUCINA

その他の家電製品

miscellaneous domestic appliances | verschiedene Haushaltsgeräte[N] | appareils[M] électroménagers divers | varios aparatos[M] electrodomésticos | elettrodomestici[M] vari

日本語 | 英語 | ドイツ語 | フランス語 | スペイン語 | イタリア語

食べ物と台所

缶切り
can opener; *tin opener*
Dosenöffner[M]
ouvre-boîtes[M]
abrelatas[M]
apriscatole[M]

突き刺しレバー
pierce lever
Einstechhebel[M]
levier[M] de perçage[M]
palanca[F] de perforación[F]
tagliente[M]

蓋(ふた)を持ち上げる磁石
magnetic lid holder
magnetischer Deckelhalter[M]
aimant[M] de retenue[F]
retén[M] imantado
magnete[M] fermacoperchio

切り刃
cutting blade
Schneidklinge[F]
lame[F] de coupe[F]
cuchilla[F]
lama[F]

駆動歯車
drive wheel
Druckzahnrädchen[N]
molette[F] d'entraînement[M]
engranaje[M] de avance[M]
ingranaggio[M] di trascinamento

コーヒー・ミル
coffee mill
Kaffeemühle[F]
moulin[M] à café[M]
molinillo[M] de café[M]
macinacaffè[M]

蓋(ふた)
lid
Deckel[M]
couvercle[M]
tapa[F]
coperchio[M]

刃
blade
Messer[N]
couteau[M]
cuchilla[F]
lama[F]

電源スイッチ・ボタン
on-off button
Ein- und Ausschalter[M]
bouton[M] marche[F]/arrêt[M]
interruptor[M]
interruttore[M]

モーター内蔵部
motor unit
Motorblock[M]
bloc[M]-moteur[M]
motor[M]
blocco[M] motore[M]

やかん
kettle
Wasserkessel[M]
bouilloire[F]
hervidor[M]
bollitore[M]

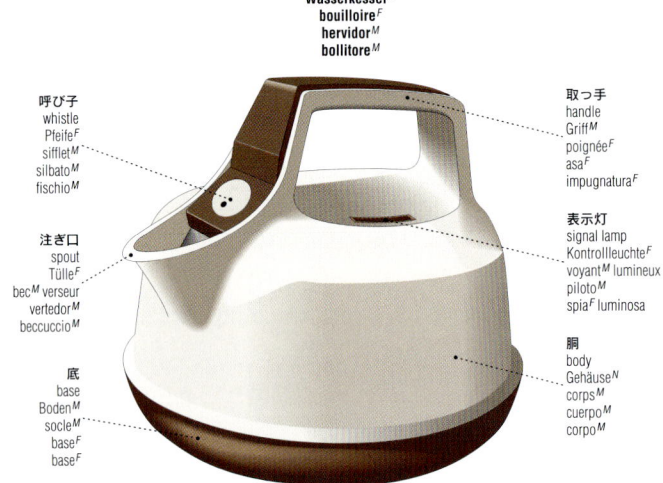

呼び子
whistle
Pfeife[F]
sifflet[M]
silbato[M]
fischio[M]

注ぎ口
spout
Tülle[F]
bec[M] verseur
vertedor[M]
beccuccio[M]

取っ手
handle
Griff[M]
poignée[F]
asa[F]
impugnatura[F]

表示灯
signal lamp
Kontrollleuchte[F]
voyant[M] lumineux
piloto[M]
spia[F] luminosa

胴
body
Gehäuse[N]
corps[M]
cuerpo[M]
corpo[M]

底
base
Boden[M]
socle[M]
base[F]
base[F]

アイスクリーム製造機
ice cream freezer
Eismaschine[F]
sorbetière[F]
heladera[F]
gelatiera[F]

モーター内蔵部
motor unit
Motorblock[M]
bloc[M]-moteur[M]
motor[M]
blocco[M] motore[M]

カバー
cover
Deckel[M]
couvercle[M]
cubierta[F]
coperchio[M]

取っ手
handle
Griff[M]
poignée[F]
asa[F]
impugnatura[F]

フリーザー容器
freezer bucket
Eisbehälter[M]
seau[M] isotherme
cubeta[F] congeladora
cestello[M] di refrigerazione[F]

ジューサー
juicer; *juice extractor*
Entsafter[M]
centrifugeuse[F]
licuadora[F]
centrifuga[F]

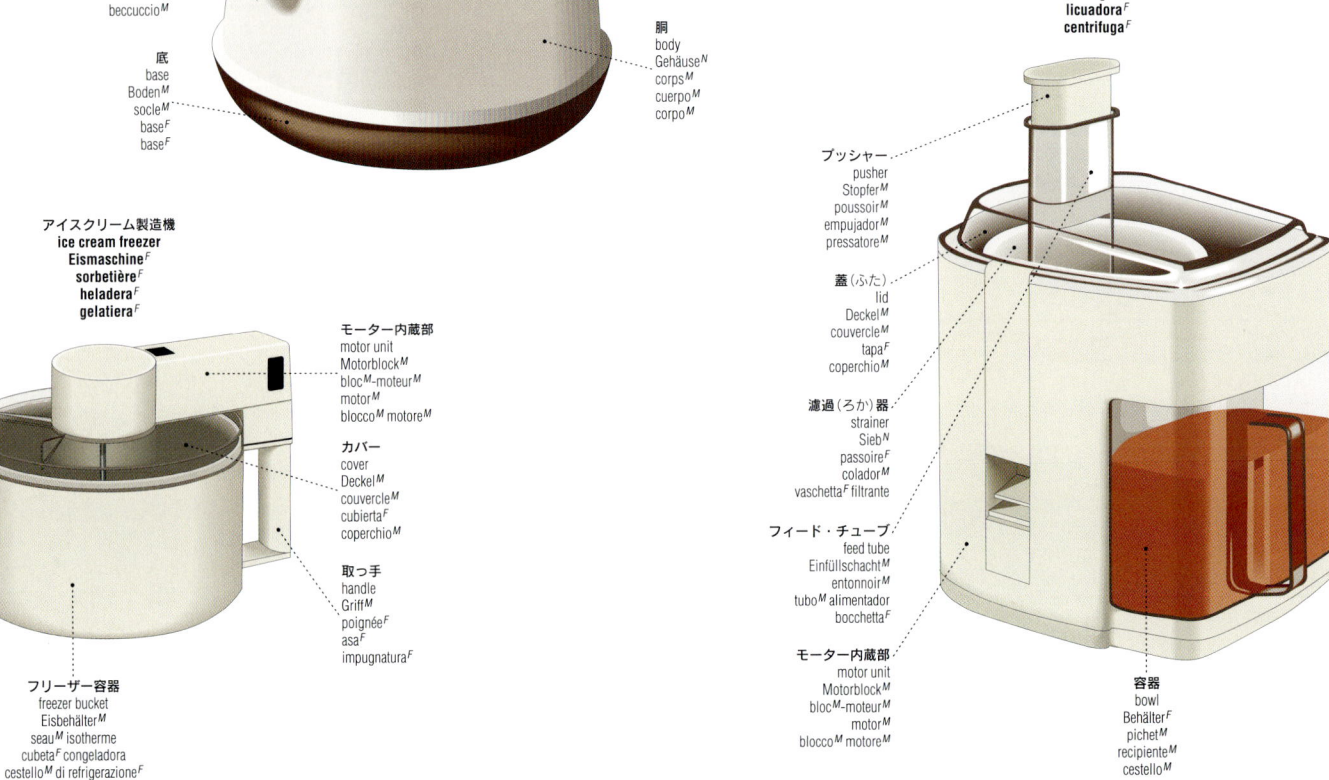

プッシャー
pusher
Stopfer[M]
poussoir[M]
empujador[M]
pressatore[M]

蓋(ふた)
lid
Deckel[M]
couvercle[M]
tapa[F]
coperchio[M]

濾過(ろか)器
strainer
Sieb[N]
passoire[F]
colador[M]
vaschetta[F] filtrante

フィード・チューブ
feed tube
Einfüllschacht[M]
entonnoir[M]
tubo[M] alimentador
bocchetta[F]

モーター内蔵部
motor unit
Motorblock[M]
bloc[M]-moteur[M]
motor[M]
blocco[M] motore[M]

容器
bowl
Behälter[M]
pichet[M]
recipiente[M]
cestello[M]

台所 | KITCHEN
KÜCHE | CUISINE | COCINA | CUCINA

コーヒー・メーカー

coffee makers | Kaffeemaschinen^F | cafetières^F | cafeteras^F | macchine^F da caffè^M

ドリップ式コーヒー・メーカー
automatic drip coffee maker; *automatic filter coffee maker*
Kaffeemaschine^F
cafetière^F filtre^M
cafetera^F de filtro^M automática
macchina^F da caffè^M a filtro^M

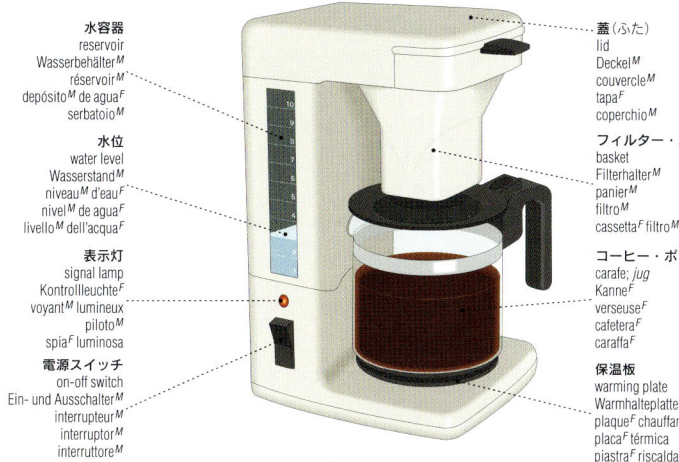

- 水容器 / reservoir / Wasserbehälter^M / réservoir^M / depósito^M de agua^F / serbatoio^M
- 水位 / water level / Wasserstand^M / niveau^M d'eau^F / nivel^M de agua^F / livello^M dell'acqua^F
- 表示灯 / signal lamp / Kontrollleuchte^F / voyant^M lumineux / piloto^M / spia^F luminosa
- 電源スイッチ / on-off switch / Ein- und Ausschalter^M / interrupteur^M / interruptor^M / interruttore^M
- 蓋（ふた）/ lid / Deckel^M / couvercle^M / tapa^F / coperchio^M
- フィルター・バスケット / basket / Filterhalter^M / panier^M / filtro^M / cassetta^F filtro^M
- コーヒー・ポット／カラフ／デカンタ / carafe; *jug* / Kanne^F / verseuse^F / cafetera^F / caraffa^F
- 保温板 / warming plate / Warmhalteplatte^F / plaque^F chauffante / placa^F térmica / piastra^F riscaldante

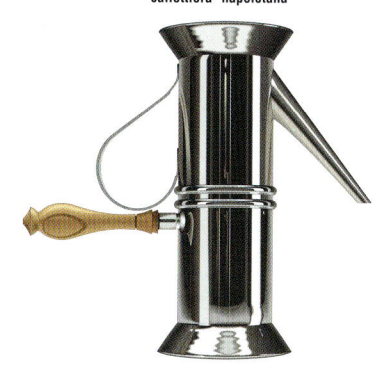

エスプレッソ・マシーン
espresso machine
Espressomaschine^F
machine^F à espresso^M
máquina^F de café^M exprés
macchina^F per espresso^M

- 電源スイッチ / on-off switch / Ein- und Ausschalter^M / interrupteur^M / interruptor^M / interruttore^M
- タンパー / tamper / Kaffeepresser^M / presse-café^M / prensa-café^M / pressacaffè^M
- ドリップ・トレー / drip tray / Auffangschale^F / cuvette^F ramasse-gouttes^M / cubeta^F colectora de gotas^M / vaschetta^F di raccolta^F
- スチーム・ノズル / steam nozzle / Aufschäumdüse^F / buse^F vapeur^F / tubo^M de vapor^M / ugello^M vaporizzatore^M
- スチーム調節つまみ / steam control knob / Dampfregler^M / manette^F vapeur^F / manecilla^F de vapor^M / regolazione^F del vapore^M
- フィルター・ホルダー / filter holder / Filterhalter^M / porte-filtre^M / porta-filtro^M / portafiltro^M
- 水タンク / water tank / Wassertank^M / réservoir^M d'eau^F / depósito^M de agua^M / serbatoio^M dell'acqua^F

コーヒー［フレンチ］プレス
plunger
Pressfilterkanne^F
cafetière^F à piston^M
cafetera^F de émbolo^M
caffettiera^F a pistone^M

エスプレッソ・コーヒー・メーカー
espresso coffee maker
Espresso-Maschine^F
cafetière^F espresso^M
cafetera^F italiana
caffettiera^F per espresso^M

ナポリタン・コーヒー・メーカー
Neapolitan coffee maker
Neapolitanische Tropfkanne^F
cafetière^F napolitaine
cafetera^F napolitana
caffettiera^F napoletana

サイフォン
vacuum coffee maker
Vakuum-Kaffeemaschine^F
cafetière^F à infusion^F
cafetera^F de infusión^F
caffettiera^F a infusione^F

- 漏斗（ろうと）/ upper bowl / oberer Glaskolben^M / tulipe^F / recipiente^M superior / coppa^F superiore
- 管 / stem / Röhre^F / tige^F / tubo^M de subida^F del agua^F / gambo^M
- フラスコ / lower bowl / unterer Glaskolben^M / ballon^M / recipiente^M inferior / coppa^F inferiore

パーコレーター
percolator
Kaffee-Filterkanne^M
percolateur^M
percoladora^F
caffettiera^F a filtro^M

- 注ぎ口 / spout / Tülle^F / bec^M verseur / pitorro^M / beccuccio^M
- 表示灯 / signal lamp / Kontrollleuchte^F / voyant^M lumineux / piloto^M / spia^F luminosa

食べ物と台所

244 敷地

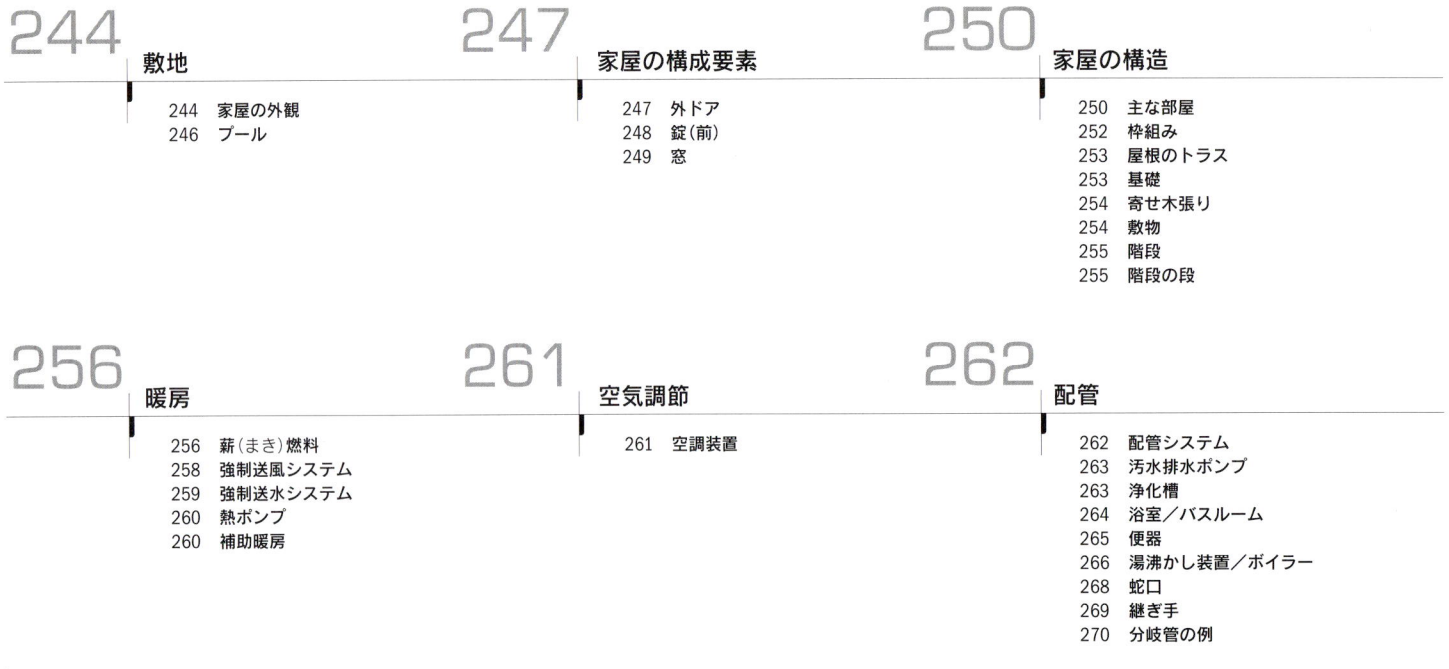

244 家屋の外観
246 プール

247 家屋の構成要素

247 外ドア
248 錠（前）
249 窓

250 家屋の構造

250 主な部屋
252 枠組み
253 屋根のトラス
253 基礎
254 寄せ木張り
254 敷物
255 階段
255 階段の段

256 暖房

256 薪（まき）燃料
258 強制送風システム
259 強制送水システム
260 熱ポンプ
260 補助暖房

261 空気調節

261 空調装置

262 配管

262 配管システム
263 汚水排水ポンプ
263 浄化槽
264 浴室／バスルーム
265 便器
266 湯沸かし装置／ボイラー
268 蛇口
269 継ぎ手
270 分岐管の例

家屋

HOUSE | HAUS | MAISON | CASA | CASA

272 電気

- 272 配電盤
- 273 ネットワーク接続
- 273 電気メーター
- 274 接続装置
- 274 照明具

276 家具調度

- 276 肘掛け椅子
- 277 背もたれ椅子
- 277 椅子
- 278 テーブル
- 278 収納家具
- 280 ベッド
- 281 幼児用家具
- 282 窓付属品
- 286 照明器具
- 288 家電製品
- 295 家事用品

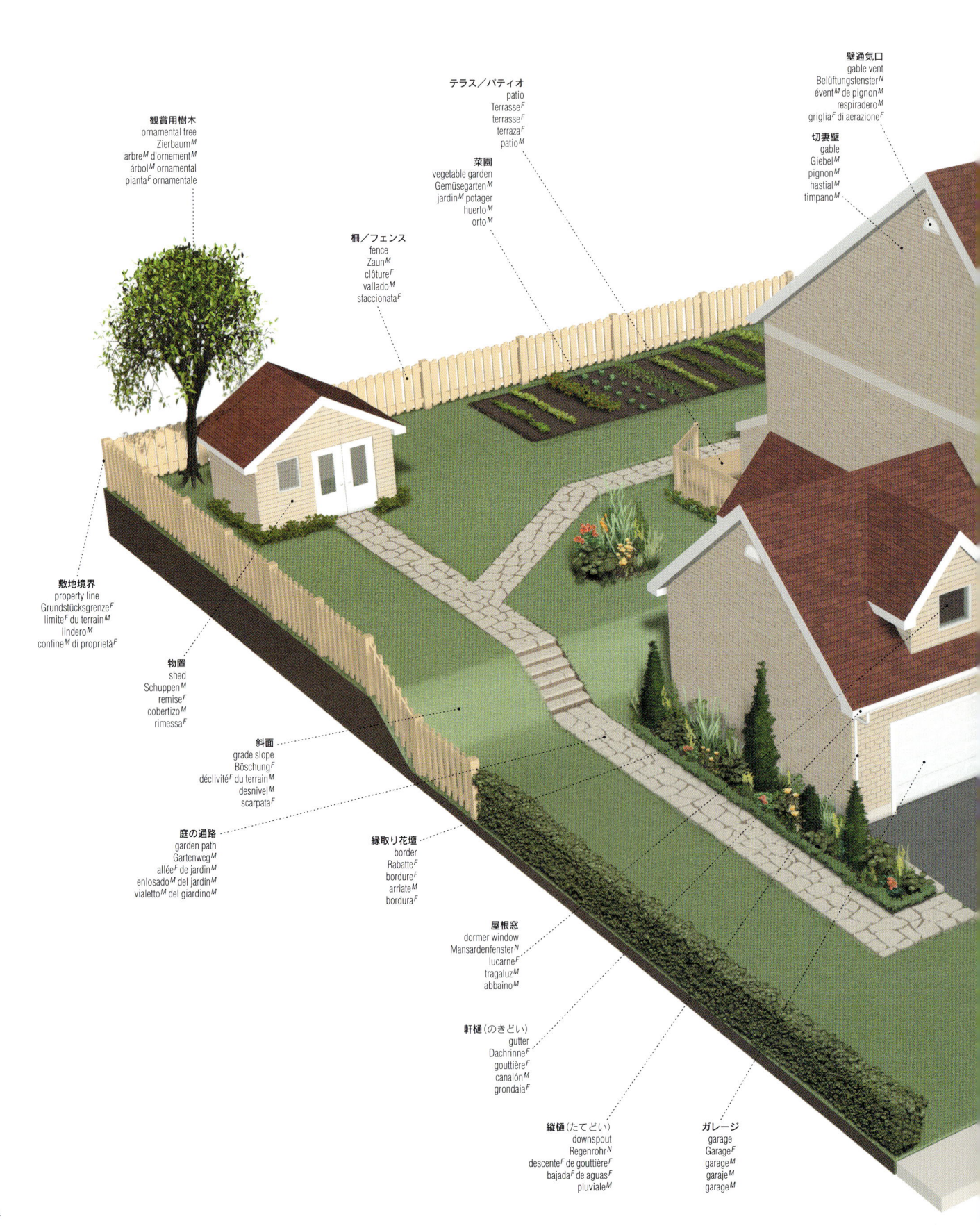

敷地 | LOCATION
ANLAGE | EMPLACEMENT | DISPOSICIÓN | DISPOSIZIONE

家屋の外観

exterior of a house | Außenansicht^F eines Hauses^N | extérieur^M d'une maison^F | exterior^M de una casa^F | esterno^M di una casa^F

日本語 | 英語 | ドイツ語 | フランス語 | スペイン語 | イタリア語

観賞用樹木
ornamental tree
Zierbaum^M
arbre^M d'ornement^M
árbol^M ornamental
pianta^F ornamentale

テラス／パティオ
patio
Terrasse^F
terrasse^F
terraza^F
patio^M

菜園
vegetable garden
Gemüsegarten^M
jardin^M potager
huerto^M
orto^M

柵／フェンス
fence
Zaun^M
clôture^F
vallado^M
staccionata^F

壁通気口
gable vent
Belüftungsfenster^N
évent^M de pignon
respiradero^M
griglia^F di aerazione^F

切妻壁
gable
Giebel^M
pignon^M
hastial^M
timpano^M

敷地境界
property line
Grundstücksgrenze^F
limite^F du terrain^M
lindero^M
confine^M di proprietà^F

物置
shed
Schuppen^M
remise^F
cobertizo^M
rimessa^F

斜面
grade slope
Böschung^F
déclivité^F du terrain^M
desnivel^M
scarpata^F

庭の通路
garden path
Gartenweg^M
allée^F de jardin^M
enlosado^M del jardín^M
vialetto^M del giardino^M

縁取り花壇
border
Rabatte^F
bordure^F
arriate^M
bordura^F

屋根窓
dormer window
Mansardenfenster^N
lucarne^F
tragaluz^M
abbaino^M

軒樋（のきどい）
gutter
Dachrinne^F
gouttière^F
canalón^M
grondaia^F

縦樋（たてどい）
downspout
Regenrohr^N
descente^F de gouttière^F
bajada^F de aguas^F
pluviale^M

ガレージ
garage
Garage^F
garage^M
garaje^M
garage^M

敷地 | LOCATION
ANLAGE | EMPLACEMENT | DISPOSICIÓN | DISPOSIZIONE

家屋の外観

天窓／明かり取り
skylight
Dachfenster^N
lanterneau^M
lucernario^M
lucernario^M

避雷針
lightning rod
Blitzableiter^M
paratonnerre^M
pararrayos^M
parafulmine^M

煙突陶冠(とうかん)
chimney pot
Kaminaufsatz^M
mitron^M
caperuza^F de la chimenea
comignolo^M

煙突
chimney
Schornstein^M
cheminée^F
chimenea^F
camino^M

屋根
roof
Dach^N
toit^M
tejado^M
tetto^M

軒蛇腹
cornice
Gesims^N
corniche^F
cornisa^F
cornicione^M

階段
steps
Treppenvorbau^M
perron^M
escalinata^F
scala^F esterna

地下窓
basement window
Kellerfenster^N
fenêtre^F de sous-sol^M
ventana^F del semisótano
finestra^F del seminterrato

敷地平面図
site plan
Lageplan^M
plan^M du terrain^M
plano^M del terreno^M
pianta^F

家屋

生け垣
hedge
Hecke^F
haie^F
seto^M
siepe^F

芝生
lawn
Rasen^M
pelouse^F
césped^M
prato^M

花壇
flower bed
Beet^N
massif^M
cuadro^M
aiuola^F

歩道
sidewalk
Gehweg^M
trottoir^M
acera^F
marciapiede^M

ポーチ
porch
Vorbau^M
porche^M
porche^M
portico^M

私有車道
driveway
Zufahrtsweg^M
entrée^F de garage^M
entrada^F del garaje^M
vialetto^M di accesso^M

245

敷地 | LOCATION
ANLAGE | EMPLACEMENT | DISPOSICIÓN | DISPOSIZIONE

プール

日本語 | 英語 | ドイツ語 | フランス語 | スペイン語 | イタリア語

pool | Schwimmbecken[N] | piscine[F] | piscina[F] | piscina[F]

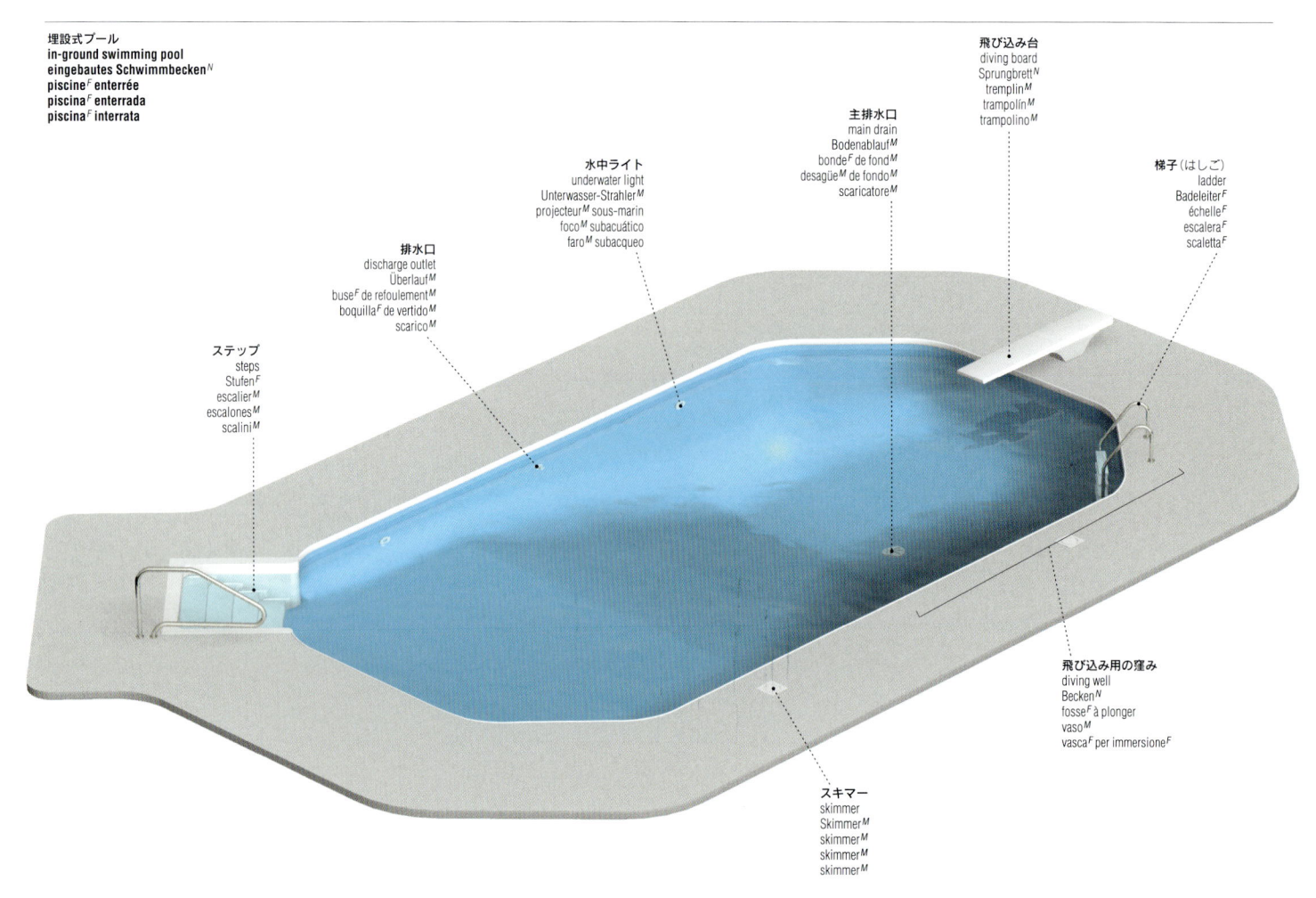

据え置き式プール
above ground swimming pool
freistehendes Schwimmbecken[N]
piscine[F] hors sol[M]
piscina[F] elevada
piscina[F] fuori terra[F]

スキマー
skimmer
Skimmer[M]
skimmer[M]
skimmer[M]

フィルター
filter
Filter[M]
filtre[M]
filtro[M]
filtro[M]

ポンプ
pump
Pumpe[F]
pompe[F]
bomba[F]
pompa[F]

支柱
upright
Stütze[F]
montant[M]
montante[M]
montante[M]

壁
wall
Wand[F]
mur[M]
muro[M]
parete[F]

埋設式プール
in-ground swimming pool
eingebautes Schwimmbecken[N]
piscine[F] enterrée
piscina[F] enterrada
piscina[F] interrata

飛び込み台
diving board
Sprungbrett[N]
tremplin[M]
trampolín[M]
trampolino[M]

主排水口
main drain
Bodenablauf[M]
bonde[F] de fond[M]
desagüe[M] de fondo[M]
scaricatore[M]

水中ライト
underwater light
Unterwasser-Strahler[M]
projecteur[M] sous-marin
foco[M] subacuático
faro[M] subacqueo

梯子（はしご）
ladder
Badeleiter[F]
échelle[F]
escalera[F]
scaletta[F]

排水口
discharge outlet
Überlauf[M]
buse[F] de refoulement[M]
boquilla[F] de vertido[M]
scarico[M]

ステップ
steps
Stufen[F]
escalier[M]
escalones[M]
scalini[M]

飛び込み用の窪み
diving well
Becken[N]
fosse[F] à plonger
vaso[M]
vasca[F] per immersione[F]

スキマー
skimmer
Skimmer[M]
skimmer[M]
skimmer[M]
skimmer[M]

家屋

246

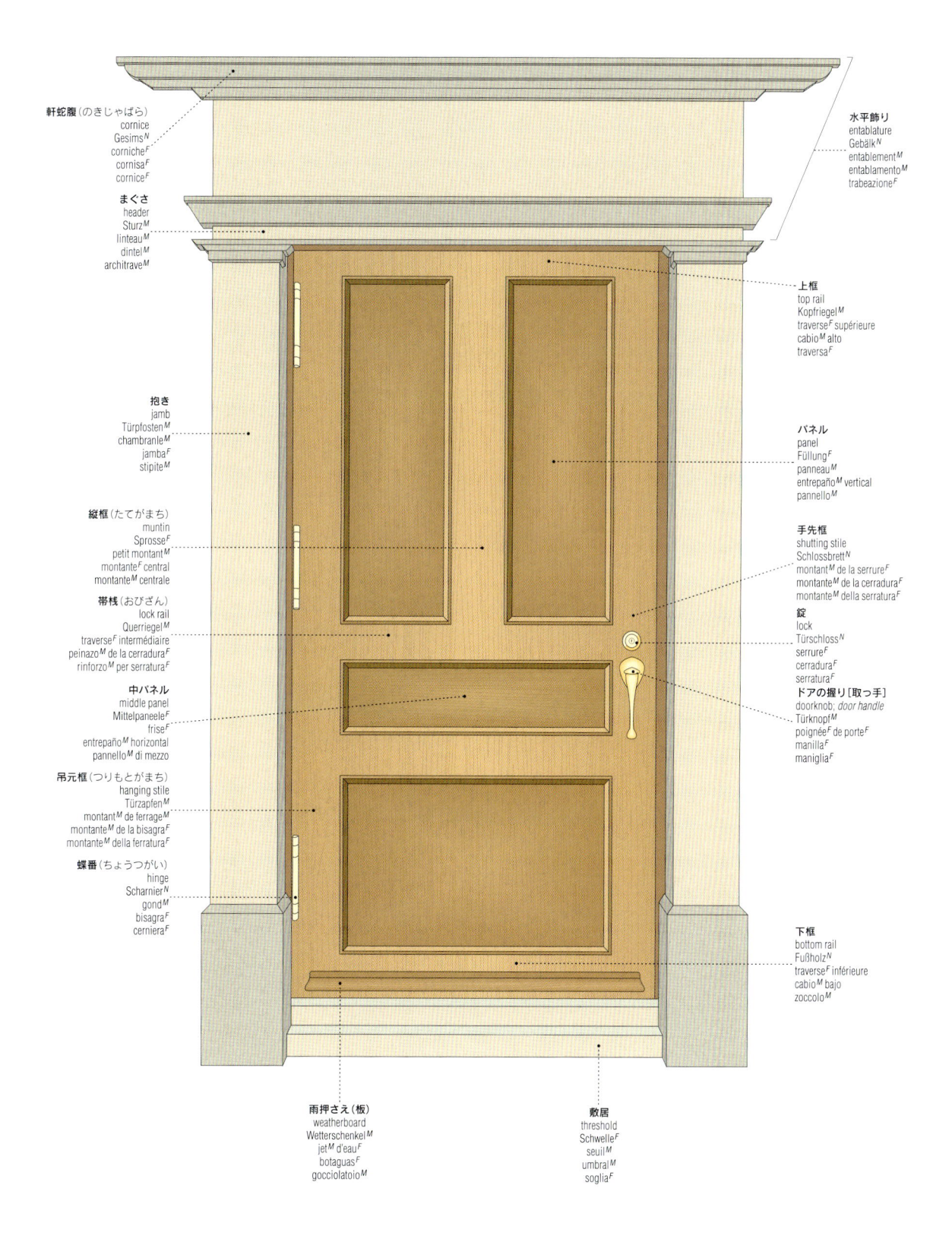

家屋の構成要素 | ELEMENTS OF A HOUSE
TEILE EINES HAUSES | ÉLÉMENTS DE LA MAISON | ELEMENTOS DE LA CASA | ELEMENTI DELLA CASA

外ドア

exterior door | Haustür^F | porte^F extérieure | puerta^F de entrada | porta^F esterna

家屋

軒蛇腹（のきじゃばら）
cornice
Gesims^N
corniche^F
cornisa^F
cornice^F

水平飾り
entablature
Gebälk^N
entablement^M
entablamento^M
trabeazione^F

まぐさ
header
Sturz^M
linteau^M
dintel^M
architrave^M

上框
top rail
Kopfriegel^M
traverse^F supérieure
cabio^M alto
traversa^F

抱き
jamb
Türpfosten^M
chambranle^M
jamba^F
stipite^M

パネル
panel
Füllung^F
panneau^M
entrepaño^M vertical
pannello^M

縦框（たてがまち）
muntin
Sprosse^F
petit montant^M
montante^F central
montante^M centrale

手先框
shutting stile
Schlossbrett^N
montant^M de la serrure^F
montante^M de la cerradura^F
montante^M della serratura^F

帯桟（おびざん）
lock rail
Querriegel^M
traverse^F intermédiaire
peinazo^M de la cerradura^F
rinforzo^M per serratura^F

錠
lock
Türschloss^N
serrure^F
cerradura^F
serratura^F

中パネル
middle panel
Mittelpaneele^F
frise^F
entrepaño^M horizontal
pannello^M di mezzo

ドアの握り[取っ手]
doorknob; door handle
Türknopf^M
poignée^F de porte^F
manilla^F
maniglia^F

吊元框（つりもとがまち）
hanging stile
Türzapfen^M
montant^M de ferrage^M
montante^M de la bisagra^F
montante^M della ferratura^F

蝶番（ちょうつがい）
hinge
Scharnier^N
gond^M
bisagra^F
cerniera^F

下框
bottom rail
Fußholz^N
traverse^F inférieure
cabio^M bajo
zoccolo^M

雨押さえ（板）
weatherboard
Wetterschenkel^M
jet^M d'eau^F
botaguas^F
gocciolatoio^M

敷居
threshold
Schwelle^F
seuil^M
umbral^M
soglia^F

247

家屋の構成要素 | ELEMENTS OF A HOUSE
TEILE EINES HAUSES | ÉLÉMENTS DE LA MAISON | ELEMENTOS DE LA CASA | ELEMENTI DELLA CASA

錠（前）

日本語 | 英語 | ドイツ語 | フランス語 | スペイン語 | イタリア語

lock | Schloss[N] | serrure[F] | cerrajería[F] | serratura[F]

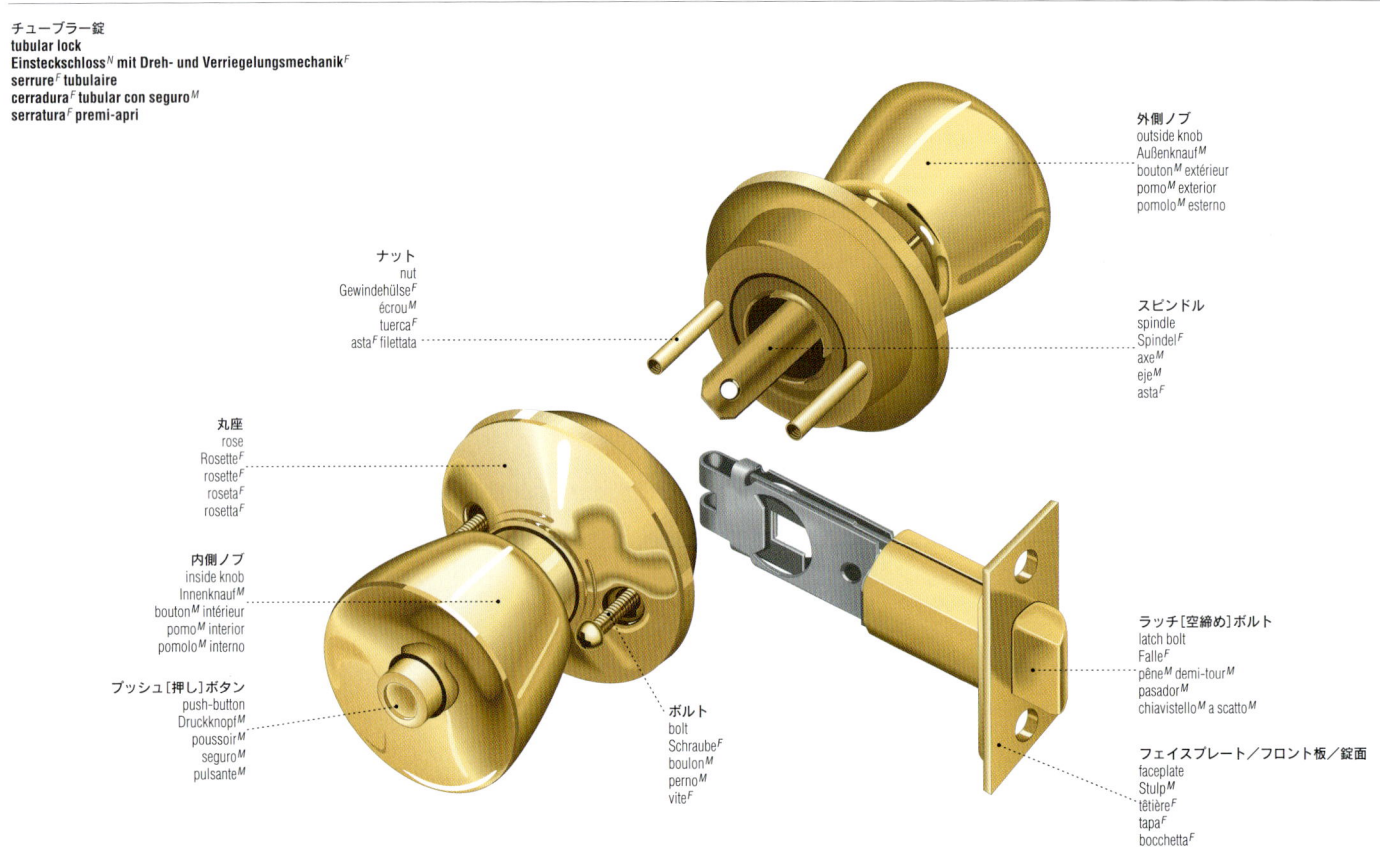

概観
general view
Gesamtansicht[F]
vue[F] d'ensemble[M]
vista[F] general
visione[F] di insieme[M]

デッド[本締め]ボルト
dead bolt
Riegel[M]
pêne[M] dormant
pestillo[M]
chiavistello[M] senza scatto[M]

鍵座／長座
escutcheon
Schlüsselschild[N]
écusson[M]
chapa[F]
piastrina[F]

フェイスプレート／フロント板／錠面
faceplate
Stulp[M]
têtière[F]
tapa[F]
bocchetta[F]

ラッチ[空締め]ボルト
latch bolt
Falle[F]
pêne[M] demi-tour
pasador[M]
chiavistello[M] a scatto[M]

錠
lock
Schloss[N]
serrure[F]
cerradura[F]
serratura[F]

丸座
rose
Rosette[F]
rosette[F]
roseta[F]
rosetta[F]

取っ手／ドアノブ
doorknob; door handle
Türgriff[M]
bec-de-cane[M]
manilla[F]
maniglia[F]

チューブラー錠
tubular lock
Einsteckschloss[N] mit Dreh- und Verriegelungsmechanik[F]
serrure[F] tubulaire
cerradura[F] tubular con seguro[M]
serratura[F] premi-apri

ナット
nut
Gewindehülse[F]
écrou[M]
tuerca[F]
asta[F] filettata

丸座
rose
Rosette[F]
rosette[F]
roseta[F]
rosetta[F]

内側ノブ
inside knob
Innenknauf[M]
bouton[M] intérieur
pomo[M] interior
pomolo[M] interno

プッシュ[押し]ボタン
push-button
Druckknopf[M]
poussoir[M]
seguro[M]
pulsante[M]

外側ノブ
outside knob
Außenknauf[M]
bouton[M] extérieur
pomo[M] exterior
pomolo[M] esterno

スピンドル
spindle
Spindel[F]
axe[M]
eje[M]
asta[F]

ボルト
bolt
Schraube[F]
boulon[M]
perno[M]
vite[F]

ラッチ[空締め]ボルト
latch bolt
Falle[F]
pêne[M] demi-tour
pasador[M]
chiavistello[M] a scatto[M]

フェイスプレート／フロント板／錠面
faceplate
Stulp[M]
têtière[F]
tapa[F]
bocchetta[F]

家屋の構成要素 | ELEMENTS OF A HOUSE
TEILE EINES HAUSES | ÉLÉMENTS DE LA MAISON | ELEMENTOS DE LA CASA | ELEMENTI DELLA CASA

錠（前）

彫り込み錠／箱錠
mortise lock
Zylinderschloss^N
serrure^F à mortaiser
cerradura^F embutida
serratura^F a pomolo^M

シリンダー
cylinder
Schließzylinder^M
barillet^M
cilindro^M
cilindro^M

外筒
stator
Stator^M
stator^M
estator^M
statore^M

スプリング
spring
Feder^F
ressort^M
muelle^M
molla^F

鍵
key
Schlüssel^M
clé^F
llave^F
chiave^F

コッター・ピン
cotter pin
Splint^M
clavette^F
pasador^M
copiglia^F

内筒
rotor
Rotor^M
rotor^M
rotor^M
rotore^M

シリンダー・ケース
cylinder case
Zylindergehäuse^N
logement^M du barillet^M
caja^F del cilindro^M
cassa^F del cilindro^M

鍵穴／鍵溝
keyway
Schlüsselloch^N
entrée^F de clé^F
bocallave^F
toppa^F

受け座
strike plate
Schließblech^N
gâche^F
cajetín^M
controbocchetta^F

リング
ring
Rosette^F
anneau^M
anillo^M
anello^M

デッド［本締め］ボルト
dead bolt
Riegel^M
pêne^M dormant
pestillo^M
chiavistello^M senza scatto^M

フェイスプレート／フロント板／錠面
faceplate
Stulp^M
têtière^F
tapa^F
bocchetta^F

窓

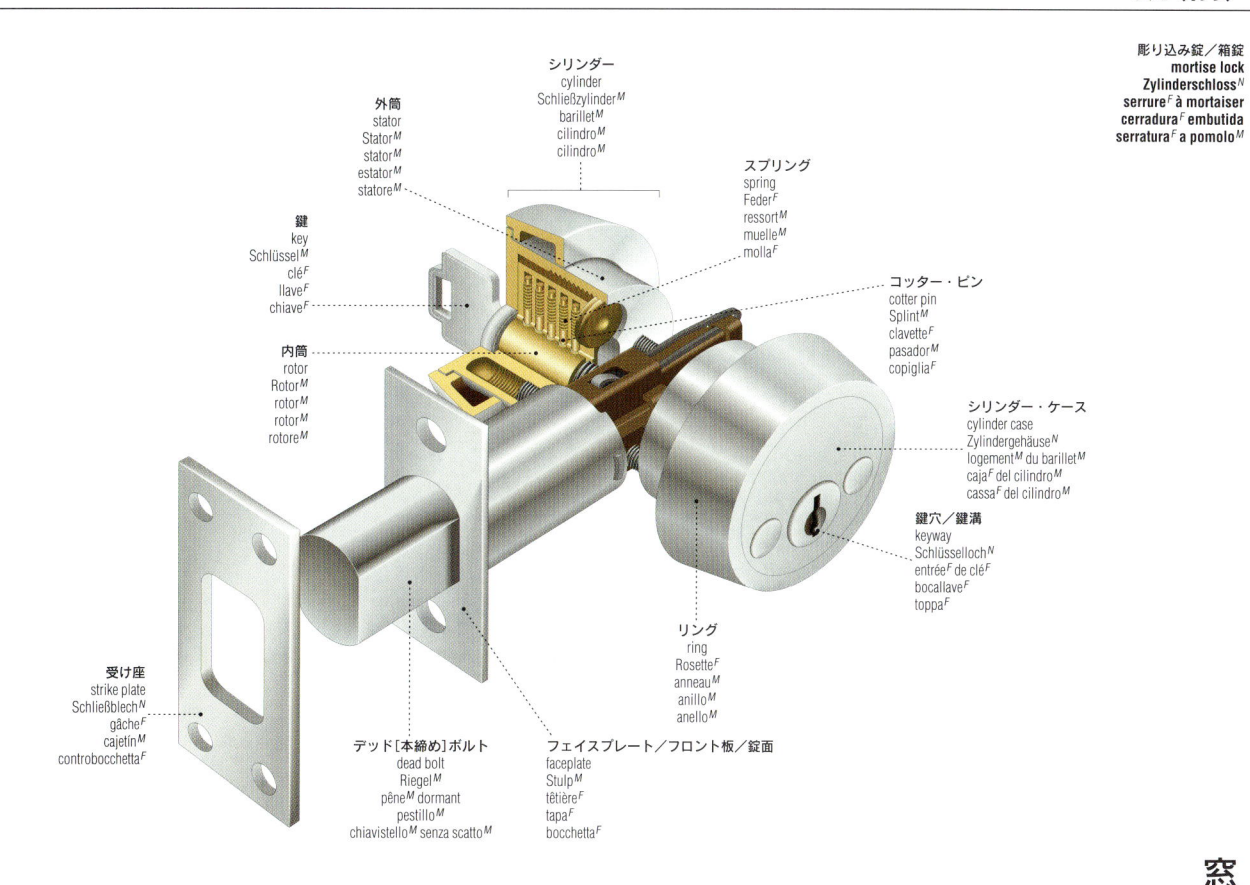

window | Fenster^N | fenêtre^F | ventana^F | finestra^F

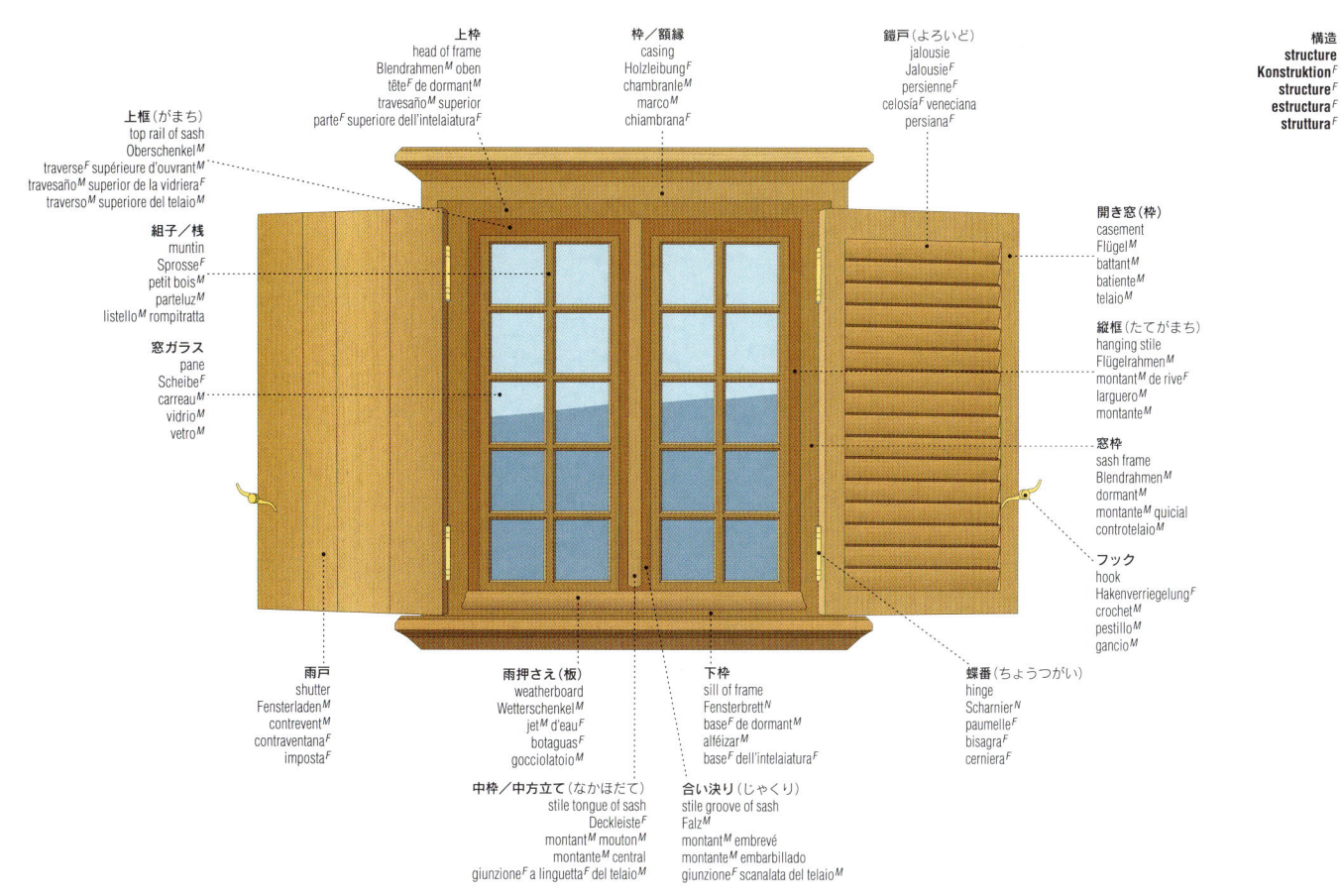

家屋

構造
structure
Konstruktion^F
structure^F
estructura^F
struttura^F

上枠
head of frame
Blendrahmen^M oben
tête^F de dormant^M
travesaño^M superior
parte^F superiore dell'intelaiatura^F

枠／額縁
casing
Holzleibung^F
chambranle^M
marco^M
chiambrana^F

鎧戸（よろいど）
jalousie
Jalousie^F
persienne^F
celosía^F veneciana
persiana^F

上框（がまち）
top rail of sash
Oberschenkel^M
traverse^F supérieure d'ouvrant^M
travesaño^M superior de la vidriera^F
traverso^M superiore del telaio^M

開き窓（枠）
casement
Flügel^M
battant^M
batiente^M
telaio^M

組子／桟
muntin
Sprosse^F
petit bois^M
parteluz^M
listello^M rompitratta

縦框（たてがまち）
hanging stile
Flügelrahmen^M
montant^M de rive^F
larguero^M
montante^M

窓ガラス
pane
Scheibe^F
carreau^M
vidrio^M
vetro^M

窓枠
sash frame
Blendrahmen^M
dormant^M
montante^M quicial
controtelaio^M

フック
hook
Hakenverriegelung^F
crochet^M
pestillo^M
gancio^M

雨戸
shutter
Fensterladen^M
contrevent^M
contraventana^F
imposta^F

雨押さえ（板）
weatherboard
Wetterschenkel^M
jet^M d'eau^F
botaguas^F
gocciolatoio^M

下枠
sill of frame
Fensterbrett^N
base^F de dormant^M
alféizar^M
base^F dell'intelaiatura^F

蝶番（ちょうつがい）
hinge
Scharnier^N
paumelle^F
bisagra^F
cerniera^F

中枠／中方立て（なかほだて）
stile tongue of sash
Deckleiste^F
montant^M mouton
montante^M central
giunzione^F a linguetta^F del telaio^M

合い決り（じゃくり）
stile groove of sash
Falz^F
montant^M embrevé
montante^M embarbillado
giunzione^F scanalata del telaio^M

249

家屋の構造 | STRUCTURE OF A HOUSE
KONSTRUKTION EINES HAUSES | STRUCTURE D'UNE MAISON | ESTRUCTURA DE UNA CASA | STRUTTURA DI UNA CASA

主な部屋

main rooms | Haupträume[M] | principales pièces[F] d'une maison | habitaciones[M] principales | stanze[F] principali

日本語 | 英語 | ドイツ語 | フランス語 | スペイン語 | イタリア語

立面図
elevation
Ansicht[F]
élévation[F]
alzado[M]
prospetto[M]

中二階
mezzanine floor
Zwischengeschoß[N]
mezzanine[F]
entresuelo[M]
piano[M] mansardato

二階
second floor; *first floor*
erster Stock[M]
étage[M]
planta[F] alta
primo piano[M]

一階
first floor; *ground floor*
Erdgeschoß[N]
rez-de-chaussée[M]
planta[F] baja
pianterreno[M]

地階
basement
Keller[M]
sous-sol[M]
semisótano[M]
seminterrato[M]

一階
first floor; *ground floor*
Erdgeschoß[N]
rez-de-chaussée[M]
planta[F] baja
pianterreno[M]

テラス・ドア
patio door
Terrassentür[F]
porte[F]-fenêtre[F]
puerta[F] trasera
porta[F] del patio[M]

台所
kitchen
Küche[F]
cuisine[F]
cocina[F]
cucina[F]

ガラス屋根
glassed roof
Glasdach[N]
verrière[F]
techo[M] de vidrio
tetto[M] a vetro[M]

食事コーナー
dinette
Wohnküche[F]
coin[M]-repas[M]
office[M]
tinello[M]

配膳室
pantry
Speisekammer[F]
garde-manger[M]
despensa[F]
dispensa[F]

居間
sitting room
Wohnzimmer[N]
salle[F] de séjour[M]
sala[F]
salotto[M]

食堂
dining room
Esszimmer[N]
salle[F] à manger
comedor[M]
sala[F] da pranzo[M]

洗濯室
laundry room
Waschküche[F]
buanderie[F]
lavandería[F]
lavanderia[F]

暖炉
fireplace
Kamin[M]
cheminée[F]
chimenea[F]
camino[M]

洗面所
toilet
WC[N]
w.-c.[M]
aseo[M]
stanza[F] da bagno[M]

居間
living room
Wohnzimmer[N]
salon[M]
cuarto[M] de estar
soggiorno[M]

手すり
banister
Geländer[N]
rampe[F]
barandilla[F]
balaustra[F]

玄関ホール
entrance hall
Eingangshalle[F]
hall[M] d'entrée[F]
recibidor[M]
sala[F] di ingresso[M]

階段
stairs
Treppe[F]
escalier[M]
escaleras[F]
scala[F]

玄関
main entrance
Haupteingang[M]
entrée[F] principale
entrada[F] principal
entrata[F] principale

玄関広間
hall
Diele[F]
vestibule[M]
vestíbulo[M]
ingresso[M]

クロゼット
closet
Garderobe[F]
vestiaire[M]
guardarropa[F]
guardaroba[M]

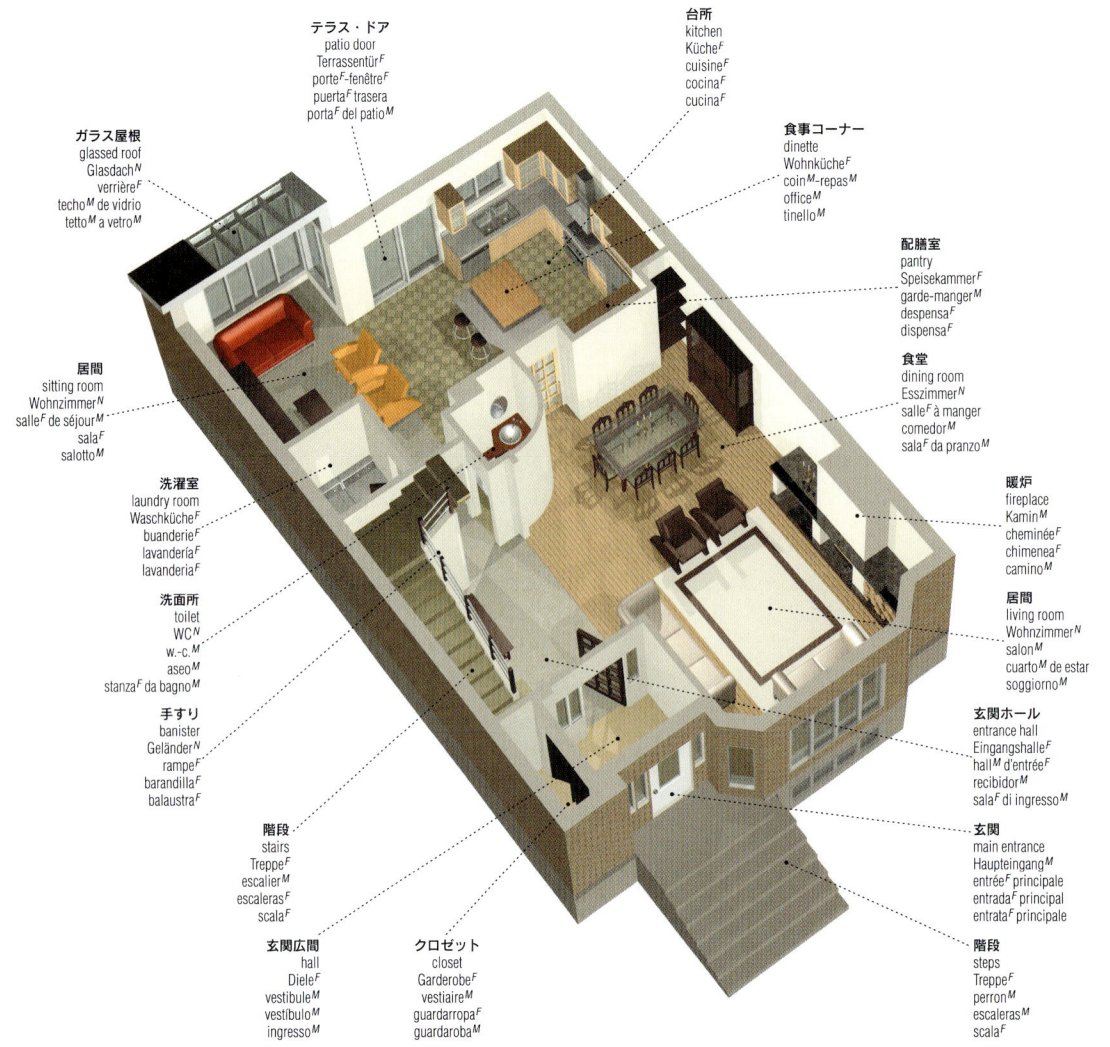

階段
steps
Treppe[F]
perron[M]
escaleras[F]
scala[F]

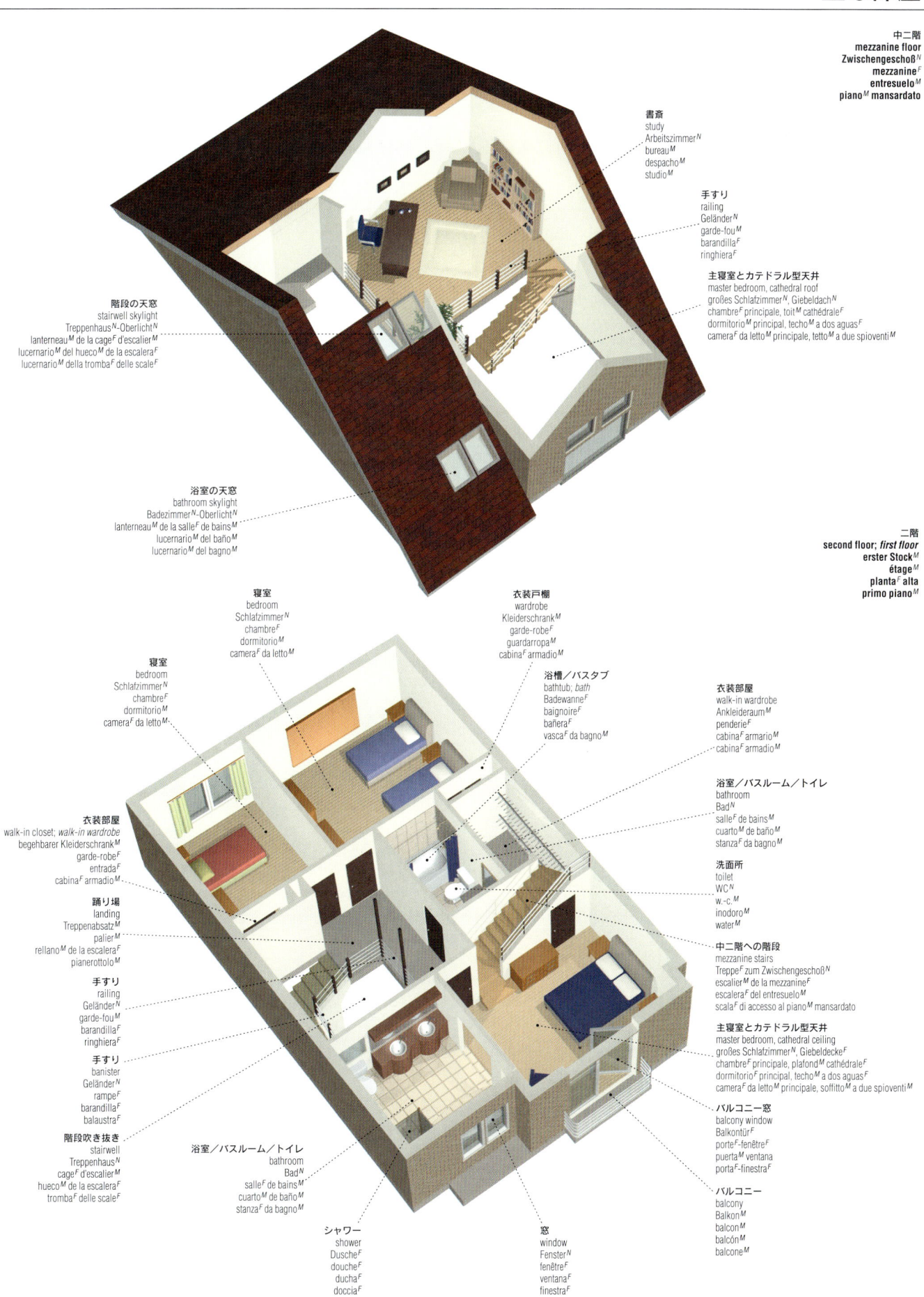

家屋の構造 | STRUCTURE OF A HOUSE
KONSTRUKTION EINES HAUSES | STRUCTURE D'UNE MAISON | ESTRUCTURA DE UNA CASA | STRUTTURA DI UNA CASA

主な部屋

中二階
mezzanine floor
Zwischengeschoß^N
mezzanine^F
entresuelo^M
piano^M mansardato

書斎
study
Arbeitszimmer^N
bureau^M
despacho^M
studio^M

手すり
railing
Geländer^N
garde-fou^M
barandilla^F
ringhiera^F

主寝室とカテドラル型天井
master bedroom, cathedral roof
großes Schlafzimmer^N, Giebeldach^N
chambre^F principale, toit^M cathédrale^F
dormitorio^M principal, techo^M a dos aguas^F
camera^F da letto^M principale, tetto^M a due spioventi^M

階段の天窓
stairwell skylight
Treppenhaus^N-Oberlicht^N
lanterneau^M de la cage^F d'escalier^M
lucernario^M del hueco^M de la escalera^F
lucernario^M della tromba^F delle scale^F

浴室の天窓
bathroom skylight
Badezimmer^N-Oberlicht^N
lanterneau^M de la salle^F de bains^M
lucernario^M del baño^M
lucernario^M del bagno^M

二階
second floor; *first floor*
erster Stock^M
étage^M
planta^F alta
primo piano^M

寝室
bedroom
Schlafzimmer^N
chambre^F
dormitorio^M
camera^F da letto^M

衣装戸棚
wardrobe
Kleiderschrank^N
garde-robe^F
guardarropa^M
cabina^F armadio^M

浴槽／バスタブ
bathtub; *bath*
Badewanne^F
baignoire^F
bañera^F
vasca^F da bagno^M

衣装部屋
walk-in wardrobe
Ankleideraum^M
penderie^F
cabina^F armario^M
cabina^F armadio^M

寝室
bedroom
Schlafzimmer^N
chambre^F
dormitorio^M
camera^F da letto^M

浴室／バスルーム／トイレ
bathroom
Bad^N
salle^F de bains^M
cuarto^M de baño^M
stanza^F da bagno^M

衣装部屋
walk-in closet; *walk-in wardrobe*
begehbarer Kleiderschrank^M
garde-robe^F
entrada^F
cabina^F armadio^M

洗面所
toilet
WC^N
w.-c.^M
inodoro^M
water^M

踊り場
landing
Treppenabsatz^M
palier^M
rellano^M de la escalera^F
pianerottolo^M

中二階への階段
mezzanine stairs
Treppe^F zum Zwischengeschoß^N
escalier^M de la mezzanine^F
escalera^F del entresuelo^M
scala^F di accesso al piano^M mansardato

手すり
railing
Geländer^N
garde-fou^M
barandilla^F
ringhiera^F

主寝室とカテドラル型天井
master bedroom, cathedral ceiling
großes Schlafzimmer^N, Giebeldecke^F
chambre^F principale, plafond^M cathédrale^F
dormitorio^M principal, techo^M a dos aguas^F
camera^F da letto^M principale, soffitto^M a due spioventi^M

手すり
banister
Geländer^N
rampe^F
barandilla^F
balaustra^F

バルコニー窓
balcony window
Balkontür^F
porte^F-fenêtre^F
puerta^F ventana
porta^F-finestra^F

階段吹き抜き
stairwell
Treppenhaus^N
cage^F d'escalier^M
hueco^M de la escalera^F
tromba^F delle scale^F

浴室／バスルーム／トイレ
bathroom
Bad^N
salle^F de bains^M
cuarto^M de baño^M
stanza^F da bagno^M

バルコニー
balcony
Balkon^M
balcon^M
balcón^M
balcone^M

シャワー
shower
Dusche^F
douche^F
ducha^F
doccia^F

窓
window
Fenster^N
fenêtre^F
ventana^F
finestra^F

251

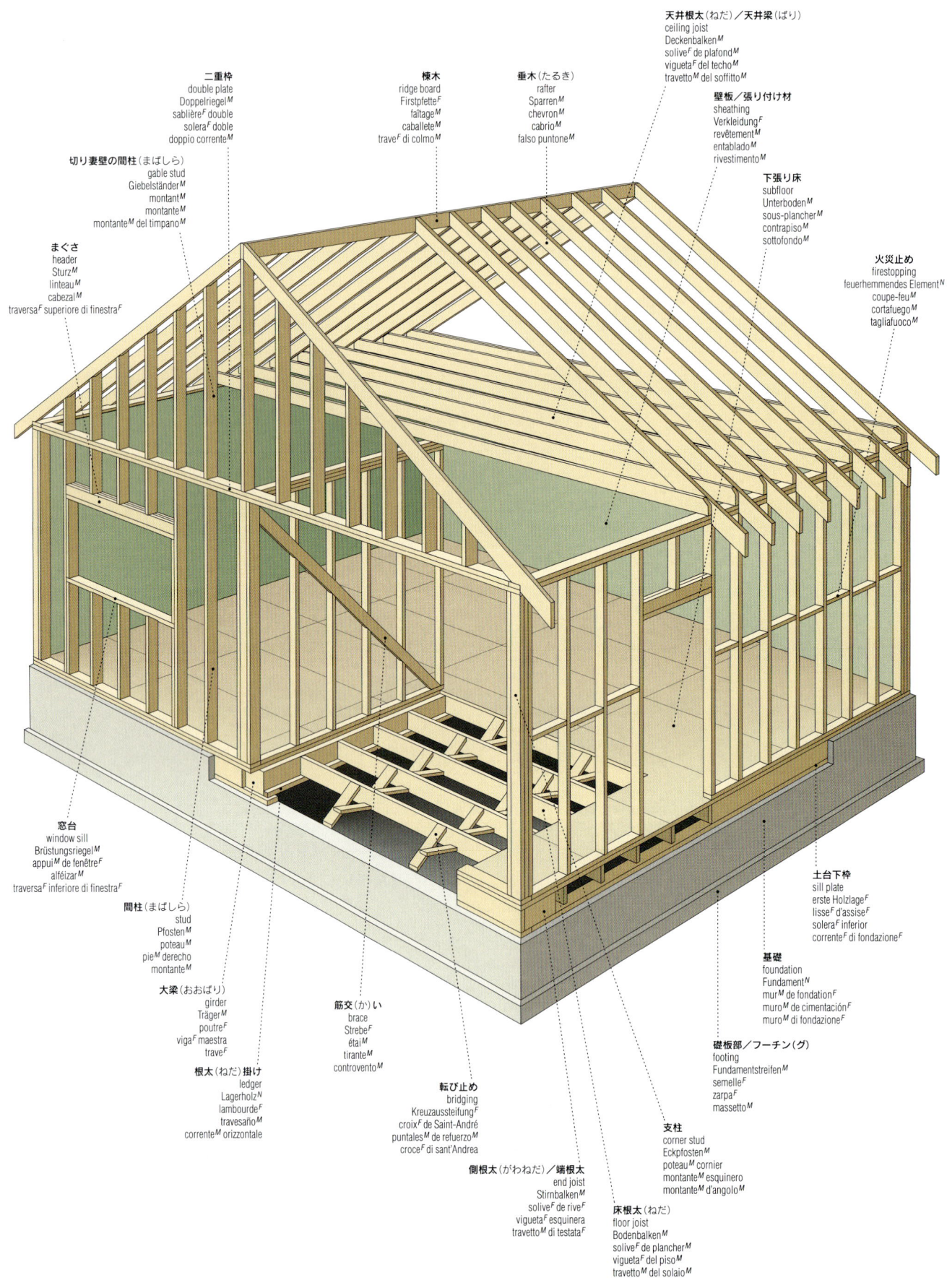

家屋の構造 | STRUCTURE OF A HOUSE
KONSTRUKTION EINES HAUSES | STRUCTURE D'UNE MAISON | ESTRUCTURA DE UNA CASA | STRUTTURA DI UNA CASA

枠組み

frame | Rahmen^M | charpente^F | armazón^M | struttura^F

日本語 | 英語 | ドイツ語 | フランス語 | スペイン語 | イタリア語

家屋

天井根太（ねだ）／天井梁（ばり）
ceiling joist
Deckenbalken^M
solive^F de plafond^M
vigueta^F del techo^M
travetto^M del soffitto^M

二重枠
double plate
Doppelriegel^M
sablière^F double
solera^F doble
doppio corrente^M

棟木
ridge board
Firstpfette^F
faîtage^M
caballete^M
trave^F di colmo^M

垂木（たるき）
rafter
Sparren^M
chevron^M
cabrio^M
falso puntone^M

壁板／張り付け材
sheathing
Verkleidung^F
revêtement^M
entablado^M
rivestimento^M

切り妻壁の間柱（まばしら）
gable stud
Giebelständer^M
montant^M
montante^M
montante^M del timpano^M

下張り床
subfloor
Unterboden^M
sous-plancher^M
contrapiso^M
sottofondo^M

まぐさ
header
Sturz^M
linteau^M
cabezal^M
traversa^F superiore di finestra^F

火災止め
firestopping
feuerhemmendes Element^N
coupe-feu^M
cortafuego^M
tagliafuoco^M

窓台
window sill
Brüstungsriegel^M
appui^M de fenêtre^F
alféizar^M
traversa^F inferiore di finestra^F

土台下枠
sill plate
erste Holzlage^F
lisse^F d'assise^F
solera^F inferior
corrente^F di fondazione^F

間柱（まばしら）
stud
Pfosten^M
poteau^M
pie^M derecho
montante^M

大梁（おおばり）
girder
Träger^M
poutre^F
viga^F maestra
trave^F

筋交（かい）
brace
Strebe^F
étai^M
tirante^M
controvento^M

基礎
foundation
Fundament^N
mur^M de fondation^F
muro^M de cimentación^F
muro^M di fondazione^F

根太（ねだ）掛け
ledger
Lagerholz^N
lambourde^F
travesaño^M
corrente^F orizzontale

転び止め
bridging
Kreuzaussteifung^F
croix^F de Saint-André
puntales^M de refuerzo^M
croce^F di sant'Andrea

礎板部／フーチン（グ）
footing
Fundamentstreifen^M
semelle^F
zarpa^F
massetto^M

支柱
corner stud
Eckpfosten^M
poteau^M cornier
montante^M esquinero
montante^M d'angolo^M

側根太（がわねだ）／端根太
end joist
Stirnbalken^M
solive^F de rive^F
vigueta^F esquinera
travetto^M di testata^F

床根太（ねだ）
floor joist
Bodenbalken^M
solive^F de plancher^M
vigueta^F del piso^M
travetto^M del solaio^M

252

家屋の構造 | STRUCTURE OF A HOUSE
KONSTRUKTION EINES HAUSES | STRUCTURE D'UNE MAISON | ESTRUCTURA DE UNA CASA | STRUTTURA DI UNA CASA

屋根のトラス

roof truss | Dachbinder^M | ferme^F de toit | armadura^F del techo^M | capriata^F

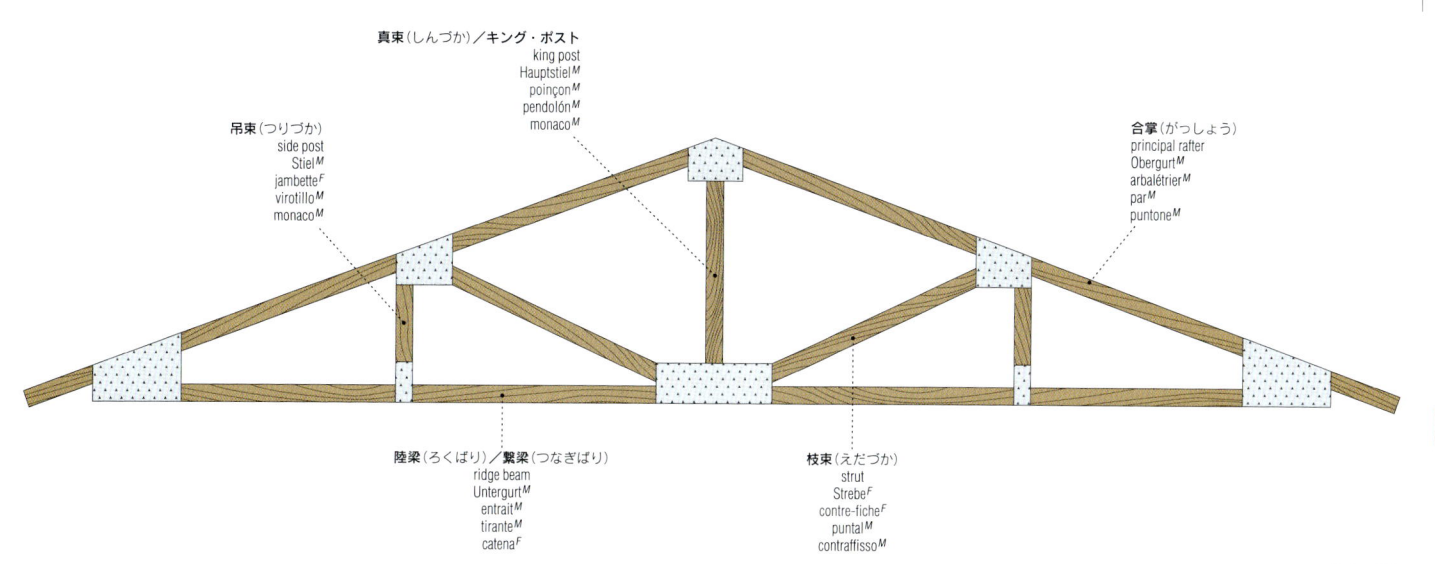

真束（しんづか）／キング・ポスト
king post
Hauptstiel^M
poinçon^M
pendolón^M
monaco^M

吊束（つりづか）
side post
Stiel^M
jambette^F
virotillo^M
monaco^M

合掌（がっしょう）
principal rafter
Obergurt^M
arbalétrier^M
par^M
puntone^M

陸梁（ろくばり）／繋梁（つなぎばり）
ridge beam
Untergurt^M
entrait^M
tirante^M
catena^F

枝束（えだづか）
strut
Strebe^F
contre-fiche^F
puntal^M
contraffisso^M

基礎

foundation | Fundament^N | fondations^F | cimientos^M | fondazioni^F

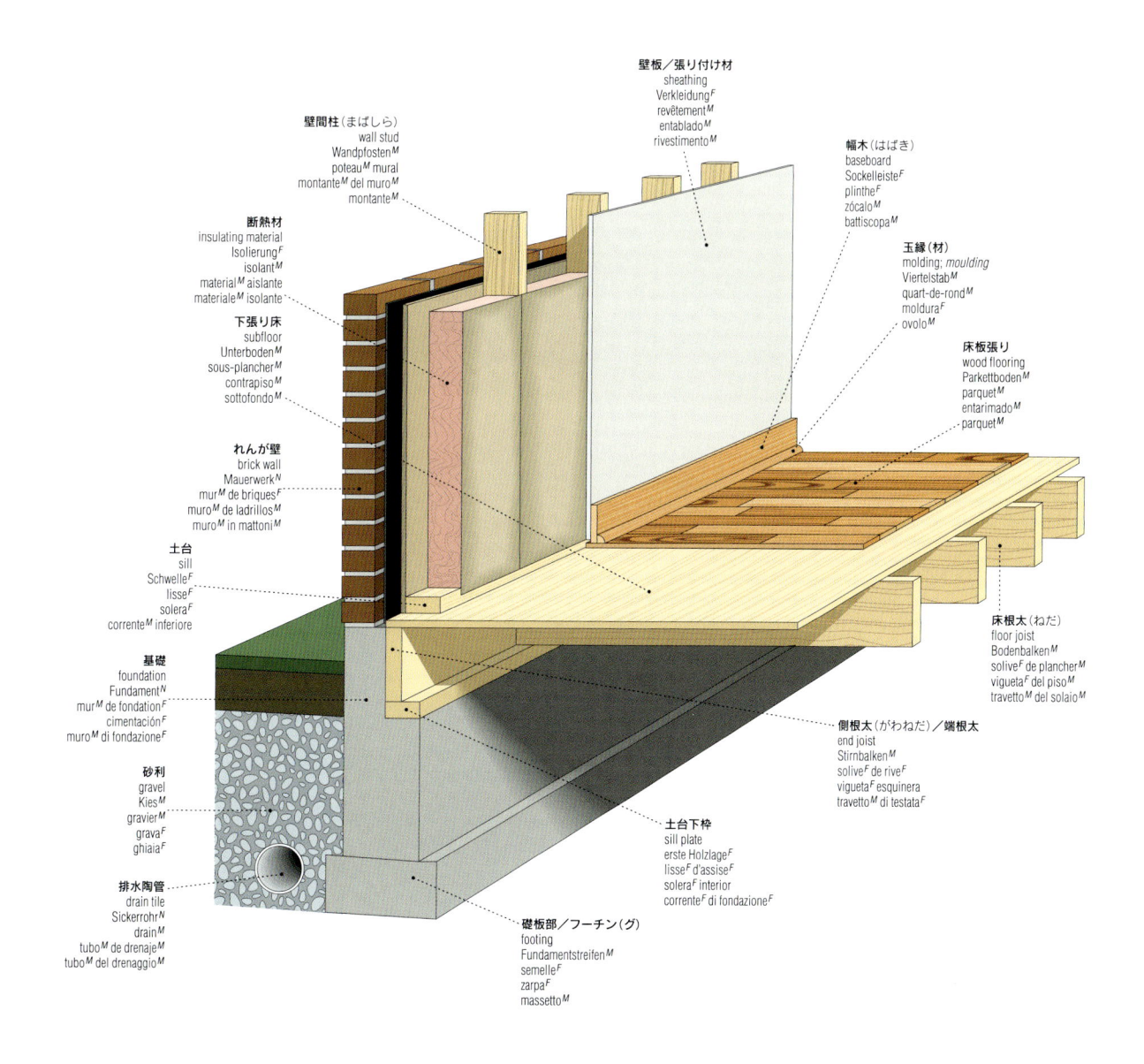

壁板／張り付け材
sheathing
Verkleidung^F
revêtement^M
entablado^M
rivestimento^M

壁間柱（まばしら）
wall stud
Wandpfosten^M
poteau^M mural
montante^M del muro^M
montante^M

幅木（はばき）
baseboard
Sockelleiste^F
plinthe^F
zócalo^M
battiscopa^M

断熱材
insulating material
Isolierung^F
isolant^M
material^M aislante
materiale^M isolante

玉縁（材）
molding; moulding
Viertelstab^M
quart-de-rond^M
moldura^F
ovolo^M

下張り床
subfloor
Unterboden^M
sous-plancher^M
contrapiso^M
sottofondo^M

床板張り
wood flooring
Parkettboden^M
parquet^M
entarimado^M
parquet^M

れんが壁
brick wall
Mauerwerk^N
mur^M de briques^F
muro^M de ladrillos^M
muro^M in mattoni^M

土台
sill
Schwelle^F
lisse^F
solera^F
corrente^M inferiore

床根太（ねだ）
floor joist
Bodenbalken^M
solive^F de plancher^M
vigueta^F del piso^M
travetto^M del solaio^M

基礎
foundation
Fundament^N
mur^M de fondation^F
cimentación^F
muro^M di fondazione^F

側根太（がわねだ）／端根太
end joist
Stirnbalken^M
solive^F de rive^F
vigueta^F esquinera
travetto^M di testata^F

砂利
gravel
Kies^M
gravier^M
grava^F
ghiaia^F

土台下枠
sill plate
erste Holzlage^F
lisse^F d'assise^F
solera^F interior
corrente^M di fondazione^F

排水陶管
drain tile
Sickerrohr^N
drain^M
tubo^M de drenaje^M
tubo^M di drenaggio^M

礎板部／フーチング（グ）
footing
Fundamentstreifen^M
semelle^F
zarpa^F
massetto^M

家屋の構造 | STRUCTURE OF A HOUSE
KONSTRUKTION EINES HAUSES | STRUCTURE D'UNE MAISON | ESTRUCTURA DE UNA CASA | STRUTTURA DI UNA CASA

寄せ木張り

wood flooring | Parkettboden^M | parquet^M | pisos^M de madera^F | parquet^M

日本語 | 英語 | ドイツ語 | フランス語 | スペイン語 | イタリア語

セメント・スクリード上の寄せ木張り
wood flooring on cement screed
Parkettboden^M auf Zementestrich
parquet^M sur chape^F de ciment^M
parqué^M sobre base^F de cemento^M
parquet^M su sottofondo^M di cemento^M

木構造上の寄せ木張り
wood flooring on wooden structure
Parkettboden^M auf Holzunterbau
parquet^M sur ossature^F de bois^M
entarimado^M sobre estructura^F de madera^F
parquet^M su struttura^F lignea

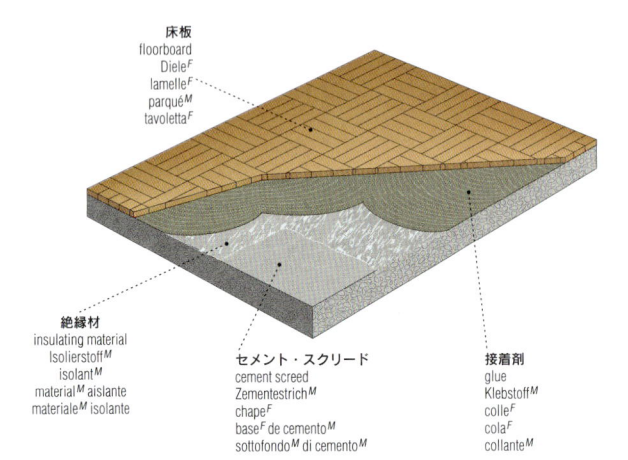

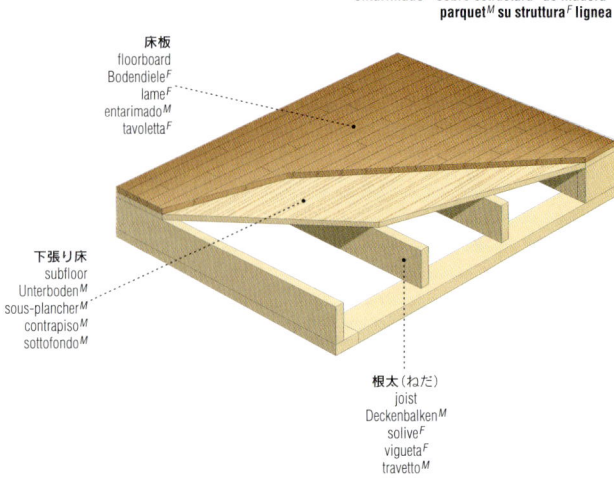

床板
floorboard
Diele^F
lamelle^F
parqué^M
tavoletta^F

床板
floorboard
Bodendiele^F
lame^F
entarimado^M
tavoletta^F

絶縁材
insulating material
Isolierstoff^M
isolant^M
material^M aislante
materiale^M isolante

セメント・スクリード
cement screed
Zementestrich^M
chape^F
base^F de cemento^M
sottofondo^M di cemento^M

接着剤
glue
Klebstoff^M
colle^F
cola^F
collante^M

下張り床
subfloor
Unterboden^M
sous-plancher^M
contrapiso^M
sottofondo^M

根太（ねだ）
joist
Deckenbalken^M
solive^F
vigueta^F
travetto^M

寄せ木張りの配列
wood flooring arrangements
Parkettmuster^N
arrangements^M des parquets^M
tipos^M de parqué^M
tipi^M di parquet^M

乱継ぎ張り
overlay flooring
Stabparkett^N im Schiffsbodenverband^M
parquet^M à coupe^F perdue
parqué^M sobrepuesto
parquet^M a listoni^M

縁甲板張り
strip flooring with alternate joints
Stabparkett^N
parquet^M à coupe^F de pierre^F
parqué^M alternado a la inglesa
parquet^M a listelli^M

矢筈（やはず）寄せ木張り
herringbone parquet
Fischgrätparkett^N
parquet^M à bâtons^M rompus
parqué^M espinapez^M
parquet^M a spina^F di pesce^M

矢筈模様
herringbone pattern
Fischgrätmuster^N
parquet^M en chevrons^M
parqué^M en punta^F de Hungría
parquet^M a spina^F di pesce^M

モザイク寄せ木張り
inlaid parquet
Mosaikparkett^N
parquet^M mosaïque^F
parqué^M de mosaico^M
parquet^M a mosaico^M

斜子（ななこ）織り模様
basket weave pattern
Würfelmusterparkett^N
parquet^M en vannerie^F
parqué^M de cestería^F
parquet^M a tessitura^F di vimini^M

アランベール寄せ木張り
Arenberg parquet
Arenberg-Parkett^N
parquet^M d'Arenberg
parqué^M Arenberg
parquet^M Arenberg

シャンティイ寄せ木張り
Chantilly parquet
Chantilly-Parkett^N
parquet^M Chantilly
parqué^M Chantilly
parquet^M Chantilly

ベルサイユ寄せ木張り
Versailles parquet
Versailles-Parkett^N
parquet^M Versailles
parqué^M Versalles
parquet^M Versailles

敷物

textile floor coverings | textile Bodenbeläge^M | revêtements^M de sol^M textiles | revestimientos^M textiles del suelo^M | rivestimenti^M in tessuto^M per pavimento^M

カーペット／絨毯（じゅうたん）
rug
Teppich^M
tapis^M
alfombra^F
tappeto^M

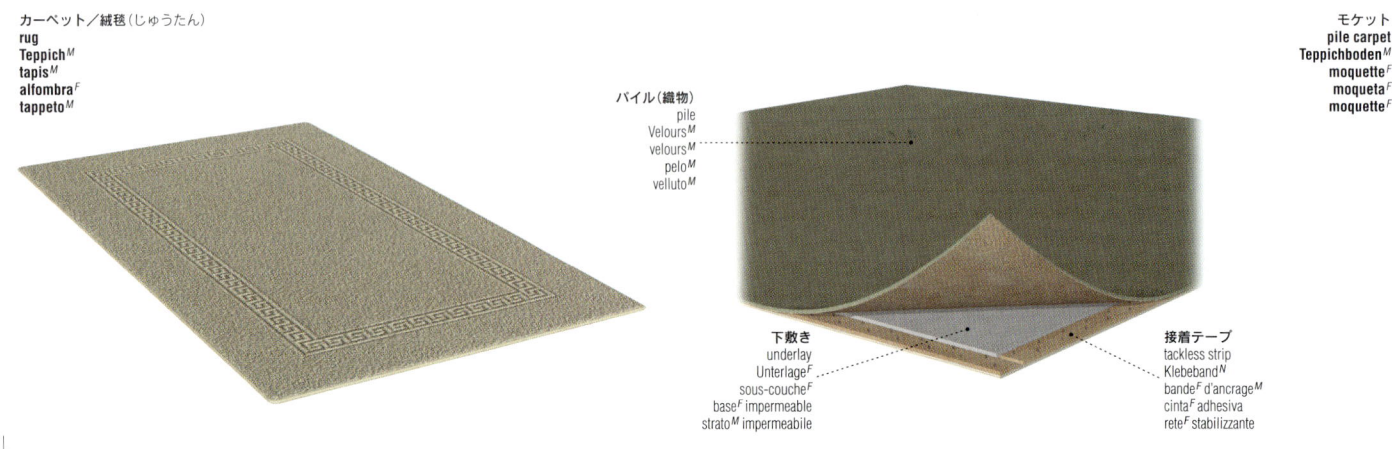

モケット
pile carpet
Teppichboden^M
moquette^F
moqueta^F
moquette^F

パイル（織物）
pile
Velours^M
velours^M
pelo^M
velluto^M

下敷き
underlay
Unterlage^F
sous-couche^F
base^F impermeable
strato^M impermeabile

接着テープ
tackless strip
Klebeband^N
bande^F d'ancrage^M
cinta^F adhesiva
rete^F stabilizzante

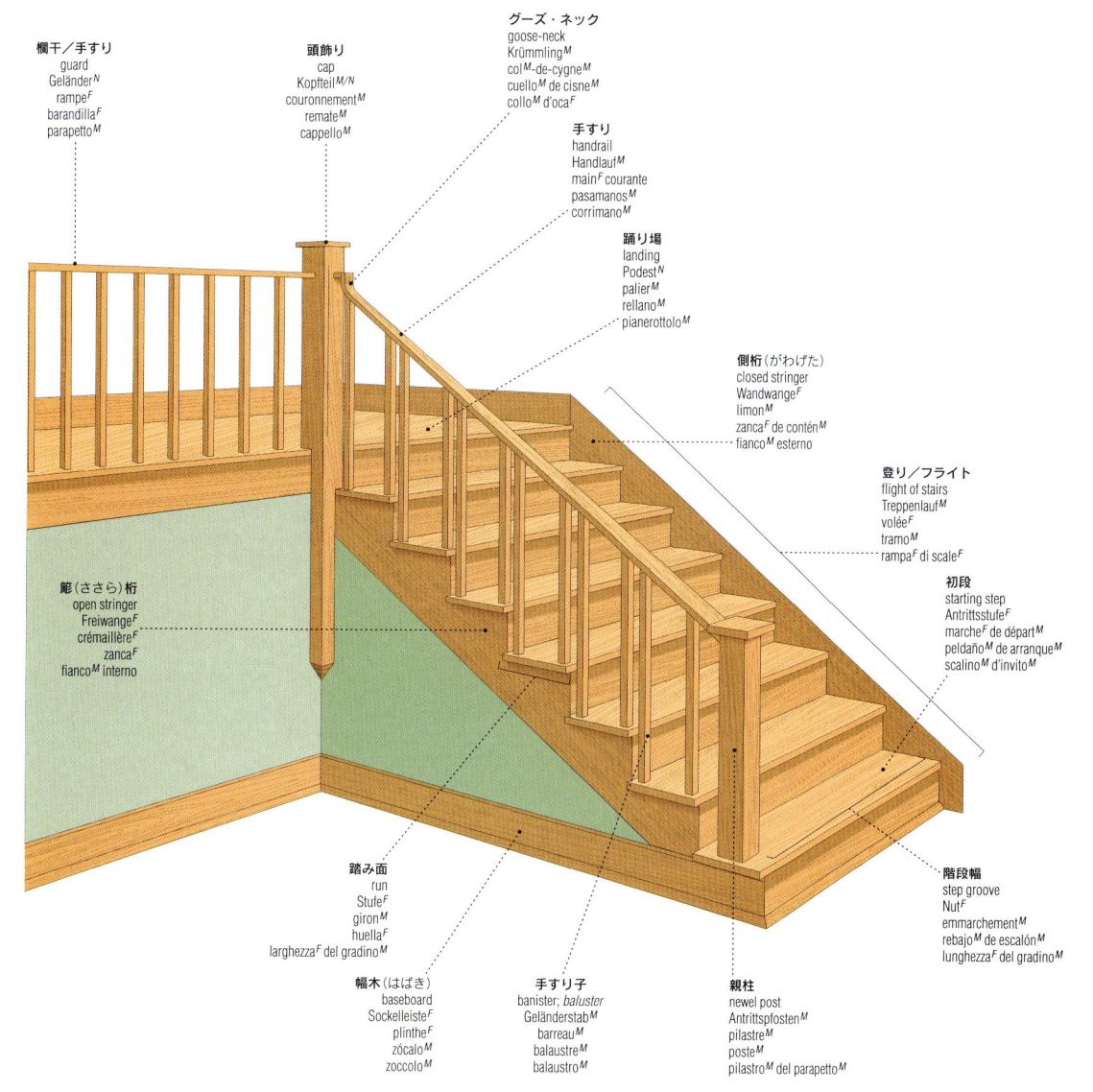

家屋の構造 | STRUCTURE OF A HOUSE
KONSTRUKTION EINES HAUSES | STRUCTURE D'UNE MAISON | ESTRUCTURA DE UNA CASA | STRUTTURA DI UNA CASA

階段

stairs | Treppe^F | escalier^M | escalera^F | scale^F

欄干／手すり
guard
Geländer^N
rampe^F
barandilla^F
parapetto^F

頭飾り
cap
Kopfteil^M/N
couronnement^M
remate^M
cappello^M

グーズ・ネック
goose-neck
Krümmling^M
col^M-de-cygne^M
cuello^M de cisne^M
collo^M d'oca^F

手すり
handrail
Handlauf^M
main^F courante
pasamanos^M
corrimano^M

踊り場
landing
Podest^N
palier^M
rellano^M
pianerottolo^M

側桁（がわげた）
closed stringer
Wandwange^F
limon^M
zanca^F de contén^M
fianco^M esterno

登り／フライト
flight of stairs
Treppenlauf^M
volée^F
tramo^M
rampa^F di scale^F

初段
starting step
Antrittsstufe^F
marche^F de départ^M
peldaño^M de arranque^M
scalino^M d'invito^M

簓（ささら）桁
open stringer
Freiwange^F
crémaillère^F
zanca^F
fianco^M interno

踏み面
run
Stufe^F
giron^M
huella^F
larghezza^F del gradino^M

幅木（はばき）
baseboard
Sockelleiste^F
plinthe^F
zócalo^M
zoccolo^M

手すり子
banister; *baluster*
Geländerstab^M
barreau^M
balaustre^M
balaustro^M

親柱
newel post
Antrittspfosten^M
pilastre^M
poste^M
pilastro^M del parapetto^M

階段幅
step groove
Nut^F
emmarchement^M
rebajo^M de escalón^M
lunghezza^F del gradino^M

階段の段

step | Treppenstufe^F | marche^F | peldaño^M | gradino^M

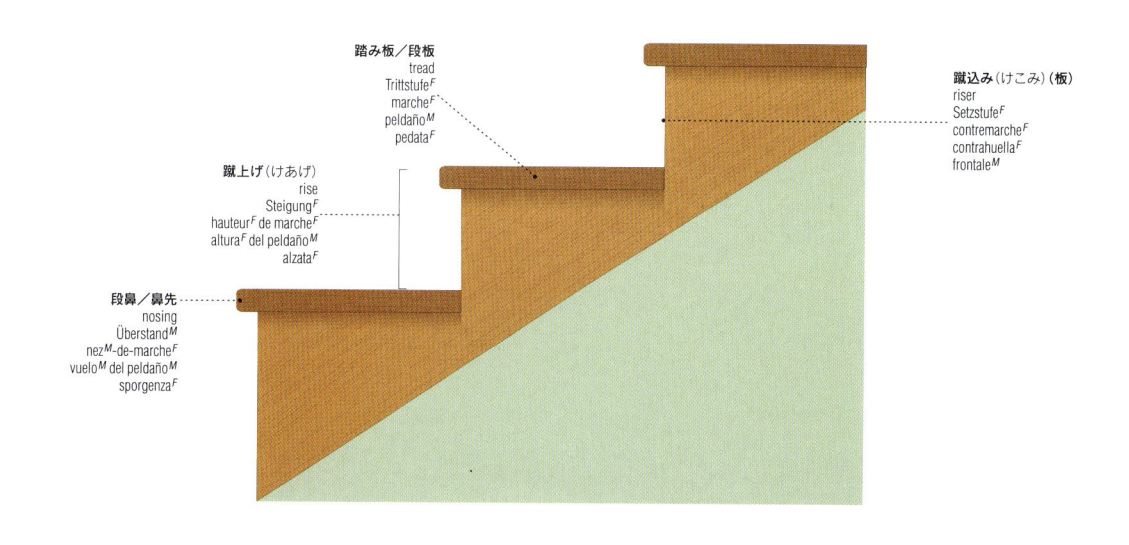

踏み板／段板
tread
Trittstufe^F
marche^F
peldaño^M
pedata^F

蹴込み（けこみ）（板）
riser
Setzstufe^F
contremarche^F
contrahuella^F
frontale^M

蹴上げ（けあげ）
rise
Steigung^F
hauteur^F de marche^F
altura^F del peldaño^M
alzata^F

段鼻／鼻先
nosing
Überstand^M
nez^M-de-marche^F
vuelo^M del peldaño^M
sporgenza^F

暖房 | HEATING
HEIZUNG | CHAUFFAGE | CALEFACCIÓN | RISCALDAMENTO

薪（まき）燃料

日本語 | 英語 | ドイツ語 | フランス語 | スペイン語 | イタリア語

wood firing | Holzbeheizung^F | chauffage^M au bois^M | calefacción^F de leña^F | riscaldamento^M a legna^F

暖炉
fireplace
Kamin^M
cheminée^F à foyer^M ouvert
chimenea^F
camino^M

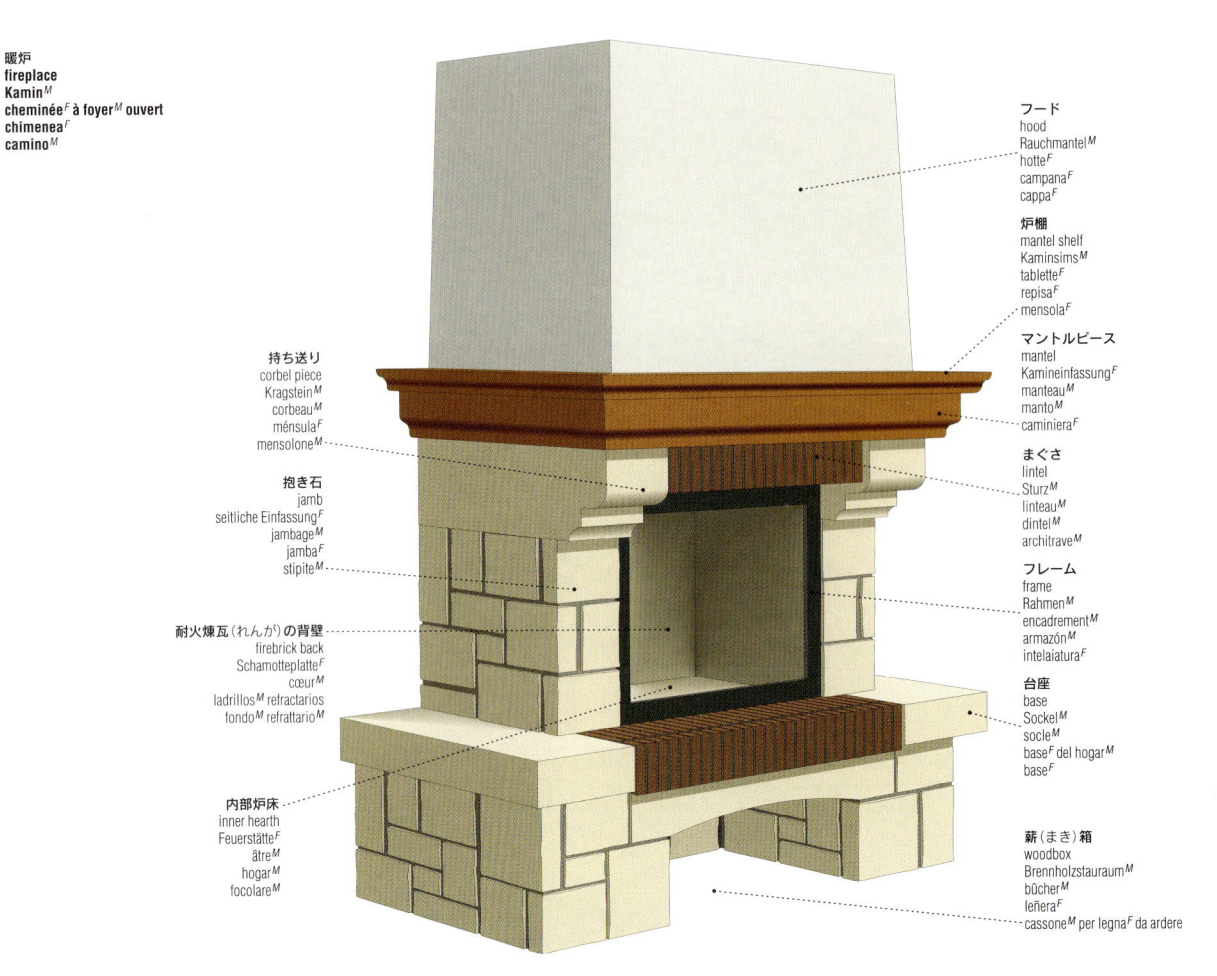

持ち送り
corbel piece
Kragstein^M
corbeau^M
ménsula^F
mensolone^M

抱き石
jamb
seitliche Einfassung^F
jambage^M
jamba^F
stipite^M

耐火煉瓦（れんが）の背壁
firebrick back
Schamotteplatte^F
cœur^M
ladrillos^M refractarios
fondo^M refrattario^M

内部炉床
inner hearth
Feuerstätte^F
âtre^M
hogar^M
focolare^M

フード
hood
Rauchmantel^M
hotte^F
campana^F
cappa^F

炉棚
mantel shelf
Kaminsims^M
tablette^F
repisa^F
mensola^F

マントルピース
mantel
Kamineinfassung^F
manteau^M
manto^M
caminiera^F

まぐさ
lintel
Sturz^M
linteau^M
dintel^M
architrave^M

フレーム
frame
Rahmen^M
encadrement^M
armazón^M
intelaiatura^F

台座
base
Sockel^M
socle^M
base^F del hogar^M
base^F

薪（まき）箱
woodbox
Brennholzstauraum^M
bûcher^M
leñera^F
cassone^M per legna^F da ardere

貯炭式ストーブ
slow-burning stove
Dauerbrandofen^M
poêle^M à combustion^F lente
estufa^F de leña^M a fuego^M lento
stufa^F a combustione^F lenta

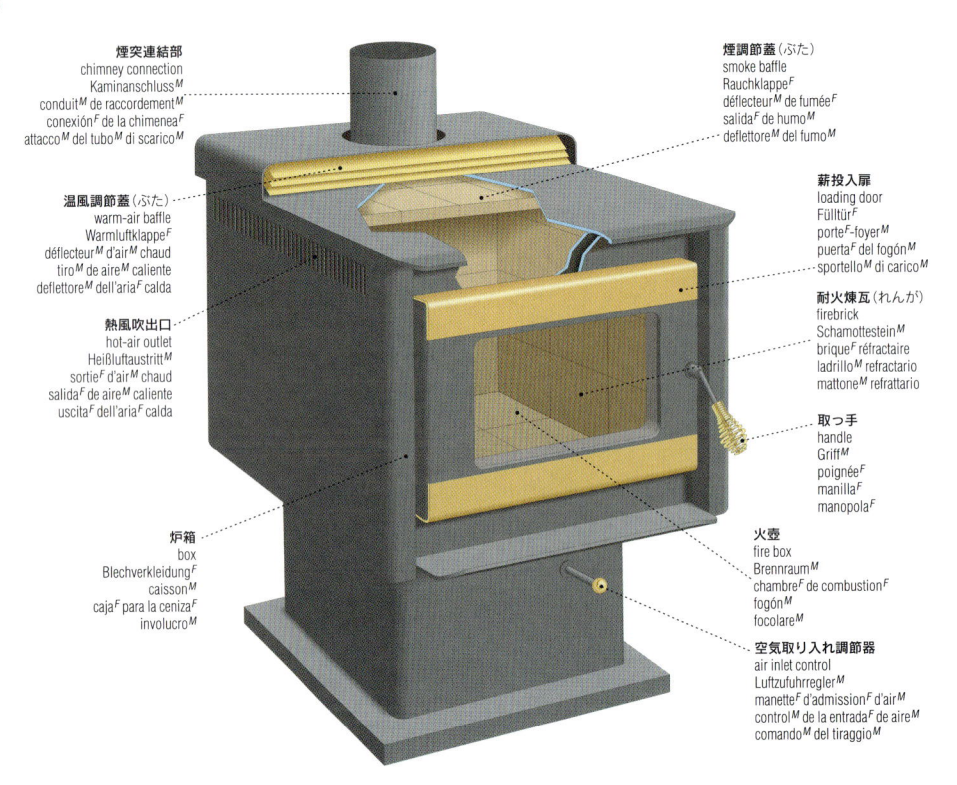

煙突連結部
chimney connection
Kaminanschluss^M
conduit^M de raccordement^M
conexión^F de la chimenea^F
attacco^M del tubo^M di scarico^M

温風調節蓋（ふた）
warm-air baffle
Warmluftklappe^F
déflecteur^M d'air^M chaud
tiro^M de aire^M caliente
deflettore^M dell'aria^F calda

熱風吹出口
hot-air outlet
Heißluftaustritt^M
sortie^F d'air^M chaud
salida^F de aire^M caliente
uscita^F dell'aria^F calda

炉箱
box
Blechverkleidung^F
caisson^M
caja^F para la ceniza^F
involucro^M

煙調節蓋（ふた）
smoke baffle
Rauchklappe^F
déflecteur^M de fumée^F
salida^F de humo^M
deflettore^M del fumo^M

薪投入扉
loading door
Fülltür^F
porte^F-foyer^M
puerta^F del fogón^M
sportello^M di carico^M

耐火煉瓦（れんが）
firebrick
Schamottestein^M
brique^F réfractaire
ladrillo^M refractario
mattone^M refrattario

取っ手
handle
Griff^M
poignée^F
manilla^F
manopola^F

火壺
fire box
Brennraum^M
chambre^F de combustion^F
fogón^M
focolare^M

空気取り入れ調節器
air inlet control
Luftzufuhrregler^M
manette^F d'admission^F d'air^M
control^M de la entrada^F de aire^M
comando^M del tiraggio^M

家屋

256

暖房 | HEATING
HEIZUNG | CHAUFFAGE | CALEFACCIÓN | RISCALDAMENTO

薪（まき）燃料

煙突
chimney
Kamin^M
cheminée^F
chimenea^F
camino^M

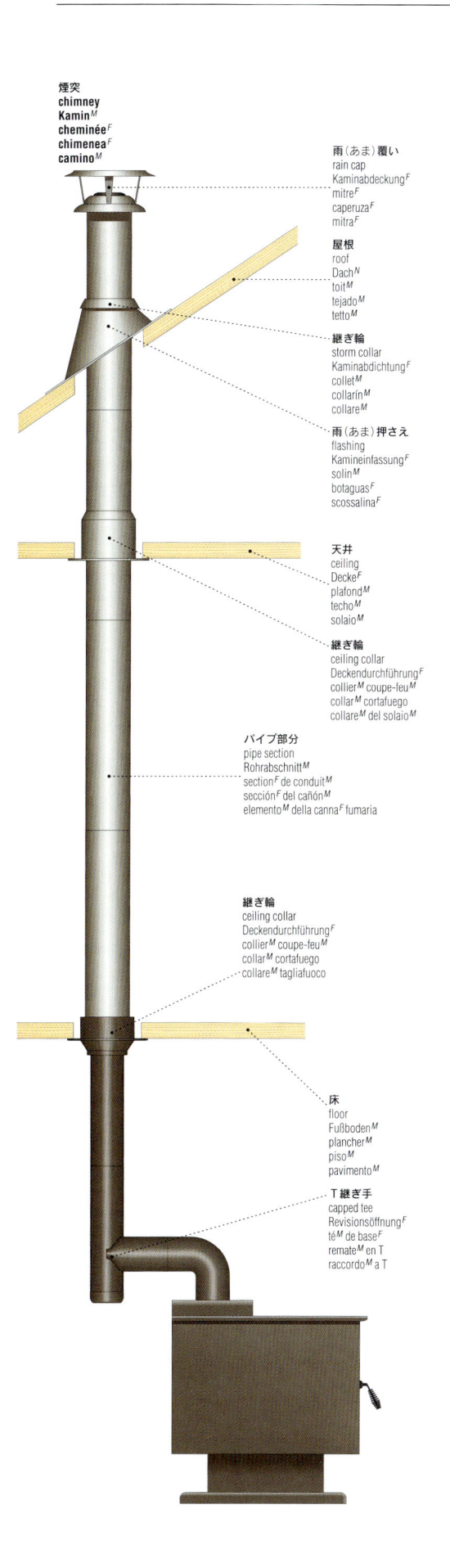

雨（あま）覆い
rain cap
Kaminabdeckung^F
mitre^M
caperuza^F
mitra^F

屋根
roof
Dach^N
toit^M
tejado^M
tetto^M

継ぎ輪
storm collar
Kaminabdichtung^F
collet^M
collarín^M
collare^M

雨（あま）押さえ
flashing
Kamineinfassung^F
solin^M
botaguas^F
scossalina^F

天井
ceiling
Decke^F
plafond^M
techo^M
solaio^M

継ぎ輪
ceiling collar
Deckendurchführung^F
collier^F coupe-feu^M
collar^M cortafuego
collare^M del solaio^M

パイプ部分
pipe section
Rohrabschnitt^M
section^F de conduit^M
sección^F del cañón^M
elemento^M della canna^F fumaria

継ぎ輪
ceiling collar
Deckendurchführung^F
collier^M coupe-feu^M
collar^M cortafuego
collare^M tagliafuoco

床
floor
Fußboden^M
plancher^M
piso^M
pavimento^M

T継ぎ手
capped tee
Revisionsöffnung^F
té^M de base^F
remate^M en T
raccordo^M a T

炉辺用鉄器具
fire irons
Kaminbesteck^N
accessoires^M de foyer^M
utensilios^M para la chimenea^F
ferri^M per il camino^M

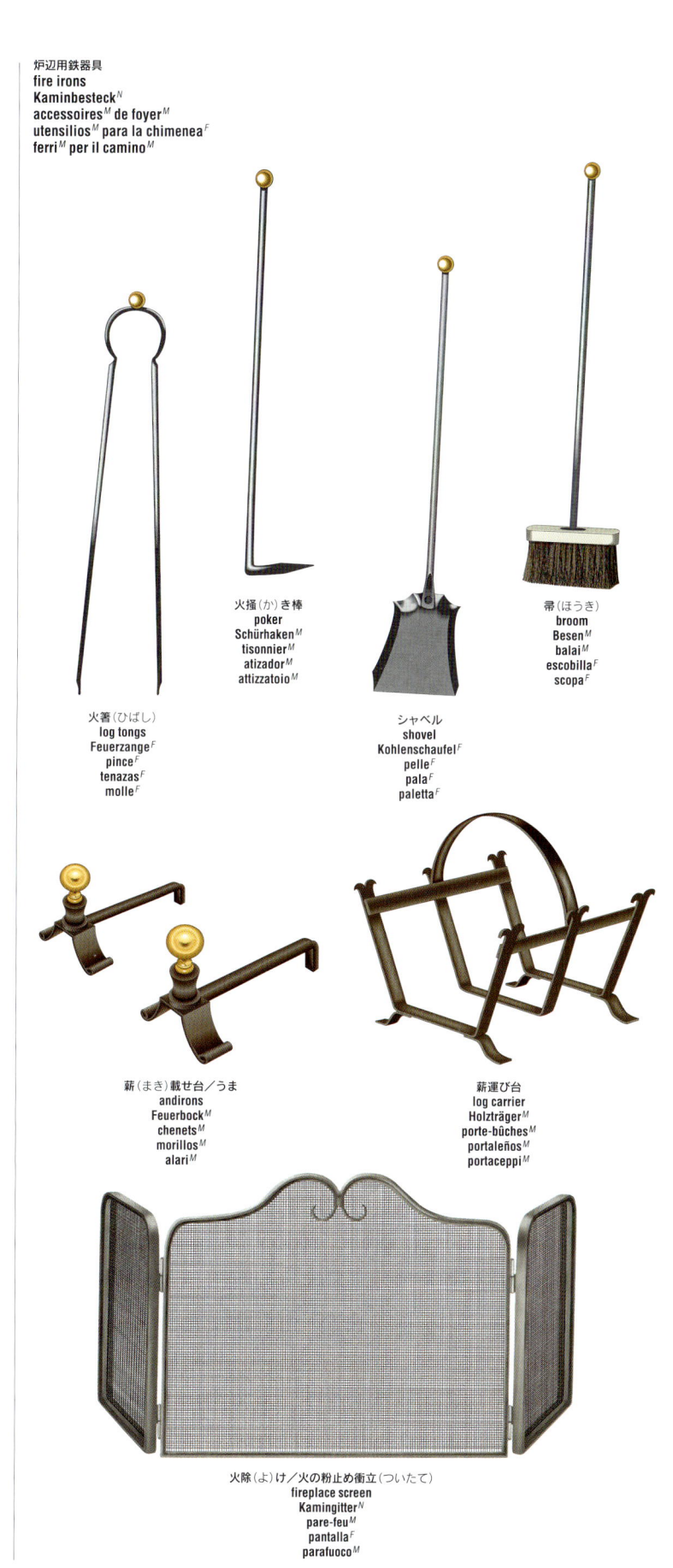

火掻（か）き棒
poker
Schürhaken^M
tisonnier^M
atizador^M
attizzatoio^M

火箸（ひばし）
log tongs
Feuerzange^F
pince^F
tenazas^F
molle^F

シャベル
shovel
Kohlenschaufel^F
pelle^F
pala^F
paletta^F

帚（ほうき）
broom
Besen^M
balai^M
escobilla^F
scopa^F

薪（まき）載せ台／うま
andirons
Feuerbock^M
chenets^M
morillos^M
alari^M

薪運び台
log carrier
Holzträger^M
porte-bûches^M
portaleños^M
portaceppi^M

火除（よ）け／火の粉止め衝立（ついたて）
fireplace screen
Kamingitter^N
pare-feu^M
pantalla^F
parafuoco^M

家屋

257

暖房 | HEATING
HEIZUNG | CHAUFFAGE | CALEFACCIÓN | RISCALDAMENTO

強制送風システム

日本語 | 英語 | ドイツ語 | フランス語 | スペイン語 | イタリア語

forced warm-air system | Warmluftsystem^N mit Zwangsumlauf^M | installation^F à air^M chaud pulsé | sistema^M de aire^M caliente a presión^F | impianto^M di riscaldamento^M ad aria^F calda

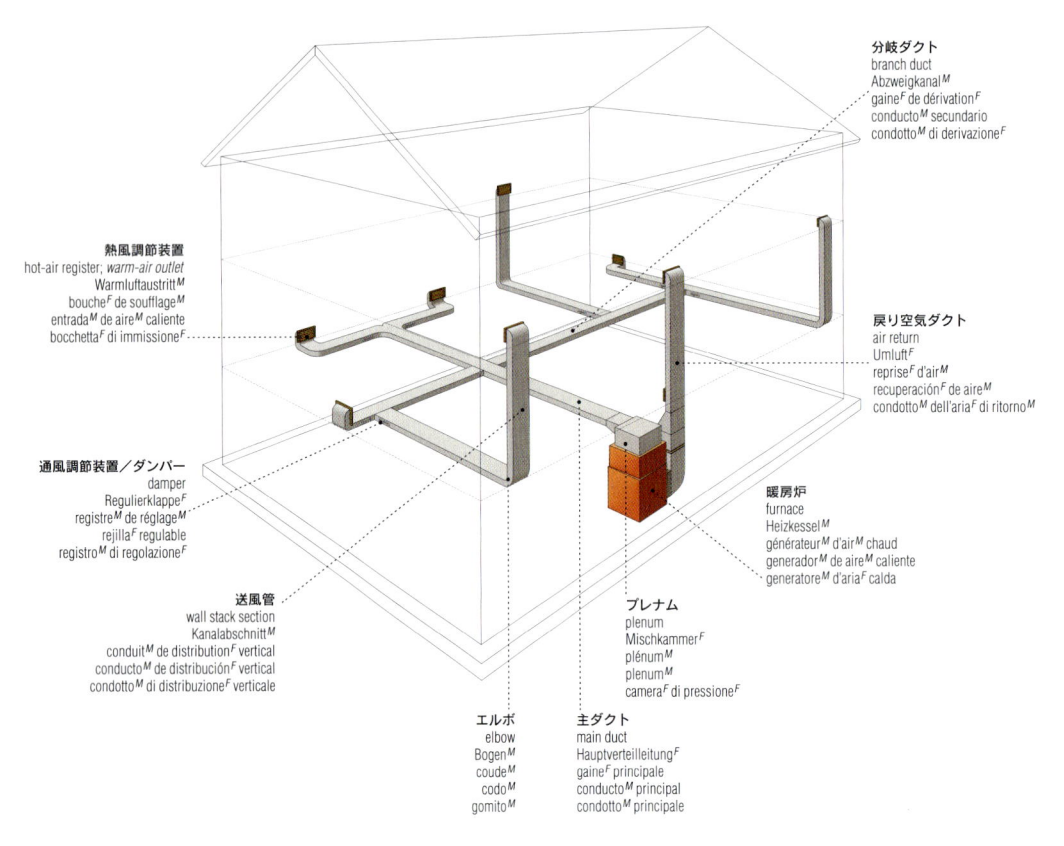

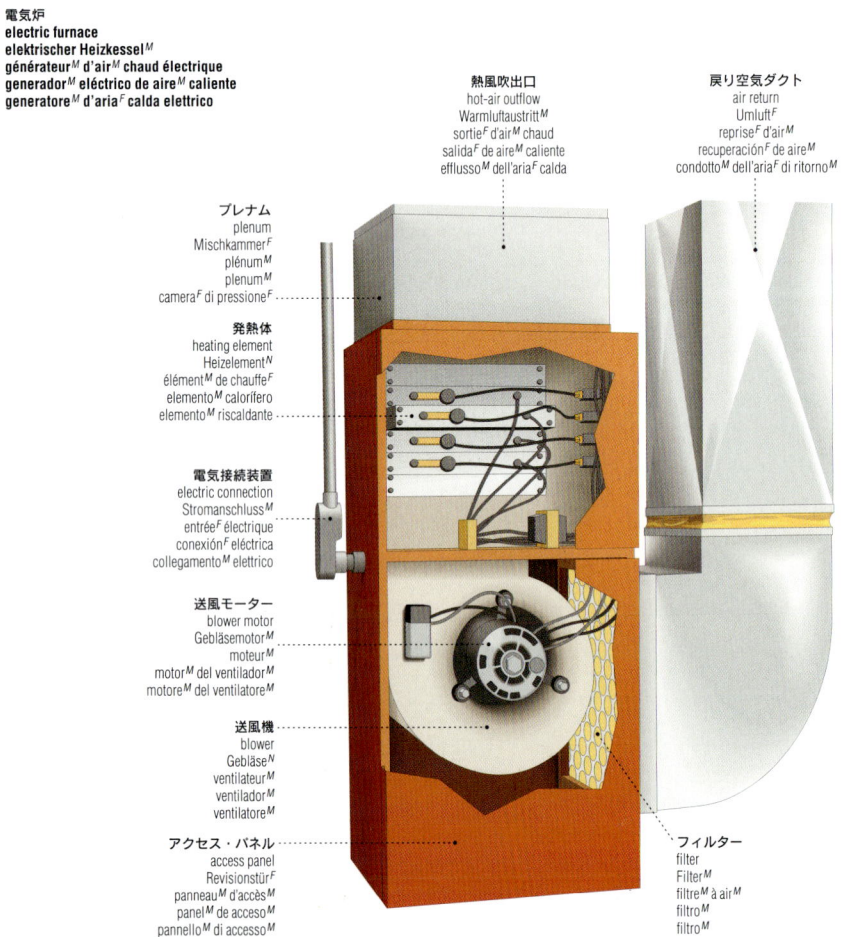

家屋

分岐ダクト
branch duct
Abzweigkanal^M
gaine^F de dérivation^F
conducto^M secundario
condotto^M di derivazione^F

熱風調節装置
hot-air register; *warm-air outlet*
Warmluftaustritt^M
bouche^F de soufflage^M
entrada^F de aire^M caliente
bocchetta^F di immissione^F

戻り空気ダクト
air return
Umluft^F
reprise^F d'air^M
recuperación^F de aire^M
condotto^M dell'aria^F di ritorno^M

通風調節装置／ダンパー
damper
Regulierklappe^F
registre^M de réglage^M
rejilla^F regulable
registro^M di regolazione^F

暖房炉
furnace
Heizkessel^M
générateur^M d'air^M chaud
generador^M de aire^M caliente
generatore^M d'aria^F calda

送風管
wall stack section
Kanalabschnitt^M
conduit^M de distribution^F vertical
conducto^M de distribución^F vertical
condotto^M di distribuzione^F verticale

エルボ
elbow
Bogen^M
coude^M
codo^M
gomito^M

プレナム
plenum
Mischkammer^F
plénum^F
plenum^M
camera^F di pressione^F

主ダクト
main duct
Hauptverteilleitung^F
gaine^F principale
conducto^M principal
condotto^M principale

電気炉
electric furnace
elektrischer Heizkessel^M
générateur^M d'air^M chaud électrique
generador^M eléctrico de aire^M caliente
generatore^M d'aria^F calda elettrico

熱風吹出口
hot-air outflow
Warmluftaustritt^M
sortie^F d'air^M chaud
salida^F de aire^M caliente
efflusso^M dell'aria^F calda

戻り空気ダクト
air return
Umluft^F
reprise^F d'air^M
recuperación^F de aire^M
condotto^M dell'aria^F di ritorno^M

調節装置の種類
types of registers; *types of outlets*
verschiedene Abzüge^M
types^M de bouches^F
tipos^M de rejillas^F
tipi^M di bocchette^F

プレナム
plenum
Mischkammer^F
plénum^F
plenum^M
camera^F di pressione^F

発熱体
heating element
Heizelement^N
élément^M de chauffe^F
elemento^M calorífero
elemento^M riscaldante

電気接続装置
electric connection
Stromanschluss^M
entrée^F électrique
conexión^F eléctrica
collegamento^M elettrico

送風モーター
blower motor
Gebläsemotor^M
moteur^M
motor^M del ventilador^M
motore^M del ventilatore^M

送風機
blower
Gebläse^N
ventilateur^M
ventilador^M
ventilatore^M

アクセス・パネル
access panel
Revisionstür^F
panneau^M d'accès^M
panel^M de acceso^M
pannello^M di accesso^M

フィルター
filter
Filter^M
filtre^F à air^M
filtro^M
filtro^M

幅木（はばき）用調節装置
baseboard register; *skirting outlet*
Lüftungsgitter^N
bouche^F de soufflage^M
rejilla^F de piso^M
bocchetta^F di immissione^F

壁用調節装置
wall register; *wall grille*
Wandgitter^N
bouche^F d'extraction^F
rejilla^F de pared^F
bocchetta^F di estrazione^F

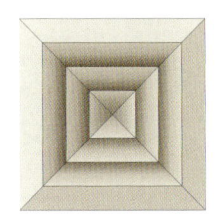

天井用調節装置
ceiling register; *ceiling outlet*
Deckendurchlass^M
bouche^F à induction^F
rejilla^F de techo^M
bocchetta^F a soffitto^M

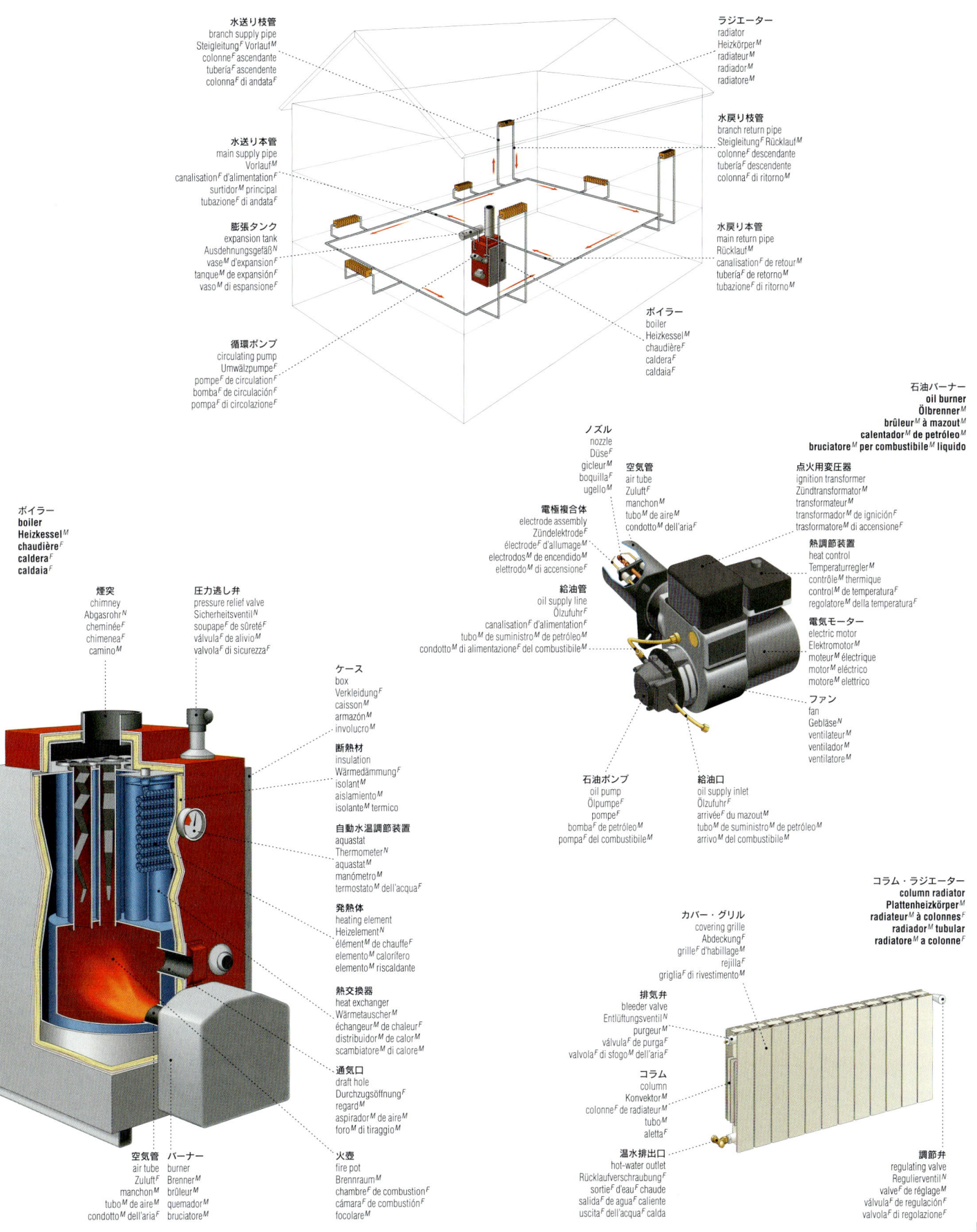

暖房 | HEATING
HEIZUNG | CHAUFFAGE | CALEFACCIÓN | RISCALDAMENTO

強制送水システム

forced hot-water system | Warmwasserheizung^F mit Zwangsumlauf^M | installation^F à eau^F chaude | sistema^M de agua^F caliente a presión^F | impianto^M di riscaldamento^M ad acqua^F calda

水送り枝管
branch supply pipe
Steigleitung^F Vorlauf^M
colonne^F ascendante
tubería^F ascendente
colonna^F di andata

水送り本管
main supply pipe
Vorlauf^M
canalisation^F d'alimentation^F
surtidor^M principal
tubazione^F di andata

膨張タンク
expansion tank
Ausdehnungsgefäß^N
vase^F d'expansion^F
tanque^M de expansión^F
vaso^M di espansione^F

循環ポンプ
circulating pump
Umwälzpumpe^F
pompe^F de circulation^F
bomba^F de circulación^F
pompa^F di circolazione^F

ラジエーター
radiator
Heizkörper^M
radiateur^M
radiador^M
radiatore^M

水戻り枝管
branch return pipe
Steigleitung^F Rücklauf^M
colonne^F descendante
tubería^F descendente
colonna^F di ritorno

水戻り本管
main return pipe
Rücklauf^M
canalisation^F de retour^M
tubería^F de retorno
tubazione^F di ritorno

ボイラー
boiler
Heizkessel^M
chaudière^F
caldera^F
caldaia^F

ボイラー
boiler
Heizkessel^M
chaudière^F
caldera^F
caldaia^F

煙突
chimney
Abgasrohr^N
cheminée^F
chimenea^F
camino^M

圧力逃し弁
pressure relief valve
Sicherheitsventil^N
soupape^F de sûreté^F
válvula^F de alivio^M
valvola^F di sicurezza^F

ケース
box
Verkleidung^F
caisson^M
armazón^M
involucro^M

断熱材
insulation
Wärmedämmung^F
isolant^M
aislamiento^M
isolante^M termico

自動水温調節装置
aquastat
Thermometer^N
aquastat^M
manómetro^M
termostato^M dell'acqua^F

発熱体
heating element
Heizelement^N
élément^M de chauffe^F
elemento^M calorífero
elemento^M riscaldante

熱交換器
heat exchanger
Wärmetauscher^M
échangeur^M de chaleur^F
distribuidor^M de calor^M
scambiatore^M di calore^M

通気口
draft hole
Durchzugsöffnung^F
regard^M
aspirador^M de aire^M
foro^M di tiraggio^M

火壺
fire pot
Brennraum^M
chambre^F de combustion^F
cámara^F de combustión^F
focolare^M

空気管
air tube
Zuluft^F
manchon^M
tubo^M de aire^M
condotto^M dell'aria^F

バーナー
burner
Brenner^M
brûleur^M
quemador^M
bruciatore^M

ノズル
nozzle
Düse^F
gicleur^M
boquilla^F
ugello^M

電極複合体
electrode assembly
Zündelektrode^F
électrode^F d'allumage^F
electrodos^M de encendido^M
elettrodo^M di accensione^F

給油管
oil supply line
Ölzufuhr^F
canalisation^F d'alimentation^F
tubo^M de suministro^M de petróleo^M
condotto^M di alimentazione^F del combustibile^M

石油ポンプ
oil pump
Ölpumpe^F
pompe^F
bomba^F de petróleo^M
pompa^F del combustibile^M

空気管
air tube
Zuluft^F
manchon^M
tubo^M de aire^M
condotto^M dell'aria^F

給油口
oil supply inlet
Ölzufuhr^F
arrivée^F du mazout^M
tubo^M de suministro^M de petróleo^M
arrivo^M del combustibile^M

カバー・グリル
covering grille
Abdeckung^F
grille^F d'habillage^M
rejilla^F
griglia^F di rivestimento^M

排気弁
bleeder valve
Entlüftungsventil^N
purgeur^M
válvula^F de purga^F
valvola^F di sfogo^M dell'aria^F

コラム
column
Konvektor^M
colonne^F de radiateur^M
tubo^M
aletta^F

温水排出口
hot-water outlet
Rücklaufverschraubung^F
sortie^F d'eau^F chaude
salida^F de agua^F caliente
uscita^F dell'acqua^F calda

石油バーナー
oil burner
Ölbrenner^M
brûleur^M à mazout^M
calentador^M de petróleo^M
bruciatore^M per combustibile^M liquido

点火用変圧器
ignition transformer
Zündtransformator^M
transformateur^M
transformador^M de ignición^F
trasformatore^M di accensione^F

熱調節装置
heat control
Temperaturregler^M
contrôle^M thermique
control^M de temperatura^F
regolatore^M della temperatura^F

電気モーター
electric motor
Elektromotor^M
moteur^M électrique
motor^M eléctrico
motore^M elettrico

ファン
fan
Gebläse^N
ventilateur^M
ventilador^M
ventilatore^M

コラム・ラジエーター
column radiator
Plattenheizkörper^M
radiateur^M à colonnes^F
radiador^M tubular
radiatore^M a colonne^F

調節弁
regulating valve
Regulierventil^N
valve^F de réglage^M
válvula^F de regulación^F
valvola^F di regolazione^F

家屋

259

暖房 | HEATING
HEIZUNG | CHAUFFAGE | CALEFACCIÓN | RISCALDAMENTO

熱ポンプ

heat pump | Wärmepumpe F | pompe F à chaleur F | sistema M de bomba F de calor M | pompa F di calore M

日本語 | 英語 | ドイツ語 | フランス語 | スペイン語 | イタリア語

（回路）遮断器／ブレーカー
circuit breaker
Sicherungsautomat M
disjoncteur M
interruptor M automático
interruttore M automatico

送風機／ファン
fan
Ventilator M
ventilateur M hélicoïde
ventilador M
ventilatore M

屋外装置
outdoor unit
Anlage F für Außenaufstellung
module M extérieur
unidad F exterior
impianto M esterno

コンプレッサー
compressor
Kompressor M
compresseur M
compresor M
compressore M

供給ダクト
supply duct
Zuluftkanal M
gaine F de distribution F
manga F de distribución F
condotto M di alimentazione F

屋内装置
indoor unit
Anlage F für Innenaufstellung F
module M intérieur
unidad F interior
impianto M interno

冷却管
refrigerant tubing
Kältemittelleitung F
liaison F frigorifique
tubería F de refrigeración F
tubo M del refrigerante M

電気接続装置
electric connection
Stromanschluss M
liaison F électrique
conexión F eléctrica
collegamento M elettrico

冷却管
refrigerant tubing
Kältemittelleitung F
liaison F frigorifique
tubería F de refrigeración F
tubo M del refrigerante M

補助暖房

auxiliary heating | Zusatzheizung F | chauffage M d'appoint M | calefacción F auxiliar | mezzi M integrativi di riscaldamento M

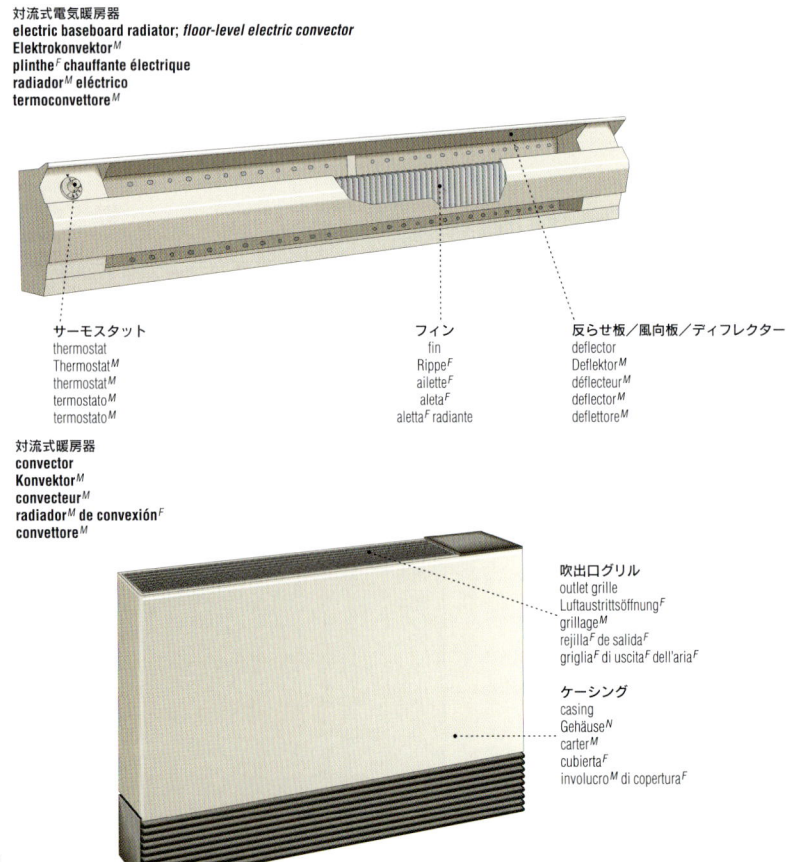

対流式電気暖房器
electric baseboard radiator; *floor-level electric convector*
Elektrokonvektor M
plinthe F **chauffante électrique**
radiador M **eléctrico**
termoconvettore M

サーモスタット
thermostat
Thermostat M
thermostat M
termostato M
termostato M

フィン
fin
Rippe F
ailette F
aleta F
aletta F radiante

反らせ板／風向板／ディフレクター
deflector
Deflektor M
déflecteur M
deflector M
deflettore M

対流式暖房器
convector
Konvektor M
convecteur M
radiador M **de convexión** F
convettore M

吹出口グリル
outlet grille
Luftaustrittsöffnung F
grillage M
rejilla F de salida F
griglia F di uscita F dell'aria F

ケーシング
casing
Gehäuse N
carter M
cubierta F
involucro M di copertura F

ファン・ヒーター／温風器
fan heater
Heizlüfter M
radiateur M **soufflant**
ventilador M **de aire** M **caliente**
termoventilatore M

放射［輻射式］暖房器
radiant heater
Heizstrahler M
radiateur M **rayonnant**
calefactor M **eléctrico a infrarrojos** M
stufa F **radiante**

石油［オイル］ヒーター
oil-filled heater; *oil-filled radiator*
ölgefüllter Heizkörper M
radiateur M **bain** M **d'huile** F
calefactor M **de aceite** M
radiatore M **elettrico a olio** M

260

空気調節 | AIR CONDITIONING
LUFTAUFBEREITUNG | CONDITIONNEMENT DE L'AIR | ACONDICIONADOR DE AIRE | CONDIZIONAMENTO DELL'ARIA

空調装置

air conditioning appliances | Klimageräte[N] | appareils[M] de conditionnement[M] de l'air[M] | aparatos[M] acondicionadores[M] | apparecchi[M] per il condizionamento[M] dell'aria[F]

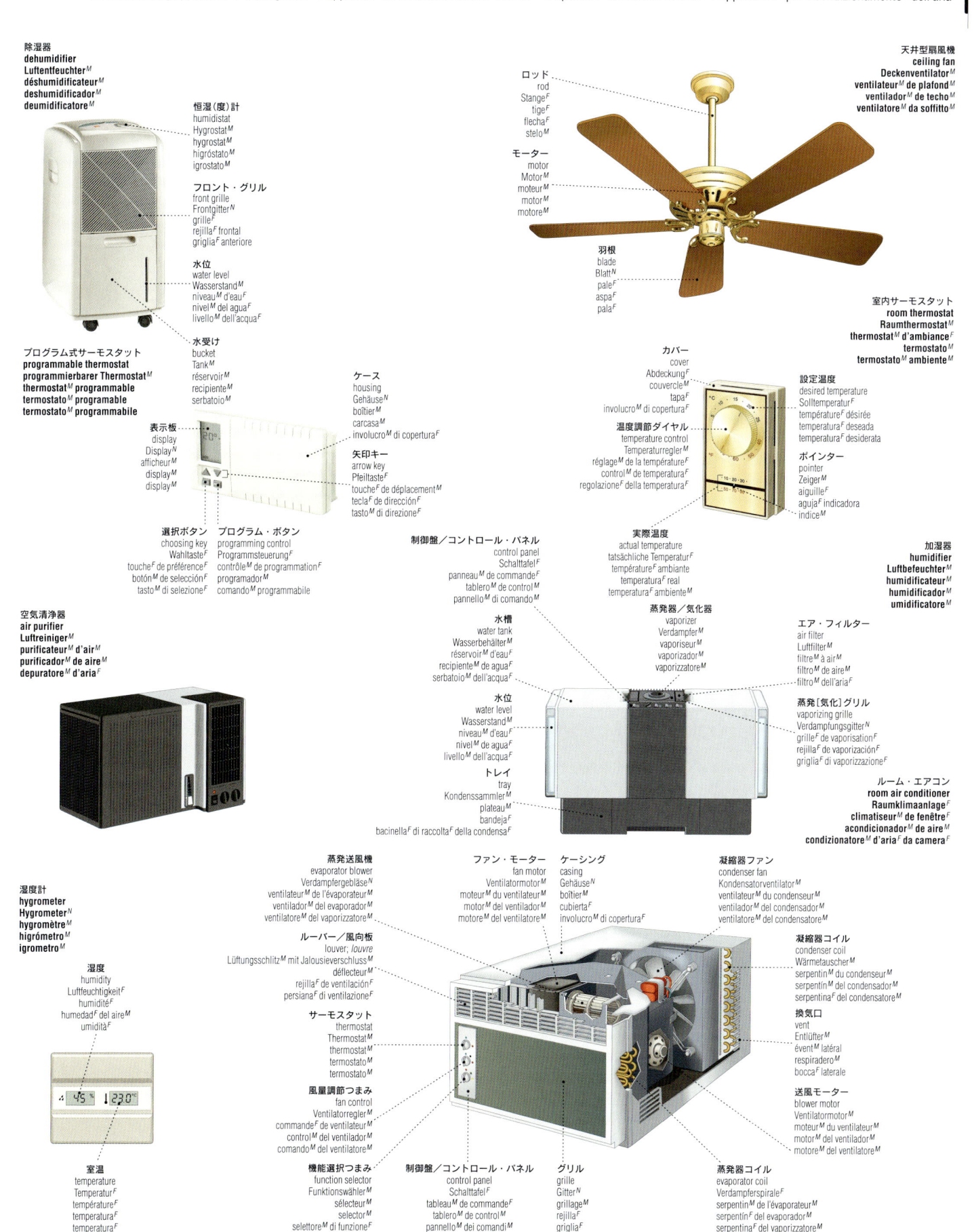

家屋

除湿器
dehumidifier
Luftentfeuchter[M]
déshumidificateur[M]
deshumidificador[M]
deumidificatore[M]

恒湿(度)計
humidistat
Hygrostat[M]
hygrostat[M]
higróstato[M]
igrostato[M]

フロント・グリル
front grille
Frontgitter[N]
grille[F]
rejilla[F] frontal
griglia[F] anteriore

水位
water level
Wasserstand[M]
niveau[M] d'eau[F]
nivel[M] del agua[F]
livello[M] dell'acqua[F]

水受け
bucket
Tank[M]
réservoir[M]
recipiente[M]
serbatoio[M]

プログラム式サーモスタット
programmable thermostat
programmierbarer Thermostat[M]
thermostat[M] programable
termostato[M] programable
termostato[M] programmabile

表示板
display
Display[N]
afficheur[M]
display[M]
display[M]

選択ボタン
choosing key
Wahltaste[F]
touche[F] de préférence[F]
botón[M] de selección[M]
tasto[M] di selezione[F]

プログラム・ボタン
programming control
Programmsteuerung[F]
contrôle[M] de programmation[F]
programador[M]
comando[M] programmabile

矢印キー
arrow key
Pfeiltaste[F]
touche[F] de déplacement[M]
tecla[F] de dirección[F]
tasto[M] di direzione[F]

ケース
housing
Gehäuse[N]
boîtier[M]
carcasa[M]
involucro[M] di copertura[F]

制御盤/コントロール・パネル
control panel
Schalttafel[F]
panneau[M] de commande[F]
tablero[M] de control[M]
pannello[M] di comando[M]

カバー
cover
Abdeckung[F]
couvercle[M]
tapa[F]
involucro[M] di copertura[F]

温度調節ダイヤル
temperature control
Temperaturregler[M]
réglage[M] de la température[F]
control[M] de temperatura[F]
regolazione[F] della temperatura[F]

実際温度
actual temperature
tatsächliche Temperatur[F]
température[F] ambiante
temperatura[F] real
temperatura[F] ambiente[F]

ロッド
rod
Stange[F]
tige[F]
flecha[F]
stelo[M]

モーター
motor
Motor[M]
moteur[M]
motor[M]
motore[M]

羽根
blade
Blatt[N]
pale[F]
aspa[F]
pala[F]

天井型扇風機
ceiling fan
Deckenventilator[M]
ventilateur[M] de plafond[M]
ventilador[M] de techo[M]
ventilatore[M] da soffitto[M]

室内サーモスタット
room thermostat
Raumthermostat[M]
thermostat[M] d'ambiance[F]
termostato[M]
termostato[M] ambiente[M]

設定温度
desired temperature
Solltemperatur[F]
température[F] désirée
temperatura[F] deseada
temperatura[F] desiderata

ポインター
pointer
Zeiger[M]
aiguille[F]
aguja[F] indicadora
indice[M]

加湿器
humidifier
Luftbefeuchter[M]
humidificateur[M]
humidificador[M]
umidificatore[M]

空気清浄器
air purifier
Luftreiniger[M]
purificateur[M] d'air[M]
purificador[M] de aire[M]
depuratore[M] d'aria[F]

水槽
water tank
Wasserbehälter[M]
réservoir[M] d'eau[F]
recipiente[M] de agua[F]
serbatoio[M] dell'acqua[F]

水位
water level
Wasserstand[M]
niveau[M] d'eau[F]
nivel[M] de agua[F]
livello[M] dell'acqua[F]

トレイ
tray
Kondenssammler[M]
plateau[M]
bandeja[F]
bacinella[F] di raccolta[F] della condensa[F]

蒸発器/気化器
vaporizer
Verdampfer[M]
vaporiseur[M]
vaporizador[M]
vaporizzatore[M]

エア・フィルター
air filter
Luftfilter[M]
filtre[M] à air[M]
filtro[M] de aire[M]
filtro[M] dell'aria[F]

蒸発[気化]グリル
vaporizing grille
Verdampfungsgitter[N]
grille[F] de vaporisation[F]
rejilla[F] de vaporización[F]
griglia[F] di vaporizzazione[F]

ルーム・エアコン
room air conditioner
Raumklimaanlage[F]
climatiseur[M] de fenêtre[F]
acondicionador[M] de aire[M]
condizionatore[M] d'aria[F] da camera[F]

湿度計
hygrometer
Hygrometer[N]
hygromètre[M]
higrómetro[M]
igrometro[M]

湿度
humidity
Luftfeuchtigkeit[F]
humidité[F]
humedad[F] del aire[M]
umidità[F]

室温
temperature
Temperatur[F]
température[F]
temperatura[F]
temperatura[F]

蒸発送風機
evaporator blower
Verdampfergebläse[N]
ventilateur[M] de l'évaporateur[M]
ventilador[M] del evaporador[M]
ventilatore[M] del vaporizzatore[M]

ルーバー/風向板
louver; louvre
Lüftungsschlitz[M] mit Jalousieverschluss[M]
déflecteur[M]
rejilla[F] de ventilación[F]
persiana[F] di ventilazione[F]

サーモスタット
thermostat
Thermostat[M]
thermostat[M]
termostato[M]
termostato[M]

風量調節つまみ
fan control
Ventilatorregler[M]
commande[F] de ventilateur[M]
control[M] del ventilador[M]
comando[M] del ventilatore[M]

機能選択つまみ
function selector
Funktionswähler[M]
sélecteur[M]
selector[M]
selettore[M] di funzione[F]

ファン・モーター
fan motor
Ventilatormotor[M]
moteur[M] du ventilateur[M]
motor[M] del ventilador[M]
motore[M] del ventilatore[M]

ケーシング
casing
Gehäuse[N]
boîtier[M]
cubierta[F]
involucro[M] di copertura[F]

制御盤/コントロール・パネル
control panel
Schalttafel[F]
tableau[M] de commande[F]
tablero[M] de control[M]
pannello[M] dei comandi[M]

グリル
grille
Gitter[N]
grillage[M]
rejilla[F]
griglia[F]

凝縮器ファン
condenser fan
Kondensatorventilator[M]
ventilateur[M] du condenseur[M]
ventilador[M] del condensador[M]
ventilatore[M] del condensatore[M]

凝縮器コイル
condenser coil
Wärmetauscher[M]
serpentin[M] du condenseur[M]
serpentín[M] del condensador[M]
serpentina[F] del condensatore[M]

換気口
vent
Entlüfter[M]
évent[M] latéral
respiradero[M]
bocca[F] laterale

送風モーター
blower motor
Ventilatormotor[M]
moteur[M] du ventilateur[M]
motor[M] del ventilador[M]
motore[M] del ventilatore[M]

蒸発器コイル
evaporator coil
Verdampferspirale[F]
serpentin[M] de l'évaporateur[M]
serpentín[M] del evaporador[M]
serpentina[F] del vaporizzatore[M]

261

配管 | PLUMBING
SANITÄRINSTALLATION | PLOMBERIE | FONTANERÍA | IDRAULICA

配管システム

plumbing system | Sanitärinstallationssystem^N | circuit^M de plomberie^F | cañerías^F | impianto^M idraulico

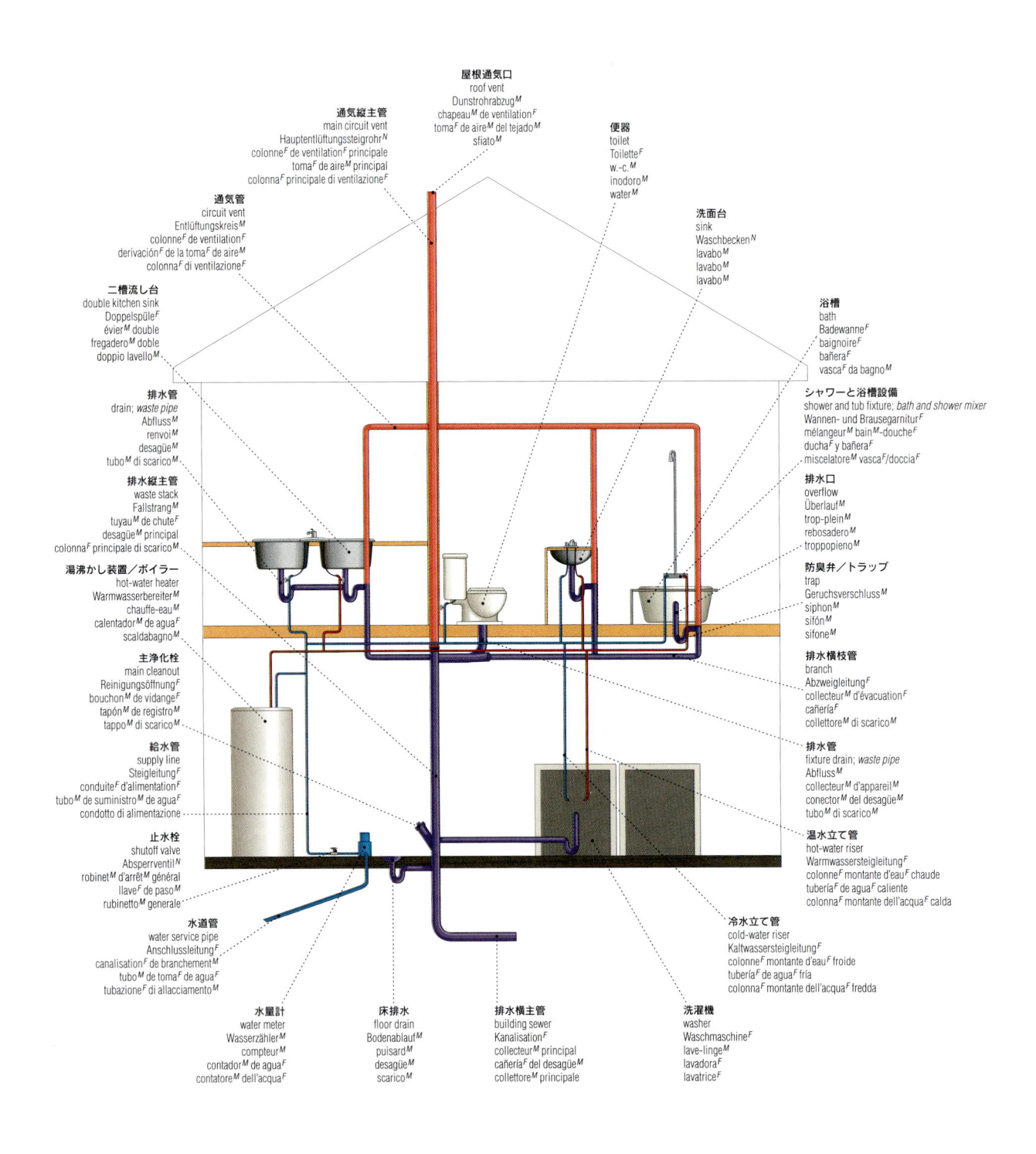

家屋

屋根通気口
roof vent
Dunstrohrabzug^M
chapeau^M de ventilation^F
toma^F de aire^M del tejado^M
sfiato^M

通気縦主管
main circuit vent
Hauptentlüftungssteigrohr^N
colonne^F de ventilation^F principale
toma^F de aire^M principal
colonna^F principale di ventilazione^F

便器
toilet
Toilette^F
w.-c.^M
inodoro^M
water^M

通気管
circuit vent
Entlüftungskreis^M
colonne^F de ventilation^F
derivación^F de la toma^F de aire^M
colonna^F di ventilazione^F

洗面台
sink
Waschbecken^N
lavabo^M
lavabo^M
lavabo^M

二槽流し台
double kitchen sink
Doppelspüle^F
évier^M double
fregadero^M doble
doppio lavello^M

浴槽
bath
Badewanne^F
baignoire^F
bañera^F
vasca^F da bagno^M

排水管
drain; waste pipe
Abfluss^M
renvoi^M
desagüe^M
tubo^M di scarico^M

シャワーと浴槽設備
shower and tub fixture; bath and shower mixer
Wannen- und Brausegarnitur^F
mélangeur^M bain^M-douche^F
ducha^F y bañera^F
miscelatore^M vasca^F/doccia^F

排水縦主管
waste stack
Fallstrang^M
tuyau^M de chute^F
desagüe^M principal
colonna^F principale di scarico^M

排水口
overflow
Überlauf^M
trop-plein^M
rebosadero^M
troppopieno^M

湯沸かし装置／ボイラー
hot-water heater
Warmwasserbereiter^M
chauffe-eau^M
calentador^M de agua^F
scaldabagno^M

防臭弁／トラップ
trap
Geruchsverschluss^M
siphon^M
sifón^M
sifone^M

主浄化栓
main cleanout
Reinigungsöffnung^F
bouchon^M de vidange^F
tapón^M de registro^M
tappo^M di scarico^M

排水横枝管
branch
Abzweigleitung^F
collecteur^M d'évacuation^F
cañería^F
collettore^M di scarico^M

給水管
supply line
Steigleitung^F
conduite^F d'alimentation^F
tubo^M de suministro^M de agua^F
condotto di alimentazione

排水管
fixture drain; waste pipe
Abfluss^M
collecteur^M d'appareil^M
conector^M del desagüe^M
tubo^M di scarico^M

止水栓
shutoff valve
Absperrventil^N
robinet^M d'arrêt^M général
llave^F de paso^F
rubinetto^M generale

温水立て管
hot-water riser
Warmwassersteigleitung^F
colonne^F montante d'eau^F chaude
tubería^F de agua^F caliente
colonna^F montante dell'acqua^F calda

水道管
water service pipe
Anschlussleitung^F
canalisation^F de branchement^M
tubo^M de toma^F de agua^F
tubazione^F di allacciamento^M

冷水立て管
cold-water riser
Kaltwassersteigleitung^F
colonne^F montante d'eau^F froide
tubería^F de agua^F fría
colonna^F montante dell'acqua^F fredda

水量計
water meter
Wasserzähler^M
compteur^M
contador^M de agua^F
contatore^M dell'acqua^F

床排水
floor drain
Bodenablauf^M
puisard^M
desagüe^M
scarico^M

排水横主管
building sewer
Kanalisation^F
collecteur^F principal
cañería^F del desagüe^M
collettore^M principale

洗濯機
washer
Waschmaschine^F
lave-linge^M
lavadora^F
lavatrice^F

通気循環
ventilating circuit
Entlüftungskreislauf^M
circuit^M de ventilation^F
circuito^M de ventilación^F
rete^F di ventilazione^F

排水循環
draining circuit
Abflusskreislauf^M
circuit^M d'évacuation^F
circuito^M de desagüe^M
rete^F di scarico^M

冷水循環
cold-water circuit
Kaltwasserkreislauf^M
circuit^M d'eau^F froide
circuito^M de agua^F fría
rete^F di distribuzione^F dell'acqua^F fredda

温水循環
hot-water circuit
Warmwasserkreislauf^M
circuit^M d'eau^F chaude
circuito^M de agua^F caliente
rete^F di distribuzione^F dell'acqua^F calda

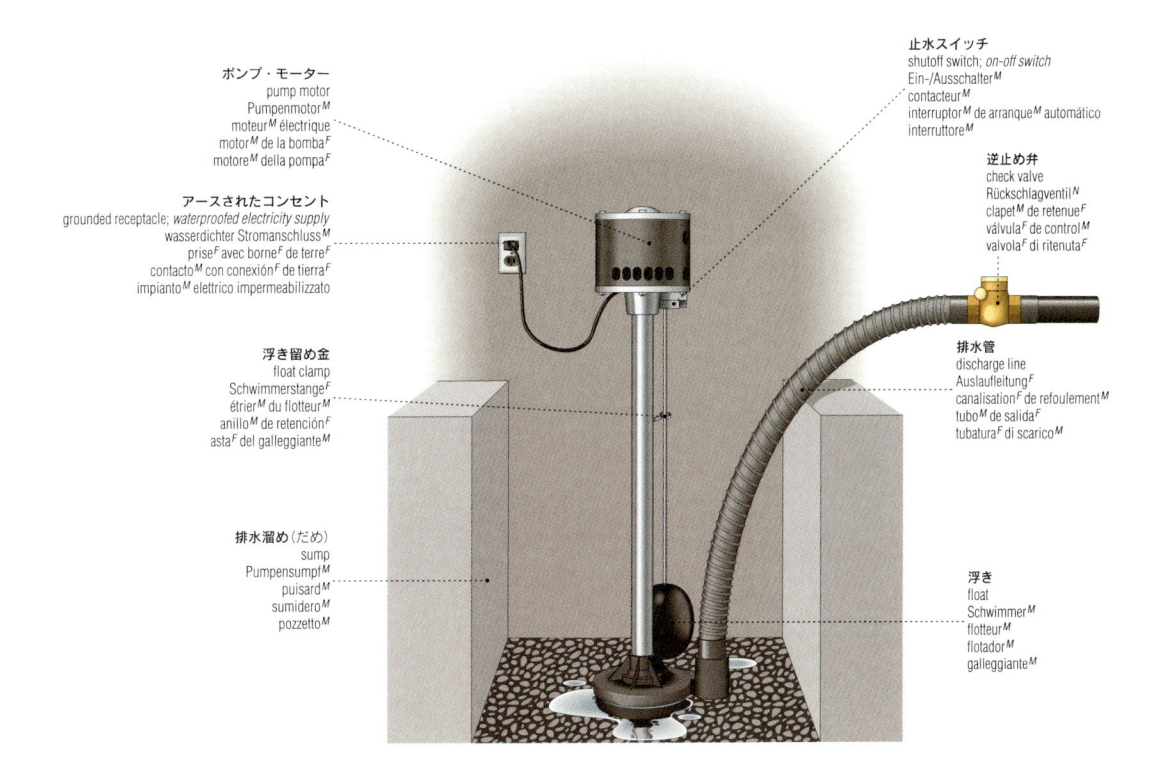

配管 | PLUMBING
SANITÄRINSTALLATION | PLOMBERIE | FONTANERÍA | IDRAULICA

汚水排水ポンプ

pedestal-type sump pump | SchmutzwasserhebeanlageF | pompeF de puisardM | bombaF tipoM pedestalM para sumideroM | pompaF di spurgoM

ポンプ・モーター
pump motor
PumpenmotorM
moteurM électrique
motorM de la bombaF
motoreM della pompaF

アースされたコンセント
grounded receptacle; *waterproofed electricity supply*
wasserdichter StromanschlussM
priseF avec borneF de terreF
contactoM con conexiónF de tierraF
impiantoM elettrico impermeabilizzato

浮き留め金
float clamp
SchwimmerstangeF
étrierM du flotteurM
anilloM de retenciónF
astaF del galleggianteM

排水溜め（だめ）
sump
PumpensumpfM
puisardM
sumideroM
pozzettoM

止水スイッチ
shutoff switch; *on-off switch*
Ein-/AusschalterM
contacteurM
interruptorM de arranqueM automático
interruttoreM

逆止め弁
check valve
RückschlagventilN
clapetM de retenueF
válvulaF de controlM
valvolaF di ritenutaF

排水管
discharge line
AuslaufleitungF
canalisationF de refoulementM
tuboM de salidaF
tubaturaF di scaricoM

浮き
float
SchwimmerM
flotteurM
flotadorM
galleggianteM

浄化槽

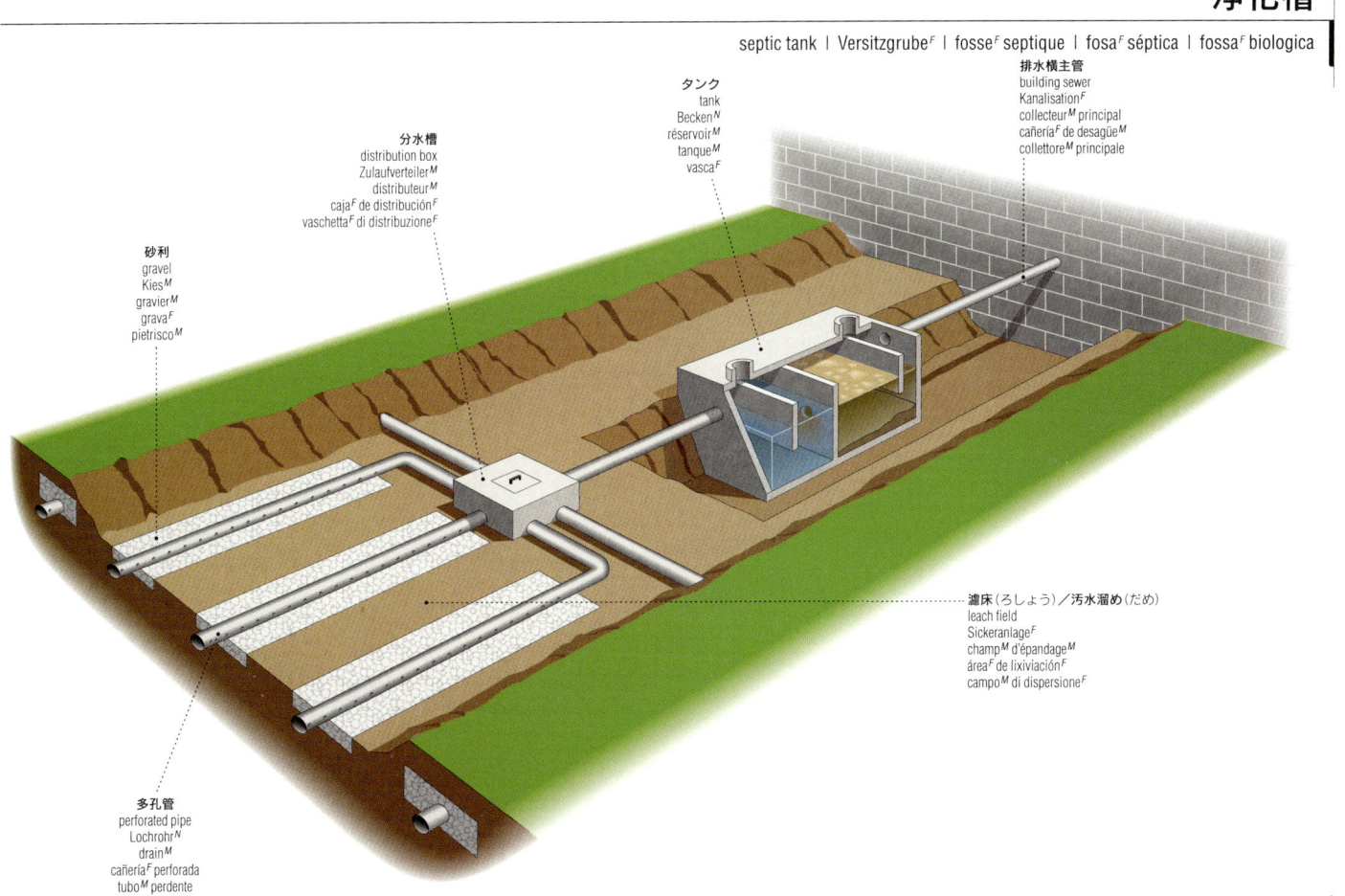

septic tank | VersitzgrubeF | fosseF septique | fosaF séptica | fossaF biologica

タンク
tank
BeckenN
réservoirM
tanqueM
vascaF

排水横主管
building sewer
KanalisationF
collecteurM principal
cañeríaF de desagüeM
collettoreM principale

分水槽
distribution box
ZulaufverteilerM
distributeurM
cajaF de distribuciónF
vaschettaF di distribuzioneF

砂利
gravel
KiesM
gravierM
gravaF
pietriscoM

濾床（ろしょう）／汚水溜め（だめ）
leach field
SickeranlageF
champM d'épandageM
áreaF de lixiviaciónF
campoM di dispersioneF

多孔管
perforated pipe
LochrohrN
drainM
cañeríaF perforada
tuboM perdente

家屋

263

配管 | PLUMBING
SANITÄRINSTALLATION | PLOMBERIE | FONTANERÍA | IDRAULICA

浴室／バスルーム

bathroom | Badezimmer^N | salle^F de bains^M | cuarto^M de baño^M | stanza^F da bagno^M

日本語 | 英語 | ドイツ語 | フランス語 | スペイン語 | イタリア語

家屋

引き戸
sliding door
Schiebetür^F
porte^F coulissante
puerta^F plegable
porta^F scorrevole

スプレー・ホース
spray hose
Brauseschlauch^M
flexible^M
manguera^F
tubo^M flessibile

シャワー・ヘッド
shower head
Brausenkopf^M
pomme^F de douche^F
alcachofa^F de la ducha^F
doccia^F

シャワー室
shower stall
Duschkabine^F
cabine^F de douche^F
cabina^F de la ducha^F
box^M doccia^F

ポータブル・シャワー・ヘッド
portable shower head
Handbrause^F
douchette^F
ducha^F de teléfono^M
doccia^F a telefono^M

蛇口
faucet; tap
Wasserhahn^M
robinet^M
grifo^M
rubinetto^M

溢（あふ）れ口／オーバーフロー
overflow
Überlauf^M
trop-plein^M
desagüe^M
troppopieno^M

鏡
mirror
Spiegel^M
miroir^M
espejo^M
specchio^M

トイレット・ペーパー・ホルダー
tissue holder
Toilettenpapierhalter^M
porte-rouleau^M
portarrollos^M de papel^M higiénico
portarotolo^M

水槽
toilet tank; cistern
Spülkasten^M
réservoir^M de chasse^F d'eau^F
cisterna^F del inodoro^M
sciacquone^M

便器
toilet
Toilette^F
w.-c.^M
inodoro^M
water^M

ビデ
bidet
Bidet^N
bidet^M
bidé^M
bidè^M

便座
seat
Sitz^M
abattant^M
asiento^M
sedile^M

入浴台
tub platform
Podest^N
banquette^F
zócalo^M de la bañera^F
piattaforma^F della vasca^F

浴槽
bathtub; bath
Badewanne^F
baignoire^F
bañera^F
vasca^F da bagno^M

流し
sink
Waschbecken^N
lavabo^M
lavabo^M
lavandino^M

石鹸（せっけん）皿
soap dish
Seifenschale^F
porte-savon^M
jabonera^F
portasapone^M

バニティー・キャビネット
vanity cabinet
Einbauwaschtisch^M
coiffeuse^F
armario^M del lavabo^M
mobile^M portaccessori

タオル掛け
towel bar; towel rail
Handtuchhalter^M
porte-serviettes^M
toallero^M
portasciugamano^M

264

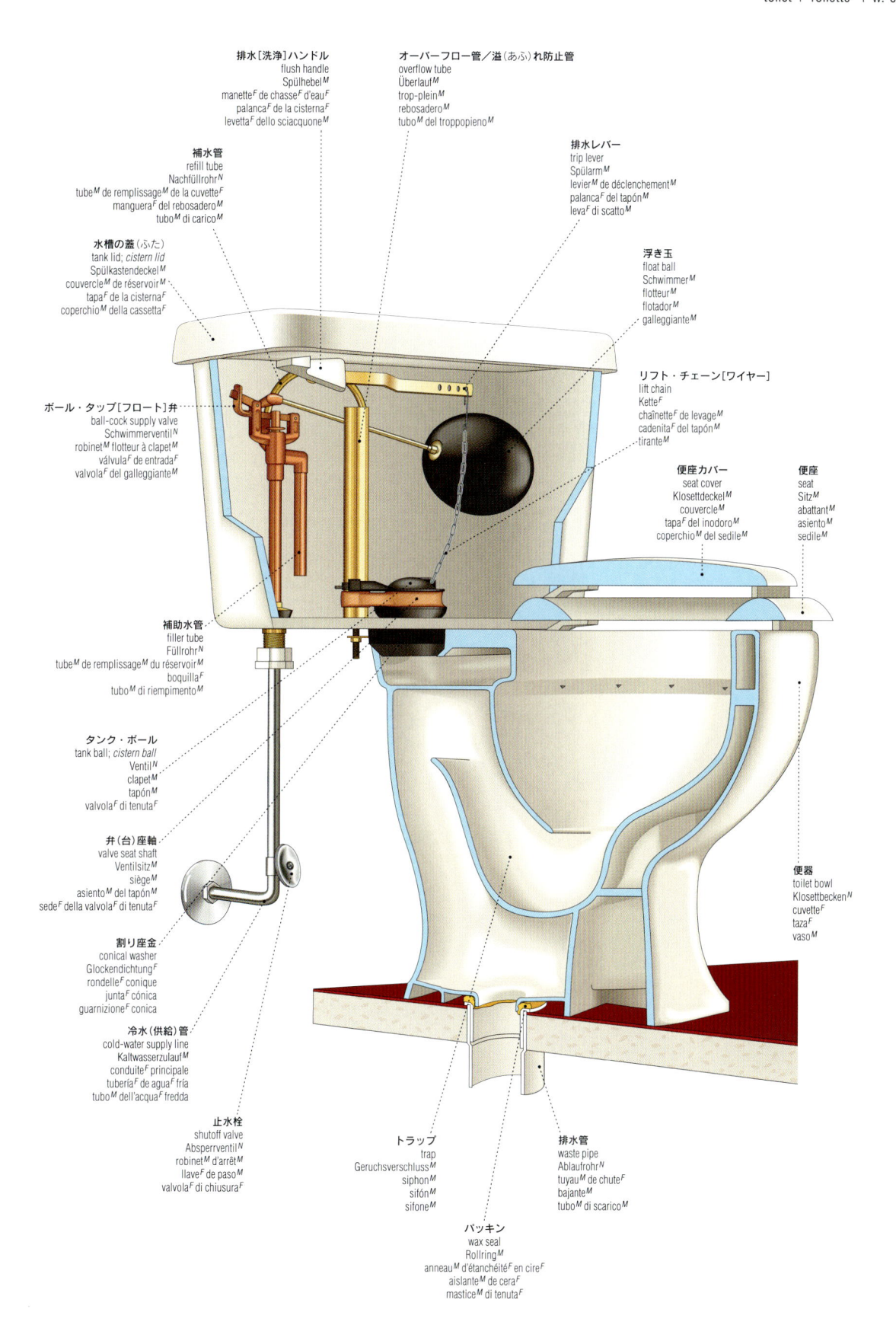

配管 | PLUMBING
SANITÄRINSTALLATION | PLOMBERIE | FONTANERÍA | IDRAULICA

便器

toilet | Toilette^F | w.-c.^M | inodoro^M | water^M

家屋

排水[洗浄]ハンドル
flush handle
Spülhebel
manette^F de chasse^F d'eau^F
palanca^F de la cisterna^F
levetta^F dello sciacquone^M

オーバーフロー管／溢(あふ)れ防止管
overflow tube
Überlauf
trop-plein^M
rebosadero^M
tubo^M del troppopieno^M

補水管
refill tube
Nachfüllrohr^N
tube^M de remplissage^M de la cuvette^F
manguera^F del rebosadero^M
tubo^M di carico^M

排水レバー
trip lever
Spülarm^M
levier^M de déclenchement^M
palanca^F del tapón^M
leva^F di scatto^M

水槽の蓋(ふた)
tank lid; cistern lid
Spülkastendeckel^M
couvercle^M de réservoir^M
tapa^F de la cisterna^F
coperchio^M della cassetta^F

浮き玉
float ball
Schwimmer^M
flotteur^M
flotador^M
galleggiante^M

ボール・タップ[フロート]弁
ball-cock supply valve
Schwimmerventil^N
robinet^M flotteur à clapet^M
válvula^F de entrada^F
valvola^F del galleggiante^M

リフト・チェーン[ワイヤー]
lift chain
Kette^F
chaînette^F de levage^M
cadenita^F del tapón^M
tirante^M

便座カバー
seat cover
Klosettdeckel^M
couvercle^M
tapa^F del inodoro^M
coperchio^M del sedile^M

便座
seat
Sitz^M
abattant^M
asiento^M
sedile^M

補助水管
filler tube
Füllrohr^N
tube^M de remplissage^M du réservoir^M
boquilla^F
tubo^M di riempimento^M

タンク・ボール
tank ball; cistern ball
Ventil^N
clapet^M
tapón^M
valvola^F di tenuta^F

弁(台)座軸
valve seat shaft
Ventilsitz^M
siège^M
asiento^M del tapón^M
sede^F della valvola^F di tenuta^F

便器
toilet bowl
Klosettbecken^N
cuvette^F
taza^F
vaso^M

割り座金
conical washer
Glockendichtung^F
rondelle^F conique
junta^F cónica
guarnizione^F conica

冷水(供給)管
cold-water supply line
Kaltwasserzulauf^M
conduite^F principale
tubería^F de agua^F fría
tubo^M dell'acqua^F fredda

止水栓
shutoff valve
Absperrventil^N
robinet^M d'arrêt^M
llave^F de paso^M
valvola^F di chiusura^F

トラップ
trap
Geruchsverschluss^M
siphon^M
sifón^M
sifone^M

排水管
waste pipe
Ablaufrohr^N
tuyau^M de chute^F
bajante^F
tubo^M di scarico^M

パッキン
wax seal
Rollring^M
anneau^M d'étanchéité^F en cire^F
aislante^M de cera^F
mastice^M di tenuta^F

配管 | PLUMBING
SANITÄRINSTALLATION | PLOMBERIE | FONTANERÍA | IDRAULICA

湯沸かし装置／ボイラー

日本語 | 英語 | ドイツ語 | フランス語 | スペイン語 | イタリア語

water-heater tank | Wasserheizkessel^M | chauffe-eau^M | calentador^M de agua^F eléctrico | scaldabagno^M

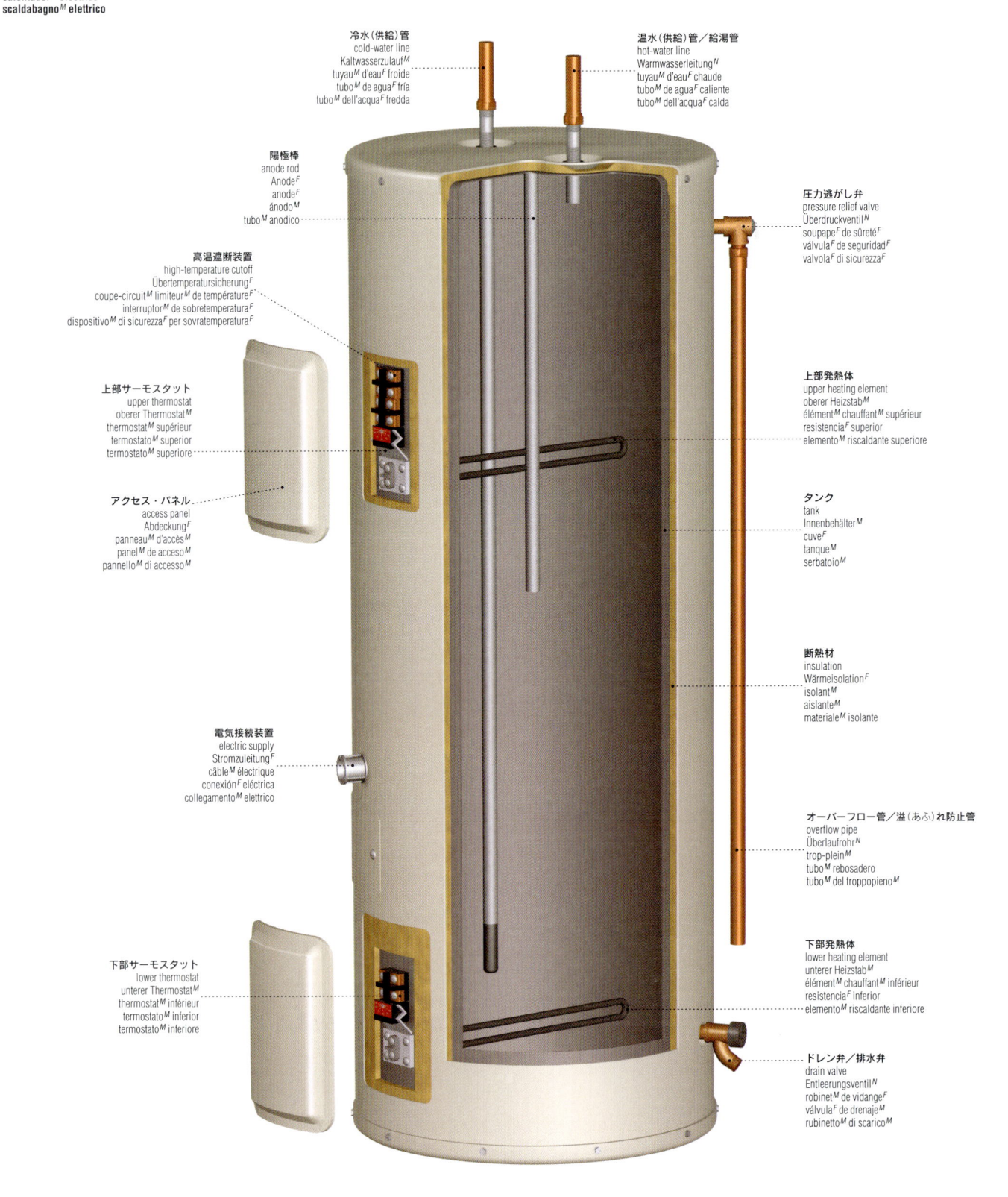

電気湯沸かし装置
electric water-heater tank
elektrischer Heißwasserbereiter^M
chauffe-eau^M électrique
calentador^M eléctrico
scaldabagno^M elettrico

家屋

冷水（供給）管
cold-water line
Kaltwasserzulauf^M
tuyau^M d'eau^F froide
tubo^M de agua^F fría
tubo^M dell'acqua^F fredda

温水（供給）管／給湯管
hot-water line
Warmwasserleitung^N
tuyau^M d'eau^F chaude
tubo^M de agua^F caliente
tubo^M dell'acqua^F calda

陽極棒
anode rod
Anode^F
anode^F
ánodo^M
tubo^M anodico

圧力逃がし弁
pressure relief valve
Überdruckventil^N
soupape^F de sûreté^F
válvula^F de seguridad^F
valvola^F di sicurezza^F

高温遮断装置
high-temperature cutoff
Übertemperatursicherung^F
coupe-circuit^M limiteur de température^F
interruptor^M de sobretemperatura^F
dispositivo^M di sicurezza^F per sovratemperatura^F

上部発熱体
upper heating element
oberer Heizstab^M
élément chauffant^M supérieur
resistencia^F superior
elemento^M riscaldante superiore

上部サーモスタット
upper thermostat
oberer Thermostat^M
thermostat^M supérieur
termostato^M superior
termostato^M superiore

アクセス・パネル
access panel
Abdeckung^F
panneau^M d'accès^M
panel^M de acceso^M
pannello^M di accesso^M

タンク
tank
Innenbehälter^M
cuve^F
tanque^M
serbatoio^M

断熱材
insulation
Wärmeisolation^F
isolant^M
aislante^M
materiale^M isolante

電気接続装置
electric supply
Stromzuleitung^F
câble^M électrique
conexión^F eléctrica
collegamento^M elettrico

オーバーフロー管／溢（あふ）れ防止管
overflow pipe
Überlaufrohr^N
trop-plein^M
tubo^M rebosadero
tubo^M del troppopieno^M

下部サーモスタット
lower thermostat
unterer Thermostat^M
thermostat^M inférieur
termostato^M inferior
termostato^M inferiore

下部発熱体
lower heating element
unterer Heizstab^M
élément^M chauffant^M inférieur
resistencia^F inferior
elemento^M riscaldante inferiore

ドレン弁／排水弁
drain valve
Entleerungsventil^N
robinet^M de vidange^F
válvula^F de drenaje^M
rubinetto^M di scarico^M

配管 | PLUMBING
SANITÄRINSTALLATION | PLOMBERIE | FONTANERÍA | IDRAULICA

湯沸かし装置／ボイラー

ガス湯沸かし装置
gas water-heater tank; *geyser*
Gaswarmwasserbereiter^M
chauffe-eau^F au gaz^M
caldera^F de gas^M
scaldabagno^M a gas^M

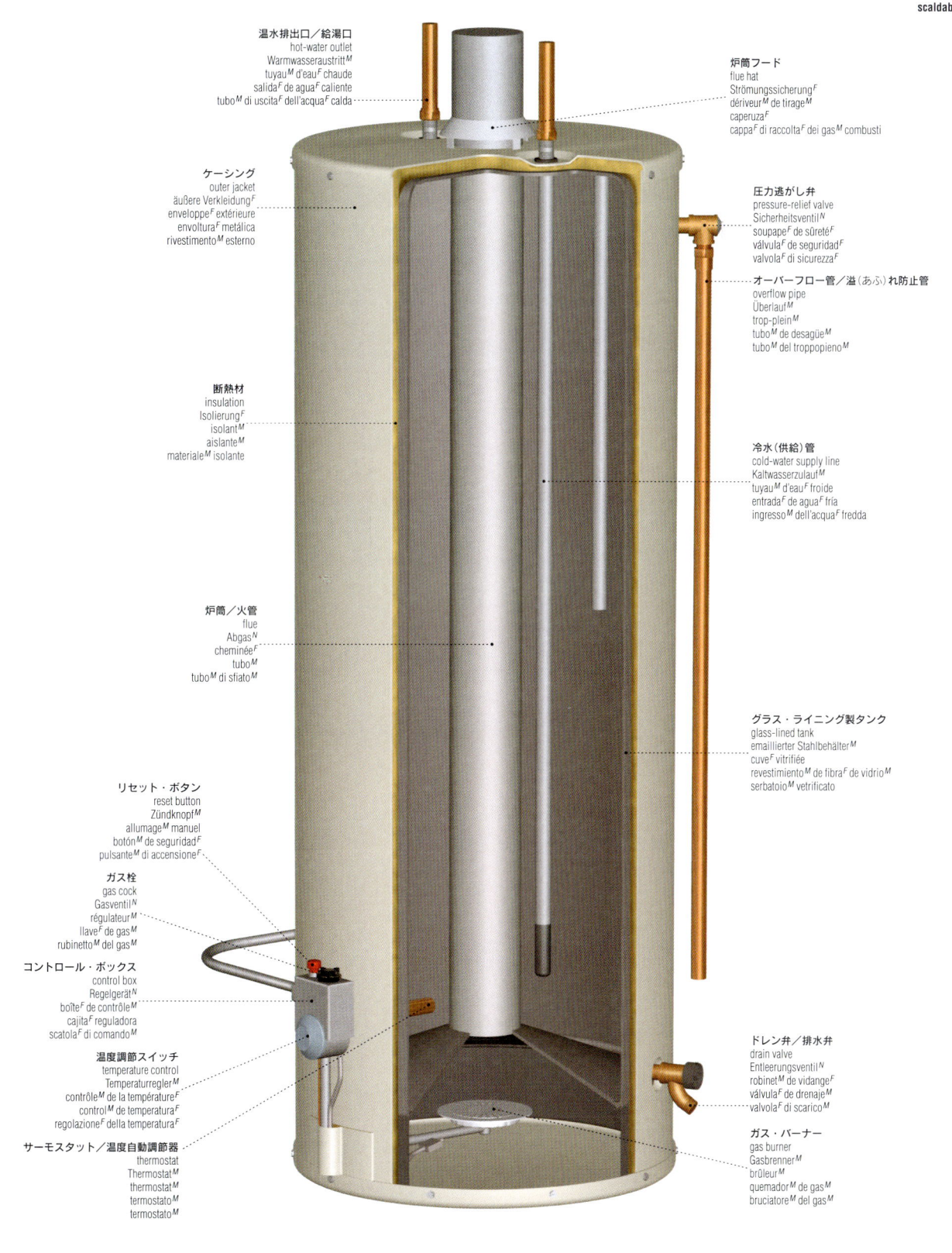

温水排出口／給湯口
hot-water outlet
Warmwasseraustritt^M
tuyau^M d'eau^F chaude
salida^F de agua^F caliente
tubo^M di uscita^F dell'acqua^F calda

炉筒フード
flue hat
Strömungssicherung^F
dériveur^M de tirage^M
caperuza^F
cappa^F di raccolta^F dei gas^M combusti

ケーシング
outer jacket
äußere Verkleidung^F
enveloppe^F extérieure
envoltura^F metálica
rivestimento^M esterno

圧力逃がし弁
pressure-relief valve
Sicherheitsventil^N
soupape^F de sûreté^F
válvula^F de seguridad^F
valvola^F di sicurezza^F

オーバーフロー管／溢(あふ)れ防止管
overflow pipe
Überlauf^M
trop-plein^M
tubo^M de desagüe^M
tubo^M del troppopieno^M

断熱材
insulation
Isolierung^F
isolant^M
aislante^M
materiale^M isolante

冷水（供給）管
cold-water supply line
Kaltwasserzulauf^M
tuyau^M d'eau^F froide
entrada^F de agua^F fría
ingresso^M dell'acqua^F fredda

炉筒／火管
flue
Abgas^N
cheminée^F
tubo^M
tubo^M di sfiato^M

グラス・ライニング製タンク
glass-lined tank
emaillierter Stahlbehälter^M
cuve^F vitrifiée
revestimiento^M de fibra^F de vidrio^M
serbatoio^M vetrificato

リセット・ボタン
reset button
Zündknopf^M
allumage^M manuel
botón^M de seguridad^F
pulsante^M di accensione^F

ガス栓
gas cock
Gasventil^N
régulateur^M
llave^F de gas^M
rubinetto^M del gas^M

コントロール・ボックス
control box
Regelgerät^N
boîte^F de contrôle^M
cajita^F reguladora
scatola^F di comando^M

ドレン弁／排水弁
drain valve
Entleerungsventil^N
robinet^M de vidange^F
válvula^F de drenaje^M
valvola^F di scarico^M

温度調節スイッチ
temperature control
Temperaturregler^M
contrôle^M de la température^F
control^M de temperatura^F
regolazione^F della temperatura^F

ガス・バーナー
gas burner
Gasbrenner^M
brûleur^M
quemador^M de gas^M
bruciatore^M del gas^M

サーモスタット／温度自動調節器
thermostat
Thermostat^M
thermostat^M
termostato^M
termostato^M

家屋

267

配管 | PLUMBING
SANITÄRINSTALLATION | PLOMBERIE | FONTANERÍA | IDRAULICA

蛇口

日本語 | 英語 | ドイツ語 | フランス語 | スペイン語 | イタリア語

faucets | Armaturen^F | robinet^M et mitigeurs^M | grifos^M y mezcladores^M | rubinetti^M e miscelatori^M

家屋

横水栓
stem faucet; *bib tap*
Wandauslaufventil^N
robinet^M
grifo^M de plato^M
rubinetto^M a valvola^F

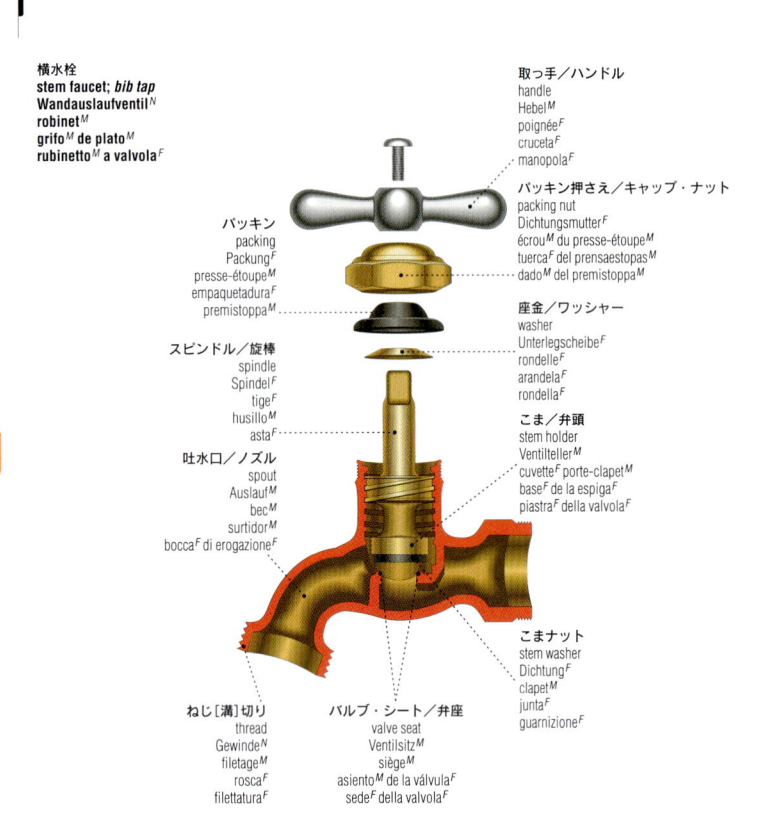

パッキン
packing
Packung^F
presse-étoupe^M
empaquetadura^F
premistoppa^M

スピンドル／旋棒
spindle
Spindel^F
tige^F
husillo^M
asta^F

吐水口／ノズル
spout
Auslauf^M
bec^M
surtidor^M
bocca^F di erogazione^F

取っ手／ハンドル
handle
Hebel^M
poignée^F
cruceta^F
manopola^F

パッキン押さえ／キャップ・ナット
packing nut
Dichtungsmutter^F
écrou^M du presse-étoupe^M
tuerca^F del prensaestopas^M
dado^M del premistoppa^M

座金／ワッシャー
washer
Unterlegscheibe^F
rondelle^F
arandela^F
rondella^F

こま／弁頭
stem holder
Ventilteller^M
cuvette^F porte-clapet^M
base^F de la espiga^F
piastra^F della valvola^F

こまナット
stem washer
Dichtung^F
clapet^M
junta^F
guarnizione^F

ねじ[溝]切り
thread
Gewinde^N
filetage^M
rosca^F
filettatura^F

バルブ・シート／弁座
valve seat
Ventilsitz^M
siège^M
asiento^M de la válvula^F
sede^F della valvola^F

ディスク式水栓
disc faucet; *disc mixer*
Mischbatterie^F mit Keramikdichtung^F
mitigeur^M à disque^M
mezclador^M de disco^M
miscelatore^M a disco^M

取っ手／ハンドル
handle
Hebel^M
levier^M
palanca^F
leva^F

ボンネット
bonnet
Rosette^F
enjoliveur^M
casquete^M
cappuccio^M

シリンダー
cylinder
Zylinder^M
cylindre^M
cilindro^M
cilindro^M

パッキン
seal
Dichtung^F
anneau^M d'étanchéité^F
junta^F de estanquidad^F
guarnizione^F

水取り入れ口
water inlet
Wasserzulauf^M
entrée^F d'eau^F
entrada^F de agua^F
entrata^F dell'acqua^F

泡沫器
aerator
Luftsprudler^M
aérateur^M
filtro^M
aeratore^M

台座
escutcheon
Messingkörper^M
applique^F du robinet^M
placa^F
base^F

ボール式水栓
ball-type faucet; *ball-type mixer tap*
Mischbatterie^F mit Kugeldichtung^F
mitigeur^M à bille^F creuse
grifo^M de bola^F
miscelatore^M a sfera^F

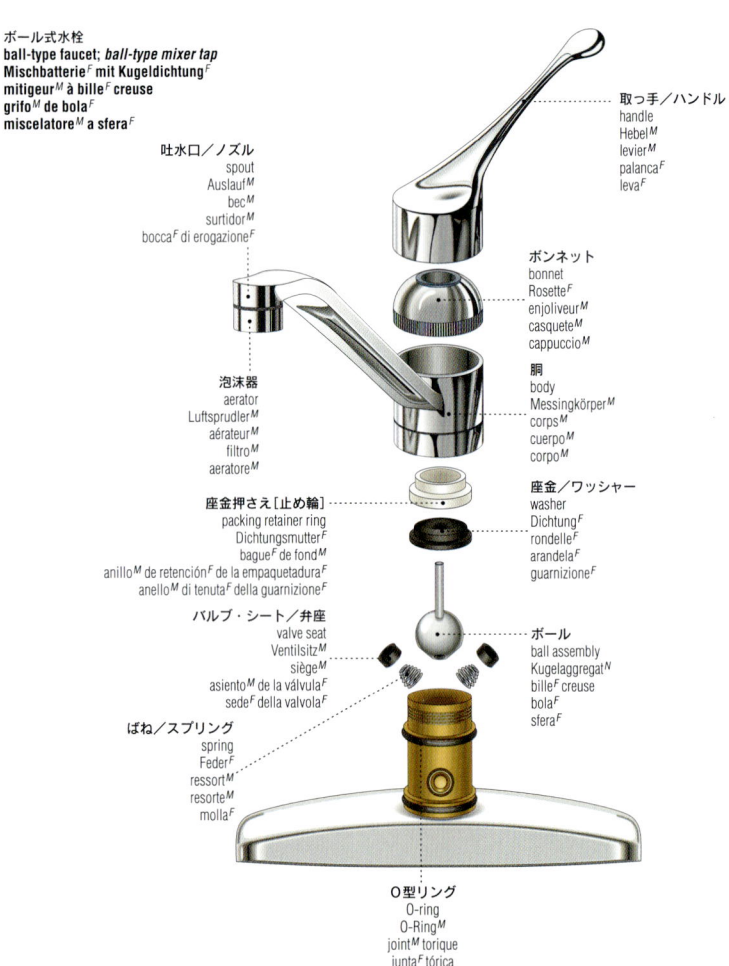

吐水口／ノズル
spout
Auslauf^M
bec^M
surtidor^M
bocca^F di erogazione^F

泡沫器
aerator
Luftsprudler^M
aérateur^M
filtro^M
aeratore^M

座金押さえ[止め輪]
packing retainer ring
Dichtungsmutter^F
bague^F de fond^M
anillo^M de retención^F de la empaquetadura^F
anello^M di tenuta^F della guarnizione^F

バルブ・シート／弁座
valve seat
Ventilsitz^M
siège^M
asiento^M de la válvula^F
sede^F della valvola^F

ばね／スプリング
spring
Feder^F
ressort^M
resorte^M
molla^F

取っ手／ハンドル
handle
Hebel^M
levier^M
palanca^F
leva^F

ボンネット
bonnet
Rosette^F
enjoliveur^M
casquete^M
cappuccio^M

胴
body
Messingkörper^M
corps^M
cuerpo^M
corpo^M

座金／ワッシャー
washer
Dichtung^F
rondelle^F
arandela^F
guarnizione^F

ボール
ball assembly
Kugelaggregat^N
bille^F creuse
bola^F
sfera^F

O型リング
O-ring
O-Ring^M
joint^M torique
junta^F tórica
guarnizione^F ad anello^M

カートリッジ式水栓
cartridge faucet; *cartridge mixer*
Mischbatterie^F mit Kartuschendichtung^F
mitigeur^M à cartouche^F
grifo^M de cartucho^M
miscelatore^M a cartuccia^F

取っ手カバー
lever cover
Deckel^M
capuchon^M du levier^M
casquete^M de la palanca^F
cappuccio^M della leva^F

カートリッジ
cartridge
Kartusche^F
cartouche^F
cartucho^M
cartuccia^F

吐水口／ノズル
spout
Auslauf^M
bec^M
surtidor^M
bocca^F di erogazione^F

泡沫器
aerator
Luftsprudler^M
aérateur^M
filtro^M
aeratore^M

取っ手／レバー
lever
Hebel^M
levier^M
palanca^F
leva^F

カートリッジ軸
cartridge stem
Kartuschenkolben^M
tige^F
espiga^F del cartucho^M
perno^M della cartuccia^F

カートリッジ受け[止め輪]
retaining ring
Dichtung^F
bague^F de serrage^M
anillo^M de retención^F
anello^M di tenuta^F

胴
body
Messingkörper^M
corps^M
cuerpo^M
corpo^M

O型リング
O-ring
O-Ring^M
joint^M torique
junta^F tórica
guarnizione^F ad anello^M

配管 | PLUMBING
SANITÄRINSTALLATION | PLOMBERIE | FONTANERÍA | IDRAULICA

継ぎ手

fittings | Fittings[N] | adaptateurs[M] et raccords[M] | conexiones[F] | adattatori[M] e raccordi[M]

滑り嵌(ば)め[滑合]の例
examples of transition fittings
Beispiele[N] für Übergangsfittings[N]
exemples[M] d'adaptateurs[M]
ejemplos[M] de adaptadores[M]
esempi[M] di adattatori[M]

鋼とプラスチック
steel to plastic
Stahl[M] auf Kunststoff[M]
plastique[M] et acier[M]
de acero[M] a plástico[M]
plastica[F]-acciaio[M]

銅とプラスチック
copper to plastic
Kupfer[N] auf Kunststoff[M]
plastique[M] et cuivre[M]
de cobre[M] a plástico[M]
rame[M]-plastica[F]

銅と鋼
copper to steel
Kupfer[N] auf Stahl[M]
cuivre[M] et acier[M]
de cobre[M] a acero[M]
rame[M]-acciaio[M]

継ぎ手の例
examples of fittings
Beispiele[N] für Fittings[N]
exemples[M] de raccords[M]
ejemplos[M] de racores[M]
esempi[M] di raccordi[M]

オフセット[食い違い]継ぎ手
offset
Etagenbogen[M]
coude[M] de renvoi[M]
codo[M] de cambio[M] de eje[M]
deviatore[M]

T継ぎ手
tee
Strömungs-T[N]
té[M]
derivación[F] en T
raccordo[M] a T

Y継ぎ手
Y-branch
Abzweig[M] 45°
culotte[F]
derivación[F] en Y
raccordo[M] a Y

トラップ継ぎ手
trap
Siphonwinkel[M]
siphon[M]
sifón[M]
sifone[M]

キャップ継ぎ手
cap
Kappe[F]
bouchon[M] femelle
tapón[M]
tappo[M] femmina

U継ぎ手
U-bend
Doppelbogen[M]
coude[M] à 180°
derivación[F] en U
raccordo[M] a U

ねじ切りキャップ継ぎ手
threaded cap
Gewindekappe[F]
bouchon[M] femelle à visser
tapón[M] hembra
tappo[M] femmina a vite[F]

エルボ継ぎ手
elbow
Winkel[M]
coude[M]
codo[M] de 90 grados[M]
raccordo[M] a gomito[M]

45度エルボ継ぎ手
45° elbow
Winkel[M] 45°
coude[M] à 45°
codo[M] de 45 grados[M]
raccordo[M] a gomito[M] di 45°

管継ぎ手
pipe coupling
Rohrverschraubung[F]
manchon[M]
unión[M]
manicotto[M]

六角頭ブッシュ継ぎ手
hexagon bushing
Sechskantreduzierhülse[F]
réduction[F] mâle-femelle hexagonale
reductor[M] con cabeza[F] hexagonal
riduzione[F] esagonale

皿頭ブッシュ継ぎ手
flush bushing
Muffe[F]
réduction[F] mâle-femelle
reductor[M]
riduzione[F] maschio/femmina

ニップル継ぎ手
nipple
Nippel[M]
mamelon[M] double
entrerrosca[F]
nipplo[M]

径違い継ぎ手
reducing coupling
Reduziermuffennippel[M]
raccord[M] de réduction[F]
reductor[M] de calibre[M]
manicotto[M] di riduzione[F]

プラグ継ぎ手
square head plug
Vierkantstopfen[M]
bouchon[M] mâle sans bourrelet[M]
tapón[M] macho[M]
tappo[M] maschio a testa[F] quadra

機械継ぎ手
mechanical connectors
mechanische Verbindungen[F]
raccords[M] mécaniques
racores[M] mecánicas
raccordi[M] meccanici

ユニオン継ぎ手
union
Verschraubung[F]
raccord[M] union[F]
unión[F]
raccordo[M] per unione[F] meccanica

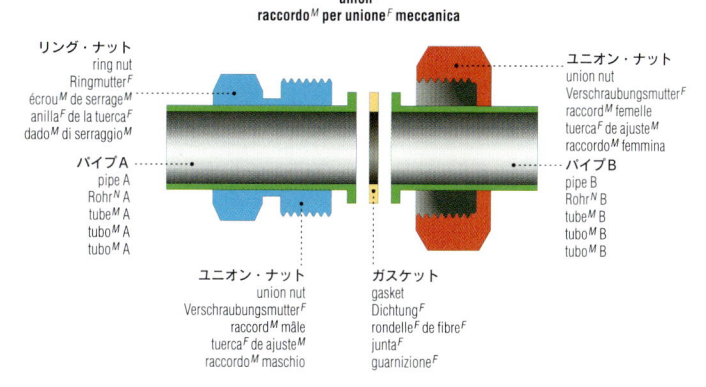

リング・ナット
ring nut
Ringmutter[F]
écrou[M] de serrage[M]
anilla[F] de la tuerca[F]
dado[M] di serraggio[M]

ユニオン・ナット
union nut
Verschraubungsmutter[F]
raccord[M] femelle
tuerca[F] de ajuste[M]
raccordo[M] femmina

パイプA
pipe A
Rohr[N] A
tube[M] A
tubo[M] A
tubo[M] A

パイプB
pipe B
Rohr[N] B
tube[M] B
tubo[M] B
tubo[M] B

ユニオン・ナット
union nut
Verschraubungsmutter[F]
raccord[M] mâle
tuerca[F] de ajuste[M]
raccordo[M] maschio

ガスケット
gasket
Dichtung[F]
rondelle[F] de fibre[F]
junta[F]
guarnizione[F]

圧縮継ぎ手
compression fitting
Quetschverschraubung[F]
raccord[M] à compression[F]
racor[M] por compresión[F]
raccordo[M] a compressione[F]

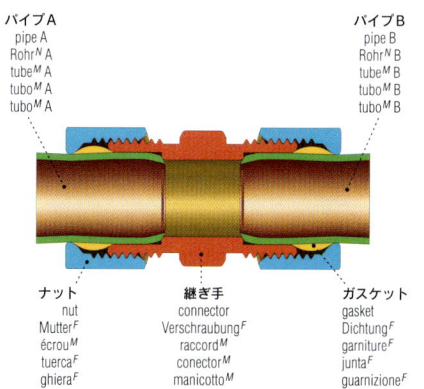

フレア継ぎ手
flare joint
Bördelverbindung[F]
raccord[M] à collet[M] repoussé
racor[M] abocinado
raccordo[M] a collarino[M] pressato

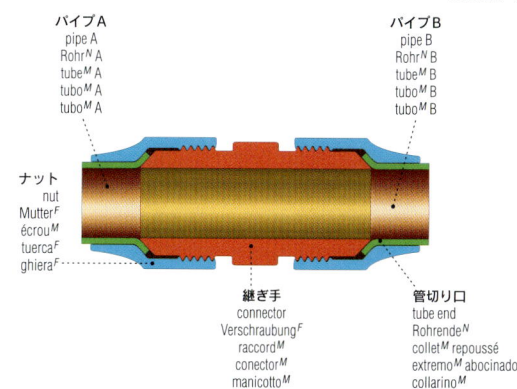

パイプA
pipe A
Rohr[N] A
tube[M] A
tubo[M] A
tubo[M] A

パイプB
pipe B
Rohr[N] B
tube[M] B
tubo[M] B
tubo[M] B

パイプA
pipe A
Rohr[N] A
tube[M] A
tubo[M] A
tubo[M] A

パイプB
pipe B
Rohr[N] B
tube[M] B
tubo[M] B
tubo[M] B

ナット
nut
Mutter[F]
écrou[M]
tuerca[F]
ghiera[F]

継ぎ手
connector
Verschraubung[F]
raccord[M]
conector[M]
manicotto[M]

ガスケット
gasket
Dichtung[F]
garniture[F]
junta[F]
guarnizione[F]

ナット
nut
Mutter[F]
écrou[M]
tuerca[F]
ghiera[F]

継ぎ手
connector
Verschraubung[F]
raccord[M]
conector[M]
manicotto[M]

管切り口
tube end
Rohrende[N]
collet[M] repoussé
extremo[M] abocinado
collarino[M]

家屋

269

配管 | PLUMBING
SANITÄRINSTALLATION | PLOMBERIE | FONTANERÍA | IDRAULICA

分岐管の例

examples of branching | Beispiele^N für Anschlüsse^M | exemples^M de branchement^M | ejemplos^M de conexiones^M | esempi^M di allacciamento^M

生ごみ処理機組み込み流し台
garbage disposal sink; *sink with waste disposal unit*
Spüle^F mit Müllschlucker^M
évier^M-broyeur^M
fregadero^M con triturador de basura^F
lavello^M con tritarifiuti^M

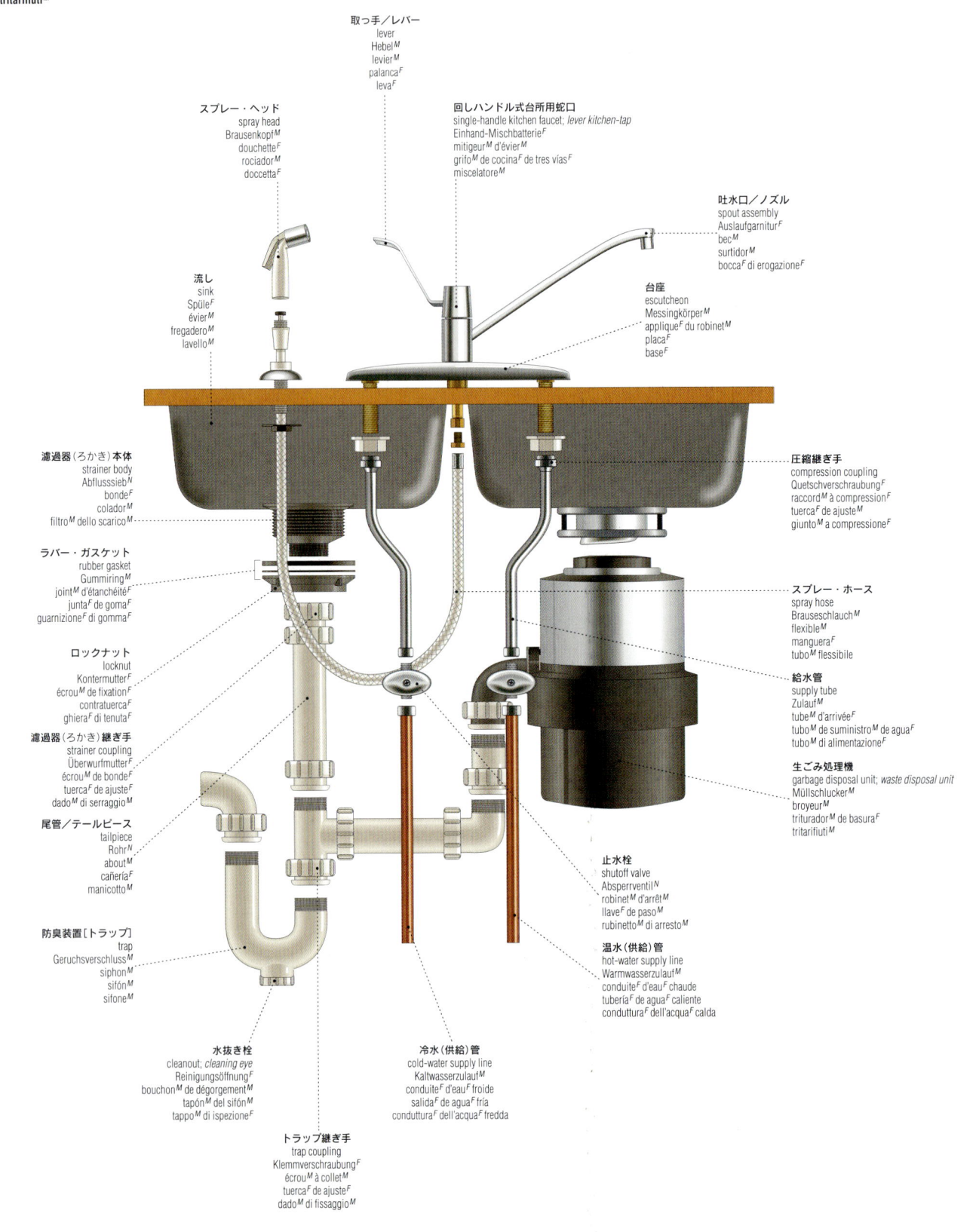

家屋

取っ手／レバー
lever
Hebel^M
levier^M
palanca^F
leva^F

スプレー・ヘッド
spray head
Brausenkopf^M
douchette^F
rociador^M
doccetta^F

回しハンドル式台所用蛇口
single-handle kitchen faucet; *lever kitchen-tap*
Einhand-Mischbatterie^F
mitigeur^M d'évier^M
grifo^M de cocina^F de tres vías^F
miscelatore^M

吐水口／ノズル
spout assembly
Auslaufgarnitur^F
bec^M
surtidor^M
bocca^F di erogazione^F

流し
sink
Spüle^F
évier^M
fregadero^M
lavello^M

台座
escutcheon
Messingkörper^M
applique^F du robinet^M
placa^F
base^F

濾過器（ろかき）本体
strainer body
Abflusssieb^N
bonde^F
colador^M
filtro^M dello scarico^M

圧縮継ぎ手
compression coupling
Quetschverschraubung^F
raccord^M à compression^F
tuerca^F de ajuste^M
giunto^M a compressione^F

ラバー・ガスケット
rubber gasket
Gummiring^M
joint^M d'étanchéité^F
junta^F de goma^F
guarnizione^F di gomma^F

スプレー・ホース
spray hose
Brauseschlauch^M
flexible^M
manguera^F
tubo^M flessibile

ロックナット
locknut
Kontermutter^F
écrou^M de fixation^F
contratuerca^F
ghiera^F di tenuta^F

給水管
supply tube
Zulauf^M
tube^M d'arrivée^F
tubo^M de suministro^M de agua^F
tubo^M di alimentazione^F

濾過器（ろかき）継ぎ手
strainer coupling
Überwurfmutter^F
écrou^M de bonde^F
tuerca^F de ajuste^M
dado^M di serraggio^M

生ごみ処理機
garbage disposal unit; *waste disposal unit*
Müllschlucker^M
broyeur^M
triturador^M de basura^F
tritarifiuti^M

尾管／テールピース
tailpiece
Rohr^N
about^N
cañería^F
manicotto^M

止水栓
shutoff valve
Absperrventil^N
robinet^M d'arrêt^M
llave^F de paso^M
rubinetto^M di arresto^M

防臭装置［トラップ］
trap
Geruchsverschluss^M
siphon^M
sifón^M
sifone^M

温水（供給）管
hot-water supply line
Warmwasserzulauf^M
conduite^F d'eau^F chaude
tubería^F de agua^F caliente
conduttura^F dell'acqua^F calda

水抜き栓
cleanout; *cleaning eye*
Reinigungsöffnung^F
bouchon^M de dégorgement^M
tapón^M del sifón^M
tappo^M di ispezione^F

冷水（供給）管
cold-water supply line
Kaltwasserzulauf^M
conduite^F d'eau^F froide
salida^F de agua^F fría
conduttura^F dell'acqua^F fredda

トラップ継ぎ手
trap coupling
Klemmverschraubung^F
écrou^M à collet^M
tuerca^F de ajuste^M
dado^M di fissaggio^M

配管 | PLUMBING
SANITÄRINSTALLATION | PLOMBERIE | FONTANERÍA | IDRAULICA

分岐管の例

洗濯機
washer; *washing machine*
Waschmaschine^F
lave-linge^M
lavadora^F
lavatrice^F

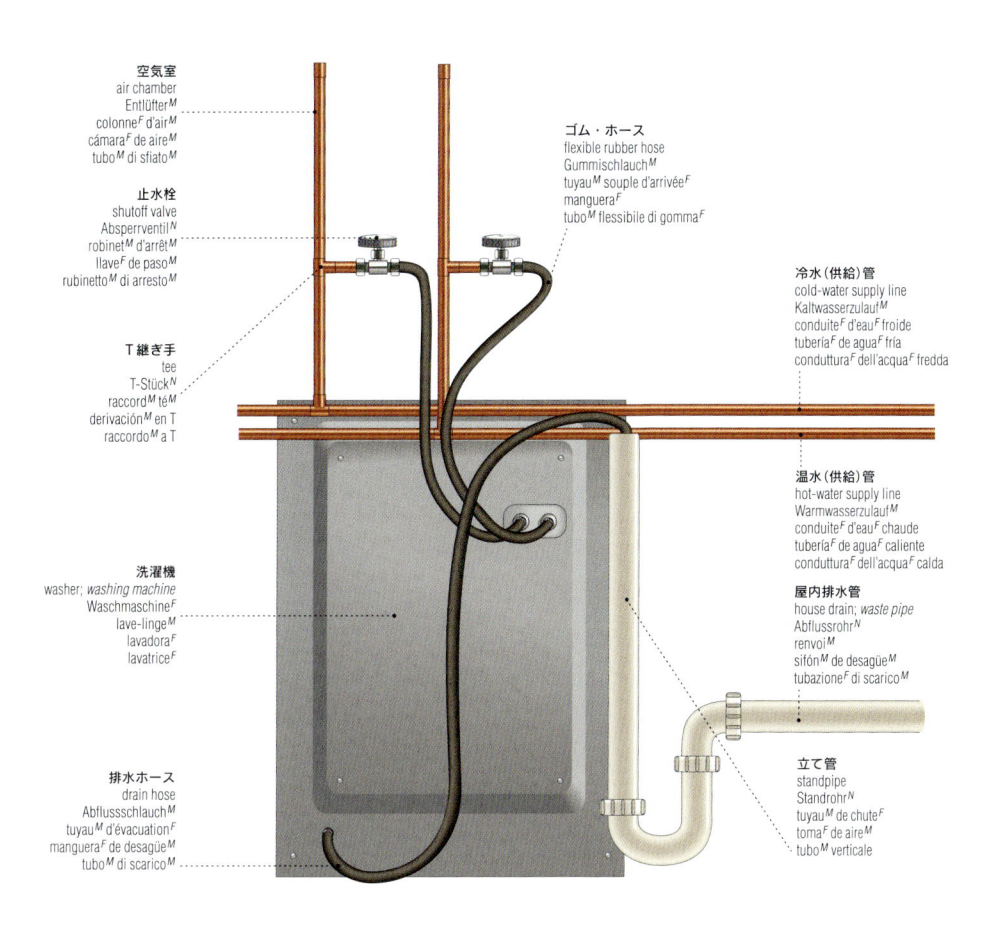

空気室
air chamber
Entlüfter^M
colonne^F d'air^M
cámara^F de aire^M
tubo^M di sfiato^M

ゴム・ホース
flexible rubber hose
Gummischlauch^M
tuyau^M souple d'arrivée^F
manguera^F
tubo^M flessibile di gomma^F

止水栓
shutoff valve
Absperrventil^N
robinet^M d'arrêt^M
llave^F de paso^M
rubinetto^M di arresto^M

冷水(供給)管
cold-water supply line
Kaltwasserzulauf^M
conduite^F d'eau^F froide
tubería^F de agua^F fría
conduttura^F dell'acqua^F fredda

T継ぎ手
tee
T-Stück^N
raccord^M té^M
derivación^M en T
raccordo^M a T

温水(供給)管
hot-water supply line
Warmwasserzulauf^M
conduite^F d'eau^F chaude
tubería^F de agua^F caliente
conduttura^F dell'acqua^F calda

洗濯機
washer; *washing machine*
Waschmaschine^F
lave-linge^M
lavadora^F
lavatrice^F

屋内排水管
house drain; waste pipe
Abflussrohr^N
renvoi^M
sifón^M de desagüe^M
tubazione^F di scarico^M

立て管
standpipe
Standrohr^N
tuyau^M de chute^F
toma^F de aire^M
tubo^M verticale

排水ホース
drain hose
Abflussschlauch^M
tuyau^M d'évacuation^F
manguera^F de desagüe^M
tubo^M di scarico^M

皿洗い機
dishwasher
Geschirrspülmaschine^F
lave-vaisselle^M
lavavajillas^F
lavastoviglie^F

排水ホース
drain hose
Ablaufschlauch^M
tuyau^M de vidange^F
manguera^F de desagüe^M
tubo^M di scarico^M

皿洗い機
dishwasher
Geschirrspülmaschine^F
lave-vaisselle^M
lavavajillas^F
lavastoviglie^F

空気室
air chamber
Entlüfter^M
colonne^F d'air^M
cámara^F de aire^M
tubo^M di sfiato^M

排水管T継ぎ手
waste tee
Abfluss-T-Stück^N
raccord^M té^M d'égout^M
derivación^F en T del desagüe^M
raccordo^M a T del tubo^M di scarico^M

温水(供給)管
hot-water supply line
Warmwasserzulauf^M
conduite^F d'eau^F chaude
tubería^F de agua^F caliente
conduttura^F dell'acqua^F calda

冷水(供給)管
cold-water supply line
Kaltwasserzulauf^M
conduite^F d'eau^F froide
cañería^F de agua^F fría
conduttura^F dell'acqua^F fredda

止水栓
shutoff valve
Absperrventil^N
robinet^M d'arrêt^M
llave^F de paso^M
rubinetto^M di arresto^M

家屋

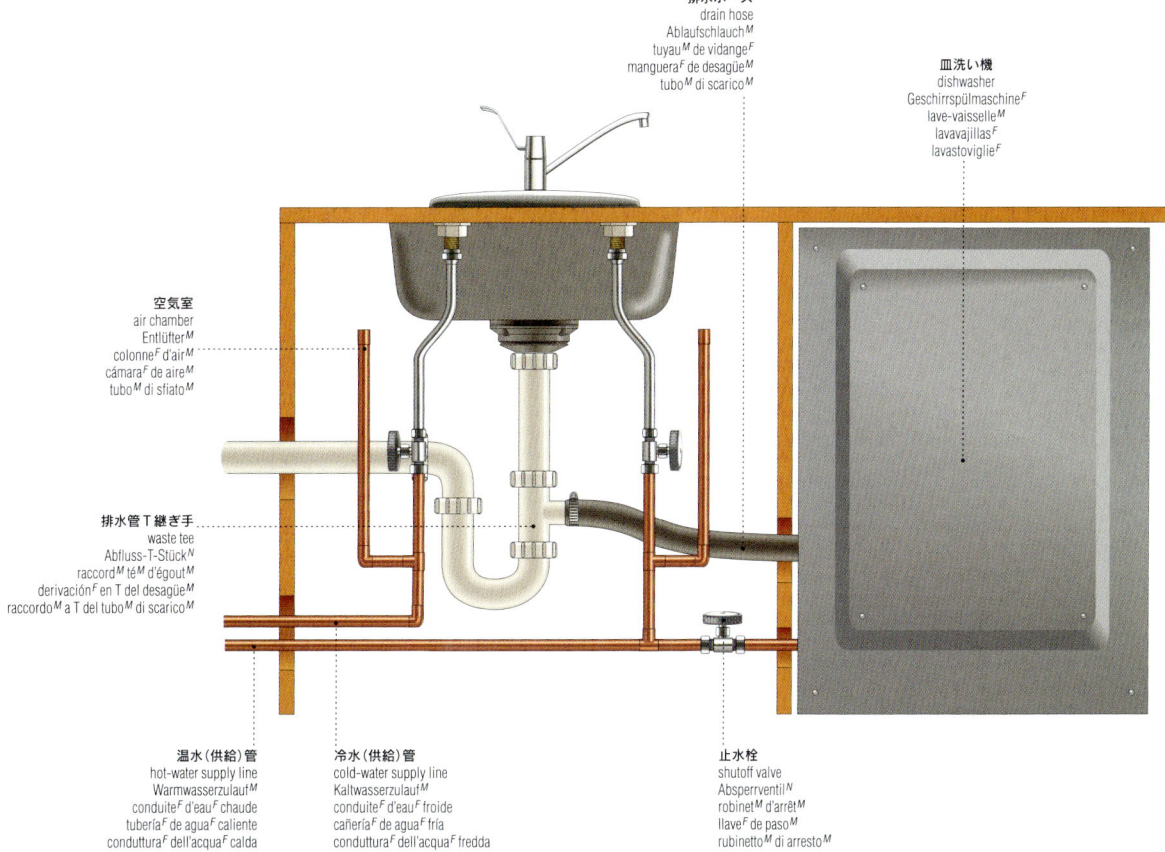

電気 | ELECTRICITY
ELEKTRIZITÄT | ÉLECTRICITÉ | ELECTRICIDAD | ELETTRICITÀ

配電盤

日本語 | 英語 | ドイツ語 | フランス語 | スペイン語 | イタリア語

distribution panel | Verteilerkasten^M | panneau^M de distribution^F | cuadro^M de distribución^F | pannello^M di distribuzione^F

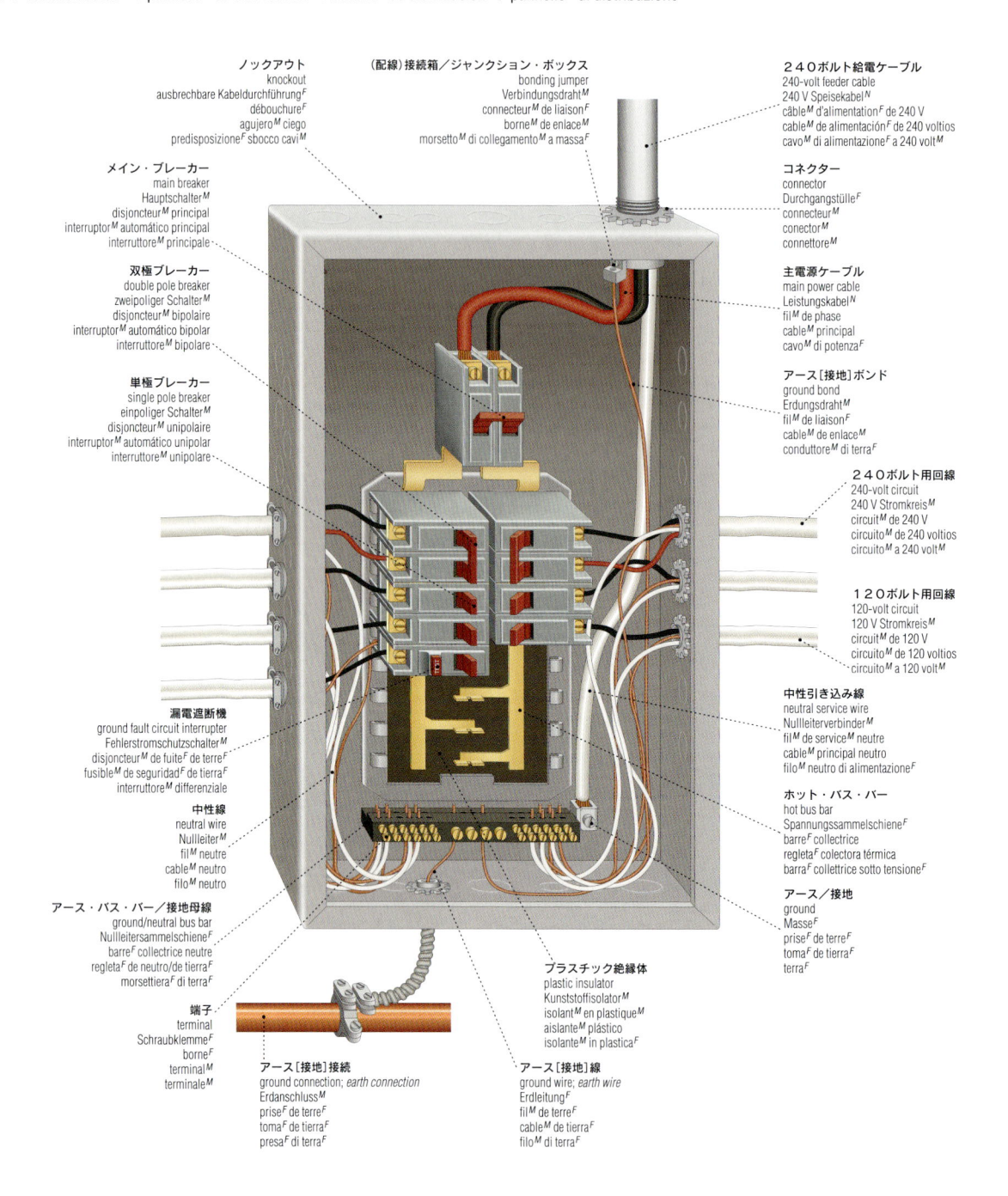

ノックアウト
knockout
ausbrechbare Kabeldurchführung^F
débouchure^F
agujero^M ciego
predisposizione^F sbocco cavi^M

（配線）接続箱／ジャンクション・ボックス
bonding jumper
Verbindungsdraht^M
connecteur de liaison^F
borne de enlace^M
morsetto^M di collegamento^F a massa^F

240ボルト給電ケーブル
240-volt feeder cable
240 V Speisekabel^N
câble^M d'alimentation^F de 240 V
cable^M de alimentación^F de 240 voltios
cavo^M di alimentazione^F a 240 volt^M

メイン・ブレーカー
main breaker
Hauptschalter^M
disjoncteur^M principal
interruptor^M automático principal
interruttore^M principale

コネクター
connector
Durchgangstülle^F
connecteur^M
conector^M
connettore^M

双極ブレーカー
double pole breaker
zweipoliger Schalter^M
disjoncteur^M bipolaire
interruptor^M automático bipolar
interruttore^M bipolare

主電源ケーブル
main power cable
Leistungskabel^N
fil^M de phase
cable^M principal
cavo^M di potenza^F

単極ブレーカー
single pole breaker
einpoliger Schalter^M
disjoncteur^M unipolaire
interruptor^M automático unipolar
interruttore^M unipolare

アース［接地］ボンド
ground bond
Erdungsdraht^M
fil^M de liaison^F
cable^M de enlace^M
conduttore^M di terra^F

240ボルト用回線
240-volt circuit
240 V Stromkreis^M
circuit^M de 240 V
circuito^M de 240 voltios
circuito^M a 240 volt^M

120ボルト用回線
120-volt circuit
120 V Stromkreis^M
circuit^M de 120 V
circuito^M de 120 voltios
circuito^M a 120 volt^M

漏電遮断機
ground fault circuit interrupter
Fehlerstromschutzschalter^M
disjoncteur^M de fuite^F de terre^F
fusible^M de seguridad^F de tierra^F
interruttore^M differenziale

中性引き込み線
neutral service wire
Nullleiterverbinder^M
fil^M de service^M neutre
cable^M principal neutro
filo^M neutro di alimentazione^F

中性線
neutral wire
Nullleiter^M
fil^M neutre
cable^M neutro
filo^M neutro

ホット・バス・バー
hot bus bar
Spannungssammelschiene^F
barre^F collectrice
regleta^F colectora térmica
barra^F collettrice sotto tensione^F

アース・バス・バー／接地母線
ground/neutral bus bar
Nullleitersammelschiene^F
barre^F collectrice neutre
regleta^F de neutro/de tierra^F
morsettiera^F di terra^F

アース／接地
ground
Masse^F
prise^F de terre^F
toma^F de tierra^F
terra^F

プラスチック絶縁体
plastic insulator
Kunststoffisolator^M
isolant^M en plastique^M
aislante^M plástico
isolante^M in plastica^F

端子
terminal
Schraubklemme^F
borne^F
terminal^M
terminale^M

アース［接地］接続
ground connection; *earth connection*
Erdanschluss^M
prise^F de terre^F
toma^F de tierra^F
presa^F di terra^F

アース［接地］線
ground wire; *earth wire*
Erdleitung^F
fil^M de terre^F
cable^M de tierra^F
filo^M di terra^F

ヒューズの例
examples of fuses
Beispiele^N für Sicherungen^F
exemples^M de fusibles^M
ejemplos^M de fusibles
esempi^M di fusibili^M

カートリッジ・ヒューズ
cartridge fuse
Patronensicherung^F
fusible^M-cartouche^F
fusible^M de cartucho^M
fusibile^M a cartuccia^F

プラグ・ヒューズ
plug fuse
Stöpselsicherung^F
fusible^M à culot^M
fusible^M de rosca^F
fusibile^M a tappo^M

刃型カートリッジ・ヒューズ
knife-blade cartridge fuse
Messersicherung^F
fusible^M-cartouche^F à lames^F
fusible^M de bayoneta^F
fusibile^M a cartuccia^F con terminali^M a coltello^M

電気 | ELECTRICITY
ELEKTRIZITÄT | ÉLECTRICITÉ | ELECTRICIDAD | ELETTRICITÀ

ネットワーク接続

network connection | Hausanschluss[M] | branchement[M] au réseau[M] | conexión[F] a la red[F] | allacciamento[M] alla rete[F]

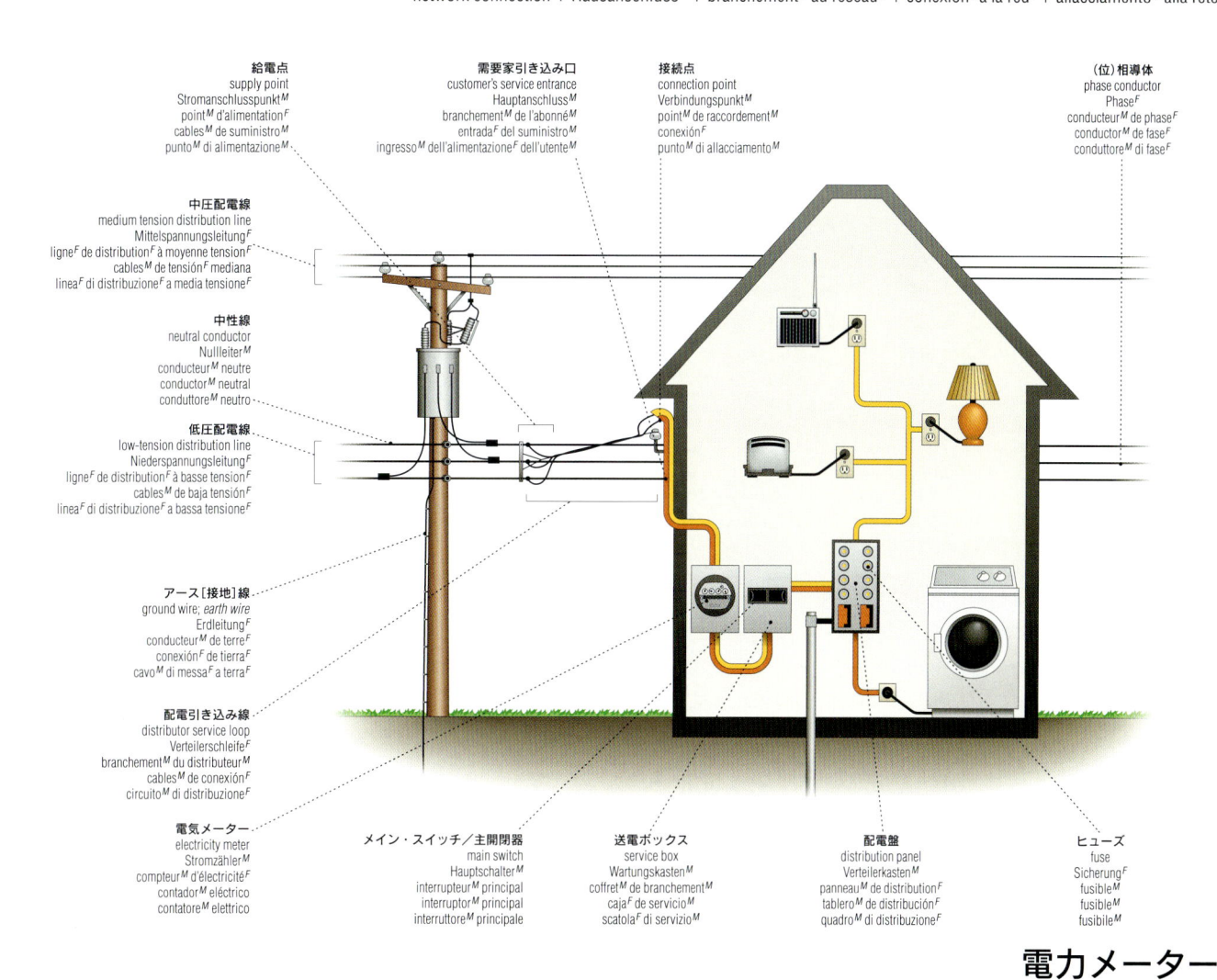

給電点
supply point
Stromanschlusspunkt[M]
point[M] d'alimentation[F]
cables[M] de suministro[M]
punto[M] di alimentazione[M]

需要家引き込み口
customer's service entrance
Hauptanschluss
branchement[M] de l'abonné[M]
entrada[F] del suministro[M]
ingresso[M] dell'alimentazione[F] dell'utente[M]

接続点
connection point
Verbindungspunkt[M]
point[M] de raccordement[M]
conexión[F]
punto[M] di allacciamento[M]

(位)相導体
phase conductor
Phase[F]
conducteur[M] de phase[F]
conductor[M] de fase[F]
conduttore[M] di fase[F]

中圧配電線
medium tension distribution line
Mittelspannungsleitung[F]
ligne[F] de distribution[F] à moyenne tension[F]
cables[M] de tensión[F] mediana
linea[F] di distribuzione[F] a media tensione[F]

中性線
neutral conductor
Nullleiter[M]
conducteur[M] neutre
conductor[M] neutral
conduttore[M] neutro

低圧配電線
low-tension distribution line
Niederspannungsleitung[F]
ligne[F] de distribution[F] à basse tension[F]
cables[M] de baja tensión[F]
linea[F] di distribuzione[F] a bassa tensione[F]

家屋

アース［接地］線
ground wire; *earth wire*
Erdleitung[F]
conducteur[M] de terre[F]
conexión[F] de tierra[F]
cavo[M] di messa[F] a terra[F]

配電引き込み線
distributor service loop
Verteilerschleife[F]
branchement[M] du distributeur[M]
cables[M] de conexión[F]
circuito[M] di distribuzione[F]

電気メーター
electricity meter
Stromzähler[M]
compteur[M] d'électricité[F]
contador[M] eléctrico
contatore[M] elettrico

メイン・スイッチ／主開閉器
main switch
Hauptschalter[M]
interrupteur[M] principal
interruptor[M] principal
interruttore[M] principale

送電ボックス
service box
Wartungskasten[M]
coffret[M] de branchement[M]
caja[F] de servicio[M]
scatola[F] di servizio[M]

配電盤
distribution panel
Verteilerkasten[M]
panneau[M] de distribution[F]
tablero[M] de distribución[F]
quadro[M] di distribuzione[F]

ヒューズ
fuse
Sicherung[F]
fusible[M]
fusible[M]
fusibile[M]

電力メーター

electricity meter | Kilowattstundenzähler[M] | compteur[M] d'électricité[F] | contador[M] de kilovatio-hora | contatore[M] di kilowattora[M]

カバー
cover
Abdeckung[F]
couvercle[M]
tapa[F]
calotta[F]

全負荷調整ねじ
full-load adjustment screw
Vollbelastungsstellschraube[F]
vis[F] de réglage[M] de grand débit[M]
tornillo[M] de regulación[F] para carga[F] completa
vite[F] di regolazione[F] a pieno carico[M]

目盛り板
dial
Ziffernblatt[N]
cadran[M]
cuadrante[M]
quadrante[M]

計器
register
Registriereinheit[F]
minuterie[F]
registro[M]
numeratore[M]

回転円板
disk; *disc*
Drehscheibe[F]
disque[M]
disco[M]
disco[M]

銘板
name plate
Kennplakette[F]
plaque[F] signalétique
placa[F] indicadora
piastrina[F] dei dati[M]

需要家番号
consumer number
Stromverbrauchernummer[F]
numéro[M] de l'abonné[F]
número[M] del consumidor[M]
numero[M] dell'utente[M]

軽負荷調整ねじ
light-load adjustment screw
Leichtbelastungsstellschraube[F]
vis[F] de réglage[M] de petit débit[M]
tornillo[M] de regulación[F] para carga[F] ligera
vite[F] di regolazione[F] a basso carico[M]

台
base
Grundplatte[F]
socle[M]
base[F]
base[F]

273

電気 | ELECTRICITY
ELEKTRIZITÄT | ÉLECTRICITÉ | ELECTRICIDAD | ELETTRICITÀ

接続装置

contact devices | Kontaktelemente^N | dispositifs^M de contact^M | dispositivos^M de contacto^M | dispositivi^M di contatto^M

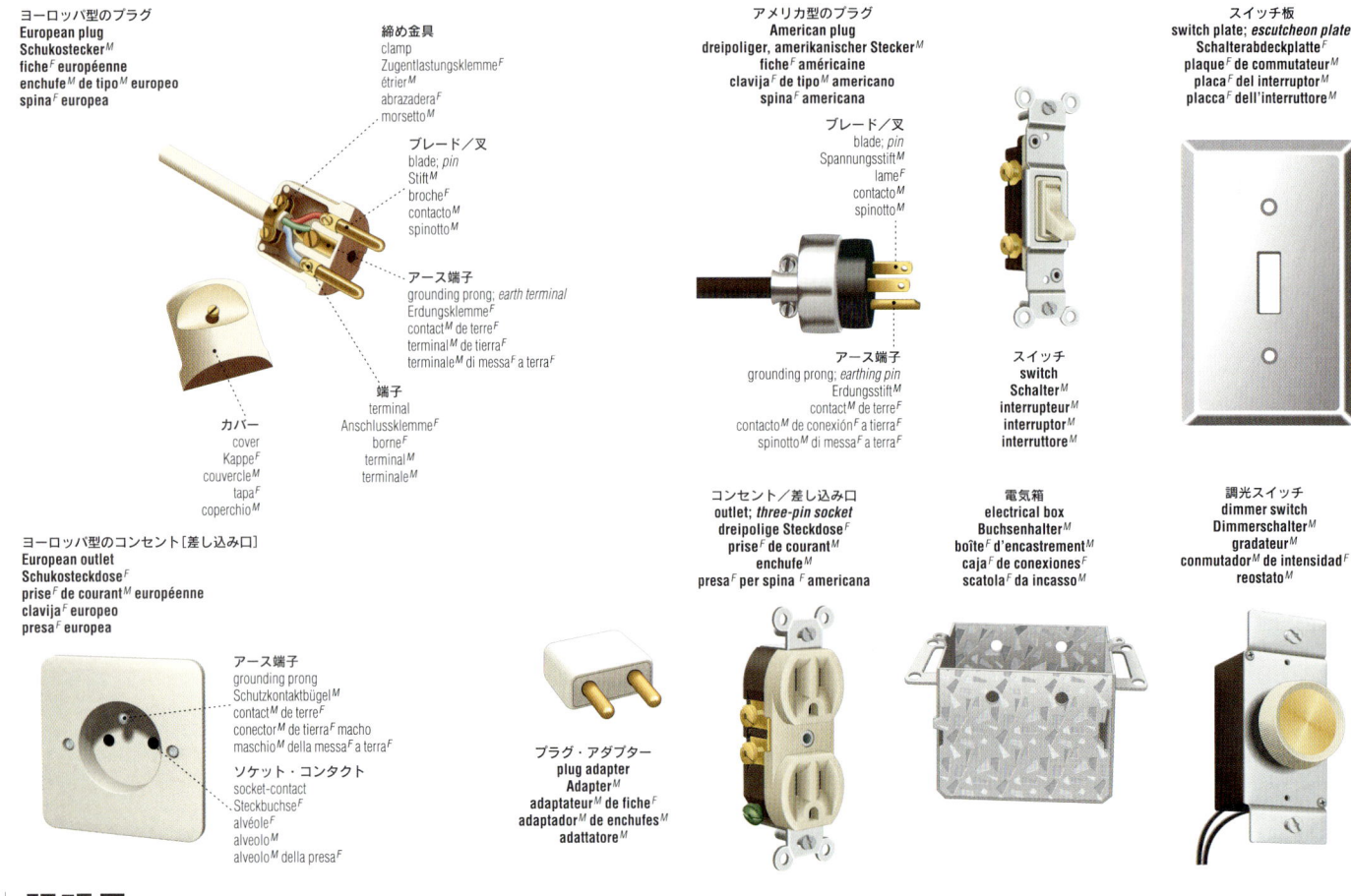

日本語 | 英語 | ドイツ語 | フランス語 | スペイン語 | イタリア語

ヨーロッパ型のプラグ
European plug
Schukostecker^M
fiche^F européenne
enchufe^F de tipo^M europeo
spina^F europea

締め金具
clamp
Zugentlastungsklemme^F
étrier^M
abrazadera^F
morsetto^M

ブレード／叉
blade; pin
Stift^M
broche^F
contacto^M
spinotto^M

アース端子
grounding prong; earth terminal
Erdungsklemme^F
contact^M de terre^F
terminal^M de tierra^F
terminale^M di messa^F a terra^F

端子
terminal
Anschlussklemme^F
borne^F
terminal^M
terminale^M

カバー
cover
Kappe^F
couvercle^M
tapa^F
coperchio^M

アメリカ型のプラグ
American plug
dreipoliger, amerikanischer Stecker^M
fiche^F américaine
clavija^F de tipo^M americano
spina^F americana

ブレード／叉
blade; pin
Spannungsstift^M
lame^F
contacto^M
spinotto^M

アース端子
grounding prong; earthing pin
Erdungsstift^M
contact^M de terre^F
contacto^M de conexión^F a tierra^F
spinotto^M di messa^F a terra^F

スイッチ
switch
Schalter^M
interrupteur^M
interruptor^M
interruttore^M

スイッチ板
switch plate; escutcheon plate
Schalterabdeckplatte^F
plaque^F de commutateur^M
placa^F del interruptor^M
placca^F dell'interruttore^M

ヨーロッパ型のコンセント［差し込み口］
European outlet
Schukosteckdose^F
prise^F de courant^M européenne
clavija^F europeo
presa^F europea

アース端子
grounding prong
Schutzkontaktbügel^M
contact^M de terre^F
conector^M de tierra^F macho
maschio^M della messa^F a terra^F

ソケット・コンタクト
socket-contact
Steckbuchse^F
alvéole^F
alveolo^M
alveolo^M della presa^F

プラグ・アダプター
plug adapter
Adapter^M
adaptateur^M de fiche^F
adaptador^M de enchufes^F
adattatore^M

コンセント／差し込み口
outlet; three-pin socket
dreipolige Steckdose^F
prise^F de courant^M
enchufe^F
presa^F per spina^F americana

電気箱
electrical box
Buchsenhalter^M
boîte^F d'encastrement^M
caja^F de conexiones^F
scatola^F da incasso^F

調光スイッチ
dimmer switch
Dimmerschalter^M
gradateur^M
conmutador^M de intensidad^F
reostato^M

照明具

lighting | Beleuchtung^F | éclairage^M | iluminación^F | illuminazione^F

白熱電球
incandescent lamp
Glühlampe^F
lampe^F à incandescence^F
bombilla^F incandescente
lampadina^F a incandescenza^F

フィラメント
filament
Glühfaden^M
filament^M
filamento^M
filamento^M

支持線／アンカー
support
Halter^M
support^M
soporte^M
supporto^M

ステム管
stem
Stab^M
pied^M
varilla^F
asta^F

遮熱板
heat deflecting disc
Wärmedeflektorscheibe^F
déflecteur^M de chaleur^F
disco^M desviador de calor^M
disco^M deflettore^M del calore^M

排気管
exhaust tube
Entladungsröhre^F
queusot^M
tubo de escape^M
tubo^M di estrazione^F dell'aria^F

不活性ガス
inert gas
Edelgas^N
gaz^M inerte
gas^M inerte
gas^M inerte

ボタン
button
Knopf^M
bouton^M
botón^M
bottone^M

導入線
lead-in wire
Zuleitungsdraht^M
entrée^F de courant^M
entrada^F de corriente^F
filo^M conduttore

つまみ
pinch
Quetschfuß^M
pincement^M
pie^M
codetta^F

口金
base
Sockel^M
culot^M
casquillo^M
attacco^M

ハロゲン電球
tungsten-halogen lamp
Wolfram-Halogenlampe^F
lampe^F à halogène^M
lámpara^F halógena
lampada^F alogena al tungsteno^M

フィラメント支持線
filament support
Wendelhalter^M
support^M du filament^M
filamento^M
supporto^M del filamento^M

ガラス球
bulb
Kolben^M
ampoule^F
ampolla^F
bulbo^M

タングステン・フィラメント
tungsten filament
Wolframwendel^F
filament^M de tungstène^M
filamento^M de tungsteno^M
filamento^M di tungsteno^M

電気回路
electric circuit
elektrischer Kreislauf^M
circuit^M électrique
circuito^M eléctrico
circuito^M elettrico

不活性ガス
inert gas
Edelgas^N
gaz^M inerte
gas^M inerte
gas^M inerte

接点／接触部
contact
Kontakt^M
plot^M
contacto^M
contatto^M

口金
base
Sockel^M
culot^M
casquillo^M
attacco^M

274

電気 | ELECTRICITY
ELEKTRIZITÄT | ÉLECTRICITÉ | ELECTRICIDAD | ELETTRICITÀ

照明具

ソケットの各部分
parts of a lamp socket
Teile M/N einer Lampenfassung F
éléments M d'une douille F de lampe F
componentes F del portalámpara M
componenti M del portalampada M

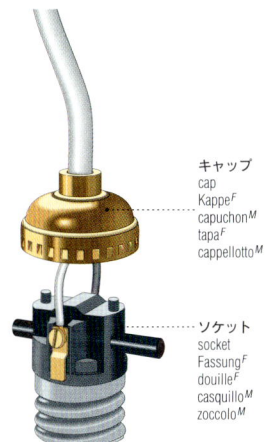

キャップ
cap
Kappe F
capuchon M
tapa F
cappellotto M

ソケット
socket
Fassung F
douille F
casquillo M
zoccolo M

絶縁スリーブ
insulating sleeve
Isolierhülse F
gaine F isolante
manga F de aislamiento M
manicotto M isolante

ソケット・シェル
outer shell
äußere Hülse F
enveloppe F
cubierta F
protezione F esterna

ソケット
lamp socket
Lampenfassung F
douille F de lampe F
portalámparas M
portalampada F

蛍光管
fluorescent tube
Leuchtstoffröhre F
tube M fluorescent
tubo M fluorescente
tubo M fluorescente

蛍光管固定クリップ
tube retention clip
Cliphalterung M
attache F du tube M
clip M de ajuste M
dispositivo M di fissaggio M del tubo M

取り付け台
mounting plate
Röhrenfassung F
plaque F de montage M
placa F de instalación F
piastra F di supporto M

ケース
housing
Gehäuse N
boîtier M
pantalla F
alloggiamento M

差し込み口金
bayonet base
Bajonettfassung F
culot M à baïonnette F
bombilla F de bayoneta F
attacco M a baionetta F

ねじ込み口金
screw base
Schraubfassung F
culot M à vis F
bombilla F de rosca F
attacco M a vite F

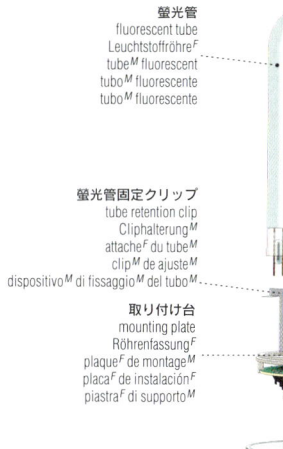

電子安定器
electronic ballast
elektronisches Vorschaltgerät N
ballast M électronique
electrodos M
regolatore M di corrente F

口金
base
Sockel M
culot M
casquillo M
attacco M

電球
bulb
Kolben M
ampoule F
ampolla F de vidrio M
bulbo M

省エネ電球
energy saving bulb
Energiesparlampe F
lampe F à économie F d'énergie F
bombilla F económica
lampadina F a risparmio M di energia F

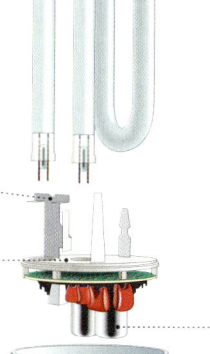

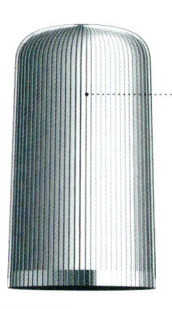

外球
bulb
Kolben M
ampoule F
ampolla F
bulbo M

家屋

蛍光灯
fluorescent tube
Leuchtstoffröhre F
tube M fluorescent
tubo M fluorescente
tubo M fluorescente

導入線
lead-in wire
Zuleitungsdraht M
entrée F de courant M
entrada F de corriente F
filo M conduttore

排気管
exhaust tube
Entladungsröhre F
queusot M
tubo M de escape M
tubo M di estrazione F dell'aria F

つまみ
pinch
Quetschfuß M
pincement M
pie M del electrodo M
codetta F

電極
electrode
Elektrode F
électrode F
electrodo M
elettrodo M

水銀
mercury
Quecksilber N
mercure M
mercurio M
mercurio M

蛍光塗料
phosphorescent coating
Phosphorschicht F
couche F fluorescente
revestimiento M de fósforo M
rivestimento M fluorescente

ガス
gas
Gas N
gaz M
gas M inerte
gas M

口金
pin base
Stiftsockel M
culot M à broches F
base F del tubo M
attacco M a spina F

ガラス球
bulb
Kolben M
tube M
tubo M
tubo M

ピン
pin
Stift M
broche F
pata F
spinotto M

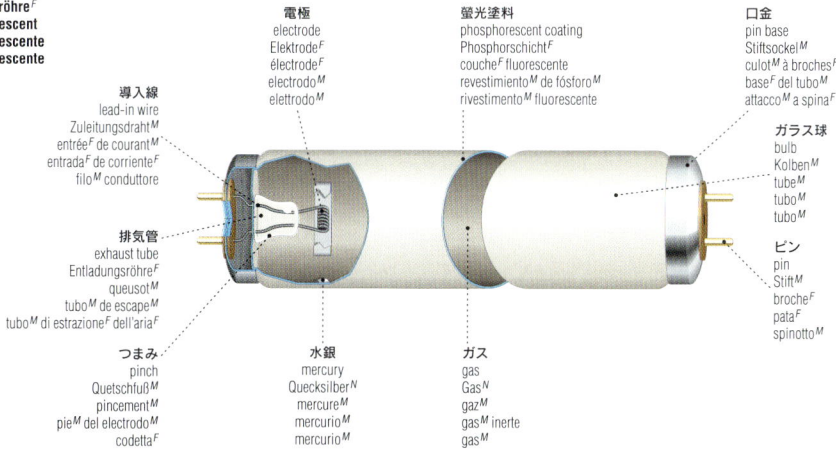

ハロゲン電球
tungsten-halogen lamp
Wolfram-Halogenlampe F
lampe F à halogène M
lámpara F halógena
lampada F alogena al tungsteno M

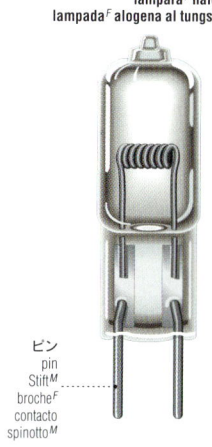

ピン
pin
Stift M
broche F
contacto
spinotto M

275

家具調度 | HOUSE FURNITURE
HAUSEINRICHTUNG | AMEUBLEMENT DE LA MAISON | MOBILIARIO PARA EL HOGAR | ARREDAMENTO PER LA CASA

肘掛け椅子

日本語 | 英語 | ドイツ語 | フランス語 | スペイン語 | イタリア語

armchair | Armlehnstuhl^M | fauteuil^M | silla^F de brazos^M | poltrona^F

各部
parts
Teile$^{M/N}$
parties^F
partes^F
parti^F

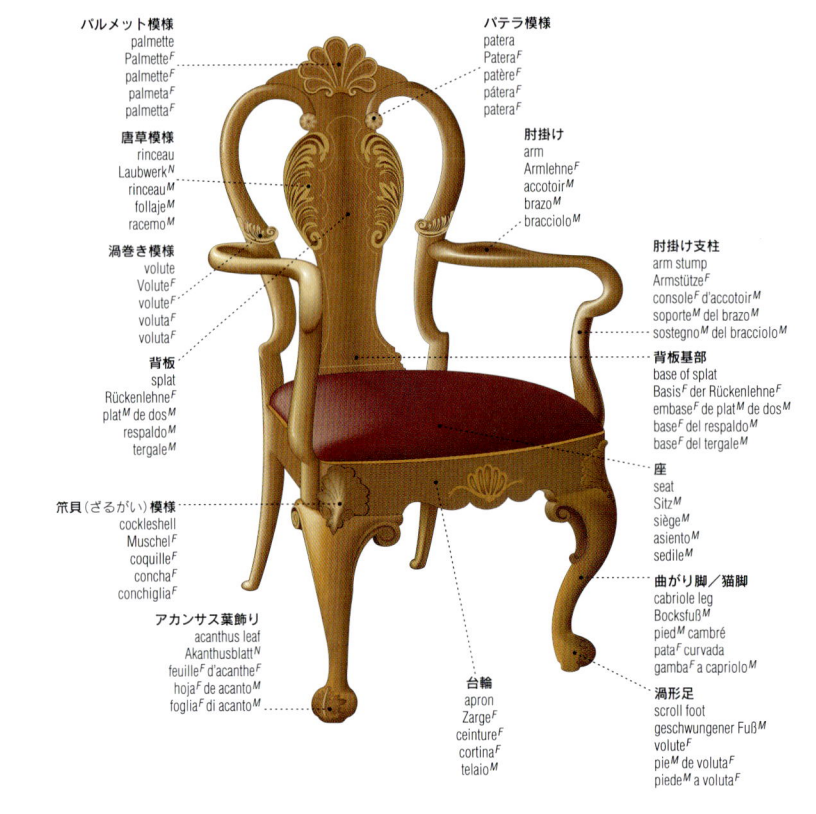

パルメット模様
palmette
Palmette^F
palmette^F
palmeta^F
palmetta^F

唐草模様
rinceau
Laubwerk^N
rinceau^M
follaje^M
racemo^M

渦巻き模様
volute
Volute^F
volute^F
voluta^F
voluta^F

背板
splat
Rückenlehne^F
plat^M de dos
respaldo^M
tergale^M

笊貝（ざるがい）模様
cockleshell
Muschel^F
coquille^F
concha^F
conchiglia^F

アカンサス葉飾り
acanthus leaf
Akanthusblatt^N
feuille^F d'acanthe
hoja^F de acanto^M
foglia^F di acanto^M

パテラ模様
patera
Patera^F
patère^F
pátera^F
patera^F

肘掛け
arm
Armlehne^F
accotoir^M
brazo^M
bracciolo^M

肘掛け支柱
arm stump
Armstütze^F
console^F d'accotoir^M
soporte^M del brazo^M
sostegno^M del bracciolo^M

背板基部
base of splat
Basis^F der Rückenlehne^F
embase^F de plat^M de dos^M
base^F del respaldo^M
base^F del tergale^M

座
seat
Sitz^M
siège^M
asiento^M
sedile^M

曲がり脚／猫脚
cabriole leg
Bocksfuß^M
pied^M cambré
pata^F curvada
gamba^F a capriolo^M

台輪
apron
Zarge^F
ceinture^F
cortina^F
telaio^M

渦形足
scroll foot
geschwungener Fuß^M
volute^F
pie^M de voluta^F
piede^M a voluta^F

肘掛け椅子の例
examples of armchairs
Beispiele^N für Armstühle^M
exemples^M de fauteuils^M
ejemplos^M de divanes^M y butacas^F
esempi^M di poltrone^F e divani^M

ワシリー・チェア
Wassily chair
Wassily-Stuhl^M
fauteuil^M Wassily
silla^F Wassily
poltrona^F Wassily

ディレクター・チェア／監督椅子
director's chair
Regiestuhl^M
fauteuil^M metteur^M en scène^F
silla^F plegable de lona^F
sedia^F da regista^M

ロッキング・チェア
rocking chair
Schaukelstuhl^M
berceuse^F
mecedora^F
sedia^F a dondolo^M

カブリオレ
cabriolet
kleiner Lehnstuhl^M
cabriolet^M
silla^F cabriolé
cabriolet^M

メリディエンヌ／休息用ソファー
méridienne
Kanapee^N
méridienne^F
meridiana^F
méridienne^F

レカミエ
récamier
Chaiselongue^F
récamier^M
sofá^M tipo^M imperio
agrippina^F

クラブ・チェア
club chair
Clubsessel^M
fauteuil^M club^M
butaca^F
poltrona^F da salotto^M

ベルジェール
bergère
Bergère^F
bergère^F
silla^F poltrona
bergère^F

ソファ／長椅子
sofa
Sofa^N
canapé^M
sofá^F
divano^M

ラブ・チェア
love seat; *two-seater settee*
Zweisitzer^M
causeuse^F
sofá^M de dos plazas^F
divano^M a due posti^M

チェスターフィールド
chesterfield
Chesterfieldsofa^N
canapé^M capitonné
chesterfield
divano^M Chesterfield

家具調度 | HOUSE FURNITURE
HAUSEINRICHTUNG | AMEUBLEMENT DE LA MAISON | MOBILIARIO PARA EL HOGAR | ARREDAMENTO PER LA CASA

背もたれ椅子

side chair | Stuhl^M | chaise^F | silla^F sin brazos^M | sedia^F

各部
parts
Teile$^{M/N}$
parties^F
partes^F
parti^F

笠木
top rail
obere Sprosse^F
traverse^F supérieure
peinazo^M superior
traversa^F superiore

耳
ear
Knauf^M
oreille^F
pomo^M
pomo^M

背
back
Rückenlehne^F
dossier^M
respaldo^M
schienale^M

横木／横板
cross rail
Querholz^N
traverse^F médiane
peinazo^M inferior
traversa^F mediana

座
seat
Sitz^M
siège^M
asiento^M
sedile^M

背柱
stile
Seitenstück^N
montant^M
larguero^M
montante^M verticale

台輪
apron
Zarge^F
ceinture^F
guarnición^F
telaio^M

脚
support
Fußgestell^N
piètement^M
pata^F
sostegno^M

貫（ぬき）
spindle
Steg^M
barreau^M
travesaño^M
traversa^F

後脚
rear leg
Hinterbein^N
pied^M arrière
pata^F trasera
gamba^F posteriore

前脚
front leg
Vorderbein^N
pied^M avant
pata^F delantera
gamba^F anteriore

椅子の例
examples of chairs
Beispiele^N für Stühle^M
exemples^M de chaises^F
ejemplos^M de sillas^F
esempi^M di sedie^F

ロッキング・チェア
rocking chair
Schaukelstuhl^M
chaise^F berçante
mecedora^F
sedia^F a dondolo^M

スタッキング・チェア
stacking chairs
Stapelstühle^M
chaises^F empilables
sillas^F apilables
sedie^F impilabili

折り畳み椅子
folding chair
Klappstuhl^M
chaise^F pliante
silla^F plegable
sedia^F pieghevole

デッキ・チェア
chaise longue
Liegestuhl^M
chaise^F longue
tumbona^F
sedia^F a sdraio^M

椅子

seats | Sitzmöbel^N | sièges^M | asientos^M | sedili^M

ビーン・バッグ（チェア）
bean bag chair
Sitzsack^M
fauteuil^M-sac^M
silla^F cojín^M
poltrona^F sacco^M

オットマン（チェア）
ottoman
Puff^M
pouf^M
puf^M
pouf^M

ステップ・チェア／はしご兼用椅子
step chair
Tritthocker^M
chaise^F-escabeau^M
silla^F escalera^F
sedia^F scala^F

ベンチ
bench
Bank^F
banc^M
banco^F
panchina^F

フットスツール／足（載せ）台
footstool
Hocker^M
tabouret^M
escabel^M
sgabello^M

バンケット
banquette
Sitzbank^F
banquette^F
banqueta^F
divanetto^M

バー・スツール
bar stool
Barhocker^M
tabouret^M-bar^M
taburete^M
sgabello^M alto

家屋

277

家具調度 | HOUSE FURNITURE
HAUSEINRICHTUNG | AMEUBLEMENT DE LA MAISON | MOBILIARIO PARA EL HOGAR | ARREDAMENTO PER LA CASA

テーブル

table | Tisch^M | table^F | mesa^F | tavolo^M

日本語 | 英語 | ドイツ語 | フランス語 | スペイン語 | イタリア語

家屋

折り畳み式[ゲート・レッグ]テーブル
gate-leg table
Klapptisch^M
table^F à abattants^M
mesa^F de hojas^F abatibles
tavolo^M a cancello^M

甲板（こういた）
top
Tischplatte^F
plateau
tablero^M
piano^M

引き出し
drawer
Schublade^F
tiroir^M
cajón^M
cassetto^M

つまみ／ノブ
knob
Knauf^M
bouton^M
pomo^M
pomello^M

テーブルの例
examples of tables
Beispiele^N für Tische^M
exemples^M de tables^F
ejemplos^M de mesas^F
esempi^M di tavoli^M

甲板（こういた）
top
Tischplatte^F
plateau
tablero^M
piano^M

伸縮[伸長式]テーブル
extension table
Ausziehtisch^M
table^F à rallonges^F
mesa^F plegable
tavolo^M allungabile

垂れ板
drop-leaf
Klappe^F
abattant^M
extensión^F plegable
ribalta^F

拡張板／伸長板
extension
Auszug^M
rallonge^F
extensión^F
prolunga^F

貫（ぬき）
stretcher
Traverse^F
traverse^F
travesaño^M
traversa^F del cancello^M

脚
leg
Bein^N
pied^M
pata^F
gamba^F

ゲート・レッグ
gate-leg
Ausziehbein^N
tréteau^M
pata^F móvil
cancello^M

台輪
apron
Zarge^F
ceinture^F
guarnición^F
telaio^M

横木／横材
crosspiece
Querstück^N
entrejambe^M
travesaño^M
traversa^F

重ねテーブル
nest of tables
Satztische^M
tables^F gigognes
juego^M de mesas^F
tavolini^M sovrapponibili

サービス・ワゴン
serving cart; serving trolley
Servierwagen^M
desserte^F
mesita^F de servicio^M
carrello^M portavivande

収納家具

storage furniture | Aufbewahrungsmöbel^N | meubles^M de rangement^M | muebles^M contenedores | mobili^M contenitori

大型衣装だんす
armoire
Kleiderschrank^M
armoire^F
armario^M
armadio^M

装飾帯
frieze
Fries^M
frise^F
friso^M
cimasa^F

上部縁飾り
cornice
Kranzprofil^N
corniche^F
cornisa^F
cornice^F

上框（がまち）
top rail
obere Querleiste^F
traverse^F supérieure
peinazo^M superior
traversa^F superiore

扉パネル
door panel
Türfüllung^F
panneau^M de vantail^M
entrepaño^M
pannello^M dell'anta^F

中枠／中方立て（なかほだて）
center post; centre post
Setzholz^N
dormant^M
montante^M central
montante^M centrale

吊元框（つりもとがまち）
hanging stile
Anschlagrahmen^M
montant^M de ferrage^F
larguero^M de la bisagra^F
montante^M verticale

枠
frame
Rahmen^M
bâti^M
armazón^M
telaio^M

ダイヤモンド・ポイント彫り
diamond point
Rautenspitze^F
pointe^F de diamant^M
punta^F de diamante^M
punta^F di diamante^M

錠
lock
Schloss^N
serrure^F
cerradura^F
serratura^F

横框
rail
Querleiste^F
traverse^F
peinazo^M
traversa^F

枠框
frame stile
Rahmenleiste^F
montant^M de bâti^M
larguero^M del marco^M
montante^M del telaio^M

下框
bottom rail
untere Querleiste^F
traverse^F inférieure
peinazo^M inferior
traversa^F inferiore

蝶番（ちょうつがい）
hinge
Scharnier^N
gond^M
bisagra^F
cerniera^F

扉
door
Tür^F
vantail^M
puerta^F
porta^F

脚
foot
Fuß^M
pied^M
pata^F
piede^M

持ち送り台
bracket base
Sockelprofil^N
soubassement^M
rodapié^M
base^F di sostegno^M

木釘
peg
Zapfen^M
cheville^F
espiga^F
tassello^M

家具調度 | HOUSE FURNITURE
HAUSEINRICHTUNG | AMEUBLEMENT DE LA MAISON | MOBILIARIO PARA EL HOGAR | ARREDAMENTO PER LA CASA

収納家具

家屋

仕切り箱／トレー
tray
Schubfach^N
casier^M
casillero^M
cassetto^M

落とし板／落下式甲板（こういた）
fall front
herausklappbare Schreibplatte^F
abattant^M
escritorio^M
ribalta^F

長持ち／櫃（ひつ）
linen chest
Truhe^F
coffre^M
baúl^M
cassapanca^F

クロゼット
closet; *hanging cupboard*
Schrankteil^{M/N}
penderie^F
guardarropa^M
armadio^M appendiabiti

棚
shelf
Fach^N
tablette^F
anaquel^M
ripiano^M

書き物机
secretary; *bureau*
Sekretär^M
secrétaire^M
bufete^M
secrétaire^M

ドレッサー
dresser; *dressing table*
Kommode^F
commode^F
cómoda^F
comò^M

洋服だんす／衣装戸棚
wardrobe
Kleiderschrank^M
armoire^F-penderie^F
ropero^M
guardaroba^M

引き出し
drawer
Schublade^F
tiroir^M
cajón^M
cassetto^M

西洋だんす
chiffonier
Chiffonière^F
chiffonnier^M
chifonier^M
cassettiera^F

陳列棚
display cabinet
Vitrine^F
vitrine^F
vitrina^F
vetrina^F

コーナー用食器棚
corner cupboard
Eckschrank^M
encoignure^F
rinconera^F
angoliera^F

ガラス戸棚
glass-fronted display cabinet
Vitrinenschrank^M
buffet^M-vaisselier^M
aparador^M con vitrina^F
credenza^F con vetrina^F

サイドボード
buffet; *sideboard*
Büfett^N
buffet^M
aparador^M
credenza^F

カクテル・キャビネット
cocktail cabinet
Cocktailschrank^M
bar^F
mueble^M bar^M
mobile^M bar^M

279

家具調度 | HOUSE FURNITURE
HAUSEINRICHTUNG | AMEUBLEMENT DE LA MAISON | MOBILIARIO PARA EL HOGAR | ARREDAMENTO PER LA CASA

ベッド

日本語 | 英語 | ドイツ語 | フランス語 | スペイン語 | イタリア語

bed | Bett[N] | lit[M] | cama[F] | letto[M]

ソファー・ベッド
sofa bed
Schlafcouch[F]
canapé[M] convertible
sofá cama[M]
divano-letto[M]

フートン／布団
futon
Auflage[F]
futon[M]
futón[M]
futon[M]

フレーム
frame
Rahmen[M]
cadre[M]
armazón[M]
telaio[M]

各部
parts
Teile[M/N]
parties[F]
partes[F]
parti[F]

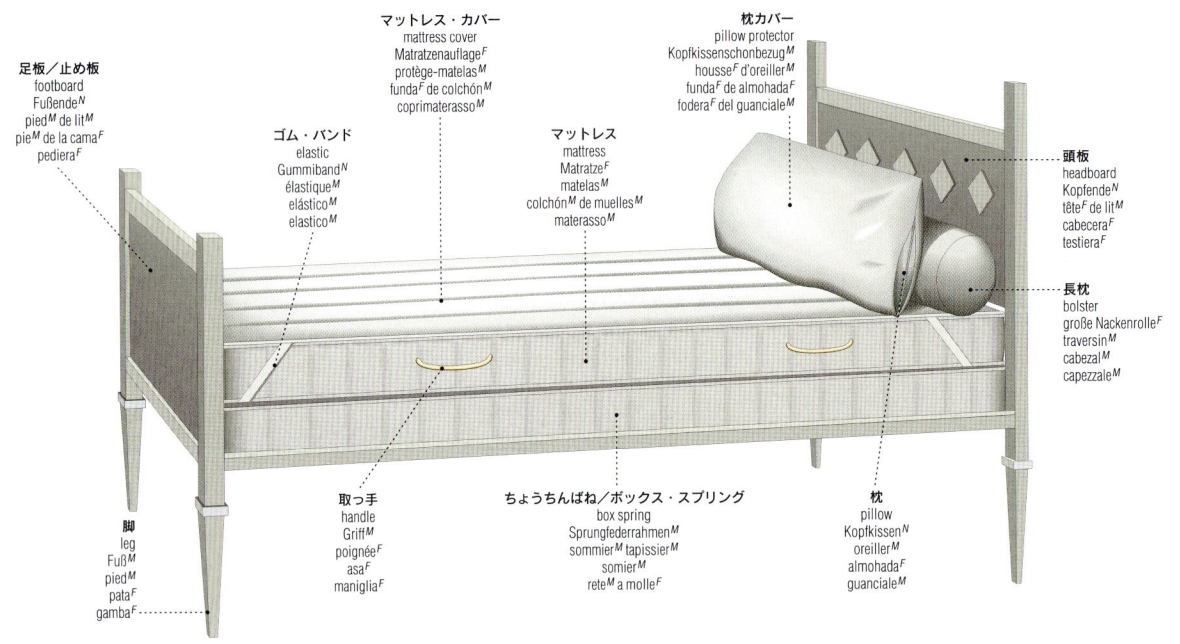

足板／止め板
footboard
Fußende[N]
pied[M] de lit[M]
pie[M] de la cama[F]
pediera[F]

ゴム・バンド
elastic
Gummiband[N]
élastique[M]
elástico[M]
elastico[M]

マットレス・カバー
mattress cover
Matratzenauflage[F]
protège-matelas[M]
funda[F] de colchón[M]
coprimaterasso[M]

マットレス
mattress
Matratze[F]
matelas[M]
colchón[M] de muelles[M]
materasso[M]

枕カバー
pillow protector
Kopfkissenschonbezug[M]
housse[F] d'oreiller[M]
funda[F] de almohada[F]
fodera[F] del guanciale[M]

頭板
headboard
Kopfende[N]
tête[F] de lit[M]
cabecera[F]
testiera[F]

長枕
bolster
große Nackenrolle[F]
traversin[M]
cabezal[M]
capezzale[M]

脚
leg
Fuß[M]
pied[M]
pata[F]
gamba[F]

取っ手
handle
Griff[M]
poignée[F]
asa[F]
maniglia[F]

ちょうちんばね／ボックス・スプリング
box spring
Sprungfederrahmen[M]
sommier[M] tapissier[M]
somier[M]
rete[F] a molle[F]

枕
pillow
Kopfkissen[N]
oreiller[M]
almohada[F]
guanciale[M]

リネン[リンネル]類
linen
Bettwäsche[F]
literie[F]
ropa[F] de cama[F]
biancheria[F] da letto[M]

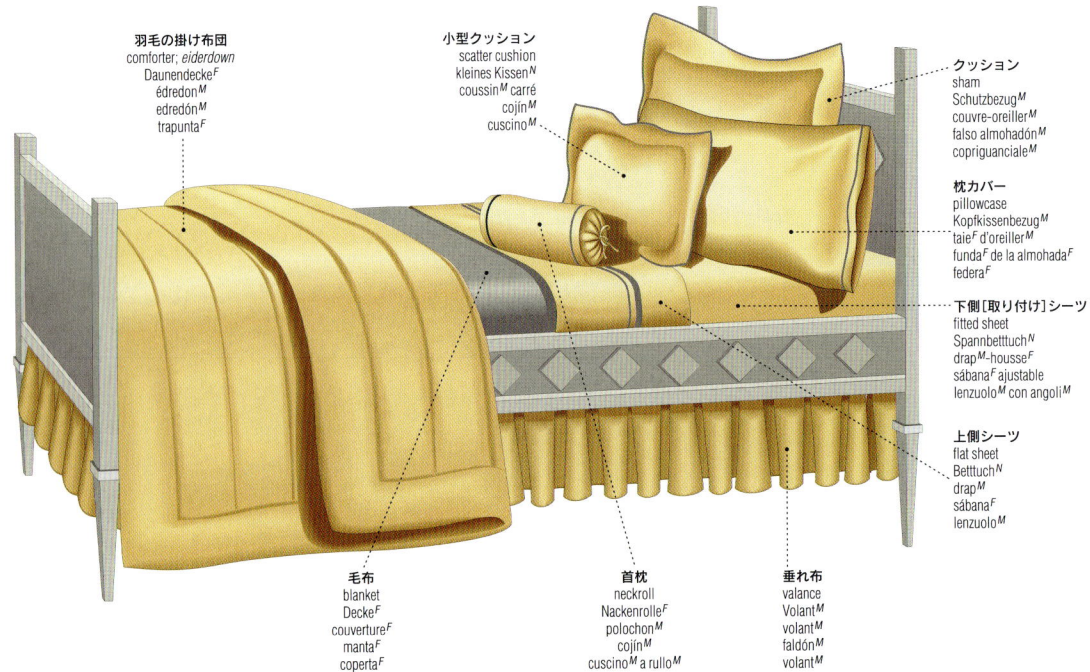

羽毛の掛け布団
comforter; eiderdown
Daunendecke[F]
édredon[M]
edredón[M]
trapunta[F]

小型クッション
scatter cushion
kleines Kissen[N]
coussin[M] carré
cojín[M]
cuscino[M]

クッション
sham
Schutzbezug[M]
couvre-oreiller[M]
falso almohadón[M]
copriguanciale[M]

枕カバー
pillowcase
Kopfkissenbezug[M]
taie[F] d'oreiller[M]
funda[F] de la almohada[F]
federa[F]

下側[取り付け]シーツ
fitted sheet
Spannbetttuch[N]
drap[M]-housse[F]
sábana[F] ajustable
lenzuolo[M] con angoli[M]

上側シーツ
flat sheet
Betttuch[N]
drap[M]
sábana[F]
lenzuolo[M]

毛布
blanket
Decke[F]
couverture[F]
manta[F]
coperta[F]

首枕
neckroll
Nackenrolle[F]
polochon[M]
cojín[M]
cuscino[M] a rullo[M]

垂れ布
valance
Volant[M]
volant[M]
faldón[M]
volant[M]

家具調度 | HOUSE FURNITURE
HAUSEINRICHTUNG | AMEUBLEMENT DE LA MAISON | MOBILIARIO PARA EL HOGAR | ARREDAMENTO PER LA CASA

幼児用家具

children's furniture | Kindermöbel[N] | meubles[M] d'enfants[M] | muebles[M] infantiles | mobili[M] per bambini

ベビー・サークル／プレイペン
playpen
Reisebett[N] mit Wickelauflage[F]
lit[M] pliant
cuna[M] plegable
lettino[M] pieghevole con fasciatoio[M]

着せ替えテーブル
changing table
Wickelauflage[F]
plan[M] à langer
cambiador[M]
fasciatoio[M]

手すり
top rail
oberer Abschluss[M]
bordure[F]
borde[M]
bordo[M]

肘掛け
armrest
Armlehne[F]
accoudoir[M]
brazos[M]
bracciolo[M]

ブースター・シート
booster seat
Kindersessel[M]
rehausseur[M]
silla[F] alzadora
poltroncina[F] per bambini

背（もたれ）
back
Rückenlehne[F]
dossier[M]
respaldo[M]
schienale[M]

座
seat
Sitz[M]
siège[M]
asiento[M]
sedile[M]

着せ替えテーブル
changing table
Wickelkommode[F]
table[F] à langer
cambiador[M]
fasciatoio[M]

メッシュ
mesh
Netz[N]
filet[M]
red[F]
retina[F]

マットレス
mattress
Matratze[F]
matelas[M]
colchón[M]
materassino[M]

ベビー・チェア
high chair
Hochstuhl[M]
chaise[F] haute
trona[F]
seggiolone[M]

背（もたれ）
back
Rückenlehne[F]
dossier[M]
respaldo[M]
schienale[M]

トレー
tray
Esstablett[N]
plateau[M]
bandeja[F]
vassoio[M]

頭板
headboard
Kopfteil[M/N]
tête[F] de lit[M]
cabecera[F]
testiera[F]

柵
barrier
Schutzgitter[N]
barrière[F]
barrera[F]
sponda[F] protettiva

ベビー・ベッド
crib
Gitterbett[N]
lit[M] à barreaux[M]
cuna[F]
lettino[M] a sponde[F]

羽根板
slat
Sprosse[F]
barreau[M]
barrote[M]
sbarra[F]

腰［安全］ベルト
waist belt
Gurt[M]
ceinture[F] ventrale
cinturón[M] de seguridad[F]
cintura[F] di ritenuta[F]

足置き
footrest
Fußstütze[F]
repose-pieds[M]
reposapies[M]
poggiapiedi[M]

脚
leg
Gestell[N]
pied[M]
pata[F]
gamba[F]

キャスター
caster
Laufrolle[F]
roulette[F]
rueda[F] giratoria
ruota[F] girevole

引き出し
drawer
Schubkasten[M]
tiroir[M]
cajón[M]
cassetto[M]

マットレス
mattress
Matratze[F]
matelas[M]
colchón[M]
materasso[M]

家屋

281

家具調度 | HOUSE FURNITURE
HAUSEINRICHTUNG | AMEUBLEMENT DE LA MAISON | MOBILIARIO PARA EL HOGAR | ARREDAMENTO PER LA CASA

窓付属品

日本語 | 英語 | ドイツ語 | フランス語 | スペイン語 | イタリア語

window accessories | Dekorationen^F | parures^F de fenêtre^F | accesorios^M para las ventanas^F | accessori^M per finestre^F

室内シャッター
indoor shutters
Innenläden^M
volets^M d'intérieur^M
postigos^M interiores
imposte^F ripiegabili

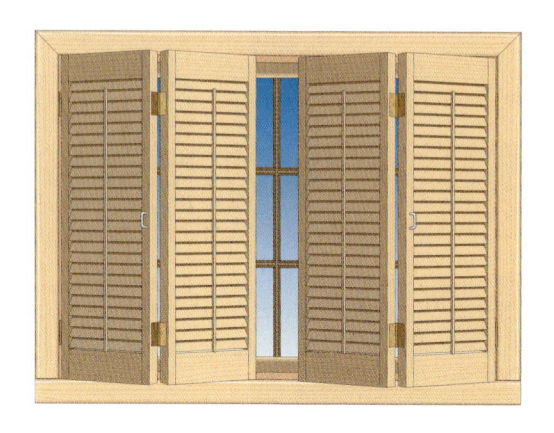

ガラス（窓用）カーテン
glass curtain
Fenstergardine^F
rideau^M de vitrage^M
cortina^F de ventana^F
tenda^F per finestra^F

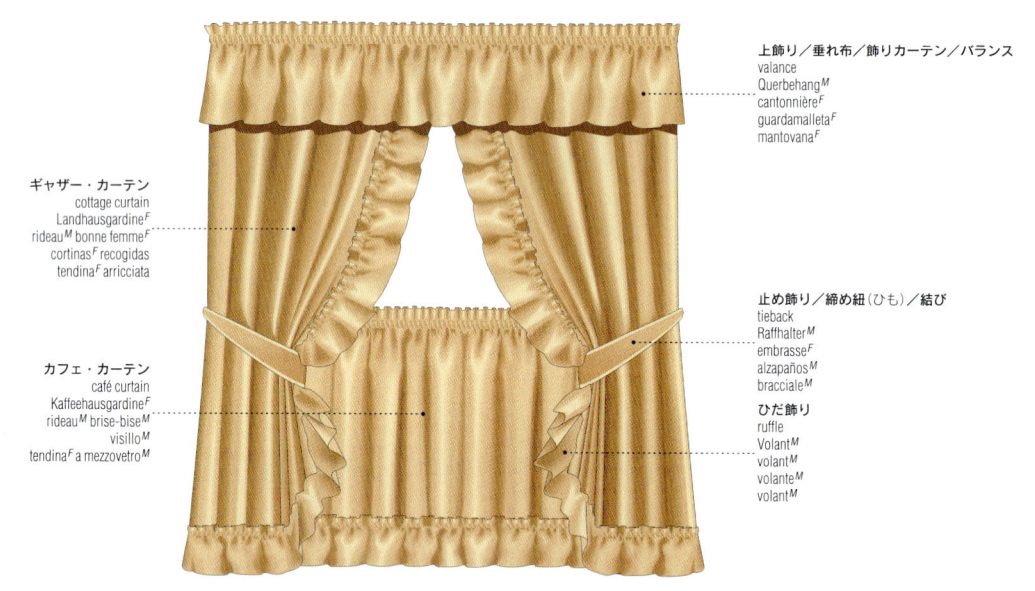

上飾り／垂れ布／飾りカーテン／バランス
valance
Querbehang^M
cantonnière^F
guardamalleta^F
mantovana^F

ギャザー・カーテン
cottage curtain
Landhausgardine^F
rideau^M bonne femme^F
cortinas^M recogidas
tendina^F arricciata

止め飾り／締め紐／結び
tieback
Raffhalter^M
embrasse^F
alzapaños^M
bracciale^F

カフェ・カーテン
café curtain
Kaffeehausgardine^F
rideau^M brise-bise^M
visillo^M
tendina^F a mezzovetro^M

ひだ飾り
ruffle
Volant^M
volant^M
volante^M
volant^M

カーテン
curtain
Vorhang^M
rideau^M
cortina^F
tenda^F

上飾り／縁飾り／バランス
cornice
Schabracke^F
bandeau^M
cenefa^F
riloga^F sagomata

オーバー・カーテン
overdrapery; *over curtain*
Übergardine^F
double rideau^M
doble cortina^F
soprattenda^F

吊りカーテン
draw drapery; *draw curtain*
Zugvorhang^M
rideau^M
cortinas^F corredera
tendone^M oscurante

止め飾り／止め具
holdback
Raffhalter^M
patère^F à embrasse^F
anilla^F del cordón^M
portabracciale^M

止め紐（ひも）／結び
cord tieback
Kordel^F
cordelière^F
cordón^M
bracciale^M a cordoncino^M

飾り房／タッセル
tassel
Troddel^F
gland^M
borla^F
nappa^F

レース（の）カーテン
sheer curtain
Store^M
voilage^M
visillos^M
tenda^F trasparente

家屋

家具調度 | HOUSE FURNITURE
HAUSEINRICHTUNG | AMEUBLEMENT DE LA MAISON | MOBILIARIO PARA EL HOGAR | ARREDAMENTO PER LA CASA

窓付属品

ひだ[プリーツ]の例
examples of pleats
Beispiele[N] für Kräuselfalten[F]
exemples[M] de plis[M]
ejemplos[M] de fruncidos[M]
esempi[M] di arricciature[F]

箱ひだ
box pleat
Schachtelfalte[F]
pli[M] creux
pliegue[M] de cajón[M]
sfondo[M] piega[F]

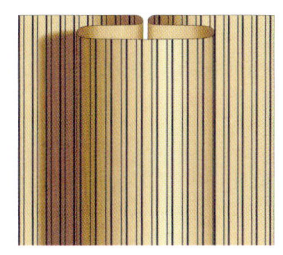

逆ひだ
inverted pleat
eingelegte Falte[F]
pli[M] rond
pliegue[M] de cajón[M] invertido
cannone[M]

山ひだ
pinch pleat
Kirsorfalte[F]
pli[M] pincé
pliegue[M] de pinza[M]
arricciatura[F] a pince[F]

家屋

カーテン・ヘッドの例
examples of headings
Beispiele[N] für Vorhangköpfe[M]
exemples[M] de têtes[F]
ejemplos[M] de cenefas[F]
esempi[M] di fettucce[F]

プリーツ
pleated heading
Kirschband[N]
tête[F] plissée
cenefa[F] plisada
fettuccia[F] plissettata

ペンシル・プリーツ
pencil pleat heading
Bleistiftfaltenband[N]
fronçage[M] tuyauté
cenefa[F] plisada de canotillo[M]
arricciatura[F] a cannoncino[M]

シャーリング
shirred heading
Durchzug[M]
tête[F] froncée
cenefa[F] fruncida
fettuccia[F] arricciata

ドレープ
draped swag
Freihand-Dekoration[F]
cantonnière[F] drapée
cenefa[F] drapeada
festone[M] drappeggiato

カーテンの例
examples of curtains
Beispiele[N] für Vorhänge[M]
exemples[M] de rideaux[M]
ejemplos[M] de cortinas[F]
esempi[M] di tende[F]

アタッチ・カーテン
attached curtain
Spanner[M]
rideau[M] coulissé
cortina[F] sujeta de doble barra[F]
tenda[F] a vetro[M]

ルース・カーテン
loose curtain
loser Vorhang[M]
rideau[M] flottant
cortina[F] suelta corrediza
tenda[F] a strappo[M]

クロスオーバー・カーテン
crisscross curtains
Raffgardine[F]
rideaux[M] croisés
cortinas[F] cruzadas
tende[F] con sormonto[M] totale

バルーン・カーテン
balloon curtain
Wolkenstore[M]
rideau[M] ballon[M]
cortina[F] abombada
tenda[F] a palloncino[M]

283

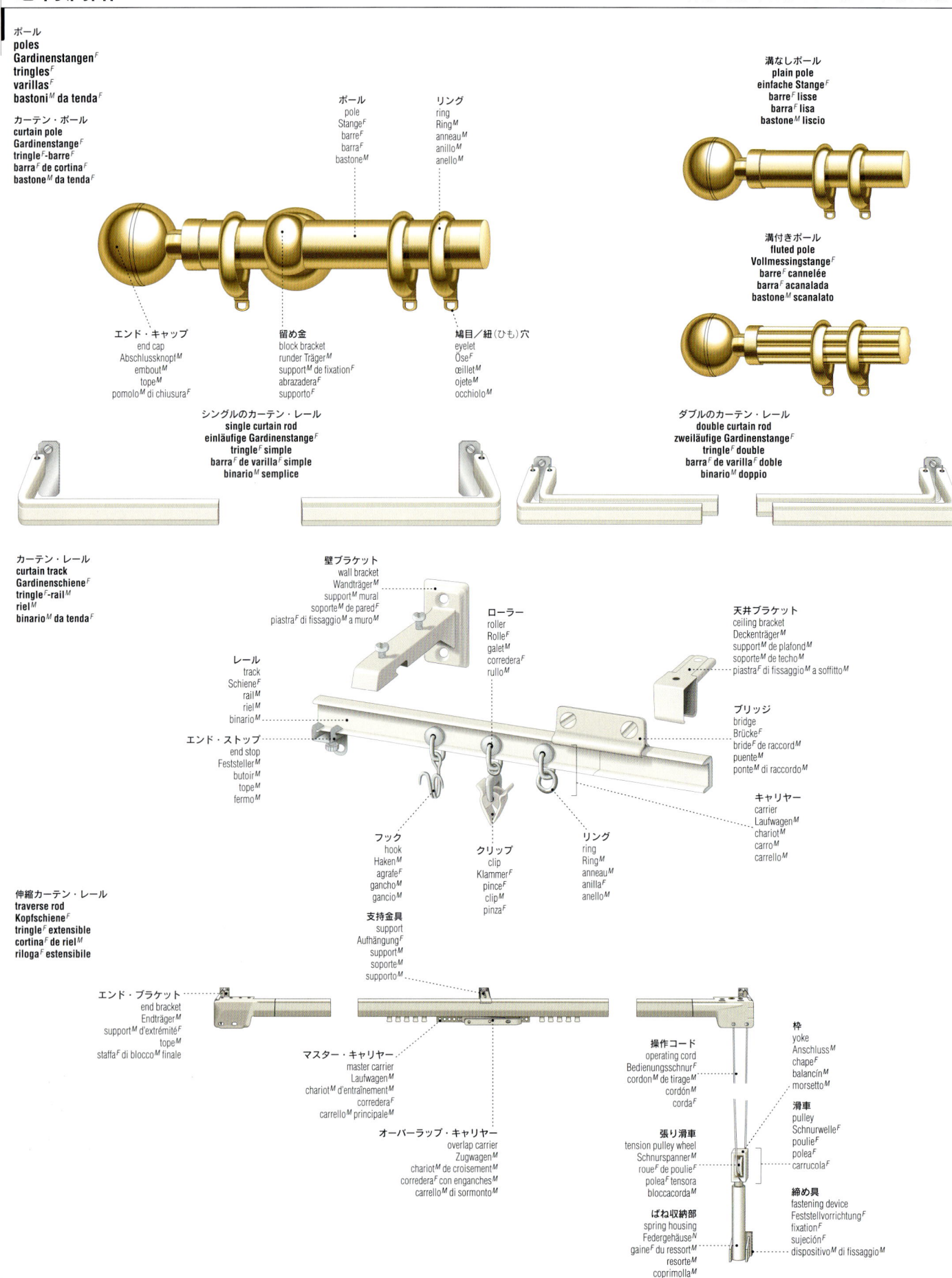

家具調度 | HOUSE FURNITURE
HAUSEINRICHTUNG | AMEUBLEMENT DE LA MAISON | MOBILIARIO PARA EL HOGAR | ARREDAMENTO PER LA CASA

窓付属品

日本語 | 英語 | ドイツ語 | フランス語 | スペイン語 | イタリア語

ポール
poles
Gardinenstangen^F
tringles^F
varillas^F
bastoni^M da tenda^F

カーテン・ポール
curtain pole
Gardinenstange^F
tringle^F-barre^F
barra^F de cortina^F
bastone^M da tenda^F

ポール
pole
Stange^F
barre^F
barra^F
bastone^M

リング
ring
Ring^M
anneau^M
anillo^M
anello^M

溝なしポール
plain pole
einfache Stange^F
barre^F lisse
barra^F lisa
bastone^M liscio

溝付きポール
fluted pole
Vollmessingstange^F
barre^F cannelée
barra^F acanalada
bastone^M scanalato

エンド・キャップ
end cap
Abschlussknopf^M
embout^M
tope^M
pomolo^M di chiusura^F

留め金
block bracket
runder Träger^M
support^M de fixation^F
abrazadera^F
supporto^F

鳩目／紐（ひも）穴
eyelet
Öse^F
œillet^M
ojete^M
occhiolo^M

シングルのカーテン・レール
single curtain rod
einläufige Gardinenstange^F
tringle^F simple
barra^F de varilla^F simple
binario^M semplice

ダブルのカーテン・レール
double curtain rod
zweiläufige Gardinenstange^F
tringle^F double
barra^F de varilla^F doble
binario^M doppio

カーテン・レール
curtain track
Gardinenschiene^F
tringle^F-rail^M
riel^M
binario^M da tenda^F

壁ブラケット
wall bracket
Wandträger^M
support^M mural
soporte^M de pared^F
piastra^F di fissaggio^M a muro^M

ローラー
roller
Rolle^F
galet^M
corredera^F
rullo^M

天井ブラケット
ceiling bracket
Deckenträger^M
support^M de plafond^M
soporte^M de techo^M
piastra^F di fissaggio^M a soffitto^M

レール
track
Schiene^F
rail^M
riel^M
binario^M

ブリッジ
bridge
Brücke^F
bride^F de raccord^M
puente^M
ponte^M di raccordo^M

エンド・ストップ
end stop
Feststeller^M
butoir^M
tope^M
fermo^M

キャリヤー
carrier
Laufwagen^M
chariot^M
carro^M
carrello^M

フック
hook
Haken^M
agrafe^F
gancho^M
gancio^M

クリップ
clip
Klammer^F
pince^F
clip^M
pinza^F

リング
ring
Ring^M
anneau^M
anilla^F
anello^M

伸縮カーテン・レール
traverse rod
Kopfschiene^F
tringle^F extensible
cortina^F de riel^M
riloga^F estensibile

支持金具
support
Aufhängung^F
support^M
soporte^M
supporto^M

エンド・ブラケット
end bracket
Endträger^M
support^M d'extrémité^F
tope^M
staffa^F di blocco^M finale

マスター・キャリヤー
master carrier
Laufwagen^M
chariot^M d'entraînement^M
corredera^F
carrello^M principale

オーバーラップ・キャリヤー
overlap carrier
Zugwagen^M
chariot^M de croisement^M
corredera^F con enganches^M
carrello^M di sormonto^M

操作コード
operating cord
Bedienungsschnur^F
cordon^M de tirage^M
cordón^M
corda^F

張り滑車
tension pulley wheel
Schnurspanner^M
roue^F de poulie^F
polea^F tensora
bloccacorda^F

ばね収納部
spring housing
Federgehäuse^N
gaine^F du ressort^M
resorte^M
coprimolla^F

枠
yoke
Anschluss^M
chape^F
balancín^M
morsetto^M

滑車
pulley
Schnurwelle^F
poulie^F
polea^F
carrucola^F

締め具
fastening device
Feststellvorrichtung^F
fixation^F
sujeción^F
dispositivo^M di fissaggio^M

家具調度 | HOUSE FURNITURE
HAUSEINRICHTUNG | AMEUBLEMENT DE LA MAISON | MOBILIARIO PARA EL HOGAR | ARREDAMENTO PER LA CASA

窓付属品

ブラインド
blinds
Rollo^N und Jalousie^F
stores^M
persianas^F enrollables
tende^F avvolgibili

巻き上げ式ブラインド
roller shade; *roller blind*
Rollo^N
store^M à enroulement^M automatique
persiana^F enrollable automática
tenda^F avvolgibile

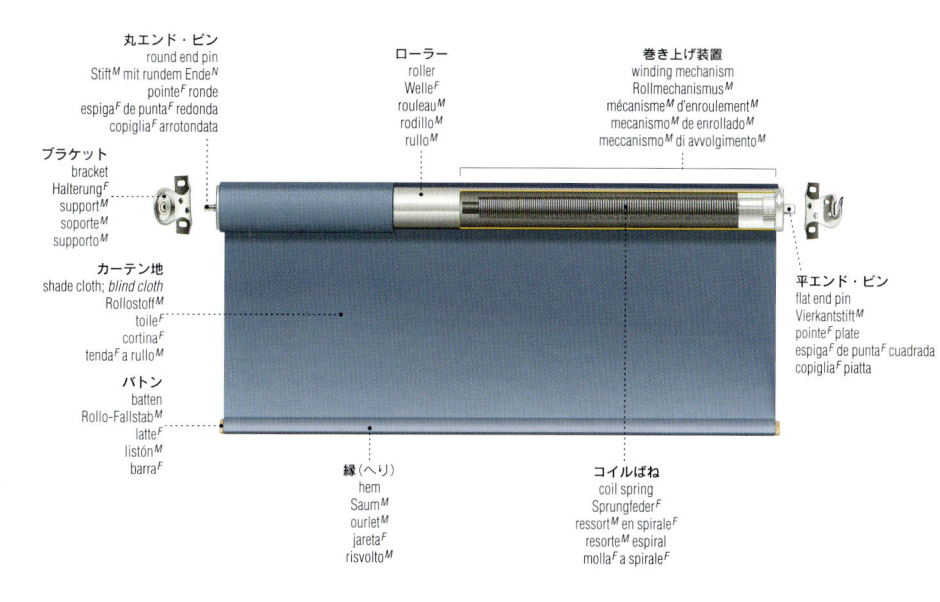

丸エンド・ピン
round end pin
Stift^M mit rundem Ende^N
pointe^F ronde
espiga^F de punta^F redonda
copiglia^F arrotondata

ローラー
roller
Welle^F
rouleau^M
rodillo^M
rullo^M

巻き上げ装置
winding mechanism
Rollmechanismus^M
mécanisme^M d'enroulement^M
mecanismo^M de enrollado
meccanismo^M di avvolgimento^M

ブラケット
bracket
Halterung^F
support^M
soporte^M
supporto^M

カーテン地
shade cloth; *blind cloth*
Rollostoff^M
toile^F
cortina^F
tenda^F a rullo^M

平エンド・ピン
flat end pin
Vierkantstift^M
pointe^F plate
espiga^F de punta^F cuadrada
copiglia^F piatta

バトン
batten
Rollo-Fallstab^M
latte^F
listón^M
barra^F

縁(へり)
hem
Saum^M
ourlet^M
jareta^F
risvolto^M

コイルばね
coil spring
Sprungfeder^F
ressort^M en spirale^F
resorte^M espiral
molla^F a spirale^F

ベネチアン・ブラインド
Venetian blind
Jalousie^F
store^M vénitien
persiana^F veneciana
veneziana^F

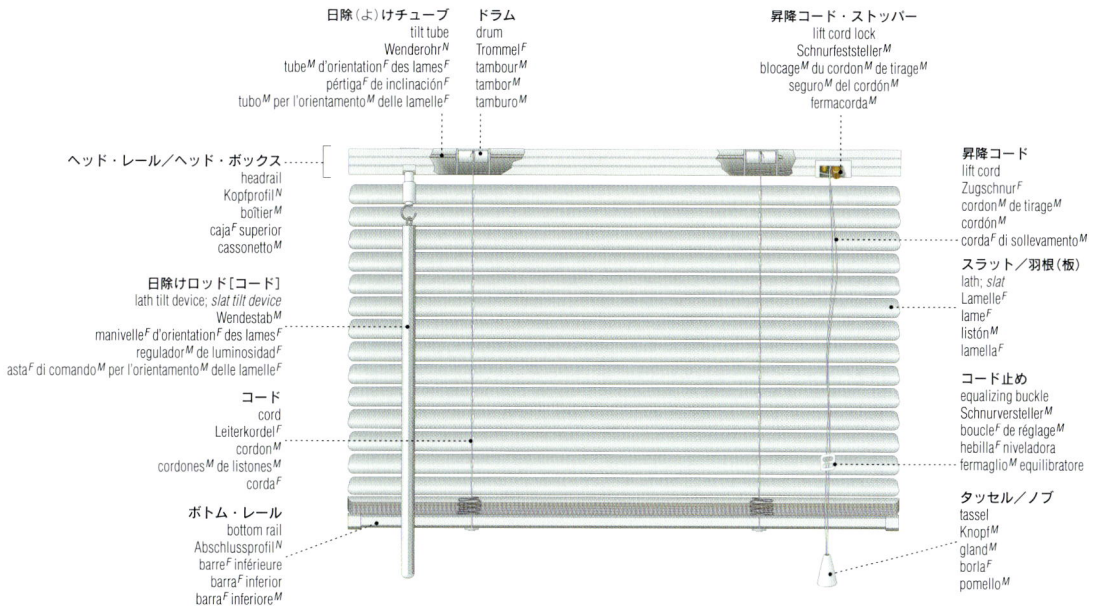

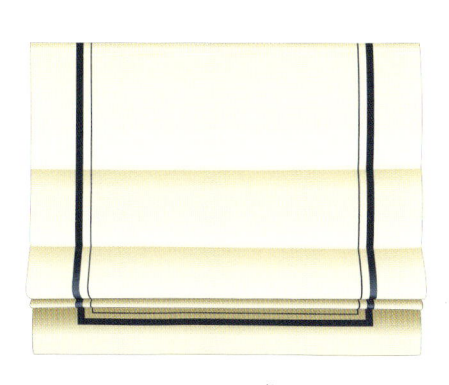

日除(よ)けチューブ
tilt tube
Wenderohr^N
tube^M d'orientation^F des lames^F
pértiga^F de inclinación^F
tubo^M per l'orientamento^M delle lamelle^F

ドラム
drum
Trommel^F
tambour^M
tambor^M
tamburo^M

昇降コード・ストッパー
lift cord lock
Schnurfeststeller^M
blocage^M du cordon^M de tirage^M
seguro^M del cordón^M
fermacorda^F

ヘッド・レール／ヘッド・ボックス
headrail
Kopfprofil^N
boîtier^M
caja^F superior
cassonetto^M

昇降コード
lift cord
Zugschnur^F
cordon^M de tirage^M
cordón^M
corda^F di sollevamento^M

日除けロッド[コード]
lath tilt device; *slat tilt device*
Wendestab^M
manivelle^F d'orientation^F des lames^F
regulador^M de luminosidad^F
asta^F di comando^M per l'orientamento^M delle lamelle^F

スラット／羽根(板)
lath; *slat*
Lamelle^F
lame^F
listón^M
lamella^F

コード
cord
Leiterkordel^F
cordon^M
cordones^M de listones^M
corda^F

コード止め
equalizing buckle
Schnurversteller^M
boucle^F de réglage^M
hebilla^F niveladora
fermaglio^M equilibratore

ボトム・レール
bottom rail
Abschlussprofil^N
barre^F inférieure
barra^F inferior
barra^F inferiore

タッセル／ノブ
tassel
Knopf^M
gland^M
borla^F
pomello^M

ローマン・シェード
roman shade
Raffrollo^N
store^M bateau^M
persianas^F romana
tenda^F a pacchetto^M

ロールアップ・ブラインド／ロール・スクリーン
roll-up blind
Zugrollo^N
store^M à enroulement^M manuel
persiana^F enrollable
tenda^F avvolgibile

285

家具調度 | HOUSE FURNITURE
HAUSEINRICHTUNG | AMEUBLEMENT DE LA MAISON | MOBILIARIO PARA EL HOGAR | ARREDAMENTO PER LA CASA

照明器具

日本語 | 英語 | ドイツ語 | フランス語 | スペイン語 | イタリア語

lights | Lampen F | luminaires M | lámparas F | luci F

クリップ式スポットライト
clamp spotlight
Klemmspot M
spot M à pince F
lámpara de pinza F
faretto M a pinza F

天井（付け）灯／シーリング・ライト
ceiling fitting
Deckenleuchte F
plafonnier M
plafón M
plafoniera F

ハロゲン・デスク・ランプ
halogen desk lamp
Halogen N-Tischleuchte F
lampe F de bureau M halogène
lámpara de despacho M halógena
lampada F alogena da tavolo M

アーム
arm
Arm M
bras M
brazo M
braccio M

台
base
Fuß M
socle M
base M
base F

吊り下げ灯／ペンダント
hanging pendant
Hängeleuchte F
suspension F
lámpara F de techo M
lampada F a sospensione F

アーム・ライト［ランプ］
adjustable lamp
Arbeitsleuchte F
lampe F d'architecte F
flexo M
lampada F a braccio M regolabile

電源スイッチ
on-off switch
Ein-/Ausschalter M
interrupteur M
interruptor M
interruttore M

アーム
arm
Arm M
bras M
brazo M
braccio M

シェード
shade
Schirm M
abat-jour M
pantalla F
paralume M

ばね
spring
Feder F
ressort M
resorte M
molla F

調節クランプ
adjustable clamp
verstellbare Klemme F
support M de fixation F
tornillo M de ajuste M
morsetto M regolabile

ベッド・ランプ
bed lamp
Leseleuchte F
lampe F liseuse
lámpara F de cabecera F
lampada F da lettura F

シェード
shade
Schirm M
abat-jour M
pantalla F
paralume M

台
base
Sockel M
socle M
base F
base F

台
stand
Fuß M
pied M
pedestal M
base F

フロア・スタンド［ランプ］
floor lamp; *standard lamp*
Standleuchte F
lampadaire M
lámpara F de pie M
lampada F a stelo M

テーブル・ランプ
table lamp
Tischleuchte F
lampe F de table F
lámpara F de mesa F
lampada F da tavolo M

デスク・ランプ
desk lamp
Schreibtischleuchte F
lampe F de bureau M
lámpara F de escritorio M
lampada F da tavolo M

家屋

286

家具調度 | HOUSE FURNITURE
HAUSEINRICHTUNG | AMEUBLEMENT DE LA MAISON | MOBILIARIO PARA EL HOGAR | ARREDAMENTO PER LA CASA

照明器具

家屋

シャンデリア
chandelier
Kronleuchter^M
lustre^M
araña^F de luces^F
lampadario^M

ろう皿
bobeche; *sconce*
Teller^M
coupelle^F
arandela^F
coppetta^F

垂れ飾り
crystal drop
Kristalltropfen^M
pendeloque^F
colgante^M
goccia^F di cristallo^M

クリスタル・ボタン
crystal button
Koppen^M
pampille^F
gota^F
perlina^F di cristallo^M

灯柱
column
Mittelsäule^F
fût^M
columna^F
colonna^F

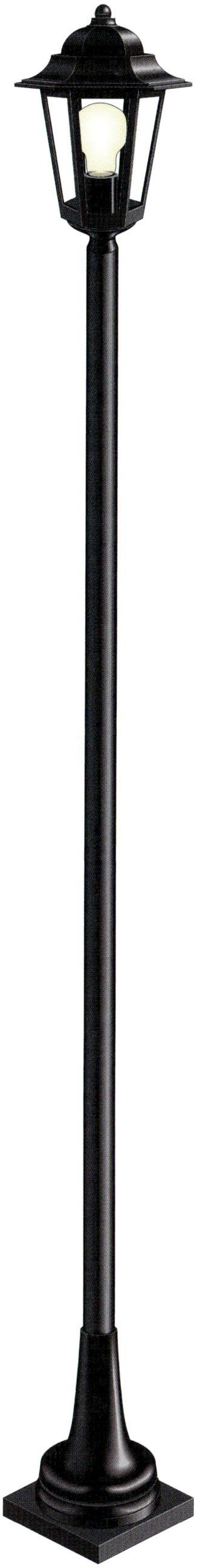

可動照明器具
track lighting
Beleuchtungsschiene^F
rail^M d'éclairage^M
riel^M de iluminación^F
faretto^M da binario^M

ライティング・レール
bar frame
Schiene^F
gouttière^F
armazón^M
binario^M

コンタクト・レバー
contact lever
Befestigungshebel^M
manette^F de contact^M
interruptor^M
leva^F di contatto^M

変圧器
transformer
Transformator^M
transformateur^M
transformador^M
trasformatore^M

スポットライト
spot
Spot^M
spot^M
foco^M
faretto^M orientabile

壁(付け)灯
wall lantern
Wandlaterne^F
lanterne^F murale
farol^M
lampione^M da parete^F

壁(付け)灯／ブラケット(灯)
wall fitting
Wandleuchte^F
applique^F
aplique^M
lampada^F da parete^F

回転式壁灯
swivel wall lamp
Scherenleuchte^F
applique^F orientable
lámpara^F orientable de pared^F
lampada^F da parete^F con braccio^F estensibile

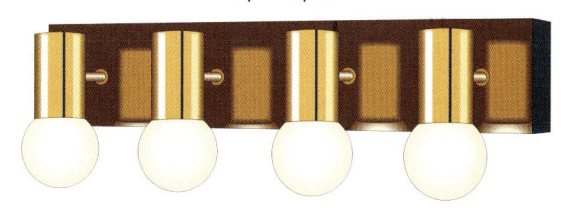

ストリップ・ライト
strip light
Lampenreihe^F
rampe^F d'éclairage^M
lámparas^F en serie^F
lampade^F in serie^F

街灯／ポール・ライト
post lantern
Straßenlaterne^F
lanterne^F de pied^M
farola^F
lampione^M

287

家具調度 | HOUSE FURNITURE
HAUSEINRICHTUNG | AMEUBLEMENT DE LA MAISON | MOBILIARIO PARA EL HOGAR | ARREDAMENTO PER LA CASA

家電製品

日本語 | 英語 | ドイツ語 | フランス語 | スペイン語 | イタリア語

domestic appliances | Haushaltsgeräte[N] | appareils[M] électroménagers | aparatos[M] electrodomésticos | elettrodomestici[M]

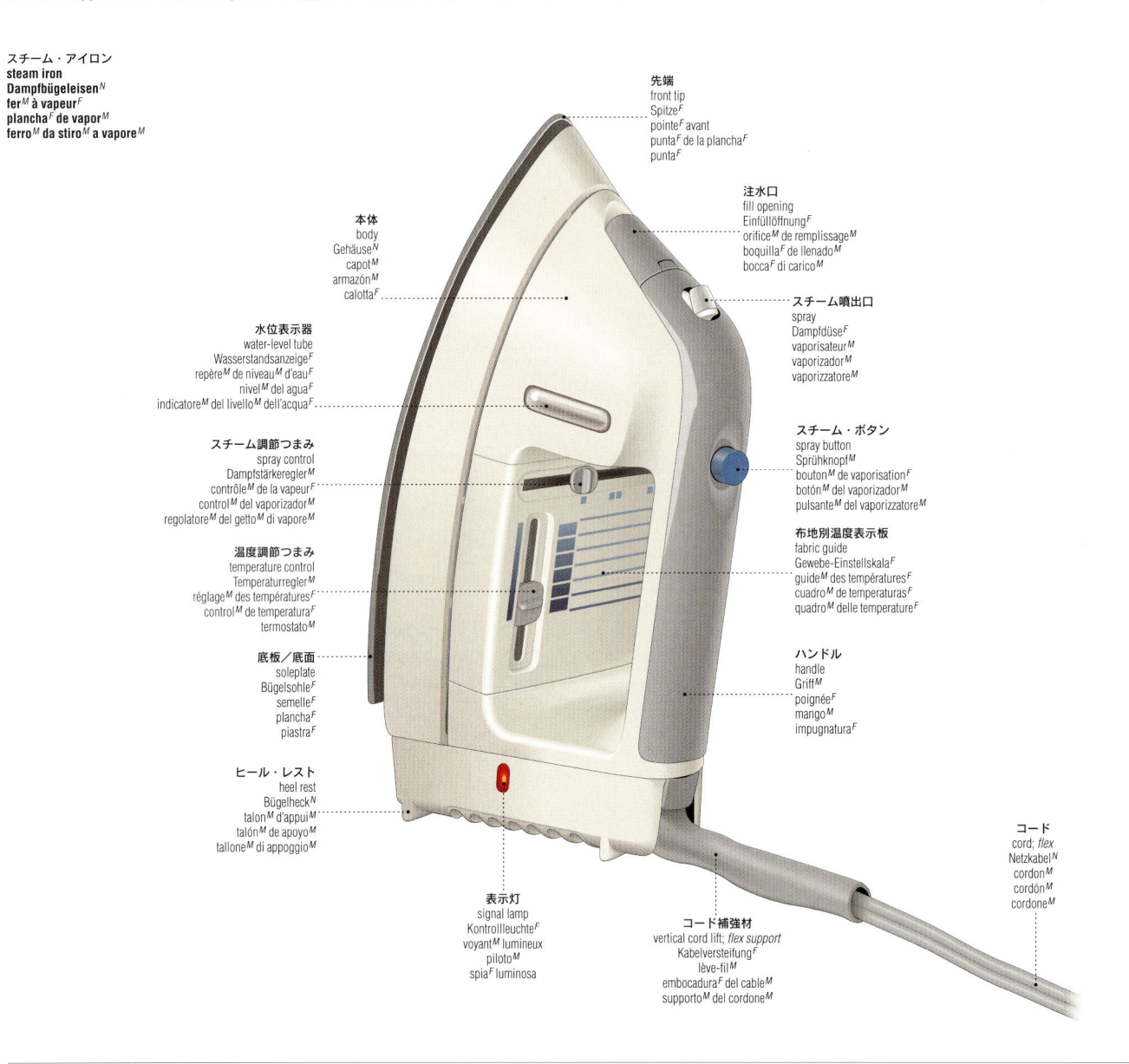

スチーム・アイロン
steam iron
Dampfbügeleisen[N]
fer[M] à vapeur[F]
plancha[F] de vapor[M]
ferro[M] da stiro[M] a vapore[M]

先端
front tip
Spitze[F]
pointe[F] avant
punta[F] de la plancha[F]
punta[F]

本体
body
Gehäuse[N]
capot[M]
armazón[M]
calotta[F]

注水口
fill opening
Einfüllöffnung[F]
orifice[M] de remplissage[M]
boquilla[F] de llenado[M]
bocca[F] di carico[M]

水位表示器
water-level tube
Wasserstandsanzeige[F]
repère[M] de niveau[M] d'eau[F]
nivel[M] del agua[F]
indicatore[M] del livello[M] dell'acqua[F]

スチーム噴出口
spray
Dampfdüse[F]
vaporisateur[M]
vaporizador[M]
vaporizzatore[M]

スチーム調節つまみ
spray control
Dampfstärkeregler[M]
contrôle[M] de la vapeur[F]
control[M] del vaporizador[M]
regolatore[M] del getto[M] di vapore[M]

スチーム・ボタン
spray button
Sprühknopf[M]
bouton[M] de vaporisation[F]
botón[M] del vaporizador[M]
pulsante[M] del vaporizzatore[M]

温度調節つまみ
temperature control
Temperaturregler[M]
réglage[M] des températures[F]
control[M] de temperatura[F]
termostato[M]

布地別温度表示板
fabric guide
Gewebe-Einstellskala[F]
guide[M] des températures[F]
cuadro[M] de temperaturas[F]
quadro[M] delle temperature[F]

底板／底面
soleplate
Bügelsohle[F]
semelle[F]
plancha[F]
piastra[F]

ハンドル
handle
Griff[M]
poignée[F]
mango[M]
impugnatura[F]

ヒール・レスト
heel rest
Bügelheck[N]
talon[M] d'appui[M]
talón[M] de apoyo[M]
tallone[M] di appoggio[M]

コード
cord; *flex*
Netzkabel[N]
cordon[M]
cordón[M]
cordone[M]

表示灯
signal lamp
Kontrollleuchte[F]
voyant[M] lumineux
piloto[M]
spia[F] luminosa

コード補強材
vertical cord lift; *flex support*
Kabelversteifung[F]
lève-fil[M]
embocadura[F] del cable[M]
supporto[M] del cordone[M]

ハンド・クリーナー
hand vacuum cleaner
Akku-Mini-Staubsauger[M]
aspirateur[M] à main[F]
aspirador[M] manual
miniaspiratutto[M]

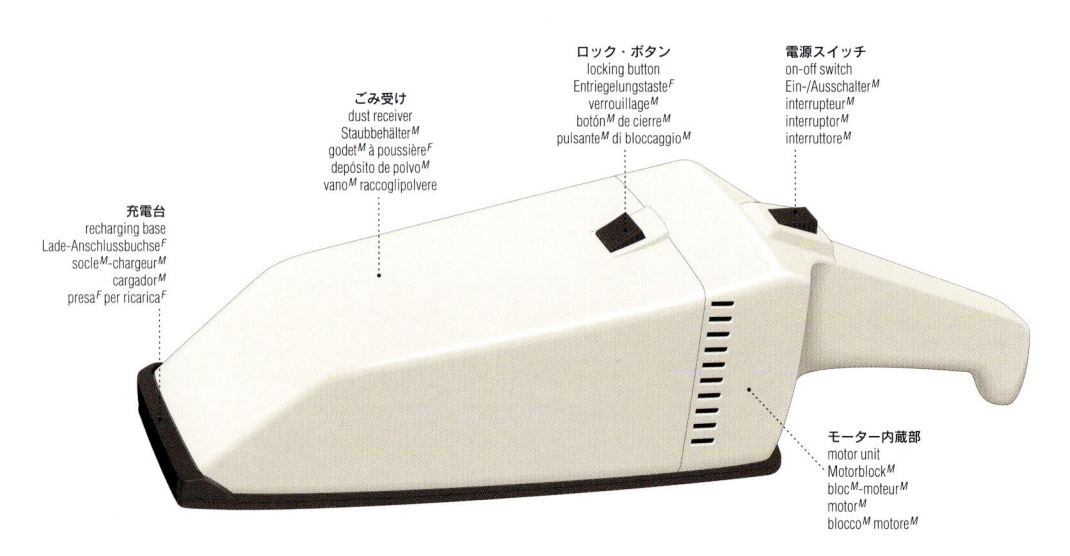

ごみ受け
dust receiver
Staubbehälter[M]
godet[M] à poussière[F]
depósito de polvo[M]
vano[M] raccoglipolvere

ロック・ボタン
locking button
Entriegelungstaste[F]
verrouillage[M]
botón[M] de cierre[M]
pulsante[M] di bloccaggio[M]

電源スイッチ
on-off switch
Ein-/Ausschalter[M]
interrupteur[M]
interruptor[M]
interruttore[M]

充電台
recharging base
Lade-Anschlussbuchse[F]
socle[M]-chargeur[M]
cargador[M]
presa[F] per ricarica[F]

モーター内蔵部
motor unit
Motorblock[M]
bloc[M]-moteur[M]
motor[M]
blocco[M] motore[M]

家具調度 | HOUSE FURNITURE
HAUSEINRICHTUNG | AMEUBLEMENT DE LA MAISON | MOBILIARIO PARA EL HOGAR | ARREDAMENTO PER LA CASA

家電製品

家屋

縦型[スティック・タイプの]電気掃除機
upright vacuum cleaner
Handstaubsauger^M
aspirateur^M-balai^M
escoba^F eléctrica
aspirapolvere^F verticale

電源スイッチ
on/off switch
Ein-/Ausschalter^M
interrupteur^M
interruptor^M on/off
interruttore^M

付属品収納部
tool storage area
Zubehörfach^N
compartiment^M d'accessoires^M
cajetín^M de accesorios
scomparto^M degli accessori^M

ホース
hose
Schlauch^M
tuyau^M flexible
tubo^M flexible
tubo^M flessibile

ごみ袋部
bag compartment
Beutelfach^N
compartiment^M de sac^M
cajetín^M portabolsa
scomparto^M del sacchetto^M

高さ調節つまみ
cleaner height adjustment knob
Höhenverstellung^F
sélecteur^M de hauteur^F
palanca^F de regulación^F de altura^F
manopola^F di regolazione^F dell'altezza^F

ブラシ
brush
Bürste^F
brosse^F
cepillo^M
spazzola^F

付属品[ノズル]
tools
Zubehör^N
accessoires^M
accesorios^M
accessori^M

シリンダー・タイプの電気掃除機
cylinder vacuum cleaner
Bodenstaubsauger^M
aspirateur^M-traîneau^M
aspirador^M
aspirapolvere^F

ロック装置
locking device
Verschluss^M
système^M de verrouillage^M
seguro^M
dispositivo^M di bloccaggio^M

パイプ
pipe
Saugrohr^N
tube^M droit
tubo^M rígido
tubo^M rigido

伸縮(自在)ホース
flexible hose
flexibler Schlauch^M
tuyau^M flexible
tubo^M flexible
tubo^M flessibile

換気口
ventilating grille
Luftaustrittsschlitz^M
grille^F de ventilation^F
rejilla^F del ventilador^M
griglia^F di ventilazione^F

バンパー
bumper
Stoßleiste^F
pare-chocs^M
tope^M amortiguador
protezione^F antiurto

キャスター
caster
Lenkrolle^F
roulette^F
ruedecilla^F
ruota^F orientabile

電源スイッチ
on-off switch
Ein-/Ausschalter^M
interrupteur^M
interruptor^M
interruttore^M

延長パイプ
extension pipe
Ansatzrohr^N
rallonge^F
tubo^M de extensión^F
tubo^M rigido di prolunga^F

コード
cord; *flex*
Kabel^N
cordon^M
cordón^M
cordone^M

取っ手
handle
Tragegriff^M
poignée^F
asa^F
maniglia^F

絨毯(じゅうたん)・床用ブラシ
rug and floor brush
Bodendüse^F
suceur^M à tapis^M et planchers^M
boquilla^F para pisos^M y alfombras^F
spazzola^F per tappeti^M e pavimenti^M

フード
hood
Haube^F
capot^M
tapa^F
calotta^F

付属品
cleaning tools
Saugzubehör^N
accessoires^M
accesorios^M
accessori^M di pulitura^F

家具ノズル
upholstery nozzle
Polsterdüse^F
suceur^M triangulaire à tissus^M
boquilla^F para tapicería^F
bocchetta^F per tappezzeria^F

ごみブラシ
dusting brush
Saugbürste^F
brosse^F à épousseter
cepillo^M-plumero^M
spazzola^F a pennello^M

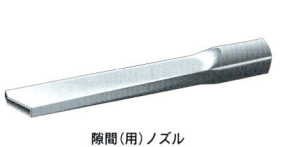

隙間(用)ノズル
crevice tool
Fugendüse^F
suceur^M plat
boquilla^F rinconera
bocchetta^F per fessure^F

床ブラシ
floor brush
Bürste^F
brosse^F à planchers^M
cepillo^M para pisos^M
spazzola^F per pavimenti^M

家電製品

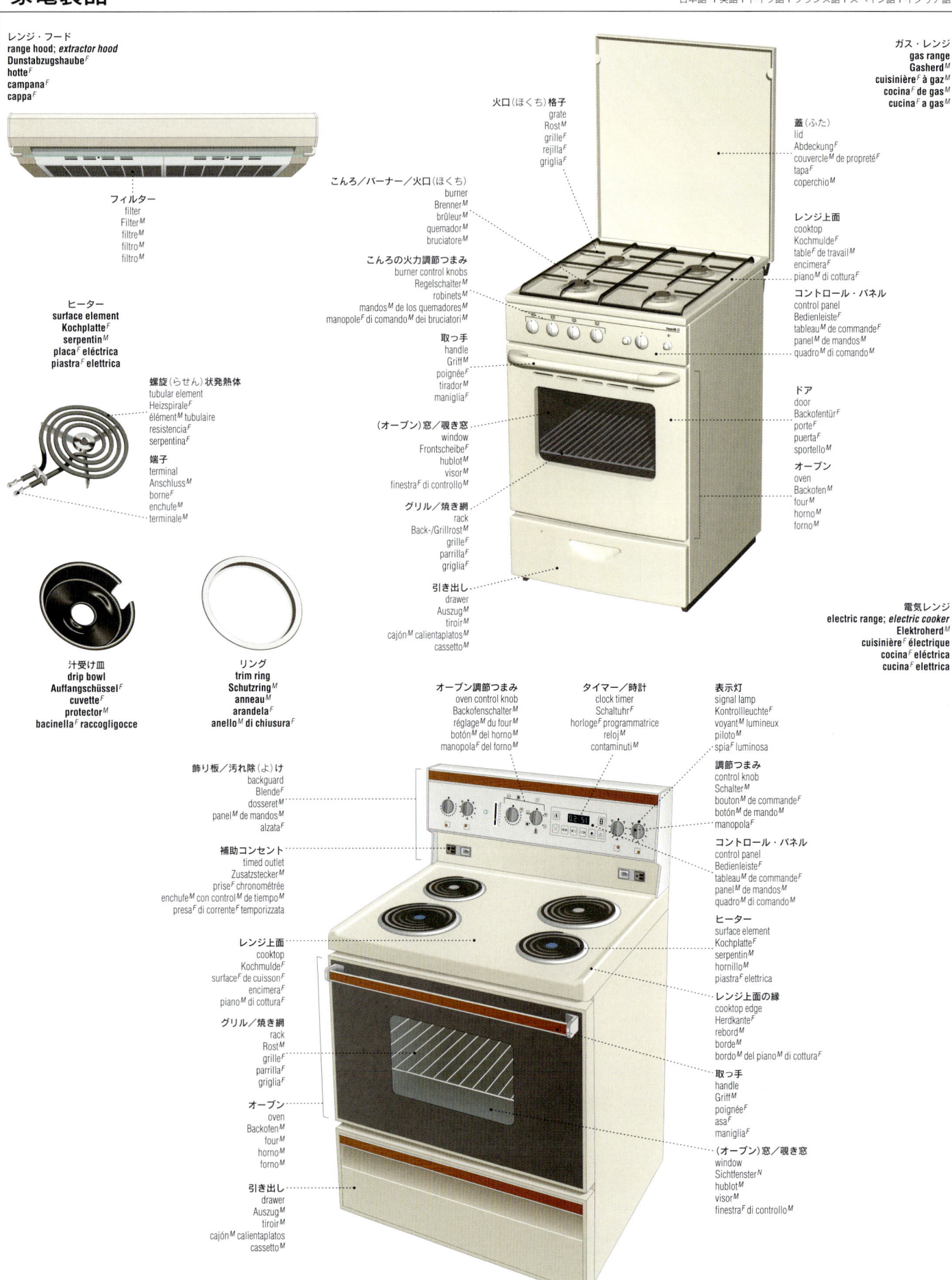

家具調度 | HOUSE FURNITURE
HAUSEINRICHTUNG | AMEUBLEMENT DE LA MAISON | MOBILIARIO PARA EL HOGAR | ARREDAMENTO PER LA CASA

日本語 | 英語 | ドイツ語 | フランス語 | スペイン語 | イタリア語

レンジ・フード
range hood; *extractor hood*
Dunstabzugshaube^F
hotte^F
campana^F
cappa^F

フィルター
filter
Filter^M
filtre^M
filtro^M
filtro^M

ヒーター
surface element
Kochplatte^F
serpentin^M
placa^F eléctrica
piastra^F elettrica

螺旋（らせん）状発熱体
tubular element
Heizspirale^F
élément^M tubulaire
resistencia^F
serpentina^F

端子
terminal
Anschluss^M
borne^F
enchufe^M
terminale^M

汁受け皿
drip bowl
Auffangschüssel^F
cuvette^F
protector^M
bacinella^F raccogligocce

リング
trim ring
Schutzring^M
anneau^M
arandela^F
anello^M di chiusura^F

火口（ほくち）格子
grate
Rost^M
grille^F
rejilla^F
griglia^F

こんろ／バーナー／火口（ほくち）
burner
Brenner^M
brûleur^M
quemador^M
bruciatore^M

こんろの火力調節つまみ
burner control knobs
Regelschalter^M
robinets^M
mandos^M de los quemadores^M
manopole^F di comando^M dei bruciatori^M

取っ手
handle
Griff^M
poignée^F
tirador^M
maniglia^F

（オーブン）窓／覗き窓
window
Frontscheibe^F
hublot^M
visor^M
finestra^F di controllo^M

グリル／焼き網
rack
Back-/Grillrost^M
grille^F
parrilla^F
griglia^F

引き出し
drawer
Auszug^M
tiroir^M
cajón^M calientaplatos^M
cassetto^M

オーブン調節つまみ
oven control knob
Backofenschalter^M
réglage^F du four^M
botón^M del horno^M
manopola^F del forno^M

タイマー／時計
clock timer
Schaltuhr^F
horloge^F programmatrice
reloj^M
contaminuti^M

飾り板／汚れ除（よ）け
backguard
Blende^F
dosseret^M
panel^M de mandos^M
alzata^F

補助コンセント
timed outlet
Zusatzstecker^M
prise^F chronométrée
enchufe^M con control^M de tiempo^M
presa^F di corrente^F temporizzata

レンジ上面
cooktop
Kochmulde^F
surface^F de cuisson^M
encimera^F
piano^M di cottura^F

グリル／焼き網
rack
Rost^M
grille^F
parrilla^F
griglia^F

オーブン
oven
Backofen^M
four^M
horno^M
forno^M

引き出し
drawer
Auszug^M
tiroir^M
cajón^M calientaplatos^M
cassetto^M

ガス・レンジ
gas range
Gasherd^M
cuisinière^F à gaz^M
cocina^F de gas^M
cucina^F a gas^M

蓋（ふた）
lid
Abdeckung^F
couvercle^M de propreté^F
tapa^F
coperchio^M

レンジ上面
cooktop
Kochmulde^F
table^F de travail^M
encimera^F
piano^M di cottura^F

コントロール・パネル
control panel
Bedienleiste^F
tableau^M de commande^F
panel^M de mandos^M
quadro^M di comando^M

ドア
door
Backofentür^F
porte^F
puerta^F
sportello^M

オーブン
oven
Backofen^M
four^M
horno^M
forno^M

電気レンジ
electric range; *electric cooker*
Elektroherd^M
cuisinière^F électrique
cocina^F eléctrica
cucina^F elettrica

表示灯
signal lamp
Kontrollleuchte^F
voyant^M lumineux
piloto^M
spia^F luminosa

調節つまみ
control knob
Schalter^M
bouton^M de commande^F
botón^M de mando^M
manopola^F

コントロール・パネル
control panel
Bedienleiste^F
tableau^M de commande^F
panel^M de mandos^M
quadro^M di comando^M

ヒーター
surface element
Kochplatte^F
serpentin^M
hornillo^M
piastra^F elettrica

レンジ上面の縁
cooktop edge
Herdkante^F
rebord^M
borde^M
bordo^M del piano^M di cottura^F

取っ手
handle
Griff^M
poignée^F
asa^M
maniglia^F

（オーブン）窓／覗き窓
window
Sichtfenster^M
hublot^M
visor^M
finestra^F di controllo^M

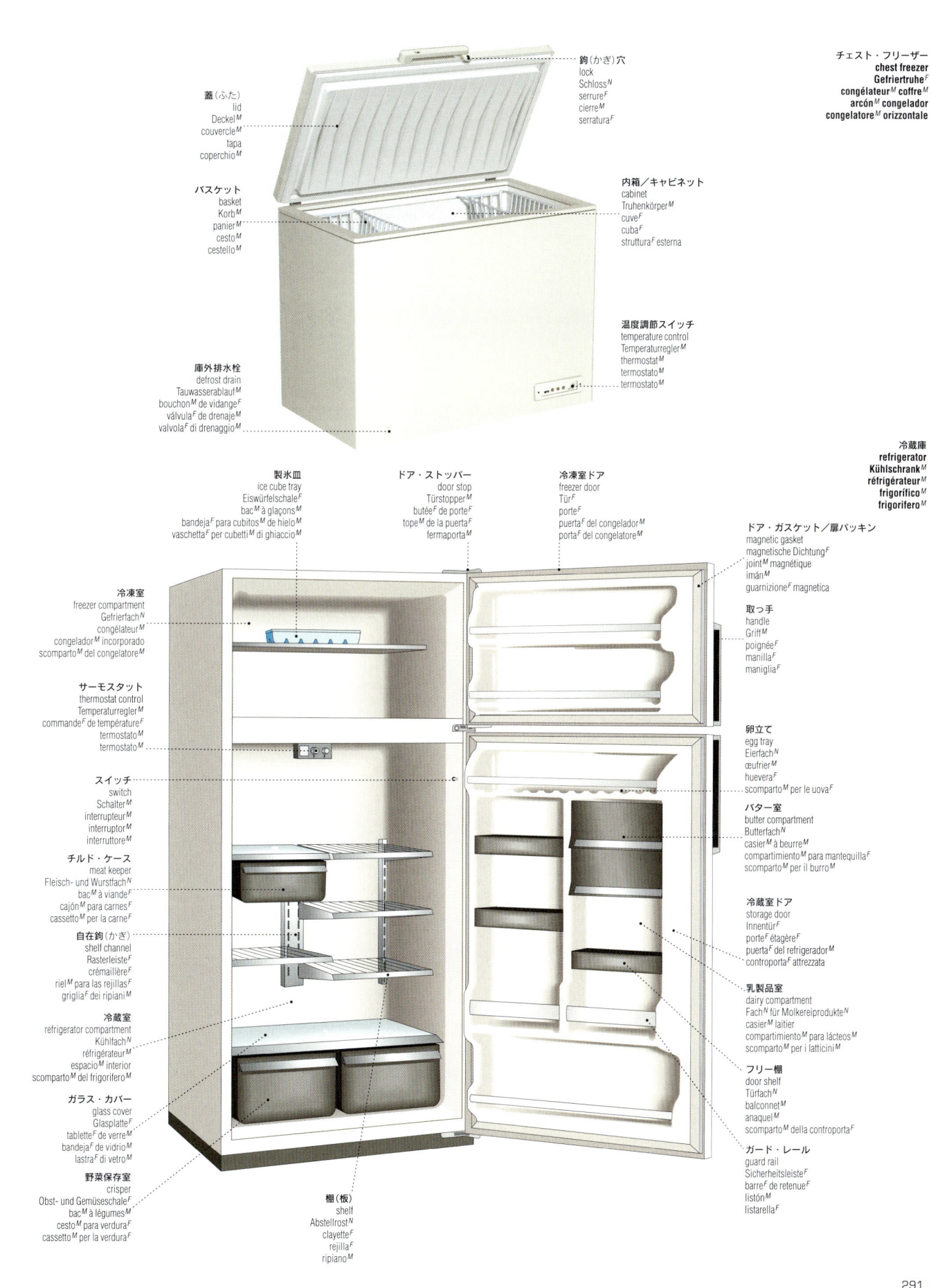

家具調度 | HOUSE FURNITURE
HAUSEINRICHTUNG | AMEUBLEMENT DE LA MAISON | MOBILIARIO PARA EL HOGAR | ARREDAMENTO PER LA CASA

家電製品

家屋

チェスト・フリーザー
chest freezer
Gefriertruhe F
congélateur M coffre M
arcón M congelador
congelatore M orizzontale

鍵(かぎ)穴
lock
Schloss N
serrure F
cierre M
serratura F

蓋(ふた)
lid
Deckel M
couvercle M
tapa
coperchio M

バスケット
basket
Korb M
panier M
cesto M
cestello M

内箱／キャビネット
cabinet
Truhenkörper M
cuve F
cuba F
struttura F esterna

温度調節スイッチ
temperature control
Temperaturregler M
thermostat M
termostato M
termostato M

庫外排水栓
defrost drain
Tauwasserablauf M
bouchon M de vidange F
válvula F de drenaje M
valvola F di drenaggio M

冷蔵庫
refrigerator
Kühlschrank M
réfrigérateur M
frigorífico M
frigorifero M

製氷皿
ice cube tray
Eiswürfelschale F
bac M à glaçons M
bandeja F para cubitos M de hielo M
vaschetta F per cubetti M di ghiaccio M

ドア・ストッパー
door stop
Türstopper M
butée F de porte F
tope M de la puerta F
fermaporta M

冷凍室ドア
freezer door
Tür F
porte F
puerta F del congelador M
porta F del congelatore M

ドア・ガスケット／扉パッキン
magnetic gasket
magnetische Dichtung F
joint M magnétique
imán M
guarnizione F magnetica

取っ手
handle
Griff M
poignée F
manilla F
maniglia F

冷凍室
freezer compartment
Gefrierfach N
congélateur M
congelador M incorporado
scomparto M del congelatore M

サーモスタット
thermostat control
Temperaturregler M
commande F de température F
termostato M
termostato M

卵立て
egg tray
Eierfach N
œufrier M
huevera F
scomparto M per le uova F

スイッチ
switch
Schalter M
interrupteur M
interruptor M
interruttore M

バター室
butter compartment
Butterfach N
casier M à beurre M
compartimiento M para mantequilla F
scomparto M per il burro M

チルド・ケース
meat keeper
Fleisch- und Wurstfach N
bac M à viande M
cajón M para carnes M
cassetto M per la carne F

冷蔵室ドア
storage door
Innentür F
porte F étagère F
puerta F del refrigerador M
controporta F attrezzata

自在鍵(かぎ)
shelf channel
Rasterleiste F
crémaillère F
riel M para las rejillas F
griglia F dei ripiani M

乳製品室
dairy compartment
Fach N für Molkereiprodukte N
casier M laitier
compartimiento M para lácteos M
scomparto M per i latticini M

冷蔵室
refrigerator compartment
Kühlfach N
réfrigérateur M
espacio M interior
scomparto M del frigorifero M

フリー棚
door shelf
Türfach N
balconnet M
anaquel M
scomparto M della controporta F

ガラス・カバー
glass cover
Glasplatte F
tablette F de verre M
bandeja F de vidrio M
lastra F di vetro M

ガード・レール
guard rail
Sicherheitsleiste F
barre F de retenue F
listón M
listarella F

野菜保存室
crisper
Obst- und Gemüseschale F
bac M à légumes M
cesto M para verdura F
cassetto M per la verdura F

棚(板)
shelf
Abstellrost N
clayette F
rejilla F
ripiano M

291

家電製品

家具調度 | HOUSE FURNITURE
HAUSEINRICHTUNG | AMEUBLEMENT DE LA MAISON | MOBILIARIO PARA EL HOGAR | ARREDAMENTO PER LA CASA

日本語 | 英語 | ドイツ語 | フランス語 | スペイン語 | イタリア語

家屋

（電気）洗濯機
washer
Waschmaschine^F
lave-linge^M
lavadora^F
lavatrice^F

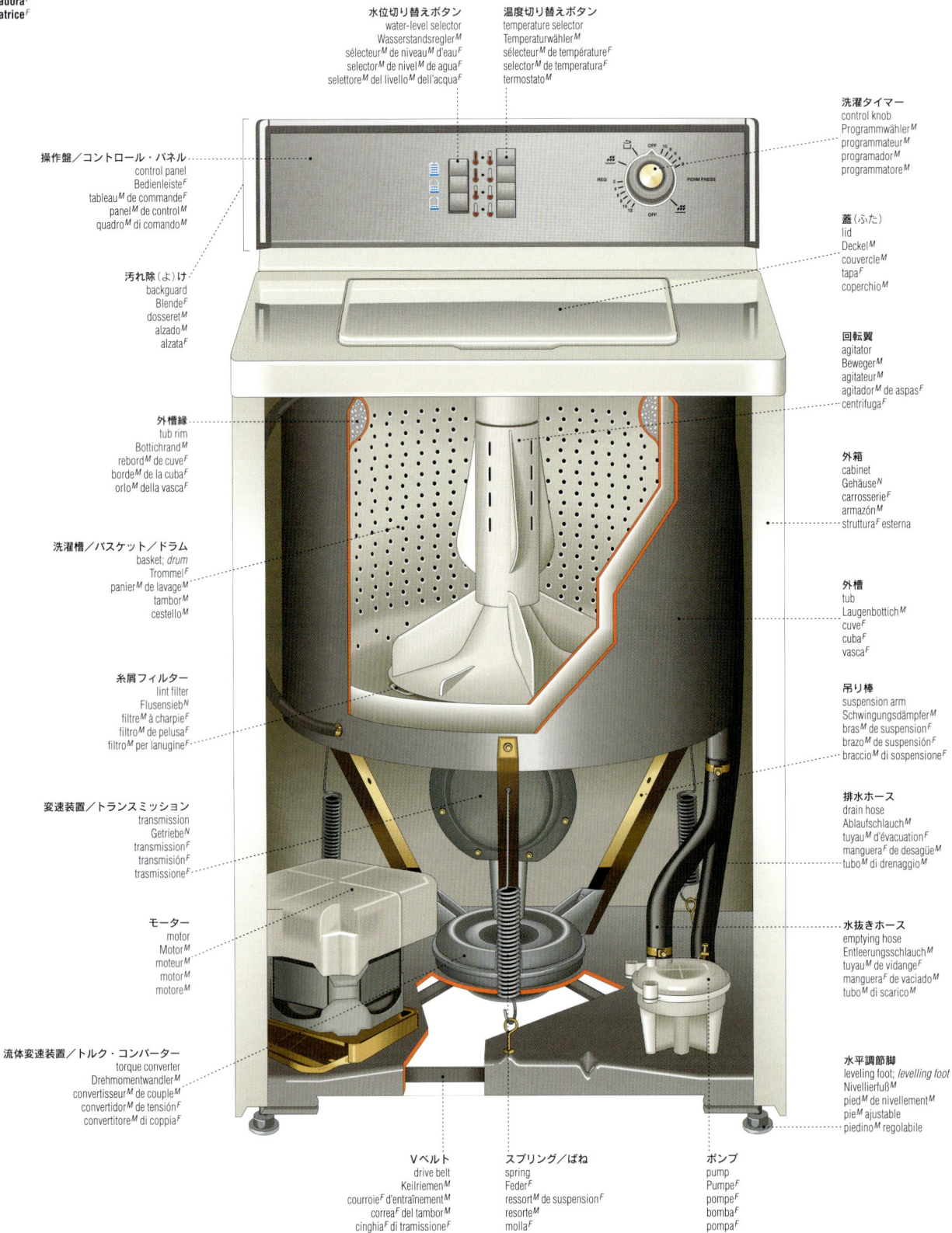

水位切り替えボタン
water-level selector
Wasserstandsregler^M
sélecteur^M de niveau^M d'eau^F
selector^M de nivel^M de agua^F
selettore^M del livello^M dell'acqua^F

温度切り替えボタン
temperature selector
Temperaturwähler^M
sélecteur^M de température^F
selector^M de temperatura^F
termostato^M

洗濯タイマー
control knob
Programmwähler^M
programmateur^M
programador^M
programmatore^M

操作盤／コントロール・パネル
control panel
Bedienleiste^F
tableau^M de commande^F
panel^M de control^M
quadro^M di comando^M

蓋（ふた）
lid
Deckel^M
couvercle^M
tapa^F
coperchio^M

汚れ除（よ）け
backguard
Blende^F
dosseret^M
alzado^M
alzata^F

回転翼
agitator
Beweger^M
agitateur^M
agitador^M de aspas^F
centrifuga^F

外槽縁
tub rim
Bottichrand^M
rebord^M de cuve^F
borde^M de la cuba^F
orlo^M della vasca^F

外箱
cabinet
Gehäuse^N
carrosserie^F
armazón^M
struttura^F esterna

洗濯槽／バスケット／ドラム
basket; drum
Trommel^F
panier^M de lavage^M
tambor^M
cestello^M

外槽
tub
Laugenbottich^M
cuve^F
cuba^F
vasca^F

糸屑フィルター
lint filter
Flusensieb^N
filtre^M à charpie^F
filtro^M de pelusa^F
filtro^M per lanugine^F

吊り棒
suspension arm
Schwingungsdämpfer^M
bras^M de suspension^F
brazo^M de suspensión^F
braccio^M di sospensione^F

変速装置／トランスミッション
transmission
Getriebe^N
transmission^F
transmisión^F
trasmissione^F

排水ホース
drain hose
Ablaufschlauch^M
tuyau^M d'évacuation^F
manguera^F de desagüe^M
tubo^M di drenaggio^M

モーター
motor
Motor^M
moteur^M
motor^M
motore^M

水抜きホース
emptying hose
Entleerungsschlauch^M
tuyau^F de vidange^F
manguera^F de vaciado^M
tubo^M di scarico^M

流体変速装置／トルク・コンバーター
torque converter
Drehmomentwandler^M
convertisseur^M de couple^M
convertidor^M de tensión^F
convertitore^M di coppia^F

水平調節脚
leveling foot; levelling foot
Nivellierfuß^M
pied^M de nivellement^M
pie^M ajustable
piedino^M regolabile

Vベルト
drive belt
Keilriemen^M
courroie^F d'entraînement^M
correa^F del tambor^M
cinghia^F di tramissione^F

スプリング／ばね
spring
Feder^F
ressort^M de suspension^F
resorte^M
molla^F

ポンプ
pump
Pumpe^F
pompe^F
bomba^F
pompa^F

292

家具調度 | HOUSE FURNITURE
HAUSEINRICHTUNG | AMEUBLEMENT DE LA MAISON | MOBILIARIO PARA EL HOGAR | ARREDAMENTO PER LA CASA

家電製品

(電気)乾燥機
electric dryer
Wäschetrockner^M
sèche-linge^M électrique
secadora^F de ropa^F
asciugatrice^F

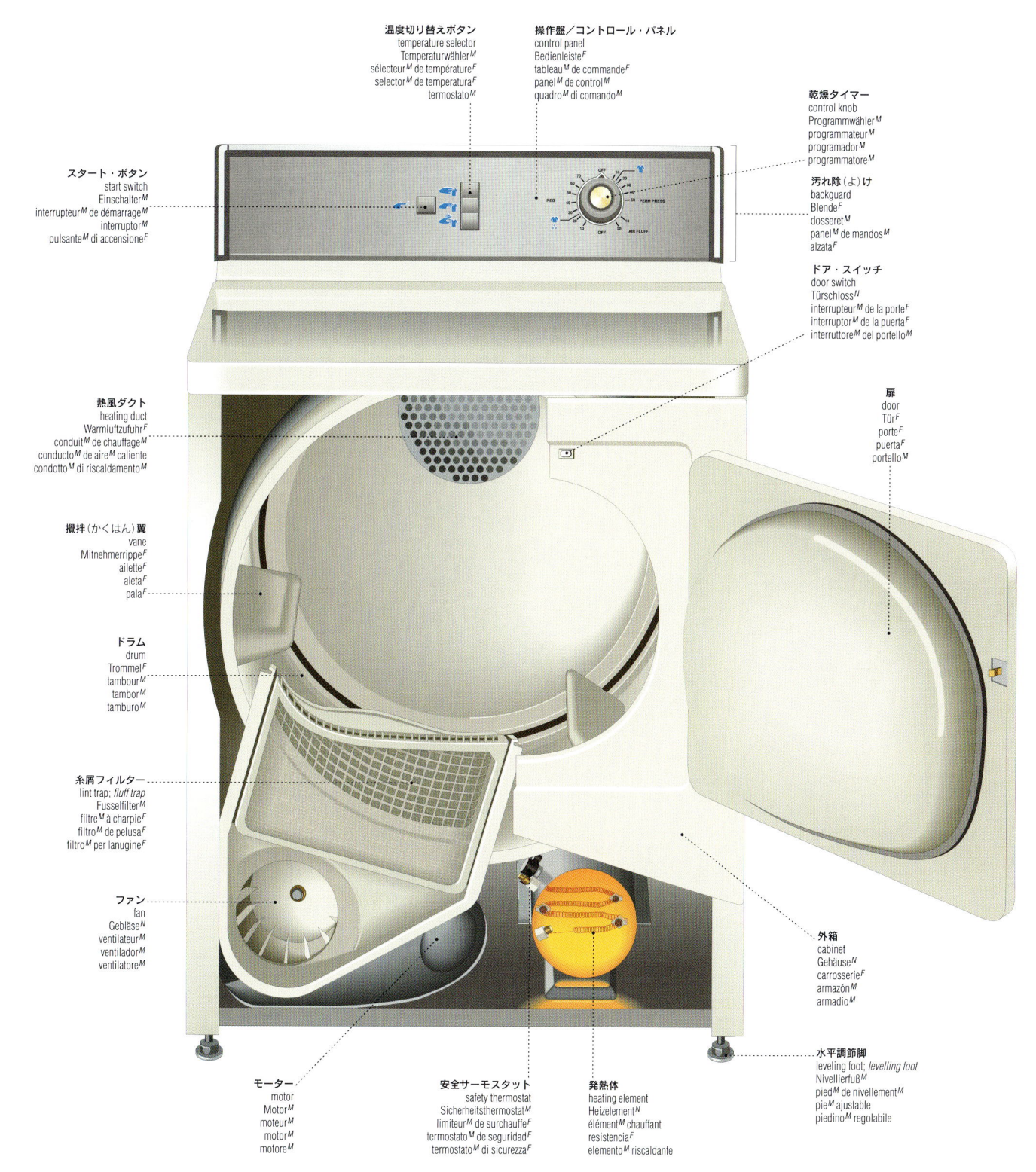

温度切り替えボタン
temperature selector
Temperaturwähler^M
sélecteur^M de température^F
selector^M de temperatura^F
termostato^M

操作盤／コントロール・パネル
control panel
Bedienleiste^F
tableau^M de commande^F
panel^M de control^M
quadro^M di comando^M

乾燥タイマー
control knob
Programmwähler^M
programmateur^M
programador^M
programmatore^M

スタート・ボタン
start switch
Einschalter^M
interrupteur^M de démarrage^M
interruptor^M
pulsante^M di accensione^F

汚れ除(よ)け
backguard
Blende^F
dosseret^M
panel^M de mandos^M
alzata^F

ドア・スイッチ
door switch
Türschloss^N
interrupteur^M de la porte^F
interruptor^M de la puerta^F
interruttore^M del portello^M

熱風ダクト
heating duct
Warmluftzufuhr^F
conduit^M de chauffage^M
conducto^M de aire^M caliente
condotto^M di riscaldamento^M

扉
door
Tür^F
porte^F
puerta^F
portello^M

攪拌(かくはん)翼
vane
Mitnehmerrippe^F
ailette^F
aleta^F
pala^F

ドラム
drum
Trommel^F
tambour^M
tambor^M
tamburo^M

糸屑フィルター
lint trap; *fluff trap*
Fusselfilter^M
filtre^M à charpie^F
filtro^M de pelusa^F
filtro^M per lanugine^F

ファン
fan
Gebläse^N
ventilateur^M
ventilador^M
ventilatore^M

外箱
cabinet
Gehäuse^N
carrosserie^F
armazón^M
armadio^M

水平調節脚
leveling foot; *levelling foot*
Nivellierfuß^M
pied^M de nivellement^M
pie^M ajustable
piedino^M regolabile

モーター
motor
Motor^M
moteur^M
motor^M
motore^M

安全サーモスタット
safety thermostat
Sicherheitsthermostat^M
limiteur^M de surchauffe^F
termostato^M de seguridad^F
termostato^M di sicurezza^F

発熱体
heating element
Heizelement^N
élément^M chauffant
resistencia^F
elemento^M riscaldante

家屋

293

家具調度 | HOUSE FURNITURE
HAUSEINRICHTUNG | AMEUBLEMENT DE LA MAISON | MOBILIARIO PARA EL HOGAR | ARREDAMENTO PER LA CASA

家電製品

日本語 | 英語 | ドイツ語 | フランス語 | スペイン語 | イタリア語

操作盤／コントロール・パネル
control panel
Bedienleiste^F
tableau^M de commande^F
panel^M de control^M
quadro^M di comando^M

表示灯
signal lamp
Kontrollleuchte^F
voyant^M lumineux
piloto^M
spia^F luminosa

調節つまみ／タイマー
control knob
Programmwähler^M
programmateur^M
programador^M
programmatore^M

押しボタン
push button
Drucktaste^F
bouton^M-poussoir
botón^M selector
pulsante^M

通気孔
air vent
Belüftungsschlitz^M
grille^F d'aération
rejilla^F de ventilación
sfiatatoio^M

掛け金
latch
Riegel^M
loquet^M
palanca^F de cierre^M
chiusura^F a scatto

かご／ラック
rack
Korb^M
panier^M
cesto^M
cestello^M

ウォッシュ・タワー／洗浄塔／ノズル
wash tower
Wascherarm^M
tourelle^F
torrecilla^F de lavado^M
torre^F di lavaggio^M

(自動)食器洗い機
dishwasher
Geschirrspülmaschine^F
lave-vaisselle^M
lavavajillas^M
lavastoviglie^F

回転ノズル／スプレー・アーム
spray arm
Sprüharm^M
bras^M gicleur^M
pulverizador^M
braccio^M spruzzante

溢(あふ)れ防止スイッチ
overflow protection switch
Überlaufschutz^M
dispositif^M antidébordement
regulador^M de entrada^F de agua^F
dispositivo^M antiallagamento

蝶番(ちょうつがい)
hinge
Scharnier^N
charnière^F
bisagra^F
cerniera^F

洗剤注入口
detergent dispenser
Reinigungsmittelbehälter^M
distributeur^M de détergent^M
recipiente^M del detergente^M
vaschetta^F per il detersivo

断熱材
insulating material
Isoliermaterial^N
isolant^M
aislante^M
materiale^M isolante

洗槽／タブ
tub
Bottich^M
cuve^F
cuba^F de lavado^M
vasca^F

スライド
slide
Schiene^F
glissière^F
riel^M corredizo
guida^F

給水ホース
water hose
Wasserschlauch^M
conduite^F d'eau^F
manguera^F de alimentación^F
tubo^M di alimentazione^F dell'acqua^F

発熱体
heating element
Heizelement^N
élément^M chauffant
resistencia^F
elemento^M riscaldante

排水ホース
drain hose
Ablaufschlauch^M
tuyau^M de vidange^F
manguera^F de desagüe^M
tubo^M di drenaggio^M

ポンプ
pump
Pumpe^F
pompe^F
bomba^F
pompa^F

ガスケット
gasket
Dichtungsring^M
joint^M
junta^F
guarnizione^F

水平調節脚
leveling foot; levelling foot
Nivellierfuß^M
pied^M de nivellement^M
pie^M ajustable
piedino^M regolabile

すすぎ水注入口
rinse-aid dispenser
Klarspülmittelbehälter^M
distributeur^M de produit^M de rinçage^M
recipiente^M del abrillantador^M
serbatoio^M per il brillantante^M

小物入れ／カトラリー・バスケット
cutlery basket
Besteckkorb^M
panier^M à couverts^M
cesto^M para cubiertos^M
cestello^M per le posate^F

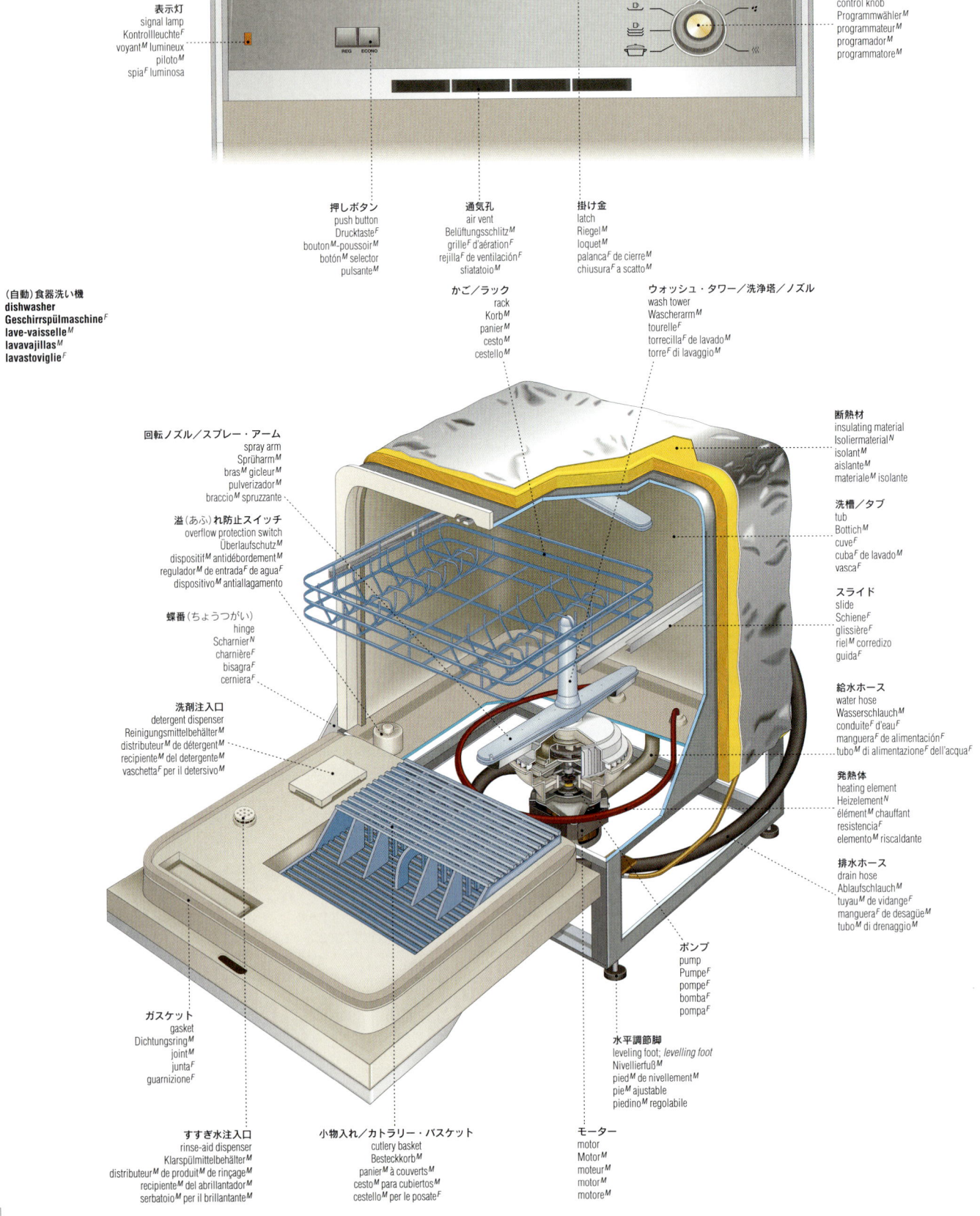

モーター
motor
Motor^M
moteur^M
motor^M
motore^M

家具調度 | HOUSE FURNITURE
HAUSEINRICHTUNG | AMEUBLEMENT DE LA MAISON | MOBILIARIO PARA EL HOGAR | ARREDAMENTO PER LA CASA

家事用品

household equipment | HaushaltsgegenständeM | articlesM ménagers | artículosM de limpiezaF | attrezziM domestici

キッチン・タオル
kitchen towel
GeschirrtuchN
torchonM
bayetaF de cocinaF
strofinaccioM da cucinaF

ちり取り
dustpan
KehrschaufelF
pelleF à poussièreF
recogedorM
palettaF

帚（ほうき）
broom
BesenM
balaiM
escobaF
scopaF

モップ
mop
MopM
balaiM à frangesF
fregonaF
scopaF a frangiaF

家屋

台所用スポンジ
scouring pad
PutzschwammM
épongeF à récurer
estropajoM con esponjaF
spugnaF abrasiva

ブラシ
brush
BürsteF
brosseF
cepilloM
spazzolaF

背
block
BürstenkörperM
montureF
lomoM
dorsoM

柄
handle
StielM
mancheM
paloM
manicoM

ごみ箱
refuse container
AbfalleimerM
poubelleF
cuboM de basuraF
bidoneM dei rifiutiM

毛
fibers
BorstenF
fibresF
cerdasF
setoleF

蓋（ふた）
lid
DeckelM
couvercleM
tapaF
coperchioM

毛
fibers
BorstenF
fibresF
cerdasF
setoleF

取っ手
handle
GriffM
poignéeF
asaF
manicoM

バケツ
pail
EimerM
seauM
cuboM
secchioM

注ぎ口
pouring spout
AusgussM
becM verseur
pitorroM
beccuccioM

取っ手
handle
HenkelM
anseF
asaF
manicoM

295

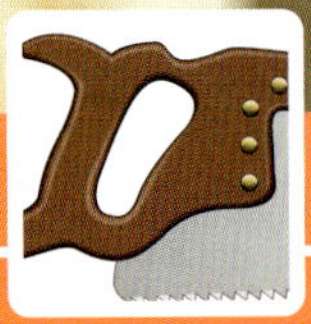

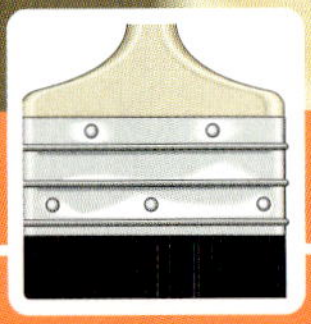

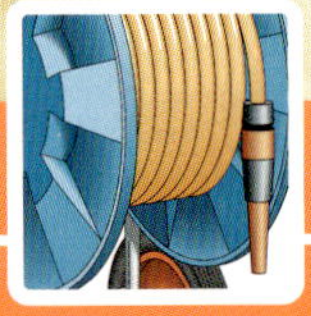

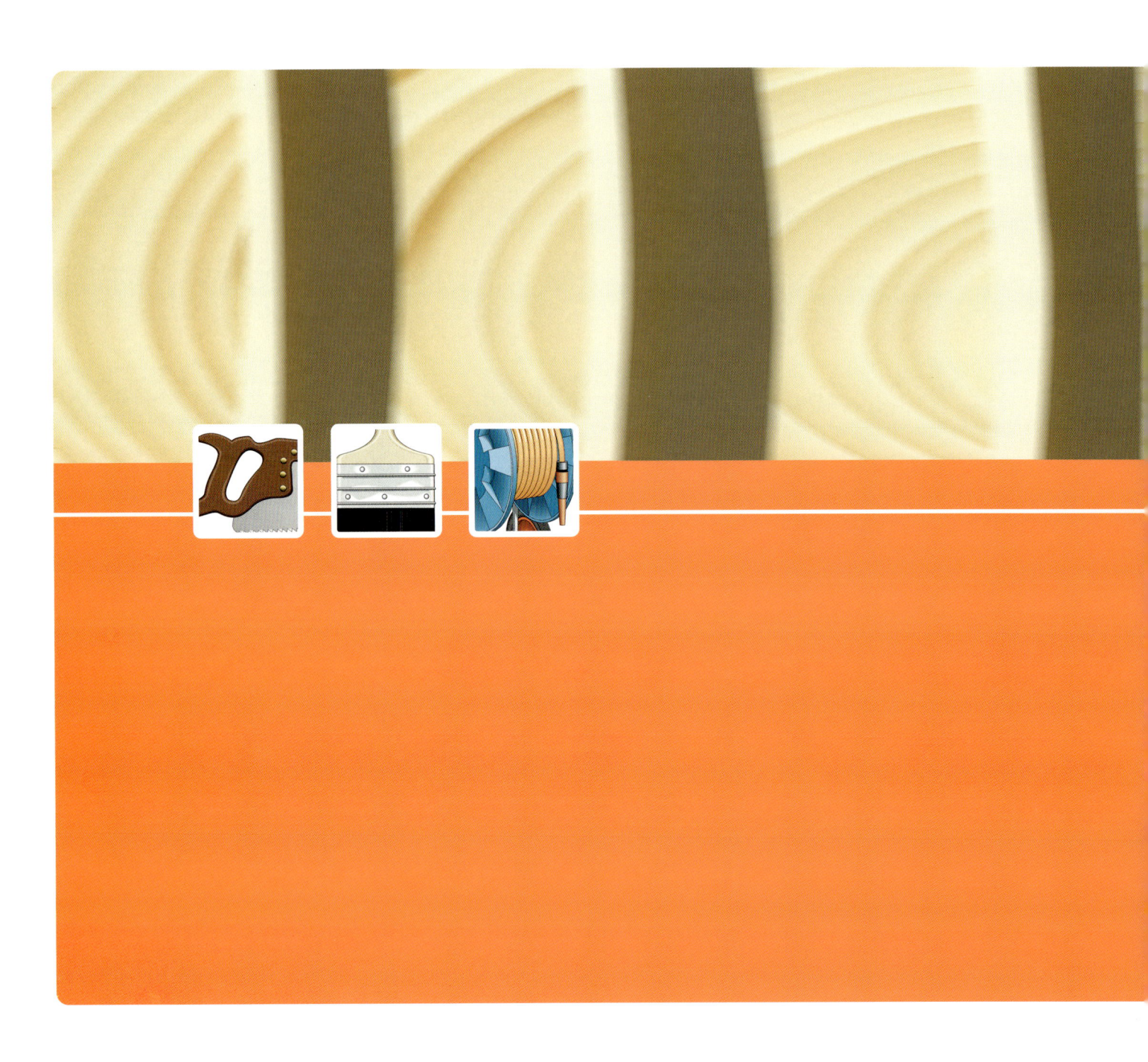

日曜大工・園芸

DO-IT-YOURSELF AND GARDENING I HEIMWERKEN UND GARTENARBEIT I BRICOLAGE ET JARDINAGE
I BRICOLAJE Y JARDINERÍA I FAI DA TE E GIARDINAGGIO

298 日曜大工

- 298 基礎建材
- 299 被覆材
- 299 断熱材
- 300 木材
- 301 木工：釘を打つ道具
- 302 木工：ねじを締める道具
- 303 木工：木材を切る道具
- 306 木工：穴を空ける道具
- 308 木工：成形する道具
- 310 木工：つかむ［締める］道具
- 313 木工：測定して印を付ける道具
- 313 木工：その他の道具
- 314 配管工具
- 315 石工用の工具
- 316 電設工具
- 318 はんだ付け・溶接工具
- 320 塗装
- 321 はしごと脚立（きゃたつ）

322 園芸

- 322 庭
- 323 いろいろな器具
- 324 種播（ま）き・植え付け用具
- 325 小型園芸用具
- 326 土をほぐす用具
- 328 水撒（ま）き用具
- 330 剪定（せんてい）用具
- 332 芝の手入れ

基礎建材 | DO-IT-YOURSELF
HEIMWERKEN | BRICOLAGE | BRICOLAJE | FAI DA TE

日本語 | 英語 | ドイツ語 | フランス語 | スペイン語 | イタリア語

basic building materials | die wichtigsten Baumaterialienᴺ | matériauxᴹ de baseꜰ | materialesᴹ básicos | materialiᴹ da costruzioneꜰ di baseꜰ

煉瓦（れんが）
brick
Ziegelsteinᴹ
briqueꜰ
ladrilloᴹ
mattoneᴹ

普通煉瓦／ソリッド・ブリック
solid brick
Vollziegelᴹ
briqueꜰ pleine
ladrilloᴹ macizo
mattoneᴹ pieno

穴空き煉瓦
perforated brick
Lochziegelᴹ
briqueꜰ perforée
ladrilloᴹ perforado
mattoneᴹ perforato

空洞煉瓦
hollow brick
Hohlziegelᴹ
briqueꜰ creuse
ladrilloᴹ hueco
mattoneᴹ forato

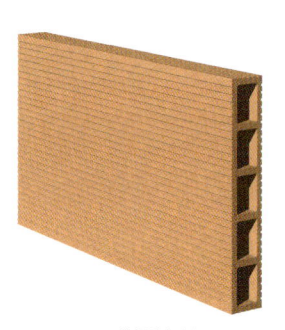

仕切りタイル
partition tile
Tonhohlplatteꜰ
briqueꜰ plâtrière
ladrilloᴹ tabiquero
mattoneᴹ forato per tramezzoᴹ

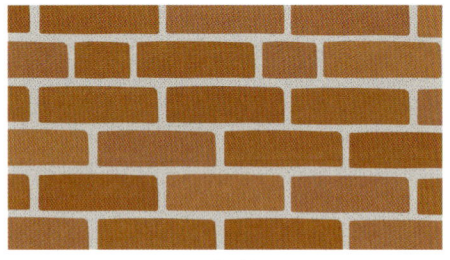

煉瓦壁
brick wall
Ziegelmauerꜰ
murᴹ de briquesꜰ
muroᴹ de ladrillosᴹ
muroᴹ di mattoniᴹ

耐火煉瓦
firebrick
feuerfester Ziegelᴹ
briqueꜰ réfractaire
ladrilloᴹ refractario
mattoneᴹ refrattario

モルタル
mortar
Mörtelᴹ
mortierᴹ
morteroᴹ
maltaꜰ

石
stone
Steinᴹ
pierreꜰ
piedraꜰ
pietraꜰ

板石（いたいし）
flagstone
Pflastersteinᴹ
dalleꜰ de pierreꜰ
losaꜰ de piedraꜰ
pietraꜰ da lastricoᴹ

粗石（あらいし）／割り栗石
rubble
Bruchsteinᴹ
moellonᴹ
morrilloᴹ
pietraꜰ da costruzioneꜰ

切石（きりいし）
cut stone
Hausteinᴹ
pierreꜰ de tailleꜰ
piedraꜰ tallada
pietraꜰ da taglioᴹ

石壁
stone wall
Steinmauerꜰ
murᴹ de pierresꜰ
muroᴹ de piedrasꜰ
muroᴹ di pietraꜰ

コンクリート
concrete
Betonᴹ
bétonᴹ
hormigónᴹ
calcestruzzoᴹ

コンクリート・ブロック
concrete block
Betonblockᴹ
blocᴹ de bétonᴹ
bloqueᴹ de hormigónᴹ
bloccoᴹ di calcestruzzoᴹ

プレストレスト・コンクリート
prestressed concrete
Spannbetonᴹ
bétonᴹ précontraint
hormigónᴹ pretensado
calcestruzzoᴹ precompresso

鉄筋コンクリート
reinforced concrete
Stahlbetonᴹ
bétonᴹ armé
hormigónᴹ armado
cementoᴹ armato

鋼（こう）
steel
Stahlᴹ
acierᴹ
aceroᴹ
acciaioᴹ

日曜大工 | DO-IT-YOURSELF
HEIMWERKEN | BRICOLAGE | BRICOLAJE | FAI DA TE

被覆材

covering materials | Verkleidungsmaterialien^N | matériaux^M de revêtement^M | materiales^M de revestimiento^M | materiali di rivestimento^M

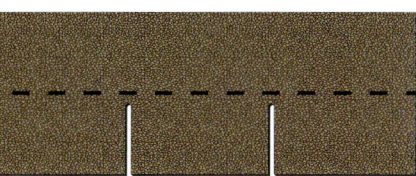

アスファルト・シングル[こけら板]
asphalt shingle
Asphaltschindel^F
bardeau^M d'asphalte^M
teja^F de asfalto^M
listello^M di cartonfeltro^M bitumato

シングル／こけら板
shingle
Schindel^F
bardeau^M
ripia^F
scandola^F

ダイヤモンド形ラス
diamond mesh metal lath
Streckmetall^N-Unterlage^F
lattis^M métallique à losanges^M
mallas^F de metal^M expandido
reticella^F metallica a maglie^F esagonali

タール紙／アスファルト・フェルト
tar paper; *roofing felt*
Teerpappe^F
papier^M goudronné
fieltro^M asfáltico
carta^F catramata

瓦
tile
Dachziegel^M
tuile^F
teja^F
tegola^F

石膏(せっこう)タイル
gypsum tile
Gipskartonplatte^F
carreau^M de plâtre^M
panel^M de yeso^M
piastrella^F di gesso^M

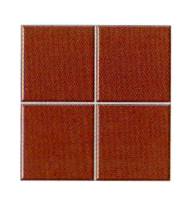

床タイル
floor tile
Fliese^F
carreau^M
baldosa^F
piastrella^F per pavimenti^M

石膏ボード
gypsum board
Gipskarton^M-Bauplatte^F
plaque^F de plâtre^M
tablero^M de yeso^M
pannello^M di gesso^M

断熱材

insulating materials | Isoliermaterialien^N | isolants^M | materiales^M aislantes | materiali^M isolanti

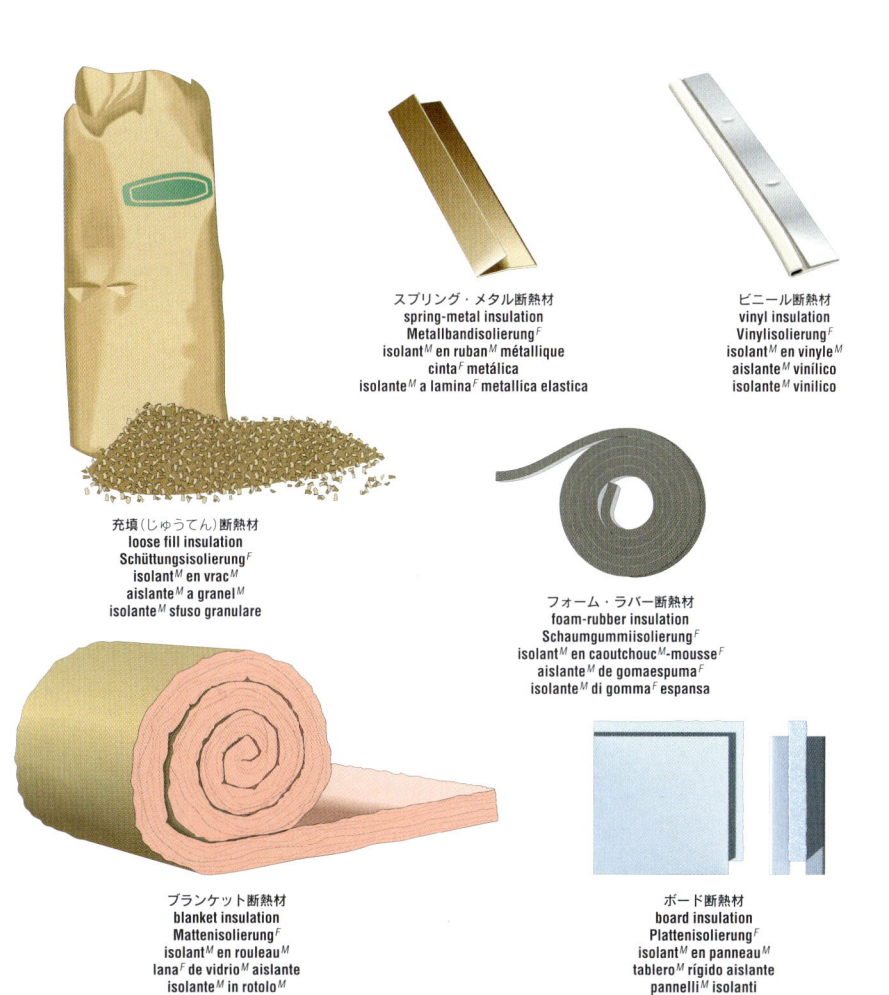

充填(じゅうてん)断熱材
loose fill insulation
Schüttungsisolierung^F
isolant^M en vrac^M
aislante^M a granel^M
isolante^M sfuso granulare

スプリング・メタル断熱材
spring-metal insulation
Metallbandisolierung^F
isolant^M en ruban^M métallique
cinta^F metálica
isolante^M a lamina^F metallica elastica

ビニール断熱材
vinyl insulation
Vinylisolierung^F
isolant^M en vinyle^M
aislante^M vinílico
isolante^M vinilico

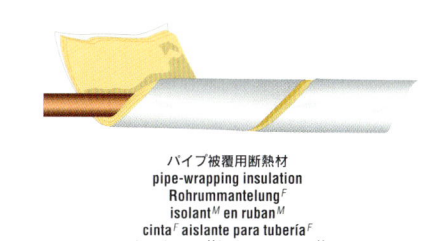

パイプ被覆用断熱材
pipe-wrapping insulation
Rohrummantelung^F
isolant^M en ruban^M
cinta^F aislante para tubería^F
rivestimento^M isolante per tubi^M

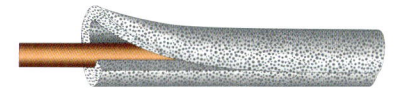

成形断熱材
molded insulation; *moulded insulation*
vorgeformte Rohrummantelung^F
isolant^M en coquille^F
aislante^M premoldeado
isolante^M preformato

フォーム・ラバー断熱材
foam-rubber insulation
Schaumgummiisolierung^F
isolant^M en caoutchouc^M-mousse^F
aislante^M de gomaespuma^F
isolante^M di gomma^F espansa

ブランケット断熱材
blanket insulation
Mattenisolierung^F
isolant^M en rouleau^M
lana^F de vidrio^M aislante
isolante^M in rotolo^M

ボード断熱材
board insulation
Plattenisolierung^F
isolant^M en panneau^M
tablero^M rígido aislante
pannelli^M isolanti

発泡断熱材
foam insulation
Bauschaumisolierung^F
espuma^F aislante
schiuma^F isolante

日曜大工 | DO-IT-YOURSELF
HEIMWERKEN | BRICOLAGE | BRICOLAJE | FAI DA TE

木材

wood | Holz^N | bois^M | madera^F | legno^M

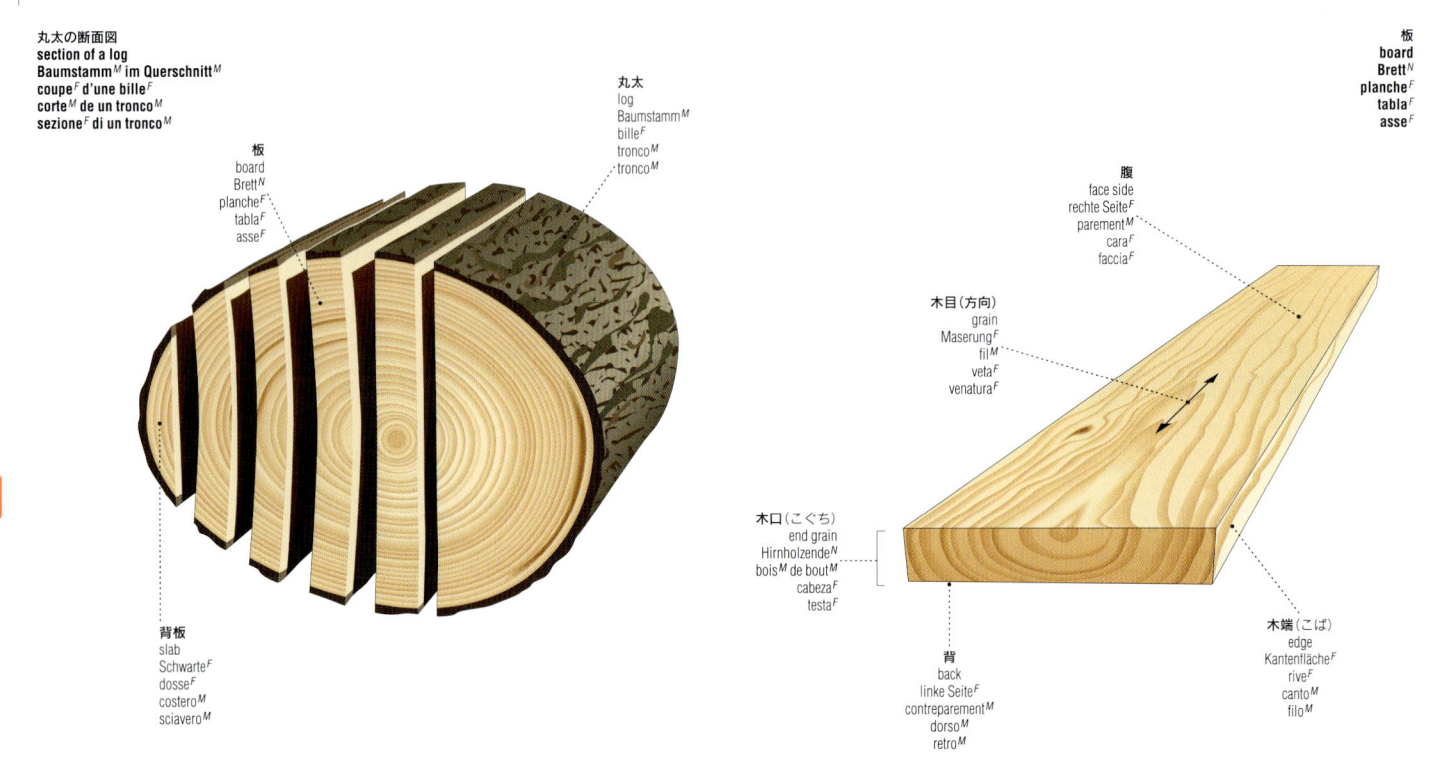

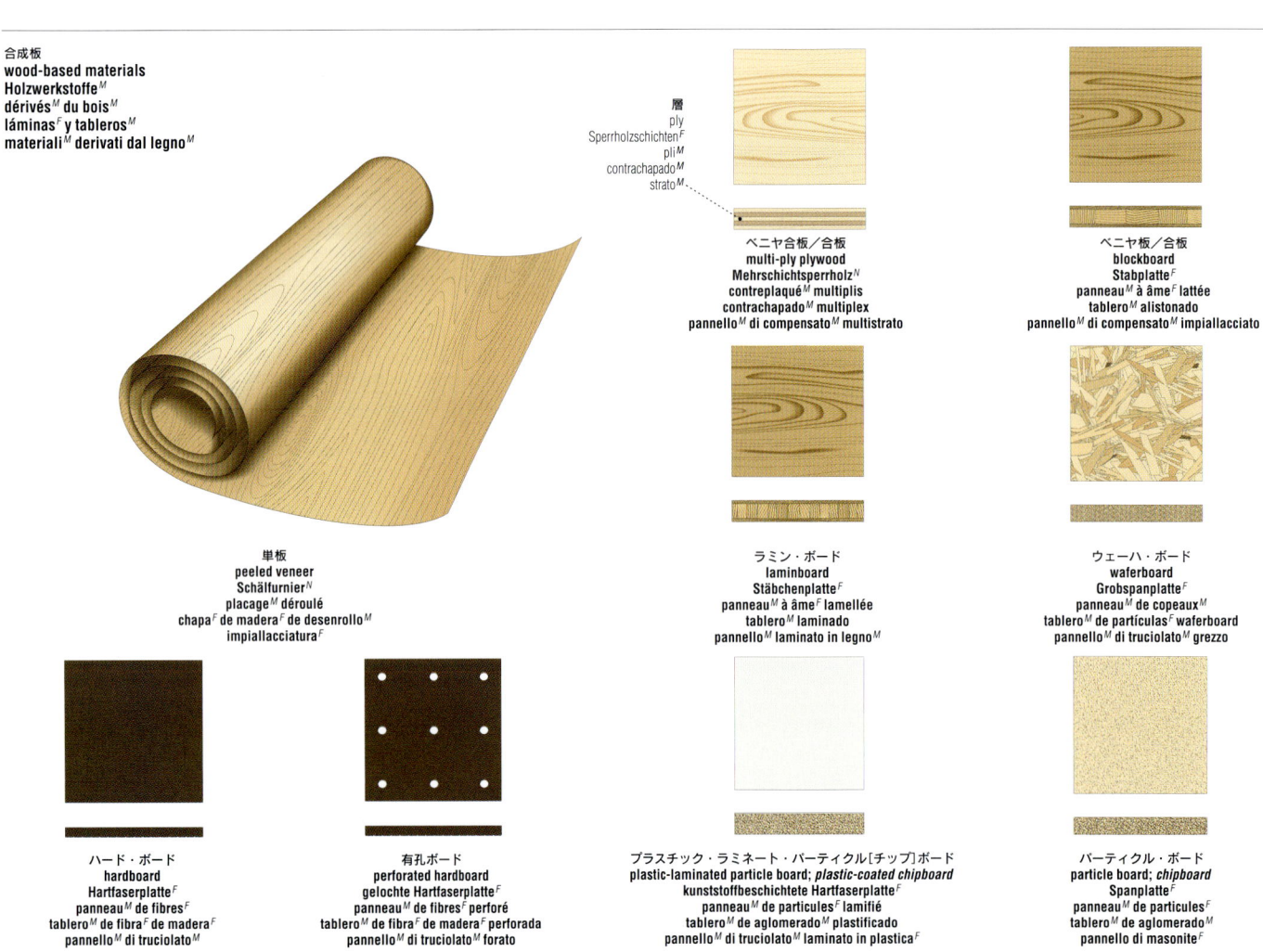

日本語 | 英語 | ドイツ語 | フランス語 | スペイン語 | イタリア語

丸太の断面図
section of a log
Baumstamm^M im Querschnitt^M
coupe^F d'une bille^F
corte^M de un tronco^M
sezione^F di un tronco^M

板
board
Brett^N
planche^F
tabla^F
asse^F

丸太
log
Baumstamm^M
bille^F
tronco^M
tronco^M

板
board
Brett^N
planche^F
tabla^F
asse^F

腹
face side
rechte Seite^F
parement^M
cara^F
faccia^F

木目（方向）
grain
Maserung^F
fil^M
veta^F
venatura^F

木口（こぐち）
end grain
Hirnholzende^N
bois^M de bout^M
cabeza^F
testa^F

木端（こば）
edge
Kantenfläche^F
rive^F
canto^M
filo^M

背板
slab
Schwarte^F
dosse^F
costero^M
sciavero^M

背
back
linke Seite^F
contreparement^M
dorso^M
retro^M

合成板
wood-based materials
Holzwerkstoffe^M
dérivés^M du bois^M
láminas^F y tableros^M
materiali^M derivati dal legno^M

層
ply
Sperrholzschichten^F
pli^M
contrachapado^M
strato^M

ベニヤ合板／合板
multi-ply plywood
Mehrschichtsperrholz^N
contreplaqué^M multiplis
contrachapado^M multiplex
pannello^M di compensato^M multistrato

ベニヤ板／合板
blockboard
Stabplatte^F
panneau^M à âme^F lattée
tablero^M alistonado
pannello^M di compensato^M impiallacciato

単板
peeled veneer
Schälfurnier^N
placage^M déroulé
chapa^F de madera^F de desenrollo^M
impiallacciatura^F

ラミン・ボード
laminboard
Stäbchenplatte^F
panneau^M à âme^F lamellée
tablero^M laminado
pannello^M laminato in legno^M

ウェーハ・ボード
waferboard
Grobspanplatte^F
panneau^M de copeaux^M
tablero^M de partículas^F waferboard
pannello^M di truciolato^M grezzo

ハード・ボード
hardboard
Hartfaserplatte^F
panneau^M de fibres^F
tablero^M de fibra^F de madera^F
pannello^M di truciolato^M

有孔ボード
perforated hardboard
gelochte Hartfaserplatte^F
panneau^M de fibres^F perforé
tablero^M de fibra^F de madera^F perforada
pannello^M di truciolato^M forato

プラスチック・ラミネート・パーティクル［チップ］ボード
plastic-laminated particle board; *plastic-coated chipboard*
kunststoffbeschichtete Hartfaserplatte^F
panneau^M de particules^F lamifié
tablero^M de aglomerado^M plastificado
pannello^M di truciolato^M laminato in plastica^F

パーティクル・ボード
particle board; *chipboard*
Spanplatte^F
panneau^M de particules^F
tablero^M de aglomerado^M
pannello di masonite^F

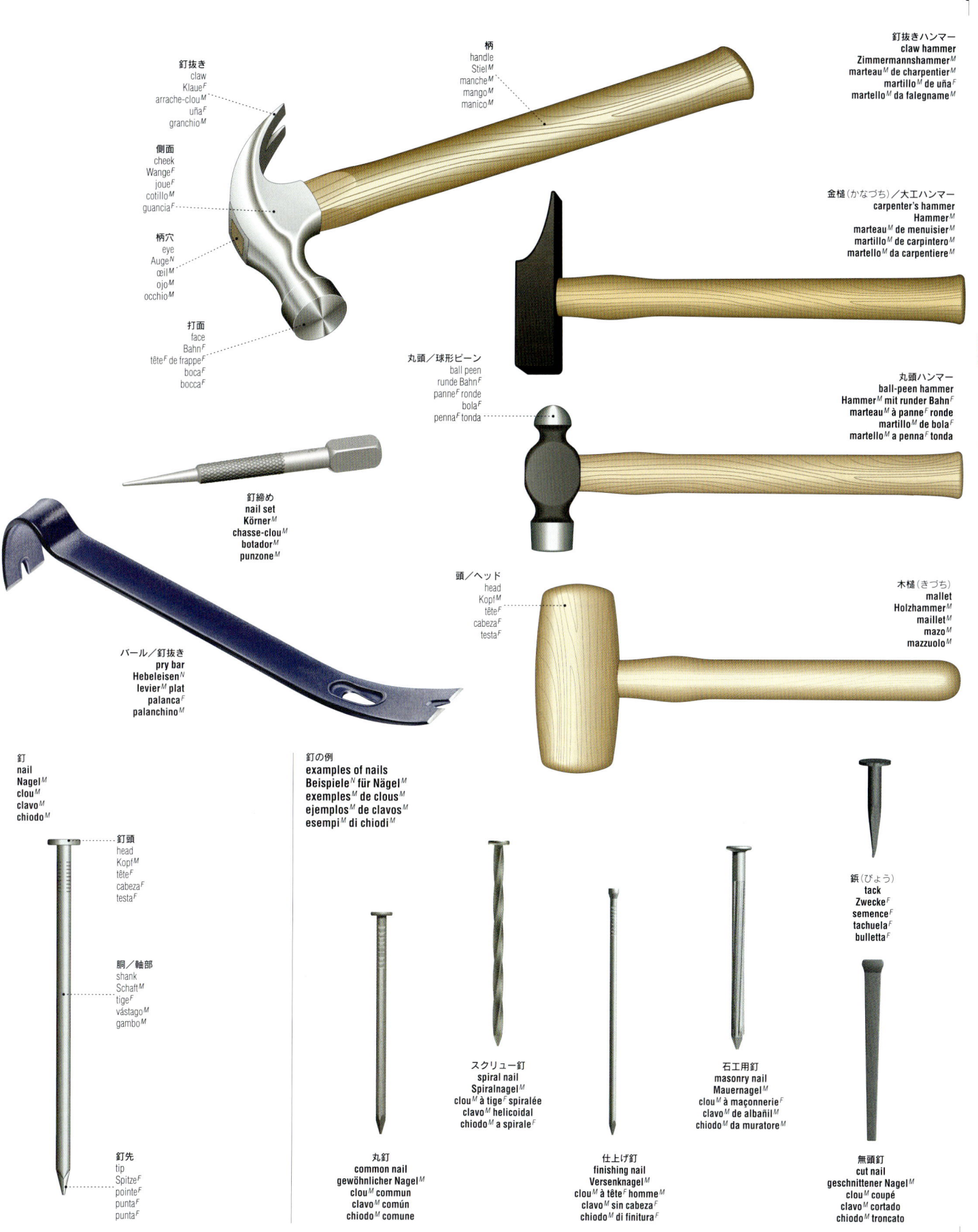

日曜大工 | DO-IT-YOURSELF
HEIMWERKEN | BRICOLAGE | BRICOLAJE | FAI DA TE

木工：釘を打つ道具

carpentry: nailing tools | Bautischlerei^F: Nagelwerkzeuge^N | menuiserie^F : outils^M pour clouer | carpintería: herramientas^F para clavar | carpenteria^F: attrezzi^M per chiodare

柄
handle
Stiel^M
manche^M
mango^M
manico^M

釘抜き
claw
Klaue^F
arrache-clou^M
uña^F
granchio^M

側面
cheek
Wange^F
joue^F
cotillo^M
guancia^F

柄穴
eye
Auge^N
œil^M
ojo^M
occhio^M

打面
face
Bahn^F
tête^F de frappe^F
boca^F
bocca^F

釘抜きハンマー
claw hammer
Zimmermannshammer^M
marteau^M de charpentier^M
martillo^M de uña^F
martello^M da falegname^M

金槌（かなづち）／大工ハンマー
carpenter's hammer
Hammer^M
marteau^M de menuisier^M
martillo^M de carpintero^M
martello^M da carpentiere^M

丸頭／球形ピーン
ball peen
runde Bahn^F
panne^F ronde
bola^F
penna^F tonda

丸頭ハンマー
ball-peen hammer
Hammer^M mit runder Bahn^F
marteau^M à panne^F ronde
martillo^M de bola^F
martello^M a penna^F tonda

釘締め
nail set
Körner^M
chasse-clou^M
botador^M
punzone^M

バール／釘抜き
pry bar
Hebeleisen^N
levier^M plat
palanca^F
palanchino^M

頭／ヘッド
head
Kopf^M
tête^F
cabeza^F
testa^F

木槌（きづち）
mallet
Holzhammer^M
maillet^M
mazo^M
mazzuolo^M

釘
nail
Nagel^M
clou^M
clavo^M
chiodo^M

釘頭
head
Kopf^M
tête^F
cabeza^F
testa^F

胴／軸部
shank
Schaft^M
tige^F
vástago^M
gambo^M

釘先
tip
Spitze^F
pointe^F
punta^F
punta^F

釘の例
examples of nails
Beispiele^N für Nägel^M
exemples^M de clous^M
ejemplos^M de clavos^M
esempi^M di chiodi^M

スクリュー釘
spiral nail
Spiralnagel^M
clou^M à tige^F spiralée
clavo^M helicoidal
chiodo^M a spirale^F

石工用釘
masonry nail
Mauernagel^M
clou^M à maçonnerie^F
clavo^M de albañil^M
chiodo^M da muratore^M

鋲（びょう）
tack
Zwecke^F
semence^F
tachuela^F
bulletta^F

丸釘
common nail
gewöhnlicher Nagel^M
clou^M commun
clavo^M común
chiodo^M comune

仕上げ釘
finishing nail
Versenknagel^M
clou^M à tête^F homme^M
clavo^M sin cabeza^F
chiodo^M di finitura^F

無頭釘
cut nail
geschnittener Nagel^M
clou^M coupé
clavo^M cortado
chiodo^M troncato

日曜大工 | DO-IT-YOURSELF
HEIMWERKEN | BRICOLAGE | BRICOLAJE | FAI DA TE

木工：ねじを締める道具

carpentry: screwing tools | Bautischlerei: Schraubwerkzeuge^N | menuiserie^F: outils^M pour visser | carpintería^F: herramientas^F para atornillar | carpenteria^F: utensili^M per avvitare

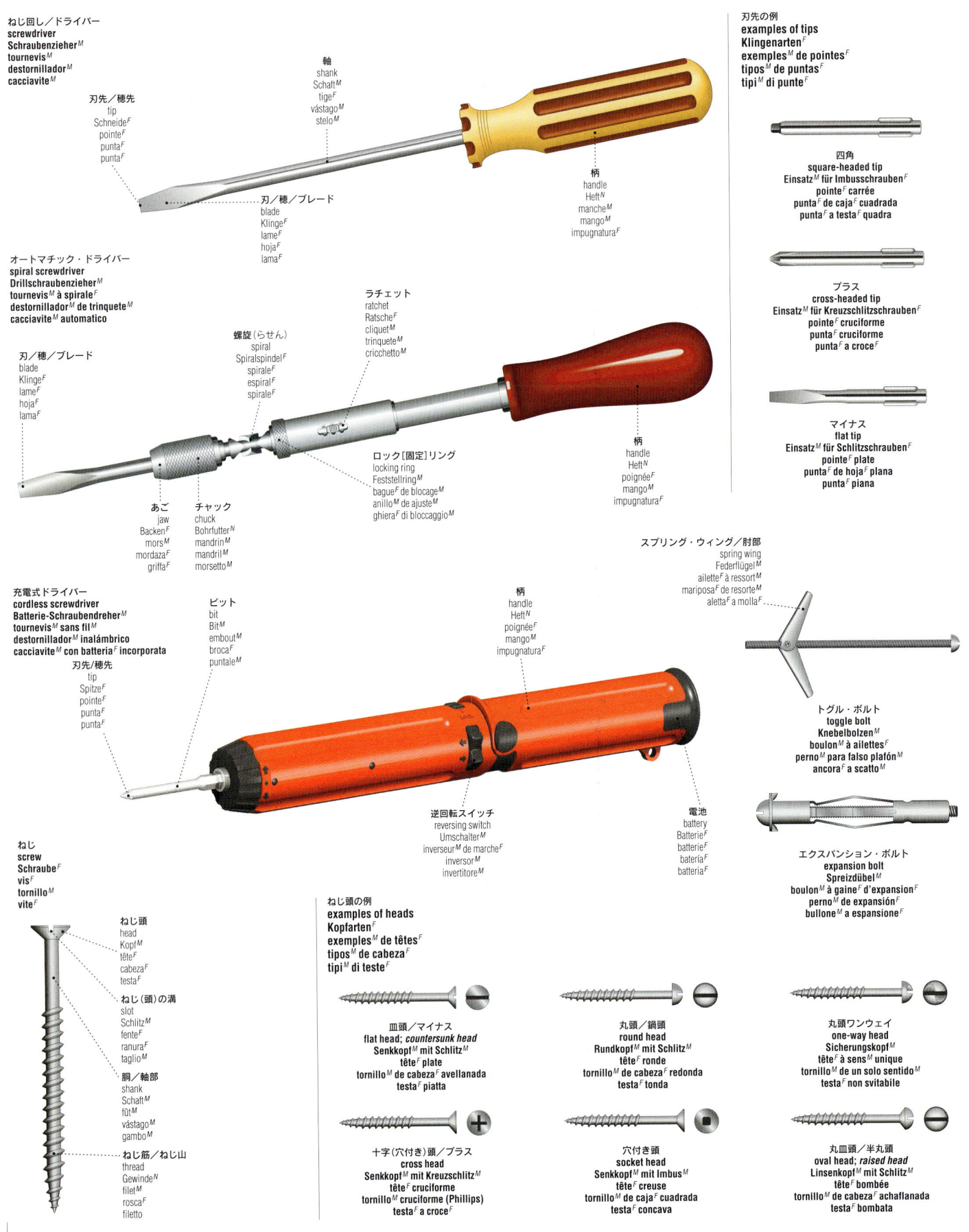

ねじ回し／ドライバー
screwdriver
Schraubenzieher^M
tournevis^M
destornillador^M
cacciavite^M

刃先／穂先 — tip / Schneide^F / pointe^F / punta^F / punta^F

軸 — shank / Schaft^M / tige^F / vástago^M / stelo^M

刃／穂／ブレード — blade / Klinge^F / lame^F / hoja^F / lama^F

柄 — handle / Heft^N / manche^M / mango^M / impugnatura^F

刃先の例
examples of tips
Klingenarten^F
exemples^M de pointes^F
tipos^M de puntas^F
tipi^M di punte^F

四角 — square-headed tip / Einsatz^M für Imbusschrauben^F / pointe^F carrée / punta^F de caja^F cuadrada / punta^F a testa^F quadra

オートマチック・ドライバー
spiral screwdriver
Drillschraubenzieher^M
tournevis^M à spirale^F
destornillador^M de trinquete^M
cacciavite^M automatico

刃／穂／ブレード — blade / Klinge^F / lame^F / hoja^F / lama^F

螺旋（らせん） — spiral / Spiralspindel^F / spirale^F / espiral^F / spirale^F

ラチェット — ratchet / Ratsche^F / cliquet^M / trinquete^M / cricchetto^M

ロック[固定]リング — locking ring / Feststellring^M / bague^F de blocage^M / anillo^M de ajuste^M / ghiera^F di bloccaggio^M

柄 — handle / Heft^N / poignée^F / mango^M / impugnatura^F

あご — jaw / Backen^F / mors^M / mordaza^M / griffa^F

チャック — chuck / Bohrfutter^N / mandrin^M / mandril^M / morsetto^M

プラス — cross-headed tip / Einsatz^M für Kreuzschlitzschrauben^F / pointe^F cruciforme / punta^F cruciforme / punta^F a croce^F

マイナス — flat tip / Einsatz^M für Schlitzschrauben^F / pointe^F plate / punta^F de hoja^F plana / punta^F piana

充電式ドライバー
cordless screwdriver
Batterie-Schraubendreher^M
tournevis^M sans fil^M
destornillador^M inalámbrico
cacciavite^M con batteria^F incorporata

ビット — bit / Bit^M / embout^M / broca^F / puntale^M

刃先／穂先 — tip / Spitze^F / pointe^F / punta^F / punta^F

柄 — handle / Heft^N / poignée^F / mango^M / impugnatura^F

逆回転スイッチ — reversing switch / Umschalter^M / inverseur^M de marche^F / inversor^M / invertitore^M

電池 — battery / Batterie^F / batterie^F / batería^F / batteria^F

スプリング・ウィング／肘部 — spring wing / Federflügel^M / ailette^F à ressort^M / mariposa^F de resorte^M / aletta^F a molla^F

トグル・ボルト — toggle bolt / Knebelbolzen^M / boulon^M à ailettes^F / perno^M para falso plafón^M / ancora^F a scatto^M

エクスパンション・ボルト — expansion bolt / Spreizdübel^M / boulon^M à gaine^F d'expansion^F / perno^M de expansión^F / bullone^M a espansione^F

ねじ
screw
Schraube^F
vis^F
tornillo^M
vite^F

ねじ頭 — head / Kopf^M / tête^F / cabeza^F / testa^F

ねじ(頭)の溝 — slot / Schlitz^M / fente^F / ranura^F / taglio^M

胴／軸部 — shank / Schaft^M / fût^M / vástago^M / gambo^M

ねじ筋／ねじ山 — thread / Gewinde^N / filet^M / rosca^F / filetto^M

ねじ頭の例
examples of heads
Kopfarten^F
exemples^M de têtes^F
tipos^M de cabeza^F
tipi^M di teste^F

皿頭／マイナス — flat head; *countersunk head* / Senkkopf^M mit Schlitz^M / tête^F plate / tornillo^M de cabeza^F avellanada / testa^F piatta

丸頭／鍋頭 — round head / Rundkopf^M mit Schlitz^M / tête^F ronde / tornillo^M de cabeza^F redonda / testa^F tonda

丸頭ワンウェイ — one-way head / Sicherungskopf^M / tête^F à sens^M unique / tornillo^M de un solo sentido^M / testa^F non svitabile

十字(穴付き)頭／プラス — cross head / Senkkopf^M mit Kreuzschlitz^M / tête^F cruciforme / tornillo^M cruciforme (Phillips) / testa^F a croce^F

穴付き頭 — socket head / Senkkopf^M mit Imbus^M / tête^F creuse / tornillo^M de caja^F cuadrada / testa^F concava

丸皿頭／半丸頭 — oval head; *raised head* / Linsenkopf^M mit Schlitz^M / tête^F bombée / tornillo^M de cabeza^F achaflanada / testa^F bombata

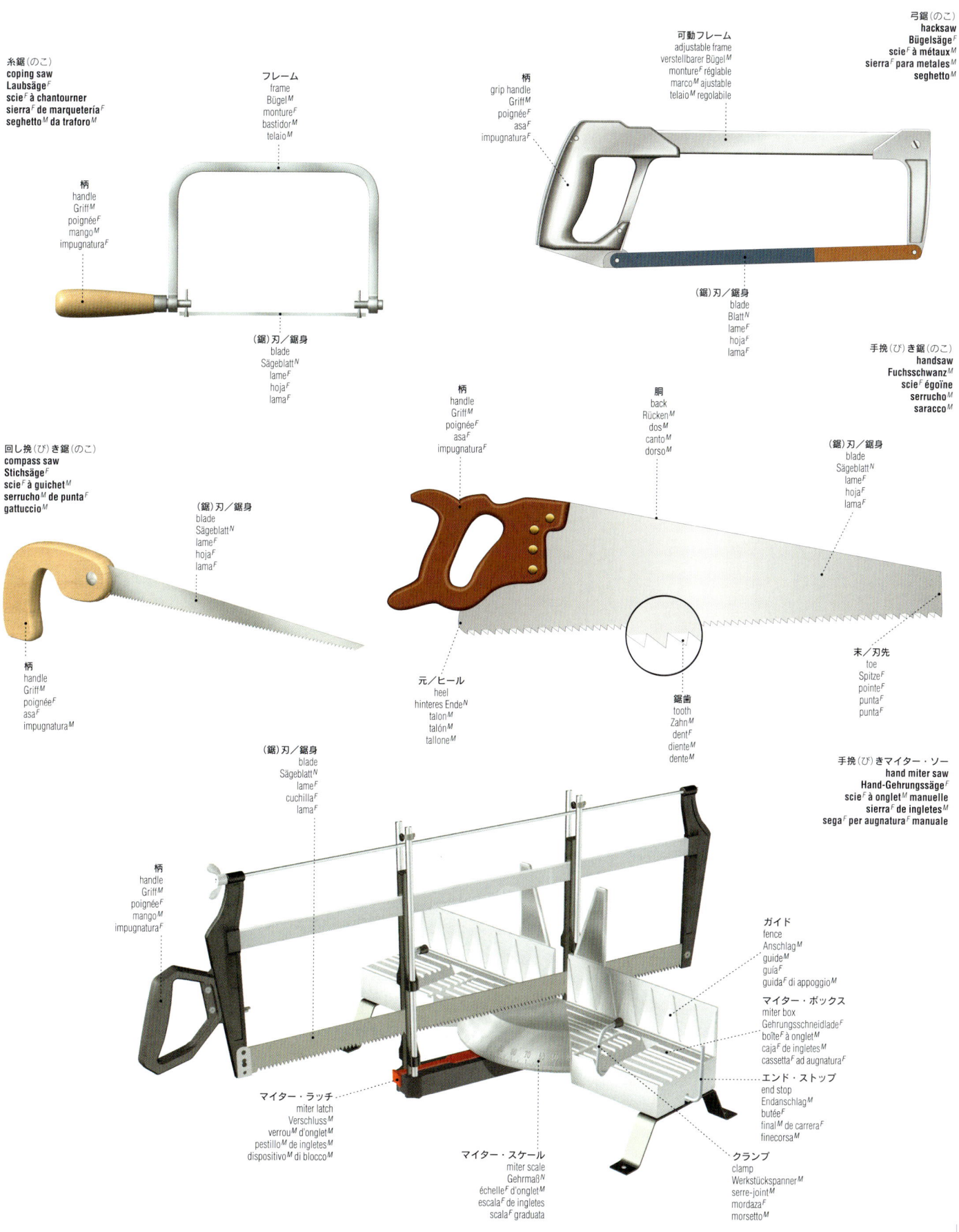

日曜大工 | DO-IT-YOURSELF
HEIMWERKEN | BRICOLAGE | BRICOLAJE | FAI DA TE

木工：木材を切る道具

carpentry: sawing tools | Bautischlerei^F: Sägewerkzeuge^N | menuiserie^F: outils^M pour scier | carpintería: herramientas^F para serrar | carpenteria: utensili^M per segare

糸鋸（のこ）
coping saw
Laubsäge^F
scie^F à chantourner
sierra^F de marquetería^F
seghetto^M da traforo^M

柄
handle
Griff^M
poignée^F
mango^M
impugnatura^F

フレーム
frame
Bügel^M
monture^F
bastidor^M
telaio^M

（鋸）刃／鋸身
blade
Sägeblatt^N
lame^F
hoja^F
lama^F

弓鋸（のこ）
hacksaw
Bügelsäge^F
scie^F à métaux^M
sierra^F para metales^M
seghetto^M

可動フレーム
adjustable frame
verstellbarer Bügel^M
monture^F réglable
marco^M ajustable
telaio^M regolabile

柄
grip handle
Griff^M
poignée^F
asa^F
impugnatura^F

（鋸）刃／鋸身
blade
Blatt^N
lame^F
hoja^F
lama^F

手挽（び）き鋸（のこ）
handsaw
Fuchsschwanz^M
scie^F égoïne
serrucho^M
saracco^M

回し挽（び）き鋸（のこ）
compass saw
Stichsäge^F
scie^F à guichet^M
serrucho^M de punta^F
gattuccio^M

（鋸）刃／鋸身
blade
Sägeblatt^N
lame^F
hoja^F
lama^F

柄
handle
Griff^M
poignée^F
asa^F
impugnatura^M

柄
handle
Griff^M
poignée^F
asa^F
impugnatura^F

胴
back
Rücken^M
dos^M
canto^M
dorso^M

（鋸）刃／鋸身
blade
Sägeblatt^N
lame^F
hoja^F
lama^F

元／ヒール
heel
hinteres Ende^N
talon^M
talón^M
tallone^M

鋸歯
tooth
Zahn^M
dent^F
diente^M
dente^M

末／刃先
toe
Spitze^F
pointe^F
punta^F
punta^F

手挽（び）きマイター・ソー
hand miter saw
Hand-Gehrungssäge^F
scie^F à onglet^M manuelle
sierra^F de ingletes^M
sega^F per augnatura^F manuale

柄
handle
Griff^M
poignée^F
mango^M
impugnatura^F

（鋸）刃／鋸身
blade
Sägeblatt^N
lame^F
cuchilla^F
lama^F

ガイド
fence
Anschlag^M
guide^M
guía^F
guida^F di appoggio^M

マイター・ボックス
miter box
Gehrungsschneidlade^F
boîte^F à onglet^M
caja^F de ingletes^M
cassetta^F ad augnatura^F

エンド・ストップ
end stop
Endanschlag^M
butée^F
final^M de carrera^F
finecorsa^F

マイター・ラッチ
miter latch
Verschluss^M
verrou^M d'onglet^M
pestillo^M de ingletes^M
dispositivo^M di blocco^M

マイター・スケール
miter scale
Gehrmaß^N
échelle^F d'onglet^M
escala^F de ingletes^M
scala^F graduata

クランプ
clamp
Werkstückspanner^M
serre-joint^M
mordaza^F
morsetto^M

日曜大工 / DO-IT-YOURSELF
HEIMWERKEN | BRICOLAGE | BRICOLAJE | FAI DA TE

木工：木材を切る道具

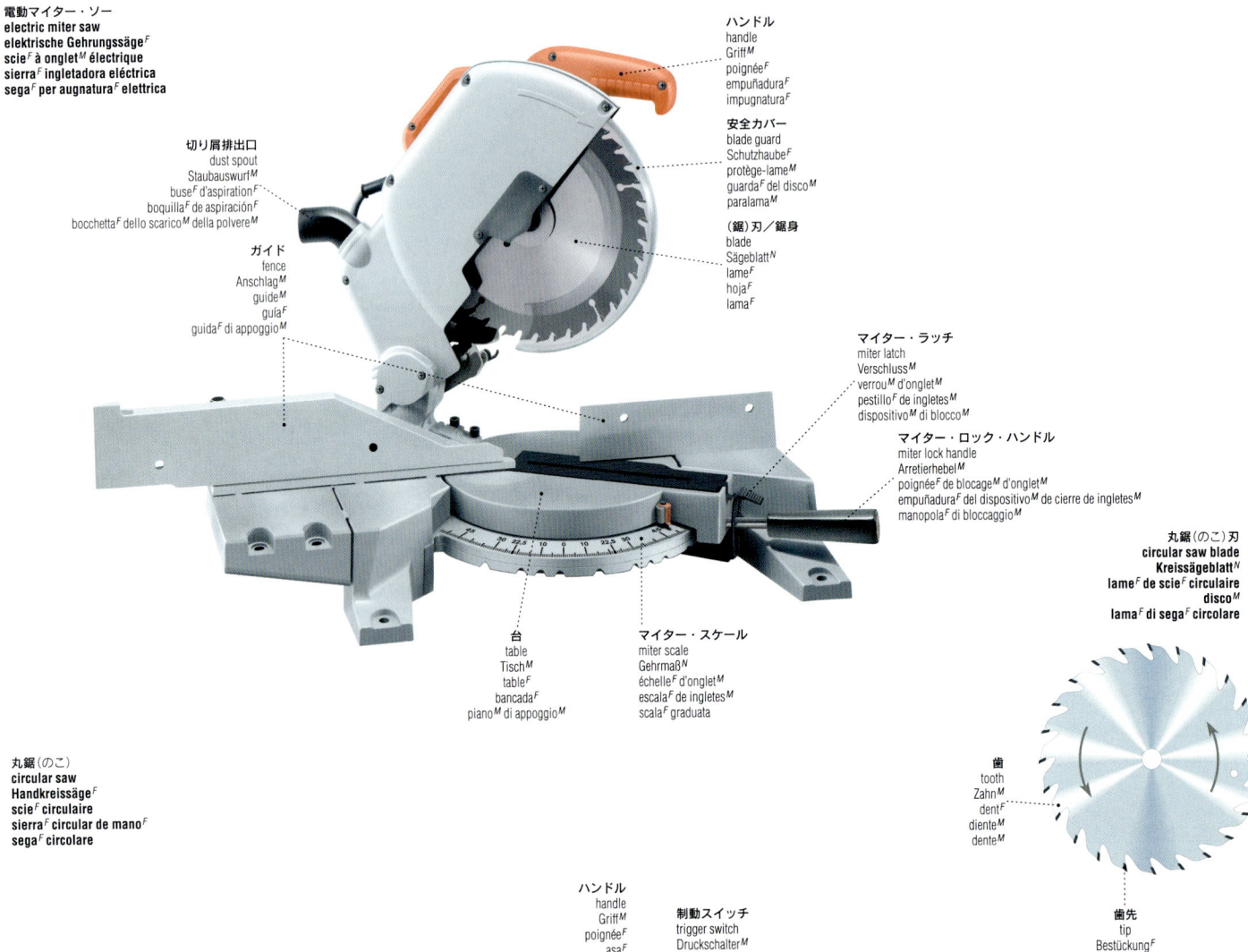

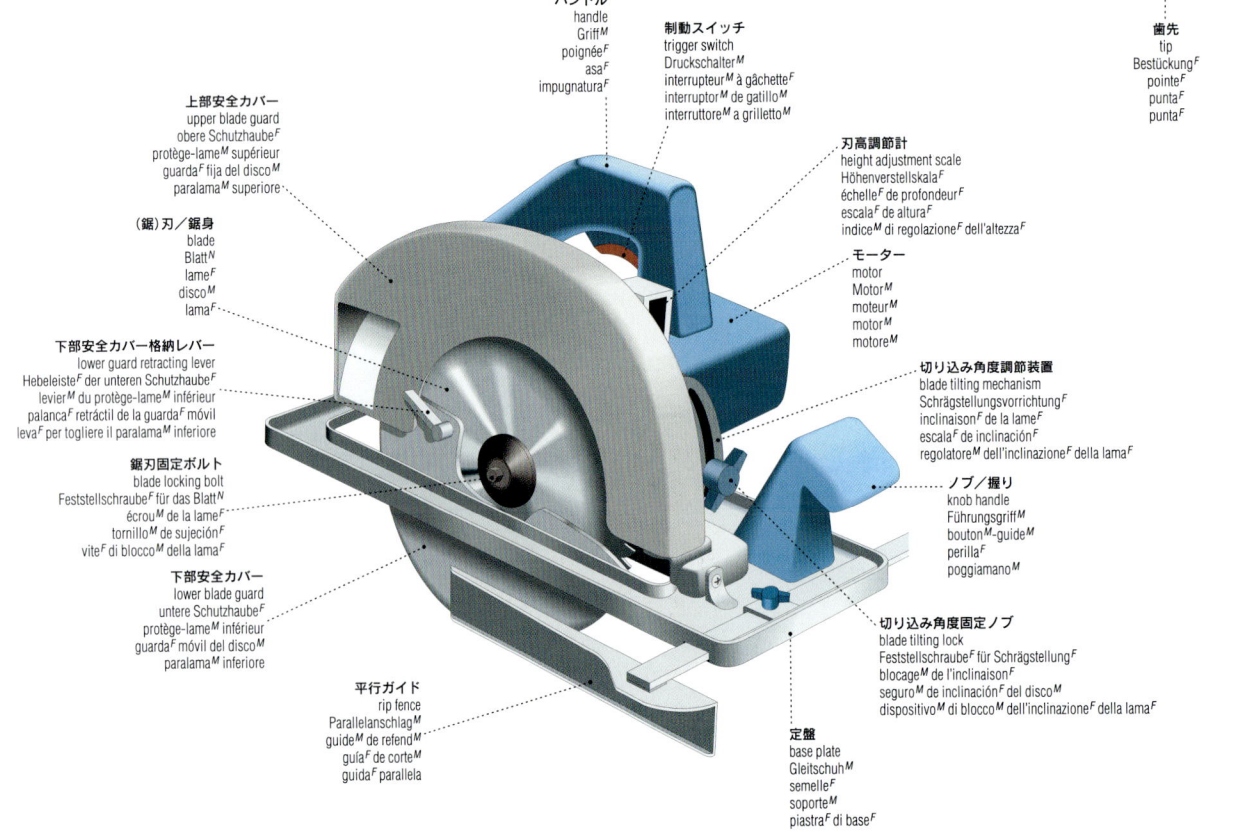

日本語 | 英語 | ドイツ語 | フランス語 | スペイン語 | イタリア語

電動マイター・ソー
electric miter saw
elektrische Gehrungssäge^F
scie^F à onglet^M électrique
sierra^F ingletadora eléctrica
sega^F per augnatura^F elettrica

切り屑排出口
dust spout
Staubauswurf^M
buse^F d'aspiration^F
boquilla^F de aspiración
bocchetta^F dello scarico^M della polvere^M

ガイド
fence
Anschlag^M
guide^M
guía^F
guida^F di appoggio^M

ハンドル
handle
Griff^M
poignée^F
empuñadura^F
impugnatura^F

安全カバー
blade guard
Schutzhaube^F
protège-lame^M
guarda^F del disco^M
paralama^M

(鋸)刃／鋸身
blade
Sägeblatt^N
lame^F
hoja^F
lama^F

マイター・ラッチ
miter latch
Verschluss^M
verrou^M d'onglet^M
pestillo^F de ingletes^M
dispositivo^M di blocco^M

マイター・ロック・ハンドル
miter lock handle
Arretierhebel^M
poignée^F de blocage^M d'onglet^M
empuñadura^F del dispositivo^M de cierre de ingletes^M
manopola^F di bloccaggio^M

台
table
Tisch^M
table^F
bancada^F
piano^M di appoggio^M

マイター・スケール
miter scale
Gehrmaß^N
échelle^F d'onglet^M
escala^F de ingletes^M
scala^F graduata

丸鋸(のこ)刃
circular saw blade
Kreissägeblatt^N
lame^F de scie^F circulaire
disco^M
lama^F di sega^F circolare

歯
tooth
Zahn^M
dent^F
diente^M
dente^M

歯先
tip
Bestückung^F
pointe^F
punta^F
punta^F

丸鋸(のこ)
circular saw
Handkreissäge^F
scie^F circulaire
sierra^F circular de mano^F
sega^F circolare

上部安全カバー
upper blade guard
obere Schutzhaube^F
protège-lame^M supérieur
guarda^F fija del disco^M
paralama^M superiore

(鋸)刃／鋸身
blade
Blatt^N
lame^F
disco^M
lama^F

下部安全カバー格納レバー
lower guard retracting lever
Hebeleiste^F der unteren Schutzhaube^F
levier^M du protège-lame^M inférieur
palanca^F retráctil de la guarda^F móvil
leva^F per togliere il paralama^M inferiore

鋸刃固定ボルト
blade locking bolt
Feststellschraube^F für das Blatt^N
écrou^M de la lame^F
tornillo^M de sujeción^F
vite^F di blocco^M della lama^F

下部安全カバー
lower blade guard
untere Schutzhaube^F
protège-lame^M inférieur
guarda^F móvil del disco^M
paralama^M inferiore

平行ガイド
rip fence
Parallelanschlag^M
guide^M de refend^M
guía^F de corte^M
guida^F parallela

ハンドル
handle
Griff^M
poignée^F
asa^F
impugnatura^F

制動スイッチ
trigger switch
Druckschalter^M
interrupteur^M à gâchette^F
interruptor^M de gatillo^M
interruttore^M a grilletto^M

刃高調節計
height adjustment scale
Höhenverstellskala^F
échelle^F de profondeur^F
escala^F de altura^F
indice^M di regolazione^F dell'altezza^F

モーター
motor
Motor^M
moteur^M
motor^M
motore^M

切り込み角度調節装置
blade tilting mechanism
Schrägstellungsvorrichtung^F
inclinaison^F de la lame^F
escala^F de inclinación^F
regolatore^M dell'inclinazione^F della lama^F

ノブ／握り
knob handle
Führungsgriff^M
bouton^M-guide^M
perilla^F
poggiamano^M

切り込み角度固定ノブ
blade tilting lock
Feststellschraube^F für Schrägstellung^F
blocage^M de l'inclinaison^F
seguro^M de inclinación^F del disco^M
dispositivo^M di blocco^M dell'inclinazione^F della lama^F

定盤
base plate
Gleitschuh^M
semelle^F
soporte^M
piastra^F di base^F

日曜大工・園芸

304

日曜大工 | DO-IT-YOURSELF
HEIMWERKEN | BRICOLAGE | BRICOLAJE | FAI DA TE

木工：木材を切る道具

ジグ・ソー
jig saw
elektrische Stichsäge^F
scie^F sauteuse
sierra^F de calar
seghetto^M alternativo

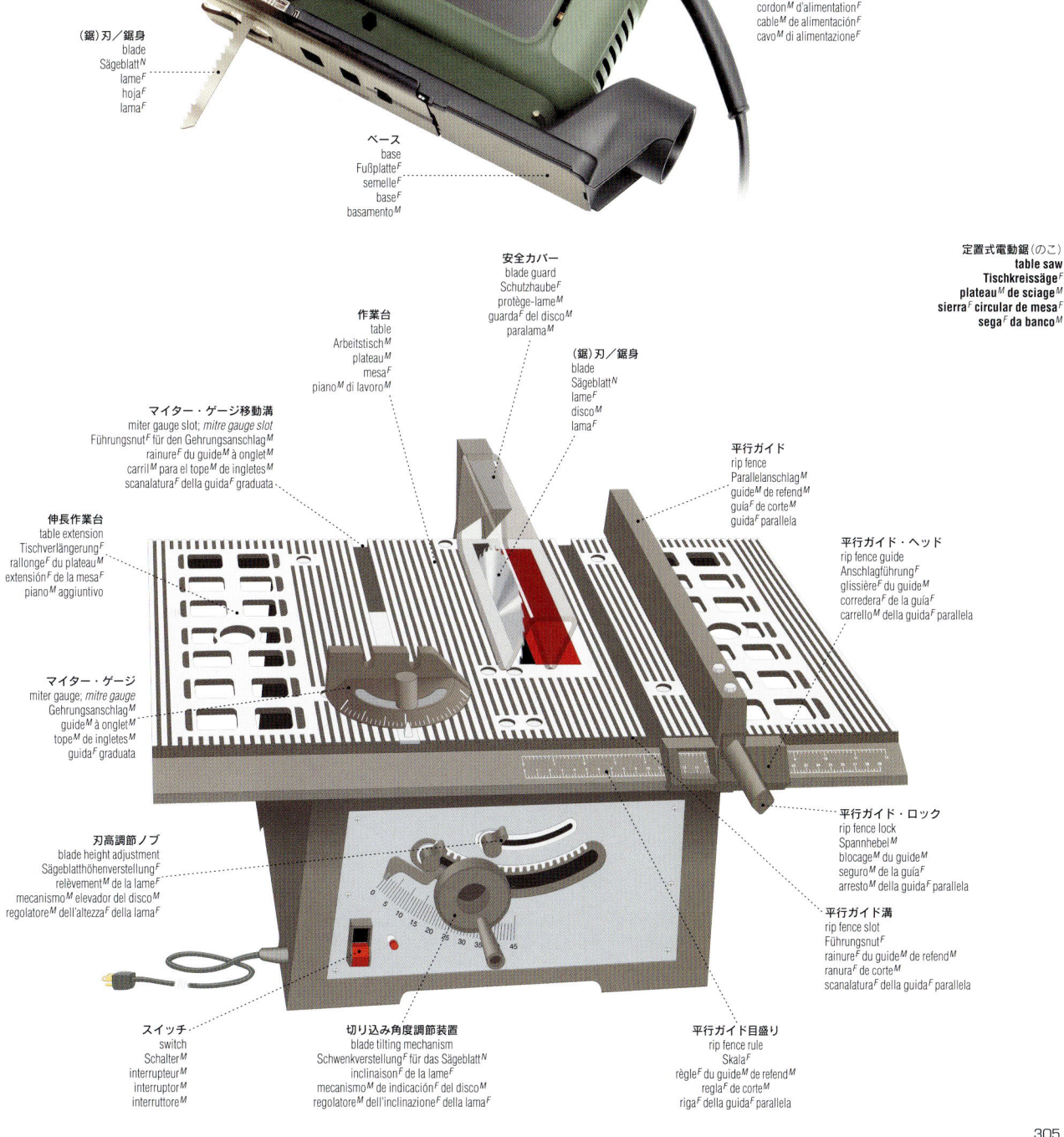

速度切り替えスイッチ
speed selector switch
Hubzahlvorwahl^F
sélecteur^M de vitesse^F
interruptor^M selector de velocidad^F
selettore^M di velocità^F

制動スイッチ
trigger switch
Druckschalter^M
interrupteur^M à gâchette^F
interruptor^M de gatillo^M
interruttore^M a grilletto^M

オービタル・アクション・セレクター
orbital-action selector
Pendelhub-Einstellung^F
sélecteur^M d'inclinaison^F de la lame^F
selector^M de movimiento^M orbital
selettore^M del movimento^M orbitale

チップ・カバー
chip cover
Späneschutz^M
déflecteur^M de copeaux^M
protector^M contra virutas^F
paratrucioli^M

（鋸）刃／鋸身
blade
Sägeblatt^N
lame^F
hoja^F
lama^F

ロック・ボタン
lock-on button
Feststellknopf^M
bouton^M de verrouillage^M de l'interrupteur^M
botón^M de bloqueo
pulsante^M di aggancio

ハンドル
handle
Griff^M
poignée^F
empuñadura^F
impugnatura^F

電源コード
power cord
Anschlusskabel^M
cordon^M d'alimentation^F
cable^M de alimentación^F
cavo^M di alimentazione^F

ベース
base
Fußplatte^F
semelle^F
base^F
basamento^M

定置式電動鋸（のこ）
table saw
Tischkreissäge^F
plateau^M de sciage^M
sierra^F circular de mesa^F
sega^F da banco^M

安全カバー
blade guard
Schutzhaube^F
protège-lame^M
guarda^F del disco^M
paralama^F

作業台
table
Arbeitstisch^M
plateau^M
mesa^F
piano^M di lavoro^M

（鋸）刃／鋸身
blade
Sägeblatt^N
lame^F
disco^M
lama^F

マイター・ゲージ移動溝
miter gauge slot; *mitre gauge slot*
Führungsnut^F für den Gehrungsanschlag^M
rainure^F du guide^M à onglet^M
carril^M para el tope^M de ingletes^M
scanalatura^F della guida^F graduata

伸長作業台
table extension
Tischverlängerung^F
rallonge^F du plateau^M
extensión^F de la mesa^F
piano^M aggiuntivo

マイター・ゲージ
miter gauge; *mitre gauge*
Gehrungsanschlag^M
guide^M à onglet^M
tope^M de ingletes^M
guida^F graduata

刃高調節ノブ
blade height adjustment
Sägeblatthöhenverstellung^F
relèvement^M de la lame^F
mecanismo^M elevador del disco^M
regolatore^M dell'altezza^F della lama^F

平行ガイド
rip fence
Parallelanschlag^M
guide^M de refend^M
guía^F de corte^M
guida^F parallela

平行ガイド・ヘッド
rip fence guide
Anschlagführung^F
glissière^F du guide^M
corredera^F de la guía^F
carrello^M della guida^F parallela

平行ガイド・ロック
rip fence lock
Spannhebel^M
blocage^M du guide^M
seguro^M de la guía^F
arresto^M della guida^F parallela

平行ガイド溝
rip fence slot
Führungsnut^F
rainure^F du guide^M de refend^M
ranura^F de corte^M
scanalatura^F della guida^F parallela

スイッチ
switch
Schalter^M
interrupteur^M
interruptor^M
interruttore^M

切り込み角度調節装置
blade tilting mechanism
Schwenkverstellung^F für das Sägeblatt^N
inclinaison^F de la lame^F
mecanismo^M de indicación del disco^M
regolatore^M dell'inclinazione^F della lama^F

平行ガイド目盛り
rip fence rule
Skala^F
règle^F du guide^M de refend^M
regla^F de corte^M
riga^F della guida^F parallela

日曜大工・園芸

305

日曜大工 | DO-IT-YOURSELF
HEIMWERKEN | BRICOLAGE | BRICOLAJE | FAI DA TE

木工：穴を空ける道具

日本語 | 英語 | ドイツ語 | フランス語 | スペイン語 | イタリア語

carpentry: drilling tools | Bautischlerei^F: Bohrwerkzeuge^N | menuiserie^F : outils^M pour percer | carpintería^F : herramientas^F percutoras | carpenteria^F: attrezzi^M per trapanare

充電式ドリル・ドライバー
cordless drill-driver
Akku^M-Bohrschrauber^M
perceuse^F-visseuse^F sans fil^M
taladro^M percutor inalámbrico
trapano^M senza fili^M

キーレス・チャック
keyless chuck
Schnellspannbohrfutter^N
mandrin^M autoserrant
mandril^M de sujeción^F
mandrino^M autoserrante

速度切り替えスイッチ
speed selector switch
Drehzahlschalter^M
sélecteur de vitesse^F de rotation^F
selector^M de velocidad^F
selettore^M di velocità^F

スクリュードライバー・ビット
screwdriver bit
Schrauberbit^M
embout^M de vissage^M
broca^F de atornillado
mecchia^F

トルク調整カラー
torque adjustment collar
Drehmoment^M-Einstellring^M
bague^F de réglage^M du couple^M de serrage^M
anillo^M de reglaje^M del par^M de apriete^M
anello^M di regolazione^F della coppia^F di serraggio^M

充電池
battery pack
Akku^M
batterie^F
batería^F
batteria^F

制動スイッチ
trigger switch
Druckschalter^M
interrupteur^M à gâchette^F
interruptor^M de gatillo^M
interruttore^M a grilletto^M

逆回転スイッチ
reversing switch
Umschalter^M
inverseur^M de marche^F
inversor^M
invertitore^M

充電池
battery pack
Akku^M
batterie^F
batería^F
batteria^F

充電器
charger
Ladegerät^N
chargeur^M
cargador^M
caricabatteria^M

電気ドリル
electric drill
elektrische Bohrmaschine^F
perceuse^F électrique
taladro^M eléctrico
trapano^M elettrico

注意書き
warning plate
Sicherheitshinweisschild^N
plaque^F d'instructions^F
placa^F de advertencias^F
targhetta^F delle avvertenze^F

銘板
name plate
Typenschild^N
plaque^F signalétique
placa^F de especificaciones^F
targhetta^F del costruttore^M

チャック・キー
chuck key
Bohrfutterschlüssel^M
clé^F de mandrin^M
llave^F del mandril^M
chiave^F del mandrino^M

ハウジング
housing
Gehäuse^N
boîtier^M
cárter^M
carcassa^F

スイッチ・ロック
switch lock
Feststellknopf^M
blocage^M de l'interrupteur^M
seguro^M del interruptor^M
dispositivo^M di blocco dell'interruttore^M

チャック
chuck
Bohrfutter^N
mandrin^M
mandril^M
mandrino^M

制動スイッチ
trigger switch
Druckschalter^M
interrupteur^M à gâchette^F
interruptor^M de gatillo^M
interruttore^M a grilletto^M

ピストル型グリップ
pistol grip handle
Pistolengriff^M
poignée^F-pistolet^M
emango^M
impugnatura^F a pistola^F

あご／くわえ部
jaw
Backen^F
mors^M
mordaza^F
griffa^F

補助ハンドル
auxiliary handle
zusätzlicher Griff^M
poignée^F auxiliaire
mango^M auxiliar
impugnatura^F laterale

プラグ
plug
Stecker^M
fiche^F
enchufe^M
spina^F

ケーブル・スリーブ
cable sleeve
Kabelmuffe^F
manchon^M de câble^M
protector^M del cable^M
manicotto^M del cavo^M

電気ケーブル
cable
Kabel^N
câble^M
cable^M
cavo^M

ビットとドリルの例
examples of bits and drills
Beispiele^N für Bits^M und Bohrer^M
exemples^M de mèches^F et de forets^M
ejemplos^M de brocas^F y barrenas^F
esempi^M di mecchie^F e punte^F da trapano^M

ねじれ錐
twist bit
Spiralbohrer^M
mèche^F hélicoïdale
broca^F helicoidal
mecchia^F elicoidale

軸
shank
Schaft^M
queue^F
talón^M
codolo^M

螺旋（らせん）形溝
flute
Spangang^M
goujure^F
canal^M
scanalatura^F

本体
body
Bohrkörper^M
corps^M
cuerpo^M
corpo^M

切れ刃
fluted land
Rücken^M
lèvre^F
lomo^M con canal^M
faccetta^F scanalata

ランド
land
Fase^F
listel^M
borde^M del lomo^M
faccetta

案内ねじ
lead screw
Zentrierspitze^F
pointe^F de centrage^M
borde^M de la punta^F
punta^F di centratura^F

螺旋（らせん）錐
solid center auger bit
Schneckenbohrer^M
mèche^F hélicoïdale à âme^F centrale
broca^F helicoidal central
mecchia^F a tortiglione^M

軸
shank
Schaft^M
queue^F
talón^M
codolo^M

ねじれ
twist
Spirale^F
torsade^F
torsión^F
elica^F

尖端
spur
Vorschneider^M
traçoir^M
espolón^M
tagliente^M

案内ねじ
lead screw
Zentrierspitze^F
pointe^F de centrage^M
tornillo^M guía
punta^F di centratura^F

メーソンリー・ドリル
masonry drill
Steinbohrer^M
foret^M de maçonnerie^F
barrena^F de muro^M
punta^F da muro^M

ねじれ錐
twist drill
Spiralbohrer^M
foret^M hélicoïdal
broca^F helicoidal
punta^F elicoidale

スペード・ビット
spade bit
Flachfräsbohrer^M
mèche^F à centre^M plat
broca^F de pala^F
mecchia^F a lancia

二重ねじれ錐
double-twist auger bit
Schlangenbohrer^M mit doppeltem Gewindegang
mèche^F hélicoïdale à double torsade^F
broca^F salomónica de canal^M angosto
mecchia^F a doppia elica^F

日曜大工 | DO-IT-YOURSELF
HEIMWERKEN | BRICOLAGE | BRICOLAJE | FAI DA TE

木工：穴を空ける道具

ハンド・ドリル
hand drill
Handbohrer^M
chignole^F
taladro^M de mano
trapano^M a mano

ターニング[回転]ハンドル — turning handle / Kurbel^F / manivelle^F / manivela^F / manovella^F

サイド[補助]ハンドル — side handle / Seitengriff^M / poignée^F latérale / perilla^F / impugnatura^F laterale

握り — main handle / Hauptgriff^M / poignée^F supérieure / mango^M / impugnatura^F principale

あご／くわえ部 — jaw / Backe^F / mors^M / mordaza^F / griffa^F

ドライブ・ホイール／傘歯車 — drive wheel / Stirnzahnrad^N / roue^F d'engrenage^M / cremallera^F / ruota^F dell'ingranaggio^M

刃先／穂先／錐先 — drill / Bohrer^M / foret^M / broca^F / punta^F

チャック — chuck / Bohrfutter^N / mandrin^M / mandril^M / mandrino^M

ピニオン・ギア／傘歯車 — pinion / Ritzel^N / pignon^M / piñón^M / pignone^M

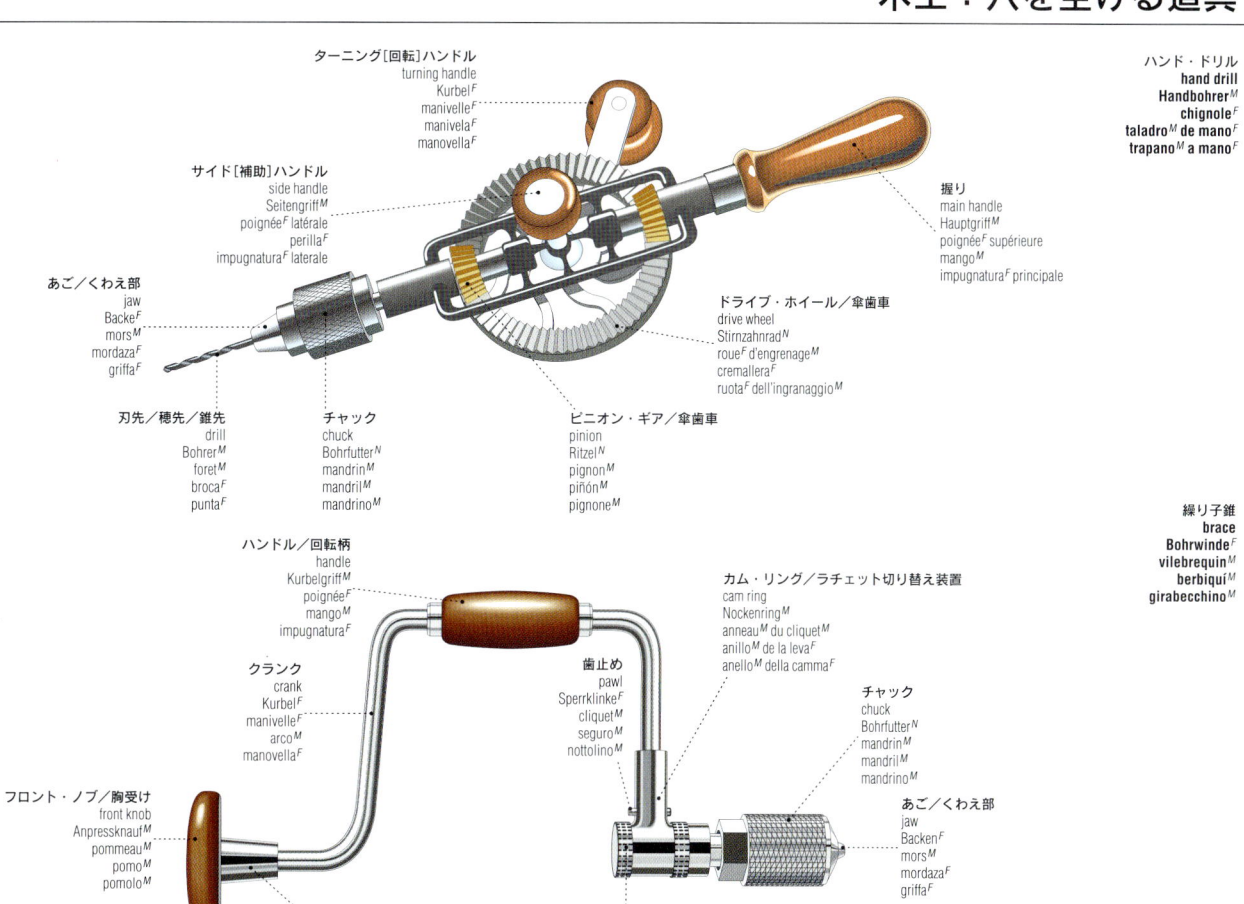

繰り子錐
brace
Bohrwinde^F
vilebrequin^M
berbiquí^M
girabecchino^M

ハンドル／回転柄 — handle / Kurbelgriff^M / poignée^F / mango^M / impugnatura^F

カム・リング／ラチェット切り替え装置 — cam ring / Nockenring^M / anneau^M du cliquet^M / anillo^M de la leva^F / anello^M della camma^F

クランク — crank / Kurbel^F / manivelle^F / arco^M / manovella^F

歯止め — pawl / Sperrklinke^F / cliquet^M / seguro^M / nottolino^M

チャック — chuck / Bohrfutter^N / mandrin^M / mandril^M / mandrino^M

フロント・ノブ／胸受け — front knob / Anpressknauf^M / pommeau^M / pomo^M / pomolo^M

あご／くわえ部 — jaw / Backen^F / mors^M / mordaza^F / griffa^F

軸受け — quill / Scheide^F / fourreau^M / manguito^M / manicotto^M cavo^M

ラチェット — ratchet / Knarre^F / rochet^M / trinquete^M / cricco^M

ボール盤
drill press
Ständerbohrmaschine^F
perceuse^F à colonne^F
taladro^M vertical
trapano^M a colonna^F

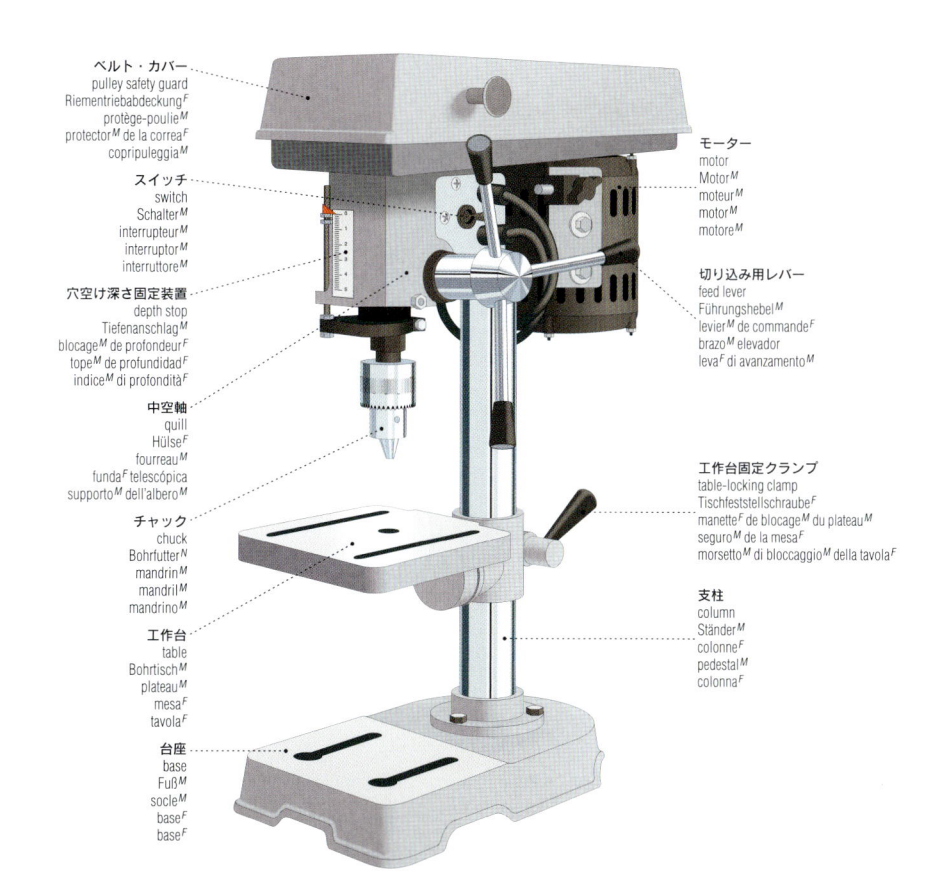

ベルト・カバー — pulley safety guard / Riementriebabdeckung^F / protège-poulie^M / protector^M de la correa^F / copripuleggia^F

スイッチ — switch / Schalter^M / interrupteur^M / interruptor^M / interruttore^M

穴空け深さ固定装置 — depth stop / Tiefenanschlag^M / blocage^M de profondeur^F / tope^M de profundidad^F / indice^M di profondità^F

中空軸 — quill / Hülse^F / fourreau^M / funda^F telescópica / supporto^M dell'albero^M

チャック — chuck / Bohrfutter^N / mandrin^M / mandril^M / mandrino^M

工作台 — table / Bohrtisch^M / plateau^M / mesa^F / tavola^F

モーター — motor / Motor^M / moteur^M / motor^M / motore^M

切り込み用レバー — feed lever / Führungshebel^M / levier^M de commande^F / brazo^M elevador / leva^F di avanzamento^M

工作台固定クランプ — table-locking clamp / Tischfeststellschraube^F / manette^F de blocage^M du plateau^M / seguro^M de la mesa^F / morsetto^M di bloccaggio^M della tavola^F

支柱 — column / Ständer^M / colonne^F / pedestal^M / colonna^F

台座 — base / Fuß^M / socle^M / base^F / base^F

307

日曜大工 | DO-IT-YOURSELF
HEIMWERKEN | BRICOLAGE | BRICOLAJE | FAI DA TE

木工：成形する道具

carpentry: shaping tools | Bautischlerei^F: Formwerkzeuge^N | menuiserie^F: outils^M pour façonner | carpintería^F: herramientas^F de perfilado^M | carpenteria^F: attrezzi^M per sagomare

日本語 | 英語 | ドイツ語 | フランス語 | スペイン語 | イタリア語

アングル・グラインダー
angle grinder
Winkelschleifer^M
meuleuse^F d'angle^M
amoladora^F de ángulo
molatrice^F angolare

スピンドル・ロック・ボタン
spindle lock button
Spindelarretierknopf^M
bouton^M de blocage^M de l'arbre^M
botón^M de bloqueo^M del eje^M
pulsante^M blocca-mandrino^M

電源コード
power cord
Netzkabel^N
cordon^M d'alimentation^F
cordón^M de alimentación^F
cavo^M d'alimentazione^F

スイッチ
switch
Schalter^M
interrupteur^M
interruptor^M
interruttore^M

サイド・ハンドル
side handle
Zusatzgriff^M
poignée^F latérale
empuñadura^F lateral
impugnatura^F laterale

研削砥石（といし）／砥石車
grinding wheel
Schleifscheibe^F
meule^F
muela^F
mola^F

砥石カバー
wheel guard
Schutzhaube^F
carter^M de meule^F
cárter^M del disco^M
carter^M della mola^F

ランダム・オービット・サンダー
random orbit sander
Exzenterschleifer^M
ponceuse^F excentrique
lijadora^F excéntrica
smerigliatrice^F eccentrica

ハウジング
housing
Gehäuse^N
boîtier^M
armazón^M
carcassa^F

ロック・ボタン
lock-on button
Arretierknopf^M
bouton^M de blocage^M
botón^M de enclavamiento^M
pulsante^M di arresto^M

ハンドル
handle
Griff^M
poignée^F
empuñadura^F
impugnatura^F

電源コード
power cord
Netzkabel^N
cordon^M d'alimentation^F
cordón^M de alimentación^F
cavo^M d'alimentazione^F

サンディング・パッド
sanding pad
Schleifteller^M
plateau^M de ponçage^M
plato^M lijador
supporto^M del disco^M abrasivo

ダスト・バッグ
dust canister
Staubbehälter^M
boîte^F à poussière^F
caja^F colectora de polvo^M
raccoglipolvere^M

サンディング・ディスク
sanding disc
Schleifblatt^N
disque^M abrasif
disco^M abrasivo
disco^M abrasivo

制動スイッチ
trigger switch
Druckschalter^M
interrupteur^M à gâchette^F
interruptor^M de gatillo^M
interruttore^M a grilletto^M

研削砥石（といし）／砥石車
grinding wheel
Schleifscheibe^F
meule^F
muela^F
mola^F

サンディング・ディスク
sanding disc
Schleifblatt^N
disque^M abrasif
disco^M abrasivo
disco^M abrasivo

サンド・ペーパー
sand paper
Schleifpapier^N
papier^M de verre^M
lija^F
carta^F vetrata

ビットの例
examples of bits
Beispiele^N für Fräser^M
exemples^M de fraises^F
ejemplos^M de fresas^F
esempi^M di frese^F

ルーター／溝鉋（かんな）
router
Oberfräse^F
défonceuse^F
fresadora^F
fresatrice^F verticale

モーター
motor
Motor^M
moteur^M
motor^M
motore^M

ヘッド
head
Kopf^M
tête^F
cabeza^F
testa^F

スイッチ
switch
Schalter^M
interrupteur^M
interruptor^M
interruttore^M

コード・スリーブ
cord sleeve; flex sleeve
Kabelmantel^M
manchon^M du cordon^M
protector^M del cable^M
manicotto^M del cordone^M

コロ付き丸面ビット
rounding-over bit
Viertelstabfräser^M
fraise^F à quart de rond^M
fresa^F de pecho^M de paloma^F
fresa^F a quarto di anello^M

ラベット・ビット
rabbet bit
Falzfräser^M
fraise^F à feuillure^F
fresa^F de acanalar
fresa^F per scanalare

深さ調節装置
depth adjustment
Tiefeneinstellung^F
réglage^M de profondeur^F
ajuste^M de profundidad^F
regolatore^M di profondità^F

コア・ボックス・ビット
core box bit
Hohlkehlfräser^M
fraise^F à gorge^F
fresa^F de enrasar
fresa^F a corona^F

蟻（あり）溝ビット
dovetail bit
Zinkenfräser^M
fraise^F à queue^F d'aronde^F
fresa^F de cola^F de milano^M
fresa^F a coda^F di rondine^F

ガイド・ハンドル
guide handle
Führungsgriff^M
poignée^F de guidage^M
asa^F
impugnatura^F

コレット
collet
Anlaufhülse^F
collet^M
collarín^M
collare^M

台座
base
Fuß^M
base^F
base^F
base^F

ツール・ホルダー
tool holder
Werkzeugfutter^N
porte-outil^M
mordaza^F
portautensili^M

コーブ・ビット
cove bit
Hohlkehlfräser^M mit Anlaufzapfen^N
fraise^F à congé^M
fresa^F de caveto^M
fresa^F di raccordo^M

面取りビット
chamfer bit
Faserfräser^M
fraise^F à chanfrein^M
fresa^F de biselar
fresa^F per smussare

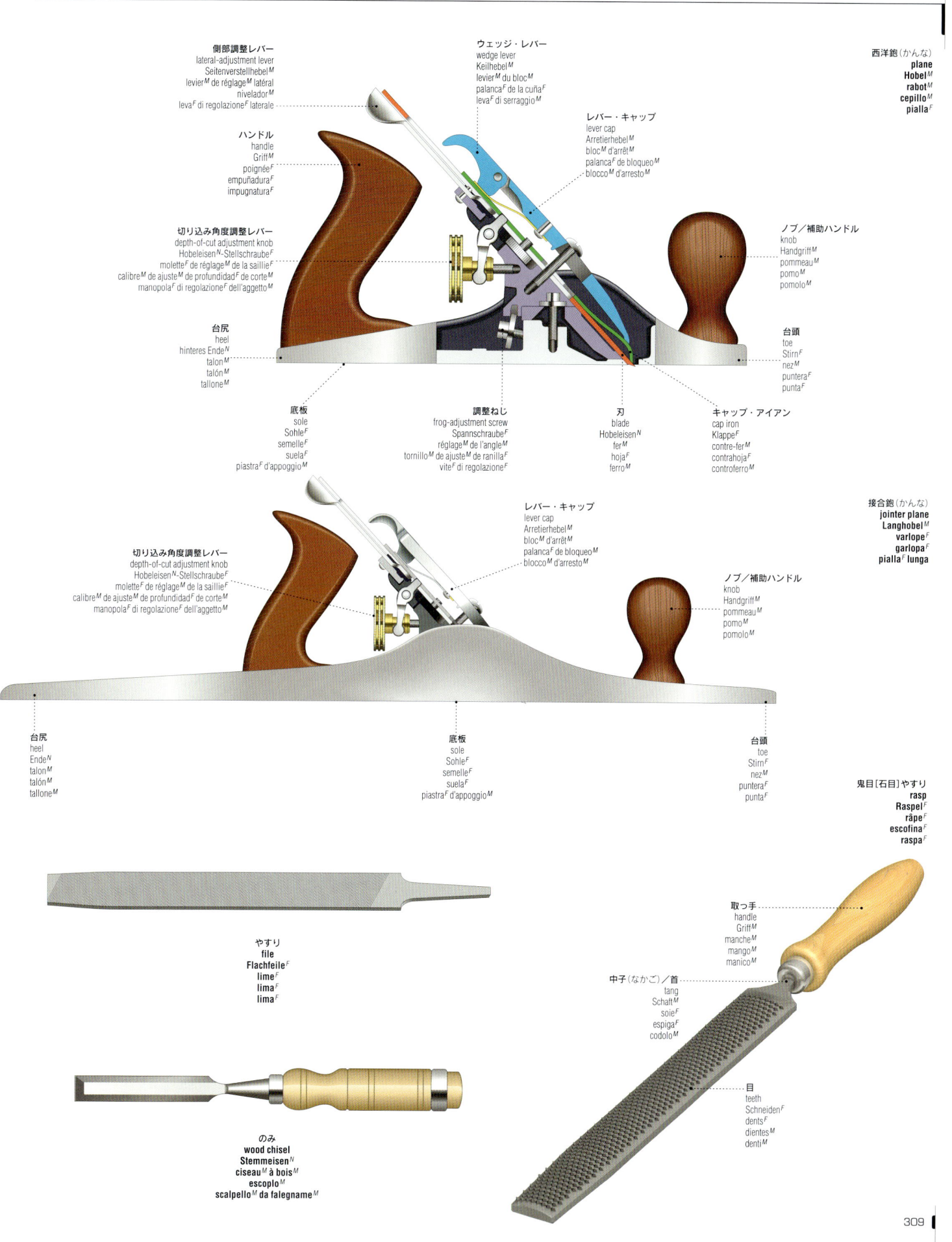

日曜大工 | DO-IT-YOURSELF
HEIMWERKEN | BRICOLAGE | BRICOLAJE | FAI DA TE

木工：成形する道具

側部調整レバー
lateral-adjustment lever
SeitenverstellhebelM
levierM de réglageM latéral
niveladorM
levaF di regolazione laterale

ウェッジ・レバー
wedge lever
KeilhebelM
levierM du blocM
palancaF de la cuñaF
levaF di serraggioM

レバー・キャップ
lever cap
ArretierhebelM
blocM d'arrêtM
palancaF de bloqueoM
bloccoM d'arrestoM

西洋鉋（かんな）
plane
HobelM
rabotM
cepilloM
piallaF

ハンドル
handle
GriffM
poignéeF
empuñaduraF
impugnaturaF

ノブ／補助ハンドル
knob
HandgriffM
pommeauM
pomoM
pomoloM

切り込み角度調整レバー
depth-of-cut adjustment knob
HobeleisenN-StellschraubeF
moletteF de réglageM de la saillieF
calibreM de ajusteM de profundidadF de corteM
manopolaF di regolazioneF dell'aggettoM

台尻
heel
hinteres EndeN
talonM
talónM
talloneM

台頭
toe
StirnF
nezM
punteraF
puntaF

底板
sole
SohleF
semelleF
suelaF
piastraF d'appoggioM

調整ねじ
frog-adjustment screw
SpannschraubeF
réglageM de l'angleM
tornilloM de ajusteM de ranillaF
viteF di regolazioneF

刃
blade
HobeleisenN
ferM
hojaF
ferroM

キャップ・アイアン
cap iron
KlappeF
contre-ferM
contrahojaF
controferroM

レバー・キャップ
lever cap
ArretierhebelM
blocM d'arrêtM
palancaF de bloqueoM
bloccoM d'arrestoM

接合鉋（かんな）
jointer plane
LanghobelM
varlopeF
garlopaF
piallaF lunga

切り込み角度調整レバー
depth-of-cut adjustment knob
HobeleisenN-StellschraubeF
moletteF de réglageM de la saillieF
calibreM de ajusteM de profundidadF de corteM
manopolaF di regolazioneF dell'aggettoM

ノブ／補助ハンドル
knob
HandgriffM
pommeauM
pomoM
pomoloM

台尻
heel
EndeN
talonM
talónM
talloneM

底板
sole
SohleF
semelleF
suelaF
piastraF d'appoggioM

台頭
toe
StirnF
nezM
punteraF
puntaF

鬼目［石目］やすり
rasp
RaspelF
râpeF
escofinaF
raspaF

やすり
file
FlachfeileF
limeF
limaF
limaF

取っ手
handle
GriffM
mancheM
mangoM
manicoM

中子（なかご）／首
tang
SchaftM
soieF
espigaF
codoloM

目
teeth
SchneidenF
dentsF
dientesM
dentiM

のみ
wood chisel
StemmeisenN
ciseauM à boisM
escoploM
scalpelloM da falegnameM

日曜大工・園芸

309

日曜大工 | DO-IT-YOURSELF
HEIMWERKEN | BRICOLAGE | BRICOLAJE | FAI DA TE

木工：つかむ［締める］道具

日本語 | 英語 | ドイツ語 | フランス語 | スペイン語 | イタリア語

carpentry: gripping and tightening tools | Bautischlerei^F: Greif- und Spannwerkzeuge^N | menuiserie^F: outils^M pour serrer | carpintería^F: herramientas^F para apretar | carpenteria^F: attrezzi^M di serraggio^M

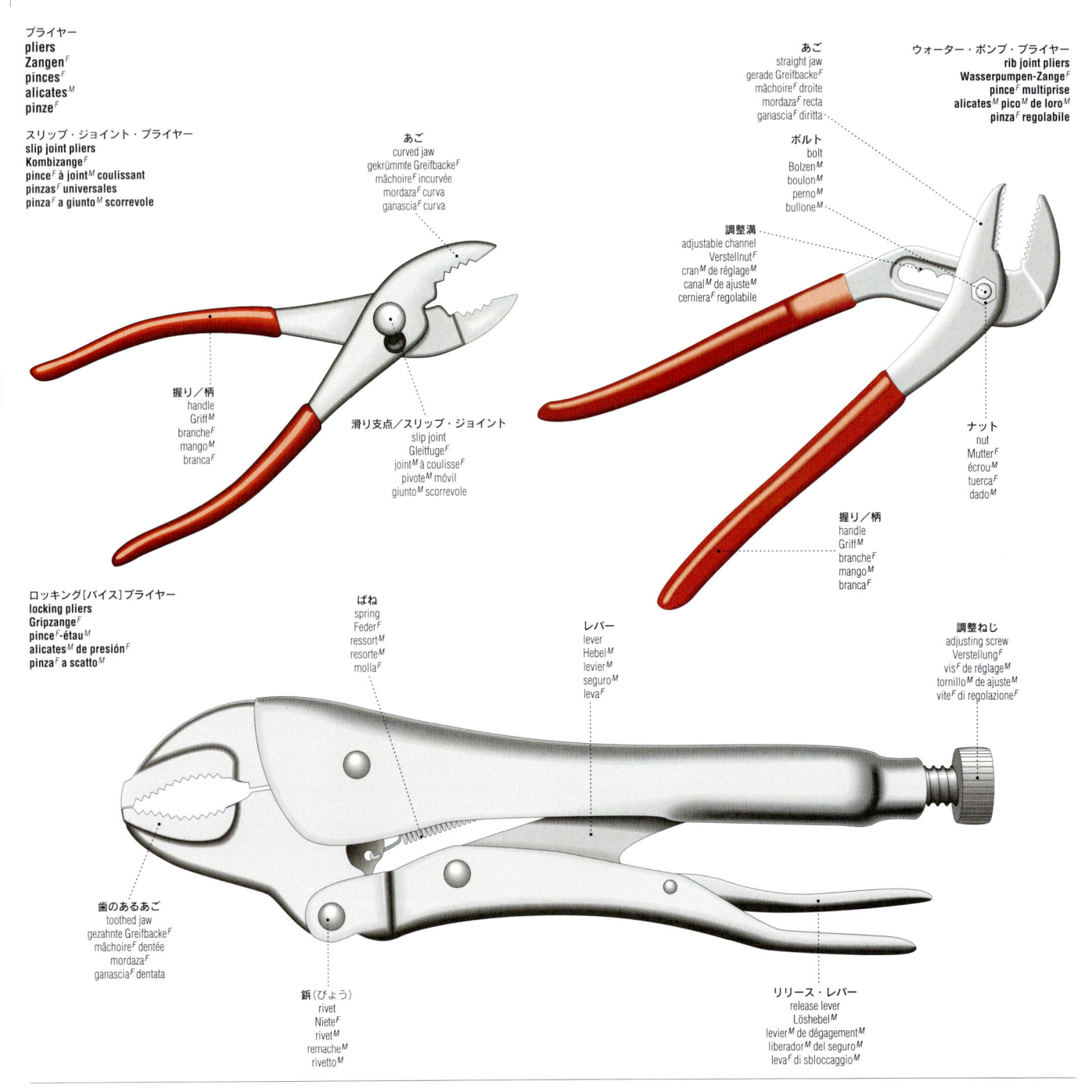

プライヤー
pliers
Zangen^F
pinces^F
alicates^M
pinze^F

スリップ・ジョイント・プライヤー
slip joint pliers
Kombizange^F
pince^F à joint^M coulissant
pinzas^F universales
pinza^F a giunto^M scorrevole

あご
curved jaw
gekrümmte Greifbacke^F
mâchoire^F incurvée
mordaza^F curva
ganascia^F curva

握り／柄
handle
Griff^M
branche^F
mango^M
branca^F

滑り支点／スリップ・ジョイント
slip joint
Gleitfuge^F
joint^M à coulisse^F
pivote^M móvil
giunto^M scorrevole

あご
straight jaw
gerade Greifbacke^F
mâchoire^F droite
mordaza^F recta
ganascia^F diritta

ウォーター・ポンプ・プライヤー
rib joint pliers
Wasserpumpen-Zange^F
pince^F multiprise
alicates^M pico de loro^M
pinza^F regolabile

ボルト
bolt
Bolzen^M
boulon^M
perno^M
bullone^M

調整溝
adjustable channel
Verstellnut^F
cran^M de réglage^M
canal^M de ajuste^M
cerniera^F regolabile

ナット
nut
Mutter^F
écrou^M
tuerca^F
dado^M

握り／柄
handle
Griff^M
branche^F
mango^M
branca^F

ロッキング［バイス］プライヤー
locking pliers
Gripzange^F
pince^F-étau^M
alicates^M de presión^F
pinza^F a scatto^M

ばね
spring
Feder^F
ressort^M
resorte^M
molla^F

レバー
lever
Hebel^M
levier^M
seguro^M
leva^F

調整ねじ
adjusting screw
Verstellung^F
vis^F de réglage^M
tornillo^M de ajuste^M
vite^F di regolazione^F

歯のあるあご
toothed jaw
gezahnte Greifbacke^F
mâchoire^F dentée
mordaza^F
ganascia^F dentata

鋲（びょう）
rivet
Niete^F
rivet^M
remache^M
rivetto^M

リリース・レバー
release lever
Lösehebel^M
levier^M de dégagement^M
liberador^M del seguro^M
leva^F di sbloccaggio^M

座金／ワッシャー
washers
Unterlegscheiben^F
rondelles^F
arandelas^F
rosette^F

平座金／平ワッシャー
flat washer
Unterlegscheibe^F
rondelle^F plate
arandela^F plana
rosetta^F piatta

ばね座金／スプリング・ワッシャー
lock washer; spring washer
Federring^M
rondelle^F à ressort^M
arandela^F de presión^F
rosetta^F elastica

外歯付き座金／外歯ワッシャー
external tooth lock washer
außengezahnte Fächerscheibe^F
rondelle^F à denture^F extérieure
arandela^F de presión^F de dientes^M externos
rosetta^F a dentatura^F esterna

内歯付き座金／内歯ワッシャー
internal tooth lock washer
innengezahnte Fächerscheibe^F
rondelle^F à denture^F intérieure
arandela^F de presión^F de dientes^M internos
rosetta^F a dentatura^F interna

日曜大工 | DO-IT-YOURSELF
HEIMWERKEN | BRICOLAGE | BRICOLAJE | FAI DA TE

木工：つかむ［締める］道具

レンチ
wrenches
Schlüssel^M
clés^F
llaves^F
chiavi^F

固定あご
fixed jaw
feste Backe^F
mâchoire^F fixe
mordaza^F fija
ganascia^F fissa

自在スパナ［レンチ］
crescent wrench; *adjustable spanner*
Rollgabelschlüssel^M
clé^F à molette^F
llave^F inglesa
chiave^F a rullino^M

可動あご
movable jaw
bewegliche Backe^F
mâchoire^F mobile
mordaza^F móvil
ganascia^F mobile

調整ねじ
thumbscrew
Rädelung^F
molette^F
tornillo^M
rullino^M

柄
handle
Griff^M
manche^M
mango^M
manico^M

ラチェット・リング・スパナ
ratchet box end wrench; *ratchet ring spanner*
Ratschenringschlüssel^M
clé^F polygonale à cliquet^M
llave^F de estrella^F hexagonal
chiave^F poligonale a cricco^M

フレア・ナット・スパナ
flare nut wrench; *flare nut spanner*
offener Doppelringschlüssel^M
clé^F polygonale à têtes^F fendues
llave^F de estrella^F abierta
chiave^F poligonale doppia ad anello^M aperto

両口スパナ
open end wrench; *open-ended spanner*
Doppelmaulschlüssel^M
clé^F à fourches^F
llave^F de tuercas^F española
chiave^F a forchetta^F doppia

眼鏡スパナ
box end wrench; *ring spanner*
Doppelringschlüssel^M
clé^F polygonale
llave^F de estrella^F común
chiave^F poligonale doppia

片口スパナ
combination box and open end wrench; *combination spanner*
Maul-Ringschlüssel^M
clé^F mixte
llave^F combinada
chiave^F combinata

ラチェット・ハンドル
ratchet socket wrench
Knarre^F
clé^F à douille^F à cliquet^M
llave^F de carraca^F
chiave^F a bussola^F a cricchetto^M

ボルト
bolts
Schrauben^F
boulons^M
pernos^M
bulloni^M

ボルト
bolt
Schraubenbolzen^M
boulon^M
perno^M
bullone^M

ソケット・セット
socket set
Steckschlüsselsatz^M
jeu^M de douilles^F
juego^M de casquillos^M
set^M di bussole^F

ナット
nut
Mutter^F
écrou^M
tuerca^F
dado^M

頭／ヘッド
head
Kopf^M
tête^F
cabeza^F
testa^F

ショルダー・ボルト
shoulder bolt
Schraubenbolzen^M mit Ansatz^M
boulon^M à épaulement^M
perno^M con collarín^M
bullone^M di spallamento^M

ナット
nuts
Muttern^F
écrous^M
tuercas^F
dadi^M

六角ナット
hexagon nut
Sechskantmutter^F
écrou^M hexagonal
tuerca^F hexagonal
dado^M esagonale

袋ナット
acorn nut
Hutmutter^F
écrou^M borgne
tuerca^F cerrada
dado^M cieco

蝶ナット
wing nut
Flügelmutter^F
écrou^M à oreilles^F
tuerca^F de mariposa^F
galletto^M

ねじ山
threaded rod
Gewindeschaft^M
tige^F filetée
rosca^F
gambo^M filettato

肩
shoulder
Ansatz^M
épaulement^M
collarín^M
spallamento^M

311

日曜大工 | DO-IT-YOURSELF
HEIMWERKEN | BRICOLAGE | BRICOLAJE | FAI DA TE

木工：つかむ[締める]道具

日本語 | 英語 | ドイツ語 | フランス語 | スペイン語 | イタリア語

C型クランプ
C-clamp
Zwinge^F
serre-joint^M
prensa^M en C
morsetto^M a C

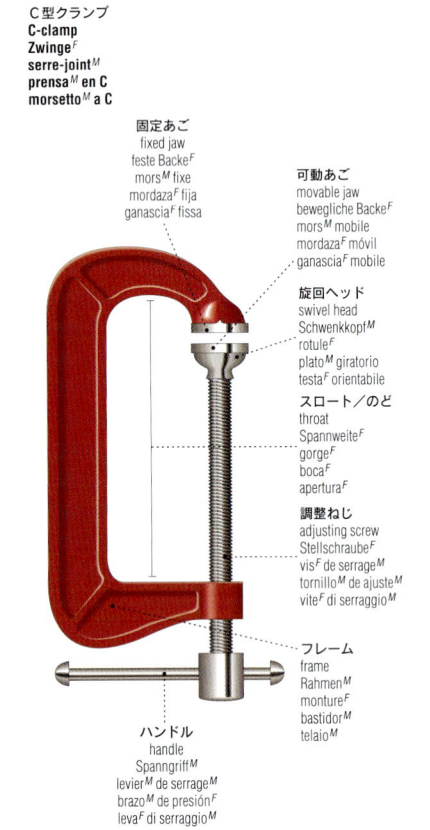

固定あご
fixed jaw
feste Backe^F
mors^M fixe
mordaza^F fija
ganascia^F fissa

可動あご
movable jaw
bewegliche Backe^F
mors^M mobile
mordaza^M móvil
ganascia^F mobile

旋回ヘッド
swivel head
Schwenkkopf^M
rotule^F
plato^M giratorio
testa^F orientabile

スロート／のど
throat
Spannweite^F
gorge^F
boca^F
apertura^F

調整ねじ
adjusting screw
Stellschraube^F
vis^F de serrage^M
tornillo^M de ajuste^M
vite^F di serraggio^M

フレーム
frame
Rahmen^M
monture^F
bastidor^M
telaio^M

ハンドル
handle
Spanngriff^M
levier^M de serrage^M
brazo^M de presión^F
leva^F di serraggio^M

パイプ・クランプ
pipe clamp
Rohrschraubstock^M
serre-joint^M à tuyau^M
sargento^M
morsa^F serratubi^M

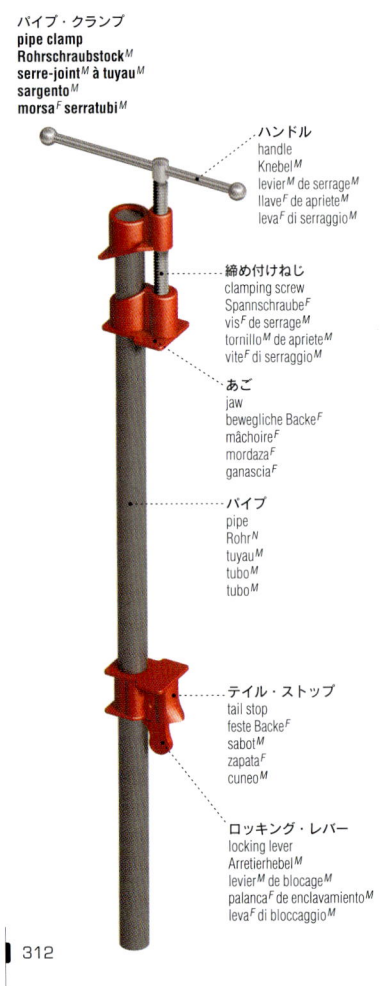

ハンドル
handle
Knebel^M
levier^M de serrage^M
llave^F de apriete^M
leva^F di serraggio^M

締め付けねじ
clamping screw
Spannschraube^F
vis^F de serrage^M
tornillo^M de apriete^M
vite^F di serraggio^M

あご
jaw
bewegliche Backe^F
mâchoire^F
mordaza^F
ganascia^F

パイプ
pipe
Rohr^N
tuyau^M
tubo^M
tubo^M

テイル・ストップ
tail stop
feste Backe^F
sabot^M
zapata^F
cuneo^M

ロッキング・レバー
locking lever
Arretierhebel^M
levier^M de blocage^M
palanca^F de enclavamiento^M
leva^F di bloccaggio^M

ハンドル
handle
Spanngriff^M
levier^M de serrage^M
mango^M
leva^F di serraggio^M

可動あご
movable jaw
bewegliche Backe^F
mors^M mobile
mordaza^F móvil
ganascia^F mobile

固定あご
fixed jaw
feste Backe^F
mors^M fixe
mordaza^F fija
ganascia^F fissa

万力
vise; *vice*
Schraubstock^M
étau^M
torno^M de banco^M
morsa^F

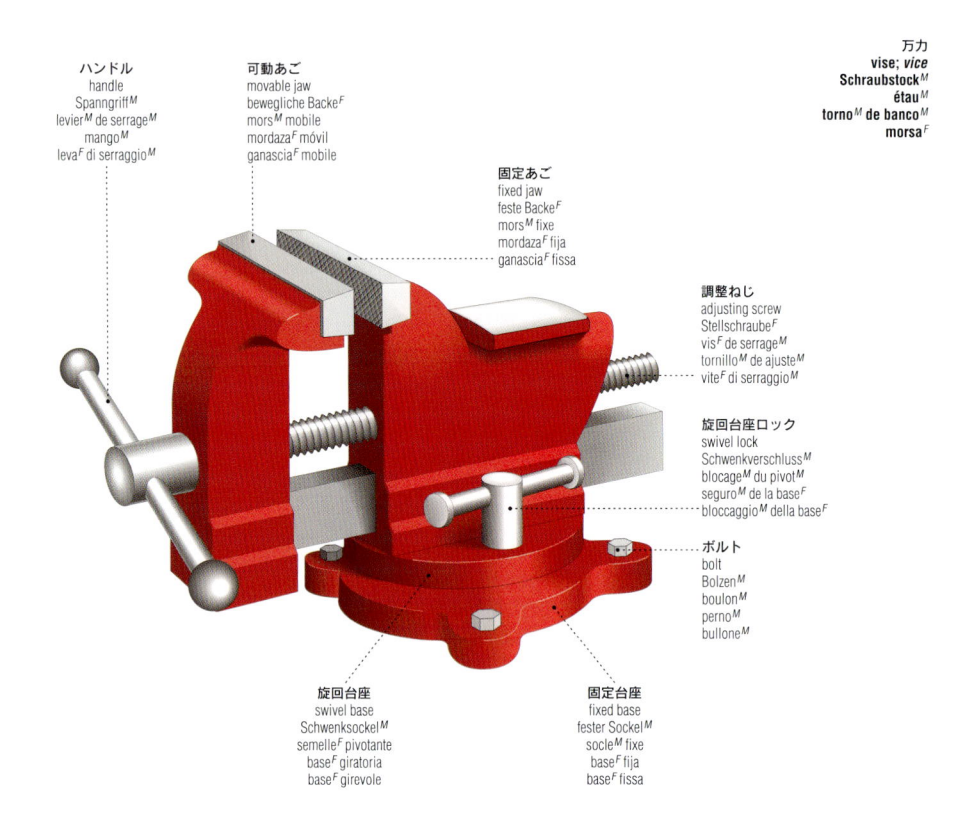

調整ねじ
adjusting screw
Stellschraube^F
vis^F de serrage^M
tornillo^M de ajuste^M
vite^F di serraggio^M

旋回台座ロック
swivel lock
Schwenkverschluss^M
blocage^M du pivot^M
seguro^M de la base^F
bloccaggio^M della base^F

ボルト
bolt
Bolzen^M
boulon^M
perno^M
bullone^M

旋回台座
swivel base
Schwenksockel^M
semelle^F pivotante
base^F giratoria
base^F girevole

固定台座
fixed base
fester Sockel^M
socle^M fixe
base^F fija
base^F fissa

押さえ
peg
Spannpratze^F
cale^F
tope^M
spessore^M

あご
jaws
Backen^F
mâchoires^F
mordazas^F
ganasce^F

作業台と万力
work bench and vise
Werkbank^F und Schraubstock^M
établi^M étau^M
banco^M de trabajo^M
piano^M di lavoro^M a morsa^F

作業面
working surface
Arbeitsplatte^F
plateau^M
tablero^M
piano^M di lavoro^M

クランク
crank
Kurbel^F
manivelle^F
manivela^F
manovella^F

足台
footrest
Fußstütze^F
appui-pieds^M
reposapiés^M
appoggiapiedi^M

日曜大工 | DO-IT-YOURSELF
HEIMWERKEN | BRICOLAGE | BRICOLAJE | FAI DA TE

木工：測定して印を付ける道具

carpentry: measuring and marking tools | Bautischlerei^F: Mess- und Markierinstrumente^N | menuiserie^F: instruments^M de traçage^M et de mesure^F | carpintería^F: instrumentos^M de trazado^M y de medición^F | carpenteria^F: strumenti^M di misurazione^F e tracciamento^M

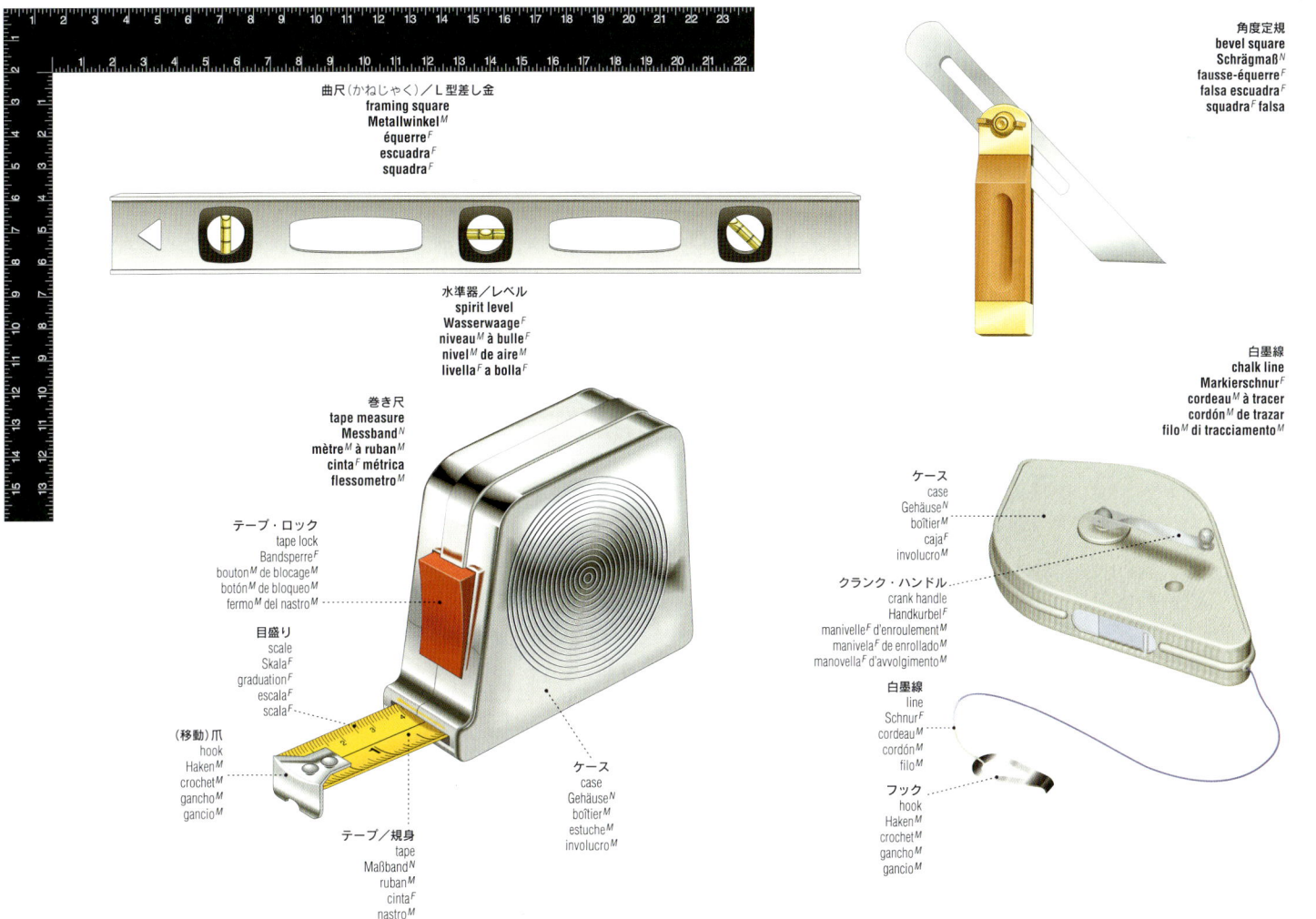

曲尺（かねじゃく）／L型差し金
framing square
Metallwinkel^M
équerre^F
escuadra^F
squadra^F

水準器／レベル
spirit level
Wasserwaage^F
niveau^M à bulle^F
nivel^M de aire^M
livella^F a bolla^F

巻き尺
tape measure
Messband^N
mètre^M à ruban^M
cinta^F métrica
flessometro^M

テープ・ロック
tape lock
Bandsperre^F
bouton^M de blocage^M
botón^M de bloqueo^M
fermo^M del nastro^M

目盛り
scale
Skala^F
graduation^F
escala^F
scala^F

(移動)爪
hook
Haken^M
crochet^M
gancho^M
gancio^M

テープ／規身
tape
Maßband^N
ruban^M
cinta^F
nastro^M

ケース
case
Gehäuse^N
boîtier^M
estuche^M
involucro^M

角度定規
bevel square
Schrägmaß^N
fausse-équerre^F
falsa escuadra^F
squadra^F falsa

白墨線
chalk line
Markierschnur^F
cordeau^M à tracer
cordón^M de trazar
filo^M di tracciamento^M

ケース
case
Gehäuse^N
boîtier^M
caja^F
involucro^M

クランク・ハンドル
crank handle
Handkurbel^F
manivelle^F d'enroulement^M
manivela^F de enrollado^M
manovella^F d'avvolgimento^M

白墨線
line
Schnur^F
cordeau^M
cordón^M
filo^M

フック
hook
Haken^M
crochet^M
gancho^M
gancio^M

木工：その他の道具

carpentry: miscellaneous material | Bautischlerei^F: verschiedenes Zubehör^N | menuiserie^F: matériel^M divers | carpintería^F: materiales^M varios | carpenteria^F: materiale^M vario

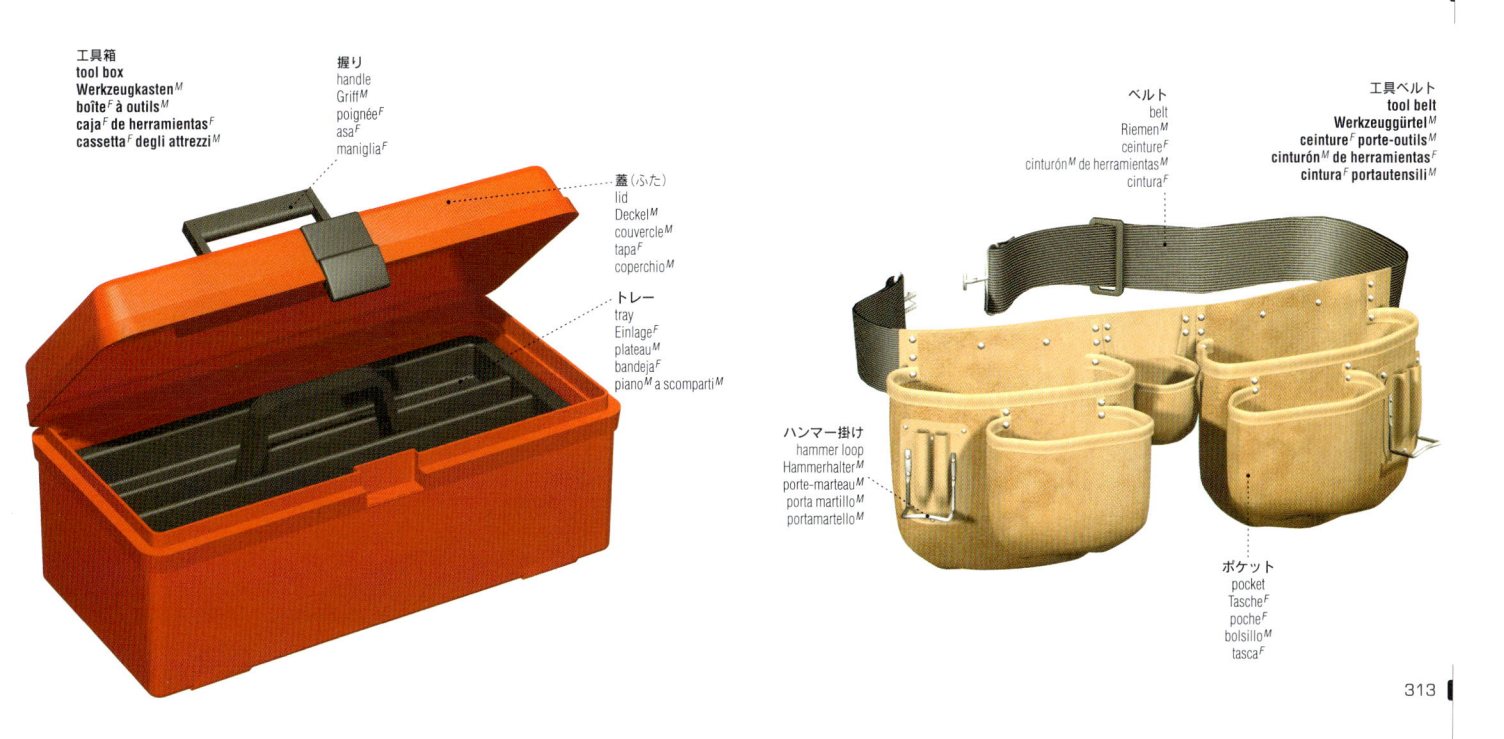

工具箱
tool box
Werkzeugkasten^M
boîte^F à outils^M
caja^F de herramientas^F
cassetta^F degli attrezzi^M

握り
handle
Griff^M
poignée^F
asa^F
maniglia^F

蓋(ふた)
lid
Deckel^M
couvercle^M
tapa^F
coperchio^M

トレー
tray
Einlage^F
plateau^M
bandeja^F
piano^M a scomparti^M

ベルト
belt
Riemen^M
ceinture^F
cinturón^M de herramientas^F
cintura^F

工具ベルト
tool belt
Werkzeuggürtel^M
ceinture^F porte-outils^F
cinturón^M de herramientas^F
cintura^F portautensili^M

ハンマー掛け
hammer loop
Hammerhalter^M
porte-marteau^M
porta martillo^M
portamartello^M

ポケット
pocket
Tasche^F
poche^F
bolsillo^M
tasca^F

313

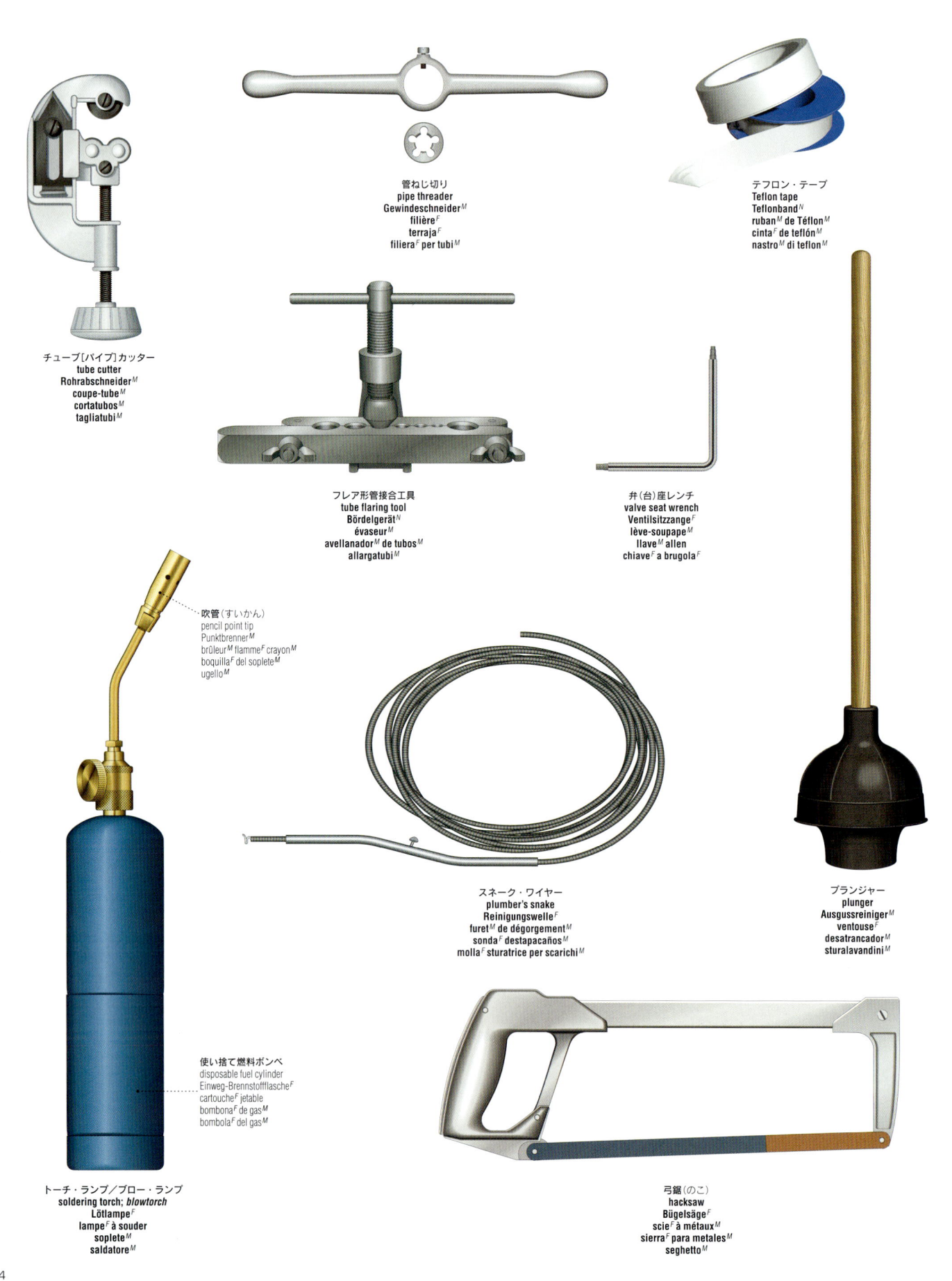

配管工具 | plumbing tools | Klempnerwerkzeuge^N | plomberie^F : outils^M | fontanería^F : herramientas^F | attrezzi^M idraulici

日曜大工 | DO-IT-YOURSELF
HEIMWERKEN | BRICOLAGE | BRICOLAJE | FAI DA TE

日本語 | 英語 | ドイツ語 | フランス語 | スペイン語 | イタリア語

管ねじ切り
pipe threader
Gewindeschneider^M
filière^F
terraja^F
filiera^F per tubi^M

テフロン・テープ
Teflon tape
Teflonband^N
ruban^M de Téflon^M
cinta^F de teflón^M
nastro^M di teflon^M

チューブ[パイプ]カッター
tube cutter
Rohrabschneider^M
coupe-tube^M
cortatubos^M
tagliatubi^M

フレア形管接合工具
tube flaring tool
Bördelgerät^N
évaseur^M
avellanador^M de tubos^M
allargatubi^M

弁(台)座レンチ
valve seat wrench
Ventilsitzzange^F
lève-soupape^M
llave^M allen
chiave^F a brugola^F

吹管(すいかん)
pencil point tip
Punktbrenner^M
brûleur^M flamme^F crayon^M
boquilla^F del soplete^M
ugello^M

スネーク・ワイヤー
plumber's snake
Reinigungswelle^F
furet^M de dégorgement^M
sonda^F destapacaños^M
molla^F sturatrice per scarichi^M

プランジャー
plunger
Ausgussreiniger^M
ventouse^F
desatrancador^M
sturalavandini^M

使い捨て燃料ボンベ
disposable fuel cylinder
Einweg-Brennstoffflasche^F
cartouche^F jetable
bombona^F de gas^M
bombola^F del gas^M

トーチ・ランプ／ブロー・ランプ
soldering torch; *blowtorch*
Lötlampe^F
lampe^F à souder
soplete^M
saldatore^M

弓鋸(のこ)
hacksaw
Bügelsäge^F
scie^F à métaux^M
sierra^F para metales^M
seghetto^M

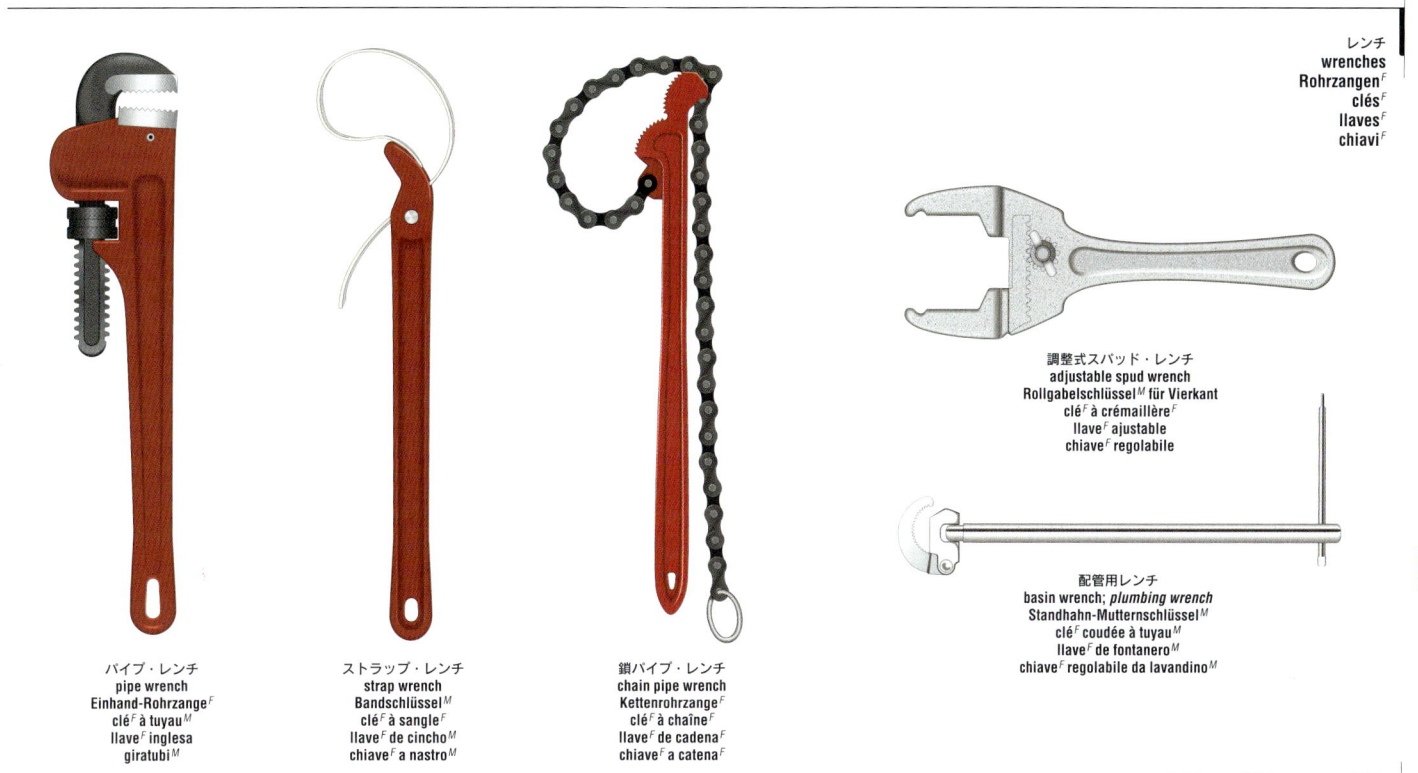

日曜大工 | DO-IT-YOURSELF
HEIMWERKEN | BRICOLAGE | BRICOLAJE | FAI DA TE

配管工具

レンチ
wrenches
Rohrzangen^F
clés^F
llaves^F
chiavi^F

調整式スパッド・レンチ
adjustable spud wrench
Rollgabelschlüssel^M für Vierkant
clé^F à crémaillère^F
llave^F ajustable
chiave^F regolabile

配管用レンチ
basin wrench; *plumbing wrench*
Standhahn-Mutternschlüssel^M
clé^F coudée à tuyau^M
llave^F de fontanero^M
chiave^F regolabile da lavandino^M

パイプ・レンチ
pipe wrench
Einhand-Rohrzange^F
clé^F à tuyau^M
llave^F inglesa
giratubi^M

ストラップ・レンチ
strap wrench
Bandschlüssel^M
clé^F à sangle^F
llave^F de cincho^M
chiave^F a nastro^M

鎖パイプ・レンチ
chain pipe wrench
Kettenrohrzange^F
clé^F à chaîne^F
llave^F de cadena^F
chiave^F a catena^F

石工用の工具

masonry tools | Maurerwerkzeuge^N | maçonnerie^F : outils^M | albañilería^F : herramientas^F | attrezzi^M da muratore^M

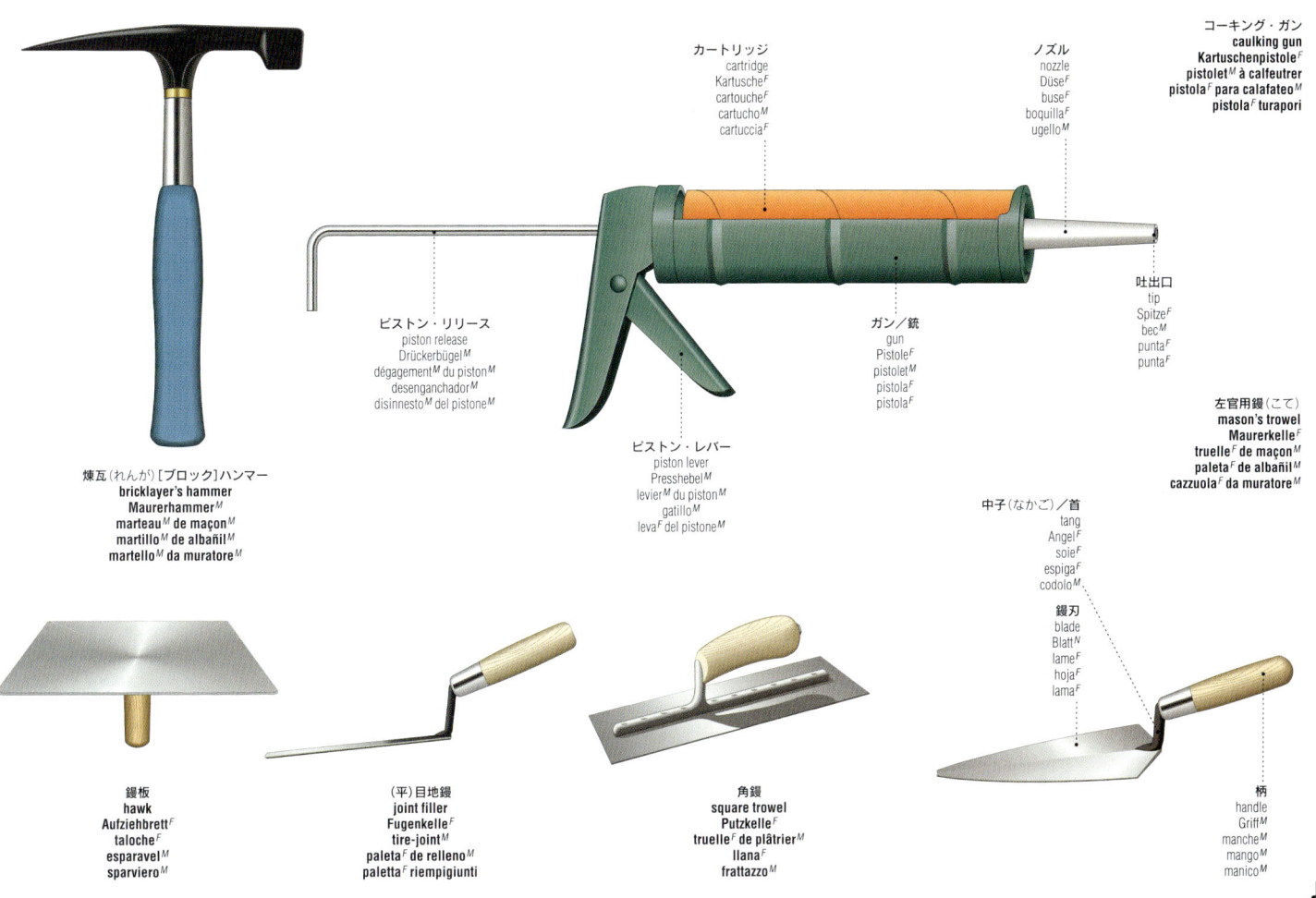

カートリッジ
cartridge
Kartusche^F
cartouche^F
cartucho^M
cartuccia^F

ノズル
nozzle
Düse^F
buse^F
boquilla^F
ugello^M

コーキング・ガン
caulking gun
Kartuschenpistole^F
pistolet^M à calfeutrer
pistola^F para calafateo^M
pistola^F turapori

吐出口
tip
Spitze^F
bec^M
punta^F
punta^F

ピストン・リリース
piston release
Drückerbügel^M
dégagement^M du piston^M
desenganchador^M
disinnesto^M del pistone^M

ガン／銃
gun
Pistole^F
pistolet^M
pistola^F
pistola^F

煉瓦（れんが）［ブロック］ハンマー
bricklayer's hammer
Maurerhammer^M
marteau^M de maçon^M
martillo^M de albañil^M
martello^M da muratore^M

ピストン・レバー
piston lever
Presshebel^M
levier^M du piston^M
gatillo^M
leva^F del pistone^M

左官用鏝（こて）
mason's trowel
Maurerkelle^F
truelle^F de maçon^M
paleta^F de albañil^M
cazzuola^F da muratore^M

中子（なかご）／首
tang
Angel^F
soie^F
espiga^F
codolo^M

鏝刃
blade
Blatt^N
lame^F
hoja^F
lama^F

鏝板
hawk
Aufziehbrett^F
taloche^F
esparavel^M
sparviero^M

（平）目地鏝
joint filler
Fugenkelle^F
tire-joint^M
paleta^F de relleno^M
paletta^F riempigiunti

角鏝
square trowel
Putzkelle^F
truelle^F de plâtrier^M
llana^F
frattazzo^M

柄
handle
Griff^M
manche^M
mango^M
manico^M

315

日曜大工 | DO-IT-YOURSELF
HEIMWERKEN | BRICOLAGE | BRICOLAJE | FAI DA TE

電設工具

日本語 | 英語 | ドイツ語 | フランス語 | スペイン語 | イタリア語

electricity tools | Elektroinstallateurwerkzeuge^N | électricité^F : outils^M | electricidad^F : herramientas^F | attrezzatura^F elettrica

マルチメーター
multimeter
Multimeter^N
multimètre^M
voltímetro^M
multimetro^M

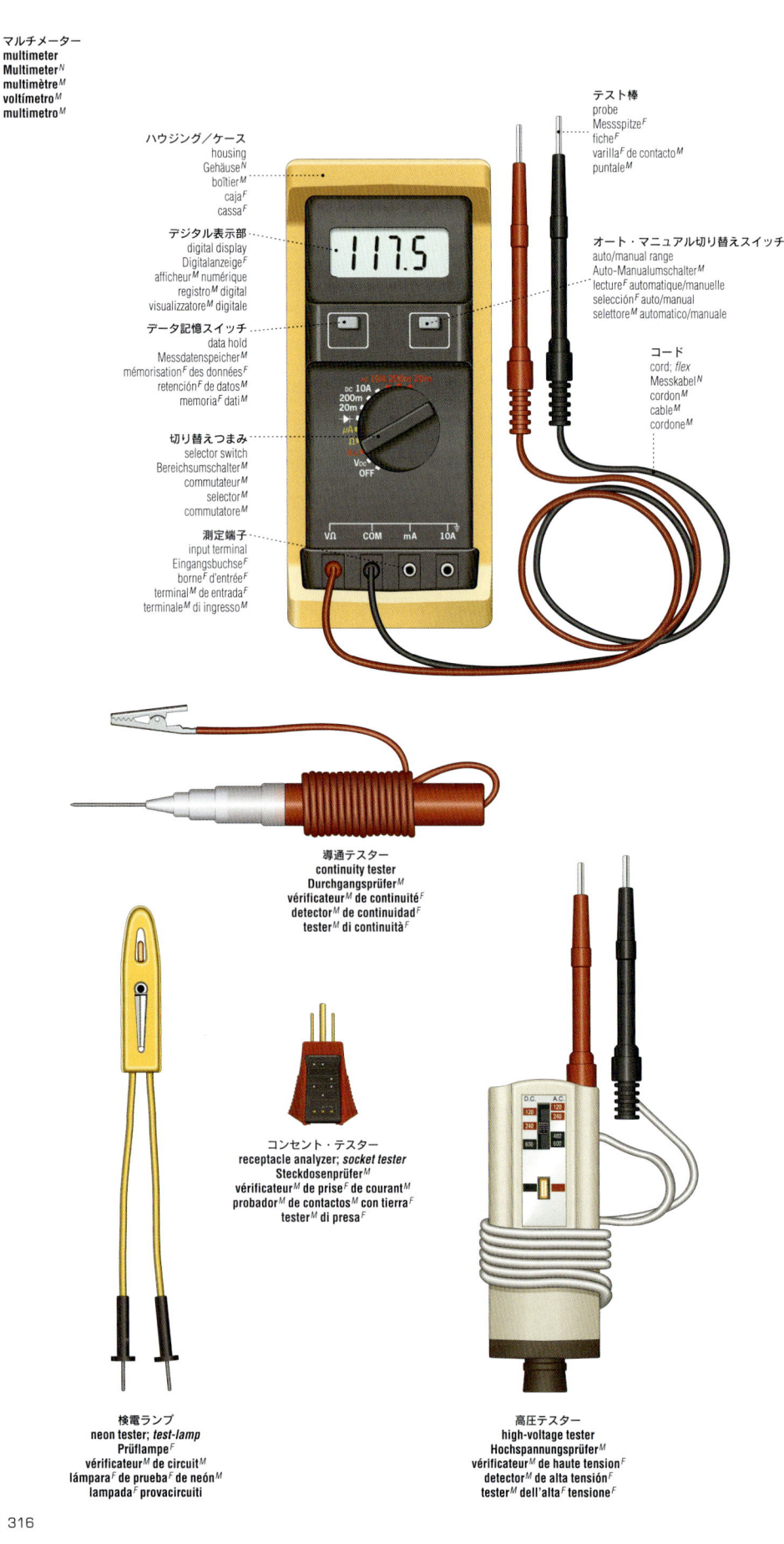

ハウジング／ケース
housing
Gehäuse^N
boîtier^M
caja^F
cassa^F

デジタル表示部
digital display
Digitalanzeige^F
afficheur^M numérique
registro^M digital
visualizzatore^M digitale

データ記憶スイッチ
data hold
Messdatenspeicher^M
mémorisation^F des données^F
retención^F de datos^M
memoria^F dati^M

切り替えつまみ
selector switch
Bereichsumschalter^M
commutateur^M
selector^M
commutatore^M

測定端子
input terminal
Eingangsbuchse^F
borne^F d'entrée^F
terminal^M de entrada^F
terminale^M di ingresso^M

テスト棒
probe
Messspitze^F
fiche^F
varilla^F de contacto^M
puntale^M

オート・マニュアル切り替えスイッチ
auto/manual range
Auto-Manualumschalter^M
lecture^F automatique/manuelle
selección^F auto/manual
selettore^M automatico/manuale

コード
cord; *flex*
Messkabel^N
cordon^M
cable^M
cordone^M

検電ドライバー
voltage tester; *tester screwdriver*
Spannungsprüfer^M
vérificateur^M de tension^F
detector^M de tensión^F
cercafase^M

絶縁刃
insulated blade
isolierte Klinge^F
lame^F isolée
vástago^M aislado
lama^F isolata

絶縁グリップ
insulated handle
isolierter Griff^M
manche^M isolé
mango^M aislado
manico^M isolato

ネオン・ランプ
neon lamp
Glimmlampe^F
lampe^F au néon^M
lámpara^F de neón^M
lampada^F al neon^M

ドロップ・ライト
drop light
Handlampe^F
baladeuse^F
linterna^F movible
lampada^F portatile a gabbia^F

導通テスター
continuity tester
Durchgangsprüfer^M
vérificateur^M de continuité^F
detector^M de continuidad^F
tester^M di continuità^F

フック
hook
Haken^M
crochet^M
gancho^M
gancio^M

反射板
reflector
Reflektor^M
réflecteur^M
reflector^M
riflettore^M

電球
bulb
Glühbirne^F
lampe^F
bombilla^F
lampadina^F

ガード
guard
Schutzgitter^N
grillage^M de protection^F
reja^F
gabbia^F di protezione^F

コンセント／差込口
convenience outlet
Zusatzsteckdose^F
prise^F de courant^M
enchufe^M
presa^F di corrente^F

取っ手
handle
Griff^M
manche^M
mango^M
impugnatura^F

電気コード
cord; *flex*
Kabel^N
cordon^M
cable^M
cordone^M

コンセント・テスター
receptacle analyzer; *socket tester*
Steckdosenprüfer^M
vérificateur^M de prise^F de courant^M
probador^M de contactos^M con tierra^F
tester^M di presa^F

検電ランプ
neon tester; *test-lamp*
Prüflampe^F
vérificateur^M de circuit^M
lámpara^F de prueba^F de neón^M
lampada^F provacircuiti

高圧テスター
high-voltage tester
Hochspannungsprüfer^M
vérificateur^M de haute tension^F
detector^M de alta tensión^F
tester^M dell'alta^F tensione^F

316

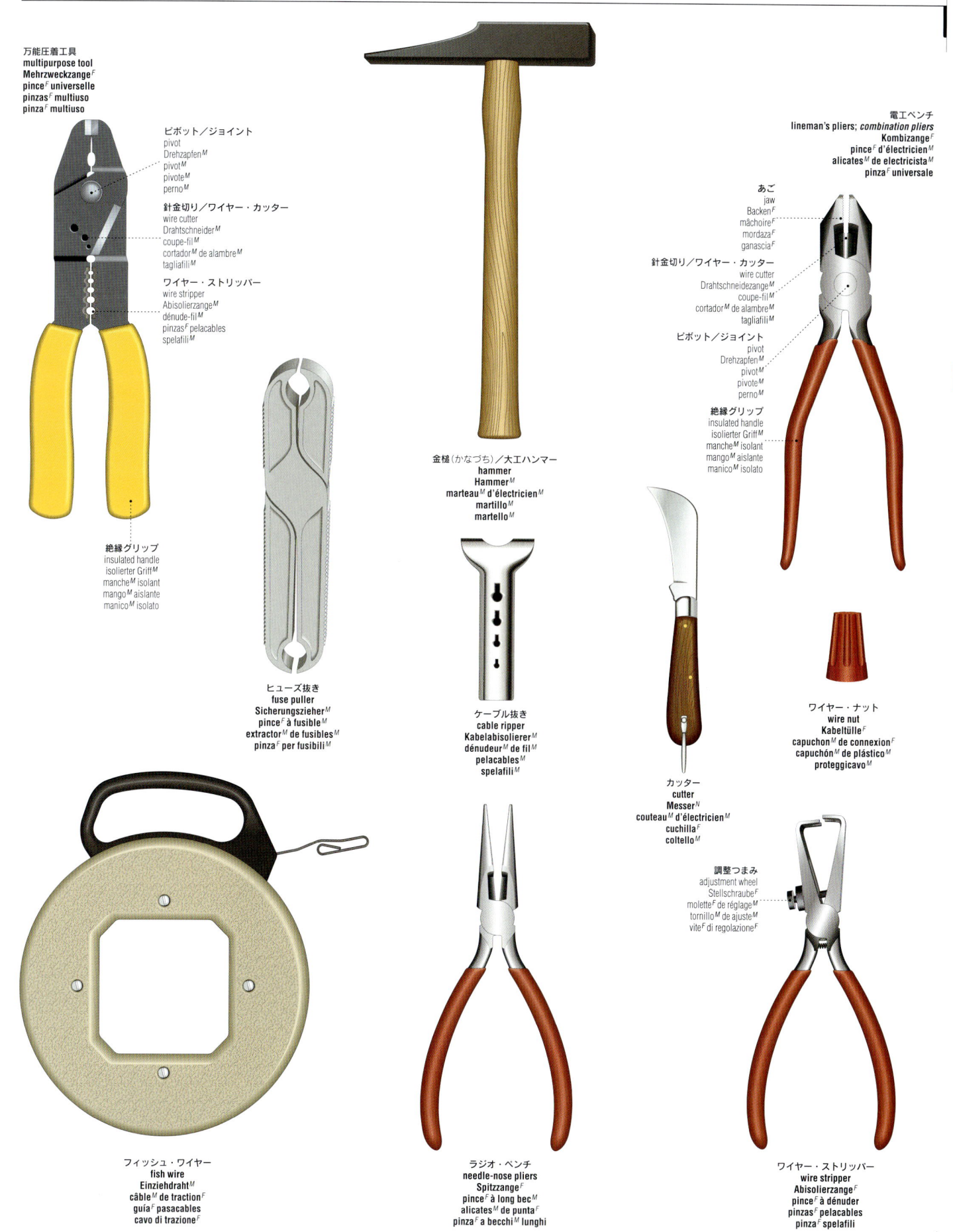

日曜大工 | DO-IT-YOURSELF
HEIMWERKEN | BRICOLAGE | BRICOLAJE | FAI DA TE

電設工具

万能圧着工具
multipurpose tool
Mehrzweckzange^F
pince^F universelle
pinzas^F multiuso
pinza^F multiuso

ピボット／ジョイント
pivot
Drehzapfen^M
pivot^M
pivote^M
perno^M

針金切り／ワイヤー・カッター
wire cutter
Drahtschneider^M
coupe-fil^M
cortador^M de alambre^M
tagliafili^M

ワイヤー・ストリッパー
wire stripper
Abisolierzange^F
dénude-fil^M
pinzas^F pelacables
spelafili^M

絶縁グリップ
insulated handle
isolierter Griff^M
manche^F isolant
mango^M aislante
manico^M isolato

電工ペンチ
lineman's pliers; combination pliers
Kombizange^F
pince^F d'électricien^M
alicates^M de electricista^M
pinza^F universale

あご
jaw
Backen^F
mâchoire^F
mordaza^F
ganascia^F

針金切り／ワイヤー・カッター
wire cutter
Drahtschneidezange^M
coupe-fil^M
cortador^M de alambre^M
tagliafili^M

ピボット／ジョイント
pivot
Drehzapfen^M
pivot^M
pivote^M
perno^M

絶縁グリップ
insulated handle
isolierter Griff^M
manche^F isolant
mango^M aislante
manico^M isolato

金槌（かなづち）／大工ハンマー
hammer
Hammer^M
marteau^M d'électricien^M
martillo^M
martello^M

ヒューズ抜き
fuse puller
Sicherungszieher^M
pince^F à fusible^M
extractor^M de fusibles^M
pinza^F per fusibili^M

ケーブル抜き
cable ripper
Kabelabisolierer^M
dénudeur^M de fil^M
pelacables^M
spelafili^M

カッター
cutter
Messer^N
couteau^M d'électricien^M
cuchilla^F
coltello^M

ワイヤー・ナット
wire nut
Kabeltülle^F
capuchon^M de connexion^F
capuchón^M de plástico^M
proteggicavo^M

調整つまみ
adjustment wheel
Stellschraube^F
molette^F de réglage^M
tornillo^M de ajuste^M
vite^F di regolazione^F

フィッシュ・ワイヤー
fish wire
Einziehdraht^M
câble^M de traction^F
guía^F pasacables
cavo^M di trazione^F

ラジオ・ペンチ
needle-nose pliers
Spitzzange^F
pince^F à long bec^M
alicates^M de punta^F
pinza^F a becchi^M lunghi

ワイヤー・ストリッパー
wire stripper
Abisolierzange^F
pince^F à dénuder
pinzas^F pelacables
pinza^F spelafili

日曜大工 | DO-IT-YOURSELF
HEIMWERKEN | BRICOLAGE | BRICOLAJE | FAI DA TE

はんだ付け・溶接工具

日本語 | 英語 | ドイツ語 | フランス語 | スペイン語 | イタリア語

soldering and welding tools | Löt- und Schweißwerkzeuge^N | soudage^M : outils^M | herramientas^F de soldadura^F | attrezzi^M di brasatura^F e saldatura^F

ソルダリング・ガン／はんだ銃
soldering gun
Lötpistole^F
pistolet^M à souder
pistola^F para soldar
saldatore^M a pistola^F

先端
tip
Lötspitze^F
panne^F
punta^F
punta^F

ハウジング
housing
Gehäuse^N
boîtier^M
caja^F
cassa^F

発熱体
heating element
Heizelement^N
élément^M chauffant
resistencia^F
elemento^M riscaldante

ピストル型グリップ
pistol grip handle
Pistolengriff^M
poignée^F pistolet^M
mango^M
impugnatura^F a pistola^F

電源スイッチ
on-off switch
Ein-/Ausschalter^M
interrupteur^M
interruptor^M
interruttore^M

コード・スリーブ
cord sleeve; *flex sleeve*
Kabelmantel^M
manchon^M du cordon^M
protector^M del cable^M
manicotto^M del cordone^M

防護装備
protective clothing
Schutzkleidung^F
équipement^M de protection^F
ropa^F de protección^F
abbigliamento^M antinfortunistico

ゴーグル
goggles
Schutzbrille^F
lunettes^F
gafas^F protectoras
occhiali^M di protezione^F

溶接カーテン
welding curtain
Schutzschirm^M
écran^M de soudeur^M
biombo^M para soldar
schermo^M di protezione^F

フェイス・シールド
face shield
Gesichtsschutz^M
casque^M
careta^F
maschera^F da saldatore^M

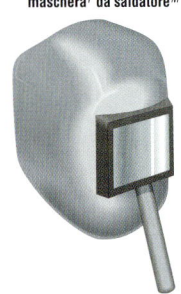

はんだ鏝（ごて）
soldering iron
Lötkolben^M
fer^M à souder
hierro^M para soldar
saldatore^M elettrico

はんだ
solder
Lötzinn^M
soudure^F
soldadura^F
filo^M per saldatura^F

掃除棒
tip cleaners
Düsenreiniger^M
aiguilles^F de nettoyage^M
limpiador^M de boquillas^F
alesatori^M per la pulizia^F degli ugelli^M

点火器
striker
Anzünder^M
briquet^M
encendedor^M
acciarino^M

摩擦ストリップ
friction strip
Reibefläche^F
frottoir^M
frotador^M
striscia^F di sfregamento^M

発火石
flint
Feuerstein^M
pierre^F
pedernal^M
pietra^F focaia

ハンド・シールド
hand shield
Handchild^N
écran^M à main^F
careta^F de mano^F
schermo^M a impugnatura^F

アーク溶接
arc welding
Elektroschweißen^N
soudage^M à l'arc^M
equipo^M de soldadura^F eléctrica
saldatura^F ad arco^M

電極ホルダー
electrode holder
Elektrodenhalter^M
porte-électrode^F
pinza^F del electrodo^M
portaelettrodo^M

電極リード
electrode lead
Elektrodenkabel^N
câble^M d'alimentation^F de l'électrode^F
cable^M de corriente^F
cavo^M di alimentazione^F dell'elettrodo^M

溶接棒
electrode
Elektrode^F
électrode^F
electrodo^M
elettrodo^M

長手袋
gauntlet
fünffingriger Schweißerhandschuh^M
gant^M à crispin^M
guantes^M
guanti^M di protezione^F

アース[接地]クランプ
ground clamp; *earth clamp*
Massezange^F
prise^F de masse^F
pinza^F de conexión^F a tierra^F
morsetto^M di messa^F a terra^F

アース・リード
work lead
Massekabel^N
câble^M de masse^F
cable^M de tierra^F
cavo^M di messa^F a terra^F

アーク溶接機
arc welding machine
Schweißtransformator^M
poste^M de soudage^M
máquina^F de soldar eléctrica
saldatrice^F ad arco^M

ミトン
mitten
Fausthandschuh^M
moufle^F
manoplas^F
manopole^F

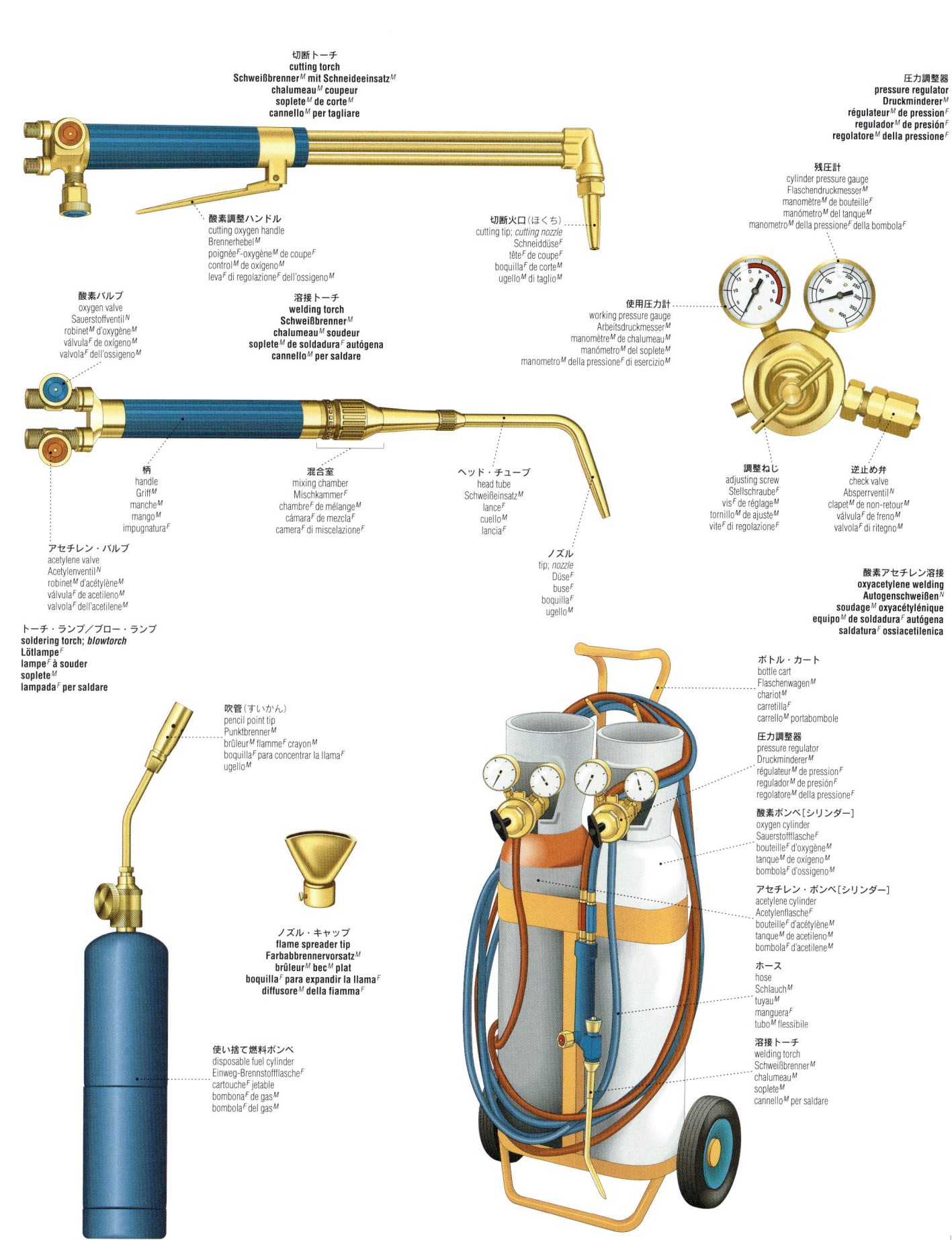

日曜大工 | DO-IT-YOURSELF
HEIMWERKEN | BRICOLAGE | BRICOLAJE | FAI DA TE

はんだ付け・溶接工具

切断トーチ
cutting torch
Schweißbrenner^M mit Schneideeinsatz^M
chalumeau^M coupeur
soplete^M de corte^M
cannello^M per tagliare

酸素調整ハンドル
cutting oxygen handle
Brennerhebel^M
poignée^F-oxygène^M de coupe^F
control^M de oxígeno^M
leva^F di regolazione^F dell'ossigeno^M

切断火口（ほくち）
cutting tip; cutting nozzle
Schneiddüse^F
tête^F de coupe^F
boquilla^F de corte^M
ugello^M di taglio^M

圧力調整器
pressure regulator
Druckminderer^M
régulateur^M de pression^F
regulador^M de presión^F
regolatore^M della pressione^F

残圧計
cylinder pressure gauge
Flaschendruckmesser^M
manomètre^M de bouteille^F
manómetro^M del tanque^M
manometro della pressione^F della bombola^F

酸素バルブ
oxygen valve
Sauerstoffventil^N
robinet^F d'oxygène^M
válvula^F de oxígeno^M
valvola^F dell'ossigeno^M

溶接トーチ
welding torch
Schweißbrenner^M
chalumeau^M soudeur
soplete^M de soldadura^F autógena
cannello^M per saldare

使用圧力計
working pressure gauge
Arbeitsdruckmesser^M
manomètre^M de chalumeau^M
manómetro^M del soplete^M
manometro della pressione^F di esercizio^M

柄
handle
Griff^M
manche^M
mango^M
impugnatura^F

混合室
mixing chamber
Mischkammer^F
chambre^F de mélange^M
cámara^F de mezcla^F
camera^F di miscelazione^F

ヘッド・チューブ
head tube
Schweißeinsatz^M
lance^F
cuello^M
lancia^F

調整ねじ
adjusting screw
Stellschraube^F
vis^F de réglage^M
tornillo^M de ajuste^M
vite^F di regolazione^F

逆止め弁
check valve
Absperrventil^N
clapet^M de non-retour^M
válvula^F de freno^M
valvola^F di ritegno^M

アセチレン・バルブ
acetylene valve
Acetylenventil^N
robinet^M d'acétylène^M
válvula^F de acetileno^M
valvola^F dell'acetilene^M

ノズル
tip; nozzle
Düse^F
buse^F
boquilla^F
ugello^M

酸素アセチレン溶接
oxyacetylene welding
Autogenschweißen^N
soudage^M oxyacétylénique
equipo^M de soldadura^F autógena
saldatura^F ossiacetilenica

トーチ・ランプ／ブロー・ランプ
soldering torch; blowtorch
Lötlampe^F
lampe^F à souder
soplete^M
lampada^F per saldare

ボトル・カート
bottle cart
Flaschenwagen^M
chariot^M
carretilla^F
carrello^M portabombole

吹管（すいかん）
pencil point tip
Punktbrenner^M
brûleur^F flamme^F crayon^M
boquilla^F para concentrar la llama^F
ugello^M

圧力調整器
pressure regulator
Druckminderer^M
régulateur^M de pression^F
regulador^M de presión^F
regolatore^M della pressione^F

酸素ボンベ［シリンダー］
oxygen cylinder
Sauerstoffflasche^F
bouteille^F d'oxygène^M
tanque^M de oxígeno^M
bombola^F d'ossigeno^M

アセチレン・ボンベ［シリンダー］
acetylene cylinder
Acetylenflasche^F
bouteille^F d'acétylène^M
tanque^M de acetileno^M
bombola^F d'acetileno^M

ノズル・キャップ
flame spreader tip
Farbabbrennervorsatz^M
brûleur^M bec^M plat
boquilla^F para expandir la llama^F
diffusore^M della fiamma^F

ホース
hose
Schlauch^M
tuyau^M
manguera^F
tubo^M flessibile

使い捨て燃料ボンベ
disposable fuel cylinder
Einweg-Brennstoffflasche^F
cartouche^F jetable
bombona^F de gas^M
bombola^F del gas^M

溶接トーチ
welding torch
Schweißbrenner^M
chalumeau^M
soplete^M
cannello^M per saldare

日曜大工・園芸

319

日曜大工 | DO-IT-YOURSELF
HEIMWERKEN | BRICOLAGE | BRICOLAJE | FAI DA TE

塗装

| 日本語 | 英語 | ドイツ語 | フランス語 | スペイン語 | イタリア語 |

painting upkeep | Anstreichen^N und Lackieren^N | peinture^F d'entretien^M | mantenimiento^M de pinturas^F | verniciatura^F: manutenzione^F

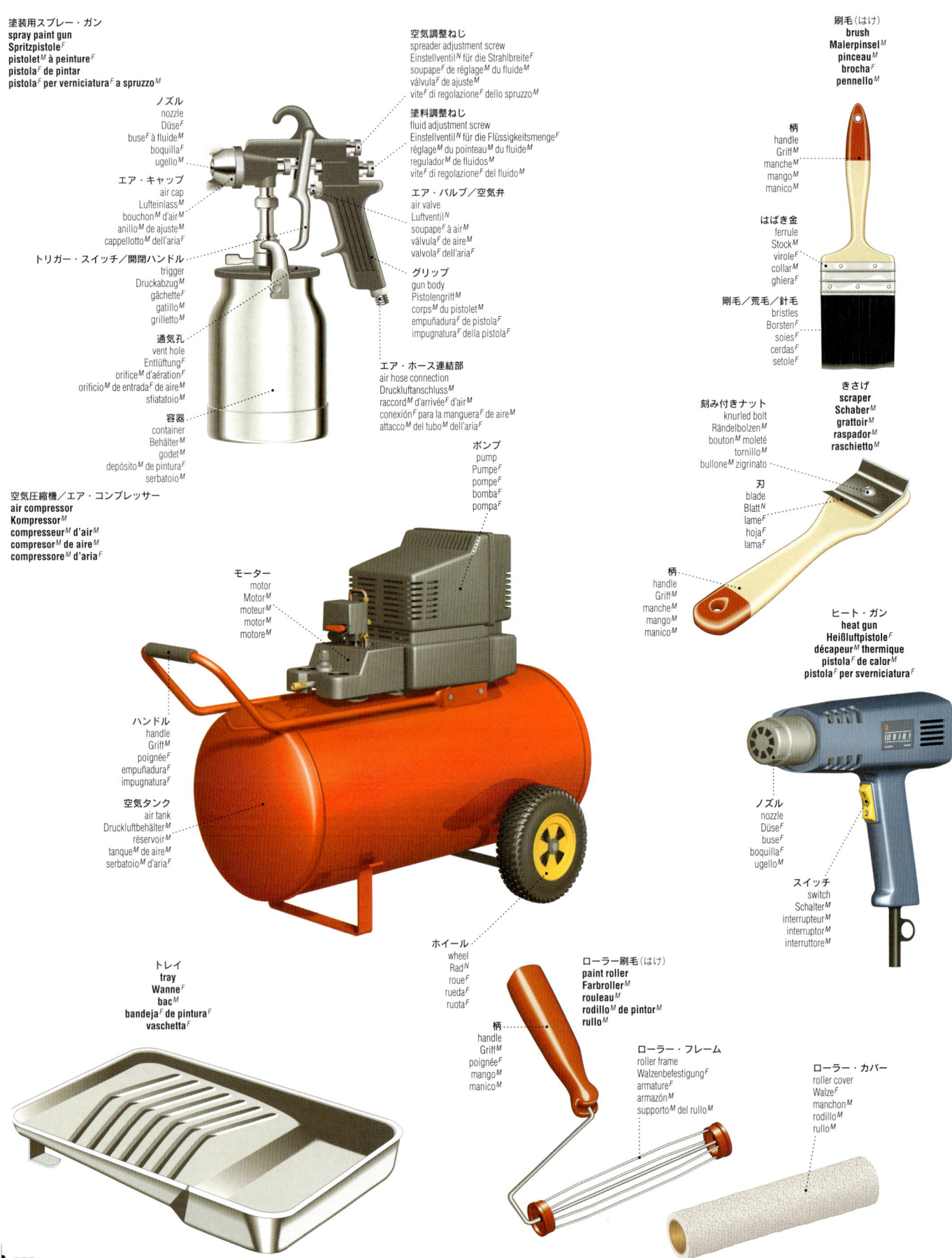

塗装用スプレー・ガン
spray paint gun
Spritzpistole^F
pistolet^M à peinture^F
pistola^F de pintar
pistola^F per verniciatura^F a spruzzo^M

ノズル
nozzle
Düse^F
buse^F à fluide^M
boquilla^F
ugello^M

エア・キャップ
air cap
Lufteinlass^M
bouchon^M d'air^M
anillo^M de ajuste^F
cappellotto^M dell'aria^F

トリガー・スイッチ／開閉ハンドル
trigger
Druckabzug^M
gâchette^F
gatillo^M
grilletto^M

通気孔
vent hole
Entlüftung^F
orifice^M d'aération^F
orificio^M de entrada^F de aire^M
sfiatatoio^M

容器
container
Behälter^M
godet^M
depósito^M de pintura^F
serbatoio^M

空気圧縮機／エア・コンプレッサー
air compressor
Kompressor^M
compresseur^M d'air^M
compresor^M de aire^M
compressore^M d'aria^F

空気調整ねじ
spreader adjustment screw
Einstellventil^N für die Strahlbreite^F
soupape^F de réglage^M du fluide^M
válvula^F de ajuste^M
vite^F di regolazione^F dello spruzzo^M

塗料調整ねじ
fluid adjustment screw
Einstellventil^N für die Flüssigkeitsmenge^F
réglage^M du pointeau^M du fluide^M
regulador^M de fluidos^M
vite^F di regolazione^F del fluido^M

エア・バルブ／空気弁
air valve
Luftventil^N
soupape^F de aire^M
válvula^F de aire^M
valvola^F dell'aria^F

グリップ
gun body
Pistolengriff^M
corps^M du pistolet^M
empuñadura^F de pistola^F
impugnatura^F della pistola^F

エア・ホース連結部
air hose connection
Druckluftanschluss^M
raccord^M d'arrivée^F d'air^M
conexión^F para la manguera^F de aire^M
attacco^M del tubo^M dell'aria^F

ポンプ
pump
Pumpe^F
pompe^F
bomba^F
pompa^F

モーター
motor
Motor^M
moteur^M
motor^M
motore^M

ハンドル
handle
Griff^M
poignée^F
empuñadura^F
impugnatura^F

空気タンク
air tank
Druckluftbehälter^M
réservoir^M
tanque^M de aire^M
serbatoio^M d'aria^F

ホイール
wheel
Rad^N
roue^F
rueda^F
ruota^F

トレイ
tray
Wanne^F
bac^M
bandeja^F de pintura^F
vaschetta^F

刷毛（はけ）
brush
Malerpinsel^M
pinceau^M
brocha^F
pennello^M

柄
handle
Griff^M
manche^M
mango^M
manico^M

はばき金
ferrule
Stock^M
virole^F
collar^M
ghiera^F

剛毛／荒毛／針毛
bristles
Borsten^F
soies^F
cerdas^F
setole^F

きさげ
scraper
Schaber^M
grattoir^M
raspador^M
raschietto^M

刻み付きナット
knurled bolt
Rändelbolzen^M
bouton^M moleté
tornillo^M
bullone^M zigrinato

刃
blade
Blatt^N
lame^F
hoja^F
lama^F

柄
handle
Griff^M
manche^M
mango^M
manico^M

ヒート・ガン
heat gun
Heißluftpistole^F
décapeur^M thermique
pistola^F de calor^M
pistola^F per sverniciatura^F

ノズル
nozzle
Düse^F
buse^F
boquilla^F
ugello^M

スイッチ
switch
Schalter^M
interrupteur^M
interruptor^M
interruttore^M

ローラー刷毛（はけ）
paint roller
Farbroller^M
rouleau^M
rodillo^M de pintor^M
rullo^M

柄
handle
Griff^M
poignée^F
mango^M
manico^M

ローラー・フレーム
roller frame
Walzenbefestigung^F
armature^F
armazón^M
supporto^M del rullo^M

ローラー・カバー
roller cover
Walze^F
manchon^M
rodillo^M
rullo^M

日曜大工 | DO-IT-YOURSELF
HEIMWERKEN | BRICOLAGE | BRICOLAJE | FAI DA TE

はしごと脚立（きゃたつ）

ladders and stepladders | Leitern[F] und Stehleitern[F] | échelles[F] et escabeaux[M] | escaleras[F] de mano | scale[F] e scale[F] a libretto[M]

引き込みばしご
foldaway ladder
Dachbodenleiter[F]
échelle[F] escamotable
escalera[F] extensible de buhardilla[F]
scala[F] retrattile

垂直ばしご
straight ladder
Anlegeleiter[F]
échelle[F] droite
escalera[F] común
scala[F] a pioli[M]

フック付きはしご
hook ladder
Einhängeleiter[F]
échelle[F] à crochets[M]
escalera[F] de gancho[M]
scala[F] a pioli[M] con ganci[M]

延長[伸展／繰り出し]はしご
extension ladder
Ausziehleiter[F]
échelle[F] coulissante
escalera[F] extensible
scala[F] estensibile

横桟
rung
Sprosse[F]
échelon[M]
travesaño[M]
piolo[M]

支柱
side rail
Holm[M]
montant[M]
larguero[M]
staggio[M]

滑車
pulley
Seilzug[M]
poulie[F]
polea[F]
puleggia[F]

固定装置
locking device
Sprossenarretierung[F]
dispositif[M] de blocage[M]
dispositivo[M] de bloqueo[M]
dispositivo[M] di blocco[M]

ローリング・タワー
ladder scaffold
Leitergerüst[N]
échelle[F] d'échafaudage[M]
andamio[M] sobre ruedas[F]
trabattello[M]

縄ばしご
rope ladder
Strickleiter[F]
échelle[F] de corde[F]
escalera[F] de cuerda[F]
biscaglina[F]

巻き上げロープ
hoisting rope
Seil[N]
corde[F] de tirage[M]
cuerda[F] de elevación[F]
fune[F] di sollevamento[F]

滑り止め付きシュー[石突き]
antislip shoe
rutschfester Fuß[M]
patin[M] antidérapant
zapata[F] antideslizante
piedino[M] snodato antiscivolo

果樹園用はしご
fruit-picking ladder
landwirtschaftliche Nutzleiter[F]
échelle[F] fruitière
escalera[F] de recolección[F] de fruta[F]
scala[F] per agricoltura[F]

伸縮自在はしご
multipurpose ladder
Mehrzweckleiter[F]
échelle[F] transformable
escalera[F] multiuso
scala[F] multiuso

回転はしご
rolling ladder
Rollenleiter[F]
échelle[F] roulante
escalera[F] rodante
scala[F] a palchetto[M] con ruote[F]

脚立（きゃたつ）
stepladder
Stehleiter[F]
escabeau[M]
escalera[F] de tijera[F]
scala[F] a libretto[M]

踏み段付き椅子
step stool
Tritthocker[M]
tabouret[M]-escabeau[M]
taburete[M] escalera[F]
scala[F] sgabello[M]

足場付きはしご
platform ladder
Trittleiter[F]
marchepied[M]
escalera[F] de plataforma[F]
scala[F] con piattaforma[F]

天板
top
Podest[N]
plateau[M]
parte[F] superior
cima[F]

バケツ台
tool shelf
Arbeitsbrett[N]
tablette[F] porte-outil[M]
bandeja[F] para herramientas[F]
mensola[F] portautensili

留め金具
brace
Ausklapparretierung[F]
entretoise[F]
tirante[M]
braccio[M] distanziatore

踏み台[段]／ステップ
step
Stufe[F]
marche[F]
peldaño[M]
gradino[M]

安全手すり
safety rail
Sicherheitsholm[M]
garde-corps[M]
barandilla[F]
barra[F] d'appoggio[M]

フレーム
frame
Gestell[N]
piètement[M]
armazón[M]
montante[M]

ゴム・キャップ／ゴム・ストッパー
rubber tip; rubber stopper
Gummistöpsel[M]
embout[M]
zapata[F] de goma[F]
piedino[M] di gomma[F]

棚
shelf
Ablage[F]
tablette[F]
entrepaño[M]
ripiano[M]

台
platform
Plattform[F]
plate-forme[F]
plataforma[F]
piattaforma[F]

踏み台[段]／ステップ
step
Tritt[M]
marche[F]
peldaño[M]
gradino[M]

日曜大工・園芸

321

園芸 | GARDENING
GARTENARBEIT | JARDINAGE | JARDINERÍA | GIARDINAGGIO

庭

日本語 | 英語 | ドイツ語 | フランス語 | スペイン語 | イタリア語

pleasure garden | Ziergarten^M | jardin^M d'agrément^M | jardín^M | giardino^M

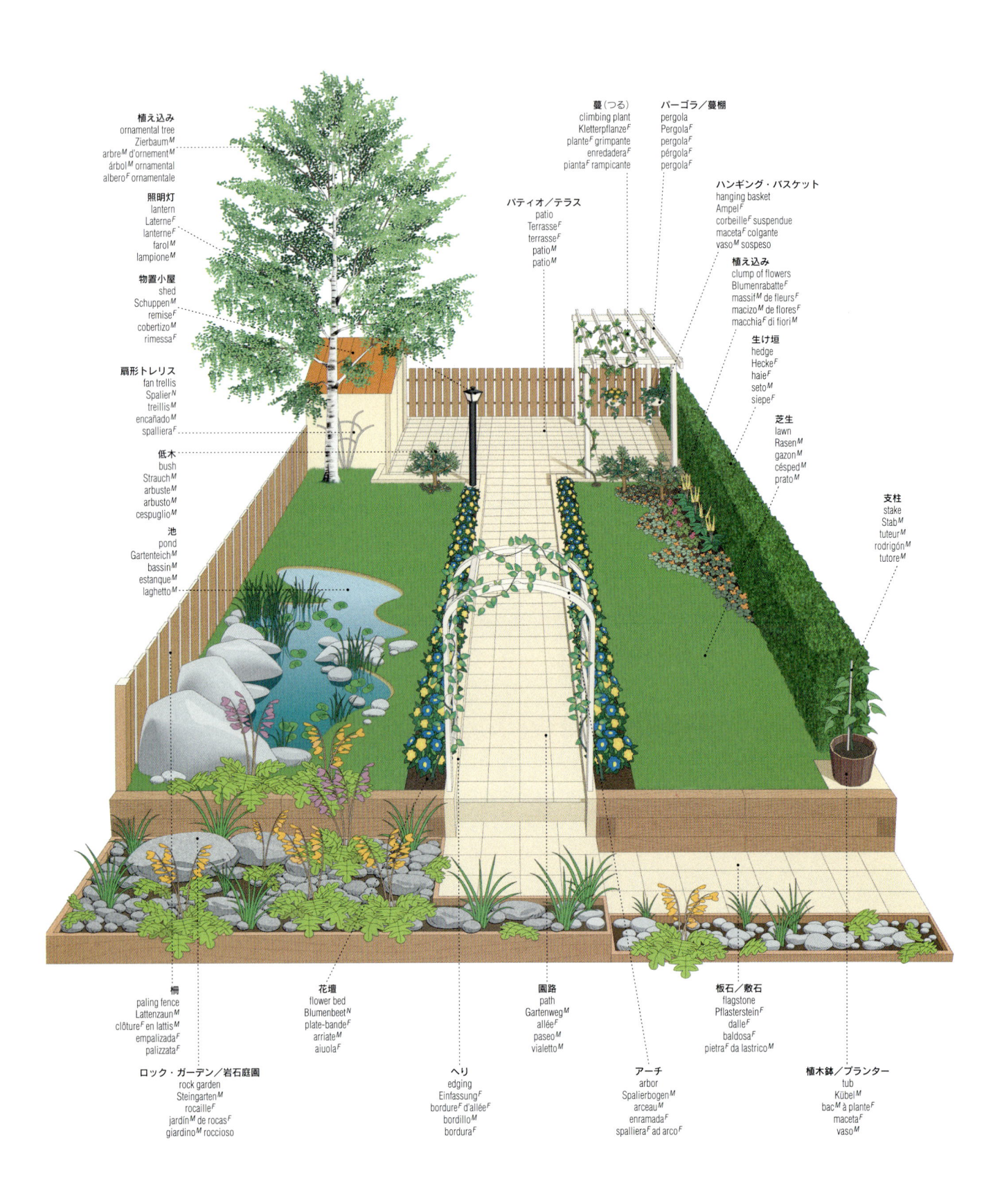

植え込み
ornamental tree
Zierbaum^M
arbre^M d'ornement^M
árbol^M ornamental
albero^F ornamentale

照明灯
lantern
Laterne^F
lanterne^F
farol^M
lampione^M

物置小屋
shed
Schuppen^M
remise^F
cobertizo^M
rimessa^F

扇形トレリス
fan trellis
Spalier^N
treillis^M
encañado^M
spalliera^F

低木
bush
Strauch^M
arbuste^F
arbusto^M
cespuglio^M

池
pond
Gartenteich^M
bassin^M
estanque^M
laghetto^M

蔓(つる)
climbing plant
Kletterpflanze^F
plante^F grimpante
enredadera^F
pianta^F rampicante

パティオ／テラス
patio
Terrasse^F
terrasse^F
patio^M
patio^M

パーゴラ／蔓棚
pergola
Pergola^F
pergola^F
pérgola^F
pergola^F

ハンギング・バスケット
hanging basket
Ampel^F
corbeille^F suspendue
maceta^F colgante
vaso^M sospeso

植え込み
clump of flowers
Blumenrabatte^F
massif^M de fleurs^F
macizo^M de flores^F
macchia^F di fiori^M

生け垣
hedge
Hecke^F
haie^F
seto^M
siepe^F

芝生
lawn
Rasen^M
gazon^M
césped^M
prato^M

支柱
stake
Stab^M
tuteur^M
rodrigón^M
tutore^M

柵
paling fence
Lattenzaun^M
clôture^F en lattis^M
empalizada^F
palizzata^F

花壇
flower bed
Blumenbeet^N
plate-bande^F
arriate^M
aiuola^F

園路
path
Gartenweg^M
allée^F
paseo^M
vialetto^M

板石／敷石
flagstone
Pflasterstein^M
dalle^F
baldosa^F
pietra^F da lastrico^M

ロック・ガーデン／岩石庭園
rock garden
Steingarten^M
rocaille^F
jardín^M de rocas^F
giardino^M roccioso

ヘリ
edging
Einfassung^F
bordure^F d'allée^F
bordillo^M
bordura^F

アーチ
arbor
Spalierbogen^M
arceau^M
enramada^F
spalliera^F ad arco^M

植木鉢／プランター
tub
Kübel^M
bac^M à plante^F
maceta^F
vaso^M

日曜大工・園芸

園芸 | GARDENING
GARTENARBEIT | JARDINAGE | JARDINERÍA | GIARDINAGGIO

いろいろな器具

miscellaneous equipment | verschiedene Geräte | équipement divers | equipamiento vario | attrezzatura varia

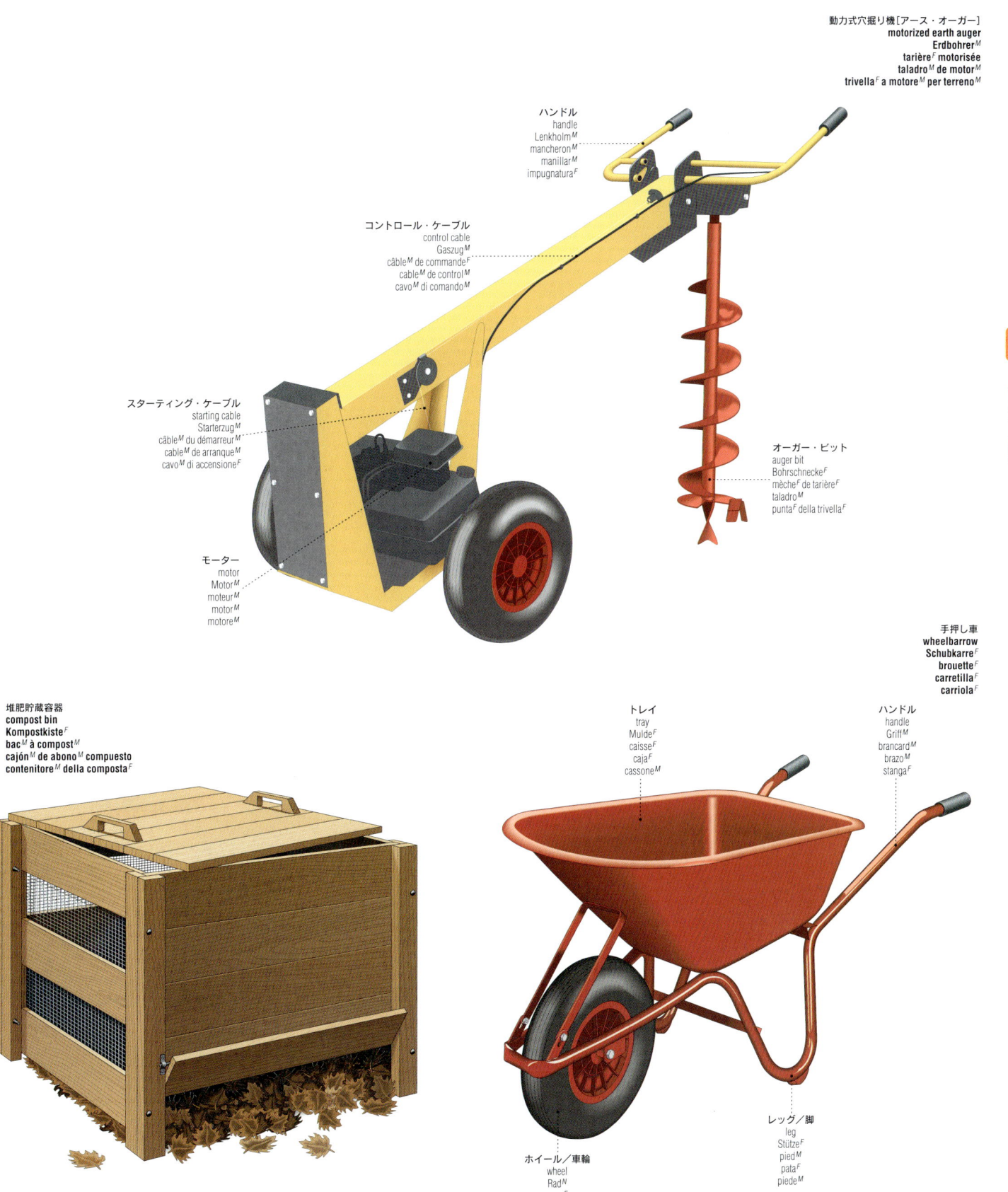

動力式穴掘り機［アース・オーガー］
motorized earth auger
Erdbohrer^M
tarière^F motorisée
taladro^M de motor^M
trivella^F a motore^M per terreno^M

ハンドル
handle
Lenkholm^M
mancheron^M
manillar^M
impugnatura^F

コントロール・ケーブル
control cable
Gaszug^M
câble^M de commande^F
cable^M de control^M
cavo^M di comando^M

スターティング・ケーブル
starting cable
Starterzug^M
câble^M du démarreur^M
cable^M de arranque^M
cavo^M di accensione^F

オーガー・ビット
auger bit
Bohrschnecke^F
mèche^F de tarière^F
taladro^M
punta^F della trivella^F

モーター
motor
Motor^M
moteur^M
motor^M
motore^M

手押し車
wheelbarrow
Schubkarre^F
brouette^F
carretilla^F
carriola^F

堆肥貯蔵容器
compost bin
Kompostkiste^F
bac^M à compost^M
cajón^M de abono^M compuesto
contenitore^M della composta^F

トレイ
tray
Mulde^F
caisse^F
caja^F
cassone^M

ハンドル
handle
Griff^M
brancard^M
brazo^M
stanga^F

ホイール／車輪
wheel
Rad^N
roue^F
rueda^F
ruota^F

レッグ／脚
leg
Stütze^F
pied^M
pata^F
piede^M

日曜大工・園芸

323

園芸 | GARDENING
GARTENARBEIT | JARDINAGE | JARDINERÍA | GIARDINAGGIO

種播(ま)き・植え付け用具

seeding and planting tools | Werkzeuge^N zum Säen^N und Pflanzen^N | outils^M pour semer et planter | herramientas^F para sembrar y plantar | attrezzi^M per seminare e piantare

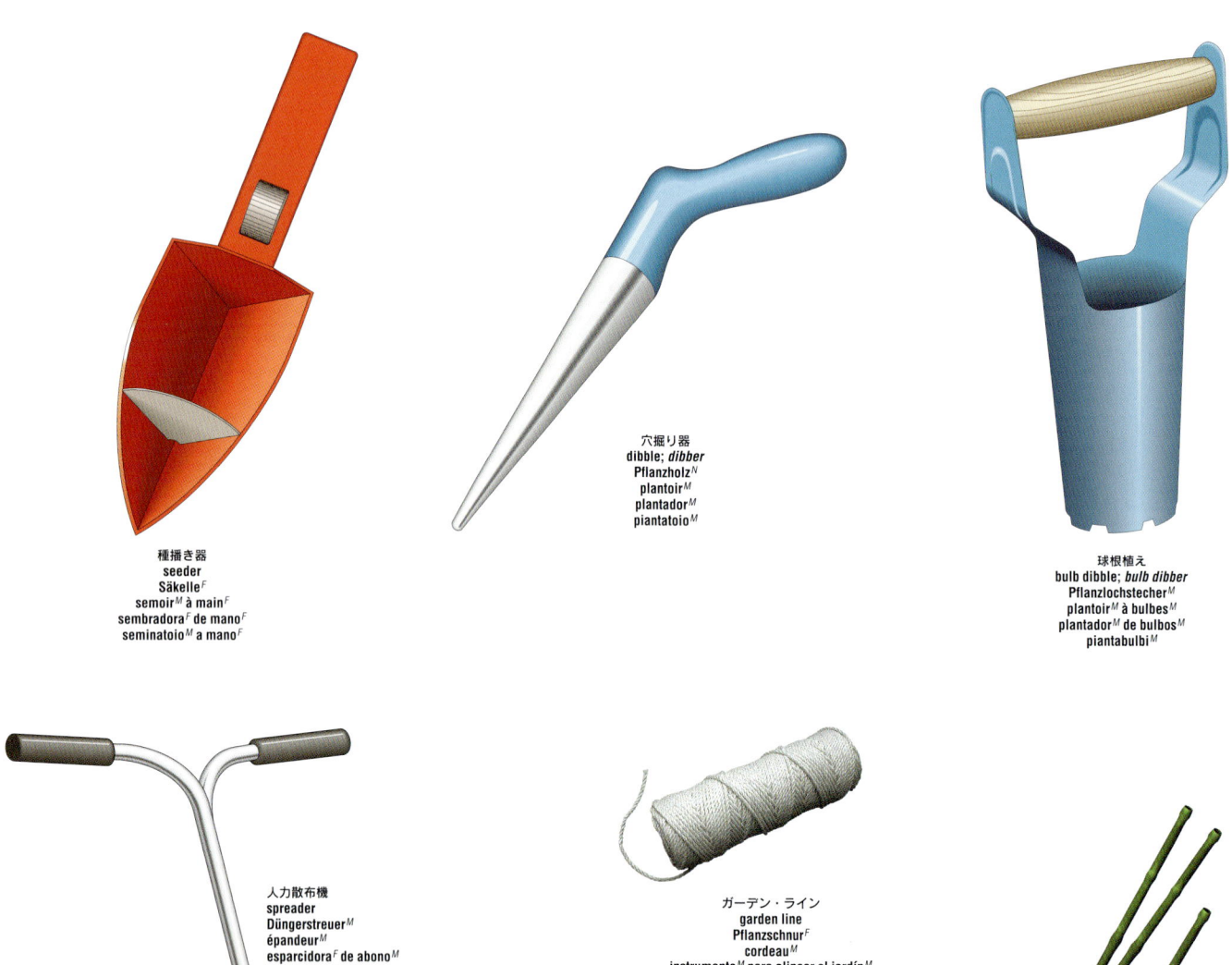

日本語 | 英語 | ドイツ語 | フランス語 | スペイン語 | イタリア語

日曜大工・園芸

穴掘り器
dibble; *dibber*
Pflanzholz^N
plantoir^M
plantador^M
piantatoio^M

種播き器
seeder
Säkelle^F
semoir^M à main^F
sembradora^F de mano^F
seminatoio^M a mano^F

球根植え
bulb dibble; *bulb dibber*
Pflanzlochstecher^M
plantoir^M à bulbes^M
plantador^M de bulbos^M
piantabulbi^M

人力散布機
spreader
Düngerstreuer^M
épandeur^M
esparcidora^F de abono^M
spandiconcime^M

ガーデン・ライン
garden line
Pflanzschnur^F
cordeau^M
instrumento^M para alinear el jardín^M
filo^M da giardino^M

支柱
stake
Baumstütze^F
tuteur^M
rodrigón^M
tutore^M

園芸 | GARDENING
GARTENARBEIT | JARDINAGE | JARDINERÍA | GIARDINAGGIO

小型園芸用具

hand tools | Handwerkzeuge[N] | jeu[M] de petits outils[M] | juego[M] de pequeñas herramientas[F] | attrezzi[M] per piccoli lavori[M] di giardinaggio[M]

小型草かき
small hand cultivator
Kralle[F]
griffe[F] à fleurs[F]
cultivador[M] de mano[F]
sarchiello[M] a mano[F]

移植鏝（ごて）
trowel
Pflanzkelle[F]
transplantoir[M]
desplantador[M]
trapiantatoio[M]

草取り／除草器
weeder
Unkrautstecher[M]
tire-racine[M]
desyerbador[M]
estirpatore[M]

園芸用手袋
gardening gloves
Gartenhandschuhe[M]
gants[M] de jardinage[M]
guantes[M] de jardinería[F]
guanti[M] da giardinaggio[M]

ハンド・フォーク
hand fork
Handgabel[F]
fourche[F] à fleurs[F]
horquilla[F] de mano[F]
piccola forca[F] a mano[F]

日曜大工・園芸

園芸 | GARDENING
GARTENARBEIT | JARDINAGE | JARDINERÍA | GIARDINAGGIO

土をほぐす用具

tools for loosening the earth | Geräte[N] zur Erdbewegung[F] | outils[M] pour remuer la terre[F] | herramientas[F] para remover la tierra[F] | attrezzi[M] per smuovere la terra[F]

日本語 | 英語 | ドイツ語 | フランス語 | スペイン語 | イタリア語

日曜大工・園芸

シャベル／スコップ
shovel
Grabschaufel[F]
pelle[F]
pala[F]
badile[M]

シャベル／スコップ
spade
Spaten[M]
bêche[F]
laya[F]
vanga[F]

掘り起こし［堆肥／干し草］用熊手
spading fork; *digging fork*
Grabgabel[F]
fourche[F] à bêcher
horca[F]
forcone[F]

芝切り
lawn edger
Kantenstecher[M]
coupe-bordures[M]
cuchilla[F] para delimitar el césped[M]
tagliabordi[M]

除草鍬（ぐわ）
weeding hoe
Handkultivator[M]
sarcloir[M]
cultivador[M]
coltivatore[M]

ホー・フォーク
hoe-fork
Kombihacke[F]
serfouette[F]
azuela[F]
zappetta[F] tridente

引き鍬
draw hoe
Rübenhacke[F]
binette[F]
azada[F]
sarchiello[M]

手押し鍬
scuffle hoe
Ziehhacke[F]
ratissoire[F]
azada[F] de doble filo[M]
sarchio[M]

園芸 | GARDENING
GARTENARBEIT | JARDINAGE | JARDINERÍA | GIARDINAGGIO

土をほぐす用具

鍬（くわ）
hoe
Rodehacke^F
houe^F
azadón^M
zappa^F

つるはし
pick
Kreuzhacke^F
pioche^F
pico^M
piccone^M

日曜大工・園芸

熊手／レーキ
rake
Rechen^M
râteau^M
rastrillo^M
rastrello^M

股鍬
hook
Krail^M
croc^M à défricher
garabato^M
zappa^F a quattro denti^M

耕耘（こううん）機
tiller; Rotavator
Gartenfräse^F
motoculteur^M
motocultor^M
motocoltivatore^M

ハンドルバー／操作レバー
handlebar
Lenkholm^M
mancheron^M
manillar^F
manubrio^M

クラッチ・レバー
clutch lever
Kupplungshebel^M
levier^M d'embrayage^M
palanca^F del embrague^M
leva^F d'innesto^M della frizione^F

フレーム
frame
Rahmen^M
châssis^M
chasis^M
telaio^M

走行変速レバー
forward/reverse
vorwärts/rückwärts
marche^F avant/marche^F arrière
palanca^F de avance^M/marcha^F atrás
innesto^M marcia^F avanti/marcia^F indietro

スターター
starter
Anlasser^M
démarreur^M manuel
arranque^M
motorino^M d'avviamento^M

歯杆（しかん）／刃／タイン
tine
Zinken^N
dent^F
púa^F de muelle^M
rebbio^M

モーター
motor
Motor^M
moteur^M
motor^M
motore^M

327

園芸 | GARDENING
GARTENARBEIT | JARDINAGE | JARDINERÍA | GIARDINAGGIO

水撒(ま)き用具

watering tools | Gießgeräte^N | outils^M pour arroser | herramientas^F para regar | attrezzi^M per annaffiare

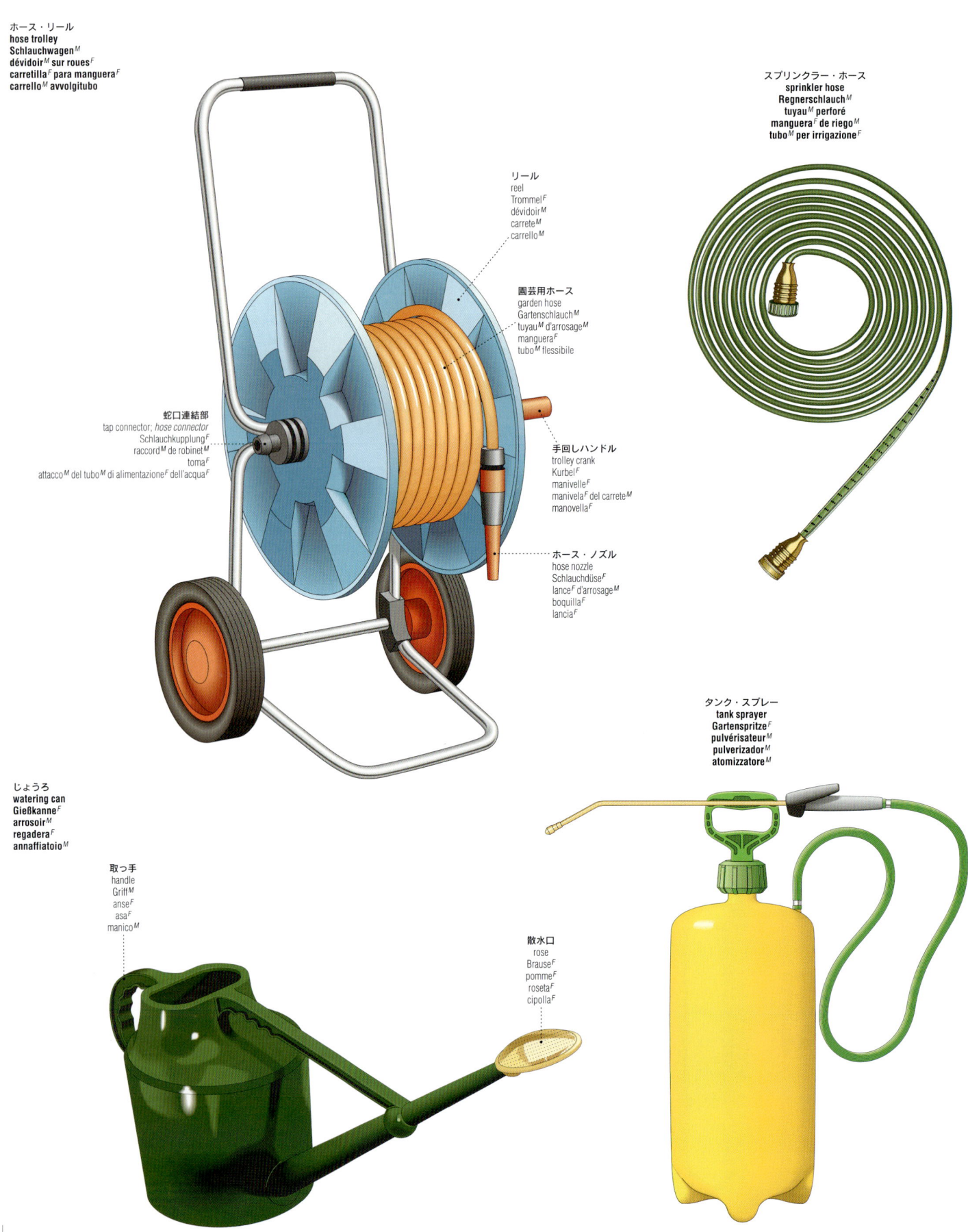

日本語 | 英語 | ドイツ語 | フランス語 | スペイン語 | イタリア語

ホース・リール
hose trolley
Schlauchwagen^M
dévidoir^M sur roues^F
carretilla^F para manguera^F
carrello^M avvolgitubo

リール
reel
Trommel^F
dévidoir^M
carrete^M
carrello^M

園芸用ホース
garden hose
Gartenschlauch^M
tuyau^M d'arrosage^M
manguera^F
tubo^M flessibile

蛇口連結部
tap connector; hose connector
Schlauchkupplung^F
raccord^M de robinet^M
toma^F
attacco^M del tubo^M di alimentazione^F dell'acqua^F

手回しハンドル
trolley crank
Kurbel^F
manivelle^F
manivela^F del carrete^M
manovella^F

ホース・ノズル
hose nozzle
Schlauchdüse^F
lance^F d'arrosage^M
boquilla^F
lancia^F

スプリンクラー・ホース
sprinkler hose
Regnerschlauch^M
tuyau^M perforé
manguera^F de riego^M
tubo^M per irrigazione^F

タンク・スプレー
tank sprayer
Gartenspritze^F
pulvérisateur^M
pulverizador^M
atomizzatore^M

じょうろ
watering can
Gießkanne^F
arrosoir^M
regadera^F
annaffiatoio^M

取っ手
handle
Griff^M
anse^F
asa^F
manico^M

散水口
rose
Brause^F
pomme^F
roseta^F
cipolla^F

日曜大工・園芸

328

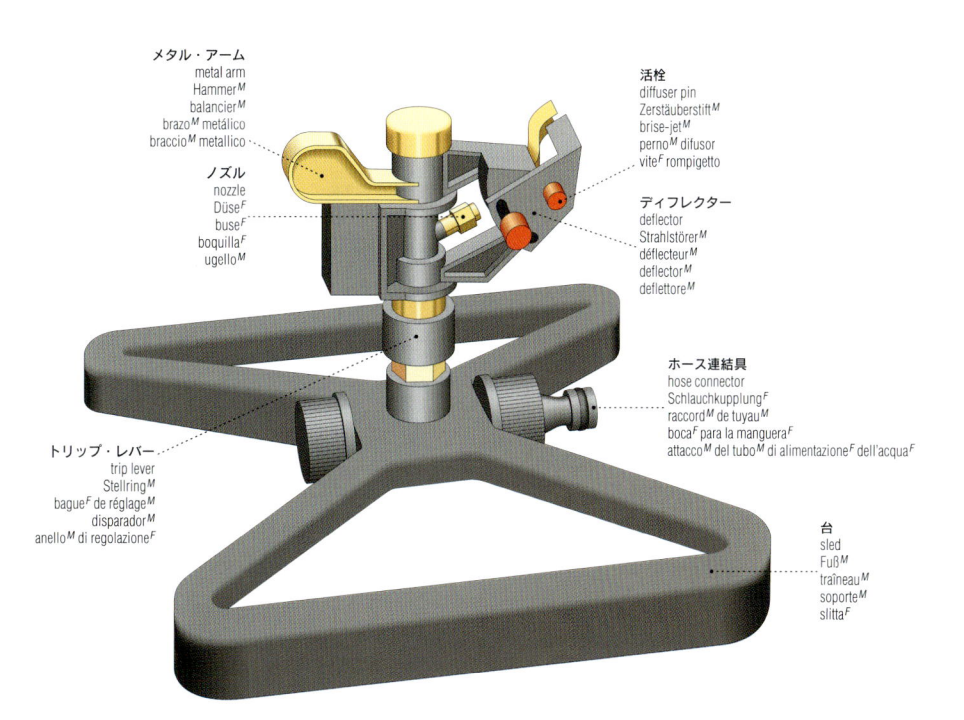

園芸 | GARDENING
GARTENARBEIT | JARDINAGE | JARDINERÍA | GIARDINAGGIO

水撒(ま)き用具

ピストル・ノズル
pistol nozzle
Gießpistole^F
pistolet^M d'arrosage^M
pistola^F pulverizadora
polverizzatore^M a pistola^F

ハンド・スプレー
sprayer
Sprühflasche^F
vaporisateur^M
pulverizador^M
spruzzatore^M

スプレー・ノズル
spray nozzle
Gießbrause^F
pistolet^M arrosoir^M
boquilla^F pulverizadora
nebulizzatore^M

アーム
arm
Drehdüse^F
bras^M
brazo^M
braccio^M

振動式[旋回式]スプリンクラー
oscillating sprinkler
Viereckregner^M
arroseur^M oscillant
irrigador^M oscilante
irrigatore^M oscillante

回転式スプリンクラー
revolving sprinkler
Kreisregner^M
arroseur^M rotatif
irrigador^M giratorio
irrigatore^M rotativo a pioggia^F

メタル・アーム
metal arm
Hammer^M
balancier^M
brazo^M metálico
braccio^M metallico

ノズル
nozzle
Düse^F
buse^F
boquilla^F
ugello^M

活栓
diffuser pin
Zerstäuberstift^M
brise-jet^M
perno^M difusor
vite^F rompigetto

ディフレクター
deflector
Strahlstörer^M
déflecteur^M
deflector^M
deflettore^M

ホース連結具
hose connector
Schlauchkupplung^F
raccord^M de tuyau^M
boca^F para la manguera^F
attacco^M del tubo^M di alimentazione^F dell'acqua^F

反発式スプリンクラー
impulse sprinkler
Impulsregner^M
arroseur^M canon^M
irrigador^M de impulso^M
irrigatore^M a impulsi^M

トリップ・レバー
trip lever
Stellring^M
bague^F de réglage^M
disparador^M
anello^M di regolazione^F

台
sled
Fuß^M
traîneau^M
soporte^M
slitta^F

園芸 | GARDENING
GARTENARBEIT | JARDINAGE | JARDINERÍA | GIARDINAGGIO

剪定(せんてい)用具

pruning and cutting tools | Schneidwerkzeuge^N | outils^M pour couper | herramientas^F para cortar | attrezzi^M per potare e tagliare

日本語 | 英語 | ドイツ語 | フランス語 | スペイン語 | イタリア語

(生け垣用の)刈り込み鋏(ばさみ)
hedge shears
Heckenschere^F
cisaille^F à haies^F
cizallas^F para setos^M
forbici^F tagliasiepi

斧／鉞(まさかり)
axe
Axt^F
hache^F
hacha^F
accetta^F

剪定(せんてい)鋏
lopping shears
Astschere^F
ébrancheur^M
podadera^F
cesoie^F

剪定鋸(のこ)
pruning saw
Baumsäge^F
scie^F d'élagage^M
sierra^F de podar
sega^F da giardiniere^M

剪定[植木]鋏
pruning shears; *secateurs*
Baumschere^F
sécateur^M
tijeras^F de podar
cesoie^F da giardino^M

接(つ)ぎ木用ナイフ
grafting knife
Veredelungsmesser^N
greffoir^M
navaja^F de injertar
innestatoio^M

円形鎌
sickle
Sichel^F
faucille^F
hoz^F
falcetto^M

園丁ナイフ／剪枝刀(せんしとう)
pruning knife
Baumhippe^F
serpette^F
podón^M
potatoio^M

高所剪定鋏
tree pruner
Raupenschere^F mit Teleskopstiel^M
échenilloir^M-élagueur^M
podadera^F de árboles^M
svettatoio^M

大鎌
scythe
Sense^F
faux^F
guadaña^F
falce^F

鉈(なた)鎌
billhook
Hippe^F
serpe^F
navaja^F jardinera
roncola^F

園芸 | GARDENING
GARTENARBEIT | JARDINAGE | JARDINERÍA | GIARDINAGGIO

剪定(せんてい)用具

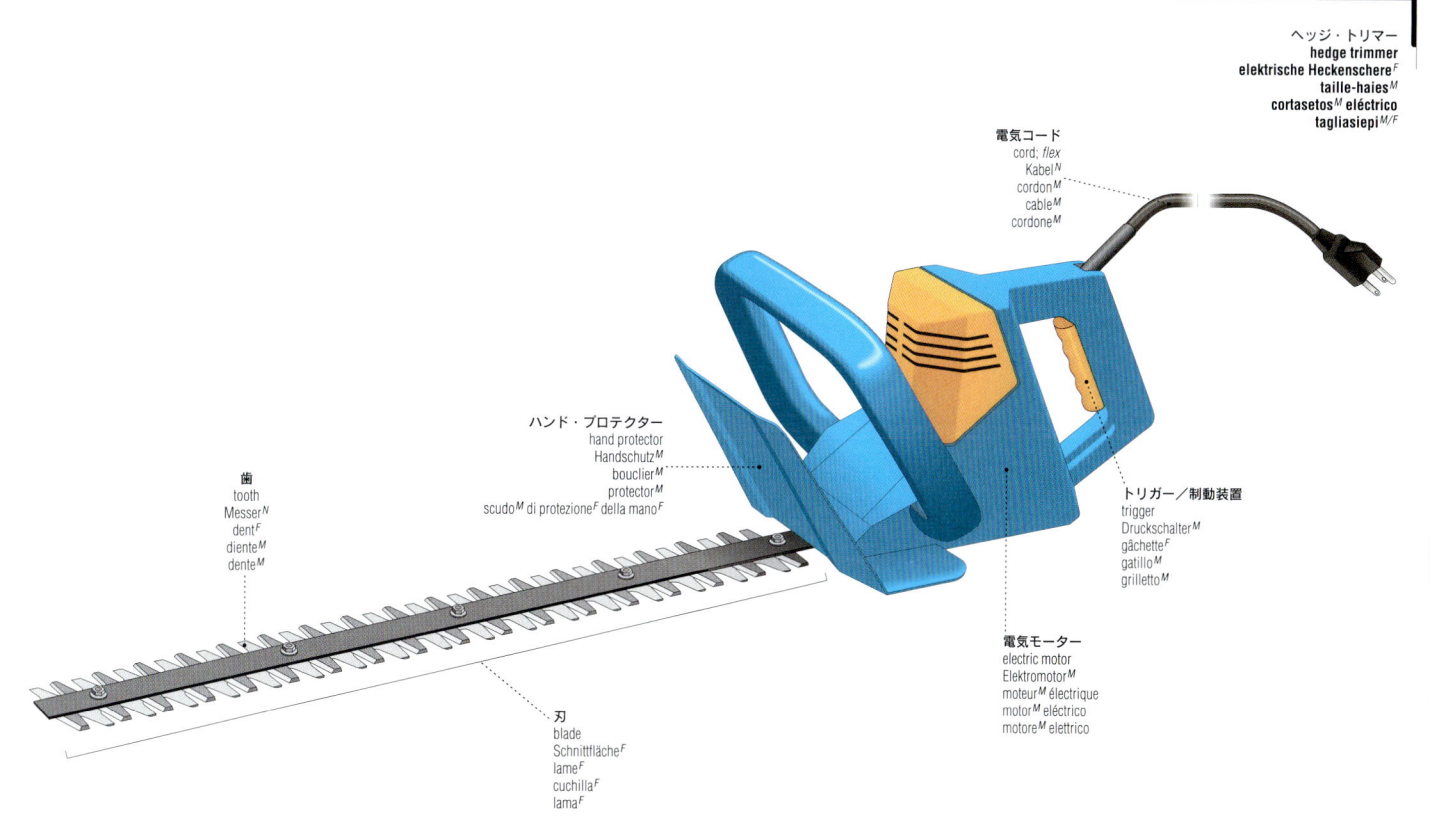

ヘッジ・トリマー
hedge trimmer
elektrische Heckenschere F
taille-haies M
cortasetos M eléctrico
tagliasiepi M/F

電気コード
cord; flex
Kabel N
cordon M
cable M
cordone M

ハンド・プロテクター
hand protector
Handschutz M
bouclier M
protector M
scudo M di protezione F della mano F

歯
tooth
Messer N
dent F
diente M
dente M

トリガー／制動装置
trigger
Druckschalter M
gâchette F
gatillo M
grilletto M

電気モーター
electric motor
Elektromotor M
moteur M électrique
motor M eléctrico
motore M elettrico

刃
blade
Schnittfläche F
lame F
cuchilla F
lama F

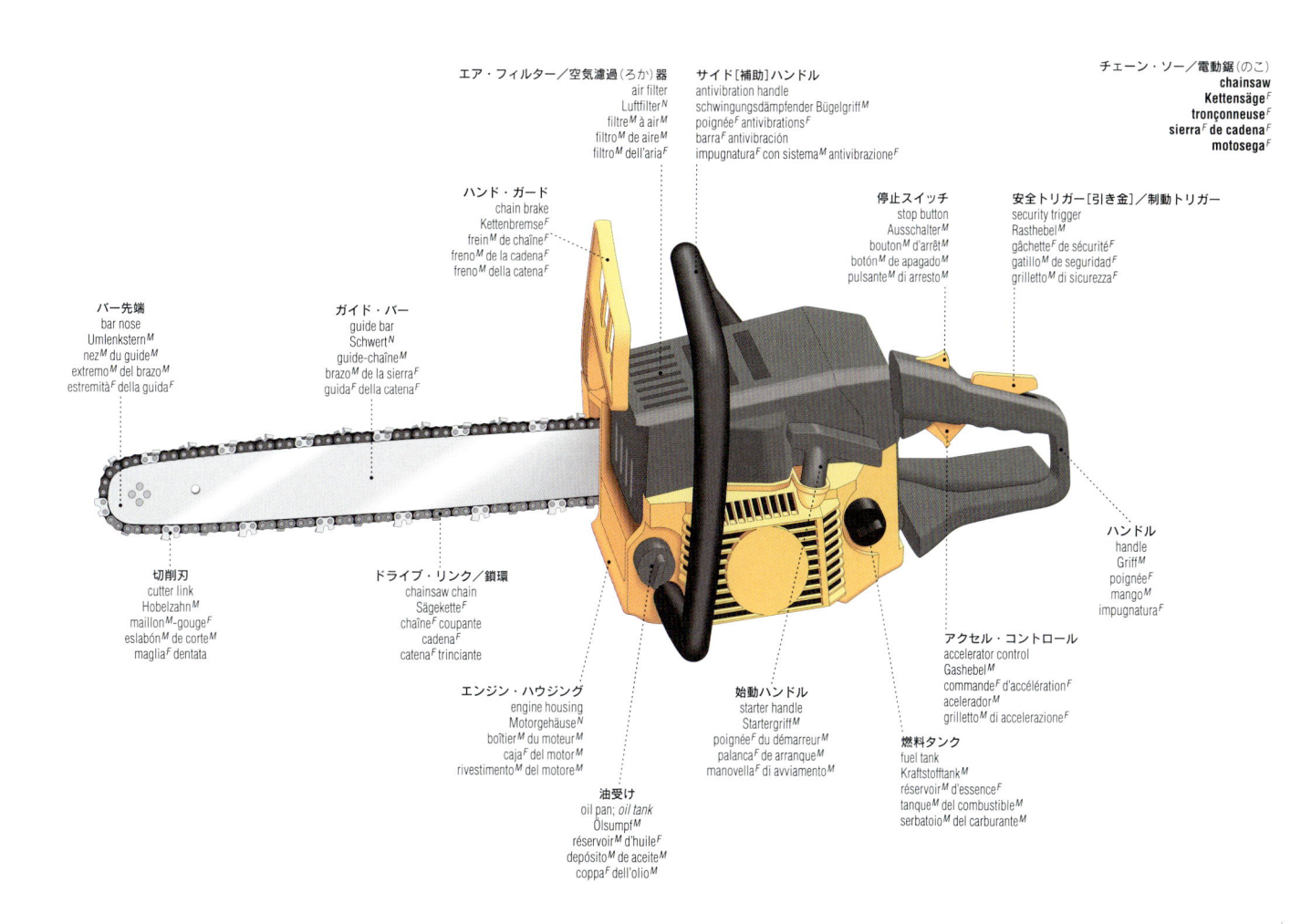

エア・フィルター／空気濾過(ろか)器
air filter
Luftfilter N
filtre M à air
filtro M de aire M
filtro M dell'aria F

サイド[補助]ハンドル
antivibration handle
schwingungsdämpfender Bügelgriff M
poignée F antivibrations
barra M antivibración
impugnatura F con sistema M antivibrazione F

チェーン・ソー／電動鋸(のこ)
chainsaw
Kettensäge F
tronçonneuse F
sierra F de cadena F
motosega F

ハンド・ガード
chain brake
Kettenbremse F
frein M de chaîne F
freno M de la cadena F
freno M della catena F

停止スイッチ
stop button
Ausschalter M
bouton M d'arrêt M
botón M de apagado M
pulsante M di arresto M

安全トリガー[引き金]／制動トリガー
security trigger
Rasthebel M
gâchette F de sécurité F
gatillo M de seguridad F
grilletto M di sicurezza F

バー先端
bar nose
Umlenkstern M
nez M du guide M
extremo M del brazo M
estremità F della guida F

ガイド・バー
guide bar
Schwert N
guide-chaîne M
brazo M de la sierra F
guida F della catena F

ハンドル
handle
Griff M
poignée F
mango M
impugnatura F

切削刃
cutter link
Hobelzahn M
maillon M-gouge F
eslabón M de corte M
maglia F dentata

ドライブ・リンク／鎖環
chainsaw chain
Sägekette F
chaîne F coupante
cadena F
catena F trinciante

アクセル・コントロール
accelerator control
Gashebel M
commande F d'accélération F
acelerador M
grilletto M di accelerazione F

エンジン・ハウジング
engine housing
Motorgehäuse N
boîtier M du moteur M
caja F del motor M
rivestimento M del motore M

始動ハンドル
starter handle
Startergriff M
poignée F du démarreur M
palanca F de arranque M
manovella F di avviamento M

燃料タンク
fuel tank
Kraftstofftank M
réservoir M d'essence F
tanque M del combustible M
serbatoio M del carburante M

油受け
oil pan; oil tank
Ölsumpf M
réservoir M d'huile F
depósito M de aceite M
coppa F dell'olio M

日曜大工・園芸

331

園芸 | GARDENING
GARTENARBEIT | JARDINAGE | JARDINERÍA | GIARDINAGGIO

芝の手入れ

lawn care | RasenpflegeF | soinsM de la pelouseF | cuidadoM del céspedM | curaF del pratoM

日本語 | 英語 | ドイツ語 | フランス語 | スペイン語 | イタリア語

(芝)縁刈り機
edger
RasentrimmerM
taille-borduresM
podadoraF de bordesM
tagliabordiM

コード
cord; *flex*
KabelN
cordonM
cableM
cordoneM

電動モーター
electric motor
ElektromotorM
moteurM électrique
motorM eléctrico
motoreM elettrico

安全ケース
security casing
SchutzgehäuseN
carterM de sécuritéF
cubiertaF de seguridadF
calottaF di sicurezzaF

ナイロン・ヤーン
nylon yarn
NylonschnurF
filM de nylonM
hiloM de nailonM
filoM di nylonM

手押し式[手動式]芝刈り機
hand mower
HandrasenmäherM
tondeuseF mécanique
cortacéspedM
falciatriceF a manoM

刃
blade
MesserN
lameF
cuchillaF
lamaF

回転刃
cutting cylinder
MesserwalzeF
cylindreM de coupeF
cilindroM de corteF
cilindroM di taglioM

動力式芝刈り機
power mower
MotorrasenmäherM
tondeuseF à moteurM
cortacéspedM eléctrico
motofalciatriceF

ハンドル
handle
GriffM
guidonM
barraF
impugnaturaF

イグニッション・キー
ignition key
ZündschlüsselM
cléF de contactM
encendidoM
chiaveF dell'accensioneF

速度調整つまみ
speed control
GeschwindigkeitsreglerM
sélecteurM de régimeM
controlM de velocidadF
regolatoreM della velocitàF

安全ハンドル
safety handle
SicherheitsgriffM
poignéeF de sécuritéF
palancaF de seguridadF
impugnaturaF di sicurezzaF

集草箱
grassbox
GrasfangM
bacM de ramassageM
cajaF para el céspedM
raccoglierbaM

スターター
starter
AnlasserM
démarreurM manuel
motorM de arranqueM
motorinoM d'avviamentoM

モーター
motor
MotorM
moteurM
motorM
motoreM

燃料注入口キャップ
filler cap
EinfüllstutzenM
bouchonM de remplissageM
bocaF del tanqueM de combustibleM
bocchettaF del serbatoioM

アクセル・ケーブル
accelerator cable
GaszugM
câbleM d'accélérationF
cableM del aceleradorM
cavoM di accelerazioneF

点火プラグ
spark plug; *sparking plug*
ZündkerzeF
bougieF
bujíaF
candelaF di accensioneF

ディフレクター
deflector
SchwadenblechN
déflecteurM
deflectorM
deflettoreM

ケーシング
casing
GehäuseN
carterM
cajaF
scoccaF

332

園芸 | GARDENING
GARTENARBEIT | JARDINAGE | JARDINERÍA | GIARDINAGGIO

芝の手入れ

整地ローラー
roller
Walze^F
rouleau^M
rodillo^M
rullo^M

熊手／芝生レーキ
lawn rake
Rasenbesen^M
balai^M à feuilles^F
rastrillo^M
rastrello^M scopa^F

芝生中耕機
lawn aerator
Vertikutierer^M
aérateur^M à gazon^M
ventilador^M de césped^M
frangizolle^M

芝刈りトラクター
lawn tractor
Aufsitzmäher^M
tondeuse^F autoportée
tractor^M cortacésped
trattore^M tosaerba^M

座席
seat
Sitz^M
siège^M
asiento^M
sedile^M

イグニッション・キー
ignition key
Zündschlüssel^M
clé^F de contact^M
llave^F de inyección^F
chiave^F dell'accensione^F

ハンドル
steering wheel
Lenkrad^N
volant^M
volante^F
volante^M

速度制御レバー
cruise control lever
Fahrtregler^M
régulateur^M de vitesse^F
regulador^M de velocidad^F
leva^F di regolazione^F della velocità^F

カッター・デッキ・リフト・レバー
mower deck lift lever
Mähwerkaushebung^F
levier^M de relevage^M du plateau^M de coupe^F
palanca^F de levantamiento^M del tablero^M de corte^M
leva^F di sollevamento^M della piastra^F di taglio^M

ブレーキ・ペダル
brake pedal
Bremspedal^N
pédale^F de frein^M
pedal^M del freno^M
pedale^M del freno^M

フード
hood
Motorhaube^F
capot^M
capó^M
cofano^M

後輪
rear wheel
Hinterrad^N
roue^F arrière
rueda^F trasera
ruota^F posteriore

前進ペダル
forward travel pedal
Vorwärtsantrieb^M
pédale^F de marche^F avant
pedal^M de marcha^F atrás
pedale^M della marcia^F avanti

ヘッドライト
headlight
Scheinwerfer^M
phare^M
faro^M
fanale^M

後退ペダル
reverse travel pedal
Rückwärtsantrieb^M
pédale^F de marche^F arrière
pedal^M de marcha^F adelante
pedale^M della retromarcia^F

ディフレクター
deflector
Schwadenblech^N
déflecteur^M
deflector^M
deflettore^M

カッター・デッキ
mower deck
Mähwerk^N
plateau^M de coupe^F
plataforma^F de corte^M
piastra^F di taglio^M

定規車／導輪
gauge wheel
Schnitthöhenverstellung^F
roue^F de jauge^F
rueda^F de calibrado^M
ruota^F di calibratura^F

前輪
front wheel
Vorderrad^N
roue^F avant
rueda^F frontal
ruota^F anteriore

日曜大工・園芸

333

334

衣 服

CLOTHING | KLEIDUNG | VÊTEMENTS | VESTIDO | ABBIGLIAMENTO

336 昔の衣装
339 伝統的衣装
340 帽子
342 靴
346 手袋
347 繊維製品取り扱い表示［マーク］
348 男性用衣類
354 セーター
355 女性用衣類
368 ベビー服
369 子供服
370 スポーツウエア

昔の衣装

elements of ancient costume | Elemente^N historischer Kostüme^N | éléments^M du costume^M ancien | indumentaria^F antigua | capi^M antichi

ペプロス
peplos
Peplos^M
péplos^M
peplo^M
peplo^M

留め針
fibula
Fibel^F
fibule^F
fíbula^F
fibula^F

ひだ
fold
Umschlag^M
repli^M
pliegue^M
piega^F

トーガ
toga
Toga^F
toge^F
toga^F
toga^F

サイナス
sinus
Sinus^M
sinus^M
seno^M
seno^M

紫の縁飾り
purple border
Purpursaum^M
bande^F de pourpre^F
orla^F de púrpura^F
bordo^M di porpora^F

ストラ
stola
Stola^F
stola^F
stola^F
stola^F

パラ
palla
Palla^F
palla^F
palla^F
palla^F

クラミス
chlamys
Chlamys^F
chlamyde^F
clámide^F
clamide^F

キトン
chiton
Chiton^M
chiton^M
quitón^M
chitone^M

昔の衣装

フローティング・スリーブ
floating sleeve
HängeärmelM
mancheF flottante
mangaF flotante
manicaF svolazzante

バーティカル・ポケット
vertical pocket
senkrechte TascheF
pocheF verticale
bolsilloM vertical
tascaF verticale

キャップ・スリーブ
short sleeve
ÄrmelpuffM
mancheronM
mangaF corta
manicaF corta

袖
sleeve
ÄrmelM
mancheF
mangaF
manicaF

縁飾り／房縁（ふさべり）
fringe
FranseF
frangeF
orlaF
frangiaF

コタルディ
cotehardie
CotardieF
cotardieF
túnicaF de mangaF larga
cottarditaF

クリノリンの入ったドレス
dress with crinoline
KleidN mit KrinolinenrockM
robeF à crinolineF
vestidoM con crinolinaF
abitoM con crinolinaF

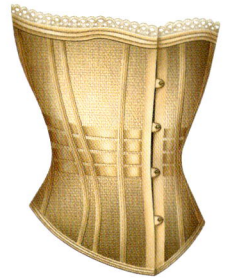

コルセット
corset
KorsettN
corsetM
corséM
corsettoM

アンダースカート
underskirt
UnterrockM
juponM
enaguasF
sottogonnaF

ショール
shawl
SchalM
châleM
chalM
scialleM

キャラコ地のジャケット
caraco jacket
CaracoM
caracoM
blusaF caracó
giaccaF attillata

ひだ飾り
ruffle
SpitzenvolantN
engageanteF
mangaF de volanteM
balzeF increspate

ストマッカー
stomacher
MiederN
pièceF d'estomacM
petoM
pettorinaF

バッスル
bustle
TurnüreF
tournureF
polisónM
sellinoM

サーコート
surcoat
ÜberkleidN
surcotM
sobrevesteM
sopravvesteF

パニエの入ったドレス
dress with panniers
KleidN mit flachem ReifrockM
robeF à paniersM
vestidoM con miriñaqueM
abitoM con panieriM

バッスルの入ったドレス
dress with bustle
KleidN mit TurnüreF
robeF à tournureF
vestidoM con polisónM
abitoM con sellinoM

衣服

337

昔の衣装

日本語 | 英語 | ドイツ語 | フランス語 | スペイン語 | イタリア語

フロック・コート
frock coat
Schoßrock^M
frac^M
levita^F
marsina^F

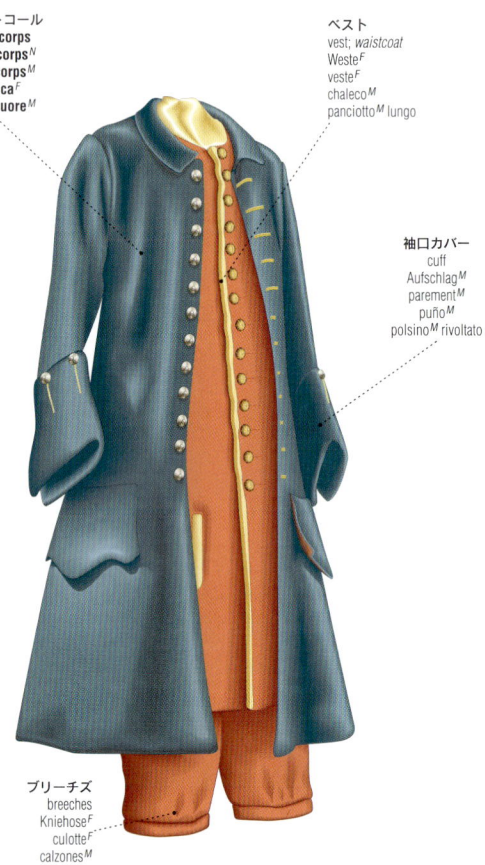

ジュストコール
justaucorps
Justaucorps^N
justaucorps^M
casaca^F
giustacuore^M

ベスト
vest; waistcoat
Weste^F
veste^F
chaleco^M
panciotto^M lungo

ケープ
cape
Umhang^M
cape^F
capa^F
cappa^F

チョッキ／ベスト／胴着
waistcoat
Weste^F
gilet^M
chaleco^M
panciotto^M

袖口カバー
cuff
Aufschlag^M
parement^M
puño^M
polsino^M rivoltato

ジャケット
jacket
Jacke^F
jaquette^F
aljuba^F
giubba^F

ブリーチズ
breeches
Kniehose^F
culotte^F
calzones^M
culottes^F

ブリーチズ
breeches
Kniehose^F
culotte^F
calzones^M
culottes^F

ダブレット
doublet
Wams^N
pourpoint^M
jubón^M
farsetto^M

翼形
wing
Achselstück^N
aileron^M
hombrera^F
ala^F

ハンギング・スリーブ
hanging sleeve
Hängeärmel^M
manche pendante
manga^F colgante
manica^F pendente

ウプランド
houppelande
Houppelande^F
houppelande^F
toga^F
pelanda^F

トランク・ホーズ
trunk hose
Pluderhose^F
haut-de-chausse^M
greguescos^M
calzoni^M a palloncino

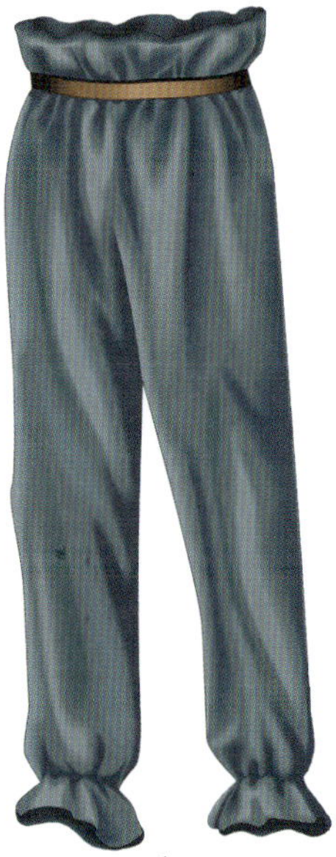

ブレー
braies
Beinlinge^M
braies^F
calzas^F
brache^F

衣服

昔の衣装

エナン
hennin
Hennin^M
hennin^M
cofia^F cónica
cappello^M a cono^M

三角帽
tricorne
Dreispitz^M
tricorne^M
tricornio^M
tricorno^M

二角帽
bicorne
Zweispitz^M
bicorne^M
bicornio^M
bicorno^M

ヒール・シューズ
heeled shoe
Absatzschuh^M
soulier^M à talon^M
zapato^M de tacón^M
scarpa^F con tacco^M

プーレーヌ
crakow
Schnabelschuh^M
soulier^M à la poulaine^F
zapato^M a la polaca
scarpa^F alla polacca

カラーレット
collaret
kleiner Kragen^M
collerette^F
cuello^M de Holanda^F
colletto^M

フレーズ／ひだ襟
fraise
Halskrause^F
fraise^F
gorguera^F
gorgiera^F

ゲートル
gaiter
Gamasche^F
guêtre^F
polaina^F
ghetta^F

衣服

伝統的衣装

traditional clothing | traditionelle Kleidung^F | vêtements^M traditionnels | indumentaria^F tradicional | abiti^M tradizionali

ブーブー
boubou
Boubou^M
boubou^M
boubou^M
boubou^M

カフタン
caftan
Kaftan^M
cafetan^M
caftán^M
caffettano^M

腰布
loincloth
Wickelrock^M
pagne^M
pareo^M
pareo^M

ターバン
turban
Turban^M
turban^M
turbante^M
turbante^M

フェズ／トルコ帽
fez
Fes^M
fez^M
fez^M
fez^M

339

帽子

headgear | Kopfbedeckungen^F | coiffure^F | sombreros^M | copricapi^M

日本語 | 英語 | ドイツ語 | フランス語 | スペイン語 | イタリア語

紳士帽
men's headgear
Herrenkopfbedeckungen^F
coiffures^F d'homme^M
sombreros^M de hombre^M
copricapi^M maschili

フェルト帽
felt hat; *trilby*
Filzhut^M
chapeau^M de feutre^M
sombrero^M de fieltro^M
cappello^M di feltro^M

ハット[帽子の]バンド
hatband
Hutband^N
bourdalou^M
cinta^F
nastro^M

縁取り
binding
Einfassband^N
galon^M
ribete^M
orlo^M

クラウン
crown
Kopfteil$^{M/N}$
calotte^F
copa^F
calotta^F

つば
brim
Krempe^F
bord^M
ala^F
tesa^F

蝶結び／ボー
bow
Schleife^F
nœud^M plat
lazo^M
fiocco^M

ボーター／カンカン帽
boater
Strohhut^M
canotier^M
canotier^M
paglietta^F

キャロット／スカルキャップ／頭蓋帽
skullcap
Käppchen^N
calotte^F
solideo
papalina^F

ダービー・ハット／山高帽
derby; *bowler*
Melone^F
melon^M
sombrero^M de hongo^M
bombetta^F

舟形略帽
garrison cap; *astrakhan cap*
Fellmütze^F
calot^M
gorra^F de cuartel^M
bustina^F

シルク・ハット
top hat
Zylinder^M
haut-de-forme^M
chistera
cilindro

シャプカ
shapka
Kosakenmütze^F
chapka^M
chapka^F
colbacco^M

ハンティング・キャップ／狩猟帽
hunting cap
Jagdkappe^F
casquette^F norvégienne
gorra^F noruega
berretto^M da cacciatore

耳隠し／耳覆い
ear flap
Ohrenschützer^M
cache-oreilles^M abattant
orejera^F
paraorecchi^M

キャスケット／鳥打ち帽
cap
Schirmmütze^F
casquette^F
gorra^F
berretto^M

パナマ帽
panama
Panamahut^M
panama^M
panamá^M
panama

つば
peak
Mützenschirm^M
visière^F
visera^F
visiera^F

衣服

340

帽子

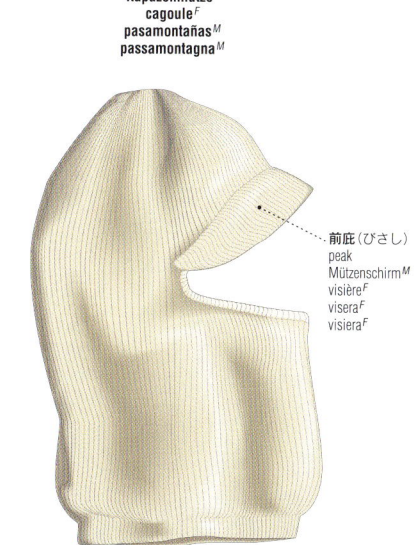

ピルボックス
pillbox hat
Pillbox^F
tambourin^M
sombrero^M sin alas^F
tocco^M

カートウィール
cartwheel hat
Wagenradhut^M
capeline^F
pamela^F
cappello^M a falda^F larga

婦人帽
women's headgear
Damenkopfbedeckungen^F
coiffures^F de femme
sombreros^M de mujer^F
copricapi^M femminili

クローシュ
cloche
Topfhut^M
cloche^F
sombrero^M de campana^F
cloche^F

トーク
toque
Toque^F
toque^F
toca^F
toque^F

ゴブ・ハット
gob hat
Regenhut^M
bob^M
gorro^M de marinero^M
cappello^M da marinaio^M

クラウン
crown
Kopfteil$^{M/N}$
calotte^F
copa^F
calotta^F

ターバン
turban
Turban^M
turban^M
turbante^M
turbante^M

サウ(ス)ウェスター／暴風雨帽
southwester; sou'wester
Südwester^M
suroît^M
sueste^M
berretto^M impermeabile

つば
brim
Krempe^F
bord^M
ala^F
tesa^F

衣服

バラクラバ帽
balaclava
Kapuzenmütze^F
cagoule^F
pasamontañas^M
passamontagna^M

ベレー帽
beret
Baskenmütze^F
béret^M
boina^F
basco^M

男女兼用の帽子
unisex headgear
Unisex-Kopfbedeckungen^F
coiffures^F unisexes
sombreros^M unisex
copricapi^M unisex

ストッキング・キャップ
stocking cap
Pudelmütze^F
bonnet^M pompon^M
gorro^M de punto^M
berretto^M con pompon^M

前庇（びさし）
peak
Mützenschirm^M
visière^F
visera^F
visiera^F

フェルト帽
felt hat; trilby
Filzhut^M
feutre^M
sombrero^M de fieltro^M
cappello^M di feltro^M

341

靴

shoes | Schuhe^M | chaussures^F | calzado^M | scarpe^F

日本語 | 英語 | ドイツ語 | フランス語 | スペイン語 | イタリア語

紳士靴
men's shoes
Herrenschuhe^M
chaussures^F d'homme^M
zapatos^M de hombre^M
scarpe^F da uomo^M

裏当て
lining
Futter^N
doublure^F
forro^M
fodera^F

靴の各部名称
parts of a shoe
Teile$^{M/N}$ des Schuhs^M
parties^F d'une chaussure^F
partes^F de un zapato^M
parti^F di una scarpa^F

靴紐（ひも）
shoelace
Schnürsenkel^M
lacet^M
cordón^M
stringa^F

カフ
cuff
Einfassung^F
revers^M
ribete^M
collo^M

舌革／べろ
tongue
Zunge^F
languette^F
lengüeta^F
linguetta^F

爪（先）革／甲革／バンプ
vamp
Vorderblatt^N
claque^F
empella^F
tomaia^F

ヒール・グリップ
heel grip
Fersenhalter^M
glissoir^M
refuerzo^M del talón^M
rinforzo^M interno del calcagno^M

ステッチ
stitch
Naht^F
surpiqûre^F
costura^F
impuntura^F

腰革／クウォーター
quarter
Quartier^N
quartier^M
cuarto^M
quartiere^M

飾り穴
punch hole
gestanztes Loch^N
perforation^F
perforaciones^F
foro^M

外側カウンター
outside counter
äußere Kappe^F
talonnette^F de dessus^M
contrafuerte^M del talón^M
rinforzo^M esterno del calcagno^M

踵（かかと）
heel
Absatz^M
talon^M
talón^M
tacco^M

トップ・リフト
top lift
Absatzoberflecken^M
bonbout^M
tapa^F
salvatacchi^M

土踏まず
waist
Gelenk^N
cambrure^F
enfranque^M
fiosso^M

腰革前部
nose of the quarter
Vorderteil$^{M/N}$
aile^F de quartier^M
ala^F del cuarto^M
parte^F anteriore del quartiere^M

アイレット・タブ
eyelet tab
Schnürlochteil$^{M/N}$
garant^M
oreja^F
lunetta^F

本底／外底／表底／アウトソール
outsole
Laufsohle^F
semelle^F d'usure^F
suela^F
suola^F

爪先飾り革
perforated toe cap
perforierte Vorderkappe^F
bout^M fleuri
puntera^F perforada
mascherina^F perforata

紐先金具／タグ
tag
Schnürsenkelende^N
ferret^M
herrete^M
puntale^M

鳩目／紐穴／アイレット
eyelet
Schnürloch^N
œillet^M
ojete^M
occhiello^M

細革／ウェルト
welt
Rahmen^M
trépointe^F
vira^F
guardolo^M

ヘビー・デューティー・ブーツ
heavy duty boot
Arbeitsstiefel^M
brodequin^M de travail^M
bota^F de trabajo^M
scarpone^M

チャッカー・ブーツ
chukka
Boot^N
chukka^M
media bota^F
scarpa^F a collo^M alto

ゴム製オーバー・シューズ
rubber; galosh
Überziehschuh^M
claque^F
chanclo^M de goma^F
galoscia^F

ショート・ブーツ／ブーティー
bootee
Halbstiefel^M
bottillon^M
botina^F
scarponcino^M

オックスフォード・シューズ
oxford shoe
Herrenhalbschuh^M
richelieu^M
zapato^M oxford
scarpa^F oxford

ブラッチャー／ダービー・シューズ
blucher oxford; lace-up
Schnürschuh^M
derby^M
zapato^M de cordones^M
scarpa^F stringata

衣服

靴

婦人靴
women's shoes
Damenschuhe^M
chaussures^F de femme^F
zapatos^M de mujer^F
scarpe^F da donna^F

サンダル
sandal; ankle-strap
Sandalette^F mit Fersenriemen^M
sandale^F
sandalia^F
sandalo^M

バレリーナ・シューズ
ballerina; pump
Ballerinaschuh^M
ballerine^F
bailarina^F
ballerina^F

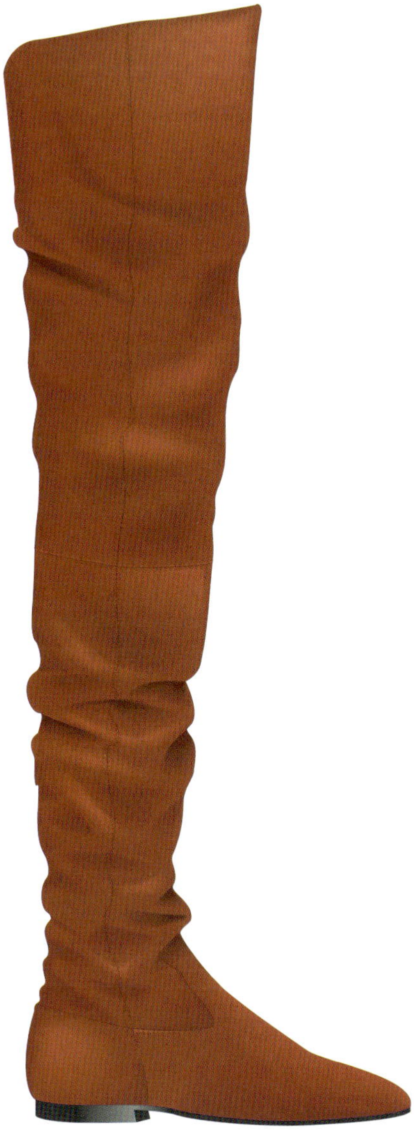

バックレス（パンプス）
sling back shoe
Slingpumps^M
escarpin^M-sandale^F
mules
scarpa^F chanel

パンプス
pump; court
Pumps^M
escarpin^M
zapato^M de salón^M
scarpa^F décolleté^M

ストラップ・パンプス
one-bar shoe
Einspangenschuh^M
Charles IX^M
zapato^M de tacón^M con correa^F
scarpa^F con cinturino^M

Tストラップ・ハイヒール
T-strap shoe
Stegspangenschuh^M
salomé^M
zapato^M de correa^F
scarpa^F con cinturino^M a T

カジュアル・シューズ
casual shoe
Straßenschuh^M
trotteur^M
zapato^M con cordones^M
francesina^F

サイ・ブーツ
thigh-boot
Schaftstiefel^M
cuissarde^F
bota^F de medio muslo^M
stivale^M alla moschettiera

ブーツ
boot
Stiefel^M
botte^F
bota^F
stivale^M

アンクル・ブーツ
ankle boot
knöchelhohe Stiefelette^F
bottine^F
botín^M
polacchina^F

衣服

靴

|日本語|英語|ドイツ語|フランス語|スペイン語|イタリア語|

男女兼用の靴
unisex shoes
Unisex-Schuhe[M]
chaussures[F] unisexes
calzado[M] unisex
scarpe[F] unisex

ミュール
mule
Pantoffel[M]
mule[F]
pantufla[F]
pianella[F]

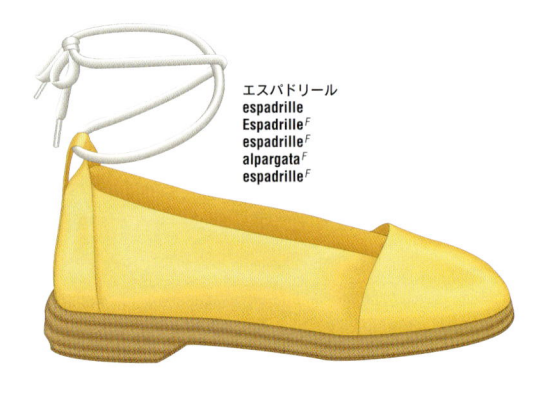

エスパドリール
espadrille
Espadrille[F]
espadrille[F]
alpargata[F]
espadrille[F]

スニーカー
tennis shoe; *plimsoll*
Tennisschuh[M]
tennis[M]
zapatilla[F] de tenis[M]
scarpa[F] da tennis[M]

ローファー
loafer; *slip-on*
Slipper[M]
loafer[M]
mocasín[M] de calle[F]
mocassino[M] classico

サンダル／草履（ぞうり）
sandal; *toe-strap*
Sandale[F] mit Zehenriemchen[N]
nu-pied[M]
sandalia[F]
sandalo[M] indiano

モカシン
moccasin
Mokassin[M]
mocassin[M]
mocasín[M]
mocassino[M]

ゴム底草履
thong; *flip-flop*
Römerpantolette[F]
tong[M]
sandalia[F] playera
infradito[M]

つっかけ
clog
Pantolette[F]
socque[M]
chancleta[F]
zoccolo[M]

サンダル
sandal
Sandale[F]
sandalette[F]
sandalia[F]
sandalo[M]

ハイキング・ブーツ
hiking boot
Wanderschuh[M]
brodequin[M] de randonnée[F]
botas[F] de caminar
pedula[F]

靴

靴磨きセット
shoeshine kit
Schuhputzzeug{N}
nécessaire{M} à chaussures{F}
juego{M} limpiabotas{M}
kit{M} per la pulizia{F} delle scarpe{F}

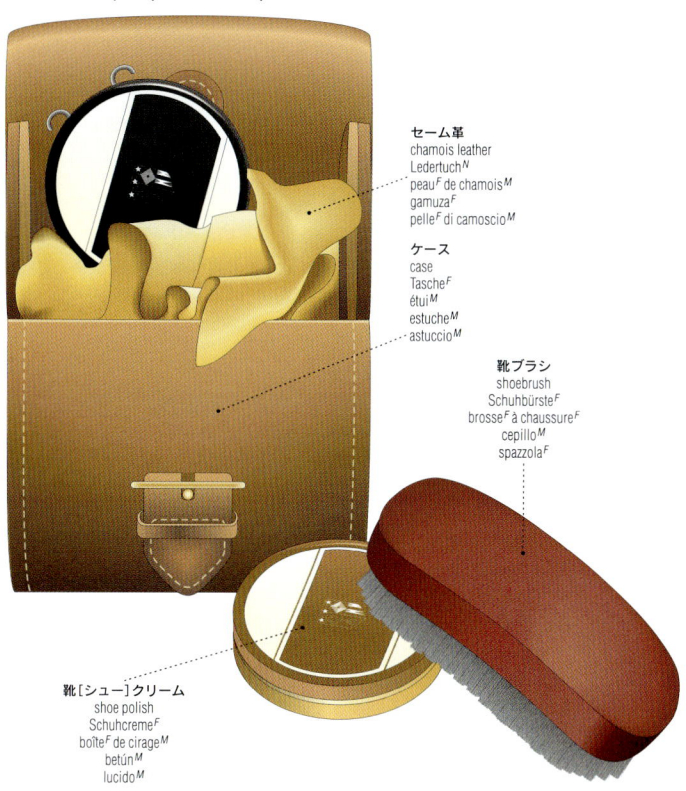

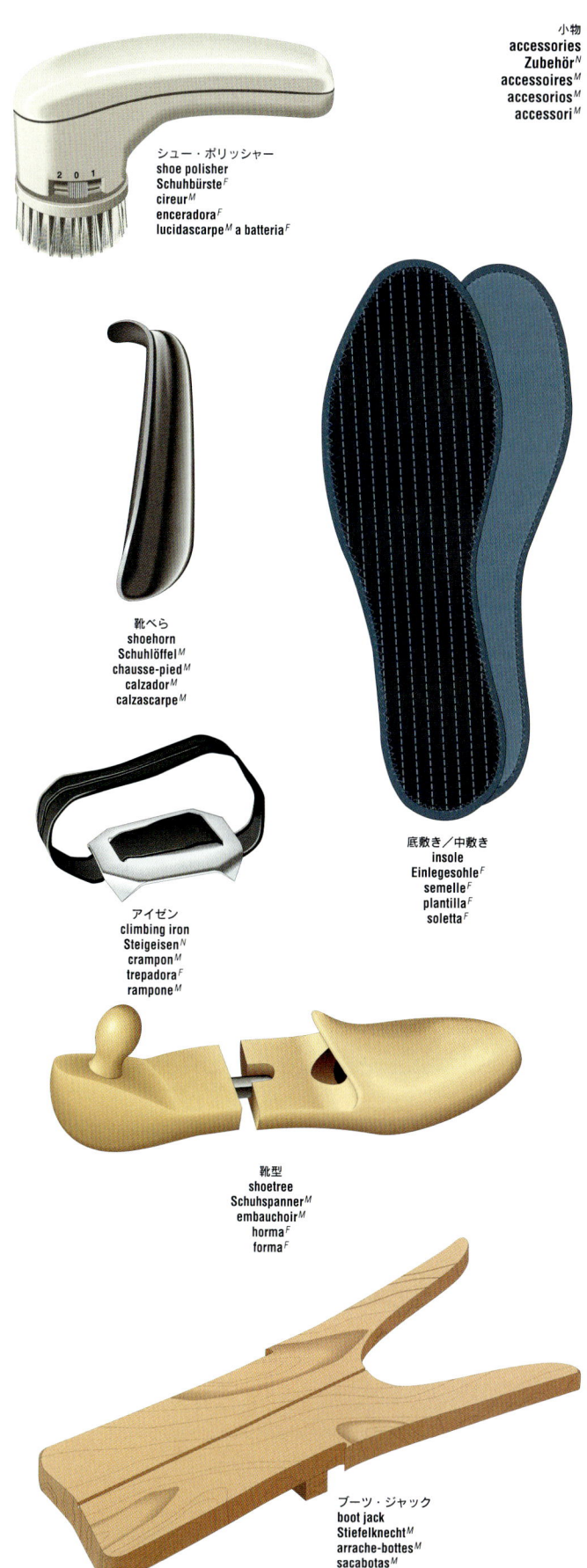

セーム革
chamois leather
Ledertuch{N}
peau{F} de chamois{M}
gamuza{F}
pelle{F} di camoscio{M}

ケース
case
Tasche{F}
étui{M}
estuche{M}
astuccio{M}

靴ブラシ
shoebrush
Schuhbürste{F}
brosse{F} à chaussure{F}
cepillo{M}
spazzola{F}

靴［シュー］クリーム
shoe polish
Schuhcreme{F}
boîte{F} de cirage{M}
betún{M}
lucido{M}

シューズ・ラック
shoe rack
Schuhständer{M}
porte-chaussures{M}
zapatero{M} de alambre{M}
scarpiera{F}

シュー・ポリッシャー
shoe polisher
Schuhbürste{F}
cireur{M}
enceradora{F}
lucidascarpe{M} a batteria{F}

靴べら
shoehorn
Schuhlöffel{M}
chausse-pied{M}
calzador{M}
calzascarpe{M}

アイゼン
climbing iron
Steigeisen{N}
crampon{M}
trepadora{F}
rampone{M}

靴型
shoetree
Schuhspanner{M}
embauchoir{M}
horma{F}
forma{F}

ブーツ・ジャック
boot jack
Stiefelknecht{M}
arrache-bottes{M}
sacabotas{M}
cavastivali{M}

小物
accessories
Zubehör{N}
accessoires{M}
accesorios{M}
accessori{M}

底敷き／中敷き
insole
Einlegesohle{F}
semelle{F}
plantilla{F}
soletta{F}

衣服

手袋

gloves | Handschuhe{M} | gants{M} | guantes{M} | guanti{M}

日本語 | 英語 | ドイツ語 | フランス語 | スペイン語 | イタリア語

紳士手袋
men's gloves
Herrenhandschuhe{M}
gants{M} d'homme{M}
guantes{M} de hombre{M}
guanti{M} da uomo{M}

手袋の甲側
back of a glove
Handschuh{M}-Außenseite{F}
dos{M} d'un gant{M}
dorso{M} de un guante{M}
dorso{M} del guanto{M}

手袋の手のひら側
palm of a glove
Handschuh{M}-Innenseite{F}
paume{F} d'un gant{M}
palma{F} de un guante{M}
palmo{M} del guanto{M}

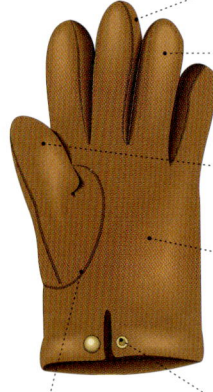

指の襠(まち)／ファシェット
fourchette
Keil{M}
fourchette{F}
horquilla{F}
linguella{F}

（手袋の）指
glove finger
Finger{M}
doigt{M}
dedo{M}
dito{M} del guanto{M}

親指
thumb
Daumen{M}
pouce{M}
pulgar{M}
pollice{M}

ひら
palm
Innenfläche{F}
paume{F}
palma{F}
palmo{M}

スナップ・ボタン
snap fastener
Druckknopf{M}
bouton{M}-pression{F}
botón{M} de presión{F}
bottone{M} a pressione{F}

ステッチ
stitching
Ziernaht{F}
baguette{F}
pespunte{M}
impuntura{F}

縫い目
seam
Naht{F}
couture{F} d'assemblage{M}
costura{F}
cucitura{F}

オープニング
opening
Öffnung{F}
fenêtre{F}
aberturas{F} para los nudillos{M}
apertura{F}

孔
perforation
Perforierung{F}
perforation{F}
perforaciones{F}
foro{M}

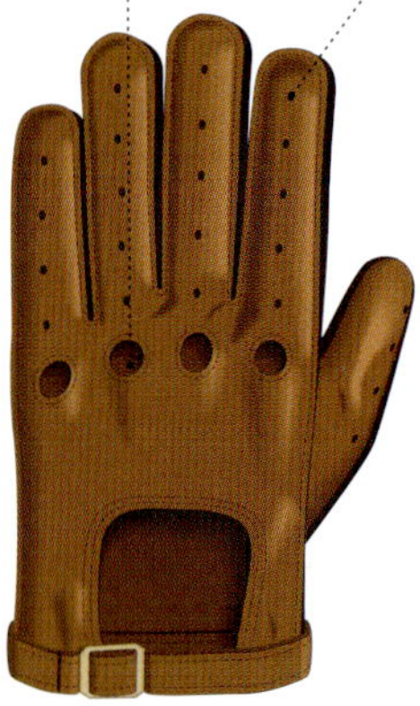

運転用手袋
driving glove
Autohandschuh{M}
gant{M} de conduite{F}
guante{M} para conducir
guanto{M} da guida{F}

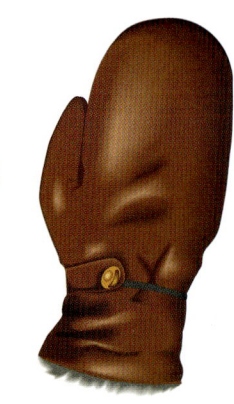

ミトン
mitten
Fäustling{M}
moufle{F}
manopla{F}
muffola{F}

婦人手袋
women's gloves
Damenhandschuhe{M}
gants{M} de femme{F}
guantes{M} de mujer{F}
guanti{M} da donna{F}

ゴーントリット
gauntlet
Stulpenhandschuh{M}
gant{M} à crispin{M}
manopla{F}
guanto{M} alla scudiera{F}

イブニング・グラブ
evening glove
langer Abendhandschuh{M}
gant{M} long
guante{M} largo
guanto{M} da sera{F}

ミット／指なしアーム・ロング
mitt; *fingerless mitt*
fingerloser Spitzenhandschuh{M}
mitaine{F}
mitón{M} sin dedos{M}
mezzoguanto{M}

ゴーントリット
gauntlet
Stulpe{F}
rebras{M}
brazo{M}
manopola{F}

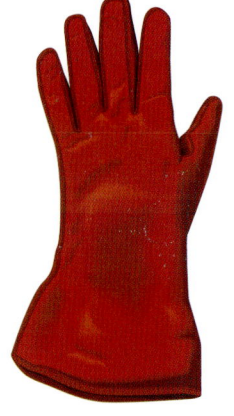

ショーティ
short glove
Kurzhandschuh{M}
gant{M} court
guante{M} corto
guanto{M} corto

手首丈グラブ
wrist-length glove
Langhandschuh{M}
gant{M} saxe
guante{M} a la muñeca{F}
guanto{M} lungo

繊維製品取り扱い表示[マーク]

fabric care symbols | Wasch- und Pflegesymbole[N] | symboles[M] d'entretien[M] des tissus[M] | símbolos[M] del cuidado[M] de los tejidos[M] | simboli[M] delle istruzioni[F] sui tessuti[M]

washing
水洗い / washing / Waschen[N] / lavage[M] / lavado[M] / lavaggio[M]

水洗い不可[禁止]
do not wash
nicht waschen
ne pas laver
no lavar
non lavare

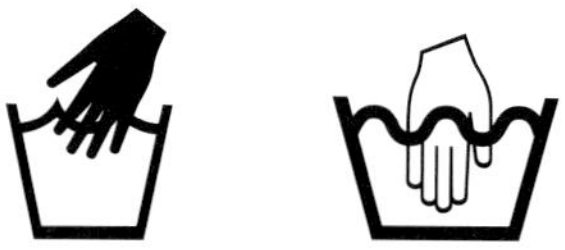

ぬるま湯で手洗い
hand wash in lukewarm water
Handwäsche[F], handwarme
laver à la main[F] à l'eau[F] tiède
lavar a mano[F] con agua[F] tibia
lavare a mano[F] in acqua[F] tiepida

40度以下の湯で、弱水流による洗濯機洗い可
machine wash in lukewarm water at a gentle setting/reduced agitation
Maschinenwäsche[F], Schonwaschgang[M], 40 Grad
laver à la machine[F] à l'eau[F] tiède avec agitation[F] réduite
lavar a máquina[F] con agua[F] tibia en el ciclo[M] para ropa[F] delicada
lavare in lavatrice[F] in acqua[F] tiepida e velocità[F] ridotta

60度以下の湯で、弱水流による洗濯機洗い可
machine wash in warm water at a gentle setting/reduced agitation
Maschinenwäsche[F], Schonwaschgang[M], 60 Grad
laver à la machine[F] à l'eau[F] chaude avec agitation[F] réduite
lavar a máquina[F] con agua[F] caliente en el ciclo[M] para ropa[F] delicada
lavare in lavatrice[F] in acqua[F] calda e velocità[F] ridotta

60度以下の湯で、通常の洗濯機洗い可
machine wash in warm water at a normal setting
Maschinenwäsche[F], Normalwaschgang[M], 60 Grad
laver à la machine[F] à l'eau[F] chaude avec agitation[F] normale
lavar a máquina[F] con agua[F] caliente, en el ciclo[M] normal
lavare in lavatrice[F] in acqua[F] calda e velocità[F] normale

95度以下の湯で、通常の洗濯機洗い可
machine wash in hot water at a normal setting
Maschinenwäsche[F], Normalwaschgang[M], 90 Grad
laver à la machine[F] à l'eau[F] très chaude avec agitation[F] normale
lavar en lavadora[F] con agua[F] muy caliente, en el ciclo[M] normal
lavare in lavatrice[F] in acqua[F] molto calda e velocità[F] normale

塩素系漂白剤の使用不可[禁止]／漂白禁止
do not use chlorine bleach
Chlorbleiche nicht möglich
ne pas utiliser de chlorure[M] décolorant
no blanquear con cloro
non candeggiare

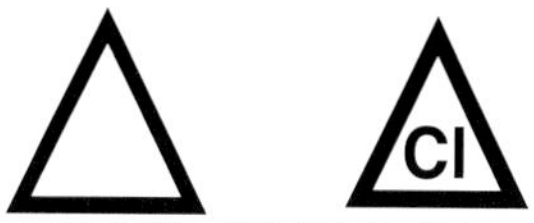

表示に従い、塩素系漂白剤の使用可
use chlorine bleach as directed
Chlorbleiche möglich
utiliser un chlorure[M] décolorant suivant les indications[F]
blanquear con cloro[M], siguiendo las indicaciones[F]
usare il candeggiante[M] secondo le istruzioni[F]

drying
乾燥 / drying / Trocknen[N] / séchage[M] / secado[M] / asciugatura[F]

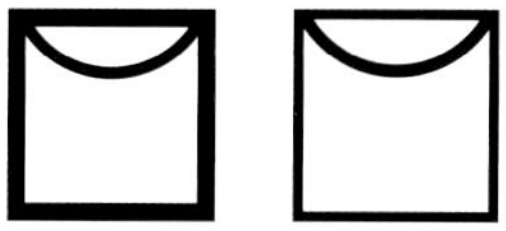

吊り干し
hang to dry
zum Trocknen[N] hängen
suspendre pour sécher
colgar al aire[M] libre después de escurrir
appendere per asciugare

平干し
dry flat
zum Trocknen[N] legen
sécher à plat
secar extendido sobre una toalla[F] después de escurrir
distendere per asciugare

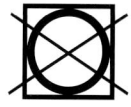

回転[タンブル]乾燥不可
do not tumble dry
Nicht in die Trockenmaschine[F] geben
ne pas sécher par culbutage[M]
no secar en secadora[F] mecánica
non centrifugare

中温で回転[タンブル]乾燥可
tumble dry at medium temperature
Bei mittlerer Temperatur[F] in den Wäschetrockner[M] geben
sécher par culbutage[M] à moyenne température[F]
secar en secadora[F] a temperatura[F] media
centrifugare a temperatura[F] media

低温で回転[タンブル]乾燥可
tumble dry at low temperature
Bei niedriger Temperatur[F] in den Wäschetrockner[M] geben
sécher par culbutage[M] à basse température[F]
secar en secadora[F] a baja temperatura[F]
centrifugare a bassa temperatura[F]

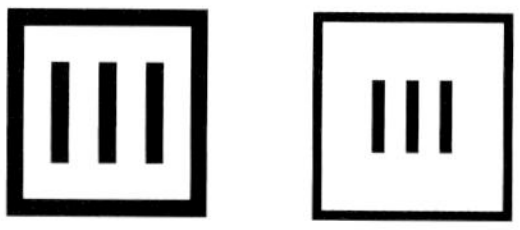

絞らずに吊り干し[乾燥]
drip dry
tropfnass hängen
suspendre pour sécher sans essorer
secar sin escurrir
appendere senza strizzare

ironing
アイロン掛け / ironing / Bügeln[N] / repassage[M] / planchado[M] / stiratura[F]

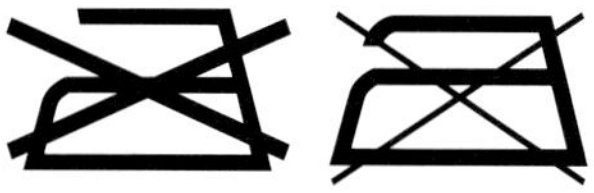

アイロン禁止
do not iron
nicht bügeln
ne pas repasser
no planchar
non stirare

低温アイロン
iron at low setting
bei niedriger Temperatur[F] bügeln
repasser à basse température[F]
usar plancha[F] tibia
stirare a bassa temperatura[F]

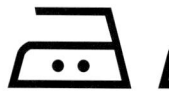

中温アイロン
iron at medium setting
bei mittlerer Temperatur[F] bügeln
repasser à moyenne température[F]
usar plancha[F] caliente
stirare a media temperatura[F]

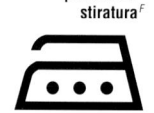

高温アイロン
iron at high setting
bei hoher Temperatur[F] bügeln
repasser à haute température[F]
usar plancha[F] muy caliente
stirare ad alta temperatura[F]

左：アメリカで用いられている表示
left: American symbols
links: amerikanische Symbole[N]
gauche: symboles[M] américains
izquierda: símbolos[M] americanos
sinistra[F]: simboli[M] americani

右：ヨーロッパで用いられている表示
right: European symbols
rechts: europäische Symbole[N]
droite[F]: symboles[M] européens
derecha: símbolos[M] europeos
destra[F]: simboli[M] europei

衣服

男性用衣類

men's clothing | Herrenkleidung^F | vêtements^M d'homme^M | ropa^F de hombre^M | abbigliamento^M maschile

日本語 | 英語 | ドイツ語 | フランス語 | スペイン語 | イタリア語

上着
jackets
Jackett^N und Weste^F
veston^M et veste^F
chaquetas^F y chalecos^M
giacche^F e gilè^M

ダブル・ジャケット
double-breasted jacket
Zweireiher^M
veston^M croisé
chaqueta^F cruzada
giacca^F a doppiopetto^M

- 襟 / collar / Kragen^M / col^M / cuello^M / collo^M
- ピークト・ラペル / peaked lapel / steigendes Revers^N / revers^M à cran^M aigu / solapa^F puntiaguda / revers^M a punta^F
- 裏地 / lining / Futter^N / doublure^F / forro^M / fodera^F
- 箱形胸ポケット / breast welt pocket / Brustleistentasche^F / pochette^F / bolsillo^M de ojal^M / taschino^M tagliato con aletta^F
- 袖 / sleeve / Ärmel^M / manche^F / manga^F / manica^F
- チケット・ポケット / outside ticket pocket / Billettasche^F / poche^F-ticket^M / bolsillo^M del cambio^M / taschino^M con aletta^F
- パッチ・ポケット / patch pocket / aufgesetzte Tasche^F / poche^F plaquée / bolsillo^M de parche^M / tasca^F applicata
- フラップ / flap / Klappe^F / rabat^M / solapa^F / aletta^F

シングル・ジャケット
single-breasted jacket
Einreiher^M
veste^F droite
chaqueta^F recta
giacca^F a un petto^M

- 下襟／折り返し／ラペル / lapel / Revers^N / revers^M / solapa^F / revers^M
- 前身(頃)(まえみごろ) / front / Vorderseite^F / devant^M / delantero^M / davanti^M
- ノッチ／Vカット / notch / Crochetwinkel^M / cran^M / muesca^F / dente^M
- 裏地 / lining / Futter^N / doublure^F / forro^M / fodera^F
- ポケット・チーフ / pocket handkerchief / Einstecktuch^N / pochette^F / pañuelo^M de bolsillo^M / fazzoletto^M da taschino^M
- フラップ・ポケット / flap pocket / Klappentasche^F / poche^F tiroir^M / bolsillo^M con cartera^F / tasca^F profilata con aletta^F

ベスト
vest; waistcoat
Weste^F
gilet^M
chaleco^M
gilè^M

- Vネック / V-neck / V-Ausschnitt^M / encolure^F en V / cuello^M en V / scollo^M a V
- 裏地 / lining / Futter^N / doublure^F / forro^M / fodera^F
- 玉縁 / welt / Patte^F / patte^F / ribete^M / aletta^F
- 前身(頃)(まえみごろ) / front / Vorderseite^F / devant^M / delantero^M / davanti^M
- 箱形ポケット / welt pocket / Leistentasche^F / poche^F gilet^M / bolsillo^M de ribete^M / tasca^F interna con aletta^F
- 切り替え(線)／縫い目 / seam / Teilungsnaht^F / découpe^F / costura^F / cucitura^F
- 調節用ウエスト・タブ / adjustable waist tab / Rückenspange^F / tirant^M de réglage^M / trincha^F / cinturino^M regolabile
- 後身(頃)(うしろみごろ) / back / Rücken^M / dos^M / espalda^F / dietro^M

サイド・ベンツ
side back vent
seitlicher Rückenschlitz^M
fente^F latérale
abertura^F trasera lateral
spacco^M laterale

- 袖 / sleeve / Ärmel^M / manche^F / manga^F / manica^F
- センター・ベンツ / center back vent; centre back vent / Rückenmittelschlitz^M / fente^F médiane / abertura^F trasera central / spacco^M centrale

男性用衣類

シャツ
shirt
Hemd^N
chemise^F
camisa^F
camicia^F

襟
collar
Kragen^M
col^M
cuello^M
colletto^M

ヨーク
yoke
Sattel^M
empiècement^M
canesú^M
sprone^M

セット・イン・スリーブ
set-in sleeve
eingesetzter Ärmel^M
manche^F montée
manga^F empotrada
manica^F a giro^M

襟先
collar point
Kragenspitze^F
pointe^F de col^M
punta^F del cuello^M
punta^F del colletto^M

胸ポケット
breast pocket
Brusttasche^F
poche^F poitrine^F
bolsillo^M superior
tasca^F applicata con aletta^F

前身(頃)(まえみごろ)
front
Vorderseite^F
devant^M
delantero^M
davanti^M

ボタン付き前開き
buttoned placket
Knopfleiste^F
patte^F de boutonnage^M
tirilla^F
cannoncino^M

ボタン
button
Knopf^M
bouton^M
botón^M
bottone^M

剣ぼろ
pointed tab end
Ärmelschlitz^M
patte^F capucin^M
abertura^F con tirilla^F
profilo^M dello spacco^M

裾
shirttail
Schoß^M
pan^M
faldón^M de la camisa^F
lembo^M della camicia^F

袖口／カフス
cuff
Manschette^F
poignet^M
puño^M
polsino^M

襟芯
collar stay
Kragenstäbchen^N
baleine^F de col^M
ballena^F
tendicollo^M

ボタンダウン・カラー
buttondown collar
Button-Down-Kragen^M
col^M pointes^F boutonnées
cuello^M con botones^M
collo^M button-down

アスコット・タイ
ascot tie; cravat
Krawattenschal^M
lavallière^F
corbata^F inglesa
lavallière^F

ボー・タイ
bow tie
Fliege^F
nœud^M papillon^M
pajarita^F
papillon^M

スプレッド・カラー
spread collar
gespreizter Kragen^M
col^M italien
cuello^M italiano
collo^M a camicia^F

ネクタイ
necktie
Krawatte^F
cravate^F
corbata^F
cravatta^F

前の垂れ／大剣
front apron
Vorderteil^M/N
pan^M avant
faldón^M delantero
lembo^M anteriore

ネック・エンド
neck end
Bindeteil^M/N
tour^M de cou^M
contorno^M del cuello^M
annodatura^F

後ろの垂れ／小剣
rear apron
Endteil^M/N
pan^M arrière
faldón^M trasero
lembo^M posteriore

裏地
lining
Futter^N
doublure^F
forro^M
fodera^F

小剣通し
loop
Schlaufe^F
passant^M
presilla^F
passante^M

くけ／隠し縫い
slip-stitched seam
Verziehnaht^F
couture^F médiane
costura^F invisible
cucitura^F a sottopunto^M

衣服

349

男性用衣類

日本語 | 英語 | ドイツ語 | フランス語 | スペイン語 | イタリア語

ズボン
pants; trousers
Hose^F
pantalon^M
pantalones^M
pantaloni^M

ベルト通し
belt loop; *belt loop*
Gürtelschlaufe^F
passant^M
trabilla^F
passante^M

ウエストバンド
waistband
Hosenbund^M
ceinture^F montée
pretina^F
cintura^F

前ポケット
front top pocket
Flügeltasche^F
poche^F cavalière
bolsillo^M delantero
tasca^F anteriore

タック・プリーツ
knife pleat
einfache Falte^F
pli^M plat
pinza^F
piega^F piatta

ウエストバンド留め
waistband extension
Bundverlängerung^F
patte^F boutonnée
trabilla^F de la pretina^F
abbottonatura^F della cintura^F

ファスナー隠し／前立て
fly
Hosenschlitz^M
braguette^F
bragueta^F
patta^F

折り目
crease
Bügelfalte^F
pli^M
raya^F
piega^F

バック・ポケット
back pocket
Gesäßtasche^F
poche^F-revolver^M
bolsillo^M trasero
tasca^F posteriore

サスペンダー・クリップ／挟み金具
suspender clip; brace clip
Klips^M
pince^F
pinza^F
fermaglio^M

サスペンダー／ズボン吊り
suspenders; braces
Hosenträger^M
bretelles^F
tirantes^M
bretelle^F

弾性帯／ゴムの吊り紐（ひも）
elastic webbing
Gummiband^N
bande^F élastique
banda^F elástica
tessuto^M elastico

調節スライド
adjustment slide
Versteller^M
coulisse^F
corredera^F de ajuste^M
cursore^M

革の端／ボタン留め
leather end
Lederstrippe^F
patte^F
lengüeta^F de cuero^M
laccio^M di pelle^F

裾折り返し／カフ
cuff; *turn-up*
Aufschlag^M
revers^M
vuelta^F
risvolto^M

ボタン穴
button loop
Knopflasche^F
boutonnière^F
presilla^F
asola^F

ベルト
belt
Gürtel^M
ceinture^F
cinturón^M
cintura^F

端縫い
top stitching
Zier-Steppnaht^F
surpiqûre^F
pespunte^M
impuntura^F

パネル
panel
Gürtelband^N
croûte^F de cuir^M
cuero^M
fascia^F di cuoio^M

先
tip
Gürtelspitze^F
capucin^M
punta^F
punta^F

パンチ穴
punch hole
gestanztes Loch^N
cran^M
ojete^M
foro^M

ベルト通し
belt loop; *belt loop*
Gürtelschlaufe^F
passant^M
trabilla^F
passante^M

タング／留めピン
tongue
Dorn^M
ardillon^M
pasador^M
ardiglione^M

バックル／留め金
buckle
Gürtelschnalle^F
boucle^F
hebilla^F
fibbia^F

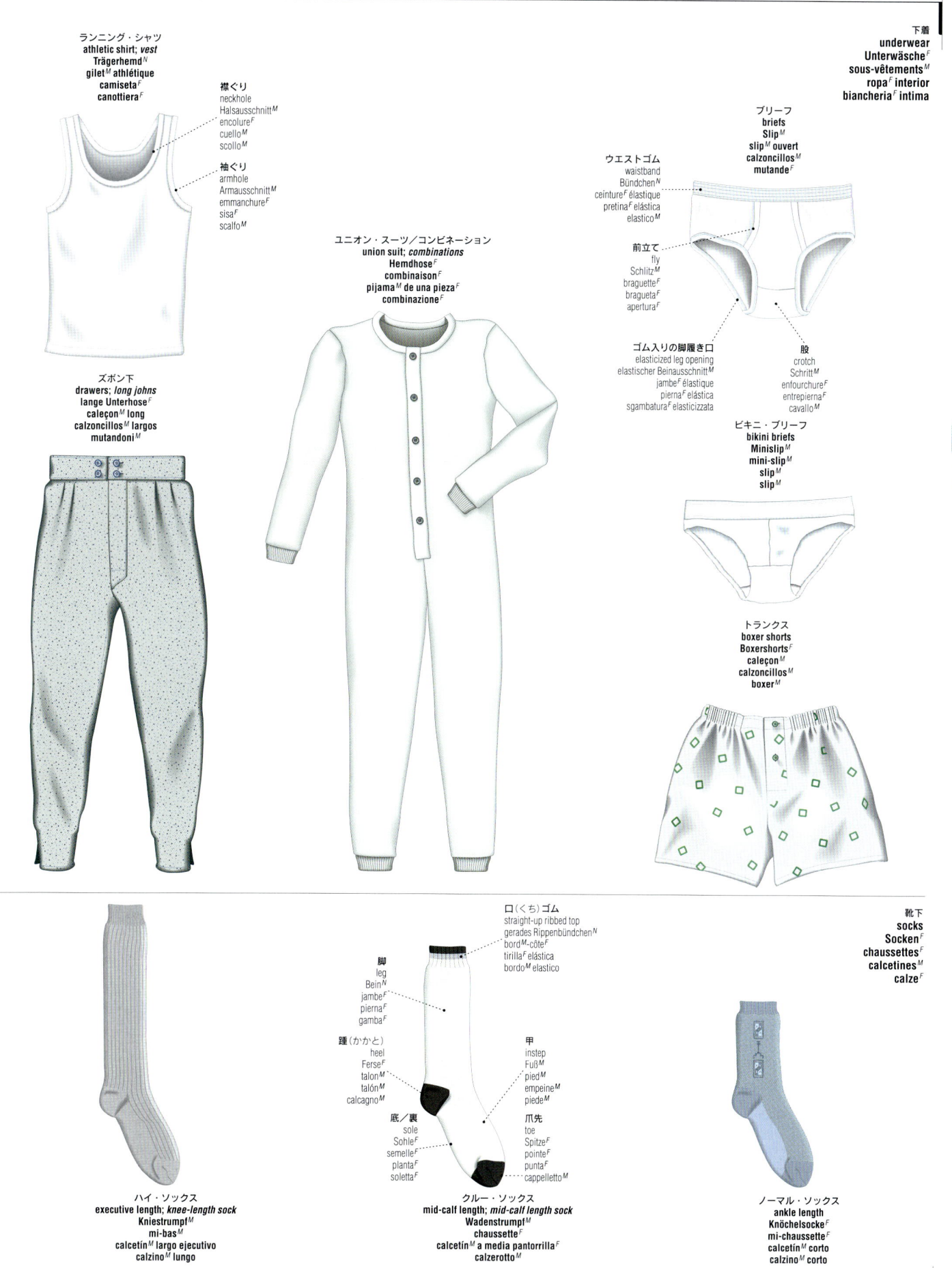

男性用衣類

下着
underwear
UnterwäscheF
sous-vêtementsM
ropaF interior
biancheriaF intima

ランニング・シャツ
athletic shirt; *vest*
TrägerhemdN
giletM athlétique
camisetaF
canottieraF

- 襟ぐり / neckhole / HalsausschnittM / encolureF / cuelloM / scolloM
- 袖ぐり / armhole / ArmausschnittM / emmanchureF / sisaF / scalfoM

ズボン下
drawers; *long johns*
lange UnterhoseF
caleçonM long
calzoncillosM largos
mutandoniM

ユニオン・スーツ／コンビネーション
union suit; *combinations*
HemdhoseF
combinaisonF
pijamaM de una piezaF
combinazioneF

ブリーフ
briefs
SlipM
slipM ouvert
calzoncillosM
mutandeF

- ウエストゴム / waistband / BündchenN / ceintureF élastique / pretinaF elástica / elasticoM
- 前立て / fly / SchlitzM / braguetteF / braguetaF / aperturaF
- ゴム入りの脚履き口 / elasticized leg opening / elastischer BeinausschnittM / jambeF élastique / piernaF elástica / sgambaturaF elasticizzata
- 股 / crotch / SchrittM / enfourchureF / entrepiernaF / cavalloM

ビキニ・ブリーフ
bikini briefs
MinislipM
mini-slipM
slipM
slipM

トランクス
boxer shorts
BoxershortsF
caleçonM
calzoncillosM
boxerM

靴下
socks
SockenF
chaussettesF
calcetinesM
calzeF

ハイ・ソックス
executive length; knee-length sock
KniestrumpfM
mi-basM
calcetínM largo ejecutivo
calzinoM lungo

クルー・ソックス
mid-calf length; mid-calf length sock
WadenstrumpfM
chaussetteF
calcetínM a media pantorrillaF
calzerottoM

- 口（くち）ゴム / straight-up ribbed top / gerades RippenbündchenN / bordM-côte / tirillaF elástica / bordoM elastico
- 脚 / leg / BeinN / jambeF / piernaF / gambaF
- 踵（かかと）/ heel / FerseF / talonM / talónM / calcagnoM
- 甲 / instep / FußM / piedM / empeineM / piedeM
- 底／裏 / sole / SohleF / semelleF / plantaF / solettaF
- 爪先 / toe / SpitzeF / pointeF / puntaF / cappellettoM

ノーマル・ソックス
ankle length
KnöchelsockeF
mi-chaussetteF
calcetínM corto
calzinoM corto

衣服

男性用衣類

日本語 | 英語 | ドイツ語 | フランス語 | スペイン語 | イタリア語

コート
coats
Mäntel^M und Jacken^F
manteaux^M et blousons^M
abrigos^M e impermeables^F
esempi^M di giacconi e cappotti^M

レインコート
raincoat
Regenmantel^M
imperméable^M
impermeable^M
impermeabile^M

オーバーコート
overcoat
Mantel^M
pardessus^M
abrigo^M
cappotto^M

襟
collar
Kragen^M
col^M
cuello^M
collo^M

ラグラン袖
raglan sleeve
Raglanärmel^M
manche^F raglan
manga^F raglán
manica^F alla raglan^M

ノッチト・ラベル
notched lapel
abfallendes Revers^N
revers^M cranté
solapa^F con ojal^M
revers^M

タブ
tab
Spange^F
patte^F
lengüeta^F
linguetta^F

箱形サイド・ポケット
broad welt side pocket
schräge Pattentasche^F
poche^F raglan
bolsillo^M de ribete^M ancho
tasca^F interna con aletta^F

ボタンホール
buttonhole
Knopfloch^N
boutonnière^F
ojal^M
occhiello^M

前身(頃)(まえみごろ)
side panel
Seitenteil$^{M/N}$
pan^M
paño^M lateral
falda^F

ノッチト・ラベル
notched lapel
abfallendes Revers^N
revers^M cranté
solapa^F con ojal^M
revers^M

胸ポケット
breast pocket
Brusttasche^F
poche^F poitrine
bolsillo^M superior
taschino^M

胸ダーツ
breast dart
Taillenabnäher^M
pince^F de taille
pinza^F
ripresa^F

フラップ・ポケット
flap pocket
Klappentasche^F
poche^F à rabat^M
bolsillo^M con cartera
tasca^F profilata con aletta^F

トレンチコート
trench coat
Trenchcoat^M
trench^M
trinchera^F
trench^M

エポレット／肩飾り
epaulet
Schulterklappe^F
patte^F d'épaule
hombrera^F
spallina^F

七分コート
three-quarter coat
dreiviertellange Jacke^F
paletot^M
abrigo^M de tres cuartos
trequarti^M

ツー・ウェイ・カラー
two-way collar
Wendekragen^M
col^M transformable
cuello^M de doble vista^F
collo^M

ガン・フラップ
gun flap
Koller^N
bavolet^M
protector^M
aletta^F staccata

ラグラン袖
raglan sleeve
Raglanärmel^M
manche^F raglan
manga^F raglán
manica^F alla raglan^M

袖バンド通し
sleeve strap loop
Riegel^M
passant^M
presilla^F de la manga
passante^M del cinturino^M

ダブル・ボタン
double-breasted buttoning
zweireihig
double boutonnage^M
botonadura^F cruzada
abbottonatura^F a doppiopetto^M

ベルト
belt
Gürtel^M
ceinture^F
cinturón^M
cintura^F

袖バンド
sleeve strap
Ärmellasche^F
patte^F de serrage
correa^F de la manga
cinturino^M della manica

箱形サイド・ポケット
broad welt side pocket
schräge Pattentasche^F
poche^F raglan
bolsillo^M de ribete^M ancho
tasca^F interna con aletta^F

ベルト通し
belt loop; belt loop
Gürtelschlaufe^F
passant^M
presilla^F del cinturón^M
passante^M della cintura

フレーム
frame
Schnalle^F
boucle^F de ceinture
hebilla^F
fibbia^F

衣服

352

男性用衣類

パーカー
parka
ParkaM
parka
parkaF
parkaM

スナップ付き前立て
snap-fastening tab
DruckknopfleisteF
patteF à boutonsM-pressionF
botónM de presiónF
allacciaturaF con bottoniM a pressioneF

ファスナー
zipper
ReißverschlussM
fermetureF à glissièreF
cremalleraF
chiusuraF lampo

羊革ジャケット
sheepskin jacket
LammfelljackeF
canadienneF
zamarraF
montoneM

ダッフル・コート
duffle coat
DufflecoatM
duffle-coatM
trencaF
montgomeryM

フード
hood
KapuzeF
capuchonM
capuchaF
cappuccioM

ヨーク
yoke
SattelM
empiècementM
hombrilloM
carréM

フロッグ
frog
LascheF
brandebourgM
alamarM
alamaroM

パッチ・ポケット
patch pocket
aufgesetzte TascheF
pocheF plaquée
bolsilloM de parcheM
tascaF applicata

トグル・ボタン
toggle fastening
KnebelverschlussM
bûchetteF
botónM de maderaF
olivettaF

ブルゾン
jacket; *windcheater*
BlousonM
blousonM court
cazadoraF
giaccaF a ventoM

ウインドブレーカー
windbreaker; *windcheater*
WindjackeF
blousonM long
cazadoraF
giaccaF a ventoM

スナップ／ホック
snap fastener
DruckknopfM
boutonM-pressionF
botónM de presiónF
bottoneM a pressioneF

ハンドウォーマー・ポケット
hand-warmer pocket
MufftascheF
pocheF repose-brasM
bolsilloM de ojalM
tascaF interna con alettaF

ゴム入りウエストバンド
elastic waistband
elastischer BundM
ceintureF élastique
pretinaF elástica
fasciaF elastica

ウエストバンド
waistband
BundM
ceintureF montée
pretinaF
coulisseF

引き締め紐（ひも）
drawstring
DurchziehschnurF
cordonM coulissant
cordónM
cordoncinoM

衣服

セーター

sweaters | Pullover^M | tricots^M | jerseys^M | maglioni^M

衣服

Vネック・カーディガン
V-neck cardigan
Strickjacke^F mit V-Ausschnitt^M
gilet^M de laine^F
cárdigan
cardigan^M con scollo^M a V

ハンガー・ループ
hanger loop
Aufhänger^M
bride^F de suspension^F
trabilla^F de suspensión^F
passante^M

Vネック
V-neck
V-Ausschnitt^M
encolure^F en V
cuello^M de pico^M
scollo^M a V

ゴム編みカフス
ribbing
Patent-Strickbündchen^N
bord^M-côte
tirilla^F elástica
bordo^M a coste^F

玉縁ポケット
welt pocket
Paspeltasche^F
poche^F passepoilée
bolsillo^M
tasca^F profilata

ボタン
button
Knopf^M
bouton^M
botón^M
bottone^M

ボタン付き前開き
buttoned placket
Knopfleiste^F
patte^F polo^M
tirilla^F
abbottonatura^F a polo^F

ニット・ベスト
sweater vest; *slipover*
Pullunder^M
débardeur^M
chaleco^M de punto^M
gilè^M

ポロ・シャツ
knit shirt
Poloshirt^N
polo^M
polo^M
polo^F

タートルネック
turtleneck
Rollkragenpullover^M
col^M roulé
jersey^M de cuello^M de tortuga^F
maglione^M dolcevita^M

クルー・ネック・セーター
crew neck sweater
Pullover^M mit halsnahem Ausschnitt^M
ras-de-cou^M
jersey^M de cuello^M redondo
maglione^M girocollo^M

カーディガン
cardigan
Strickjacke^F
cardigan^M
chaqueta^F de punto^M
cardigan^M

354

女性用衣類

women's clothing | Damenkleidung^F | vêtements^M de femme | ropa^F de mujer | abbigliamento^M femminile

スーツ
suit
Kostüm^N
tailleur^M
traje^M de chaqueta^F
tailleur^M

ジャケット
jacket
Jacke^F
veste^F
chaqueta^F
giacca^F

スカート
skirt
Rock^M
jupe^F
falda^F
gonna^F

ラグラン(コート)
raglan
Raglanmantel^M
raglan^M
abrigo^M ranglan
cappotto^M alla raglan

ラグラン袖
raglan sleeve
Raglanärmel^M
manche^F raglan
manga^F raglán
manica^F alla raglan^M

比翼式打ち合わせ[打ち合い]
fly front closing
verdeckte Knopfleiste^F
boutonnage^M sous patte^F
pestaña^F
finta^F

箱形サイド・ポケット
broad welt side pocket
schräge Pattentasche^F
poche^F raglan
bolsillo^M de ribete^M ancho
tasca^F interna con aletta^F

コート
coats
Mäntel^M und Jacken^F
manteaux^M
chaquetones^M y abrigos^M
esempi^M di giacche^F e cappotti^M

トップ・コート
top coat; riding coat
Redingote^F
redingote^F
abrigo^M redingote
redingote^F

ペルリーヌ
pelerine
Pelerine^F
pèlerine^F
abrigo^M con esclavina^F
cappotto^M con pellegrina^F

ケープ/ペルリーヌ
pelerine
Pelerine^F
pèlerine^F
esclavina^F
pellegrina^F

ケープ
cape
Cape^N
cape^F
capa^F
mantella^F

ピー・ジャケット
pea jacket
Cabanjacke^F
caban^M
chaquetón^M marinero
giacca^F alla marinara^F

テーラード・カラー
tailored collar
Schneiderkragen^M
col^M tailleur
cuello^M hechura^F sastre^M
collo^M a uomo^M

ハンドウォーマー・ポケット
hand-warmer pocket
Mufftasche^F
poche^F repose-bras^M
bolsillo^M de ojal^M
tasca^F tagliata in verticale

アーム・スリット
arm slit
Durchgrifftasche^F
passe-bras^M
abertura^F para el brazo^M
apertura^F per le braccia^F

シーム・ポケット
seam pocket
Nahttasche^F
poche^F prise dans une couture^F
bolsillo^M disimulado
tasca^F inserita nella cucitura^F

偽ポケット
mock pocket
blinde Tasche^F
fausse poche^F
bolsillo^M simulado
tasca^F finta

オーバーコート
overcoat
Mantel^M
manteau^M
abrigo^M
cappotto^M

カー・コート
car coat
Autocoat^M
paletot^M
chaquetón^M de tres cuartos
giaccone^M

ジャケット
jacket
Blazer^M
veste^F
chaquetón^M
giacca^F

ポンチョ
poncho
Poncho^M
poncho^M
poncho^M
poncho^M

衣服

355

女性用衣類

| 日本語 | 英語 | ドイツ語 | フランス語 | スペイン語 | イタリア語 |

ドレスの例
examples of dresses
Beispiele^N für Kleider^N
exemples^M de robes^F
ejemplos^M de vestidos^M
esempi^M di abiti^M

シース・ドレス
sheath dress
Schlauchkleid^N
robe^F fourreau^M
recto^M entallado
tubino^M

プリンセス・ドレス
princess dress
Prinzesskleid^N
robe^F princesse^F
corte^M princesa^F
princesse^F

コート・ドレス
coat dress
Mantelkleid^N
robe^F-manteau
traje^M cruzado
robe-manteau$^{F/M}$

ポロ・ドレス
polo dress
Polokleid^N
robe^F-polo^M
vestido^M de camiseta^F
abito^M a polo^F

ハウス・ドレス
house dress
Hauskleid^N
robe^F de maison^F
vestido^M casero
abito^M da casa^F

シャツウエスト・ドレス
shirtwaist dress
Hemdblusenkleid^N
robe^F chemisier^M
vestido^M camisero
chemisier^M

ドロップト・トルソー・ドレス
drop waist dress
Kleid^N mit angesetztem Schoß^M
robe^F taille^F basse
vestido de talle^M bajo
abito^M a vita^F bassa

トラペーズ・ドレス
trapeze dress
Kleid^N in Trapez-Form^F
robe^F trapèze
vestido^M acampanado
abito^M a trapezio^M

サンドレス
sundress
leichtes Sonnenkleid^N
robe^F bain^M-de-soleil^F
vestido^M de tirantes^M
prendisole^M

ラップアラウンド・ドレス
wraparound dress; *wrapover dress*
Wickelkleid^N
robe^F enveloppe^F
vestido^M cruzado
abito^M a vestaglia^F

チュニック・ドレス
tunic dress
Tunikakleid^N
robe^F tunique^F
túnica^F
abito^M a tunica^F

ジャンパー・スカート［ドレス］
jumper; *pinafore*
Trägerrock^M
chasuble^F
pichi^M
scamiciato^M

女性用衣類

スカートの例
examples of skirts
Beispiele^N für Röcke^M
exemples^M de jupes^F
ejemplos^M de faldas^F
esempi^M di gonne^F

ゴアー(ド)・スカート
gored skirt
Bahnenrock^M
jupe^F à lés^M
falda^F de piezas^F
gonna^F a teli^M

キルト・スカート
kilt
Schottenrock^M
kilt^M
falda^F escocesa
kilt^M

サロン
sarong
Sarong
paréo^M
falda^F sarong^M
sarong^M

巻き[ラップ]スカート
wraparound skirt; *wrapover skirt*
Wickelrock^M
jupe^F portefeuille^M
falda^F cruzada
gonna^F a portafoglio^M

タイト・スカート
sheath skirt
Etuirock^M
jupe^F fourreau^M
falda^F de tubo^M
gonna^F ad anfora^F

ティアード・スカート
ruffled skirt
Stufenrock^M
jupe^F à volants^M étagés
falda^F de volantes^M
gonna^F a balze^F

セミタイト・スカート
straight skirt
gerader Rock^M
jupe^F droite
falda^F recta
gonna^F diritta

ヨーク・スカート
yoke skirt
Sattelrock^M
jupe^F à empiècement^M
falda^F acampanada
gonna^F con baschina^F

ギャザー・フレアー・スカート
gather skirt
Kräuselrock^M
jupe^F froncée
falda^F fruncida
gonna^F arricciata

キュロット
culottes
Hosenrock^M
jupe^F-culotte^F
falda^F pantalón^M
gonna^F pantalone^M

プリーツの例
examples of pleats
Beispiele^N für Falten^F
exemples^M de plis^M
ejemplos^M de tablas^F
esempi^M di pieghe^F

インバーテッド・プリーツ
inverted pleat
Kellerfalte^F
pli^M creux
tabla^F delantera
piega^F invertita

キック・プリーツ
kick pleat
Gehfalte^F
pli^M d'aisance^F
tabla^F abierta
piega^M sovrapposta

アコーディオン・プリーツ
accordion pleat
Bahnenplissee^N
plissé^M accordéon^M
plisada
plissé^M

トップ・ステッチト・プリーツ
top stitched pleat
abgesteppte Falte^F
pli^M surpiqué
pespunteada
piega^F impunturata

ナイフ・プリーツ
knife pleat
einfache Falte^F
pli^M plat
tablas^F
piega^F a coltello^M

衣服

女性用衣類

| 日本語 | 英語 | ドイツ語 | フランス語 | スペイン語 | イタリア語 |

パンツの例
examples of pants; *examples of trousers*
Beispiele^N für Hosen^F
exemples^M de pantalons^M
ejemplos^M de pantalones^M
esempi^M di pantaloni^M

ショート・パンツ
shorts
Shorts^F
short^M
pantalón^M corto
shorts^M

バミューダ・パンツ
Bermuda shorts
Bermudashorts^F
bermuda^M
bermudas^M
bermuda^M

ニッカボッカーズ
knickers; *knickerbockers*
Kniebundhose^F
knicker^M
bombachos^M
pantaloni^M alla zuava^F

ペダル・プッシャー・パンツ
pedal pushers
Caprihose^F
corsaire^M
pirata^M
pantaloni^M alla pescatora

ジーンズ
jeans
Jeans^F
jean^M
vaqueros^M
jeans^M

スキー・パンツ
ski pants
Steghose^F
fuseau^M
pantalones^M de tubo^M
fuseau^M

フットストラップ
footstrap
Steg^M
sous-pied^M
trabilla^F
staffa^F

ジャンプスーツ
jumpsuit
Overall^M
combinaison^F-pantalon^M
buzo^M
tuta^F

オーバーオール
overalls; *dungarees*
Latzhose^F
salopette^F
pantalones^M conpeto^M
salopette^F

ベル・ボトム
bell bottoms
Schlaghose^F
pantalon^M pattes^F d'éléphant^M
pantalones^M acampanados
pantaloni^M a zampa^F di elefante^M

ジャケット、ベストとセーター
jackets, vest and sweaters; *waistcoats and jackets*
Westen^F und Jacken^F
vestes^F et pulls^F
chalecos^M, jerseys^M y chaquetas^F
esempi^M di giacche^F e pullover^M

ボレロ
bolero
Bolero^M
boléro^M
bolero^M
bolero^M

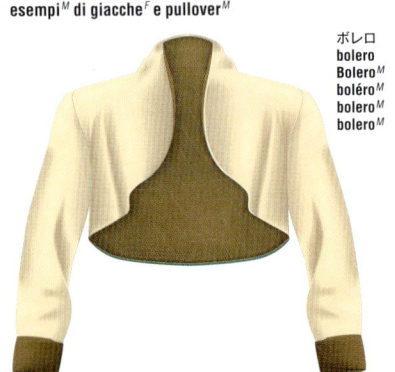

スペンサー・ジャケット
spencer
Spenzer^M
spencer^M
bolero^M con botones^M
spencer^M

ブレザー
blazer
Blazer^M
blazer^M
americana^F
blazer^M

衣服

女性用衣類

サファリ・ジャケット
safari jacket
Safarijacke^F
saharienne^F
sahariana^F
sahariana^F

ベスト
vest; *waistcoat*
Weste^F
gilet^M
chaleco^M
gilè^M

ニット・アンサンブル
twin-set
Twinset^N
tandem^M
jerseys^M combinados
twin-set^M

クルー・ネック・セーター
crew neck sweater
Pullover^M mit halsnahem Ausschnitt^M
ras-de-cou^M
jersey^M de cuello^M redondo
maglia^F girocollo^M

襠(まち)付きポケット
gusset pocket
Blasebalgtasche^F
poche^F soufflet^M
bolsillo^M de fuelle^M
tasca^F applicata a soffietto^M

カーディガン
cardigan
Cardigan^M
cardigan^M
chaqueta^F de punto^M
cardigan^M

ボディー・シャツ
body shirt
Bodyshirt^N
corsage^M-culotte^F
body^M
body^M

セーラー・ブラウス
middy; *sailor tunic*
Matrosenbluse^F
marinière^F
camisa^F marinera
maglietta^F alla marinara

ブラウスの例
examples of blouses
Beispiele^N für Blusen^F und Hemden^N
exemples^M de chemisiers^M
ejemplos^M de blusas^F
esempi^M di camicette^F

股当て
crotch piece
Schritt^M
patte^F d'entrejambe^M
entrepierna^F
cavallo^M

ヨーク
yoke
Sattel^M
empiècement^M
canesú^M
carré^M

ギャザー
gather
Kräuselfalte^F
fronce^F
fruncido^M
arricciatura^F

裾
shirttail
Schoß^M
pan^M
faldón^M
lembo^M

クラシック・ブラウス
classic blouse
klassische Bluse^F
chemisier^M classique
camisera clásica
camicetta^F classica

スモック
smock; *button-through smock*
Kittelbluse^F
tablier^M-blouse^F
blusón^M
sopravveste^F a grembiule^M

シャツ・ブラウス
mini shirtdress; *overshirt*
Hosenbluse^F
liquette^F
camisa^F
camicione^M

チュニック・シャツ
tunic; *smock*
Arbeitskittel^M
tunique^F
blusón^M con tirilla^F
camiciotto^M

ラップ・ブラウス
wrapover top
Wickelbluse^F
cache-cœur^M
chaqueta^F cruzada
camicetta^F incrociata

ポロ・シャツ
polo shirt; *polo shirt*
Polohemd^N
polo^M
polo^M
polo^F

オーバー・ブラウス
over-blouse; *tunic*
Tunika^F
casaque^F
casaca^F
casacca^F

衣服

女性用衣類

日本語 | 英語 | ドイツ語 | フランス語 | スペイン語 | イタリア語

ポケットの例
examples of pockets
Beispiele^N für Taschen^F
exemples^M de poches^F
ejemplos^M de bolsillos^M
esempi^M di tasche^F

襠(まち)付きポケット
gusset pocket
Blasebalgtasche^F
poche^F soufflet^M
bolsillo^M de fuelle^M
tasca^F applicata a soffietto^M

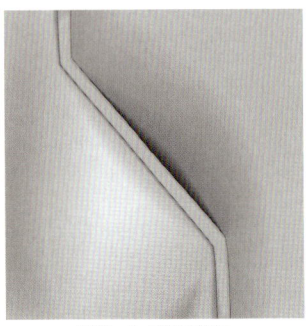

内ポケット／内隠(がく)し
inset pocket
eingesetzte Tasche^F
poche^F prise dans une découpe^F
bolsillo^M simulado
tasca^F sagomata

玉縁ポケット
welt pocket
Paspeltasche^F
poche^F passepoilée
bolsillo^M de ojal^M de sastre^M
tasca^F profilata

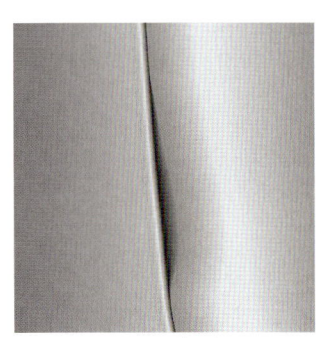

シーム・ポケット
seam pocket
Nahttasche^F
poche^F prise dans une couture^F
bolsillo^M disimulado
tasca^F inserita nella cucitura^F

フラップ・ポケット
flap pocket
Klappentasche^F
poche^F à rabat^M
bolsillo^M de parche^M con cartera^F
tasca^F applicata con aletta^F

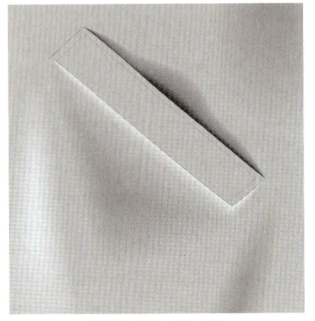

箱形サイド・ポケット
broad welt side pocket
schräge Pattentasche^F
poche^F raglan
bolsillo^M de ojal^M con ribete^M
tasca^F interna con aletta^F

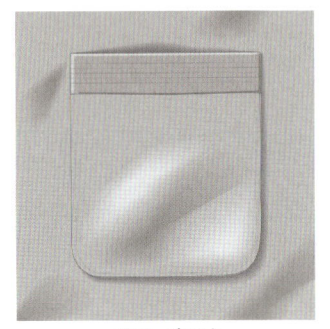

パッチ・ポケット
patch pocket
aufgesetzte Tasche^F
poche^F plaquée
bolsillo^M de parche^M
tasca^F applicata

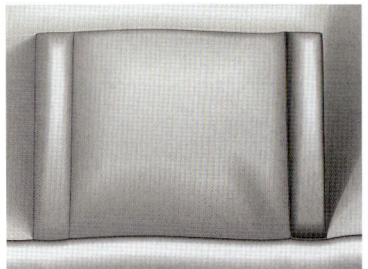

マフ・ポケット
hand-warmer pouch
Mufftasche^F
poche^F manchon^M
bolsillo^M de manguito^M
manicotto^M

袖の例
examples of sleeves
Beispiele^N für Ärmel^M
exemples^M de manches^F
ejemplos^M de mangas^F
esempi^M di maniche^F

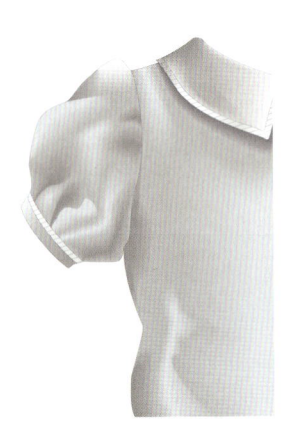

パフ・スリーブ
puff sleeve
Puffärmel^M
manche^F ballon^M
manga^F farol
manica^F a palloncino^M

キャップ・スリーブ
cap sleeve
angeschnittener Ärmel^M
mancheron^M
manga^F corta sencilla
manica^F ad aletta^F

七分袖
three-quarter sleeve
Dreiviertelarm^M
manche^F trois-quarts
manga^F recta de tres cuartos^M
manica^F tre quarti^M

エポーレット・スリーブ
epaulet sleeve
Zungenraglan^M
manche^F marteau^M
con hombrera^F
manica^F con spallina^F

女性用衣類

フレンチ・カフス
French cuff
Doppelmanschette^F
poignet^M mousquetaire^M
puño^M para gemelos^M
polsino^M doppio

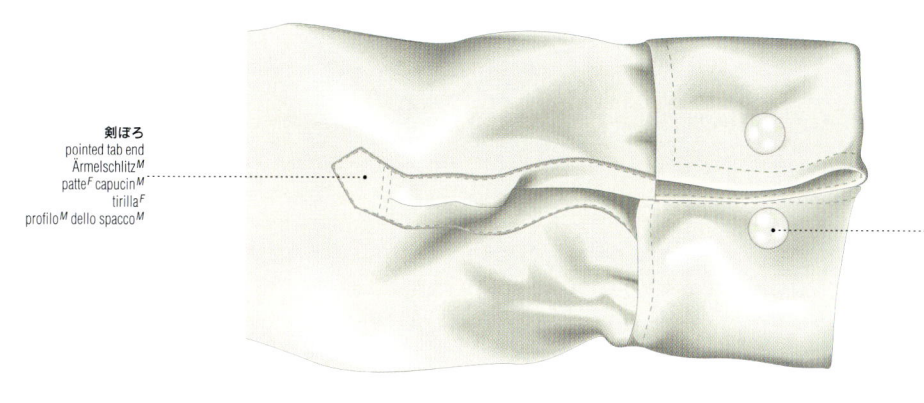

剣ぼろ
pointed tab end
Ärmelschlitz^M
patte^F capucin^M
tirilla^F
profilo^M dello spacco^M

カフス・ボタン／カフ・リンク
cuff link
Manschettenknopf^M
bouton^M de manchette^F
gemelos^M
gemello^M

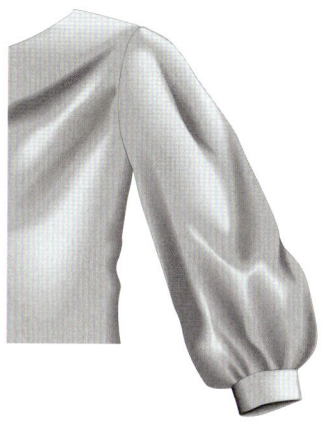

バットウィング[バタフライ]スリーブ
batwing sleeve
Fledermausärmel^M
manche^F chauve-souris^F
manga^F de murciélago^M
manica^F a pipistrello^M

レッグ・オブ・マトン・スリーブ
leg-of-mutton sleeve
Keulenärmel^M
manche^F gigot^M
manga^F de jamón^M
manica^F a prosciutto^M

ビショップ[ブラウス]スリーブ
bishop sleeve
Bauschärmel^M
manche^F bouffante
manga^F común fruncida
manica^F da vescovo^M

キモノ[着物]スリーブ
kimono sleeve
Kimonoärmel^M
manche^F kimono^M
manga^F kimono
manica^F a kimono^M

ラグラン・スリーブ
raglan sleeve
Raglanärmel^M
manche^F raglan
manga^F raglán
manica^F alla raglan^M

パゴダ・スリーブ
pagoda sleeve
Pagodenärmel^M
manche^F pagode^F
manga^F de pagoda^F
manica^F a pagoda^F

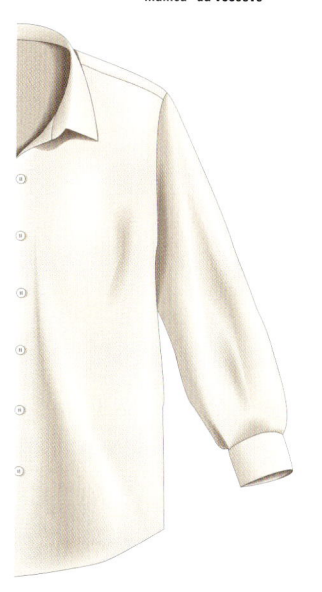

シャツ・スリーブ
shirt sleeve
Hemdblusenärmel^M
manche^F chemisier^M
manga^F camisera^F
manica^F di camicia^F

テーラード・スリーブ
tailored sleeve
Schneiderärmel^M
manche^F tailleur^M
manga^F de hechura^F sastre^M
manica^F a giro^M

衣服

女性用衣類

日本語 | 英語 | ドイツ語 | フランス語 | スペイン語 | イタリア語

襟の例
examples of collars
Beispiele^N für Kragen^M
exemples^M de cols
ejemplos^M de cuellos
esempi^M di colli^M

スタンド
stand
Stand^M
montant
doblez^M
montante^M

上襟
fall
Fall^M
tombant
caída^F
parte^F superiore del collo^M

襟先
collar point
Kragenecke^F
pointe
punta^F del cuello^M
punta^F del collo^M

ノッチ
notch
Crochetwinkel^M
cran^M
muesca^F
dente^M

襟腰
roll
Kragensteg^M
chute^F
alzada^F
risvolto^M

折り目
break line
Umschlag^M
cassure
línea de caída^F
linea^F di spezzatura^F

折り襟／ラペル
lapel
Revers^N
revers^M
solapa^F
revers^M

合わせ目
leading edge
Fassonübertritt^M
bord^M de pli^M
escote^M
bordo^M del risvolto^M

襟
collar
Kragen^M
col^M
cuello^M
collo^M

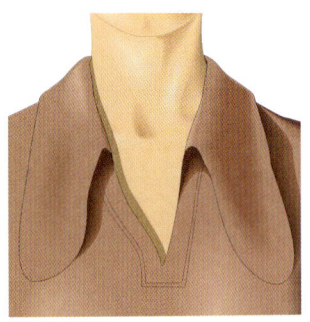

ドッグ・イヤー・カラー
dog ear collar
Dackelohrkragen^M
col^M banane^F
cuello^M plano con orejas^F
collo^M a orecchie^F di cane^M

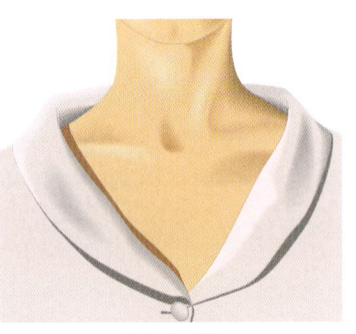

ショール・カラー
shawl collar
Schalkragen^M
col^M châle^M
cuello^M de chal^M
collo^M a scialle^M

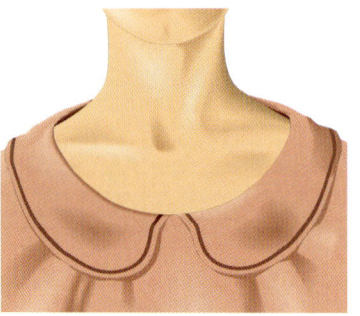

ピーター・パン・カラー
Peter Pan collar
Bubikragen^M
col^M Claudine
cuello^M plano tipo^M Peter Pan
collo^M alla Peter Pan

開襟（かいきん）／オープン・カラー
shirt collar
Hemdblusenkragen^M
col^M chemisier^M
cuello^M camisero
collo^M a camicia^F

テーラード・カラー
tailored collar
Schneiderkragen^M
col^M tailleur^M
cuello^M de hechura^F de sastre^M
collo^M a uomo^M

ボウ・カラー
bow collar
Schleifenkragen^M
col^M cravate^F
cuello^M de lazo^M
collo^M con sciarpa^F

ジャボ
jabot
Jabot^N
jabot^M
chorrera^F
jabot^M

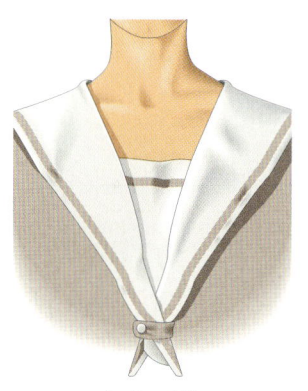

セーラー・カラー
sailor collar
Matrosenkragen^M
col^M marin^M
cuello^M marinero
collo^M alla marinara^F

衣服

女性用衣類

マンダリン・カラー
mandarin collar
Chinesenkragen^M
col^M chinois
cuello^M chino
collo^M alla coreana^F

カラーレット
collaret
Halskrause^F
collerette^F
cuello^M de volantes^M
collaretto^F

バーサ・カラー
bertha collar
Berthe^F
col^M berthe^F
cuello^M Berta
berta^F

タートルネック
turtleneck
Rollkragen^M
col^M roulé
cuello^M de tortuga^F
dolcevita^M

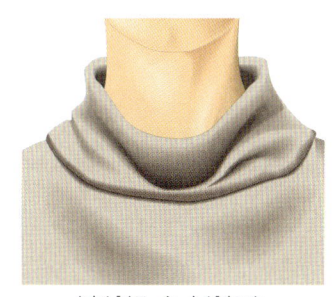

カウル[オフ・タートル]ネック
cowl neck
Kuttenkragen^M
col^M cagoule
cuello^M tipo cogulla^F
collo^M a cappuccio^M

ポロ・カラー
polo collar
Polokragen^M
col^M polo^M
cuello^M de polo^M
collo^M a polo^F

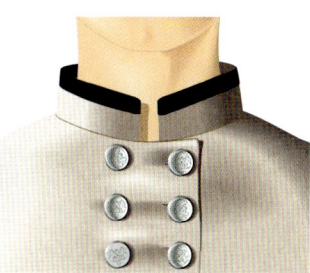

スタンダップ・カラー
stand-up collar
Stehbundkragen^M
col^M officier^M
cuello^M Mao
collo^M a listino^M

ネックライン
necklines and necks
Dekolletés^N und Ausschnitte^M
décolletés^M et encolures^F
escotes^M
scollature^F

プランジング・ネックライン
plunging neckline
spitzes Dekolleté^N
décolleté^M plongeant
escote^M bajo
scollatura^F profonda a V

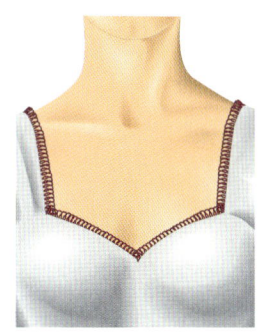

スイートハート・ネックライン
sweetheart neckline
Coeur-Dekolleté^N
décolleté^M en cœur^M
escote^M de corazón^M
scollatura^F a cuore^M

Vネック
V-shaped neck
V-Ausschnitt^M
décolleté^M en V
escote^M de pico^M
scollatura^F a V

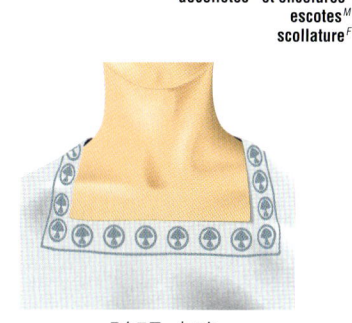

スクエア・ネック
square neck
viereckiger Ausschnitt^M
décolleté^M carré
escote^M cuadrado
scollatura^F quadrata

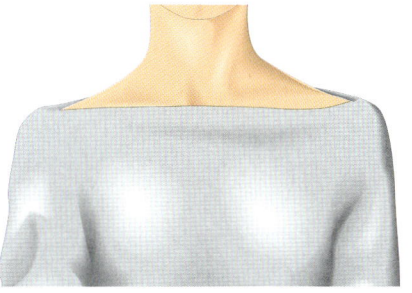

ボート・ネック
bateau neck
Bateau-Kragen^M
encolure^F bateau^M
escote^M de barco^M
scollatura^F a barchetta^F

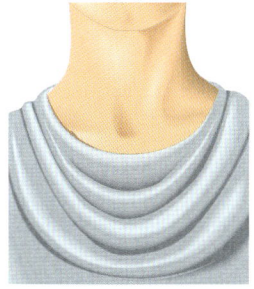

ドレープト・ネック
draped neck
drapierter Kragen^M
encolure^F drapée
cuello^M drapeado
girocollo^M drappeggiato

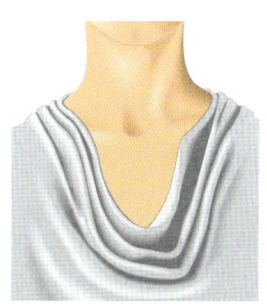

ドレープト・ネックライン
draped neckline
drapierter Ausschnitt^M
décolleté^M drapé
descote^M rapeado
scollatura^F drappeggiata

ラウンド・ネック
round neck
runder Ausschnitt^M
encolure^F ras-de-cou^M
cuello^M redondo
girocollo^M

衣服

女性用衣類

| 日本語 | 英語 | ドイツ語 | フランス語 | スペイン語 | イタリア語 |

ナイトウエア
nightwear
Nachtwäsche^F
vêtements^M de nuit^F
lencería^F
biancheria^F da notte^F

ナイトドレス
nightgown
Nachthemd^N
chemise^F de nuit^F
camisón^M
camicia^F da notte^F

ベビー・ドール
baby doll
Baby-Doll^N
nuisette^F
picardía^M
baby-doll^M

着物
kimono
Kimono^M
kimono^M
kimono^M
kimono^M

バジャマ
pajamas; *pyjamas*
Schlafanzug^M
pyjama^M
pijama^M
pigiama^M

ナイトガウン
negligee
Negligé^N
déshabillé^M
bata^F
vestaglia^F

バスローブ
bathrobe
Bademantel^M
peignoir^M
albornoz^M
accappatoio^M

衣服

364

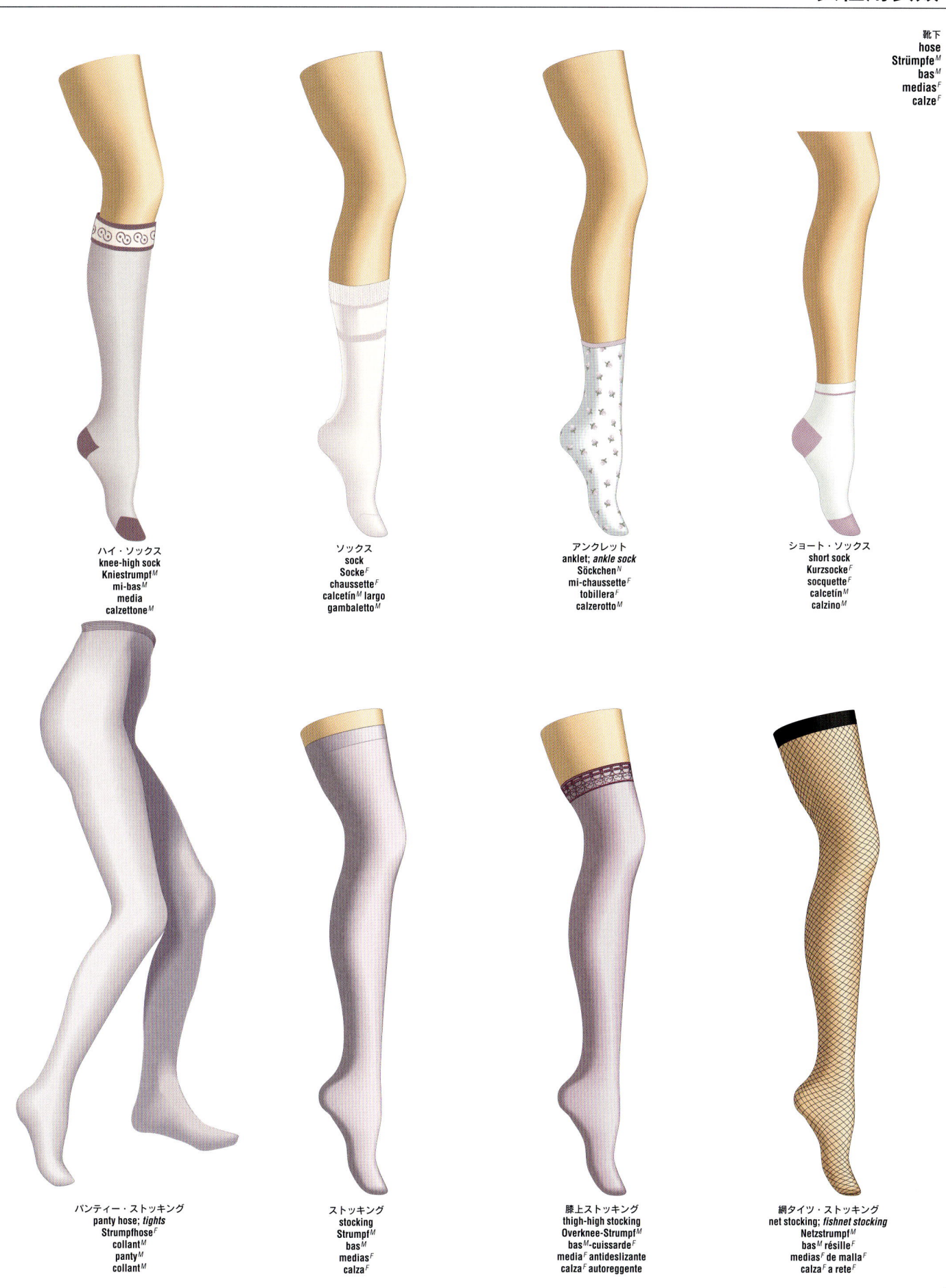

女性用衣類

靴下
hose
Strümpfe^M
bas^M
medias^F
calze^F

衣服

ハイ・ソックス
knee-high sock
Kniestrumpf^M
mi-bas^M
media
calzettone^M

ソックス
sock
Socke^F
chaussette^F
calcetín^M largo
gambaletto^M

アンクレット
anklet; *ankle sock*
Söckchen^N
mi-chaussette^F
tobillera^F
calzerotto^M

ショート・ソックス
short sock
Kurzsocke^F
socquette^F
calcetín^M
calzino^M

パンティー・ストッキング
panty hose; *tights*
Strumpfhose^F
collant^M
panty^M
collant^M

ストッキング
stocking
Strumpf^M
bas^M
medias^F
calza^F

膝上ストッキング
thigh-high stocking
Overknee-Strumpf^M
bas^M-cuissarde^F
media^F antideslizante
calza^F autoreggente

網タイツ・ストッキング
net stocking; *fishnet stocking*
Netzstrumpf^M
bas^M résille^F
medias^F de malla^F
calza^F a rete^F

女性用衣類

日本語 | 英語 | ドイツ語 | フランス語 | スペイン語 | イタリア語

下着
underwear
Unterwäsche^F
sous-vêtements^M
ropa^F interior
biancheria^F intima

コースレット
corselette
Korselett^N
combiné^M
faja^F con sostén^M
modellatore^M aperto

キャミソール
camisole
Camisol^N
caraco^M
camisola^F
top^M

テディー
teddy
Teddy^M
teddy^M
canesú^M
pagliaccetto^M

ボディー・スーツ
body suit
Bodysuit^M
body^M
body^M
body^M

パンティー・コースレット／ボディー・スーツ
panty corselette
Panty-Korselett^N
combiné^M-culotte^F
faja^F corsé^M
modellatore^M sgambato

ハーフ・スリップ／ペティコート
half-slip
Unterrock^M
jupon^M
falda^F combinación^F
sottogonna^F

プリンセス・シーム
princess seaming
Prinzessnaht^F
découpe^F princesse^F
costura^F de corte^M princesa^F
cucitura^F a princesse^F

ファンデーション・スリップ
foundation slip
Vollachsel-Unterkleid^N
fond^M de robe^F
combinación^F
sottoveste^F

スリップ
slip
Unterkleid^N
combinaison^F-jupon^M
combinación^F con sujetador^M
sottoveste^F con reggiseno^M

衣服

366

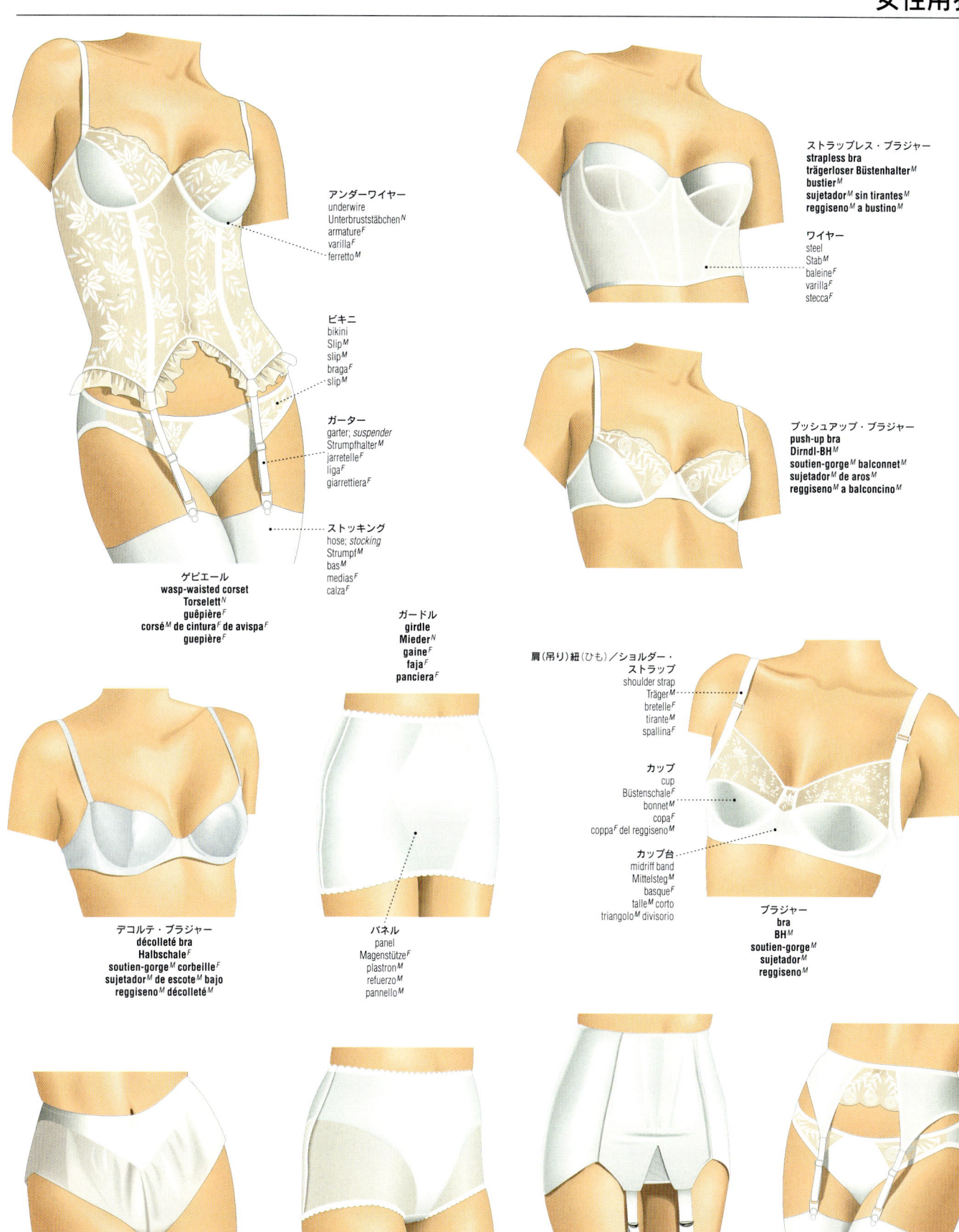

女性用衣類

アンダーワイヤー
underwire
Unterbruststäbchen^N
armature^F
varilla^F
ferretto^M

ビキニ
bikini
Slip^M
slip^M
braga^F
slip^M

ガーター
garter; *suspender*
Strumpfhalter^M
jarretelle^F
liga^F
giarrettiera^F

ストッキング
hose; *stocking*
Strumpf^M
bas^M
medias^F
calza^F

ゲピエール
wasp-waisted corset
Torselett^N
guêpière^F
corsé^M de cintura^F de avispa^F
guepière^F

ストラップレス・ブラジャー
strapless bra
trägerloser Büstenhalter^M
bustier^M
sujetador^M sin tirantes^M
reggiseno^M a bustino^M

ワイヤー
steel
Stab^M
baleine^F
varilla^F
stecca^F

プッシュアップ・ブラジャー
push-up bra
Dirndl-BH^M
soutien-gorge^M balconnet^M
sujetador^M de aros^M
reggiseno^M a balconcino^M

ガードル
girdle
Mieder^N
gaine^F
faja^F
panciera^F

肩(吊り)紐(ひも)／ショルダー・ストラップ
shoulder strap
Träger^M
bretelle^F
tirante^M
spallina^F

カップ
cup
Büstenschale^F
bonnet^M
copa^F
coppa^F del reggiseno^M

カップ台
midriff band
Mittelsteg^M
basque^F
talle^M corto
triangolo^M divisorio

デコルテ・ブラジャー
décolleté bra
Halbschale^F
soutien-gorge^M corbeille^F
sujetador^M de escote^M bajo
reggiseno^M décolleté^M

パネル
panel
Magenstütze^F
plastron^M
refuerzo^M
pannello^M

ブラジャー
bra
BH^M
soutien-gorge^M
sujetador^M
reggiseno^M

ブリーフス
briefs
Slip^M
culotte^F
braga^F
mutandina^F

パンティー・ガードル
panty girdle
Miederhose^F
gaine^F-culotte^F
faja^M braga
mutandina^F elastica

コルセット
corset
Korsett^N
corset^M
faja^F con liguero^M
corsetto^M

ガーター・ベルト
garter belt; *suspender belt*
Strumpfhaltergürtel^M
porte-jarretelles^M
liguero^M
reggicalze^M

ベビー服

newborn children's clothing | Babybekleidung^F | vêtements^M de nouveau-né^M | ropa^F de bebé^M | vestiti^M per neonati^M

日本語 | 英語 | ドイツ語 | フランス語 | スペイン語 | イタリア語

ジャンプスーツ
jumpsuit; *rompers*
Strampelhöschen^N
grenouillère^F
pantalón^M de peto^M
salopette^F a tutina^F

おくるみ
bunting bag
Schneesack^M
nid^M d'ange^M
saco^M portabebé^M
tutina^F a sacco^M

ベビー・フード・タオル
bathing wrap; *hooded towelling robe*
Badetuch^N mit Kapuze^F
cape^F de bain^M
toalla^F con capuchón^M
telo^M di spugna^F con cappuccio^M

- フード / hood / Kapuze^F / capuche^F / capuchón^M / cappuccio^M
- 飾りテープ / decorative braid / Zierborte^F / galon^M d'ornement^M / orla^F decorativa / guarnizione^F
- バイアス・テープ / false tuck / Paspel^F / biais^M / falsa doblez^F / profilo^M sbieco

ナイロン製フリル・タイツ
nylon rumba tights; *frilly nylon tights*
Rüschenstrumpfhose^F
collant^M fantaisie^F
mallas^F con volantes^M
ghettina^F con ruches^F

ベビーグロウ
grow sleepers; *babygro*
zweiteiliger Schlafanzug^M
dormeuse^F de croissance^F
pelele^M de dos piezas^F
pigiamino^M a due pezzi^M

- クルー・ネック / crew neck / halsnaher Ausschnitt^M / encolure^F ras-de-cou^M / cuello^M redondo / girocollo^M
- スクリーン・プリント / screen print / Aufdruck^M / motif^M / dibujo^M / disegno^M stampato
- ウエスト・スナップ / snap-fastening waist / Bund^M mit Druckknöpfen^M / pression^F à la taille / pretina^F con botones^M de presión^F / abbottonatura^F a pressione^F
- 足 / foot / Fuß^M / pied^M / pie^M / piede^M

調節可能な肩紐 (ひも)
adjustable strap
verstellbarer Träger^M
bretelle^F réglable
tirante^M ajustable
bretella^F regolabile

オーバーオール／サロペット
high-back overalls; *high-back dungarees*
Latzhose^F mit hohem Rückenteil^M/N
salopette^F à dos^M montant
pantalón^M de peto^M
salopette^F

- 胸当て / bib / Lätzchen^N / bavette^F / peto^M / pettorina^F
- パッチ・ポケット / patch pocket / aufgesetzte Tasche^F / poche^F plaquée / bolsillo^M de parche^M / tasca^F applicata
- ミシン・ステッチ / top stitching / Zier-Steppnaht^F / surpiqûre^F / pespunte^M / impuntura^F
- 前立て / fly / Schlitz^M / braguette^F / bragueta^F / patta^F
- 股下スナップ・ボタン / inside-leg snap-fastening / Druckknopfleiste^F an der Beininnenseite^F / entrejambe^M pressionné / botón^M de presión^F / interno^M gamba^F con abbottonatura^F a pressione^F

シャツ
shirt
Hemdchen^N
brassière^F
camiseta^F
maglietta^F intima

おむつ
diaper; *nappy*
Windel^F
couche^F
pañal^M
pannolino^M

フリル・パンツ
ruffled rumba pants; *frilly pants*
Rüschenhöschen^N
culotte^F à ruchés^M
braga^F de volantes^M
mutandina^F con ruches^F

- ルーシュ / ruching / Rüschen^F / ruché^M / volantes^M / ruches^F

よだれ掛け
bib
Lätzchen^N
bavoir^M
babero^M
bavaglino^M

紙おむつ
disposable diaper
Gummihöschen^N
couche^F-culotte^F
bragas^F de hule^M
pannolino^M usa e getta

- マジック・テープ / Velcro® closure / Haftgurtband^N / fermeture^F Velcro® / tirita^F Velcro® / velcro®^M
- 防水カバー / waterproof pants / dichtes Windelhöschen^N / poche^F intérieure isolante / material^M impermeable / mutandina^F impermeabile

ベビー服

カバーオール
blanket sleepers; *blanket sleepsuit*
Wagenanzug^M
dormeuse^F-couverture^F
pelele
pigiamino^M

ゴム編みカフス
ribbing
Rippenbündchen^N
bord^M-côte^F
tirilla^F elástica
bordo^F a coste

カバーオール
sleepers; *sleepsuit*
Schlafanzug^M
combinaison^F de nuit
pelele
pigiamino^M

ラグラン・スリーブ
raglan sleeve
Raglanärmel^M
manche^F raglan
manga^F raglán
manica^F alla raglan

スナップ付き前身(頃)(まえみごろ)
snap-fastening front
vordere Druckknopfleiste^F
pression^F devant
botones^M de presión^F delanteros
abbottonatura^F anteriore a pressione^F

ゴム編みカフス
ribbing
Rippenbündchen^N
bord^M-côte^F
tirilla^F elástica
bordo^F a coste

ファスナー
zipper; *zip*
Reißverschluss^M
fermeture^F à glissière^F
cremallera^F
chiusura^F lampo

スクリーン・プリント
screen print
Druckmotiv^N
motif^M
dibujo^M
disegno^M stampato

滑り防止加工の足裏
vinyl grip sole
Vinyl-Laufsohle^F
semelle^F antidérapante
suela^F de hule
soletta^F antiscivolo

股下スナップ・ボタン
inside-leg snap-fastening
Druckknopfleiste^F an der Beininnenseite^F
entrejambe^M pressionné
botones^M de presión^F de la pierna^F
interno^M gamba^F con abbottonatura^F a pressione^F

子供服

children's clothing | Kinderbekleidung^F | vêtements^M d'enfant^M | ropa^F de niños^M | vestiti^M per bambini^M

衣服

肩紐(ひも)クロス式オーバーオール
crossover back straps overalls; *dungarees with crossover back straps*
Latzhose^F mit gekreuzten Rückenträgern^M
salopette^F à bretelles^F croisées
pantalones^M de peto^M
salopette^F con bretelle^F incrociate

スノースーツ
snowsuit
Schneeanzug^M
esquimau^M
mono^M de esquí^M con capuchón^M
tuta^F da sci^M

パジャマ
pajama; *slip-on pyjamas*
Schlafanzug^M in Schlupfform^F
polojama^M
pijama^M
pigiama^M

ボタン・ストラップ
button strap
Träger^M mit Knopf^M
bretelle^F boutonnée
tirante^M con botones^M
bretella^F abbottonabile

絞り紐(ひも)付きフード
drawstring hood
Kapuze^F mit Zugband^N
capuche^F coulissée
capuchón^M con cordón^M
cappuccio^M con cordoncino^M

胸当て
bib
Lätzchen^N
bavette^F
peto^M
pettorina^F

比翼式打合わせ[打ち合い]
fly front closing
Verschluss^M mit verdeckter Knopfleiste^F
fermeture^F sous patte^F
cremallera^F
finta^F

Tシャツ・ドレス
T-shirt dress
T-Shirt Kleid^N
robe^F tee-shirt^M
camiseta^F de cuerpo^M entero
abito^M a T-shirt^F

ロンパース
rompers
Spielanzug^M
barboteuse^F
ranita^F
pagliaccetto^M

運動着
training set
Sportset^N
tenue^F d'exercice^M
conjunto^M deportivo
completo^M da ginnastica^F

タンク・トップ
tank top
Trägerhemdchen^N
débardeur^M
camiseta^F
canottiera^F

短パン
shorts
kurze Hose^F
short^M
pantalón^M corto
pantaloncini^M

ジャンプスーツ
jumpsuit
Overall^M
combinaison^F
mono^M
tuta^F

スポーツウエア

sportswear | Sportkleidung^F | tenue^F d'exercice^M | ropa^F deportiva | abbigliamento^M sportivo

ランニング・シューズ
running shoe
Joggingschuh^M
chaussure^F de sport^M
zapatilla^F deportivo
scarpa^F da corsa^F

裏当て
lining
Futter^N
doublure^F
forro^M
fodera^F

舌革／べろ
tongue
Zunge^F
languette^F
lengüeta^F
linguetta^F

腰革前部
nose of the quarter
Vorderteil^{M/N}
aile^F de quartier^M
ala^F del cuarto^M
parte^F anteriore del quartiere^M

カラー
collar
Fersenrand^M
col^M
ribete^M
collo^M

カウンター
counter
Hinterkappe^F
contrefort^M
contrafuerte^M
rinforzo^M del calcagno^M

腰革／クォーター
quarter
Quartier^N
quartier^M
cuarto^M
quartiere^M

ステッチ
stitch
Naht^F
surpiqûre^F
pespunteado^M
impuntura^F

踵（かかと）
heel
Absatz^M
talon^M
talón^M
tallone^M

ミッドソール
middle sole
Zwischensohle^F
semelle^F intercalaire
cambrillón^M
intersuola^F

エア・ユニット
air unit
Luftpolster^N
coussin^M d'air^M
cámara^F de aire^M
cuscinetto^M ad aria^F

紐先金具／タグ
tag
Schnürsenkelende^N
ferret^M
herrete^M
puntale^M

靴紐（ひも）
shoelace
Schnürsenkel^M
lacet^M
cordón^M
laccio^M

トレーニング・スーツ
training suit
Trainingsanzug^M
survêtement^M
traje^M de entrenamiento^M
tuta^F sportiva

スウェット・パーカー
hooded sweat shirt
Sweatshirt^N mit Kapuze^F
pull^M à capuche^F
sudadera con capucha^F
felpa^F con cappuccio^M

トレーナー
sweat shirt
Sweatshirt^N
pull^M d'entraînement^M
sudadera^F
felpa^F

スウェット・パンツ
sweat pants; jogging pants
Trainingshose^F
pantalon^M molleton
pantalones^M de chándal^M
pantaloni^M felpati

スポーツウエア

海水パンツ
swimming trunks
Badehose^F
slip^M de bain^M
traje^M de baño^M
slip^M da bagno^M

水着
swimsuit
Badeanzug^M
maillot^M de bain^M
traje^M de baño^M
costume^M da bagno^M

エクササイズ・ウエア
exercise wear
Sportkleidung^F
vêtement^M d'exercice^M
ropa^F para ejercicio^M
abbigliamento^M da ginnastica^F

鳩目／紐穴／アイレット
eyelet
Öse^F
œillet^M
ojete^M
occhiello^M

爪（先）革／甲革／バンプ
vamp
Vorderblatt^N
claque^F
empella^F
tomaia^F

飾り穴
punch hole
gestanztes Loch^N
perforation^F
perforación^F
foro^M

レオタード
leotard
Trikot^N
justaucorps^M
body^M
body^M

スパッツ
footless tights
Leggins^F
collant^M sans pied^M
mallas^F
pantacollant^M

レッグ・ウォーマー
leg-warmer
Legwarmer^M
jambière^F
calentador^M de pierna^M
scaldamuscoli^M

本底／外底／表底／アウトソール
outsole
Laufsohle^F
semelle^F d'usure^F
suela^F
suola^F

スタッド
stud
Stollen^M
crampon^M
montante^M
tacchetto^M

ズボン
pants; trousers
Hose^F
pantalon^M
pantalones^M
pantaloni^M

アノラック
anorak
Anorak^M
anorak^M
anorak^M
k-way^M

ボクサー・ショーツ
boxer shorts
Shorts^F
short^M boxeur^M
pantalón^M de boxeo^M
pantaloncini^M da corsa^F

タンク・トップ
tank top
Trägerhemd^N
débardeur^M
camiseta^F
canottiera^F

衣服

371

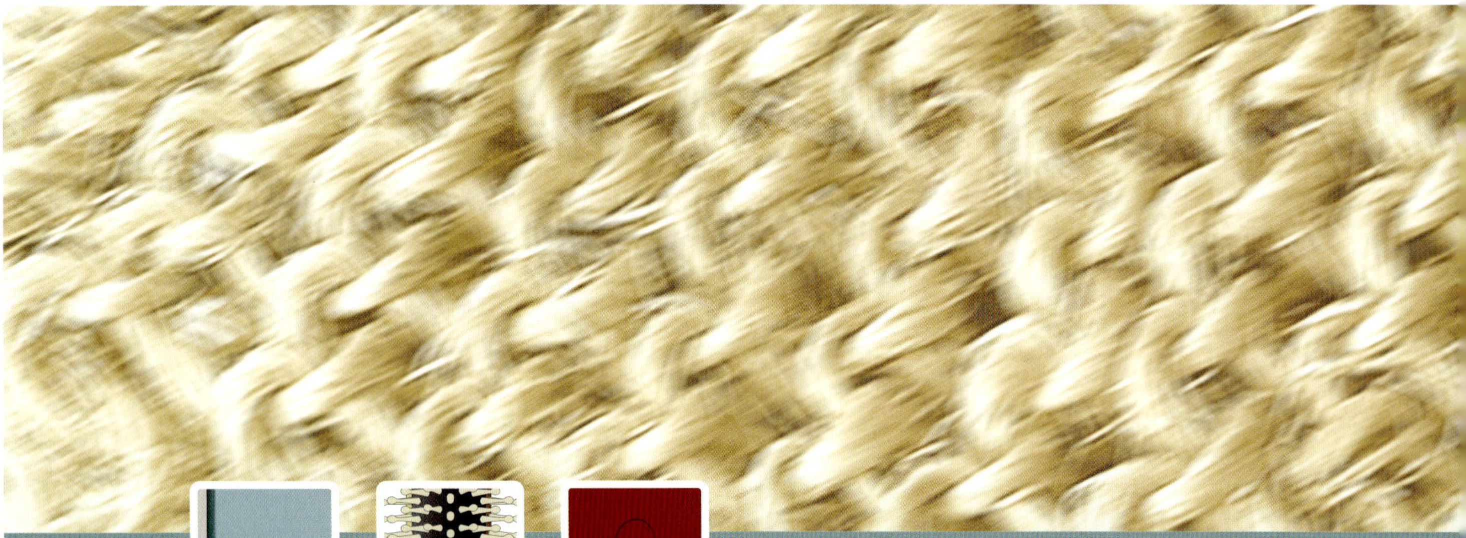
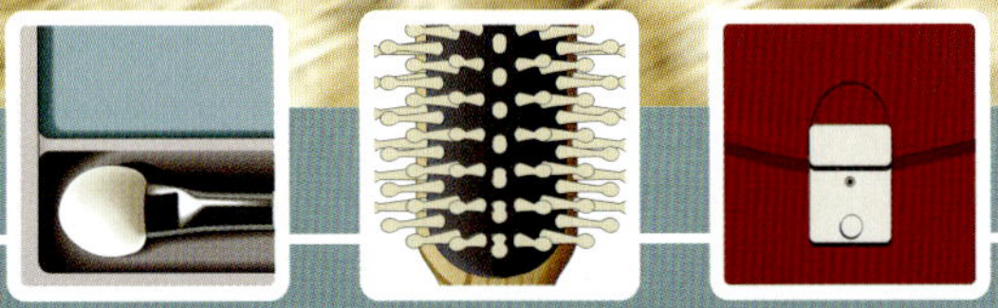

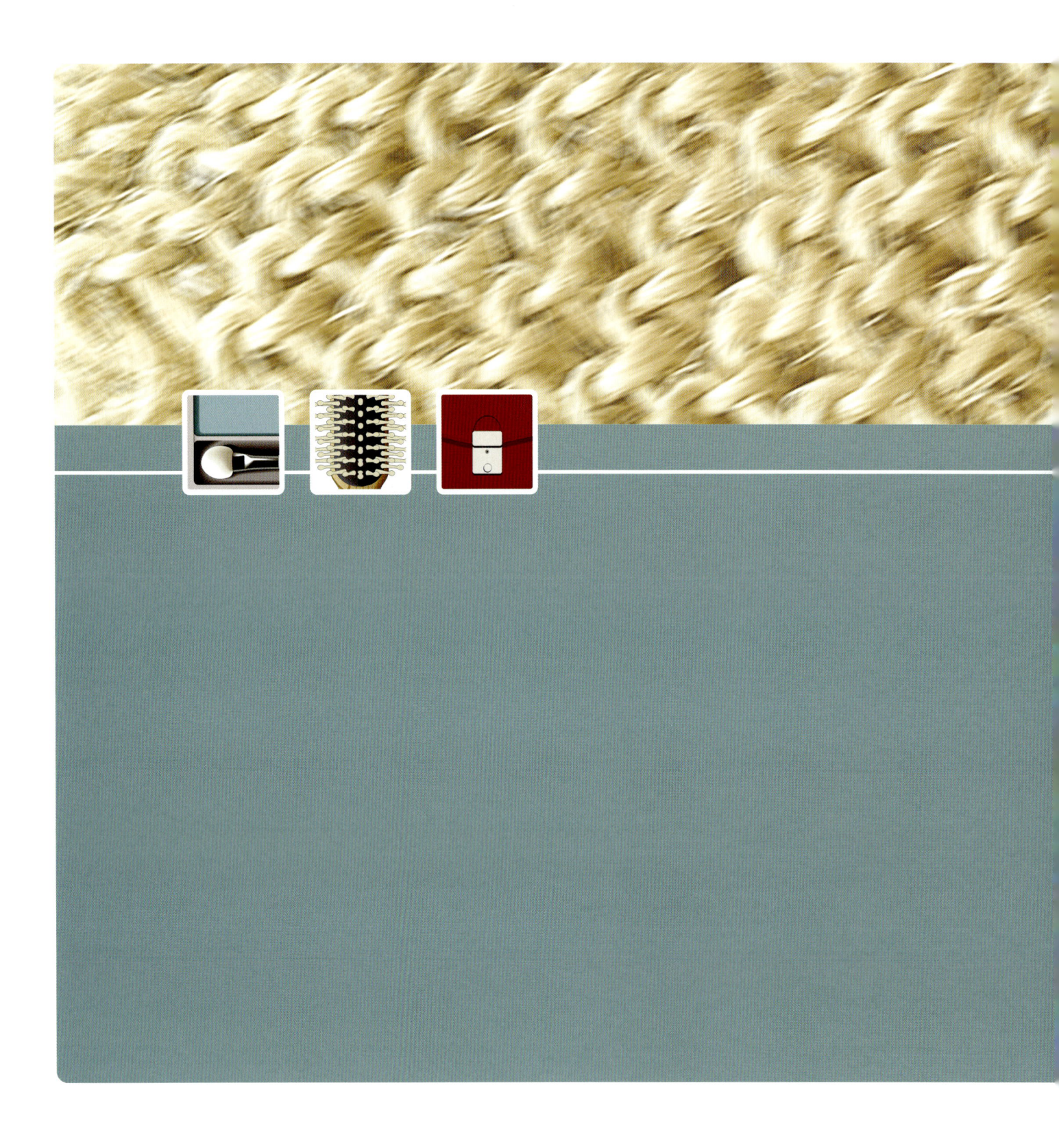

装身具類と日用品

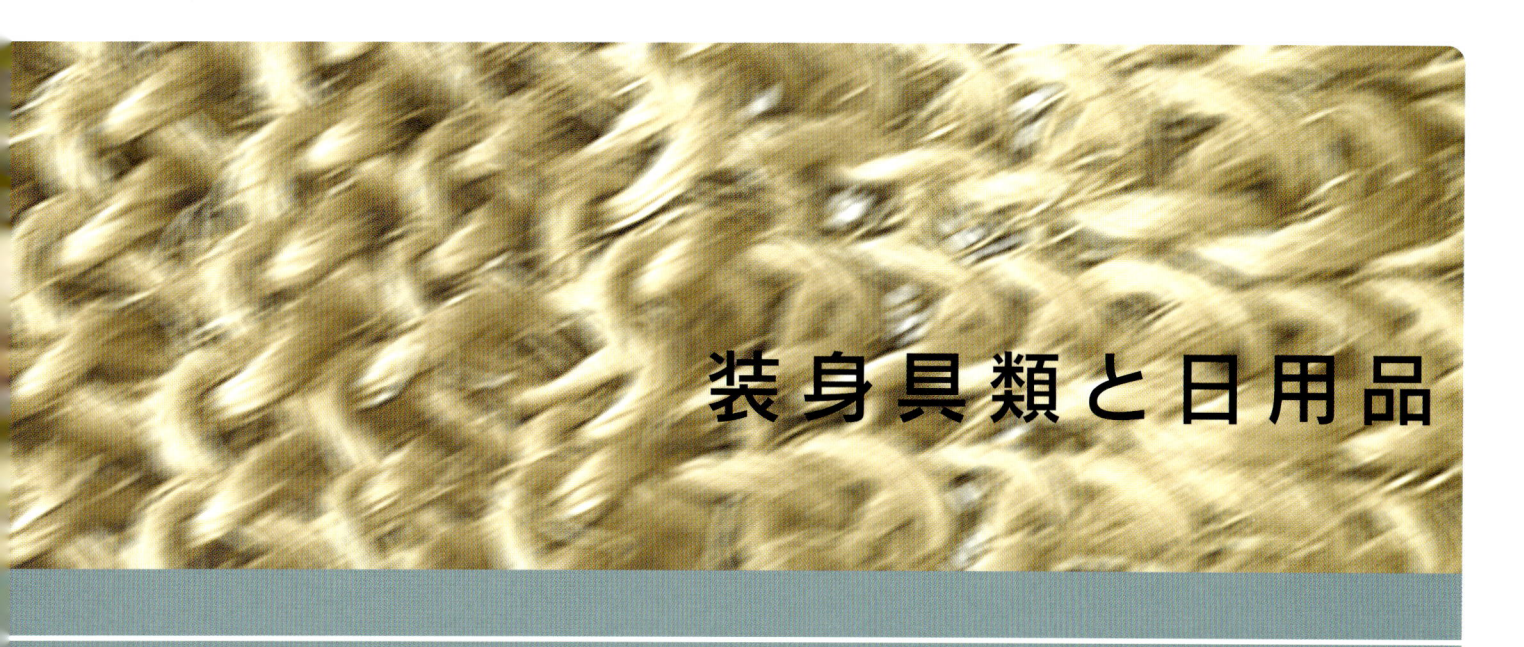

PERSONAL ADORNMENT AND ARTICLES I PERSÖNLICHE AUSSTATTUNG I PARURE ET OBJETS PERSONNELS I ACCESORIOS Y ARTÍCULOS PERSONALES I ACCESSORI E ARTICOLI PERSONALI

374 装身具類

- 374 宝飾品
- 377 ネイル・ケア
- 378 化粧用品
- 379 ボディー・ケア
- 380 整髪

383 日用品

- 383 髭（ひげ）剃り
- 384 歯磨き
- 384 コンタクト・レンズ
- 385 眼鏡
- 386 革製品
- 387 ハンドバッグ
- 388 旅行用鞄
- 390 喫煙具
- 391 傘とステッキ

宝飾品

装身具類 | PERSONAL ADORNMENT
SCHMUCK UND SCHÖNHEITSPFLEGE | PARURE | ACCESORIOS PERSONALES | ACCESSORI DI BELLEZZA

日本語 | 英語 | ドイツ語 | フランス語 | スペイン語 | イタリア語

jewelry; *jewellery* | Schmuck^M | bijouterie^F | joyería^F | gioielli^M

イヤリング
earrings
Ohrringe^M
boucles^F d'oreille^F
pendientes^M
orecchini^M

クリップ式イヤリング
clip earrings
Klips^M
boucles^F d'oreille^F à pince^F
pendientes^M de clip^M
orecchini^M a clip^F

ねじ式イヤリング
screw earrings
Ohrringe^M mit Schraubverschluss^M
boucles^F d'oreille^F à vis^F
pendientes^M de tornillo^M
orecchini^M a vite^F

ピアス・イヤリング
pierced earrings
Ohrstecker^M
boucles^F d'oreille^F à tige^F
pendientes^M de espiga^F
orecchini^M a perno^M

ドロップ・イヤリング
drop earrings
Ohrgehänge^N
pendants^M d'oreille^F
pendientes^M
orecchini^M pendenti

フープ・イヤリング
hoop earrings
Kreolen^F
anneaux^M
pendientes^M de aro^M
orecchini^M ad anello^M

ネックレス
necklaces
Halsketten^F
colliers^M
collares^M
collane^F

ロープ・ネックレス
rope
Endlosperlenkette^F
sautoir^M
lazo^M
collana^F lunga alla vita^F

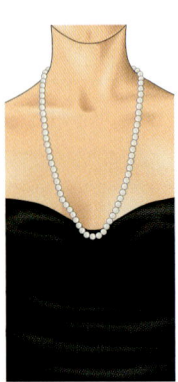

オペラ・レングス・ネックレス
opera-length necklace
Halskette^F in Opernlänge^F
sautoir^M, longueur^F opéra^F
collar^M de una vuelta^F, ópera^F
collana^F lunga

マチネ・レングス・ネックレス
matinee-length necklace
Halskette^F in Matineelänge^F
collier^M de perles^F, longueur^F matinée^F
collar^M de una vuelta^F, matinée^F
collana^F

ビブ・ネックレス
bib necklace
mehrreihige Halskette^F
collier^M de soirée^F
collar^M de 5 vueltas^F, peto^M
collana^F a cinque giri^M

ベルベット・チョーカー
velvet-band choker
Samtkropfband^N
collier^M-de-chien^M
gargantilla^F de terciopelo^M
collarino^M di velluto^M

チョーカー
choker
Chokerkette^F
ras-de-cou^M
gargantilla^F
girocollo^M

ペンダント
pendant
Anhänger^M
pendentif^M
pendiente^M
pendenti^M

ロケット
locket
Medaillon^N
médaillon^M
medallón^M
medaglione^M

ブリリアント・カットのカット面
brilliant cut facets
Facetten^F des Brillantschliffs^M
taille^F d'un diamant^M
talla^F brillante de un diamante^M
sfaccettature^F del taglio^M a brillante^M

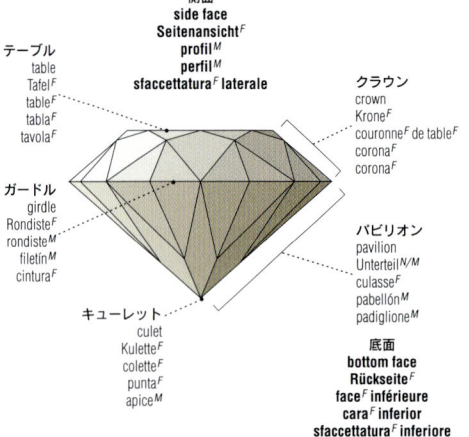

側面
side face
Seitenansicht^F
profil^M
perfil^M
sfaccettatura^F laterale

- テーブル / table / Tafel^F / table / tabla^F / tavola^F
- クラウン / crown / Krone^F / couronne^F de table^F / corona^F / corona^F
- ガードル / girdle / Rondiste^F / rondiste^M / filetín^M / cintura^F
- パビリオン / pavilion / Unterteil$^{N/M}$ / culasse^F / pabellón^M / padiglione^M
- キューレット / culet / Kulette^F / colette^F / punta^F / apice^M

上面
top face
Vorderseite^F
face^F supérieure
cara^F superior
sfaccettatura^F superiore

- スター・ファセット（8） / star facet (8) / Tafelfacette^F (8) / étoile^F (8) / faceta^F estrella^F (8) / faccia^F della stella^F (8)
- テーブル / table / Tafel^F / table / tabla^F / tavola^F
- ベゼル・ファセット（8） / bezel facet (8) / Oberteilhauptfacette^F (8) / bezel (8) / faceta^F fundamental exterior (8) / faccia^F principale della corona^F (8)
- アッパー・ガードル・ファセット（16） / upper girdle facet (16) / obere Rondistenfacette^F (16) / halefis^F de table^F (16) / media faceta^F superior / faccia^F superiore della cintura^F (16)

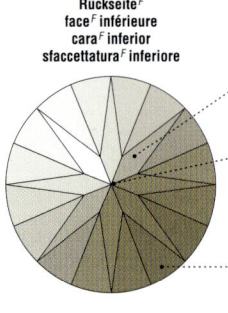

底面
bottom face
Rückseite^F
face^F inférieure
cara^F inferior
sfaccettatura^F inferiore

- パビリオン・ファセット（8） / pavilion facet (8) / Unterteilhauptfacette^F (8) / pavillon^M (8) / faceta^F de pabellón^M / faccia^F del padiglione^M (8)
- キューレット / culet / Kulette^F / colette^F / culata^F / apice^M
- ロワー・ガードル・ファセット（16） / lower girdle facet (16) / untere Rondistenfacette^F (16) / halefis^F de culasse^F (16) / faceta^F inferior del contorno^M / faccia^F inferiore della cintura^F (16)

装身具類 | PERSONAL ADORNMENT
SCHMUCK UND SCHÖNHEITSPFLEGE | PARURE | ACCESORIOS PERSONALES | ACCESSORI DI BELLEZZA

宝飾品

宝石のカット
cut for gemstones
Schliffformen^F für Edelsteine^M
taille^F des pierres^F
tallas^F de piedras^F preciosas
tagli^M di pietre^F preziose

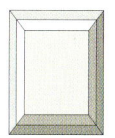

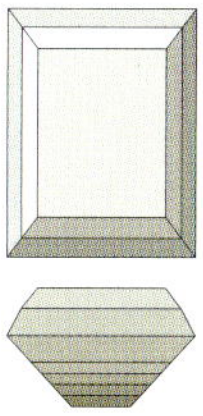

ステップ・カット
step cut
Treppenschliff^M
taille^F en escalier^M
talla^F escalonada
taglio^M a gradini^M

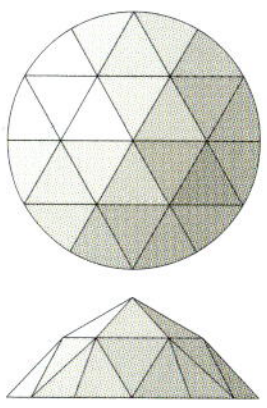

ローズ・カット
rose cut
Rosenschliff^M
taille^F en rose^F
talla^F en rosa^F holandesa
taglio^M a rosetta^F

テーブル・カット
table cut
Tafelschliff^M
taille^F en table^F
talla^F en tabla^F
taglio^M a tavola^F

カボション・カット
cabochon cut
Cabochonschliff^M
taille^F cabochon
talla^F en cabujón^M
taglio^M a cabochon^M

ペア・シェイプ・カット
pear-shaped cut
Pendeloque-Schliff^M
taille^F en poire^F
talla^F en pera^F
taglio^M a pera^F

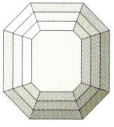

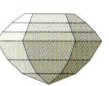

エメラルド・カット
emerald cut
Emeraldcut^M
taille^F émeraude^F
esmeralda^F
taglio^M a smeraldo^M

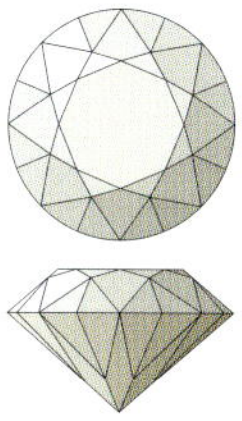

ブリリアント・フル・カット
brilliant full cut
Vollbrillantschliff^M
taille^F brillant
brillante^F
taglio^M a brillante^M

エイト・カット
eight cut
Achtkantschliff^M
taille^F huit facettes^F
talla^F octógono
taglio^M ottagonale

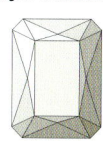

シザーズ・カット
scissors cut
Scherenschliff^M
taille^F en ciseaux^M
en tijera^F
taglio^M a forbice^F

ブリオレット・カット
briolette cut
Briolettschliff^M
taille^F en goutte^F
talla^F en briolette^F
taglio^M a briolette

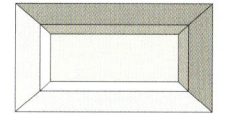

バゲット・カット
baguette cut
Baguetteform^F
taille^F baguette^F
talla^F en baguette^F
taglio^M a baguette^F

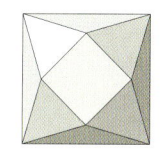

フレンチ・カット
French cut
Frenchcut^M
taille^F française
talla^F francesa
taglio^M francese

オーバル・カット
oval cut
ovale Form^F
taille^F ovale
talla^F oval
taglio^M ovale

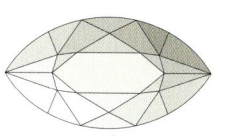

マーキーズ・カット
navette cut
Navette^F
taille^F marquise^F
marquesa^F
taglio^M a marquise^F

準貴石[宝石]
semiprecious stones
Halbedelsteine^M
pierres^F fines
piedras^F semipreciosas
pietre^F semipreziose

アメシスト
amethyst
Amethyst^M
améthyste^F
amatista^F
ametista^F

ラピス・ラズリ
lapis lazuli
Lapislazuli^M
lapis-lazuli^M
lapislázuli^M
lapislazzuli^M

アクアマリン
aquamarine
Aquamarin^M
aigue-marine^F
aguamarina^F
acquamarina^F

トパーズ
topaz
Topas^M
topaze^F
topacio^F
topazio^M

トルマリン
tourmaline
Turmalin^M
tourmaline^F
turmalina^F
tormalina^F

オパール
opal
Opal^M
opale^F
ópalo^F
opale^M

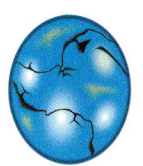

トルコ石
turquoise
Türkis^M
turquoise^F
turquesa^F
turchese^M

ガーネット
garnet
Granat^M
grenat^M
granate^M
granato^M

貴石
precious stones
Edelsteine^M
pierres^F précieuses
piedras^F preciosas
pietre^F preziose

エメラルド
emerald
Smaragd^M
émeraude^F
esmeralda^F
smeraldo^M

サファイア
sapphire
Saphir^M
saphir^M
zafiro^M
zaffiro^M

ダイヤモンド
diamond
Diamant^M
diamant^M
diamante^M
diamante^M

ルビー
ruby
Rubin^M
rubis^M
rubí^M
rubino^M

375

装身具類 | PERSONAL ADORNMENT
SCHMUCK UND SCHÖNHEITSPFLEGE | PARURE | ACCESORIOS PERSONALES | ACCESSORI DI BELLEZZA

宝飾品

指輪
rings
Ringe^M
bagues^F
anillos^M
anelli^M

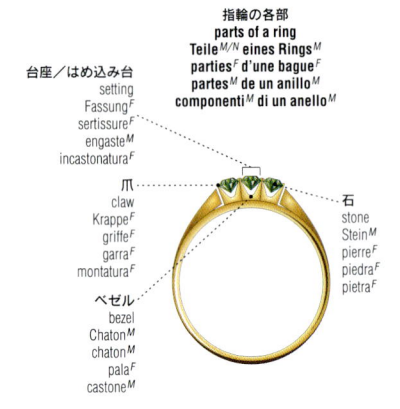

指輪の各部
parts of a ring
Teile^{M/N} eines Rings^M
parties^F d'une bague^F
partes^M de un anillo^M
componenti^M di un anello^M

台座／はめ込み台
setting
Fassung^F
sertissure^F
engaste^M
incastonatura^F

爪
claw
Krappe^F
griffe^F
garra^F
montatura^F

石
stone
Stein^M
pierre^F
piedra^F
pietra^F

ベゼル
bezel
Chaton^M
chaton^M
pala^F
castone^M

シグネット・リング
signet ring
Herrenring^M
chevalière^F
sortija^F de sello^M
anello^M con sigillo^M

クラス・リング
class ring
Collegering^M
bague^F de finissant^M
anillo^M de graduación^F
anello^M studentesco

バンド（型）リング
band ring
Bandring^M
jonc^M
alianza^F
anello^M a fascia^F

婚約指輪
engagement ring
Verlobungsring^M
bague^F de fiançailles^F
anillo^M de compromiso^M
anello^M di fidanzamento^M

結婚指輪
wedding ring
Ehering^M
alliance^F
alianza^F
fede^F nuziale

ソリテール・リング
solitaire ring
Solitärring^M
bague^F solitaire^M
solitario^M
solitario^M

ブレスレット
bracelets
Armbänder^N
bracelets^M
brazaletes^M
bracciali^M

バングル
bangle
Armreif^M
bracelet^M tubulaire
brazalete^M tubular
bracciale^M tubolare

チャーム・ブレスレット
charm bracelet
Armband^N
gourmette^F
pulsera^F de dijes^M
bracciale^M con ciondoli^M

ネーム・ブレスレット
identification bracelet
Identitätsband^N
gourmette^F d'identité^F
brazalete^M de identificación^F
bracciale^M con piastrina^F

チャーム
charms
Anhänger^M
breloques^F
dijes^M
ciondoli^M

角（つの）形チャーム
horn
Horn^N
corne^F
cuerno^M
corno^M

蹄鉄形チャーム
horseshoe
Hufeisen^N
fer^M à cheval^M
herradura^F
ferro^M di cavallo^M

ネームプレート
nameplate
Gravurplatte^F
plaque^F d'identité^F
placa^F de identificación^F
piastrina^F d'identità^F

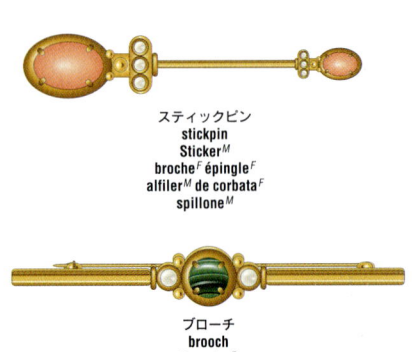

ピン
pins
Anstecknadeln^F
épingles^F
alfileres^M
spille^F

スティックピン
stickpin
Sticker^M
broche^F épingle^F
alfiler^M de corbata^F
spillone^M

ブローチ
brooch
Brosche^F
broche^F
broche^M
spilla^F

タイ・バー
tie bar
Krawattenklemme^F
pince^F à cravate^F
pisacorbatas^M
fermacravatta^M

タイピン
tiepin
Krawattennadel^F
épingle^F à cravate^F
alfiler^M de corbata^F
spillo^M fermacravatta^M

カラー・バー
collar bar
Kragenklammer^F
tige^F pour col^M
yugo^M
fermacolletto^M

装身具類 | PERSONAL ADORNMENT
SCHMUCK UND SCHÖNHEITSPFLEGE | PARURE | ACCESORIOS PERSONALES | ACCESSORI DI BELLEZZA

ネイル・ケア

nail care | Maniküre^F | manucure^F | manicura^F | manicure^F

マニキュア・セット
manicure set
Nagelnecessaire^N
trousse^F de manucure
estuche^M de manicura
set^M per manicure

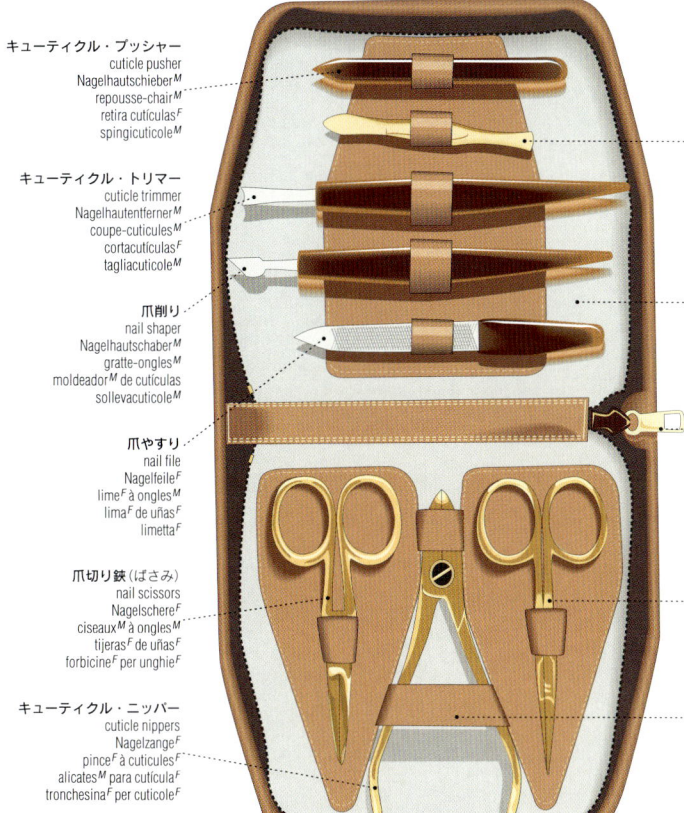

キューティクル・プッシャー
cuticle pusher
Nagelhautschieber^M
repousse-chair^M
retira cutículas^F
spingicuticole^M

キューティクル・トリマー
cuticle trimmer
Nagelhautentferner^M
coupe-cuticules^M
cortacutículas^M
tagliacuticole^M

爪削り
nail shaper
Nagelhautschaber^M
gratte-ongles^M
moldeador^M de cutículas
sollevacuticole^M

爪やすり
nail file
Nagelfeile^F
lime^F à ongles
lima^F de uñas
limetta^F

爪切り鋏（ばさみ）
nail scissors
Nagelschere^F
ciseaux^M à ongles
tijeras^F de uñas
forbicine^F per unghie

キューティクル・ニッパー
cuticle nippers
Nagelzange^F
pince^F à cuticules
alicates^M para cutícula
tronchesina^F per cuticole

眉毛抜き
eyebrow tweezers
Augenbrauenpinzette^F
pince^F à épiler
pinzas^F para depilar cejas^F
pinzette^F per sopracciglia

ケース
case
Etui^N
étui^M
estuche^M
astuccio^M

ジッパー
zipper; zip
Reißverschluss^M
fermeture^F à glissière
cremallera^F
cerniera^F lampo

キューティクル・シザー
cuticle scissors
Nagelhautschere^F
ciseaux^M à cuticules
tijeras^F para cutícula
forbicine^F per cuticole

ストラップ
strap
Schlaufe^F
bride^F
correa^F
fascetta^F

ネイル・バッファー
nail buffer
Nagelfeile^F
polissoir^M d'ongles
lima^F de uñas
lucidaunghie^M

ネイル・エナメル
nail enamel
Nagellack^M
vernis^M à ongles
esmalte^M de uñas
smalto^M per unghie

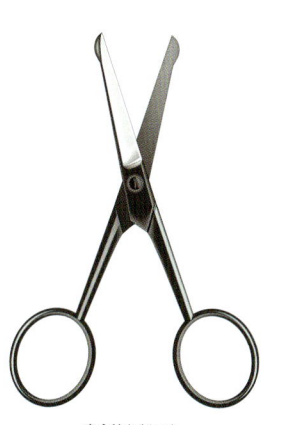

安全鋏（ばさみ）
safety scissors
Nasen-Bartschere^F
ciseaux^M de sûreté
tijeras^F de punta^F roma
forbici^F di sicurezza

爪切り
nail clippers
Nagelknipser^M
coupe-ongles^M
cortaúñas^M
tronchesina^F per unghie

爪磨き
nail cleaner
Nagelreiniger^M
cure-ongles^M
limpiador^M de uñas
pulisci unghie^M

持ち手／レバー
lever
Hebel^M
levier^M
palanca^F
leva^F

刃
jaw
Klemmbacke^F
mors^M
mordaza^F
ganascia^F

折り畳み式やすり
folding nail file
klappbare Nagelfeile^F
lime^F
lima^F de uñas
limetta^F pieghevole

セーム革
chamois leather
Wildleder^N
peau^F de chamois^M
piel^F de gamuza
pelle^F di camoscio

ネイル・ホワイト・ペンシル
nail whitener pencil
Nagelweißstift^M
crayon^M blanchisseur d'ongles^M
lápiz^M blanco para uñas
matita^F sbiancante per unghie

爪磨き／爪やすり／エメリー板
emery boards
Sandblattfeilen^F
limes^F-émeri^M
lima^F de uñas
limetta^F di cartoncino^M vetrato

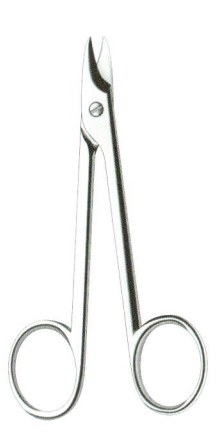

足指用爪切り鋏（ばさみ）
toenail scissors
Fußnagelschere^F
ciseaux^M de pédicure
tijeras^F de pedicura
forbici^F per unghie dei piedi^M

装身具類と日用品

377

装身具類 | PERSONAL ADORNMENT
SCHMUCK UND SCHÖNHEITSPFLEGE | PARURE | ACCESORIOS PERSONALES | ACCESSORI DI BELLEZZA

化粧用品

makeup; *make-up* | Make-up[N] | maquillage[M] | maquillaje[M] | trucco[M]

日本語 | 英語 | ドイツ語 | フランス語 | スペイン語 | イタリア語

顔のメーキャップ
facial makeup; *make-up*
Make-up[N]
maquillage[M]
maquillaje[M] facial
trucco[M] per il viso[M]

ファン・ブラシ
fan brush
Fächerpinsel[M]
pinceau[M] éventail
brocha[F] en forma[F] de abanico[M]
pennello[M] a ventaglio[M]

パウダー・パフ
powder puff
Puderkissen[N]
houpette[F]
borla[F]
piumino[M] da cipria[F]

合成スポンジ
synthetic sponge
Kunstschwamm[M]
éponge[F] synthétique
pincel[M] de esponja[F] sintética
spugna[F] sintetica

ブラッシュ・ブラシ／チーク・ブラシ
blusher brush
Rougepinsel[M]
pinceau[M] pour fard[M] à joues[F]
brocha[F] aplicadora de colorete[M]
pennello[M] da fard[M]

頰(ほお)紅
powder blusher
Puderrouge[N]
fard[M] à joues[F] en poudre[F]
colorete[M] en polvo[M]
fard[M] in polvere[F]

パウダー
loose powder
loser Puder[M]
poudre[F] libre
polvos[M] sueltos
cipria[F] in polvere[F]

パウダー・ブラシ
loose powder brush
Puderpinsel[M]
pinceau[M] pour poudre[F] libre
brocha[F]
pennello[M] da cipria[F] in polvere[F]

コンパクト
compact
Puderdose[F]
poudrier[M]
polvera[F]
portacipria[M]

固形パウダー
pressed powder
Kompaktpuder[M]
poudre[F] pressée
polvo[M] compacto
cipria[F] compatta

リキッド・ファンデーション
liquid foundation
flüssige Grundierung[F]
fond[M] de teint[M] liquide
base[F] líquida
fondotinta[M] fluido

目元のメーキャップ
eye makeup; *eye make-up*
Augen-Make-up[N]
maquillage[M] des yeux[M]
maquillaje[M] para ojos[M]
trucco[M] per gli occhi[M]

アイブロウ・ペンシル
eyebrow pencil
Augenbrauenstift[M]
crayon[M] à sourcils[M]
lápiz[M] de cejas[F]
matita[F] per sopracciglia[F]

アイ・カーラー
eyelash curler
Wimpernzange[F]
recourbe-cils[M]
rizador de pestañas[F]
piegaciglia[M]

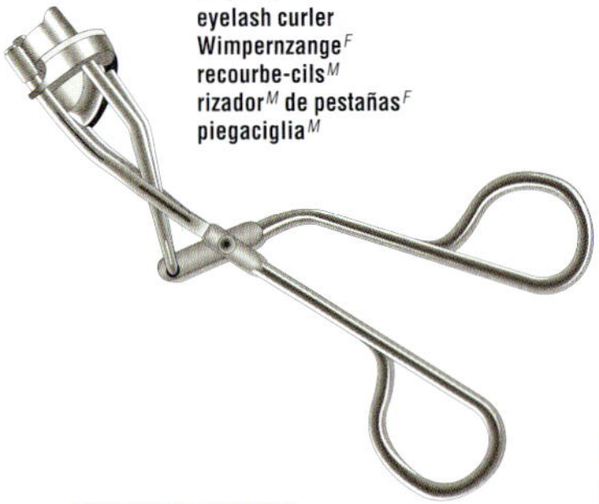

(アイ)ブロウ・ブラシとアイ・ラッシュ・コーム
brow brush and lash comb
Brauenbürstchen[N] und Wimpernkämmchen[N]
brosse[F]-peigne[M] pour cils[M] et sourcils[M]
cepillo[M] para cejas[F] y pestañas[F]
pettinino[M] per ciglia[F] e spazzolino[M] per sopracciglia[F]

マスカラ・ブラシ
mascara brush
Mascarabürstchen[N]
brosse[F] à mascara[M]
cepillo[M] aplicador de rímel[M]
spazzolino[M] per mascara[M]

固形マスカラ
cake mascara
Mascarastein[M]
mascara[M] en pain[M]
rímel[M] en pasta[F]
mascara[M] compatto

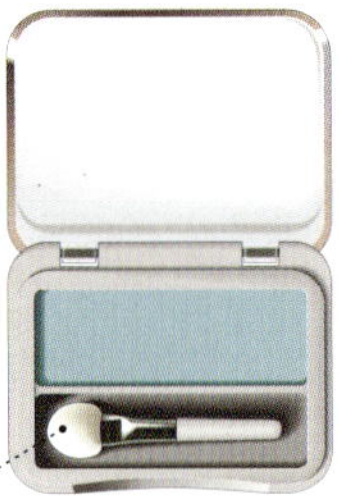

スポンジ・チップ
sponge-tipped applicator
Schwammstäbchen[N]
applicateur[M]-mousse[F]
aplicador[M] de esponja[F]
applicatore[M] a spugnetta[F]

アイシャドー
eyeshadow
Lidschatten[M]
ombre[F] à paupières[F]
sombra[F] de ojos[M]
ombretto[M]

リキッド・アイライナー
liquid eyeliner
flüssiger Eyeliner[M]
eye-liner[M] liquide
delineador[M]
eye-liner[M]

リキッド・マスカラ
liquid mascara
flüssiges Mascara[M]
mascara[M] liquide
rímel[M] líquido
mascara[M] liquido

唇のメーキャップ
lip makeup; *lip make-up*
Lippen-Make-up[N]
maquillage[M] des lèvres[F]
maquillaje[M] labial
trucco[M] per le labbra[F]

リップブラシ
lipbrush
Lippenpinsel[M]
pinceau[M] à lèvres[F]
pincel[M] para labios[M]
pennellino[M] per labbra[F]

リップライナー／カラー・スティック
lipliner
Lippenkonturenstift[M]
crayon[M] contour[M] des lèvres[F]
delineador[M] de labios[M]
matite[F] per il contorno[M] delle labbra[F]

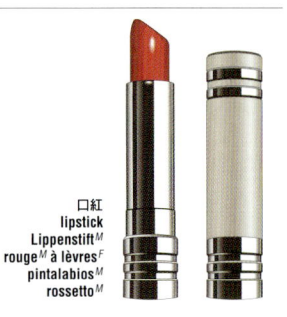

口紅
lipstick
Lippenstift[M]
rouge[M] à lèvres[F]
pintalabios[M]
rossetto[M]

装身具類 | PERSONAL ADORNMENT
SCHMUCK UND SCHÖNHEITSPFLEGE | PARURE | ACCESORIOS PERSONALES | ACCESSORI DI BELLEZZA

ボディー・ケア

body care | Körperpflege^F | soins^M du corps | cuidado^M personal | cura^F del corpo^M

栓
stopper
Stopfen^M
bouchon^M
tapón^M
tappo^M

瓶
bottle
Flasche^F
flacon^M
botella^F
bottiglia^F

オー・ド・パルファン
eau de parfum
Eau de parfum^N
eau^F de parfum^M
agua^F de perfume^M
profumo^M

化粧石鹸（せっけん）
toilet soap
Toilettenseife^F
savon^M de toilette^F
jabón^M de tocador^M
saponetta^F

ヘア・コンディショナー
hair conditioner
Haarspülung^F
revitalisant^M capillaire
acondicionador^M
balsamo^M per capelli^M

シャンプー
shampoo
Shampoo^N
shampooing^M
champú^M
shampoo^M

オー・ド・トワレ
eau de toilette
Eau de toilette^N
eau^F de toilette^F
eau^F de toilette^F
eau de toilette^F

バブル・バス
bubble bath
Schaumbad^N
bain^M moussant
gel^M de baño^M
bagnoschiuma^M

ヘアカラー
haircolor
Haarfärbemittel^N
colorant^M capillaire
tinte^M para el cabello^M
tintura^F per capelli^M

デオドラント／脱臭剤
deodorant
Deodorant^N
déodorant^N
desodorante^M
deodorante^M

（手袋形）洗顔[浴用]タオル
washcloth
Waschhandschuh^M
gant^M de toilette^F
manopla^F de baño^M
manopola^F

洗顔[浴用]タオル
washcloth
Waschlappen^M
débarbouillette^F
toalla^F para la cara^F
ospite^M

マッサージ・グローブ
massage glove
Massagehandschuh^M
gant^M de crin^M
guante^M de crin^M
guanto^M di crine^M

へちまスポンジ
vegetable sponge
Luffaschwamm^M
éponge^F végétale
esponja^F vegetal
spugna^F vegetale

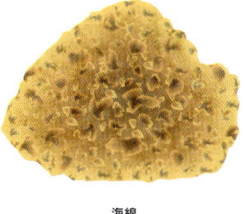

海綿
natural sponge
Naturschwamm^M
éponge^F de mer^F
esponja^F natural
spugna^F naturale

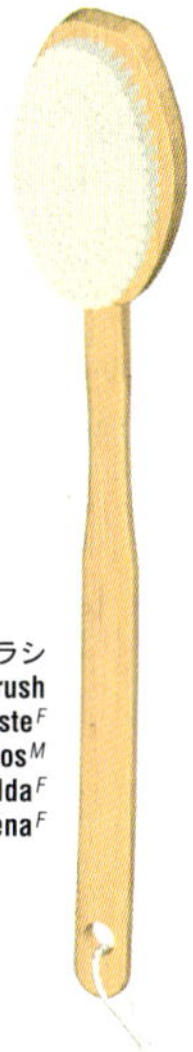

背中洗い用[長柄]ボディー・ブラシ
back brush
Massagebürste^F
brosse^F pour le dos^M
cepillo^M de espalda^F
spazzola^F per la schiena^F

大型バス・タオル
bath sheet
Badetuch^N
drap^M de bain^M
toalla^F de baño^M
asciugamano^M da bagno^M

バス・タオル
bath towel
Handtuch^N
serviette^F de toilette^F
toalla^F de lavabo^M
asciugamano^M

バス・ブラシ
bath brush
Badebürste^F
brosse^F pour le bain^M
cepillo^M de baño^M
spazzola^F da bagno^M

装身具類と日用品

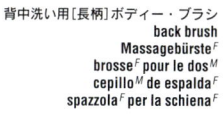

379

装身具類 | PERSONAL ADORNMENT
SCHMUCK UND SCHÖNHEITSPFLEGE | PARURE | ACCESORIOS PERSONALES | ACCESSORI DI BELLEZZA

整髪　　　　　　　　　　　　　　　　　　　　　　　　　　　　　　　　　　　　日本語 | 英語 | ドイツ語 | フランス語 | スペイン語 | イタリア語

hairdressing | Haarpflege^F | coiffure^F | peinado^M | articoli^M per acconciatura^F

ヘアブラシ
hairbrushes
Haarbürsten^F
brosses^F à cheveux^M
cepillos^M
spazzole^F per capelli^M

フラット・バック・ブラシ
flat-back brush
flache Frisierbürste^F
brosse^F pneumatique
cepillo^M con base^F de goma^F
spazzola^F a dorso^M piatto

回転ブラシ
round brush
Rundbürste^F
brosse^F ronde
cepillo^M redondo
spazzola^F rotonda

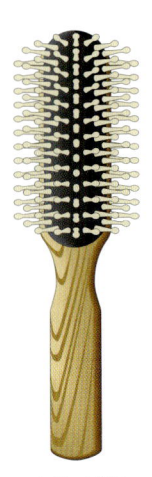

クイル・ブラシ
quill brush
Drahtbürste^F
brosse^F anglaise
cepillo^M de púas
spazzola^F antistatica

ベント・ブラシ
vent brush
Skelettbürste^F
brosse^F-araignée^F
cepillo^M de esqueleto^M
spazzola^F ragno

櫛（くし）
combs
Kämme^M
peignes^M
peines^M
pettini^M

アフロ・ピック
Afro pick
Strähnenkamm^M
peigne^M afro
peine^M afro
pettine^M afro

ティーザー・コーム
teaser comb
Toupierkamm^M
peigne^M à crêper
peine^M de cardar
pettine^M per cotonare

テール・コーム
tail comb
Stielkamm^M
peigne^M à tige^F
peine^M de mango^M
pettine^M a coda^F

バーバー・コーム
barber comb
Haarschneidekamm^M
peigne^M de coiffeur^M
peine^M de peluquero^M
pettine^M da barbiere^M

ピッチフォーク・コーム
pitchfork comb
Haarliftkamm^M
combiné^M 2 dans 1
peine^M combinado
pettine^M a forchetta^F

レーキ・コーム
rake comb
Griffkamm^M
démêloir^M
peine^M para desenredar
pettine^M rado

ヘア・カーラー
hair roller
Lockenwickler^M
bigoudi^M
rulo^M para el cabello^M
bigodino^M

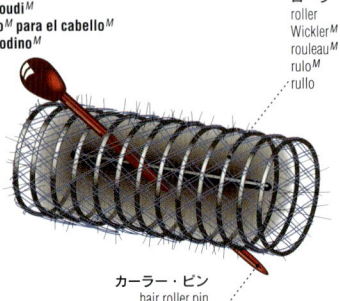

ローラー
roller
Wickler^M
rouleau^M
rulo^M
rullo

カーラー・ピン
hair roller pin
Haarstecker^M
épingle^F à bigoudi^M
alfiler^M
spillone^M

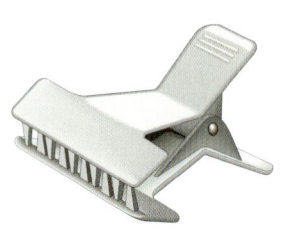

ウエーブ・クリップ
wave clip
Abteilklammer^F
pince^F à boucles^F de cheveux^M
pinza^F para rizar
pinza^F per capelli^M

ヘアピン
hairpin
Lockennadel^F
épingle^F à cheveux^M
horquilla^F de moño^M
forcina^F

ヘア・クリップ
hair clip
Haarclip^M
pince^F de mise^F en plis^M
pinza^F para el cabello^M
beccuccio^M

ボビー・ピン/ヘアピン
bobby pin; *hair grip*
Haarklemme^F
pince^F à cheveux^M
horquilla^F
molletta^F

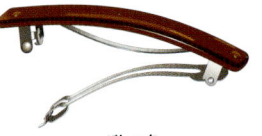

バレッタ
barrette; *hair slide*
Haarspange^F
barrette^F
pasador^M
fermacapelli^M

装身具類 | PERSONAL ADORNMENT
SCHMUCK UND SCHÖNHEITSPFLEGE | PARURE | ACCESORIOS PERSONALES | ACCESSORI DI BELLEZZA

整髪

照明付き鏡台
lighted mirror
beleuchteter Spiegel^M
miroir^M **lumineux**
espejo^M **luminoso**
specchio^M **luminoso**

照明
lighting
Beleuchtung^F
éclairage^M
iluminación^F
luce^F

三面鏡
dual swivel mirror
Drehspiegel^M
miroir^M double pivotant
espejo^M doble giratorio
specchio^M doppio girevole

サイド・ミラー
side mirror
Seitenspiegel^M
miroir^M latéral
espejo^M lateral
specchio^M laterale

台
base
Sockel^M
base^F
base^F
base^F

電源スイッチ
on-off switch
Schalter^M
interrupteur^M d'éclairage^M
interruptor^M
interruttore^M

ストレート・アイロン
straightening iron
Haarglätter^M
pince^F **à défriser**
plancha^F **de pelo**
piastra^F **stiracapelli**

グリップ
handle
Griff^M
poignée^F
mango^M
impugnatura^F

電源コード
power cord
Netzkabel^N
cordon^M d'alimentation^F
cordón^M de alimentación^F
cavo^M di alimentazione^F

毛梳(す)き用レザー
thinning razor
Effiliermesser^N
rasoir^M **effileur**
navaja^F **para entresacar**
rasoio^M **sfoltitore**

プレート
plate
Platte^F
plaque^F
plancha^F
piastra^F

カール・アイロン／電気鏝(ごて)
curling iron
Lockenstab^M
fer^M **à friser**
tenacillas^F
arricciacapelli^M

押さえレバー
clamp lever
Hebel^M für den Klemmbügel^M
levier^M
palanca^F
leva^F della pinza^F

電源スイッチ
on-off switch
Schalter^M
interrupteur^M
interruptor^M
interruttore^M

グリップ／取っ手
handle
Griff^M
poignée^F profilée
mango^M
impugnatura^F sagomata

回転コード
swivel cord; swivel flex
Knickschutztülle^F
cordon^M d'alimentation^F pivotant
cable^M de alimentación^M
cavo^M di alimentazione^F

温度表示器
heat ready indicator
Bereitschaftsanzeige^F
point^M indicateur^M de température^F
indicador^M de temperatura^F
indicatore^M di temperatura^F

押さえ
clamp
Klemmbügel^M
pince^F
pinza^F
pinza^F

電源表示灯
on-off indicator
Kontrolllampe^F
voyant^M lumineux
luz^F piloto^M
spia^F

スタンド／台
stand
Ständer^M
support^M
soporte^M
supporto^M

バレル／胴部
barrel
Zylinder^M
tube^M
varilla^F rizadora
rullo^M

クール・チップ
cool tip
nicht wärmeleitende Spitze^F
embout^M isolant
punta^F de plástico^M
punta^F fredda

バリカン
clippers
Haarschneider^M
tondeuse^F
maquinilla^F **para cortar el cabello**^{M}
macchinetta^F

装身具類と日用品

装身具類 | PERSONAL ADORNMENT
SCHMUCK UND SCHÖNHEITSPFLEGE | PARURE | ACCESORIOS PERSONALES | ACCESSORI DI BELLEZZA

整髪

日本語 | 英語 | ドイツ語 | フランス語 | スペイン語 | イタリア語

理髪鋏（ばさみ）
haircutting scissors
Haarschneideschere^F
ciseaux^M de coiffeur^M
tijeras^F de peluquero^M
forbici^F da parrucchiere^M

小刃
cutting edge
Schneide^F
tranchant^M
filo^M
filo^M della lama^F

切り刃
blade
Blatt^N
lame^F
hoja^F
lama^F

支軸
pivot
Bolzen^M
pivot^M
pivote^M
perno^M

柄
shank
Halm^M
branche^F
brazo^M
braccio^M

指輪
ringhandle
Auge^N
anneau^M
ojo^M
anello^M

接点突起
blade close stop
Klingenstopper^M
amortisseur^M
tope^M
fermo^M della lama^F

片梳（す）き用梳き鋏
notched single-edged thinning scissors
einseitig gezahnte Effilierschere^F
ciseaux^M sculpteurs
tijeras^F con filo^M simple para entresacar
forbice^F sfoltitrice a lama^F singola dentellata

梳き刃
notched edge
gekerbtes Scherenblatt^N
lame^F dentée
hoja^F dentada
lama^F dentellata

切り刃
blade
Blatt^N
lame^F droite
cuchilla^F
lama^F dritta

両梳（す）き用梳き鋏
notched double-edged thinning scissors
zweiseitig gezahnte Effilierschere^F
ciseaux^M à effiler
tijeras^F con doble filo^M para entresacar
forbice^F sfoltitrice a doppia lama^F dentellata

歯
tooth
Zahn^M
dent^F
diente^M
dente^M

ヘア・ドライヤー
hair dryer
Fön^M
sèche-cheveux^M
secador^F de mano^M
asciugacapelli^M

本体
barrel
Zylinder^M
corps^M
tubo^M de aire^F
corpo^M

吹き出し口グリル
air-outlet grille
Luftaustrittsöffnung^F
grille^F de sortie^F d'air^M
rejilla^F de salida^F de aire^M
griglia^F di uscita^F dell'aria^F

（送風）ファン内蔵部
fan housing
Föngehäuse^N
boîtier^M du ventilateur^M
caja^F del ventilador^M
alloggiamento^M del ventilatore^M

吸い込み口グリル
air-inlet grille
Ansauggitter^N
grille^F d'aspiration^F
rejilla^F de entrada^F de aire^M
presa^F d'aria^F posteriore

風量切り替えスイッチ
speed selector switch
Luftstromschalter^M
sélecteur^M de vitesse^F
botón^M selector de velocidad^F
selettore^M della velocità^F

電源スイッチ
on-off switch
Schalter^M
interrupteur^M
interruptor^M
interruttore^M

温度切り替えスイッチ
heat selector switch
Temperaturschalter^M
sélecteur^M de température^F
botón^M selector de temperatura^F
selettore^M della temperatura^F

取っ手
handle
Griff^M
poignée^F
mango^M
manico^M

フック
hang-up ring
Aufhängeöse^F
anneau^M de suspension^F
anilla^F para colgar
anello^M di sospensione^F

フード
air concentrator
Luftstromrichtdüse^F
buse^F
concentrador^M de aire^M
riduttore^M

電気コード
power supply cord; flex
Netzkabel^N
cordon^M d'alimentation^F
cable^M de alimentación^F
cavo^M di alimentazione^F

日用品 | PERSONAL ARTICLES
PERSÖNLICHE ARTIKEL | OBJETS PERSONNELS | ARTÍCULOS PERSONALES | ARTICOLI PERSONALI

髭（ひげ）剃り

shaving | Rasur^F | rasage^M | afeitado^M | rasatura^F

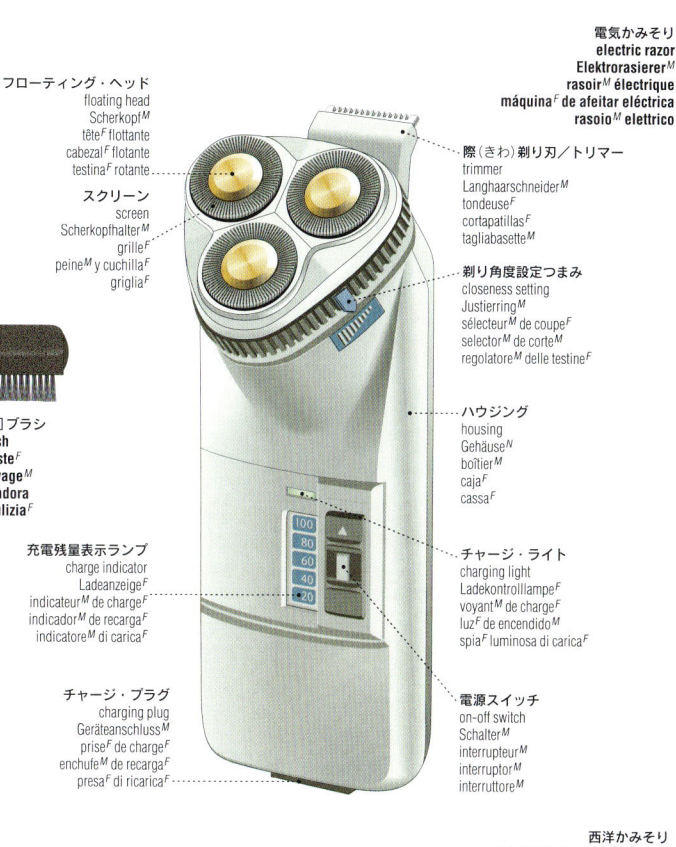

フローティング・ヘッド
floating head
Scherkopf^M
tête^F flottante
cabezal^F flotante
testina^F rotante

スクリーン
screen
Scherkopfhalter^M
grille^F
peine^M y cuchilla^F
griglia^F

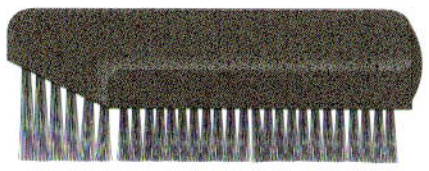

掃除[クリーニング]ブラシ
cleaning brush
Reinigungsbürste^F
brosse^F de nettoyage^M
escobilla^F limpiadora
spazzolino^M di pulizia^F

充電残量表示ランプ
charge indicator
Ladeanzeige^F
indicateur^M de charge^F
indicador^M de recarga^F
indicatore^M di carica^F

チャージ・プラグ
charging plug
Geräteanschluss^M
prise^F de charge^F
enchufe^M de recarga^F
presa^F di ricarica^F

電気かみそり
electric razor
Elektrorasierer^M
rasoir^M électrique
máquina^F de afeitar eléctrica
rasoio^M elettrico

際（きわ）剃り刃／トリマー
trimmer
Langhaarschneider^M
tondeuse^F
cortapatillas^F
tagliabasette^M

剃り角度設定つまみ
closeness setting
Justierring^M
sélecteur^M de coupe^F
selector^M de corte^M
regolatore^M delle testine^F

ハウジング
housing
Gehäuse^N
boîtier^M
caja^F
cassa^F

チャージ・ライト
charging light
Ladekontrolllampe^F
voyant^M de charge^F
luz^F de encendido^M
spia^F luminosa di carica^F

電源スイッチ
on-off switch
Schalter^M
interrupteur^M
interruptor^M
interruttore^M

シェービング・フォーム
shaving foam
Rasierschaum^M
mousse^F à raser
espuma^F de afeitar
schiuma^F da barba^F

電源コード
power cord; flex
Netzkabel^N
cordon^M d'alimentation^F
cable^M de alimentación^F
cordone^M dell'alimentazione^F

シェービング・ブラシ
shaving brush
Rasierpinsel^M
blaireau^M
brocha^F de afeitar
pennello^M da barba^F

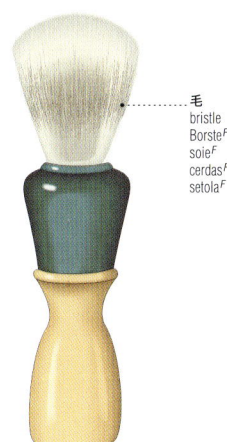

プラグ・アダプター
plug adapter
Adapter^M
adaptateur^M de fiche^F
adaptador^M
adattatore^M

毛
bristle
Borste^F
soie^F
cerdas^F
setola^F

アフター・シェーブ・ローション
after shave
Rasierwasser^N
après-rasage^M
loción^F para después del afeitado^M
dopobarba^M

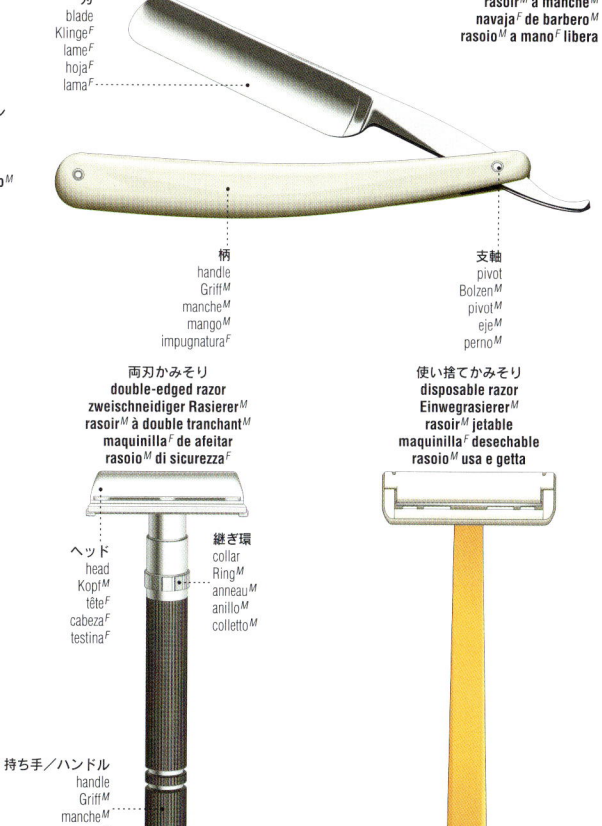

刃
blade
Klinge^F
lame^F
hoja^F
lama^F

西洋かみそり
straight razor; cut-throat razor
Rasiermesser^N
rasoir^M à manche^M
navaja^F de barbero^M
rasoio^M a mano^F libera

柄
handle
Griff^M
manche^M
mango^M
impugnatura^F

支軸
pivot
Bolzen^M
pivot^M
eje^M
perno^M

両刃かみそり
double-edged razor
zweischneidiger Rasierer^M
rasoir^M à double tranchant^M
maquinilla^F de afeitar
rasoio^M di sicurezza^F

使い捨てかみそり
disposable razor
Einwegrasierer^M
rasoir^M jetable
maquinilla^F desechable
rasoio^M usa e getta

ヘッド
head
Kopf^M
tête^F
cabeza^F
testina^F

継ぎ環
collar
Ring^M
anneau^M
anillo^M
colletto^M

シェービング・カップ
shaving mug
Seifenbecher^M
bol^M à raser
jabonera^F
tazza^F per sapone^M da barba^F

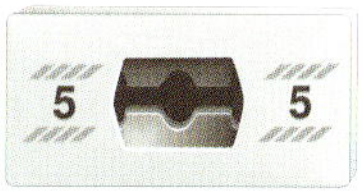

インジェクター
blade injector
Klingendose^F
distributeur^M de lames^F
distribuidor^M de hojas^F de afeitar
caricatore^M di lamette^F

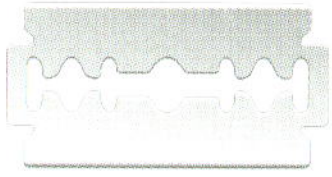

両刃
double-edged blade
zweischneidige Klinge^F
lame^F à double tranchant^M
hoja^F de afeitar
lametta^F a due tagli^M

持ち手／ハンドル
handle
Griff^M
manche^M
mango^M
manico^M

383

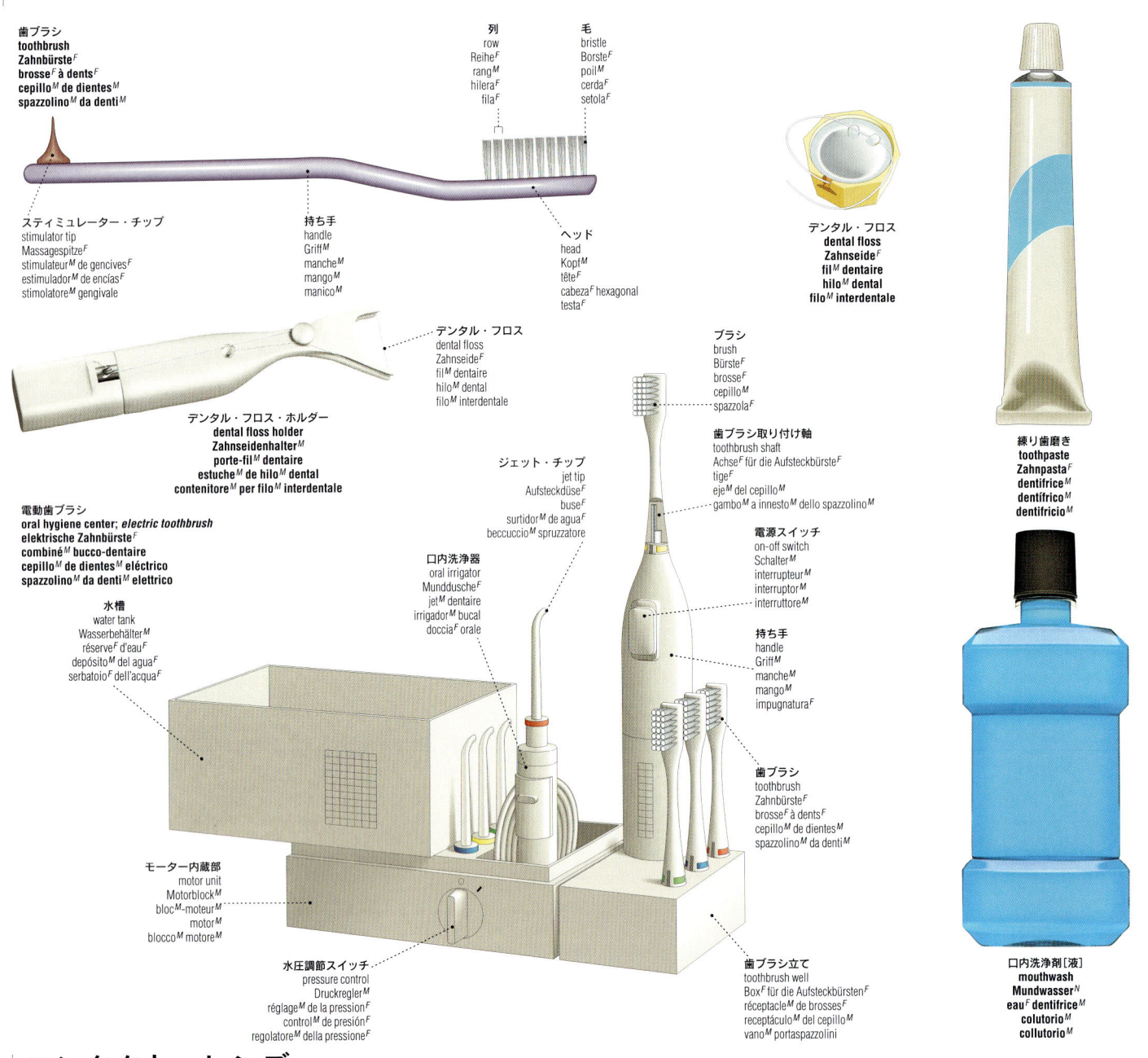

日用品 | PERSONAL ARTICLES
PERSÖNLICHE ARTIKEL | OBJETS PERSONNELS | ARTÍCULOS PERSONALES | ARTICOLI PERSONALI

歯磨き

dental care | Zahnpflege^F | hygiène^F dentaire | higiene^F dental | igiene^F orale

日本語 | 英語 | ドイツ語 | フランス語 | スペイン語 | イタリア語

歯ブラシ
toothbrush
Zahnbürste^F
brosse^F à dents^F
cepillo^M de dientes^M
spazzolino^M da denti^M

列
row
Reihe^F
rang^M
hilera^F
fila^F

毛
bristle
Borste^F
poil^M
cerda^F
setola^F

スティミュレーター・チップ
stimulator tip
Massagespitze^F
stimulateur^M de gencives^F
estimulador^M de encías^F
stimolatore^M gengivale

持ち手
handle
Griff^M
manche^M
mango^M
manico^M

ヘッド
head
Kopf^M
tête^F
cabeza^F hexagonal
testa^F

デンタル・フロス
dental floss
Zahnseide^F
fil^M dentaire
hilo^M dental
filo^M interdentale

デンタル・フロス
dental floss
Zahnseide^F
fil^M dentaire
hilo^M dental
filo^M interdentale

デンタル・フロス・ホルダー
dental floss holder
Zahnseidenhalter^M
porte-fil^M dentaire
estuche^M de hilo^M dental
contenitore^M per filo^M interdentale

ブラシ
brush
Bürste^F
brosse^F
cepillo^M
spazzola^F

歯ブラシ取り付け軸
toothbrush shaft
Achse^F für die Aufsteckbürste^F
tige^F
eje^M del cepillo^M
gambo^M a innesto^M dello spazzolino^M

練り歯磨き
toothpaste
Zahnpasta^F
dentifrice^M
dentífrico^M
dentifricio^M

電動歯ブラシ
oral hygiene center; electric toothbrush
elektrische Zahnbürste^F
combiné^M bucco-dentaire
cepillo^M de dientes^M eléctrico
spazzolino^M da denti^M elettrico

ジェット・チップ
jet tip
Aufsteckdüse^F
buse^F
surtidor^M de agua^F
beccuccio^M spruzzatore

電源スイッチ
on-off switch
Schalter^M
interrupteur^M
interruptor^M
interruttore^M

水槽
water tank
Wasserbehälter^M
réserve^F d'eau^F
depósito^M del agua^F
serbatoio^M dell'acqua^F

口内洗浄器
oral irrigator
Munddusche^F
jet^M dentaire
irrigador^M bucal
doccia^F orale

持ち手
handle
Griff^M
manche^M
mango^M
impugnatura^F

歯ブラシ
toothbrush
Zahnbürste^F
brosse^F à dents^F
cepillo^M de dientes^M
spazzolino^M da denti^M

モーター内蔵部
motor unit
Motorblock^M
bloc^M-moteur
motor^M
blocco^M motore^M

水圧調節スイッチ
pressure control
Druckregler^M
réglage^M de la pression^F
control^M de presión^F
regolatore^M della pressione^F

歯ブラシ立て
toothbrush well
Box^F für die Aufsteckbürsten^F
réceptacle^M de brosses^F
receptáculo^M del cepillo^M
vano^M portaspazzolini

口内洗浄剤［液］
mouthwash
Mundwasser^N
eau^F dentifrice^M
colutorio^M
collutorio^M

コンタクト・レンズ

contact lenses | Kontaktlinsen^F | lentilles^F de contact^M | lentes^F de contacto^M | lenti^F a contatto^M

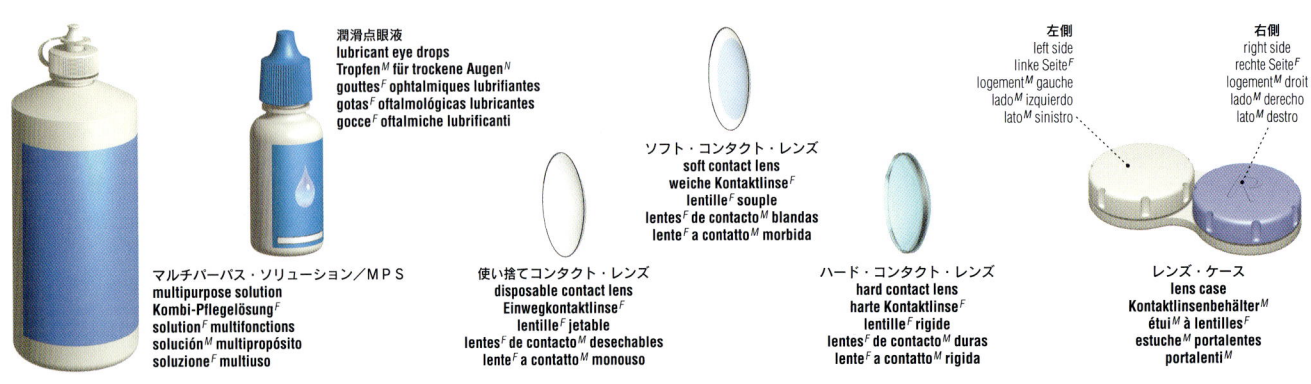

潤滑点眼液
lubricant eye drops
Tropfen^M für trockene Augen^N
gouttes^F ophtalmiques lubrifiantes
gotas^F oftalmológicas lubricantes
gocce^F oftalmiche lubricanti

ソフト・コンタクト・レンズ
soft contact lens
weiche Kontaktlinse^F
lentille^F souple
lentes^F de contacto^M blandas
lente^F a contatto^M morbida

左側
left side
linke Seite^F
logement^M gauche
lado^M izquierdo
lato^M sinistro

右側
right side
rechte Seite^F
logement^M droit
lado^M derecho
lato^M destro

マルチパーパス・ソリューション／MPS
multipurpose solution
Kombi-Pflegelösung^F
solution^F multifonctions
solución^M multipropósito
soluzione^F multiuso

使い捨てコンタクト・レンズ
disposable contact lens
Einwegkontaktlinse^F
lentille^F jetable
lentes^F de contacto^M desechables
lente^F a contatto^M monouso

ハード・コンタクト・レンズ
hard contact lens
harte Kontaktlinse^F
lentille^F rigide
lentes^F de contacto^M duras
lente^F a contatto^M rigida

レンズ・ケース
lens case
Kontaktlinsenbehälter^M
étui^M à lentilles^F
estuche^M portalentes
portalenti

日用品 | PERSONAL ARTICLES
PERSÖNLICHE ARTIKEL | OBJETS PERSONNELS | ARTÍCULOS PERSONALES | ARTICOLI PERSONALI

眼鏡

eyeglasses | Brille^F | lunettes^F | gafas^F | occhiali^M

眼鏡の各部名称
eyeglasses parts
Teile^{M/N} der Brille^F
parties^F des lunettes^F
gafas^F : partes^F
parti^F degli occhiali^M

山（わたり） — bar / Steg^M / barre^F / barra^F / barretta^F

ブリッジ — bridge / Brücke^F / pont^M / puente^M / ponticello^M

眼鏡レンズ — glass lens / Glas^N / verre^F / lente^F / lente^F

智（ち） — endpiece / Backe^F / tenon^M / espiga^F / attacco^M

テンプル — temple / Bügel^M / branche^F / patilla^F / stanghetta^F

丁番／ヒンジ — butt-strap / Bügelanschlag^M / talon^M / extremo^M / copricerniera^F

ベンド — bend / Bügelrundung^F / coude^M / codo^M / curvatura^F

縁／リム — rim / Rand^M / cercle^M / aro^M / montatura^F

耳当て — earpiece / Bügelende^N / cambre^M / gafa^F / terminale^M

パッド・プレート — pad plate / Stegplättchen^N / support^M de plaquette^F / soporte^M de la plaqueta^F / placchetta^F del portanasello^M

パッド・アーム — pad arm / Stegstütze^F / bras^M de plaquette^F / brazo^M de la plaqueta^F / portanaso^M

(鼻)パッド／鼻当て — nose pad / Seitensteg^M / plaquette^F / plaqueta^F / nasello^M

フレーム
frames
Fassungen^F
monture^F
montura^F
montatura^F

遠視用 — distance / Fernteil^{M/N} / segment^M de loin / enfoque^M de lejos / lente^F da distanza^F

遠近両用レンズ — bifocal lens / Zweistärkenglas^N / verre^M bifocal / lente^F bifocal / lente^F bifocale

読書用 — reading / Nahteil^{M/N} / segment^M de près / enfoque^M de cerca / lente^F da lettura^F

縁／リム — rim / Rand^M / cercle^M / aro^M / montatura^F

眼鏡の例
examples of eyeglasses
Beispiele^N für Augengläser^N
exemples^M de lunettes^F
ejemplos^M de gafas^F
esempi^M di occhiali^M

鼻眼鏡 — pince-nez / Kneifer^M / bésicles^F à pont^M élastique / quevedos^M / pince-nez^M

ハーフ・グラス／読書用眼鏡 — half-glasses / Halbbrille^F / demi-lune^F / media luna^F / mezzi occhiali^M

ローネット — lorgnette / Lorgnette^F / face-à-main^M / impertinentes^M / lorgnette^F

サングラス — sunglasses / Sonnenbrille^F / lunettes^F de soleil^M / gafas^F de sol^M / occhiali^M da sole^M

鼻眼鏡 — scissors-glasses / Scherenbrille^F / binocle^M / binóculos^M de tijera^F / occhiali^M a forbice^F

モノクル／片眼鏡 — monocle / Monokel^N / monocle^M / monóculo^M / monocolo^M

オペラ・グラス — opera glasses / Opernglas^N / lorgnette^F / gemelos^M de teatro^M / binocolo^M da teatro^M

装身具類と日用品

385

日用品 | PERSONAL ARTICLES
PERSÖNLICHE ARTIKEL | OBJETS PERSONNELS | ARTÍCULOS PERSONALES | ARTICOLI PERSONALI

革製品
leather goods | Lederwaren^F | articles^M de maroquinerie^F | artículos^M de marroquinería^F | articoli^M di pelletteria^F

日本語 | 英語 | ドイツ語 | フランス語 | スペイン語 | イタリア語

アタッシュ・ケース
attaché case
Aktenkoffer^M
mallette^F porte-documents^M
maletín^M
ventiquattrore^F

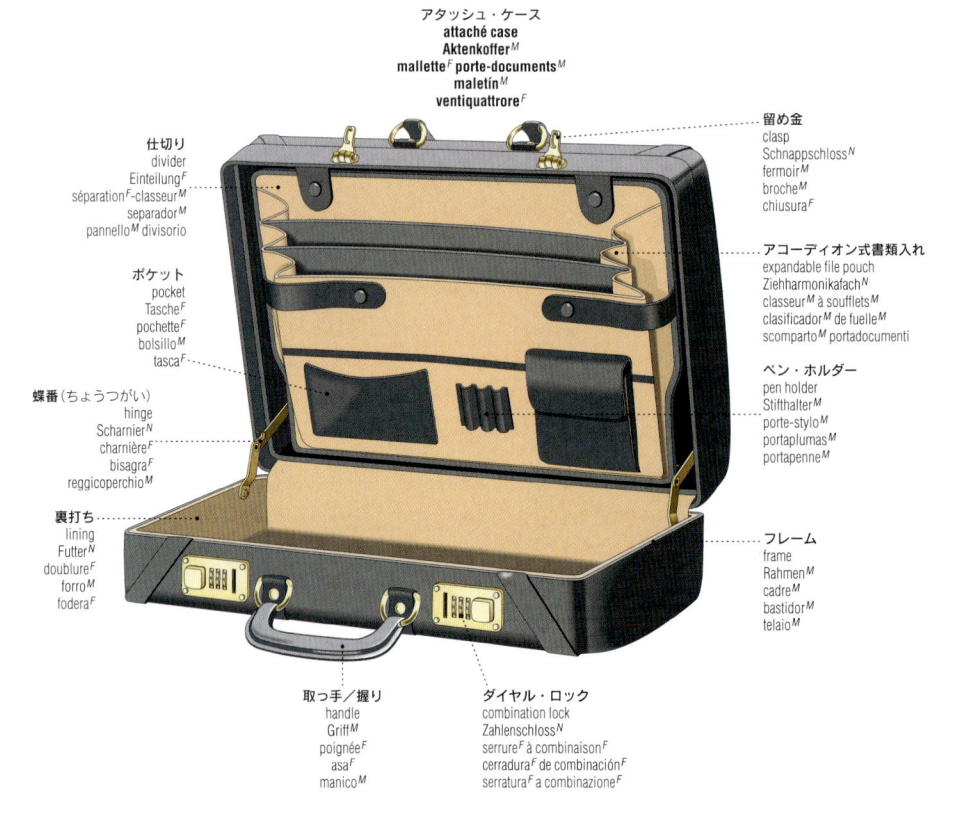

仕切り
divider
Einteilung^F
séparation^F-classeur^M
separador^M
pannello^M divisorio

ポケット
pocket
Tasche^F
pochette^F
bolsillo^M
tasca^F

蝶番（ちょうつがい）
hinge
Scharnier^N
charnière^F
bisagra^F
reggicoperchio^M

裏打ち
lining
Futter^N
doublure^F
forro^M
fodera^F

留め金
clasp
Schnappschloss^N
fermoir^M
broche^M
chiusura^F

アコーディオン式書類入れ
expandable file pouch
Ziehharmonikafach^N
classeur^M à soufflets^M
clasificador^M de fuelle
scomparto^M portadocumenti

ペン・ホルダー
pen holder
Stifthalter^M
porte-stylo^M
portaplumas^M
portapenne^M

フレーム
frame
Rahmen^M
cadre^M
bastidor^M
telaio^M

取っ手／握り
handle
Griff^M
poignée^F
asa^F
manico^M

ダイヤル・ロック
combination lock
Zahlenschloss^N
serrure^F à combinaison^F
cerradura^F de combinación^F
serratura^F a combinazione^F

襠（まち）付きの折り鞄
bottom-fold portfolio
Kollegmappe^F mit Griff^M
porte-documents^M à soufflet^M
cartera^F de fondo^M plegable
portacarte^M a soffietto^M

格納式の取っ手［握り］
retractable handle
ausziehbarer Griff^M
poignée^F rentrante
asa^F extensible
manico^M a scomparsa^F

外ポケット
exterior pocket
Außentasche^F
poche^F extérieure
bolsillo^M delantero
tasca^F esterna

襠（まち）
gusset
Keil^M
soufflet^M
fuelle^M
soffietto^M

ブリーフケース
briefcase
Aktentasche^F
serviette^F
cartera^F
borsa^F a soffietto^M

タブ／べろ
tab
Lasche^F
patte^F
lengüeta^F
linguetta^F

キー・ロック
key lock
Schlüsselschloss^N
serrure^F à clé^F
cerradura^F
serratura^F a chiave^F

小切手帳入れ
checkbook/secretary clutch; calculator/cheque book holder
Etui^N für Taschenrechner^M und Scheckheft^N
portefeuille^M chéquier^M
chequera^F con calculadora^F
portassegni^M/portacalcolatrice^F

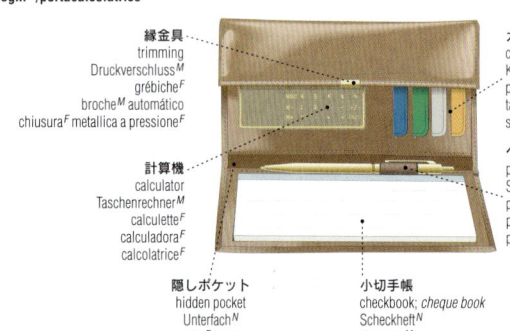

縁金具
trimming
Druckverschluss^M
grébiche^F
broche^M automático
chiusura^F metallica a pressione^F

計算機
calculator
Taschenrechner^M
calculette^F
calculadora^F
calcolatrice^F

隠しポケット
hidden pocket
Unterfach^N
poche^F secrète
bolsillo^M secreto
tasca^F nascosta

カード挿（さ）し
card case; credit card wallet
Kreditkartenfach^N
porte-cartes^M
tarjetero^M
scomparto^M per carte^F di credito^M

ペン・ホルダー
pen holder
Stifthalter^M
porte-stylo^M
portaplumas^M
portapenne^M

小切手帳
checkbook; cheque book
Scheckheft^N
chéquier^M
talonario^M de cheques^M
libretto^M degli assegni^M

札入れ
bill compartment; wallet section
Geldscheinfach^N
poche^F américaine
billetera^F
scomparto^M per banconote^F

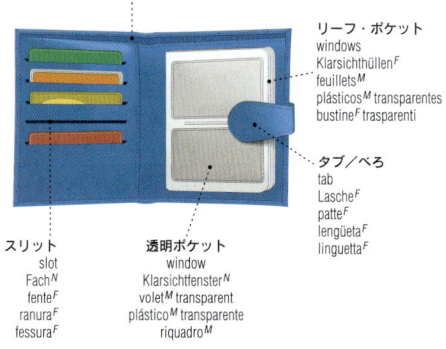

スリット
slot
Fach^N
fente^F
ranura^F
fessura^F

透明ポケット
window
Klarsichtfenster^N
volet^M transparent
plástico^M transparente
riquadro^M

カード挿（さ）し付き札入れ
card case; credit card wallet
Kreditkartenetui^N
porte-cartes^M
tarjetero^M
portafoglio^M per carte^F di credito^M

リーフ・ポケット
windows
Klarsichthüllen^F
feuillets^M
plásticos^M transparentes
bustine^F trasparenti

タブ／べろ
tab
Lasche^F
patte^F
lengüeta^F
linguetta^F

装身具類と日用品

386

日用品 | PERSONAL ARTICLES
PERSÖNLICHE ARTIKEL | OBJETS PERSONNELS | ARTÍCULOS PERSONALES | ARTICOLI PERSONALI

革製品

二つ折り札入れ
wallet
Brieftasche[F]
portefeuille[M]
billetero[M]
portafoglio[M]

小銭入れ
coin purse
Geldbeutel[M] für Münzen[F]
porte-monnaie[M]
portamonedas[M]
portamonete[M]

キー・ケース
key case
Schlüsseletui[N]
porte-clés[M]
llavero[M]
portachiavi[M]

がま口／小銭入れ
purse
Geldbeutel[M]
bourse[F] à monnaie[F]
monedero[M]
borsellino[M]

パスポート・ケース
passport case
Brieftasche[F]
porte-passeport[M]
porta pasaportes[M]
portapassaporto[M]

札入れ
billfold; *wallet*
Brieftasche[F]
porte-coupures[M]
billetera[F]
portafoglio[M]

ライティング・ケース
writing case
Schreibmappe[F]
écritoire[F]
agenda[M]
portablocco[M]

小切手帳カバー
checkbook; *cheque book cover*
Scheckhülle[F]
porte-chéquier[M]
talonario[M] de cheques[M]
portassegni[M]

眼鏡ケース
eyeglasses case
Brillenetui[N]
étui[M] à lunettes[F]
funda[F] de gafas[F]
astuccio[M] per occhiali[M]

クラッチ・バッグ式の折り鞄
underarm portfolio
Unterarmmappe[F]
porte-documents[M] plat
cartera[F] porta documentos[M]
busta[F] portadocumenti

装身具類と日用品

ハンドバッグ

handbags | Handtaschen[F] | sacs[M] à main[F] | bolsos[M] | borse[F]

ドローストリング・バッグ
drawstring bag
Beuteltasche[F]
sac[M] seau[M]
bolso[M] tipo cubo[M]
secchiello[M] con cordoncino[M]

鳩目
eyelet
Öse[F]
œillet[M]
ojal[M]
occhiello[M]

絞り紐（ひも）
drawstring
Zugschnur[F]
lacet[M] de serrage[M]
cordón[M]
cordoncino[M] di chiusura[F]

前ポケット
front pocket
Vortasche[F]
poche[F] frontale
bolsillo[M] exterior
tasca[F] frontale

サッチェル・バッグ
satchel bag
Aktentasche[F]
sac[M] cartable[M]
bolso[M] clásico
cartella[F]

取っ手／握り
handle
Griff[M]
poignée[F]
asa[F]
manico[M]

フラップ／被せ
flap
Überschlag[M]
rabat[M]
ala[F]
aletta[F]

留め金
clasp
Schnappverschluss[M]
fermoir[M]
broche[M]
chiusura[F]

ロック
lock
Schloss[N]
serrure[F]
cierre[M]
serratura[F]

387

日用品 | PERSONAL ARTICLES
PERSÖNLICHE ARTIKEL | OBJETS PERSONNELS | ARTÍCULOS PERSONALES | ARTICOLI PERSONALI

ハンドバッグ

日本語 | 英語 | ドイツ語 | フランス語 | スペイン語 | イタリア語

ボックス・バッグ
box bag
Boxtasche^F
sac^M boîte^F
bolso^M de vestir
borsa^F a telaio^M rigido

ドローストリング・バッグ
drawstring bag
kleine Beuteltasche^F
balluchon^M
bolso^M saco
secchiello^M piccolo con cordoncino^M

ショルダー・バッグ
shoulder bag
Schultertasche^F
sac^M à bandoulière^F
bolso^M de bandolera^F
borsa^F a tracolla^F

バックル
buckle
Schnalle^F
boucle^F
hebilla^F
fibbia^F

マフ
muff
Mufftasche^F
manchon^M
bolso^M manguito^M
borsa^F a manicotto^M

肩紐（ひも）
shoulder strap
Schulterriemen^M
bandoulière^F
bandolera^F
tracolla^F

ホーボー・バッグ
hobo bag
Umhängetasche^F mit Reißverschluss^M
sac^M besace^F
morral^M
sacca^F a tracolla^F

アコーディオン・バッグ
accordion bag
Umhängetasche^F mit Dehnfalte^F
sac^M accordéon^M
bolso^M de fuelle^F
borsa^F da postino^M

襠（まち）
gusset
Keil^M
soufflet^M
fuelle^M
soffietto^M

トート・バッグ
tote bag
Einkaufstasche^F
sac^M fourre-tout^M
bolsa^F de lona^F
sporta^F

メンズ・バッグ
men's bag
Herrentasche^F
pochette^F d'homme^M
mariconera^F
borsello^M

シー・バッグ
sea bag
Matchbeutel^M
sac^M marin
saco^M de marinero^M
sacca^F da marinaio^M

ダッフル・バッグ
duffel bag
geräumige Tasche^F
sac^M polochon^M
bolso^M de viaje^M
borsone^M da viaggio^M

キャリア・バッグ
carrier bag
Einkaufstasche^F
sac^M à provisions^F
bolso^M de la compra^F
borsa^F della spesa^F

ショッピング・バッグ
shopping bag
große Einkaufstasche^F
cabas^M
capazo^M
borsa^F della spesa^F

旅行用鞄

luggage | Gepäck^N | bagages^M | equipaje^M | bagagli^M

化粧ポーチ／洗面具入れ
utility case
Kulturbeutel^M
trousse^F de toilette^F
neceser^M
trousse^F

キャリー・オン・バッグ
carry-on bag; *travel bag*
Reisetasche^F
sac^M de vol^M
bolso^M de viaje^M
borsa^F da viaggio^M

取っ手／握り
handle
Griff^M
poignée^F
asa^F
manico^M

航空バッグ
tote bag; *flight bag*
Flugtasche^F
sac^M fourre-tout^M
maletín^M
bagaglio^M a mano^F

外ポケット
exterior pocket
Außentasche^F
poche^F extérieure
bolsillo^M exterior
tasca^F esterna

肩紐（ひも）
shoulder strap
Schulterriemen^M
bandoulière^F
bandolera^F
tracolla^F

日用品 | PERSONAL ARTICLES
PERSÖNLICHE ARTIKEL | OBJETS PERSONNELS | ARTÍCULOS PERSONALES | ARTICOLI PERSONALI

旅行用鞄

ガーメント[スーツ携帯用衣装]バッグ
garment bag
Kleidersackᴹ
housseᶠ à vêtementsᴹ
bolsaᶠ para trajesᴹ
portabitiᴹ

取っ手／握り
handle
Griffᴹ
poignéeᶠ
asaᶠ
manicoᴹ

フレーム
frame
Rahmenᴹ
cadreᶠ
bastidorᴹ
telaioᴹ

引き紐（ひも）
pull strap
Zugriemenᴹ
dragonneᶠ
correaᶠ
manigliaᶠ di trainoᴹ

スーツケース／旅行鞄
Pullman case; *suitcase*
Kofferᴹ
valiseᶠ pullman
maletaᶠ clásica
valigiaᶠ

キャスター
wheel
Rolleᶠ
rouletteᶠ
ruedecillaᶠ
ruotaᶠ

ジッパー
zipper; *zip*
Reißverschlussᴹ
fermetureᶠ à glissièreᶠ
cremalleraᶠ
cernieraᶠ lampo

名札
identification tag; *identity tag*
Gepäckanhängerᴹ
porte-adresseᶠ
etiquetaᶠ de identificaciónᶠ
etichettaᶠ portaindirizzo

当て布
trim
Blendeᶠ
garnitureᶠ
guarniciónᶠ
bordoᴹ di rifinituraᶠ

化粧鞄
vanity case
Kosmetikkofferᴹ
malletteᶠ de toiletteᶠ
neceserᴹ
beauty-caseᴹ

鏡
mirror
Spiegelᴹ
miroirᴹ
espejoᴹ
specchioᴹ

蝶番（ちょうつがい）
hinge
Scharnierᴺ
charnièreᶠ
bisagraᶠ
reggicoperchioᴹ

化粧用トレイ
cosmetic tray
Kosmetikeinsatzᴹ
plateauᴹ
bandejaᶠ para cosméticosᴹ
portatrucchiᴹ

小型スーツケース
weekender; *weekend case*
Wochenendkofferᴹ
valiseᶠ finᴹ de semaineᶠ
maletaᶠ de finᴹ de semanaᶠ
quarantottoreᴹ

内ポケット
interior pocket
Innentascheᶠ
pocheᶠ intérieure
bolsoᴹ interior
tascaᶠ interna

中仕切り
curtain; *divider*
Trennklappeᶠ
panneauᴹ de séparationᶠ
panelᴹ de separaciónᶠ
pannelloᴹ divisorio

クロス・ベルト
garment strap
Packriemenᴹ
sangleᶠ serre-vêtementsᴹ
correaᶠ de retenciónᶠ
elasticoᴹ ferma abitiᴹ

錠／ロック
lock
Schlossᴺ
serrureᶠ
cerraduraᶠ
serraturaᶠ

ケース／外枠
shell
Schaleᶠ
coqueᶠ
tapaᶠ
guscioᴹ

キャリア
luggage carrier; *luggage trolley*
Gepäckrollerᴹ
porte-bagagesᴹ
carritoᴹ portamaletasᶠ
carrelloᴹ portabagagli

フレーム
frame
Rahmenᴹ
armatureᶠ
armazónᴹ
telaioᴹ

ゴム・バンド
luggage elastic
Gepäckschnurᶠ
sangleᶠ élastique
correaᶠ elástico
legabagagliᴹ elastico

スタンド
stand
Ständerᴹ
béquilleᶠ
soporteᴹ
baseᶠ

掛け金
hasp
Überfallschlossᴺ
moraillonᴹ
aldabillaᶠ
chiusuraᶠ a occhielloᴹ

掛け金
latch
Riegelᴹ
cramponᴹ de fermetureᶠ
abrazaderaᶠ
gancioᴹ di chiusuraᶠ

隅金／隅金具
cornerpiece
Eckstückᴺ
cantonnièreᶠ
conteraᶠ
angolareᴹ

トランク
trunk
Überseekofferᴹ
malleᶠ
baúlᴹ
bauleᴹ

トレイ
tray
Einsatzᴹ
plateauᴹ
bandejaᶠ
vassoioᴹ

取っ手／握り
handle
Griffᴹ
poignéeᶠ
asaᶠ
manigliaᶠ

止め金具
fittings
Schutzkanteᶠ
ferrureᶠ
herrajeᴹ
bandellaᶠ di rinforzoᴹ

日用品 | PERSONAL ARTICLES
PERSÖNLICHE ARTIKEL | OBJETS PERSONNELS | ARTÍCULOS PERSONALES | ARTICOLI PERSONALI

喫煙具

日本語 | 英語 | ドイツ語 | フランス語 | スペイン語 | イタリア語

smoking accessories | Raucherbedarf^M | articles^M de fumeur^M | artículos^M de fumador^M | accessori^M per fumatori^M

パイプ
pipe
Pfeife^F
pipe^F
pipa^F
pipa^F

ボウル／雁首（がんくび）
bowl
Pfeifenkopf^M
talon^M
cazoleta^F
fornello^M

シャンク／軸
shank
Holm^M
tige^F
caña^F
cannuccia^F

ビット／吸い口
bit
Biss^M
lentille^F
boquilla^F
dente^M

ブライヤー
stummel
Pfeifenstummel^M
tête^F
barba^F
testa^F

ステム／柄
stem
Pfeifenmundstück^N
tuyau^M
cañón^M
bocchino^M

パイプ・ツール／コンパニオン
pipe tools
Pfeifenbesteck^N
bourre-pipe^M
accesorios^M para la pipa^F
curapipe^M

タンパー／プレッサー
tamper
Stopfer^M
bourre-pipe^M
pisón^M
premitabacco^M

スプーン／スクープ
scoop
Auskratzer^M
curette^F
raspador^M
cucchiaino^M

ピック
pick
Dorn^M
pointe^F
palillo^M
stilo^M

パイプ・クリーナー
pipe cleaners
Pfeifenputzer^M
nettoie-pipes^M
escobillas^F
scovolini^M

パイプの断面図
cross section of a pipe
Pfeife^F im Querschnitt^M
coupe^F d'une pipe^F
corte^M transversal de una pipa^F
sezione^F di una pipa^F

火皿
tobacco hole
Tabakkammer^F
fourneau^M
hornillo^M
cavo^M per la combustione^F del tabacco^M

タボ
peg
Zapfen^M
tenon^M
espiga^F
perno^M

タボ穴
mortise
Zapfenloch^N
mortaise^F
tiro^F
mortasa^F

フィルター
filter
Filter^M
système^M filtre^M
filtro^M
filtro^M

煙道
air hole
Luftloch^N
trou^M de l'embout^M
tiraje^M
foro^M per l'aria^F

タバコ・ポーチ
tobacco pouch
Tabaksbeutel^M
blague^F à tabac^M
tabaquera^F
borsa^F del tabacco^M

パイプ・ラック
pipe rack
Pfeifenständer^M
porte-pipes^M
porta pipas^M
portapipe^M

シガー・カッター
cigar cutter
Zigarrenschneider^M
coupe-cigare^M
cortapuros^M
tagliasigari^M

刃
blade
Klinge^F
lame^F
cuchilla^F
lama^F

リング・ハンドル
ring handle
Ring^M
anneau^M
anillo^M
impugnatura^F a anello^M

葉巻
cigar
Zigarre^F
cigare^M
puro^M
sigaro^M

リング／シガー・バンド
cigar band
Banderole^F
bague^F
vitola^F
fascetta^F del sigaro^M

ラッパー／上［外］巻き葉
wrapper
Deckblatt^N
cape^F
capa^F
fascia^F

タバコの葉
tobacco
Tabak^M
tabac^M
tabaco^M
tabacco^M

フィラー／填充（てんじゅう）葉
filler
Einlage^F
tripe^F
tripa^F
ripieno^M

ヘッド／吸い口
head
Spitze^F
tête^F
cabeza^F
testa^F

バンチ
bunch
Mittelstück^N
corps^M
cuerpo^M
corpo^M

タック
tuck
Endstück^N
pied^M
punta^F
piede^M

シガレット・ペーパー
cigarette papers
Zigarettenpapier^N
papier^M à cigarettes^F
papel^M de fumar
cartine^F per sigarette^F

カートン
carton
Stange^F
cartouche^F
cartón^M de cigarrillos^M
stecca^F

紙巻きタバコ
cigarette
Zigarette^F
cigarette^F
cigarrillo^M
sigaretta^F

巻き紙
paper
Papier^N
papier^M
papel^M
carta^F

紙巻きタバコのパッケージ
cigarette pack
Zigarettenschachtel^F
paquet^M de cigarettes^F
paquete^M de cigarrillos^M
pacchetto^M di sigarette^F

封
stamp
Steuermarke^F
timbre^F
timbre^M
bollo^M del monopolio^M

フィルター
filter tip
Filterspitze^F
bout^M-filtre^M
filtro^M
filtro^M

開封テープ
tear tape
Aufreißband^N
bandelette^F d'arrachage^M
tira^F para rasgar la envoltura^F
linguetta^F a strappo^M

シーム
seam
Naht^F
couture^F
costura^F
giuntura^F

タバコの葉
tobacco
Tabak^M
tabac^M
tabaco^M
tabacco^M

商標
trade name
Markenname^M
marque^F déposée
marca^F registrada
marca^F

日用品 | PERSONAL ARTICLES
PERSÖNLICHE ARTIKEL | OBJETS PERSONNELS | ARTÍCULOS PERSONALES | ARTICOLI PERSONALI

喫煙具

ガス・ライター
gas lighter
GasfeuerzeugN
briquetM à gazM
encendedorM
accendinoM a gasM

蓋(ふた)
cover
AbdeckkappeF
couvercleM
tapaF
coperchioM

やすり
striker wheel
ZahnrädchenN
moletteF
ruedecillaF de la piedraF
rotellaF della pietrinaF

炎調整つまみ
flame adjustment wheel
FlammenregulierungF
moletteF de réglageM de la flammeF
ajusteM de la llamaF
regolatoreM della fiammaF

タンク
butane tank
ButangastankM
réservoirM
depósitoM de gasM
serbatoioM del gasM

紙マッチ／ブックマッチ
matchbook
StreichholzheftchenN
pochetteF d'allumettesF
carteritaF de cerillasF
bustinaF di fiammiferiM

カバー
cover
DeckelM
grand rabatM
tapaF
copertinaF

折り返し
front flap
VorderflächeF
petit rabatM
solapaF
alettaF frontale

軸頭
head
KopfM
têteF
cabezaF
capocchiaF

軸木
matchstick
StreichholzN
tigeF
cerillaF
fiammiferoM minerva

マッチ箱
matchbox
StreichholzschachtelF
boîteF d'allumettesF
cajaF de cerillasF
scatolaF di fiammiferiM

安全マッチ
safety match
SicherheitsstreichholzN
allumetteF de sûretéF
cerillasF de seguridadF
fiammiferoM svedese

背面
back
RückenM
dosM
respaldoM
dorsoM

側薬帯
friction strip
ReibeflächeF
frottoirM
frotadorM de fósforoM
strisciaF di sfregamentoM

灰皿
ashtray
AschenbecherM
cendrierM
ceniceroM
portacenereM

吸い殻
butt
StummelM
mégotM
colillaF
mozziconeM

灰
ash
AscheF
cendreF
cenizaF
cenereF

傘とステッキ

umbrella and stick | SchirmM und StockM | parapluieM et canneF | paraguasM y bastonesM | ombrelloM e bastoneM

傘立て
umbrella stand
SchirmständerM
porte-parapluiesM
paragüeroM
portaombrelliM

折り畳み式傘
telescopic umbrella
TaschenschirmM
parapluieM télescopique
paraguasM plegable
ombrelloM pieghevole

プッシュ・ボタン
push button
AuslöseknopfM
poussoirM d'ouvertureF
botónM de presiónF
pulsanteM

カバー
cover
FutteralN
fourreauM
fundaF
foderoM

長傘
stick umbrella
StockschirmM
parapluieM-canneF
paraguasM de bastónM
ombrelloM a bastoneM

石突き
ferrule
StahlspitzeF
emboutM
conteraF
puntaleM

バンド
tie closure
LitzeF
courroieF d'attacheF
cierreM con brocheM
cinturinoM di chiusuraF

肩紐(ひも)
shoulder strap
SchulterriemenM
bandoulièreF
bandoleraF
tracollaF

散歩用ステッキ
walking stick
SpazierstockM
canneF
bastónM
bastoneM da passeggioM

受け骨
spreader
GestellN
rayonM
extensorM
controsteccaF

バンド
tie
LitzeF
attacheF
cierreM
cinturinoM

下ろくろ／骨受け
ring
SchieberM
coulantM
anilloM
collareM

傘布
canopy
BezugsstoffM
toileF
telaF impermeable
coperturaF

下弾(はじ)き
tab
FederF
ferretM
resorteM
fermoM a mollaF

雨傘
umbrella
SchirmM
parapluieM
paraguasM
ombrelloM

(親)骨
rib
StangeF
baleineF
varillaF
steccaF

露先
tip
SpitzeF
emboutM de baleineF
puntaF
copripuntaF

中棒
shank
UnterstockM
mancheM
bastónM
fustoM

手元
handle
GriffM
poignéeF
empuñaduraF
manicoM

394 美術

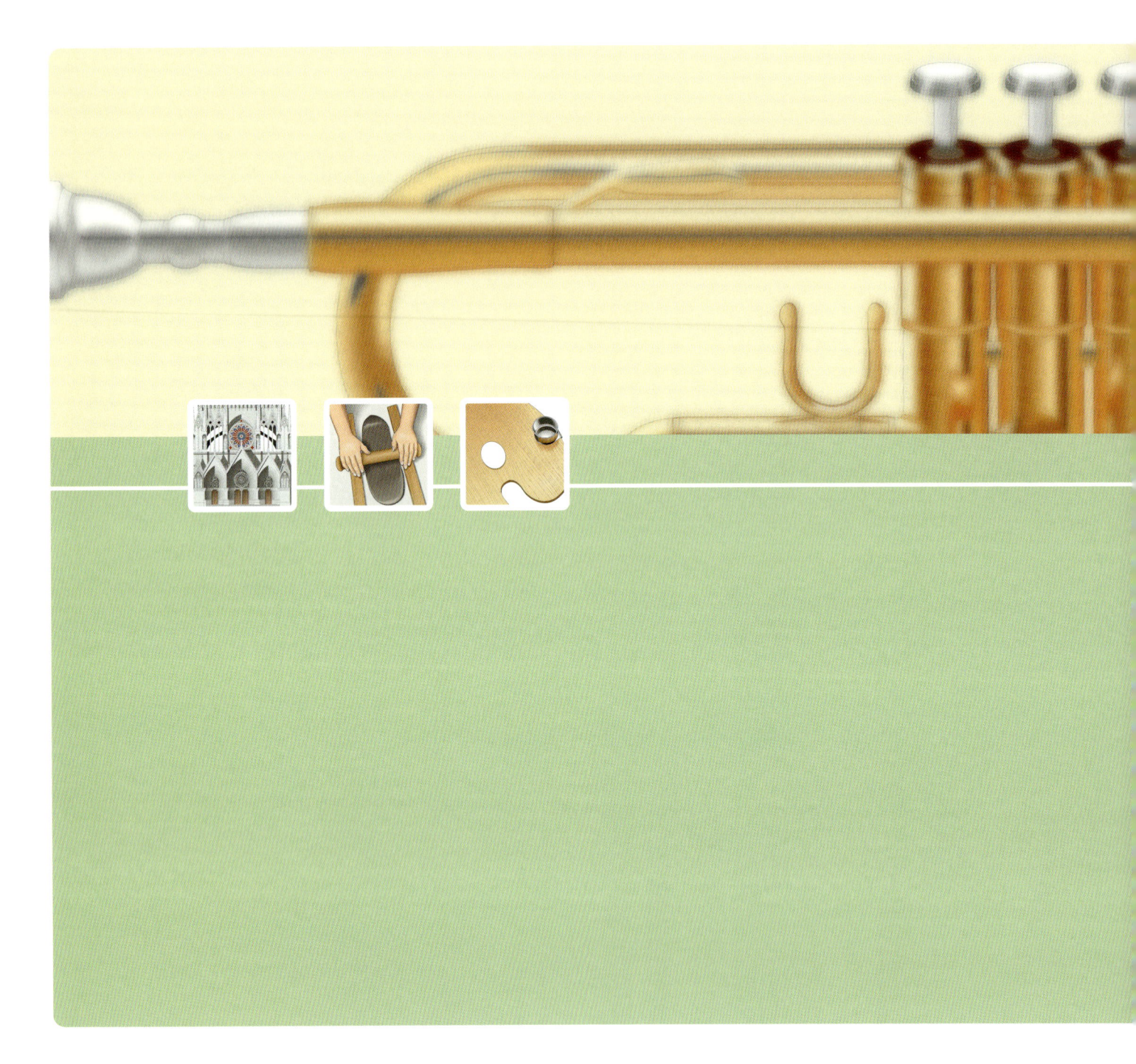

- 394 美術館
- 396 絵画と線画
- 401 木彫

402 建築

- 402 ピラミッド
- 402 ギリシャ劇場
- 403 ギリシャ神殿
- 404 建築様式
- 406 古代ローマの住宅
- 407 古代ローマの円形闘技場
- 408 城
- 409 ボーバン式要塞
- 410 大聖堂
- 412 仏塔
- 412 アステカ神殿
- 413 建築の要素
- 417 エスカレーター
- 417 エレベーター
- 418 伝統的な家屋
- 419 都市の住宅

420 グラフィック・アート

- 420 印刷
- 421 凸版印刷方式
- 422 凹版印刷方式
- 423 平版印刷方式
- 424 製本

芸術と建築

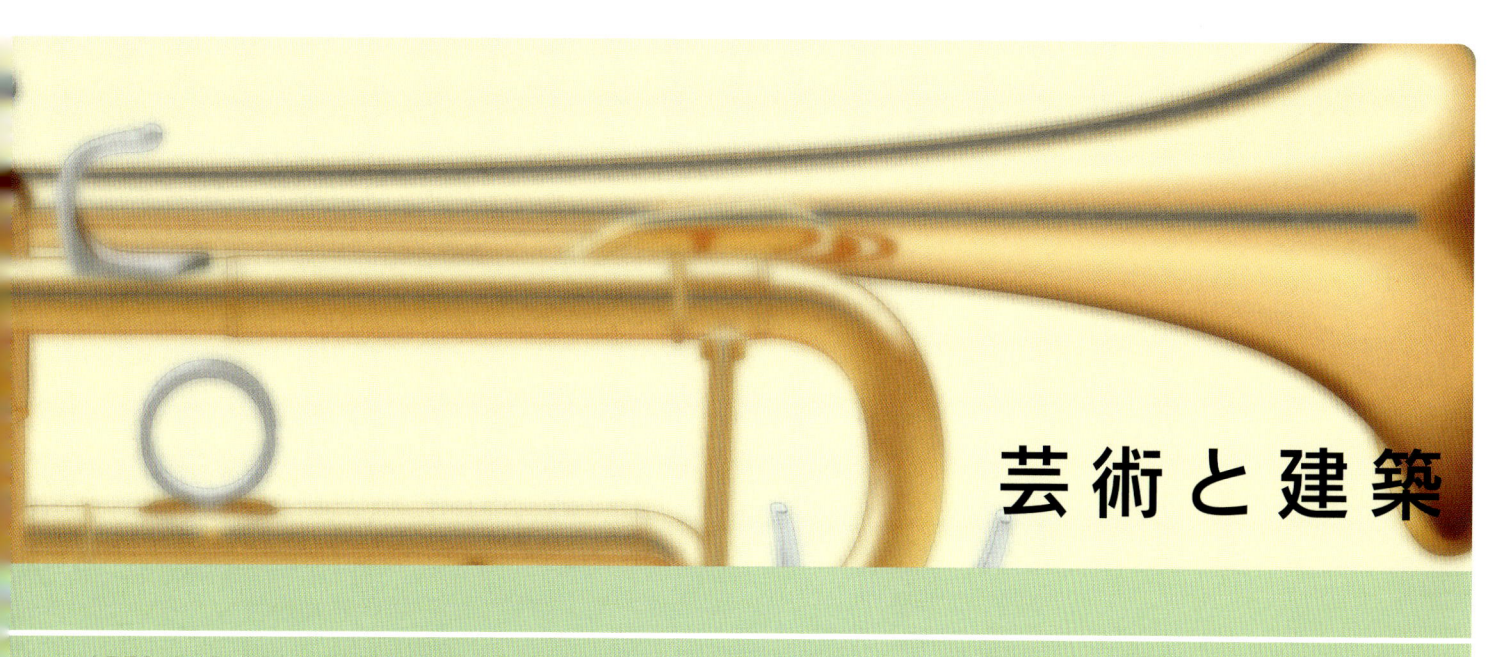

ARTS AND ARCHITECTURE I KUNST UND ARCHITEKTUR I ARTS ET ARCHITECTURE I ARTE Y ARQUITECTURA I ARTE E ARCHITETTURA

427 舞台芸術
- 427　映画館
- 428　映画のセット
- 430　劇場

432 音楽
- 432　伝統[民族]楽器
- 434　楽譜記号
- 436　演奏用付属品
- 437　交響[管弦]楽団
- 438　楽器編成の例
- 439　弦楽器
- 442　鍵盤楽器
- 446　管楽器
- 448　打楽器
- 450　電子楽器

452 工芸
- 452　裁縫
- 456　編み機
- 457　編み物
- 458　ボビン・レース
- 459　刺繍（ししゅう）
- 460　紡織
- 464　陶芸

美術 | FINE ARTS
BILDENDE KÜNSTE | BEAUX-ARTS | BELLAS ARTES | BELLE ARTI

美術館

日本語 | 英語 | ドイツ語 | フランス語 | スペイン語 | イタリア語

museum | Museum^N | musée^M | museo^M | museo^M

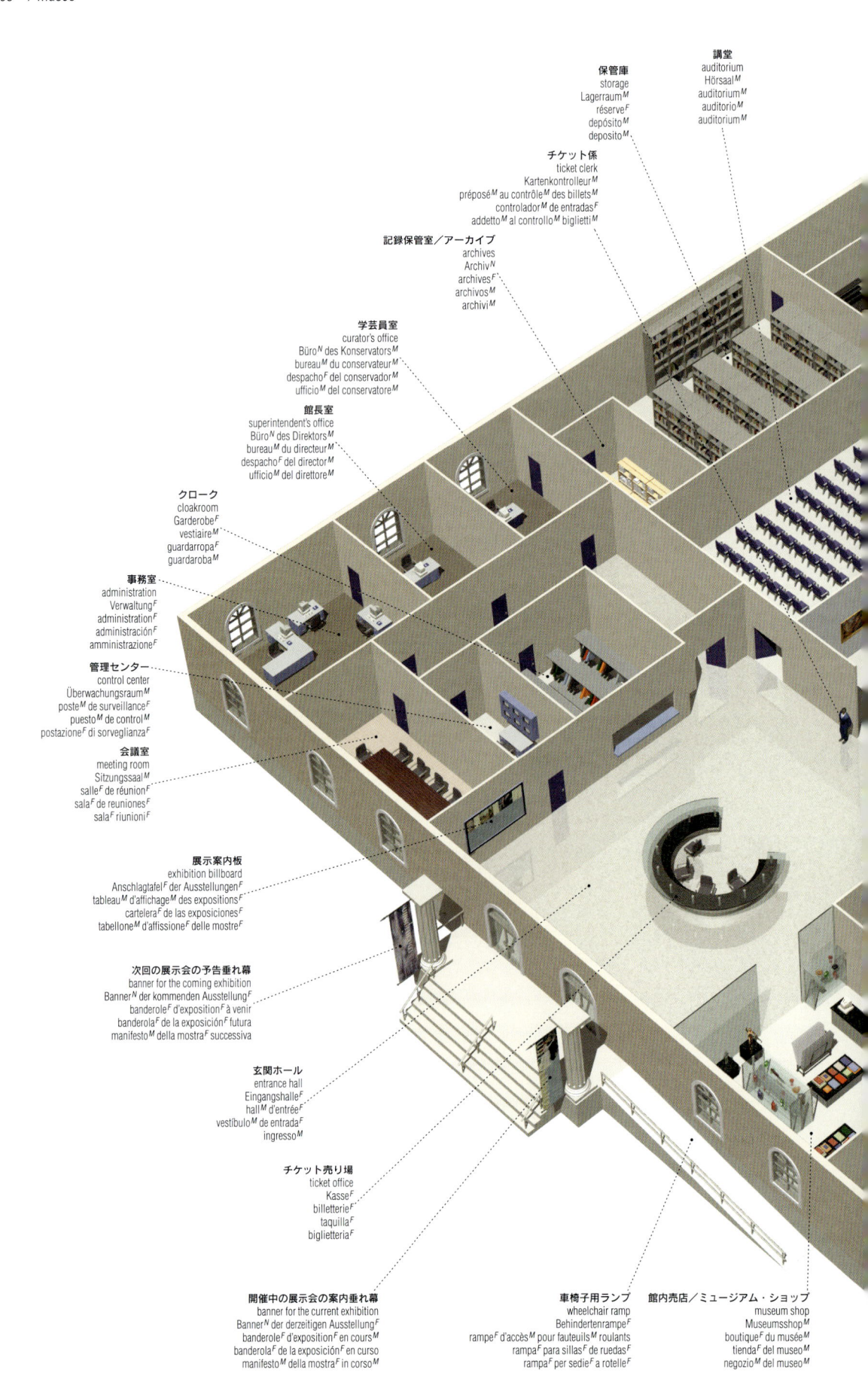

保管庫
storage
Lagerraum^M
réserve^F
depósito^M
deposito^M

講堂
auditorium
Hörsaal^M
auditorium^M
auditorio^M
auditorium^M

チケット係
ticket clerk
Kartenkontrolleur^M
préposé^M au contrôle^M des billets^M
controlador^M de entradas^F
addetto^M al controllo^M biglietti^M

記録保管室／アーカイブ
archives
Archiv^N
archives^F
archivos^M
archivi^M

学芸員室
curator's office
Büro^N des Konservators^M
bureau^M du conservateur^M
despacho^F del conservador^M
ufficio^M del conservatore^M

館長室
superintendent's office
Büro^N des Direktors^M
bureau^M du directeur^M
despacho^F del director^M
ufficio^M del direttore^M

クローク
cloakroom
Garderobe^F
vestiaire^M
guardarropa^F
guardaroba^M

事務室
administration
Verwaltung^F
administration^F
administración^F
amministrazione^F

管理センター
control center
Überwachungsraum^M
poste^M de surveillance^F
puesto^M de control^M
postazione^F di sorveglianza^F

会議室
meeting room
Sitzungssaal^M
salle^F de réunion^F
sala^F de reuniones^F
sala^F riunioni^F

展示案内板
exhibition billboard
Anschlagtafel^F der Ausstellungen^F
tableau^M d'affichage^M des expositions^F
cartelera^F de las exposiciones^F
tabellone^M d'affissione^F delle mostre^F

次回の展示会の予告垂れ幕
banner for the coming exhibition
Banner^N der kommenden Ausstellung^F
banderole^F d'exposition^F à venir
banderola^F de la exposición^F futura
manifesto^M della mostra^F successiva

玄関ホール
entrance hall
Eingangshalle^F
hall^M d'entrée^F
vestíbulo^M de entrada^F
ingresso^M

チケット売り場
ticket office
Kasse^F
billetterie^F
taquilla^F
biglietteria^F

音声ガイド
audioguide
Audioführer^M
audioguide^M
audioguía^F
audioguida^F

開催中の展示会の案内垂れ幕
banner for the current exhibition
Banner^N der derzeitigen Ausstellung^F
banderole^F d'exposition^F en cours
banderola^F de la exposición^F en curso
manifesto^M della mostra^F in corso^M

車椅子用ランプ
wheelchair ramp
Behindertenrampe^F
rampe^F d'accès^M pour fauteuils^M roulants
rampa^F para sillas^F de ruedas^F
rampa^F per sedie^F a rotelle^F

館内売店／ミュージアム・ショップ
museum shop
Museumsshop^M
boutique^F du musée^M
tienda^F del museo^M
negozio^M del museo^M

芸術と建築

394

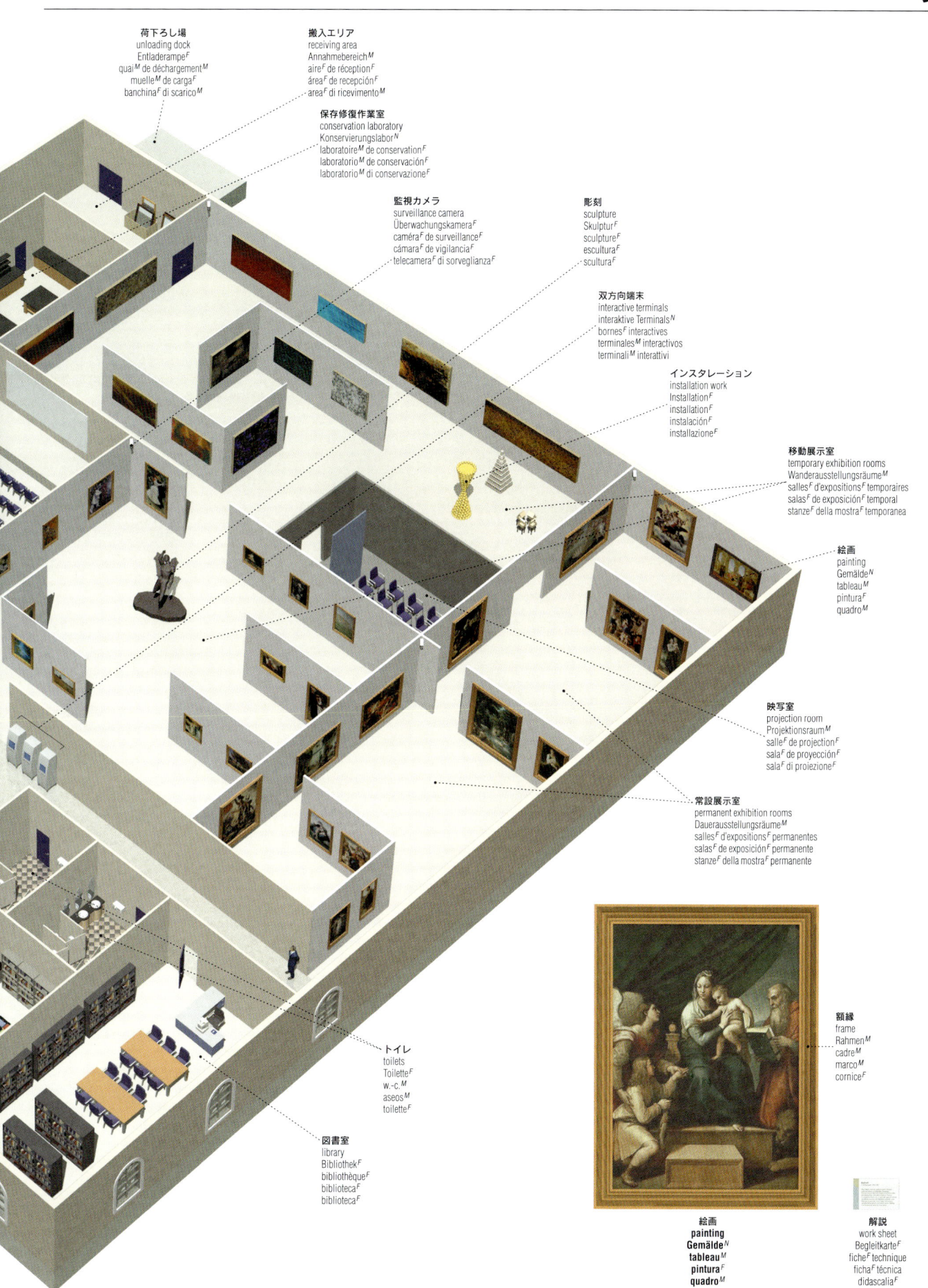

美術 | FINE ARTS
BILDENDE KÜNSTE | BEAUX-ARTS | BELLAS ARTES | BELLE ARTI

美術館

荷下ろし場
unloading dock
EntladerampeF
quaiM de déchargementM
muelleM de cargaF
banchinaF di scaricoM

搬入エリア
receiving area
AnnahmebereichM
aireF de réceptionF
áreaF de recepciónF
areaF di ricevimentoM

保存修復作業室
conservation laboratory
KonservierungslaborN
laboratoireM de conservationF
laboratorioM de conservaciónF
laboratorioM di conservazioneF

監視カメラ
surveillance camera
ÜberwachungskameraF
caméraF de surveillanceF
cámaraF de vigilanciaF
telecameraF di sorveglianzaF

彫刻
sculpture
SkulpturF
sculptureF
esculturaF
sculturaF

双方向端末
interactive terminals
interaktive TerminalsN
bornesF interactives
terminalesM interactivos
terminaliM interattivi

インスタレーション
installation work
InstallationF
installationF
instalaciónF
installazioneF

移動展示室
temporary exhibition rooms
WanderausstellungsräumeM
sallesF d'expositionsF temporaires
salasF de exposiciónF temporal
stanzeF della mostraF temporanea

絵画
painting
GemäldeN
tableauM
pinturaF
quadroM

映写室
projection room
ProjektionsraumM
salleF de projectionF
salaF de proyecciónF
salaF di proiezioneF

常設展示室
permanent exhibition rooms
DauerausstellungsräumeM
sallesF d'expositionsF permanentes
salasF de exposiciónF permanente
stanzeF della mostraF permanente

トイレ
toilets
ToiletteF
w.-c.M
aseosM
toiletteF

図書室
library
BibliothekF
bibliothèqueF
bibliotecaF
bibliotecaF

額縁
frame
RahmenM
cadreM
marcoM
corniceF

絵画
painting
GemäldeN
tableauM
pinturaF
quadroM

解説
work sheet
BegleitkarteF
ficheF technique
fichaF técnica
didascaliaF

芸術と建築

395

美術 | FINE ARTS
BILDENDE KÜNSTE | BEAUX-ARTS | BELLAS ARTES | BELLE ARTI

絵画と線画

painting and drawing | Malen^N und Zeichnen^N | peinture^F et dessin^M | pintura^F y dibujo^M | disegno^M e pittura^F

日本語 | 英語 | ドイツ語 | フランス語 | スペイン語 | イタリア語

主な技法
major techniques
die wichtigsten Techniken^F
principales techniques^F
técnicas^F principales
tecniche^F principali

インク画法
ink drawing
Tuschezeichnung^F
dessin^M à l'encre^F
dibujo^M de tinta^F china
disegno^M a inchiostro^M

木炭画法
charcoal drawing
Kohlezeichnung^F
dessin^M au fusain^M
dibujo^M al carboncillo^M
disegno^M a carboncino^M

油彩
oil painting
Ölmalerei^F
peinture^F à l'huile^F
pintura^F al óleo^M
pittura^F a olio^M

水彩
watercolor
Aquarell^N
aquarelle^F
acuarela^F
acquerello^M

グワッシュ画法
gouache
Gouache^F
gouache^F
guache
pittura^F a guazzo^M

フェルト・ペン画法
felt tip pen drawing
Filzstiftzeichnung^F
dessin^M au feutre^M
pintura^F con rotuladores^M
disegno^M a pennarelli^M

ドライ・パステル画法
dry pastel drawing
Trockenpastell^N
dessin^M au pastel^M sec
pintura^F al pastel^M blando
disegno^M a pastelli secchi

オイル・パステル画法
oil pastel drawing
Ölpastell^N
dessin^M au pastel^M gras
pintura^F al pastel^M al óleo^M
disegno^M a pastelli^M a olio^M

色鉛筆画法
colored pencil drawing
Buntstiftzeichnung^F
dessin^M au crayon^M de couleur^F
dibujo^M de lápices^M de colores^M
disegno^M a matite^F colorate

ワックス・クレヨン画法
wax crayon drawing
Wachsmalerei^F
dessin^M au crayon^M de cire^F
dibujo^M a la cera^F
disegno^M a pastelli^M a cera^F

画材
equipment
Ausstattung^F
matériel^M
equipo^M
attrezzatura^F

オイル［油性］パステル
oil pastel
Ölpastell^N
pastels^M gras
pastel^M al óleo^M
pastelli^M a olio^M

ワックス・クレヨン
wax crayons
Wachsfarbstifte^M
crayons^M de cire^F
ceras^F
pastelli^M a cera^F

ソフト・パステル
soft pastel
Pastell^N
pastels^M secs
pastel^M
pastelli^M morbidi

色鉛筆
colored pencils; colouring pencils
Buntstifte^M
crayons^M de couleur^F
lápices^M de colores^M
matite^F colorate

美術 | FINE ARTS
BILDENDE KÜNSTE | BEAUX-ARTS | BELLAS ARTES | BELLE ARTI

絵画と線画

フェルト・ペン
felt tip pen
Filzstift^M
feutre^F
rotulador^M
pennarello^M

インク
ink
Tinte^F
encre^F
tinta^F china
inchiostro^M

油絵の具
oil paint
Ölfarbe^F
couleur^F à l'huile^F
óleo^M
colore^M a olio^M

水彩[グワッシュ]チューブ入り絵の具
watercolor/gouache tube
Tube^F mit Aquarellfarbe^F/Gouachefarbe^F
tube^M d'aquarelle^F/ gouache^F
tubo^M de acuarela^F/de guache^M
tubo^M d'acquerello^M/guazzo^M

マーカー・ペン
marker pen
Marker^M
marqueur^M
marcador^M
evidenziatore^M

木炭
charcoal
Kohle^F
fusain^M
carboncillo^M
carboncino^M

水彩[グワッシュ]ケーキ・カラー
watercolor/gouache cakes
Näpfchen^N mit Aquarellfarbe^F/Gouachefarbe^F
pastilles^F d'aquarelle^F/ gouache^F
pastillas^F de acuarela^F /de guaches^M
pastiglie^F d'acquerello^M/guazzo^M

芸術と建築

画用ペン
reservoir-nib pen
Graphosfeder^F
plume^F
pluma^F
pennino^M

墨絵筆
sumi-e brush
Japanpinsel^M
pinceau^M à sumie^M
sumie^M
penna^F sumi

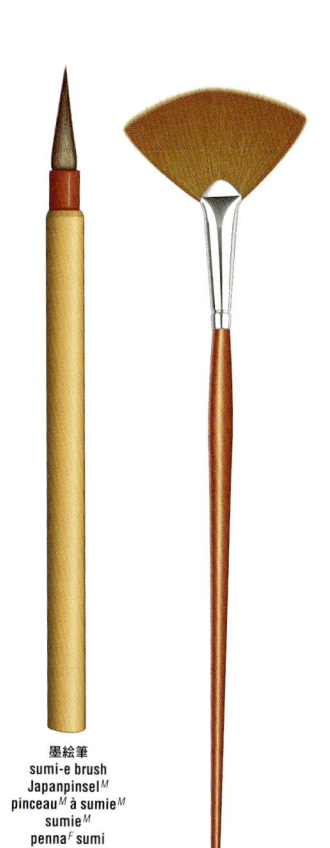

パレット・ナイフ／スパチュラ
spatula
Palettmesser^N
spatule^F
espátula^F
spatola^F

ペインティング・ナイフ
painting knife
Malspachtel^M
couteau^M à peindre
cuchillo^M paleta^F
mestichino^M

平筆（ひらふで）
flat brush
Flachpinsel^M
brosse^F
pincel^M plano
pennello^M piatto^M

扇形筆
fan brush
Fächerpinsel^M
brosse^F éventail^M
brocha^F
pennello^M a ventaglio^M

丸筆
brush
Pinsel^M
pinceau^M
pincel^M
pennello^M

397

美術 | FINE ARTS
BILDENDE KÜNSTE | BEAUX-ARTS | BELLAS ARTES | BELLE ARTI

絵画と線画

日本語 | 英語 | ドイツ語 | フランス語 | スペイン語 | イタリア語

窪み付きパレット
palette with hollows
Palette^F mit Vertiefungen
palette^F à alvéoles
paleta^F con huecos^M para pintura
tavolozza^F con vaschette

油壺
dipper
Palettstecker^M
godet^M
tarrito^M para pincel^M
vasetto^M

カラー・チャート／色見本
color chart; *colour chart*
Farbtafel^F
nuancier^M
gama^F de colores^M
tabella^F dei colori^M

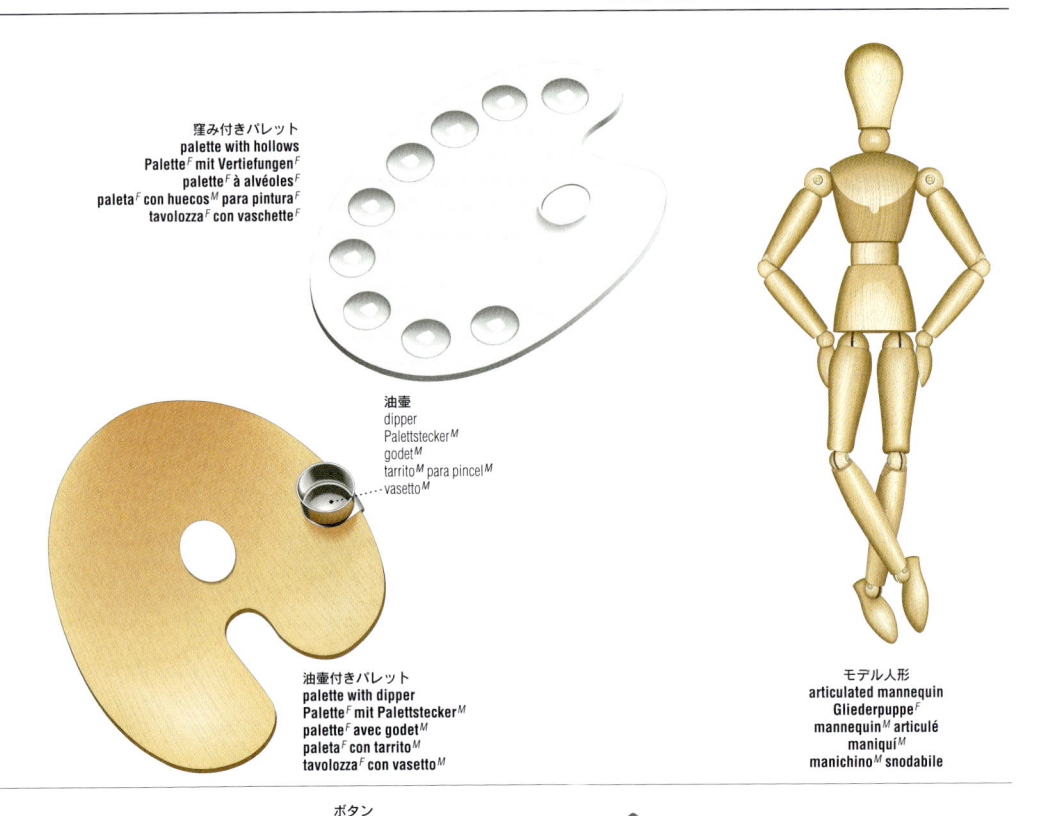

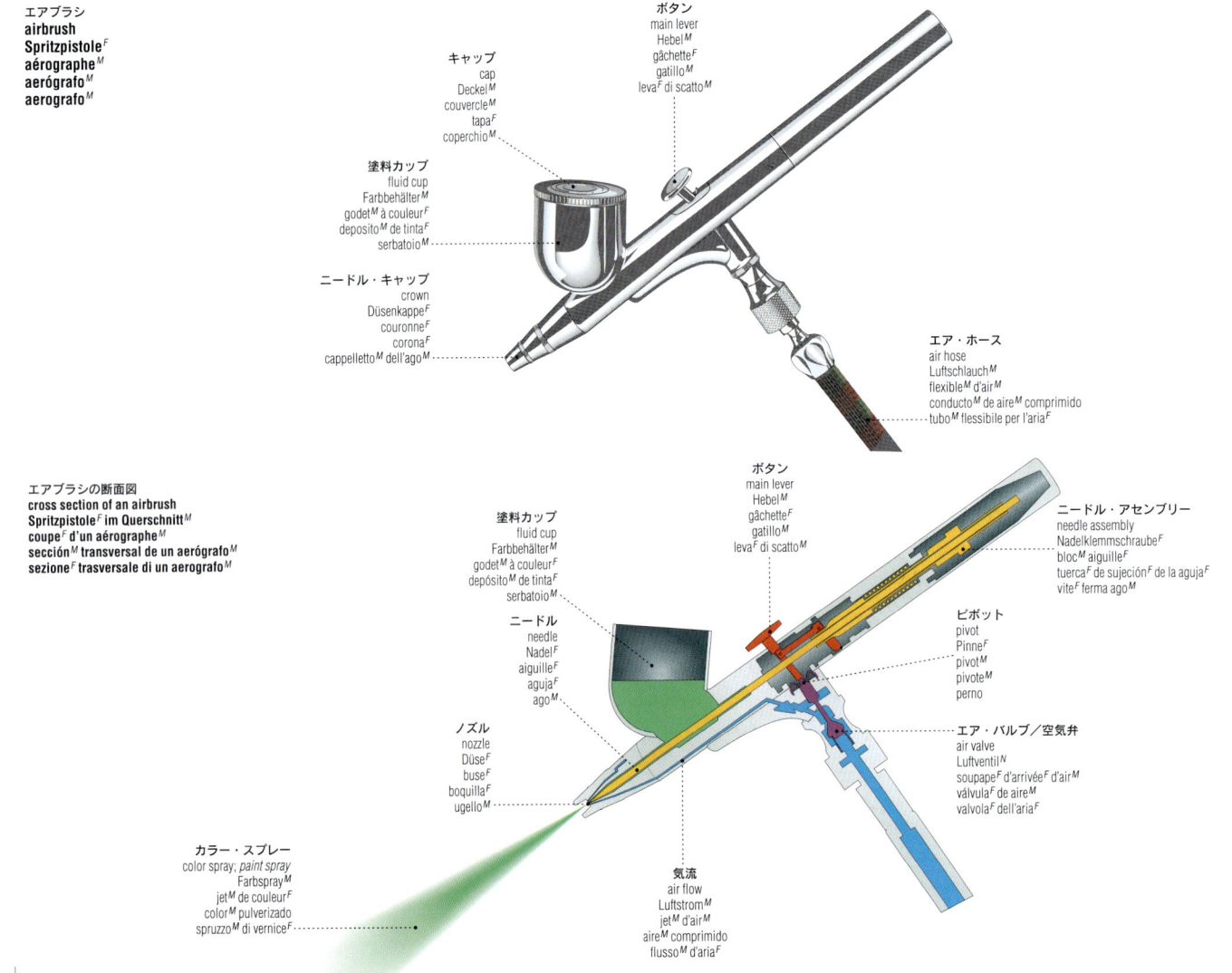

油壺付きパレット
palette with dipper
Palette^F mit Palettstecker^M
palette^F avec godet^M
paleta^F con tarrito^M
tavolozza^F con vasetto^M

モデル人形
articulated mannequin
Gliederpuppe^F
mannequin^M articulé
maniquí^M
manichino^M snodabile

エアブラシ
airbrush
Spritzpistole^F
aérographe^M
aerógrafo^M
aerografo^M

キャップ
cap
Deckel^M
couvercle^M
tapa^F
coperchio^M

ボタン
main lever
Hebel^M
gâchette^F
gatillo^M
leva^F di scatto^M

塗料カップ
fluid cup
Farbbehälter^M
godet^M à couleur^F
deposito^M de tinta^F
serbatoio^M

ニードル・キャップ
crown
Düsenkappe^F
couronne^F
corona^F
cappelletto^M dell'ago^M

エア・ホース
air hose
Luftschlauch^M
flexible^M d'air^M
conducto^M de aire^M comprimido
tubo^M flessibile per l'aria^F

エアブラシの断面図
cross section of an airbrush
Spritzpistole^F im Querschnitt^M
coupe^F d'un aérographe^M
sección^M transversal de un aerógrafo^M
sezione^F trasversale di un aerografo^M

塗料カップ
fluid cup
Farbbehälter^M
godet^M à couleur^F
depósito^M de tinta^F
serbatoio^M

ボタン
main lever
Hebel^M
gâchette^F
gatillo^M
leva^F di scatto^M

ニードル・アセンブリー
needle assembly
Nadelklemmschraube^F
bloc^M aiguille^F
tuerca^F de sujeción^F de la aguja^F
vite^F ferma ago^M

ニードル
needle
Nadel^F
aiguille^F
aguja^F
ago^M

ピボット
pivot
Pinne^F
pivot^F
pivote^M
perno

ノズル
nozzle
Düse^F
buse^F
boquilla^F
ugello^M

エア・バルブ／空気弁
air valve
Luftventil^N
soupape^F d'arrivée^F d'air^M
válvula^F de aire^M
valvola^F dell'aria^F

カラー・スプレー
color spray; *paint spray*
Farbspray^M
jet^M de couleur^F
color^M pulverizado
spruzzo^M di vernice^F

気流
air flow
Luftstrom^M
jet^M d'air^M
aire^M comprimido
flusso^M d'aria^F

美術 | FINE ARTS
BILDENDE KÜNSTE | BEAUX-ARTS | BELLAS ARTES | BELLE ARTI

絵画と線画

付属品
accessories
Zubehör^N
accessoires^M
accesorios^M
accessori^M

製図台
drafting table; *drawing board*
Reißbrett^N
table^F à dessin^M
tablero^M de dibujo^M
tavolo^M da disegno^M

可動ライト
adjustable lamp
Arbeitslampe^F
lampe^F d'architecte^M
flexo^M extensible
lampada^F orientabile

製図板
drawing board
Reißbrett^N
planche^F à dessin^M
tablero^M de dibujo^M
piano^M da disegno^M

小物入れ
storage tray
Ablagebrett^N
plateau^M de rangement^M
bandeja^F de accesorios^M
vaschette^F portaaccessori

定規
ruler
Lineal^N
règle^F
regla^F de escuadra^F
riga^F

縦レール
track
Laufschiene^F
rail^M de guidage^M
guía^F de la máquina^F de dibujar
binario^M

ドラフター
drafting machine
Zeichenmaschine^F
appareil^M à dessiner
máquina^F de dibujar con guía^F
tecnigrafo^M

調節ペダル
adjustment pedal
Pedal^N zur Verstellung^F
pédale^F d'ajustement^M
pedal^M de ajuste^M
pedale^M di regolazione^F

腕木／腕支え／腕枝／マールスティック
maulstick
Malstock^M
appui^M-main^F
tiento^M
appoggiamano^M

画架／イーゼル
easel
Staffelei^F
chevalet^M
caballete^M
cavalletto^M

芸術と建築

399

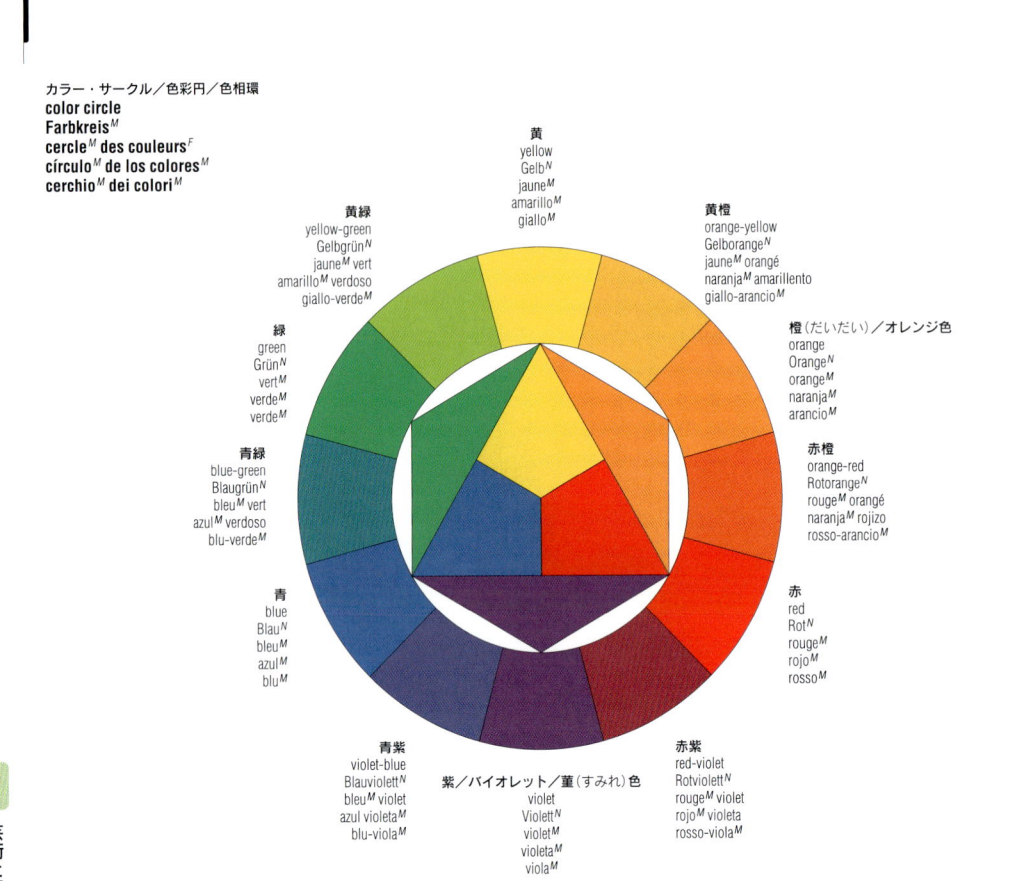

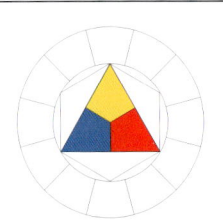

美術 | FINE ARTS
BILDENDE KÜNSTE | BEAUX-ARTS | BELLAS ARTES | BELLE ARTI

絵画と線画

日本語 | 英語 | ドイツ語 | フランス語 | スペイン語 | イタリア語

カラー・サークル／色彩円／色相環
color circle
Farbkreis^M
cercle^M des couleurs^F
círculo^M de los colores^M
cerchio^M dei colori^M

黄
yellow
Gelb^N
jaune^M
amarillo^M
giallo^M

黄緑
yellow-green
Gelbgrün^N
jaune^M vert
amarillo^M verdoso
giallo-verde^M

黄橙
orange-yellow
Gelborange^N
jaune^M orangé
naranja^M amarillento
giallo-arancio^M

緑
green
Grün^N
vert^M
verde^M
verde^M

橙（だいだい）／オレンジ色
orange
Orange^N
orange^M
naranja^M
arancio^M

青緑
blue-green
Blaugrün^N
bleu^M vert
azul^M verdoso
blu-verde^M

赤橙
orange-red
Rotorange^N
rouge^M orangé
naranja^M rojizo
rosso-arancio^M

青
blue
Blau^N
bleu^M
azul^M
blu^M

赤
red
Rot^N
rouge^M
rojo^M
rosso^M

青紫
violet-blue
Blauviolett^N
bleu^M violet
azul^M violeta
blu-viola^M

紫／バイオレット／菫（すみれ）色
violet
Violett^N
violet^M
violeta^M
viola^M

赤紫
red-violet
Rotviolett^N
rouge^M violet
rojo^M violeta
rosso-viola^M

原色
primary colors
Farben^F erster Ordnung^F
couleurs^F primaires
colores^M primarios
colori^M primari

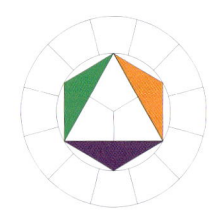

第二色／等和色
secondary colors
Farben^F zweiter Ordnung^F
couleurs^F secondaires
colores^M secundarios
colori^M secondari

第三色
tertiary colors
Farben^F dritter Ordnung^F
couleurs^F tertiaires
colores^M terciarios
colori^M terziari

画溶液
utility liquids
Hilfsmittel^N
liquides^M d'appoint^M
líquidos^M accesorios
liquidi^M utilizzabili

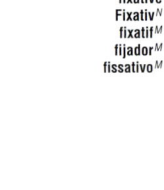

リンシード・オイル
linseed oil
Leinöl^N
huile^F de lin^M
aceite^M de linaza^F
olio^M di semi^M di lino^M

ワニス
varnish
Firnis^M
vernis^M
barniz^M
lacca^F

フィクサチーフ
fixative
Fixativ^N
fixatif^M
fijador^M
fissativo^M

テレピン油
turpentine
Terpentin^N
térébenthine^F
aguarrás^M
acquaragia^F

支持体／基底材／画布
supports
Bildträger^M
supports^M
soportes^M
supporti^M

紙
paper
Papier^N
papier^M
papel^M
carta^F

厚紙／ボール紙
cardboard
Malpappe^F
carton^M
cartón^M
cartoncino^M

カンバス
canvas
Leinwand^F
toile^F
lienzo^M
tela^F

パネル
panel
Platte^F
panneau^M
tabla^F
pannello^M

美術 | FINE ARTS
BILDENDE KÜNSTE | BEAUX-ARTS | BELLAS ARTES | BELLE ARTI

木彫

wood carving | Holzschnitzerei^F | sculpture^F sur bois^M | talla^F en madera^F | scultura^F in legno^M

工程
steps
Schritte^M
étapes^F
etapas^F
fasi^F

下絵
drawing
Zeichnen^N
traçage^M
diseño^M
tracciatura^F

粗[荒]取り
roughing out
Aussägen^N
dégrossissage^M
desbaste^M
sgrossatura^F

彫刻／粗[荒]彫り
carving
Schnitzen^N
sculpture^F
talla^F
intaglio^M

完成／仕上げ
finishing
Herausarbeiten^N
finition^F
acabado^M
finitura^F

彫刻具の例
examples of tools
Beispiele^N für Werkzeuge^N
exemples^M d'outils^M
ejemplos^M de utensilios^M
esempi^M di utensili^M

薄のみ
firmer chisel
gerades Balleisen^N
fermoir^M
formón^M
unghia^F

切り出しナイフ
knife
Messer^N
couteau^M
cuchillo^M de contornear
coltello^M

波目[波形]やすり
riffler
Riffelfeile^F
rifloir^M
bruñidor^M con rascador^M
lima^F curva^F

ビュラン
block cutter
gerades Hohleisen^N
burin^M
escoplo^M redondo
bulino^M

フルテロニ
fluteroni
Kasteneisen^N
fluteroni^M
escoplo^M de acanalar
sgorbia^F diritta

マカロニ
macaroni
gebogenes Hohleisen^N
macaroni^M
escoplo^M de macarrón^M
sgorbia^F incurvata

丸のみ
gouge
Hohlbeitel^M
gouge^F
gubia^F
sgorbia^F

石目[鬼目]やすり
rasp
Raspel^F
râpe^F
escofina^F
raspa^F

手斧（ておの／ちょうな）
adze
Dechsel^F
herminette^F
azuela^F para desbastar
ascia^F

主な刃の種類
major types of blades
die wichtigsten Schnitzeisen^N
principales formes^F de lames^F
principales tipos^M de cuchillas^F
tipi^M principali di lame^F

浅丸曲型
bent blade
gebogenes Eisen^N
lame^F coudée curvada
lama^F ricurva

丸曲型
spoon blade
Löffeleisen^N
lame^F en cuiller^F
cuchara^F
lama^F a cucchiaio^M

三角型
straight blade
gerades Eisen^N
lame^F droite
plana
lama^F diritta

平型
blade with two beveled edges; *blade with two bevelled edges*
Eisen^N mit zwei schrägen Seiten^F
lame^F à deux biseaux^M
escoplo^M
lama^F smussata

作業台
stand
Bock^M
sellette^F
taburete^M
trespolo^M

ベンチ・スクリュー
carver's bench screw
Schnitzbankschraube^F
queue^F-de-cochon^M
tornillo^M de banco^M
vite^F di banco^M da scultore^M

たがねと図案
punch and pattern
Prägung^F und Muster^M
poinçon^M et fond^M
punteo^M
punzone e motivo^M

小道具
accessories
Zubehör^N
accessoires^M
accesorios^M
accessori^M

木槌／丸才（まるさい）
mallet
Schlegel^M
maillet^M
mazo^M
mazzuolo^M

建築 | ARCHITECTURE
ARCHITEKTUR | ARCHITECTURE | ARQUITECTURA | ARCHITETTURA

ピラミッド

pyramid | Pyramide^F | pyramide^F | pirámide^F | piramide^F

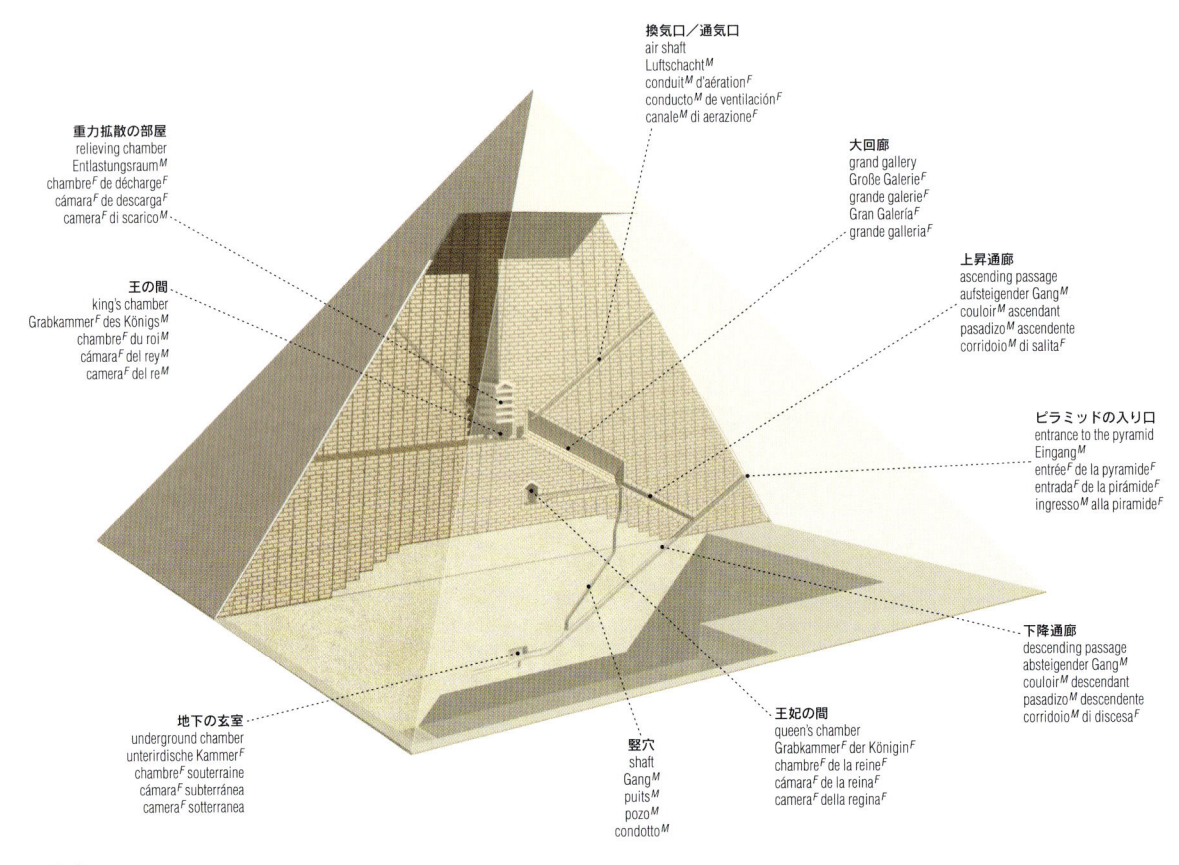

日本語 | 英語 | ドイツ語 | フランス語 | スペイン語 | イタリア語

換気口／通気口
air shaft
Luftschacht^M
conduit^M d'aération^F
conducto^M de ventilación^F
canale^F di aerazione^F

重力拡散の部屋
relieving chamber
Entlastungsraum^M
chambre^F de décharge^F
cámara^F de descarga^F
camera^F di scarico^F

大回廊
grand gallery
Große Galerie^F
grande galerie^F
Gran Galería^F
grande galleria^F

王の間
king's chamber
Grabkammer^F des Königs^M
chambre^F du roi^M
cámara^F del rey^M
camera^F del re^M

上昇通廊
ascending passage
aufsteigender Gang^M
couloir^M ascendant
pasadizo^M ascendente
corridoio^M di salita^F

ピラミッドの入り口
entrance to the pyramid
Eingang^M
entrée^F de la pyramide^F
entrada^F de la pirámide^F
ingresso^M alla piramide^F

下降通廊
descending passage
absteigender Gang^M
couloir^M descendant
pasadizo^M descendente
corridoio^M di discesa^F

地下の玄室
underground chamber
unterirdische Kammer^F
chambre^F souterraine
cámara^F subterránea
camera^F sotterranea

竪穴
shaft
Gang^M
puits^M
pozo^M
condotto^M

王妃の間
queen's chamber
Grabkammer^F der Königin^F
chambre^F de la reine^F
cámara^F de la reina^F
camera^F della regina^F

ギリシャ劇場

Greek theater | griechisches Theater^N | théâtre^M grec | teatro^M griego | teatro^M greco

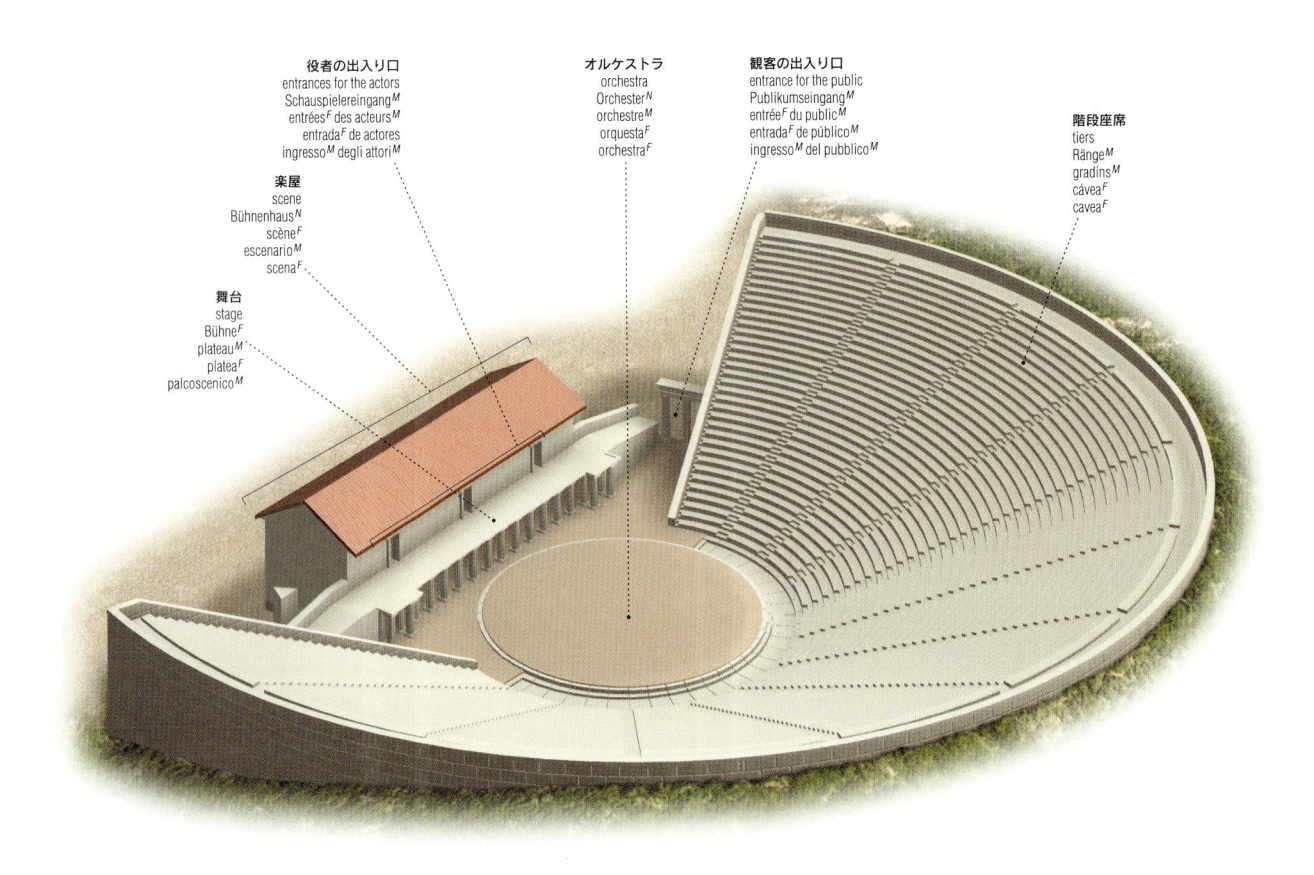

役者の出入り口
entrances for the actors
Schauspielereingang^M
entrées^F des acteurs^M
entrada^F de actores^M
ingresso^M degli attori^M

オルケストラ
orchestra
Orchester^N
orchestre^M
orquesta^F
orchestra^F

観客の出入り口
entrance for the public
Publikumseingang^M
entrée^F du public^M
entrada^F de público^M
ingresso^M del pubblico^M

階段座席
tiers
Ränge^M
gradins^M
cávea^F
cavea^F

楽屋
scene
Bühnenhaus^N
scène^F
escenario^M
scena^F

舞台
stage
Bühne^F
plateau^M
platea^F
palcoscenico^M

芸術と建築

402

建築 | ARCHITECTURE
ARCHITEKTUR | ARCHITECTURE | ARQUITECTURA | ARCHITETTURA

ギリシャ神殿

Greek temple | griechischer Tempel[M] | temple[M] grec | templo[M] griego | tempio[M] greco

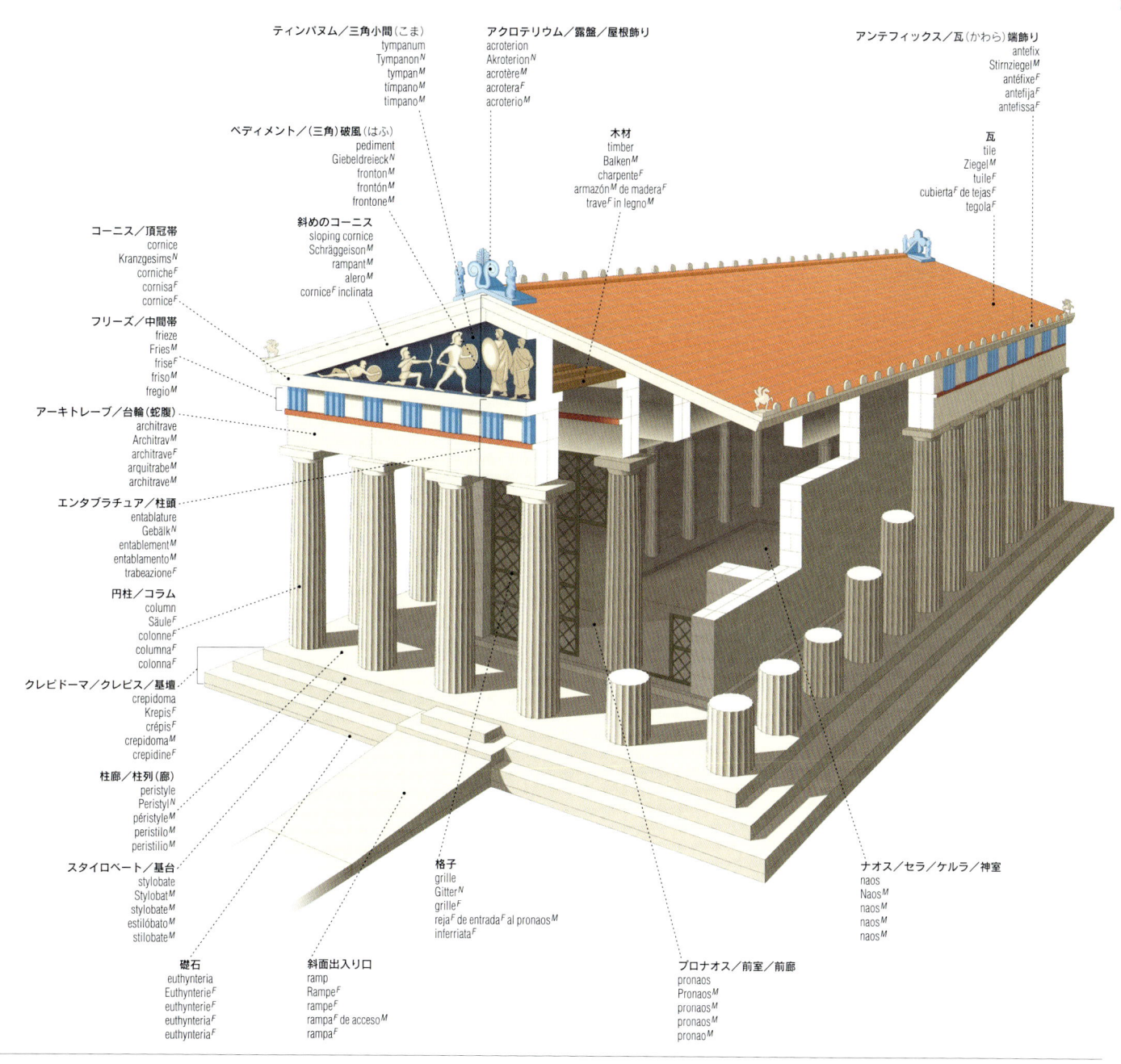

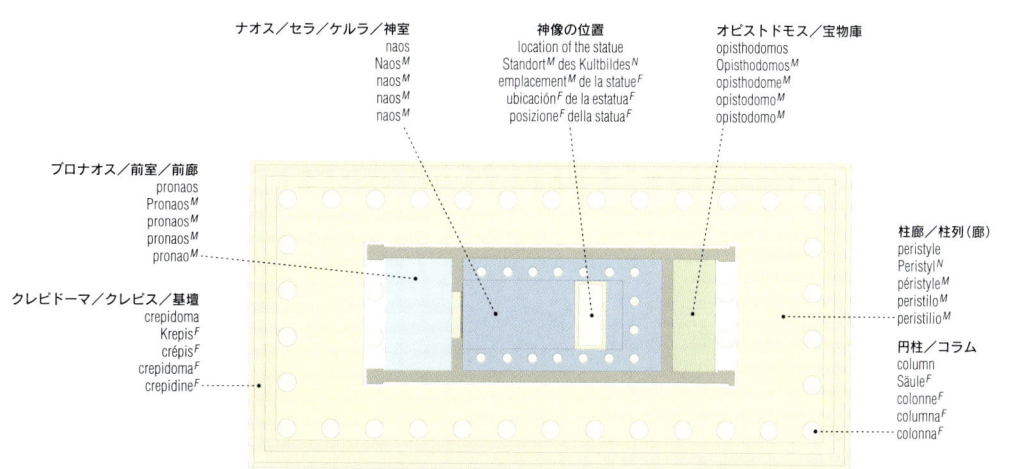

ティンパヌム／三角小間（こま）
tympanum
Tympanon[N]
tympan[M]
tímpano[M]
timpano[M]

アクロテリウム／露盤／屋根飾り
acroterion
Akroterion[N]
acrotère[M]
acrotera[F]
acroterio[M]

アンテフィックス／瓦（かわら）端飾り
antefix
Stirnziegel[M]
antéfixe[F]
antefija[F]
antefissa[F]

ペディメント／（三角）破風（はふ）
pediment
Giebeldreieck[N]
fronton[M]
frontón[M]
frontone[M]

木材
timber
Balken[M]
charpente[F]
armazón[M] de madera[F]
trave[F] in legno[M]

瓦
tile
Ziegel[M]
tuile[F]
cubierta[F] de tejas[F]
tegola[F]

コーニス／頂冠帯
cornice
Kranzgesims[N]
corniche[F]
cornisa[F]
cornice[F]

斜めのコーニス
sloping cornice
Schräggeison[N]
rampant[M]
alero[M]
cornice[F] inclinata

フリーズ／中間帯
frieze
Fries[M]
frise[F]
friso[M]
fregio[M]

アーキトレーブ／台輪（蛇腹）
architrave
Architrav[M]
architrave[F]
arquitrabe[M]
architrave[M]

エンタブラチュア／柱頭
entablature
Gebälk[N]
entablement[M]
entablamento[M]
trabeazione[F]

円柱／コラム
column
Säule[F]
colonne[F]
columna[F]
colonna[F]

クレピドーマ／クレピス／基壇
crepidoma
Krepis[F]
crépis[F]
crepidoma[M]
crepidine[F]

柱廊／柱列（廊）
peristyle
Peristyl[N]
péristyle[M]
peristilo[M]
peristilio[M]

スタイロベート／基台
stylobate
Stylobat[M]
stylobate[M]
estilóbato[M]
stilobate[M]

礎石
euthynteria
Euthynterie[F]
euthynteria[F]
euthynteria[F]
euthynteria[F]

斜面出入口
ramp
Rampe[F]
rampe[F]
rampa[F] de acceso[M]
rampa[F]

格子
grille
Gitter[N]
grille[F]
reja[F] de entrada[F] al pronaos[M]
inferriata[F]

プロナオス／前室／前廊
pronaos
Pronaos[M]
pronaos[M]
pronaos[M]
pronao[M]

ナオス／セラ／ケルラ／神室
naos
Naos[M]
naos[M]
naos[M]
naos[M]

ナオス／セラ／ケルラ／神室
naos
Naos[M]
naos[M]
naos[M]
naos[M]

神像の位置
location of the statue
Standort[M] des Kultbildes[N]
emplacement[M] de la statue[F]
ubicación[F] de la estatua[F]
posizione[F] della statua[F]

オピストドモス／宝物庫
opisthodomos
Opisthodomos[M]
opisthodome[M]
opistodomo[M]
opistodomo[M]

見取り図
plan
Grundriss[M]
plan[M]
plano[M]
pianta[F]

プロナオス／前室／前廊
pronaos
Pronaos[M]
pronaos[M]
pronaos[M]
pronao[M]

クレピドーマ／クレピス／基壇
crepidoma
Krepis[F]
crépis[F]
crepidoma[M]
crepidine[F]

柱廊／柱列（廊）
peristyle
Peristyl[N]
péristyle[M]
peristilo[M]
peristilio[M]

円柱／コラム
column
Säule[F]
colonne[F]
columna[F]
colonna[F]

芸術と建築

403

建築 | ARCHITECTURE
ARCHITEKTUR | ARCHITECTURE | ARQUITECTURA | ARCHITETTURA

建築様式

日本語 | 英語 | ドイツ語 | フランス語 | スペイン語 | イタリア語

architectural styles | Baustile^M | styles^M d'architecture^F | estilos^M arquitectónicos | stili^M architettonici

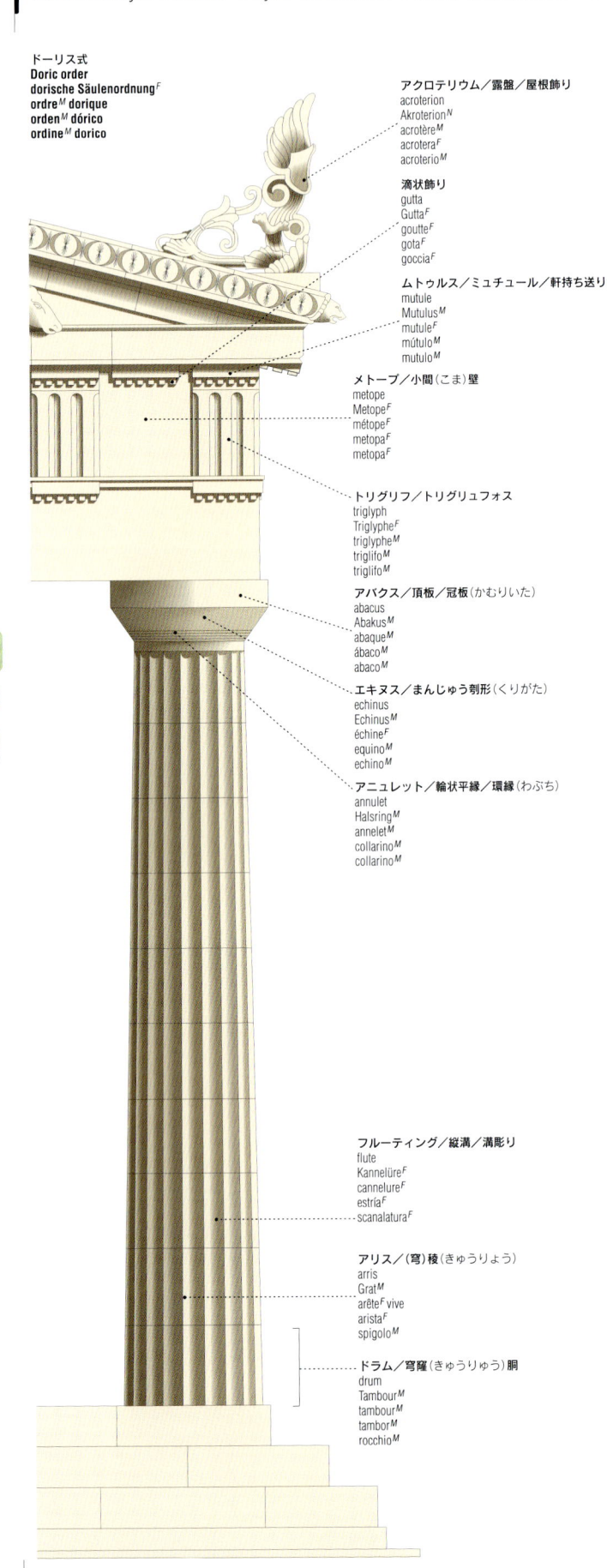

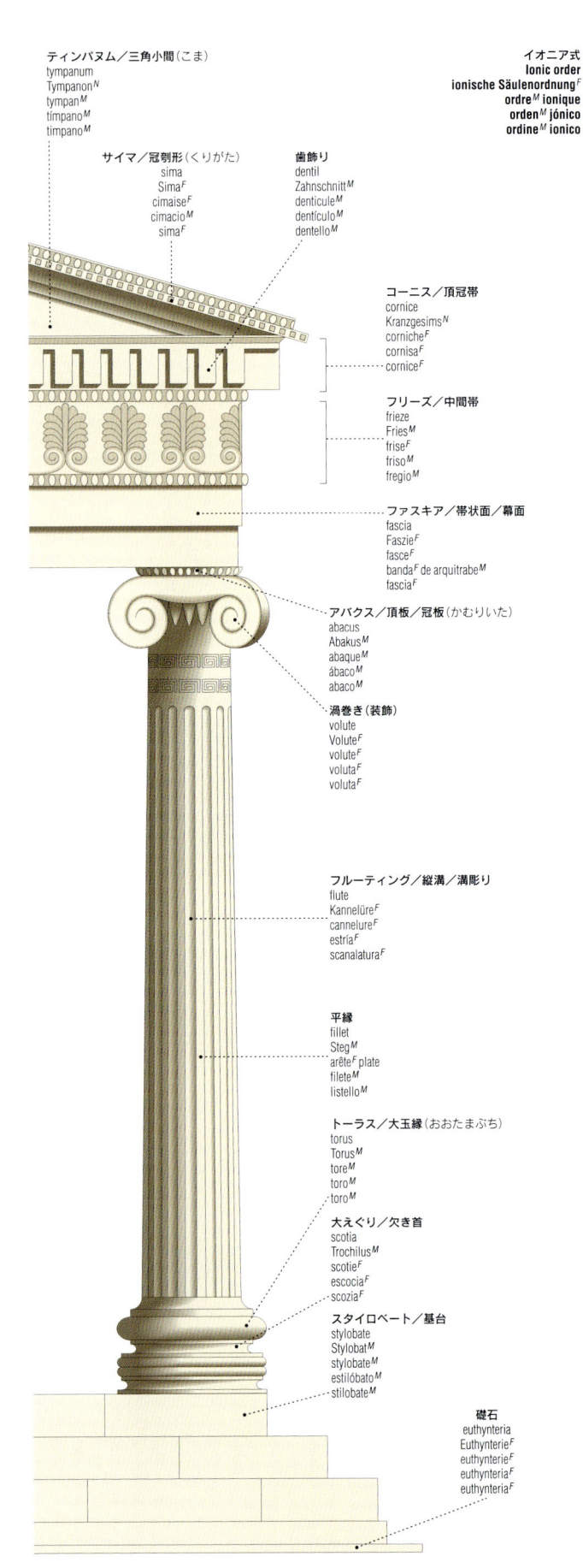

ドーリス式
Doric order
dorische Säulenordnung^F
ordre^M dorique
orden^M dórico
ordine^M dorico

アクロテリウム／露盤／屋根飾り
acroterion
Akroterion^N
acrotère^M
acrotera^F
acroterio^M

滴状飾り
gutta
Gutta^F
goutte^F
gota^F
goccia^F

ムトゥルス／ミュチュール／軒持ち送り
mutule
Mutulus^M
mutule^F
mútulo^M
mutulo^M

メトープ／小間（こま）壁
metope
Metope^F
métope^F
metopa^F
metopa^F

トリグリフ／トリグリュフォス
triglyph
Triglyphe^F
triglyphe^M
triglifo^M
triglifo^M

アバクス／頂板／冠板（かむりいた）
abacus
Abakus^M
abaque^M
ábaco^M
abaco^M

エキヌス／まんじゅう刳形（くりがた）
echinus
Echinus^M
échine^F
equino^M
echino^M

アニュレット／輪状平縁／環縁（わぶち）
annulet
Halsring^M
annelet^M
collarino^M
collarino^M

フルーティング／縦溝／溝彫り
flute
Kannelüre^F
cannelure^F
estría^F
scanalatura^F

アリス／(穹)稜（きゅうりょう）
arris
Grat^M
arête^F vive
arista^F
spigolo^M

ドラム／穹窿（きゅうりゅう）胴
drum
Tambour^M
tambour^M
tambor^M
rocchio^M

ティンパヌム／三角小間（こま）
tympanum
Tympanon^N
tympan^M
tímpano^M
timpano^M

サイマ／冠刳形（くりがた）
sima
Sima^F
cimaise^F
cimacio^M
sima^F

歯飾り
dentil
Zahnschnitt^M
denticule^M
dentículo^M
dentello^M

コーニス／頂冠帯
cornice
Kranzgesims^N
corniche^F
cornisa^F
cornice^F

フリーズ／中間帯
frieze
Fries^M
frise^F
friso^M
fregio^M

ファスキア／帯状面／幕面
fascia
Faszie^F
fasce^F
banda^F de arquitrabe^M
fascia^F

アバクス／頂板／冠板（かむりいた）
abacus
Abakus^M
abaque^M
ábaco^M
abaco^M

渦巻き（装飾）
volute
Volute^F
volute^F
voluta^F
voluta^F

イオニア式
Ionic order
ionische Säulenordnung^F
ordre^M ionique
orden^M jónico
ordine^M ionico

フルーティング／縦溝／溝彫り
flute
Kannelüre^F
cannelure^F
estría^F
scanalatura^F

平縁
fillet
Steg^M
arête^F plate
filete^M
listello^M

トーラス／大玉縁（おおたまぶち）
torus
Torus^M
tore^M
toro^M
toro^M

大えぐり／欠き首
scotia
Trochilus^M
scotie^F
escocia^F
scozia^F

スタイロベート／基台
stylobate
Stylobat^M
stylobate^M
estilóbato^M
stilobate^M

礎石
euthynteria
Euthynterie^F
euthynteria^F
euthynteria^F
euthynteria^F

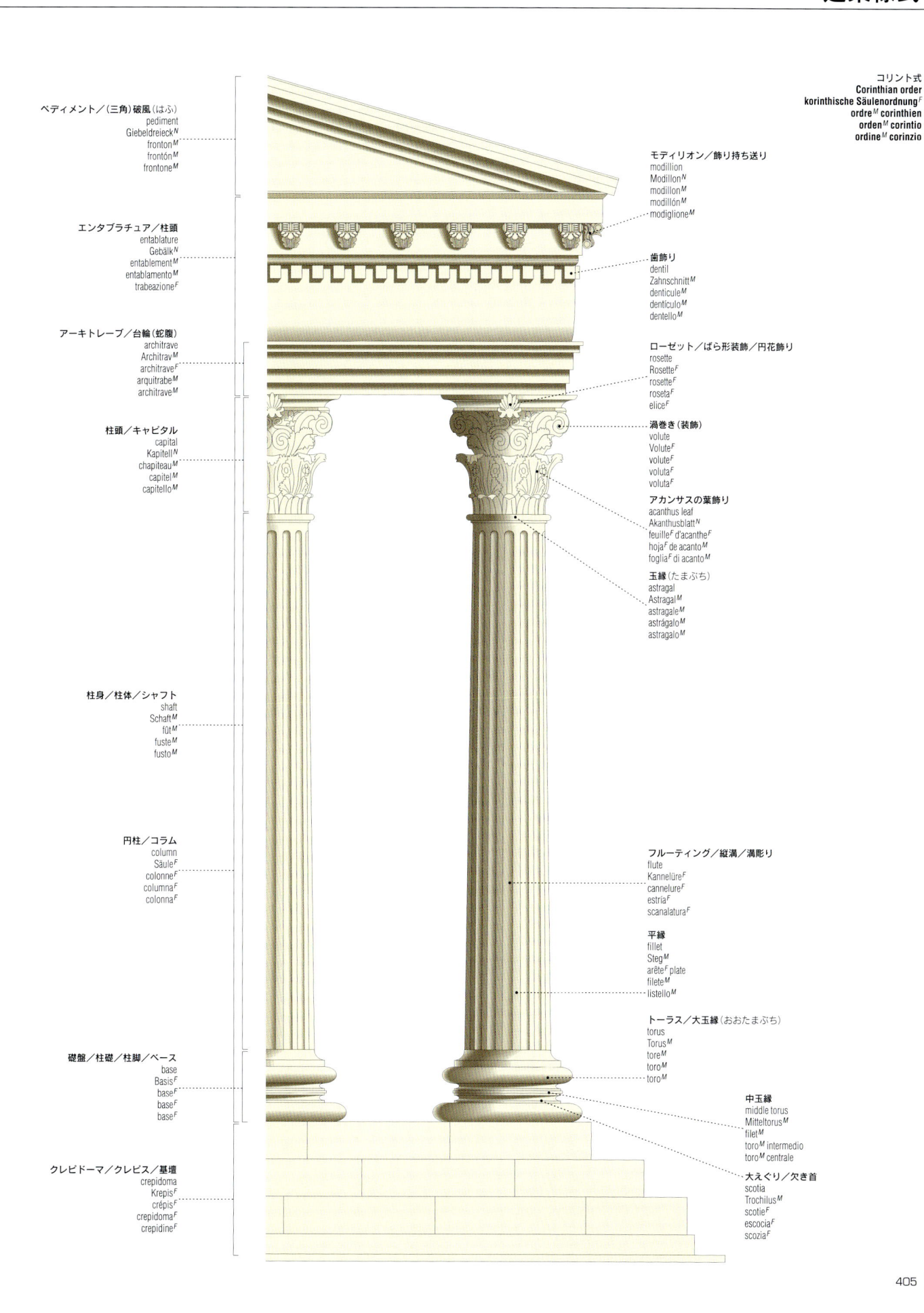

建築 | ARCHITECTURE
ARCHITEKTUR | ARCHITECTURE | ARQUITECTURA | ARCHITETTURA

建築様式

コリント式
Corinthian order
korinthische SäulenordnungF
ordreM corinthien
ordenM corintio
ordineM corinzio

ペディメント／(三角)破風(はふ)
pediment
GiebeldreieckN
frontonM
frontónM
frontoneM

モディリオン／飾り持ち送り
modillion
ModillonN
modillonM
modillónM
modiglioneM

エンタブラチュア／柱頭
entablature
GebälkN
entablementM
entablamentoM
trabeazioneF

歯飾り
dentil
ZahnschnittM
denticuleM
dentículoM
dentelloM

アーキトレーブ／台輪(蛇腹)
architrave
ArchitravM
architraveF
arquitrabeM
architraveM

ローゼット／ばら形装飾／円花飾り
rosette
RosetteF
rosetteF
rosetaF
eliceF

柱頭／キャピタル
capital
KapitellN
chapiteauM
capitelM
capitelloM

渦巻き(装飾)
volute
VoluteF
voluteF
volutaF
volutaF

アカンサスの葉飾り
acanthus leaf
AkanthusblattN
feuilleF d'acantheF
hojaF de acantoM
fogliaF di acantoM

玉縁(たまぶち)
astragal
AstragalM
astragaleM
astrágaloM
astragaloM

柱身／柱体／シャフト
shaft
SchaftM
fûtM
fusteM
fustoM

円柱／コラム
column
SäuleF
colonneF
columnaF
colonnaF

フルーティング／縦溝／溝彫り
flute
KannelüreF
cannelureF
estríaF
scanalaturaF

平縁
fillet
StegM
arêteF plate
fileteM
listelloM

トーラス／大玉縁(おおたまぶち)
torus
TorusM
toreM
toroM
toroM

礎盤／柱礎／柱脚／ベース
base
BasisF
baseF
baseF
baseF

中玉縁
middle torus
MitteltorusM
filetM
toroM intermedio
toroM centrale

クレピドーマ／クレピス／基壇
crepidoma
KrepisF
crépisF
crepidomaF
crepidineF

大えぐり／欠き首
scotia
TrochilusM
scotieF
escociaF
scoziaF

芸術と建築

405

建築 | ARCHITECTURE
ARCHITEKTUR | ARCHITECTURE | ARQUITECTURA | ARCHITETTURA

古代ローマの住宅

Roman house | römisches Wohnhaus[N] | maison[F] romaine | casa[F] romana | casa[F] romana

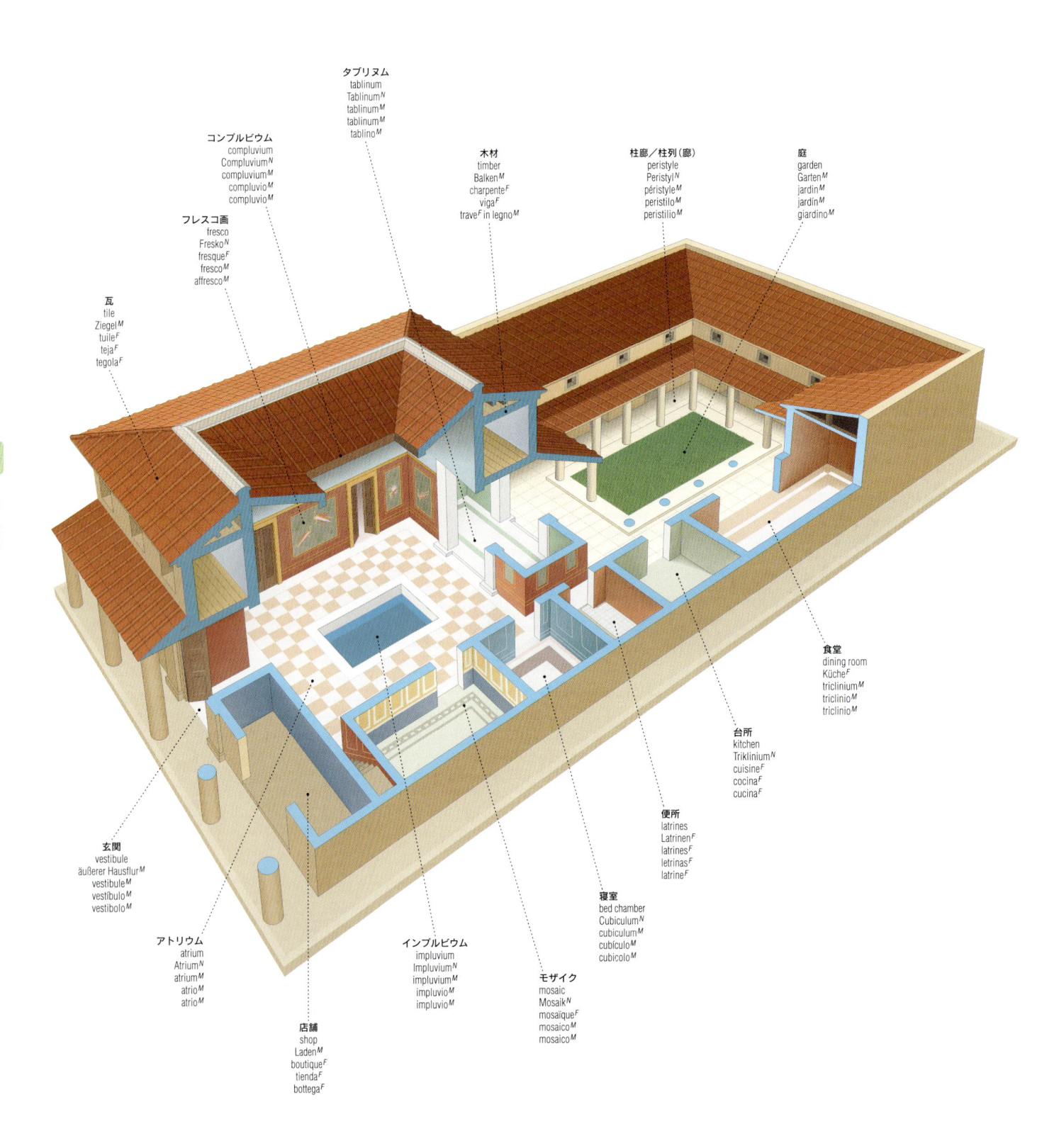

日本語 | 英語 | ドイツ語 | フランス語 | スペイン語 | イタリア語

タブリヌム
tablinum
Tablinum[N]
tablinum[M]
tablinum[M]
tablino[M]

コンプルビウム
compluvium
Compluvium[N]
compluvium[M]
compluvio[M]
compluvio[M]

木材
timber
Balken[M]
charpente[F]
viga[F]
trave[F] in legno[M]

柱廊／柱列(廊)
peristyle
Peristyl[N]
péristyle[M]
peristilo[M]
peristilio[M]

庭
garden
Garten[M]
jardin[M]
jardín[M]
giardino[M]

フレスコ画
fresco
Fresko[N]
fresque[F]
fresco[M]
affresco[M]

瓦
tile
Ziegel[M]
tuile[F]
teja[F]
tegola[F]

食堂
dining room
Küche[F]
triclinium[M]
triclinio[M]
triclinio[M]

台所
kitchen
Triklinium[N]
cuisine[F]
cocina[F]
cucina[F]

便所
latrines
Latrinen[F]
latrines[F]
letrinas[F]
latrine[F]

玄関
vestibule
äußerer Hausflur[M]
vestibule[M]
vestíbulo[M]
vestibolo[M]

寝室
bed chamber
Cubiculum[N]
cubiculum[M]
cubículo[M]
cubicolo[M]

アトリウム
atrium
Atrium[N]
atrium[M]
atrio[M]
atrio[M]

インプルビウム
impluvium
Impluvium[N]
impluvium[M]
impluvio[M]
impluvio[M]

モザイク
mosaic
Mosaik[N]
mosaïque[F]
mosaico[M]
mosaico[M]

店舗
shop
Laden[M]
boutique[F]
tienda[F]
bottega[F]

芸術と建築

406

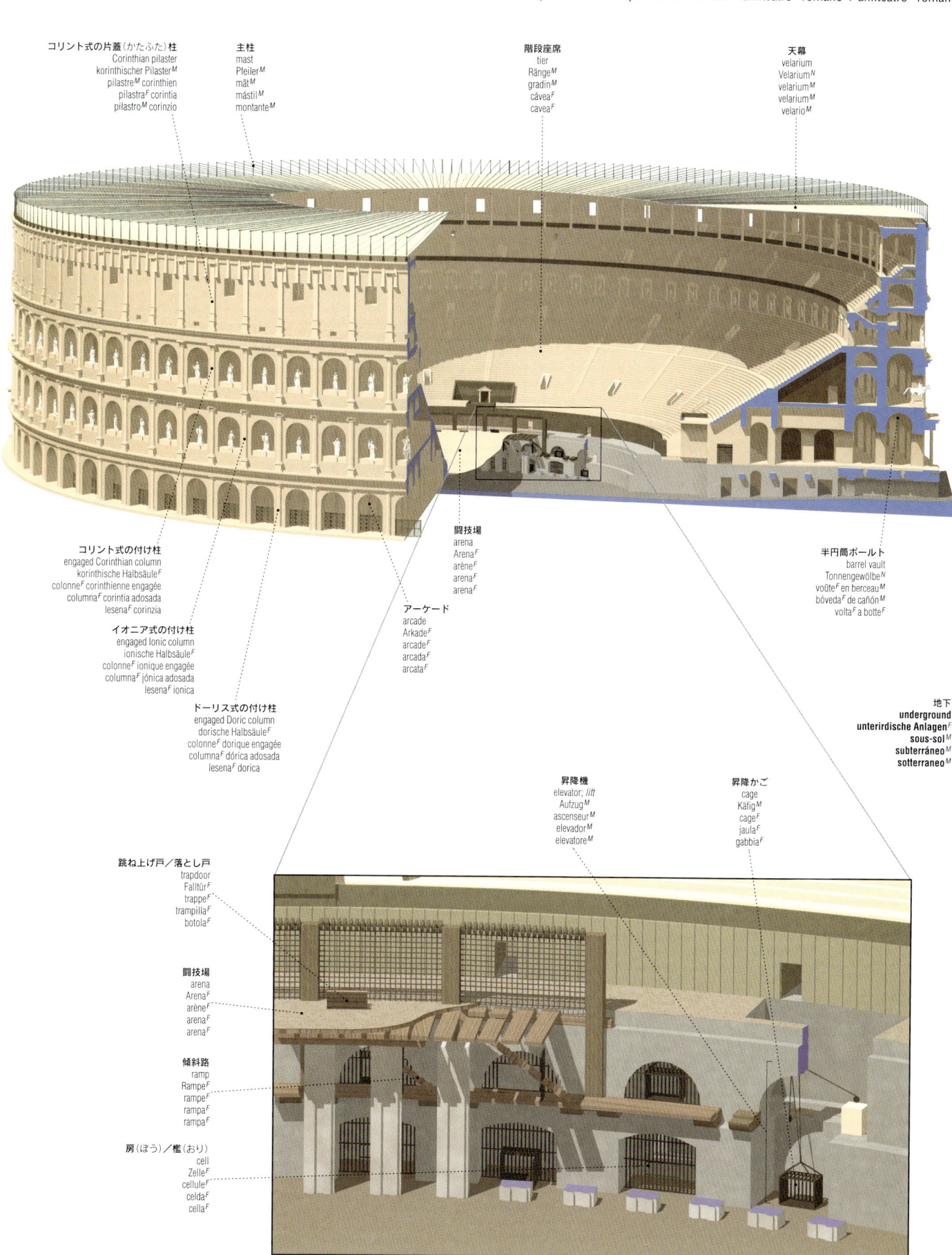

建築 | ARCHITECTURE
ARCHITEKTUR | ARCHITECTURE | ARQUITECTURA | ARCHITETTURA

古代ローマの円形闘技場

Roman amphitheater | römisches Amphitheater^N | amphithéâtre^M romain | anfiteatro^M romano | anfiteatro^M romano

コリント式の片蓋（かたふた）柱
Corinthian pilaster
korinthischer Pilaster^M
pilastre^M corinthien
pilastra^F corintia
pilastro^M corinzio

主柱
mast
Pfeiler^M
mât^M
mástil^M
montante^M

階段座席
tier
Ränge^M
gradin^M
cávea^F
cavea^F

天幕
velarium
Velarium^N
velarium^M
velarium^M
velario^M

コリント式の付け柱
engaged Corinthian column
korinthische Halbsäule^F
colonne^F corinthienne engagée
columna^F corintia adosada
lesena^F corinzia

イオニア式の付け柱
engaged Ionic column
ionische Halbsäule^F
colonne^F ionique engagée
columna^F jónica adosada
lesena^F ionica

闘技場
arena
Arena^F
arène^F
arena^F
arena^F

アーケード
arcade
Arkade^F
arcade^F
arcada^F
arcata^F

半円筒ボールト
barrel vault
Tonnengewölbe^N
voûte^F en berceau^M
bóveda^F de cañón^M
volta^F a botte^F

芸術と建築

ドーリス式の付け柱
engaged Doric column
dorische Halbsäule^F
colonne^F dorique engagée
columna^F dórica adosada
lesena^F dorica

地下
underground
unterirdische Anlagen^F
sous-sol^M
subterráneo^M
sotterraneo^M

昇降機
elevator; lift
Aufzug^M
ascenseur^M
elevador^M
elevatore^M

昇降かご
cage
Käfig^M
cage^F
jaula^F
gabbia^F

跳ね上げ戸／落とし戸
trapdoor
Falltür^F
trappe^F
trampilla^F
botola^F

闘技場
arena
Arena^F
arène^F
arena^F
arena^F

傾斜路
ramp
Rampe^F
rampe^F
rampa^F
rampa^F

房（ぼう）／檻（おり）
cell
Zelle^F
cellule^F
celda^F
cella^F

407

建築 | ARCHITECTURE
ARCHITEKTUR | ARCHITECTURE | ARQUITECTURA | ARCHITETTURA

城

castle | Burg^F | château^M fort | castillo^M | castello^M

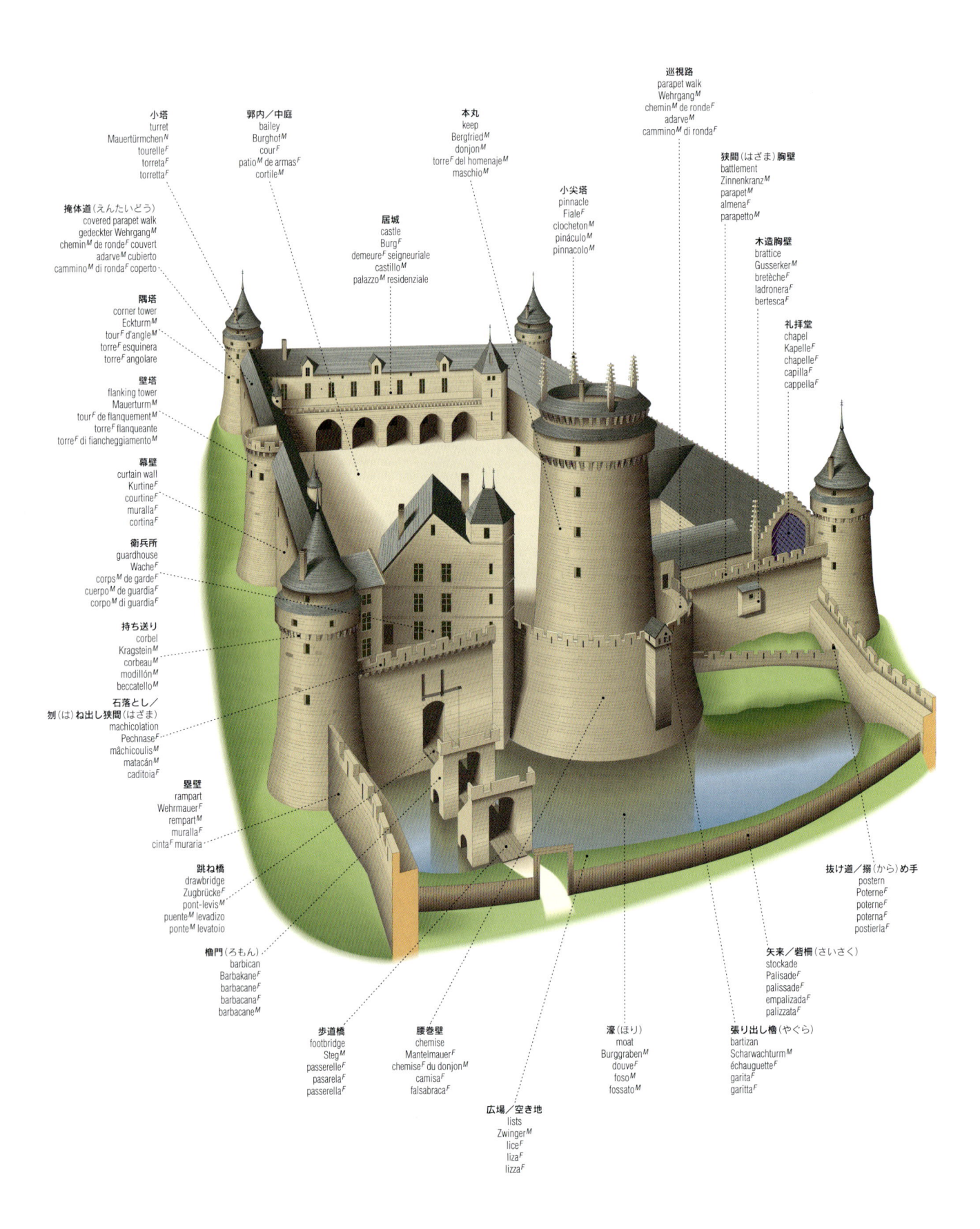

日本語 | 英語 | ドイツ語 | フランス語 | スペイン語 | イタリア語

小塔
turret
Mauertürmchen^N
tourelle^F
torreta^F
torretta^F

郭内／中庭
bailey
Burghof^M
cour^F
patio^M de armas^F
cortile^M

本丸
keep
Bergfried^M
donjon^M
torre^F del homenaje^M
maschio^M

巡視路
parapet walk
Wehrgang^M
chemin^M de ronde^F
adarve^M
cammino^M di ronda^F

小尖塔
pinnacle
Fiale^F
clocheton^M
pináculo^M
pinnacolo^M

狭間（はざま）胸壁
battlement
Zinnenkranz^M
parapet^M
almena^F
parapetto^M

掩体道（えんたいどう）
covered parapet walk
gedeckter Wehrgang^M
chemin^M de ronde^F couvert
adarve^M cubierto
cammino^M di ronda^F coperto

居城
castle
Burg^F
demeure^F seigneuriale
castillo^M
palazzo^M residenziale

木造胸壁
brattice
Gusserker^M
bretèche^F
ladronera^F
bertesca^F

隅塔
corner tower
Eckturm^M
tour^F d'angle^M
torre^F esquinera
torre^F angolare

礼拝堂
chapel
Kapelle^F
chapelle^F
capilla^F
cappella^F

壁塔
flanking tower
Mauerturm^M
tour^F de flanquement^M
torre^F flanqueante
torre^F di fiancheggiamento^M

幕壁
curtain wall
Kurtine^F
courtine^F
muralla^F
cortina^F

衛兵所
guardhouse
Wache^F
corps^M de garde^F
cuerpo^M de guardia^F
corpo^M di guardia^F

持ち送り
corbel
Kragstein^M
corbeau^M
modillón^M
beccatello^M

石落とし／刎（は）ね出し狭間（はざま）
machicolation
Pechnase^F
mâchicoulis^M
matacán^M
caditoia^F

塁壁
rampart
Wehrmauer^F
rempart^M
muralla^F
cinta^F muraria

跳ね橋
drawbridge
Zugbrücke^F
pont-levis^M
puente^M levadizo
ponte^M levatoio

抜け道／搦（から）め手
postern
Poterne^F
poterne^F
poterna^F
postierla^F

櫓門（ろもん）
barbican
Barbakane^F
barbacane^F
barbacana^F
barbacane^F

矢来／砦柵（さいさく）
stockade
Palisade^F
palissade^F
empalizada^F
palizzata^F

歩道橋
footbridge
Steg^M
passerelle^F
pasarela^F
passerella^F

腰巻壁
chemise
Mantelmauer^F
chemise^F du donjon^M
camisa^F
falsabraca^F

濠（ほり）
moat
Burggraben^M
douve^F
foso^M
fossato^M

張り出し櫓（やぐら）
bartizan
Scharwachturm^M
échauguette^F
garita^F
garitta^F

広場／空き地
lists
Zwinger^M
lice^F
liza^F
lizza^F

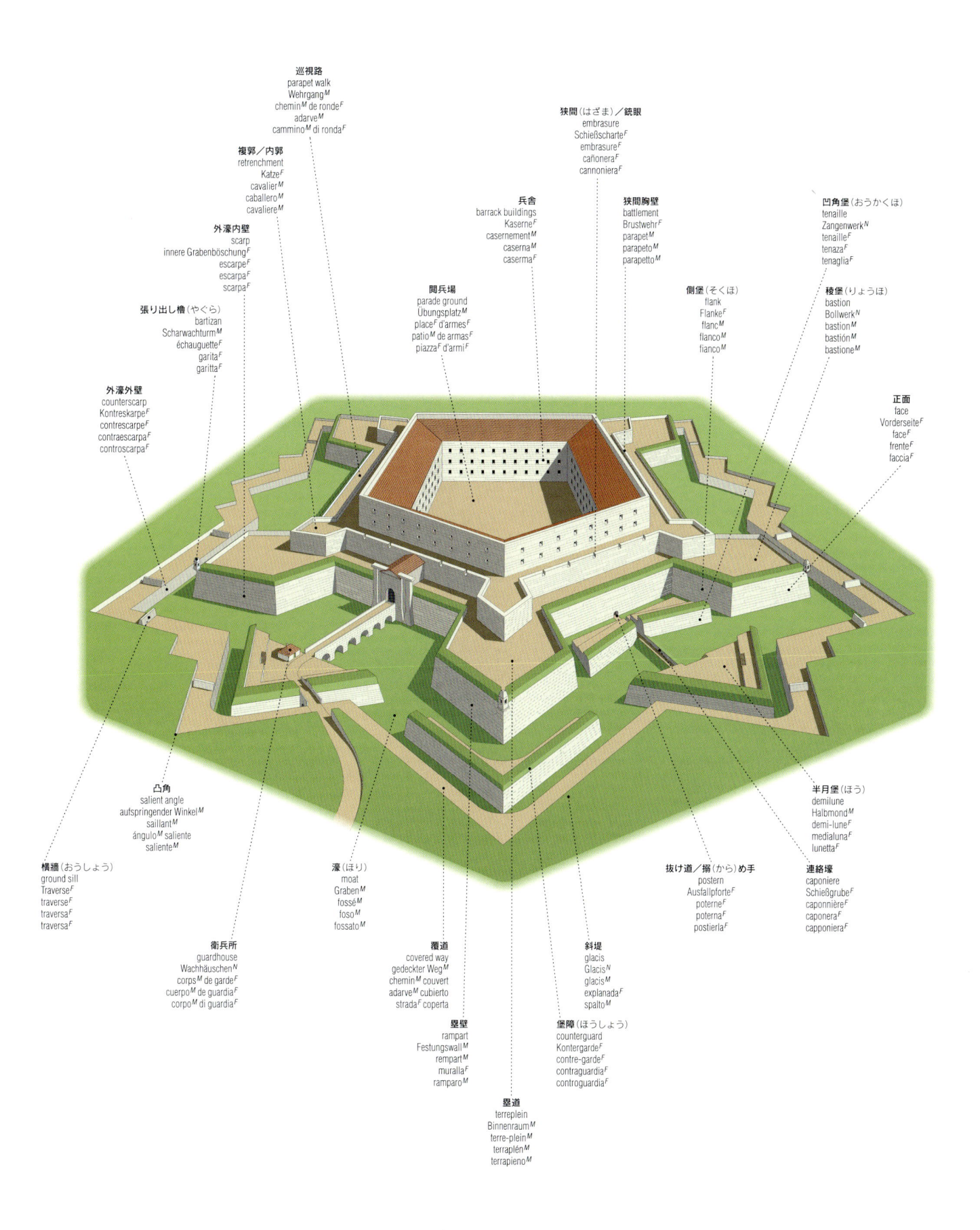

建築 | ARCHITECTURE
ARCHITEKTUR | ARCHITECTURE | ARQUITECTURA | ARCHITETTURA

ボーバン式要塞

Vauban fortification | Festung^F | fortification^F à la Vauban | fortificación^F de Vauban | fortificazione^F alla Vauban

巡視路
parapet walk
Wehrgang^M
chemin^M de ronde^F
adarve^M
cammino^M di ronda^F

狭間(はざま)／銃眼
embrasure
Schießscharte^F
embrasure^F
cañonera^F
cannoniera^F

複郭／内郭
retrenchment
Katze^F
cavalier^M
caballero^M
cavaliere^M

兵舎
barrack buildings
Kaserne^F
casernement^M
caserna^M
caserma^F

狭間胸壁
battlement
Brustwehr^F
parapet
parapeto^M
parapetto^M

凹角堡(おうかくほ)
tenaille
Zangenwerk^N
tenaille^F
tenaza^F
tenaglia^F

外濠内壁
scarp
innere Grabenböschung^F
escarpe^F
escarpa^F
scarpa^F

閲兵場
parade ground
Übungsplatz^M
place^F d'armes^F
patio^M de armas^F
piazza^F d'armi^F

側堡(そくほ)
flank
Flanke^F
flanc^M
flanco^M
fianco^M

稜堡(りょうほ)
bastion
Bollwerk^N
bastion
bastión^M
bastione^M

張り出し櫓(やぐら)
bartizan
Scharwachturm^M
échauguette^F
garita^F
garitta^F

正面
face
Vorderseite^F
face^F
frente^F
faccia^F

外濠外壁
counterscarp
Kontreskarpe^F
contrescarpe^F
contraescarpa^F
controscarpa^F

半月堡(ほう)
demilune
Halbmond^M
demi-lune^F
medialuna^F
lunetta^F

凸角
salient angle
aufspringender Winkel^M
saillant^M
ángulo^M saliente
saliente^M

横牆(おうしょう)
ground sill
Traverse^F
traverse^F
traversa^F
traversa^F

濠(ほり)
moat
Graben^M
fossé^M
foso^M
fossato^M

抜け道／搦(から)め手
postern
Ausfallpforte^F
poterne^F
poterna^F
postierla^F

連絡壕
caponiere
Schießgrube^F
caponnière^F
caponera^F
capponiera^F

衛兵所
guardhouse
Wachhäuschen^N
corps^M de garde^F
cuerpo^M de guardia^F
corpo^M di guardia^F

覆道
covered way
gedeckter Weg^M
chemin^M couvert
adarve^M cubierto
strada^F coperta

斜堤
glacis
Glacis^N
glacis^M
explanada^F
spalto^M

堡障(ほうしょう)
counterguard
Kontergarde^F
contre-garde^F
contraguardia^F
controguardia^F

塁壁
rampart
Festungswall^M
rempart^M
muralla^F
ramparo^M

塁道
terreplein
Binnenraum^M
terre-plein^M
terraplén^M
terrapieno^M

芸術と建築

409

建築 | ARCHITECTURE
ARCHITEKTUR | ARCHITECTURE | ARQUITECTURA | ARCHITETTURA

大聖堂

cathedral | Dom^M | cathédrale^F | catedral^F | cattedrale^F

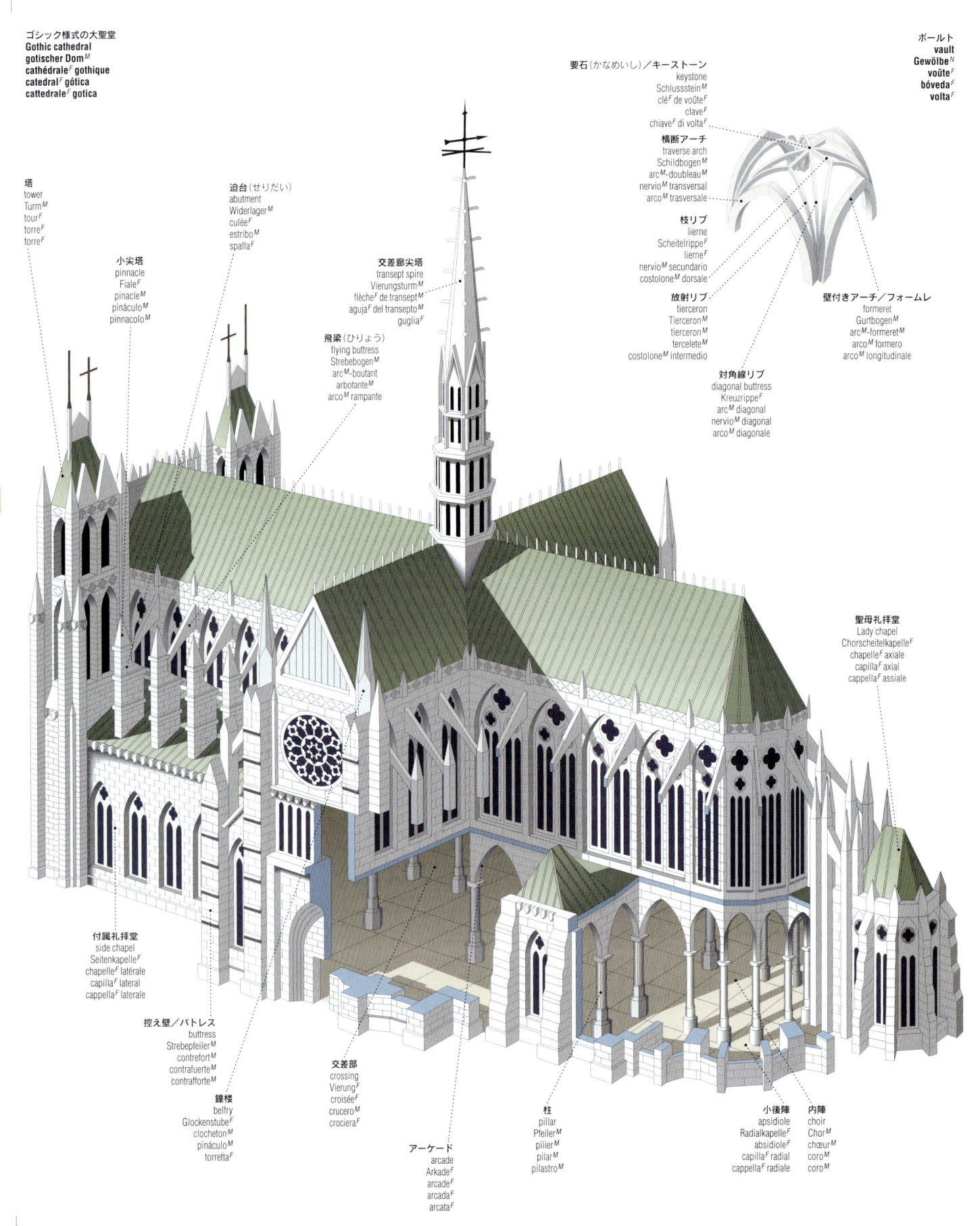

日本語 | 英語 | ドイツ語 | フランス語 | スペイン語 | イタリア語

ゴシック様式の大聖堂
Gothic cathedral
gotischer Dom^M
cathédrale^F **gothique**
catedral^F **gótica**
cattedrale^F **gotica**

要石(かなめいし)／キーストーン
keystone
Schlussstein^M
clé^F de voûte^F
clave^F
chiave^F di volta^F

ボールト
vault
Gewölbe^N
voûte^F
bóveda^F
volta^F

横断アーチ
traverse arch
Schildbogen^M
arc^M-doubleau
nervio^M transversal
arco^M trasversale

塔
tower
Turm^M
tour^F
torre^F
torre^F

迫台(せりだい)
abutment
Widerlager^M
culée^F
estribo^M
spalla^F

枝リブ
lierne
Scheitelrippe^F
lierne^F
nervio^M secundario
costolone^M dorsale

小尖塔
pinnacle
Fiale^F
pinacle^M
pináculo^M
pinnacolo^M

交差廊尖塔
transept spire
Vierungsturm^M
flèche^F de transept^M
aguja^F del transepto^M
guglia^F

放射リブ
tierceron
Tierceron^M
tierceron^M
tercelete^M
costolone^M intermedio

壁付きアーチ／フォームレ
formeret
Gurtbogen^M
arc^M-formeret
arco^M formero
arco^M longitudinale

飛梁(ひりょう)
flying buttress
Strebebogen^M
arc^M-boutant
arbotante^M
arco^M rampante

対角線リブ
diagonal buttress
Kreuzrippe^F
arc^M diagonal
nervio^M diagonal
arco^M diagonale

聖母礼拝堂
Lady chapel
Chorscheitelkapelle^F
chapelle^F axiale
capilla^F axial
cappella^F assiale

付属礼拝堂
side chapel
Seitenkapelle^F
chapelle^F latérale
capilla^F lateral
cappella^F laterale

控え壁／バトレス
buttress
Strebepfeiler^M
contrefort^M
contrafuerte^M
contrafforte^M

交差部
crossing
Vierung^F
croisée^F
crucero^M
crociera^F

鐘楼
belfry
Glockenstube^F
clocheton^M
pináculo^M
torretta^F

アーケード
arcade
Arkade^F
arcade^F
arcada^F
arcata^F

柱
pillar
Pfeiler^M
pilier^M
pilar^M
pilastro^M

小後陣
apsidiole
Radialkapelle^F
absidiole^F
capilla^F radial
cappella^F radiale

内陣
choir
Chor^M
chœur^M
coro^M
coro^M

芸術と建築

建築 | ARCHITECTURE
ARCHITEKTUR | ARCHITECTURE | ARQUITECTURA | ARCHITETTURA

大聖堂

正面図
façade
Fassade^F
façade^F
fachada^F
facciata^F

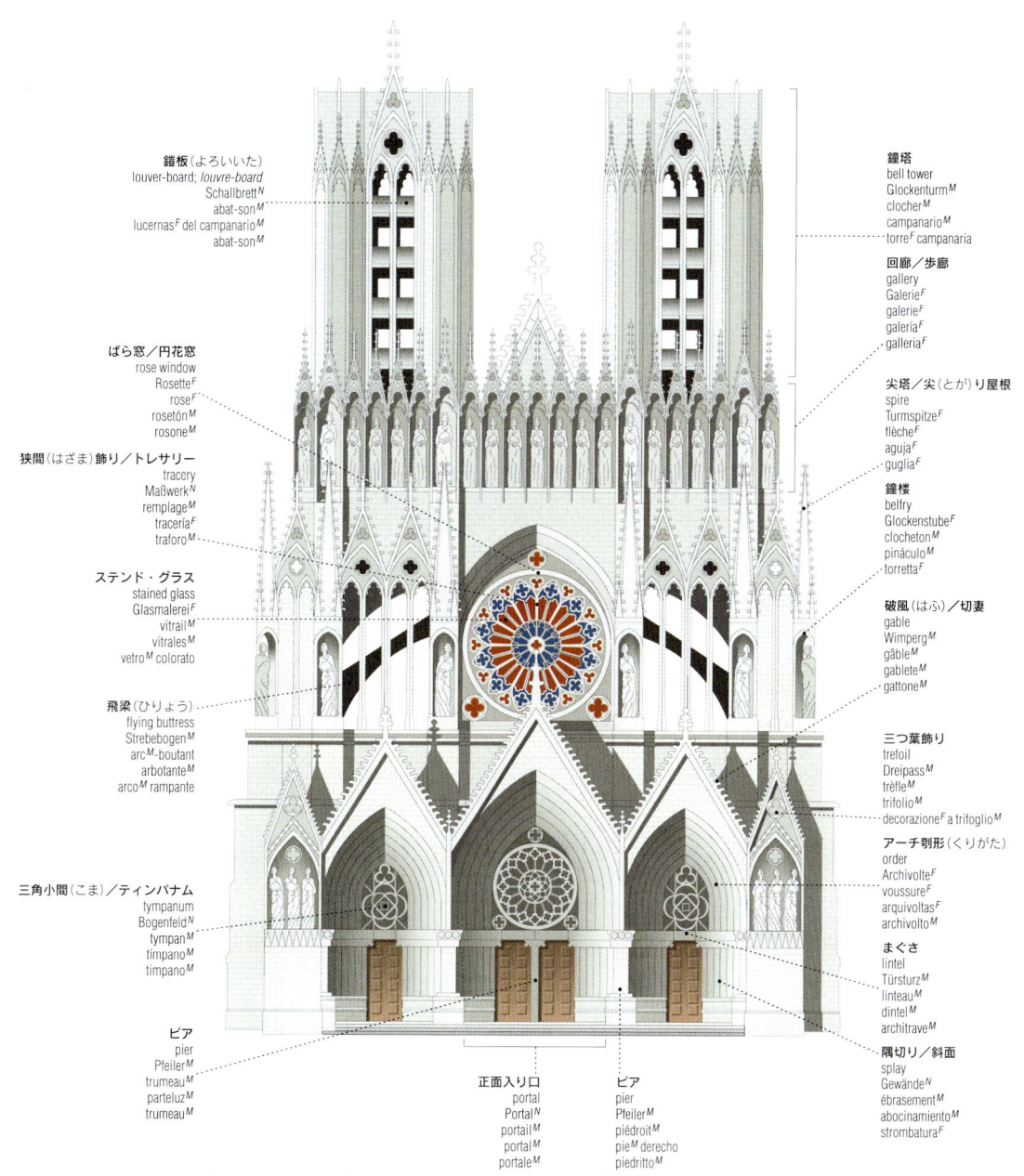

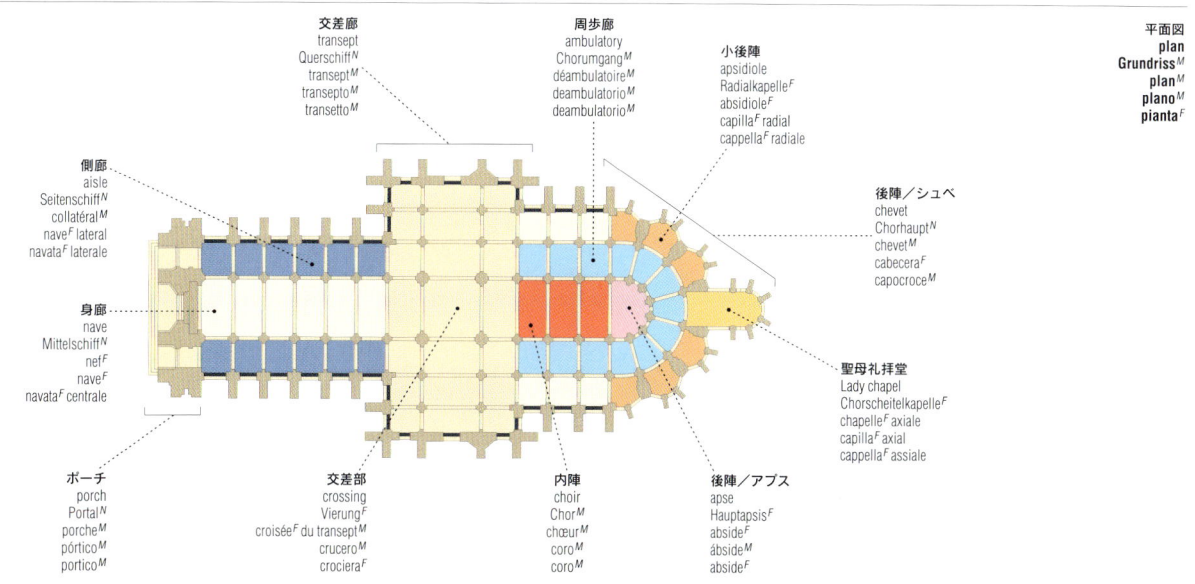

鎧板（よろいいた）
louver-board; *louvre-board*
Schallbrett^N
abat-son^M
lucernas^F del campanario^M
abat-son

ばら窓／円花窓
rose window
Rosette^F
rose^F
rosetón^M
rosone^M

狭間（はざま）飾り／トレサリー
tracery
Maßwerk^N
remplage^M
tracería^F
traforo^M

ステンド・グラス
stained glass
Glasmalerei^F
vitrail^M
vitrales^M
vetro^M colorato

飛梁（ひりょう）
flying buttress
Strebebogen^M
arc^M-boutant
arbotante^M
arco^M rampante

三角小間（こま）／ティンパナム
tympanum
Bogenfeld^N
tympan^M
tímpano^M
timpano^M

ピア
pier
Pfeiler^M
trumeau^M
parteluz^M
trumeau^M

正面入り口
portal
Portal^N
portail^M
portal^M
portale^M

ピア
pier
Pfeiler^M
piédroit^M
pie^M derecho
piedritto^M

鐘塔
bell tower
Glockenturm^M
clocher^M
campanario^M
torre^F campanaria

回廊／歩廊
gallery
Galerie^F
galerie^F
galería^F
galleria^F

尖塔／尖（とが）り屋根
spire
Turmspitze^F
flèche^F
aguja^F
guglia^F

鐘楼
belfry
Glockenstube^F
clocheton^M
pináculo^M
torretta^F

破風（はふ）／切妻
gable
Wimperg^M
gâble^M
gablete^M
gattone^M

三つ葉飾り
trefoil
Dreipass^M
trèfle^M
trifolio^M
decorazione^F a trifoglio^M

アーチ刳形（くりがた）
order
Archivolte^F
voussure^F
arquivoltas^F
archivolto^M

まぐさ
lintel
Türsturz^M
linteau^M
dintel^M
architrave^F

隅切り／斜面
splay
Gewände^N
ébrasement^M
abocinamiento^M
strombatura^F

平面図
plan
Grundriss^M
plan^M
plano^M
pianta^F

交差廊
transept
Querschiff^N
transept^M
transepto^M
transetto^M

周歩廊
ambulatory
Chorumgang^M
déambulatoire^M
deambulatorio^M
deambulatorio^M

小後陣
apsidiole
Radialkapelle^F
absidiole^F
capilla^F radial
cappella^F radiale

側廊
aisle
Seitenschiff^N
collatéral^M
nave^F lateral
navata^F laterale

身廊
nave
Mittelschiff^N
nef^F
nave^F
navata^F centrale

後陣／シュベ
chevet
Chorhaupt^N
chevet^M
cabecera^F
capocroce^M

聖母礼拝堂
Lady chapel
Chorscheitelkapelle^F
chapelle^F axiale
capilla^F axial
cappella^F assiale

ポーチ
porch
Portal^N
porche^F
pórtico^M
portico^M

交差部
crossing
Vierung^F
croisée^F du transept
crucero^M
crociera^F

内陣
choir
Chor^M
chœur^M
coro^M
coro^M

後陣／アプス
apse
Hauptapsis^F
abside^F
ábside^M
abside^F

芸術と建築

建築 | ARCHITECTURE
ARCHITEKTUR | ARCHITECTURE | ARQUITECTURA | ARCHITETTURA

仏塔

日本語 | 英語 | ドイツ語 | フランス語 | スペイン語 | イタリア語

pagoda | Pagode^F | pagode^F | pagoda^F | pagoda^F

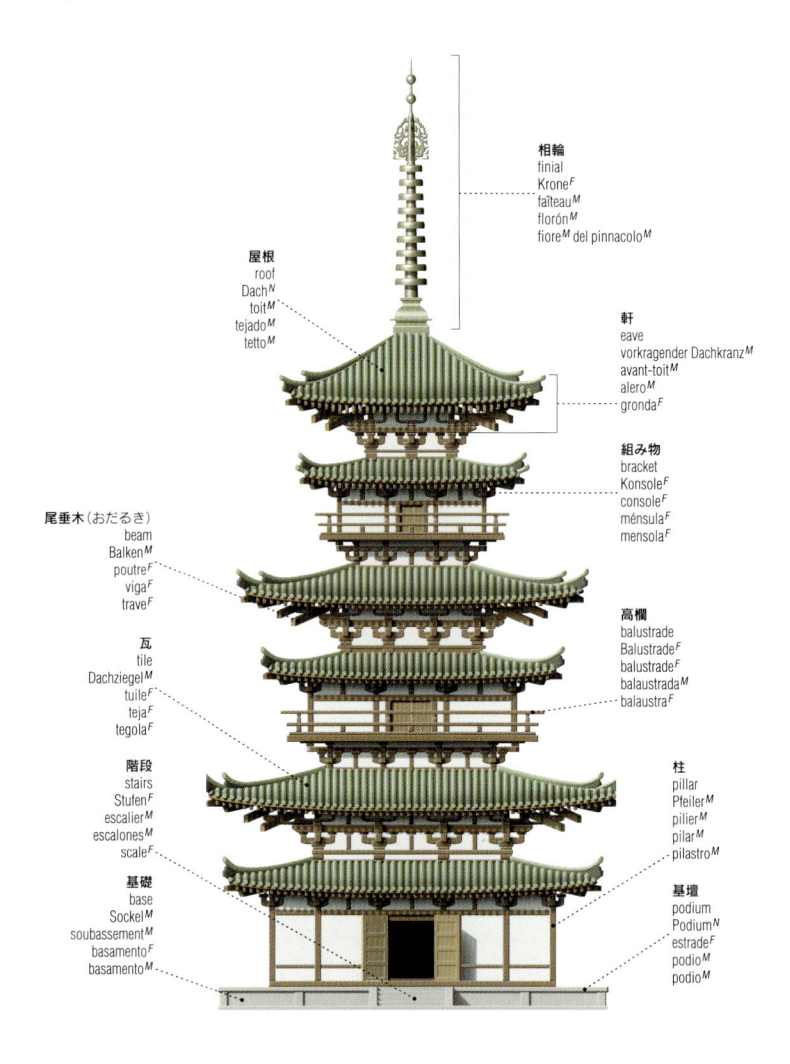

相輪
finial
Krone^F
faîteau^M
florón^M
fiore del pinnacolo^M

屋根
roof
Dach^N
toit^M
tejado^M
tetto^M

軒
eave
vorkragender Dachkranz^M
avant-toit^M
alero^M
gronda^F

組み物
bracket
Konsole^F
console^F
ménsula^F
mensola^F

尾垂木（おだるき）
beam
Balken^M
poutre^F
viga^F
trave^F

高欄
balustrade
Balustrade^F
balustrade^F
balaustrada^M
balaustra^F

瓦
tile
Dachziegel^M
tuile^F
teja^F
tegola^F

柱
pillar
Pfeiler^M
pilier^M
pilar^M
pilastro^M

階段
stairs
Stufen^F
escalier^M
escalones^M
scale^F

基礎
base
Sockel^M
soubassement^M
basamento^F
basamento^M

基壇
podium
Podium^N
estrade^F
podio^M
podio^M

アステカ神殿

Aztec temple | aztekischer Tempel^M | temple^M aztèque | templo^M azteca | tempio^M azteco

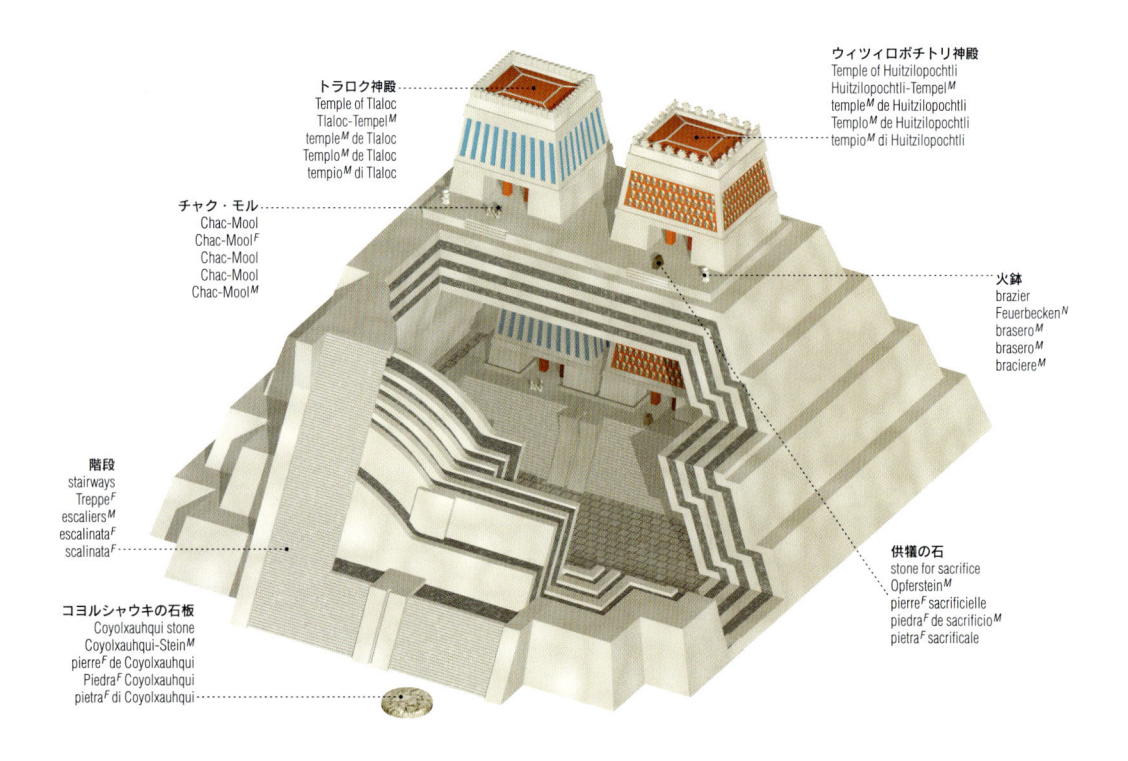

トラロク神殿
Temple of Tlaloc
Tlaloc-Tempel^M
temple^M de Tlaloc
Templo^M de Tlaloc
tempio^M di Tlaloc

ウィツィロポチトリ神殿
Temple of Huitzilopochtli
Huitzilopochtli-Tempel^M
temple^M de Huitzilopochtli
Templo^M de Huitzilopochtli
tempio^M di Huitzilopochtli

チャク・モル
Chac-Mool
Chac-Mool^F
Chac-Mool
Chac-Mool
Chac-Mool^M

火鉢
brazier
Feuerbecken^N
brasero^M
brasero^M
braciere^M

階段
stairways
Treppe^F
escaliers^M
escalones^M
scalinata^F

供犠の石
stone for sacrifice
Opferstein^M
pierre^F sacrificielle
piedra^F de sacrificio^M
pietra^F sacrificale

コヨルシャウキの石板
Coyolxauhqui stone
Coyolxauhqui-Stein^M
pierre^F de Coyolxauhqui
Piedra^F Coyolxauhqui
pietra^F di Coyolxauhqui

建築 | ARCHITECTURE
ARCHITEKTUR | ARCHITECTURE | ARQUITECTURA | ARCHITETTURA

建築の要素
elements of architecture | Architekturelemente[N] | éléments[M] d'architecture[F] | elementos[M] arquitectónicos | elementi[M] architettonici

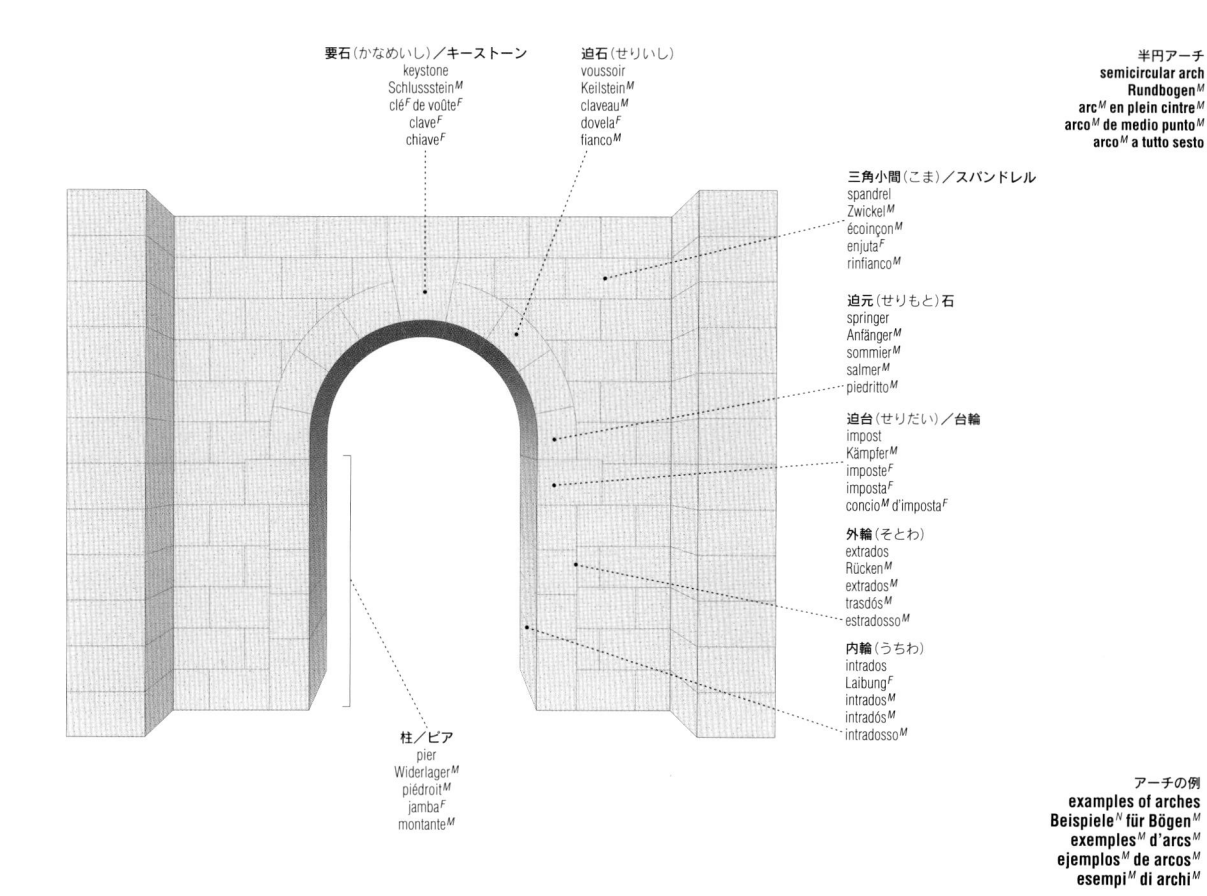

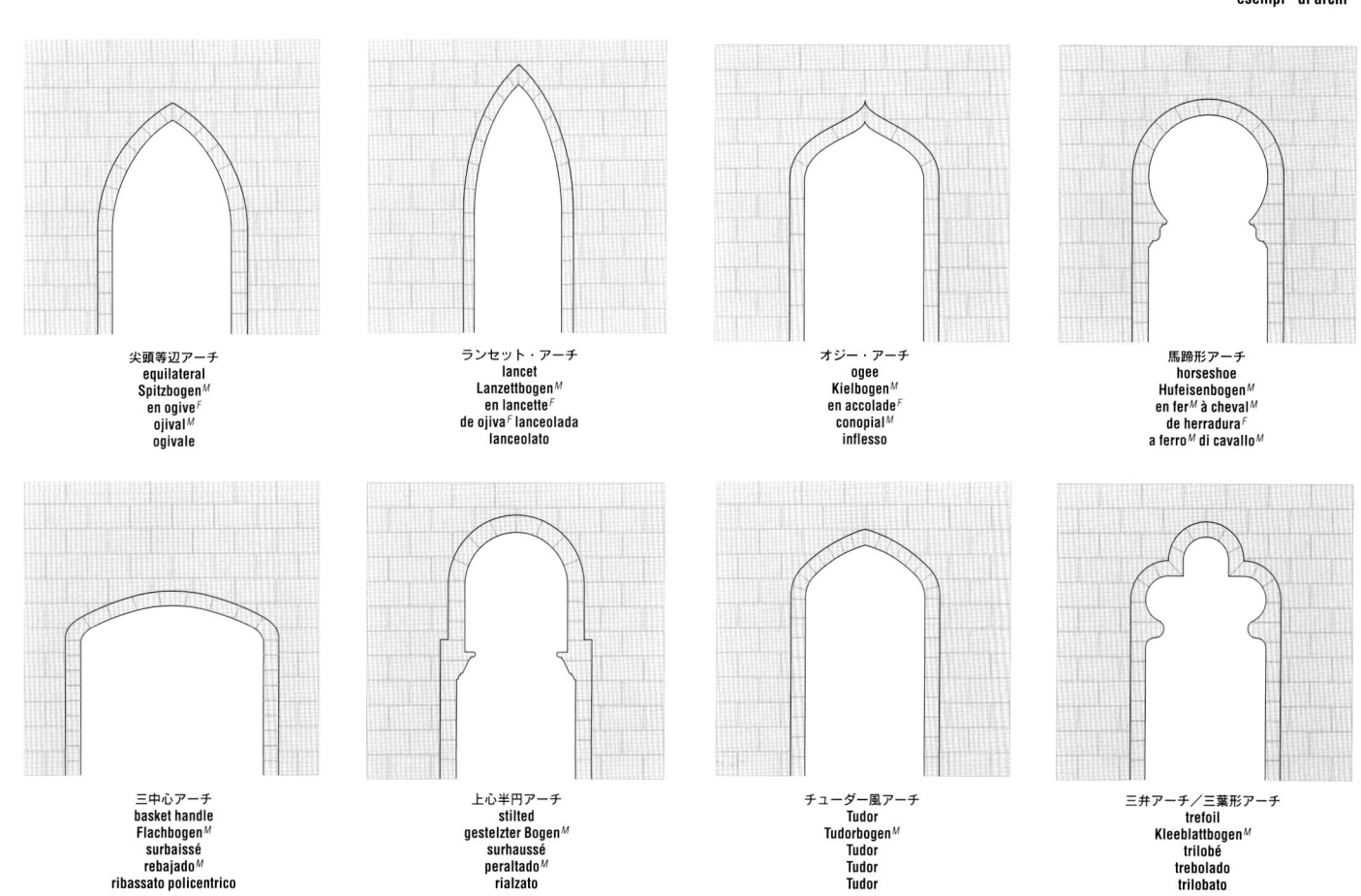

要石（かなめいし）／キーストーン
keystone
Schlussstein[M]
clé[F] de voûte[F]
clave[F]
chiave[F]

迫石（せりいし）
voussoir
Keilstein[M]
claveau[M]
dovela[F]
fianco[M]

半円アーチ
semicircular arch
Rundbogen[M]
arc[M] en plein cintre[M]
arco[M] de medio punto[M]
arco[M] a tutto sesto

三角小間（こま）／スパンドレル
spandrel
Zwickel[M]
écoinçon[M]
enjuta[F]
rinfianco[M]

迫元（せりもと）石
springer
Anfänger[M]
sommier[M]
salmer[M]
piedritto[M]

迫台（せりだい）／台輪
impost
Kämpfer[M]
imposte[F]
imposta[F]
concio[M] d'imposta[F]

外輪（そとわ）
extrados
Rücken[M]
extradós[M]
trasdós[M]
estradosso[M]

内輪（うちわ）
intrados
Laibung[F]
intrados[M]
intradós[M]
intradosso[M]

柱／ピア
pier
Widerlager[M]
piédroit[M]
jamba[F]
montante[M]

アーチの例
examples of arches
Beispiele[N] für Bögen[M]
exemples[M] d'arcs[M]
ejemplos[M] de arcos[M]
esempi[M] di archi[M]

尖頭等辺アーチ
equilateral
Spitzbogen[M]
en ogive[F]
ojival[M]
ogivale

ランセット・アーチ
lancet
Lanzettbogen[M]
en lancette[F]
de ojiva[F] lanceolada
lanceolato

オジー・アーチ
ogee
Kielbogen[M]
en accolade[F]
conopial[M]
inflesso

馬蹄形アーチ
horseshoe
Hufeisenbogen[M]
en fer[M] à cheval[M]
de herradura[F]
a ferro[M] di cavallo[M]

三中心アーチ
basket handle
Flachbogen[M]
surbaissé
rebajado[M]
ribassato policentrico

上心半円アーチ
stilted
gestelzter Bogen[M]
surhaussé
peraltado[M]
rialzato

チューダー風アーチ
Tudor
Tudorbogen[M]
Tudor
Tudor
Tudor

三弁アーチ／三葉形アーチ
trefoil
Kleeblattbogen[M]
trilobé
trebolado
trilobato

芸術と建築

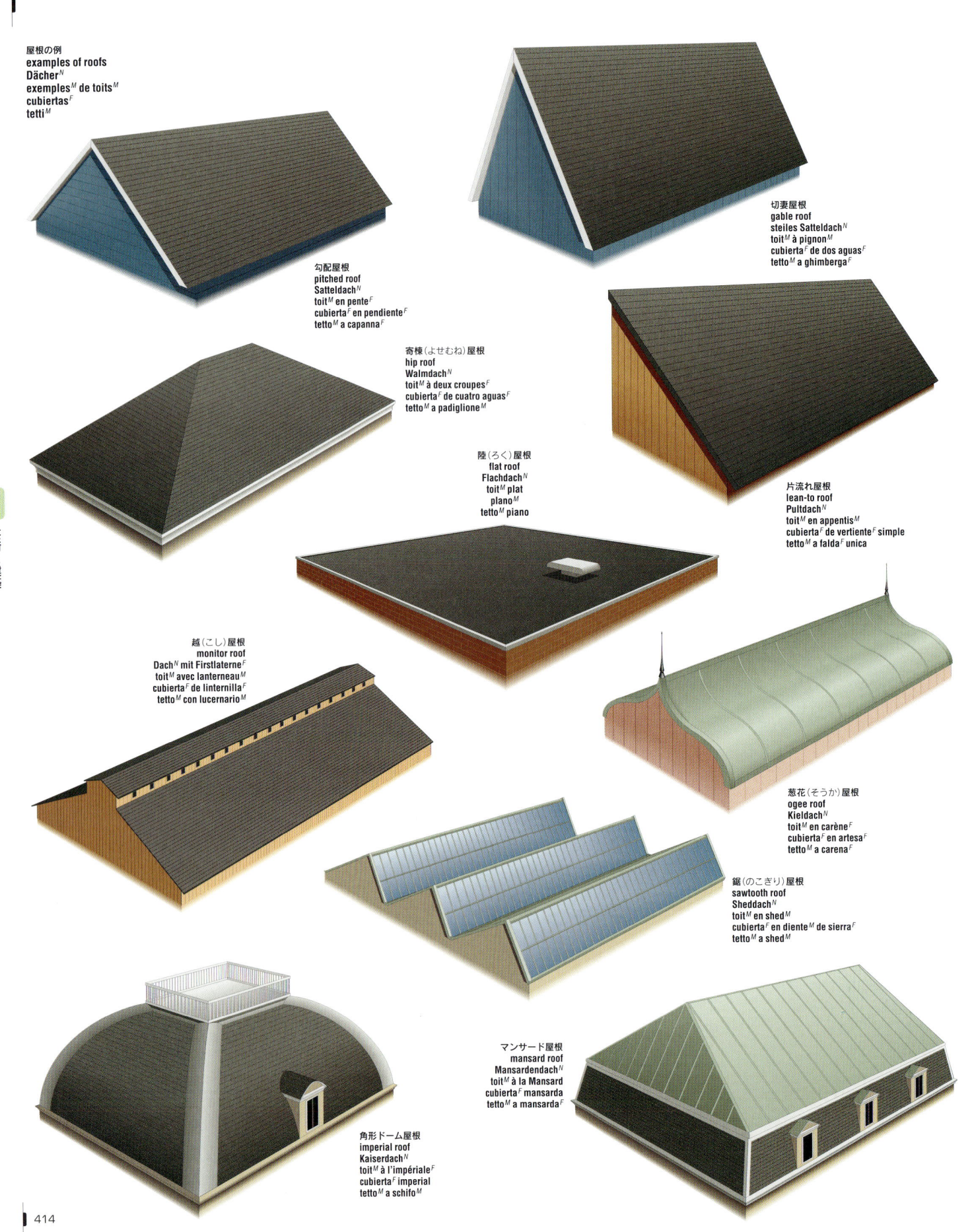

建築 | ARCHITECTURE
ARCHITEKTUR | ARCHITECTURE | ARQUITECTURA | ARCHITETTURA

建築の要素

日本語 | 英語 | ドイツ語 | フランス語 | スペイン語 | イタリア語

屋根の例
examples of roofs
Dächer^N
exemples^M de toits^M
cubiertas^F
tetti^M

勾配屋根
pitched roof
Satteldach^N
toit^M en pente^F
cubierta^F en pendiente^F
tetto^M a capanna^F

切妻屋根
gable roof
steiles Satteldach^N
toit^M à pignon^M
cubierta^F de dos aguas^F
tetto^M a ghimberga^F

寄棟(よせむね)屋根
hip roof
Walmdach^N
toit^M à deux croupes^F
cubierta^F de cuatro aguas^F
tetto^M a padiglione^M

陸(ろく)屋根
flat roof
Flachdach^N
toit^M plat
plano^M
tetto^M piano

片流れ屋根
lean-to roof
Pultdach^N
toit^M en appentis^M
cubierta^F de vertiente^F simple
tetto^M a falda^F unica

越(こし)屋根
monitor roof
Dach^N mit Firstlaterne^F
toit^M avec lanterneau^M
cubierta^F de linternilla^F
tetto^M con lucernario^M

葱花(そうか)屋根
ogee roof
Kieldach^N
toit^M en carène^F
cubierta^F en artesa^F
tetto^M a carena^F

鋸(のこぎり)屋根
sawtooth roof
Sheddach^N
toit^M en shed^M
cubierta^F en diente^M de sierra^F
tetto^M a shed^M

角形ドーム屋根
imperial roof
Kaiserdach^N
toit^M à l'impériale^F
cubierta^F imperial
tetto^M a schifo^M

マンサード屋根
mansard roof
Mansardendach^N
toit^M à la Mansard
cubierta^F mansarda
tetto^M a mansarda^F

建築 | ARCHITECTURE
ARCHITEKTUR | ARCHITECTURE | ARQUITECTURA | ARCHITETTURA

建築の要素

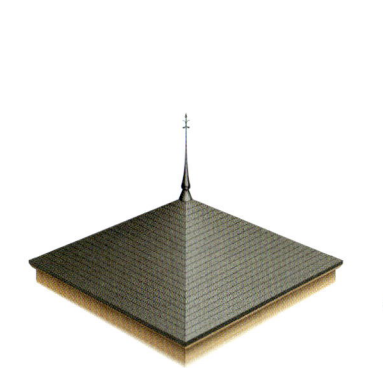

方形屋根
pavilion roof
Pavillondach^N
toit^M en pavillon^M
cubierta^F de pabellón^M
tetto^M a piramide^F

小塔屋根
sloped turret
Faltkegeldach^N
toit^M à tourelle^F à pans^M
cubierta^F de torrecilla^F
torretta^F spiovente

兜（かぶと）屋根
helm roof
Helmdach^N
toit^M en flèche^F
cubierta^F piramidal
tetto^M a padiglione^M da torre^F

ベル屋根
bell roof
Glockendach^N
toit^M en coupole^F
cubierta^F de cúpula^F peraltada
cupola^F ovoide rialzata

円錐形尖塔屋根
conical broach roof
Kegeldach^N
toit^M en poivrière^F
cubierta^F cónica
tetto^M a cono^M

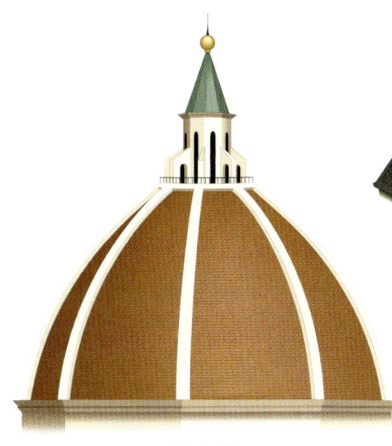

ドーム屋根
dome roof
Kuppeldach^N
toit^M en dôme^M
cúpula^F
cupola^F

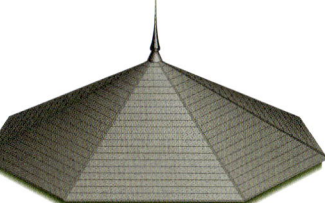

傘形［八角］屋根
rotunda roof
Pyramidendach^N
toit^M en rotonde^F
cubierta^F de rotonda^F
tetto^M a ombrello^M

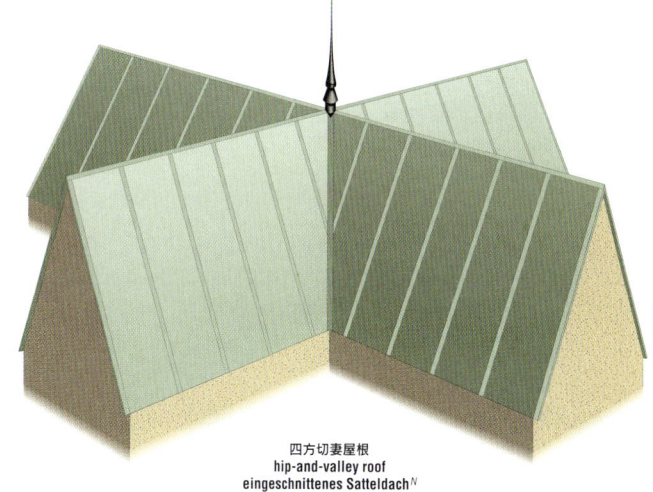

四方切妻屋根
hip-and-valley roof
eingeschnittenes Satteldach^N
toit^M à quatre versants^M
cubierta^F de cuatro aguas^F con canalera^F
tetto^M a bracci^M

窓の例
examples of windows
Beispiele^N für Fenster^N
exemples^M de fenêtres^F
ejemplos^M de ventanas^F
esempi^M di finestre^F

アコーディオン窓
sliding folding window
Faltfenster^N
fenêtre^F en accordéon^M
ventana^F de librillo^M
finestra^F a libro^M

フランス窓
French window
Drehflügel^M nach innen
fenêtre^F à la française^F
ventana^F a la francesa
finestra^F a battenti^M con apertura^F all'interno^M

両開き窓
casement window
Drehflügel^M nach außen
fenêtre^F à l'anglaise^F
ventana^F a la inglesa^F
finestra^F a battenti^M

鎧（よろい）窓
louvered window; *louvred window*
Jalousiefenster^N
fenêtre^F à jalousies^F
ventana^F de celosía^F
finestra^F a gelosia^F

引き違い窓
sliding window
horizontales Schiebefenster^N
fenêtre^F coulissante
ventana^F corredera
finestra^F scorrevole

上げ下げ窓／サッシ窓
sash window
vertikales Schiebefenster^N
fenêtre^F à guillotine^F
ventana^F de guillotina^F
finestra^F a ghigliottina^F

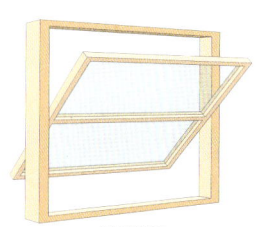

水平回転窓
horizontal pivoting window
Schwingflügel^M
fenêtre^F basculante
ventana^F basculante
finestra^F a bilico^M orizzontale

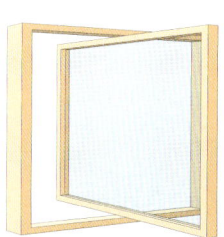

垂直回転窓
vertical pivoting window
Wendeflügel^M
fenêtre^F pivotante
ventana^F pivotante
finestra^F a bilico^M verticale

芸術と建築

建築 | ARCHITECTURE
ARCHITEKTUR | ARCHITECTURE | ARQUITECTURA | ARCHITETTURA

建築の要素

日本語 | 英語 | ドイツ語 | フランス語 | スペイン語 | イタリア語

ドアの例
examples of doors
Beispiele^N für Türen^F
exemples^M de portes^F
ejemplos^M de puertas^F
esempi^M di porte^F

手動式回転ドア
manual revolving door
Drehtür^F
porte^F à tambour^M manuelle
puerta^F giratoria manual
porta^F girevole manuale

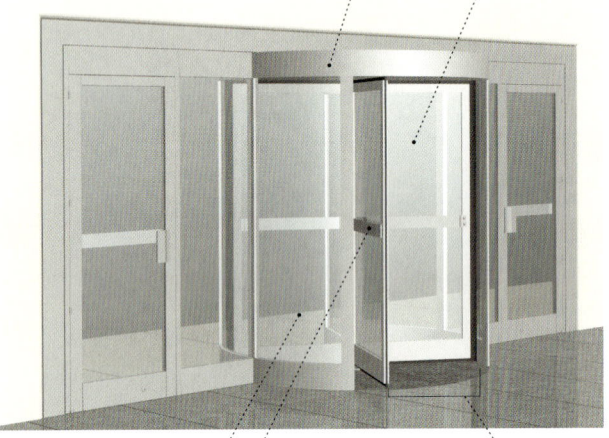

庇（ひさし）／キャノピー
canopy
Gehäusedach^N
couronne^F
tambor^M
cappello^M

扉／ウイング
wing
Flügel^M
vantail^M
hoja^F
battente^M

センサー
motion detector
Bewegungsmelder^M
détecteur^M de mouvement^M
sensor^M de movimiento
rilevatore^M di movimento^M

自動式引き戸／自動ドア
automatic sliding door
automatische Schiebetür^F
porte^F coulissante automatique
puerta^F corredera automática
porta^F scorrevole automatica

囲い
enclosure
Drehgehäuse^N
sas^M
estructura^F interior
alloggiamento

押し棒
push bar
Handgriff^M
barre^F de poussée^F
tirador^M
maniglia^F di spinta^F

区画／コンパートメント
compartment
Zelle^F
compartiment^M
compartimiento^M
vano^F

扉／ウイング
wing
Flügel^M
vantail^M
hoja^F
battente^M

ストリップ
strip
Streifen^M
lanière^F
tira^F
banda^F

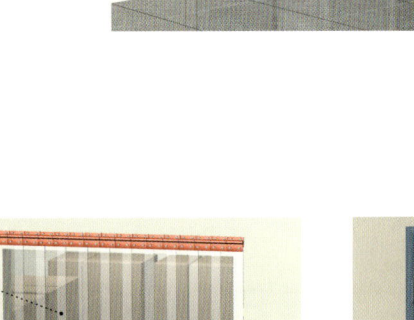

開き戸
conventional door
Drehflügeltür^F
porte^F classique
puerta^F convencional
porta^F a un battente^M

折り畳みドア
folding door
Falttür^F
porte^F pliante
puerta^F plegable
porta^M a libro^M

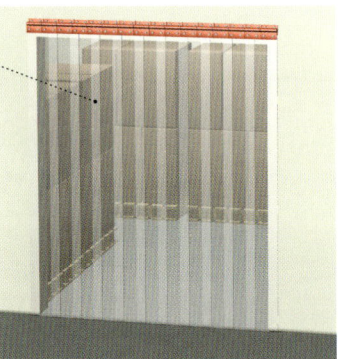

ストリップ・ドア
strip door
Streifenvorhang^M
porte^F à lanières^F
puerta^F de tiras^F
porta^F a bande^F verticali

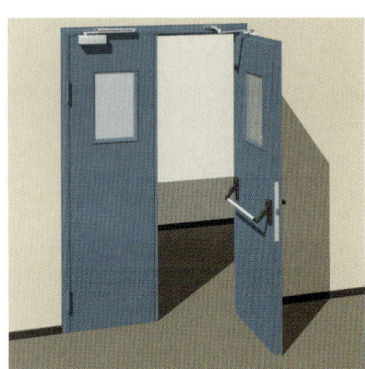

防火扉
fire door
Feuerschutztür^F
porte^F coupe-feu
puerta^F cortafuego
porta^F antincendio

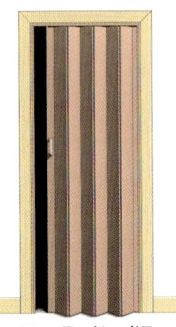

アコーディオン・ドア
sliding folding door
Harmonikatür^F
porte^F accordéon^M
puerta^F de librillo^M
porta^F a fisarmonica^F

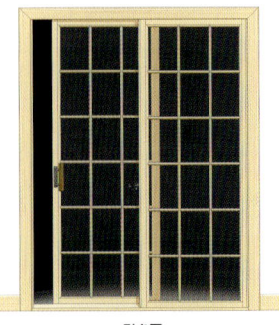

引き戸
sliding door
Schiebetür^F
porte^F coulissante
puerta^F corredera
porta^F scorrevole

オーバー・スライド式車庫扉
sectional garage door
Sektionalgaragentor^N
porte^F de garage^M sectionnelle
puerta^F de garaje^M seccional
porta^F sezionale del garage^M

跳ね上げ式車庫扉
up and over garage door
Schwinggaragentor^N
porte^F de garage^M basculante
puerta^F basculante de garaje^M
porta^F basculante del garage^M

芸術と建築

建築 | ARCHITECTURE
ARCHITEKTUR | ARCHITECTURE | ARQUITECTURA | ARCHITETTURA

エスカレーター

escalator | Rolltreppe[F] | escalier[M] mécanique | escalera[F] mecánica | scala[F] mobile

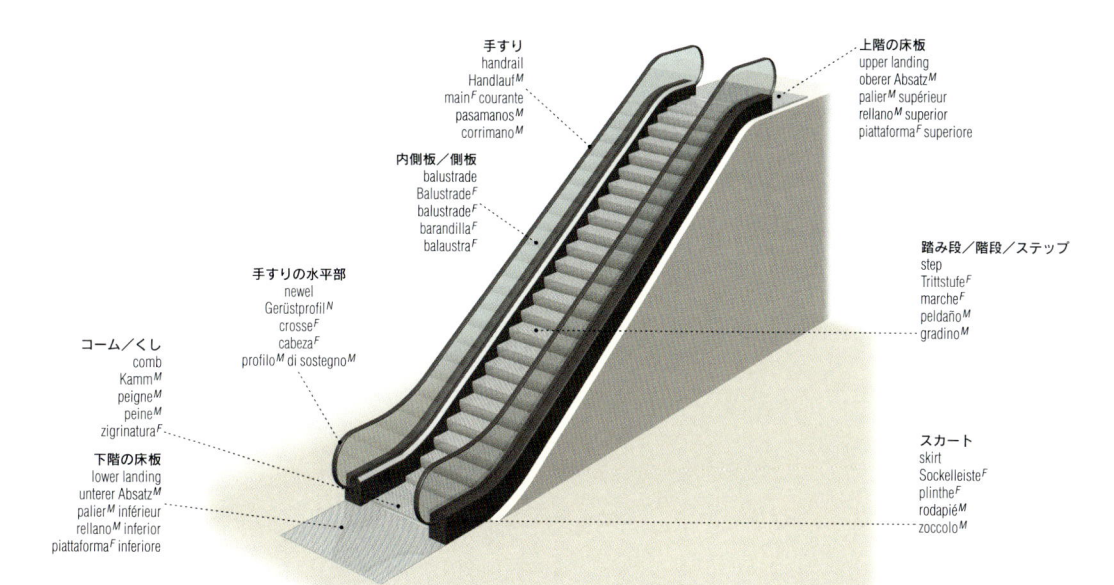

手すり
handrail
Handlauf[M]
main[F] courante
pasamanos[M]
corrimano[M]

上階の床板
upper landing
oberer Absatz[M]
palier[M] supérieur
rellano[M] superior
piattaforma[F] superiore

内側板／側板
balustrade
Balustrade[F]
balustrade[F]
barandilla[F]
balaustra[F]

踏み段／階段／ステップ
step
Trittstufe[F]
marche[F]
peldaño[M]
gradino[M]

手すりの水平部
newel
Gerüstprofil[N]
crosse[F]
cabeza[F]
profilo[M] di sostegno[M]

コーム／くし
comb
Kamm[M]
peigne[M]
peine[M]
zigrinatura[F]

スカート
skirt
Sockelleiste[F]
plinthe[F]
rodapié[M]
zoccolo[M]

下階の床板
lower landing
unterer Absatz[M]
palier[M] inférieur
rellano[M] inferior
piattaforma[F] inferiore

エレベーター

elevator | Aufzug[M] | ascenseur[M] | ascensor[M] | ascensore[M]

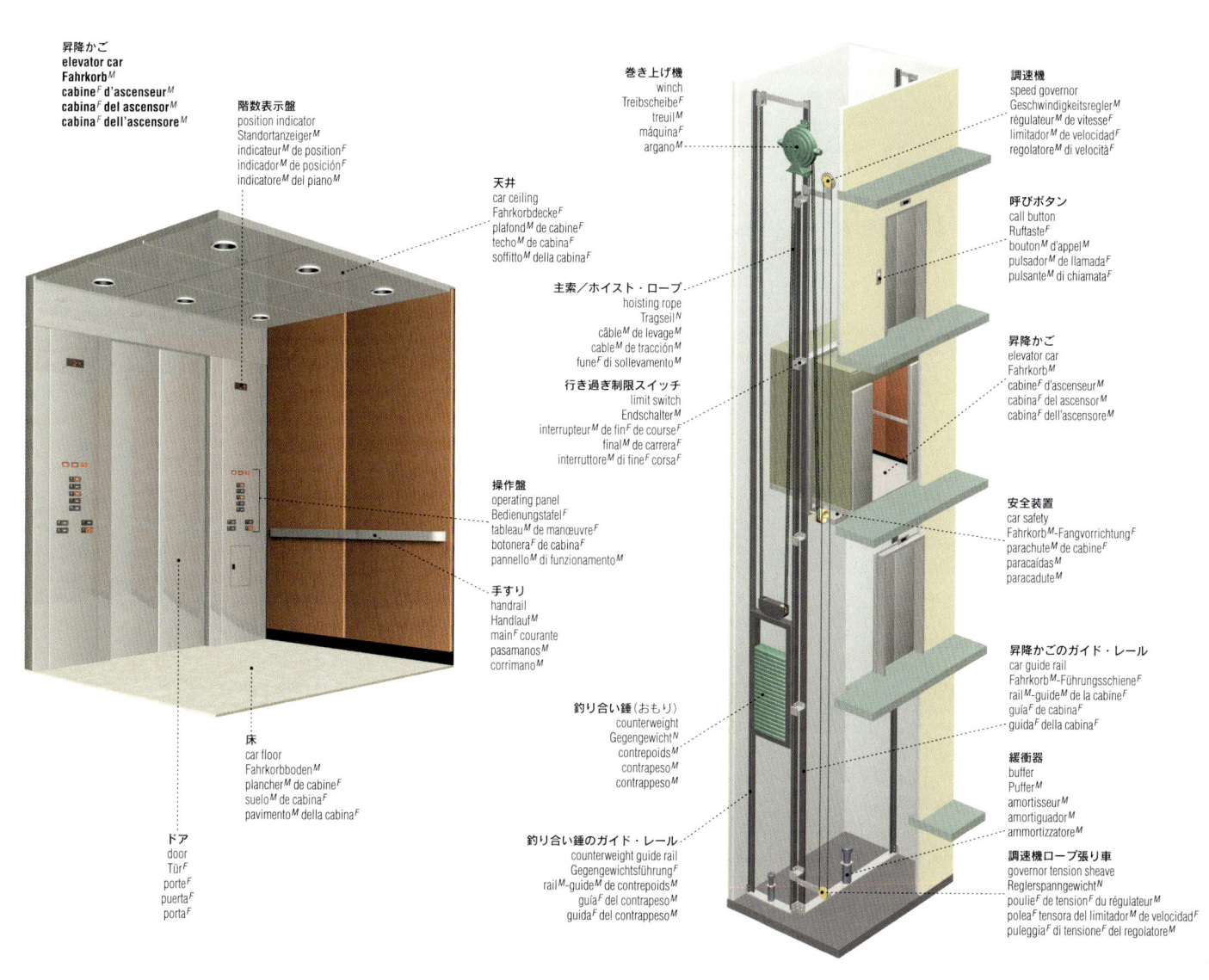

昇降かご
elevator car
Fahrkorb[M]
cabine[F] d'ascenseur[M]
cabina[F] del ascensor[M]
cabina[F] dell'ascensore[M]

階数表示盤
position indicator
Standortanzeiger[M]
indicateur[M] de position[F]
indicador[M] de posición[F]
indicatore[M] del piano[M]

巻き上げ機
winch
Treibscheibe[F]
treuil[M]
máquina[F]
argano[M]

調速機
speed governor
Geschwindigkeitsregler[M]
régulateur[M] de vitesse[F]
limitador[M] de velocidad[F]
regolatore[M] di velocità[F]

天井
car ceiling
Fahrkorbdecke[F]
plafond[M] de cabine[F]
techo[M] de cabina[F]
soffitto[M] della cabina[F]

呼びボタン
call button
Ruftaste[F]
bouton[M] d'appel[M]
pulsador[M] de llamada[F]
pulsante[M] di chiamata[F]

主索／ホイスト・ロープ
hoisting rope
Tragseil[N]
câble[M] de levage[M]
cable[M] de tracción[F]
fune[F] di sollevamento[M]

昇降かご
elevator car
Fahrkorb[M]
cabine[F] d'ascenseur[M]
cabina[F] del ascensor[M]
cabina[F] dell'ascensore[M]

行き過ぎ制限スイッチ
limit switch
Endschalter[M]
interrupteur[M] de fin[F] de course[F]
final[M] de carrera[F]
interruttore[M] di fine[F] corsa[F]

操作盤
operating panel
Bedienungstafel[F]
tableau[M] de manœuvre[F]
botonera[F] de cabina[F]
pannello[M] di funzionamento[M]

安全装置
car safety
Fahrkorb[M]-Fangvorrichtung[F]
parachute[M] de cabine[F]
paracaídas[M]
paracadute[M]

手すり
handrail
Handlauf[M]
main[F] courante
pasamanos[M]
corrimano[M]

昇降かごのガイド・レール
car guide rail
Fahrkorb[M]-Führungsschiene[F]
rail[M]-guide[M] de la cabine[F]
guía[F] de cabina[F]
guida[F] della cabina[F]

釣り合い錘（おもり）
counterweight
Gegengewicht[N]
contrepoids[M]
contrapeso[M]
contrappeso[M]

緩衝器
buffer
Puffer[M]
amortisseur[M]
amortiguador[M]
ammortizzatore[M]

床
car floor
Fahrkorbboden[M]
plancher[M] de cabine[F]
suelo[M] de cabina[F]
pavimento[M] della cabina[F]

ドア
door
Tür[F]
porte[F]
puerta[F]
porta[F]

釣り合い錘のガイド・レール
counterweight guide rail
Gegengewichtsführung[F]
rail[M]-guide[M] de contrepoids[M]
guía[F] del contrapeso[M]
guida[F] del contrappeso[M]

調速機ロープ張り車
governor tension sheave
Reglerspanngewicht[N]
poulie[F] de tension[F] du régulateur[M]
polea[F] tensora del limitador[M] de velocidad[F]
puleggia[F] di tensione[F] del regolatore[M]

芸術と建築

建築 | ARCHITECTURE
ARCHITEKTUR | ARCHITECTURE | ARQUITECTURA | ARCHITETTURA

伝統的な家屋

日本語 | 英語 | ドイツ語 | フランス語 | スペイン語 | イタリア語

traditional houses | traditionelle Wohnhäuser[N] | maisons[F] traditionnelles | viviendas[F] tradicionales | case[F] tradizionali

イグルー
igloo
Iglu[M]
igloo[M]
iglú[M]
igloo[M]

ユルト／パオ
yurt
Jurte[F]
yourte[F]
yurta[F]
iurta[F]

わら葺(ぶ)き小屋
hut
Strohhütte[F]
hutte[F]
choza[F] indígena
capanna[F] di paglia

ウィグワム
wigwam
Wigwam[M]
wigwam[M]
wigwam[M]
wigwam[M]

土小屋
hut
Lehmhütte[F]
case[F]
choza[F]
capanna[F] di fango[M]

イズバ
isba
Isba[F]
isba[F]
isba[F]
isba[F]

ティピー
tepee
Tipi[N]
tipi[M]
tipi[M]
tepee

高床(式)住居
pile dwelling
Pfahlbau[M]
maison[F] sur pilotis[M]
habitación[F] lacustre
palafitta[F]

梁(りょう)
beam
Balken[M]
poutre[F]
viga[F]
trave[F]

アドービ・ハウス
adobe house
Backsteinhaus[N]
maison[F] en adobe[M]
casa[F] de adobes[M]
casa[F] in mattoni[M] cotti

はしご
ladder
Leiter[F]
échelle[F]
escalera[F]
scala[F]

芸術と建築

建築 | ARCHITECTURE
ARCHITEKTUR | ARCHITECTURE | ARQUITECTURA | ARCHITETTURA

都市の住宅

city houses | Häuserformen^F in der Stadt^F | maisons^F de ville^F | viviendas^F urbanas | abitazioni^F urbane

二階建て住宅
two-storey house
zweistöckiges Haus^N
maison^F à deux étages^M
casa^F de dos plantas^M
casa^F a due piani^M

平屋住宅
one-storey house
einstöckiges Haus^N
maison^F de plain-pied^M
casa^F de una planta^F
casa^F a un piano^M

棟割り住宅
semi-detached cottage
Doppelhaus^N
maison^F jumelée
casas^F pareadas
villetta^F bifamiliare

連棟住宅
town houses
Reihenhaus^N
maisons^F en rangée^F
casas^F adosadas
case^F a schiera^F

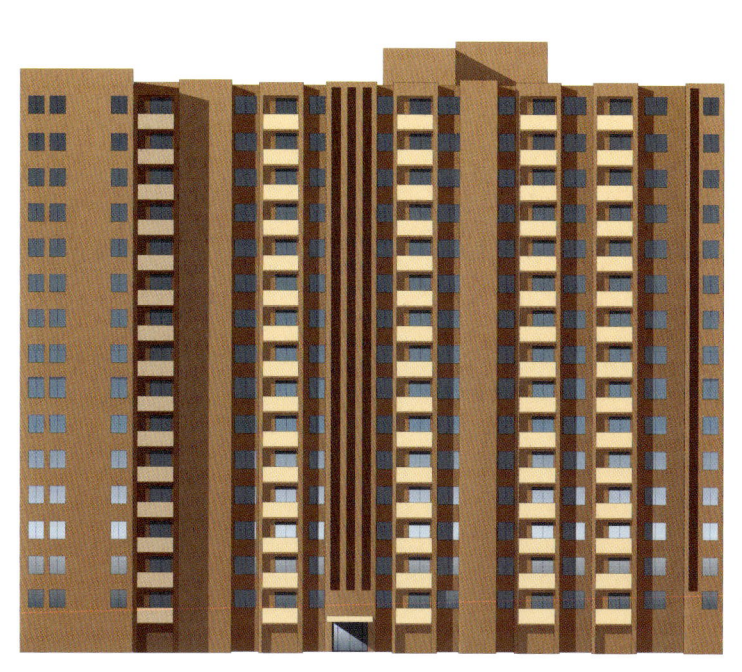

共同住宅
condominiums
Eigentumswohnungen^F
appartements^M en copropriété^F
viviendas^F plurifamiliares
palazzo^M in condominio^M

高層アパート
high-rise apartment; *high-rise block*
Wohnblock^M
tour^F d'habitation^F
bloque^M de apartamentos^M
casatorre^F

芸術と建築

グラフィック・アート | GRAPHIC ARTS
GRAFISCHE KÜNSTE | ARTS GRAPHIQUES | ARTES GRÁFICAS | ARTI GRAFICHE

印刷

日本語 | 英語 | ドイツ語 | フランス語 | スペイン語 | イタリア語

printing | Drucken^N | impression^F | impresión^F | stampa^F

凸版印刷
relief printing
Hochdruck^M
impression^F en relief^M
impresión^F en relieve^M
stampa^F in rilievo^M

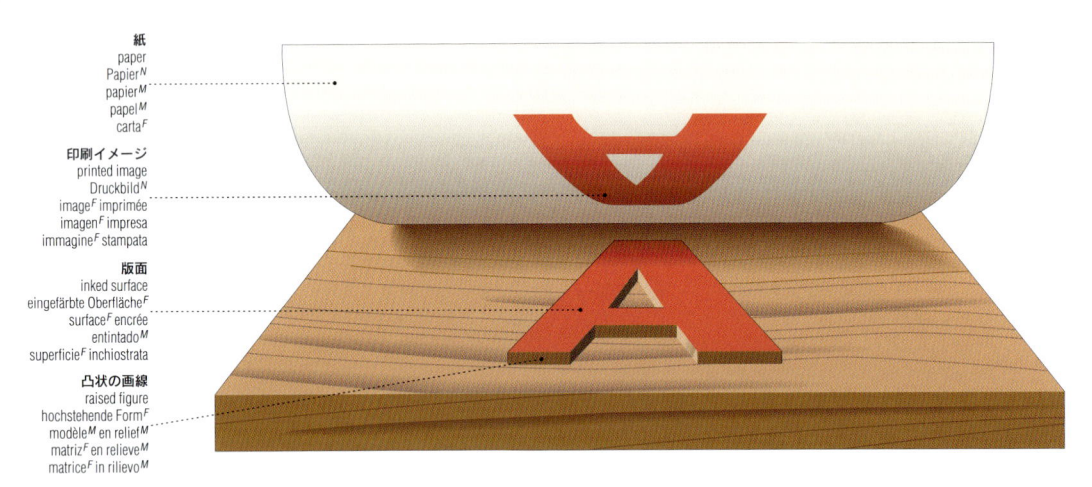

紙
paper
Papier^N
papier^M
papel^M
carta^F

印刷イメージ
printed image
Druckbild^N
image^F imprimée
imagen^F impresa
immagine^F stampata

版面
inked surface
eingefärbte Oberfläche^F
surface^F encrée
entintado^M
superficie^F inchiostrata

凸状の画線
raised figure
hochstehende Form^F
modèle^M en relief^M
matriz^F en relieve^M
matrice^F in rilievo^M

凹版印刷
intaglio printing
Tiefdruck^M
impression^F en creux^M
huecograbado^M
stampa^F in cavo^M

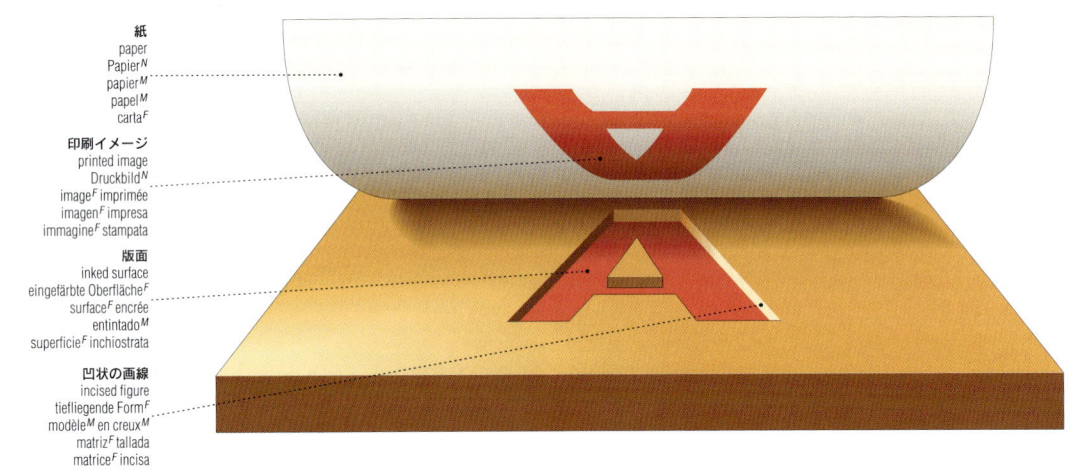

紙
paper
Papier^N
papier^M
papel^M
carta^F

印刷イメージ
printed image
Druckbild^N
image^F imprimée
imagen^F impresa
immagine^F stampata

版面
inked surface
eingefärbte Oberfläche^F
surface^F encrée
entintado^M
superficie^F inchiostrata

凹状の画線
incised figure
tiefliegende Form^F
modèle^M en creux^M
matriz^F tallada
matrice^F incisa

平版（へいはん）印刷
lithographic printing
Lithografie^F
impression^F à plat^M
impresión^F litográfica
litografia^F

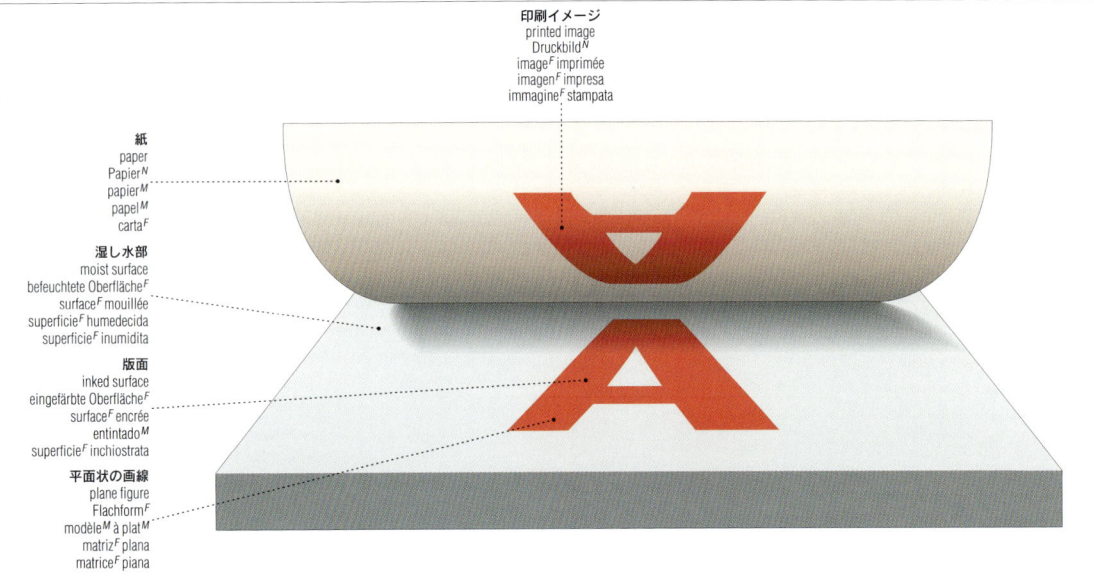

印刷イメージ
printed image
Druckbild^N
image^F imprimée
imagen^F impresa
immagine^F stampata

紙
paper
Papier^N
papier^M
papel^M
carta^F

湿し水部
moist surface
befeuchtete Oberfläche^F
surface^F mouillée
superficie^F humedecida
superficie^F inumidita

版面
inked surface
eingefärbte Oberfläche^F
surface^F encrée
entintado^M
superficie^F inchiostrata

平面状の画線
plane figure
Flachform^F
modèle^M à plat^M
matriz^F plana
matrice^F piana

芸術と建築

グラフィック・アート | GRAPHIC ARTS
GRAFISCHE KÜNSTE | ARTS GRAPHIQUES | ARTES GRÁFICAS | ARTI GRAFICHE

凸版印刷方式

relief printing process | Hochdruckverfahren[N] | gravure[F] en relief[M] | impresión[F] en relieve[F] | metodo[M] di stampa[F] in rilievo[M]

器具
equipment
Ausstattung[F]
matériel[M]
equipo[M]
attrezzatura[F]

木槌／丸才（まるさい）
mallet
Schlegel[M]
maillet[M]
maza[F]
mazzuolo[M]

丸のみ
U-shaped gouge
Rundeisen[N]
gouge[F] creuse
gubia[F]
sgorbia[F] a U

三角のみ
V-shaped gouge
Geißfuß[M]
gouge[F] en V
cincel[M] de rincón[M]
sgorbia[F] a V

平のみ
chisel
Beitel[M]
ciseau[M]
escoplo[M]
scalpello[M]

小刀
knife
Messer[N]
canif[M]
cuchillo[M] de contornear
coltello[M]

たがね
block cutter
gerades Hohleisen[N]
burin[M]
buril[M]
bulino[M]

インク
ink
Farbe[F]
encre[F]
tinta[F]
inchiostro[M]

へら
spatula
Spachtel[M]
spatule[F]
espátula[F]
spatola[F]

練り盤
inking slab
Farbstein[M]
marbre[M]
plancha[F] de entintado[M]
lastra[F] inchiostratrice

インク
ink
Farbe[F]
encre[F]
tinta[F]
inchiostro[M]

インク・ローラー
brayer; ink roller
Farbwalze[F]
rouleau[M] d'encrage[M]
rodillo[M] entintador
rullo[M] inchiostratore

バレン
baren
Baren[M]
baren[M]
frotador[M]
tampone[M]

板目木版用版木
woodcut
Holzstock[M]
gravure[F] sur bois[M] de fil[M]
bloque[M] de madera[F] grabado
xilografia[F] di filo[M]

木口（こぐち）木版用版木
wood engraving
Holzschnitt[M]
gravure[F] sur bois[M] debout
bloque[M] de madera[F] para grabar
xilografia[F] di testa[F]

圧力調整ねじ
pressure screw
Pressspindel[F]
vis[F] de pression[F]
tornillo[M] de presión[F]
vite[F] di pressione[F]

フェルト
felt; blanket
Druckbogen[M]
lange[M]
fieltro[M]
tessuto[M] gommato

版面台／ベッド・プレート
press bed
Drucktisch[M]
table[F]
tímpano[M]
piano[M]

エッチング・プレス機
etching press
Zylinderdruckpresse[F]
presse[F] à taille-douce[F]
prensa[F] de aguafuerte[F]
torchio[M] di stampa[F] a due cilindri[M]

上部ローラー
top cylinder
Oberwalze[F]
cylindre[M] supérieur
cilindro[M] superior
cilindro[M] superiore

下部ローラー
bottom cylinder
Antriebswalze[F]
cylindre[M] inférieur
cilindro[M] inferior
cilindro[M] inferiore

ハンドル／回転棒
flywheel; capstan
Drehkreuz[N]
moulinet[M]
volante[M] de aspas[F]
maniglia[F] a crociera[F]

芸術と建築

421

グラフィック・アート | GRAPHIC ARTS
GRAFISCHE KÜNSTE | ARTS GRAPHIQUES | ARTES GRÁFICAS | ARTI GRAFICHE

凹版印刷方式

intaglio printing process | Tiefdruckverfahren^N | gravure^F en creux^M | impresión^F en huecograbado^M | metodo^M di stampa^F in cavo^M

日本語 | 英語 | ドイツ語 | フランス語 | スペイン語 | イタリア語

器具
equipment
Ausstattung^F
matériel^M
equipo^M
attrezzatura^F

刷毛（はけ）
brush
Pinsel^M
pinceau^M
bruza^F
pennello^M

ロッカー／ベルソー
rocking tool
Wiegestahl^M
berceau^M
graneador^M
rocker^M

ルーレット
roulette
Roulette^F
roulette^F
ruedecilla^F
roulette^F

銅板
copper plate; copperplate
Kupferplatte^F
plaque^F de cuivre^M
placa^F de cobre^M
lastra^F di rame^M

ドライポイント
drypoint
Kaltnadel^F
pointe^F sèche
punta^F seca
puntasecca^F

つやべら／バニッシャー
burnisher
Polierstahl^M
brunissoir^M
bruñidor^M
brunitoio^M

蝋（ろう）引き灯芯
smoking candle; taper
dünne Wachskerze^F
rat^M de cave^F
cabo^F
candelotto^M

手万力／ハンド・バイス
hand vice
Plattenhalter^M
étau^M
pinza^F
morsetto^M a mano^F

角刃引き／スクレーパー
scraper
Schaber^M
ébarboir^M
rascador^M
raschietto^M

燻煙（くんえん）器
smoking-apparatus
Räucherapparat^M
enfumoir^M
ahumador^M
bruciatore^M

寒冷紗／ターラタン／薄地モスリン
tarlatan
Tarlatan^M
tarlatane^F
tarlatana^M
tarlatana^F

タンポン／ダバー
dabber
Tampon^M
tampon^M
tampón^M
tampone^M

ニス・ローラー
varnish-roller
Lederwalze^F
rouleau^M à vernir
rodillo^M para barnizar
rullo^M per verniciare

油砥石（といし）
oilstone
Ölstein^M
pierre^F à aiguiser
piedra^F al aceite^M
pietra^F da cote^F

芸術と建築

422

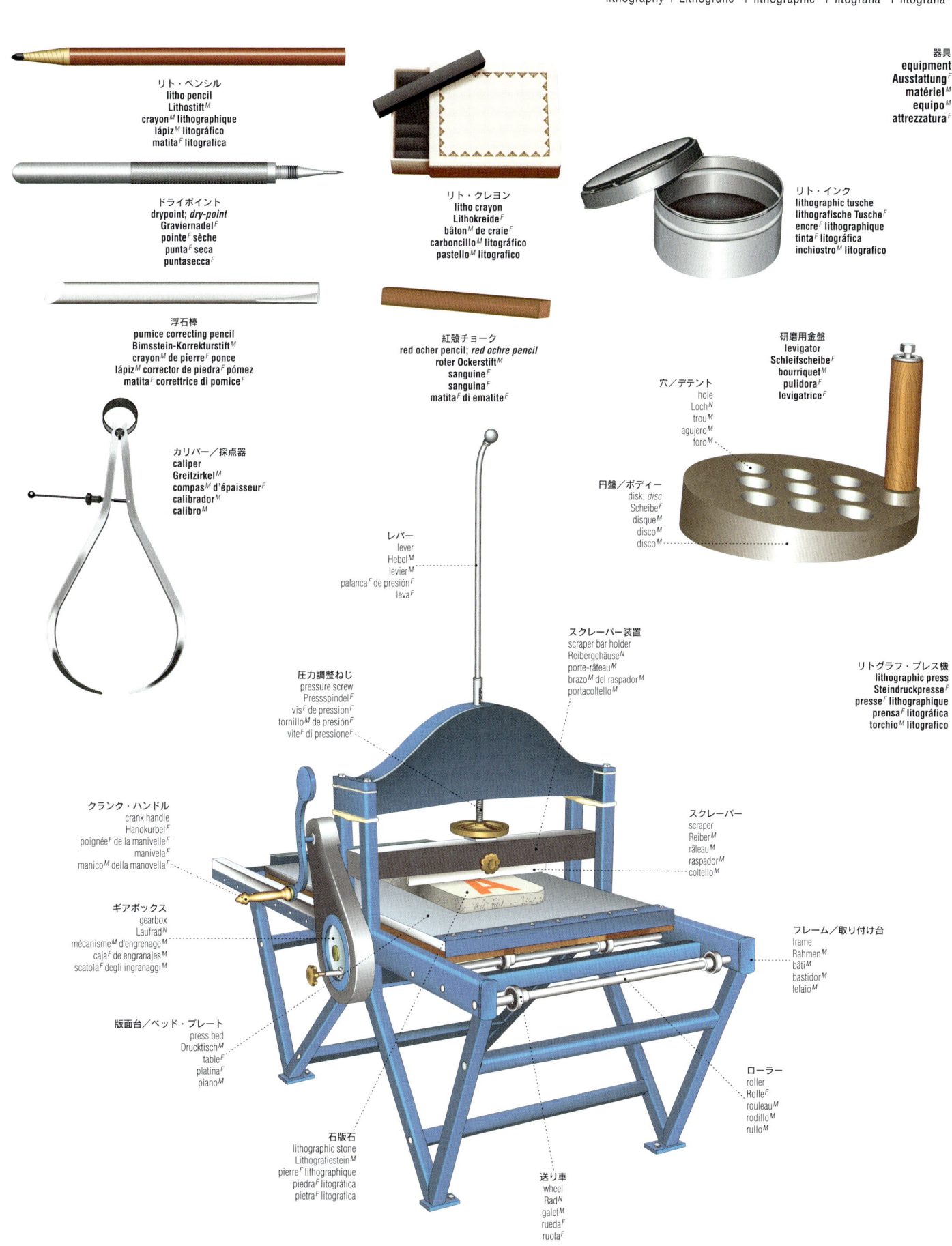

グラフィック・アート | GRAPHIC ARTS
GRAFISCHE KÜNSTE | ARTS GRAPHIQUES | ARTES GRÁFICAS | ARTI GRAFICHE

平版印刷方式

lithography | Lithografie^F | lithographie^F | litografía^F | litografia^F

リト・ペンシル
litho pencil
Lithostift^M
crayon^M lithographique
lápiz^M litográfico
matita^F litografica

ドライポイント
drypoint; dry-point
Graviernadel^F
pointe^F sèche
punta^F seca
puntasecca^F

浮石棒
pumice correcting pencil
Bimsstein-Korrekturstift^M
crayon^M de pierre^F ponce
lápiz^M corrector de piedra^F pómez
matita^F correttrice di pomice^F

リト・クレヨン
litho crayon
Lithokreide^F
bâton^M de craie^F
carboncillo^M litográfico
pastello^M litografico

紅殻チョーク
red ocher pencil; red ochre pencil
roter Ockerstift^M
sanguine^F
sanguina^F
matita^F di ematite^F

器具
equipment
Ausstattung^F
matériel^M
equipo^M
attrezzatura^F

リト・インク
lithographic tusche
lithografische Tusche^F
encre^F lithographique
tinta^F litográfica
inchiostro^M litografico

研磨用金盤
levigator
Schleifscheibe^F
bourriquet^M
pulidora^F
levigatrice^F

穴／デテント
hole
Loch^N
trou^M
agujero^M
foro^M

円盤／ボディー
disk; disc
Scheibe^F
disque^M
disco^M
disco^M

カリバー／採点器
caliper
Greifzirkel^M
compas^M d'épaisseur^F
calibrador^M
calibro^M

レバー
lever
Hebel^M
levier^M
palanca^F de presión^F
leva^F

スクレーパー装置
scraper bar holder
Reibergehäuse^N
porte-râteau^M
brazo^M del raspador^M
portacoltello^M

リトグラフ・プレス機
lithographic press
Steindruckpresse^F
presse^F lithographique
prensa^F litográfica
torchio^M litografico

圧力調整ねじ
pressure screw
Pressspindel^F
vis^F de pression^F
tornillo^M de presión^F
vite^F di pressione^F

クランク・ハンドル
crank handle
Handkurbel^F
poignée^F de la manivelle^F
manivela^F
manico^M della manovella^F

ギアボックス
gearbox
Laufrad^N
mécanisme^M d'engrenage^M
caja^F de engranajes^M
scatola^F degli ingranaggi^M

版面台／ベッド・プレート
press bed
Drucktisch^M
table^F
platina^F
piano^M

スクレーパー
scraper
Reiber^M
râteau^M
raspador^M
coltello^M

フレーム／取り付け台
frame
Rahmen^M
bâti^M
bastidor^M
telaio^M

ローラー
roller
Rolle^F
rouleau^M
rodillo^M
rullo^M

石版石
lithographic stone
Lithografiestein^M
pierre^F lithographique
piedra^F litográfica
pietra^F litografica

送り車
wheel
Rad^N
galet^M
rueda^F
ruota^F

芸術と建築

423

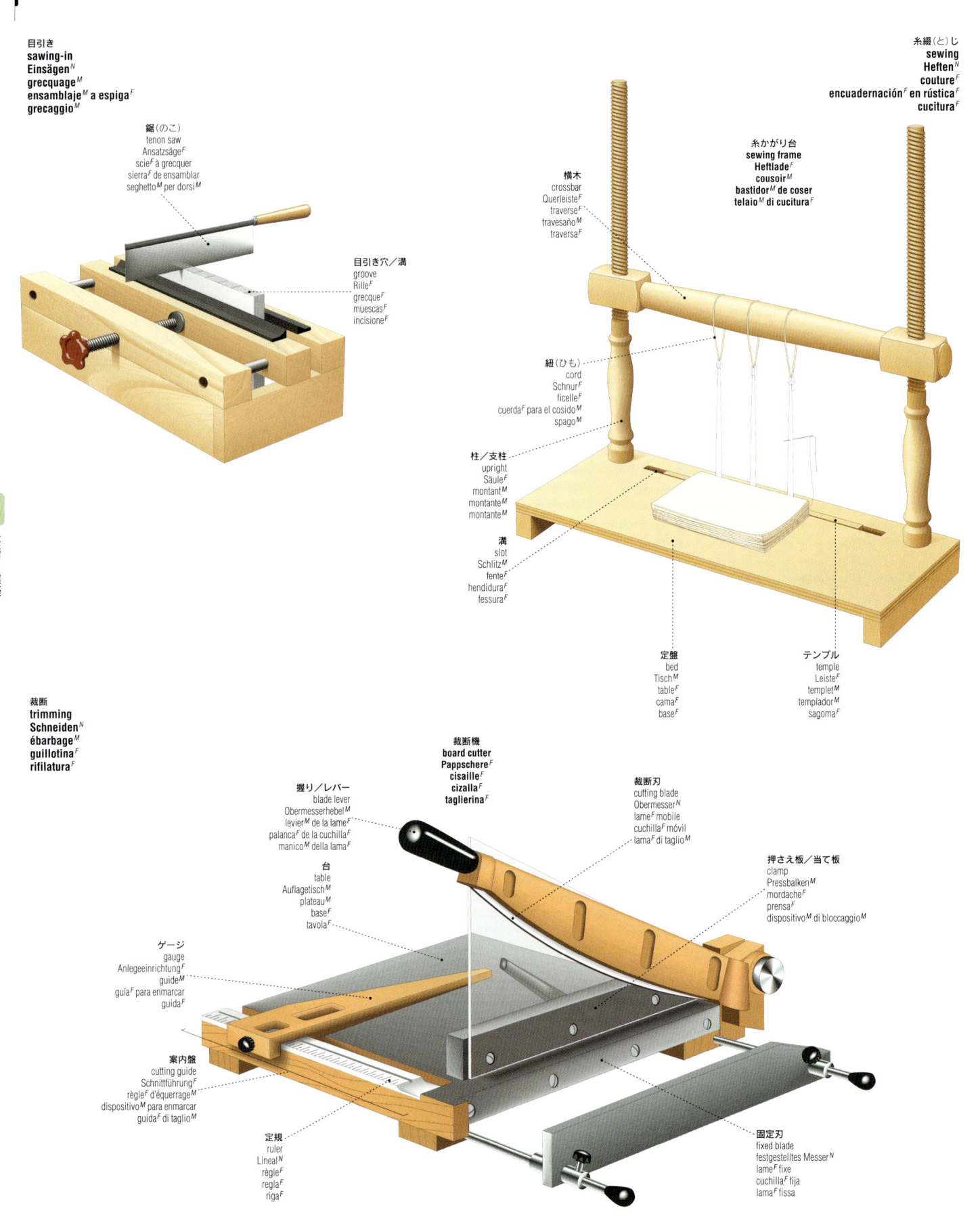

グラフィック・アート | GRAPHIC ARTS
GRAFISCHE KÜNSTE | ARTS GRAPHIQUES | ARTES GRÁFICAS | ARTI GRAFICHE

製本

日本語 | 英語 | ドイツ語 | フランス語 | スペイン語 | イタリア語

fine bookbinding | Handbuchbinderei^F | reliure^F d'art^M | encuadernación^F a mano^F | rilegatura^F a mano^F

目引き
sawing-in
Einsägen^N
grecquage^M
ensamblaje^M a espiga^F
grecaggio^M

鋸（のこ）
tenon saw
Ansatzsäge^F
scie^F à grecquer
sierra^F de ensamblar
seghetto^M per dorsi^M

目引き穴／溝
groove
Rille^F
grecque^F
muescas^F
incisione^F

糸綴（と）じ
sewing
Heften^N
couture^F
encuadernación^F en rústica^F
cucitura^F

糸かがり台
sewing frame
Heftlade^F
cousoir^M
bastidor^M de coser
telaio^M di cucitura^F

横木
crossbar
Querleiste^F
traverse^F
travesaño^M
traversa^F

紐（ひも）
cord
Schnur^F
ficelle^F
cuerda^F para el cosido^M
spago^M

柱／支柱
upright
Säule^F
montant^M
montante^M
montante^M

溝
slot
Schlitz^M
fente^F
hendidura^F
fessura^F

定盤
bed
Tisch^M
table^F
cama^F
base^F

テンプル
temple
Leiste^F
templet^M
templador^M
sagoma^F

裁断
trimming
Schneiden^N
ébarbage^M
guillotina^F
rifilatura^F

裁断機
board cutter
Pappschere^F
cisaille^F
cizalla^F
taglierina^F

裁断刃
cutting blade
Obermesser^N
lame^F mobile
cuchilla^F móvil
lama^F di taglio^M

握り／レバー
blade lever
Obermesserhebel^M
levier^M de la lame
palanca^F de la cuchilla^F
manico^M della lama^F

押さえ板／当て板
clamp
Pressbalken^M
mordache^F
prensa^F
dispositivo^M di bloccaggio^M

台
table
Auflagetisch^M
plateau^M
base^F
tavola^F

ゲージ
gauge
Anlegeeinrichtung^F
guide^M
guía^F para enmarcar
guida^F

案内盤
cutting guide
Schnittführung^F
règle^F d'équerrage^M
dispositivo^M para enmarcar
guida^F di taglio^M

定規
ruler
Lineal^N
règle^F
regla^F
riga^F

固定刃
fixed blade
festgestelltes Messer^N
lame^F fixe
cuchilla^F fija
lama^F fissa

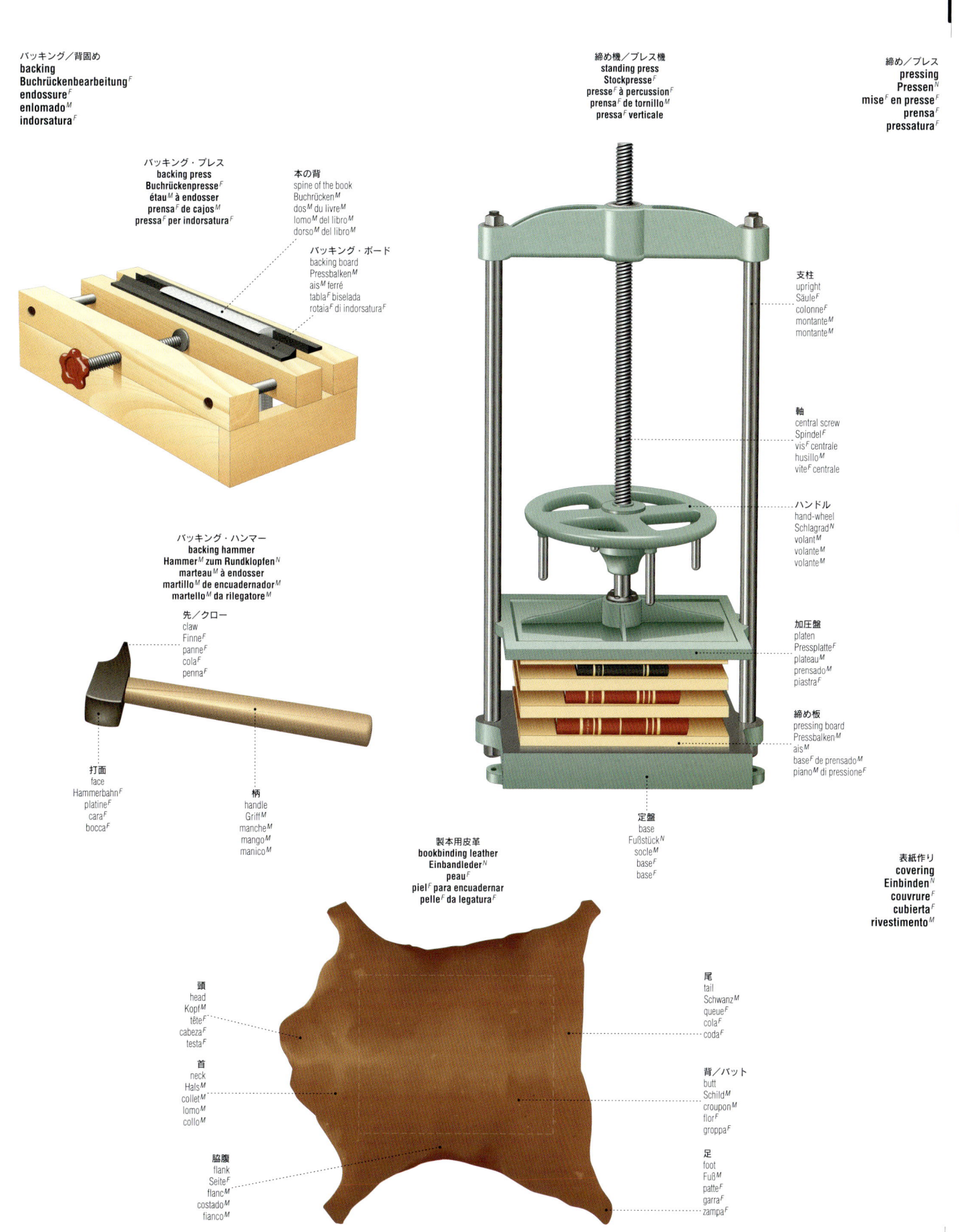

グラフィック・アート | GRAPHIC ARTS
GRAFISCHE KÜNSTE | ARTS GRAPHIQUES | ARTES GRÁFICAS | ARTI GRAFICHE

製本

バッキング／背固め
backing
Buchrückenbearbeitung^F
endossure^F
enlomado^M
indorsatura^F

バッキング・プレス
backing press
Buchrückenpresse^F
étau^M à endosser
prensa^F de cajos^M
pressa^F per indorsatura^F

本の背
spine of the book
Buchrücken^M
dos^M du livre^M
lomo^M del libro^M
dorso^M del libro^M

バッキング・ボード
backing board
Pressbalken^M
ais^M ferré
tabla^F biselada
rotaia^F di indorsatura^F

バッキング・ハンマー
backing hammer
Hammer^M zum Rundklopfen^N
marteau^M à endosser
martillo^M de encuadernador^M
martello^M da rilegatore^M

先／クロー
claw
Finne^F
panne^F
cola^F
penna^F

打面
face
Hammerbahn^F
platine^F
cara^F
bocca^F

柄
handle
Griff^M
manche^M
mango^M
manico^M

締め機／プレス機
standing press
Stockpresse^F
presse^F à percussion^F
prensa^F de tornillo^M
pressa^F verticale

支柱
upright
Säule^F
colonne^F
montante^M
montante^M

軸
central screw
Spindel^F
vis^F centrale
husillo^M
vite^F centrale

ハンドル
hand-wheel
Schlagrad^N
volant^M
volante^M
volante^M

加圧盤
platen
Pressplatte^F
plateau^M
prensado^M
piastra^F

締め板
pressing board
Pressbalken^M
ais^M
base^F de prensado^M
piano^M di pressione^F

定盤
base
Fußstück^N
socle^M
base^F
base^F

製本用皮革
bookbinding leather
Einbandleder^N
peau^F
piel^F para encuadernar
pelle^F da legatura^F

締め／プレス
pressing
Pressen^N
mise^F en presse^F
prensa^F
pressatura^F

表紙作り
covering
Einbinden^N
couvrure^F
cubierta^F
rivestimento^M

頭
head
Kopf^M
tête^F
cabeza^F
testa^F

首
neck
Hals^M
collet^M
lomo^M
collo^M

脇腹
flank
Seite^F
flanc^M
costado^M
fianco^M

尾
tail
Schwanz^M
queue^F
cola^F
coda^F

背／バット
butt
Schild^M
croupon^M
flor^F
groppa^F

足
foot
Fuß^M
patte^F
garra^F
zampa^F

芸術と建築

425

グラフィック・アート | GRAPHIC ARTS
GRAFISCHE KÜNSTE | ARTS GRAPHIQUES | ARTES GRÁFICAS | ARTI GRAFICHE

製本

日本語 | 英語 | ドイツ語 | フランス語 | スペイン語 | イタリア語

装丁本
bound book
gebundenes Buch[N]
livre[M] relié
libro[M] encuadernado
libro[M] rilegato

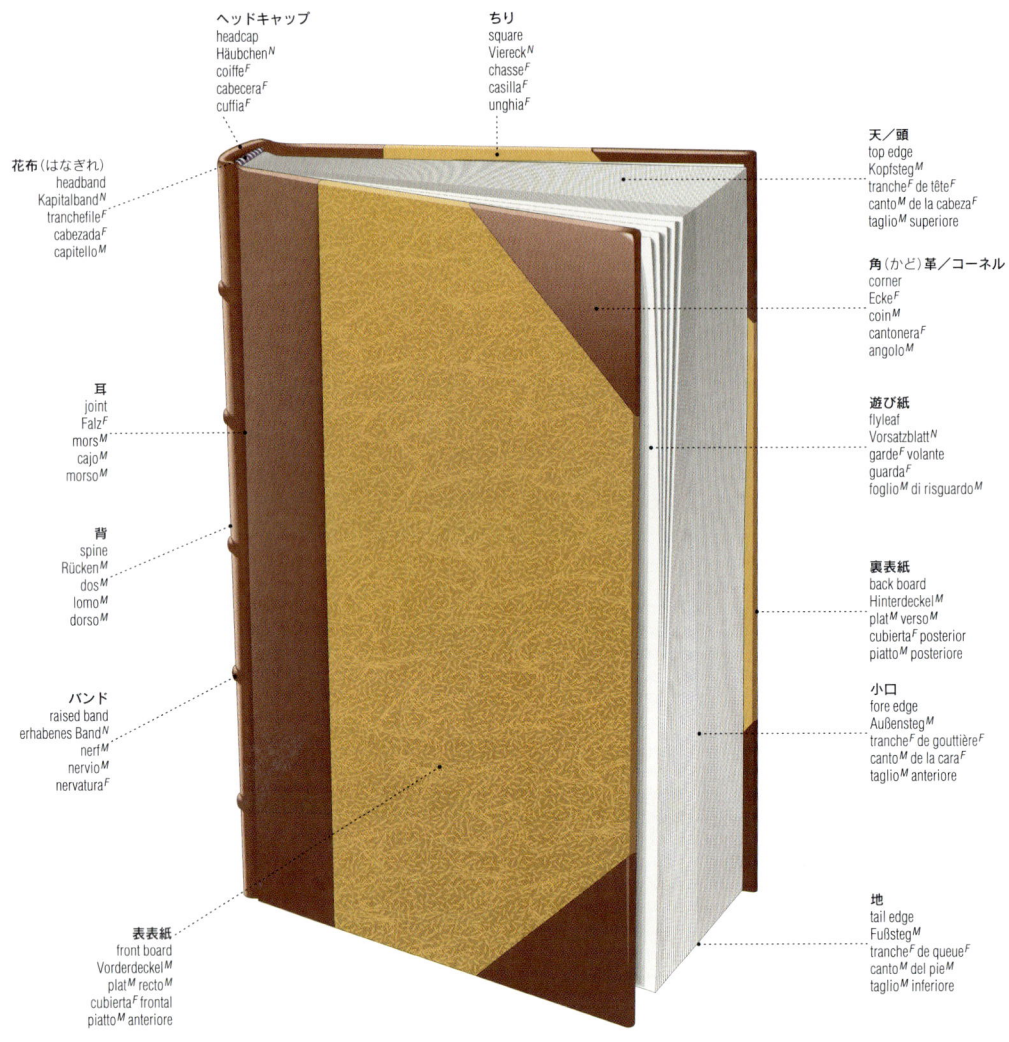

ヘッドキャップ
headcap
Häubchen[N]
coiffe[F]
cabecera[F]
cuffia[F]

ちり
square
Viereck[N]
chasse[F]
casilla[F]
unghia[F]

天／頭
top edge
Kopfsteg[M]
tranche[F] de tête[F]
canto[M] de la cabeza[F]
taglio[M] superiore

花布（はなぎれ）
headband
Kapitalband[N]
tranchefile[F]
cabezada[F]
capitello[M]

角（かど）革／コーネル
corner
Ecke[F]
coin[M]
cantonera[F]
angolo[M]

耳
joint
Falz[F]
mors[M]
cajo[M]
morso[M]

遊び紙
flyleaf
Vorsatzblatt[N]
garde[F] volante
guarda[F]
foglio[M] di risguardo[M]

背
spine
Rücken[M]
dos[M]
lomo[M]
dorso[M]

裏表紙
back board
Hinterdeckel[M]
plat[M] verso[M]
cubierta[F] posterior
piatto[M] posteriore

バンド
raised band
erhabenes Band[N]
nerf[M]
nervio[M]
nervatura[F]

小口
fore edge
Außensteg[M]
tranche[F] de gouttière[F]
canto[M] de la cara[F]
taglio[M] anteriore

表表紙
front board
Vorderdeckel[M]
plat[M] recto[M]
cubierta[F] frontal
piatto[M] anteriore

地
tail edge
Fußsteg[M]
tranche[F] de queue[F]
canto[M] del pie[M]
taglio[M] inferiore

丁合い
gathering
Zusammentragen[N]
plaçure[F]
cosido[M]
raccolta[F]

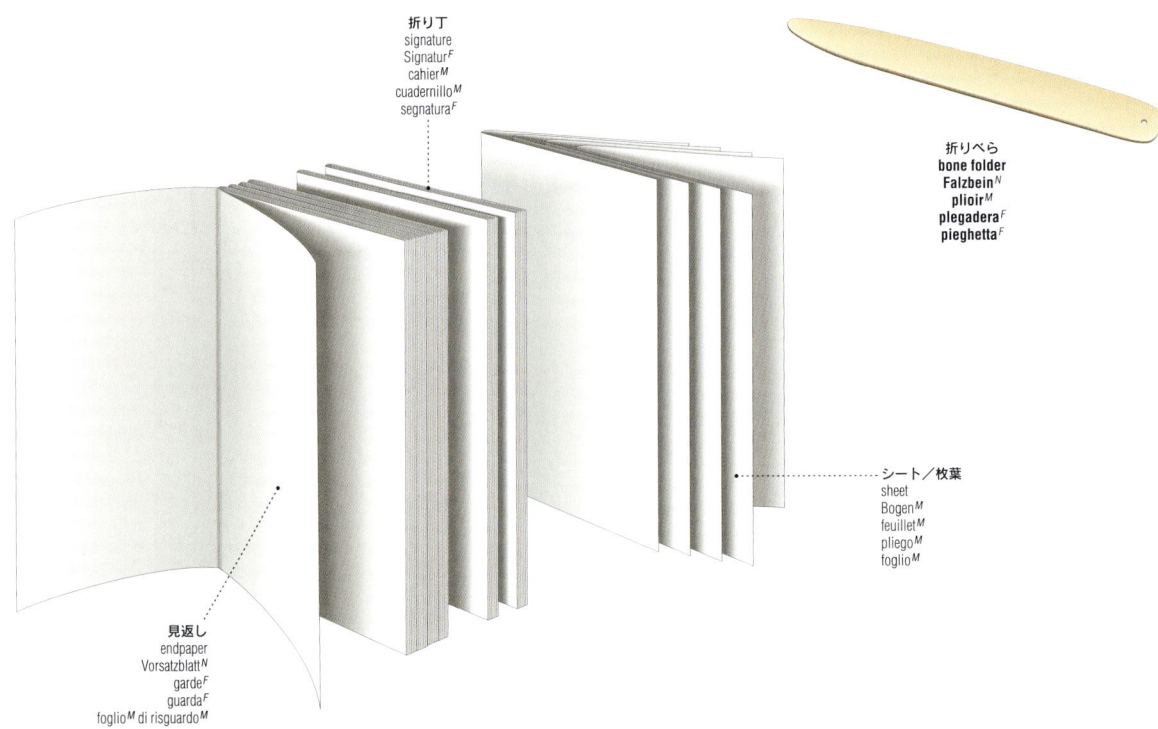

折り丁
signature
Signatur[F]
cahier[M]
cuadernillo[M]
segnatura[F]

折りべら
bone folder
Falzbein[N]
plioir[M]
plegadera[F]
pieghetta[F]

シート／枚葉
sheet
Bogen[M]
feuillet[M]
pliego[M]
foglio[M]

見返し
endpaper
Vorsatzblatt[N]
garde[F]
guarda[F]
foglio[M] di risguardo[M]

芸術と建築

426

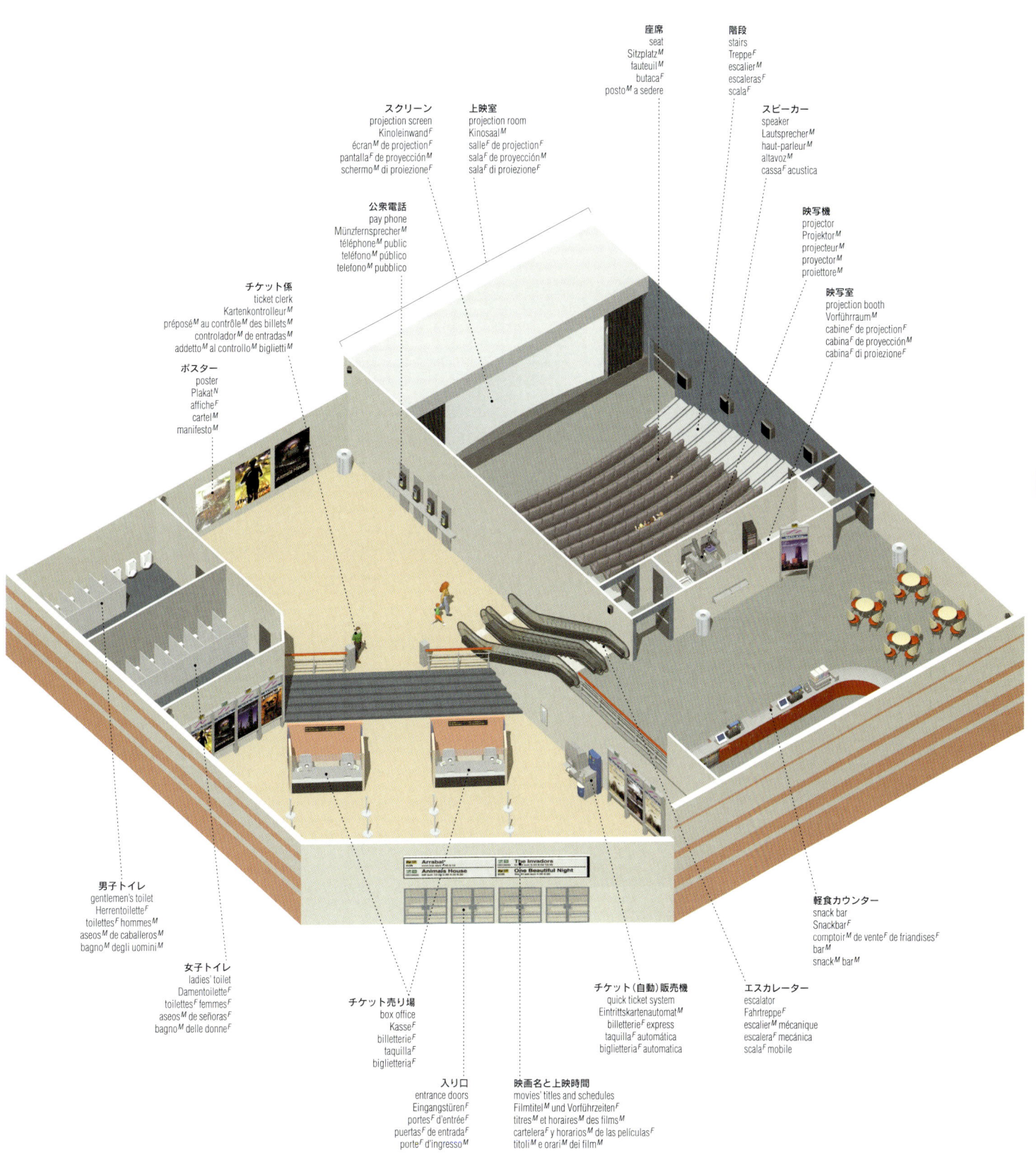

舞台芸術 | PERFORMING ARTS
DARSTELLENDE KÜNSTE | ARTS DE LA SCÈNE | ARTES ESCÉNICAS | ARTI SCENICHE

映画館

movie theater | Kino[N] | cinéma[M] | cine[M] | cinema[M]

座席
seat
Sitzplatz[M]
fauteuil[M]
butaca[F]
posto[M] a sedere

階段
stairs
Treppe[F]
escalier[M]
escaleras[F]
scala[F]

スクリーン
projection screen
Kinoleinwand[F]
écran[M] de projection[F]
pantalla[F] de proyección[F]
schermo[M] di proiezione[F]

上映室
projection room
Kinosaal[M]
salle[F] de projection[F]
sala[F] de proyección[F]
sala[F] di proiezione[F]

スピーカー
speaker
Lautsprecher[M]
haut-parleur[M]
altavoz[M]
cassa[F] acustica

公衆電話
pay phone
Münzfernsprecher[M]
téléphone[M] public
teléfono[M] público
telefono[M] pubblico

映写機
projector
Projektor[M]
projecteur[M]
proyector[M]
proiettore[M]

チケット係
ticket clerk
Kartenkontrolleur[M]
préposé[M] au contrôle[M] des billets[M]
controlador[M] de entradas[F]
addetto[M] al controllo[M] biglietti[M]

映写室
projection booth
Vorführraum[M]
cabine[F] de projection[F]
cabina[F] de proyección[F]
cabina[F] di proiezione[F]

ポスター
poster
Plakat[N]
affiche[F]
cartel[M]
manifesto[M]

芸術と建築

男子トイレ
gentlemen's toilet
Herrentoilette[F]
toilettes[F] hommes[M]
aseos[M] de caballeros[M]
bagno[M] degli uomini[M]

女子トイレ
ladies' toilet
Damentoilette[F]
toilettes[F] femmes[F]
aseos[M] de señoras[F]
bagno[M] delle donne[F]

チケット売り場
box office
Kasse[F]
billetterie[F]
taquilla[F]
biglietteria[F]

チケット(自動)販売機
quick ticket system
Eintrittskartenautomat[M]
billetterie[F] express
taquilla[F] automática
biglietteria[F] automatica

エスカレーター
escalator
Fahrtreppe[F]
escalier[M] mécanique
escalera[F] mecánica
scala[F] mobile

軽食カウンター
snack bar
Snackbar[F]
comptoir[M] de vente[F] de friandises[F]
bar[M]
snack[M] bar[M]

入り口
entrance doors
Eingangstüren[F]
portes[F] d'entrée[F]
puertas[F] de entrada[F]
porte[F] d'ingresso[M]

映画名と上映時間
movies' titles and schedules
Filmtitel[M] und Vorführzeiten[F]
titres[M] et horaires[M] des films[M]
cartelera[F] y horarios[M] de las películas[F]
titoli[M] e orari[M] dei film[M]

427

映画のセット

movie set | Aufnahmebühne[F] | plateau[M] de tournage | plató[M] de rodaje[M] | set[M] delle riprese[F]

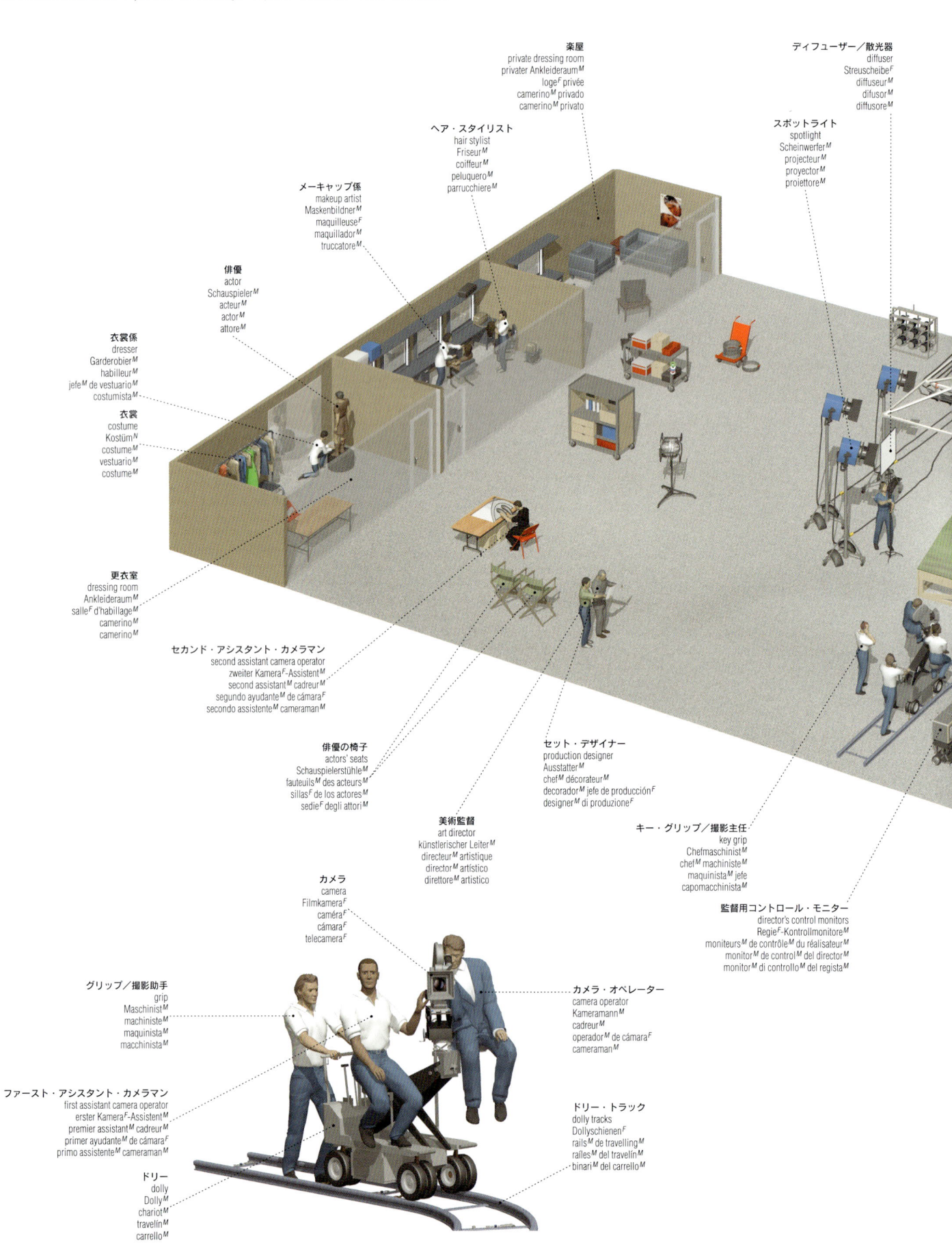

舞台芸術 | PERFORMING ARTS
DARSTELLENDE KÜNSTE | ARTS DE LA SCÈNE | ARTES ESCÉNICAS | ARTI SCENICHE

日本語 | 英語 | ドイツ語 | フランス語 | スペイン語 | イタリア語

- 楽屋 / private dressing room / privater Ankleideraum[M] / loge[F] privée / camerino[M] privado / camerino[M] privato
- ヘア・スタイリスト / hair stylist / Friseur[M] / coiffeur[M] / peluquero[M] / parrucchiere[M]
- メーキャップ係 / makeup artist / Maskenbildner[M] / maquilleuse[F] / maquillador[M] / truccatore[M]
- 俳優 / actor / Schauspieler[M] / acteur[M] / actor[M] / attore[M]
- 衣裳係 / dresser / Garderobier[M] / habilleur[M] / jefe[M] de vestuario[M] / costumista[M]
- 衣裳 / costume / Kostüm[N] / costume[M] / vestuario[M] / costume[M]
- 更衣室 / dressing room / Ankleideraum[M] / salle[F] d'habillage[M] / camerino[M] / camerino[M]
- セカンド・アシスタント・カメラマン / second assistant camera operator / zweiter Kamera[F]-Assistent[M] / second assistant[M] cadreur[M] / segundo ayudante[M] de cámara[F] / secondo assistente[M] cameraman[M]
- 俳優の椅子 / actors' seats / Schauspielerstühle[M] / fauteuils[M] des acteurs[M] / sillas[F] de los actores[M] / sedie[F] degli attori[M]
- セット・デザイナー / production designer / Ausstatter[M] / chef[M] décorateur[M] / decorador[M] jefe de producción[F] / designer[M] di produzione[F]
- 美術監督 / art director / künstlerischer Leiter[M] / directeur[M] artistique / director[M] artístico / direttore[M] artistico
- カメラ / camera / Filmkamera[F] / caméra[F] / cámara[F] / telecamera[F]
- グリップ／撮影助手 / grip / Maschinist[M] / machiniste[M] / maquinista[M] / macchinista[M]
- ファースト・アシスタント・カメラマン / first assistant camera operator / erster Kamera[F]-Assistent[M] / premier assistant[M] cadreur[M] / primer ayudante[M] de cámara[F] / primo assistente[M] cameraman[M]
- ドリー / dolly / Dolly[M] / chariot[M] / travelín[M] / carrello[M]
- カメラ・オペレーター / camera operator / Kameramann[M] / cadreur[M] / operador[M] de cámara[F] / cameraman[M]
- ドリー・トラック / dolly tracks / Dollyschienen[F] / rails[M] de travelling[M] / raíles[M] del travelín[M] / binari[M] del carrello[M]
- 監督用コントロール・モニター / director's control monitors / Regie[F]-Kontrollmonitore[M] / moniteurs[M] de contrôle[M] du réalisateur[M] / monitor[M] de control[M] del director[M] / monitor[M] di controllo[M] del regista[M]
- キー・グリップ／撮影主任 / key grip / Chefmaschinist[M] / chef[M] machiniste[M] / maquinista[M] jefe / capomacchinista[M]
- スポットライト / spotlight / Scheinwerfer[M] / projecteur[M] / proyector[M] / proiettore[M]
- ディフューザー／散光器 / diffuser / Streuscheibe[F] / diffuseur[M] / difusor[M] / diffusore[M]

芸術と建築

428

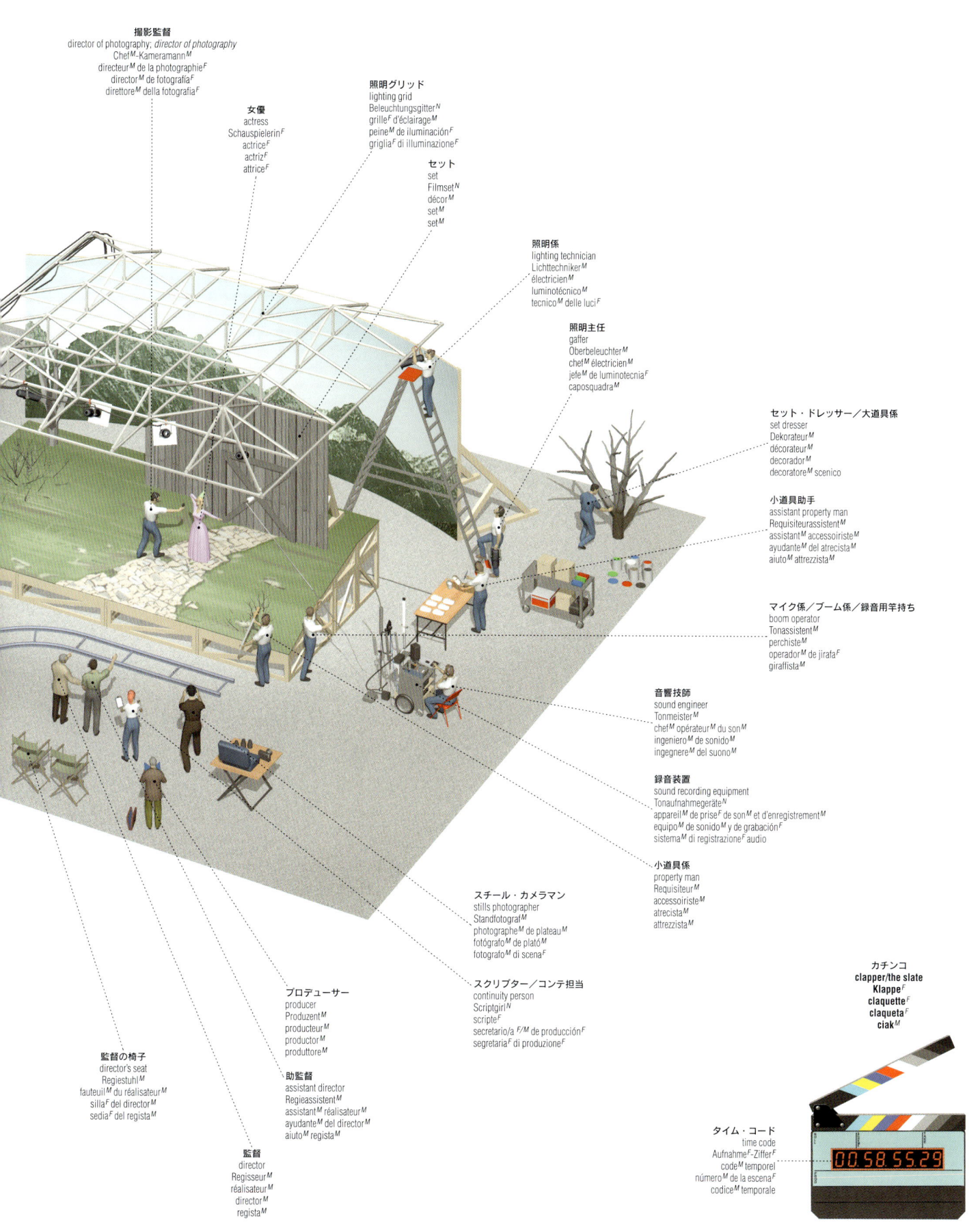

舞台芸術 | PERFORMING ARTS
DARSTELLENDE KÜNSTE | ARTS DE LA SCÈNE | ARTES ESCÉNICAS | ARTI SCENICHE

映画のセット

撮影監督
director of photography; *director of photography*
Chef^M-Kameramann^M
directeur^M de la photographie^F
director^M de fotografía^F
direttore^M della fotografia^F

女優
actress
Schauspielerin^F
actrice^F
actriz^F
attrice^F

照明グリッド
lighting grid
Beleuchtungsgitter^N
grille^F d'éclairage^M
peine^M de iluminación^F
griglia^F di illuminazione^F

セット
set
Filmset^N
décor^M
set^M
set^M

照明係
lighting technician
Lichttechniker^M
électricien^M
luminotécnico^M
tecnico^M delle luci^F

照明主任
gaffer
Oberbeleuchter^M
chef^M électricien^M
jefe^M de luminotecnia^F
caposquadra^M

セット・ドレッサー／大道具係
set dresser
Dekorateur^M
décorateur^M
decorador^M
decoratore^M scenico

小道具助手
assistant property man
Requisiteurassistent^M
assistant^M accessoiriste^M
ayudante^M del atrecista^M
aiuto^M attrezzista^M

マイク係／ブーム係／録音用竿持ち
boom operator
Tonassistent^M
perchiste^M
operador^M de jirafa^F
giraffista^M

音響技師
sound engineer
Tonmeister^M
chef^M opérateur^M du son^M
ingeniero^M de sonido^M
ingegnere^M del suono^M

録音装置
sound recording equipment
Tonaufnahmegeräte^N
appareil^M de prise^F de son^M et d'enregistrement^M
equipo^M de sonido^M y de grabación^F
sistema^M di registrazione^F audio

小道具係
property man
Requisiteur^M
accessoiriste^M
atrecista^M
attrezzista^M

スチール・カメラマン
stills photographer
Standfotograf^M
photographe^M de plateau^M
fotógrafo^M de plató^M
fotografo^M di scena^F

カチンコ
clapper/the slate
Klappe^F
claquette^F
claqueta^F
ciak^M

プロデューサー
producer
Produzent^M
producteur^M
productor^M
produttore^M

スクリプター／コンテ担当
continuity person
Scriptgirl^N
scripte^F
secretario/a ^{F/M} de producción^F
segretaria^F di produzione^F

監督の椅子
director's seat
Regiestuhl^M
fauteuil^M du réalisateur^M
silla^F del director^M
sedia^F del regista^M

助監督
assistant director
Regieassistent^M
assistant^M réalisateur^M
ayudante^M del director^M
aiuto^M regista^M

タイム・コード
time code
Aufnahme^F-Ziffer^F
code^M temporel
número^M de la escena^F
codice^M temporale

監督
director
Regisseur^M
réalisateur^M
director^M
regista^M

芸術と建築

舞台芸術 | PERFORMING ARTS
DARSTELLENDE KÜNSTE | ARTS DE LA SCÈNE | ARTES ESCÉNICAS | ARTI SCENICHE

劇場

日本語 | 英語 | ドイツ語 | フランス語 | スペイン語 | イタリア語

theater; *theatre* | Theater^N | salle^F de spectacle^M | teatro^M | teatro^M

吊り物
borders
Soffitten^F
frises^F
bambalina^F
cieletti^M

背景幕
backdrop
Prospektzug^M
toile^F de fond^M
telón^M de fondo^M
fondale^M

バトン
batten
Beleuchterbrücke^F
herse^F
rastrillos^M
bilancia^F

フライ
flies
Obermaschinerie^F
cintres^M
telares^M
ballatoi^M

ステージ・ハウス
stage-house
Bühnenhaus^N
cage^F de scène^F
escenario^M
gabbia^F del palcoscenico^M

常設歩路
catwalk
Galerie^F
passerelle^F
pasarela^F
passerella^F

防火幕
iron curtain
eiserner Vorhang^M
rideau^M de fer^M
telón^M cortafuegos^M
sipario^M tagliafuoco

舞台後方壁
upstage
Bühnenhintergrund^M
lointain^M
fondo^M
muro^M di fondo^M

袖
wings
Kulissen^F
coulisses^F
bastidores^M
quinte^F

緞帳(どんちょう)／幕
stage curtain
Hauptvorhang^M
rideau^M de scène^F
telón^M de boca^F
sipario^M

迫(せ)り／昇降舞台
trap
Versenkpodium^N
trappe^F
trampilla^F
botola^F

舞台下／奈落
below-stage
Unterbühne^F
dessous^M
foso^M de escenario^M
sottopalco^M

舞台
stage
Bühne^F
scène^F
escenario^M
palcoscenico^M

前舞台
proscenium
Vorbühne^F
avant-scène^F
proscenio^M
proscenio^M

オーケストラ・ボックス
orchestra pit
Orchestergraben^M
fosse^F d'orchestre^M
foso^M de orquesta^F
golfo^M mistico

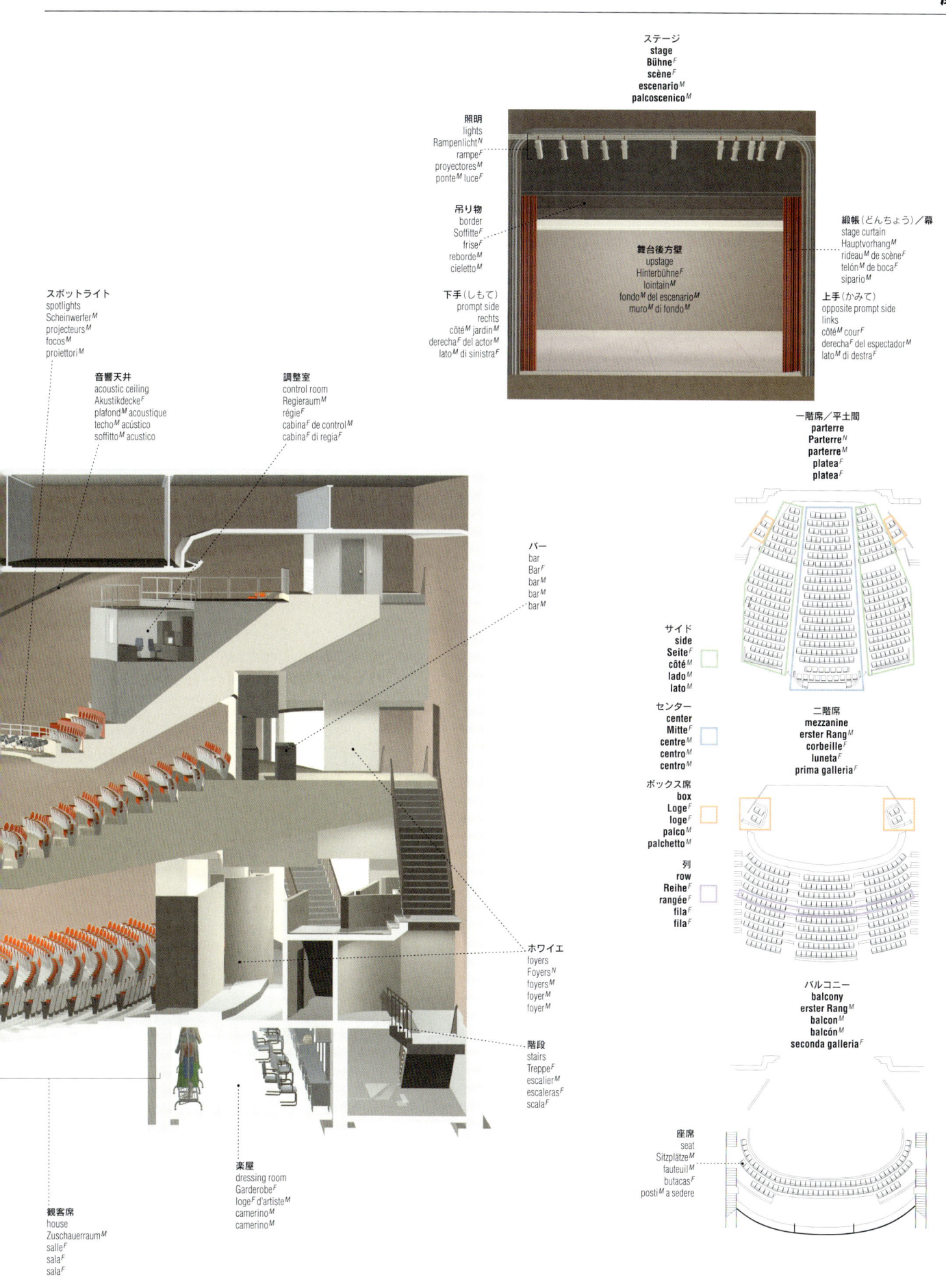

舞台芸術 | PERFORMING ARTS
DARSTELLENDE KÜNSTE | ARTS DE LA SCÈNE | ARTES ESCÉNICAS | ARTI SCENICHE

劇場

ステージ
stage
Bühne^F
scène^F
escenario^M
palcoscenico^M

照明
lights
Rampenlicht^N
rampe^F
proyectores^M
ponte^M luce^F

吊り物
border
Soffitte^F
frise^F
reborde^M
cieletto^M

緞帳（どんちょう）／幕
stage curtain
Hauptvorhang^M
rideau^M de scène^F
telón^M de boca^F
sipario^M

舞台後方壁
upstage
Hinterbühne^F
lointain^M
fondo^M del escenario^M
muro^M di fondo^M

下手（しもて）
prompt side
rechts
côté^M jardin^M
derecha^F del actor^M
lato^M di sinistra^F

上手（かみて）
opposite prompt side
links
côté^M cour^F
derecha^F del espectador^M
lato^M di destra^F

スポットライト
spotlights
Scheinwerfer^M
projecteurs^M
focos^M
proiettori^M

音響天井
acoustic ceiling
Akustikdecke^F
plafond^M acoustique
techo^M acústico
soffitto^M acustico

調整室
control room
Regieraum^M
régie^F
cabina^F de control^M
cabina^F di regia^F

バー
bar
Bar^F
bar^M
bar^M
bar^M

一階席／平土間
parterre
Parterre^N
parterre^M
platea^F
platea^F

サイド
side
Seite^F
côté^M
lado^M
lato^M

センター
center
Mitte^F
centre^M
centro^M
centro^M

二階席
mezzanine
erster Rang^M
corbeille^F
luneta^F
prima galleria^F

ボックス席
box
Loge^F
loge^F
palco^M
palchetto^M

列
row
Reihe^F
rangée^F
fila^F
fila^F

ホワイエ
foyers
Foyers^N
foyers^M
foyer^M
foyer^M

階段
stairs
Treppe^F
escalier^M
escaleras^F
scala^F

バルコニー
balcony
erster Rang^M
balcon^M
balcón^M
seconda galleria^F

楽屋
dressing room
Garderobe^F
loge^F d'artiste^M
camerino^M
camerino^M

観客席
house
Zuschauerraum^M
salle^F
sala^F
sala^F

座席
seat
Sitzplätze^M
fauteuil^M
butacas^F
posti^M a sedere

芸術と建築

431

音楽｜MUSIC
MUSIK｜MUSIQUE｜MÚSICA｜MUSICA

伝統[民族]楽器

日本語｜英語｜ドイツ語｜フランス語｜スペイン語｜イタリア語

traditional musical instruments | traditionelle Musikinstrumente^N | instruments^M traditionnels | instrumentos^M musicales tradicionales | strumenti^M musicali tradizionali

アコーディオン
accordion
Akkordeon^N
accordéon^M
acordeón^M
fisarmonica^F

蛇腹バンド
bellows strap
Balgenverschluss^M
fermeture^F du soufflet^M
seguro^M del fuelle^M
cinghia^F del mantice^M

ハーモニカ
harmonica
Mundharmonika^F
harmonica^M
armónica^F
armonica^F a bocca^F

高音[トレブル]レジスター
treble register
Diskantregister^N
registre^M des aigus^M
registro^M de altos^M
registro^M degli acuti^M

(空気)ボタン
button
Knopf^M
bouton^M
botón^M
bottone^M

高音(域)用鍵盤
treble keyboard
Diskanttastatur^F
clavier^M chant^M
teclado^M triple
tastiera^F degli acuti^M

低音(域)用指盤[ボタン部]
bass keyboard
Basstastatur^F
clavier^M accompagnement^M
teclado^M de bajos^M
bottoniera^F dei bassi^M

鍵(けん)／キー
key
Taste^F
touche^F
tecla^F
tasto^M

低音[バス]レジスター
bass register
Bassregister^N
registre^M des basses^F
registros^M de bajos^M
registro^M dei bassi^M

飾り板／グリル
grille
Gitter^N
grille^F
rejilla^F
mascherina^F

蛇腹
bellows
Balg^M
soufflet^M
doble fuelle^M
mantice^M a soffietto^M

チター
zither
Zither^F
cithare^F
cítara^F
zither^M

バグパイプ
bagpipes
Dudelsack^M
cornemuse^F
gaita^F
cornamusa^F

共鳴板／響板
soundboard
Resonanzdecke^F
caisse^F de résonance^F
caja^F de resonancia^F
tavola^F armonica

ドローン(管)
drone pipe
Bordunpfeife^F
bourdon^M
gran roncón^M
bordone^M

指板／ゆびいた
fingerboard
Griffbrett^N
touche^F
traste^M
tastiera^F

吹き込み管／ブロー・パイプ
blow pipe
Blaspfeife^F
tuyau^M d'insufflation^F
portaviento^M
cannello^M

接続管／ストック
stock
Aufsatzstück^N
monture^F
cabo^M
base^F

空気袋／バッグ
windbag
Windsack^M
sac^M
saco^M de piel^F
sacco^M

伴奏弦
open strings
Freisaiten^F
cordes^F d'accompagnement^M
cuerdas^F de acompañamiento^M
corde^F per l'accompagnamento^M

旋律弦
melody strings
Melodiesaiten^F
cordes^F de mélodie^F
cuerdas^F melódicas
corde^F per la melodia^F

バンジョー
banjo
Banjo^N
banjo^M
banjo^M
banjo^M

指笛／チャンター
chanter
Melodiepfeife^F
chalumeau^M
caramillo^M
canna^F della melodia^F

円形の胴
circular body
runder Korpus^M
caisse^F circulaire
caja^F circular
cassa^F armonica circolare

芸術と建築

音楽 | MUSIC
MUSIK | MUSIQUE | MÚSICA | MUSICA

伝統[民族]楽器

マンドリン
mandolin
Mandoline^F
mandoline^F
mandolina^F
mandolino^M

バラライカ
balalaika
Balalaika^F
balalaïka^F
balalaica^F
balalaica^F

コーラ
kora
Kora^F
kora^F
kora^M
kora^F

棹
neck
Hals^M
manche^M
mástil^M
manico^M

弦
strings
Saiten^F
cordes^F
cuerdas^F
corde^F

三角形の胴
triangular body
dreieckiger Korpus^M
caisse^F triangulaire
caja^F triangular
cassa^F armonica triangolare

取っ手
hand post
Handgriff^M
support^M de main
soporte^M de la mano
poggiamano^M

調律リング
tuning ring
Stimmring^M
attache^F d'accordage^M
anillos^M de sonido^M
anello^M d'accordatura^F

共鳴箱／響箱
sound box
Resonanzkörper^M
caisse^F de résonance
caja^F de resonancia
cassa^F di risonanza

鼓面
snare head
Klangfell^N
peau^F de timbre^M
piel^F armónica
pelle^F armonica

洋梨形の胴
pear-shaped body
birnenförmiger Korpus^M
caisse^F bombée
caja^F media pera^F
cassa^F armonica piriforme

駒
bridge
Steg^M
chevalet^M
puente^M
ponticello^M

緒止め(板)
tailpiece
Saitenhalterung^F
cordier^M
cordal^M
cordiera^F

リラ
lyre
Lyra^F
lyre^F
lira^F
lira^F

枠
frame
Rahmen^M
cadre^M
estructura^F
telaio^M

舌
tongue
Zunge^F
lame^F
lengüeta^F de la caña^F
linguetta^F

横木
crossbar
Querjoch^N
traverse^F
travesaño^M
traversa^F

枹（ばち）
drumstick
Trommelschlegel^M
mailloche^F
baqueta^F
mazzuolo^M

腕木
arm
Jocharm^M
montant^M
brazo^M
braccio^M

口琴（こうきん）／琵琶笛（びやほん）／
ジューズ・ハープ
Jew's harp
Maultrommel^F
guimbarde^F
birimbao^M
scacciapensieri

ピック
plectrum
Plektron^N
médiator^M
púa^F
plettro^M

ジェンベ／ジャンベ／ジンベ
djembe
Djembe^F
djembé^M
yembé^M
djembè^M

共鳴板／響板
soundboard
Resonanzdecke^F
caisse^F de résonance
caja^F de resonancia
tavola^F armonica

トーキング・ドラム
talking drum
Sprechtrommel^F
tambour^M d'aisselle^F
tambor^M hablante
tamburo^M parlante

鼓面の皮
batter skin
Trommelfell^N
peau^F de batterie
piel^F
battitoia^F

パンの笛／パンパイプ
panpipe
Panflöte^F
flûte^F de Pan
zampoña^F
flauto^M di Pan

共鳴箱／響箱
sound box
Resonanzkörper^M
caisse^F de résonance
caja^F de resonancia
cassa^F di risonanza

張り縄
tension rope
Spannschnur^F
corde^F de tension
cuerda^F de tensión
corda^F di tensione

芸術と建築

433

音楽 | MUSIC
MUSIK | MUSIQUE | MÚSICA | MUSICA

楽譜記号

日本語 | 英語 | ドイツ語 | フランス語 | スペイン語 | イタリア語

musical notation | Musiknotation[F] | notation[F] musicale | notación[F] musical | notazione[F] musicale

譜表
staff
Liniensystem[N]
portée[F]
pentagrama[F]
pentagramma[M]

(線)間
space
Zwischenraum[M]
interligne[M]
espacio[M]
spazio[M]

線
line
Notenlinie[F]
ligne[F]
línea[F]
linea[F]

加線
ledger line
Hilfslinie[F]
ligne[F] supplémentaire
línea[F] suplementaria
taglio[M] addizionale

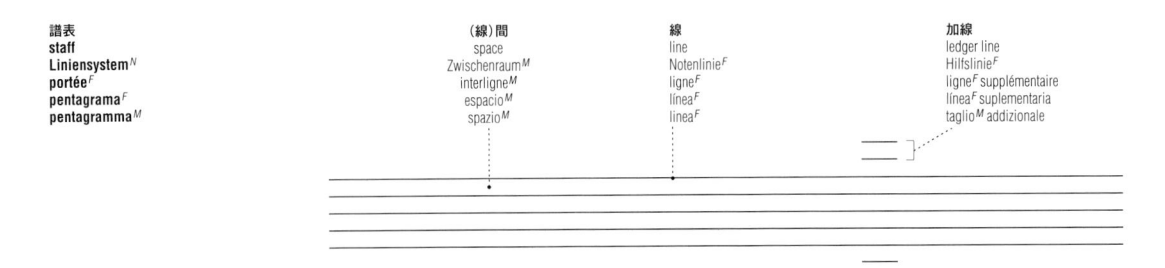

音部記号
clefs
Notenschlüssel[M]
clés[F]
claves[F]
chiavi[F]

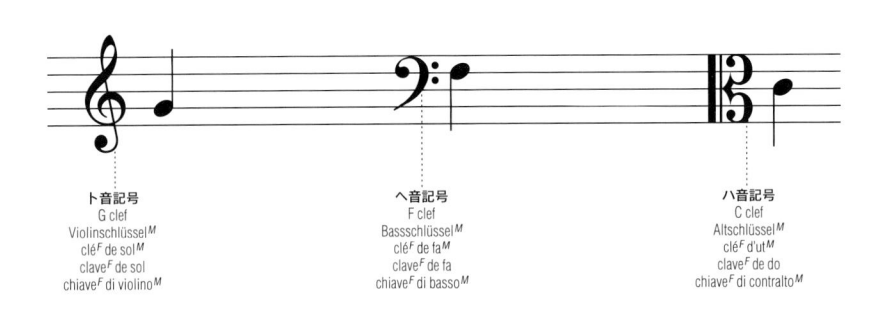

ト音記号
G clef
Violinschlüssel[M]
clé[F] de sol[M]
clave[F] de sol
chiave[F] di violino[M]

ヘ音記号
F clef
Bassschlüssel[M]
clé[F] de fa[M]
clave[F] de fa
chiave[F] di basso[M]

ハ音記号
C clef
Altschlüssel[M]
clé[F] d'ut[M]
clave[F] de do
chiave[F] di contralto[M]

拍子記号
time signatures
Taktarten[F]
mesures[F]
compás[M]
indicazioni[F] di tempo[M]

2分の2拍子
two-two time
Zweihalbetakt[M]
mesure[F] à deux temps[M]
de dos mitades[F]
tempo[M] di due metà[F]

4分の3拍子
three-four time
Dreivierteltakt[M]
mesure[F] à trois temps[M]
de tres cuartos[M]
tempo[M] di tre quarti[M]

4分の4拍子
four-four time
Viervierteltakt[M]
mesure[F] à quatre temps[M]
de cuatro cuartos[M]
tempo[M] di quattro quarti[M]

縦線（じゅうせん）／小節線
bar line
Taktstrich[M]
barre[F] de mesure[F]
barra[F] de compás[M]
stanghetta[F]

繰り返し記号
repeat mark
Wiederholungszeichen[N]
barre[F] de reprise[F]
barra[F] de repetición[F]
ritornello

音程
intervals
Intervalle[N]
intervalles[M]
intervalos[M]
intervalli[M]

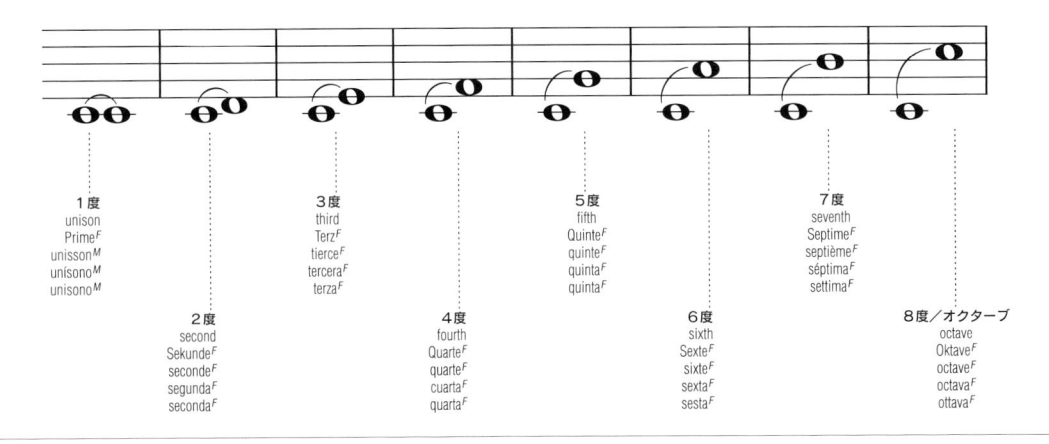

1度
unison
Prime[F]
unisson[M]
unísono[M]
unisono[M]

2度
second
Sekunde[F]
seconde[F]
segunda[F]
seconda[F]

3度
third
Terz[F]
tierce[F]
tercera[F]
terza[F]

4度
fourth
Quarte[F]
quarte[F]
cuarta[F]
quarta[F]

5度
fifth
Quinte[F]
quinte[F]
quinta[F]
quinta[F]

6度
sixth
Sexte[F]
sixte[F]
sexta[F]
sesta[F]

7度
seventh
Septime[F]
septième[F]
séptima[F]
settima[F]

8度／オクターブ
octave
Oktave[F]
octave[F]
octava[F]
ottava[F]

音階
scale
Tonleiter[F]
gamme[F]
escala[F]
scala[F]

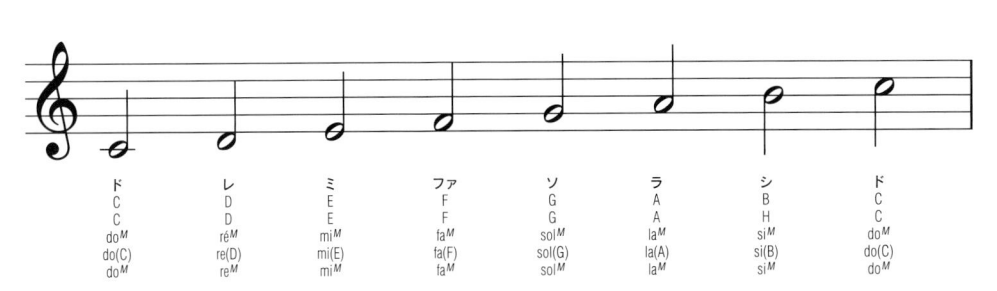

ド
C
C
do[M]
do(C)
do[M]

レ
D
D
ré[M]
re(D)
re[M]

ミ
E
E
mi[M]
mi(E)
mi[M]

ファ
F
F
fa[M]
fa(F)
fa[M]

ソ
G
G
sol[M]
sol(G)
sol[M]

ラ
A
A
la[M]
la(A)
la[M]

シ
B
H
si[M]
si(B)
si[M]

ド
C
C
do[M]
do(C)
do[M]

音楽 | MUSIC
MUSIK | MUSIQUE | MÚSICA | MUSICA

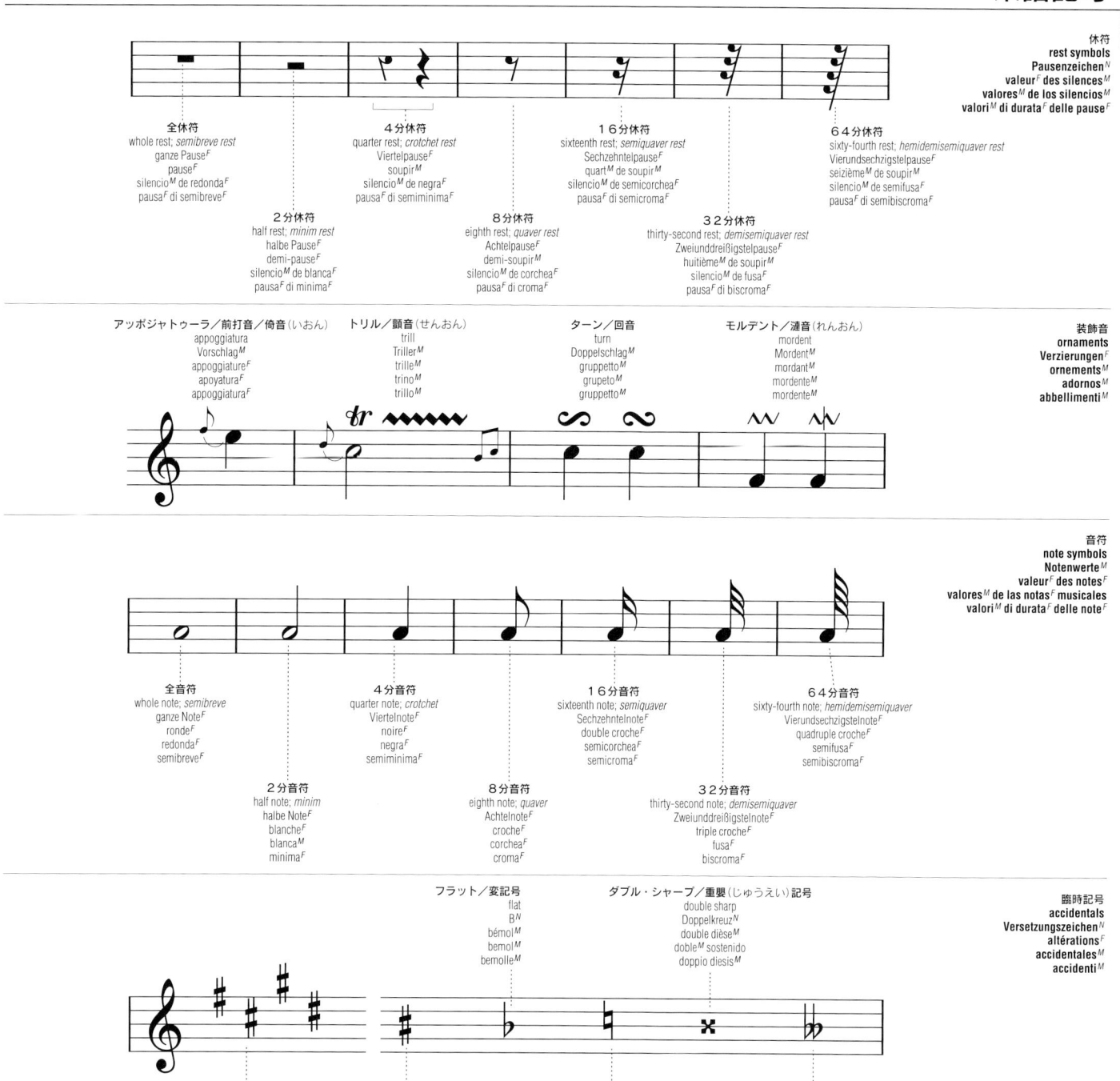

楽譜記号

休符
rest symbols
Pausenzeichen^N
valeur^F des silences^M
valores^M de los silencios^M
valori^M di durata^F delle pause^F

全休符
whole rest; *semibreve rest*
ganze Pause^F
pause^F
silencio^M de redonda^F
pausa^F di semibreve^F

2分休符
half rest; *minim rest*
halbe Pause^F
demi-pause^F
silencio^M de blanca^F
pausa^F di minima^F

4分休符
quarter rest; *crotchet rest*
Viertelpause^F
soupir^M
silencio^M de negra^F
pausa^F di semiminima^F

8分休符
eighth rest; *quaver rest*
Achtelpause^F
demi-soupir^M
silencio^M de corchea^F
pausa^F di croma^F

16分休符
sixteenth rest; *semiquaver rest*
Sechzehntelpause^F
quart^M de soupir^M
silencio^M de semicorchea^F
pausa^F di semicroma^F

32分休符
thirty-second rest; *demisemiquaver rest*
Zweiunddreißigstelpause^F
huitième^M de soupir^M
silencio^M de fusa^F
pausa^F di biscroma^F

64分休符
sixty-fourth rest; *hemidemisemiquaver rest*
Vierundsechzigstelpause^F
seizième^M de soupir^M
silencio^M de semifusa^F
pausa^F di semibiscroma^F

装飾音
ornaments
Verzierungen^F
ornements^M
adornos^M
abbellimenti^M

アッポジャトゥーラ／前打音／倚音（いおん）
appoggiatura
Vorschlag^M
appoggiature^M
apoyatura^F
appoggiatura^F

トリル／顫音（せんおん）
trill
Triller^M
trille^M
trino^M
trillo^M

ターン／回音
turn
Doppelschlag^M
gruppetto^M
grupeto^M
gruppetto^M

モルデント／漣音（れんおん）
mordent
Mordent^M
mordant^M
mordente^M
mordente^M

音符
note symbols
Notenwerte^M
valeur^F des notes^F
valores^M de las notas^F musicales
valori^M di durata^F delle note^F

全音符
whole note; *semibreve*
ganze Note^F
ronde^F
redonda^F
semibreve^F

2分音符
half note; *minim*
halbe Note^F
blanche^F
blanca^M
minima^F

4分音符
quarter note; *crotchet*
Viertelnote^F
noire^F
negra^F
semiminima^F

8分音符
eighth note; *quaver*
Achtelnote^F
croche^F
corchea^F
croma^F

16分音符
sixteenth note; *semiquaver*
Sechzehntelnote^F
double croche^F
semicorchea^F
semicroma^F

32分音符
thirty-second note; *demisemiquaver*
Zweiunddreißigstelnote^F
triple croche^F
fusa^F
biscroma^F

64分音符
sixty-fourth note; *hemidemisemiquaver*
Vierundsechzigstelnote^F
quadruple croche^F
semifusa^F
semibiscroma^F

臨時記号
accidentals
Versetzungszeichen^N
altérations^F
accidentales^M
accidenti^M

調号
key signature
Tonartvorzeichen^N
armature^F de la clé^F
armadura^F
armatura^F di chiave^F

シャープ／嬰（えい）記号
sharp
Kreuz^N
dièse^M
sostenido^M
diesis^M

フラット／変記号
flat
B^N
bémol^M
bemol^M
bemolle^M

ナチュラル／本位記号
natural
Auflösungszeichen^N
bécarre^M
becuadro^M
bequadro^M

ダブル・シャープ／重嬰（じゅうえい）記号
double sharp
Doppelkreuz^N
double dièse^M
doble^M sostenido
doppio diesis^M

ダブル・フラット／重変記号
double flat
Doppel-B^N
double bémol^M
doble^M bemol
doppio bemolle^M

その他の記号
other signs
andere Zeichen^N
autres signes^M
otros signos^M
altri segni^M

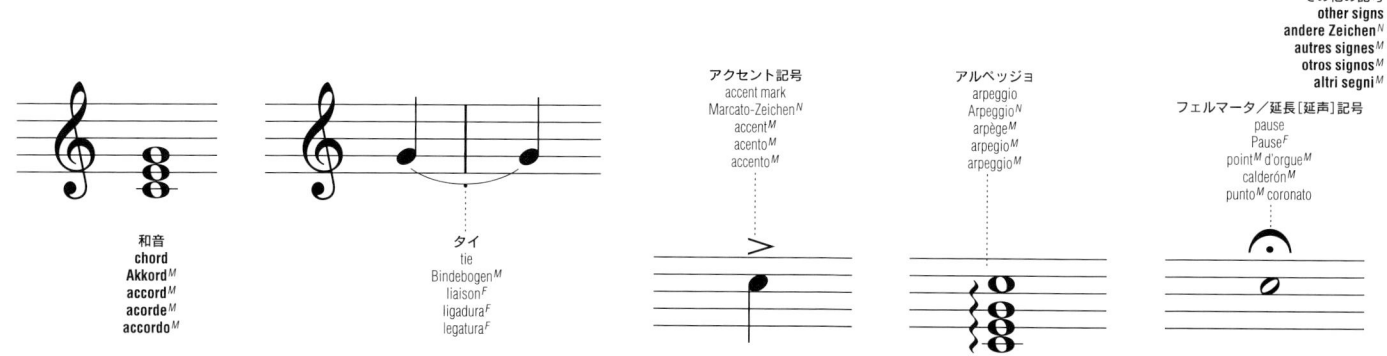

和音
chord
Akkord^M
accord^M
acorde^M
accordo^M

タイ
tie
Bindebogen^M
liaison^F
ligadura^F
legatura^F

アクセント記号
accent mark
Marcato-Zeichen^N
accent^M
acento^M
accento^M

アルペッジョ
arpeggio
Arpeggio^N
arpège^M
arpegio^M
arpeggio^M

フェルマータ／延長［延声］記号
pause
Pause^F
point^M d'orgue^M
calderón^M
punto^M coronato

芸術と建築

音楽 | MUSIC
MUSIK | MUSIQUE | MÚSICA | MUSICA

演奏用付属品

日本語 | 英語 | ドイツ語 | フランス語 | スペイン語 | イタリア語

musical accessories | Musikzubehör^N | accessoires^M | accesorios^M musicales | accessori^M musicali

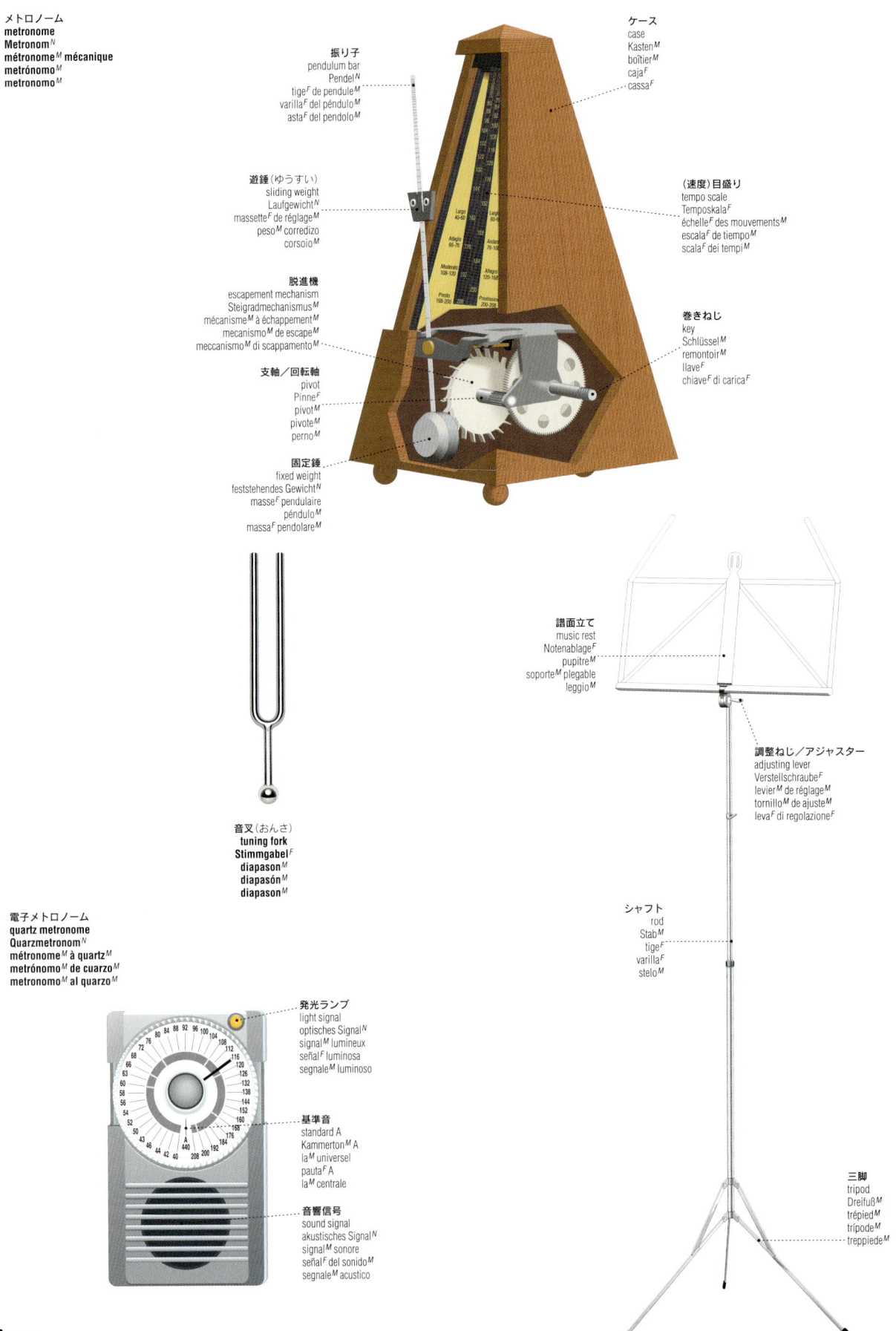

メトロノーム
metronome
Metronom^N
métronome^M mécanique
metrónomo^M
metronomo^M

振り子
pendulum bar
Pendel^N
tige^F de pendule
varilla^F del péndulo^M
asta^F del pendolo^M

ケース
case
Kasten^M
boîtier^M
caja^F
cassa^F

遊錘（ゆうすい）
sliding weight
Laufgewicht^N
massette^F de réglage^M
peso^M corredizo
corsoio^M

（速度）目盛り
tempo scale
Temposkala^F
échelle^F des mouvements^M
escala^F de tiempo^M
scala^F dei tempi^M

脱進機
escapement mechanism
Steigradmechanismus^M
mécanisme^M à échappement^M
mecanismo^M de escape^M
meccanismo^M di scappamento^M

巻きねじ
key
Schlüssel^M
remontoir^M
llave^F
chiave^F di carica^F

支軸／回転軸
pivot
Pinne^F
pivot^M
pivote^M
perno^M

固定錘
fixed weight
feststehendes Gewicht^N
masse^F pendulaire
péndulo^M
massa^F pendolare^M

譜面台
music stand
Notenständer^M
pupitre^M à musique^F
atril^M
leggio^M da orchestra^F

譜面立て
music rest
Notenablage^F
pupitre^M
soporte^M plegable
leggio^M

音叉（おんさ）
tuning fork
Stimmgabel^F
diapason^M
diapasón^M
diapason^M

調整ねじ／アジャスター
adjusting lever
Verstellschraube^F
levier^M de réglage^M
tornillo^M de ajuste^M
leva^F di regolazione^F

電子メトロノーム
quartz metronome
Quarzmetronom^N
métronome^M à quartz^M
metrónomo^M de cuarzo^M
metronomo^M al quarzo^M

シャフト
rod
Stab^M
tige^F
varilla^F
stelo^M

発光ランプ
light signal
optisches Signal^N
signal^M lumineux
señal^F luminosa
segnale^M luminoso

基準音
standard A
Kammerton^M A
la^M universel
pauta^F A
la^M centrale

音響信号
sound signal
akustisches Signal^N
signal^M sonore
señal^F del sonido^M
segnale^M acustico

三脚
tripod
Dreifuß^M
trépied^M
trípode^M
treppiede^M

音楽 | MUSIC
MUSIK | MUSIQUE | MÚSICA | MUSICA

交響[管弦]楽団

symphony orchestra | Sinfonieorchester[N] | orchestre[M] symphonique | orquesta[F] sinfónica | orchestra[F] sinfonica

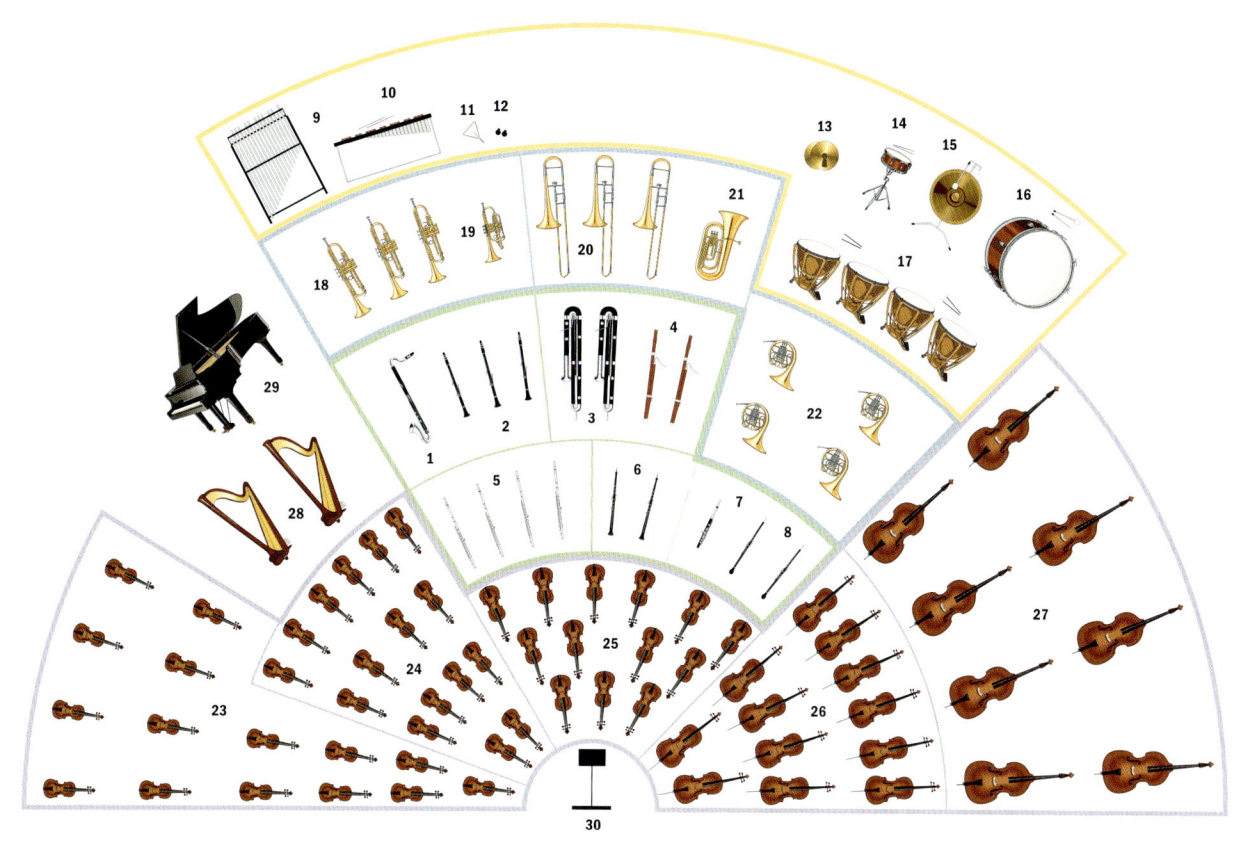

芸術と建築

木管楽器の仲間
woodwind family
Familie[F] der Holzblasinstrumente[N]
famille[F] des bois[M]
familia[F] de instrumentos[M] de madera[F]
famiglia[F] dei legni[M]

1 バス・クラリネット
bass clarinet
Bassklarinette[F]
clarinette[F] basse
clarinete[M] bajo
clarinetto[M] basso

2 クラリネット
clarinets
Klarinetten[F]
clarinettes[F]
clarinetes[M]
clarinetti[M]

3 コントラ・バスーン[ファゴット]
contrabassoons
Kontrafagotte[N]
contrebassons[M]
contrafagot[M]
controfagotti[M]

4 バスーン／ファゴット
bassoons
Fagotte[N]
bassons[M]
fagotes[M]
fagotti[M]

5 フルート
flutes
Querflöten[F]
flûtes[F]
flautas[F] traverseras
flauti[M]

6 オーボエ
oboes
Oboen[F]
hautbois[M]
oboes[M]
oboi[M]

7 ピッコロ
piccolo
Pikkoloflöte[F]
piccolo[M]
píccolo[M]
ottavino[M]

8 イングリッシュ・ホルン／
コーラングレ
English horns; cors anglais
Englischhörner[N]
cors[M] anglais
cornos[M] ingleses
corni[M] inglesi

打楽器
percussion instruments
Schlaginstrumente[N]
instruments[M] à percussion[F]
instrumentos[M] de percusión[F]
strumenti[M] a percussione[F]

9 チューブ・ベル／組み鐘
tubular bells
Röhrenglocken[F]
carillon[M] tubulaire
campanas[F] tubulares
campane[F] tubolari

10 シロ[ザイロ]フォーン／木琴
xylophone
Xylophon[N]
xylophone[M]
xilófono[M]
xilofono[M]

11 トライアングル
triangle
Triangel[M]
triangle[M]
triángulo[M]
triangolo[M]

12 カスタネット
castanets
Kastagnetten[F]
castagnettes[F]
castañuelas[F]
nacchere[F]

13 シンバル
cymbals
Becken[N]
cymbales[F]
platillos[M]
piatti[M]

14 スネア・ドラム／小太鼓
snare drum
kleine Trommel[F]
caisse[F] claire
caja[F] clara
cassa[F] chiara

15 どら／ゴング
gong
Gong[M]
gong[M]
gong[M]
gong[M]

16 バス・ドラム／大太鼓
bass drum
Basstrommel[F]
grosse caisse[F]
bombo[M]
grancassa[F]

17 ティンパニ
timpani
Pauken[F]
timbales[F]
timbales[M]
timpani[M]

金管楽器の仲間
brass family
Familie[F] der Blechbläser[M]
famille[F] des cuivres[M]
familia[F] de los metales[M]
famiglia[F] degli ottoni[M]

18 トランペット
trumpets
Trompeten[F]
trompettes[F]
trompetas[F]
trombe[F]

19 コルネット
cornet
Kornett[N]
cornet[M] à pistons[M]
cornetín[M]
cornetta[F]

20 トロンボーン
trombones
Posaunen[F]
trombones[M]
trombones[M]
tromboni[M]

21 チューバ
tuba
Tuba[F]
tuba[M]
tuba[F]
tuba[F]

22 フレンチ・ホルン
French horns
Waldhörner[N]
cors[M] d'harmonie[F]
cornos[M] franceses
corni[M]

バイオリンの仲間
violin family
Geigenfamilie[F]
famille[F] du violon[M]
familia[F] de los violines[M]
famiglia[F] degli archi[M]

23 第一バイオリン
first violins
erste Violinen[F]
premiers violons[M]
primeros violines[M]
primi violini[M]

24 第二バイオリン
second violins
zweite Violinen[F]
seconds violons[M]
segundos violines[M]
secondi violini[M]

25 ビオラ
violas
Bratschen[F]
altos[M]
violas[F]
viole[F]

26 チェロ
cellos
Celli[N]
violoncelles[M]
violoncelos[M]
violoncelli[M]

27 ダブル・ベース／コントラバス
double basses
Kontrabässe[M]
contrebasses[F]
contrabajos[M]
contrabbassi[M]

28 ハープ
harps
Harfen[F]
harpes[F]
arpas[F]
arpe[F]

29 ピアノ
piano
Flügel[M]
piano[M]
piano[M]
pianoforte[M]

30 指揮台
conductor's podium
Dirigentenpult[N]
pupitre[M] du chef[M] d'orchestre[M]
estrado[M] del director[M]
podio[M] del direttore[M] d'orchestra[F]

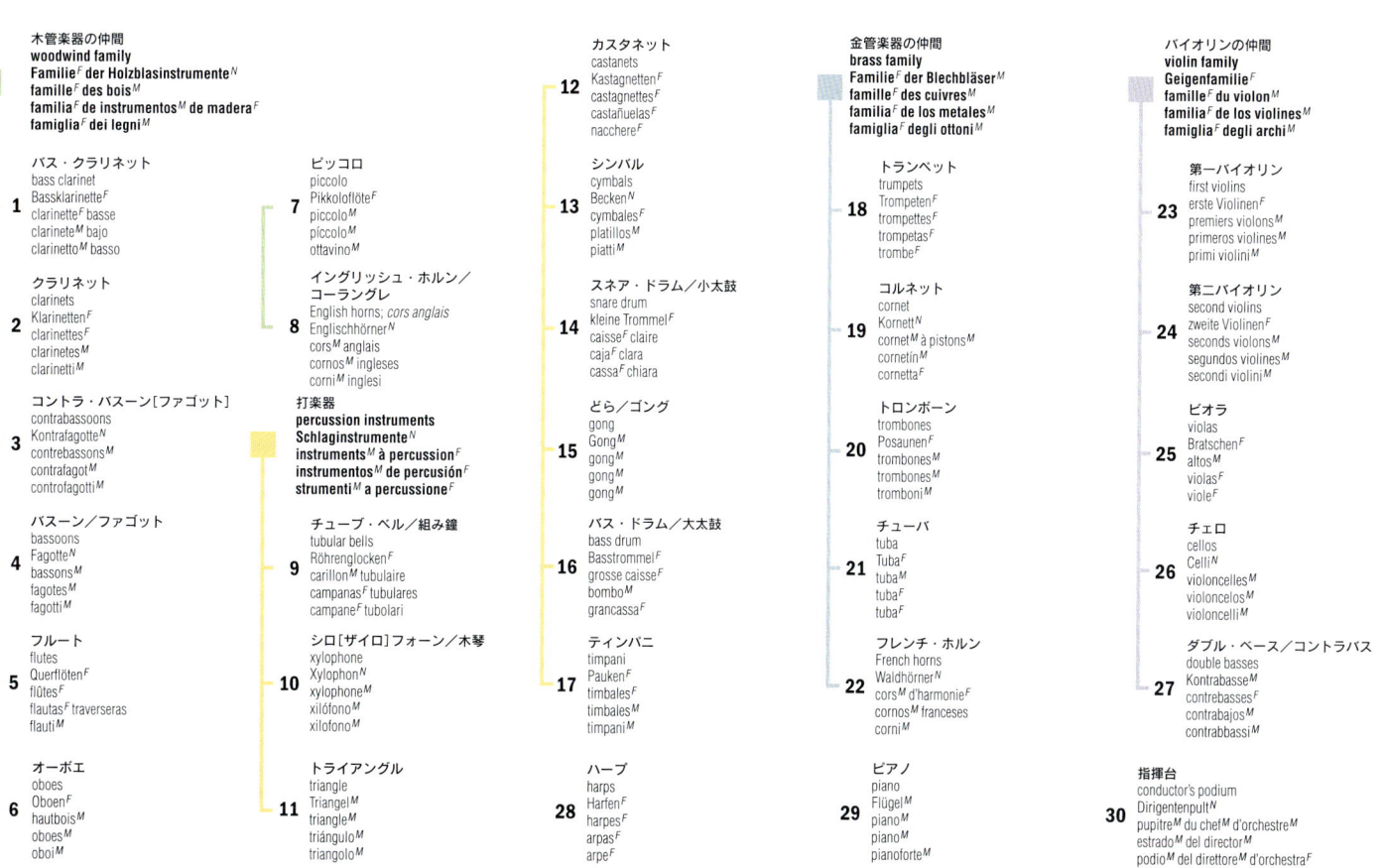

437

音楽｜MUSIC
MUSIK｜MUSIQUE｜MÚSICA｜MUSICA

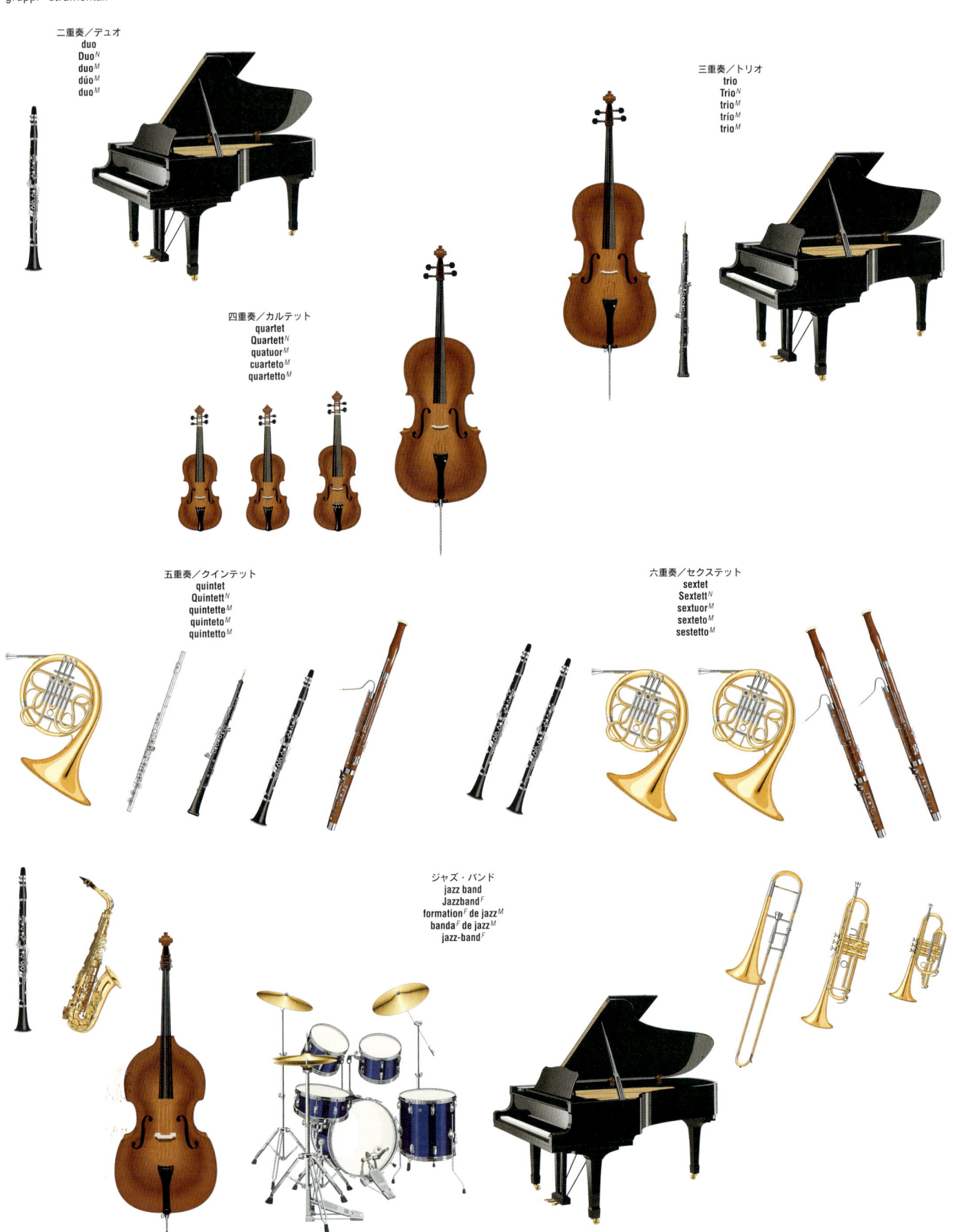

楽器編成の例

日本語｜英語｜ドイツ語｜フランス語｜スペイン語｜イタリア語

examples of instrumental groups ｜ Beispiele[N] für Instrumentalgruppierungen[F] ｜ exemples[M] de groupes[M] instrumentaux ｜ ejemplos[M] de conjuntos[M] instrumentales ｜ esempi[M] di gruppi[M] strumentali

二重奏／デュオ
duo
Duo[N]
duo[M]
dúo[M]
duo[M]

三重奏／トリオ
trio
Trio[N]
trio[M]
trío[M]
trio[M]

四重奏／カルテット
quartet
Quartett[N]
quatuor[M]
cuarteto[M]
quartetto[M]

五重奏／クインテット
quintet
Quintett[N]
quintette[M]
quinteto[M]
quintetto[M]

六重奏／セクステット
sextet
Sextett[N]
sextuor[M]
sexteto[M]
sestetto[M]

ジャズ・バンド
jazz band
Jazzband[F]
formation[F] de jazz[M]
banda[F] de jazz[M]
jazz-band[F]

芸術と建築

438

音楽 | MUSIC
MUSIK | MUSIQUE | MÚSICA | MUSICA

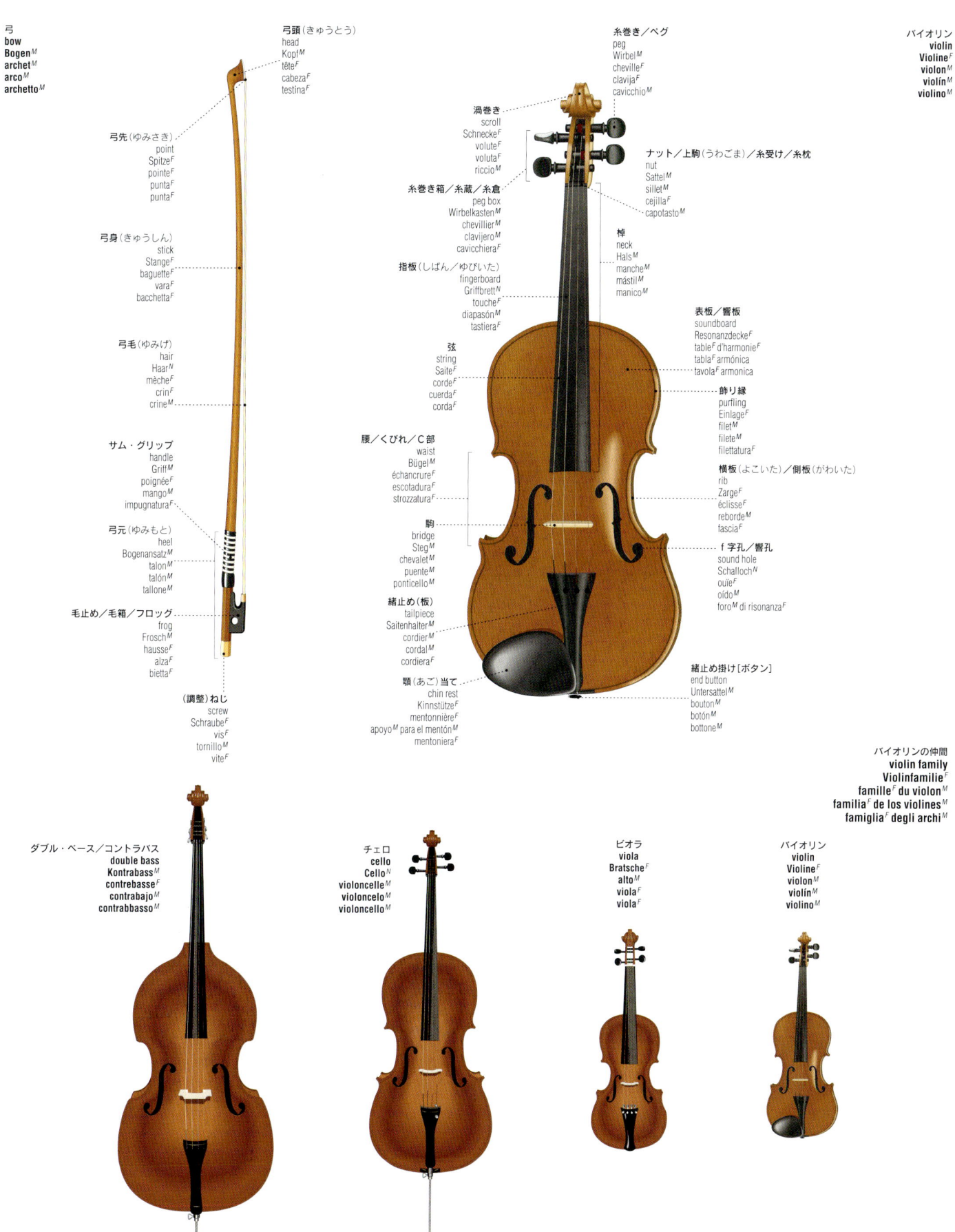

弦楽器

stringed instruments | Saiteninstrumente[N] | instruments[M] à cordes[F] | instrumentos[M] de cuerda[F] | strumenti[M] a corde[F]

弓
bow
Bogen[M]
archet[M]
arco[M]
archetto[M]

弓先（ゆみさき）
point
Spitze[F]
pointe[F]
punta[F]
punta[F]

弓身（きゅうしん）
stick
Stange[F]
baguette[F]
vara[F]
bacchetta[F]

弓毛（ゆみげ）
hair
Haar[N]
mèche[F]
crin[F]
crine[M]

サム・グリップ
handle
Griff[M]
poignée[F]
mango[M]
impugnatura[F]

弓元（ゆみもと）
heel
Bogenansatz[M]
talon[M]
talón[M]
tallone[M]

毛止め／毛箱／フロッグ
frog
Frosch[M]
hausse[F]
alza[F]
bietta[F]

（調整）ねじ
screw
Schraube[F]
vis[F]
tornillo[M]
vite[F]

弓頭（きゅうとう）
head
Kopf[M]
tête[F]
cabeza[F]
testina[F]

渦巻き
scroll
Schnecke[F]
volute[F]
voluta[F]
riccio[M]

糸巻き箱／糸蔵／糸倉
peg box
Wirbelkasten[M]
chevillier[M]
clavijero[M]
cavicchiera[F]

指板（しばん／ゆびいた）
fingerboard
Griffbrett[N]
touche[F]
diapasón[M]
tastiera[F]

弦
string
Saite[F]
corde[F]
cuerda[F]
corda[F]

腰／くびれ／C部
waist
Bügel[M]
échancrure[F]
escotadura[F]
strozzatura[F]

駒
bridge
Steg[M]
chevalet[M]
puente[M]
ponticello[M]

緒止め（板）
tailpiece
Saitenhalter[M]
cordier[M]
cordal[M]
cordiera[F]

顎（あご）当て
chin rest
Kinnstütze[F]
mentonnière[F]
apoyo[M] para el mentón[M]
mentoniera[F]

糸巻き／ペグ
peg
Wirbel[M]
cheville[F]
clavija[F]
cavicchio[M]

ナット／上駒（うわごま）／糸受け／糸枕
nut
Sattel[M]
sillet[M]
cejilla[F]
capotasto[M]

棹
neck
Hals[M]
manche[M]
mástil[M]
manico[M]

表板／響板
soundboard
Resonanzdecke[F]
table[F] d'harmonie[F]
tabla[F] armónica
tavola[F] armonica

飾り縁
purfling
Einlage[F]
filet[M]
filete[M]
filettatura[F]

横板（よこいた）／側板（がわいた）
rib
Zarge[F]
éclisse[F]
reborde[M]
fascia[F]

f字孔／響孔
sound hole
Schalloch[N]
ouïe[F]
oído[M]
foro[M] di risonanza[F]

緒止め掛け［ボタン］
end button
Untersattel[M]
bouton[M]
botón[M]
bottone[M]

バイオリン
violin
Violine[F]
violon[M]
violín[M]
violino[M]

バイオリンの仲間
violin family
Violinfamilie[F]
famille[F] du violon[M]
familia[F] de los violines[M]
famiglia[F] degli archi[M]

ダブル・ベース／コントラバス
double bass
Kontrabass[M]
contrebasse[F]
contrabajo[M]
contrabbasso[M]

チェロ
cello
Cello[N]
violoncelle[M]
violoncelo[M]
violoncello[M]

ビオラ
viola
Bratsche[F]
alto[M]
viola[F]

バイオリン
violin
Violine[F]
violon[M]
violín[M]
violino[M]

芸術と建築

弦楽器

音楽 | MUSIC
MUSIK | MUSIQUE | MÚSICA | MUSICA

日本語 | 英語 | ドイツ語 | フランス語 | スペイン語 | イタリア語

ハープ
harp
Harfe F
harpe F
arpa F
arpa F

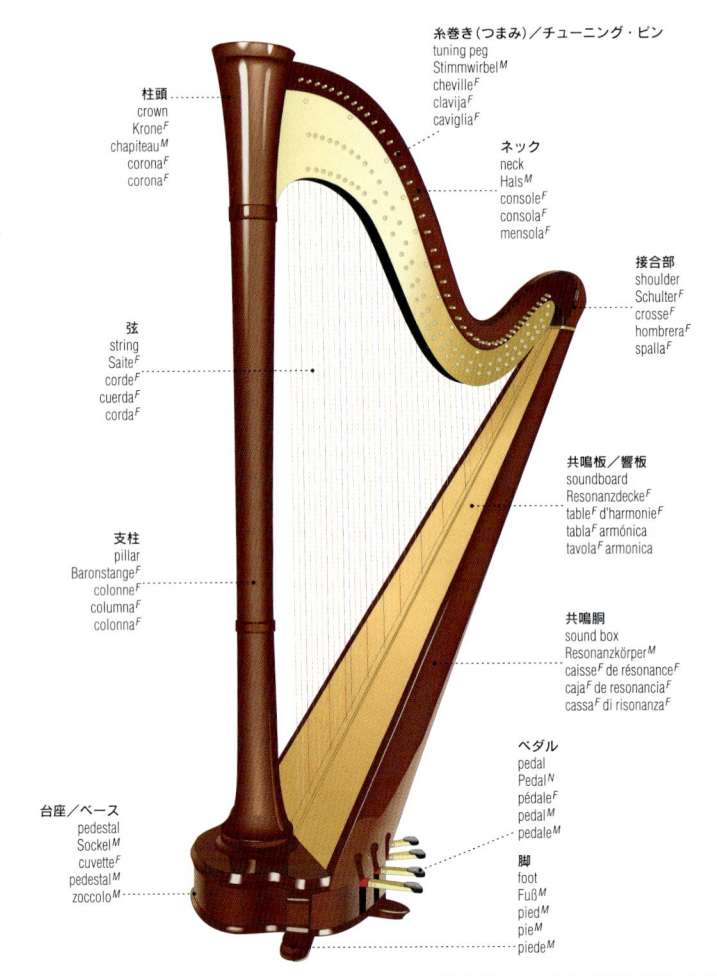

柱頭
crown
Krone F
chapiteau M
corona F
corona F

糸巻き(つまみ)／チューニング・ピン
tuning peg
Stimmwirbel M
cheville F
clavija F
caviglia F

ネック
neck
Hals M
console F
consola F
mensola F

接合部
shoulder
Schulter F
crosse F
hombrera F
spalla F

弦
string
Saite F
corde F
cuerda F
corda F

共鳴板／響板
soundboard
Resonanzdecke F
table F d'harmonie F
tabla F armónica
tavola F armonica

支柱
pillar
Baronstange F
colonne F
columna F
colonna F

共鳴胴
sound box
Resonanzkörper M
caisse F de résonance F
caja F de resonancia F
cassa F di risonanza F

ペダル
pedal
Pedal N
pédale F
pedal M
pedale M

台座／ベース
pedestal
Sockel M
cuvette F
pedestal M
zoccolo M

脚
foot
Fuß M
pied M
pie M
piede M

アコースティック・ギター
acoustic guitar
akustische Gitarre F
guitare F acoustique
guitarra F clásica
chitarra F acustica

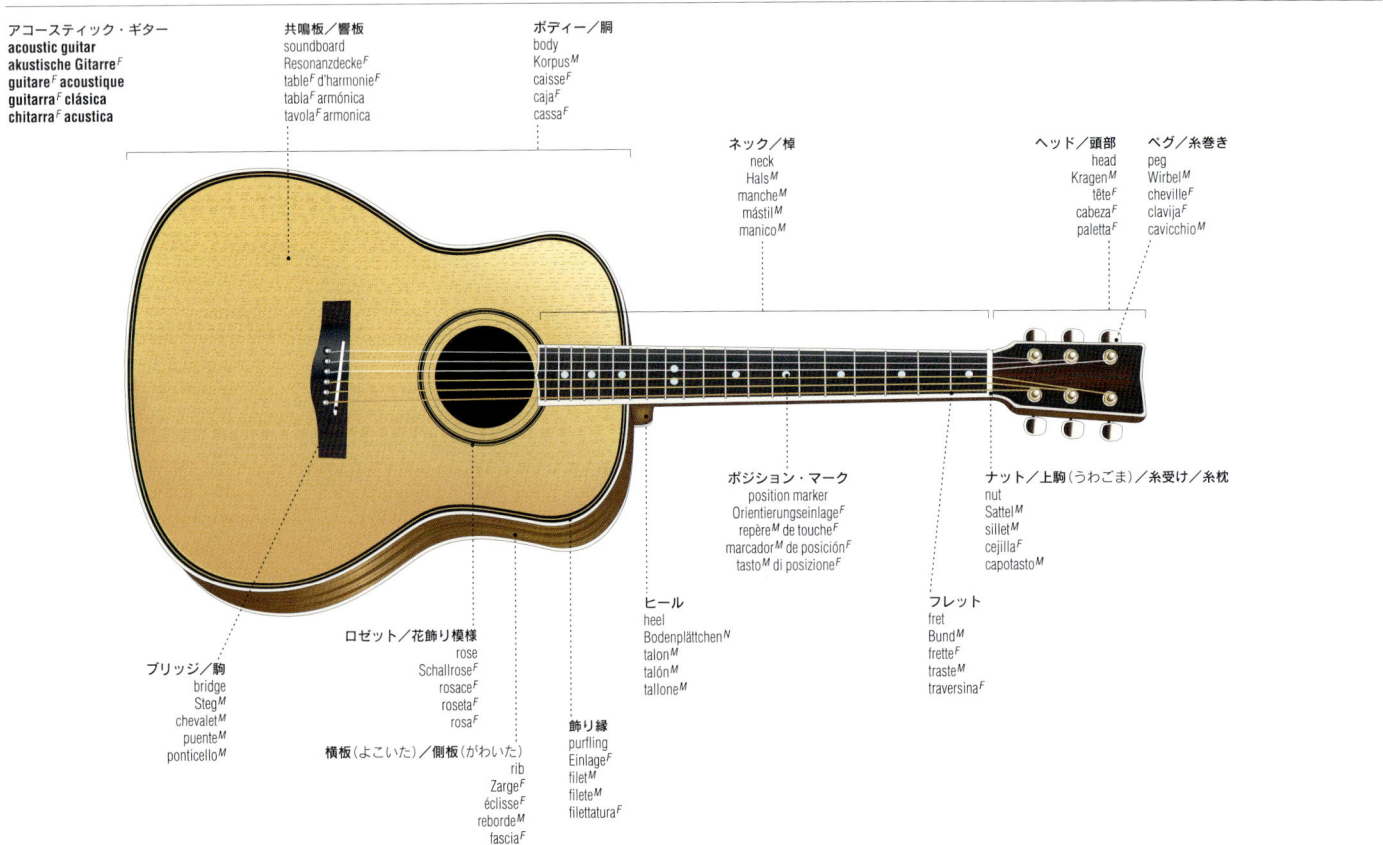

共鳴板／響板
soundboard
Resonanzdecke F
table F d'harmonie F
tabla F armónica
tavola F armonica

ボディー／胴
body
Korpus M
caisse F
caja F
cassa F

ネック／棹
neck
Hals M
manche M
mástil M
manico M

ヘッド／頭部
head
Kragen M
tête F
cabeza F
paletta F

ペグ／糸巻き
peg
Wirbel M
cheville F
clavija F
cavicchio M

ポジション・マーク
position marker
Orientierungseinlage F
repère M de touche F
marcador M de posición F
tasto M di posizione F

ナット／上駒(うわごま)／糸受け／糸枕
nut
Sattel M
sillet M
cejilla F
capotasto M

ヒール
heel
Bodenplättchen N
talon M
talón M
tallone M

フレット
fret
Bund M
frette F
traste M
traversina F

ブリッジ／駒
bridge
Steg M
chevalet M
puente M
ponticello M

ロゼット／花飾り模様
rose
Schallrose F
rosace F
roseta F
rosa F

横板(よこいた)／側板(がわいた)
rib
Zarge F
éclisse F
reborde M
fascia F

飾り縁
purfling
Einlage F
filet M
filete M
filettatura F

芸術と建築

440

音楽 ｜ MUSIC
MUSIK ｜ MUSIQUE ｜ MÚSICA ｜ MUSICA

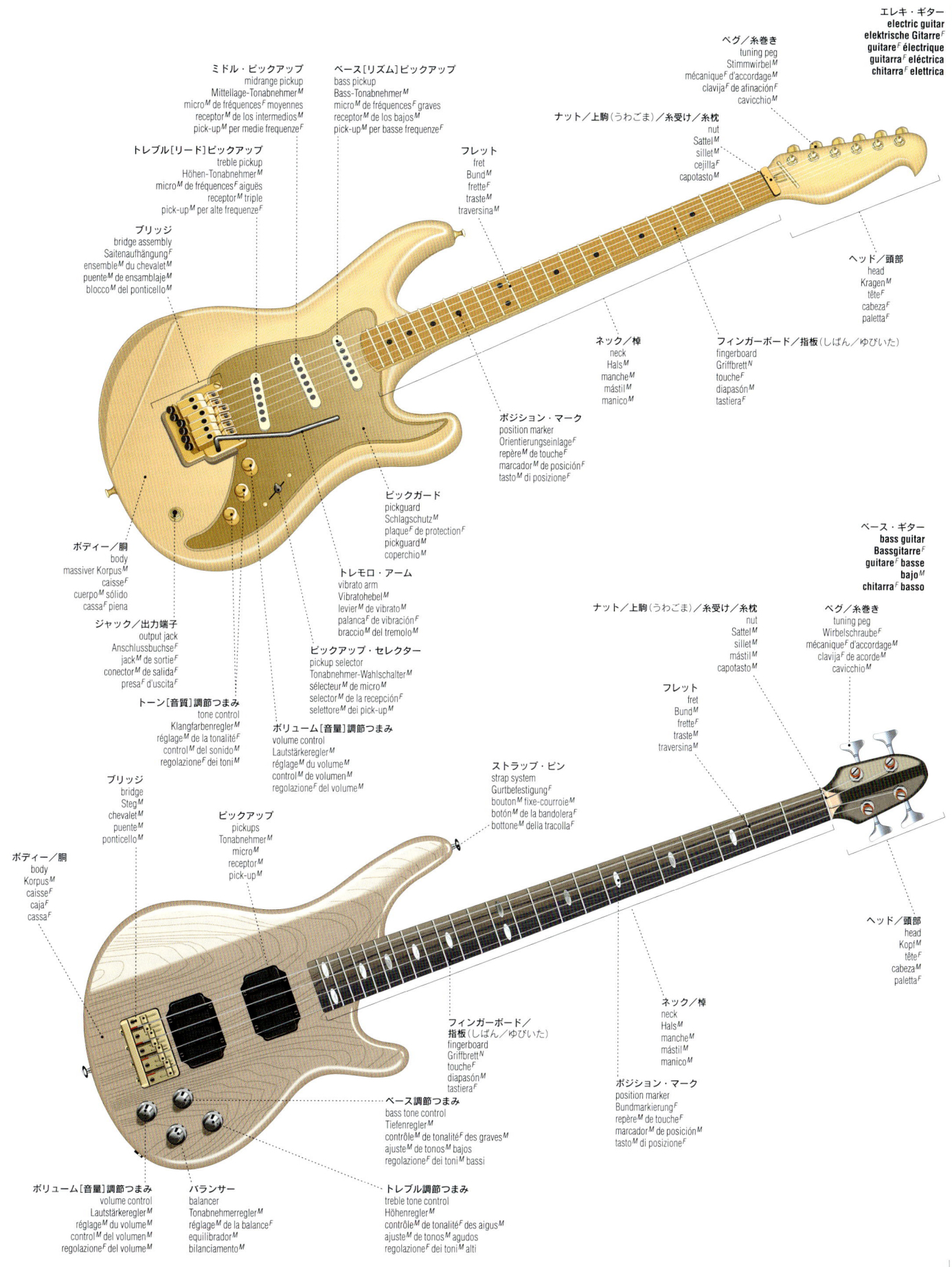

弦楽器

エレキ・ギター
electric guitar
elektrische Gitarre^F
guitare^F électrique
guitarra^F eléctrica
chitarra^F elettrica

ベグ／糸巻き
tuning peg
Stimmwirbel^M
mécanique^F d'accordage
clavija^F de afinación^F
cavicchio^M

ミドル・ピックアップ
midrange pickup
Mittellage-Tonabnehmer^M
micro^M de fréquences^F moyennes
receptor^M de los intermedios^M
pick-up^M per medie frequenze^F

ベース[リズム]ピックアップ
bass pickup
Bass-Tonabnehmer^M
micro^M de fréquences^F graves
receptor^M de los bajos^M
pick-up^M per basse frequenze^F

ナット／上駒（うわごま）／糸受け／糸枕
nut
Sattel^M
sillet^M
cejilla^F
capotasto^M

トレブル[リード]ピックアップ
treble pickup
Höhen-Tonabnehmer^M
micro^M de fréquences^F aiguës
receptor^M triple
pick-up^M per alte frequenze^F

フレット
fret
Bund^M
frette^F
traste^M
traversina^F

ブリッジ
bridge assembly
Saitenaufhängung^F
ensemble^M du chevalet^M
puente^F de ensamblaje^M
blocco^M del ponticello^M

ヘッド／頭部
head
Kragen^M
tête^F
cabeza^F
paletta^F

ネック／棹
neck
Hals^M
manche^F
mástil^M
manico^M

フィンガーボード／指板（しばん／ゆびいた）
fingerboard
Griffbrett^N
touche^F
diapasón^M
tastiera^F

ポジション・マーク
position marker
Orientierungseinlage^F
repère^F de touche^F
marcador^M de posición^F
tasto^M di posizione^F

ピックガード
pickguard
Schlagschutz^M
plaque^F de protection^F
pickguard^M
coperchio^M

ボディー／胴
body
massiver Korpus^M
caisse^F
cuerpo^M sólido
cassa^F piena

トレモロ・アーム
vibrato arm
Vibratohebel^M
levier^F de vibrato^M
palanca^F de vibración^F
braccio^M del tremolo^M

ジャック／出力端子
output jack
Anschlussbuchse^F
jack^M de sortie^F
conector^M de salida^F
presa^F d'uscita^F

ピックアップ・セレクター
pickup selector
Tonabnehmer-Wahlschalter^M
sélecteur^M de micro^M
selector^M de la recepción^F
selettore^M dei pick-up^M

ベース・ギター
bass guitar
Bassgitarre^F
guitare^F basse
bajo^M
chitarra^F basso

ナット／上駒（うわごま）／糸受け／糸枕
nut
Sattel^M
sillet^M
mástil^M
capotasto^M

ベグ／糸巻き
tuning peg
Wirbelschraube^F
mécanique^F d'accordage^M
clavija^F de acorde^M
cavicchio^M

トーン[音質]調節つまみ
tone control
Klangfarbenregler^M
réglage^F de la tonalité^F
control^M del sonido^M
regolazione^F dei toni^M

ボリューム[音量]調節つまみ
volume control
Lautstärkeregler^M
réglage^F du volume^M
control^M de volumen^M
regolazione^F del volume^M

フレット
fret
Bund^M
frette^F
traste^M
traversina^F

ストラップ・ピン
strap system
Gurtbefestigung^F
bouton^M fixe-courroie^F
botón^M de la bandolera^F
bottone^M della tracolla^F

ブリッジ
bridge
Steg^M
chevalet^M
puente^M
ponticello^M

ピックアップ
pickups
Tonabnehmer^M
micro^M
receptor^M
pick-up^M

ヘッド／頭部
head
Kopf^M
tête^F
cabeza^M
paletta^F

ボディー／胴
body
Korpus^M
caisse^F
caja^F
cassa^F

ネック／棹
neck
Hals^M
manche^F
mástil^M
manico^M

フィンガーボード／指板（しばん／ゆびいた）
fingerboard
Griffbrett^N
touche^F
diapasón^M
tastiera^F

ポジション・マーク
position marker
Bundmarkierung^F
repère^F de touche^F
marcador^M de posición^F
tasto^M di posizione^F

ベース調節つまみ
bass tone control
Tiefenregler^M
contrôle^M de tonalité^F des graves^M
ajuste^M de tonos^M bajos
regolazione^F dei toni^M bassi

ボリューム[音量]調節つまみ
volume control
Lautstärkeregler^M
réglage^F du volume^M
control^M del volumen^M
regolazione^F del volume^M

バランサー
balancer
Tonabnehmerregler^M
réglage^F de la balance^F
equilibrador^M
bilanciamento^M

トレブル調節つまみ
treble tone control
Höhenregler^M
contrôle^M de tonalité^F des aigus^M
ajuste^M de tonos^M agudos
regolazione^F dei toni^M alti

芸術と建築

441

音楽 | MUSIC
MUSIK | MUSIQUE | MÚSICA | MUSICA

鍵盤楽器

日本語 | 英語 | ドイツ語 | フランス語 | スペイン語 | イタリア語

keyboard instruments | Tasteninstrumente^N | instruments^M à clavier^M | instrumentos^M de teclado^M | strumenti^M a tastiera^F

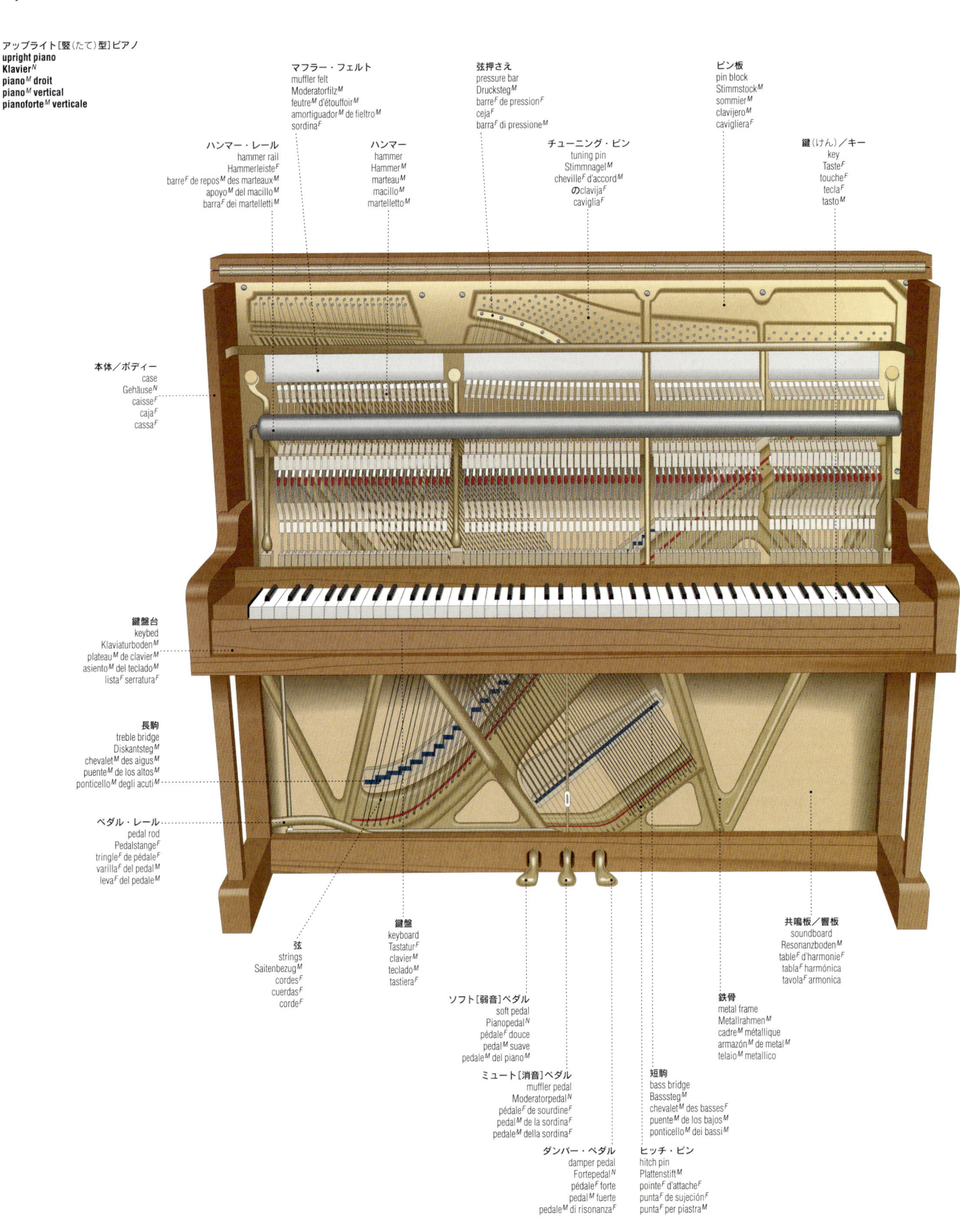

アップライト[竪(たて)型]ピアノ
upright piano
Klavier^N
piano^M droit
piano^M vertical
pianoforte^M verticale

マフラー・フェルト
muffler felt
Moderatorfilz^M
feutre^M d'étouffoir^M
amortiguador^M de fieltro^M
sordina^F

弦押さえ
pressure bar
Drucksteg^M
barre^F de pression^F
ceja^F
barra^F di pressione^M

ピン板
pin block
Stimmstock^M
sommier^M
clavijero^M
cavigliera^F

ハンマー・レール
hammer rail
Hammerleiste^F
barre^F de repos^M des marteaux^M
apoyo^M del macillo^M
barra^F dei martelletti^M

ハンマー
hammer
Hammer^M
marteau^M
macillo^M
martelletto^M

チューニング・ピン
tuning pin
Stimmnagel^M
cheville^F d'accord^M
clavija^F de
caviglia^F

鍵(けん)／キー
key
Taste^F
touche^F
tecla^F
tasto^M

本体／ボディー
case
Gehäuse^N
caisse^F
caja^F
cassa^F

鍵盤台
keybed
Klaviaturboden^M
plateau^M de clavier^M
asiento^M del teclado^M
lista^F serratura^F

長駒
treble bridge
Diskantsteg^M
chevalet^M des aigus^M
puente^M de los altos^M
ponticello^M degli acuti^M

ペダル・レール
pedal rod
Pedalstange^F
tringle^F de pédale^F
varilla^F del pedal^M
leva^F del pedale^M

弦
strings
Saitenbezug^M
cordes^F
cuerdas^F
corde^F

鍵盤
keyboard
Tastatur^F
clavier^M
teclado^M
tastiera^F

ソフト[弱音]ペダル
soft pedal
Pianopedal^N
pédale^F douce
pedal^M suave
pedale^M del piano^M

ミュート[消音]ペダル
muffler pedal
Moderatorpedal^N
pédale^F de sourdine^F
pedal^M de la sordina^F
pedale^M della sordina^F

ダンパー・ペダル
damper pedal
Fortepedal^N
pédale^F forte
pedal^M fuerte
pedale^M di risonanza^F

共鳴板／響板
soundboard
Resonanzboden^M
table^F d'harmonie^F
tabla^F harmónica
tavola^F armonica

鉄骨
metal frame
Metallrahmen^M
cadre^M métallique
armazón^M de metal^M
telaio^M metallico

短駒
bass bridge
Basssteg^M
chevalet^M des basses^F
puente^M de los bajos^M
ponticello^M dei bassi^M

ヒッチ・ピン
hitch pin
Plattenstift^M
pointe^F d'attache^F
punta^F de sujeción^F
punta^F per piastra^M

芸術と建築

音楽 | MUSIC
MUSIK | MUSIQUE | MÚSICA | MUSICA

鍵盤楽器

アップライト・ピアノのアクション[打弦機構]
upright piano action
Klaviermechanik^F
mécanique^F du piano^M droit
mecanismo^M del piano^M vertical
meccanica^F del pianoforte^M verticale

弦
string
Saite^F
corde^F
cuerda^F
corda^F

ダンパー
damper
Dämpfer^M
étouffoir^M
apagador^M
smorzatore^M

ダンパー・レール
damper rail
Dämpferpralleiste^F
barre^F d'étouffoir^M
apoyo^M de la sordina^F
barra^F dello smorzatore^M

ハンマー・バット
hammer butt
Hammernuss^F
noix^F
cabo^M del macillo^M
salterello^M

ダンパー・レバー
damper lever
Dämpferarm^M
lame^F d'étouffoir^M
palanca^F del apagador^M
leva^F dello smorzatore^M

ジャック／弾機
jack
Stoßzunge^F
levier^M d'échappement^M
martinete^M
scappamento^M

調節ボタン
regulating button
Auslösepuppe^F
bouton^M d'échappement^M
regulador^M
bottone^M di regolazione^F

ジャック・スプリング
jack spring
Stoßzungenschraubenfeder^F
ressort^M d'échappement^M
resorte^M del martinete^M
molla^F dello scappamento^M

ハンマー・フェルト
hammer felt
Hammerfilz^M
feutre^M
macillo^M de fieltro^M
feltro^M del martelletto^M

ハンマー（ヘッド）
hammer
Hammer^M
marteau^M
macillo^M
martelletto^M

ハンマー・レール
hammer rail
Hammerruheleiste^F
barre^F de repos^M des marteaux^M
apoyo^M del macillo^M
barra^F del martelletto^M

ハンマー・シャンク
hammer shank
Hammerstiel^M
manche^M
vástago^M del macillo^M
asta^F del martelletto^M

キャッチャー
catcher
Gegenfänger^M
contre-attrape^F
receptor^M
nasello^M del paramartello^M

バック・チェック
back check
Fänger^M
attrape^F
descanso^M del macillo^M
paramartello^M

ブライドル・テープ
bridle tape
Bändchen^N
lanière^F
tirante^M
tirante^M

鍵（けん）／キー
key
Taste^F
touche^F
tecla^F
tasto^M

キャプスタン
capstan button
Pilote^F
pilote^M
cabrestante^M
perno^M

ウィペン
action lever; *action lever*
Hebeglied^N
chevalet^M
mecanismo^M de la palanca^F
cavalletto^M

バランス・レール
balance rail
Waagebalken^M
pointe^F
fulcro^M
bilanciere^M

鍵盤楽器の例
examples of keyboard instruments
Beispiele^N für Tasteninstrumente^N
exemples^M d'instruments^M à clavier^M
ejemplos^M de instrumentos^M de teclado^M
esempi^M di strumenti^M a tastiera^F

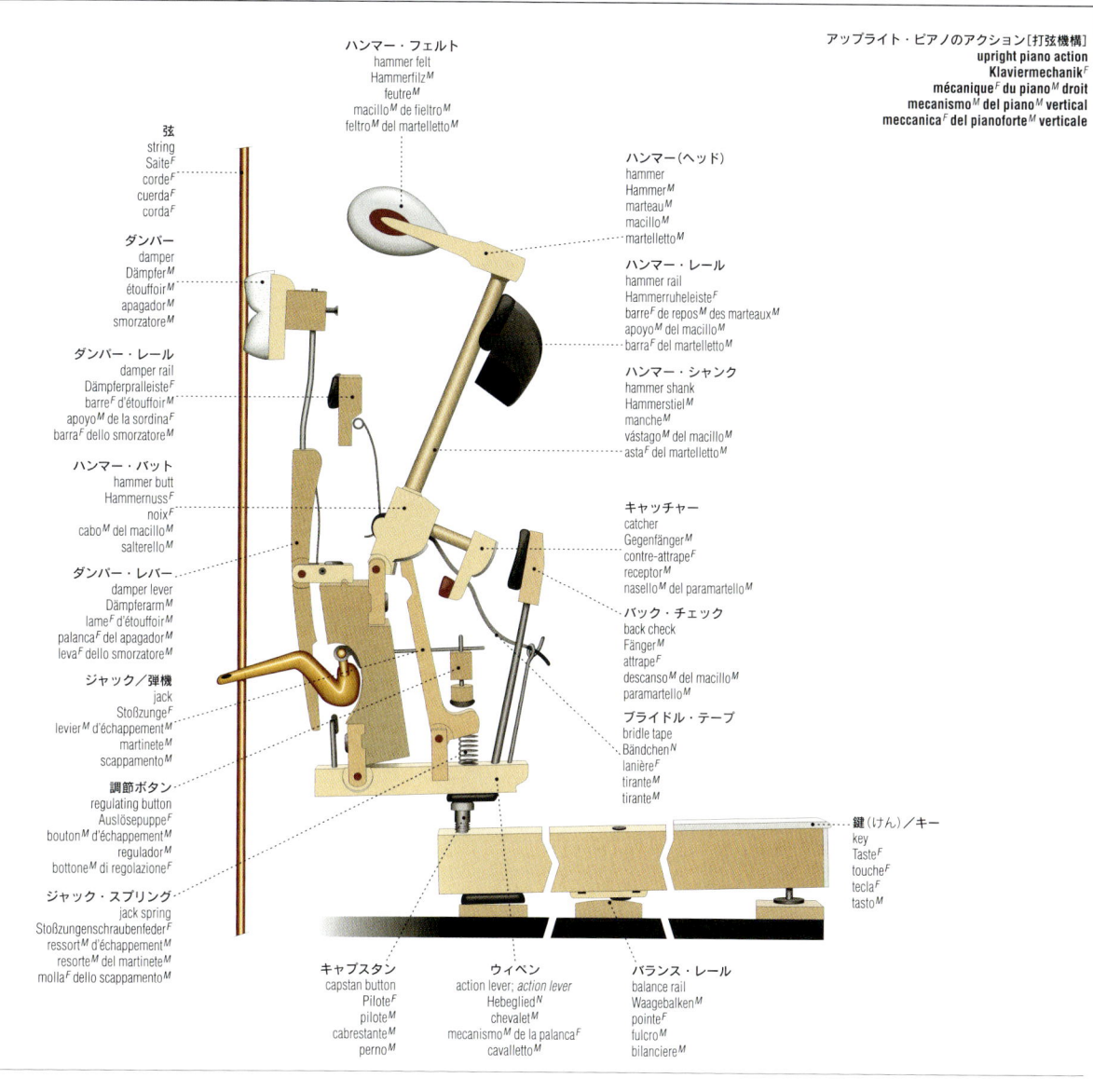

コンサート・グランド
concert grand
Konzertflügel^M
piano^M à queue^F de concert^M
piano^M de cola^F de concierto^M
pianoforte^M a coda^F da concerto^M

ベビー・グランド
baby grand
Kleinflügel^M
piano^M quart-de-queue^F
piano^M cuarto de cola^F
pianoforte^M a un quarto^M di coda^F

家庭用グランド
boudoir grand
Salonflügel^M
piano^M demi-queue^M
piano^M de media cola^F
pianoforte^M a mezza coda^F

ハープシコード／チェンバロ／クラブサン
harpsichord
Cembalo^N
clavecin^M
clavecín^M
clavicembalo^M

芸術と建築

音楽 | MUSIC
MUSIK | MUSIQUE | MÚSICA | MUSICA

鍵盤楽器

オルガン
organ
Orgel^F
orgue^M
órgano^M
organo^M

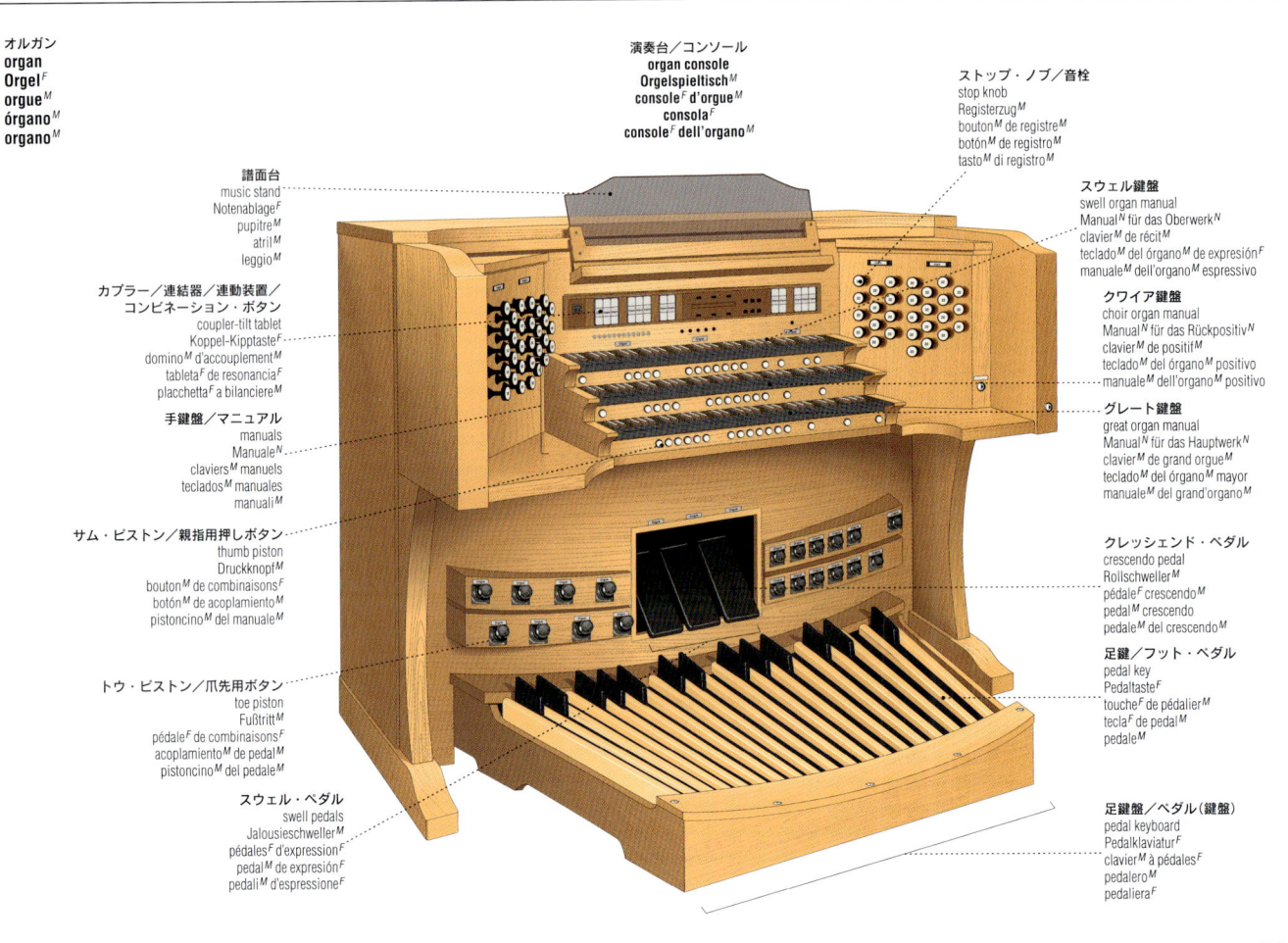

演奏台／コンソール
organ console
Orgelspieltisch^M
console^F d'orgue^M
consola^F
console^F dell'organo^M

ストップ・ノブ／音栓
stop knob
Registerzug^M
bouton^M de registre^M
botón^M de registro^M
tasto^M di registro^M

譜面台
music stand
Notenablage^F
pupitre^M
atril^M
leggio^M

スウェル鍵盤
swell organ manual
Manual^N für das Oberwerk^N
clavier^M de récit^M
teclado^M del órgano^M de expresión^F
manuale^M dell'organo^M espressivo

カプラー／連結器／連動装置／コンビネーション・ボタン
coupler-tilt tablet
Koppel-Kipptaste^F
domino^M d'accouplement^M
tableta^F de resonancia^F
placchetta^F a bilanciere^M

クワイア鍵盤
choir organ manual
Manual^N für das Rückpositiv^N
clavier^M de positif^M
teclado^M del órgano^M positivo
manuale^M dell'organo^M positivo

手鍵盤／マニュアル
manuals
Manuale^N
claviers^M manuels
teclados^M manuales
manuali^M

グレート鍵盤
great organ manual
Manual^N für das Hauptwerk^N
clavier^M de grand orgue^M
teclado^M del órgano^M mayor
manuale^M del grand'organo^M

サム・ピストン／親指用押しボタン
thumb piston
Druckknopf^M
bouton^M de combinaisons^M
botón^M de acoplamiento^M
pistoncino^M del manuale^M

クレッシェンド・ペダル
crescendo pedal
Rollschweller^M
pédale^F crescendo^M
pedal^M crescendo
pedale^M del crescendo^M

足鍵／フット・ペダル
pedal key
Pedaltaste^F
touche^F de pédalier^M
tecla^F de pedal^M
pedale^M

トウ・ピストン／爪先用ボタン
toe piston
Fußtritt^M
pédale^F de combinaisons^F
acoplamiento^M de pedal^M
pistoncino^M del pedale^M

スウェル・ペダル
swell pedals
Jalousieschweller^M
pédales^F d'expression^F
pedal de expresión^F
pedali^M d'espressione^F

足鍵盤／ペダル(鍵盤)
pedal keyboard
Pedalklaviatur^F
clavier^M à pédales^F
pedalero^M
pedaliera^F

リード・パイプ
reed pipe
Zungenpfeife^F
tuyau^M à anche^F
tubo^M de lengüeta^F
canna^F ad ancia^F

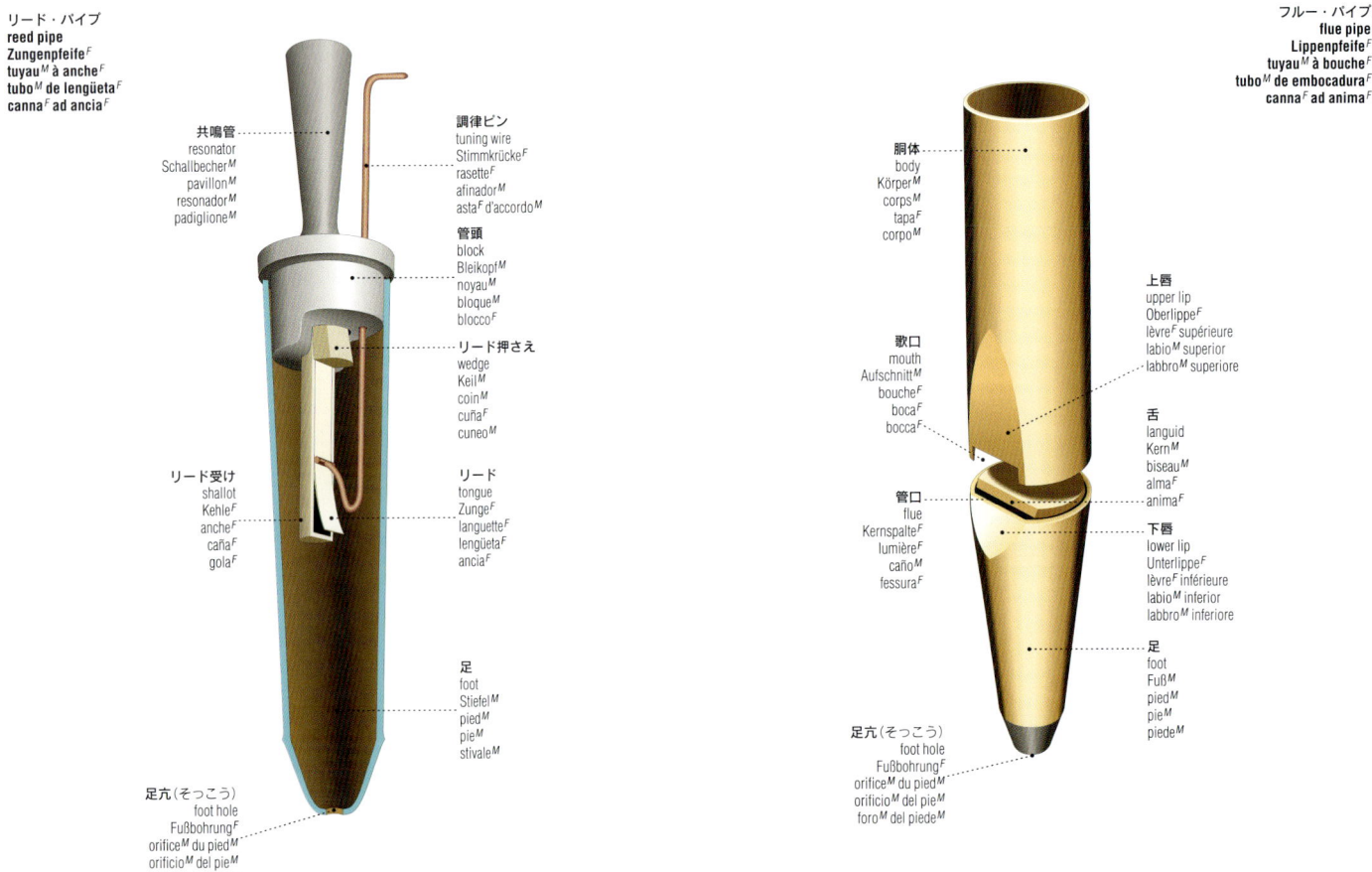

フルー・パイプ
flue pipe
Lippenpfeife^F
tuyau^M à bouche^F
tubo^M de embocadura^F
canna^F ad anima^F

共鳴管
resonator
Schallbecher^M
pavillon^M
resonador^M
padiglione^M

調律ピン
tuning wire
Stimmkrücke^F
rasette^F
afinador^M
asta^F d'accordo^M

胴体
body
Körper^M
corps^M
tapa^F
corpo^M

管頭
block
Bleikopf^M
noyau^M
bloque^M
blocco^M

上唇
upper lip
Oberlippe^F
lèvre^F supérieure
labio^M superior
labbro^M superiore

リード押さえ
wedge
Keil^M
coin^M
cuña^F
cuneo^M

歌口
mouth
Aufschnitt^M
bouche^F
boca^F
bocca^F

舌
languid
Kern^M
biseau^M
alma^F
anima^F

リード受け
shallot
Kehle^F
anche^F
caña^F
gola^F

リード
tongue
Zunge^F
languette^F
lengüeta^F
ancia^F

管口
flue
Kernspalte^F
lumière^F
caño^M
fessura^F

下唇
lower lip
Unterlippe^F
lèvre^F inférieure
labio^M inferior
labbro^M inferiore

足
foot
Fuß^M
pied^M
pie^M
piede^M

足
foot
Stiefel^M
pied^M
pie^M
stivale^M

足穴（そっこう）
foot hole
Fußbohrung^F
orifice^M du pied^M
orificio^M del pie^M
foro^M del piede^M

足穴（そっこう）
foot hole
Fußbohrung^F
orifice^M du pied^M
orificio^M del pie^M
foro^M del piede^M

音楽 | MUSIC
MUSIK | MUSIQUE | MÚSICA | MUSICA

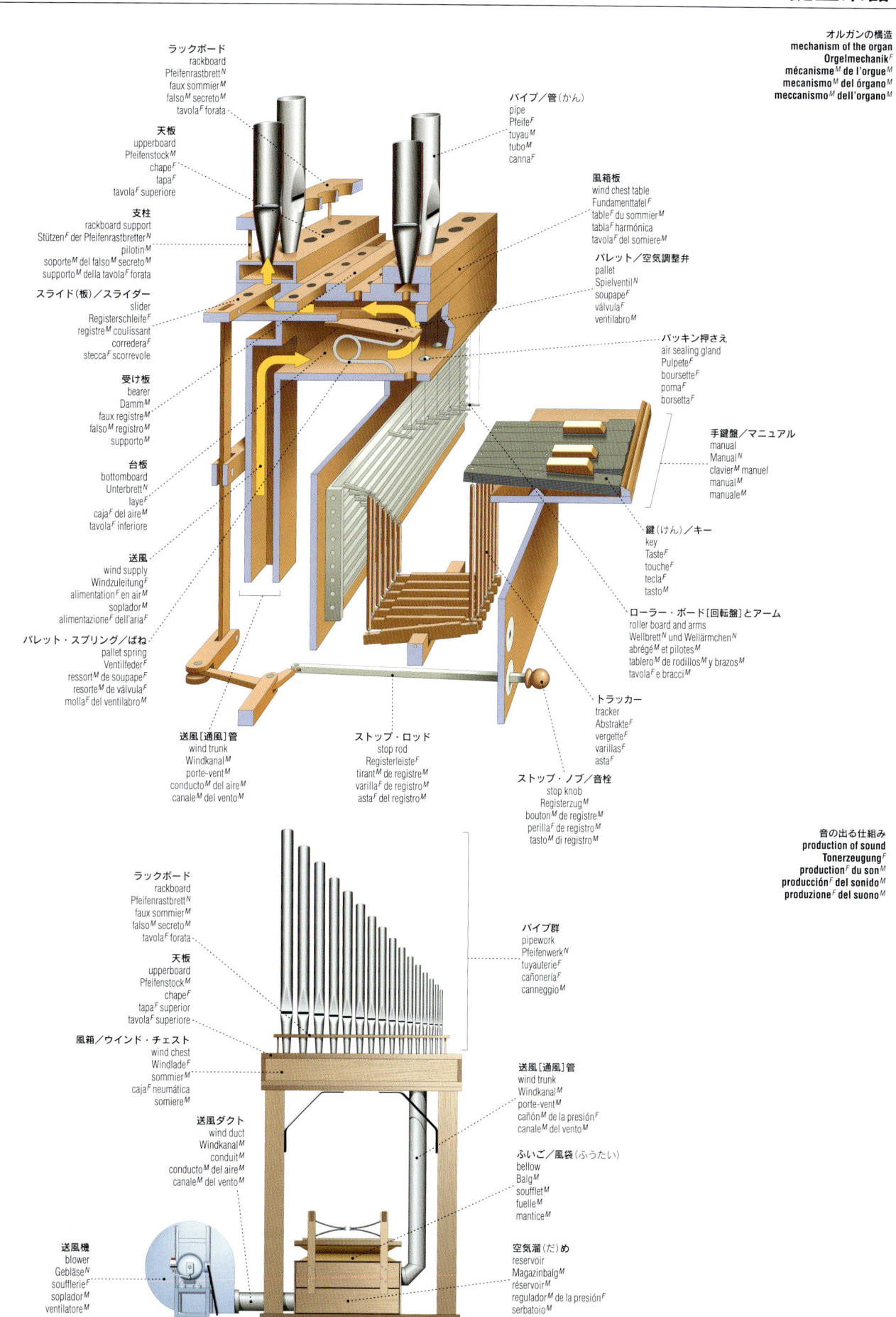

鍵盤楽器

オルガンの構造
mechanism of the organ
Orgelmechanik^F
mécanisme^M de l'orgue^M
mecanismo^M del órgano^M
meccanismo^M dell'organo^M

ラックボード
rackboard
Pfeifenrastbrett^N
faux sommier^M
falso^M secreto^M
tavola^F forata

天板
upperboard
Pfeifenstock^M
chape^F
tapa^F
tavola^F superiore

支柱
rackboard support
Stützen^F der Pfeifenrastbretter^N
pilotin^M
soporte^M del falso^M secreto^M
supporto^M della tavola^F forata

スライド(板)／スライダー
slider
Registerschleife^F
registre^M coulissant
corredera^F
stecca^F scorrevole

受け板
bearer
Damm^M
faux registre^M
falso^M registro^M
supporto^M

台板
bottomboard
Unterbrett^N
laye^F
caja^F del aire^M
tavola^F inferiore

送風
wind supply
Windzuleitung^F
alimentation^F en air^M
soplador^M
alimentazione^F dell'aria^M

パレット・スプリング／ばね
pallet spring
Ventilfeder^F
ressort^M de soupape^F
resorte^M de válvula^F
molla^F del ventilabro^M

パイプ／管(かん)
pipe
Pfeife^F
tuyau^M
tubo^M
canna^F

風箱板
wind chest table
Fundamenttafel^F
table^F du sommier^M
tabla^F harmónica
tavola^F del somiere^M

パレット／空気調整弁
pallet
Spielventil^N
soupape^F
válvula^F
ventilabro^M

パッキン押さえ
air sealing gland
Pulpete^F
boursette^F
poma^F
borsetta^F

手鍵盤／マニュアル
manual
Manual^N
clavier^M manuel
manual^M
manuale^M

鍵(けん)／キー
key
Taste^F
touche^F
tecla^F
tasto^M

ローラー・ボード[回転盤]とアーム
roller board and arms
Wellbrett^N und Wellärmchen^N
abrégé^M et pilotes^M
tablero^M de rodillos^M y brazos^M
tavola^F e bracci^M

トラッカー
tracker
Abstrakte^F
vergette^F
varillas^F
asta^F

送風[通風]管
wind trunk
Windkanal^M
porte-vent^M
conducto^M del aire^M
canale^M del vento^M

ストップ・ロッド
stop rod
Registerleiste^F
tirant^M de registre^M
varilla^F de registro^M
asta^F del registro^M

ストップ・ノブ／音栓
stop knob
Registerzug^M
bouton^M de registre^M
perilla^F de registro^M
tasto^M di registro^M

音の出る仕組み
production of sound
Tonerzeugung^F
production^F du son^M
producción^F del sonido^M
produzione^F del suono^M

ラックボード
rackboard
Pfeifenrastbrett^N
faux sommier^M
falso^M secreto^M
tavola^F forata

天板
upperboard
Pfeifenstock^M
chape^F
tapa^F superior
tavola^F superiore

風箱／ウインド・チェスト
wind chest
Windlade^F
sommier^M
caja^F neumática
somiere^M

送風ダクト
wind duct
Windkanal^M
conduit^M
conducto^M del aire^M
canale^M del vento^M

パイプ群
pipework
Pfeifenwerk^N
tuyauterie^F
cañonería^F
canneggio^M

送風[通風]管
wind trunk
Windkanal^M
porte-vent^M
cañón^M de la presión^F
canale^M del vento^M

ふいご／風袋(ふうたい)
bellow
Balg^M
soufflet^M
fuelle^M
mantice^M

送風機
blower
Gebläse^N
soufflerie^F
soplador^M
ventilatore^M

空気溜(だ)め
reservoir
Magazinbalg^M
réservoir^M
regulador^M de la presión^F
serbatoio^M

芸術と建築

445

音楽 | MUSIC
MUSIK | MUSIQUE | MÚSICA | MUSICA

管楽器

日本語 | 英語 | ドイツ語 | フランス語 | スペイン語 | イタリア語

wind instruments | Blasinstrumente^N | instruments^M à vent^M | instrumentos^M de viento^M | strumenti^M a fiato^M

サクソフォン
saxophone
Saxophon^N
saxophone^M
saxofón^M
sassofono^M

マウスピース／吹き口／歌口
mouthpiece
Mundstück^N
bec^M
boquilla^F
bocchino

クルック／吹き込み管
crook
S-Bogen^M
bocal^M
embocadura^F
chiver^M

クルック・キー
crook key
Griffhebel^M für S-Bogen^M
clé^F de bocal^M
llave^F de embocadura^F
chiave^F del chiver^M

キー・レバー
key lever
Klappenstiel^M
levier^M de clé^F
palanca^F
leva^F della chiave^F

ダブル・リード
double reed
Doppelblatt^N
anche^F double
doble caña^F
ancia^F doppia

シングル・リード
single reed
Rohrblatt^N
anche^F simple
caña^F simple
ancia^F semplice

リガチャー／留め金／締め金
ligature
Blattschraube^F
bague^F de serrage^M
anillo^M de ajuste^M
legatura^F

リード
reed
Rohrblatt^N
anche^F
lengüeta^F
ancia^F

オクターブ・レバー
octave mechanism
Oktavmechanik^F
mécanisme^M d'octave^F
mecanismo^M para las octavas^F
meccanismo^M dell'ottava^F

ベル／朝顔
bell
Trichter^M
pavillon^M
pabellón^M
campana^F

ベルの留め金／ベル支柱
bell brace
Schallbecherstütze^F
attache^F de pavillon^M
sujetador^M del pabellón^M
attacco^M della campana^F

ボディー／本体
body
Korpus^M
corps^M
cuerpo^M
corpo^M

キー
key
Klappe^F
clé^F
llave^F
chiave^F

指当て
key finger button
Klappendrücker^M
bouton^M de clé^F
botón^M de la llave^F
tasto^M

キー・ガード
key guard
Klappenschutz^M
garde^F de clé^F
dispositivo^M de protección^F
protezione^F delle chiavi^F

親指掛け
thumb rest
Daumenauflage^F
support^M de pouce^M
gancho^M del pulgar^M
appoggio^M del pollice^M

ブリーチ／下部
breech
Bogen^M
culasse^F
culata^F
curva^F

ブリーチ・ガード
breech guard
Bogenschutz^M
garde^F de culasse^F
protector^M de la culata^F
rinforzo^M della curva^F

ピッコロ
piccolo
Pikkoloflöte^F
piccolo^M
píccolo^M
ottavino^M

バスーン／ファゴット
bassoon
Fagott^N
basson^M
fagot^M
fagotto^M

クラリネット
clarinet
Klarinette^F
clarinette^F
clarinete^M
clarinetto^M

オーボエ
oboe
Oboe^F
hautbois^M
oboe^M
oboe^M

フルート
tranverse flute
Querflöte^F
flûte^F traversière
flauta^F
flauto^M

イングリッシュ・ホルン／コーラングレ
English horn; *cor anglais*
Englischhorn^N
cor^M anglais
corno^M inglés
corno^M inglese

446

音楽 | MUSIC
MUSIK | MUSIQUE | MÚSICA | MUSICA

管楽器

トランペット
trumpet
Trompete^F
trompette^F
trompeta^F
tromba^F

ピストン／バルブ・ボタン
finger button
Drücker^M
bouton^F de piston^M
llave^F
pistone^M

小指掛け
little finger hook
Kleinfingerhaken^M
crochet^F de petit doigt^M
gancho^M del meñique^M
appoggio^M del mignolo^M

ベル／朝顔
bell
Trichter^M
pavillon^M
pabellón^M
campana^F

マウスピース・レシーバー
mouthpiece receiver
Mundstückaufnahme^F
boisseau^F d'embouchure^F
empate^M de la boquilla^F
alloggiamento^M del bocchino^F

マウスパイプ／吹き込み管
mouthpipe
Mundrohr^N
branche^F d'embouchure^F
tubo^M
canna^F di imboccatura^F

指掛けリング
ring
Ring^M
bague^F
anillo^M
anello^M

マウスピース／吹き口／歌口
mouthpiece
Mundstück^N
embouchure^F
boquilla^F
bocchino^M

第1抜き差し管
first valve slide
erster Ventilzug^M
coulisse^F du premier piston^M
primer pistón^M móvil
tubo^M della prima valvola^F

親指掛け
thumb hook
Daumenring^M
crochet^M de pouce^M
gancho^M del pulgar^M
appoggio^M del pollice^M

第3抜き差し管
third valve slide
dritter Ventilzug^M
coulisse^F du troisième piston^M
tercer pistón^M móvil
tubo^M della terza valvola^F

主管／チューニング・スライド
tuning slide
Stimmzug^M
coulisse^F d'accord^M
corredera^F de afinamiento^M
tubo^M di accordo^M

ウォーター・キー／唾（つば）抜き
water key
Wasserklappe^F
soupape^F d'évacuation^F
llave^F para agua^F
chiave^F dell'acqua^F

バルブ
valve
Ventil^N
piston^M
pistón^M
valvola^F

バルブ・ケース
valve casing
Ventilbüchse^F
corps^M de piston^M
tubo^M del pistón^M
corpo^M della valvola^F

第2抜き差し管
second valve slide
zweiter Ventilzug^M
coulisse^F du deuxième piston^M
segundo pistón^M móvil
tubo^M della seconda valvola^F

ミュート／弱音器
mute
Dämpfer^M
sourdine^F
sordina^F
sordina^F

コルネット
cornet
Kornett^N
cornet^M à pistons^M
cornetín^M
cornetta^F

フレンチ・ホルン
French horn
Waldhorn^N
cor^M d'harmonie^F
corno^M francés
corno^M

ビューグル
bugle
Bügelhorn^N
clairon^M
clarín^M
tromba^F militare

サクソルン
saxhorn
Saxhorn^N
saxhorn^M
bombardino^M
saxhorn^M

チューバ
tuba
Tuba^F
tuba^M
tuba^F
tuba^F

トロンボーン
trombone
Posaune^F
trombone^M
trombón^M
trombone^M

芸術と建築

音楽 | MUSIC
MUSIK | MUSIQUE | MÚSICA | MUSICA

打楽器

日本語 | 英語 | ドイツ語 | フランス語 | スペイン語 | イタリア語

percussion instruments | Schlaginstrumente[N] | instruments[M] à percussion[F] | instrumentos[M] de percusión[F] | strumenti[M] a percussione[F]

ドラム
drums
Trommeln[F]
batterie[F]
batería[F]
batteria[F]

シンバル
cymbal
Becken[N]
cymbale[F] suspendue
platillo[M] suspendido
piatto[M]

ハイ・ハット・シンバル
high-hat cymbal
Charlestonmaschine[F]
cymbale[F] charleston
platillo[M] high hat
charleston[M]

トップ・ハイ・ハット
superior cymbal
oberes Becken[N]
cymbale[F] supérieure
platillo[M] superior
piatto[M] superiore

ボトム・ハイ・ハット
inferior cymbal
unteres Becken[N]
cymbale[F] inférieure
platillo[M] inferior
piatto[M] inferiore

ヘッド／打面
batter head
Trommelfell[N]
peau[F] de batterie
parche[M] superior
battitoia[F]

スネア・ドラム／小太鼓
snare drum
kleine Trommel[F]
caisse[F] claire
caja[F] clara
cassa[F] chiara

三脚
tripod stand
Dreifußständer[M]
trépied[M]
trípode[M]
treppiede[M]

バス・ドラム
bass drum
Basstrommel[F]
grosse caisse[F]
bombo[M]
grancassa[F]

タム・タム
tom-tom
Tomtom[N]
tam-tam[M]
tam-tam[M]
tom tom[M]

チューニング・ボルト
tension screw
Stellschraube[F]
vis[F] de tension[F]
clavija[F] de tensión[F]
tirante[M] a vite[F]

スタンド
stand
Ständer[M]
support[M]
soporte[M]
supporto[M]

ビーター
mallet
Schlegel[M]
mailloche[F]
palillo[M]
mazza[F]

フロア・タム／テナー・ドラム
tenor drum
Standtom[N]
caisse[F] roulante
tamboril[M]
tamburo[M] tenore[M]

脚
spur
Feststellspitze[F]
éperon[M]
espolón[M]
piedino[M]

ペダル
pedal
Pedal[N]
pédale[F]
pedal[M]
pedale[M]

脚
leg
Bein[N]
pied[M]
pata[F]
piedino[M]

ティンパニ／ケトル・ドラム
kettledrum
Kesselpauke[F]
timbale[F]
timbal[M]
timpano[M]

スネア・ドラム／小太鼓
snare drum
kleine Trommel[F]
caisse[F] claire
caja[F] clara
cassa[F] chiara

ラグ／つまみ
lug
Böckchen[N]
attache[F]
sujetador[M]
blocchetto[M]

テンション・ボルト
tension rod
Stimmeinrichtung[F]
tringle[F] de tension[F]
varilla[F] de tensión[F]
tirante[M]

ストレーナー／響き線スイッチ
snare strainer
Schnarrsaitenspanner[M]
tendeur[M] de timbre[M]
tensor[M] de las cuerdas[F]
tirante[M] della cordiera[F]

スナッピー／響き線／触り弦
snare
Schnarrsaite[F]
cordes[F] de timbre[M]
cuerdas[F]
cordiera[F]

スネア・ヘッド
snare head
Resonanzfell[N]
peau[F] de timbre[M]
parche[M] inferior
bordoniera[F]

締めボルト
tie rod
Spannschraube[F]
tirant[M]
barra[F] sujetadora
tirante[M] a vite[F]

ヘッド／打面
batter head
Trommelfell[N]
peau[F] de batterie
parche[M] superior
battitoia[F]

キャスター
caster
Rolle[F]
roulette[F]
ruedecilla[F]
rotella[F] orientabile

台／脚／ベース
foot
Bodenplatte[F]
pied[M]
pata[F]
base[F]

締め枠／カウンターフープ
metal counterhoop
Metallspannreifen[M]
cercle[M] de serrage[M]
arco[M] tensor
cerchio[M] di serraggio[M]

チューニング・ゲージ
tuning gauge
Stimmanzeiger[M]
manomètre[M] d'accord[M]
afinación[F]
chiavi[F] di tensione[F]

ケトル／シェル／胴
shell
Kessel[M]
fût[M]
concha[F]
caldaia[F]

支柱
strut
Strebe[F]
châssis[M]
puntal[M]
gabbia[F]

テンション・ロッド
tension rod
Stimmeinrichtung[F]
tringle[F] de tension[F]
varilla[F] de tensión[F]
tirante[M]

スパイダー・ナット
crown
Aufhängung[F]
couronne[F]
corona[F]
corona[F]

ペダル
pedal
Pedal[N]
pédale[F]
pedal[M]
pedale[M]

芸術と建築

音楽 | MUSIC
MUSIK | MUSIQUE | MÚSICA | MUSICA

打楽器

橇（そり）の鈴
sleigh bells
Schellen^F
grelots^M
cascabeles^M
sonagli^M

釣り鐘状の鈴
set of bells
Glockenband^N
clochettes^F
campanillas^F
campanelle^F

シストルム
sistrum
Sistrum^N
sistre^M
sistro^M
sistro^M

カスタネット
castanets
Kastagnetten^F
castagnettes^F
castañuelas^F
nacchere^F

シンバル
cymbals
Becken^N
cymbales^F
platillos^M
piatti^M

タンバリン
tambourine
Tamburin^N
tambour^M de basque^M
pandereta^F
tamburello^M

トライアングル
triangle
Triangel^M
triangle^M
triángulo^M
triangolo^M

ボンゴ
bongos
Bongos^N
bongo^M
bongos^M
bongos^M

ヘッド／打面
head
Fell^N
peau^F
parche^M
membrana^F

ジングル
jingle
Schelle^F
cymbalette^F
cascabel^M
sonagli^M

ビーター／打棒
metal rod
Stahlstab^M
battant^M
varilla^F de acero^M
bacchetta^F di metallo^M

どら／ゴング
gong
Gong^M
gong^M
gong^M
gong^M

ワイヤー・ブラシ
wire brush
Jazzbesen^M
balai^M métallique
escobilla^F metálica
spazzola^F metallica

シロフォン／ザイロフォン／木琴
xylophone
Xylophon^N
xylophone^M
xilófono^M
xilofono^M

ばち／スティック
sticks
Stöcke^M
baguettes^F
baquetas^F
bacchette^F

共鳴管
resonator
Resonanzröhren^F
tube^M de résonance^F
resonador^M
risonatore^M

枠／フレーム
frame
Rahmen^M
châssis^M
armazón^M
telaio^M

音板
bar
Platte^F
lame^F
barra^F
piastra^F

オーケストラ・チャイム／
チューブ・ベル／組み鐘
tubular bells
Röhrenglocken^F
carillon^M tubulaire
campanas^F tubulares
campane^F tubolari

ばち／マレット
mallets
Schlegel^M
mailloches^F
maza^F
mazze^F

芸術と建築

449

音楽 | MUSIC
MUSIK | MUSIQUE | MÚSICA | MUSICA

電子楽器

日本語 | 英語 | ドイツ語 | フランス語 | スペイン語 | イタリア語

electronic instruments | elektronische Instrumente[N] | instruments[M] électroniques | instrumentos[M] electrónicos | strumenti[M] elettronici

シーケンサー
sequencer
Sequencer[M]
séquenceur[M]
secuenciador[M]
sequencer[M]

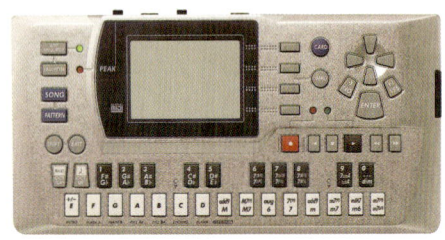

サンプラー
sampler
Sampler[M]
échantillonneur[M]
muestreador[M]
campionatore[M]

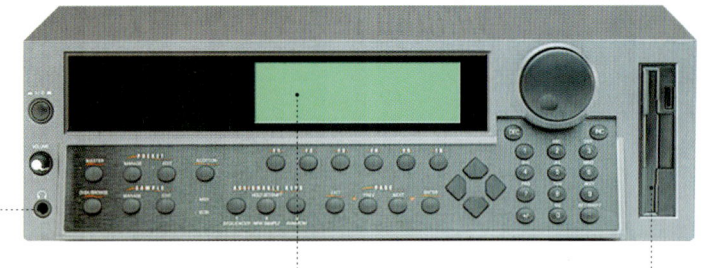

エクスパンダー
expander
Expander[M]
expandeur[M]
amplificador[M]
expander[M]

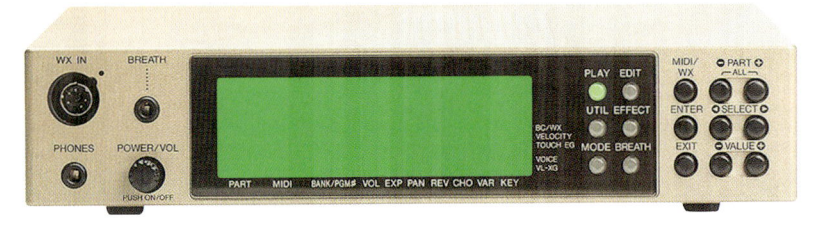

ヘッドホン端子
headphone jack
Kopfhöreranschlussbuchse[F]
prise[F] casque[M]
toma[F] para auriculares[M]
presa[F] per cuffia[F]

機能表示窓［画面］
function display
Funktionsdisplay[N]
affichage[M] des fonctions[F]
display[M] de las funciones[F]
display[M] delle funzioni[F]

ディスク・ドライブ
disk drive; disc drive
Diskettenlaufwerk[N]
lecteur[M] de disquette[F]
lector[M] de CD[M]
unità[F] a disco[M]

シンセサイザー
synthesizer
Synthesizer[M]
synthétiseur[M]
sintetizador[M]
sintetizzatore[M]

ディスク・ドライブ
disk drive; disc drive
Diskettenlaufwerk[N]
lecteur[M] de disquette[F]
unidad[F] de discos[M]
unità[F] a disco[M]

システム・ボタン
system buttons
Systemschalter[M]
fonctions[F] système[M]
sistema[M] de botones[M]
tasti[M] di sistema[M]

ボリューム・コントローラー
volume control
Lautstärkeregler[M]
contrôle[M] du volume[M]
control[M] de volumen[M]
controllo[M] del volume[M]

機能表示窓［画面］
function display
Funktionsanzeige[F]
affichage[M] des fonctions[F]
display[M] de funciones[F]
display[M] delle funzioni[F]

ファイン・データ・エントリー・コントロール
fine data entry control
Feinregler[M] für Dateneingabe[F]
modification[F] fine des variables[F]
control[M] de entrada[F] de información[F] fina
controllo[M] fine dei dati[M]

シーケンサー・コントロール
sequencer control
Sequenzerregler[M]
contrôle[M] du séquenceur[M]
control[M] de secuencias[F]
controllo[M] del sequencer[M]

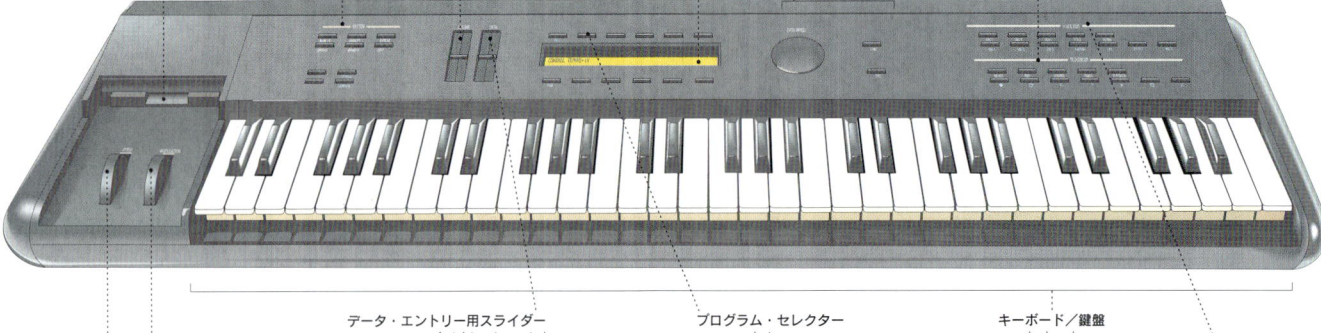

データ・エントリー用スライダー
fast data entry control
Grobregler[M] für Dateneingabe[F]
modification[F] rapide des variables[F]
control[M] de entrada[F] de información[F] rápida
controllo[M] veloce dei dati[M]

プログラム・セレクター
program selector
Programmwahlschalter[M]
sélecteur[M] de programme[M]
selector[M] de programa[M]
selettore[M] di programma[M]

キーボード／鍵盤
keyboard
Tastatur[F]
clavier[M]
teclado[M]
tastiera[F]

モジュレーション・ホイール
modulation wheel
Modulationsrad[N]
modulation[F] du timbre[M] du son[M]
rueda[F] de modulación[F]
rotella[F] di modulazione[F]

音声編集ボタン
voice edit buttons
Stimmenwahlschalter[M]
programmation[F] des voix[F]
botones[M] para editar la voz[F]
tasti[M] per l'editing[M] del suono[M]

ピッチ・ホイール
pitch wheel
Tonhöhenrad[N]
modulation[F] de la hauteur[F] du son[M]
rueda[F] para ajustar el tono[M]
rotella[F] di intonazione[F]

音楽 | MUSIC
MUSIK | MUSIQUE | MÚSICA | MUSICA

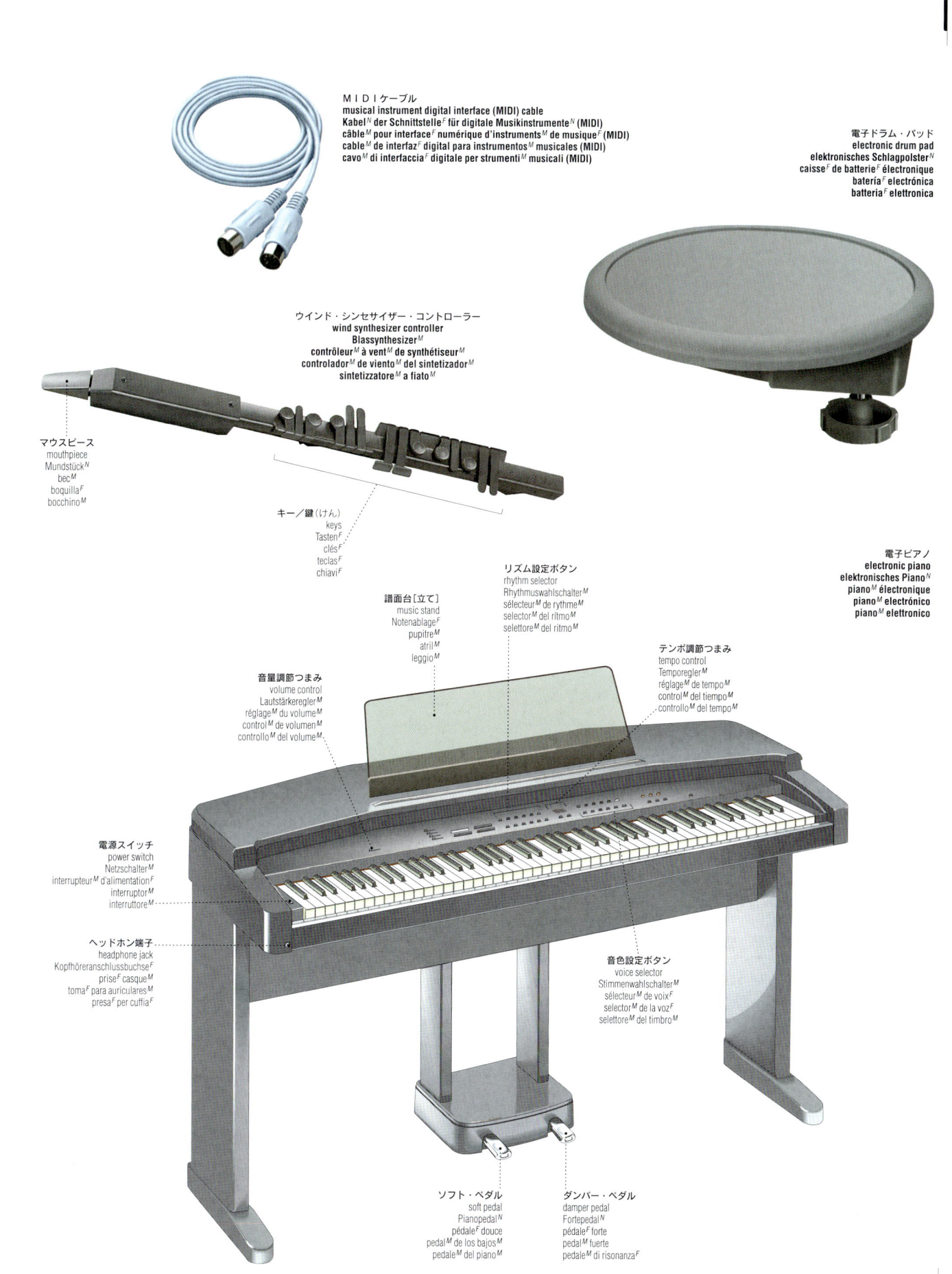

電子楽器

MIDIケーブル
musical instrument digital interface (MIDI) cable
Kabel^N der Schnittstelle^F für digitale Musikinstrumente^N (MIDI)
câble^M pour interface^F numérique d'instruments^M de musique^F (MIDI)
cable^M de interfaz^F digital para instrumentos^M musicales (MIDI)
cavo^M di interfaccia^F digitale per strumenti^M musicali (MIDI)

電子ドラム・パッド
electronic drum pad
elektronisches Schlagpolster^N
caisse^F de batterie^F électronique
batería^F electrónica
batteria^F elettronica

ウインド・シンセサイザー・コントローラー
wind synthesizer controller
Blassynthesizer^M
contrôleur^M à vent^M de synthétiseur^M
controlador^M de viento^M del sintetizador^M
sintetizzatore^M a fiato^M

マウスピース
mouthpiece
Mundstück^N
bec^M
boquilla^F
bocchino^M

キー／鍵（けん）
keys
Tasten^F
clés^F
teclas^F
chiavi^F

譜面台［立て］
music stand
Notenablage^F
pupitre^M
atril^M
leggio^M

リズム設定ボタン
rhythm selector
Rhythmuswahlschalter^M
sélecteur^M de rythme^M
selector^M del ritmo^M
selettore^M del ritmo^M

テンポ調節つまみ
tempo control
Temporegler^M
réglage^M de tempo^M
control^M del tiempo^M
controllo^M del tempo^M

電子ピアノ
electronic piano
elektronisches Piano^N
piano^M électronique
piano^M electrónico
piano^M elettronico

音量調節つまみ
volume control
Lautstärkeregler^M
réglage^M du volume^M
control^M de volumen^M
controllo^M del volume^M

電源スイッチ
power switch
Netzschalter^M
interrupteur^M d'alimentation^F
interruptor^M
interruttore^M

ヘッドホン端子
headphone jack
Kopfhöreranschlussbuchse^F
prise^F casque^M
toma^F para auriculares^M
presa^F per cuffia^F

音色設定ボタン
voice selector
Stimmenwahlschalter^M
sélecteur^M de voix^F
selector^M de la voz^F
selettore^M del timbro^M

ソフト・ペダル
soft pedal
Pianopedal^N
pédale^F douce
pedal^M de los bajos^M
pedale^M del piano^M

ダンパー・ペダル
damper pedal
Fortepedal^N
pédale^F forte
pedal^M fuerte
pedale^M di risonanza^F

芸術と建築

裁縫
sewing | Nähen^N | couture^F | costura^F | cucito^M

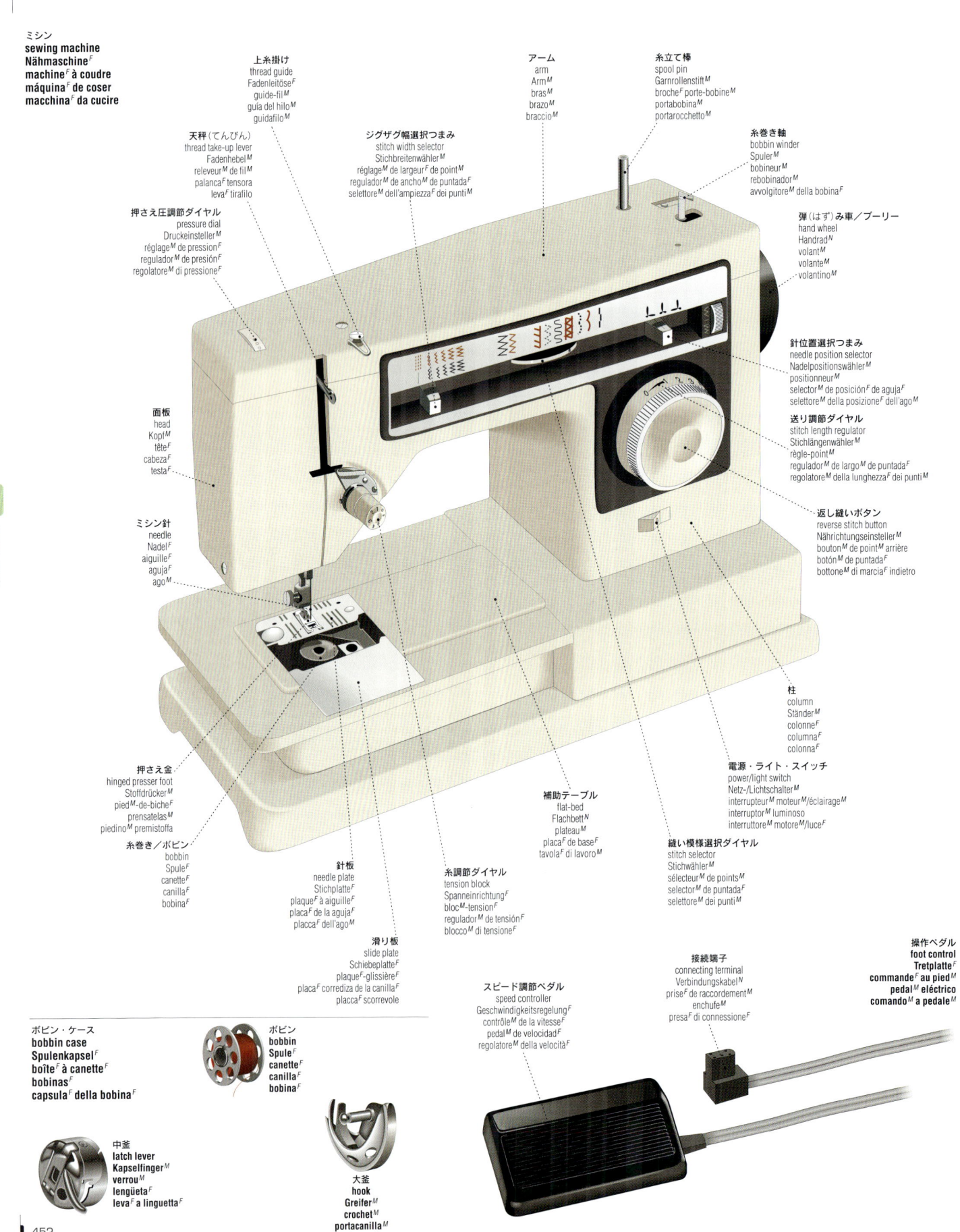

| 日本語 | 英語 | ドイツ語 | フランス語 | スペイン語 | イタリア語 |

ミシン — sewing machine / Nähmaschine^F / machine^F à coudre / máquina^F de coser / macchina^F da cucire

上糸掛け — thread guide / Fadenleitöse^F / guide-fil^M / guía del hilo^M / guidafilo^M

アーム — arm / Arm^M / bras^M / brazo^M / braccio^M

糸立て棒 — spool pin / Garnrollenstift^M / broche^F porte-bobine^F / portabobina^M / portarocchetto^M

天秤（てんびん） — thread take-up lever / Fadenhebel^M / releveur^M de fil^M / palanca^F tensora / leva^F tirafilo

ジグザグ幅選択つまみ — stitch width selector / Stichbreitenwähler^M / réglage^M de largeur^F de point^M / regulador^M de ancho de puntada^F / selettore^M dell'ampiezza^F dei punti^M

糸巻き軸 — bobbin winder / Spuler^M / bobineur^M / rebobinador^M / avvolgitore^M della bobina^F

押さえ圧調節ダイヤル — pressure dial / Druckeinsteller^M / réglage^M de pression^F / regulador^M de presión^F / regolatore^M di pressione^F

弾（はず）み車／プーリー — hand wheel / Handrad^N / volant^M / volante^M / volantino^M

針位置選択つまみ — needle position selector / Nadelpositionswähler^M / positionneur^M / selector^M de posición^F de aguja^F / selettore^M della posizione^F dell'ago^M

面板 — head / Kopf^M / tête^F / cabeza^F / testa^F

送り調節ダイヤル — stitch length regulator / Stichlängenwähler^M / règle-point^M / regulador^M de largo^M de puntada^F / regolatore^M della lunghezza^F dei punti^M

ミシン針 — needle / Nadel^F / aiguille^F / aguja^F / ago^M

返し縫いボタン — reverse stitch button / Nährichtungseinsteller^M / bouton^M de point^M arrière / botón^M de puntada^F / bottone^M di marcia^F indietro

柱 — column / Ständer^M / colonne^F / columna^F / colonna^F

押さえ金 — hinged presser foot / Stoffdrücker^M / pied^M-de-biche^F / prensatelas^M / piedino^M premistoffa

電源・ライト・スイッチ — power/light switch / Netz-/Lichtschalter^M / interrupteur^M moteur^M/éclairage^M / interruptor^M luminoso / interruttore^M motore^M/luce^F

補助テーブル — flat-bed / Flachbett^N / plateau^M / placa^F de base^F / tavola^F di lavoro^M

縫い模様選択ダイヤル — stitch selector / Stichwähler^M / sélecteur^M de points^M / selector^M de puntada^F / selettore^M dei punti^M

糸巻き／ボビン — bobbin / Spule^F / canette^F / canilla^F / bobina^F

針板 — needle plate / Stichplatte^F / plaque^F à aiguille^F / placa^F de la aguja^F / placca^F dell'ago^M

糸調節ダイヤル — tension block / Spanneinrichtung^F / bloc^M-tension^F / regulador^M de tensión^F / blocco^M di tensione^F

滑り板 — slide plate / Schiebeplatte^F / plaque^F-glissière^F / placa^F corrediza de la canilla^F / placca^F scorrevole

接続端子 — connecting terminal / Verbindungskabel^N / prise^F de raccordement^M / enchufe^M / presa^F di connessione^F

操作ペダル — foot control / Tretplatte^F / commande^F au pied^M / pedal^M eléctrico / comando^M a pedale^M

スピード調節ペダル — speed controller / Geschwindigkeitsregelung^F / contrôle^M de la vitesse^F / pedal^M de velocidad^F / regolatore^M della velocità^F

ボビン・ケース — bobbin case / Spulenkapsel^F / boîte^F à canette^F / bobinas^F / capsula^F della bobina^F

ボビン — bobbin / Spule^F / canette^F / canilla^F / bobina^F

中釜 — latch lever / Kapselfinger^M / verrou^M / lengüeta^F / leva^F a linguetta^F

大釜 — hook / Greifer^M / crochet^M / portacanilla^M / crochet^M

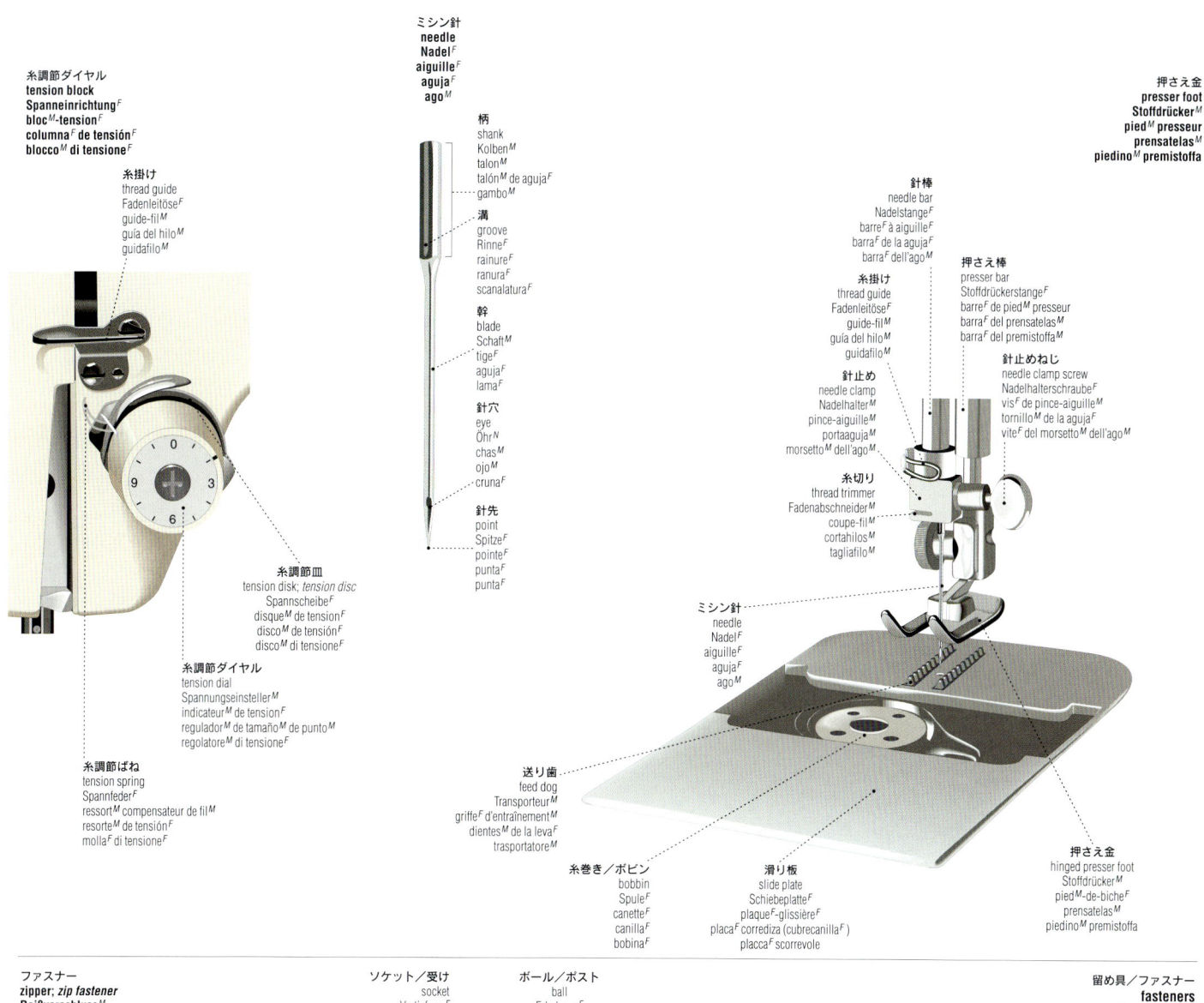

工芸 | CRAFTS
KUNSTGEWERBE | ARTISANAT | OFICIOS | MESTIERI

裁縫

糸調節ダイヤル
tension block
Spanneinrichtung^F
bloc^M-tension^F
columna^F de tensión
blocco^M di tensione^F

糸掛け
thread guide
Fadenleitöse^F
guide-fil^M
guía del hilo^M
guidafilo^M

糸調節皿
tension disk; tension disc
Spannscheibe^F
disque^M de tension^F
disco^M de tensión^F
disco^M di tensione^F

糸調節ダイヤル
tension dial
Spannungseinsteller^M
indicateur^M de tension^F
regulador^M de tamaño^M de punto^M
regolatore^M di tensione^F

糸調節ばね
tension spring
Spannfeder^F
ressort^M compensateur de fil^M
resorte^M de tensión^F
molla^F di tensione^F

ミシン針
needle
Nadel^F
aiguille^F
aguja^F
ago^M

柄
shank
Kolben^M
talon^M
talón^M de aguja^F
gambo^M

溝
groove
Rinne^F
rainure^F
ranura^F
scanalatura^F

幹
blade
Schaft^M
tige^F
aguja^F
lama^F

針穴
eye
Öhr^N
Nadelhalter^M
chas^M
ojo^M
cruna^F

針先
point
Spitze^F
pointe^F
punta^F
punta^F

送り歯
feed dog
Transporteur^M
griffe^F d'entraînement^M
dientes^M de la leva^F
trasportatore^M

糸巻き／ボビン
bobbin
Spule^F
canette^F
canilla^F
bobina^F

針棒
needle bar
Nadelstange^F
barre^F à aiguille^F
barra^F de la aguja^F
barra^F dell'ago^M

糸掛け
thread guide
Fadenleitöse^F
guide-fil^M
guía del hilo^M
guidafilo^M

針止め
needle clamp
Nadelhalter^M
pince-aiguille^M
portaaguja^M
morsetto^M dell'ago^M

糸切り
thread trimmer
Fadenabschneider^M
coupe-fil^M
cortahilos^M
tagliafilo^M

ミシン針
needle
Nadel^F
aiguille^F
aguja^F
ago^M

滑り板
slide plate
Schiebeplatte^F
plaque^F-glissière^F
placa^F corrediza (cubrecanilla^F)
placca^F scorrevole

押さえ金
presser foot
Stoffdrücker^M
pied^M presseur
prensatelas^M
piedino^M premistoffa

押さえ棒
presser bar
Stoffdrückerstange^F
barre^F de pied^M presseur
barra^F del prensatelas^M
barra^F del premistoffa

針止めねじ
needle clamp screw
Nadelhalterschraube^F
vis^F de pince-aiguille^M
tornillo^M de la aguja^F
vite^F del morsetto^M dell'ago^M

押さえ金
hinged presser foot
Stoffdrücker^M
pied^M-de-biche^F
prensatelas^M
piedino^M premistoffa

ファスナー
zipper; zip fastener
Reißverschluss^M
fermeture^F à glissière^F
cremallera^F
chiusura^F lampo^F

務歯
tooth
Zähne^M
dent^F
dientes^M
dentini^M

滑り金具／スライダー
slide
Schieber^M
curseur^M
corredera^F
cursore^M

引き手／プル・タブ
tab
Griff^M
tirette^F
lengüeta^F
tirante^M

テープ
tape
Band^N
ruban^M
cinta^F
lembo^M

下止め
stop
Endklammer^F
butée^F
tope^M
arresto^M

ソケット／受け
socket
Vertiefung^F
côté^M femelle
hembra^F
femmina^F

スナップ［プレス］ボタン
snap
Druckknopf^M
bouton^M-pression^F
automático^M
bottone^M automatico

穴ボタン
sew-through buttons
gelochte Knöpfe^M
boutons^M à trous^M
botones^M comunes
bottoni^M forati

ボール／ポスト
ball
Erhebung^F
côté^M mâle
macho^M
maschio^M

安全ピン
safety pin
Sicherheitsnadel^F
épingle^F de sûreté^F
imperdible^M
spilla^F di sicurezza^F

フック
hook
Haken^M
crochet^M
macho^M
gancio^M

受け金／アイ
straight eye
gerade Öse^F
bride^F
enganche^M
occhiello^M diritto

留め具／ファスナー
fasteners
Verschlüsse^M
attaches^F
accesorios^M para cerrar
chiusure^F

シャンク・ボタン
shank button
Ösenknopf^M
bouton^M à tige^F
botón^M de fantasía^F
bottone^M a gambo^M

鉤（かぎ）ホック
hook and eyes
Haken^M und Ösen^F
agrafes^F
corchetes^M
gancio^M e occhielli^M

受け金／アイ
round eye
runde Öse^F
porte^F
hembra^F
occhiello^M rotondo

縫い付け穴
ring
Ring^M
boucle^F
ojo^M
anello^M

453

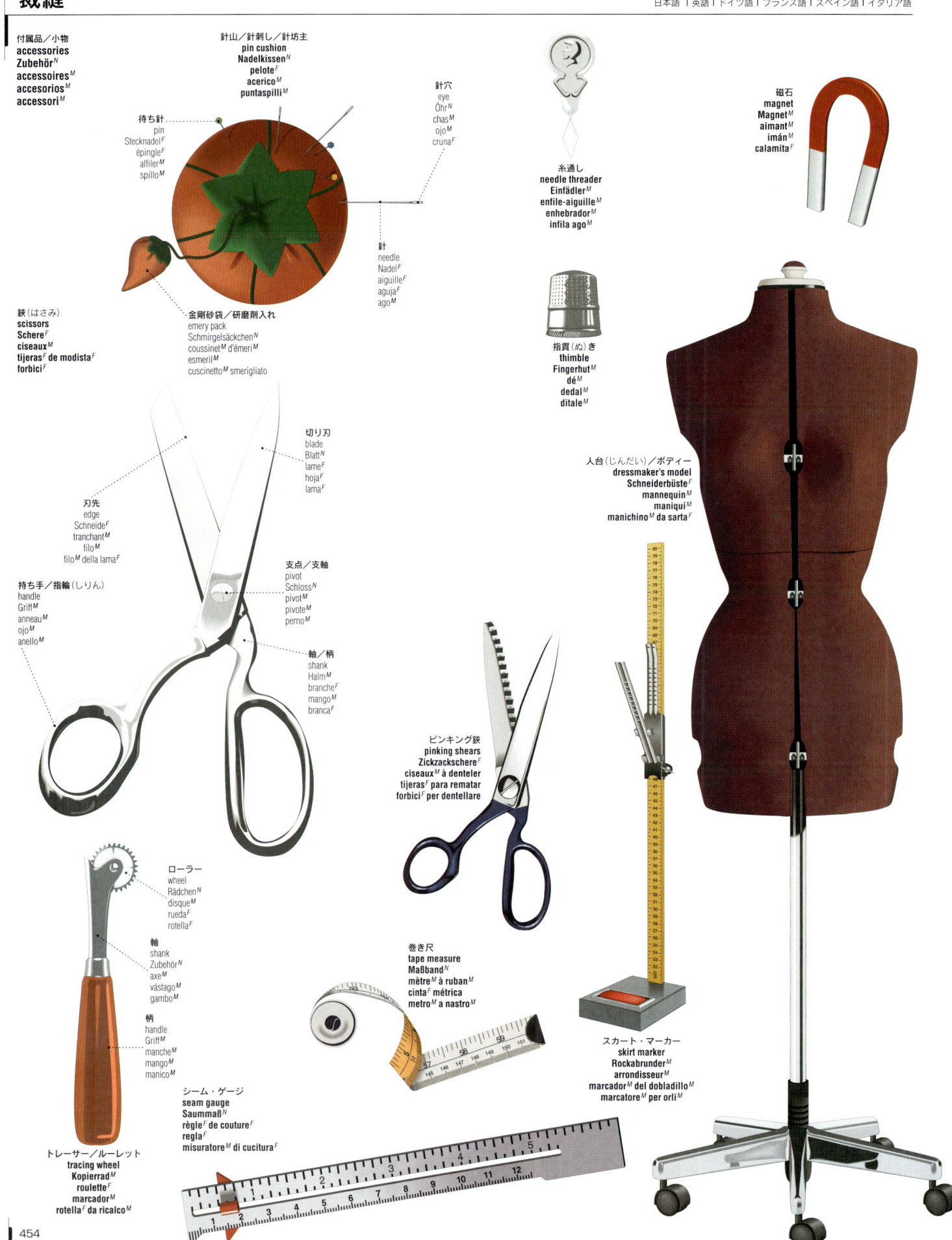

工芸 | CRAFTS
KUNSTGEWERBE | ARTISANAT | OFICIOS | MESTIERI

裁縫

日本語 | 英語 | ドイツ語 | フランス語 | スペイン語 | イタリア語

付属品／小物
accessories
Zubehör[N]
accessoires[M]
accesorios[M]
accessori[M]

針山／針刺し／針坊主
pin cushion
Nadelkissen[N]
pelote[F]
acerico[M]
puntaspilli[M]

針穴
eye
Öhr[N]
chas[M]
ojo[M]
cruna[F]

磁石
magnet
Magnet[M]
aimant[M]
imán[M]
calamita[F]

待ち針
pin
Stecknadel[F]
épingle[F]
alfiler[M]
spillo[M]

糸通し
needle threader
Einfädler[M]
enfile-aiguille[M]
enhebrador[M]
infila ago[M]

針
needle
Nadel[F]
aiguille[F]
aguja[F]
ago[F]

鋏（はさみ）
scissors
Schere[F]
ciseaux[M]
tijeras[F] de modista[F]
forbici[F]

金剛砂袋／研磨剤入れ
emery pack
Schmirgelsäckchen[N]
coussinet[M] d'émeri[M]
esmeril[M]
cuscinetto[M] smerigliato

指貫（ぬ）き
thimble
Fingerhut[M]
dé[M]
dedal[M]
ditale[M]

切り刃
blade
Blatt[N]
lame[F]
hoja[F]
lama[F]

人台（じんだい）／ボディー
dressmaker's model
Schneiderbüste[F]
mannequin[M]
maniquí[M]
manichino[M] da sarta[F]

刃先
edge
Schneide[F]
tranchant[M]
filo[M]
filo[M] della lama[F]

支点／支軸
pivot
Schloss[N]
pivot[M]
pivote[M]
perno[M]

持ち手／指輪（しりん）
handle
Griff[M]
anneau[M]
ojo[M]
anello[M]

軸／柄
shank
Halm[M]
branche[F]
mango[M]
branca[F]

ピンキング鋏
pinking shears
Zickzackschere[F]
ciseaux[M] à denteler
tijeras[F] para rematar
forbici[F] per dentellare

ローラー
wheel
Rädchen[N]
disque[M]
rueda[F]
rotella[F]

軸
shank
Zubehör[N]
axe[M]
vástago[M]
gambo[M]

巻き尺
tape measure
Maßband[N]
mètre[M] à ruban[M]
cinta[F] métrica
metro[M] a nastro[M]

柄
handle
Griff[M]
manche[M]
mango[M]
manico[M]

スカート・マーカー
skirt marker
Rockabrunder[M]
arrondisseur[M]
marcador[M] del dobladillo[M]
marcatore[M] per orli[M]

シーム・ゲージ
seam gauge
Saummaß[N]
règle[F] de couture[F]
regla[F]
misuratore[M] di cucitura[F]

トレーサー／ルーレット
tracing wheel
Kopierrad[M]
roulette[F]
marcador[M]
rotella[F] da ricalco[M]

芸術と建築

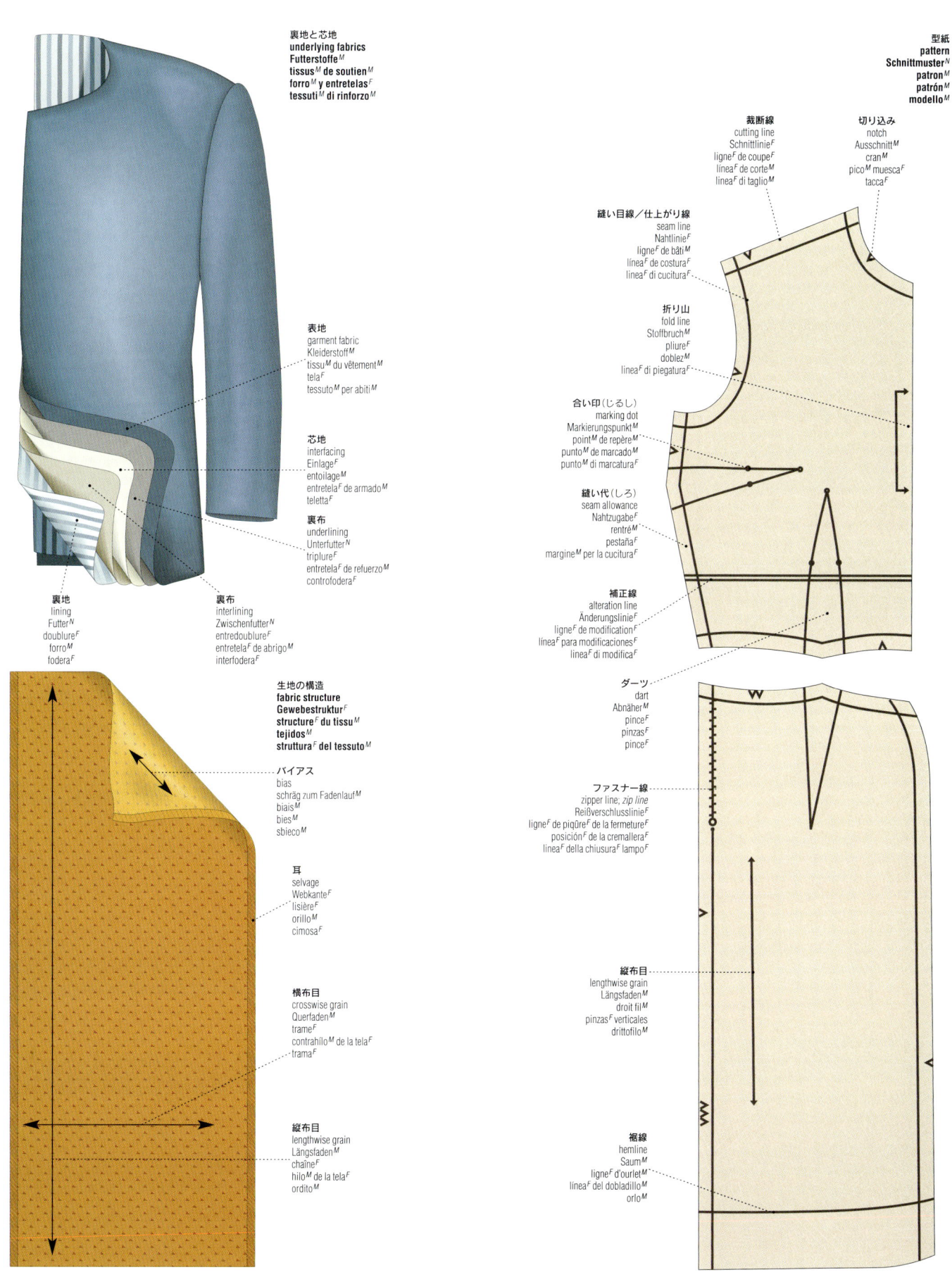

工芸 | CRAFTS
KUNSTGEWERBE | ARTISANAT | OFICIOS | MESTIERI

裁縫

裏地と芯地
underlying fabrics
Futterstoffe[M]
tissus[M] de soutien[M]
forro[M] y entretelas[F]
tessuti[M] di rinforzo[M]

表地
garment fabric
Kleiderstoff[M]
tissu[M] du vêtement[M]
tela[F]
tessuto[M] per abiti[M]

芯地
interfacing
Einlage[F]
entoilage[M]
entretela[F] de armado[M]
teletta[F]

裏布
underlining
Unterfutter[N]
triplure[F]
entretela[F] de refuerzo[M]
controfodera[F]

裏地
lining
Futter[N]
doublure[F]
forro[M]
fodera[F]

裏布
interlining
Zwischenfutter[N]
entredoublure[F]
entretela[F] de abrigo[M]
interfodera[F]

生地の構造
fabric structure
Gewebestruktur[F]
structure[F] du tissu[M]
tejidos[M]
struttura[F] del tessuto[M]

バイアス
bias
schräg zum Fadenlauf[M]
biais[M]
bies[M]
sbieco[M]

耳
selvage
Webkante[F]
lisière[F]
orillo[M]
cimosa[F]

横布目
crosswise grain
Querfaden[M]
trame[F]
contrahilo[M] de la tela[F]
trama[F]

縦布目
lengthwise grain
Längsfaden[M]
chaîne[F]
hilo[M] de la tela[F]
ordito[M]

型紙
pattern
Schnittmuster[N]
patron[M]
patrón[M]
modello[M]

裁断線
cutting line
Schnittlinie[F]
ligne[F] de coupe[F]
línea[F] de corte[M]
linea[F] di taglio[M]

切り込み
notch
Ausschnitt[M]
cran[M]
pico[M] muesca[F]
tacca[F]

縫い目線／仕上がり線
seam line
Nahtlinie[F]
ligne[F] de bâti[M]
línea[F] de costura[F]
linea[F] di cucitura[F]

折り山
fold line
Stoffbruch[M]
pliure[F]
doblez[M]
linea[F] di piegatura[F]

合い印（じるし）
marking dot
Markierungspunkt[M]
point[M] de repère[M]
punto[M] de marcado[M]
punto[M] di marcatura[F]

縫い代（しろ）
seam allowance
Nahtzugabe[F]
rentré[M]
pestaña[F]
margine[M] per la cucitura[F]

補正線
alteration line
Änderungslinie[F]
ligne[F] de modification[F]
línea[F] para modificaciones[F]
linea[F] di modifica[F]

ダーツ
dart
Abnäher[M]
pince[F]
pinzas[F]
pince[F]

ファスナー線
zipper line; zip line
Reißverschlusslinie[F]
ligne[F] de piqûre[F] de la fermeture[F]
posición[F] de la cremallera[F]
linea[F] della chiusura[F] lampo[F]

縦布目
lengthwise grain
Längsfaden[M]
droit fil[M]
pinzas[F] verticales
drittofilo[M]

裾線
hemline
Saum[M]
ligne[F] d'ourlet[M]
linea[F] del dobladillo[M]
orlo[M]

芸術と建築

455

工芸 | CRAFTS
KUNSTGEWERBE | ARTISANAT | OFICIOS | MESTIERI

編み機
knitting machine | Strickmaschine^F | machine^F à tricoter | máquina^F tricotar | macchina^F da maglieria^F

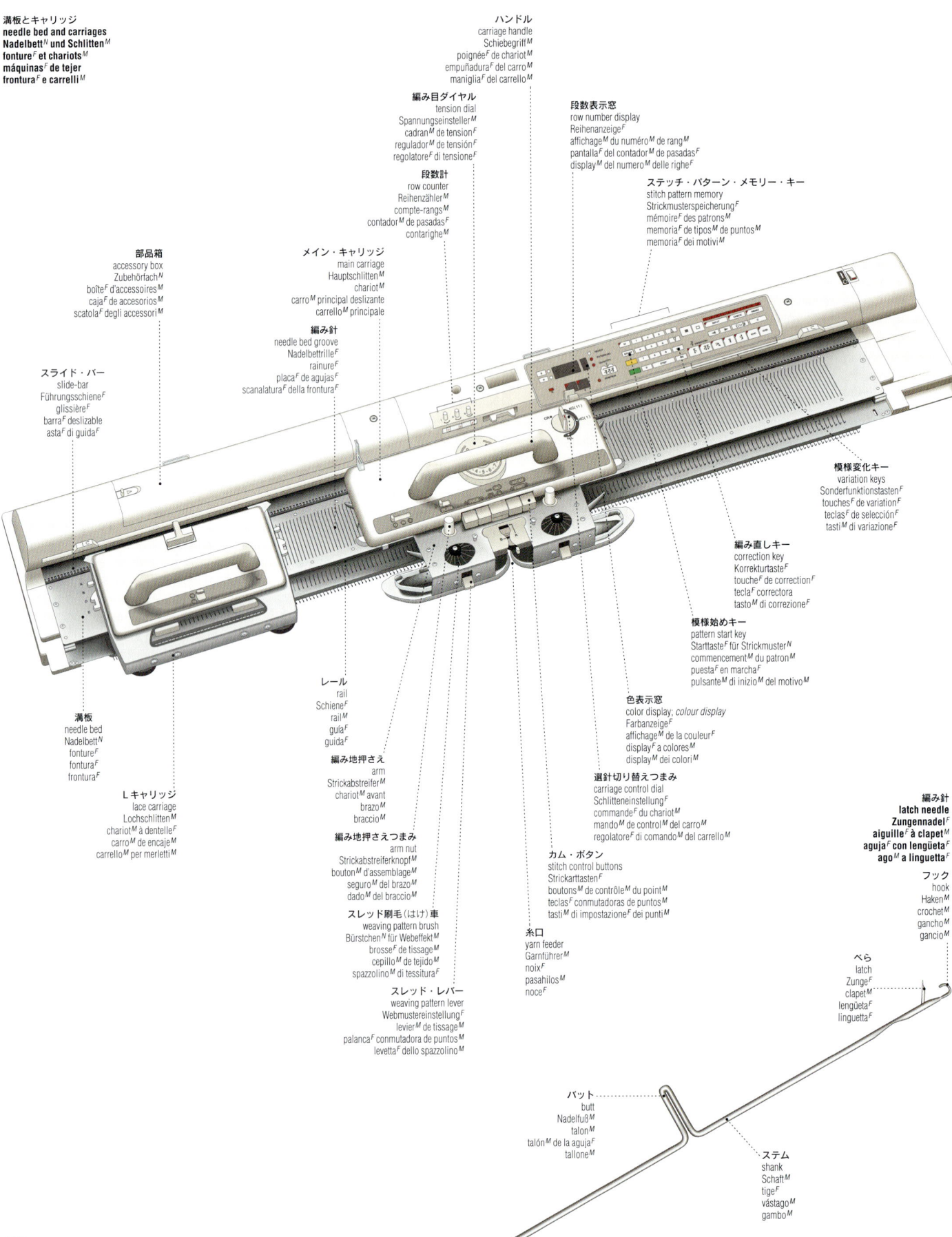

溝板とキャリッジ — needle bed and carriages; Nadelbett^N und Schlitten^M; fonture^F et chariots^M; máquinas^F de tejer; frontura^F e carrelli^M

編み目ダイヤル — tension dial; Spannungseinsteller^M; cadran^M de tension^F; regulador^M de tensión^F; regolatore^M di tensione^F

ハンドル — carriage handle; Schiebegriff^M; poignée^F de chariot^M; empuñadura^F del carro^M; maniglia^F del carrello^M

段数表示窓 — row number display; Reihenanzeige^F; affichage^M du numéro^M de rang^M; pantalla^F del contador^M de pasadas^F; display^M del numero^M delle righe^F

段数計 — row counter; Reihenzähler^M; compte-rangs^M; contador^M de pasadas^F; contarighe^M

ステッチ・パターン・メモリー・キー — stitch pattern memory; Strickmusterspeicherung^F; mémoire^F des patrons^M; memoria^F de tipos^M de puntos^M; memoria^F dei motivi^M

部品箱 — accessory box; Zubehörfach^N; boîte^F d'accessoires^M; caja^F de accesorios^M; scatola^F degli accessori^M

メイン・キャリッジ — main carriage; Hauptschlitten^M; chariot^M; carro^M principal deslizante; carrello^M principale

編み針 — needle bed groove; Nadelbettrille^F; rainure^F; placa^F de agujas^F; scanalatura^F della frontura^F

スライド・バー — slide-bar; Führungsschiene^F; glissière^F; barra^F deslizable; asta^F di guida^F

模様変化キー — variation keys; Sonderfunktionstasten^F; touches^F de variation^F; teclas^F de selección^F; tasti^M di variazione^F

編み直しキー — correction key; Korrekturtaste^F; touche^F de correction^F; tecla^F correctora; tasto^M di correzione^F

模様始めキー — pattern start key; Starttaste^F für Strickmuster^N; commencement^M du patron^M; puesta^F en marcha^F; pulsante^M di inizio del motivo^M

レール — rail; Schiene^F; rail^M; guía^F; guida^F

色表示窓 — color display; colour display; Farbanzeige^F; affichage^M de la couleur^F; display^F a colores^M; display^M dei colori^M

溝板 — needle bed; Nadelbett^N; fonture^F; fontura^F; frontura^F

編み地押さえ — arm; Strickabstreifer^M; chariot^M avant; brazo^M; braccio^M

選針切り替えつまみ — carriage control dial; Schlitteneinstellung^F; commande^F du chariot^M; mando^M de control del carro^M; regolatore^M di comando^M del carrello^M

Lキャリッジ — lace carriage; Lochschlitten^M; chariot^M à dentelle^F; carro^M de encaje^M; carrello^M per merletti^M

編み地押さえつまみ — arm nut; Strickabstreiferknopf^M; bouton^M d'assemblage^M; seguro^M del brazo^M; dado^M del braccio^M

カム・ボタン — stitch control buttons; Strickarttasten^F; boutons^M de contrôle^M du point^M; teclas^F conmutadoras de puntos^M; tasti^M di impostazione^F dei punti^M

編み針 — latch needle; Zungennadel^F; aiguille^F à clapet^M; aguja^F con lengüeta^F; ago^M a linguetta^F

スレッド刷毛(はけ)車 — weaving pattern brush; Bürstchen^N für Webeffekt^M; brosse^F de tissage^M; cepillo^M de tejido^M; spazzolino^M di tessitura^F

糸口 — yarn feeder; Garnführer^M; noix^F; pasahilos^M; noce^F

フック — hook; Haken^M; crochet^M; gancho^M; gancio^M

スレッド・レバー — weaving pattern lever; Webmustereinstellung^F; levier^M de tissage^M; palanca^F conmutadora de puntos^M; levetta^F dello spazzolino^M

べら — latch; Zunge^F; clapet^M; lengüeta^F; linguetta^F

バット — butt; Nadelfuß^M; talon^M; talón^M de la aguja^F; tallone^M

ステム — shank; Schaft^M; tige^F; vástago^M; gambo^M

工芸 | CRAFTS
KUNSTGEWERBE | ARTISANAT | OFICIOS | MESTIERI

編み機

糸取り装置
tension block
SpanneinrichtungF
blocM-tensionF
sistemaM de tensiónF
bloccoM di tensioneF

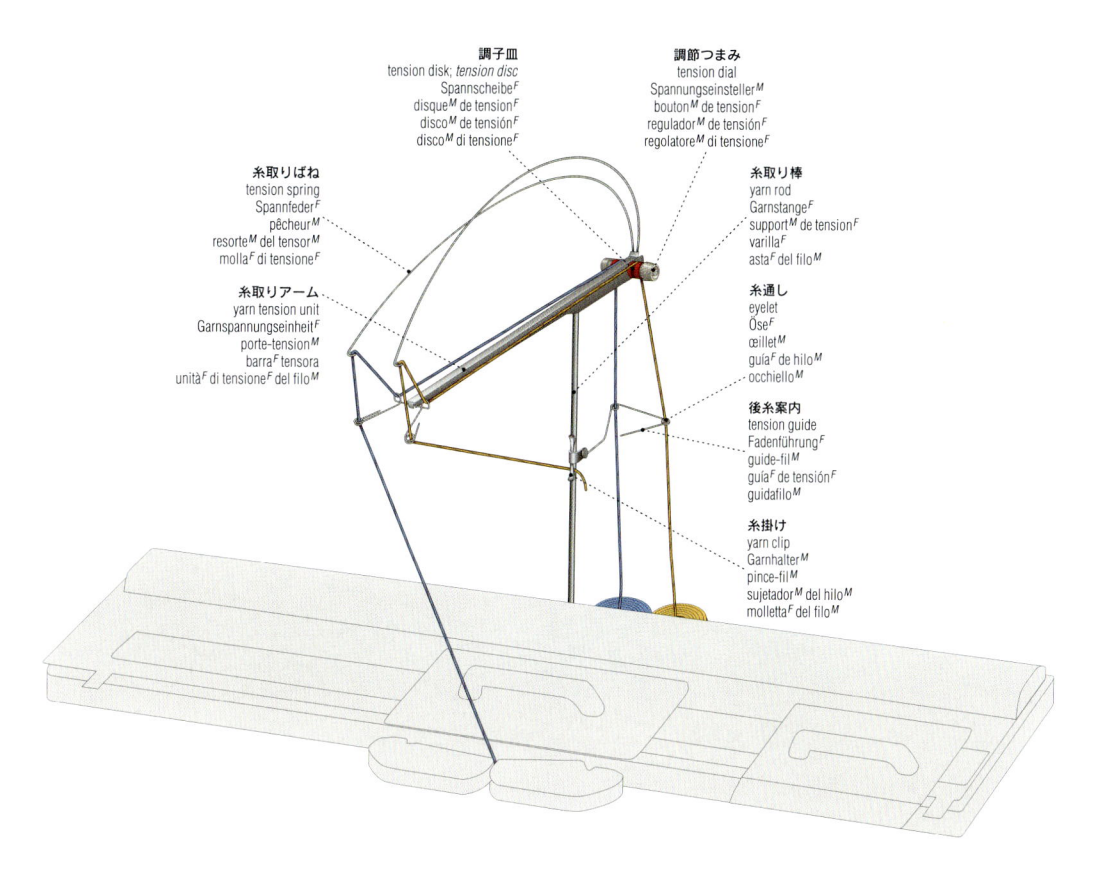

調子皿 — tension disk; tension disc / SpannscheibeF / disqueM de tensionF / discoM de tensiónF / discoM di tensioneF

調節つまみ — tension dial / SpannungseinstellerM / boutonM de tensionF / reguladorM de tensiónF / regolatoreM di tensioneF

糸取りばね — tension spring / SpannfederF / pêcheurM / resorteM del tensorM / mollaF di tensioneF

糸取り棒 — yarn rod / GarnstangeF / supportM de tensionF / varillaF / astaF del filoM

糸取りアーム — yarn tension unit / GarnspannungseinheitF / porte-tensionM / barraF tensora / unitàF di tensioneF del filoM

糸通し — eyelet / ÖseF / œilletM / guíaF de hiloM / occhielloM

後糸案内 — tension guide / FadenführungF / guide-filM / guíaF de tensiónF / guidafiloM

糸掛け — yarn clip / GarnhalterM / pince-filM / sujetadorM del hiloM / mollettaF del filoM

編み物

knitting | StrickenN | tricotM | tejidoM de puntoM | lavoroM a magliaF

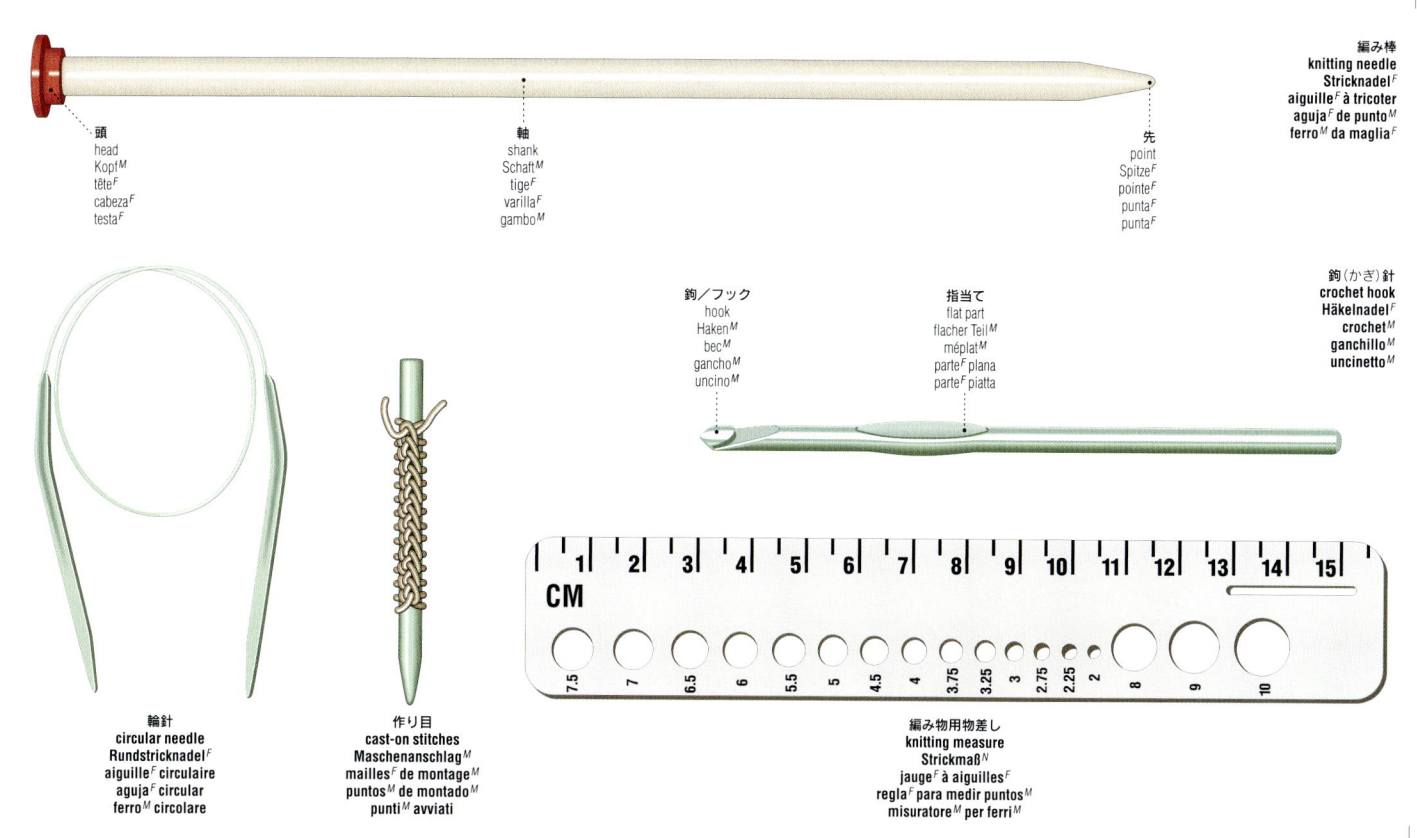

編み棒
knitting needle
StricknadelF
aiguilleF à tricoter
agujaF de puntoM
ferroM da magliaF

頭 — head / KopfM / têteF / cabezaF / testaF

軸 — shank / SchaftM / tigeF / varillaF / gamboM

先 — point / SpitzeF / pointeF / puntaF / puntaF

鉤（かぎ）針
crochet hook
HäkelnadelF
crochetM
ganchilloM
uncinettoM

鉤/フック — hook / HakenM / becM / ganchoM / uncinoM

指当て — flat part / flacher TeilM / méplatM / parteF plana / parteF piatta

輪針 — circular needle / RundstricknadelF / aiguilleF circulaire / agujaF circular / ferroM circolare

作り目 — cast-on stitches / MaschenanschlagM / maillesF de montage / puntosM de montado / puntiM avviati

編み物用物差し — knitting measure / StrickmaßN / jaugeF à aiguilles / reglaF para medir puntosM / misuratoreM per ferriM

芸術と建築

457

工芸 | CRAFTS
KUNSTGEWERBE | ARTISANAT | OFICIOS | MESTIERI

編み物

日本語 | 英語 | ドイツ語 | フランス語 | スペイン語 | イタリア語

編み方
stitch patterns
Strickmuster[N]
points[M] de tricot[M]
tipos[M] de punto[M]
motivi[M]

試し編み
sample
Maschenprobe[F]
échantillon[M]
muestra[F]
campione[M]

メリヤス編み
stocking stitch
Glattstrick[M]
point[M] de jersey[M]
punto[M] del derecho[M]
maglia[F] diritta

ガーター編み
garter stitch
Krausstrick[M]
point[M] mousse[F]
punto[M] del revés[M]
maglia[F] rovescia

鹿の子（かのこ）編み
moss stitch
Gerstenkornmuster[N]
point[M] de riz[M]
punto[M] de arroz[M]
punto[M] riso[M]

ゴム［リブ／ダブル］編み
rib stitch
Perlrippen[F]
point[M] de côtes[F]
punto[M] de respiguilla[F]
maglia[F] a coste[F]

バスケット編み
basket stitch
Wabenstrick[M]
point[M] de damier[M]
punto[M] de malla[F]
scacchi[M]

縄編み
cable stitch
Zopfmuster[N]
point[M] de torsades[F]
punto[M] de ochos[M]
treccia[F]

ボビン・レース

bobbin lace | Klöppelspitze[F] | dentelle[F] aux fuseaux[M] | encaje[M] de bolillos[M] | pizzo[M] al tombolo[M]

織り台／ピロー／クッサン
pillow
Klöppelkissen[N]
carreau[M]
bolillos[M]
tombolo[M]

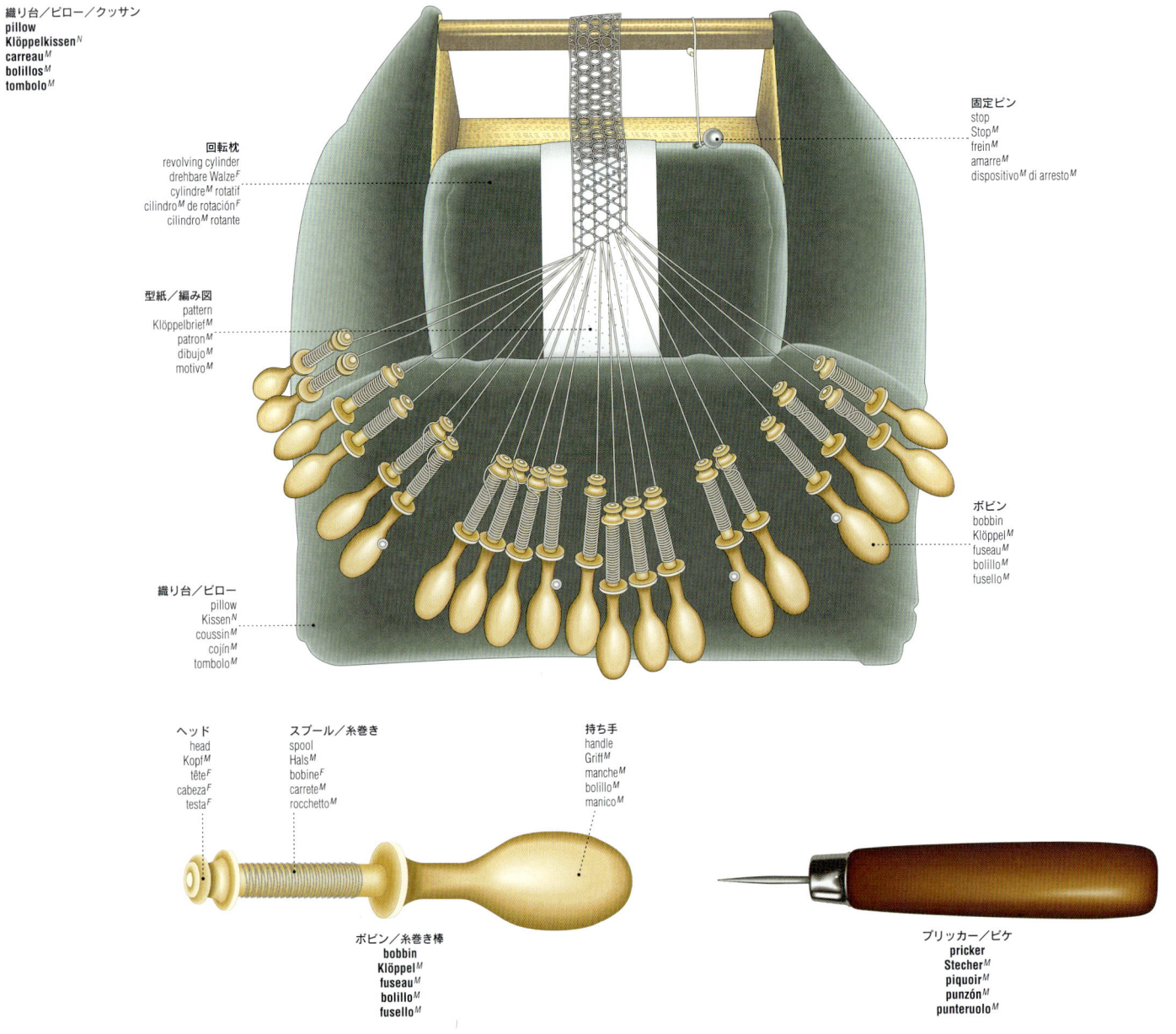

回転枕
revolving cylinder
drehbare Walze[F]
cylindre[M] rotatif
cilindro[M] de rotación[F]
cilindro[M] rotante

固定ピン
stop
Stop[M]
frein[M]
amarre[M]
dispositivo[M] di arresto[M]

型紙／編み図
pattern
Klöppelbrief[M]
patron[M]
dibujo[M]
motivo[M]

ボビン
bobbin
Klöppel[M]
fuseau[M]
bolillo[M]
fusello[M]

織り台／ピロー
pillow
Kissen[N]
coussin[M]
cojín[M]
tombolo[M]

ヘッド
head
Kopf[M]
tête[F]
cabeza[F]
testa[F]

スプール／糸巻き
spool
Hals[M]
bobine[F]
carrete[M]
rocchetto[M]

持ち手
handle
Griff[M]
manche[M]
bolillo[M]
manico[M]

ボビン／糸巻き棒
bobbin
Klöppel[M]
fuseau[M]
bolillo[M]
fusello[M]

プリッカー／ピケ
pricker
Stecher[M]
piquoir[M]
punzón[M]
punteruolo[M]

工芸 | CRAFTS
KUNSTGEWERBE | ARTISANAT | OFICIOS | MESTIERI

刺繡（ししゅう）

embroidery | Stickerei[F] | broderie[F] | bordado[M] | ricamo[M]

円型枠
hoop
runder Stickrahmen[M]
tambour[M]
aro[M]
telaio[M] circolare

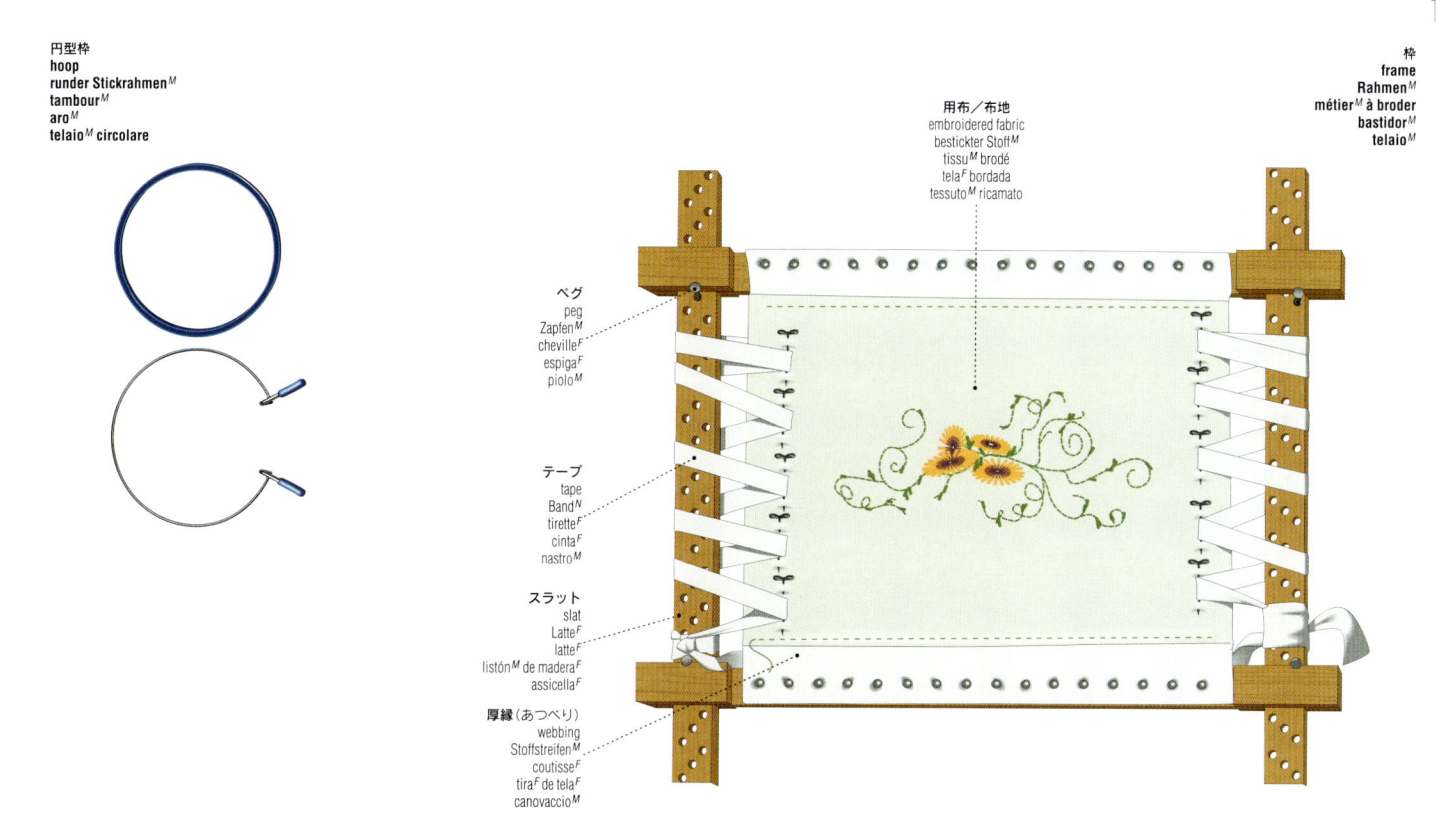

用布／布地
embroidered fabric
bestickter Stoff[M]
tissu[M] brodé
tela[F] bordada
tessuto[M] ricamato

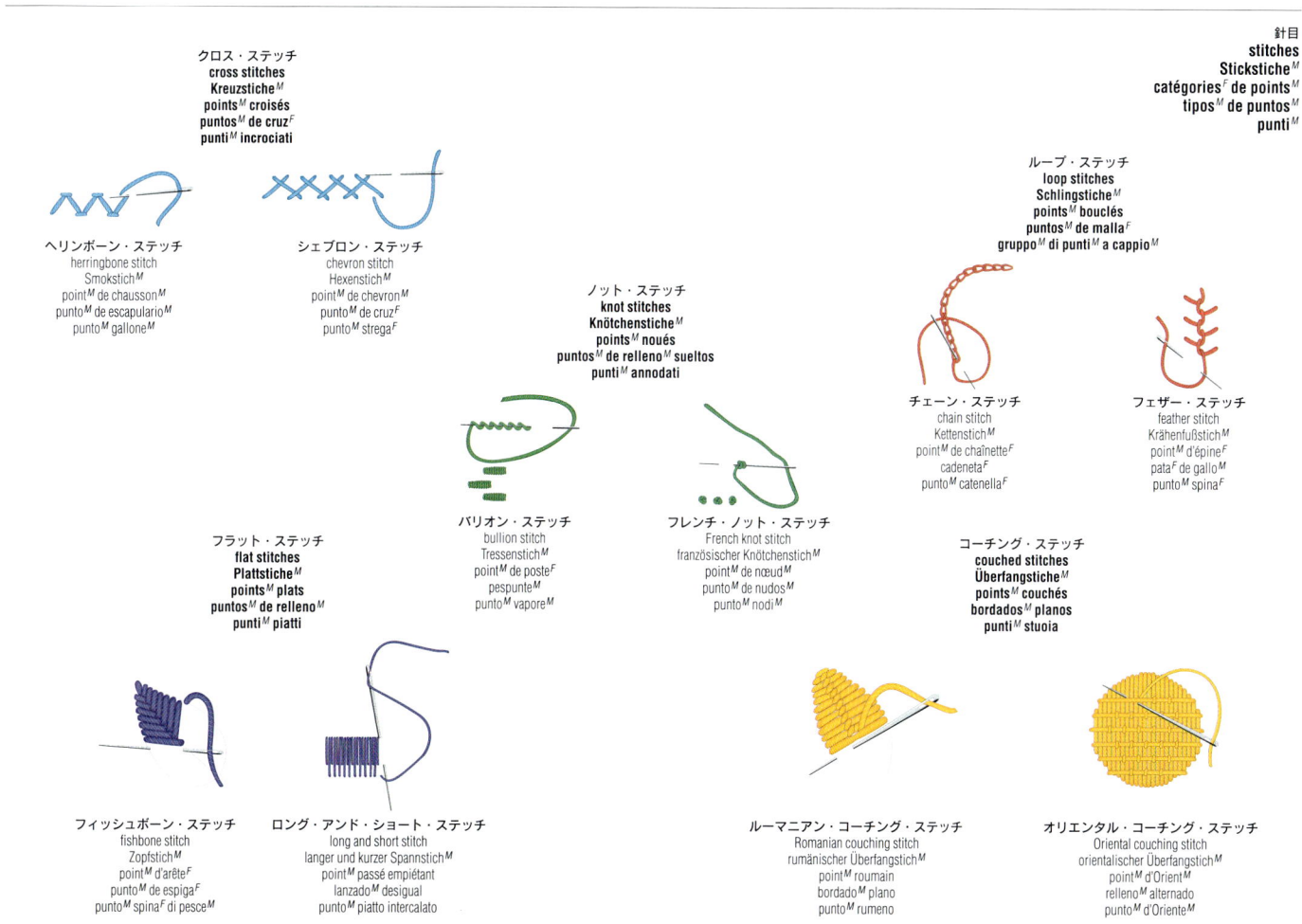

枠
frame
Rahmen[M]
métier[M] à broder
bastidor[M]
telaio[M]

ペグ
peg
Zapfen[M]
cheville[F]
espiga[F]
piolo[M]

テープ
tape
Band[N]
tirette[F]
cinta[F]
nastro[M]

スラット
slat
Latte[F]
latte[F]
listón[M] de madera[F]
assicella[F]

厚縁（あつべり）
webbing
Stoffstreifen[M]
coutisse[F]
tira[F] de tela[F]
canovaccio[M]

針目
stitches
Stickstiche[M]
catégories[F] de points[M]
tipos[M] de puntos[M]
punti[M]

クロス・ステッチ
cross stitches
Kreuzstiche[M]
points[M] croisés
puntos[M] de cruz[F]
punti[M] incrociati

ヘリンボーン・ステッチ
herringbone stitch
Smokstich[M]
point[M] de chausson[M]
punto[M] de escapulario[M]
punto[M] gallone[M]

シェブロン・ステッチ
chevron stitch
Hexenstich[M]
point[M] de chevron[M]
punto[M] de cruz[F]
punto[M] strega[F]

ループ・ステッチ
loop stitches
Schlingstiche[M]
points[M] bouclés
puntos[M] de malla[F]
gruppo[M] di punti[M] a cappio[M]

チェーン・ステッチ
chain stitch
Kettenstich[M]
point[M] de chaînette[F]
cadeneta[F]
punto[M] catenella[F]

フェザー・ステッチ
feather stitch
Krähenfußstich[M]
point[M] d'épine[F]
pata[F] de gallo[M]
punto[M] spina[F]

ノット・ステッチ
knot stitches
Knötchenstiche[M]
points[M] noués
puntos[M] de relleno[M] sueltos
punti[M] annodati

バリオン・ステッチ
bullion stitch
Tressenstich[M]
point[M] de poste[F]
pespunte[M]
punto[M] vapore[M]

フレンチ・ノット・ステッチ
French knot stitch
französischer Knötchenstich[M]
point[M] de nœud[M]
punto[M] de nudos[M]
punto[M] nodi[M]

コーチング・ステッチ
couched stitches
Überfangstiche[M]
points[M] couchés
bordados[M] planos
punti[M] stuoia

フラット・ステッチ
flat stitches
Plattstiche[M]
points[M] plats
puntos[M] de relleno[M]
punti[M] piatti

フィッシュボーン・ステッチ
fishbone stitch
Zopfstich[M]
point[M] d'arête[F]
punto[M] de espiga[F]
punto[M] spina[F] di pesce[M]

ロング・アンド・ショート・ステッチ
long and short stitch
langer und kurzer Spannstich[M]
point[M] passé empiétant
lanzado desigual
punto[M] piatto intercalato

ルーマニアン・コーチング・ステッチ
Romanian couching stitch
rumänischer Überfangstich[M]
point[M] roumain
bordado[M] plano
punto[M] rumeno

オリエンタル・コーチング・ステッチ
Oriental couching stitch
orientalischer Überfangstich[M]
point[M] d'Orient[M]
relleno[M] alternado
punto[M] d'Oriente[M]

芸術と建築

459

工芸 | CRAFTS
KUNSTGEWERBE | ARTISANAT | OFICIOS | MESTIERI

紡織

weaving | Weben^N | tissage^M | tejido^M | tessitura^F

日本語 | 英語 | ドイツ語 | フランス語 | スペイン語 | イタリア語

臥機（ねばた）
low warp loom
Flachwebstuhl^M
métier^M de basse lisse^F
telar^M de cuatro marcos^M
telaio^M a ordito^M basso

綜絖（そうこう）／ヘドル
heddles
Litzen^F
lisses^F
lizos^M
licci^M

上段ろくろ
head roller
obere Rolle^F
rouleau^M principal
tambor^M principal
subbio^M superiore

緯糸（よこいと）
weft
Schuss^M
trame^F
trama^F
trama^F

筬框脚（おさがまちあし）
upright
Säule^F
support^M du rouleau^M
soporte^M del juego^M de marcos^M
piantana^F

綜絖枠
harnesses
Geschirr^N
harnais^M
marcos^M
gioco^M di liccioli^M

綜絖通糸（そうこうつうじ）
harness
Schaft^M
lame^F
marco^M
licciolo^M

筬（おさ）
reed
Riet^N
ros^M
peine^M
pettine^M

筬柄（おさづか）横木
beater handtree
Schwenklade^F
chapeau^M du battant^M
travesaño^M superior del batán^M
impugnatura^F della cassa^F battente

筬柄（おさづか）
beater
Kammlade^F
battant^M
batán^M
cassa^F battente

間丁（けんちょう）
back beam
Streichbaum^M
porte-fils^M
plegador^M posterior
portafili^M

胸木（むなぎ）
breast beam
Brustbaum^M
poitrinière^F
travesaño^M frontal
pettorale^M

経糸（たていと）
warp
Kette^F
chaîne^F
urdimbre^F
ordito^M

筬框（おさがまち）
beater sley
Ladenbahn^F
semelle^F du battant^M
travesaño^M intermedio del batán^M
traversa^F della cassa^F battente

ハンドル
handle
Griff^M
manivelle^F
manivela^F
manovella^F

千巻（ちまき）／布巻
cloth roller
Warenbaum^M
ensouple^F de tissu^M
plegador^M del tejido^M
subbio^M del tessuto^M

緒巻（おまき）／
経糸巻（たていとまき）
warp roller
Kettbaum^M
ensouple^F de chaîne^F
plegador^M de urdimbre^F
subbio^M dell'ordito^M

招木（まねき）
lam
Seitenschwinge^F
contremarche^F
travesaño^M
contromarce^F

爪／ラチェット
ratchet
Klinke^F
cliquet^M
leva^F
dente^M d'arresto^M

ポスト
post
Pfosten^M
montant^M
montante^M
montante^M

横木
crosspiece
Querholz^N
entretoise^F
travesaño^M
traversa^F laterale

踏み木
treadle
Tritt^M
marche^F
pedal^M
calcola^F

爪車
ratchet wheel
Sperrrad^N
roue^F dentée
engranaje^M
ruota^F dentata d'arresto^M

踏み木紐（ひも）
treadle cord
Schnur^F am Tritt^M
corde^F d'accrochage^M
cordón^M del pedal^M
corda^F della calcola^F

踏み木レバー
release treadle
Trittlöser^M
pédale^F de frein^M
pedal del freno^M
calcola^F di disinnesto^M

横木
crossbeam
Kantholz^N
traverse^F
travesaño^M frontal interior
traversa^F anteriore

巻き上げハンドル
take-up handle
Spannhandgriff^M
tentoir^M
palanca^F de compensación^F
regolatore^M della tensione^F

枠
frame
Rahmen^M
bâti^M
armazón^M
incastellatura^F

工芸 | CRAFTS
KUNSTGEWERBE | ARTISANAT | OFICIOS | MESTIERI

紡織

杼（ひ）
shuttle
Webschütz^M
navette^F
lanzadera^F
navetta^F

心棒
rod
Dorn^M
tige^F
varilla^F
asticella^F

管巻き
bobbin
Spule^F
canette^F
canilla^F
spola^F

伸子（しんし）／テンプル
temple
Breithalter^M
templet^M
templazo^M
tempiale^M

綜絖（そうこう）／ヘドル
heddles
Litzen^F
lisses^F
lizos^M
licci^M

綜目（あやめ）
eye
Fadenauge^N
œil^M
ojal^M
occhiello^M

糸通し穴
eye
Fadenauge^N
œil^M
ojal^M
cruna^F

筬（おさ）通し／通し針
reed hooks
Blattstecher^M
passettes^F
ganchos^M peinadores
ganci^M del pettine

杼（ひ）
flat shuttle
Webnadel^F
réglette^F
lanzadera^F plana
navetta^F piana

堅機（たてばた）
high warp loom
Hochwebstuhl^M
métier^M de haute lisse^F
telar^M de tapicería^F
telaio^M a ordito^M alto

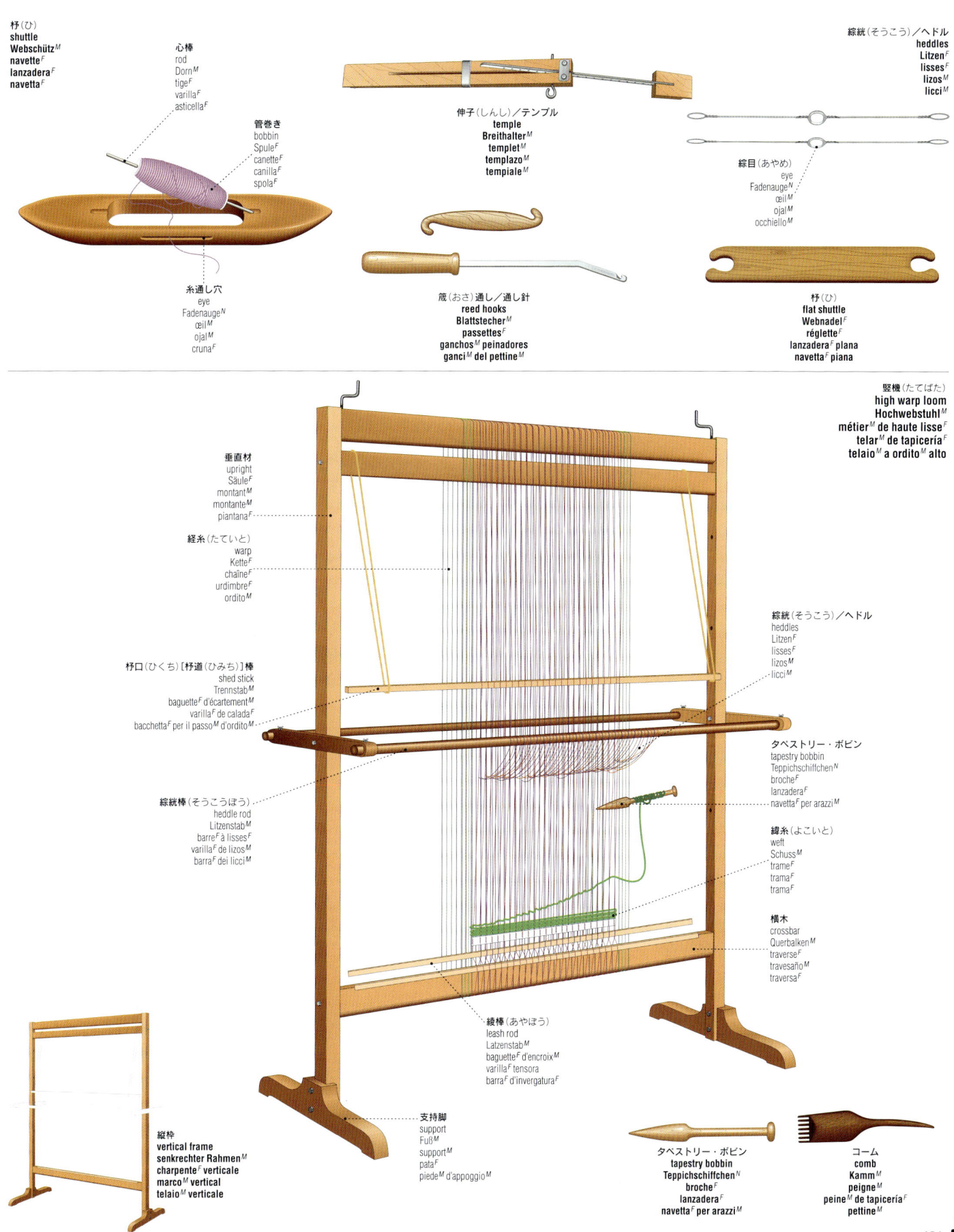

垂直材
upright
Säule^F
montant^M
montante^M
piantana^F

経糸（たていと）
warp
Kette^F
chaîne^F
urdimbre^F
ordito^M

杼口（ひくち）[杼道（ひみち）]棒
shed stick
Trennstab^M
baguette^F d'écartement^M
varilla^F de calada
bacchetta^F per il passo^M d'ordito^M

綜絖棒（そうこうぼう）
heddle rod
Litzenstab^M
barre^F à lisses^F
varilla^F de lizos^M
barra^F dei licci^M

綜絖（そうこう）／ヘドル
heddles
Litzen^F
lisses^F
lizos^M
licci^M

タペストリー・ボビン
tapestry bobbin
Teppichschiffchen^N
broche^F
lanzadera^F
navetta^F per arazzi^M

緯糸（よこいと）
weft
Schuss^M
trame^F
trama^F
trama^F

横木
crossbar
Querbalken^M
traverse^F
travesaño^M
traversa^F

綾棒（あやぼう）
leash rod
Latzenstab^M
baguette^F d'encroix^M
varilla^F tensora
barra^F d'invergatura^F

縦枠
vertical frame
senkrechter Rahmen^M
charpente^F verticale
marco^M vertical
telaio^M verticale

支持脚
support
Fuß^M
support^M
pata^F
piede^M d'appoggio^M

タペストリー・ボビン
tapestry bobbin
Teppichschiffchen^N
broche^F
lanzadera^F
navetta^F per arazzi^M

コーム
comb
Kamm^M
peigne^M
peine^M de tapicería^F
pettine^M

芸術と建築

461

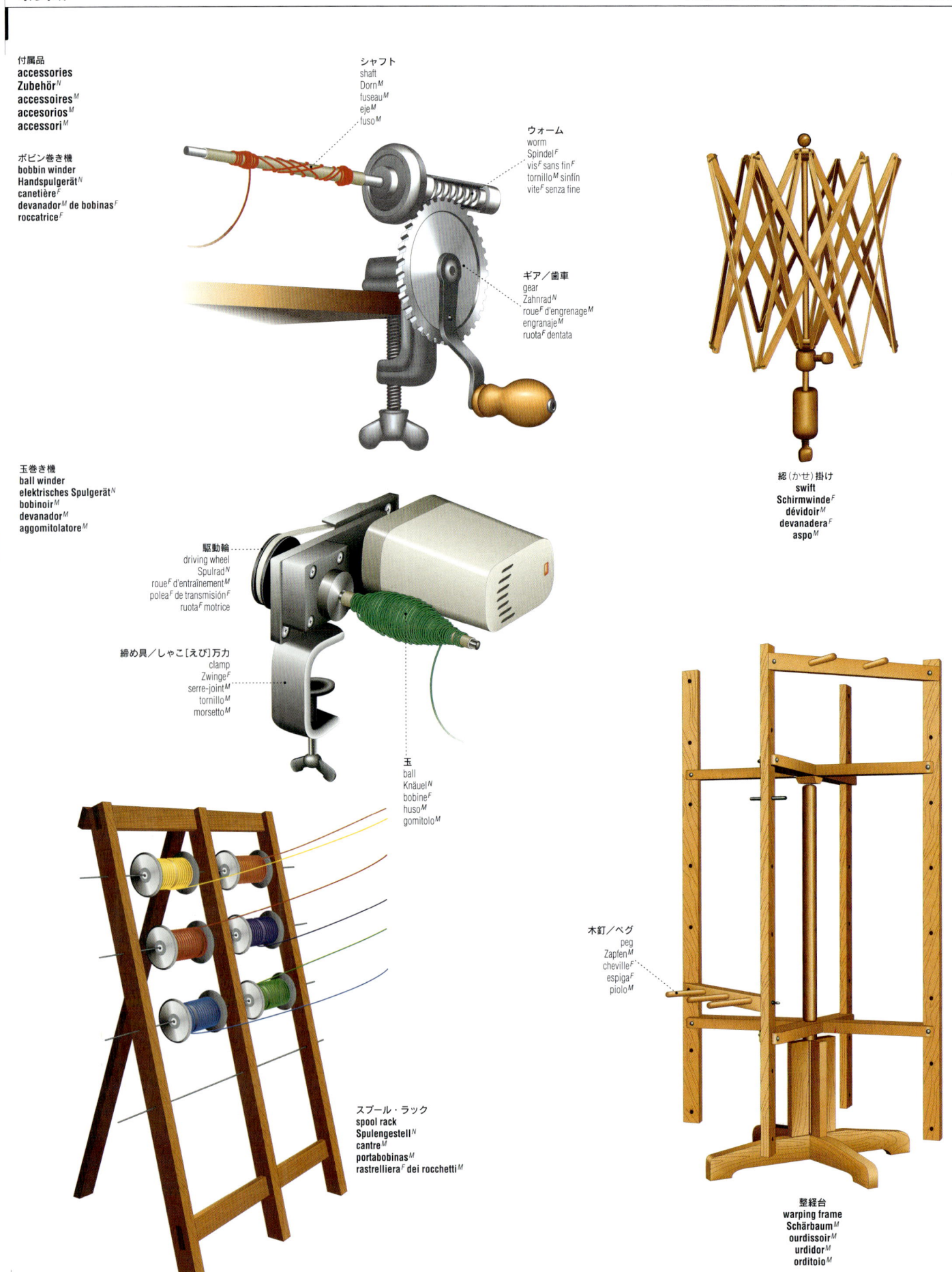

工芸 | CRAFTS
KUNSTGEWERBE | ARTISANAT | OFICIOS | MESTIERI

紡織

日本語 | 英語 | ドイツ語 | フランス語 | スペイン語 | イタリア語

付属品
accessories
Zubehör^N
accessoires^M
accesorios^M
accessori^M

ボビン巻き機
bobbin winder
Handspulgerät^N
canetière^F
devanador^M de bobinas^F
roccatrice^F

シャフト
shaft
Dorn^M
fuseau^M
eje^M
fuso^M

ウォーム
worm
Spindel^F
vis^F sans fin^F
tornillo^M sinfín
vite^F senza fine

ギア／歯車
gear
Zahnrad^N
roue^F d'engrenage^M
engranaje^M
ruota^F dentata

綛（かせ）掛け
swift
Schirmwinde^F
dévidoir^M
devanadera^F
aspo^M

玉巻き機
ball winder
elektrisches Spulgerät^N
bobinoir^M
devanador^M
aggomitolatore^M

駆動輪
driving wheel
Spulrad^N
roue^F d'entraînement^M
polea^F de transmisión^F
ruota^F motrice

締め具／しゃこ[えび]万力
clamp
Zwinge^F
serre-joint^M
tornillo^M
morsetto^M

玉
ball
Knäuel^N
bobine^F
huso^M
gomitolo^M

木釘／ペグ
peg
Zapfen^M
cheville^F
espiga^F
piolo^M

スプール・ラック
spool rack
Spulengestell^N
cantre^M
portabobinas^M
rastrelliera^F dei rocchetti^M

整経台
warping frame
Schärbaum^M
ourdissoir^M
urdidor^M
orditoio^M

芸術と建築

462

工芸 | CRAFTS
KUNSTGEWERBE | ARTISANAT | OFICIOS | MESTIERI

紡織

織りの原理
diagram of weaving principle
SchaubildN für das WebprinzipN
schémaM du principeM du tissageM
diagramasM de tejidosM
schemaM della tessituraF

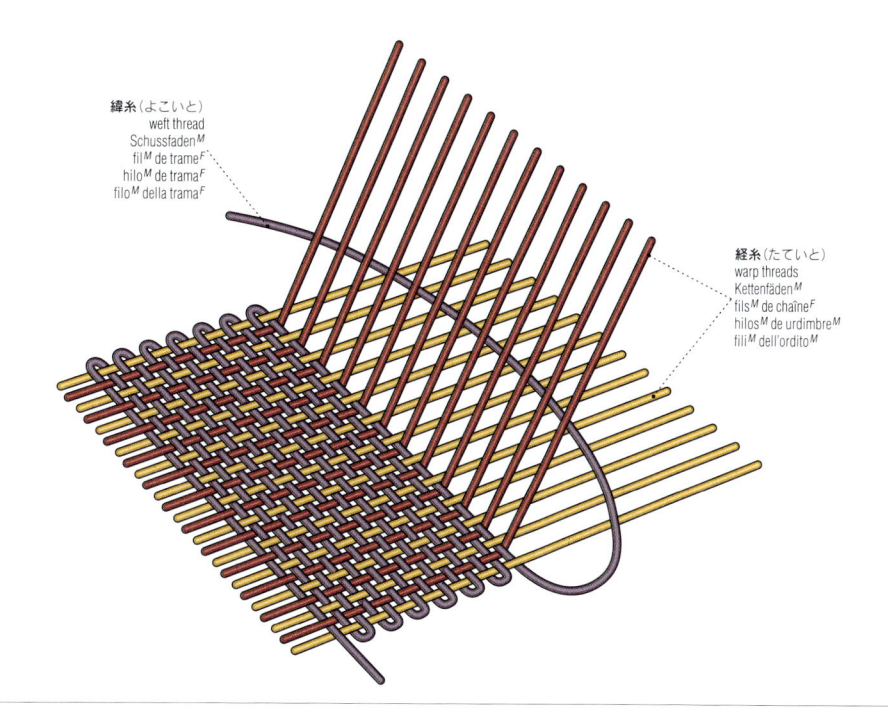

緯糸（よこいと）
weft thread
SchussfadenM
filM de trameF
hiloM de tramaF
filoM della tramaF

経糸（たていと）
warp threads
KettenfädenM
filsM de chaîneF
hilosM de urdimbreM
filiM dell'orditoM

原（げん）組織
basic weaves
GrundbindungenF
armuresF de baseF
ligamentosM textiles básicos
armatureF di baseF

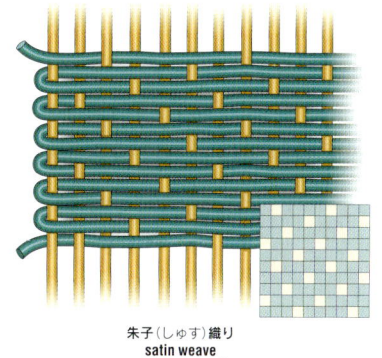

朱子（しゅす）織り
satin weave
AtlasbindungF
satinM
saténM
rasoM

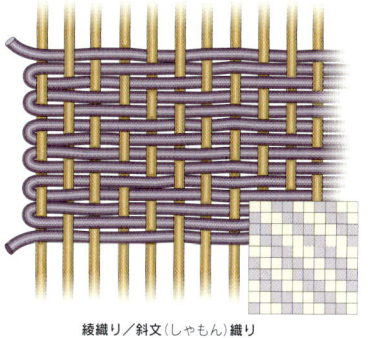

綾織り／斜文（しゃもん）織り
twill weave
KöperbindungF
sergéM
sargaF
saiaF

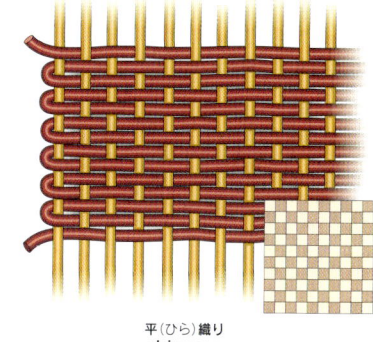

平（ひら）織り
plain weave
LeinwandbindungF
toileF
tafetánM
telaF

その他の織り方
other techniques
andere TechnikenF
autres techniquesF
otros ligamentosM textiles
altre tecnicheF

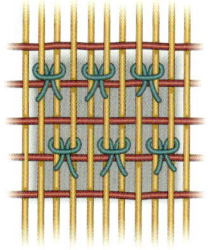

ノット
knot
KnotenM
nœudM
anudado
annodaturaF

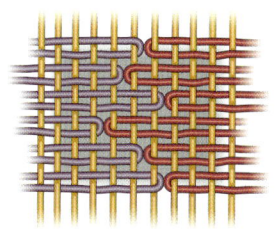

ハッチング
hatching
KelimbindungF mit wechselnden WendenF
hachureF
punteado
ombreggiaturaF

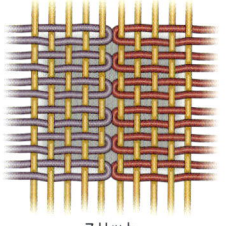

スリット
slit
senkrechte KelimbindungF
fenteF
vertical
fessuraF

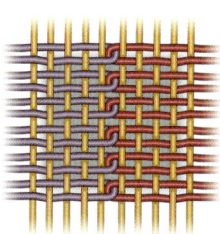

インターロック
interlock
GobelinbindungF
croisementM
entrecruzado
incrocioM

芸術と建築

463

工芸 | CRAFTS
KUNSTGEWERBE | ARTISANAT | OFICIOS | MESTIERI

陶芸

pottery | Töpferei^F | poterie^F | cerámica^F | ceramica^F

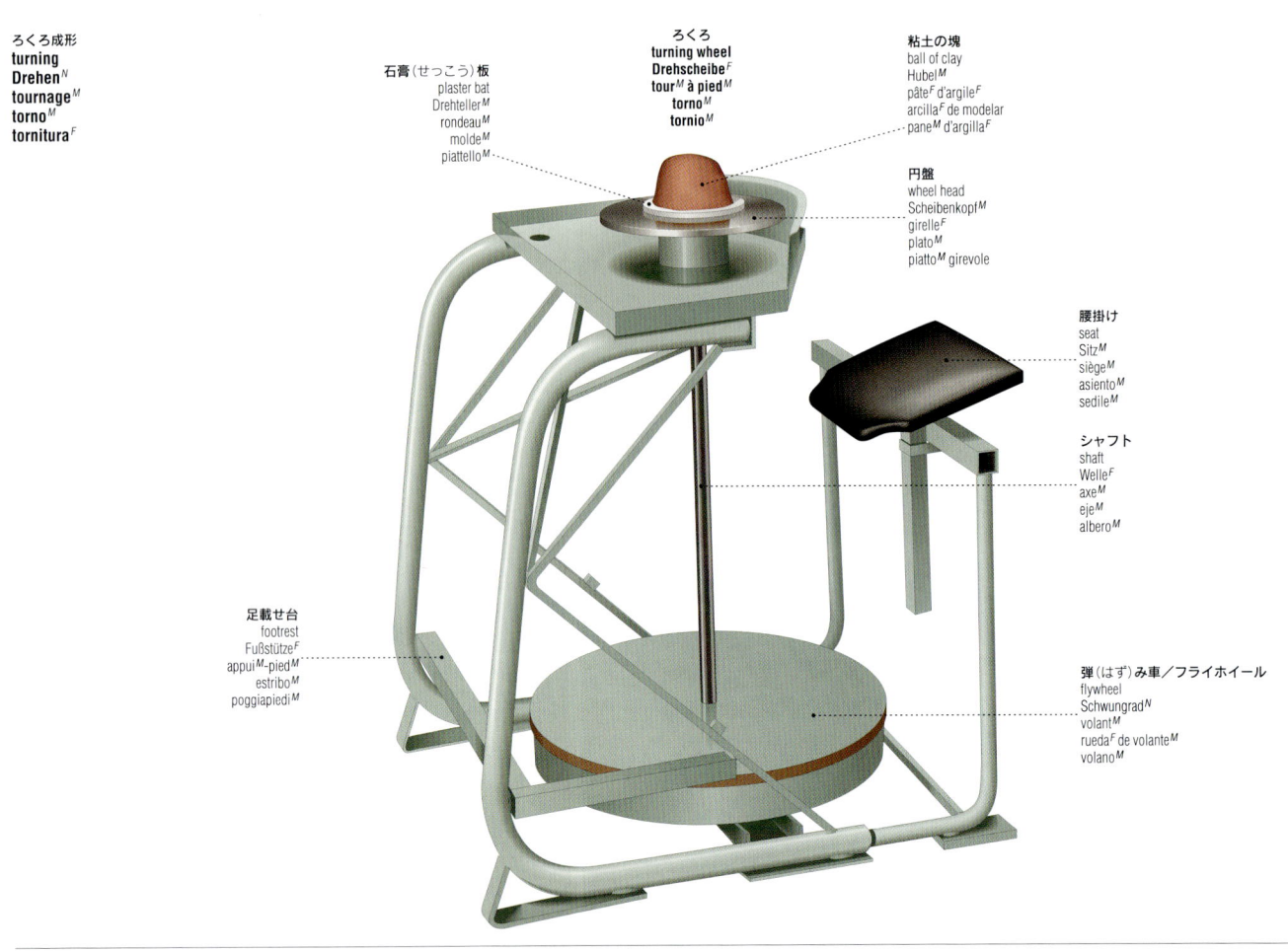

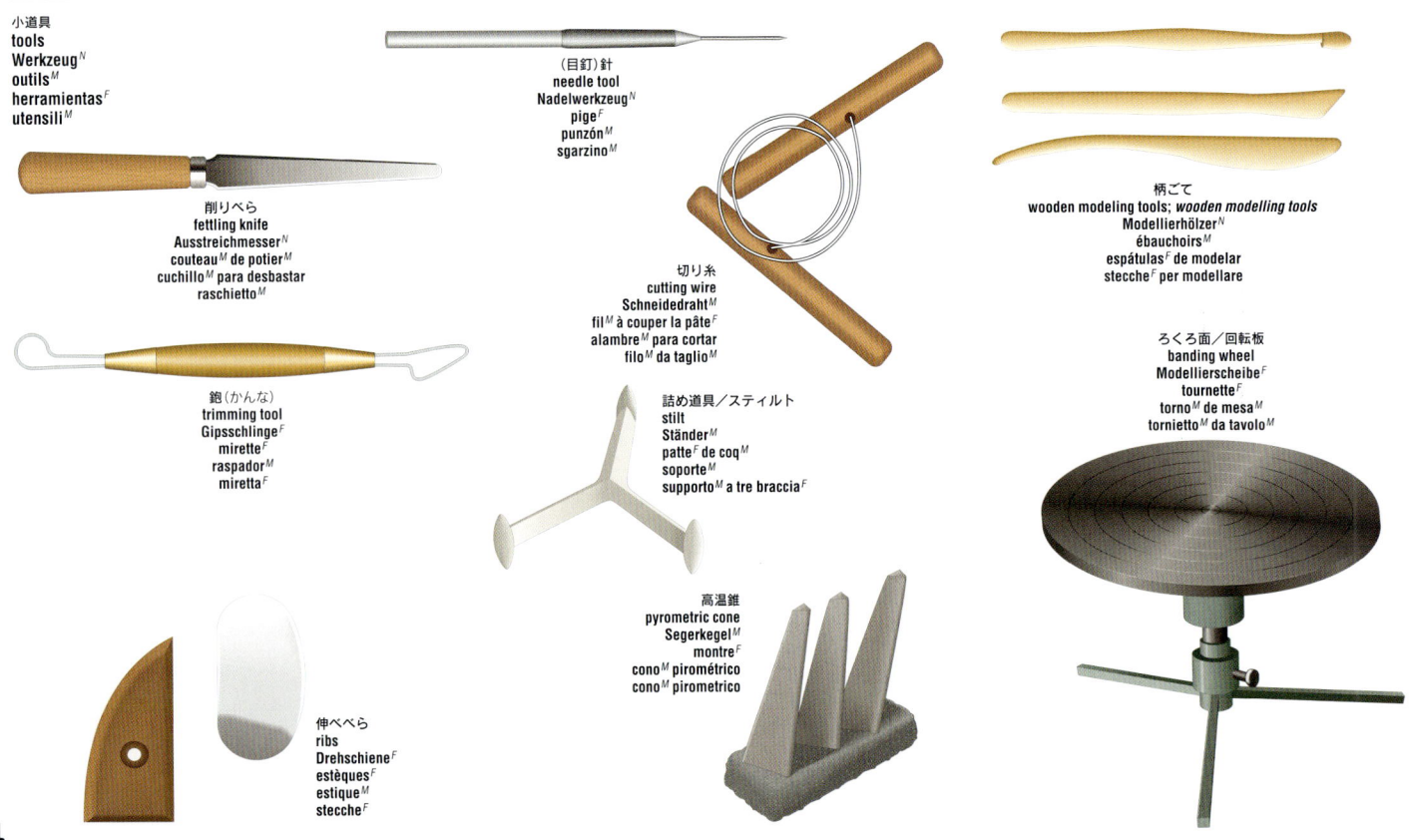

日本語 | 英語 | ドイツ語 | フランス語 | スペイン語 | イタリア語

ろくろ成形
turning
Drehen^N
tournage^M
torno^M
tornitura^F

石膏（せっこう）板
plaster bat
Drehteller^M
rondeau^M
molde^M
piattello^M

ろくろ
turning wheel
Drehscheibe^F
tour^M à pied^F
torno^M
tornio^M

粘土の塊
ball of clay
Hubel^M
pâte^F d'argile^F
arcilla^F de modelar
pane^M d'argilla^F

円盤
wheel head
Scheibenkopf^M
girelle^F
plato^M
piatto^M girevole

腰掛け
seat
Sitz^M
siège^M
asiento^M
sedile^M

シャフト
shaft
Welle^F
axe^M
eje^M
albero^M

足載せ台
footrest
Fußstütze^F
appui^M-pied^M
estribo^M
poggiapiedi^M

弾（はず）み車／フライホイール
flywheel
Schwungrad^N
volant^M
rueda^F de volante^M
volano^M

小道具
tools
Werkzeug^N
outils^M
herramientas^F
utensili^M

（目釘）針
needle tool
Nadelwerkzeug^N
pige^F
punzón^M
sgarzino^M

柄ごて
wooden modeling tools; wooden modelling tools
Modellierhölzer^N
ébauchoirs^M
espátulas^F de modelar
stecche^F per modellare

削りべら
fettling knife
Ausstreichmesser^N
couteau^M de potier^M
cuchillo^M para desbastar
raschietto^M

切り糸
cutting wire
Schneidedraht^M
fil^M à couper la pâte^F
alambre^M para cortar
filo^M da taglio^M

ろくろ面／回転板
banding wheel
Modellierscheibe^F
tournette^F
torno^M de mesa^M
tornietto^M da tavolo^M

鉋（かんな）
trimming tool
Gipsschlinge^F
mirette^F
raspador^M
miretta^F

詰め道具／スティルト
stilt
Ständer^M
patte^F de coq^M
soporte^M
supporto^M a tre braccia^F

高温錐
pyrometric cone
Segerkegel^M
montre^F
cono^M pirométrico
cono^M pirometrico

伸べべら
ribs
Drehschiene^F
estèques^F
estique^M
stecche^F

芸術と建築

464

工芸 | CRAFTS
KUNSTGEWERBE | ARTISANAT | OFICIOS | MESTIERI

陶芸

たたら作り
slab building
Platten^F ausrollen
galettage^M
rodillo^M
tecnica^F a nastro^M

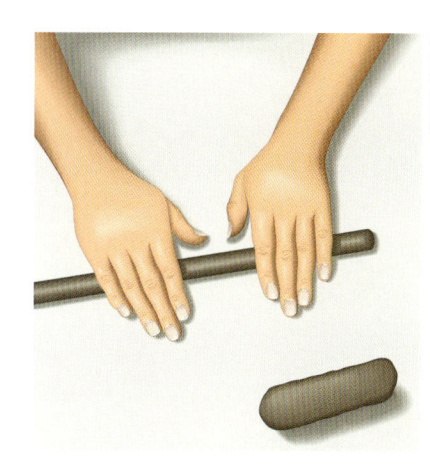

ひも作り
coiling
Spiralwülste^F rollen
colombin^M
cordón^M para espirales^F
tecnica^F a colombino^M

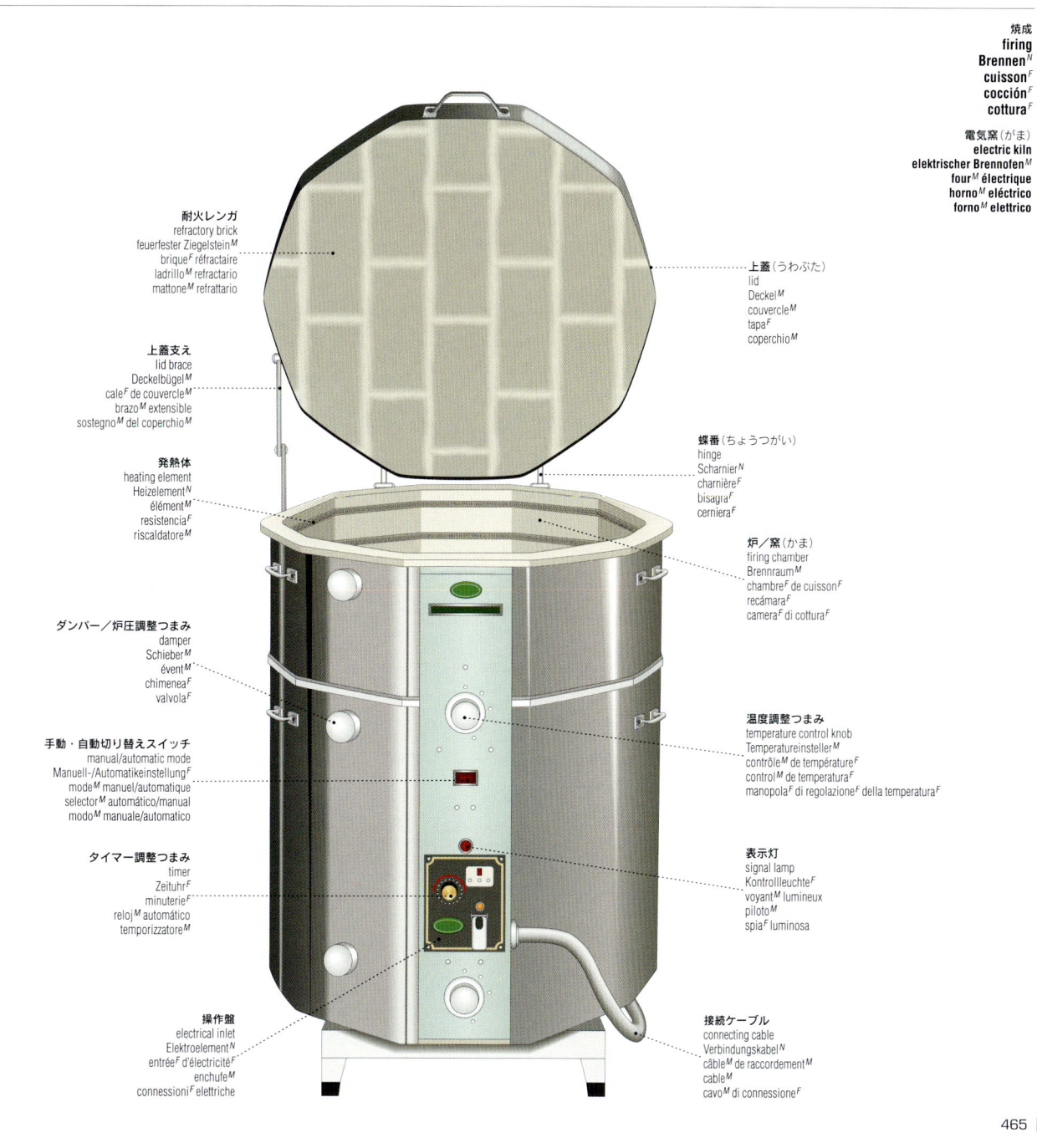

焼成
firing
Brennen^N
cuisson^F
cocción^F
cottura^F

電気窯（がま）
electric kiln
elektrischer Brennofen^M
four^M électrique
horno^M eléctrico
forno^M elettrico

耐火レンガ
refractory brick
feuerfester Ziegelstein^M
brique^F réfractaire
ladrillo^M refractario
mattone^M refrattario

上蓋（うわぶた）
lid
Deckel^M
couvercle^M
tapa^F
coperchio^M

上蓋支え
lid brace
Deckelbügel^M
cale^F de couvercle^M
brazo^M extensible
sostegno^M del coperchio^M

蝶番（ちょうつがい）
hinge
Scharnier^N
charnière^F
bisagra^F
cerniera^F

発熱体
heating element
Heizelement^N
élément^M
resistencia^F
riscaldatore^M

炉／窯（かま）
firing chamber
Brennraum^M
chambre^F de cuisson^F
recámara^F
camera^F di cottura^F

ダンパー／炉圧調整つまみ
damper
Schieber^M
évent^M
chimenea^F
valvola^F

温度調整つまみ
temperature control knob
Temperatureinsteller^M
contrôle^M de température^F
control^M de temperatura^F
manopola^F di regolazione^F della temperatura^F

手動・自動切り替えスイッチ
manual/automatic mode
Manuell-/Automatikeinstellung^F
mode^M manuel/automatique
selector^M automático/manual
modo^M manuale/automatico

タイマー調整つまみ
timer
Zeituhr^F
minuterie^F
reloj^M automático
temporizzatore^M

表示灯
signal lamp
Kontrollleuchte^F
voyant^M lumineux
piloto^M
spia^F luminosa

操作盤
electrical inlet
Elektroelement^N
entrée^F d'électricité^F
enchufe^M
connessioni^F elettriche

接続ケーブル
connecting cable
Verbindungskabel^N
câble^M de raccordement^M
cable^M
cavo^M di connessione^F

芸術と建築

465

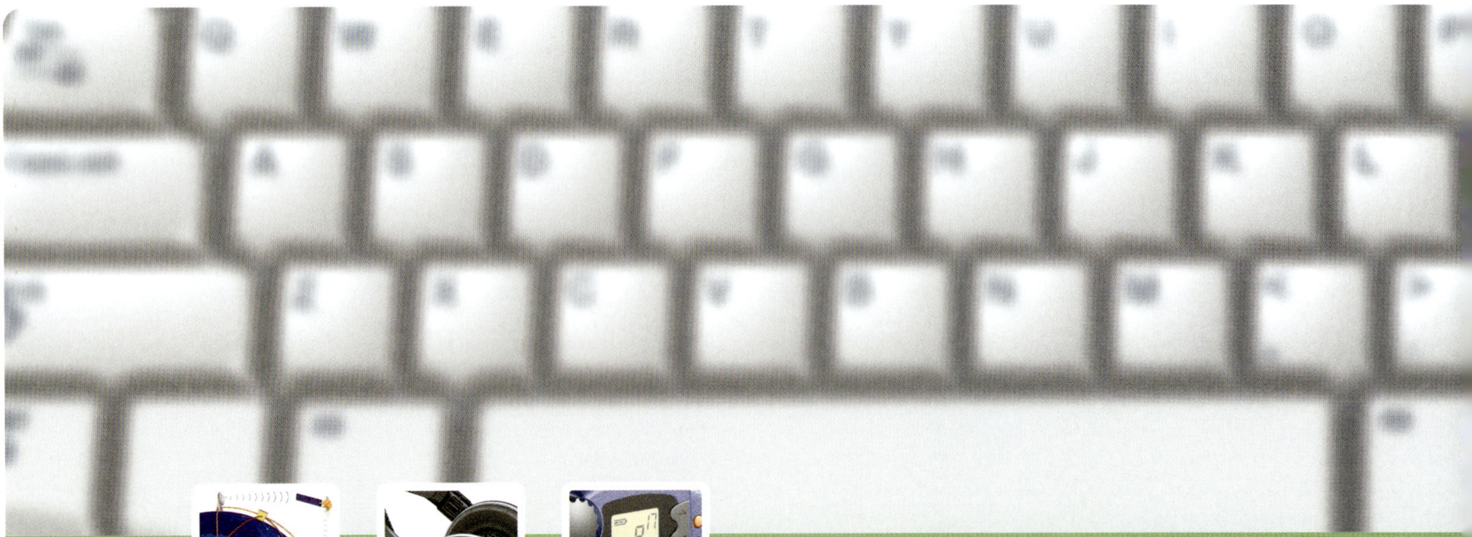

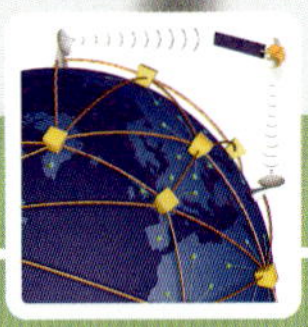

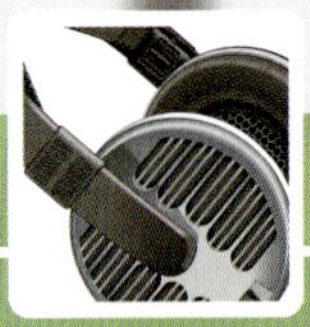

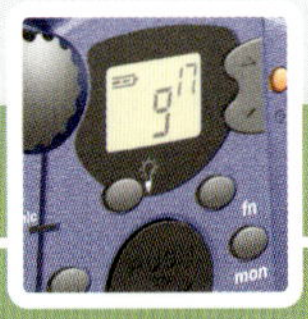
fn
mon

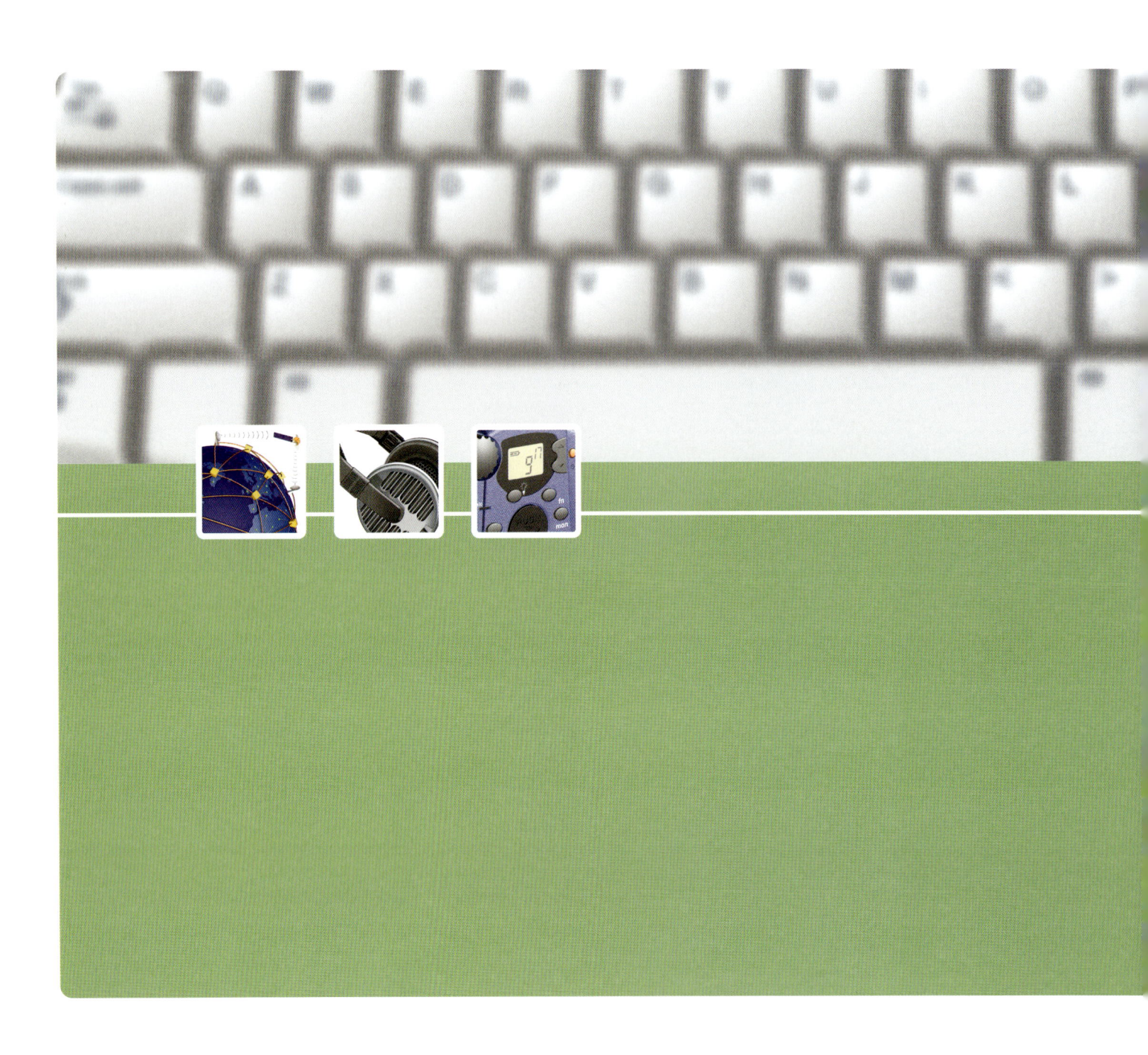

情報伝達とオフィス・オートメーション

COMMUNICATIONS AND OFFICE AUTOMATION | KOMMUNIKATION UND BÜROTECHNIK | COMMUNICATIONS ET BUREAUTIQUE | COMUNICACIONES Y AUTOMATIZACIÓN DE OFICINA | COMUNICAZIONI E BUROTICA

468 情報伝達

- 468 世界の言語
- 470 筆記用具
- 471 新聞
- 472 活版印刷／タイポグラフィー
- 473 区別的発音符／区分表示符
- 473 その他の符号
- 473 句読点／句読符号
- 474 郵便網［ネットワーク］
- 476 写真
- 486 衛星中継
- 486 通信衛星
- 487 衛星通信
- 488 ダイナミック・マイク
- 488 ラジオ：スタジオとコントロール・ルーム
- 489 テレビ
- 497 音声再生装置
- 503 ステレオ・コンポ
- 503 ポータブル音響装置
- 505 無線通信
- 506 電話

509 オフィス・オートメーション

- 509 オフィス／事務所
- 510 オフィス家具
- 513 パーソナル・コンピューター／パソコン
- 514 入力装置
- 518 出力装置
- 520 補助［無停電］電源装置（UPS）
- 521 データ記憶装置
- 522 通信装置
- 522 ネットワークの例
- 523 コンピューター・ネットワーク
- 524 インターネット
- 525 インターネットの利用
- 526 ラップトップ（型）コンピューター
- 527 電子ブック
- 527 ポケット・コンピューター
- 528 文房具

情報伝達 | COMMUNICATIONS
KOMMUNIKATION | COMMUNICATIONS | COMUNICACIONES | COMUNICAZIONI

世界の言語

日本語 | 英語 | ドイツ語 | フランス語 | スペイン語 | イタリア語

languages of the world | Sprachen^F der Erde^F | langues^F du monde^M | lenguas^F del mundo^M | lingue^F del mondo^M

主要な語族
major language families
wichtigste Sprachgruppen^F
grandes familles^F **de langues**^{F}
grandes familias^F **linguisticas**
principali famiglie^F **linguistiche**

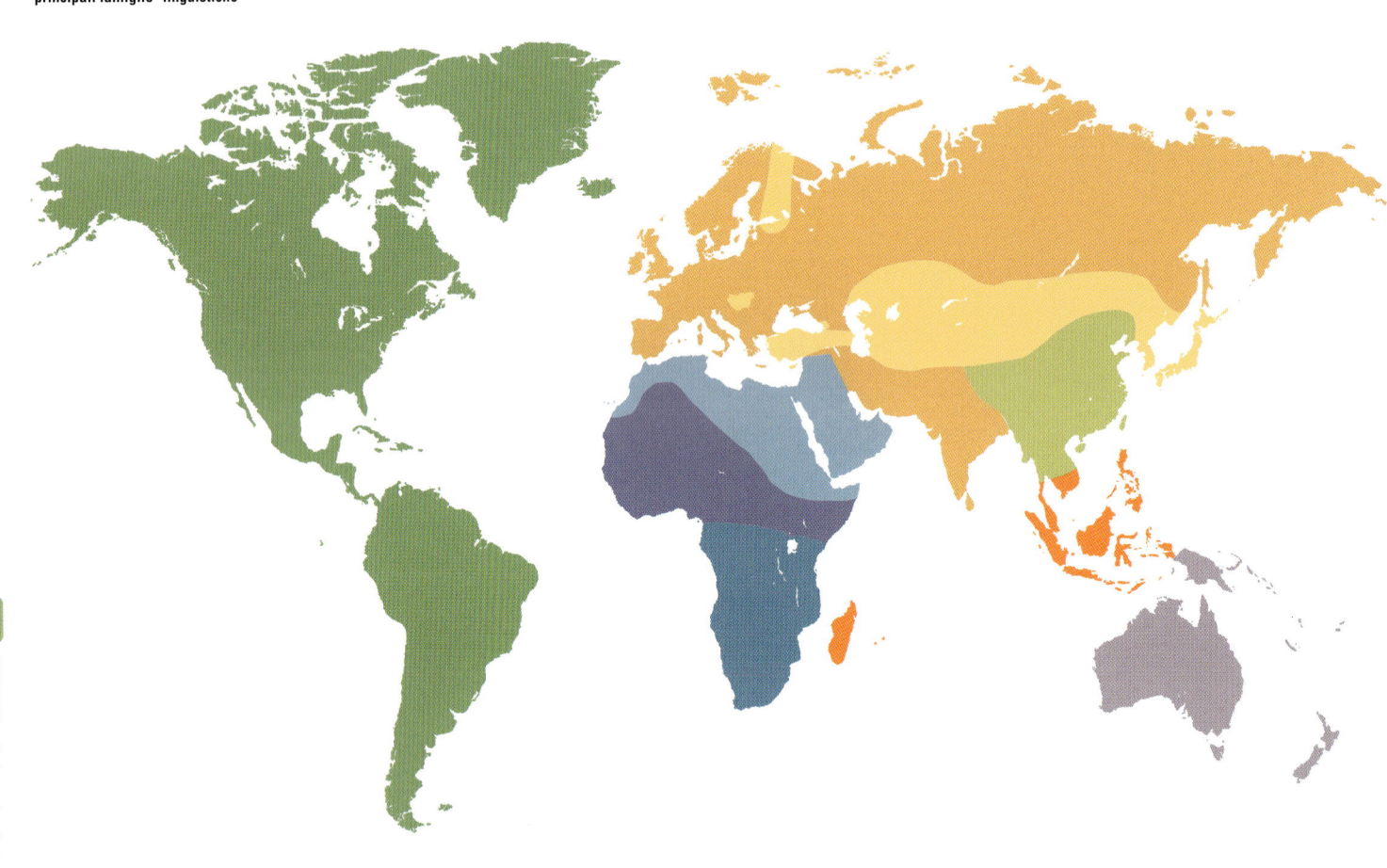

アフロ・アジア語族
Afro-Asiatic languages
afroasiatische Sprachen^F
langues^F **afro-asiatiques**
lenguas^F **afro-asiáticas**
lingue^F **afroasiatiche**

アラビア語
Arabic
Arabisch^N
arabe^M
árabe^M
arabo^M

ヘブライ語
Hebrew
Hebräisch^N
hébreu^M
hebreo^M
ebraico^M

アラム語
Aramaic
Aramäisch^N
araméen^M
arameo^M
aramaico^M

アムハラ語
Amharic
Amharisch^N
amharique^M
amárico^M
amarico^M

ベルベル語群
Berber
Berbersprache^F
berbère^M
bereber^M
berbero^M

中央アフリカ語族
Central African languages
zentralafrikanische Sprachen^F
langues^F **d'Afrique**^{F} **centrale**
lenguas^F **centro-africanas**
lingue^F **centrafricane**

フラニ語
Fulani
Ful^N
peul^M
fulani^M
fulani^M

ウォロフ語
Wolof
Wolof^N
wolof^M
Wolof^M
wolof^M

バンバラ語
Bambara
Bambara^N
bambara^M
Bambara^M
bambara^M

ハウサ語
Hausa
Hausa^N
haoussa^M
hausa^F
hausa^M

ヨルバ語
Yoruba
Yoruba^N
yoruba^M
yoruba^M
yoruba^M

バントゥー語族
Bantu languages
Bantusprachen^F
langues^F **bantoues**
lenguas^F **bantúes**
lingue^F **bantu**

スワヒリ語
Swahili
Suaheli^N
swahili^M
swahili^M
swahili^M

キルンディ語
Kirundi
Kirundi^N
kirundi^M
kirundi^M
kirundi^M

キニャルワンダ語
Kinyarwanda
Kinyarwanda^N
kinyarwanda^M
Kinyarwanda^M
Kinyarwanda^M

リンガラ語
Lingala
Lingala^N
lingala^M
lingala^M
lingala^M

ズールー語
Zulu
Zulu^N
zoulou^M
zulú^M
zulu^M

シナ・チベット語族
Sino-Tibetan languages
sinotibetische Sprachen^F
langues^F **sino-tibétaines**
lenguas^F **chinotibetanas**
lingue^F **sinotibetane**

中国語
Chinese
Chinesisch^N
chinois^M
chino^M
cinese^M

タイ語
Thai
Thai^N
thaï^M
thai^M
tailandese^M

ベトナム語
Vietnamese
Vietnamesisch^N
vietnamien^M
vietnamita^M
vietnamita^M

ビルマ語
Burmese
Birmanisch^N
birman^M
birmano^M
birmano^M

チベット語
Tibetan
Tibetisch^N
tibétain^M
tibetano^M
tibetano^M

情報伝達 | COMMUNICATIONS
KOMMUNIKATION | COMMUNICATIONS | COMUNICACIONES | COMUNICAZIONI

世界の言語

インド・ヨーロッパ語族
Indo-European languages
indoeuropäische Sprachen^F
langues^F **indo-européennes**
lenguas^F **indoeuropeas**
lingue^F **indoeuropee**

ロマンス諸語
Romance languages
romanische Sprachen^F
langues^F **romanes**
lenguas^F **romances**
lingue^F **romanze**

フランス語
French
Französisch^N
français^M
francés^M
francese

スペイン語
Spanish
Spanisch^N
espagnol^M
español^M
spagnolo

カタロニア語
Catalan
Katalanisch^N
catalan^M
catalán^M
catalano^M

ポルトガル語
Portuguese
Portugiesisch^N
portugais^M
portugués^M
portoghese^M

イタリア語
Italian
Italienisch^N
italien^M
italiano^M
italiano^M

ルーマニア語
Romanian
Rumänisch^N
roumain^M
rumano^M
rumeno^M

ゲルマン諸語
Germanic languages
germanische Sprachen^F
langues^F **germaniques**
lenguas^F **germánicas**
lingue^F **germaniche**

英語
English
Englisch^N
anglais^M
inglés^M
inglese

ドイツ語
German
Deutsch^N
allemand^M
alemán^M
tedesco^M

オランダ語
Dutch
Niederländisch^N
néerlandais^M
holandés^M
olandese^M

デンマーク語
Danish
Dänisch^N
danois^M
danés^M
danese^M

スウェーデン語
Swedish
Schwedisch^N
suédois^M
sueco^M
svedese^M

ノルウェー語
Norwegian
Norwegisch^N
norvégien^M
noruego^M
norvegese^M

アイスランド語
Icelandic
Isländisch^N
islandais^M
islandés^M
islandese^M

イディッシュ語
Yiddish
Jiddisch^N
yiddish^M
yidish^M
yiddish^M

ケルト諸語
Celtic languages
keltische Sprachen^F
langues^F **celtiques**
lenguas^F **célticas**
lingue^F **celtiche**

ブルトン語
Breton
Bretonisch^N
breton^M
bretón^M
bretone^M

ウェールズ語
Welsh
Walisisch^N
gallois^M
galés^M
gallese^M

スコットランド語
Scottish
Schottisch-Gälisch^N
écossais^M
escocés^M
scozzese^M

アイルランド語
Irish
Irisch^N
irlandais^M
irlandés^M
irlandese^M

孤立した諸言語
isolated languages
isolierte Sprachen^F
langues^F **isolées**
lenguas^F **aisladas**
lingue^F **isolate**

ギリシャ語
Greek
Griechisch^N
grec^M
griego^M
greco^M

アルバニア語
Albanian
Albanisch^N
albanais^M
albanés^M
albanese^M

アルメニア語
Armenian
Armenisch^N
arménien^M
armenio^M
armeno^M

スラブ諸語
Slavic languages
slawische Sprachen^F
langues^F **slaves**
lenguas^F **eslavas**
lingue^F **slave**

チェコ語
Czech
Tschechisch^N
tchèque^M
checo^M
ceco^M

スロバキア語
Slovak
Slowakisch^N
slovaque^M
eslovaco^M
slovacco^M

ポーランド語
Polish
Polnisch^N
polonais^M
polaco^M
polacco^M

ロシア語
Russian
Russisch^N
russe^M
ruso^M
russo^M

ウクライナ語
Ukrainian
Ukrainisch^N
ukrainien^M
ucranio^M
ucraino^M

ブルガリア語
Bulgarian
Bulgarisch^N
bulgare^M
búlgaro^M
bulgaro^M

スロベニア語
Slovene
Slowenisch^N
slovène^M
esloveno^M
sloveno^M

セルボ・クロアチア語
Serbo-Croatian
Serbokroatisch^N
serbo-croate^M
serbocroata^M
serbo-croato^M

インド・イラン諸語
Indo-Iranian languages
indoarische Sprachen^F
langues^F **indo-iraniennes**
lenguas^F **indoiranias**
lingue^F **indoiraniche**

ペルシャ語
Persian
Persisch^N
persan^M
persa^M
persiano^M

ウルドゥー語
Urdu
Urdu^N
ourdou^M
urdu^M
urdu^M

ヒンディー語
Hindi
Hindi^N
hindi^M
Hindi^M
hindi^M

アメリカインディアン語族
Amerindian languages
Indianersprachen^F
langues^F **amérindiennes**
lenguas^F **amerindias**
lingue^F **amerindie**

イヌクティトット語
Inuktitut
Inuktikut^N
inuktitut^M
inuktitut^M
inuktitut^M

クリー語
Cree
Cree^N
cri^M
cree^M
cree^M

モンタニェ語
Montagnais
Montagnais^N
montagnais^M
montagnais^N
montagnais^M

ナバホ語
Navajo
Navajo^N
navaho^M
navajo^M
navajo^M

ナワトル語
Nahuatl
Nahuatl^N
nahuatl^M
nahuatl^M
nahuatl^M

マヤ語
Maya
Maya^N
maya^M
maya^M
maya^M

ケチュア語
Quechua
Ketschua^N
quechua^M
quechua^M
quechua^M

アイマラ語
Aymara
Aimara^N
aymara^M
aymara^M
aymara^M

グワラニ語
Guarani
Guaraní^N
guarani^M
guaraní^M
guarani^M

ウラル・アルタイ語族
Ural-Altaic languages
altaische Sprachen^F
langues^F **ouralo-altaïques**
lenguas^F **uraloaltaicas**
lingue^F **uralo-altaiche**

日本語
Japanese
Japanisch^N
japonais^M
japonés^M
giapponese^M

韓国[朝鮮]語
Korean
Koreanisch^N
coréen^M
coreano^M
coreano^M

モンゴル語
Mongolian
Mongolisch^N
mongol^M
mogol^M
mongolo^M

トルコ語
Turkish
Türkisch^N
turc^M
turco^M
turco^M

マレー・ポリネシア語族
Malayo-Polynesian languages
malaiopolynesische Sprachen^F
langues^F **malayo-polynésiennes**
lenguas^F **malayo-polinesias**
lingue^F **maleopolinesiane**

インドネシア語
Indonesian
Indonesisch^N
indonésien^M
indonesio^M
indonesiano^M

タガログ語
Tagalog
Tagalog^N
tagalog^M
tagalo^M
tagalog^M

マラガシー語
Malagasy
Malagasy^N
malgache^M
malgache^M
malgascio^M

サモア語
Samoan
Samoanisch^N
samoan^M
samoano^M
samoano^M

タヒチ語
Tahitian
Tahitianisch^N
tahitien^M
tahitiano^M
tahitiano^M

ハワイ語
Hawaiian
Hawaiianisch^N
hawaïen^M
hawaiano^M
hawaiano^M

マオリ語
Maori
Maori^N
maori^M
maorí^M
maori^M

オセアニア語族
Oceanian languages
ozeanische Sprachen^F
langues^F **d'Océanie**
lenguas^F **oceánicas**
lingue^F **dell'Oceania**

メラネシア語
Melanesian
Melanesisch^N
mélanésien^M
melanesia^M
melanesiano^M

パプア諸語
Papuan languages
Papuasprachen^F
langues^F papoues
lenguas^F papúas
lingue^F papuane

オーストラリア先住民の諸言語
Australian aboriginal languages
australische Sprachen^F
langues^F aborigènes d'Australie^F
lenguas^F australianas aborígenas
lingue^F aborigene dell'Australia

情報伝達とオフィス・オートメーション

情報伝達 | COMMUNICATIONS
KOMMUNIKATION | COMMUNICATIONS | COMUNICACIONES | COMUNICAZIONI

筆記用具
writing instruments | Schreibgeräte^N | instruments^M d'écriture^F | instrumentos^M para escribir | strumenti^M scrittori

日本語 | 英語 | ドイツ語 | フランス語 | スペイン語 | イタリア語

羽ペン
quill
Federkiel^F
plume^F d'oie^F
pluma^F de ave^F
penna^F d'oca^F

茎ペン
cane pen
Rohrfeder^F
plume^F creuse de roseau^M
pluma^F de caña^F
calamo^M vegetale

筆
writing brush
Schreibpinsel^M
pinceau^M
pincel^M
pennello^M per scrivere

(古代エジプトの)葦(あし)ペン
Egyptian reed pen
Binsenstängel^M
calame^M
cálamo^M egipcio
stilo^M di canna^F

万年筆
fountain pen
Füllfederhalter^M
stylo^M-plume^F
pluma^F estilográfica
penna^F stilografica

ペン先
nib
Feder^F
plume^F
punta^F
pennino^M

キャップ
cap
Kappe^F
capuchon^M
tapa^F
cappuccio^M

空気孔
air hole
Luftloch^N
évent^M
orificio^M
occhio^M

軸
barrel
Tintenraum^M
corps^M
caña^F
corpo^M

ボール・ペン
ballpoint pen
Kugelschreiber^M
stylo^M-bille^F
bolígrafo^M
penna^F a sfera^F

カートリッジ
cartridge
Mine^F
cartouche^F
carga^F
cartuccia^F

ジョイント
joint
Verbindung^F
joint^M
unión^F
raccordo^M

(古代ローマの)金属ペン
Roman metal pen
römische Metallfeder^F
plume^F métallique romaine
pluma^F metálica romana
stilo^M metallico romano

黒鉛鉛筆
lead pencil
Graphitstift^M
crayon^M en plomb^M
lápiz^M de grafito^M
stilo^M di piombo^M

尖筆／鉄筆
stylus
Stilus^M
stylet^M
estilo^M
stilo^M

スチール・ペン
steel pen
Stahlschreibfeder^F
plume^F métallique
pluma^F metálica
penna^F con pennino^M metallico

マーカー
marker
Marker^M
marqueur^M
marcador^M
evidenziatore^M

シャープ・ペンシル®
mechanical pencil
Druckbleistift^M
porte-mine^M
portaminas^M
portamine^M

鉛筆
pencil
Bleistift^M
crayon^M
lápiz^M
matita^F

ポケット・クリップ
clip
Clip^M
agrafe^F
pinza^F
fermaglio^M

ペン先
point
Spitze^F
pointe^F
punta^F
punta^F

ばね／スプリング
spring
Feder^F
ressort^M
resorte^M
molla^F

押し出し装置
thrust device
Druckmechanik^F
dispositif^M de poussée^F
mecanismo^M de empuje^M
meccanismo^M a scatto^M

押し圧チューブ
thrust tube
Druckrohr^N
tube^M de poussée^F
tubo^M de empuje^M
asta^F del meccanismo^M a scatto^M

押しボタン
push-button
Druckknopf^M
bouton^M-poussoir^M
botón^M de presión^F
pulsante^M

ボール・ベアリング
ball bearing
Kugel^F
bille^F
bola^F de rodamiento^M
sfera^F

インク
ink
Farbmasse^F
encre^F
tinta^F
inchiostro^M

詰め替え芯
refill
Nachfüllmine^F
recharge^F
repuesto^M
refill^M

情報伝達とオフィス・オートメーション

470

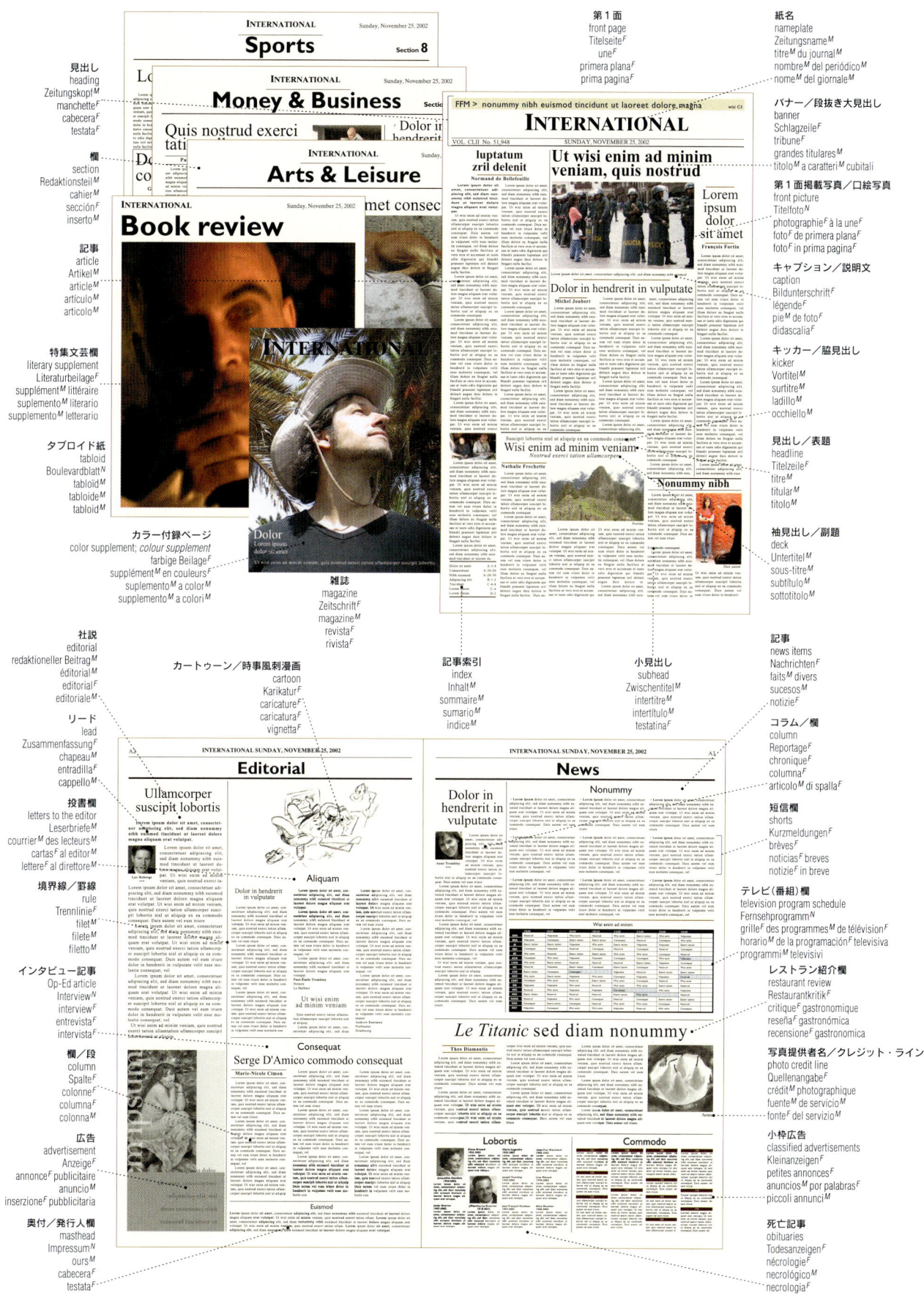

情報伝達 | COMMUNICATIONS
KOMMUNIKATION | COMMUNICATIONS | COMUNICACIONES | COMUNICAZIONI

新聞

newspaper | Zeitung^F | journal^M | periódico^M | giornale^M

見出し
heading
Zeitungskopf^M
manchette^F
cabecera^F
testata^F

欄
section
Redaktionsteil^M
cahier^M
sección^F
inserto^M

記事
article
Artikel^M
article^M
artículo^M
articolo^M

特集文芸欄
literary supplement
Literaturbeilage^F
supplément^M littéraire
suplemento^M literario
supplemento^M letterario

タブロイド紙
tabloid
Boulevardblatt^N
tabloïd^M
tabloide^M
tabloid^M

カラー付録ページ
color supplement; *colour supplement*
farbige Beilage^F
supplément^M en couleurs
suplemento^M a color^M
supplemento^M a colori^M

社説
editorial
redaktioneller Beitrag^M
éditorial^M
editorial^F
editoriale^F

リード
lead
Zusammenfassung^F
chapeau^M
entradilla^F
cappello^M

投書欄
letters to the editor
Leserbriefe^M
courrier^M des lecteurs
cartas^F al editor^M
lettere^F al direttore^M

境界線／罫線
rule
Trennlinie^F
filet^M
filete^M
filetto^M

インタビュー記事
Op-Ed article
Interview^N
interview^F
entrevista^F
intervista^F

欄／段
column
Spalte^F
colonne^F
columna^F
colonna^F

広告
advertisement
Anzeige^F
annonce^F publicitaire
anuncio^M
inserzione^F pubblicitaria

奥付／発行人欄
masthead
Impressum^N
ours^M
cabecera^F
testata^F

第1面
front page
Titelseite^F
une^F
primera plana^F
prima pagina^F

雑誌
magazine
Zeitschrift^F
magazine^M
revista^F
rivista^F

カートゥーン／時事風刺漫画
cartoon
Karikatur^F
caricature^F
caricatura^F
vignetta^F

記事引
index
Inhalt^M
sommaire^M
sumario^M
indice^M

紙名
nameplate
Zeitungsname^M
titre^M du journal^M
nombre^M del periódico^M
nome^M del giornale^M

バナー／段抜き大見出し
banner
Schlagzeile^F
tribune^F
grandes titulares^M
titolo^M a caratteri cubitali

第1面掲載写真／口絵写真
front picture
Titelfoto^N
photographie^F à la une^F
foto^F de primera plana^F
foto^F in prima pagina^F

キャプション／説明文
caption
Bildunterschrift^F
légende^F
pie^M de foto^F
didascalia^F

キッカー／脇見出し
kicker
Vortitel^M
surtitre^M
ladillo^M
occhiello^M

見出し／表題
headline
Titelzeile^F
titre^M
titular^M
titolo^M

袖見出し／副題
deck
Untertitel^M
sous-titre^M
subtítulo^M
sottotitolo^M

記事
news items
Nachrichten^F
faits^M divers
sucesos^M
notizie^F

コラム／欄
column
Reportage^F
chronique^F
columna^F
articolo^M di spalla^F

短信欄
shorts
Kurzmeldungen^F
brèves^F
noticias^F breves
notizie^F in breve

テレビ（番組）欄
television program schedule
Fernsehprogramm^N
grille^F des programmes^M de télévision^F
horario^M de la programación^F televisiva
programmi^M televisivi

レストラン紹介欄
restaurant review
Restaurantkritik^F
critique^F gastronomique
reseña^F gastronómica
recensione^F gastronomica

写真提供者名／クレジット・ライン
photo credit line
Quellenangabe^F
crédit^M photographique
fuente^M de servicio^M
fonte^F del servizio^M

小枠広告
classified advertisements
Kleinanzeigen^F
petites annonces^F
anuncios^M por palabras^F
piccoli annunci^M

死亡記事
obituaries
Todesanzeigen^F
nécrologie^F
necrológico^M
necrologia^F

情報伝達とオフィス・オートメーション

471

情報伝達 | COMMUNICATIONS
KOMMUNIKATION | COMMUNICATIONS | COMUNICACIONES | COMUNICAZIONI

活版印刷／タイポグラフィー

日本語 | 英語 | ドイツ語 | フランス語 | スペイン語 | イタリア語

typography | Typografie[F] | typographie[F] | tipografía[F] | tipografia[F]

フォントのタイプ
characters of a font
Schriftarten[F]
caractères[M] d'une police[F]
caracteres[M] de una fundición[F]
caratteri[M] di un font[M]

サン・セリフ書体
sans serif type
Groteskschrift[F]
caractère[M] sans empattement[M]
tipo[M] sans serif
carattere senza grazie

セリフ書体
serif type
Serifenschrift[F]
caractère[M] avec empattements[M]
tipo[M] serif
carattere con grazie

abcdefghijklmnopqrstuvwxyz 0123456789   abcdefghijklmnopqrstuvwxyz 0123456789

文字／アルファベット
letters
Buchstaben[M]
lettres[F]
letras[F]
lettere[F]

数字
figures
Ziffern[F]
chiffres[M]
cifras[F]
cifre[F]

字体
shape of characters
Zeichenform[F]
forme[F] des caractères[M]
forma[F] de los caracteres[M]
forma[F] dei caratteri[M]

ABCDEF   ABCDEF   abcdef   *abcdef*

大文字
uppercase
Majuskel[F]
capitale[F]
mayúscula
maiuscolo[M]

スモール・キャピタル
small capital
Kapitälchen[N]
petite capitale[F]
versalita
maiuscoletto[M]

小文字
lowercase
Minuskel[F]
bas[M] de casse[F]
minúscula
minuscolo[M]

イタリック体／斜体
italic
kursiv
italique[M]
cursiva
corsivo[M]

線の太さ
weight
Schriftstärke[F]
graisse[F]
tamaño[M]
spessore[M]

a   a   a   a   a

エクストラ・ライト
extra-light
extra mager
extra-maigre
extra-fina
molto sottile

ライト／肉細
light
mager
maigre
fina
sottile

ミディアム
medium
normal
normal
media
medio

セミ・ボールド
semi-bold
halbfett
demi-gras
semi-negrita
semi-grassetto

ボールド／肉太
bold
fett
gras
negrita
grassetto

ブラック
black
doppelfett
noir
negro
nero

エクストラ・ボールド
extra-bold
extra fett
extra-gras
extra-negrita
extra-nero

活字幅
set width
Dickte[F]
chasse[F]
espacio[M]
spaziatura[F]

a   a   a   a   a

コンデンス／長体
condensed
extra schmal
serré
condensada
ridotta

ナロー
narrow
schmal
étroit
estrecha
piccola

ノーマル
normal
normal
normal
normal
normale

ワイド
wide
breit
large
ancha
intera

エキステンド／エキスパンド／平体
extended
extra breit
étendu
alargada
espansa

行間
leading
Durchschuss[M]
interlignage[M]
interlineado[M]
interlinea[F]

Lorem ipsum dolor sit amet, consectetuer adipiscing elit, sed

Lorem ipsum dolor sit amet, consectetuer adipiscing elit, sed

Lorem ipsum dolor sit amet, consectetuer adipiscing elit, sed

H_2SO_4 XXe

1行空き
simple spacing
einfacher Zeilenabstand[M]
interligne[M] simple
interlineado[M] sencillo
interlinea[F] singola

1.5行空き
1.5 spacing
Zeilenabstand[M] 1,5 Zeilen[F]
interligne[M] 1,5
interlineado[M] 1,5
interlinea[F] 1,5

2行空き
double spacing
doppelter Zeilenabstand[M]
interligne[M] double
interlineado[M] doble
interlinea[F] doppia

下付き
inferior
tiefgestellt
indice[M]
subíndice
pedice[M]

文字位置
position of a character
Zeichenstellung[F]
position[F] d'un caractère[M]
posición[F] de un carácter[M]
posizione[F] di un carattere[M]

肩付き／上（うわ）付き
superior
hochgestellt
exposant[M]
superíndice
apice[M]

情報伝達 | COMMUNICATIONS
KOMMUNIKATION | COMMUNICATIONS | COMUNICACIONES | COMUNICAZIONI

区別的発音符／区分表示符

diacritic symbols | diakritische Zeichen^N | signes^M diacritiques | signos^M diacríticos | simboli^M diacritici

à
アクサングラーブ／
低[抑音]アクセント
grave accent
Accent^M grave
accent^M grave
acento^M grave
accento^M grave

ü
ウムラウト
umlaut
Umlaut^M
tréma^M
diéresis^F
dieresi^F

é
アクサンテギュ／
鋭[揚音]アクセント
acute accent
Accent^M aigu
accent^M aigu
acento^M agudo
accento^M acuto

â
アクサン・シルコンフレックス／
曲折アクセント
circumflex accent
Circumflex^M
accent^M circonflexe
acento^M circunflejo
accento^M circonflesso

ç
セディーユ
cedilla
Cedille^F
cédille^F
cedilla^F
cediglia^F

ñ
ティルデ
tilde
Tilde^F
tilde^M
tilde^F
tilde$^{M/F}$

その他の符号

miscellaneous symbols | Weitere Symbole^N | symboles^M divers | varios | varie^F

®
登録商標
registered trademark
eingetragenes Warenzeichen^N
marque^F déposée
marca^F registrada
marchio^M registrato

©
著作権
copyright
Copyright^N
copyright^M
copyright (derechos^M de autor^M)
copyright^M

&
アンパーサンド
ampersand
Et-Zeichen^N
esperluette^F
y
e^F commerciale

's
アポストロフィー
apostrophe
Apostroph^M
apostrophe^F
apóstrofe^M
apostrofo^M

句読点／句読符号

punctuation marks | Satzzeichen^N | signes^M de ponctuation^F | signos^M de puntuación^F | segni^M di interpunzione^F

.
ピリオド
period; *full stop*
Punkt^M
point^M
punto^M
punto^M

;
セミコロン
semicolon
Strichpunkt^M
point^M-virgule^F
punto^M y coma^F
punto^M e virgola^F

,
カンマ／コンマ
comma
Komma^N
virgule^F
coma^F
virgola^F

...
3点リーダー
ellipses; *ellipsis*
Fortführungspunkte^M
points^M de suspension^F
puntos^M suspensivos
puntini^M di sospensione^F

:
コロン
colon
Doppelpunkt^M
deux-points^M
dos puntos^M
due punti^M

*
アステリスク／星印
asterisk
Sternchen^N
astérisque^M
asterisco^M
asterisco^M

—
ダッシュ
dash
Gedankenstrich^M
tiret^M
guión^M largo
trattino^M

( )
パーレン／(丸)括弧
parentheses
runde Klammern^F
parenthèses^F
paréntesis^M
parentesi^F

[ ]
ブラケット／角[大]括弧
square brackets
eckige Klammern^F
crochets^M
corchetes^M
parentesi^F quadre

/
スラッシュ／斜線
virgule; *slash*
Schrägstrich^M
barre^F oblique
diagonal^F
barra^F obliqua

!
感嘆符／雨垂れ／エクスクラメーション・マーク
exclamation point; *exclamation mark*
Ausrufezeichen^N
point^M d'exclamation^F
exlamación^F
punto^M esclamativo

?
疑問符／クエッション・マーク
question mark
Fragezeichen^N
point^M d'interrogation^F
interrogación^F
punto^M interrogativo

' '
引用符／シングル・
クォーテーション・マーク
single quotation marks
halbe Anführungszeichen^N
guillemets^M
comillas^F sencillas
virgolette^F semplici

" "
引用符／(ダブル)
クォーテーション・マーク
quotation marks
Anführungszeichen
guillemets^M
comillas^F
virgolette^F doppie

« »
二重ギュメ[山形]
quotation marks (French)
Anführungszeichen^N (französisch)
guillemets^M
comillas^F
caporali

情報伝達 | COMMUNICATIONS
KOMMUNIKATION | COMMUNICATIONS | COMUNICACIONES | COMUNICAZIONI

郵便網［ネットワーク］

日本語 | 英語 | ドイツ語 | フランス語 | スペイン語 | イタリア語

public postal network | öffentliches Postnetz[N] | réseau[F] public postal | red[F] de correos[M] pública | rete[F] pubblica postale

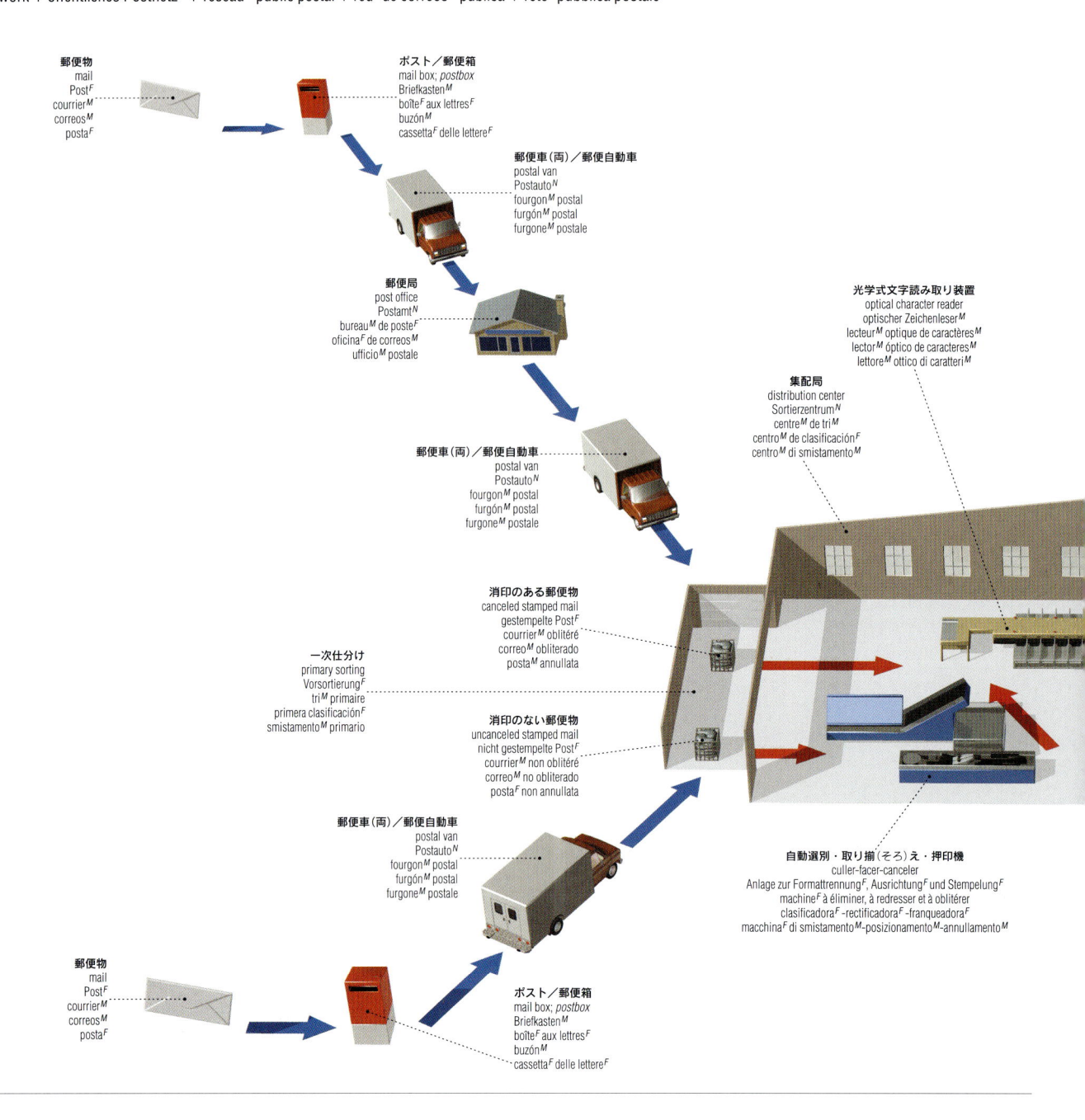

郵便物
mail
Post[F]
courrier[M]
correos[M]
posta[F]

ポスト／郵便箱
mail box; *postbox*
Briefkasten[M]
boîte[F] aux lettres[F]
buzón[M]
cassetta[F] delle lettere[F]

郵便車(両)／郵便自動車
postal van
Postauto[N]
fourgon[M] postal
furgón[M] postal
furgone[M] postale

郵便局
post office
Postamt[N]
bureau[M] de poste[F]
oficina[F] de correos[M]
ufficio[M] postale

光学式文字読み取り装置
optical character reader
optischer Zeichenleser[M]
lecteur[M] optique de caractères[M]
lector[M] óptico de caracteres[M]
lettore[M] ottico di caratteri[M]

集配局
distribution center
Sortierzentrum[N]
centre[M] de tri[M]
centro[M] de clasificación[F]
centro[M] di smistamento[M]

郵便車(両)／郵便自動車
postal van
Postauto[N]
fourgon[M] postal
furgón[M] postal
furgone[M] postale

消印のある郵便物
canceled stamped mail
gestempelte Post[F]
courrier[M] oblitéré
correo[M] obliterado
posta[F] annullata

一次仕分け
primary sorting
Vorsortierung[F]
tri[M] primaire
primera clasificación[F]
smistamento[M] primario

消印のない郵便物
uncanceled stamped mail
nicht gestempelte Post[F]
courrier[M] non oblitéré
correo[M] no obliterado
posta[F] non annullata

郵便車(両)／郵便自動車
postal van
Postauto[N]
fourgon[M] postal
furgón[M] postal
furgone[M] postale

自動選別・取り揃(そろ)え・押印機
culler-facer-canceler
Anlage zur Formattrennung[F], Ausrichtung[F] und Stempelung[F]
machine[F] à éliminer, à redresser et à oblitérer
clasificadora[F] -rectificadora[F] -franqueadora[F]
macchina[F] di smistamento[M] -posizionamento[M] -annullamento[M]

郵便物
mail
Post[F]
courrier[M]
correos[M]
posta[F]

ポスト／郵便箱
mail box; *postbox*
Briefkasten[M]
boîte[F] aux lettres[F]
buzón[M]
cassetta[F] delle lettere[F]

情報伝達とオフィス・オートメーション

郵便物
mail
Post[F]
courrier[M]
correo[M]
posta[F]

切手
postage stamp
Briefmarke[F]/Postwertzeichen[N]
timbre[M]-poste[F]
sello[M] de correos[M]
francobollo[M]

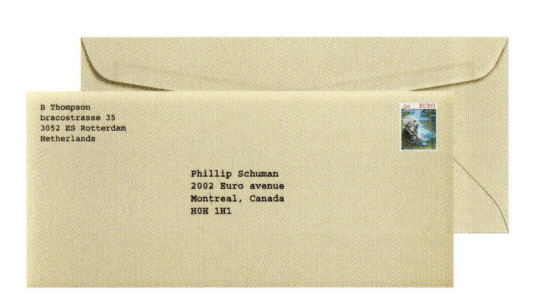

手紙／封書
letter
Brief[M]
lettre[F]
carta[F]
lettera[F]

葉書
postcard
Postkarte[F]
carte[F] postale
postal[F]
cartolina[F]

474

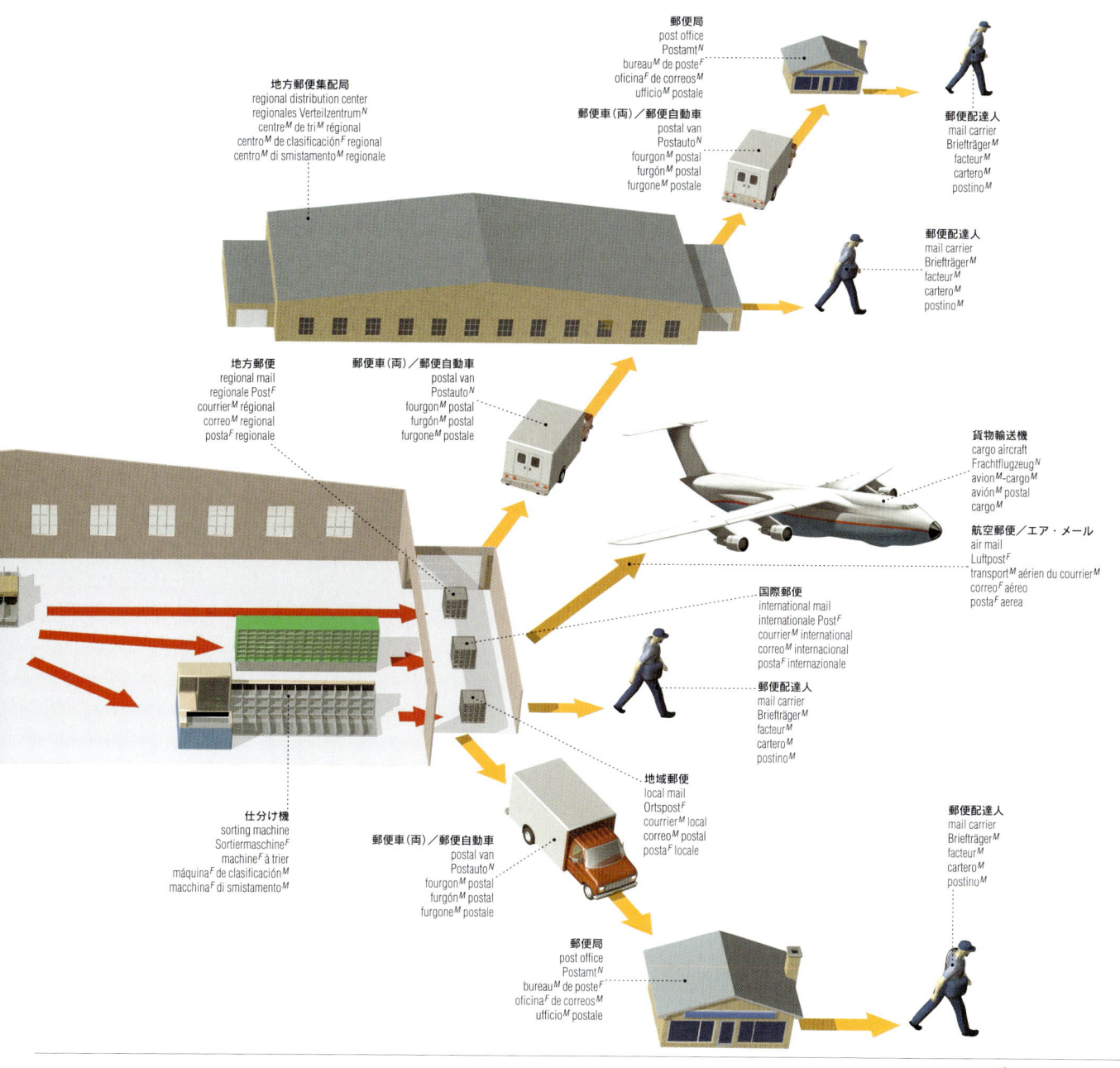

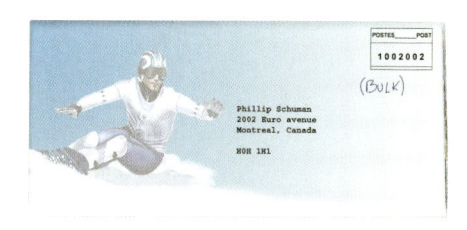

情報伝達 | COMMUNICATIONS
KOMMUNIKATION | COMMUNICATIONS | COMUNICACIONES | COMUNICAZIONI

郵便網［ネットワーク］

郵便局
post office
Postamt^N
bureau^M de poste^F
oficina^F de correos^M
ufficio^M postale

地方郵便集配局
regional distribution center
regionales Verteilzentrum^N
centre^M de tri^M régional
centro^M de clasificación^F regional
centro^M di smistamento^M regionale

郵便車(両)／郵便自動車
postal van
Postauto^N
fourgon^M postal
furgón^M postal
furgone^M postale

郵便配達人
mail carrier
Briefträger^M
facteur^M
cartero^M
postino^M

郵便配達人
mail carrier
Briefträger^M
facteur^M
cartero^M
postino^M

地方郵便
regional mail
regionale Post^F
courrier^M régional
correo^M regional
posta^F regionale

郵便車(両)／郵便自動車
postal van
Postauto^N
fourgon^M postal
furgón^M postal
furgone^M postale

貨物輸送機
cargo aircraft
Frachtflugzeug^N
avion^M-cargo^M
avión^M postal
cargo^M

航空郵便／エア・メール
air mail
Luftpost^F
transport^M aérien du courrier^M
correo^F aéreo
posta^F aerea

国際郵便
international mail
internationale Post^F
courrier^M international
correo^M internacional
posta^F internazionale

郵便配達人
mail carrier
Briefträger^M
facteur^M
cartero^M
postino^M

仕分け機
sorting machine
Sortiermaschine^F
machine^F à trier
máquina^F de clasificación^M
macchina^F di smistamento^M

郵便車(両)／郵便自動車
postal van
Postauto^N
fourgon^M postal
furgón^M postal
furgone^M postale

地域郵便
local mail
Ortspost^F
courrier^M local
correo^M postal
posta^F locale

郵便配達人
mail carrier
Briefträger^M
facteur^M
cartero^M
postino^M

郵便局
post office
Postamt^N
bureau^M de poste^F
oficina^F de correos^M
ufficio^M postale

料金別納郵便
bulk mail letter
Massenversand^M
envoi^M en nombre^M
correo^M de masa^F
posta^F a tariffa ridotta^F

郵便為替
postal order
Postanweisung^F
mandat^M-poste^F
giro^M postal
vaglia^F postale

郵便小包
postal parcel
Postpaket^N
colis^M postal
paquete^M postal
pacco^M postale

情報伝達とオフィス・オートメーション

475

情報伝達 | COMMUNICATIONS
KOMMUNIKATION | COMMUNICATIONS | COMUNICACIONES | COMUNICAZIONI

写真

日本語 | 英語 | ドイツ語 | フランス語 | スペイン語 | イタリア語

photography | Fotografie^F | photographie^F | fotografía^F | fotografia^F

一眼レフ・カメラ：正面図
single-lens reflex (SLR) camera: front view
einäugige Spiegelreflexkamera^F/SLR-Kamera^F: Vorderansicht^F
appareil^M à visée^F reflex mono-objectif^M : vue^F avant
cámara^F réflex monocular: vista^F frontal
macchina^F fotografica reflex monoculare: vista^F frontale

フィルム巻き戻しボタン
film rewind knob
Rückspulknopf^M
rebobinage^M
botón^M de rebobinado^M de la película^F
pulsante^M di riavvolgimento^M della pellicola^F

アクセサリー・シュー
accessory shoe
Zubehörschuh^M
griffe^F porte-accessoires^M
patín^M de los accesorios^M
slitta^F per accessori^M

露出補正ボタン
exposure adjustment knob
Belichtungskorrekturknopf^M
correction^F d'exposition^F
botón^M de compensación^F de la exposición^F
pulsante^M di compensazione^F dell'esposizione^F

ホット・シュー接点／ストロボ接点
hot-shoe contact
Blitzkontakt^M
contact^M électrique
contacto^M central
contatto^M caldo

フィルム巻き上げモード・ボタン
film advance mode
Filmtransporteinstellung^F
mode^M d'entraînement^M du film^M
modalidad^F de avance^M de la película^F
tasto^M per l'avanzamento^M della pellicola^F

表示パネル
control panel
Display^N
écran^M de contrôle^M
panel^M de controles^M
display^M

露出モード・ボタン
exposure mode
Belichtungseinstellung^F
mode^M d'exposition^F
modalidad^F de exposición^F
tasto^M per il modo^M di esposizione^F

機能選択ダイヤル
command control dial
Programmwählscheibe^F
sélecteur^M de fonctions^F
selector^M de programa^F
selettore^M dei programmi^M

多重露出モード・ボタン
multiple exposure mode
Belichtungsmesser^M
surimpression^F
modalidad^F de exposición^F múltiple
tasto^M per le esposizioni^M multiple

電源スイッチ
on-off switch
Ein-/Ausschalter^M
commutateur^M marche^F/arrêt^M
interruptor^M de encendido/apagado
interruttore^M di accensione^F

フィルム感度設定ボタン
film speed
Filmempfindlichkeit^F
sensibilité^F du film^M
indicador^M de velocidad^F
tasto^M per la sensibilità^F della pellicola^F

シャッター・レリーズ・ボタン
shutter release button
Auslöser^M
déclencheur^M
disparador^M
pulsante^M di scatto^M

リモコン端末
remote control terminal
Diode^F des Selbstauslösers^M
prise^F de télécommande^F
terminal^M del control^M a remoto
presa^F per il comando^M a distanza^F

セルフ・タイマー・インジケーター[ランプ]
self-timer indicator
Selbstauslöser-Lichtsignal^N
témoin^M du retardateur^M
indicador^M de tiempo^M
spia^F luminosa dell'autoscatto^M

フォーカス・モード切り換えボタン
focus mode selector
Autofocus-Umschalter^M
mode^M de mise^F au point^M
selector^M de focalización^F
selettore^M della messa^F a fuoco^M

カメラ・ボディー
camera body
Kameragehäuse^N
boîtier^M
caja^F
corpo^M della macchina^F fotografica

被写界深度確認ボタン
depth-of-field preview button
Schärfentiefenknopf^M
vérification^F de la profondeur^F de champ^M
botón^M de previsionado profundidad^F de campo^M
pulsante^M di controllo^M della profondità^F di campo^M

一眼レフ・カメラ：背面図
single-lens reflex (SLR) camera: camera back
einäugige Spiegelreflexkamera^F/SLR-Kamera^F: Rückansicht^F
appareil^M à visée^F reflex mono-objectif^M : dos^M
cámara^F réflex monocular: vista^F posterior
macchina^F fotografica reflex monoculare: dorso^M

レンズ取り外しボタン
lens release button
Objektivauswurf^M
déverrouillage^M de l'objectif^M
botón^M de desbloqueo^M del objetivo^M
pulsante^M di sblocco^M dell'obiettivo^M

(対物)レンズ
objective lens
Objektiv^N
objectif^M
objetivo^M
obiettivo^M

フィルム巻き戻し軸
film rewind system
Filmrückspulung^F
mécanisme^M de rebobinage^M
sistema^M de rebobinado^M de la película^F
sistema^M di riavvolgimento^M della pellicola^F

ファインダー
viewfinder
Bildsucher^M
viseur^M
visor^M
mirino^M

フィルム・ガイド・ローラー
film guide roller
Transportwalze^F
cylindre^M guide^M-film^M
rodillo^M guía^F de la película^F
rullo^M di guida^F della pellicola^F

フォーカル・プレーン・シャッター
focal plane shutter
Schlitzverschluss^M
rideau^M d'obturateur^M
obturador^M de plano^M focal
otturatore^M a tendina^F

吊り金具／ストラップ取り付け部
neckstrap eyelet
Öse^F für Schulterriemen^M
œillet^M d'attache^F
ojete^M para la correa^F del cuello^M
occhiello^M per la cinghia^F

巻き取りスプール
take-up spool
Filmaufrollspule^F
bobine^F réceptrice
carrete^M de rebobinado^M
rocchetto^M di avvolgimento^M

圧着板
pressure plate
Andruckplatte^F
presseur^M
placa^F de presión^F
piastra^F di pressione^F

パトローネ室
film cartridge chamber
Patronenkammer^F
logement^M de la bobine^F
cámara^F para el carrete^M de la película^F
alloggiamento^M del caricatore^M

フィルム・ガイド・レール
film guide rail
Transportschiene^F
rail^M guide^M-film^M
carril^M guía^F de la película^F
guida^F della pellicola^F

フィルム・スプロケット
film sprocket
Transporträdchen^N
tambour^M d'entraînement^M
piñón^M la rueda^F de la película^F
rocchetto^M di trascinamento^M della pellicola^F

フィルム先端インジケーター
film leader indicator
Markierung^F für Filmanfang^M
témoin^M de l'amorce^F du film^M
indicador^M de inicio^M de la película^F
spia^F della coda^F della pellicola^F

情報伝達とオフィス・オートメーション

476

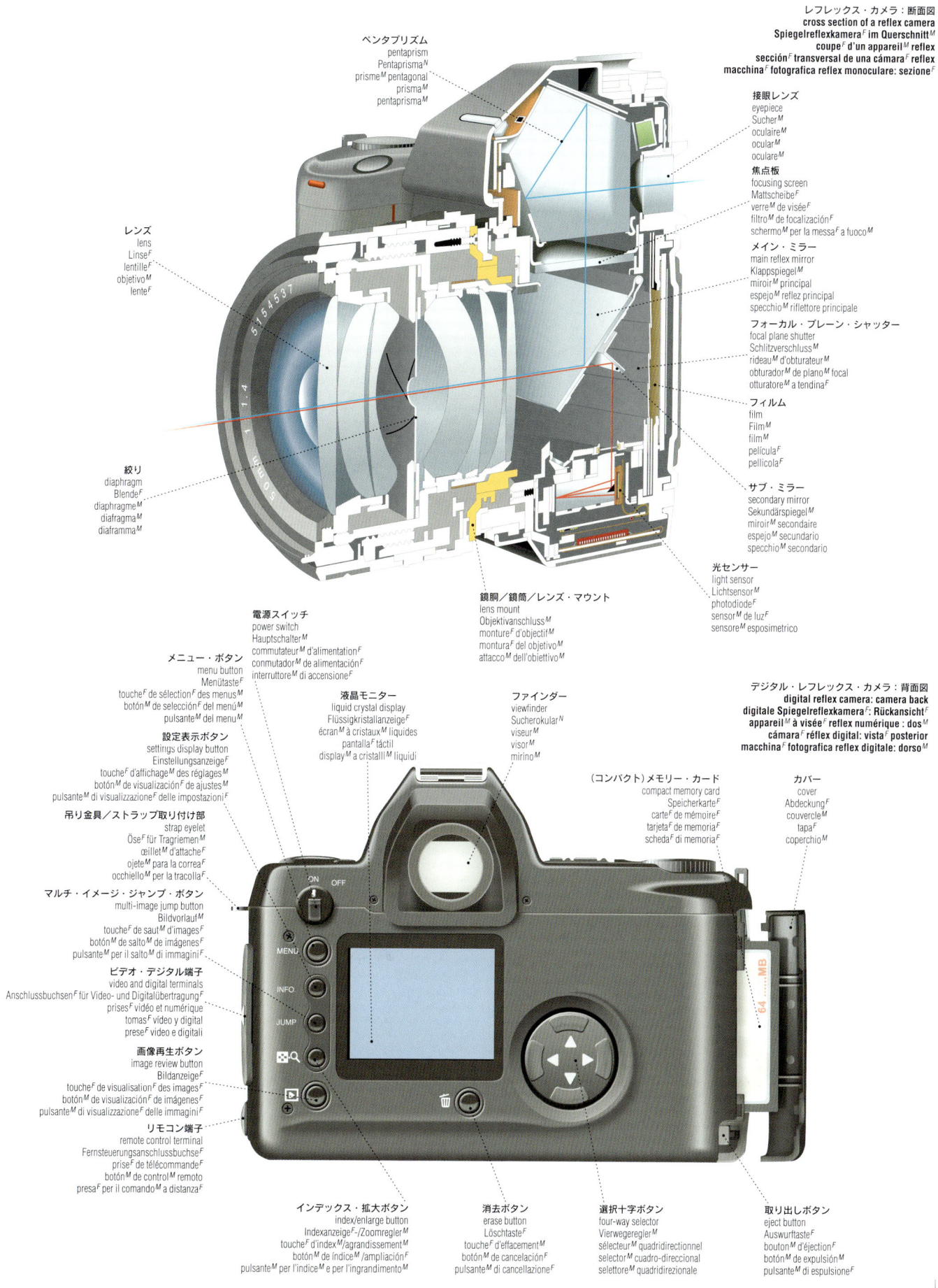

情報伝達 | COMMUNICATIONS
KOMMUNIKATION | COMMUNICATIONS | COMUNICACIONES | COMUNICAZIONI

写真

レフレックス・カメラ：断面図
cross section of a reflex camera
Spiegelreflexkamera[F] im Querschnitt[M]
coupe[F] d'un appareil[M] reflex
sección[F] transversal de una cámara[F] reflex
macchina[F] fotografica reflex monoculare: sezione[F]

ペンタプリズム
pentaprism
Pentaprisma[N]
prisme[M] pentagonal
prisma[M]
pentaprisma[M]

接眼レンズ
eyepiece
Sucher[M]
oculaire[M]
ocular[M]
oculare[M]

焦点板
focusing screen
Mattscheibe[F]
verre[M] de visée[F]
filtro[M] de focalización[F]
schermo[M] per la messa[F] a fuoco[M]

レンズ
lens
Linse[F]
lentille[F]
objetivo[M]
lente[F]

メイン・ミラー
main reflex mirror
Klappspiegel[M]
miroir[M] principal
espejo[M] reflex principal
specchio[M] riflettore principale

フォーカル・プレーン・シャッター
focal plane shutter
Schlitzverschluss[M]
rideau[M] d'obturateur[M]
obturador[M] de plano[M] focal
otturatore[M] a tendina[F]

フィルム
film
Film[M]
film[M]
película[F]
pellicola[F]

絞り
diaphragm
Blende[F]
diaphragme[M]
diafragma[M]
diaframma[M]

サブ・ミラー
secondary mirror
Sekundärspiegel[M]
miroir[M] secondaire
espejo[M] secundario
specchio[M] secondario

光センサー
light sensor
Lichtsensor[M]
photodiode[F]
sensor[M] de luz[F]
sensore[M] esposimetrico

鏡胴／鏡筒／レンズ・マウント
lens mount
Objektivanschluss[M]
monture[F] d'objectif[M]
montura[F] del objetivo[M]
attacco[M] dell'obiettivo[M]

電源スイッチ
power switch
Hauptschalter[M]
commutateur[M] d'alimentation[F]
conmutador[M] de alimentación[F]
interruttore[M] di accensione[F]

メニュー・ボタン
menu button
Menütaste[F]
touche[F] de sélection[F] des menus[M]
botón[M] de selección[F] del menú[M]
pulsante[M] del menu[M]

液晶モニター
liquid crystal display
Flüssigkristallanzeige[F]
écran[M] à cristaux[M] liquides
pantalla[F] táctil
display[M] a cristalli[M] liquidi

ファインダー
viewfinder
Sucherokular[N]
viseur[M]
visor[M]
mirino[M]

デジタル・レフレックス・カメラ：背面図
digital reflex camera: camera back
digitale Spiegelreflexkamera[F]: Rückansicht[F]
appareil[M] à visée[F] reflex numérique : dos[M]
cámara[F] reflex digital: vista[F] posterior
macchina[F] fotografica reflex digitale: dorso[M]

設定表示ボタン
settings display button
Einstellungsanzeige[F]
touche[F] d'affichage[M] des réglages[M]
botón[M] de visualización[F] de ajustes[M]
pulsante[M] di visualizzazione[F] delle impostazioni[F]

（コンパクト）メモリー・カード
compact memory card
Speicherkarte[F]
carte[F] de mémoire[F]
tarjeta[F] de memoria[F]
scheda[F] di memoria[F]

カバー
cover
Abdeckung[F]
couvercle[M]
tapa[F]
coperchio[M]

吊り金具／ストラップ取り付け部
strap eyelet
Öse[F] für Trageriemen[M]
œillet[M] d'attache[F]
ojete[M] para la correa[F]
occhiello[M] per la tracolla[F]

マルチ・イメージ・ジャンプ・ボタン
multi-image jump button
Bildvorlauf[M]
touche[F] de saut[M] d'images[F]
botón[M] de salto[M] de imágenes[F]
pulsante[M] per il salto[M] di immagini[F]

ビデオ・デジタル端子
video and digital terminals
Anschlussbuchsen[F] für Video- und Digitalübertragung[F]
prises[F] vidéo et numérique
tomas[F] vídeo y digital
prese[F] video e digitali

画像再生ボタン
image review button
Bildanzeige[F]
touche[F] de visualisation[F] des images[F]
botón[M] de visualización[F] de imágenes[F]
pulsante[M] di visualizzazione[F] delle immagini[F]

リモコン端子
remote control terminal
Fernsteuerungsanschlussbuchse[F]
prise[F] de télécommande[F]
botón[M] de control[M] remoto
presa[F] per il comando[M] a distanza[F]

インデックス・拡大ボタン
index/enlarge button
Indexanzeige[F]-/Zoomregler[M]
touche[F] d'index[M]/agrandissement[M]
botón[M] de índice[M]/ampliación[F]
pulsante[M] per l'indice[M] e per l'ingrandimento[M]

消去ボタン
erase button
Löschtaste[F]
touche[F] d'effacement[M]
botón[M] de cancelación[F]
pulsante[M] di cancellazione[F]

選択十字ボタン
four-way selector
Vierwegeregler[M]
sélecteur[M] quadridirectionnel
selector[M] cuadro-direccional
selettore[M] quadridirezionale

取り出しボタン
eject button
Auswurftaste[F]
bouton[M] d'éjection[F]
botón[M] de expulsión[M]
pulsante[M] di espulsione[F]

情報伝達とオフィス・オートメーション

477

情報伝達 | COMMUNICATIONS
KOMMUNIKATION | COMMUNICATIONS | COMUNICACIONES | COMUNICAZIONI

写真

日本語 | 英語 | ドイツ語 | フランス語 | スペイン語 | イタリア語

撮影レンズ
lenses
Objektive^N
objectifs^M
objetivos^M
obiettivi^M

標準レンズ
standard lens
Standardobjektiv^N
objectif^M normal
objetivo^M normal
obiettivo^M normale

レンズ
lens
Linse^F
lentille^F
objetivo^M
lente^F

距離目盛り
distance scale
Entfernungsskala^F
échelle^F des distances
escala^F de distancia^F
scala^F delle distanze^F

ピント合わせリング
focus setting ring
Scharfstellring^M
bague^F de mise^F au point^M
anillo^M de ajuste^M del enfoque^M
ghiera^F di messa^F a fuoco^M

被写界深度目盛り
depth-of-field scale
Schärfentiefenskala^F
échelle^F de profondeur^F de champ^M
escala^F de profundidad^F de campo^M de visión^F
scala^F delle profondità^F di campo^M

絞り目盛り
lens aperture scale
Blendenskala^F
échelle^F d'ouverture^F de diaphragme^M
escala^F de abertura^F del diafragma^M
scala^F dell'apertura^F di diaframma^M

バヨネット・マウント
bayonet mount
Bajonettanschluss^M
monture^F baïonnette^F
montura^F de bayoneta^F
attacco^M a baionetta^F

レンズ・アクセサリー
lens accessories
Objektivzubehör^N
accessoires^M de l'objectif^M
accesorios^M para el objetivo^M
accessori^M dell'obiettivo^M

レンズ・キャップ
lens cap
Objektivschutzdeckel^M
capuchon^M d'objectif^M
tapa^F del objetivo^M
coperchio^M di protezione^F dell'obiettivo^M

ズーム・レンズ
zoom lens
Zoomobjektiv^N
objectif^M zoom^M
objetivo^M zoom^M
obiettivo^M zoom

レンズ・フード
lens hood
Gegenlichtblende^F
parasoleil^M
capuchón^M
paraluce^M

広角レンズ
wide-angle lens
Weitwinkelobjektiv^N
objectif^M grand-angulaire
objetivo^M gran angular^M
obiettivo^M grandangolare

接写用レンズ／マクロ・レンズ
macro lens
Makroobjektiv^N
objectif^M macro
objetivo^M macro
obiettivo^M macro

カラー[色]フィルター
color filter; colour filter
Farbfilter^M
filtre^F de couleur^F
filtro^M de color^M
filtro^M colorato

クローズ・アップ・レンズ
close-up lens
Nahlinse^F
lentille^F de macrophotographie^F
lente^F de acercamiento^M
lente^F addizionale per macrofotografie^F

望遠レンズ
telephoto lens
Teleobjektiv^N
téléobjectif^M
teleobjetivo^M
teleobiettivo^M

偏光フィルター
polarizing filter
Polarisationsfilter^M
filtre^M de polarisation^F
filtro^M de polarización^F
filtro^M polarizzatore

（対物）レンズ
objective lens
Objektiv^N
objectif^M
objetivo^M
obiettivo^M

魚眼レンズ
fisheye lens
Fischauge^N
hypergone
lente^M de 180 grados^M
fish-eye^M

超広角レンズ
semi-fisheye lens
Super-Weitwinkelobjektiv^N
objectif^M super-grand-angle^M
objetivo^M ojo^M de pez^M
obiettivo^M supergrandangolare

接写用中間リング
tele-converter
Telekonverter^M
multiplicateur^M de focale^F
teleconvertidor^M
moltiplicatore^M di focale^F

情報伝達とオフィス・オートメーション

情報伝達 | COMMUNICATIONS
KOMMUNIKATION | COMMUNICATIONS | COMUNICACIONES | COMUNICAZIONI

写真

露出計
exposure meter
Belichtungsmesser^M
posemètre^M photoélectrique
fotómetro^M
esposimetro^M

(入射光測定用)拡散板
diffuser
Diffusionskalotte^F
tête^F diffusante
difusor^M
diffusore^M

指針
indicator needle
Anzeigenadel^F
aiguille^F
aguja^F indicadora
indice^M

指示目盛り
light-reading scale
Lichtwertskala^F
échelle^F de lecture^F de la luminosité^F
escala^F de lectura^F
scala^F della luminosità^F

露出値
exposure value
Belichtungswert^M
indice^F d'exposition^F
índices^M de exposición^F
indice^M di esposizione^F

シネ目盛り／シネ・スケール
cine scale
Cine-Skala^F
cadence^F images^F/seconde^F
escala^F de imágenes^F por segundo^M
scala^F cine

露光時間目盛り
exposure-time scale
Belichtungszeitskala^F
échelle^F des temps^F d'exposition^F
escala^F de duración^F de la exposición^F
scala^F dei tempi^M di esposizione^F

絞り目盛り
aperture scale
Blendenskala^F
échelle^F d'ouverture^F
escala^F de abertura^F
scala^F dell'apertura^F del diaframma^M

フィルム感度
film speed
Filmempfindlichkeit^F
sensibilité^F du film^M
velocidad^F de la película^F
sensibilità^F della pellicola^F

計算盤
calculator dial
Rechenscheibe^F
disque^M de réglage^M
cuadrante^M calculador
ghiera^F di calcolo^M

指示換算目盛り
transfer scale
Umrechnungsskala^F
report^M de lecture^F
escala^F de transferencia^F
scala^F di conversione^F

スポットメーター[露出計]
spotmeter
Spotmeter^M
posemètre^M à visée^F reflex
fotómetro^M spot
esposimetro^M spot

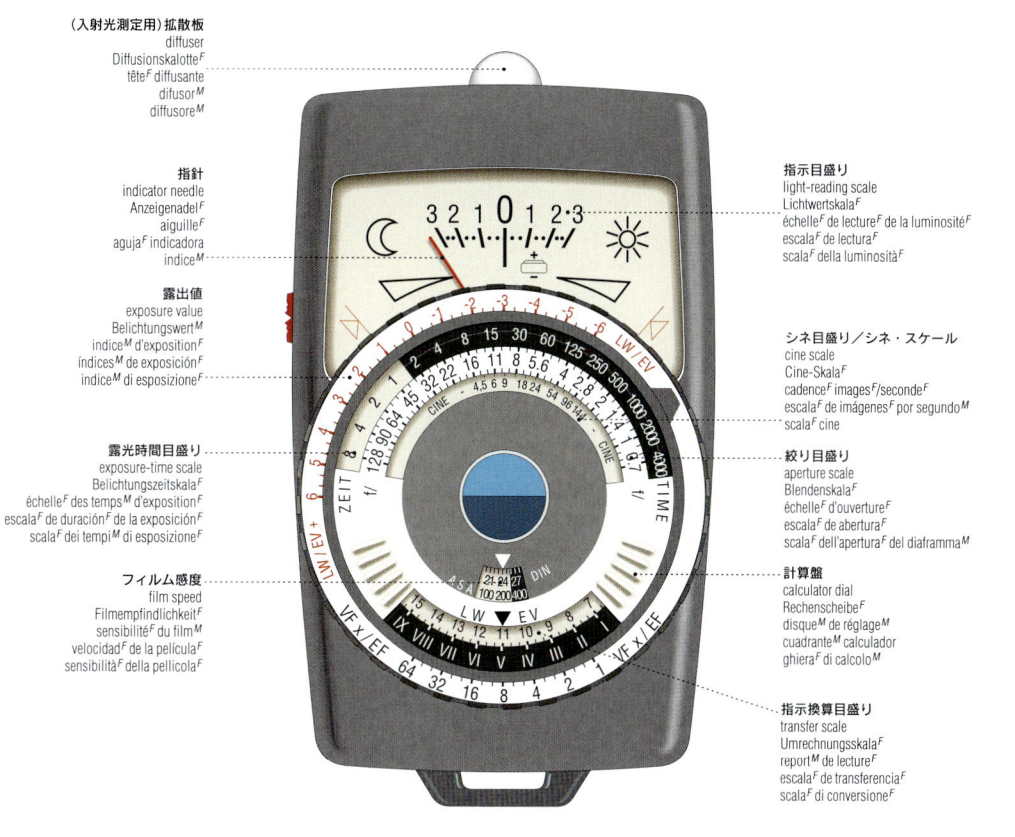

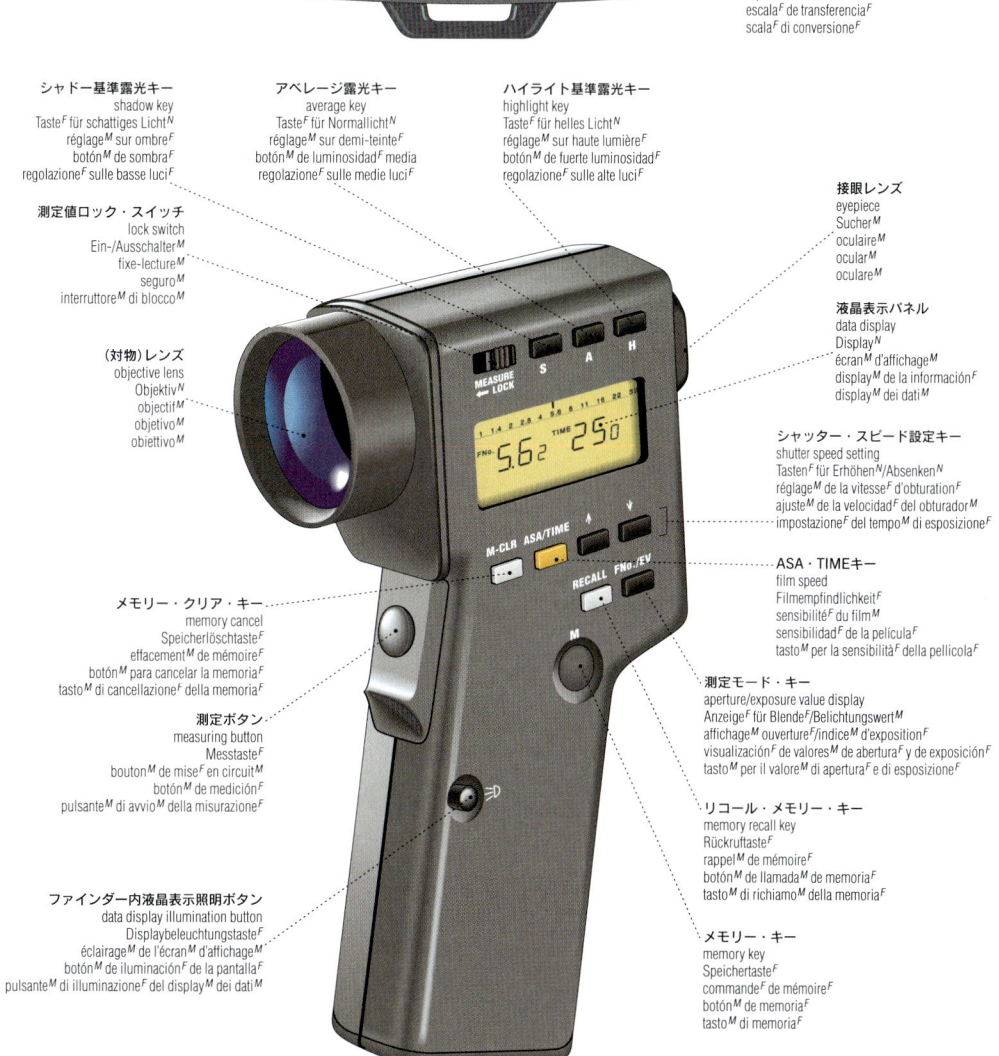

シャドー基準露光キー
shadow key
Taste^F für schattiges Licht^N
réglage^M sur ombre^F
botón^M de sombra^F
regolazione^F sulle basse luci^F

アベレージ露光キー
average key
Taste^F für Normallicht^N
réglage^M sur demi-teinte^F
botón^M de luminosidad^F media
regolazione^F sulle medie luci^F

ハイライト基準露光キー
highlight key
Taste^F für helles Licht^N
réglage^M sur haute lumière^F
botón^M de fuerte luminosidad^F
regolazione^F sulle alte luci^F

接眼レンズ
eyepiece
Sucher^M
oculaire^M
ocular^M
oculare^M

測定値ロック・スイッチ
lock switch
Ein-/Ausschalter^M
fixe-lecture^M
seguro^M
interruttore^M di blocco^M

液晶表示パネル
data display
Display^N
écran^M d'affichage^M
display^M de la información^F
display^M dei dati^M

(対物)レンズ
objective lens
Objektiv^N
objectif^M
objetivo^M
obiettivo^M

シャッター・スピード設定キー
shutter speed setting
Tasten^F für Erhöhen^N/Absenken^N
réglage^M de la vitesse^F d'obturation^F
ajuste^M de la velocidad^F del obturador^M
impostazione^F del tempo^M di esposizione^F

ASA・TIMEキー
film speed
Filmempfindlichkeit^F
sensibilité^F du film^M
sensibilidad^F de la película^F
tasto^M per la sensibilità^F della pellicola^F

メモリー・クリア・キー
memory cancel
Speicherlöschtaste^F
effacement^M de mémoire^F
botón^M para cancelar la memoria^F
tasto^M di cancellazione^F della memoria^F

測定モード・キー
aperture/exposure value display
Anzeige^F für Blende^F/Belichtungswert^M
affichage^M ouverture^F/indice^M d'exposition^F
visualización^F de valores^M de abertura^F y de exposición^F
tasto^M per il valore^M di apertura^F e di esposizione^F

測定ボタン
measuring button
Messtaste^F
bouton^M de mise^F en circuit^M
botón^M de medición^F
pulsante^M di avvio^M della misurazione^F

リコール・メモリー・キー
memory recall key
Rückruftaste^F
rappel^M de mémoire^F
botón^M de llamada^M de memoria^F
tasto^M di richiamo^M della memoria^F

ファインダー内液晶表示照明ボタン
data display illumination button
Displaybeleuchtungstaste^F
éclairage^M de l'écran^M d'affichage^M
botón^M de iluminación^F de la pantalla^F
pulsante^M di illuminazione^F del display^M dei dati^M

メモリー・キー
memory key
Speichertaste^F
commande^F de mémoire^F
botón^M de memoria^F
tasto^M di memoria^F

情報伝達とオフィス・オートメーション

情報伝達 | COMMUNICATIONS
KOMMUNIKATION | COMMUNICATIONS | COMUNICACIONES | COMUNICAZIONI

写真

日本語 | 英語 | ドイツ語 | フランス語 | スペイン語 | イタリア語

スチル・カメラ
still cameras
Fotoapparate^M
appareils^M photographiques
cámaras^M fijas
macchine^F fotografiche

レンジファインダー・カメラ
rangefinder
Sucherkamera^F
appareil^M à télémètre^M couplé
telémetro^M
macchina^F fotografica autofocus

ポラロイド®・カメラ
Polaroid® camera
Sofortbildkamera^F
Polaroid®^M
cámara^F Polaroid Land
Polaroid^F

水中カメラ
underwater camera
Unterwasserkamera^F
appareil^M de plongée^F
cámara^F submarina
macchina^F fotografica subacquea

一眼レフ・カメラ
single-lens reflex (SLR) camera
einäugige Spiegelreflexkamera^F
appareil^M à visée^F reflex mono-objectif^M
cámara^F reflex de un solo objetivo^M
macchina^F fotografica reflex

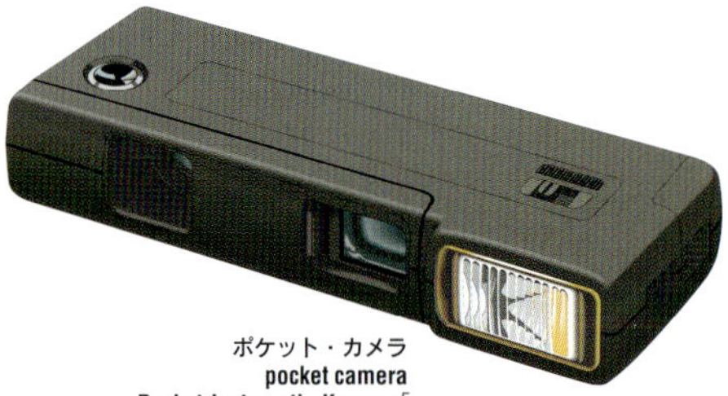

ポケット・カメラ
pocket camera
Pocket-Instamatic-Kamera^F
appareil^M petit-format^M
cámara^F de bolsillo^M
macchina^F fotografica tascabile

使い捨てカメラ／レンズ付きフィルム
disposable camera
Einwegkamera^F
appareil^M jetable
cámara^F desechable
macchina^F fotografica usa e getta

二眼レフ・カメラ
twin-lens reflex camera
Zweiäugige Spiegelreflexkamera^F
appareil^M reflex à deux objectifs^M
cámara^F réflex con dos objetivos^M
macchina^F fotografica reflex biottica

ビュー・カメラ
view camera
Großformatkamera^F
chambre^F photographique
cámara^F de fuelle^M
macchina^F fotografica a banco^M ottico

情報伝達とオフィス・オートメーション

情報伝達 | COMMUNICATIONS
KOMMUNIKATION | COMMUNICATIONS | COMUNICACIONES | COMUNICAZIONI

写真

中型一眼レフ・カメラ
medium format SLR (6 x 6)
Mittelformatkamera^F SLR (6 x 6)
appareil^M reflex 6 X 6 mono-objectif^M
cámara^F reflex de formato^M mediao SLR (6x6)
macchina^F fotografica reflex (6x6)

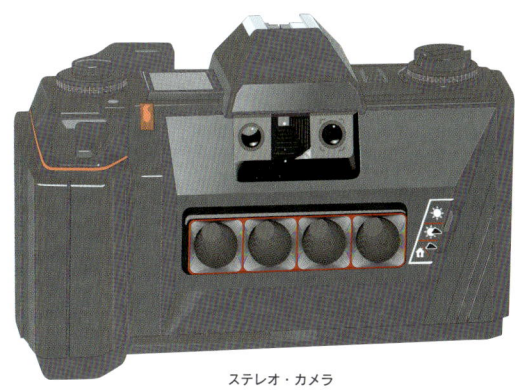

ステレオ・カメラ
stereo camera
Stereokamera^F
appareil^M stéréoscopique
cámara^F estereoscópica
macchina^F fotografica stereoscopica

デジタル・カメラ
digital camera
Digitalkamera^F
appareil^M numérique
cámara^F digital
macchina^F fotografica digitale

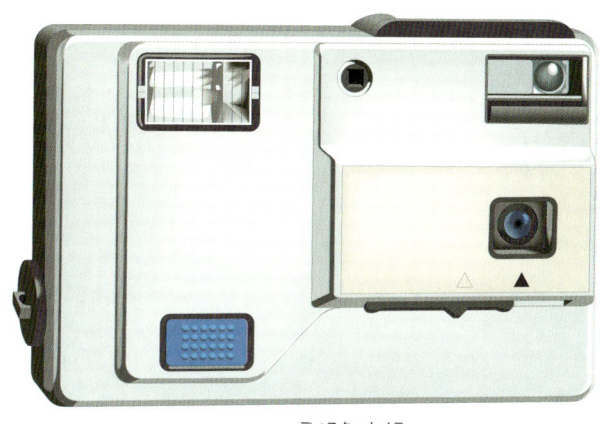

ディスク・カメラ
disk camera; *disc camera*
Disc-Kamera^F
appareil^M pour photodisque^M
cámara^F de disco^M
macchina^F fotografica a disco^M

フィルムとデジタル記憶装置
film and digital storage
Filme^M und digitale Speicher^M
pellicules^F et stockage^M numérique
películas^F y almacenamiento^M digital
pellicole^F e supporti^M digitali

ロール・フィルム
roll film
Rollfilm^M
rouleau^M de pellicule^F
rollo^M de película^F
pellicola^F in rotolo^M

シート・フィルム
sheet film
Planfilm^M
pellicule^F en feuille^F
hoja^F de la película^F
pellicola^F piana

パック・フィルム／フィルム・パック
film pack
Filmkassette^F
film^M-pack^M
paquete^M de placas^F fotográficas
filmpack^M

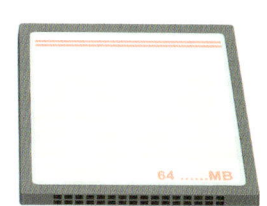

コンパクト・フラッシュ・メモリー・カード
compact flash memory card
Compact-Flash-Speicherkarte^F
carte^F de mémoire^F flash compacte
tarjeta^F de memoria^F compact flash
scheda^F di memoria^F compact flash

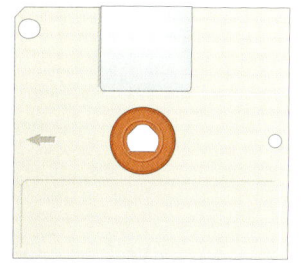

スチル・ビデオ・フィルム・ディスク
still video film disk; *still video film disc*
Videofilmdiskette^F
disque^M vidéophoto^F
disquete^F para video^M fijo
disco^M per macchina^F fotografica digitale

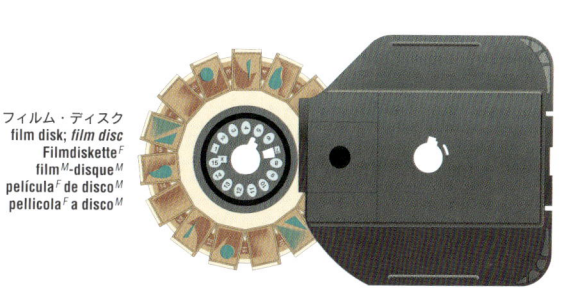

フィルム・ディスク
film disk; *film disc*
Filmdiskette^F
film^M-disque^M
película^F de disco^M
pellicola^F a disco^M

カートリッジ・フィルム
cartridge film
Kassettenfilm^M
cassette^F de pellicule^F
cartucho^M de la película^F
caricatore^M

情報伝達とオフィス・オートメーション

481

情報伝達 | COMMUNICATIONS
KOMMUNIKATION | COMMUNICATIONS | COMUNICACIONES | COMUNICAZIONI

写真

日本語 | 英語 | ドイツ語 | フランス語 | スペイン語 | イタリア語

情報伝達とオフィス・オートメーション

撮影用アクセサリー
photographic accessories
fotografisches Zubehör^N
accessoires^M photographiques
accesorios^M fotográficos
accessori^M fotografici

エア(ー)・レリーズ
air bulb shutter release
pneumatischer Auslöser^M
déclencheur^M pneumatique
disparador^M neumático
flessibile^M pneumatico

ストロボ
electronic flash
Elektronenblitz
flash^M électronique
flash^M electrónico
flash^M elettronico

フラッシュチューブ／閃光管
flashtube
Blitzröhre^F
réflecteur^M
tubo^M de flash^M
lampada^F a tubo^M per flash^M

電池
battery
Batterie^F
pile^F
pila^F
batteria^F

光電セル
photoelectric cell
Fotozelle^F
cellule^F photoélectrique
celda^F fotoeléctrica
cellula^F fotoelettrica

フラッシュ・ランプ
flash lamp
Blitzbirne^F
lampe^F-éclair^M
bombilla^F de flash^M
lampada^F per flash^M

フラッシュ・キューブ
flashcube
Blitzwürfel^M
flash^M-cube^M
cubo^M de flash^M
cuboflash^M

取り付け脚
mounting foot
Aufsteckschuh^M
pied^M de fixation^F
pie^M de montura^F
piedino^M di montaggio^M

ケーブル[ワイヤー]レリーズ
cable shutter release
Drahtauslöser^M
déclencheur^M souple
disparador^M de cable^M
flessibile^M

カメラ取り付けネジ
camera screw
Kameraschraube^F
vis^F de fixation^F
tornillo^M de fijación^F
vite^F di fissaggio^M della macchina^F fotografica

カメラ台
camera platform
Kameraplattform^F
plate-forme^F
plataforma^F
piattaforma^F per macchina^F fotografica

三脚
tripod
Stativ^N
trépied^M
trípode^M
treppiede^M

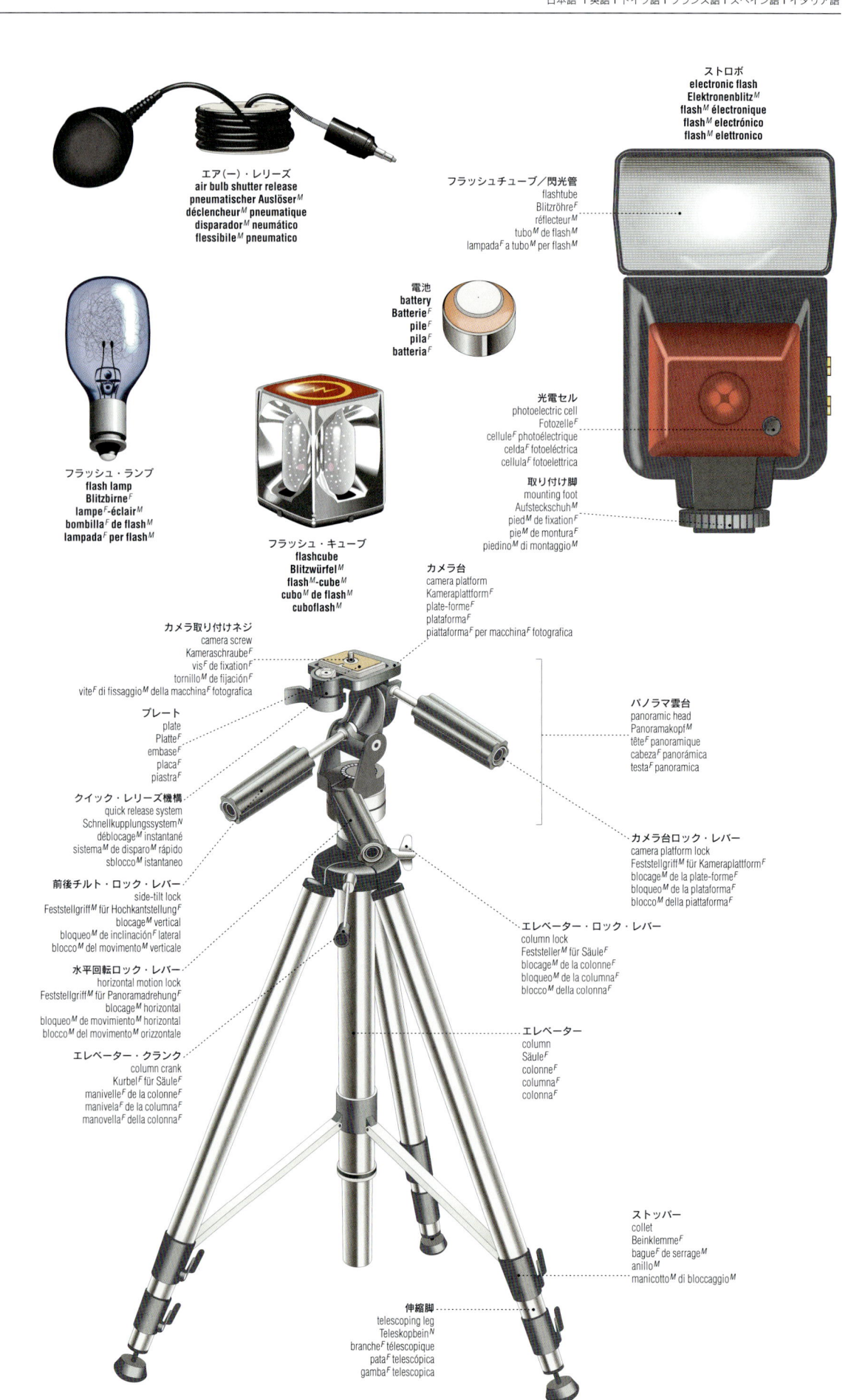

プレート
plate
Platte^F
embase^F
placa^F
piastra^F

パノラマ雲台
panoramic head
Panoramakopf^M
tête^F panoramique
cabeza^F panorámica
testa^F panoramica

クイック・レリーズ機構
quick release system
Schnellkupplungssystem^N
déblocage^M instantané
sistema^M de disparo^M rápido
sblocco^M istantaneo

カメラ台ロック・レバー
camera platform lock
Feststellgriff^M für Kameraplattform^F
blocage^M de la plate-forme^F
bloqueo^M de la plataforma^F
blocco^M della piattaforma^F

前後チルト・ロック・レバー
side-tilt lock
Feststellgriff^M für Hochkantstellung^F
blocage^M vertical
bloqueo^M de inclinación^F lateral
blocco^M del movimento^M verticale

エレベーター・ロック・レバー
column lock
Feststeller^M für Säule^F
blocage^M de la colonne^F
bloqueo^M de la columna^F
blocco^M della colonna^F

水平回転ロック・レバー
horizontal motion lock
Feststellgriff^M für Panoramadrehung^F
blocage^M horizontal
bloqueo^M de movimiento^M horizontal
blocco^M del movimento^M orizzontale

エレベーター・クランク
column crank
Kurbel^F für Säule^F
manivelle^F de la colonne^F
manivela^F de la columna^F
manovella^F della colonna^F

エレベーター
column
Säule^F
colonne^F
columna^F
colonna^F

ストッパー
collet
Beinklemme^F
bague^F de serrage^M
anillo^M
manicotto^M di bloccaggio^M

伸縮脚
telescoping leg
Teleskopbein^N
branche^F télescopique
pata^F telescópica
gamba^F telescopica

情報伝達 | COMMUNICATIONS
KOMMUNIKATION | COMMUNICATIONS | COMUNICACIONES | COMUNICAZIONI

写真

スライド映写機
slide projector
Diaprojektor^M
projecteur^M de diapositives^F
proyector^M de diapositivas^F
proiettore^M per diapositive^F

手動スライド・チェンジャー
power-off/slide-select bar
manuelle Diawahl^F
commande^F de sélection^F manuelle
palanca^F corrediza de selección^F de diapositivas^F
comando^M di selezione^F manuale

スライド
slide
Dia^N
diapositive^F
diapositiva^F
diapositiva^F

電源スイッチ
on-off switch
Ein-/Ausschalter^M
commutateur^M
interruptor^M de encendido/apagado
interruttore^M di accensione^F

ロック・リング
lock ring
Verschlussring^M
couvercle^M
anillo^M de cierre^M
anello^M di arresto^M

スライド前進ボタン
forward slide change
Diawechsel^M, vorwärts
commande^F de marche^F avant
mecanismo^M de avance^M y cambio^M de la diapositiva^F
cambio^M diapositiva^F avanti

スライド・トレイ
slide tray
Diamagazin^N
panier^M de projection^F
carrusel^M
caricatore^M

スライド後進ボタン
reverse slide change
Diawechsel^M, rückwärts
commande^F de marche^F arrière
mecanismo^M de retroceso^M y cambio^M de la diapositiva^F
cambio^M diapositiva^F indietro

収納ボックス
storage compartment
Aufbewahrungsfach^N
logement^M de rangement^M
compartimiento^M para almacenamiento^M
vano^M accessori

リモコン
remote control
Fernbedienung^F
télécommande^F
control^M a larga distancia^F
telecomando^M

水平調節脚
leveling-adjustment foot; *height adjustment foot*
Höhenverstellfuß^M
réglage^M en hauteur^F
pata^F de ajuste^M de altura^F
piedino^M di regolazione^F dell'altezza^F

オートフォーカス・スイッチ
autofocus on-off switch
Autofocus-Schalter^M
interrupteur^M de mise^F au point^M automatique
interruptor^M de focalización^F automática
interruttore^M dell'autofocus^M

手動焦点調節ノブ
manual focusing knob
manuelle Scharfeinstellung^F
bouton^M de mise^F au point^M manuelle
botón^M de enfoque^M manual
manopola^F di messa a fuoco^M manuale

(対物)レンズ
objective lens
Objektiv^N
objectif^M
objetivo^M
obiettivo^M

スライド
transparency slide; *slide*
Dia^N
diapositive^F
diapositiva^F
diapositiva^F

原版／ネガ
photographic picture
Diapositiv^N
phototype^M
fototipo^M
immagine^F fotografica

ハンガー
hanger
Aufhänger^M
crochet^M
gancho^M
gancio^M

映写スクリーン
projection screen
Projektionswand^F
écran^M de projection^F
pantalla^F de proyección^F
schermo^M di proiezione^F

サドル
saddle
Sattel^M
support^M
soporte^M
telaio^M

スクリーン
screen
Leinwand^F
toile^F
pantalla^F
schermo^M

スライド・マウント／スライド用枠
mount frame binder; *slide mount*
Diarähmchen^N
cadre^M-cache^M
montura^F de cartón^M
telaietto^M

スクリーン・ケース
screen case
Leinwandbehälter^M
carter^M
caja^F de la pantalla^F
custodia^F dello schermo^M

三脚
tripod
Stativ^N
trépied^M
trípode^M
cavalletto^M

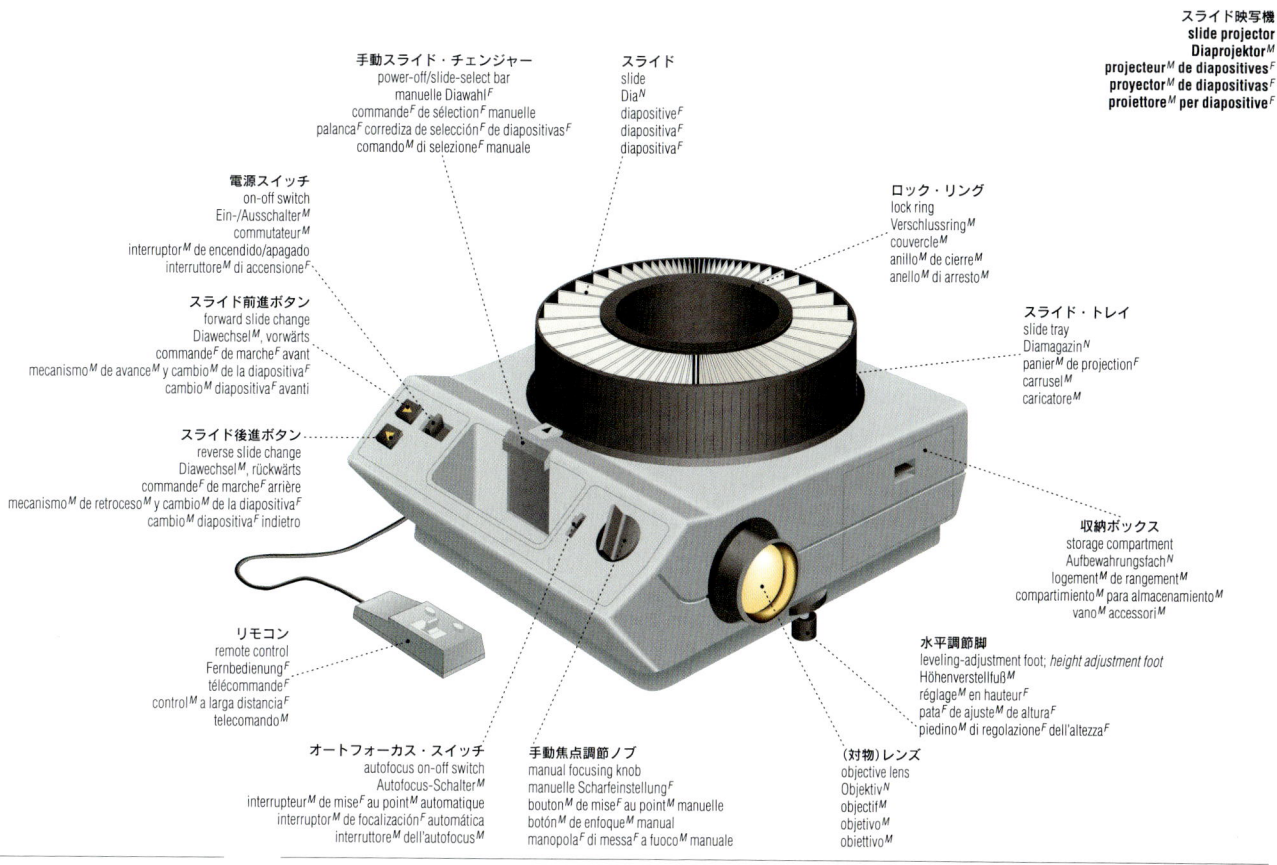

三脚足
shoe
Fuß^M
embout^M
contera^F
puntale^M

情報伝達とオフィス・オートメーション

483

情報伝達 | COMMUNICATIONS
KOMMUNIKATION | COMMUNICATIONS | COMUNICACIONES | COMUNICAZIONI

日本語 | 英語 | ドイツ語 | フランス語 | スペイン語 | イタリア語

写真

暗室
darkroom
Dunkelkammer^F
chambre^F noire
cámara^F oscura
camera^F oscura

現像タンク
developing tank
Entwicklungstrommel^F
cuve^F de développement^M
tanque^M de revelado
sviluppatrice^F

キャップ
cap
Kappe^F
capuchon^M
capuchón^M
tappo^M

タンク蓋（ぶた）
lid
Deckel^M
couvercle^M
tapa^F
coperchio^M

（現像用）リール
reel
Spirale^F
spirale^F
espiral^F
spirale^F

タンク
tank
Dose^F
cuve^F
cubeta^F
vaschetta^F

ライトボックス
lightbox
Leuchtpult^N
négatoscope^M
caja^F de luz^F
visore^M

タイマー
timer
Laboruhr^F
minuterie^F
reloj^M
temporizzatore^M

安全光
safelight
Laborleuchte^F
éclairage^M inactinique
luz^F de seguridad^F
luce^F inattinica

フィルム乾燥キャビネット
film drying cabinet
Trockenschrank^M
armoire^F de séchage^M
armario^M de secado^M de negativos^M
armadio^M essiccatore

カッター／押し切り
guillotine trimmer
Schneidegerät^N
cisaille^F
guillotina^F
taglierina^F

イーゼル
easel
Vergrößerungsrahmen^M
margeur^M
marginador^M
marginatore^M

コンタクト・プリンター
contact printer
Kontaktkopiergerät^N
châssis^M-presse^F
prensa^F de contactos^M
bromografo^M

情報伝達 | COMMUNICATIONS
KOMMUNIKATION | COMMUNICATIONS | COMUNICACIONES | COMUNICAZIONI

写真

引き伸ばし機
enlarger
Vergrößerer^M
agrandisseur^M
ampliadora^F
ingranditore^M

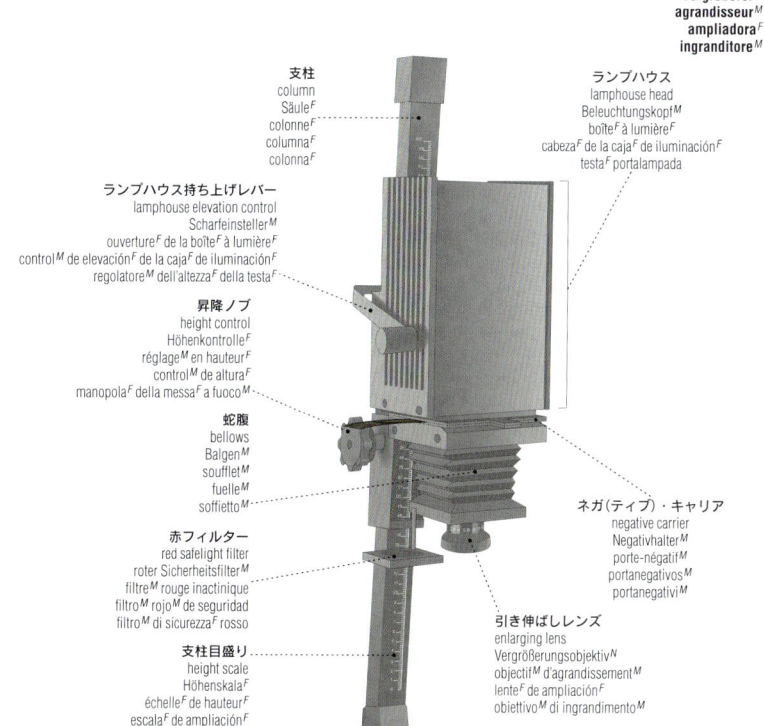

窓
window
Sichtfenster^N
fenêtre^F
ventana^F
finestra^F

ネガ
negative
Negativ^N
négatif^M
negativo^M
negativo^M

支柱
column
Säule^F
colonne^F
columna^F
colonna^F

ランプハウス
lamphouse head
Beleuchtungskopf^M
boîte^F à lumière^F
cabeza^F de la caja^F de iluminación^F
testa^F portalampada

ランプハウス持ち上げレバー
lamphouse elevation control
Scharfeinsteller^M
ouverture^F de la boîte^F à lumière^F
control^M de elevación^F de la caja^F de iluminación^F
regolatore^M dell'altezza^F della testa^F

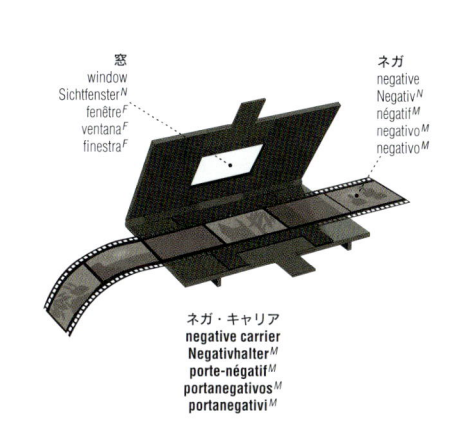

ネガ・キャリア
negative carrier
Negativhalter^M
porte-négatif^M
portanegativos^M
portanegativi^M

昇降ノブ
height control
Höhenkontrolle^F
réglage^M en hauteur^F
control^M de altura^F
manopola^F della messa^F a fuoco^M

蛇腹
bellows
Balgen^M
soufflet^M
fuelle^M
soffietto^M

引き伸ばし機タイマー
enlarger timer
Belichtungs-Schaltuhr^F
compte-pose^M
reloj^M de la ampliadora^F
temporizzatore^M dell'ingranditore^M

赤フィルター
red safelight filter
roter Sicherheitsfilter^M
filtre^M rouge inactinique
filtro^M rojo^M de seguridad
filtro^M di sicurezza^F rosso

ネガ(ティブ)・キャリア
negative carrier
Negativhalter^M
porte-négatif^M
portanegativos^M
portanegativi^M

支柱目盛り
height scale
Höhenskala^F
échelle^F de hauteur^F
escala^F de ampliación^F
scala^F dell'altezza^F

引き伸ばしレンズ
enlarging lens
Vergrößerungsobjektiv^N
objectif^M d'agrandissement^M
lente^F de ampliación^F
obiettivo^M di ingrandimento^M

台板
baseboard
Grundplatte^F
plateau^M
tablero^M de base^F
piano^M di stampa^F

印画紙水洗器／プリント・ウォッシャー
print washer
Bilderwascher^M
laveuse^F pour épreuves^F
cubeta^F para lavar impresiones^F
vasca^F di lavaggio^M delle stampe^F

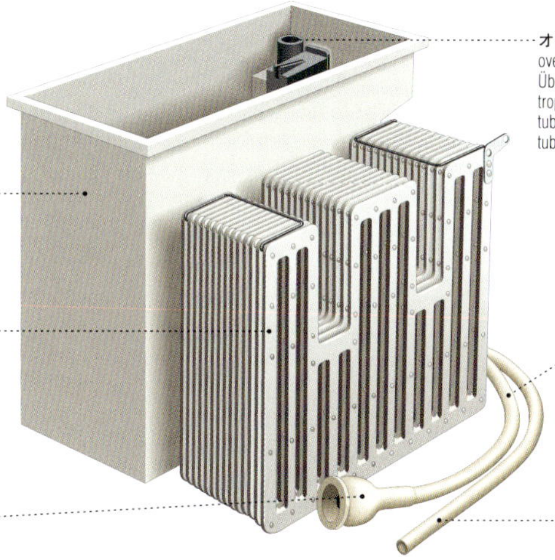

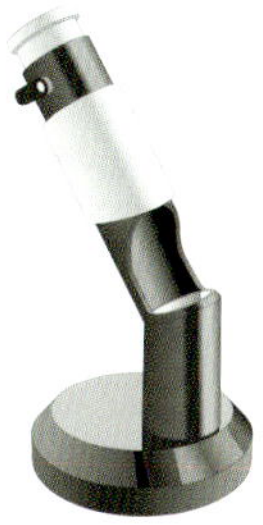

オーバーフロー管
overflow tube
Überlaufstutzen^M
trop-plein^M
tubo^M de drenaje^M
tubo^M di troppopieno^M

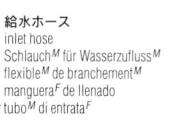

タンク
tank
Wässerungswanne^F
réservoir^M
tanque^M
vaschetta^F

水洗ラック
cradle
Fächerkorb^M
cadre^M porte-épreuves^M
soporte^M
intelaiatura^F di sostegno^M

給水ホース
inlet hose
Schlauch^M für Wasserzufluss^M
flexible^M de branchement^M
manguera^F de llenado^M
tubo^M di entrata^F

フォーカス・スコープ／ピント・ルーペ
focusing magnifier
Scharfsteller^M
loupe^F de mise^F au point^M
lupa^F de focalización^F
lente^F di ingrandimento^M per la messa^F a fuoco^M

蛇口アダプター
adaptor
Adapter^M
raccord^M
adaptador^M
adattatore^M

排水ホース
outlet hose
Schlauch^M für Wasserablauf^M
renvoi^M d'eau^F
manguera^F de vaciado^M
tubo^M di uscita^F

現像処理液
developing baths
Entwicklungsbäder^N
bains^M de développement^M
baños^M de revelado^M
bagni^M di sviluppo^M

現像液
developer bath
Entwickler^M
bain^M de révélateur^M
baño^M de revelado^M
bagno^M di sviluppo^M

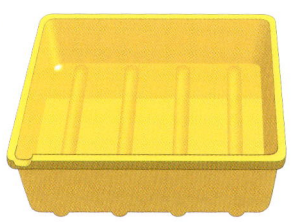

停止液
stop bath
Stoppbad^N
bain^M d'arrêt^M
baño^M de stop^M
bagno^M di arresto^M

定着液
fixing bath
Fixierbad^N
bain^M de fixation^F
baño^M de fijación^F
bagno^M di fissaggio^M

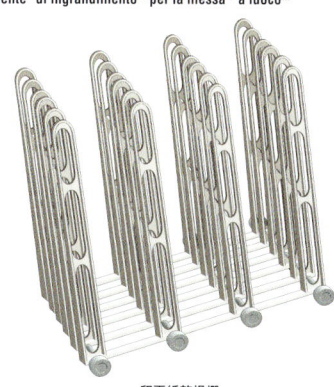

印画紙乾燥棚
print drying rack
Trockenständer^M
séchoir^M d'épreuves^F
secadora^F de pruebas^F
rastrelliera^F

情報伝達とオフィス・オートメーション

情報伝達 | COMMUNICATIONS
KOMMUNIKATION | COMMUNICATIONS | COMUNICACIONES | COMUNICAZIONI

衛星中継

broadcast satellite communication | Satellitenübertragungstechnik^F | télédiffusion^F par satellite^M | comunicación^F vía satélite^M | trasmissione^F via satellite^M

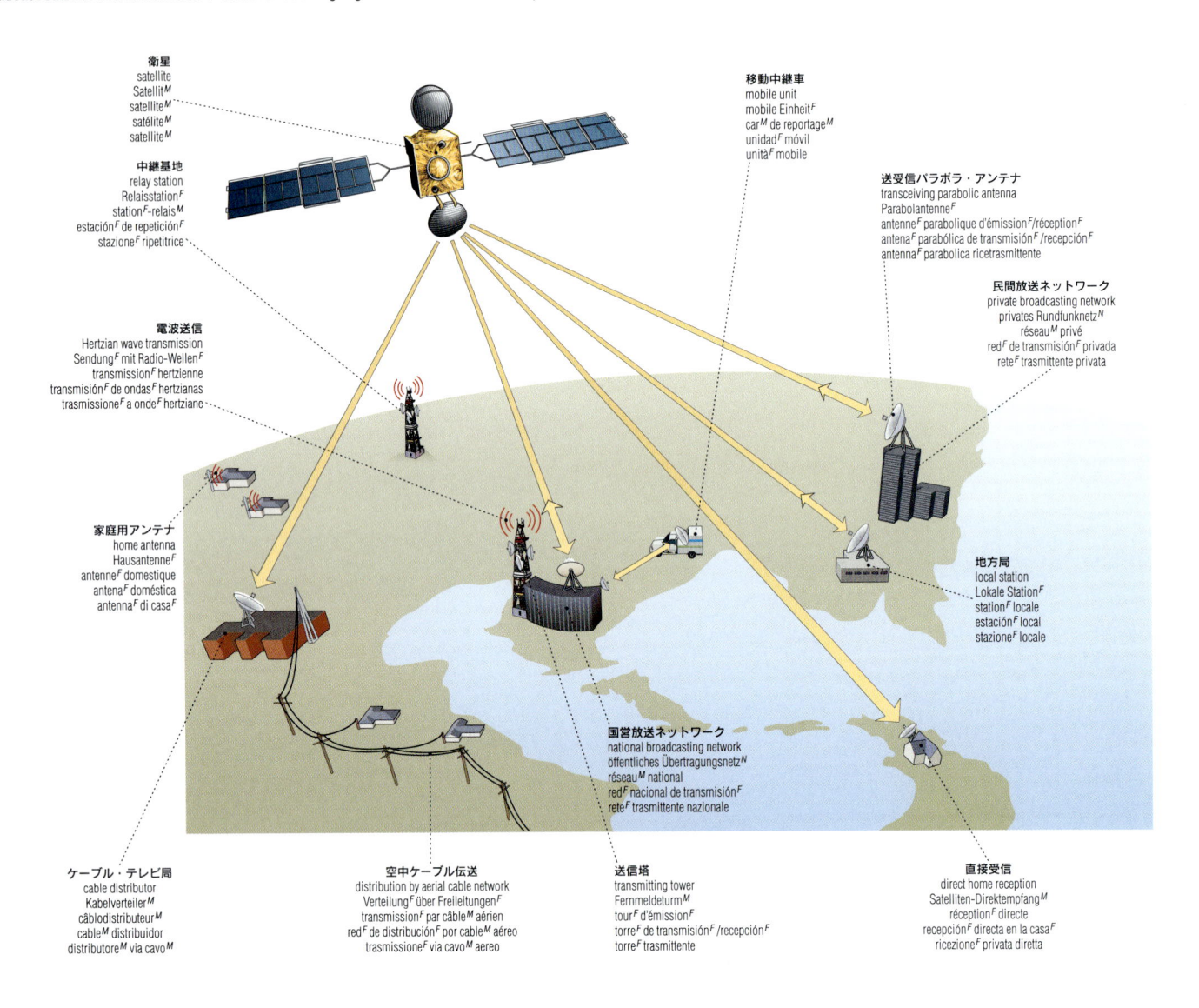

日本語 | 英語 | ドイツ語 | フランス語 | スペイン語 | イタリア語

衛星
satellite
Satellit^M
satellite^M
satélite^M
satellite^M

中継基地
relay station
Relaisstation^F
station^F-relais^M
estación^F de repetición^F
stazione^F ripetitrice

移動中継車
mobile unit
mobile Einheit^F
car^M de reportage^M
unidad^F móvil
unità^F mobile

送受信パラボラ・アンテナ
transceiving parabolic antenna
Parabolantenne^F
antenne^F parabolique d'émission^F/réception^F
antena^F parabólica de transmisión^F/recepción^F
antenna^F parabolica ricetrasmittente

民間放送ネットワーク
private broadcasting network
privates Rundfunknetz^N
réseau^F privé
red^F de transmisión^F privada
rete^F trasmittente privata

電波送信
Hertzian wave transmission
Sendung^F mit Radio-Wellen^F
transmission^F hertzienne
transmisión^F de ondas^F hertzianas
trasmissione^F a onde^F hertziane

家庭用アンテナ
home antenna
Hausantenne^F
antenne^F domestique
antena^F doméstica
antenna^F di casa^F

地方局
local station
Lokale Station^F
station^F locale
estación^F local
stazione^F locale

ケーブル・テレビ局
cable distributor
Kabelverteiler^M
câblodistributeur^M
cable^M distribuidor
distributore via cavo^M

空中ケーブル伝送
distribution by aerial cable network
Verteilung^F über Freileitungen^F
transmission^F par câble^M aérien
red^F de distribución^F por cable^M aéreo
trasmissione^F via cavo^M aereo

送信塔
transmitting tower
Fernmeldeturm^M
tour^F d'émission^F
torre^F de transmisión^F/recepción^F
torre^F trasmittente

国営放送ネットワーク
national broadcasting network
öffentliches Übertragungsnetz^N
réseau^M national
red^F nacional de transmisión^F
rete^F trasmittente nazionale

直接受信
direct home reception
Satelliten-Direktempfang^M
réception^F directe
recepción^F directa en la casa^F
ricezione^F privata diretta

通信衛星

telecommunication satellites | Fernmeldesatelliten^M | satellites^M de télécommunications^F | satélites^M de telecomunicaciones^F | satelliti^M per telecomunicazioni^F

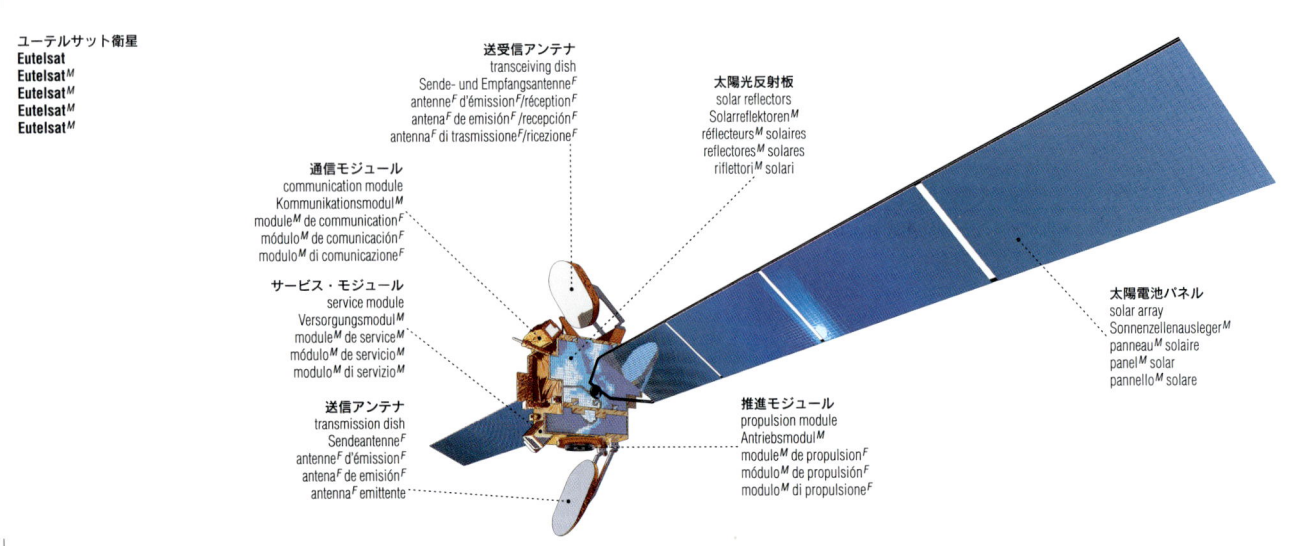

ユーテルサット衛星
Eutelsat
Eutelsat^M
Eutelsat^M
Eutelsat^M
Eutelsat^M

送受信アンテナ
transceiving dish
Sende- und Empfangsantenne^F
antenne^F d'émission^F/réception^F
antena^F de emisión^F/recepción^F
antenna^F di trasmissione^F/ricezione^F

太陽光反射板
solar reflectors
Solarreflektoren^M
réflecteurs^M solaires
reflectores^M solares
riflettori^M solari

通信モジュール
communication module
Kommunikationsmodul^M
module^M de communication^M
módulo^M de comunicación^F
modulo^M di comunicazione^F

サービス・モジュール
service module
Versorgungsmodul^M
module^M de service^M
módulo^M de servicio^M
modulo^M di servizio^M

太陽電池パネル
solar array
Sonnenzellenausleger^M
panneau^M solaire
panel^M solar
pannello^M solare

送信アンテナ
transmission dish
Sendeantenne^F
antenne^F d'émission^F
antena^F de emisión^F
antenna^F emittente

推進モジュール
propulsion module
Antriebsmodul^M
module^M de propulsion^F
módulo^M de propulsión^F
modulo^M di propulsione^F

情報伝達 | COMMUNICATIONS
KOMMUNIKATION | COMMUNICATIONS | COMUNICACIONES | COMUNICAZIONI

衛星通信

telecommunications by satellite | Telekommunikation^F über Nachrichtensatellit^M | télécommunications^F par satellite^M | telecomunicaciones^F vía satélite^M | telecomunicazioni^F via satellite^M

航空通信
air communications
Telekommunikation^F für die Luftfahrt^F
communications^F aériennes
comunicaciones^F aéreas
comunicazioni^F aeree

産業通信
industrial communications
industrielle Telekommunikation^F
communications^F industrielles
comunicaciones^F industriales
comunicazioni^F industriali

軍事通信
military communications
militärische Telekommunikation^F
communications^F militaires
comunicaciones^F militares
comunicazioni^F militari

船舶通信
maritime communications
Telekommunikation^F für die Schifffahrt^F
communications^F maritimes
comunicaciones^F maritimas
comunicazioni^F marittime

テレポート
teleport
Teleport^M
téléport^M
teleporte
porta^F di rete^F telefonica

海底ケーブル伝送
distribution by submarine cable
Verteilung^F über Tiefseekabel^N
transmission^F par câble^M sous-marin
transmisión^F por cable^M submarino
trasmissione^F via cavo^M sottomarino

電話ネットワーク
telephone network
Telefonnetz^N
réseau^M téléphonique
red^F telefónica
rete^F telefonica

道路通信
road communications
Telekommunikation^F für den Straßenverkehr^M
communications^F routières
comunicaciones^F terrestres
comunicazioni^F stradali

地下ケーブル伝送
distribution by underground cable network
Verteilung^F über unterirdisches Kabelnetz^N
transmission^F par câble^M souterrain
red de transmisión^F por cable^M subterráneo
trasmissione^F via cavo^M sotterraneo

加入者通信
personal communications
private Telekommunikation^F
communications^F individuelles
comunicaciones^F particulares
comunicazioni^F private

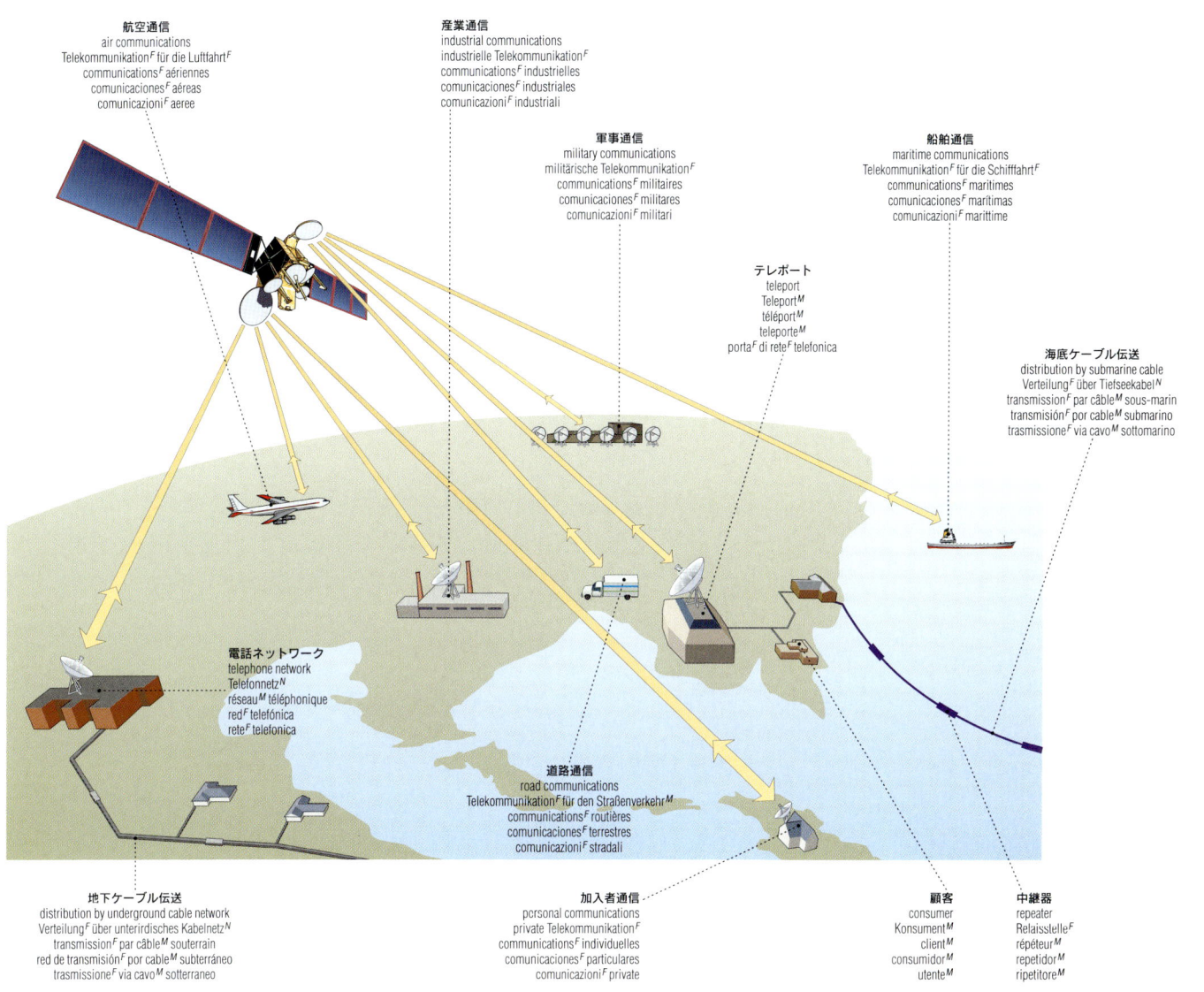

顧客
consumer
Konsument^M
client^M
consumidor^M
utente^M

中継器
repeater
Relaisstelle^F
répéteur^M
repetidor^M
ripetitore^M

情報伝達とオフィス・オートメーション

通信衛星

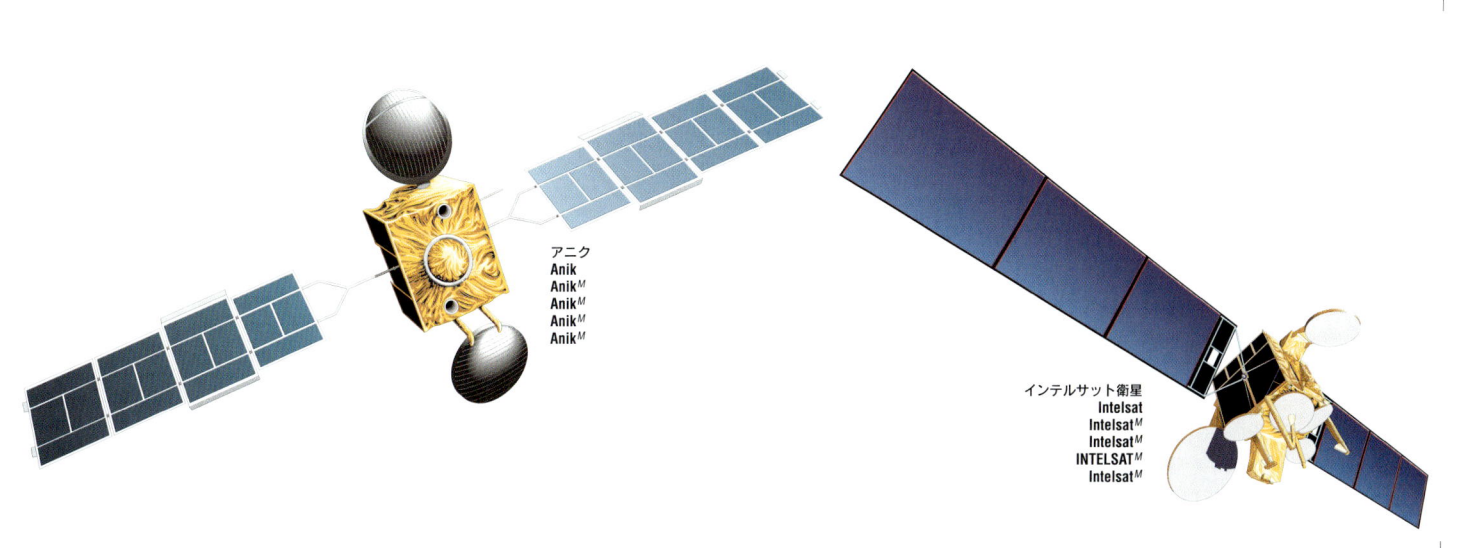

アニク
Anik
Anik^M
Anik^M
Anik^M
Anik^M

インテルサット衛星
Intelsat
Intelsat^M
Intelsat^M
INTELSAT^M
Intelsat^M

487

情報伝達 | COMMUNICATIONS
KOMMUNIKATION | COMMUNICATIONS | COMUNICACIONES | COMUNICAZIONI

ダイナミック・マイク

日本語 | 英語 | ドイツ語 | フランス語 | スペイン語 | イタリア語

dynamic microphone | elektrodynamisches Mikrofon[N] | microphone[M] dynamique | micrófono[M] electrodinámico | microfono[M] dinamico

ウインドスクリーン
windscreen
Windschutz[M]
treillis[F] de protection[F]
rejilla[F]
retino[M] di protezione[F]

振動板
diaphragm
Membrane[F]
membrane[F]
diafragma[F]
diaframma[M]

磁石
magnet
Magnet[M]
aimant[M]
imán[M]
magnete[M]

可動コイル
moving coil
Induktionsspule[F]
bobine[F] mobile
bobina[F] móvil
bobina[F] mobile

ハウジング
housing
Gehäuse[N]
boîtier[M]
caja[F]
corpo[M]

プラグ
plug
Klinkenstecker[M]
fiche[F] pour jack[M]
clavija[F]
jack[M]

電源スイッチ
on-off switch
Ein-/Ausschalter[M]
interrupteur[M]
interruptor[M]
interruttore[M] di accensione[F]

接続部
connector
Verbindungsstück[N]
connecteur[M]
conector[M]
connettore[M]

コード
cable
Kabel[N]
cordon[M]
cable[M]
cavo[M]

ラジオ：スタジオとコントロール・ルーム

radio: studio and control room | Rundfunk[M]: Sprecherraum[M] und Regieraum[M] | radio[F]: studio et régie[F] | radio[F]: estudio[M] y sala[F] de control | radio[F]: studio[M] e cabina[F] di regia[F]

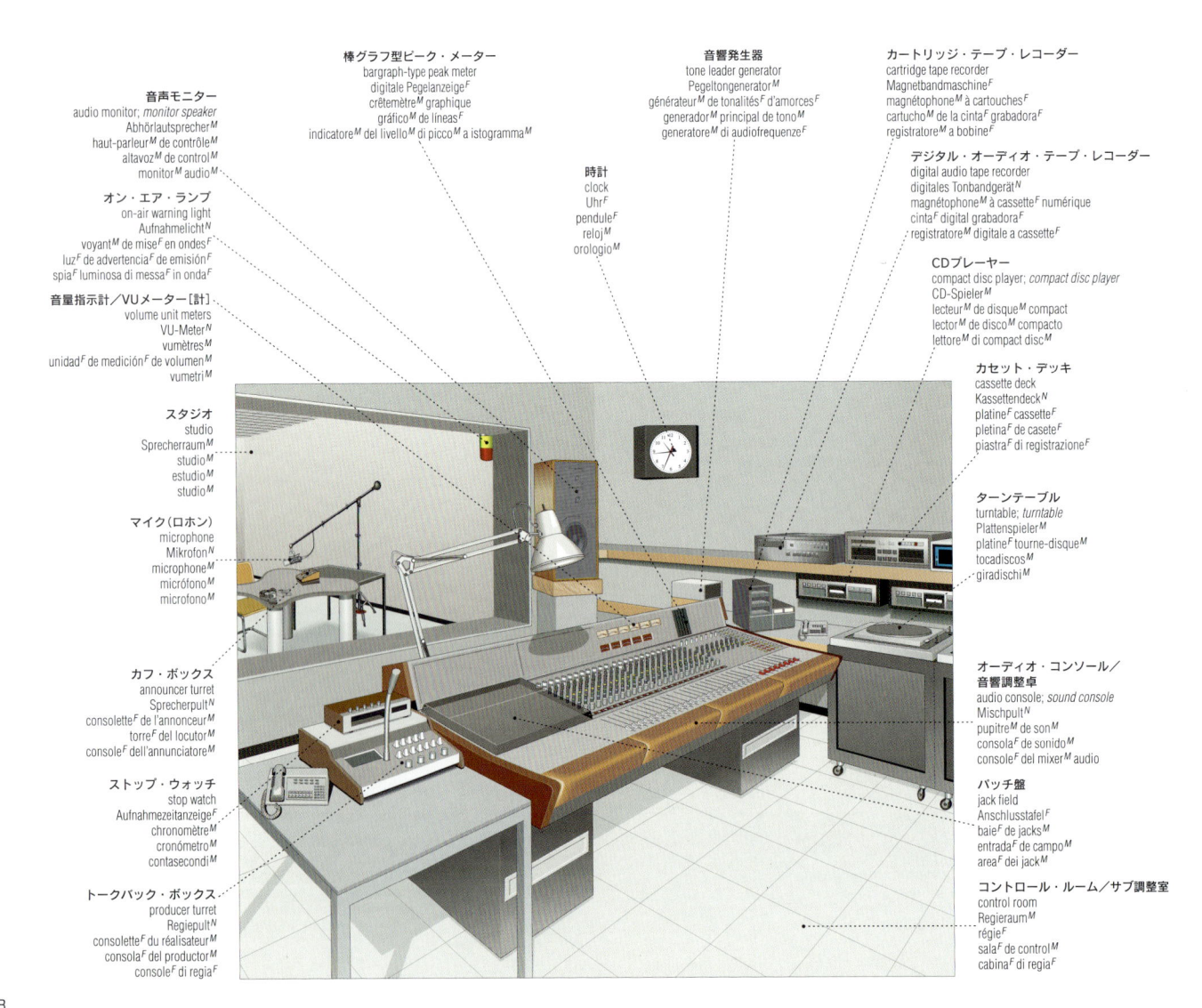

音声モニター
audio monitor; monitor speaker
Abhörlautsprecher[M]
haut-parleur[M] de contrôle[F]
altavoz[M] de control[M]
monitor[M] audio[M]

オン・エア・ランプ
on-air warning light
Aufnahmelicht[N]
voyant[M] de mise[F] en ondes[F]
luz[F] de advertencia[F] de emisión[F]
spia[F] luminosa di messa[F] in onda[F]

音量指示計／VUメーター[計]
volume unit meters
VU-Meter[N]
vumètres[M]
unidad[F] de medición[F] de volumen[M]
vumetri[M]

スタジオ
studio
Sprecherraum[M]
studio[M]
estudio[M]
studio[M]

マイク（ロホン）
microphone
Mikrofon[N]
microphone[M]
micrófono[M]
microfono[M]

カフ・ボックス
announcer turret
Sprecherpult[N]
consolette[F] de l'annonceur[M]
torre[F] del locutor[M]
console[F] dell'annunciatore[M]

ストップ・ウォッチ
stop watch
Aufnahmezeitanzeige[F]
chronomètre[M]
cronómetro[M]
contasecondi[M]

トークバック・ボックス
producer turret
Regiepult[N]
consolette[F] du réalisateur[M]
consola[F] del productor[M]
console[F] di regia[F]

棒グラフ型ピーク・メーター
bargraph-type peak meter
digitale Pegelanzeige[F]
crêtemètre[M] graphique
gráfico[M] de líneas[F]
indicatore[M] del livello[M] di picco[M] a istogramma[M]

音響発生器
tone leader generator
Pegeltongenerator[M]
générateur[M] de tonalités[F] d'amorces[F]
generador[M] principal de tono[M]
generatore[M] di audiofrequenze[F]

時計
clock
Uhr[F]
pendule[F]
reloj[M]
orologio[M]

カートリッジ・テープ・レコーダー
cartridge tape recorder
Magnetbandmaschine[F]
magnétophone[M] à cartouches[F]
cartucho[M] de la cinta[F] grabadora[F]
registratore[M] a bobine[F]

デジタル・オーディオ・テープ・レコーダー
digital audio tape recorder
digitales Tonbandgerät[N]
magnétophone[M] à cassette[F] numérique
cinta[F] digital grabadora[F]
registratore[M] digitale a cassette[F]

CDプレーヤー
compact disc player; compact disc player
CD-Spieler[M]
lecteur[M] de disque[M] compact
lector[M] de disco[M] compacto
lettore[M] di compact disc[M]

カセット・デッキ
cassette deck
Kassettendeck[N]
platine[F] cassette[F]
pletina[F] de casete[F]
piastra[F] di registrazione[F]

ターンテーブル
turntable; turntable
Plattenspieler[M]
platine[F] tourne-disque[M]
tocadiscos[M]
giradischi[M]

オーディオ・コンソール／音響調整卓
audio console; sound console
Mischpult[N]
pupitre[M] de son[M]
consola[F] de sonido[M]
console[F] del mixer[M] audio

パッチ盤
jack field
Anschlusstafel[F]
baie[F] de jacks[M]
entrada[F] de campo[M]
area[F] dei jack[M]

コントロール・ルーム／サブ調整室
control room
Regieraum[M]
régie[F]
sala[F] de control[M]
cabina[F] di regia[F]

情報伝達 | COMMUNICATIONS
KOMMUNIKATION | COMMUNICATIONS | COMUNICACIONES | COMUNICAZIONI

テレビ

television | Fernsehen[N] | télévision[F] | televisión[F] | televisione[F]

マイクロウェーブ送信機
microwave transmitter
Mikrowellensender[M]
émetteur[M] micro-ondes[F]
transmisor[M] de microondas[F]
trasmettitore[M] a microonde[F]

導波管
wave guide
Wellenleiter[M]
guide[M] d'ondes[F]
guía[F] de la onda[F]
guida[F] di onda[F]

パラボラ・アンテナ
parabolic antenna
Parabolantenne[F]
antenne[F] parabolique
antena[F] parabólica
antenna[F] parabolica

パラボラ反射鏡／ディッシュ
microwave dish
Mikrowellenschüssel[F]
réflecteur[M] parabolique
reflector[M] parabólico de microondas[F]
riflettore[M] parabolico a microonde[F]

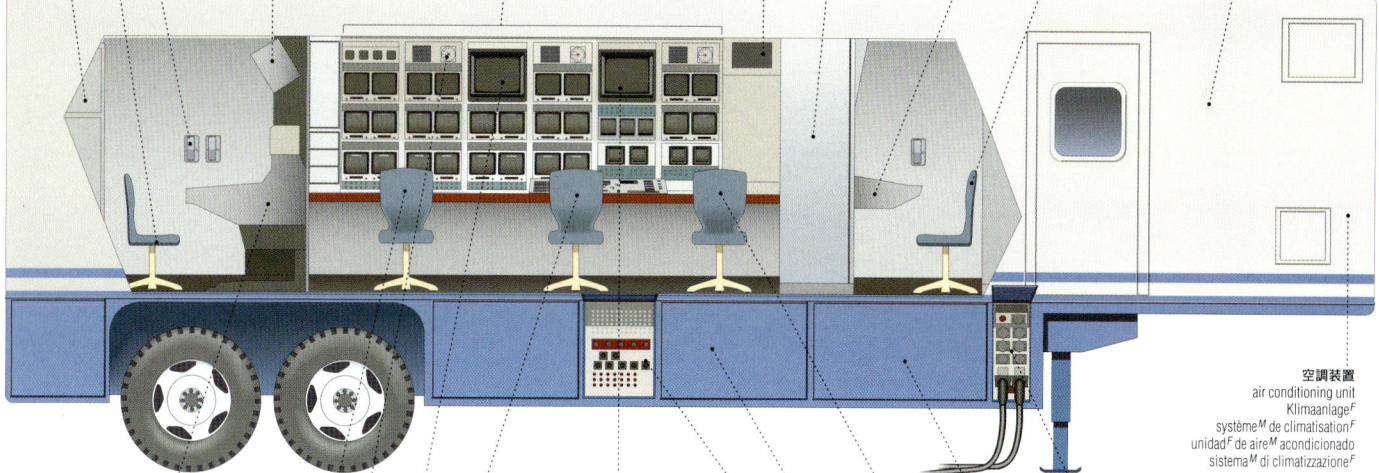

機器材ラック
equipment rack
Ausrüstungsspind[M]
bâti[M] d'équipement[M]
equipo[M] de soporte[M]
rack[M] per apparecchiature[F]

三脚
tripod
Stativ[N]
trépied[N]
trípode[M]
treppiede

移動中継車
mobile unit
Übertragungswagen[M]
car[M] de reportage[M]
unidad[F] móvil
unità[F] mobile

音響調整室
audio control room; sound control room
Tonregieraum[M]
régie[F] du son[M]
sala[F] de control[M] de sonido[M]
cabina[F] di controllo[M] audio[M]

映像調整室
camera control area
Bereich[M] der Bildkontrolle[F]
régie[F] image[F]
área[F] de control[M] de la cámara[F]
area[F] di controllo[M] delle telecamere[F]

音響担当
audio technician; sound technician
Tontechniker[M]
preneur[M] de son[M]
técnico[M] de sonido[M]
tecnico[M] audio[M]

制作調整室
production control room
Regieraum[M]
régie[F] de production[F]
sala[F] de control[M] de la producción[F]
cabina[F] di regia[F]

機器材ラック
equipment rack
Geräteschrank[M]
bâti[M] d'équipement[M]
equipo[M] de soporte[M]
rack[M] per apparecchiature[F]

映像調整装置
camera control unit
Bildkontrolle[F]
bloc[M] de commande[F] des caméras[F]
unidad[F] de control[M] de la cámara[F]
unità[F] di controllo[M] delle telecamere[F]

電話設備
telephone set
Telefonapparat[M]
poste[M] téléphonique
teléfono[M]
apparecchio[M] telefonico

モニター・ウォール
monitor wall
Kontrollmonitore[M]
baie[F] de contrôle[M]
panel[M] de control[M]
parete[F] dei monitor[M]

映像調整担当
camera control technician
Bildtechniker[M]
contrôleur[M] d'images[F]
técnico[M] de control[M] de la cámara[F]
tecnico[M] di controllo[M] delle immagini[F]

音声モニター
audio monitor; sound monitor
Abhörlautsprecher[M]
haut-parleur[M] de contrôle[M]
monitor[M] de sonido[M]
monitor[M] audio[M]

音声モニター
audio monitor; sound monitor
Abhörlautsprecher[M]
haut-parleur[M] de contrôle[M]
monitor[M] de sonido[M]
monitor[M] audio[M]

メンテナンス室
maintenance area
Eingangsbereich[M]
secteur[M] maintenance[F]
área[M] de mantenimiento[M]
area[F] di servizio[M]

オーディオ・コンソール／音響調整卓
audio console; sound console
Tonregiepult[N]
pupitre[M] de son[M]
consola[F] de sonido[M]
mixer[M] audio[M]

プレビュー(用)モニター
preview monitor
Vorschaumonitor[M]
écran[M] de précontrôle[M]
monitor[M] de visualización[F] previa
monitor[M] di anteprima[F]

空調装置
air conditioning unit
Klimaanlage[F]
système[M] de climatisation[F]
unidad[F] de aire[M] acondicionado
sistema[M] di climatizzazione[F]

プロデューサー
producer
Sendeleiter[M]
réalisateur[M]
productor[M]
responsabile[M] di regia[F]

ビデオ・スイッチャー
video switcher technician
Video-Switcher[M]
technicien[M] aiguilleur[M]
operador[M] técnico de video[M]
tecnico[M] di commutazione[F] video[M]

配電盤[パネル]
electrical connection panel
Stromverteiler[M]
panneau[M] de raccordement[M] électrique
panel[M] de conexiones[F] eléctricas
pannello[M] dei collegamenti[M] elettrici

時計
clock
Kontrolluhr[F]
pendule[F]
reloj[M]
orologio[M]

出力モニター
output monitor
Ausgangsmonitor[M]
écran[M] de sortie[F]
monitor[M] de producción[F]
monitor[M] di uscita[F]

映像接続パネル
video connection panel
Videoschalttafel[F]
panneau[M] de raccordement[M] vidéo
panel[M] de conexión[F] del video[M]
pannello[M] dei collegamenti[M] video[M]

技術機器収納庫
technical equipment compartment
Fach[N] für technische Ausrüstung[F]
soute[F] d'équipement[M] technique
compartimento[M] del equipo[M] técnico
scomparto[M] delle attrezzature[F] tecniche

テクニカル・プロデューサー
technical producer
Aufsichtsingenieur[M]
directeur[M] technique
productor[M] técnico
direttore[M] tecnico

ケーブル・ドラム収納庫
cable drum compartment
Fach[N] für Kabeltrommel[F]
soute[F] des bobines[F] de câbles[M]
compartimento[M] del cable[M] de la batería[F]
scomparto[M] delle bobine[F] dei cavi[M]

情報伝達とオフィス・オートメーション

489

テレビ

情報伝達 | COMMUNICATIONS
KOMMUNIKATION | COMMUNICATIONS | COMUNICACIONES | COMUNICAZIONI

日本語 | 英語 | ドイツ語 | フランス語 | スペイン語 | イタリア語

スタジオとコントロール・ルーム
studio and control rooms
Sprecher- und Regieräume^M
plateau^M et régies^F
estudio^M de televisión^F y cabinas^F de control^M
studio^M e cabine^F di regia^F

多目的室
auxiliary facilities room
allgemeiner Geräteraum^M
salle^F polyvalente
sala^F de instalaciones^F auxiliares
sala^F delle strutture^F ausiliarie

調光室
dimmer room
Dimmerraum^M
salle^F des gradateurs^M
sala^F de regulación^F de luces^F
sala^F di regolazione^F delle luci^F

照明スタジオへの出入り口
lighting grid access
Zugang^M zur Beleuchtungsanlage^F
accès^M à la grille^F d'éclairage^M
puerta^F de acceso^M a la rejilla^F de las luces^F
accesso^M alla griglia^F di illuminazione^F

照明担当
lighting technician
Beleuchtungstechniker^M
éclairagiste^M
técnico^M de luces^F
tecnico^M delle luci^F

映像調整担当
camera control technician
Bildtechniker^M
contrôleur^M d'images^F
técnico^M de control^M de cámaras^F
tecnico^M video^M

制作補助員
additional production personnel
zusätzliches Studiopersonal^N
personnel^M additionnel de production^F
personal^M suplementario de producción^F
personale^M ausiliario di produzione^F

照明ボード担当
lighting board operator
Oberbeleuchtungstechniker^M
opérateur^M de régie^F d'éclairage^M
operador^M del tablero^M de luces^F
operatore^M del pannello^M delle luci^F

照明ボード
lighting board
Lichtregelanlage^F
pupitre^M d'éclairage^M
tablero^M de luces^F
pannello^M delle luci^F

接続ボックス
connection box
Kamera-Steckfeld^N
boîte^F de raccordement^M
caja^F de conexiones^F
scatola^F dei collegamenti^M

映像調整装置
camera control unit
Bildkontrolle^F
bloc^M de commande^F des caméras^F
unidad^F de control^M de cámaras^F
unità^F di controllo^M video^M

カメラ
camera
Kamera^F
caméra^F
cámara^F
telecamera^F

テクニカル・ディレクター
technical producer
Aufsichtsingenieur^M
directeur^M technique
productor^M técnico
direttore^M tecnico

モニター・ウォール[壁]
monitor wall
Kontrollmonitore^M
baie^F de contrôle^M
panel^M de monitores^M
parete^F dei monitor^M

マイク(ロホン)・アーム
microphone boom
Mikrofonausleger^M
perche^F
jirafa^F del micrófono^M
giraffa^F

ビデオ・スイッチャー
video switcher technician
Video-Switch-Techniker^M
technicien^M aiguilleur^M
operador^M técnico de video^M
tecnico^M di commutazione^F video^M

プロデューサー
producer
Sendeleiter^M
réalisateur^M
productor^M
regista^M

監督助手
script assistant
Skript-Assistent^M
assistant^M à la réalisation^F
asistente^M del guionista^M
segretario^M di edizione^F

制作アドバイザー
production adviser
Regieassistent^M
conseiller^M de production^F
consejero^M de producción^F
assistente^M alla regia^F

オーディオ・コンソール
audio console; *sound desk*
Tonregiepult^N
pupitre^M de son^M
consola^F de sonido^M
console^F del mixer^M audio^M

音楽アドバイザー
musical advisers
Musikregie^F
conseillers^M musicaux
consejeros^M musicales
consulenti^M musicali

機器材ラック
equipment rack
Ausrüstungsspind^M
bâti^M d'équipement^M
soporte^M para el equipo^M
rack^M per apparecchiature^F

低音トラップ
bass trap
Bassfalle^F
trappe^F acoustique
panel^M absorbente de frecuencias^F bajas
pannello^M di assorbimento^M dei bassi^M

音響担当
audio technician; *sound technician*
Tontechniker^M
preneur^M de son^M
técnico^M de sonido^M
tecnico^M audio^M

音声モニター
audio monitor; *sound monitor*
Lautsprecher^M
haut-parleur^M de contrôle^M
monitor^M del sonido^M
monitor^M audio^M

スタジオ・フロア
studio floor
Studioebene^F
plateau^M
estudio^M
studio^M televisivo

照明・映像調整室
lighting/camera control area
Beleuchtung^F/Bildregie^F
régie^F image^F/éclairage^M
sala^F de control^M de luces^F/de cámara^F
area^F di controllo^M luci^F/video^M

音響調整室
audio control room; *sound control room*
Tonregieraum^M
régie^F du son^M
control^M de sonido^M
cabina^F di controllo^M audio^M

制作調整室
production control room
Regieraum^M
régie^F de production^F
sala^F de producción^F y control^M
cabina^F di regia^F

情報伝達 | COMMUNICATIONS
KOMMUNIKATION | COMMUNICATIONS | COMUNICACIONES | COMUNICAZIONI

テレビ

制作調整室
production control room
Regieraum^M
régie^F de production^F
sala^F de control^M de producción^F
cabina^F di regia^F

音響・映像プレビュー装置
audio/video preview unit; *sound/video preview unit*
Ton-/Bild-Vorschaueinheit^F
poste^M de contrôle^M audio/vidéo
unidad de visualización de imagen^F/sonido^M
console^F di anteprima^F audio^M/video^M

ステレオ位相モニター
stereo phase monitor
Lautsprecher^M zum Prüfen^N von Zweikanalton^M
oscilloscope de phase^F audio
control^M del sonido^M estereofónico
monitor^M di fase^F stereo

プレビュー(用)モニター
preview monitors
Vorschaumonitore^M
écrans^M de précontrôle^M
monitores^M de visualización^F previa
serie^F dei monitor^M di anteprima^F

ベクトル・波形モニター
vector/waveform monitor
Oszillograph-/Oszilloskopmonitor^M
oscilloscope^M/vectoscope^M
osciloscopio^M de control^M de las formas^F de onda^F
monitor^M per il controllo^M della forma^F d'onda^F

入力モニター
input monitors
Eingangsmonitore^M
écrans^M d'entrée^F
monitores^M de entrada^F
serie^F dei monitor^M di ingresso^M

モニター・ウォール
monitor wall
Kontrollmonitore^M
baie^F de contrôle^M
panel^M de monitores^M
parete^F dei monitor^M

デジタル映像効果モニター
digital video effects monitor
Trickmischer^M
écran^M du truqueur^M numérique
monitor^M de efectos^M video/digitales
monitor^M degli effetti^M video^M digitali

テクニカル・プロデューサー用モニター
technical producer monitor
Kontrollmonitor^M des Aufsichtsingenieurs^M
écran^M du directeur^M technique
monitor^M de la producción^F técnica
monitor^M del direttore^M tecnico

音声モニター
audio monitor; *sound monitor*
Lautsprecher^M
haut-parleur^M de contrôle^M
monitor^M de sonido^M
monitor^M audio^M

出力モニター
output monitor
Ausgangsmonitor^M
écran^M de sortie^F
monitor^M de salida^F
monitor^M di uscita^F

時計
clock
Kontrolluhr^F
pendule^F
reloj^M
orologio^M

インカム・マイク
intercom microphone
Mikrofon^N zum Studio^N
microphone^M d'interphone^M
micrófono^M del intercomunicador^M
microfono^M dell'interfono^M

インカム親機
intercom station
Studio-Kommandoanlage^F
interphone^M
intercomunicador^M
interfono^M

補助映像スイッチャー
auxiliary video switcher
zusätzlicher Video-Switcher^M
sélecteur^M vidéo auxiliaire
interruptor^M para el video^M auxiliar
mixer^M video^M ausiliario

映像モニター・セレクター
video monitoring selector
Video-Kreuzschiene^F
sélecteur^M de contrôle^M vidéo
selector^M del control^M de video^M
selettore^M di controllo^M video^M

電話
telephone
Telefon^N
poste^M téléphonique
teléfono^M
telefono^M

メイン・プレビュー(用)モニター
main preview monitor
Hauptvorschaumonitor^M
écran^M principal de précontrôle^M
monitor^M principal de visualización^F previa
monitor^M principale di anteprima^F

音響モニター・セレクター
audio monitoring selector; *sound monitoring selector*
Tonvormischung^F
sélecteur^M de contrôle^M audio
selector^M del control^M de volumen^M
selettore^M di controllo^M audio^M

制作デスク
production desk
Regiepult^N
table^F de production^F
mesa^F de producción^F
console^F di regia^F

制作ビデオ・スイッチャー
production video switcher
Video-Switcher^M
aiguilleur^M vidéo de production^F
interruptor^M para la producción^F de video^M
commutatore^M video^M di regia^F

デジタル映像特殊効果装置
digital video special effects
Trickmischer^M
truqueur^M numérique
efectos^M especiales video/digitales
effetti^M speciali video^M digitali

音量指示計／VUメーター[計]
audio volume unit meters; *VU meters*
VU-Meter^N
vumètres^M audio
vúmetro^M
vumetri^M

情報伝達とオフィス・オートメーション

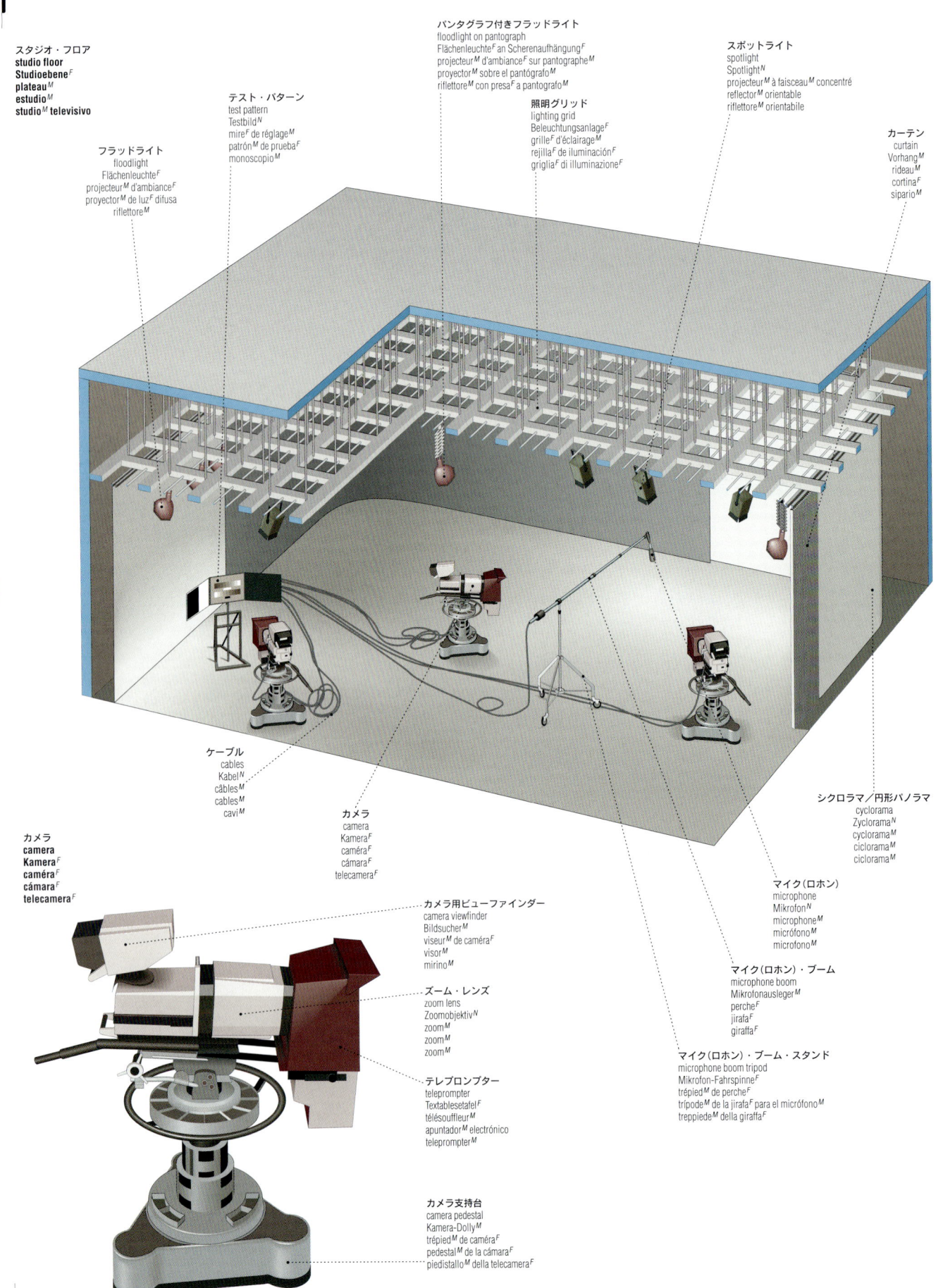

情報伝達 | COMMUNICATIONS
KOMMUNIKATION | COMMUNICATIONS | COMUNICACIONES | COMUNICAZIONI

テレビ

日本語 | 英語 | ドイツ語 | フランス語 | スペイン語 | イタリア語

スタジオ・フロア
studio floor
Studioebene^F
plateau^M
estudio^M
studio^M televisivo

パンタグラフ付きフラッドライト
floodlight on pantograph
Flächenleuchte^F an Scherenaufhängung^F
projecteur^M d'ambiance^F sur pantographe^M
proyector^M sobre el pantógrafo^M
riflettore^M con presa^F a pantografo^M

スポットライト
spotlight
Spotlight^N
projecteur^M à faisceau^M concentré
reflector^M orientable
riflettore^M orientabile

テスト・パターン
test pattern
Testbild^N
mire^F de réglage^M
patrón^M de prueba^F
monoscopio^M

照明グリッド
lighting grid
Beleuchtungsanlage^F
grille^F d'éclairage^M
rejilla^F de iluminación^F
griglia^F di illuminazione^F

カーテン
curtain
Vorhang^M
rideau^M
cortina^F
sipario^M

フラッドライト
floodlight
Flächenleuchte^F
projecteur^M d'ambiance^F
proyector^M de luz^F difusa
riflettore^M

情報伝達とオフィス・オートメーション

ケーブル
cables
Kabel^N
câbles^M
cables^M
cavi^M

カメラ
camera
Kamera^F
caméra^F
cámara^F
telecamera^F

シクロラマ／円形パノラマ
cyclorama
Zyclorama^N
cyclorama^M
ciclorama^M
ciclorama^M

カメラ
camera
Kamera^F
caméra^F
cámara^F
telecamera^F

マイク（ロホン）
microphone
Mikrofon^N
microphone^M
micrófono^M
microfono^M

カメラ用ビューファインダー
camera viewfinder
Bildsucher^M
viseur^M de caméra^F
visor^M
mirino^M

マイク（ロホン）・ブーム
microphone boom
Mikrofonausleger^M
perche^F
jirafa^F
giraffa^F

ズーム・レンズ
zoom lens
Zoomobjektiv^N
zoom^M
zoom^M
zoom^M

マイク（ロホン）・ブーム・スタンド
microphone boom tripod
Mikrofon-Fahrspinne^F
trépied^M de perche^F
trípode^M de la jirafa^F para el micrófono^M
treppiede^M della giraffa^F

テレプロンプター
teleprompter
Textablesetafel^F
télésouffleur^M
apuntador^M electrónico
teleprompter^M

カメラ支持台
camera pedestal
Kamera-Dolly^M
trépied^M de caméra^F
pedestal^M de la cámara^F
piedistallo^M della telecamera^F

492

情報伝達 | COMMUNICATIONS
KOMMUNIKATION | COMMUNICATIONS | COMUNICACIONES | COMUNICAZIONI

テレビ

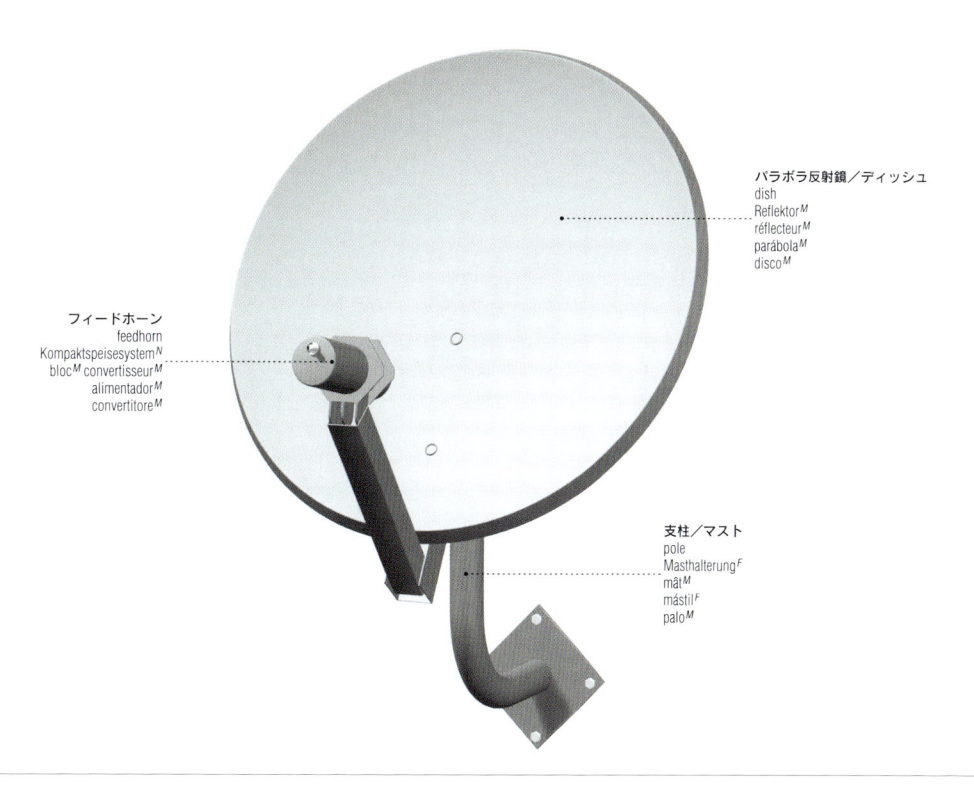

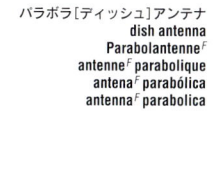

パラボラ[ディッシュ]アンテナ
dish antenna
Parabolantenne F
antenne F parabolique
antena F parabólica
antenna F parabolica

パラボラ反射鏡／ディッシュ
dish
Reflektor M
réflecteur M
parábola M
disco M

フィードホーン
feedhorn
Kompaktspeisesystem N
bloc M convertisseur M
alimentador M
convertitore M

支柱／マスト
pole
Masthalterung F
mât M
mástil F
palo M

受信機
receiver
Receiver M
terminal M numérique
receptor M
ricevitore M

カード読み取り装置／
カード・リーダー
card reader
Kartenleser M
lecteur M de carte F
lector M de tarjeta F
lettore M di schede F

リモコン（装置）
remote control
Fernbedienung F
télécommande F
mando M a distancia F
telecomando M

サラウンド・スピーカー
surround loudspeaker
Surround M-Lautsprecher M
enceinte F ambiophonique
altavoz M surround
cassa F acustica surround

センター・スピーカー
center loudspeaker
Centerlautsprecher M
enceinte F centrale
altavoz M central
cassa F acustica centrale

大型スクリーン・テレビ
large-screen television set
Breitbild N-Fernseher M
téléviseur M grand écran M
televisor M de pantalla F ancha
televisore M a grande schermo M

メイン・スピーカー
main loudspeaker
Hauptlautsprecher M
enceinte F principale
altavoz M principal
cassa F acustica principale

サブ[スーパー]ウーファー
subwoofers
Subwoofer M
enceintes F d'extrêmes graves M
altavoces M extremos de graves M
sub woofer M

ホーム・シアター
home theater; *home theatre*
Heimkino N
cinéma M maison F
home M theatre
home theatre M

情報伝達とオフィス・オートメーション

493

情報伝達 | COMMUNICATIONS
KOMMUNIKATION | COMMUNICATIONS | COMUNICACIONES | COMUNICAZIONI

テレビ

日本語 | 英語 | ドイツ語 | フランス語 | スペイン語 | イタリア語

テレビ受像機
television set
Fernsehapparat^M
téléviseur^M
televisor^M
televisore^M

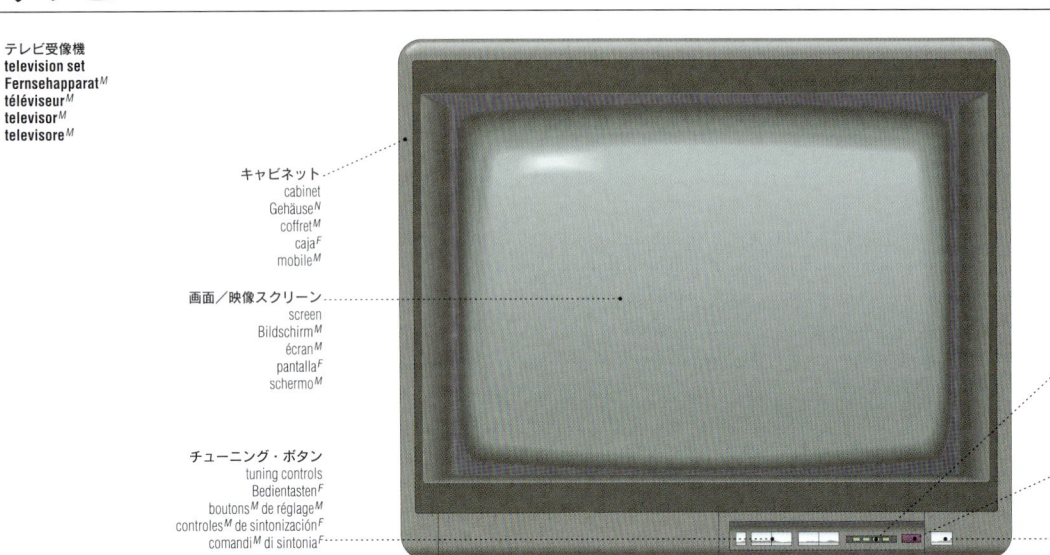

キャビネット
cabinet
Gehäuse^N
coffret^M
caja^F
mobile^M

画面／映像スクリーン
screen
Bildschirm^M
écran^M
pantalla^F
schermo^M

チューニング・ボタン
tuning controls
Bedientasten^F
boutons^M de réglage^M
controles^M de sintonización^F
comandi^M di sintonia^F

表示ランプ
indicators
Betriebsanzeigen^F
lampes^F témoins^M
indicadores^M
spie^F luminose

リモコン受光部［受信部］
remote control sensor
Sensor^M für Fernbedienung^F
capteur^M de télécommande^F
sensor^M del mando^M a distancia^F
sensore^M del telecomando^M

電源ボタン
power button
Netzschalter^M
interrupteur^M d'alimentation^F
botón^M de encendido
interruttore^M di accensione^F

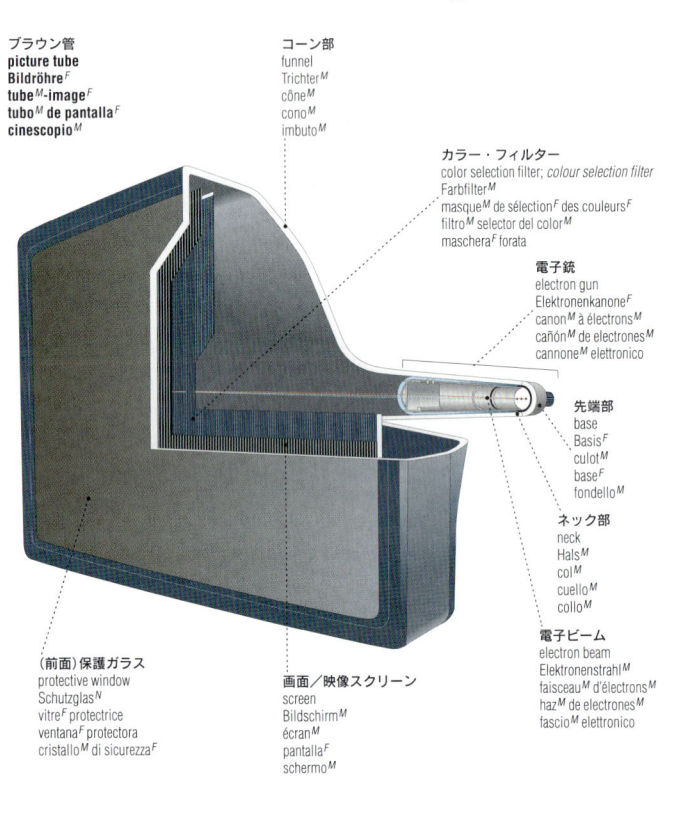

ブラウン管
picture tube
Bildröhre^F
tube^M-image^F
tubo^M de pantalla^F
cinescopio^M

コーン部
funnel
Trichter^M
cône^M
cono^M
imbuto^M

カラー・フィルター
color selection filter; colour selection filter
Farbfilter^M
masque^M de sélection^F des couleurs^F
filtro^M selector del color^M
maschera^F forata

電子銃
electron gun
Elektronenkanone^F
canon^M à électrons^M
cañón^M de electrones^M
cannone^M elettronico

電子銃
electron gun
Elektronenkanone^F
canon^M à électrons^M
cañón^M de electrones^M
cannone^M elettronico

グリッド
grid
Gitter^N
grille^F
rejilla^F
griglia^F

赤の電子ビーム
red beam
Rotstrahl^M
faisceau^M rouge
haz^M rojo
fascio^M rosso

先端部
base
Basis^F
culot^M
base^F
fondello^M

ネック部
neck
Hals^M
col^M
cuello^M
collo^M

緑の電子ビーム
green beam
Grünstrahl^M
faisceau^M vert
haz^M verde
fascio^M verde

磁場
magnetic field
magnetisches Feld^N
champ^M magnétique
campo^M magnético
campo^M magnetico

（前面）保護ガラス
protective window
Schutzglas^N
vitre^F protectrice
ventana^F protectora
cristallo^M di sicurezza^F

電子ビーム
electron beam
Elektronenstrahl^M
faisceau^M d'électrons^M
haz^M de electrones^M
fascio^M elettronico

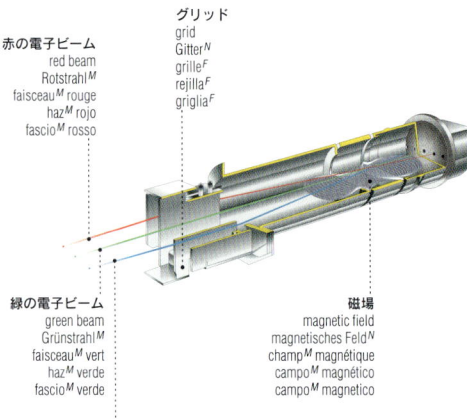

画面／映像スクリーン
screen
Bildschirm^M
écran^M
pantalla^F
schermo^M

青の電子ビーム
blue beam
Blaustrahl^M
faisceau^M bleu
haz^M azul
fascio^M blu

DVDプレーヤー
DVD player
DVD^F-Spieler^M
lecteur^M de DVD^M vidéo
reproductor^M DVD
lettore^M DVD^M

電源ボタン
power button
Ein-/Ausschalter^M
interrupteur^M d'alimentation^F
interruptor^M de alimentación^F
pulsante^M di alimentazione^F

ディスク・トレー
disc tray
DVD^F-Lade^F
plateau^M de chargement^M
bandeja^F del disco
vassoio^M portadischi

表示窓［画面］
display
Display^N
afficheur^M
pantalla^F
display^M

DVD／デジタル多用途ディスク
digital versatile disc (DVD)
DVD^F
disque^M numérique polyvalent (DVD)
disco^M versátil digital (DVD)
disco^M versatile digitale (DVD)

情報伝達とオフィス・オートメーション

494

情報伝達 | COMMUNICATIONS
KOMMUNIKATION | COMMUNICATIONS | COMUNICACIONES | COMUNICAZIONI

テレビ

テレビ・モード
TV mode
TV-Einstellung^F
mode^M télévision^F
modalidad^F TV
modo^M TV^F

テレビ・ビデオ切り替えボタン
TV/video button
TV/Video-Taste^F
sélecteur^M télé^F/vidéo^F
botón^M TV video^M
tasto^M TV^F/video^M

リモコン
remote control
Fernbedienung^F
télécommande^F
mando^M a distancia^F
telecomando^M

音量(調節)ボタン
volume control
Lautstärkeregler^M
réglage^M du volume^M
control^M de volumen^M
tasti^M di regolazione^F del volume^M

テレビ電源ボタン
TV power button
TV-Netzschalter^M
interrupteur^M du téléviseur^M
botón^M de encendido TV
interruttore^M di accensione^F della TV^F

ビデオ・モード
VCR mode
VCR-Einstellung^F
mode^M magnétoscope^M
modalidad^F VCR
modo^M VCR^M

チャンネル送りボタン
channel scan button
Kanalsuchtasten^F
recherche^F des canaux^M
botones^M de búsqueda de canales^M
tasti^M di ricerca^F emittenti^F

チャンネル選局ボタン
channel selector controls
Programmwahltasten^F
sélection^F des canaux^M
selector^M de canales^M
tasti^M di selezione^F dei canali^M

ビデオ電源ボタン
VCR power button
VCR-Netzschalter^M
interrupteur^M du magnétoscope^M
botón^M de encendido VCR
interruttore^M di accensione^F del VCR^M

(タイマー)予約設定ボタン
preset buttons
Programmiertasten^F
commandes^F de préréglage^M
botones^M de ajuste^M
tasti^M di programmazione^F

スローモーション・ボタン
slow-motion button
Zeitlupe^F
ralenti
cámara^F lenta
riproduzione^F al rallentatore^M

ビデオ操作ボタン
VCR controls
VCR-Tasten^F
commandes^F du magnétoscope^M
controles^M VCR
comandi^M del VCR^M

早送りボタン
fast-forward button
Vorspultaste^F
avance^F rapide
avance^M rápido
tasto^M di avanzamento^M rapido

磁気テープ
magnetic tape
Magnetband^N
bande^F magnétique
cinta^F magnética
nastro^M magnetico

録画ボタン
record button
Aufnahmetaste^F
enregistrement^M
grabación^F
tasto^M di registrazione^F

早戻しボタン
rewind button
Rückspultaste^F
rebobinage^M
rebobinado^M
tasto^M di riavvolgimento^M

リール
reel
Spule^F
bobine^F
bobina^F
bobina^F

再生ボタン
play button
Wiedergabetaste^F
lecture^F
funcionamiento^M
tasto^M di riproduzione^F

一時停止ボタン
pause/still button
Pausetaste^F
pause^F/arrêt^M sur l'image^F
pausa^F/imagen^F fija
tasto^M di pausa^F/fermo immagine^F

停止ボタン
stop button
Stopptaste^F
arrêt^M
botón^M de stop^M
tasto^M di arresto^M

ビデオカセット
videocassette
Videokassette^F
cassette^F vidéo
cinta^F de vídeo^M
videocassetta^F

ビデオ(カセット)・レコーダー
videocassette recorder
Videorecorder^M
magnétoscope^M
reproductor/grabador de video^M VCR
videoregistratore^M

カセット挿入口
cassette compartment
Kassettenschacht^M
logement^M de la cassette^F
alojamiento^M para la cinta^F
vano^M cassetta^F

データ表示窓[画面]
data display
Display^N
affichage^F des données^F
visualización^F de la información^F
display^M

再生ボタン
play button
Abspieltaste^F
commande^F de lecture^F
botón^M de reproducción^F
tasto^M di riproduzione^F

早送りボタン
fast-forward button
Vorspultaste^F
commande^F d'avance^F rapide
botón^M de avance^M rápido
tasto^M di avanzamento^M rapido

(タイマー)予約設定ボタン
preset buttons
Programmiertasten^F
commandes^F de préréglage^M
botones^M de ajuste^M
tasti^M di programmazione^F

リセット・ボタン
reset button
Rückstelltaste^F
commande^F de remise^F à zéro^M
botón^M del contador^M a cero
tasto^M di azzeramento^M

電源ボタン
power button
Netzschalter^M
interrupteur^M d'alimentation^F
interruptor^M
interruttore^M generale

録画ボタン
record button
Aufnahmetaste^F
commande^F d'enregistrement^M
botón^M de grabación^F
tasto^M di registrazione^F

チャンネル送りボタン
channel scan buttons
Kanalsuchtasten^F
recherche^F des canaux^M
botones^M para búsqueda de canales^M
tasti^M di ricerca delle emittenti^F

カセット取り出しボタン
cassette eject switch
Kassettenauswurfschalter^M
commande^F d'éjection^F de la cassette^F
interruptor^M de expulsión^F
tasto^M di espulsione^F

停止ボタン
stop button
Stopptaste^F
commande^F d'arrêt^M
botón^M de stop^M
tasto^M di arresto^M

早戻しボタン
rewind button
Rückspultaste^F
commande^F de rebobinage^M
botón^M de rebobinado^M
tasto^M di riavvolgimento^M

一時停止ボタン
pause/still button
Pausetaste^F
pause^F/arrêt^M sur l'image^F
pausa^F/imagen^F fija
tasto^M di pausa^F/fermo immagine^F

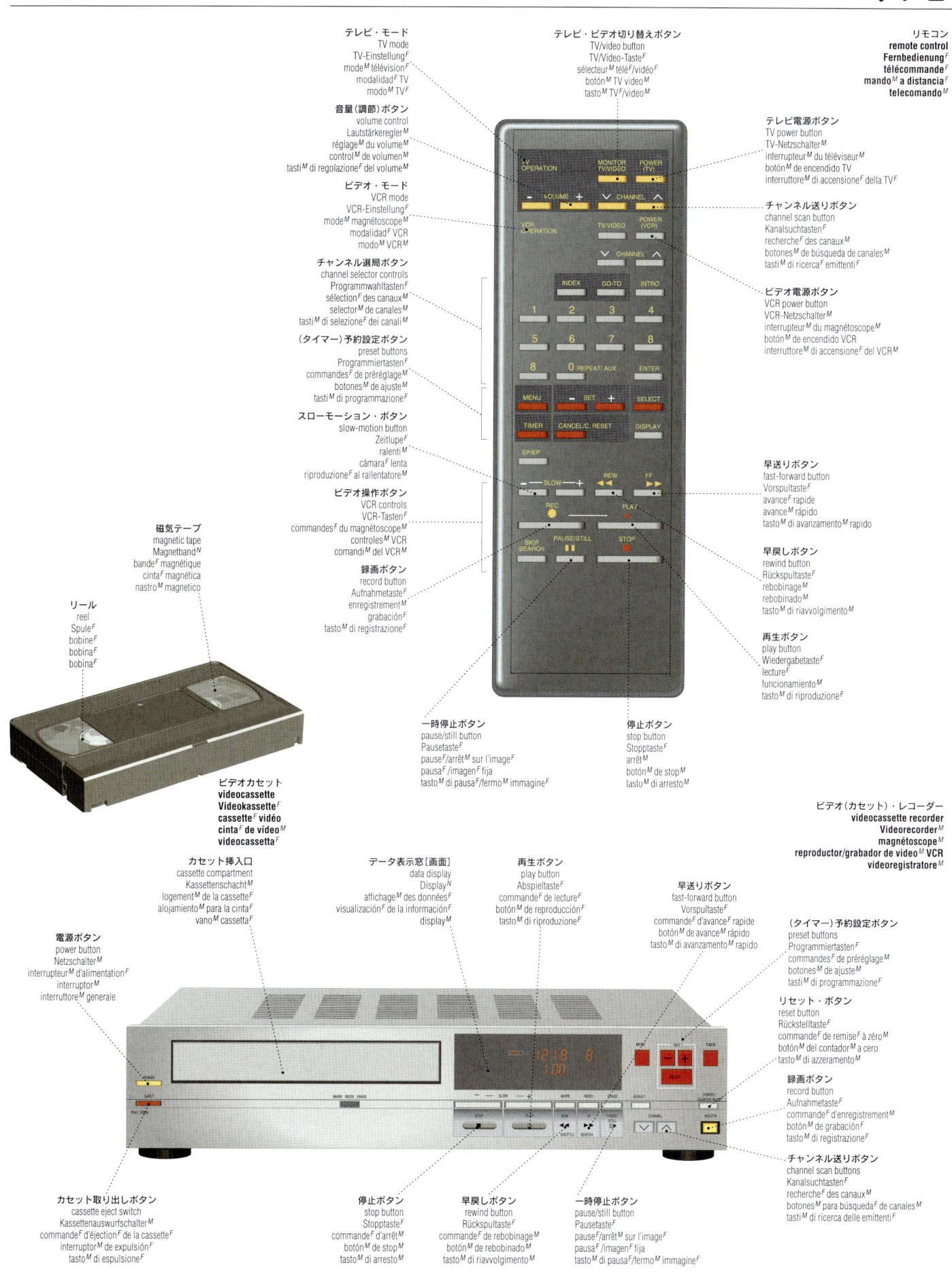

情報伝達とオフィス・オートメーション

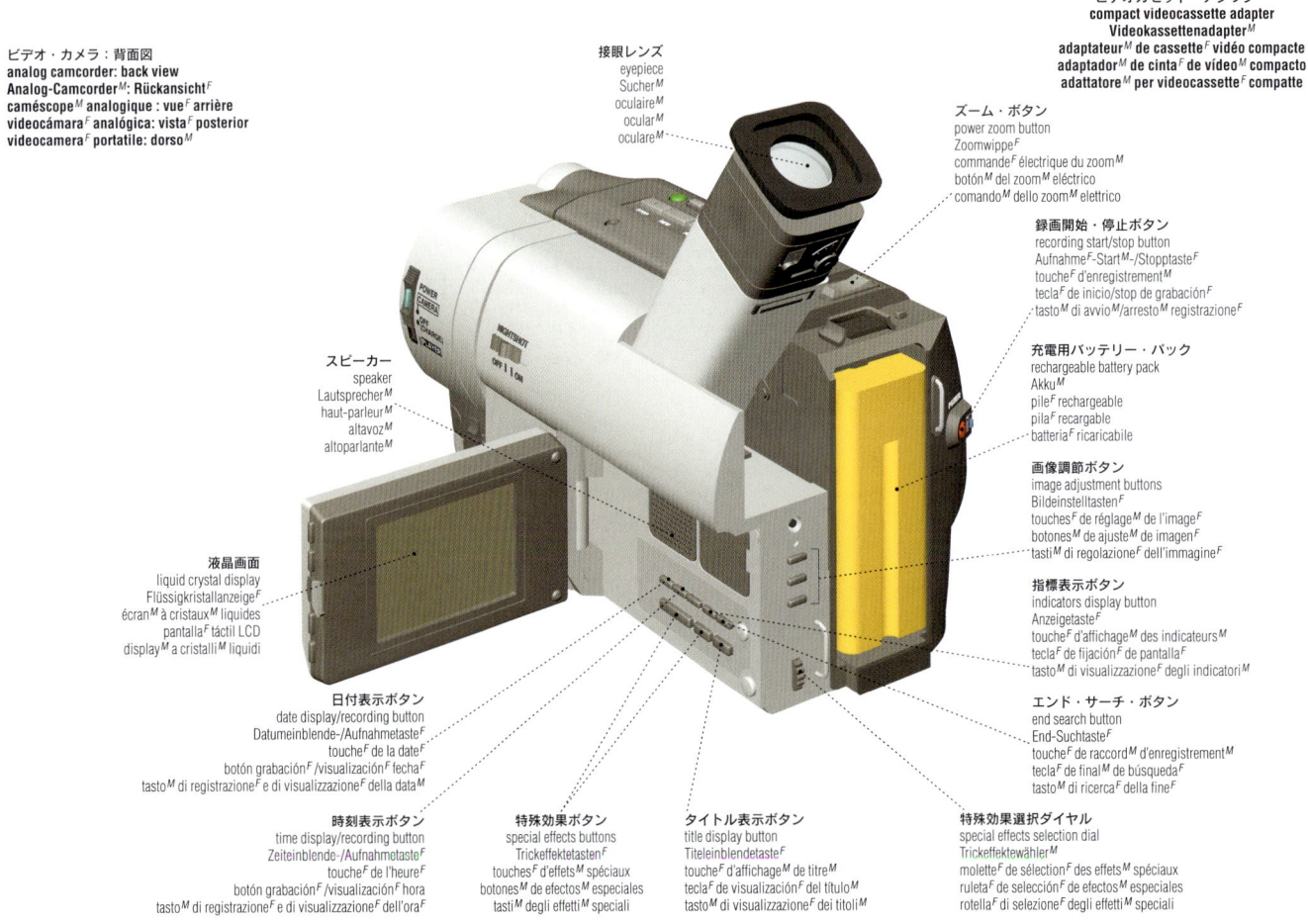

情報伝達 | COMMUNICATIONS
KOMMUNIKATION | COMMUNICATIONS | COMUNICACIONES | COMUNICAZIONI

テレビ

日本語 | 英語 | ドイツ語 | フランス語 | スペイン語 | イタリア語

ビデオ・カメラ：前面図
analog camcorder: front view
Analog-Camcorder^M: Vorderansicht^F
caméscope^M analogique : vue^F avant
videocámara^F analógica: vista^F frontal
videocamera^F portatile: vista^F frontale

録画編集ボタン
edit search button
Editier-Such-Taste^F
touche^F de raccord d'enregistrement^M
botón^M de selección^F y montaje^M
tasto^M di selezione^F e montaggio^M

ズーム・レンズ
zoom lens
Zoomobjektiv^N
objectif^M zoom^M
objetivo^M zoom
zoom^M

マイク（ロホン）
microphone
Mikrofon^N
microphone^M
micrófono^M
microfono^M

ズーム・ダイヤル
near/far dial
Zoomer^M
molette^F de réglage^M près/loin
ruleta^F de enfoque^M lejos/cerca
rotella^F regolatrice vicino/lontano

電子ビューファインダー
electronic viewfinder
elektronischer Sucher^M
viseur^F électronique
visor^M electrónico
mirino^M elettronico

電源・機能スイッチ
power/functions switch
Haupt-/Funktionsschalter^M
commutateur^M alimentation^F/fonctions^F
interruptor^M alimentación^F/funciones^F
interruttore^M di accensione^F/funzioni^F

フォーカス・キー
focus selector
Fokussiersteuerung^F
sélecteur^M de mise^F au point^M
selector^M de enfoque^M
selettore^M della messa^F a fuoco^M

アイカップ
eyecup
Sonnenschutzblende^F
œilleton^M
ojera^F
adattatore^M per oculare^M

ビデオテープ操作ボタン
videotape operation controls
Videobandsteuerungen^F
commandes^F de la bande^F vidéo
mandos^M de la cinta^F de vídeo
comandi^M della videocassetta^F

表示パネル
display panel
Display^N-Panel^F
panneau^M de l'écran^M
panel^F del display^M
pannello^M del display^M

夜間録画スイッチ
nightshot switch
Nachtaufnahmeschalter^M
commutateur^M de prise^F de vues^F nocturne
conmutador^M de grabación^F nocturna
selettore^M di registrazione^F notturna

カセット・コンパートメント
cassette compartment
Videokassettenschacht^M
logement^M de la cassette^F
alojamiento^M de la cinta^F
vano^M della videocassetta^F

ビデオカセット・アダプター
compact videocassette adapter
Videokassettenadapter^M
adaptateur^M de cassette^F vidéo compacte
adaptador^M de cinta^F de vídeo compacto
adattatore^M per videocassette^F compatte

ビデオ・カメラ：背面図
analog camcorder: back view
Analog-Camcorder^M: Rückansicht^F
caméscope^M analogique : vue^F arrière
videocámara^F analógica: vista^F posterior
videocamera^F portatile: dorso^M

スピーカー
speaker
Lautsprecher^M
haut-parleur^M
altavoz^M
altoparlante^M

液晶画面
liquid crystal display
Flüssigkristallanzeige^F
écran^M à cristaux^M liquides
pantalla^F táctil LCD
display^M a cristalli^M liquidi

接眼レンズ
eyepiece
Sucher^M
oculaire^F
ocular^M
oculare^M

日付表示ボタン
date display/recording button
Datumeinblende-/Aufnahmetaste^F
touche^F de la date^F
botón^M grabación^F/visualización^F fecha^F
tasto^M di registrazione^F e di visualizzazione^F della data^M

時刻表示ボタン
time display/recording button
Zeiteinblende-/Aufnahmetaste^F
touche^F de l'heure^F
botón^M grabación^F/visualización^F hora^F
tasto^M di registrazione^F e di visualizzazione^F dell'ora^F

特殊効果ボタン
special effects buttons
Trickeffektetasten^F
touches^F d'effets^M spéciaux
botones^M de efectos^M especiales
tasti^M degli effetti^M speciali

ズーム・ボタン
power zoom button
Zoomwippe^F
commande^F électrique du zoom^M
botón^M del zoom^M eléctrico
comando^M dello zoom^M elettrico

録画開始・停止ボタン
recording start/stop button
Aufnahme^F-Start^M-/Stopptaste^F
touche^F d'enregistrement^M
tecla^F de inicio/stop de grabación^F
tasto^M di avvio^M/arresto^M registrazione^F

充電用バッテリー・パック
rechargeable battery pack
Akku^M
pile^F rechargeable
pila^F recargable
batteria^F ricaricabile

画像調節ボタン
image adjustment buttons
Bildeinstelltasten^F
touches^F de réglage^M de l'image^F
botones^M de ajuste^M de imagen^F
tasti^M di regolazione^F dell'immagine^F

指標表示ボタン
indicators display button
Anzeigetaste^F
touche^F d'affichage des indicateurs^M
tecla^F de fijación^F de pantalla^F
tasto^M di visualizzazione^F degli indicatori^M

エンド・サーチ・ボタン
end search button
End-Suchtaste^F
touche^F de raccord d'enregistrement^M
tecla^F de final^M de búsqueda^F
tasto^M di ricerca^F della fine^F

タイトル表示ボタン
title display button
Titeleinblendetaste^F
touche^F d'affichage^M de titre^M
tecla^F de visualización^F del título^M
tasto^M di visualizzazione^F dei titoli^M

特殊効果選択ダイヤル
special effects selection dial
Trickeffektewähler^M
molette^F de sélection^F des effets^M spéciaux
ruleta^F de selección^F de efectos^M especiales
rotella^F di selezione^F degli effetti^M speciali

情報伝達とオフィス・オートメーション

496

情報伝達 | COMMUNICATIONS
KOMMUNIKATION | COMMUNICATIONS | COMUNICACIONES | COMUNICAZIONI

音声再生装置

sound reproducing system | Tonwiedergabesystem[N] | chaîne[F] stéréo | equipo[M] de alta fidelidad[F] | impianto[M] hi-fi di riproduzione[F] del suono[M]

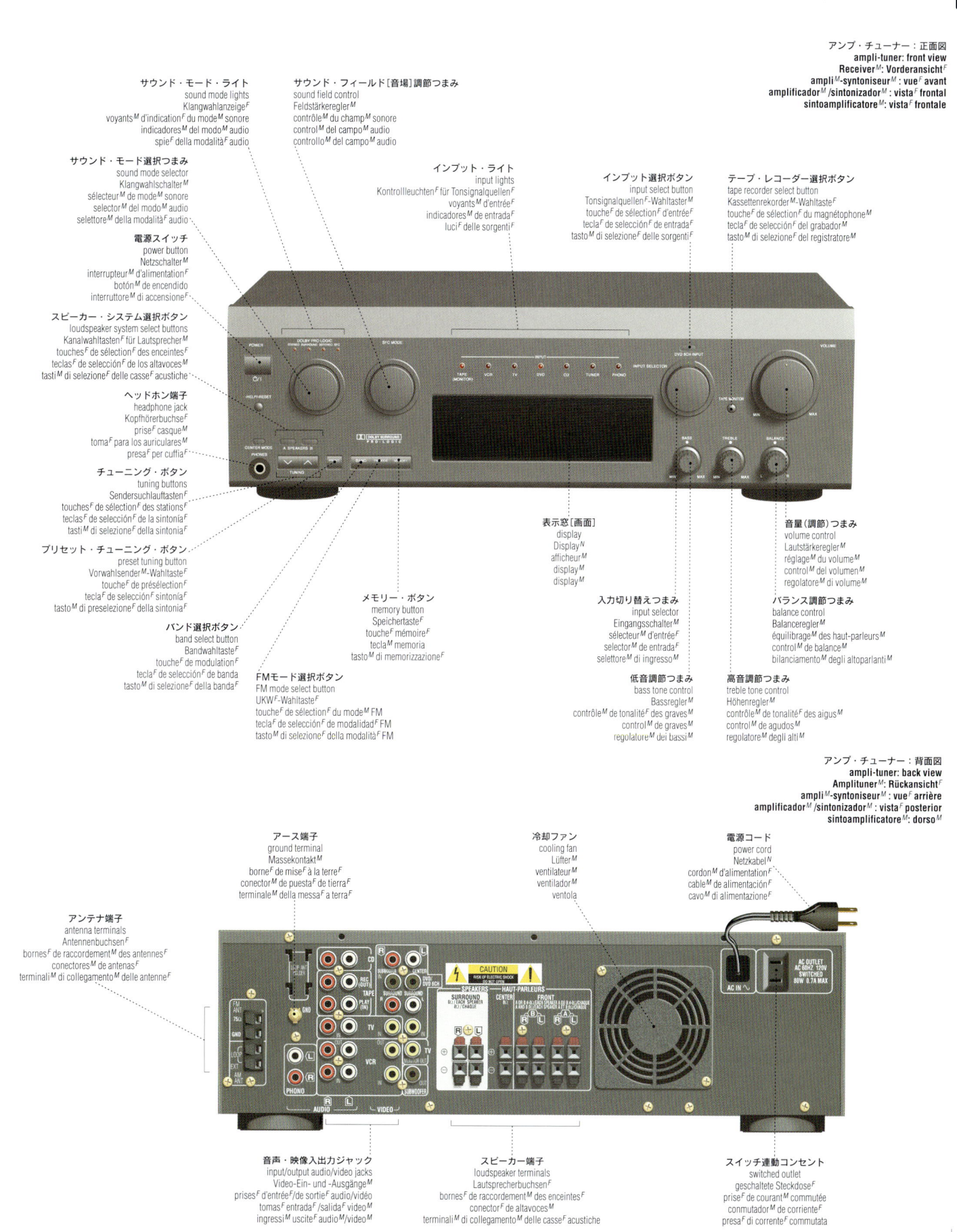

アンプ・チューナー：正面図
ampli-tuner: front view
Receiver[M]: Vorderansicht[F]
ampli[M]-syntoniseur[M] : vue[F] avant
amplificador[M] /sintonizador[M] : vista[F] frontal
sintoamplificatore[M]: vista[F] frontale

サウンド・モード・ライト
sound mode lights
Klangwahlanzeige[F]
voyants[M] d'indication[F] du mode[M] sonore
indicadores[M] del modo[M] audio
spie[F] della modalità[F] audio

サウンド・フィールド［音場］調節つまみ
sound field control
Feldstärkeregler[M]
contrôle[M] du champ[M] sonore
control[M] del campo[M] audio
controllo[M] del campo[M] audio

サウンド・モード選択つまみ
sound mode selector
Klangwahlschalter[M]
sélecteur[M] de mode[M] sonore
selector[M] del modo[M] audio
selettore[M] della modalità[F] audio

インプット・ライト
input lights
Kontrollleuchten[F] für Tonsignalquellen[F]
voyants[M] d'entrée[F]
indicadores[M] de entrada[F]
luci[F] delle sorgenti[F]

インプット選択ボタン
input select button
Tonsignalquellen[F]-Wahltaster[F]
touche[F] de sélection[F] d'entrée[F]
tecla[F] de selección[F] de entrada[F]
tasto[M] di selezione[F] delle sorgenti[F]

テープ・レコーダー選択ボタン
tape recorder select button
Kassettenrekorder[M]-Wahltaste[F]
touche[F] de sélection[F] du magnétophone[M]
tecla[F] de selección[F] del grabador[M]
tasto[M] di selezione[F] del registratore[M]

電源スイッチ
power button
Netzschalter[M]
interrupteur[M] d'alimentation[F]
botón[M] de encendido
interruttore[M] di accensione[F]

スピーカー・システム選択ボタン
loudspeaker system select buttons
Kanalwahltasten[F] für Lautsprecher[M]
touches[F] de sélection[F] des enceintes[F]
teclas[F] de selección[F] de los altavoces[M]
tasti[M] di selezione[F] delle casse[F] acustiche

ヘッドホン端子
headphone jack
Kopfhörerbuchse[F]
prise[F] casque[M]
toma[F] para los auriculares[M]
presa[F] per cuffia[F]

チューニング・ボタン
tuning buttons
Sendersuchlauftasten[F]
touches[F] de sélection[F] des stations[F]
teclas[F] de selección[F] de la sintonía[F]
tasti[M] di selezione[F] della sintonia[F]

プリセット・チューニング・ボタン
preset tuning button
Vorwahlsender[M]-Wahltaste[F]
touche[F] de présélection[F]
tecla[F] de selección[F] sintonía[F]
tasto[M] di preselezione[F] della sintonia[F]

バンド選択ボタン
band select button
Bandwahltaste[F]
touche[F] de modulation[F]
tecla[F] de selección[F] de banda[F]
tasto[M] di selezione[F] della banda[F]

メモリー・ボタン
memory button
Speichertaste[F]
touche[F] mémoire[F]
tecla[M] memoria
tasto[M] di memorizzazione[F]

FMモード選択ボタン
FM mode select button
UKW[F]-Wahltaste[F]
touche[F] de sélection[F] du mode[M] FM
tecla[F] de selección[F] de modalidad[F] FM
tasto[M] di selezione[F] della modalità[F] FM

表示窓［画面］
display
Display[N]
afficheur[M]
display[M]
display[M]

入力切り替えつまみ
input selector
Eingangsschalter[M]
sélecteur[M] d'entrée[F]
selector[M] de entrada[F]
selettore[M] di ingresso[M]

低音調節つまみ
bass tone control
Bassregler[M]
contrôle[M] de tonalité[F] des graves[M]
control[M] de graves[M]
regolatore[M] dei bassi[M]

音量（調節）つまみ
volume control
Lautstärkeregler[M]
réglage[M] du volume[M]
control[M] del volumen[M]
regolatore[M] di volume[M]

バランス調節つまみ
balance control
Balanceregler[M]
équilibrage[M] des haut-parleurs[M]
control[M] de balance[M]
bilanciamento[M] degli altoparlanti[M]

高音調節つまみ
treble tone control
Höhenregler[M]
contrôle[M] de tonalité[F] des aigus[M]
control[M] de agudos[M]
regolatore[M] degli alti[M]

アンプ・チューナー：背面図
ampli-tuner: back view
Amplituner[M]: Rückansicht[F]
ampli[M]-syntoniseur[M] : vue[F] arrière
amplificador[M] /sintonizador[M] : vista[F] posterior
sintoamplificatore[M]: dorso[M]

アース端子
ground terminal
Massekontakt[M]
borne[F] de mise[F] à la terre[F]
conector[M] de puesta[F] de tierra[F]
terminale[M] della messa[F] a terra[F]

冷却ファン
cooling fan
Lüfter[M]
ventilateur[M]
ventilador[M]
ventola

電源コード
power cord
Netzkabel[N]
cordon[M] d'alimentation[F]
cable[M] de alimentación[F]
cavo[M] di alimentazione[F]

アンテナ端子
antenna terminals
Antennenbuchsen[F]
bornes[F] de raccordement[M] des antennes[F]
conectores[M] de antenas[F]
terminali[M] di collegamento[M] delle antenne[F]

音声・映像入出力ジャック
input/output audio/video jacks
Video-Ein- und -Ausgänge[M]
prises[F] d'entrée[F]/de sortie[F] audio/vidéo
tomas[F] entrada[F] /salida[F] video[M]
ingressi[M] uscite[F] audio[M]/video[M]

スピーカー端子
loudspeaker terminals
Lautsprecherbuchsen[F]
bornes[F] de raccordement[M] des enceintes[F]
conector[M] de altavoces[M]
terminali[M] di collegamento[M] delle casse[F] acustiche

スイッチ連動コンセント
switched outlet
geschaltete Steckdose[F]
prise[F] de courant[M] commutée
conmutador[M] de corriente[F]
presa[F] di corrente[F] commutata

情報伝達とオフィス・オートメーション

情報伝達 | COMMUNICATIONS
KOMMUNIKATION | COMMUNICATIONS | COMUNICACIONES | COMUNICAZIONI

音声再生装置

日本語 | 英語 | ドイツ語 | フランス語 | スペイン語 | イタリア語

チューナー
tuner
Rundfunkempfänger^M
syntoniseur^M
sintonizador^M
sintonizzatore^M

電源スイッチ
power button
Netzschalter^M
interrupteur^M d'alimentation^F
botón^M de encendido
interruttore^M di accensione^F

メモリー・ボタン
memory button
Speichertaste^F
touche^F mémoire^F
botón^M de memoria^F
tasto^M di memorizzazione^F

モード切り替えスイッチ
mode selector
Mono-Stereo-Taste^F
commutateur^M mono^F/stéréo^F
selector^M mono/estéreo
commutatore^M mono/stereo

アクティブ・トラッキング・スイッチ
active tracking
automatischer Sendersuchlauf^M
balayage^M automatique des stations^F
búsqueda^F automática de canales^M
ricerca^F automatica

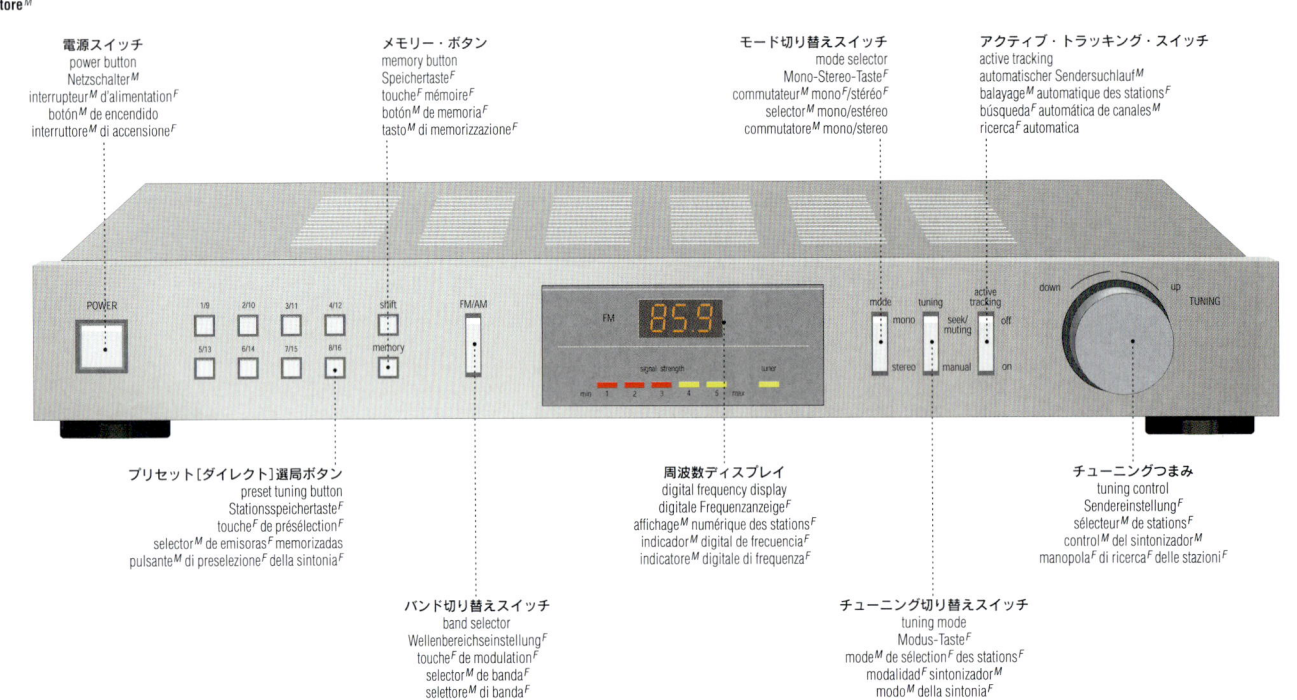

プリセット[ダイレクト]選局ボタン
preset tuning button
Stationsspeichertaste^F
touche^F de présélection^F
selector^M de emisoras^F memorizadas
pulsante^M di preselezione^F della sintonia^F

周波数ディスプレイ
digital frequency display
digitale Frequenzanzeige^F
affichage^M numérique des stations^F
indicador^M digital de frecuencia^F
indicatore^M digitale di frequenza^F

チューニングつまみ
tuning control
Sendereinstellung^F
sélecteur^M de stations^F
control^M del sintonizador^M
manopola^F di ricerca^F delle stazioni^F

バンド切り替えスイッチ
band selector
Wellenbereichseinstellung^F
touche^F de modulation^F
selector^M de banda^F
selettore^M di banda^F

チューニング切り替えスイッチ
tuning mode
Modus-Taste^F
mode^M de sélection^F des stations^F
modalidad^F sintonizador^M
modo^M della sintonia^F

グラフィック・イコライザー
graphic equalizer
Equalizer^M
égalisateur^M **graphique**
compensador^M **gráfico de sintonización**^{F}
equalizzatore^M **grafico**

周波数帯
frequency bands
Frequenzbänder^N
bandes^F de fréquences^F
bandas^F de frecuencia^F
bande^F di frequenza^F

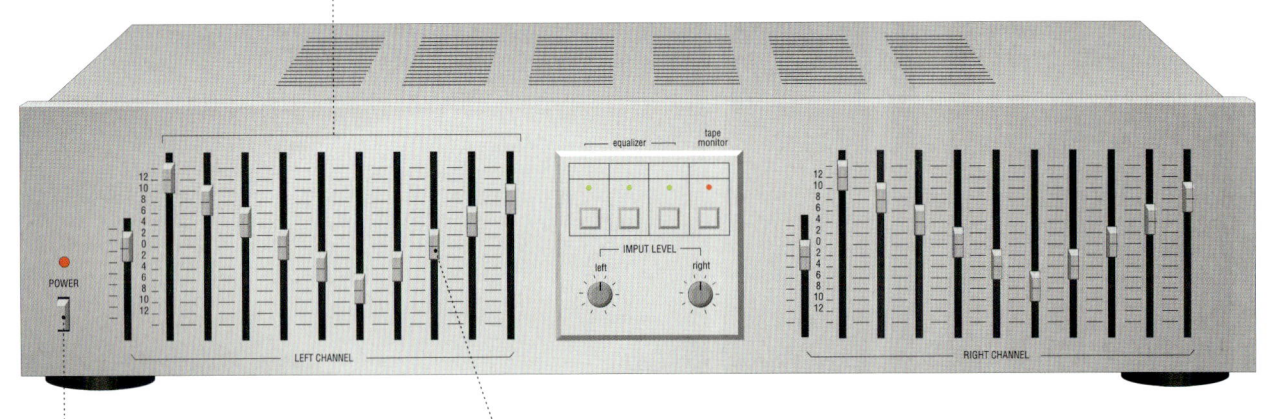

電源ボタン
power button
Ein-/Ausschalter^M
interrupteur^M d'alimentation^F
interruptor^M de alimentación^F
interruttore^M di accensione^F

周波数スライダー
frequency setting slide control
Frequenzregler^M
curseur^M de réglage^M de la fréquence^F
cursor^M de ajuste^M de la frecuencia^F
cursore^M di regolazione^F della frequenza^F

情報伝達とオフィス・オートメーション

情報伝達 | COMMUNICATIONS
KOMMUNIKATION | COMMUNICATIONS | COMUNICACIONES | COMUNICAZIONI

音声再生装置

カセット・テープ
cassette
Kassette^F
cassette^F
casete^F
cassetta^F

巻き取りリール
take-up reel
Aufwickelkern^M
bobine^F réceptrice
carrete^M receptor de la cinta^F
bobina^F di avvolgimento^M

ケース
housing
Gehäuse^N
boîtier^M
cubierta^F
caricatore^M

録音テープ
recording tape
Kassettenband^N
bande^F magnétique
cinta^F de grabación^F
nastro^M di registrazione^F

ガイド・ローラー
guide roller
Führungsrolle^F
galet^M
rodillo^M guía^F
rullo^M di guida^F

再生ヘッド用窓
playing window
Aussparung^F für Magnetköpfe^M
fenêtre^F de lecture^F
ventana^F de lectura^F
finestra^F di lettura^F

テープ・ガイド
tape-guide
Bandführung^F
guide-bande^M
guía^F para la cinta^F
guida^F del nastro^M

カセット(テープ)デッキ
cassette tape deck
Kassettendeck^N
platine^F **cassette**^{F}
pletina^F de casete^F
piastra^F di registrazione^F

カウンター・リセット・ボタン
counter reset button
Rückstelltaste^F
bouton^M de remise^F à zéro^M
botón^M de ajuste^M a cero^M del contador^M
tasto^M di azzeramento^M del contatore^M

テープ・セレクター
tape selector
Bandsortenschalter^M
sélecteur^M de bandes^F
selector^M de tipo^M de cinta^F
selettore^M del nastro^M

早送りボタン
fast-forward button
Schnellvorlauf-Taste^F
avance^M rapide
botón^M de avance^M rápido
tasto^M di avanzamento^M rapido

カセット取り出しボタン
eject button
Auswurf-Taste^F
bouton^M d'éjection^F
botón^M de expulsión^F
tasto^M di espulsione^F

テープ・カウンター
tape counter
Zählwerk^N
compteur^M
contador^M
contatore^M

再生ボタン
play button
Play-Taste^F
lecture^F
botón^M de reproducción^F
tasto^M di riproduzione^F

ピーク・レベル・メーター
peak level meter
LED-Pegelanzeige^F
indicateur^M de niveau^M
medidor^M de altos niveles^M de frecuencia^F
LED^M indicatore^M del livello^M di picco^M

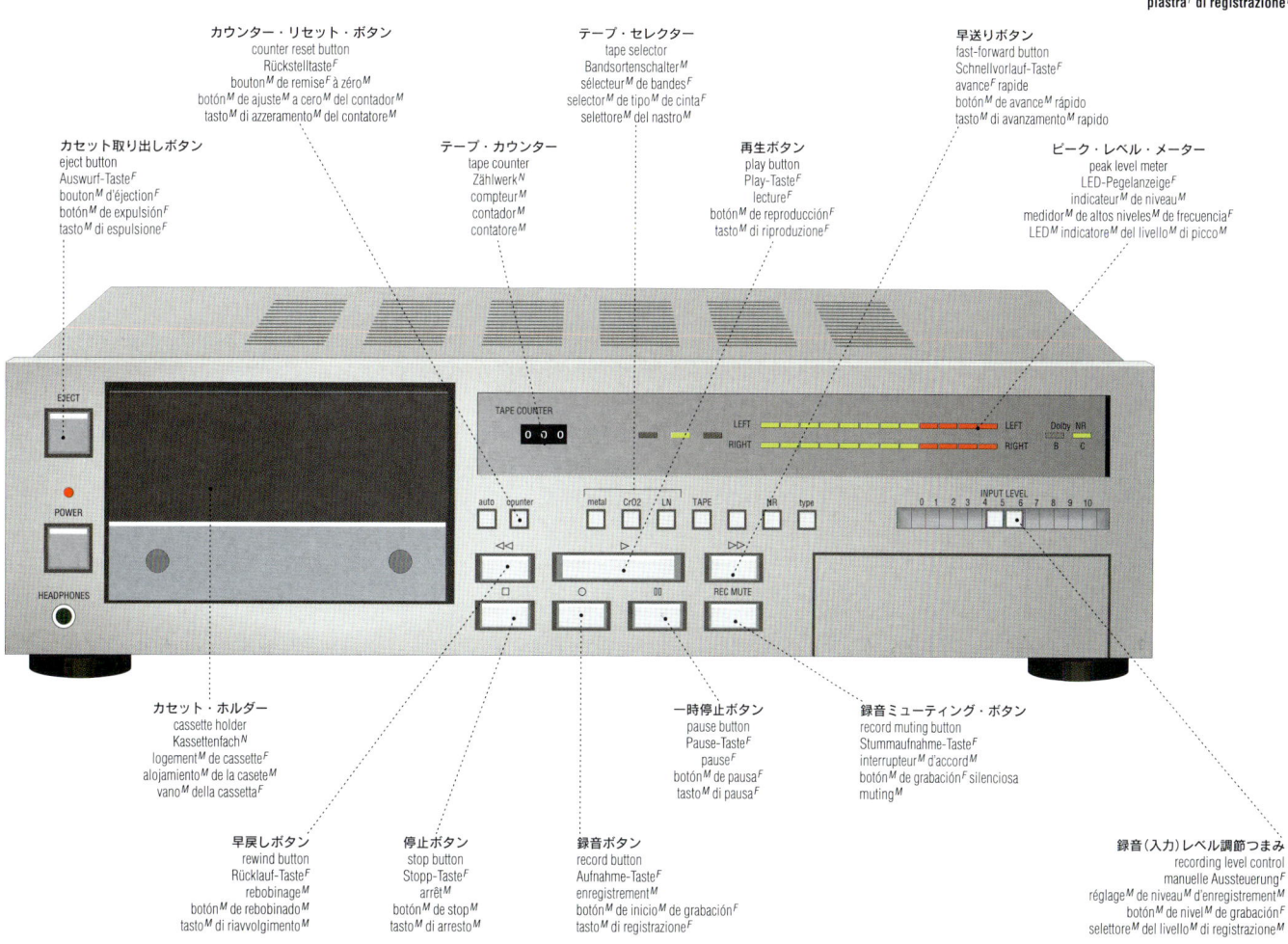

カセット・ホルダー
cassette holder
Kassettenfach^N
logement^M de cassette^F
alojamiento^M de la casete^F
vano^M della cassetta^F

早戻しボタン
rewind button
Rücklauf-Taste^F
rebobinage^M
botón^M de rebobinado^M
tasto^M di riavvolgimento^M

停止ボタン
stop button
Stopp-Taste^F
arrêt^M
botón^M de stop^M
tasto^M di arresto^M

録音ボタン
record button
Aufnahme-Taste^F
enregistrement^M
botón^M de inicio^M de grabación^F
tasto^M di registrazione^F

一時停止ボタン
pause button
Pause-Taste^F
pause^F
botón^M de pausa^F
tasto^M di pausa^F

録音ミューティング・ボタン
record muting button
Stummaufnahme-Taste^F
interrupteur^M d'accord^M
botón^M de grabación^F silenciosa
muting^M

録音(入力)レベル調節つまみ
recording level control
manuelle Aussteuerung^F
réglage^M de niveau^M d'enregistrement^M
botón^M de nivel^M de grabación^F
selettore^M del livello^M di registrazione^F

情報伝達とオフィス・オートメーション

499

情報伝達 | COMMUNICATIONS
KOMMUNIKATION | COMMUNICATIONS | COMUNICACIONES | COMUNICAZIONI

音声再生装置

日本語 | 英語 | ドイツ語 | フランス語 | スペイン語 | イタリア語

レコード
record
Schallplatte^F
disque^M
disco^M
disco^M

送り溝
spiral
Schallrille^F
plage^F de séparation^F
espiral^M de separación^F
solco^M di separazione^F

導入溝
spiral-in groove
Einlaufrille^F
sillon^M de départ^M
surco^M en espiral^M
solco^M iniziale

エンドレス
locked groove
Ausschaltrille^F
sillon^M concentrique
surco^M concéntrico
solco^M concentrico

バンド
band
Track^M
surface^F gravée
banda^F grabada
banda^F

導出溝
tail-out groove
Auslaufrille^F
sillon^M de sortie^F
surco^M de salida^F
solco^M finale

中心孔
center hole; centre hole
Mittelloch^N
trou^M central
orificio^M central
foro^M centrale

ラベル／レーベル
label
Label^N
étiquette^F
etiqueta^F
etichetta^F

レコード・プレーヤー
record player
Plattenspieler^M
platine^F tourne-disque^M
tocadiscos^M
giradischi^M

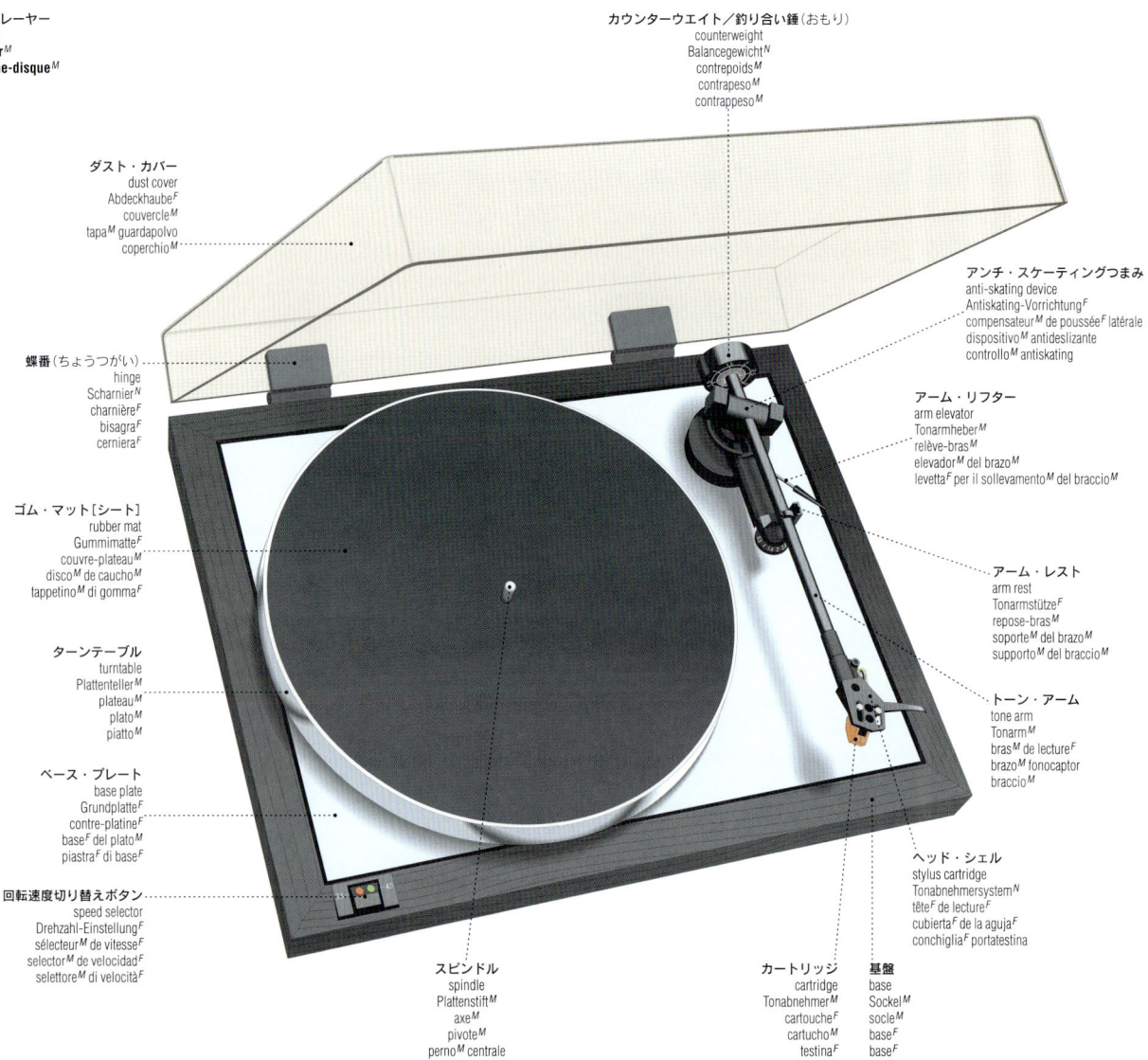

カウンターウエイト／釣り合い錘（おもり）
counterweight
Balancegewicht^N
contrepoids^M
contrapeso^M
contrappeso^M

ダスト・カバー
dust cover
Abdeckhaube^F
couvercle^M
tapa^M guardapolvo
coperchio^M

アンチ・スケーティングつまみ
anti-skating device
Antiskating-Vorrichtung^F
compensateur^M de poussée^F latérale
dispositivo^M antideslizante
controllo^M antiskating

蝶番（ちょうつがい）
hinge
Scharnier^N
charnière^F
bisagra^F
cerniera^F

アーム・リフター
arm elevator
Tonarmheber^M
relève-bras^M
elevador^M del brazo^M
levetta^F per il sollevamento^M del braccio^M

ゴム・マット［シート］
rubber mat
Gummimatte^F
couvre-plateau^M
disco^M de caucho^M
tappetino^M di gomma^F

アーム・レスト
arm rest
Tonarmstütze^F
repose-bras^M
soporte^M del brazo^M
supporto^M del braccio^M

ターンテーブル
turntable
Plattenteller^M
plateau^M
plato^M
piatto^M

トーン・アーム
tone arm
Tonarm^M
bras^M de lecture^F
brazo^M fonocaptor
braccio^M

ベース・プレート
base plate
Grundplatte^F
contre-platine^F
base^F del plato^M
piastra^F di base^F

ヘッド・シェル
stylus cartridge
Tonabnehmersystem^N
tête^F de lecture^F
cubierta^F de la aguja^F
conchiglia^F portatestina

回転速度切り替えボタン
speed selector
Drehzahl-Einstellung^F
sélecteur^M de vitesse^F
selector^M de velocidad^F
selettore^M di velocità^F

スピンドル
spindle
Plattenstift^M
axe^M
pivote^M
perno^M centrale

カートリッジ
cartridge
Tonabnehmer^M
cartouche^F
cartucho^M
testina^F

基盤
base
Sockel^M
socle^M
base^M
base^F

情報伝達とオフィス・オートメーション

500

情報伝達 | COMMUNICATIONS
KOMMUNIKATION | COMMUNICATIONS | COMUNICACIONES | COMUNICAZIONI

音声再生装置

CD／コンパクト・ディスク
compact disc; *compact disc*
CD[F]
disque[M] compact
disco[M] compacto
compact disc[M]

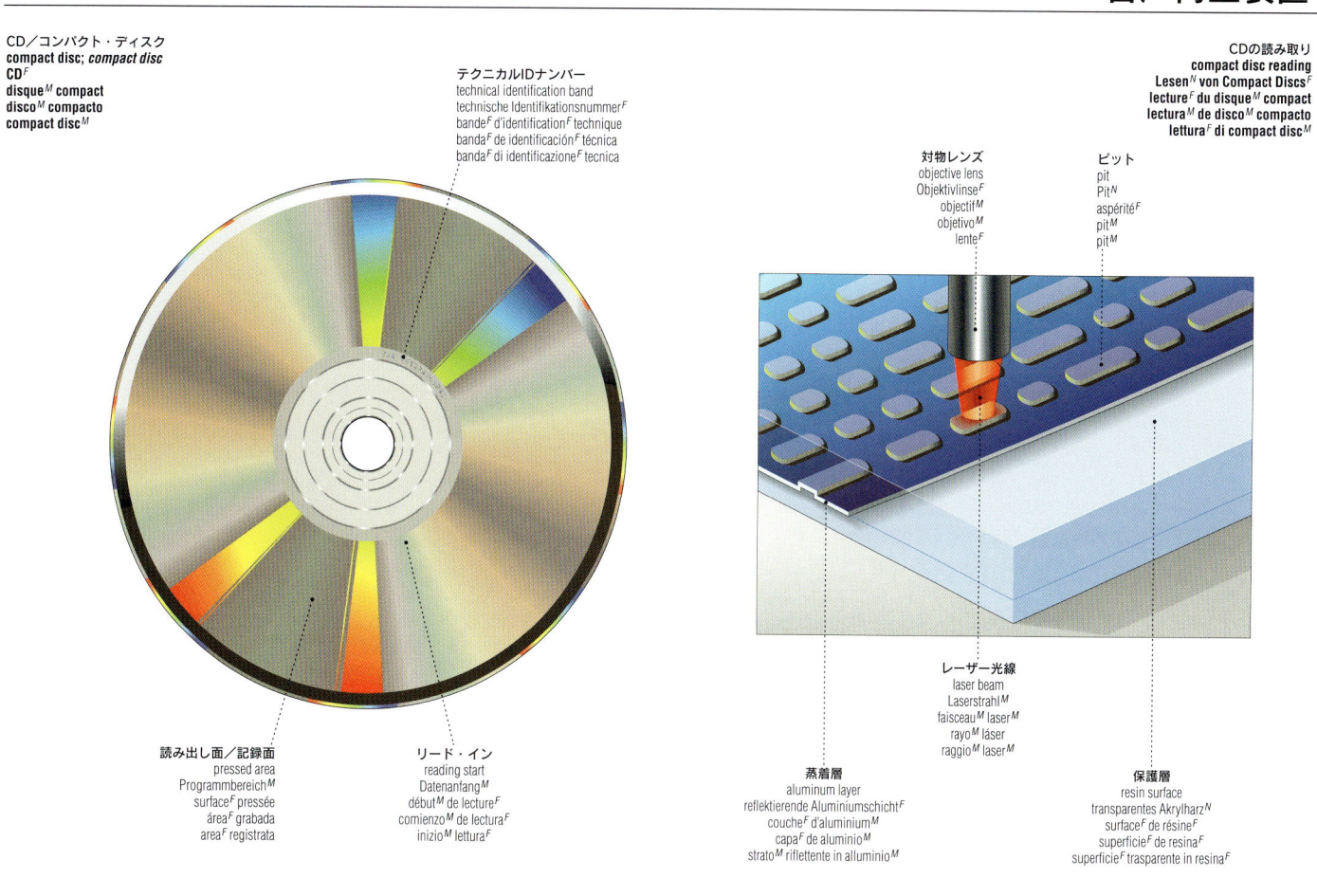

テクニカルIDナンバー
technical identification band
technische Identifikationsnummer[F]
bande[F] d'identification[F] technique
banda[F] de identificación[F] técnica
banda[F] di identificazione[F] tecnica

対物レンズ
objective lens
Objektivlinse[F]
objectif[M]
objetivo[M]
lente[F]

ピット
pit
Pit[N]
aspérité[F]
pit[M]
pit[M]

CDの読み取り
compact disc reading
Lesen[N] von Compact Discs[F]
lecture[F] du disque[M] compact
lectura[F] de disco[M] compacto
lettura[F] di compact disc[M]

読み出し面／記録面
pressed area
Programmbereich[M]
surface[F] pressée
área[F] grabada
area[F] registrata

リード・イン
reading start
Datenanfang[M]
début[M] de lecture[F]
comienzo[M] de lectura[F]
inizio[M] lettura[F]

レーザー光線
laser beam
Laserstrahl[M]
faisceau[M] laser[M]
rayo[M] láser
raggio[M] laser[M]

蒸着層
aluminum layer
reflektierende Aluminiumschicht[F]
couche[F] d'aluminium[M]
capa[F] de aluminio[M]
strato[M] riflettente in alluminio[M]

保護層
resin surface
transparentes Akrylharz[N]
surface[F] de résine[F]
superficie[F] de resina[F]
superficie[F] trasparente in resina[F]

電源ボタン
power button
Netzschalter[M]
interrupteur[M] d'alimentation[F]
interruptor[M]
interruttore[M] di accensione[F]

表示窓［画面］
indicators
Anzeigen[F]
voyants[M] de contrôle[M]
indicadores[M]
indicatori[M]

CDプレーヤー
compact disc player; *compact disc player*
CD-Spieler[M]
lecteur[M] de disque[M] compact
lector[M] de disco[M] compacto
lettore[M] di compact disc[M]

ディスク・トレイ
disc compartment; *disc compartment*
CD-Fach[N]
logement[M] du plateau[M]
alojamiento[M] para el disco[M]
vano[M] del disco[M]

トラック番号
track number
Titelnummer[F]
numéro[M] de la piste[F]
número[M] de pista[F]
numero[M] del brano[M]

メモリー・ボタン
memory button
Speichertaste[F]
touche[F] mémoire[F]
botón[M] de la memoria[F]
tasto[M] di memorizzazione[F]

リピート・ボタン
repeat buttons
Wiederholungstasten[F]
touches[F] de répétition[F]
tecla[F] de repetición[F]
tasti[M] di ripetizione[F]

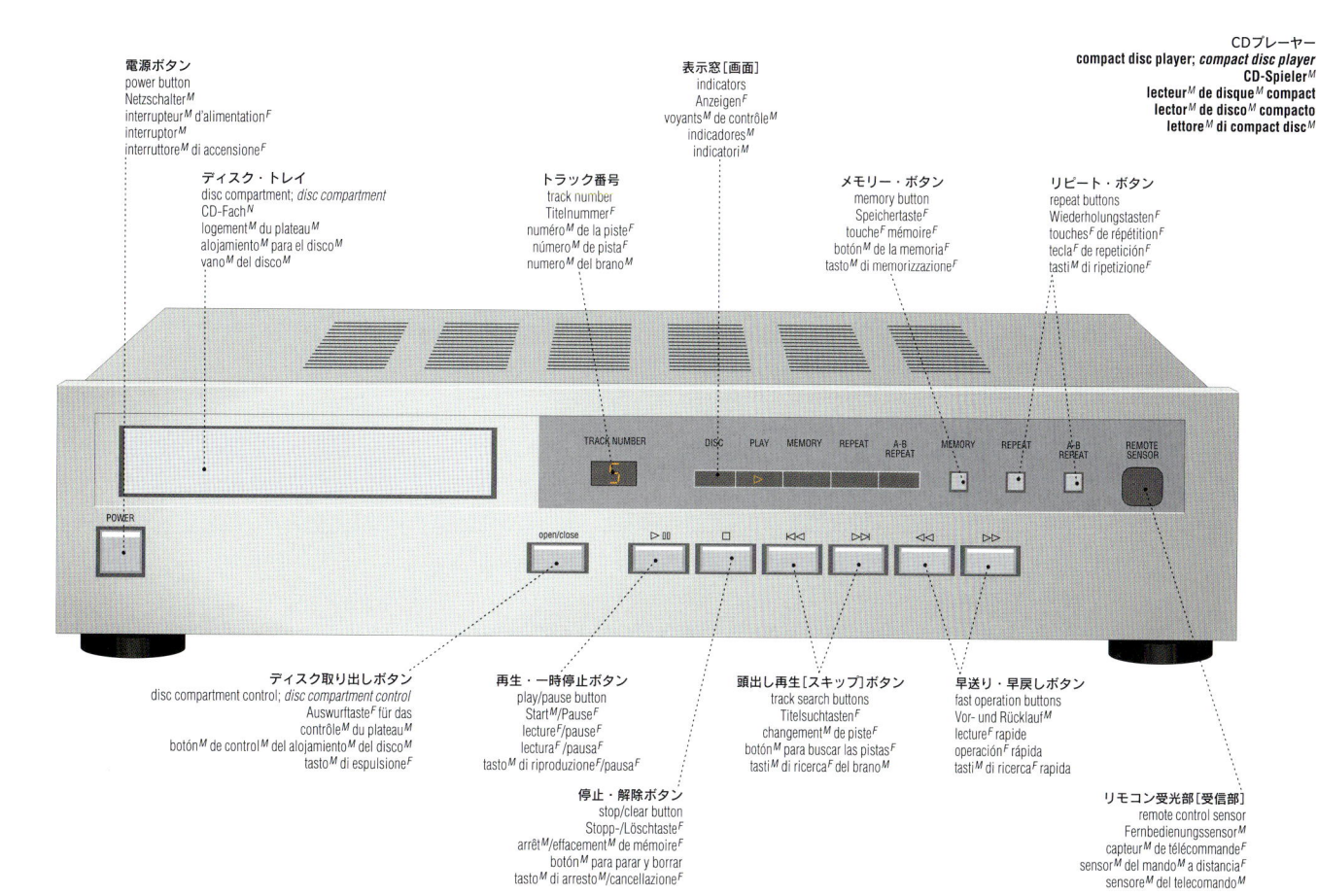

ディスク取り出しボタン
disc compartment control; *disc compartment control*
Auswurftaste[F] für das
contrôle[M] du plateau[M]
botón[M] de control[M] del alojamiento[M] del disco[M]
tasto[M] di espulsione[F]

再生・一時停止ボタン
play/pause button
Start[M]/Pause[F]
lecture[F]/pause[F]
lectura[F]/pausa[F]
tasto[M] di riproduzione[F]/pausa[F]

頭出し再生［スキップ］ボタン
track search buttons
Titelsuchtasten[F]
changement[M] de piste[F]
botón[M] para buscar las pistas[F]
tasti[M] di ricerca[F] del brano[M]

早送り・早戻しボタン
fast operation buttons
Vor- und Rücklauf[M]
lecture[F] rapide
operación[F] rápida
tasti[M] di ricerca[F] rapida

停止・解除ボタン
stop/clear button
Stopp-/Löschtaste[F]
arrêt[M]/effacement[M] de mémoire[F]
botón[M] para parar y borrar
tasto[M] di arresto[F]/cancellazione[F]

リモコン受光部［受信部］
remote control sensor
Fernbedienungssensor[M]
capteur[M] de télécommande[F]
sensor[M] del mando[M] a distancia[F]
sensore[M] del telecomando[M]

情報伝達とオフィス・オートメーション

501

情報伝達 | COMMUNICATIONS
KOMMUNIKATION | COMMUNICATIONS | COMUNICACIONES | COMUNICAZIONI

音声再生装置

日本語 | 英語 | ドイツ語 | フランス語 | スペイン語 | イタリア語

ヘッドホン
headphones
Kopfhörer^M
casque^M d'écoute^F
auriculares^M
cuffia^F

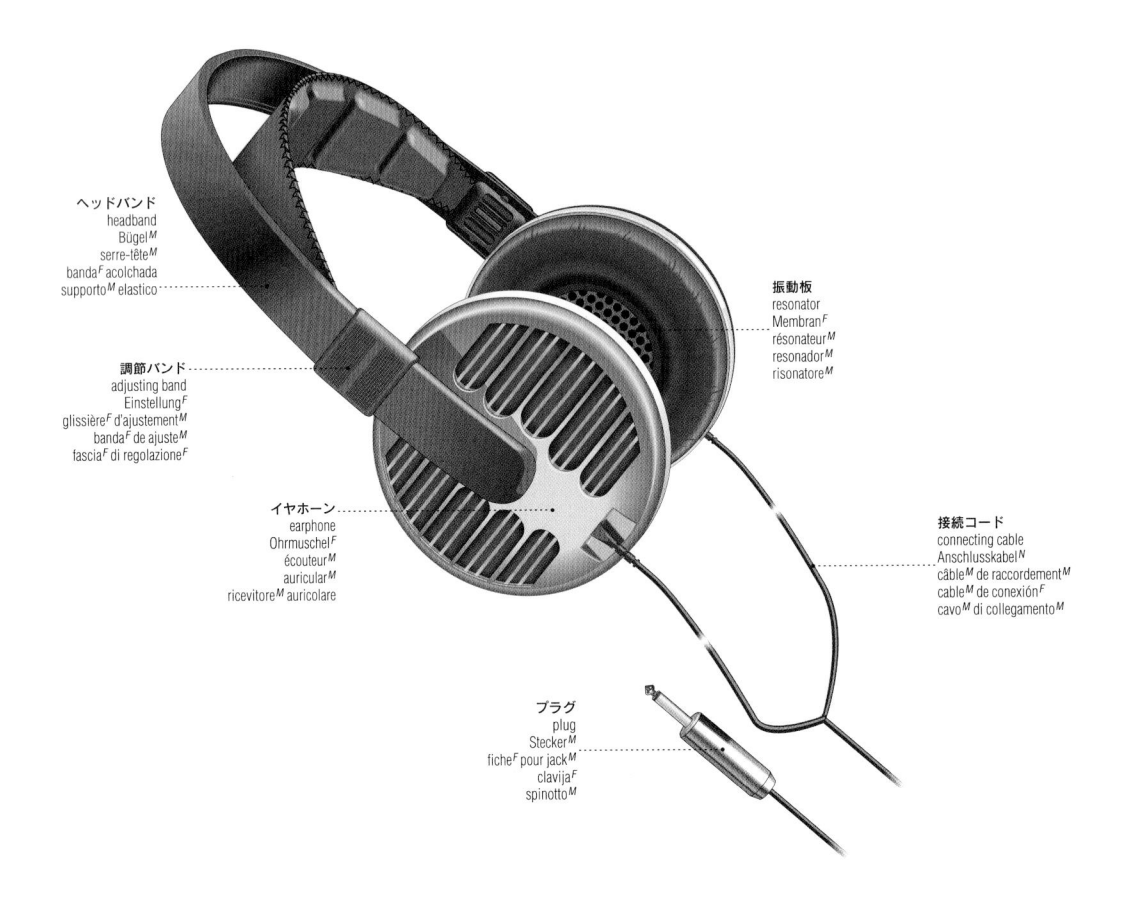

ヘッドバンド
headband
Bügel^M
serre-tête^M
banda^F acolchada
supporto^M elastico

調節バンド
adjusting band
Einstellung^F
glissière^F d'ajustement^M
banda^F de ajuste^M
fascia^F di regolazione^F

イヤホーン
earphone
Ohrmuschel^F
écouteur^M
auricular^M
ricevitore^M auriculare

振動板
resonator
Membran^F
résonateur^M
resonador^M
risonatore^M

接続コード
connecting cable
Anschlusskabel^N
câble^M de raccordement^M
cable^M de conexión^F
cavo^M di collegamento^M

プラグ
plug
Stecker^M
fiche^F pour jack^M
clavija^F
spinotto^M

スピーカー
loudspeakers
Lautsprecherbox^F
enceinte^F acoustique
altavoz^M
cassa^F acustica

右チャンネル
right channel
rechter Kanal^M
canal^M droit
canal^M derecho
canale^M destro

左チャンネル
left channel
linker Kanal^M
canal^M gauche
canal^M izquierdo
canale^M sinistro

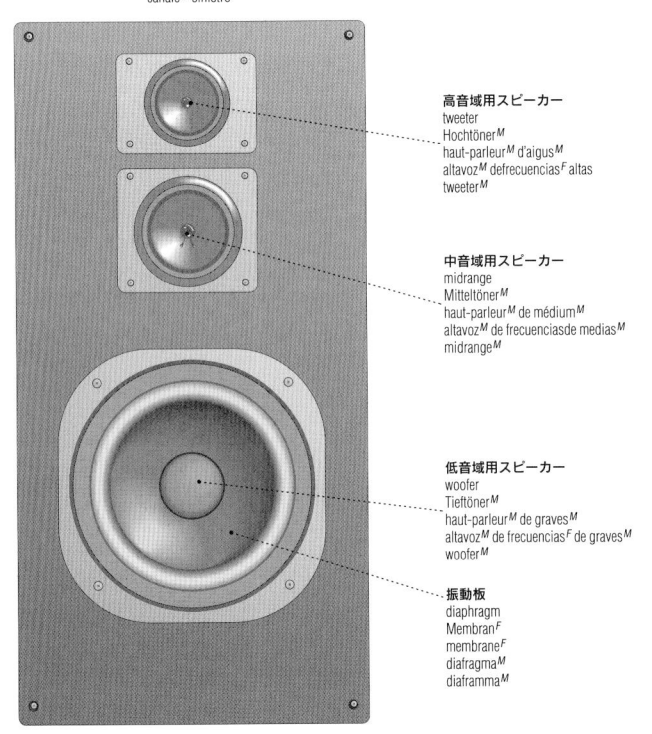

高音域用スピーカー
tweeter
Hochtöner^M
haut-parleur^M d'aigus^M
altavoz^M de frecuencias^F altas
tweeter^M

中音域用スピーカー
midrange
Mitteltöner^M
haut-parleur^M de médium^M
altavoz^M de frecuencias de medias^M
midrange^M

スピーカー・グリル
speaker cover
Abdeckung^F
treillis^M
rejilla^F protectora
griglia^F

低音域用スピーカー
woofer
Tieftöner^M
haut-parleur^M de graves^M
altavoz^M de frecuencias^F de graves^M
woofer^M

振動板
diaphragm
Membran^F
membrane^F
diafragma^M
diaframma^M

情報伝達とオフィス・オートメーション

502

情報伝達 | COMMUNICATIONS
KOMMUNIKATION | COMMUNICATIONS | COMUNICACIONES | COMUNICAZIONI

ステレオ・コンポ

mini stereo sound system | Mini-HiFi[F]-System[N] | minichaîne[F] stéréo | mini-cadena[F] estéreo | mini impianto[M] hi-fi

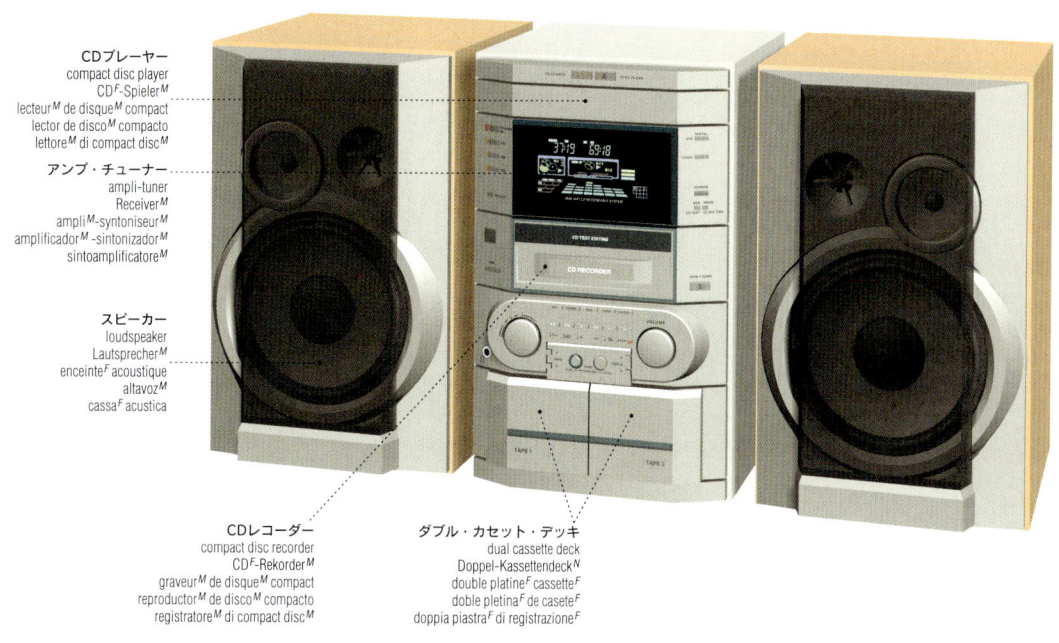

CDプレーヤー
compact disc player
CD[F]-Spieler[M]
lecteur[M] de disque[M] compact
lector de disco[M] compacto
lettore[M] di compact disc[M]

アンプ・チューナー
ampli-tuner
Receiver[M]
ampli[M]-syntoniseur[M]
amplificador[M]-sintonizador[M]
sintoamplificatore[M]

スピーカー
loudspeaker
Lautsprecher[M]
enceinte[F] acoustique
altavoz[M]
cassa[F] acustica

CDレコーダー
compact disc recorder
CD[F]-Rekorder[M]
graveur[M] de disque[M] compact
reproductor[M] de disco[M] compacto
registratore[M] di compact disc[M]

ダブル・カセット・デッキ
dual cassette deck
Doppel-Kassettendeck[N]
double platine[F] cassette[F]
doble pletina[F] de casete[F]
doppia piastra[F] di registrazione[F]

ポータブル音響装置

portable sound systems | tragbare Tonwiedergabesysteme[N] | appareils[M] de son[M] portatifs | sistemas[M] de sonido[M] portátiles | riproduttori[M] portatili

タイマー付きラジオ
clock radio
Uhrenradio[N]
radio[F]-réveil[M]
radio[M] despertador
radiosveglia[F]

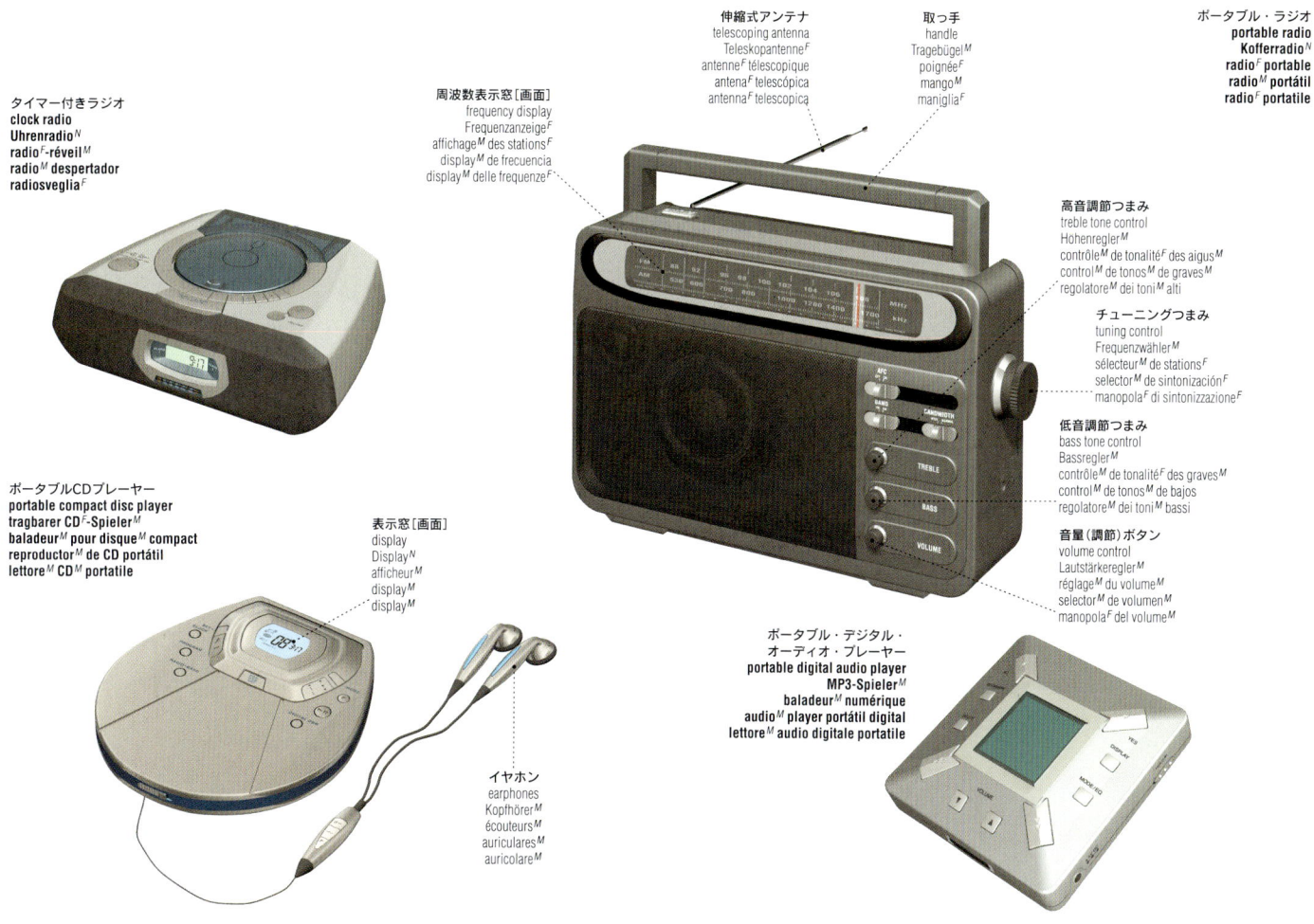

伸縮式アンテナ
telescoping antenna
Teleskopantenne[F]
antenne[F] télescopique
antena[F] telescópica
antenna[F] telescopica

取っ手
handle
Tragebügel[M]
poignée[F]
mango[M]
maniglia[F]

ポータブル・ラジオ
portable radio
Kofferradio[N]
radio[F] portable
radio[M] portátil
radio[F] portatile

周波数表示窓［画面］
frequency display
Frequenzanzeige[F]
affichage[M] des stations[F]
display[M] de frecuencia
display[M] delle frequenze[F]

高音調節つまみ
treble tone control
Höhenregler[M]
contrôle[M] de tonalité[F] des aigus[M]
control[M] de tonos[M] de graves[M]
regolatore[M] dei toni[M] alti

チューニングつまみ
tuning control
Frequenzwähler[M]
sélecteur[M] de stations[F]
selector[M] de sintonización[F]
manopola[F] di sintonizzazione[F]

低音調節つまみ
bass tone control
Bassregler[M]
contrôle[M] de tonalité[F] des graves[M]
control[M] de tonos[M] de bajos[M]
regolatore[M] dei toni[M] bassi

ポータブルCDプレーヤー
portable compact disc player
tragbarer CD[F]-Spieler[M]
baladeur[M] pour disque[M] compact
reproductor[M] de CD portátil
lettore[M] CD[M] portatile

表示窓［画面］
display
Display[N]
afficheur[M]
display[M]
display[M]

音量（調節）ボタン
volume control
Lautstärkeregler[M]
réglage[M] du volume[M]
selector[M] de volumen[M]
manopola[F] del volume[M]

ポータブル・デジタル・
オーディオ・プレーヤー
portable digital audio player
MP3-Spieler[M]
baladeur[M] numérique
audio[M] player portátil digital
lettore[M] audio digitale portatile

イヤホン
earphones
Kopfhörer[M]
écouteurs[M]
auriculares[M]
auricolare[M]

情報伝達とオフィス・オートメーション

503

情報伝達 | COMMUNICATIONS
KOMMUNIKATION | COMMUNICATIONS | COMUNICACIONES | COMUNICAZIONI

ポータブル音響装置

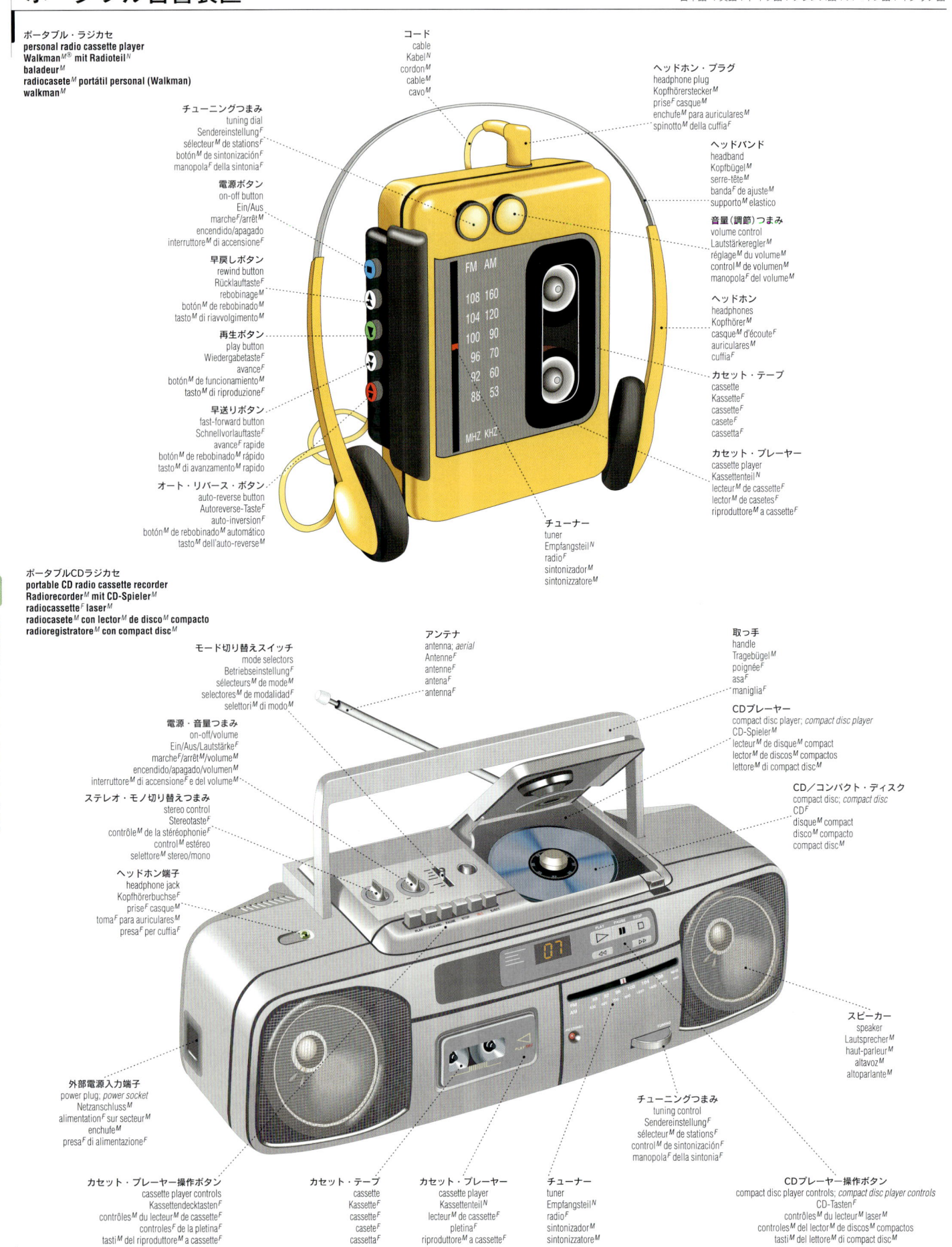

日本語 | 英語 | ドイツ語 | フランス語 | スペイン語 | イタリア語

ポータブル・ラジカセ
personal radio cassette player
Walkman^M® mit Radioteil^N
baladeur^M
radiocasete^M portátil personal (Walkman)
walkman^M

コード
cable
Kabel^N
cordon^M
cable^M
cavo^M

ヘッドホン・プラグ
headphone plug
Kopfhörerstecker^M
prise^F casque^M
enchufe^M para auriculares^M
spinotto^M della cuffia^F

チューニングつまみ
tuning dial
Sendereinstellung^F
sélecteur^M de stations^F
botón^M de sintonización^F
manopola^F della sintonia^F

ヘッドバンド
headband
Kopfbügel^M
serre-tête^M
banda^F de ajuste^M
supporto^M elastico

電源ボタン
on-off button
Ein/Aus
marche^F/arrêt^M
encendido/apagado
interruttore^M di accensione^F

音量(調節)つまみ
volume control
Lautstärkeregler^M
réglage^M du volume^M
control^M de volumen^M
manopola^F del volume^M

早戻しボタン
rewind button
Rücklauftaste^F
rebobinage^M
botón^M de rebobinado^M
tasto^M di riavvolgimento^M

ヘッドホン
headphones
Kopfhörer^M
casque^M d'écoute^F
auriculares^M
cuffia^F

再生ボタン
play button
Wiedergabetaste^F
avance^F
botón^M de funcionamiento^M
tasto^M di riproduzione^F

カセット・テープ
cassette
Kassette^F
cassette^F
casete^F
cassetta^F

早送りボタン
fast-forward button
Schnellvorlauftaste^F
avance^F rapide
botón^M de rebobinado^M rápido
tasto^M di avanzamento^M rapido

カセット・プレーヤー
cassette player
Kassettenteil^N
lecteur^M de cassette^F
lector^M de casetes^F
riproduttore^M a cassette^F

オート・リバース・ボタン
auto-reverse button
Autoreverse-Taste^F
auto-inversion^F
botón^M de rebobinado^M automático
tasto^M dell'auto-reverse^M

チューナー
tuner
Empfangsteil^N
radio^F
sintonizador^M
sintonizzatore^M

ポータブルCDラジカセ
portable CD radio cassette recorder
Radiorecorder^M mit CD-Spieler^M
radiocassette^F laser^M
radiocasete^M con lector^M de disco^M compacto
radioregistratore^M con compact disc^M

モード切り替えスイッチ
mode selectors
Betriebseinstellung^F
sélecteurs^M de mode^M
selectores^M de modalidad^F
selettori^M di modo^M

アンテナ
antenna; aerial
Antenne^F
antenne^F
antena^F
antenna^F

取っ手
handle
Tragebügel^M
poignée^F
asa^M
maniglia^F

電源・音量つまみ
on-off/volume
Ein/Aus/Lautstärke^F
marche^F/arrêt^M/volume^M
encendido/apagado/volumen^M
interruttore^M di accensione^F e del volume^M

CDプレーヤー
compact disc player; compact disc player
CD-Spieler^M
lecteur^M de disque^M compact
lector^M de discos^M compactos
lettore^M di compact disc^M

ステレオ・モノ切り替えつまみ
stereo control
Stereotaste^F
contrôle^M de la stéréophonie^F
control^M estéreo
selettore^M stereo/mono

CD/コンパクト・ディスク
compact disc; compact disc
CD^F
disque^M compact
disco^M compacto
compact disc^M

ヘッドホン端子
headphone jack
Kopfhörerbuchse^F
prise^F casque^M
toma^F para auriculares^M
presa^F per cuffia^F

スピーカー
speaker
Lautsprecher^M
haut-parleur^M
altavoz^M
altoparlante^M

外部電源入力端子
power plug; power socket
Netzanschluss^M
alimentation^F sur secteur^M
enchufe^M
presa^F di alimentazione^F

チューニングつまみ
tuning control
Sendereinstellung^F
sélecteur^M de stations^F
control^M de sintonización^F
manopola^F della sintonia^F

カセット・プレーヤー操作ボタン
cassette player controls
Kassettendecktasten^F
contrôles^M du lecteur^M de cassette^F
controles^M de la pletina^F
tasti^M del riproduttore^M a cassette^F

カセット・テープ
cassette
Kassette^F
cassette^F
casete^F
cassetta^F

カセット・プレーヤー
cassette player
Kassettenteil^N
lecteur^M de cassette^F
pletina^F
riproduttore^M a cassette^F

チューナー
tuner
Empfangsteil^N
radio^F
sintonizador^M
sintonizzatore^M

CDプレーヤー操作ボタン
compact disc player controls; compact disc player controls
CD-Tasten^F
contrôles^M du lecteur^M laser^M
controles^M del lector^M de discos^M compactos
tasti^M del lettore^M di compact disc^M

情報伝達 | COMMUNICATIONS
KOMMUNIKATION | COMMUNICATIONS | COMUNICACIONES | COMUNICAZIONI

無線通信

wireless communication | drahtlose Kommunikation[F] | communication[F] sans fil[M] | comunicación[M] sin hilos[M] | comunicazione[F] senza fili[M]

音量(調節)つまみ
volume control
Lautstärkeregler[M]
réglage[M] du volume[M]
ajuste[M] de volumen[M]
manopola[F] del volume[M]

表示窓[画面]
display
Display[N]
afficheur[M]
display[M]
display[M]

アンテナ
antenna
Antenne[F]
antenne[F]
antena[F]
antenna[F]

ウォーキー・トーキー
walkie-talkie
Walkie-Talkie[N]
talkie-walkie[M]
walkie-talkie[M]
walkie-talkie[M]

コール[呼び出し]ボタン
call button
Ruftaste[F]
touche[F] d'appel[M]
tecla[F] de llamada[F]
tasto[M] di chiamata[F]

電源ボタン
power button
Ein-/Ausschalter[M]
interrupteur[M]
interruptor[M]
interruttore[M] di accensione[F]

ライト・ボタン
light button
Helligkeitstaste[F]
touche[F] de luminosité[F]
tecla[F] de luminosidad[F]
tasto[M] di luminosità[F]

スクロール・ボタン
scroll button
Scrolltaste[F]
touche[F] de défilement[M]
tecla[F] de desplazamiento[M]
tasto[M] di scorrimento[M]

マイク(ロホン)
microphone
Mikrofon[N]
microphone[M]
micrófono[M]
microfono[M]

メニュー・ボタン
menu button
Menütaste[F]
touche[F] de menu[M]
tecla[M] del menú[M]
tasto[M] del menu[M]

ロック・ボタン
lock button
Feststelltaste[F]
touche[F] de verrouillage[M]
tecla[F] de bloqueo[M]
tasto[M] di blocco[M]

モニター・ボタン
monitor button
Kontrolltaste[F]
touche[F] de contrôle[M]
tecla[F] de menú[M]
tasto[M] di controllo[M]

通話スイッチ
push-to-talk switch
Wechselsprechschalter[M]
interrupteur[M] d'émission[F]
interruptor[M] de emisión[F]
interruttore[M] di trasmissione[F]

スピーカー
speaker
Lautsprecher[M]
haut-parleur[M]
altavoz[M]
altoparlante[M]

表示窓[画面]
display
Display[N]
afficheur[M]
display[M]
display[M]

ベルト・クリップ
belt clip
Gürtelclip[M]
pince[F] de ceinture[F]
pinza[F] de cinturón[M]
gancio[M] della cintura[F]

ページャー／ポケット・ベル
numeric pager
Pager[M]
téléavertisseur[M] numérique
buscapersonas[M]
cercapersone[M]

リード・ボタン
read button
Lesetaste[F]
touche[F] de lecture[F]
botón[M] de lectura[F]
tasto[M] di lettura[F]

メニュー・ボタン
menu button
Menütaste[F]
touche[F] de menu[M]
botón[M] del menú[M]
tasto[M] del menu[M]

セレクト[選択]ボタン
select button
Wahltaste[F]
touche[F] de sélection[F]
botón[M] de selección[F]
tasto[M] di selezione[F]

マイク(ロホン)端子
microphone jack
Mikrofonanschlussbuchse[F]
prise[F] microphone[M]
toma[F] del micrófono[M]
presa[F] del microfono[M]

通話スイッチ
push-to-talk switch
Wechselsprechschalter[M]
interrupteur[M] d'émission[F]
interruptor[M] de transmisión[F]
interruttore[M] di trasmissione[F]

マイク(ロホン)
microphone
Mikrofon[N]
microphone[M]
micrófono[M]
microfono[M]

CB無線
CB radio
CB-Funkanlage[F]
poste[M] CB[F]
radio[M] CB
radio[F] CB

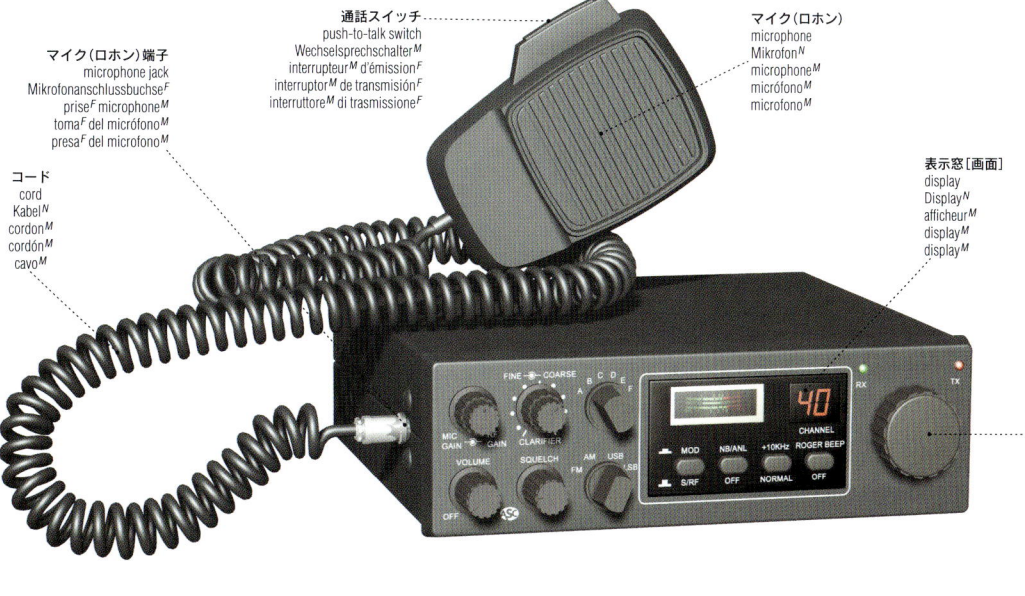

コード
cord
Kabel[N]
cordon[M]
cordón[M]
cavo[M]

表示窓[画面]
display
Display[N]
afficheur[M]
display[M]
display[M]

チャンネル・セレクター
channel selector
Kanalwahlschalter[M]
sélecteur[M] de canaux[M]
selector[M] de canales[M]
selettore[M] dei canali[M]

情報伝達とオフィス・オートメーション

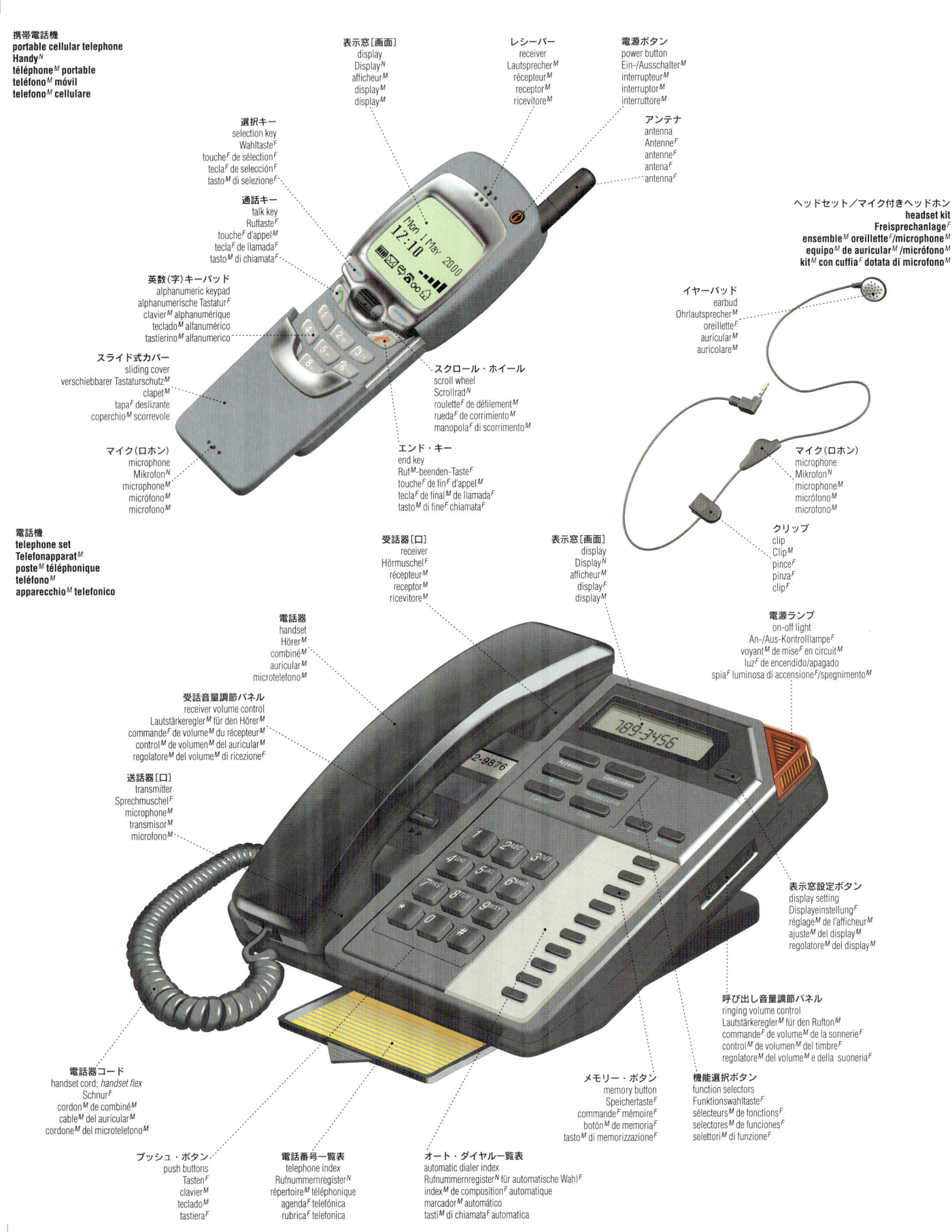

情報伝達 | COMMUNICATIONS
KOMMUNIKATION | COMMUNICATIONS | COMUNICACIONES | COMUNICAZIONI

電話

日本語 | 英語 | ドイツ語 | フランス語 | スペイン語 | イタリア語

communication by telephone | Telefonieren[N] | communication[F] par téléphone[M] | comunicación[F] por teléfono[M] | comunicazione[F] via telefono[M]

携帯電話機
portable cellular telephone
Handy[N]
téléphone[M] **portable**
teléfono[M] **móvil**
telefono[M] **cellulare**

表示窓[画面]
display
Display[N]
afficheur[M]
display[M]
display[M]

レシーバー
receiver
Lautsprecher[M]
récepteur[M]
receptor[M]
ricevitore[M]

電源ボタン
power button
Ein-/Ausschalter[M]
interrupteur[M]
interruptor[M]
interruttore[M]

選択キー
selection key
Wahltaste[F]
touche[F] de sélection[F]
tecla[F] de selección[F]
tasto[M] di selezione[F]

通話キー
talk key
Ruftaste[F]
touche[F] d'appel[M]
tecla[F] de llamada[F]
tasto[M] di chiamata[F]

アンテナ
antenna
Antenne[F]
antenne[F]
antena[F]
antenna[F]

ヘッドセット／マイク付きヘッドホン
headset kit
Freisprechanlage[F]
ensemble[M] **oreillette**[F]/**microphone**[M]
equipo[M] **de auricular**[M] /**micrófono**[M]
kit[M] **con cuffia**[F] **dotata di microfono**[M]

英数(字)キーパッド
alphanumeric keypad
alphanumerische Tastatur[F]
clavier[M] alphanumérique
teclado[M] alfanumérico
tastierino[M] alfanumerico

イヤーバッド
earbud
Ohrlautsprecher[M]
oreillette[F]
auricular[M]
auricolare[M]

スライド式カバー
sliding cover
verschiebbarer Tastaturschutz[M]
clapet[M]
tapa[F] deslizante
coperchio[M] scorrevole

スクロール・ホイール
scroll wheel
Scrollrad[N]
roulette[F] de défilement[M]
rueda[F] de corrimiento[M]
manopola[F] di scorrimento[M]

マイク(ロホン)
microphone
Mikrofon[N]
microphone[M]
micrófono[M]
microfono[M]

エンド・キー
end key
Ruf[M]-beenden-Taste[F]
touche[F] de fin[F] d'appel[M]
tecla[F] de final[M] de llamada[F]
tasto[M] di fine[F] chiamata[F]

マイク(ロホン)
microphone
Mikrofon[N]
microphone[M]
micrófono[M]
microfono[M]

電話機
telephone set
Telefonapparat[M]
poste[M] **téléphonique**
teléfono[M]
apparecchio[M] **telefonico**

受話器[口]
receiver
Hörmuschel[F]
récepteur[M]
receptor[M]
ricevitore[M]

表示窓[画面]
display
Display[N]
afficheur[M]
display[F]
display[M]

クリップ
clip
Clip[M]
pince[F]
pinza[F]
clip[F]

電話器
handset
Hörer[M]
combiné[M]
auricular[M]
microtelefono[M]

電源ランプ
on-off light
An-/Aus-Kontrolllampe[F]
voyant[M] de mise[F] en circuit[M]
luz[F] de encendido/apagado
spia[F] luminosa di accensione[F]/spegnimento[M]

受話音量調節パネル
receiver volume control
Lautstärkeregler[M] für den Hörer[M]
commande[F] de volume[M] du récepteur[M]
control[M] de volumen[M] del auricular[M]
regolatore[M] del volume[M] di ricezione[F]

送話器[口]
transmitter
Sprechmuschel[F]
microphone[M]
transmisor[M]
microfono[M]

表示窓設定ボタン
display setting
Displayeinstellung[F]
réglage[M] de l'afficheur[M]
ajuste[M] del display[M]
regolatore[M] del display[M]

呼び出し音量調節パネル
ringing volume control
Lautstärkeregler[M] für den Rufton[M]
commande[F] de volume[M] de la sonnerie[F]
control[M] de volumen[M] del timbre[M]
regolatore[M] del volume[M] e della suoneria[F]

電話器コード
handset cord; handset flex
Schnur[F]
cordon[M] de combiné[M]
cable[M] del auricular[M]
cordone[M] del microtelefono[M]

プッシュ・ボタン
push buttons
Tasten[F]
clavier[M]
teclado[M]
tastiera[F]

電話番号一覧表
telephone index
Rufnummernregister[N]
répertoire[M] téléphonique
agenda[F] telefónica
rubrica[F] telefonica

オート・ダイヤル一覧表
automatic dialer index
Rufnummernregister[N] für automatische Wahl[F]
index[M] de composition[F] automatique
marcador[M] automático
tasti[M] di chiamata[F] automatica

メモリー・ボタン
memory button
Speichertaste[F]
commande[F] mémoire[F]
botón[M] de memoria[F]
tasto[M] di memorizzazione[F]

機能選択ボタン
function selectors
Funktionswahltaste[F]
sélecteurs[M] de fonctions[F]
selectores[M] de funciones[F]
selettori[M] di funzione[F]

506

情報伝達 | COMMUNICATIONS
KOMMUNIKATION | COMMUNICATIONS | COMUNICACIONES | COMUNICAZIONI

電話

公衆電話機
pay phone
öffentlicher Fernsprecher^M
téléphone^M public
teléfono^M público
apparecchio^M telefonico a gettoni^M

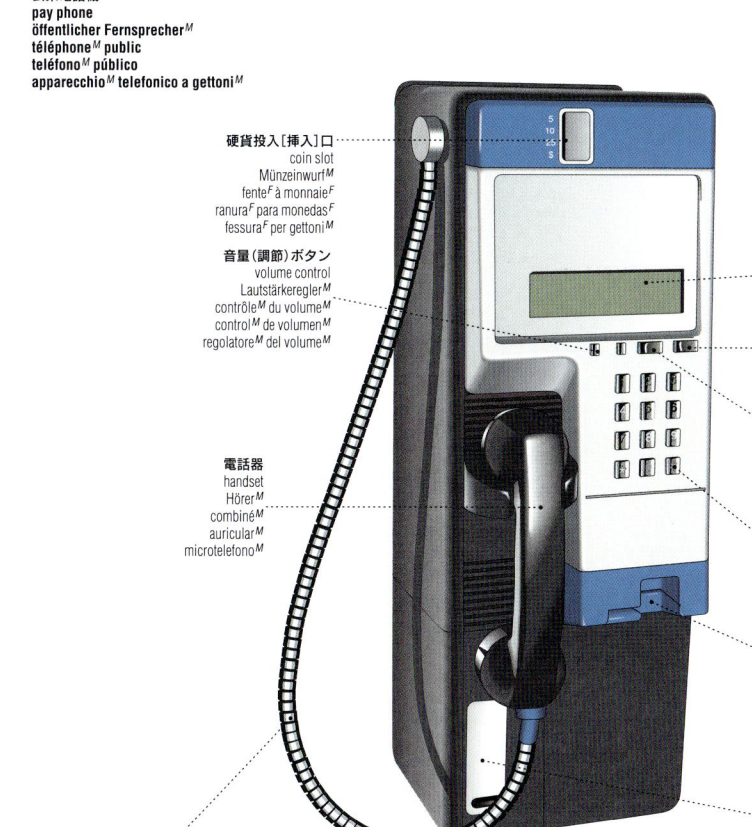

電話機の例
examples of telephones
Beispiele^N für Telefone^N
exemples^M de postes^M téléphoniques
ejemplos^M de teléfonos^M
esempi^M di telefoni^M

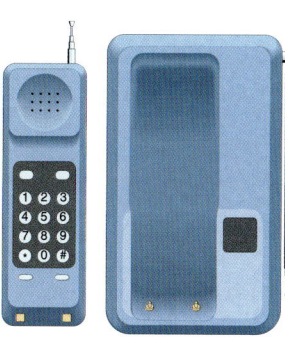

硬貨投入[挿入]口
coin slot
Münzeinwurf^M
fente^F à monnaie^F
ranura^F para monedas^F
fessura^F per gettoni^M

音量(調節)ボタン
volume control
Lautstärkeregler^M
contrôle^M du volume^M
control^M de volumen^M
regolatore^M del volume^M

電話器
handset
Hörer^M
combiné^M
auricular^M
microtelefono^M

表示窓[画面]
display
Display^N
écran^M
visualización^F
display^M

ネクスト・コール・ボタン
next call
nächster Ruf^M
appel^M suivant
próxima llamada^F
tasto^M di chiamata^F successiva

言語表示ボタン
language display button
Sprachanzeigetaste^F
choix^M de la langue^F d'affichage^M
botón^M de selección^F de idioma^M
tasto^M di selezione^F della lingua^F del display^M

プッシュ・ボタン
push button
Taste^F
clavier^M
teclado^M
tastiera^F

カード読み取り装置
card reader
Kartenschlitz^M
lecteur^M de carte^F
lector^M de tarjetas^F
lettore^M di schede^F

コードレス電話機
cordless telephone
schnurloses Telefon^N
poste^M sans cordon^M
teléfono^M inalámbrico
telefono^M senza fili^M

硬貨返却口
coin return bucket
Geldrückgabefach^F
sébile^F de remboursement^M
devolución^F de monedas^F
finestrella^F per la restituzione^F dei gettoni^M

外装コード
armored cord; *armoured flex*
Panzerschnur^F
cordon^M à gaine^F métallique
cable^M con funda^F metálica
cavo^M armato

通信端末
telecommunication terminal
Kommunikationsterminal^N
terminal^M de télécommunication^F
terminal^M de comunicaciones^F
videoterminale^F

ハウジング
housing
Gehäuse^N
boîtier^M
caja^F
monitor^M

表示画面／ディスプレイ
visual display unit
Bildschirm^N
écran^M
monitor^M
schermo^M

機能[ファンクション]キー
function keys
Funktionstasten^F
touches^F de fonctions^F
teclas^F de función^F
tasti^M funzione^F

数字キー／テン・キー
numeric keyboard
numerische Tastatur^F
clavier^M numérique
teclado^M numérico
tastiera^F numerica

英数(字)キーボード
alphanumeric keyboard
alphanumerische Tastatur^F
clavier^M alphanumérique
teclado^M alfanumérico
tastiera^F alfanumerica

プッシュ・ボタン電話機
push-button telephone
Tastentelefon^N
poste^M à clavier^M
teléfono^M de teclado^M
telefono^M a tastiera^F

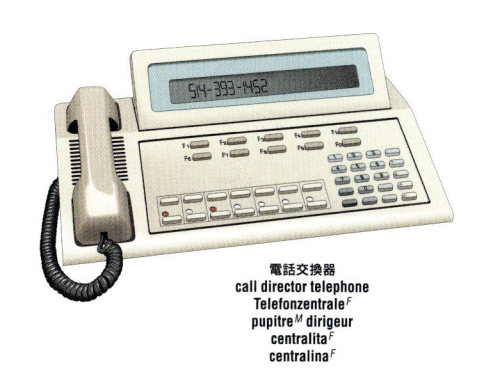

操作キー
operation keys
Bedienungstasten^F
touches^F de commande^F
teclas^F de operación^F
tasti^M di comando^M

キーボード
keyboard
Tastatur^F
clavier^M
teclado^M
tastiera^F

電話交換器
call director telephone
Telefonzentrale^F
pupitre^M dirigeur
centralita
centralina^F

情報伝達とオフィス・オートメーション

507

情報伝達 | COMMUNICATIONS
KOMMUNIKATION | COMMUNICATIONS | COMUNICACIONES | COMUNICAZIONI

電話

日本語 | 英語 | ドイツ語 | フランス語 | スペイン語 | イタリア語

留守番電話機
telephone answering machine
AnrufbeantworterM
répondeurM téléphonique
contestadorM automático
segreteriaF telefonica

着信表示ランプ
calls indicator
NachrichtenanzeigeF
voyantM de réceptionF de messagesM
indicadorM de llamadasF
indicatoreM delle telefonate

伝言録音カセット
incoming message cassette
AufzeichnungskassetteF
cassetteF messagesM
caseteF para grabar los mensajesM
cassettaF dei messaggiM in entrataF

電源表示ランプ
power-on light
NetzkontrolllampeF
voyantM de miseF en circuitM
luzF de encendido
spiaF luminosa di alimentazioneF

応答メッセージ録音カセット
outgoing announcement cassette
AnsagekassetteF
cassetteF annonceF
caseteF con saludoM
cassettaF del messaggioM registrato

自動応答表示ランプ
auto answer indicator
BereitschaftsanzeigeF
voyantM de réponseF automatique
indicadorM de respuestaF automática
indicatoreM del funzionamentoM automatico

再生ボタン
listen button
MithörtasteF
écouteF
botónM de reproducciónF
tastoM di ascoltoM diretto

早送りボタン
fast-forward button
VorlauftasteF
avanceF rapide
botónM de avanceM rápido
tastoM di avanzamentoM rapido

マイク（ロホン）
microphone
MikrofonN
microphoneM
micrófonoM
microfonoM

スピーカー
speaker
LautsprecherM
haut-parleurM
altavozM
altoparlanteM

再生ボタン
on/play button
Einschalt-/WiedergabetasteF
miseF en marcheF
botónM de encendido
tastoM di riascoltoM dei messaggiM

応答メッセージ録音ボタン
record announcement button
AufzeichnungstasteF
enregistrementM
botónM de grabaciónF
tastoM di registrazioneF del messaggioM

停止ボタン
stop button
StopptasteF
arrêtM
botónM de stopM
tastoM di arrestoM

消去ボタン
erase button
LöschtasteF
effacementM
botónM para borrar
tastoM di cancellazioneF

早戻しボタン
rewind button
RücklauftasteF
rebobinageM
botónM de rebobinado
tastoM di riavvolgimentoM

音量（調節）つまみ
volume control
LautstärkereglerM
commandeF de volumeM
controlM del volumenM
regolatoreM del volumeM

電源ボタン
power-on button
NetzschalterM
boutonM de miseF en circuitM
botónM de encendido
pulsanteM di accensioneF

ファクシミリ
facsimile machine
TelefaxgerätN
télécopieurM
faxM
telefaxM

送信トレイ
sent document tray
OriginalrückführungF
sortieF des originauxM
recuperaciónF del documentoM enviado
vassoioM dei documentiM trasmessi

原稿挿入口
document-to-be-sent position
OriginaleinzugM
entréeF des originauxM
posiciónF del documentoM a enviar
puntoM di inserimentoM dei documentiM da trasmettere

受信トレイ
receiving tray
EmpfangM von DokumentenN
réceptionF des messagesM
recepciónF de documentosM
vassoioM dei documentiM ricevuti

ペーパー［原稿］ガイド
paper guide
PapierführungF
guide-papierM
guíaF del papelM
guidaF della cartaF

機能［ファンクション］キー
function keys
FunktionstastenF
panneauM de fonctionsF
teclasF de funciónF
tastiM funzioneF

リセット・キー
reset key
RückstelltasteF
toucheF de correctionF
teclaF de reiniciaciónF
tastoM di resetM

データ表示窓
data display
DatendisplayN
écranM d'affichageM
visualizaciónF de datosM
displayM

スタート・キー
start key
StarttasteF
miseF en marcheF
teclaF de iniciaciónF
tastoM di avvioM

操作［コントロール］パネル
control keys
BedienungstastenF
panneauM de commandeF
teclasF de controlM
tastiM di comandoM

数字キー／テン・キー
number key
NummerntastenF
toucheF de compositionF automatique
tecladoM numéricas
tastieraF numerica

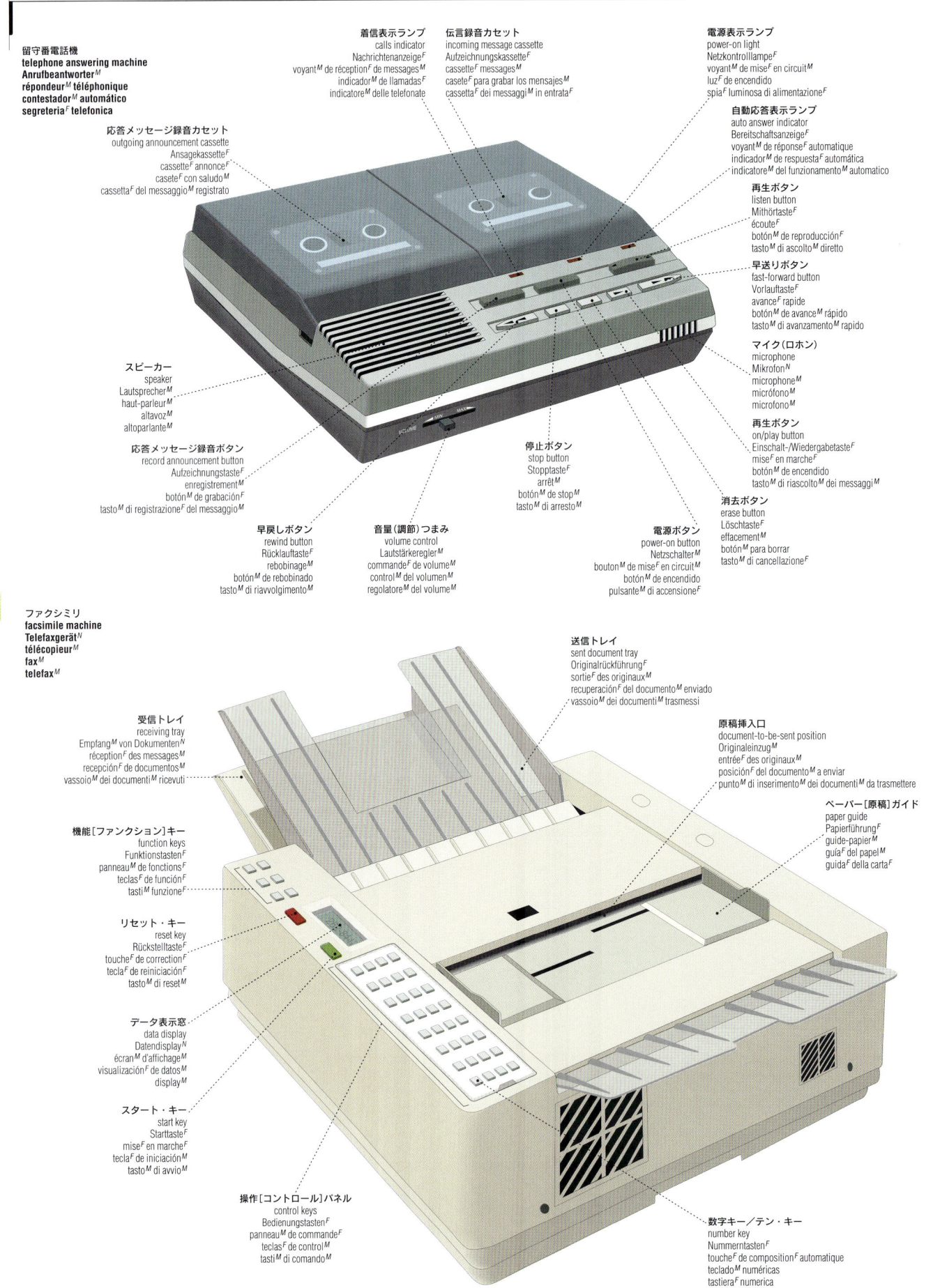

情報伝達とオフィス・オートメーション

オフィス・オートメーション | OFFICE AUTOMATION
BÜROAUTOMATION | BUREAUTIQUE | AUTOMATIZACIÓN DE LA OFICINA | BUROTICA E FORNITURE PER L'UFFICIO

オフィス／事務所

office | Büro[N] | bureau[M] | oficina[F] | ufficio[M]

物置／納戸
storeroom
Abstellraum[M]
débarras[M]
trastero[M]
ripostiglio[M]

郵便室
mail processing room
Poststelle[F]
salle[F] de courrier[M]
sala[F] de correos[M]
stanza[F] della gestione[F] della posta[F]

コピー室
photocopy room
Kopierraum[M]
salle[F] de reprographie[F]
sala[F] de reprografía[F]
stanza[F] della fotocopiatrice[F]

可動仕切り壁［パーティション］
moveable panel
bewegliche Trennwand[F]
cloison[F] mobile
tabique[M] móvil
pannello[M] mobile

会計士事務室
accountant's office
Buchhaltung[F]
comptabilité[F]
contabilidad[F]
ufficio[M] del contabile[M]

ワークステーション
workstation
Arbeitsplatz[M]
poste[M] de travail[M]
puesto[M] de trabajo[M]
postazione[F] di lavoro[M]

プロダクション・マネージャー室
production manager
Produktionsleiter[M]
directeur[M] de production[F]
director[M] de producción[F]
ufficio[M] del direttore[M] della produzione[F]

重役付き秘書室
executive secretary
Sekretärin[F]
secrétaire[M] de direction[F]
secretaría[M] de dirección[F]
stanza[F] della segretaria[F] di direzione[F]

社員食堂
employee lunchroom
Kaffeeküche[F]
cafétéria[F]
comedor[M] de los empleados[M]
sala[F] da pranzo[M] del personale[M]

システム・サポート室
system support
Datentechnik[F]
soutien[M] informatique[F]
soporte[M] informático
stanze[F] del supporto[M] informatico

書類保管室
file room
Archiv[N]
archives[F]
archivo[M]
archivio[M]

支配人室
chief executive officer's office
Büro[N] des Geschäftsführers[M]
bureau[M] du directeur[M] général
oficina[F] del gerente[M]
ufficio[M] del direttore[M] generale

配膳コーナー
kitchen facilities
Kochecke[F]
coin[M] cuisine[F]
cocina[F]
angolo[M] cucina[F]

男子トイレ
gentlemen's toilet
Herrentoilette[F]
w.-c.[M] hommes[M]
aseo[M] de caballeros[M]
bagno[M] degli uomini[M]

女子トイレ
ladies' toilet
Damentoilette[F]
w.-c.[M] femmes[F]
aseo[M] de señoras[F]
bagno[M] delle donne[F]

更衣室
dressing room
Umkleideraum[M]
vestiaire[M]
guardarropa[F]
spogliatoio[M]

非常階段
fire escape stairs
Feuertreppe[F]
escalier[M] de secours[M]
escaleras[F] de incendios[M]
scale[F] antincendio

エントランス・ホール
entrance hall
Eingangshalle[F]
hall[M] d'entrée[F]
hall[F] de entrada
ingresso[M]

エレベーター
elevator; lift
Aufzug[M]
ascenseur
ascensor[M]
ascensore[M]

受付
reception
Empfang[M]
réception[F]
recepción[F]
reception[F]

待合室
waiting room
Warteraum[M]
salle[F] d'attente[F]
sala[F] de espera[F]
sala[F] di attesa[F]

社長秘書室
president's secretary
Chefsekretärin[F]
secrétaire[M] du président[M]
secretaría[F] de dirección[F]
stanza[F] della segretaria[F] dell'amministratore[M] delegato

社長室
president's office
Chefzimmer[N]
bureau[M] du président[M]
despacho[M] del administrador[M] delegado
ufficio[M] dell'amministratore[M] delegato

会議室
conference room
Konferenzraum[M]
salle[F] de conférences[F]
sala[F] de reuniones[F]
sala[F] riunioni[F]

情報伝達とオフィス・オートメーション

オフィス・オートメーション | OFFICE AUTOMATION
BÜROAUTOMATION | BUREAUTIQUE | AUTOMATIZACIÓN DE LA OFICINA | BUROTICA E FORNITURE PER L'UFFICIO

オフィス家具
office furniture | Büromöbel[N] | mobilier[M] de bureau | muebles[M] de oficina[F] | mobili[M] per ufficio[M]

日本語 | 英語 | ドイツ語 | フランス語 | スペイン語 | イタリア語

書類整理用家具
filing furniture
Archivmöbel[N]
meubles[M] de classement[M]
archivadores[M]
mobili[M] di archivio[M]

キャスター付きファイリング・ユニット
mobile filing unit
fahrbare Aktenablage[F]
classeur[M] mobile
archivador[M] móvil
schedario[M] mobile

サイド・チェスト／脇机
mobile drawer unit
fahrbares Schubladenelement[N]
caisson[M]
cajonera[F] móvil
cassettiera[F] mobile

ラテラル・ファイリング・キャビネット
lateral filing cabinet
Hängekartei[F]
classeur[M] à clapets[M]
archivador[M] lateral
schedario[M] a visibilità[F] laterale

保管用家具
storage furniture
Aufbewahrungsmöbel[N]
meubles[M] de rangement[M]
muebles[M] contenedores
mobili[M] contenitori[M]

展示架／雑誌架[棚]
display cabinet
Ausstellungsregal[N]
présentoir[M] à revues[F]
estante[M] para revistas[F]
espositore[M]

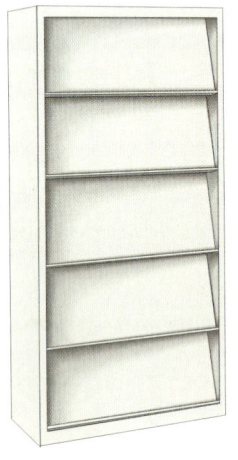

コート掛け[ハンガー／フック]
coat hook
Kleiderhaken[M]
patère[F]
perchero[M] de pared[F]
attaccapanni[M] a muro[M]

可動仕切り壁[パーティション]
movable panel
flexible Trennwand[F]
cloison[F] mobile
tabique[M] móvil
pannello[M] mobile

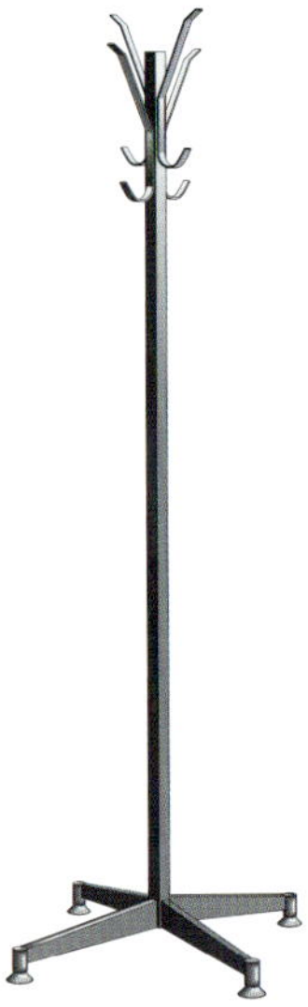

文房具キャビネット
stationery cabinet
Schrank[M]
armoire[F] à papeterie[F]
armario[M] para papelería[F]
armadietto[M] per cancelleria[F]

ロッカー
locker
Kleiderschrank[M]
armoire[F]-vestiaire[F]
guardarropa[M]
armadietto[M]

コート・ラック[置き棚／掛け]
coat rack
Garderobe[F]
vestiaire[M] de bureau[M]
perchero[M]
attaccapanni[M] a rastrelliera[F]

コート[帽子]スタンド
coat tree; hat stand
Garderobenständer[M]
porte-manteau[M]
perchero[M] de pie[M]
attaccapanni[M] a stelo[M]

サイド・キャビネット
credenza
Aktenschrank[M]
bahut[M]
armario[M] bajo
mobile[M] contenitore

情報伝達とオフィス・オートメーション

オフィス・オートメーション | OFFICE AUTOMATION
BÜROAUTOMATION | BUREAUTIQUE | AUTOMATIZACIÓN DE LA OFICINA | BUROTICA E FORNITURE PER L'UFFICIO

オフィス家具

コンピューター・テーブル[デスク]
computer table
Computertisch^M
table^F d'ordinateur^M
mesa^F del ordenador^M
tavolo^M portacomputer

作業用家具
work furniture
Arbeitsmöbel^N
meubles^M de travail^M
muebles^M de trabajo^M
mobili^M da lavoro^M

プリンター・テーブル
printer table
Druckertisch^M
table^F d'imprimante^F
mesa^F de la impresora^F
tavolo^M portastampante

用紙送り口
paper feed channel
Öffnung^F für die Papierzufuhr^F
fente^F d'alimentation
canal^M de arrastre^M del papel^M
fessura^F di alimentazione^F della carta^F

キーボード天板
adjustable platen; *adjustable shelf*
verstellbare Tastaturablage^F
support^M ajustable
plato^M ajustable
ripiano^M regolabile

用紙受け
paper catcher
Papieraufnehmer^M
panier^M de réception^F
bandeja^F para recoger el papel^M
cestello^M di uscita^F della carta^F

パネル
panel
Verblendung^F
panneau^M de modestie^F
panel^M
pannello^M frontale

用紙トレイ
paper tray
Papierablage^F
panier^M d'alimentation^F
bandeja^F para el papel^M
cestello^M di alimentazione^F della carta^F

オフィス・チェアー
typist's chair
Bürodrehstuhl^M
chaise^F dactylo^M
silla^F de secretaria^F
sedia^F dattilo

エグゼクティブ・デスク／
両袖事務机／重役机
executive desk
Chefschreibtisch^M
bureau^M de direction^F
escritorio^M de ejecutivo^M
scrivania^F direzionale

デスク・マット
desk mat; *desk pad*
Schreibunterlage^F
sous-main^M
vade^M
sottomano^M

脇机
return
Winkeltisch^M
retour^M
mesa^M auxiliar de escritorio^M
appendice^F dattilo

キャスター付き肘掛け椅子
swivel-tilter armchair
Drehsessel^M
fauteuil^M pivotant à bascule^F
sillón^M giratorio
poltrona^F girevole reclinabile

セクレタリー・デスク
secretarial desk
Arbeitsplatz^M
bureau^M secrétaire^M
escritorio^M de secretaria^F
scrivania^F operativa

情報伝達とオフィス・オートメーション

511

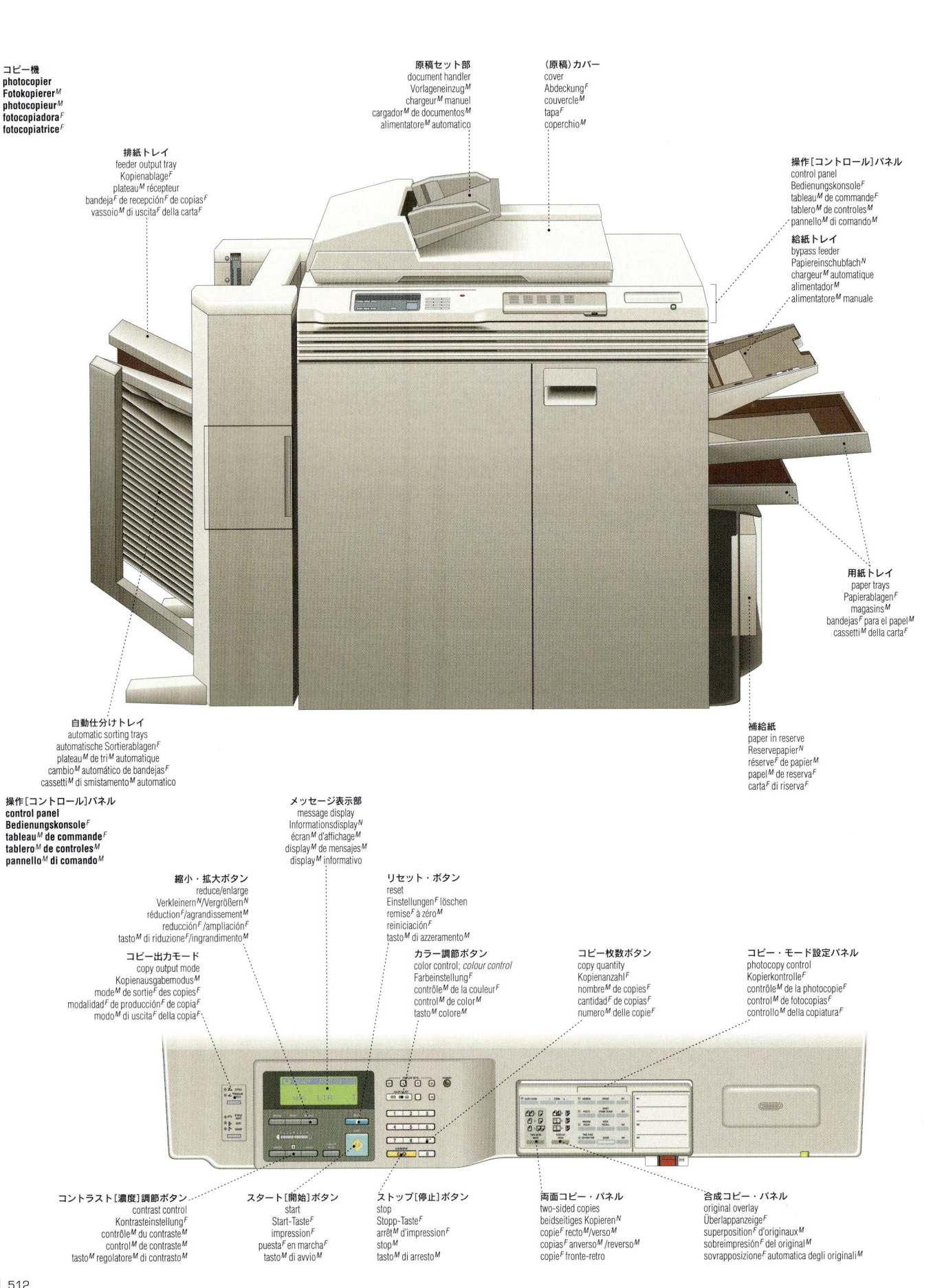

オフィス・オートメーション | OFFICE AUTOMATION
BÜROAUTOMATION | BUREAUTIQUE | AUTOMATIZACIÓN DE LA OFICINA | BUROTICA E FORNITURE PER L'UFFICIO

オフィス家具

日本語 | 英語 | ドイツ語 | フランス語 | スペイン語 | イタリア語

コピー機
photocopier
Fotokopierer^M
photocopieur^M
fotocopiadora^F
fotocopiatrice^F

排紙トレイ
feeder output tray
Kopienablage^F
plateau^M récepteur
bandeja^F de recepción^F de copias^F
vassoio^M di uscita^F della carta^F

原稿セット部
document handler
Vorlageneinzug^M
chargeur^M manuel
cargador^M de documentos^M
alimentatore^M automatico

（原稿）カバー
cover
Abdeckung^F
couvercle^M
tapa^F
coperchio^M

操作[コントロール]パネル
control panel
Bedienungskonsole^F
tableau^M de commande^F
tablero^M de controles^M
pannello^M di comando^M

給紙トレイ
bypass feeder
Papiereinschubfach^N
chargeur^M automatique
alimentador^M
alimentatore^M manuale

用紙トレイ
paper trays
Papierablagen^F
magasins^M
bandejas^F para el papel^M
cassetti^M della carta^F

自動仕分けトレイ
automatic sorting trays
automatische Sortierablagen^F
plateau^M de tri^M automatique
cambio^M automático de bandejas^F
cassetti^M di smistamento^M automatico

補給紙
paper in reserve
Reservepapier^N
réserve^F de papier^M
papel^M de reserva^F
carta^F di riserva^F

操作[コントロール]パネル
control panel
Bedienungskonsole^F
tableau^M de commande^F
tablero^M de controles^M
pannello^M di comando^M

メッセージ表示部
message display
Informationsdisplay^N
écran^M d'affichage^M
display^M de mensajes^M
display^M informativo

縮小・拡大ボタン
reduce/enlarge
Verkleinern^N/Vergrößern^N
réduction^F/agrandissement^M
reducción^F/ampliación^F
tasto^M di riduzione^F/ingrandimento^M

リセット・ボタン
reset
Einstellungen^F löschen
remise^F à zéro^M
reiniciación^F
tasto^M di azzeramento^M

コピー出力モード
copy output mode
Kopienausgabemodus^M
mode^M de sortie^F des copies^F
modalidad^F de producción^F de copia^F
modo^M di uscita^F della copia^F

カラー調節ボタン
color control; colour control
Farbeinstellung^F
contrôle^M de la couleur^F
control^M de color^M
tasto^M colore^M

コピー枚数ボタン
copy quantity
Kopienanzahl^F
nombre^M de copies^F
cantidad^F de copias^F
numero^M delle copie^F

コピー・モード設定パネル
photocopy control
Kopierkontrolle^F
contrôle^M de la photocopie^F
control^M de fotocopias^F
controllo^M della copiatura^F

コントラスト[濃度]調節ボタン
contrast control
Kontrasteinstellung^F
contrôle^M du contraste^M
control^M de contraste^M
tasto^M regolatore^M di contrasto^M

スタート[開始]ボタン
start
Start-Taste^F
impression^F
puesta^F en marcha^F
tasto^M di avvio^M

ストップ[停止]ボタン
stop
Stopp-Taste^F
arrêt^M d'impression^F
stop^M
tasto^M di arresto^M

両面コピー・パネル
two-sided copies
beidseitiges Kopieren^N
copie^F recto^M/verso^M
copias^F anverso^M/reverso^M
copie^F fronte-retro

合成コピー・パネル
original overlay
Überlappanzeige^F
superposition^F d'originaux^M
sobreimpresión^F del original^M
sovrapposizione^F automatica degli originali^M

情報伝達とオフィス・オートメーション

オフィス・オートメーション | OFFICE AUTOMATION
BÜROAUTOMATION | BUREAUTIQUE | AUTOMATIZACIÓN DE LA OFICINA | BUROTICA E FORNITURE PER L'UFFICIO

パーソナル・コンピューター／パソコン

personal computer | Personalcomputer^M | micro-ordinateur^M | ordenador^M personal | personal computer^M

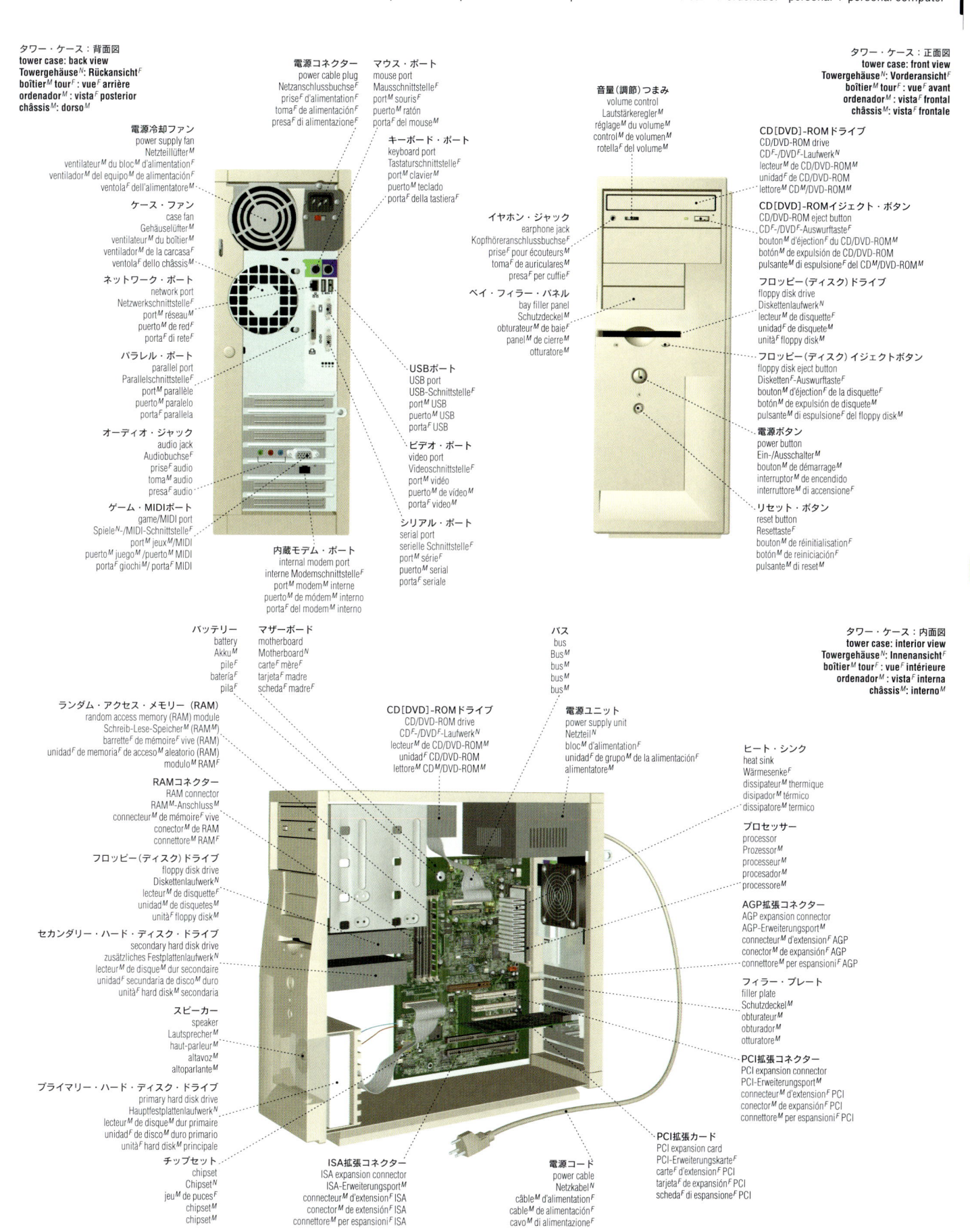

タワー・ケース：背面図
tower case: back view
Towergehäuse^N: Rückansicht^F
boîtier^M tour^F : vue^F arrière
ordenador^M : vista^F posterior
châssis^M: dorso^M

電源冷却ファン
power supply fan
Netzteillüfter^M
ventilateur^M du bloc^M d'alimentation^F
ventilador^M del equipo^M de alimentación^F
ventola^F dell'alimentatore^M

ケース・ファン
case fan
Gehäuselüfter^M
ventilateur^M du boîtier^M
ventilador^M de la carcasa^F
ventola^F dello chàssis^M

ネットワーク・ポート
network port
Netzwerkschnittstelle^F
port^M réseau
puerto^M de red^F
porta^F di rete^F

パラレル・ポート
parallel port
Parallelschnittstelle^F
port^M parallèle
puerto^M paralelo
porta^F parallela

オーディオ・ジャック
audio jack
Audiobuchse^F
prise^F audio
toma^F audio
presa^F audio

ゲーム・MIDIポート
game/MIDI port
Spiele^N-/MIDI-Schnittstelle^F
port^M jeux^M/MIDI
puerto^M juego^M /puerto^M MIDI
porta^F giochi^M/ porta^F MIDI

電源コネクター
power cable plug
Netzanschlussbuchse^F
prise^F d'alimentation^F
toma^F de alimentación^F
presa^F di alimentazione^F

マウス・ポート
mouse port
Mausschnittstelle^F
port^M souris^F
puerto^M ratón
porta^F del mouse^M

キーボード・ポート
keyboard port
Tastaturschnittstelle^F
port^M clavier^M
puerto^M teclado
porta^F della tastiera^F

イヤホン・ジャック
earphone jack
Kopfhöreranschlussbuchse^F
prise^F pour écouteurs^M
toma^F de auriculares^M
presa^F per cuffie^F

USBポート
USB port
USB-Schnittstelle^F
port^M USB
puerto^M USB
porta^F USB

ビデオ・ポート
video port
Videoschnittstelle^F
port^M vidéo
puerto^M de vídeo^M
porta^F video

シリアル・ポート
serial port
serielle Schnittstelle^F
port^M série^F
puerto^M serial
porta^F seriale

内蔵モデム・ポート
internal modem port
interne Modemschnittstelle^F
port^M modem^M interne
puerto^M de módem^M interno
porta^F del modem^M interno

音量(調節)つまみ
volume control
Lautstärkeregler^M
réglage^M du volume^M
control^M de volumen^M
rotella^F del volume^M

タワー・ケース：正面図
tower case: front view
Towergehäuse^N: Vorderansicht^F
boîtier^M tour^F : vue^F avant
ordenador^M : vista^F frontal
chàssis^M: vista^F frontale

CD[DVD]-ROMドライブ
CD/DVD-ROM drive
CD^F-/DVD^F-Laufwerk^N
lecteur^M de CD/DVD-ROM^M
unidad^F de CD/DVD-ROM
lettore^M CD^M/DVD-ROM^M

CD[DVD]-ROMイジェクト・ボタン
CD/DVD-ROM eject button
CD^F-/DVD^F-Auswurftaste^F
bouton^M d'éjection^F du CD/DVD-ROM^M
botón^M de expulsión de CD/DVD-ROM
pulsante^M di espulsione^F del CD^M/DVD-ROM^M

フロッピー(ディスク)ドライブ
floppy disk drive
Diskettenlaufwerk^N
lecteur^M de disquette^F
unidad^F de disquete^M
unità^F floppy disk^M

フロッピー(ディスク)イジェクトボタン
floppy disk eject button
Disketten^F-Auswurftaste^F
bouton^M d'éjection^F de la disquette^F
botón^M de expulsión de disquete^M
pulsante^M di espulsione^F del floppy disk^M

電源ボタン
power button
Ein-/Ausschalter^M
bouton^M de démarrage^M
interruptor^M de encendido
interruttore^M di accensione^F

リセット・ボタン
reset button
Resettaste^F
bouton^M de réinitialisation^F
botón^M de reiniciación^F
pulsante^M di reset^M

バッテリー
battery
Akku^M
pile^F
batería^F
pila^F

マザーボード
motherboard
Motherboard^N
carte^F mère^F
tarjeta^F madre
scheda^F madre

ランダム・アクセス・メモリー（RAM）
random access memory (RAM) module
Schreib-Lese-Speicher (RAM^M)
barrette^F de mémoire^F vive (RAM)
unidad^F de memoria^F de acceso^M aleatorio (RAM)
modulo^M RAM^F

RAMコネクター
RAM connector
RAM^M-Anschluss^M
connecteur^M de mémoire^F vive
conector^M de RAM
connettore^M RAM^F

フロッピー(ディスク)ドライブ
floppy disk drive
Diskettenlaufwerk^N
lecteur^M de disquette^F
unidad^M de disquetes^M
unità^F floppy disk^M

セカンダリー・ハード・ディスク・ドライブ
secondary hard disk drive
zusätzliches Festplattenlaufwerk^N
lecteur^M de disque^M dur secondaire
unidad^F secundaria de disco^M duro
unità^F hard disk^M secondaria

スピーカー
speaker
Lautsprecher^M
haut-parleur^M
altavoz^M
altoparlante^M

プライマリー・ハード・ディスク・ドライブ
primary hard disk drive
Hauptfestplattenlaufwerk^N
lecteur^M de disque^M dur primaire
unidad^F de disco^M duro primario
unità^F hard disk^M principale

チップセット
chipset
Chipset^N
jeu^M de puces^F
chipset^M
chipset^M

CD[DVD]-ROMドライブ
CD/DVD-ROM drive
CD^F-/DVD^F-Laufwerk^N
lecteur^M de CD/DVD-ROM^M
unidad^F de CD/DVD-ROM
lettore^M CD^M/DVD-ROM^M

ISA拡張コネクター
ISA expansion connector
ISA-Erweiterungsport^M
connecteur^M d'extension^F ISA
conector^M de extensión^F ISA
connettore^M per espansioni^F ISA

バス
bus
Bus^M
bus^M
bus^M
bus^M

電源ユニット
power supply unit
Netzteil^N
bloc^M d'alimentation^F
unidad^F de grupo^M de la alimentación^F
alimentatore^M

電源コード
power cable
Netzkabel^N
câble^M d'alimentation^F
cable^M de alimentación^F
cavo^M di alimentazione^F

タワー・ケース：内面図
tower case: interior view
Towergehäuse^N: Innenansicht^F
boîtier^M tour^F : vue^F intérieure
ordenador^M : vista^F interna
chàssis^M: interno^M

ヒート・シンク
heat sink
Wärmesenke^F
dissipateur^M thermique
disipador^M térmico
dissipatore^M termico

プロセッサー
processor
Prozessor^M
processeur^M
procesador^M
processore^M

AGP拡張コネクター
AGP expansion connector
AGP-Erweiterungsport^M
connecteur^M d'extension^F AGP
conector^M de expansión^F AGP
connettore^M per espansioni^F AGP

フィラー・プレート
filler plate
Schutzdeckel^M
obturateur^M
obturador^M
otturatore^M

PCI拡張コネクター
PCI expansion connector
PCI-Erweiterungsport^M
connecteur^M d'extension^F PCI
conector^M de expansión^F PCI
connettore^M per espansioni^F PCI

PCI拡張カード
PCI expansion card
PCI-Erweiterungskarte^F
carte^F d'extension^F PCI
tarjeta^F de expansión^F PCI
scheda^F di espansione^F PCI

ベイ・フィラー・パネル
bay filler panel
Schutzdeckel^M
obturateur^M de baie^F
panel^M de cierre^M
otturatore^M

情報伝達とオフィス・オートメーション

オフィス・オートメーション | OFFICE AUTOMATION
BÜROAUTOMATION | BUREAUTIQUE | AUTOMATIZACIÓN DE LA OFICINA | BUROTICA E FORNITURE PER L'UFFICIO

入力装置

日本語 | 英語 | ドイツ語 | フランス語 | スペイン語 | イタリア語

input devices | Eingabegeräte^N | périphériques^M d'entrée^F | unidades^F de entrada^F de información^F | dispositivi^M di entrata^F

キーボードとピクトグラム [絵文字]
keyboard and pictograms
Tastatur^F und Piktogramme^N
clavier^M et pictogrammes^M
teclado^M y pictogramas^M
tastiera^F e pittogrammi^M

ファンクション [機能] キー
function keys
Funktionstasten^F
touches^F de fonction^F
tecla^F de funciones^F
tasti^M funzione^F

インターネット・キー
Internet keys
Internet^N-Tasten^F
touches^F Internet^M
tecla^F Internet
tasti^M Internet

Eメール・キー
e-mail key
E-Mail^F-Taste^F
touche^F de courriel^M
tecla^F email
tasto^M email

エスケープ・キー
escape key
Escapetaste^F
touche^F d'échappement^M
tecla^F escape
tasto^M Esc

タブ・キー
tabulation key
Tabulatortaste^F
touche^F de tabulation^F
tecla^F tabulación
tasto^M di tabulazione

キャップス・ロック・キー
capitals lock key
Großschriftfeststellungstaste^F
touche^F de verrouillage^F des majuscules^F
tecla^F bloqueo^M mayúsculas
tasto^M di blocco^M delle maiuscole^F

シフト・キー
shift key
Umschalttasten^F
touche^F majuscule^F
tecla^F de mayúsculas^F
tasto^M delle maiuscole^F

コントロール・キー
control key
Steuerungstaste^F
touche^F de contrôle^M
tecla^F de servicio^M
tasto^M Control

スタート・キー
start key
Startmenütaste^F
touche^F de démarrage^M
tecla^F inicio
tasto^M Avvio^M

オルト [アルト] キー
alternative key
Alt-Taste^F
touche^F alternative
tecla^F alternativa
tasto^M Alt

取り外し式パーム・レスト
detachable palm rest
abnehmbare Handballenauflage^F
repose-poignets^M détachable
reposamanos^M
poggiamano^M amovibile

スペース・バー
space bar
Leertaste^F
barre^F d'espacement^M
barra^F espaciadora
barra^F spaziatrice

英数字キーパッド
alphanumeric keypad
alphanumerische Tastatur^F
pavé^M alphanumérique
teclado^M alfanumérico
tastiera^F alfanumerica

エスケープ
escape
Abbruch^M
échappement^M
escape^M
escape^M

左揃えタブ
tabulation left
Tabulator^M nach links
tabulation^F à gauche
tabulación^F a la izquierda^F
tabulazione^F a sinistra^F

右揃えタブ
tabulation right
Tabulator^M nach rechts
tabulation^F à droite
tabulación^F a la derecha^F
tabulazione^F a destra^F

キャップス・ロック
capitals lock
Großschriftfeststellung^F
verrouillage^M des majuscules^F
bloqueo^M mayúsculas^M
blocco^M delle maiuscole^F

オルト／アルト：レベル3セレクト
alternate: level 3 select
Alternative^F: Drittbelegung^F
alternative : sélection^F du niveau^M 3
alternado: selección^F de nivel^M 3
alternato^M: selezione^F di livello^M 3

シフト：レベル2セレクト
shift: level 2 select
Großschriftumschaltung^F: Zweitbelegung^F
majuscule^F : sélection^F du niveau^M 2
mayúscula^F : selección^F de nivel^M 2
maiuscola^F: selezione^F di livello^M 2

コントロール：グループ・セレクト
control: group select
Steuerung^F: Gruppenwahl^F
contrôle^M : sélection^F de groupe^M
control^M: selección^F de grupo^M
controllo^M: selezione^F di gruppo^M

コントロール
control
Steuerung^F
contrôle^M
control^M
controllo^M

オルト／アルト
alternate
Alternative^F
alternative
alternativa^F
alternato^M

スペース
space
Leerzeichen^N
espace^F
espacio^M
spazio^M

ノンブレーキング・スペース
nonbreaking space
geschütztes Leerzeichen^N
espace^F insécable
espacio^M sin pausa^F
spazio^M unificatore

情報伝達とオフィス・オートメーション

514

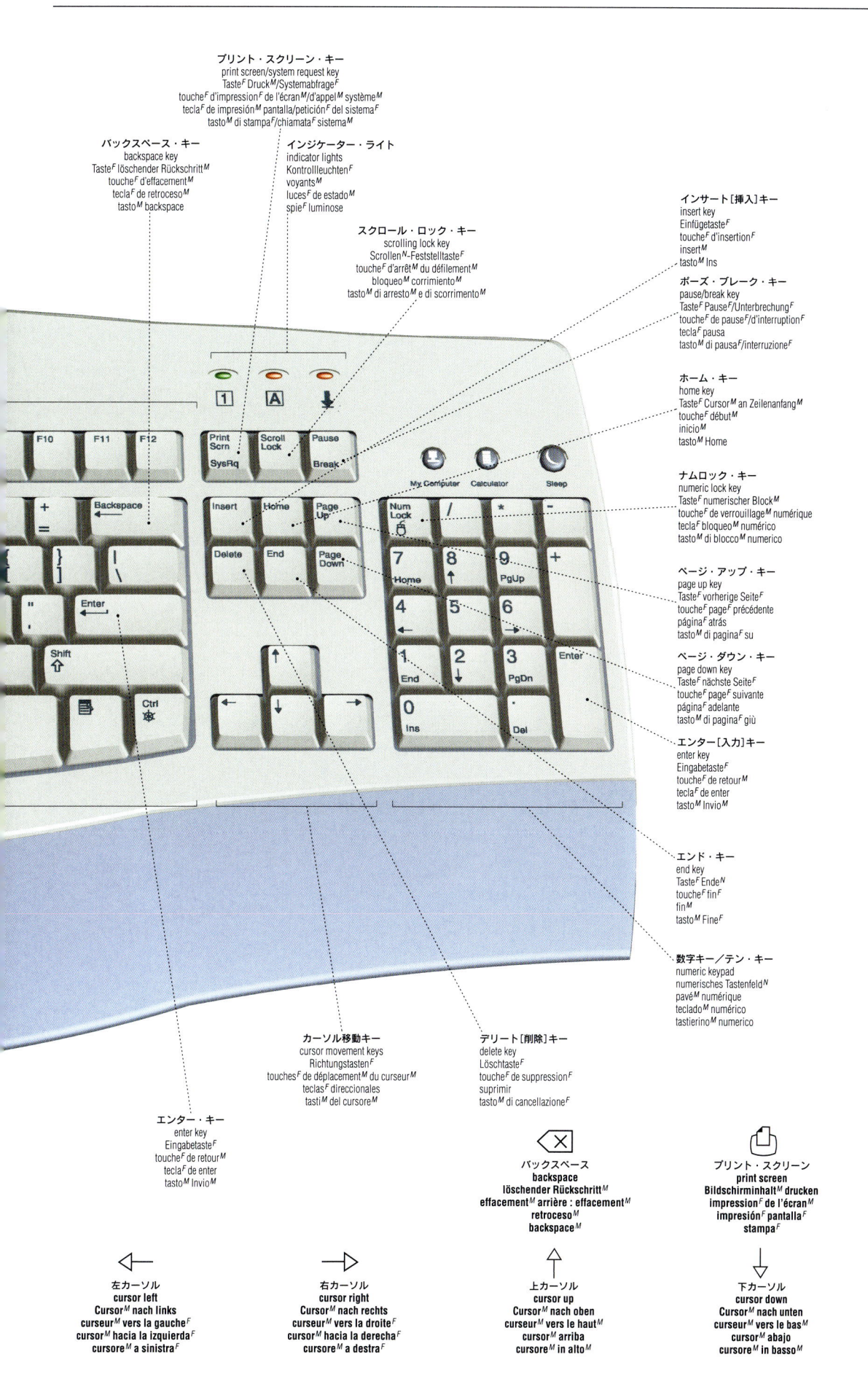

オフィス・オートメーション | OFFICE AUTOMATION
BÜROAUTOMATION | BUREAUTIQUE | AUTOMATIZACIÓN DE LA OFICINA | BUROTICA E FORNITURE PER L'UFFICIO

入力装置

プリント・スクリーン・キー
print screen/system request key
Taste^F Druck^M/Systemabfrage^F
touche^F d'impression^F de l'écran^M/d'appel^M système^M
tecla^F de impresión^M pantalla/petición^F del sistema^M
tasto^M di stampa^F/chiamata^F sistema^M

バックスペース・キー
backspace key
Taste^F löschender Rückschritt^M
touche^F d'effacement^M
tecla^F de retroceso^M
tasto^M backspace

インジケーター・ライト
indicator lights
Kontrollleuchten^F
voyants^M
luces^F de estado^M
spie^F luminose

スクロール・ロック・キー
scrolling lock key
Scrollen^N-Feststelltaste^F
touche^F d'arrêt^M du défilement^M
bloqueo^M corrimiento^M
tasto^M di arresto^M e di scorrimento^M

インサート［挿入］キー
insert key
Einfügetaste^F
touche^F d'insertion^F
insert^M
tasto^M Ins

ポーズ・ブレーク・キー
pause/break key
Taste^F Pause^F/Unterbrechung^F
touche^F de pause^F/d'interruption^F
tecla^F pausa
tasto^M di pausa^F/interruzione^F

ホーム・キー
home key
Taste^F Cursor^M an Zeilenanfang^M
touche^F début^M
inicio^M
tasto^M Home

ナムロック・キー
numeric lock key
Taste^F numerischer Block^M
touche^F de verrouillage^M numérique
tecla^F bloqueo^M numérico
tasto^M di blocco^M numerico

ページ・アップ・キー
page up key
Taste^F vorherige Seite^F
touche^F page^F précédente
página^F atrás
tasto^M di pagina^F su

ページ・ダウン・キー
page down key
Taste^F nächste Seite^F
touche^F page^F suivante
página^F adelante
tasto^M di pagina^F giù

エンター［入力］キー
enter key
Eingabetaste^F
touche^F de retour^M
tecla^F de enter
tasto^M Invio^M

エンド・キー
end key
Taste^F Ende^N
touche^F fin^F
fin^M
tasto^M Fine^F

数字キー／テン・キー
numeric keypad
numerisches Tastenfeld^N
pavé^M numérique
teclado^M numérico
tastierino^M numerico

カーソル移動キー
cursor movement keys
Richtungstasten^F
touches^F de déplacement^M du curseur^M
teclas^F direccionales
tasti^M del cursore^M

デリート［削除］キー
delete key
Löschtaste^F
touche^F de suppression^F
suprimir
tasto^M di cancellazione^F

エンター・キー
enter key
Eingabetaste^F
touche^F de retour^M
tecla^F de enter
tasto^M Invio^M

バックスペース
backspace
löschender Rückschritt^M
effacement^M arrière : effacement^M
retroceso^M
backspace^M

プリント・スクリーン
print screen
Bildschirminhalt^M drucken
impression^F de l'écran^M
impresión^F pantalla^F
stampa^F

左カーソル
cursor left
Cursor^M nach links
curseur^M vers la gauche^F
cursor^M hacia la izquierda^F
cursore^M a sinistra^F

右カーソル
cursor right
Cursor^M nach rechts
curseur^M vers la droite^F
cursor^M hacia la derecha^F
cursore^M a destra^F

上カーソル
cursor up
Cursor^M nach oben
curseur^M vers le haut^M
cursor^M arriba
cursore^M in alto^M

下カーソル
cursor down
Cursor^M nach unten
curseur^M vers le bas^M
cursor^M abajo
cursore^M in basso^M

ポーズ
pause
Pause^F
pause^F
pausa^F
pausa^F

ブレーク
break
Unterbrechung^F
interruption^F
pausa^F
interruzione^F

ナムロック
numeric lock
numerischer Block^M
verrouillage^M numérique
bloqueo^M numérico
blocco^M numerico

スクローリング
scrolling
Scrollen^N
défilement^M
desplazamiento^M
scorrimento^M

インサート／挿入
insert
Einfügen^N
insertion^F
insertar
inserimento^M

デリート／削除
delete
Löschen^N
suppression^F
borrar
cancellazione^F

ホーム
home
Cursor^M an Zeilenanfang^M
début^M
inicio^M
home^F

エンド
end
Cursor^M an Zeilenende^N
fin^F
fin^M
fine^F

ページ・アップ
page up
vorherige Seite^F
page^F précédente
ventana^F arriba
pagina^F precedente

ページ・ダウン
page down
nächste Seite^F
page^F suivante
ventana^F abajo
pagina^F successiva

リターン
return
Eingabe^F
retour^M
retorno^M
invio^M

情報伝達とオフィス・オートメーション

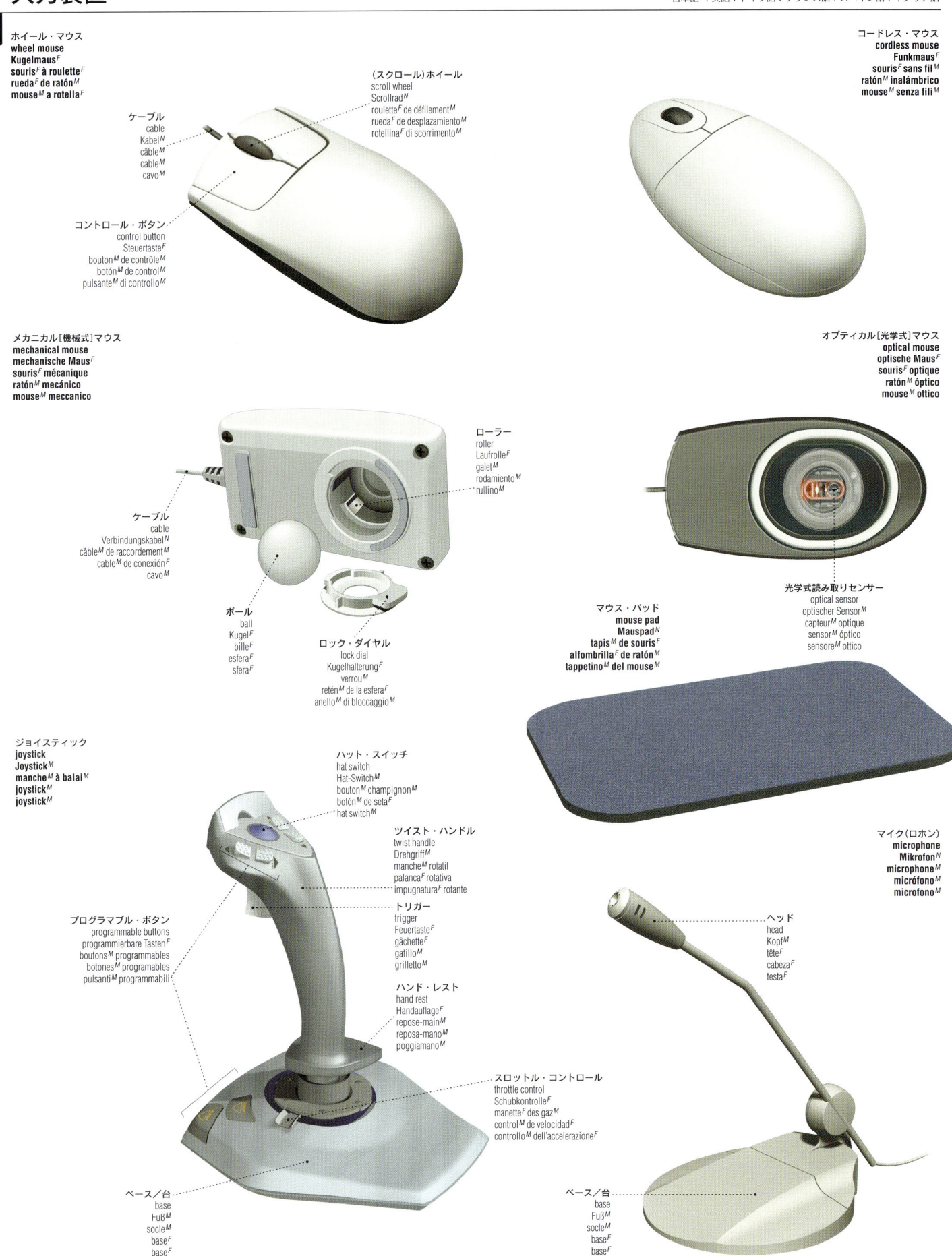

オフィス・オートメーション | OFFICE AUTOMATION
BÜROAUTOMATION | BUREAUTIQUE | AUTOMATIZACIÓN DE LA OFICINA | BUROTICA E FORNITURE PER L'UFFICIO

入力装置

日本語 | 英語 | ドイツ語 | フランス語 | スペイン語 | イタリア語

ホイール・マウス
wheel mouse
Kugelmaus^F
souris^F à roulette^F
rueda^F de ratón^M
mouse^M a rotella^F

(スクロール)ホイール
scroll wheel
Scrollrad^N
roulette^F de défilement^M
rueda^F de desplazamiento^M
rotellina^F di scorrimento^M

ケーブル
cable
Kabel^N
câble^M
cable^M
cavo^M

コントロール・ボタン
control button
Steuertaste^F
bouton^M de contrôle^M
botón^M de control^M
pulsante^M di controllo^M

コードレス・マウス
cordless mouse
Funkmaus^F
souris^F sans fil^M
ratón^M inalámbrico
mouse^M senza fili^M

メカニカル[機械式]マウス
mechanical mouse
mechanische Maus^F
souris^F mécanique
ratón^M mecánico
mouse^M meccanico

ローラー
roller
Laufrolle^F
galet^M
rodamiento^M
rullino^M

ケーブル
cable
Verbindungskabel^N
câble^M de raccordement^M
cable^M de conexión^F
cavo^M

ボール
ball
Kugel^F
bille^F
esfera^F
sfera^F

ロック・ダイヤル
lock dial
Kugelhalterung^F
verrou^M
retén^M de la esfera^F
anello^M di bloccaggio^M

オプティカル[光学式]マウス
optical mouse
optische Maus^F
souris^F optique
ratón^M óptico
mouse^M ottico

光学式読み取りセンサー
optical sensor
optischer Sensor^M
capteur^M optique
sensor^M óptico
sensore^M ottico

マウス・パッド
mouse pad
Mauspad^N
tapis^M de souris^F
alfombrilla^F de ratón^M
tappetino^M del mouse^M

ジョイスティック
joystick
Joystick^M
manche^M à balai^M
joystick^M
joystick^M

ハット・スイッチ
hat switch
Hat-Switch^M
bouton^M champignon^M
botón^M de seta^F
hat switch^M

ツイスト・ハンドル
twist handle
Drehgriff^M
manche^M rotatif
palanca^F rotativa
impugnatura^F rotante

プログラマブル・ボタン
programmable buttons
programmierbare Tasten^F
boutons^M programmables
botones^M programables
pulsanti^M programmabili

トリガー
trigger
Feuertaste^F
gâchette^F
gatillo^M
grilletto^M

ハンド・レスト
hand rest
Handauflage^F
repose-main^M
reposa-mano^M
poggiamano^M

スロットル・コントロール
throttle control
Schubkontrolle^F
manette^F des gaz^M
control^M de velocidad^F
controllo^M dell'accelerazione^F

ベース／台
base
Fuß^M
socle^M
base^F
base^F

マイク(ロホン)
microphone
Mikrofon^N
microphone^M
micrófono^M
microfono^M

ヘッド
head
Kopf^M
tête^F
cabeza^F
testa^F

ベース／台
base
Fuß^M
socle^M
base^F
base^F

情報伝達とオフィス・オートメーション

516

オフィス・オートメーション | OFFICE AUTOMATION
BÜROAUTOMATION | BUREAUTIQUE | AUTOMATIZACIÓN DE LA OFICINA | BUROTICA E FORNITURE PER L'UFFICIO

入力装置

トラックボール
trackball
Rollkugel^F
boule^F
trackball^M
trackball^M

タブレット
digitizing pad
Digitalisierungsunterlage^F
tablette^F graphique
tableta^F digitalizada
tavoletta^F grafica

スタイラス・ホルダー
stylus holder
Stifthalter^M
porte-stylet^M
porta stilus^M
portastilo^M

スタイラス（ペン）
stylus
Stift^M
stylet^M
stylus
stilo^F

CD - ROMプレーヤー
CD/ROM player
CD-ROM-Laufwerk^N
lecteur^M de disque^M compact
lector^M de CD-ROM
lettore^M di compact disc^M

ケーブル
cable
Kabel^N
câble^M
cable^M
cavo^M

レンズ
lens
Objektiv^N
objectif^M
objetivo^M
obiettivo^M

マイク（ロホン）
microphone
Mikrofon^N
microphone^M
micrófono^M
microfono^M

ウェブカメラ／ウェブカム
Webcam
Webcam^F
webcaméra^F
cámara^F web
webcam^F

ベース／台
base
Fuß^M
socle^M
base^F
base^F

バー・コード・リーダー
bar code reader
Strichcodeleser^M
lecteur^M de code-barres^M
lector^M de código^M de barras^M
lettore^M dei codici^M a barre^F

デジタル・カメラ
digital camera
Digitalkamera^F
appareil^M numérique
cámara^F digital
macchina^F fotografica digitale

デジタル・カムコーダー
digital camcorder
Digital-Camcorder^M
caméscope^M numérique
camcorder^M digital
videocamera^F digitale

（光学式）スキャナー
optical scanner
Scanner^M
scanneur^M
escáner^M
scanner^M

情報伝達とオフィス・オートメーション

オフィス・オートメーション | OFFICE AUTOMATION
BÜROAUTOMATION | BUREAUTIQUE | AUTOMATIZACIÓN DE LA OFICINA | BUROTICA E FORNITURE PER L'UFFICIO

出力装置

日本語 | 英語 | ドイツ語 | フランス語 | スペイン語 | イタリア語

output devices | Ausgabegeräte[N] | périphériques[M] de sortie[F] | unidades[F] de salida[F] de información[F] | dispositivi[M] di uscita[F]

フラット・スクリーン・モニター
flat screen monitor
Flachbildschirm[M]
écran[M] **plat**
pantalla[F] **plana**
monitor[M] **a schermo**[M] **piatto**

モニター／ディスプレイ
video monitor
Bildschirm[M]
écran[M]
monitor[M] **de vídeo**[M]
monitor[M]

垂直調節つまみ
vertical control
vertikale Einstellung[F]
réglage[M] vertical
control[M] vertical
regolazione[F] verticale

水平調節つまみ
horizontal control
horizontale Einstellung[F]
réglage[M] horizontal
control[M] horizontal
regolazione[F] orizzontale

センタリング調節つまみ
centering control; *centring control*
Zentriereinstellung[F]
réglage[M] de centrage
control[M] de centrado[M]
regolatore[M] di centratura[F]

コントラスト調節つまみ
contrast control
Kontrastregler[M]
réglage[M] du contraste
control[M] de contraste[M]
regolatore[M] di contrasto[M]

電源表示ランプ
power indicator
Leuchtanzeige[F]
témoin[M] d'alimentation[F]
indicador[M] de encendido
spia[F] di alimentazione[F]

電源スイッチ
power switch
Netzschalter[M]
interrupteur[M]
interruptor[M]
interruttore[M] di accensione[F]

輝度調節つまみ
brightness control
Helligkeitsregler[M]
réglage[M] de la luminosité[F]
control[M] de brillo[M]
regolatore[M] di luminosità[F]

プロジェクター
projector
Projektor[M]
vidéoprojecteur[M]
proyector[M]
proiettore[M]

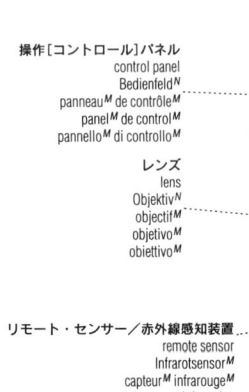

操作［コントロール］パネル
control panel
Bedienfeld[N]
panneau[M] de contrôle[M]
panel[M] de control[M]
pannello[M] di controllo[M]

レンズ
lens
Objektiv[N]
objectif[M]
objetivo[M]
obiettivo[M]

リモート・センサー／赤外線感知装置
remote sensor
Infrarotsensor[M]
capteur[M] infrarouge[M]
sensor infrarrojos
telesensore[M]

電源スイッチ
power switch
Ein-/Ausschalter[M]
interrupteur[M] d'alimentation[F]
interruptor[M] de encendido
interruttore[M] di accensione[F]

コネクター・パネル
connector panel
Anschlussfeld[N]
panneau[M] de connexions[F]
panel[M] de conexión[F]
pannello[M] di connessione[F]

コンピューター・コネクター
computer connector
Computeranschlussbuchse[F]
entrée[F] informatique
conector[M] del ordenador[M]
ingresso[M] per il computer[M]

マウス・ポート
mouse port
Mausschnittstelle[F]
port[M] souris[F]
conector[M] del ratón[M]
porta[F] del mouse[M]

情報伝達とオフィス・オートメーション

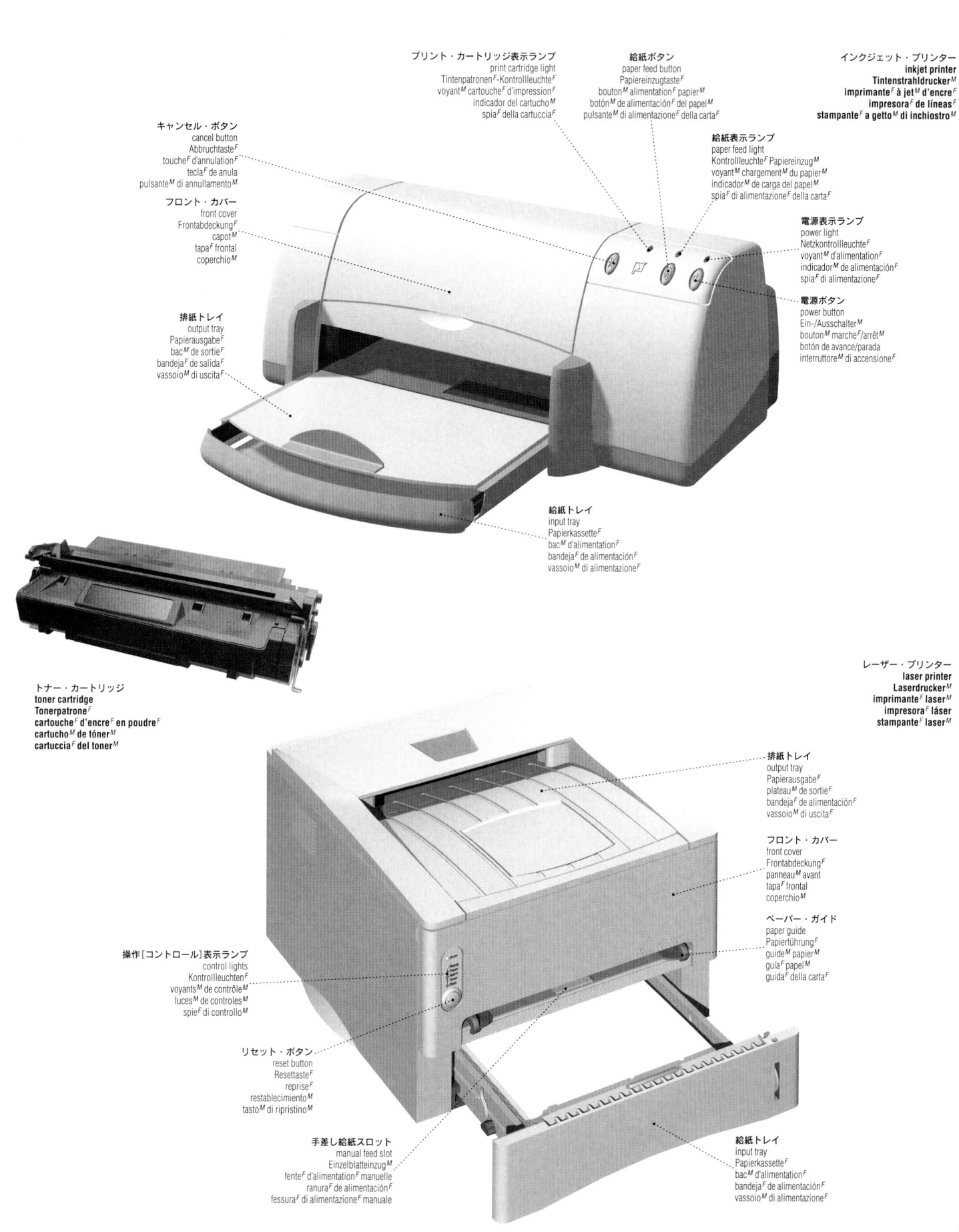

オフィス・オートメーション | OFFICE AUTOMATION
BÜROAUTOMATION | BUREAUTIQUE | AUTOMATIZACIÓN DE LA OFICINA | BUROTICA E FORNITURE PER L'UFFICIO

出力装置

プリント・カートリッジ表示ランプ
print cartridge light
Tintenpatronen^F-Kontrollleuchte^F
voyant^M cartouche^F d'impression^F
indicador del cartucho^M
spia^F della cartuccia^F

給紙ボタン
paper feed button
Papiereinzugtaste^F
bouton^M alimentation^F papier^M
botón^M de alimentación^F del papel^M
pulsante^M di alimentazione^F della carta^F

インクジェット・プリンター
inkjet printer
Tintenstrahldrucker^M
imprimante^F à jet^M d'encre^F
impresora^F de líneas^F
stampante^F a getto^M di inchiostro^M

キャンセル・ボタン
cancel button
Abbruchtaste^F
touche^F d'annullation^F
tecla^F de anula
pulsante^M di annullamento^M

給紙表示ランプ
paper feed light
Kontrollleuchte^F Papiereinzug^M
voyant^M chargement^M du papier^M
indicador^M de carga del papel^M
spia^F di alimentazione^F della carta^F

フロント・カバー
front cover
Frontabdeckung^F
capot^M
tapa^F frontal
coperchio^M

電源表示ランプ
power light
Netzkontrollleuchte^F
voyant^M d'alimentation^F
indicador^M de alimentación^F
spia^F di alimentazione^F

排紙トレイ
output tray
Papierausgabe^F
bac^M de sortie^F
bandeja^F de salida^F
vassoio^M di uscita^F

電源ボタン
power button
Ein-/Ausschalter^M
bouton^M marche^F/arrêt^M
botón de avance/parada
interruttore^F di accensione^F

給紙トレイ
input tray
Papierkassette^F
bac^M d'alimentation^F
bandeja^F de alimentación^F
vassoio^M di alimentazione^F

トナー・カートリッジ
toner cartridge
Tonerpatrone^F
cartouche^F d'encre^F en poudre^F
cartucho^M de tóner^M
cartuccia^F del toner^M

レーザー・プリンター
laser printer
Laserdrucker^M
imprimante^F laser
impresora^F láser
stampante^F laser

排紙トレイ
output tray
Papierausgabe^F
plateau^M de sortie^F
bandeja^F de alimentación^F
vassoio^M di uscita^F

フロント・カバー
front cover
Frontabdeckung^F
panneau^M avant
tapa^F frontal
coperchio^M

ペーパー・ガイド
paper guide
Papierführung^F
guide^M papier^M
guía^F papel^M
guida^F della carta^F

操作［コントロール］表示ランプ
control lights
Kontrollleuchten^F
voyants^M de contrôle^M
luces^M de controles^M
spie^F di controllo^M

リセット・ボタン
reset button
Resettaste^F
reprise^F
restablecimiento^M
tasto^M di ripristino^M

手差し給紙スロット
manual feed slot
Einzelblatteinzug^M
fente^F d'alimentation^F manuelle
ranura^F de alimentación^F
fessura^F di alimentazione^F manuale

給紙トレイ
input tray
Papierkassette^F
bac^M d'alimentation^F
bandeja^F de alimentación^F
vassoio^M di alimentazione^F

情報伝達とオフィス・オートメーション

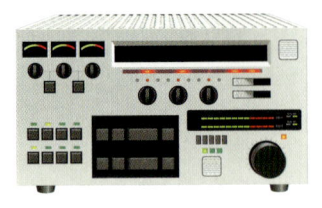

オフィス・オートメーション | OFFICE AUTOMATION
BÜROAUTOMATION | BUREAUTIQUE | AUTOMATIZACIÓN DE LA OFICINA | BUROTICA E FORNITURE PER L'UFFICIO

出力装置

日本語 | 英語 | ドイツ語 | フランス語 | スペイン語 | イタリア語

デスクトップ・ビデオ装置
desktop video unit
Schreibtisch-Videogerät^N
unité^F vidéo
consola^F de la unidad^F de vídeo^M
unità^F video^M da tavolo^M

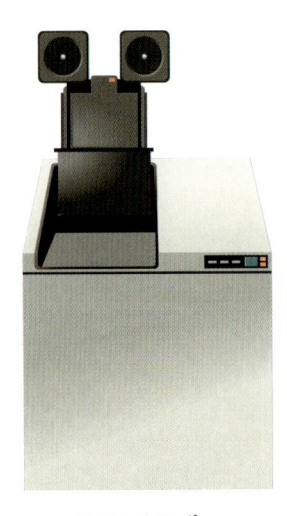

フィルム・レコーダー
film recorder
Filmaufnahmegerät^N
enregistreur^M de film^M
filmadora^F
registratore^M di microfilm^M

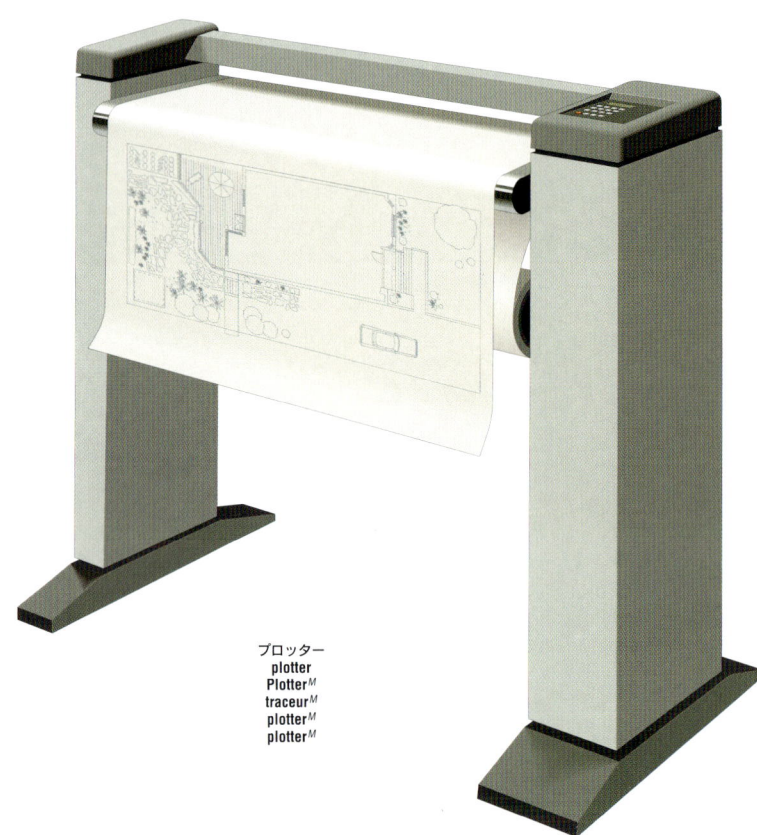

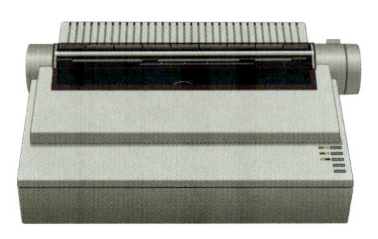

ドット・プリンター
dot matrix printer
Nadeldrucker^M
imprimante^F matricielle
impresora^F matriz
stampante^F ad aghi^M

プロッター
plotter
Plotter^M
traceur^M
plotter^M
plotter^M

補助[無停電]電源装置（UPS）

uninterruptible power supply (UPS) | unterbrechungsfreie Stromversorgung^F (USV) | onduleur^M | sistema^F de alimentación ininterrumpida (SAI/UPS) | gruppo^M di continuità^F

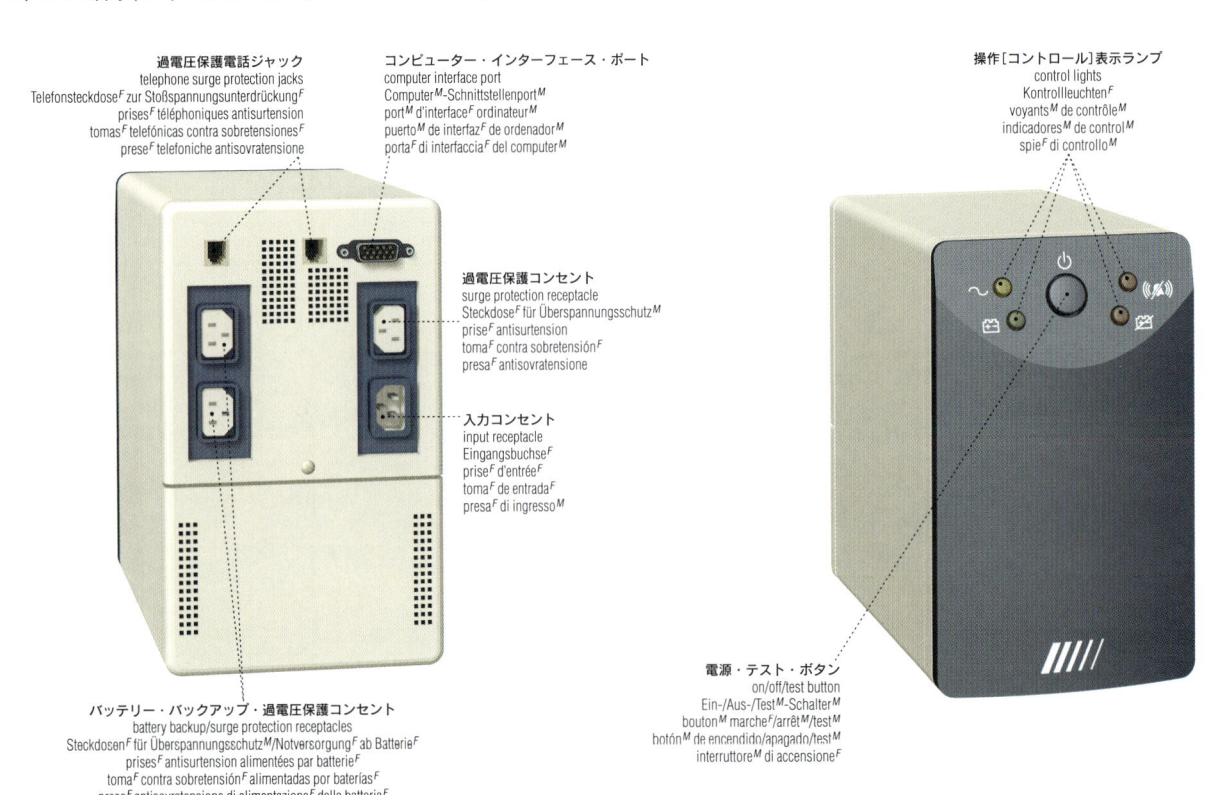

過電圧保護電話ジャック
telephone surge protection jacks
Telefonsteckdose^F zur Stoßspannungsunterdrückung^F
prises^F téléphoniques antisurtension
tomas^F telefónicas contra sobretensiones^F
prese^F telefoniche antisovratensione

コンピューター・インターフェース・ポート
computer interface port
Computer^M-Schnittstellenport^M
port^M d'interface^F ordinateur^M
puerto^M de interfaz^F de ordenador^M
porta^F di interfaccia^F del computer^M

操作[コントロール]表示ランプ
control lights
Kontrollleuchten^F
voyants^M de contrôle^M
indicadores^M de control^M
spie^F di controllo^M

過電圧保護コンセント
surge protection receptacle
Steckdose^F für Überspannungsschutz^M
prise^F antisurtension
toma^F contra sobretensión^F
presa^F antisovratensione

入力コンセント
input receptacle
Eingangsbuchse^F
prise^F d'entrée^F
toma^F de entrada^F
presa^F di ingresso^M

バッテリー・バックアップ・過電圧保護コンセント
battery backup/surge protection receptacles
Steckdosen^F für Überspannungsschutz^M/Notversorgung^F ab Batterie^F
prises^F antisurtension alimentées par batterie^F
toma^F contra sobretensión^F alimentadas por baterías^F
prese^F antisovratensione di alimentazione^F della batteria^F

電源・テスト・ボタン
on/off/test button
Ein-/Aus-/Test^M-Schalter^M
bouton^M marche/arrêt^M/test^M
botón^M de encendido/apagado/test^M
interruttore^M di accensione^F

オフィス・オートメーション | OFFICE AUTOMATION
BÜROAUTOMATION | BUREAUTIQUE | AUTOMATIZACIÓN DE LA OFICINA | BUROTICA E FORNITURE PER L'UFFICIO

データ記憶装置

data storage devices | Speichergeräte[N] | périphériques[M] de stockage[M] | unidades[F] de almacenamiento[F] de información[F] | dispositivi[M] di memorizzazione[F] dei dati[M]

外付け[取り外し可能]ハード・ディスク・ドライブ
removable hard disk drive
externes Festplattenlaufwerk[N]
lecteur[M] de disque[M] dur amovible
unidad[F] de disco[M] duro extraíble
unità[F] hard disk[M] estraibile

ハード・ディスク・ドライブ／HDD
hard disk drive; *hard disk drive*
Festplattenlaufwerk[N]
lecteur[M] de disque[M] dur
unidad[F] del disco[M] duro
unità[F] hard disk[M]

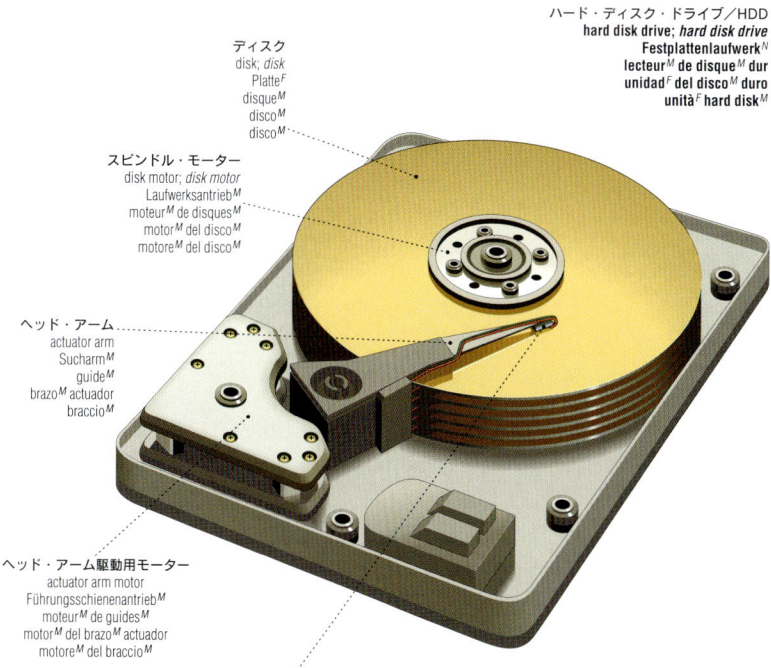

ディスク
disk; *disk*
Platte[F]
disque[M]
disco[M]
disco[M]

スピンドル・モーター
disk motor; *disk motor*
Laufwerksantrieb[M]
moteur[M] de disques[M]
motor[M] del disco[M]
motore[M] del disco[M]

ヘッド・アーム
actuator arm
Sucharm[M]
guide[M]
brazo[M] actuador
braccio[M]

ディスク・イジェクト[取り出し]ボタン
disk eject button
Diskettenauswurftaste[F]
bouton[M] d'éjection[F] du disque[M]
botón[M] de expulsión[F] del disco[M]
pulsante[M] di espulsione[F] del disco[M]

外付け[取り外し可能]
ハード・ディスク
removable hard disk
herausnehmbare Festplatte[F]
disque[M] dur amovible
disco[M] duro extraíble
hard disk[M] estraibile

ヘッド・アーム駆動用モーター
actuator arm motor
Führungsschienenantrieb[M]
moteur[M] de guides[M]
motor[M] del brazo[M] actuador
motore[M] del braccio[M]

読み取り・書き込みヘッド
read/write head
Schreib-/Lesekopf[M]
tête[F] de lecture[F]/écriture[F]
cabeza[F] de lectura[F]/escritura[F]
testina[F] di lettura[F]/scrittura[F]

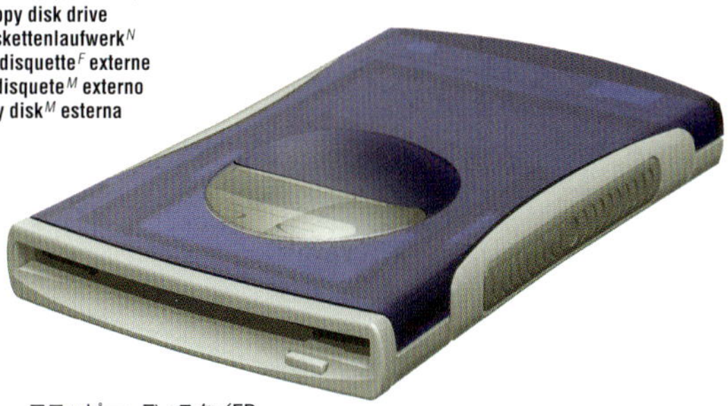

DVDレコーダー
DVD recorder
DVD[F]-Rekorder[M]
graveur[M] de DVD[M]
reproductor[M] de DVD
registratore[M] DVD

外付けフロッピー（ディスク）ドライブ
external floppy disk drive
externes Diskettenlaufwerk[N]
lecteur[M] de disquette[F] externe
unidad[F] de disquete[M] externo
unità[F] floppy disk[M] esterna

フロッピー・ディスク／FD
diskette
Diskette[F]
disquette[F]
disquete[M]
floppy disk[M]

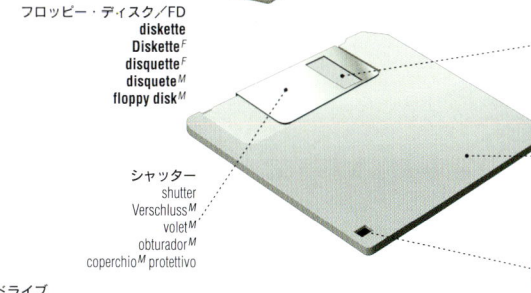

アクセス・ウインドー
access window
Zugriffsöffnung[F]
fenêtre[F] de lecture[F]
ventana[F] de acceso[M]
finestra[F] di accesso[M]

ジャケット
jacket
Hülle[F]
enveloppe[F]
carcasa[F]
involucro[M]

コンパクト・ディスク・リライタブル[CD - RW]レコーダー
compact disc rewritable recorder
Rewritable-Rekorder[M]
graveur[M] de disque[M] compact réinscriptible
grabador[M] de CD[M] compacto regrabable
registratore[M] di compact disc[M] riscrivibili

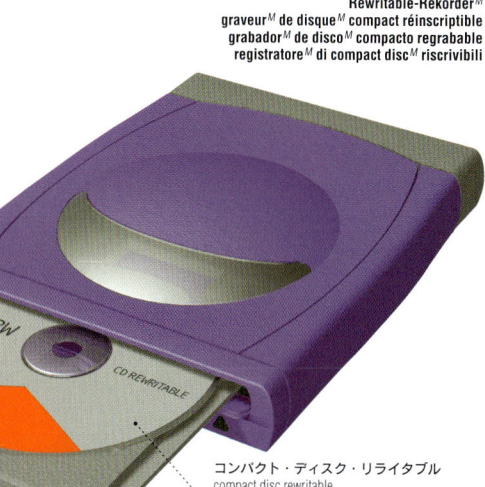

シャッター
shutter
Verschluss[M]
volet[M]
obturador[M]
coperchio[M] protettivo

書き込み禁止タブ
protect tab
Schreibschutz[M]
taquet[M] de verrouillage[M]
lengüeta[F] protectora
linguetta[F] di protezione[F]

カセット・ドライブ
cassette drive
Kassettenlaufwerk[N]
lecteur[M] de cassette[F]
unidad[F] de casetes[F]
drive[M] per cassette[F]

カセット
cassette
Kassette[F]
cassette[F]
casete[F]
cassetta[F]

ディスク・トレイ
disc tray
CD[F]-Lade[F]
plateau[M] de chargement[M]
alojamiento[F] de disco[M]
vassoio[M] portadischi

コンパクト・ディスク・リライタブル
compact disc rewritable
wiederbeschreibbare CD[F]
disque[M] compact réinscriptible
disco[M] compacto
compact disc[M] riscrivibile

情報伝達とオフィス・オートメーション

521

オフィス・オートメーション | OFFICE AUTOMATION
BÜROAUTOMATION | BUREAUTIQUE | AUTOMATIZACIÓN DE LA OFICINA | BUROTICA E FORNITURE PER L'UFFICIO

通信装置

日本語 | 英語 | ドイツ語 | フランス語 | スペイン語 | イタリア語

communication devices | Übertragungsgeräte[N] | périphériques[M] de communication[F] | unidades[F] de comunicación[F] | dispositivi[M] di comunicazione[F]

ネットワーク（インターフェース）カード
network interface card
Netzwerkkarte[F], LAN-Karte[F]
carte[F] réseau[M]
tarjeta[F] de interfaz[F] de red[F]
scheda[F] di rete[F]

ネットワーク・アクセス・
ポイント・トランシーバー
network access point transceiver
Basisstation[F] für Funknetzwerk[N]
émetteur[M]-récepteur[M] d'accès[M] réseau[M]
emisor[M]-receptor[M] de acceso[M] a la red[F]
ricetrasmittente[F] di accesso[M] alla rete[F]

ワイヤレス[無線]ネットワーク
（インターフェース）カード
wireless network interface card
Funknetzwerkkarte[F], wireless-LAN-Karte[F]
carte[F] réseau[M] sans fil[M]
tarjeta[F] de interfaz[F] de red[F] sin hilos[M]
scheda[F] di rete[F] senza fili[M]

モデム
modem
Modem[N]
modem[M]
módem[M]
modem[M]

ネットワークの例

examples of networks | Beispiele[N] für Netzwerke[N] | exemples[M] de réseaux[M] | ejemplos[M] de redes[F] | esempi[M] di reti[F]

リング型ネットワーク
ring network
Ringnetzwerk[N]
réseau[M] en anneau[M]
red[F] en anillo[M]
rete[F] ad anello[M]

サーバー
server
Server[M]
serveur[M]
servidor[M]
server[M]

リング
ring
Ringnetzwerk[N]
anneau[M]
anillo[M]
anello[M]

スター型ネットワーク
star network
Sternnetzwerk[N]
réseau[M] en étoile[F]
red[F] en estrella[F]
rete[F] a stella[F]

デスクトップ・コンピューター
desktop computer
Tischcomputer[M]
ordinateur[M] de bureau[M]
ordenador[M] de sobremesa[F]
computer[M] da tavolo[M]

デスクトップ・コンピューター
desktop computer
Tischcomputer[M]
ordinateur[M] de bureau[M]
ordenador[M] de sobremesa[F]
computer[M] da tavolo[M]

サーバー
server
Server[M]
serveur[M]
servidor[M]
server[M]

バス型ネットワーク
bus network
Busnetzwerk[N]
réseau[M] en bus[M]
red[F] en bus[M]
rete[F] a bus[M]

デスクトップ・コンピューター
desktop computer
Tischcomputer[M]
ordinateur[M] de bureau[M]
ordenador de sobremesa[F]
computer[M] da tavolo[M]

Tコネクター
T-connector
T[N]-Verbinder
connecteur[M] en T[M]
conector[M] en T[F]
connettore[M] a T[F]

ハブ
hub
Hub[M]
concentrateur[M]
concentrador[M]
hub[M]

バス
bus
Bus[M]
bus[M]
bus[M]
bus[M]

ターミネーター／終端器
terminator
Netzabschlusswiderstand[M]
terminateur[M]
terminador[M]
terminatore[M]

情報伝達とオフィス・オートメーション

オフィス・オートメーション | OFFICE AUTOMATION
BÜROAUTOMATION | BUREAUTIQUE | AUTOMATIZACIÓN DE LA OFICINA | BUROTICA E FORNITURE PER L'UFFICIO

コンピューター・ネットワーク

computer network | Rechnernetzwerk[N] | réseau[M] informatique | red[F] informática | rete[F] informatica

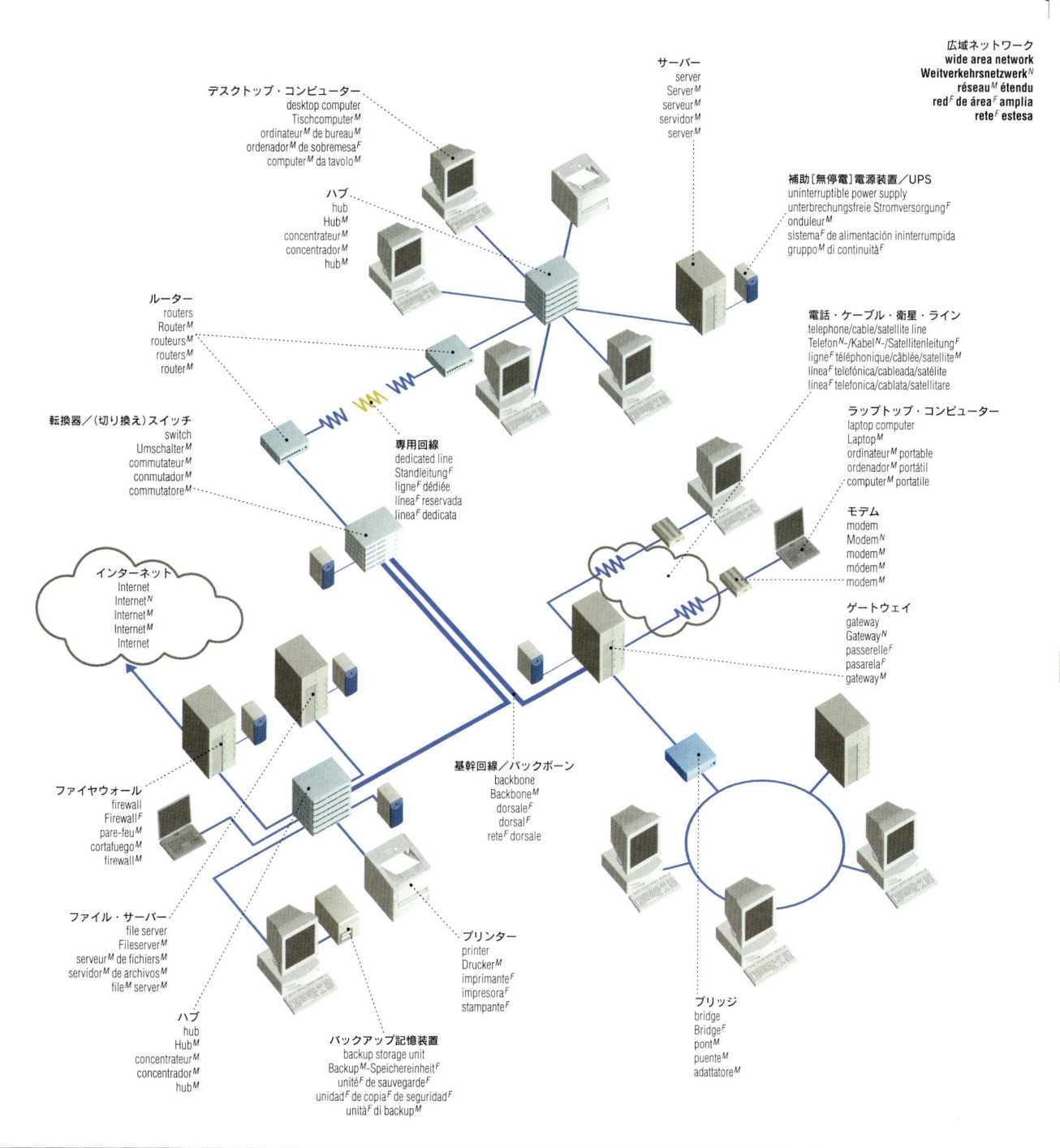

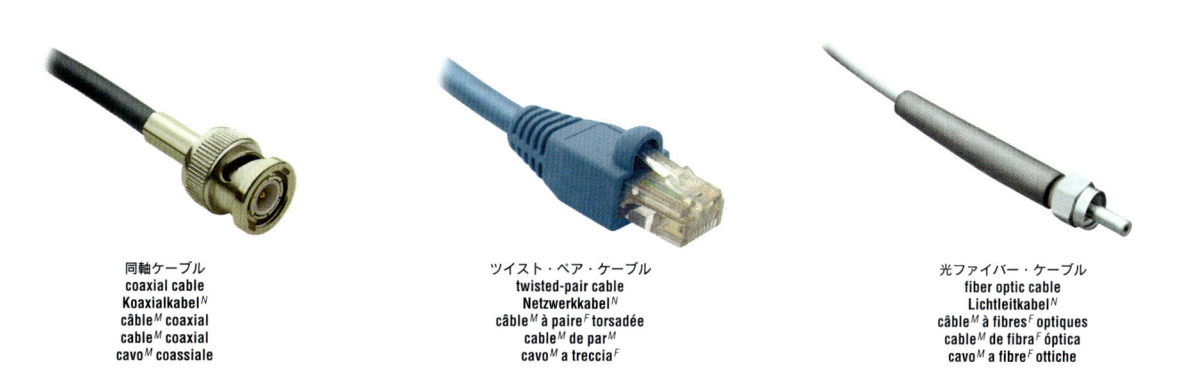

デスクトップ・コンピューター
desktop computer
Tischcomputer[M]
ordinateur[M] de bureau[M]
ordenador[M] de sobremesa[F]
computer[M] da tavolo[M]

サーバー
server
Server[M]
serveur[M]
servidor[M]
server[M]

広域ネットワーク
wide area network
Weitverkehrsnetzwerk[N]
réseau[M] étendu
red[F] de área[F] amplia
rete[F] estesa

ハブ
hub
Hub[M]
concentrateur[M]
concentrador[M]
hub[M]

補助[無停電]電源装置／UPS
uninterruptible power supply
unterbrechungsfreie Stromversorgung[F]
onduleur[M]
sistema[F] de alimentación ininterrumpida
gruppo[M] di continuità[F]

ルーター
routers
Router[M]
routeurs[M]
routers[M]
router[M]

電話・ケーブル・衛星・ライン
telephone/cable/satellite line
Telefon[N]-/Kabel[N]-/Satellitenleitung[F]
ligne[F] téléphonique/câblée/satellite[M]
línea[F] telefónica/cableada/satélite
linea[F] telefonica/cablata/satellitare

転換器／（切り換え）スイッチ
switch
Umschalter[M]
commutateur[M]
conmutador[M]
commutatore[M]

専用回線
dedicated line
Standleitung[F]
ligne[F] dédiée
línea[F] reservada
linea[F] dedicata

ラップトップ・コンピューター
laptop computer
Laptop[M]
ordinateur[M] portable
ordenador[M] portátil
computer[M] portatile

モデム
modem
Modem[N]
modem[M]
módem[M]
modem[M]

インターネット
Internet
Internet[N]
Internet[M]
Internet

ゲートウェイ
gateway
Gateway[N]
passerelle[F]
pasarela[F]
gateway[M]

ファイヤウォール
firewall
Firewall[F]
pare-feu[M]
cortafuego[M]
firewall[M]

基幹回線／バックボーン
backbone
Backbone[M]
dorsale[F]
dorsal[F]
rete[F] dorsale

ファイル・サーバー
file server
Fileserver[M]
serveur[M] de fichiers[M]
servidor[M] de archivos[M]
file[M] server

プリンター
printer
Drucker[M]
imprimante[F]
impresora[F]
stampante[F]

ブリッジ
bridge
Bridge[F]
pont[M]
puente[M]
adattatore[M]

ハブ
hub
Hub[M]
concentrateur[M]
concentrador[M]
hub[M]

バックアップ記憶装置
backup storage unit
Backup[M]-Speichereinheit[F]
unité[F] de sauvegarde[F]
unidad[F] de copia[F] de seguridad[F]
unità[F] di backup[M]

情報伝達とオフィス・オートメーション

ケーブル
cables
Kabel[N]
câbles[M]
cables[M]
cavi[M]

同軸ケーブル
coaxial cable
Koaxialkabel[N]
câble[M] coaxial
cable[M] coaxial
cavo[M] coassiale

ツイスト・ペア・ケーブル
twisted-pair cable
Netzwerkkabel[N]
câble[M] à paire[F] torsadée
cable[M] de par[M]
cavo[M] a treccia[F]

光ファイバー・ケーブル
fiber optic cable
Lichtleitkabel[N]
câble[M] à fibres[F] optiques
cable[M] de fibra[F] óptica
cavo[M] a fibre[F] ottiche

523

オフィス・オートメーション | OFFICE AUTOMATION
BÜROAUTOMATION | BUREAUTIQUE | AUTOMATIZACIÓN DE LA OFICINA | BUROTICA E FORNITURE PER L'UFFICIO

インターネット

Internet | Internet[N] | Internet[M] | Internet[M] | Internet

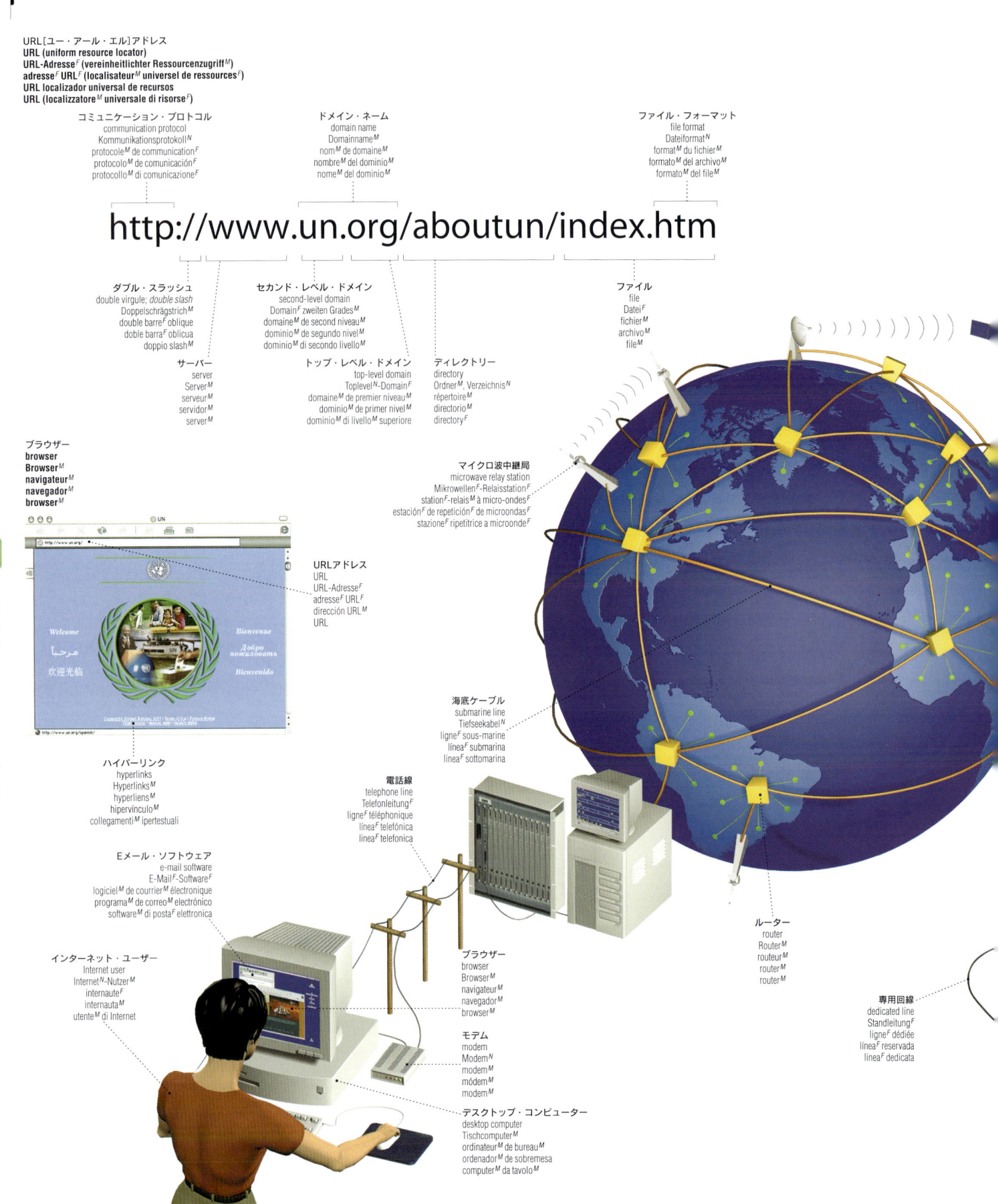

日本語 | 英語 | ドイツ語 | フランス語 | スペイン語 | イタリア語

URL[ユー・アール・エル]アドレス
URL (uniform resource locator)
URL-Adresse[F] (vereinheitlichter Ressourcenzugriff[M])
adresse[F] URL[F] (localisateur[M] universel de ressources[F])
URL localizador universal de recursos
URL (localizzatore[M] universale di risorse[F])

コミュニケーション・プロトコル
communication protocol
Kommunikationsprotokoll[N]
protocole[M] de communication[F]
protocolo[M] de comunicación[F]
protocollo[M] di comunicazione[F]

ドメイン・ネーム
domain name
Domainname[M]
nom[M] de domaine[M]
nombre[M] del dominio[M]
nome[M] del dominio[M]

ファイル・フォーマット
file format
Dateiformat[N]
format[M] du fichier[M]
formato[M] del archivo[M]
formato[M] del file[M]

http://www.un.org/aboutun/index.htm

ダブル・スラッシュ
double virgule; *double slash*
Doppelschrägstrich[M]
double barre[F] oblique
doble barra[F] oblicua
doppio slash[M]

セカンド・レベル・ドメイン
second-level domain
Domain[F] zweiten Grades[M]
domaine[M] de second niveau[M]
dominio[M] de segundo nivel[M]
dominio[M] di secondo livello[M]

ファイル
file
Datei[F]
fichier[M]
archivo[M]
file[M]

サーバー
server
Server[M]
serveur[M]
servidor[M]
server[M]

トップ・レベル・ドメイン
top-level domain
Toplevel[N]-Domain[F]
domaine[M] de premier niveau[M]
dominio[M] de primer nivel[M]
dominio[M] di livello[M] superiore

ディレクトリー
directory
Ordner[M], Verzeichnis[N]
répertoire[M]
directorio[M]
directory[F]

ブラウザー
browser
Browser[M]
navigateur[M]
navegador[M]
browser[M]

マイクロ波中継局
microwave relay station
Mikrowellen[F]-Relaisstation[F]
station[F]-relais[F] à micro-ondes[F]
estación[F] de repetición[F] de microondas[F]
stazione[F] ripetitrice a microonde[F]

URLアドレス
URL
URL-Adresse[F]
adresse[F] URL[F]
dirección URL[M]
URL

海底ケーブル
submarine line
Tiefseekabel[N]
ligne[F] sous-marine
línea[F] submarina
linea[F] sottomarina

ハイパーリンク
hyperlinks
Hyperlinks[M]
hyperliens[M]
hipervínculo[M]
collegamenti[M] ipertestuali

電話線
telephone line
Telefonleitung[F]
ligne[F] téléphonique
línea[F] telefónica
linea[F] telefonica

Eメール・ソフトウェア
e-mail software
E-Mail[F]-Software[F]
logiciel[M] de courrier[M] électronique
programa[M] de correo[M] electrónico
software[M] di posta[F] elettronica

ルーター
router
Router[M]
routeur[M]
router[M]
router[M]

インターネット・ユーザー
Internet user
Internet[N]-Nutzer[M]
internaute[F]
internauta[M]
utente[M] di Internet

ブラウザー
browser
Browser[M]
navigateur[M]
navegador[M]
browser[M]

モデム
modem
Modem[N]
modem[M]
módem[M]
modem[M]

専用回線
dedicated line
Standleitung[F]
ligne[F] dédiée
línea[F] reservada
linea[F] dedicata

デスクトップ・コンピューター
desktop computer
Tischcomputer[M]
ordinateur[M] de bureau[M]
ordenador[M] de sobremesa
computer[M] da tavolo[M]

情報伝達とオフィス・オートメーション

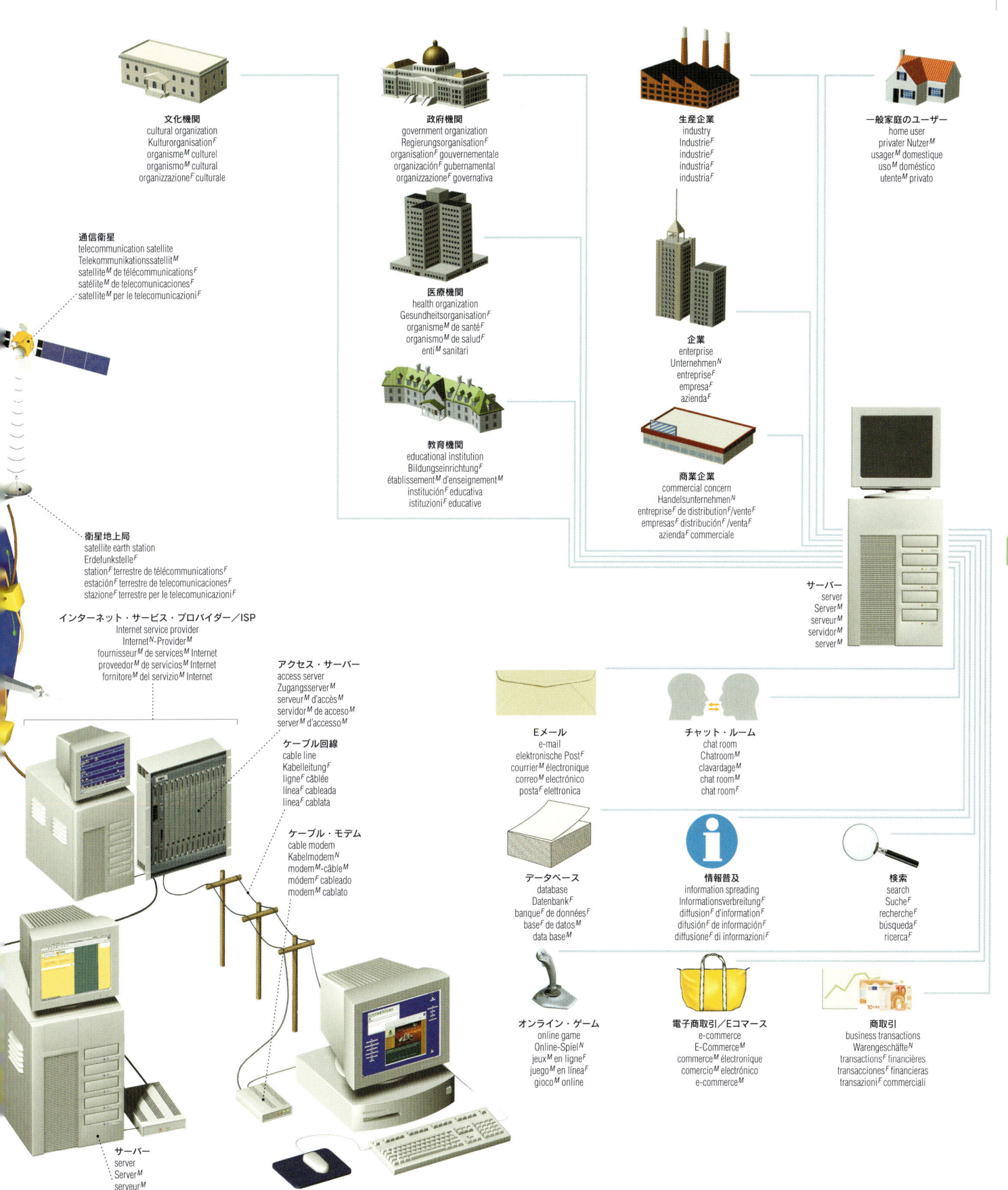

オフィス・オートメーション | OFFICE AUTOMATION
BÜROAUTOMATION | BUREAUTIQUE | AUTOMATIZACIÓN DE LA OFICINA | BUROTICA E FORNITURE PER L'UFFICIO

インターネットの利用

Internet uses | Internet^N-Nutzungen^F | utilisations^F d'Internet^M | usos^M de Internet^M | impieghi^M di Internet

文化機関
cultural organization
Kulturorganisation^F
organisme^M culturel
organismo^M cultural
organizzazione^F culturale

政府機関
government organization
Regierungsorganisation^F
organisation^F gouvernementale
organización^F gubernamental
organizzazione^F governativa

生産企業
industry
Industrie^F
industrie^F
industria^F
industria^F

一般家庭のユーザー
home user
privater Nutzer^M
usager^M domestique
uso^M doméstico
utente^M privato

通信衛星
telecommunication satellite
Telekommunikationssatellit^M
satellite^M de télécommunications^F
satélite^M de telecomunicaciones^F
satellite^M per le telecomunicazioni^F

医療機関
health organization
Gesundheitsorganisation^F
organisme^M de santé^F
organismo^M de salud^F
enti^M sanitari

企業
enterprise
Unternehmen^N
entreprise^F
empresa^F
azienda^F

教育機関
educational institution
Bildungseinrichtung^F
établissement^M d'enseignement^M
institución^F educativa
istituzioni^F educative

商業企業
commercial concern
Handelsunternehmen^N
entreprise^F de distribution^F/vente^F
empresas^F distribución^F/venta^F
azienda^F commerciale

衛星地上局
satellite earth station
Erdefunkstelle^F
station^F terrestre de télécommunications^F
estación^F terrestre de telecomunicaciones^F
stazione^F terrestre per le telecomunicazioni^F

インターネット・サービス・プロバイダー／ISP
Internet service provider
Internet^N-Provider^M
fournisseur^M de services^M Internet
proveedor^M de servicios^M Internet
fornitore^M del servizio^M Internet

アクセス・サーバー
access server
Zugangsserver^M
serveur^M d'accès^M
servidor^M de acceso^M
server^M d'accesso^M

ケーブル回線
cable line
Kabelleitung^F
ligne^F câblée
línea^F cableada
linea^F cablata

ケーブル・モデム
cable modem
Kabelmodem^N
modem^M-câble^M
módem^F cableado
modem^M cablato

サーバー
server
Server^M
serveur^M
servidor^M
server^M

Eメール
e-mail
elektronische Post^F
courrier^M électronique
correo^M electrónico
posta^F elettronica

チャット・ルーム
chat room
Chatroom^M
clavardage^M
chat room^M
chat room^F

データベース
database
Datenbank^F
banque^F de données^F
base^F de datos^M
data base^M

情報普及
information spreading
Informationsverbreitung^F
diffusion^F d'information^F
difusión^F de información^F
diffusione^F di informazioni^F

検索
search
Suche^F
recherche^F
búsqueda^F
ricerca^F

オンライン・ゲーム
online game
Online-Spiel^N
jeux^M en ligne^F
juego^M en línea^F
gioco^M online

電子商取引／Eコマース
e-commerce
E-Commerce^M
commerce^M électronique
comercio^M electrónico
e-commerce^M

商取引
business transactions
Warengeschäfte^N
transactions^F financières
transacciones^F financieras
transazioni^F commerciali

サーバー
server
Server^M
serveur^M
servidor^M
server^M

情報伝達とオフィス・オートメーション

オフィス・オートメーション | OFFICE AUTOMATION
BÜROAUTOMATION | BUREAUTIQUE | AUTOMATIZACIÓN DE LA OFICINA | BUROTICA E FORNITURE PER L'UFFICIO

ラップトップ(型)コンピューター

laptop computer | Laptop[M] | ordinateur[M] portable | ordenador[M] portátil | computer[M] portatile

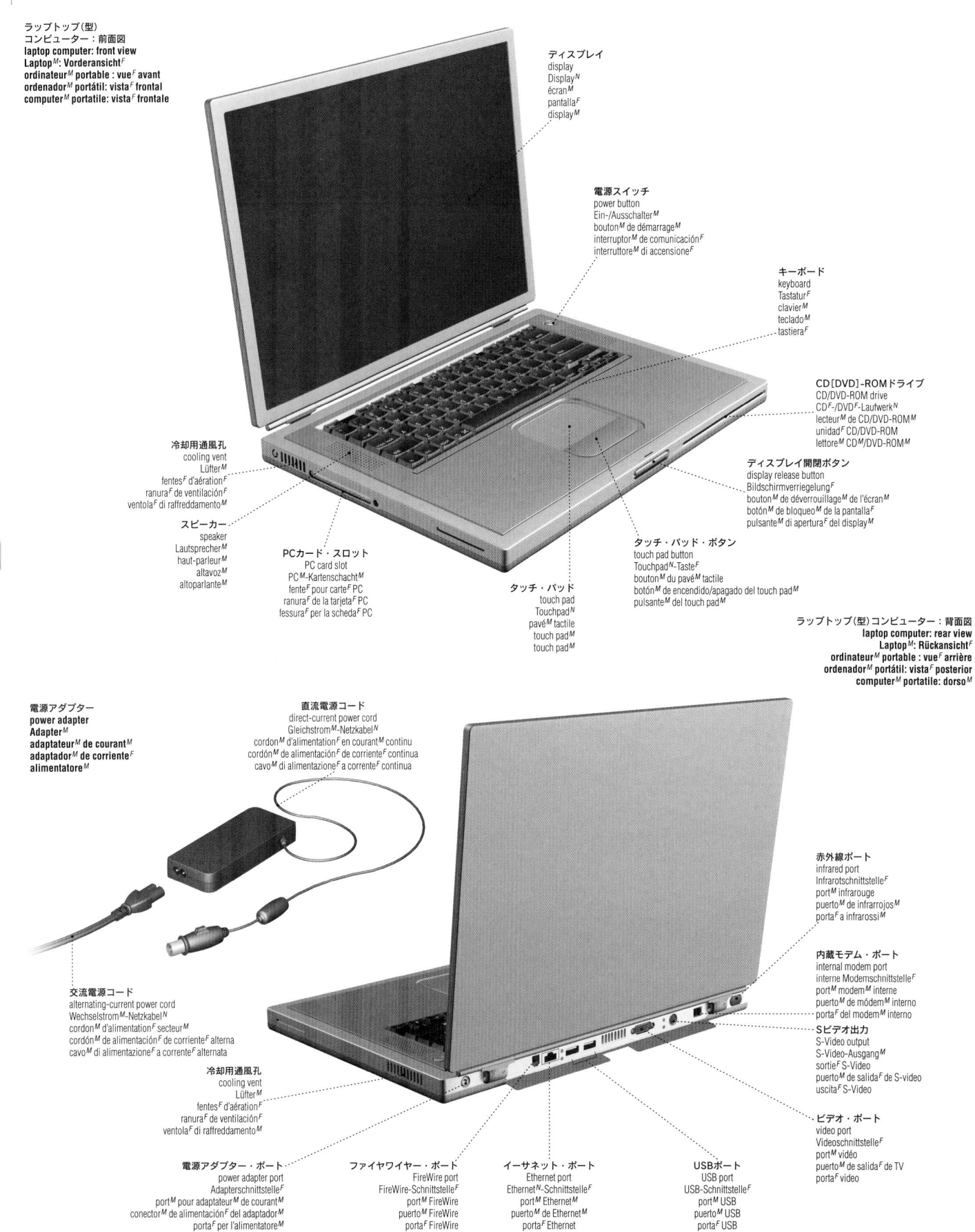

日本語 | 英語 | ドイツ語 | フランス語 | スペイン語 | イタリア語

ラップトップ(型)
コンピューター：前面図
laptop computer: front view
Laptop[M]**: Vorderansicht**[F]
ordinateur[M] **portable : vue**[F] **avant**
ordenador[M] **portátil: vista**[F] **frontal**
computer[M] **portatile: vista**[F] **frontale**

ディスプレイ
display
Display[N]
écran[M]
pantalla[F]
display[M]

電源スイッチ
power button
Ein-/Ausschalter[M]
bouton[M] de démarrage[M]
interruptor[M] de comunicación[F]
interruttore[M] di accensione[F]

キーボード
keyboard
Tastatur[F]
clavier[M]
teclado[M]
tastiera[F]

CD[DVD]-ROMドライブ
CD/DVD-ROM drive
CD[F]-/DVD[F]-Laufwerk[N]
lecteur[M] de CD/DVD-ROM[M]
unidad[F] CD/DVD-ROM
lettore[M] CD[M]/DVD-ROM[M]

ディスプレイ開閉ボタン
display release button
Bildschirmverriegelung[F]
bouton[M] de déverrouillage[M] de l'écran[M]
botón[M] de bloqueo[M] de la pantalla[F]
pulsante[M] di apertura[F] del display[M]

冷却用通風孔
cooling vent
Lüfter[M]
fentes[F] d'aération[F]
ranura[F] de ventilación[F]
ventola[F] di raffreddamento[M]

スピーカー
speaker
Lautsprecher[M]
haut-parleur[M]
altavoz[M]
altoparlante[M]

PCカード・スロット
PC card slot
PC[M]-Kartenschacht[M]
fente[F] pour carte[F] PC
ranura[F] de la tarjeta[F] PC
fessura[F] per la scheda[F] PC

タッチ・パッド・ボタン
touch pad button
Touchpad[N]-Taste[F]
bouton[M] du pavé[M] tactile
botón[M] de encendido/apagado del touch pad[M]
pulsante[M] del touch pad[M]

タッチ・パッド
touch pad
Touchpad[N]
pavé[M] tactile
touch pad[M]
touch pad[M]

ラップトップ(型)コンピューター：背面図
laptop computer: rear view
Laptop[M]**: Rückansicht**[F]
ordinateur[M] **portable : vue**[F] **arrière**
ordenador[M] **portátil: vista**[F] **posterior**
computer[M] **portatile: dorso**[M]

電源アダプター
power adapter
Adapter[M]
adaptateur[M] de courant[M]
adaptador[M] de corriente[F]
alimentatore[M]

直流電源コード
direct-current power cord
Gleichstrom[M]-Netzkabel[N]
cordon[M] d'alimentation[F] en courant[M] continu
cordón[M] de alimentación[F] de corriente[F] continua
cavo[M] di alimentazione[F] a corrente[F] continua

赤外線ポート
infrared port
Infrarotschnittstelle[F]
port[M] infrarouge
puerto[M] de infrarrojos[M]
porta[F] a infrarossi[M]

内蔵モデム・ポート
internal modem port
interne Modemschnittstelle[F]
port[M] modem[M] interne
puerto[M] de módem[M] interno
porta[F] del modem[M] interno

交流電源コード
alternating-current power cord
Wechselstrom[M]-Netzkabel[N]
cordon[M] d'alimentation[F] secteur[M]
cordón[M] de alimentación[F] de corriente[F] alterna
cavo[M] di alimentazione[F] a corrente[F] alternata

Sビデオ出力
S-Video output
S-Video-Ausgang[M]
sortie[F] S-Video
puerto[M] de salida[F] de S-video
uscita[F] S-Video

冷却用通風孔
cooling vent
Lüfter[M]
fentes[F] d'aération[F]
ranura[F] de ventilación[F]
ventola[F] di raffreddamento[M]

ビデオ・ポート
video port
Videoschnittstelle[F]
port[M] vidéo
puerto[M] de salida[F] de TV
porta[F] video

電源アダプター・ポート
power adapter port
Adapterschnittstelle[F]
port[M] pour adaptateur[M] de courant[M]
conector[M] de alimentación[F] del adaptador[M]
porta[F] per l'alimentatore[M]

ファイヤワイヤー・ポート
FireWire port
FireWire-Schnittstelle[F]
port[M] FireWire
puerto[M] FireWire
porta[F] FireWire

イーサネット・ポート
Ethernet port
Ethernet[N]-Schnittstelle[F]
port[M] Ethernet[M]
puerto[M] de Ethernet[M]
porta[F] Ethernet

USBポート
USB port
USB-Schnittstelle[F]
port[M] USB
puerto[M] USB
porta[F] USB

情報伝達とオフィス・オートメーション

526

オフィス・オートメーション | OFFICE AUTOMATION
BÜROAUTOMATION | BUREAUTIQUE | AUTOMATIZACIÓN DE LA OFICINA | BUROTICA E FORNITURE PER L'UFFICIO

ラップトップ(型)コンピューター

ラップトップ(型)
コンピューターのブリーフケース
laptop computer briefcase
Laptop^M-Tasche^F
mallette^F d'ordinateur^M portable
maletín^M para ordenador^M portátil
valigetta^F per il computer^M portatile

コンピューター・コンパートメント
computer compartment
Computerfach^N
compartiment^M pour ordinateur^M
compartimiento^M para ordenador^M
scomparto^M per il computer^M

文書コンパートメント
document compartment
Dokumentenfach^N
compartiment^M pour documents^M
compartimiento^M de documentos^M
scomparto^M per i documenti^M

肩紐(ひも)
shoulder strap
Schulterriemen^M
bandoulière^F
bandolera^F
tracolla^F

電子ブック

electronic book | elektronisches Buch^N | livre^M électronique | libro^M electrónico | libro^M elettronico

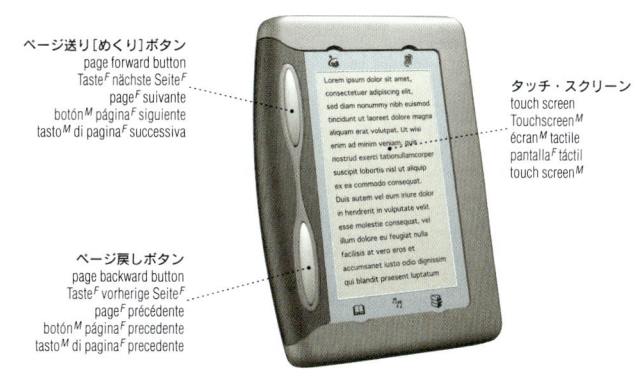

ページ送り[めくり]ボタン
page forward button
Taste^F nächste Seite^F
page^F suivante
botón^M página^F siguiente
tasto^M di pagina^F successiva

タッチ・スクリーン
touch screen
Touchscreen^M
écran^M tactile
pantalla^F táctil
touch screen^M

ページ戻しボタン
page backward button
Taste^F vorherige Seite^F
page^F précédente
botón^M página^F precedente
tasto^M di pagina^F precedente

ポケット・コンピューター

handheld computer | Handheld-Computer^M | ordinateur^M de poche^F | ordenador^M de bolsillo^M | computer^M tascabile

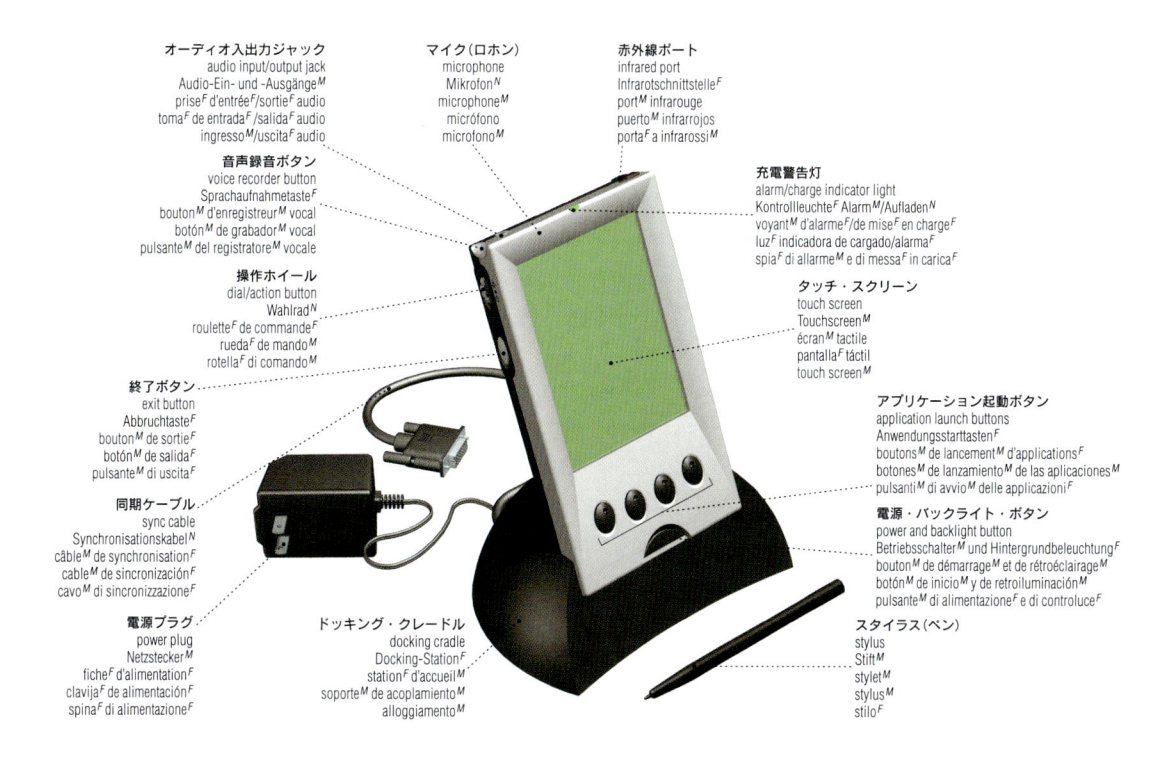

オーディオ入出力ジャック
audio input/output jack
Audio-Ein- und -Ausgänge^M
prise^F d'entrée^F/sortie^F audio
toma^F de entrada^F/salida^F audio
ingresso^M/uscita^F audio

マイク(ロホン)
microphone
Mikrofon^N
microphone^M
micrófono^M
microfono^M

赤外線ポート
infrared port
Infrarotschnittstelle^F
port^M infrarouge
puerto^M infrarrojos
porta^F a infrarossi

音声録音ボタン
voice recorder button
Sprachaufnahmetaste^F
bouton^M d'enregistreur^M vocal
botón^M de grabador^M vocal
pulsante^M del registratore^M vocale

充電警告灯
alarm/charge indicator light
Kontrollleuchte^F Alarm^M/Aufladen^N
voyant^M d'alarme^F/de mise^F en charge^F
luz^F indicadora de cargado/alarma^F
spia^F di allarme^M e di messa^F in carica^F

操作ホイール
dial/action button
Wahlrad^N
roulette^F de commande^F
rueda^F de mando^M
rotella^F di comando^M

タッチ・スクリーン
touch screen
Touchscreen^M
écran^M tactile
pantalla^F táctil
touch screen^M

終了ボタン
exit button
Abbruchtaste^F
bouton^M de sortie^F
botón^M de salida^F
pulsante^M di uscita^F

アプリケーション起動ボタン
application launch buttons
Anwendungsstarttasten^F
boutons^M de lancement^M d'applications^F
botones^M de lanzamiento^M de las aplicaciones^M
pulsanti^M di avvio^M delle applicazioni^F

同期ケーブル
sync cable
Synchronisationskabel^N
câble^M de synchronisation^F
cable^M de sincronización^F
cavo^M di sincronizzazione^F

電源・バックライト・ボタン
power and backlight button
Betriebsschalter^M und Hintergrundbeleuchtung^F
bouton^M de démarrage^M et de rétroéclairage^M
botón^M de inicio^M y de retroiluminación^F
pulsante^M di alimentazione^F e di controluce^F

電源プラグ
power plug
Netzstecker^M
fiche^F d'alimentation^F
clavija^F de alimentación^F
spina^F di alimentazione^F

ドッキング・クレードル
docking cradle
Docking-Station^F
station^F d'accueil^M
soporte^M de acoplamiento^M
alloggiamento^M

スタイラス(ペン)
stylus
Stift^M
stylet^M
stylus^M
stilo^F

527

オフィス・オートメーション | OFFICE AUTOMATION
BÜROAUTOMATION | BUREAUTIQUE | AUTOMATIZACIÓN DE LA OFICINA | BUROTICA E FORNITURE PER L'UFFICIO

文房具

stationery | Schreibwaren^F | articles^M de bureau^M | artículos^M de escritorio^M | articoli^M di cancelleria^F

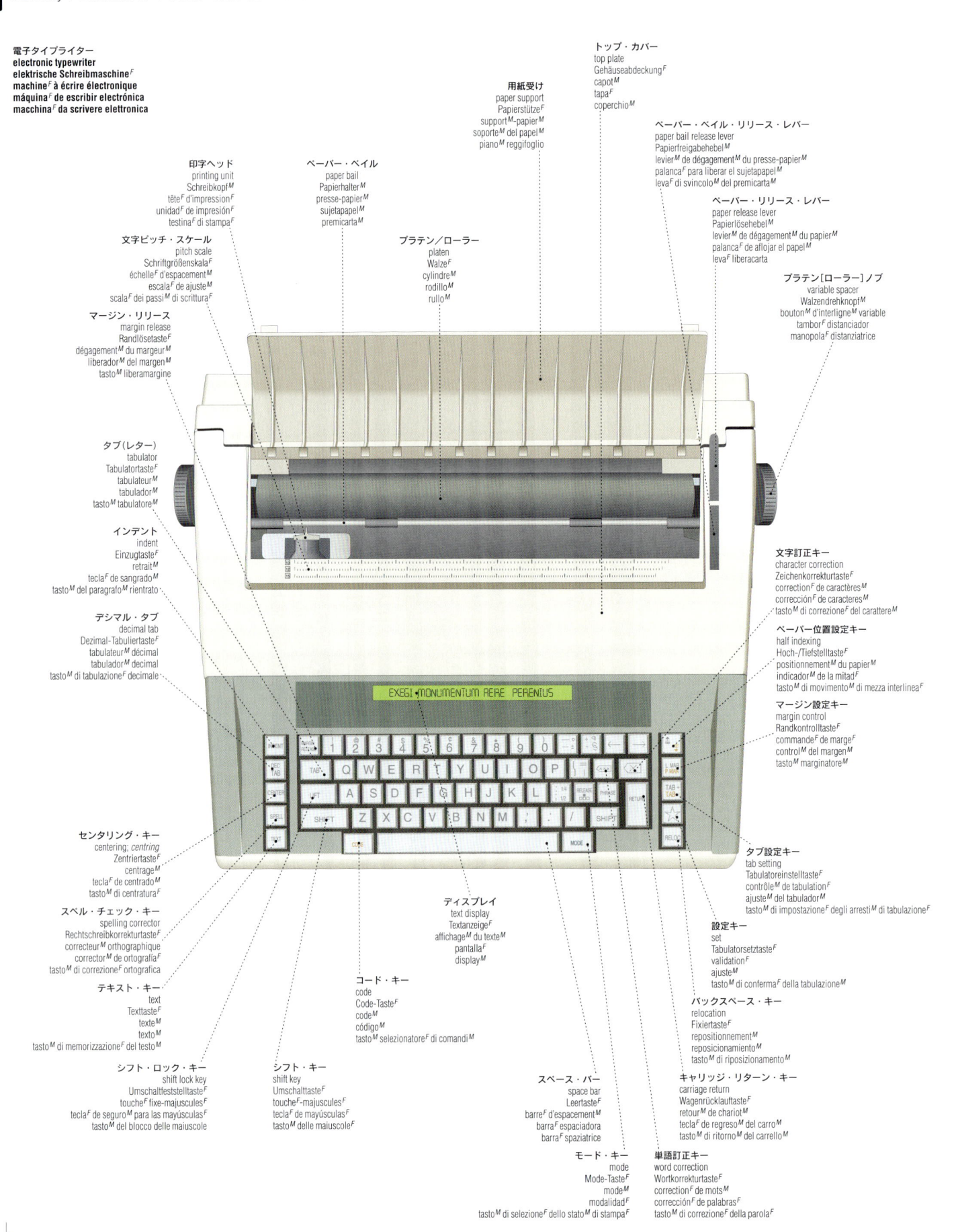

日本語 | 英語 | ドイツ語 | フランス語 | スペイン語 | イタリア語

電子タイプライター
electronic typewriter
elektrische Schreibmaschine^F
machine^F à écrire électronique
máquina^F de escribir electrónica
macchina^F da scrivere elettronica

トップ・カバー
top plate
Gehäuseabdeckung^F
capot^M
tapa^F
coperchio^M

印字ヘッド
printing unit
Schreibkopf^M
tête^F d'impression^F
unidad^F de impresión^F
testina^F di stampa^F

ペーパー・ベイル
paper bail
Papierhalter^M
presse-papier^M
sujetapapel^M
premicarta^M

用紙受け
paper support
Papierstütze^F
support^M-papier^M
soporte^M del papel^M
piano^M reggifoglio

ペーパー・ベイル・リリース・レバー
paper bail release lever
Papierfreigabehebel^M
levier^M de dégagement^M du presse-papier^M
palanca^F para liberar el sujetapapel^M
leva^F di svincolo^M del premicarta^M

文字ピッチ・スケール
pitch scale
Schriftgrößenskala^F
échelle^F d'espacement^M
escala^F de ajuste^F
scala^F dei passi di scrittura^F

プラテン/ローラー
platen
Walze^F
cylindre^M
rodillo^M
rullo^M

ペーパー・リリース・レバー
paper release lever
Papierlösehebel^M
levier^M de dégagement^M du papier^M
palanca^F de aflojar el papel^M
leva^F liberacarta

マージン・リリース
margin release
Randlösetaste^F
dégagement^M du margeur^M
liberador^M del margen^M
tasto^M liberamargine

プラテン[ローラー]ノブ
variable spacer
Walzendrehknopf^M
bouton^M d'interligne^M variable
tambor^F distanciador
manopola^F distanziatrice

タブ(レター)
tabulator
Tabulatortaste^F
tabulateur^M
tabulador^M
tasto^M tabulatore^M

インデント
indent
Einzugtaste^F
retrait^M
tecla^F de sangrado^M
tasto^M del paragrafo^M rientrato

文字訂正キー
character correction
Zeichenkorrekturtaste^F
correction^F de caractères^M
corrección^F de caracteres^M
tasto^M di correzione^F del carattere^M

デシマル・タブ
decimal tab
Dezimal-Tabuliertaste^F
tabulateur^M décimal
tabulador^M decimal
tasto^M di tabulazione^F decimale

ペーパー位置設定キー
half indexing
Hoch-/Tiefstelltaste^F
positionnement^M du papier^M
indicador^M de la mitad^F
tasto^M di movimento^M di mezza interlinea^F

マージン設定キー
margin control
Randkontrolltaste^F
commande^F de marge^F
control^M del margen^M
tasto^M marginatore^M

センタリング・キー
centering; centring
Zentriertaste^F
centrage^M
tecla^F de centrado^M
tasto^M di centratura^F

タブ設定キー
tab setting
Tabulatoreinstelltaste^F
contrôle^F de tabulation^F
ajuste^M del tabulador^M
tasto^M di impostazione^F degli arresti^M di tabulazione^F

スペル・チェック・キー
spelling corrector
Rechtschreibkorrekturtaste^F
correcteur^M orthographique
corrector^M de ortografía^F
tasto^M di correzione^F ortografica

ディスプレイ
text display
Textanzeige^F
affichage^M du texte^M
pantalla^F
display^M

設定キー
set
Tabulatorsetztaste^F
validation^F
ajuste^M
tasto^M di conferma^F della tabulazione^M

テキスト・キー
text
Texttaste^F
texte^M
texto^M
tasto^M di memorizzazione^F del testo^M

コード・キー
code
Code-Taste^F
code^M
código^M
tasto^M selezionatore^F di comandi^M

バックスペース・キー
relocation
Fixiertaste^F
repositionnement^M
reposicionamiento^M
tasto^M di riposizionamento^M

シフト・ロック・キー
shift lock key
Umschaltfeststelltaste^F
touche^F fixe-majuscules^F
tecla^F de seguro^M para las mayúsculas^F
tasto^M del blocco delle maiuscole^F

シフト・キー
shift key
Umschalttaste^F
touche^F-majuscules^F
tecla^F de mayúsculas^F
tasto^M delle maiuscole^F

スペース・バー
space bar
Leertaste^F
barre^F d'espacement^M
barra^F espaciadora
barra^F spaziatrice

キャリッジ・リターン・キー
carriage return
Wagenrücklauftaste^F
retour^M de chariot^M
tecla^F de regreso^M del carro^M
tasto^M di ritorno^M del carrello^M

モード・キー
mode
Mode-Taste^F
mode^M
modalidad^F
tasto^M di selezione^F dello stato^M di stampa^F

単語訂正キー
word correction
Wortkorrekturtaste^F
correction^F de mots^M
corrección^F de palabras^F
tasto^M di correzione^F della parola^F

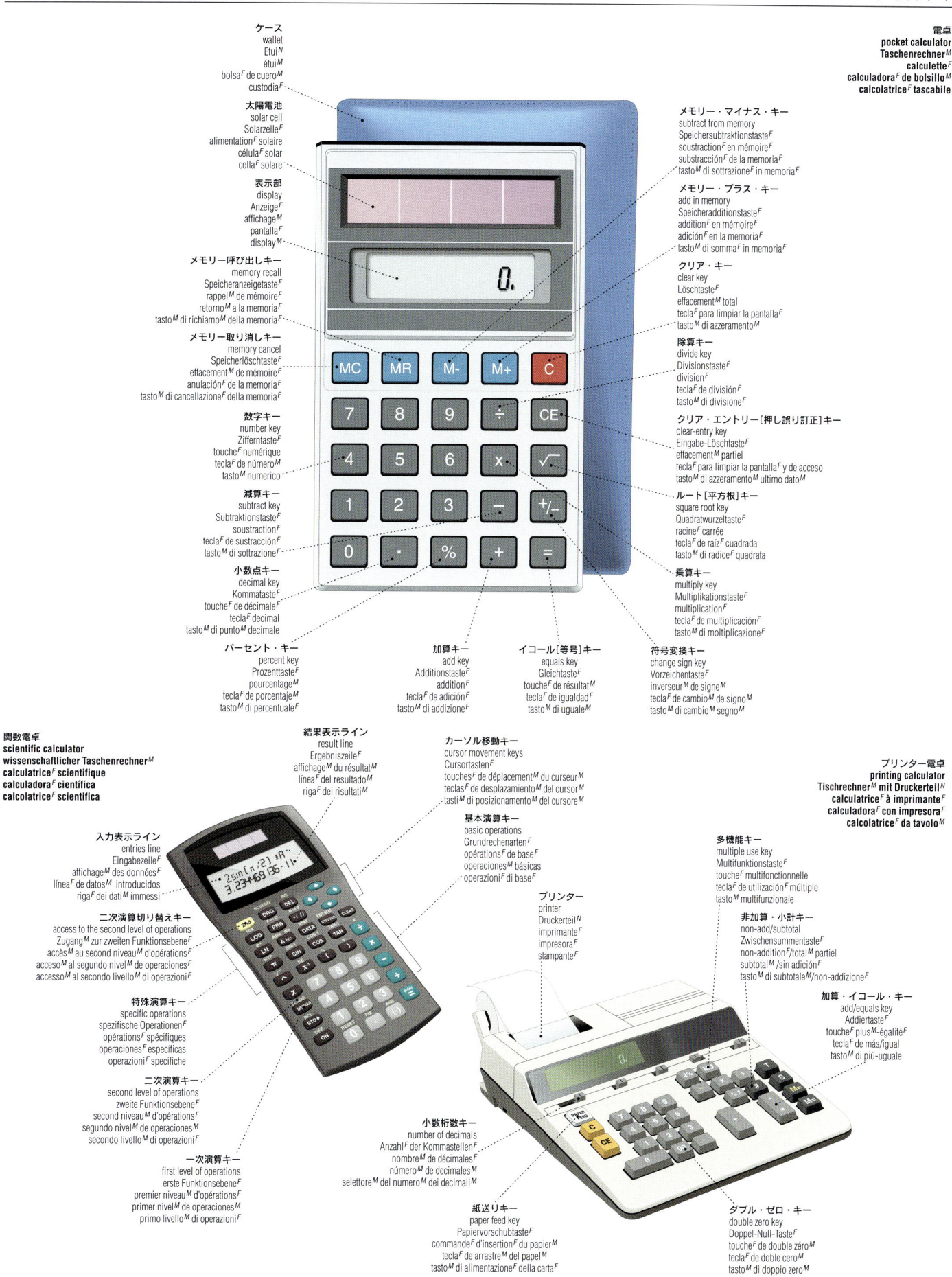

オフィス・オートメーション | OFFICE AUTOMATION
BÜROAUTOMATION | BUREAUTIQUE | AUTOMATIZACIÓN DE LA OFICINA | BUROTICA E FORNITURE PER L'UFFICIO

文房具

電卓
pocket calculator
Taschenrechner^M
calculette^F
calculadora^F de bolsillo^M
calcolatrice^F tascabile

ケース
wallet
Etui^N
étui^M
bolsa^F de cuero^M
custodia^F

太陽電池
solar cell
Solarzelle^F
alimentation^F solaire
célula^F solar
cella^F solare

表示部
display
Anzeige^F
affichage^M
pantalla^F
display^M

メモリー呼び出しキー
memory recall
Speicheranzeigetaste^F
rappel^M de mémoire^F
retorno^M a la memoria^F
tasto^M di richiamo^M della memoria^F

メモリー取り消しキー
memory cancel
Speicherlöschtaste^F
effacement^M de mémoire^F
anulación^F de la memoria^F
tasto^M di cancellazione^F della memoria^F

数字キー
number key
Zifferntaste^F
touche^F numérique
tecla^F de número^M
tasto^M numerico

減算キー
subtract key
Subtraktionstaste^F
soustraction^F
tecla^F de sustracción^F
tasto^M di sottrazione^F

小数点キー
decimal key
Kommataste^F
touche^F de décimale
tecla^F decimal
tasto^M di punto^M decimale

メモリー・マイナス・キー
subtract from memory
Speichersubtraktionstaste^F
soustraction^F en mémoire^F
substracción^F de la memoria^F
tasto^M di sottrazione^F in memoria^F

メモリー・プラス・キー
add in memory
Speicheradditionstaste^F
addition^F en mémoire^F
adición^F en la memoria^F
tasto^M di somma^F in memoria^F

クリア・キー
clear key
Löschtaste^F
effacement^M total
tecla^F para limpiar la pantalla^F
tasto^M di azzeramento^M

除算キー
divide key
Divisionstaste^F
division^F
tecla^F de división^F
tasto^M di divisione^F

クリア・エントリー［押し誤り訂正］キー
clear-entry key
Eingabe-Löschtaste^F
effacement^M partiel
tecla^F para limpiar la pantalla^F y de acceso
tasto^M di azzeramento^M ultimo dato^M

ルート［平方根］キー
square root key
Quadratwurzeltaste^F
racine^F carrée
tecla^F de raíz^F cuadrada
tasto^M di radice^F quadrata

乗算キー
multiply key
Multiplikationstaste^F
multiplication^F
tecla^F de multiplicación^F
tasto^M di moltiplicazione^F

パーセント・キー
percent key
Prozenttaste^F
pourcentage^M
tecla^F de porcentaje^M
tasto^M di percentuale^F

加算キー
add key
Additionstaste^F
addition^F
tecla^F de adición^F
tasto^M di addizione^F

イコール［等号］キー
equals key
Gleichtaste^F
touche^F de résultat^M
tecla^F de igualdad^F
tasto^M di uguale^M

符号変換キー
change sign key
Vorzeichentaste^F
inverseur^M de signe^M
tecla^F de cambio^M de signo^M
tasto^M di cambio^M segno^M

関数電卓
scientific calculator
wissenschaftlicher Taschenrechner^M
calculatrice^F scientifique
calculadora^F científica
calcolatrice^F scientifica

入力表示ライン
entries line
Eingabezeile^F
affichage^M des données^F
línea^F de datos^M introducidos
riga^F dei dati^M immessi

二次演算切り替えキー
access to the second level of operations
Zugang^M zur zweiten Funktionsebene^F
accès^M au second niveau^M d'opérations^F
acceso^M al segundo nivel^M de operaciones^F
accesso^M al secondo livello^M di operazioni^F

特殊演算キー
specific operations
spezifische Operationen^F
opérations^F spécifiques
operaciones^F específicas
operazioni^F specifiche

二次演算キー
second level of operations
zweite Funktionsebene^F
second niveau^M d'opérations^F
segundo nivel^M de operaciones^F
secondo livello^M di operazioni^F

一次演算キー
first level of operations
erste Funktionsebene^F
premier niveau^M d'opérations^F
primer nivel^M de operaciones^F
primo livello^M di operazioni^F

結果表示ライン
result line
Ergebniszeile^F
affichage^M du résultat^M
línea^F del resultado^M
riga^F dei risultati^M

カーソル移動キー
cursor movement keys
Cursortasten^F
touches^F de déplacement^M du curseur^M
teclas^F de desplazamiento^M del cursor^M
tasti^M di posizionamento^M del cursore^M

基本演算キー
basic operations
Grundrechenarten^F
opérations^F de base^F
operaciones^F básicas
operazioni^F di base^F

プリンター
printer
Druckerteil^N
imprimante^F
impresora^F
stampante^F

小数桁数キー
number of decimals
Anzahl^F der Kommastellen^F
nombre^M de décimales^F
número^M de decimales^M
selettore^M del numero^M dei decimali^M

紙送りキー
paper feed key
Papiervorschubtaste^F
commande^F d'insertion^F du papier^M
tecla^F de arrastre^M del papel^M
tasto^M di alimentazione^F della carta^F

プリンター電卓
printing calculator
Tischrechner^M mit Druckerteil^N
calculatrice^F à imprimante^F
calculadora^F con impresora^F
calcolatrice^F da tavolo^M

多機能キー
multiple use key
Multifunktionstaste^F
touche^F multifonctionnelle
tecla^F de utilización^F múltiple
tasto^M multifunzionale

非加算・小計キー
non-add/subtotal
Zwischensummentaste^F
non-addition^F/total^M partiel
subtotal^M/sin adición^F
tasto^M di subtotale^M/non-addizione^F

加算・イコール・キー
add/equals key
Addiertaste^F
touche^F plus^M-égalité^F
tecla^F de más/igual
tasto^M di più-uguale

ダブル・ゼロ・キー
double zero key
Doppel-Null-Taste^F
touche^F de double zéro^M
tecla^F de doble cero^M
tasto^M di doppio zero^M

情報伝達とオフィス・オートメーション

オフィス・オートメーション | OFFICE AUTOMATION
BÜROAUTOMATION | BUREAUTIQUE | AUTOMATIZACIÓN DE LA OFICINA | BUROTICA E FORNITURE PER L'UFFICIO

文房具

日本語 | 英語 | ドイツ語 | フランス語 | スペイン語 | イタリア語

時間管理用
for time management
für die Terminplanung^F
pour l'emploi du temps^M
para el empleo del tiempo^M
per la gestione^F del tempo^M

日めくり式卓上カレンダー
calendar pad
Ringbuchkalender^M
bloc^M-éphéméride^F
calendario^M de escritorio^M
calendario^M da tavolo^M

オーガナイザー
organizer
Organizer^M
organiseur^M
agenda^F electrónica
organizer^M

日めくりカレンダー
tear-off calendar
Abreißkalender^M
calendrier^M-mémorandum^M
calendario^M de pared^F
calendario^M a fogli^M staccabili

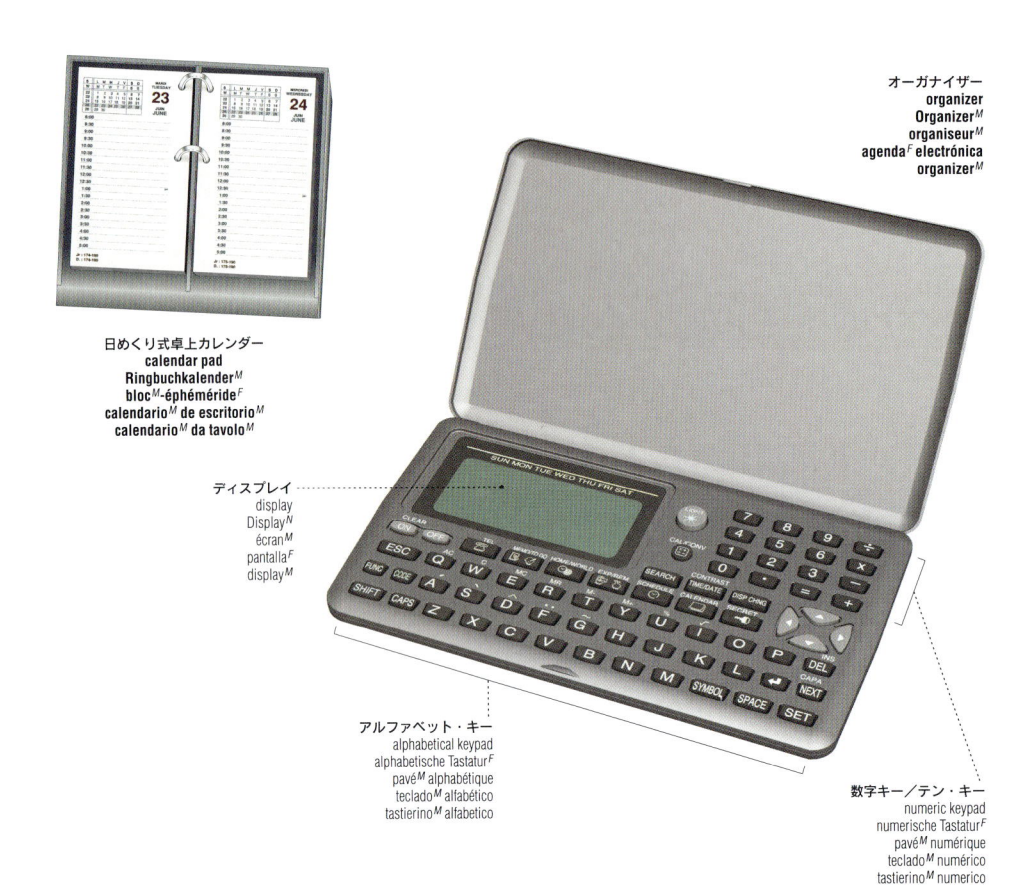

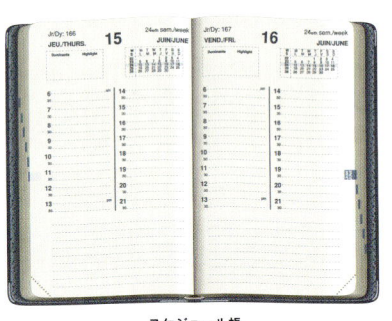

ディスプレイ
display
Display^N
écran^M
pantalla^F
display^M

アルファベット・キー
alphabetical keypad
alphabetische Tastatur^F
pavé^M alphabétique
teclado^M alfabético
tastierino^M alfabetico

数字キー／テン・キー
numeric keypad
numerische Tastatur^F
pavé^M numérique
teclado^M numérico
tastierino^M numerico

スケジュール帳
appointment book
Terminkalender^M
agenda^M
agenda^F
agenda^F

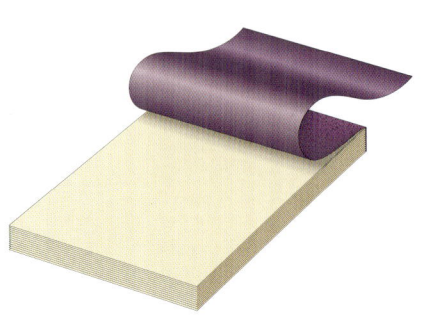

表示窓［画面］
display
Display^N
écran^M
pantalla^F
display^M

タイム・レコーダー
time clock
Stempeluhr^F
pointeuse^F
timbradora^F
orologio^M per la timbratura^F dei cartellini

情報伝達とオフィス・オートメーション

メモ・パッド
memo pad
Notizblock^M
bloc^M-notes^F
libreta^F
bloc-notes^M

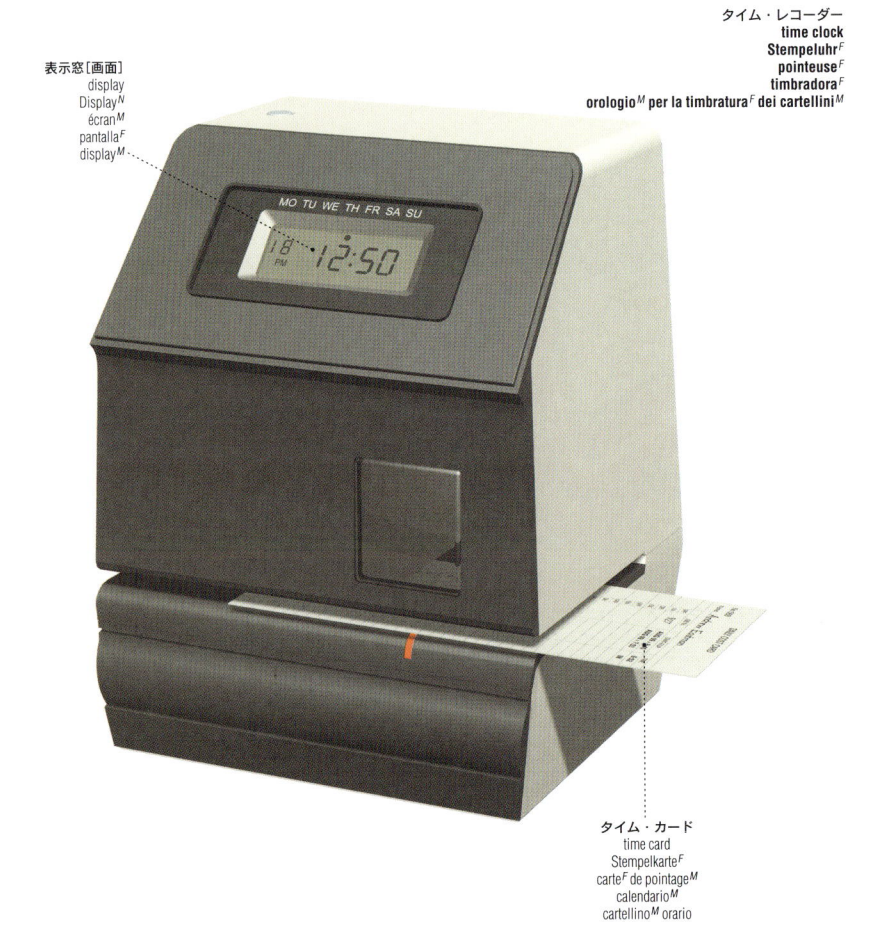

タイム・カード
time card
Stempelkarte^F
carte^F de pointage^M
calendario^M
cartellino^M orario

オフィス・オートメーション | OFFICE AUTOMATION
BÜROAUTOMATION | BUREAUTIQUE | AUTOMATIZACIÓN DE LA OFICINA | BUROTICA E FORNITURE PER L'UFFICIO

文房具

クッション封筒
padded envelope
Luftpolsterumschlag^M
enveloppe^F matelassée
sobre^M almohadillado
busta^F imbottita

接着式フラップ
self-sealing flap
selbstklebende Lasche^F
patte^F autocollante
solapa^F autoadhesiva
aletta^F autoadesiva

ペーパー・ナイフ
letter opener
Brieföffner^M
coupe-papier^M
abrecartas^M
tagliacarte^M

日付印
dater
Datumstempel^M
timbre^M dateur
fechador^M
datario^M

書状作成用
for correspondence
für die Korrespondenz^F
pour la correspondance^F
para la correspondencia^F
per la corrispondenza^F

ステノ・ブック
steno book
Stenografieblock^M
bloc^M-sténo^F
cuaderno^M de taquigrafía^F
blocchetto^M per stenografia^F

エア・バブル
air bubbles
Luftpolster^N
bulles^F d'air^M
burbujas^F de aire^M
bolle^F d'aria^F

ナンバリング
numbering machine
Nummerierstempel^M
numéroteur^M
foliador^M
numeratore^M

指サック
finger tip
elastischer Fingerhut^M
doigtier^M
dedil^M
ditale^M in gomma^F

手紙秤（ばかり）／レター・スケール
letter scale
Briefwaage^F
pèse-lettres^M
balanza^F para cartas^F
pesalettere^F

署名帳
signature book
Unterschriftenmappe^F
parapheur^M
libro^M de firmas^M
libro^M delle firme^F

切手濡らし器
moistener
Befeuchter^M
mouilleur^M
rueda^F humedecedora
spugnetta^F

スタンプ・ラック
stamp rack
Stempelrad^N
porte-timbres^M
portasellos^M
portatimbri^M

スタンプ台
stamp pad
Stempelkissen^N
tampon^M encreur
cojín^M para sellos^M
tampone^M

ゴム印
rubber stamp
Stempel^M
timbre^M caoutchouc^M
sello^M de goma^F
timbro^M di gomma^F

ロータリー式カード・ファイル
rotary file
Drehkartei^F
fichier^M rotatif
fichero^M giratorio
schedario^M rotativo

郵便料金計器
postage meter
Frankiermaschine^F
machine^F à affranchir
máquina^F franqueadora
affrancatrice^F

吸い取り紙
blotting paper
Löschpapier^N
papier^M buvard
papel^M secante
carta^F assorbente

テレホン・インデックス
telephone index
Telefonnummernverzeichnis^N
répertoire^M téléphonique
agenda^F telefónica
rubrica^F telefonica

郵便料金印字器
postmarking module
Frankiermodul^N
module^M d'affranchissement^M
módulo^M de franqueado
modulo^M di affrancamento^M

デスク・トレイ
desk tray
Dokumentenablage^F
boîte^F à courrier^M
bandeja^F de correspondencia^F
vaschetta^F portacorrispondenza

郵便物載せ皿
feed deck
Einzugsablage^F
plateau^M d'alimentation^F
plataforma^F de alimentación^F
piano^M di alimentazione^F

ベース／底部
base
Unterteil$^{M/N}$
base^F
base^F
base^F

情報伝達とオフィス・オートメーション

531

文房具

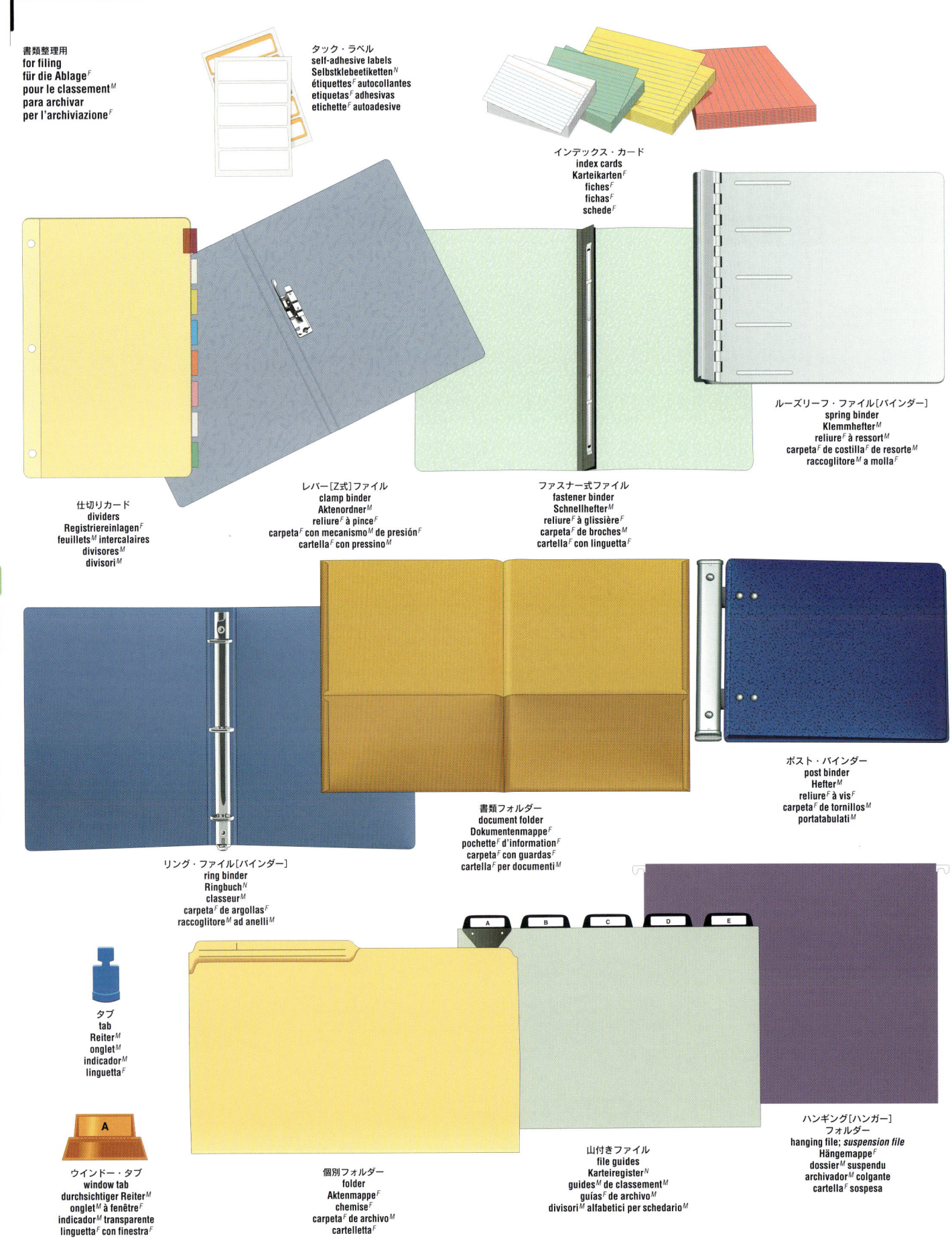

オフィス・オートメーション | OFFICE AUTOMATION
BÜROAUTOMATION | BUREAUTIQUE | AUTOMATIZACIÓN DE LA OFICINA | BUROTICA E FORNITURE PER L'UFFICIO

日本語 | 英語 | ドイツ語 | フランス語 | スペイン語 | イタリア語

書類整理用
for filing
für die Ablage^F
pour le classement^M
para archivar
per l'archiviazione^F

タック・ラベル
self-adhesive labels
Selbstklebeetiketten^N
étiquettes^F autocollantes
etiquetas^F adhesivas
etichette^F autoadesive

インデックス・カード
index cards
Karteikarten^F
fiches^F
fichas^F
schede^F

ルーズリーフ・ファイル[バインダー]
spring binder
Klemmhefter^M
reliure^F à ressort^M
carpeta^F de costilla^F de resorte^M
raccoglitore^M a molla^F

仕切りカード
dividers
Registriereinlagen^F
feuillets^M intercalaires
divisores^M
divisori^M

レバー[Z式]ファイル
clamp binder
Aktenordner^M
reliure^F à pince^F
carpeta^F con mecanismo^M de presión^F
cartella^F con pressino^M

ファスナー式ファイル
fastener binder
Schnellhefter^M
reliure^F à glissière^F
carpeta^F de broches^M
cartella^F con linguetta^F

情報伝達とオフィス・オートメーション

ポスト・バインダー
post binder
Hefter^M
reliure^F à vis^F
carpeta^F de tornillos^M
portatabulati^M

リング・ファイル[バインダー]
ring binder
Ringbuch^N
classeur^M
carpeta^F de argollas^F
raccoglitore^M ad anelli^M

書類フォルダー
document folder
Dokumentenmappe^F
pochette^F d'information^F
carpeta^F con guardas^F
cartella^F per documenti^M

タブ
tab
Reiter^M
onglet^M
indicador^M
linguetta^F

個別フォルダー
folder
Aktenmappe^F
chemise^F
carpeta^F de archivo^M
cartelletta^F

山付きファイル
file guides
Karteiregister^N
guides^M de classement^M
guías^F de archivo^M
divisori^M alfabetici per schedario^M

ハンギング[ハンガー]フォルダー
hanging file; *suspension file*
Hängemappe^F
dossier^M suspendu
archivador^M colgante
cartella^F sospesa

ウインドー・タブ
window tab
durchsichtiger Reiter^M
onglet^M à fenêtre^F
indicador^M transparente
linguetta^F con finestra^F

オフィス・オートメーション | OFFICE AUTOMATION
BÜROAUTOMATION | BUREAUTIQUE | AUTOMATIZACIÓN DE LA OFICINA | BUROTICA E FORNITURE PER L'UFFICIO

文房具

スパイラル[スプリング]ノート
spiral binder
Spiralringbuch[N]
reliure[F] spirale[F]
carpeta[F] de espiral[F]
rilegatura[F] con spirale[F]

クリップ・ボード
clipboard
Klemmbrett[N]
planchette[F] à pince[F]
tabla[F] con pinza[F]
tavoletta[F] portablocco[M]

アーチボード
archboard
Ringablage[F]
planchette[F] à arches[F]
tabla[F] con argollas[F]
portablocco[M]

インデックス・カード引き出し
index card drawer
Karteischubfach[N]
tiroir[M] de fichier[M]
gaveta[F] de archivador[M]
cassetto[M] di schedario[M]

仕切り
compressor
Begrenzungseinsatz[M]
compresseur[M]
compresor[M]
pressore[M]

金属レール
metal rail
Führungsschiene[F]
tringle[F] métallique
riel[M] metálico
guida[F] metallica

インデックス・カード・キャビネット
index card cabinet
Karteikasten[M]
fichier[M]
archivador[M] de fichas[F]
schedario[M]

ラベル[テープ]ライター
label maker
Präger[M]
pince[F] à étiqueter
rotulador[M]
etichettatrice[F]

ラベル入れ
label holder
Etikettenfenster[N]
porte-étiquette[M]
soporte[M] del rótulo[M]
portaetichetta[F]

コム・バインダー
comb binding
Spiralheftung[F]
reliure[F] à anneaux[M] plastiques
encuadernación[F] de anillas[F]
rilegatura[F] con spirale[F]

ファイル・ボックス
filing box
Aktenbox[F]
boîte[F]-classeur[F]
caja[F] archivo[M]
scatola[F] per archivio[M]

パンチ
paper punch
Locher[M]
perforatrice[F]
perforadora[F]
perforatore[M]

ドキュメント・ファイル
expanding file
Erweiterungskartei[F]
pochette[F] de classement[M]
archivador[M] de fuelle[M]
classificatore[M] a soffietto[M]

情報伝達とオフィス・オートメーション

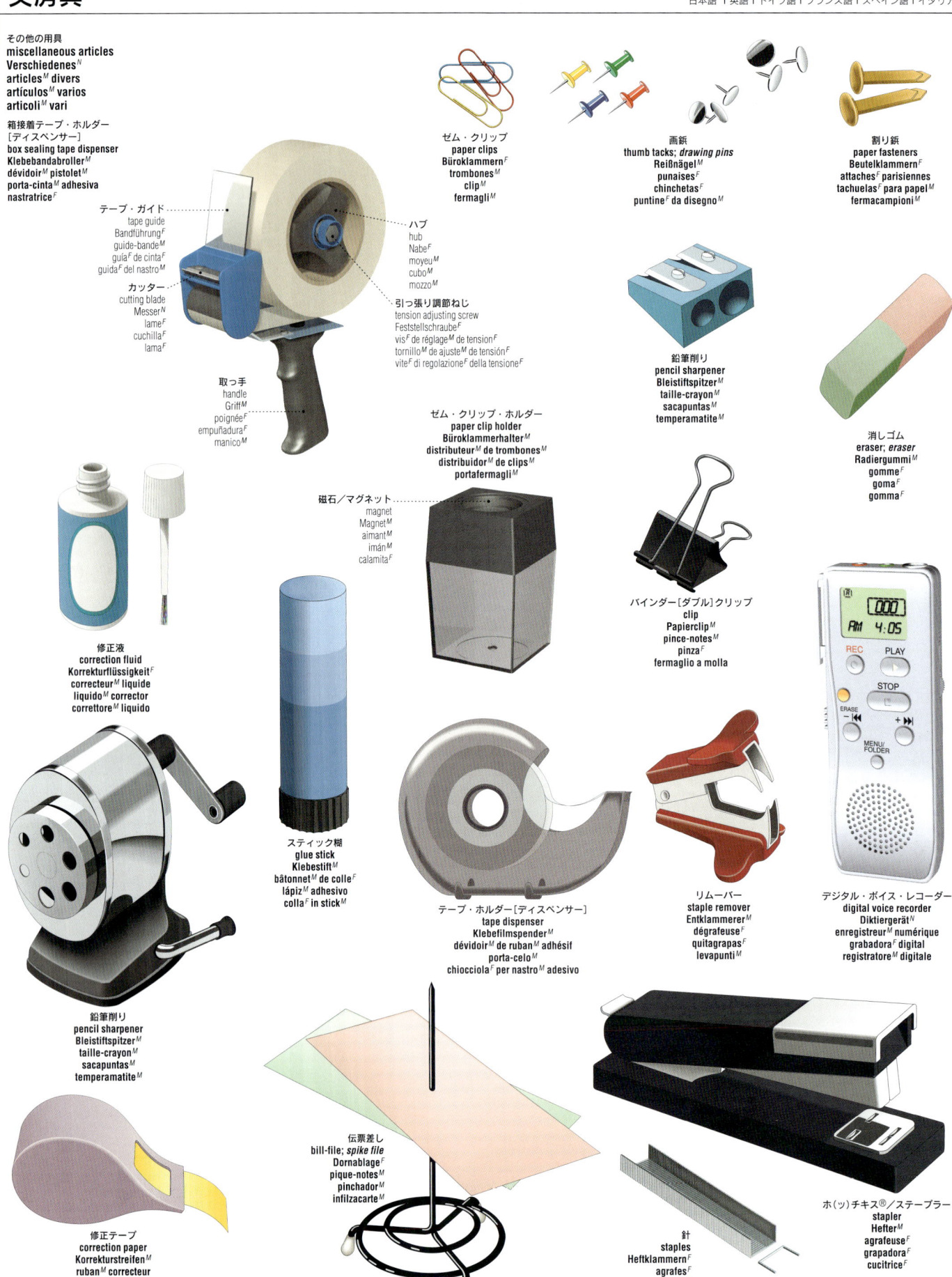

オフィス・オートメーション | OFFICE AUTOMATION
BÜROAUTOMATION | BUREAUTIQUE | AUTOMATIZACIÓN DE LA OFICINA | BUROTICA E FORNITURE PER L'UFFICIO

文房具

日本語 | 英語 | ドイツ語 | フランス語 | スペイン語 | イタリア語

その他の用具
miscellaneous articles
Verschiedenes^N
articles^M divers
artículos^M varios
articoli^M vari

箱接着テープ・ホルダー
[ディスペンサー]
box sealing tape dispenser
Klebebandabroller^M
dévidoir^M pistolet^M
porta-cinta^F adhesiva
nastratrice^F

ゼム・クリップ
paper clips
Büroklammern^F
trombones^M
clip^M
fermagli^M

画鋲
thumb tacks; drawing pins
Reißnägel^M
punaises^F
chinchetas^F
puntine^F da disegno^M

割り鋲
paper fasteners
Beutelklammern^F
attaches^F parisiennes
tachuelas^F para papel^M
fermacampioni^M

テープ・ガイド
tape guide
Bandführung^F
guide-bande^M
guía^F de cinta^F
guida^F del nastro^M

ハブ
hub
Nabe^F
moyeu^M
cubo^M
mozzo^M

カッター
cutting blade
Messer^N
lame^F
cuchilla^F
lama^F

引っ張り調節ねじ
tension adjusting screw
Feststellschraube^F
vis^F de réglage^M de tension^F
tornillo^M de ajuste^M de tensión^F
vite^F di regolazione^F della tensione^F

鉛筆削り
pencil sharpener
Bleistiftspitzer^M
taille-crayon^M
sacapuntas^M
temperamatite^M

取っ手
handle
Griff^M
poignée^F
empuñadura^F
manico^M

ゼム・クリップ・ホルダー
paper clip holder
Büroklammerhalter^M
distributeur^M de trombones^M
distribuidor^M de clips^M
portafermagli^M

消しゴム
eraser; eraser
Radiergummi^M
gomme^F
goma^F
gomma^F

磁石/マグネット
magnet
Magnet^M
aimant^M
imán^M
calamita^F

修正液
correction fluid
Korrekturflüssigkeit^F
correcteur^M liquide
líquido^M corrector
correttore^M liquido

バインダー[ダブル]クリップ
clip
Papierclip^M
pince-notes^M
pinza^F
fermaglio a molla

スティック糊
glue stick
Klebestift^M
bâtonnet^M de colle^F
lápiz^M adhesivo
colla^F in stick^M

テープ・ホルダー[ディスペンサー]
tape dispenser
Klebefilmspender^M
dévidoir^M de ruban^M adhésif
porta-celo^M
chiocciola^F per nastro^M adesivo

リムーバー
staple remover
Entklammerer^M
dégrafeuse^F
quitagrapas^F
levapunti^M

デジタル・ボイス・レコーダー
digital voice recorder
Diktiergerät^N
enregistreur^M numérique
grabadora^F digital
registratore^M digitale

鉛筆削り
pencil sharpener
Bleistiftspitzer^M
taille-crayon^M
sacapuntas^M
temperamatite^M

伝票差し
bill-file; spike file
Dornablage^F
pique-notes^M
pinchador^M
infilzacarte

修正テープ
correction paper
Korrekturstreifen^M
ruban^M correcteur
papel^M corrector
nastro^M per correzioni^F

針
staples
Heftklammern^F
agrafes^F
grapas^F
punti^M metallici

ホ(ッ)チキス®/ステープラー
stapler
Hefter^M
agrafeuse^F
grapadora^F
cucitrice^F

情報伝達とオフィス・オートメーション

534

オフィス・オートメーション | OFFICE AUTOMATION
BÜROAUTOMATION | BUREAUTIQUE | AUTOMATIZACIÓN DE LA OFICINA | BUROTICA E FORNITURE PER L'UFFICIO

文房具

オーバーヘッド・プロジェクター／OHP
overhead projector
Tageslichtprojektor^M
rétroprojecteur^M
proyector
proiettore^M

プロジェクター・ヘッド
projection head
Projektionskopf^M
tête^F de projection^F
cabeza^F de proyección^M
testa^F di proiezione^F

レンズ
optical lens
Objektiv^N
lentille^F
lente^F
lenti^F

ミラー
mirror
Spiegel^M
miroir^M
espejo^M
specchio^M

プロジェクター・ステージ
optical stage
Glasplatte^F
platine^F de projection^F
pletina^F de proyección^F
piano^M di proiezione^F

カッター・ヘッド
cutting head
Schneidkopf^M
tête^F de coupe^F
cabeza^F cortadora
testa^F di taglio^M

金銭出納（すいとう）帳
account book
Geschäftsbuch^N, Journal^N
registre^M de comptabilité^F
agenda^F de caja^F
libro^M contabile

屑（くず）入れ
waste basket
Papierkorb^M
corbeille^F à papier^M
papelera
cestino^M

紙屑（くず）かご
waste basket
Papierkorb^M
corbeille^F à papier^M
papelera
cestino^M

掲示板
bulletin board
Pinnwand^F
tableau^M d'affichage^M
tablero^M de anuncios^M
bacheca^F

ペーパー・シュレッダー
paper shredder
Aktenvernichter^M
destructeur^M de documents^M
destructora^F de documentos^M
distruggidocumenti^M

ブック・エンド
book ends
Bücherstütze^F
serre-livres^M
sujetalibros^M
reggilibri^M

ライト・ボックス
lightbox
Leuchtkasten^M
négatoscope^M
caja^F de luz^F
visore^M

掲示面
posting surface
Anschlagfläche^F
surface^F d'affichage^M
superficie^F de fijación^F
superficie^F di affissione^F

持ち手穴付き段ボール箱
slotted box
amerikanische Faltschachtel^F
caisse^F américaine
caja^F de cartón^M
scatola^F americana

蓋（ふた）
flap
Klappe^F
rabat^M
solapa^F
lembo^M

紙断裁機
paper cutter
Papierschneider^M
cisaille^F
guillotina^F
taglierina^F

持ち手穴
hand hole
Griffloch^N
poignée^F découpée
empuñadura^F recortada
fessura^F di sollevamento^M

情報伝達とオフィス・オートメーション

538 道路交通

- 538 道路網
- 540 固定橋
- 542 可動橋
- 543 道路トンネル
- 544 道路標識
- 548 ガソリン・スタンド
- 549 自動車
- 559 ブレーキ
- 560 タイヤ
- 561 ラジエーター／放熱器
- 562 点火プラグ
- 562 バッテリー／蓄電池
- 563 電気自動車
- 563 ハイブリッド（自動）車
- 564 エンジンの種類
- 567 トレーラー・ハウス
- 568 バス
- 570 トラック運送
- 574 オートバイ
- 577 四輪駆動の全地形型車両
- 578 自転車

582 鉄道輸送

- 582 旅客駅
- 583 鉄道駅
- 584 客車の種類
- 585 高速列車
- 586 ディーゼル電気機関車
- 587 貨車
- 589 操車場
- 590 鉄道線路
- 591 踏切
- 592 地下鉄
- 595 路面［市街］電車

596 海上交通

- 596 港
- 597 運河の閘門（こうもん）
- 598 昔の船
- 599 伝統的な船
- 601 帆の例
- 601 帆装の例
- 602 4本マスト・バーグ（型帆船）
- 604 ボートと船の例
- 610 錨
- 611 救命用具
- 612 航海計器
- 614 海路標識
- 616 海上浮標式

交通と機械

TRANSPORT AND MACHINERY I TRANSPORT UND FAHRZEUGE I TRANSPORT ET MACHINERIE I
TRANSPORTE Y VEHÍCULOS I TRASPORTI E VEICOLI

618 航空交通

- 618 空港
- 624 大型[長距離]ジェット機
- 626 操縦室／フライト・デッキ
- 627 ターボファン・エンジン
- 628 飛行機の例
- 629 尾翼形状の例
- 630 主翼形状の例
- 630 飛行機に作用する力
- 630 飛行機の動き
- 631 ヘリコプター
- 631 ヘリコプターの例

632 搬送

- 632 搬送装置
- 634 クレーン
- 635 コンテナ

636 重機器

- 636 ブルドーザー
- 637 ホイール・ローダー
- 638 スクレーパー
- 638 油圧式ショベル
- 639 グレーダー／地均(なら)し機
- 639 ダンプ・トラック
- 640 トラクター
- 641 農業機械

道路交通 | ROAD TRANSPORT
STRASSENVERKEHR | TRANSPORT ROUTIER | TRANSPORTE TERRESTRE | TRASPORTO SU STRADA

道路網

road system | Straßenbau[M] | système[M] routier | sistema[M] de carreteras[F] | sistema[M] stradale

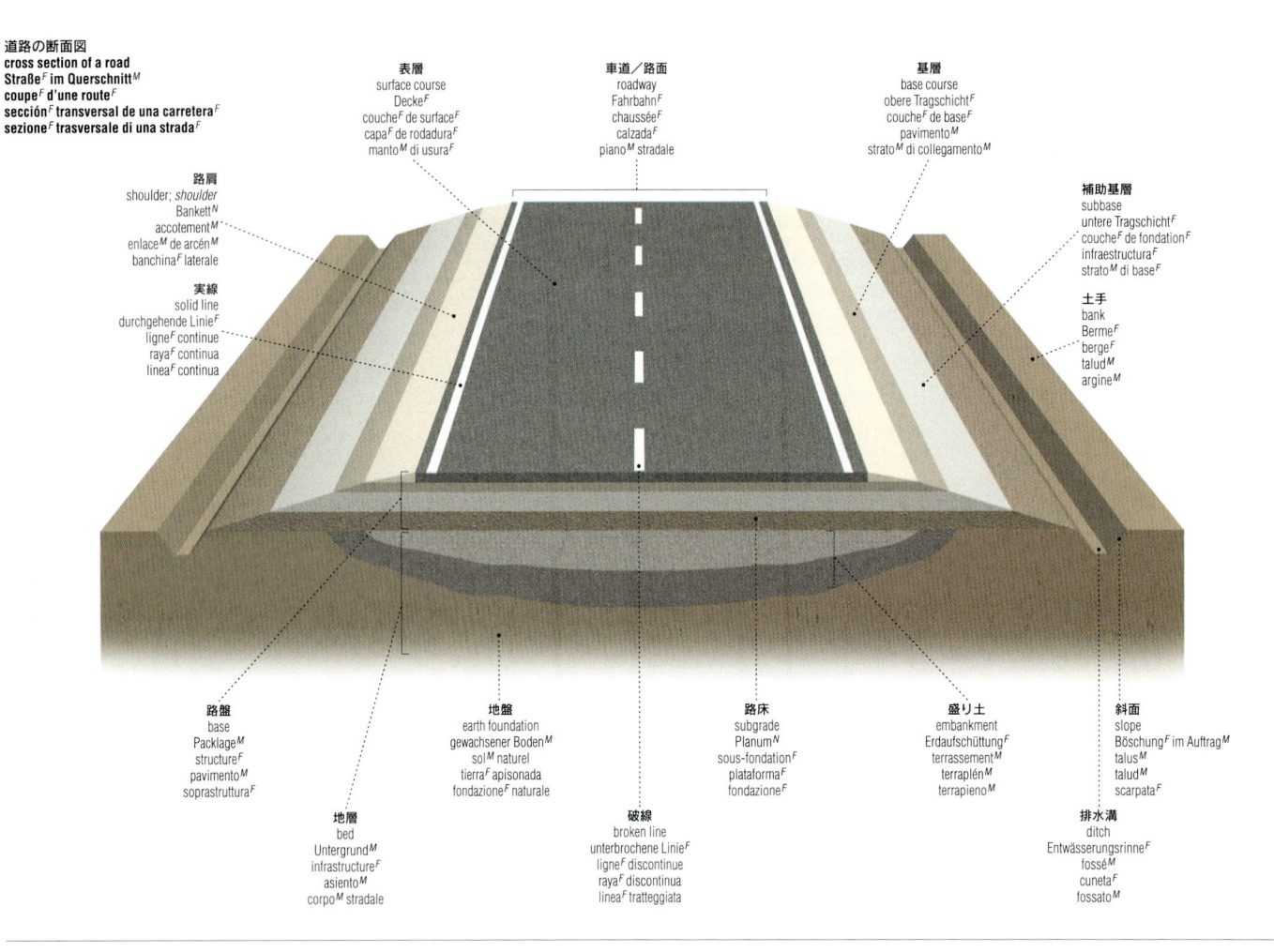

道路の断面図
cross section of a road
Straße[F] im Querschnitt[M]
coupe[F] d'une route[F]
sección[F] transversal de una carretera[F]
sezione[F] trasversale di una strada[F]

表層
surface course
Decke[F]
couche[F] de surface[F]
capa[F] de rodadura[F]
manto[M] di usura[F]

車道／路面
roadway
Fahrbahn[F]
chaussée[F]
calzada[F]
piano[M] stradale

基層
base course
obere Tragschicht[F]
couche[F] de base[F]
pavimento[M]
strato[M] di collegamento[M]

路肩
shoulder; *shoulder*
Bankett[N]
accotement[M]
enlace[M] de arcén[M]
banchina[F] laterale

補助基層
subbase
untere Tragschicht[F]
couche[F] de fondation[F]
infraestructura[F]
strato[M] di base[F]

実線
solid line
durchgehende Linie[F]
ligne[F] continue
raya[F] continua
linea[F] continua

土手
bank
Berme[F]
berge[F]
talud[M]
argine[M]

路盤
base
Packlage[M]
structure[F]
pavimento[M]
soprastruttura[F]

地盤
earth foundation
gewachsener Boden[M]
sol[M] naturel
tierra[F] apisonada
fondazione[F] naturale

路床
subgrade
Planum[N]
sous-fondation[F]
plataforma[F]
fondazione[F]

盛り土
embankment
Erdaufschüttung[F]
terrassement[M]
terraplén[M]
terrapieno[M]

斜面
slope
Böschung[F] im Auftrag[M]
talus[M]
talud[M]
scarpata[F]

地層
bed
Untergrund[M]
infrastructure[F]
asiento[M]
corpo[M] stradale

破線
broken line
unterbrochene Linie[F]
ligne[F] discontinue
raya[F] discontinua
linea[F] tratteggiata

排水溝
ditch
Entwässerungsrinne[F]
fossé[M]
cuneta[F]
fossato[M]

インターチェンジの例
examples of interchanges
Beispiele[N] für Anschlussstellen[F]
exemples[M] d'échangeurs[M]
ejemplos[M] de enlaces[M] de carreteras[F]
esempi[M] di raccordo[M]

クローバー型インターチェンジ
cloverleaf
Kleeblatt[N]
échangeur[M] en trèfle[M]
enlace[M] de trébol[M]
raccordo[M] a quadrifoglio[M]

ロータリー型インターチェンジ
traffic circle
Verteiler[M]
carrefour[M] giratoire
enlace[M] de glorieta[F]
raccordo[M] a rotatoria[F]

ダイヤモンド型インターチェンジ
diamond interchange
Raute[F]
échangeur[M] en losange[M]
enlace[M] de diamante[M]
raccordo[M] a losanga[F]

トランペット型インターチェンジ
trumpet interchange
Trompete[F]
échangeur[M] en trompette[F]
trompeta[F]
raccordo[M] a tromba[F]

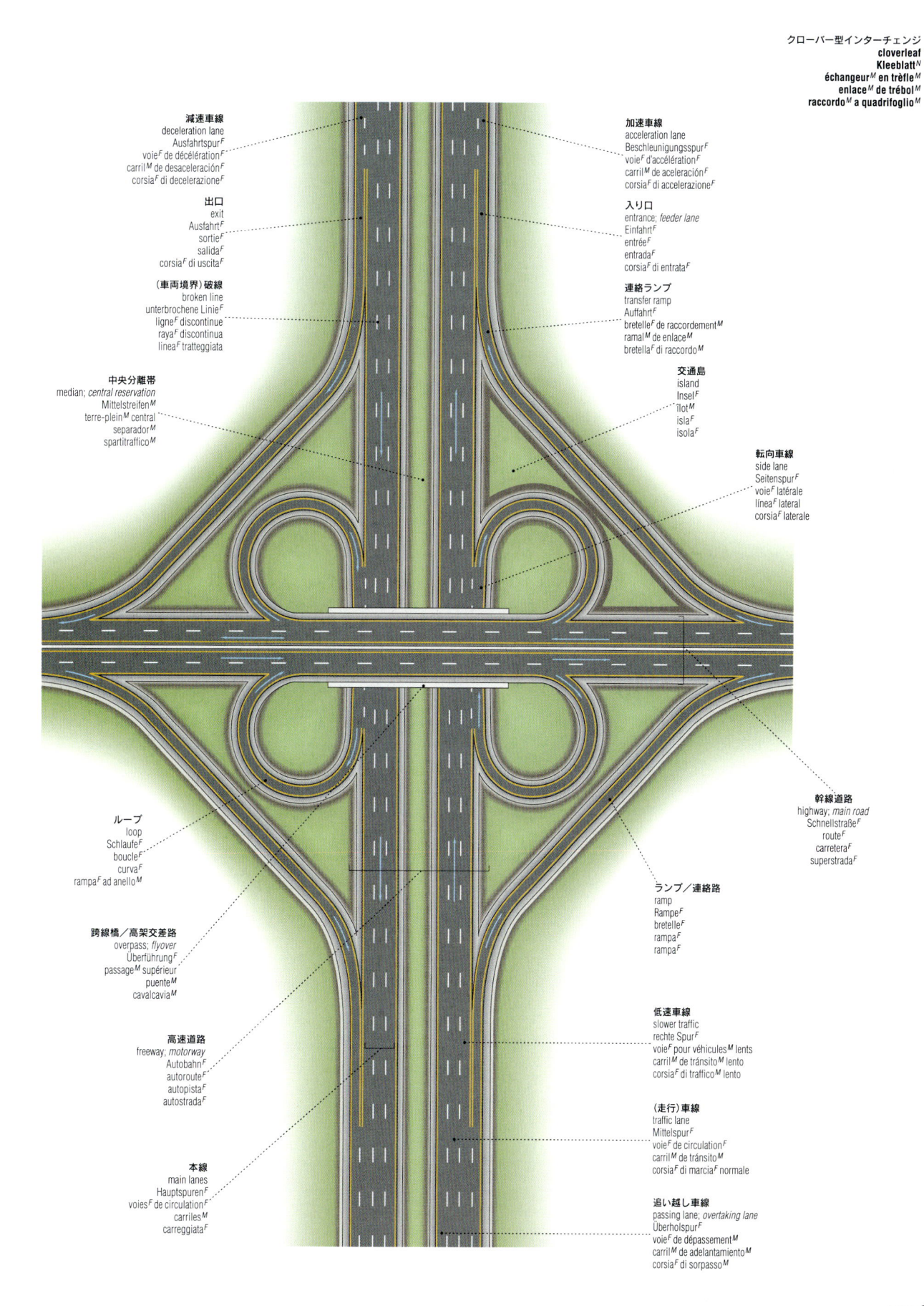

道路交通 | ROAD TRANSPORT
STRASSENVERKEHR | TRANSPORT ROUTIER | TRANSPORTE TERRESTRE | TRASPORTO SU STRADA

道路網

クローバー型インターチェンジ
cloverleaf
Kleeblatt^N
échangeur^M en trèfle^M
enlace^M de trébol^M
raccordo^M a quadrifoglio^M

減速車線
deceleration lane
Ausfahrtspur^F
voie^F de décélération^F
carril^M de desaceleración^F
corsia^F di decelerazione^F

加速車線
acceleration lane
Beschleunigungsspur^F
voie^F d'accélération^F
carril^M de aceleración^F
corsia^F di accelerazione^F

出口
exit
Ausfahrt^F
sortie^F
salida^F
corsia^F di uscita^F

入り口
entrance; *feeder lane*
Einfahrt^F
entrée^F
entrada^F
corsia^F di entrata^F

(車両境界)破線
broken line
unterbrochene Linie^F
ligne^F discontinue
raya^F discontinua
linea^F tratteggiata

連絡ランプ
transfer ramp
Auffahrt^F
bretelle^F de raccordement^M
ramal^M de enlace^M
bretella^F di raccordo^M

中央分離帯
median; *central reservation*
Mittelstreifen^M
terre-plein^M central
separador^M
spartitraffico^M

交通島
island
Insel^F
îlot^M
isla^F
isola^F

転向車線
side lane
Seitenspur^F
voie^F latérale
línea^F lateral
corsia^F laterale

ループ
loop
Schlaufe^F
boucle^F
curva^F
rampa^F ad anello^M

幹線道路
highway; *main road*
Schnellstraße^F
route^F
carretera^F
superstrada^F

跨線橋/高架交差路
overpass; *flyover*
Überführung^F
passage^M supérieur
puente^M
cavalcavia^M

ランプ/連絡路
ramp
Rampe^F
bretelle^F
rampa^F
rampa^F

高速道路
freeway; *motorway*
Autobahn^F
autoroute^F
autopista^F
autostrada^F

低速車線
slower traffic
rechte Spur^F
voie^F pour véhicules^M lents
carril^M de tránsito^M lento
corsia^F di traffico^M lento

(走行)車線
traffic lane
Mittelspur^F
voie^F de circulation^F
carril^M de tránsito^M
corsia^F di marcia^F normale

本線
main lanes
Hauptspuren^F
voies^F de circulation^F
carriles^M
carreggiata^F

追い越し車線
passing lane; *overtaking lane*
Überholspur^F
voie^F de dépassement^F
carril^M de adelantamiento^M
corsia^F di sorpasso^M

道路交通 | ROAD TRANSPORT
STRASSENVERKEHR | TRANSPORT ROUTIER | TRANSPORTE TERRESTRE | TRASPORTO SU STRADA

固定橋

日本語 | 英語 | ドイツ語 | フランス語 | スペイン語 | イタリア語

fixed bridges | starre Brücken^F | ponts^M fixes | puentes^M fijos | ponti^M fissi

桁橋
beam bridge
Balkenbrücke^F
pont^M à poutre^F
puente^M de viga^F
ponte^M a travata^F

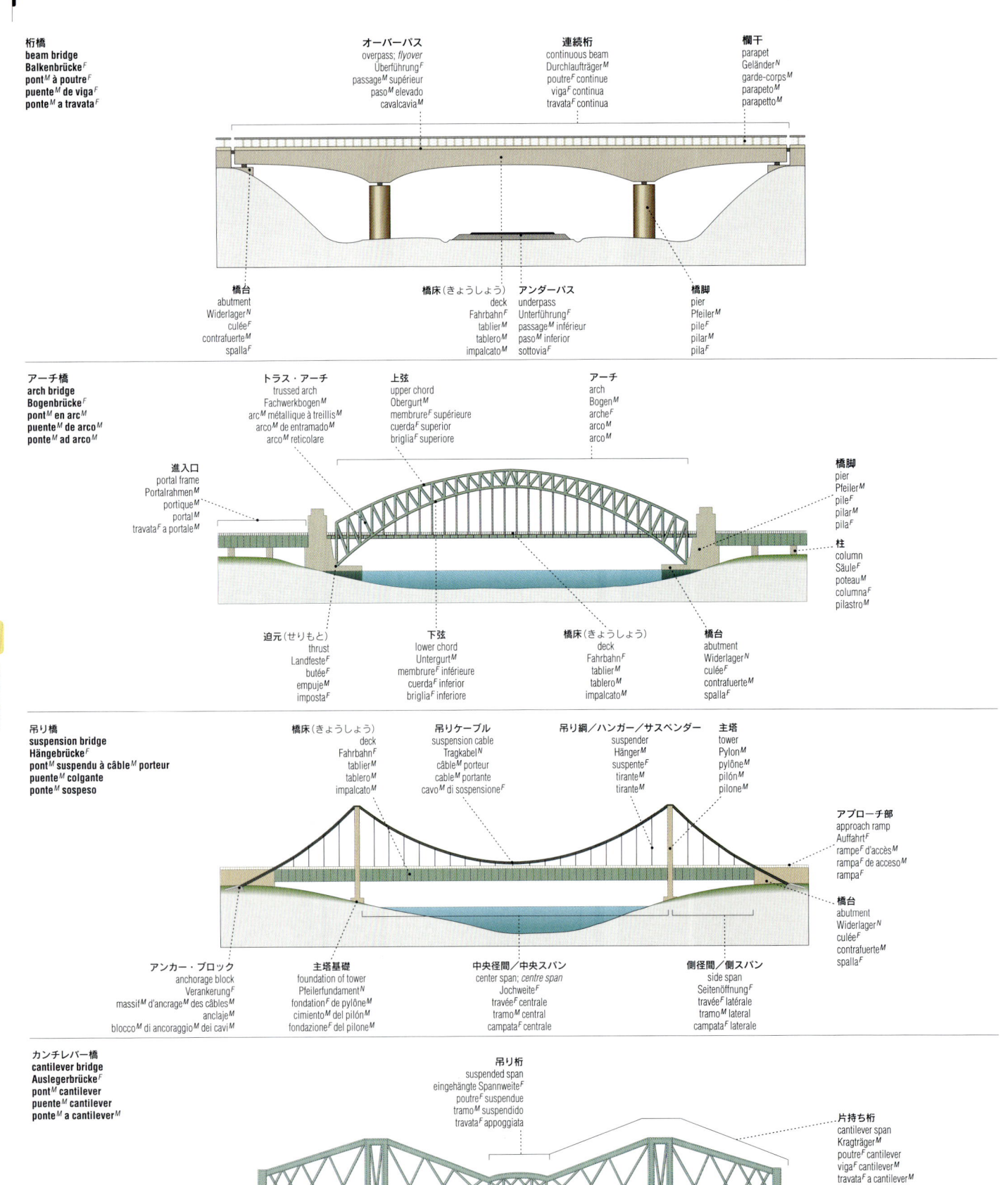

オーバーパス
overpass; flyover
Überführung^F
passage^M supérieur
paso^M elevado
cavalcavia^M

連続桁
continuous beam
Durchlaufträger^M
poutre^F continue
viga^F continua
travata^F continua

欄干
parapet
Geländer^N
garde-corps^M
parapeto^M
parapetto^M

橋台
abutment
Widerlager^N
culée^F
contrafuerte^M
spalla^F

橋床（きょうしょう）
deck
Fahrbahn^F
tablier^M
tablero^M
impalcato^M

アンダーパス
underpass
Unterführung^F
passage^M inférieur
paso^M inferior
sottovia^F

橋脚
pier
Pfeiler^M
pile^F
pilar^M
pila^F

アーチ橋
arch bridge
Bogenbrücke^F
pont^M en arc^M
puente^M de arco^M
ponte^M ad arco^M

トラス・アーチ
trussed arch
Fachwerkbogen^M
arc^M métallique à treillis^M
arco^M de entramado^M
arco^M reticolare

上弦
upper chord
Obergurt^M
membrure^F supérieure
cuerda^F superior
briglia^F superiore

アーチ
arch
Bogen^M
arche^F
arco^M
arco^M

進入口
portal frame
Portalrahmen^M
portique^M
portal^M
travata^F a portale^M

橋脚
pier
Pfeiler^M
pile^F
pilar^M
pila^F

柱
column
Säule^F
poteau^M
columna^F
pilastro^M

迫元（せりもと）
thrust
Landfeste^F
butée^F
empuje^M
imposta^F

下弦
lower chord
Untergurt^M
membrure^F inférieure
cuerda^F inferior
briglia^F inferiore

橋床（きょうしょう）
deck
Fahrbahn^F
tablier^M
tablero^M
impalcato^M

橋台
abutment
Widerlager^N
culée^F
contrafuerte^M
spalla^F

吊り橋
suspension bridge
Hängebrücke^F
pont^M suspendu à câble^M porteur
puente^M colgante
ponte^M sospeso

橋床（きょうしょう）
deck
Fahrbahn^F
tablier^M
tablero^M
impalcato^M

吊りケーブル
suspension cable
Tragkabel^N
câble^M porteur
cable^M portante
cavo^M di sospensione^F

吊り綱／ハンガー／サスペンダー
suspender
Hänger^M
suspente^F
tirante^M
tirante^M

主塔
tower
Pylon^M
pylône^F
pilón^M
pilone^M

アプローチ部
approach ramp
Auffahrt^F
rampe^F d'accès^M
rampa^F de acceso^M
rampa^F

橋台
abutment
Widerlager^N
culée^F
contrafuerte^M
spalla^F

アンカー・ブロック
anchorage block
Verankerung^F
massif^M d'ancrage^M des câbles^M
anclaje^M
blocco^M di ancoraggio^M dei cavi^M

主塔基礎
foundation of tower
Pfeilerfundament^N
fondation^F de pylône^M
cimiento^M del pilón^M
fondazione^F del pilone^M

中央径間／中央スパン
center span; centre span
Jochweite^F
travée^F centrale
tramo^M central
campata^F centrale

側径間／側スパン
side span
Seitenöffnung^F
travée^F latérale
tramo^M lateral
campata^F laterale

カンチレバー橋
cantilever bridge
Auslegerbrücke^F
pont^M cantilever
puente^M cantilever
ponte^M a cantilever^M

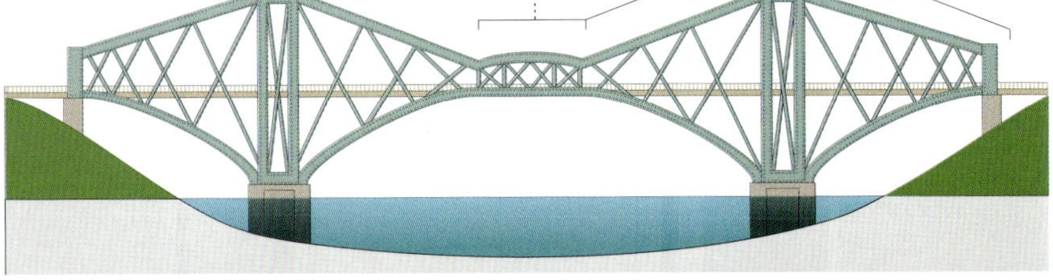

吊り桁
suspended span
eingehängte Spannweite^F
poutre^F suspendue
tramo^M suspendido
travata^F appoggiata

片持ち桁
cantilever span
Kragträger^M
poutre^F cantilever
viga^F cantilever^M
travata^F a cantilever^M

道路交通 | ROAD TRANSPORT
STRASSENVERKEHR | TRANSPORT ROUTIER | TRANSPORTE TERRESTRE | TRASPORTO SU STRADA

固定橋

斜張ケーブル定着部
cable stay anchorage
Schrägseilverankerung^F
ancrage^M des haubans^M
pilón^M de los tirantes^M
ancoraggio^M degli stralli^M

斜張ケーブル
stays
Abspannseile^N
haubans^M
tirantes^M
stralli^M

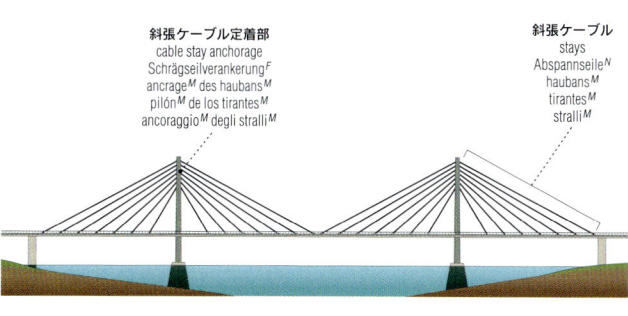

斜張橋
cable-stayed bridges
Schrägseilbrücke^F
ponts^M suspendus à haubans^M
puentes^M de tirantes^M
ponti^M strallati

扇形斜張ケーブル
fan cable stays
Zügelgurte^N
haubans^M en éventail^M
tirantes^M en abanico^M
stralli^M a ventaglio^M

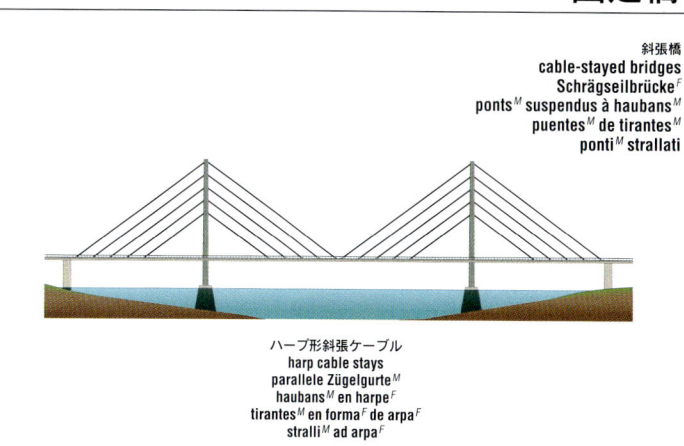

ハープ形斜張ケーブル
harp cable stays
parallele Zügelgurte^M
haubans^M en harpe^M
tirantes^M en forma^F de arpa^F
stralli^M ad arpa^F

アーチ橋の例
examples of arch bridges
Beispiele^N für Bogenbrücken^F
exemples^M de ponts^M en arc^M
ejemplos^M de puentes^M en arco^M
esempi^M di ponti^M ad arco^M

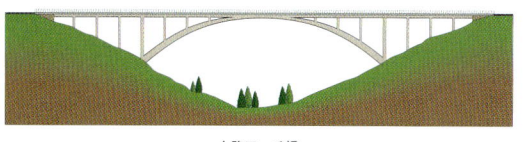

上路アーチ橋
deck arch bridge
aufgeständerte Bogenbrücke^F
pont^M à tablier^M supérieur
puente^M de tablero^M superior
ponte^M a via^F superiore

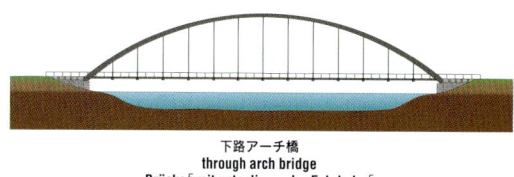

下路アーチ橋
through arch bridge
Brücke^F mit untenliegender Fahrbahn^F
pont^M à tablier^M inférieur
puente^M de tablero^M inferior
ponte^M a via^F inferiore

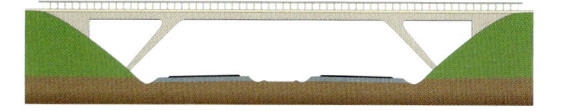

方杖（ほうづえ）橋
portal bridge
Portalbrücke^F
pont^M à béquilles^F
puente^M de portal^M
ponte^M a portale^M

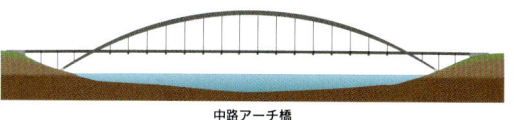

中路アーチ橋
half-through arch bridge
Halbtrogbrücke^F
pont^M à tablier^M intermédiaire
puente^M de tablero^M intermedio
ponte^M a via^F intermedia

アーチの例
examples of arches
Beispiele^N für Bögen^M
exemples^M d'arcs^M
ejemplos^M de arcos^M
esempi^M di archi^M

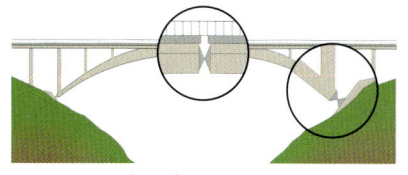

3ヒンジ・アーチ
three-hinged arch
Dreigelenkbogen^M
arc^M à trois articulations^F
arco^M de tres articulaciones^F
arco^M a tre cerniere^F

2ヒンジ・アーチ
two-hinged arch
Zweigelenkbogen^M
arc^M à deux articulations^F
arco^M de dos articulaciones^F
arco^M a due cerniere^F

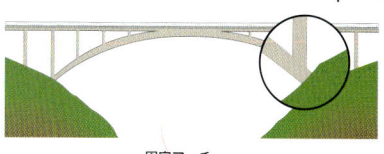

固定アーチ
fixed arch
gelenkloser Bogen^M
arc^M encastré
arco^M fijo
arco^M senza cerniere^F

桁橋の例
examples of beam bridges
Beispiele^N für Balkenbrücken^F
exemples^M de ponts^M à poutre^F
ejemplos^M de puentes^M de vigas^F
esempi^M di ponti^M a travata^F

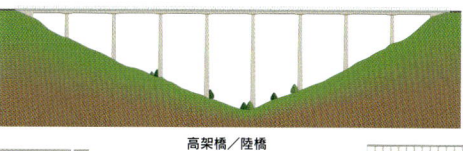

高架橋／陸橋
viaduct
Viadukt^M
viaduc^M
viaducto^M
viadotto^M

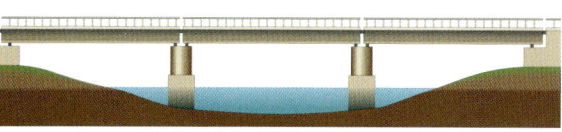

連続桁橋
multiple-span beam bridge
Mehrfeldbrücke^F
pont^M à poutres^F indépendantes
puente^M de viga^F de varios tramos^M
ponte^M a travi^F semplici indipendenti

単純桁橋
simple-span beam bridge
Einfeldbrücke^F
pont^M à poutre^F simple
puente^M de viga^F de un tramo^M
ponte^M a trave^M continua

交通と機械

道路交通 | ROAD TRANSPORT
STRASSENVERKEHR | TRANSPORT ROUTIER | TRANSPORTE TERRESTRE | TRASPORTO SU STRADA

可動橋

movable bridges | bewegliche Brücken^F | ponts^M mobiles | puentes^M móviles | ponti^M mobili

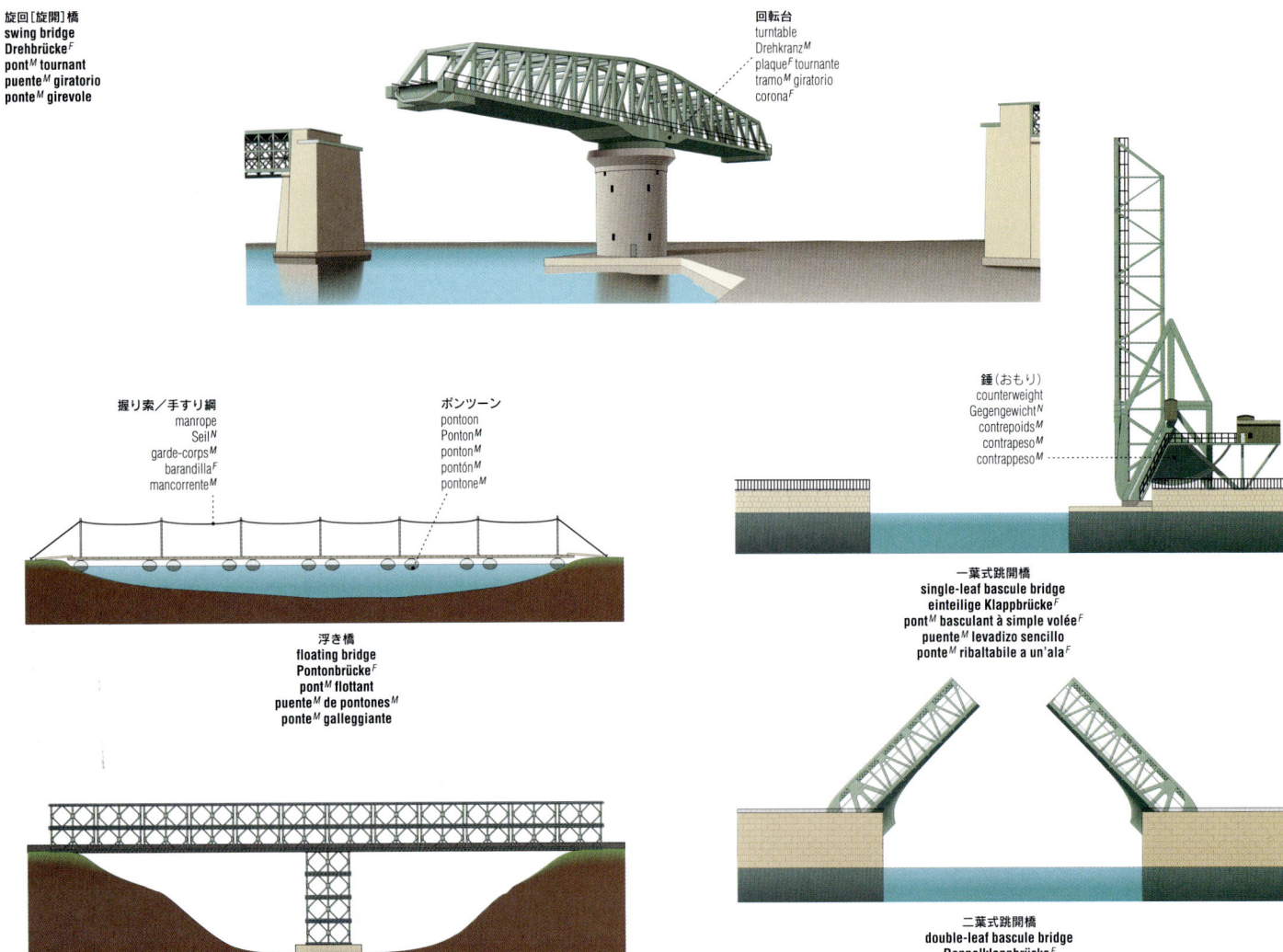

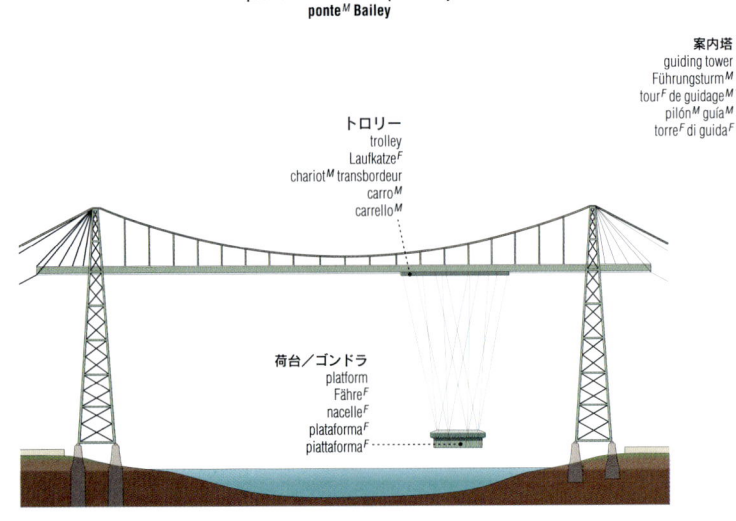

日本語 | 英語 | ドイツ語 | フランス語 | スペイン語 | イタリア語

旋回[旋開]橋
swing bridge
Drehbrücke^F
pont^M tournant
puente^M giratorio
ponte^M girevole

回転台
turntable
Drehkranz^M
plaque^F tournante
tramo^M giratorio
corona^F

握り索／手すり綱
manrope
Seil^N
garde-corps^M
barandilla^F
mancorrente^M

ポンツーン
pontoon
Ponton^M
ponton^M
pontón^M
pontone^M

錘（おもり）
counterweight
Gegengewicht^N
contrepoids^M
contrapeso^M
contrappeso^M

浮き橋
floating bridge
Pontonbrücke^F
pont^M flottant
puente^M de pontones
ponte^M galleggiante

一葉式跳開橋
single-leaf bascule bridge
einteilige Klappbrücke^F
pont^M basculant à simple volée^F
puente^M levadizo sencillo
ponte^M ribaltabile a un'ala^F

ベイリー橋
Bailey bridge
Bailey-Brücke^F
pont^M Bailey
puente^M desmontable tipo^M Bailey
ponte^M Bailey

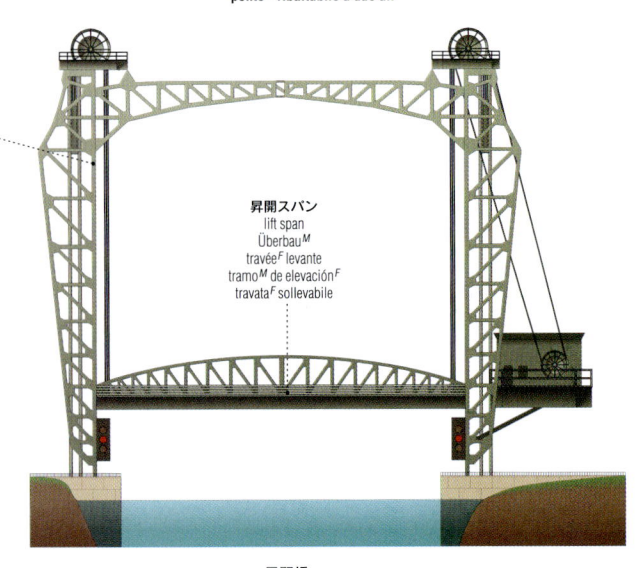

二葉式跳開橋
double-leaf bascule bridge
Doppelklappbrücke^F
pont^M basculant à double volée^F
puente^M levadizo doble
ponte^M ribaltabile a due ali^F

トロリー
trolley
Laufkatze^F
chariot^M transbordeur
carro^M
carrello^M

案内塔
guiding tower
Führungsturm^M
tour^F de guidage
pilón^M guía^M
torre^F di guida^F

昇開スパン
lift span
Überbau^M
travée^F levante
tramo^M de elevación^F
travata^F sollevabile

荷台／ゴンドラ
platform
Fähre^F
nacelle^F
plataforma^F
piattaforma^F

輸送[運搬]橋
transporter bridge
Fährbrücke^F
pont^M transbordeur
puente^M transbordador
ponte^M trasportatore

昇開橋
lift bridge
Hubbrücke^F
pont^M levant
puente^M elevador
ponte^M sollevabile

交通と機械

道路交通 | ROAD TRANSPORT
STRASSENVERKEHR | TRANSPORT ROUTIER | TRANSPORTE TERRESTRE | TRASPORTO SU STRADA

道路トンネル

road tunnel | Straßentunnel^M | tunnel^M routier | túnel^M de carretera^F | galleria^F

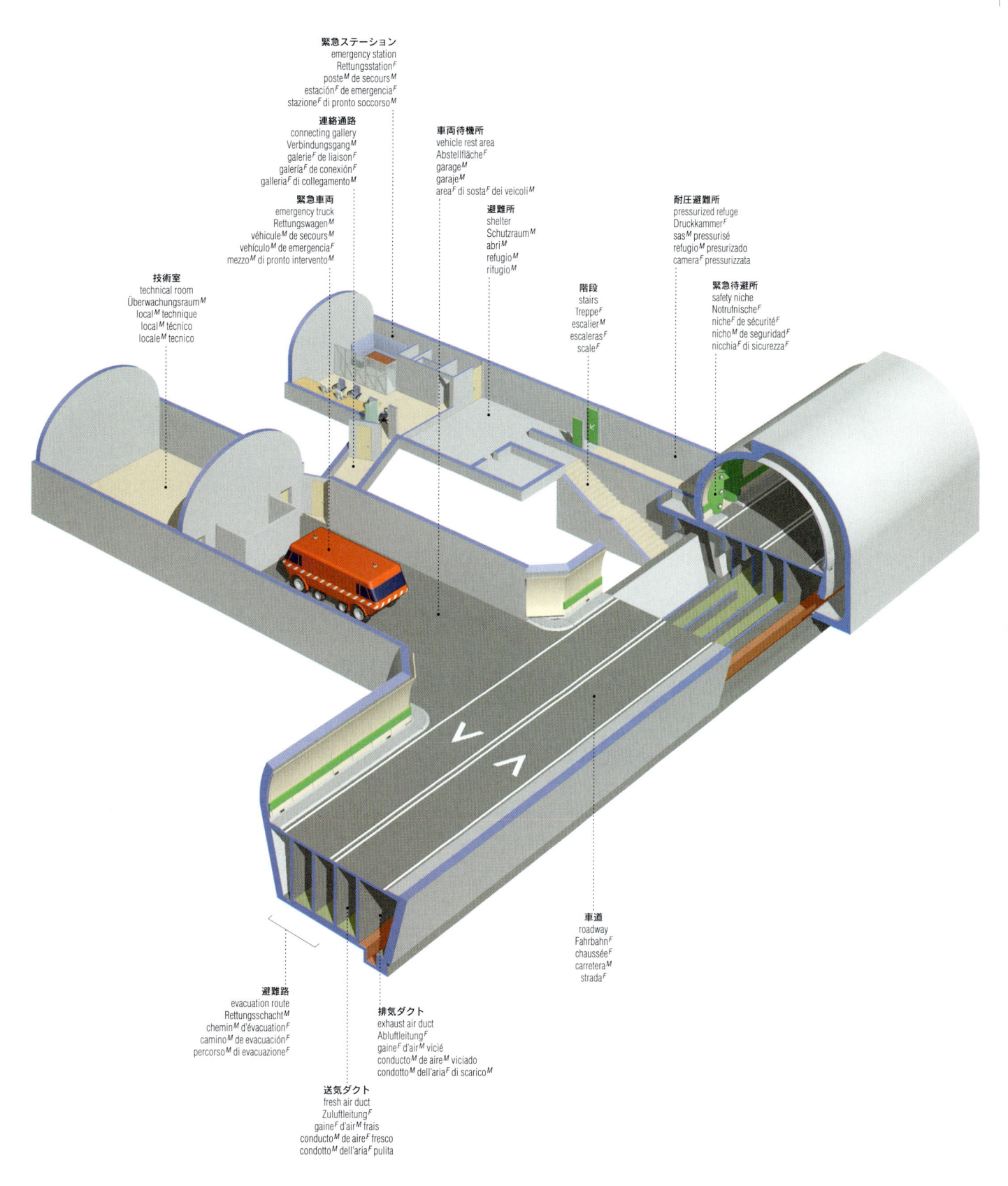

緊急ステーション
emergency station
Rettungsstation^F
poste^M de secours^M
estación^F de emergencia^F
stazione^F di pronto soccorso^M

連絡通路
connecting gallery
Verbindungsgang^M
galerie^F de liaison^F
galería^F de conexión^F
galleria^F di collegamento^M

車両待機所
vehicle rest area
Abstellfläche^F
garage^M
garaje^M
area^F di sosta^F dei veicoli^M

緊急車両
emergency truck
Rettungswagen^M
véhicule^M de secours^M
vehículo^M de emergencia^F
mezzo^M di pronto intervento^M

避難所
shelter
Schutzraum^M
abri^M
refugio^M
rifugio^M

耐圧避難所
pressurized refuge
Druckkammer^F
sas^M pressurisé
refugio^M presurizado
camera^F pressurizzata

技術室
technical room
Überwachungsraum^M
local^M technique
local^M técnico
locale^M tecnico

階段
stairs
Treppe^F
escalier^M
escaleras^F
scale^F

緊急待避所
safety niche
Notrufnische^F
niche^F de sécurité^F
nicho^M de seguridad^F
nicchia^F di sicurezza^F

車道
roadway
Fahrbahn^F
chaussée^F
carretera^M
strada^F

避難路
evacuation route
Rettungsschacht^M
chemin^M d'évacuation^F
camino^M de evacuación^F
percorso^M di evacuazione^F

排気ダクト
exhaust air duct
Abluftleitung^F
gaine^F d'air^M vicié
conducto^M de aire^M viciado
condotto^M dell'aria^F di scarico^M

送気ダクト
fresh air duct
Zuluftleitung^F
gaine^F d'air^M frais
conducto^M de aire^F fresco
condotto^M dell'aria^F pulita

交通と機械

543

道路交通 | ROAD TRANSPORT
STRASSENVERKEHR | TRANSPORT ROUTIER | TRANSPORTE TERRESTRE | TRASPORTO SU STRADA

道路標識

road signs | Verkehrszeichen[N] | signalisation[F] routière | señales[F] de circulación[F] | segnali[M] stradali

主な国際道路標識
major international road signs
die wichtigsten internationalen Verkehrszeichen[N]
principaux panneaux[M] internationaux
principales señales[F] de circulación[F] internacionales
principali segnali[M] stradali internazionali

右方屈曲あり
right bend
Rechtskurve[F]
virage[M] à droite[F]
curva[F] a la derecha[F]
curva[F] a destra

右[左]背向屈折あり
double bend
Doppelkurve[F]
double virage[M]
doble curva[F]
doppia curva[F], la prima a destra

幅員減少
roadway narrows
verengte Fahrbahn[F]
chaussée[F] rétrécie
estrechamiento[M] de la calzada[F]
strettoia[F] simmetrica

交差点につき一時停止
stop at intersection
Halt! Vorfahrt[F] gewähren
arrêt[M] à l'intersection[F]
stop[M]
fermarsi e dare precedenza[F]

車両進入禁止
no entry
Verbot[N] der Einfahrt[F]
accès[M] interdit
prohibido el paso[M]
senso[M] vietato

Uターン[車両転回]禁止
no U-turn
Wenden[N] verboten
interdiction[F] de faire demi-tour[M]
media vuelta[F] prohibida
divieto[M] di inversione[F] di marcia[F]

追い越し禁止
passing prohibited
Überholverbot[N]
interdiction[F] de dépasser
prohibido adelantar
divieto[M] di sorpasso[M]

指定方向外進行禁止
direction to be followed
vorgeschriebene Fahrtrichtung[F]
direction[F] obligatoire
dirección[F] obligatoria
preavviso[M] di direzione[F] obbligatoria a sinistra

指定方向外進行禁止
direction to be followed
vorgeschriebene Fahrtrichtung[F]
direction[F] obligatoire
dirección[F] obligatoria
direzione[F] obbligatoria a sinistra

指定方向外進行禁止
direction to be followed
vorgeschriebene Fahrtrichtung[F]
direction[F] obligatoire
dirección[F] obligatoria
direzione[F] obbligatoria diritto

指定方向外進行禁止
direction to be followed
vorgeschriebene Fahrtrichtung[F]
direction[F] obligatoire
dirección[F] obligatoria
direzioni[F] consentite diritto e a sinistra

一方通行
one-way traffic
Einbahnstraße[F]
voie[F] à sens[M] unique
una vía[F]
strada[F] a senso[M] unico

対面通行／二方向交通
two-way traffic
Gegenverkehr[M]
circulation[F] dans les deux sens[M]
doble vía[F]
doppio senso[M] di circolazione[F]

前方優先道路
yield; *give way*
Vorfahrt[F] gewähren
cédez le passage[M]
ceda el paso[M]
dare precedenza[F]

合流注意／合流交通あり
priority intersection
Vorfahrt[F] an nächster Einmündung[F]
intersection[F] avec priorité[F]
cruce[M] con preferencia[F]
confluenza[F] a destra

544

道路交通 | ROAD TRANSPORT
STRASSENVERKEHR | TRANSPORT ROUTIER | TRANSPORTE TERRESTRE | TRASPORTO SU STRADA

道路標識

交通と機械

落石注意／落石の恐れあり
falling rocks
Steinschlag^M
chutes^F de pierres^F
desprendimientos^M
caduta^F massi^M

高さ制限
overhead clearance
Verbot^N für Fahrzeuge^M mit mehr als der angegebenen Höhe^F
limitation^F de hauteur^F
altura^F máxima
transito^M vietato ai veicoli^M con altezza^F superiore a

信号機あり
signal ahead
Ampelanlage^F
signalisation^F lumineuse
semáforo^M
semaforo^M

スクール・ゾーン／学校あり
school zone
Kinder^N
zone^F scolaire
zona^F escolar
bambini^M

横断歩道
pedestrian crossing
Fußgängerüberweg^M
passage^M pour piétons^M
paso^M de peatones^M
attraversamento^M pedonale

（前方）道路工事中
road works ahead
Baustelle^F
travaux^M
obras^F
lavori^M

スリップ注意／滑りやすし
slippery road
Schleudergefahr^F
chaussée^F glissante
pavimento^M deslizante
strada^F sdrucciolevole

踏切あり
railroad crossing; *level crossing*
Bahnübergang^M
passage^M à niveau^M
paso^M a nivel^M
passaggio^M a livello^M con barriere^F

鹿（の飛び出し）に注意
deer crossing
Wildwechsel^M
passage^M d'animaux^M sauvages
cruce^M de animales^M en libertad^F
animali^M selvatici vaganti

急勾配
steep hill
Gefälle^N
descente^F dangereuse
bajada^F peligrosa
discesa^F pericolosa

路面凹凸あり
bumps
unebene Fahrbahn^F
chaussée^F cahoteuse
badén^M
strada^F deformata

自転車通行止め
closed to bicycles
Verbot^N für Radfahrer^M
accès^M interdit aux bicyclettes^F
prohibido el paso^M de bicicletas^F
transito^M vietato alle biciclette^F

自動二輪車通行止め
closed to motorcycles
Verbot^N für Krafträder^N
accès^M interdit aux motocycles^M
prohibido el paso^M de motocicletas^F
transito^M vietato ai motocicli^M

大型貨物自動車等通行止め
closed to trucks
Verbot^N für Lkws^M über einem zulässigen Gesamtgewicht^N
accès^M interdit aux camions^M
prohibido el paso^M de camiones^M
transito^M vietato agli autocarri^M

歩行者通行止め
closed to pedestrians
Verbot^N für Fußgänger^M
accès^M interdit aux piétons^M
prohibido el paso^M de peatones^M
transito^M vietato ai pedoni^M

道路交通 | ROAD TRANSPORT
STRASSENVERKEHR | TRANSPORT ROUTIER | TRANSPORTE TERRESTRE | TRASPORTO SU STRADA

道路標識

日本語 | 英語 | ドイツ語 | フランス語 | スペイン語 | イタリア語

北アメリカの主な道路標識
major North American road signs
die wichtigsten nordamerikanischen Verkehrszeichen[N]
principaux panneaux[M] nord-américains
principales señales[F] de circulación[F] norteamericanas
principali segnali[M] stradali nordamericani

交差点につき一時停止
stop at intersection
Halt! Vorfahrt[F] gewähren
arrêt[M] à l'intersection[F]
alto
fermarsi e dare precedenza[F]

車両進入禁止
no entry
Verbot[N] der Einfahrt[F]
accès[M] interdit
prohibido el paso[M]
senso[M] vietato

前方優先道路
yield; *give way*
Vorfahrt[F] gewähren
cédez le passage[M]
ceda el paso[M]
dare precedenza[F]

自動二輪車通行止め
closed to motorcycles
Verbot[N] für Krafträder[N]
accès[M] interdit aux motocycles[M]
prohibido el paso[M] de motocicletas[F]
transito[M] vietato ai motocicli[M]

歩行者通行止め
closed to pedestrians
Verbot[N] für Fußgänger[M]
accès[M] interdit aux piétons[M]
prohibido el paso[M] de peatones[M]
transito[M] vietato ai pedoni[M]

自転車通行止め
closed to bicycles
Verbot[N] für Radfahrer[M]
accès[M] interdit aux bicyclettes[F]
prohibido el paso[M] de bicicletas[F]
transito[M] vietato alle biciclette[F]

大型貨物自動車等通行止め
closed to trucks
Verbot[N] für Lkws[M] über einem zulässigen Gesamtgewicht[N]
accès[M] interdit aux camions[M]
prohibido el paso[M] de camiones[M]
transito[M] vietato agli autocarri[M]

指定方向外進行禁止
direction to be followed
vorgeschriebene Fahrtrichtung[F]
direction[F] obligatoire
dirección[F] obligatoria
direzioni[F] consentite diritto e a destra

指定方向外進行禁止
direction to be followed
vorgeschriebene Fahrtrichtung[F]
direction[F] obligatoire
dirección[F] obligatoria
direzione[F] obbligatoria a sinistra

指定方向外進行禁止
direction to be followed
vorgeschriebene Fahrtrichtung[F]
direction[F] obligatoire
dirección[F] obligatoria
direzione[F] obbligatoria a destra

指定方向外進行禁止
direction to be followed
vorgeschriebene Fahrtrichtung[F]
direction[F] obligatoire
dirección[F] obligatoria
direzione[F] obbligatoria diritto

Uターン[車両転回]禁止
no U-turn
Wenden[N] verboten
interdiction[F] de faire demi-tour[M]
prohibido[M] el cambio[M] de sentido[M]
divieto[M] di inversione[F] di marcia[F]

追い越し禁止
passing prohibited
Überholverbot[N]
interdiction[F] de dépasser
prohibido adelantar
divieto[M] di sorpasso[M]

一方通行
one-way traffic
Einbahnstraße[F]
voie[F] à sens[M] unique
una vía[F]
strada[F] a senso[M] unico

対面通行／二方向交通
two-way traffic
Gegenverkehr[M]
circulation[F] dans les deux sens[M]
doble vía[F]
doppio senso[M] di circolazione[F]

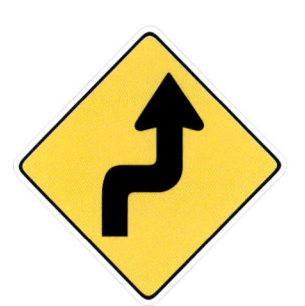

道路交通 | ROAD TRANSPORT
STRASSENVERKEHR | TRANSPORT ROUTIER | TRANSPORTE TERRESTRE | TRASPORTO SU STRADA

道路標識

右[左]背向屈折あり
double bend
Doppelkurve[F]
double virage[M]
curva[F] doble
doppia curva[F], la prima a destra

合流注意／合流交通あり
merging traffic
Vorfahrt[F] an nächster Einmündung[F]
intersection[F] avec priorité[F]
señal[F] de unión[M]
confluenza[F] a destra

右方屈曲あり
right bend
Rechtskurve[F]
virage[M] à droite[F]
curva[F] a la derecha[F]
curva[F] a destra

幅員減少
roadway narrows
verengte Fahrbahn[F]
chaussée[F] rétrécie
estrechamiento[M] de la calzada[F]
strettoia[F] simmetrica

スリップ注意／滑りやすし
slippery road
Schleudergefahr[F]
chaussée[F] glissante
pavimento[M] deslizante
strada[F] sdrucciolevole

鹿（の飛び出し）に注意
deer crossing
Wildwechsel[M]
passage[M] d'animaux sauvages
cruce[M] de animales[M] en libertad
animali[M] selvatici vaganti

（前方）道路工事中
road works ahead
Baustelle[F]
travaux[M]
obras[F]
lavori[M]

路面凹凸あり
bumps
unebene Fahrbahn[F]
chaussée[F] cahoteuse
superficie[F] irregular
strada[F] deformata

急勾配
steep hill
Gefälle[N]
descente[F] dangereuse
bajada[F] pronunciada
discesa[F] pericolosa

落石注意／落石の恐れあり
falling rocks
Steinschlag[M]
chutes[F] de pierres[F]
desprendimientos[M]
caduta[F] massi[M]

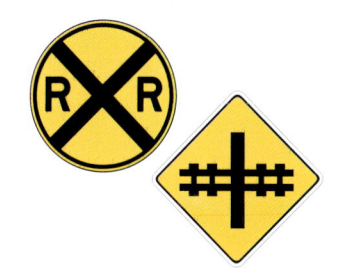

踏切あり
railroad crossing; *level crossing*
Bahnübergang[M]
passage[M] à niveau[M]
paso[M] a nivel[M]
passaggio[M] a livello[M]

高さ制限
overhead clearance
Verbot[N] für Fahrzeuge[N] mit mehr als der angegebenen Höhe[F]
limitation[F] de hauteur[F]
altura[F] máxima
transito[M] vietato ai veicoli[M] con altezza[F] superiore a

信号機あり
signal ahead
Ampelanlage[F]
signalisation[F] lumineuse
semáforo[M]
semaforo[M]

スクール・ゾーン／学校あり
school zone
Schule[F]
zone[F] scolaire
zona[F] escolar
bambini[M]

横断歩道
pedestrian crossing
Fußgängerüberweg[M]
passage[M] pour piétons[M]
paso[M] de peatones[M]
attraversamento[M] pedonale

交通と機械

547

道路交通 | ROAD TRANSPORT
STRASSENVERKEHR | TRANSPORT ROUTIER | TRANSPORTE TERRESTRE | TRASPORTO SU STRADA

ガソリン・スタンド

日本語 | 英語 | ドイツ語 | フランス語 | スペイン語 | イタリア語

service station; *service station* | Tankstelle^F | station^F-service^M | estación^F de servicio^M | stazione^F di servizio^M

ガソリン・ポンプ
gasoline pump; *petrol pump*
Zapfsäule^F
distributeur^M d'essence^F
surtidor^M de gasolina^F
pompa^F della benzina^F

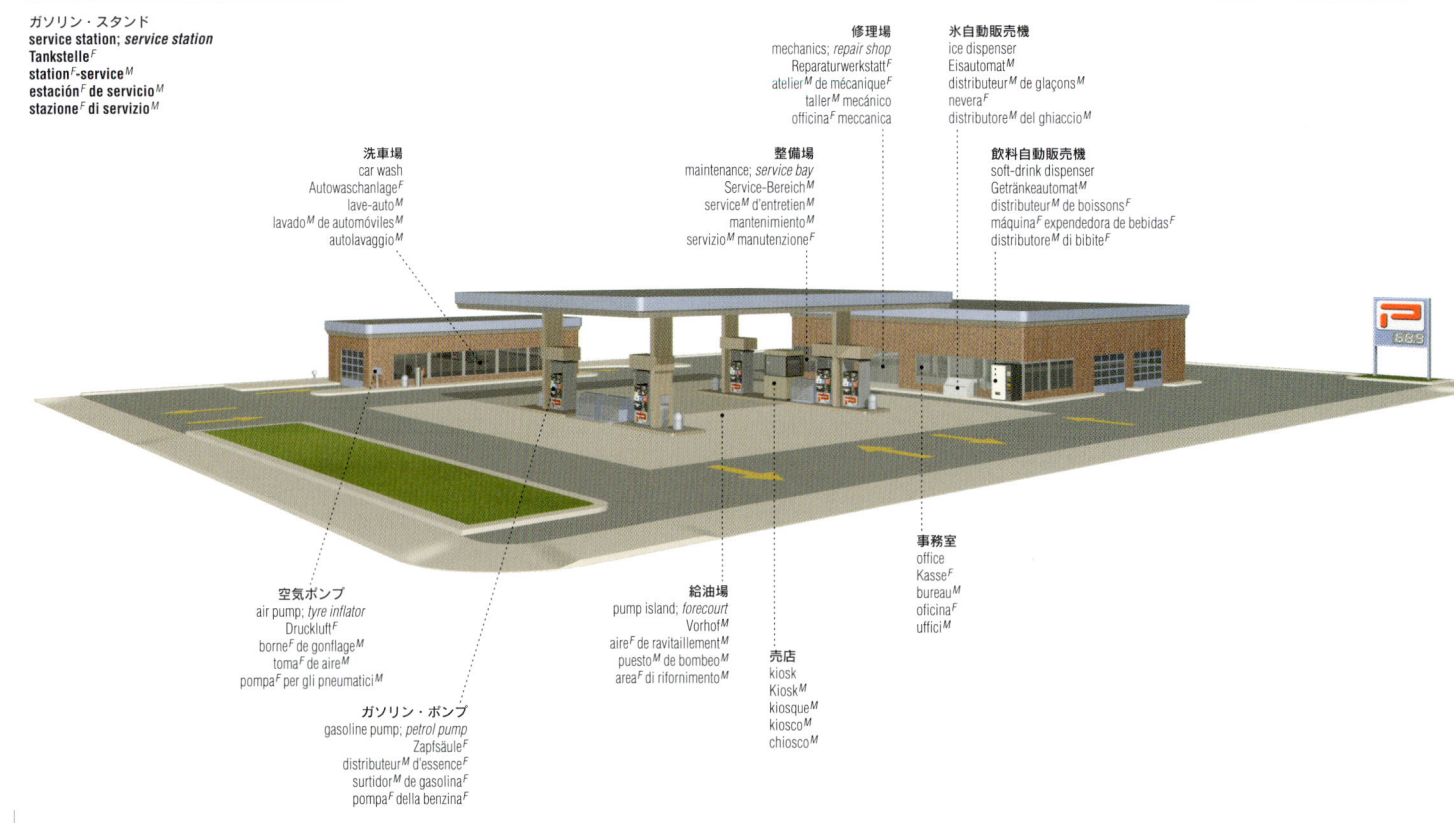

表示窓
display
Anzeige^F
écran^M
display^M
display^M

料金表示メーター
total sale display
Zahlungsbetragsanzeige^F
afficheur^M totaliseur
indicador^M del importe^M total^M
importo^M da pagare

カード読み取りスロット
card reader slot
Kartenleserschlitz^M
fente^F du lecteur^M de carte^F
ranura^F de lectura^F de tarjeta^F
lettore^M di carte^F

量表示メーター
volume display
Füllmengenanzeige^F
afficheur^M volume^M
cuentalitros^M
litri^M erogati

英数(字)キーボード
alphanumeric keyboard
alphanumerische Tastatur^F
clavier^M alphanumérique
teclado^M alfanumérico
tastiera^F alfanumerica

1ガロン[リットル]当たりの単価表示窓
price per gallon/liter; *price per gallon/litre*
Preis^M pro Liter/Gallone^F
afficheur^M prix^M
indicador^M del precio^M por litro^M/galón^M
prezzo^M per litro^M/gallone^M

伝票発行口
slip presenter
Belegausgabe^F
sortie^F des tickets^M
expedidor^F de recibo^M
emissione^F dello scontrino^M

ポンプ番号
pump number
Zapfsäulennummer^F
numéro^M de la pompe^F
número^M de la bomba^F
numero^M della pompa^F

ガソリンの種類
type of fuel
Treibstoffart^F
type^M de carburant^M
tipo^M de combustible^M
tipo^M di carburante^M

給油ノズル
pump nozzle
Zapfhahn^M
pistolet^M de distribution^F
pistola^F del surtidor^M
pistola^F di erogazione^F

操作解説図
operating instructions
Bedienungsanleitung^F
mode^M d'emploi^M
instrucciones^F operativas
istruzioni^F per l'uso^M

給油ホース
gasoline pump hose; *petrol pump hose*
Zapfschlauch^M
flexible^M de distribution^F
manguera^F de servicio^M
tubo^M della pompa^F

交通と機械

ガソリン・スタンド
service station; *service station*
Tankstelle^F
station^F-service^M
estación^F de servicio^M
stazione^F di servizio^M

修理場
mechanics; *repair shop*
Reparaturwerkstatt^F
atelier^F de mécanique^F
taller^M mecánico
officina^F meccanica

氷自動販売機
ice dispenser
Eisautomat^M
distributeur^M de glaçons^M
nevera^F
distributore^M del ghiaccio^M

洗車場
car wash
Autowaschanlage^F
lave-auto^M
lavado^M de automóviles^M
autolavaggio^M

整備場
maintenance; *service bay*
Service-Bereich^M
service^M d'entretien^M
mantenimiento^M
servizio^M manutenzione^F

飲料自動販売機
soft-drink dispenser
Getränkeautomat^M
distributeur^M de boissons^F
máquina^F expendedora de bebidas^F
distributore^M di bibite^F

事務室
office
Kasse^F
bureau^M
oficina^F
uffici^M

空気ポンプ
air pump; *tyre inflator*
Druckluft^F
borne^F de gonflage^M
toma^F de aire^M
pompa^F per gli pneumatici^M

給油場
pump island; *forecourt*
Vorhof^M
aire^F de ravitaillement^M
puesto^M de bombeo^M
area^F di rifornimento^M

売店
kiosk
Kiosk^M
kiosque^M
kiosco^M
chiosco^M

ガソリン・ポンプ
gasoline pump; *petrol pump*
Zapfsäule^F
distributeur^M d'essence^F
surtidor^M de gasolina^F
pompa^F della benzina^F

道路交通 | ROAD TRANSPORT
STRASSENVERKEHR | TRANSPORT ROUTIER | TRANSPORTE TERRESTRE | TRASPORTO SU STRADA

自動車

automobile | Auto[N] | automobile[F] | automóvil[M] | automobile[F]

車体の例
examples of bodies
Beispiele[N] für Karosserien[F]
exemples[M] de carrosseries[F]
ejemplos[M] de carrocerías[F]
esempi[M] di carrozzerie[F]

スポーツ・カー
sports car
Sportwagen[M]
voiture[F] sport
deportivo[M]
granturismo[F]

超小型車／マイクロ・コンパクト・カー
micro compact car
Kleinwagen[M]
voiture[F] micro-compacte
automóvil[M] urbanita
microvettura[F] compatta

ハッチバック
hatchback
dreitürige Kombilimousine[F]
trois-portes[F]
turismo[M] de tres puertas[F]
vettura[F] a tre porte

ツー・ドア・セダン
two-door sedan; *coupé*
Coupé[N]
coach[M]
cupé[M]
coupé[F]

コンバーチブル／オープン・カー
convertible
Kabriolett[N]
cabriolet[M]
descapotable[M]
spider[F]

フォー・ドア・セダン
four-door sedan; *four-door saloon*
viertürige Limousine[F]
berline[F]
berlina[F]
berlina[F]

ステーション・ワゴン
station wagon; *estate car*
Kombi[M]
break[M]
coche[M] familiar
station wagon[F]

ミニバン
minivan; *minibus*
Minibus[M]
fourgonnette[F]
monovolumen[M]
monovolume[F]

ワゴン車／オフ・ロード車
sport-utility vehicle; *all-terrain vehicle*
Geländewagen[M]
véhicule[M] tout-terrain[M]
vehículo[M] todo terreno[M]
fuoristrada[M]

ピックアップ・トラック
pickup truck
Pickup[M]
camionnette[F]
camioneta[F]
pickup[M]

リムジン
limousine; *stretch-limousine*
Pullman Limousine[F]
limousine[F]
limusina[F]
limousine[F]

549

道路交通 | ROAD TRANSPORT
STRASSENVERKEHR | TRANSPORT ROUTIER | TRANSPORTE TERRESTRE | TRASPORTO SU STRADA

自動車

日本語 | 英語 | ドイツ語 | フランス語 | スペイン語 | イタリア語

車体
body
Karosserie^F
carrosserie^F
carrocería^F
carrozzeria^F

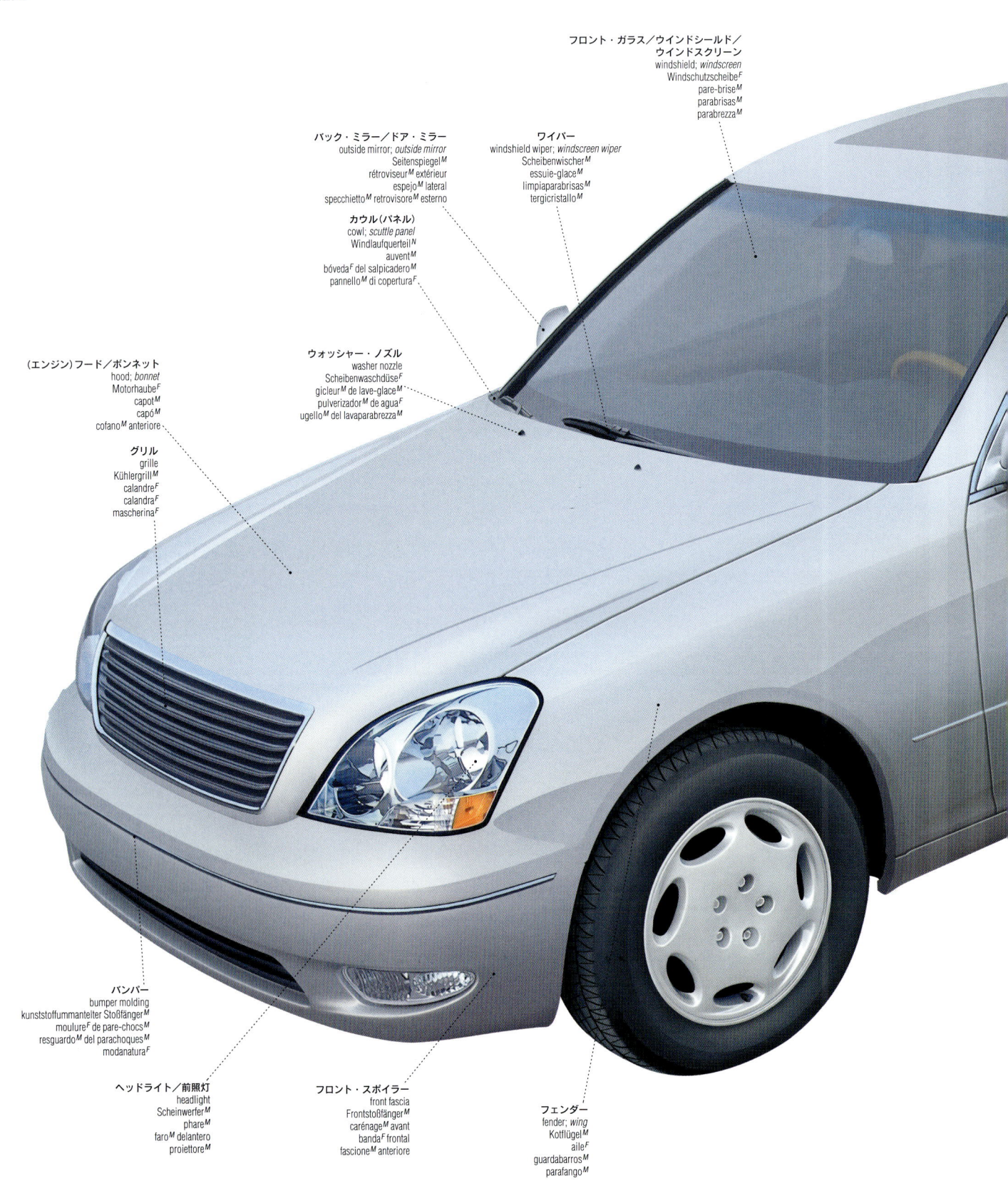

フロント・ガラス／ウインドシールド／ウインドスクリーン
windshield; *windscreen*
Windschutzscheibe^F
pare-brise^M
parabrisas^M
parabrezza^M

バック・ミラー／ドア・ミラー
outside mirror; *outside mirror*
Seitenspiegel^M
rétroviseur^M extérieur
espejo^M lateral
specchietto^M retrovisore^M esterno

ワイパー
windshield wiper; *windscreen wiper*
Scheibenwischer^M
essuie-glace^M
limpiaparabrisas^M
tergicristallo^M

カウル（パネル）
cowl; *scuttle panel*
Windlaufquerteil^N
auvent^M
bóveda^F del salpicadero^M
pannello^M di copertura^F

（エンジン）フード／ボンネット
hood; *bonnet*
Motorhaube^F
capot^M
capó^M
cofano^M anteriore

ウォッシャー・ノズル
washer nozzle
Scheibenwaschdüse^F
gicleur^M de lave-glace^M
pulverizador^M de agua^F
ugello^M del lavaparabrezza^M

グリル
grille
Kühlergrill^M
calandre^F
calandra^F
mascherina^F

バンパー
bumper molding
kunststoffummantelter Stoßfänger^M
moulure^F de pare-chocs^M
resguardo^M del parachoques^M
modanatura^F

ヘッドライト／前照灯
headlight
Scheinwerfer^M
phare^M
faro^M delantero
proiettore^M

フロント・スポイラー
front fascia
Frontstoßfänger^M
carénage^M avant
banda^F frontal
fascione^M anteriore

フェンダー
fender; *wing*
Kotflügel^M
aile^F
guardabarros^M
parafango^M

交通と機械

550

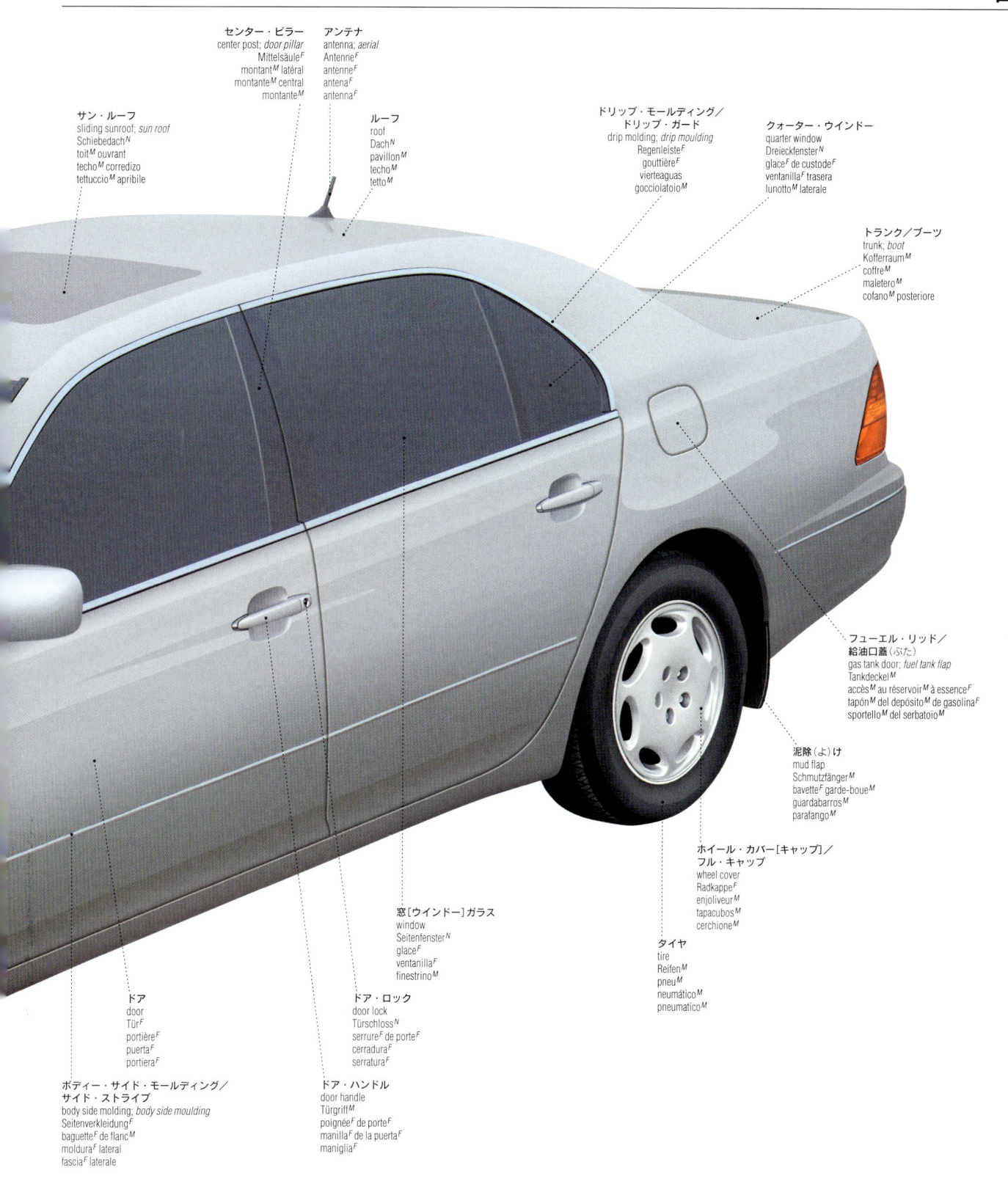

道路交通 | ROAD TRANSPORT
STRASSENVERKEHR | TRANSPORT ROUTIER | TRANSPORTE TERRESTRE | TRASPORTO SU STRADA

自動車

センター・ピラー
center post; door pillar
Mittelsäule^F
montant^M latéral
montante^M central
montante^M

アンテナ
antenna; aerial
Antenne^F
antenne^F
antena^F
antenna^F

サン・ルーフ
sliding sunroof; sun roof
Schiebedach^N
toit^M ouvrant
techo^M corredizo
tettuccio^M apribile

ルーフ
roof
Dach^N
pavillon^M
techo^M
tetto^M

ドリップ・モールディング／
ドリップ・ガード
drip molding; drip moulding
Regenleiste^F
gouttière^F
vierteaguas
gocciolatoio^M

クォーター・ウインドー
quarter window
Dreieckfenster^N
glace^F de custode^F
ventanilla^F trasera
lunotto^M laterale

トランク／ブーツ
trunk; boot
Kofferraum^M
coffre^M
maletero^M
cofano^M posteriore

フューエル・リッド／
給油口蓋 (ぶた)
gas tank door; fuel tank flap
Tankdeckel^M
accès^M au réservoir^M à essence^F
tapón^M del depósito^M de gasolina^F
sportello^M del serbatoio^M

泥除(よ)け
mud flap
Schmutzfänger^M
bavette^F garde-boue^M
guardabarros^M
parafango^M

ホイール・カバー[キャップ]／
フル・キャップ
wheel cover
Radkappe^F
enjoliveur^M
tapacubos^M
cerchione^M

タイヤ
tire
Reifen^M
pneu^M
neumático^M
pneumatico^M

窓[ウインドー]ガラス
window
Seitenfenster^N
glace^F
ventanilla^F
finestrino^M

ドア
door
Tür^F
portière^F
puerta^F
portiera^F

ドア・ロック
door lock
Türschloss^N
serrure^F de porte^F
cerradura^F
serratura^F

ボディー・サイド・モールディング／
サイド・ストライプ
body side molding; body side moulding
Seitenverkleidung^F
baguette^F de flanc^M
moldura^F lateral
fascia^F laterale

ドア・ハンドル
door handle
Türgriff^M
poignée^F de porte^F
manilla^F de la puerta^F
maniglia^F

交通と機械

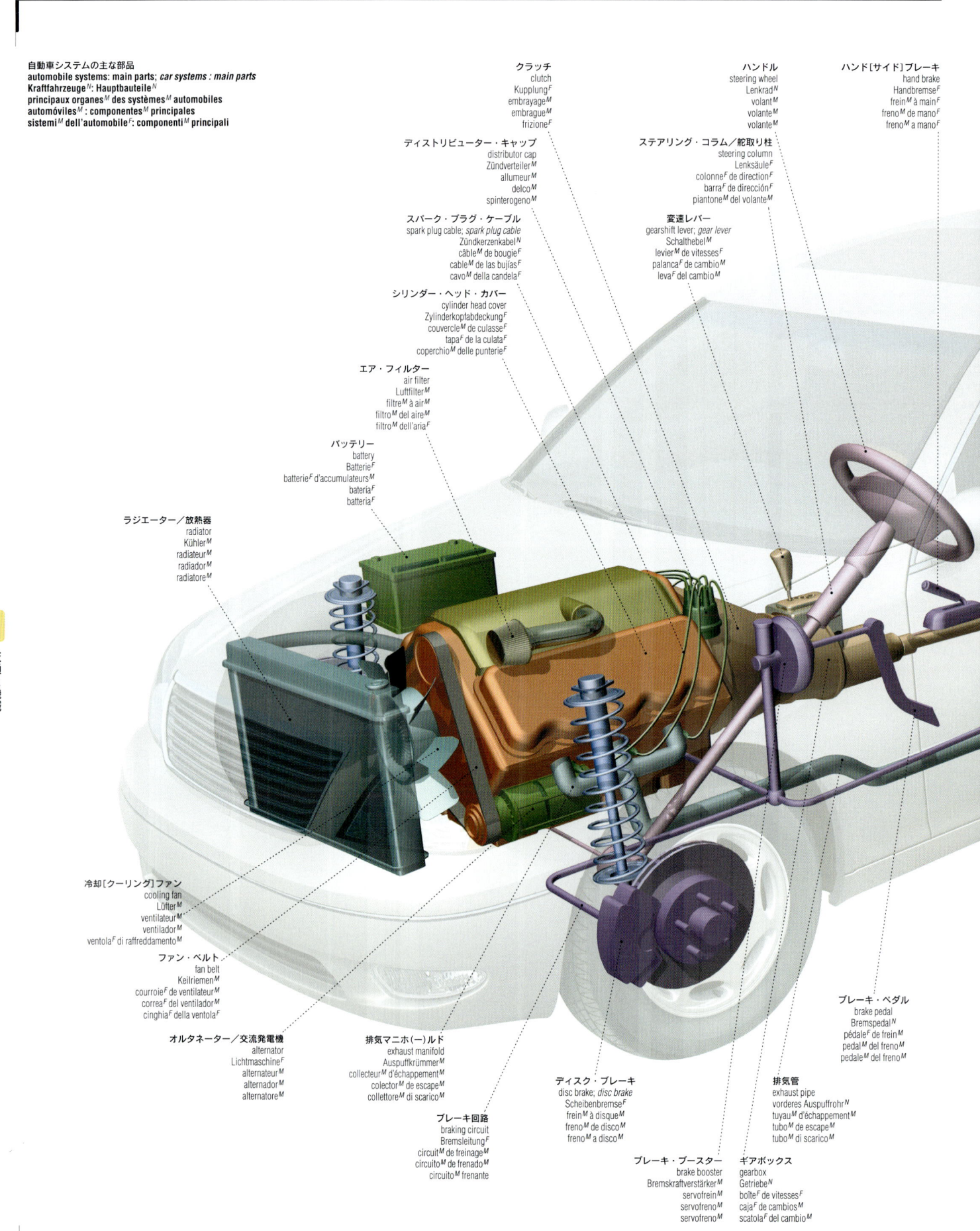

道路交通 | ROAD TRANSPORT
STRASSENVERKEHR | TRANSPORT ROUTIER | TRANSPORTE TERRESTRE | TRASPORTO SU STRADA

自動車

日本語 | 英語 | ドイツ語 | フランス語 | スペイン語 | イタリア語

自動車システムの主な部品
automobile systems: main parts; *car systems : main parts*
Kraftfahrzeuge[N]: Hauptbauteile[N]
principaux organes[M] des systèmes[M] automobiles
automóviles[M] : componentes[M] principales
sistemi[M] dell'automobile[F] : componenti[M] principali

クラッチ
clutch
Kupplung[F]
embrayage[M]
embrague[M]
frizione[F]

ハンドル
steering wheel
Lenkrad[N]
volant[M]
volante[M]
volante[M]

ハンド[サイド]ブレーキ
hand brake
Handbremse[F]
frein[M] à main[F]
freno[M] de mano[F]
freno[M] a mano[F]

ディストリビューター・キャップ
distributor cap
Zündverteiler[M]
allumeur[M]
delco[M]
spinterogeno[M]

ステアリング・コラム／舵取り柱
steering column
Lenksäule[F]
colonne[F] de direction[F]
barra[F] de dirección[F]
piantone[M] del volante[M]

スパーク・プラグ・ケーブル
spark plug cable; *spark plug cable*
Zündkerzenkabel[N]
câble[M] de bougie[F]
cable[M] de las bujías[F]
cavo[M] della candela[F]

変速レバー
gearshift lever; *gear lever*
Schalthebel[M]
levier[M] de vitesses[F]
palanca[F] de cambio[M]
leva[F] del cambio[M]

シリンダー・ヘッド・カバー
cylinder head cover
Zylinderkopfabdeckung[F]
couvercle[M] de culasse[F]
tapa[F] de la culata[F]
coperchio[M] delle punterie[F]

エア・フィルター
air filter
Luftfilter[M]
filtre[M] à air[M]
filtro[M] del aire[M]
filtro[M] dell'aria[F]

バッテリー
battery
Batterie[F]
batterie[F] d'accumulateurs[M]
batería[F]
batteria[F]

ラジエーター／放熱器
radiator
Kühler[M]
radiateur[M]
radiador[M]
radiatore[M]

冷却[クーリング]ファン
cooling fan
Lüfter[M]
ventilateur[M]
ventilador[M]
ventola[F] di raffreddamento[M]

ファン・ベルト
fan belt
Keilriemen[M]
courroie[F] de ventilateur[M]
correa[F] del ventilador[M]
cinghia[F] della ventola[F]

オルタネーター／交流発電機
alternator
Lichtmaschine[F]
alternateur[M]
alternador[M]
alternatore[M]

排気マニホ(ー)ルド
exhaust manifold
Auspuffkrümmer[M]
collecteur[M] d'échappement[M]
colector[M] de escape[M]
collettore[M] di scarico[M]

ブレーキ回路
braking circuit
Bremsleitung[F]
circuit[M] de freinage[M]
circuito[M] de frenado[M]
circuito[M] frenante[M]

ディスク・ブレーキ
disc brake; *disc brake*
Scheibenbremse[F]
frein[M] à disque[M]
freno[M] de disco[M]
freno[M] a disco[M]

ブレーキ・ブースター
brake booster
Bremskraftverstärker[M]
servofrein[M]
servofreno[M]
servofreno[M]

ブレーキ・ペダル
brake pedal
Bremspedal[N]
pédale[F] de frein[M]
pedal[M] del freno[M]
pedale[M] del freno[M]

排気管
exhaust pipe
vorderes Auspuffrohr[N]
tuyau[M] d'échappement[M]
tubo[M] de escape[M]
tubo[M] di scarico[M]

ギアボックス
gearbox
Getriebe[N]
boîte[F] de vitesses[F]
caja[F] de cambios[M]
scatola[F] del cambio[M]

交通と機械

552

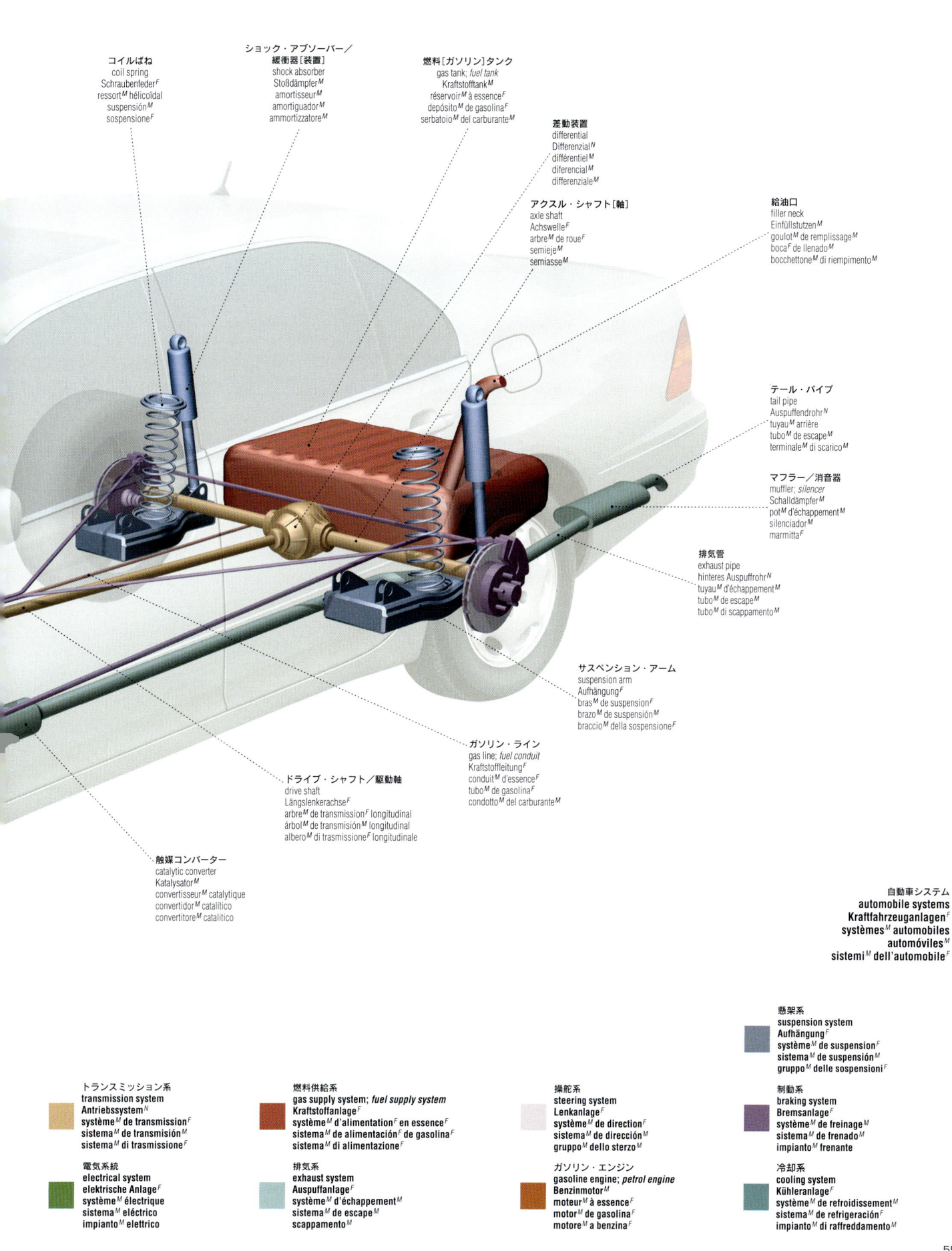

道路交通 | ROAD TRANSPORT
STRASSENVERKEHR | TRANSPORT ROUTIER | TRANSPORTE TERRESTRE | TRASPORTO SU STRADA

自動車

コイルばね
coil spring
Schraubenfeder^F
ressort^M hélicoïdal
suspensión^M
sospensione^F

ショック・アブソーバー／緩衝器［装置］
shock absorber
Stoßdämpfer^M
amortisseur^M
amortiguador^M
ammortizzatore^M

燃料［ガソリン］タンク
gas tank; *fuel tank*
Kraftstofftank^M
réservoir^M à essence^F
depósito^M de gasolina^F
serbatoio^M del carburante^M

差動装置
differential
Differenzial^N
différentiel^M
diferencial^M
differenziale^M

アクスル・シャフト［軸］
axle shaft
Achswelle^F
arbre^M de roue^F
semieje^M
semiasse^M

給油口
filler neck
Einfüllstutzen^M
goulot^M de remplissage^M
boca^F de llenado^M
bocchettone^M di riempimento^M

テール・パイプ
tail pipe
Auspuffendrohr^N
tuyau^M arrière
tubo^M de escape^M
terminale^M di scarico^M

マフラー／消音器
muffler; *silencer*
Schalldämpfer^M
pot^M d'échappement^M
silenciador^M
marmitta^F

排気管
exhaust pipe
hinteres Auspuffrohr^N
tuyau^M d'échappement^M
tubo^M de escape^M
tubo^M di scappamento^M

サスペンション・アーム
suspension arm
Aufhängung^F
bras^M de suspension^F
brazo^M de suspensión^M
braccio^M della sospensione^F

ガソリン・ライン
gas line; *fuel conduit*
Kraftstoffleitung^F
conduit^M d'essence^F
tubo^M de gasolina^F
condotto^M del carburante^M

ドライブ・シャフト／駆動軸
drive shaft
Längslenkerachse^F
arbre^M de transmission^F longitudinal
árbol^M de transmisión^M longitudinal
albero^M di trasmissione^F longitudinale

触媒コンバーター
catalytic converter
Katalysator^M
convertisseur^M catalytique
convertidor^M catalítico
convertitore^M catalitico

自動車システム
automobile systems
Kraftfahrzeuganlagen^F
systèmes^M **automobiles**
automóviles^M
sistemi^M **dell'automobile**^{F}

懸架系
suspension system
Aufhängung^F
système^M de suspension^F
sistema^M de suspensión^M
gruppo^M delle sospensioni^F

トランスミッション系
transmission system
Antriebssystem^N
système^M de transmission^F
sistema^M de transmisión^M
sistema^M di trasmissione^F

燃料供給系
gas supply system; *fuel supply system*
Kraftstoffanlage^F
système^M d'alimentation^F en essence^F
sistema^M de alimentación^F de gasolina^F
sistema^M di alimentazione^F

操舵系
steering system
Lenkanlage^F
système^M de direction^F
sistema^M de dirección^F
gruppo^M dello sterzo^M

制動系
braking system
Bremsanlage^F
système^M de freinage^M
sistema^M de frenado^M
impianto^M frenante

電気系統
electrical system
elektrische Anlage^F
système^M électrique
sistema^M eléctrico
impianto^M elettrico

排気系
exhaust system
Auspuffanlage^F
système^M d'échappement^M
sistema^M de escape^M
scappamento^M

ガソリン・エンジン
gasoline engine; *petrol engine*
Benzinmotor^M
moteur^M à essence^F
motor^M de gasolina^F
motore^M a benzina^F

冷却系
cooling system
Kühleranlage^F
système^M de refroidissement^M
sistema^M de refrigeración^F
impianto^M di raffreddamento^M

交通と機械

553

道路交通 | ROAD TRANSPORT
STRASSENVERKEHR | TRANSPORT ROUTIER | TRANSPORTE TERRESTRE | TRASPORTO SU STRADA

自動車

日本語 | 英語 | ドイツ語 | フランス語 | スペイン語 | イタリア語

ヘッドライト／前照灯
headlights; *front lights*
Frontscheinwerfer^F
feux^M avant
faros^M delanteros
luci^F anteriori

ハイ・ビーム
high beam; *main beam headlight*
Fernlicht^N
feu^M de route^F
luz^F larga
proiettore^M abbagliante e anabbagliante

ロー・ビーム
low beam; *dipped beam headlight*
Abblendlicht^N
feu^M de croisement^M
luz^F de cruce^M
luce^F di posizione^F

フォッグ・ライト［ランプ］／霧灯
fog light; *fog lamp*
Nebelleuchte^F
feu^M antibrouillard
luz^F antiniebla
faro^M fendinebbia

ウインカー／方向指示灯
turn signal; *indicator*
Blinkleuchte^F
feu^M clignotant
intermitente^M
indicatore^M di direzione^F

サイド・マーカー・ライト［ランプ］／車幅灯
side-marker light; *side marker light*
Begrenzungsleuchte^F
feu^M de gabarit
luz^F de posición^F
luce^F di ingombro^M laterale

テールライト／尾灯
taillights; *rear lights*
Heckleuchten^F
feux^M arrière
luces^F traseras
luci^F posteriori

ウインカー／方向指示灯
turn signal; *indicator*
Blinkleuchte^F
feu^M clignotant
intermitente^M
indicatore^M di direzione^F

ブレーキ・ライト［ランプ］／制動灯
brake light; *brake light*
Bremsleuchte^F
feu^M stop^M
luz^F de freno^M
luce^F di arresto^M

ナンバー・プレート・ライト［ランプ］／番号灯
license plate light; *number plate light*
Nummernschildbeleuchtung^F
feu^M de plaque
iluminación^F de la placa^F de matrícula^F
luce^F della targa^F

ハイ・マウント・ストップ・ライト［ランプ］
brake light; *brake light*
Bremsleuchte^F
feu^M stop^M
luz^F de freno^M
luce^F di arresto^M

バックアップ・ライト［ランプ］
reverse light; *reversing light*
Rückfahrscheinwerfer^M
feu^M de recul^M
luz^F de marcha^F atrás
luce^F di retromarcia^F

テールライト［ランプ］／尾灯
taillight; *rear light*
Schlussleuchte^F
feu^M rouge arrière
luz^F trasera
luce^F di posizione^F posteriore

サイド・マーカー・ライト［ランプ］／車幅灯
side-marker light; *side marker light*
Begrenzungsleuchte^F
feu^M de gabarit^M
luz^F de posición^F
luce^F di ingombro^M laterale

ドア
door
Wagentür^F
portière^F
puerta^F
portiera^F

（ドア）内側ハンドル
interior door handle
Türöffnungshebel^M
poignée^F intérieure
tirador^M de la puerta^F
maniglia^F interna

アシスト・グリップ
assist grip
Seitengriff^M
poignée^F de maintien^M
asidero^M
maniglia^F fissa

バック・ミラー・スイッチ
outside mirror control; *outside mirror control*
Seitenspiegelverstellhebel^N
commande^F du rétroviseur^M
control^M del espejo^M retrovisor exterior
regolazione^F dello specchietto^M retrovisore^M esterno

窓ガラス開閉調節ハンドル／
手動式ウインドー・レギュレーター
window regulator handle; *window winder handle*
Fensterheber^M
manivelle^F de lève-glace^M
manivela^F de la ventanilla^F
manopola^F alzacristalli^M

ドア・ヒンジ
hinge
Scharnier^N
charnière^F
bisagra^F
cardine^M

ドア・ポケット
accessory pocket
Seitenfach^N
vide-poches^M
bolsillo^M lateral
tasca^F portaoggetti^M

窓（ガラス）／ウインドー
window
Fenster^N
glace^F
ventanilla^F
finestrino^M

（ドア）内側ロック・ボタン
interior door lock button
Sicherungsknopf^M
bouton^M de verrouillage^M
botón^M del seguro^M
pomello^M della sicura^F

アームレスト／肘掛け／腕もたれ
armrest
Armstütze^F
appui^M-bras^M
soporte^M para el brazo^M
bracciolo^M

ロック
lock
Türschloss^N
serrure^F
cerradura^F
serratura^F

内装パネル
trim panel
Türverkleidung^F
panneau^M de garnissage^M
panel^M de la puerta^F
pannello^M

ドア・インナー・パネル
inner door shell
Türinnenverschalung^F
caisson^M de porte^F
revestimiento^M interior
telaio^M interno della portiera^F

道路交通 | ROAD TRANSPORT
STRASSENVERKEHR | TRANSPORT ROUTIER | TRANSPORTE TERRESTRE | TRASPORTO SU STRADA

自動車

バケット・シート：正面図
bucket seat: front view
Schalensitz^M: Vorderansicht^F
siège^M-baquet^M : vue^F de face^F
asiento^M : vista^F frontal
sedile^M: vista^F anteriore

バケット・シート：側面図
bucket seat: side view
Schalensitz^M: Seitenansicht^F
siège^M-baquet^M : vue^F de profil^F
asiento^M : vista^F lateral
sedile^M: vista^F laterale

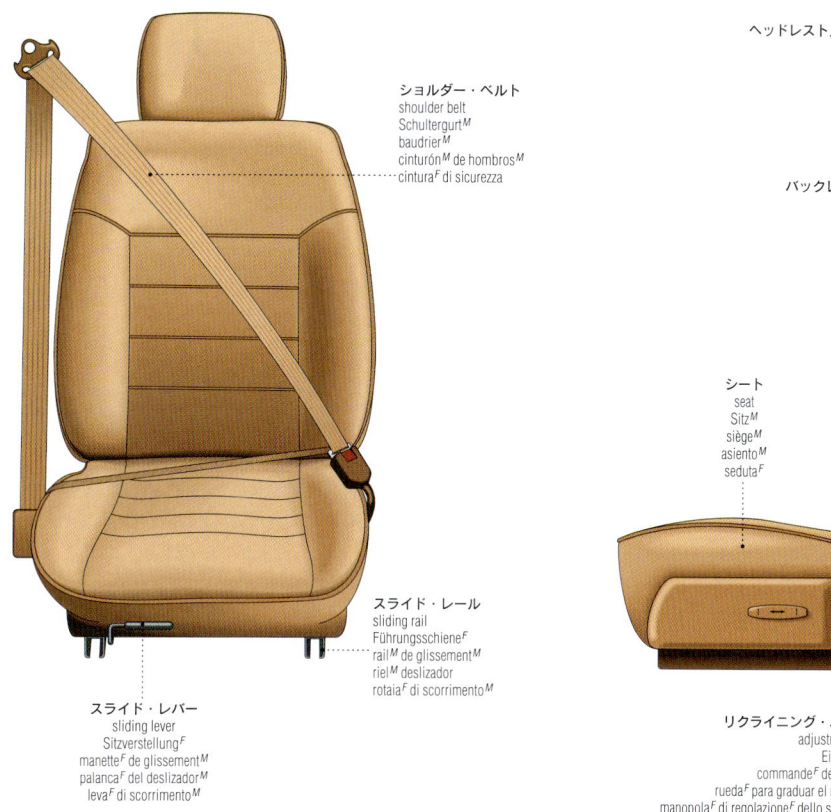

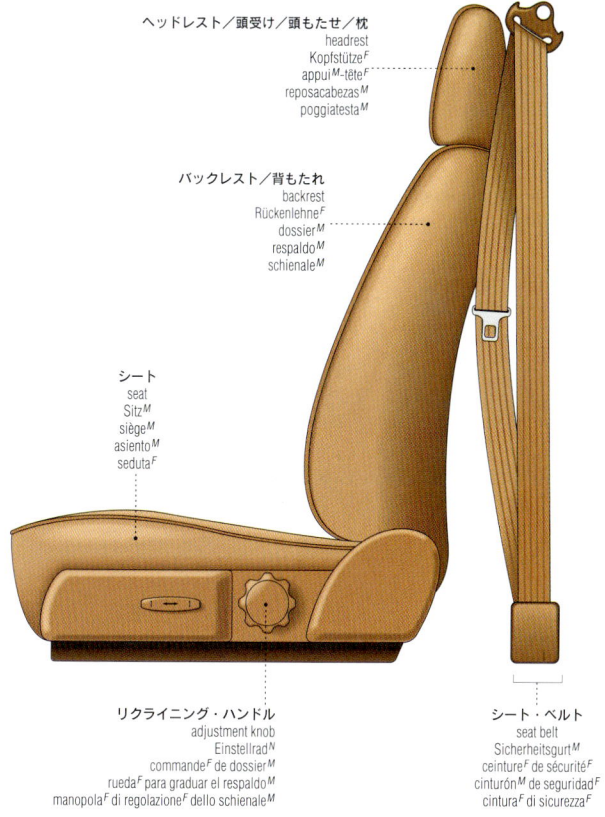

ショルダー・ベルト
shoulder belt
Schultergurt^M
baudrier^M
cinturón^M de hombros^M
cintura^F di sicurezza

ヘッドレスト／頭受け／頭もたせ／枕
headrest
Kopfstütze^F
appui^M-tête^F
reposacabezas^M
poggiatesta^M

バックレスト／背もたれ
backrest
Rückenlehne^F
dossier^M
respaldo^M
schienale

シート
seat
Sitz^M
siège^M
asiento^M
seduta^F

スライド・レール
sliding rail
Führungsschiene^F
rail^M de glissement^M
riel^M deslizador
rotaia^F di scorrimento^M

スライド・レバー
sliding lever
Sitzverstellung^F
manette^F de glissement^M
palanca^F del deslizador^M
leva^F di scorrimento^M

リクライニング・ハンドル
adjustment knob
Einstellrad^N
commande^F de dossier^M
rueda^F para graduar el respaldo^M
manopola^F di regolazione^F dello schienale^M

シート・ベルト
seat belt
Sicherheitsgurt^M
ceinture^F de sécurité^F
cinturón^M de seguridad^F
cintura^F di sicurezza^F

リア・シート／後部座席
rear seat
Rückbank^F
banquette^F arrière
asiento^M trasero
divano^M posteriore

アームレスト／肘掛け／腕もたれ
armrest
Armstütze^F
appui^M-bras^M
reposabrazo^M
bracciolo^M

リア・シート・ベルト
webbing
Beckengurt^M
sangle^F
cinturón^M subabdominal
cintura^F ventrale

バックル
buckle
Gurtschließe^F
boucle^F
enganche^M
fibbia^F

ベンチ・シート
bench seat
Sitzbank^F
banquette^F
asiento^M
seduta^F del divano^M posteriore

交通と機械

道路交通 | ROAD TRANSPORT
STRASSENVERKEHR | TRANSPORT ROUTIER | TRANSPORTE TERRESTRE | TRASPORTO SU STRADA

自動車

日本語 | 英語 | ドイツ語 | フランス語 | スペイン語 | イタリア語

計器板／ダッシュボード
dashboard
Armaturenbrett^N
tableau^M de bord^M
salpicadero^M
plancia^F

ルーム・ミラー／インナー・ミラー／防眩ミラー
rearview mirror
Rückspiegel^M
rétroviseur^M
espejo^M retrovisor^M
specchietto^M retrovisore^M

化粧鏡／バニティー・ミラー
vanity mirror
Spiegel^M
miroir^M de courtoisie^F
espejo^M de cortesía^F
specchietto^M di cortesia^F

ワイパー（ウォッシャー）スイッチ
wiper switch
Scheibenwischerhebel^M
commande^F d'essuie-glace^M
interruptor^M del limpiaparabrisas^M
comando^M del tergicristallo^M

オン・ボード・コンピューター
on-board computer
Bordcomputer^M
ordinateur^M de bord^M
ordenador^M de a bordo^M
computer^M di bordo^M

日除（よ）け（板）／サン・バイザー
sun visor
Sonnenblende^F
pare-soleil^M
parasol^M
aletta^F parasole

クルーズ・コントロール／自動速度制御装置
cruise control
Tempomat^M
régulateur^M de vitesse^F
regulador^M de velocidad^F
controllo^M della velocità^F di crociera^F

グローブ・ボックス／小物入れ
glove compartment
Handschuhfach^N
boîte^F à gants^M
guantera^F
vano^M portaoggetti^M

エンジン［イグニッション］スイッチ
ignition switch
Zündschloss^N
commutateur^M de démarrage^M
interruptor^M de encendido^M
blocchetto^M di accensione^F

吹き出し口
vent
Luftdüse^F
bouche^F d'air^M
ventilación^F
bocchetta^F di ventilazione^F

警音器／ホーン
horn
Hupe^F
avertisseur^M
claxón^M
clacson^M

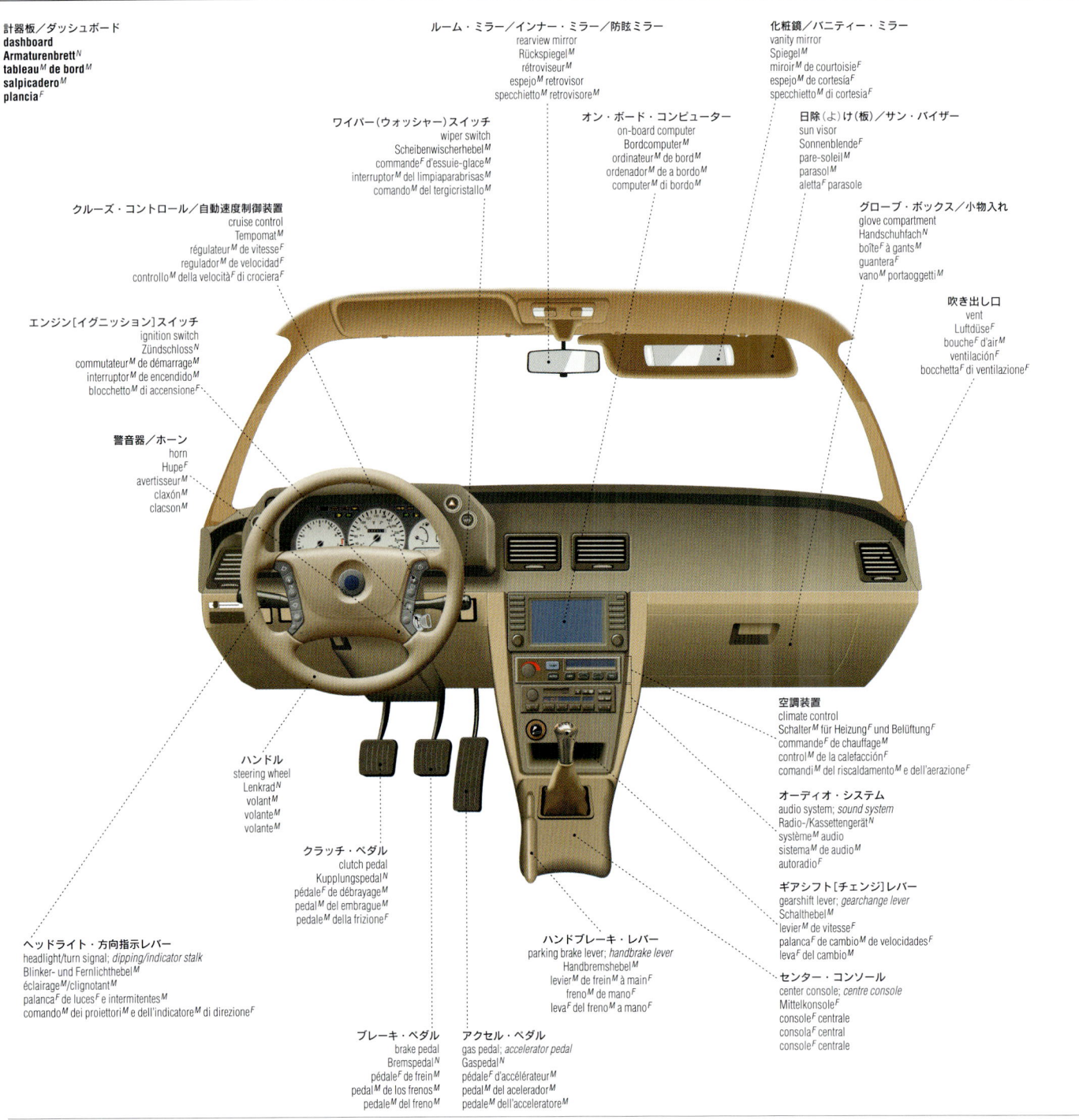

ハンドル
steering wheel
Lenkrad^N
volant^M
volante^M
volante^M

クラッチ・ペダル
clutch pedal
Kupplungspedal^N
pédale^F de débrayage^M
pedal^M del embrague^M
pedale^M della frizione^F

空調装置
climate control
Schalter^M für Heizung^F und Belüftung^F
commande^F de chauffage^M
control^M de la calefacción^F
comandi^M del riscaldamento^M e dell'aerazione^F

オーディオ・システム
audio system; *sound system*
Radio-/Kassettengerät^N
système^M audio
sistema^M de audio^M
autoradio^F

ギアシフト［チェンジ］レバー
gearshift lever; *gearchange lever*
Schalthebel^M
levier^M de vitesse^F
palanca^F de cambio^M de velocidades^F
leva^F del cambio^M

ヘッドライト・方向指示レバー
headlight/turn signal; *dipping/indicator stalk*
Blinker- und Fernlichthebel^M
éclairage^M/clignotant^M
palanca^F de luces^F e intermitentes^M
comando^M dei proiettori^M e dell'indicatore^M di direzione^F

ハンドブレーキ・レバー
parking brake lever; *handbrake lever*
Handbremshebel^M
levier^M de frein^M à main^F
freno^M de mano^M
leva^F del freno^M a mano^M

センター・コンソール
center console; *centre console*
Mittelkonsole^F
console^F centrale
consola^F central
console^F centrale

ブレーキ・ペダル
brake pedal
Bremspedal^N
pédale^F de frein^M
pedal^M de los frenos^M
pedale^M del freno^M

アクセル・ペダル
gas pedal; *accelerator pedal*
Gaspedal^N
pédale^F d'accélérateur^M
pedal^M del acelerador^M
pedale^M dell'acceleratore^M

エア・バッグ制御システム
air bag restraint system
Airbag^M-Rückhaltesystem^N
système^M de retenue^F à sacs^M gonflables
sistema^M de restricción^F del airbag^M
sistema^M di ritenuta^F degli air bag^M

セーフィング・センサー
safing sensor
Sicherheitssensor^M
détecteur^M de sécurité^F
sensor^M de seguridad^F
sensore^M di sicurezza^F

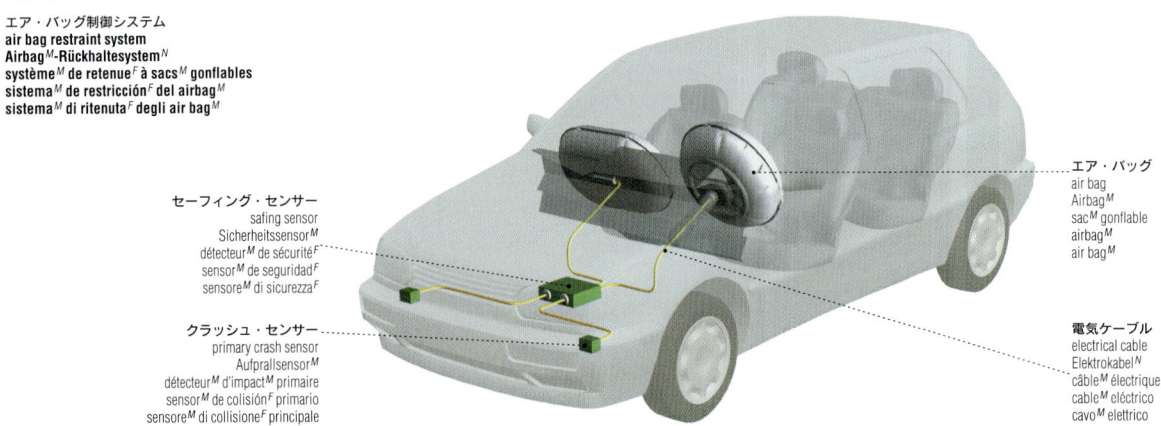

エア・バッグ
air bag
Airbag^M
sac^M gonflable
airbag^M
air bag^M

クラッシュ・センサー
primary crash sensor
Aufprallsensor^M
détecteur^M d'impact^M primaire
sensor^M de colisión^F primario
sensore^M di collisione^F principale

電気ケーブル
electrical cable
Elektrokabel^N
câble^M électrique
cable^M eléctrico
cavo^M elettrico

道路交通 | ROAD TRANSPORT
STRASSENVERKEHR | TRANSPORT ROUTIER | TRANSPORTE TERRESTRE | TRASPORTO SU STRADA

自動車

計器盤
instrument panel
Instrumententafel^F
instruments^M de bord^M
instrumentos^M del salpicadero^M
quadro^M degli strumenti^M di controllo^M

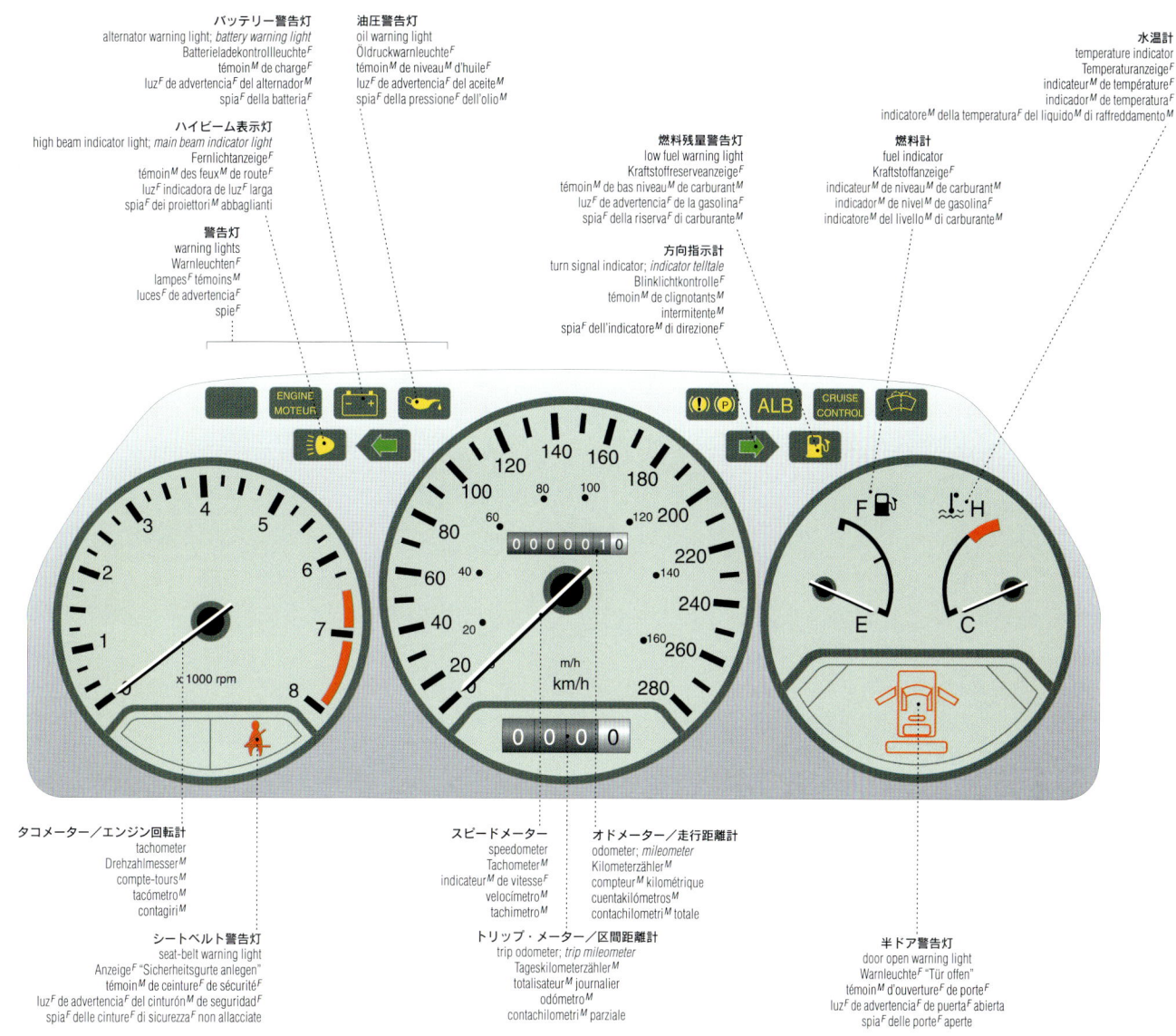

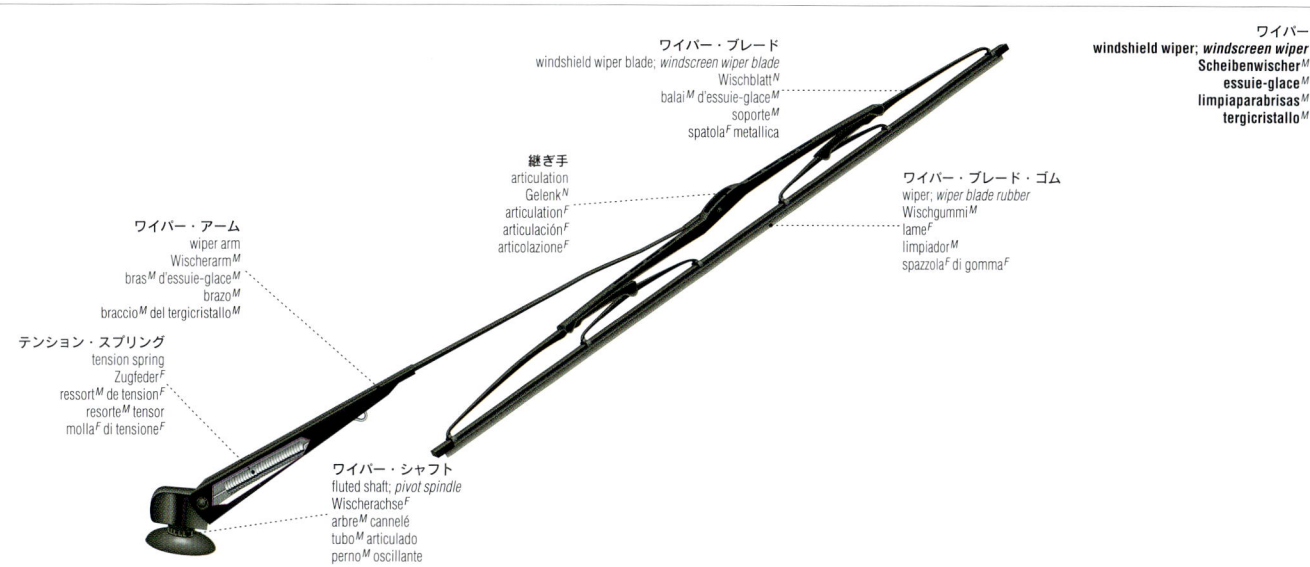

バッテリー警告灯
alternator warning light; *battery warning light*
Batterieladekontrollleuchte^F
témoin^M de charge^F
luz^F de advertencia^F del alternador^M
spia^F della batteria^F

油圧警告灯
oil warning light
Öldruckwarnleuchte^F
témoin^M de niveau^M d'huile^F
luz^F de advertencia^F del aceite^M
spia^F della pressione^F dell'olio^M

水温計
temperature indicator
Temperaturanzeige^F
indicateur^M de température^F
indicador^M de temperatura^F
indicatore^M della temperatura^F del liquido^M di raffreddamento^M

ハイビーム表示灯
high beam indicator light; *main beam indicator light*
Fernlichtanzeige^F
témoin^M des feux^M de route^F
luz^F indicadora de luz^F larga
spia^F dei proiettori^M abbaglianti

燃料残量警告灯
low fuel warning light
Kraftstoffreserveanzeige^F
témoin^M de bas niveau^M de carburant^M
luz^F de advertencia^F de la gasolina^F
spia^F della riserva^F di carburante^M

燃料計
fuel indicator
Kraftstoffanzeige^F
indicateur^M de niveau^M de carburant^M
indicador^M de nivel^M de gasolina^F
indicatore^M del livello^M di carburante^M

警告灯
warning lights
Warnleuchten^F
lampes^F témoins^M
luces^F de advertencia^F
spie^F

方向指示計
turn signal indicator; *indicator telltale*
Blinklichtkontrolle^F
témoin^M de clignotants^M
intermitente^M
spia^F dell'indicatore^M di direzione^F

タコメーター／エンジン回転計
tachometer
Drehzahlmesser^M
compte-tours^M
tacómetro^M
contagiri^M

スピードメーター
speedometer
Tachometer^M
indicateur^M de vitesse^F
velocímetro^M
tachimetro^M

オドメーター／走行距離計
odometer; *mileometer*
Kilometerzähler^M
compteur^M kilométrique
cuentakilómetros^M
contachilometri^M totale

半ドア警告灯
door open warning light
Warnleuchte^F "Tür offen"
témoin^M d'ouverture^F de porte^F
luz^F de advertencia^F de puerta^F abierta
spia^F delle porte^F aperte

シートベルト警告灯
seat-belt warning light
Anzeige^F "Sicherheitsgurte anlegen"
témoin^M de ceinture^F de sécurité^F
luz^F de advertencia^F del cinturón^M de seguridad^F
spia^F delle cinture^F di sicurezza^F non allacciate

トリップ・メーター／区間距離計
trip odometer; *trip mileometer*
Tageskilometerzähler^M
totalisateur^M journalier
odómetro^M
contachilometri^M parziale

ワイパー・ブレード
windshield wiper blade; *windscreen wiper blade*
Wischblatt^N
balai^M d'essuie-glace^F
soporte^M
spatola^F metallica

ワイパー
windshield wiper; *windscreen wiper*
Scheibenwischer^M
essuie-glace^M
limpiaparabrisas^M
tergicristallo^M

継ぎ手
articulation
Gelenk^N
articulation^F
articulación^F
articolazione^F

ワイパー・ブレード・ゴム
wiper; *wiper blade rubber*
Wischgummi^M
lame^F
limpiador^M
spazzola^F di gomma^F

ワイパー・アーム
wiper arm
Wischerarm^M
bras^M d'essuie-glace^M
brazo^M
braccio^M del tergicristallo^M

テンション・スプリング
tension spring
Zugfeder^F
ressort^M de tension^F
resorte^M tensor
molla^F di tensione^F

ワイパー・シャフト
fluted shaft; *pivot spindle*
Wischerachse^F
arbre^M cannelé
tubo^M articulado
perno^M oscillante

交通と機械

557

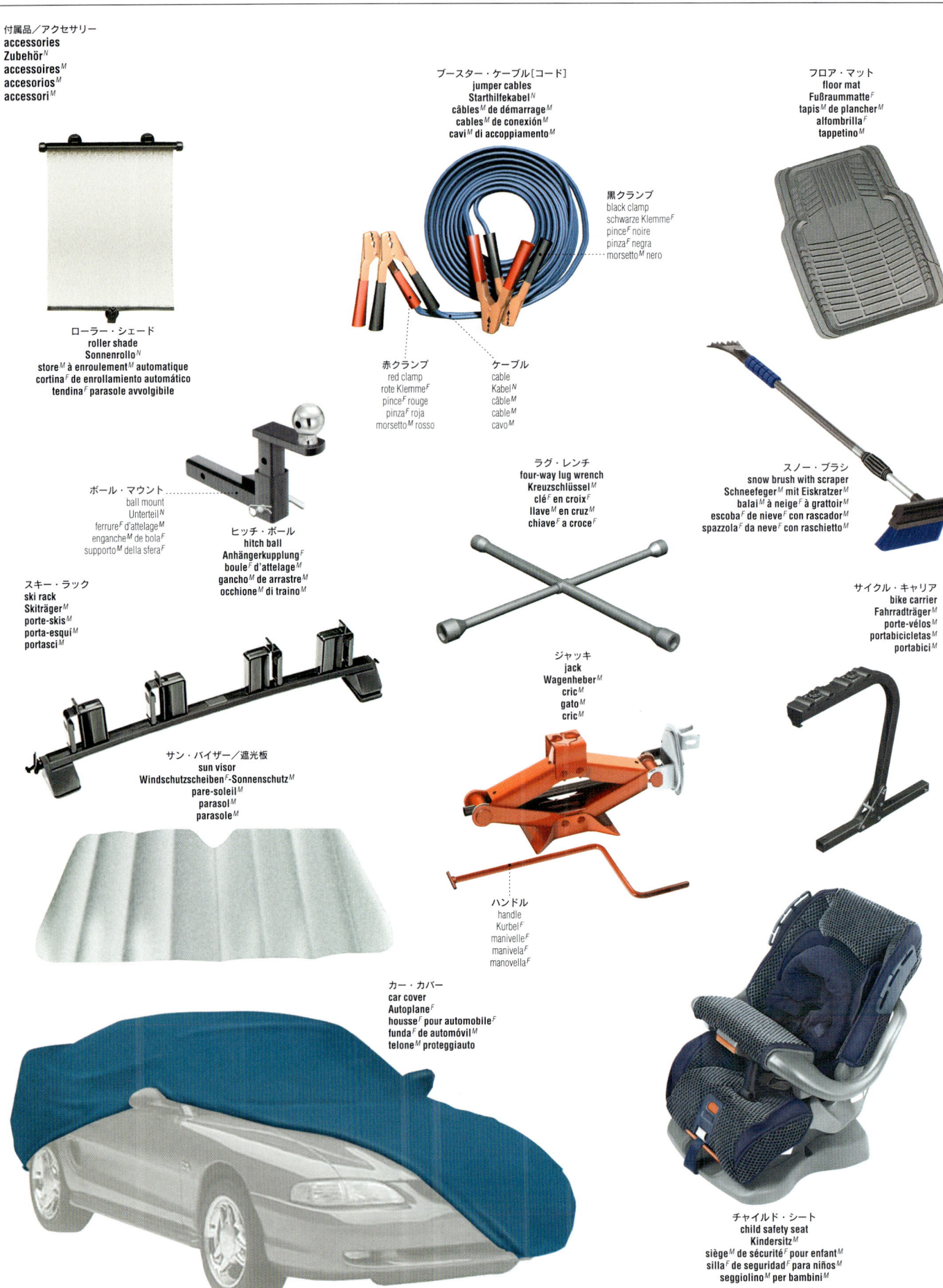

道路交通 | ROAD TRANSPORT
STRASSENVERKEHR | TRANSPORT ROUTIER | TRANSPORTE TERRESTRE | TRASPORTO SU STRADA

自動車

日本語 | 英語 | ドイツ語 | フランス語 | スペイン語 | イタリア語

付属品／アクセサリー
accessories
Zubehör^N
accessoires^M
accesorios^M
accessori^M

ブースター・ケーブル[コード]
jumper cables
Starthilfekabel^N
câbles^M de démarrage^M
cables^M de conexión^M
cavi^M di accoppiamento^M

フロア・マット
floor mat
Fußraummatte^F
tapis^M de plancher^M
alfombrilla^F
tappetino^M

黒クランプ
black clamp
schwarze Klemme^F
pince^F noire
pinza^F negra
morsetto^M nero

ローラー・シェード
roller shade
Sonnenrollo^N
store^M à enroulement^M automatique
cortina^F de enrollamiento^M automático
tendina^F parasole avvolgibile

赤クランプ
red clamp
rote Klemme^F
pince^F rouge
pinza^F roja
morsetto^M rosso

ケーブル
cable
Kabel^N
câble^M
cable^M
cavo^M

ボール・マウント
ball mount
Unterteil^N
ferrure^F d'attelage^M
enganche^M de bola^F
supporto^M della sfera^F

ラグ・レンチ
four-way lug wrench
Kreuzschlüssel^M
clé^F en croix^F
llave^M en cruz^M
chiave^F a croce^F

スノー・ブラシ
snow brush with scraper
Schneefeger^M mit Eiskratzer^M
balai^M à neige^F à grattoir^M
escoba^F de nieve^F con rascador^M
spazzola^F da neve^F con raschietto^M

ヒッチ・ボール
hitch ball
Anhängerkupplung^F
boule^F d'attelage^M
gancho^M de arrastre^M
occhione^M di traino^M

スキー・ラック
ski rack
Skiträger^M
porte-skis^M
porta-esquí^M
portasci^M

ジャッキ
jack
Wagenheber^M
cric^M
gato^M
cric^M

サイクル・キャリア
bike carrier
Fahrradträger^M
porte-vélos^M
portabicicletas^M
portabici^M

サン・バイザー／遮光板
sun visor
Windschutzscheiben^F-Sonnenschutz^M
pare-soleil^M
parasol^M
parasole^M

ハンドル
handle
Kurbel^F
manivelle^F
manivela^F
manovella^F

カー・カバー
car cover
Autoplane^F
housse^F pour automobile^F
funda^F de automóvil^M
telone^M proteggiauto

チャイルド・シート
child safety seat
Kindersitz^M
siège^M de sécurité^F pour enfant^M
silla^F de seguridad^F para niños^M
seggiolino^M per bambini^M

交通と機械

道路交通 | ROAD TRANSPORT
STRASSENVERKEHR | TRANSPORT ROUTIER | TRANSPORTE TERRESTRE | TRASPORTO SU STRADA

ブレーキ

brakes | Bremsen^F | freins^M | frenos^M | freni^M

ディスク[円板]ブレーキ
disc brake; *disc brake*
Scheibenbremse^F
frein^M à disque^M
freno^M de disco^M
freno^M a disco^M

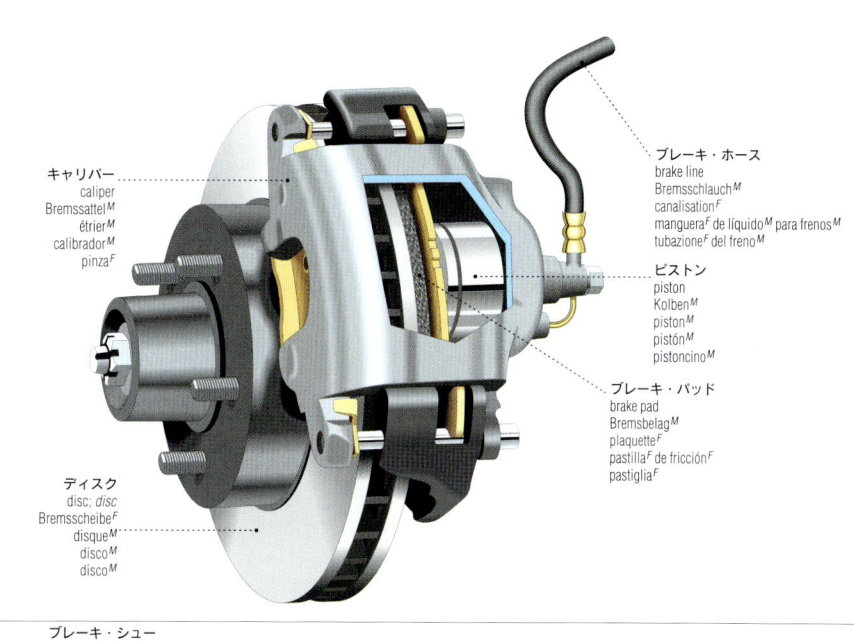

キャリパー
caliper
Bremssattel^M
étrier^M
calibrador^M
pinza^F

ブレーキ・ホース
brake line
Bremsschlauch^M
canalisation^F
manguera^F de líquido^M para frenos^M
tubazione^F del freno^M

ピストン
piston
Kolben^M
piston^M
pistón^M
pistoncino^M

ブレーキ・パッド
brake pad
Bremsbelag^M
plaquette^F
pastilla^F de fricción^F
pastiglia^F

ディスク
disc; *disc*
Bremsscheibe^F
disque^F
disco^M
disco^M

ブレーキ・シュー
brake shoe
Bremsbacke^F
segment^M
zapata^F
ganascia^F

ドラム・ブレーキ
drum brake
Trommelbremse^F
frein^M à tambour^M
freno^M de tambor^M
freno^M a tamburo^M

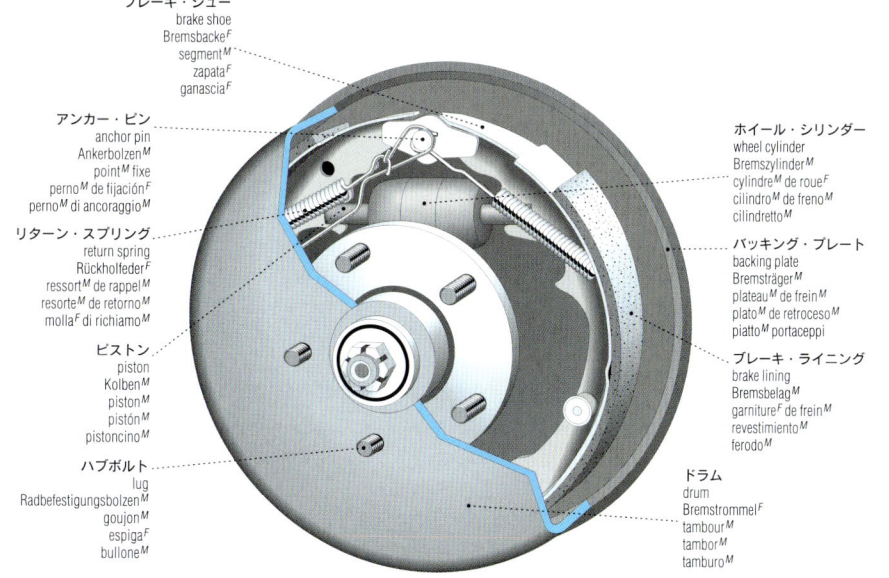

アンカー・ピン
anchor pin
Ankerbolzen^M
point^M fixe
perno^M de fijación^F
perno^M di ancoraggio^M

ホイール・シリンダー
wheel cylinder
Bremszylinder^M
cylindre^M de roue^F
cilindro^M de freno^M
cilindretto^M

リターン・スプリング
return spring
Rückholfeder^F
ressort^M de rappel^M
resorte^M de retorno^M
molla^F di richiamo^M

バッキング・プレート
backing plate
Bremsträger^M
plateau^M de frein^M
plato^M de retroceso^M
piatto^M portaceppi

ピストン
piston
Kolben^M
piston^M
pistón^M
pistoncino^M

ブレーキ・ライニング
brake lining
Bremsbelag^M
garniture^F de frein^M
revestimiento^M
ferodo^M

ハブボルト
lug
Radbefestigungsbolzen^M
goujon^M
espiga^F
bullone^M

ドラム
drum
Bremstrommel^F
tambour^M
tambor^M
tamburo^M

ブレーキ・リザーバー・タンク
brake fluid reservoir
Bremsflüssigkeitsbehälter^M
réservoir^M de liquide^M de frein^M
depósito^M del líquido^M de frenos^M
serbatoio^M del liquido^M dei freni^M

ブレーキ・ブースター
brake booster
Bremskraftverstärker^M
servofrein^M
servofreno^M
servofreno^M

アンチロック・ブレーキ・システム（ABS）
antilock braking system (ABS)
Antiblockiersystem^N (ABS)
système^M de freinage^M antiblocage
sistema^M antibloqueo de frenos^M
ABS, sistema^M frenante antibloccaggio

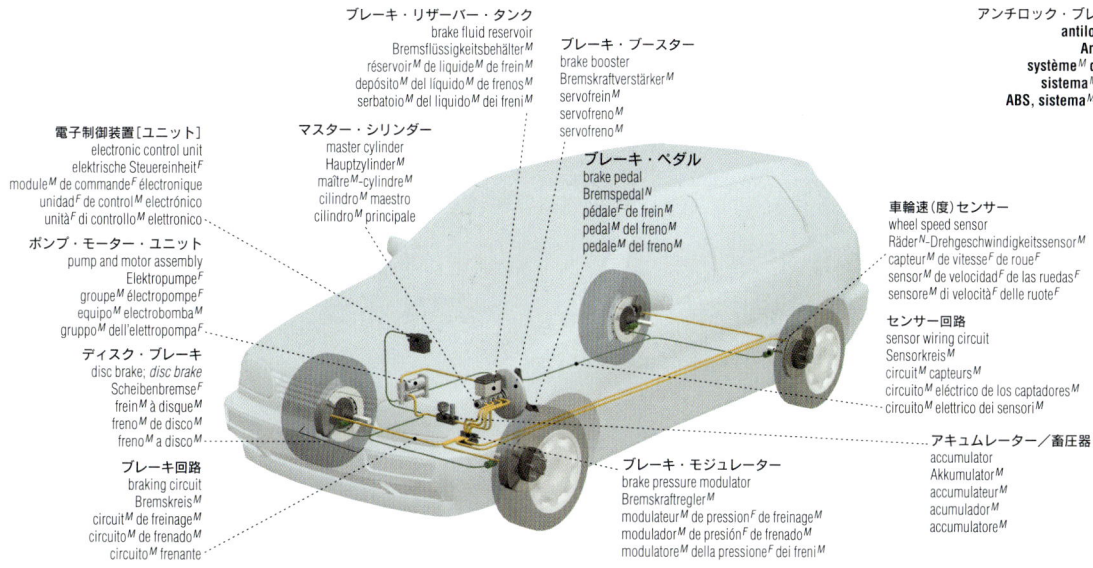

電子制御装置[ユニット]
electronic control unit
elektrische Steuereinheit^F
module^M de commande^F électronique
unidad^F de control^M electrónico
unità^F di controllo^M elettronico

マスター・シリンダー
master cylinder
Hauptzylinder^M
maître^M-cylindre^M
cilindro^M maestro
cilindro^M principale

ブレーキ・ペダル
brake pedal
Bremspedal^N
pédale^F de frein^M
pedal^M del freno^M
pedale^M del freno^M

車輪速(度)センサー
wheel speed sensor
Räder^N-Drehgeschwindigkeitssensor^M
capteur^M de vitesse^F de roue^F
sensor^M de velocidad^F de las ruedas^F
sensore^M di velocità^F delle ruote^F

ポンプ・モーター・ユニット
pump and motor assembly
Elektropumpe^F
groupe^M électropompe^F
equipo^M electrobomba^F
gruppo^M dell'elettropompa^F

センサー回路
sensor wiring circuit
Sensorkreis^M
circuit^M capteurs^M
circuito^M eléctrico de los captadores^M
circuito^M elettrico dei sensori^M

ディスク・ブレーキ
disc brake; *disc brake*
Scheibenbremse^F
frein^M à disque^M
freno^M de disco^M
freno^M a disco^M

ブレーキ回路
braking circuit
Bremskreis^M
circuit^M de freinage^M
circuito^M de frenado^M
circuito^M frenante

ブレーキ・モジュレーター
brake pressure modulator
Bremskraftregler^M
modulateur^M de pression^F de freinage^M
modulador^M de presión^F de frenado^M
modulatore^M della pressione^F dei freni^M

アキュムレーター／畜圧器
accumulator
Akkumulator^M
accumulateur^M
acumulador^M
accumulatore^M

交通と機械

559

道路交通 | ROAD TRANSPORT
STRASSENVERKEHR | TRANSPORT ROUTIER | TRANSPORTE TERRESTRE | TRASPORTO SU STRADA

タイヤ

tire; *tyre* | Reifen^M | pneu^M | neumático^M | pneumatico^M

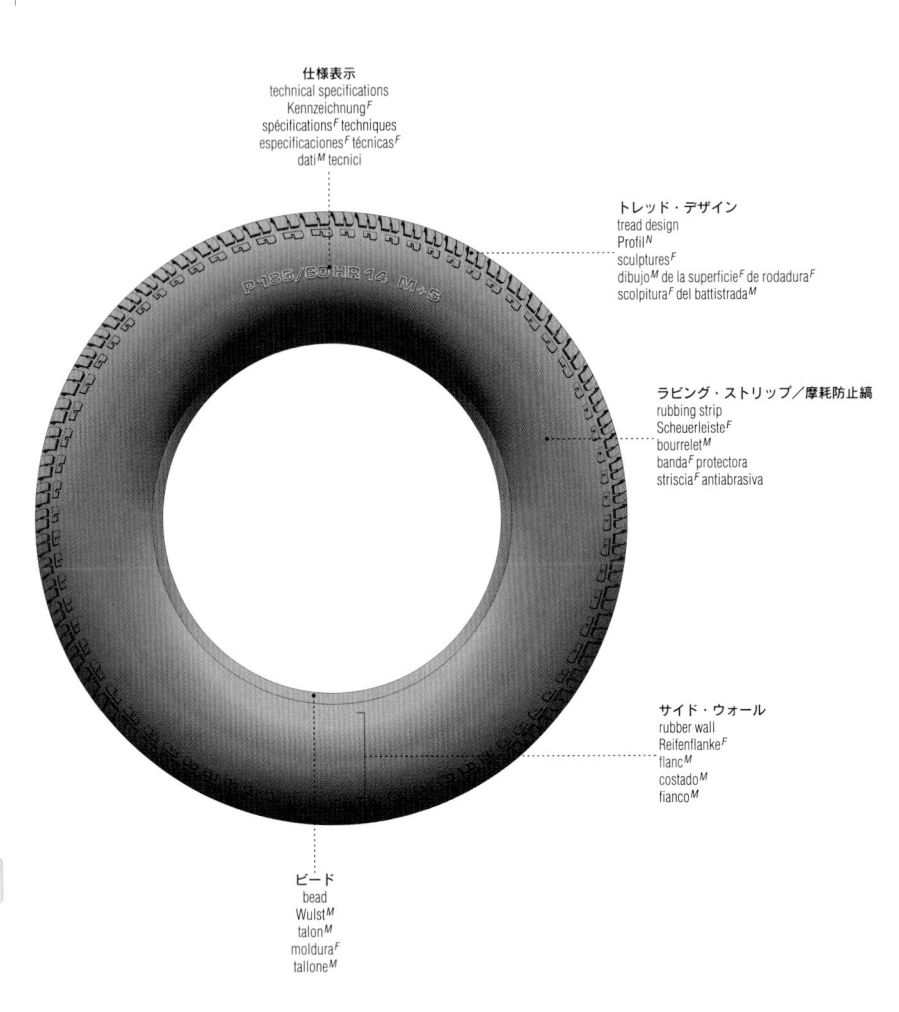

日本語 | 英語 | ドイツ語 | フランス語 | スペイン語 | イタリア語

仕様表示
technical specifications
Kennzeichnung^F
spécifications^F techniques
especificaciones^F técnicas
dati^M tecnici

トレッド・デザイン
tread design
Profil^N
sculptures^F
dibujo^M de la superficie^F de rodadura^F
scolpitura^F del battistrada^M

ラビング・ストリップ／摩耗防止縞
rubbing strip
Scheuerleiste^F
bourrelet^M
banda^F protectora
striscia^F antiabrasiva

サイド・ウォール
rubber wall
Reifenflanke^F
flanc^M
costado^M
fianco^M

ビード
bead
Wulst^M
talon^M
moldura^F
tallone^M

ディスク
disk; *disc*
Radschüssel^F
voile^M
disco^M
disco^M

ホイール
wheel
Rad^N
roue^F
rueda^F
ruota^F

リム
rim
Felge^F
jante^F
llanta^F
cerchio^M

リム・フランジ
rim flange
Felgenhorn^N
joue^F de jante^F
pestaña^F de la llanta^F
bordo^M del cerchio^M

タイヤの例
examples of tires
Reifenarten^F
exemples^M de pneus^M
ejemplos^M de neumáticos^M
esempi^M di pneumatici^M

高性能タイヤ
performance tire; *performance tyre*
Sportreifen^M
pneu^M de performance^F
neumático^M de rendimiento^M
pneumatico^M sportivo

オール・シーズン・タイヤ
all-season tire; *all-season tyre*
Ganzjahresreifen^M
pneu^M toutes saisons^F
neumáticos^M de todas las estaciones^F
pneumatico^M per tutte le stagioni^F

ウインター・タイヤ
winter tire; *winter tyre*
Winterreifen^M
pneu^M d'hiver^M
neumático^M de invierno^M
pneumatico^M invernale

ツーリング・タイヤ
touring tire; *touring tyre*
Touringreifen^M
pneu^M autoroutier
neumáticos^M de turismo^M
pneumatico^M granturismo

スパイク・タイヤ
studded tire; *studded tyre*
Spikereifen^M
pneu^M à crampons^M
neumático^M de tacos^M
pneumatico^M chiodato

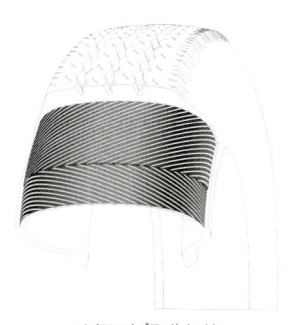

道路交通 | ROAD TRANSPORT
STRASSENVERKEHR | TRANSPORT ROUTIER | TRANSPORTE TERRESTRE | TRASPORTO SU STRADA

タイヤ

バイアス（プライ）タイヤ
bias-ply tire; *cross-ply tyre*
Diagonalreifen^M
pneu^M à carcasse^F diagonale
neumático^M de capas^F al sesgo^M
pneumatico^M con carcassa^F a struttura^F diagonale

ラジアル・タイヤ
radial tire; *radial tyre*
Radialreifen^M
pneu^M à carcasse^F radiale
neumático^M radial
pneumatico^M con carcassa^F a struttura^F radiale

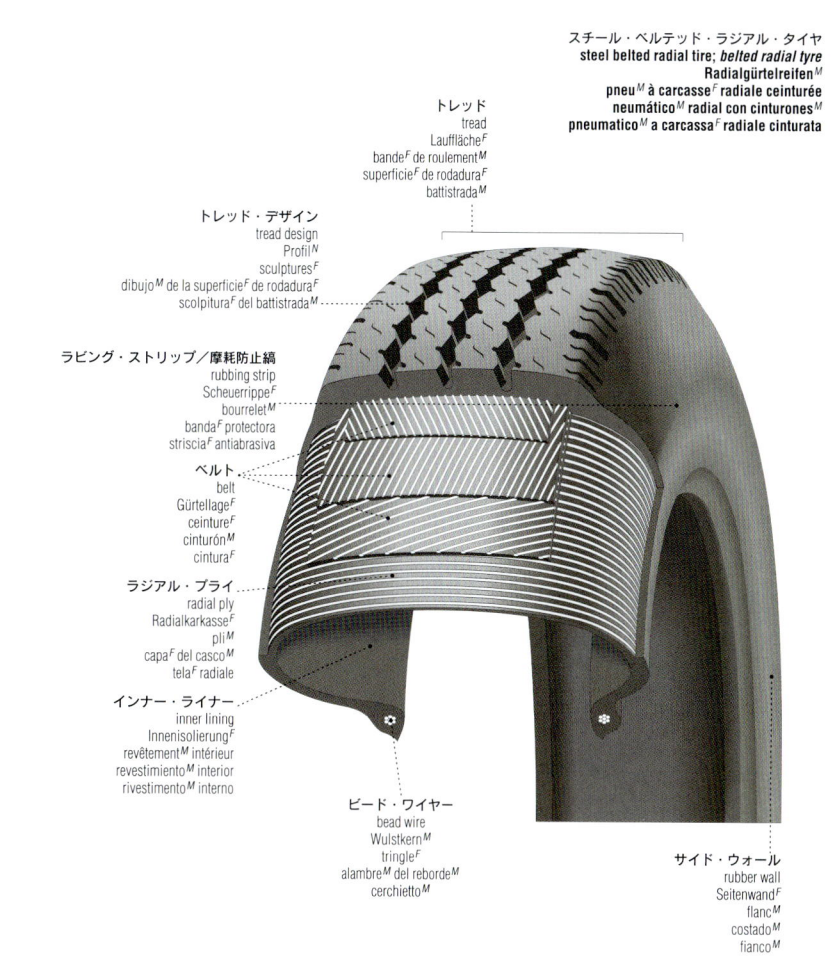

スチール・ベルテッド・ラジアル・タイヤ
steel belted radial tire; *belted radial tyre*
Radialgürtelreifen^M
pneu^M à carcasse^F radiale ceinturée
neumático^M radial con cinturones^M
pneumatico^M a carcassa^F radiale cinturata

トレッド
tread
Lauffläche^F
bande^F de roulement^M
superficie^F de rodadura^F
battistrada^M

トレッド・デザイン
tread design
Profil^N
sculptures^F
dibujo^M de la superficie^F de rodadura^F
scolpitura^F del battistrada^M

ラビング・ストリップ／摩耗防止縞
rubbing strip
Scheuerrippe^F
bourrelet^M
banda^F protectora
striscia^F antiabrasiva

ベルト
belt
Gürtellage^F
ceinture^F
cinturón^M
cintura^F

ラジアル・プライ
radial ply
Radialkarkasse^F
pli^M
capa^F del casco^M
tela^F radiale

インナー・ライナー
inner lining
Innenisolierung^F
revêtement^M intérieur
revestimiento^M interior
rivestimento^M interno

ビード・ワイヤー
bead wire
Wulstkern^M
tringle^F
alambre^M del reborde^M
cerchietto^M

サイド・ウォール
rubber wall
Seitenwand^F
flanc^M
costado^M
fianco^M

ラジエーター／放熱器

radiator | Kühler^M | radiateur^M | radiador^M | radiatore^M

ラジエーター［フィラー］キャップ／燃料補給口
filler cap
Kühlerverschlussdeckel^M
bouchon^M de remplissage^M
tapa^F
tappo^M

冷却［クーリング］ファン
cooling fan
Lüfter^M
ventilateur^M
ventilador^M
ventilatore^M

温度センサー
temperature sensor
Temperaturfühler^M
thermocontact
sensor^M de temperatura^F
sensore^M di temperatura^F

下部ラジエーター・ホース
lower radiator hose
unterer Kühleranschluss^M
durite^F de radiateur^M
manguito^M inferior del radiador^M
manicotto^M inferiore del radiatore^M

グリル
grille
Kühlerblock^M
grille^F
rejilla^F
griglia^F

電気・ファン・モーター
electric fan motor
Elektromotor^M
moteur^M électrique
motor^M eléctrico
motore^M elettrico

道路交通 | ROAD TRANSPORT
STRASSENVERKEHR | TRANSPORT ROUTIER | TRANSPORTE TERRESTRE | TRASPORTO SU STRADA

点火プラグ

日本語 | 英語 | ドイツ語 | フランス語 | スペイン語 | イタリア語

spark plug; *spark plug* | Zündkerze^F | bougie^F d'allumage^M | bujía^F | candela^F

コルゲーション
spline
Kriechstrombarriere^F
cannelure^F
ranura^F
scanalatura^F

六角ナット
hex nut
Sechskantmutter^F
écrou^M hexagonal
hexagonal
dado^M esagonale

ボディー
spark plug body; *spark plug body*
Zündkerzengehäuse^N
culot^M
cuerpo^M metálico de la bujía^F
radice^F filettata

端子
spark plug terminal; *spark plug Anschluss^M für Zündkabel^N*
borne^F
borne^M
morsetto^M terminale a spina^F

中心電極
center electrode; *centre electrode*
Mittelelektrode^F
électrode^F centrale
electrodo^M central
elettrodo^M centrale

絶縁体
insulator
Isolator^M
isolateur^M
aislador^M
corpo^M isolante

ガスケット
spark plug gasket; *spark plug seat*
Zündkerzendichtring^M
joint^M de bougie^F
junta^F
rondella^F di tenuta^F

接地電極
ground electrode
Masseelektrode^F
électrode^F de masse^F
electrodo^M de masa^F
elettrodo^M di massa^F

火花隙間（すきま）[ギャップ]
spark plug gap; *spark plug gap*
Funkenstrecke^F
écartement^M des électrodes^F
espacio^M para la chispa^F
distanza^F tra le puntine^F

バッテリー／蓄電池

battery | Batterie^F | batterie^F d'accumulateurs^M | batería^F | batteria^F

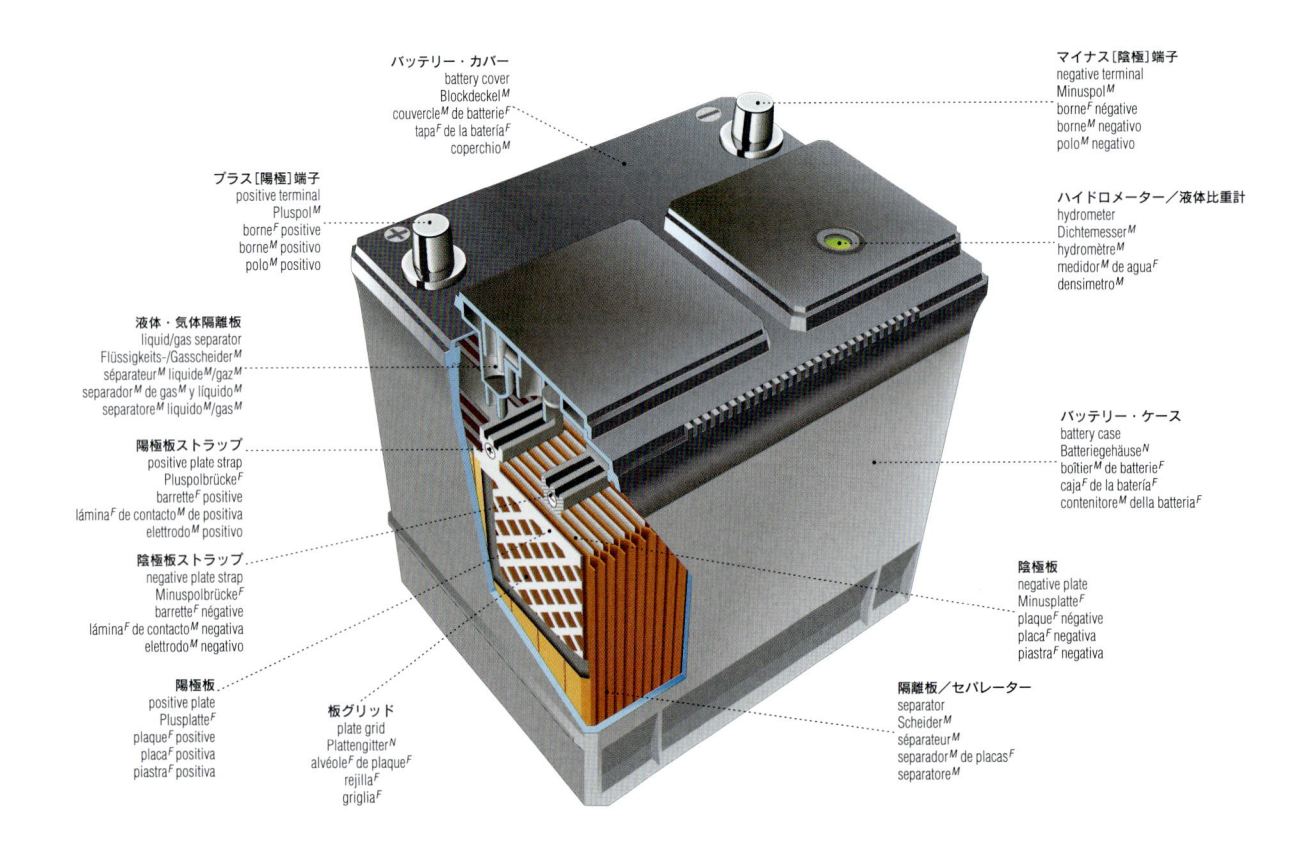

交通と機械

バッテリー・カバー
battery cover
Blockdeckel^M
couvercle^M de batterie^F
tapa^F de la batería^F
coperchio^M

プラス[陽極]端子
positive terminal
Pluspol^M
borne^F positive
borne^M positivo
polo^M positivo

液体・気体隔離板
liquid/gas separator
Flüssigkeits-/Gasscheider^M
séparateur^M liquide^M/gaz^M
separador^M de gas^M y líquido^M
separatore^M liquido^M/gas^M

陽極板ストラップ
positive plate strap
Pluspolbrücke^F
barrette^F positive
lámina^F de contacto^M de positiva
elettrodo^M positivo

陰極板ストラップ
negative plate strap
Minuspolbrücke^F
barrette^F négative
lámina^F de contacto^M negativa
elettrodo^M negativo

陽極板
positive plate
Plusplatte^F
plaque^F positive
placa^F positiva
piastra^F positiva

板グリッド
plate grid
Plattengitter^N
alvéole^F de plaque^F
rejilla^F
griglia^F

マイナス[陰極]端子
negative terminal
Minuspol^M
borne^F négative
borne^M negativo
polo^M negativo

ハイドロメーター／液体比重計
hydrometer
Dichtemesser^M
hydromètre^M
medidor^M de agua^F
densimetro^M

バッテリー・ケース
battery case
Batteriegehäuse^N
boîtier^M de batterie^F
caja^F de la batería^F
contenitore^M della batteria^F

陰極板
negative plate
Minusplatte^F
plaque^F négative
placa^F negativa
piastra^F negativa

隔離板／セパレーター
separator
Scheider^M
séparateur^M
separador^M de placas^F
separatore^M

道路交通 | ROAD TRANSPORT
STRASSENVERKEHR | TRANSPORT ROUTIER | TRANSPORTE TERRESTRE | TRASPORTO SU STRADA

電気自動車

electric automobile; *electric car* | Elektrofahrzeug^N | automobile^F électrique | automóvil^M eléctrico | automobile^F elettrica

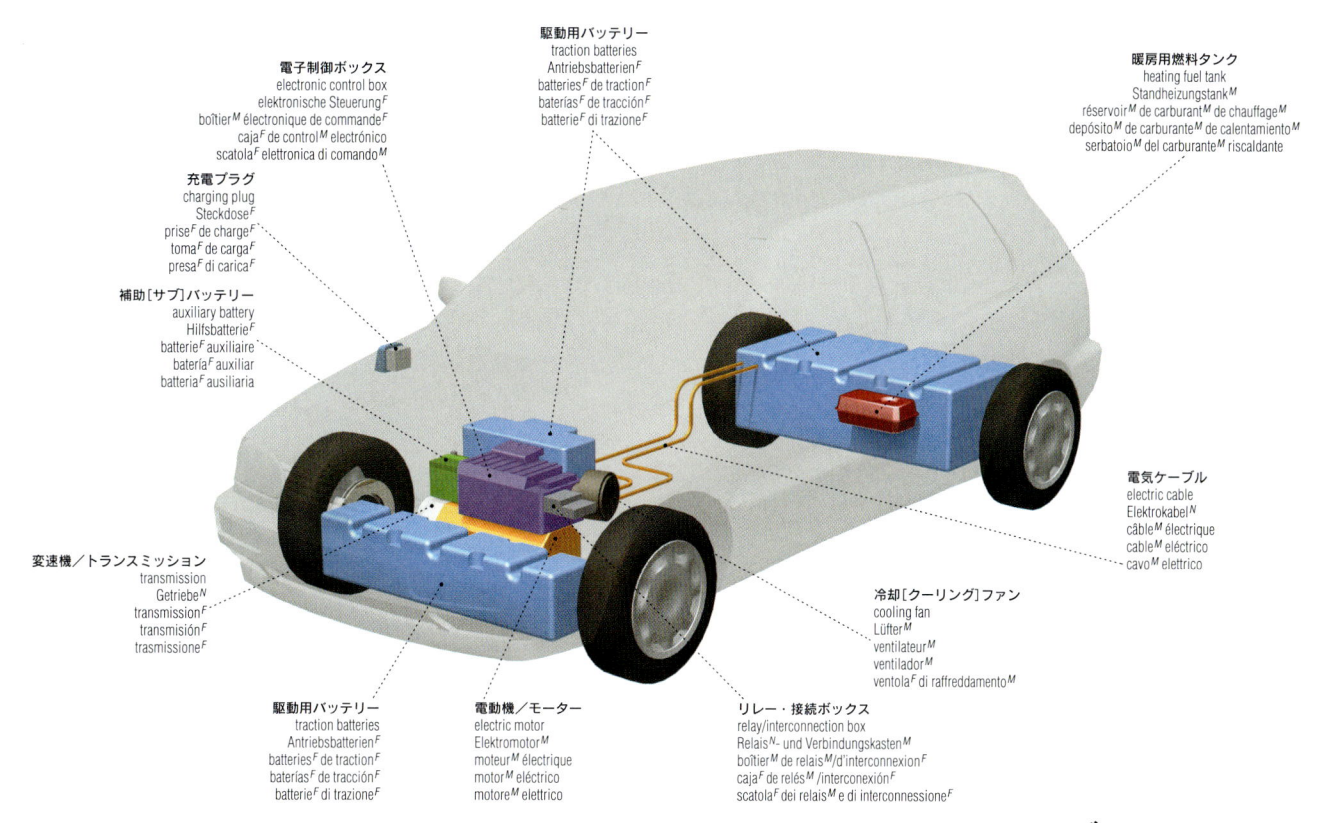

電子制御ボックス
electronic control box
elektronische Steuerung^F
boîtier^M électronique de commande^F
caja^F de control^M electrónico
scatola^F elettronica di comando^M

駆動用バッテリー
traction batteries
Antriebsbatterien^F
batteries^F de traction^F
baterías^F de tracción^F
batterie^F di trazione^F

暖房用燃料タンク
heating fuel tank
Standheizungstank^M
réservoir^M de carburant^M de chauffage^M
depósito^M de carburante^M de calentamiento^M
serbatoio^M del carburante^M riscaldante

充電プラグ
charging plug
Steckdose^F
prise^F de charge^F
toma^F de carga^F
presa^F di carica^F

補助[サブ]バッテリー
auxiliary battery
Hilfsbatterie^F
batterie^F auxiliaire
batería^F auxiliar
batteria^F ausiliaria

電気ケーブル
electric cable
Elektrokabel^N
câble^M électrique
cable^M eléctrico
cavo^M elettrico

冷却[クーリング]ファン
cooling fan
Lüfter^M
ventilateur^M
ventilador^M
ventola^F di raffreddamento^M

変速機/トランスミッション
transmission
Getriebe^N
transmission^F
transmisión^F
trasmissione^F

駆動用バッテリー
traction batteries
Antriebsbatterien^F
batteries^F de traction^F
baterías^F de tracción^F
batterie^F di trazione^F

電動機/モーター
electric motor
Elektromotor^M
moteur^M électrique
motor^M eléctrico
motore^M elettrico

リレー・接続ボックス
relay/interconnection box
Relais^N- und Verbindungskasten^M
boîtier^M de relais^M/d'interconnexion^F
caja^F de relés^M/interconexión^F
scatola^F dei relais^M e di interconnessione^F

ハイブリッド（自動）車

hybrid automobile; *hybrid car* | Hybridfahrzeug^N | automobile^F hybride | automóvil^M híbrido | automobile^F ibrida

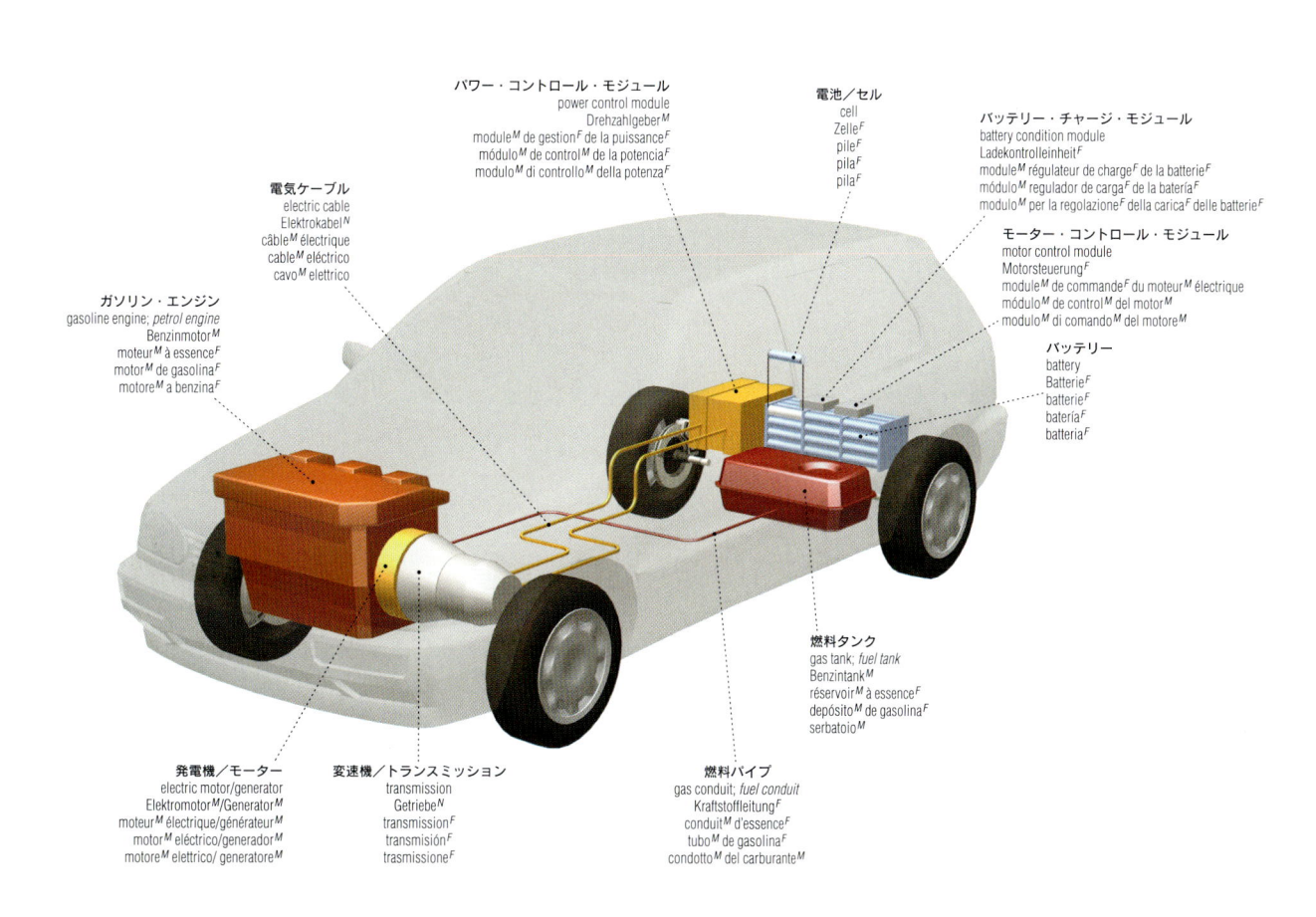

パワー・コントロール・モジュール
power control module
Drehzahlgeber^M
module^M de gestion^F de la puissance^F
módulo^M de control^M de la potencia^F
modulo^M di controllo^M della potenza^F

電池/セル
cell
Zelle^F
pile^F
pila^F
pila^F

バッテリー・チャージ・モジュール
battery condition module
Ladekontrolleinheit^F
module^M régulateur de charge^F de la batterie^F
módulo^M regulador de carga^F de la batería^F
modulo^M per la regolazione^F della carica^F delle batterie^F

電気ケーブル
electric cable
Elektrokabel^N
câble^M électrique
cable^M eléctrico
cavo^M elettrico

モーター・コントロール・モジュール
motor control module
Motorsteuerung^F
module^M de commande^F du moteur^M électrique
módulo^M de control^M del motor^M
modulo^M di comando^M del motore^M

ガソリン・エンジン
gasoline engine; *petrol engine*
Benzinmotor^M
moteur^M à essence^F
motor^M de gasolina^F
motore^M a benzina^F

バッテリー
battery
Batterie^F
batterie^F
batería^F
batteria^F

燃料タンク
gas tank; *fuel tank*
Benzintank^M
réservoir^M à essence^F
depósito^M de gasolina^F
serbatoio^M

発電機/モーター
electric motor/generator
Elektromotor^M/Generator^M
moteur^M électrique/générateur^M
motor^M eléctrico/generador^M
motore^M elettrico/generatore^M

変速機/トランスミッション
transmission
Getriebe^N
transmission^F
transmisión^F
trasmissione^F

燃料パイプ
gas conduit; *fuel conduit*
Kraftstoffleitung^F
conduit^M d'essence^F
tubo^M de gasolina^F
condotto^M del carburante^M

道路交通 | ROAD TRANSPORT
STRASSENVERKEHR | TRANSPORT ROUTIER | TRANSPORTE TERRESTRE | TRASPORTO SU STRADA

エンジンの種類

types of engines | Motortypen^M | types^M de moteurs^M | tipos^M de motores^M | tipi^M di motori^M

ターボ・チャージド・エンジン
turbo-compressor engine; *turbo-charged engine*
Motor^M mit Abgasturbolader^M
moteur^M à turbocompression^F
motor^M turbocompresor
motore^M turbocompresso

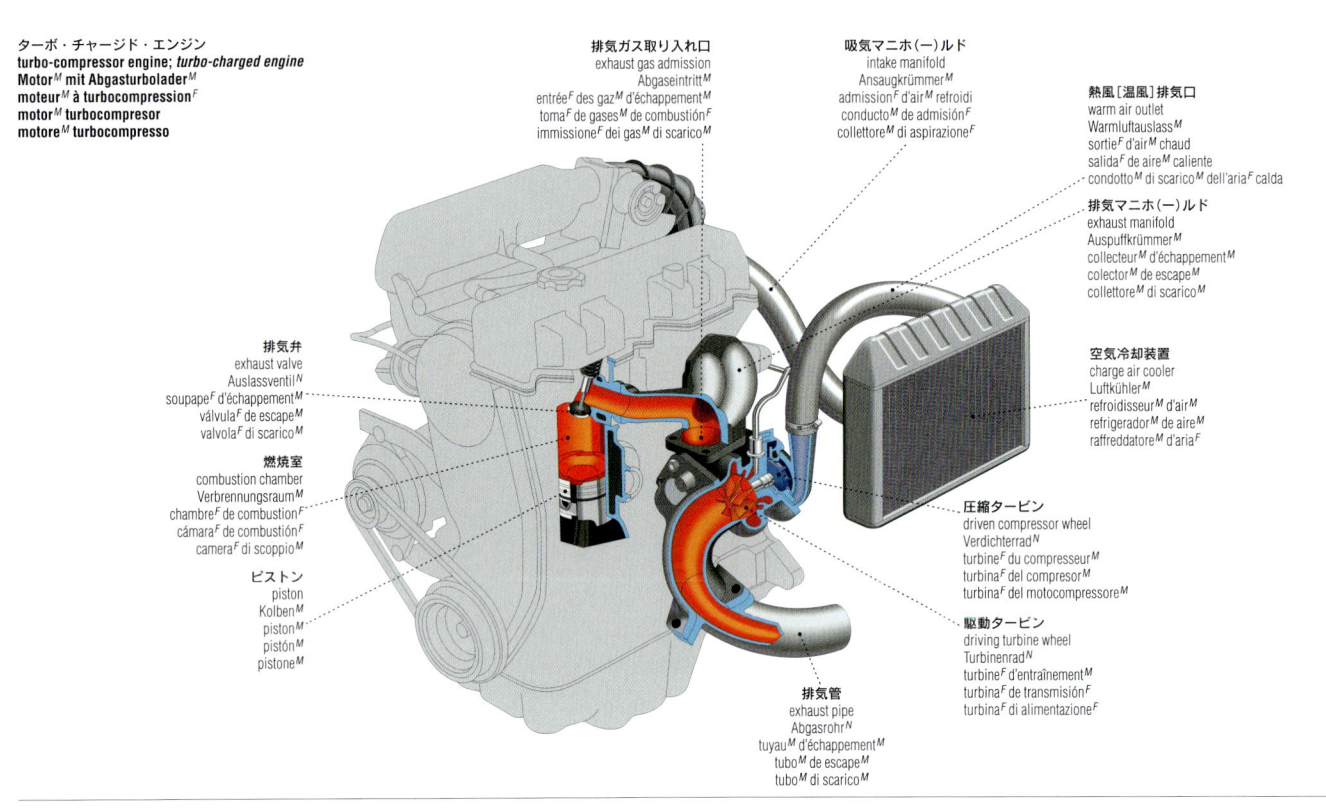

排気ガス取り入れ口
exhaust gas admission
Abgaseintritt^M
entrée^F des gaz^M d'échappement^M
toma^F de gases^M de combustión^F
immissione^F dei gas^M di scarico^M

吸気マニホ（ー）ルド
intake manifold
Ansaugkrümmer^M
admission^F d'air^M refroidi
conducto^M de admisión^F
collettore^M di aspirazione^F

熱風[温風]排気口
warm air outlet
Warmluftauslass^M
sortie^F d'air^M chaud
salida^F de aire^M caliente
condotto^M di scarico^M dell'aria^F calda

排気マニホ（ー）ルド
exhaust manifold
Auspuffkrümmer^M
collecteur^M d'échappement^M
colector^M de escape^M
collettore^M di scarico^M

排気弁
exhaust valve
Auslassventil^N
soupape^F d'échappement^M
válvula^F de escape^M
valvola^F di scarico^M

空気冷却装置
charge air cooler
Luftkühler^M
refroidisseur^M d'air^M
refrigerador^M de aire^M
raffreddatore^M d'aria^F

燃焼室
combustion chamber
Verbrennungsraum^M
chambre^F de combustion^F
cámara^F de combustión^F
camera^F di scoppio^M

圧縮タービン
driven compressor wheel
Verdichterrad^N
turbine^F du compresseur^M
turbina^F del compresor^M
turbina^F del motocompressore^M

ピストン
piston
Kolben^M
piston^M
pistón^M
pistone^M

駆動タービン
driving turbine wheel
Turbinenrad^N
turbine^F d'entraînement^M
turbina^F de transmisión^F
turbina^F di alimentazione^F

排気管
exhaust pipe
Abgasrohr^N
tuyau^M d'échappement^M
tubo^M de escape^M
tubo^M di scarico^M

4（ストローク）サイクル［4行程］エンジン
four-stroke-cycle engine
Viertaktmotor^M
moteur^M à quatre temps^M
motor^M de cuatro tiempos^M
motore^M a quattro tempi^M

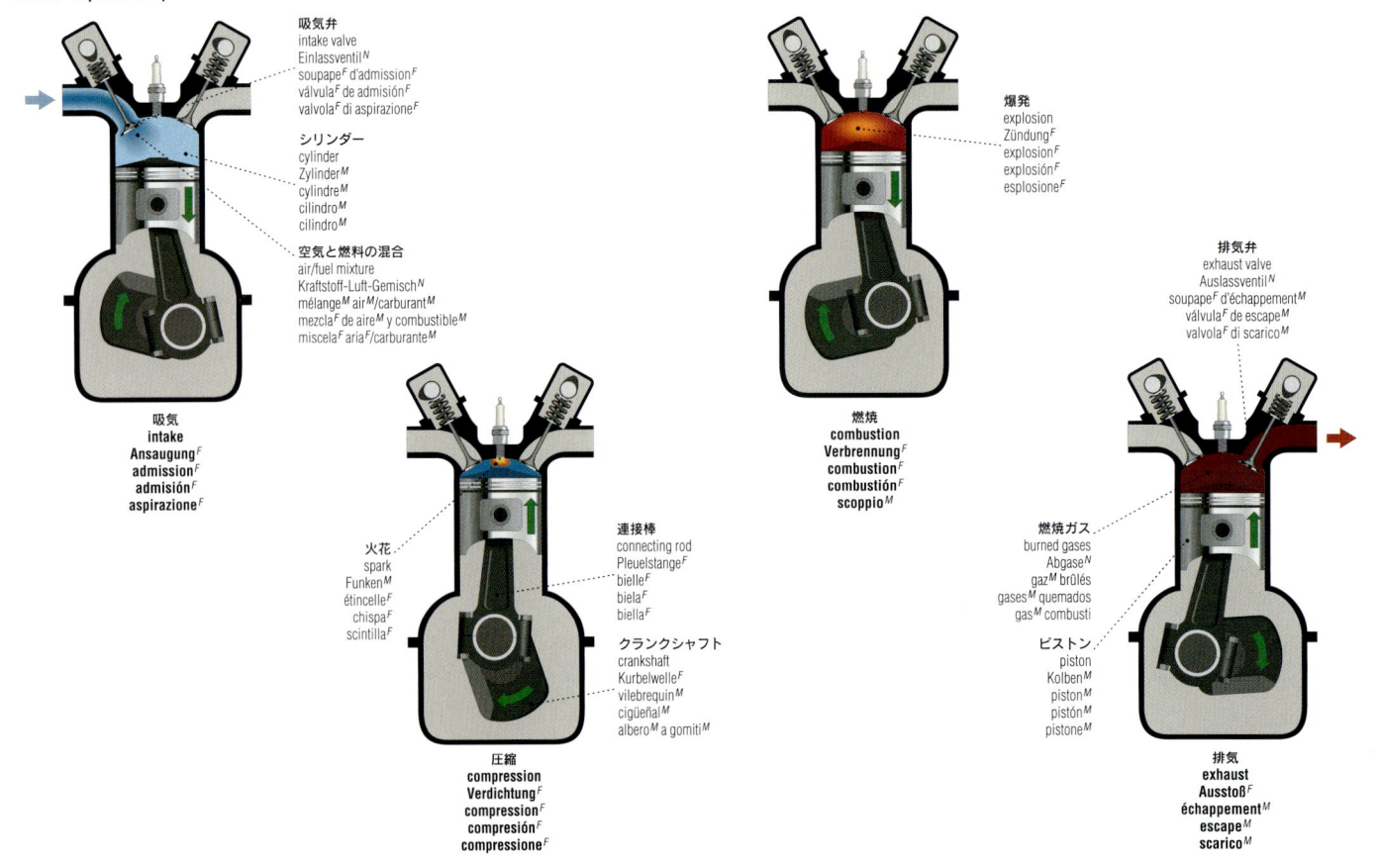

吸気弁
intake valve
Einlassventil^N
soupape^F d'admission^F
válvula^F de admisión^F
valvola^F di aspirazione^F

シリンダー
cylinder
Zylinder^M
cylindre^M
cilindro^M
cilindro^M

空気と燃料の混合
air/fuel mixture
Kraftstoff-Luft-Gemisch^N
mélange^M air^M/carburant^M
mezcla^F de aire^M y combustible^M
miscela^F aria^F/carburante^M

爆発
explosion
Zündung^F
explosion^F
explosión^F
esplosione^F

排気弁
exhaust valve
Auslassventil^N
soupape^F d'échappement^M
válvula^F de escape^M
valvola^F di scarico^M

吸気
intake
Ansaugung^F
admission^F
admisión^F
aspirazione^F

火花
spark
Funken^M
étincelle^F
chispa^F
scintilla^F

連接棒
connecting rod
Pleuelstange^F
bielle^F
biela^F
biella^F

燃焼
combustion
Verbrennung^F
combustion^F
combustión^F
scoppio^M

燃焼ガス
burned gases
Abgase^N
gaz^M brûlés
gases^M quemados
gas^M combusti

ピストン
piston
Kolben^M
piston^M
pistón^M
pistone^M

クランクシャフト
crankshaft
Kurbelwelle^F
vilebrequin^M
cigüeñal^M
albero^M a gomiti^M

圧縮
compression
Verdichtung^F
compression^F
compresión^F
compressione^F

排気
exhaust
Ausstoß^F
échappement^F
escape^M
scarico^M

道路交通 | ROAD TRANSPORT
STRASSENVERKEHR | TRANSPORT ROUTIER | TRANSPORTE TERRESTRE | TRASPORTO SU STRADA

エンジンの種類

2（ストローク）サイクル［2行程］エンジンの周期
two-stroke-cycle engine cycle
Arbeitsprozess^M des Zweitaktmotors^M
cycle^M d'un moteur^M à deux temps^M
ciclo^M de un motor^M de dos tiempos^M
ciclo^M del motore^M a due tempi^M

点火［スパーク］プラグ
spark plug; *spark plug*
Zündkerze^F
bougie^F d'allumage^M
bujía^F
candela^F

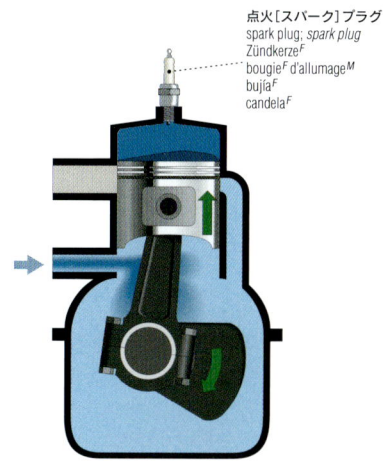

排気管
exhaust port
Auspuffkanal^M
canal^M d'échappement^M
lumbrera^F de escape^M
luce^F di scarico^M

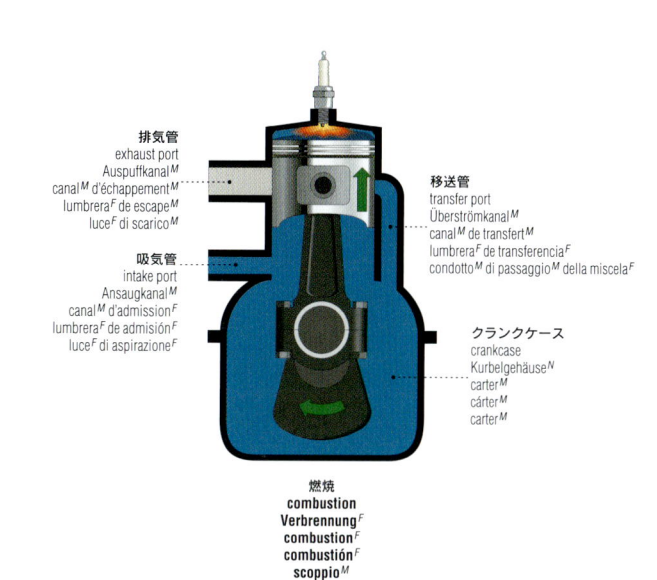

移送管
transfer port
Überströmkanal^M
canal^M de transfert^M
lumbrera^F de transferencia^F
condotto^M di passaggio^M della miscela^F

吸気管
intake port
Ansaugkanal^M
canal^M d'admission^F
lumbrera^F de admisión^F
luce^F di aspirazione^F

クランクケース
crankcase
Kurbelgehäuse^N
carter^M
cárter^M
carter^M

圧縮・吸気
compression/intake
Verdichtung^F/Ansaugung^F
compression^F/admission^F
compresión^F/admisión^F
compressione^F/aspirazione^F

燃焼
combustion
Verbrennung^F
combustion^F
combustión^F
scoppio^M

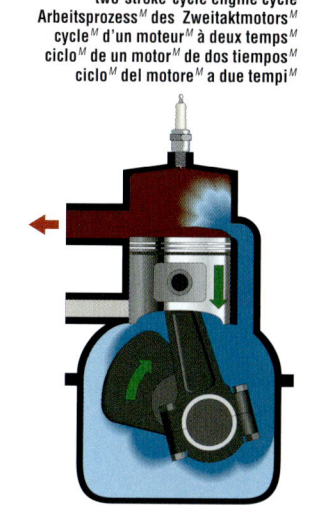

排気・掃気
exhaust/scavaging
Ausstoß^M
échappement^M
escape^M
scarico^M

吸気マニホ（ー）ルド
intake manifold
Einlasskanal^M
tubulure^F d'admission^F
colector^M de admisión^F
collettore^M di aspirazione^F

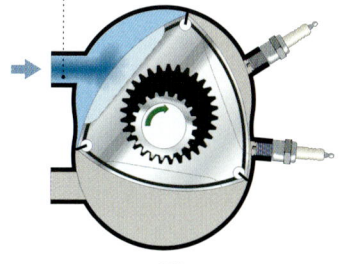

排気マニホ（ー）ルド
exhaust manifold
Auslasskanal^M
tubulure^F d'échappement^M
colector^M de escape^M
collettore^M di scarico^M

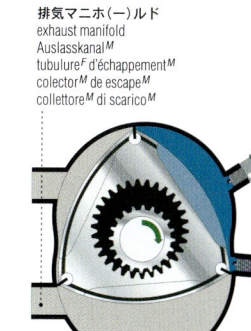

ローター
rotor
Kolben^M
rotor^M
rotor^M
rotore^M

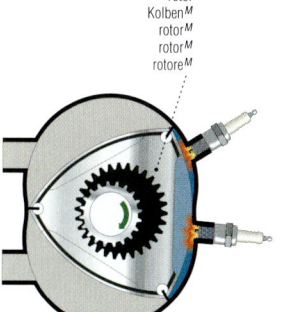

ロータリー・エンジンの周期
rotary engine cycle
Arbeitsprozess^M des Kreiskolbenmotors^M
cycle^M d'un moteur^M rotatif
ciclo^M de un motor^M rotatorio
ciclo^M del motore^M rotativo

吸気
intake
Ansaugung^F
admission^F
admisión^F
aspirazione^F

圧縮
compression
Verdichtung^F
compression^F
compresión^F
compressione^F

燃焼
power
Verbrennung^F
combustion^F
combustión^F
scoppio^M

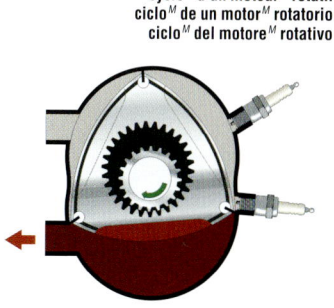

排気
exhaust
Ausstoß^M
échappement^M
escape^M
scarico^M

空気
air
Luft^F
air^M
aire^M
aria^F

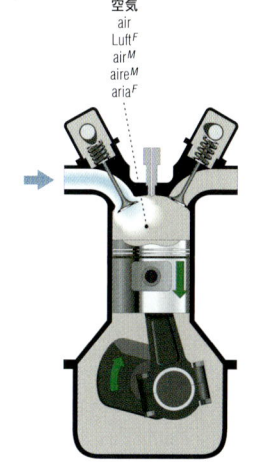

噴射・爆発
injection/combustion
Einspritzung^F/Verbrennung^F
injection^F/explosion^F
inyección^F/combustión^F
iniezione^F/combustione^F

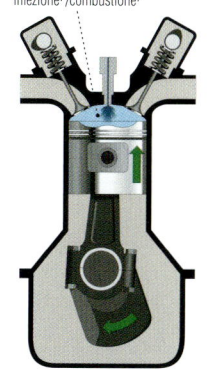

燃料噴射器［インジェクター］
fuel injector
Einspritzdüse^F
injecteur^M
inyector^M de combustible^M
iniettore^M

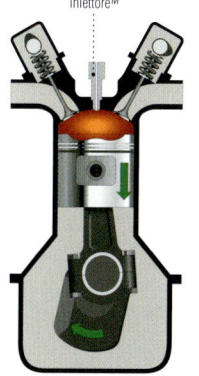

ディーゼル・エンジンの周期
diesel engine cycle
Arbeitsprozess^M des Dieselmotors^M
cycle^M d'un moteur^M diesel
ciclo^M de un motor^M diesel
ciclo^M del motore^M diesel

吸気
intake
Ansaugung^F
admission^F
admisión^F
aspirazione^F

圧縮
compression
Verdichten^N
compression^F
compresión^F
compressione^F

燃焼
power
Verbrennung^F
combustion^F
combustión^F
combustione^F

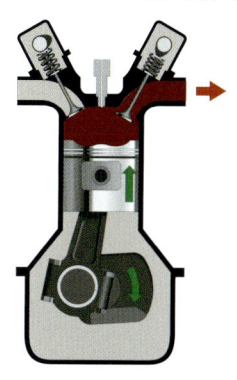

排気
exhaust
Ausstoß^M
échappement^M
escape^M
scarico^M

交通と機械

565

道路交通 | ROAD TRANSPORT
STRASSENVERKEHR | TRANSPORT ROUTIER | TRANSPORTE TERRESTRE | TRASPORTO SU STRADA

エンジンの種類

日本語 | 英語 | ドイツ語 | フランス語 | スペイン語 | イタリア語

ガソリン・エンジン
gasoline engine; *petrol engine*
Ottomotor[M]
moteur[M] à essence[F]
motor[M] de gasolina[F]
motore[M] a benzina[F]

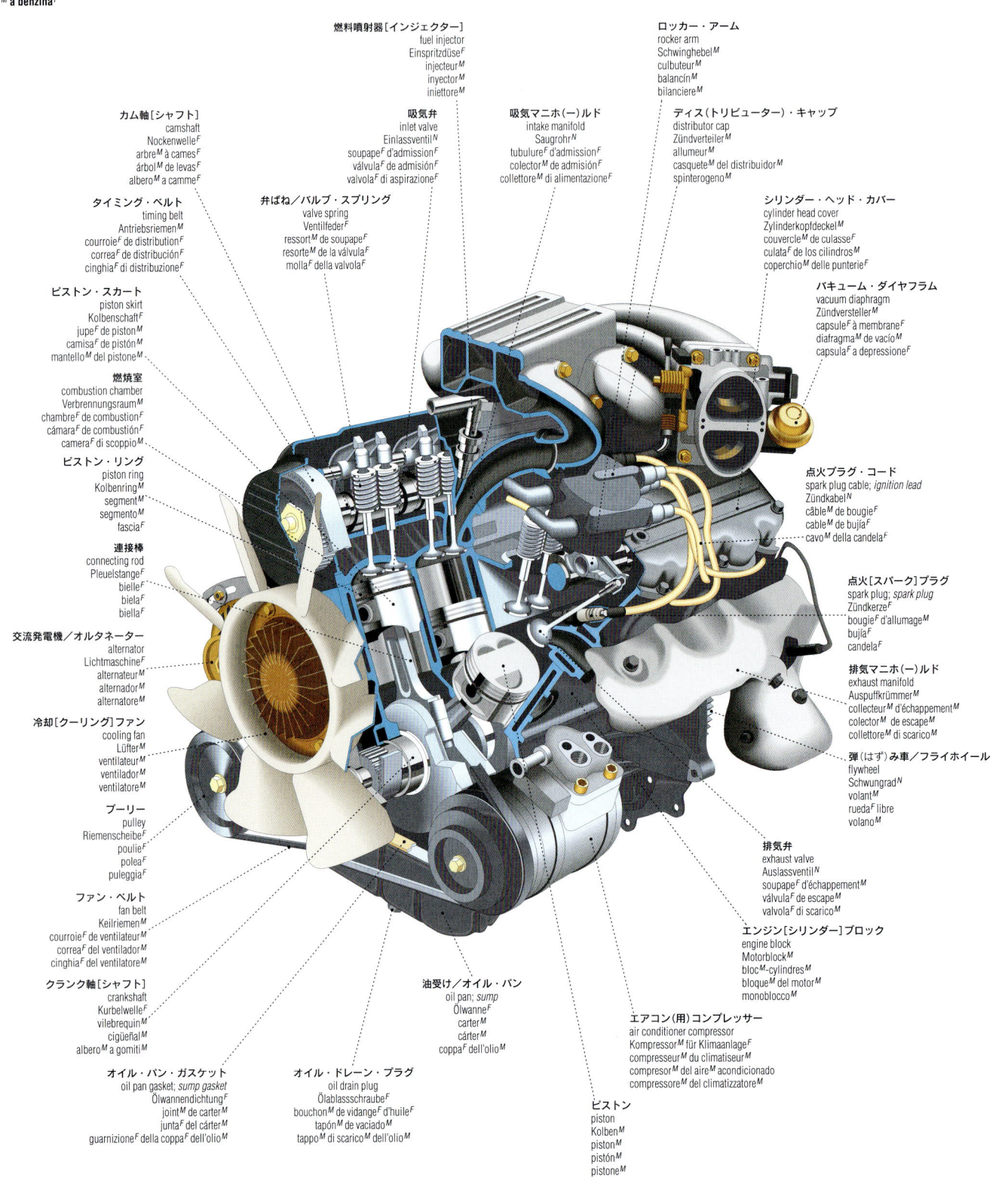

カム軸[シャフト]
camshaft
Nockenwelle[F]
arbre[M] à cames[F]
árbol[M] de levas[F]
albero[M] a camme[F]

タイミング・ベルト
timing belt
Antriebsriemen[M]
courroie[F] de distribution[F]
correa[F] de distribución[F]
cinghia[F] di distribuzione[F]

ピストン・スカート
piston skirt
Kolbenschaft[F]
jupe[F] de piston[M]
camisa[F] de pistón[M]
mantello[M] del pistone[M]

燃焼室
combustion chamber
Verbrennungsraum[M]
chambre[F] de combustion[F]
cámara[F] de combustión[F]
camera[F] di scoppio[M]

ピストン・リング
piston ring
Kolbenring[M]
segment[M]
segmento[M]
fascia[F]

連接棒
connecting rod
Pleuelstange[F]
bielle[F]
biela[F]
biella[F]

交流発電機／オルタネーター
alternator
Lichtmaschine[F]
alternateur[M]
alternador[M]
alternatore[M]

冷却[クーリング]ファン
cooling fan
Lüfter[M]
ventilateur[M]
ventilador[M]
ventilatore[M]

プーリー
pulley
Riemenscheibe[F]
poulie[F]
polea[F]
puleggia[F]

ファン・ベルト
fan belt
Keilriemen[M]
courroie[F] de ventilateur[M]
correa[F] del ventilador[M]
cinghia[F] del ventilatore[M]

クランク軸[シャフト]
crankshaft
Kurbelwelle[F]
vilebrequin[M]
cigüeñal[M]
albero[M] a gomiti[M]

オイル・パン・ガスケット
oil pan gasket; *sump gasket*
Ölwannendichtung[F]
joint[M] de carter[M]
junta[F] del cárter[M]
guarnizione[F] della coppa[F] dell'olio[M]

燃料噴射器[インジェクター]
fuel injector
Einspritzdüse[F]
injecteur[M]
inyector[M]
iniettore[M]

吸気弁
inlet valve
Einlassventil[N]
soupape[F] d'admission[F]
válvula[F] de admisión[F]
valvola[F] di aspirazione[F]

弁ばね／バルブ・スプリング
valve spring
Ventilfeder[F]
ressort[M] de soupape[F]
resorte[M] de la válvula[F]
molla[F] della valvola[F]

吸気マニホ(ー)ルド
intake manifold
Saugrohr[N]
tubulure[F] d'admission[F]
colector[M] de admisión[F]
collettore[M] di alimentazione[F]

油受け／オイル・パン
oil pan; *sump*
Ölwanne[F]
carter[M]
cárter[M]
coppa[F] dell'olio[M]

オイル・ドレーン・プラグ
oil drain plug
Ölablassschraube[F]
bouchon[M] de vidange[F] d'huile[F]
tapón[M] de vaciado[M]
tappo[M] di scarico[M] dell'olio[M]

ピストン
piston
Kolben[M]
piston[M]
pistón[M]
pistone[M]

ロッカー・アーム
rocker arm
Schwinghebel[M]
culbuteur[M]
balancín[M]
bilanciere[M]

ディス(トリビューター)・キャップ
distributor cap
Zündverteiler[M]
allumeur[M]
casquete[M] del distribuidor[M]
spinterogeno[M]

シリンダー・ヘッド・カバー
cylinder head cover
Zylinderkopfdeckel[M]
couvercle[M] de culasse[F]
culata[F] de los cilindros[M]
coperchio[M] delle punterie[F]

バキューム・ダイヤフラム
vacuum diaphragm
Zündversteller[M]
capsule[F] à membrane[F]
diafragma[M] de vacío[M]
capsula[F] a depressione[F]

点火プラグ・コード
spark plug cable; *ignition lead*
Zündkabel[N]
câble[M] de bougie[F]
cable[M] de bujía[F]
cavo[M] della candela[F]

点火[スパーク]プラグ
spark plug; *spark plug*
Zündkerze[F]
bougie[F] d'allumage[M]
bujía[F]
candela[F]

排気マニホ(ー)ルド
exhaust manifold
Auspuffkrümmer[M]
collecteur[M] d'échappement[M]
colector[M] de escape[M]
collettore[M] di scarico[M]

弾(はず)み車／フライホイール
flywheel
Schwungrad[N]
volant[M]
rueda[F] libre
volano[M]

排気弁
exhaust valve
Auslassventil[N]
soupape[F] d'échappement[M]
válvula[F] de escape[M]
valvola[F] di scarico[M]

エンジン[シリンダー]ブロック
engine block
Motorblock[M]
bloc[M]-cylindres[M]
bloque[M] del motor[M]
monoblocco[M]

エアコン(用)コンプレッサー
air conditioner compressor
Kompressor[M] für Klimaanlage[F]
compresseur[M] du climatiseur[M]
compresor[M] del aire[M] acondicionado
compressore[M] del climatizzatore[M]

道路交通 | ROAD TRANSPORT
STRASSENVERKEHR | TRANSPORT ROUTIER | TRANSPORTE TERRESTRE | TRASPORTO SU STRADA

トレーラー・ハウス

caravan | Wohnwagen^M | caravane^F | caravana^F | rimorchi^M e autocaravan^M

キャンピング・カー
trailer; *trailer caravan*
Wohnwagen^M
caravane^F tractée
remolque^M
roulotte^F

屋根換気口 — roof vent / Dachluke^F / aérateur^M de toit / ventanilla^F de ventilación^F del techo^M / presa^F d'aria^F sul tetto^M

側壁換気口 — side vent / Lufteinlass^M / aérateur^M latéral / respiradero^M lateral / presa^F d'aria^F laterale

車体 — body / Karosserie^F / coque^F / carrocería^F / carrozzeria^F

日除(よ)け/サン・バイザー — sun visor / Sonnenblende^F / pare-soleil^M / parasol^M / visiera^F parasole

プロパン・ガス・ボンベ — propane gas cylinder / Propanflasche^F / réservoir^M propane / tanque^M de gas^M propano^M / bombola^F di gas^M propano

滴除(よ)け — awning channel / Vordachrille^F / glissière^F d'auvent / ranura^F para toldo^M / telaio^M per tenda^F esterna

取っ手 — grab handle / Haltegriff^F / poignée^F montoir^M / asidero^M / maniglia^F

油圧式ジャッキ — hydraulic jack / Hydraulik-Heber^M / vérin^M hydraulique / gato^M hidráulico / martinetto^M idraulico

コンセント — outlet; *external socket* / Steckdose^F / prise^F électrique / toma^F de corriente^F / presa^F di corrente^F

連結器 — towing hitch / Anhängerkupplung^F / tête^F d'attelage^M / enganche^M del remolque^M / gancio^M di traino^M

収納庫 — storage compartment / Stauraum^M / coffre^M à bagages^M / compartimento^M para almacenamiento^M / vano^M portattrezzi^M

ドア — door / Tür^F / porte^F / puerta^F / porta^F

連結棒/トウ・バー — tow bar / Anhängerkupplung^F / timon^M / barra^F de remolque^M / barra^F di traino^M

格納式ステップ — retractable step / Klappstufe^F / marchepied^M escamotable / escalón^M retráctil / gradino^M rientrabile

安全チェーン — tow safety chain / Sicherheitskette^F / chaîne^F de sûreté^F / cadena^F de seguridad^F / catena^F di sicurezza^F

補助脚 — landing gear / Stützfuß^M / béquille^F d'appui^M / amarre^M anterior retráctil / supporto^M anteriore retrattile

照明用電気コード — lighting cable / Stromanschlusskabel^N / raccord^M de signalisation^F / cable^M de alumbrado^M / cavo^M di raccordo^M per luci^F di segnalazione^F

テント・トレーラー
tent trailer
Zeltwagen^M
tente^F-caravane^F
caravana^F plegable
carrello^M tenda^F

屋根/ルーフ — roof / Dach^N / toit^M / techo^M / tetto^M

キャノピー — canopy / Vordach^N / auvent^M / toldo^M / tettuccio^M

窓 — window / Fenster^N / fenêtre^F / ventana^F / finestrino^M

バンク — bunk / Bett^N / lit^M / litera^F / letto^M

スペア・タイヤ — spare tire / Reserverad^N / roue^F de secours^M / rueda^F de repuesto^M / ruota^F di scorta^F

車体 — body / Aufbau^M / coque^F / carrocería^F / scocca^F

安定[固定]ジャッキ — stabilizer jack / Stütze^F / béquille^F d'appoint^M / gato^M estabilizador / supporto^M stabilizzatore^M

網戸 — screen door / Fliegengittertür^F / porte^F moustiquaire / puerta^F mosquitera / porta^F a zanzariera^F

モーター・ホーム
motor home; *camper*
Wohnmobil^N
auto^F-caravane^F
autocaravana^M
autocaravan^M

エア・コン — air conditioner / Klimaanlage^F / climatiseur^M / aire^M acondicionado / condizionatore^M

荷物台/ルーフ・ラック — luggage rack / Gepäckträger^M / porte-bagages^M / portaequipajes^M / portabagagli^M

はしご — ladder / Leiter^F / échelle^F / escalerilla^F / scala^F

交通と機械

567

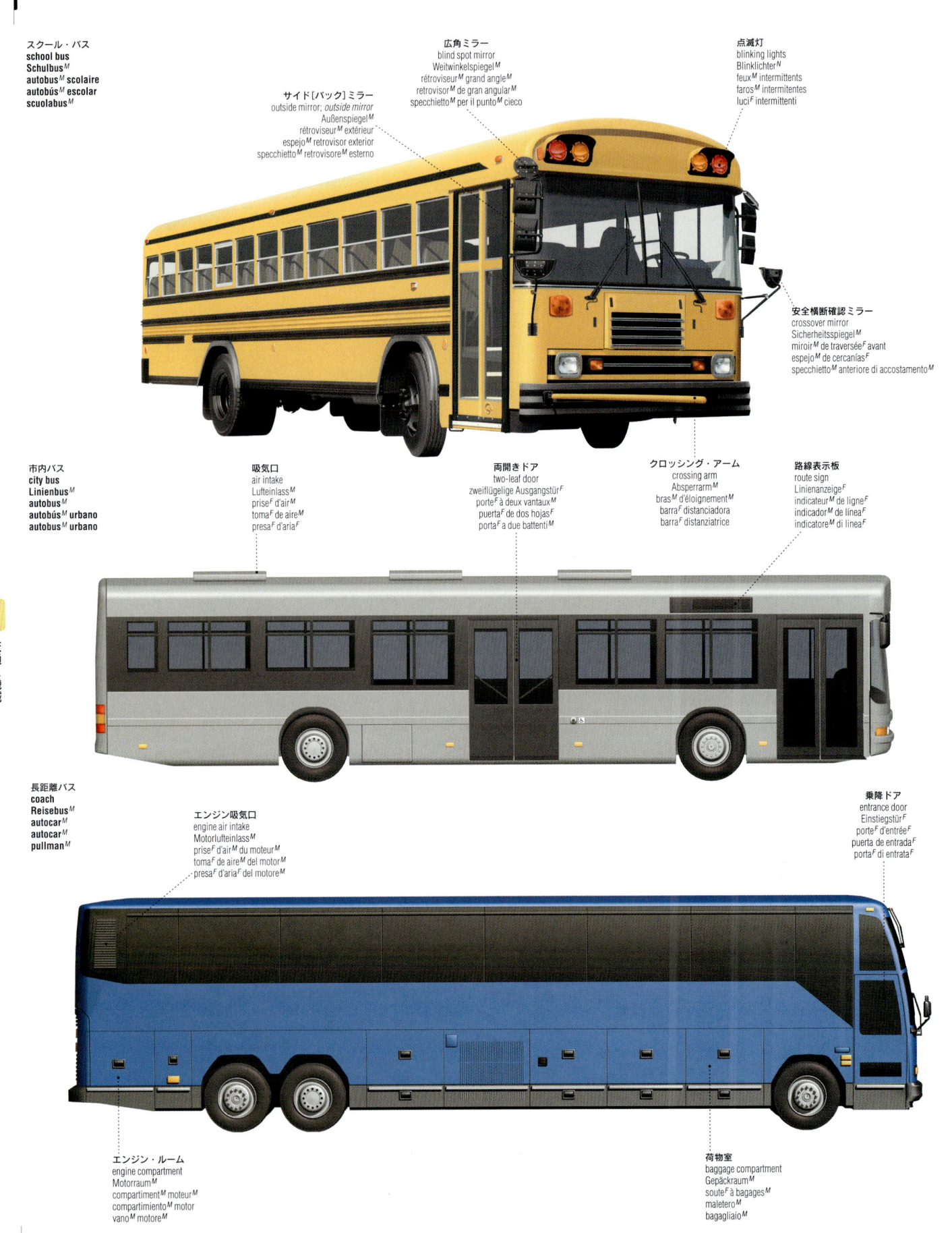

道路交通 | ROAD TRANSPORT
STRASSENVERKEHR | TRANSPORT ROUTIER | TRANSPORTE TERRESTRE | TRASPORTO SU STRADA

バス

日本語 | 英語 | ドイツ語 | フランス語 | スペイン語 | イタリア語

bus | Bus^M | autobus^M | autobús^M | autobus^M

スクール・バス
school bus
Schulbus^M
autobus^M scolaire
autobús^M escolar
scuolabus^M

サイド[バック]ミラー
outside mirror; *outside mirror*
Außenspiegel^M
rétroviseur^M extérieur
espejo^M retrovisor exterior
specchietto^M retrovisore^M esterno

広角ミラー
blind spot mirror
Weitwinkelspiegel^M
rétroviseur^M grand angle^M
retrovisor^M de gran angular^M
specchietto^M per il punto^M cieco

点滅灯
blinking lights
Blinklichter^N
feux^M intermittents
faros^M intermitentes
luci^F intermittenti

安全横断確認ミラー
crossover mirror
Sicherheitsspiegel^M
miroir^M de traversée^F avant
espejo^M de cercanías^F
specchietto^M anteriore di accostamento^M

市内バス
city bus
Linienbus^M
autobus^M
autobús^M urbano
autobus^M urbano

吸気口
air intake
Lufteinlass^M
prise^F d'air^M
toma^F de aire^M
presa^F d'aria^F

両開きドア
two-leaf door
zweiflügelige Ausgangstür^F
porte^F à deux vantaux^M
puerta^F de dos hojas^F
porta^F a due battenti^M

クロッシング・アーム
crossing arm
Absperrarm^M
bras^M d'éloignement^M
barra^F distanciadora
barra^F distanziatrice

路線表示板
route sign
Linienanzeige^F
indicateur^M de ligne^F
indicador^M de línea^F
indicatore^M di linea^F

長距離バス
coach
Reisebus^M
autocar^M
autocar^M
pullman^M

エンジン吸気口
engine air intake
Motorlufteinlass^M
prise^F d'air^M du moteur^M
toma^F de aire^M del motor^M
presa^F d'aria^F del motore^M

乗降ドア
entrance door
Einstiegstür^F
porte^F d'entrée^F
puerta^F de entrada
porta^F di entrata^F

エンジン・ルーム
engine compartment
Motorraum^M
compartiment^M moteur
compartimento^M motor
vano^M motore^M

荷物室
baggage compartment
Gepäckraum^M
soute^F à bagages^M
maletero^M
bagagliaio^M

568

道路交通 | ROAD TRANSPORT
STRASSENVERKEHR | TRANSPORT ROUTIER | TRANSPORTE TERRESTRE | TRASPORTO SU STRADA

バス

二階建てバス
double-deck bus
Doppeldeckerbus^M
autocar^M à impériale^F
autocar^M de dos pisos^M
autobus^M a due piani^M

二階
upper deck
Oberdeck^N
impériale^F
piso^M superior
piano^M superiore

路線表示板
route sign
Linienanzeige^F
indicateur^M de ligne^F
indicador^M de línea^F
indicatore^M di linea^F

小型バス／マイクロバス
minibus
Kleinbus^M
minibus^M
minibús^M
minibus^M

リフト・ドア
lift door
elektrische Schiebetür^F
porte^F de l'élévateur^M
puerta^F de la plataforma^F elevadora
porta^F dell'elevatore^M

広角ミラー
blind spot mirror
Weitwinkelspiegel^M
rétroviseur^M grand angle^M
retrovisor^M gran angular
specchietto^M per il punto^M cieco

カリフォルニア[サイド]ミラー／後写鏡
West Coast mirror; *West Coast mirror*
Außenspiegel^M
rétroviseur^M
espejo^M retrovisor
specchietto^M retrovisore^M

手すり
handrail
Haltegriff^M
barre^F de maintien^M
pasamano^M
corrimano^M

段差解消機／車椅子用リフト
wheelchair lift
Rollstuhllift^M
élévateur^M pour fauteuils^M roulants
plataforma^F elevadora para silla^F de ruedas^F
elevatore^M per sedie^F a rotelle^F

乗降ドア
entrance door
Einstiegstür^F
porte^F d'entrée^F
puerta^F de entrada^F
porta^F di entrata^F

プラットホーム
platform
Plattform^F
plate-forme^F
plataforma^F
piattaforma^F

連結[連接]バス
articulated bus
Gelenkbus^M
autobus^M articulé
autobús^M articulado
autobus^M articolato

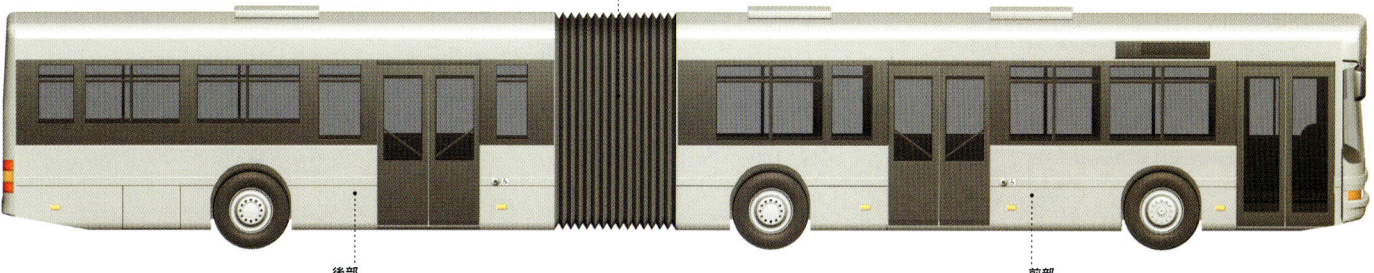

自在連結部／蛇腹
articulated joint
Gelenk^N
section^F articulée
sección^F articulada
passaggio^M a soffietto^M

後部
rear rigid section
steifer Nachläufer^M
tronçon^M rigide arrière
remolque^M rígido trasero
sezione^F rigida posteriore

前部
front rigid section
steifes Vorderteil^N
tronçon^M rigide avant
sección^F rígida de tracción^F delantera
sezione^F rigida anteriore

交通と機械

569

道路交通 | ROAD TRANSPORT
STRASSENVERKEHR | TRANSPORT ROUTIER | TRANSPORTE TERRESTRE | TRASPORTO SU STRADA

トラック運送

日本語 | 英語 | ドイツ語 | フランス語 | スペイン語 | イタリア語

trucking | Lastkraftfahrzeuge[N] | camionnage[M] | camiones[M] | autoveicoli[M] industriali

トラック・トラクター
truck tractor; *tractor unit*
Sattelschlepper[M]
tracteur[M] routier
camión[M] tractor[M]
motrice[F]

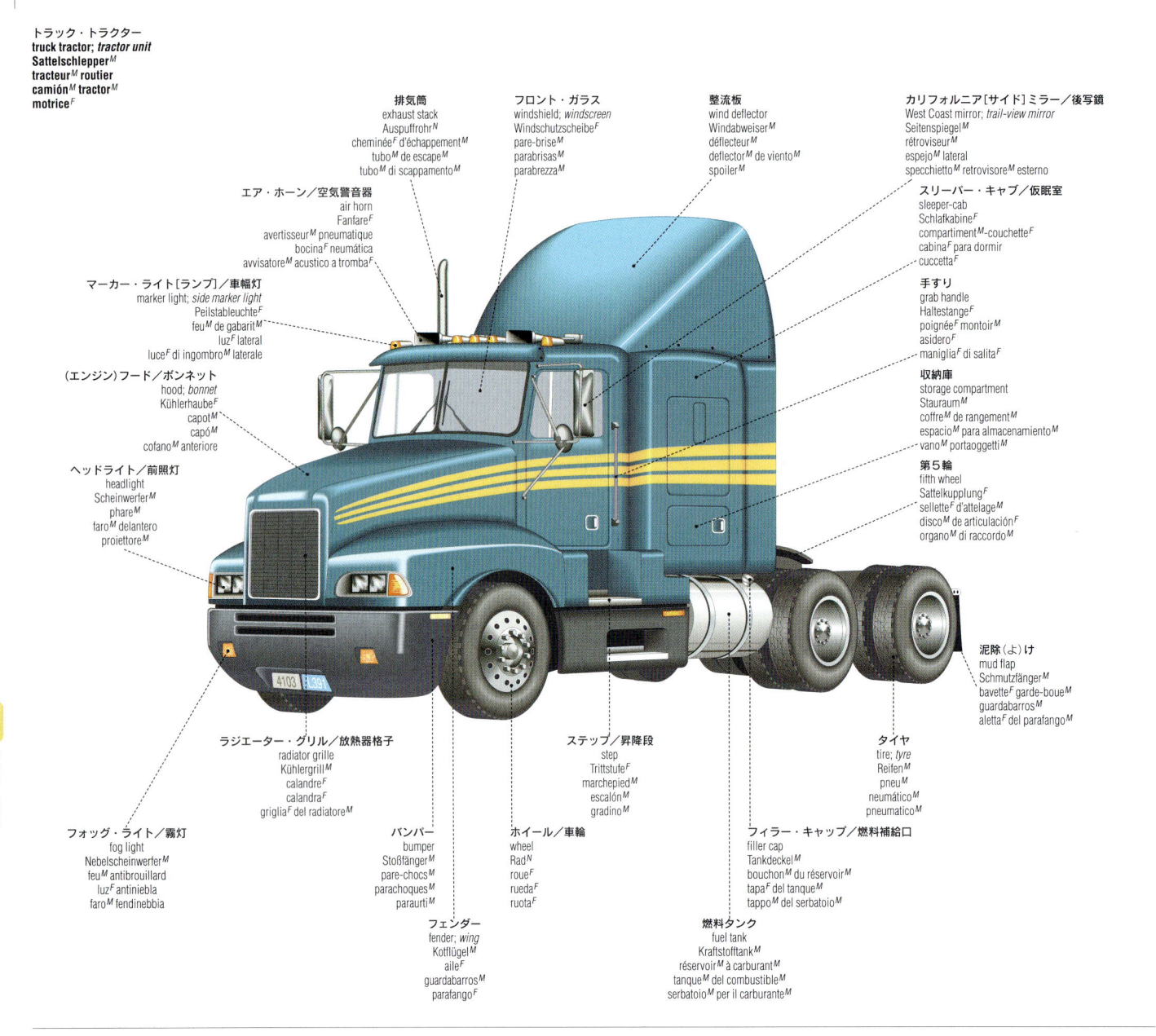

排気筒
exhaust stack
Auspuffrohr[N]
cheminée[F] d'échappement[M]
tubo[M] de escape[M]
tubo[M] di scappamento[M]

フロント・ガラス
windshield; *windscreen*
Windschutzscheibe[F]
pare-brise[M]
parabrisas[M]
parabrezza[M]

整流板
wind deflector
Windabweiser[M]
déflecteur[M]
deflector[M] de viento[M]
spoiler[M]

カリフォルニア[サイド]ミラー／後写鏡
West Coast mirror; *trail-view mirror*
Seitenspiegel[M]
rétroviseur[M]
espejo[M] lateral
specchietto[M] retrovisore[M] esterno

エア・ホーン／空気警音器
air horn
Fanfare[F]
avertisseur[M] pneumatique
bocina[F] neumática
avvisatore[M] acustico a tromba[F]

スリーパー・キャブ／仮眠室
sleeper-cab
Schlafkabine[F]
compartiment[M]-couchette[F]
cabina[F] para dormir
cuccetta[F]

マーカー・ライト[ランプ]／車幅灯
marker light; *side marker light*
Peilstableuchte[F]
feu[M] de gabarit[M]
luz[F] lateral
luce[F] di ingombro[M] laterale

手すり
grab handle
Haltestange[F]
poignée[F] montoir[M]
asidero[M]
maniglia[F] di salita[F]

（エンジン）フード／ボンネット
hood; *bonnet*
Kühlerhaube[F]
capot[M]
capó[M]
cofano[M] anteriore

収納庫
storage compartment
Stauraum[M]
coffre[M] de rangement[M]
espacio[M] para almacenamiento[M]
vano[M] portaoggetti[M]

ヘッドライト／前照灯
headlight
Scheinwerfer[M]
phare[M]
faro[M] delantero
proiettore[M]

第5輪
fifth wheel
Sattelkupplung[F]
sellette[F] d'attelage[M]
disco[M] de articulación[F]
organo[M] di raccordo[M]

泥除（よ）け
mud flap
Schmutzfänger[M]
bavette[F] garde-boue[M]
guardabarros[M]
aletta[F] del parafango[M]

ラジエーター・グリル／放熱器格子
radiator grille
Kühlergrill[M]
calandre[F]
calandra[F]
griglia[F] del radiatore[M]

ステップ／昇降段
step
Trittstufe[F]
marchepied[M]
escalón[M]
gradino[M]

タイヤ
tire; *tyre*
Reifen[M]
pneu[M]
neumático[M]
pneumatico[M]

フォッグ・ライト／霧灯
fog light
Nebelscheinwerfer[M]
feu[M] antibrouillard
luz[F] antiniebla
faro[M] fendinebbia

バンパー
bumper
Stoßfänger[M]
pare-chocs[M]
parachoques[M]
paraurti[M]

ホイール／車輪
wheel
Rad[N]
roue[F]
rueda[F]
ruota[F]

フィラー・キャップ／燃料補給口
filler cap
Tankdeckel[M]
bouchon[M] du réservoir[M]
tapa[F] del tanque[M]
tappo[M] del serbatoio[M]

フェンダー
fender; *wing*
Kotflügel[M]
aile[F]
guardabarros[M]
parafango[M]

燃料タンク
fuel tank
Kraftstofftank[M]
réservoir[M] à carburant[M]
tanque[M] del combustible[M]
serbatoio[M] per il carburante[M]

タンデム・トレーラー
tandem tractor trailer; *articulated lorry with trailer*
Sattelzug[M]
train[M] routier
camión[M] articulado
autoarticolato[M]

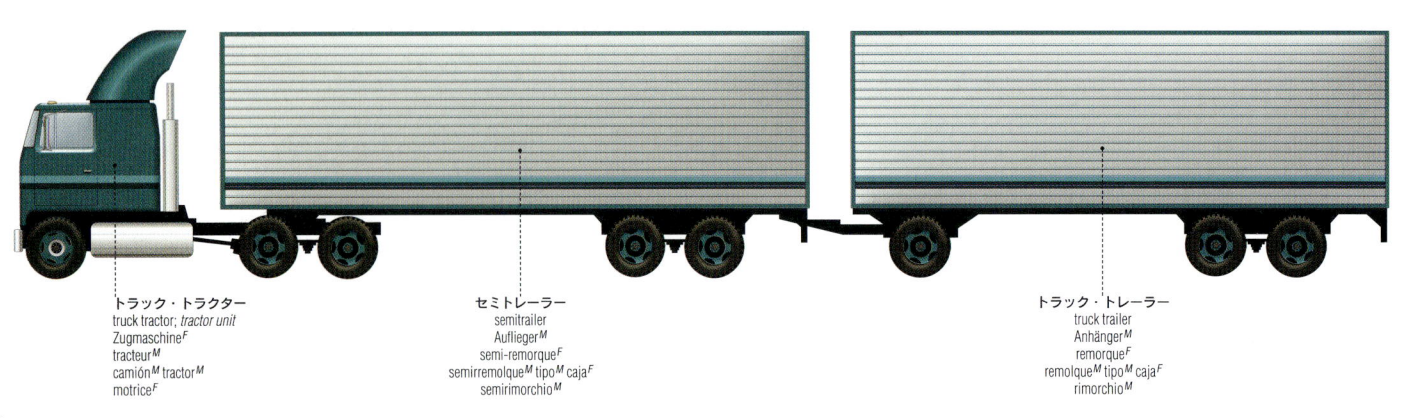

トラック・トラクター
truck tractor; *tractor unit*
Zugmaschine[F]
tracteur[M]
camión[M] tractor[M]
motrice[F]

セミトレーラー
semitrailer
Auflieger[M]
semi-remorque[F]
semirremolque[M] tipo[M] caja[F]
semirimorchio[M]

トラック・トレーラー
truck trailer
Anhänger[M]
remorque[F]
remolque[M] tipo[M] caja[F]
rimorchio[M]

570

道路交通 | ROAD TRANSPORT
STRASSENVERKEHR | TRANSPORT ROUTIER | TRANSPORTE TERRESTRE | TRASPORTO SU STRADA

トラック運送

マーカー・ライト［ランプ］／車幅灯
marker light; side marker light
Peilstableuchte^F
feu^M de gabarit^M
luz^F lateral
luce^F di ingombro^M laterale

冷凍ユニット
refrigeration unit
Kühlaggregat^N
groupe^M frigorifique
unidad^F de refrigeración^F
gruppo^M frigorifero^M

前壁
frontwall
Stirnwand^F
paroi^F avant
panel^M frontal
parete^F anteriore

側壁
sidewall
Seitenwand^F
paroi^F latérale
panel^M lateral
parete^F laterale

セミトレーラー
semitrailer
Auflieger^M
semi-remorque^F
semirremolque^M tipo^M caja^F
semirimorchio^M

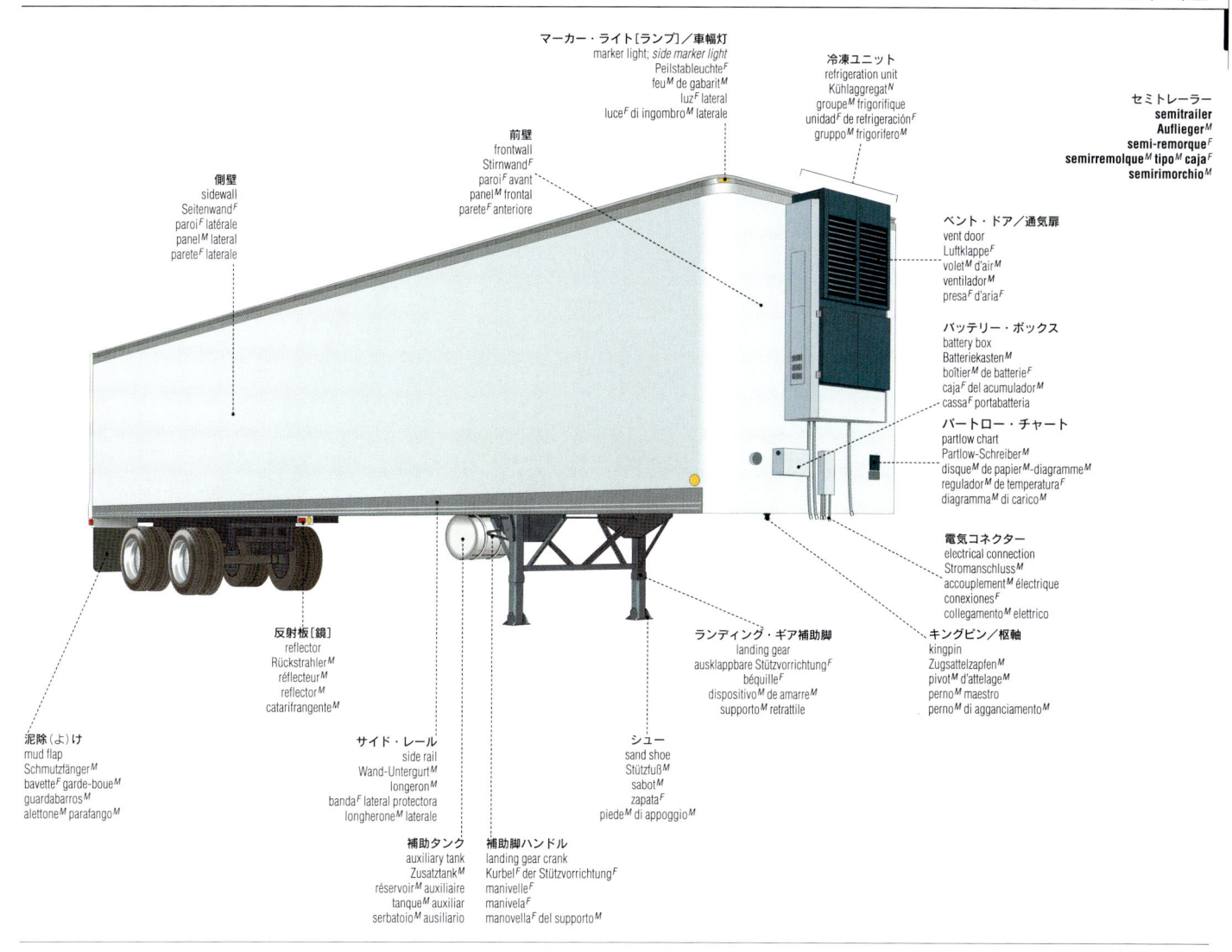

ベント・ドア／通気扉
vent door
Luftklappe^F
volet^M d'air^M
ventilador^M
presa^F d'aria^F

バッテリー・ボックス
battery box
Batteriekasten^M
boîtier^M de batterie^F
caja^F del acumulador^M
cassa^F portabatteria

パートロー・チャート
partlow chart
Partlow-Schreiber^M
disque^M de papier^M-diagramme^M
regulador^M de temperatura^F
diagramma^M di carico^M

電気コネクター
electrical connection
Stromanschluss^M
accouplement^M électrique
conexiones^F
collegamento^M elettrico

反射板［鏡］
reflector
Rückstrahler^M
réflecteur^M
reflector^M
catarifrangente^M

サイド・レール
side rail
Wand-Untergurt^M
longeron^M
banda^F lateral protectora
longherone^M laterale

ランディング・ギア補助脚
landing gear
ausklappbare Stützvorrichtung^F
béquille^F
dispositivo^M de amarre^M
supporto^M retrattile

シュー
sand shoe
Stützfuß^M
sabot^M
zapata^F
piede^M di appoggio^M

キングピン／枢軸
kingpin
Zugsattelzapfen^M
pivot^M d'attelage^M
perno^M maestro
perno^M di agganciamento^M

泥除（よ）け
mud flap
Schmutzfänger^M
bavette^F garde-boue^M
guardabarros^M
alettone^M parafango^M

補助タンク
auxiliary tank
Zusatztank^M
réservoir^M auxiliaire
tanque^M auxiliar
serbatoio^M ausiliario

補助脚ハンドル
landing gear crank
Kurbel^F der Stützvorrichtung^F
manivelle^F
manivela^F
manovella^F del supporto^M

平床（式）トレーラー
flatbed semitrailer
Sattelpritschenanhänger^M
semi-remorque^F plateau^M
semirremolque^M tipo plataforma^F
autocarro^M a pianale^M

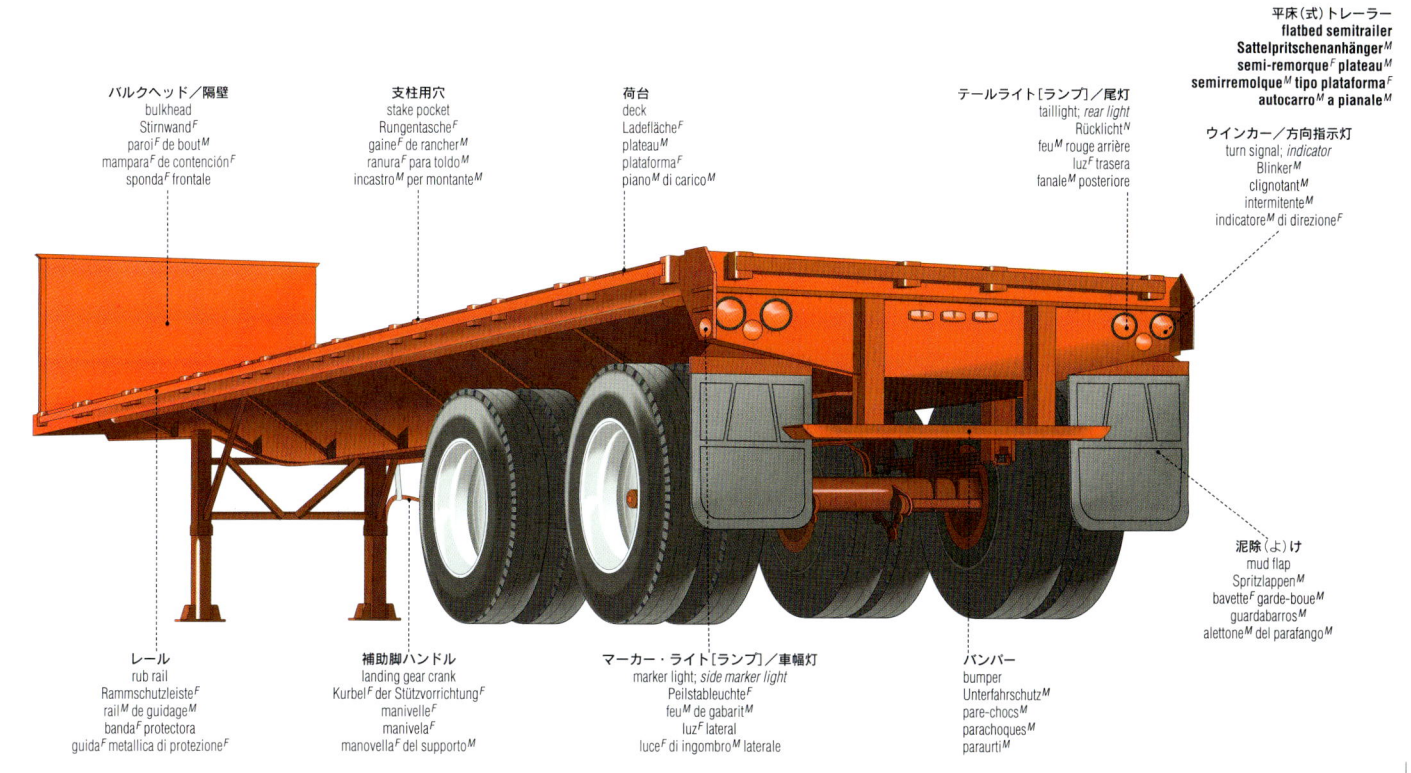

バルクヘッド／隔壁
bulkhead
Stirnwand^F
paroi^F de bout^M
mampara^F de contención^F
sponda^F frontale

支柱用穴
stake pocket
Rungentasche^F
gaîne^F de rancher^M
ranura^F para toldo^M
incastro^M per montante^M

荷台
deck
Ladefläche^F
plateau^M
plataforma^F
piano^M di carico^M

テールライト［ランプ］／尾灯
taillight; rear light
Rücklicht^N
feu^M rouge arrière
luz^F trasera
fanale^M posteriore

ウインカー／方向指示灯
turn signal; indicator
Blinker^M
clignotant^M
intermitente^M
indicatore^M di direzione^F

レール
rub rail
Rammschutzleiste^F
rail^M de guidage^M
banda^F protectora
guida^F metallica di protezione^F

補助脚ハンドル
landing gear crank
Kurbel^F der Stützvorrichtung^F
manivelle^F
manivela^F
manovella^F del supporto^M

マーカー・ライト［ランプ］／車幅灯
marker light; side marker light
Peilstableuchte^F
feu^M de gabarit^M
luz^F lateral
luce^F di ingombro^M laterale

バンパー
bumper
Unterfahrschutz^M
pare-chocs^M
parachoques^M
paraurti^M

泥除（よ）け
mud flap
Spritzlappen^M
bavette^F garde-boue^M
guardabarros^M
alettone^M del parafango^M

571

道路交通 | ROAD TRANSPORT
STRASSENVERKEHR | TRANSPORT ROUTIER | TRANSPORTE TERRESTRE | TRASPORTO SU STRADA

トラック運送

日本語 | 英語 | ドイツ語 | フランス語 | スペイン語 | イタリア語

セミトレーラーの例
examples of semitrailers
Beispiele[N] für Sattelkraftfahrzeuge[N]
exemples[M] de semi-remorques[F]
ejemplos[M] de camiones[M] articulados
esempi[M] di autoarticolati[M]

タンク・トレーラー
tank trailer; road tanker
Tanklastzug[M]
semi-remorque[F] citerne[F]
camión[M] cisterna[F]
autocisterna[F]

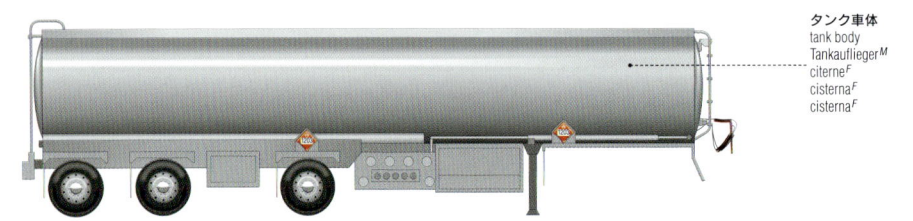

タンク車体
tank body
Tankauflieger[M]
citerne[F]
cisterna[F]
cisterna[F]

ダンプ車体
dump body
aufgesatelter Kippanhänger[M]
benne[F] basculante
volquete[M] basculante
cassone[M] ribaltabile

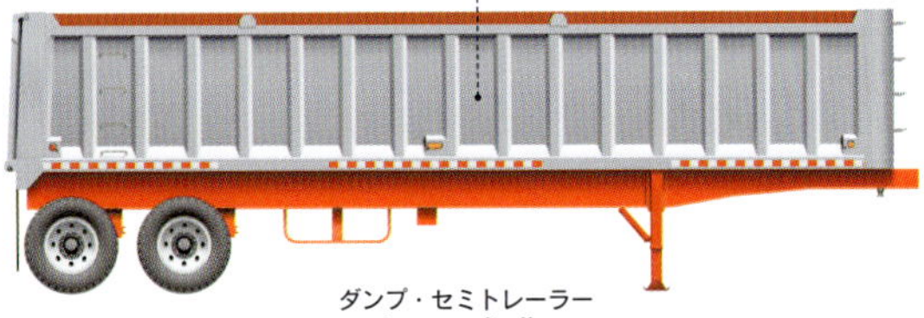

車両運搬セミトレーラー
automobile transport semitrailer
Autotransporter[M]
semi-remorque[F] porte-véhicules[M]
trailer[M] para transporte[M] de vehículos[M]
bisarca[F]

コンテナ緊締装置
twist lock
Drehfeststeller[M]
verrou[M] tournant
bloqueo[M] giratorio
fermo[M] girevole

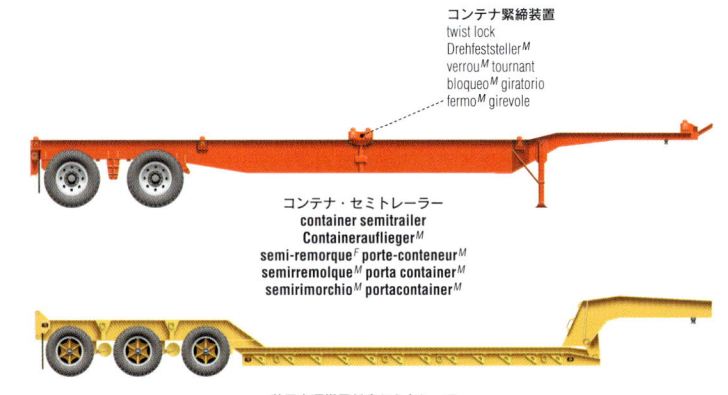

ダンプ・セミトレーラー
dump semitrailer
Kipplader[M]
semi-remorque[F] benne[F]
camión[M] volquete
ribaltabile[M]

コンテナ・セミトレーラー
container semitrailer
Containerauflieger[M]
semi-remorque[F] porte-conteneur[M]
semirremolque[M] porta container[M]
semirimorchio[M] portacontainer[M]

チップ・セミトレーラー
chip van
Sattelanhänger[M] für den Spantransport[M]
semi-remorque[F] à copeaux[M]
semirremolque[M] con lona[F]
autocarro[M] per trucioli[M]

装甲車運搬用低床セミトレーラー
double drop lowbed semitrailer
Satteltiefladeanhänger[M] für den Transport[M] von Panzerfahrzeugen[N]
semi-remorque[F] porte-engins[M] surbaissée
semirremolque[M] bajo portamáquinas[M]
semirimorchio[M] ribassato per il trasporto[M] di mezzi[M] corazzati

バン・セミトレーラー
van body semitrailer
Kofferauflieger[M]
semi-remorque[F] fourgon[M]
semirremolque[M] furgón
semirimorchio[M] furgonato

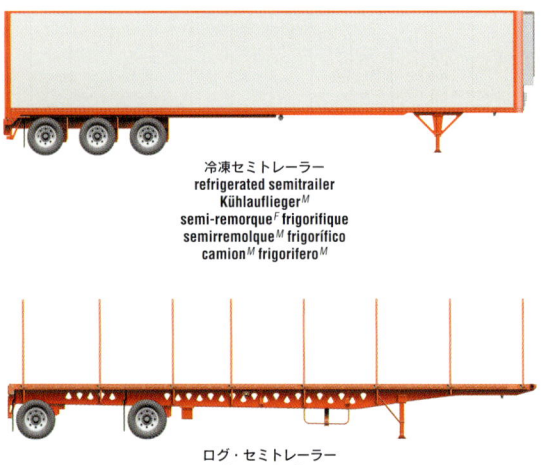

冷凍セミトレーラー
refrigerated semitrailer
Kühlauflieger[M]
semi-remorque[F] frigorifique
semirremolque[M] frigorífico
camion[M] frigorifero[M]

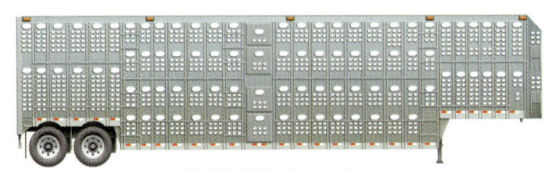

家畜移送用低床セミトレーラー
possum-belly body semitrailer
Satteltiefladeanhänger[M] für den Tiertransport[M]
semi-remorque[F] bétaillère surbaissée
semirremolque[M] jaula[F] bajo para transporte[M] ganadero
semirimorchio[M] ribassato per il trasporto[M] del bestiame[M]

ログ・セミトレーラー
log semitrailer
Sattelanhänger[M] für den Baumstammtransport[M]
semi-remorque[F] à grumes[F]
semirremolque[M] para el transporte[M] de troncos[M]
autocarro[M] per il trasporto[M] dei tronchi[M]

交通と機械

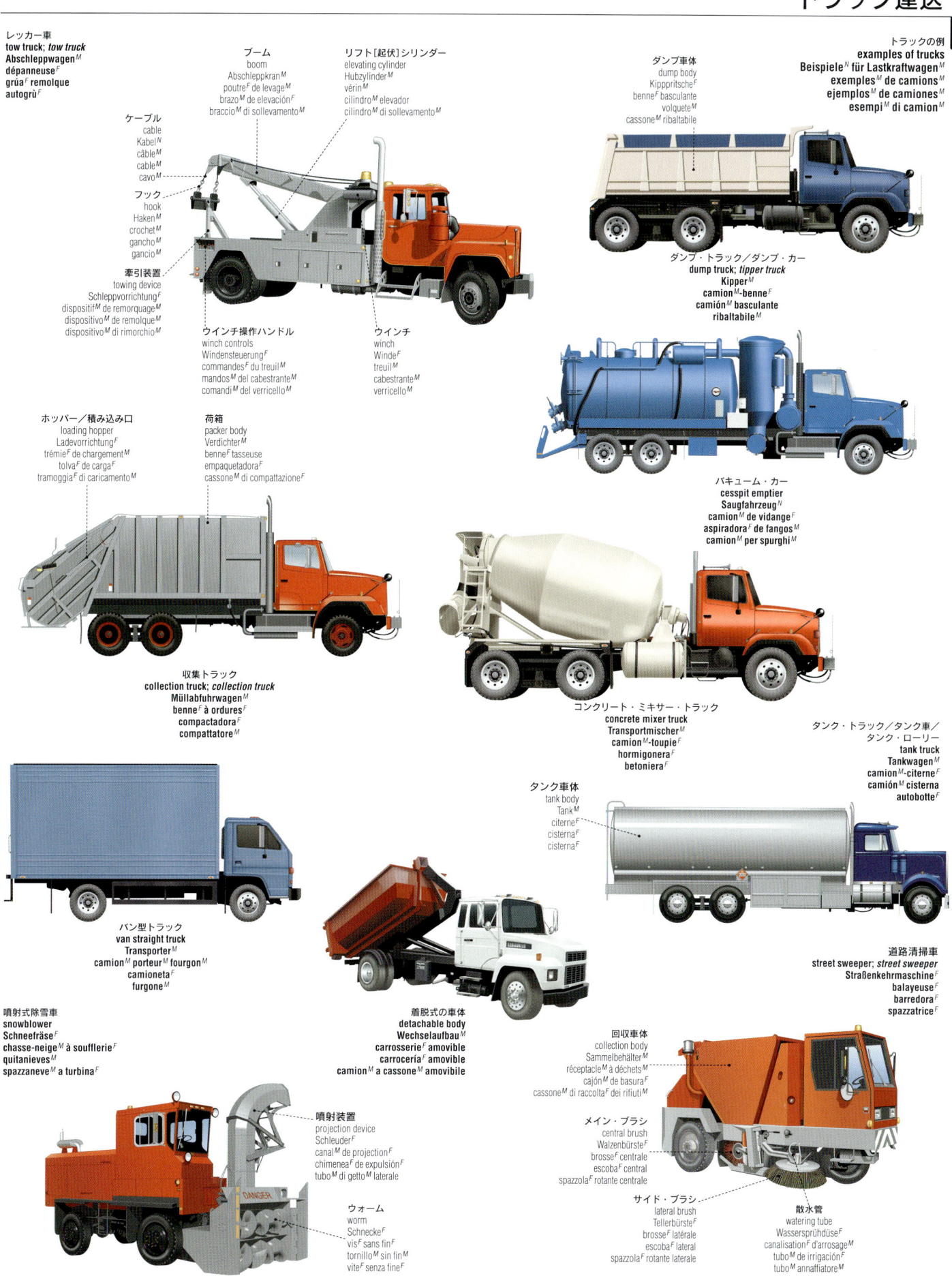

道路交通 | ROAD TRANSPORT
STRASSENVERKEHR | TRANSPORT ROUTIER | TRANSPORTE TERRESTRE | TRASPORTO SU STRADA

トラック運送

レッカー車
tow truck; tow truck
Abschleppwagen^M
dépanneuse^F
grúa^F remolque
autogrù^F

ブーム
boom
Abschleppkran^M
poutre^F de levage^M
brazo^M de elevación^F
braccio^M di sollevamento^M

リフト[起伏]シリンダー
elevating cylinder
Hubzylinder^M
vérin^M
cilindro^M elevador
cilindro^M di sollevamento^M

ダンプ車体
dump body
Kipppritsche^F
benne^F basculante
volquete^M
cassone^M ribaltabile

トラックの例
examples of trucks
Beispiele^N für Lastkraftwagen^M
exemples^M de camions
ejemplos^M de camiones
esempi^M di camion

ケーブル
cable
Kabel^N
câble^M
cable^M
cavo^M

フック
hook
Haken^M
crochet^M
gancho^M
gancio^M

牽引装置
towing device
Schleppvorrichtung^F
dispositif^M de remorquage^M
dispositivo^M de remolque^M
dispositivo^M di rimorchio^M

ウインチ操作ハンドル
winch controls
Windensteuerung^F
commandes^F du treuil^M
mandos^M del cabestrante^M
comandi^M del verricello^M

ウインチ
winch
Winde^F
treuil^M
cabestrante^M
verricello^M

ダンプ・トラック／ダンプ・カー
dump truck; tipper truck
Kipper^M
camion^M-benne^F
camión^M basculante
ribaltabile^M

ホッパー／積み込み口
loading hopper
Ladevorrichtung^F
trémie^F de chargement^M
tolva^F de carga^F
tramoggia^F di caricamento^M

荷箱
packer body
Verdichter^M
benne^F tasseuse
empaquetadora^F
cassone^M di compattazione^F

バキューム・カー
cesspit emptier
Saugfahrzeug^N
camion^M de vidange^F
aspiradora^F de fangos^M
camion^M per spurghi^M

収集トラック
collection truck; collection truck
Müllabfuhrwagen^M
benne^F à ordures^F
compactadora^F
compattatore^M

コンクリート・ミキサー・トラック
concrete mixer truck
Transportmischer^M
camion^M-toupie^F
hormigonera^F
betoniera^F

タンク・トラック／タンク車／タンク・ローリー
tank truck
Tankwagen^M
camion^M-citerne^F
camión^M cisterna
autobotte^F

タンク車体
tank body
Tank^M
citerne^F
cisterna^F
cisterna^F

バン型トラック
van straight truck
Transporter^M
camion^M porteur^M fourgon^M
camioneta^F
furgone^M

着脱式の車体
detachable body
Wechselaufbau^M
carrosserie^F amovible
carrocería^F amovible
camion^M a cassone^M amovibile

道路清掃車
street sweeper; street sweeper
Straßenkehrmaschine^F
balayeuse^F
barredora^F
spazzatrice^F

噴射式除雪車
snowblower
Schneefräse^F
chasse-neige^M à soufflerie^F
quitanieves^M
spazzaneve^M a turbina^F

噴射装置
projection device
Schleuder^F
canal^M de projection^F
chimenea^F de expulsión^F
tubo^M di getto^M laterale

ウォーム
worm
Schnecke^F
vis^F sans fin^F
tornillo^M sin fin^M
vite^F senza fine^F

回収車体
collection body
Sammelbehälter^M
réceptacle^M à déchets^M
cajón^M de basura^F
cassone^M di raccolta^F dei rifiuti^M

メイン・ブラシ
central brush
Walzenbürste^F
brosse^F centrale
escoba^F central
spazzola^F rotante centrale

サイド・ブラシ
lateral brush
Tellerbürste^F
brosse^F latérale
escoba^F lateral
spazzola^F rotante laterale

散水管
watering tube
Wassersprühdüse^F
canalisation^F d'arrosage^M
tubo^M de irrigación^F
tubo^M annaffiatore^M

交通と機械

573

道路交通 | ROAD TRANSPORT
STRASSENVERKEHR | TRANSPORT ROUTIER | TRANSPORTE TERRESTRE | TRASPORTO SU STRADA

オートバイ

motorcycle | Motorrad[N] | moto[F] | motocicleta[F] | motocicletta[F]

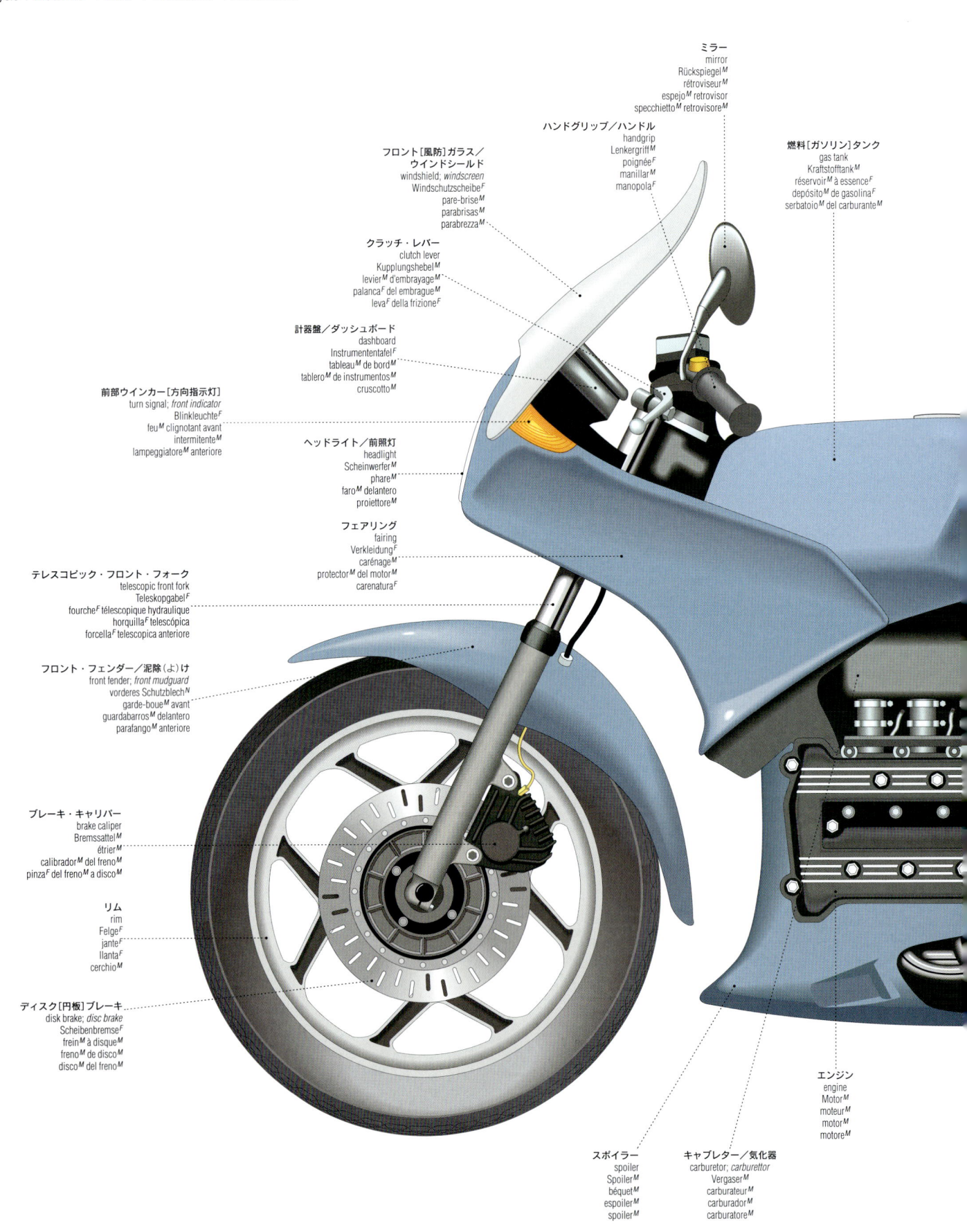

ミラー
mirror
Rückspiegel[M]
rétroviseur[M]
espejo[M] retrovisor
specchietto[M] retrovisore[M]

ハンドグリップ／ハンドル
handgrip
Lenkergriff[M]
poignée[F]
manillar[F]
manopola[F]

燃料［ガソリン］タンク
gas tank
Kraftstofftank[M]
réservoir[M] à essence[F]
depósito[M] de gasolina[F]
serbatoio[M] del carburante[M]

フロント［風防］ガラス／ウインドシールド
windshield; windscreen
Windschutzscheibe[F]
pare-brise[M]
parabrisas[M]
parabrezza[M]

クラッチ・レバー
clutch lever
Kupplungshebel[M]
levier[M] d'embrayage[M]
palanca[F] del embrague[M]
leva[F] della frizione[F]

計器盤／ダッシュボード
dashboard
Instrumententafel[F]
tableau[M] de bord[M]
tablero[M] de instrumentos[M]
cruscotto[M]

前部ウインカー［方向指示灯］
turn signal; front indicator
Blinkleuchte[F]
feu[M] clignotant avant
intermitente[M]
lampeggiatore[M] anteriore

ヘッドライト／前照灯
headlight
Scheinwerfer[M]
phare[M]
faro[M] delantero
proiettore[M]

フェアリング
fairing
Verkleidung[F]
carénage[M]
protector[M] del motor[M]
carenatura[F]

テレスコピック・フロント・フォーク
telescopic front fork
Teleskopgabel[F]
fourche[F] télescopique hydraulique
horquilla[F] telescópica
forcella[F] telescopica anteriore

フロント・フェンダー／泥除（よ）け
front fender; front mudguard
vorderes Schutzblech[N]
garde-boue[M] avant
guardabarros[M] delantero
parafango[M] anteriore

ブレーキ・キャリパー
brake caliper
Bremssattel[M]
étrier[M]
calibrador[M] del freno[M]
pinza[F] del freno[M] a disco[M]

リム
rim
Felge[F]
jante[F]
llanta[F]
cerchio[M]

ディスク［円板］ブレーキ
disk brake; disc brake
Scheibenbremse[F]
frein[M] à disque[M]
freno[M] de disco[M]
disco[M] del freno[M]

スポイラー
spoiler
Spoiler[M]
béquet[M]
espoiler[M]
spoiler[M]

キャブレター／気化器
carburetor; carburettor
Vergaser[M]
carburateur[M]
carburador[M]
carburatore[M]

エンジン
engine
Motor[M]
moteur[M]
motor[M]
motore[M]

交通と機械

574

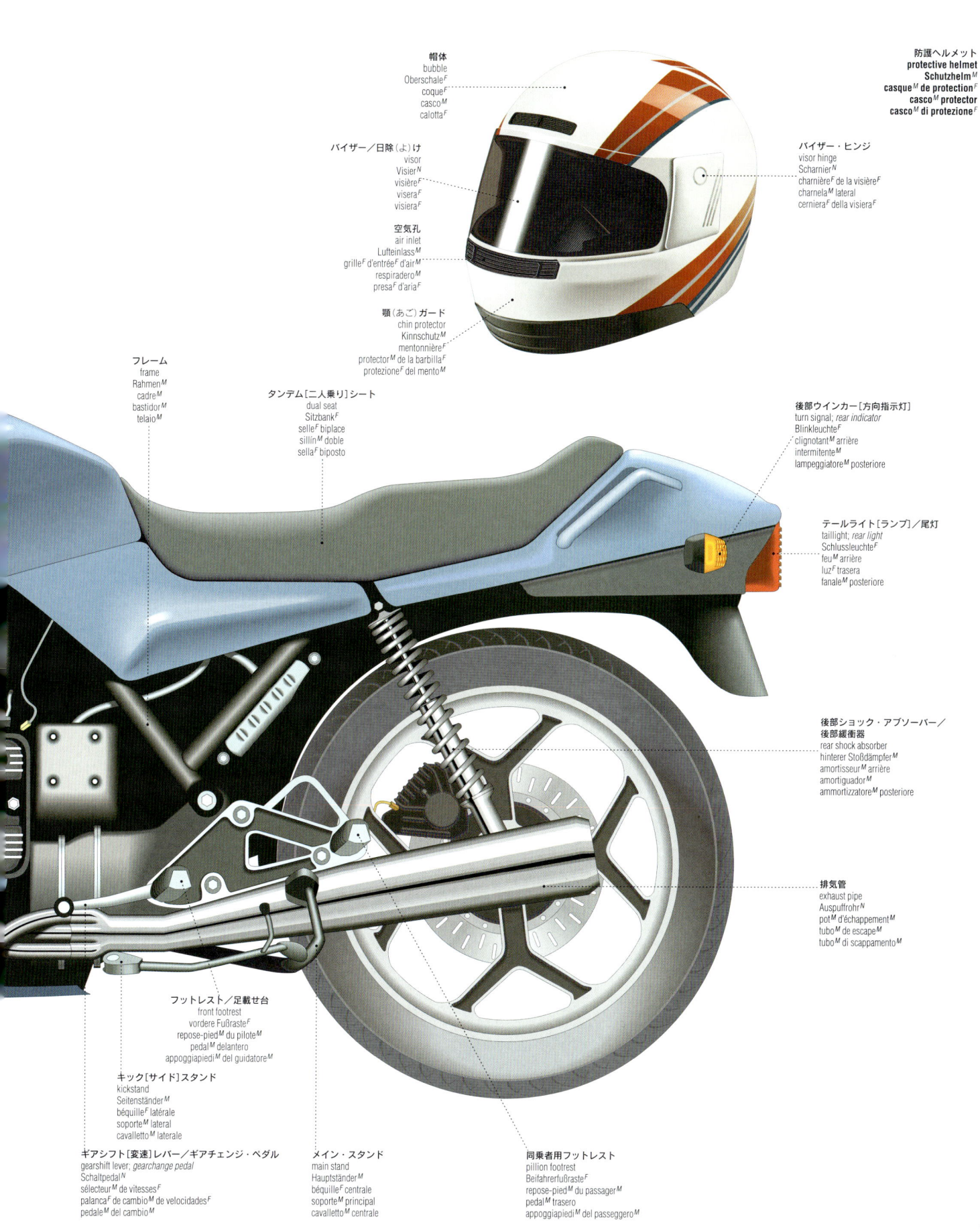

道路交通 | ROAD TRANSPORT
STRASSENVERKEHR | TRANSPORT ROUTIER | TRANSPORTE TERRESTRE | TRASPORTO SU STRADA

オートバイ

帽体
bubble
Oberschale^F
coque^F
casco^M
calotta^F

防護ヘルメット
protective helmet
Schutzhelm^M
casque^M de protection^F
casco^M protector
casco^M di protezione^F

バイザー／日除(よ)け
visor
Visier^N
visière^F
visera^F
visiera^F

バイザー・ヒンジ
visor hinge
Scharnier^N
charnière^F de la visière^F
charnela^F lateral
cerniera^F della visiera^F

空気孔
air inlet
Lufteinlass^M
grille^F d'entrée^F d'air^M
respiradero^M
presa^F d'aria^F

顎(あご)ガード
chin protector
Kinnschutz^M
mentonnière^F
protector^M de la barbilla^F
protezione^F del mento^M

フレーム
frame
Rahmen^M
cadre^M
bastidor^M
telaio^M

タンデム[二人乗り]シート
dual seat
Sitzbank^F
selle^F biplace
sillín^M doble
sella^F biposto

後部ウインカー[方向指示灯]
turn signal; rear indicator
Blinkleuchte^F
clignotant^M arrière
intermitente^M
lampeggiatore^M posteriore

テールライト[ランプ]／尾灯
taillight; rear light
Schlussleuchte^F
feu^M arrière
luz^F trasera
fanale^M posteriore

後部ショック・アブソーバー／後部緩衝器
rear shock absorber
hinterer Stoßdämpfer^M
amortisseur^M arrière
amortiguador^M
ammortizzatore^M posteriore

排気管
exhaust pipe
Auspuffrohr^N
pot^M d'échappement^M
tubo^M de escape^M
tubo^M di scappamento^M

フットレスト／足載せ台
front footrest
vordere Fußraste^F
repose-pied^M du pilote^M
pedal^M delantero
appoggiapiedi^M del guidatore^M

キック[サイド]スタンド
kickstand
Seitenständer^M
béquille^F latérale
soporte^M lateral
cavalletto^M laterale

ギアシフト[変速]レバー／ギアチェンジ・ペダル
gearshift lever; gearchange pedal
Schaltpedal^N
sélecteur^M de vitesses^F
palanca^F de cambio^M de velocidades^F
pedale^M del cambio^M

メイン・スタンド
main stand
Hauptständer^M
béquille^F centrale
soporte^M principal
cavalletto^M centrale

同乗者用フットレスト
pillion footrest
Beifahrerfußraste^F
repose-pied^M du passager^M
pedal^M trasero
appoggiapiedi^M del passeggero^M

交通と機械

575

道路交通 | ROAD TRANSPORT
STRASSENVERKEHR | TRANSPORT ROUTIER | TRANSPORTE TERRESTRE | TRASPORTO SU STRADA

オートバイ

日本語 | 英語 | ドイツ語 | フランス語 | スペイン語 | イタリア語

オートバイの計器盤
motorcycle dashboard
Instrumententafel^F
tableau^M de bord^M
tablero^M de instrumentos^M
cruscotto^M

スピードメーター
speedometer
Tachometer^M
indicateur^M de vitesse^F
velocímetro^M
tachimetro^M

タコメーター／回転速度計
tachometer
Drehzahlmesser^M
tachymètre^M
tacómetro^M
contagiri^M

油圧警告灯
oil pressure warning indicator
Öldruckkontrollleuchte^F
témoin^M de pression^F d'huile^F
luz^F indicadora de la presión^F del aceite^M
spia^F della pressione^F dell'olio^M

ハイ・ビーム警告灯
high beam warning indicator; *main beam warning light*
Fernlichtkontrollleuchte^F
témoin^M de phare^M
indicador^M de luz^F larga
spia^F delle luci^F abbaglianti

ニュートラル表示灯
neutral indicator
Leerlaufanzeige^N
témoin^M de position^F neutre
indicador^M neutro
spia^F della posizione^F di folle

ウインカー／方向指示灯
turn signal indicator; *indicator telltale*
Blinkerkontrollleuchte^F
témoin^M de clignotants^M
indicador^M del intermitente^M
spia^F dell'indicatore^M di direzione^F

エンジン[イグニッション]スイッチ
ignition switch
Zündschalter^M
démarreur^M électrique
interruptor^M de encendido^M
blocchetto^M di avviamento^M

オートバイ：上面図
motorcycle: view from above
Motorrad^N: Draufsicht^F
moto^F: vue^F en plongée^F
motocicleta^F: vista^F desde lo alto^M
motocicletta^F: vista^F dall'alto^M

ヘッドライト／前照灯
headlight
Scheinwerfer^M
phare^M
faro^M delantero
proiettore^M

前部ウインカー[方向指示灯]
turn signal; *front indicator*
Blinkleuchte^F
feu^M clignotant avant
intermitente^M delantero
lampeggiatore^M anteriore

ミラー
mirror
Seitenspiegel^M
rétroviseur^M
espejo^M
specchietto^M retrovisore^M

前[前輪]ブレーキ・レバー
front brake lever
Hebel^M für Vorderbremse^F
levier^M de frein^M avant
palanca^F del freno^M delantero
leva^F del freno^M anteriore

クラッチ・レバー
clutch lever
Kupplungshebel^M
levier^M d'embrayage^M
palanca^F del embrague^M
leva^F della frizione^F

スロットル・グリップ
twist grip throttle
Gashebel^M
poignée^F des gaz^M
acelerador^M
manopola^F dell'acceleratore^M

減光スイッチ
dip switch
Abblendschalter^M
inverseur^M route^F-croisement^M
interruptor^M
commutatore^M delle luci^F

エンジン・ストップ・スイッチ
emergency switch
Notschalter^M
coupe-circuit^M d'urgence^F
interruptor^M de emergencia^F
interruttore^M di emergenza^F

ホーン[警音器]ボタン
horn
Hupe^F
avertisseur^M
claxon^M
clacson^M

エンジン[イグニッション]スイッチ
starter button
Zündschalter^M
bouton^M de démarreur^M
interruptor^M de encendido^M
interruttore^M di avviamento^M

燃料タンク・キャップ
gas tank cap; *petrol tank cap*
Benzintankverschluss^M
bouchon^M de remplissage^M
tapa^F del tanque^M de la gasolina^F
tappo^M del serbatoio^M

クラッチ・ハウジング
clutch housing
Kupplungsgehäuse^N
carter^M d'embrayage^M
cubierta^F del embrague^M
scatola^F della frizione^F

ギアシフト[変速]レバー／ギアチェンジ・ペダル
gear shift; *gearchange pedal*
Schaltpedal^N
sélecteur^M de vitesses^F
pedal^M de cambio^M de velocidades^F
pedale^M del cambio^M

後ろ[後輪]ブレーキ・ペダル
rear brake pedal
Bremspedal^N
pédale^F de frein^M arrière
pedal^M del freno^M trasero
pedale^M del freno^M posteriore

フットレスト／足載せ台
front footrest
vordere Fußraste^F
repose-pied^M du pilote^M
pedal^M delantero
appoggiapiedi^M del guidatore^M

同乗者用フットレスト
pillion footrest
Beifahrer-Fußraste^F
repose-pied^M du passager^M
pedal^M trasero
appoggiapiedi^M del passeggero^M

排気管
exhaust pipe
Auspuffrohr^N
pot^M d'échappement^M
tubo^M de escape^M
tubo^M di scappamento^M

テールライト[ランプ]／尾灯
taillight; *rear light*
Schlussleuchte^F
feu^M arrière
luz^F trasera
fanale^M posteriore

後部ウインカー[方向指示灯]
turn signal; *rear indicator*
Blinkleuchte^F
feu^M clignotant arrière
intermitente^M trasero
lampeggiatore^M posteriore

交通と機械

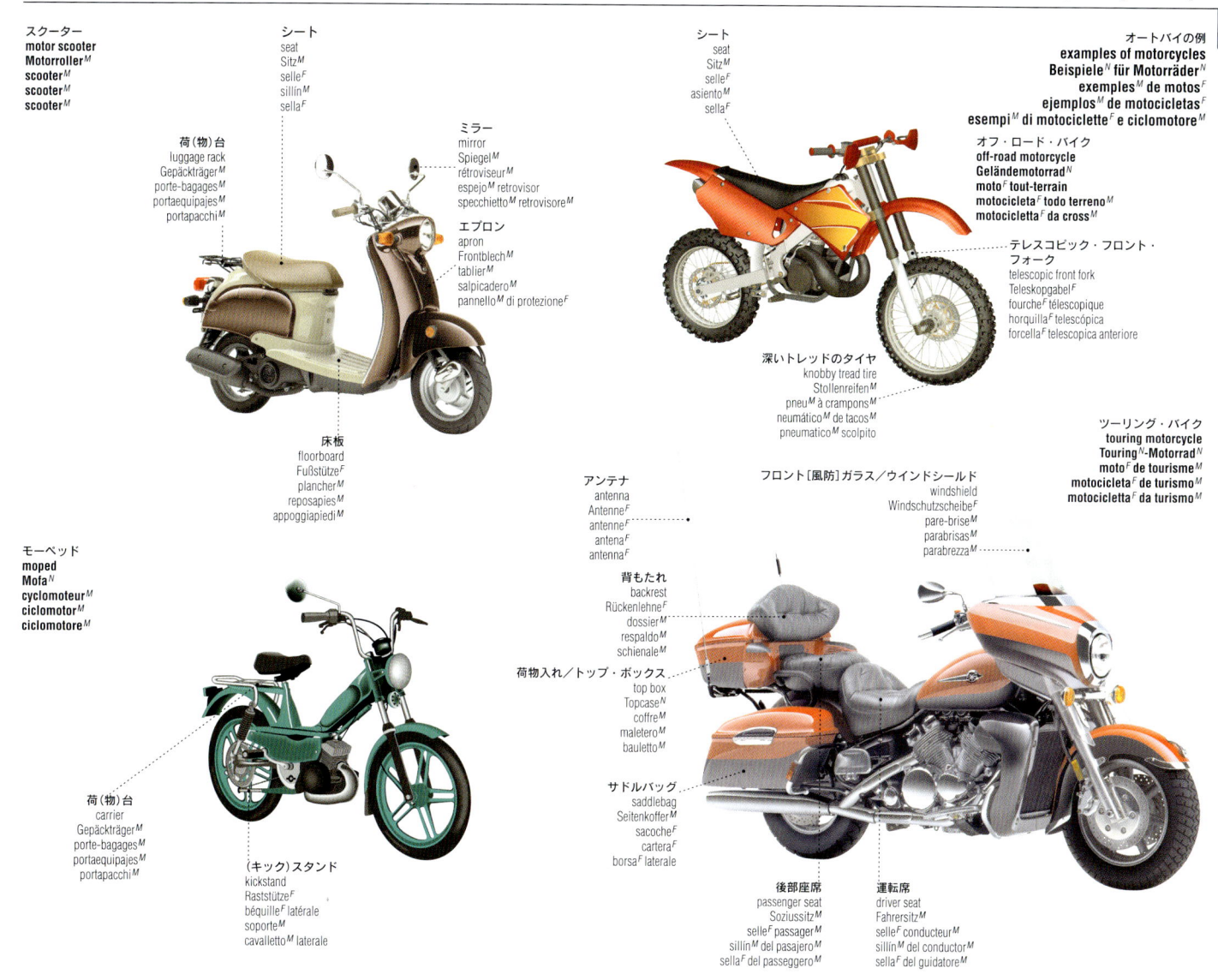

道路交通 | ROAD TRANSPORT
STRASSENVERKEHR | TRANSPORT ROUTIER | TRANSPORTE TERRESTRE | TRASPORTO SU STRADA

オートバイ

スクーター
motor scooter
Motorroller^M
scooter^M
scooter^M
scooter^M

シート
seat
Sitz^M
selle^F
sillín^M
sella^F

シート
seat
Sitz^M
selle^F
asiento^M
sella^F

オートバイの例
examples of motorcycles
Beispiele^N für Motorräder^N
exemples^M de motos^F
ejemplos^M de motocicletas^F
esempi^M di motociclette^F e ciclomotore^M

荷(物)台
luggage rack
Gepäckträger^M
porte-bagages^M
portaequipajes^M
portapacchi^M

ミラー
mirror
Spiegel^M
rétroviseur^M
espejo^M retrovisor
specchietto^M retrovisore^M

オフ・ロード・バイク
off-road motorcycle
Geländemotorrad^N
moto^F tout-terrain
motocicleta^F todo terreno^M
motocicletta^F da cross^M

エプロン
apron
Frontblech^N
tablier^M
salpicadero^M
pannello^M di protezione^F

テレスコピック・フロント・フォーク
telescopic front fork
Teleskopgabel^F
fourche^F télescopique
horquilla^F telescópica
forcella^F telescopica anteriore

深いトレッドのタイヤ
knobby tread tire
Stollenreifen^M
pneu^M à crampons^M
neumático^M de tacos^M
pneumatico^M scolpito

床板
floorboard
Fußstütze^F
plancher^M
reposapies^M
appoggiapiedi^M

ツーリング・バイク
touring motorcycle
Touring^N-Motorrad^N
moto^F de tourisme^M
motocicleta^F de turismo^M
motocicletta^F da turismo^M

アンテナ
antenna
Antenne^F
antenne^F
antena^F
antenna^F

フロント[風防]ガラス／ウインドシールド
windshield
Windschutzscheibe^F
pare-brise^M
parabrisas^M
parabrezza^M

モーペッド
moped
Mofa^N
cyclomoteur^M
ciclomotor^M
ciclomotore^M

背もたれ
backrest
Rückenlehne^F
dossier^M
respaldo^M
schienale^M

荷物入れ／トップ・ボックス
top box
Topcase^N
coffre^M
maletero^M
bauletto^M

荷(物)台
carrier
Gepäckträger^M
porte-bagages^M
portaequipajes^M
portapacchi^M

サドルバッグ
saddlebag
Seitenkoffer^M
sacoche^F
cartera^F
borsa^F laterale

(キック)スタンド
kickstand
Raststütze^F
béquille^F latérale
soporte^M
cavalletto^M laterale

後部座席
passenger seat
Soziussitz^M
selle^F passager^M
sillín^M del pasajero^M
sella^F del passeggero^M

運転席
driver seat
Fahrersitz^M
selle^F conducteur^M
sillín^M del conductor^M
sella^F del guidatore^M

四輪駆動の全地形型車両

4 X 4 all-terrain vehicle | 4x4-Geländemotorrad^N | quad^M | quad^M | veicolo^M a trazione^F integrale 4x4

後部荷台
rear cargo rack
Gepäckträger^M
porte-bagages^M arrière
portaequipajes^M posterior
portapacchi^M posteriore

シート
seat
Sitz^M
selle^F
sillín^M
sella^F

燃料[ガソリン]タンク
gas tank; fuel tank
Kraftstofftank^M
réservoir^M à essence^F
depósito^M de gasolina^F
serbatoio^M del carburante^M

ハンドグリップ／ハンドル
handgrip
Lenkergriff^M
poignée^F
manillar^M
manopola^F

リア・フェンダー
rear fender; rear bumper
hinterer Kotflügel^M
garde-boue^M arrière
parachoques^M posterior
paraurti^M posteriore

バンパー
bumper
Stoßfänger^M
pare-chocs^M
parachoques^M
paraurti^M

マフラー／消音器
muffler
Auspuffrohr^N
pot^M d'échappement^M
silenciador^M
tubo^M di scappamento^M

前部ショック・アブソーバー／前部緩衝器
front shock absorber
Frontstoßdämpfer^M
amortisseur^M avant
amortiguador^M delantero
ammortizzatore^M anteriore

ギアシフト[変速]レバー／ギアチェンジ・ペダル
gearshift lever
Schalthebel^M
sélecteur^M de vitesses^F
palanca^F de velocidad^F
pedale^M del cambio^M

道路交通 | ROAD TRANSPORT
STRASSENVERKEHR | TRANSPORT ROUTIER | TRANSPORTE TERRESTRE | TRASPORTO SU STRADA

自転車

日本語 | 英語 | ドイツ語 | フランス語 | スペイン語 | イタリア語

bicycle | Fahrrad[N] | bicyclette[F] | bicicleta[F] | bicicletta[F]

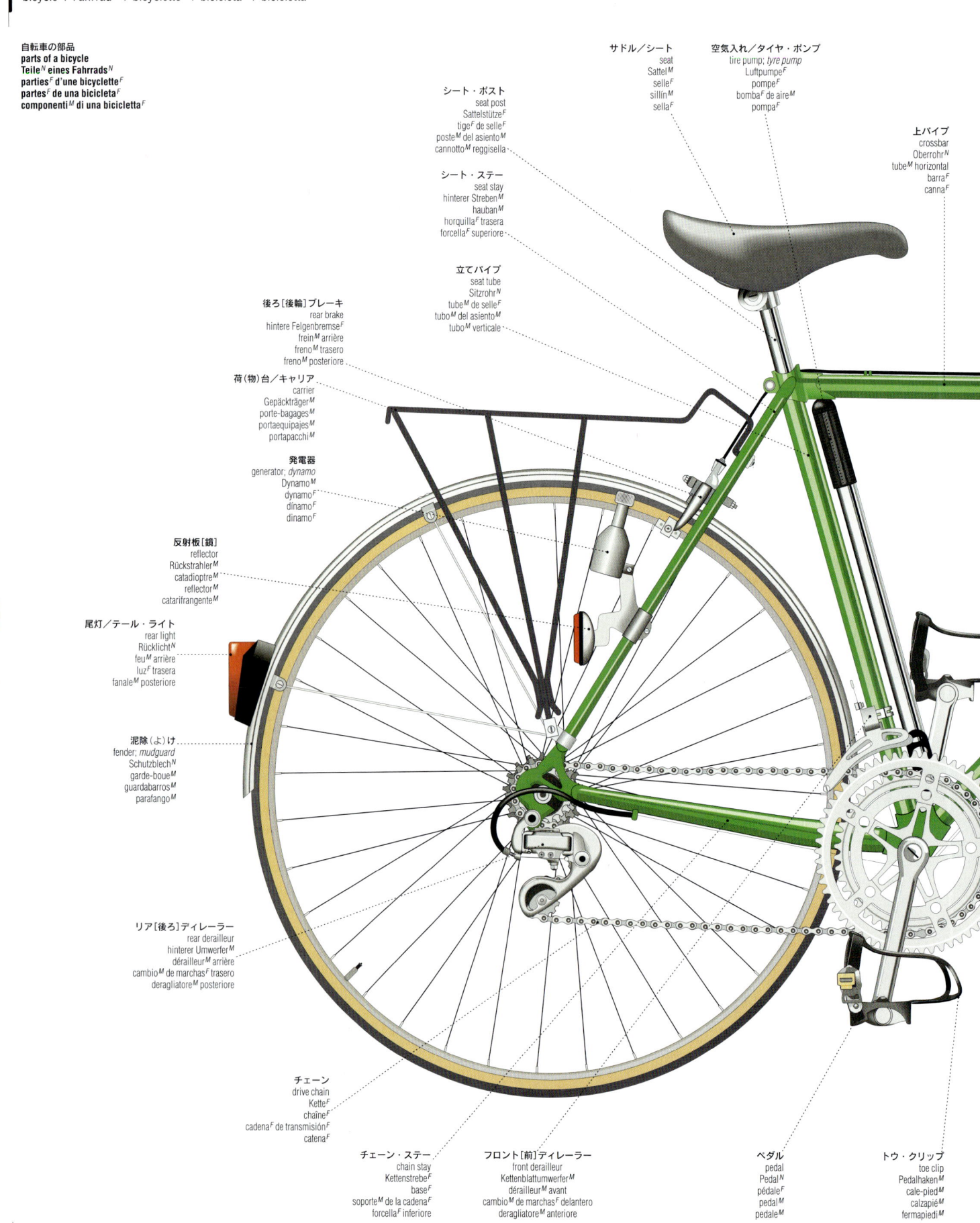

自転車の部品
parts of a bicycle
Teile[N] eines Fahrrads[N]
parties[F] d'une bicyclette[F]
partes[F] de una bicicleta[F]
componenti[M] di una bicicletta[F]

サドル／シート
seat
Sattel[M]
selle[F]
sillín[M]
sella[F]

空気入れ／タイヤ・ポンプ
tire pump; *tyre pump*
Luftpumpe[F]
pompe[F]
bomba[F] de aire[M]
pompa[F]

シート・ポスト
seat post
Sattelstütze[F]
tige[F] de selle[F]
poste[M] del asiento[M]
cannotto[M] reggisella

上パイプ
crossbar
Oberrohr[N]
tube[M] horizontal
barra[F]
canna[F]

シート・ステー
seat stay
hinterer Streben[M]
hauban[M]
horquilla[F] trasera
forcella[F] superiore

立てパイプ
seat tube
Sitzrohr[N]
tube[M] de selle[F]
tubo[M] del asiento[M]
tubo[M] verticale

後ろ[後輪]ブレーキ
rear brake
hintere Felgenbremse[F]
frein[M] arrière
freno[M] trasero
freno[M] posteriore

荷(物)台／キャリア
carrier
Gepäckträger[M]
porte-bagages[M]
portaequipajes[M]
portapacchi[M]

発電器
generator; *dynamo*
Dynamo[M]
dynamo[F]
dínamo[F]
dinamo[F]

反射板[鏡]
reflector
Rückstrahler[M]
catadioptre[M]
reflector[M]
catarifrangente[M]

尾灯／テール・ライト
rear light
Rücklicht[N]
feu[M] arrière
luz[F] trasera
fanale[M] posteriore

泥除(よ)け
fender; *mudguard*
Schutzblech[N]
garde-boue[M]
guardabarros[M]
parafango[M]

リア[後ろ]ディレーラー
rear derailleur
hinterer Umwerfer[M]
dérailleur[M] arrière
cambio[M] de marchas[F] trasero
deragliatore[M] posteriore

チェーン
drive chain
Kette[F]
chaîne[F]
cadena[F] de transmisión[F]
catena[F]

チェーン・ステー
chain stay
Kettenstrebe[F]
base[F]
soporte[M] de la cadena[F]
forcella[F] inferiore

フロント[前]ディレーラー
front derailleur
Kettenblattumwerfer[M]
dérailleur[M] avant
cambio[M] de marchas[F] delantero
deragliatore[M] anteriore

ペダル
pedal
Pedal[N]
pédale[F]
pedal[M]
pedale[M]

トウ・クリップ
toe clip
Pedalhaken[M]
cale-pied[M]
calzapié[M]
fermapiedi[M]

交通と機械

578

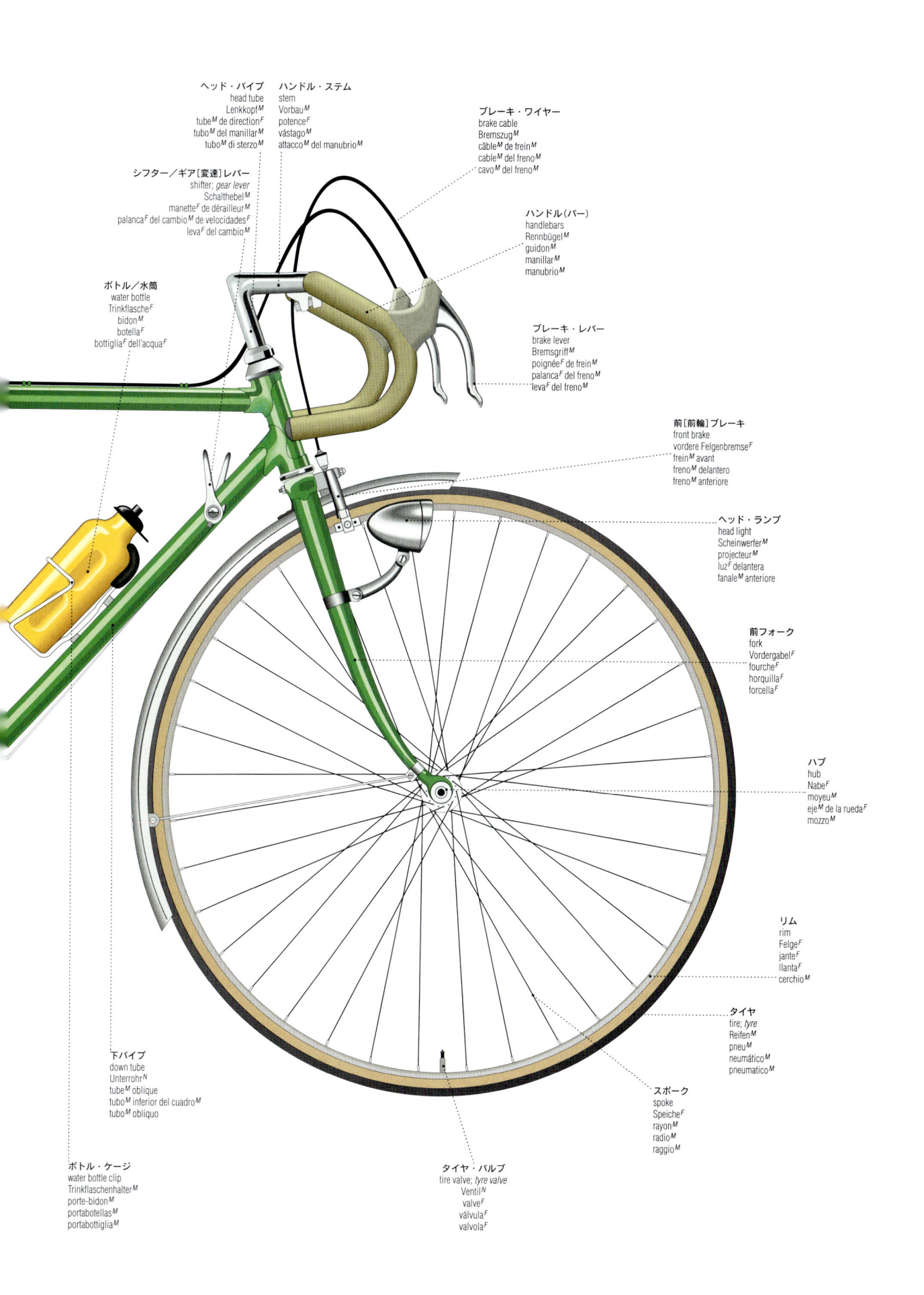

道路交通 | ROAD TRANSPORT
STRASSENVERKEHR | TRANSPORT ROUTIER | TRANSPORTE TERRESTRE | TRASPORTO SU STRADA

自転車

ヘッド・パイプ
head tube
Lenkkopf^M
tube^M de direction^F
tubo^M del manillar^M
tubo^M di sterzo^M

ハンドル・ステム
stem
Vorbau^M
potence^F
vástago^M
attacco^M del manubrio^M

ブレーキ・ワイヤー
brake cable
Bremszug^M
câble^M de frein^M
cable^M del freno^M
cavo^M del freno^M

シフター／ギア[変速]レバー
shifter; *gear lever*
Schalthebel^M
manette^F de dérailleur^M
palanca^F del cambio^M de velocidades^F
leva^F del cambio^M

ハンドル(バー)
handlebars
Rennbügel^M
guidon^M
manillar^M
manubrio^M

ボトル／水筒
water bottle
Trinkflasche^F
bidon^M
botella^F
bottiglia^F dell'acqua^F

ブレーキ・レバー
brake lever
Bremsgriff^M
poignée^F de frein^M
palanca^F del freno^M
leva^F del freno^M

前[前輪]ブレーキ
front brake
vordere Felgenbremse^F
frein^M avant
freno^M delantero
freno^M anteriore

ヘッド・ランプ
head light
Scheinwerfer^M
projecteur^M
luz^F delantera
fanale^M anteriore

前フォーク
fork
Vordergabel^F
fourche^F
horquilla^F
forcella^F

ハブ
hub
Nabe^F
moyeu^M
eje^M de la rueda^F
mozzo^M

リム
rim
Felge^F
jante^F
llanta^F
cerchio^M

タイヤ
tire; *tyre*
Reifen^M
pneu
neumático^M
pneumatico^M

下パイプ
down tube
Unterrohr^N
tube^M oblique
tubo^M inferior del cuadro^M
tubo^M obliquo

スポーク
spoke
Speiche^F
rayon^M
radio^M
raggio^M

ボトル・ケージ
water bottle clip
Trinkflaschenhalter^M
porte-bidon^M
portabotellas^M
portabottiglia^M

タイヤ・バルブ
tire valve; *tyre valve*
Ventil^N
valve^F
válvula^F
valvola^F

交通と機械

579

自転車

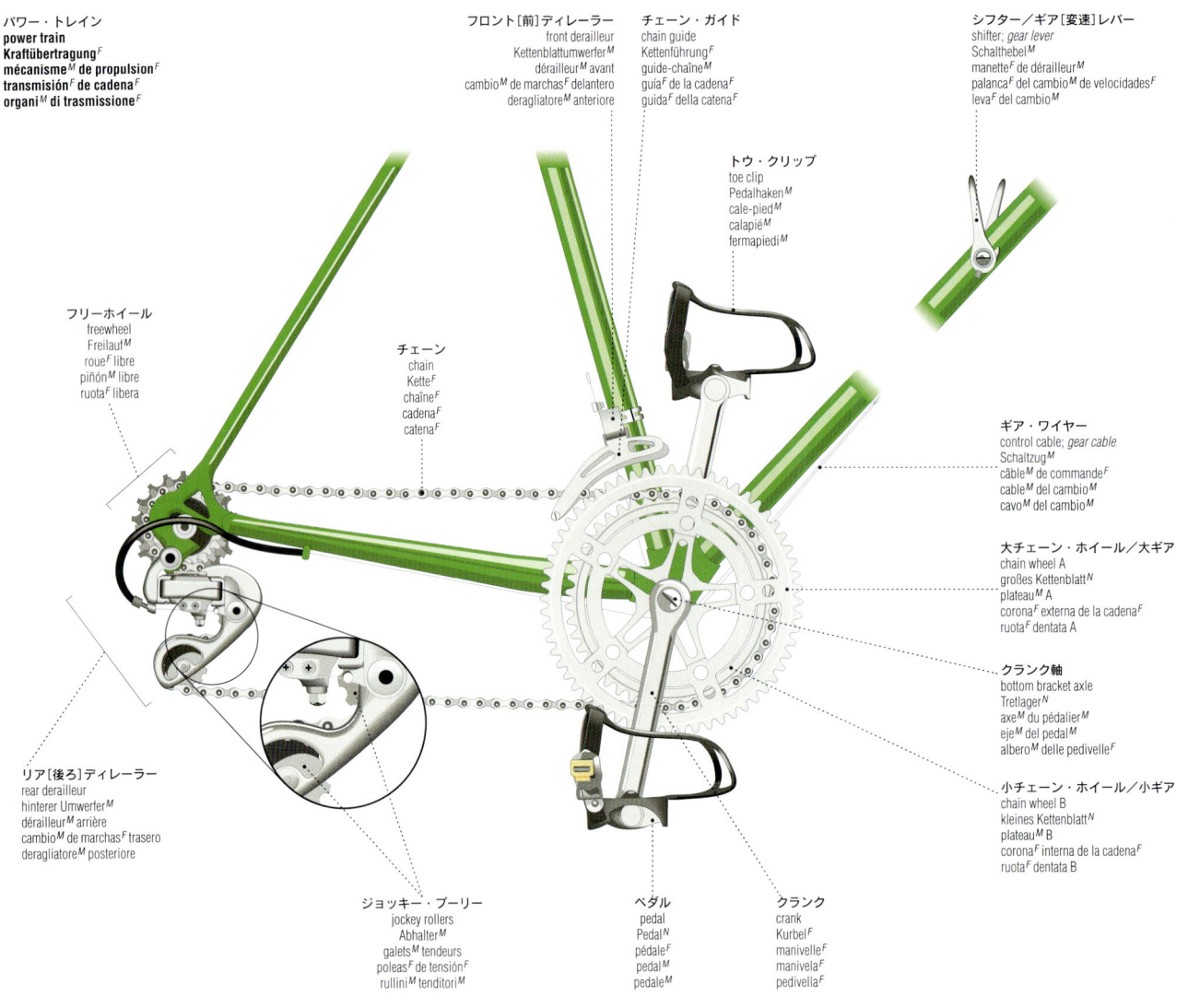

道路交通 | ROAD TRANSPORT
STRASSENVERKEHR | TRANSPORT ROUTIER | TRANSPORTE TERRESTRE | TRASPORTO SU STRADA

日本語 | 英語 | ドイツ語 | フランス語 | スペイン語 | イタリア語

パワー・トレイン
power train
Kraftübertragung F
mécanisme M de propulsion F
transmisión F de cadena F
organi M di trasmissione F

フロント[前]ディレーラー
front derailleur
Kettenblattumwerfer M
dérailleur M avant
cambio M de marchas F delantero
deragliatore M anteriore

チェーン・ガイド
chain guide
Kettenführung F
guide-chaîne F
guía F de la cadena F
guida F della catena F

シフター／ギア[変速]レバー
shifter; gear lever
Schalthebel M
manette F de dérailleur M
palanca F del cambio M de velocidades F
leva F del cambio M

トウ・クリップ
toe clip
Pedalhaken M
cale-pied M
calapié M
fermapiedi M

フリーホイール
freewheel
Freilauf M
roue F libre
piñón M libre
ruota F libera

チェーン
chain
Kette F
chaîne F
cadena F
catena F

ギア・ワイヤー
control cable; gear cable
Schaltzug M
câble M de commande F
cable M del cambio M
cavo M del cambio M

大チェーン・ホイール／大ギア
chain wheel A
großes Kettenblatt N
plateau M A
corona F externa de la cadena F
ruota F dentata A

クランク軸
bottom bracket axle
Tretlager N
axe M du pédalier M
eje M del pedal M
albero M delle pedivelle F

小チェーン・ホイール／小ギア
chain wheel B
kleines Kettenblatt N
plateau M B
corona F interna de la cadena F
ruota F dentata B

リア[後ろ]ディレーラー
rear derailleur
hinterer Umwerfer M
dérailleur M arrière
cambio M de marchas F trasero
deragliatore M posteriore

ジョッキー・プーリー
jockey rollers
Abhalter M
galets M tendeurs
poleas F de tensión F
rullini M tenditori M

ペダル
pedal
Pedal N
pédale F
pedal M
pedale M

クランク
crank
Kurbel F
manivelle F
manivela F
pedivella F

付属品／アクセサリー
accessories
Zubehör N
accessoires M
accesorios M
accessori M

ロック
lock
Schloss N
cadenas M
candado M para bicicleta F
lucchetto M

防護ヘルメット
protective helmet
Fahrradhelm M
casque M de protection F
casco M protector
casco M di protezione F

工具一式
tool kit
Werkzeugsatz M
trousse F de dépannage M
herramientas F
kit M di attrezzi M

自転車[サイド]バッグ
bicycle bag; pannier bag
Satteltasche F
sacoche F
cartera F
zaino M

自転車用チャイルド・シート
child carrier
Kindersitz M
siège M de vélo M pour enfant M
silla F porta-niño M
seggiolino M per bambini M

交通と機械

580

道路交通 | ROAD TRANSPORT
STRASSENVERKEHR | TRANSPORT ROUTIER | TRANSPORTE TERRESTRE | TRASPORTO SU STRADA

自転車

BMX自転車
BMX bike
BMX-RadN, MountainbikeN
véloM crossM
bicicletaF BMX
mountain bikeF da crossM

子供用三輪車
child's tricycle
DreiradN
tricycleM d'enfantM
tricicloM
tricicloM

自転車の例
examples of bicycles
BeispieleN für FahrräderN
exemplesM de bicyclettesF
ejemplosM de bicicletasF
esempiM di bicicletteF

マウンテン・バイク
mountain bike
Mountain BikeN
bicycletteF tout-terrain
bicicletaF todo terrenoM
mountain bikeF

ダッチ・バイク
Dutch bicycle
HollandradN
bicycletteF hollandaise
bicicletaF holandesa
biciclettaF olandese

ロード・バイク
road bicycle
RennradN
bicycletteF de courseF
bicicletaF de carreteraF
biciclettaF da corsaF

シティ・サイクル
city bicycle
StadtradN
bicycletteF de villeF
bicicletaF de ciudadF
city bikeF

ツーリング・バイク
touring bicycle
TourenradN
bicycletteF de tourismeM
bicicletaF de turismoM
biciclettaF da turismoM

タンデム自転車
tandem bicycle
TandemN
tandemM
tándemM
tandemM

交通と機械

581

鉄道輸送 | RAIL TRANSPORT
SCHIENENVERKEHR | TRANSPORT FERROVIAIRE | TRANSPORTE FERROVIARIO | TRASPORTO SU ROTAIA

旅客駅
passenger station | Bahnhof^M | gare^F de voyageurs^M | estación^F de ferrocarril^M | stazione^F dei viaggiatori^M

日本語 | 英語 | ドイツ語 | フランス語 | スペイン語 | イタリア語

事務室
office
Büro^N
locaux^M administratifs
oficina^F
uffici^M

ガラス屋根
glassed roof
Glasüberdachung^F
verrière^F
techo^M de vidiro^M
tettoia^F vetrata

案内板
indicator board
Fahrplan^M
panneau^M indicateur
tablero^M de información^F
tabellone^M degli orari^M

手押し車
baggage cart; luggage trolley
Förderwagen^M
chariot^M à bagages^M
carro^M portaequipaje
carrello^M portabagagli

鉄骨架構
metal structure
Eisenträger^M
structure^F métallique
estrucutra^F de metal^M
struttura^F metallica

手荷物ロッカー
baggage lockers; luggage lockers
Gepäckschließfächer^M
consigne^F automatique
taquillas^F de consigna^F automática
cassette^F di deposito^M per bagagli^M

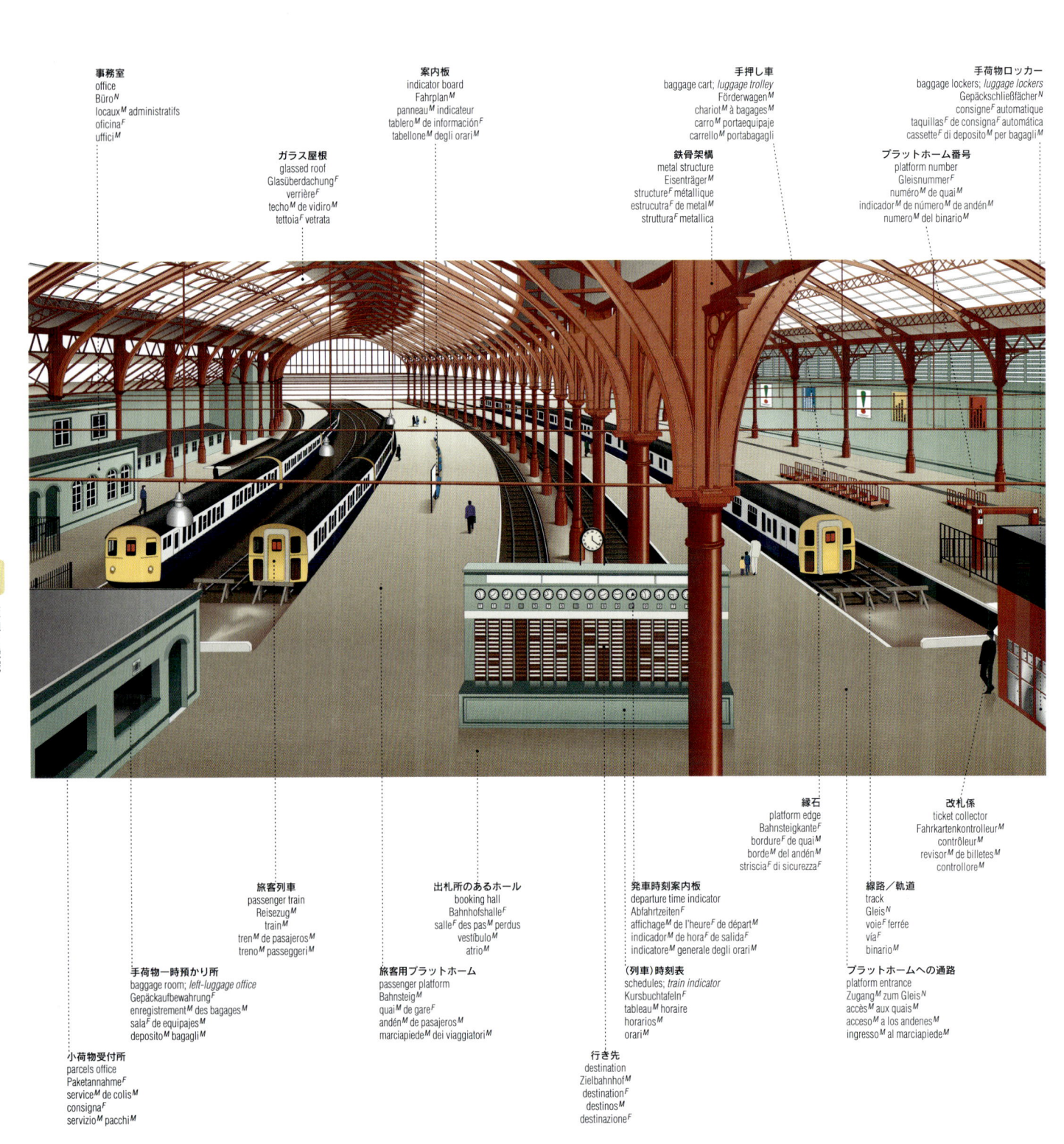

プラットホーム番号
platform number
Gleisnummer^F
numéro^M de quai^M
indicador^M de número^M de andén^M
numero^M del binario^M

旅客列車
passenger train
Reisezug^M
train^M
tren^M de pasajeros^M
treno^M passeggeri^M

出札所のあるホール
booking hall
Bahnhofshalle^F
salle^F des pas^M perdus
vestíbulo^M
atrio^M

発車時刻案内板
departure time indicator
Abfahrtzeiten^F
affichage^M de l'heure^F de départ^M
indicador^M de hora^F de salida^F
indicatore^M generale degli orari^M

縁石
platform edge
Bahnsteigkante^F
bordure^F de quai^M
borde^M del andén^M
striscia^F di sicurezza^F

改札係
ticket collector
Fahrkartenkontrolleur^M
contrôleur^M
revisor^M de billetes^M
controllore^M

手荷物一時預かり所
baggage room; left-luggage office
Gepäckkaufbewahrung^F
enregistrement^M des bagages^M
sala^F de equipajes^M
deposito^M bagagli^M

旅客用プラットホーム
passenger platform
Bahnsteig^M
quai^M de gare^F
andén^M de pasajeros^M
marciapiede^M dei viaggiatori^M

(列車)時刻表
schedules; train indicator
Kursbuchtafeln^F
tableau^M horaire
horarios^M
orari^M

線路／軌道
track
Gleis^N
voie^F ferrée
vía^F
binario^M

プラットホームへの通路
platform entrance
Zugang^M zum Gleis^N
accès^M aux quais^M
acceso^M a los andenes^M
ingresso^M al marciapiede^M

小荷物受付所
parcels office
Paketannahme^F
service^M de colis^M
consigna^F
servizio^M pacchi^M

行き先
destination
Zielbahnhof^M
destination^F
destinos^M
destinazione^F

交通と機械

582

鉄道輸送 | RAIL TRANSPORT
SCHIENENVERKEHR | TRANSPORT FERROVIAIRE | TRANSPORTE FERROVIARIO | TRASPORTO SU ROTAIA

鉄道駅

railroad station; *railway station* | Bahnhof[M] | gare[F] | estación[F] de ferrocarril | stazione[F] ferroviaria

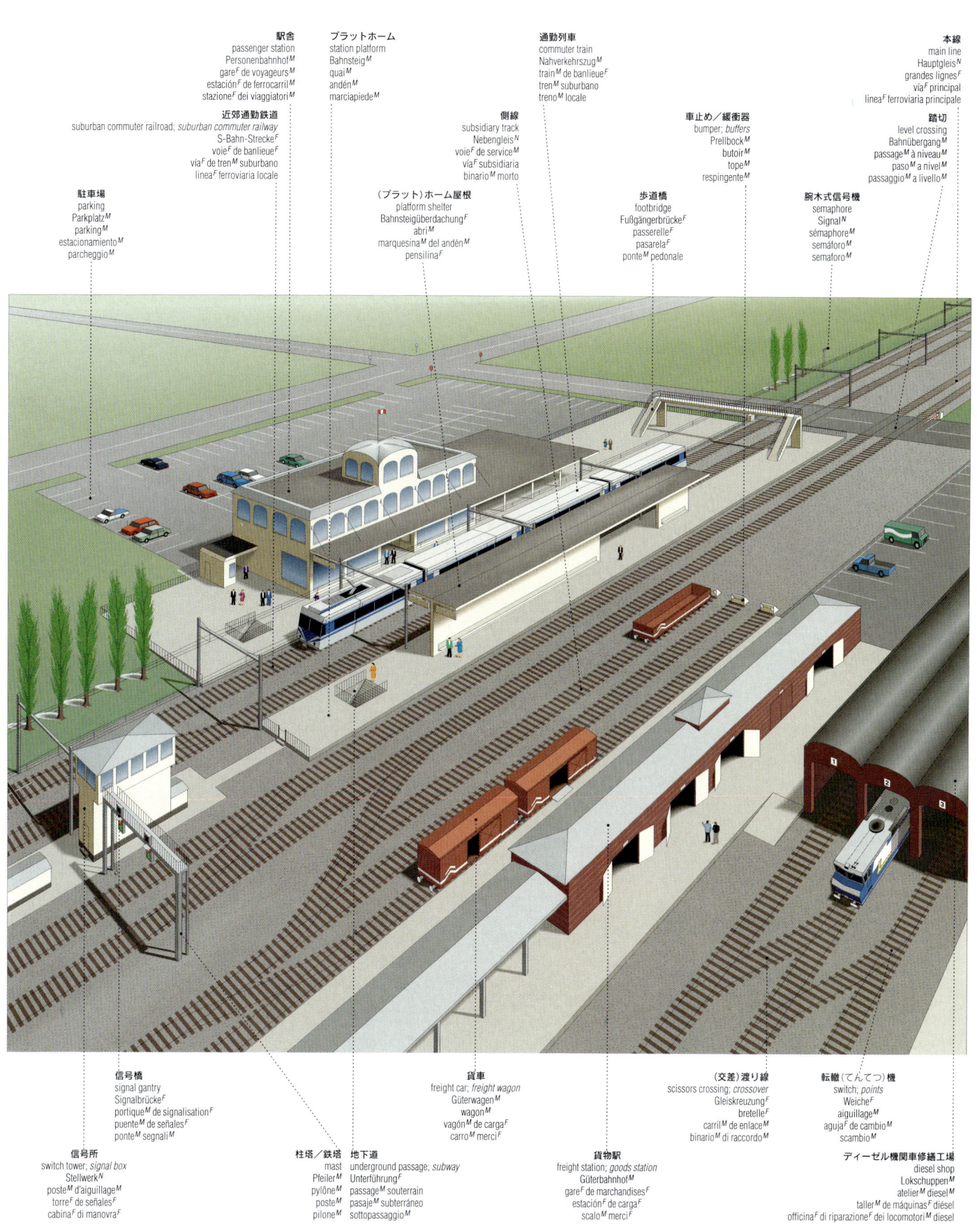

駅舎
passenger station
Personenbahnhof[M]
gare[F] de voyageurs[M]
estación[F] de ferrocarril[M]
stazione[F] dei viaggiatori[M]

プラットホーム
station platform
Bahnsteig[M]
quai[M]
andén[M]
marciapiede[M]

通勤列車
commuter train
Nahverkehrszug[M]
train[M] de banlieue[F]
tren[M] suburbano
treno[M] locale

本線
main line
Hauptgleis[N]
grandes lignes[F]
vía[F] principal
linea[F] ferroviaria principale

近郊通勤鉄道
suburban commuter railroad; *suburban commuter railway*
S-Bahn-Strecke[F]
voie[F] de banlieue[F]
vía[F] de tren[M] suburbano
linea[F] ferroviaria locale

側線
subsidiary track
Nebengleis[N]
voie[F] de service[M]
vía[F] subsidiaria
binario[M] morto

車止め／緩衝器
bumper; *buffers*
Prellbock[M]
butoir[M]
tope[M]
respingente[M]

踏切
level crossing
Bahnübergang[M]
passage[M] à niveau[M]
paso[M] a nivel[M]
passaggio[M] a livello[M]

駐車場
parking
Parkplatz[M]
parking[M]
estacionamiento[M]
parcheggio[M]

（プラット）ホーム屋根
platform shelter
Bahnsteigüberdachung[F]
abri[M]
marquesina[F] del andén[M]
pensilina[F]

歩道橋
footbridge
Fußgängerbrücke[F]
passerelle[F]
pasarela[F]
ponte[M] pedonale

腕木式信号機
semaphore
Signal[N]
sémaphore[M]
semáforo[M]
semaforo[M]

信号橋
signal gantry
Signalbrücke[F]
portique[M] de signalisation[F]
puente[M] de señales[F]
ponte[M] segnali[M]

貨車
freight car; *freight wagon*
Güterwagen[M]
wagon[M]
vagón[M] de carga[F]
carro[M] merci[F]

（交差）渡り線
scissors crossing; *crossover*
Gleiskreuzung[F]
bretelle[F]
carril[M] de enlace[M]
binario[M] di raccordo[M]

転轍（てんてつ）機
switch; *points*
Weiche[F]
aiguillage[M]
aguja[F] de cambio[M]
scambio[M]

信号所
switch tower; *signal box*
Stellwerk[N]
poste[M] d'aiguillage[M]
torre[F] de señales[F]
cabina[F] di manovra[F]

柱塔／鉄塔
mast
Pfeiler[M]
pylône[M]
poste[M]
pilone[M]

地下道
underground passage; *subway*
Unterführung[F]
passage[M] souterrain
pasaje[M] subterráneo
sottopassaggio[M]

貨物駅
freight station; *goods station*
Güterbahnhof[M]
gare[F] de marchandises[F]
estación[F] de carga[F]
scalo[M] merci[F]

ディーゼル機関車修繕工場
diesel shop
Lokschuppen[M]
atelier[M] diesel[M]
taller[M] de máquinas[F] diésel
officina[F] di riparazione[F] dei locomotori[M] diesel

583

鉄道輸送 | RAIL TRANSPORT
SCHIENENVERKEHR | TRANSPORT FERROVIAIRE | TRANSPORTE FERROVIARIO | TRASPORTO SU ROTAIA

客車の種類

types of passenger cars; *types of passenger coach* | Personenzüge^M: Wagentypen^M | types^M de voitures^F | vagones^M de pasajeros^M | tipi^M di vagoni^M passeggeri^M

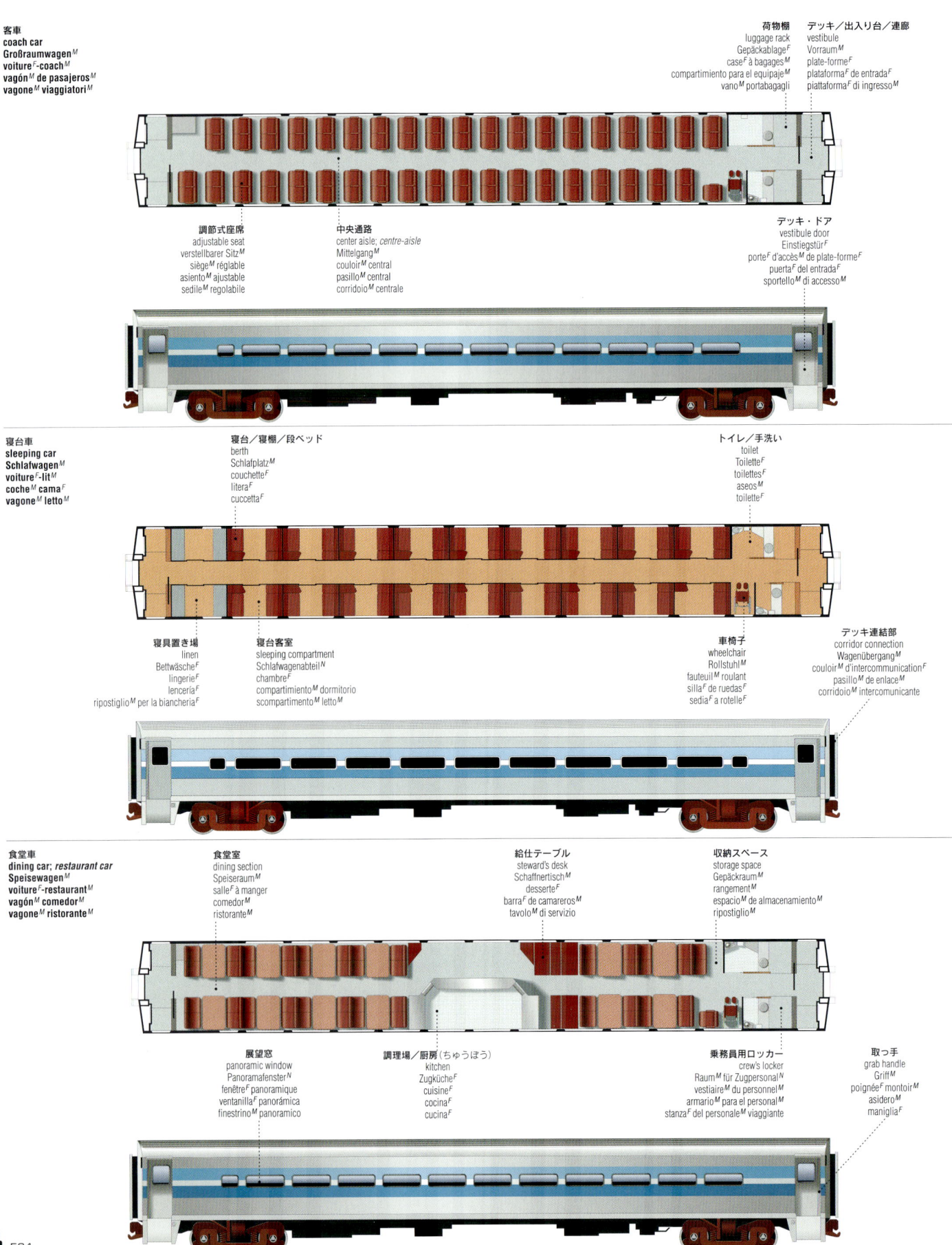

日本語 | 英語 | ドイツ語 | フランス語 | スペイン語 | イタリア語

客車
coach car
Großraumwagen^M
voiture^F-coach^M
vagón^M de pasajeros^M
vagone^M viaggiatori^M

荷物棚
luggage rack
Gepäckablage^F
case^F à bagages^M
compartimiento para el equipaje^M
vano^M portabagagli

デッキ／出入り台／連廊
vestibule
Vorraum^M
plate-forme^F
plataforma^F de entrada^F
piattaforma^F di ingresso^M

調節式座席
adjustable seat
verstellbarer Sitz^M
siège^M réglable
asiento^M ajustable
sedile^M regolabile

中央通路
center aisle; *centre-aisle*
Mittelgang^M
couloir^M central
pasillo^M central
corridoio^M centrale

デッキ・ドア
vestibule door
Einstiegstür^F
porte^F d'accès^M de plate-forme^F
puerta^F del entrada^F
sportello^M di accesso^M

寝台車
sleeping car
Schlafwagen^M
voiture^F-lit^M
coche^M cama^F
vagone^M letto^M

寝台／寝棚／段ベッド
berth
Schlafplatz^M
couchette^F
litera^F
cuccetta^F

トイレ／手洗い
toilet
Toilette^F
toilettes^F
aseos^M
toilette^F

寝具置き場
linen
Bettwäsche^F
lingerie^F
lencería^F
ripostiglio^M per la biancheria^F

寝台客室
sleeping compartment
Schlafwagenabteil^N
chambre^F
compartimiento^M dormitorio
scompartimento^M letto^M

車椅子
wheelchair
Rollstuhl^M
fauteuil^M roulant
silla^F de ruedas^F
sedia^F a rotelle^F

デッキ連結部
corridor connection
Wagenübergang^M
couloir^M d'intercommunication^F
pasillo^M de enlace^M
corridoio^M intercomunicante

食堂車
dining car; *restaurant car*
Speisewagen^M
voiture^F-restaurant^M
vagón^M comedor^M
vagone^M ristorante^M

食堂室
dining section
Speiseraum^M
salle^F à manger
comedor^M
ristorante^M

給仕テーブル
steward's desk
Schaffnertisch^M
desserte^F
barra^F de camareros^M
tavolo^M di servizio

収納スペース
storage space
Gepäckraum^M
rangement^M
espacio^M de almacenamiento^M
ripostiglio^M

展望窓
panoramic window
Panoramafenster^N
fenêtre^F panoramique
ventanilla^F panorámica
finestrino^M panoramico

調理場／厨房（ちゅうぼう）
kitchen
Zugküche^F
cuisine^F
cocina^F
cucina^F

乗務員用ロッカー
crew's locker
Raum^M für Zugpersonal^N
vestiaire^F du personnel^M
armario^M para el personal^M
stanza^F del personale^M viaggiante

取っ手
grab handle
Griff^M
poignée^F montoir^M
asidero^M
maniglia^F

交通と機械

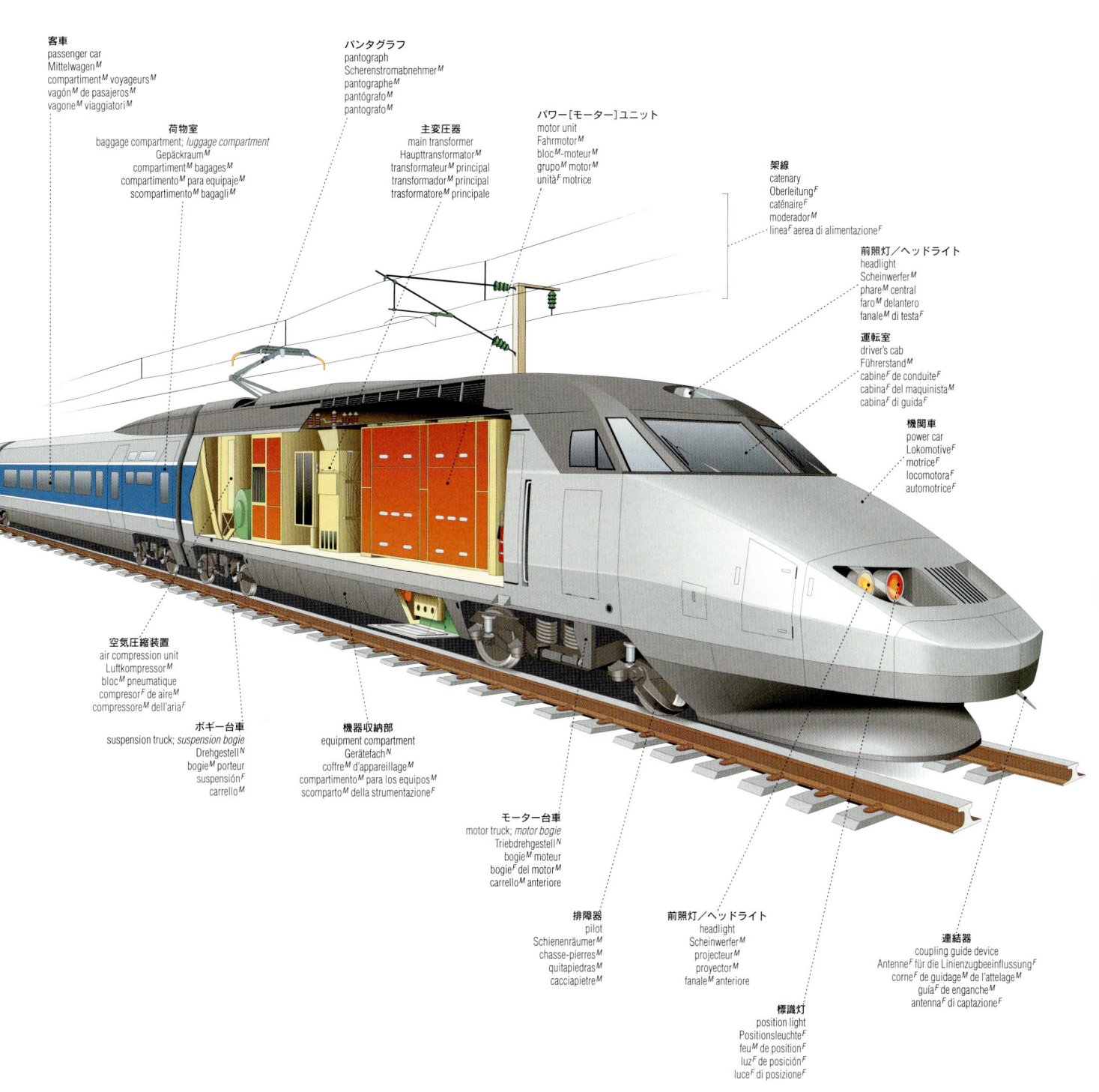

鉄道輸送 | RAIL TRANSPORT
SCHIENENVERKEHR | TRANSPORT FERROVIAIRE | TRANSPORTE FERROVIARIO | TRASPORTO SU ROTAIA

高速列車

high-speed train | Hochgeschwindigkeitszug[M] | train[M] à grande vitesse[F] (T.G.V.) | tren[M] de alta velocidad[F] | treno[M] ad alta velocità[F]

客車
passenger car
Mittelwagen[M]
compartiment[M] voyageurs[M]
vagón[M] de pasajeros[M]
vagone[M] viaggiatori[M]

荷物室
baggage compartment; *luggage compartment*
Gepäckraum[M]
compartiment[M] bagages[M]
compartimento[M] para equipaje[M]
scompartimento[M] bagagli[M]

パンタグラフ
pantograph
Scherenstromabnehmer[M]
pantographe[M]
pantógrafo[M]
pantografo[M]

主変圧器
main transformer
Haupttransformator[M]
transformateur[M] principal
transformador[M] principal
trasformatore[M] principale

パワー[モーター]ユニット
motor unit
Fahrmotor[M]
bloc[M]-moteur[M]
grupo[M] motor[M]
unità[F] motrice

架線
catenary
Oberleitung[F]
caténaire[F]
moderador[M]
linea[F] aerea di alimentazione[F]

前照灯／ヘッドライト
headlight
Scheinwerfer[M]
phare[M] central
faro[M] delantero
fanale[M] di testa[F]

運転室
driver's cab
Führerstand[M]
cabine[F] de conduite[F]
cabina[F] del maquinista[M]
cabina[F] di guida[F]

機関車
power car
Lokomotive[F]
motrice[F]
locomotora[F]
automotrice[F]

空気圧縮装置
air compression unit
Luftkompressor[M]
bloc[M] pneumatique
compresor[F] de aire[M]
compressore[M] dell'aria[F]

ボギー台車
suspension truck; *suspension bogie*
Drehgestell[N]
bogie[M] porteur
suspensión[F]
carrello[M]

機器収納部
equipment compartment
Gerätefach[N]
coffre[M] d'appareillage[M]
compartimento[M] para los equipos[M]
scomparto[M] della strumentazione[F]

モーター台車
motor truck; *motor bogie*
Triebdrehgestell[N]
bogie[M] moteur
bogie[F] del motor[M]
carrello[M] anteriore

排障器
pilot
Schienenräumer[M]
chasse-pierres[M]
quitapiedras[M]
cacciapietre[M]

前照灯／ヘッドライト
headlight
Scheinwerfer[M]
projecteur[M]
proyector[M]
fanale[M] anteriore

標識灯
position light
Positionsleuchte[F]
feu[M] de position[F]
luz[F] de posición[F]
luce[F] di posizione[F]

連結器
coupling guide device
Antenne[F] für die Linienzugbeeinflussung[F]
corne[F] de guidage[M] de l'attelage[M]
guía[F] de enganche[M]
antenna[F] di captazione[F]

交通と機械

585

鉄道輸送 | RAIL TRANSPORT
SCHIENENVERKEHR | TRANSPORT FERROVIAIRE | TRANSPORTE FERROVIARIO | TRASPORTO SU ROTAIA

ディーゼル電気機関車

日本語 | 英語 | ドイツ語 | フランス語 | スペイン語 | イタリア語

diesel-electric locomotive | dieselelektrische Lokomotive^F | locomotive^F diesel-électrique | locomotora^F diésel eléctrica | locomotiva^F diesel-elettrica

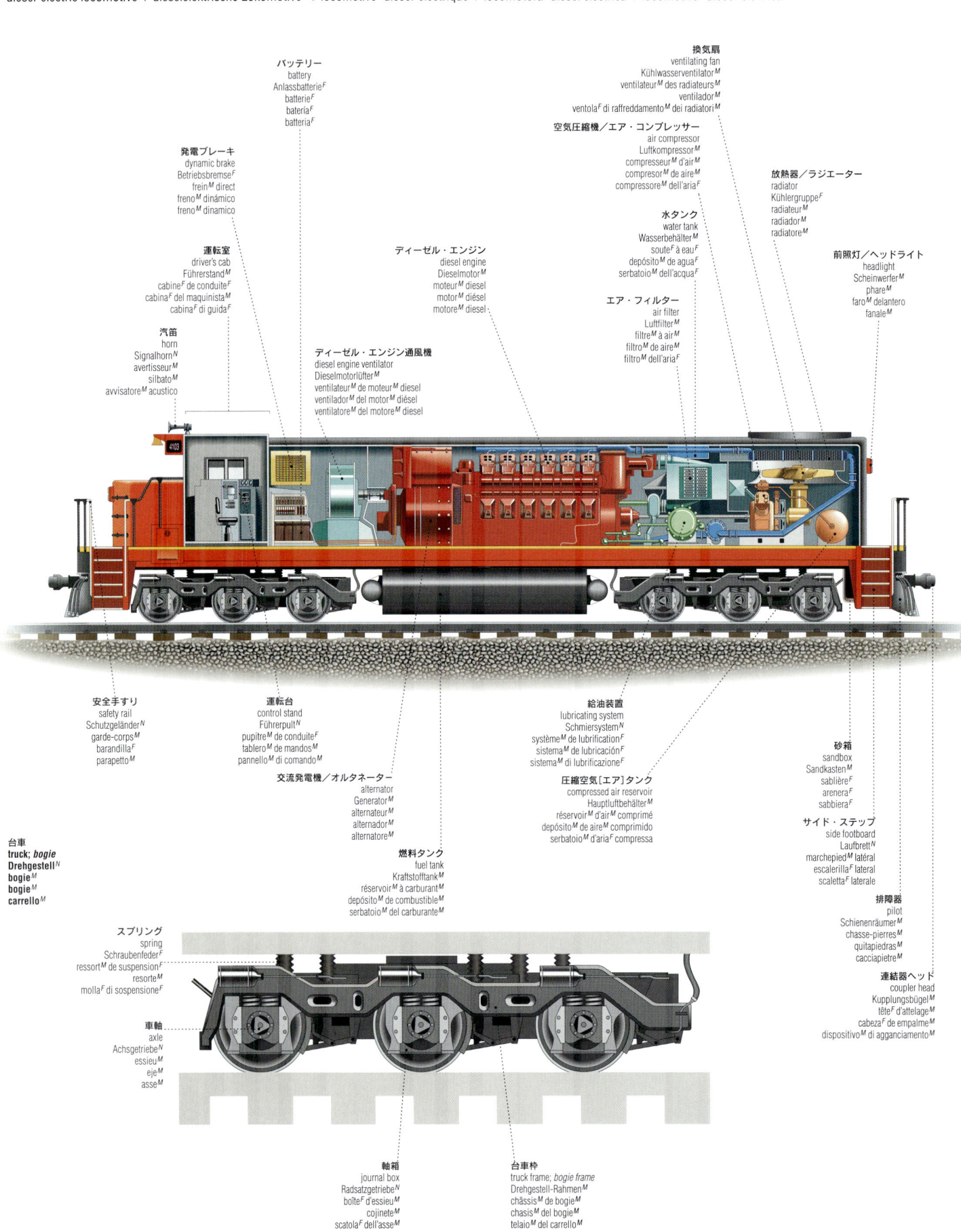

バッテリー
battery
Anlassbatterie^F
batterie^F
batería^F
batteria^F

換気扇
ventilating fan
Kühlwasserventilator^M
ventilateur^M des radiateurs^M
ventilador^M
ventola^F di raffreddamento^M dei radiatori^M

発電ブレーキ
dynamic brake
Betriebsbremse^F
frein^M direct
freno^M dinámico
freno^M dinamico

空気圧縮機／エア・コンプレッサー
air compressor
Luftkompressor^M
compresseur^M d'air^M
compresor^M de aire^M
compressore^M dell'aria^F

放熱器／ラジエーター
radiator
Kühlergruppe^F
radiateur^M
radiador^M
radiatore^M

運転室
driver's cab
Führerstand^M
cabine^F de conduite^F
cabina^F del maquinista^M
cabina^F di guida^F

ディーゼル・エンジン
diesel engine
Dieselmotor^M
moteur^M diesel
motor^M diésel
motore^M diesel

水タンク
water tank
Wasserbehälter^M
soute^F à eau^F
depósito^M de agua^M
serbatoio^M dell'acqua^F

前照灯／ヘッドライト
headlight
Scheinwerfer^M
phare^M
faro^M delantero
fanale^M

汽笛
horn
Signalhorn^N
avertisseur^M
silbato^M
avvisatore^M acustico

ディーゼル・エンジン通風機
diesel engine ventilator
Dieselmotorlüfter^M
ventilateur^M de moteur^M diesel
ventilador^M del motor^M diésel
ventilatore^M del motore^M diesel

エア・フィルター
air filter
Luftfilter^M
filtre^M à air^M
filtro^M de aire^M
filtro^M dell'aria^F

安全手すり
safety rail
Schutzgeländer^N
garde-corps^M
barandilla^F
parapetto^M

運転台
control stand
Führerpult^N
pupitre^M de conduite^F
tablero^M de mandos^M
pannello^M di comando^M

給油装置
lubricating system
Schmiersystem^N
système^M de lubrification^F
sistema^M de lubricación^F
sistema^M di lubrificazione^F

砂箱
sandbox
Sandkasten^M
sablière^F
arenera^F
sabbiera^F

交流発電機／オルタネーター
alternator
Generator^M
alternateur^M
alternador^M
alternatore^M

圧縮空気［エア］タンク
compressed air reservoir
Hauptluftbehälter^M
réservoir^M d'air^M comprimé
depósito^M de aire^M comprimido
serbatoio^M d'aria^F compressa

サイド・ステップ
side footboard
Laufbrett^N
marchepied^M latéral
escalerilla^F lateral
scaletta^F laterale

台車
truck; bogie
Drehgestell^N
bogie^M
bogie^M
carrello^M

燃料タンク
fuel tank
Kraftstofftank^M
réservoir^M à carburant^M
depósito^M de combustible^M
serbatoio^M del carburante^M

排障器
pilot
Schienenräumer^M
chasse-pierres^M
quitapiedras^M
cacciapietre^M

スプリング
spring
Schraubenfeder^F
ressort^M de suspension^F
resorte^M
molla^F di sospensione^F

連結器ヘッド
coupler head
Kupplungsbügel^M
tête^F d'attelage^M
cabeza^F de empalme^M
dispositivo^M di agganciamento^M

車軸
axle
Achsgetriebe^N
essieu^M
eje^M
asse^M

軸箱
journal box
Radsatzgetriebe^N
boîte^F d'essieu^M
cojinete^M
scatola^F dell'asse^M

台車枠
truck frame; bogie frame
Drehgestell-Rahmen^M
châssis^M de bogie^M
chasis^M del bogie^M
telaio^M del carrello^M

交通と機械

586

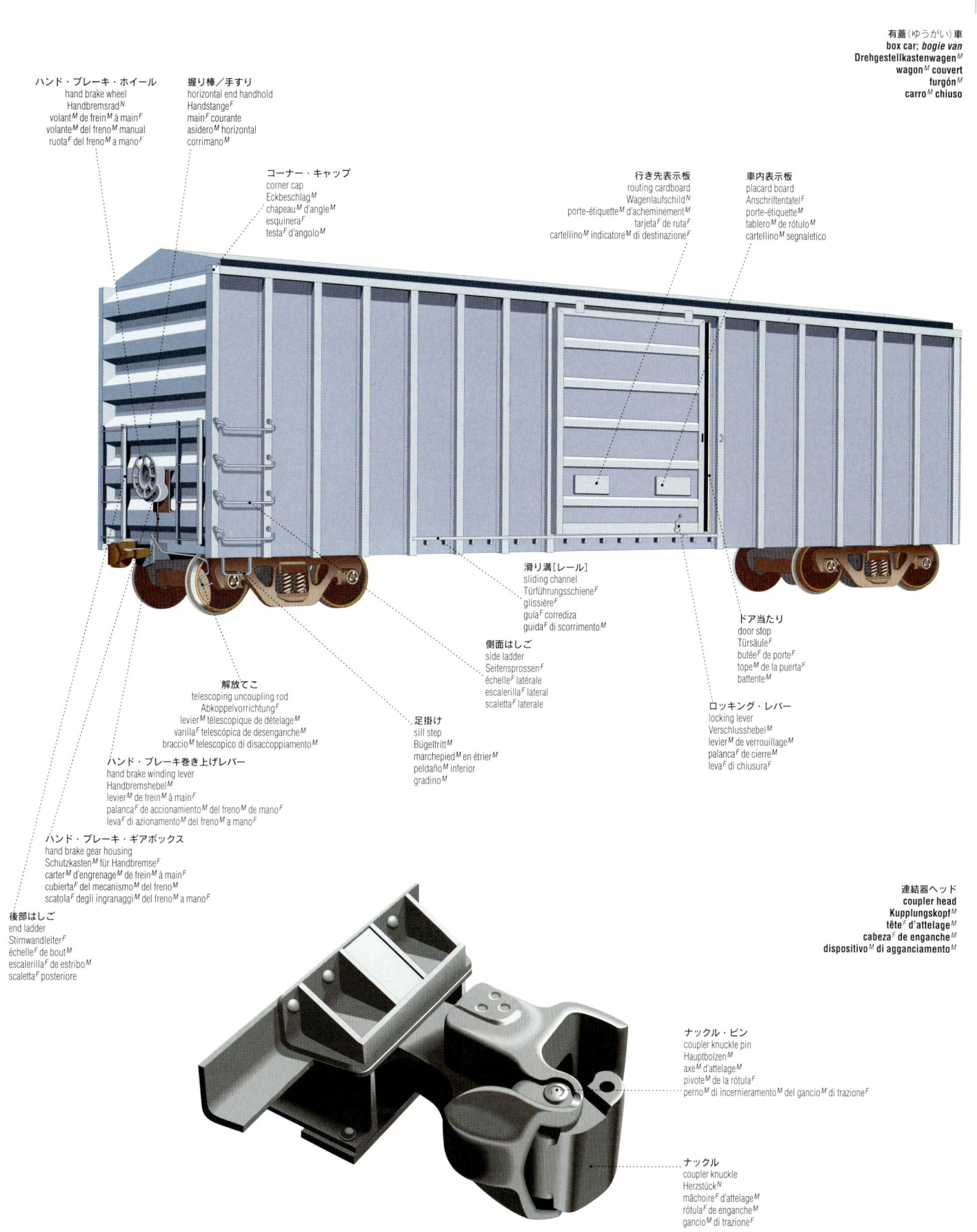

鉄道輸送 | RAIL TRANSPORT
SCHIENENVERKEHR | TRANSPORT FERROVIAIRE | TRANSPORTE FERROVIARIO | TRASPORTO SU ROTAIA

貨車

car; *goods van* | Waggon^M | wagon^M | vagón^M | carro^M merci^M

有蓋(ゆうがい)車
box car; *bogie van*
Drehgestellkastenwagen^M
wagon^M couvert
furgón^M
carro^M chiuso

ハンド・ブレーキ・ホイール
hand brake wheel
Handbremsrad^N
volant^M de frein^F à main^F
volante^M del freno^M manual
ruota^F del freno^M a mano^F

握り棒／手すり
horizontal end handhold
Handstange^F
main^F courante
asidero^M horizontal
corrimano^M

コーナー・キャップ
corner cap
Eckbeschlag^M
chapeau^M d'angle^M
esquinera^F
testa^F d'angolo^M

行き先表示板
routing cardboard
Wagenlaufschild^N
porte-étiquette^M d'acheminement^M
tarjeta^F de ruta^F
cartellino^M indicatore^M di destinazione^F

車内表示板
placard board
Anschriftentafel^F
porte-étiquette^M
tablero^M de rótulo^M
cartellino^M segnaletico

滑り溝[レール]
sliding channel
Türführungsschiene^F
glissière^F
guía^F corrediza
guida^F di scorrimento^M

ドア当たり
door stop
Türsäule^F
butée^F de porte^F
tope^M de la puerta^F
battente^M

側面はしご
side ladder
Seitensprossen^F
échelle^F latérale
escalerilla^F lateral
scaletta^F laterale

解放てこ
telescoping uncoupling rod
Abkoppelvorrichtung^F
levier^M télescopique de dételage^M
varilla^F telescópica de desenganche^M
braccio^M telescopico di disaccoppiamento^M

足掛け
sill step
Bügeltritt^M
marchepied^M en étrier^M
peldaño^M inferior
gradino^M

ロッキング・レバー
locking lever
Verschlusshebel^M
levier^M de verrouillage^M
palanca^F de cierre^M
leva^F di chiusura^F

ハンド・ブレーキ巻き上げレバー
hand brake winding lever
Handbremshebel^M
levier^M de frein^M à main^F
palanca^F de accionamiento^M del freno^M de mano^F
leva^F di azionamento^M del freno^M a mano^F

ハンド・ブレーキ・ギアボックス
hand brake gear housing
Schutzkasten^M für Handbremse^F
carter^M d'engrenage^M de frein^M à main^F
cubierta^F del mecanismo^M del freno^M
scatola^F degli ingranaggi^M del freno^M a mano^F

連結器ヘッド
coupler head
Kupplungskopf^M
tête^F d'attelage^M
cabeza^F de enganche^M
dispositivo^M di agganciamento^M

後部はしご
end ladder
Stirnwandleiter^F
échelle^F de bout^M
escalerilla^F de estribo^M
scaletta^F posteriore

ナックル・ピン
coupler knuckle pin
Hauptbolzen^M
axe^M d'attelage^M
pivote^M de la rótula^F
perno^M di incernieramento^M del gancio^M di trazione^F

ナックル
coupler knuckle
Herzstück^N
mâchoire^F d'attelage^M
rótula^F de enganche^M
gancio^M di trazione^F

交通と機械

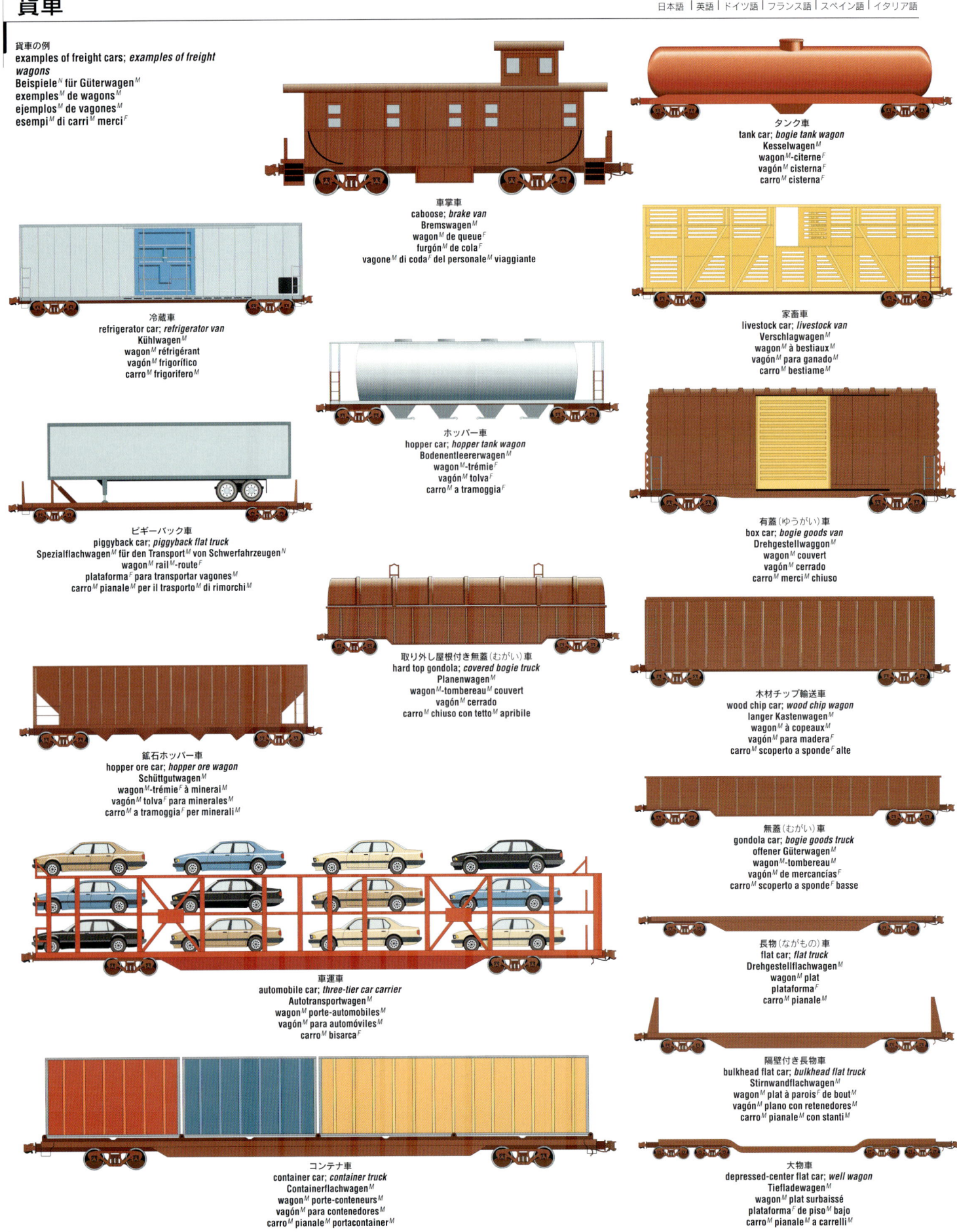

鉄道輸送 | RAIL TRANSPORT
SCHIENENVERKEHR | TRANSPORT FERROVIAIRE | TRANSPORTE FERROVIARIO | TRASPORTO SU ROTAIA

貨車

貨車の例
examples of freight cars; *examples of freight wagons*
Beispiele[N] für Güterwagen[M]
exemples[M] de wagons[M]
ejemplos[M] de vagones[M]
esempi[M] di carri[M] merci[F]

日本語 | 英語 | ドイツ語 | フランス語 | スペイン語 | イタリア語

車掌車
caboose; *brake van*
Bremswagen[M]
wagon[M] de queue[F]
furgón[M] de cola[F]
vagone[F] di coda[F] del personale[M] viaggiante

タンク車
tank car; *bogie tank wagon*
Kesselwagen[M]
wagon[M]-citerne[F]
vagón[M] cisterna[F]
carro[M] cisterna[F]

冷蔵車
refrigerator car; *refrigerator van*
Kühlwagen[M]
wagon[M] réfrigérant
vagón[M] frigorífico
carro[M] frigorifero[M]

家畜車
livestock car; *livestock van*
Verschlagwagen[M]
wagon[M] à bestiaux[M]
vagón[M] para ganado[M]
carro[M] bestiame[M]

ホッパー車
hopper car; *hopper tank wagon*
Bodenentleererwagen[M]
wagon[M]-trémie[F]
vagón[M] tolva[F]
carro[M] a tramoggia[F]

ピギーバック車
piggyback car; *piggyback flat truck*
Spezialflachwagen[M] für den Transport[M] von Schwerfahrzeugen[N]
wagon[M] rail[M]-route[F]
plataforma[F] para transportar vagones[M]
carro[M] pianale[M] per il trasporto[M] di rimorchi[M]

有蓋(ゆうがい)車
box car; *bogie goods van*
Drehgestellwaggon[M]
wagon[M] couvert
vagón[M] cerrado
carro[M] merci[M] chiuso

取り外し屋根付き無蓋(むがい)車
hard top gondola; *covered bogie truck*
Planenwagen[M]
wagon[M]-tombereau[M] couvert
vagón[M] cerrado
carro[M] chiuso con tetto[M] apribile

木材チップ輸送車
wood chip car; *wood chip wagon*
langer Kastenwagen[M]
wagon[M] à copeaux[M]
vagón[M] para madera[F]
carro[M] scoperto a sponde[F] alte

鉱石ホッパー車
hopper ore car; *hopper ore wagon*
Schüttgutwagen[M]
wagon[M]-trémie[F] à minerai[M]
vagón[M] tolva[F] para minerales[M]
carro[M] a tramoggia[F] per minerali[M]

無蓋(むがい)車
gondola car; *bogie goods truck*
offener Güterwagen[M]
wagon[M]-tombereau[M]
vagón[M] de mercancías[F]
carro[M] scoperto a sponde[F] basse

車運車
automobile car; *three-tier car carrier*
Autotransportwagen[M]
wagon[M] porte-automobiles[M]
vagón[M] para automóviles[M]
carro[M] bisarca[F]

長物(ながもの)車
flat car; *flat truck*
Drehgestellflachwagen[M]
wagon[M] plat
plataforma[F]
carro[M] pianale[M]

隔壁付き長物車
bulkhead flat car; *bulkhead flat truck*
Stirnwandflachwagen[M]
wagon[M] plat à parois[F] de bout[M]
vagón[M] plano con retenedores[M]
carro[M] pianale[M] con stanti[M]

コンテナ車
container car; *container truck*
Containerflachwagen[M]
wagon[M] porte-conteneurs[M]
vagón[M] para contenedores[M]
carro[M] pianale[M] portacontainer[M]

大物車
depressed-center flat car; *well wagon*
Tiefladewagen[M]
wagon[M] plat surbaissé
plataforma[F] de piso[M] bajo
carro[M] pianale[M] a carrelli[M]

交通と機械

鉄道輸送 | RAIL TRANSPORT
SCHIENENVERKEHR | TRANSPORT FERROVIAIRE | TRANSPORTE FERROVIARIO | TRASPORTO SU ROTAIA

操車場

yard | Rangierbahnhof^M | gare^F de triage^M | estación^M de clasificación^F | stazione^F di smistamento^M

第2仕分け[仕訳]線
second classification track; *secondary marshalling track*
Richtungsgleis^N
voie^F de tri^M secondaire
segunda vía^F de clasificación^F
binario^M di secondo smistamento^M

仕分け[仕訳]場
classification yard; *marshalling yard*
Ordnungsgleis^N
zone^F de triage^M
zona^F de clasificación^F
area^F di smistamento^M

洗車場
car cleaning yard; *rolling stock cleaning yard*
Waschplatte^F
zone^F de lavage^M des wagons^M
zona^F de lavado^M de vagones^M
area^F di lavaggio^M delle carrozze^F

給水塔
water tower
Wasserturm^M
château^M d'eau^F
tanque^M de agua^F
serbatoio^M dell'acqua^F

出発線
outbound track
Ausfahrgleis^N
voie^F de sortie^F
vía^F de salida^F
binario^M di uscita^M

検修庫
car repair shop; *rolling stock repair shop*
Wagenausbesserungshalle^F
atelier^M de réparation^F des wagons^M
taller^M de reparación^F de vagones^M
officina^F di manutenzione^F dei vagoni^M

到着線
receiving yard
Empfangsgleise^N
zone^F de réception^F
zona^F de recepción^F
area^F ricevitrice

交通と機械

ハンプ／操車用丘状地
hump
Ablaufberg^M
butte^F de débranchement^M
terraplén^M de desenganche^M
parigina^F

ハンプ仕分け[仕訳]室
hump office
Ablaufstellwerk^N
poste^M de débranchement^M
puesto^M de clasificación^F
cabina^F di controllo^F della parigina^F

ハンプ引き上げ線
hump lead
Auffahrgleis^N
voie^F de butte^F
dirección^F
binario^M di rampa^F

第1仕分け[仕訳]線
first classification track; *primary marshalling track*
Einfahrgleis^N
voie^F de tri^M primaire
primera vía^F de clasificación^F
binario^M di primo smistamento^M

機関車線
locomotive track
Lokverkehrsgleis^N
voie^F de circulation^F des locomotives^F
vía^F locomotriz
binario^M per le locomotive^F

589

鉄道輸送 | RAIL TRANSPORT
SCHIENENVERKEHR | TRANSPORT FERROVIAIRE | TRANSPORTE FERROVIARIO | TRASPORTO SU ROTAIA

鉄道線路

日本語 | 英語 | ドイツ語 | フランス語 | スペイン語 | イタリア語

railroad track; *railway track* | Eisenbahn-Oberbau^M | voie^F ferrée | vía^F férrea | strada^F ferrata

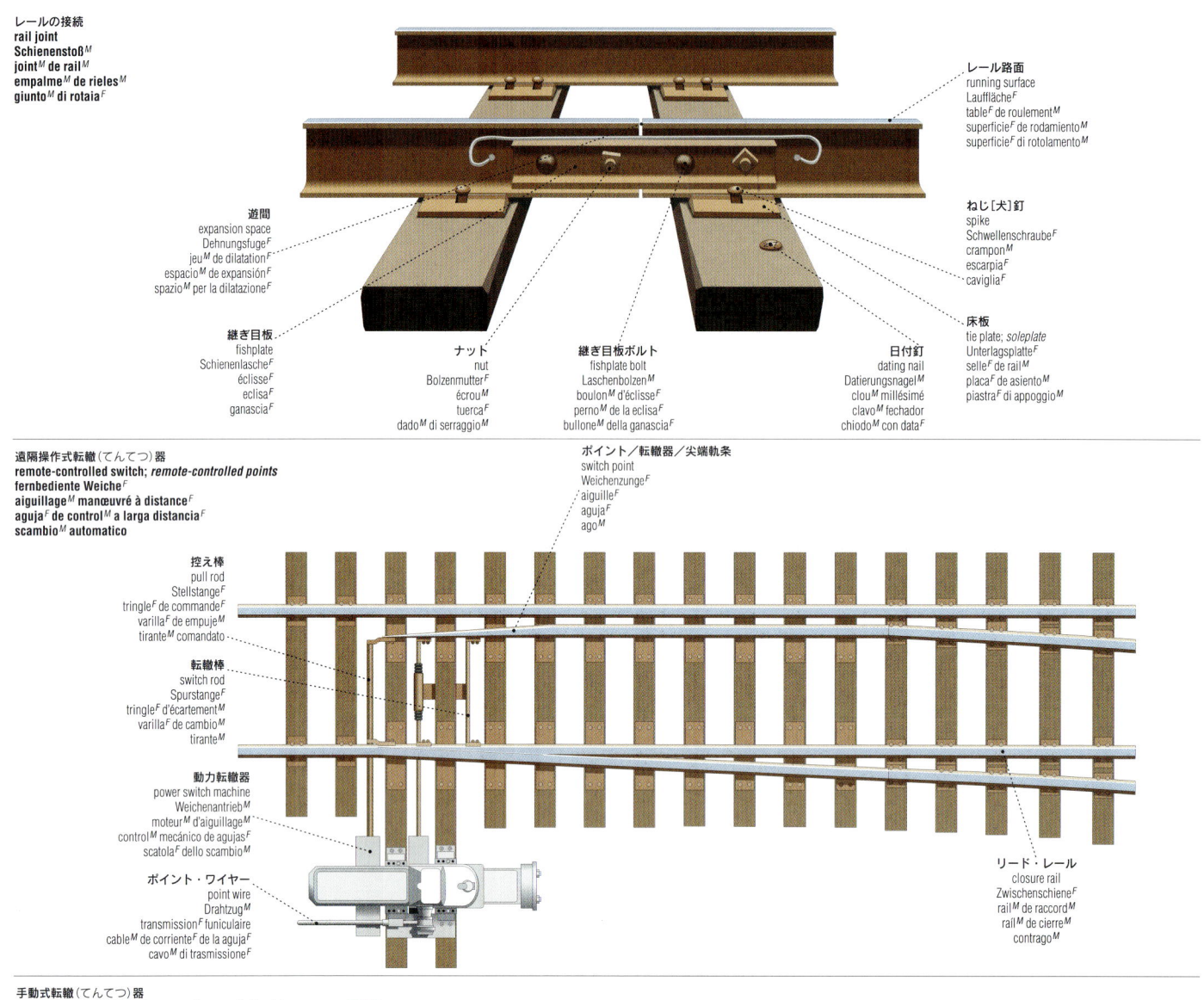

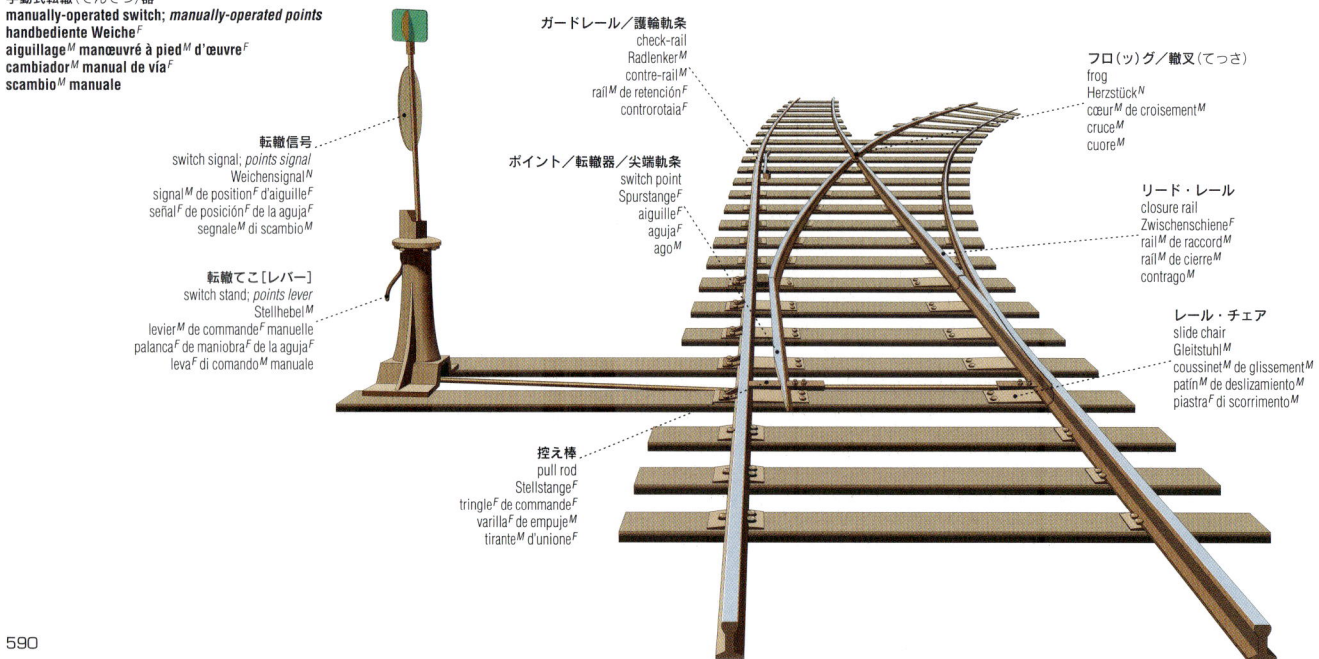

レールの接続 / rail joint / Schienenstoß^M / joint^M de rail^M / empalme^M de rieles^M / giunto^M di rotaia^F

- レール路面 / running surface / Lauffläche^F / table^F de roulement^F / superficie^F de rodamiento^M / superficie^F di rotolamento^M
- 遊間 / expansion space / Dehnungsfuge^F / jeu^F de dilatation^F / espacio^M de expansión^F / spazio^M per la dilatazione^F
- ねじ[犬]釘 / spike / Schwellenschraube^F / crampon^M / escarpia^F / caviglia^F
- 継ぎ目板 / fishplate / Schienenlasche^F / éclisse^F / eclisa^F / ganascia^F
- ナット / nut / Bolzenmutter^F / écrou^M / tuerca^F / dado^M di serraggio^M
- 継ぎ目板ボルト / fishplate bolt / Laschenbolzen^M / boulon^M d'éclisse^F / perno^M de la eclisa^F / bullone^M della ganascia^F
- 日付釘 / dating nail / Datierungsnagel^M / clou^M millésimé / clavo^M fechador / chiodo^M con data^F
- 床板 / tie plate; *soleplate* / Unterlagsplatte^F / selle^F de rail^M / placa^F de asiento^M / piastra^F di appoggio^M

遠隔操作式転轍(てんてつ)器 / remote-controlled switch; *remote-controlled points* / fernbediente Weiche^F / aiguillage^M manœuvré à distance^F / aguja^F de control^M a larga distancia^F / scambio^M automatico

- ポイント／転轍器／尖端軌条 / switch point / Weichenzunge^F / aiguille^F / aguja^F / ago^M
- 控え棒 / pull rod / Stellstange^F / tringle^F de commande^F / varilla^F de empuje^M / tirante^M comandato
- 転轍棒 / switch rod / Spurstange^F / tringle^F d'écartement^F / varilla^F de cambio^M / tirante^M
- 動力転轍器 / power switch machine / Weichenantrieb^M / moteur^M d'aiguillage^M / control^M mecánico de agujas^F / scatola^F dello scambio^M
- ポイント・ワイヤー / point wire / Drahtzug^M / transmission^F funiculaire / cable^M de corriente^F de la aguja^F / cavo^M di trasmissione^F
- リード・レール / closure rail / Zwischenschiene^F / rail^M de raccord^M / rail^M de cierre^M / contrago^M

手動式転轍(てんてつ)器 / manually-operated switch; *manually-operated points* / handbediente Weiche^F / aiguillage^M manœuvré à pied^M d'œuvre^F / cambiador^M manual de vía^F / scambio^M manuale

- ガードレール／護輪軌条 / check-rail / Radlenker^M / contre-rail^M / rail^M de retención^F / controrotaia^F
- 転轍信号 / switch signal; *points signal* / Weichensignal^N / signal^M de position^F d'aiguille^F / señal^F de posición^F de la aguja^F / segnale^M di scambio^M
- ポイント／転轍器／尖端軌条 / switch point / Spurstange^F / aiguille^F / aguja^F / ago^M
- フロ(ッ)グ／轍叉(てっさ) / frog / Herzstück^N / cœur^M de croisement^M / cruce^M / cuore^M
- 転轍てこ[レバー] / switch stand; *points lever* / Stellhebel^M / levier^M de commande^F manuelle / palanca^F de maniobra^F de la aguja^F / leva^F di comando^M manuale
- リード・レール / closure rail / Zwischenschiene^F / rail^M de raccord^M / rail^M de cierre^M / contrago^M
- レール・チェア / slide chair / Gleitstuhl^M / coussinet^M de glissement^M / patín^M de deslizamiento^M / piastra^F di scorrimento^M
- 控え棒 / pull rod / Stellstange^F / tringle^F de commande^F / varilla^F de empuje^M / tirante^M d'unione^F

交通と機械

鉄道輸送 | RAIL TRANSPORT
SCHIENENVERKEHR | TRANSPORT FERROVIAIRE | TRASPORTE FERROVIARIO | TRASPORTO SU ROTAIA

鉄道線路

鉄道線路
railroad track; *railway track*
Oberbau^M
voie^F ferrée
vía^F férrea
strada^F ferrata

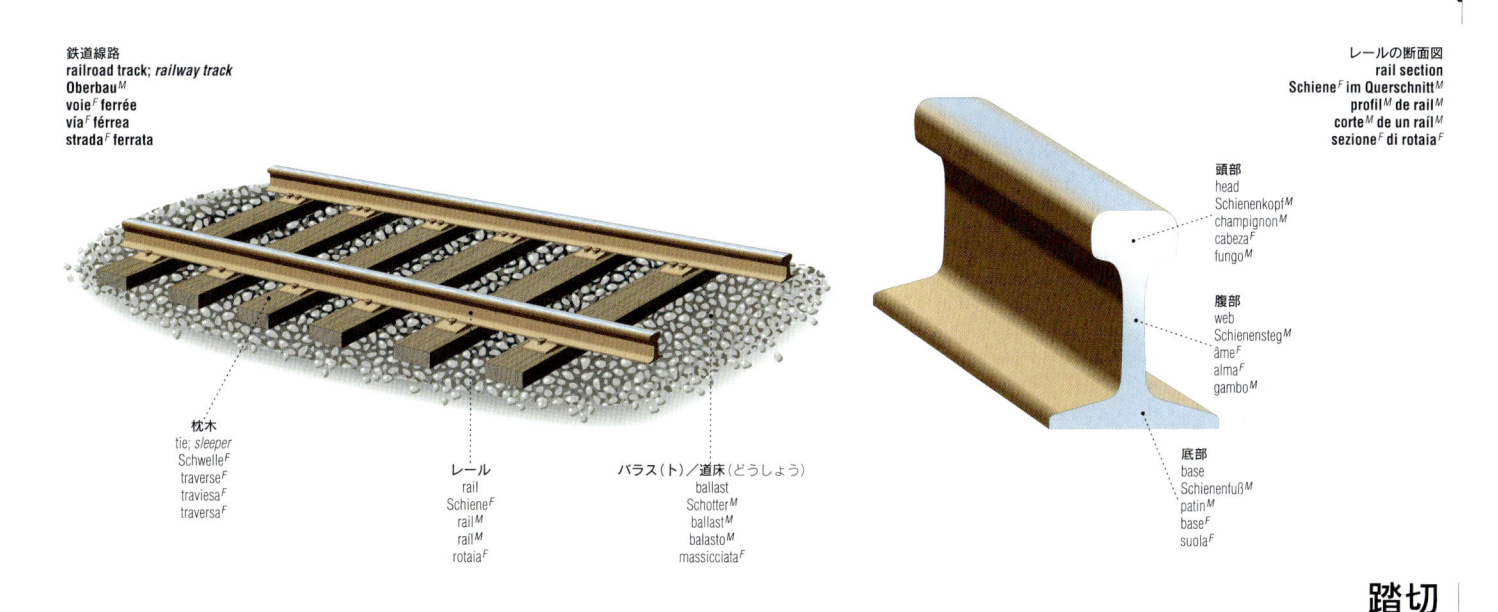

レールの断面図
rail section
Schiene^F im Querschnitt^M
profil^M de rail^M
corte^M de un rail^M
sezione^F di rotaia^F

頭部
head
Schienenkopf^M
champignon^M
cabeza^F
fungo^M

腹部
web
Schienensteg^M
âme^F
alma^F
gambo^M

底部
base
Schienenfuß^M
patin^M
base^F
suola^F

枕木
tie; *sleeper*
Schwelle^F
traverse^F
traviesa^F
traversa^F

レール
rail
Schiene^F
rail^M
rail^M
rotaia^F

バラス(ト)／道床(どうしょう)
ballast
Schotter^M
ballast^M
balasto^M
massicciata^F

踏切

highway crossing; *level crossing* | schienengleicher, gesicherter Bahnübergang^M | passage^M à niveau^M | paso^M a nivel^M | passaggio^M a livello^M

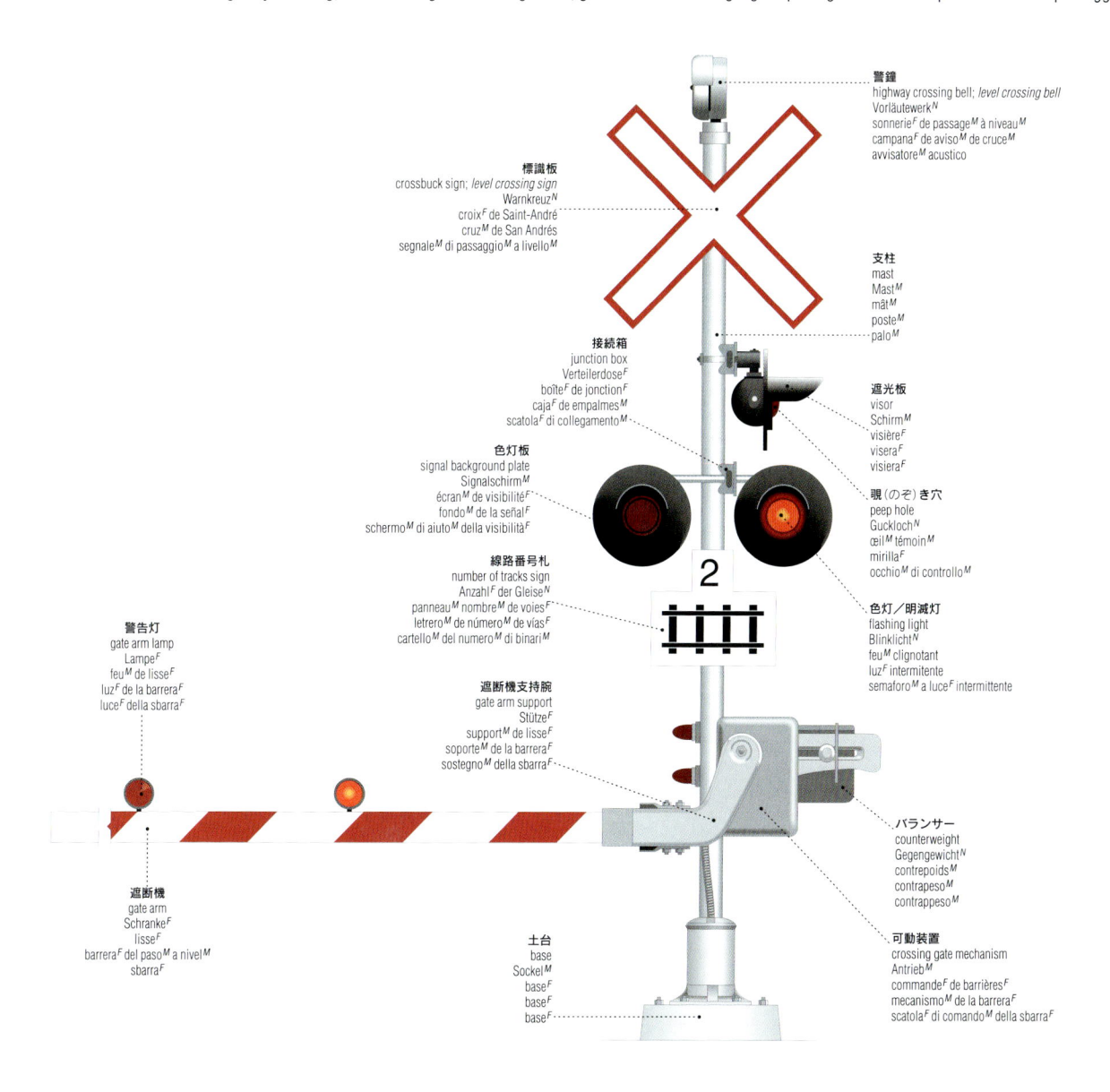

警鐘
highway crossing bell; *level crossing bell*
Vorläutewerk^N
sonnerie^F de passage^M à niveau^M
campana^F de aviso^M de cruce^M
avvisatore^M acustico

標識板
crossbuck sign; *level crossing sign*
Warnkreuz^N
croix^F de Saint-André
cruz^M de San Andrés
segnale^M di passaggio^M a livello^M

支柱
mast
Mast^M
mât^M
poste^M
palo^M

接続箱
junction box
Verteilerdose^F
boîte^F de jonction^F
caja^F de empalmes^M
scatola^F di collegamento^M

遮光板
visor
Schirm^M
visière^F
visera^F
visiera^F

色灯板
signal background plate
Signalschirm^M
écran^M de visibilité^F
fondo^M de la señal^F
schermo^M di aiuto^M della visibilità^F

覗(のぞ)き穴
peep hole
Guckloch^N
œil^M témoin^M
mirilla^F
occhio^M di controllo^M

線路番号札
number of tracks sign
Anzahl^F der Gleise^N
panneau^M nombre^M de voies^F
letrero^M de número^M de vías^F
cartello^M del numero^M di binari^M

色灯／明滅灯
flashing light
Blinklicht^N
feu^M clignotant
luz^F intermitente
semaforo^M a luce^F intermittente

警告灯
gate arm lamp
Lampe^F
feu^M de lisse^F
luz^F de la barrera^F
luce^F della sbarra^F

遮断機支持腕
gate arm support
Stütze^F
support^M de lisse^F
soporte^M de la barrera^F
sostegno^M della sbarra^F

バランサー
counterweight
Gegengewicht^N
contrepoids^M
contrapeso^M
contrappeso^M

遮断機
gate arm
Schranke^F
lisse^F
barrera^F del paso^M a nivel^M
sbarra^F

土台
base
Sockel^M
base^F
base^F
base^F

可動装置
crossing gate mechanism
Antrieb^M
commande^F de barrières^F
mecanismo^M de la barrera^F
scatola^F di comando^M della sbarra^F

591

交通と機械

鉄道輸送 | RAIL TRANSPORT
SCHIENENVERKEHR | TRANSPORT FERROVIAIRE | TRANSPORTE FERROVIARIO | TRASPORTO SU ROTAIA

地下鉄

日本語 | 英語 | ドイツ語 | フランス語 | スペイン語 | イタリア語

subway; *underground railway* | U-Bahn^F | chemin^M de fer^M métropolitain | metro^M | metropolitana^F

地下鉄駅
subway station; *underground station*
U-Bahn-Station^F
station^F de métro^M
estación^F de metro^M
stazione^F della metropolitana^F

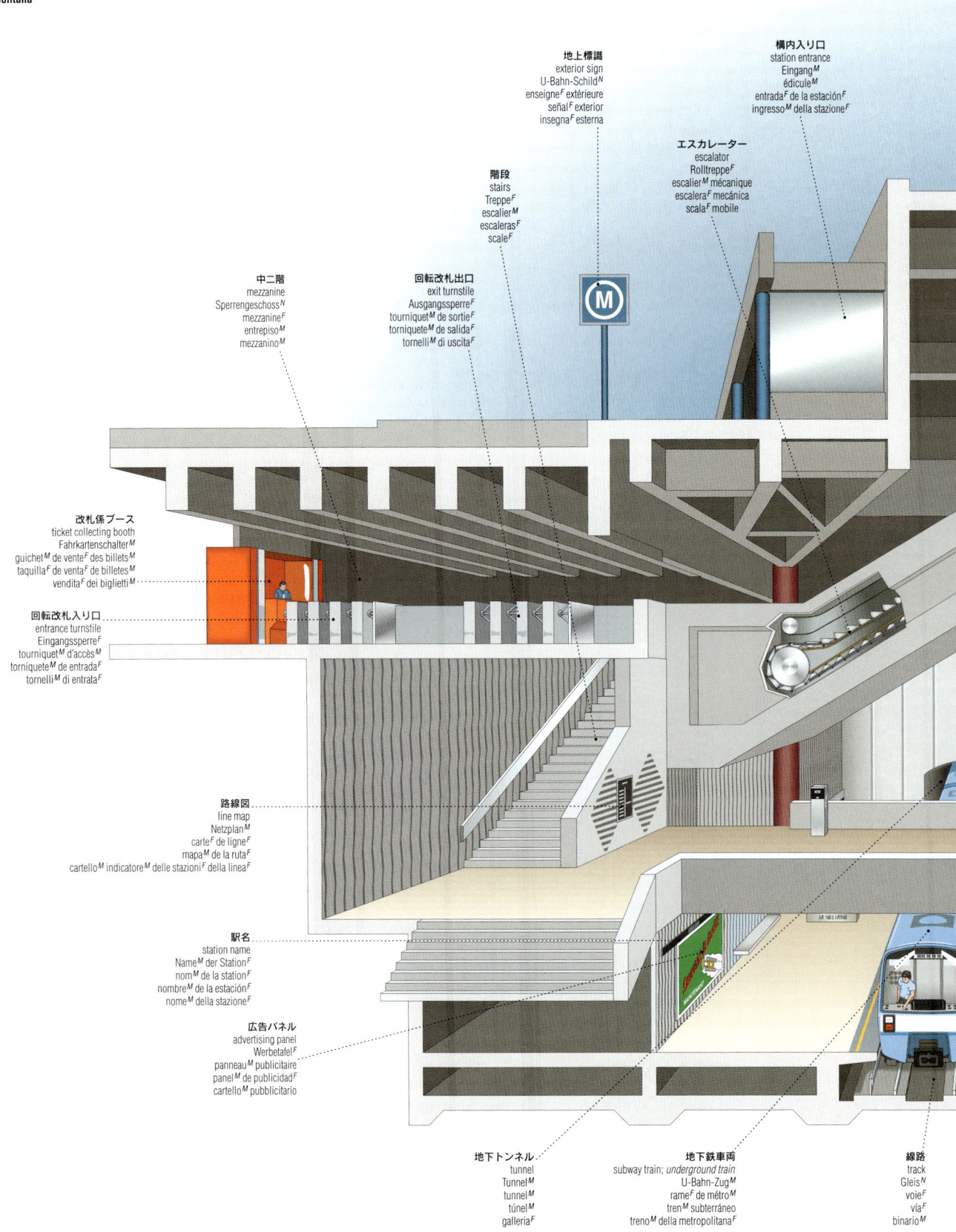

地上標識
exterior sign
U-Bahn-Schild^N
enseigne^F extérieure
señal^F exterior
insegna^F esterna

構内入り口
station entrance
Eingang^M
édicule^M
entrada^F de la estación^F
ingresso^M della stazione^F

エスカレーター
escalator
Rolltreppe^F
escalier^M mécanique
escalera^F mecánica
scala^F mobile

階段
stairs
Treppe^F
escalier^M
escaleras^F
scale^F

回転改札出口
exit turnstile
Ausgangssperre^F
tourniquet^M de sortie^F
torniquete^M de salida^F
tornelli^M di uscita^F

中二階
mezzanine
Sperrengeschoss^N
mezzanine^F
entrepiso^M
mezzanino^M

改札係ブース
ticket collecting booth
Fahrkartenschalter^M
guichet^M de vente^F des billets^M
taquilla^F de venta^F de billetes^M
vendita^F dei biglietti^M

回転改札入り口
entrance turnstile
Eingangssperre^F
tourniquet^M d'accès^M
torniquete^M de entrada^F
tornelli^M di entrata^F

路線図
line map
Netzplan^M
carte^F de ligne^F
mapa^M de la ruta^F
cartello^M indicatore^M delle stazioni^F della linea^F

駅名
station name
Name^M der Station^F
nom^M de la station^F
nombre^M de la estación^F
nome^M della stazione^F

広告パネル
advertising panel
Werbetafel^F
panneau^M publicitaire
panel^M de publicidad^F
cartello^M pubblicitario

地下トンネル
tunnel
Tunnel^M
tunnel^M
túnel^M
galleria^F

地下鉄車両
subway train; *underground train*
U-Bahn-Zug^M
rame^F de métro^M
tren^M subterráneo
treno^M della metropolitana^F

線路
track
Gleis^N
voie^F
vía^F
binario^M

交通と機械

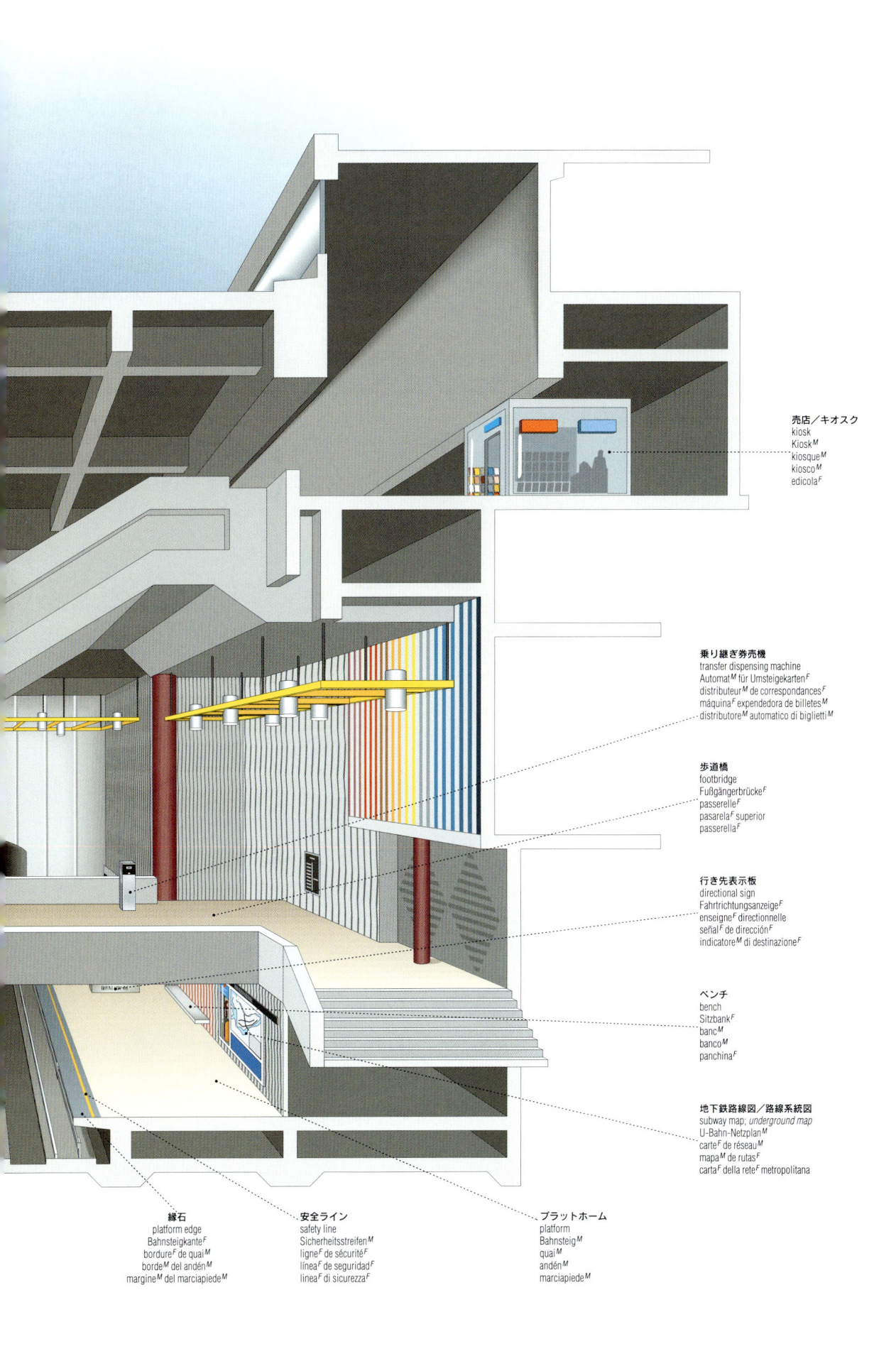

鉄道輸送 | RAIL TRANSPORT
SCHIENENVERKEHR | TRANSPORT FERROVIAIRE | TRANSPORTE FERROVIARIO | TRASPORTO SU ROTAIA

地下鉄

売店／キオスク
kiosk
KioskM
kiosqueM
kioscoM
edicolaF

乗り継ぎ券売機
transfer dispensing machine
AutomatM für UmsteigekartenF
distributeurM de correspondancesF
máquinaF expendedora de billetesM
distributoreM automatico di bigliettiM

歩道橋
footbridge
FußgängerbrückeF
passerelleF
pasarelaF superior
passerellaF

行き先表示板
directional sign
FahrtrichtungsanzeigeF
enseigneF directionnelle
señalF de direcciónF
indicatoreM di destinazioneF

ベンチ
bench
SitzbankF
bancM
bancoM
panchinaF

地下鉄路線図／路線系統図
subway map; *underground map*
U-Bahn-NetzplanM
carteF de réseauM
mapaM de rutasF
cartaF della reteF metropolitana

交通と機械

縁石
platform edge
BahnsteigkanteF
bordureF de quaiM
bordeM del andénM
margineM del marciapiedeM

安全ライン
safety line
SicherheitsstreifenM
ligneF de sécuritéF
líneaF de seguridadF
lineaF di sicurezzaF

プラットホーム
platform
BahnsteigM
quaiM
andénM
marciapiedeM

593

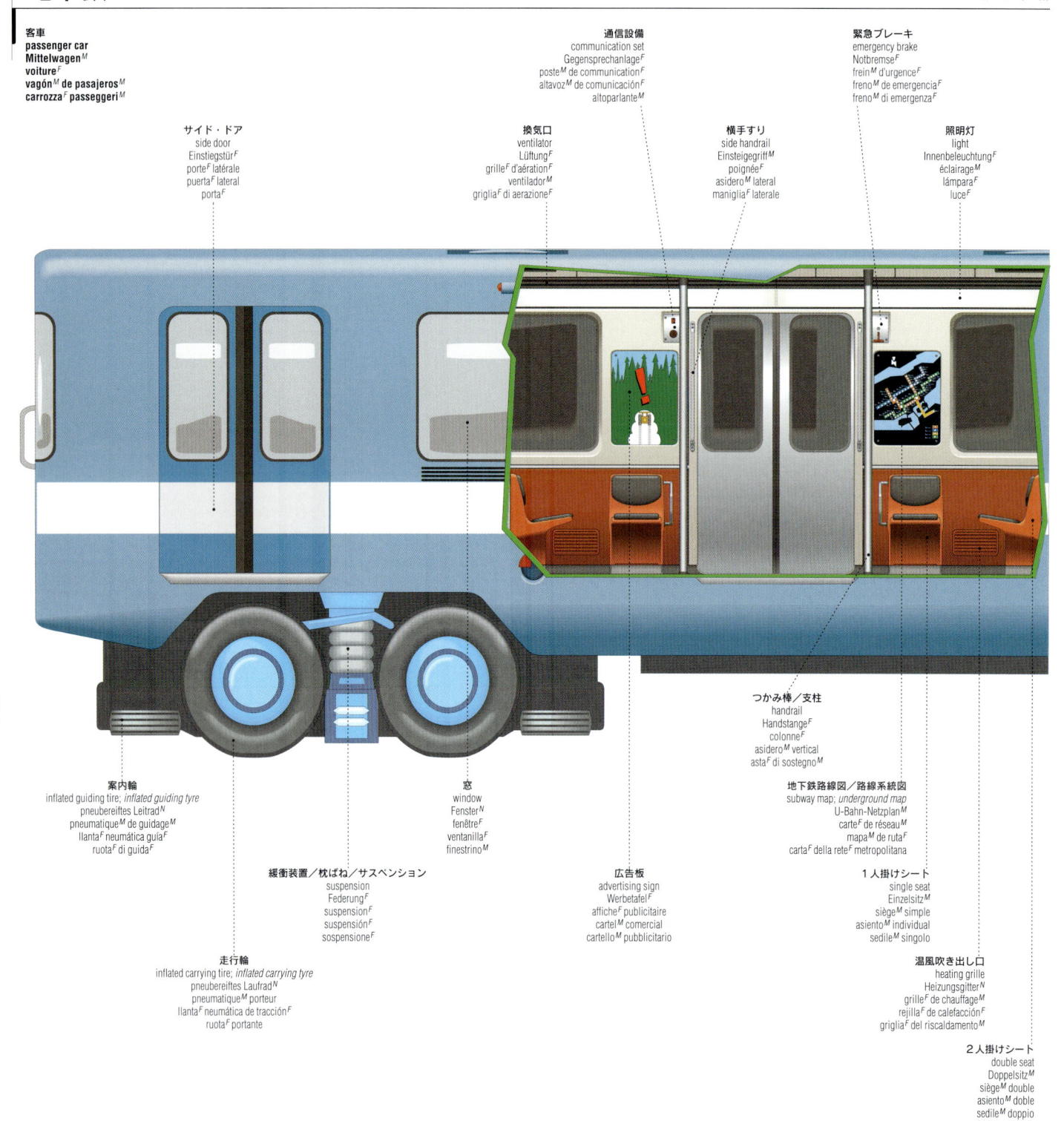

鉄道輸送 | RAIL TRANSPORT
SCHIENENVERKEHR | TRANSPORT FERROVIAIRE | TRANSPORTE FERROVIARIO | TRASPORTO SU ROTAIA

地下鉄

日本語 | 英語 | ドイツ語 | フランス語 | スペイン語 | イタリア語

客車
passenger car
Mittelwagen^M
voiture^F
vagón^M de pasajeros^M
carrozza^F passeggeri^M

サイド・ドア
side door
Einstiegstür^F
porte^F latérale
puerta^F lateral
porta^F

通信設備
communication set
Gegensprechanlage^F
poste^M de communication^F
altavoz^M de comunicación^F
altoparlante^M

緊急ブレーキ
emergency brake
Notbremse^F
frein^M d'urgence^F
freno^M de emergencia^F
freno^M di emergenza^F

換気口
ventilator
Lüftung^F
grille^F d'aération^F
ventilador^M
griglia^F di aerazione^F

横手すり
side handrail
Einsteigegriff^M
poignée^F
asidero^M lateral
maniglia^F laterale

照明灯
light
Innenbeleuchtung^F
éclairage^M
lámpara^F
luce^F

案内輪
inflated guiding tire; *inflated guiding tyre*
pneubereiftes Leitrad^N
pneumatique^M de guidage^M
llanta^F neumática guía^F
ruota^F di guida^F

窓
window
Fenster^N
fenêtre^F
ventanilla^F
finestrino^M

つかみ棒／支柱
handrail
Handstange^F
colonne^F
asidero^M vertical
asta^F di sostegno^M

地下鉄路線図／路線系統図
subway map; *underground map*
U-Bahn-Netzplan^M
carte^F de réseau^M
mapa^M de ruta^F
carta^F della rete^F metropolitana

緩衝装置／枕ばね／サスペンション
suspension
Federung^F
suspension^F
suspensión^F
sospensione^F

広告板
advertising sign
Werbetafel^F
affiche^F publicitaire
cartel^M comercial
cartello^M pubblicitario

1人掛けシート
single seat
Einzelsitz^M
siège^M simple
asiento^M individual
sedile^M singolo

走行輪
inflated carrying tire; *inflated carrying tyre*
pneubereiftes Laufrad^N
pneumatique^M porteur
llanta^F neumática de tracción^F
ruota^F portante

温風吹き出し口
heating grille
Heizungsgitter^N
grille^F de chauffage^M
rejilla^F de calefacción^F
griglia^F del riscaldamento^M

2人掛けシート
double seat
Doppelsitz^M
siège^M double
asiento^M doble
sedile^M doppio

地下鉄車両
subway train; *underground train*
U-Bahn-Zug^M
rame^F de métro^M
tren^M subterráneo
metropolitana^F

動力車
motor car
Triebwagen^M
motrice^F
vagón^M máquina^F
motrice^F

トレーラー客車／付随車
trailer car
Beiwagen^M
remorque^F
coche^M de tracción^F
rimorchio^M

動力車
motor car
Triebwagen^M
motrice^F
vagón^M máquina^F
motrice^F

交通と機械

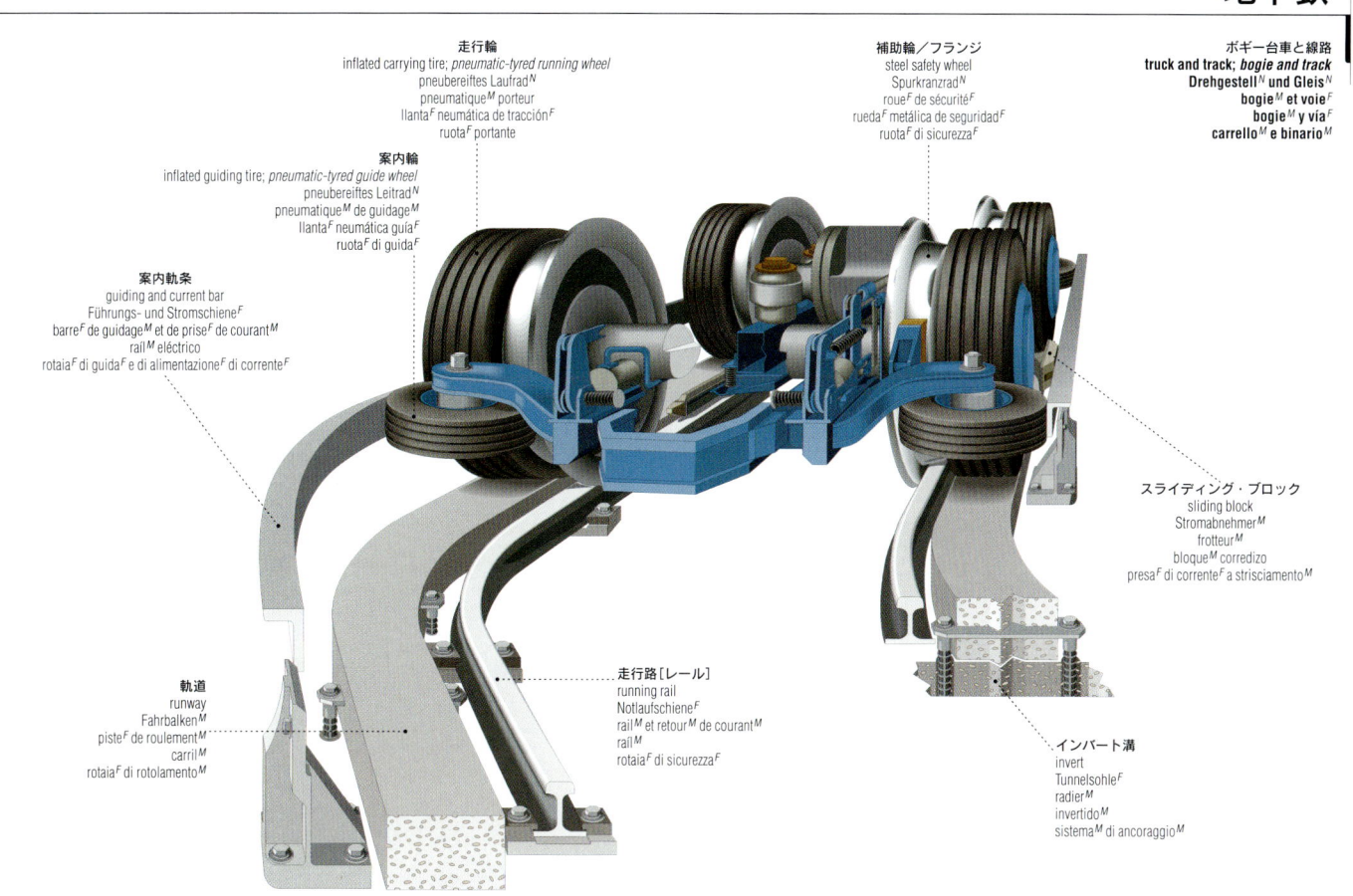

鉄道輸送 | RAIL TRANSPORT
SCHIENENVERKEHR | TRANSPORT FERROVIAIRE | TRANSPORTE FERROVIARIO | TRASPORTO SU ROTAIA

地下鉄

ボギー台車と線路
truck and track; *bogie and track*
Drehgestell^N und Gleis^N
bogie^M et voie^F
bogie^M y vía^F
carrello^M e binario^M

走行輪
inflated carrying tire; *pneumatic-tyred running wheel*
pneubereiftes Laufrad^N
pneumatique^M porteur
llanta^F neumática de tracción^F
ruota^F portante

補助輪／フランジ
steel safety wheel
Spurkranzrad^N
roue^F de sécurité^F
rueda^F metálica de seguridad^F
ruota^F di sicurezza^F

案内輪
inflated guiding tire; *pneumatic-tyred guide wheel*
pneubereiftes Leitrad^N
pneumatique^M de guidage^M
llanta^F neumática guía^F
ruota^F di guida^F

案内軌条
guiding and current bar
Führungs- und Stromschiene^F
barre^F de guidage^M et de prise^F de courant^M
rail^M eléctrico
rotaia^F di guida^F e di alimentazione^F di corrente^F

スライディング・ブロック
sliding block
Stromabnehmer^M
frotteur^M
bloque^M corredizo
presa^F di corrente^F a strisciamento^M

軌道
runway
Fahrbalken^M
piste^F de roulement^M
carril^M
rotaia^F di rotolamento^M

走行路［レール］
running rail
Notlaufschiene^F
rail^M et retour^M de courant^M
rail^M
rotaia^F di sicurezza^F

インバート溝
invert
Tunnelsohle^F
radier^M
invertido^M
sistema^M di ancoraggio^M

路面［市街］電車

streetcar; *streetcar* | Straßenbahn^F | tramway^M | tranvía^F | tram^M

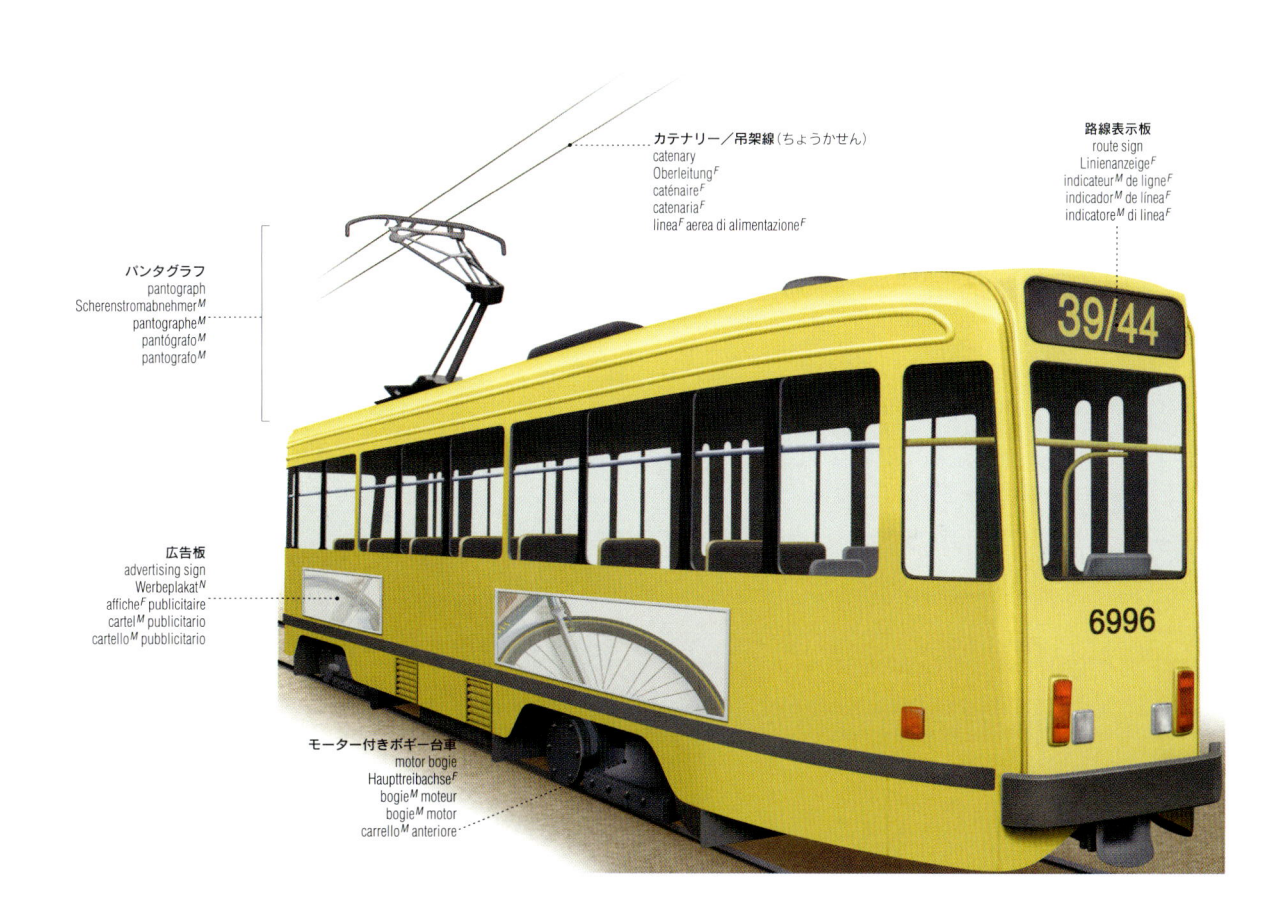

カテナリー／吊架線（ちょうかせん）
catenary
Oberleitung^F
caténaire^F
catenaria^F
linea^F aerea di alimentazione^F

路線表示板
route sign
Linienanzeige^F
indicateur^M de ligne^F
indicador^M de línea^F
indicatore^M di linea^F

パンタグラフ
pantograph
Scherenstromabnehmer^M
pantographe^M
pantógrafo^M
pantografo^M

広告板
advertising sign
Werbeplakat^N
affiche^F publicitaire
cartel^M publicitario
cartello^M pubblicitario

モーター付きボギー台車
motor bogie
Haupttreibachse^F
bogie^M moteur
bogie^M motor
carrello^M anteriore

交通と機械

595

海上交通 | MARITIME TRANSPORT
SCHIFFFAHRT | TRANSPORT MARITIME | TRANSPORTE MARÍTIMO | TRASPORTO MARITTIMO

港

日本語 | 英語 | ドイツ語 | フランス語 | スペイン語 | イタリア語

harbor; *harbour* | Hafen[M] | port[M] maritime | puerto[M] | porto[M] marittimo

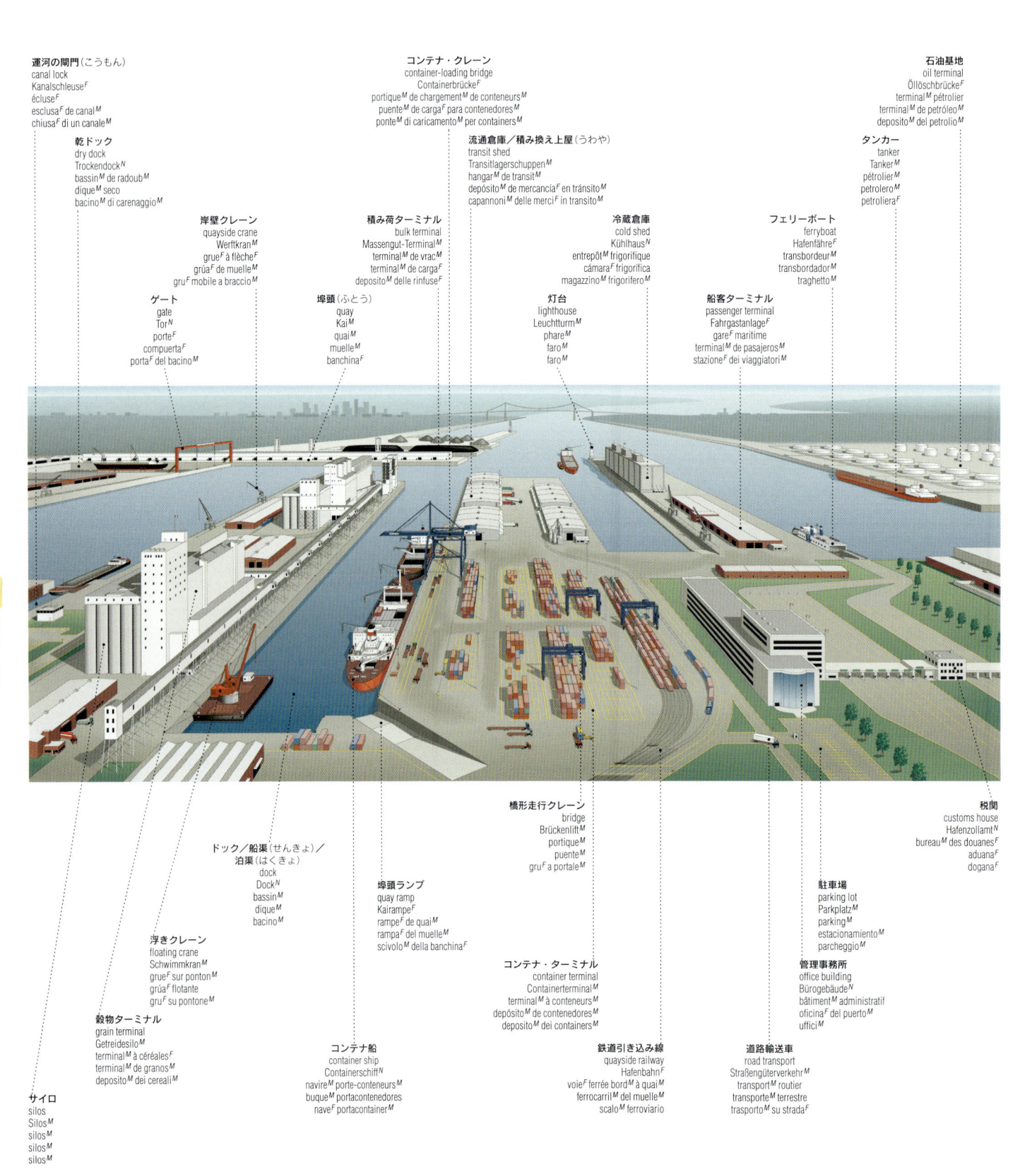

運河の閘門（こうもん）
canal lock
Kanalschleuse[F]
écluse[F]
esclusa[F] de canal[M]
chiusa[F] di un canale[M]

乾ドック
dry dock
Trockendock[N]
bassin[M] de radoub[M]
dique[M] seco
bacino[M] di carenaggio[M]

岸壁クレーン
quayside crane
Werftkran[M]
grue[F] à flèche[F]
grúa[F] de muelle[M]
gru[F] mobile a braccio[M]

ゲート
gate
Tor[N]
porte[F]
compuerta[F]
porta[F] del bacino[M]

コンテナ・クレーン
container-loading bridge
Containerbrücke[F]
portique[M] de chargement[M] de conteneurs[M]
puente[M] de carga[F] para contenedores[M]
ponte[M] di caricamento[M] per containers[M]

流通倉庫／積み換え上屋（うわや）
transit shed
Transitlagerschuppen[M]
hangar[M] de transit[M]
depósito[M] de mercancía[F] en tránsito[M]
capannoni[M] delle merci[F] in transito[M]

積み荷ターミナル
bulk terminal
Massengut-Terminal[M]
terminal[M] de vrac[M]
terminal[M] de carga[F]
deposito[M] delle rinfuse[F]

埠頭（ふとう）
quay
Kai[M]
quai[M]
muelle[M]
banchina[F]

冷蔵倉庫
cold shed
Kühlhaus[N]
entrepôt[M] frigorifique
cámara[F] frigorífica
magazzino[M] frigorifero

灯台
lighthouse
Leuchtturm[M]
phare[M]
faro[M]
faro[M]

石油基地
oil terminal
Öllöschbrücke[F]
terminal[M] pétrolier
terminal[M] de petróleo[M]
deposito[M] del petrolio[M]

タンカー
tanker
Tanker[M]
pétrolier[M]
petrolero[M]
petroliera[F]

フェリーボート
ferryboat
Hafenfähre[F]
transbordeur[M]
transbordador[M]
traghetto[M]

船客ターミナル
passenger terminal
Fahrgastanlage[F]
gare[F] maritime
terminal[M] de pasajeros[M]
stazione[F] dei viaggiatori[M]

橋形走行クレーン
bridge
Brückenlift[M]
portique[M]
puente[M]
gru[F] a portale[M]

ドック／船渠（せんきょ）／
泊渠（はくきょ）
dock
Dock[N]
bassin[M]
dique[M]
bacino[M]

埠頭ランプ
quay ramp
Kairampe[F]
rampe[F] de quai[M]
rampa[F] del muelle[M]
scivolo[M] della banchina[F]

コンテナ・ターミナル
container terminal
Containerterminal[M]
terminal[M] à conteneurs[M]
depósito[M] de contenedores[M]
deposito[M] dei containers[M]

税関
customs house
Hafenzollamt[N]
bureau[M] des douanes[F]
aduana[F]
dogana[F]

駐車場
parking lot
Parkplatz[M]
parking[M]
estacionamiento[M]
parcheggio[M]

管理事務所
office building
Bürogebäude[N]
bâtiment[M] administratif
oficina[F] del puerto[M]
uffici[M]

浮きクレーン
floating crane
Schwimmkran[M]
grue[F] sur ponton[M]
grúa[F] flotante
gru[F] su pontone[M]

穀物ターミナル
grain terminal
Getreidesilo[M]
terminal[M] à céréales[F]
terminal[M] de granos[M]
deposito[M] dei cereali[M]

コンテナ船
container ship
Containerschiff[N]
navire[M] porte-conteneurs[M]
buque[M] portacontenedores[M]
nave[F] portacontainer[M]

鉄道引き込み線
quayside railway
Hafenbahn[F]
voie[F] ferrée bord[M] à quai[M]
ferrocarril[M] del muelle[M]
scalo[M] ferroviario

道路輸送車
road transport
Straßengüterverkehr[M]
transport[M] routier
transporte[M] terrestre
trasporto[M] su strada[F]

サイロ
silos
Silos[M]
silos[M]
silos[M]
silos[M]

交通と機械

596

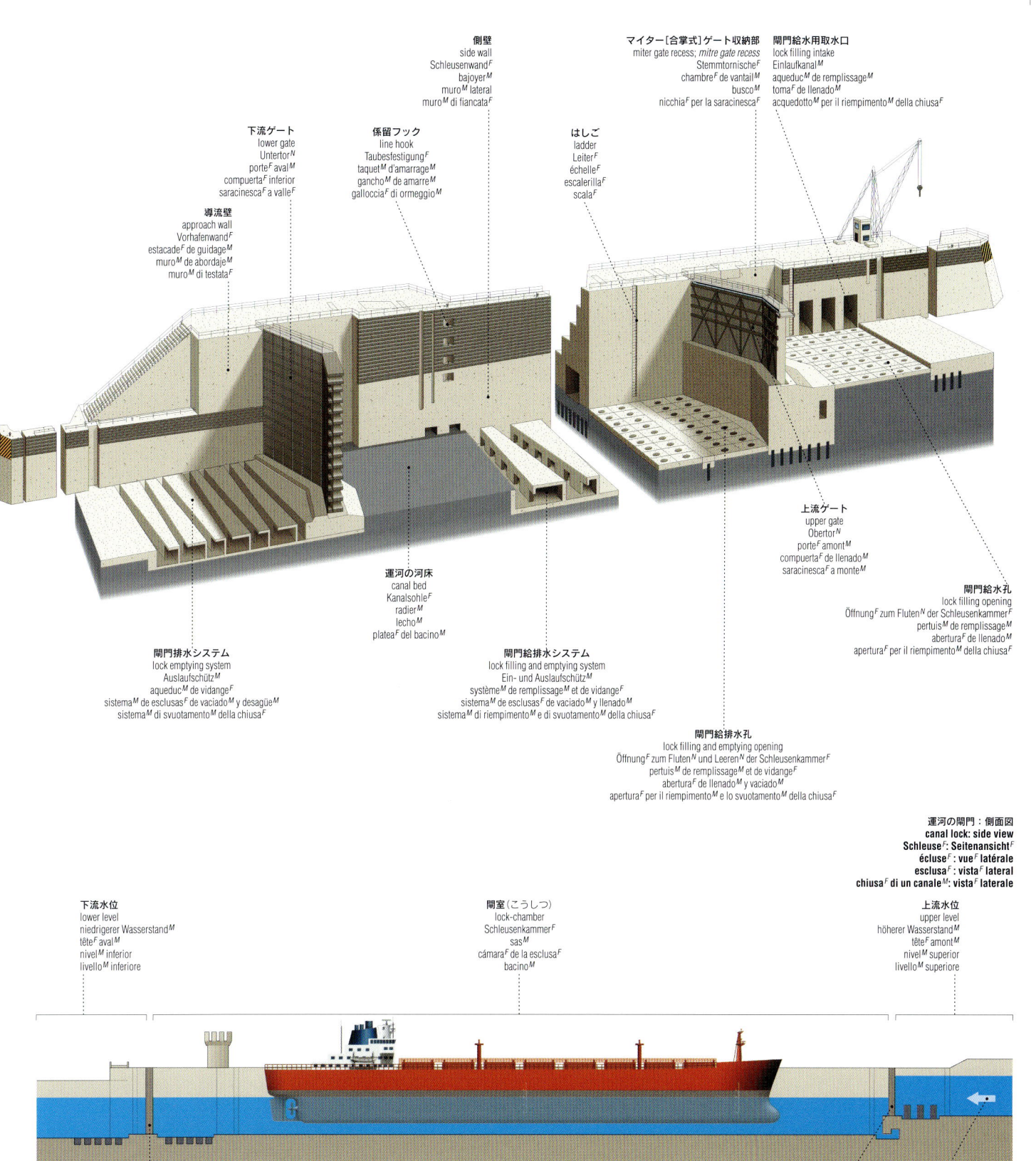

海上交通 | MARITIME TRANSPORT
SCHIFFFAHRT | TRANSPORT MARITIME | TRANSPORTE MARÍTIMO | TRASPORTO MARITTIMO

運河の閘門（こうもん）

canal lock | Kanalschleuse^F | écluse^F | esclusa^F de canal^M | chiusa^F di un canale^M

側壁
side wall
Schleusenwand^F
bajoyer^M
muro^M lateral
muro^M di fiancata^F

マイター[合掌式]ゲート収納部
miter gate recess; *mitre gate recess*
Stemmtornische^F
chambre^F de vantail^M
busco^M
nicchia^F per la saracinesca^F

閘門給水用取水口
lock filling intake
Einlaufkanal^M
aqueduc^M de remplissage^F
toma^F de llenado^M
acquedotto^M per il riempimento della chiusa^F

下流ゲート
lower gate
Untertor^N
porte^F aval^M
compuerta^F inferior
saracinesca^F a valle^F

係留フック
line hook
Taubesfestigung^F
taquet^M d'amarrage^M
gancho^M de amarre^M
galloccia^F di ormeggio^M

はしご
ladder
Leiter^F
échelle^F
escalerilla^F
scala^F

導流壁
approach wall
Vorhafenwand^F
estacade^F de guidage^M
muro^M de abordaje^M
muro^M di testata^F

上流ゲート
upper gate
Obertor^N
porte^F amont^M
compuerta^F de llenado^M
saracinesca^F a monte^M

運河の河床
canal bed
Kanalsohle^F
radier^M
lecho^M
platea^F del bacino^M

閘門給水孔
lock filling opening
Öffnung^F zum Fluten^N der Schleusenkammer^F
pertuis^M de remplissage^F
abertura^F de llenado^M
apertura^F per il riempimento della chiusa^F

閘門排水システム
lock emptying system
Auslaufschütz^N
aqueduc^M de vidange^F
sistema^M de esclusas^F de vaciado^M y desagüe^M
sistema^M di svuotamento^M della chiusa^F

閘門給排水システム
lock filling and emptying system
Ein- und Auslaufschütz^N
système^M de remplissage^F et de vidange^F
sistema^M de esclusas^F de vaciado^M y llenado^M
sistema^M di riempimento^M e di svuotamento^M della chiusa^F

閘門給排水孔
lock filling and emptying opening
Öffnung^F zum Fluten^N und Leeren^N der Schleusenkammer^F
pertuis^M de remplissage^F et de vidange^F
abertura^F de llenado^M y vaciado^M
apertura^F per il riempimento^M e lo svuotamento^M della chiusa^F

運河の閘門：側面図
canal lock: side view
Schleuse^F: Seitenansicht^F
écluse^F: vue^F latérale
esclusa^F: vista^F lateral
chiusa^F di un canale^M: vista^F laterale

下流水位
lower level
niedrigerer Wasserstand^M
tête^F aval
nivel^M inferior
livello^M inferiore

閘室（こうしつ）
lock-chamber
Schleusenkammer^F
sas^M
cámara^F de la esclusa^F
bacino^M

上流水位
upper level
höherer Wasserstand^M
tête^F amont
nivel^M superior
livello^M superiore

下流ゲート
lower gate
unteres Schleusentor^N
porte^F aval^M
puerta^F inferior
saracinesca^F a valle^F

上流ゲート
upper gate
oberes Schleusentor^N
porte^F amont^M
puerta^F superior
saracinesca^F a monte^M

（水の）流れ
flow
Strömung^F
courant^M
corriente^M
corrente^F

交通と機械

海上交通 | MARITIME TRANSPORT
SCHIFFFAHRT | TRANSPORT MARITIME | TRANSPORTE MARÍTIMO | TRASPORTO MARITTIMO

昔の船

日本語 | 英語 | ドイツ語 | フランス語 | スペイン語 | イタリア語

ancient ships | historische Schiffe[N] | embarcations[F] anciennes | embarcaciones[F] antiguas | imbarcazioni[F] antiche

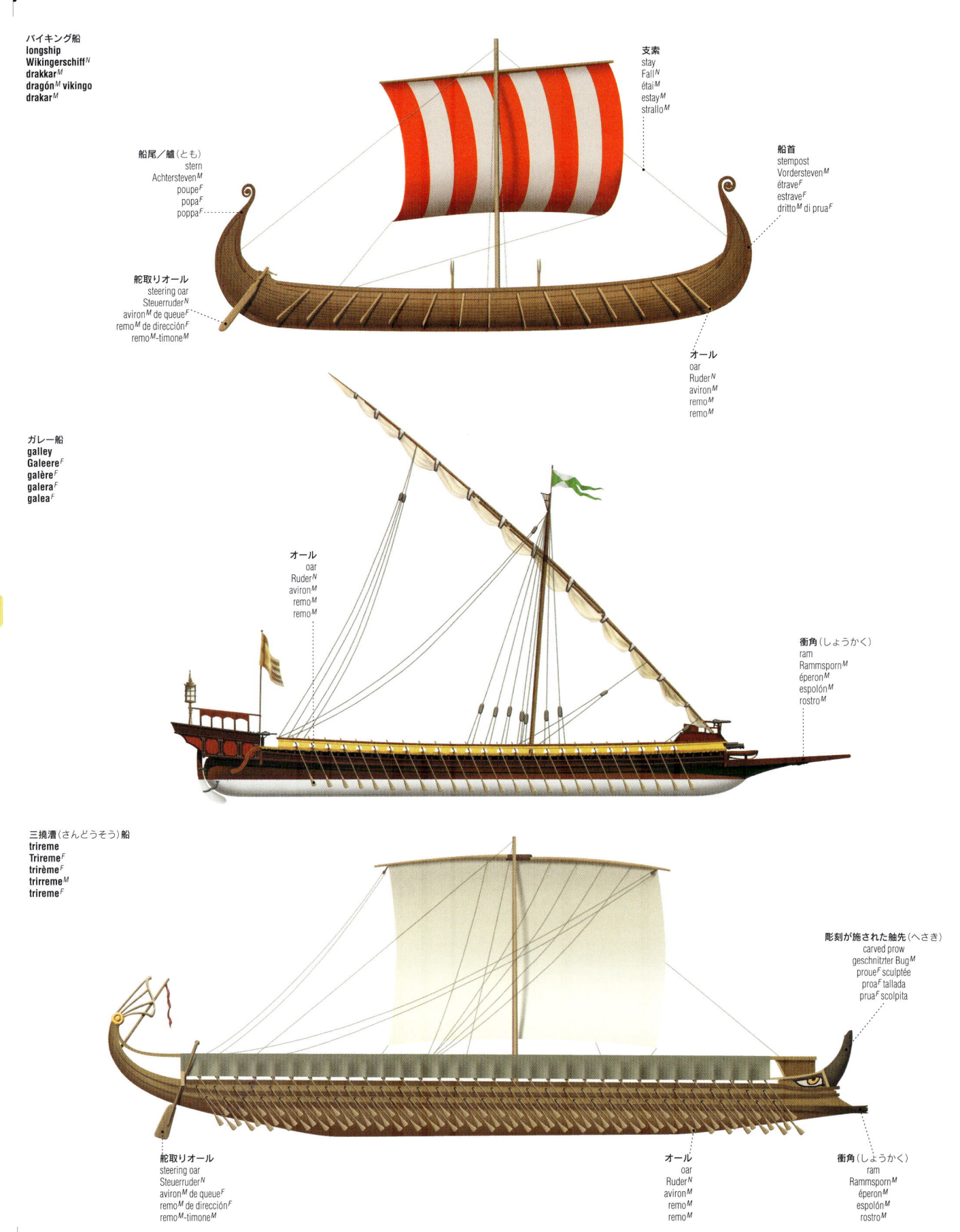

バイキング船
longship
Wikingerschiff[N]
drakkar[M]
dragón[M] vikingo
drakar[M]

支索
stay
Fall[N]
étai[M]
estay[M]
strallo[M]

船尾／艫（とも）
stern
Achtersteven[M]
poupe[F]
popa[F]
poppa[F]

船首
stempost
Vordersteven[M]
étrave[F]
estrave[F]
dritto[M] di prua[F]

舵取りオール
steering oar
Steuerruder[N]
aviron[M] de queue[F]
remo de dirección[F]
remo[M]-timone[M]

オール
oar
Ruder[N]
aviron[M]
remo[M]
remo[M]

ガレー船
galley
Galeere[F]
galère[F]
galera[F]
galea[F]

オール
oar
Ruder[N]
aviron[M]
remo[M]
remo[M]

衝角（しょうかく）
ram
Rammsporn[M]
éperon[M]
espolón[M]
rostro[M]

三撓漕（さんどうそう）船
trireme
Trireme[F]
trirème[F]
trirreme[M]
trireme[F]

彫刻が施された舳先（へさき）
carved prow
geschnitzter Bug[M]
proue[F] sculptée
proa[F] tallada
prua[F] scolpita

舵取りオール
steering oar
Steuerruder[N]
aviron[M] de queue[F]
remo[M] de dirección[F]
remo[M]-timone[M]

オール
oar
Ruder[N]
aviron[M]
remo[M]
remo[M]

衝角（しょうかく）
ram
Rammsporn[M]
éperon[M]
espolón[M]
rostro[M]

交通と機械

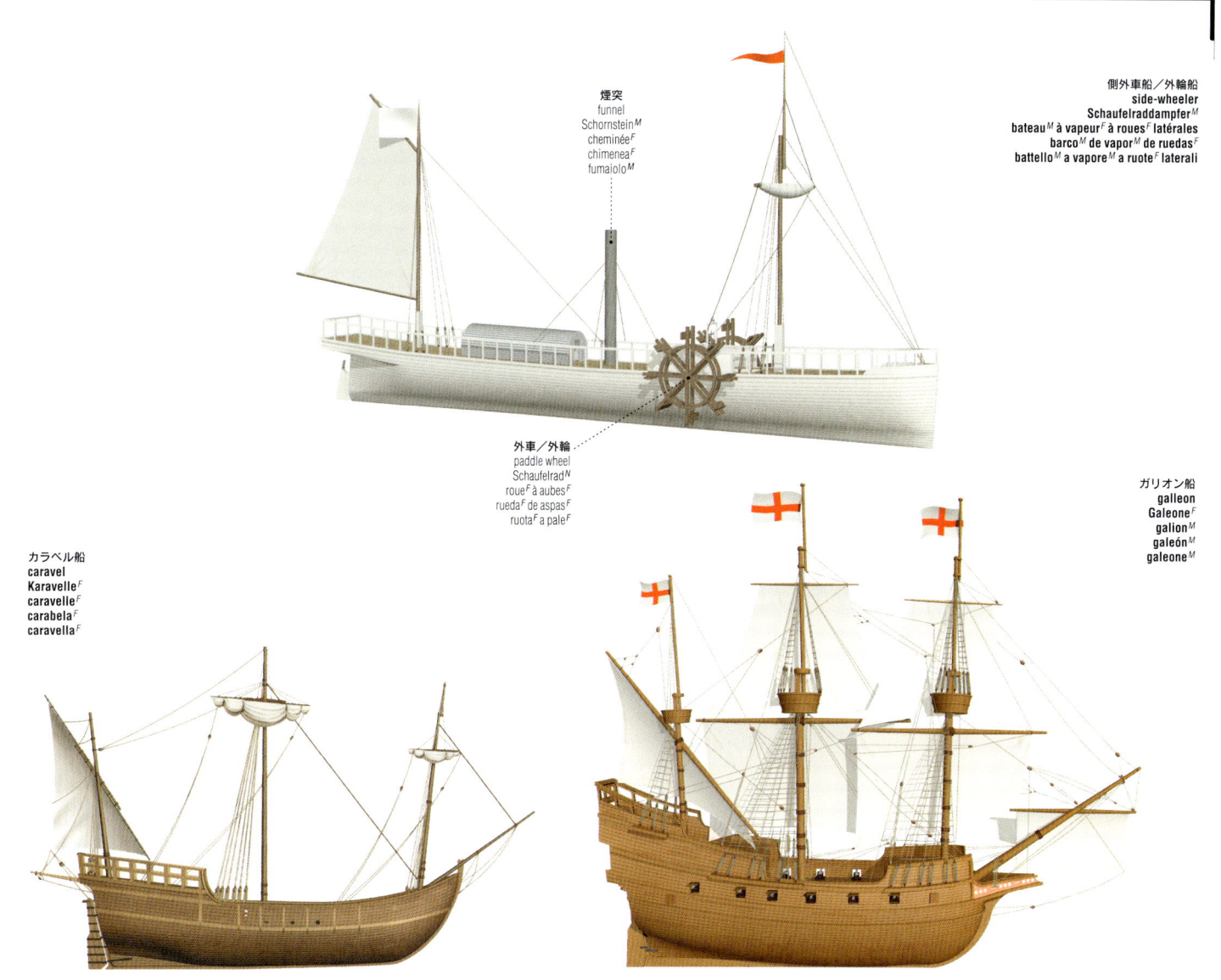

海上交通 | MARITIME TRANSPORT
SCHIFFFAHRT | TRANSPORT MARITIME | TRASPORTE MARÍTIMO | TRASPORTO MARITTIMO

昔の船

煙突
funnel
Schornstein^M
cheminée^F
chimenea^F
fumaiolo^M

側外車船／外輪船
side-wheeler
Schaufelraddampfer^M
bateau^M à vapeur^F à roues^F latérales
barco^M de vapor^M de ruedas^F
battello^M a vapore^M a ruote^F laterali

外車／外輪
paddle wheel
Schaufelrad^N
roue^F à aubes^F
rueda^F de aspas^F
ruota^F a pale^F

カラベル船
caravel
Karavelle^F
caravelle^F
carabela^F
caravella^F

ガリオン船
galleon
Galeone^F
galion^M
galeón^M
galeone^M

伝統的な船

traditional ships | traditionelle Boote^N | embarcations^F traditionnelles | embarcaciones^F tradicionales | imbarcazioni^F tradizionali

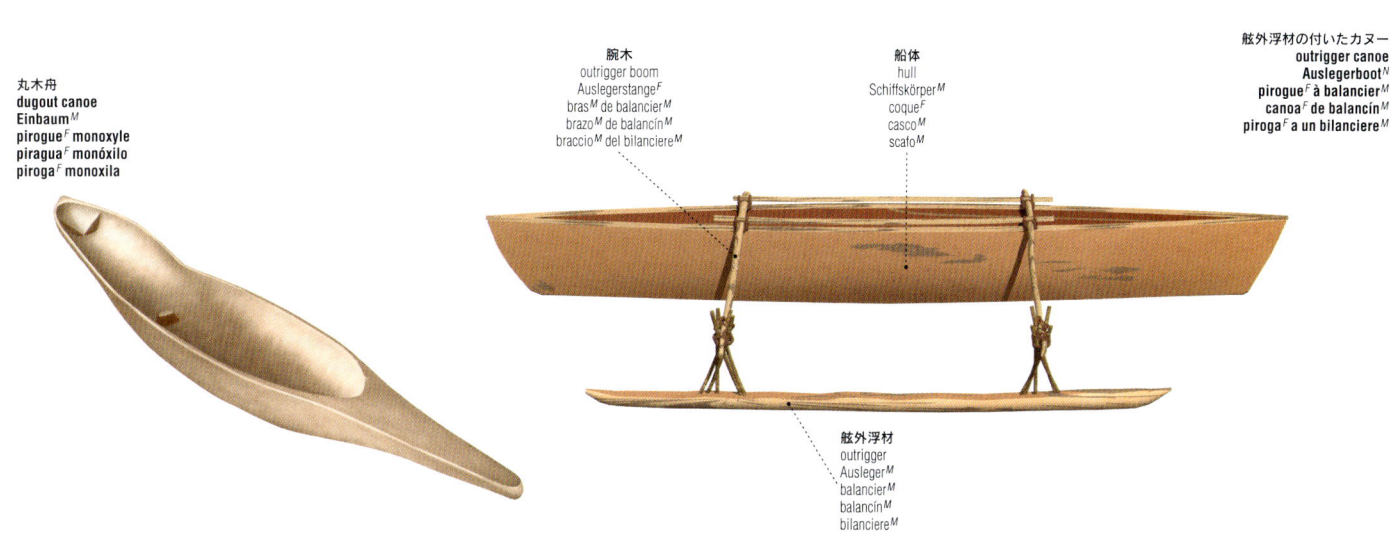

丸木舟
dugout canoe
Einbaum^M
pirogue^F monoxyle
piragua^F monóxilo
piroga^F monoxila

腕木
outrigger boom
Auslegerstange^F
bras^M de balancier^M
brazo^M de balancín^M
braccio^M del bilanciere^M

船体
hull
Schiffskörper^M
coque^F
casco^M
scafo^M

舷外浮材の付いたカヌー
outrigger canoe
Auslegerboot^N
pirogue^F à balancier^M
canoa^F de balancín^M
piroga^F a un bilanciere^M

舷外浮材
outrigger
Ausleger^M
balancier^M
balancín^M
bilanciere^M

599

伝統的な船

海上交通 | MARITIME TRANSPORT
SCHIFFFAHRT | TRANSPORT MARITIME | TRANSPORTE MARÍTIMO | TRASPORTO MARITTIMO

日本語 | 英語 | ドイツ語 | フランス語 | スペイン語 | イタリア語

ジャンク船
junk
Dschunke^F
jonque^F
junco^M
giunca^F

ミズンマスト／後檣（こうしょう）
mizzenmast
Besanmast^M
mât^M d'artimon^M
palo^M de mesana^F
albero^M di mezzana^F

メインマスト／大檣（だいしょう）／主檣
mainmast
Großmast^M
grand mât^M
palo^M mayor
albero^M di maestra^F

フォアマスト／前檣（ぜんしょう）
foremast
Fockmast^M
mât^M de misaine^F
palo^M de trinquete^M
albero^M di trinchetto^M

バッテン／当て木
batten
Segellatte^F
latte^F
quilla^F
canna^F

舵
rudder
Ruder^N
gouvernail^M
timón^M
timone^M

マスト
mast
Mast^M
mât^M
mástil^M
albero^M

オール
oar
Ruder^N
aviron^M
remo^M
remo^M

舳先（へさき）の装飾
prow ornament
Bugverzierung^F
ornement^M de proue^F
ornamento^M de proa^F
ornamento^M di prua^F

ゴンドラ
gondola
Gondel^F
gondole^F
góndola^F
gondola^F

舵
rudder
Ruder^N
gouvernail^M
timón^M
timone^M

大三角帆の帆桁
lateen yard
Rahe^F
antenne^F
entena^F
antenna^F

フェラッカ船
felucca
Feluke^F
felouque^F
falucho^M
feluca^F

カヌー
canoe
Kanu^N
canoë^M
canoa^F
canoa^F

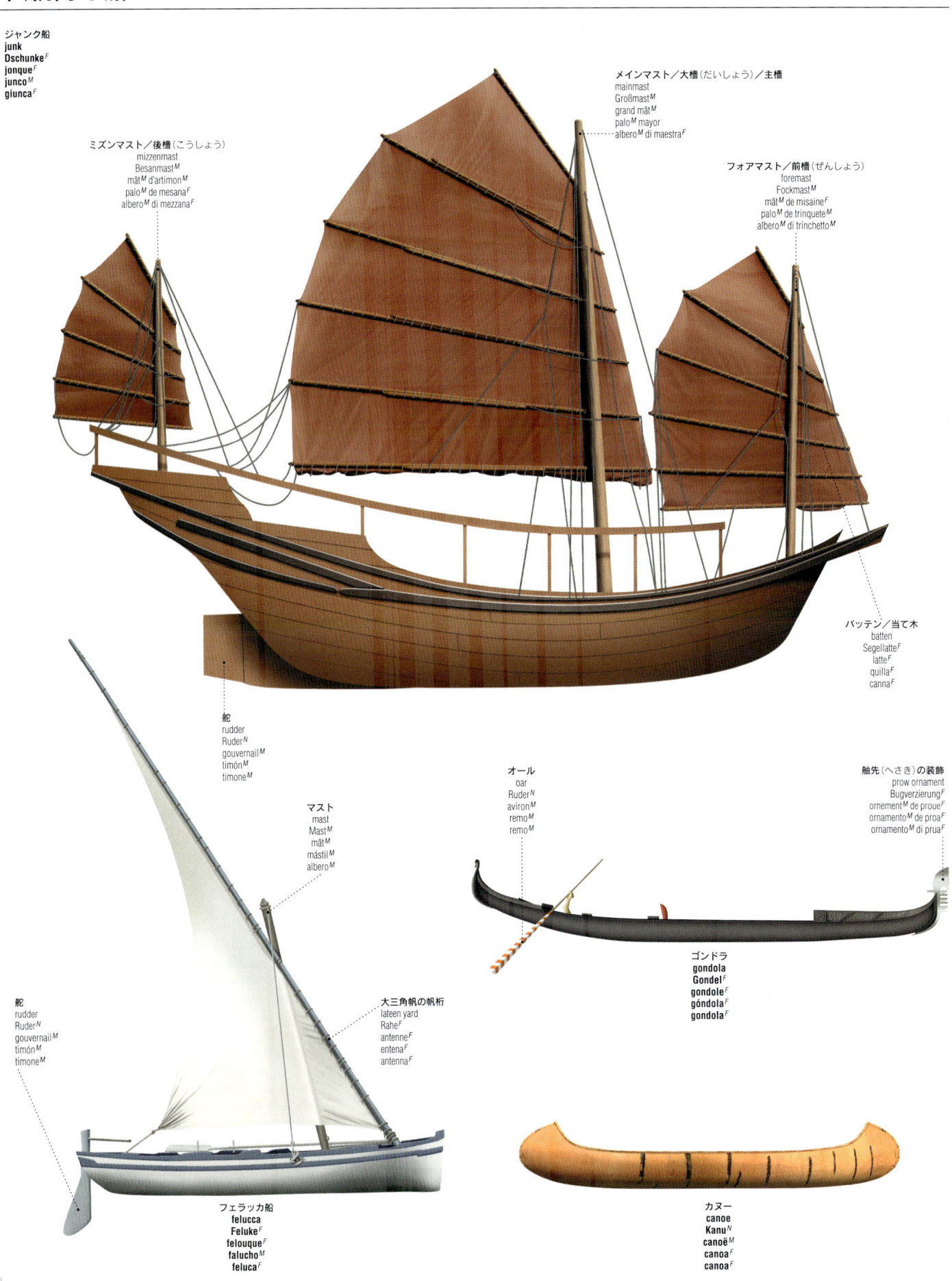

交通と機械

海上交通 | MARITIME TRANSPORT
SCHIFFFAHRT | TRANSPORT MARITIME | TRANSPORTE MARÍTIMO | TRASPORTO MARITTIMO

帆の例

examples of sails | Beispiele[N] für Segel[N] | exemples[M] de voiles[F] | ejemplos[M] de velas[F] | esempi[M] di vele[F]

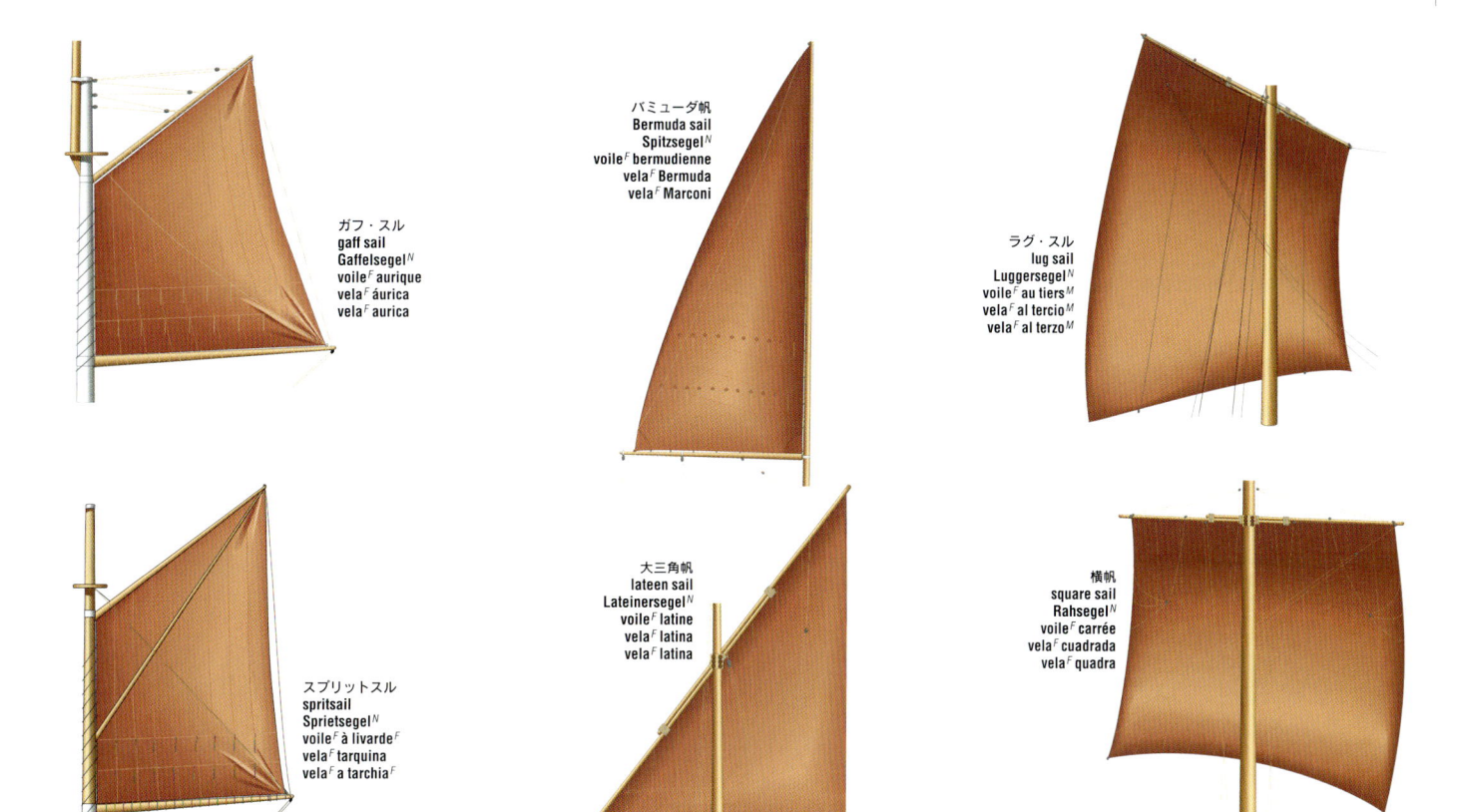

ガフ・スル
gaff sail
Gaffelsegel[N]
voile[F] aurique
vela[F] áurica
vela[F] aurica

バミューダ帆
Bermuda sail
Spitzsegel[N]
voile[F] bermudienne
vela[F] Bermuda
vela[F] Marconi

ラグ・スル
lug sail
Luggersegel[N]
voile[F] au tiers[M]
vela[F] al tercio[M]
vela[F] al terzo[M]

スプリットスル
spritsail
Sprietsegel[N]
voile[F] à livarde[F]
vela[F] tarquina
vela[F] a tarchia[F]

大三角帆
lateen sail
Lateinersegel[N]
voile[F] latine
vela[F] latina
vela[F] latina

横帆
square sail
Rahsegel[N]
voile[F] carrée
vela[F] cuadrada
vela[F] quadra

帆装の例

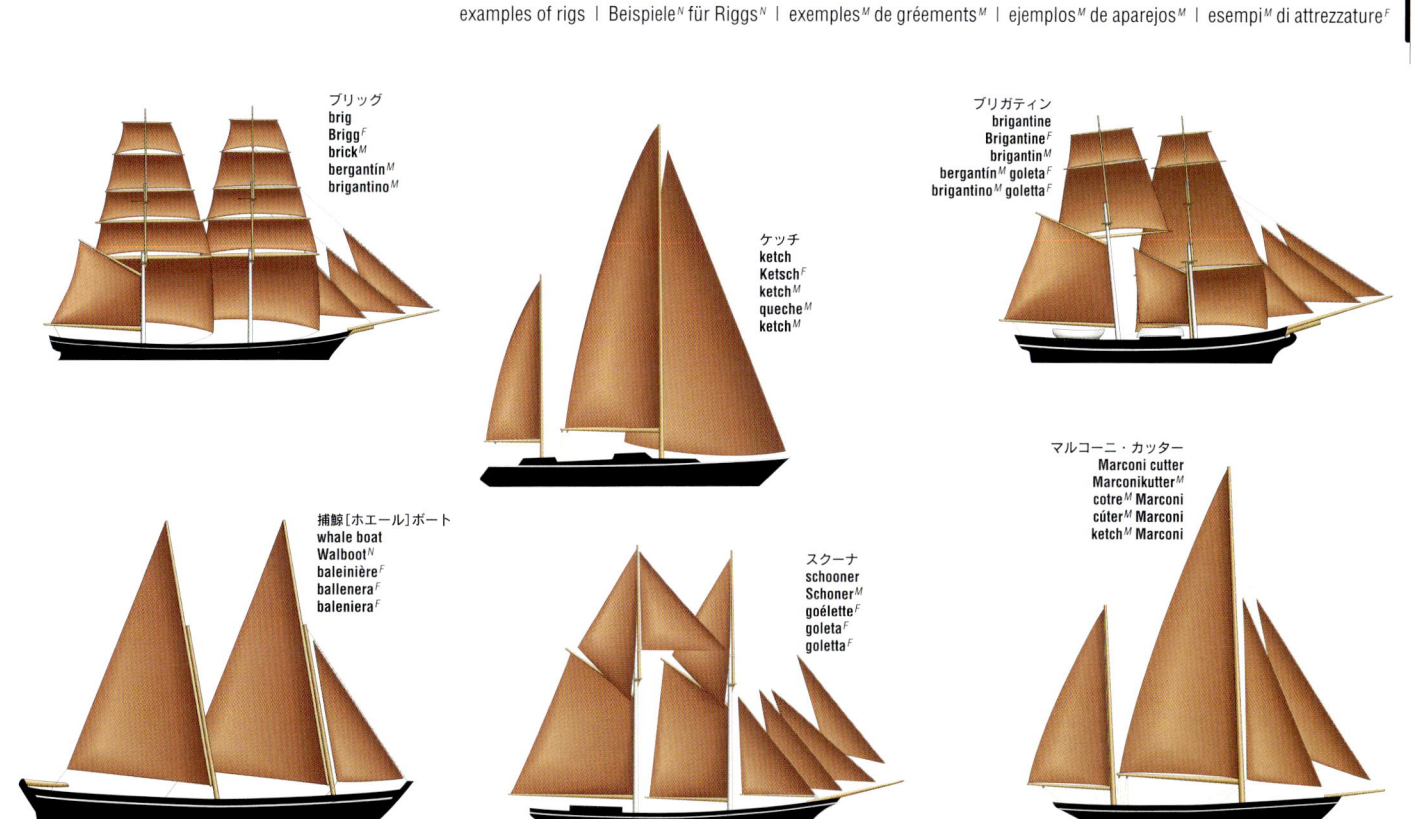

examples of rigs | Beispiele[N] für Riggs[N] | exemples[M] de gréements[M] | ejemplos[M] de aparejos[M] | esempi[M] di attrezzature[F]

ブリッグ
brig
Brigg[F]
brick[M]
bergantín[M]
brigantino[M]

ケッチ
ketch
Ketsch[F]
ketch[M]
queche[M]
ketch[M]

ブリガンティン
brigantine
Brigantine[F]
brigantin[M]
bergantín[M] goleta[F]
brigantino[M] goletta[F]

捕鯨［ホエール］ボート
whale boat
Walboot[N]
baleinière[F]
ballenera[F]
baleniera[F]

スクーナ
schooner
Schoner[M]
goélette[F]
goleta[F]
goletta[F]

マルコーニ・カッター
Marconi cutter
Marconikutter[M]
cotre[M] Marconi
cúter[M] Marconi
ketch[M] Marconi

601

海上交通 | MARITIME TRANSPORT
SCHIFFFAHRT | TRANSPORT MARITIME | TRANSPORTE MARÍTIMO | TRASPORTO MARITTIMO

4本マスト・バーク（型帆船）

日本語 | 英語 | ドイツ語 | フランス語 | スペイン語 | イタリア語

four-masted bark | Viermastbark^F | quatre-mâts^M barque^F | barco^M de vela^F de cuatro palos^M | veliero^M a quattro alberi^M

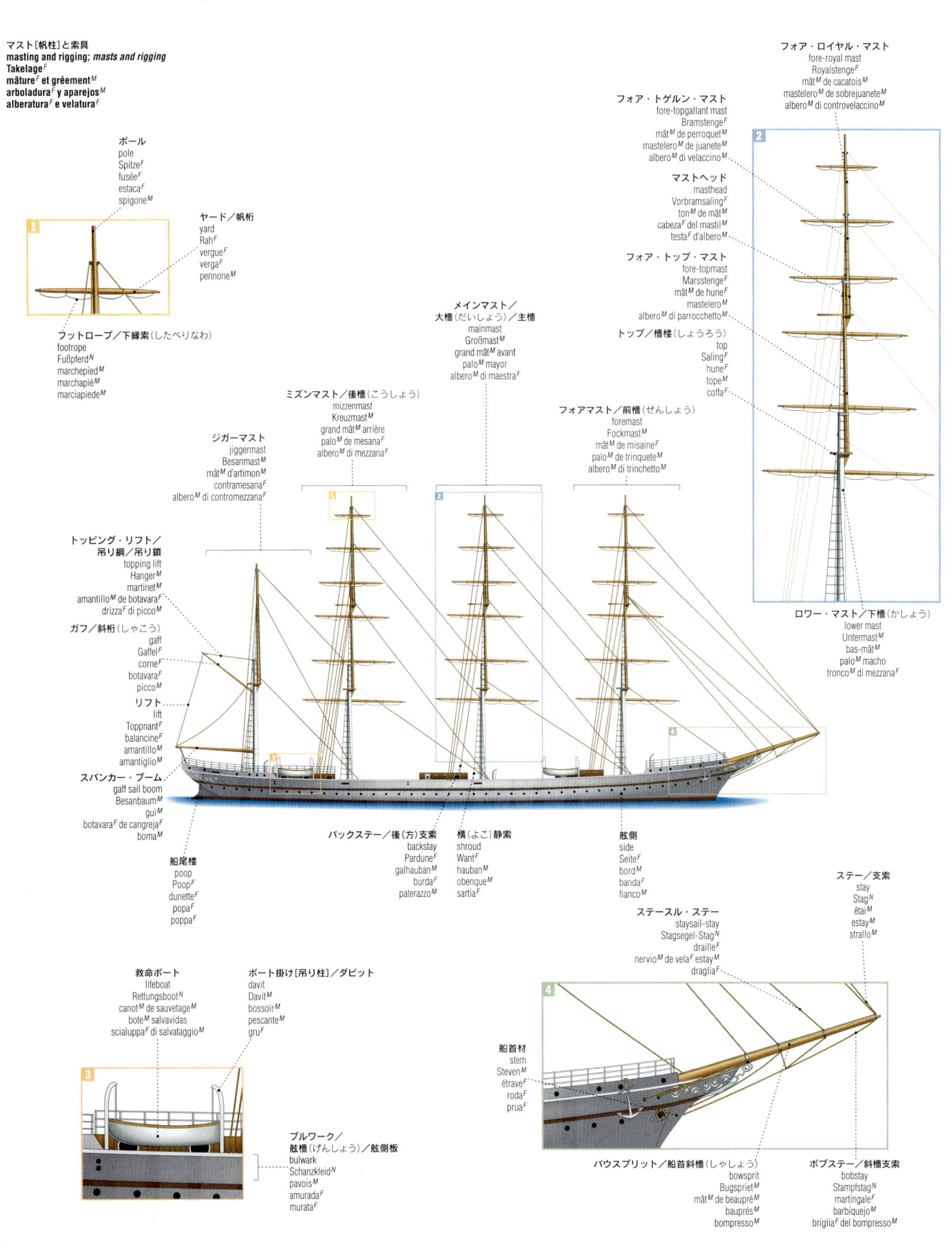

マスト[帆柱]と索具
masting and rigging; *masts and rigging*
Takelage^F
mâture^F et gréement^M
arboladura^F y aparejos^M
alberatura^F e velatura^F

ポール
pole
Spitze^F
fusée^F
estaca^F
spigone^M

ヤード／帆桁
yard
Rah^F
vergue^F
verga^F
pennone^M

フットロープ／下縁索（したべりなわ）
footrope
Fußpferd^N
marchepied^M
marchapié^M
marciapiede^M

メインマスト／
大檣（だいしょう）／主檣
mainmast
Großmast^M
grand mât avant
palo^M mayor
albero^M di maestra^F

ミズンマスト／後檣（こうしょう）
mizzenmast
Kreuzmast^M
grand mât arrière
palo^M de mesana^F
albero^M di mezzana^F

ジガーマスト
jiggermast
Besanmast^M
mât^M d'artimon^M
contramesana^F
albero^M di contromezzana^F

トッピング・リフト／吊り綱／吊り鎖
topping lift
Hanger^M
martinet
amantillo^M de botavara^F
drizza^F di picco^M

ガフ／斜桁（しゃこう）
gaff
Gaffel^F
corne^F
botavara^F
picco^M

リフト
lift
Toppnant^F
balancine^F
amantillo^M
amantiglio^M

スパンカー・ブーム
gaff sail boom
Besanbaum^M
gui^M
botavara^F de cangreja^F
boma^M

フォアマスト／前檣（ぜんしょう）
foremast
Fockmast^M
mât^M de misaine^F
palo^M de trinquete^M
albero^M di trinchetto^M

フォア・ロイヤル・マスト
fore-royal mast
Royalstenge^F
mât^M de cacatois
mastelero de sobrejuanete^M
albero^M di controvelaccino^M

フォア・トゲルン・マスト
fore-topgallant mast
Bramstenge^F
mât^M de perroquet^M
mastelero de juanete^M
albero^M di velaccino^M

マストヘッド
masthead
Vorbramsaling^F
ton^M de mât^M
cabeza^F del mastil^M
testa^F d'albero^M

フォア・トップ・マスト
fore-topmast
Marsstenge^F
mât^M de hune^F
mastelero
albero^M di parrocchetto^M

トップ／檣楼（しょうろう）
top
Saling^F
hune^F
tope^M
coffa^F

ロワー・マスト／下檣（かしょう）
lower mast
Untermast^M
bas-mât
palo^M macho
tronco^M di mezzana^F

バックステー／後(方)支索
backstay
Pardune^F
galhauban^M
burda^F
paterazzo^M

横（よこ）静索
shroud
Want^F
hauban^M
obenque^M
sartia^F

舷側
side
Seite^F
bord^M
banda^F
fianco^M

ステー／支索
stay
Stag^N
étai^M
estay^M
strallo^M

船尾楼
poop
Poop^F
dunette^F
popa^F
poppa^F

ステースル・ステー
staysail-stay
Stagsegel-Stag^N
draille^F
nervio^M de vela^F estay^M
draglia^F

救命ボート
lifeboat
Rettungsboot^N
canot^M de sauvetage^M
bote^M salvavidas
scialuppa^F di salvataggio^M

ボート掛け[吊り柱]／ダビット
davit
Davit^M
bossoir^M
pescante^M
gru^F

船首材
stem
Steven^M
étrave^F
roda^F
prua^F

ブルワーク／舷檣（げんしょう）／舷側板
bulwark
Schanzkleid^N
pavois^M
amurada^F
murata^F

バウスプリット／船首斜檣（しゃしょう）
bowsprit
Bugspriet^M
mât^M de beaupré^M
baupré^M
bompresso^M

ボブステー／斜檣支索
bobstay
Stampfstag^N
martingale^F
barbiquejo^M
briglia^F del bompresso^M

海上交通 | MARITIME TRANSPORT
SCHIFFFAHRT | TRANSPORT MARITIME | TRANSPORTE MARÍTIMO | TRASPORTO MARITTIMO

4本マスト・バーク（型帆船）

帆
sails
Segel^N
voilure^F
velamen^M
vele^F

ミズン・ロイヤル・ステースル
mizzen royal staysail
Kreuz-Royalstagsegel^N
voile^F d'étai^M de grand perroquet^M arrière
sobrejuanete^M de mesana^F de estay^M
vela^F di strallo^M di controvelaccio^M

ミズン・トゲルン・ステースル
mizzen topgallant staysail
Kreuz-Bramstagsegel^N
voile^F d'étai^M de hune^F arrière
juanete^M de mesana^F de estay^M
vela^F di strallo^M di velaccio^M

ミズン・トップマスト・ステースル
mizzen topmast staysail
Kreuz-Stengestagsegel^N
grand-voile^F d'étai^M arrière
mastelero^M de mesana^F de estay^M
vela^F di strallo^M di gabbia^F

ジガー・トゲルン・ステースル
jigger topgallant staysail
Besan-Bramstagsegel^N
voile^F d'étai^M de flèche^F
aparejo^M de juanete^M de estay^M
vela^F di strallo^M di belvedere^M

ジガー・トップマスト・ステースル
jigger topmast staysail
Besan-Stengestagsegel^N
marquise^F
aparejo^M de mastelero^M de estay^M
vela^F di strallo^M di mezzana^F

ミズン・ロイヤル・ブレース
mizzen royal brace
Kreuz-Royalbrasse^F
bras^M de grand cacatois^M arrière
brazas^M de sobrejuanete^M de mesana^F
braccio^M del pennone^M di controbelvedere^M

ガフ・トップスル
gaff topsail
Besantoppsegel^N
voile^F de flèche^F
escandalosa^F
controranda^F

スパンカー
spanker
Besan^M
brigantine^F
cangreja^F de popa^F
randa^F

メイン・ロイヤル・スル
main royal sail
Groß-Royalsegel^N
grand cacatois^M avant
sobrejuanete^M mayor
controvelaccio^M

メイン・アッパー・トゲルン・スル
main upper topgallant sail
Groß-Oberbramsegel^N
grand perroquet^M volant avant
juanete^M mayor proel alto
velaccio^M volante

メイン・ロワー・トゲルン・スル
main lower topgallant sail
Groß-Unterbramsegel^N
grand perroquet^M fixe avant
juanete^M mayor bajo
velaccio^M fisso

メイン・アッパー・トップスル
main upper topsail
Groß-Obermarssegel^N
grand hunier^M volant avant
gavia^F mayor alta
gabbia^F volante

フォア・ロイヤル・スル
fore royal sail
Vor-Royalsegel^N
petit cacatois^M
sobrejuanete^M de proa^F
controvelaccino^M

フォア・アッパー・トゲルン・スル
upper fore topgallant sail
Vor-Oberbramsegel^N
petit perroquet^M volant
juanete^M de proa^F alto
velaccino^M volante

フォア・ロワー・トゲルン・スル
lower fore topgallant sail
Vor-Unterbramsegel^N
petit perroquet^M fixe
juanete^M de proa^F bajo
velaccino^M fisso

フォア・アッパー・トップスル
upper fore topsail
Vor-Obermarssegel^N
petit hunier^M volant
gavia^F proel alta
parrocchetto^M volante

フライング・ジブ
flying jib
Flieger^M
clinfoc^M
petifoque^M
controfiocco^M

交通と機械

ミズン・スル
mizzen sail
Kreuzsegel^N
grand-voile^F arrière
cangreja^F mayor popel
vela^F di mezzana^F

メイン・スル
main sail
Großsegel^N
grand-voile^F avant
vela^F mayor proel
vela^F di maestra^F

ハリヤード
halyard
Fall^N
drisse^F
driza^F
drizza^F

シート／操帆索
sheet
Schot^F
écoute^F
escota^F
scotta^F

フォースル／フォアスル
foresail
Fock^F
misaine^F
trinquete^M
vela^F di trinchetto^M

メイン・ロワー・トップスル
main lower topsail
Groß-Untermarssegel^N
grand hunier^M fixe avant
gavia^F mayor baja
gabbia^F fissa

フォア・ロワー・トップスル
lower fore topsail
Vor-Untermarssegel^N
petit hunier^M fixe
gavia^F inferior proel
parrocchetto^M fisso

アウター・ジブ
outer jib
Außenklüver^M
grand foc^M
foque^M
fiocco^M

ミドル・ジブ
middle jib
Binnenklüver^M
faux foc^M
fofoque^M
fiocco^M di dentro

インナー・ジブ
inner jib
Vorstenge-Stagsegel^N
petit foc^M
contrafoque^M
trinchettina^F

リーフ・バンド／縮帆帯
reef band
Reffband^N
bande^F de ris^M
envergue^M de rizo^M
benda^F di terzarolo^M

リーフ・ポイント／縮帆索
reef point
Reffbänsel^N
garcette^F de ris^M
tomarrizos^M
matafione^M di terzarolo^M

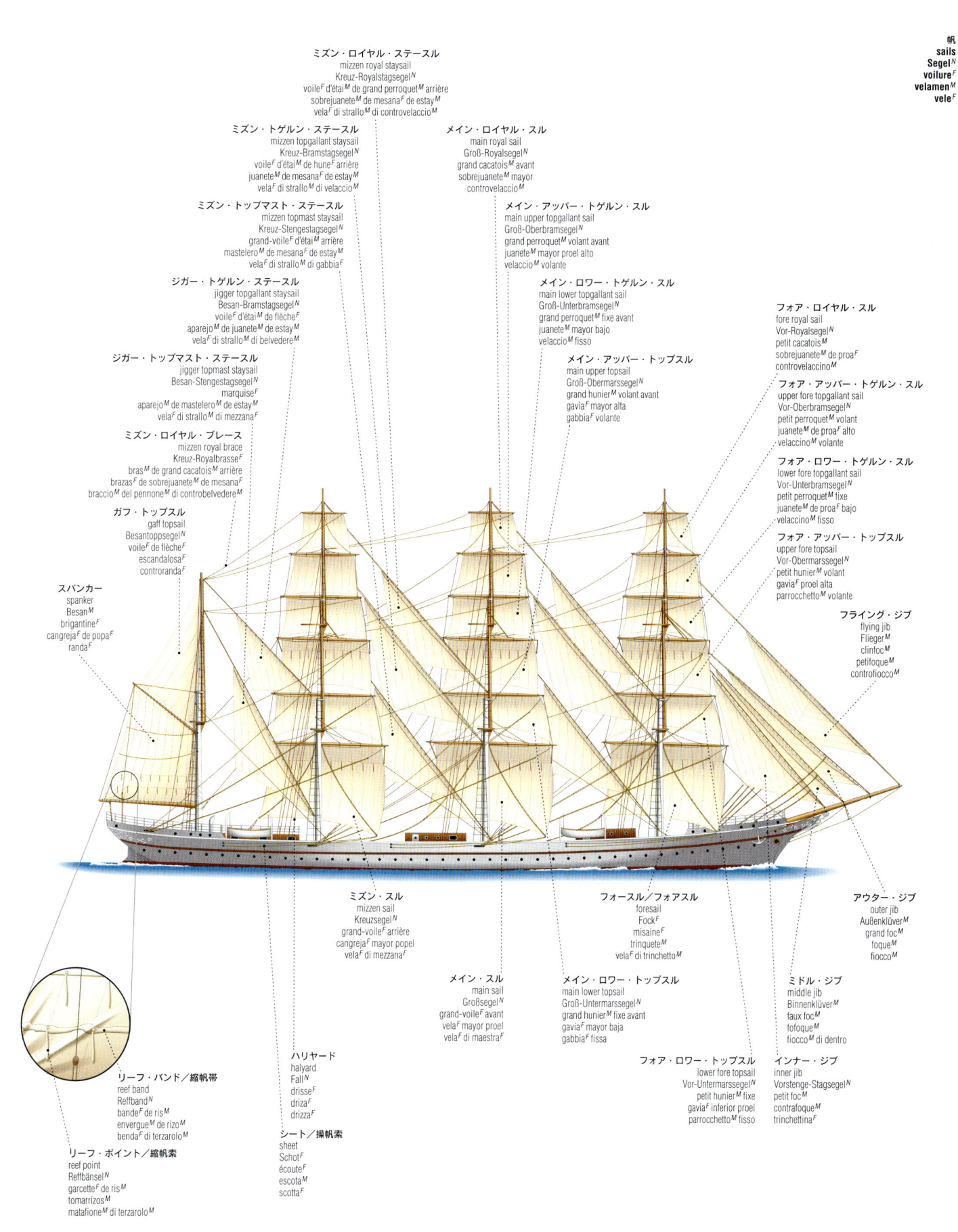

603

海上交通 | MARITIME TRANSPORT
SCHIFFFAHRT | TRANSPORT MARITIME | TRANSPORTE MARÍTIMO | TRASPORTO MARITTIMO

ボートと船の例

日本語 | 英語 | ドイツ語 | フランス語 | スペイン語 | イタリア語

examples of boats and ships | Beispiele^N für Boote^N und Schiffe^N | exemples^M de bateaux^M et d'embarcations^F | ejemplos^M de barcos^M y embarcaciones^M | esempi^M di barche^F e navi^F

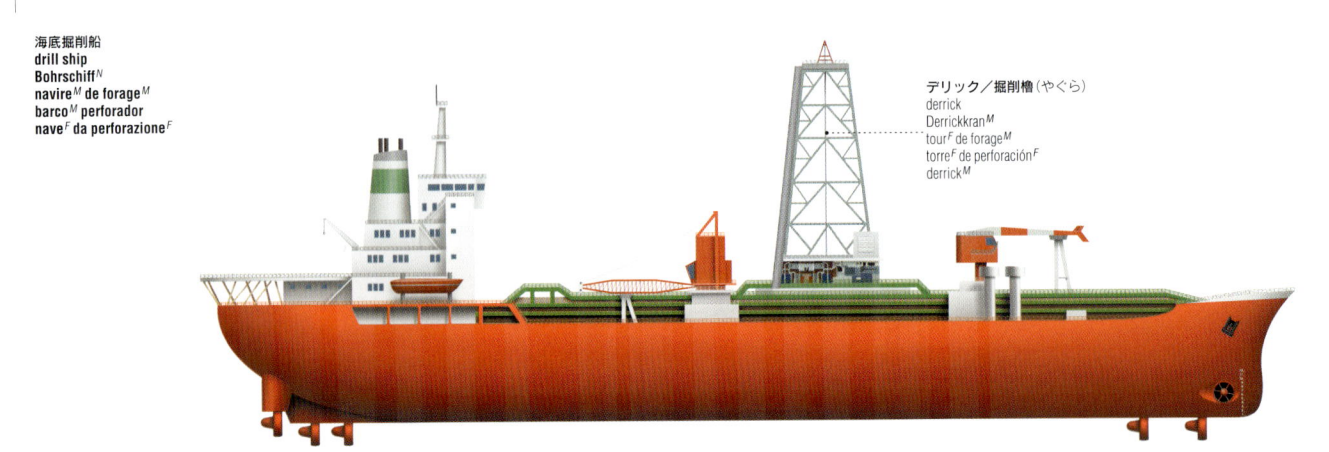

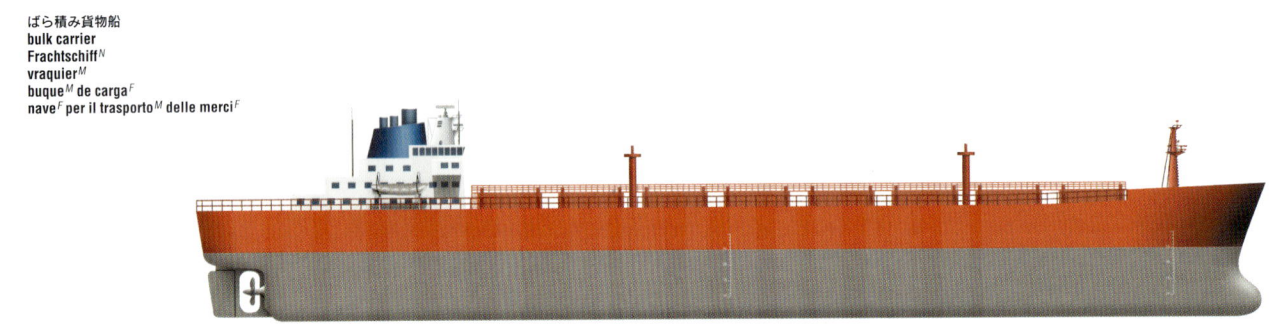

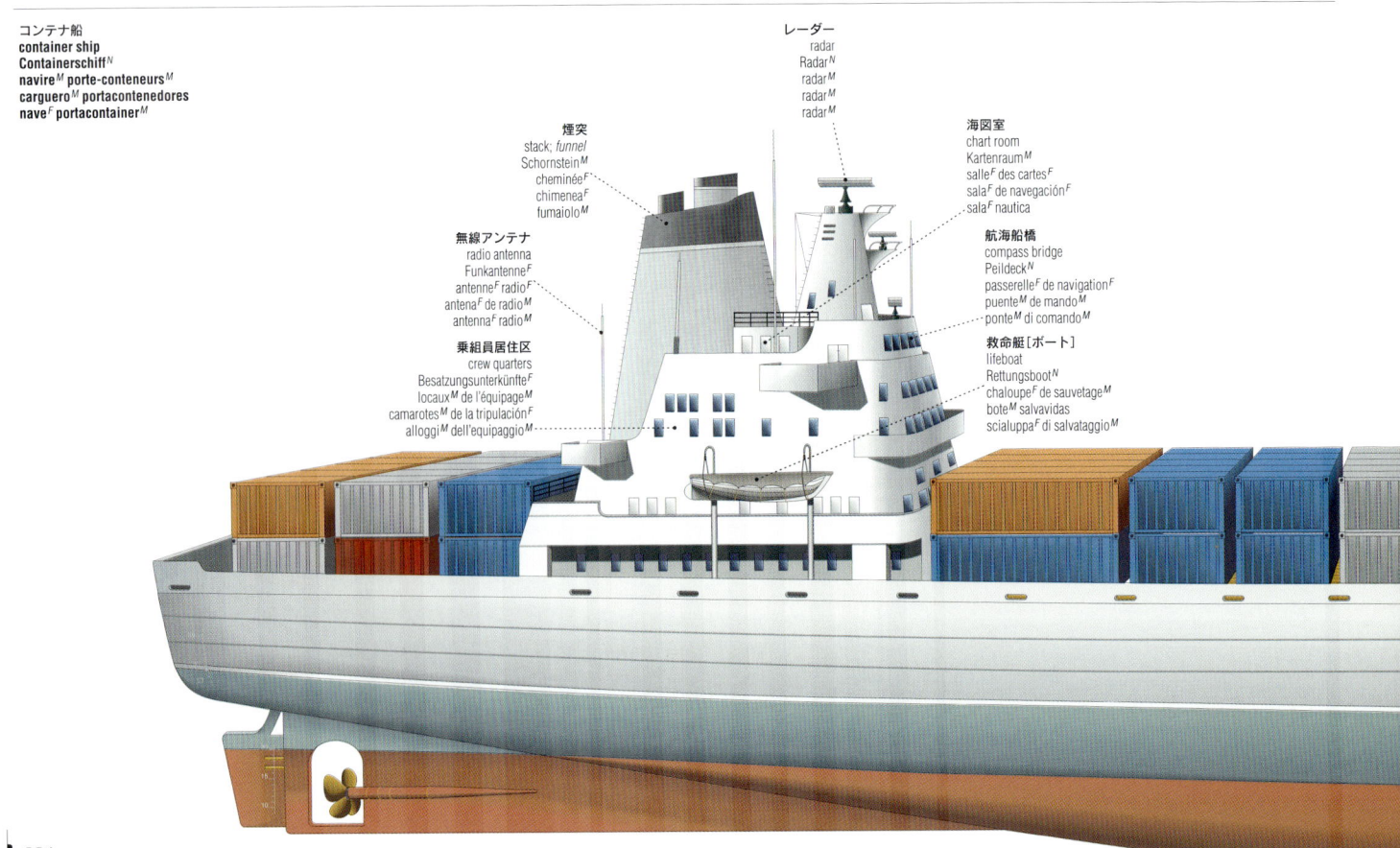

海底掘削船
drill ship
Bohrschiff^N
navire^M de forage^M
barco^M perforador
nave^F da perforazione^F

デリック／掘削櫓（やぐら）
derrick
Derrickkran^M
tour^F de forage^M
torre^F de perforación^F
derrick^M

ばら積み貨物船
bulk carrier
Frachtschiff^N
vraquier^M
buque^M de carga^F
nave^F per il trasporto^M delle merci^F

コンテナ船
container ship
Containerschiff^N
navire^M porte-conteneurs^M
carguero^M portacontenedores
nave^F portacontainer^M

レーダー
radar
Radar^N
radar^M
radar^M
radar^M

煙突
stack; funnel
Schornstein^M
cheminée^F
chimenea^F
fumaiolo^M

海図室
chart room
Kartenraum^M
salle^F des cartes^F
sala^F de navegación^F
sala^F nautica

無線アンテナ
radio antenna
Funkantenne^F
antenne^F radio^M
antena^F de radio^M
antenna^F radio^M

航海船橋
compass bridge
Peildeck^N
passerelle^F de navigation^F
puente^M de mando^M
ponte^M di comando^M

乗組員居住区
crew quarters
Besatzungsunterkünfte^F
locaux^M de l'équipage^M
camarotes^M de la tripulación^F
alloggi^M dell'equipaggio^M

救命艇［ボート］
lifeboat
Rettungsboot^N
chaloupe^F de sauvetage^M
bote^M salvavidas
scialuppa^F di salvataggio^M

交通と機械

604

海上交通 | MARITIME TRANSPORT
SCHIFFFAHRT | TRANSPORT MARITIME | TRANSPORTE MARÍTIMO | TRASPORTO MARITTIMO

ボートと船の例

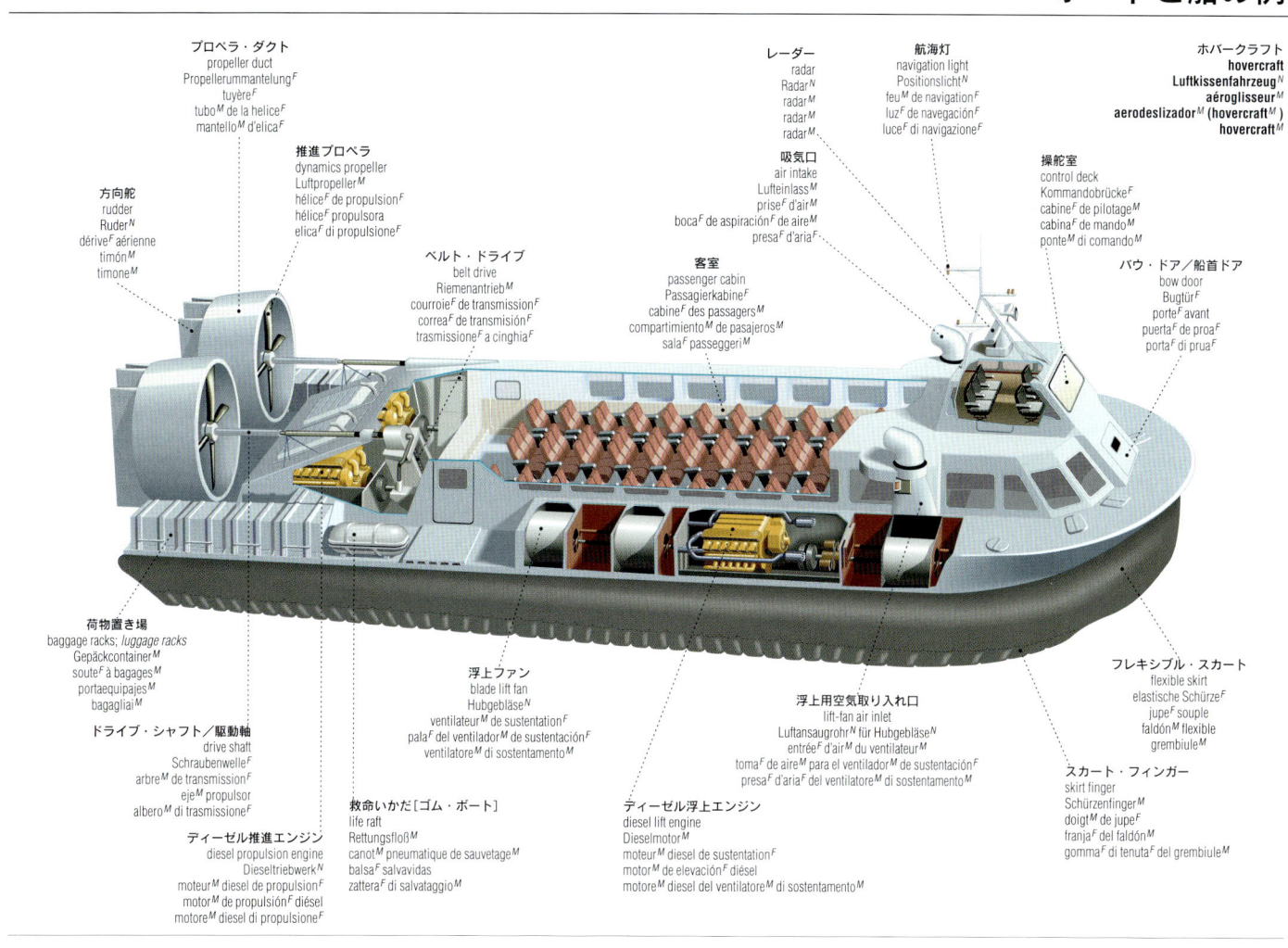

ホバークラフト
hovercraft
Luftkissenfahrzeug[N]
aéroglisseur[M]
aerodeslizador[M] (hovercraft[M])
hovercraft

プロペラ・ダクト
propeller duct
Propellerummantelung[F]
tuyère[F]
tubo[M] de la hélice[F]
mantello[M] d'elica[F]

推進プロペラ
dynamics propeller
Luftpropeller[M]
hélice[F] de propulsion[F]
hélice[F] propulsora
elica[F] di propulsione[F]

レーダー
radar
Radar[N]
radar[M]
radar[M]
radar[M]

航海灯
navigation light
Positionslicht[N]
feu[M] de navigation[F]
luz[F] de navegación[F]
luce[F] di navigazione[F]

方向舵
rudder
Ruder[N]
dérive[F] aérienne
timón[M]
timone[M]

吸気口
air intake
Lufteinlass[M]
prise[F] d'air[M]
boca[F] de aspiración[F] de aire[M]
presa[F] d'aria[F]

操舵室
control deck
Kommandobrücke[F]
cabine[F] de pilotage[F]
cabina[F] de mando[M]
ponte[M] di comando[M]

ベルト・ドライブ
belt drive
Riemenantrieb[M]
courroie[F] de transmission[F]
correa[F] de transmisión[F]
trasmissione[F] a cinghia[F]

客室
passenger cabin
Passagierkabine[F]
cabine[F] des passagers[M]
compartimiento[M] de pasajeros[M]
sala[F] passeggeri[M]

バウ・ドア／船首ドア
bow door
Bugtür[F]
porte[F] avant
puerta[F] de proa[F]
porta[F] di prua[F]

荷物置き場
baggage racks; luggage racks
Gepäckcontainer[M]
soute[F] à bagages[M]
portaequipajes[M]
bagagliai[M]

浮上ファン
blade lift fan
Hubgebläse[N]
ventilateur[M] de sustentation[F]
pala[F] del ventilador[M] de sustentación[F]
ventilatore[M] di sostentamento[M]

浮上用空気取り入れ口
lift-fan air inlet
Luftansaugrohr[N] für Hubgebläse[N]
entrée[F] d'air[M] du ventilateur[M]
toma[F] de aire[M] para el ventilador[M] de sustentación[F]
presa[F] d'aria[F] del ventilatore[M] di sostentamento[M]

フレキシブル・スカート
flexible skirt
elastische Schürze[F]
jupe[F] souple
faldón[M] flexible
grembiule[M]

ドライブ・シャフト／駆動軸
drive shaft
Schraubenwelle[F]
arbre[M] de transmission[F]
eje[M] propulsor
albero[M] di trasmissione[F]

救命いかだ［ゴム・ボート］
life raft
Rettungsfloß[N]
canot[M] pneumatique de sauvetage[M]
balsa[F] salvavidas
zattera[F] di salvataggio[M]

ディーゼル浮上エンジン
diesel lift engine
Dieselmotor[M]
moteur[M] diesel de sustentation[F]
motor[M] de elevación[F] diésel
motore[M] diesel del ventilatore[M] di sostentamento[M]

スカート・フィンガー
skirt finger
Schürzenfinger[M]
doigt[M] de jupe[F]
franja[F] del faldón[M]
gomma[F] di tenuta[F] del grembiule[M]

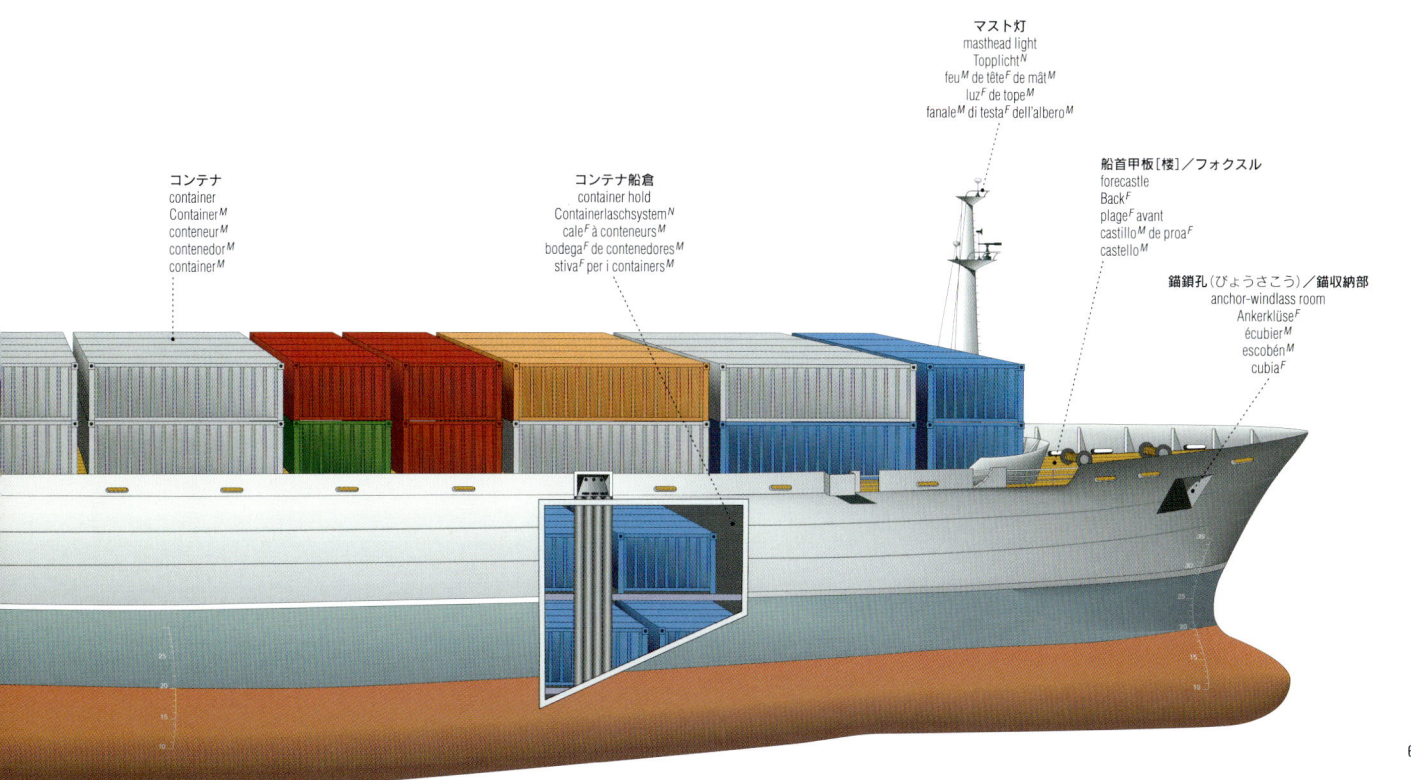

ディーゼル推進エンジン
diesel propulsion engine
Dieseltriebwerk[N]
moteur[M] diesel de propulsion[F]
motor[M] de propulsión[F] diésel
motore[M] diesel di propulsione[F]

コンテナ
container
Container[M]
conteneur[M]
contenedor[M]
container[M]

コンテナ船倉
container hold
Containerlaschsystem[N]
cale[F] à conteneurs[M]
bodega[F] de contenedores[M]
stiva[F] per i containers[M]

マスト灯
masthead light
Topplicht[N]
feu[M] de tête[F] de mât[M]
luz[F] de tope[M]
fanale[M] di testa[F] dell'albero[M]

船首甲板［楼］／フォクスル
forecastle
Back[F]
plage[F] avant
castillo[M] de proa[F]
castello

錨鎖孔（びょうさこう）／錨収納部
anchor-windlass room
Ankerklüse[F]
écubier[M]
escobén[M]
cubia[F]

605

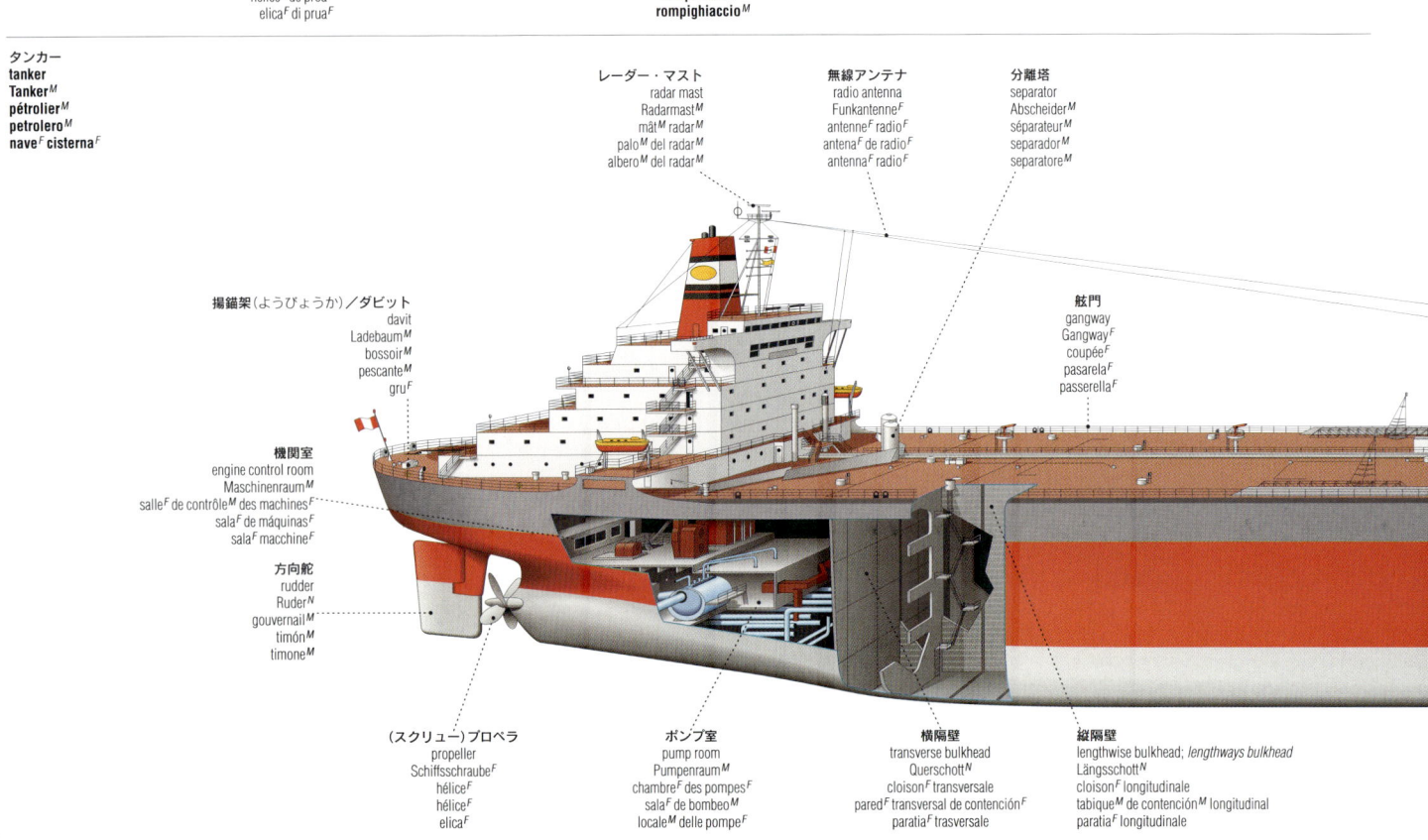

海上交通 | MARITIME TRANSPORT
SCHIFFFAHRT | TRANSPORT MARITIME | TRANSPORTE MARÍTIMO | TRASPORTO MARITTIMO

ボートと船の例

日本語 | 英語 | ドイツ語 | フランス語 | スペイン語 | イタリア語

トロール船
trawler
Trawler^M
chalutier^M
trainera^F
peschereccio^M

操舵室
wheelhouse
Ruderhaus^N
timonerie^F
cámara^F del timón^M
timoneria^F

引き船／タグボート
tug
Schlepper^M
remorqueur^M
remolcador^M
rimorchiatore^M

プロペラ
propeller
Schraube^F
hélice^F
hélice^F
elica^F

舵板
rudder blade
Ruderblatt^N
safran^M
pala^F de timón^M
pala^F del timone^M

船首
stem
Bug^M
étrave^F
proa^F
prua^F

船首プロペラ
stem propeller
Bugpropeller^M
hélice^F d'étrave^F
hélice^F de proa^F
elica^F di prua^F

砕氷船
ice breaker
Eisbrecher^M
brise-glace^M
rompehielos^M
rompighiaccio^M

後部プロペラ
rear propeller
Heckpropeller^M
hélice^F arrière
hélice^F posterior
elica^F posteriore

タンカー
tanker
Tanker^M
pétrolier^M
petrolero^M
nave^F cisterna^F

レーダー・マスト
radar mast
Radarmast^M
mât^M radar
palo^M del radar^M
albero^M del radar^M

無線アンテナ
radio antenna
Funkantenne^F
antenne^F radio^F
antena^F de radio^F
antenna^F radio^F

分離塔
separator
Abscheider^M
séparateur^M
separador^M
separatore^M

揚錨架（ようびょうか）／ダビット
davit
Ladebaum^M
bossoir^M
pescante^M
gru^F

舷門
gangway
Gangway^F
coupée^F
pasarela^F
passerella^F

機関室
engine control room
Maschinenraum^M
salle^F de contrôle^M des machines^F
sala^F de máquinas^F
sala^F macchine^F

方向舵
rudder
Ruder^N
gouvernail^M
timón^M
timone^M

（スクリュー）プロペラ
propeller
Schiffsschraube^F
hélice^F
hélice^F
elica^F

ポンプ室
pump room
Pumpenraum^M
chambre^F des pompes^F
sala^F de bombeo^M
locale^M delle pompe^F

横隔壁
transverse bulkhead
Querschott^N
cloison^F transversale
pared^F transversal de contención^F
paratia^F trasversale

縦隔壁
lengthwise bulkhead; lengthways bulkhead
Längsschott^N
cloison^F longitudinale
tabique^M de contención^M longitudinal
paratia^F longitudinale

海上交通 | MARITIME TRANSPORT
SCHIFFFAHRT | TRANSPORT MARITIME | TRANSPORTE MARÍTIMO | TRASPORTO MARITTIMO

ボートと船の例

甲板通路
fore and aft passage
Laufbrücke^F
passavant^M
paso^M de popa^F a proa
passavanti^M

操舵室
pilot house
Steuerhaus^N
cabine^F de pilotage^M
cabina^F de pilotaje^M
cabina^F di pilotaggio^M

操舵輪／(舵取り)ハンドル
steering wheel
Lenkrad^N
volant^M
volante^M
volante^M

船外機
outboard engine; *outboard engine*
Außenbordmotor^M
moteur^M hors-bord
motor^M fueraborda^M
motore^M fuoribordo^M

ハウスボート
houseboat
Hausboot^N
caravane^F flottante
casa^F flotante
casa^F galleggiante

風防ガラス／ウインドシールド
windshield
Windschutzscheibe^F
pare-brise^M
parabrisas^F
parabrezza^M

手すり
handrail
Reling^F
main^F courante
pasamano^M
corrimano^M

サン・デッキ
sun deck
Sonnendeck^N
solarium^M
cubierta^F de sol^M
solarium^M

手すり
handrail
Reling^F
main^F courante
pasamano^M
corrimano^M

小型モーターボート
runabout
Motorboot^N
canot^M automobile
lancha^F pequeña
motoscafo^M da diporto^M

モーター・ヨット
motor yacht
Motorjacht^F
yacht^M à moteur^M
yate^M de motor^M
yacht^M a motore^M

デリック／荷役マスト
derrick
Ladebaum^M
mât^M de charge^F
grúa^F
derrick^M

デリック[門型]ポスト／小マスト
derrick mast
Lademast^M
mâtereau^M
poste^M de la grúa^F
albero^M del derrick^M

タンクのハッチ
tank hatch
Tankluke^F
panneau^M de citerne^F
compuerta^F de la cisterna^F
portello^M di accesso^M

空気逃がし弁
air relief valve
Entlüftungsventil^N
dégagement^M d'air^M des citernes^F
válvula^F de liberación^F de aire^M
valvola^F di sfiato^M

消火泡モニター
foam monitor
Schaumanzeiger^M
canon^M à mousse^F
cañón^M expulsor de espuma^F
lancia^F antincendio^M schiumogena

前部マスト
foremast
Vordermast^M
mât^M avant
palo^M de proa^F
albero^M prodiero

係船ウィンチ
mooring winch
Verhol-Winde^F
treuil^M d'amarrage^M
amarra^F
verricello^M di ormeggio^M

タンク
tank
Tank^M
citerne^F
tanque^M
cisterna^F

メイン・デッキ
main deck
Hauptdeck^N
pont^M principal
cubierta^F principal
ponte^M di coperta^F

係柱／ビット
bitt
Poller^M
bitte^F
bita^F
bitta^F

船荷用横梁（おうりょう）
crossover cargo deck line
Umladeabschnitt^M
traverse^F de chargement^M
zona^F de traspaso^M de carga^F
tubolatura^F di carico^M trasversale

船側
wall side
Geradseite^F
muraille^F
pared^F lateral
murata^F

ウェブ・フレーム
web frame
Rahmenspant^M
porque^F
cuaderna^F
ordinata^F rinforzata

中央ケルソン[キルソン]
center keelson; *centre Keelson*
Mittelkielschwein^N
carlingue^F centrale
contraquilla^F
paramezzale^M centrale

球状船首
bulb
Bugwulst^F
bulbe^M d'étrave^F
bulbo^M
bulbo^M

交通と機械

607

海上交通 | MARITIME TRANSPORT
SCHIFFFAHRT | TRANSPORT MARITIME | TRANSPORTE MARÍTIMO | TRASPORTO MARITTIMO

ボートと船の例

日本語 | 英語 | ドイツ語 | フランス語 | スペイン語 | イタリア語

フェリー
ferry
Fähre^F
transbordeur^M
transbordador^M
nave^F **traghetto**^{M}

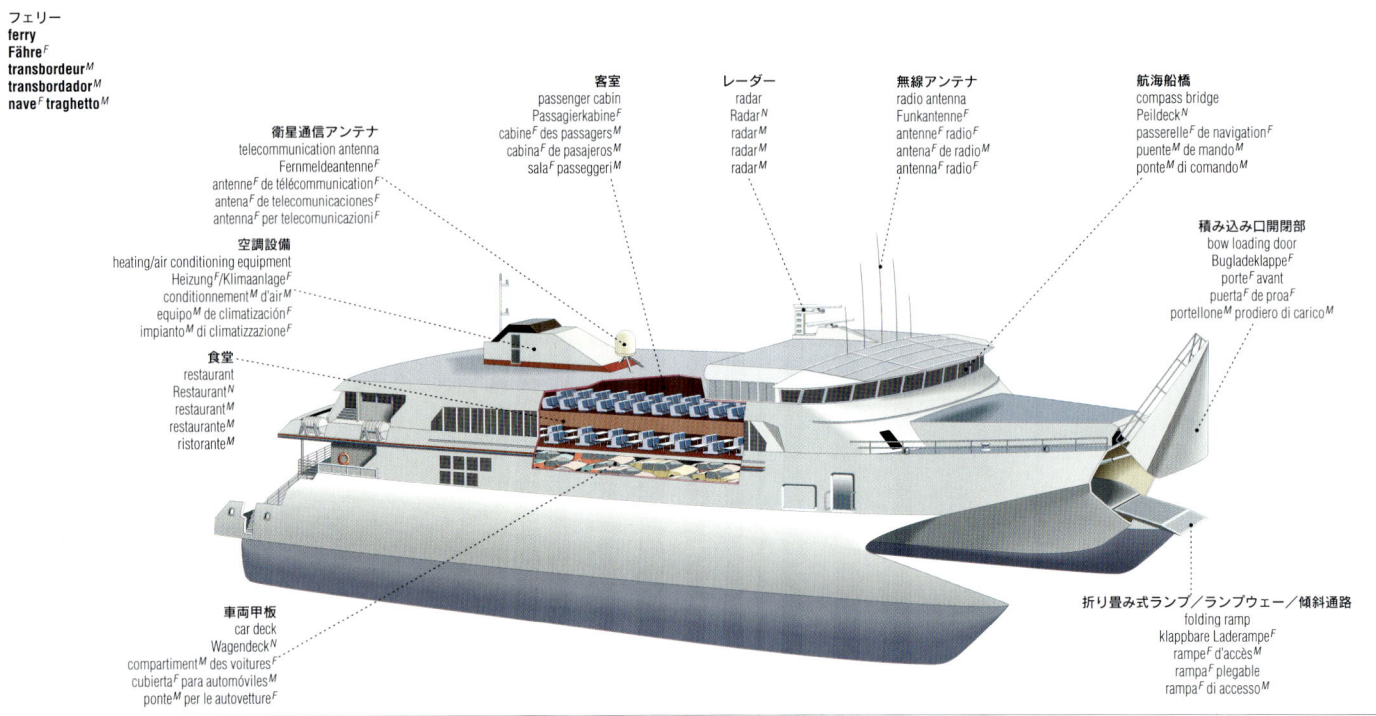

客室
passenger cabin
Passagierkabine^F
cabine^F des passagers
cabina^F de pasajeros^M
sala^F passeggeri^M

レーダー
radar
Radar^N
radar^M
radar^M
radar^M

無線アンテナ
radio antenna
Funkantenne^F
antenne^F radio^M
antena^F de radio^M
antenna^F radio^M

航海船橋
compass bridge
Peildeck^N
passerelle^F de navigation^F
puente^M de mando^M
ponte^M di comando^M

衛星通信アンテナ
telecommunication antenna
Fernmeldeantenne^F
antenne^F de télécommunication
antena^F de telecomunicaciones^F
antenna^F per telecomunicazioni^F

積み込み口開閉部
bow loading door
Bugladeklappe^F
porte^F avant
puerta^F de proa^F
portellone^M prodiero di carico^M

空調設備
heating/air conditioning equipment
Heizung^F/Klimaanlage^F
conditionnement^M d'air^M
equipo^M de climatización^F
impianto^M di climatizzazione^F

食堂
restaurant
Restaurant^N
restaurant^M
restaurante^M
ristorante^M

車両甲板
car deck
Wagendeck^N
compartiment^M des voitures^F
cubierta^F para automóviles^M
ponte^M per le autovetture^F

折り畳み式ランプ／ランプウェー／傾斜通路
folding ramp
klappbare Laderampe^F
rampe^F d'accès^M
rampa^F plegable
rampa^F di accesso^M

客船
passenger liner; *cruiseliner*
Passagierdampfer^M
paquebot^M
buque^M **trasatlántico**
transatlantico^M

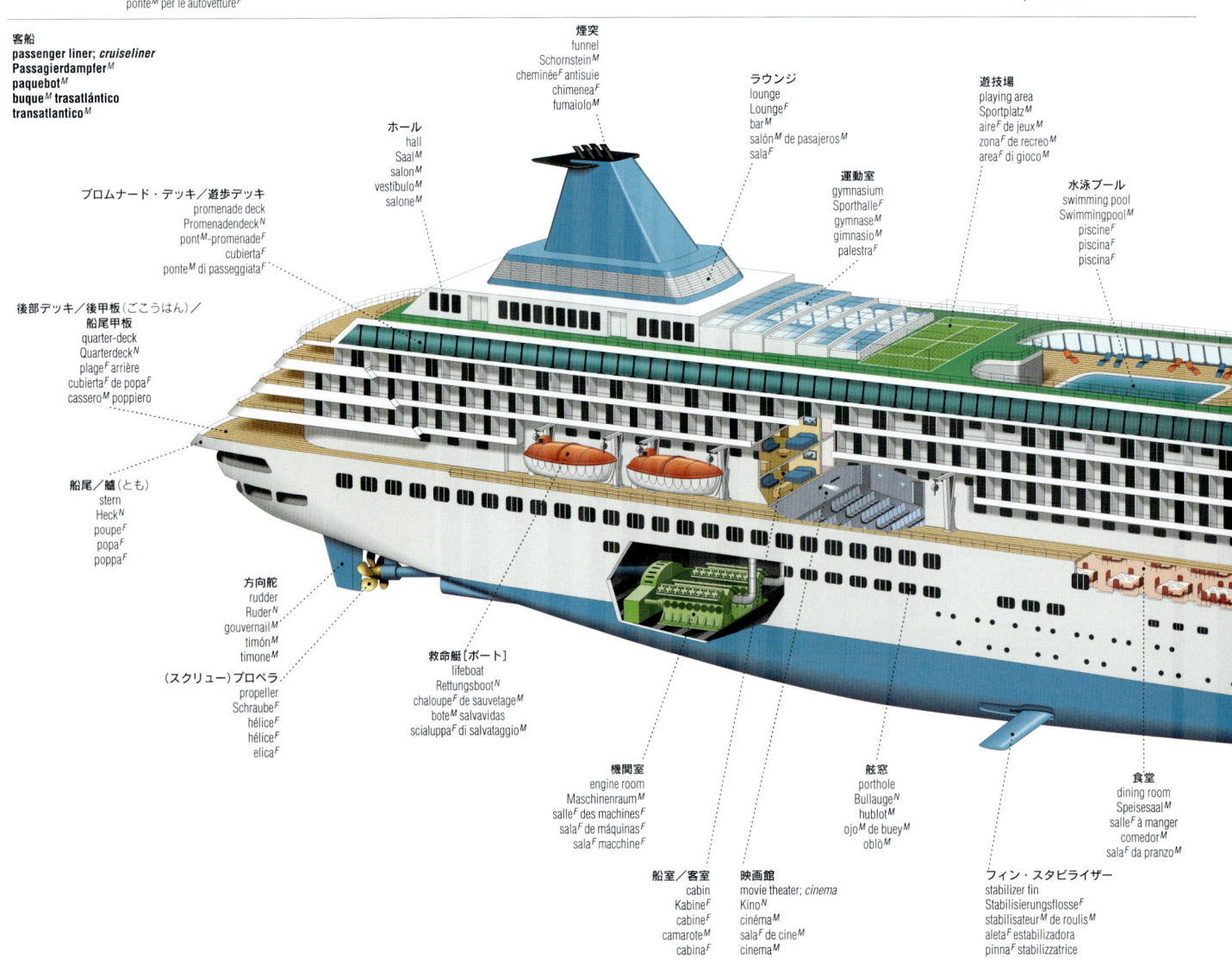

煙突
funnel
Schornstein^M
cheminée^F antisuie
chimenea^F
fumaiolo^M

ラウンジ
lounge
Lounge^F
bar^M
salón^M de pasajeros^M
sala^F

遊技場
playing area
Sportplatz^M
aire^F de jeux^M
zona^F de recreo^M
area^F di gioco^M

ホール
hall
Saal^M
salon^M
vestíbulo^M
salone^M

運動室
gymnasium
Sporthalle^F
gymnase^M
gimnasio^M
palestra^F

水泳プール
swimming pool
Swimmingpool^M
piscine^F
piscina^F
piscina^F

プロムナード・デッキ／遊歩デッキ
promenade deck
Promenadendeck^N
pont^M-promenade^F
cubierta^F
ponte^M di passeggiata^F

後部デッキ／後甲板（こうこうはん）／船尾甲板
quarter-deck
Quarterdeck^N
plage^F arrière
cubierta^F de popa^F
cassero^M poppiero

船尾／艫（とも）
stern
Heck^N
poupe^F
popa^F
poppa^F

方向舵
rudder
Ruder^N
gouvernail^M
timón^M
timone^M

（スクリュー）プロペラ
propeller
Schraube^F
hélice^F
hélice^F
elica^F

救命艇［ボート］
lifeboat
Rettungsboot^N
chaloupe^F de sauvetage^M
bote^M salvavidas
scialuppa^F di salvataggio^M

機関室
engine room
Maschinenraum^M
salle^F des machines^F
sala^F de máquinas^F
sala^F macchine^F

舷窓
porthole
Bullauge^N
hublot^M
ojo^M de buey^M
oblò^M

船室／客室
cabin
Kabine^F
cabine^F
camarote^M
cabina^F

映画館
movie theater; *cinema*
Kino^N
cinéma^M
sala^F de cine^M
cinema^M

フィン・スタビライザー
stabilizer fin
Stabilisierungsflosse^F
stabilisateur^M de roulis^M
aleta^F estabilizadora
pinna^F stabilizzatrice

食堂
dining room
Speisesaal^M
salle^F à manger
comedor^M
sala^F da pranzo^M

海上交通 | MARITIME TRANSPORT
SCHIFFFAHRT | TRANSPORT MARITIME | TRANSPORTE MARÍTIMO | TRASPORTO MARITTIMO

ボートと船の例

水中翼船
hydrofoil boat
Tragflügelschiff^N
hydroptère^M
hidróptero^M
aliscafo^M

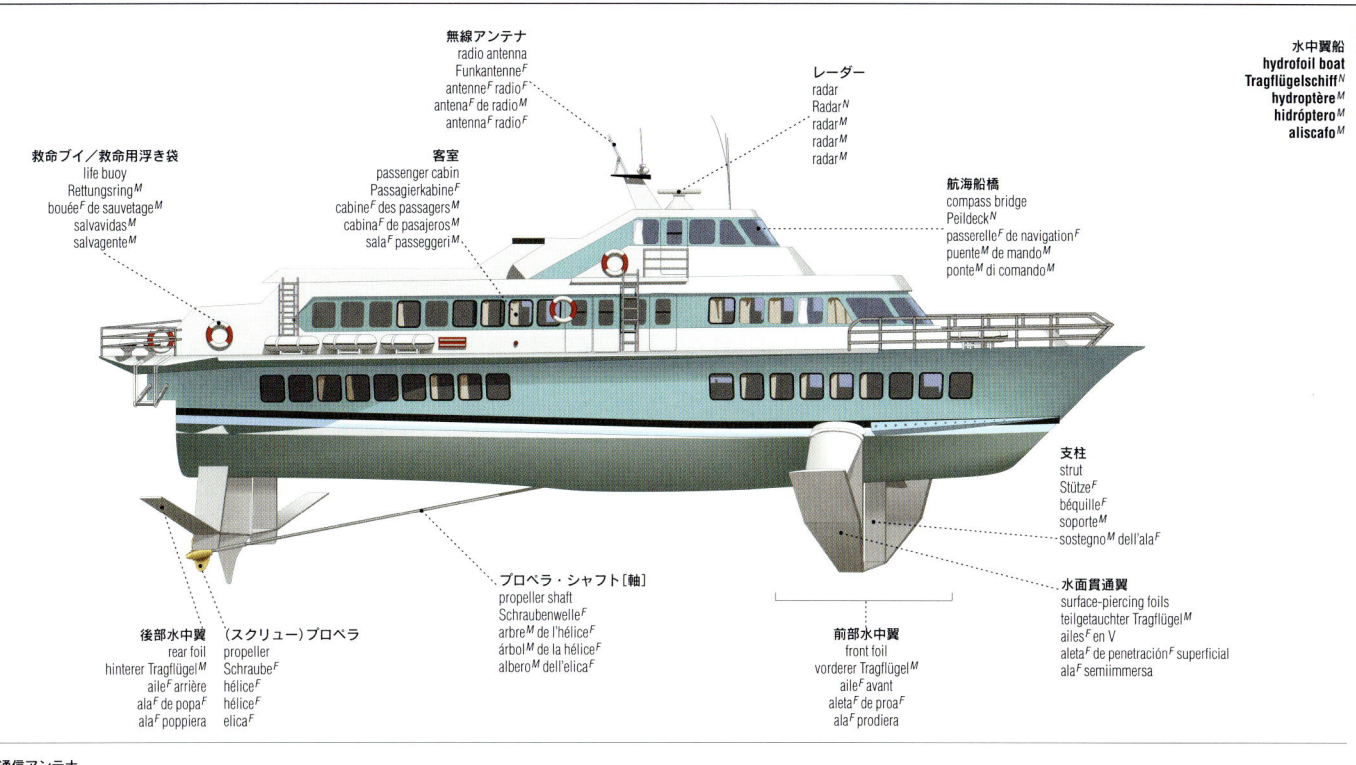

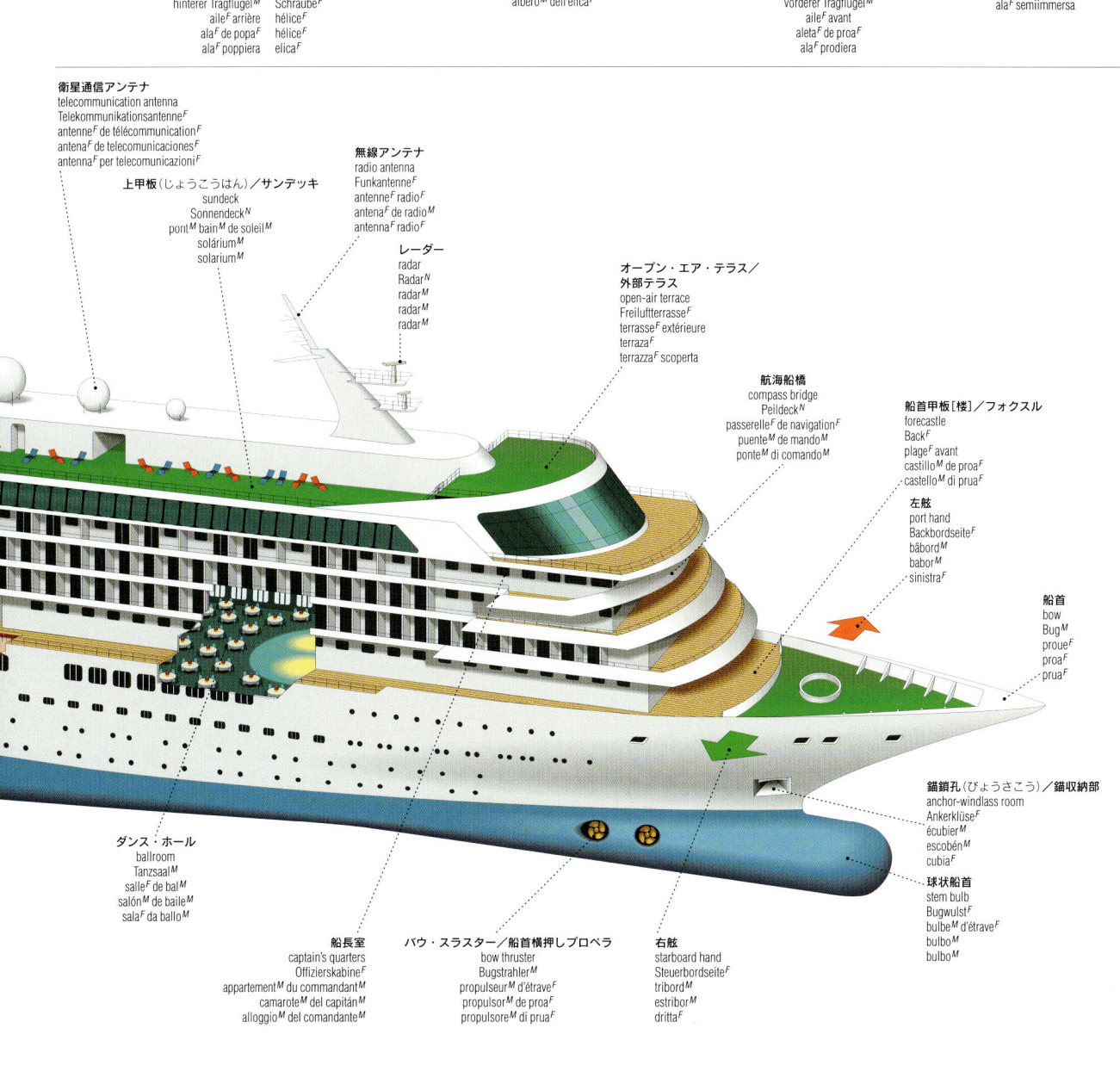

無線アンテナ
radio antenna
Funkantenne^F
antenne^F radio
antena^F de radio
antenna^F radio

レーダー
radar
Radar^N
radar^M
radar^M
radar^M

客室
passenger cabin
Passagierkabine^F
cabine^F des passagers
cabina^F de pasajeros
sala^F passeggeri

救命ブイ／救命用浮き袋
life buoy
Rettungsring^M
bouée^F de sauvetage
salvavidas^M
salvagente^M

航海船橋
compass bridge
Peildeck^N
passerelle^F de navigation
puente^M de mando
ponte^M di comando

支柱
strut
Stütze^F
béquille^F
soporte^M
sostegno^M dell'ala^F

プロペラ・シャフト［軸］
propeller shaft
Schraubenwelle^F
arbre^M de l'hélice^F
árbol^M de la hélice^F
albero^M dell'elica^F

前部水中翼
front foil
vorderer Tragflügel^M
aile^F avant
aleta^F de proa
ala^F prodiera

水面貫通翼
surface-piercing foils
teilgetauchter Tragflügel^M
ailes^F en V
aleta^F de penetración^F superficial
ala^F semiimmersa

後部水中翼
rear foil
hinterer Tragflügel^M
aile^F arrière
ala^F de popa
ala^F poppiera

（スクリュー）プロペラ
propeller
Schraube^F
hélice^F
hélice^F
elica^F

衛星通信アンテナ
telecommunication antenna
Telekommunikationsantenne^F
antenne^F de télécommunication
antena^F de telecomunicaciones
antenna^F per telecomunicazioni

上甲板（じょうこうはん）／サンデッキ
sundeck
Sonnendeck^N
pont^M bain de soleil^M
solárium^M
solarium^M

無線アンテナ
radio antenna
Funkantenne^F
antenne^F radio
antena^F de radio
antenna^F radio

レーダー
radar
Radar^N
radar^M
radar^M
radar^M

オープン・エア・テラス／外部テラス
open-air terrace
Freiluftterrasse^F
terrasse^F extérieure
terraza^F
terrazza^F scoperta

航海船橋
compass bridge
Peildeck^N
passerelle^F de navigation
puente^M de mando
ponte^M di comando

船首甲板［楼］／フォクスル
forecastle
Back^F
plage^F avant
castillo^M de proa
castello^M di prua

左舷
port hand
Backbordseite^F
bâbord^M
babor^M
sinistra^F

船首
bow
Bug^M
proue^F
proa^F
prua^F

錨鎖孔（びょうさこう）／錨収納部
anchor-windlass room
Ankerklüse^F
écubier^M
escobén^M
cubia^F

球状船首
stem bulb
Bugwulst^F
bulbe^M d'étrave
bulbo^M
bulbo^M

ダンス・ホール
ballroom
Tanzsaal^M
salle^F de bal
salón^M de baile
sala^F da ballo

船長室
captain's quarters
Offizierskabine^F
appartement^M du commandant
camarote^M del capitán
alloggio^M del comandante

バウ・スラスター／船首横押しプロペラ
bow thruster
Bugstrahler^M
propulseur^M d'étrave
propulsor^M de proa
propulsore^M di prua

右舷
starboard hand
Steuerbordseite^F
tribord^M
estribor^M
dritta^F

交通と機械

609

海上交通 | MARITIME TRANSPORT
SCHIFFFAHRT | TRANSPORT MARITIME | TRANSPORTE MARÍTIMO | TRASPORTO MARITTIMO

錨

anchor | Anker^M | ancre^F | ancla^F | ancora^F

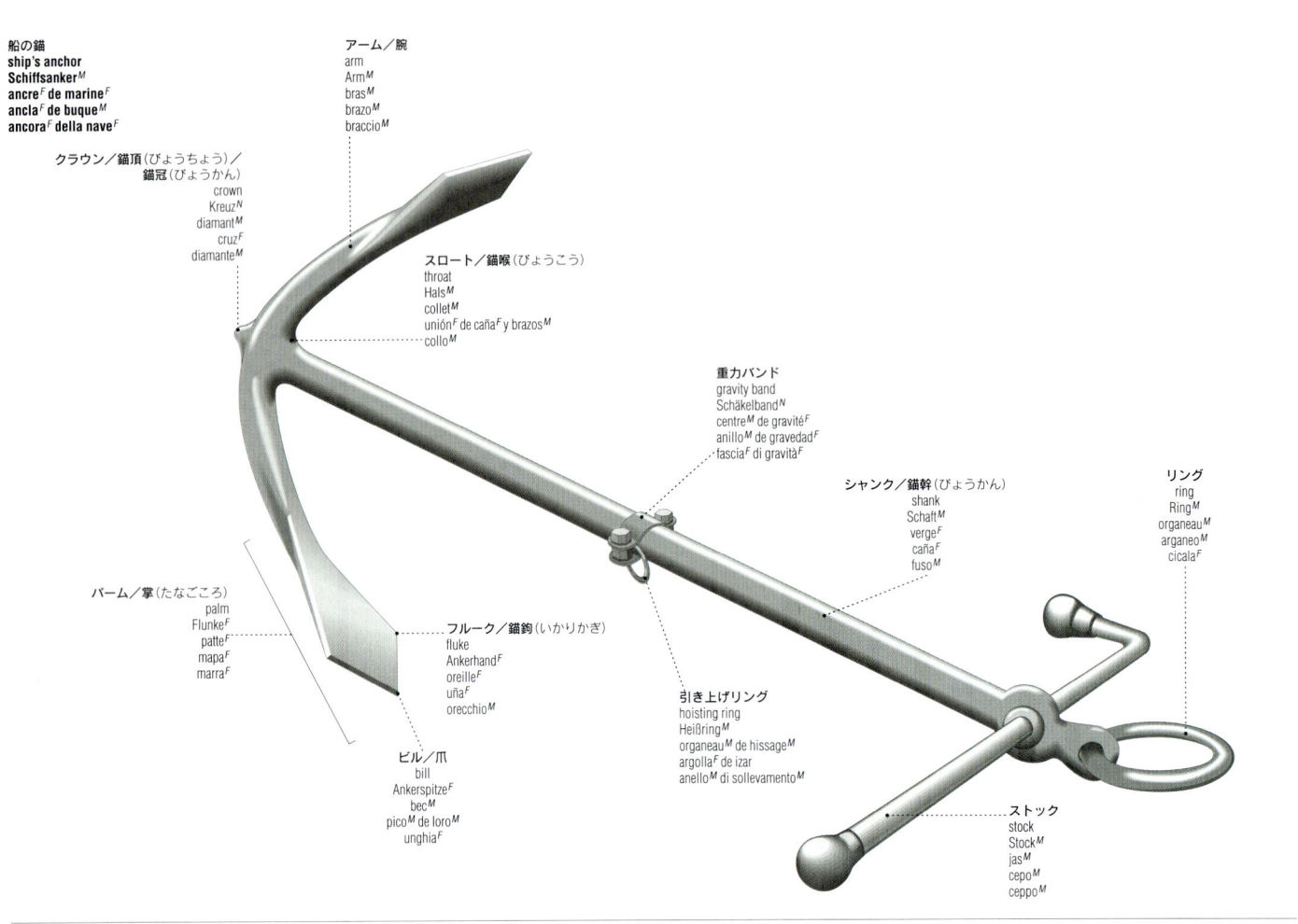

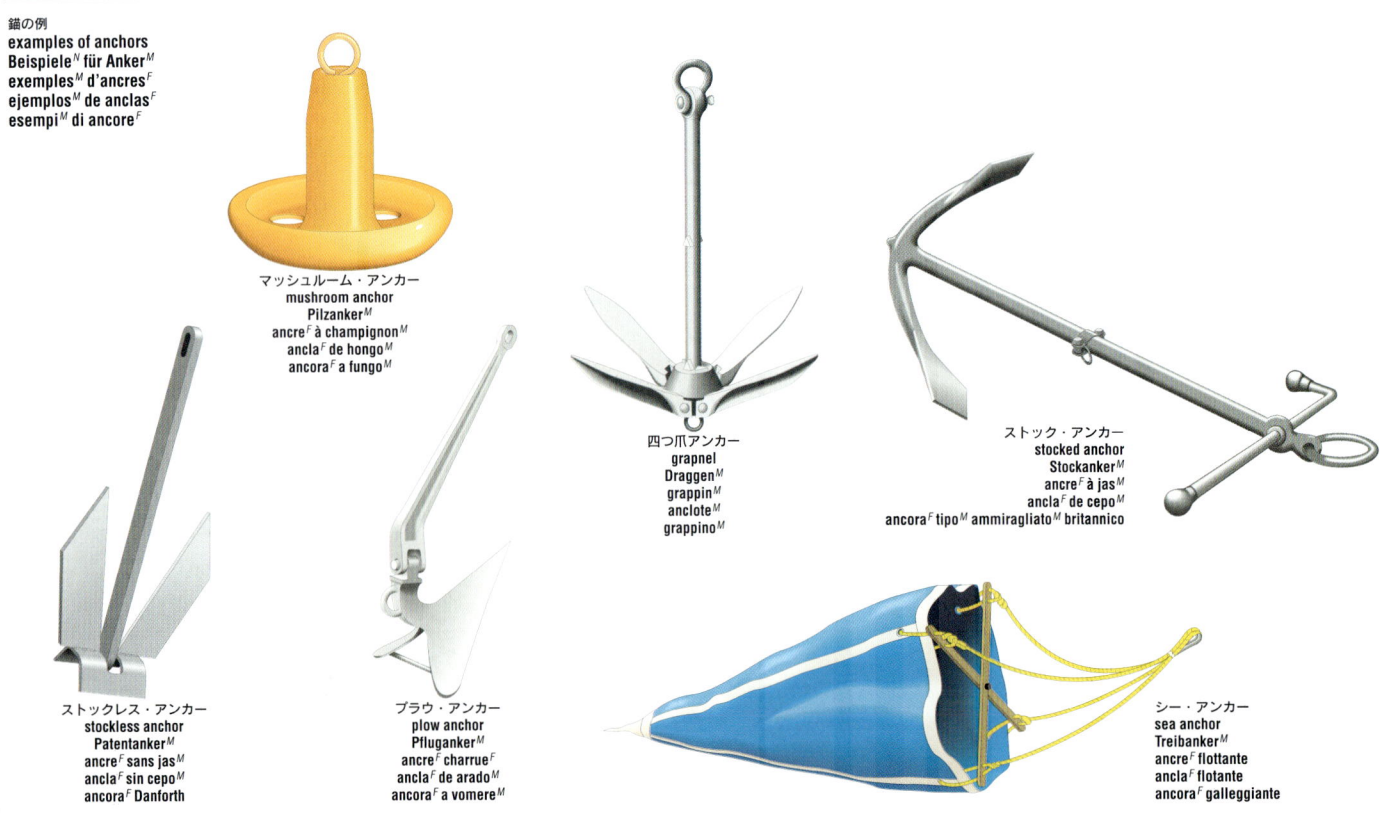

船の錨
ship's anchor
Schiffsanker^M
ancre^F de marine^F
ancla^F de buque^M
ancora^F della nave^F

アーム／腕
arm
Arm^M
bras^M
brazo^M
braccio^M

クラウン／錨頂（びょうちょう）／錨冠（びょうかん）
crown
Kreuz^N
diamant^M
cruz^F
diamante^M

スロート／錨喉（びょうこう）
throat
Hals^M
collet^M
unión^F de caña^F y brazos^M
collo^M

重力バンド
gravity band
Schäkelband^N
centre^M de gravité^F
anillo^M de gravedad^F
fascia^F di gravità^F

シャンク／錨幹（びょうかん）
shank
Schaft^M
verge^F
caña^F
fuso^M

リング
ring
Ring^M
organeau^M
arganeo^M
cicala^F

パーム／掌（たなごころ）
palm
Flunke^F
patte^F
mapa^F
marra^F

フルーク／錨鉤（いかりかぎ）
fluke
Ankerhand^F
oreille^F
uña^F
orecchio^M

引き上げリング
hoisting ring
Heißring^M
organeau^M de hissage^M
argolla^F de izar
anello^M di sollevamento^M

ビル／爪
bill
Ankerspitze^F
bec^M
pico^M de loro^M
unghia^F

ストック
stock
Stock^M
jas^M
cepo^M
ceppo^M

錨の例
examples of anchors
Beispiele^N für Anker^M
exemples^M d'ancres^F
ejemplos^M de anclas^F
esempi^M di ancore^F

マッシュルーム・アンカー
mushroom anchor
Pilzanker^M
ancre^F à champignon^M
ancla^F de hongo^M
ancora^F a fungo^M

四つ爪アンカー
grapnel
Draggen^M
grappin^M
anclote^M
grappino^M

ストック・アンカー
stocked anchor
Stockanker^M
ancre^F à jas^M
ancla^F de cepo^M
ancora^F tipo^M ammiragliato^M britannico

ストックレス・アンカー
stockless anchor
Patentanker^M
ancre^F sans jas^M
ancla^F sin cepo^M
ancora^F Danforth

プラウ・アンカー
plow anchor
Pfluganker^M
ancre^F charrue^F
ancla^F de arado^M
ancora^F a vomere^M

シー・アンカー
sea anchor
Treibanker^M
ancre^F flottante
ancla^F flotante
ancora^F galleggiante

海上交通 | MARITIME TRANSPORT
SCHIFFFAHRT | TRANSPORT MARITIME | TRANSPORTE MARÍTIMO | TRASPORTO MARITTIMO

救命用具

life-saving equipment | Rettungsgeräte^N | équipement^M de sauvetage^M | equipo^M salvavidas | equipaggiamento^M di salvataggio^M

アンテナ
antenna
Antenne^F
antenne^F
antena^F
antenna^F

ストロボスコープ
strobe
Stroboskop^N
stroboscope^M
estroboscopio^M
stroboscopio^M

救難ビーコン
distress beacon
Rettungsboje^F
balise^F de détresse^F
baliza^F de socorro^M
boa^F di salvataggio^M

ラッパ
trumpet
Sirene^F
trompe^F
trompeta^F
tromba^F

缶
canister
Dose^F
cartouche^F
cilindro^M
bomboletta^F

霧笛／フォグ・ホーン
fog horn
Nebelhorn^N
avertisseur^M de brume^F
bocina^F de niebla^F
segnalatore^M di nebbia^F

バックル
buckle
Schnalle^F
boucle^F
hebilla^F
fibbia^F

ベルト
belt
Gurt^M
ceinture^F
cinturón^M
cintura^F

股紐（ひも）
leg strap
Beingurt^M
sangle^F sous-cutale
arnés^M
cinghia^F di sicurezza^F sottogamba

救命胴衣
life jacket
Rettungsweste^F
gilet^M de sauvetage^M
chaleco^M salvavidas
giubbotto^M di salvataggio^M

天蓋（てんがい）／キャノピー
canopy
Abdeckung^F
tente^F
toldo^M
tenda^F

乗り込み用はしご
boarding ladder
Leiter^F
échelle^F d'accès^M
escalera^F de embarque^M
scaletta^F di imbarco^M

浮力チューブ
buoyancy tube
Wassertank^M
flotteur^M
flotador^M
galleggiante^M

ガス充気装置
inflation system
Aufblassystem^N
dispositif^M de gonflement^M
dispositivo^M de inflado^M
dispositivo^M di gonfiaggio^M

救命いかだ
life raft
Rettungsinsel^F
radeau^M de sauvetage^M
balsa^F salvavidas
zattera^F di salvataggio^M

浮き輪
ring
Ring^M
anneau^M
aro^M
anello^F

ロープ
rope
Greifleine^F
filin^M
cuerda^F
corda^F

再帰性反射テープ
retro-reflective tape
reflektierendes Band^N
bande^F rétro-réfléchissante
banda^F reflectante
fascia^F catarifrangente

救命ブイ［浮き輪］
life buoy
Rettungsring^M
bouée^F de sauvetage^M
salvavidas^M
salvagente^M

柄／取っ手
handle
Stange^F
manche^M
mango^M
manico^M

爪竿／ボート・フック
boat hook
Bootshaken^M
gaffe^F
bichero^M
gaffa^F

爪／フック
hook
Haken^M
crochet^M
garfio^M
uncino^M

交通と機械

611

海上交通 | MARITIME TRANSPORT
SCHIFFFAHRT | TRANSPORT MARITIME | TRANSPORTE MARÍTIMO | TRASPORTO MARITTIMO

航海計器

日本語 | 英語 | ドイツ語 | フランス語 | スペイン語 | イタリア語

navigation devices | Navigationsinstrumente^N | appareils^M de navigation^F | instrumentos^M de navegación^F | strumenti^M per la navigazione^F

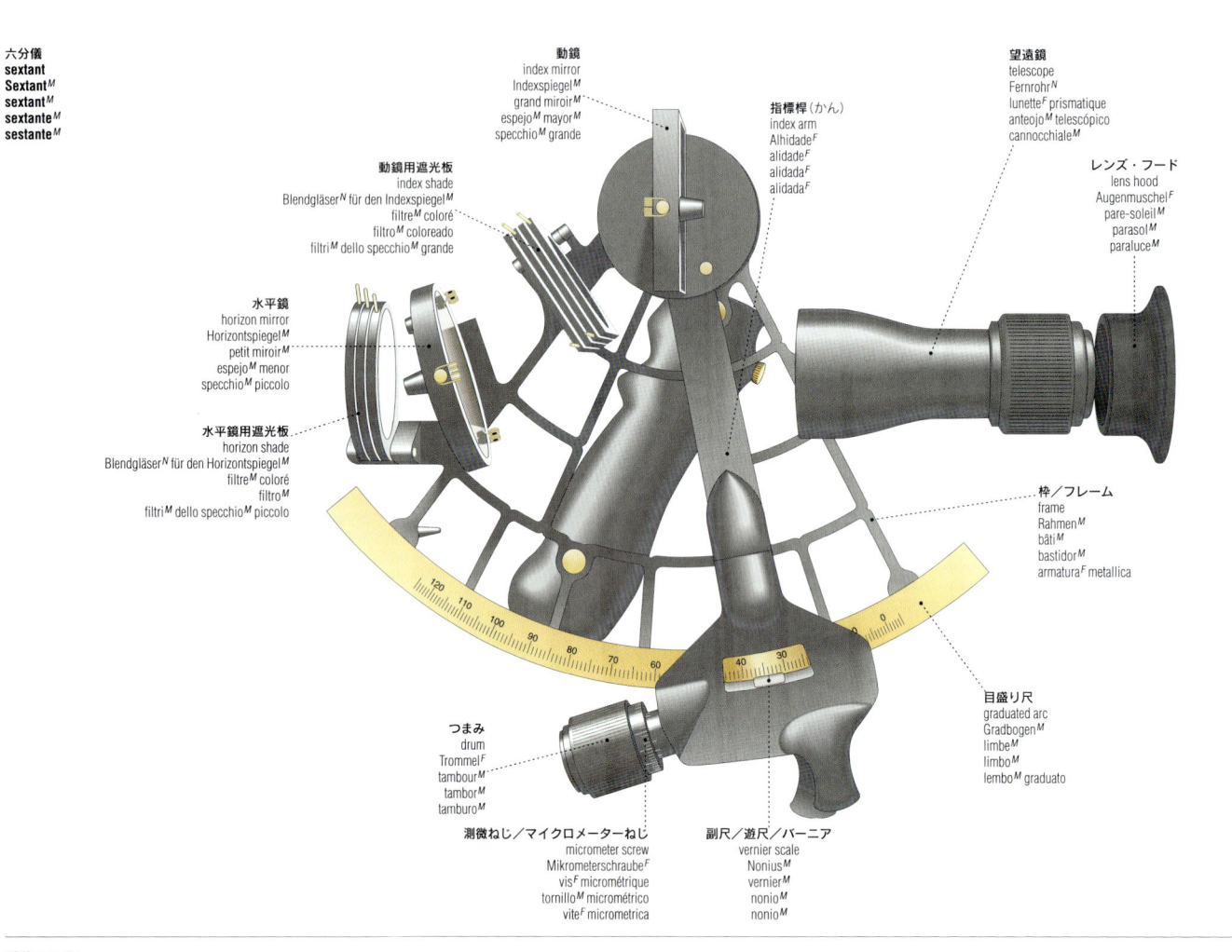

六分儀
sextant
Sextant^M
sextant^M
sextante^M
sestante^M

動鏡
index mirror
Indexspiegel^M
grand miroir^M
espejo^M mayor^M
specchio^M grande

指標桿（かん）
index arm
Alhidade^F
alidade^F
alidada^F
alidada^F

望遠鏡
telescope
Fernrohr^N
lunette^F prismatique
anteojo^M telescópico
cannocchiale^M

動鏡用遮光板
index shade
Blendgläser^N für den Indexspiegel^M
filtre^M coloré
filtro^M coloreado
filtri^M dello specchio^M grande

レンズ・フード
lens hood
Augenmuschel^F
pare-soleil^M
parasol^M
paraluce^M

水平鏡
horizon mirror
Horizontspiegel^M
petit miroir^M
espejo^M menor
specchio^M piccolo

水平鏡用遮光板
horizon shade
Blendgläser^N für den Horizontspiegel^M
filtre^M coloré
filtro^M
filtri^M dello specchio^M piccolo

枠／フレーム
frame
Rahmen^M
bâti^M
bastidor^M
armatura^F metallica

目盛り尺
graduated arc
Gradbogen^M
limbe^M
limbo^M
lembo^M graduato

つまみ
drum
Trommel^F
tambour^M
tambor^M
tamburo^M

測微ねじ／マイクロメーターねじ
micrometer screw
Mikrometerschraube^F
vis^F micrométrique
tornillo^M micrométrico
vite^F micrometrica

副尺／遊尺／バーニア
vernier scale
Nonius^M
vernier^M
nonio^M
nonio^M

液体コンパス
liquid compass
Flüssigkeitskompass^M
compas^M magnétique liquide
brújula^F líquida
bussola^F a liquido^M

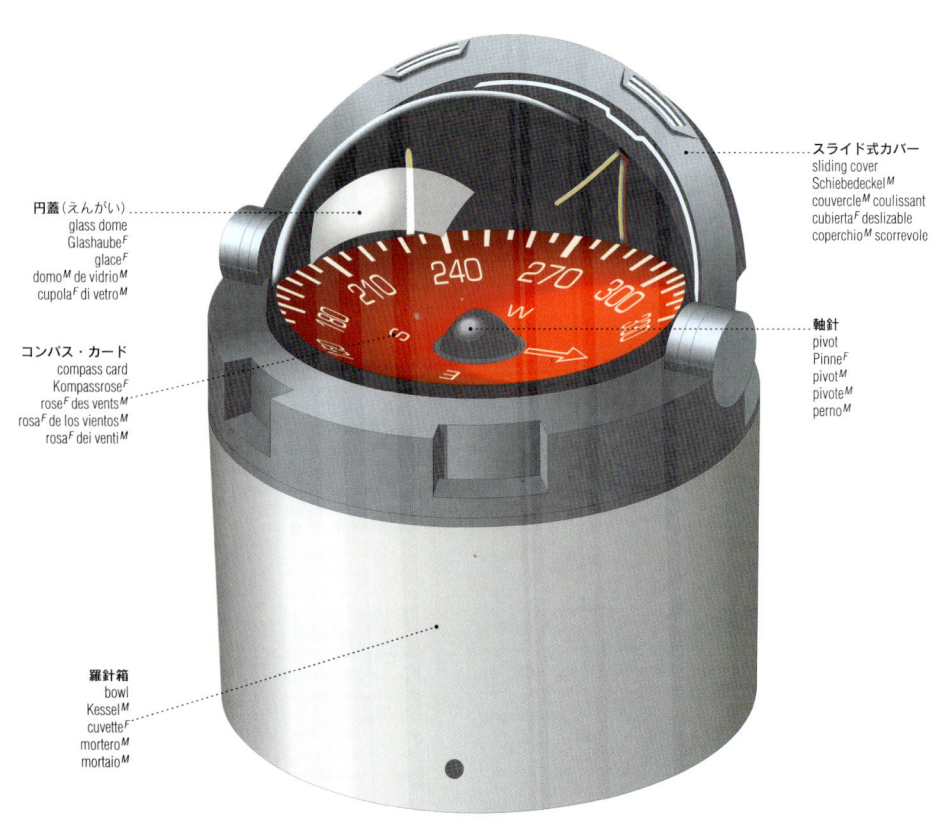

スライド式カバー
sliding cover
Schiebedeckel^M
couvercle^M coulissant
cubierta^F deslizable
coperchio^M scorrevole

円蓋（えんがい）
glass dome
Glashaube^F
glace^F
domo^M de vidrio^M
cupola^F di vetro^M

軸針
pivot
Pinne^F
pivot^M
pivote^M
perno^M

コンパス・カード
compass card
Kompassrose^F
rose^F des vents^M
rosa^F de los vientos^M
rosa^F dei venti^M

羅針箱
bowl
Kessel^M
cuvette^F
mortero^M
mortaio^M

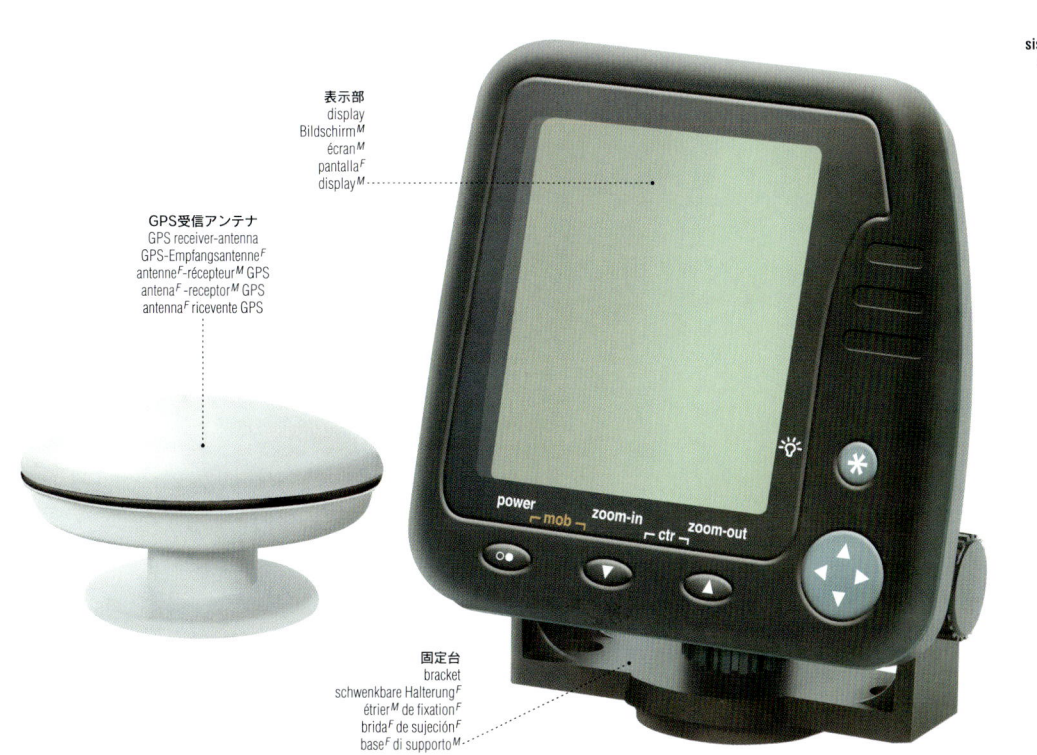

海上交通 | MARITIME TRANSPORT
SCHIFFFAHRT | TRANSPORT MARITIME | TRANSPORTE MARÍTIMO | TRASPORTO MARITTIMO

航海計器

音響測深機[器]
echo sounder
Echolot^N
sondeur^M à éclats^M
sonar^M
ecoscandaglio^M

水深目盛り
depth scale
Tiefenskala^F in m
échelle^F de profondeur^F
escala^F de profundidad^F
scala^F di profondità^F in metri^M

ダイヤル式表示盤
dial-type display
Anzeigeskala^F
écran^M
indicador^M del cuadrante^M
quadrante^M indicatore^M

アラーム閾値（しきいち）設定つまみ
alarm threshold setting
Alarmschwellenwert-Einstellung^F
réglage^M du seuil^M d'alarme^F
control^M del nivel^M de alarma^F
regolazione^F della soglia^F di allarme^M

ケース
housing
Gehäuse^N
boîtier^M
caja^F
contenitore^M

音声アラーム
sound alarm
Lautsprecher^M
alarme^F sonore
alarma^F sonora
allarme^M acustico

電源スイッチ
on-off switch
Ein-/Ausschalter^M
interrupteur^M
interruptor^M
interruttore^M

音響測深機[器]送受波器
echo sounder probe
Schwinger^M
sonde^F
sonda^F
sonda^F dell'ecoscandaglio^M

アラーム閾値表示ボタン
alarm threshold display button
Knopf^M für Alarmschwellenwert-Anzeige^F
visualisation^F du seuil^M d'alarme^F
botón^M de visualización^F del nivel^M de alarma^F
pulsante^M per la visualizzazione^F della soglia^F di allarme^M

利得調整つまみ
gain control
Verstärkerregler^M
contrôle^M du gain^M
control^M de ganancia^F
regolatore^M di amplificazione^F

伝送ケーブル
transmission cable
Übertragungskabel^N
câble^M de transmission^F
cable^M de transmisión^F
cavo^M di trasmissione^F

変換器
transducer
Messwandler^M
émetteur^M/récepteur^M
transductor^M
trasduttore^M

プラグ
plug
Stecker^M
fiche^F
clavija^F
spinotto^M

衛星航法装置
satellite navigation system
Satelliten^M-Navigationssystem^N
traceur^M de route^F
sistema^M de navegación^F por satélite^M
sistema^M di navigazione^F satellitare

表示部
display
Bildschirm^M
écran^M
pantalla^F
display^M

GPS受信アンテナ
GPS receiver-antenna
GPS-Empfangsantenne^F
antenne^F-récepteur^M GPS
antena^F-receptor^M GPS
antenna^F ricevente GPS

固定台
bracket
schwenkbare Halterung^F
étrier^M de fixation^F
brida^F de sujeción^F
base^F di supporto^M

交通と機械

海上交通 | MARITIME TRANSPORT
SCHIFFFAHRT | TRANSPORT MARITIME | TRANSPORTE MARÍTIMO | TRASPORTO MARITTIMO

海路標識

maritime signals | Seezeichen[N] | signalisation[F] maritime | señales[F] marítimas | segnali[M] marittimi

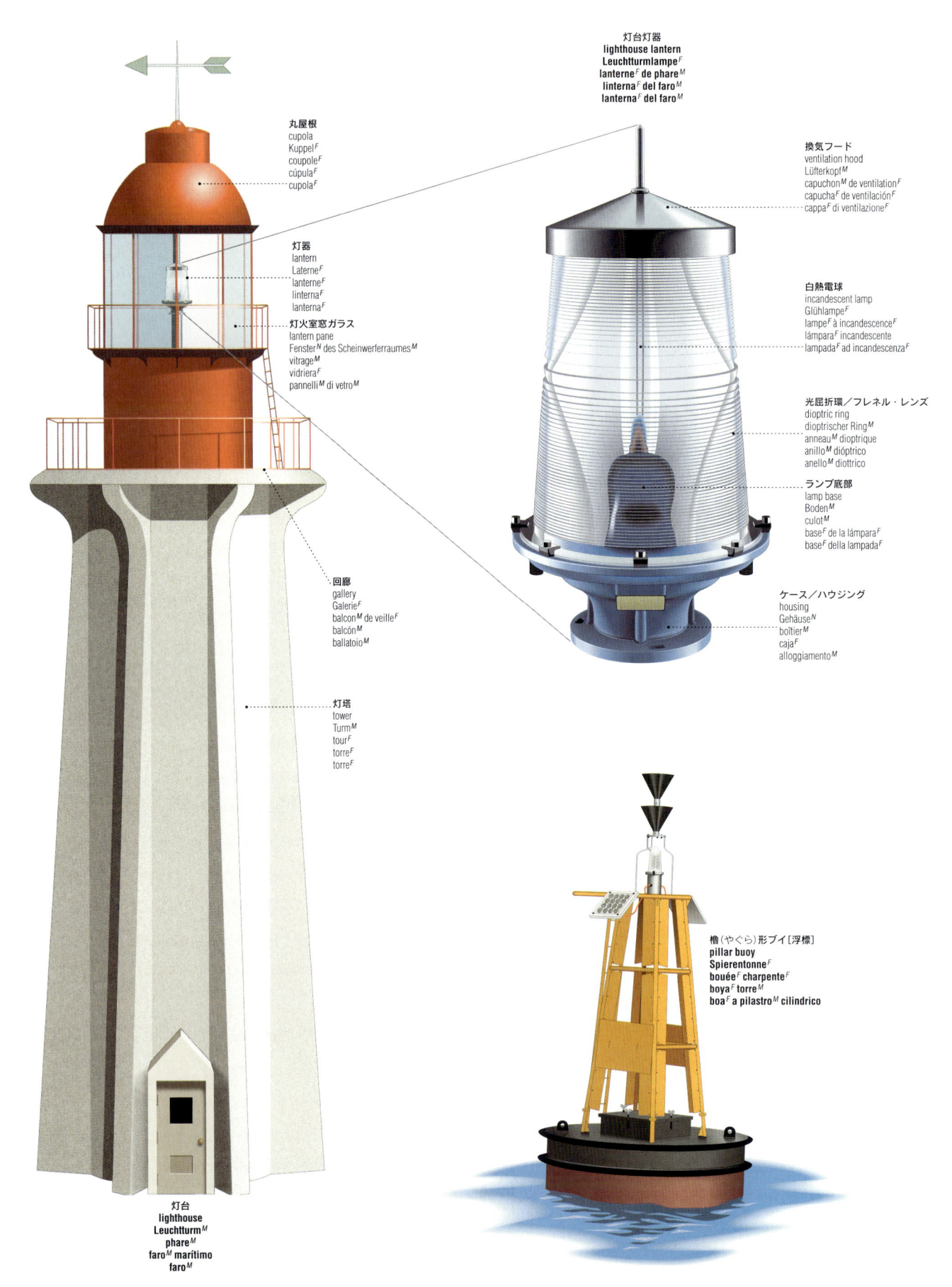

日本語 | 英語 | ドイツ語 | フランス語 | スペイン語 | イタリア語

灯台灯器
lighthouse lantern
Leuchtturmlampe[F]
lanterne[F] de phare[M]
linterna[F] del faro[M]
lanterna[F] del faro[M]

丸屋根
cupola
Kuppel[F]
coupole[F]
cúpula[F]
cupola[F]

換気フード
ventilation hood
Lüfterkopf[M]
capuchon[M] de ventilation[F]
capucha[F] de ventilación[F]
cappa[F] di ventilazione[F]

灯器
lantern
Laterne[F]
lanterne[F]
linterna[F]
lanterna[F]

白熱電球
incandescent lamp
Glühlampe[F]
lampe[F] à incandescence[F]
lámpara[F] incandescente
lampada[F] ad incandescenza[F]

灯火室窓ガラス
lantern pane
Fenster[N] des Scheinwerferraumes[M]
vitrage[M]
vidriera[F]
pannelli[M] di vetro[M]

光屈折環／フレネル・レンズ
dioptric ring
dioptrischer Ring[M]
anneau[M] dioptrique
anillo[M] dióptrico
anello[M] diottrico

ランプ底部
lamp base
Boden[M]
culot[M]
base[F] de la lámpara[F]
base[F] della lampada[F]

回廊
gallery
Galerie[F]
balcon[M] de veille[F]
balcón[M]
ballatoio[M]

ケース／ハウジング
housing
Gehäuse[N]
boîtier[M]
caja[F]
alloggiamento[M]

灯塔
tower
Turm[M]
tour[F]
torre[F]
torre[F]

櫓（やぐら）形ブイ［浮標］
pillar buoy
Spierentonne[F]
bouée[F] charpente[F]
boya[F] torre[M]
boa[F] a pilastro[M] cilindrico

灯台
lighthouse
Leuchtturm[M]
phare[M]
faro[M] marítimo
faro[M]

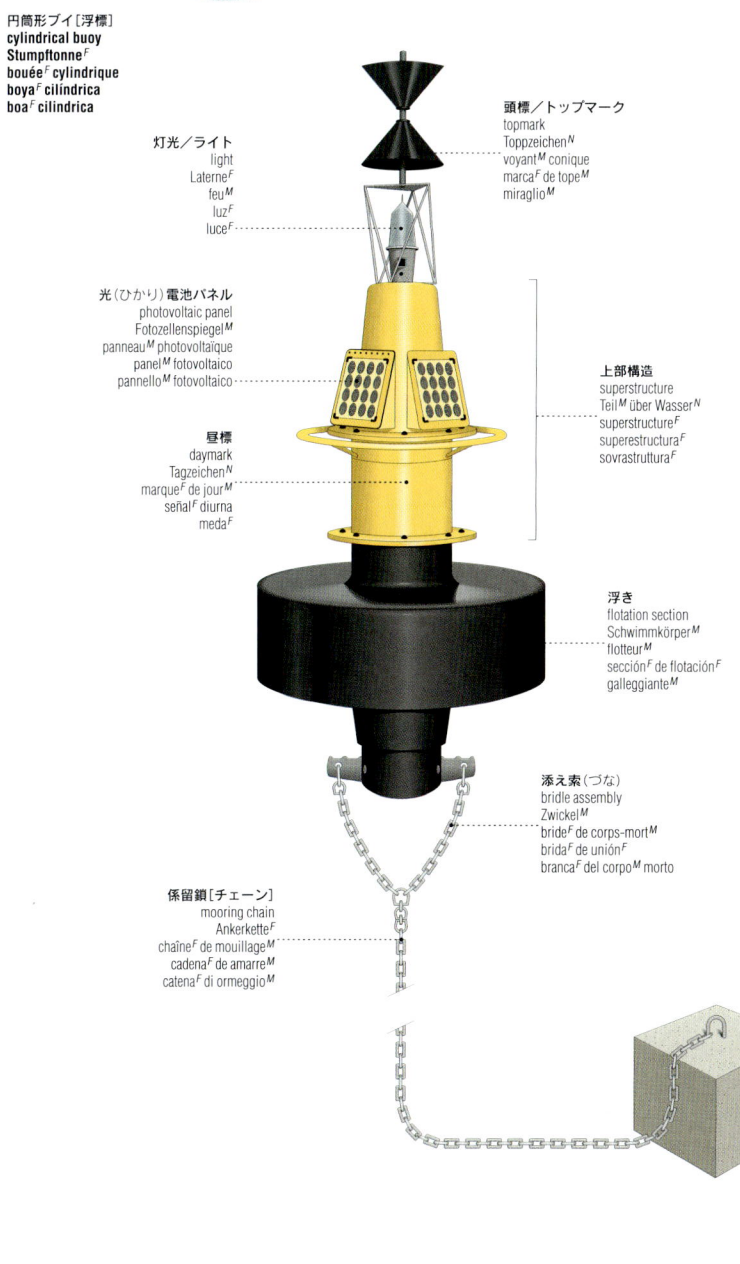

海上交通 | MARITIME TRANSPORT
SCHIFFFAHRT | TRANSPORT MARITIME | TRANSPORTE MARÍTIMO | TRASPORTO MARITTIMO

海路標識

円錐形ブイ［浮標］
conical buoy
Spitztonne^F
bouée^F conique
boya^F cónica
boa^F conica

高焦点水面ブイ［浮標］
high focal plane buoy
Großtonne^F
bouée^F à plan^M focal élevé
boya^F de plano^M focal elevado
boa^F a piano^M focale elevato

灯光／ライト
light
Laterne^F
feu^M
luz^F
luce^F

レーダー反射器
radar reflector
Radarreflektor^M
réflecteur^M radar^M
reflector^M del radar^M
riflettore^M radar^M passivo

光（ひかり）電池パネル
photovoltaic panel
Fotozellenspiegel^M
panneau^M photovoltaïque
panel^M fotovoltaico
pannello^M fotovoltaico

昼標
daymark
Tagzeichen^N
marque^F de jour^M
señal^F diurna
meda^F

円筒形ブイ［浮標］
cylindrical buoy
Stumpftonne^F
bouée^F cylindrique
boya^F cilíndrica
boa^F cilindrica

はしご
ladder
Leiter^F
échelle^F
escalerilla^F
scala^F

灯光／ライト
light
Laterne^F
feu^M
luz^F
luce^F

頭標／トップマーク
topmark
Toppzeichen^N
voyant^M conique
marca^F de tope^M
miraglio^M

管状支柱
tubular structure
Rohrstütze^F
structure^F tubulaire
estructura^F tubular
struttura^F tubolare

光（ひかり）電池パネル
photovoltaic panel
Fotozellenspiegel^M
panneau^M photovoltaïque
panel^M fotovoltaico
pannello^M fotovoltaico

上部構造
superstructure
Teil^M über Wasser^N
superstructure^F
superestructura^F
sovrastruttura^F

昼標
daymark
Tagzeichen^N
marque^F de jour^M
señal^F diurna
meda^F

水線
waterline
Wasserlinie^F
surface^F de l'eau^F
línea^F de flotación^F
linea^F dell'acqua^M

浮き
flotation section
Schwimmkörper^M
flotteur^M
sección^F de flotación^F
galleggiante^M

添え索（づな）
bridle assembly
Zwickel^M
bride^F de corps-mort^M
brida^F de unión^F
branca^F del corpo^M morto

係留鎖［チェーン］
mooring chain
Ankerkette^F
chaîne^F de mouillage^M
cadena^F de amarre^M
catena^F di ormeggio^M

錘（おもり）
sinker
Tonnenstein^M
corps-mort^M
plomo^M
corpo^M morto

海上交通 | MARITIME TRANSPORT
SCHIFFFAHRT | TRANSPORT MARITIME | TRANSPORTE MARÍTIMO | TRASPORTO MARITTIMO

海上浮標式

maritime buoyage system | Betonnungssystem^N | système^M de balisage^M maritime | sistema^M de boyas^F marítimas | sistema^M di segnalamento^M marittimo per mezzo di boe^F

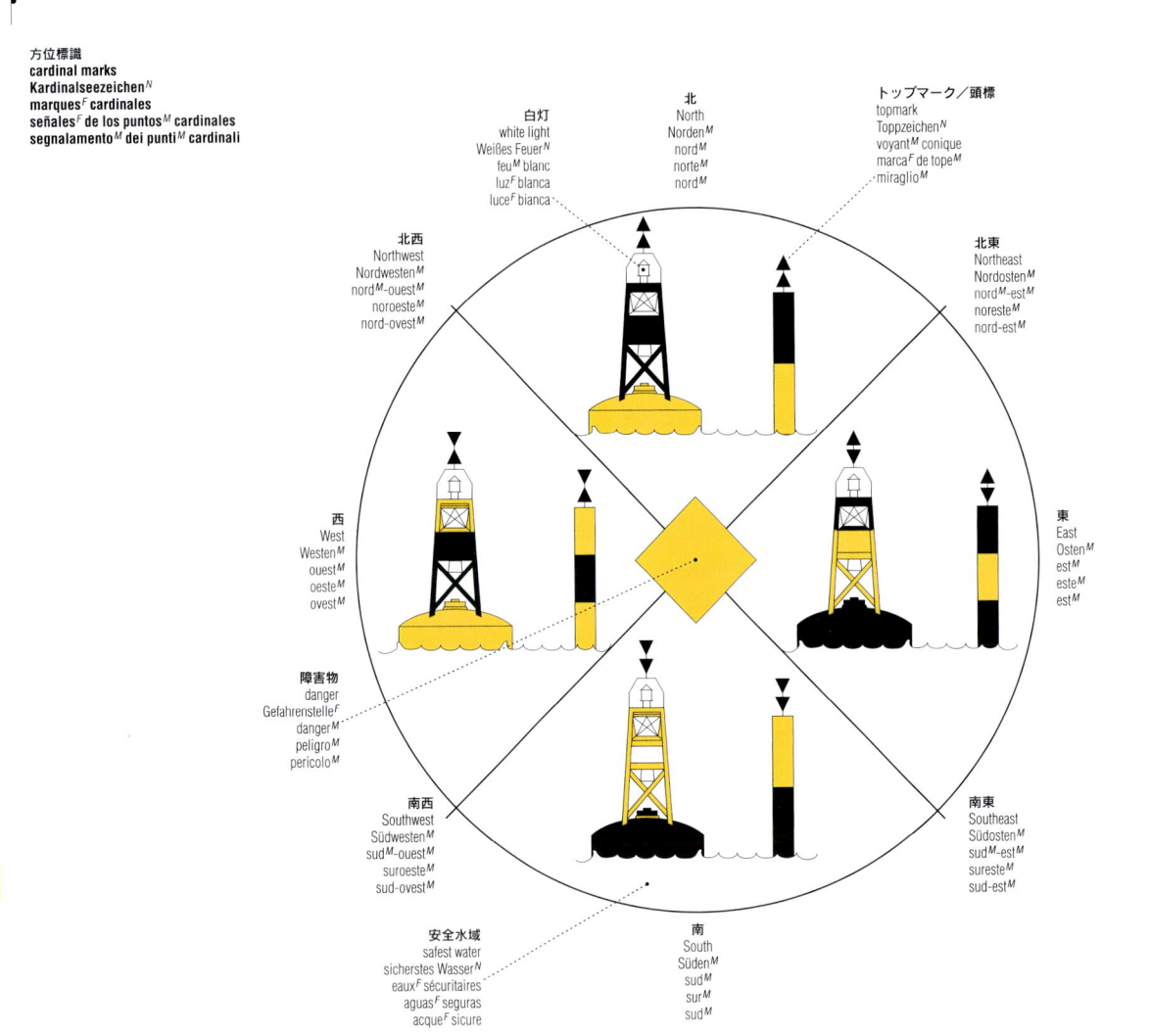

方位標識
cardinal marks
Kardinalseezeichen^N
marques^F cardinales
señales^F de los puntos^M cardinales
segnalamento^M dei punti^M cardinali

白灯
white light
Weißes Feuer^N
feu^M blanc
luz^F blanca
luce^F bianca

北
North
Norden^M
nord^M
norte^M
nord^M

トップマーク／頭標
topmark
Toppzeichen^N
voyant^M conique
marca^F de tope^M
miraglio^M

北西
Northwest
Nordwesten^M
nord^M-ouest^M
noroeste^M
nord-ovest^M

北東
Northeast
Nordosten^M
nord^M-est^M
noreste^M
nord-est^M

西
West
Westen^M
ouest^M
oeste^M
ovest^M

東
East
Osten^M
est^M
este^M
est^M

障害物
danger
Gefahrenstelle^F
danger^M
peligro^M
pericolo^M

南西
Southwest
Südwesten^M
sud^M-ouest^M
suroeste^M
sud-ovest^M

南東
Southeast
Südosten^M
sud^M-est^M
sureste^M
sud-est^M

安全水域
safest water
sicherstes Wasser^N
eaux^F sécuritaires
aguas^F seguras
acque^F sicure

南
South
Süden^M
sud^M
sur^M
sud^M

浮標式地域
buoyage regions
Betonnte Fahrwasser^N
régions^F de balisage^M
regiones^F de boyas^F
regioni^F con segnalamento^M mediante boe^F

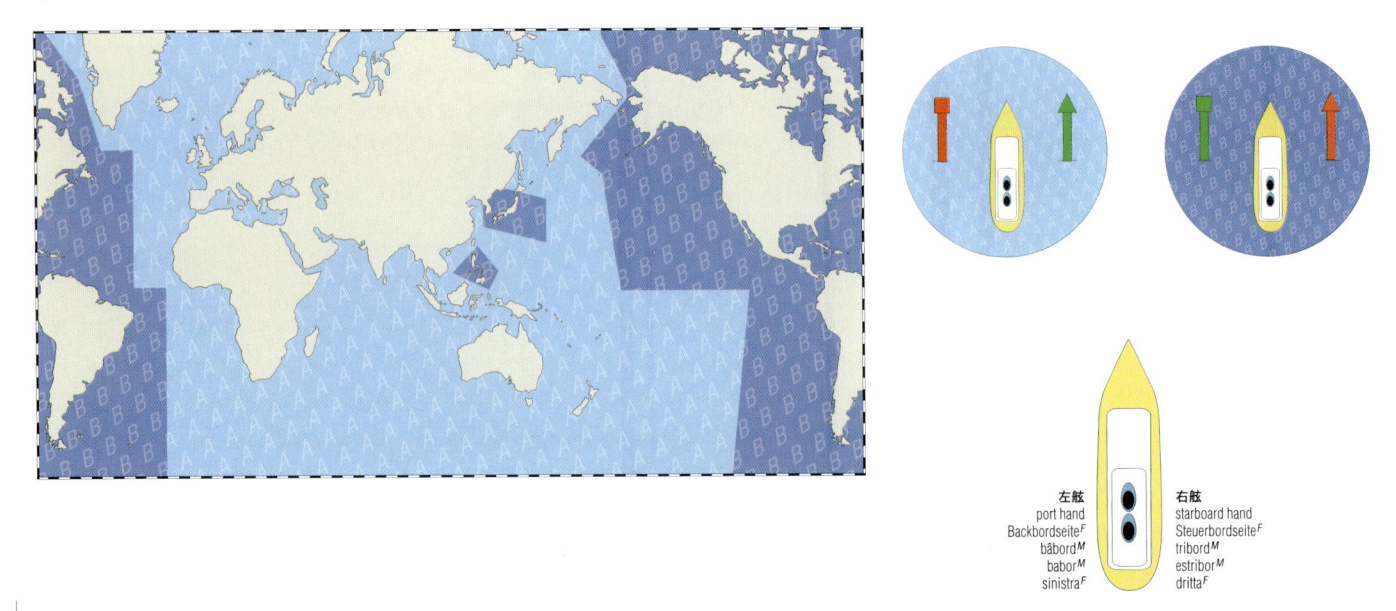

左舷
port hand
Backbordseite^F
bâbord^M
babor^M
sinistra^F

右舷
starboard hand
Steuerbordseite^F
tribord^M
estribor^M
dritta^F

交通と機械

616

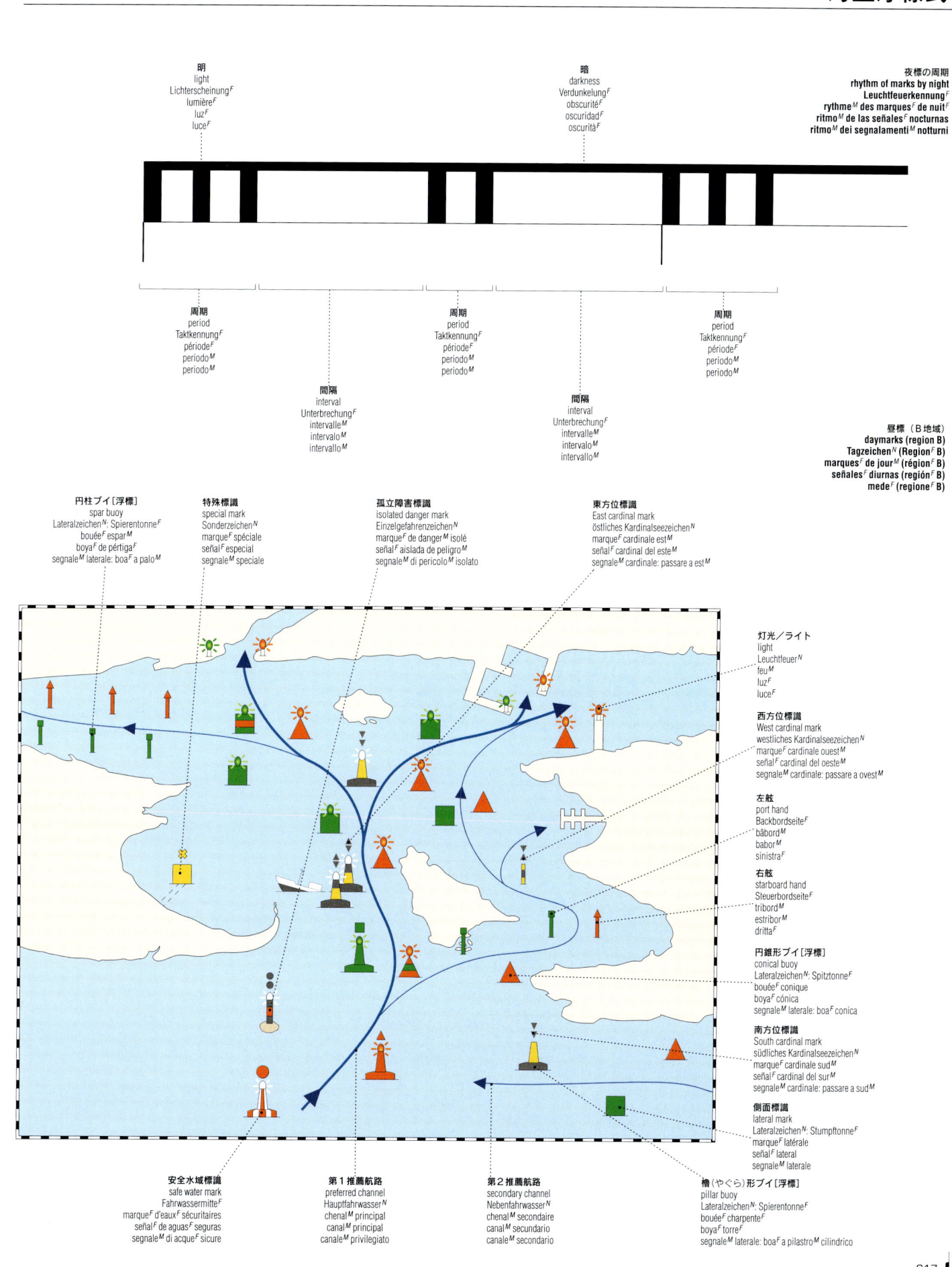

海上交通 | MARITIME TRANSPORT
SCHIFFFAHRT | TRANSPORT MARITIME | TRANSPORTE MARÍTIMO | TRASPORTO MARITTIMO

海上浮標式

明
light
Lichterscheinung^F
lumière^F
luz^F
luce^F

暗
darkness
Verdunkelung^F
obscurité^F
oscuridad^F
oscurità^F

夜標の周期
rhythm of marks by night
Leuchtfeuerkennung^F
rythme^M des marques^F de nuit^F
ritmo^M de las señales^F nocturnas
ritmo^M dei segnalamenti^M notturni

周期
period
Taktkennung^F
période^F
periodo^M
periodo^M

間隔
interval
Unterbrechung^F
intervalle^M
intervalo^M
intervallo^M

昼標（B地域）
daymarks (region B)
Tagzeichen^N (Region^F B)
marques^F de jour^M (région^F B)
señales^F diurnas (región^F B)
mede^F (regione^F B)

円柱ブイ［浮標］
spar buoy
Lateralzeichen^N: Spierentonne^F
bouée^F espar^M
boya^F de pértiga^F
segnale^M laterale: boa^F a palo^M

特殊標識
special mark
Sonderzeichen^N
marque^F spéciale
señal^F especial
segnale^M speciale

孤立障害標識
isolated danger mark
Einzelgefahrenzeichen^N
marque^F de danger^M isolé
señal^F aislada de peligro^M
segnale^M di pericolo^M isolato

東方位標識
East cardinal mark
östliches Kardinalseezeichen^N
marque^F cardinale est^M
señal^F cardinal del este^M
segnale^M cardinale: passare a est^M

灯光／ライト
light
Leuchtfeuer^N
feu^M
luz^F
luce^F

西方位標識
West cardinal mark
westliches Kardinalseezeichen^N
marque^F cardinale ouest^M
señal^F cardinal del oeste^M
segnale^M cardinale: passare a ovest^M

左舷
port hand
Backbordseite^F
bâbord^M
babor^M
sinistra^F

右舷
starboard hand
Steuerbordseite^F
tribord^M
estribor^M
dritta^F

円錐形ブイ［浮標］
conical buoy
Lateralzeichen^N: Spitztonne^F
bouée^F conique
boya^F cónica
segnale^M laterale: boa^F conica

南方位標識
South cardinal mark
südliches Kardinalseezeichen^N
marque^F cardinale sud^M
señal^F cardinal del sur^M
segnale^M cardinale: passare a sud^M

側面標識
lateral mark
Lateralzeichen^N: Stumpftonne^F
marque^F latérale
señal^F lateral
segnale^M laterale

安全水域標識
safe water mark
Fahrwassermitte^F
marque^F d'eaux^F sécuritaires
señal^F de aguas^F seguras
segnale^M di acque^F sicure

第1推薦航路
preferred channel
Hauptfahrwasser^N
chenal^M principal
canal^M principal
canale^M privilegiato

第2推薦航路
secondary channel
Nebenfahrwasser^N
chenal^M secondaire
canal^M secundario
canale^M secondario

櫓(やぐら)形ブイ［浮標］
pillar buoy
Lateralzeichen^N: Spierentonne^F
bouée^F charpente
boya^F torre
segnale^M laterale: boa^F a pilastro^M cilindrico

航空交通 | AIR TRANSPORT
LUFTVERKEHR | TRANSPORT AÉRIEN | TRANSPORTE AÉREO | TRASPORTO AEREO

空港

airport | Flughafen^M | aéroport^M | aeropuerto^M | aeroporto^M

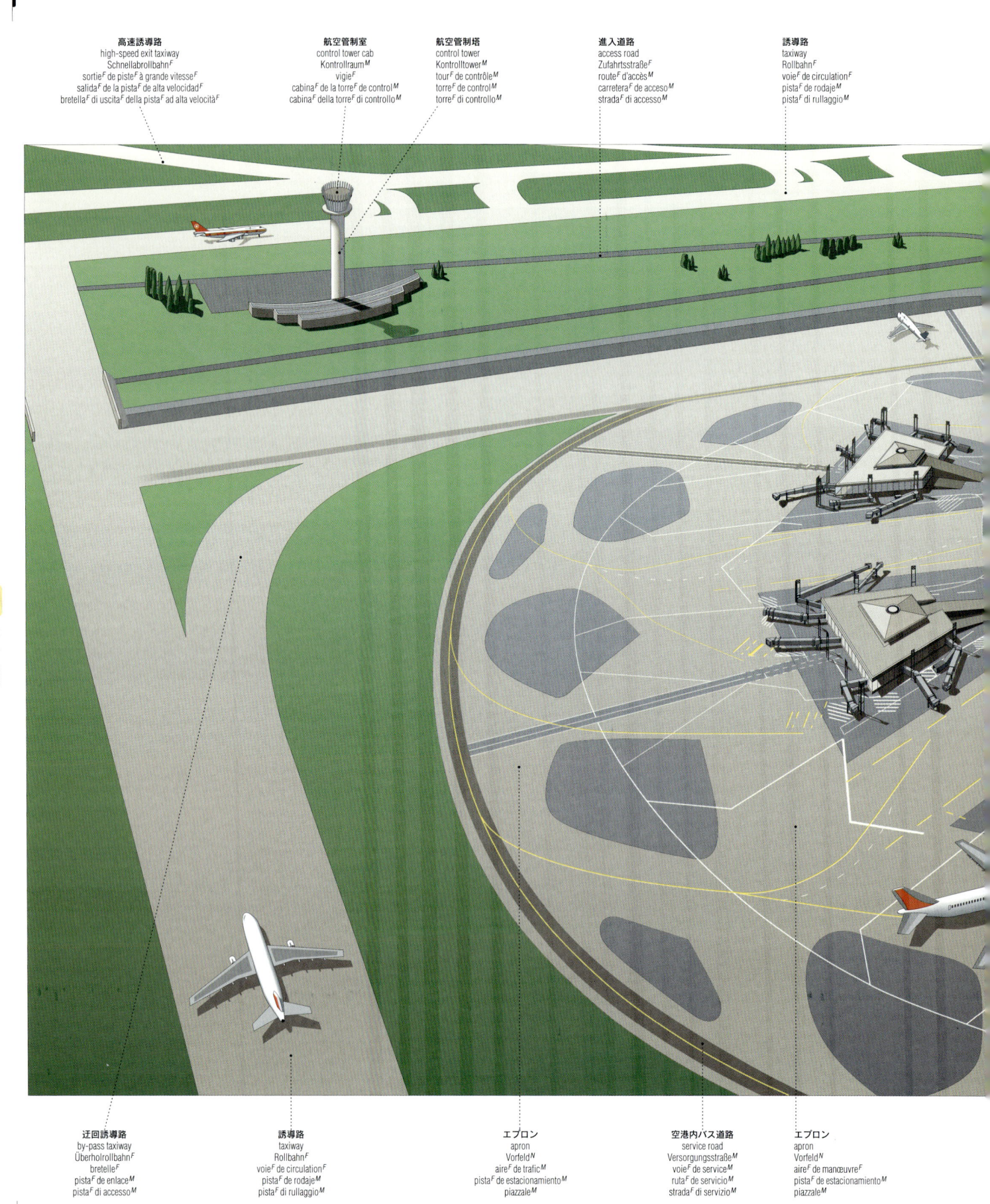

日本語 | 英語 | ドイツ語 | フランス語 | スペイン語 | イタリア語

高速誘導路
high-speed exit taxiway
Schnellabrollbahn^F
sortie^F de piste^F à grande vitesse^F
salida^F de la pista^F de alta velocidad^F
bretella^F di uscita^F della pista^F ad alta velocità^F

航空管制室
control tower cab
Kontrollraum^M
vigie^F
cabina^F de la torre^F de control^M
cabina^F della torre^F di controllo^M

航空管制塔
control tower
Kontrolltower^M
tour^F de contrôle^M
torre^F de control^M
torre^F di controllo^M

進入道路
access road
Zufahrtsstraße^F
route^F d'accès^M
carretera^F de acceso^M
strada^F di accesso^M

誘導路
taxiway
Rollbahn^F
voie^F de circulation^F
pista^F de rodaje^M
pista^F di rullaggio^M

迂回誘導路
by-pass taxiway
Überholrollbahn^F
bretelle^F
pista^F de enlace^M
pista^F di accesso^M

誘導路
taxiway
Rollbahn^F
voie^F de circulation^F
pista^F de rodaje^M
pista^F di rullaggio^M

エプロン
apron
Vorfeld^N
aire^F de trafic^M
pista^F de estacionamiento^M
piazzale^M

空港内バス道路
service road
Versorgungsstraße^F
voie^F de service^M
ruta^F de servicio^M
strada^F di servizio^M

エプロン
apron
Vorfeld^N
aire^F de manœuvre^F
pista^F de estacionamiento^M
piazzale^M

交通と機械

航空交通 | AIR TRANSPORT
LUFTVERKEHR | TRANSPORT AÉRIEN | TRANSPORTE AÉREO | TRASPORTO AEREO

空港

旅客ターミナル
passenger terminal
Passagierterminal^M
aérogare^F de passagers
terminal^M de pasajeros
terminal^M dei passeggeri

整備格納庫
maintenance hangar
Flugzeugwartungshalle^F
hangar^M
hangar^M de mantenimiento
aviorimessa^F

駐機場
parking area
Abstellplatz^M
aire^F de stationnement
parque^M de estacionamiento
area^F di parcheggio

交通と機械

可動式搭乗橋
telescopic corridor
ausziehbare Fluggastbrücke^F
passerelle^F télescopique
pasarela^F telescópico
corridoio^M telescopico

サービス・エリア
service area
Versorgungsbereich^M
aire^F de service
zona^F de servicio
area^F di servizio

旅客通路
boarding walkway
Fluggastbrücke^F
quai^M d'embarquement
túnel^M de embarque
passerella^F di imbarco

誘導ライン
taxiway line
Rolbahnmarkierung^F
marques^F de circulation
línea^F de pista
linea^F di rullaggio

サテライト・ターミナル
radial passenger loading area
radiale Einsteigestation^F
aérogare^F satellite
terminal^M satélite de pasajeros
terminal^M satellite dei passeggeri

619

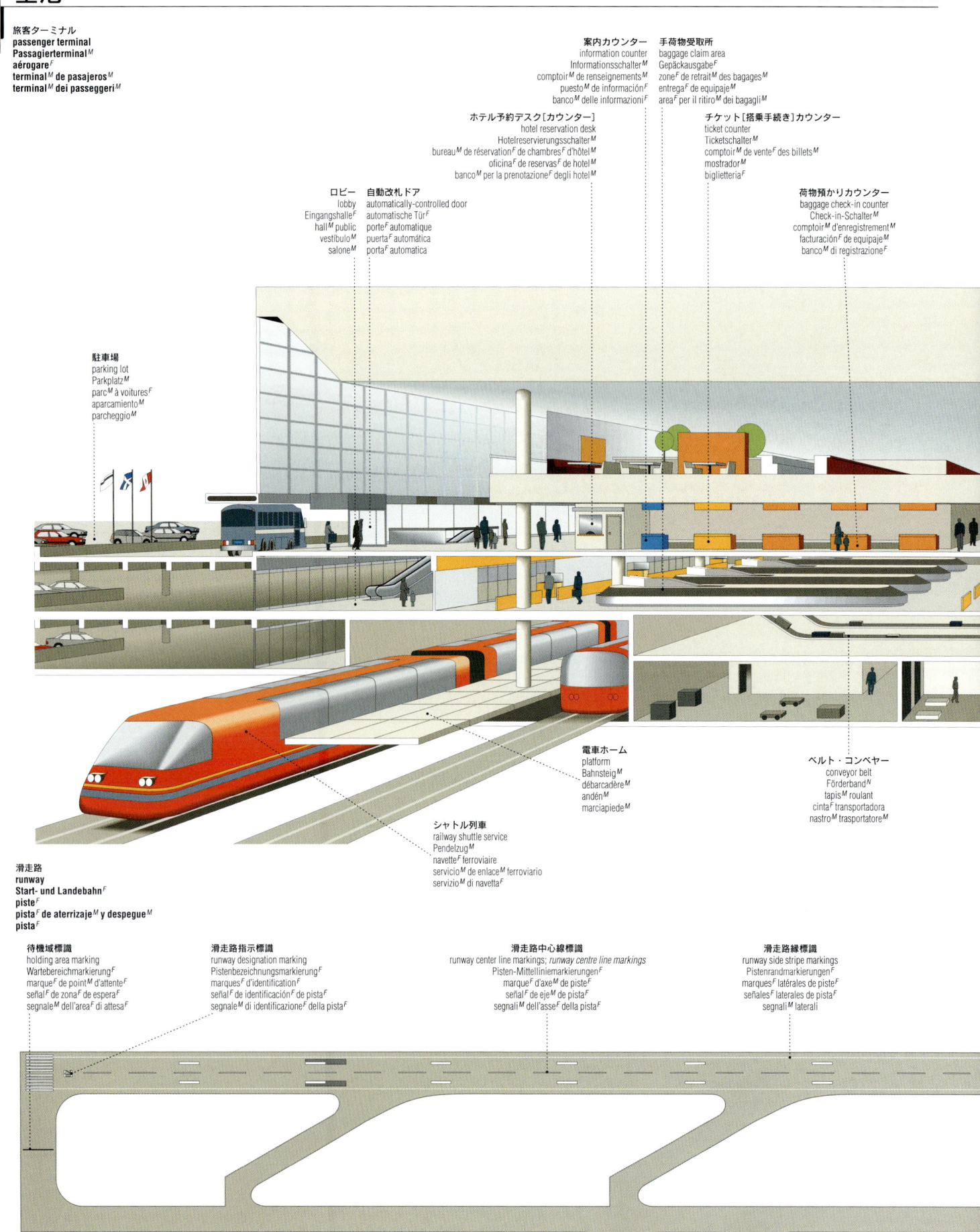

航空交通 | AIR TRANSPORT
LUFTVERKEHR | TRANSPORT AÉRIEN | TRANSPORTE AÉREO | TRASPORTO AEREO

空港

日本語 | 英語 | ドイツ語 | フランス語 | スペイン語 | イタリア語

旅客ターミナル
passenger terminal
Passagierterminal^M
aérogare^F
terminal^M de pasajeros^M
terminal^M dei passeggeri^M

案内カウンター
information counter
Informationsschalter^M
comptoir^M de renseignements^M
puesto^M de información^F
banco^M delle informazioni^F

手荷物受取所
baggage claim area
Gepäckausgabe^F
zone^F de retrait^M des bagages^M
entrega^F de equipaje^M
area^F per il ritiro^M dei bagagli^M

ホテル予約デスク[カウンター]
hotel reservation desk
Hotelreservierungsschalter^M
bureau^M de réservation^F de chambres^F d'hôtel^M
oficina^F de reservas^F de hotel^M
banco^M per la prenotazione^F degli hotel^M

チケット[搭乗手続き]カウンター
ticket counter
Ticketschalter^M
comptoir^M de vente^F des billets^M
mostrador^M
biglietteria^F

ロビー
lobby
Eingangshalle^F
hall^M public
vestíbulo^M
salone^M

自動改札ドア
automatically-controlled door
automatische Tür^F
porte^F automatique
puerta^F automática
porta^F automatica

荷物預かりカウンター
baggage check-in counter
Check-in-Schalter^M
comptoir^M d'enregistrement^M
facturación^F de equipaje^M
banco^M di registrazione^F

駐車場
parking lot
Parkplatz^M
parc^M à voitures^F
aparcamiento^M
parcheggio^M

電車ホーム
platform
Bahnsteig^M
débarcadère^M
andén^M
marciapiede^M

ベルト・コンベヤー
conveyor belt
Förderband^N
tapis^M roulant
cinta^F transportadora
nastro^M trasportatore^M

シャトル列車
railway shuttle service
Pendelzug^M
navette^F ferroviaire
servicio^M de enlace^M ferroviario
servizio^M di navetta^F

滑走路
runway
Start- und Landebahn^F
piste^F
pista^F de aterrizaje^M y despegue^M
pista^F

待機域標識
holding area marking
Wartebereichmarkierung^F
marque^F de point^M d'attente^F
señal^F de zona^F de espera^F
segnale^M dell'area^F di attesa^F

滑走路指示標識
runway designation marking
Pistenbezeichnungsmarkierung^F
marques^F d'identification^F
señal^F de identificación^F de pista^F
segnale^M di identificazione^F della pista^F

滑走路中心線標識
runway center line markings; *runway centre line markings*
Pisten-Mittellinienmarkierungen^F
marque^F d'axe^M de piste^F
señal^F de eje^M de pista^F
segnali^M dell'asse^M della pista^F

滑走路縁標識
runway side stripe markings
Pistenrandmarkierungen^F
marques^F latérales de piste^F
señales^F laterales de pista^F
segnali^M laterali

交通と機械

航空交通 | AIR TRANSPORT
LUFTVERKEHR | TRANSPORT AÉRIEN | TRANSPORTE AÉREO | TRASPORTO AEREO

空港

手荷物検査場
security check
Sicherheitskontrolle^F
contrôle^M de sécurité^F
control^M de seguridad^F
controllo^M di sicurezza^F

免税店
duty-free shop
Duty-free-Shop^M
boutique^F hors taxe^F
tienda^F libre de impuestos^M
duty free^M

送迎デッキ
observation deck
Besucherterrasse^F
terrasse^F
mirador^M
terrazza^F

発着案内板
flight information board
Fluginformationsanzeige^F
tableau^M d'affichage^M des vols^M
tablero^M de llegadas^F y salidas^F
tabellone^M degli arrivi^M e delle partenze^F

荷物発送所
freight expedition; cargo dispatch
Frachtversand^M
expédition^F du fret^M
expedición^F de carga^F
spedizione^F merci^F

出国審査場
passport control
Passkontrolle^F
contrôle^M des passeports^M
control^M de pasaportes^M
controllo^M dei passaporti^M

搭乗控え室
boarding room
Abflugwartehalle^F
salle^F d'embarquement^M
sala^F de espera^F de embarque^M
sala^F di imbarco^M

旅客運搬橋
passenger transfer vehicle
Passagiertransferfahrzeug^N
transbordeur^M
transbordador^M
navetta^F per il trasbordo^M dei passeggeri^M

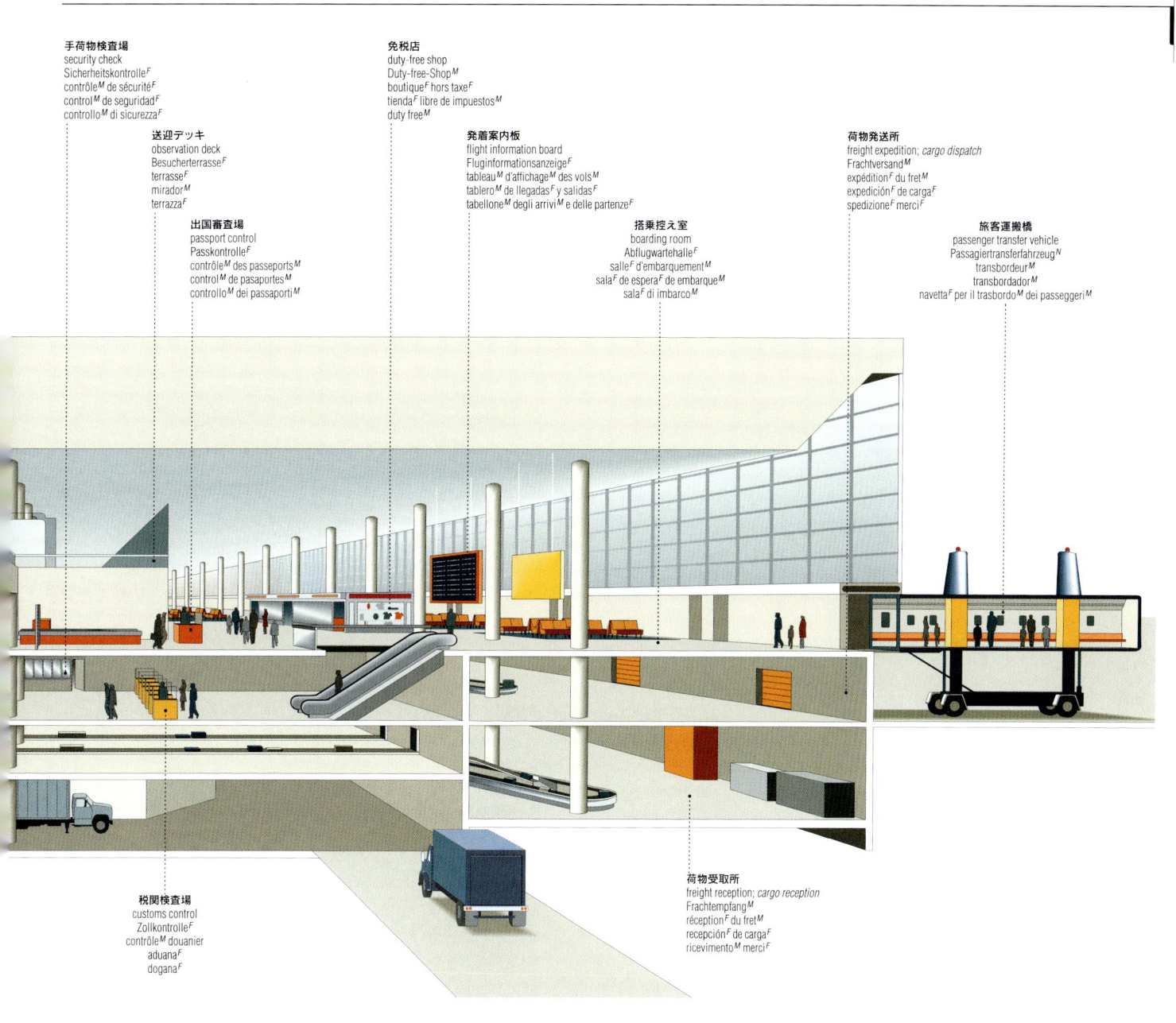

税関検査場
customs control
Zollkontrolle^F
contrôle^M douanier
aduana^F
dogana^F

荷物受取所
freight reception; cargo reception
Frachtempfang^M
réception^F du fret^M
recepción^F de carga^F
ricevimento^M merci^F

交通と機械

出口誘導路
exit taxiway
Abrollbahn^F
sortie^F de piste^F
salida^F de la pista^F
bretella^F di uscita^F

滑走路着陸接地点標識
runway touchdown zone marking
Aufsetzzonenmarkierungen^F
marque^F d'aire^F de prise^F de contact^M
señal^F de zona^F de contacto^M de pista^F
segnale^M di zona^F di contatto^M

滑走路末端標識
runway threshold markings
Schwellenmarkierungen^F
marques^F de seuil^M de piste^F
señales de límite^M de la pista^F
segnali^M della soglia^F della pista^F

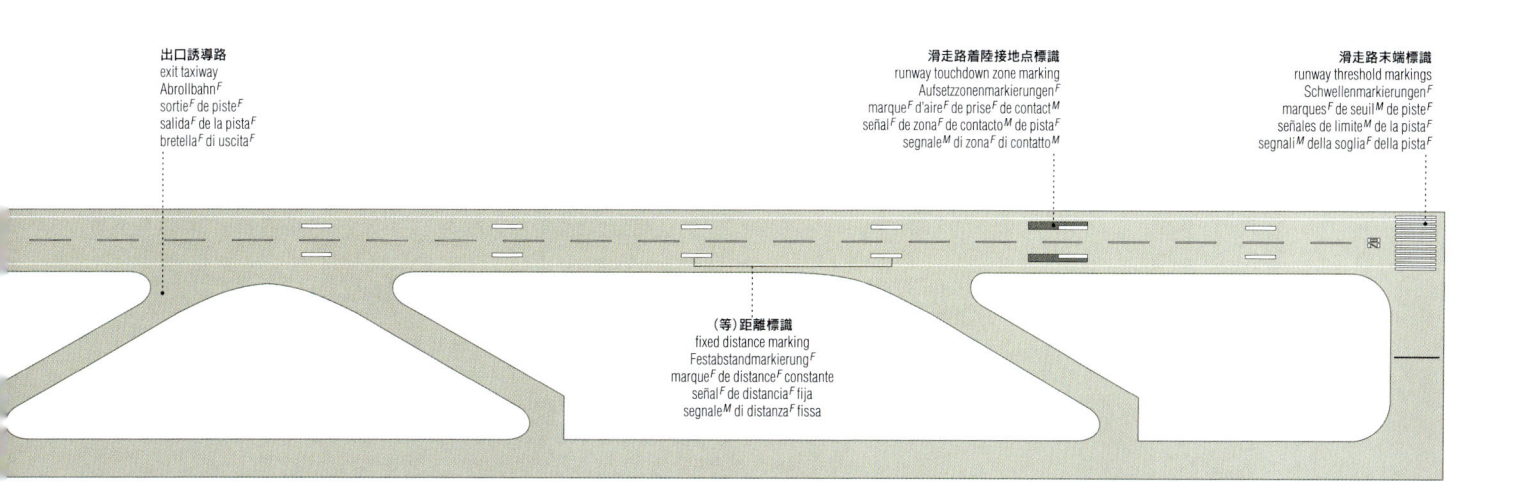

(等)距離標識
fixed distance marking
Festabstandmarkierung^F
marque^F de distance^F constante
señal^F de distancia^F fija
segnale^M di distanza^F fissa

621

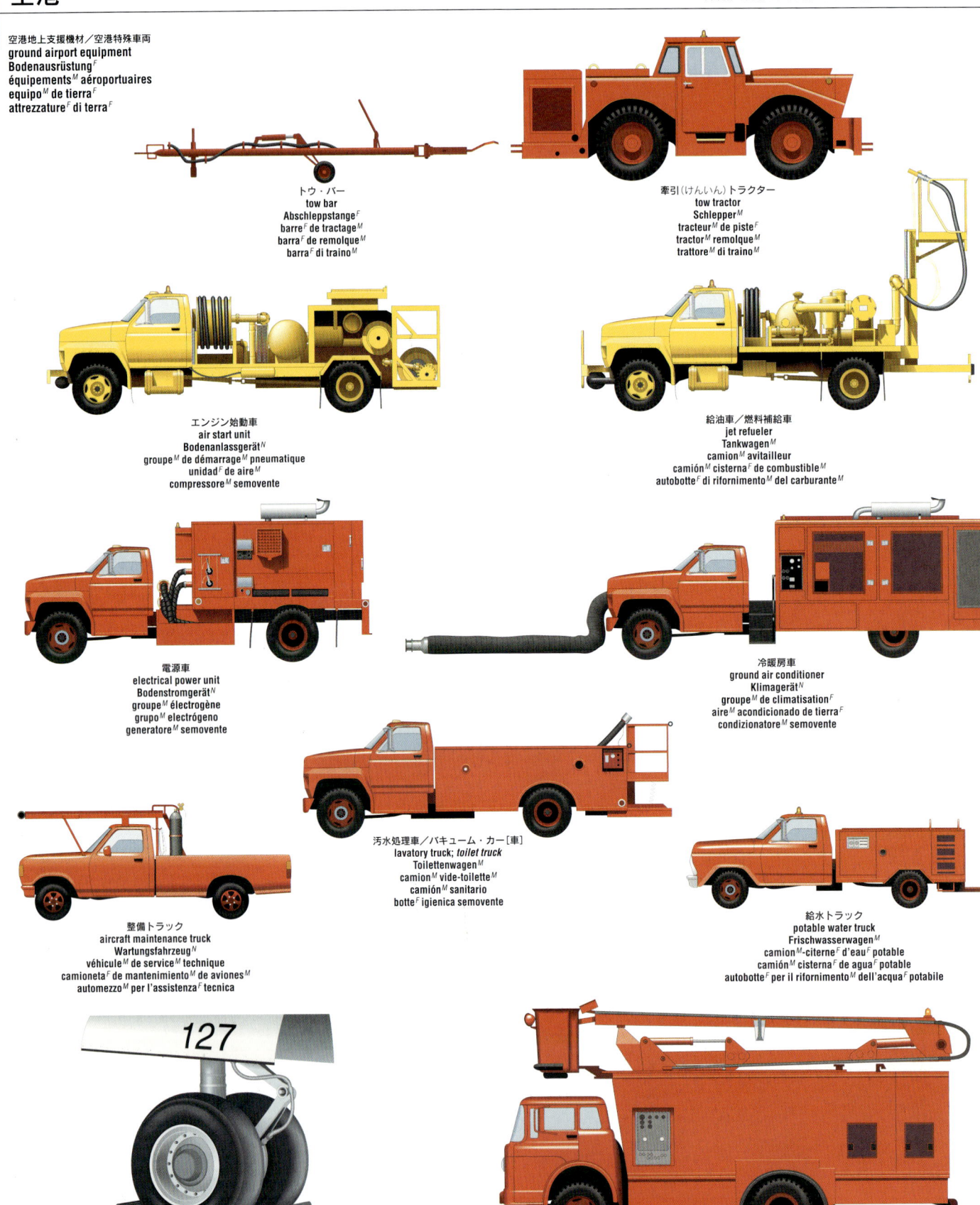

航空交通 | AIR TRANSPORT
LUFTVERKEHR | TRANSPORT AÉRIEN | TRANSPORTE AÉREO | TRASPORTO AEREO

空港

日本語 | 英語 | ドイツ語 | フランス語 | スペイン語 | イタリア語

空港地上支援機材／空港特殊車両
ground airport equipment
Bodenausrüstung^F
équipements^M aéroportuaires
equipo^M de tierra^F
attrezzature^F di terra^F

トウ・バー
tow bar
Abschleppstange^F
barre^F de tractage^M
barra^F de remolque^M
barra^F di traino^M

牽引(けんいん)トラクター
tow tractor
Schlepper^M
tracteur^M de piste^F
tractor^M remolque^M
trattore^M di traino^M

エンジン始動車
air start unit
Bodenanlassgerät^N
groupe^M de démarrage^M pneumatique
unidad^F de aire^M
compressore^M semovente

給油車／燃料補給車
jet refueler
Tankwagen^M
camion^M avitailleur
camión^M cisterna^F de combustible^M
autobotte^F di rifornimento^M del carburante^M

電源車
electrical power unit
Bodenstromgerät^N
groupe^M électrogène
grupo^M electrógeno
generatore^M semovente

冷暖房車
ground air conditioner
Klimagerät^N
groupe^M de climatisation^F
aire^M acondicionado de tierra^F
condizionatore^M semovente

整備トラック
aircraft maintenance truck
Wartungsfahrzeug^N
véhicule^M de service^M technique
camioneta^F de mantenimiento^M de aviones^M
automezzo^M per l'assistenza^F tecnica

汚水処理車／バキューム・カー[車]
lavatory truck; toilet truck
Toilettenwagen^M
camion^M vide-toilette
camión^M sanitario
botte^F igienica semovente

給水トラック
potable water truck
Frischwasserwagen^M
camion^M-citerne^F d'eau^F potable
camión^M cisterna^F de agua^F potable
autobotte^F per il rifornimento^M dell'acqua^F potabile

車輪止め
wheel chock
Bremsklotz^M
cale^F
calzo^M de la rueda^F
tacco^M

ゴンドラ付き高所作業車
boom truck
Tankwagen^M mit beweglichem Ausleger^M
nacelle^F élévatrice
camioneta^F con canastilla^F telescópica
automezzo^M con braccio^M mobile

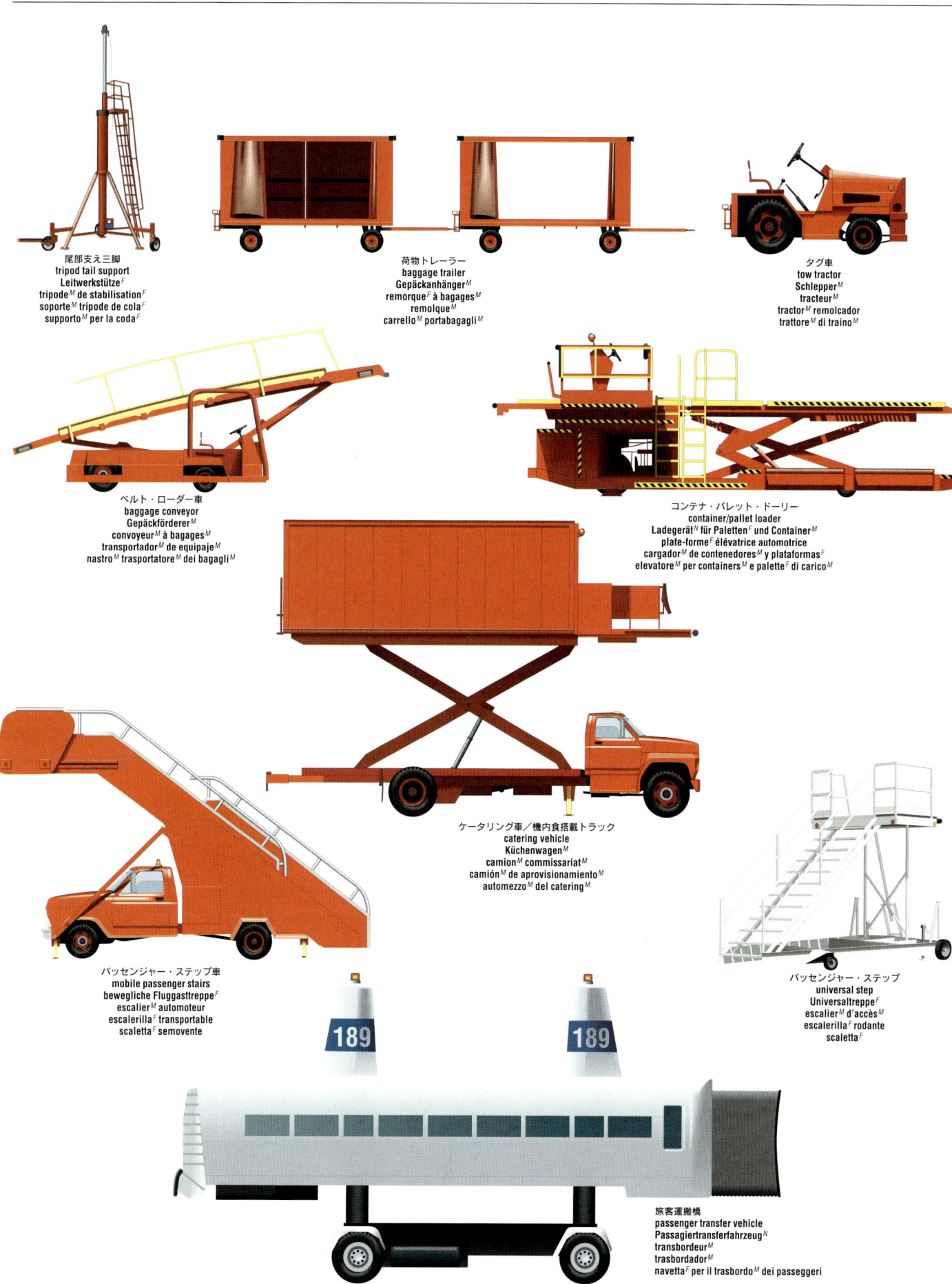

航空交通 | AIR TRANSPORT
LUFTVERKEHR | TRANSPORT AÉRIEN | TRANSPORTE AÉREO | TRASPORTO AEREO

空港

尾部支え三脚
tripod tail support
Leitwerkstütze^F
tripode^M de stabilisation^F
soporte^M trípode de cola^F
supporto^M per la coda^F

荷物トレーラー
baggage trailer
Gepäckanhänger^M
remorque^F à bagages^M
remolque^M
carrello^M portabagagli^M

タグ車
tow tractor
Schlepper^M
tracteur^M
tractor^M remolcador
trattore^M di traino^M

ベルト・ローダー車
baggage conveyor
Gepäckförderer^M
convoyeur^M à bagages^M
transportador^M de equipaje^M
nastro^M trasportatore dei bagagli^M

コンテナ・パレット・ドーリー
container/pallet loader
Ladegerät^N für Paletten^F und Container^M
plate-forme^F élévatrice automotrice
cargador^M de contenedores^M y plataformas^F
elevatore^M per containers^M e palette^F di carico^M

ケータリング車／機内食搭載トラック
catering vehicle
Küchenwagen^M
camion^M commissariat^M
camión^M de aprovisionamiento^M
automezzo^M del catering^M

パッセンジャー・ステップ車
mobile passenger stairs
bewegliche Fluggasttreppe^F
escalier^M automoteur
escalerilla^F transportable
scaletta^F semovente

パッセンジャー・ステップ
universal step
Universaltreppe^F
escalier^M d'accès^M
escalerilla^F rodante
scaletta^F

交通と機械

旅客運搬機
passenger transfer vehicle
Passagiertransferfahrzeug^N
transbordeur^M
trasbordador^M
navetta^F per il trasbordo^M dei passeggeri^M

航空交通 | AIR TRANSPORT
LUFTVERKEHR | TRANSPORT AÉRIEN | TRANSPORTE AÉREO | TRASPORTO AEREO

大型[長距離]ジェット機

日本語 | 英語 | ドイツ語 | フランス語 | スペイン語 | イタリア語

long-range jet | Langstrecken-Düsenflugzeug[N] | avion[M] long-courrier[M] | avión[M] turborreactor de pasajeros[M] | aviogetto[M] a lungo raggio[M]

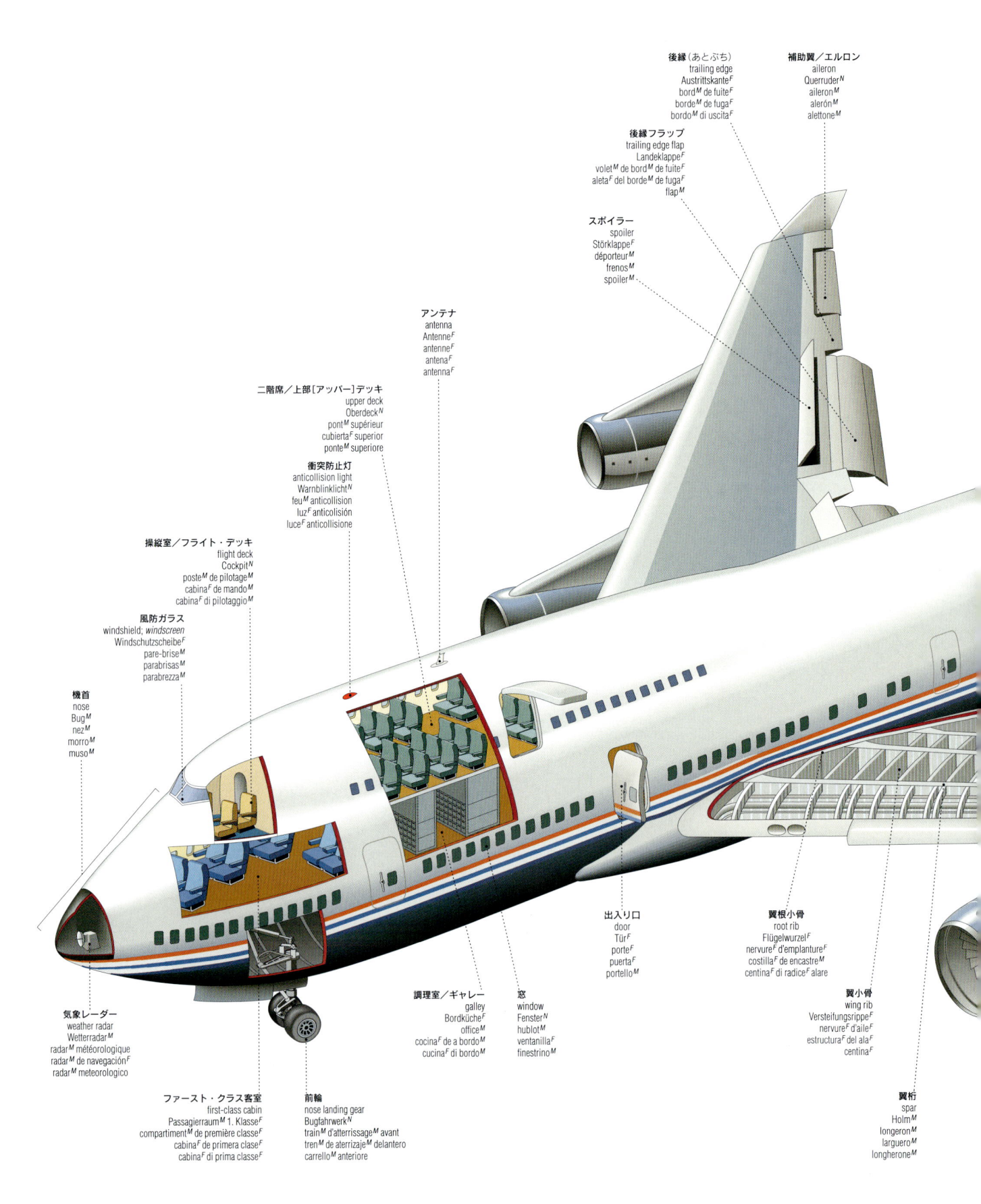

後縁(あとぶち)
trailing edge
Austrittskante[F]
bord[M] de fuite[F]
borde[M] de fuga[F]
bordo[M] di uscita[F]

補助翼／エルロン
aileron
Querruder[N]
aileron[M]
alerón[M]
alettone[M]

後縁フラップ
trailing edge flap
Landeklappe[F]
volet[M] de bord[M] de fuite[F]
aleta[F] del borde[M] de fuga[F]
flap[M]

スポイラー
spoiler
Störklappe[F]
déporteur[M]
frenos[M]
spoiler[M]

アンテナ
antenna
Antenne[F]
antenne[F]
antena[F]
antenna[F]

二階席／上部[アッパー]デッキ
upper deck
Oberdeck[N]
pont[M] supérieur
cubierta[F] superior
ponte[M] superiore

衝突防止灯
anticollision light
Warnblinklicht[N]
feu[M] anticollision
luz[F] anticolisión
luce[F] anticollisione

操縦室／フライト・デッキ
flight deck
Cockpit[N]
poste[M] de pilotage[M]
cabina[F] de mando[M]
cabina[F] di pilotaggio[M]

風防ガラス
windshield; *windscreen*
Windschutzscheibe[F]
pare-brise[M]
parabrisas[M]
parabrezza[M]

機首
nose
Bug[M]
nez[M]
morro[M]
muso[M]

気象レーダー
weather radar
Wetterradar[M]
radar[M] météorologique
radar[M] de navegación[F]
radar[M] meteorologico

ファースト・クラス客室
first-class cabin
Passagierraum[M] 1. Klasse[F]
compartiment[M] de première classe[F]
cabina[F] de primera clase[F]
cabina[F] di prima classe[F]

前輪
nose landing gear
Bugfahrwerk[N]
train[M] d'atterrissage[M] avant
tren[M] de aterrizaje[M] delantero
carrello[M] anteriore

調理室／ギャレー
galley
Bordküche[F]
office[M]
cocina[F] de a bordo[M]
cucina[F] di bordo[M]

窓
window
Fenster[N]
hublot[M]
ventanilla[F]
finestrino[M]

出入リロ
door
Tür[F]
porte[F]
puerta[F]
portello[M]

翼根小骨
root rib
Flügelwurzel[F]
nervure[F] d'emplanture[F]
costilla[F] de encastre[M]
centina[F] di radice[F] alare

翼小骨
wing rib
Versteifungsrippe[F]
nervure[F] d'aile[F]
estructura[F] del ala[F]
centina[F]

翼桁
spar
Holm[M]
longeron[M]
larguero[M]
longherone[M]

624

航空交通 | AIR TRANSPORT
LUFTVERKEHR | TRANSPORT AÉRIEN | TRANSPORTE AÉREO | TRASPORTO AEREO

大型[長距離]ジェット機

尾翼／尾部
tail assembly
Leitwerk^N
empennage^M
plano^M vertical
impennaggio^M verticale

胴体
fuselage
Rumpf^M
fuselage^M
fuselaje^M
fusoliera^F

客室
passenger cabin
Passagierraum^M
compartiment^M touriste^M
cabina^F de clase^F turista
cabina^F di classe^F turistica

貨物室
freight hold; *cargo hold*
Frachtraum^M
compartiment^M à fret^M
bodega^F de equipaje^M
bagagliaio^M

主車輪／主脚
main landing gear
Hauptfahrwerk^N
train^M d'atterrissage^M principal
tren^M de aterrizaje^M principal
carrello^M principale

前縁（まえぶち）
leading edge
Eintrittskante^F
bord^M d'attaque^F
borde^M de ataque^M
bordo^M di attacco^M

エンジン支柱／パイロン
engine mounting pylon
Pylon^M zur Aufhängung^F des Triebwerks^N
pylône^M du moteur^M
pilón^M del turborreactor^M
castello^M motore^M

ターボジェット・エンジン
turbojet engine
TL-Triebwerk^N
turboréacteur^M
turborreactor^M
turboreattore^M

垂直安定板
fin
Seitenflosse^F
dérive^F
plano^M de deriva^F
deriva^F

方向舵／ラダー
rudder
Seitenruder^N
gouverne^F de direction^F
timón^M
timone^M di direzione^F

尾
tail
Heck^N
queue^F
cola^F
coda^F

昇降舵／エレベーター
elevator
Höhenruder^N
gouverne^F de profondeur^F
timón^M de profundidad^F
timone^M di profondità^F

水平安定板
horizontal stabilizer; *tailplane*
Höhenflosse^F
stabilisateur^M
plano^M horizontal
stabilizzatore^M

（翼端）小翼／ウイングレット
winglet
Winglet^N
ailette^F
aleta^F
aletta^F

主翼
wing
Tragflügel^M
aile^F
ala^F
ala^F

航行灯／標識灯／ナビゲーション・ライト
navigation light
Positionslicht^N
feu^M de navigation^F
luz^F de navegación^F
luce^F di navigazione^F

前縁フラップ
wing slat
Vorflügel^M
bec^M de bord^M d'attaque^F
aleta^F hipersustentadora
ipersostentatore^M sul bordo^M di attacco^M

交通と機械

航空交通 | AIR TRANSPORT
LUFTVERKEHR | TRANSPORT AÉRIEN | TRANSPORTE AÉREO | TRASPORTO AEREO

操縦室／フライト・デッキ

日本語 | 英語 | ドイツ語 | フランス語 | スペイン語 | イタリア語

flight deck | Cockpit[N] | poste[M] de pilotage[M] | puente[M] de mando[M] | cabina[F] di pilotaggio[M]

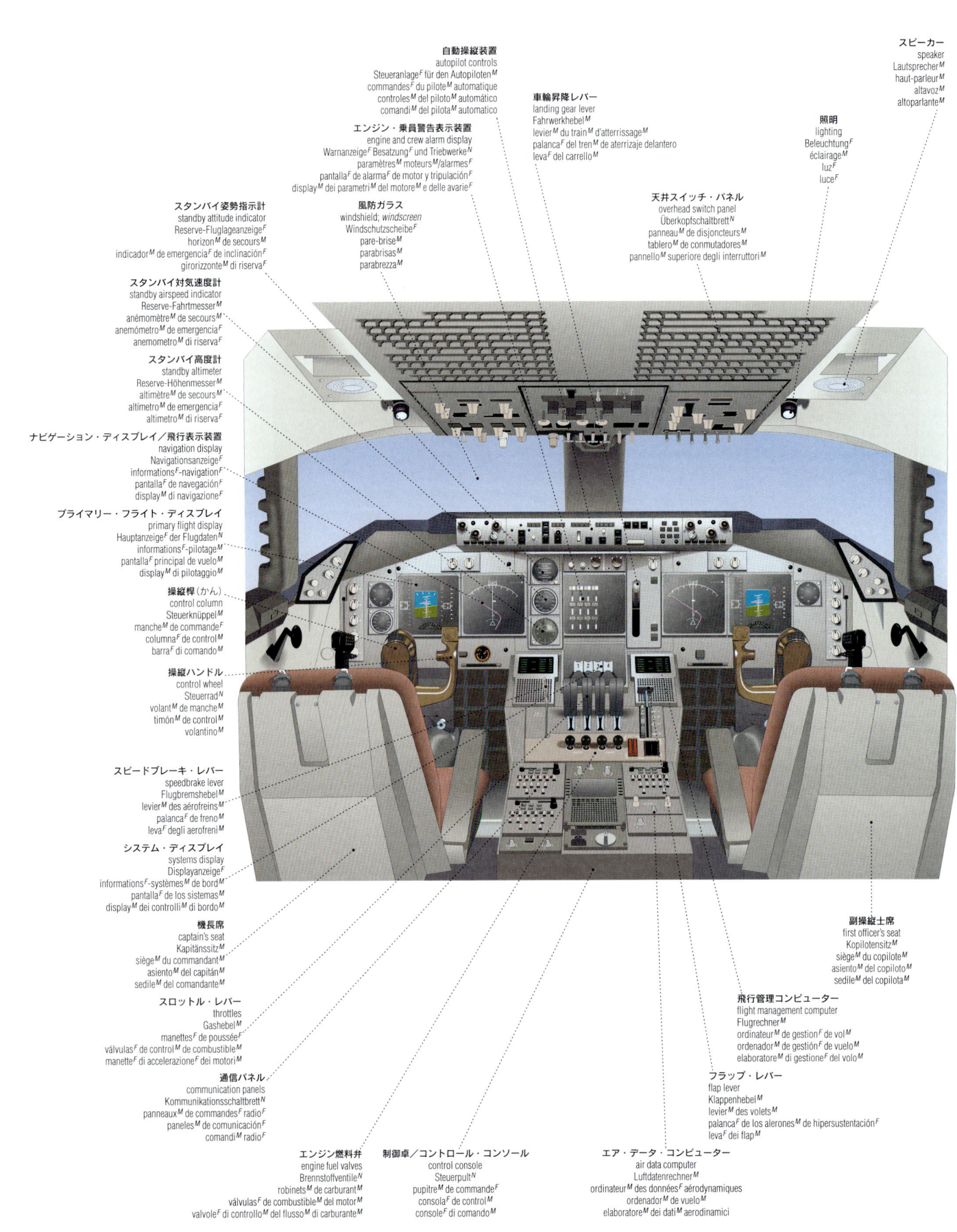

交通と機械

自動操縦装置
autopilot controls
Steueranlage[F] für den Autopiloten[M]
commandes[F] du pilote[M] automatique
controles[M] del piloto[M] automático
comandi[M] del pilota[M] automatico

エンジン・乗員警告表示装置
engine and crew alarm display
Warnanzeige[F] Besatzung[F] und Triebwerke[N]
paramètres[M] moteurs/alarmes[F]
pantalla[F] de alarma[F] de motor[M] y tripulación[F]
display[M] dei parametri[M] del motore[M] e delle avarie[F]

車輪昇降レバー
landing gear lever
Fahrwerkhebel[M]
levier[M] du train[M] d'atterrissage[M]
palanca[F] del tren[M] de aterrizaje delantero
leva[F] del carrello[M]

スピーカー
speaker
Lautsprecher[M]
haut-parleur[M]
altavoz[M]
altoparlante[M]

照明
lighting
Beleuchtung[F]
éclairage[M]
luz[F]
luce[F]

スタンバイ姿勢指示計
standby attitude indicator
Reserve-Fluglageanzeige[F]
horizon[M] de secours[M]
indicador[M] de emergencia[F] de inclinación[F]
girorizzonte[M] di riserva[F]

風防ガラス
windshield; windscreen
Windschutzscheibe[F]
pare-brise[M]
parabrisas[M]
parabrezza[M]

天井スイッチ・パネル
overhead switch panel
Überkopfschaltbrett[N]
panneau[M] de disjoncteurs[M]
tablero[M] de conmutadores[M]
pannello[M] superiore degli interruttori[M]

スタンバイ対気速度計
standby airspeed indicator
Reserve-Fahrtmesser[M]
anémomètre[M] de secours[M]
anemómetro[M] de emergencia[F]
anemometro[M] di riserva[F]

スタンバイ高度計
standby altimeter
Reserve-Höhenmesser[M]
altimètre[M] de secours[M]
altímetro[M] de emergencia[F]
altimetro[M] di riserva[F]

ナビゲーション・ディスプレイ／飛行表示装置
navigation display
Navigationsanzeige[F]
informations[F]-navigation[F]
pantalla[F] de navegación[F]
display[M] di navigazione[F]

プライマリー・フライト・ディスプレイ
primary flight display
Hauptanzeige[F] der Flugdaten[F]
informations[F]-pilotage[F]
pantalla[F] principal de vuelo[M]
display[M] di pilotaggio[M]

操縦桿（かん）
control column
Steuerknüppel[M]
manche[M] de commande[F]
columna[F] de control[M]
barra[F] di comando[M]

操縦ハンドル
control wheel
Steuerrad[N]
volant[M] de manche[M]
timón[M] de control[M]
volantino[M]

スピードブレーキ・レバー
speedbrake lever
Flugbremshebel[M]
levier[M] des aérofreins[M]
palanca[F] de freno[M]
leva[F] degli aerofreni[M]

システム・ディスプレイ
systems display
Displayanzeige[F]
informations[F]-systèmes[M] de bord[M]
pantalla[F] de los sistemas[M]
display[M] dei controlli[M] di bordo[M]

機長席
captain's seat
Kapitänssitz[M]
siège[M] du commandant[M]
asiento[M] del capitán[M]
sedile[M] del comandante[M]

スロットル・レバー
throttles
Gashebel[M]
manettes[F] de poussée[F]
válvulas[F] de control[M] de combustible[M]
manette[F] di accelerazione[F] dei motori[M]

通信パネル
communication panels
Kommunikationsschaltbrett[N]
panneaux[M] de commandes[F] radio[F]
paneles[M] de comunicación[F]
comandi[M] radio[M]

副操縦士席
first officer's seat
Kopilotensitz[M]
siège[M] du copilote[M]
asiento[M] del copiloto[M]
sedile[M] del copilota[M]

飛行管理コンピューター
flight management computer
Flugrechner[M]
ordinateur[M] de gestion[F] de vol[M]
ordenador[M] de gestión[F] de vuelo[M]
elaboratore[M] di gestione[F] del volo[M]

フラップ・レバー
flap lever
Klappenhebel[M]
levier[M] des volets[M]
palanca[F] de los alerones[M] de hipersustentación[F]
leva[F] dei flap[M]

エンジン燃料弁
engine fuel valves
Brennstoffventile[N]
robinets[M] de carburant[M]
válvulas[F] de combustible[M] del motor[M]
valvole[F] di controllo[M] del flusso[M] di carburante[M]

制御卓／コントロール・コンソール
control console
Steuerpult[N]
pupitre[M] de commande[F]
consola[F] de control[M]
console[M] di comando[M]

エア・データ・コンピューター
air data computer
Luftdatenrechner[M]
ordinateur[M] des données[F] aérodynamiques
ordenador[M] de vuelo[M]
elaboratore[M] dei dati[M] aerodinamici

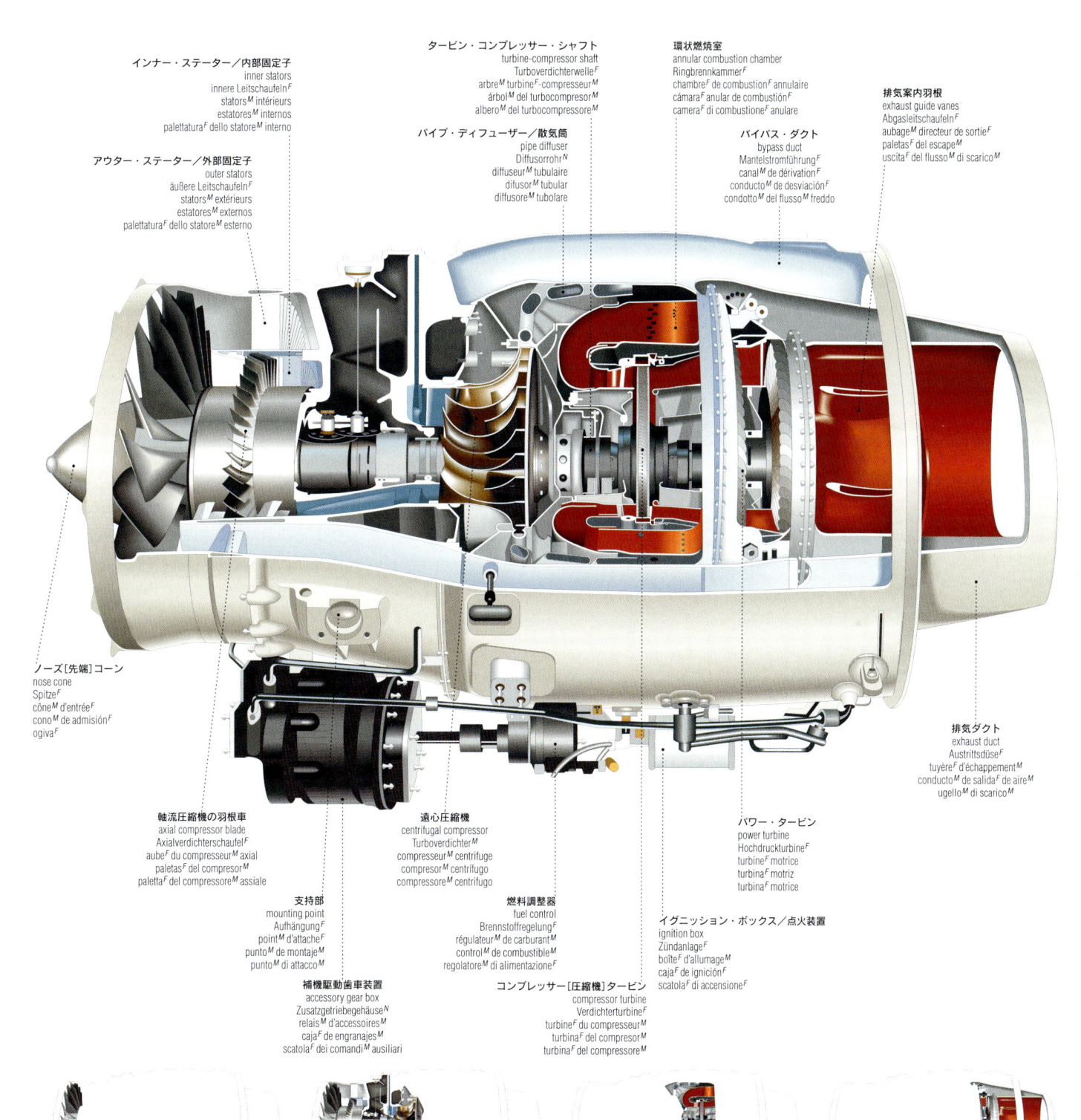

航空交通 | AIR TRANSPORT
LUFTVERKEHR | TRANSPORT AÉRIEN | TRANSPORTE AÉREO | TRASPORTO AEREO

ターボファン・エンジン

turbofan engine | Zweistromtriebwerk^N | turboréacteur^M à double flux^M | turborreactor^M | turboreattore^M a doppio flusso^M

インナー・ステーター／内部固定子
inner stators
innere Leitschaufeln^F
stators^M intérieurs
estatores^M internos
palettatura^F dello statore^M interno

アウター・ステーター／外部固定子
outer stators
äußere Leitschaufeln^F
stators^M extérieurs
estatores^M externos
palettatura^F dello statore^M esterno

タービン・コンプレッサー・シャフト
turbine-compressor shaft
Turboverdichterwelle^F
arbre^M turbine^F-compresseur^M
árbol^M del turbocompresor
albero^M del turbocompressore

パイプ・ディフューザー／散気筒
pipe diffuser
Diffusorrohr^N
diffuseur^M tubulaire
difusor^M tubular
diffusore^M tubolare

環状燃焼室
annular combustion chamber
Ringbrennkammer^F
chambre^F de combustion^F annulaire
cámara^F anular de combustión^F
camera^F di combustione^F anulare

バイパス・ダクト
bypass duct
Mantelstromführung^F
canal^M de dérivation^F
conducto^M de desviación^F
condotto^M del flusso^M freddo

排気案内羽根
exhaust guide vanes
Abgasleitschaufeln^F
aubage^M directeur de sortie^F
paletas^F del escape^M
uscita^F del flusso^M di scarico^M

ノーズ［先端］コーン
nose cone
Spitze^F
cône^M d'entrée^F
cono^M de admisión^F
ogiva^F

軸流圧縮機の羽根車
axial compressor blade
Axialverdichterschaufel^F
aube^F du compresseur^M axial
paletas^F del compresor^M
paletta^F del compressore^M assiale

支持部
mounting point
Aufhängung^F
point^M d'attache^F
punto^M de montaje^M
punto^M di attacco^M

遠心圧縮機
centrifugal compressor
Turboverdichter^M
compresseur^M centrifuge
compresor^M centrífugo
compressore^M centrifugo

燃料調整器
fuel control
Brennstoffregelung^F
régulateur^M de carburant^M
control^M de combustible^M
regolatore^M di alimentazione^F

パワー・タービン
power turbine
Hochdruckturbine^F
turbine^F motrice
turbina^F motriz
turbina^F motrice

イグニッション・ボックス／点火装置
ignition box
Zündanlage^F
boîte^F d'allumage^M
caja^F de ignición^F
scatola^F di accensione^F

補機駆動歯車装置
accessory gear box
Zusatzgetriebegehäuse^N
relais^M d'accessoires^M
caja^F de engranajes^M
scatola^F dei comandi^M ausiliari

コンプレッサー［圧縮機］タービン
compressor turbine
Verdichterturbine^F
turbine^F du compresseur^M
turbina^F del compresor^M
turbina^F del compressore^M

排気ダクト
exhaust duct
Austrittsdüse^F
tuyère^F d'échappement^M
conducto^M de salida^F de aire^M
ugello^M di scarico^M

ファン
fan
Niederdruckverdichtung^F
soufflante^F
ventilador^M
soffiante^M

圧縮
compression
Verdichtung^F
compression^F
compresión^F
compressione^F

燃焼
combustion
Verbrennung^F
combustion^F
combustión^F
combustione^F

排気
exhaust
Abgas^N
échappement^M
escape^M
scarico^M

交通と機械

航空交通 | AIR TRANSPORT
LUFTVERKEHR | TRANSPORT AÉRIEN | TRANSPORTE AÉREO | TRASPORTO AEREO

飛行機の例

examples of airplanes | Beispiele^N für Flugzeuge^N | exemples^M d'avions^M | ejemplos^M de aviones^M | esempi^M di aeroplani^M

日本語 | 英語 | ドイツ語 | フランス語 | スペイン語 | イタリア語

フロート水上機
float seaplane
Wasserflugzeug^N
hydravion^M à flotteurs^M
hidroavión^M de flotadores^M
idrovolante^M a due galleggianti^M

3枚羽根プロペラ
three-blade propeller
dreiflügeliger Propeller^M
hélice^F tripale
hélice^F de tres aspas^F
elica^F tripala

高翼
high wing
Tragflügel^M
aile^F haute
ala^F alta
ala^F alta

上翼
upper wing
oberer Flügel^M
aile^F supérieure
ala^F superior
ala^F superiore

複葉機
biplane
Doppeldecker^M
biplan^M
biplano^M
biplano^M

翼
wings
Flügel^M
voilure^F
alas^F
ali^F

フロート
float
Schwimmkörper^M
flotteur^M
flotador^M
galleggiante^M

下翼
lower wing
unterer Flügel^M
aile^F inférieure
ala^F alta
ala^F inferiore

軽飛行機
light aircraft
Leichtflugzeug^N
avion^M léger
avión^M ligero
aeroplano^M leggero

翼支柱
wing strut
Flügelstrebe^F
hauban^M
montante^M
montante^M dell'ala^F

高周波アンテナ・ケーブル
high frequency antenna cable
Funkantenne^F
câble^M de l'antenne^F haute fréquence^F
cable^M de la antena^F de alta frecuencia^F
cavo^M dell'antenna^F ad alta frequenza^F

ビジネス機
business aircraft
Privatflugzeug^N
avion^M d'affaires^M
avión^M particular
aeroplano^M privato

2枚羽根プロペラ
two-blade propeller
zweiflügeliger Propeller^M
hélice^F bipale
hélice^F de dos aspas^F
elica^F bipala

キャノピー
canopy
Kuppel^F
verrière^F
parabrisas^M
parabrezza^M

垂直離着陸機
vertical take-off and landing aircraft
Senkrechtstartflugzeug^N
avion^M à décollage^M et atterrissage^M verticaux
avión^M de despegue^M y aterrizaje^M verticales
aeroplano^M a decollo^M e atterraggio^M verticale

(翼端)小翼／ウイングレット
winglet
Flosse^F
ailette^F
aleta^F
aletta^F

消防飛行艇
amphibious firefighting aircraft
Amphibien^F-Löschflugzeug^N
avion^M-citerne^F amphibie
hidroavión^M cisterna
aeroplano^M anfibio antincendio

推力偏向ノズル
swiveling nozzle
Schwenkdüse^F
tuyère^F orientable
tobera^F orientable
ugello^M orientabile

3枚羽根プロペラ
three-blade propeller
dreiflügeliger Propeller^M
hélice^F tripale
hélice^F de tres aspas^F
elica^F tripala

水タンク
water-tank area
Wassertank^M
compartiment^M de réservoir^M d'eau^F
compartimento^M del depósito^M del agua^F
vano^M del serbatoio^M dell'acqua^F

フロート
float
Schwimmkörper^M
flotteur^M
flotador^M
galleggiante^M

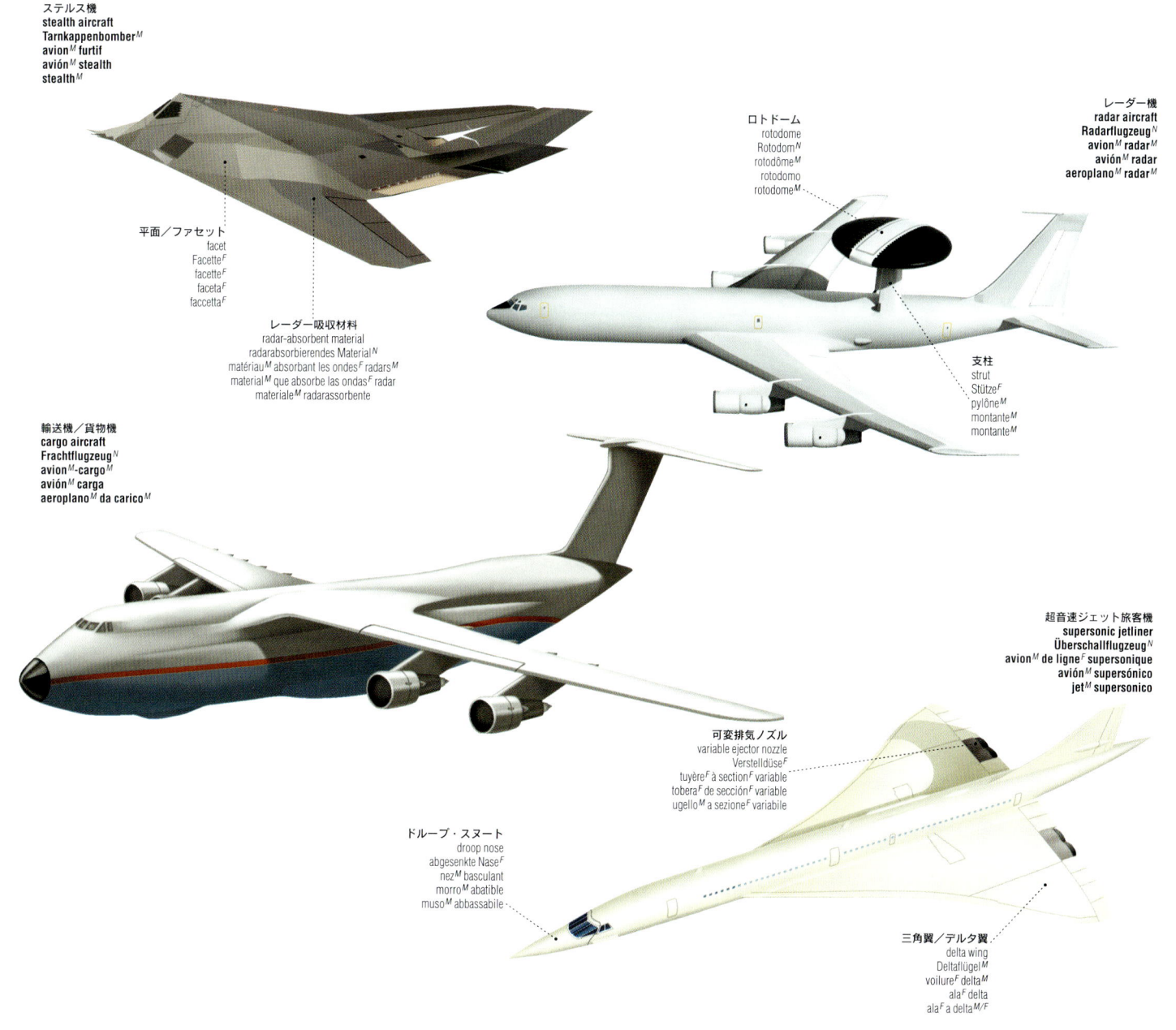

航空交通 | AIR TRANSPORT
LUFTVERKEHR | TRANSPORT AÉRIEN | TRANSPORTE AÉREO | TRASPORTO AEREO

飛行機の例

ステルス機
stealth aircraft
Tarnkappenbomber^M
avion^M furtif
avión^M stealth
stealth^M

レーダー機
radar aircraft
Radarflugzeug^N
avion^M radar^M
avión^M radar
aeroplano^M radar^M

平面／ファセット
facet
Facette^F
facette^F
faceta^F
faccetta^F

ロトドーム
rotodome
Rotodom^N
rotodôme^M
rotodomo
rotodome

レーダー吸収材料
radar-absorbent material
radarabsorbierendes Material^N
matériau^M absorbant les ondes^F radars^M
material^M que absorbe las ondas^F radar
materiale^M radarassorbente

支柱
strut
Stütze^F
pylône^M
montante^M
montante^M

輸送機／貨物機
cargo aircraft
Frachtflugzeug^N
avion^M-cargo^M
avión^M carga
aeroplano^M da carico^M

超音速ジェット旅客機
supersonic jetliner
Überschallflugzeug^N
avion^M de ligne^F supersonique
avión^M supersónico
jet^M supersonico

可変排気ノズル
variable ejector nozzle
Verstelldüse^F
tuyère^F à section^F variable
tobera^F de sección^F variable
ugello^M a sezione^F variabile

ドループ・スヌート
droop nose
abgesenkte Nase^F
nez^M basculant
morro^M abatible
muso^M abbassabile

三角翼／デルタ翼
delta wing
Deltaflügel^M
voilure^F delta^M
ala^F delta
ala^F a delta$^{M/F}$

尾翼形状の例

examples of tail shapes | Beispiele^N für Leitwerke^N | exemples^M d'empennages^M | ejemplos de empenajes^M de cola^F | esempi^M di impennaggi^M

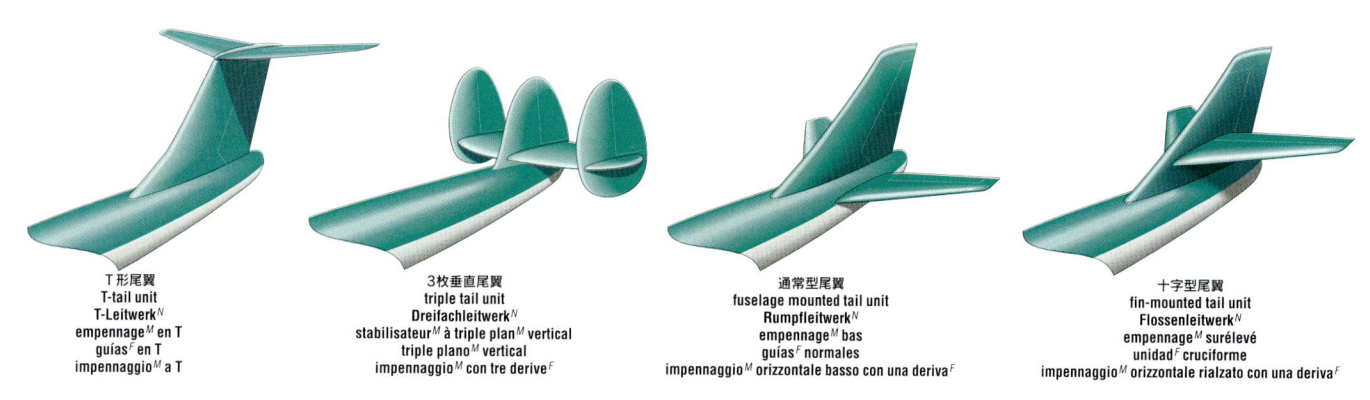

T形尾翼
T-tail unit
T-Leitwerk^N
empennage^M en T
guías^F en T
impennaggio^M a T

3枚垂直尾翼
triple tail unit
Dreifachleitwerk^N
stabilisateur^M à triple plan^M vertical
triple plano^M vertical
impennaggio^M con tre derive^F

通常型尾翼
fuselage mounted tail unit
Rumpfleitwerk^N
empennage^M bas
guías^F normales
impennaggio^M orizzontale basso con una deriva^F

十字型尾翼
fin-mounted tail unit
Flossenleitwerk^N
empennage^M surélevé
unidad^F cruciforme
impennaggio^M orizzontale rialzato con una deriva^F

航空交通 | AIR TRANSPORT
LUFTVERKEHR | TRANSPORT AÉRIEN | TRANSPORTE AÉREO | TRASPORTO AEREO

主翼形状の例

日本語 | 英語 | ドイツ語 | フランス語 | スペイン語 | イタリア語

examples of wing shapes | Tragflügelformen^F | exemples^M de voilures^F | diferentes formas^F de alas^F | tipi^M di ali^F

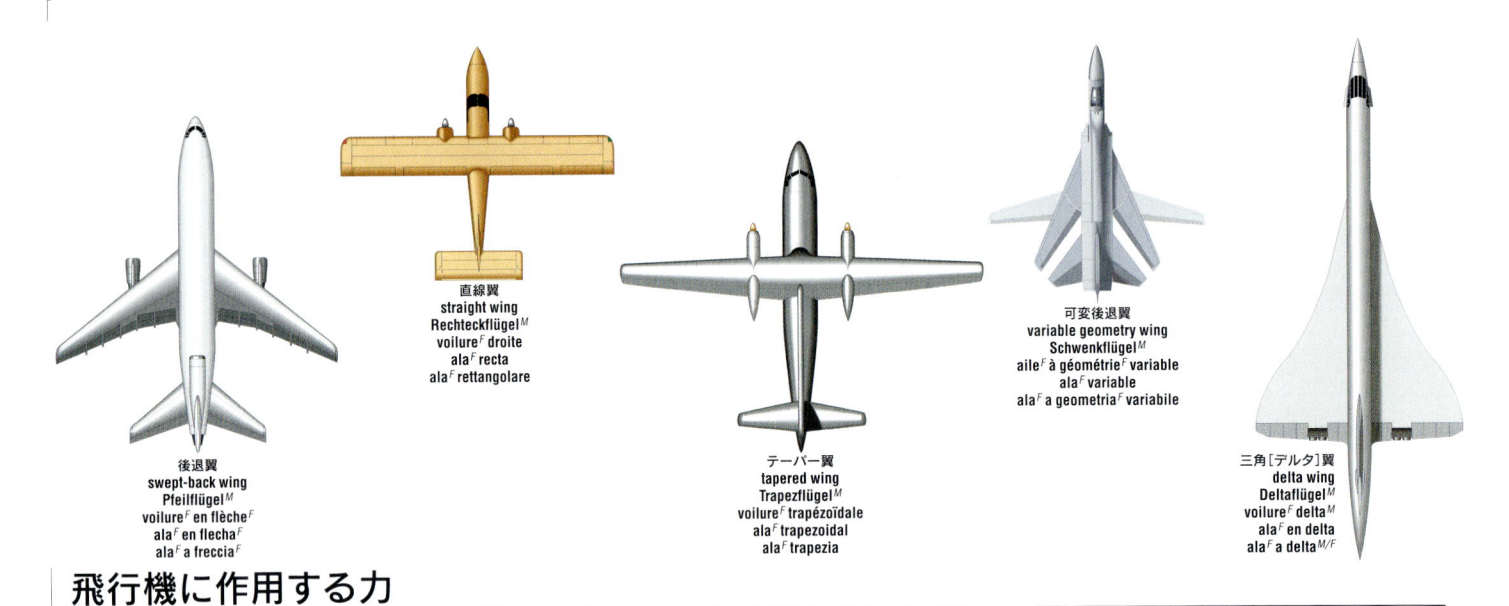

直線翼
straight wing
Rechteckflügel^M
voilure^F droite
ala^F recta
ala^F rettangolare

可変後退翼
variable geometry wing
Schwenkflügel^M
aile^F à géométrie^F variable
ala^F variable
ala^F a geometria^F variabile

後退翼
swept-back wing
Pfeilflügel^M
voilure^F en flèche^F
ala^F en flecha^F
ala^F a freccia^F

テーパー翼
tapered wing
Trapezflügel^M
voilure^F trapézoïdale
ala^F trapezoidal
ala^F trapezia

三角［デルタ］翼
delta wing
Deltaflügel^M
voilure^F delta^M
ala^F en delta
ala^F a delta$^{M/F}$

飛行機に作用する力

forces acting on an airplane | auf Flugzeuge^N wirkende Kräfte^F | forces^F agissant sur un avion^M | fuerzas^F que actúan sobre un avión^M | forze^F che agiscono su un aeroplano^M

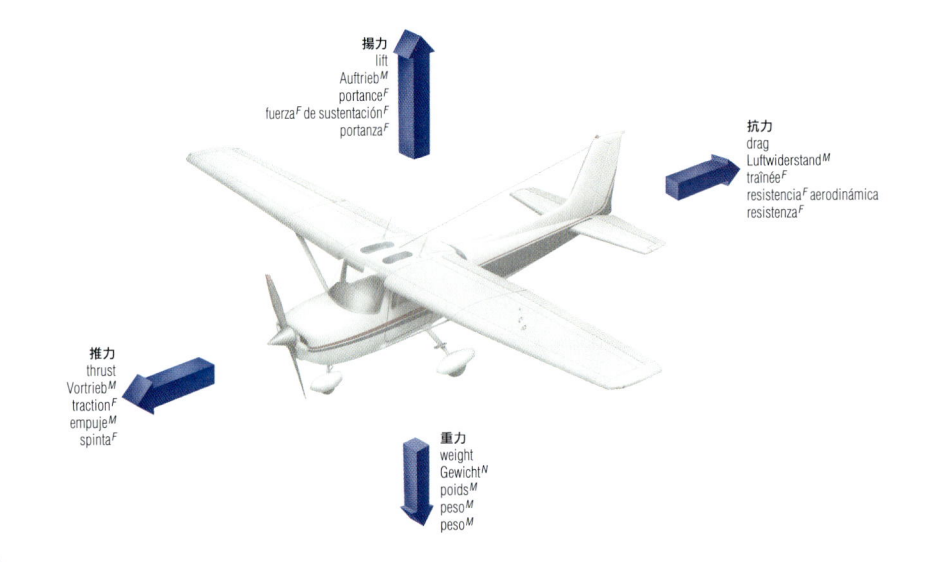

揚力
lift
Auftrieb^M
portance^F
fuerza^F de sustentación^F
portanza^F

抗力
drag
Luftwiderstand^M
traînée^F
resistencia^F aerodinámica
resistenza^F

推力
thrust
Vortrieb^M
traction^F
empuje^M
spinta^F

重力
weight
Gewicht^N
poids^M
peso^M
peso^M

飛行機の動き

movements of an airplane | Bewegungen^F eines Flugzeugs^N | mouvements^M de l'avion^M | movimientos^M de un avión^M | movimenti^M di un aeroplano^M

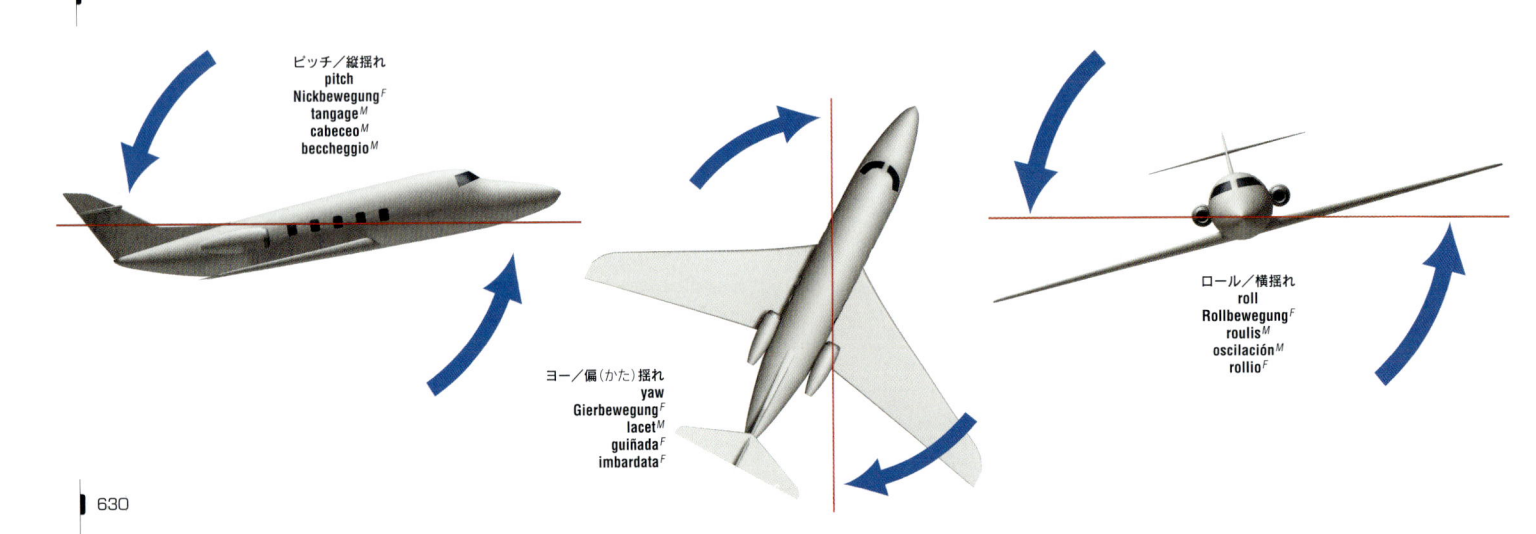

ピッチ／縦揺れ
pitch
Nickbewegung^F
tangage^M
cabeceo^M
beccheggio^M

ヨー／偏（かた）揺れ
yaw
Gierbewegung^F
lacet^M
guiñada^F
imbardata^F

ロール／横揺れ
roll
Rollbewegung^F
roulis^M
oscilación^M
rollio^F

航空交通 | AIR TRANSPORT
LUFTVERKEHR | TRANSPORT AÉRIEN | TRANSPORTE AÉREO | TRASPORTO AEREO

ヘリコプター

helicopter | Hubschrauber^M | hélicoptère^M | helicóptero^M | elicottero^M

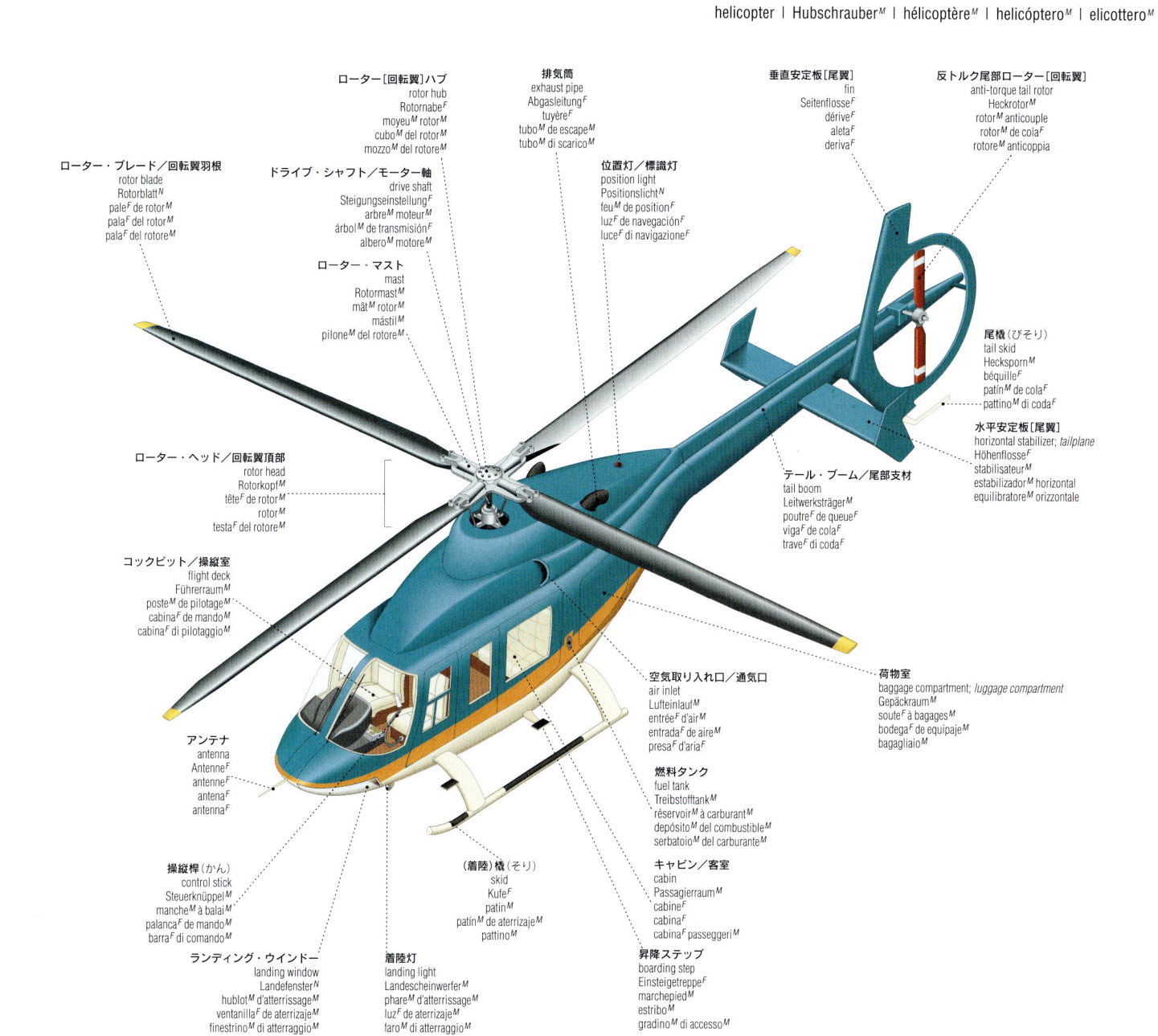

ローター[回転翼]ハブ
rotor hub
Rotornabe
moyeu^M rotor
cubo^M del rotor
mozzo^M del rotore

排気筒
exhaust pipe
Abgasleitung^F
tuyère^F
tubo^M de escape
tubo^M di scarico

垂直安定板[尾翼]
fin
Seitenflosse
dérive^F
aleta^F
deriva^F

反トルク尾部ローター[回転翼]
anti-torque tail rotor
Heckrotor
rotor^M anticouple
rotor^F de cola
rotore^M anticoppia

ローター・ブレード／回転翼羽根
rotor blade
Rotorblatt^N
pale^F de rotor
pala^F del rotor
pala^F del rotore

ドライブ・シャフト／モーター軸
drive shaft
Steigungseinstellung
arbre^F moteur
árbol^M de transmisión^F
albero^M motore

位置灯／標識灯
position light
Positionslicht^N
feu^M de position
luz^F de navegación
luce^F di navigazione

尾橇（びそり）
tail skid
Hecksporn^M
béquille^F
patín^M de cola^F
pattino^M di coda^F

ローター・マスト
mast
Rotormast^M
mât^M rotor
mástil^M
pilone^M del rotore

水平安定板[尾翼]
horizontal stabilizer; *tailplane*
Höhenflosse^F
stabilisateur
estabilizador^M horizontal
equilibratore^M orizzontale

ローター・ヘッド／回転翼頂部
rotor head
Rotorkopf
tête^F de rotor^M
rotor
testa^F del rotore^M

テール・ブーム／尾部支材
tail boom
Leitwerksträger^M
poutre^F de queue^F
viga^F de cola^F
trave^F di coda^F

コックピット／操縦室
flight deck
Führerraum
poste^M de pilotage^M
cabina^F de mando^M
cabina^F di pilotaggio^M

荷物室
baggage compartment; *luggage compartment*
Gepäckraum^M
soute^F à bagages^M
bodega^F de equipaje^M
bagagliaio^M

空気取り入れ口／通気口
air inlet
Lufteinlauf^M
entrée^F d'air^M
entrada^F de aire^M
presa^F d'aria^F

アンテナ
antenna
Antenne^F
antenne^F
antena^F
antenna^F

燃料タンク
fuel tank
Treibstofftank^M
réservoir^M à carburant^M
depósito^M del combustible^M
serbatoio^M del carburante^M

操縦桿（かん）
control stick
Steuerknüppel
manche^M à balai^M
palanca^F de mando^M
barra^F di comando^M

（着陸）橇（そり）
skid
Kufe^F
patin
patín^M de aterrizaje^M
pattino^M

キャビン／客室
cabin
Passagierraum^M
cabine^F
cabina^F
cabina^F passeggeri^M

ランディング・ウインドー
landing window
Landefenster^N
hublot^M d'atterrissage^M
ventanilla^F de aterrizaje^M
finestrino^M di atterraggio^M

着陸灯
landing light
Landescheinwerfer^M
phare^M d'atterrissage^M
luz^F de aterrizaje^M
faro^M di atterraggio^M

昇降ステップ
boarding step
Einsteigetreppe^F
marchepied^M
estribo^M
gradino^M di accesso^M

ヘリコプターの例

examples of helicopters | Beispiele^N für Hubschrauber^M | exemples^M d'hélicoptères^M | ejemplos^M de helicópteros^M | esempi^M di elicotteri^M

戦術輸送ヘリコプター
tactical transport helicopter
taktischer Transporthubschrauber^M
hélicoptère^M de transport^M tactique
helicóptero^M de transporte^M táctico
elicottero^M da trasporto^M tattico

消防ヘリコプター
water bomber helicopter
Löschhubschrauber^M
hélicoptère^M bombardier^M d'eau^F
helicóptero^M contraincendios
elicottero^M antincendio

消火タンク／ベリー・タンク
belly tank
Bauchtank^M
réservoir^M ventral
depósito^M ventral
serbatoio^M ventrale

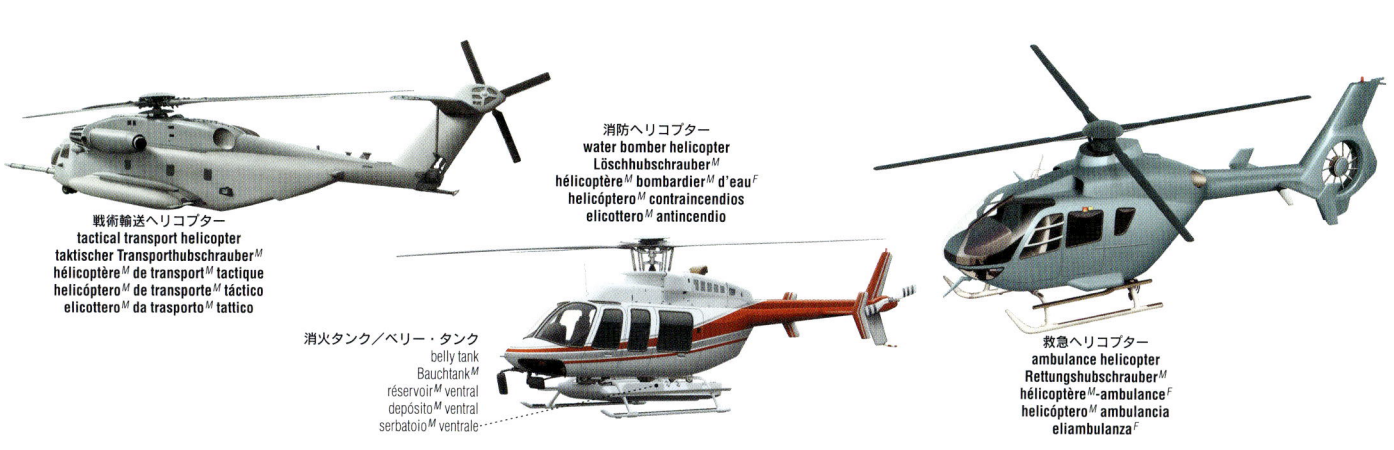

救急ヘリコプター
ambulance helicopter
Rettungshubschrauber^M
hélicoptère^M-ambulance^F
helicóptero^M ambulancia
eliambulanza^F

搬送 | HANDLING
HANDHABUNG | MANUTENTION | MANIPULACIÓN | MOVIMENTAZIONE

搬送装置

日本語 | 英語 | ドイツ語 | フランス語 | スペイン語 | イタリア語

material handling | Lastenfortbewegung^F | manutention^F | manejo^M de materiales^M | movimentazione^F dei materiali^M

フォークリフト
forklift truck
Gabelstapler^M
chariot^M élévateur
carretilla^F elevadora de horquilla^F
carrello^M elevatore^M

マスト／フォーク支柱
mast
Führungsständer^M
mât^M
mástil^M
guida^F

水平材／横材
crosshead
Kreuzkopf^M
tête^F du vérin de levage^M
cabeza^F del gato^M elevador
testa^F del martinetto^M elevatore^M

リフト・チェーン
lifting chain
Hubkette^F
chaîne^F de levage^M
cadena^F de elevación^F
catena^F di sollevamento^M

油圧装置
hydraulic system
Hydraulik^F
système^M hydraulique
sistema^M hidráulico
sistema^M idraulico

キャリッジ
carriage
Träger^M
tablier^M
portahorquilla^F
piastra^F portaforche

フォーク（アーム）
fork
Gabel^F
bras^M de fourche^F
horquilla^F
braccio^M della forca^F

フォーク
forks
Gabeln^F
fourches^F
horquillas^F
forche^F

ヘッド・ガード／庇（ひさし）
overhead guard
Schutzdach^N
toit^M de protection^F
techo^M de protección^F
tettuccio^M di protezione^F

マスト操作レバー
mast operating lever; *mast operating lever*
Maststeuerhebel^M
levier^M de manœuvre^F du mât^M
palanca^F de maniobra^F
leva^F di manovra^F della guida^F

エンジン収納部
engine compartment
Motorraum^M
moteur^M
hueco^M del motor^M
vano^M motore^M

フレーム
frame
Rahmen^M
châssis^M
chasis^M
telaio^M

交通と機械

パレット
pallets
Paletten^F
palettes^F
palés^M
palette^F di carico^M

翼形パレット
wing pallet
Rücksprungpalette^F
palette^F à ailes^F
palé^M con alas^F
paletta^F di carico^M ad alette^F

差し込み口
entry
Einfahröffnung^F
entrée^F
entrada^F
tasca^F di inforcamento^M

下面デッキボード
bottom deckboard
untere Vertäfelung^F
plancher^M inférieur
plataforma^F inferior
piano^M di appoggio^M

上面デッキボード
top deckboard
obere Vertäfelung^F
plancher^M supérieur
plataforma^F
piano^M di carico^M

桁／水平材／横材
stringer
Träger^M
entretoise^F
larguerillo^M
traversa^F orizzontale

両面（使用形）パレット
double-decked pallet
Doppeldeck-Flachpalette^F
palette^F à double face^F
palé^M de plataforma^F doble
paletta^F di carico^M a due piani^M

ボックス・パレット
box pallet
Gitterboxpalette^F
palette^F-caisse^F
palé^M de caja^F
paletta^F di carico^M a cassa^F

サイド／側壁
side
Seitenteil^N
paroi^F
costado^M
lato^M

パレット
pallet
Palette^F
palette^F
palé^M
paletta^F di carico^M

単面（形）パレット
single-decked pallet
Einfachdeck-Flachpalette^F
palette^F à simple face^F
palé^M de plataforma^F sencilla
paletta^F di carico^M a un piano^M

ブロック／支え
block
Klotz^M
support^M
soporte^M
blocco^M

ハーフ・サイド／半側壁
half-side
Halbseite^F
demi-panneau^M
medio lado^M
mezzo lato^M

搬送 | HANDLING
HANDHABUNG | MANUTENTION | MANIPULACIÓN | MOVIMENTAZIONE

搬送装置

油圧式パレット・トラック
hydraulic pallet truck
hydraulischer Palettenhubwagen^M
gerbeur^M
apilador hidráulico
carrello^M idraulico per palette^F di carico^M

マスト／フォーク支柱
mast
Führungsständer^M
mât^M
mástil^M
guida^F

ハンド・トラック／手押し荷物運搬車
hand truck; *barrow*
Sackkarren^M
diable^M
carretilla^F
carrello^M

油圧シリンダー
hydraulic cylinder
Hydraulikzylinder^M
vérin^M hydraulique
cilindro^M hidráulico
cilindro^M idraulico

ステアリング［舵取り］レバー
steering lever
Lenkhebel^M
levier^M de conduite^F
palanca^F de dirección^F
leva^F direzionale

フォーク
forks
Gabeln^F
fourches^F
horquillas^F
forche^F

マスト操作レバー
mast control lever; *mast control lever*
Maststeuerhebel^M
levier^M de manœuvre^F du mât^M
palanca^F de maniobra^F
leva^F di manovra^F della guida^F

フレーム
frame
Rahmen^M
châssis^M
chasis^M
telaio^M

ゴム・タイヤ
solid rubber tire; *solid rubber tyre*
Vollgummirad^N
bandage^M de roue^F caoutchoutée
llanta^F maciza
gomma^F piena

ステアリング・アクスル／舵取り車軸
steering axle
Lenkachse^F
essieu^M directeur
eje^M de dirección^F
asse^M sterzante

アウトリガー（フォーク）
stabilizing shaft
Stabilisator^M
longeron^M stabilisateur
barra^F estabilizadora
barra^F di stabilizzazione^F

ローラー／キャスター
roller
Rolle^F
roulette^F
rueda^F
rotella^F

ハンド・パレット・リフト
pallet truck
Palettenhubwagen^M
transpalette^F manuelle
transpaleta^F
carrello^M a forca^F per palette^F di carico^M

パレット台車
platform pallet truck
Flachpalettenwagen^M
chariot^M à palette^F
carretilla^F transportadora
carrello^M a piattaforma^F per palette^F di carico^M

（手押し）台車
flatbed pushcart; *platform trolley*
Handwagen^M
chariot^M à plateau^M
plataforma^F móvil
carrello^M a piattaforma^F

交通と機械

搬送 | HANDLING
HANDHABUNG | MANUTENTION | MANIPULACIÓN | MOVIMENTAZIONE

クレーン

日本語 | 英語 | ドイツ語 | フランス語 | スペイン語 | イタリア語

cranes | Kräne^M | grues^F et portique^M | grúas^F | gru^F

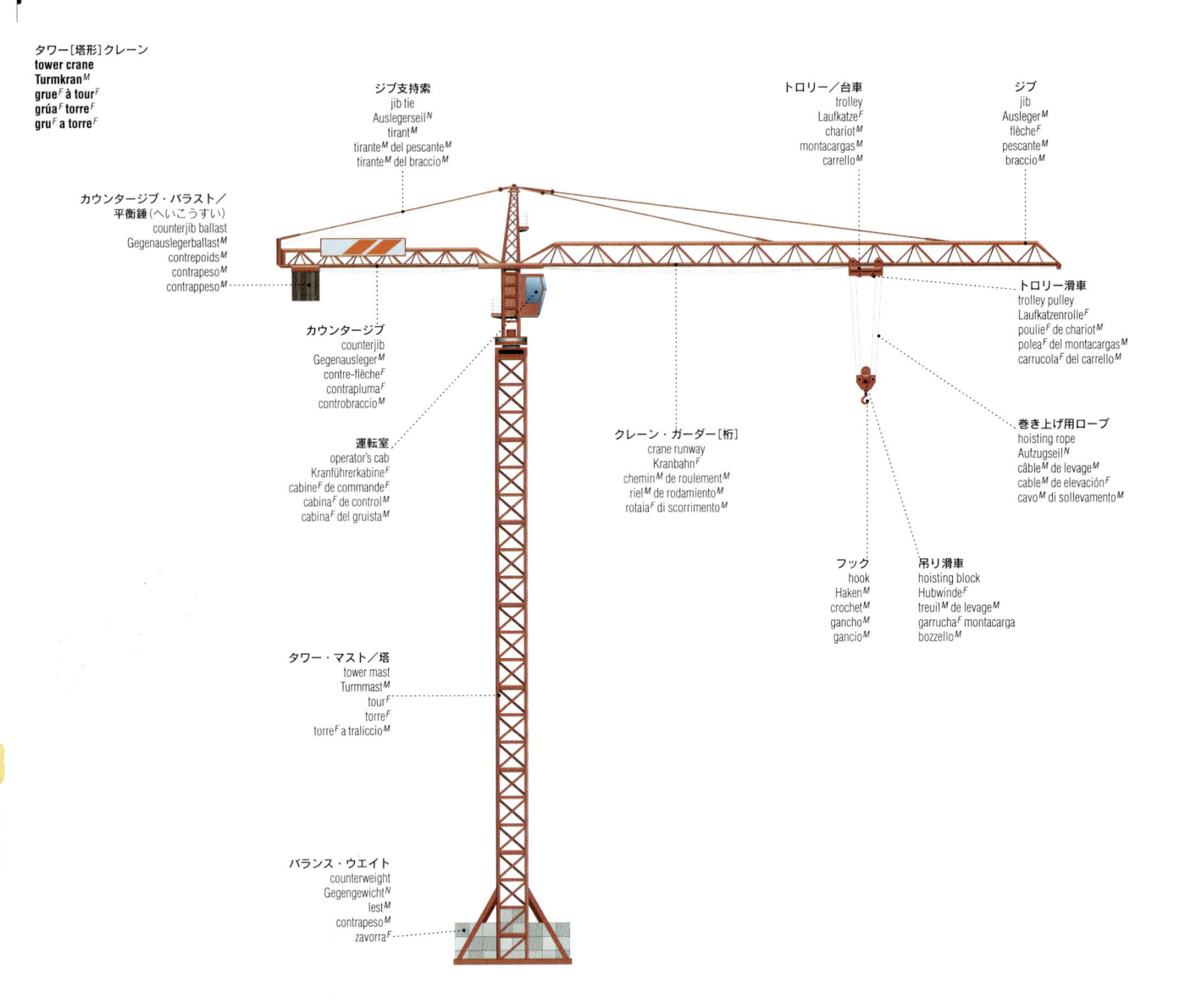

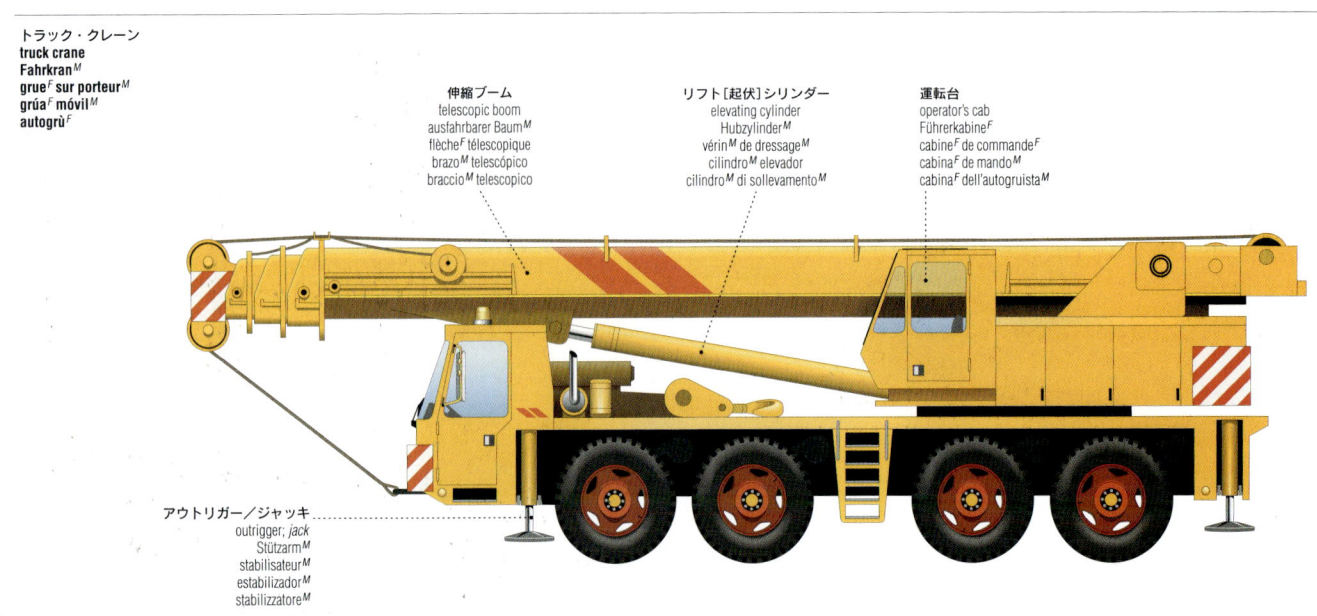

タワー[塔形]クレーン
tower crane
Turmkran^M
grue^F à tour^F
grúa^F torre^F
gru^F a torre^F

ジブ支持索
jib tie
Auslegerseil^N
tirant^M
tirante del pescante^M
tirante^M del braccio^M

トロリー／台車
trolley
Laufkatze^F
chariot^M
montacargas^M
carrello^M

ジブ
jib
Ausleger^M
flèche^F
pescante^M
braccio^M

カウンタージブ・バラスト／
平衡錘（へいこうすい）
counterjib ballast
Gegenauslegerballast^M
contrepoids^M
contrapeso^M
contrappeso^M

カウンタージブ
counterjib
Gegenausleger^M
contre-flèche^F
contrapluma^F
controbraccio^M

トロリー滑車
trolley pulley
Laufkatzenrolle^F
poulie^F de chariot^M
polea^F del montacargas^M
carrucola^F del carrello^M

運転室
operator's cab
Kranführerkabine^F
cabine^F de commande^F
cabina^F de control^M
cabina^F del gruista^M

クレーン・ガーダー[桁]
crane runway
Kranbahn^F
chemin^M de roulement^M
riel^M de rodamiento^M
rotaia^F di scorrimento^M

巻き上げ用ロープ
hoisting rope
Aufzugseil^N
câble^M de levage^M
cable^M de elevación^F
cavo^M di sollevamento^M

フック
hook
Haken^M
crochet^M
gancho^M
gancio^M

吊り滑車
hoisting block
Hubwinde^F
treuil^M de levage^M
garrucha^F montacarga
bozzello^M

タワー・マスト／塔
tower mast
Turmmast^M
tour^F
torre^F
torre^F a traliccio^M

バランス・ウエイト
counterweight
Gegengewicht^N
lest^M
contrapeso^M
zavorra^F

交通と機械

トラック・クレーン
truck crane
Fahrkran^M
grue^F sur porteur^M
grúa^F móvil^M
autogrù^F

伸縮ブーム
telescopic boom
ausfahrbarer Baum^M
flèche^F télescopique
brazo^M telescópico
braccio^M telescopico

リフト[起伏]シリンダー
elevating cylinder
Hubzylinder^M
vérin^M de dressage^M
cilindro^M elevador
cilindro^M di sollevamento^M

運転台
operator's cab
Führerkabine^F
cabine^F de commande^F
cabina^F de mando^M
cabina^F dell'autogruista^M

アウトリガー／ジャッキ
outrigger; jack
Stützarm^M
stabilisateur^M
estabilizador^M
stabilizzatore^M

634

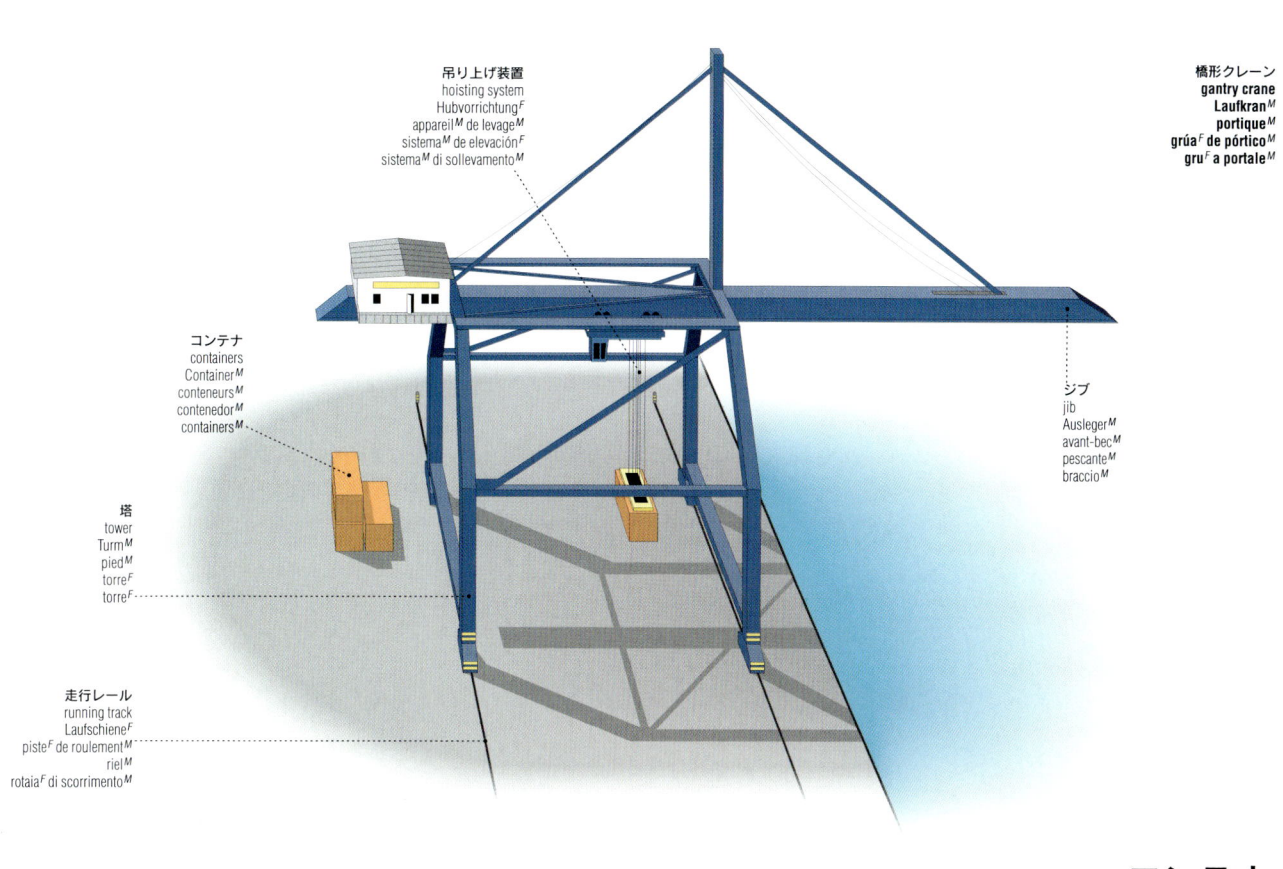

搬送 | HANDLING
HANDHABUNG | MANUTENTION | MANIPULACIÓN | MOVIMENTAZIONE

クレーン

橋形クレーン
gantry crane
Laufkran^M
portique^M
grúa^F de pórtico^M
gru^F a portale^M

吊り上げ装置
hoisting system
Hubvorrichtung^F
appareil^M de levage^M
sistema^M de elevación^F
sistema^M di sollevamento^M

コンテナ
containers
Container^M
conteneurs^M
contenedor^M
containers^M

ジブ
jib
Ausleger^M
avant-bec^M
pescante^M
braccio^M

塔
tower
Turm^M
pied^M
torre^F
torre^F

走行レール
running track
Laufschiene^F
piste^F de roulement^M
riel^M
rotaia^F di scorrimento^M

コンテナ

container | Container^M | conteneur^M | contenedor^M | container^M

側壁
side wall
Seitenwand^F
paroi^F latérale
panel^M lateral
parete^F laterale

屋根
roof
Dach^N
toit^M
techo^M
tetto^M

上部緩衝梁（ばり）
top-end transverse member
oberer Querträger^M
traverse^F d'extrémité^F supérieure
travesaño^M superior
traversa^F terminale superiore

隅金具
corner fitting
Eckbeschlag^M
pièce^F de coin^M
herraje^M de la esquina^F
giunto^M angolare

端部扉
end door
Stirntür^F
porte^F d'extrémité^F
puerta^F trasera
porta^F terminale

隅構造物
corner structure
Ecksäule^F
montant^M d'angle^M
esquina^F
montante^M angolare

フォーク・ポケット
fork pocket
Gabelstaplertasche^F
passage^M de fourche^F
abertura^F para horquilla^F
incastro^M per la forca^F di sollevamento^M

下部側梁（がわばり）
bottom side rail
unterer Längsträger^M
longeron^M latéral inférieur
larguero^M inferior
longherone^M laterale inferiore

下部緩衝梁
bottom-end transverse member
unterer Querträger^M
traverse^F d'extrémité^F inférieure
travesaño^M inferior
traversa^F terminale inferiore

交通と機械

635

重機器 | HEAVY MACHINERY
SCHWERMASCHINEN | MACHINERIE LOURDE | MAQUINARIA PESADA | MACCHINE PESANTI

ブルドーザー

日本語 | 英語 | ドイツ語 | フランス語 | スペイン語 | イタリア語

bulldozer | Planierraupe^F | bouteur^M | bulldozer^M | bulldozer^M

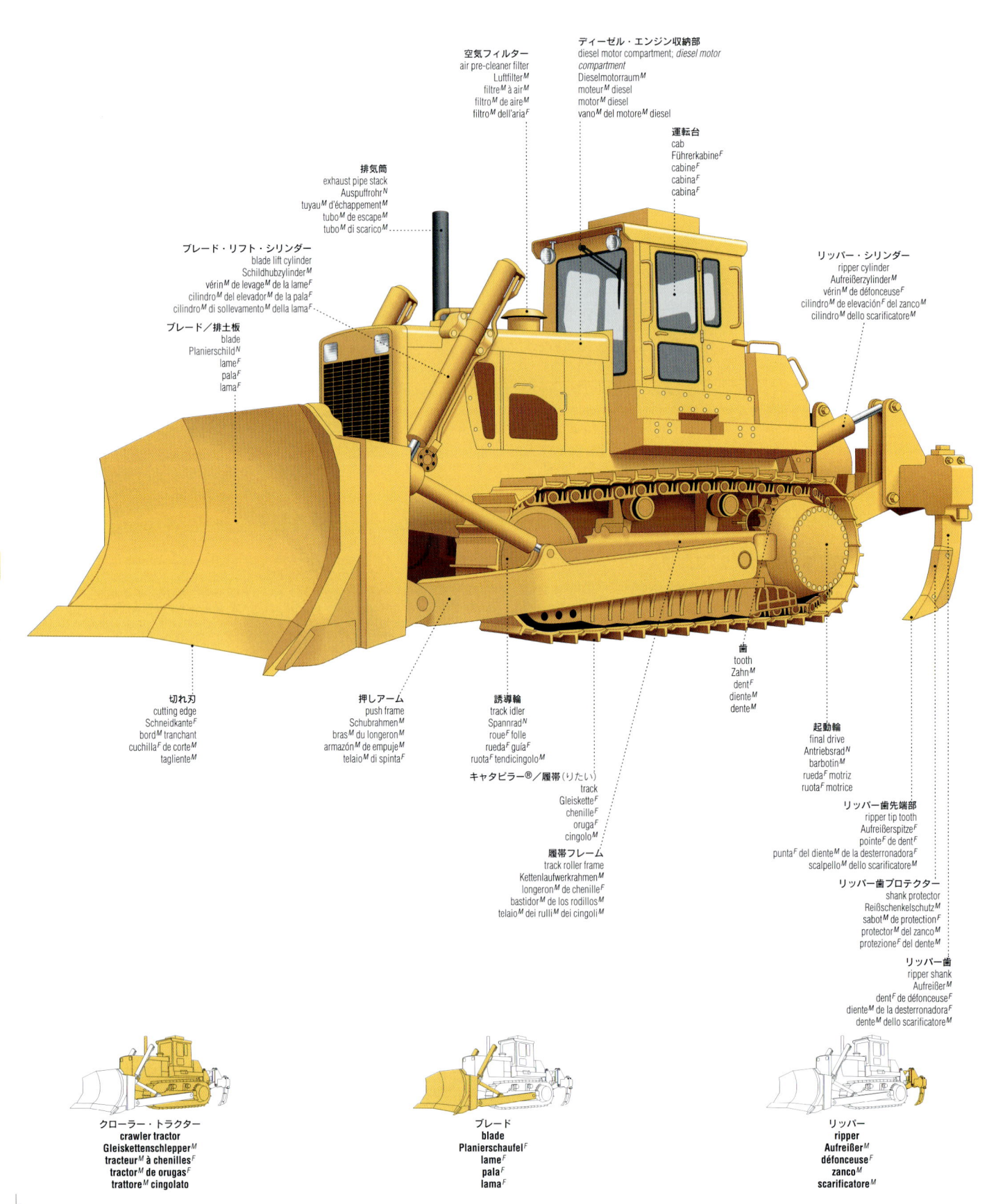

空気フィルター
air pre-cleaner filter
Luftfilter^M
filtre^M à air^M
filtro^M de aire^M
filtro^M dell'aria^F

ディーゼル・エンジン収納部
diesel motor compartment; *diesel motor compartment*
Dieselmotorraum^M
moteur^M diesel
motor^M diesel
vano^M del motore^M diesel

運転台
cab
Führerkabine^F
cabine^F
cabina^F
cabina^F

排気筒
exhaust pipe stack
Auspuffrohr^N
tuyau^M d'échappement^M
tubo^M de escape^M
tubo^M di scarico^M

ブレード・リフト・シリンダー
blade lift cylinder
Schildhubzylinder^M
vérin^M de levage^M de la lame^F
cilindro^M del elevador^M de la pala^F
cilindro^M di sollevamento^M della lama^F

リッパー・シリンダー
ripper cylinder
Aufreißerzylinder^M
vérin^M de défonceuse^F
cilindro^M de elevación^F del zanco^M
cilindro^M dello scarificatore^M

ブレード／排土板
blade
Planierschild^N
lame^F
pala^F
lama^F

切れ刃
cutting edge
Schneidkante^F
bord^M tranchant
cuchilla^F de corte^M
tagliente^M

押しアーム
push frame
Schubrahmen^M
bras^M du longeron^M
armazón^M de empuje^M
telaio^M di spinta^F

誘導輪
track idler
Spannrad^N
roue^F folle
rueda^F guía
ruota^F tendicingolo^M

キャタピラー®／履帯（りたい）
track
Gleiskette^F
chenille^F
oruga^F
cingolo^M

履帯フレーム
track roller frame
Kettenlaufwerkrahmen^M
longeron^M de chenille^F
bastidor^M de los rodillos^M
telaio^M dei rulli^M dei cingoli^M

歯
tooth
Zahn^M
dent^F
diente^M
dente^M

起動輪
final drive
Antriebsrad^N
barbotin^M
rueda^F motriz
ruota^F motrice

リッパー歯先端部
ripper tip tooth
Aufreißerspitze^F
pointe^F de dent^F
punta^F del diente^M de la desterronadora^F
scalpello^M dello scarificatore^M

リッパー歯プロテクター
shank protector
Reißschenkelschutz^M
sabot^M de protection^F
protector^M del zanco^M
protezione^F del dente^M

リッパー歯
ripper shank
Aufreißer^M
dent^F de défonceuse^F
diente^M de la desterronadora^F
dente^M dello scarificatore^M

クローラー・トラクター
crawler tractor
Gleiskettenschlepper^M
tracteur^M à chenilles^F
tractor^M de orugas^F
trattore^M cingolato

ブレード
blade
Planierschaufel^F
lame^F
pala^F
lama^F

リッパー
ripper
Aufreißer^M
défonceuse^F
zanco^M
scarificatore^M

636

重機器 | HEAVY MACHINERY
SCHWERMASCHINEN | MACHINERIE LOURDE | MAQUINARIA PESADA | MACCHINE PESANTI

ホイール・ローダー

wheel loader | Radlader^M | chargeuse^F-pelleteuse^F | cargadora^F-retroexcavadora^F | terna^F

ディッパー・アーム
dipper arm
Löffelstiel^M
bras^M
brazo^M del cucharón^M
braccio^M della pala^F caricatrice

ディッパー・アーム・シリンダー
dipper arm cylinder
Löffelstielzylinder^M
vérin^M du bras^M
cilindro^M del brazo^M elevador
cilindro^M della pala^F caricatrice

ブーム
boom
Ausleger^M
flèche^F
elevador^M
braccio^M di sollevamento^M

バケット・シリンダー
bucket cylinder
Schaufelzylinder^M
vérin^M du godet^M
cilindro^M del cucharón^M
cilindro^M della pala^F caricatrice

後部バケット
backward bucket
hintere Schaufel^F
godet^M rétro
cucharón^M trasero
pala^F caricatrice posteriore

運転台
cab
Führerkabine^F
cabine^F
cabina^F
cabina^F

バケット・レバー
bucket lever
Schaufelarm^M
levier^M coudé
palanca^F del cucharón^M
braccio^M della pala^F caricatrice

バックホー操縦装置
backhoe controls
Tieflöffelsteuerung^F
manœuvre^F de la pelleteuse^F
maniobra^F de la excavadora^F
comandi^M del retroescavatore^M

バケット
bucket
Schaufel^F
godet^M
cucharón^M
pala^F caricatrice anteriore

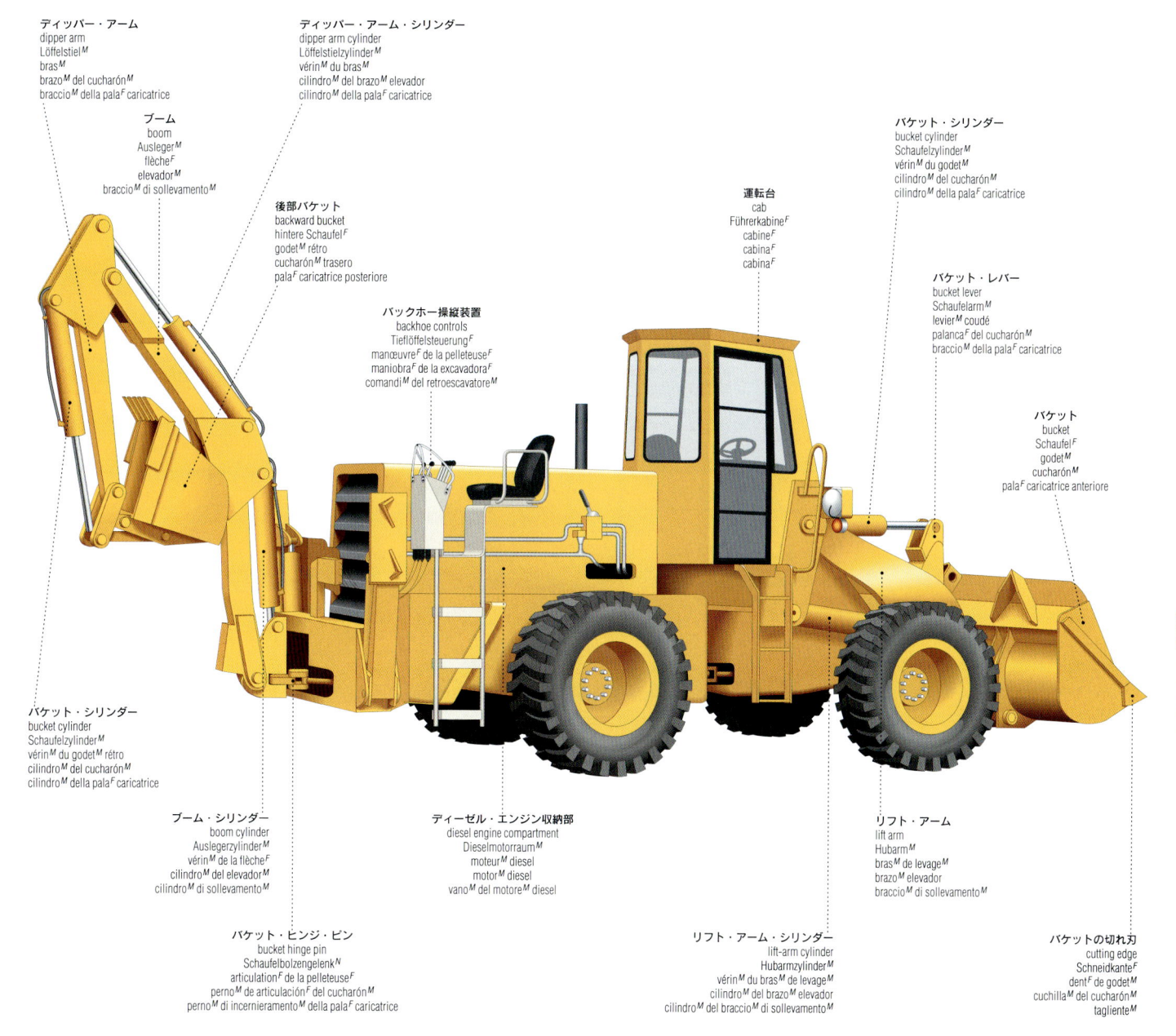

バケット・シリンダー
bucket cylinder
Schaufelzylinder^M
vérin^M du godet^M rétro
cilindro^M del cucharón^M
cilindro^M della pala^F caricatrice

ブーム・シリンダー
boom cylinder
Auslegerzylinder^M
vérin^M de la flèche^F
cilindro^M del elevador^M
cilindro^M di sollevamento^M

ディーゼル・エンジン収納部
diesel engine compartment
Dieselmotorraum^M
moteur^M diesel
motor^M diesel
vano^M del motore^M diesel

リフト・アーム
lift arm
Hubarm^M
bras^M de levage^M
brazo^M elevador
braccio^M di sollevamento^M

バケット・ヒンジ・ピン
bucket hinge pin
Schaufelbolzengelenk^N
articulation^F de la pelleteuse^F
perno^M de articulación^F del cucharón^M
perno^M di incernieramento^M della pala^F caricatrice

リフト・アーム・シリンダー
lift-arm cylinder
Hubarmzylinder^M
vérin^M du bras^M de levage^M
cilindro^M del brazo^M elevador
cilindro^M del braccio^M di sollevamento^M

バケットの切れ刃
cutting edge
Schneidkante^F
dent^F de godet^M
cuchilla^F del cucharón^M
tagliente^M

交通と機械

フロント・エンド・ローダー
front-end loader
Schaufellader^M
chargeuse^F frontale
cargador^M delantero
pala^F caricatrice anteriore

ホイール・トラクター
wheel tractor
Radtraktor^M
tracteur^M
tractor^M de ruedas^F
trattore^M gommato

バックホー
backhoe
Tieflöffel^M
pelleteuse^F
excavadora^F
retroescavatore^M

重機器 | HEAVY MACHINERY
SCHWERMASCHINEN | MACHINERIE LOURDE | MAQUINARIA PESADA | MACCHINE PESANTI

スクレーパー

scraper | Schrapper^M | décapeuse^F | raspador^M | ruspa^F

日本語 | 英語 | ドイツ語 | フランス語 | スペイン語 | イタリア語

グーズネック
gooseneck
Schwanenhals^M
col^M-de-cygne^M
cuello^M de ganso^M
collo^M d'oca^F

ステアリング・シリンダー
steering cylinder
Lenkzylinder^M
vérin^M de direction^F
cilindro^M de dirección^F
cilindro^M direzionale

トラクター・エンジン収納部
tractor engine compartment
Motorraum^M
tracteur^M-remorqueur^M
motor^M del tractor^M
vano^M del motore^M di traino^M

エジェクター
ejector
Auswerfer^M
éjecteur^M
eyector^M
eiettore^M

ドラフト・チューブ／吸い出し管
draft tube; *draught tube*
Saugrohr^N
palonnier^M
barra^F de arrastre^M
tubo^M di posizionamento^M

ボウル
bowl
Schürfkübel^M
benne^F
contenedor^M
cassone^M

切れ刃
cutting edge
Schneidkante^F
lame^F racleuse
cuchilla^F de corte^M
tagliente^M

ドラフト・アーム
draft arm; *draught arm*
Saugarm^M
brancard^M
brazo^M de arrastre^M
braccio^M di posizionamento^M

油圧式ショベル

hydraulic shovel | Hydraulik-Hochlöffelbagger^M | pelle^F hydraulique | pala^F hidráulica | escavatore^M idraulico

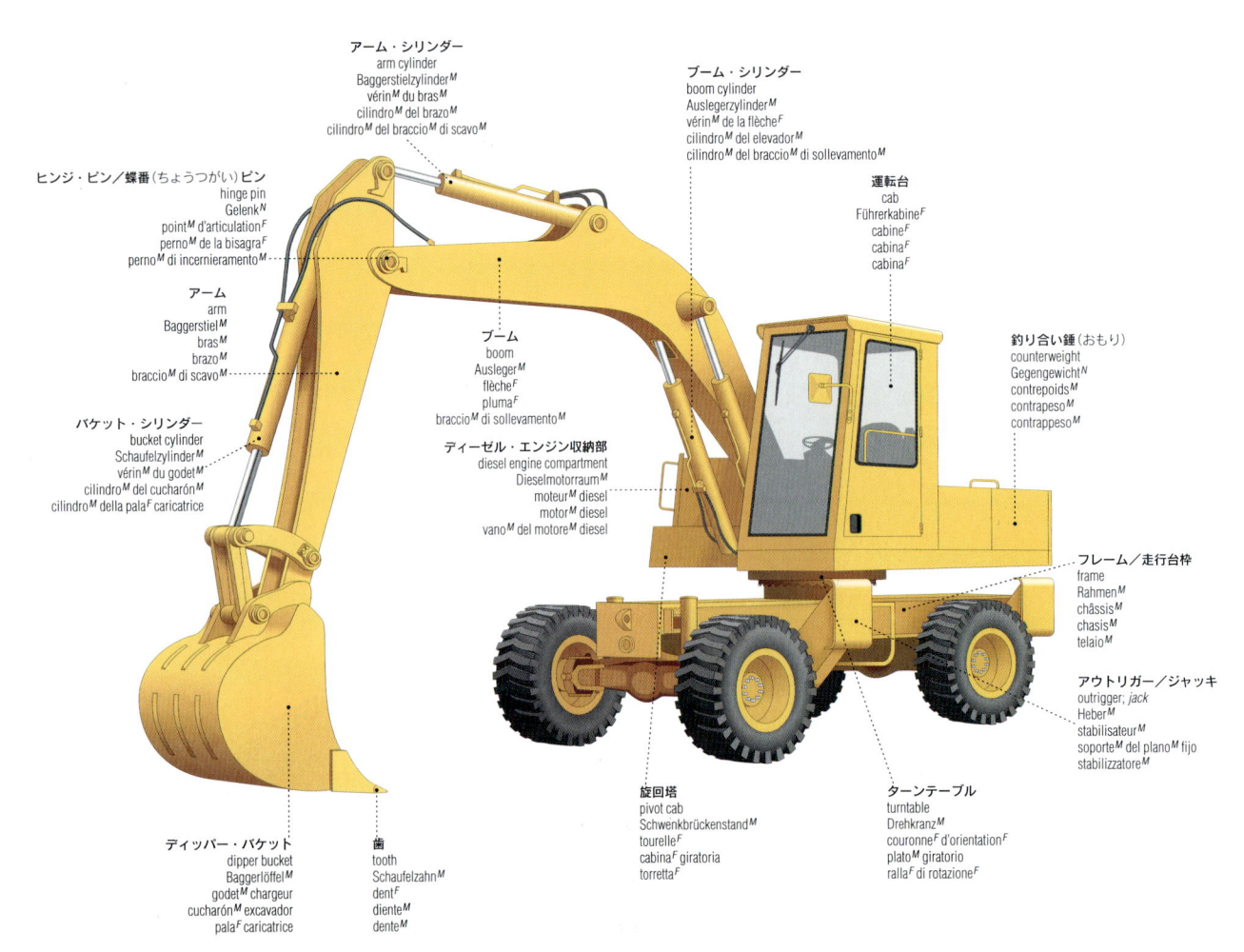

アーム・シリンダー
arm cylinder
Baggerstielzylinder^M
vérin^M du bras^M
cilindro^M del brazo^M
cilindro^M del braccio^M di scavo^M

ブーム・シリンダー
boom cylinder
Auslegerzylinder^M
vérin^M de la flèche^F
cilindro^M del elevador^M
cilindro^M del braccio^M di sollevamento^M

ヒンジ・ピン／蝶番（ちょうつがい）ピン
hinge pin
Gelenk^N
point^M d'articulation^F
perno^M de la bisagra^F
perno^M di incernieramento^M

運転台
cab
Führerkabine^F
cabine^F
cabina^F
cabina^F

アーム
arm
Baggerstiel^M
bras^M
brazo^M
braccio^M di scavo^M

ブーム
boom
Ausleger^M
flèche^F
pluma^F
braccio^M di sollevamento^M

釣り合い錘（おもり）
counterweight
Gegengewicht^N
contrepoids^M
contrapeso^M
contrappeso^M

バケット・シリンダー
bucket cylinder
Schaufelzylinder^M
vérin^M du godet^M
cilindro^M del cucharón^M
cilindro^M della pala^F caricatrice

ディーゼル・エンジン収納部
diesel engine compartment
Dieselmotorraum^M
moteur^M diesel
motor^M diesel
vano^M del motore^M diesel

フレーム／走行台枠
frame
Rahmen^M
châssis^M
chasis^M
telaio^M

アウトリガー／ジャッキ
outrigger; *jack*
Heber^M
stabilisateur^M
soporte^M del plano^M fijo
stabilizzatore^M

ディッパー・バケット
dipper bucket
Baggerlöffel^M
godet^M chargeur
cucharón^M excavador
pala^F caricatrice

歯
tooth
Schaufelzahn^M
dent^F
diente^M
dente^M

旋回塔
pivot cab
Schwenkbrückenstand^M
tourelle^F
cabina^F giratoria
torretta^F

ターンテーブル
turntable
Drehkranz^M
couronne^F d'orientation^F
plato^M giratorio
ralla^F di rotazione^F

交通と機械

638

重機器 | HEAVY MACHINERY
SCHWERMASCHINEN | MACHINERIE LOURDE | MAQUINARIA PESADA | MACCHINE PESANTI

グレーダー／地均(なら)し機

grader | Straßenhobel[M] | niveleuse[F] | niveladora[F] | livellatrice[F]

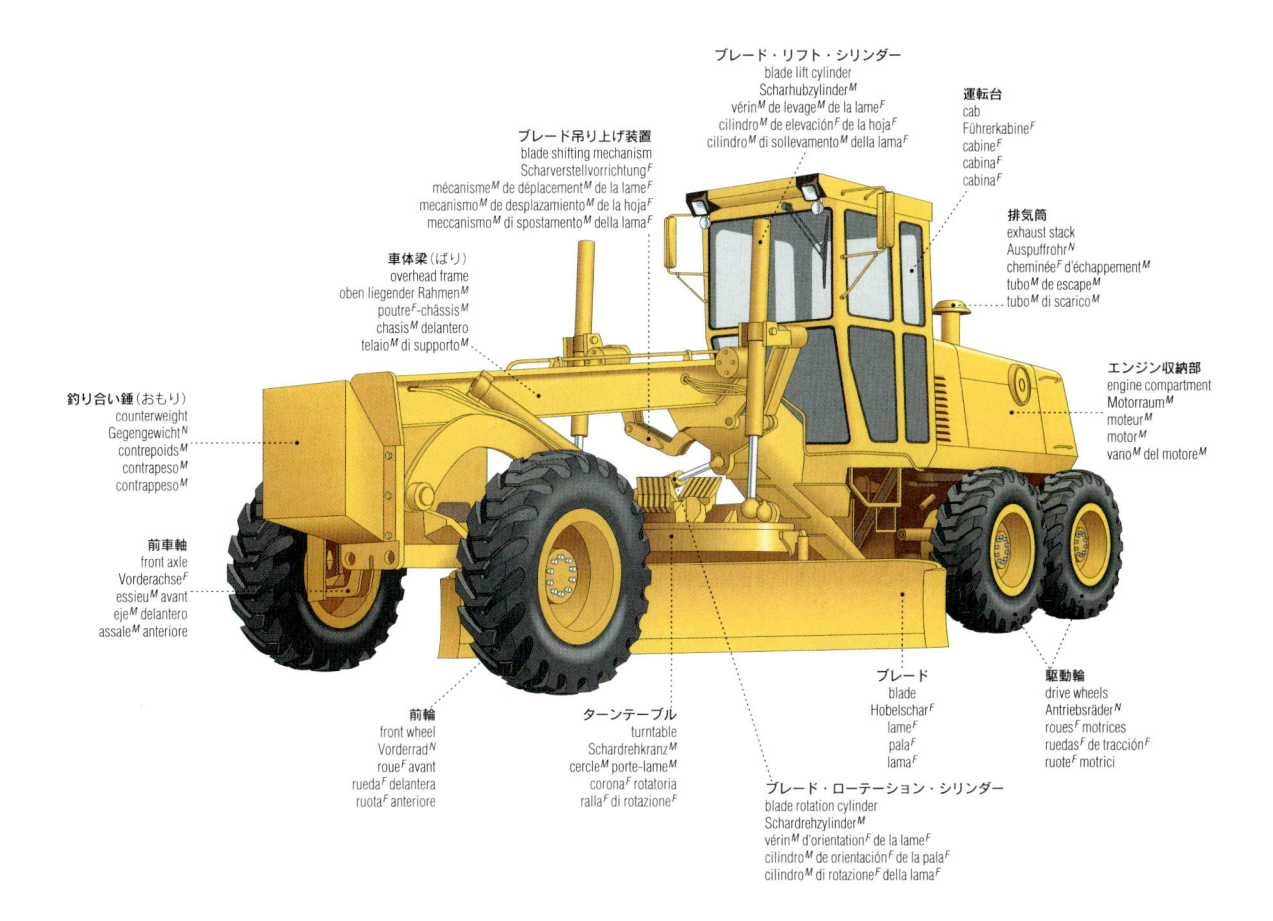

ブレード・リフト・シリンダー
blade lift cylinder
Scharhubzylinder[M]
vérin de levage de la lame[F]
cilindro[M] de elevación[F] de la hoja[F]
cilindro[M] di sollevamento[M] della lama[F]

ブレード吊り上げ装置
blade shifting mechanism
Scharverstellvorrichtung[F]
mécanisme[M] de déplacement[M] de la lame[F]
mecanismo[M] de desplazamiento[M] de la hoja[F]
meccanismo[M] di spostamento[M] della lama[F]

運転台
cab
Führerkabine[F]
cabine[F]
cabina[F]
cabina[F]

車体梁(ばり)
overhead frame
oben liegender Rahmen[M]
poutre[F]-châssis[M]
chasis[M] delantero
telaio[M] di supporto[M]

排気筒
exhaust stack
Auspuffrohr[N]
cheminée[F] d'échappement[M]
tubo[M] de escape[M]
tubo[M] di scarico[M]

釣り合い錘(おもり)
counterweight
Gegengewicht[N]
contrepoids[M]
contrapeso[M]
contrappeso[M]

エンジン収納部
engine compartment
Motorraum[M]
moteur[M]
motor[M]
vano[M] del motore[M]

前車軸
front axle
Vorderachse[F]
essieu[M] avant
eje[M] delantero
assale[M] anteriore

駆動輪
drive wheels
Antriebsräder[N]
roues[F] motrices
ruedas[F] de tracción[F]
ruote[F] motrici

前輪
front wheel
Vorderrad[N]
roue[F] avant
rueda[F] delantera
ruota[F] anteriore

ターンテーブル
turntable
Schardrehkranz[M]
cercle[M] porte-lame[M]
corona[F] rotatoria
ralla[F] di rotazione[F]

ブレード
blade
Hobelschar[F]
lame[F]
pala[F]
lama[F]

ブレード・ローテーション・シリンダー
blade rotation cylinder
Schardrehzylinder[M]
vérin[M] d'orientation[F] de la lame[F]
cilindro[M] de orientación[F] de la pala[F]
cilindro[M] di rotazione[F] della lama[F]

ダンプ・トラック

dump truck; *tipper truck* | Muldenkipper[M] | camion[M]-benne[F] | volcadora[F] | autocarro[M] a cassone[M] ribaltabile

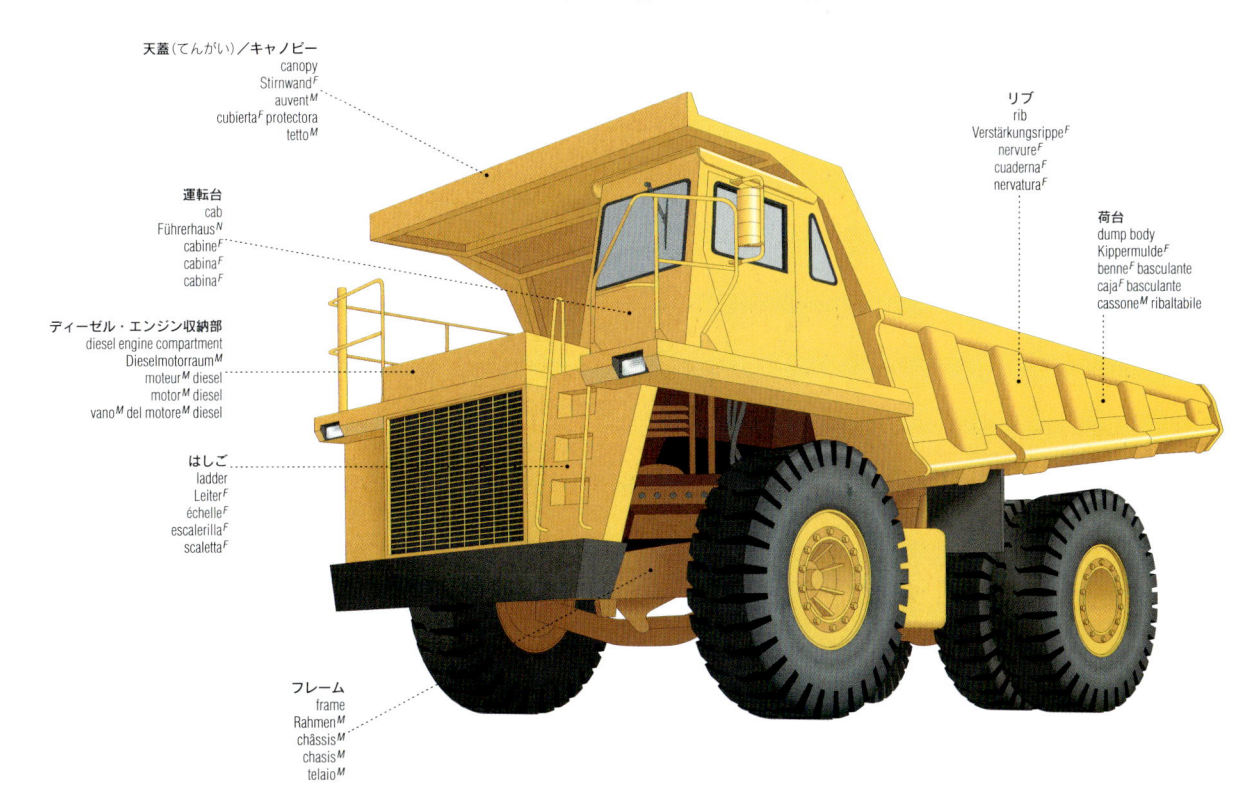

天蓋(てんがい)／キャノピー
canopy
Stirnwand[F]
auvent[M]
cubierta[F] protectora
tetto[M]

運転台
cab
Führerhaus[N]
cabine[F]
cabina[F]
cabina[F]

ティーゼル・エンジン収納部
diesel engine compartment
Dieselmotorraum[M]
moteur[M] diesel
motor[M] diesel
vano[M] del motore[M] diesel

はしご
ladder
Leiter[F]
échelle[F]
escalerilla[F]
scaletta[F]

リブ
rib
Verstärkungsrippe[F]
nervure[F]
cuaderna[F]
nervatura[F]

荷台
dump body
Kippermulde[F]
benne[F] basculante
caja[F] basculante
cassone[M] ribaltabile

フレーム
frame
Rahmen[M]
châssis[M]
chasis[M]
telaio[M]

交通と機械

重機器 | HEAVY MACHINERY
SCHWERMASCHINEN | MACHINERIE LOURDE | MAQUINARIA PESADA | MACCHINE PESANTI

トラクター

日本語 | 英語 | ドイツ語 | フランス語 | スペイン語 | イタリア語

tractor | Traktor^M | tracteur^M agricole | tractor^M | trattore^M

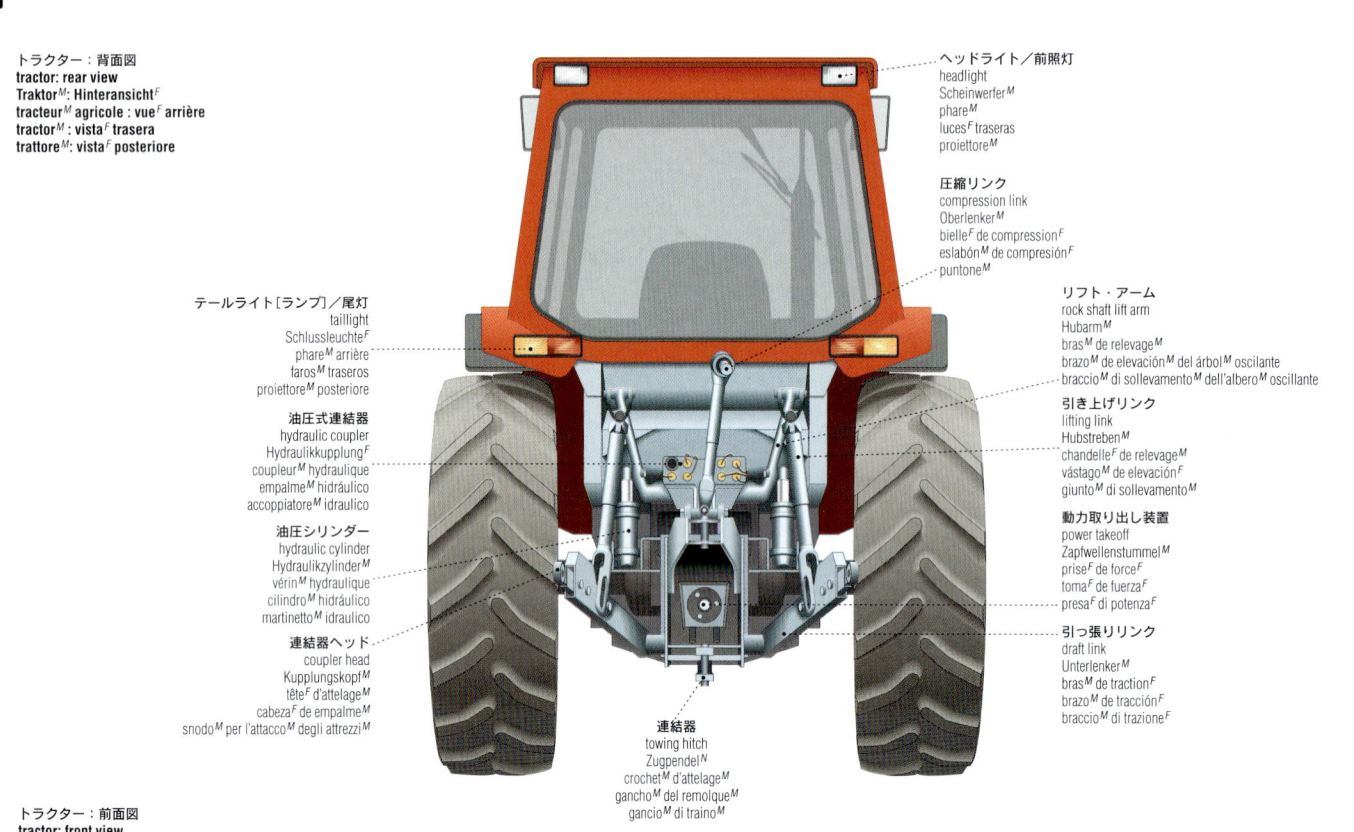

トラクター：背面図
tractor: rear view
Traktor^M: Hinteransicht^F
tracteur^M agricole : vue^F arrière
tractor^M : vista^F trasera
trattore^M : vista^F posteriore

ヘッドライト／前照灯
headlight
Scheinwerfer^M
phare^M
luces^F traseras
proiettore^M

圧縮リンク
compression link
Oberlenker^M
bielle^F de compression^F
eslabón^M de compresión^F
puntone^M

リフト・アーム
rock shaft lift arm
Hubarm^M
bras^M de relevage^M
brazo^M de elevación^F del árbol^M oscilante
braccio^M di sollevamento^M dell'albero^M oscillante

テールライト［ランプ］／尾灯
taillight
Schlussleuchte^F
phare^M arrière
faros^M traseros
proiettore^M posteriore

引き上げリンク
lifting link
Hubstreben^M
chandelle^F de relevage^M
vástago^M de elevación^F
giunto^M di sollevamento^M

油圧式連結器
hydraulic coupler
Hydraulikkupplung^F
coupleur^M hydraulique
empalme^M hidráulico
accoppiatore^M idraulico

動力取り出し装置
power takeoff
Zapfwellenstummel^M
prise^F de force^F
toma^F de fuerza^F
presa^F di potenza^F

油圧シリンダー
hydraulic cylinder
Hydraulikzylinder^M
vérin^M hydraulique
cilindro^M hidráulico
martinetto^M idraulico

引っ張りリンク
draft link
Unterlenker^M
bras^M de traction^F
brazo^M de tracción^F
braccio^M di trazione^F

連結器ヘッド
coupler head
Kupplungskopf^M
tête^F d'attelage^M
cabeza^F de empalme^M
snodo^M per l'attacco^M degli attrezzi^M

連結器
towing hitch
Zugpendel^N
crochet^M d'attelage^M
gancho^M del remolque^M
gancio^M di traino^M

トラクター：前面図
tractor: front view
Traktor^M: Vorderansicht^F
tracteur^M agricole : vue^F avant
tractor^M : vista^F frontal
trattore^M : vista^F anteriore

ハンドル
steering wheel
Lenkrad^N
volant^M
volante^M
volante^M

排気筒
exhaust stack
Auspuff^M
cheminée^F d'échappement^M
tubo^M de escape^M
tubo^M di scappamento^M

フェンダー／泥除（よ）け
fender
Spritzschutz^M
garde-boue^M
guardabarros^M
parafango^M

運転台
cab
Kabine^F
cabine^F de conduite^F
cabina^F
cabina^F

リム／外輪
rim
Felge^F
jante^F
llanta^F
cerchione^M

ヘッドライト／前照灯
headlight
Scheinwerfer^M
phare^M
faro^F delantero
proiettore^M

スパイク
tread bar
Stollen^M
sculpture^F
banda^F de rodamiento^M
scolpitura^F del battistrada^M

釣り合い錘（おもり）
counterweight
Frontgewicht^N
contrepoids^M
contrapeso^M
contrappeso^F

エンジン収納部
engine compartment
Motor^M
moteur^M
motor^M
motore^M

前輪
front wheel
Vorderrad^N
roue^F avant
rueda^F delantera
ruota^F anteriore

ステップ
step
Aufstieg^M
marchepied^M
peldaño^M
predellino^M

駆動輪
driving wheel
Antriebsrad^N
roue^F motrice
rueda^F motriz
ruota^F motrice

交通と機械

640

重機器 | HEAVY MACHINERY
SCHWERMASCHINEN | MACHINERIE LOURDE | MAQUINARIA PESADA | MACCHINE PESANTI

農業機械

agricultural machinery | landwirtschaftliche Maschinen^F | machinerie^F agricole | maquinaria^F agrícola | macchine^F agricole

畝(うね)立てプラウ / ribbing plow; ribbing plough / Beetpflug / charrue^F à soc^M / arado^M de vertedera^F / aratro^M a vomere-versoio^M

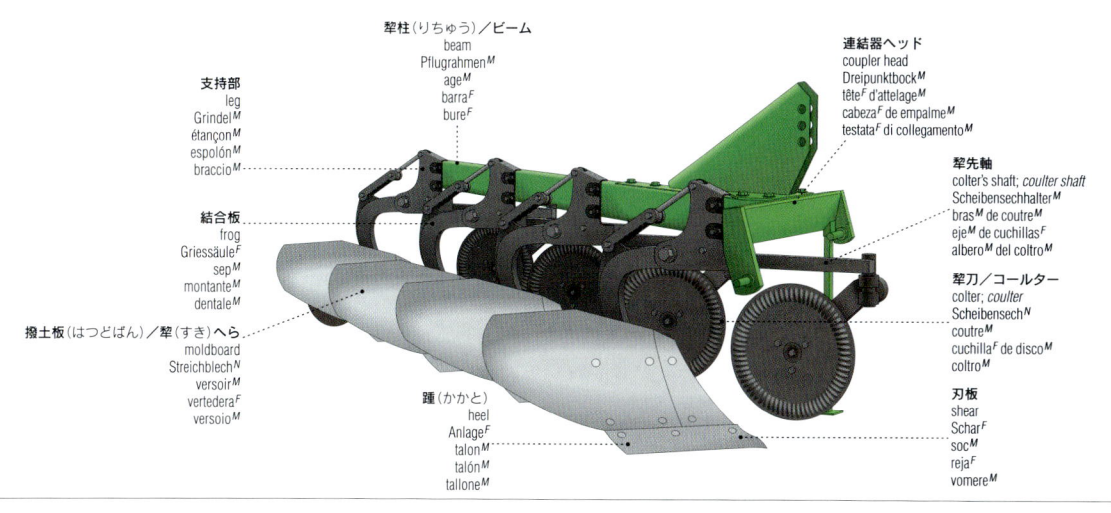

- 犂柱(りちゅう)／ビーム — beam / Pflugrahmen^M / age^M / barra^F / bure^F
- 支持部 — leg / Grindel^M / étançon^M / espolón^M / braccio^M
- 結合板 — frog / Griessäule^F / sep^F / montante^M / dentale^M
- 撥土板(はつどばん)／犂(すき)へら — moldboard / Streichblech^N / versoir^M / vertedera^F / versoio^M
- 連結器ヘッド — coupler head / Dreipunktbock^M / tête^F d'attelage^M / cabeza^F de empalme^M / testata^F di collegamento^M
- 犂先軸 — colter's shaft; coulter shaft / Scheibensechhalter^M / bras^M de coutre^M / eje^M de cuchillas^F / albero^M del coltro^M
- 犂刀／コールター — colter; coulter / Scheibensech^N / coutre^M / cuchilla^F de disco^M / coltro^M
- 踵(かかと) — heel / Anlage^F / talon^M / talón^M / tallone^M
- 刃板 — shear / Schar^F / soc^M / reja^F / vomere^M

タンデム・ディスク・ハロー / tandem disc harrow; tandem disc harrow / Tandemscheibenegge^F / pulvériseur^M tandem / pulverizador^M tándem / erpice^M doppio a dischi^M

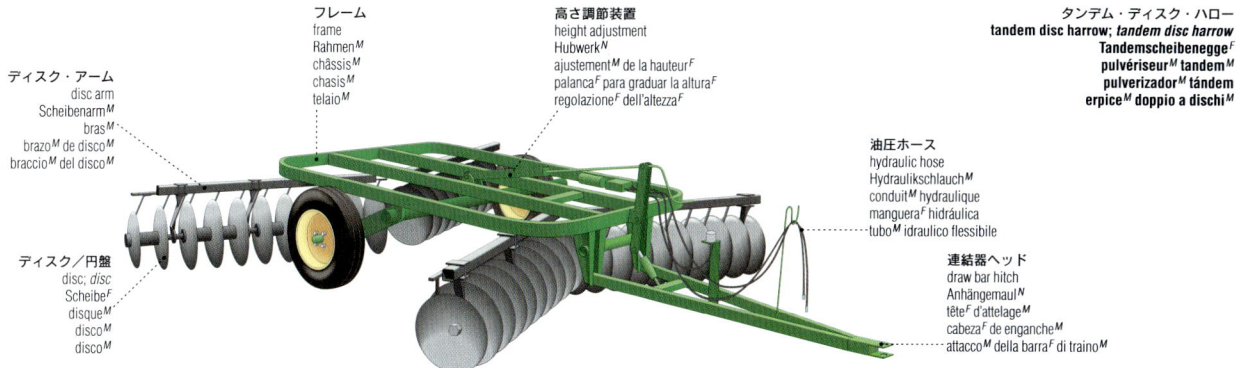

- フレーム — frame / Rahmen^M / châssis^M / chasis^M / telaio^M
- 高さ調節装置 — height adjustment / Hubwerk^N / ajustement^M de la hauteur^F / palanca^F para graduar la altura^F / regolazione^F dell'altezza^F
- ディスク・アーム — disc arm / Scheibenarm^M / bras^M / brazo^M de disco^M / braccio^M del disco^M
- ディスク／円盤 — disc; disc / Scheibe^F / disque^M / disco^M / disco^M
- 油圧ホース — hydraulic hose / Hydraulikschlauch^M / conduit^M hydraulique / manguera^F hidráulica / tubo^M idraulico flessibile
- 連結器ヘッド — draw bar hitch / Anhängemaul^N / tête^F d'attelage^M / cabeza^F de enganche^M / attacco^M della barra^F di traino^M

除草耕耘機(こううんき) / cultivator / Grubber^M / cultivateur^M / cultivador^M / coltivatore^M

- フレーム — frame / Rahmen^M / châssis^M / bastidor^M / telaio^M
- 回転鍬(ぐわ) — rotary hoe / Sternscheibe^F / houe^F rotative / azadón^M rotatorio / zappa^F rotante
- 歯(先) — tine / Zinke^F / dent^F / púa^F de muelle^M / rebbio^M

堆肥(たいひ)散布機 / manure spreader / Dungstreuer^M / épandeur^M de fumier^M / esparcidora^F de estiércol^M / spandiletame^M

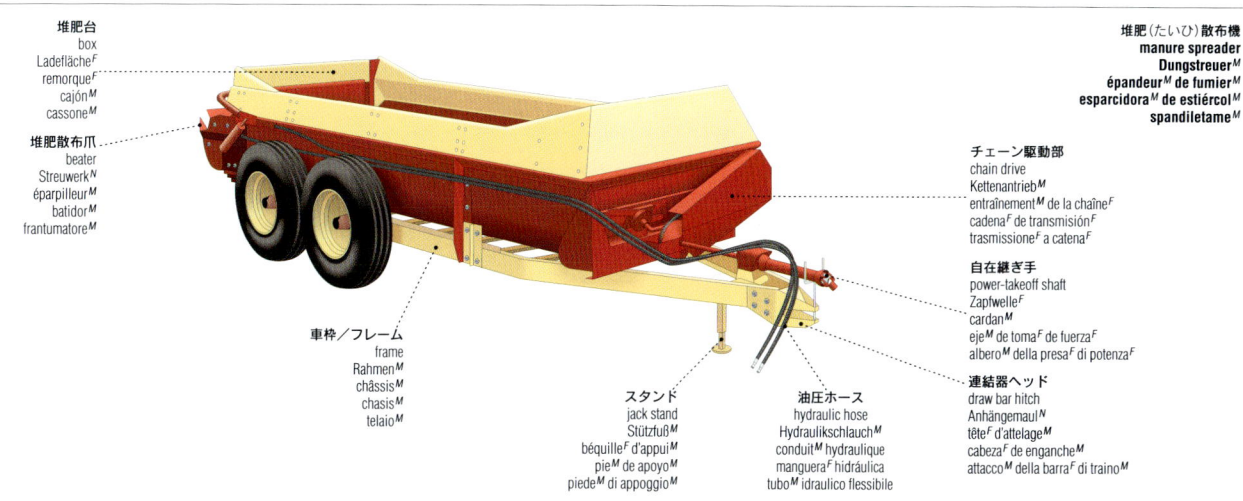

- 堆肥台 — box / Ladefläche^F / remorque^F / cajón^M / cassone^M
- 堆肥散布爪 — beater / Streuwerk^N / éparpilleur^M / batidor^M / frantumatore^M
- 車枠／フレーム — frame / Rahmen^M / châssis^M / chasis^M / telaio^M
- スタンド — jack stand / Stützfuß^M / béquille^F d'appui^M / pie^M de apoyo^M / piede^M di appoggio^M
- 油圧ホース — hydraulic hose / Hydraulikschlauch^M / conduit^M hydraulique / manguera^F hidráulica / tubo^M idraulico flessibile
- チェーン駆動部 — chain drive / Kettenantrieb^M / entraînement^M de la chaîne^F / cadena^F de transmisión^F / trasmissione^F a catena^F
- 自在継ぎ手 — power-takeoff shaft / Zapfwelle^F / cardan^M / eje^M de toma^F de fuerza^F / albero^M della presa^F di potenza^F
- 連結器ヘッド — draw bar hitch / Anhängemaul^N / tête^F d'attelage^M / cabeza^F de enganche^M / attacco^M della barra^F di traino^M

交通と機械

641

重機器 | HEAVY MACHINERY
SCHWERMASCHINEN | MACHINERIE LOURDE | MAQUINARIA PESADA | MACCHINE PESANTI

農業機械

日本語 | 英語 | ドイツ語 | フランス語 | スペイン語 | イタリア語

ドラッグ式集草レーキ
rake
Schubrechwender^M
râteau^M
rastrillo^M
rastrello^M meccanico

高さ調節ハンドル
height adjustment
Verstellspindel^F
ajustement^M de la hauteur^F
palanca^F para graduar la altura^F
regolazione^F dell'altezza^F

フレーム
frame
Rahmen^M
châssis^M
chasis^M
telaio^M

歯杆（しかん）
tooth
Zinke^F
dent^F
diente^M
dente^M

レーキ棒
rake bar
Rechenbalken^M
peigne^M
barra^F de rastrillos^M
traversa^F portadenti

フレール式草刈り機
flail mower
Anhängemähwerk^N
faucheuse^F-conditionneuse^F
segadora^F
falciacondizionatrice^F

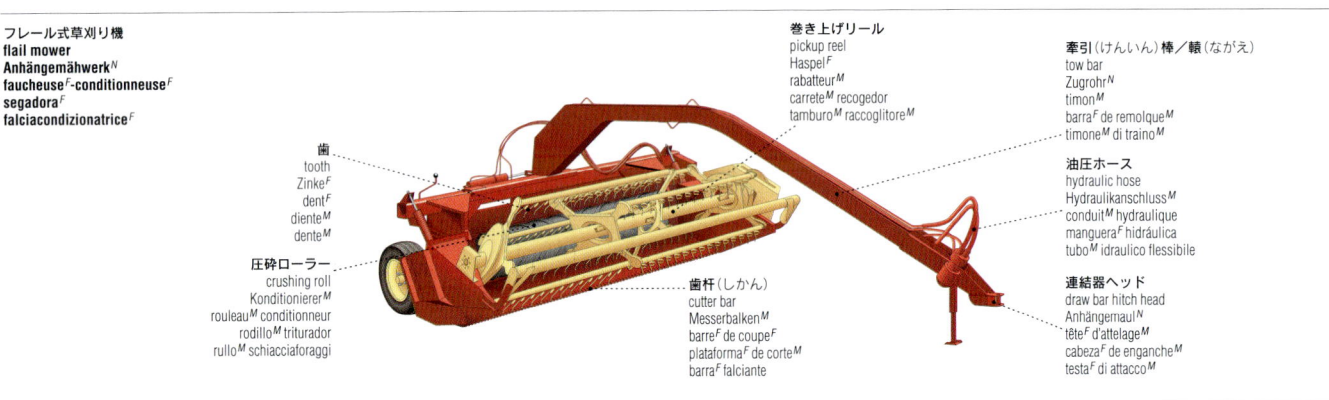

歯
tooth
Zinke^F
dent^F
diente^M
dente^M

圧砕ローラー
crushing roll
Konditionierer^M
rouleau^M conditionneur
rodillo^M triturador
rullo^M schiacciaforaggi

巻き上げリール
pickup reel
Haspel^F
rabatteur^M
carrete^M recogedor
tamburo^M raccoglitore^M

歯杆（しかん）
cutter bar
Messerbalken^M
barre^F de coupe^F
plataforma^F de corte^M
barra^F falciante

牽引（けんいん）棒／轅（ながえ）
tow bar
Zugrohr^N
timon^M
barra^F de remolque^M
timone^M di traino^M

油圧ホース
hydraulic hose
Hydraulikanschluss^M
conduit^M hydraulique
manguera^F hidráulica
tubo^M idraulico flessibile

連結器ヘッド
draw bar hitch head
Anhängemaul^N
tête^F d'attelage^M
cabeza^F de enganche^M
testa^F di attacco^M

乾草梱包機
hay baler
Hochdruckpresse^F
ramasseuse^F-presse^F
empacadora^F de heno^M
imballatrice^F

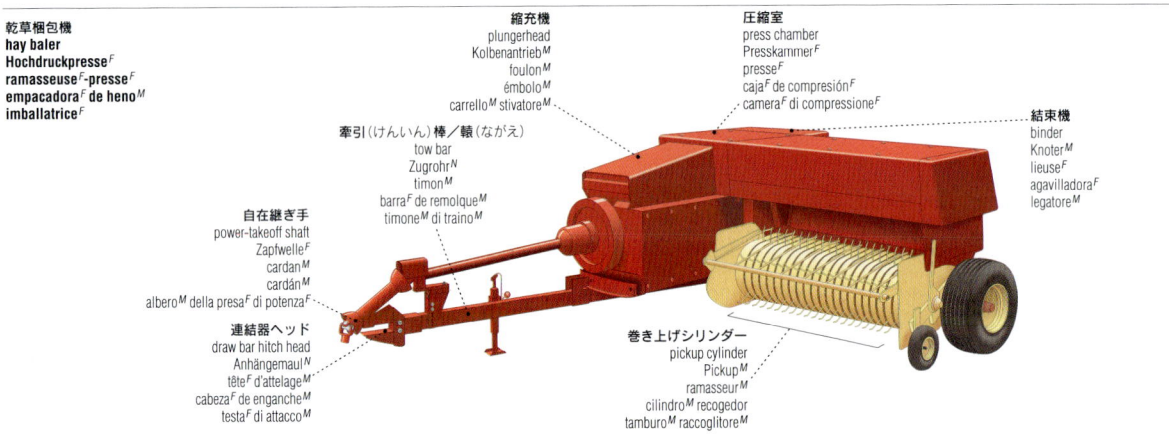

縮充機
plungerhead
Kolbenantrieb^M
foulon^M
émbolo^M
carrello^M stivatore^M

圧縮室
press chamber
Presskammer^F
presse^F
caja^F de compresión^F
camera^F di compressione^F

牽引（けんいん）棒／轅（ながえ）
tow bar
Zugrohr^N
timon^M
barra^F de remolque^M
timone^M di traino^M

結束機
binder
Knoter^M
lieuse^F
agavilladora^F
legatore^M

自在継ぎ手
power-takeoff shaft
Zapfwelle^F
cardan^M
cardán^M
albero^M della presa di potenza^F

連結器ヘッド
draw bar hitch head
Anhängemaul^N
tête^F d'attelage^M
cabeza^F de enganche^M
testa^F di attacco^M

巻き上げシリンダー
pickup cylinder
Pickup
ramasseur^M
cilindro^M recogedor
tamburo^M raccoglitore^M

秣（まぐさ）運搬車
forage harvester
Feldhäcksler^M
fourragère^F
cosechera^F de forraje^M
raccoglitrice^F di foraggio^M

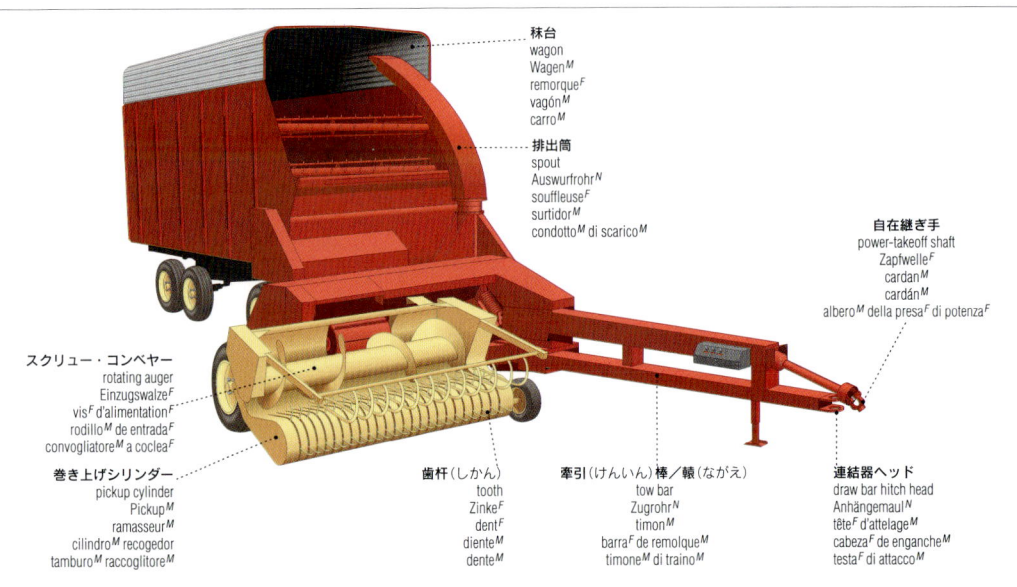

秣台
wagon
Wagen^M
remorque^F
vagón^M
carro^M

排出筒
spout
Auswurfrohr^N
souffleuse^F
surtidor^M
condotto^M di scarico^M

自在継ぎ手
power-takeoff shaft
Zapfwelle^F
cardan^M
cardán^M
albero^M della presa di potenza^F

スクリュー・コンベヤー
rotating auger
Einzugswalze^F
vis^F d'alimentation^F
rodillo^M de entrada^F
convogliatore^M a coclea^F

巻き上げシリンダー
pickup cylinder
Pickup
ramasseur^M
cilindro^M recogedor
tamburo^M raccoglitore^M

歯杆（しかん）
tooth
Zinke^F
dent^F
diente^M
dente^M

牽引（けんいん）棒／轅（ながえ）
tow bar
Zugrohr^N
timon^M
barra^F de remolque^M
timone^M di traino^M

連結器ヘッド
draw bar hitch head
Anhängemaul^N
tête^F d'attelage^M
cabeza^F de enganche^M
testa^F di attacco^M

交通と機械

重機器 | HEAVY MACHINERY
SCHWERMASCHINEN | MACHINERIE LOURDE | MAQUINARIA PESADA | MACCHINE PESANTI

農業機械

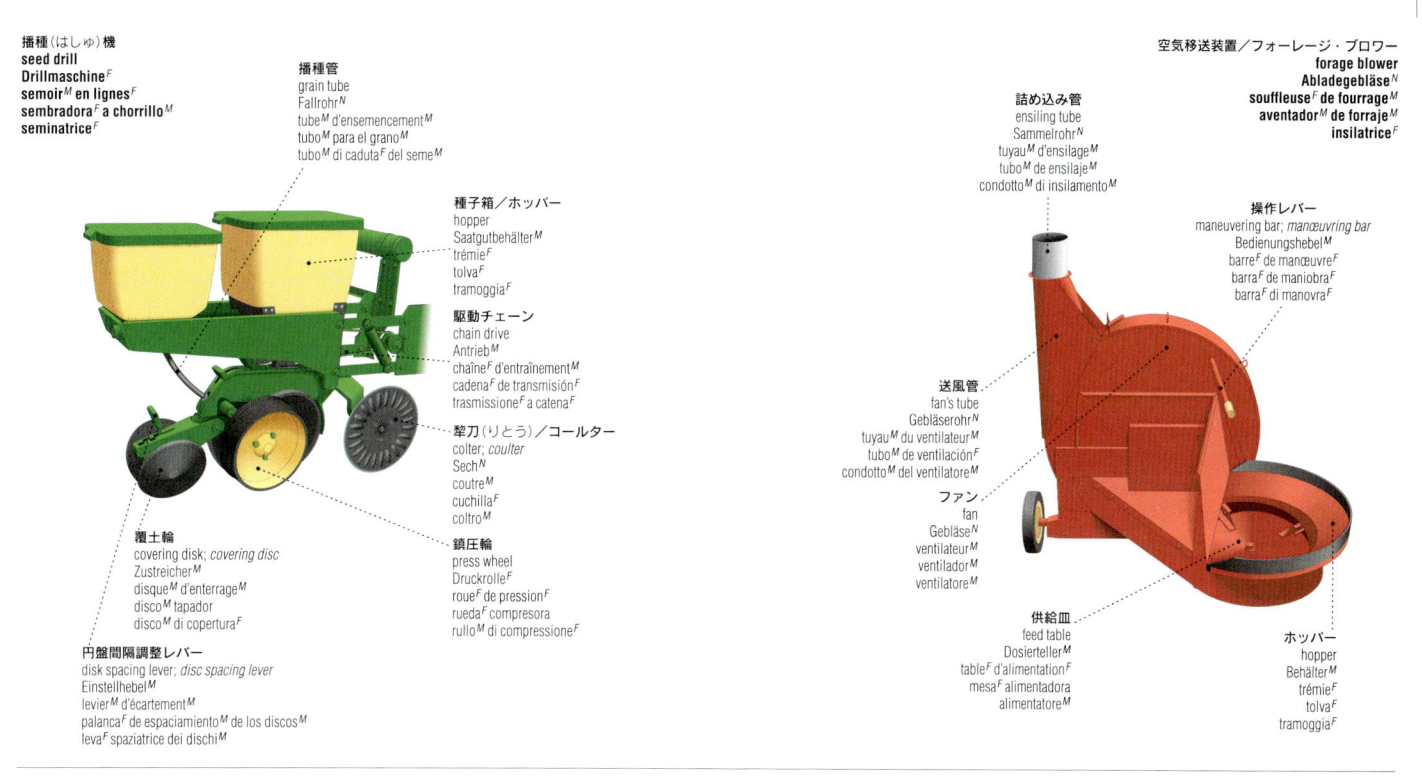

播種（はしゅ）機
seed drill
Drillmaschine^F
semoir^M en lignes^F
sembradora^F a chorrillo^M
seminatrice^F

播種管
grain tube
Fallrohr^N
tube^M d'ensemencement^M
tubo^M para el grano^M
tubo^M di caduta^F del seme^M

種子箱／ホッパー
hopper
Saatgutbehälter^M
trémie^F
tolva^F
tramoggia^F

駆動チェーン
chain drive
Antrieb^M
chaîne^F d'entraînement^M
cadena^F de transmisión^F
trasmissione^F a catena^F

犂刀（りとう）／コールター
colter; coulter
Sech^N
coutre^M
cuchilla^F
coltro^M

覆土輪
covering disk; covering disc
Zustreicher^M
disque^M d'enterrage^M
disco^M tapador
disco^M di copertura^F

鎮圧輪
press wheel
Druckrolle^F
roue^F de pression^F
rueda^F compresora
rullo^M di compressione^F

円盤間隔調整レバー
disk spacing lever; disc spacing lever
Einstellhebel^M
levier^M d'écartement^M
palanca^F de espaciamiento^M de los discos^M
leva^F spaziatrice dei dischi^M

空気移送装置／フォーレージ・ブロワー
forage blower
Ablagegebläse^N
souffleuse^F de fourrage^M
aventador^M de forraje^M
insilatrice^F

詰め込み管
ensiling tube
Sammelrohr^N
tuyau^M d'ensilage^M
tubo^M de ensilaje^M
condotto^M di insilamento^M

操作レバー
maneuvering bar; manœuvring bar
Bedienungshebel^M
barre^F de manœuvre^F
barra^F de maniobra^F
barra^F di manovra^F

送風管
fan's tube
Gebläserohr^N
tuyau^M du ventilateur^M
tubo^M de ventilación^F
condotto^M del ventilatore^M

ファン
fan
Gebläse^N
ventilateur^M
ventilador^M
ventilatore^M

供給皿
feed table
Dosierteller^M
table^F d'alimentation^F
mesa^F alimentadora
alimentatore^M

ホッパー
hopper
Behälter^M
trémie^F
tolva^F
tramoggia^F

スクリュー・コンベヤー
rotating auger
Einzugsschnecke^F
vis^F d'alimentation^F
rodillo^M de entrada^F
convogliatore^M a coclea^F

ディバイダー
divider
Halmteiler^M
diviseur^M
separador^M
separatore^M

運転台
cab
Kabine^F
cabine^F de conduite^F
cabina^F
cabina^F

穀粒昇降機
grain elevator
Kornelevator^M
élévateur^M à grain^M
elevador^M
elevatore^M della granella^F

穀粒タンク
grain tank
Korntank^M
réservoir^M à grain^M
depósito^M del grano^M
serbatoio^M della granella^F

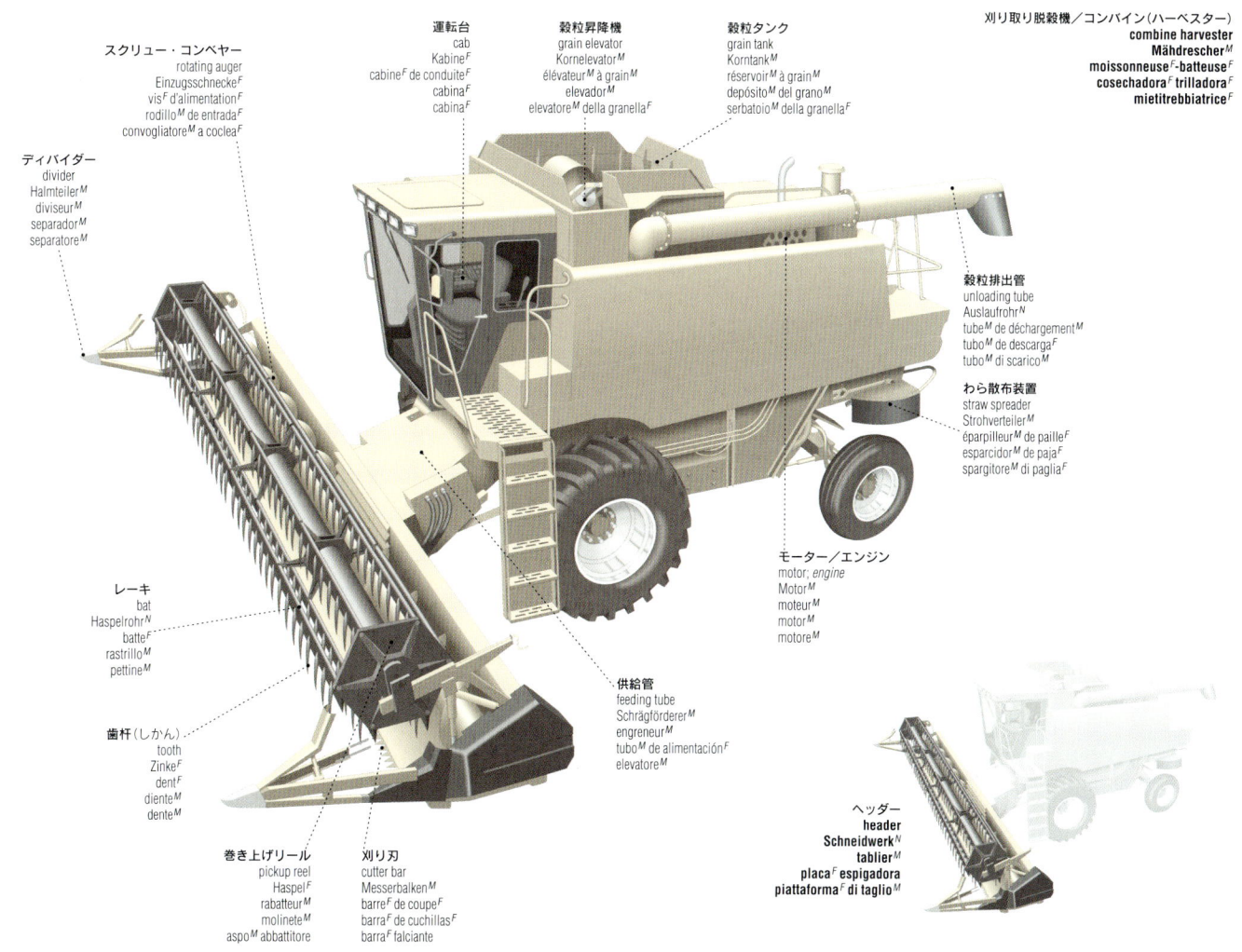

刈り取り脱穀機／コンバイン（ハーベスター）
combine harvester
Mähdrescher^M
moissonneuse^F-batteuse^F
cosechadora^F trilladora^F
mietitrebbiatrice^F

穀粒排出管
unloading tube
Auslaufrohr^N
tube^M de déchargement^M
tubo^M de descarga^F
tubo^M di scarico^M

わら散布装置
straw spreader
Strohverteiler^M
éparpilleur^M de paille^F
esparcidor^M de paja^F
spargitore^M di paglia^F

モーター／エンジン
motor; engine
Motor^M
moteur^M
motor^M
motore^M

レーキ
bat
Haspelrohr^N
batte^F
rastrillo^M
pettine^M

歯杆（しかん）
tooth
Zinke^F
dent^F
diente^M
dente^M

巻き上げリール
pickup reel
Haspel^F
rabatteur^M
molinete^M
aspo^M abbattitore^M

刈り刃
cutter bar
Messerbalken^M
barre^F de coupe^F
barra^F de cuchillas^F
barra^F falciante

供給管
feeding tube
Schrägförderer^M
engreneur^M
tubo^M de alimentación^F
elevatore^M

ヘッダー
header
Schneidwerk^N
tablier^M
placa^F espigadora
piattaforma^F di taglio^M

交通と機械

643

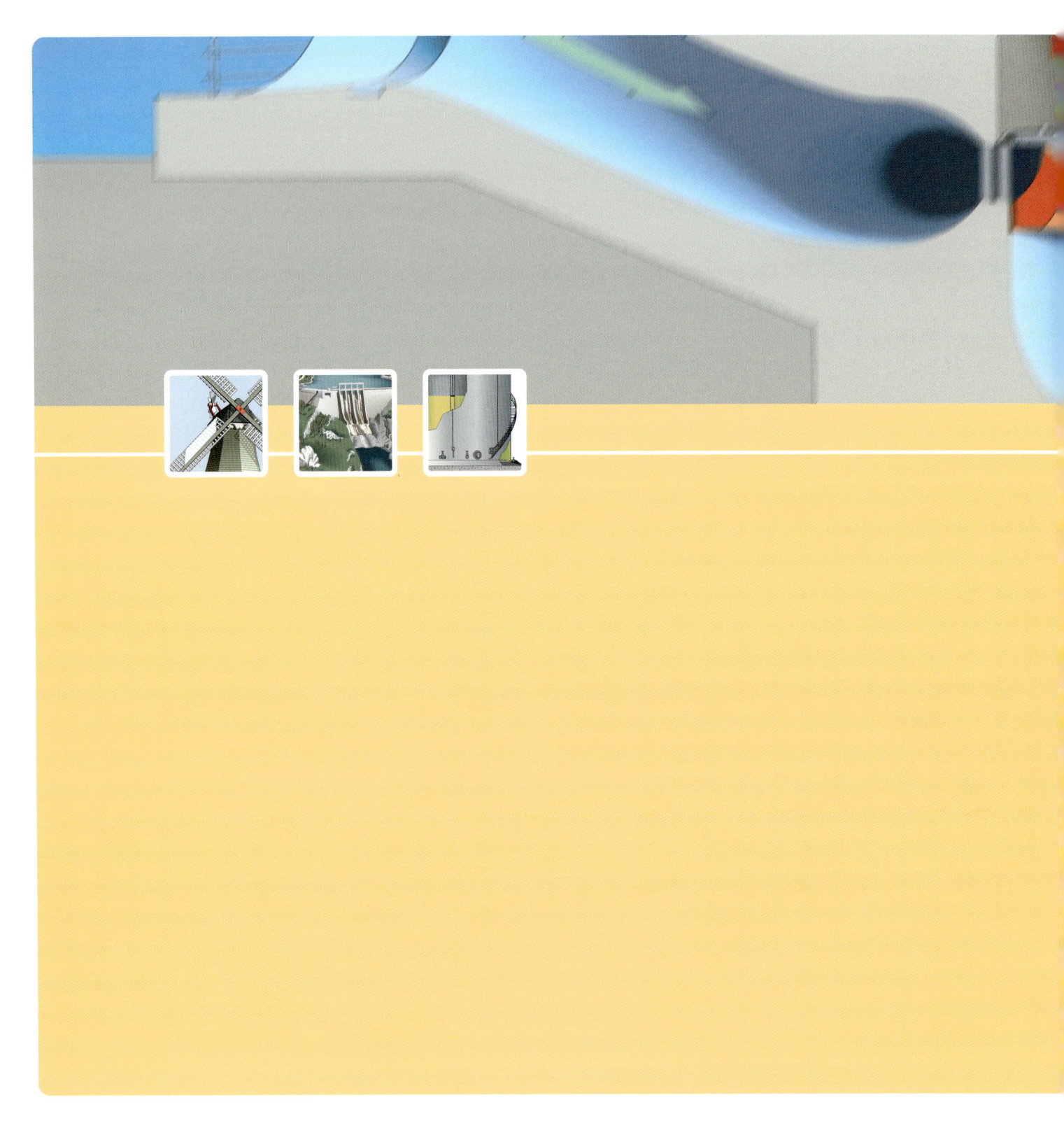

646 地熱・化石エネルギー

- 646 地熱発電
- 646 熱エネルギー
- 647 炭鉱
- 651 石油

657 水力電気

- 657 水力発電所
- 659 発電装置
- 660 ダムの例
- 662 電気の発生過程
- 663 送電
- 664 潮汐[潮力]発電所

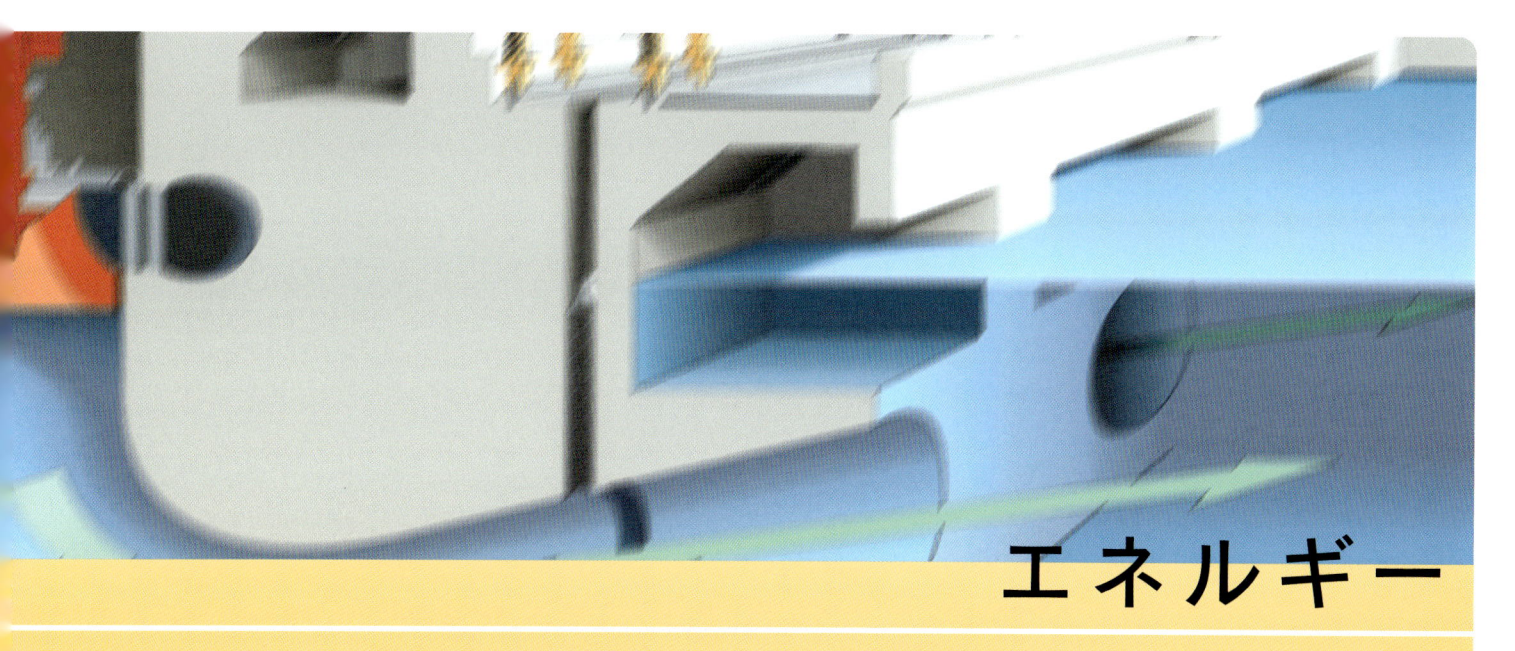

エネルギー

ENERGY | ENERGIE | ÉNERGIES | ENERGÍA | ENERGIA

665 核エネルギー

- 665 核エネルギー発電
- 666 燃料取り扱いの流れ
- 667 燃料集合体
- 667 原子炉
- 668 原子力発電所
- 670 炭酸ガス炉
- 670 重水路
- 671 加圧水型炉
- 671 沸騰水型炉

672 太陽エネルギー

- 672 太陽電池
- 672 平板型太陽(熱)集熱器
- 673 太陽電池の仕組み
- 674 太陽炉
- 674 太陽エネルギー発電
- 675 ソーラー・ハウス

676 風力エネルギー

- 676 風車
- 676 風力タービンと発電

地熱・化石エネルギー | GEOTHERMAL AND FOSSIL ENERGY
GEOTHERMISCHE UND FOSSILE ENERGIE | ÉNERGIE GÉOTHERMIQUE ET ÉNERGIE FOSSILE | ENERGÍA GEOTÉRMICA Y FÓSIL | ENERGIA GEOTERMICA E FOSSILE

地熱発電

日本語 | 英語 | ドイツ語 | フランス語 | スペイン語 | イタリア語

production of electricity from geothermal energy | Elektrizitätserzeugung^F aus geothermischer Energie^F | production^F d'électricité^F par énergie^F géothermique | producción^F de electricidad^F por energía^F geotérmica | produzione^F di elettricità^F da energia^F geotermica

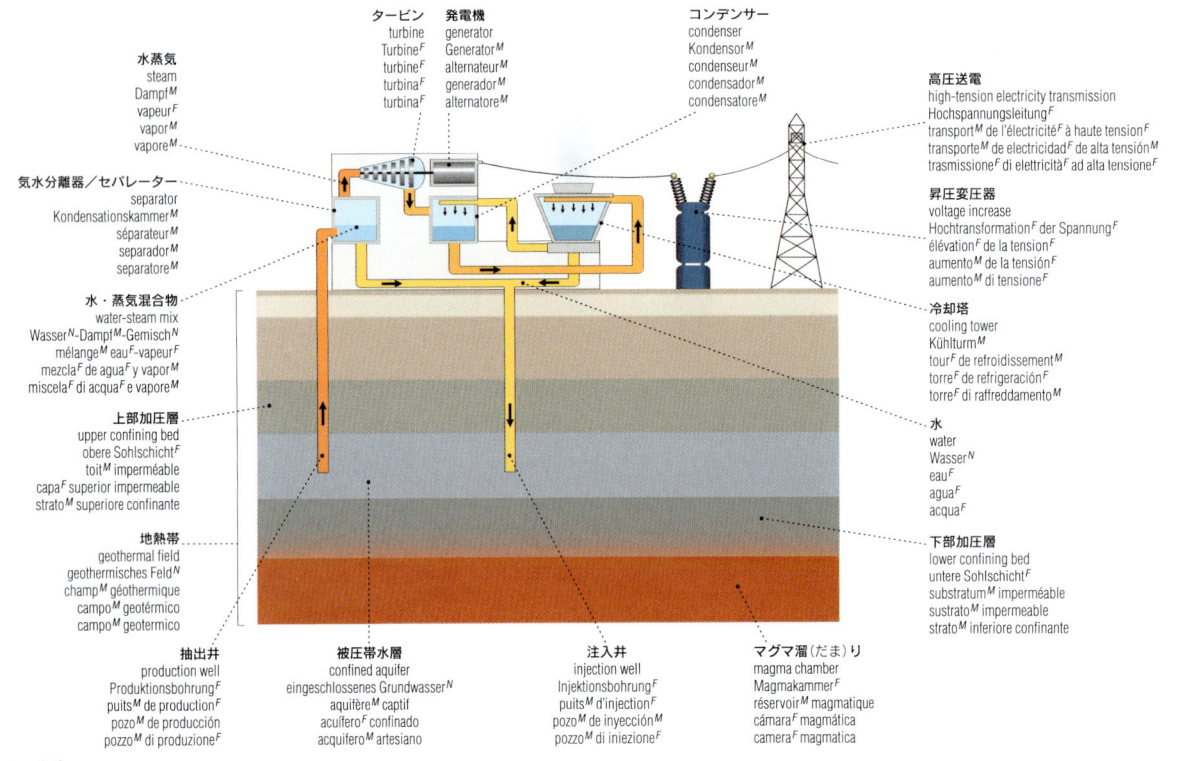

タービン
turbine
Turbine^F
turbine^F
turbina^F
turbina^F

発電機
generator
Generator^M
alternateur^M
generador^M
alternatore^M

コンデンサー
condenser
Kondensor^M
condenseur^M
condensador^M
condensatore^M

水蒸気
steam
Dampf^M
vapeur^F
vapor^M
vapore^M

高圧送電
high-tension electricity transmission
Hochspannungsleitung^F
transport^M de l'électricité^F à haute tension^F
transporte^M de electricidad^F de alta tensión^M
trasmissione^F di elettricità^F ad alta tensione^F

気水分離器／セパレーター
separator
Kondensationskammer^M
séparateur^M
separador^M
separatore^M

昇圧変圧器
voltage increase
Hochtransformation^F der Spannung^F
élévation^F de la tension^F
aumento^M de la tensión^F
aumento^M di tensione^F

水・蒸気混合物
water-steam mix
Wasser^N-Dampf^M-Gemisch^N
mélange^M eau^F-vapeur^F
mezcla^F de agua^F y vapor^M
miscela^F di acqua^F e vapore^M

冷却塔
cooling tower
Kühlturm^M
tour^F de refroidissement^M
torre^F de refrigeración^F
torre^F di raffreddamento^M

上部加圧層
upper confining bed
obere Sohlschicht^F
toit^M imperméable
capa^F superior impermeable
strato^M superiore confinante

水
water
Wasser^N
eau^F
agua^F
acqua^F

地熱帯
geothermal field
geothermisches Feld^N
champ^M géothermique
campo^M geotérmico
campo^M geotermico

下部加圧層
lower confining bed
untere Sohlschicht^F
substratum^M imperméable
sustrato^M impermeable
strato^M inferiore confinante

抽出井
production well
Produktionsbohrung^F
puits^M de production^F
pozo^M de producción
pozzo^M di produzione^F

被圧帯水層
confined aquifer
eingeschlossenes Grundwasser^N
aquifère^M captif
acuífero^M confinado
acquifero^M artesiano

注入井
injection well
Injektionsbohrung^F
puits^M d'injection^F
pozo^M de inyección^F
pozzo^M di iniezione^F

マグマ溜（だま）り
magma chamber
Magmakammer^F
réservoir^M magmatique
cámara^F magmática
camera^F magmatica

熱エネルギー

thermal energy | Wärmeenergie^F | énergie^F thermique | energía^F térmica | energia^F termica

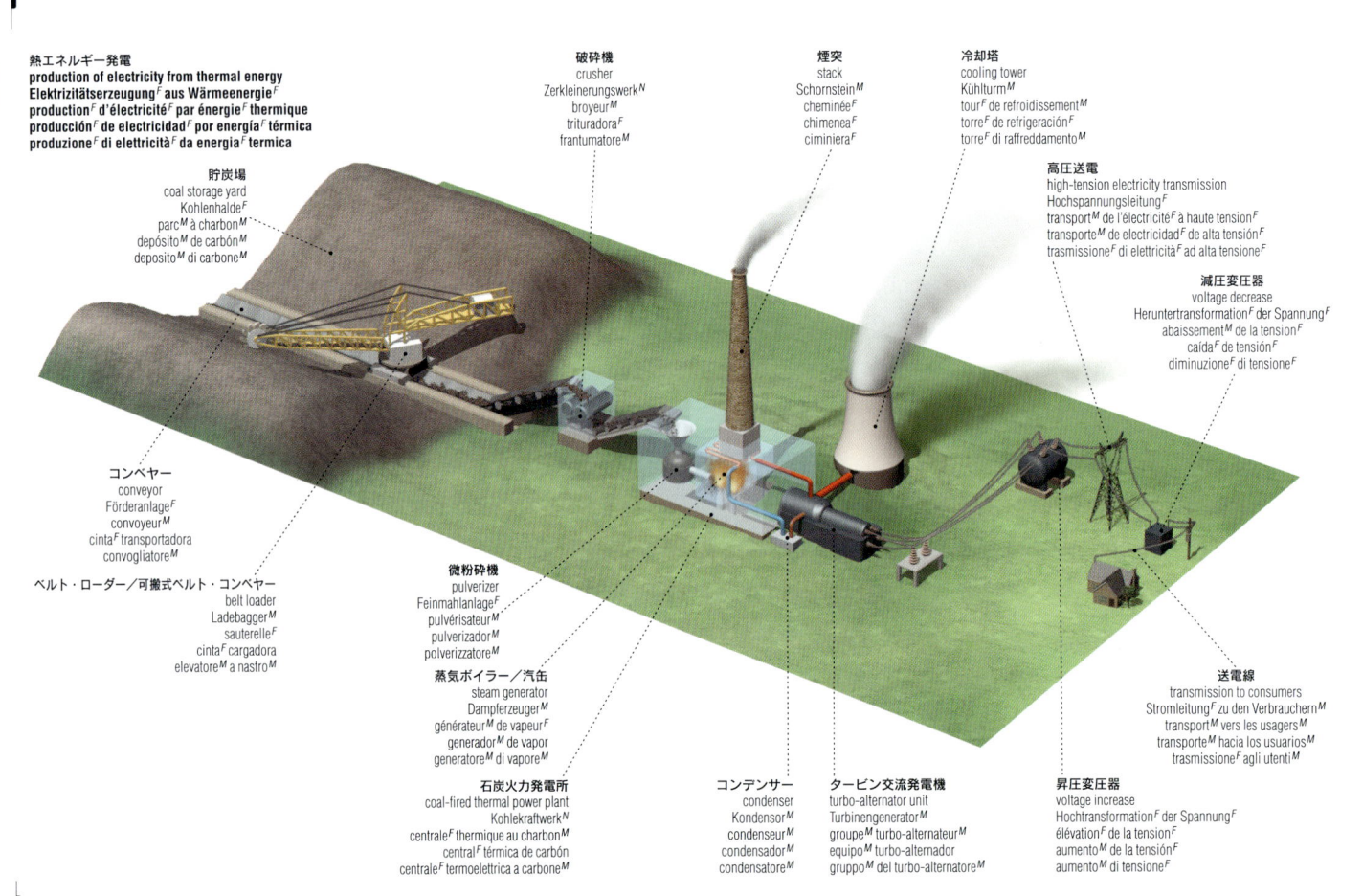

熱エネルギー発電
production of electricity from thermal energy
Elektrizitätserzeugung^F aus Wärmeenergie^F
production^F d'électricité^F par énergie^F thermique
producción^F de electricidad^F por energía^F térmica
produzione^F di elettricità^F da energia^F termica

破砕機
crusher
Zerkleinerungswerk^N
broyeur^M
trituradora^F
frantumatore^M

煙突
stack
Schornstein^M
cheminée^F
chimenea^F
ciminiera^F

冷却塔
cooling tower
Kühlturm^M
tour^F de refroidissement^M
torre^F de refrigeración^F
torre^F di raffreddamento^M

貯炭場
coal storage yard
Kohlenhalde^F
parc^M à charbon^M
depósito^M de carbón^M
deposito^M di carbone^M

高圧送電
high-tension electricity transmission
Hochspannungsleitung^F
transport^M de l'électricité^F à haute tension^F
transporte^M de electricidad^F de alta tensión^F
trasmissione^F di elettricità^F ad alta tensione^F

減圧変圧器
voltage decrease
Heruntertransformation^F der Spannung^F
abaissement^M de la tension^F
caída^F de tensión^F
diminuzione^F di tensione^F

コンベヤー
conveyor
Förderanlage^F
convoyeur^M
cinta^F transportadora
convogliatore^M

ベルト・ローダー／可搬式ベルト・コンベヤー
belt loader
Ladebagger^M
sauterelle^F
cinta^F cargadora
elevatore^M a nastro^M

微粉砕機
pulverizer
Feinmahlanlage^F
pulvérisateur^M
pulverizador^M
polverizzatore^M

蒸気ボイラー／汽缶
steam generator
Dampferzeuger^M
générateur^M de vapeur^F
generador^M de vapor^M
generatore^M di vapore^M

送電線
transmission to consumers
Stromleitung^F zu den Verbrauchern^M
transport^M vers les usagers^M
transporte^M hacia los usuarios^M
trasmissione^F agli utenti^M

石炭火力発電所
coal-fired thermal power plant
Kohlekraftwerk^N
centrale^F thermique au charbon^M
central^F térmica de carbón^M
centrale^F termoelettrica a carbone^M

コンデンサー
condenser
Kondensor^M
condenseur^M
condensador^M
condensatore^M

タービン交流発電機
turbo-alternator unit
Turbinengenerator^M
groupe^M turbo-alternateur^M
equipo^M turbo-alternador^M
gruppo^M del turbo-alternatore^M

昇圧変圧器
voltage increase
Hochtransformation^F der Spannung^F
élévation^F de la tension^F
aumento^M de la tensión^F
aumento^M di tensione^F

地熱・化石エネルギー | GEOTHERMAL AND FOSSIL ENERGY
GEOTHERMISCHE UND FOSSILE ENERGIE | GÉOTHERMIE ET ÉNERGIE FOSSILE | ENERGÍA GEOTÉRMICA Y FÓSIL | ENERGIA GEOTERMICA E FOSSILE

炭鉱
coal mine | Kohlebergwerk^N | mine^F de charbon^M | minas^F de carbón^M | miniera^F di carbone^M

段丘
bench
Bank^F
gradin^M
banco^M
gradino^M

地表
ground surface
Erdoberfläche^F
terrain^M naturel
superficie^F del terreno^M
livello^M del suolo^M

露天掘り炭鉱［鉱山］
open-pit mine
offene Grube^F
carrière^F en entonnoir^M
mina^F a cielo^M abierto
miniera^F a cielo^M aperto

表土
overburden
Obergestein^N
morts-terrains^M
relleno^M exterior
strato^M sterile

切羽（きりは）
face
Stroße^F
front^M de taille^F
frente^M de corte^M
fronte^M di abbattimento^M

段丘の高さ
bench height
Bankhöhe^F
hauteur^F du gradin^M
altura^F del banco^M
altezza^F del gradino^M

原鉱
ore
Erz^N
minerai^M
mineral^M
giacimento^M minerale

運搬坑道
haulage road
Transportstrecke^F
voie^F de transport^M
camino^M de arrastre^M
via^F di carreggio^M

傾斜路
ramp
Rampe^F
rampe^F
talud^M
rampa^F

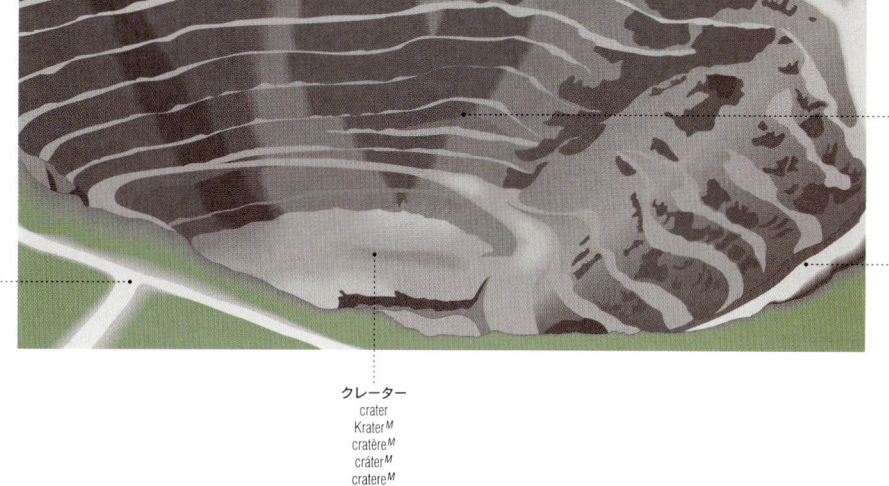

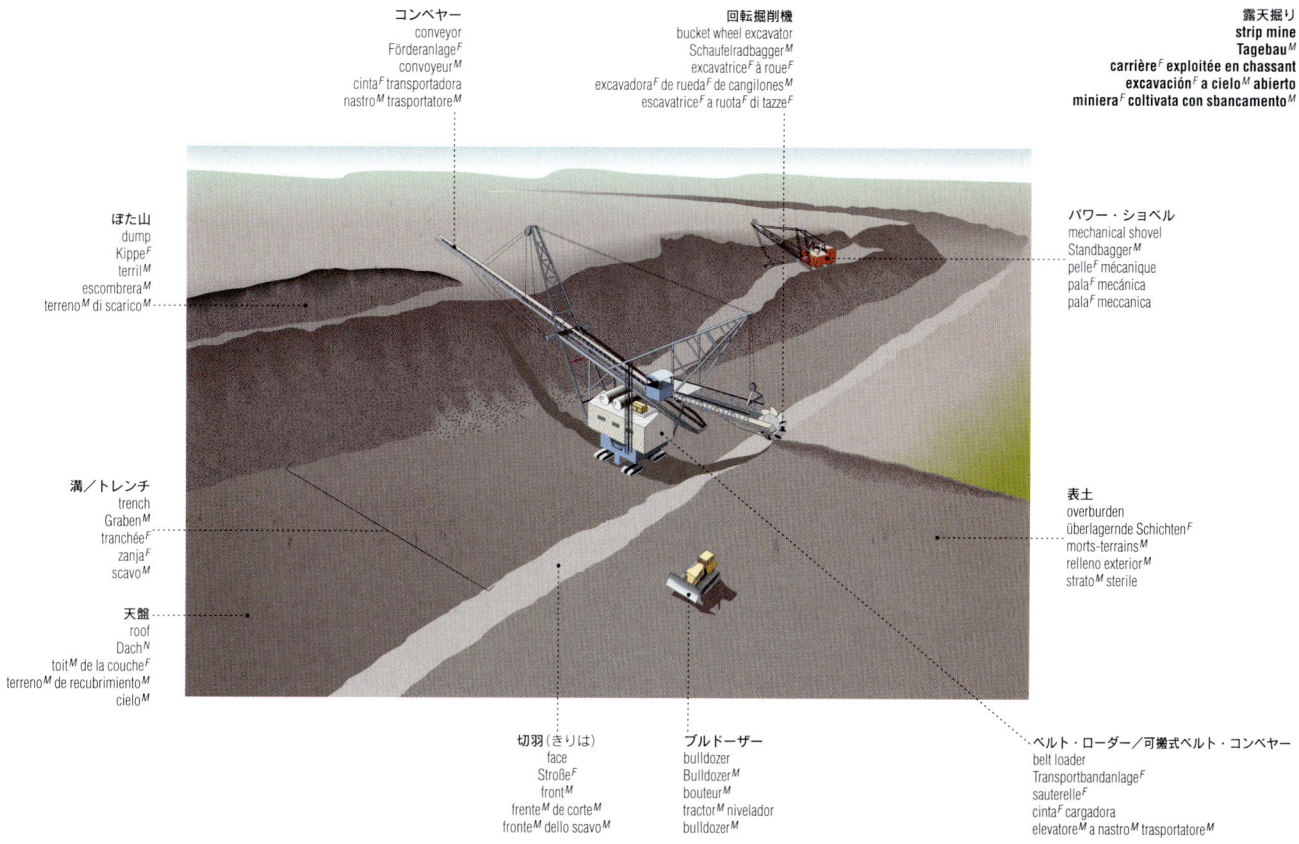

クレーター
crater
Krater^M
cratère^M
cráter^M
cratere^M

コンベヤー
conveyor
Förderanlage^F
convoyeur^M
cinta^F transportadora
nastro^M trasportatore^M

回転掘削機
bucket wheel excavator
Schaufelradbagger^M
excavatrice^F à roue^F
excavadora^F de rueda^F de cangilones^M
escavatrice^F a ruota^F di tazze^F

露天掘り
strip mine
Tagebau^M
carrière^F exploitée en chassant
excavación^F a cielo^M abierto
miniera^F coltivata con sbancamento^M

ぼた山
dump
Kippe^F
terril^M
escombrera^F
terreno^M di scarico^M

パワー・ショベル
mechanical shovel
Standbagger^M
pelle^F mécanique
pala^F mecánica
pala^F meccanica

溝／トレンチ
trench
Graben^M
tranchée^F
zanja^F
scavo^M

天盤
roof
Dach^N
toit^M de la couche^F
terreno^M de recubrimiento^M
cielo^M

表土
overburden
überlagernde Schichten^F
morts-terrains^M
relleno exterior^M
strato^M sterile

切羽（きりは）
face
Stroße^F
front^M
frente^M de corte^M
fronte^M dello scavo^M

ブルドーザー
bulldozer
Bulldozer^M
bouteur^M
tractor^M nivelador
bulldozer^M

ベルト・ローダー／可搬式ベルト・コンベヤー
belt loader
Transportbandanlage^F
sauterelle^F
cinta^F cargadora
elevatore^M a nastro^M trasportatore^M

エネルギー

647

地熱・化石エネルギー | GEOTHERMAL AND FOSSIL ENERGY
GEOTHERMISCHE UND FOSSILE ENERGIE | GÉOTHERMIE ET ÉNERGIE FOSSILE | ENERGÍA GEOTÉRMICA Y FÓSIL | ENERGIA GEOTERMICA E FOSSILE

炭鉱

日本語 | 英語 | ドイツ語 | フランス語 | スペイン語 | イタリア語

ジャックレッグ・ドリル
jackleg drill
Bohrhammer^M
marteau^M perforateur à poussoir^M pneumatique
perforadora^F con empujador^M neumático
martello^M perforatore con servosostegno^M

ハンマー・ドリル
hammer drill
Schlagbohrer^M
marteau^M perforateur
taladro^M percutor
martello^M perforatore

刃先／ビット
bit
Bohrkopf^M
taillant^M
broca^F
tagliente^M

軸／ドリル・ロッド
drill rod
Bohrstange^F
fleuret^M
barrena^F
fioretto^M

水ホース
water hose
Wasserschlauch^M
flexible^M d'eau^F
manguera^F de agua^F
tubo^M flessibile per l'acqua^F

エア・レッグ
air leg
Druckluft-Bohrknecht^M
poussoir^M pneumatique
cilindro^M neumático
servosostegno^M

空気ホース
air hose
Luftschlauch^M
flexible^M d'air^M
manguera^F de aire^M
tubo^M flessibile per l'aria^F compressa

水分離器
water separator
Wasserabscheider^M
séparateur^M d'eau^F
separador^M de agua^F
separatore^M dell'acqua^F

油差し
oiler
Öler^M
graisseur^M
aceitera^F
oliatore^M

整修工場
maintenance shop
Maschinenhaus^N
atelier^M d'entretien^M
taller^M de mantenimiento^M
officina^F riparazioni^F

坑道入り口周辺
pithead
Übertageanlage^F
carreau^M de mine^F
planta^F exterior de una mina^F
esterno^M della miniera^F

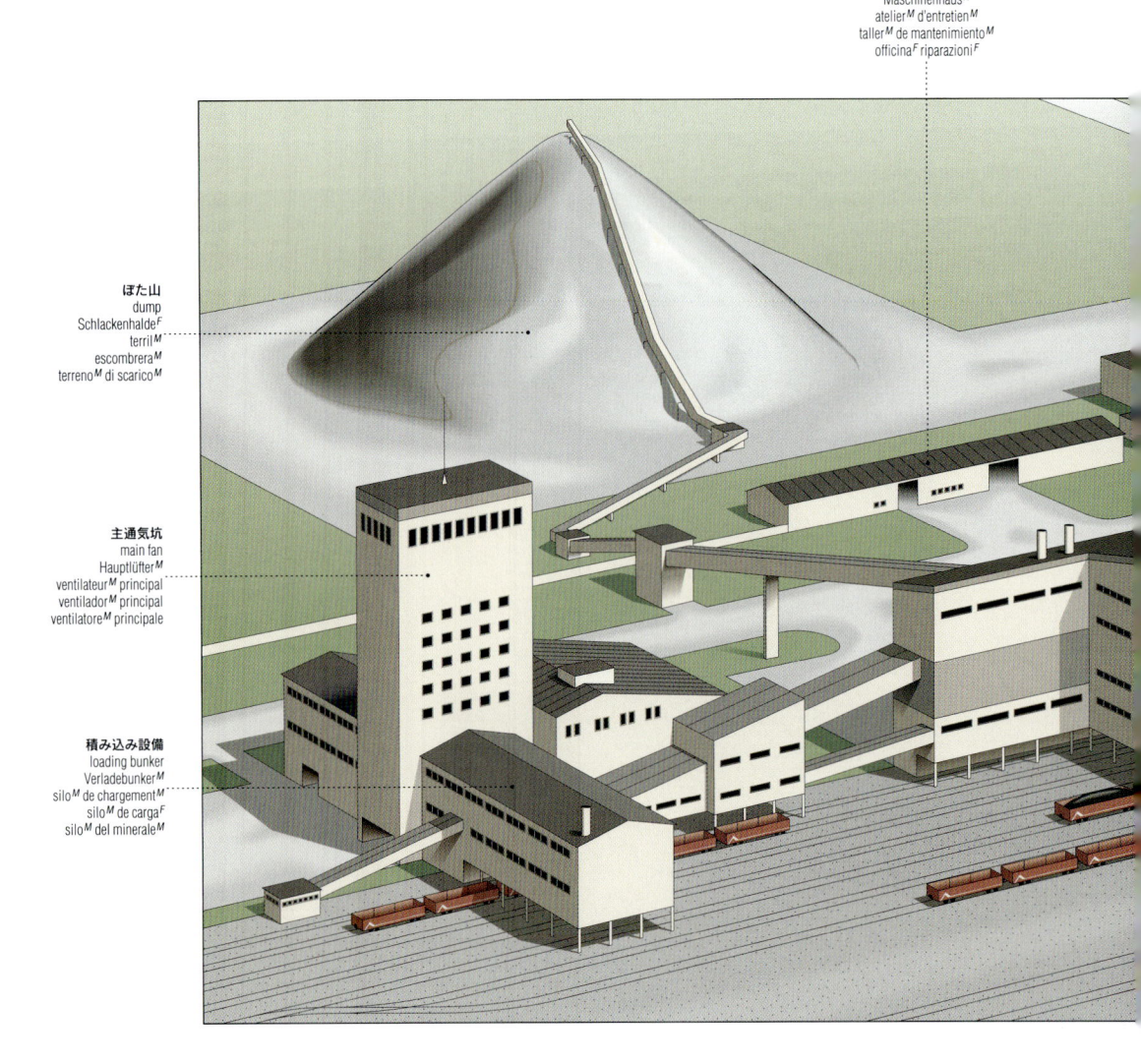

ぼた山
dump
Schlackenhalde^F
terril^M
escombrera^F
terreno^M di scarico^M

主通気坑
main fan
Hauptlüfter^M
ventilateur^M principal
ventilador^M principal
ventilatore^M principale

積み込み設備
loading bunker
Verladebunker^M
silo^M de chargement^M
silo^M de carga^F
silo^M del minerale^M

エネルギー

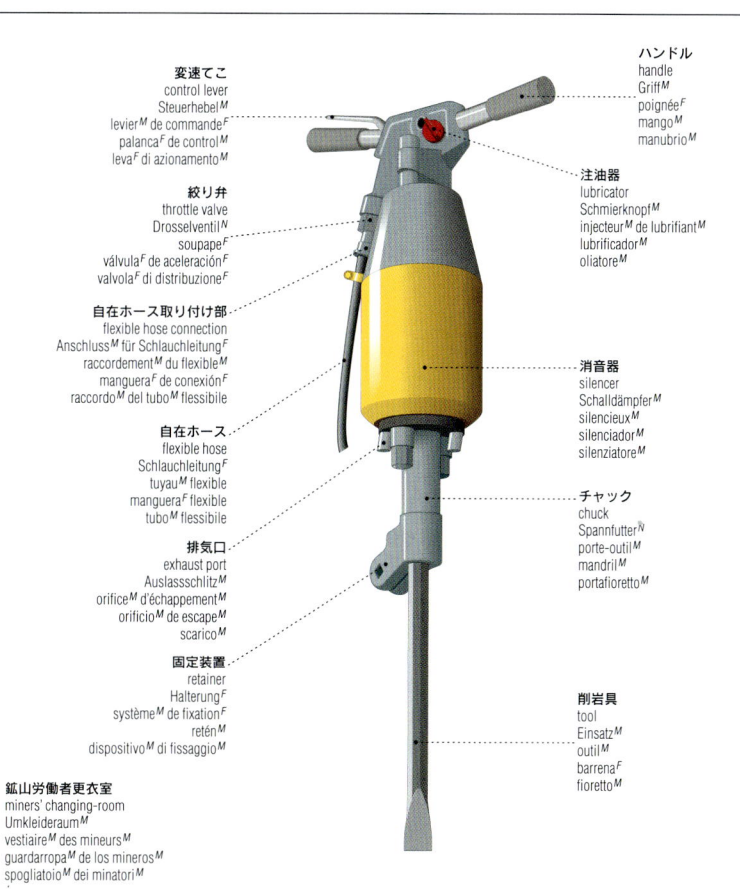

地熱・化石エネルギー | GEOTHERMAL AND FOSSIL ENERGY
GEOTHERMISCHE UND FOSSILE ENERGIE | GÉOTHERMIE ET ÉNERGIE FOSSILE | ENERGÍA GEOTÉRMICA Y FÓSIL | ENERGIA GEOTERMICA E FOSSILE

炭鉱

空気ハンマー
pneumatic hammer
Pressluftbohrer^M
marteau^M pneumatique
martillo^M neumático
piccone^M pneumatico

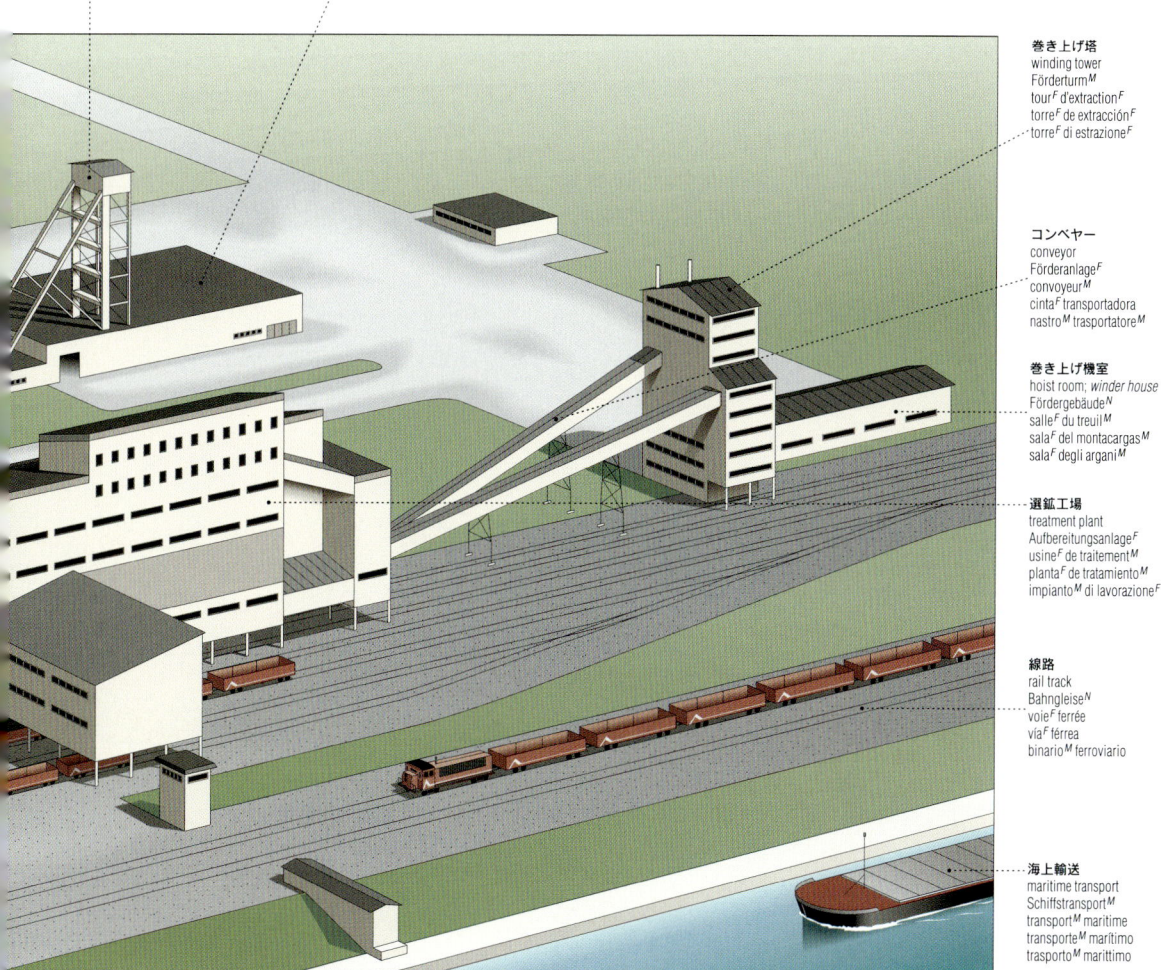

変速てこ
control lever
Steuerhebel^M
levier^M de commande^F
palanca^F de control^M
leva^F di azionamento^M

ハンドル
handle
Griff^M
poignée^F
mango^M
manubrio^M

絞り弁
throttle valve
Drosselventil^N
soupape^F
válvula^F de aceleración^F
valvola^F di distribuzione^F

注油器
lubricator
Schmierknopf^M
injecteur^M de lubrifiant^M
lubrificador^M
oliatore^M

自在ホース取り付け部
flexible hose connection
Anschluss^M für Schlauchleitung^F
raccordement^M du flexible^M
manguera^F de conexión^F
raccordo^M del tubo^M flessibile

消音器
silencer
Schalldämpfer^M
silencieux^M
silenciador^M
silenziatore^M

自在ホース
flexible hose
Schlauchleitung^F
tuyau^M flexible
manguera^F flexible
tubo^M flessibile

チャック
chuck
Spannfutter^N
porte-outil^M
mandril^M
portafioretto^M

排気口
exhaust port
Auslassschlitz^M
orifice^M d'échappement^M
orificio^M de escape^M
scarico^M

固定装置
retainer
Halterung^F
système^M de fixation^F
retén^M
dispositivo^M di fissaggio^M

削岩具
tool
Einsatz^M
outil^M
barrena^F
fioretto^M

立て坑口
shaft head
Schachtgerüsteingang^M
tête^F de puits^M
pozo^M principal
entrata^F del pozzo^M

鉱山労働者更衣室
miners' changing-room
Umkleideraum^M
vestiaire^M des mineurs^M
guardarropa^M de los mineros^M
spogliatoio^M dei minatori^M

巻き上げ塔
winding tower
Förderturm^M
tour^F d'extraction^F
torre^F de extracción^F
torre^F di estrazione^F

コンベヤー
conveyor
Förderanlage^F
convoyeur^M
cinta^F transportadora
nastro^M trasportatore^M

巻き上げ機室
hoist room; *winder house*
Fördergebäude^N
salle^F du treuil^M
sala^F del montacargas^M
sala^F degli argani^M

選鉱工場
treatment plant
Aufbereitungsanlage^F
usine^F de traitement^M
planta^F de tratamiento^M
impianto^M di lavorazione^F

線路
rail track
Bahngleise^N
voie^F ferrée
vía^F férrea
binario^M ferroviario

海上輸送
maritime transport
Schiffstransport^M
transport^M maritime
transporte^M marítimo
trasporto^M marittimo

エネルギー

地熱・化石エネルギー | GEOTHERMAL AND FOSSIL ENERGY
GEOTHERMISCHE UND FOSSILE ENERGIE | GÉOTHERMIE ET ÉNERGIE FOSSILE | ENERGÍA GEOTÉRMICA Y FÓSIL | ENERGIA GEOTERMICA E FOSSILE

炭鉱

日本語 | 英語 | ドイツ語 | フランス語 | スペイン語 | イタリア語

坑内掘り炭鉱
underground mine
Grube^F
mine^F souterraine
mina^F subterránea
miniera^F sotterranea

巻き上げ塔
headframe
Schachtgerüst^N
chevalement^M
castillete^M de extracción^F
castelletto^M di testa^F del pozzo^M

（垂直）立て坑
vertical shaft
Richtschacht^M
puits^M vertical
tiro^M vertical
pozzo^M verticale

エレベーター
elevator; lift
Aufzug^M
ascenseur^M
montacargas^M
ascensore^M

シュート
chute
Rutsche^F
cheminée^F
chimenea^F
fornello^M di getto^M

立て入れ坑道
cross cut
Querschlag^M
travers-banc^M
galería^F transversal
traversa^F

人員専用通路
manway
Einstiegschacht^M
galerie^F de circulation^F
galería^F de acceso^M
fornello^M di accesso^M

沿層坑道
drift
Seitenstollen^M
galerie^F en direction^F
galería^F de arrastre^M
galleria^F in direzione^F

切羽（きりは）
face
Abbaufront^F
front^M de taille^F
frente^M de corte^M
fronte^M

坑口
pithead
Übertageanlage^F
tour^F d'extraction^F
bocamina^F
torre^F di estrazione^F

運搬立て坑
winding shaft
Förderschacht^M
puits^M d'extraction^F
pozo^M de extracción^F
pozzo^M di estrazione^F

鉱柱／炭柱／残柱
pillar
Abbaupfeiler^M
pilier^M
pilar^M
pilastro^M

居住室
room
Kammer^F
chambre^F
cámara^F
camera^F

水平坑道／水準
level
Sohle^F
niveau^M
nivel^M
livello^M

第一水平坑道
top road
Kopfstrecke^F
voie^F de tête^F
galería^F superior
galleria^F di testa^F

レベル
deck
Förderstockwerk^N
étage^M
plataforma^F de jaula^F
strato^M di tetto^M

装入バスケット／スキップ
skip
Förderkübel^M
skip^M
jaula^F
benna^F di caricamento^M

鉱柱／鉱筒
ore pass
Erzgang^M
cheminée^F à minerai^M
chimenea^F de evacuación^F
pozzo^M del minerale^M

区画
panel
Feld^M im Abbau^M
panneau^M
pared^F
sezione^F

坑底操作場／石炭置き場
landing
Schacht^M-Hängebank^F
recette^F
estación^F de carga^F
stazione^F di caricamento^M

集水坑
sump
Schachtsumpf^M
puisard^M
sumidero^M
pozzo^M di drenaggio^M

最下路
bottom road
Fußstrecke^F
voie^F de fond^M
galería^M inferior
galleria^F di fondo^M

坑井（こうせい）／掘り下がり
winze
Blindschacht^M
descenderie^F
pozo^M ciego^M
discenderia^F

地熱・化石エネルギー | GEOTHERMAL AND FOSSIL ENERGY
GEOTHERMISCHE UND FOSSILE ENERGIE | GÉOTHERMIE ET ÉNERGIE FOSSILE | ENERGÍA GEOTÉRMICA Y FÓSIL | ENERGIA GEOTERMICA E FOSSILE

石油

oil | Erdöl[N] | pétrole[M] | petróleo[M] | petrolio[M]

陸上の物理探鉱
surface prospecting
Oberflächenerkundung[F]
prospection[F] terrestre
prospección[F] terrestre
prospezione[F] terrestre

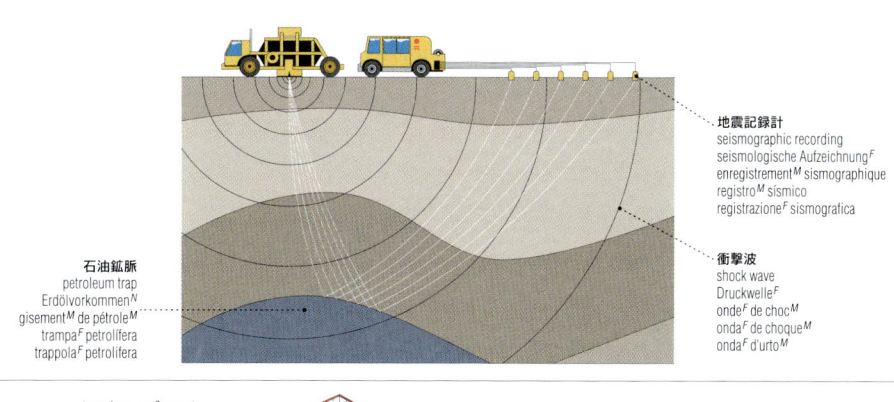

地震記録計
seismographic recording
seismologische Aufzeichnung[F]
enregistrement[M] sismographique
registro[M] sísmico
registrazione[F] sismografica

衝撃波
shock wave
Druckwelle[F]
onde[F] de choc
onda[F] de choque
onda[F] d'urto[M]

石油鉱脈
petroleum trap
Erdölvorkommen[N]
gisement[M] de pétrole[M]
trampa[F] petrolífera
trappola[F] petrolifera

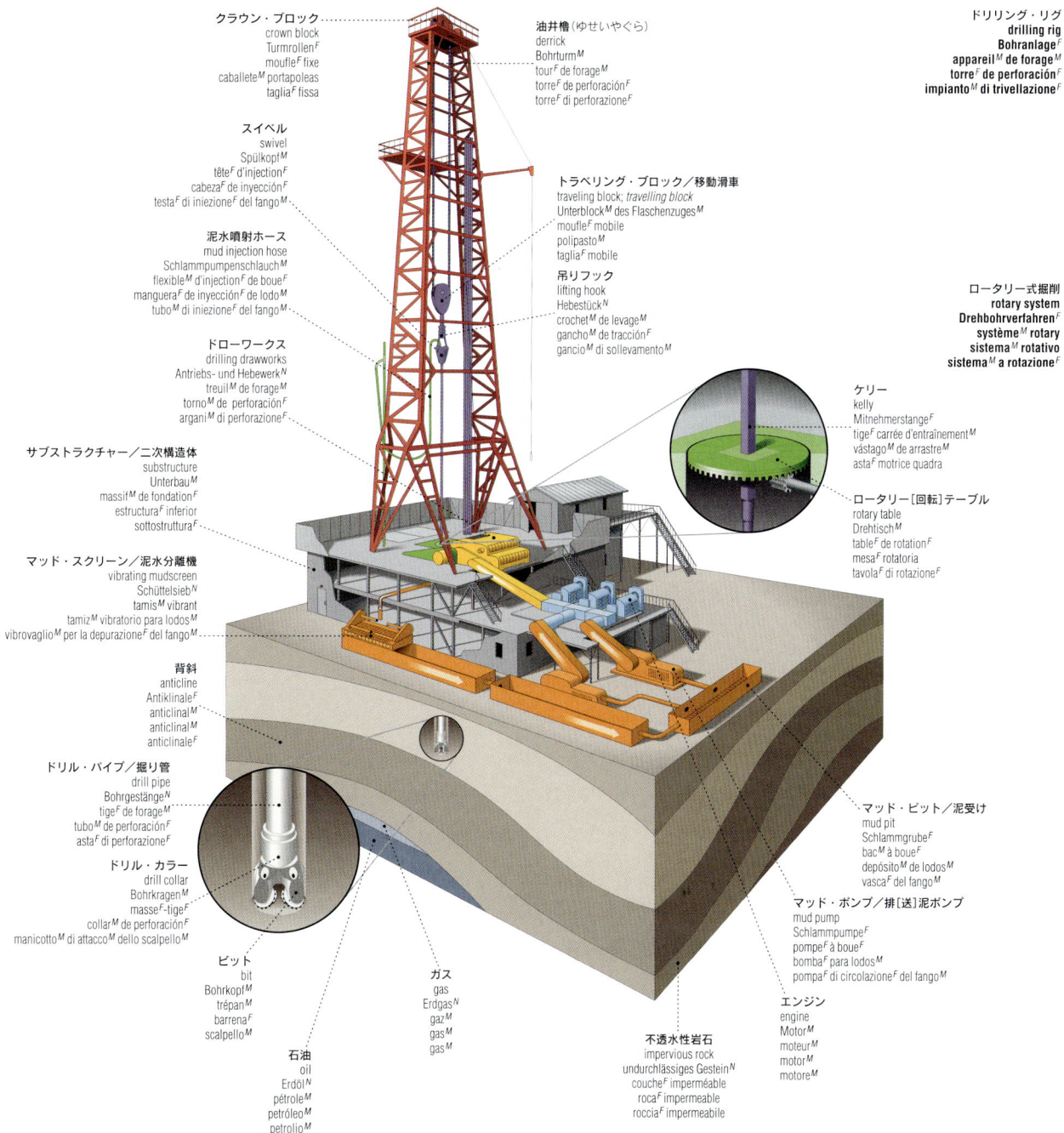

クラウン・ブロック
crown block
Turmrollen[F]
moufle[F] fixe
caballete[M] portapoleas
taglia[F] fissa

油井櫓（ゆせいやぐら）
derrick
Bohrturm[M]
tour[F] de forage[M]
torre[F] de perforación[F]
torre[F] di perforazione[F]

ドリリング・リグ
drilling rig
Bohranlage[F]
appareil[M] de forage[M]
torre[F] de perforación[F]
impianto[M] di trivellazione[F]

スイベル
swivel
Spülkopf[M]
tête[F] d'injection[F]
cabeza[F] de inyección[F]
testa[F] di iniezione[F] del fango[M]

トラベリング・ブロック／移動滑車
traveling block; travelling block
Unterblock[M] des Flaschenzuges[M]
moufle[M] mobile
polipasto[M]
taglia[F] mobile

泥水噴射ホース
mud injection hose
Schlammpumpenschlauch[M]
flexible[M] d'injection[F] de boue[F]
manguera[F] de inyección[F] de lodo[M]
tubo[M] di iniezione[F] del fango[M]

吊りフック
lifting hook
Hebestück[N]
crochet[M] de levage[M]
gancho[M] de tracción[F]
gancio[M] di sollevamento[M]

ロータリー式掘削
rotary system
Drehbohrverfahren[F]
système[M] rotary
sistema[M] rotativo
sistema[M] a rotazione[F]

ドローワークス
drilling drawworks
Antriebs- und Hebewerk[N]
treuil[M] de forage[M]
torno[M] de perforación[F]
argani[M] di perforazione[F]

ケリー
kelly
Mitnehmerstange[F]
tige[F] carrée d'entraînement[M]
vástago[M] de arrastre[M]
asta[F] motrice quadra

サブストラクチャー／二次構造体
substructure
Unterbau[M]
massif[M] de fondation[F]
estructura[F] inferior
sottostruttura[F]

ロータリー[回転]テーブル
rotary table
Drehtisch[M]
table[F] de rotation[F]
mesa[F] rotatoria
tavola[F] di rotazione[F]

マッド・スクリーン／泥水分離機
vibrating mudscreen
Schüttelsieb[N]
tamis[M] vibrant
tamiz[M] vibratorio para lodos[M]
vibrovaglio[M] per la depurazione[F] del fango[M]

背斜
anticline
Antiklinale[F]
anticlinal[F]
anticlinal[M]
anticlinale[F]

ドリル・パイプ／掘り管
drill pipe
Bohrgestänge[N]
tige[F] de forage[M]
tubo[M] de perforación[F]
asta[F] di perforazione[F]

マッド・ピット／泥受け
mud pit
Schlammgrube[F]
bac[M] à boue[F]
depósito[M] de lodos[M]
vasca[F] del fango[M]

ドリル・カラー
drill collar
Bohrkragen[M]
masse[F]-tige[F]
collar[M] de perforación[F]
manicotto[M] di attacco[M] dello scalpello[M]

マッド・ポンプ／排[送]泥ポンプ
mud pump
Schlammpumpe[F]
pompe[F] à boue[F]
bomba[F] para lodos[M]
pompa[F] di circolazione[F] del fango[M]

ビット
bit
Bohrkopf[M]
trépan[M]
barrena[F]
scalpello[M]

ガス
gas
Erdgas[N]
gaz[M]
gas[M]
gas[M]

エンジン
engine
Motor[M]
moteur[M]
motor[M]
motore[M]

石油
oil
Erdöl[N]
pétrole[M]
petróleo[M]
petrolio[M]

不透水性岩石
impervious rock
undurchlässiges Gestein[N]
couche[F] imperméable
roca[F] impermeable
roccia[F] impermeabile

エネルギー

651

地熱・化石エネルギー | GEOTHERMAL AND FOSSIL ENERGY
GEOTHERMISCHE UND FOSSILE ENERGIE | GÉOTHERMIE ET ÉNERGIE FOSSILE | ENERGÍA GEOTÉRMICA Y FÓSIL | ENERGIA GEOTERMICA E FOSSILE

石油

日本語 | 英語 | ドイツ語 | フランス語 | スペイン語 | イタリア語

生産プラットフォーム
production platform
Förderplattform^F
plate-forme^F de production^F
plataforma^F de producción^F
piattaforma^F di produzione^F

クレーン
crane
Kran^M
grue^F
grúa^F
gru^F

油井櫓（ゆせいやぐら）
derrick
Bohrturm^M
tour^F de forage^M
torre^F de perforación^F
torre^F di perforazione^F

原油・ガス分離器
oil/gas separator
Öl-/Gasabscheider^M
séparateur^M de gaz^M
separador^M de petróleo^M y gas^M
separatore^M gas^M / petrolio^M

ガス圧入モジュール
gas lift module
Druckgasförderanlage^F
module^M d'injection^F de gaz^M
módulo^M de inyección^F de gas^M
modulo^M di sollevamento^M a mezzo gas^M

精油区画
oil processing area
Ölverarbeitungsbereich^M
section^F raffinerie^F
área^F de procesamiento^M del petróleo^M
area^F di lavorazione^F del greggio^M

炎
flare
Abfackelung^F
torche^F
quemador^M
torcia^F

ヘリポート
helipad
Hubschrauberlandeplatz^M
hélisurface^F
helipuerto^M
eliporto^M

無線アンテナ
radio mast
Funkmast^M
antenne^F radio^F
antena^F de radio^M
antenna^F radio^F

救命艇［ボート］
lifeboat
Rettungsboot^N
canot^M de sauvetage^M
bote^M salvavidas
lancia^F di salvataggio^M

船体柱
hull column
Tragsäule^F
colonne^F de stabilisation^F
columna^F de estabilización^F
colonna^F di stabilizzazione^F

アンカー・ワイヤー
anchor wires
Ankerketten^F
chaînes^F d'ancrage^M
cables^M de anclaje^M
cavi^M di ancoraggio^M

支材／管状部材
tubular member
Rohrquerstrebe^F
section^F tubulaire
estructura^F tubular
elemento^M tubolare

ポンツーン
pontoon
Ponton^M, Schwimmkörper^M
ponton^M
pontón^M
galleggiante^M

生産・輸送立ち管システム
production/export riser system
Förder-/Exportsteigsystem^N
tubage^M de production^F/expédition^F
sistema^M de tubería de producción^F /expedición^F
tubazione^F di produzione^F e di spedizione^F

マニホールド
manifold
Rohrverteilerstück^N
manifold^M
colector^M
collettore^M

輸送管
export pipeline
Exportpipeline^F
oléoduc^M d'évacuation^F
oleoducto^M de exportación^M
oleodotto^M di spedizione^F

ガイド・チューブ
surface pipe
Leitrohr^N
tube^M conducteur
tubería^F del caudal^M del pozo^M
tubazione^F di superficie^F

クリスマス・ツリー
Christmas tree
Erdöleruptionskreuz^N
arbre^M de Noël
árbol^M de Navidad^F
albero^M di Natale^F

油井フロー・ライン
well flow line
Produktionsbohrung^F
tubage^M de production^F
línea^F de flujo^M del pozo^M
condotta^F di raccolta^F

GEOTHERMAL AND FOSSIL ENERGY | 地熱・化石エネルギー
GEOTHERMISCHE UND FOSSILE ENERGIE | GÉOTHERMIE ET ÉNERGIE FOSSILE | ENERGÍA GEOTÉRMICA Y FÓSIL | ENERGIA GEOTERMICA E FOSSILE

石油

海上の物理探鉱
offshore prospecting
Offshore-Erkundung^F
prospection^F en mer^F
prospección^F marina
prospezione^F off-shore

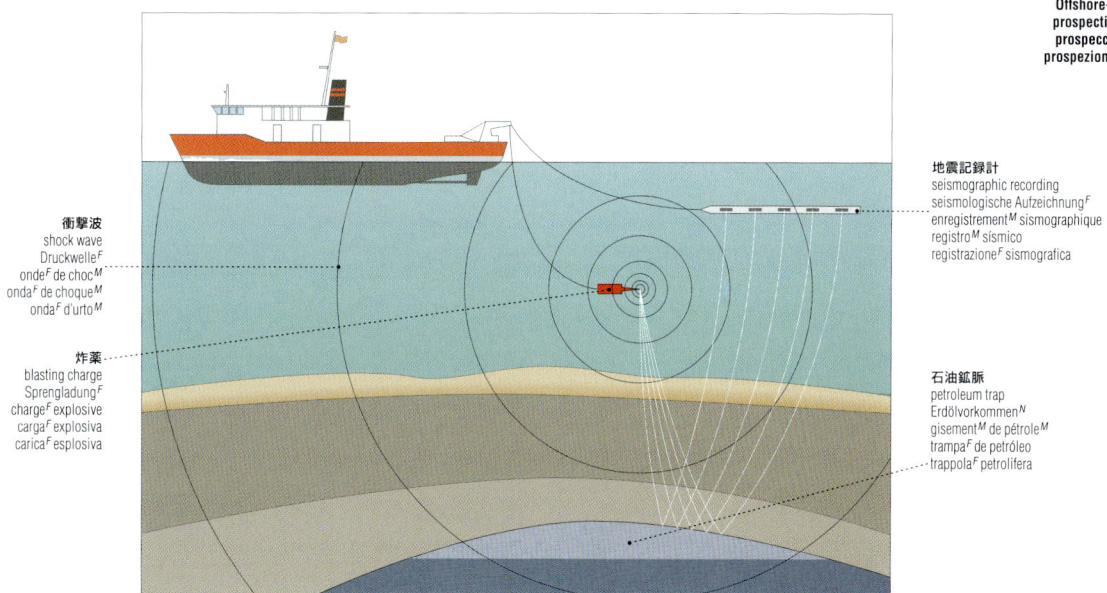

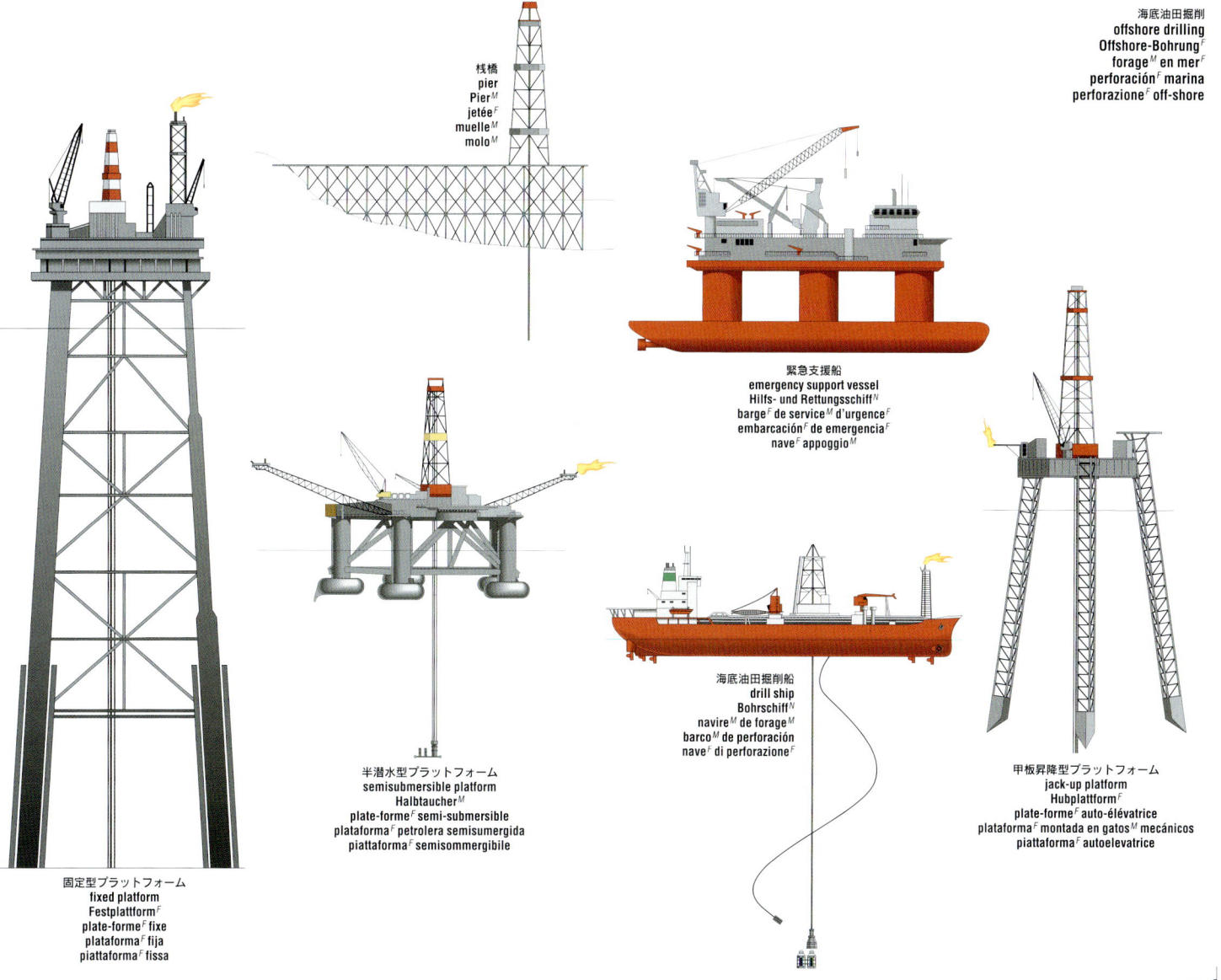

地震記録計
seismographic recording
seismologische Aufzeichnung^F
enregistrement^M sismographique
registro^M sísmico
registrazione^F sismografica

衝撃波
shock wave
Druckwelle^F
onde^F de choc^M
onda^F de choque^M
onda^F d'urto^M

炸薬
blasting charge
Sprengladung^F
charge^F explosive
carga^F explosiva
carica^F esplosiva

石油鉱脈
petroleum trap
Erdölvorkommen^N
gisement^M de pétrole^M
trampa^F de petróleo
trappola^F petrolifera

海底油田掘削
offshore drilling
Offshore-Bohrung^F
forage^M en mer^F
perforación^F marina
perforazione^F off-shore

桟橋
pier
Pier^M
jetée^F
muelle^M
molo^M

緊急支援船
emergency support vessel
Hilfs- und Rettungsschiff^N
barge^M de service^M d'urgence^F
embarcación^F de emergencia^F
nave^F appoggio^M

海底油田掘削船
drill ship
Bohrschiff^N
navire^M de forage^M
barco^M de perforación
nave^F di perforazione^F

半潜水型プラットフォーム
semisubmersible platform
Halbtaucher^M
plate-forme^F semi-submersible
plataforma^F petrolera semisumergida
piattaforma^F semisommergibile

甲板昇降型プラットフォーム
jack-up platform
Hubplattform^F
plate-forme^F auto-élévatrice
plataforma^F montada en gatos^M mecánicos
piattaforma^F autoelevatrice

固定型プラットフォーム
fixed platform
Festplattform^F
plate-forme^F fixe
plataforma^F fija
piattaforma^F fissa

エネルギー

653

地熱・化石エネルギー | GEOTHERMAL AND FOSSIL ENERGY
GEOTHERMISCHE UND FOSSILE ENERGIE | GÉOTHERMIE ET ÉNERGIE FOSSILE | ENERGÍA GEOTÉRMICA Y FÓSIL | ENERGIA GEOTERMICA E FOSSILE

石油

日本語 | 英語 | ドイツ語 | フランス語 | スペイン語 | イタリア語

クリスマス・ツリー
Christmas tree
Erdöleruptionskreuz^N
arbre^M de Noël^M
árbol^M de Navidad^F
albero^M di Natale^M

圧力計
pressure gauge
Druckmesser^M
manomètre^M
manómetro^M
manometro^M

流量調節ノズル
flow bean
Eruptionsdüse^F
duse^F
reductor^M de flujo^M
valvola^F di regolazione^F

元栓
master gate valve
Hauptschieberventil^N
vanne^F maîtresse
válvula^F maestra
valvola^F a saracinesca^F principale

パイプライン
pipeline
Pipeline^F
oléoduc^M
oleoducto^M
oleodotto^M

配管口
tubing head
Steigrohrkopf^M
tête^F de puits^M
cabeza^F de la tubería^F
testa^F della condotta di produzione^F

配管バルブ
tubing valve
Steigrohrventil^N
vanne^F de production^F
válvula^F de la tubería^F
valvola^F di produzione^F

配管
tubing
Steigrohr^N
colonne^F de production^F
tubería^F
condotta^F di produzione^F

ケーシング・ファースト・ストリング
casing first string
Rohrfahrteingang^M
tubage^M de surface^F
recubrimiento^M de la primera tubería^F
colonna^F di superficie^F

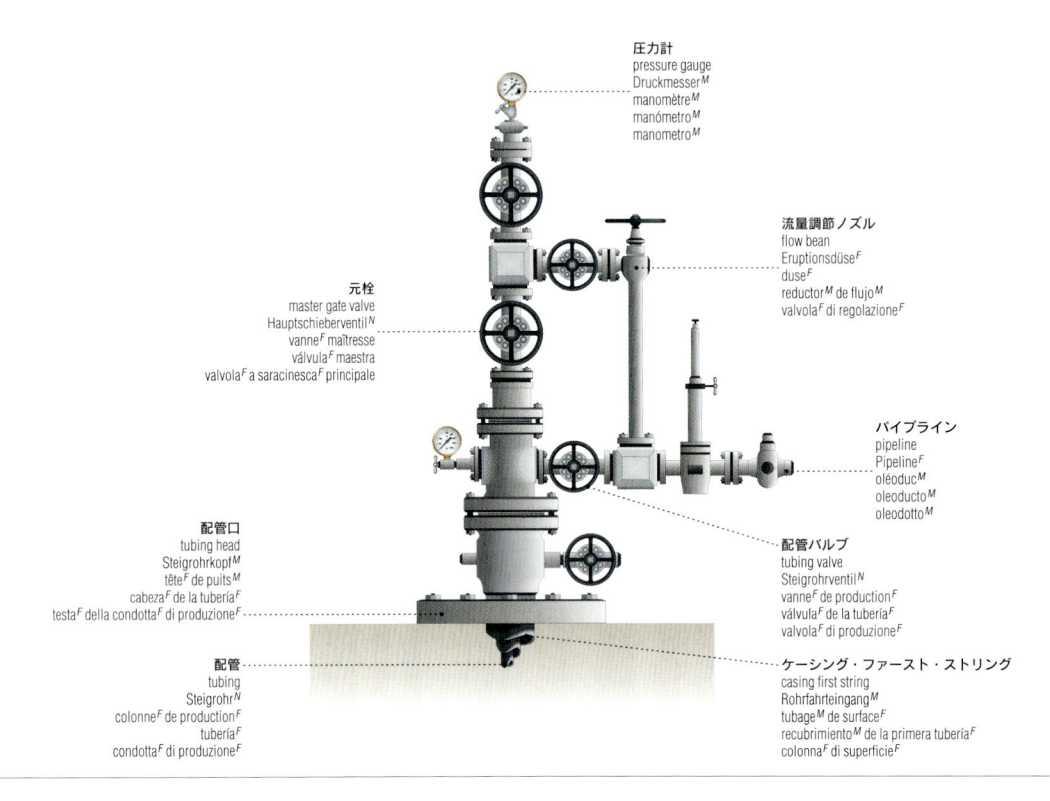

原油パイプライン
crude-oil pipeline
Rohölpipeline^F
réseau^M d'oléoducs^M
oleoducto^M para crudo^M
rete^F di oleodotti^M

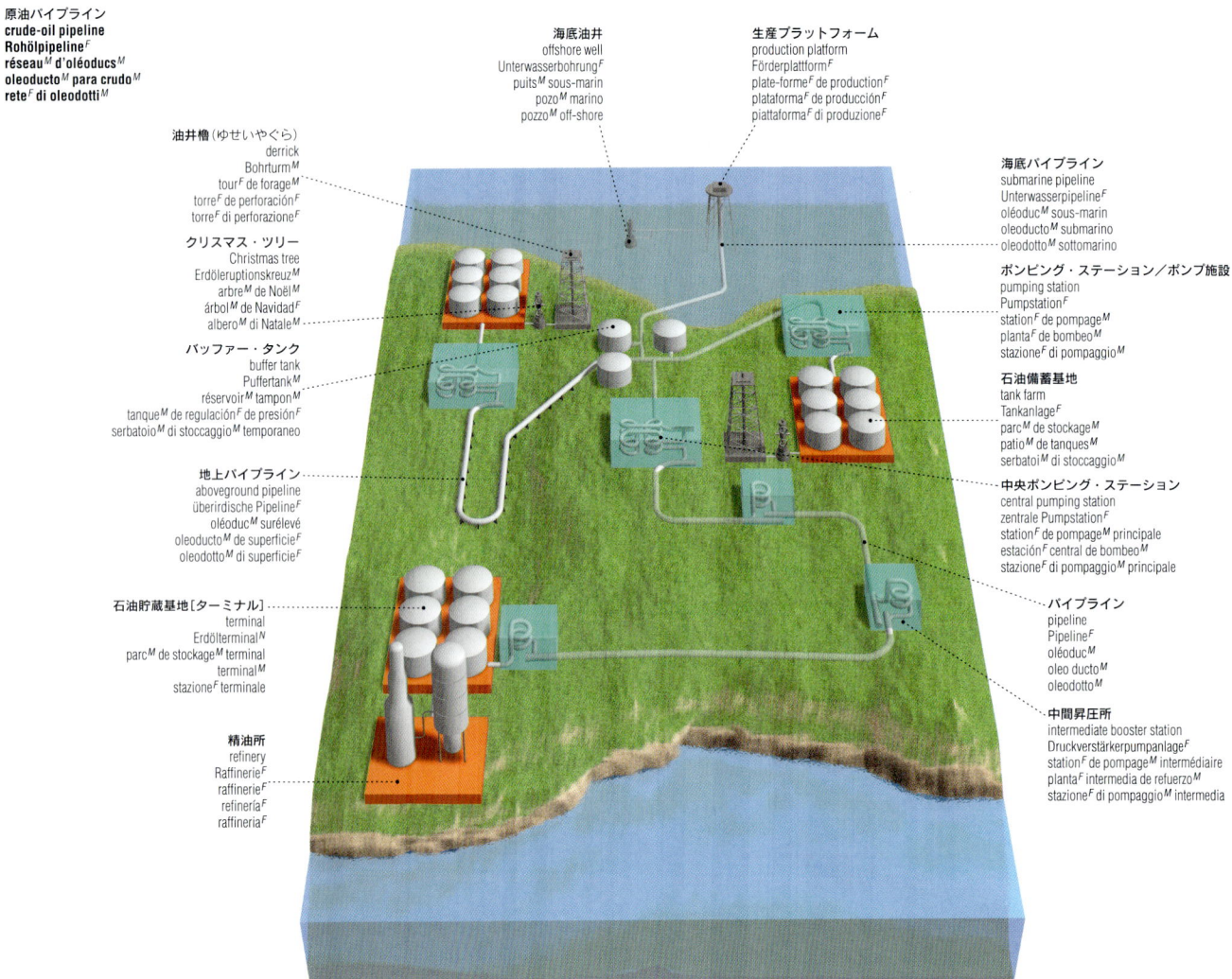

海底油井
offshore well
Unterwasserbohrung^F
puits^M sous-marin
pozo^M marino
pozzo^M off-shore

生産プラットフォーム
production platform
Förderplattform^F
plate-forme^F de production^F
plataforma^F de producción^F
piattaforma^F di produzione^F

油井櫓（ゆせいやぐら）
derrick
Bohrturm^M
tour^F de forage^M
torre^F de perforación^F
torre^F di perforazione^F

クリスマス・ツリー
Christmas tree
Erdöleruptionskreuz^N
arbre^M de Noël^M
árbol^M de Navidad^F
albero^M di Natale^M

海底パイプライン
submarine pipeline
Unterwasserpipeline^F
oléoduc^M sous-marin
oleoducto^M submarino
oleodotto^M sottomarino

ポンピング・ステーション／ポンプ施設
pumping station
Pumpstation^F
station^F de pompage^M
planta^F de bombeo^M
stazione^F di pompaggio^M

バッファー・タンク
buffer tank
Puffertank^M
réservoir^M tampon
tanque^M de regulación^F de presión^F
serbatoio^M di stoccaggio^M temporaneo

石油備蓄基地
tank farm
Tankanlage^F
parc^M de stockage^M
patio^M de tanques^M
serbatoi^M di stoccaggio^M

地上パイプライン
aboveground pipeline
überirdische Pipeline^F
oléoduc^M surélevé
oleoducto^M de superficie^F
oleodotto^M di superficie^F

中央ポンピング・ステーション
central pumping station
zentrale Pumpstation^F
station^F de pompage^M principale
estación^F central de bombeo^M
stazione^F di pompaggio^M principale

石油貯蔵基地［ターミナル］
terminal
Erdölterminal^M
parc^M de stockage^M terminal
terminal^M
stazione^F terminale

パイプライン
pipeline
Pipeline^F
oléoduc^M
oleo ducto^M
oleodotto^M

中間昇圧所
intermediate booster station
Druckverstärkerpumpanlage^F
station^F de pompage^M intermédiaire
planta^F intermedia de refuerzo^M
stazione^F di pompaggio^M intermedia

精油所
refinery
Raffinerie^F
raffinerie^F
refinería^F
raffineria^F

地熱・化石エネルギー | GEOTHERMAL AND FOSSIL ENERGY
GEOTHERMISCHE UND FOSSILE ENERGIE | GÉOTHERMIE ET ÉNERGIE FOSSILE | ENERGÍA GEOTÉRMICA Y FÓSIL | ENERGIA GEOTERMICA E FOSSILE

石油

タンク
tanks
TanksM
réservoirsM
tanquesM
serbatoiM

固定蓋式貯蔵タンク
fixed-roof tank
FestdachtankM
réservoirM à toitM fixe
tanqueM de techoM fijo
serbatoioM a tettoM fisso

スプレー・ノズル[管]
spray nozzle
ZerstäuberM
gicleurM
boquillaF rociadora
spruzzatoreM d'acquaM

呼吸弁／大気弁／ブリーザー[アトモス]バルブ
breather valve
EntlüftungsventilN
soupapeF à pressionF et dépressionF
respiraderoM
valvolaF di sfiatoM

マンホール
manhole
EinstiegslukeF
trouM d'hommeM
bocaF de accesoM
passoM d'uomoM

液位フロート
tank gauge float
FüllanzeigeschwimmerM
flotteurM
flotadorM del medidorM
galleggianteM dell'indicatoreM di livelloM

マンホール
manhole
EinstiegslukeF
trouM d'hommeM
bocaF de accesoM
passoM d'uomoM

自動測量計
automatic tank gauge
automatische FüllanzeigeF
jaugeF magnétique à lectureF directe
medidorM automático
indicatoreM di livelloM automatico

二次取り入れ口
secondary inlet
NebeneinfüllstutzenM
conduiteF d'admissionF secondaire
tomaF secundaria
tubazioneF di immissioneF secondaria

ラギング
lagging
IsoliermaterialN
revêtementM
empaqueM
rivestimentoM isolante

スプラッシュ・プレート
splash plate
SpritzblechN
tôleF pare-gouttesM
protecciónF contra salpicadurasF
paraspruzziM

螺旋（らせん）階段
spiral staircase
WendeltreppeF
escalierM en spiraleF
escaleraF de caracolM
scalaF a chiocciolaF

圧力計
manometer
ManometerN
manomètreM
manómetroM
manometroM

ドレン弁
drain valve
AblassventilN
robinetM de vidangeF
válvulaF de vaciadoM
valvolaF di spurgoM

石油貯蔵タンク防壁
bund wall
TankwallM
merlonM de protectionF
tabiqueM cortafuego
plateaF

主取り入れ口
main inlet
HaupteinfüllstutzenM
conduiteF d'admissionF principale
tomaF principal de llenadoM
tubazioneF di immissioneF principale

コンクリート・ドレン
concrete drain
BetonauslaufM
canalM d'écoulementM
canalM de drenajeM
canaleM di scoloM

浮蓋式貯蔵タンク
floating-roof tank
SchwimmdachtankM
réservoirM à toitM flottant
tanqueM de techoM pontón
serbatoioM a tettoM galleggiante

エネルギー

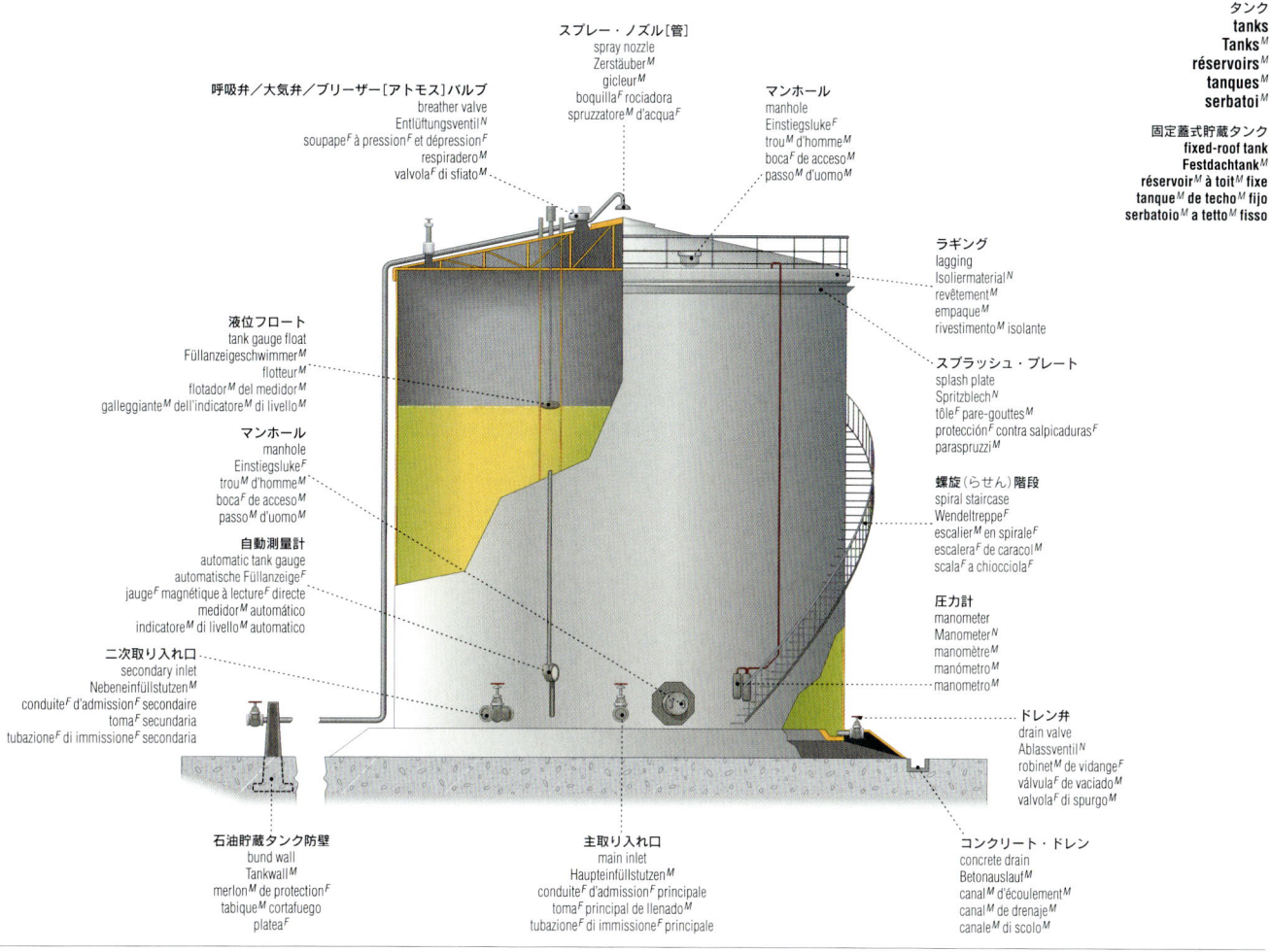

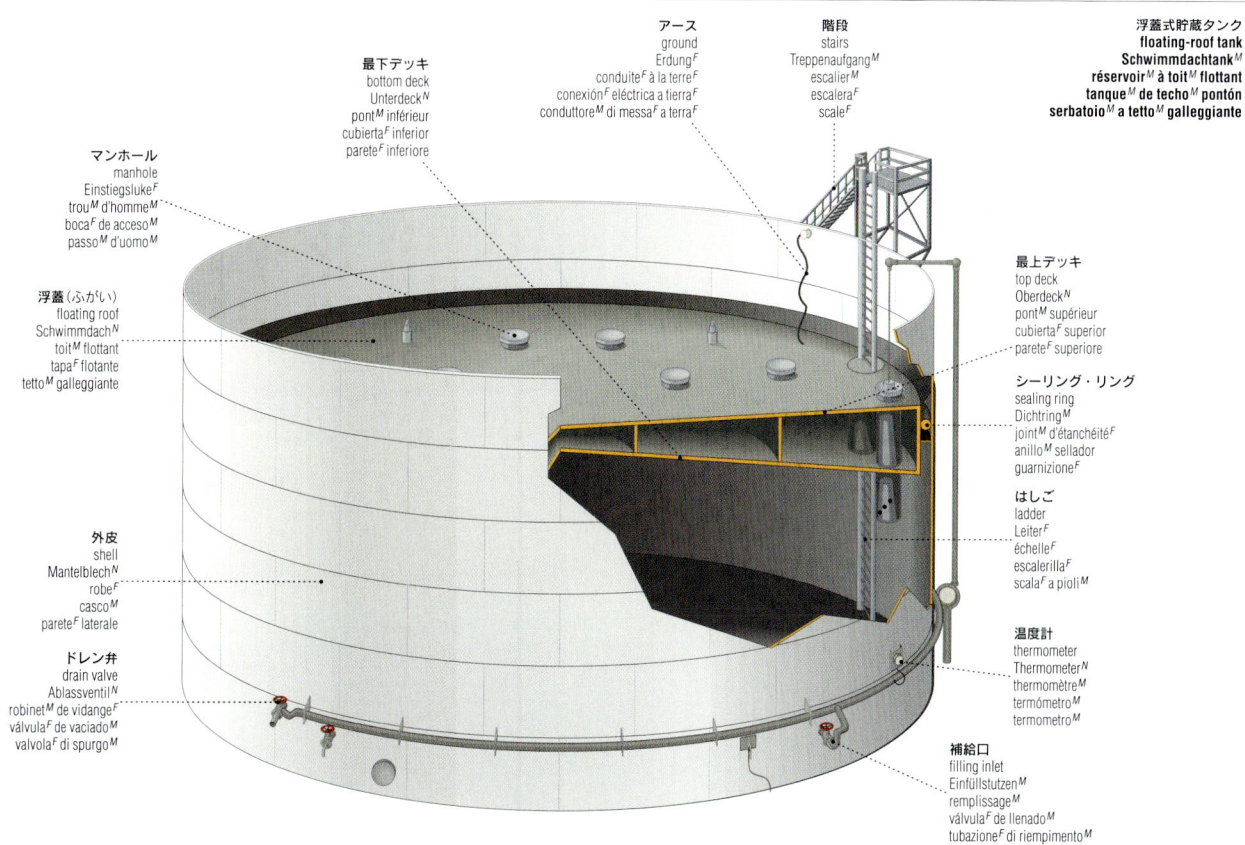

最下デッキ
bottom deck
UnterdeckN
pontM inférieur
cubiertaF inferior
pareteF inferiore

アース
ground
ErdungF
conduiteF à la terreF
conexiónF eléctrica a tierraF
conduttoreM di messaF a terraF

階段
stairs
TreppenaufgangM
escalierM
escaleraF
scaleF

マンホール
manhole
EinstiegslukeF
trouM d'hommeM
bocaF de accesoM
passoM d'uomoM

浮蓋（ふがい）
floating roof
SchwimmdachN
toitF flottant
tapaF flotante
tettoM galleggiante

最上デッキ
top deck
OberdeckN
pontM supérieur
cubiertaF superior
pareteF superiore

シーリング・リング
sealing ring
DichtringM
jointM d'étanchéitéF
anilloM sellador
guarnizioneF

外皮
shell
MantelblechN
robeF
cascoM
pareteF laterale

はしご
ladder
LeiterF
échelleF
escalerillaF
scalaF a pioliM

温度計
thermometer
ThermometerN
thermomètreM
termómetroM
termometroM

ドレン弁
drain valve
AblassventilN
robinetM de vidangeF
válvulaF de vaciadoM
valvolaF di spurgoM

補給口
filling inlet
EinfüllstutzenM
remplissageM
válvulaF de llenadoM
tubazioneF di riempimentoM

655

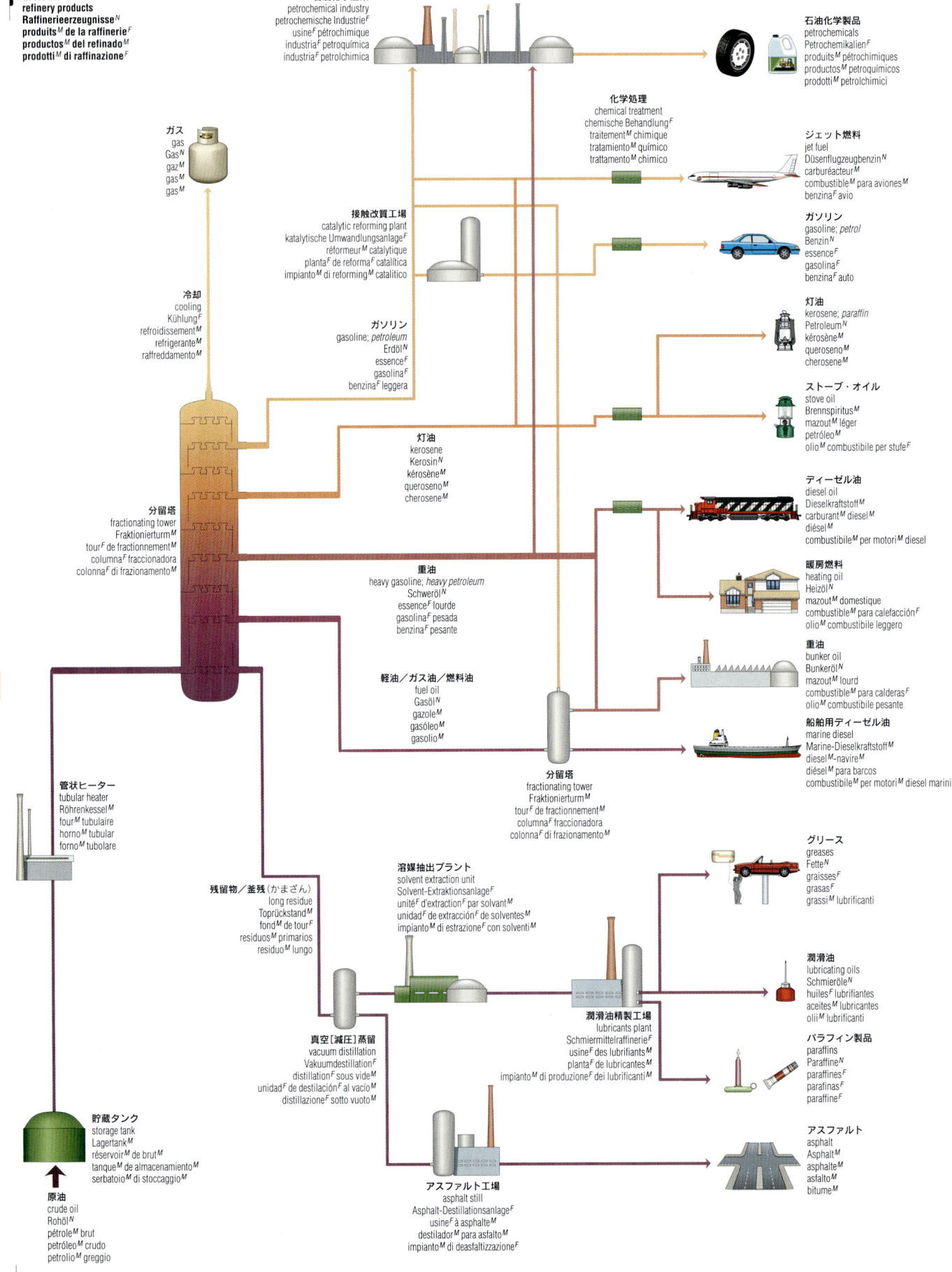

地熱・化石エネルギー | GEOTHERMAL AND FOSSIL ENERGY
GEOTHERMISCHE UND FOSSILE ENERGIE | GÉOTHERMIE ET ÉNERGIE FOSSILE | ENERGÍA GEOTÉRMICA Y FÓSIL | ENERGIA GEOTERMICA E FOSSILE

石油

日本語 | 英語 | ドイツ語 | フランス語 | スペイン語 | イタリア語

精油製品
refinery products
Raffinerieerzeugnisse[N]
produits[M] de la raffinerie[F]
productos[M] del refinado[M]
prodotti di raffinazione[F]

石油化学産業
petrochemical industry
petrochemische Industrie[F]
usine[F] pétrochimique
industria[F] petroquímica
industria petrolchimica

石油化学製品
petrochemicals
Petrochemikalien[F]
produits[M] pétrochimiques
productos[M] petroquímicos
prodotti petrolchimici

化学処理
chemical treatment
chemische Behandlung[F]
traitement[M] chimique
tratamiento[M] químico
trattamento[M] chimico

ガス
gas
Gas[N]
gaz[M]
gas[M]
gas[M]

ジェット燃料
jet fuel
Düsenflugzeugbenzin[N]
carburéacteur[M]
combustible[M] para aviones[M]
benzina[F] avio

接触改質工場
catalytic reforming plant
katalytische Umwandlungsanlage[F]
réformeur[M] catalytique
planta[F] de reforma[F] catalítica
impianto[M] di reforming[M] catalitico

ガソリン
gasoline; petrol
Benzin[N]
essence[F]
gasolina[F]
benzina[F] auto

冷却
cooling
Kühlung[F]
refroidissement[M]
refrigerante[M]
raffreddamento[M]

ガソリン
gasoline; *petroleum*
Erdöl[N]
essence[F]
gasolina[F]
benzina[F] leggera

灯油
kerosene; *paraffin*
Petroleum[N]
kérosène[M]
queroseno[M]
cherosene[M]

ストーブ・オイル
stove oil
Brennspiritus[M]
mazout[M] léger
petróleo[M]
olio[M] combustibile per stufe[F]

灯油
kerosene
Kerosin[N]
kérosène[M]
queroseno[M]
cherosene[M]

ディーゼル油
diesel oil
Dieselkraftstoff[M]
carburant[M] diesel
diésel[M]
combustibile[M] per motori diesel

分留塔
fractionating tower
Fraktionierturm[M]
tour[F] de fractionnement[M]
columna[F] fraccionadora
colonna[F] di frazionamento[M]

重油
heavy gasoline; *heavy petroleum*
Schweröl[N]
essence[F] lourde
gasolina[F] pesada
benzina[F] pesante

暖房燃料
heating oil
Heizöl[N]
mazout[M] domestique
combustible[M] para calefacción[F]
olio[M] combustibile leggero

軽油／ガス油／燃料油
fuel oil
Gasöl[N]
gazole[M]
gasóleo[M]
gasolio[M]

重油
bunker oil
Bunkeröl[N]
mazout[M] lourd
combustible[M] para calderas[F]
olio[M] combustibile pesante

船舶用ディーゼル油
marine diesel
Marine-Dieselkraftstoff[M]
diésel[M]-navire[M]
diésel[M] para barcos
combustibile[M] per motori[M] diesel marini

分留塔
fractionating tower
Fraktionierturm[M]
tour[F] de fractionnement[M]
columna[F] fraccionadora
colonna[F] di frazionamento[M]

管状ヒーター
tubular heater
Röhrenkessel[M]
four[M] tubulaire
horno[M] tubular
forno[M] tubolare

残留物／釜残（かまざん）
long residue
Toprückstand[M]
fond[M] de tour[M]
residuos[M] primarios
residuo[M] lungo

溶媒抽出プラント
solvent extraction unit
Solvent-Extraktionsanlage[F]
unité[F] d'extraction[F] par solvant[M]
unidad[F] de extracción[F] de solventes[M]
impianto[M] di estrazione[F] con solventi[M]

グリース
greases
Fette[N]
graisses[F]
grasas[F]
grassi lubrificanti

潤滑油
lubricating oils
Schmieröle[N]
huiles[F] lubrifiantes
aceites[M] lubricantes
olii lubrificanti

真空[減圧]蒸留
vacuum distillation
Vakuumdestillation[F]
distillation[F] sous vide[M]
unidad[F] de destilación[F] al vacío[M]
distillazione[F] sotto vuoto[M]

潤滑油精製工場
lubricants plant
Schmiermittelraffinerie[F]
usine[F] des lubrifiants[M]
planta[F] de lubricantes[M]
impianto[M] di produzione[F] dei lubrificanti[M]

パラフィン製品
paraffins
Paraffine[N]
paraffines[F]
parafinas[F]
paraffine[F]

貯蔵タンク
storage tank
Lagertank[M]
réservoir[M] de brut[M]
tanque[M] de almacenamiento[M]
serbatoio[M] di stoccaggio[M]

原油
crude oil
Rohöl[N]
pétrole[M] brut
petróleo[M] crudo
petrolio[M] greggio

アスファルト工場
asphalt still
Asphalt-Destillationsanlage[F]
usine[F] à asphalte[M]
destilador[M] para asfalto[M]
impianto[M] di deasfaltizzazione[F]

アスファルト
asphalt
Asphalt[M]
asphalte[F]
asfalto[M]
bitume[M]

エネルギー

水力電気 | HYDROELECTRICITY
ELEKTRIZITÄT AUS WASSERKRAFT | HYDROÉLECTRICITÉ | HIDROELECTRICIDAD | IDROELETTRICITÀ

水力発電所

hydroelectric complex | Wasserkraftwerkⁿ | complexeᴹ hydroélectrique | complejoᴹ hidroeléctrico | impiantoᴹ idroelettrico

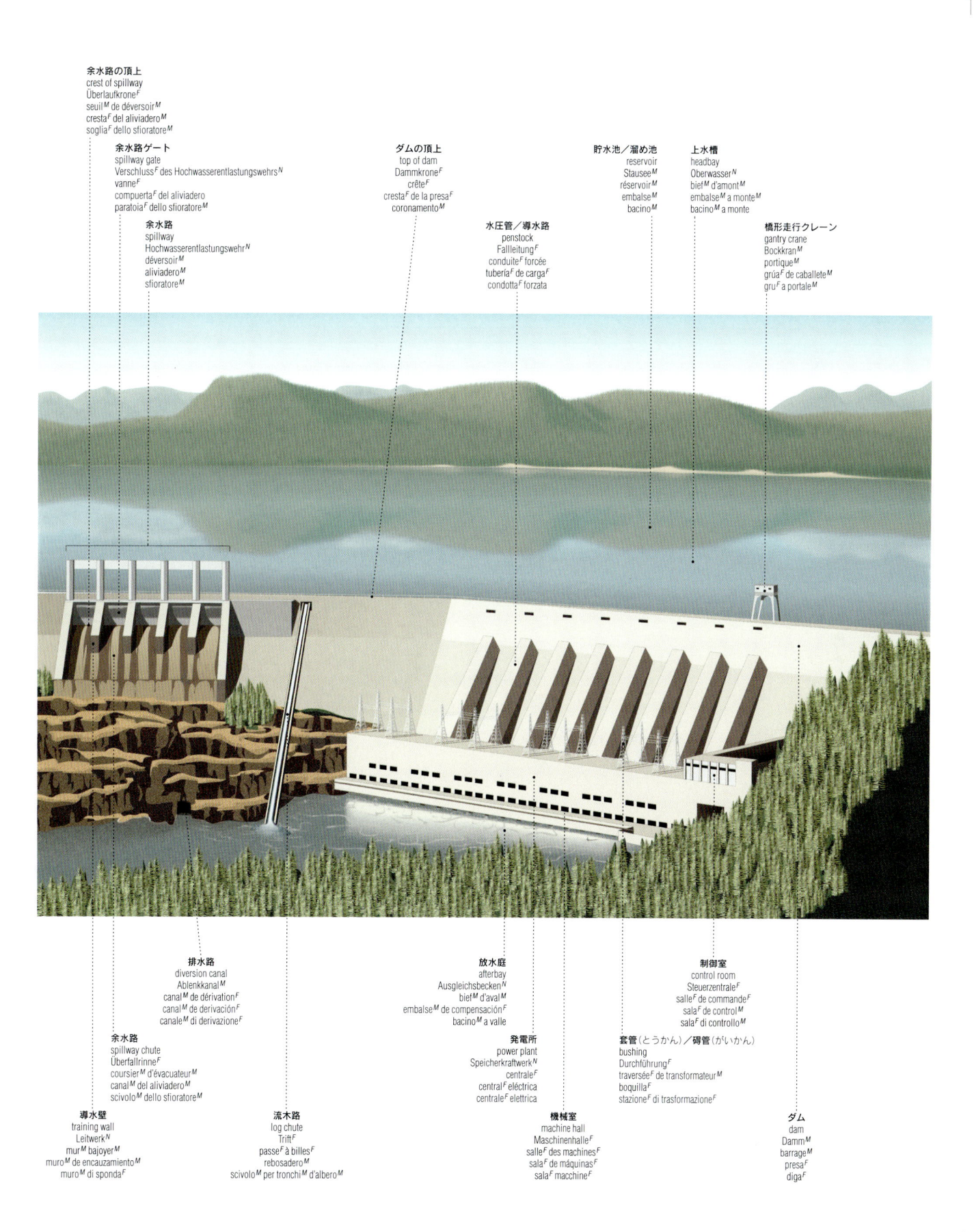

余水路の頂上
crest of spillway
Überlaufkroneꜰ
seuilᴹ de déversoirᴹ
crestaꜰ del aliviaderoᴹ
sogliaꜰ dello sfioratoreᴹ

余水路ゲート
spillway gate
Verschlussꜰ des Hochwasserentlastungswehrsɴ
vanneꜰ
compuertaꜰ del aliviadero
paratoiaꜰ dello sfioratoreᴹ

余水路
spillway
Hochwasserentlastungswehrɴ
déversoirᴹ
aliviaderoᴹ
sfioratoreᴹ

ダムの頂上
top of dam
Dammkroneꜰ
crêteꜰ
crestaꜰ de la presaꜰ
coronamentoᴹ

水圧管／導水路
penstock
Fallleitungꜰ
conduiteꜰ forcée
tuberíaꜰ de cargaꜰ
condottaꜰ forzata

貯水池／溜め池
reservoir
Stauseeᴹ
réservoirᴹ
embalseᴹ
bacinoᴹ

上水槽
headbay
Oberwasserɴ
biefᴹ d'amontᴹ
embalseᴹ a monteᴹ
bacinoᴹ a monteᴹ

橋形走行クレーン
gantry crane
Bockkranᴹ
portiqueᴹ
grúaꜰ de caballeteᴹ
gruꜰ a portaleᴹ

排水路
diversion canal
Ablenkkanalᴹ
canalᴹ de dérivationꜰ
canalᴹ de derivaciónꜰ
canaleᴹ di derivazioneꜰ

放水庭
afterbay
Ausgleichsbeckenɴ
biefᴹ d'avalᴹ
embalseᴹ de compensaciónꜰ
bacinoᴹ a valle

制御室
control room
Steuerzentraleꜰ
salleꜰ de commandeꜰ
salaꜰ de controlᴹ
salaꜰ di controlloᴹ

余水路
spillway chute
Überfallrinneꜰ
coursierᴹ d'évacuateurᴹ
canalᴹ del aliviaderoᴹ
scivoloᴹ dello sfioratoreᴹ

発電所
power plant
Speicherkraftwerkɴ
centraleꜰ
centralꜰ eléctrica
centraleꜰ elettrica

套管（とうかん）／碍管（がいかん）
bushing
Durchführungꜰ
traverséeꜰ de transformateurᴹ
boquillaꜰ
stazioneꜰ di trasformazioneꜰ

導水壁
training wall
Leitwerkɴ
murᴹ bajoyerᴹ
muroᴹ de encauzamientoᴹ
muroᴹ di spondaꜰ

流木路
log chute
Triftꜰ
passeꜰ à billesꜰ
rebosaderoᴹ
scivoloᴹ per tronchiᴹ d'alberoᴹ

機械室
machine hall
Maschinenhalleꜰ
salleꜰ des machinesꜰ
salaꜰ de máquinasꜰ
salaꜰ macchineꜰ

ダム
dam
Dammᴹ
barrageᴹ
presaꜰ
digaꜰ

エネルギー

657

水力発電所

水力電気 | HYDROELECTRICITY
ELEKTRIZITÄT AUS WASSERKRAFT | HYDROÉLECTRICITÉ | HIDROELECTRICIDAD | IDROELETTRICITÀ

日本語 | 英語 | ドイツ語 | フランス語 | スペイン語 | イタリア語

水力発電所の断面図
cross section of a hydroelectric power plant
Wasserkraftwerk^N im Querschnitt^M
coupe^F d'une centrale^F hydroélectrique
sección^F transversal de una central^F hidroeléctrica
sezione^F trasversale di una centrale^F idroelettrica

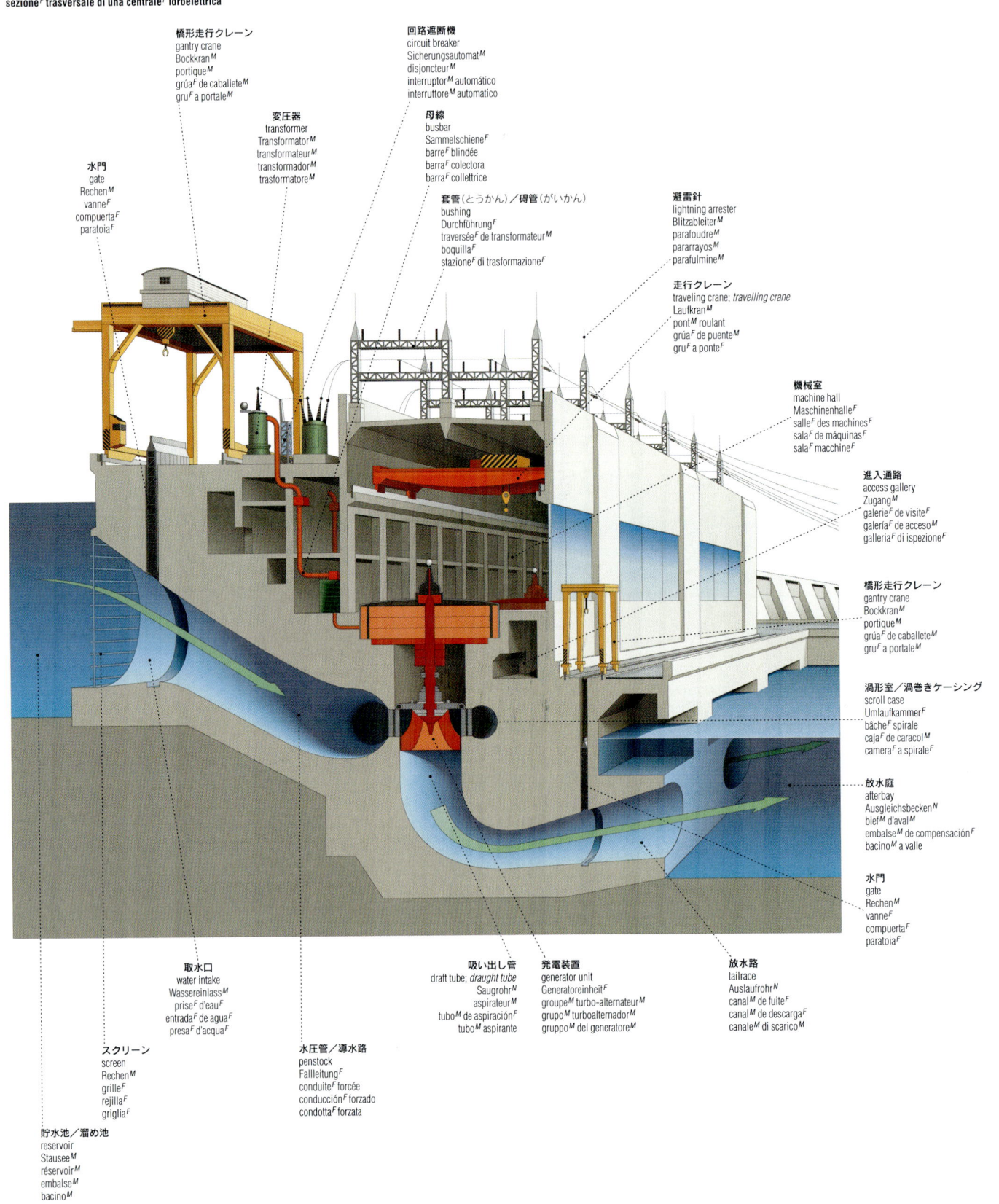

橋形走行クレーン
gantry crane
Bockkran^M
portique^M
grúa^F de caballete^M
gru^F a portale^M

回路遮断機
circuit breaker
Sicherungsautomat^M
disjoncteur^M
interruptor^M automático
interruttore^M automatico

変圧器
transformer
Transformator^M
transformateur^M
transformador^M
trasformatore^M

母線
busbar
Sammelschiene^F
barre^F blindée
barra^F colectora
barra^F collettrice

水門
gate
Rechen^M
vanne^F
compuerta^F
paratoia^F

套管(とうかん)／碍管(がいかん)
bushing
Durchführung^F
traversée^F de transformateur^M
boquilla^F
stazione^F di trasformazione^F

避雷針
lightning arrester
Blitzableiter^M
parafoudre^M
pararrayos^M
parafulmine^M

走行クレーン
traveling crane; *travelling crane*
Laufkran^M
pont^M roulant
grúa^F de puente^M
gru^F a ponte^F

機械室
machine hall
Maschinenhalle^F
salle^F des machines^F
sala^F de máquinas^F
sala^F macchine^F

進入通路
access gallery
Zugang^M
galerie^F de visite^F
galería^F de acceso^M
galleria^F di ispezione^F

橋形走行クレーン
gantry crane
Bockkran^M
portique^M
grúa^F de caballete^M
gru^F a portale^M

渦形室／渦巻きケーシング
scroll case
Umlaufkammer^F
bâche^F spirale
caja^F de caracol^M
camera^F a spirale^F

放水庭
afterbay
Ausgleichsbecken^N
bief^M d'aval^M
embalse^M de compensación^F
bacino^F a valle

水門
gate
Rechen^M
vanne^F
compuerta^F
paratoia^F

取水口
water intake
Wassereinlass^M
prise^F d'eau^F
entrada^F de agua^F
presa^F d'acqua^F

吸い出し管
draft tube; *draught tube*
Saugrohr^N
aspirateur^M
tubo^M de aspiración^F
tubo^M aspirante

発電装置
generator unit
Generatoreinheit^F
groupe^M turbo-alternateur^M
grupo^M turboalternador^M
gruppo^M del generatore^M

放水路
tailrace
Auslaufrohr^N
canal^M de fuite^F
canal^M de descarga^F
canale^M di scarico^M

スクリーン
screen
Rechen^M
grille^F
rejilla^F
griglia^F

水圧管／導水路
penstock
Fallleitung^F
conduite^F forcée
conducción^F forzado
condotta^F forzata

貯水池／溜め池
reservoir
Stausee^M
réservoir^M
embalse^M
bacino^M

エネルギー

水力電気 | HYDROELECTRICITY
ELEKTRIZITÄT AUS WASSERKRAFT | HYDROÉLECTRICITÉ | HIDROELECTRICIDAD | IDROELETTRICITÀ

発電装置

generator unit | Stromgenerator^M | groupe^M turbo-alternateur^M | grupo^M turboalternador^M | gruppo^M generatore^M

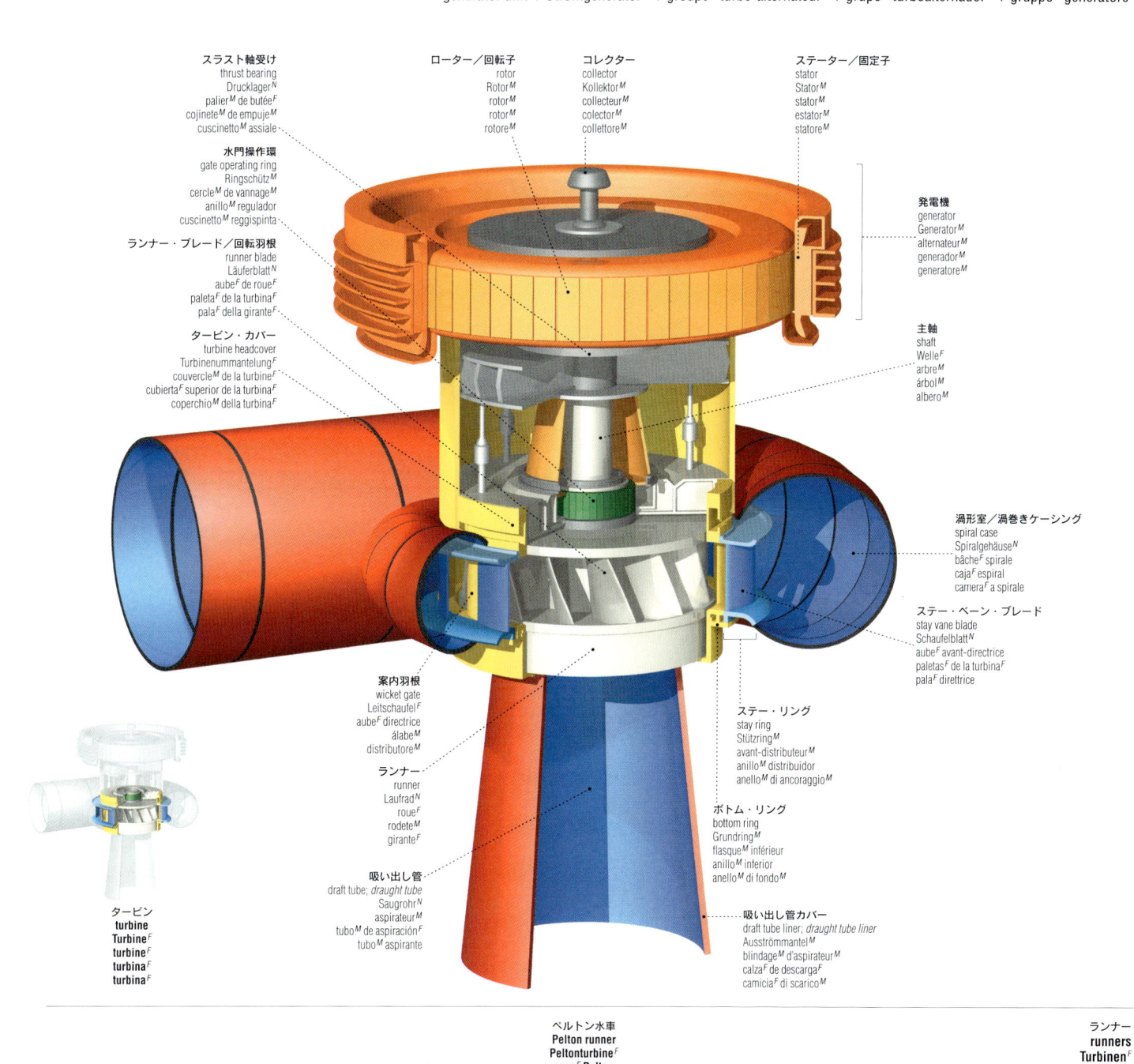

スラスト軸受け
thrust bearing
Drucklager^N
palier^M de butée^F
cojinete^M de empuje^M
cuscinetto^M assiale

ローター／回転子
rotor
Rotor^M
rotor^M
rotor^M
rotore^M

コレクター
collector
Kollektor^M
collecteur^M
colector^M
collettore^M

ステーター／固定子
stator
Stator^M
stator^M
estator^M
statore^M

水門操作環
gate operating ring
Ringschütz^M
cercle de vannage^M
anillo^M regulador
cuscinetto^M reggispinta

発電機
generator
Generator^M
alternateur^M
generador^M
generatore^M

ランナー・ブレード／回転羽根
runner blade
Läuferblatt^N
aube^F de roue^F
paleta^F de la turbina^F
pala^F della girante^F

主軸
shaft
Welle^F
arbre^M
árbol^M
albero^M

タービン・カバー
turbine headcover
Turbinenummantelung^F
couvercle^M de la turbine^F
cubierta^F superior de la turbina^F
coperchio^M della turbina^F

渦形室／渦巻きケーシング
spiral case
Spiralgehäuse^N
bâche^F spirale
caja^F espiral
camera^F a spirale

ステー・ベーン・ブレード
stay vane blade
Schaufelblatt^N
aube^F avant-directrice
paletas^F de la turbina^F
pala^F direttrice

案内羽根
wicket gate
Leitschaufel^F
aube^F directrice
álabe^M
distributore^M

ステー・リング
stay ring
Stützring^M
avant-distributeur^M
anillo^M distribuidor
anello^M di ancoraggio^M

ランナー
runner
Laufrad^N
roue^F
rodete^M
girante^F

ボトム・リング
bottom ring
Grundring^M
flasque^F inférieur
anillo^M inferior
anello^M di fondo^M

吸い出し管
draft tube; draught tube
Saugrohr^N
aspirateur^M
tubo^M de aspiración^F
tubo^M aspirante

吸い出し管カバー
draft tube liner; draught tube liner
Ausströmmantel^M
blindage^M d'aspirateur^M
calza^F de descarga^F
camicia^F di scarico^M

タービン
turbine
Turbine^F
turbine^F
turbina^F
turbina^F

カプラン水車
Kaplan runner
Kaplanturbine^F
roue^F Kaplan
turbina^F Kaplan
turbina^F Kaplan

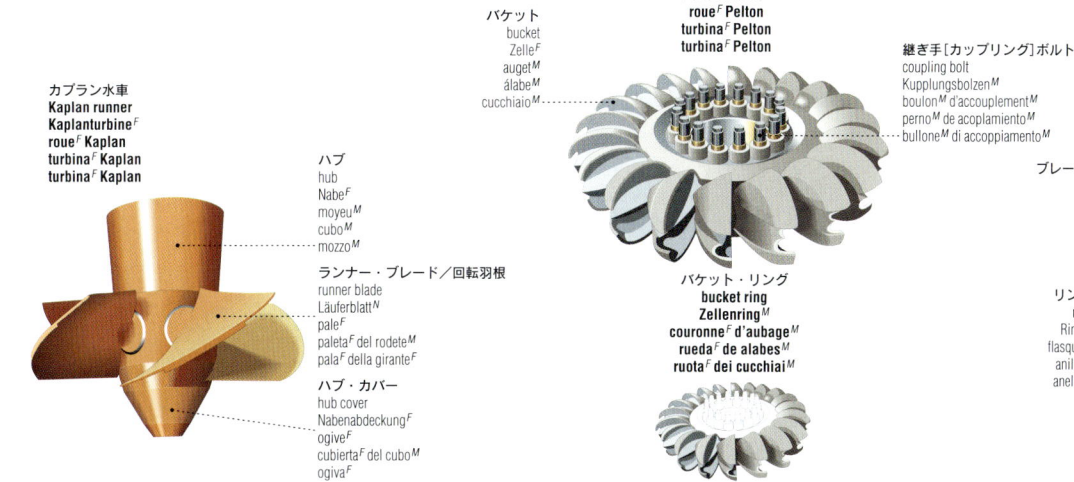

ハブ
hub
Nabe^F
moyeu^M
cubo^M
mozzo^M

ランナー・ブレード／回転羽根
runner blade
Läuferblatt^N
pale^F
paleta^F del rodete^M
pala^F della girante^F

ハブ・カバー
hub cover
Nabenabdeckung^F
ogive^F
cubierta^F del cubo^M
ogiva^F

ペルトン水車
Pelton runner
Peltonturbine^F
roue^F Pelton
turbina^F Pelton
turbina^F Pelton

バケット
bucket
Zelle^F
auget^M
álabe^M
cucchiaio^M

継ぎ手［カップリング］ボルト
coupling bolt
Kupplungsbolzen^M
boulon^M d'accouplement^M
perno^M de acoplamiento^M
bullone^M di accoppiamento^M

バケット・リング
bucket ring
Zellenring^M
couronne^F d'aubage^M
rueda^F de alabes^M
ruota^F dei cucchiai^M

ランナー
runners
Turbinen^F
roues^F
rodetes^M
giranti^F

フランシス水車
Francis runner
Francisturbine^F
roue^F Francis
turbina^F Francis
turbina^F Francis

ブレード／羽根
blade
Blatt^N
aube^F
paleta^F
pala^F

リング
ring
Ring^M
flasque^F
anillo^M
anello^M

エネルギー

659

水力電気 | HYDROELECTRICITY
ELEKTRIZITÄT AUS WASSERKRAFT | HYDROÉLECTRICITÉ | HIDROELECTRICIDAD | IDROELETTRICITÀ

ダムの例

日本語 | 英語 | ドイツ語 | フランス語 | スペイン語 | イタリア語

examples of dams | Beispiele^N für Staudämme^M | exemples^M de barrages^M | ejemplos^M de presas^F | esempi^M di dighe^F

バットレス[扶壁]ダム
buttress dam
Stützpfeilerstaudamm^M
barrage^M à contreforts^M
presa^F de contrafuertes^M
diga^F a contrafforti^M

バットレス・ダムの断面図
cross section of a buttress dam
Stützpfeilerstaudamm^M im Querschnitt^M
coupe^F d'un barrage^M à contreforts^M
sección^F transversal de una presa^F de contrafuerte^M
sezione^F trasversale di una diga^F a contrafforti^M

貯水池／溜め池
reservoir
Stausee^M
réservoir^M
embalse^M
bacino^M

バットレス／扶壁
buttress
Stützpfeiler^M
contrefort^M
contrafuerte^M
contrafuerte^M

基礎ブロック
foundation blockage
Fundamentklotz^M
blocage^F
bloqueo^M de los cimientos^M
rinforzo^M della fondazione^F

基礎
foundation
Fundament^N
fondation^F
cimientos^M
fondazione^F

表面遮水壁型ダム
embankment dam
Uferdamm^M
barrage^M en remblai^M
presa^F de tierra^F
diga^F in terra^F

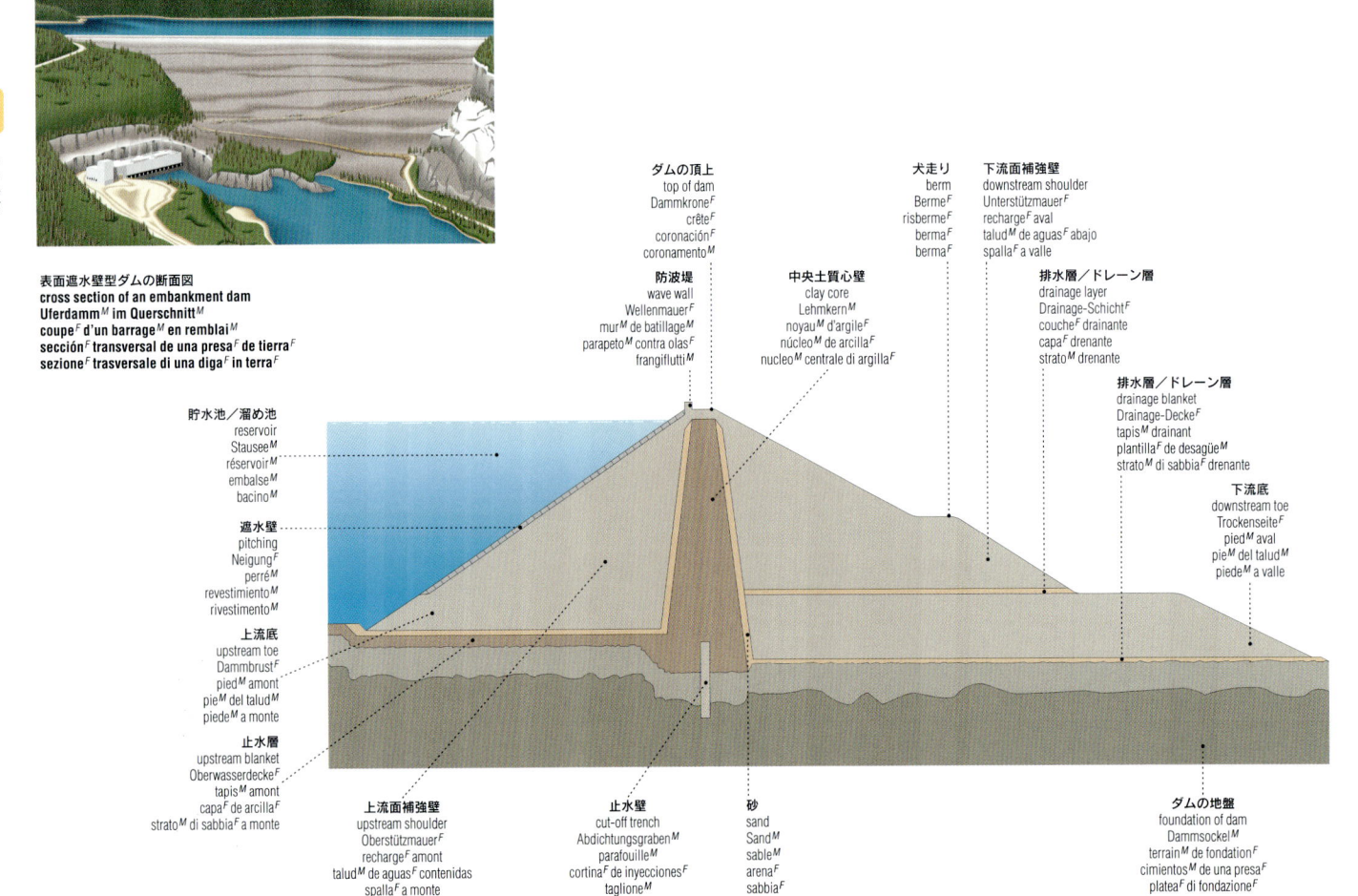

表面遮水壁型ダムの断面図
cross section of an embankment dam
Uferdamm^M im Querschnitt^M
coupe^F d'un barrage^M en remblai^M
sección^F transversal de una presa^F de tierra^F
sezione^F trasversale di una diga^F in terra^F

ダムの頂上
top of dam
Dammkrone^F
crête^F
coronación^F
coronamento^M

犬走り
berm
Berme^F
risberme^F
berma^F
berma^F

下流面補強壁
downstream shoulder
Unterstützmauer^F
recharge^F aval
talud^M de aguas^F abajo
spalla^F a valle

防波堤
wave wall
Wellenmauer^F
mur^M de batillage^M
parapeto^M contra olas^F
frangiflutti^M

中央土質心壁
clay core
Lehmkern^M
noyau^M d'argile^F
núcleo^M de arcilla^F
nucleo^M centrale di argilla^F

排水層／ドレーン層
drainage layer
Drainage-Schicht^F
couche^F drainante
capa^F drenante
strato^M drenante

排水層／ドレーン層
drainage blanket
Drainage-Decke^F
tapis^M drainant
plantilla^F de desagüe^M
strato^M di sabbia^F drenante

貯水池／溜め池
reservoir
Stausee^M
réservoir^M
embalse^M
bacino^M

遮水壁
pitching
Neigung^F
perré^M
revestimiento^M
rivestimento^M

下流底
downstream toe
Trockenseite^F
pied^M aval
pie^M del talud^M
piede^M a valle

上流底
upstream toe
Dammbrust^F
pied^M amont
pie^M del talud^M
piede^M a monte

止水層
upstream blanket
Oberwasserdecke^F
tapis^M amont
capa^F de arcilla^F
strato^M di sabbia^F a monte

上流面補強壁
upstream shoulder
Oberstützmauer^F
recharge^F amont
talud^M de aguas^F contenidas
spalla^F a monte

止水壁
cut-off trench
Abdichtungsgraben^M
parafouille^M
cortina^F de inyecciones^F
taglione^M

砂
sand
Sand^M
sable^M
arena^F
sabbia^F

ダムの地盤
foundation of dam
Dammsockel^M
terrain^M de fondation^F
cimientos^M de una presa^F
platea^F di fondazione^F

水力電気 | HYDROELECTRICITY
ELEKTRIZITÄT AUS WASSERKRAFT | HYDROÉLECTRICITÉ | HIDROELECTRICIDAD | IDROELETTRICITÀ

ダムの例

アーチ・ダムの断面図
cross section of an arch dam
Bogenstaudamm^M im Querschnitt^M
coupe^F d'un barrage^M-voûte^F
sección^F transversal de una presa^F de bóveda
sezione^F trasversale di una diga^F a volta^F

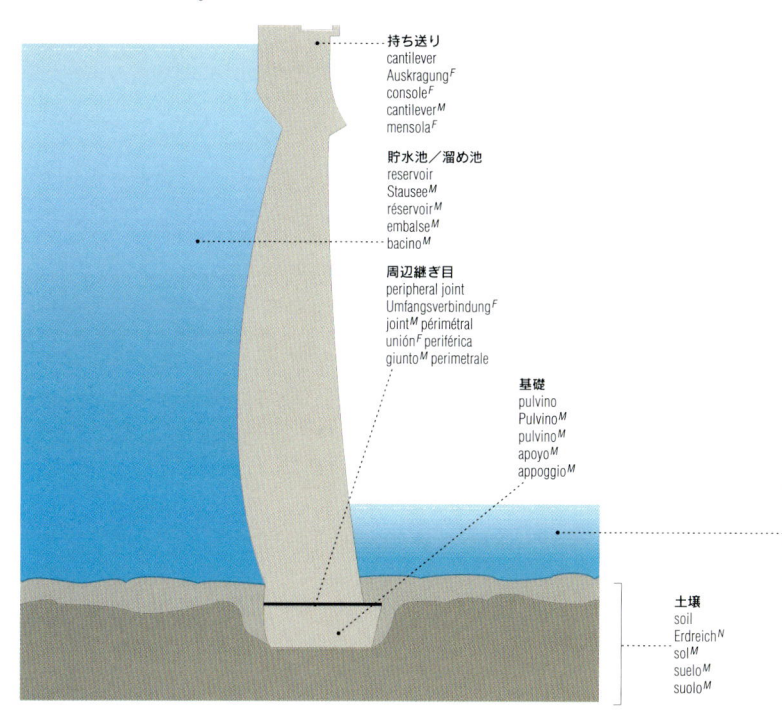

アーチ・ダム
arch dam
Bogenstaudamm^M
barrage^M-voûte^F
presa^F de bóveda^F
diga^F a volta^F

持ち送り / cantilever / Auskragung^F / console^F / cantilever^M / mensola^F

貯水池／溜め池 / reservoir / Stausee^M / réservoir^M / embalse^M / bacino^M

周辺継ぎ目 / peripheral joint / Umfangsverbindung^F / joint^M périmétral / unión^F periférica / giunto^M perimetrale

基礎 / pulvino / Pulvino^M / pulvino^M / apoyo^M / appoggio^M

放水庭 / afterbay / Ausgleichsbecken^N / bief^M aval / embalse^M de compensación^F / bacino^M a valle

土壌 / soil / Erdreich^N / sol^M / suelo^M / suolo^M

重力式ダムの断面図
cross section of a gravity dam
Schwergewichtsstaudamm^M im Querschnitt^M
coupe^F d'un barrage^M-poids^M
sección^F transversal de una presa^F de gravedad^F
sezione^F trasversale di una diga^F a gravità^F

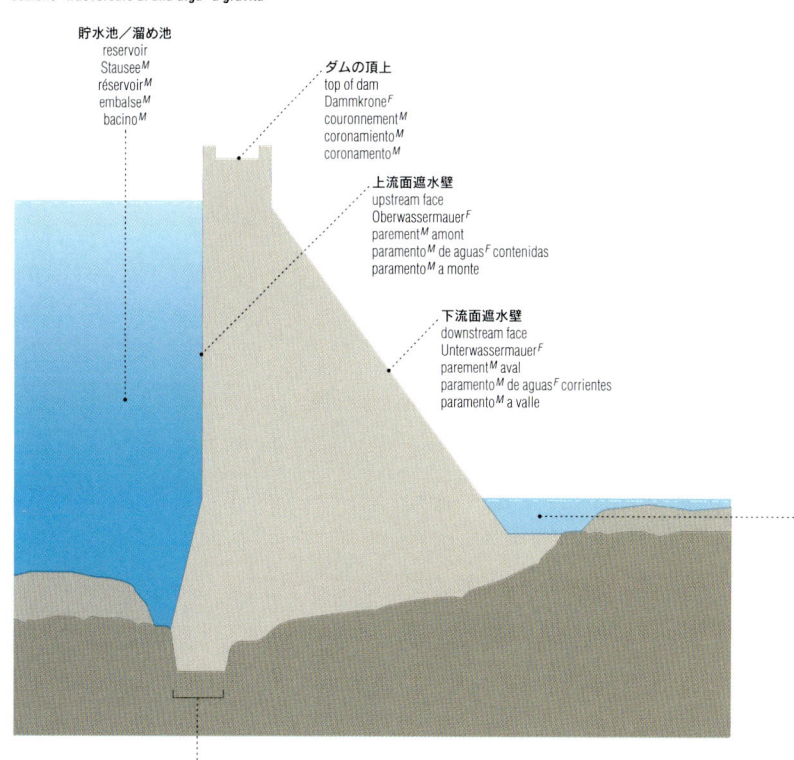

重力式ダム
gravity dam
Gewichtsstaudamm^M
barrage^M-poids^M
presa^F
diga^F a gravità^F

貯水池／溜め池 / reservoir / Stausee^M / réservoir^M / embalse^M / bacino^M

ダムの頂上 / top of dam / Dammkrone^F / couronnement^M / coronamiento^M / coronamento^M

上流面遮水壁 / upstream face / Oberwassermauer^F / parement^M amont / paramento^M de aguas^F contenidas / paramento^M a monte

下流面遮水壁 / downstream face / Unterwassermauer^F / parement^M aval / paramento^M de aguas^F corrientes / paramento^M a valle

放水庭 / afterbay / Ausgleichsbecken^N / bief^M aval / embalse^M de compensación^F / bacino^M a valle

止水壁 / cut-off trench / Dichtungsschleier^M / parafouille^F / cortina^F de inyecciones^F / taglione^M

エネルギー

水力電気 | HYDROELECTRICITY
ELEKTRIZITÄT AUS WASSERKRAFT | HYDROÉLECTRICITÉ | HIDROELECTRICIDAD | IDROELETTRICITÀ

電気の発生過程

日本語 | 英語 | ドイツ語 | フランス語 | スペイン語 | イタリア語

steps in production of electricity | Einzelschritte^M bei der Elektrizitätserzeugung^F | étapes^F de production^F de l'électricité^F | etapas^F de la producción^F de electricidad^F | fasi^F della produzione^F di elettricità^F

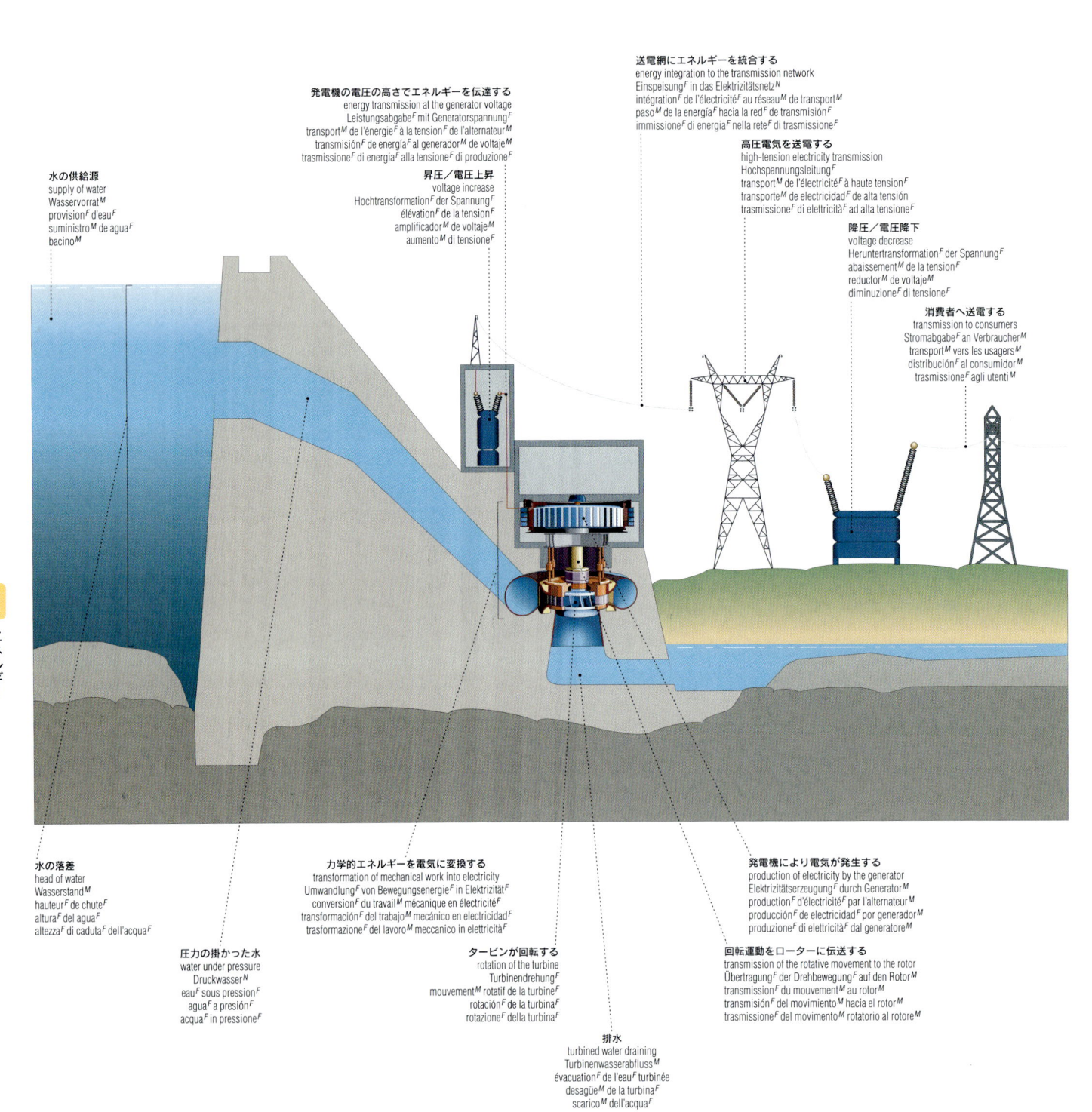

送電網にエネルギーを統合する
energy integration to the transmission network
Einspeisung^F in das Elektrizitätsnetz^N
intégration^F de l'électricité^F au réseau^M de transport^M
paso^M de la energía^F hacia la red^F de transmisión^F
immissione^F di energia^F nella rete^F di trasmissione^F

発電機の電圧の高さでエネルギーを伝達する
energy transmission at the generator voltage
Leistungsabgabe^F mit Generatorspannung^F
transport^M de l'énergie^F à la tension^F de l'alternateur^M
transmisión^F de energía^F al generador^M de voltaje^M
trasmissione^F di energia^F alla tensione^F di produzione^F

高圧電気を送電する
high-tension electricity transmission
Hochspannungsleitung^F
transport^M de l'électricité^F à haute tension^F
transporte^M de electricidad^F de alta tensión^F
trasmissione^F di elettricità^F ad alta tensione^F

昇圧／電圧上昇
voltage increase
Hochtransformation^F der Spannung^F
élévation^F de la tension^F
amplificador^M de voltaje^M
aumento^M di tensione^F

降圧／電圧降下
voltage decrease
Heruntertransformation^F der Spannung^F
abaissement^M de la tension^F
reductor^M de voltaje^M
diminuzione^F di tensione^F

水の供給源
supply of water
Wasservorrat^M
provision^F d'eau^F
suministro^M de agua^F
bacino^M

消費者へ送電する
transmission to consumers
Stromabgabe^F an Verbraucher^M
transport^M vers les usagers^M
distribución^F al consumidor^M
trasmissione^F agli utenti^M

水の落差
head of water
Wasserstand^M
hauteur^F de chute^F
altura^F del agua^F
altezza^F di caduta^F dell'acqua^F

力学的エネルギーを電気に変換する
transformation of mechanical work into electricity
Umwandlung^F von Bewegungsenergie^F in Elektrizität^F
conversion^F du travail^M mécanique en électricité^F
transformación^F del trabajo^M mecánico en electricidad^F
trasformazione^F del lavoro^M meccanico in elettricità^F

発電機により電気が発生する
production of electricity by the generator
Elektrizitätserzeugung^F durch Generator^M
production^F d'électricité^F par l'alternateur^M
producción^F de electricidad^F por generador^M
produzione^F di elettricità^F dal generatore^M

圧力の掛かった水
water under pressure
Druckwasser^N
eau^F sous pression^F
agua^F a presión^F
acqua^F in pressione^F

タービンが回転する
rotation of the turbine
Turbinendrehung^F
mouvement^M rotatif de la turbine^F
rotación^F de la turbina^F
rotazione^F della turbina^F

回転運動をローターに伝送する
transmission of the rotative movement to the rotor
Übertragung^F der Drehbewegung^F auf den Rotor^M
transmission^F du mouvement^M au rotor^M
transmisión^F del movimiento^M hacia el rotor^M
trasmissione^F del movimento^M rotatorio al rotore^M

排水
turbined water draining
Turbinenwasserabfluss^M
évacuation^F de l'eau^F turbinée
desagüe^M de la turbina^F
scarico^M dell'acqua^F

エネルギー

水力電気 | HYDROELECTRICITY
ELEKTRIZITÄT AUS WASSERKRAFT | HYDROÉLECTRICITÉ | HIDROELECTRICIDAD | IDROELETTRICITÀ

送電

electricity transmission | Elektrizitätsverteilung F | transport M de l'électricité F | transporte M de electricidad F | trasmissione F di elettricità F

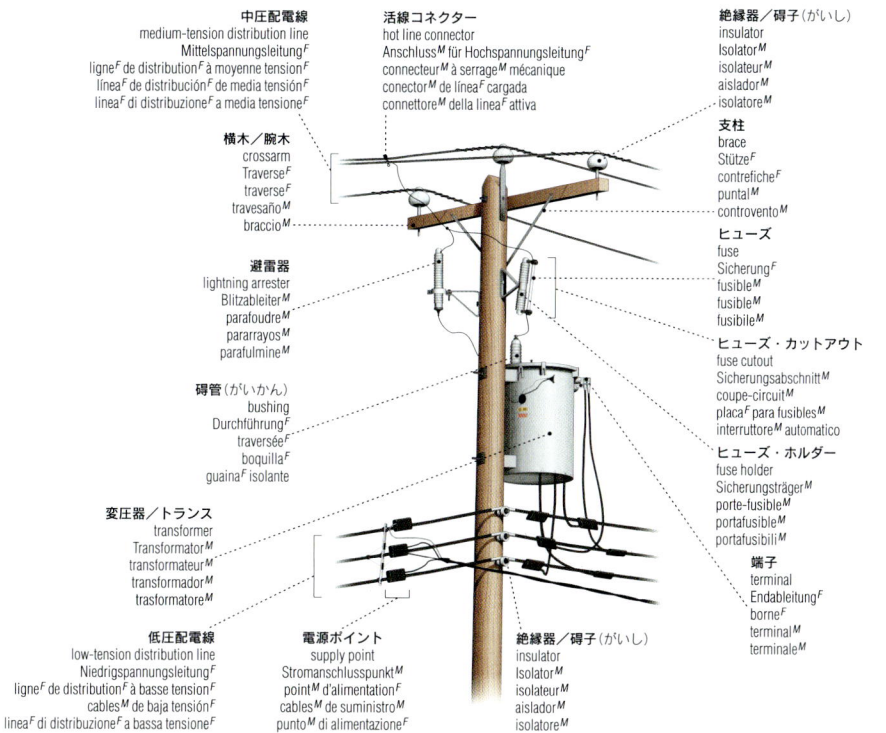

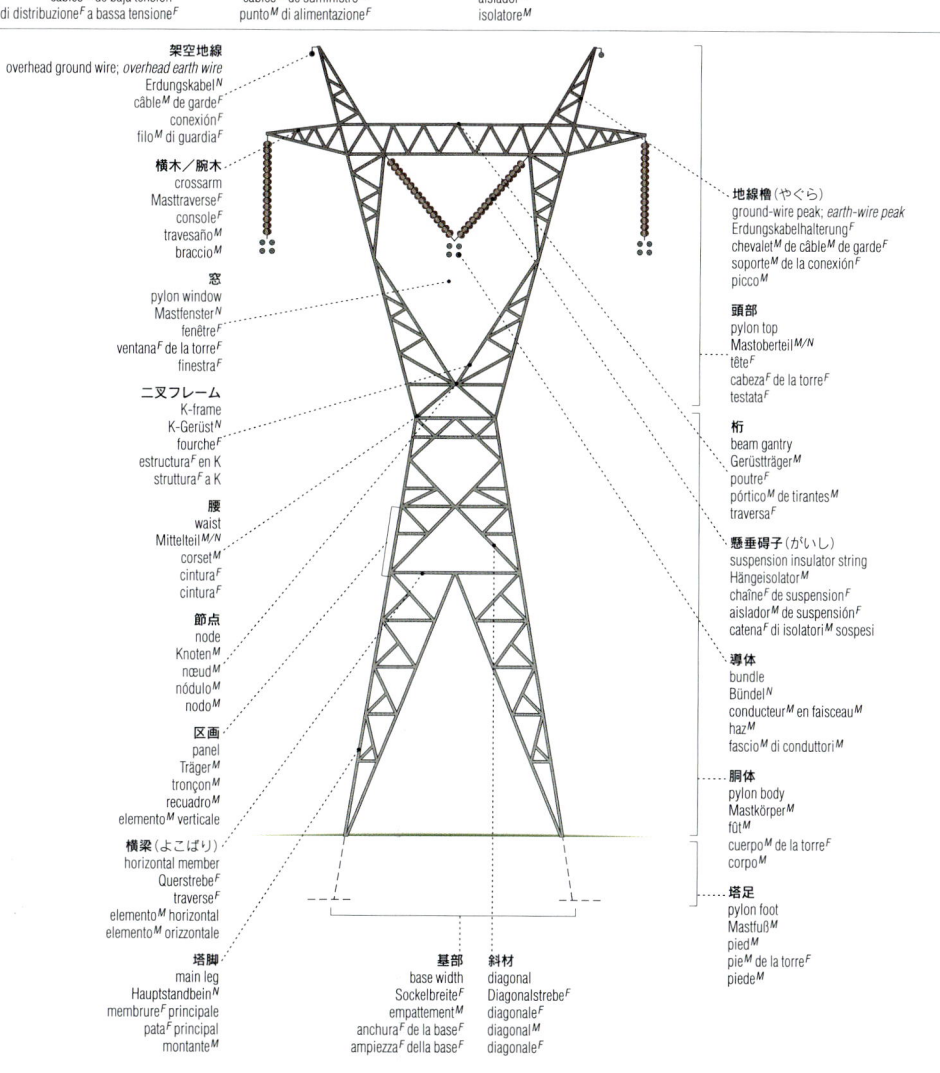

中圧配電線 — medium-tension distribution line / Mittelspannungsleitung F / ligne F de distribution F à moyenne tension F / línea F de distribución F de media tensión F / linea F di distribuzione F a media tensione F

活線コネクター — hot line connector / Anschluss M für Hochspannungsleitung F / connecteur F à serrage M mécanique / conector M de línea F cargada / connettore M della linea F attiva

絶縁器／碍子（がいし） — insulator / Isolator M / isolateur M / aislador M / isolatore M

架空（送）電線 — overhead connection / Freileitung F / branchement M aérien / acometida F aérea / connessione F aerea

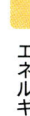

横木／腕木 — crossarm / Traverse F / traverse F / travesaño M / braccio M

支柱 — brace / Stütze F / contrefiche F / puntal M / controvento M

避雷器 — lightning arrester / Blitzableiter M / parafoudre M / pararrayos M / parafulmine M

ヒューズ — fuse / Sicherung F / fusible M / fusible M / fusibile M

碍管（がいかん） — bushing / Durchführung F / traversée F / boquilla F / guaina F isolante

ヒューズ・カットアウト — fuse cutout / Sicherungsabschnitt M / coupe-circuit M / placa F para fusibles M / interruttore M automatico

ヒューズ・ホルダー — fuse holder / Sicherungsträger M / porte-fusible M / portafusible M / portafusibili M

変圧器／トランス — transformer / Transformator M / transformateur M / transformador M / trasformatore M

端子 — terminal / Endableitung F / borne F / terminal M / terminale M

低圧配電線 — low-tension distribution line / Niedrigspannungsleitung F / ligne F de distribution F à basse tension F / cables M de baja tensión F / linea F di distribuzione F a bassa tensione F

電源ポイント — supply point / Stromanschlusspunkt M / point M d'alimentation F / cables M de suministro M / punto M di alimentazione F

絶縁器／碍子（がいし） — insulator / Isolator M / isolateur M / aislador M / isolatore M

架空地線 — overhead ground wire; *overhead earth wire* / Erdungskabel N / câble M de garde F / conexión F / filo M di guardia F

送電（鉄）塔 — pylon / Hochspannungsmast M / pylône M / torre F de alta tensión F / traliccio M per alta tensione F

横木／腕木 — crossarm / Masttraverse F / console F / travesaño M / braccio M

地線櫓（やぐら） — ground-wire peak; *earth-wire peak* / Erdungskabelhalterung F / chevalet M de câble M de garde F / soporte M de la conexión F / picco M

窓 — pylon window / Mastfenster N / fenêtre F / ventana F de la torre F / finestra F

頭部 — pylon top / Mastoberteil M/N / tête F / cabeza F de la torre F / testata F

二叉フレーム — K-frame / K-Gerüst N / fourche F / estructura F en K / struttura F a K

桁 — beam gantry / Gerüstträger M / poutre F / pórtico M de tirantes M / traversa F

腰 — waist / Mittelteil M/N / corset M / cintura F / cintura F

懸垂碍子（がいし） — suspension insulator string / Hängeisolator M / chaîne F de suspension F / aislador M de suspensión F / catena F di isolatori M sospesi

節点 — node / Knoten M / nœud M / nódulo M / nodo M

導体 — bundle / Bündel N / conducteur M en faisceau M / haz M / fascio M di conduttori M

区画 — panel / Träger M / tronçon M / recuadro M / elemento M verticale

胴体 — pylon body / Mastkörper M / fût M / cuerpo M de la torre F / corpo M

横梁（よこばり） — horizontal member / Querstrebe F / traverse F / elemento M horizontal / elemento M orizzontale

塔足 — pylon foot / Mastfuß M / pied M / pie M de la torre F / piede M

塔脚 — main leg / Hauptstandbein N / membrure F principale / pata F principal / montante M

基部 — base width / Sockelbreite F / empattement M / anchura F de la base F / ampiezza F della base F

斜材 — diagonal / Diagonalstrebe F / diagonale F / diagonal M / diagonale M

エネルギー

663

水力電気 | HYDROELECTRICITY
ELEKTRIZITÄT AUS WASSERKRAFT | HYDROÉLECTRICITÉ | HIDROELECTRICIDAD | IDROELETTRICITÀ

潮汐［潮力］発電所

日本語 | 英語 | ドイツ語 | フランス語 | スペイン語 | イタリア語

tidal power plant | Gezeitenkraftwerk^N | usine^F marémotrice | planta^F de energía^F maremotriz | centrale^F elettrica mareomotrice

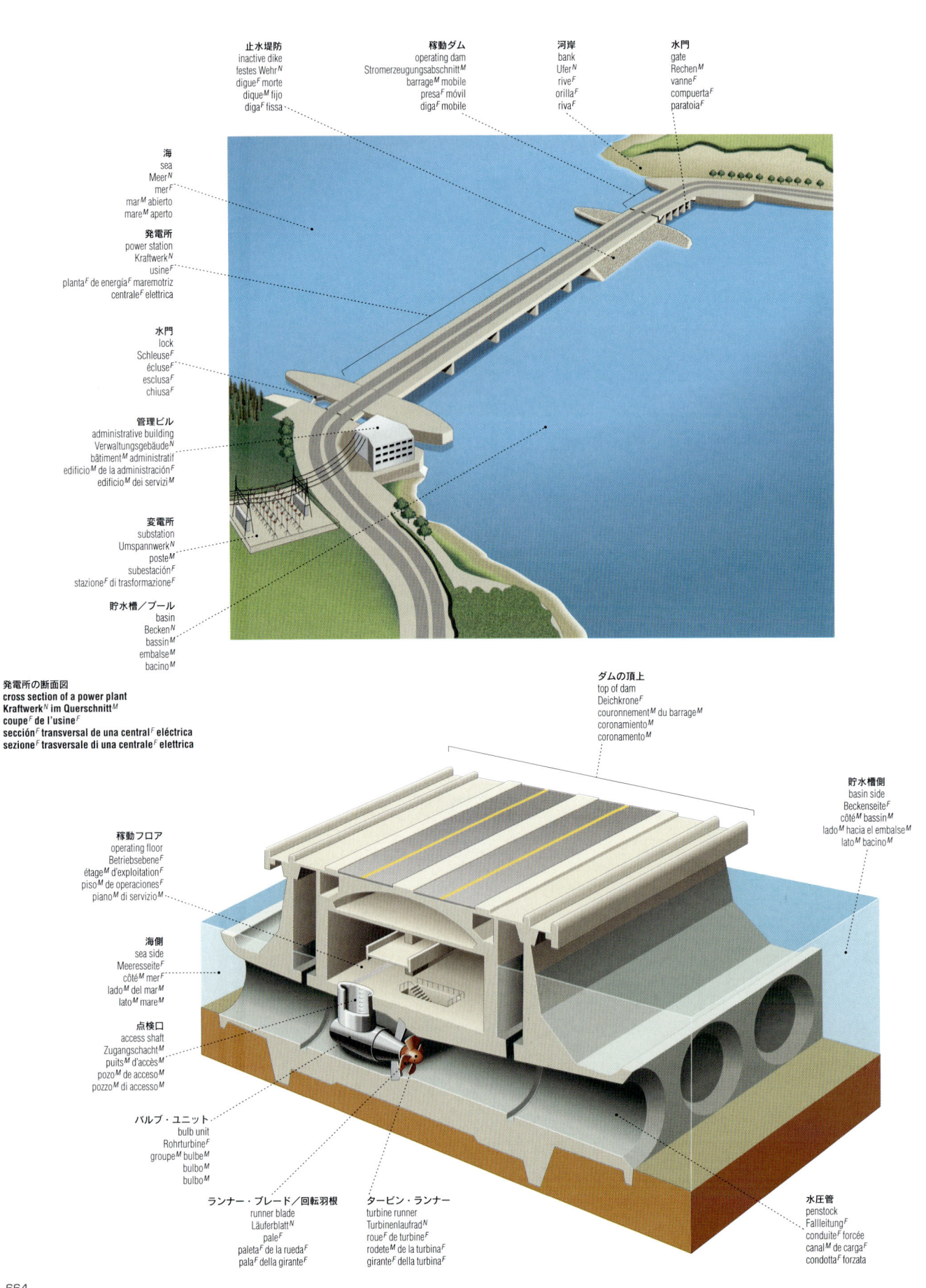

止水堤防
inactive dike
festes Wehr^N
digue^F morte
dique^F fijo
diga^F fissa

移動ダム
operating dam
Stromerzeugungsabschnitt^M
barrage^M mobile
presa^F móvil
diga^F mobile

河岸
bank
Ufer^N
rive^F
orilla^F
riva^F

水門
gate
Rechen^M
vanne^F
compuerta^F
paratoia^F

海
sea
Meer^N
mer^F
mar^M abierto
mare^M aperto

発電所
power station
Kraftwerk^N
usine^F
planta^F de energía^F maremotriz
centrale^F elettrica

水門
lock
Schleuse^F
écluse^F
esclusa^F
chiusa^F

管理ビル
administrative building
Verwaltungsgebäude^N
bâtiment^M administratif
edificio^M de la administración^F
edificio^M dei servizi^M

変電所
substation
Umspannwerk^N
poste^M
subestación^F
stazione^F di trasformazione^F

貯水槽／プール
basin
Becken^N
bassin^M
embalse^M
bacino^M

発電所の断面図
cross section of a power plant
Kraftwerk^N im Querschnitt^M
coupe^F de l'usine^F
sección^F transversal de una central^F eléctrica
sezione^F trasversale di una centrale^F elettrica

ダムの頂上
top of dam
Deichkrone^F
couronnement^M du barrage^M
coronamiento^M
coronamento^M

貯水槽側
basin side
Beckenseite^F
côté^M bassin^M
lado^M hacia el embalse^M
lato^M bacino^M

移動フロア
operating floor
Betriebsebene^F
étage^M d'exploitation^F
piso^M de operaciones^F
piano^M di servizio^M

海側
sea side
Meeresseite^F
côté^M mer^F
lado^M del mar^M
lato^M mare^M

点検口
access shaft
Zugangschacht^M
puits^M d'accès^M
pozo^M de acceso^M
pozzo^M di accesso^M

バルブ・ユニット
bulb unit
Rohrturbine^F
groupe^M bulbe^M
bulbo^M
bulbo^M

ランナー・ブレード／回転羽根
runner blade
Läuferblatt^N
pale^F
paleta^F de la rueda^F
pala^F della girante^F

タービン・ランナー
turbine runner
Turbinenlaufrad^N
roue^F de turbine^F
rodete^M de la turbina^F
girante^F della turbina^F

水圧管
penstock
Fallleitung^F
conduite^F forcée
canal^M de carga^F
condotta^F forzata

核エネルギー | NUCLEAR ENERGY
KERNENERGIE | ÉNERGIE NUCLÉAIRE | ENERGÍA NUCLEAR | ENERGIA NUCLEARE

核エネルギー発電

production of electricity from nuclear energy | Elektrizitätserzeugung^F aus Kernenergie^F | production^F d'électricité^F par énergie^F nucléaire | producción de electricidad^F por energía^F nuclear | produzione^F di elettricità^F da energia^F nucleare

灌水（かんすい）タンク
dousing water tank
Kühlwassertank^M
réservoir^M d'arrosage^F
tanque^M de agua^F de rociado^M
serbatoio^M dell'acqua^F di raffreddamento^M

原子炉格納建屋
containment building
Sicherheitshülle^F
enceinte^F de confinement^M
edificio^M de hormigón^M
contenitore^M in calcestruzzo^M

安全弁
safety valve
Sicherheitsventil^N
soupape^F de sûreté^F
válvula^F de seguridad^F
valvola^F di sicurezza^F

冷却材
coolant
Kühlmittel^N
caloporteur^M
refrigerante^M
refrigerante^M

減速材
moderator
Moderator^M
modérateur^M
moderador^M
moderatore^M

燃料
fuel
Brennstoff^M
combustible^M
combustible^M
combustibile^M

水が蒸気になる
water turns into steam
Wasser^N verdampft
transformation^F de l'eau^F en vapeur^F
conversión^F del agua^F en vapor^M
l'acqua^F si trasforma in vapore^M

原子炉
reactor
Reaktor^M
réacteur^M
reactor^M
reattore^M

ウラン燃料が核分裂を起こす
fission of uranium fuel
Kernspaltung^F des Uranbrennstoffs^M
fission^F de l'uranium^M
uranio^M en fisión^F
fissione^F dell'uranio^M

スプリンクラー
sprinklers
Sprinkler^M
gicleurs^M
rociadores^M
spruzzatori^M

熱を水に伝える
transfer of heat to water
Wärmeabgabe^F an Wasser^N
transmission^F de la chaleur^F à l'eau^F
transferencia^F de calor^M al agua^F
trasferimento^M del calore^M all'acqua^F

熱が発生する
heat production
Wärmeerzeugung^F
production^F de chaleur^F
producción^F de calor^M
produzione^F di calore^M

熱せられた冷却液
hot coolant
erwärmtes Kühlmittel^N
caloporteur^M chaud
refrigerante^M caliente
fluido^M vettore^M caldo

冷やされた冷却液
cold coolant
kaltes Kühlmittel^N
caloporteur^M refroidi
refrigerante^M frío
fluido^M vettore^M freddo

蒸気の圧力でタービンを回転させる
steam pressure drives turbine
Dampfdruck^M treibt Turbine^F an
entraînement^M de la turbine^F par la vapeur^F
la presión^F del vapor^M impulsa las turbinas^F
la pressione^F del vapore^M aziona la turbina

タービン軸が回転して発電機を回転させる
turbine shaft turns generator
Turbinenwelle^F treibt Generator^M an
entraînement^M du rotor^M de l'alternateur^M
el eje^M de la turbina^F hace girar el generador^M
l'albero^M della turbina^F fa ruotare il generatore^M

発電機から電気が発生する
production of electricity by the generator
Elektrizitätserzeugung^F durch den Generator^M
production^F d'électricité^F par l'alternateur^M
producción^F de electricidad^F por generador^M
produzione^F di elettricità^F da alternatore^M

送電する
electricity transmission
Stromfortleitung^F
transport^M de l'électricité^F
transmisión^F de electricidad^F
trasmissione^F dell'elettricità^F

電圧を上げる
voltage increase
Hochtransformation^F der Spannung^F
élévation^F de la tension^F
ampliación^F del voltaje^M
aumento^M di tensione^F

ポンプで水を再び蒸気発生器へ送る
water is pumped back into the steam generator
Wasser^N wird zum Dampfgenerator^M zurückgepumpt
retour^M de l'eau^F au générateur^M de vapeur^F
el agua^F regresa al generador^M de vapor^M
l'acqua^F di condensazione^F ritorna nel generatore^M di vapore^M

蒸気を凝縮して水に戻す
condensation of steam into water
Dampf^M kondensiert zu Wasser^N
condensation^F de la vapeur^F
el vapor^M se condensa en agua^F
il vapore^M condensa in acqua^F

使用後の蒸気を水で冷却する
water cools the used steam
Wasser^N kühlt Brauchdampf^M ab
refroidissement^M de la vapeur^F par l'eau^F
el agua^F enfría el vapor^M utilizado
l'acqua^F raffredda il vapore^M utilizzato

エネルギー

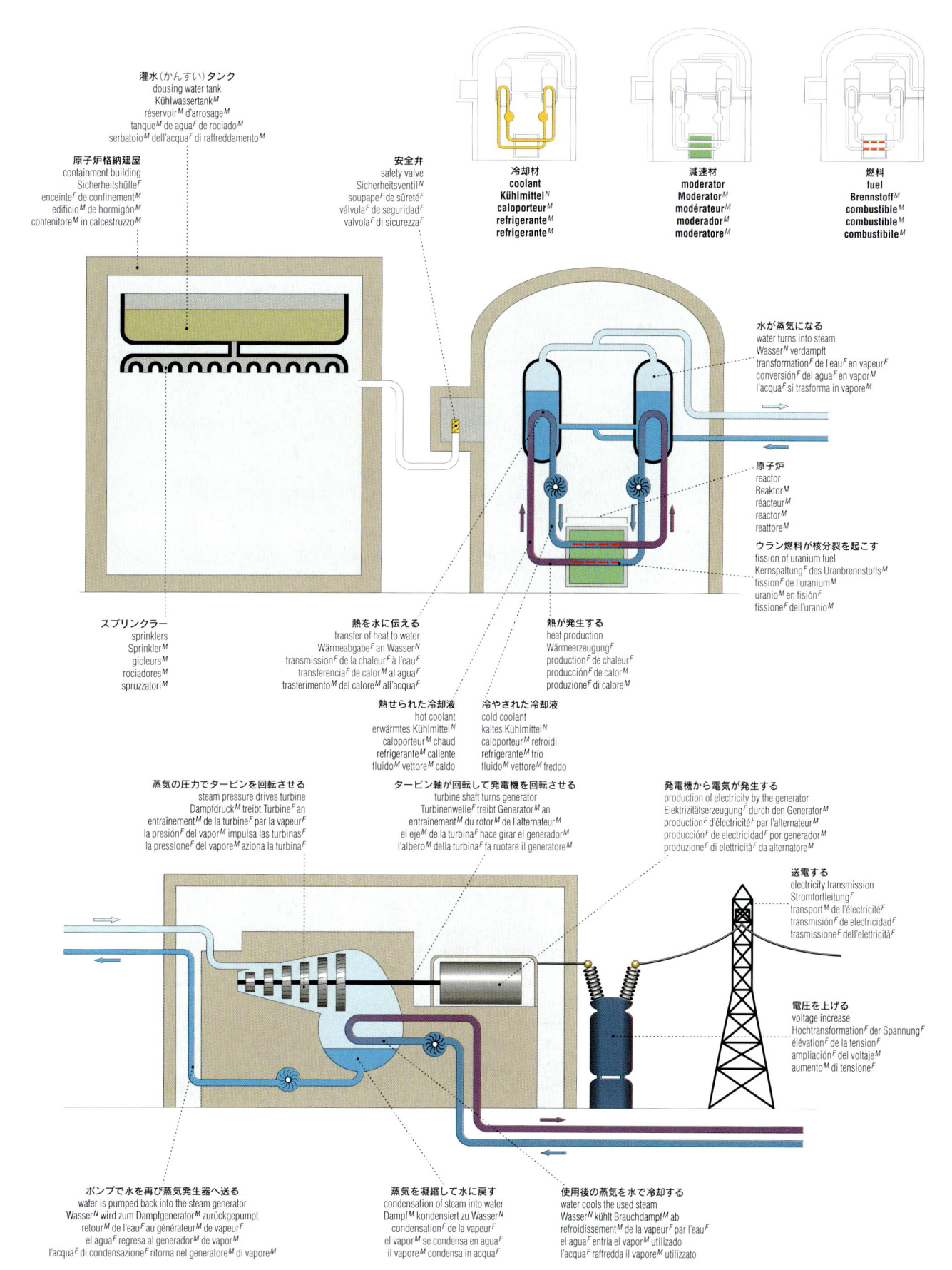

核エネルギー | NUCLEAR ENERGY
KERNENERGIE | ÉNERGIE NUCLÉAIRE | ENERGÍA NUCLEAR | ENERGIA NUCLEARE

燃料取り扱いの流れ

日本語 | 英語 | ドイツ語 | フランス語 | スペイン語 | イタリア語

fuel handling sequence | Brennstabbeschickung^F | séquence^F de manipulation^F du combustible^M | secuencia^F en el manejo^M de combustible^M | manipolazione^F del combustibile^M

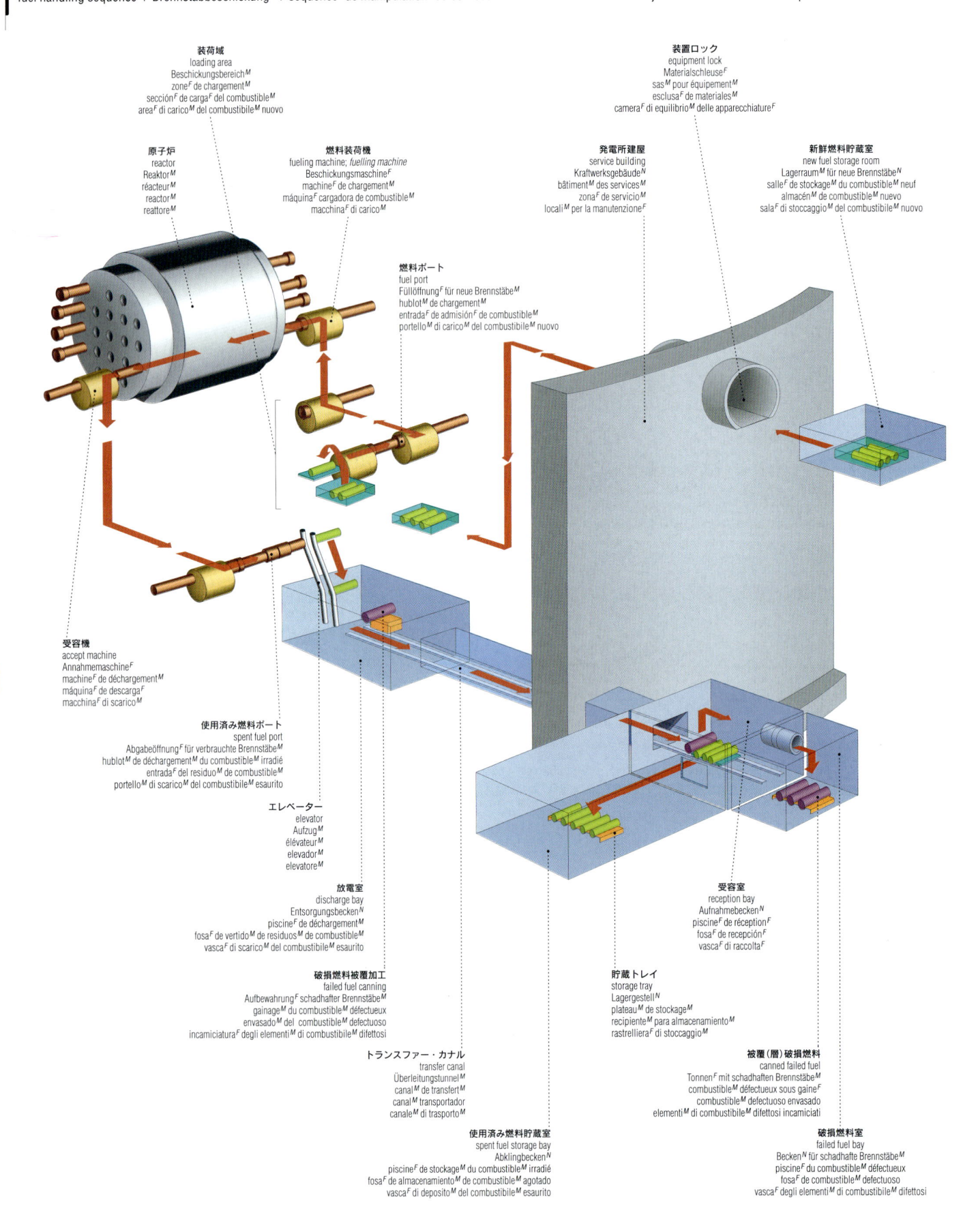

装荷域
loading area
Beschickungsbereich^M
zone^F de chargement^M
sección^F de carga^F del combustible^M
area^F di carico^M del combustibile^M nuovo

装置ロック
equipment lock
Materialschleuse^F
sas^M pour équipement^M
esclusa^F de materiales^M
camera^F di equilibrio^M delle apparecchiature^F

原子炉
reactor
Reaktor^M
réacteur^M
reactor^M
reattore^M

燃料装荷機
fueling machine; fuelling machine
Beschickungsmaschine^F
machine^F de chargement^M
máquina^F cargadora de combustible^M
macchina^F di carico^M

発電所建屋
service building
Kraftwerksgebäude^N
bâtiment^M des services^M
zona^F de servicio^M
locali^M per la manutenzione^F

新鮮燃料貯蔵室
new fuel storage room
Lagerraum^M für neue Brennstäbe^N
salle^F de stockage^M du combustible^M neuf
almacén^M de combustible^M nuevo
sala^F di stoccaggio^M del combustibile^M nuovo

燃料ポート
fuel port
Füllöffnung^F für neue Brennstäbe^M
hublot^M de chargement^M
entrada^F de admisión^F de combustible^M
portello^M di carico^M del combustibile^M nuovo

受容機
accept machine
Annahmemaschine^F
machine^F de déchargement^M
máquina^F de descarga^F
macchina^F di scarico^M

使用済み燃料ポート
spent fuel port
Abgabeöffnung^F für verbrauchte Brennstäbe^M
hublot^M de déchargement^M du combustible^M irradié
entrada^F del residuo^M de combustible^M
portello^M di scarico^M del combustibile^M esaurito

エレベーター
elevator
Aufzug^M
élévateur^M
elevador^M
elevatore^M

放電室
discharge bay
Entsorgungsbecken^N
piscine^F de déchargement^M
fosa^F de vertido^M de residuos^M de combustible^M
vasca^F di scarico^M del combustibile^M esaurito

受容室
reception bay
Aufnahmebecken^N
piscine^F de réception^F
fosa^F de recepción^F
vasca^F di raccolta^F

破損燃料被覆加工
failed fuel canning
Aufbewahrung^F schadhafter Brennstäbe^M
gainage^M du combustible^M défectueux
envasado^M del combustible^M defectuoso
incamiciatura^F degli elementi^M di combustibile^M difettosi

貯蔵トレイ
storage tray
Lagergestell^N
plateau^M de stockage^M
recipiente^M para almacenamiento^M
rastrelliera^F di stoccaggio^M

トランスファー・カナル
transfer canal
Überleitungstunnel^M
canal^M de transfert^M
canal^M transportador
canale^M di trasporto^M

被覆(層)破損燃料
canned failed fuel
Tonnen^M mit schadhaften Brennstäbe^M
combustible^M défectueux sous gaine^F
combustible^M defectuoso envasado
elementi^M di combustibile^M difettosi incamiciati

使用済み燃料貯蔵室
spent fuel storage bay
Abklingbecken^N
piscine^F de stockage^M du combustible^M irradié
fosa^F de almacenamiento^M de combustible^M agotado
vasca^F di deposito^M del combustibile^M esaurito

破損燃料室
failed fuel bay
Becken^N für schadhafte Brennstäbe^M
piscine^F du combustible^M défectueux
fosa^F de combustible^M defectuoso
vasca^F degli elementi^M di combustibile^M difettosi

エネルギー

核エネルギー | NUCLEAR ENERGY
KERNENERGIE | ÉNERGIE NUCLÉAIRE | ENERGÍA NUCLEAR | ENERGIA NUCLEARE

燃料集合体

fuel bundle | Brennstabbündel^N | grappe^F de combustible^M | elemento^M de combustible^M | elemento^M di combustibile^M

圧力管
pressure tube
druckfestes Außenrohr^N
tube^M de force^F
tubo^M de presión^F
tubo^M in pressione^F

スペーサー
spacer
Distanzstück^N
patin^M d'espacement^M
separador^M
spaziatore^M

端[エンド]プレート
end plate
Abschlussplatte^F
grille^F d'extrémité^F
placa^F terminal
griglia^F terminale

(燃料)棒
pencil
Brennstab^M
crayon^M
barra^F de combustible^M
barretta^F di combustibile^M

ベアリング・パッド
bearing pad
Lagerraster^N
patin^M d'appui^M
soporte^M
pattino^M distanziatore^M

端栓／エンド・キャップ
end cap
Endstück^N
bouchon^M
tapa^F terminal
cappello^M terminale

端[エンド]プレート
end plate
Abschlussplatte^F
grille^F d'extrémité^F
placa^F terminal
griglia^F terminale

(燃料)棒
pencil
Brennstab^M
crayon^M
barra^F de combustible^M
barretta^F di combustibile^M

燃料ペレット
fuel pellet
Brennstofftablette^F
pastille^F de combustible^M
pastilla^F de combustible^M
pastiglia^F di combustibile^M

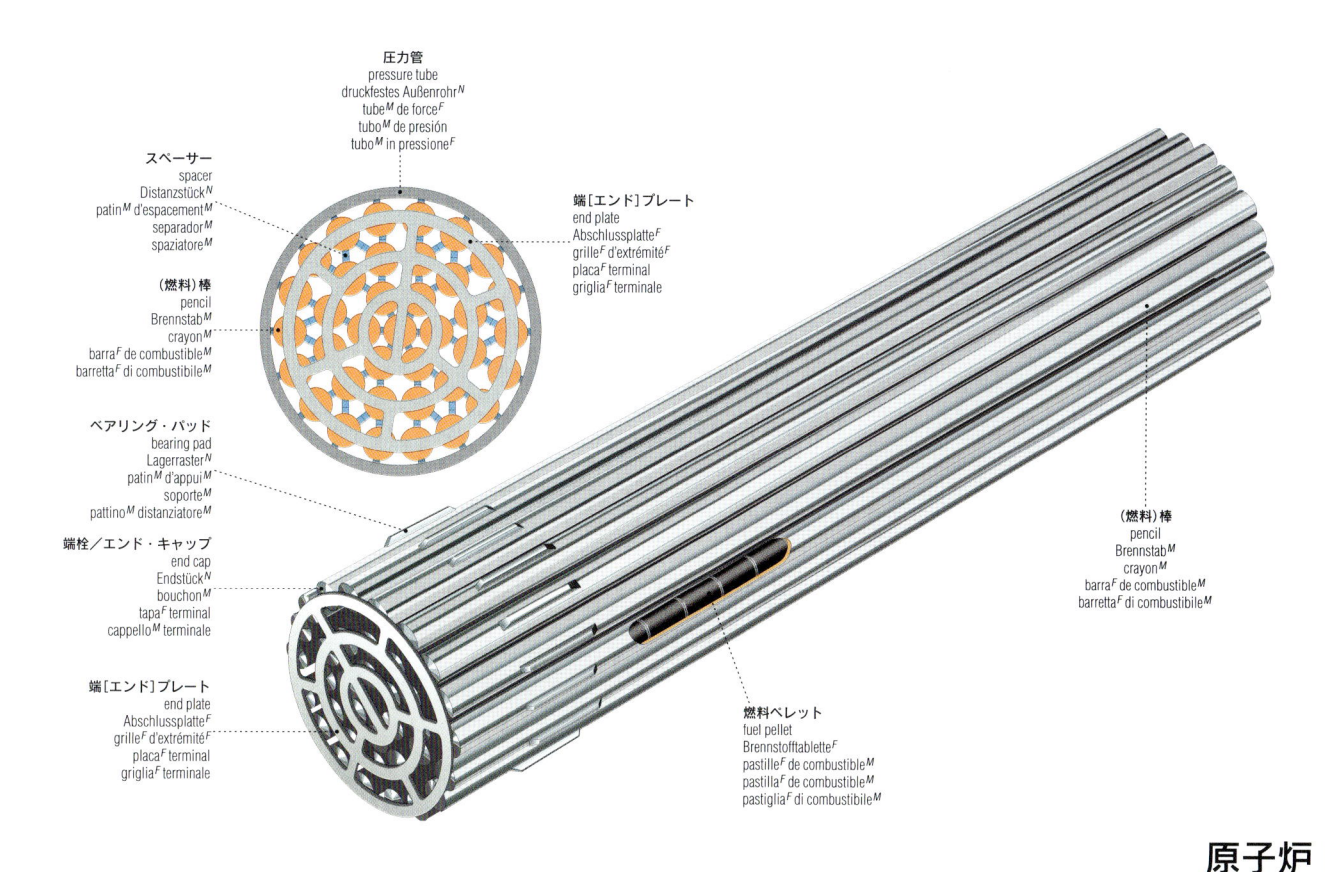

原子炉

nuclear reactor | Kernreaktor^M | réacteur^M nucléaire | carga^F del reactor^M nuclear | reattore^M nucleare

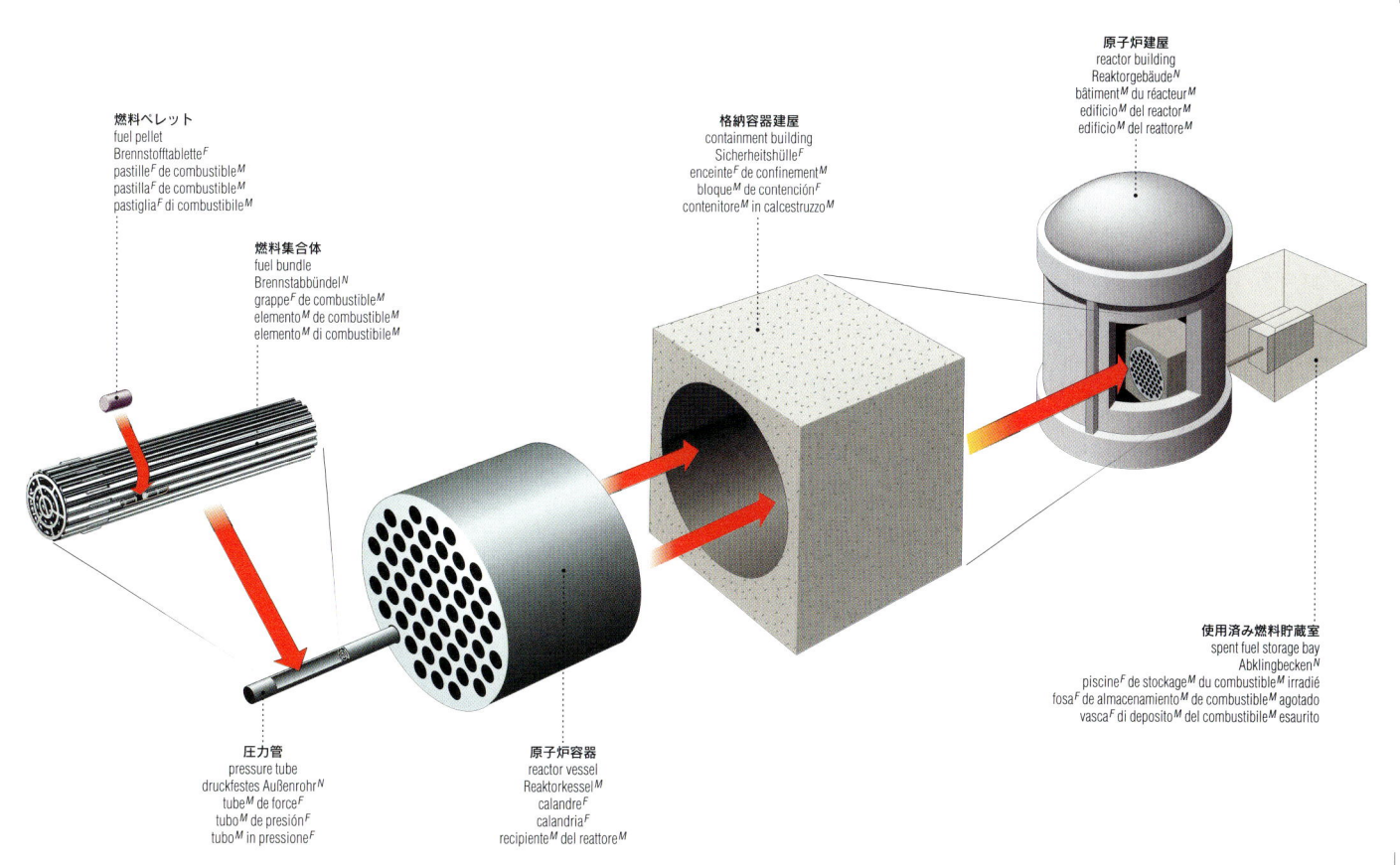

燃料ペレット
fuel pellet
Brennstofftablette^F
pastilla^F de combustible^M
pastilla^F de combustible^M
pastiglia^F di combustibile^M

燃料集合体
fuel bundle
Brennstabbündel^N
grappe^F de combustible^M
elemento^M de combustible^M
elemento^M di combustibile^M

格納容器建屋
containment building
Sicherheitshülle^F
enceinte^F de confinement^M
bloque^M de contención^F
contenitore^M in calcestruzzo^M

原子炉建屋
reactor building
Reaktorgebäude^N
bâtiment^M du réacteur^M
edificio^M del reactor^M
edificio^M del reattore^M

使用済み燃料貯蔵室
spent fuel storage bay
Abklingbecken^N
piscine^F de stockage^M du combustible^M irradié
fosa^F de almacenamiento^M de combustible^M agotado
vasca^F di deposito^M del combustibile^M esaurito

圧力管
pressure tube
druckfestes Außenrohr^N
tube^M de force^F
tubo^M de presión^F
tubo^M in pressione^F

原子炉容器
reactor vessel
Reaktorkessel^M
calandre^F
calandria^F
recipiente^M del reattore^M

エネルギー

667

核エネルギー | NUCLEAR ENERGY
KERNENERGIE | ÉNERGIE NUCLÉAIRE | ENERGÍA NUCLEAR | ENERGIA NUCLEARE

原子力発電所

nuclear generating station; *nuclear power station* | Kernkraftwerk[N] | centrale[F] nucléaire | central[F] nuclear | centrale[F] elettronucleare

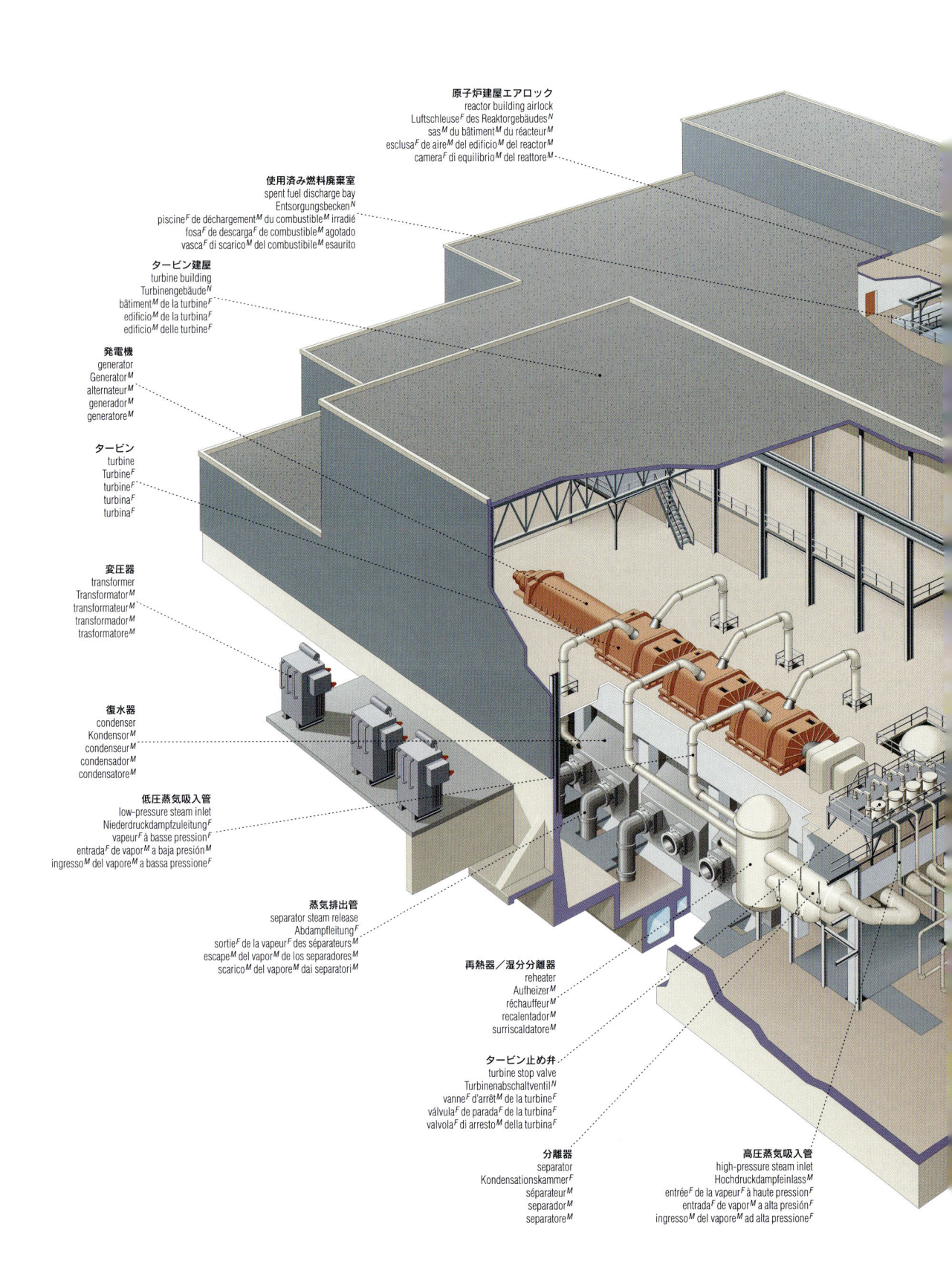

日本語 | 英語 | ドイツ語 | フランス語 | スペイン語 | イタリア語

原子炉建屋エアロック
reactor building airlock
Luftschleuse[F] des Reaktorgebäudes[N]
sas[M] du bâtiment[M] du réacteur[M]
esclusa[F] de aire[M] del edificio[M] del reactor[M]
camera[F] di equilibrio[M] del reattore[M]

使用済み燃料廃棄室
spent fuel discharge bay
Entsorgungsbecken[N]
piscine[F] de déchargement[M] du combustible[M] irradié
fosa[F] de descarga de combustible[M] agotado
vasca[F] di scarico[M] del combustibile[M] esaurito

タービン建屋
turbine building
Turbinengebäude[N]
bâtiment[M] de la turbine[F]
edificio[M] de la turbina[F]
edificio[M] delle turbine[F]

発電機
generator
Generator[M]
alternateur[M]
generador[M]
generatore[M]

タービン
turbine
Turbine[F]
turbine[F]
turbina[F]
turbina[F]

変圧器
transformer
Transformator[M]
transformateur[M]
transformador[M]
trasformatore[M]

復水器
condenser
Kondensor[M]
condenseur[M]
condensador[M]
condensatore[M]

低圧蒸気吸入管
low-pressure steam inlet
Niederdruckdampfzuleitung[F]
vapeur[F] à basse pression[F]
entrada[F] de vapor[M] a baja presión[M]
ingresso[M] del vapore[M] a bassa pressione[F]

蒸気排出管
separator steam release
Abdampfleitung[F]
sortie[F] de la vapeur[F] des séparateurs[M]
escape[M] del vapor[M] de los separadores[M]
scarico[M] del vapore[M] dai separatori[M]

再熱器／湿分分離器
reheater
Aufheizer[M]
réchauffeur[M]
recalentador[M]
surriscaldatore[M]

タービン止め弁
turbine stop valve
Turbinenabschaltventil[N]
vanne[F] d'arrêt[M] de la turbine[F]
válvula[F] de parada[F] de la turbina[F]
valvola[F] di arresto[M] della turbina[F]

分離器
separator
Kondensationskammer[F]
séparateur[M]
separador[M]
separatore[M]

高圧蒸気吸入管
high-pressure steam inlet
Hochdruckdampfeinlass[M]
entrée[F] de la vapeur[F] à haute pression[F]
entrada[F] de vapor[M] a alta presión[F]
ingresso[M] del vapore[M] ad alta pressione[F]

エネルギー

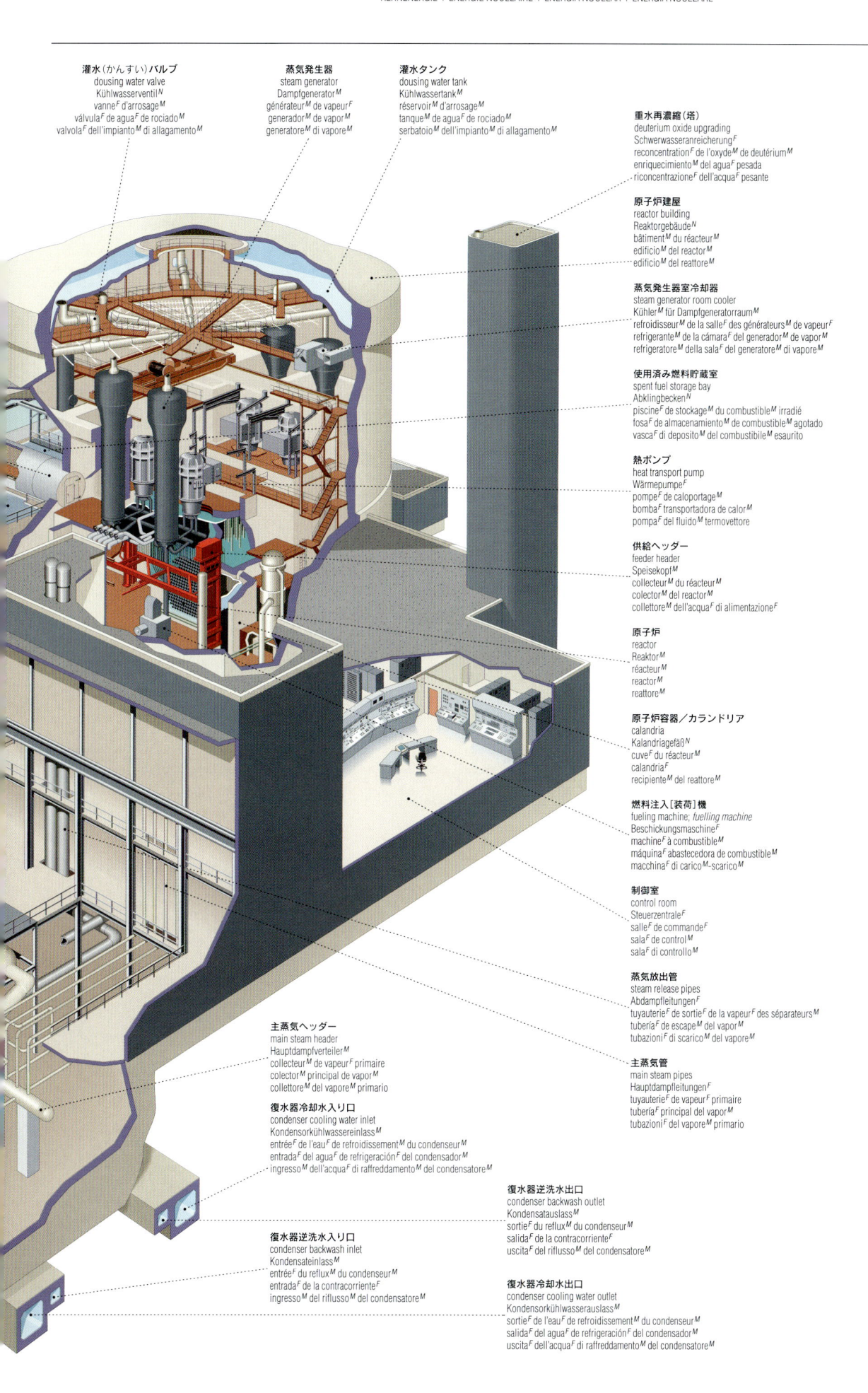

核エネルギー | NUCLEAR ENERGY
KERNENERGIE | ÉNERGIE NUCLÉAIRE | ENERGÍA NUCLEAR | ENERGIA NUCLEARE

原子力発電所

灌水（かんすい）バルブ
dousing water valve
Kühlwasserventil^N
vanne^F d'arrosage^M
válvula^F de agua^F de rociado^M
valvola^F dell'impianto di allagamento^M

蒸気発生器
steam generator
Dampfgenerator^M
générateur^M de vapeur^F
generador^M de vapor^M
generatore^M di vapore^M

灌水タンク
dousing water tank
Kühlwassertank^M
réservoir^M d'arrosage^M
tanque^M de agua^F de rociado^M
serbatoio^M dell'impianto di allagamento^M

重水再濃縮（塔）
deuterium oxide upgrading
Schwerwasseranreicherung^F
reconcentration^F de l'oxyde^M de deutérium^M
enriquecimiento^M del agua^F pesada
riconcentrazione^F dell'acqua^F pesante

原子炉建屋
reactor building
Reaktorgebäude^N
bâtiment^M du réacteur^M
edificio^M del reactor^M
edificio^M del reattore^M

蒸気発生器室冷却器
steam generator room cooler
Kühler^M für Dampfgeneratorraum^M
refroidisseur^M de la salle^F des générateurs^M de vapeur^F
refrigerante^M de la cámara^F del generador^M de vapor^M
refrigeratore^M della sala^F del generatore^M di vapore^M

使用済み燃料貯蔵室
spent fuel storage bay
Abklingbecken^N
piscine^F de stockage^M du combustible^M irradié
fosa^F de almacenamiento^M de combustible^M agotado
vasca^F di deposito^M del combustibile^M esaurito

熱ポンプ
heat transport pump
Wärmepumpe^F
pompe^F de caloportage^M
bomba^F transportadora de calor^M
pompa^F del fluido^M termovettore

供給ヘッダー
feeder header
Speisekopf^M
collecteur^M du réacteur^M
colector^M del reactor^M
collettore^M dell'acqua^F di alimentazione^F

原子炉
reactor
Reaktor^M
réacteur^M
reactor^M
reattore^M

原子炉容器／カランドリア
calandria
Kalandriagefäß^N
cuve^F du réacteur^M
calandria^F
recipiente^M del reattore^M

燃料注入[装荷]機
fueling machine; *fuelling machine*
Beschickungsmaschine^F
machine^F à combustible^M
máquina^F abastecedora de combustible^M
macchina^F di carico^M-scarico^M

制御室
control room
Steuerzentrale^F
salle^F de commande^F
sala^F de control^M
sala^F di controllo^M

蒸気放出管
steam release pipes
Abdampfleitungen^F
tuyauterie^F de sortie^F de la vapeur^F des séparateurs^M
tubería^F de escape^M del vapor^M
tubazioni^F di scarico^M del vapore^M

主蒸気管
main steam pipes
Hauptdampfleitungen^F
tuyauterie^F de vapeur^F primaire
tubería^F principal del vapor^M
tubazioni^F del vapore^M primario

主蒸気ヘッダー
main steam header
Hauptdampfverteiler^M
collecteur^M de vapeur^F primaire
colector^M principal de vapor^M
collettore^M del vapore^M primario

復水器冷却水入り口
condenser cooling water inlet
Kondensorkühlwassereinlass^M
entrée^F de l'eau^F de refroidissement^M du condenseur^M
entrada^F del agua^F de refrigeración^F del condensador^M
ingresso^M dell'acqua^F di raffreddamento^M del condensatore^M

復水器逆洗水出口
condenser backwash outlet
Kondensatauslass^M
sortie^F du reflux^M du condenseur^M
salida^F de la contracorriente^F
uscita^F del riflusso^M del condensatore^M

復水器逆洗水入り口
condenser backwash inlet
Kondensateinlass^M
entrée^F du reflux^M du condenseur^M
entrada^F de la contracorriente^F
ingresso^M del riflusso^M del condensatore^M

復水器冷却水出口
condenser cooling water outlet
Kondensorkühlwasserauslass^M
sortie^F de l'eau^F de refroidissement^M du condenseur^M
salida^F del agua^F de refrigeración^F del condensador^M
uscita^F dell'acqua^F di raffreddamento^M del condensatore^M

エネルギー

核エネルギー | NUCLEAR ENERGY
KERNENERGIE | ÉNERGIE NUCLÉAIRE | ENERGÍA NUCLEAR | ENERGIA NUCLEARE

炭酸ガス炉

carbon dioxide reactor | Kohlendioxidreaktor^M | réacteur^M au gaz^M carbonique | reactor^M de bióxido^M de carbono^M | reattore^M ad anidride^F carbonica

日本語 | 英語 | ドイツ語 | フランス語 | スペイン語 | イタリア語

燃料注入[装荷]機
fueling machine; *fuelling machine*
Beschickungsmaschine^F
machine^F de chargement^M
máquina^F cargadora del combustible^M
macchina^F di carico^M-scarico^M

コンクリート遮蔽(しゃへい)体[壁]
concrete shielding
Betonmantel^M
enceinte^F en béton^M
blindaje^M de hormigón^M
schermatura^F in calcestruzzo^M

炭酸ガス冷却材
carbon dioxide gas coolant
Kohlendioxidkühlgas^N
gaz^M carbonique de refroidissement^M
gas^M refrigerante de dióxido^M de carbono^M
anidride^F carbonica di raffreddamento^M

熱交換器
heat exchanger
Wärmetauscher^M
échangeur^M de chaleur^F
intercambiador^M de calor^M
scambiatore^M di calore^M

蒸気排出口
steam outlet
Dampfauslass^M
sortie^F de la vapeur^F
salida^F de vapor^M
uscita^F del vapore^M

給水管
feedwater
Speisewasser^N
alimentation^F en eau^F
alimentación^F de agua^F
acqua^F di alimentazione^F

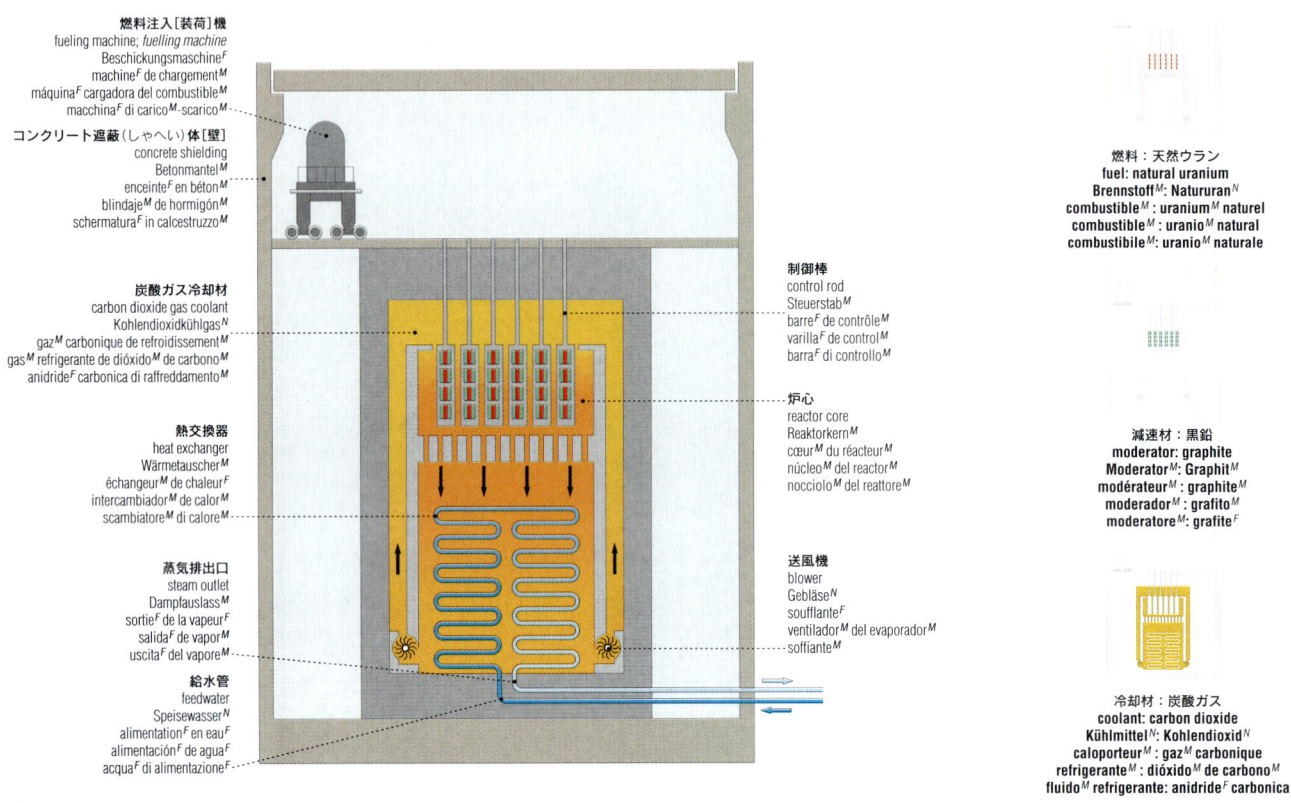

制御棒
control rod
Steuerstab^M
barre^F de contrôle^M
varilla^F de control^M
barra^F di controllo^M

炉心
reactor core
Reaktorkern^M
cœur^M du réacteur^M
núcleo^M del reactor^M
nocciolo^M del reattore^M

送風機
blower
Gebläse^N
soufflante^F
ventilador^M del evaporador^M
soffiante^F

燃料:天然ウラン
fuel: natural uranium
Brennstoff^M: Natururan^N
combustible^M: uranium^M naturel
combustible^M: uranio^M natural
combustibile^M: uranio^M naturale

減速材:黒鉛
moderator: graphite
Moderator^M: Graphit^M
modérateur^M: graphite^M
moderador^M: grafito^M
moderatore^M: grafite^F

冷却材:炭酸ガス
coolant: carbon dioxide
Kühlmittel^N: Kohlendioxid^M
caloporteur^M: gaz^M carbonique
refrigerante^M: dióxido^M de carbono^M
fluido^M refrigerante: anidride^F carbonica

重水炉

heavy-water reactor | Schwerwasserreaktor^M | réacteur^M à eau^F lourde | reactor^M de agua^F pesada | reattore^M ad acqua^F pesante

ポンプ
pump
Pumpe^F
pompe^F
bomba^F
pompa^F

制御棒
control rod
Steuerstab^M
barre^F de contrôle^M
varilla^F de control^M
barra^F di controllo^M

加圧重水
pressurized heavy water
Schwerwasser^N unter Druck^M
eau^F lourde sous pression^F
agua^F pesada a presión^F
acqua^F pesante pressurizzata

燃料
fuel
Brennstoff^M
combustible^M
combustible^M
combustibile^M

燃料注入[装荷]機
fueling machine; *fuelling machine*
Beschickungsmaschine^F
machine^F de chargement^M
máquina^F cargadora del combustible^M
macchina^F di carico^M-scarico^M

減速材タンク
moderator tank
Moderatortank^M
cuve^F du modérateur^M
tanque^M moderador
recipiente^M del moderatore^M

安全タンク
safety tank
Sicherheitstank^M
réservoir^M de sécurité^F
tanque^M de seguridad^F
serbatoio^M di sicurezza^F

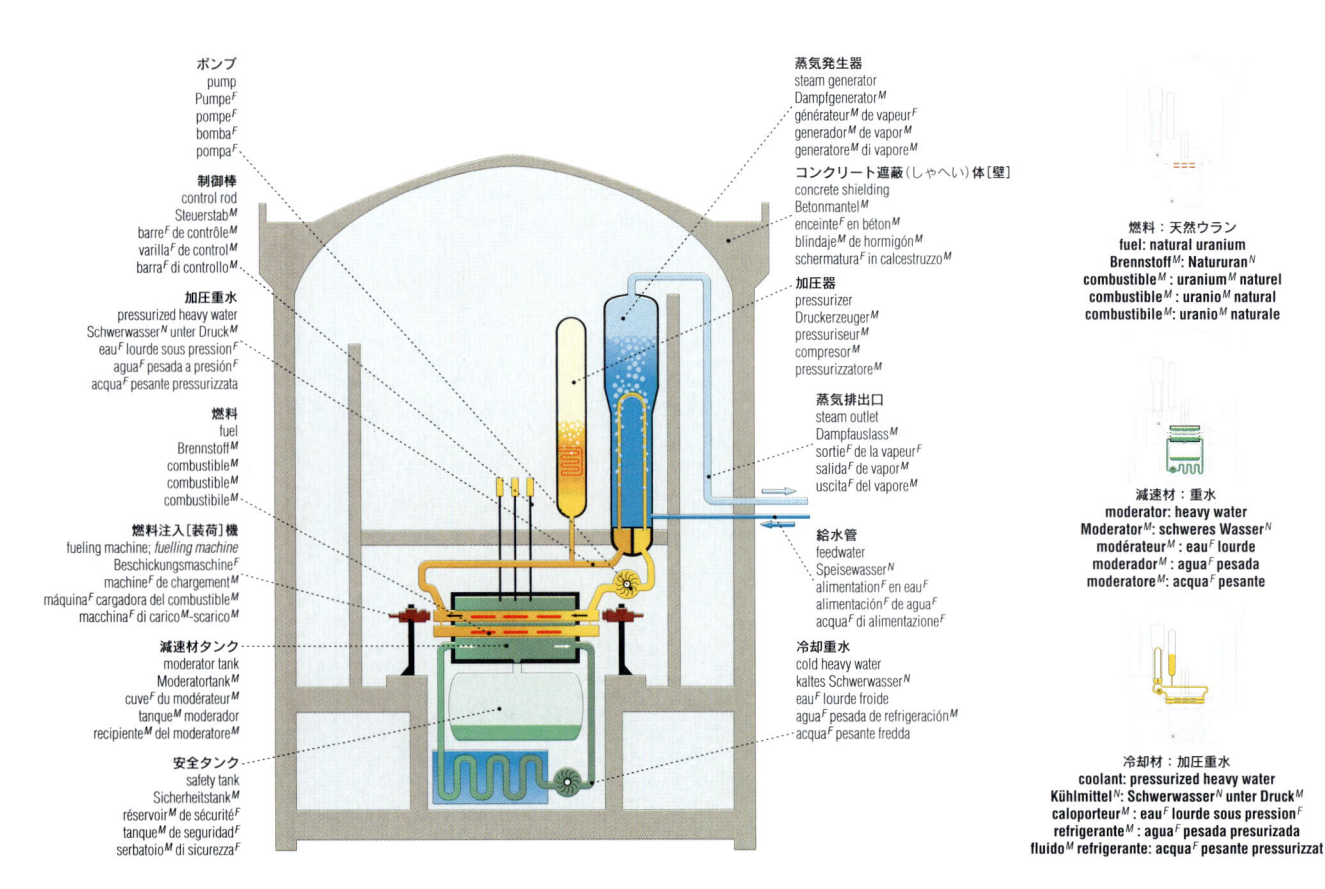

蒸気発生器
steam generator
Dampfgenerator^M
générateur^M de vapeur^F
generador^M de vapor^M
generatore^M di vapore^M

コンクリート遮蔽(しゃへい)体[壁]
concrete shielding
Betonmantel^M
enceinte^F en béton^M
blindaje^M de hormigón^M
schermatura^F in calcestruzzo^M

加圧器
pressurizer
Druckerzeuger^M
pressuriseur^M
compresor^M
pressurizzatore^M

蒸気排出口
steam outlet
Dampfauslass^M
sortie^F de la vapeur^F
salida^F de vapor^M
uscita^F del vapore^M

給水管
feedwater
Speisewasser^N
alimentation^F en eau^F
alimentación^F de agua^F
acqua^F di alimentazione^F

冷却重水
cold heavy water
kaltes Schwerwasser^N
eau^F lourde froide
agua^F pesada de refrigeración^M
acqua^F pesante fredda

燃料:天然ウラン
fuel: natural uranium
Brennstoff^M: Natururan^N
combustible^M: uranium^M naturel
combustible^M: uranio^M natural
combustibile^M: uranio^M naturale

減速材:重水
moderator: heavy water
Moderator^M: schweres Wasser^N
modérateur^M: eau^F lourde
moderador^M: agua^F pesada
moderatore^M: acqua^F pesante

冷却材:加圧重水
coolant: pressurized heavy water
Kühlmittel^N: Schwerwasser^N unter Druck^M
caloporteur^M: eau^F lourde sous pression^F
refrigerante^M: agua^F pesada presurizada
fluido^M refrigerante: acqua^F pesante pressurizzat

核エネルギー | NUCLEAR ENERGY
KERNENERGIE | ÉNERGIE NUCLÉAIRE | ENERGÍA NUCLEAR | ENERGIA NUCLEARE

加圧水型炉

pressurized-water reactor | Druckwasserreaktor^M | réacteur^M à eau^F sous pression^F | reactor^M de agua^F a presión^F | reattore^M ad acqua^F pressurizzata

燃料：濃縮ウラン
fuel: enriched uranium
Brennstoff^M: angereichertes Uran^N
combustible^M: uranium^M enrichi
combustible^M: uranio^M enriquecido
combustibile^M: uranio^M arricchito

減速材：天然水／軽水
moderator: natural water
Moderator^M: leichtes Wasser^N
modérateur^M: eau^F naturelle
moderador^M: agua^F natural
moderatore^M: acqua^F naturale

冷却材：加圧水
coolant: pressurized water
Kühlmittel^N: Druckwasser^N
caloporteur^M: eau^F sous pression^F
refrigerante^M: agua^F presurizada
fluido^M refrigerante: acqua^F pressurizzata

コンクリート遮蔽（しゃへい）体［壁］
concrete shielding
Betonmantel^M
enceinte^F en béton^M
blindaje^M de hormigón^M
schermatura^F in calcestruzzo^M

加圧器
pressurizer
Druckbehälter^M
pressuriseur^M
presurizador^M
pressurizzatore^M

蒸気発生器
steam generator
Dampfgenerator^M
générateur^M de vapeur^F
generador^M de vapor^M
generatore^M di vapore^M

制御棒
control rod
Steuerstab^M
barre^F de contrôle^M
varilla^F de control^M
barra^F di controllo^M

蒸気排出口
steam outlet
Dampfauslass^M
sortie^F de la vapeur^F
salida^F de vapor^M
uscita^F del vapore^M

炉心
reactor core
Reaktorkern^M
cœur^F du réacteur^M
núcleo^M del reactor^M
nocciolo^M del reattore^M

給水管
feedwater
Speisewasser^N
alimentation^F en eau^F
alimentación^F de agua^F
acqua^F di alimentazione^F

ポンプ
pump
Pumpe^F
pompe^F
bomba^F
pompa^F

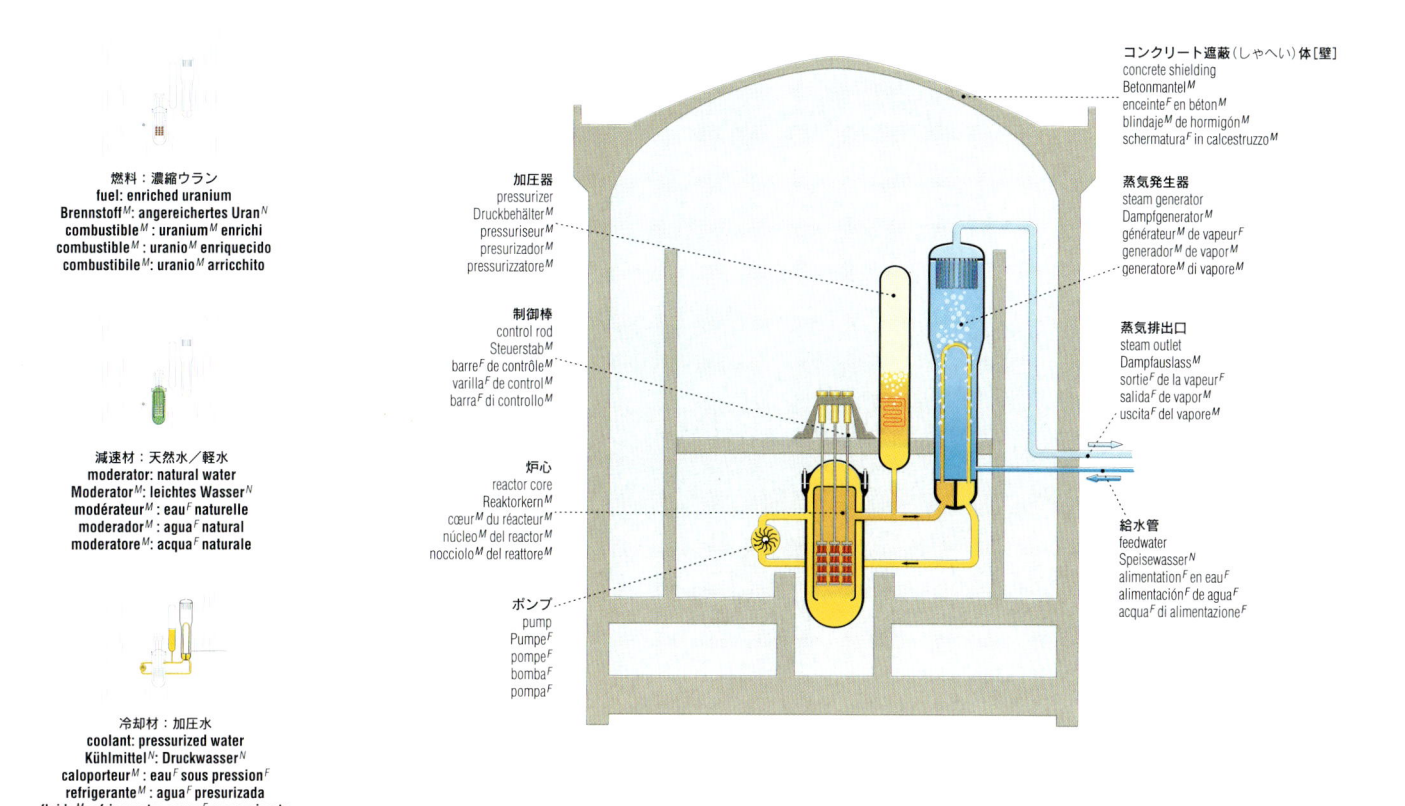

沸騰水型炉

boiling-water reactor | Siedewasserreaktor^M | réacteur^M à eau^F bouillante | reactor^M de agua^F hirviente | reattore^M ad acqua^F bollente

燃料：濃縮ウラン
fuel: enriched uranium
Brennstoff^M: angereichertes Uran^N
combustible^M: uranium^M enrichi
combustible^M: uranio^M enriquecido
combustibile^M: uranio^M arricchito

減速材：天然水／軽水
moderator: natural water
Moderator^M: leichtes Wasser^N
modérateur^M: eau^F naturelle
moderador^M: agua^F natural
moderatore^M: acqua^F naturale

冷却材：熱湯
coolant: boiling water
Kühlmittel^N: Siedewasser^N
caloporteur^M: eau^F bouillante
refrigerante^M: agua^F hirviente
fluido^M refrigerante: acqua^F bollente

原子炉（圧力）容器
reactor tank
Reaktortank^M
cuve^F du réacteur^M
tanque^M del reactor^M
recipiente^M del reattore^M

炉心
reactor core
Reaktorkern^M
cœur^F du réacteur^M
núcleo^M del reactor^M
nocciolo^M del reattore^M

（再循環）ポンプ
pump
Pumpe^F
pompe^F de recirculation^F
bomba^F
pompa^F

制御棒
control rod
Steuerstab^M
barre^F de contrôle^M
varilla^F de control^M
barra^F di controllo^M

乾式セル
dry well
Druckkammer^F
enceinte^F sèche
pozo^M seco
camera^F a secco

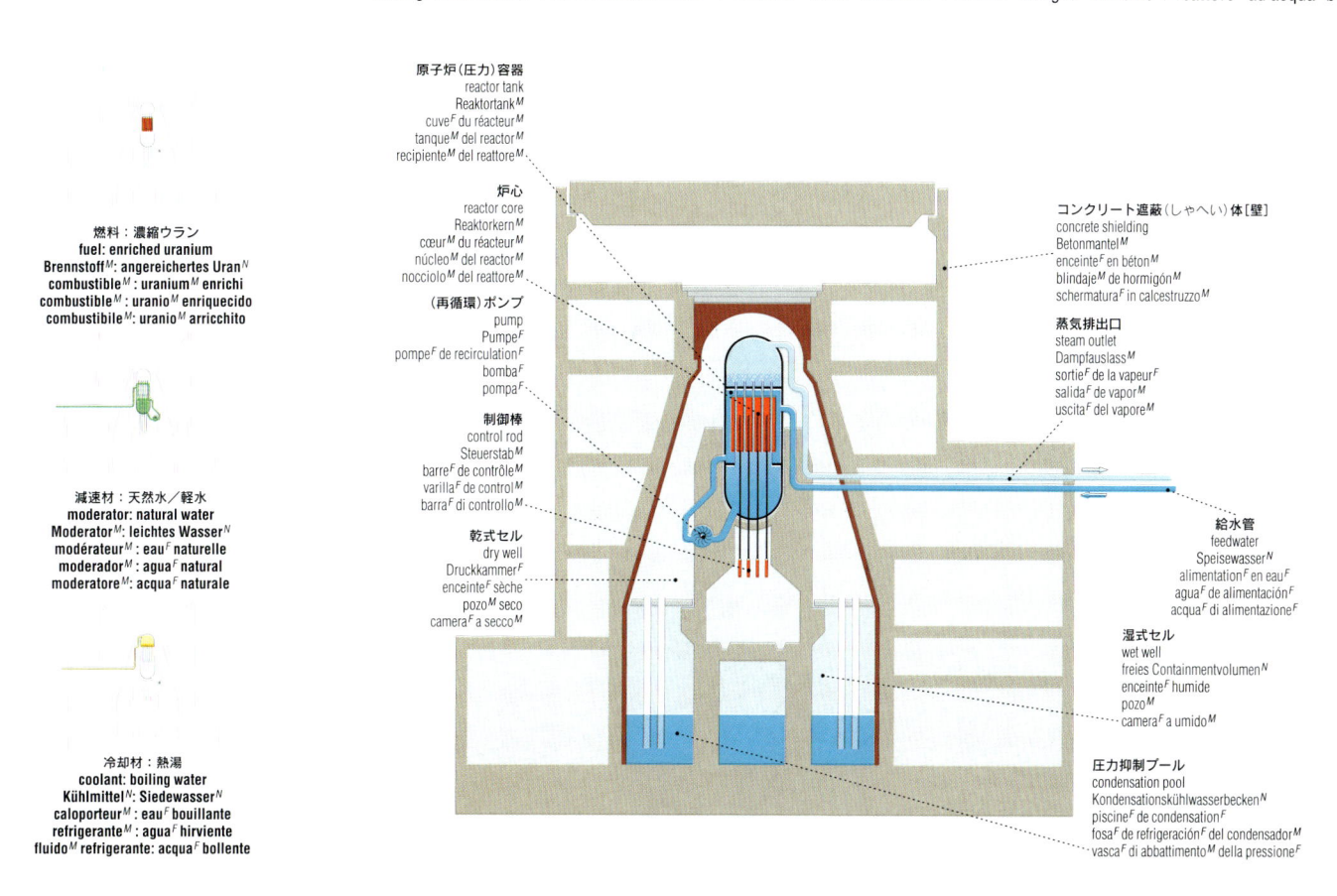

コンクリート遮蔽（しゃへい）体［壁］
concrete shielding
Betonmantel^M
enceinte^F en béton^M
blindaje^M de hormigón^M
schermatura^F in calcestruzzo^M

蒸気排出口
steam outlet
Dampfauslass^M
sortie^F de la vapeur^F
salida^F de vapor^M
uscita^F del vapore^M

給水管
feedwater
Speisewasser^N
alimentation^F en eau^F
agua^F de alimentación^F
acqua^F di alimentazione^F

湿式セル
wet well
freies Containmentvolumen^N
enceinte^F humide
pozo^M
camera^F a umido^M

圧力抑制プール
condensation pool
Kondensationskühlwasserbecken^N
piscine^F de condensation^F
fosa^F de refrigeración^F del condensador^M
vasca^F di abbattimento^M della pressione^F

エネルギー

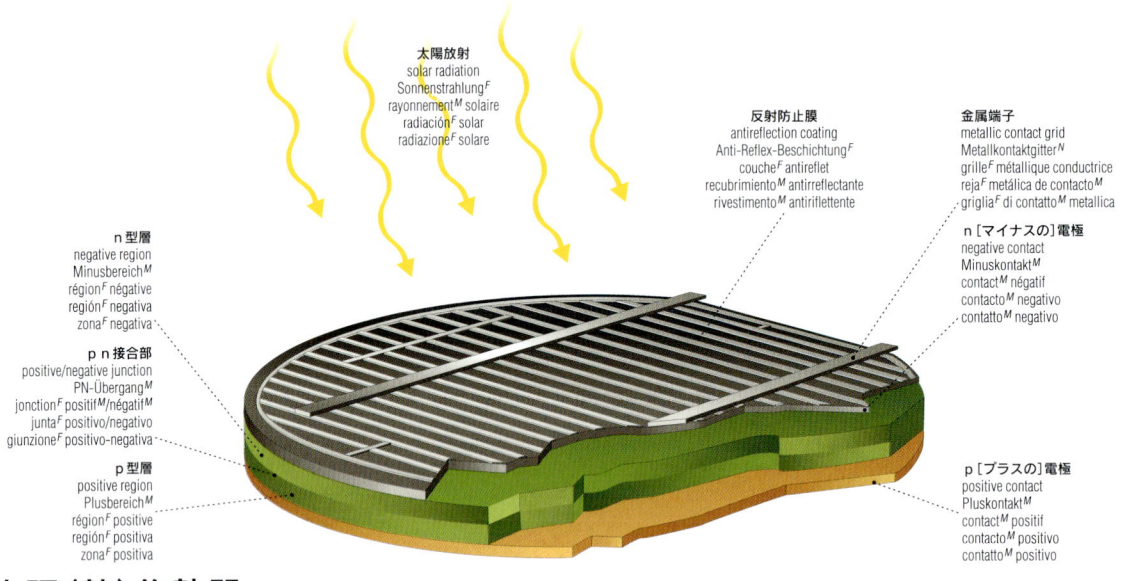

太陽エネルギー | SOLAR ENERGY
SONNENENERGIE | ÉNERGIE SOLAIRE | ENERGÍA SOLAR | ENERGIA SOLARE

太陽電池
solar cell | Solarzelle^F | photopile^F | célula^F solar | cella^F solare

太陽放射 — solar radiation / Sonnenstrahlung^F / rayonnement^M solaire / radiación^F solar / radiazione^F solare

反射防止膜 — antireflection coating / Anti-Reflex-Beschichtung^F / couche^F antireflet / recubrimiento^M antirreflectante / rivestimento^M antiriflettente

金属端子 — metallic contact grid / Metallkontaktgitter^N / grille^F métallique conductrice / reja^F metálica de contacto^M / griglia^F di contatto^M metallica

n 型層 — negative region / Minusbereich^M / région^F négative / región^F negativa / zona^F negativa

n [マイナスの] 電極 — negative contact / Minuskontakt^M / contact^M négatif / contacto^M negativo / contatto^M negativo

p n 接合部 — positive/negative junction / PN-Übergang^M / jonction^F positif/négatif^M / junta^F positivo/negativo / giunzione^F positivo-negativa

p 型層 — positive region / Plusbereich^M / région^F positive / región^F positiva / zona^F positiva

p [プラスの] 電極 — positive contact / Pluskontakt^M / contact^M positif / contacto^M positivo / contatto^M positivo

平板型太陽(熱)集熱器
flat-plate solar collector | Flachkollektor^M | capteur^M solaire plan | colector^M solar plano | collettore^M solare piatto

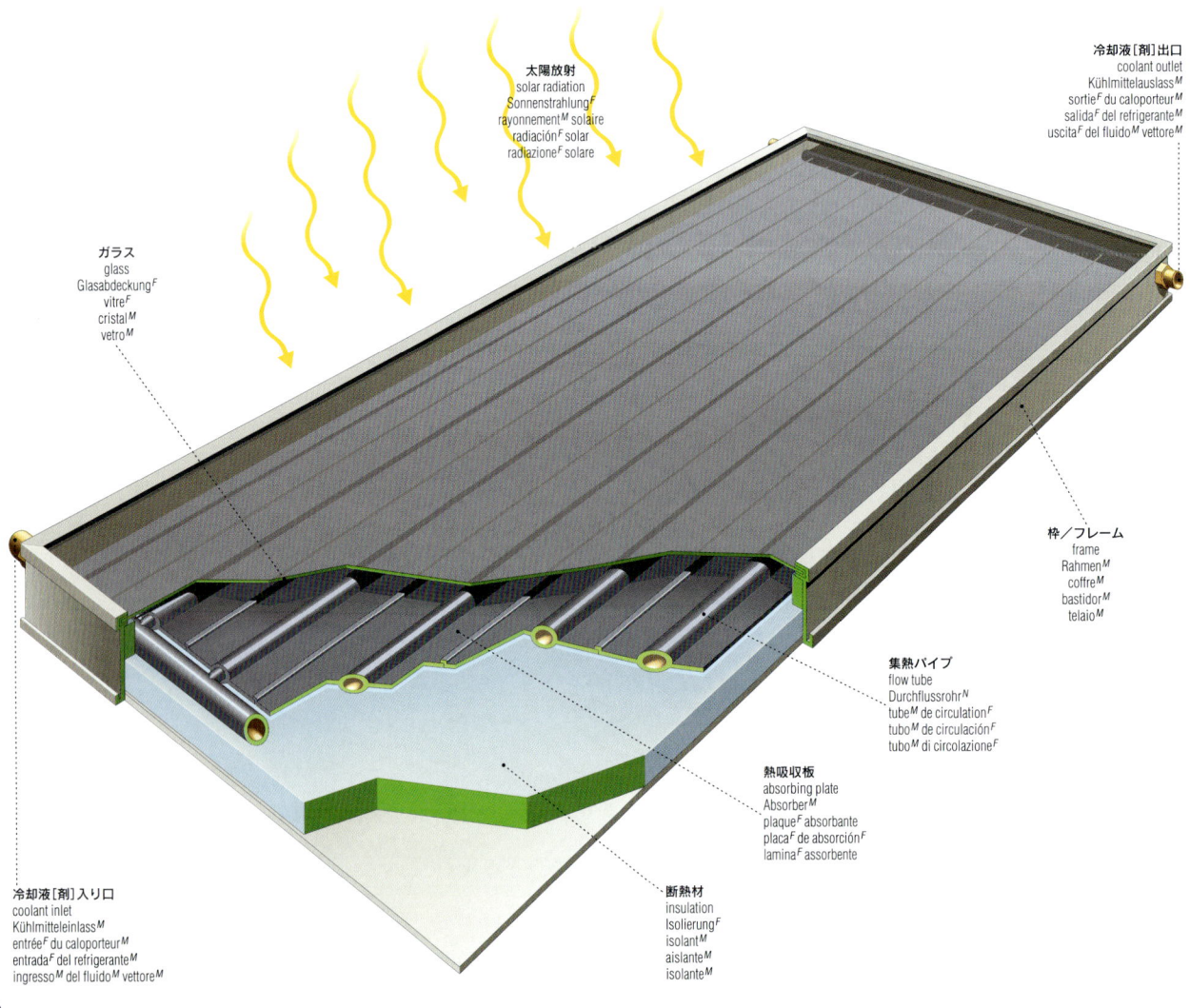

太陽放射 — solar radiation / Sonnenstrahlung^F / rayonnement^M solaire / radiación^F solar / radiazione^F solare

冷却液[剤]出口 — coolant outlet / Kühlmittelauslass^M / sortie^F du caloporteur^M / salida^F del refrigerante^M / uscita^F del fluido^M vettore

ガラス — glass / Glasabdeckung^F / vitre^F / cristal^M / vetro^M

枠／フレーム — frame / Rahmen^M / coffre^M / bastidor^M / telaio^M

集熱パイプ — flow tube / Durchflussrohr^N / tube^M de circulation^F / tubo^M de circulación^F / tubo^M di circolazione^F

熱吸収板 — absorbing plate / Absorber^M / plaque^F absorbante / placa^F de absorción^F / lamina^F assorbente

断熱材 — insulation / Isolierung^F / isolant^M / aislante^M / isolante^M

冷却液[剤]入り口 — coolant inlet / Kühlmitteleinlass^M / entrée^F du caloporteur^M / entrada^F del refrigerante^M / ingresso^M del fluido^M vettore

太陽エネルギー | SOLAR ENERGY
SONNENENERGIE | ÉNERGIE SOLAIRE | ENERGÍA SOLAR | ENERGIA SOLARE

太陽電池の仕組み

solar-cell system | Solarzellensystem^N | circuit^M de photopiles^F | sistema^M de células^F solares | sistema^M a celle^F solari

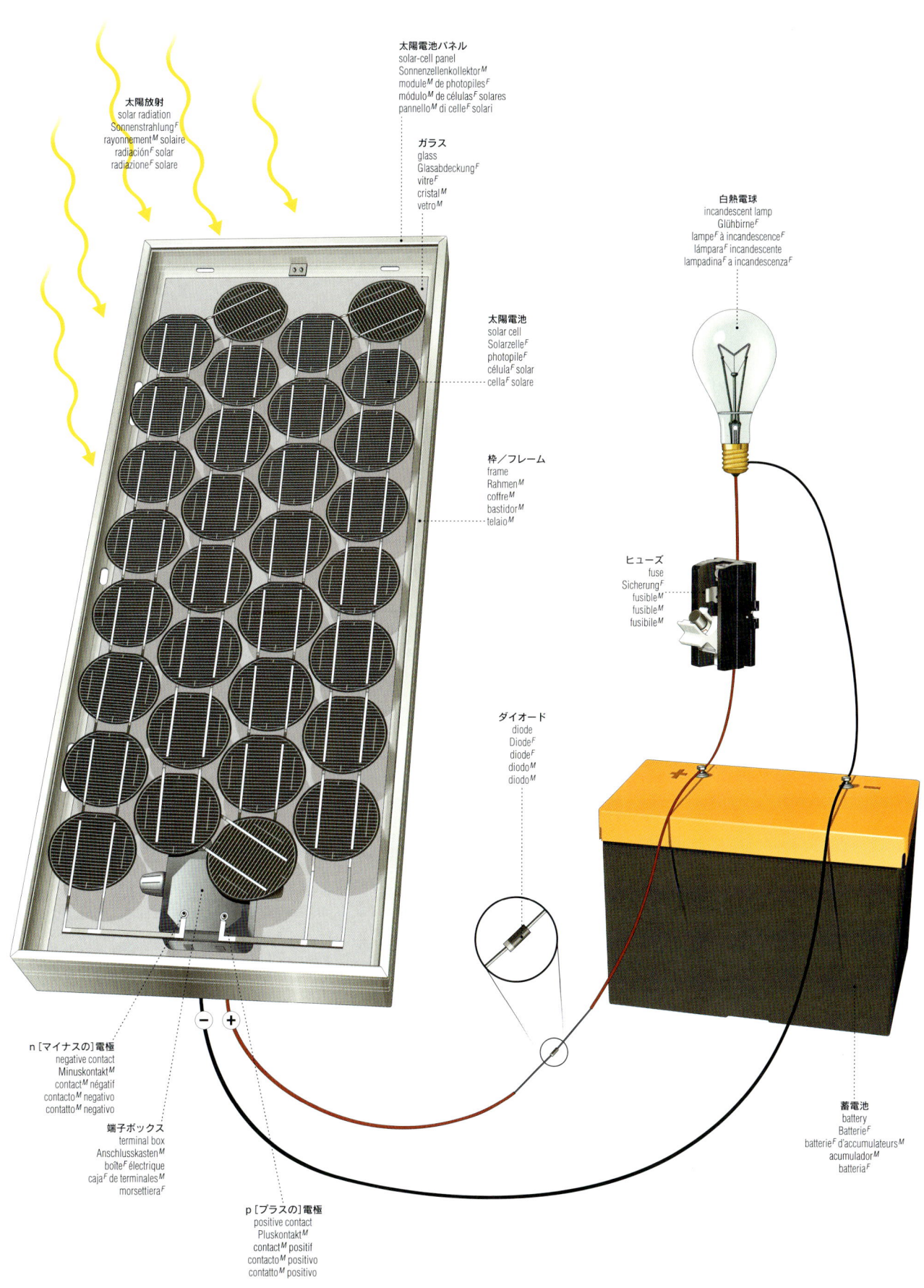

太陽電池パネル
solar-cell panel
Sonnenzellenkollektor^M
module^M de photopiles^F
módulo^M de células^F solares
pannello^M di celle^F solari

太陽放射
solar radiation
Sonnenstrahlung^F
rayonnement^M solaire
radiación^F solar
radiazione^F solare

ガラス
glass
Glasabdeckung^F
vitre^F
cristal^M
vetro^M

白熱電球
incandescent lamp
Glühbirne^F
lampe^F à incandescence^F
lámpara^F incandescente
lampadina^F a incandescenza^F

太陽電池
solar cell
Solarzelle^F
photopile^F
célula^F solar
cella^F solare

枠／フレーム
frame
Rahmen^M
coffre^M
bastidor^M
telaio^M

ヒューズ
fuse
Sicherung^F
fusible^M
fusible^M
fusibile^M

ダイオード
diode
Diode^F
diode^F
diodo^M
diodo^M

n［マイナスの］電極
negative contact
Minuskontakt^M
contact^M négatif
contacto^M negativo
contatto^M negativo

端子ボックス
terminal box
Anschlusskasten^M
boîte^F électrique
caja^F de terminales^F
morsettiera^F

蓄電池
battery
Batterie^F
batterie^F d'accumulateurs^M
acumulador^M
batteria^F

p［プラスの］電極
positive contact
Pluskontakt^M
contact^M positif
contacto^M positivo
contatto^M positivo

エネルギー

673

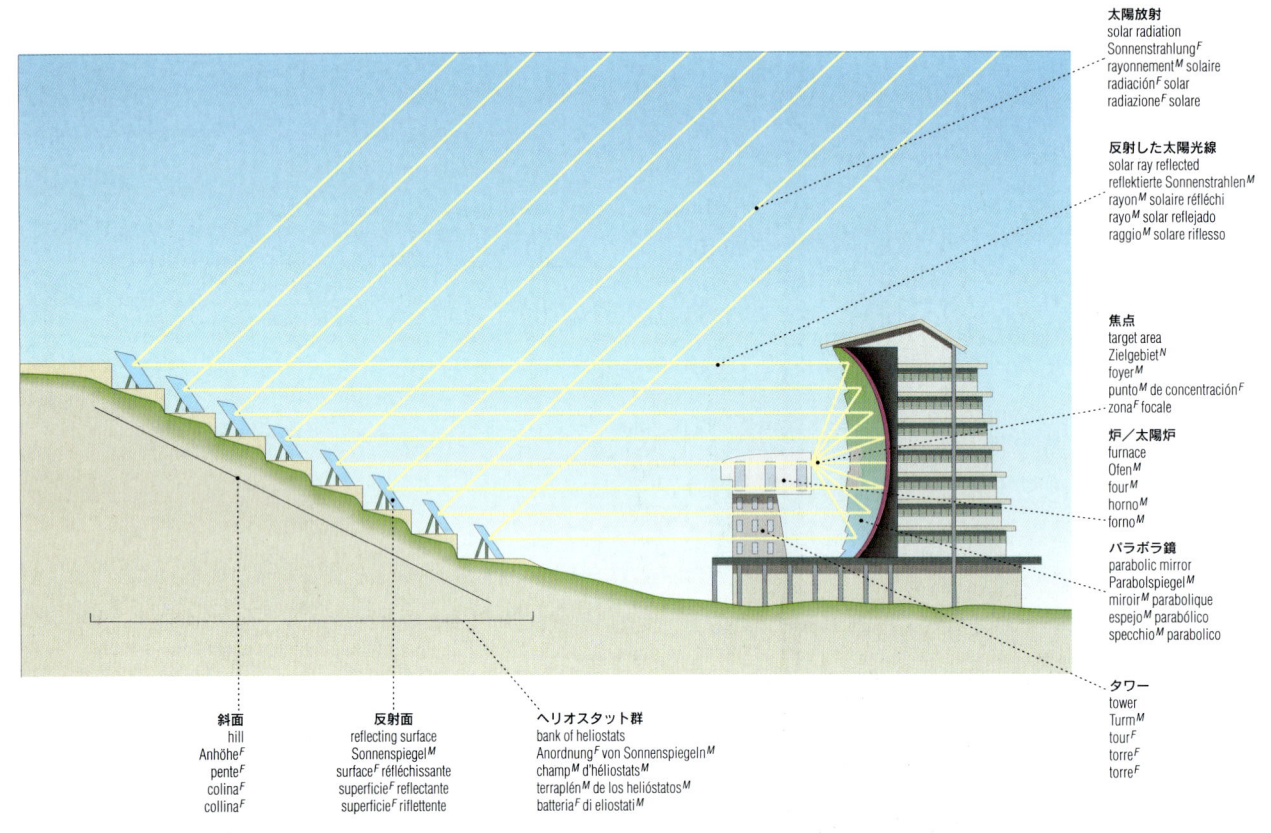

太陽エネルギー | SOLAR ENERGY
SONNENENERGIE | ÉNERGIE SOLAIRE | ENERGÍA SOLAR | ENERGIA SOLARE

太陽炉
solar furnace | Sonnenofen^M | four^M solaire | horno^M solar | forno^M solare

日本語 | 英語 | ドイツ語 | フランス語 | スペイン語 | イタリア語

太陽放射
solar radiation
Sonnenstrahlung^F
rayonnement^M solaire
radiación^F solar
radiazione^F solare

反射した太陽光線
solar ray reflected
reflektierte Sonnenstrahlen^M
rayon^M solaire réfléchi
rayo^M solar reflejado
raggio^M solare riflesso

焦点
target area
Zielgebiet^N
foyer^M
punto^M de concentración^F
zona^F focale

炉／太陽炉
furnace
Ofen^M
four^M
horno^M
forno^M

パラボラ鏡
parabolic mirror
Parabolspiegel^M
miroir^M parabolique
espejo^M parabólico
specchio^M parabolico

タワー
tower
Turm^M
tour^F
torre^F
torre^F

斜面
hill
Anhöhe^F
pente^F
colina^F
collina^F

反射面
reflecting surface
Sonnenspiegel^M
surface^F réfléchissante
superficie^F reflectante
superficie^F riflettente

ヘリオスタット群
bank of heliostats
Anordnung^F von Sonnenspiegeln^M
champ^M d'héliostats^M
terraplén^M de los helióstatos^M
batteria^F di eliostati^M

太陽エネルギー発電
production of electricity from solar energy | Elektrizitätserzeugung^F aus Sonnenenergie^F | production^F d'électricité^F par énergie^F solaire | producción^F de electricidad^F por energía^F solar | produzione^F di elettricità^F da energia^F solare

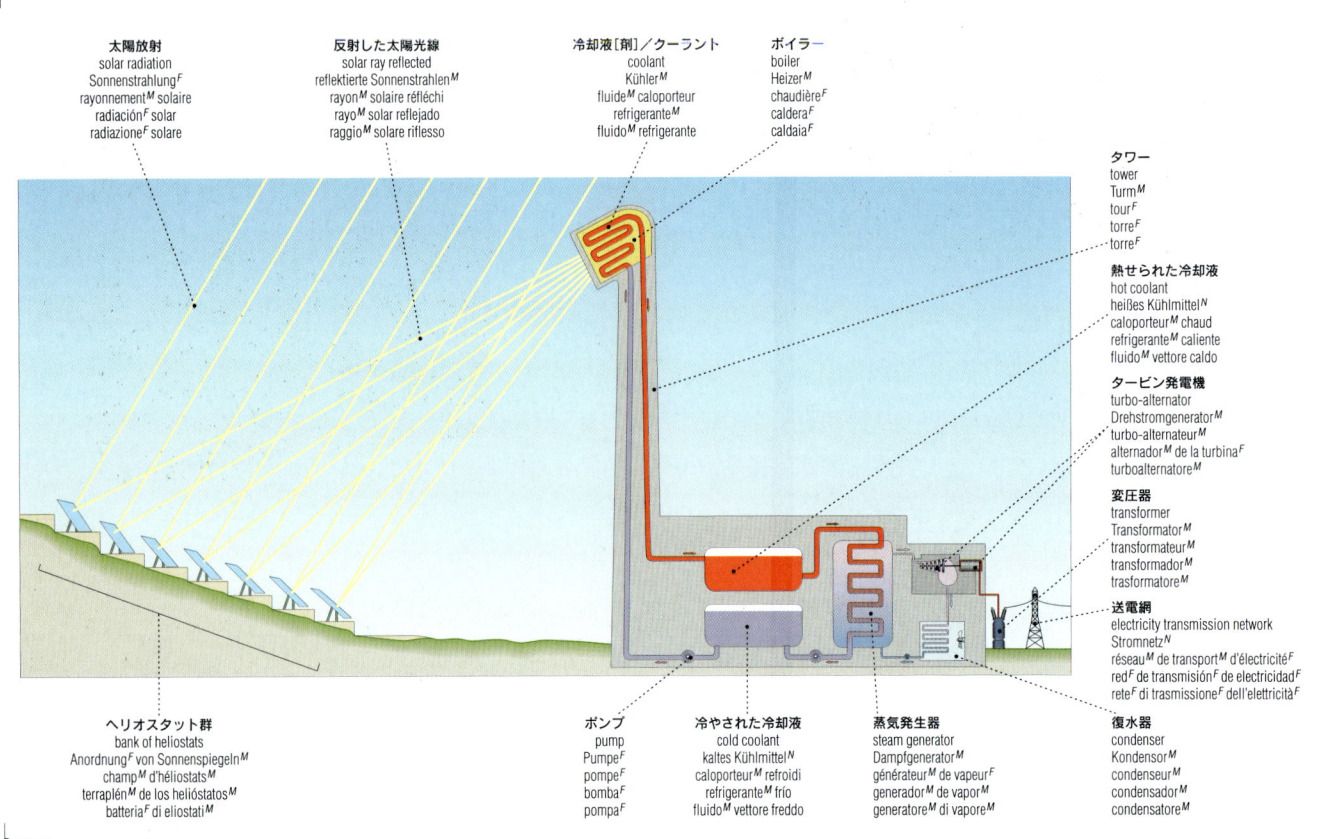

太陽放射
solar radiation
Sonnenstrahlung^F
rayonnement^M solaire
radiación^F solar
radiazione^F solare

反射した太陽光線
solar ray reflected
reflektierte Sonnenstrahlen^M
rayon^M solaire réfléchi
rayo^M solar reflejado
raggio^M solare riflesso

冷却液[剤]／クーラント
coolant
Kühler^M
fluide^M caloporteur
refrigerante^M
fluido^M refrigerante

ボイラー
boiler
Heizer^M
chaudière^F
caldera^F
caldaia^F

タワー
tower
Turm^M
tour^F
torre^F
torre^F

熱せられた冷却液
hot coolant
heißes Kühlmittel^N
caloporteur^M chaud
refrigerante^M caliente
fluido^M vettore caldo

タービン発電機
turbo-alternator
Drehstromgenerator^M
turbo-alternateur^M
alternador^M de la turbina^F
turboalternatore^M

変圧器
transformer
Transformator^M
transformateur^M
transformador^M
trasformatore^M

送電網
electricity transmission network
Stromnetz^N
réseau^M de transport^M d'électricité^F
red^F de transmisión^F de electricidad^F
rete^F di trasmissione^F dell'elettricità^F

ヘリオスタット群
bank of heliostats
Anordnung^F von Sonnenspiegeln^M
champ^M d'héliostats^M
terraplén^M de los helióstatos^M
batteria^F di eliostati^M

ポンプ
pump
Pumpe^F
pompe^F
bomba^F
pompa^F

冷やされた冷却液
cold coolant
kaltes Kühlmittel^N
caloporteur^M refroidi
refrigerante^M frío
fluido^M vettore freddo

蒸気発生器
steam generator
Dampfgenerator^M
générateur^M de vapeur^F
generador^M de vapor^M
generatore^M di vapore^M

復水器
condenser
Kondensor^M
condenseur^M
condensador^M
condensatore^M

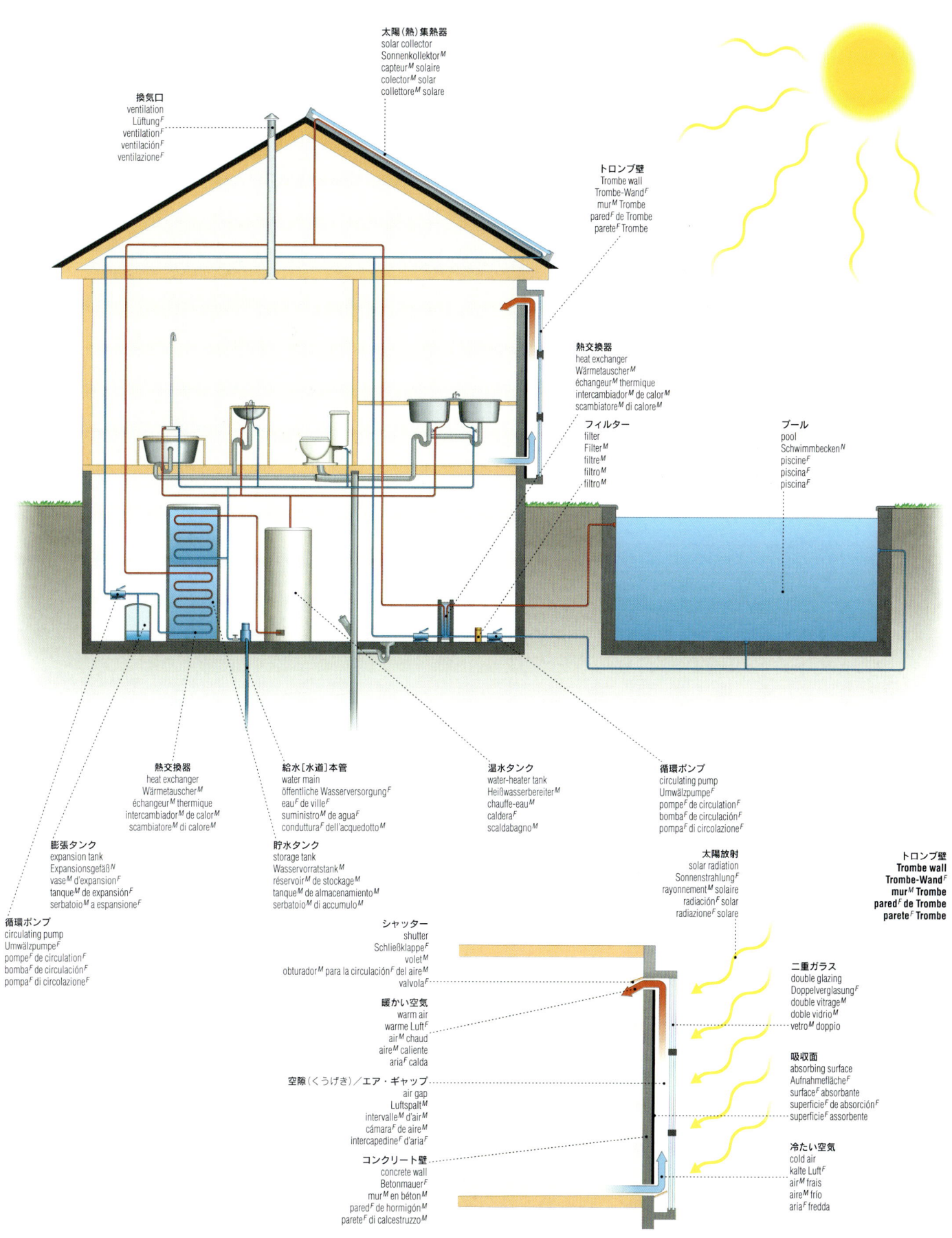

太陽エネルギー | SOLAR ENERGY
SONNENENERGIE | ÉNERGIE SOLAIRE | ENERGÍA SOLAR | ENERGIA SOLARE

ソーラー・ハウス

solar house | Solarhaus[N] | maison[F] solaire | casa[F] solar | casa[F] solare

太陽(熱)集熱器
solar collector
Sonnenkollektor[M]
capteur[M] solaire
colector[M] solar
collettore[M] solare

換気口
ventilation
Lüftung[F]
ventilation[F]
ventilación[F]
ventilazione[F]

トロンブ壁
Trombe wall
Trombe-Wand[F]
mur[M] Trombe
pared[F] de Trombe
parete[F] Trombe

熱交換器
heat exchanger
Wärmetauscher[M]
échangeur[M] thermique
intercambiador[M] de calor[M]
scambiatore[M] di calore[M]

フィルター
filter
Filter[M]
filtre[M]
filtro[M]
filtro[M]

プール
pool
Schwimmbecken[N]
piscine[F]
piscina[F]
piscina[F]

熱交換器
heat exchanger
Wärmetauscher[M]
échangeur[M] thermique
intercambiador[M] de calor[M]
scambiatore[M] di calore[M]

給水[水道]本管
water main
öffentliche Wasserversorgung[F]
eau[F] de ville[F]
suministro[M] de agua[F]
conduttura[F] dell'acquedotto[M]

温水タンク
water-heater tank
Heißwasserbereiter[M]
chauffe-eau[M]
caldera[F]
scaldabagno[M]

循環ポンプ
circulating pump
Umwälzpumpe[F]
pompe[F] de circulation[F]
bomba[F] de circulación[F]
pompa[F] di circolazione[F]

膨張タンク
expansion tank
Expansionsgefäß[N]
vase[M] d'expansion[F]
tanque[M] de expansión[F]
serbatoio[M] a espansione[F]

貯水タンク
storage tank
Wasservorratstank[M]
réservoir[M] de stockage[M]
tanque[M] de almacenamiento[M]
serbatoio[M] di accumulo[M]

太陽放射
solar radiation
Sonnenstrahlung[F]
rayonnement[M] solaire
radiación[F] solar
radiazione[F] solare

トロンブ壁
Trombe wall
Trombe-Wand[F]
mur[M] Trombe
pared[F] de Trombe
parete[F] Trombe

循環ポンプ
circulating pump
Umwälzpumpe[F]
pompe[F] de circulation[F]
bomba[F] de circulación[F]
pompa[F] di circolazione[F]

シャッター
shutter
Schließklappe[F]
volet[M]
obturador[M] para la circulación[F] del aire[M]
valvola[F]

暖かい空気
warm air
warme Luft[F]
air[M] chaud
aire[M] caliente
aria[F] calda

二重ガラス
double glazing
Doppelverglasung[F]
double vitrage[M]
doble vidrio[M]
vetro[M] doppio

吸収面
absorbing surface
Aufnahmefläche[F]
surface[F] absorbante
superficie[F] de absorción[F]
superficie[F] assorbente

空隙(くうげき)／エア・ギャップ
air gap
Luftspalt[M]
intervalle[M] d'air[M]
cámara[F] de aire[M]
intercapedine[F] d'aria[F]

冷たい空気
cold air
kalte Luft[F]
air[M] frais
aire[M] frío
aria[F] fredda

コンクリート壁
concrete wall
Betonmauer[F]
mur[M] en béton[M]
pared[F] de hormigón[M]
parete[F] di calcestruzzo[M]

エネルギー

風力エネルギー | WIND ENERGY
WINDENERGIE | ÉNERGIE ÉOLIENNE | ENERGÍA EÓLICA | ENERGIA EOLICA

風車

日本語 | 英語 | ドイツ語 | フランス語 | スペイン語 | イタリア語

windmill | Windmühle^F | moulin^M à vent^M | molino^M de viento^M | mulino^M a vento^M

塔形[型]風車
tower mill
Turmwindmühle^F
moulin^M tour^F
molino^M de torre^F
mulino^M a torre^F

キャップ
cap
Windmühlenhaube^F
calotte^F
casquete^M
calotta^F

回転翼／ローター
rotor
Rotor^M
rotor^M
rotor^M
rotore^M

回転式風車
post mill
Bockmühle^F
moulin^M pivot^M
molino^M de plataforma^F giratoria
mulino^M a pilastro^M

横木／ストック
stock
Windrute^F
bras^M
larguero^M
braccio^M

車翼／翼板／羽根／帆
sail
Flügel^M
aile^F
aspa^F
pala^F

後部支柱
tail pole
Stert^M
queue^F
puntal^M trasero
timone^M

(方向舵)尾翼
fantail
Seitenrad^N
gouvernail^M
molinete^M
pala^F ausiliaria

ヘルマス
hemlath
Saumlatte^F
cotret^M
lama^F
barra^F

風車軸／シャフト
windshaft
Welle^F
arbre^M
eje^M de las aspas^F
albero^M

帆布
sail cloth
Segeltuchbespannung^F
voile^F
lona^F
tela^F

帆骨
sailbar
Segelstange^F
latte^F
travesaño^M
listello^M

床(部)
floor
Sockelgeschoß^N
étage^M
piso^M
piano^M

回廊
gallery
Galerie^F
galerie^F
corredor^M
balcone^M

塔
tower
Turm^M
tour^F
torre^F
torre^F

フレーム
frame
Rahmen^M
cadre^M
armazón^M
telaio^M

回転軸
post
Königsbaum^M
pivot^M
soporte^M de la plataforma^F
pilastro^M

踏み段
steps
Treppe^F
escalier^M
escalera^F
scala^F

風力タービンと発電

wind turbines and electricity production | Windkraftwerke^N und Elektrizitätserzeugung^F | éoliennes^F et production^F d'électricité^F | turbinas^F de viento^M y producción^F eléctrica | turbine^F eoliche e produzione^F di elettricità^F

垂直軸型風力タービン
vertical-axis wind turbine
Windkraftwerk mit vertikaler Achse^F
éolienne^F à axe^M vertical
turbina^F de viento^M de eje^M vertical
turbina^F ad asse^M verticale

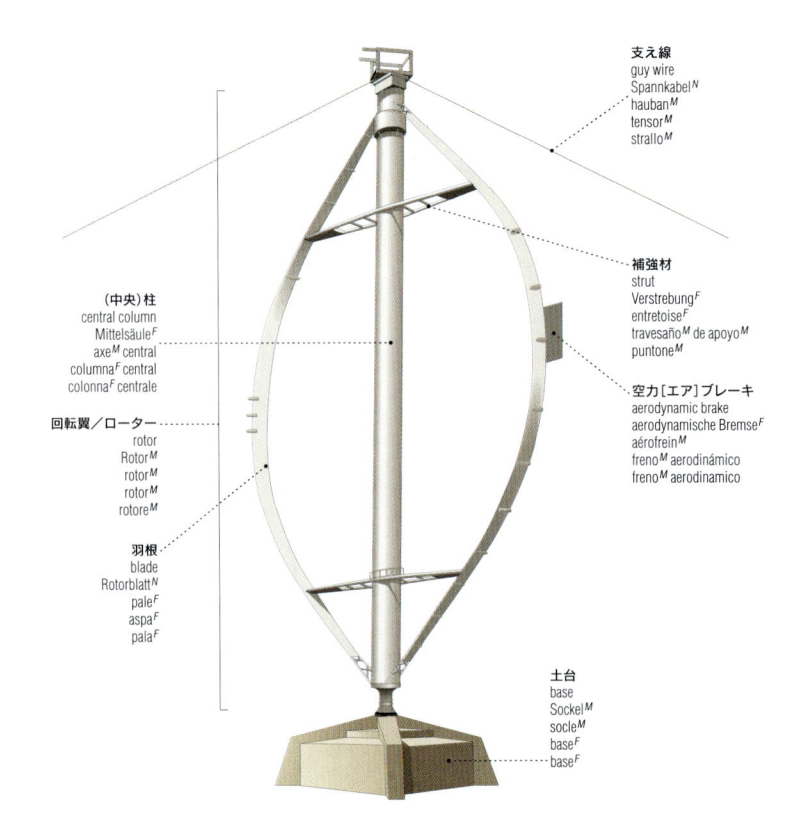

支え線
guy wire
Spannkabel^N
hauban^M
tensor^M
strallo^M

補強材
strut
Verstrebung^F
entretoise^F
travesaño^M de apoyo^M
puntone^M

(中央)柱
central column
Mittelsäule^F
axe^M central
columna^F central
colonna^F centrale

空力[エア]ブレーキ
aerodynamic brake
aerodynamische Bremse^F
aérofrein^M
freno^M aerodinámico
freno^M aerodinamico

回転翼／ローター
rotor
Rotor^M
rotor^M
rotor^M
rotore^M

羽根
blade
Rotorblatt^N
pale^F
aspa^F
pala^F

土台
base
Sockel^M
socle^M
base^F
base^F

エネルギー

676

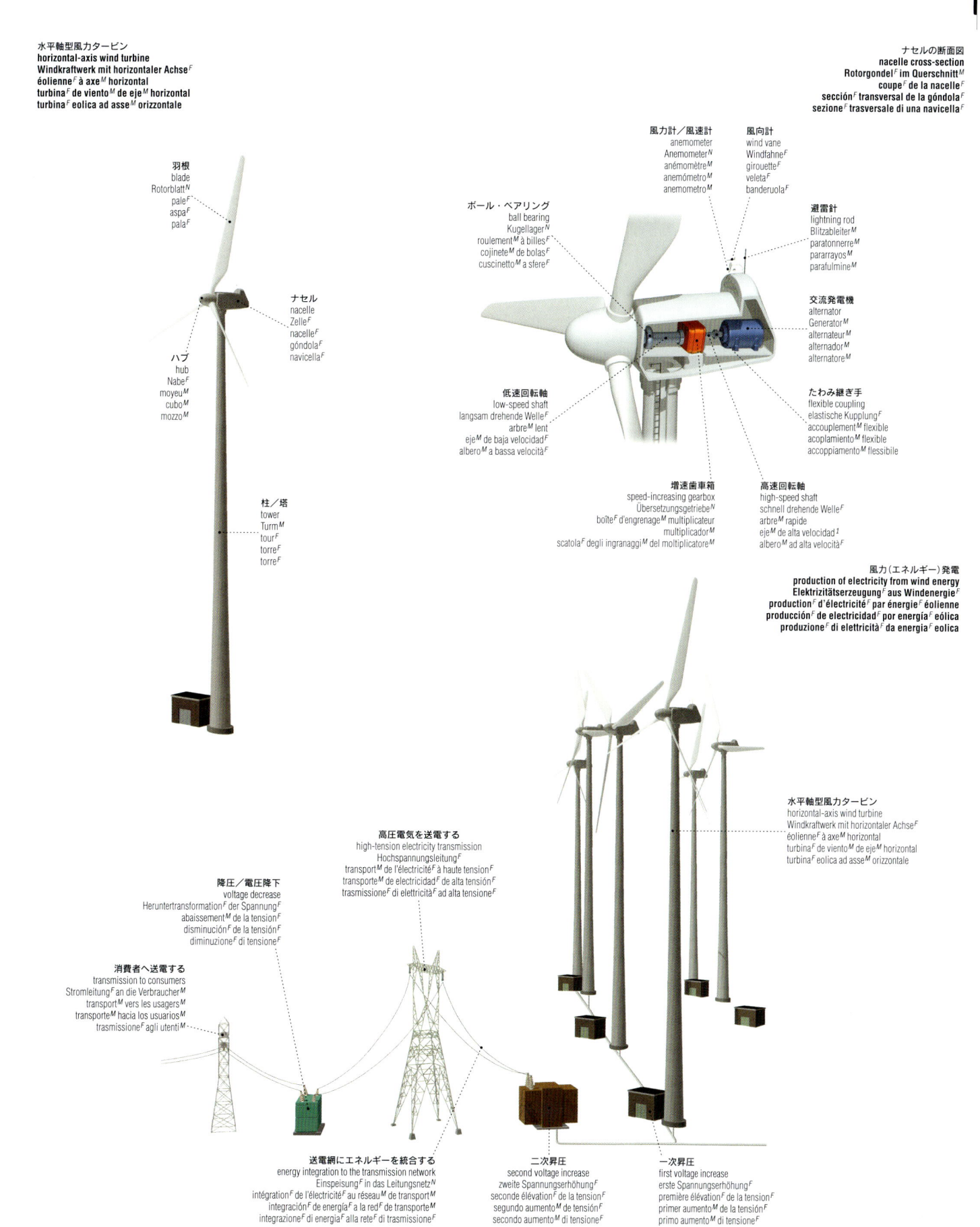

風力エネルギー | WIND ENERGY
WINDENERGIE | ÉNERGIE ÉOLIENNE | ENERGÍA EÓLICA | ENERGIA EOLICA

風力タービンと発電

水平軸型風力タービン
horizontal-axis wind turbine
Windkraftwerk mit horizontaler Achse^F
éolienne^F à axe^M horizontal
turbina^F de viento^M de eje^M horizontal
turbina^F eolica ad asse^M orizzontale

ナセルの断面図
nacelle cross-section
Rotorgondel^F im Querschnitt^M
coupe^F de la nacelle^F
sección^F transversal de la góndola^F
sezione^F trasversale di una navicella^F

羽根
blade
Rotorblatt^N
pale^F
aspa^F
pala^F

風力計／風速計
anemometer
Anemometer^N
anémomètre^M
anemómetro^M
anemometro^M

風向計
wind vane
Windfahne^F
girouette^F
veleta^F
banderuola^F

ボール・ベアリング
ball bearing
Kugellager^N
roulement^M à billes^F
cojinete^F de bolas^F
cuscinetto^M a sfere^F

避雷針
lightning rod
Blitzableiter^M
paratonnerre^M
pararrayos^M
parafulmine^M

ナセル
nacelle
Zelle^F
nacelle^F
góndola^F
navicella^F

交流発電機
alternator
Generator^M
alternateur^M
alternador^M
alternatore^M

ハブ
hub
Nabe^F
moyeu^M
cubo^M
mozzo^M

たわみ継ぎ手
flexible coupling
elastische Kupplung^F
accouplement^M flexible
acoplamiento^M flexible
accoppiamento^M flessibile

低速回転軸
low-speed shaft
langsam drehende Welle^F
arbre^M lent
eje^M de baja velocidad^F
albero^M a bassa velocità^F

増速歯車箱
speed-increasing gearbox
Übersetzungsgetriebe^N
boîte^F d'engrenage^M multiplicateur
multiplicador^M
scatola^F degli ingranaggi^M del moltiplicatore^M

高速回転軸
high-speed shaft
schnell drehende Welle^F
arbre^M rapide
eje^M de alta velocidad^F
albero^M ad alta velocità^F

柱／塔
tower
Turm^M
tour^F
torre^F
torre^F

風力（エネルギー）発電
production of electricity from wind energy
Elektrizitätserzeugung^F aus Windenergie^F
production^F d'électricité^F par énergie^F éolienne
producción^F de electricidad^F por energía^F eólica
produzione^F di elettricità^F da energia^F eolica

水平軸型風力タービン
horizontal-axis wind turbine
Windkraftwerk mit horizontaler Achse^F
éolienne^F à axe^M horizontal
turbina^F de viento^M de eje^M horizontal
turbina^F eolica ad asse^M orizzontale

高圧電気を送電する
high-tension electricity transmission
Hochspannungsleitung^F
transport^M de l'électricité^F à haute tension^F
transporte^M de electricidad^F de alta tensión^F
trasmissione^F di elettricità^F ad alta tensione^F

降圧／電圧降下
voltage decrease
Heruntertransformation^F der Spannung^F
abaissement^M de la tension^F
disminución^F de la tensión^F
diminuzione^F di tensione^F

消費者へ送電する
transmission to consumers
Stromleitung^F an die Verbraucher^M
transport^M vers les usagers^M
transporte^M hacia los usuarios^M
trasmissione^F agli utenti^M

送電網にエネルギーを統合する
energy integration to the transmission network
Einspeisung^F in das Leitungsnetz^N
intégration^F de l'électricité^F au réseau^M de transport^M
integración^F de energía^F a la red^F de transporte^M
integrazione^F di energia^F alla rete^F di trasmissione^F

二次昇圧
second voltage increase
zweite Spannungserhöhung^F
seconde élévation^F de la tension^F
segundo aumento^M de tensión^F
secondo aumento^M di tensione^F

一次昇圧
first voltage increase
erste Spannungserhöhung^F
première élévation^F de la tension^F
primer aumento^M de la tensión^F
primo aumento^M di tensione^F

エネルギー

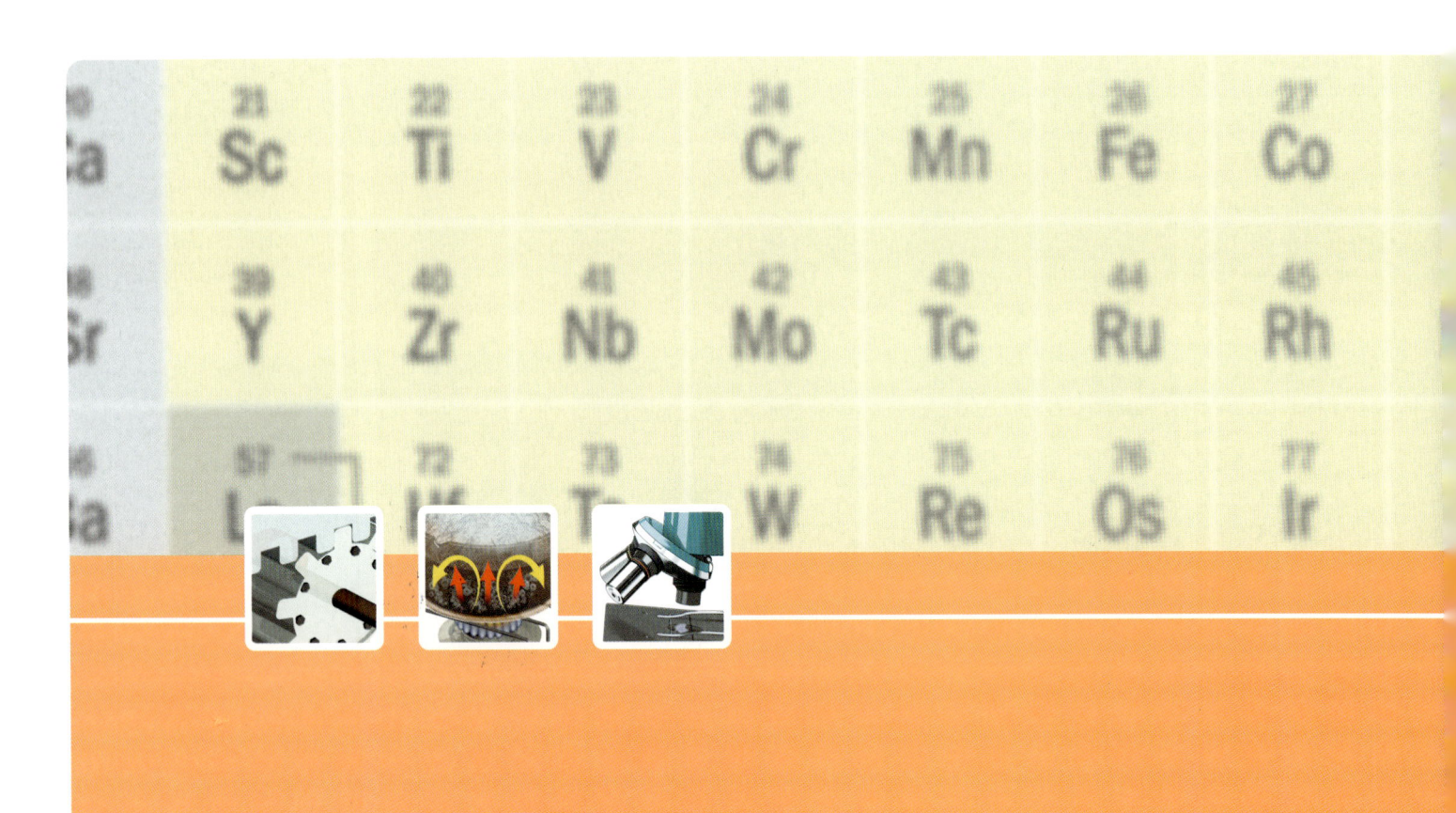

680	686	687
化学	物理：力学	物理：電気学と磁気学
680 物質	686 歯車装置	687 磁気
682 化学元素	686 定滑車と動滑車の組み合わせ	687 並列電気回路
684 化学記号	686 てこ	688 発電機
685 実験器具		689 乾電池
		689 電子工学／エレクトロニクス

科学

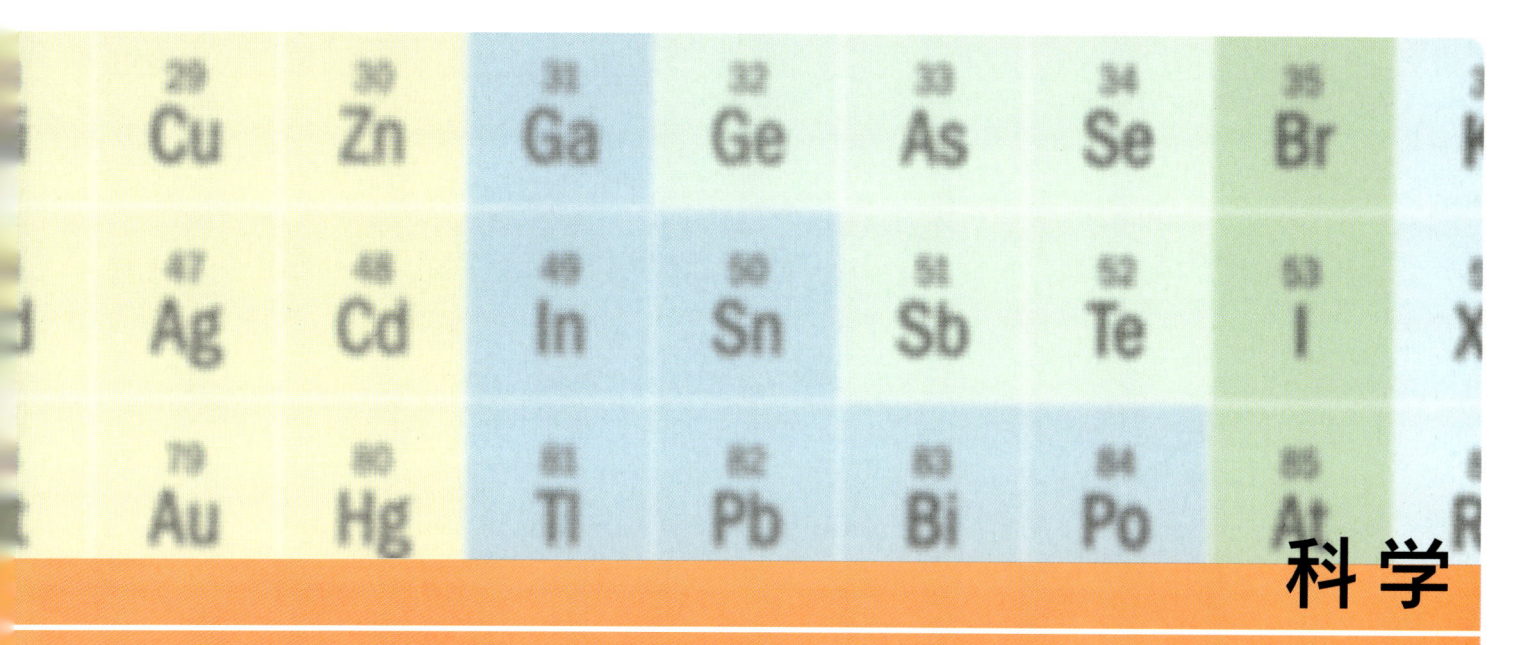

SCIENCE | WISSENSCHAFT | SCIENCE | CIENCIA | SCIENZA

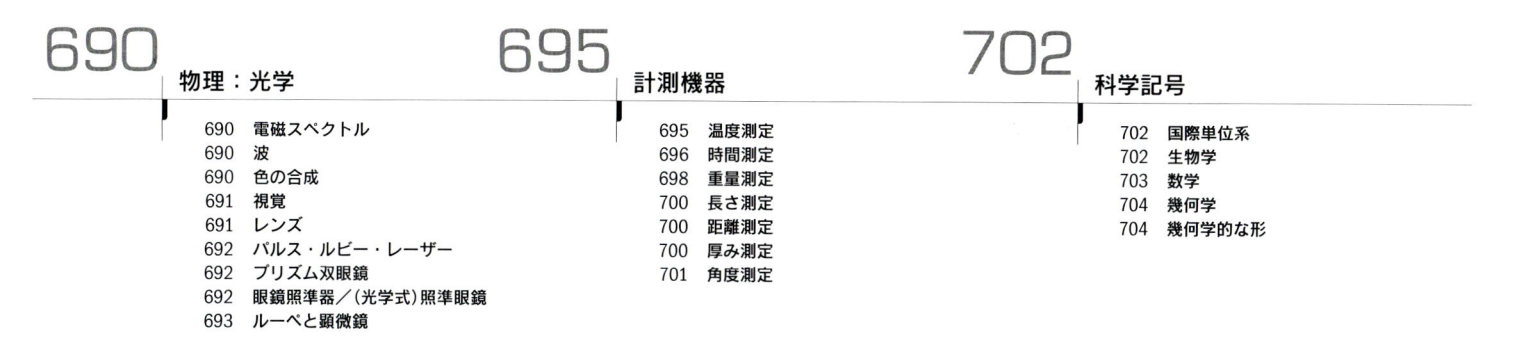

690 物理：光学

- 690 電磁スペクトル
- 690 波
- 690 色の合成
- 691 視覚
- 691 レンズ
- 692 パルス・ルビー・レーザー
- 692 プリズム双眼鏡
- 692 眼鏡照準器／（光学式）照準眼鏡
- 693 ルーペと顕微鏡

695 計測機器

- 695 温度測定
- 696 時間測定
- 698 重量測定
- 700 長さ測定
- 700 距離測定
- 700 厚み測定
- 701 角度測定

702 科学記号

- 702 国際単位系
- 702 生物学
- 703 数学
- 704 幾何学
- 704 幾何学的な形

化学 | CHEMISTRY
CHEMIE | CHIMIE | QUÍMICA | CHIMICA

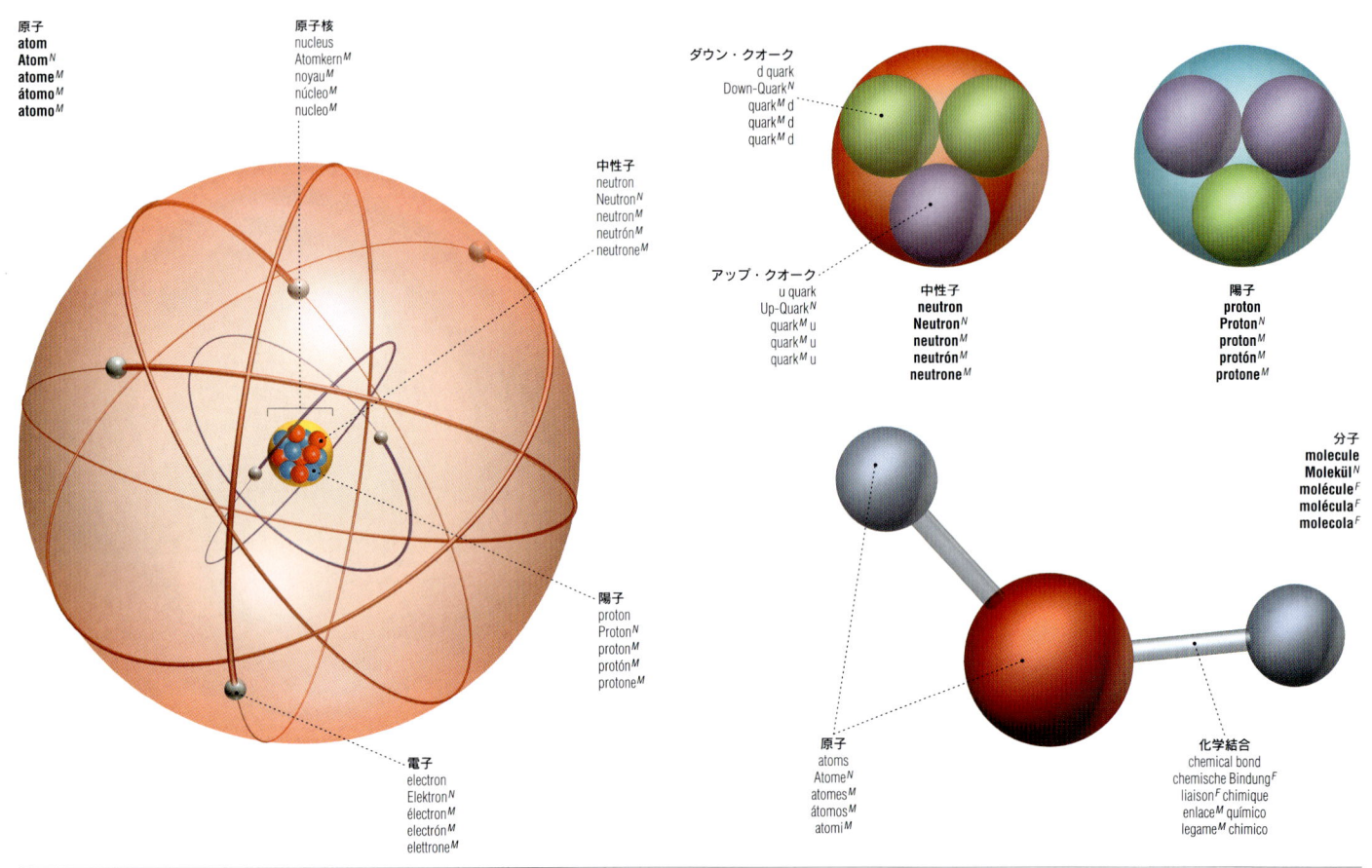

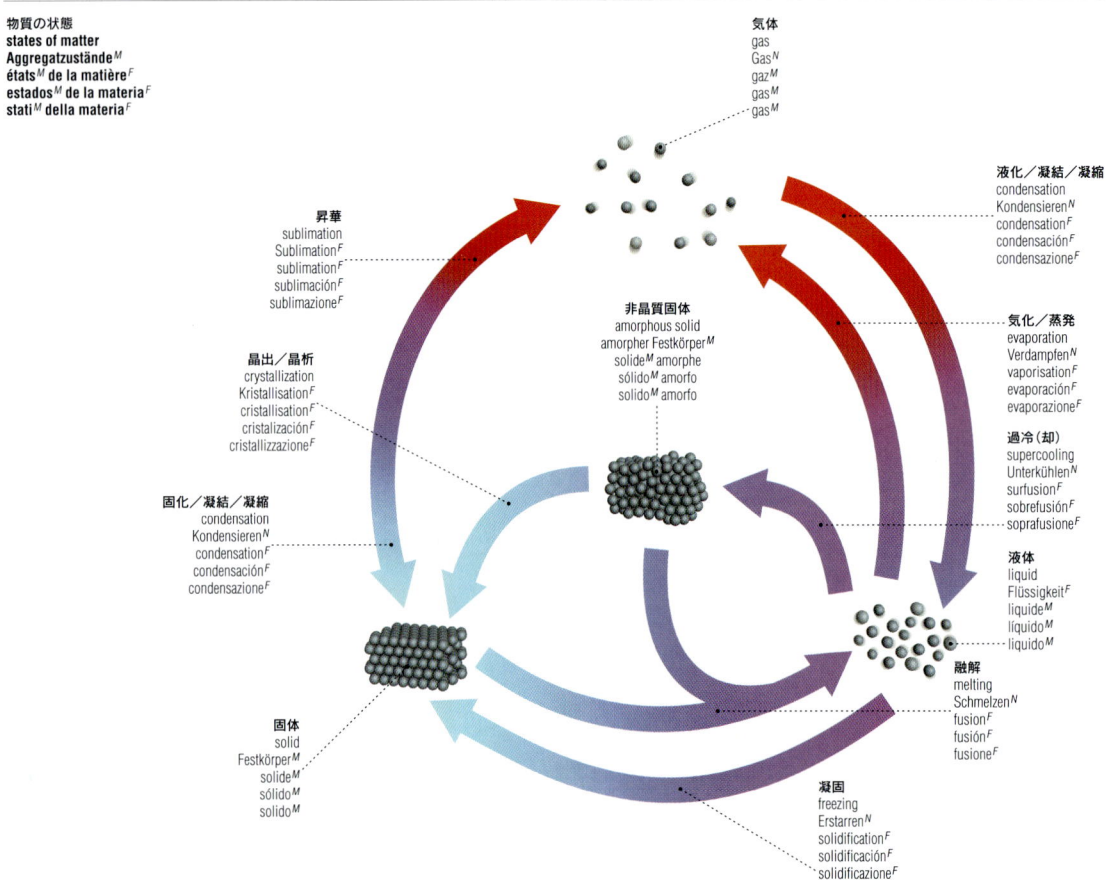

物質
matter | Materie^F | matière^F | materia^F | materia^F

日本語 | 英語 | ドイツ語 | フランス語 | スペイン語 | イタリア語

原子
atom
Atom^N
atome^M
átomo^M
atomo^M

原子核
nucleus
Atomkern^M
noyau^M
núcleo^M
nucleo^M

中性子
neutron
Neutron^N
neutron^M
neutrón^M
neutrone^M

ダウン・クオーク
d quark
Down-Quark^N
quark^M d
quark^M d
quark^M d

アップ・クオーク
u quark
Up-Quark^N
quark^M u
quark^M u
quark^M u

中性子
neutron
Neutron^N
neutron^M
neutrón^M
neutrone^M

陽子
proton
Proton^N
proton^M
protón^M
protone^M

陽子
proton
Proton^N
proton^M
protón^M
protone^M

分子
molecule
Molekül^N
molécule^F
molécula^F
molecola^F

電子
electron
Elektron^N
électron^M
electrón^M
elettrone^M

原子
atoms
Atome^N
atomes^M
átomos^M
atomi^M

化学結合
chemical bond
chemische Bindung^F
liaison^F chimique
enlace^M químico
legame^M chimico

物質の状態
states of matter
Aggregatzustände^M
états^M de la matière^F
estados^M de la materia^F
stati^M della materia^F

気体
gas
Gas^N
gaz^M
gas^M
gas^M

昇華
sublimation
Sublimation^F
sublimation^F
sublimación^F
sublimazione^F

液化／凝結／凝縮
condensation
Kondensieren^N
condensation^F
condensación^F
condensazione^F

非晶質固体
amorphous solid
amorpher Festkörper^M
solide^M amorphe
sólido^M amorfo
solido^M amorfo

気化／蒸発
evaporation
Verdampfen^N
vaporisation^F
evaporación^F
evaporazione^F

晶出／晶析
crystallization
Kristallisation^F
cristallisation^F
cristalización^F
cristallizzazione^F

過冷(却)
supercooling
Unterkühlen^N
surfusion^F
sobrefusión^F
soprafusione^F

固化／凝結／凝縮
condensation
Kondensieren^N
condensation^F
condensación^F
condensazione^F

液体
liquid
Flüssigkeit^F
liquide^M
líquido^M
liquido^M

融解
melting
Schmelzen^N
fusion^F
fusión^F
fusione^F

固体
solid
Festkörper^M
solide^M
sólido^M
solido^M

凝固
freezing
Erstarren^N
solidification^F
solidificación^F
solidificazione^F

科学

化学 | CHEMISTRY
CHEMIE | CHIMIE | QUÍMICA | CHIMICA

物質

核分裂
nuclear fission
Kernspaltung^F
fission^F nucléaire
fisión^M nuclear
fissione^F nucleare

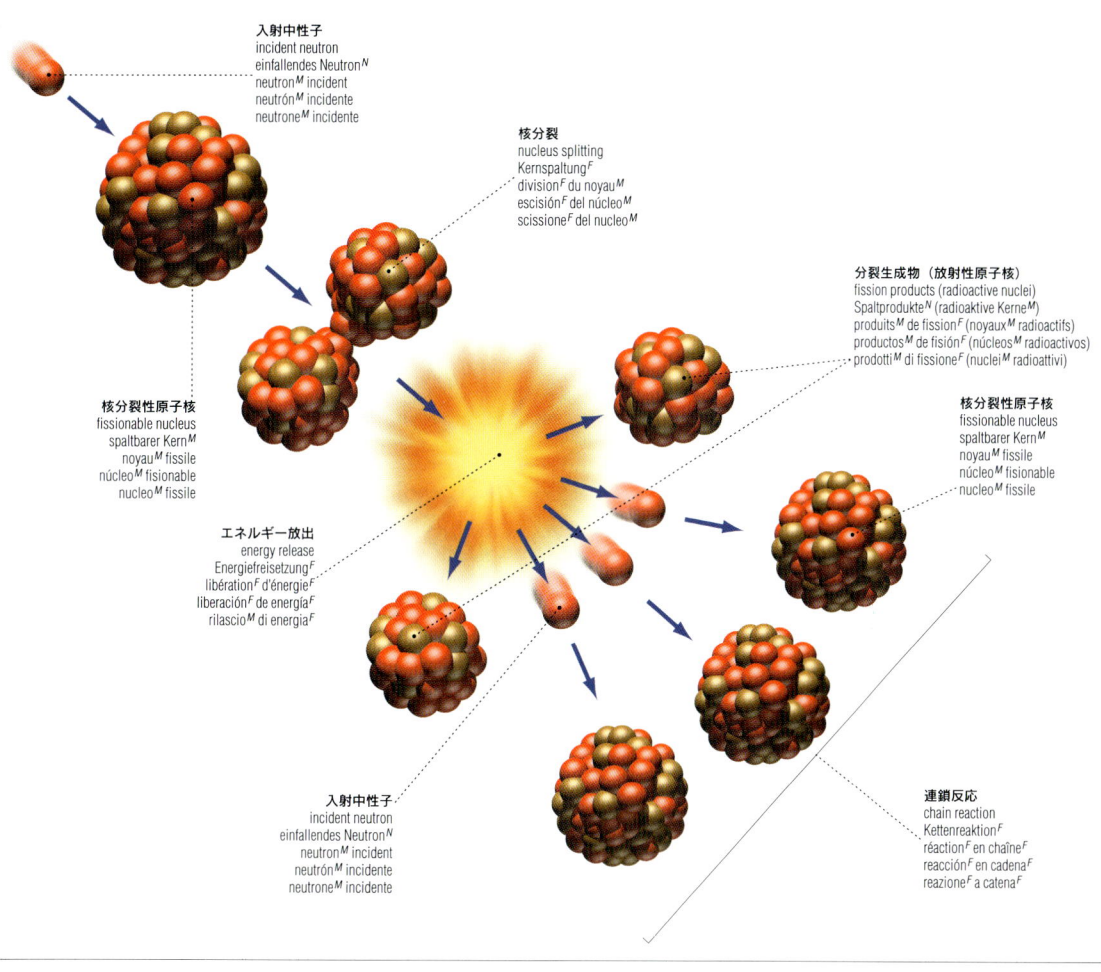

入射中性子
incident neutron
einfallendes Neutron^N
neutron^M incident
neutrón^M incidente
neutrone^M incidente

核分裂
nucleus splitting
Kernspaltung^F
division^F du noyau^M
escisión^F del núcleo^M
scissione^F del nucleo^M

分裂生成物（放射性原子核）
fission products (radioactive nuclei)
Spaltprodukte^N (radioaktive Kerne^M)
produits^M de fission^F (noyaux^M radioactifs)
productos^M de fisión^F (núcleos^M radioactivos)
prodotti^M di fissione^F (nuclei^M radioattivi)

核分裂性原子核
fissionable nucleus
spaltbarer Kern^M
noyau^M fissile
núcleo^M fisionable
nucleo^M fissile

核分裂性原子核
fissionable nucleus
spaltbarer Kern^M
noyau^M fissile
núcleo^M fisionable
nucleo^M fissile

エネルギー放出
energy release
Energiefreisetzung^F
libération^F d'énergie^F
liberación^F de energía^F
rilascio^M di energia^F

入射中性子
incident neutron
einfallendes Neutron^N
neutron^M incident
neutrón^M incidente
neutrone^M incidente

連鎖反応
chain reaction
Kettenreaktion^F
réaction^F en chaîne^F
reacción^F en cadena^F
reazione^F a catena^F

熱伝達
heat transfer
Wärmeübertragung^F
transfert^M de la chaleur^F
transmisión^F de calor^M
trasferimento^M di calore^M

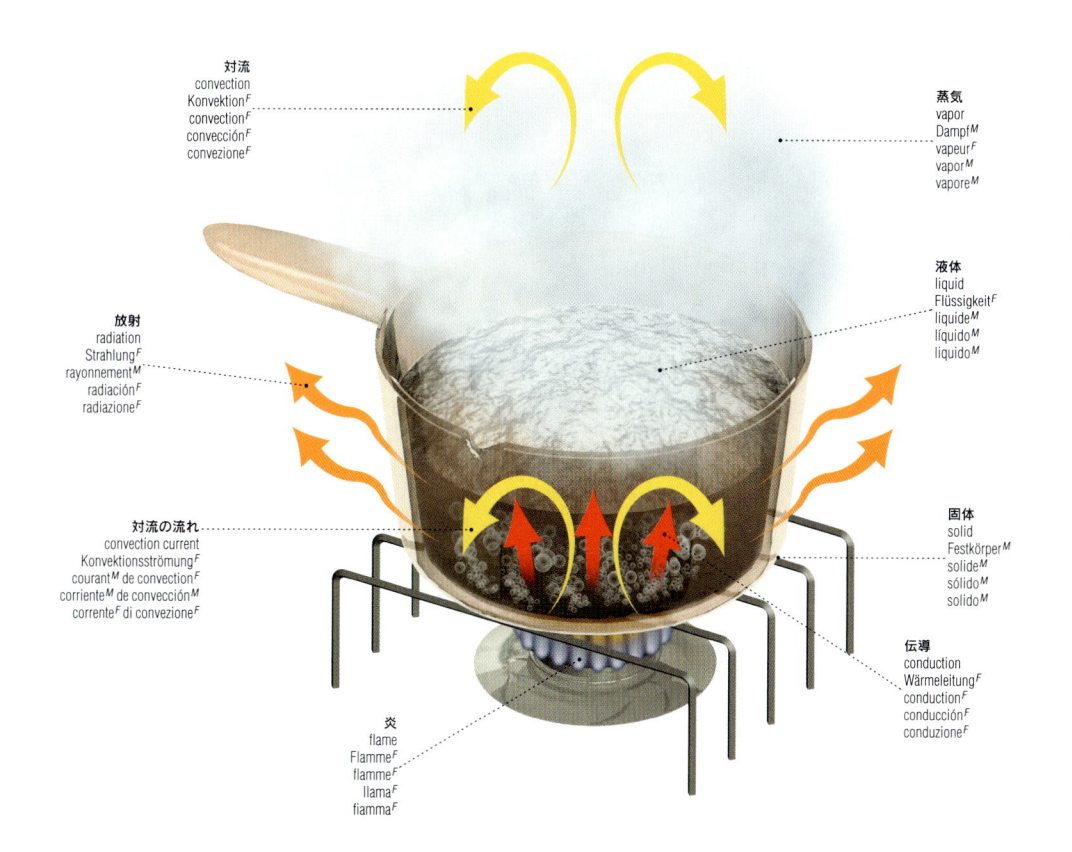

対流
convection
Konvektion^F
convection^F
convección^F
convezione^F

蒸気
vapor
Dampf^M
vapeur^F
vapor^M
vapore^M

放射
radiation
Strahlung^F
rayonnement^M
radiación^F
radiazione^F

液体
liquid
Flüssigkeit^F
liquide^M
líquido^M
liquido^M

対流の流れ
convection current
Konvektionsströmung^F
courant^M de convection^F
corriente^M de convección^M
corrente^F di convezione^F

固体
solid
Festkörper^M
solide^M
sólido^M
solido^M

伝導
conduction
Wärmeleitung^F
conduction^F
conducción^F
conduzione^F

炎
flame
Flamme^F
flamme^F
llama^F
fiamma^F

科学

化学 | CHEMISTRY
CHEMIE | CHIMIE | QUÍMICA | CHIMICA

化学元素

日本語 | 英語 | ドイツ語 | フランス語 | スペイン語 | イタリア語

chemical elements | chemische Elemente[N] | éléments[M] chimiques | elementos[M] químicos | elementi[M] chimici

周期表
table of elements
Periodensystem[N]
tableau[M] périodique des éléments[M]
tabla[F] periódica de los elementos[M]
tavola[F] periodica degli elementi[M]

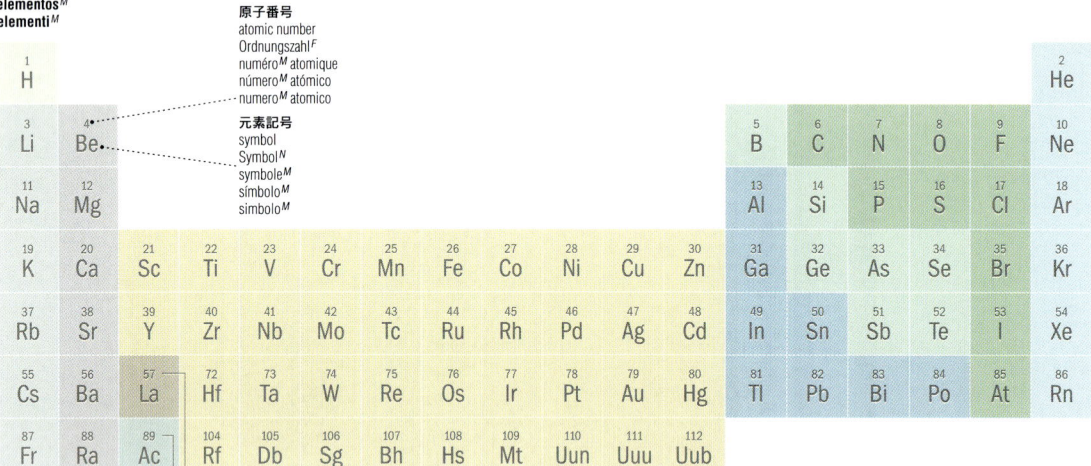

原子番号
atomic number
Ordnungszahl[F]
numéro[M] atomique
número[M] atómico
numero[M] atomico

元素記号
symbol
Symbol[N]
symbole[M]
símbolo[M]
simbolo[M]

1 H																	2 He
3 Li	4 Be											5 B	6 C	7 N	8 O	9 F	10 Ne
11 Na	12 Mg											13 Al	14 Si	15 P	16 S	17 Cl	18 Ar
19 K	20 Ca	21 Sc	22 Ti	23 V	24 Cr	25 Mn	26 Fe	27 Co	28 Ni	29 Cu	30 Zn	31 Ga	32 Ge	33 As	34 Se	35 Br	36 Kr
37 Rb	38 Sr	39 Y	40 Zr	41 Nb	42 Mo	43 Tc	44 Ru	45 Rh	46 Pd	47 Ag	48 Cd	49 In	50 Sn	51 Sb	52 Te	53 I	54 Xe
55 Cs	56 Ba	57 La	72 Hf	73 Ta	74 W	75 Re	76 Os	77 Ir	78 Pt	79 Au	80 Hg	81 Tl	82 Pb	83 Bi	84 Po	85 At	86 Rn
87 Fr	88 Ra	89 Ac	104 Rf	105 Db	106 Sg	107 Bh	108 Hs	109 Mt	110 Uun	111 Uuu	112 Uub						

58 Ce	59 Pr	60 Nd	61 Pm	62 Sm	63 Eu	64 Gd	65 Tb	66 Dy	67 Ho	68 Er	69 Tm	70 Yb	71 Lu
90 Th	91 Pa	92 U	93 Np	94 Pu	95 Am	96 Cm	97 Bk	98 Cf	99 Es	100 Fm	101 Md	102 No	103 Lr

水素
hydrogen
Wasserstoff[M]
hydrogène[M]
hidrógeno[M]
idrogeno[M]

1 H

その他の金属
other metals
andere Metalle[N]
autres métaux[M]
otros metales[M]
altri metalli[M]

アルカリ金属
alkali metals
Alkalimetalle[N]
métaux[M] alcalins
metales[M] alcalinos
metalli[M] alcalini

アルカリ土類金属
alkaline earth metals
Erdalkalimetalle[N]
métaux[M] alcalino-terreux
metales[M] alcalinotérreos
metalli[M] alcalino-terrosi

半金属／メタロイド
semi-metals (metalloids)
Halbmetalle (Metalloide[N])
semi-métaux[M] (métalloïdes[M])
semimetales[M] (metaloides[M])
semimetalli[M] (metalloidi[M])

アルミニウム
aluminum; *aluminium*
Aluminium[N]
aluminium[M]
aluminio[M]
alluminio[M]

13 Al

リチウム
lithium
Lithium[N]
lithium[M]
litio[M]
litio[M]

3 Li

ベリリウム
beryllium
Beryllium[N]
béryllium[M]
berilio[M]
berillio[M]

4 Be

ホウ素
boron
Bor[N]
bore[M]
boro[M]
boro[M]

5 B

ガリウム
gallium
Gallium[N]
gallium[M]
galio[M]
gallio[M]

31 Ga

ナトリウム
sodium
Natrium[N]
sodium[M]
sodio[M]
sodio[M]

11 Na

マグネシウム
magnesium
Magnesium[N]
magnésium[M]
magnesio[M]
magnesio[M]

12 Mg

ケイ素
silicon
Silizium[N]
silicium[M]
silicio[M]
silicio[M]

14 Si

インジウム
indium
Indium[N]
indium[M]
indio[M]
indio[M]

49 In

カリウム
potassium
Kalium[N]
potassium[M]
potasio[M]
potassio[M]

19 K

カルシウム
calcium
Kalzium[N]
calcium[M]
calcio[M]
calcio[M]

20 Ca

ゲルマニウム
germanium
Germanium[N]
germanium[M]
germanio[M]
germanio[M]

32 Ge

錫（すず）
tin
Zinn[N]
étain[M]
estaño[M]
stagno[M]

50 Sn

ルビジウム
rubidium
Rubidium[N]
rubidium[M]
rubidio[M]
rubidio[M]

37 Rb

ストロンチウム
strontium
Strontium[N]
strontium[M]
estroncio[M]
stronzio[M]

38 Sr

ヒ素
arsenic
Arsen[N]
arsenic[M]
arsénico[M]
arsenico[M]

33 As

タリウム
thallium
Thallium[N]
thallium[M]
talio[M]
tallio[M]

81 Tl

セシウム
cesium
Cäsium[N]
césium[M]
cesio[M]
cesio[M]

55 Cs

バリウム
barium
Barium[N]
baryum[M]
bario[M]
bario[M]

56 Ba

セレン／セレニウム
selenium
Selen[N]
sélénium[M]
selenio[M]
selenio[M]

34 Se

鉛
lead
Blei[N]
plomb[M]
plomo[M]
piombo[M]

82 Pb

フランシウム
francium
Franzium[N]
francium[M]
francio[M]
francio[M]

87 Fr

ラジウム
radium
Radium[N]
radium[M]
radio[M]
radio[M]

88 Ra

アンチモン
antimony
Antimon[N]
antimoine[M]
antimonio[M]
antimonio[M]

51 Sb

ビスマス
bismuth
Wismut[N]
bismuth[M]
bismuto[M]
bismuto[M]

83 Bi

テルル
tellurium
Tellur[N]
tellure[M]
telurio[M]
tellurio[M]

52 Te

ポロニウム
polonium
Polonium[N]
polonium[M]
polonio[M]
polonio[M]

84 Po

化学 | CHEMISTRY
CHEMIE | CHIMIE | QUÍMICA | CHIMICA

化学元素

遷移金属[元素]
transition metals
Übergangsmetalle[N]
métaux[M] **de transition**[F]
metales[M] **de transición**
metalli[M] **di transizione**[F]

21 Sc スカンジウム / scandium / Scandium[N] / scandium[M] / escandio[M] / scandio[M]	**39 Y** イットリウム / yttrium / Yttrium[N] / yttrium[M] / itrio[M] / ittrio[M]	**72 Hf** ハフニウム / hafnium / Hafnium[N] / hafnium[M] / hafnio[M] / afnio[M]	**104 Rf** ラザフォルジウム / rutherfordium / Rutherfordium[N] / rutherfordium[M] / rutherfodio[M] / rutherfordio[M]
22 Ti チタン / titanium / Titan[N] / titane[M] / titanio[M] / titanio[M]	**40 Zr** ジルコニウム / zirconium / Zirkonium[N] / zirconium[M] / zirconio[M] / zirconio[M]	**73 Ta** タンタル / tantalum / Tantal[N] / tantale[M] / tántalo[M] / tantalio[M]	**105 Db** ドブニウム / dubnium / Dubnium[N] / dubnium[M] / dubnio[M] / dubnio[M]
23 V バナジウム / vanadium / Vanadium[N] / vanadium[M] / vanadio[M] / vanadio[M]	**41 Nb** ニオブ / niobium / Niob[N] / niobium[M] / niobio[M] / niobio[M]	**74 W** タングステン / tungsten / Wolfram[N] / tungstène[M] / tungsteno[M] / tungsteno[M]	**106 Sg** シーボーギウム / seaborgium / Seaborgium[N] / seaborgium[M] / seaborgio[M] / seaborgio[M]
24 Cr クロム / chromium / Chrom[N] / chrome[M] / cromo[M] / cromo[M]	**42 Mo** モリブデン / molybdenum / Molybdän[N] / molybdène[M] / molibdeno[M] / molibdeno[M]	**75 Re** レニウム / rhenium / Rhenium[N] / rhénium[M] / renio[M] / renio[M]	**107 Bh** ボーリウム / bohrium / Bohrium[N] / bohrium[M] / bohrio[M] / bohrio[M]
25 Mn マンガン / manganese / Mangan[N] / manganèse[M] / manganeso[M] / manganese[M]	**43 Tc** テクネチウム / technetium / Technetium[N] / technétium[M] / tecnecio[M] / tecnezio[M]	**76 Os** オスミウム / osmium / Osmium[N] / osmium[M] / osmio[M] / osmio[M]	**108 Hs** ハッシウム / hassium / Hassium[N] / hassium[M] / hassio[M] / hassio[M]
26 Fe 鉄 / iron / Eisen[N] / fer[M] / hierro[M] / ferro[M]	**44 Ru** ルテニウム / ruthenium / Ruthenium[N] / ruthénium[M] / rutenio[M] / rutenio[M]	**77 Ir** イリジウム / iridium / Iridium[N] / iridium[M] / iridio[M] / iridio[M]	**109 Mt** マイトネリウム / meitnerium / Meitnerium[N] / meitnerium[M] / meitnerio[M] / meitnerio[M]
27 Co コバルト / cobalt / Kobalt[N] / cobalt[M] / cobalto[M] / cobalto[M]	**45 Rh** ロジウム / rhodium / Rhodium[N] / rhodium[M] / rodio[M] / rodio[M]	**78 Pt** 白金 / platinum / Platin[N] / platine[M] / platino[M] / platino[M]	**110 Uun** ウンウンニリウム / ununnilium / Ununnilium[N] / ununnilium[M] / ununnilio[M] / ununnilio[M]
28 Ni ニッケル / nickel / Nickel[N] / nickel[M] / niquel[M] / nichel[M]	**46 Pd** パラジウム / palladium / Palladium[N] / palladium[M] / paladio[M] / palladio[M]	**79 Au** 金 / gold / Gold[N] / or[M] / oro[M] / oro[M]	**111 Uuu** ウンウンウニウム / unununium / Unununium[N] / unununium[M] / unununio[M] / unununio[M]
29 Cu 銅 / copper / Kupfer[N] / cuivre[M] / cobre[M] / rame[M]	**47 Ag** 銀 / silver / Silber[N] / argent[M] / plata[F] / argento[M]	**80 Hg** 水銀 / mercury / Quecksilber[N] / mercure[M] / mercurio[M] / mercurio[M]	**112 Uub** ウンウンビウム / ununbium / Ununbium[N] / ununbium[M] / ununbio[M] / ununbio[M]
30 Zn 亜鉛 / zinc / Zink[N] / zinc[M] / cinc[M] / zinco[M]	**48 Cd** カドミウム / cadmium / Cadmium[N] / cadmium[M] / cadmio[M] / cadmio[M]		

非金属
non-metals
Nichtmetalle[N]
non-métaux[M]
no metales[M]
non metalli[M]

6 C 炭素 / carbon / Kohlenstoff[M] / carbone[M] / carbón[M] / carbonio	**9 F** 弗素 (ふっそ) / fluorine / Fluor[N] / fluor[M] / flúor[M] / fluoro[M]	**17 Cl** 塩素 / chlorine / Chlor[N] / chlore[M] / cloro[M] / cloro[M]	**53 I** ヨウ素 / iodine / Jod[N] / iode[M] / yodo[M] / iodio[M]
7 N 窒素 / nitrogen / Stickstoff[M] / azote[M] / nitrógeno[M] / azoto[M]	**15 P** 燐 (りん) / phosphorus / Phosphor[M] / phosphore[M] / fósforo[M] / fosforo[M]	**35 Br** 臭素 / bromine / Brom[N] / brome[M] / bromo[M] / bromo[M]	**85 At** アスタチン / astatine / Astat[N] / astate[M] / ástato[M] / astato[M]
8 O 酸素 / oxygen / Sauerstoff[M] / oxygène[M] / oxígeno[M] / ossigeno[M]	**16 S** 硫黄 (いおう) / sulfur / Schwefel[M] / soufre[M] / azufre[M] / zolfo[M]		

科学

化学元素

希ガス
noble gases
Edelgase[N]
gaz[M] rares
gases[M] nobles
gas[M] nobili

He 2 ヘリウム helium Helium[N] hélium[M] helio[M] elio[M]	**Ne** 10 ネオン neon Neon[N] néon[M] neón[M] neon[M]	**Ar** 18 アルゴン argon Argon[N] argon[M] argón[M] argo[M]	**Kr** 36 クリプトン krypton Krypton[N] krypton[M] criptón[M] cripto[M]
		Xe 54 キセノン xenon Xenon[N] xénon[M] xenón[M] xeno[M]	**Rn** 86 ラドン radon Radon[N] radon[M] radón[M] radon[M]

ランタノイド[ランタナイド]元素/希土類元素
lanthanides (rare earth)
Lanthanoide[N] (Seltenerdmetalle[N])
lanthanides[M] (terres[F] rares)
lantánidos[M] (tierras[F] raras)
lantanidi[M] (terre[F] rare)

La 57 ランタン lanthanum Lanthan[N] lanthane[M] lantano[M] lantanio[M]	**Pm** 61 プロメチウム promethium Promethium[N] prométhium[M] promecio[M] promezio[M]	**Tb** 65 テルビウム terbium Terbium[N] terbium[M] terbio[M] terbio[M]	**Tm** 69 ツリウム thulium Thulium[N] thulium[M] tulio[M] tulio[M]
Ce 58 セリウム cerium Cer[N] cérium[M] cerio[M] cerio[M]	**Sm** 62 サマリウム samarium Samarium[N] samarium[M] samario[M] samario[M]	**Dy** 66 ジスプロシウム dysprosium Dysprosium[N] dysprosium[M] disprosio[M] disprosio[M]	**Yb** 70 イッテルビウム ytterbium Ytterbium[N] ytterbium[M] iterbio[M] itterbio[M]
Pr 59 プラセオジム praseodymium Praseodym[N] praséodyme[M] praseodimio[M] praseodimio[M]	**Eu** 63 ユウロピウム europium Europium[N] europium[M] europio[M] europio[M]	**Ho** 67 ホルミウム holmium Holmium[N] holmium[M] holmio[M] olmio[M]	**Lu** 71 ルテチウム lutetium Lutetium[N] lutécium[M] lutecio[M] lutezio[M]
Nd 60 ネオジム neodymium Neodym[N] néodyme[M] neodimio[M] neodimio[M]	**Gd** 64 ガドリニウム gadolinium Gadolinium[N] gadolinium[M] gadolinio[M] gadolinio[M]	**Er** 68 エルビウム erbium Erbium[N] erbium[M] erbio[M] erbio[M]	

アクチノイド元素
actinides
Actinoide[N] (Seltenerdmetalle[N])
actinides[M]
actínidos[M] (tierras[F] raras)
attinidi

Ac 89 アクチニウム actinium Actinium[N] actinium[M] actino[M] attinio[M]	**Np** 93 ネプツニウム neptunium Neptunium[N] neptunium[M] neptunio[M] nettunio[M]	**Bk** 97 バークリウム berkelium Berkelium[N] berkélium[M] berquelio[M] berchelio[M]	**Md** 101 メンデレビウム mendelevium Mendelevium[N] mendélévium[M] mendelevio[M] mendelevio[M]
Th 90 トリウム thorium Thorium[N] thorium[M] torio[M] torio[M]	**Pu** 94 プルトニウム plutonium Plutonium[N] plutonium[M] plutonio[M] plutonio[M]	**Cf** 98 カリホルニウム californium Californium[N] californium[M] californio[M] californio[M]	**No** 102 ノーベリウム nobelium Nobelium[N] nobélium[M] nobelio[M] nobelio[M]
Pa 91 プロトアクチニウム protactinium Protactinium[N] protactinium[M] protactinio[M] protoattinio[M]	**Am** 95 アメリシウム americium Americium[N] américium[M] americio[M] americio[M]	**Es** 99 アインスタイニウム einsteinium Einsteinium[N] einsteinium[M] einstenio[M] einsteinio[M]	**Lr** 103 ローレンシウム lawrencium Lawrencium[N] lawrencium[M] laurencio[M] laurenzio[M]
U 92 ウラン uranium Uran[N] uranium[M] uranio[M] uranio[M]	**Cm** 96 キュリウム curium Curium[N] curium[M] curio[M] curio[M]	**Fm** 100 フェルミウム fermium Fermium[N] fermium[M] fermio[M] fermio[M]	

化学記号

chemistry symbols | chemische Symbole[N] | symboles[M] de chimie[F] | símbolos[M] químicos | simboli[M] chimici

—	+	⇌	→
陰電荷 negative charge negativ geladen négatif[M] elemento[M] negativo carica[F] negativa	陽電荷 positive charge positiv geladen positif[M] elemento[M] positivo carica[F] positiva	可逆反応 reversible reaction reversible Reaktion[F] réaction[F] réversible reacción[F] reazione[F] reversibile	反応の方向 reaction direction Reaktionsrichtung[F] direction[F] d'une réaction[F] dirección[F] direzione[F] della reazione[F]

化学 | CHEMISTRY
CHEMIE | CHIMIE | QUÍMICA | CHIMICA

実験器具

laboratory equipment | Laborgeräte[N] | matériel[M] de laboratoire[M] | material[M] de laboratorio[M] | strumenti[M] di laboratorio[M]

支柱
rod
Stativstange[F]
tige[F]
varilla[F]
asta[F]

試験管挟み
holder
Klemmhalter[M]
noix[F] de serrage[M]
nuez[M]
dispositivo[M] di serraggio[M]

メス・シリンダー
graduated cylinder
Messzylinder[M]
éprouvette[F] graduée
probeta[F] graduada
cilindro[M] graduato

コック付きビュレット
straight stopcock burette
Bürette[F]
burette[F] à robinet[M] droit
bureta[F] con llave a la derecha
buretta[F] con rubinetto[M] a destra

血清用ピペット
serological pipette
Pipette[F]
pipette[F] sérologique
pipeta[F]
pipetta[F] sierologica

クランプ／ホルダー／自在挟み
clamp/holder
Stativklemme[F]/Klemmhalter[M]
pince[F] avec noix[F] de serrage[M]
pinzas[F] con nuez[F]
pinze[F] di serraggio[M]

台
base
Fuß[M]
socle[M]
base[F]
base[F]

シャーレ／ペトリ皿／培養皿
Petri dish
Petri-Schale[F]
boîte[F] de Pétri
cápsula[F] de Petri
capsula[F] di Petri

試験管
test tube
Reagenzglas[N]
tube[M] à essai[M]
tubo[M] de ensayo[M]
provetta[F]

スタンド
stand
Stativ[N]
statif[M]
soporte[M]
stativo[M]

ガス・バーナー
gas burner
Bunsenbrenner[M]
brûleur[M] à gaz[M]
mechero[M] de gas[M]
becco[M] Bunsen

瓶／ボトル
bottle
Flasche[F]
bouteille[F]
botella[F]
bottiglia[F]

洗(浄)瓶／噴射瓶
wash bottle
Spritzflasche[F]
pissette[F]
frasco[M] lavador
spruzzetta[F]

丸底フラスコ
round-bottom flask
Rundkolben[M]
ballon[M] à fond[M] rond
balón[M]
pallone[M]

ビーカー
beaker
Becherglas[N]
bécher[M]
cubeta[F] de precipitación[M]
becher[M]

三角フラスコ
Erlenmeyer flask
Erlenmeyer-Kolben[M]
erlenmeyer[M]
frasco[M] Erlenmeyer
beuta[F] di Erlenmeyer

科学

物理：力学 | PHYSICS: MECHANICS
PHYSIK: MECHANIK | PHYSIQUE : MÉCANIQUE | FÍSICA: MECÁNICA | FISICA: MECCANICA

歯車装置

gearing systems | Zahnradgetriebe^N | engrenages^M | sistemas^M de engranajes^M | sistemi^M di ingranaggio^M

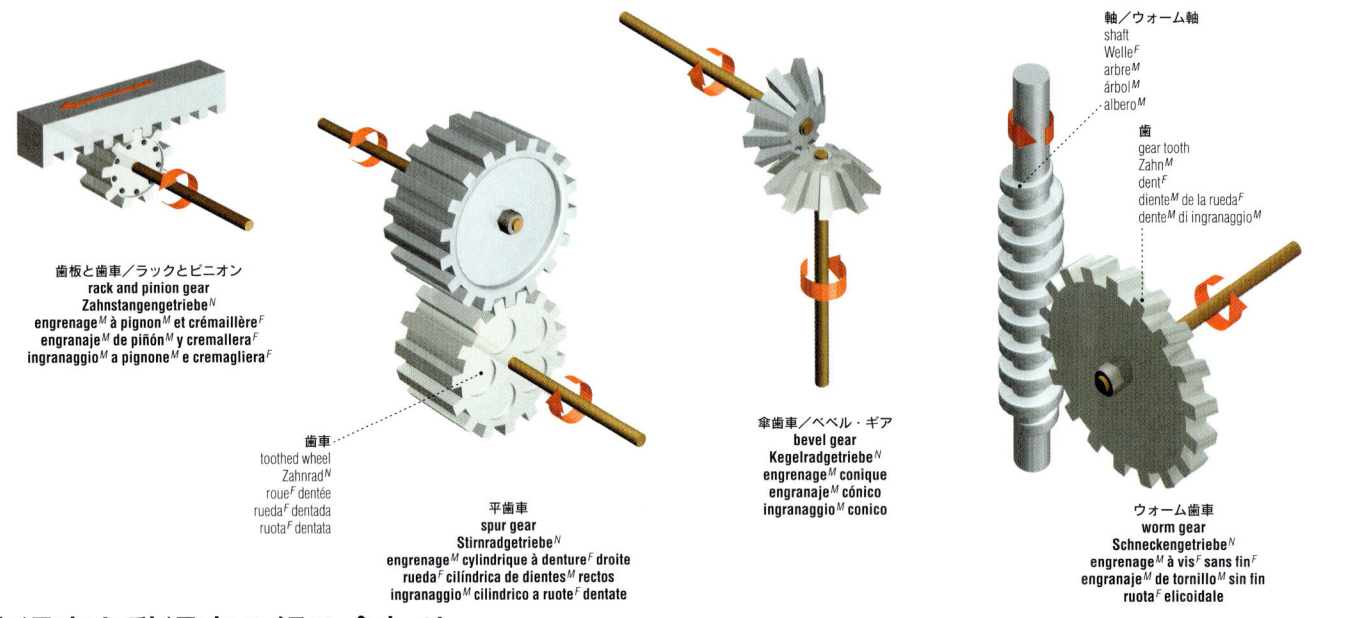

軸／ウォーム軸
shaft
Welle^F
arbre^M
árbol^M
albero^M

歯
gear tooth
Zahn^M
dent^F
diente^M de la rueda^F
dente^M di ingranaggio^M

歯板と歯車／ラックとピニオン
rack and pinion gear
Zahnstangengetriebe^N
engrenage^M à pignon^M et crémaillère^F
engranaje^M de piñón^M y cremallera^F
ingranaggio^M a pignone^M e cremagliera^F

歯車
toothed wheel
Zahnrad^N
roue^F dentée
rueda^F dentada
ruota^F dentata

平歯車
spur gear
Stirnradgetriebe^N
engrenage^M cylindrique à denture^F droite
rueda^F cilíndrica de dientes^M rectos
ingranaggio^M cilindrico a ruote^F dentate

傘歯車／ベベル・ギア
bevel gear
Kegelradgetriebe^N
engrenage^M conique
engranaje^M cónico
ingranaggio^M conico

ウォーム歯車
worm gear
Schneckengetriebe^N
engrenage^M à vis^F sans fin^F
engranaje^M de tornillo^M sin fin
ruota^F elicoidale

定滑車と動滑車の組み合わせ

double pulley system | einfacher Flaschenzug^M | système^M à deux poulies^F | sistema^F de doble polea^F | sistema^M a doppia puleggia^F

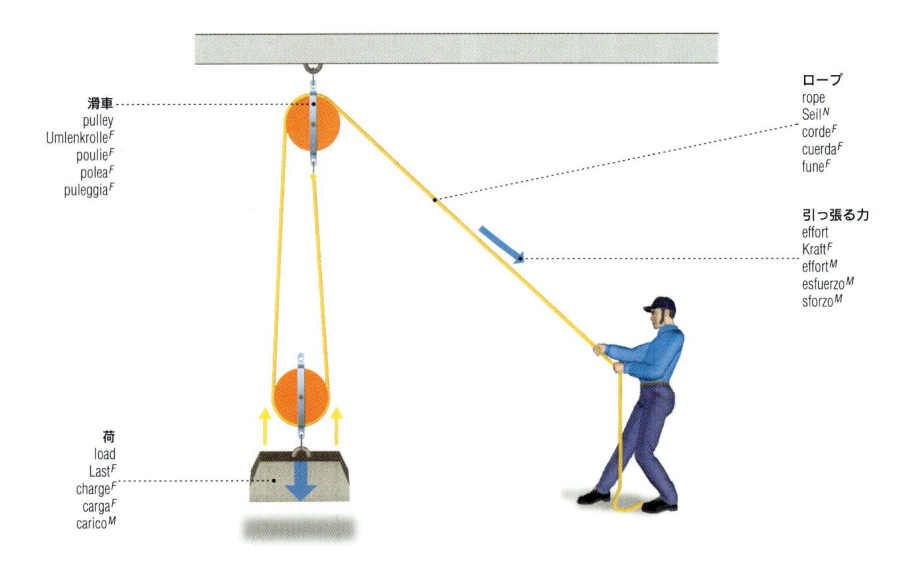

滑車
pulley
Umlenkrolle^F
poulie^F
polea^F
puleggia^F

ロープ
rope
Seil^N
corde^F
cuerda^F
fune^F

引っ張る力
effort
Kraft^F
effort^M
esfuerzo^M
sforzo^M

荷
load
Last^F
charge^F
carga^F
carico^M

てこ

lever | Hebel^M | levier^M | palanca^F | leva^F

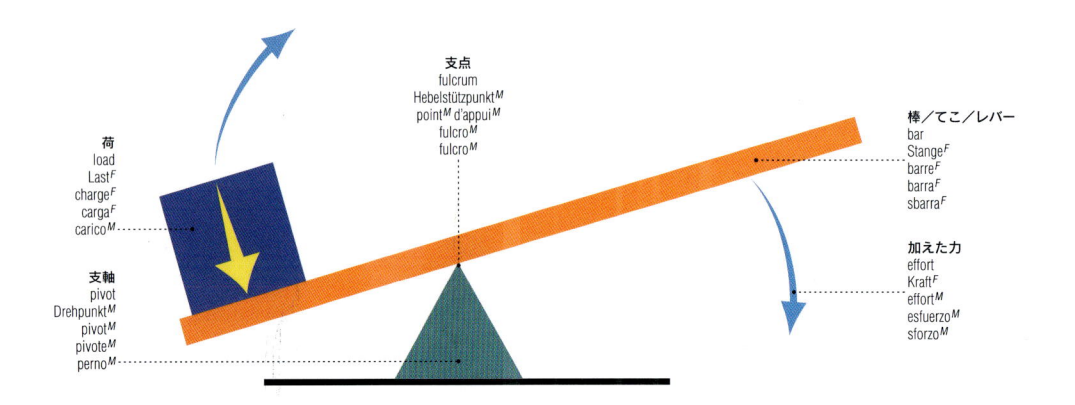

荷
load
Last^F
charge^F
carga^F
carico^M

支点
fulcrum
Hebelstützpunkt^M
point^M d'appui^M
fulcro^M
fulcro^M

棒／てこ／レバー
bar
Stange^F
barre^F
barra^F
sbarra^F

支軸
pivot
Drehpunkt^M
pivot^M
pivote^M
perno^M

加えた力
effort
Kraft^F
effort^M
esfuerzo^M
sforzo^M

物理：電気学と磁気学 | PHYSICS: ELECTRICITY AND MAGNETISM
PHYSIK: ELEKTRIZITÄT UND MAGNETISMUS | PHYSIQUE : ÉLECTRICITÉ ET MAGNÉTISME | FÍSICA : ELECTRICIDAD Y MAGNETISMO | FISICA: ELETTRICITÀ E MAGNETISMO

磁気

magnetism | Magnetismus^M | magnétisme^M | magnetismo^M | magnetismo^M

斥力（せきりょく） — repulsion / Abstoßung^F / répulsion^F / repulsión^F / repulsione^F

N極 — north pole / Nordpol^M / pôle^M nord / polo^M norte / polo^M nord^M

磁石 — magnet / Magnet^M / aimant^M / imán^M / magnete^M

磁壁 — neutral line / neutrale Linie^F / ligne^F neutre / línea^F neutra / linea^F neutra

磁場／磁界 — magnetic field / magnetisches Feld^N / champ^M magnétique / campo^M magnético / campo^M magnetico

磁力線 — field line / Feldlinie^F / ligne^F de force / línea^F de campo^M / linea^F di forza

S極 — south pole / Südpol^M / pôle^M sud / polo^M sur / polo^M sud^M

引力 — attraction / Anziehung^F / attraction^F / atracción^M / attrazione^F

並列電気回路

parallel electrical circuit | Parallelschaltung^F | circuit^M électrique en parallèle^F | circuito^M eléctrico en paralelo^M | circuito^M elettrico parallelo

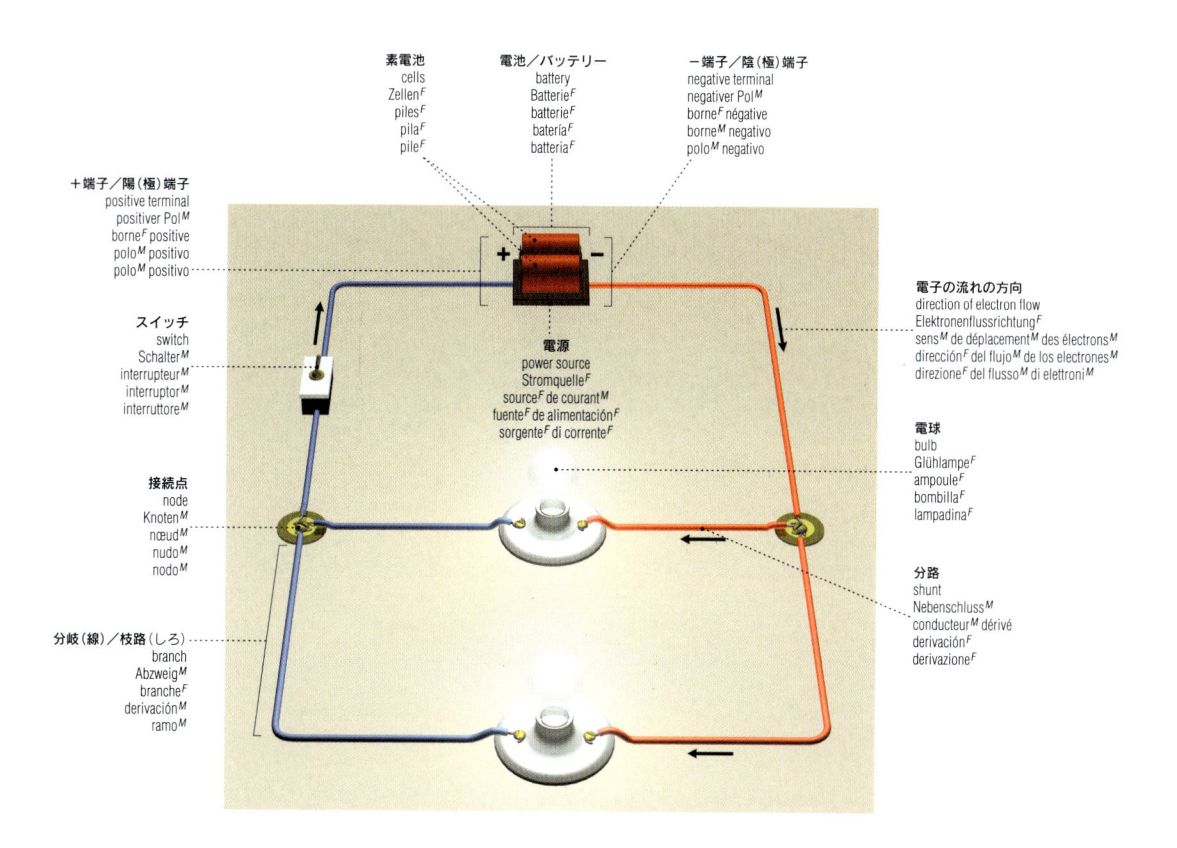

素電池 — cells / Zellen^F / piles^F / pila^F / pile^F

電池／バッテリー — battery / Batterie^F / batterie^F / batería^F / batteria^F

−端子／陰（極）端子 — negative terminal / negativer Pol^M / borne^F négative / borne^M negativo / polo^M negativo

＋端子／陽（極）端子 — positive terminal / positiver Pol^M / borne^F positive / polo^M positivo

スイッチ — switch / Schalter^M / interrupteur^M / interruptor^M / interruttore^M

電源 — power source / Stromquelle^F / source^F de courant^M / fuente^F de alimentación^F / sorgente^F di corrente^F

電子の流れの方向 — direction of electron flow / Elektronenflussrichtung^F / sens^M de déplacement^M des électrons^M / dirección^F del flujo^M de los electrones^M / direzione^F del flusso^M di elettroni

電球 — bulb / Glühlampe^F / ampoule^F / bombilla^F / lampadina^F

接続点 — node / Knoten^M / nœud^M / nudo^M / nodo^M

分路 — shunt / Nebenschluss^M / conducteur^M dérivé / derivación^F / derivazione^F

分岐（線）／枝路（しろ） — branch / Abzweig^M / branche^F / derivación^M / ramo^M

687

物理：電気学と磁気学 | PHYSICS: ELECTRICITY AND MAGNETISM
PHYSIK: ELEKTRIZITÄT UND MAGNETISMUS | PHYSIQUE : ÉLECTRICITÉ ET MAGNÉTISME | FÍSICA : ELECTRICIDAD Y MAGNETISMO | FISICA : ELETTRICITÀ E MAGNETISMO

発電機

日本語 | 英語 | ドイツ語 | フランス語 | スペイン語 | イタリア語

generators | Generatoren^M | générateurs^M | generadores^M | generatori^M

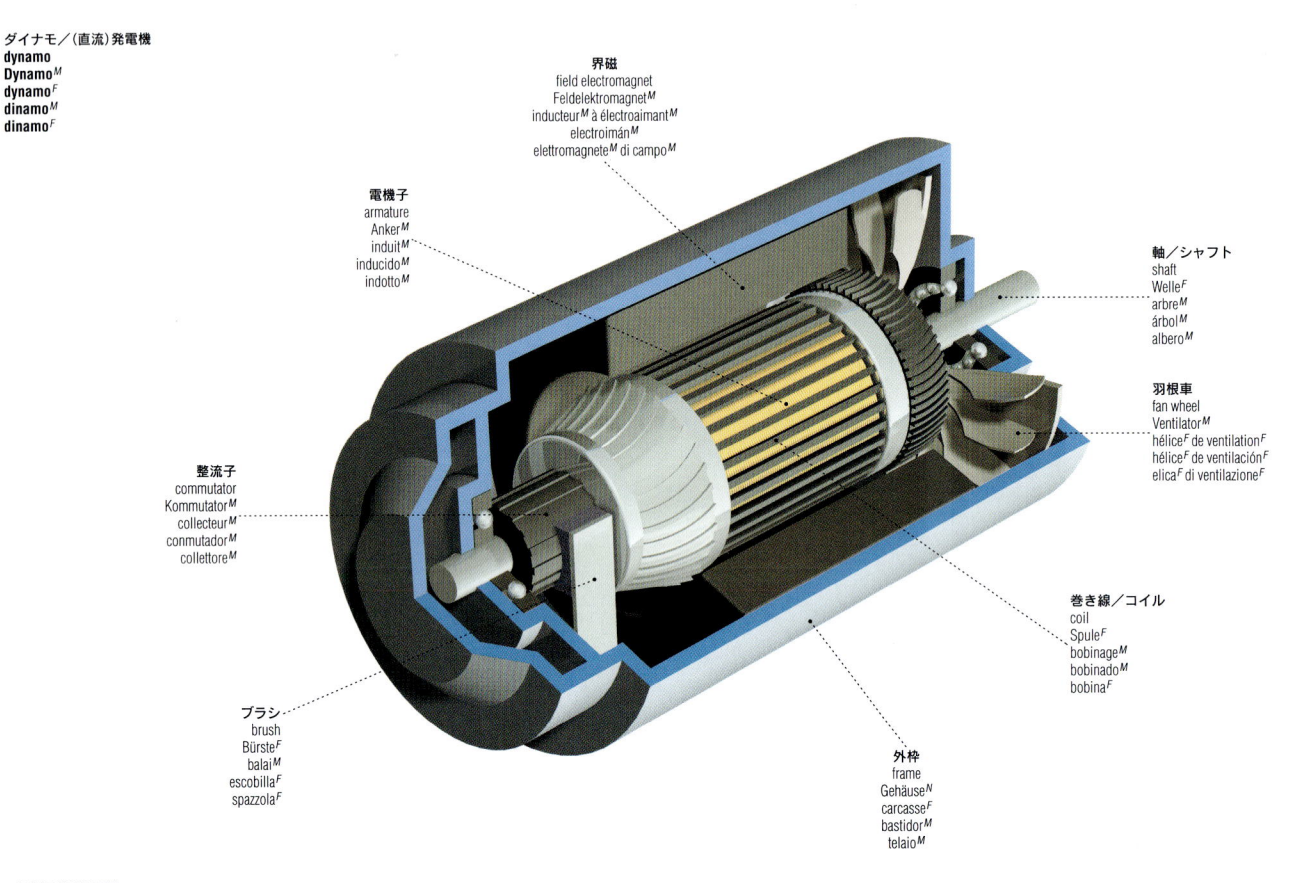

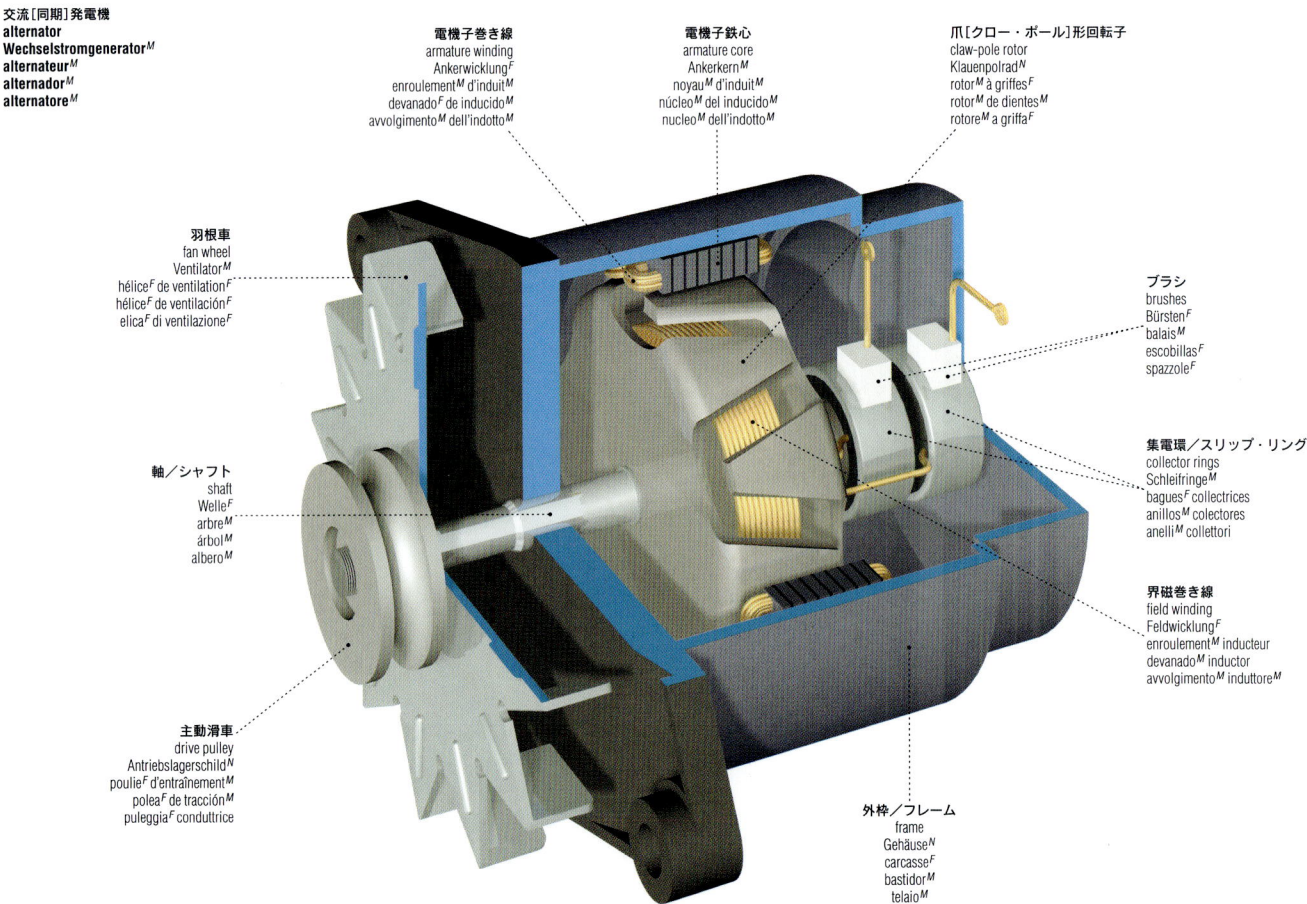

ダイナモ／（直流）発電機
dynamo
Dynamo^M
dynamo^F
dinamo^M
dinamo^F

界磁
field electromagnet
Feldelektromagnet^M
inducteur^M à électroaimant^M
electroimán^M
elettromagnete^M di campo^M

電機子
armature
Anker^M
induit^M
inducido^M
indotto^M

軸／シャフト
shaft
Welle^F
arbre^M
árbol^M
albero^M

羽根車
fan wheel
Ventilator^M
hélice^F de ventilation^F
hélice^F de ventilación^F
elica^F di ventilazione^F

整流子
commutator
Kommutator^M
collecteur^M
conmutador^M
collettore^M

巻き線／コイル
coil
Spule^F
bobinage^M
bobinado^M
bobina^F

ブラシ
brush
Bürste^F
balai^M
escobilla^F
spazzola^F

外枠
frame
Gehäuse^N
carcasse^F
bastidor^M
telaio^M

交流［同期］発電機
alternator
Wechselstromgenerator^M
alternateur^M
alternador^M
alternatore^M

電機子巻き線
armature winding
Ankerwicklung^F
enroulement^M d'induit^M
devanado^F de inducido^M
avvolgimento^M dell'indotto^M

電機子鉄心
armature core
Ankerkern^M
noyau^M d'induit^M
núcleo^M del inducido^M
nucleo^M dell'indotto^M

爪［クロー・ポール］形回転子
claw-pole rotor
Klauenpolrad^N
rotor^M à griffes^F
rotor^M de dientes^M
rotore^M a griffa^F

羽根車
fan wheel
Ventilator^M
hélice^F de ventilation^F
hélice^F de ventilación^F
elica^F di ventilazione^F

ブラシ
brushes
Bürsten^F
balais^M
escobillas^F
spazzole^F

軸／シャフト
shaft
Welle^F
arbre^M
árbol^M
albero^M

集電環／スリップ・リング
collector rings
Schleifringe^M
bagues^F collectrices
anillos^M colectores
anelli^M collettori

主動滑車
drive pulley
Antriebslagerschild^N
poulie^F d'entraînement^M
polea^F de tracción^F
puleggia^F conduttrice

界磁巻き線
field winding
Feldwicklung^F
enroulement^M inducteur
devanado^M inductor
avvolgimento^M induttore^M

外枠／フレーム
frame
Gehäuse^N
carcasse^F
bastidor^M
telaio^M

科学

688

物理：電気学と磁気学 | PHYSICS: ELECTRICITY AND MAGNETISM
PHYSIK: ELEKTRIZITÄT UND MAGNETISMUS | PHYSIQUE : ÉLECTRICITÉ ET MAGNÉTISME | FÍSICA : ELECTRICIDAD Y MAGNETISMO | FISICA : ELETTRICITÀ E MAGNETISMO

乾電池

dry cells | Trockenelemente[N] | piles[F] sèches | pilas[F] secas | pile[F] a secco[M]

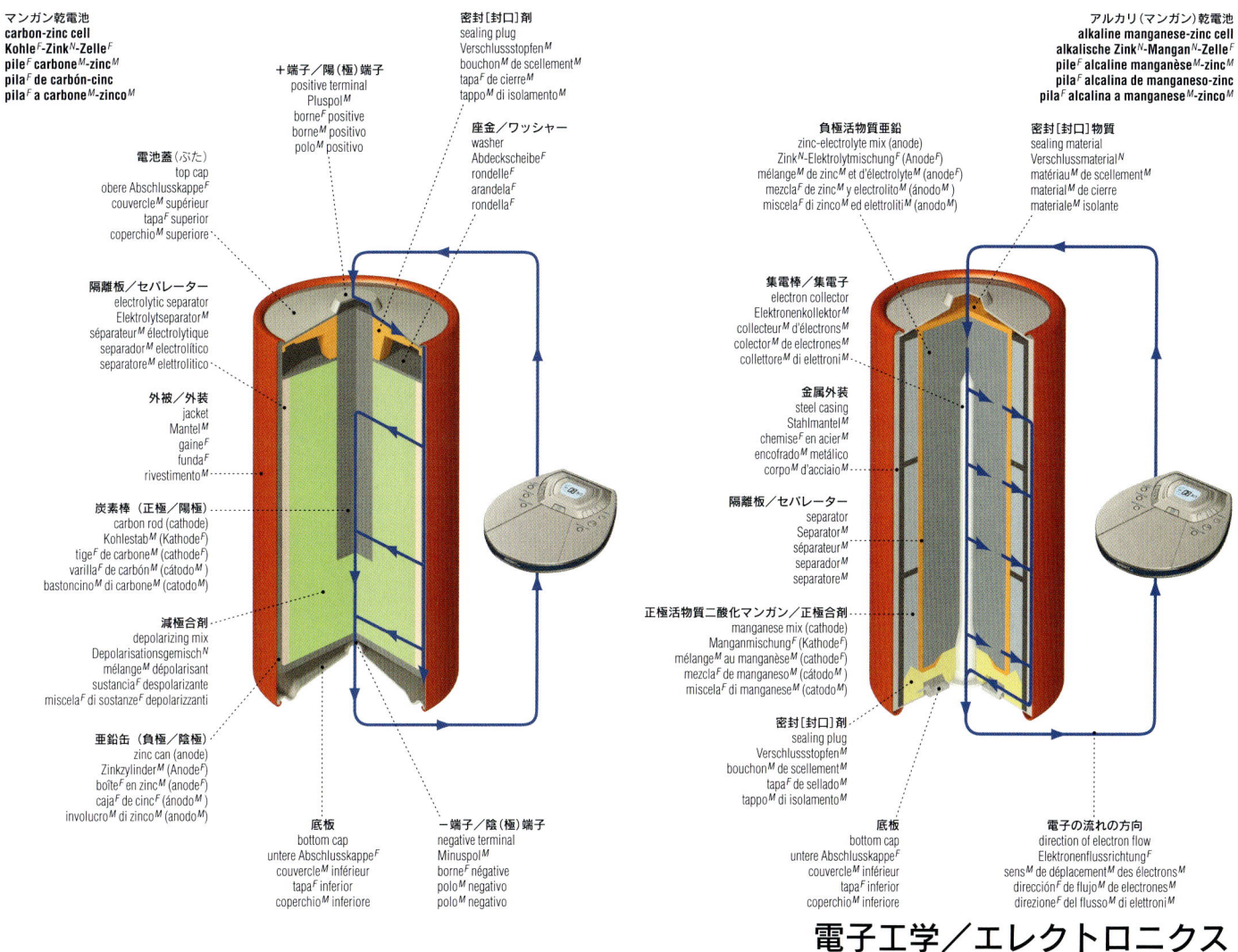

マンガン乾電池
carbon-zinc cell
Kohle[F]-Zink[N]-Zelle[F]
pile[F] carbone[M]-zinc[M]
pila[F] de carbón-cinc
pila[F] a carbone[M]-zinco[M]

電池蓋（ふた）
top cap
obere Abschlusskappe[F]
couvercle[M] supérieur
tapa[F] superior
coperchio[M] superiore

隔離板／セパレーター
electrolytic separator
Elektrolytseparator[M]
séparateur[M] électrolytique
separador[M] electrolítico
separatore[M] elettrolitico

外被／外装
jacket
Mantel[M]
gaine[F]
funda[F]
rivestimento[M]

炭素棒（正極／陽極）
carbon rod (cathode)
Kohlestab[M] (Kathode[F])
tige[F] de carbone[M] (cathode[F])
varilla[F] de carbón[M] (cátodo[M])
bastoncino[M] di carbone[M] (catodo[M])

減極合剤
depolarizing mix
Depolarisationsgemisch[N]
mélange[M] dépolarisant
sustancia[F] despolarizante
miscela[F] di sostanze[F] depolarizzanti

亜鉛缶（負極／陰極）
zinc can (anode)
Zinkzylinder[M] (Anode[F])
boîte[F] en zinc[M] (anode[F])
caja[F] de cinc[F] (ánodo[M])
involucro[M] di zinco[M] (anodo[M])

密封［封口］剤
sealing plug
Verschlussstopfen[M]
bouchon[M] de scellement[M]
tapa[F] de cierre[M]
tappo[M] di isolamento[M]

＋端子／陽（極）端子
positive terminal
Pluspol[M]
borne[F] positive
borne[M] positivo
polo[M] positivo

座金／ワッシャー
washer
Abdeckscheibe[F]
rondelle[F]
arandela[F]
rondella[F]

底板
bottom cap
untere Abschlusskappe[F]
couvercle[M] inférieur
tapa[F] inferior
coperchio[M] inferiore

－端子／陰（極）端子
negative terminal
Minuspol[M]
borne[F] négative
polo[M] negativo

負極活物質亜鉛
zinc-electrolyte mix (anode)
Zink[N]-Elektrolytmischung[F] (Anode[F])
mélange[M] de zinc[M] et d'électrolyte[M] (anode[F])
mezcla[F] de zinc[M] y electrolito[M] (ánodo[M])
miscela[F] di zinco[M] ed elettroliti[M] (anodo[M])

集電棒／集電子
electron collector
Elektronenkollektor[M]
collecteur[M] d'électrons[M]
colector[M] de electrones[M]
collettore[M] di elettroni[M]

金属外装
steel casing
Stahlmantel[M]
chemise[F] en acier[M]
encofrado[M] metálico
corpo[M] d'acciaio[M]

隔離板／セパレーター
separator
Separator[M]
séparateur[M]
separador[M]
separatore[M]

正極活物質二酸化マンガン／正極合剤
manganese mix (cathode)
Manganmischung[F] (Kathode[F])
mélange[M] au manganèse[M] (cathode[F])
mezcla[F] de manganeso[M] (cátodo[M])
miscela[F] di manganese[M] (catodo[M])

密封［封口］剤
sealing plug
Verschlussstopfen[M]
bouchon[M] de scellement[M]
tapa[F] de sellado[M]
tappo[M] di isolamento[M]

底板
bottom cap
untere Abschlusskappe[F]
couvercle[M] inférieur
tapa[F] inferior
coperchio[M] inferiore

アルカリ（マンガン）乾電池
alkaline manganese-zinc cell
alkalische Zink[N]-Mangan[N]-Zelle[F]
pile[F] alcaline manganèse[M]-zinc[M]
pila[F] alcalina de manganeso-zinc
pila[F] alcalina a manganese[M]-zinco[M]

密封［封口］物質
sealing material
Verschlussmaterial[N]
matériau[M] de scellement[M]
material[M] de cierre[M]
materiale[M] isolante

電子の流れの方向
direction of electron flow
Elektronenflussrichtung[F]
sens[M] de déplacement[M] des électrons[M]
dirección[F] de flujo[M] de electrones[M]
direzione[F] del flusso[M] di elettroni[M]

電子工学／エレクトロニクス

electronics | Elektronik[F] | électronique[F] | electrónica[F] | elettronica[F]

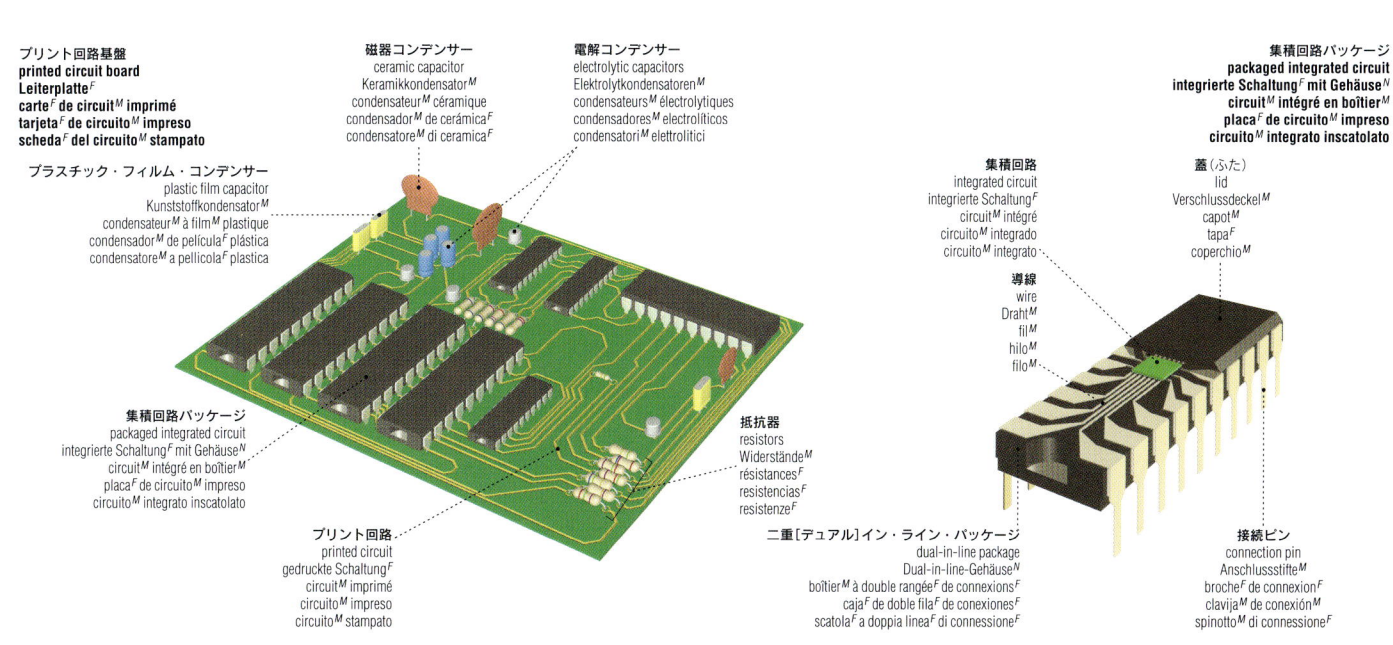

プリント回路基盤
printed circuit board
Leiterplatte[F]
carte[F] de circuit[M] imprimé
tarjeta[F] de circuito[M] impreso
scheda[F] del circuito[M] stampato

プラスチック・フィルム・コンデンサー
plastic film capacitor
Kunststoffkondensator[M]
condensateur[M] à film[M] plastique
condensador[M] de película[F] plástica
condensatore[M] a pellicola[F] plastica

集積回路パッケージ
packaged integrated circuit
integrierte Schaltung[F] mit Gehäuse[N]
circuit[M] intégré en boîtier[M]
placa[F] de circuito[M] impreso
circuito[M] integrato inscatolato

磁器コンデンサー
ceramic capacitor
Keramikkondensator[M]
condensateur[M] céramique
condensador[M] de cerámica[F]
condensatore[M] di ceramica[F]

電解コンデンサー
electrolytic capacitors
Elektrolytkondensatoren[M]
condensateurs[M] électrolytiques
condensadores[M] electrolíticos
condensatori[M] elettrolitici

抵抗器
resistors
Widerstände[M]
résistances[F]
resistencias[F]
resistenze[F]

プリント回路
printed circuit
gedruckte Schaltung[F]
circuit[M] imprimé
circuito[M] impreso
circuito[M] stampato

二重［デュアル］イン・ライン・パッケージ
dual-in-line package
Dual-in-line-Gehäuse[N]
boîtier[M] à double rangée[F] de connexions[F]
caja[F] de doble fila[F] de conexiones[F]
scatola[F] a doppia linea[F] di connessione[F]

集積回路パッケージ
packaged integrated circuit
integrierte Schaltung[F] mit Gehäuse[N]
circuit[M] intégré en boîtier[M]
placa[F] de circuito[M] impreso
circuito[M] integrato inscatolato

集積回路
integrated circuit
integrierte Schaltung[F]
circuit[M] intégré
circuito[M] integrado
circuito[M] integrato

蓋（ふた）
lid
Verschlussdeckel[M]
capot[M]
tapa[F]
coperchio[M]

導線
wire
Draht[M]
fil[M]
hilo[M]
filo[M]

接続ピン
connection pin
Anschlussstifte[M]
broche[F] de connexion[F]
clavija[M] de conexión[M]
spinotto[M] di connessione[F]

科学

物理：光学 | PHYSICS: OPTICS
PHYSIK: OPTIK | PHYSIQUE : OPTIQUE | FÍSICA : ÓPTICA | FISICA: OTTICA

電磁スペクトル

日本語 | 英語 | ドイツ語 | フランス語 | スペイン語 | イタリア語

electromagnetic spectrum | elektromagnetisches Spektrum[N] | spectre[M] électromagnétique | espectro[M] electromagnético | spettro[M] elettromagnetico

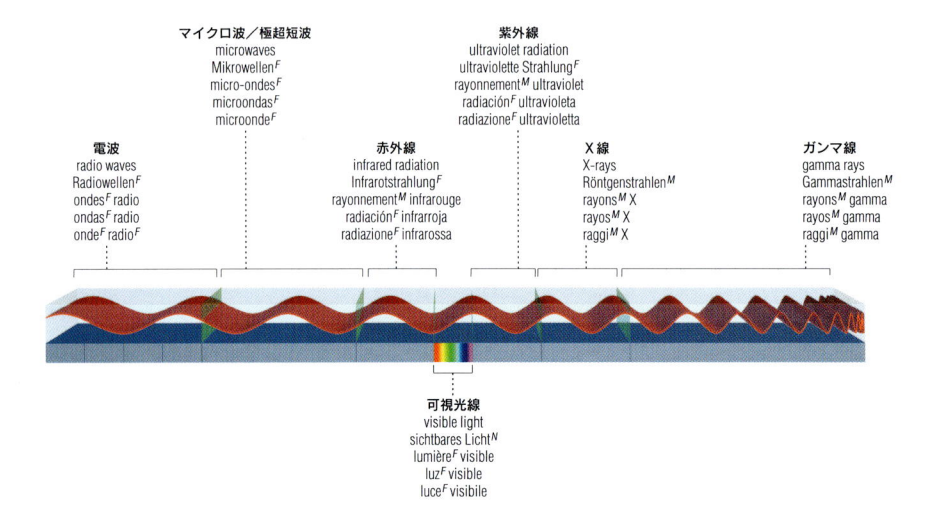

マイクロ波／極超短波
microwaves
Mikrowellen[F]
micro-ondes[F]
microondas[F]
microonde[F]

紫外線
ultraviolet radiation
ultraviolette Strahlung[F]
rayonnement[M] ultraviolet
radiación[F] ultravioleta
radiazione[F] ultravioletta

電波
radio waves
Radiowellen[F]
ondes[F] radio
ondas[F] radio
onde[F] radio

赤外線
infrared radiation
Infrarotstrahlung[F]
rayonnement[M] infrarouge
radiación[F] infrarroja
radiazione[F] infrarossa

X線
X-rays
Röntgenstrahlen[M]
rayons[M] X
rayos[M] X
raggi[M] X

ガンマ線
gamma rays
Gammastrahlen[M]
rayons[M] gamma
rayos[M] gamma
raggi[M] gamma

可視光線
visible light
sichtbares Licht[N]
lumière[F] visible
luz[F] visible
luce[F] visibile

波

wave | Welle[F] | onde[F] | onda[F] | onda[F]

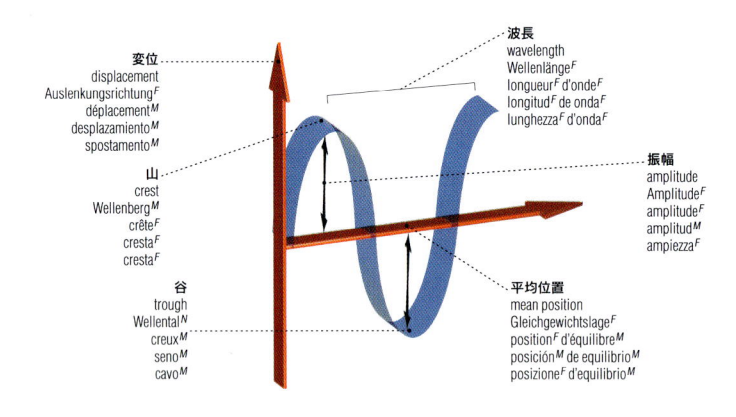

変位
displacement
Auslenkungsrichtung[F]
déplacement[M]
desplazamiento[M]
spostamento[M]

波長
wavelength
Wellenlänge[F]
longueur[F] d'onde[F]
longitud[F] de onda[F]
lunghezza[F] d'onda[F]

山
crest
Wellenberg[M]
crête[F]
cresta[F]
cresta[F]

振幅
amplitude
Amplitude[F]
amplitude[F]
amplitud[M]
ampiezza[F]

谷
trough
Wellental[N]
creux[M]
seno[M]
cavo[M]

平均位置
mean position
Gleichgewichtslage[F]
position[F] d'équilibre[M]
posición[M] de equilibrio[M]
posizione[F] d'equilibrio[M]

色の合成

color synthesis | Farbmischung[F] | synthèse[F] des couleurs[F] | síntesis[F] de los colores[M] | sintesi[F] dei colori[M]

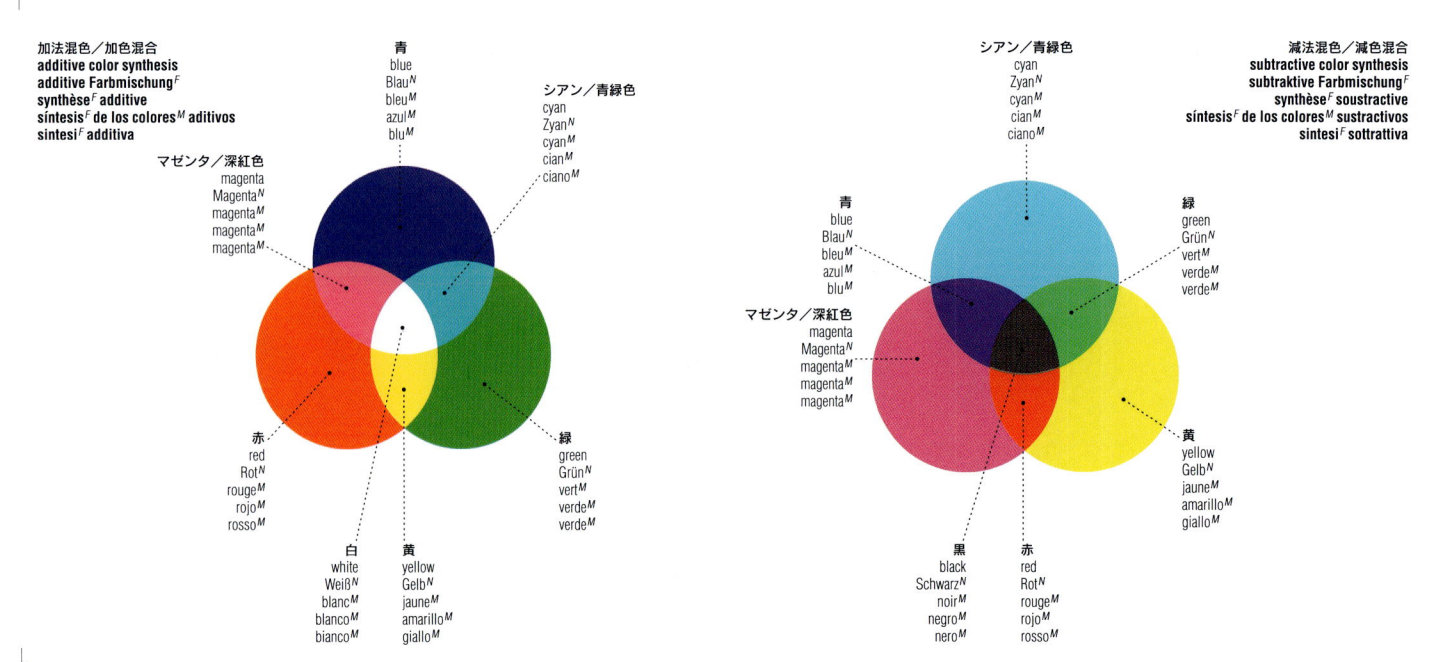

加法混色／加色混合
additive color synthesis
additive Farbmischung[F]
synthèse[F] additive
síntesis[F] de los colores[M] aditivos
sintesi[F] additiva

青
blue
Blau[N]
bleu[M]
azul[M]
blu[M]

シアン／青緑色
cyan
Zyan[N]
cyan[M]
cian[M]
ciano[M]

シアン／青緑色
cyan
Zyan[N]
cyan[M]
cian[M]
ciano[M]

減法混色／減色混合
subtractive color synthesis
subtraktive Farbmischung[F]
synthèse[F] soustractive
síntesis[F] de los colores[M] sustractivos
sintesi[F] sottrattiva

マゼンタ／深紅色
magenta
Magenta[N]
magenta[M]
magenta[M]
magenta[M]

青
blue
Blau[N]
bleu[M]
azul[M]
blu[M]

緑
green
Grün[N]
vert[M]
verde[M]
verde[M]

マゼンタ／深紅色
magenta
Magenta[N]
magenta[M]
magenta[M]
magenta[M]

赤
red
Rot[N]
rouge[M]
rojo[M]
rosso[M]

緑
green
Grün[N]
vert[M]
verde[M]
verde[M]

黄
yellow
Gelb[N]
jaune[M]
amarillo[M]
giallo[M]

白
white
Weiß[N]
blanc[M]
blanco[M]
bianco[M]

黄
yellow
Gelb[N]
jaune[M]
amarillo[M]
giallo[M]

黒
black
Schwarz[N]
noir[M]
negro[M]
nero[M]

赤
red
Rot[N]
rouge[M]
rojo[M]
rosso[M]

科学

物理：光学 | PHYSICS: OPTICS
PHYSIK: OPTIK | PHYSIQUE : OPTIQUE | FÍSICA : ÓPTICA | FISICA: OTTICA

視覚

vision | Sehen^N | vision^F | visión^F | vista^F

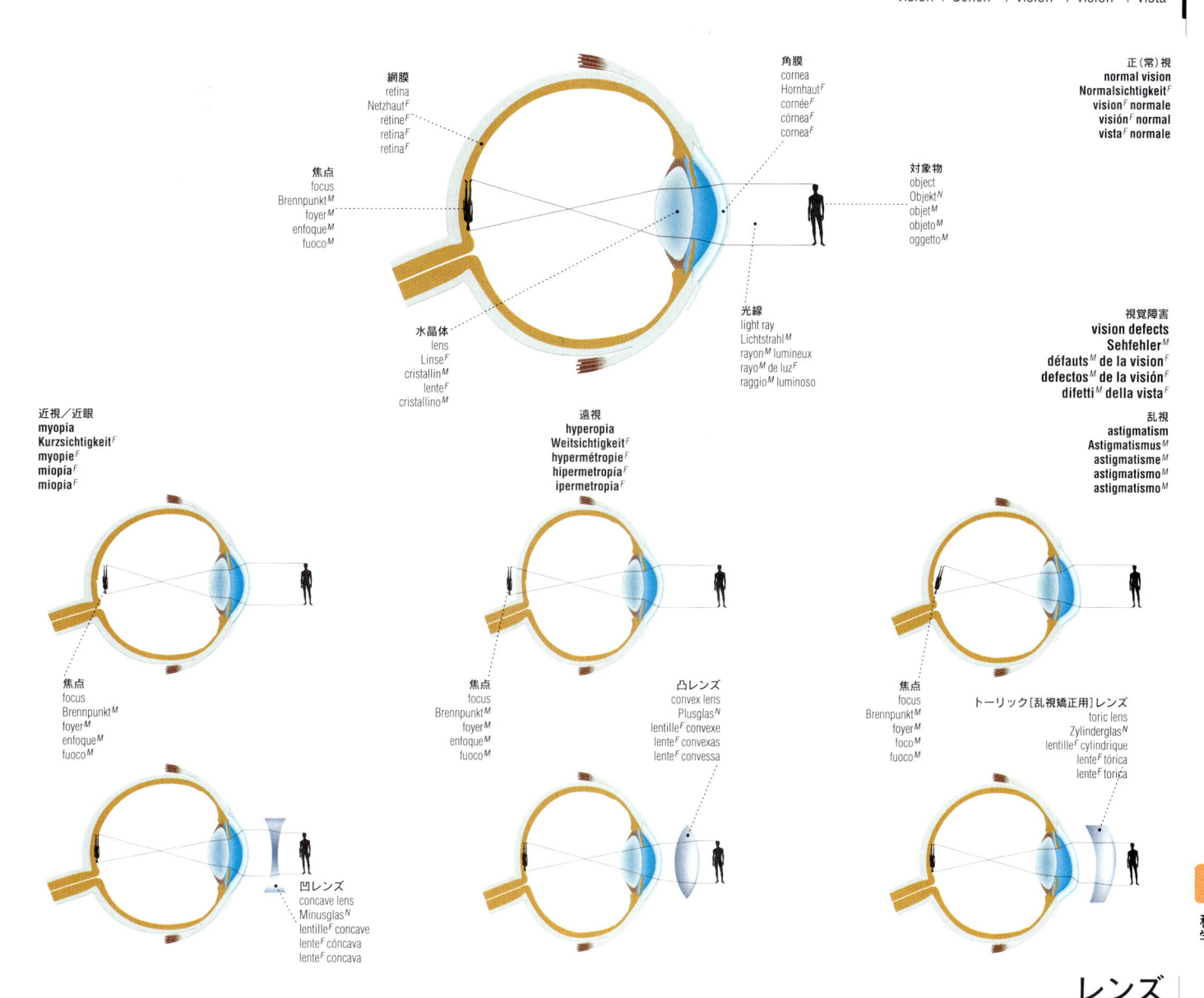

網膜 retina / Netzhaut^F / rétine^F / retina^F / retina^F

角膜 cornea / Hornhaut^F / cornée^F / córnea^F / cornea^F

焦点 focus / Brennpunkt^M / foyer^M / enfoque^M / fuoco^M

対象物 object / Objekt^N / objet^M / objeto^M / oggetto^M

水晶体 lens / Linse^F / cristallin^M / lente^F / cristallino^M

光線 light ray / Lichtstrahl^M / rayon^M lumineux / rayo^M de luz^F / raggio^M luminoso

正（常）視 normal vision / Normalsichtigkeit^F / vision^F normale / visión^F normal / vista^F normale

視覚障害 vision defects / Sehfehler^M / défauts^M de la vision^F / defectos^M de la visión^F / difetti^M della vista^F

近視／近眼 myopia / Kurzsichtigkeit^F / myopie^F / miopía^F / miopia^F

遠視 hyperopia / Weitsichtigkeit^F / hypermétropie^F / hipermetropía^F / ipermetropia^F

乱視 astigmatism / Astigmatismus^M / astigmatisme^M / astigmatismo^M / astigmatismo^M

焦点 focus / Brennpunkt^M / foyer^M / enfoque^M / fuoco^M

焦点 focus / Brennpunkt^M / foyer^M / enfoque^M / fuoco^M

焦点 focus / Brennpunkt^M / foyer^M / foco^M / fuoco^M

凸レンズ convex lens / Plusglas^N / lentille^F convexe / lente^F convexas / lente^F convessa

トーリック[乱視矯正用]レンズ toric lens / Zylinderglas^N / lentille^F cylindrique / lente^F tórica / lente^F torica

凹レンズ concave lens / Minusglas^N / lentille^F concave / lente^F cóncava / lente^F concava

レンズ

lenses | Linsen^F | lentilles^F | lentes^F | lenti^F

収束レンズ converging lenses / Sammellinsen^F / lentilles^F convergentes / lentes^F convergentes / lenti^F convergenti

両凸レンズ biconvex lens / bikonvexe Linse^F / lentille^F biconvexe / lentes^F biconvexas / lente^F biconvessa

凸メニスカス・レンズ positive meniscus / konkavkonvexe Linse^F / ménisque^M convergent / menisco^M convergente / menisco^M convergente

凸レンズ convex lens / konvexe Linse^F / lentille^F convexe / lentes^F convexas / lente^F convessa

平凸レンズ plano-convex lens / plankonvexe Linse^F / lentille^F plan^M-convexe / lente^F convexo-plana / lente^F piano-convessa

発散レンズ diverging lenses / Zerstreuungslinsen^F / lentilles^F divergentes / lentes^F divergentes / lenti^F divergenti

平凹レンズ plano-concave lens / plankonkave Linse^F / lentille^F plan^M-concave / lentes^F cóncavo-planas / lente^F piano-concava

凹レンズ concave lens / konkave Linse^F / lentille^F concave / lentes^F cóncavas / lente^F concava

両凹レンズ biconcave lens / bikonkave Linse^F / lentille^F biconcave / lentes^F bicóncavas / lente^F biconcava

凹メニスカス・レンズ negative meniscus / konvexkonkave Linse^F / ménisque^M divergent / menisco^M divergente / menisco^M divergente

科学

物理：光学｜PHYSICS: OPTICS
PHYSIK: OPTIK｜PHYSIQUE : OPTIQUE｜FÍSICA : ÓPTICA｜FISICA: OTTICA

パルス・ルビー・レーザー

日本語｜英語｜ドイツ語｜フランス語｜スペイン語｜イタリア語

pulsed ruby laser ｜ Rubin^M-Impulslaser^M ｜ laser^M à rubis^M pulsé ｜ láser^M de rubí^M pulsado ｜ laser^M a rubino^M pulsato

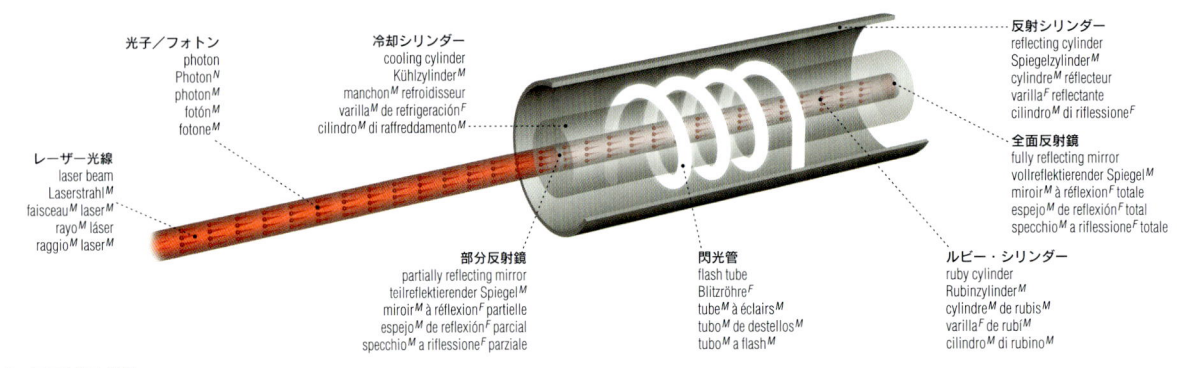

光子／フォトン
photon
Photon^N
photon^M
fotón^M
fotone^M

冷却シリンダー
cooling cylinder
Kühlzylinder^M
manchon^M refroidisseur
varilla^F de refrigeración
cilindro^M di raffreddamento

反射シリンダー
reflecting cylinder
Spiegelzylinder^M
cylindre^M réflecteur
varilla^F reflectante
cilindro^M di riflessione

レーザー光線
laser beam
Laserstrahl^M
faisceau^M laser^M
rayo^M láser
raggio^M laser

全面反射鏡
fully reflecting mirror
vollreflektierender Spiegel^M
miroir^M à réflexion^F totale
espejo^M de reflexión^F total
specchio^M a riflessione^F totale

部分反射鏡
partially reflecting mirror
teilreflektierender Spiegel^M
miroir^M à réflexion^F partielle
espejo^M de reflexión^F parcial
specchio^M a riflessione^F parziale

閃光管
flash tube
Blitzröhre^F
tube^M à éclairs^M
tubo^M de destellos^M
tubo^M a flash^M

ルビー・シリンダー
ruby cylinder
Rubinzylinder^M
cylindre^M de rubis^M
varilla^F de rubí^M
cilindro^M di rubino^M

プリズム双眼鏡

prism binoculars ｜ Prismenfernglas^N ｜ jumelles^F à prismes^M ｜ prismáticos^M binoculares ｜ binocolo^M prismatico

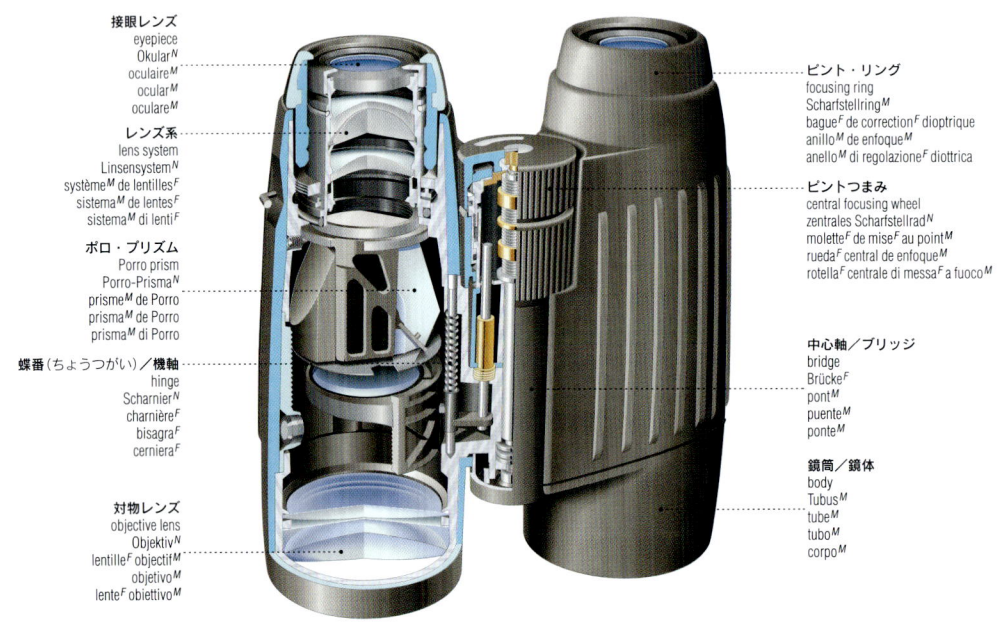

接眼レンズ
eyepiece
Okular^N
oculaire^M
ocular^M
oculare^M

レンズ系
lens system
Linsensystem^N
système^M de lentilles^F
sistema^M de lentes^F
sistema^M di lenti^F

ポロ・プリズム
Porro prism
Porro-Prisma^N
prisme^M de Porro
prisma^M de Porro
prisma^M di Porro

蝶番（ちょうつがい）／機軸
hinge
Scharnier^N
charnière^F
bisagra^F
cerniera^F

対物レンズ
objective lens
Objektiv^N
lentille^F objectif^M
objetivo^M
lente^F obiettivo^M

ピント・リング
focusing ring
Scharfstellring^M
bague^F de correction^F dioptrique
anillo^M de enfoque^M
anello^M di regolazione^F diottrica

ピントつまみ
central focusing wheel
zentrales Scharfstellrad^N
molette^F de mise^F au point^M
rueda^F central de enfoque^M
rotella^F centrale di messa^F a fuoco^M

中心軸／ブリッジ
bridge
Brücke^F
pont^M
puente^M
ponte^M

鏡筒／鏡体
body
Tubus^M
tube^M
tubo^M
corpo^M

眼鏡照準器／（光学式）照準眼鏡

telescopic sight ｜ Zielfernrohr^N ｜ lunette^F de visée^F ｜ visor^M telescópico ｜ cannocchiale^M di mira^F

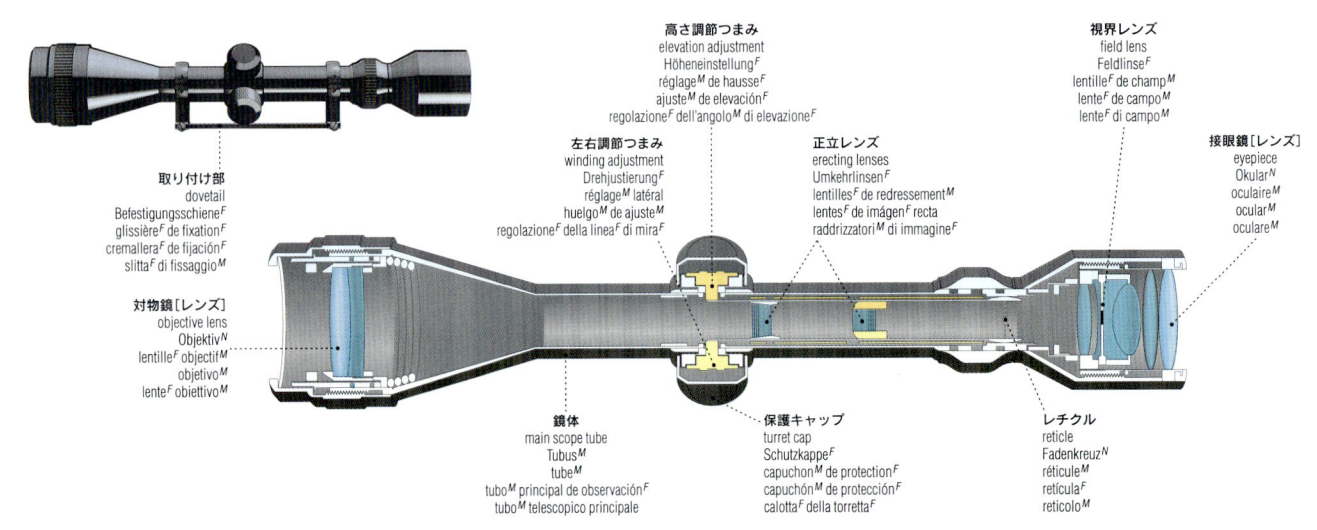

高さ調節つまみ
elevation adjustment
Höheneinstellung^F
réglage^M de hausse^F
ajuste^M de elevación^F
regolazione^F dell'angolo^M di elevazione^F

左右調節つまみ
winding adjustment
Drehjustierung^F
réglage^M latéral
huelgo^M de ajuste^M
regolazione^F della linea^F di mira^F

正立レンズ
erecting lenses
Umkehrlinsen^F
lentilles^F de redressement^M
lentes^F de imágen^F recta
raddrizzatori^M di immagine^F

視界レンズ
field lens
Feldlinse^F
lentille^F de champ^M
lente^F de campo^M
lente^F di campo^M

接眼鏡［レンズ］
eyepiece
Okular^N
oculaire^M
ocular^M
oculare^M

取り付け部
dovetail
Befestigungsschiene^F
glissière^F de fixation^F
cremallera^F de fijación^F
slitta^F di fissaggio^M

対物鏡［レンズ］
objective lens
Objektiv^N
lentille^F objectif^M
objetivo^M
lente^F obiettivo^M

鏡体
main scope tube
Tubus^M
tube^M
tubo^M principal de observación^F
tubo^M telescopico principale

保護キャップ
turret cap
Schutzkappe^F
capuchon^M de protection^F
capuchón^M de protección^F
calotta^F della torretta^F

レチクル
reticle
Fadenkreuz^N
réticule^M
retícula^F
reticolo^M

物理：光学 | PHYSICS: OPTICS
PHYSIK: OPTIK | PHYSIQUE : OPTIQUE | FÍSICA : ÓPTICA | FISICA: OTTICA

ルーペと顕微鏡

magnifying glass and microscopes | Lupe^F und Mikroskope^N | loupe^F et microscopes^M | lupa^F y microscopios^M | lente^F di ingrandimento^M e microscopi^M

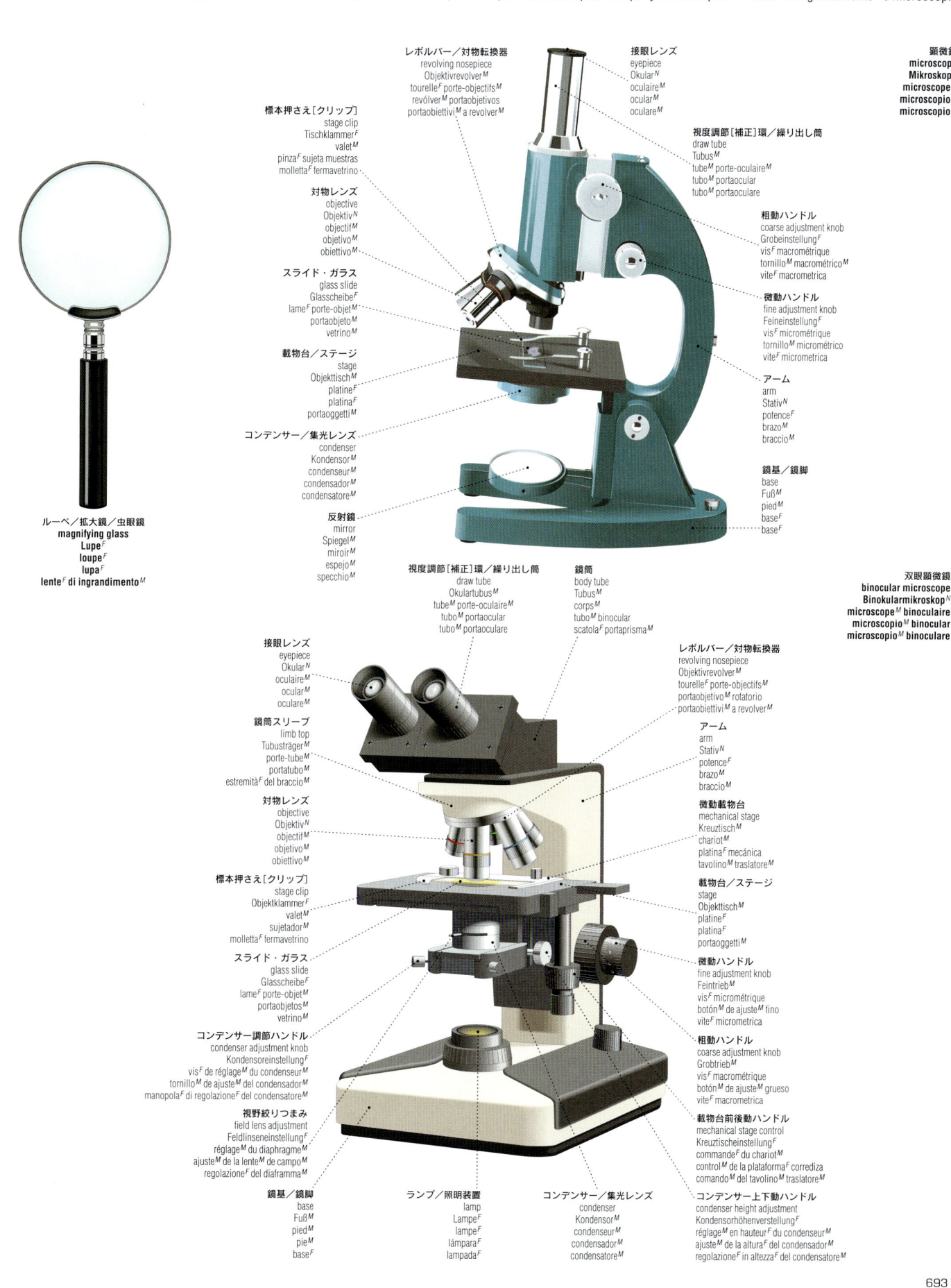

顕微鏡
microscope
Mikroskop^N
microscope^M
microscopio^M
microscopio^M

レボルバー／対物転換器
revolving nosepiece
Objektivrevolver^M
tourelle^F porte-objectifs^M
revólver^M portaobjetivos
portaobiettivi^M a revolver^M

接眼レンズ
eyepiece
Okular^N
oculaire^M
ocular^M
oculare^M

視度調節［補正］環／繰り出し筒
draw tube
Tubus^M
tube^M porte-oculaire^M
tubo^M portaocular
tubo^M portaoculare

標本押さえ［クリップ］
stage clip
Tischklammer^F
valet^M
pinza^F sujeta muestras
molletta^F fermavetrino

対物レンズ
objective
Objektiv^N
objectif^M
objetivo^M
obiettivo^M

粗動ハンドル
coarse adjustment knob
Grobeinstellung^F
vis^F macrométrique
tornillo^M macrométrico
vite^F macrometrica

スライド・ガラス
glass slide
Glasscheibe^F
lame^F porte-objet^M
portaobjeto^M
vetrino^M

微動ハンドル
fine adjustment knob
Feineinstellung^F
vis^F micrométrique
tornillo^M micrométrico
vite^F micrometrica

載物台／ステージ
stage
Objekttisch^M
platine^F
platina^F
portaoggetti^M

アーム
arm
Stativ^N
potence^F
brazo^M
braccio^M

コンデンサー／集光レンズ
condenser
Kondensor^M
condenseur^M
condensador^M
condensatore^M

鏡基／鏡脚
base
Fuß^M
pied^M
base^F
base^F

反射鏡
mirror
Spiegel^M
miroir^M
espejo^M
specchio^M

ルーペ／拡大鏡／虫眼鏡
magnifying glass
Lupe^F
loupe^F
lupa^F
lente^F di ingrandimento^M

視度調節［補正］環／繰り出し筒
draw tube
Okulartubus^M
tube^M porte-oculaire^M
tubo^M portaocular
tubo^M portaoculare

鏡筒
body tube
Tubus^M
corps^M
tubo^M binocular
scatola^F portaprisma^M

双眼顕微鏡
binocular microscope
Binokularmikroskop^N
microscope^M binoculaire
microscopio^M binocular
microscopio^M binoculare

接眼レンズ
eyepiece
Okular^N
oculaire^M
ocular^M
oculare^M

レボルバー／対物転換器
revolving nosepiece
Objektivrevolver^M
tourelle^F porte-objectifs^M
portaobjetivo^M rotatorio
portaobiettivi^M a revolver^M

鏡筒スリーブ
limb top
Tubusträger^M
porte-tube^M
portatubo^M
estremità^F del braccio^M

アーム
arm
Stativ^N
potence^F
brazo^M
braccio^M

対物レンズ
objective
Objektiv^N
objectif^M
objetivo^M
obiettivo^M

微動載物台
mechanical stage
Kreuztisch^M
chariot^M
platina^F mecánica
tavolino^M traslatore^M

標本押さえ［クリップ］
stage clip
Objektklammer^F
valet^M
sujetador^M
molletta^F fermavetrino

載物台／ステージ
stage
Objekttisch^M
platine^F
platina^F
portaoggetti^M

スライド・ガラス
glass slide
Glasscheibe^F
lame^F porte-objet^M
portaobjetos^M
vetrino^M

微動ハンドル
fine adjustment knob
Feintrieb^M
vis^F micrométrique
botón^M de ajuste^M fino
vite^F micrometrica

コンデンサー調節ハンドル
condenser adjustment knob
Kondensoreinstellung^F
vis^F de réglage^M du condenseur^M
tornillo^M de ajuste^M del condensador^M
manopola^F di regolazione^F del condensatore^M

粗動ハンドル
coarse adjustment knob
Grobtrieb^M
vis^F macrométrique
botón^M de ajuste^M grueso
vite^F macrometrica

視野絞りつまみ
field lens adjustment
Feldlinseneinstellung^F
réglage^M du diaphragme^M
ajuste^M de la lente^F de campo^M
regolazione^F del diaframma^M

載物台前後動ハンドル
mechanical stage control
Kreuztischeinstellung^F
commande^F du chariot^M
control^M de la plataforma^F corrediza
comando^M del tavolino^M traslatore^M

鏡基／鏡脚
base
Fuß^M
pied^M
pie^M
base^F

ランプ／照明装置
lamp
Lampe^F
lampe^F
lámpara^F
lampada^F

コンデンサー／集光レンズ
condenser
Kondensor^M
condenseur^M
condensador^M
condensatore^M

コンデンサー上下動ハンドル
condenser height adjustment
Kondensorhöhenverstellung^F
réglage^M en hauteur^F du condenseur^M
ajuste^M de la altura^F del condensador^M
regolazione^F in altezza^F del condensatore^M

科学

物理：光学 | PHYSICS: OPTICS
PHYSIK: OPTIK | PHYSIQUE : OPTIQUE | FÍSICA : ÓPTICA | FISICA : OTTICA

ルーペと顕微鏡

日本語 | 英語 | ドイツ語 | フランス語 | スペイン語 | イタリア語

電子顕微鏡の断面図
cross section of an electron microscope
Elektronenmikroskop^N im Querschnitt^M
coupe^F d'un microscope^M électronique
corte^M transversal de un microscopio^M de electrones^M
sezione^F di un microscopio^M elettronico

電子銃
electron gun
Elektronenkanone^F
canon^M à électrons^M
cañón^M de electrones^M
cannone^M elettronico

電子ビーム［線］
electron beam
Elektronenstrahl^M
faisceau^M d'électrons^M
haz^M de electrones^M
fascio^M elettronico

真空マニホルド
vacuum manifold
Vakuumrohr^N
canalisation^F de pompage^M
canalización^F de vacío^M
collettore^M a vuoto^M

電子ビーム軸合わせ部
electron beam positioning
Elektronenstrahljustierung^F
alignement^M du faisceau^M dans l'axe^M
posición^F del haz^M de electrones^M
posizionamento^M del fascio^M rispetto all'asse^F

ビーム径の絞り込み部
beam diameter reduction
Verminderung^F des Strahldurchmessers^M
concentration^F du faisceau^M
reducción^F del diámetro^M del haz^M
riduzione^F del diametro^M del fascio^M

コンデンサー
condenser
Kondensor^M
condenseur^M
condensador^M
condensatore^M

開口絞り調節つまみ
aperture changer
Blendeneinstellung^F
commande^F de sélection^F de l'ouverture^F
abertura^F para el cambio^M de gases^M
cambiaaperture^M

集束レンズ
focusing lenses
elektronenoptische Linsen^F
lentilles^F de mise^F au point^M
lentes^F de enfoque^M
lenti^F di focalizzazione^F

開口絞り
aperture diaphragm
Aperturblende^F
diaphragme^M d'ouverture^F
abertura^F del diafragma^M
diaframma^M di apertura^F

検出器
visual transmission
Einblicklupe^F
transmission^F de l'image^F
transmisión^F visual
trasmissione^F dell'immagine^F

試料ステージ
stage
Objekttisch^M
porte-spécimen^M
platina^F
portaoggetti^M

真空［試料］室
vacuum chamber
Vakuumkammer^F
chambre^F à vide^M
cámara^F de vacío^M
camera^F a vuoto^M

電子顕微鏡の構成部品
electron microscope elements
Teile^N des Elektronenmikroskops^N
composantes^F d'un microscope^M électronique
elementos^M del microscopio^M de electrones^M
elementi^M del microscopio^M elettronico

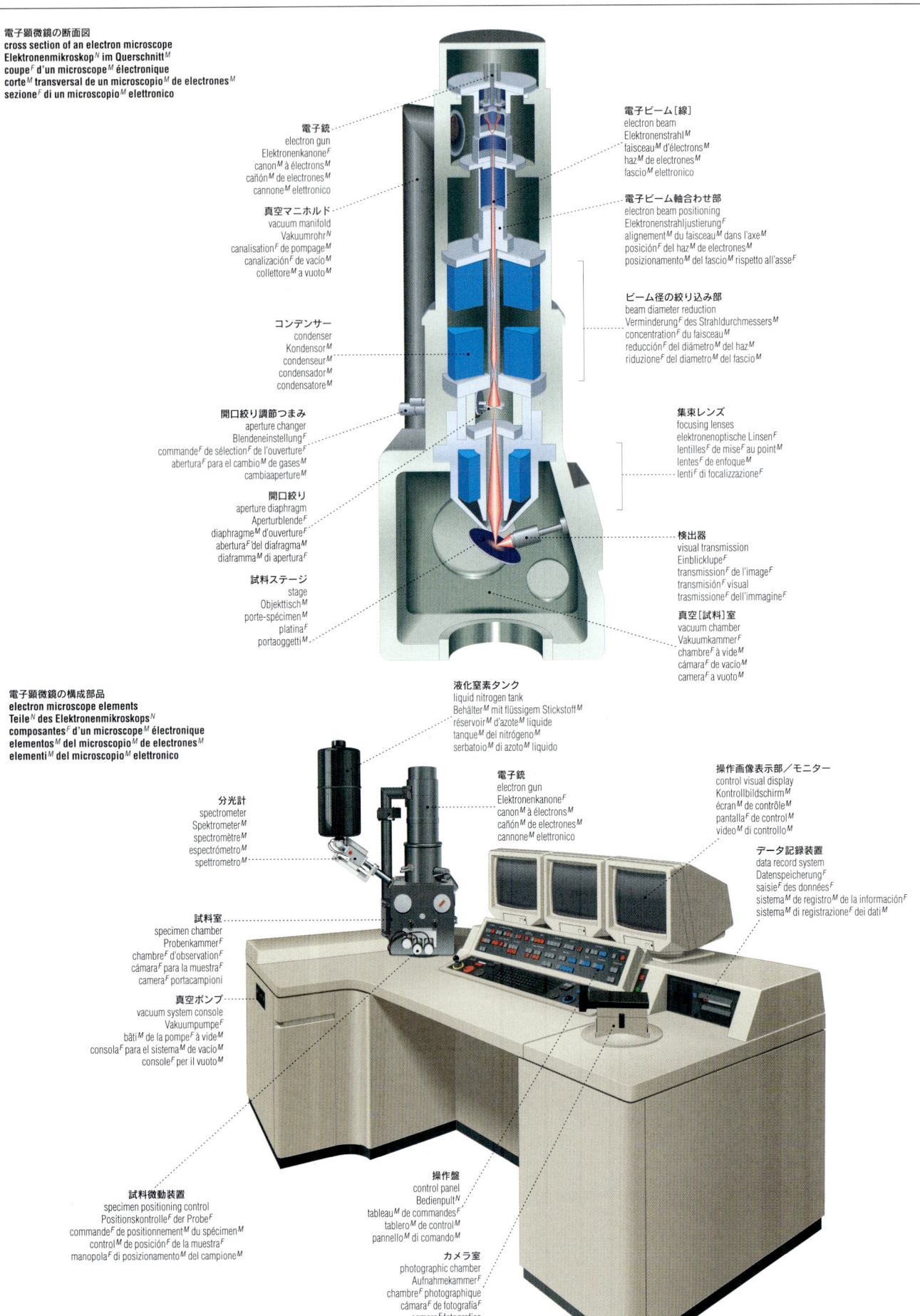

液化窒素タンク
liquid nitrogen tank
Behälter^M mit flüssigem Stickstoff^M
réservoir^M d'azote^M liquide
tanque^M del nitrógeno^M
serbatoio^M di azoto^M liquido

電子銃
electron gun
Elektronenkanone^F
canon^M à électrons^M
cañón^M de electrones^M
cannone^M elettronico

操作画像表示部／モニター
control visual display
Kontrollbildschirm^M
écran^M de contrôle^M
pantalla^F de control^M
video^M di controllo^M

分光計
spectrometer
Spektrometer^M
spectromètre^M
espectrómetro^M
spettrometro^M

データ記録装置
data record system
Datenspeicherung^F
saisie^F des données^F
sistema^M de registro^M de la información^F
sistema^M di registrazione^F dei dati^M

試料室
specimen chamber
Probenkammer^F
chambre^F d'observation^F
cámara^F para la muestra^F
camera^F portacampioni

真空ポンプ
vacuum system console
Vakuumpumpe^F
bâti^M de la pompe^F à vide^M
consola^F para el sistema^M de vacío^M
console^F per il vuoto^M

試料微動装置
specimen positioning control
Positionskontrolle^F der Probe^F
commande^F de positionnement^M du spécimen^M
control^M de posición^F de la muestra^F
manopola^F di posizionamento^M del campione^M

操作盤
control panel
Bedienpult^N
tableau^M de commandes^F
tablero^M de control^M
pannello^M di comando^M

カメラ室
photographic chamber
Aufnahmekammer^F
chambre^F photographique
cámara^F de fotografía^F
camera^F fotografica

科学

計測機器 | MEASURING DEVICES
MESSINSTRUMENTE | APPAREILS DE MESURE | APARATOS DE MEDICIÓN | STRUMENTI DI MISURA

温度測定

measure of temperature | Temperaturmessung^F | mesure^F de la température^F | medición^F de la temperatura^F | misura^F della temperatura^F

温度計
thermometer
Thermometer^N
thermomètre^M
termómetro^M
termometro^M

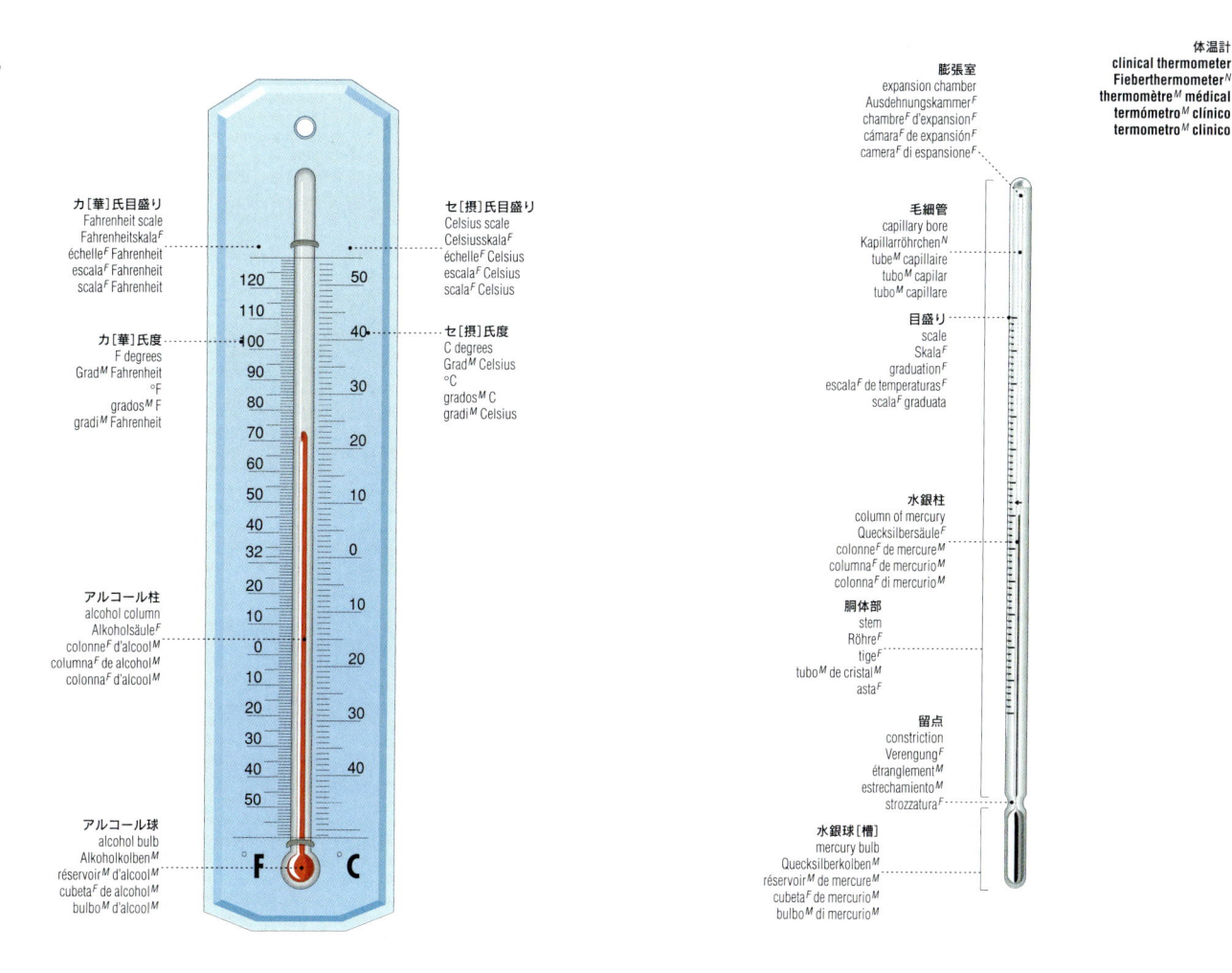

カ[華]氏目盛り
Fahrenheit scale
Fahrenheitskala^F
échelle^F Fahrenheit
escala^F Fahrenheit
scala^F Fahrenheit

カ[華]氏度
F degrees
Grad^M Fahrenheit
°F
grados^M F
gradi^M Fahrenheit

アルコール柱
alcohol column
Alkoholsäule^F
colonne^F d'alcool^M
columna^F de alcohol^M
colonna^F d'alcool^M

アルコール球
alcohol bulb
Alkoholkolben^M
réservoir^M d'alcool^M
cubeta^F de alcohol^M
bulbo^M d'alcool^M

セ[摂]氏目盛り
Celsius scale
Celsiusskala^F
échelle^F Celsius
escala^F Celsius
scala^F Celsius

セ[摂]氏度
C degrees
Grad^M Celsius
°C
grados^M C
gradi^M Celsius

膨張室
expansion chamber
Ausdehnungskammer^F
chambre^F d'expansion^F
cámara^F de expansión^F
camera^F di espansione^F

毛細管
capillary bore
Kapillarröhrchen^N
tube^M capillaire
tubo^M capilar
tubo^M capillare

目盛り
scale
Skala^F
graduation^F
escala^F de temperaturas^F
scala^F graduata

水銀柱
column of mercury
Quecksilbersäule^F
colonne^F de mercure^M
columna^F de mercurio^M
colonna^F di mercurio^M

胴体部
stem
Röhre^F
tige^F
tubo^M de cristal^M
asta^F

留点
constriction
Verengung^F
étranglement^M
estrechamiento^M
strozzatura^F

水銀球[槽]
mercury bulb
Quecksilberkolben^M
réservoir^M de mercure^M
cubeta^F de mercurio^M
bulbo^M di mercurio^M

体温計
clinical thermometer
Fieberthermometer^N
thermomètre^M **médical**
termómetro^M **clínico**
termometro^M **clinico**

バイメタル温度計
bimetallic thermometer
Bimetall-Thermometer^N
thermomètre^M **bimétallique**
termómetro^M **bimetálico**
termometro^M **a lamina**^{F} **bimetallica**

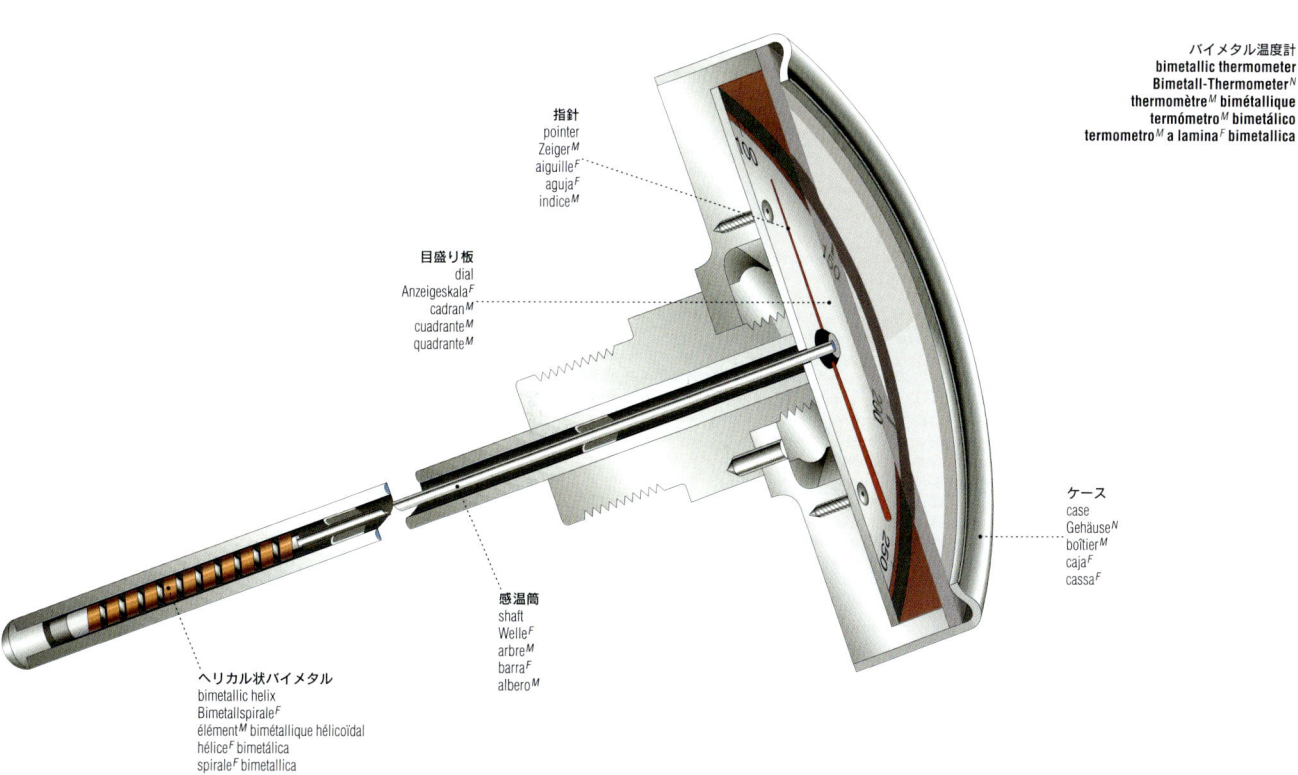

指針
pointer
Zeiger^M
aiguille^F
aguja^F
indice^M

目盛り板
dial
Anzeigeskala^F
cadran^M
cuadrante^M
quadrante^M

感温筒
shaft
Welle^F
arbre^M
barra^F
albero^M

ヘリカル状バイメタル
bimetallic helix
Bimetallspirale^F
élément^M bimétallique hélicoïdal
hélice^F bimetálica
spirale^F bimetallica

ケース
case
Gehäuse^N
boîtier^M
caja^F
cassa^F

科学

695

計測機器 | MEASURING DEVICES
MESSINSTRUMENTE | APPAREILS DE MESURE | APARATOS DE MEDICIÓN | STRUMENTI DI MISURA

時間測定

日本語 | 英語 | ドイツ語 | フランス語 | スペイン語 | イタリア語

measure of time | Zeitmessung^F | mesure^F du temps^M | medición^F del tiempo^M | misura^F del tempo^M

ストップウォッチ
stopwatch
Stoppuhr^F
chronomètre^M
cronómetro^M
cronometro^M

分針
minute hand
Minutenzeiger^M
aiguille^F des minutes^F
minutero^M
lancetta^F dei minuti^M

リセット・ボタン
reset button
Rückstellknopf^M
poussoir^M de remise^F à zéro^M
botón^M de inicio^M del contador^M
pulsante^M di azzeramento^M

秒針
second hand
Sekundenzeiger^M
trotteuse^F
segundero^M
lancetta^F dei secondi^M

10分の1秒針
1/10th second hand
Zehntelsekundenzeiger^M
aiguille^F des dixièmes^F de seconde^F
aguja^F de décimas^F de segundo^M
lancetta^F dei decimi^M di secondo^M

リング
ring
Ring^M
anneau^M
anilla^F
anello^M

スタート・ボタン
start button
Startknopf^M
poussoir^M de mise^F en marche^F
botón^M de inicio^M de marcha^F
pulsante^M di partenza^M

ストップ・ボタン
stop button
Stoppknopf^M
poussoir^M d'arrêt^M
botón^M de parada^M
pulsante^M di arresto^M

ケース
case
Gehäuse^N
boîtier^M
estuche^M
cassa^F

デジタル時計
digital watch
Digitaluhr^F
montre^F à affichage^M numérique
reloj^M digital
orologio^M digitale

液晶ディスプレイ
liquid-crystal display
LCD-Anzeige^F
cristaux^M liquides
registro^M de cristal^M líquido
quadrante^M a cristalli^M liquidi

アナログ時計
analog watch; *analogue watch*
Analoguhr^F
montre^F à affichage^M analogique
reloj^M de pulsera^F
orologio^M analogico

文字盤
dial
Zifferblatt^N
cadran^M
cuadrante^M
quadrante^M

機械式時計
mechanical watch
mechanische Uhr^F
montre^F mécanique
reloj^M mecánico
orologio^M meccanico

四番車
fourth wheel
Ankerrad^N
roue^F de champ^M
rueda^F de los segundos^M
ruota^F dei secondi^M

三番車
third wheel
Antriebswerk^N
roue^F petite moyenne
rueda^F media
ruota^F intermedia

貴石
jewel
Stein^M
rubis^M
rubí^M
rubino^M

雁木（がんぎ）車
escape wheel
Hemmungsrad^N
roue^F d'échappement^M
rueda^F de escape^M
ruota^F di scappamento^M

ひげぜんまい
hairspring
Spiralfeder^F
spiral^M
espiral^M
molla^F a spirale^F

二番車
center wheel; *centre wheel*
Spannrad^N
roue^F de centre^M
rueda^F central
ruota^F di centro^M

巻き上げ装置
winder
Aufzugsrad^N
remontoir^M
cuerda^F
ruota^F di carica^F

小鉤（こはぜ）
click
Sperrstift^M
cliquet^M
trinquete^M
cricchetto^M

香箱（こうばこ）車／一番車
ratchet wheel; *barrel*
Federhaus^N
rochet^M
rueda^F de trinquete^M
barilletto^M

竜頭（りゅうず）
crown
Krone^F
couronne^F
corona^F
corona^F

革バンド
strap
Uhrband^N
bracelet^M
correa^F
cinturino^M

日時計
sundial
Sonnenuhr^F
cadran^M solaire
reloj^M de sol^M
meridiana^F

指時計／指柱
gnomon
Gnomon^M
style^M
estilo^M
gnomone^M

文字盤
dial
Zifferblatt^N
cadran^M
cuadrante^M
quadrante^M

影
shadow
Schatten^M
ombre^F
sombra^F
ombra^F

科学

計測機器 | MEASURING DEVICES
MESSINSTRUMENTE | APPAREILS DE MESURE | APARATOS DE MEDICIÓN | STRUMENTI DI MISURA

時間測定

振り子式箱型大時計
grandfather clock
Standuhr^F
horloge^F de parquet^M
reloj^M de péndulo^M
orologio^M a pendolo^M

頭飾り
pediment
Giebeldreieck^N
corniche^F
frontón^M
frontone^M

外箱／ケーシング
body
Uhrkasten^M
caisse^F
caja^F
cassa^F

時針
hour hand
Sekundenzeiger^M
aiguille^F des heures^F
manecilla^F de las horas^F
lancetta^F delle ore^F

文字盤
dial
Zifferblatt^N
cadran^M
esfera^F
quadrante^M

月齢盤
Moon dial
Mondphasenzeiger^M
cadran^M des phases^F de la Lune^F
esfera^F lunar
quadrante^M a fasi^F lunari

分針
minute hand
Minutenzeiger^M
aiguille^F des minutes^F
minutero^M
lancetta^F dei minuti^M

錘（おもり）
weight
Gewicht^N
poids^M
pesa^F
peso^M

振り子
pendulum
Pendel^N
pendule^F
péndulo^M
pendolo^M

鎖
chain
Kette^F
chaîne^F
cadena^F
catena^F

台足
plinth
Plinthe^F
socle^M
zócalo^M
piedistallo^M

振り子時計の仕組み
weight-driven clock mechanism
Uhrwerk^N mit Gewichtsantrieb^M
mécanisme^M de l'horloge^F à poids^M
mecanismo^M del reloj^M de pesas^F
meccanismo^M dell'orologio^M a peso^M

ピニオン
pinion
Ritzel^N
pignon^M
piñón^M
pignone^M

アンクル／パレット
pallet
Hemmungslappen^M
ancre^F
áncora^F
ancora^F

吊りばね
suspension spring
Aufhängefeder^F
lame^F de suspension^F
resorte^M de suspensión^F
molla^F di sospensione^F

アンクル竿
fork
Gabel^F
fourchette^F
diapasón^M
forchetta^F

二番車
center wheel; centre wheel
Spannrad^N
roue^F de centre^F
rueda^F central
ruota^F di centro^M

小鉤（こはぜ）
click
Sperrstift^M
cliquet^M
trinquete^M
cricchetto^M

振り竿
pendulum rod
Pendelstab^M
tige^F
varilla^F del péndulo^M
asta^F del pendolo^M

振り子
pendulum
Pendel^N
lentille^F
péndulo^M
lente^F del pendolo^M

雁木（がんぎ）車
escape wheel
Hemmungsrad^N
roue^F d'échappement^M
rueda^F de escape^M
ruota^F di scappamento^M

回転軸
spindle
Spindel^F
arbre^M
eje^M
albero^M

三番車
third wheel
Antriebswerk^N
roue^F petite moyenne
rueda^F de corona^F
ruota^F intermedia

分針
minute hand
Minutenzeiger^M
aiguille^F des minutes^F
minutero^M
lancetta^F dei minuti^M

時針
hour hand
Stundenzeiger^M
aiguille^F des heures^F
manecilla^F de las horas^F
lancetta^F delle ore^F

巻き上げ装置
winding mechanism
Aufzugsmechanismus^M
remontoir^M
mecanismo^M de cuerda^F
meccanismo^M di carica^F

一番車
main wheel
Hauptrad^M
roue^F motrice
rueda^F motriz
ruota^F motrice

角穴車
ratchet wheel
Sperrrad^N
rochet^M
rueda^F de trinquete^M
ruota^F a denti^M di sega^F

錘（おもり）
weight
Gewicht^N
poids^M
pesa^F
peso^M

ドラム
drum
Trommel^F
tambour^M
cilindro^M
tamburo^M

科学

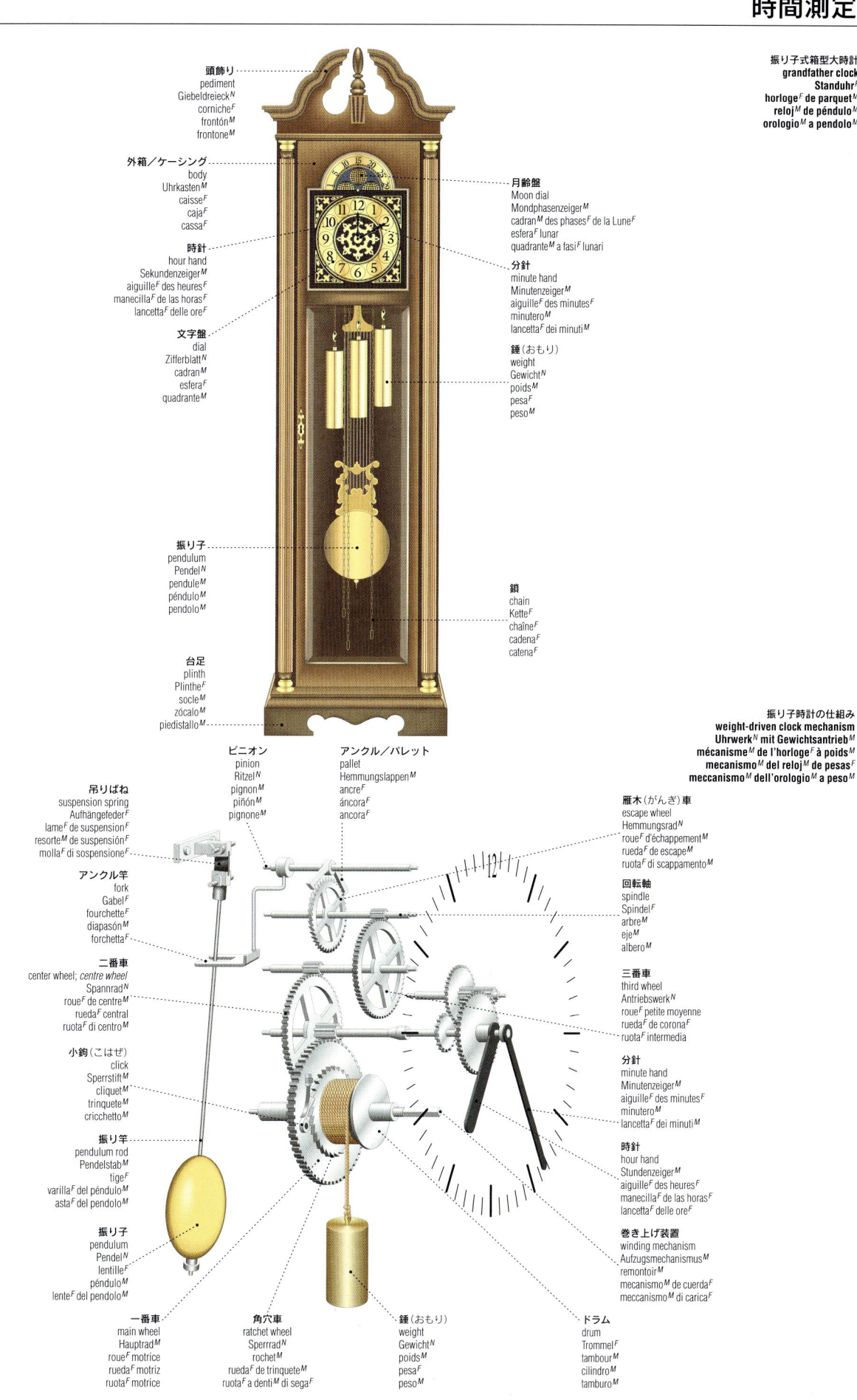

697

計測機器 | MEASURING DEVICES
MESSINSTRUMENTE | APPAREILS DE MESURE | APARATOS DE MEDICIÓN | STRUMENTI DI MISURA

重量測定

日本語 | 英語 | ドイツ語 | フランス語 | スペイン語 | イタリア語

measure of weight | Wiegen^N | mesure^F de la masse^F | medición^F del peso^M | misura^F del peso^M

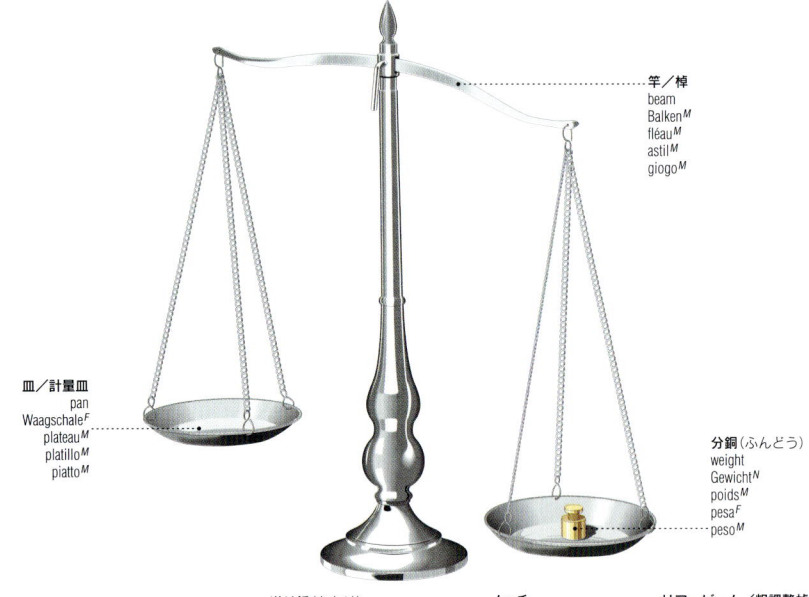

天秤
beam balance
Balkenwaage^F
balance^F à fléau^M
balanza^F de astil^M
bilancia^F di precisione^F

竿／棹
beam
Balken^M
fléau^M
astil^M
giogo^M

皿／計量皿
pan
Waagschale^F
plateau^M
platillo^M
piatto^M

分銅（ふんどう）
weight
Gewicht^N
poids^M
pesa^F
peso^M

竿[棹]秤
steelyard
Handwaage^F
balance^F romaine
báscula^F romana
stadera^F

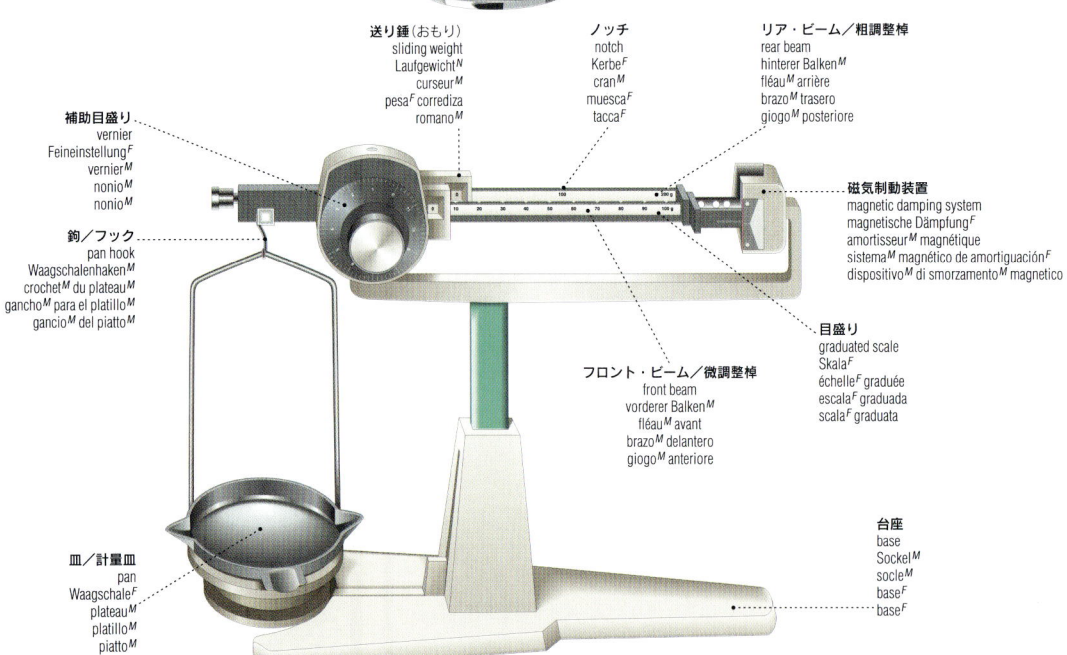

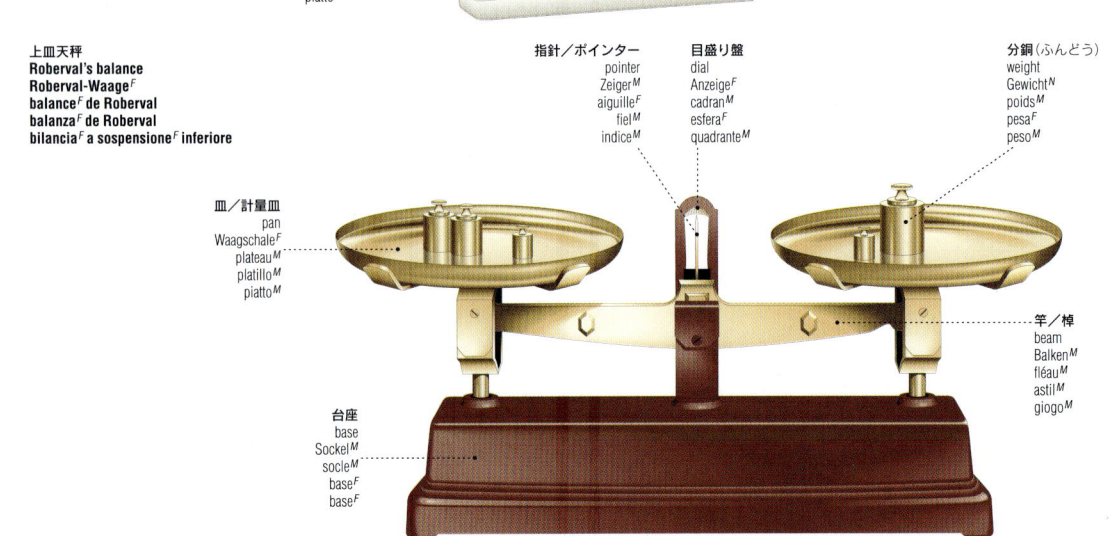

送り錘（おもり）
sliding weight
Laufgewicht^N
curseur^M
pesa^F corrediza
romano^M

ノッチ
notch
Kerbe^F
cran^M
muesca^F
tacca^F

リア・ビーム／粗調整棹
rear beam
hinterer Balken^M
fléau^M arrière
brazo^M trasero
giogo^M posteriore

補助目盛り
vernier
Feineinstellung^F
vernier^M
nonio^M
nonio^M

磁気制動装置
magnetic damping system
magnetische Dämpfung^F
amortisseur^M magnétique
sistema^M magnético de amortiguación^F
dispositivo^M di smorzamento magnetico

鉤／フック
pan hook
Waagschalenhaken^M
crochet^M du plateau^M
gancho^M para el platillo^M
gancio^M del piatto^M

目盛り
graduated scale
Skala^F
échelle^F graduée
escala^F graduada
scala^F graduata

フロント・ビーム／微調整棹
front beam
vorderer Balken^M
fléau^M avant
brazo^M delantero
giogo^M anteriore

皿／計量皿
pan
Waagschale^F
plateau^M
platillo^M
piatto^M

台座
base
Sockel^M
socle^M
base^F
base^F

上皿天秤
Roberval's balance
Roberval-Waage^F
balance^F de Roberval
balanza^F de Roberval
bilancia^F a sospensione^F inferiore

指針／ポインター
pointer
Zeiger^M
aiguille^F
fiel^M
indice^M

目盛り盤
dial
Anzeige^F
cadran^M
esfera^F
quadrante^M

分銅（ふんどう）
weight
Gewicht^N
poids^M
pesa^F
peso^M

皿／計量皿
pan
Waagschale^F
plateau^M
platillo^M
piatto^M

竿／棹
beam
Balken^M
fléau^M
astil^M
giogo^M

台座
base
Sockel^M
socle^M
base^F
base^F

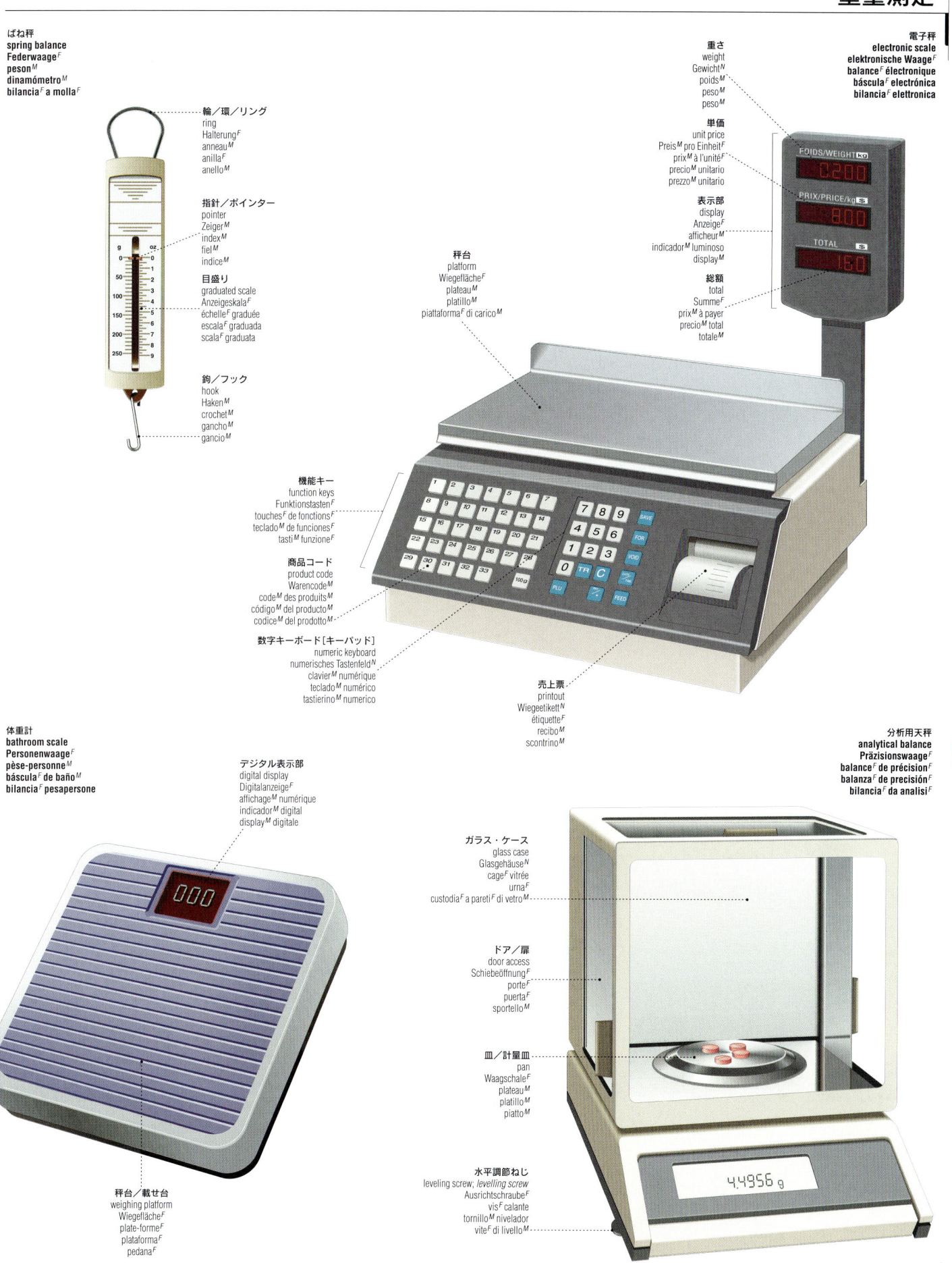

計測機器 | MEASURING DEVICES
MESSINSTRUMENTE | APPAREILS DE MESURE | APARATOS DE MEDICIÓN | STRUMENTI DI MISURA

重量測定

ばね秤
spring balance
Federwaage^F
peson^M
dinamómetro^M
bilancia^F a molla^F

輪／環／リング
ring
Halterung^F
anneau^M
anilla^F
anello^M

指針／ポインター
pointer
Zeiger^M
index^M
fiel^M
indice^M

目盛り
graduated scale
Anzeigeskala^F
échelle^F graduée
escala^F graduada
scala^F graduata

鉤／フック
hook
Haken^M
crochet^M
gancho^M
gancio^M

秤台
platform
Wiegefläche^F
plateau^M
platillo^M
piattaforma^F di carico^M

重さ
weight
Gewicht^N
poids^M
peso^M
peso^M

単価
unit price
Preis^M pro Einheit^F
prix^M à l'unité^F
precio^M unitario
prezzo^M unitario

表示部
display
Anzeige^F
afficheur^M
indicador^M luminoso
display^M

総額
total
Summe^F
prix^M à payer
precio^M total
totale^M

電子秤
electronic scale
elektronische Waage^F
balance^F électronique
báscula^F electrónica
bilancia^F elettronica

機能キー
function keys
Funktionstasten^F
touches^F de fonctions^F
teclado^M de funciones^F
tasti^M funzione^F

商品コード
product code
Warencode^M
code^M des produits^M
código^M del producto^M
codice^M del prodotto^M

数字キーボード［キーパッド］
numeric keyboard
numerisches Tastenfeld^N
clavier^M numérique
teclado^M numérico
tastierino^M numerico

売上票
printout
Wiegeetikett^N
étiquette^F
recibo^M
scontrino^M

体重計
bathroom scale
Personenwaage^F
pèse-personne^M
báscula^F de baño^M
bilancia^F pesapersone

デジタル表示部
digital display
Digitalanzeige^F
affichage^M numérique
indicador^M digital
display^M digitale

分析用天秤
analytical balance
Präzisionswaage^F
balance^F de précision^F
balanza^F de precisión^F
bilancia^F da analisi^F

ガラス・ケース
glass case
Glasgehäuse^N
cage^F vitrée
urna^F
custodia^F a pareti^M di vetro^M

ドア／扉
door access
Schiebeöffnung^F
porte^F
puerta^F
sportello^M

皿／計量皿
pan
Waagschale^F
plateau^M
platillo^M
piatto^M

秤台／載せ台
weighing platform
Wiegefläche^F
plate-forme^F
plataforma^F
pedana^F

水平調節ねじ
leveling screw; levelling screw
Ausrichtschraube^F
vis^F calante
tornillo^M nivelador
vite^F di livello^M

科学

計測機器 | MEASURING DEVICES
MESSINSTRUMENTE | APPAREILS DE MESURE | APARATOS DE MEDICIÓN | STRUMENTI DI MISURA

長さ測定

日本語 | 英語 | ドイツ語 | フランス語 | スペイン語 | イタリア語

measure of length | Längenmessung^F | mesure^F de la longueur^F | medición^F de la longitud^F | misura^F della lunghezza^F

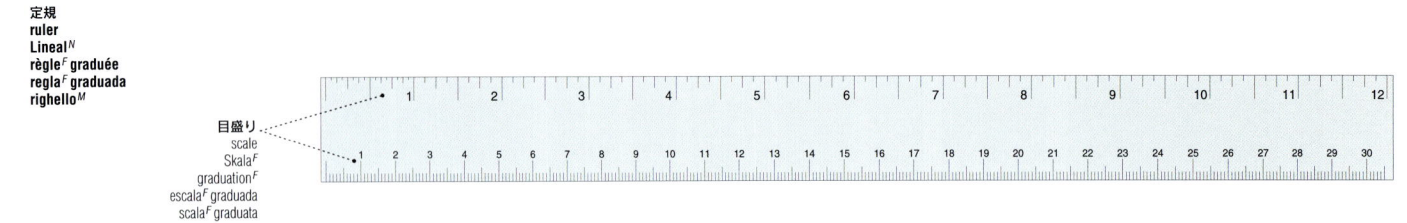

定規
ruler
Lineal^N
règle^F graduée
regla^F graduada
righello^M

目盛り
scale
Skala^F
graduation^F
escala^F graduada
scala^F graduata

距離測定

measure of distance | Entfernungsmessung^F | mesure^F de la distance^F | medición^F de la distancia^F | misura^F della distanza^F

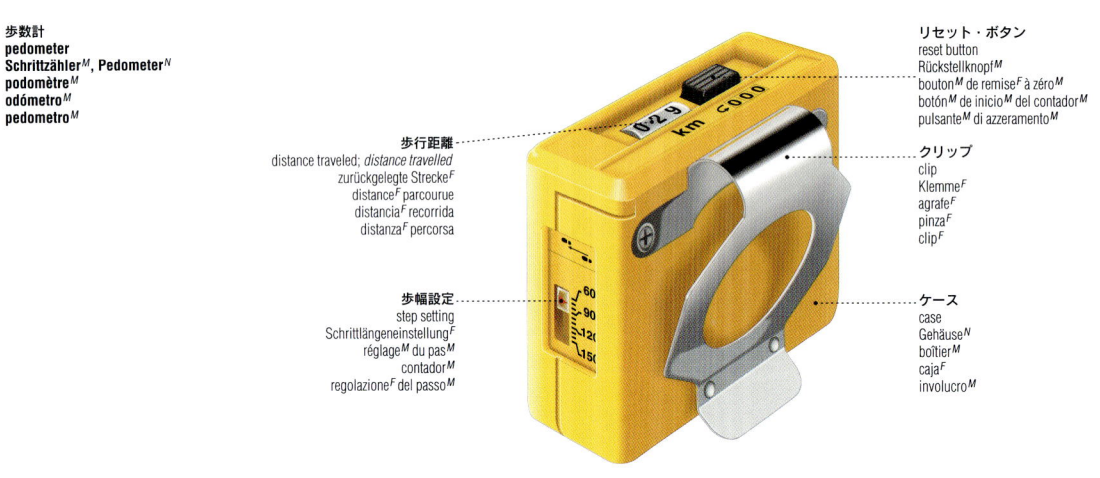

歩数計
pedometer
Schrittzähler^M, Pedometer^N
podomètre^M
odómetro^M
pedometro^M

歩行距離
distance traveled; distance travelled
zurückgelegte Strecke^F
distance^F parcourue
distancia^F recorrida
distanza^F percorsa

歩幅設定
step setting
Schrittlängeneinstellung^F
réglage^M du pas^M
contador^M
regolazione^F del passo^M

リセット・ボタン
reset button
Rückstellknopf^M
bouton^M de remise^F à zéro^M
botón^M de inicio^M del contador^M
pulsante^M di azzeramento^M

クリップ
clip
Klemme^F
agrafe^F
pinza^F
clip^F

ケース
case
Gehäuse^N
boîtier^M
caja^F
involucro^M

厚み測定

measure of thickness | Dickemessung^F | mesure^F de l'épaisseur^F | medición^F del espesor^M | misura^F dello spessore^M

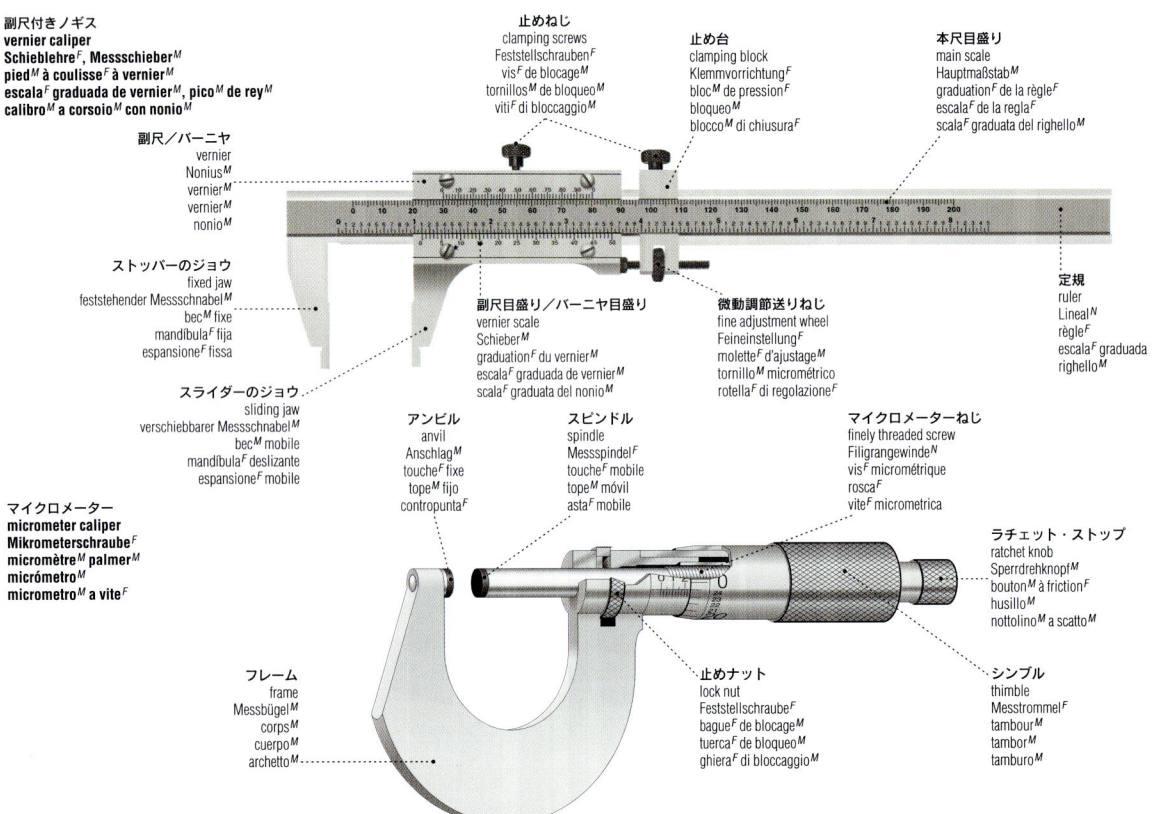

副尺付きノギス
vernier caliper
Schieblehre^F, Messschieber^M
pied^M à coulisse^F à vernier^M
escala^F graduada de vernier^M, pico de rey^M
calibro^M a corsoio^M con nonio^M

副尺／バーニヤ
vernier
Nonius^M
vernier^M
vernier^M
nonio^M

ストッパーのジョウ
fixed jaw
feststehender Messschnabel^M
bec^M fixe
mandíbula^F fija
espansione^F fissa

スライダーのジョウ
sliding jaw
verschiebbarer Messschnabel^M
bec^M mobile
mandíbula^F deslizante
espansione^F mobile

止めねじ
clamping screws
Feststellschrauben^F
vis^F de blocage^M
tornillos^M de bloqueo^M
viti^F di bloccaggio^M

副尺目盛り／バーニヤ目盛り
vernier scale
Schieber^M
graduation^F du vernier^M
escala^F graduada de vernier^M
scala^F graduata del nonio^M

止め台
clamping block
Klemmvorrichtung^F
bloc^M de pression^F
bloqueo^M
blocco^M di chiusura^F

微動調節送りねじ
fine adjustment wheel
Feineinstellung^F
molette^F d'ajustage^M
tornillo^M micrométrico
rotella^F di regolazione^M

本尺目盛り
main scale
Hauptmaßstab^M
graduation^F de la règle^F
escala^F de la regla^F
scala^F graduata del righello^M

定規
ruler
Lineal^N
règle^F
escala^F graduada
righello^M

マイクロメーター
micrometer caliper
Mikrometerschraube^F
micromètre^M palmer
micrómetro^M
micrometro^M a vite^F

アンビル
anvil
Anschlag^M
touche^F fixe
tope^M fijo
contropunta^F

スピンドル
spindle
Messspindel^F
touche^F mobile
tope^M móvil
asta^M mobile

マイクロメーターねじ
finely threaded screw
Filigrangewinde^N
vis^F micrométrique
rosca^F
vite^F micrometrica

ラチェット・ストップ
ratchet knob
Sperrdrehknopf^M
bouton^M à friction^F
husillo^M
nottolino^M a scatto^M

シンブル
thimble
Messtrommel^F
tambour^M
tambor^M
tamburo^M

フレーム
frame
Messbügel^M
corps^M
cuerpo^M
archetto^M

止めナット
lock nut
Feststellschraube^F
bague^F de blocage^M
tuerca^F de bloqueo^M
ghiera^F di bloccaggio^M

科学

計測機器 | MEASURING DEVICES
MESSINSTRUMENTE | APPAREILS DE MESURE | APARATOS DE MEDICIÓN | STRUMENTI DI MISURA

角度測定
measure of angles | Winkelmessung^F | mesure^F des angles^M | medición^F de ángulos^M | misura^F degli angoli^M

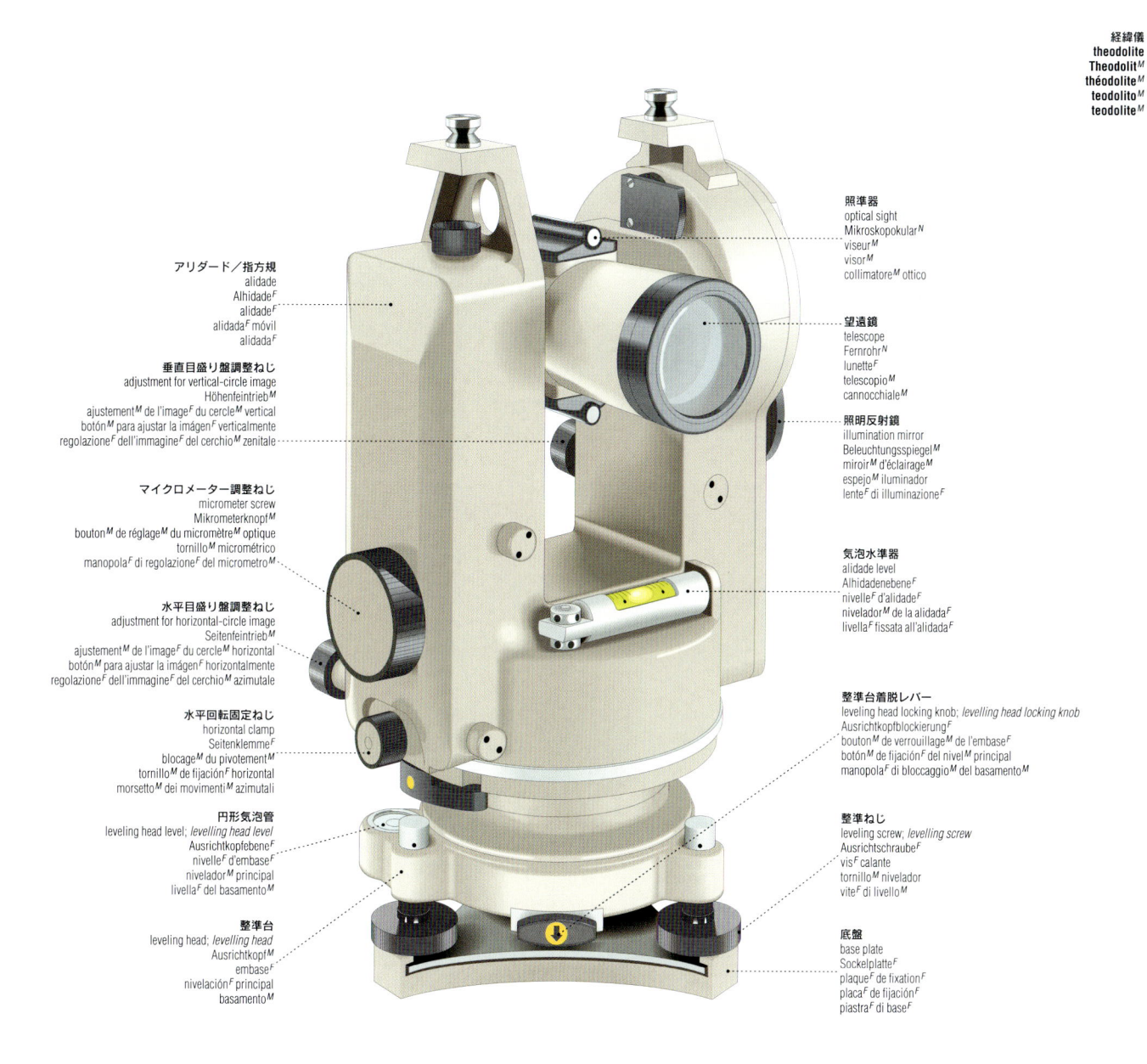

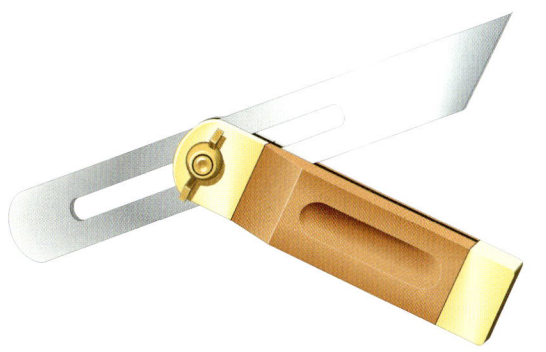

経緯儀
theodolite
Theodolit^M
théodolite^M
teodolito^M
teodolite^M

照準器
optical sight
Mikroskopokular^N
viseur^M
visor^M
collimatore^M ottico

アリダード／指方規
alidade
Alhidade^F
alidade^F
alidada^F móvil
alidada^F

望遠鏡
telescope
Fernrohr^N
lunette^F
telescopio^M
cannocchiale^M

垂直目盛り盤調整ねじ
adjustment for vertical-circle image
Höhenfeintrieb^M
ajustement^M de l'image^F du cercle^M vertical
botón^M para ajustar la imágen^F verticalmente
regolazione^F dell'immagine^F del cerchio^M zenitale

照明反射鏡
illumination mirror
Beleuchtungsspiegel^M
miroir^M d'éclairage^M
espejo^M iluminador
lente^F di illuminazione^F

マイクロメーター調整ねじ
micrometer screw
Mikrometerknopf^M
bouton^M de réglage^M du micromètre^M optique
tornillo^M micrométrico
manopola^F di regolazione^F del micrometro^M

気泡水準器
alidade level
Alhidadenebene^F
nivelle^F d'alidade^F
nivelador^M de la alidada^F
livella^F fissata all'alidada^F

水平目盛り盤調整ねじ
adjustment for horizontal-circle image
Seitenfeintrieb^M
ajustement^M de l'image^F du cercle^M horizontal
botón^M para ajustar la imágen^F horizontalmente
regolazione^F dell'immagine^F del cerchio^M azimutale

整準台着脱レバー
leveling head locking knob; *levelling head locking knob*
Ausrichtkopfblockierung^F
bouton^M de verrouillage^M de l'embase^F
botón^M de fijación^F del nivel^M principal
manopola^M di bloccaggio^M del basamento^M

水平回転固定ねじ
horizontal clamp
Seitenklemme^F
blocage^M du pivotement^M
tornillo^M de fijación^F horizontal
morsetto^M dei movimenti^M azimutali

整準ねじ
leveling screw; *levelling screw*
Ausrichtschraube^F
vis^F calante
tornillo^M nivelador
vite^F di livello^M

円形気泡管
leveling head level; *levelling head level*
Ausrichtkopfebene^F
nivelle^F d'embase^F
nivelador^M principal
livella^F del basamento^M

底盤
base plate
Sockelplatte^F
plaque^F de fixation^F
placa^F de fijación^F
piastra^F di base^F

整準台
leveling head; *levelling head*
Ausrichtkopf^M
embase^F
nivelación^F principal
basamento^M

角度定規
bevel square
Schmiege^F
fausse-équerre^F
falsa escuadra^F
squadra^F falsa

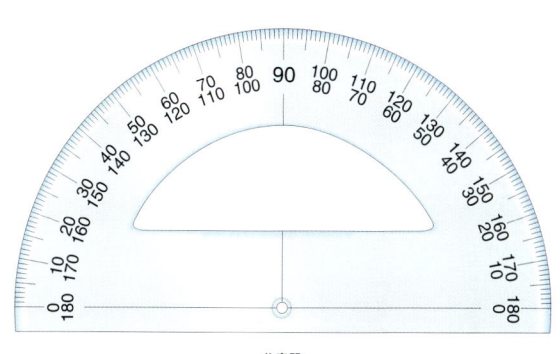

分度器
protractor
Winkelmesser^M
rapporteur^M d'angle^M
transportador
goniometro^M

科学

科学記号 | SCIENTIFIC SYMBOLS
WISSENSCHAFTLICHE SYMBOLE | SYMBOLES SCIENTIFIQUES USUELS | SÍMBOLOS CIENTÍFICOS | SIMBOLI SCIENTIFICI

国際単位系

日本語 | 英語 | ドイツ語 | フランス語 | スペイン語 | イタリア語

international system of units | internationales Einheitensystem^N | système^M international d'unités^F | sistema^M internacional de unidades^F de medida^F | sistema^M internazionale di unità^F di misura^F

周波数[振動数]の単位
measurement of frequency
Maßeinheit^F der Frequenz^F
mesure^F de la fréquence^F
unidad^F de medida^F de frecuencia^F
unità^F di misura^F della frequenza^F

Hz
ヘルツ
hertz
Hertz^N
hertz^M
hertz^M

電圧[電位差]の単位
measurement of electric potential difference
Maßeinheit^F der elektrischen Spannung^F
mesure^F de la différence^F de potentiel^M électrique
unidad^F de medida^F de la diferencia^F de potencial^M eléctrico
unità^F di misura^F della differenza^F di potenziale^M elettrico

V
ボルト
volt
Volt^N
volt^M
voltio^M, volt^M
volt^M

電荷の単位
measurement of electric charge
Maßeinheit^F der elektrischen Ladung^F
mesure^F de la charge^F électrique
unidad^F de medida^F de carga^F eléctrica
unità^F di misura^F della carica^F elettrica

C
クーロン
coulomb
Coulomb^N
coulomb^M
culombio^M
coulomb^M

エネルギーの単位
measurement of energy
Maßeinheit^F der Energie^F
mesure^F de l'énergie^F
unidad^F de medida^F de energía^F
unità^F di misura^F dell'energia^F

J
ジュール
joule
Joule^N
joule^M
joule^M
joule^M

電力の単位
measurement of power
Maßeinheit^F der Leistung^F
mesure^F de la puissance^F
medida^F de potencia^F eléctrica
unità^F di misura^F della potenza^F elettrica

W
ワット
watt
Watt^N
watt^M
vatt^M
watt^M

力の単位
measurement of force
Maßeinheit^F der Kraft^F
mesure^F de la force^F
unidad^F de medida^F de fuerza^F
unità^F di misura^F della forza^F

N
ニュートン
newton
Newton^N
newton^M
newton^M
newton^M

電気抵抗の単位
measurement of electric resistance
Maßeinheit^F des elektrischen Widerstands^M
mesure^F de la résistance^F électrique
unidad^F de medida^F de resistencia^F eléctrica
unità^F di misura^F della resistenza^F elettrica

Ω
オーム
ohm
Ohm^N
ohm^M
ohmnio^M, ohm^M
ohm^M

電流の単位
measurement of electric current
Maßeinheit^F der elektrischen Stromstärke^F
mesure^F du courant^M électrique
unidad^F de medida^F de corriente^F eléctrica
unità^F di misura^F della corrente^F elettrica

A
アンペア
ampere
Ampere^N
ampère^M
amperio^M
ampere^M

長さの単位
measurement of length
Maßeinheit^F der Länge^F
mesure^F de la longueur^F
unidad^F de medida^F de longitud^F
unità^F di misura^F della lunghezza^F

m
メーター
meter; *metre*
Meter^M
mètre^M
metro^M
metro^M

質量の単位
measurement of mass
Maßeinheit^F der Masse^F
mesure^F de la masse^F
unidad^F de medida^F de masa^F
unità^F di misura^F della massa^F

kg
キログラム
kilogram
Kilogramm^N
kilogramme^M
kilogramo^M
kilogrammo^M

セルシウス温度の単位
measurement of Celsius temperature
Maßeinheit^F der Celsius-Temperatur^F
mesure^F de la température^F Celsius
unidad^F de medida^F de la temperatura^F Celsius
unità^F di misura^F della temperatura^F Celsius

°C
セ[摂]氏度
degree Celsius
Grad^M Celsius
degré^M Celsius
grado^M Celsius
grado^M Celsius

熱力学温度の単位
measurement of thermodynamic temperature
Maßeinheit^F der thermodynamischen Temperatur^F
mesure^F de la température^F thermodynamique
unidad^F de medida^F de temperatura^F termodinámica
unità^F di misura^F della temperatura^F termodinamica

K
ケルビン
kelvin
Kelvin^N
kelvin^M
kelvin^M
kelvin^M

物質量の単位
measurement of amount of substance
Maßeinheit^F der Stoffmenge^F
mesure^F de la quantité^F de matière^F
unidad^F de medida^F de cantidad^F de materia^F
unità^F di misura^F della quantità^F di sostanza^F

mol
モル
mole
Mol^N
mole^F
mole^F
mole^F

放射能の単位
measurement of radioactivity
Maßeinheit^F der Radioaktivität^F
mesure^F de la radioactivité^F
unidad^F de medida^F de radioactividad^F
unità^F di misura^F della radioattività^F

Bq
ベクレル
becquerel
Becquerel^N
becquerel^M
becquerel^M
becquerel^M

圧力の単位
measurement of pressure
Maßeinheit^F des Drucks^M
mesure^F de la pression^F
unidad^F de medida^F de presión^F
unità^F di misura^F della pressione^F

Pa
パスカル
pascal
Pascal^N
pascal^M
pascal^M
pascal^M

光度の単位
measurement of luminous intensity
Maßeinheit^F der Lichtstärke^F
mesure^F de l'intensité^F lumineuse
unidad^F de medida^F de intensidad^F luminosa
unità^F di misura^F dell'intensità^F luminosa

cd
カンデラ
candela
Candela^F
candela^F
candela^F
candela^F

生物学

biology | Biologie^F | biologie^F | biología^F | biologia^F

♀
雌
female
weiblich
femelle^F
femenino^M
femminile

♂
雄
male
männlich
mâle^M
masculino^M
maschile

Rh+
血液因子陽性／Ｒｈプラス［陽性］
blood factor positive
Rhesusfaktor^M positiv
facteur^M Rhésus positif
factor^M RH positivo
fattore^M Rh positivo

Rh-
血液因子陰性／Ｒｈマイナス［陰性］
blood factor negative
Rhesusfaktor^M negativ
facteur^M Rhésus négatif
factor^M RH negativo
fattore^M Rh negativo

†
死／死亡
death
gestorben
mort^F
muerte^F
morte^F

*
生／誕生
birth
geboren
naissance^F
nacimiento^M
nascita^F

科学記号 | SCIENTIFIC SYMBOLS
WISSENSCHAFTLICHE SYMBOLE | SYMBOLES SCIENTIFIQUES USUELS | SÍMBOLOS CIENTÍFICOS | SIMBOLI SCIENTIFICI

数学
mathematics | Mathematik^F | mathématiques^F | matemáticas^F | matematica^F

−
マイナス／負／引く／減じる
minus/negative
Subtraktion^F
soustraction^F
menos^M
sottrazione^F

+
プラス／正／足す／加える
plus/positive
Addition^F
addition^F
más^M
addizione^F

×
掛ける
multiplied by
Multiplikation^F
multiplication^F
por^M
moltiplicazione^F

÷
割る
divided by
Division^F
division^F
entre^M
divisione^F

=
等しい／イコール
equals
ist gleich
égale
igual a
uguale a

≠
等しくない
is not equal to
ist ungleich
n'égale pas
desigual a
diverso da

≈
ほとんど等しい
is approximately equal to
ist annähernd gleich
égale à peu près
casi igual a
approssimativamente uguale a

∼
同値である
is equivalent to
ist äquivalent mit
équivaut à
equivalente a
equivalente a

≡
合同［同一］である／常に等しい
is identical with
ist identisch mit
est identique à
idéntico a
coincide con

≢
合同［同一］ではない
is not identical with
ist nicht identisch mit
n'est pas identique à
no es idéntico a
non coincide con

±
プラス・マイナス
plus or minus
plus oder minus
plus ou moins
más^M o menos^M
più o meno

≤
より小さいか等しい
is less than or equal to
ist gleich oder kleiner als
égal ou plus petit que
igual o menor que
minore o uguale a

>
より大きい
is greater than
ist größer als
plus grand que
mayor que
maggiore di

≥
より大きいか等しい
is greater than or equal to
ist gleich oder größer als
égal ou plus grand que
igual o mayor que
maggiore o uguale a

<
より小さい
is less than
ist kleiner als
plus petit que
menor que
minore di

∅
空集合
empty set
leere Menge^F
ensemble^M vide
conjunto^M vacío
insieme^M vuoto

∪
和集合
union of two sets
Mengenvereinigung^F
réunion^F
unión^F
unione^F

∩
積［共通］集合／共通部分
intersection of two sets
Mengenschnitt^M
intersection
intersección^F
intersezione^F

⊂
部分集合である
is included in/is a subset of
echte Teilmenge^F von
inclusion
contenido en
contenuto in

%
パーセント
percent
Prozent^N
pourcentage^M
porcentaje^M
percento^M

∈
属する／元である
is an element of
Element^N von
appartenance^F
pertenece a
appartiene a

∉
属さない／元でない
is not an element of
nicht Element^N von
non-appartenance^F
no pertenece a
non appartiene a

Σ
総和／シグマ
sum
Summe^F
sommation^F
suma^F
sommatoria^F

√
…の平方根／ルート…
square root of
Quadratwurzel^F aus
racine^F carrée de
raíz^F cuadrada de
radice^F quadrata di

½
分数
fraction
Bruch^M
fraction^F
fracción^F
frazione^F

∞
無限大
infinity
unendlich
infini^M
infinito^M
infinito^M

∫
積分／インテグラル
integral
Integral^N
intégrale^F
integral
integrale^M

!
階乗
factorial
Fakultät^F
factorielle^F
factorial
fattoriale^M

ローマ数字
Roman numerals
römische Ziffern^F
chiffres^M romains
números^M romanos
numeri^M romani

I
1
one
Eins^F
un^M
uno
uno

V
5
five
Fünf^F
cinq^M
cinco
cinque

X
10
ten
Zehn^F
dix^M
diez
dieci

L
50
fifty
Fünfzig^F
cinquante^M
cincuenta
cinquanta

C
100
one hundred
Hundert^F
cent^M
mil
cento

D
500
five hundred
Fünfhundert^F
cinq cents^M
quinientos
cinquecento

M
1,000
one thousand
Tausend^F
mille^M
cien
mille

科学記号 | SCIENTIFIC SYMBOLS
WISSENSCHAFTLICHE SYMBOLE | SYMBOLES SCIENTIFIQUES USUELS | SÍMBOLOS CIENTÍFICOS | SIMBOLI SCIENTIFICI

幾何学

日本語 | 英語 | ドイツ語 | フランス語 | スペイン語 | イタリア語

geometry | Geometrie^F | géométrie^F | geometría^F | geometria^F

○
度
degree
Grad^M
degré^M
grado^M
grado^M

′
分
minute
Bogenminute^F
minute^F
minuto^M
primo^M

″
秒
second
Bogensekunde^F
seconde^F
segundo^M
secondo^M

π
バイ
pi
Pi^N
pi^M
pi
pi^M greco

⊥
垂直である
perpendicular
ist senkrecht zu
perpendiculaire^F
perpendicular
perpendicolare

∥
平行である
is parallel to
ist parallel zu
parallèle
es paralelo a
parallelo a

∦
平行でない
is not parallel to
ist nicht parallel zu
non-parallèle
no es paralelo a
non parallelo a

∟
直角
right angle
rechter Winkel^M
angle^M droit
ángulo^M recto
angolo^M retto

∠
鈍角
obtuse angle
stumpfer Winkel^M
angle^M obtus
ángulo^M obtuso
angolo^M ottuso

∠
鋭角
acute angle
spitzer Winkel^M
angle^M aigu
ángulo^M agudo
angolo^M acuto

幾何学的な形

geometrical shapes | geometrische Formen^F | formes^F géométriques | formas^F geométricas | forme^F geometriche

角度の例
examples of angles
Beispiele^N für Winkel^M
exemples^M d'angles^M
ejemplos^M de ángulos^M
esempi^M di angoli^M

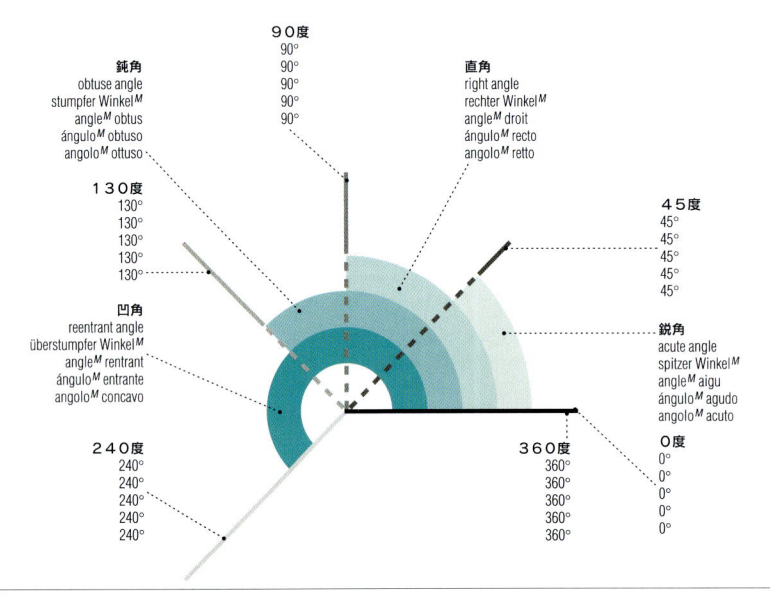

鈍角
obtuse angle
stumpfer Winkel^M
angle^M obtus
ángulo^M obtuso
angolo^M ottuso

90度
90°
90°
90°
90°
90°

直角
right angle
rechter Winkel^M
angle^M droit
ángulo^M recto
angolo^M retto

130度
130°
130°
130°
130°
130°

45度
45°
45°
45°
45°
45°

凹角
reentrant angle
überstumpfer Winkel^M
angle^M rentrant
ángulo^M entrante
angolo^M concavo

鋭角
acute angle
spitzer Winkel^M
angle^M aigu
ángulo^M agudo
angolo^M acuto

240度
240°
240°
240°
240°
240°

360度
360°
360°
360°
360°
360°

0度
0°
0°
0°
0°
0°

平面
plane surfaces
ebene Flächen^F
surfaces^F
superficies^F
superfici^F

円の部分
parts of a circle
Teile^M eines Kreises^M
parties^F d'un cercle^M
partes^M de círculo^M
parti^F di un cerchio^M

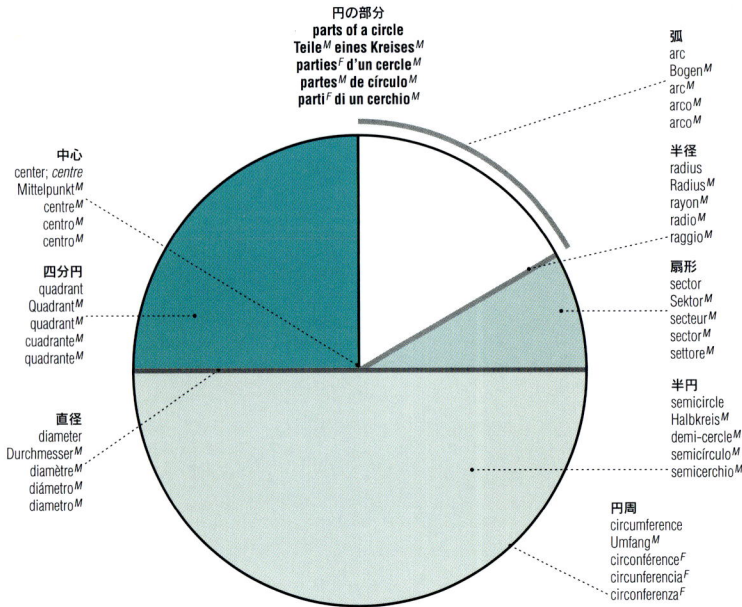

弧
arc
Bogen^M
arc^M
arco^M
arco^M

中心
center; centre
Mittelpunkt^M
centre^M
centro^M
centro^M

半径
radius
Radius^M
rayon^M
radio^M
raggio^M

四分円
quadrant
Quadrant^M
quadrant^M
cuadrante^M
quadrante^M

扇形
sector
Sektor^M
secteur^M
sector^M
settore^M

直径
diameter
Durchmesser^M
diamètre^M
diámetro^M
diametro^M

半円
semicircle
Halbkreis^M
demi-cercle^M
semicírculo^M
semicerchio^M

円周
circumference
Umfang^M
circonférence^F
circunferencia^F
circonferenza^F

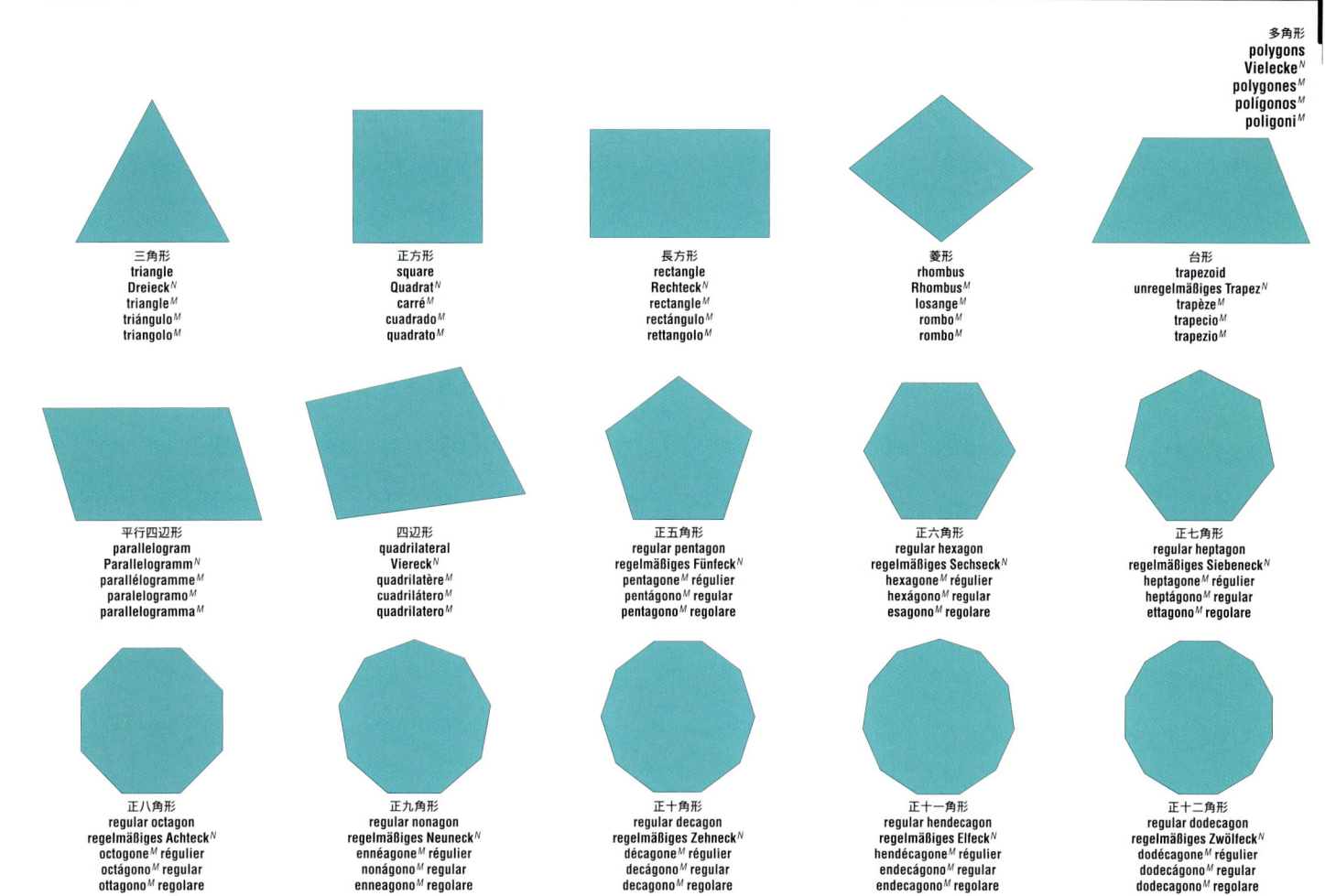

科学記号 | SCIENTIFIC SYMBOLS
WISSENSCHAFTLICHE SYMBOLE | SYMBOLES SCIENTIFIQUES USUELS | SÍMBOLOS CIENTÍFICOS | SIMBOLI SCIENTIFICI

幾何学的な形

多角形
polygons
Vielecke^N
polygones^M
polígonos^M
poligoni^M

三角形
triangle
Dreieck^N
triangle^M
triángulo^M
triangolo^M

正方形
square
Quadrat^N
carré^M
cuadrado^M
quadrato^M

長方形
rectangle
Rechteck^N
rectangle^M
rectángulo^M
rettangolo^M

菱形
rhombus
Rhombus^M
losange^M
rombo^M
rombo^M

台形
trapezoid
unregelmäßiges Trapez^N
trapèze^M
trapecio^M
trapezio^M

平行四辺形
parallelogram
Parallelogramm^N
parallélogramme^M
paralelogramo^M
parallelogramma^M

四辺形
quadrilateral
Viereck^N
quadrilatère^M
cuadrilátero^M
quadrilatero^M

正五角形
regular pentagon
regelmäßiges Fünfeck^N
pentagone^M régulier
pentágono^M regular
pentagono^M regolare

正六角形
regular hexagon
regelmäßiges Sechseck^N
hexagone^M régulier
hexágono^M regular
esagono^M regolare

正七角形
regular heptagon
regelmäßiges Siebeneck^N
heptagone^M régulier
heptágono^M regular
ettagono^M regolare

正八角形
regular octagon
regelmäßiges Achteck^N
octogone^M régulier
octágono^M regular
ottagono^M regolare

正九角形
regular nonagon
regelmäßiges Neuneck^N
ennéagone^M régulier
nonágono^M regular
enneagono^M regolare

正十角形
regular decagon
regelmäßiges Zehneck^N
décagone^M régulier
decágono^M regular
decagono^M regolare

正十一角形
regular hendecagon
regelmäßiges Elfeck^N
hendécagone^M régulier
endecágono^M regular
endecagono^M regolare

正十二角形
regular dodecagon
regelmäßiges Zwölfeck^N
dodécagone^M régulier
dodecágono^M regular
dodecagono^M regolare

立体
solids
Körper^M
volumes^M
cuerpos^M sólidos^M
solidi^M

螺旋（らせん）
helix
Helix^F
hélice^F
hélice^F
elica^F

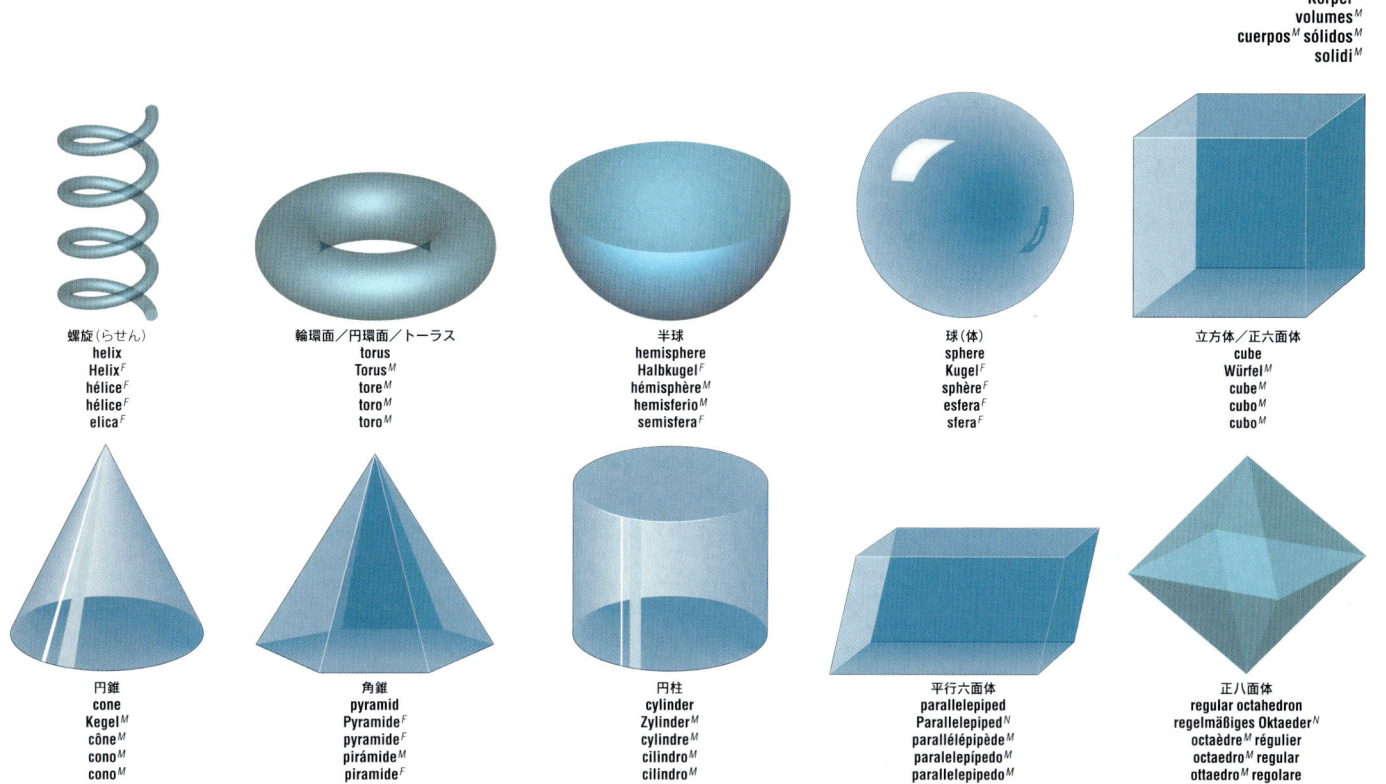

輪環面／円環面／トーラス
torus
Torus^M
tore^M
toro^M
toro^M

半球
hemisphere
Halbkugel^F
hémisphère^M
hemisferio^M
semisfera^F

球（体）
sphere
Kugel^F
sphère^F
esfera^F
sfera^F

立方体／正六面体
cube
Würfel^M
cube^M
cubo^M
cubo^M

円錐
cone
Kegel^M
cône^M
cono^M
cono^M

角錐
pyramid
Pyramide^F
pyramide^F
pirámide^F
piramide^F

円柱
cylinder
Zylinder^M
cylindre^M
cilindro^M
cilindro^M

平行六面体
parallelepiped
Parallelepiped^N
parallélépipède^M
paralelepípedo^M
parallelepipedo^M

正八面体
regular octahedron
regelmäßiges Oktaeder^N
octaèdre^M régulier
octaedro^M regular
ottaedro^M regolare

科学

708 都市

- 708 都市圏
- 710 中心街
- 712 道の断面図
- 713 オフィス・ビル
- 714 ショッピング・センター
- 716 デパート
- 718 コンベンション・センター
- 720 レストラン
- 722 セルフ・サービス式レストラン
- 724 ホテル
- 725 一般的な案内標識

726 司法

- 726 刑務所
- 728 裁判所

728 経済と金融

- 728 通貨省略記号の例
- 729 貨幣と支払い形態
- 730 銀行

732 教育

- 732 図書館
- 734 学校

736 宗教

- 736 宗教年表
- 737 教会
- 738 シナゴーグ
- 738 モスク

739 政治

- 739 紋章
- 742 旗

社会

SOCIETY | GESELLSCHAFT | SOCIÉTÉ | SOCIEDAD | SOCIETÀ

748 兵器

- 748 石器時代の武器
- 748 ローマ時代の武器
- 749 鎧(兜)(よろいかぶと)／甲冑(かっちゅう)
- 750 弓と石弓
- 751 刀剣
- 752 火打ち石銃
- 752 １７世紀の大砲と臼砲(きゅうほう)
- 754 短機関銃
- 754 ピストル
- 754 回転式(連発)拳銃／リボルバー
- 755 自動小銃
- 755 軽機関銃
- 756 現代の榴弾砲
- 756 現代の迫撃砲
- 757 手榴弾
- 757 バズーカ砲
- 757 無反動ライフル
- 758 対人地雷
- 758 戦車
- 759 ミサイル
- 760 戦闘機
- 761 航空母艦／空母
- 762 フリゲート艦
- 763 原子力潜水艦

764 安全

- 764 火災予防
- 768 犯罪防止
- 772 耳の保護具
- 772 目の保護具
- 772 頭部の保護具
- 773 呼吸器系の保護具
- 773 足の保護具
- 774 安全標識

775 健康

- 775 救急車
- 775 救急処置の用具
- 777 救急箱
- 777 体温計
- 777 血圧計
- 778 病院
- 782 歩行補助具
- 783 車椅子
- 783 薬の様々な形態

784 親族

- 784 家族関係

都市 | CITY
STADT | VILLE | CIUDAD | CITTÀ

都市圏

日本語 | 英語 | ドイツ語 | フランス語 | スペイン語 | イタリア語

agglomeration | Ballungsgebiet^N | agglomération^F | conurbación^F | conurbazione^F

村
village
Dorf^N
village^M
pueblo^M
paese^M

道路
road
Straße^F
route^F
carretera^F
strada^F

ゴルフ・コース
golf course
Golfplatz^M
terrain^M de golf^M
campo^M de golf^M
campo^M da golf^M

空港
airport
Flughafen^M
aéroport^M
aeropuerto^M
aeroporto^M

ビジネス街
business district
Geschäftsviertel^N
quartier^M des affaires^F
centro^M de negocios^M
quartiere^M degli affari^M

操車場
railyard
Güterbahnhof^M
gare^F de triage^M
terminal^M de mercancías^F
scalo^M merci^F

工場
factory
Fabrik^F
usine^F
fábrica^F
stabilimento^M industriale

鉄道駅
railroad station; *railway station*
Bahnhof^M
gare^F
estación^F de ferrocarriles^M
stazione^F ferroviaria

倉庫
warehouse
Lagerhaus^N
entrepôt^M
depósito^M de mercancías^F
magazzino^M

埠頭（ふとう）
quay
Kaianlage^F
quai^M
muelle^M
molo^M

展示場
exhibition center; *exhibition centre*
Messezentrum^N
parc^M des expositions^F
recinto^M ferial
quartiere^M fieristico

駐車場
parking area; *parking area*
Parkplatz^M
parc^M de stationnement^M
área^F de estacionamiento^M
parcheggio^M

コンテナ・ターミナル
container terminal
Containerterminal^N
terminal^M à conteneurs^M
terminal^F de contenedores^M
deposito^M per containers^M

社会

708

都市 | CITY
STADT | VILLE | CIUDAD | CITTÀ

都市圏

鉄道線路
track
Eisenbahnstrecke^F
voie^F ferrée
vía^F ferroviaria
binario^M

連絡道路
peripheral
Zubringer^M
périphérique^M
carretera^F secundaria
tangenziale^F

高速道路
freeway; *motorway*
Autobahn^F
autoroute^F
autopista^F
autostrada^F

ごみ廃棄場［埋立地］
landfill
Mülldeponie^F
décharge^F
vertedero^M
discarica^F

インターチェンジ
interchange
Anschlussstelle^F
échangeur^M
nudo^M viario
svincolo^M

ショッピング・センター
shopping center; *shopping centre*
Einkaufszentrum^N
centre^M commercial
centro^M comercial
centro^M commerciale

住宅地域
residential district
Wohngebiet^N
zone^F résidentielle
zona^F residencial
quartiere^M residenziale

田園
country
Land^N
campagne^F
campo^M
campagna^F

商業地区
commercial zone
Gewerbegebiet^N
zone^F commerciale
zona^F comercial
zona^F commerciale

郊外
suburb
Vorstadt^F
banlieue^F
suburbio^M
suburbio^M

スタジアム
stadium
Stadion^N
stade^M
estadio^M
stadio^M

中心街
downtown; *city centre*
Innenstadt^F
centre^M-ville
centro^M ciudad
centro^M della città

工業地区
industrial area
Industriegebiet^N
zone^F industrielle
polígono^M industrial
zona^F industriale

精油所
refinery
Raffinerie^F
raffinerie^F
refinería^F
raffineria^F

港
port
Hafen^M
port^M
puerto^M
porto^M

スポーツ複合施設
sports complex
Sportanlagen^F
complexe^M sportif
polideportivo^M
complesso^M sportivo

社会

中心街

都市 | CITY
STADT | VILLE | CIUDAD | CITTÀ

日本語 | 英語 | ドイツ語 | フランス語 | スペイン語 | イタリア語

downtown; *city centre* | Innenstadt[F] | centre[M]-ville[F] | centro[M] ciudad[F] | centro[M] della città[F]

裁判所
courthouse
Gerichtsgebäude[N]
palais[M] de justice[F]
Palacio[M] de Justicia[F]
palazzo[M] di giustizia[F]

ビジネス街
business district
Geschäftsviertel[N]
quartier[M] des affaires[F]
centro[M] de negocios[M]
quartiere[M] degli affari[M]

ホテル
hotel
Hotel[N]
hôtel[M]
hotel[M]
albergo[M]

オフィス・ビル
office building
Bürogebäude[N]
édifice[M] à bureaux[M]
edificio[M] de oficinas[F]
edificio[M] per uffici[M]

鉄道駅
railroad station; *railway station*
Bahnhof[M]
gare[F]
estación[F] de ferrocarriles[M]
stazione[F] ferroviaria

オペラ劇場
opera house
Opernhaus[N]
opéra[M]
opera[F]
Opera[F]

バス・ターミナル
bus station
Busbahnhof[M]
gare[F] routière
estación[F] de autobuses[M]
stazione[F] degli autobus[M]

鉄道線路
railroad track
Gleis[N]
voie[F] ferrée
vía[F] ferroviaria
binario[M] ferroviario

パビリオン
pavilion
Pavillon[M]
pavillon[M]
pabellón[M]
padiglione[M]

大学
university
Universität[F]
université[F]
universidad[F]
università[F]

市庁舎
city hall
Rathaus[N]
hôtel[M] de ville[F]
ayuntamiento[M]
municipio[M]

劇場
theater; *theatre*
Theater[N]
salle[F] de spectacle[M]
teatro[M]
teatro[M]

商店街
shopping street
Einkaufsstraße[F]
rue[F] commerçante
calle[F] comercial
via[F] commerciale

バー
bar
Bar[F]
bar[M]
bar[M]
bar[M]

店／商店
store
Geschäft[N]
magasin[M]
tienda[F]
negozio[M]

レストラン
restaurant
Restaurant[N]
restaurant[M]
restaurante[M]
ristorante[M]

銀行
bank
Bank[F]
banque[F]
banco[M]
banca[F]

喫茶店
coffee shop
Café[N]
café[M]
cafetería[F]
caffè[M]

地下鉄駅
subway station; *underground railway station*
U-Bahn[F]-Station[F]
station[F] de métro[M]
estación[F] de metro[M]
stazione[F] della metropolitana[F]

映画館
movie theater; *cinema*
Kino[N]
cinéma[M]
cine[M]
cinema[M]

社会

710

都市 | CITY
STADT | VILLE | CIUDAD | CITTÀ

中心街

コンベンション・センター
convention center; *convention centre*
Kongresszentrum[N]
palais[M] des congrès[M]
palacio[M] de Congresos[M]
palazzo[M] dei congressi[M]

教育施設
educational institution
Bildungseinrichtung[F]
établissement[M] scolaire
centro[M] educacional
complesso[M] scolastico

ブルバード／大通り
boulevard
Boulevard[M]
boulevard[M]
bulevar[M]
boulevard

通り／街路
street
Straße[F]
rue[F]
calle[F]
via[F]

アベニュー／大通り／本通り
avenue
Querstraße[F], Allee[F]
avenue[F]
avenida[F]
avenue

消防署
fire station
Feuerwache[F]
caserne[F] de pompiers[M]
parque[M] de bomberos[M]
caserma[F] dei vigili[M] del fuoco[M]

墓地
cemetery
Friedhof[M]
cimetière[M]
cementerio[M]
cimitero[M]

教会
church
Kirche[F]
église[F]
iglesia[F]
chiesa[F]

小道
lane
Gasse[F]
ruelle[F]
callejón[M]
vicolo[M]

アパート
apartment building
Wohnblock[M]
immeuble[M] résidentiel
bloque[M] de apartamentos[M]
condominio[M]

警察署
police station
Polizeirevier[N]
poste[M] de police[F]
estación[F] de policía[F]
stazione[F] di polizia[F]

公園
park
Park[M]
parc[M]
parque[M]
parco[M]

図書館
library
Bibliothek[F]
bibliothèque[F]
biblioteca[F]
biblioteca[F]

郵便局
post office
Postamt[N]
bureau[M] de poste[F]
oficina[F] de Correos[M]
ufficio[M] postale

ガソリン・スタンド
service station; *service station*
Tankstelle[F]
station[F]-service[F]
estación[F] de servicio[M]
stazione[F] di servizio[M]

スーパーマーケット
supermarket
Supermarkt[M]
supermarché[M]
supermercado[M]
supermercato[M]

自動車ディーラー
car dealer
Autohaus[N]
concessionnaire[M] d'automobiles[F]
concesionario[M] automovilístico
concessionaria[F] di automobili[M]

博物館
museum
Museum[N]
musée[M]
museo[M]
museo[M]

劇場
theater; *theatre*
Theater[N]
théâtre[M]
teatro[M]
teatro[M]

病院
hospital
Krankenhaus[N]
hôpital[M]
hospital[M]
ospedale[M]

社会

711

都市 | CITY
STADT | VILLE | CIUDAD | CITTÀ

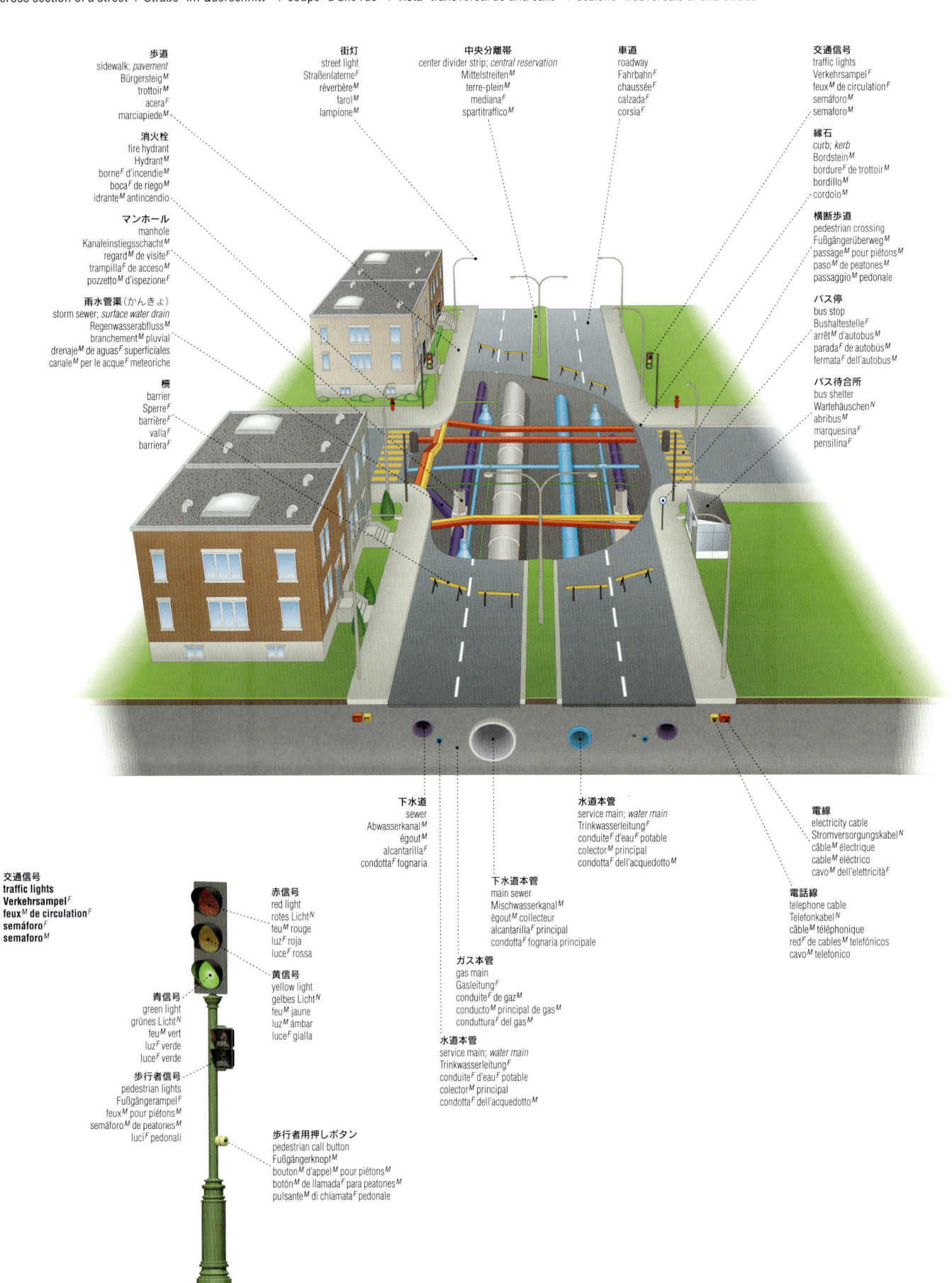

道の断面図

cross section of a street | Straße^F im Querschnitt^M | coupe^F d'une rue^F | vista^F transversal de una calle^F | sezione^F trasversale di una strada^F

日本語 | 英語 | ドイツ語 | フランス語 | スペイン語 | イタリア語

歩道
sidewalk; *pavement*
Bürgersteig^M
trottoir^M
acera^F
marciapiede^M

消火栓
fire hydrant
Hydrant^M
borne^F d'incendie^M
boca^F de riego^M
idrante^M antincendio

マンホール
manhole
Kanaleinstiegsschacht^M
regard^M de visite^F
trampilla^F de acceso^M
pozzetto^M d'ispezione^F

雨水管渠（かんきょ）
storm sewer; *surface water drain*
Regenwasserabfluss^M
branchement^M pluvial
drenaje^M de aguas^F superficiales
canale^M per le acque^F meteoriche

柵
barrier
Sperre^F
barrière^F
valla^F
barriera^F

街灯
street light
Straßenlaterne^F
réverbère^M
farol^M
lampione^M

中央分離帯
center divider strip; *central reservation*
Mittelstreifen^M
terre-plein^M
mediana^F
spartitraffico^M

車道
roadway
Fahrbahn^F
chaussée^F
calzada^F
corsia^F

交通信号
traffic lights
Verkehrsampel^F
feux^M de circulation^F
semáforo^F
semaforo^M

縁石
curb; *kerb*
Bordstein^M
bordure^F de trottoir^M
bordillo^M
cordolo^M

横断歩道
pedestrian crossing
Fußgängerüberweg^M
passage^M pour piétons^M
paso^M de peatones^M
passaggio^M pedonale

バス停
bus stop
Bushaltestelle^F
arrêt^M d'autobus^M
parada^F de autobús^M
fermata^F dell'autobus^M

バス待合所
bus shelter
Wartehäuschen^N
abribus^M
marquesina^F
pensilina^F

下水道
sewer
Abwasserkanal^M
égout^M
alcantarilla^F
condotta^F fognaria

水道本管
service main; *water main*
Trinkwasserleitung^F
conduite^F d'eau^F potable
colector^M principal
condotta^F dell'acquedotto^M

電線
electricity cable
Stromversorgungskabel^N
câble^M électrique
cable^M eléctrico
cavo^M dell'elettricità^F

下水道本管
main sewer
Mischwasserkanal^M
égout^M collecteur
alcantarilla^F principal
condotta^F fognaria principale

ガス本管
gas main
Gasleitung^F
conduite^F de gaz^M
conducto^M principal de gas^M
conduttura^F del gas^M

水道本管
service main; *water main*
Trinkwasserleitung^F
conduite^F d'eau^F potable
colector^M principal
condotta^F dell'acquedotto^M

電話線
telephone cable
Telefonkabel^N
câble^M téléphonique
red^F de cables^M telefónicos
cavo^M telefonico

交通信号
traffic lights
Verkehrsampel^F
feux^M de circulation^F
semáforo^F
semaforo^M

赤信号
red light
rotes Licht^N
feu^M rouge
luz^F roja
luce^F rossa

黄信号
yellow light
gelbes Licht^N
feu^M jaune
luz^M ámbar
luce^F gialla

青信号
green light
grünes Licht^N
feu^M vert
luz^F verde
luce^F verde

歩行者信号
pedestrian lights
Fußgängerampel^F
feux^M pour piétons^M
semáforo^M de peatones^M
luci^F pedonali

歩行者用押しボタン
pedestrian call button
Fußgängerknopf^M
bouton^M d'appel^M pour piétons^M
botón^M de llamada^F para peatones^M
pulsante^M di chiamata^F pedonale

都市 | CITY
STADT | VILLE | CIUDAD | CITTÀ

オフィス・ビル

office building | Bürogebäude[N] | édifice[M] à bureaux[M] | edificio[M] de oficinas[F] | edificio[M] per uffici[M]

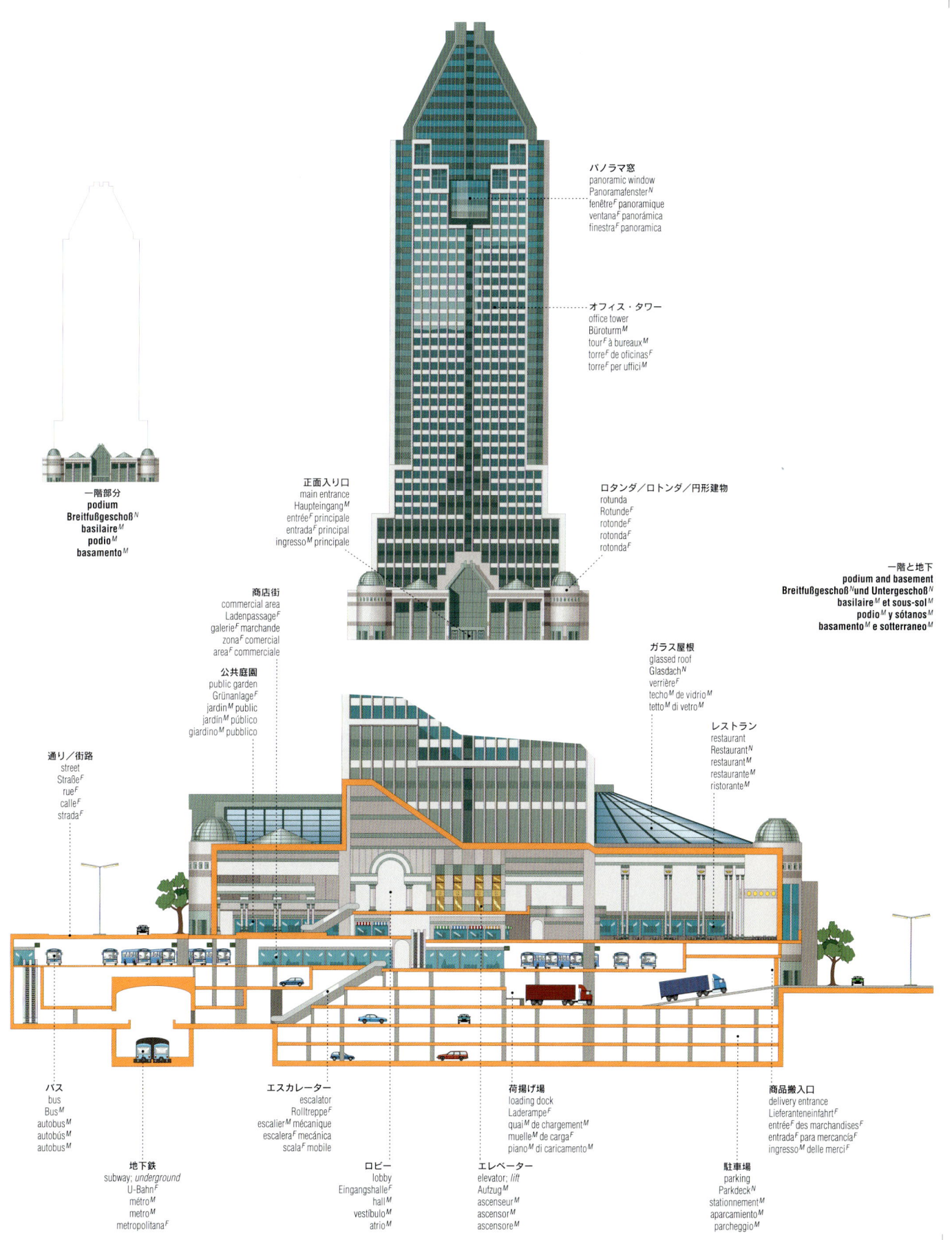

パノラマ窓
panoramic window
Panoramafenster[N]
fenêtre[F] panoramique
ventana[F] panorámica
finestra[F] panoramica

オフィス・タワー
office tower
Büroturm[M]
tour[F] à bureaux[M]
torre[F] de oficinas[F]
torre[F] per uffici[M]

一階部分
podium
Breitfußgeschoß[N]
basilaire[M]
podio[M]
basamento[M]

正面入口
main entrance
Haupteingang[M]
entrée[F] principale
entrada[F] principal
ingresso[M] principale

ロタンダ/ロトンダ/円形建物
rotunda
Rotunde[F]
rotonde[F]
rotonda[F]
rotonda[F]

一階と地下
podium and basement
Breitfußgeschoß[N] und Untergeschoß[N]
basilaire[M] et sous-sol[M]
podio[M] y sótanos[M]
basamento[M] e sotterraneo[M]

商店街
commercial area
Ladenpassage[F]
galerie[F] marchande
zona[F] comercial
area[F] commerciale

ガラス屋根
glassed roof
Glasdach[N]
verrière[F]
techo[M] de vidrio[M]
tetto[M] di vetro[M]

公共庭園
public garden
Grünanlage[F]
jardin[M] public
jardín[M] público
giardino[M] pubblico

レストラン
restaurant
Restaurant[N]
restaurant[M]
restaurante[M]
ristorante[M]

通り/街路
street
Straße[F]
rue[F]
calle[F]
strada[F]

社会

バス
bus
Bus[M]
autobus[M]
autobús[M]
autobus[M]

地下鉄
subway; *underground*
U-Bahn[F]
métro[M]
metro[M]
metropolitana[F]

エスカレーター
escalator
Rolltreppe[F]
escalier[M] mécanique
escalera[F] mecánica
scala[F] mobile

ロビー
lobby
Eingangshalle[F]
hall[M]
vestíbulo[M]
atrio[M]

荷揚げ場
loading dock
Laderampe[F]
quai[M] de chargement[M]
muelle[M] de carga[F]
piano[M] di caricamento[M]

エレベーター
elevator; *lift*
Aufzug[M]
ascenseur[M]
ascensor[M]
ascensore[M]

商品搬入口
delivery entrance
Lieferanteneinfahrt[F]
entrée[F] des marchandises[F]
entrada[F] para mercancía[F]
ingresso[M] delle merci[F]

駐車場
parking
Parkdeck[N]
stationnement[M]
aparcamiento[M]
parcheggio[M]

713

都市 | CITY
STADT | VILLE | CIUDAD | CITTÀ

ショッピング・センター

shopping center; *shopping centre* | Einkaufszentrum[N] | centre[M] commercial | centro[M] comercial | centro[M] commerciale

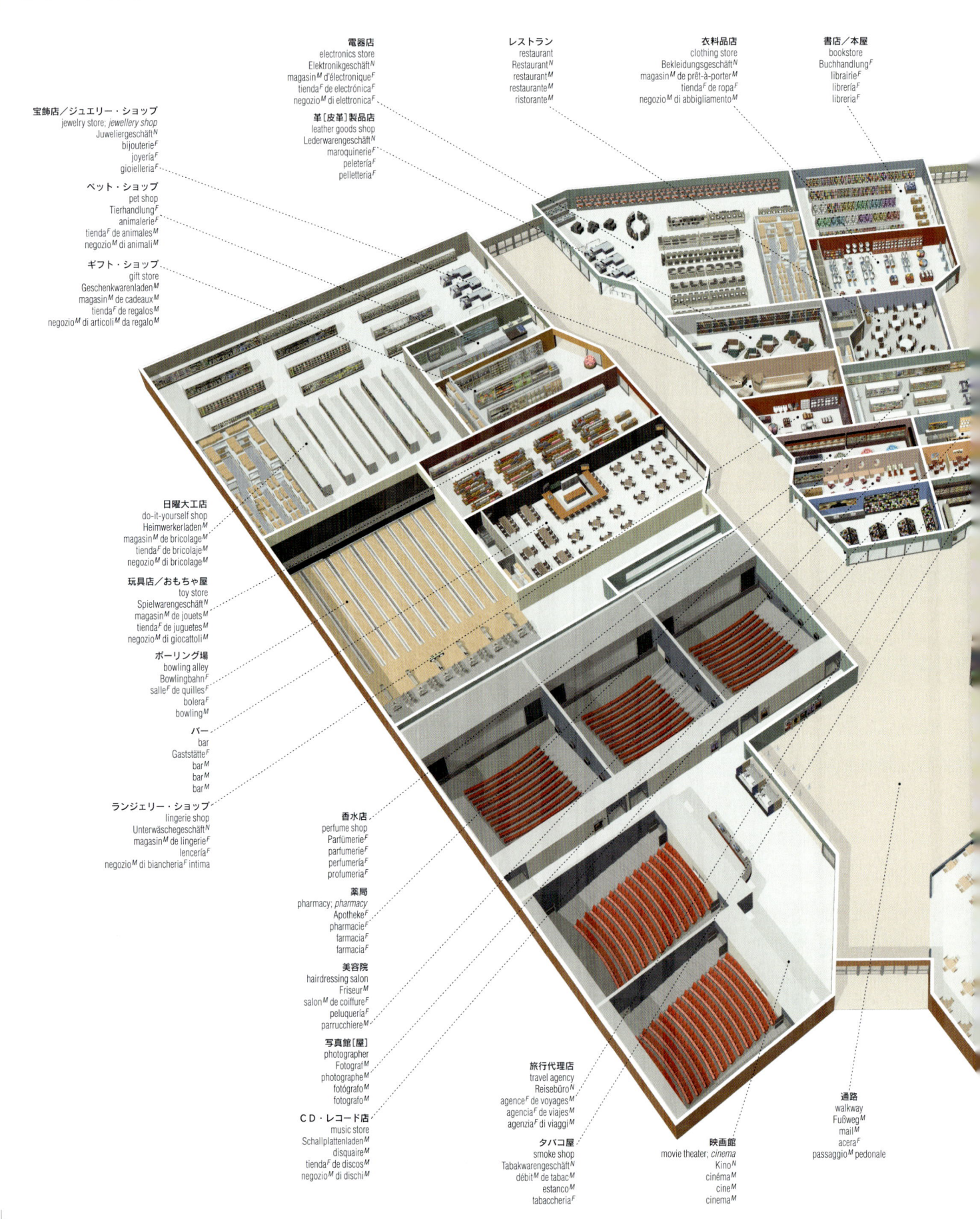

日本語 | 英語 | ドイツ語 | フランス語 | スペイン語 | イタリア語

電器店
electronics store
Elektronikgeschäft[N]
magasin[M] d'électronique
tienda[F] de electrónica
negozio[M] di elettronica

レストラン
restaurant
Restaurant[N]
restaurant[M]
restaurante[M]
ristorante[M]

衣料品店
clothing store
Bekleidungsgeschäft[N]
magasin[M] de prêt-à-porter
tienda[F] de ropa
negozio[M] di abbigliamento

書店／本屋
bookstore
Buchhandlung[F]
librairie[F]
librería[F]
libreria

宝飾店／ジュエリー・ショップ
jewelry store; *jewellery shop*
Juweliergeschäft[N]
bijouterie[F]
joyería[F]
gioielleria[F]

革[皮革]製品店
leather goods shop
Lederwarengeschäft[N]
maroquinerie[F]
peletería[F]
pelletteria[F]

ペット・ショップ
pet shop
Tierhandlung[F]
animalerie[F]
tienda[F] de animales[M]
negozio[M] di animali

ギフト・ショップ
gift store
Geschenkwarenladen[M]
magasin[M] de cadeaux
tienda[F] de regalos
negozio[M] di articoli[M] da regalo[M]

日曜大工店
do-it-yourself shop
Heimwerkerladen[M]
magasin[M] de bricolage
tienda[F] de bricolaje
negozio[M] di bricolage

玩具店／おもちゃ屋
toy store
Spielwarengeschäft[N]
magasin[M] de jouets
tienda[F] de juguetes
negozio[M] di giocattoli

ボーリング場
bowling alley
Bowlingbahn[F]
salle[F] de quilles
bolera[F]
bowling[M]

バー
bar
Gaststätte[F]
bar[M]
bar[M]
bar[M]

ランジェリー・ショップ
lingerie shop
Unterwäschegeschäft[N]
magasin[M] de lingerie
lencería[F]
negozio[M] di biancheria[F] intima

香水店
perfume shop
Parfümerie[F]
parfumerie[F]
perfumería[F]
profumeria[F]

薬局
pharmacy; *pharmacy*
Apotheke[F]
pharmacie[F]
farmacia[F]
farmacia[F]

美容院
hairdressing salon
Friseur[M]
salon[M] de coiffure
peluquería[F]
parrucchiere[M]

写真館[屋]
photographer
Fotograf[M]
photographe[M]
fotógrafo[M]
fotografo[M]

旅行代理店
travel agency
Reisebüro[N]
agence[F] de voyages
agencia[F] de viajes
agenzia[F] di viaggi

CD・レコード店
music store
Schallplattenladen[M]
disquaire[M]
tienda[F] de discos
negozio[M] di dischi

タバコ屋
smoke shop
Tabakwarengeschäft[N]
débit[M] de tabac
estanco[M]
tabaccheria[F]

映画館
movie theater; *cinema*
Kino[N]
cinéma[M]
cine[M]
cinema[M]

通路
walkway
Fußweg[M]
mail[M]
acera[F]
passaggio[M] pedonale

社会

714

都市 | CITY
STADT | VILLE | CIUDAD | CITTÀ

ショッピング・センター

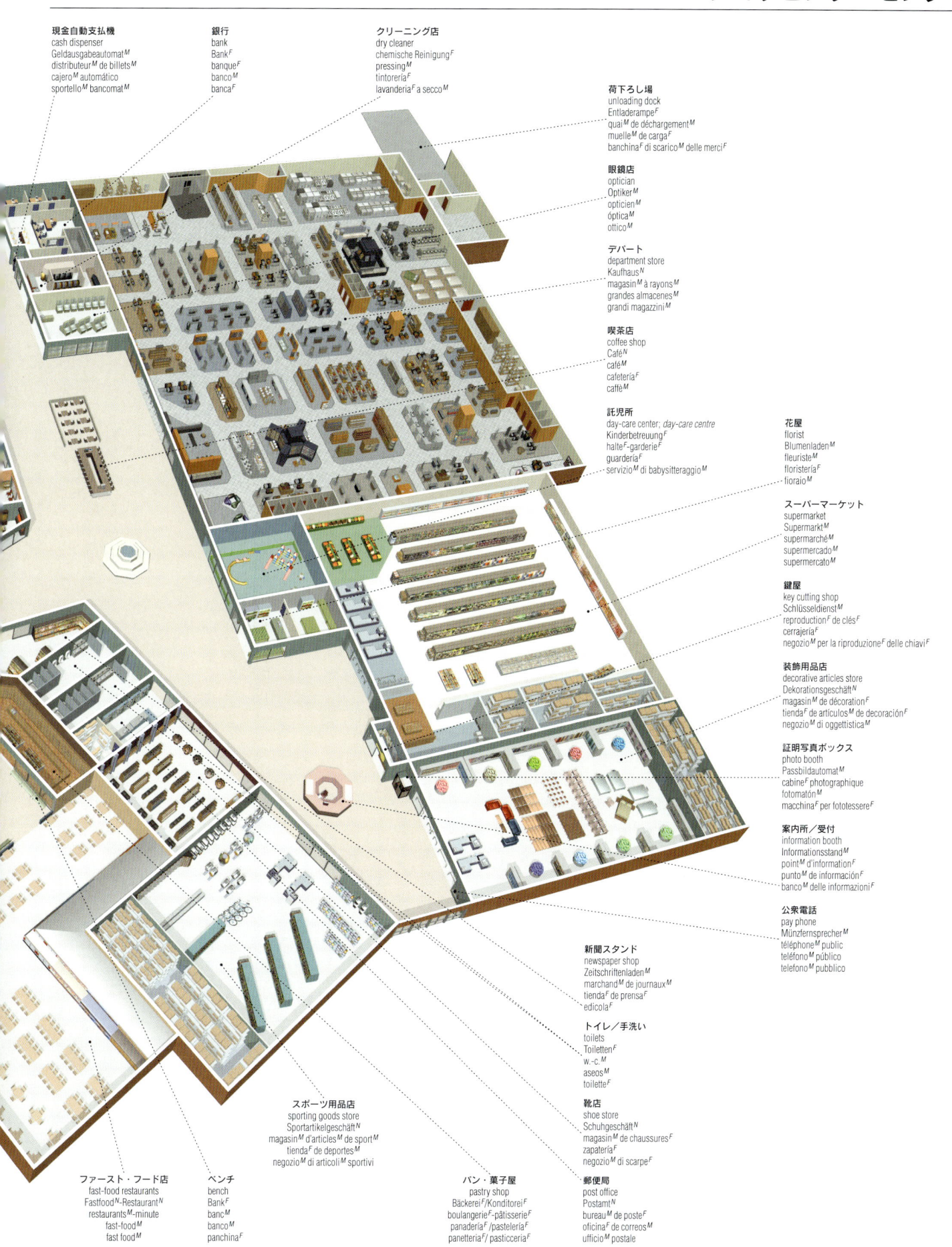

現金自動支払機
cash dispenser
Geldausgabeautomat^M
distributeur^M de billets^M
cajero^M automático
sportello^M bancomat^M

銀行
bank
Bank^F
banque^F
banco^M
banca^F

クリーニング店
dry cleaner
chemische Reinigung^F
pressing^M
tintorería^F
lavandería^F a secco^M

荷下ろし場
unloading dock
Entladerampe^F
quai^M de déchargement^M
muelle^M de carga^F
banchina^F di scarico^M delle merci^F

眼鏡店
optician
Optiker^M
opticien^M
óptica^M
ottico^M

デパート
department store
Kaufhaus^N
magasin^M à rayons^M
grandes almacenes^M
grandi magazzini^M

喫茶店
coffee shop
Café^N
café^M
cafetería^F
caffè^M

託児所
day-care center; day-care centre
Kinderbetreuung^F
halte^F-garderie^F
guardería^F
servizio^M di babysitteraggio^M

花屋
florist
Blumenladen^M
fleuriste^M
floristería^F
fioraio^M

スーパーマーケット
supermarket
Supermarkt^M
supermarché^M
supermercado^M
supermercato^M

鍵屋
key cutting shop
Schlüsseldienst^M
reproduction^F de clés^F
cerrajería^F
negozio^M per la riproduzione^F delle chiavi^F

装飾用品店
decorative articles store
Dekorationsgeschäft^N
magasin^M de décoration^F
tienda^F de artículos^M de decoración^F
negozio^M di oggettistica^F

証明写真ボックス
photo booth
Passbildautomat^M
cabine^F photographique
fotomatón^M
macchina^F per fototessere^F

案内所／受付
information booth
Informationsstand^M
point^M d'information^F
punto^M de información^F
banco^M delle informazioni^F

公衆電話
pay phone
Münzfernsprecher^M
téléphone^M public
teléfono^M público
telefono^M pubblico

新聞スタンド
newspaper shop
Zeitschriftenladen^M
marchand^M de journaux^M
tienda^F de prensa^F
edicola^F

トイレ／手洗い
toilets
Toiletten^F
w.-c.^{M}
aseos^M
toilette^F

靴店
shoe store
Schuhgeschäft^N
magasin^M de chaussures^F
zapatería^F
negozio^M di scarpe^F

ファースト・フード店
fast-food restaurants
Fastfood^N-Restaurant^N
restaurants^M-minute
fast-food
fast food^M

ベンチ
bench
Bank^F
banc^M
banco^M
panchina^F

スポーツ用品店
sporting goods store
Sportartikelgeschäft^N
magasin^M d'articles^M de sport^M
tienda^F de deportes^M
negozio^M di articoli^M sportivi

パン・菓子屋
pastry shop
Bäckerei^F/Konditorei^F
boulangerie^F-pâtisserie^F
panadería^F/pastelería^F
panetteria^F/pasticceria^F

郵便局
post office
Postamt^N
bureau^M de poste^F
oficina^F de correos^M
ufficio^M postale

社会

715

都市 | CITY
STADT | VILLE | CIUDAD | CITTÀ

デパート

日本語 | 英語 | ドイツ語 | フランス語 | スペイン語 | イタリア語

department store | Kaufhaus^N | magasin^M à rayons^M | grandes almacenes^M | grandi magazzini^M

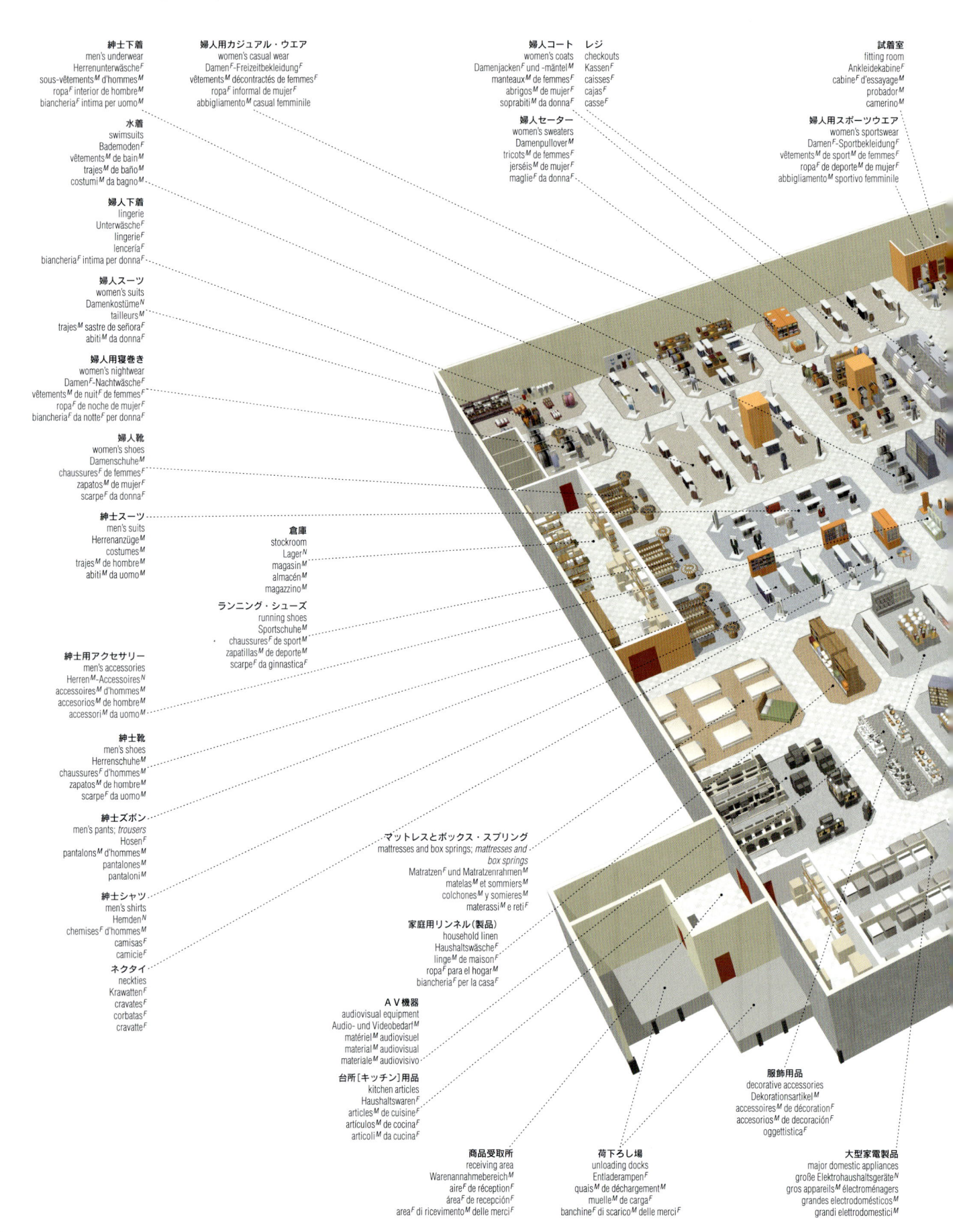

紳士下着
men's underwear
Herrenunterwäsche^F
sous-vêtements^M d'hommes^M
ropa^F interior de hombre^M
biancheria^F intima per uomo^M

婦人用カジュアル・ウエア
women's casual wear
Damen^F-Freizeitbekleidung^F
vêtements^M décontractés de femmes^F
ropa^F informal de mujer^F
abbigliamento^M casual femminile

婦人コート
women's coats
Damenjacken^F und -mäntel^M
manteaux^M de femmes^F
abrigos^M de mujer^F
soprabiti^M da donna^F

レジ
checkouts
Kassen^F
caisses^F
cajas^F
casse^F

試着室
fitting room
Ankleidekabine^F
cabine^F d'essayage^M
probador^M
camerino^M

水着
swimsuits
Bademoden^F
vêtements^M de bain^M
trajes^M de baño^M
costumi^M da bagno^M

婦人セーター
women's sweaters
Damenpullover^M
tricots^M de femmes^F
jerséis^M de mujer^F
maglie^F da donna^F

婦人用スポーツウエア
women's sportswear
Damen^F-Sportbekleidung^F
vêtements^M de sport^M de femmes^F
ropa^F de deporte^M de mujer^F
abbigliamento^M sportivo femminile

婦人下着
lingerie
Unterwäsche^F
lingerie^F
lencería^F
biancheria^F intima per donna^F

婦人スーツ
women's suits
Damenkostüme^N
tailleurs^M
trajes^M sastre de señora^F
abiti^M da donna^F

婦人用寝巻き
women's nightwear
Damen^F-Nachtwäsche^F
vêtements^M de nuit^F de femmes^F
ropa^F de noche de mujer^F
biancheria^F da notte^F per donna^F

婦人靴
women's shoes
Damenschuhe^M
chaussures^F de femmes^F
zapatos^M de mujer^F
scarpe^F da donna^F

紳士スーツ
men's suits
Herrenanzüge^M
costumes^M
trajes^M de hombre^M
abiti^M da uomo^M

倉庫
stockroom
Lager^N
magasin^M
almacén^M
magazzino^M

ランニング・シューズ
running shoes
Sportschuhe^M
chaussures^F de sport^M
zapatillas^M de deporte^M
scarpe^F da ginnastica^F

紳士用アクセサリー
men's accessories
Herren^M-Accessoires^N
accessoires^M d'hommes^M
accesorios^M de hombre^M
accessori^M da uomo^M

紳士靴
men's shoes
Herrenschuhe^M
chaussures^F d'hommes^M
zapatos^M de hombre^M
scarpe^F da uomo^M

紳士ズボン
men's pants; *trousers*
Hosen^F
pantalons^M d'hommes^M
pantalones^M
pantaloni^M

マットレスとボックス・スプリング
mattresses and box springs; *mattresses and box springs*
Matratzen^F und Matratzenrahmen^M
matelas^M et sommiers^M
colchones^M y somieres^M
materassi^M e reti^F

紳士シャツ
men's shirts
Hemden^N
chemises^F d'hommes^M
camisas^F
camicie^F

家庭用リンネル（製品）
household linen
Haushaltswäsche^F
linge^M de maison^F
ropa^F para el hogar^M
biancheria^F per la casa^F

ネクタイ
neckties
Krawatten^F
cravates^F
corbatas^F
cravatte^F

AV機器
audiovisual equipment
Audio- und Videobedarf^M
matériel^M audiovisuel
material^M audiovisual
materiale^M audiovisivo

服飾用品
decorative accessories
Dekorationsartikel^M
accessoires^M de décoration^F
accesorios^M de decoración^F
oggettistica^F

台所[キッチン]用品
kitchen articles
Haushaltswaren^F
articles^M de cuisine^F
artículos^M de cocina^F
articoli^M da cucina^F

商品受取所
receiving area
Warenannahmebereich^M
aire^F de réception^F
área^F de recepción^F
area^F di ricevimento^M delle merci^F

荷下ろし場
unloading docks
Entladerampen^F
quais^M de déchargement^M
muelle^M de carga^F
banchine^F di scarico^M delle merci^F

大型家電製品
major domestic appliances
große Elektrohaushaltsgeräte^N
gros appareils^M électroménagers
grandes electrodomésticos^M
grandi elettrodomestici^M

社会

716

都市 | CITY
STADT | VILLE | CIUDAD | CITTÀ

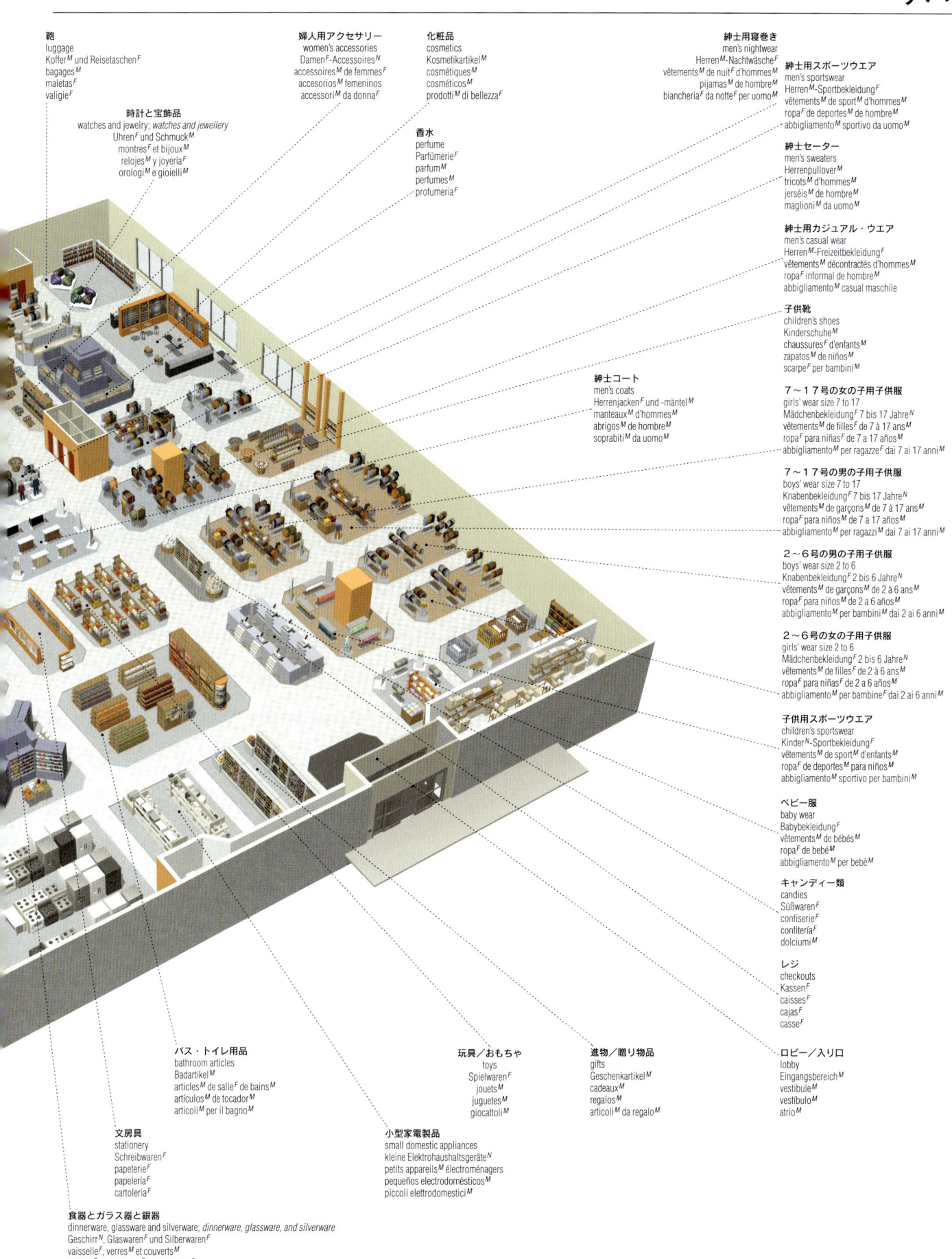

デパート

鞄
luggage
Koffer^M und Reisetaschen^F
bagages^M
maletas^F
valigie^F

時計と宝飾品
watches and jewelry; watches and jewellery
Uhren^F und Schmuck^M
montres^F et bijoux^M
relojes^M y joyería^F
orologi^M e gioielli^M

婦人用アクセサリー
women's accessories
Damen^F-Accessoires^N
accessoires^M de femmes^F
accesorios^M femeninos
accessori^M da donna^F

化粧品
cosmetics
Kosmetikartikel^M
cosmétiques^M
cosméticos^M
prodotti^M di bellezza^F

香水
perfume
Parfümerie^F
parfum^M
perfumes^M
profumeria^F

紳士用寝巻き
men's nightwear
Herren^M-Nachtwäsche^F
vêtements^M de nuit^F d'hommes^M
pijamas^M de hombre^M
biancheria^F da notte^F per uomo^M

紳士用スポーツウエア
men's sportswear
Herren^M-Sportbekleidung^F
vêtements^M de sport^M d'hommes^M
ropa^F de deportes^M de hombre^M
abbigliamento^M sportivo da uomo^M

紳士セーター
men's sweaters
Herrenpullover^M
tricots^M d'hommes^M
jerséis^M de hombre^M
maglioni^M da uomo^M

紳士用カジュアル・ウエア
men's casual wear
Herren^M-Freizeitbekleidung^F
vêtements^M décontractés d'hommes^M
ropa^F informal de hombre^M
abbigliamento^M casual maschile

子供靴
children's shoes
Kinderschuhe^M
chaussures^F d'enfants^M
zapatos^F de niños^M
scarpe^F per bambini^M

紳士コート
men's coats
Herrenjacken^F und -mäntel^M
manteaux^M d'hommes^M
abrigos^M de hombre^M
soprabiti^M da uomo^M

7〜17号の女の子用子供服
girls' wear size 7 to 17
Mädchenbekleidung^F 7 bis 17 Jahre^N
vêtements^M de filles^F de 7 à 17 ans^M
ropa^F para niñas^F de 7 a 17 años^M
abbigliamento^M per ragazze^F dai 7 ai 17 anni^M

7〜17号の男の子用子供服
boys' wear size 7 to 17
Knabenbekleidung^F 7 bis 17 Jahre^N
vêtements^M de garçons^M de 7 à 17 ans^M
ropa^F para niños^M de 7 a 17 años^M
abbigliamento^M per ragazzi^M dai 7 ai 17 anni^M

2〜6号の男の子用子供服
boys' wear size 2 to 6
Knabenbekleidung^F 2 bis 6 Jahre^N
vêtements^M de garçons^M de 2 à 6 ans^M
ropa^F para niños^M de 2 a 6 años^M
abbigliamento^M per bambini^M dai 2 ai 6 anni^M

2〜6号の女の子用子供服
girls' wear size 2 to 6
Mädchenbekleidung^F 2 bis 6 Jahre^N
vêtements^M de filles^F de 2 à 6 ans^M
ropa^F para niñas^F de 2 a 6 años^M
abbigliamento^M per bambine^F dai 2 ai 6 anni^M

子供用スポーツウエア
children's sportswear
Kinder^N-Sportbekleidung^F
vêtements^M de sport^M d'enfants^M
ropa^F de deportes^M para niños^M
abbigliamento^M sportivo per bambini^M

ベビー服
baby wear
Babybekleidung^F
vêtements^M de bébés^M
ropa^F de bebé^M
abbigliamento^M per bebè^M

キャンディー類
candies
Süßwaren^F
confiserie
confitería^F
dolciumi^M

レジ
checkouts
Kassen^F
caisses^F
cajas^F
casse^F

ロビー／入り口
lobby
Eingangsbereich^M
vestibule
vestíbulo^M
atrio^M

バス・トイレ用品
bathroom articles
Badartikel^M
articles^M de salle^F de bains^M
artículos^M de tocador^M
articoli^M per il bagno^M

文房具
stationery
Schreibwaren^F
papeterie^F
papelería^F
cartoleria^F

玩具／おもちゃ
toys
Spielwaren^F
jouets^M
juguetes^M
giocattoli^M

進物／贈り物品
gifts
Geschenkartikel^M
cadeaux^M
regalos^M
articoli^M da regalo^M

小型家電製品
small domestic appliances
kleine Elektrohaushaltsgeräte^N
petits appareils^M électroménagers
pequeños electrodomésticos^M
piccoli elettrodomestici^M

食器とガラス器と銀器
dinnerware, glassware and silverware; dinnerware, glassware, and silverware
Geschirr^N, Glaswaren^F und Silberwaren^F
vaisselle^F, verres^M et couverts^M
vajillas^F, cristalerías^F y cuberterías^F
vasellame^M, cristalleria^F e argenteria^F

社会

都市 | CITY
STADT | VILLE | CIUDAD | CITTÀ

コンベンション・センター

convention center; *convention centre* | Kongresszentrum[N] | palais[M] des congrès[M] | palacio[M] de congresos[M] | palazzo[M] dei congressi[M]

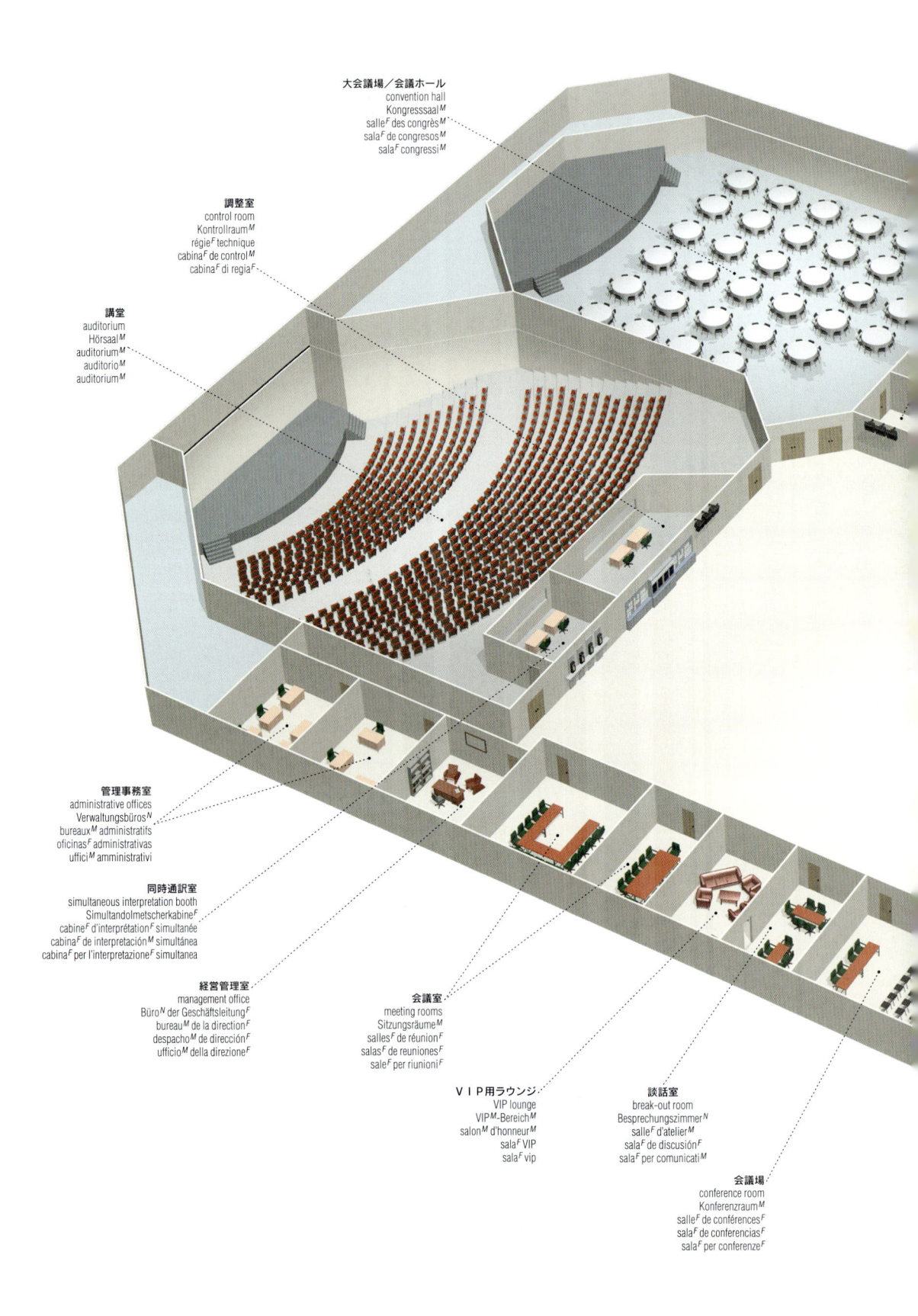

日本語 | 英語 | ドイツ語 | フランス語 | スペイン語 | イタリア語

大会議場／会議ホール
convention hall
Kongresssaal[M]
salle[F] des congrès[M]
sala[F] de congresos[M]
sala[F] congressi[M]

調整室
control room
Kontrollraum[M]
régie[F] technique
cabina[F] de control[M]
cabina[F] di regia[F]

講堂
auditorium
Hörsaal[M]
auditorium[M]
auditorio[M]
auditorium[M]

管理事務室
administrative offices
Verwaltungsbüros[N]
bureaux[M] administratifs
oficinas[F] administrativas
uffici[M] amministrativi

同時通訳室
simultaneous interpretation booth
Simultandolmetscherkabine[F]
cabine[F] d'interprétation[F] simultanée
cabina[F] de interpretación[M] simultánea
cabina[F] per l'interpretazione[F] simultanea

経営管理室
management office
Büro[N] der Geschäftsleitung[F]
bureau[M] de la direction[F]
despacho[M] de dirección[F]
ufficio[M] della direzione[F]

会議室
meeting rooms
Sitzungsräume[M]
salles[F] de réunion[F]
salas[F] de reuniones[F]
sale[F] per riunioni[F]

VIP用ラウンジ
VIP lounge
VIP[M]-Bereich[M]
salon[M] d'honneur[M]
sala[F] VIP
sala[F] vip

談話室
break-out room
Besprechungszimmer[N]
salle[F] d'atelier[M]
sala[F] de discusión[F]
sala[F] per comunicati[M]

会議場
conference room
Konferenzraum[M]
salle[F] de conférences[F]
sala[F] de conferencias[F]
sala[F] per conferenze[F]

718

都市 | CITY
STADT | VILLE | CIUDAD | CITTÀ

コンベンション・センター

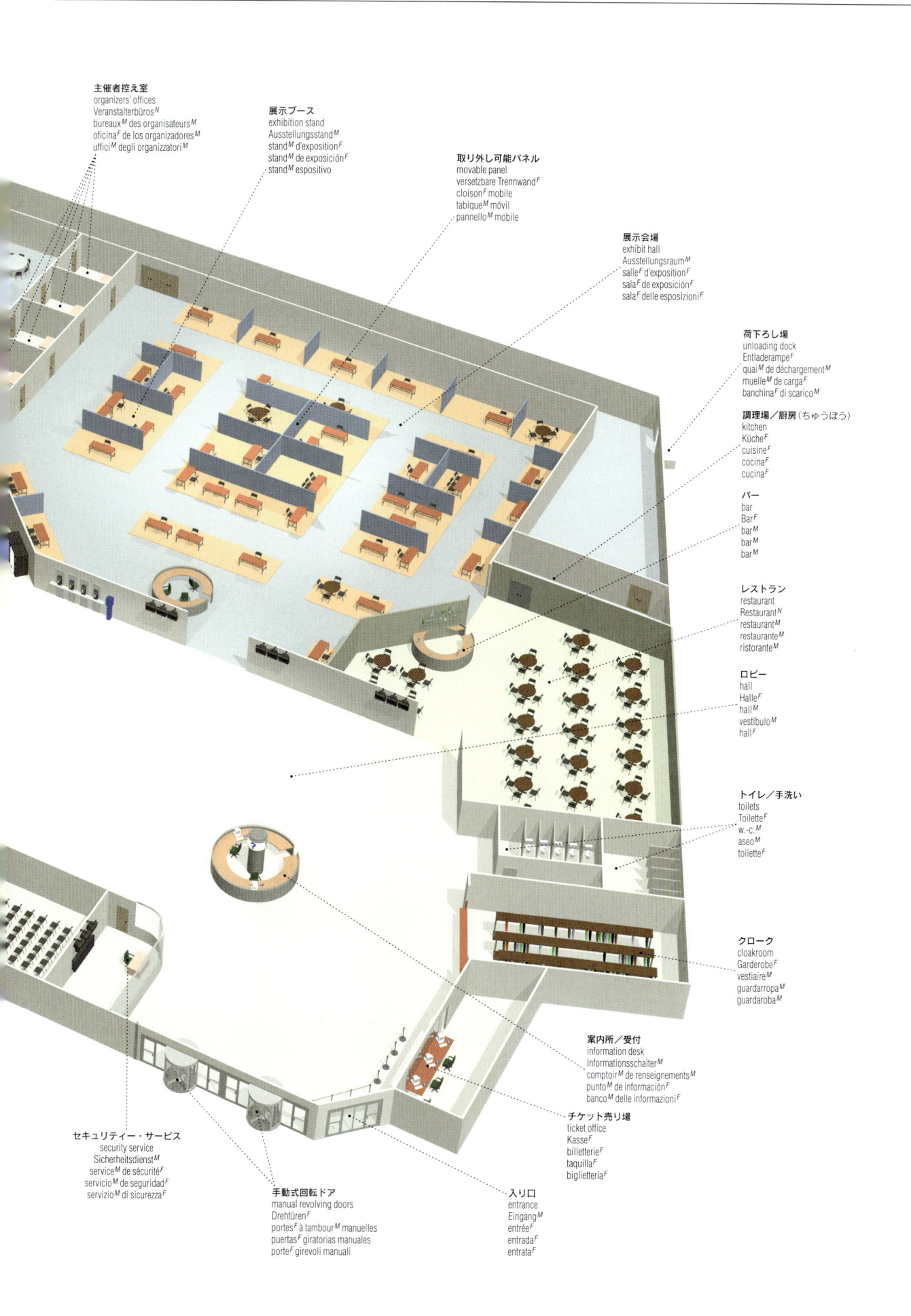

主催者控え室
organizers' offices
Veranstalterbüros[N]
bureaux[M] des organisateurs[M]
oficina[F] de los organizadores[M]
uffici[M] degli organizzatori[M]

展示ブース
exhibition stand
Ausstellungsstand[M]
stand[M] d'exposition[F]
stand[M] de exposición[F]
stand[M] espositivo

取り外し可能パネル
movable panel
versetzbare Trennwand[F]
cloison[F] mobile
tabique[M] móvil
pannello[M] mobile

展示会場
exhibit hall
Ausstellungsraum[M]
salle[F] d'exposition[F]
sala[F] de exposición[F]
sala[F] delle esposizioni[F]

荷下ろし場
unloading dock
Entladerampe[F]
quai[M] de déchargement[M]
muelle[M] de carga[F]
banchina[F] di scarico[M]

調理場／厨房（ちゅうぼう）
kitchen
Küche[F]
cuisine[F]
cocina[F]
cucina[F]

バー
bar
Bar[F]
bar[M]
bar[M]
bar[M]

レストラン
restaurant
Restaurant[N]
restaurant[M]
restaurante[M]
ristorante[M]

ロビー
hall
Halle[F]
hall[M]
vestíbulo[M]
hall[F]

トイレ／手洗い
toilets
Toilette[F]
w.-c.[M]
aseo[M]
toilette[F]

クローク
cloakroom
Garderobe[F]
vestiaire[M]
guardarropa[M]
guardaroba[M]

案内所／受付
information desk
Informationsschalter[M]
comptoir[M] de renseignements[M]
punto[M] de información[F]
banco[M] delle informazioni[F]

チケット売り場
ticket office
Kasse[F]
billetterie[F]
taquilla[F]
biglietteria[F]

セキュリティー・サービス
security service
Sicherheitsdienst[M]
service[M] de sécurité[F]
servicio[M] de seguridad[F]
servizio[M] di sicurezza[F]

手動式回転ドア
manual revolving doors
Drehtüren[F]
portes[F] à tambour[M] manuelles
puertas[F] giratorias manuales
porte[F] girevoli manuali

入り口
entrance
Eingang[M]
entrée[F]
entrada[F]
entrata[F]

社会

719

都市 | CITY
STADT | VILLE | CIUDAD | CITTÀ

レストラン

restaurant | Restaurant^M | restaurant^M | restaurante^M | ristorante^M

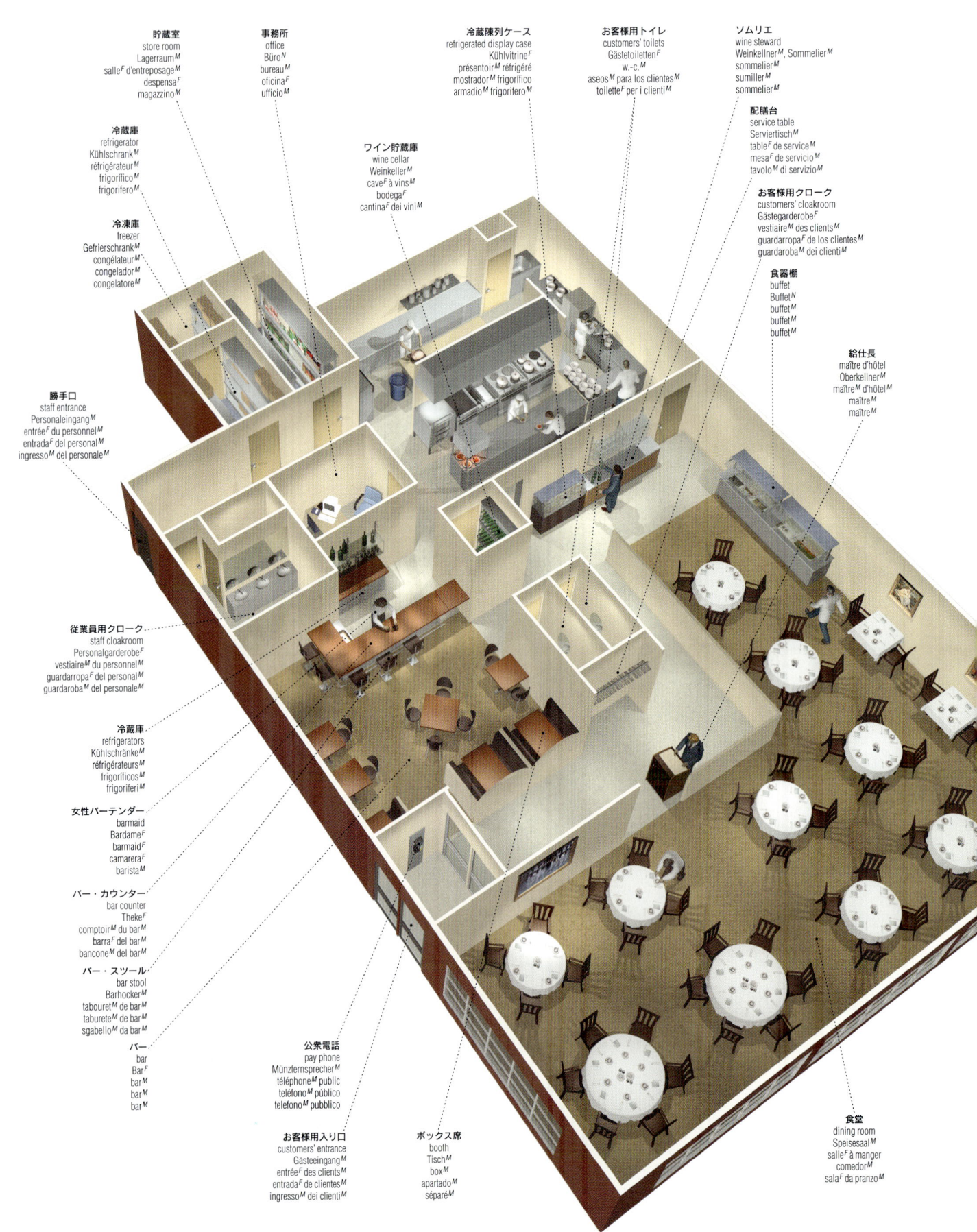

貯蔵室
store room
Lagerraum^M
salle^F d'entreposage^M
despensa^F
magazzino^M

事務所
office
Büro^N
bureau^M
oficina^F
ufficio^M

冷蔵陳列ケース
refrigerated display case
Kühlvitrine^F
présentoir^M réfrigéré
mostrador^M frigorífico
armadio^M frigorifero

お客様用トイレ
customers' toilets
Gästetoiletten^F
w.-c.^M
aseos^M para los clientes
toilette^F per i clienti

ソムリエ
wine steward
Weinkellner^M, Sommelier^M
sommelier^M
sumiller^M
sommelier^M

冷蔵庫
refrigerator
Kühlschrank^M
réfrigérateur^M
frigorífico^M
frigorifero^M

ワイン貯蔵庫
wine cellar
Weinkeller^M
cave^F à vins^M
bodega^F
cantina^F dei vini^M

配膳台
service table
Serviertisch^M
table^F de service^M
mesa^F de servicio^M
tavolo^M di servizio^M

お客様用クローク
customers' cloakroom
Gästegarderobe^F
vestiaire^M des clients^M
guardarropa^F de los clientes^M
guardaroba^M dei clienti^M

冷凍庫
freezer
Gefrierschrank^M
congélateur^M
congelador^M
congelatore^M

食器棚
buffet
Buffet^N
buffet^M
buffet^M
buffet^M

勝手口
staff entrance
Personaleingang^M
entrée^F du personnel^M
entrada^F del personal^M
ingresso^M del personale

給仕長
maître d'hôtel
Oberkellner^M
maître^M d'hôtel^M
maître^M
maître^M

従業員用クローク
staff cloakroom
Personalgarderobe^F
vestiaire^M du personnel^M
guardarropa^F del personal^M
guardaroba^M del personale^M

冷蔵庫
refrigerators
Kühlschränke^M
réfrigérateurs^M
frigoríficos^M
frigoriferi^M

女性バーテンダー
barmaid
Bardame^F
barmaid^F
camarera^F
barista^M

バー・カウンター
bar counter
Theke^F
comptoir^M du bar^M
barra^F del bar^M
bancone^M del bar^M

バー・スツール
bar stool
Barhocker^M
tabouret^M de bar^M
taburete^M de bar^M
sgabello^M da bar^M

バー
bar
Bar^F
bar^M
bar^M
bar^M

公衆電話
pay phone
Münzfernsprecher^M
téléphone^M public
teléfono^M público
telefono^M pubblico

お客様用入り口
customers' entrance
Gästeeingang^M
entrée^F des clients^M
entrada^F de clientes^M
ingresso^M dei clienti^M

ボックス席
booth
Tisch^M
box^M
apartado^M
séparé^M

食堂
dining room
Speisesaal^M
salle^F à manger
comedor^M
sala^F da pranzo^M

都市 | CITY
STADT | VILLE | CIUDAD | CITTÀ

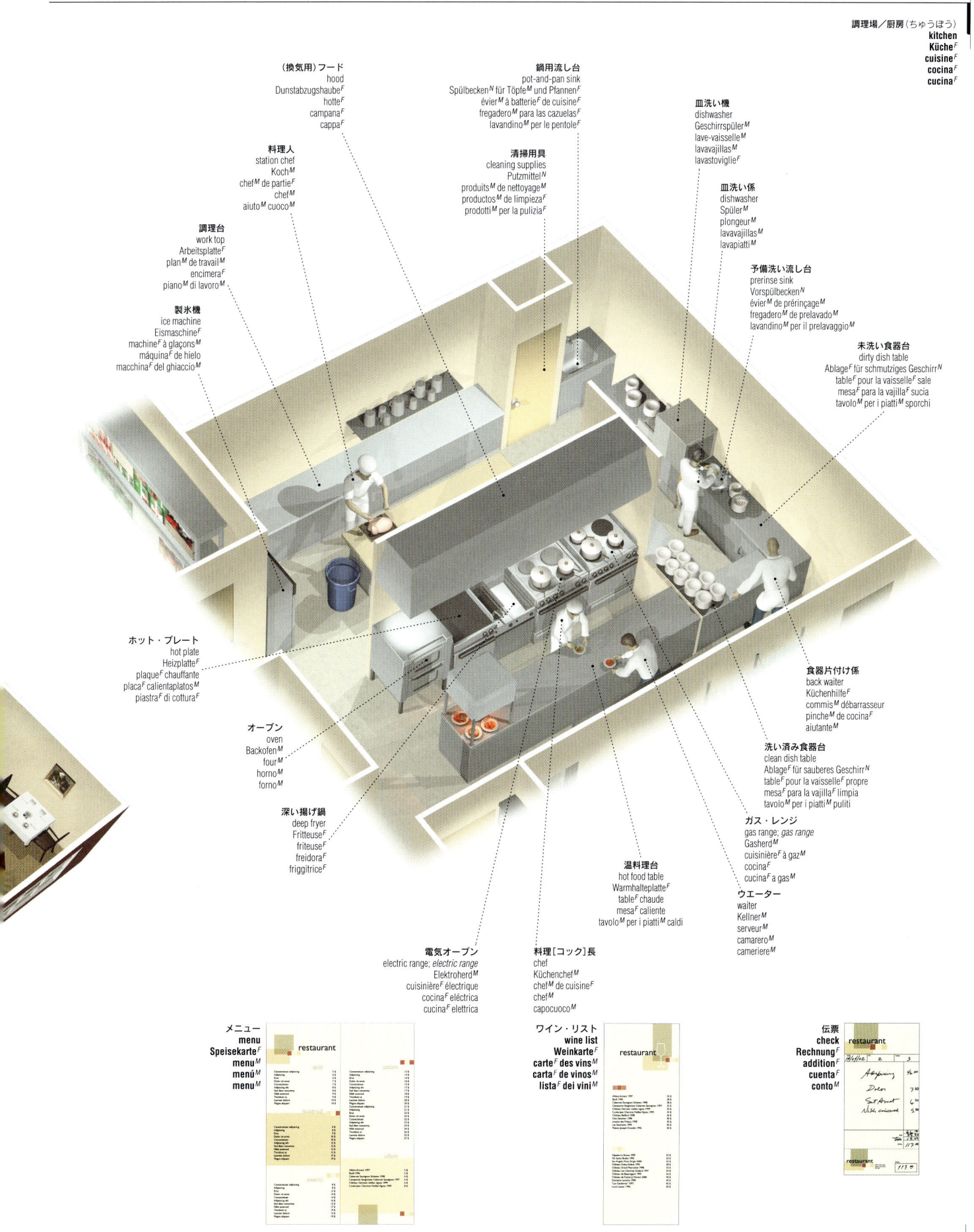

レストラン

調理場／厨房（ちゅうぼう）
kitchen
Küche^F
cuisine^F
cocina^F
cucina^F

(換気用)フード
hood
Dunstabzugshaube^F
hotte^F
campana^F
cappa^F

鍋用流し台
pot-and-pan sink
Spülbecken^N für Töpfe^M und Pfannen^F
évier^M à batterie^F de cuisine^F
fregadero^M para las cazuelas^F
lavandino^M per le pentole^F

皿洗い機
dishwasher
Geschirrspüler^M
lave-vaisselle^M
lavavajillas^M
lavastoviglie^F

料理人
station chef
Koch^M
chef^M de partie^F
chef^M
aiuto^M cuoco^M

清掃用具
cleaning supplies
Putzmittel^N
produits^M de nettoyage^M
productos^M de limpieza^F
prodotti^M per la pulizia^F

皿洗い係
dishwasher
Spüler^M
plongeur^M
lavavajillas^M
lavapiatti^M

調理台
work top
Arbeitsplatte^F
plan^M de travail^M
encimera^F
piano^M di lavoro^M

予備洗い流し台
prerinse sink
Vorspülbecken^N
évier^M de prérinçage^M
fregadero^M de prelavado^M
lavandino^M per il prelavaggio^M

製氷機
ice machine
Eismaschine^F
machine^F à glaçons^M
máquina^F de hielo^M
macchina^F del ghiaccio^M

未洗い食器台
dirty dish table
Ablage^F für schmutziges Geschirr^N
table^F pour la vaisselle^F sale
mesa^F para la vajilla^F sucia
tavolo^M per i piatti^M sporchi

ホット・プレート
hot plate
Heizplatte^F
plaque^F chauffante
placa^F calientaplatos^M
piastra^F di cottura^F

食器片付け係
back waiter
Küchenhilfe^F
commis^M débarrasseur
pinche^M de cocina^F
aiutante^M

オーブン
oven
Backofen^M
four^M
horno^M
forno^M

洗い済み食器台
clean dish table
Ablage^F für sauberes Geschirr^N
table^F pour la vaisselle^F propre
mesa^F para la vajilla^F limpia
tavolo^M per i piatti^M puliti

深い揚げ鍋
deep fryer
Fritteuse^F
friteuse^F
freidora^F
friggitrice^F

ガス・レンジ
gas range; gas range
Gasherd^M
cuisinière^F à gaz^M
cocina^F
cucina^F a gas^M

温料理台
hot food table
Warmhalteplatte^F
table^F chaude
mesa^F caliente
tavolo^M per i piatti^M caldi

ウエーター
waiter
Kellner^M
serveur^M
camarero^M
cameriere^M

電気オーブン
electric range; electric range
Elektroherd^M
cuisinière^F électrique
cocina^F eléctrica
cucina^F elettrica

料理[コック]長
chef
Küchenchef^M
chef^M de cuisine^F
chef^M
capocuoco^M

メニュー
menu
Speisekarte^F
menu^F
menú^M
menu^M

ワイン・リスト
wine list
Weinkarte^F
carte^F des vins^M
carta^F de vinos^M
lista^F dei vini^M

伝票
check
Rechnung^F
addition^F
cuenta^F
conto^M

社会

721

セルフ・サービス式レストラン

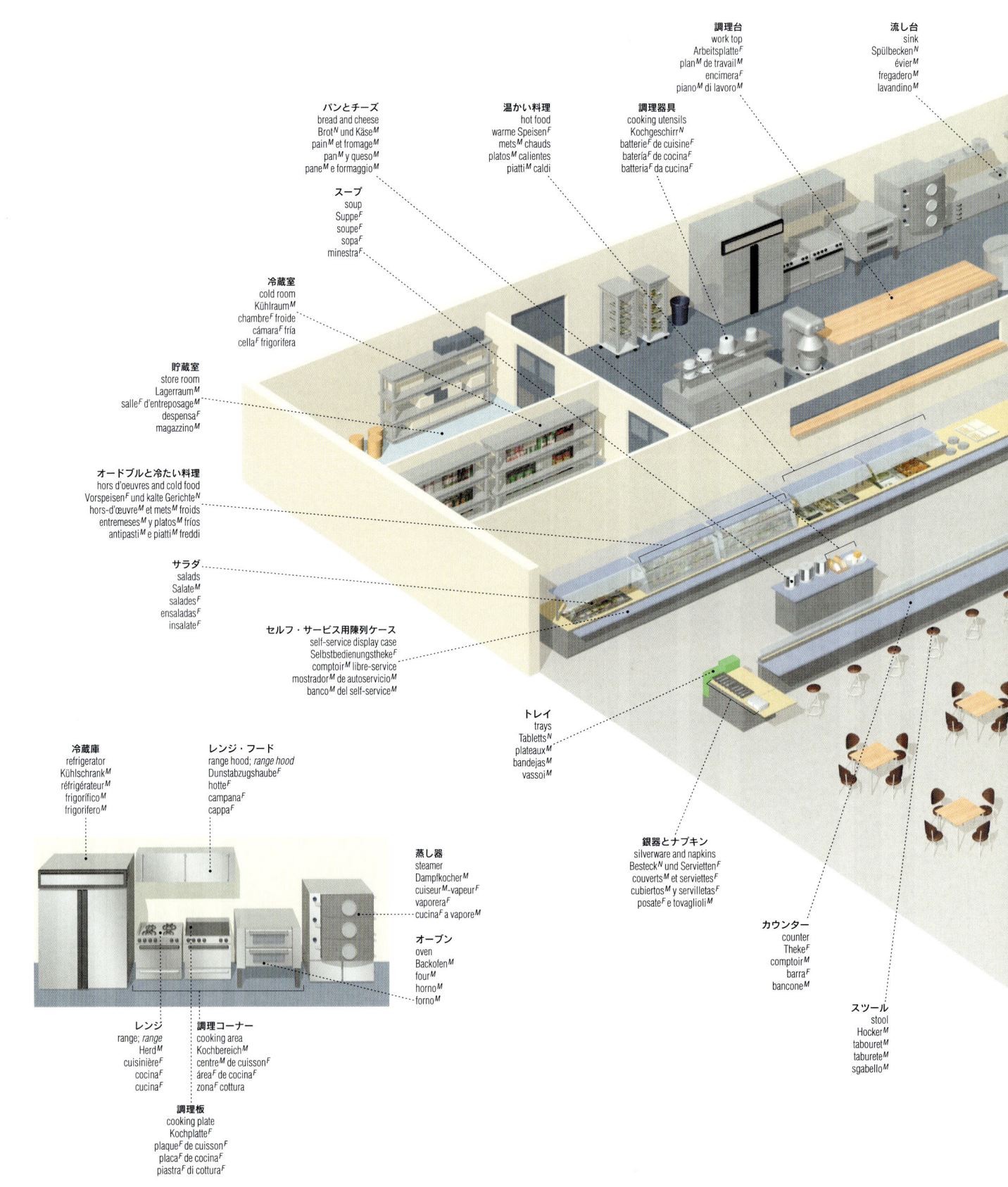

都市 | CITY
STADT | VILLE | CIUDAD | CITTÀ

日本語 | 英語 | ドイツ語 | フランス語 | スペイン語 | イタリア語

self-service restaurant | Selbstbedienungsrestaurant^N | restaurant^M libre-service | restaurante^M de autoservicio^M | self-service^M

調理台 — work top / Arbeitsplatte^F / plan^M de travail / encimera^F / piano^M di lavoro^M

流し台 — sink / Spülbecken^N / évier^M / fregadero^M / lavandino^M

パンとチーズ — bread and cheese / Brot^N und Käse^M / pain^M et fromage^M / pan^M y queso^M / pane^M e formaggio^M

温かい料理 — hot food / warme Speisen^F / mets^M chauds / platos^M calientes / piatti^M caldi

調理器具 — cooking utensils / Kochgeschirr^N / batterie^F de cuisine^F / batería^F de cocina^F / batteria^F da cucina^F

スープ — soup / Suppe^F / soupe^F / sopa^F / minestra^F

冷蔵室 — cold room / Kühlraum^M / chambre^F froide / cámara^F fría / cella^F frigorifera

貯蔵室 — store room / Lagerraum^M / salle^F d'entreposage^M / despensa^F / magazzino^M

オードブルと冷たい料理 — hors d'oeuvres and cold food / Vorspeisen^F und kalte Gerichte^N / hors-d'œuvre^M et mets^M froids / entremeses^M y platos^M fríos / antipasti^M e piatti^M freddi

サラダ — salads / Salate^M / salades^F / ensaladas^F / insalate^F

セルフ・サービス用陳列ケース — self-service display case / Selbstbedienungstheke^F / comptoir^M libre-service / mostrador^M de autoservicio^M / banco^M del self-service^M

冷蔵庫 — refrigerator / Kühlschrank^M / réfrigérateur^M / frigorífico^M / frigorifero^M

レンジ・フード — range hood; range hood / Dunstabzugshaube^F / hotte^F / campana^F / cappa^F

トレイ — trays / Tabletts^N / plateaux^M / bandejas^M / vassoi^M

蒸し器 — steamer / Dampfkocher^M / cuiseur^M-vapeur^F / vaporera^F / cucina^F a vapore^M

オーブン — oven / Backofen^M / four^M / horno^M / forno^M

銀器とナプキン — silverware and napkins / Besteck^N und Servietten^F / couverts^M et serviettes^F / cubiertos^M y servilletas^F / posate^F e tovaglioli^M

カウンター — counter / Theke^F / comptoir^M / barra^F / bancone^M

スツール — stool / Hocker^M / tabouret^M / taburete^M / sgabello^M

レンジ — range; range / Herd^M / cuisinière^F / cocina^F / cucina^F

調理コーナー — cooking area / Kochbereich^M / centre^M de cuisson^F / área^F de cocina^F / zona^F cottura

調理板 — cooking plate / Kochplatte^F / plaque^F de cuisson^F / placa^F de cocina^F / piastra^F di cottura^F

都市 | CITY
STADT | VILLE | CIUDAD | CITTÀ

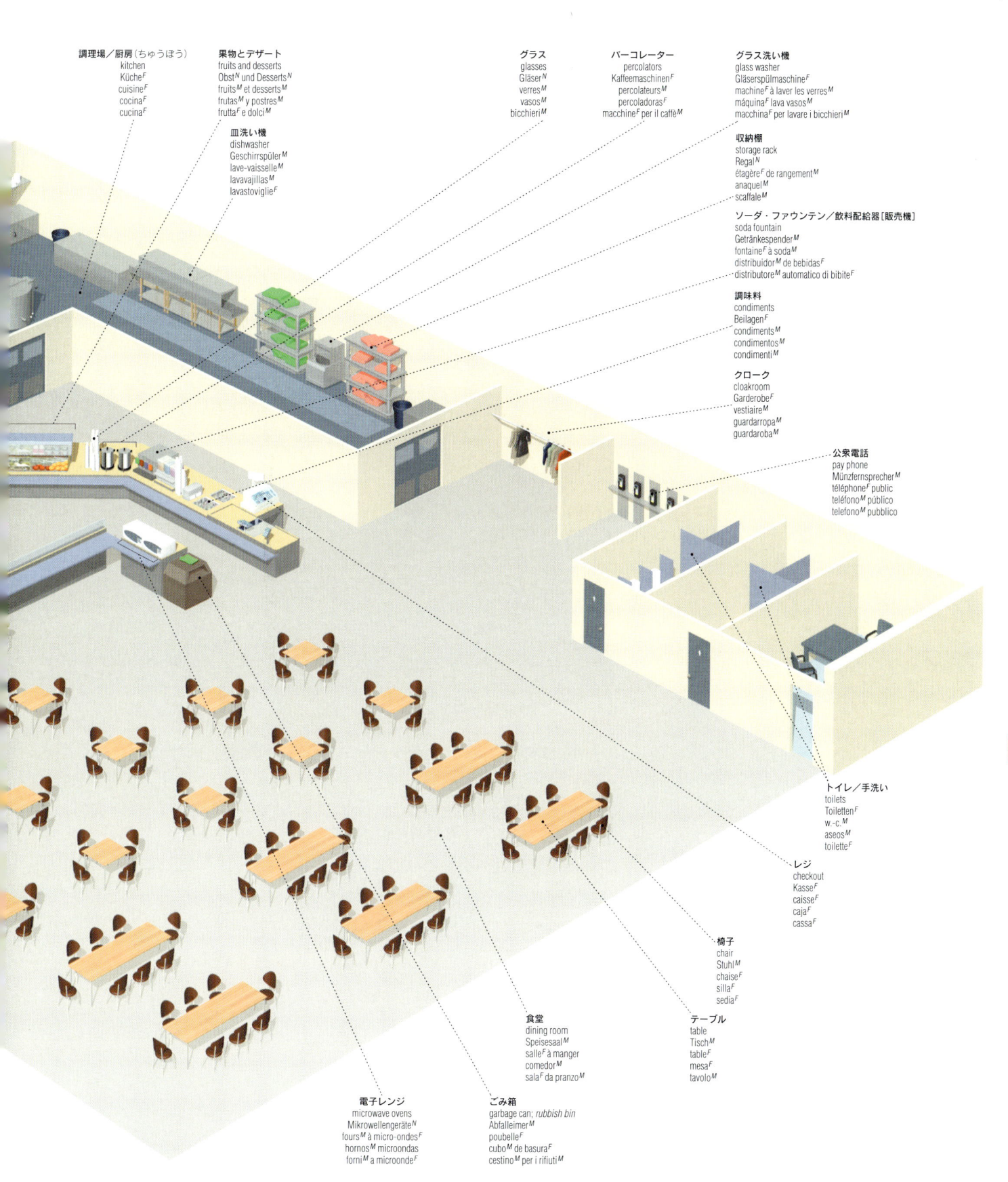

セルフ・サービス式レストラン

調理場／厨房（ちゅうぼう）
kitchen
Küche F
cuisine F
cocina F
cucina F

果物とデザート
fruits and desserts
Obst N und Desserts N
fruits M et desserts M
frutas F y postres M
frutta F e dolci M

皿洗い機
dishwasher
Geschirrspüler M
lave-vaisselle F
lavavajillas M
lavastoviglie F

グラス
glasses
Gläser N
verres M
vasos M
bicchieri M

パーコレーター
percolators
Kaffeemaschinen F
percolateurs M
percoladoras F
macchine F per il caffè M

グラス洗い機
glass washer
Gläserspülmaschine F
machine F à laver les verres M
máquina F lava vasos M
macchina F per lavare i bicchieri M

収納棚
storage rack
Regal N
étagère F de rangement M
anaquel M
scaffale M

ソーダ・ファウンテン／飲料配給器［販売機］
soda fountain
Getränkespender M
fontaine F à soda M
distribuidor M de bebidas F
distributore M automatico di bibite F

調味料
condiments
Beilagen F
condiments M
condimentos M
condimenti M

クローク
cloakroom
Garderobe F
vestiaire M
guardarropa M
guardaroba M

公衆電話
pay phone
Münzfernsprecher M
téléphone F public
teléfono M público
telefono M pubblico

トイレ／手洗い
toilets
Toiletten F
w.-c. M
aseos M
toilette F

レジ
checkout
Kasse F
caisse F
caja F
cassa F

椅子
chair
Stuhl M
chaise F
silla F
sedia F

テーブル
table
Tisch M
table F
mesa F
tavolo M

食堂
dining room
Speisesaal M
salle F à manger
comedor M
sala F da pranzo M

電子レンジ
microwave ovens
Mikrowellengeräte N
fours M à micro-ondes F
hornos M microondas
forni M a microonde F

ごみ箱
garbage can; rubbish bin
Abfalleimer M
poubelle F
cubo M de basura F
cestino M per i rifiuti M

社会

723

都市 | CITY
STADT | VILLE | CIUDAD | CITTÀ

ホテル
hotel | Hotel^N | hôtel^M | hotel^M | albergo^M

日本語 | 英語 | ドイツ語 | フランス語 | スペイン語 | イタリア語

ロビー階
reception level
Empfangsebene^F
niveau^M de la réception^F
nivel^M de la recepción^F
piano^M della reception^F

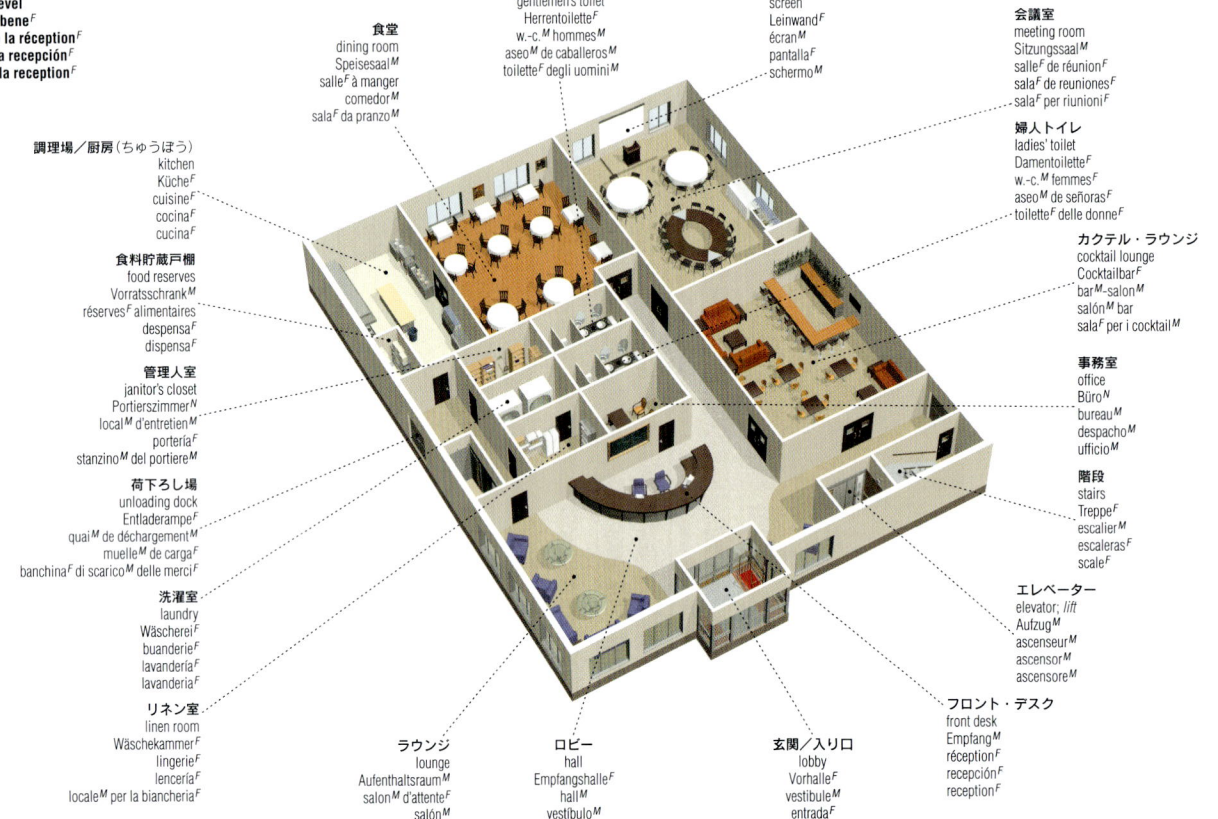

調理場／厨房（ちゅうぼう）
kitchen
Küche^F
cuisine^F
cocina^F
cucina^F

食料貯蔵戸棚
food reserves
Vorratsschrank^M
réserves^F alimentaires
despensa^F
dispensa^F

管理人室
janitor's closet
Portierszimmer^N
local^M d'entretien
portería^F
stanzino^M del portiere^M

荷下ろし場
unloading dock
Entladerampe^F
quai^M de déchargement
muelle^M de carga^F
banchina^F di scarico^F delle merci^F

洗濯室
laundry
Wäscherei^F
buanderie^F
lavandería^F
lavanderia^F

リネン室
linen room
Wäschekammer^F
lingerie^F
lencería^F
locale^M per la biancheria^F

食堂
dining room
Speisesaal^M
salle^F à manger
comedor^M
sala^F da pranzo^M

紳士トイレ
gentlemen's toilet
Herrentoilette^F
w.-c.^M hommes^F
aseo^M de caballeros^M
toilette^F degli uomini^M

スクリーン
screen
Leinwand^F
écran^M
pantalla^F
schermo^M

ラウンジ
lounge
Aufenthaltsraum^M
salon^M d'attente^F
salón^M
salotto^M

ロビー
hall
Empfangshalle^F
hall^M
vestíbulo^M
hall^F

玄関／入り口
lobby
Vorhalle^F
vestibule^M
entrada^F
atrio^M

会議室
meeting room
Sitzungssaal^M
salle^F de réunion^F
sala^F de reuniones^F
sala^F per riunioni^F

婦人トイレ
ladies' toilet
Damentoilette^F
w.-c.^M femmes^F
aseo^M de señoras^F
toilette^F delle donne^F

カクテル・ラウンジ
cocktail lounge
Cocktailbar^F
bar^M-salon^M
salón^M bar
sala^F per i cocktail^M

事務室
office
Büro^N
bureau^M
despacho^M
ufficio^M

階段
stairs
Treppe^F
escalier^M
escaleras^F
scale^F

エレベーター
elevator; lift
Aufzug^M
ascenseur^M
ascensor^M
ascensore^M

フロント・デスク
front desk
Empfang^M
réception^F
recepción^F
reception^F

ホテルの客室
hotel rooms
Hotelzimmer^N
chambres^F d'hôtel^M
habitación^F de hotel^M
camera^F d'albergo^M

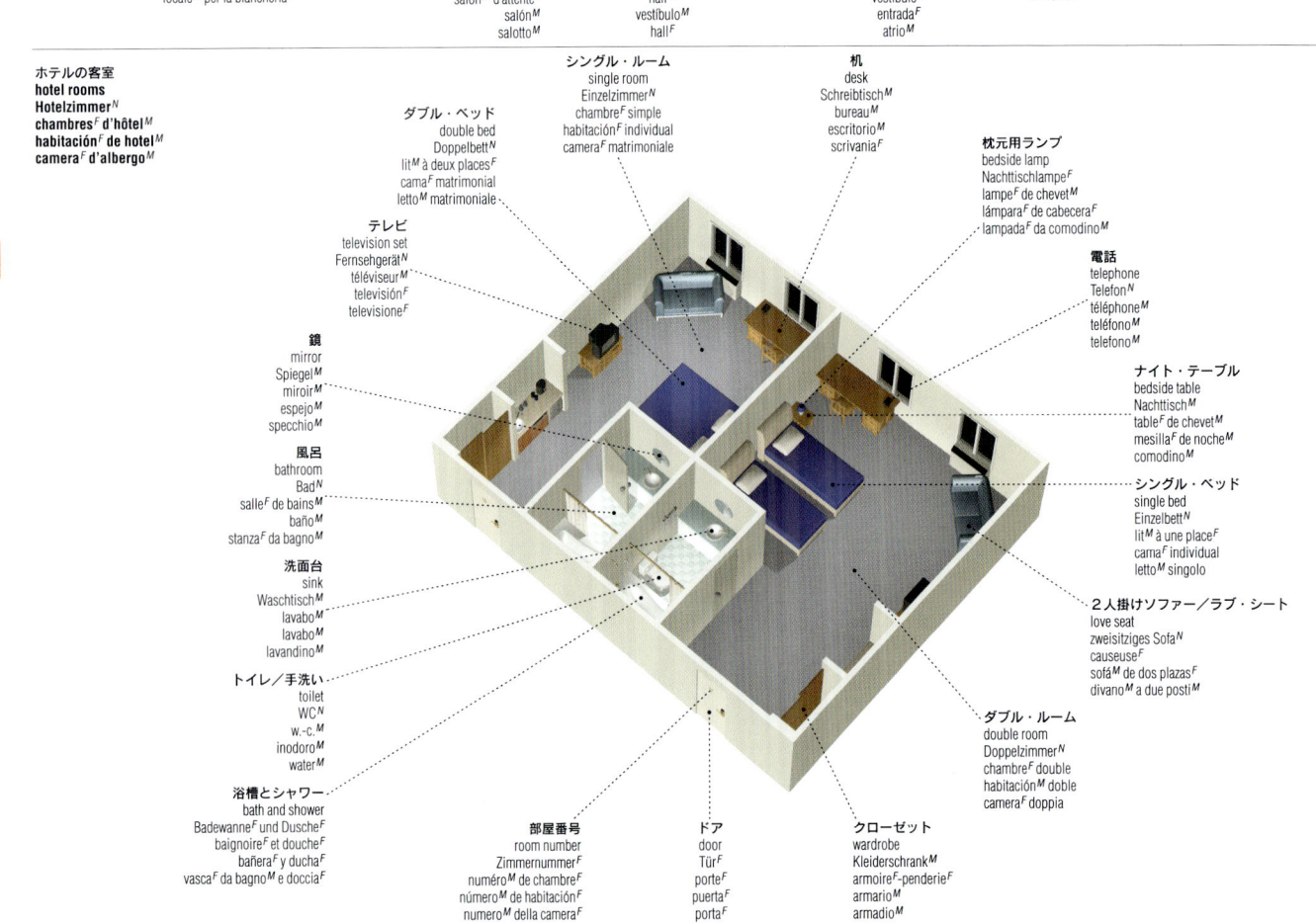

シングル・ルーム
single room
Einzelzimmer^N
chambre^F simple
habitación^F individual
camera^F matrimoniale

ダブル・ベッド
double bed
Doppelbett^N
lit^M à deux places^F
cama^F matrimonial
letto^M matrimoniale

テレビ
television set
Fernsehgerät^N
téléviseur^M
televisión^F
televisione^F

鏡
mirror
Spiegel^M
miroir^M
espejo^M
specchio^M

風呂
bathroom
Bad^N
salle^F de bains^M
baño^M
stanza^F da bagno^M

洗面台
sink
Waschtisch^M
lavabo^M
lavabo^M
lavandino^M

トイレ／手洗い
toilet
WC^N
w.-c.^M
inodoro^M
water^M

浴槽とシャワー
bath and shower
Badewanne^F und Dusche^F
baignoire^F et douche^F
bañera^F y ducha^F
vasca^F da bagno^M e doccia^F

部屋番号
room number
Zimmernummer^F
numéro^M de chambre^F
número^M de habitación^F
numero^M della camera^F

ドア
door
Tür^F
porte^F
puerta^F
porta^F

机
desk
Schreibtisch^M
bureau^M
escritorio^M
scrivania^F

枕元用ランプ
bedside lamp
Nachttischlampe^F
lampe^F de chevet^M
lámpara^F de cabecera^F
lampada^F da comodino^M

電話
telephone
Telefon^N
téléphone^M
teléfono^M
telefono^M

ナイト・テーブル
bedside table
Nachttisch^M
table^F de chevet^M
mesilla^F de noche^F
comodino^M

シングル・ベッド
single bed
Einzelbett^N
lit^M à une place^F
cama^F individual
letto^M singolo

2人掛けソファー／ラブ・シート
love seat
zweisitziges Sofa^N
causeuse^F
sofá^M de dos plazas^F
divano^M a due posti^M

ダブル・ルーム
double room
Doppelzimmer^N
chambre^F double
habitación^F doble
camera^F doppia

クローゼット
wardrobe
Kleiderschrank^M
armoire^F-penderie^F
armario^M
armadio^M

社会

724

都市 | CITY
STADT | VILLE | CIUDAD | CITTÀ

一般的な案内標識

common symbols | allgemeine Zeichen[N] | symboles[M] d'usage[M] courant | símbolos[M] de uso[M] común | simboli[M] comuni

男子トイレ
men's rest room; *men's toilet*
Toiletten[F] (Herren[M])
toilettes[F] pour hommes[M]
aseoss[M] de caballeros[M]
toilette[F] (uomini[M])

女子トイレ
women's rest room; *women's toilet*
Toiletten[F] (Damen[F])
toilettes[F] pour dames[F]
aseos[M] de señoras[F]
toilette[F] (donne[F])

車椅子乗り入れ可能
wheelchair access
Zugang[M] für Behinderte[M]
accès[M] pour handicapés[M] physiques
acceso[M] para minusválidos[M]
accesso[M] per i portatori[M] di handicap[M]

車椅子乗り入れ禁止
no wheelchair access
Verbot[M] für Rollstuhlfahrer[M]
ne pas utiliser avec un fauteuil[M] roulant
prohibido usar silla[F] de ruedas[F]
accesso[M] non consentito alle sedie[F] a rotelle[M]

キャンプ可（キャンピング・カーおよびテント）
camping (trailer and tent); *camping (caravan and tent)*
Camping[N] für Zelte[N] und Wohnwagen[M]
camping et caravaning[M]
zona[F] para acampar y para caravanas[F]
area[F] per campeggio[M] e caravan[M]

ピクニック地域
picnic area
Rastplatz[M]
pique-nique[M]
zona[F] de comidas[F] campestres
area[F] per pic-nic[M]

ピクニック禁止
picnics prohibited
Picknick[N] verboten
pique-nique[M] interdit
prohibido hacer comidas[F] campestres
vietato fare pic-nic[M]

キャンプ可（テント）
camping (tent)
Zeltplatz[M]
camping[M]
zona[F] para acampar
campeggio[M]

キャンプ禁止
camping prohibited
Zelten[N] verboten
camping[M] interdit
prohibido acampar
vietato fare campeggio[M]

キャンプ可（キャンピング・カー）
camping (trailer); *camping (caravan)*
Camping[N] für Wohnwagen[M]
caravaning[M]
zona[F] para caravanas[F]
area[F] per caravan[M]

病院
hospital
Krankenhaus[N]
hôpital[M]
hospital[M]
ospedale[M]

コーヒー・ショップ／喫茶店
coffee shop; *buffet*
Cafeteria[F]
casse-croûte[M]
cafetería[F]
punto[M] di ristoro[M]

公衆電話／電話ボックス
telephone
Telefon[N]
téléphone[M]
teléfono[M]
telefono[M]

レストラン
restaurant
Restaurant[N]
restaurant[M]
restaurante[M]
ristorante[M]

薬局
pharmacy; *chemist's shop*
Apotheke[F]
pharmacie[F]
farmacia[F]
farmacia[F]

警察
police
Polizei[F]
police[F]
policía[F]
polizia[F]

救急（室）／救護所
first aid
Erste Hilfe[F]
premiers soins[M]
puesto[M] de socorro[M]
pronto soccorso[M]

ガソリン・スタンド
service station; *petrol station*
Tankstelle[F]
poste[M] de carburant[M]
gasolinera[F]
stazione[F] di rifornimento[M]

消火器
fire extinguisher
Feuerlöscher[M]
extincteur[M] d'incendie[M]
extintor[M] de incendios[M]
estintore[M]

案内所
information
Information[F]
renseignements[M]
información[F]
informazioni[F]

案内所
information
Information[F]
renseignements[M]
información[F]
informazioni[F]

遺失物取扱所
lost and found articles; *lost property*
Fundbüro[N]
articles[M] perdus et retrouvés
oficina[F] de objetos[M] perdidos
oggetti[M] smarriti

両替所
currency exchange
Geldwechsel[M]
change[M]
cambio[M]
cambio[M]

タクシー乗り場
taxi transportation; *taxi rank*
Taxi[N]
transport[M] par taxi[M]
servicio[M] de taxis[M]
taxi[M]

社会

725

司法 | JUSTICE
JUSTIZ | JUSTICE | JUSTICIA | GIUSTIZIA

刑務所

prison | Justizvollzugsanstalt^F | prison^F | cárcel^F | carcere^M

日本語 | 英語 | ドイツ語 | フランス語 | スペイン語 | イタリア語

職員出入り管理室
control of staff entries and exits
Personalein- und -ausgangskontrolle^F
contrôle^M des entrées^F et sorties^F du personnel^M
control^M de entrada^F y salida^F del personal^M
controllo^M dell'entrata^F e dell'uscita^F del personale^M

作業場
workshop
Werkstatt^F
atelier^M
taller^M
laboratorio^M

礼拝所
chapel
Kapelle^F
chapelle^F
capilla^M
cappella^F

職員出入り口
staff entrance
Personaleingang^M
entrée^F du personnel^M
entrada^F del personal^M
ingresso^M del personale^M

図書室
library
Bibliothek^F
bibliothèque^F
biblioteca^F
biblioteca^F

刑務所長室
governor's office
Büro^N des Direktors^M
bureau^M du directeur^M
despacho^M del director^M
ufficio^M del direttore^M

副刑務所長室
assistant governor's office
Büro^N des stellvertretenden Direktors^M
bureau^M du directeur^M adjoint
despacho^F del subdirector^M
ufficio^M del vicedirettore^M

事務室
office
Büro^N
bureau^M
oficina^F
ufficio^M

面会者受付
visitors' front office; visitors' front office
Empfangsraum^M für Besucher^M
bureau^M d'accueil^M des visiteurs^M
oficina^F de recepción^F de visitantes^M
ufficio^M di accettazione^F dei visitatori^M

面会室
visiting room
Sprechzimmer^N
parloir^M
locutorio^M
parlatorio^M

面会者出入り口
visitors' entrance
Besuchereingang^M
entrée^F des visiteurs^M
entrada^F de los visitantes^M
ingresso^M dei visitatori^M

通り抜け式金属探知器
walk-through metal detector
Durchgangsmetalldetektor^M
portique^M détecteur de métal^M
pórtico^M detector^M de metales^M
metal detector^M a porta^F

面会者待合室
visitors' waiting room
Warteraum^M für Besucher^M
salle^F d'attente^F des visiteurs^M
sala^F de espera^F de visitantes^M
sala^F d'attesa^F dei visitatori^M

クローク
coatroom
Garderobe^F
vestiaire^M
guardarropa^M
guardaroba^M

囚人護送車
patrol wagon
Gefangenentransporter^M
voiture^F cellulaire
coche^M celular
cellulare^M

車庫
garage
Garage^F
garage^M
garaje^M
garage^M

在監者出入り口
inmates' entrance
Insasseneingang^M
entrée^F des détenus^M
entrada^F de detenidos^M
ingresso^M dei detenuti^M

医務室
infirmary
Krankenstation^F
infirmerie^F
enfermería^F
infermeria^F

調理場／厨房（ちゅうぼう）
kitchen
Küche^F
cuisine^F
cocina^M
cucina^F

囚人受入室
inmates' admission office
Insassenaufnahme^F
bureau^M d'admission^F des détenus^M
oficina^F de admisión^F de los detenidos^M
ufficio^M d'ammissione^F dei detenuti^M

洗濯室
laundry
Wäscherei^F
buanderie^F
lavandería^F
lavanderia^F

シャワー
shower
Dusche^F
douche^F
ducha^F
doccia^F

司法 | JUSTICE
JUSTIZ | JUSTICE | JUSTICIA | GIUSTIZIA

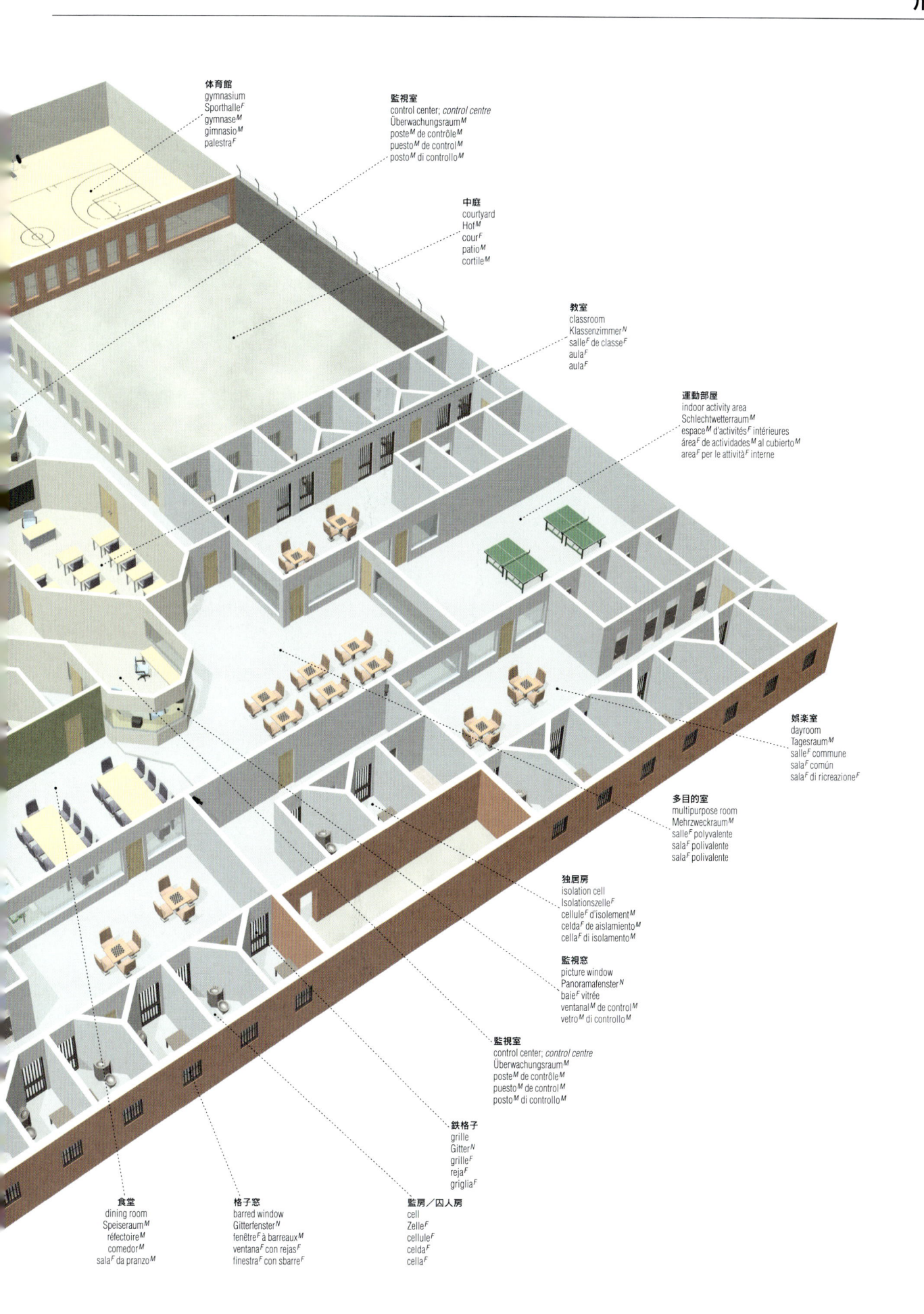

刑務所

体育館
gymnasium
Sporthalle^F
gymnase^M
gimnasio^M
palestra^F

監視室
control center; control centre
Überwachungsraum^M
poste^M de contrôle^M
puesto^M de control^M
posto^M di controllo^M

中庭
courtyard
Hof^M
cour^F
patio^M
cortile^M

教室
classroom
Klassenzimmer^N
salle^F de classe^F
aula^F
aula^F

運動部屋
indoor activity area
Schlechtwetterraum^M
espace^M d'activités^F intérieures
área^F de actividades^M al cubierto^M
area^F per le attività^F interne

娯楽室
dayroom
Tagesraum^M
salle^F commune
sala^F común
sala^F di ricreazione^F

多目的室
multipurpose room
Mehrzweckraum^M
salle^F polyvalente
sala^F polivalente
sala^F polivalente

独居房
isolation cell
Isolationszelle^F
cellule^F d'isolement^M
celda^F de aislamiento^M
cella^F di isolamento^M

監視窓
picture window
Panoramafenster^N
baie^F vitrée
ventanal^M de control^M
vetro^M di controllo^M

監視室
control center; control centre
Überwachungsraum^M
poste^M de contrôle^M
puesto^M de control^M
posto^M di controllo^M

鉄格子
grille
Gitter^N
grille^F
reja^F
griglia^F

食堂
dining room
Speiseraum^M
réfectoire^M
comedor^M
sala^F da pranzo^M

格子窓
barred window
Gitterfenster^N
fenêtre^F à barreaux^M
ventana^F con rejas^F
finestra^F con sbarre^F

監房／囚人房
cell
Zelle^F
cellule^F
celda^F
cella^F

社会

経済と金融 | ECONOMY AND FINANCE
WIRTSCHAFT UND FINANZWESEN | ÉCONOMIE ET FINANCE | ECONOMÍA Y FINANZAS | ECONOMIA E FINANZA

裁判所

日本語 | 英語 | ドイツ語 | フランス語 | スペイン語 | イタリア語

court | Gericht^N | tribunal^M | tribunal^M | tribunale^M

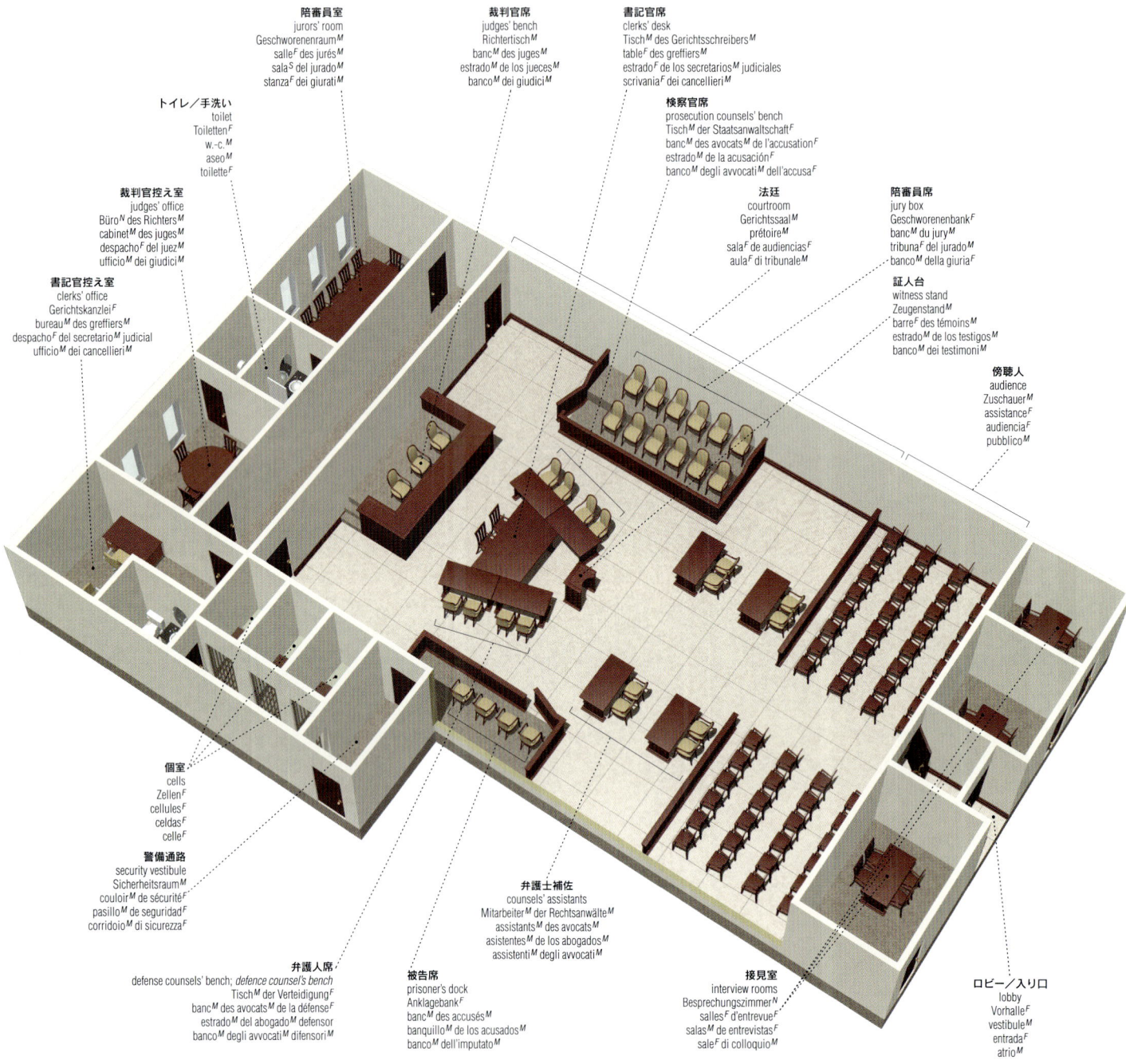

陪審員室
jurors' room
Geschworenenraum^M
salle^F des jurés^M
sala^S del jurado^M
stanza^F dei giurati^M

裁判官席
judges' bench
Richtertisch^M
banc^M des juges^M
estrado^M de los jueces^M
banco^M dei giudici^M

書記官席
clerks' desk
Tisch^M des Gerichtsschreibers^M
table^F des greffiers^M
estrado^F de los secretarios^M judiciales
scrivania^F dei cancellieri^M

トイレ／手洗い
toilet
Toiletten^F
w.-c.^M
aseo^M
toilette^F

検察官席
prosecution counsels' bench
Tisch^M der Staatsanwaltschaft^F
banc^M des avocats^M de l'accusation^F
estrado^M de la acusación^F
banco^M degli avvocati^M dell'accusa^F

裁判官控え室
judges' office
Büro^N des Richters^M
cabinet^M des juges^M
despacho^F del juez^M
ufficio^M dei giudici^M

法廷
courtroom
Gerichtssaal^M
prétoire^M
sala^F de audiencias^F
aula^F di tribunale^M

陪審員席
jury box
Geschworenenbank^F
banc^M du jury^M
tribuna^F del jurado^M
banco^M della giuria^F

書記官控え室
clerks' office
Gerichtskanzlei^F
bureau^M des greffiers^M
despacho^F del secretario^M judicial
ufficio^M dei cancellieri^M

証人台
witness stand
Zeugenstand^M
barre^F des témoins^M
estrado^M de los testigos^M
banco^M dei testimoni^M

傍聴人
audience
Zuschauer^M
assistance^F
audiencia^F
pubblico^M

個室
cells
Zellen^F
cellules^F
celdas^F
celle^F

警備通路
security vestibule
Sicherheitsraum^M
couloir^M de sécurité^F
pasillo^M de seguridad^F
corridoio^M di sicurezza^F

弁護士補佐
counsels' assistants
Mitarbeiter^M der Rechtsanwälte^M
assistants^M des avocats^M
asistentes^M de los abogados^M
assistenti^M degli avvocati^M

接見室
interview rooms
Besprechungszimmer^N
salles^F d'entrevue^F
salas^M de entrevistas^F
sale^F di colloquio^M

ロビー／入り口
lobby
Vorhalle^F
vestibule^M
entrada^F
atrio^M

弁護人席
defense counsels' bench; defence counsel's bench
Tisch^M der Verteidigung^F
banc^M des avocats^M de la défense^F
estrado^M del abogado^M defensor
banco^M degli avvocati^M difensori^M

被告席
prisoner's dock
Anklagebank^F
banc^M des accusés^M
banquillo^M de los acusados^M
banco^M dell'imputato^M

通貨省略記号の例

examples of currency abbreviations | Beispiele^N für Währungsabkürzungen^F | exemples^M d'unités^F monétaires | ejemplos^M de abreviaciones^F de monedas^F | esempi^M di simboli^M di valute^F

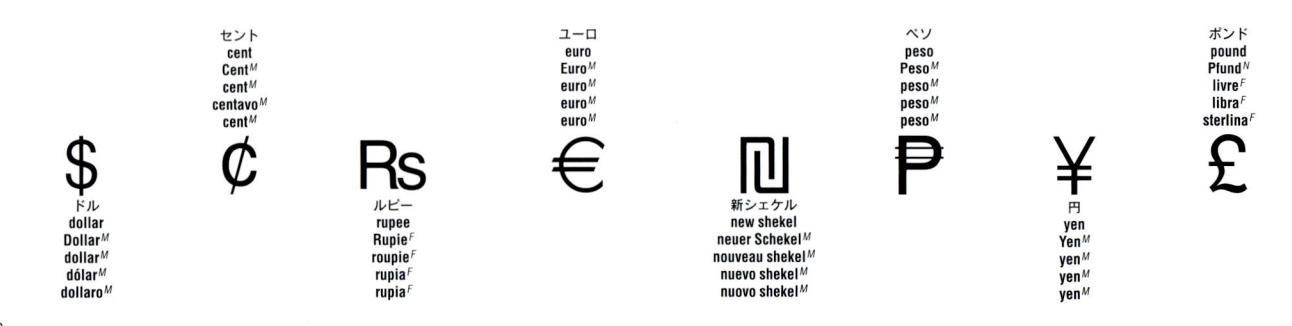

$
ドル
dollar
Dollar^M
dollar^M
dólar^M
dollaro^M

¢
セント
cent
Cent^M
cent^M
centavo^M
cent^M

Rs
ルピー
rupee
Rupie^F
roupie^F
rupia^F
rupia^F

€
ユーロ
euro
Euro^M
euro^M
euro^M
euro^M

₪
新シェケル
new shekel
neuer Schekel^M
nouveau shekel^M
nuevo shekel^M
nuovo shekel^M

P
ペソ
peso
Peso^M
peso^M
peso^M
peso^M

¥
円
yen
Yen^M
yen^M
yen^M
yen^M

£
ポンド
pound
Pfund^N
livre^F
libra^F
sterlina^F

経済と金融 | ECONOMY AND FINANCE
WIRTSCHAFT UND FINANZWESEN | ÉCONOMIE ET FINANCE | ECONOMÍA Y FINANZAS | ECONOMIA E FINANZA

貨幣と支払い形態

money and modes of payment | Geld^N und Zahlungsmodalitäten^F | monnaie^F et modes^M de paiement^M | dinero^M y modos^M de pago^M | denaro^M e metodi^M di pagamento^M

硬貨：表面
coin: obverse
Münze^F: Vorderseite^F
pièce^F : avers^M
moneda^F : anverso^M
moneta^F : diritto^M

発行銀行名の頭文字
initials of the issuing bank
Kürzel^N der Ausgabebank^F
initiales^F de la banque^F émettrice
iniciales^F del banco^M emisor
iniziali^F della banca^F di emissione

紙幣：表面
banknote: front
Banknote^F: Vorderseite^F
billet^M de banque^F : recto^M
billete^M : recto^M
banconota^F : dritto^M

安全線／偽造防止糸
security thread
Sicherheitsfaden^M
fil^M de sécurité^F
filigrana^F
filo^M di sicurezza^F

ホログラム箔
hologram foil strip
metallisiertes Hologramm^N
bande^F métallisée holographique
banda^F holográfica metalizada
banda^F olografica

鋳造年
date
Jahreszahl^F
millésime^M
fecha^F
anno^M

透かし（模様）
watermark
Wasserzeichen^N
filigrane^M
filigrana^F
filigrana^F

正式署名
official signature
amtliche Unterschrift^F
signature^F officielle
firma^F oficial
firma^F ufficiale

縁
edge
Rand^M
tranche^F
canto^M
contorno^M

カラー・シフティング・インク
color shifting ink
metallische Tinte^F
encre^F à couleur^F changeante
tinta^F de color^M cambiante
inchiostro^M a colori^M cangianti

肖像（画）
portrait
Porträt^N
effigie^F
retrato^M
effigie^F

製造番号
serial number
Seriennummer^F
numéro^M de série^F
número^M de serie^F
numero^M di serie^F

硬貨：裏面
coin: reverse
Münze^F : Rückseite^F
pièce^F : revers^M
moneda^F : reverso^M
moneta^F : rovescio^M

紙幣：裏面
banknote: back
Banknote^F: Rückseite^F
billet^M de banque^F : verso^M
billete^M : verso^M
banconota^F : rovescio^M

欧州連合旗
flag of the European Union
Flagge^F der Europäischen Union^F
drapeau^M de l'Union^F Européenne
bandera^F de la Unión^F Europea
bandiera^F dell'Unione^F Europea

製造番号
serial number
Seriennummer^F
numéro^M de série^F
número^M de serie^F
numero^M di serie^F

外縁
outer ring
Außenring^M
couronne^F
cordoncillo^M
corona^F

標語／銘
motto
Leitspruch^M
devise^F
lema^F
motto^M

額面金額
denomination
Wertangabe^F
valeur^F
valor^M
indicazione^F del valore^M

額面金額
denomination
Wertangabe^F
valeur^F
valor^M
indicazione^F del valore^M

通貨の名称
name of the currency
Währungsangabe^F
nom^M de la monnaie^F
nombre^M moneda^F
nome^M della valuta^F

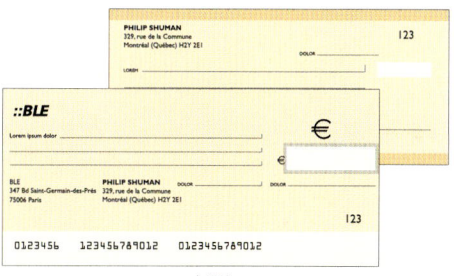

磁気帯
magnetic stripe
Magnetstreifen^M
bande^F magnétique
banda^F magnética
banda^F magnetica

クレジット・カード
credit card
Kreditkarte^F
carte^F de crédit^M
tarjeta^F de crédito^M
carta^F di credito^M

カード保有者のサイン
cardholder's signature
Unterschrift^F des Inhabers^M
signature^F du titulaire^M
firma^M del titular^M
firma^F del titolare^M

小切手
checks
Schecks^M
chèques^M
cheques^M
assegni^M

カード番号
card number
Kartennummer^F
numéro^M de carte^F
número^M de la tarjeta^F
numero^M della carta^F

トラベラーズ・チェック／旅行者用小切手
traveler's check
Travellerscheck^M
chèque^M de voyage^M
cheque^M de viaje^M
traveller's cheque^M

カード保有者名
cardholder's name
Name^M des Inhabers^M
nom^M du titulaire^M
nombre^M del titular^M
nome^M del titolare^M

有効期限
expiration date
Verfallsdatum^N
date^F d'expiration^F
fecha^F de vencimiento^M
data^F di scadenza^F

経済と金融 | ECONOMY AND FINANCE
WIRTSCHAFT UND FINANZWESEN | ÉCONOMIE ET FINANCE | ECONOMÍA Y FINANZAS | ECONOMIA E FINANZA

銀行

bank | Bank^F | banque^F | banco^M | banca^F

日本語 | 英語 | ドイツ語 | フランス語 | スペイン語 | イタリア語

現金自動支払機
cash dispenser
Geldausgabeautomat^M
distributeur^M de billets^M
cajero^M automático
sportello^M bancomat^M

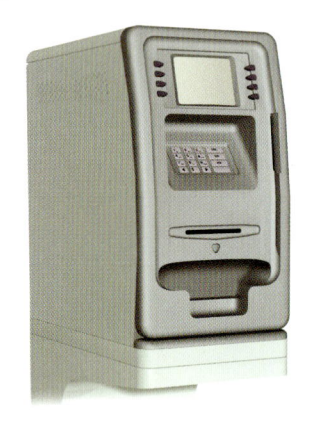

職業訓練室
professional training office
Fortbildungsbüro^N
bureau^M de formation^F professionnelle
oficina^F de formación^F profesional
ufficio^M di formazione^F professionale

待合所
waiting area
Wartebereich^M
aire^F d'attente^F
zona^F de espera^F
area^F d'attesa^F

保険業務部門
insurance services
Versicherungsabteilung^F
services^M d'assurance^F
servicios^M de seguros^M
servizi^M assicurativi

パンフレット棚
brochure rack
Prospektständer^M
présentoir^M de brochures^F
expositor^M de folletos^M
espositore^M di brochure^F

コピー機
photocopier
Fotokopiergerät^N
reprographie^F
fotocopiadora^F
fotocopiatrice^F

金融サービス部門
financial services
Finanzabteilung^F
services^M financiers
servicios^M financieros^M
servizi^M finanziari

案内窓口／受付
information desk
Informationsschalter^M
comptoir^M de renseignements^M
información^F
banco^M delle informazioni^F

大会議室
conference room
Konferenzraum^M
salle^F de conférences^F
sala^F de conferencias^F
sala^F per conferenze^F

現金自動預入支払機（ＡＴＭ）
automatic teller machine (ATM)
automatischer Bankschalter^M
guichet^M automatique bancaire
cajero^M automático
sportello^M automatico

受付デスク
reception desk
Empfang^M
accueil^M
recepción^F
banco^M della reception^F

操作キー
operation keys
Funktionstasten^F
touches^F d'opérations^F
teclas^F de operación^F
tasti^M funzione^F

預金投入口
deposit slot
Einzahlungsschlitz^M
fente^F de dépôt^M
ranura^F de depósito^M
fessura^F per il deposito^M

融資業務部門
loan services
Kreditabteilung^F
services^M de crédit^M
servicios^M de crédito^M
servizi^M di credito^M

小会議室
meeting room
Sitzungsraum^M
salle^F de réunion^F
sala^F de reuniones^F
sala^F per riunioni^F

ディスプレイ／表示板
display
Display^N
écran^M
pantalla^F
display^M

カード読み取り口
card reader slot
Kartenlesegerät^N
fente^F du lecteur^M de carte^F
lector^M de tarjeta^F
lettore^M di carte^F

取引明細書受取口
transaction record slot
Quittungsausgabe^F
fente^F de relevé^M d'opération^F
ranura^F de registro^M de la transacción^F
fessura^F di registrazione^F della transazione^F

英数(字)キーボード
alphanumeric keyboard
alphanumerische Tastatur^F
clavier^M alphanumérique
teclado^M alfanumérico
tastiera^F alfanumerica

防犯用鉄格子
security grille
Schutzgitter^N
grille^F de sécurité^F
reja^F de seguridad^F
griglia^F di sicurezza^F

紙幣受取口
bill presenter
Geldscheinausgabe^F
sortie^F des billets^M
emisión^F de billetes^M
emissione^F di banconote^F

通帳記入口
passbook update slot
Sparbuchnachtrag^M
fente^F de mise^F à jour^M du livret^M bancaire
ranura^F de puesta^F al día^M de la cartilla^F
fessura^F di aggiornamento^M dell'estratto^M conto^M

ロビー／入り口
lobby
Vorhalle^F
vestibule^M
entrada^F
atrio^M

社会

経済と金融 | ECONOMY AND FINANCE
WIRTSCHAFT UND FINANZWESEN | ÉCONOMIE ET FINANCE | ECONOMÍA Y FINANZAS | ECONOMIA E FINANZA

銀行

従業員ラウンジ
staff lounge
Personalraum^M
salon^F des employés^M
sala^F del personal^M
sala^F del personale^M

守衛室
janitor's closet
Hausmeisterraum^M
local^M d'entretien^M
cuarto^M de limpieza^F
stanzino^M della guardia^F giurata

クローク
cloakroom
Garderobe^F
vestiaire^M
guardarropa^M
guardaroba^M

顧客サービス
customer service
Kundenbetreuung^F
service^M à la clientèle^F
servicio^M clientes^M
servizio^M di assistenza^F ai clienti^M

トイレ／手洗い
toilet
Toiletten^F
w.-c.^{M}
aseo^M
toilette^F

支店長室
director's office
Büro^N des Direktors^M
bureau^M du directeur^M
despacho^M del director^M
ufficio^M del direttore^M

秘書室
secretary's office
Sekretariat^N
secrétariat^M
secretaría^F
ufficio^M della segretaria^F

貸し金庫
safe deposit box
Schließfach^N
coffret^M de sûreté^F
caja^F de seguridad^F
cassetta^F di sicurezza^F

金庫
safe
Tresor^M
coffre-fort^M
caja^F fuerte
cassaforte^F

デビット・カード
debit card
Scheckkarte^F
carte^F de débit^M
tarjeta^F de débito^M
carta^F di addebito^M

カード番号
card number
Kartennummer^F
numéro^M de carte^F
número^M de tarjeta^F
numero^M della carta^F

金庫室
vault
Tresorraum^M
chambre^F forte
cámara^F acorazada
camera^F blindata

クーポン[利札]ブース
coupon booth
Kabine^F
isoloir^M
cabina^F
cabina^F

窓口
wicket
Schalter^M
guichet^M
ventanilla^F
sportello^M

（待ち）列
line; line
Warteschlange^F
file^F d'attente^F
fila^F
linea^F della fila^F di attesa

電源・用紙感知ライト
power-on/paper-detect light
Kontrollleuchte^F Netzspannung^F/Papierabtastung^F
voyant^M de mise^F sous tension^F/détection^F du papier^M
indicador^M de puesta^F en marcha^F/detección^F de papel^M
spia^F di accensione^F e rilevamento^M della carta^F

電子支払い端末
electronic payment terminal
elektronisches Zahlungsterminal^N
terminal^M de paiement^M électronique
terminal^M de pago^M electrónico
terminale^M di pagamento^M elettronico^M

給紙ボタン
paper feed button
Papiereinzugstaste^F
bouton^M d'alimentation^F papier^M
botón^M de alimentación^F del papel^M
tasto^M di avanzamento^M della carta^F

取引明細書
transaction receipt
Geschäftsbeleg^M
relevé^M de transaction^F
recibo^M de transacción^F
ricevuta^F della transazione^F

法人窓口
business wicket
Firmenkundenschalter^M
guichet^M commercial
ventanilla^F comercial
sportello^M commerciale

ディスプレイ／表示板
display
Display^N
écran^M
display^F
display^M

口座識別キー
account identification
Kontoidentifikation^F
identification^F du compte^M
identificación^F de cuenta^F
tasti^M di identificazione^F del conto^M

操作キー
operation keys
Funktionstasten^F
touches^F d'opérations^F
teclas^F de operación^F
tasti^M funzione

カード読み取り口
card reader slot
Kartenlesegerät^N
fente^F du lecteur^M de carte^F
lector^M de tarjeta^F
lettore^M di carte^F

現金装填
cash supply
Bargeldbestückung^F
approvisionnement^M en numéraire^M
provisión^F de dinero^M en efectivo^M
rifornimento^M di contanti^M

拡張機能キー
programmable function keys
programmierbare Funktionstasten^F
touches^F de fonctions^F programmables
teclas^F de funciones^F programables
tasti^M funzione programmabili

現金自動預入支払機
automatic teller machine
automatischer Bankschalter^M
guichet^M automatique bancaire
cajero^M automático
sportello^M automatico

夜間金庫
night deposit box
Nachtschalter^M
guichet^M de nuit^F
buzón^M de depósito^M nocturno
sportello^M notturno

暗証番号入力パッド
personal identification number (PIN) pad
Eingabegerät^N für persönliche Identifikationsnummer^F (PIN)
clavier^M d'identification^F personnelle
teclado^M del número^M de identificación^F personal(PIN)
tastierina^F per il codice^M di identificazione^F personale (PIN)

確認キー
confirmation key
Eingabetaste^F
touche^F de confirmation^F
tecla^F de confirmación^F
tasto^M di conferma

英数(字)キーボード
alphanumeric keyboard
alphanumerische Tastatur^F
clavier^M alphanumérique
teclado^M alfanumérico
tastiera^F alfanumerica

社会

731

教育 | EDUCATION
BILDUNG | ÉDUCATION | EDUCACIÓN | ISTRUZIONE

図書館

日本語 | 英語 | ドイツ語 | フランス語 | スペイン語 | イタリア語

library | Bibliothek^F | bibliothèque^F | biblioteca^F | biblioteca^F

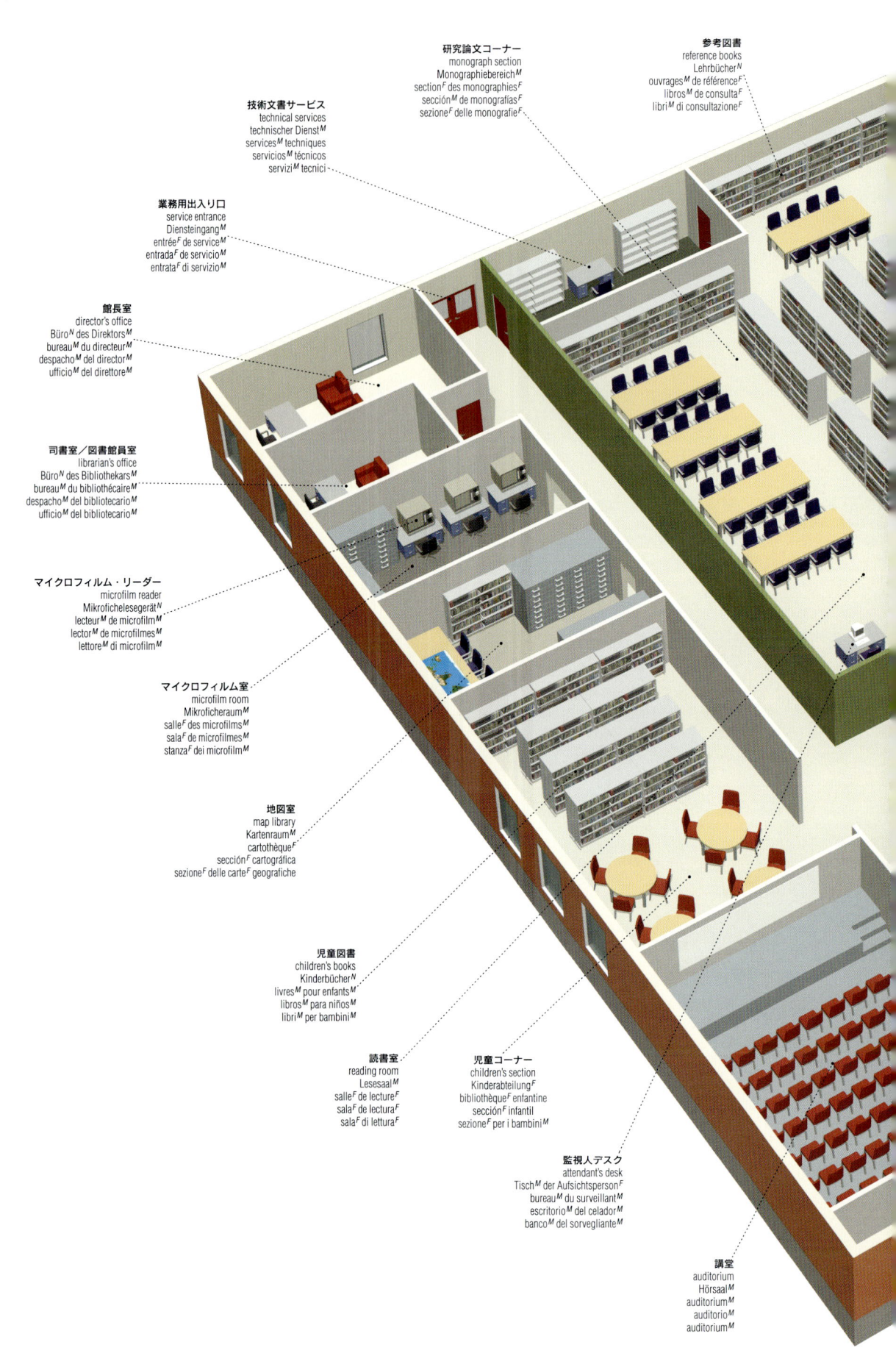

研究論文コーナー
monograph section
Monographiebereich^M
section^F des monographies^F
sección^F de monografías^F
sezione^F delle monografie^F

参考図書
reference books
Lehrbücher^N
ouvrages^M de référence^F
libros^M de consulta^F
libri^M di consultazione^F

技術文書サービス
technical services
technischer Dienst^M
services^F techniques
servicios^M técnicos
servizi^M tecnici

業務用出入り口
service entrance
Diensteingang^M
entrée^F de service^M
entrada^F de servicio^M
entrata^F di servizio^M

館長室
director's office
Büro^N des Direktors^M
bureau^M du directeur^M
despacho^M del director^M
ufficio^M del direttore^M

司書室／図書館員室
librarian's office
Büro^N des Bibliothekars^M
bureau^M du bibliothécaire^M
despacho^M del bibliotecario^M
ufficio^M del bibliotecario^M

マイクロフィルム・リーダー
microfilm reader
Mikrofichelesegerät^N
lecteur^M de microfilm^M
lector^M de microfilmes^M
lettore^M di microfilm^M

マイクロフィルム室
microfilm room
Mikroficheraum^M
salle^F des microfilms^M
sala^F de microfilmes^M
stanza^F dei microfilm^M

地図室
map library
Kartenraum^M
cartothèque^F
sección^F cartográfica
sezione^F delle carte^F geografiche

児童図書
children's books
Kinderbücher^N
livres^M pour enfants
libros^M para niños^M
libri^M per bambini^M

読書室
reading room
Lesesaal^M
salle^F de lecture^F
sala^F de lectura^F
sala^F di lettura^F

児童コーナー
children's section
Kinderabteilung^F
bibliothèque^F enfantine
sección^F infantil
sezione^F per i bambini^M

監視人デスク
attendant's desk
Tisch^M der Aufsichtsperson^F
bureau^M du surveillant^M
escritorio^M del celador^M
banco^M del sorvegliante^M

講堂
auditorium
Hörsaal^M
auditorium^M
auditorio^M
auditorium^M

社会

教育 | EDUCATION
BILDUNG | ÉDUCATION | EDUCACIÓN | ISTRUZIONE

図書館

閲覧室
reference room
Lehrbuchsaal^M
salle^F de référence^F
sala^F de consulta^F
sala^F di consultazione^F

サウンド・ライブラリー
sound library
Phonothek^F
phonothèque^F
fonoteca^F
fonoteca^F

オンライン目録
online catalogue
Online-Katalog^M
catalogue^M informatisé
catalogo^M online
catalogo^M on-line

試聴ブース
listening posts
Hörplätze^M
postes^M d'écoute^F
puestos^M de escucha^F
postazioni^F di ascolto^M

コピー機
photocopier
Fotokopiergerät^N
photocopieur^M
fotocopiadora^F
fotocopiatrice^F

ビデオ・ライブラリー
videotape library
Videothek^F
vidéothèque^F
videoteca^F
videoteca^F

返却ワゴン
book truck
Bücherwagen^M
chariot^M à livres^M
carrito^M de libros^M
carrello^M per i libri^M

フィルム・スライド室
viewing room
Ansichtsraum^M
salle^F de visionnement^M
sala^F de visión^F
sala^F audiovisiva

新着図書棚
acquisition rack
Regal^N der Neuzugänge^M
présentoir^M des nouveautés^F
expositor^M de nuevas adquisiciones^F
scaffale^M delle novità^F

雑誌室
periodicals room
Zeitschriftensaal^M
salle^F des périodiques^M
sala^F periódicos^M
sala^F dei periodici^M

雑誌棚
periodicals rack
Zeitschriftenständer^M
présentoir^M des périodiques^M
estantería^F de periódicos^M
scaffale^M dei periodici^M

図書返却デスク
book return desk
Bücherrückgabe^F
comptoir^M de retour^M des livres^M
mostrador^M de devolución^F de libros^M
banco^M per la restituzione^F dei libri^M

守衛室
security guard's office
Büro^N des Wachpersonals^N
bureau^M de l'agent^M de sécurité^F
despacho^M de la guardia^F de seguridad^F
ufficio^M dell'agente^M di sicurezza^F

正面入リ口
main entrance
Haupteingang^M
entrée^F principale
entrada^F principal
ingresso^M principale

案内所／受付
information desk
Informationsschalter^M
comptoir^M de renseignements^M
punto^M de información^F
banco^M delle informazioni^F

トイレ／手洗い
toilets
Toiletten^F
w.-c.^M
aseo^M
toilette^F

貸し出しデスク
circulation desk
Ausleihe^F
comptoir^M de prêt^M
mostrador^M de préstamo^M
banco^M per il prestito^M dei libri^M

社会

教育 | EDUCATION
BILDUNG | ÉDUCATION | EDUCACIÓN | ISTRUZIONE

学校

school | Schule^F | école^F | colegio^M | scuola^F

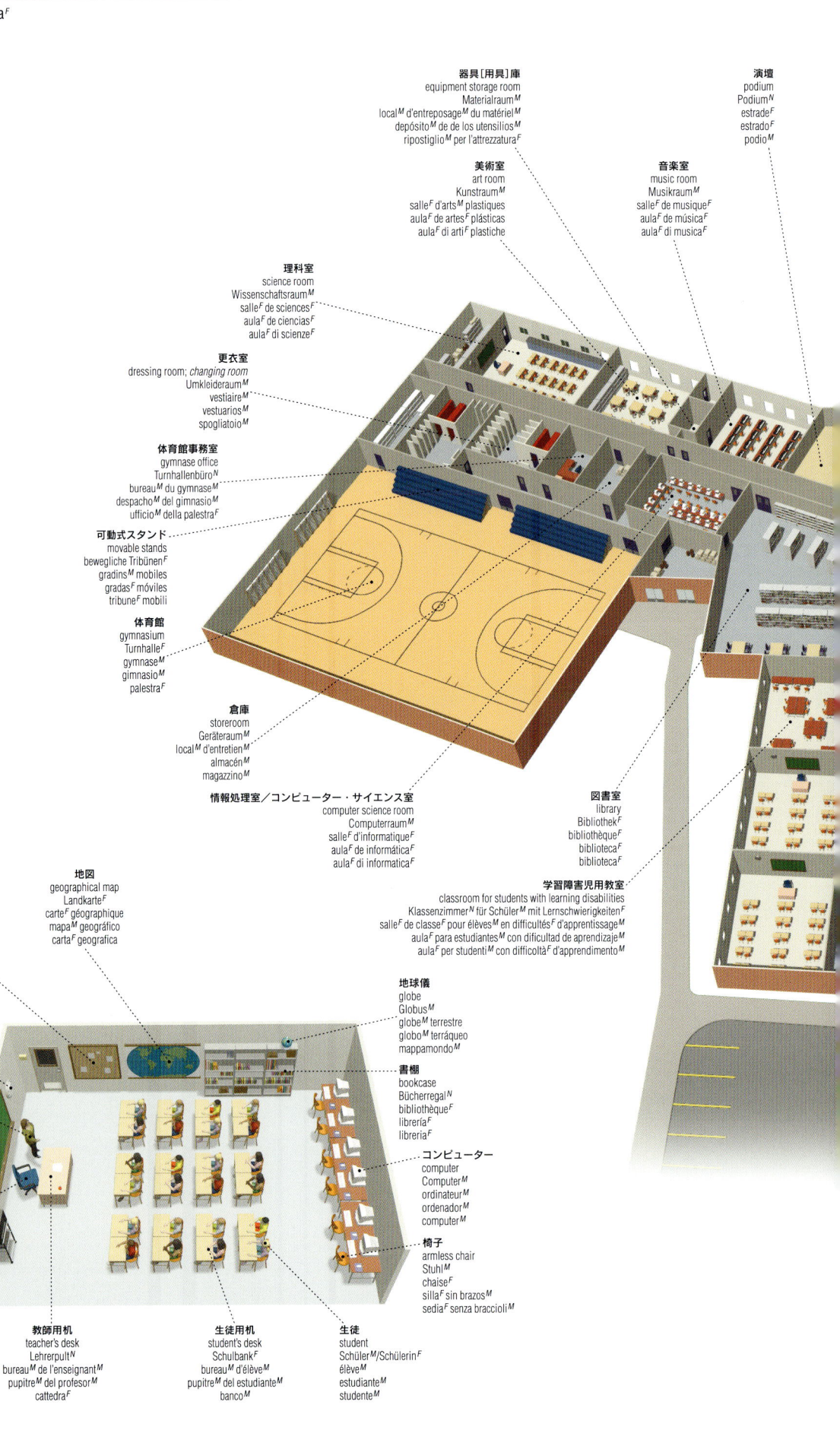

日本語 | 英語 | ドイツ語 | フランス語 | スペイン語 | イタリア語

器具[用具]庫
equipment storage room
Materialraum^M
local^M d'entreposage^M du matériel^M
depósito^M de los utensilios^M
ripostiglio^M per l'attrezzatura^F

美術室
art room
Kunstraum^M
salle^F d'arts^M plastiques
aula^F de artes^F plásticas
aula^F di arti^F plastiche

音楽室
music room
Musikraum^M
salle^F de musique^F
aula^F de música^F
aula^F di musica^F

演壇
podium
Podium^N
estrade^F
estrado^F
podio^M

理科室
science room
Wissenschaftsraum^M
salle^F de sciences^F
aula^F de ciencias^F
aula^F di scienze^F

更衣室
dressing room; changing room
Umkleideraum^M
vestiaire^M
vestuarios^M
spogliatoio^M

体育館事務室
gymnase office
Turnhallenbüro^N
bureau^M du gymnase^M
despacho^M del gimnasio^M
ufficio^M della palestra^F

可動式スタンド
movable stands
bewegliche Tribünen^F
gradins^M mobiles
gradas^F móviles
tribune^F mobili

体育館
gymnasium
Turnhalle^F
gymnase^M
gimnasio^M
palestra^F

倉庫
storeroom
Geräteraum^M
local^M d'entretien^M
almacén^M
magazzino^M

情報処理室／コンピューター・サイエンス室
computer science room
Computerraum^M
salle^F d'informatique^F
aula^F de informática^F
aula^F di informatica^F

図書室
library
Bibliothek^F
bibliothèque^F
biblioteca^F
biblioteca^F

学習障害児用教室
classroom for students with learning disabilities
Klassenzimmer^N für Schüler^M mit Lernschwierigkeiten^F
salle^F de classe^F pour élèves^M en difficultés^F d'apprentissage^M
aula^F para estudiantes^M con dificultad de aprendizaje^M
aula^F per studenti^M con difficoltà^F d'apprendimento^M

教室
classroom
Klassenzimmer^N
salle^F de classe^F
clase^F
aula^F

掲示板
bulletin board; *bulletin board*
schwarzes Brett^N
tableau^M d'affichage^M
tablón^M de anuncios^M
bacheca^F

地図
geographical map
Landkarte^F
carte^F géographique
mapa^M geográfico
carta^F geografica

時計
clock
Uhr^F
pendule^F
reloj^M
orologio^M

教師
teacher
Lehrer^M/Lehrerin^F
enseignant^M
profesor^M
insegnante^{F/M}

黒板
blackboard
Tafel^F
tableau^M
pizarra^F
lavagna^F

肘掛け椅子
armchair
Armstuhl^M
fauteuil^M
sillón^M
sedia^F con braccioli^M

地球儀
globe
Globus^M
globe^M terrestre
globo^M terráqueo
mappamondo^M

書棚
bookcase
Bücherregal^N
bibliothèque^F
librería^F
libreria^F

コンピューター
computer
Computer^M
ordinateur^M
ordenador^M
computer^M

椅子
armless chair
Stuhl^M
chaise^F
silla^F sin brazos^M
sedia^F senza braccioli^M

テレビ
television set
Fernsehgerät^N
téléviseur^M
televisión^F
televisione^F

教師用机
teacher's desk
Lehrerpult^N
bureau^M de l'enseignant^M
pupitre^M del profesor^M
cattedra^F

生徒用机
student's desk
Schulbank^F
bureau^M d'élève^M
pupitre^M del estudiante^M
banco^M

生徒
student
Schüler^M/Schülerin^F
élève^M
estudiante^M
studente^M

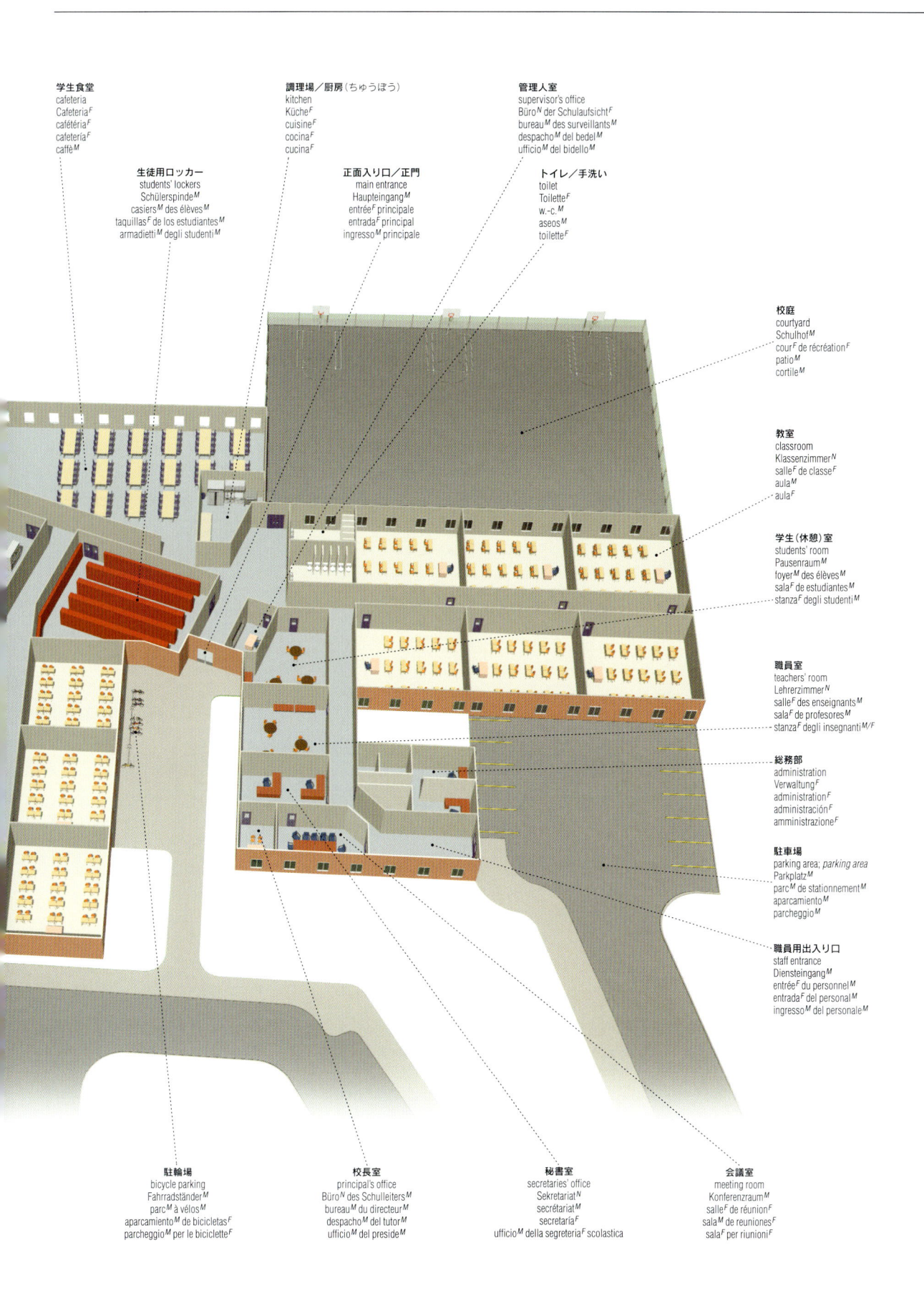

教育 | EDUCATION
BILDUNG | ÉDUCATION | EDUCACIÓN | ISTRUZIONE

学校

学生食堂
cafeteria
Cafeteria^F
cafétéria^F
cafetería^F
caffè^M

調理場／厨房（ちゅうぼう）
kitchen
Küche^F
cuisine^F
cocina^F
cucina^F

管理人室
supervisor's office
Büro^N der Schulaufsicht^F
bureau^M des surveillants^M
despacho^M del bedel^M
ufficio^M del bidello^M

生徒用ロッカー
students' lockers
Schülerspinde^M
casiers^F des élèves^M
taquillas^F de los estudiantes^M
armadietti^M degli studenti^M

正面入り口／正門
main entrance
Haupteingang^M
entrée^F principale
entrada^F principal
ingresso^M principale

トイレ／手洗い
toilet
Toilette^F
w.-c.^{M}
aseos^M
toilette^F

校庭
courtyard
Schulhof^M
cour^F de récréation^F
patio^M
cortile^M

教室
classroom
Klassenzimmer^N
salle^F de classe^F
aula^M
aula^F

学生(休憩)室
students' room
Pausenraum^M
foyer^M des élèves^M
sala^F de estudiantes^M
stanza^F degli studenti^M

職員室
teachers' room
Lehrerzimmer^N
salle^F des enseignants^M
sala^F de profesores^M
stanza^F degli insegnanti$^{M/F}$

総務部
administration
Verwaltung^F
administration^F
administración^F
amministrazione^F

駐車場
parking area; parking area
Parkplatz^M
parc^M de stationnement^M
aparcamiento^M
parcheggio^M

職員用出入り口
staff entrance
Diensteingang^M
entrée^F du personnel^M
entrada^F del personal^M
ingresso^M del personale^M

駐輪場
bicycle parking
Fahrradständer^M
parc^M à vélos^M
aparcamiento^M de bicicletas^F
parcheggio^M per le biciclette^F

校長室
principal's office
Büro^N des Schulleiters^M
bureau^M du directeur^M
despacho^M del tutor^M
ufficio^M del preside^M

秘書室
secretaries' office
Sekretariat^N
secrétariat^M
secretaría^F
ufficio^M della segreteria^F scolastica

会議室
meeting room
Konferenzraum^M
salle^F de réunion^F
sala^F de reuniones^F
sala^F per riunioni^F

社会

宗教 | RELIGION
RELIGION | RELIGION | RELIGION | RELIGIÓN | RELIGIONE

宗教年表

日本語 | 英語 | ドイツ語 | フランス語 | スペイン語 | イタリア語

chronology of religions | Chronologie^F der Religionen^F | chronologie^F des religions^F | Cronología^F de las Religiones^F | cronologia^F delle religioni^F

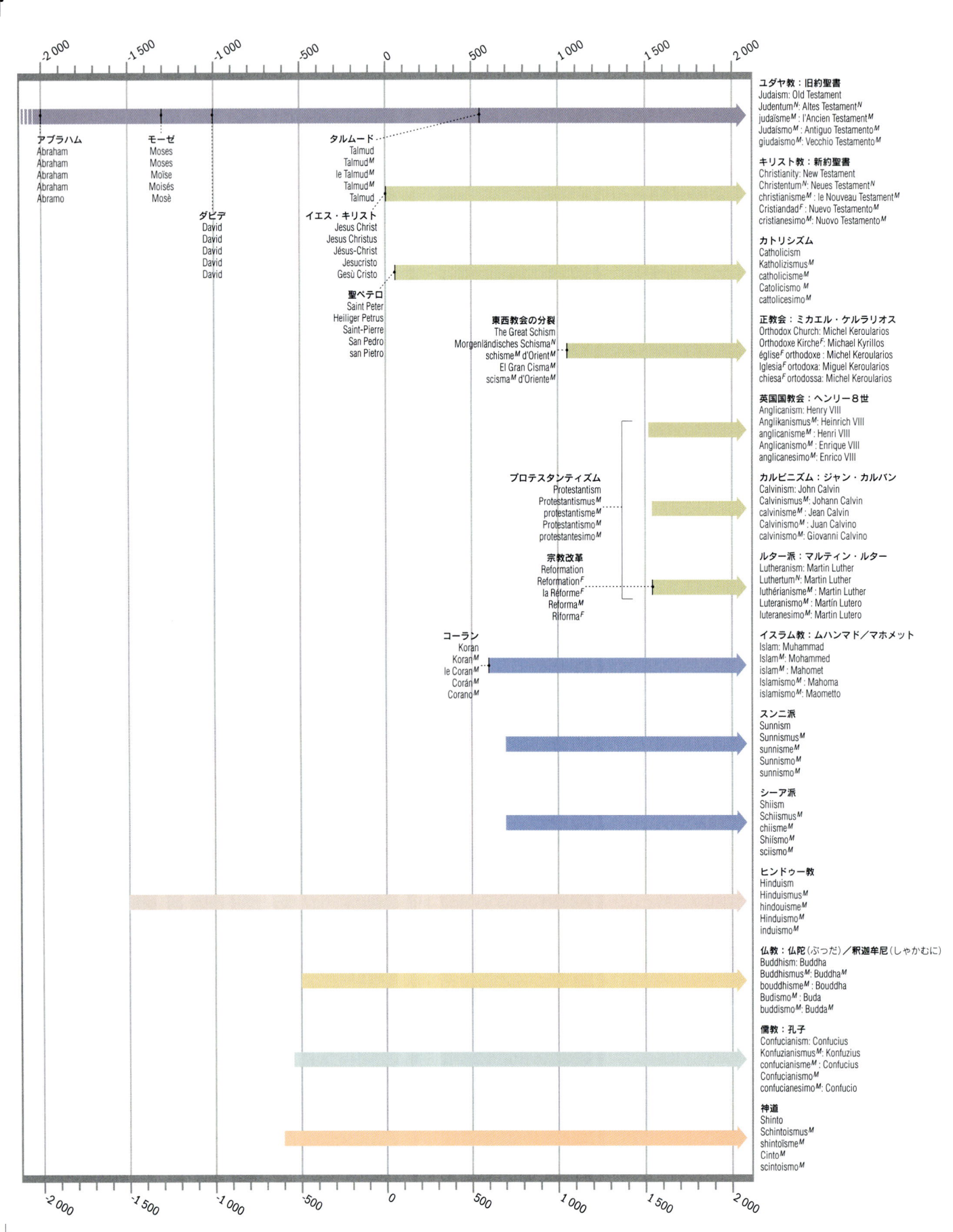

日本語	英語	ドイツ語	フランス語	スペイン語	イタリア語
アブラハム	Abraham	Abraham	Abraham	Abraham	Abramo
モーゼ	Moses	Moses	Moïse	Moisés	Mosè
ダビデ	David	David	David	David	David
タルムード	Talmud	Talmud^M	le Talmud^M	Talmud^M	Talmud
イエス・キリスト	Jesus Christ	Jesus Christus	Jésus-Christ	Jesucristo	Gesù Cristo
聖ペテロ	Saint Peter	Heiliger Petrus	Saint-Pierre	San Pedro	san Pietro
東西教会の分裂	The Great Schism	Morgenländisches Schisma^N	schisme^M d'Orient^M	El Gran Cisma^M	scisma^M d'Oriente^M
コーラン	Koran	Koran^M	le Coran^M	Corán^M	Corano^M

ユダヤ教：旧約聖書	Judaism: Old Testament	Judentum^N: Altes Testament^N	judaïsme^M: l'Ancien Testament^M	Judaísmo^M: Antiguo Testamento^M	giudaismo^M: Vecchio Testamento^M
キリスト教：新約聖書	Christianity: New Testament	Christentum^N: Neues Testament^N	christianisme^M: le Nouveau Testament^M	Cristiandad^F: Nuevo Testamento^M	cristianesimo^M: Nuovo Testamento^M
カトリシズム	Catholicism	Katholizismus^M	catholicisme^M	Catolicismo^M	cattolicesimo^M
正教会：ミカエル・ケルラリオス	Orthodox Church: Michel Keroularios	Orthodoxe Kirche^F: Michael Kyrillos	église^F orthodoxe : Michel Keroularios	Iglesia^F ortodoxa: Miguel Keroularios	chiesa^F ortodossa: Michel Keroularios
英国国教会：ヘンリー8世	Anglicanism: Henry VIII	Anglikanismus^M: Heinrich VIII	anglicanisme^M : Henri VIII	Anglicanismo^M: Enrique VIII	anglicanesimo^M: Enrico VIII
プロテスタンティズム	Protestantism	Protestantismus^M	protestantisme^M	Protestantismo^M	protestantesimo^M
カルビニズム：ジャン・カルバン	Calvinism: John Calvin	Calvinismus^M: Johann Calvin	calvinisme^M : Jean Calvin	Calvinismo^M : Juan Calvino	calvinismo^M: Giovanni Calvino
宗教改革	Reformation	Reformation^F	la Réforme^F	Reforma^M	Riforma^F
ルター派：マルティン・ルター	Lutheranism: Martin Luther	Luthertum^N: Martin Luther	luthérianisme^M : Martin Luther	Luteranismo^M : Martín Lutero	luteranesimo^M: Martin Lutero
イスラム教：ムハンマド／マホメット	Islam: Muhammad	Islam^M: Mohammed	islam^M : Mahomet	Islamismo^M: Mahoma	islamismo^M: Maometto
スンニ派	Sunnism	Sunnismus^M	sunnisme^M	Sunnismo^M	sunnismo^M
シーア派	Shiism	Schiismus^M	chiisme^M	Shiísmo^M	sciismo^M
ヒンドゥー教	Hinduism	Hinduismus^M	hindouisme^M	Hinduismo^M	induismo^M
仏教：仏陀（ぶっだ）／釈迦牟尼（しゃかむに）	Buddhism: Buddha	Buddhismus^M: Buddha^M	bouddhisme^M : Bouddha	Budismo^M : Buda	buddismo^M: Budda^M
儒教：孔子	Confucianism: Confucius	Konfuzianismus^M: Konfuzius	confucianisme^M : Confucius	Confucianismo^M	confucianesimo^M: Confucio
神道	Shinto	Schintoismus^M	shintoïsme^M	Cinto^M	scintoismo^M

社会

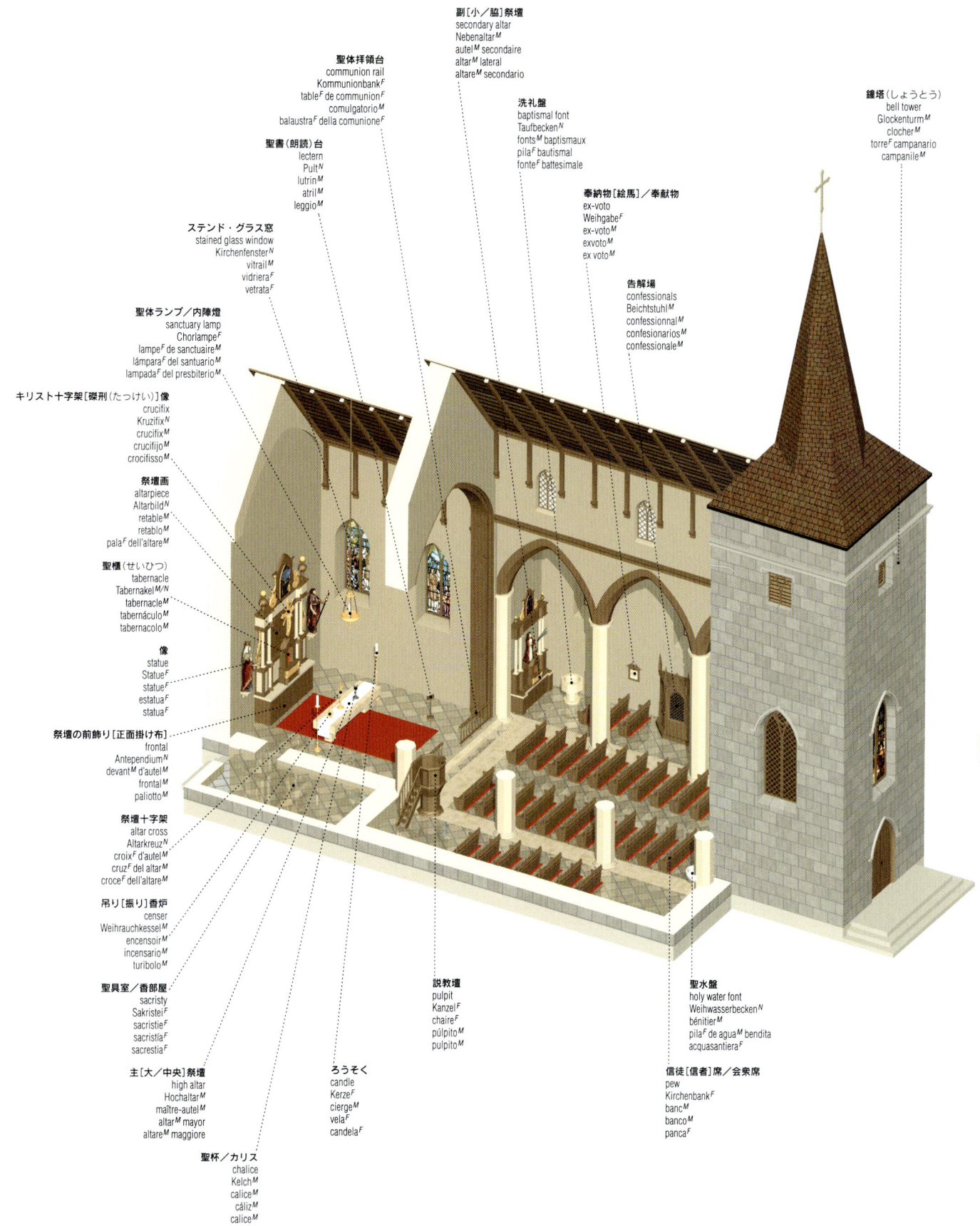

宗教 | RELIGION
RELIGION | RELIGION | RELIGIÓN | RELIGIONE

教会

church | Kirche^F | église^F | iglesia^M | chiesa^F

副[小／脇]祭壇
secondary altar
Nebenaltar^M
autel^M secondaire
altar^M lateral
altare^M secondario

聖体拝領台
communion rail
Kommunionbank^F
table^F de communion^F
comulgatorio^M
balaustra^F della comunione^F

洗礼盤
baptismal font
Taufbecken^N
fonts^M baptismaux
pila^F bautismal
fonte^F battesimale

鐘塔（しょうとう）
bell tower
Glockenturm^M
clocher^M
torre^F campanario
campanile^M

聖書（朗読）台
lectern
Pult^N
lutrin^M
atril^M
leggio^M

奉納物[絵馬]／奉献物
ex-voto
Weihgabe^F
ex-voto^M
exvoto^M
ex voto^M

ステンド・グラス窓
stained glass window
Kirchenfenster^N
vitrail^M
vidriera^F
vetrata^F

告解場
confessionals
Beichtstuhl^M
confessionnal
confesionarios^M
confessionale^M

聖体ランプ／内陣燈
sanctuary lamp
Chorlampe^F
lampe^F de sanctuaire^M
lámpara^F del santuario^M
lampada^F del presbiterio^M

キリスト十字架［磔刑（たっけい）］像
crucifix
Kruzifix^N
crucifix^M
crucifijo^M
crocifisso^M

祭壇画
altarpiece
Altarbild^N
retable^M
retablo^M
pala^F dell'altare^M

聖櫃（せいひつ）
tabernacle
Tabernakel^M/N
tabernacle^M
tabernáculo^M
tabernacolo^M

像
statue
Statue^F
statue^F
estatua^F
statua^F

祭壇の前飾り[正面掛け布]
frontal
Antependium^N
devant^M d'autel^M
frontal^M
paliotto^M

祭壇十字架
altar cross
Altarkreuz^N
croix^F d'autel^M
cruz^F del altar^M
croce^F dell'altare^M

吊り[振り]香炉
censer
Weihrauchkessel^M
encensoir^M
incensario^M
turibolo^M

聖具室／香部屋
sacristy
Sakristei^F
sacristie^F
sacristía^F
sacrestia^F

説教壇
pulpit
Kanzel^F
chaire^F
púlpito^M
pulpito^M

聖水盤
holy water font
Weihwasserbecken^N
bénitier^M
pila^F de agua^M bendita
acquasantiera^F

主[大／中央]祭壇
high altar
Hochaltar^M
maître-autel^M
altar^M mayor
altare^M maggiore

ろうそく
candle
Kerze^F
cierge^M
vela^F
candela^F

信徒[信者]席／会衆席
pew
Kirchenbank^F
banc^M
banco^M
panca^F

聖杯／カリス
chalice
Kelch^M
calice^F
cáliz^M
calice^M

社会

737

宗教 | RELIGION
RELIGION | RELIGION | RELIGIÓN | RELIGIONE

シナゴーグ

synagogue | Synagoge^F | synagogue^F | sinagoga^F | sinagoga^F

日本語 | 英語 | ドイツ語 | フランス語 | スペイン語 | イタリア語

七枝の燭台／メノラー
menorah
Menora^F
menora^F
menorah^F
menorah^F

二階席
balcony
Galerie^F
balcon^M
balcón^M
balconata^F

記念銘板
memorial board
Gedenktafel^F
tableau^M du souvenir
lápida^F conmemorativa
lapide^F commemorativa

説教壇
pulpit
Kanzel^F
table^F de lecture
púlpito^M
pulpito^M

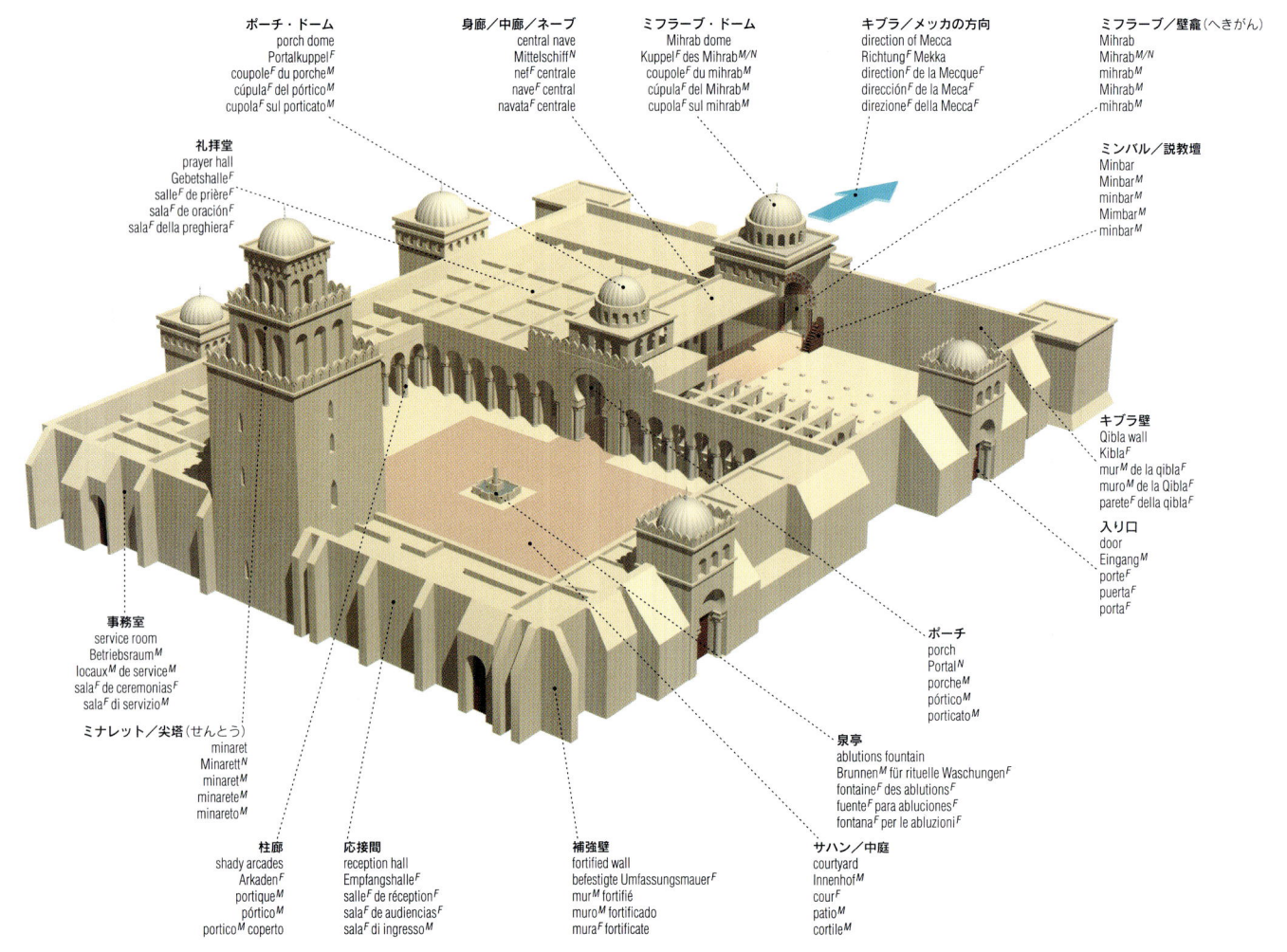

講壇／ビーマー
bimah
Bimah^F
bimah^F
bimah^F
bimah^F

永遠の灯
eternal light
Ewiges Licht^N
lumière^F perpétuelle
llama^F perpetua
luce^F perpetua

トーラーの巻き物
Torah scrolls
Thorarollen^F
rouleaux^M de la Torah^F
rollos^M de la Torá^F
rotoli^M della Torah^F

ダビデの星
Star of David
Davidstern^M
étoile^F de David
estrella^F de David
stella^F di David

十戒
Ten Commandments
Zehn Gebote^N
les Dix commandements^M
diez mandamientos^M
dieci comandamenti^M

契約の聖櫃（せいひつ）
ark
Thoraschrein^M
arche^F
arca^M
arca^F

祭司の席
rabbi's seat
steinerner Ehrensessel^M
siège^M du rabbin^M
asiento^M del rabino^M
seggio^M del rabbino^M

モスク

mosque | Moschee^F | mosquée^F | mezquita^F | moschea^F

ポーチ・ドーム
porch dome
Portalkuppel^F
coupole^F du porche
cúpula^F del pórtico^M
cupola^F sul porticato^M

身廊／中廊／ネーブ
central nave
Mittelschiff^N
nef^F centrale
nave^F central
navata^F centrale

ミフラーブ・ドーム
Mihrab dome
Kuppel^F des Mihrab^M/N
coupole^F du mihrab^M
cúpula^F del Mihrab^M
cupola^F sul mihrab^M

キブラ／メッカの方向
direction of Mecca
Richtung^F Mekka
direction^F de la Mecque
dirección^F de la Meca^F
direzione^F della Mecca^F

ミフラーブ／壁龕（へきがん）
Mihrab
Mihrab^M/N
mihrab^M
Mihrab^M
mihrab^M

礼拝堂
prayer hall
Gebetshalle^F
salle^F de prière
sala^F de oración^F
sala^F della preghiera^F

ミンバル／説教壇
Minbar
Minbar^M
minbar^M
Mimbar^M
minbar^M

キブラ壁
Qibla wall
Kibla
mur^M de la qibla^F
muro^M de la Qibla^F
parete^F della qibla^F

入口
door
Eingang^M
porte^F
puerta^F
porta^F

事務室
service room
Betriebsraum^M
locaux^M de service
sala^F de ceremonias^F
sala^F di servizio^M

ミナレット／尖塔（せんとう）
minaret
Minarett^N
minaret^M
minarete^M
minareto^M

柱廊
shady arcades
Arkaden^F
portique^F
pórtico^M
portico^M coperto

応接間
reception hall
Empfangshalle^F
salle^F de réception
sala^F de audiencias^F
sala^F di ingresso^M

補強壁
fortified wall
befestigte Umfassungsmauer^F
mur^M fortifié
muro^M fortificado
mura^F fortificate

ポーチ
porch
Portal^N
porche^F
pórtico^M
porticato^M

泉亭
ablutions fountain
Brunnen^M für rituelle Waschungen^F
fontaine^F des ablutions
fuente^F para abluciones^F
fontana^F per le abluzioni^F

サハン／中庭
courtyard
Innenhof^M
cour^F
patio^M
cortile^M

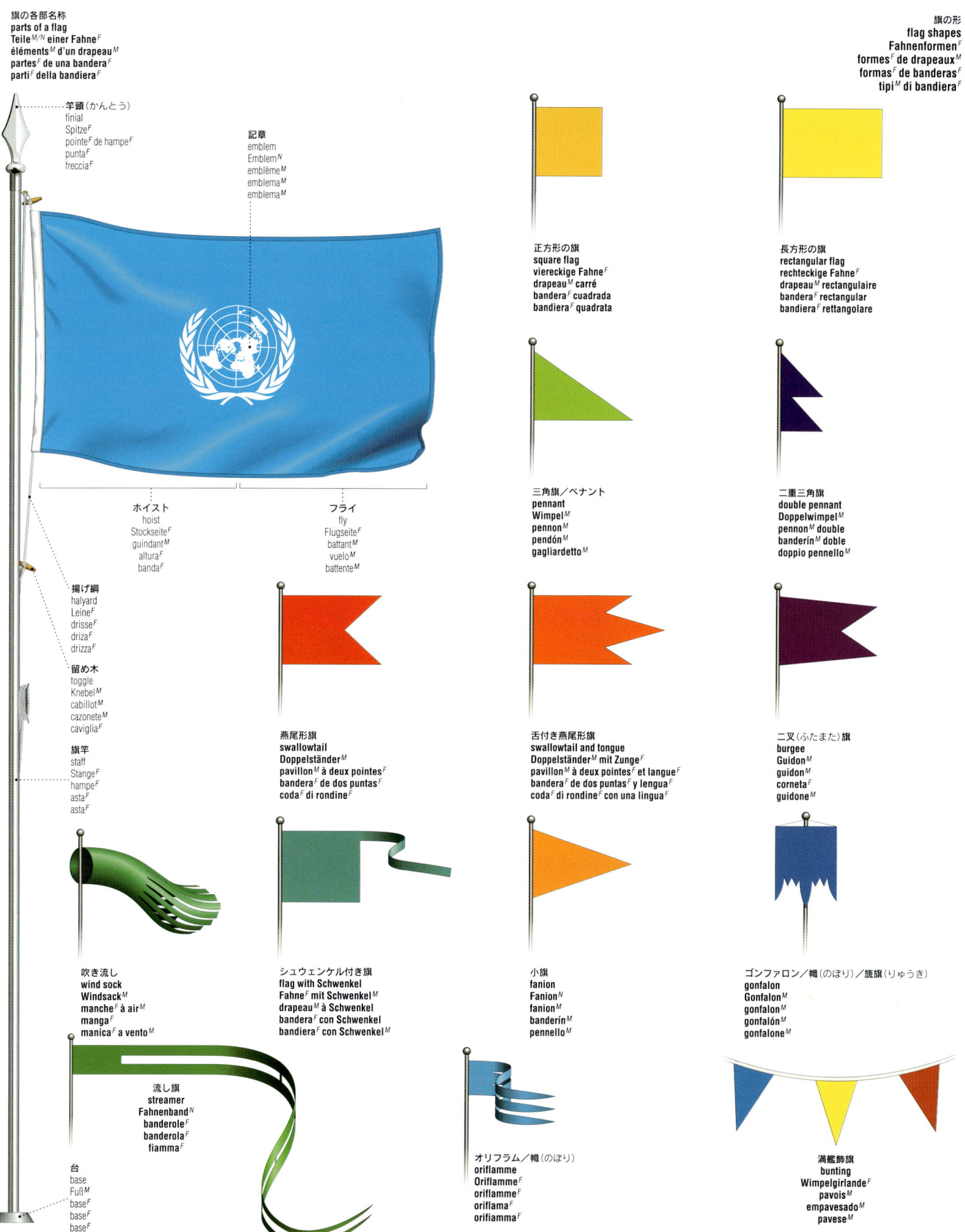

政治 | POLITICS
POLITIK | POLITIQUE | POLÍTICA | POLITICA

紋章

heraldry | Heraldik[F] | héraldique[F] | heráldica[F] | araldica[F]

旗の各部名称
parts of a flag
Teile[M/N] einer Fahne[F]
éléments[M] d'un drapeau[M]
partes[F] de una bandera[F]
parti[F] della bandiera[F]

竿頭（かんとう）
finial
Spitze[F]
pointe[F] de hampe[F]
punta[F]
freccia[F]

記章
emblem
Emblem[N]
emblème[M]
emblema[M]
emblema[M]

ホイスト
hoist
Stockseite[F]
guindant[M]
altura[F]
banda[F]

フライ
fly
Flugseite[F]
battant[M]
vuelo[M]
battente[M]

揚げ綱
halyard
Leine[F]
drisse[F]
driza[F]
drizza[F]

留め木
toggle
Knebel[M]
cabillot[M]
cazonete[M]
caviglia[F]

旗竿
staff
Stange[F]
hampe[F]
asta[F]
asta[F]

吹き流し
wind sock
Windsack[M]
manche[F] à air[M]
manga[F]
manica[F] a vento[M]

流し旗
streamer
Fahnenband[N]
banderole[F]
banderola[F]
fiamma[F]

台
base
Fuß[M]
base[F]
base[F]
base[F]

旗の形
flag shapes
Fahnenformen[F]
formes[F] de drapeaux[M]
formas[F] de banderas[F]
tipi[M] di bandiera[F]

正方形の旗
square flag
viereckige Fahne[F]
drapeau[M] carré
bandera[F] cuadrada
bandiera[F] quadrata

長方形の旗
rectangular flag
rechteckige Fahne[F]
drapeau[M] rectangulaire
bandera[F] rectangular
bandiera[F] rettangolare

三角旗／ペナント
pennant
Wimpel[M]
pennon[M]
pendón[M]
gagliardetto[M]

二重三角旗
double pennant
Doppelwimpel[M]
pennon[M] double
banderín[M] doble
doppio pennello[M]

燕尾形旗
swallowtail
Doppelständer[M]
pavillon[M] à deux pointes[F]
bandera[F] de dos puntas[F]
coda[F] di rondine[F]

舌付き燕尾形旗
swallowtail and tongue
Doppelständer[M] mit Zunge[F]
pavillon[M] à deux pointes[F] et langue[F]
bandera[F] de dos puntas[F] y lengua[F]
coda[F] di rondine[F] con una lingua[F]

二叉（ふたまた）旗
burgee
Guidon[M]
guidon[M]
corneta[F]
guidone[M]

シュウェンケル付き旗
flag with Schwenkel
Fahne[F] mit Schwenkel[M]
drapeau[M] à Schwenkel
bandera[F] con Schwenkel
bandiera[F] con Schwenkel

小旗
fanion
Fanion[N]
fanion[M]
banderín[M]
pennello[M]

ゴンファロン／幟（のぼり）／旒旗（りゅうき）
gonfalon
Gonfalon[M]
gonfalon[M]
gonfalón[M]
gonfalone[M]

オリフラム／幟（のぼり）
oriflamme
Oriflamme[F]
oriflamme[F]
oriflama[F]
orifiamma[F]

満艦飾旗
bunting
Wimpelgirlande[F]
pavois[M]
empavesado[M]
pavese[M]

社会

739

政治 | POLITICS
POLITIK | POLITIQUE | POLÍTICA | POLITICA

紋章

日本語 | 英語 | ドイツ語 | フランス語 | スペイン語 | イタリア語

楯形紋章[楯紋]の区分
shield divisions
Schildplätze^M
divisions^F de l'écu^M
divisiones^F de los escudos^M
divisioni^M dello scudo^M

デクスター／デキスター／右側の
dexter
rechte Flanke^F
dextre^F
tercio^M diestro
destra^F

シニスター／左側の
sinister
linke Flanke^F
senestre^F
tercio^M siniestro
sinistra^F

デクスター・チーフ
dexter chief
rechtes Obereck^N
canton^M dextre du chef^M
cantón^M diestro del jefe^M
cantone^M destro del capo^M

シニスター・チーフ
sinister chief
linkes Obereck^N
canton^M senestre du chef^M
cantón^M siniestro del jefe^M
cantone^M sinistro del capo^M

チーフ
chief
Schildhaupt^N
chef^M
jefe^M
capo^M

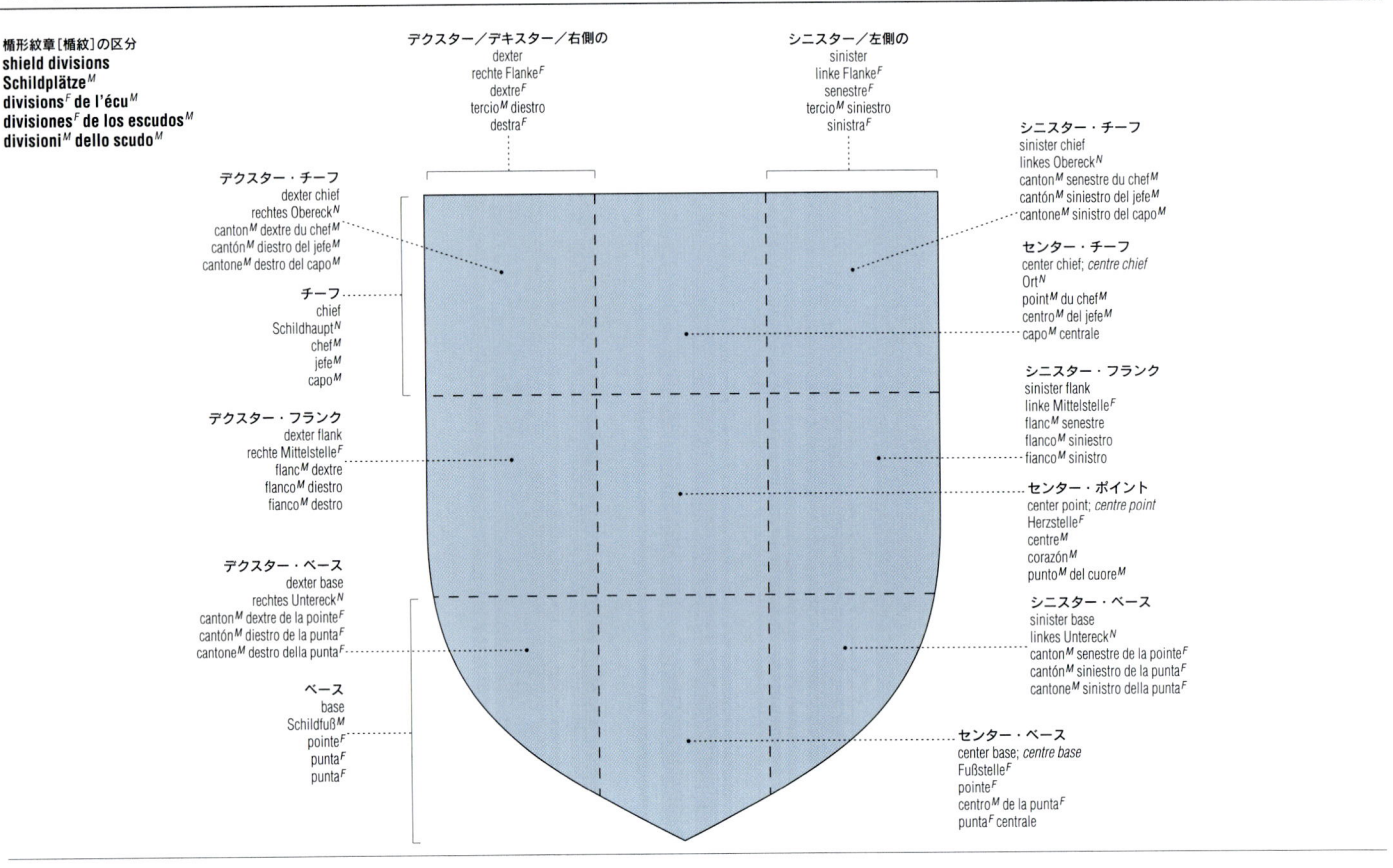

センター・チーフ
center chief; centre chief
Ort^N
point^M du chef^M
centro^M del jefe^M
capo^M centrale

デクスター・フランク
dexter flank
rechte Mittelstelle^F
flanc^M dextre
flanco^M diestro
fianco^M destro

シニスター・フランク
sinister flank
linke Mittelstelle^F
flanc^M senestre
flanco^M siniestro
fianco^M sinistro

センター・ポイント
center point; centre point
Herzstelle^F
centre^M
corazón^M
punto^M del cuore^M

デクスター・ベース
dexter base
rechtes Untereck^N
canton^M dextre de la pointe^F
cantón^M diestro de la punta^F
cantone^M destro della punta^F

シニスター・ベース
sinister base
linkes Untereck^N
canton^M senestre de la pointe^F
cantón^M siniestro de la punta^F
cantone^M sinistro della punta^F

ベース
base
Schildfuß^M
pointe^F
punta^F
punta^F

センター・ベース
center base; centre base
Fußstelle^F
pointe^F
centro^M de la punta^F
punta^F centrale

分割図形の例
examples of partitions
Teilungsbeispiele^N
exemples^M de partitions^F
ejemplos^M de particiones^F
esempi^M di partizioni^F

バー・フェス／横二分割
per fess
blaues Schildhaupt^N in Silber
coupé
escudo^M cortado
troncato

バー・ペイル／縦二分割
party; per pale
gespalten
parti
escudo^M partido
partito

バー・ベンド／斜め分割
per bend
schräg geteilt
tranché
escudo^M tronchado
trinciato

クォータリー／複数分割
quarterly
geviert
écartelé
escudo^M acuartelado
inquartato

抽象図形の例
examples of ordinaries
Beispiele^N für Heroldsbilder^N
exemples^M de pièces^F honorables
ejemplos^M de piezas^F honorables
esempi^M di pezze^F onorevoli^M

チーフ／横帯
chief
Hauptrand^M
chef^M
jefe^M
capo^M

シェブロン／山形
chevron
Sparren^M
chevron^M
cheurón^M
scaglione^M

ペイル／縦帯
pale
Pfahl^M
pal^M
palo^M
palo^M

クロス／十字形
cross
Kreuz^N
croix^F
cruz^F
croce^F

政治 | POLITICS
POLITIK | POLITIQUE | POLÍTICA | POLITICA

紋章

金属色の例
examples of metals
Beispiele^N für Metall^N
exemples^M de métaux^M
ejemplos^M de metales^M
esempi^M di metalli^M

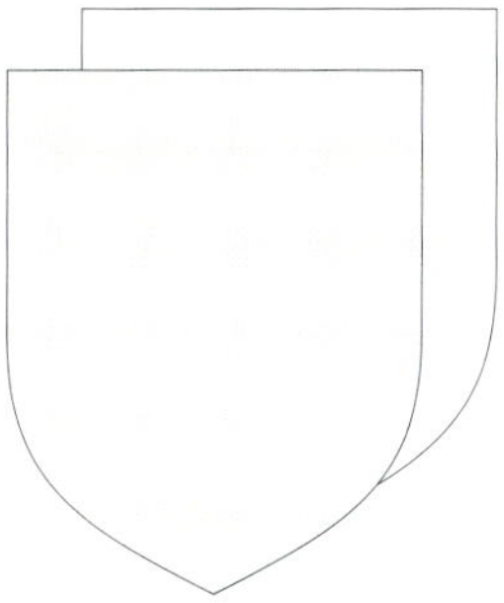

毛皮模様の例
examples of furs
Beispiele^N für Pelzwerk^N
exemples^M de fourrures^F
ejemplos^M de forros^M
esempi^M di pellicce^F

銀
argent
Silber^N
argent^M
plata^F
argento^M

金
or
Gold^N
or^M
oro^M
oro^M

アーミン
ermine
Hermelin^M
hermine^F
armiño^M
ermellino^M

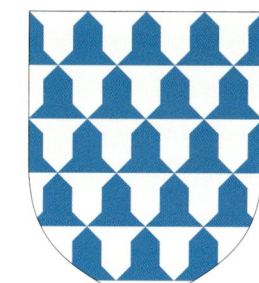

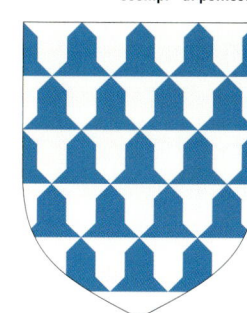

ベア／ベール
vair
Eishutfeh^N
vair^M
cerros^M
vaio^M

チャージ[具象図形]の例
examples of charges
Beispiele^N für Wappenzeichen^N
exemples^M de meubles^M
ejemplos^M de muebles^M
esempi^M di figure^F

百合の花
fleur-de-lis
Lilie^F
fleur^F de lis^M
flor^F de lis^F
giglio^M

三日月
crescent
Mondsichel^F
croissant^M
creciente^M
crescente^M

歩行姿勢のライオン
lion passant
schreitender Löwe^M
lion^M passant
león^M rampante
leone^M passante

鷲（わし）
eagle
Adler^M
aigle^F
águila^F
aquila^F

五光星
mullet
Stern^M
étoile^F
estrella^F
stella^F

配色の例
examples of colors; *examples of colours*
Farbbeispiele^N
exemples^M de couleurs^F
ejemplos^M de colores^M
esempi^M di colori^M

青
azure
blau
azur^M
azur^M
azzurro^M

赤
gules
rot
gueules^M
gules^M
rosso^M

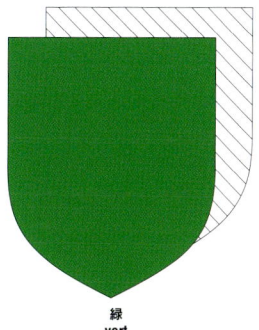

緑
vert
grün
sinople^M
sinople^M
verde^M

紫
purpure
purpurn
pourpre^M
púrpura^M
porpora^M

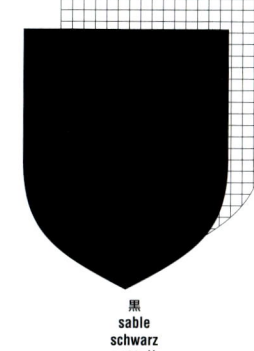

黒
sable
schwarz
sable^M
sable^M
nero^M

社会

741

政治 | POLITICS
POLITIK | POLITIQUE | POLÍTICA | POLITICA

旗

flags | Flaggen^F | drapeaux^M | banderas^F | bandiere^F

日本語 | 英語 | ドイツ語 | フランス語 | スペイン語 | イタリア語

南北アメリカ
Americas
Amerika
Amériques^F
Américas^F
Americhe^F

1 カナダ / Canada / Kanada / Canada^M / Canadá^M / Canada^M

2 アメリカ合衆国 / United States of America / Vereinigte Staaten^M von Amerika / États-Unis^M d'Amérique^F / Estados^M Unidos de América^F / Stati^M Uniti d'America^F

3 メキシコ / Mexico / Mexiko / Mexique^M / México^M / Messico^M

4 ホンジュラス / Honduras / Honduras / Honduras^M / Honduras^M / Honduras^M

5 グアテマラ / Guatemala / Guatemala / Guatemala^M / Guatemala^M / Guatemala^M

6 ベリーズ / Belize / Belize / Belize^M / Belice^M / Belize^M

7 エルサルバドル / El Salvador / El Salvador / El Salvador^M / El Salvador^M / El Salvador^M

8 ニカラグア / Nicaragua / Nicaragua / Nicaragua^M / Nicaragua^M / Nicaragua^M

9 コスタリカ / Costa Rica / Costa Rica / Costa Rica^M / Costa Rica^M / Costa Rica^M

10 パナマ / Panama / Panama / Panama^M / Panamá^M / Panama^M

11 コロンビア / Colombia / Kolumbien / Colombie^F / Colombia^F / Colombia^F

12 ベネズエラ / Venezuela / Venezuela / Venezuela^M / Venezuela^M / Venezuela^M

13 ガイアナ / Guyana / Guyana / Guyana^F / Guyana^F / Guyana^F

14 スリナム / Suriname / Surinam / Suriname^M / Surinam^M / Suriname^M

15 エクアドル / Ecuador / Ecuador / Équateur^M / Ecuador^M / Ecuador^M

16 ペルー / Peru / Peru / Pérou^M / Perú^M / Perù^M

17 ブラジル / Brazil / Brasilien / Brésil^M / Brasil^M / Brasile^M

18 ボリビア / Bolivia / Bolivien / Bolivie^F / Bolivia^F / Bolivia^F

19 パラグアイ / Paraguay / Paraguay / Paraguay^M / Paraguay^M / Paraguay^M

20 チリ / Chile / Chile / Chili^M / Chile^M / Cile^M

21 アルゼンチン / Argentina / Argentinien / Argentine^F / Argentina^F / Argentina^F

22 ウルグアイ / Uruguay / Uruguay / Uruguay^M / Uruguay^M / Uruguay^M

カリブ海諸島
Caribbean Islands
Karibische Inseln^F
Antilles^F
Islas^F del Caribe^M
Isole^F delle Antille^F

23 バハマ / Bahamas / Bahamas^F / Bahamas^F / Bahamas^F / Bahama

24 キューバ / Cuba / Kuba / Cuba^F / Cuba^F / Cuba^F

25 ジャマイカ / Jamaica / Jamaika / Jamaïque^F / Jamaica^F / Giamaica^F

26 ハイチ / Haiti / Haiti / Haïti^M / Haití^M / Haiti^F

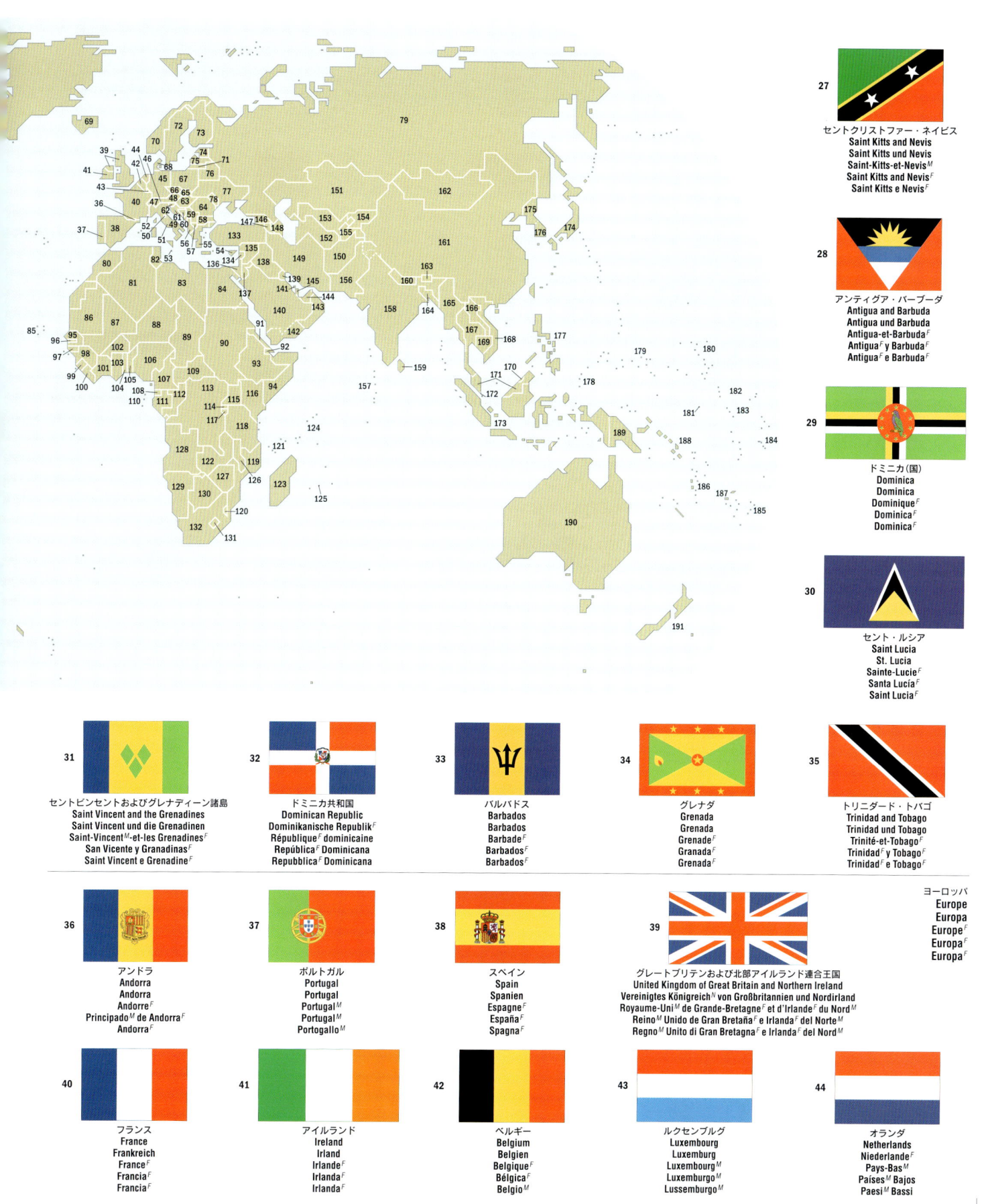

政治 | POLITICS
POLITIK | POLITIQUE | POLÍTICA | POLITICA

旗

27
セントクリストファー・ネイビス
Saint Kitts and Nevis
Saint Kitts und Nevis
Saint-Kitts-et-Nevis^M
Saint Kitts and Nevis^F
Saint Kitts e Nevis^F

28
アンティグア・バーブーダ
Antigua and Barbuda
Antigua und Barbuda
Antigua-et-Barbuda^F
Antigua y Barbuda^F
Antigua e Barbuda^F

29
ドミニカ(国)
Dominica
Dominica
Dominique^F
Dominica^F
Dominica^F

30
セント・ルシア
Saint Lucia
St. Lucia
Sainte-Lucie^F
Santa Lucía^F
Saint Lucia^F

31
セントビンセントおよびグレナディーン諸島
Saint Vincent and the Grenadines
Saint Vincent und die Grenadinen
Saint-Vincent^M-et-les Grenadines^F
San Vicente y Granadinas^F
Saint Vincent e Grenadine^F

32
ドミニカ共和国
Dominican Republic
Dominikanische Republik^F
République^F dominicaine
República^F Dominicana
Repubblica^F Dominicana

33
バルバドス
Barbados
Barbados
Barbade^F
Barbados^F
Barbados^F

34
グレナダ
Grenada
Grenada
Grenade^F
Granada^F
Grenada^F

35
トリニダード・トバゴ
Trinidad and Tobago
Trinidad und Tobago
Trinité-et-Tobago^F
Trinidad y Tobago^F
Trinidad e Tobago^F

ヨーロッパ
Europe
Europa
Europe^F
Europa^F
Europa^F

36
アンドラ
Andorra
Andorra
Andorre^F
Principado^M de Andorra^F
Andorra^F

37
ポルトガル
Portugal
Portugal
Portugal^M
Portugal^M
Portogallo^M

38
スペイン
Spain
Spanien
Espagne^F
España^F
Spagna^F

39
グレートブリテンおよび北部アイルランド連合王国
United Kingdom of Great Britain and Northern Ireland
Vereinigtes Königreich^N von Großbritannien und Nordirland
Royaume-Uni^M de Grande-Bretagne^F et d'Irlande^F du Nord^M
Reino^M Unido de Gran Bretaña^F e Irlanda^F del Norte^M
Regno^M Unito di Gran Bretagna^F e Irlanda^F del Nord^M

40
フランス
France
Frankreich
France^F
Francia^F
Francia^F

41
アイルランド
Ireland
Irland
Irlande^F
Irlanda^F
Irlanda^F

42
ベルギー
Belgium
Belgien
Belgique^F
Bélgica^F
Belgio^M

43
ルクセンブルグ
Luxembourg
Luxemburg
Luxembourg^M
Luxemburgo^M
Lussemburgo^M

44
オランダ
Netherlands
Niederlande^F
Pays-Bas^M
Países^M Bajos
Paesi^M Bassi

社会

743

政治 | POLITICS
POLITIK | POLITIQUE | POLÍTICA | POLITICA

旗

45
ドイツ
Germany
Deutschland
Allemagne^F
Alemania^F
Germania^F

46
リヒテンシュタイン
Liechtenstein
Liechtenstein
Liechtenstein^M
Liechtenstein^M
Liechtenstein^M

47
スイス
Switzerland
Schweiz^F
Suisse^F
Suiza^F
Svizzera^F

48
オーストリア
Austria
Österreich
Autriche^F
Austria^F
Austria^F

49
イタリア
Italy
Italien
Italie^F
Italia^F
Italia^F

50
サンマリノ
San Marino
San Marino
Saint-Marin^M
República^F de San Marino^M
Repubblica^F di San Marino^M

51
バチカン市国
Vatican City State
Vatikanstaat
État^M de la cité^F du Vatican^M
Ciudad^F del Vaticano^M
Città^F del Vaticano^M

52
モナコ
Monaco
Monaco
Monaco^M
Principado^M de Mónaco^M
Principato^M di Monaco^M

53
マルタ
Malta
Malta
Malte^F
Malta^F
Malta^F

54
キプロス
Cyprus
Zypern
Chypre^F
Chipre^M
Cipro^M

55
ギリシャ
Greece
Griechenland
Grèce^F
Grecia^F
Grecia^F

56
アルバニア
Albania
Albanien
Albanie^F
Albania^F
Albania^F

57
マケドニア旧ユーゴースラビア共和国
The Former Yugoslav Republic of Macedonia
Mazedonien
Ex-République^F yougoslave de Macédoine^F
Macedonia^F
Macedonia^F

58
ブルガリア
Bulgaria
Bulgarien
Bulgarie^F
Bulgaria^F
Bulgaria^F

59
ユーゴスラビア
Yugoslavia
Jugoslawien
Yougoslavie^F
Yugoslavia^F
Iugoslavia^F

60
ボスニア・ヘルツェゴビナ
Bosnia and Herzegovina
Bosnien und Herzegowina^F
Bosnie-Herzégovine^F
Bosnia-Herzegovina^F
Bosnia^F ed Erzegovina^F

61
クロアチア
Croatia
Kroatien
Croatie^F
Croacia^F
Croazia^F

62
スロベニア
Slovenia
Slowenien
Slovénie^F
Eslovenia^F
Slovenia^F

63
ハンガリー
Hungary
Ungarn
Hongrie^F
Hungría^F
Ungheria^F

64
ルーマニア
Romania
Rumänien
Roumanie^F
Rumania^F
Romania^F

65
スロバキア
Slovakia
Slowakische Republik^F
Slovaquie^F
Eslovaquia^F
Slovacchia^F

66
チェコ共和国
Czech Republic
Tschechische Republik^F
République^F tchèque
República^F Checa
Repubblica^F Ceca

67
ポーランド
Poland
Polen
Pologne^F
Polonia^F
Polonia^F

68
デンマーク
Denmark
Dänemark
Danemark^M
Dinamarca^F
Danimarca^F

69
アイスランド
Iceland
Island
Islande^F
Islandia^F
Islanda^F

70
ノルウェー
Norway
Norwegen
Norvège^F
Noruega^F
Norvegia^F

71
リトアニア
Lithuania
Litauen
Lituanie^F
Lituania^F
Lituania^F

72
スウェーデン
Sweden
Schweden
Suède^F
Suecia^F
Svezia^F

73
フィンランド
Finland
Finnland
Finlande^F
Finlandia^F
Finlandia^F

74
エストニア
Estonia
Estland
Estonie^F
Estonia^F
Estonia^F

75
ラトビア
Latvia
Lettland
Lettonie^F
Letonia^F
Lettonia^F

76
ベラルーシ
Belarus
Weißrussland
Bélarus^M
Bielorrusia^F
Bielorussia^F

77
ウクライナ
Ukraine
Ukraine^F
Ukraine^F
Ucrania^F
Ucraina^F

78
モルドバ共和国
Republic of Moldova
Moldawien
République^F de Moldova^F
Moldavia^F
Moldavia^F

79
ロシア連邦
Russian Federation
Russland
Fédération^F de Russie^F
Federación^F Rusa
Federazione^F Russa

社会

政治 | POLITICS
POLITIK | POLITIQUE | POLÍTICA | POLITICA

旗

アフリカ
Africa
Afrika
Afrique[F]
África[F]
Africa[F]

80
モロッコ
Morocco
Marokko
Maroc[M]
Marruecos[M]
Marocco[M]

81
アルジェリア
Algeria
Algerien
Algérie[F]
Argelia[F]
Algeria[F]

82
チュニジア
Tunisia
Tunesien
Tunisie[F]
Túnez[M]
Tunisia[F]

83
リビア
Libyan Arab Jamahiriya
Libyen
Jamahiriya[F] arabe libyenne
Libia
Libia[F]

84
エジプト
Egypt
Ägypten
Égypte[F]
Egipto[M]
Egitto[M]

85
カーボベルデ
Cape Verde
Kap Verde
Cap-Vert[M]
Islas[F] de Cabo[M] Verde
Capo Verde[M]

86
モーリタニア
Mauritania
Mauretanien
Mauritanie[F]
Mauritania[F]
Mauritania[F]

87
マリ
Mali
Mali
Mali[M]
República[F] de Malí
Repubblica[F] del Mali[M]

88
ニジェール
Niger
Niger[M]
Niger[M]
Nigeria[F]
Niger[M]

89
チャド
Chad
Tschad[M]
Tchad[M]
Chad[M]
Ciad[M]

90
スーダン
Sudan
Sudan[M]
Soudan[M]
Sudán[M]
Sudan[M]

91
エリトリア
Eritrea
Eritrea
Érythrée[F]
Eritrea
Eritrea[F]

92
ジブチ
Djibouti
Dschibuti
Djibouti[M]
Djibouti[M]
Gibuti[M]

93
エチオピア
Ethiopia
Äthiopien
Éthiopie[F]
Etiopía[F]
Etiopia[F]

94
ソマリア
Somalia
Somalia
Somalie[F]
Somalia[F]
Somalia[F]

95
セネガル
Senegal
Senegal
Sénégal[M]
Senegal[M]
Senegal[M]

96
ガンビア
Gambia
Gambia
Gambie[F]
Gambia[M]
Gambia[M]

97
ギニアビサウ
Guinea-Bissau
Guinea-Bissau
Guinée-Bissau[F]
Guinea-Bissau[F]
Guinea Bissau[F]

98
ギニア
Guinea
Guinea
Guinée[F]
Guinea[F]
Guinea[F]

99
シエラレオネ
Sierra Leone
Sierra Leone
Sierra Leone[F]
Sierra[F] León
Sierra Leone[F]

100
リベリア
Liberia
Liberia
Libéria[M]
Liberia[F]
Liberia[F]

101
コートジボワール
Côte d'Ivoire
Elfenbeinküste[F]
Côte d'Ivoire[F]
Costa de Marfil[F]
Costa d'Avorio[F]

102
ブルキナファソ
Burkina Faso
Burkina Faso
Burkina Faso[M]
Burkina Faso[M]
Burkina Faso[M]

103
ガーナ
Ghana
Ghana
Ghana[M]
Ghana[M]
Ghana[M]

104
トーゴ
Togo
Togo
Togo[M]
Togo[M]
Togo[M]

105
ベナン
Benin
Benin
Bénin[M]
Benín[M]
Benin[M]

106
ナイジェリア
Nigeria
Nigeria
Nigeria[M]
Nigeria[M]
Nigeria[F]

107
カメルーン
Cameroon
Kamerun
Cameroun[M]
Camerún[M]
Camerun[M]

108
赤道ギニア
Equatorial Guinea
Äquatorialguinea
Guinée[F] équatoriale
Guinea[F] Ecuatorial
Guinea[F] Equatoriale

109
中央アフリカ共和国
Central African Republic
Zentralafrikanische Republik[F]
République[F] centrafricaine
República[F] Centroafricana
Repubblica[F] Centrafricana

110
サントメ・プリンシペ
Sao Tome and Principe
São Tomé und Príncipe
São Tomé-et-Príncipe[M]
Santo Tomé y Príncipe[M]
São Tomé e Príncipe[M]

111
ガボン
Gabon
Gabun
Gabon[M]
Gabón[M]
Gabon[M]

112
コンゴ（共和国）
Congo
Kongo[M]
Congo[M]
Congo[M]
Congo[M]

113
コンゴ民主共和国
Democratic Republic of the Congo
Republik[F] Kongo[M]
République[F] démocratique du Congo[M]
República[F] Democrática del Congo[M]
Repubblica[F] Democratica del Congo[M]

114
ルワンダ
Rwanda
Ruanda
Rwanda[M]
Ruanda[M]
Ruanda[M]

115
ウガンダ
Uganda
Uganda
Ouganda[M]
Uganda[M]
Uganda[F]

116
ケニア
Kenya
Kenia
Kenya[M]
Kenia[F]
Kenya[M]

117
ブルンジ
Burundi
Burundi
Burundi[M]
Burundi[M]
Burundi[M]

118
タンザニア連合共和国
United Republic of Tanzania
Tansania
République[F]-Unie de Tanzanie[F]
Tanzania[F]
Tanzania[F]

社会

政治 | POLITICS
POLITIK | POLITIQUE | POLÍTICA | POLITICA

旗

日本語 | 英語 | ドイツ語 | フランス語 | スペイン語 | イタリア語

119 モザンビーク / Mozambique / Mosambik / Mozambique^F / Mozambique^M / Mozambico^M

120 スワジランド / Swaziland / Swasiland^N / Swaziland^M / Swazilandia^M / Swaziland^M

121 コモロ / Comoros / Komoren^F / Comores^F / Comores^F / Comore^F

122 ザンビア / Zambia / Sambia / Zambie^F / Zambia^M / Zambia^M

123 マダガスカル / Madagascar / Madagaskar / Madagascar^F / Madagascar^M / Madagascar^M

124 セイシェル / Seychelles / Seychellen^F / Seychelles^F / Seychelles^F / Seychelles^F

125 モーリシャス / Mauritius / Mauritius / Maurice^F / Mauricio^M / Maurizio^M

126 マラウイ / Malawi / Malawi / Malawi^F / Malawi^M / Malawi^M

127 ジンバブエ / Zimbabwe / Simbabwe / Zimbabwe^M / Zimbabwe^M / Zimbabwe^M

128 アンゴラ / Angola / Angola / Angola^M / Angola^F / Angola^F

129 ナミビア / Namibia / Namibia / Namibie^F / Namibia^F / Namibia^F

130 ボツワナ / Botswana / Botswana / Botswana^M / Bostwana^M / Botswana^M

131 レソト / Lesotho / Lesotho / Lesotho^M / Lesotho^M / Lesotho^M

132 南アフリカ / South Africa / Südafrika / Afrique^F du Sud / Suráfrica^M / Repubblica^F Sudafricana

アジア / Asia / Asien / Asie^F / Asia^F / Asia^F

133 トルコ / Turkey / Türkei^F / Turquie^F / Turquía^F / Turchia^F

134 レバノン / Lebanon / Libanon^M / Liban^M / Líbano^M / Libano^M

135 シリア・アラブ共和国 / Syrian Arab Republic / Syrien / République^F arabe syrienne / Siria^F / Siria^F

136 イスラエル / Israel / Israel / Israël^M / Israel^M / Israele^M

137 ヨルダン / Jordan / Jordanien / Jordanie^F / Jordania^F / Giordania^F

138 イラク / Iraq / Irak^M / Iraq^M / Iraq^M / Iraq^M

139 クウェート / Kuwait / Kuwait / Koweït^M / Kuwait^M / Kuwait^M

140 サウジアラビア / Saudi Arabia / Saudi-Arabien / Arabie^F saoudite / Arabia Saudí^F / Arabia Saudita^F

141 バーレーン / Bahrain / Bahrain / Bahreïn^M / Bahrain^M / Bahrein^M

142 イエメン / Yemen / Jemen^M / Yémen^M / Yemen^M / Yemen^M

143 オマーン / Oman / Oman / Oman^M / Omán^M / Oman^M

144 アラブ首長国連邦 / United Arab Emirates / Vereinigte Arabische Emirate^N / Émirats^M arabes unis / Emiratos^M Árabes Unidos / Emirati Arabi Uniti^M

145 カタール / Qatar / Katar / Qatar^M / Qatar^M / Qatar^M

146 グルジア / Georgia / Georgien / Géorgie^F / Georgia^F / Georgia^F

147 アルメニア / Armenia / Armenien / Arménie^F / Armenia^F / Armenia^F

148 アゼルバイジャン / Azerbaijan / Aserbeidschan / Azerbaïdjan^M / Azerbaiyán^M / Azerbaigian^M

149 イラン / Iran / Iran / Iran^M / Irán^M / Iran^M

150 アフガニスタン / Afghanistan / Afghanistan / Afghanistan^M / Afganistán^M / Afghanistan^M

151 カザフスタン / Kazakhstan / Kasachstan / Kazakhstan^M / Kazastán^M / Kazakistan^M

152 トルクメニスタン / Turkmenistan / Turkmenistan / Turkménistan^M / Turkmenistán^M / Turkmenistan^M

153 ウズベキスタン / Uzbekistan / Usbekistan / Ouzbékistan^M / Uzbekistán^M / Uzbekistan^M

154 キルギス / Kyrgyzstan / Kirgisistan / Kirghizistan^M / Kirguizistán^M / Kirghizistan^M

155 タジキスタン / Tajikistan / Tadschikistan / Tadjikistan^M / Tayikistán^M / Tagikistan^M

156 パキスタン / Pakistan / Pakistan / Pakistan^M / Pakistán^M / Pakistan^M

社会

政治 | POLITICS
POLITIK | POLITIQUE | POLÍTICA | POLITICA

旗

| 157 | モルディブ
Maldives
Malediven^F
Maldives^F
Maldivas^F
Maldive^F | 158 | インド
India
Indien
Inde^F
India^F
India^F | 159 | スリランカ
Sri Lanka
Sri Lanka
Sri Lanka^M
Sri Lanka^M
Sri Lanka^M | 160 | ネパール
Nepal
Nepal
Népal^M
Nepal^M
Nepal^M | 161 | 中華人民共和国
China
China
Chine^F
China^F
Cina^F |

162 モンゴル国 / Mongolia / Mongolei^F / Mongolie^F / Mongolia^F / Mongolia^F

163 ブータン / Bhutan / Bhutan / Bhoutan^M / Buthán^M / Bhutan^M

164 バングラデシュ / Bangladesh / Bangladesch / Bangladesh^M / Bangladesh^M / Bangladesh^M

165 ミャンマー / Myanmar / Myanmar / Myanmar^F / Myanmar^M / Myanmar^M

166 ラオス人民民主共和国 / Lao People's Democratic Republic / Laos / République^F démocratique populaire lao / Laos^M / Laos^M

167 タイ / Thailand / Thailand / Thaïlande^F / Tailandia^F / Tailandia^F

168 ベトナム / Viet Nam / Vietnam / Viet Nam^M / Vietnam^M / Vietnam^M

169 カンボジア / Cambodia / Kambodscha / Cambodge^M / Camboya^F / Cambogia^F

170 ブルネイダルサラーム(国) / Brunei Darussalam / Brunei / Brunéi Darussalam^M / Brunei^M / Brunei^M

171 マレーシア / Malaysia / Malaysia / Malaisie^F / Malasia^F / Malaysia^F

172 シンガポール / Singapore / Singapur / Singapour^F / Singapur^M / Singapore^F

173 インドネシア / Indonesia / Indonesien / Indonésie^F / Indonesia^F / Indonesia^F

174 日本 / Japan / Japan / Japon^M / Japón^M / Giappone^M

175 朝鮮民主主義人民共和国 / Democratic People's Republic of Korea / Nord-Korea / République^F populaire démocratique de Corée^F / Republica Democrática Popular de Corea^F / Repubblica^F Democratica Popolare di Corea^F

176 大韓民国 / Republic of Korea / Süd-Korea / République^F de Corée^F / República^F de Corea^F / Repubblica^F di Corea^F

オセアニア・ポリネシア
Oceania and Polynesia
Ozeanien und Polynesien
Océanie^F et Polynésie^F
Oceanía^F y Polinesia^F
Oceania^F e Polinesia^F

177 フィリピン / Philippines / Philippinen / Philippines^F / Filipinas^F / Filippine^F

178 パラオ / Palau / Palau / Palaos^M / Palau^M / Palau^M

179 ミクロネシア / Micronesia / Mikronesien / Micronésie^F / Micronesia^F / Micronesia^F

180 マーシャル諸島 / Marshall Islands / Marshallinseln^F / Îles^F Marshall / Islas Marshall^F / Isole Marshall^F

181 ナウル / Nauru / Nauru / Nauru^F / Nauru^M / Nauru^M

182 キリバス / Kiribati / Kiribati / Kiribati^F / Kiribati^M / Kiribati^M

183 ツバル / Tuvalu / Tuvalu / Tuvalu^F / Tuvalu^M / Tuvalu^M

184 サモア / Samoa / Samoa / Samoa^F / Samoa^F / Samoa^F

185 トンガ / Tonga / Tonga / Tonga^F / Tonga^F / Tonga^M

186 バヌアツ / Vanuatu / Vanuatu / Vanuatu^M / Vanuatu^M / Vanuatu^M

187 フィジー / Fiji / Fidschi / Fidji^F / Fiji^F / Figi^F

188 ソロモン諸島 / Solomon Islands / Salomoninseln^F / Îles^F Salomon / Islas Salomón^F / Isole Salomone^F

189 パプアニューギニア / Papua New Guinea / Papua-Neuguinea / Papouasie-Nouvelle-Guinée^F / Papúa Nueva Guinea^F / Papua Nuova Guinea^F

190 オーストラリア / Australia / Australien / Australie^F / Australia^F / Australia^F

191 ニュージーランド / New Zealand / Neuseeland / Nouvelle-Zélande^F / Nueva Zelanda^F / Nuova Zelanda^F

社会

兵器 | WEAPONS
WAFFEN | ARMES | ARMAS | ARMI

石器時代の武器

weapons in the Stone Age | Steinzeitwaffen^F | armes^F de l'âge^M de pierre^F | armas^F de la Edad^F de Piedra^F | armi^F dell'età^F della pietra^F

日本語 | 英語 | ドイツ語 | フランス語 | スペイン語 | イタリア語

磨かれた石の手斧（ておの）［握斧（あくふ）］
polished stone hand axe
polierter Steinfaustkeil^M
hache^F en pierre^F polie
hacha^F de piedra^F pulida
ascia^F levigata

火打ち石でできた矢尻
flint arrowhead
Pfeilspitze^F aus Feuerstein^M
pointe^F de flèche^F en silex^M
punta^F de flecha^F de sílex^M
punta^F di freccia^F in selce^F

火打ち石でできたナイフ
flint knife
Messer^N aus Feuerstein^M
couteau^M en silex^M
cuchillo^M de sílex^M
coltello^M di selce^F

ローマ時代の武器

weapons in the age of the Romans | Waffen^F in der Römerzeit^F | armes^F de l'époque^F romaine | armas^F del imperio^M romano | armi^F al tempo^M dei Romani^M

軍団［レギオン］の兵士
Roman legionary
römischer Legionär^M
légionnaire^M romain
legionario^M romano
legionario^M romano

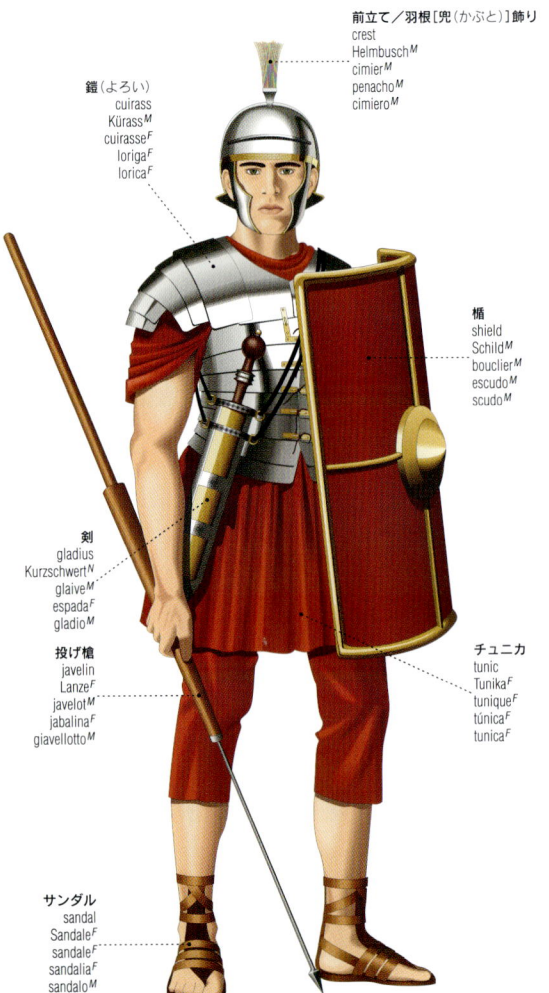

前立て／羽根［兜（かぶと）］飾り
crest
Helmbusch^M
cimier^M
penacho^M
cimiero^M

鎧（よろい）
cuirass
Küraß^M
cuirasse^F
loriga^F
lorica^F

楯
shield
Schild^M
bouclier^M
escudo^M
scudo^M

剣
gladius
Kurzschwert^N
glaive^M
espada^F
gladio^M

投げ槍
javelin
Lanze^F
javelot^M
jabalina^F
giavellotto^M

チュニカ
tunic
Tunika^F
tunique^F
túnica^F
tunica^F

サンダル
sandal
Sandale^F
sandale^F
sandalia^F
sandalo^M

ガリア［ゴール］人の戦士
Gallic warrior
gallischer Krieger^M
guerrier^M gaulois
guerrero^M galo
guerriero^M gallico

兜（かぶと）／ヘルメット
helmet
Helm^M
casque^M
casco^M
elmo^M

楯
shield
Schild^M
bouclier^M
escudo^M
scudo^M

ズボン
breeches
Hose^F
braies^F
pantalones^M
calzoni^M

槍
spear
Speer^M
lance^F
lanza^F
lancia^F

社会

748

兵器 | WEAPONS
WAFFEN | ARMES | ARMAS | ARMI

鎧(兜)(よろいかぶと)／甲冑(かっちゅう)

armor; *armour* | Rüstung^F | armure^F | armadura^F | armatura^F

兜／ヘルメット
armet
Helm^M
armet^M
celada^F
celata^F

覗(のぞ)き穴
vision slit
Sehschlitz^M
fente^F de vision^F
ranura^F de visión^F
lessura^F oculare

顎(あご)当て
beaver
Kinnreff^N
mentonnière^F
barbote^M
barbozza^F

肩甲
pauldron
Vorderflug^M
épaulière^F
espaldarón^M
spallaccio^M

上腕甲
rerebrace
Oberarmschiene^F
brassard^M
brafonera^F
cannone^M di braccio^M

胸甲／胸当て
breastplate
Bruststück^N
plastron^M
peto^M
petto^M

肘当て
couter
Armkachel^F
cubitière^F
codal^M
cubitiera^F

腰当て
skirt
Vorderschürze^F
braconnière^F
faldar^M
falda^F

腕甲
vambrace
Unterarmschiene^F
canon^M d'avant-bras^M
avambrazo^M
cannone^M di antibraccio^M

草摺(くさずり)
tasset
Bauchreifen^M
tassette^F
escarcela^F
fiancale^M

鎖帷子(かたびら)
chain mail
Panzerschurz^M
cotte^F de mailles^F
cota^F de malla^F
cotta^F di maglia^F

籠手(こて)／小手当て
gauntlet
Panzerhandschuh^M
gantelet^M
guantelete^M
manopola^F

腿(もも)当て
cuisse
Diechling^M
cuissard^M
quijote^M
cosciale^M

膝覆い
poleyn
Kniebuckel^M
genouillère^F
rodillera^F
ginocchiera^M

脛(すね)当て
greave
Beinröhre^F
grève^F
greba^F
schiniere^M

鉄靴
sabaton
Bärlatsch^M
soleret^M
escarpe^M
scarpa^F a lame^F

プレーヌ
poulaine
Schnabel^M
poulaine^F
escarpín^M
punta^F articolata

兜
armet
Helm^M
armet^M
yelmo^M
elmo^M

飾冠／頂飾／峰
comb
Scheitelstück^N
crête^F
crestón^M
cresta^F

面頬(めんぽお)
visor
Visier^N
visière^F
visera^F
visiera^F

鉢
skull
Helmglocke^F
timbre^M
celada^F
coppo^M

鼻当て
nose
Nase^F
nasal^M
nasal^M
nasale^M

眉庇(まびさし)
brow reinforce
Stirn^F
frontal^M
frontal^M
frontale^M

息抜き
vent-tail
Luftlöcher^N
ventail^M
ventalle^M
ventaglia^F

頸甲(けいこう)／喉(のど)当て
gorget
Halsberge^F
gorgerin^M
gola^F
goletta^F

顎(あご)当て
beaver
Kinnreff^N
mentonnière^F
babera^F
barbozza^F

社会

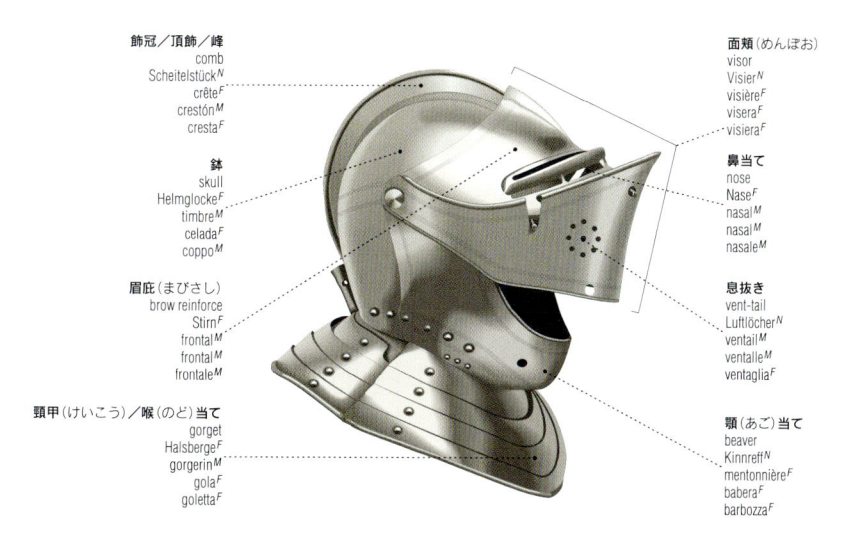

兵器 | WEAPONS
WAFFEN | ARMES | ARMAS | ARMI

弓と石弓

日本語 | 英語 | ドイツ語 | フランス語 | スペイン語 | イタリア語

bows and crossbow | Bogen^M und Armbrust^F | arcs^M et arbalète^F | arcos^M y ballesta^F | archi^M e balestra^F

石弓／弩（おおゆみ）
crossbow
Armbrust^F
arbalète^F
ballesta^F
balestra^F

柱身
tiller
Abzugstange^F
arbrier^M
cureña^F
teniere^M

止め金／ナット
nut
Nuss^F
noix^F
nuez^F
noce^F

弓
bow
Bügel^M
arc^M
arco^M
arco^M

踏み輪／鐙金（あぶみがね）
stirrup
Steigbügel^M
étrier^M
estribera^F
staffa^F

滑車装置／プーリー・ブロック
pulley block
Rollkloben^M
moufle^F
cierre^M de polea^F
ponte^M

引き金／トリガー
trigger
Abzug^M
détente^F
gatillo^M
manetta^F

四角矢／太矢
bolt
Bolzen^M
carreau^M d'arbalète^F
flecha^F
dardo^M

矢溝
groove
Rinne^F
rainure^F
canal^M
scanalatura^F

手回しハンドル／クランク
crank
Drehschwengel^M
manivelle^F
manivela^F
manovella^F

滑車／プーリー
pulley
Winde^F
poulie^F
polea^F
carrucola^F

弦（つる）
bowstring
Bogensehne^F
corde^F
cuerda^F
corda^F

現代の弓
modern bow
moderner Bogen^M
arc^M **moderne**
arco^M **moderno**
arco^M **moderno**

弓
bow
Bogen^M
arc^M
arco^M
arco^M

弓筈（ゆはず）／ノック
nock
Nocke^F
encoche^F
muesca^F
cocca^F

上部／アッパー・リム
upper limb
oberer Wurfarm^M
branche^F supérieure
rama^F superior
braccio^M superiore

背
back
Bogen^M
dos^M
dorso^M
dorso^M

握り部／ハンドル／グリップ
handle
Handgriff^M
poignée^F
empuñadura^F
impugnatura^F

下部／ロワー・リム
lower limb
unterer Wurfarm^M
branche^F inférieure
rama^F inferior
braccio^M inferiore

弦（つる）
bowstring
Bogensehne^F
corde^F
cuerda^F
corda^F

矢
arrow
Pfeil^M
flèche^F
flecha^F
freccia^F

750

兵器 | WEAPONS
WAFFEN | ARMES | ARMAS | ARMI

刀剣

thrusting and cutting weapons | Hieb- und Stichwaffen^F | armes^F blanches | armas^F blancas | armi^F da lancio^M e da taglio^M

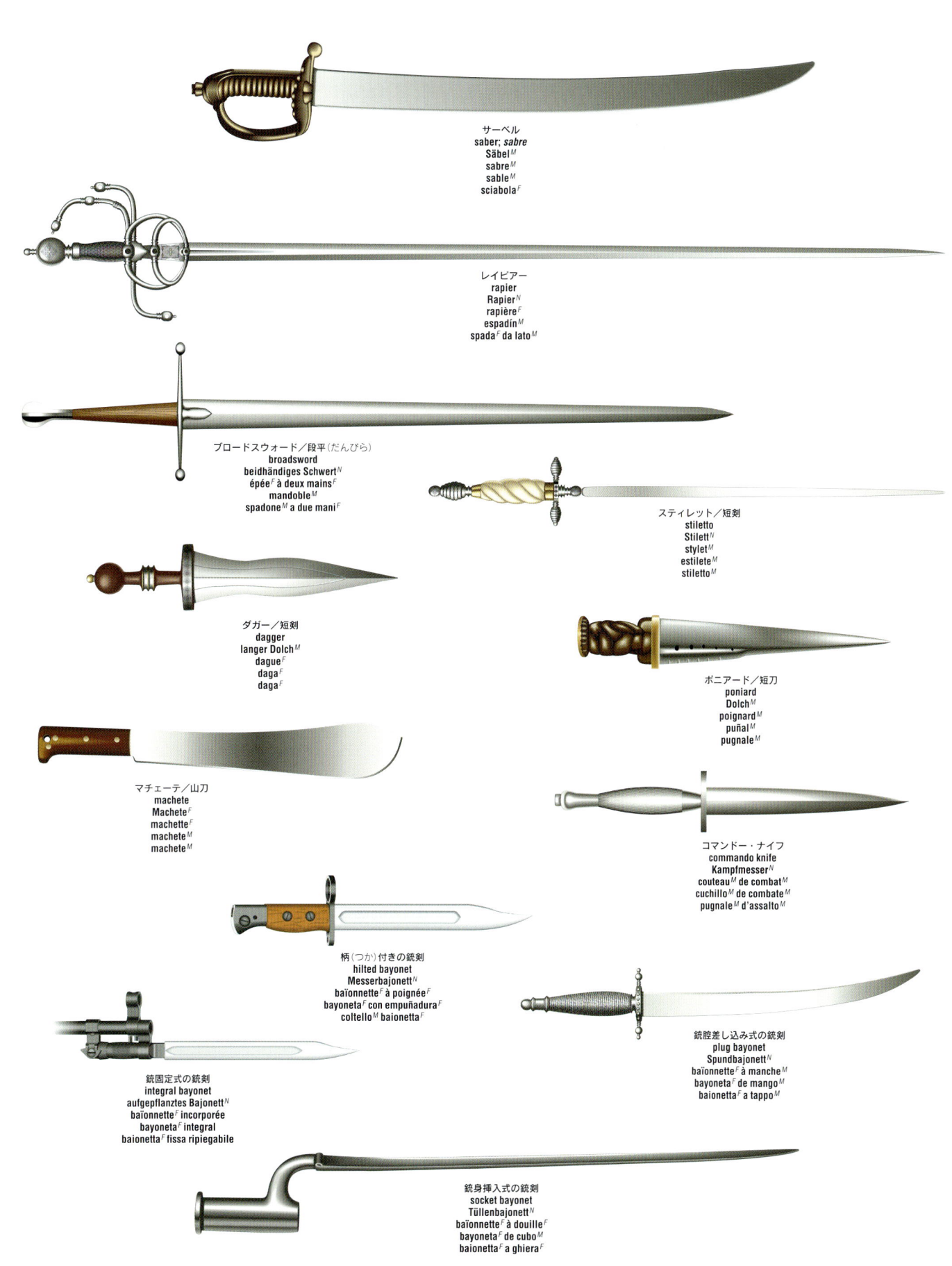

サーベル
saber; *sabre*
Säbel^M
sabre^M
sable^M
sciabola^F

レイピアー
rapier
Rapier^N
rapière^F
espadín^M
spada^F da lato^M

ブロードスウォード／段平（だんびら）
broadsword
beidhändiges Schwert^N
épée^F à deux mains^F
mandoble^M
spadone^M a due mani^F

スティレット／短剣
stiletto
Stilett^N
stylet^M
estilete^M
stiletto^M

ダガー／短剣
dagger
langer Dolch^M
dague^F
daga^F
daga^F

ポニアード／短刀
poniard
Dolch^M
poignard^M
puñal^M
pugnale^M

マチェーテ／山刀
machete
Machete^F
machette^F
machete^M
machete^M

コマンドー・ナイフ
commando knife
Kampfmesser^N
couteau^M de combat^M
cuchillo^M de combate^M
pugnale^M d'assalto^M

柄（つか）付きの銃剣
hilted bayonet
Messerbajonett^N
baïonnette^F à poignée^F
bayoneta^F con empuñadura^F
coltello^M baionetta^F

銃腔差し込み式の銃剣
plug bayonet
Spundbajonett^N
baïonnette^F à manche^M
bayoneta^F de mango^M
baionetta^F a tappo^M

銃固定式の銃剣
integral bayonet
aufgepflanztes Bajonett^N
baïonnette^F incorporée
bayoneta^F integral
baionetta^F fissa ripiegabile

銃身挿入式の銃剣
socket bayonet
Tüllenbajonett^N
baïonnette^F à douille^F
bayoneta^F de cubo^M
baionetta^F a ghiera^F

社会

751

兵器 | WEAPONS
WAFFEN | ARMES | ARMAS | ARMI

火打ち石銃

harquebus; *arquebus* | Arkebuse^F | arquebuse^F | arcabuz^M | archibugio^M

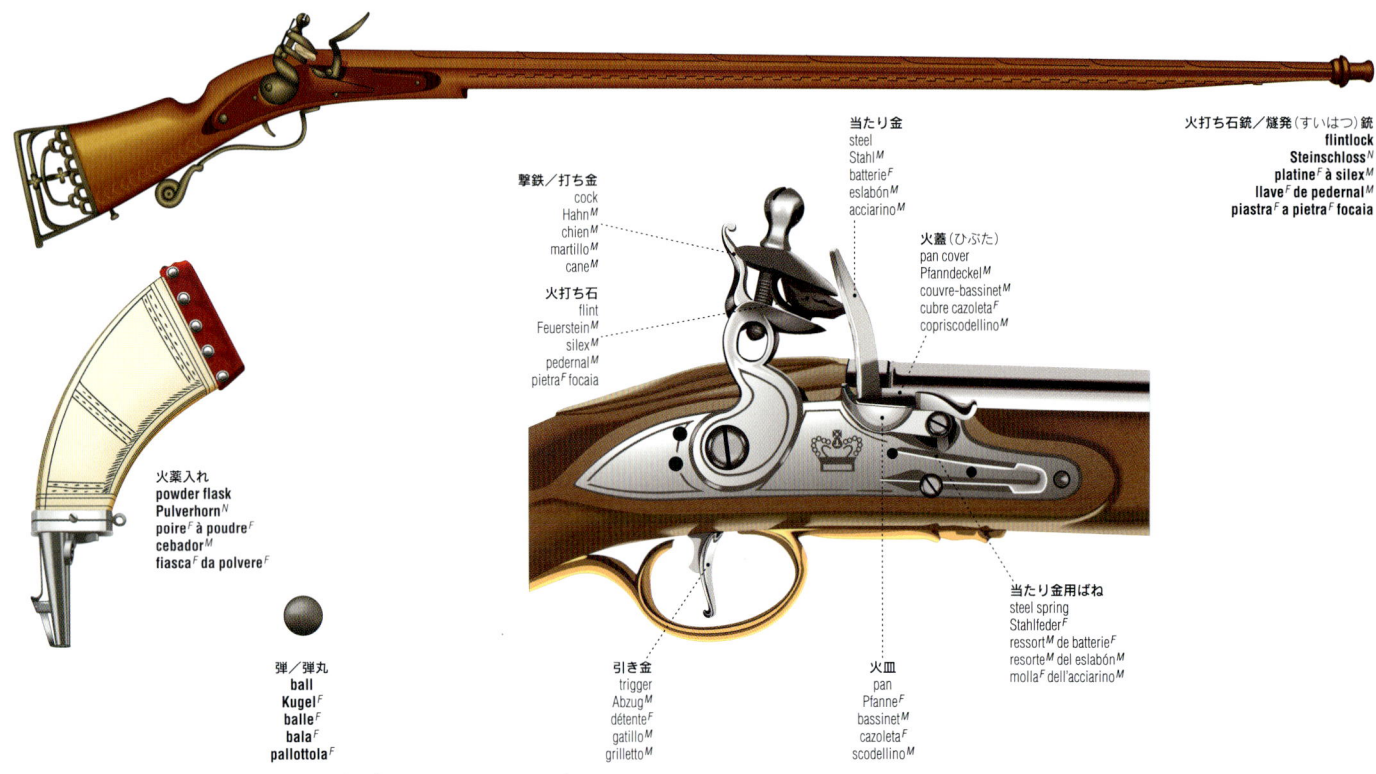

日本語 | 英語 | ドイツ語 | フランス語 | スペイン語 | イタリア語

当たり金
steel
Stahl^M
batterie^F
eslabón^M
acciarino^M

撃鉄／打ち金
cock
Hahn^M
chien^M
martillo^M
cane^M

火打ち石
flint
Feuerstein^M
silex^M
pedernal^M
pietra^F focaia

火蓋（ひぶた）
pan cover
Pfanndeckel^M
couvre-bassinet^M
cubre cazoleta^F
copriscodellino^M

火打ち石銃／燧発（すいはつ）銃
flintlock
Steinschloss^N
platine^F à silex^M
llave^F de pedernal^M
piastra^F a pietra^F focaia

火薬入れ
powder flask
Pulverhorn^N
poire^F à poudre^F
cebador^M
fiasca^F da polvere^F

弾／弾丸
ball
Kugel^F
balle^F
bala^F
pallottola^F

引き金
trigger
Abzug^M
détente^F
gatillo^M
grilletto^M

火皿
pan
Pfanne^F
bassinet^M
cazoleta^F
scodellino^M

当たり金用ばね
steel spring
Stahlfeder^F
ressort^M de batterie^F
resorte^M del eslabón^M
molla^F dell'acciarino^M

１７世紀の大砲と臼砲（きゅうほう）

seventeenth century cannon and mortar; *seventeenth-century cannon and mortar* | Kanone^F und Mörser^M aus dem 17. Jahrhundert^N | canon^M et mortier^M du XVIIe siÈcle^M | cañón^M y mortero^M del siglo^M XVII | cannone^M e mortaio^M del XVII° secolo^M

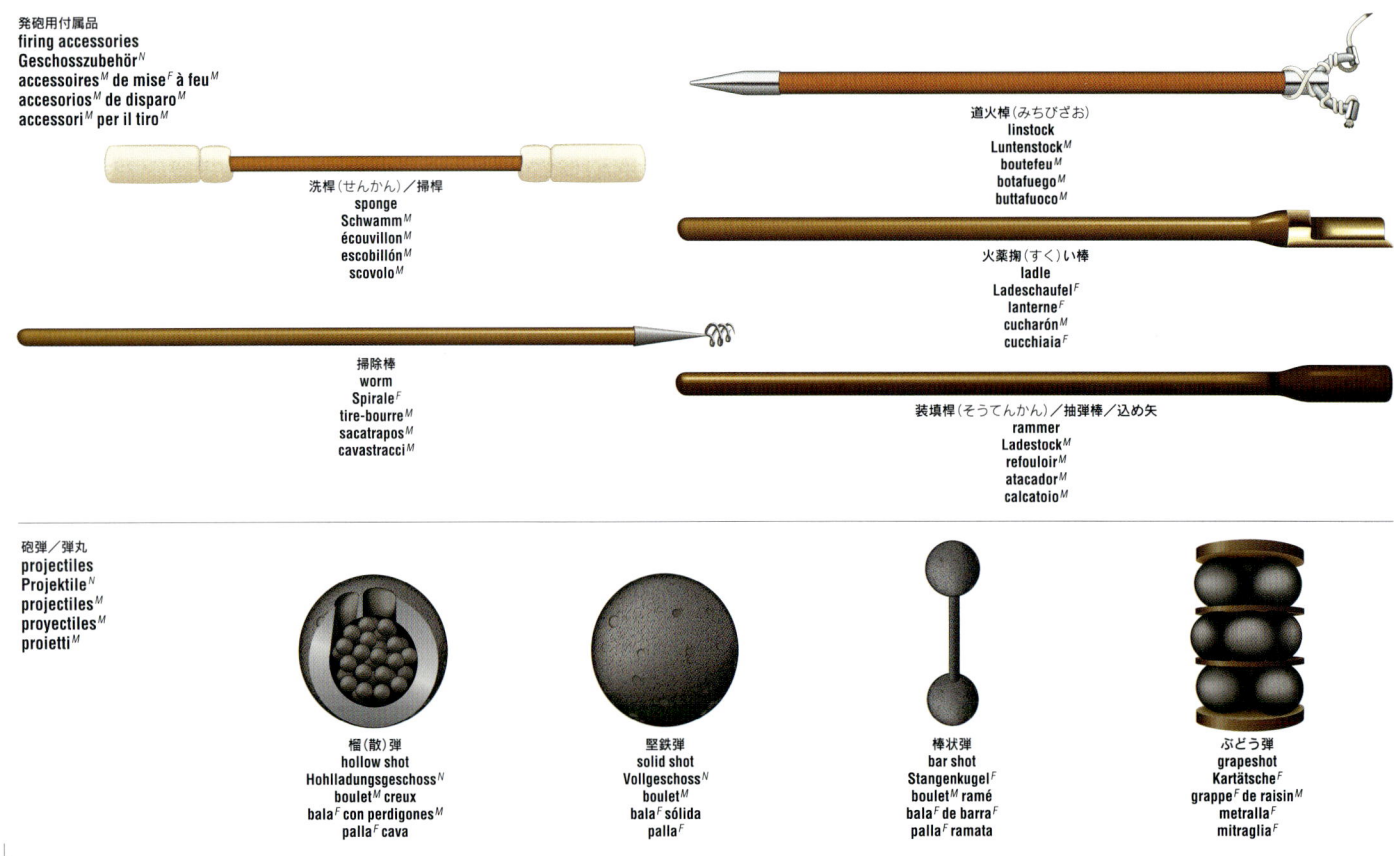

発砲用付属品
firing accessories
Geschosszubehör^N
accessoires^M de mise^F à feu^M
accesorios^M de disparo^M
accessori^M per il tiro^M

洗桿（せんかん）／掃桿
sponge
Schwamm^M
écouvillon^M
escobillón^M
scovolo^M

道火棒（みちびざお）
linstock
Luntenstock^M
boutefeu^M
botafuego^M
buttafuoco^M

火薬掬（すく）い棒
ladle
Ladeschaufel^F
lanterne^F
cucharón^M
cucchiaia^F

掃除棒
worm
Spirale^F
tire-bourre^M
sacatrapos^M
cavastracci^M

装填桿（そうてんかん）／抽弾棒／込め矢
rammer
Ladestock^M
refouloir^M
atacador^M
calcatoio^M

砲弾／弾丸
projectiles
Projektile^N
projectiles^M
proyectiles^M
proietti^M

榴（散）弾
hollow shot
Hohlladungsgeschoss^N
boulet^M creux
bala^F con perdigones^M
palla^F cava

堅鉄弾
solid shot
Vollgeschoss^N
boulet^M
bala^F sólida
palla^F

棒状弾
bar shot
Stangenkugel^F
boulet^M ramé
bala^F de barra^F
palla^F ramata

ぶどう弾
grapeshot
Kartätsche^F
grappe^F de raisin^M
metralla^F
mitraglia^F

社会

752

兵器 | WEAPONS
WAFFEN | ARMES | ARMAS | ARMI

１７世紀の大砲と臼砲（きゅうほう）

前装式砲身の断面図
cross section of a muzzle loading
Vorderlade-Geschütz^N im Querschnitt^M
coupe^F d'une bouche^F à feu^M
sección^F transversal de un cañón^M de avancarga^F
sezione^F di un cannone^M ad avancarica^F

火門
vent
Zündloch^N
lumière^F
cazoleta^F
focone^M

薬室
powder chamber
Pulverkammer^F
chambre^F à poudre^F
cámara^F de la pólvora^F
camera^F di scoppio^M

砲弾
shot
Geschoss^N
boulet^M
bala^F
palla^F

砲弾詰め材
wad
Pfropf^M
bourre^F
taco^M
stoppaccio^M

銃腔
bore
Bohrungsdurchmesser^M
âme^F
alma^F
anima^F

第二補強部［薬室覆い］
second reinforce
zweiter Ring^M
second renfort^M
segundo refuerzo^M
secondo rinforzo^M

前身
chase
langes Feld^N
volée^F
caña^F
volata^F

砲口
muzzle
Mündung^F
bouche^F
boca^F
bocca^F

前装式砲身
muzzle loading
Vorderlade-Geschütz^N
bouche^F à feu^M
cañón^M de avancarga^F
cannone^M ad avancarica^F

火門
vent
Zündloch^N
lumière^F
cazoleta^F
focone^M

第一補強部［薬室覆い］
first reinforce
erster Ring^M
renfort^M de culasse^F
refuerzo^M de la culata^F
rinforzo^M di culatta^F

砲尾環［輪帯］
base ring
Bodengesims^M
plate-bande^F de culasse^F
faja^F de la culata^F
plinto^M di culatta^F

砲尾把手［取っ手］／鈴玉／ボタン
button
Knopf^M
bouton^M de culasse^F
botón^M de la culata^F
bottone^M

砲口凸縁［凸状（装飾）刳形（くりがた）］／装飾環
astragal
Band^N
astragale^M
astrágalo^M
astragalo^M

砲耳
trunnion
Lagerzapfen^M
tourillon^M
gorrón^M
orecchione^M

車輪／ホイール
wheel
Rad^N
roue^F
rueda^F
ruota^F

楔（くさび）材／ウェッジ
wedge
Keil^M
cale^F
calce^M
cuneo^M di mira^F

側板／チーク
cheek
Lafettenwand^F
flasque^M
gualdera^F
coscia^F

砲架
carriage
Fahrgestell^N
affût^M
cureña^F
affusto^M

砲身／バレル
barrel
Rohr^N
tube^M
tubo^M
bocca^F da fuoco^M

臼砲（きゅうほう）
mortar
Mörser^M
mortier^M
mortero^M
mortaio^M

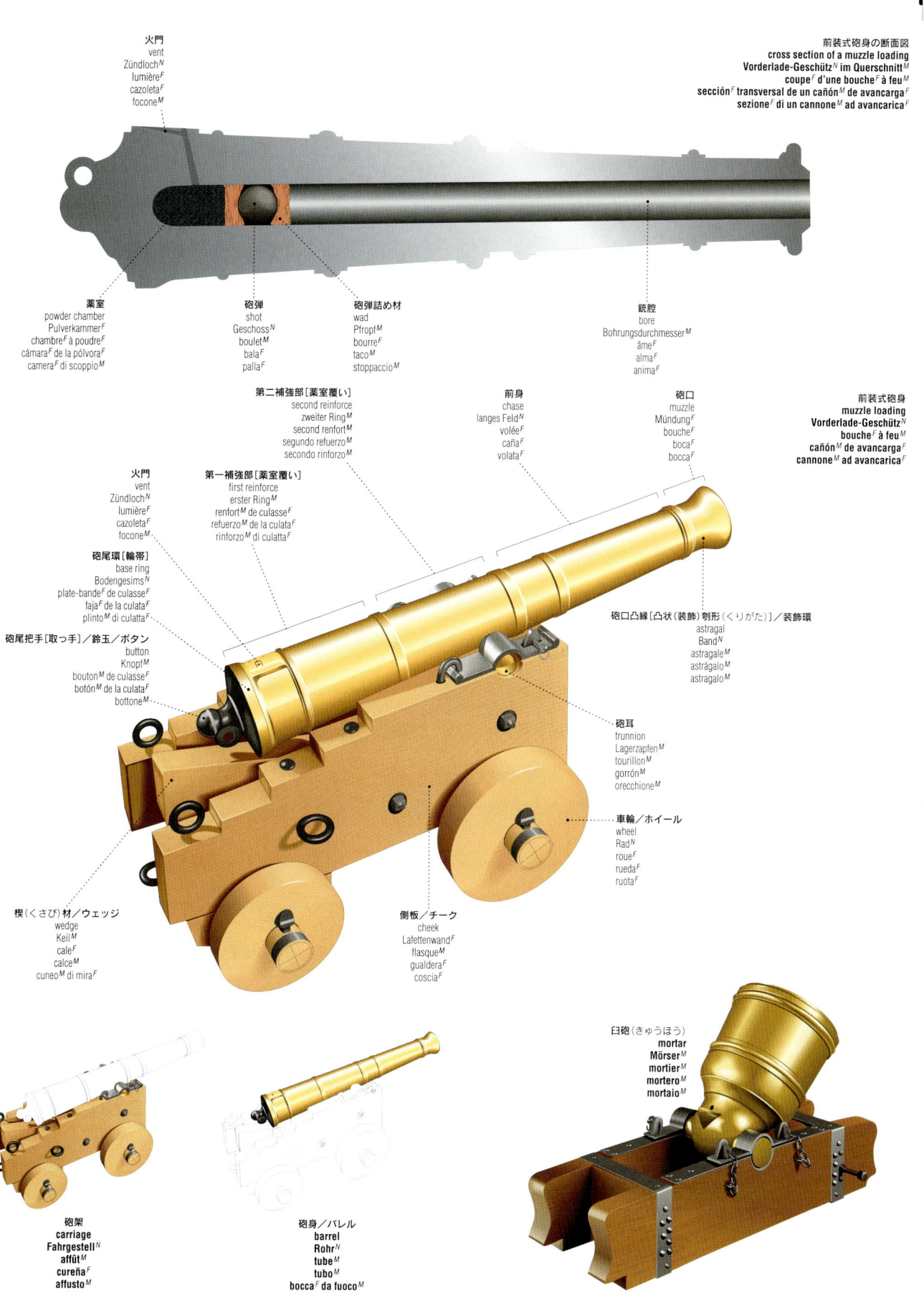

753

兵器｜WEAPONS
WAFFEN｜ARMES｜ARMAS｜ARMI

短機関銃

日本語｜英語｜ドイツ語｜フランス語｜スペイン語｜イタリア語

submachine gun ｜ Maschinenpistole F ｜ pistolet M mitrailleur M ｜ metralleta F ｜ pistola F mitragliatrice F

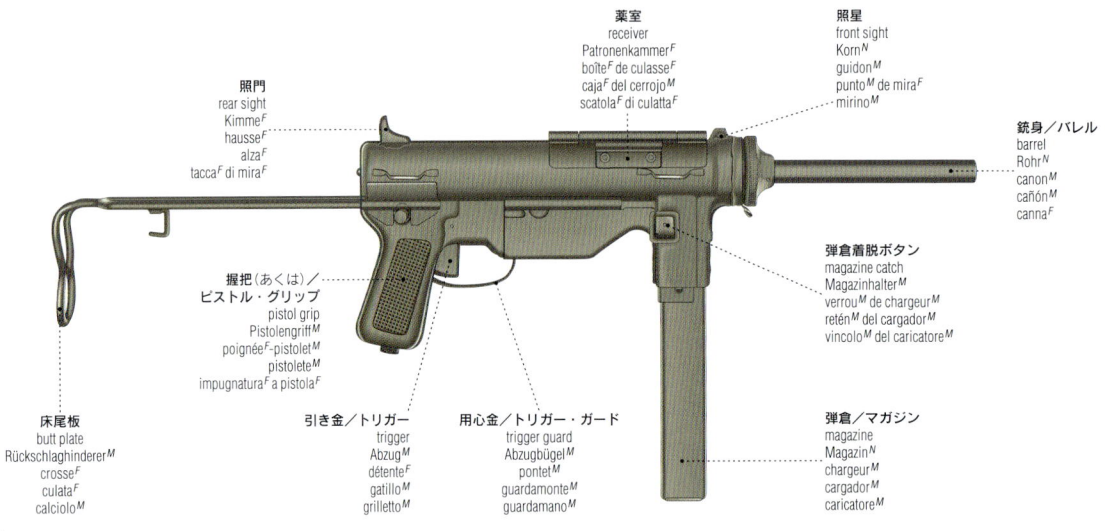

薬室
receiver
Patronenkammer F
boîte F de culasse F
caja F del cerrojo M
scatola F di culatta F

照星
front sight
Korn N
guidon M
punto M de mira F
mirino M

照門
rear sight
Kimme F
hausse F
alza F
tacca F di mira F

銃身／バレル
barrel
Rohr N
canon M
cañón M
canna F

握把（あくは）／
ピストル・グリップ
pistol grip
Pistolengriff M
poignée F-pistolet M
pistolete M
impugnatura F a pistola F

弾倉着脱ボタン
magazine catch
Magazinhalter M
verrou M de chargeur M
retén M del cargador M
vincolo M del caricatore M

床尾板
butt plate
Rückschlaghinderer M
crosse F
culata F
calciolo M

引き金／トリガー
trigger
Abzug M
détente F
gatillo M
grilletto M

用心金／トリガー・ガード
trigger guard
Abzugbügel M
pontet M
guardamonte M
guardamano M

弾倉／マガジン
magazine
Magazin N
chargeur M
cargador M
caricatore M

ピストル

pistol ｜ Pistole F ｜ pistolet M ｜ pistola F ｜ pistola F semiautomatica

照門
rear sight
Kimme F
cran M de mire F
mira F
tacca F di mira F

銃身／バレル
barrel
Rohr N
canon M
cañón M
canna F

照星
front sight
Korn N
guidon M
punto M de mira F
mirino M

撃鉄
hammer
Schlaghebel M
chien M
percutor M
cane M

遊底／スライド
slide
Schieber M
glissière F
guía F
carrello M

弾倉／マガジン
magazine
Magazin N
chargeur M
cargador M
caricatore M

用心金／トリガー・ガード
trigger guard
Abzugbügel M
pontet M
guardamonte M
guardamano M

引き金／トリガー
trigger
Abzug M
détente F
gatillo M
grilletto M

弾薬筒／薬包／カートリッジ
cartridge
Patrone F
cartouche F
cartucho M
cartuccia F

弾倉底板
magazine base
Magazinboden M
semelle F de chargeur M
base F del cargador M
fondello M del caricatore M

握り
butt
Kolben M
crosse F
culata F
impugnatura F

弾倉止め
magazine catch
Magazinhalter M
arrêtoir M de chargeur M
seguro M del cargador M
vincolo M del caricatore M

回転式（連発）拳銃／リボルバー

revolver ｜ Revolver M ｜ revolver M ｜ revólver M ｜ pistola F a tamburo M

撃鉄
hammer
Hahn M
chien M
percutor M
cane M

銃身／バレル
barrel
Rohr N
canon M
cañón M
canna F

照星
front sight
Korn N
guidon M
punto M de mira F
mirino M

回転弾倉／シリンダー
cylinder
Trommel F
barillet M
tambor M
tamburo M

銃口／銃腔
muzzle
Mündung F
bouche F
boca F
bocca F

握り
butt
Kolben M
crosse F
culata F
impugnatura F

引き金／トリガー
trigger
Abzug M
détente F
gatillo M
grilletto M

用心金／トリガー・ガード
trigger guard
Abzugbügel M
pontet M
guardamonte M
guardamano M

社会

兵器 | WEAPONS
WAFFEN | ARMES | ARMAS | ARMI

自動小銃

automatic rifle | automatisches Gewehrⁿ | fusilᴹ automatique | fusilᴹ automático | fucileᴹ automatico

- 薬室 — receiver / Patronenkammerᶠ / boîteᶠ de culasseᶠ / cajaᶠ del cerrojoᴹ / scatolaᶠ di culattaᶠ
- 照門 — rear sight / Kimmeᶠ / hausseᶠ / alzaᶠ / taccaᴹ di miraᶠ
- 銃身／バレル — barrel / Rohrᴺ / canonᴹ / cañónᴹ / cannaᶠ
- 尾筒部補助装置 — bolt assist mechanism / Schlagbolzenmechanismusᴹ / mécanismeᴹ d'assistanceᶠ de la culasseᶠ / mecanismoᴹ asistido de descargaᶠ / meccanismoᴹ di chiusuraᶠ, caricamentoᴹ e sparoᴹ
- 空薬莢（からやっきょう）排出口 — ejection port / Hülsenauswurfᴹ / fenêtreᶠ d'éjectionᶠ / ventanaᶠ de eyecciónᶠ / feritoiaᶠ di espulsioneᶠ
- 銃身被筒［覆い］ — barrel jacket / Kühlmantelᴹ für den Laufᴹ / manchonᴹ de refroidissementᴹ / manguitoᴹ de enfriamientoᴹ / manicottoᴹ di raffreddamentoᴹ
- 照星覆い — front sight housing / Kornhalterᴹ mit Kornᴺ / protège-guidonᴹ / puntoᴹ de miraᶠ / mirinoᴹ
- 槓桿（こうかん） charging handle / Durchladegriffᴹ / levierᶠ d'armementᴹ / palancaᶠ del cerrojoᴹ / manettaᶠ di caricamentoᴹ
- 握把（あくは）／ハンドガード — handguard / Handschutzᴹ / garde-mainᴹ / guardamanoᴹ / copricannaᶠ
- 消炎器 — flash hider / Feuerdämpferᴹ / cache-flammesᴹ / apagallamaᶠ / spegnifiammaᴹ
- 握把（あくは）／ピストル・グリップ — pistol grip / Pistolengriffᴹ / poignéeᶠ-pistoletᴹ / pistoleteᴹ / impugnaturaᶠ a pistolaᶠ
- 弾倉／マガジン — magazine / Magazinᴺ / chargeurᴹ / cargadorᴹ / caricatoreᴹ
- 床尾／台尻 — butt / Schulterstützeᶠ / crosseᶠ / culataᶠ / calcioloᴹ
- 引き金／トリガー — trigger / Abzugᴹ / détenteᶠ / gatilloᴹ / grillettoᴹ
- 安全装置 — safety / Sicherungᶠ / verrouᴹ de sûretéᶠ / seguroᴹ / sicuraᶠ

軽機関銃

light machine gun | leichtes Maschinengewehrᴺ | fusilᴹ mitrailleurᴹ | fusilᴹ ametralladorᴹ | mitragliatriceᶠ leggera

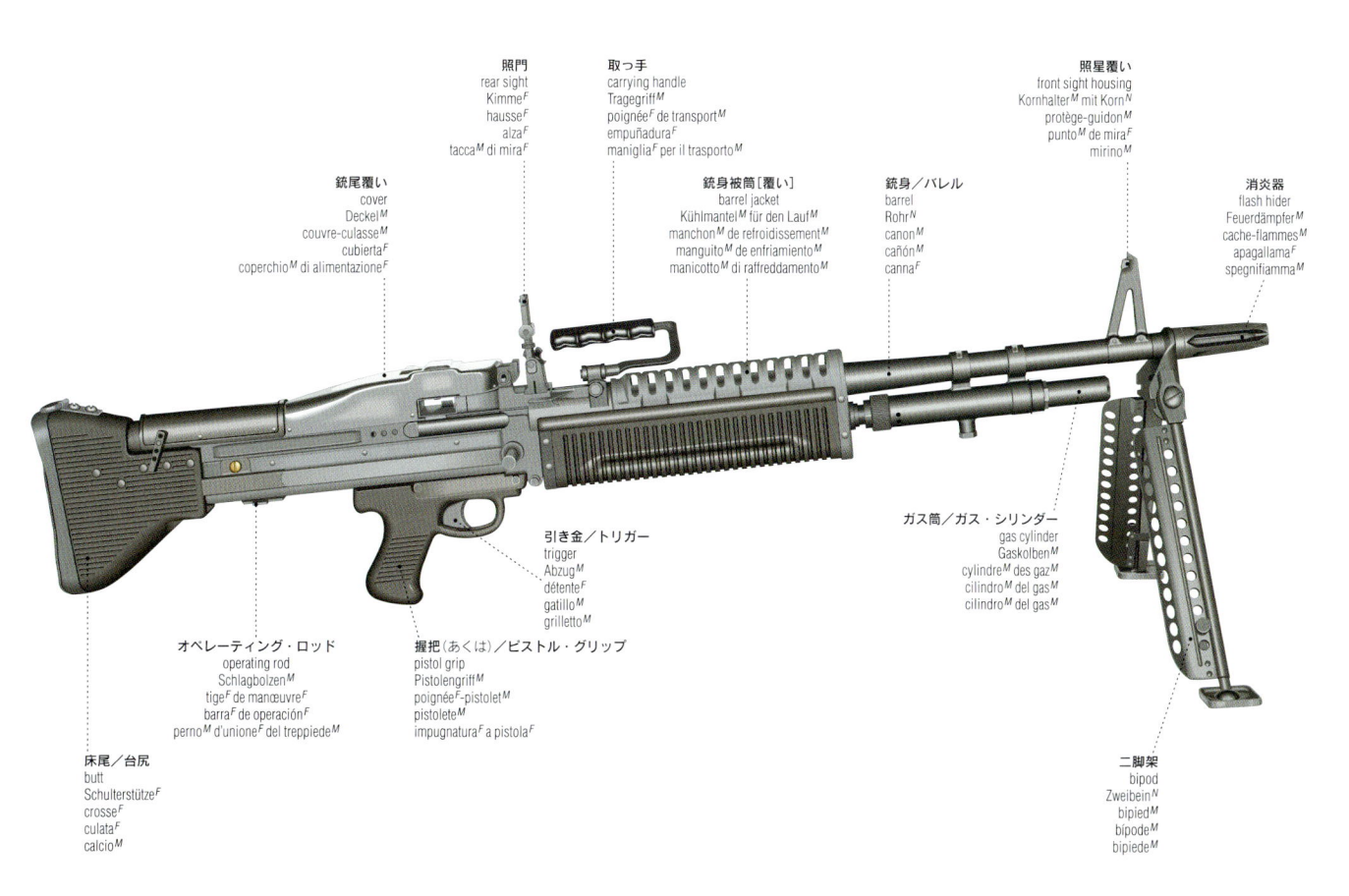

- 照門 — rear sight / Kimmeᶠ / hausseᶠ / alzaᶠ / taccaᴹ di miraᶠ
- 取っ手 — carrying handle / Tragegriffᴹ / poignéeᶠ de transportᴹ / empuñaduraᶠ / manigliaᶠ per il trasportoᴹ
- 照星覆い — front sight housing / Kornhalterᴹ mit Kornᴺ / protège-guidonᴹ / puntoᴹ de miraᶠ / mirinoᴹ
- 銃尾覆い — cover / Deckelᴹ / couvre-culasseᶠ / cubiertaᶠ / coperchioᴹ di alimentazioneᶠ
- 銃身被筒［覆い］ — barrel jacket / Kühlmantelᴹ für den Laufᴹ / manchonᴹ de refroidissementᴹ / manguitoᴹ de enfriamientoᴹ / manicottoᴹ di raffreddamentoᴹ
- 銃身／バレル — barrel / Rohrᴺ / canonᴹ / cañónᴹ / cannaᶠ
- 消炎器 — flash hider / Feuerdämpferᴹ / cache-flammesᴹ / apagallamaᶠ / spegnifiammaᴹ
- ガス筒／ガス・シリンダー — gas cylinder / Gaskolbenᴹ / cylindreᴹ des gazᴹ / cilindroᴹ del gasᴹ / cilindroᴹ del gasᴹ
- オペレーティング・ロッド — operating rod / Schlagbolzenᴹ / tigeᶠ de manœuvreᶠ / barraᶠ de operaciónᶠ / pernoᴹ d'unioneᶠ del treppiedeᴹ
- 引き金／トリガー — trigger / Abzugᴹ / détenteᶠ / gatilloᴹ / grillettoᴹ
- 握把（あくは）／ピストル・グリップ — pistol grip / Pistolengriffᴹ / poignéeᶠ-pistoletᴹ / pistoleteᴹ / impugnaturaᶠ a pistolaᶠ
- 床尾／台尻 — butt / Schulterstützeᶠ / crosseᶠ / culataᶠ / calcioᴹ
- 二脚架 — bipod / Zweibeinᴺ / bipiedᴹ / bípodeᴹ / bipiedeᴹ

社会

兵器 | WEAPONS
WAFFEN | ARMES | ARMAS | ARMI

現代の榴弾砲

modern howitzer | moderne Haubitze^F | obusier^M moderne | obús^M moderno | obice^M moderno

閉鎖機操作桿（かん）
breechblock operating lever assembly
Bedienungshebel^M für Verschlussblock^M
levier^M de manœuvre^F de la culasse^F
palanca^F de accionamiento de la recámara^F
leva^F di manovra^F dell'otturatore^M

復座機
recuperator cylinder
Vorholer^M
cylindre^M récupérateur
cilindro^M de recuperación^F
cilindro^M ricuperatore

滑動部
recoil sleigh
Rohrrücklauf^M
glissoire^F de recul^M
patín^M de retroceso^M
slitta^F di rinculo^M

牽引棒止め具
drawbar lock
Zugstangenverschluss^M
verrou^M de barre^F d'attelage^M
seguro^M de la barra^F de tracción^F
fermo^M del braccio^M d'attacco^M dell'occhione^M

閉鎖機
breechblock
Verschlussblock^M
culasse^F
bloque^M de cierre^M de la recámara^F
prisma^M otturatore

俯仰（ふぎょう）装置／高低照準装置
elevating arc
Zahnbogen^M
crémaillère^F de pointage^M
arco^M de elevación^F
arco^M dentato di elevazione^F

復座管先端部
recuperator cylinder front head
Vorholervorderteil^N
tête^F avant du cylindre^M récupérateur
cabeza^F delantera del cilindro^M de recuperación^F
testa^F del cilindro^M ricuperatore

牽引棒
drawbar
Zugstange^F
barre^F d'attelage^M
barra^F de tracción^F
braccio^M d'attacco^M dell'occhione^M

可動砲尾
sliding breech
Schubkurbelverschluss^M
manchon^M de culasse^F
placa^F de la culata^F
culatta^F mobile

架尾環（かん）
towing eye
Auge^N
lunette^F
argolla^F de remolque^M
occhione^M

発射桿（かん）
firing shaft
Schlagbolzenschaft^M
arbre^M de mise^F à feu^M
eje^M de tiro^M
asta^F di sparo^M

砲身／バレル
barrel
Rohr^N
canon^M
cañón^M
bocca^F da fuoco^M

揺架（ようか）
cradle
Wiege^F
berceau^M
cuña^F
culla^F

緊締環
locking ring
Verschlussring^M
cercle^M de verrouillage^F
anillo^M de bloqueo^M
ghiera^F di bloccaggio^M

架尾／脚
trail
Schleppstange^F
crosse^F
gualdera^F
coda^F

砲架
carriage
Fahrgestell^N
affût^M
afuste^M
affusto^M

可動板
float
Schwimmer^M
flotteur^M
flotador^M
dente^M di roccia^F

把手
lifting handle
Hebegriff^M
poignée^F de soulèvement^M
asa^F de levantamiento^M
maniglia^F di sollevamento^M

平衡機
equilibrator
Gewichtsausgleicher^M
équilibreur^M
estabilizador^M
equilibratore^M

俯仰（ふぎょう）ハンドル
elevating hand-wheel
Höhenrichtwerk^N
manivelle^F de pointage^M en hauteur^F
rueda^F de elevación^F
volantino^M di puntamento^M in elevazione^F

駐鋤（ちゅうじょ）
spade
Spaten^M
bêche^F
pala^F
vomere^M

引き綱
firing lanyard
Abzugsleine^F
cordon^M tire-feu^M
cuerda^F de disparo^M
funicella^F di sparo^M

現代の迫撃砲

modern mortar | Granatwerfer^M | mortier^M moderne | mortero^M moderno | mortaio^M moderno

砲口
muzzle
Mündung^F
bouche^F
boca^F
bocca^F

照準器
sight
Richtaufsatz^M
appareil^M de pointage^M
mira^F
congegno^M di puntamento^M

俯仰（ふぎょう）ハンドル
elevating handle
Höheneinstellhebel^M
manivelle^F de pointage^M en hauteur^F
manivela^F de elevación^F
volantino^M di puntamento^M in elevazione^F

旋回ハンドル
traversing handle
Richtkurbel^F
manivelle^F de pointage^M en direction^F
manivela^F de dirección^F
volantino^M di puntamento^M in direzione^F

砲身
tube
Rohr^N
tube^M
tubo^M
tubo^M di lancio^M

二脚架
bipod
Zweibein^N
bipied^M
bípode^M
bipiede^M

底板
base plate
Grundplatte^F
plaque^F de base^F
placa^F de apoyo^M
piastra^F di appoggio^M

兵器 | WEAPONS
WAFFEN | ARMES | ARMAS | ARMI

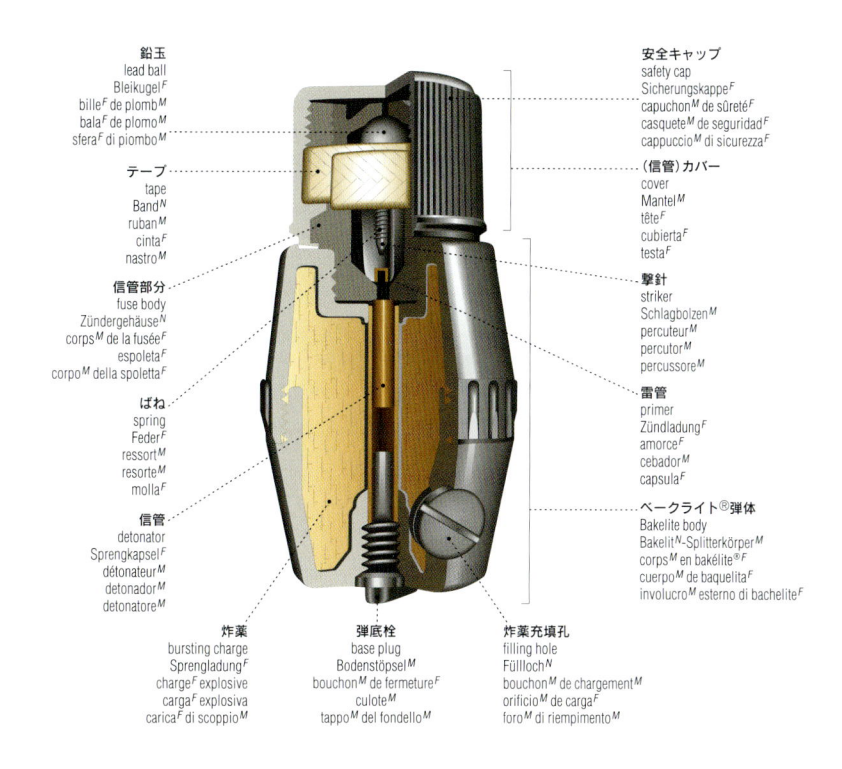

手榴弾

hand grenade | Handgranate^F | grenade^F à main^F | granada^F de mano^F | bomba^F a mano^F

鉛玉
lead ball
Bleikugel^F
bille^F de plomb^M
bala^F de plomo^M
sfera^F di piombo^M

テープ
tape
Band^N
ruban^M
cinta^F
nastro^M

信管部分
fuse body
Zündergehäuse^N
corps^M de la fusée^F
espoleta^F
corpo^M della spoletta^F

ばね
spring
Feder^F
ressort^M
resorte^M
molla^F

信管
detonator
Sprengkapsel^F
détonateur^M
detonador^M
detonatore^M

安全キャップ
safety cap
Sicherungskappe^F
capuchon^M de sûreté^F
casquete^M de seguridad^F
cappuccio^M di sicurezza^F

(信管)カバー
cover
Mantel^M
tête^F
cubierta^F
testa^F

撃針
striker
Schlagbolzen^M
percuteur^M
percutor^M
percussore^M

雷管
primer
Zündladung^F
amorce^F
cebador^M
capsula^F

ベークライト®弾体
Bakelite body
Bakelit^N-Splitterkörper^M
corps^M en bakélite^{®F}
cuerpo^M de baquelita^F
involucro^M esterno di bachelite^F

炸薬
bursting charge
Sprengladung^F
charge^F explosive
carga^F explosiva
carica^F di scoppio^M

弾底栓
base plug
Bodenstöpsel^M
bouchon^M de fermeture^F
culote^M
tappo^M del fondello^M

炸薬充填孔
filling hole
Füllloch^N
bouchon^M de chargement^M
orificio^M de carga^F
foro^M di riempimento^M

バズーカ砲

bazooka | Panzerfaust^F | bazooka^M | bazuca^F | bazooka^M

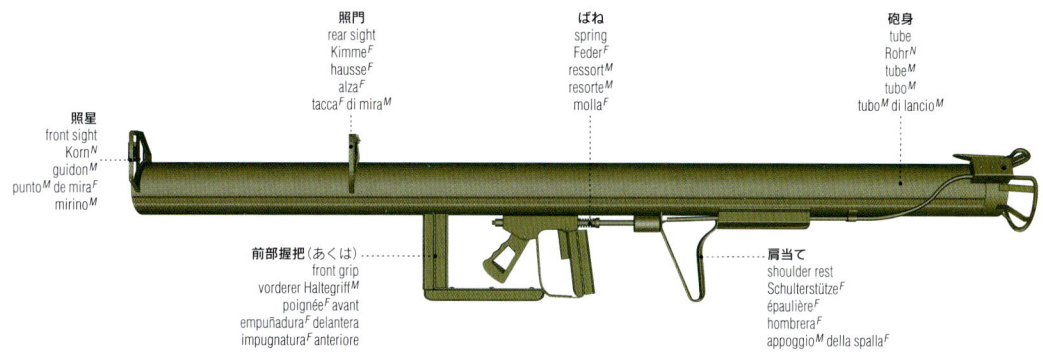

照門
rear sight
Kimme^F
hausse^F
alza^F
tacca^F di mira^M

ばね
spring
Feder^F
ressort^M
resorte^M
molla^F

砲身
tube
Rohr^N
tube^M
tubo^M
tubo^M di lancio^M

照星
front sight
Korn^N
guidon^M
punto^M de mira^F
mirino^M

前部握把（あくは）
front grip
vorderer Haltegriff^M
poignée^F avant
empuñadura^F delantera
impugnatura^F anteriore

肩当て
shoulder rest
Schulterstütze^F
épaulière^F
hombrera^F
appoggio^M della spalla^F

無反動ライフル

recoilless rifle | rückstoßfreies Geschütz^N | canon^M sans recul^M | cañón^M sin retroceso^M | cannone^M senza rinculo^M

砲身
barrel
Rohr^N
tube^M
cañón^M
tubo^M di lancio^M

肩当て
shoulder rest
Schulterstütze^F
épaulière^F
apoyo^M de espalda^M
appoggio^M della spalla^F

ベンチュリ管固定レバー
venturi fastening lever
Feststellhebel^M für Venturidüse^F
levier^M de fixation^F de venturi^M
palanca^F de fijación^F del venturi^M
leva^F di fissaggio^M del venturi^M

ベンチュリ管
venturi
Venturidüse^F
venturi^M
venturi^M
venturi^M

前部握把（あくは）
front grip
vorderer Haltegriff^M
poignée^F avant
empuñadura^F delantera
impugnatura^F anteriore

引き金／トリガー
trigger
Abzug^M
détente^F
gatillo^M
grilletto^M

槓桿（こうかん）
cocking lever
Spannhebel^M
levier^M d'armement^M
palanca^F de armar
leva^F d'armamento^M

撃発装置
firing mechanism
Zündmechanismus^M
mécanisme^M de tir^M
mecanismo^M de disparo^M
congegno^M di sparo^M

対戦車ロケット弾
antitank rocket
Panzerabwehrgeschoss^N
projectile^M antichar
cohete^M anticarro
proiettile^M anticarro

兵器 | WEAPONS
WAFFEN | ARMES | ARMAS | ARMI

対人地雷

antipersonnel mine | Antipersonenmine^F | mine^F antipersonnel | minas^M antipersonas | mina^F antiuomo

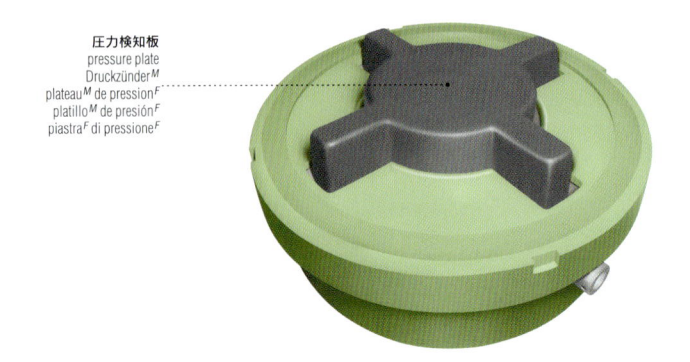

日本語 | 英語 | ドイツ語 | フランス語 | スペイン語 | イタリア語

圧力検知板
pressure plate
Druckzünder^M
plateau^M de pression
platillo^M de presión^F
piastra^F di pressione^F

戦車

tank | Panzer^M | char^M d'assaut^M | carro^M de combate^M | carro^M armato

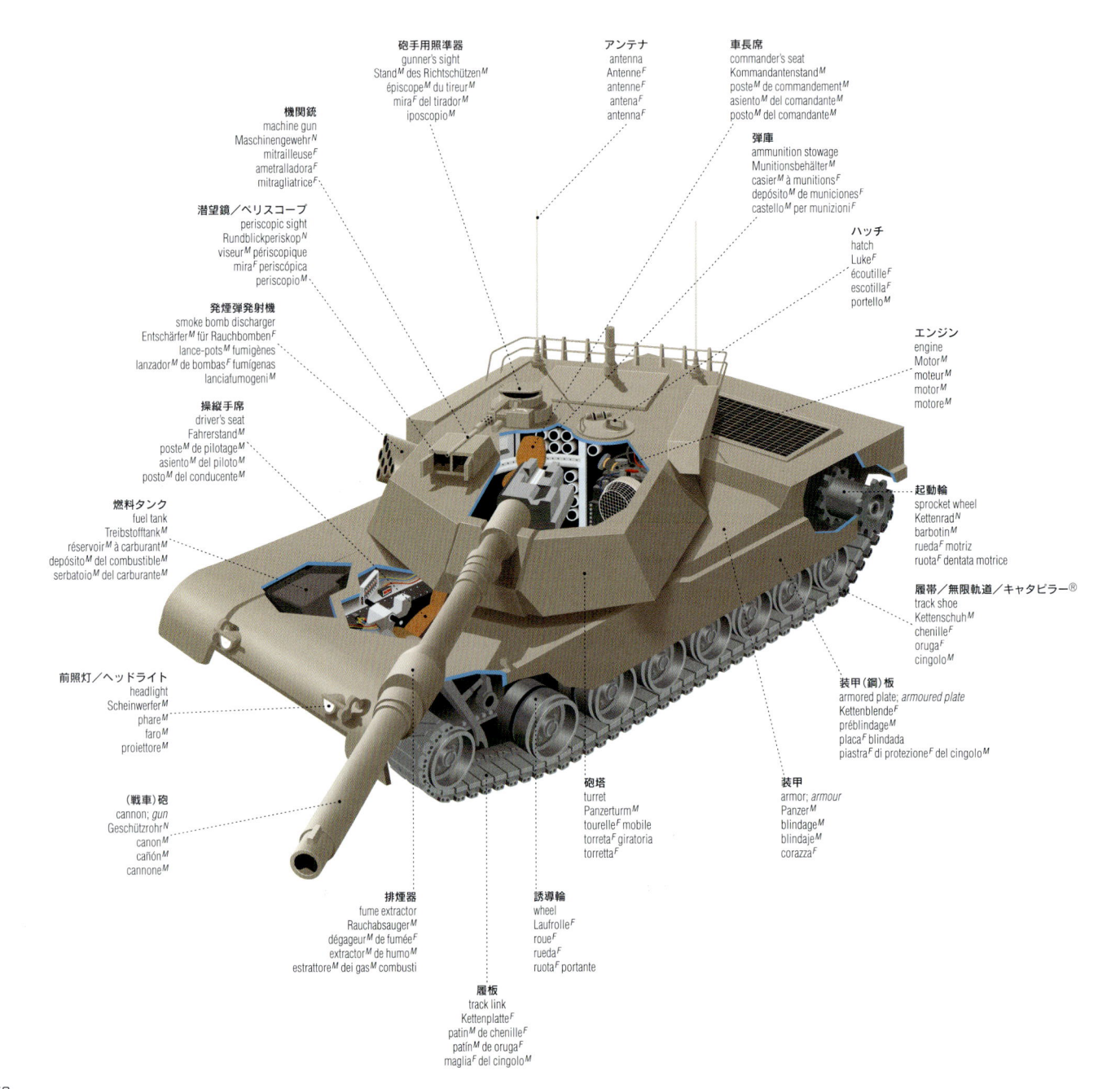

砲手用照準器
gunner's sight
Stand^M des Richtschützen^M
épiscope^M du tireur^M
mira^F del tirador^M
iposcopio^M

アンテナ
antenna
Antenne^F
antenne^F
antena^F
antenna^F

車長席
commander's seat
Kommandantenstand^M
poste^M de commandement^M
asiento^M del comandante^M
posto^M del comandante^M

機関銃
machine gun
Maschinengewehr^N
mitrailleuse^F
ametralladora^F
mitragliatrice^F

弾庫
ammunition stowage
Munitionsbehälter^M
casier^M à munitions^F
depósito^M de municiones^F
castello^M per munizioni^F

潜望鏡／ペリスコープ
periscopic sight
Rundblickperiskop^N
viseur^M périscopique
mira^F periscópica
periscopio^M

ハッチ
hatch
Luke^F
écoutille^F
escotilla^F
portello^M

発煙弾発射機
smoke bomb discharger
Entschärfer^M für Rauchbomben^F
lance-pots^M fumigènes
lanzador^M de bombas^F fumígenas
lanciafumogeni^M

エンジン
engine
Motor^M
moteur^M
motor^M
motore^M

操縦手席
driver's seat
Fahrerstand
poste^M de pilotage^M
asiento^M del piloto^M
posto^M del conducente^M

起動輪
sprocket wheel
Kettenrad^N
barbotin^F
rueda^F motriz
ruota^F dentata motrice

燃料タンク
fuel tank
Treibstofftank^M
réservoir^M à carburant^M
depósito^M del combustible^M
serbatoio^M del carburante^M

履帯／無限軌道／キャタピラー®
track shoe
Kettenschuh^M
chenille^F
oruga^F
cingolo^M

装甲(鋼)板
armored plate; armoured plate
Kettenblende^F
préblindage^M
placa^F blindada
piastra^F di protezione^F del cingolo

前照灯／ヘッドライト
headlight
Scheinwerfer^M
phare^M
faro^M
proiettore^M

装甲
armor; armour
Panzer^M
blindage^M
blindaje^M
corazza^F

(戦車)砲
cannon; gun
Geschützrohr^N
canon^M
cañón^M
cannone^M

砲塔
turret
Panzerturm^M
tourelle^F mobile
torreta^F giratoria
torretta^F

排煙器
fume extractor
Rauchabsauger^M
dégageur^M de fumée^F
extractor^M de humo^M
estrattore^M dei gas^M combusti

誘導輪
wheel
Laufrolle^F
roue^F
rueda^F
ruota^F portante

履板
track link
Kettenplatte^F
patin^M de chenille^F
patín^M de oruga^F
maglia^F del cingolo^M

兵器 | WEAPONS
WAFFEN | ARMES | ARMAS | ARMI

ミサイル

missiles | Flugkörper[M] | missiles[M] | proyectiles[M] | missili[M]

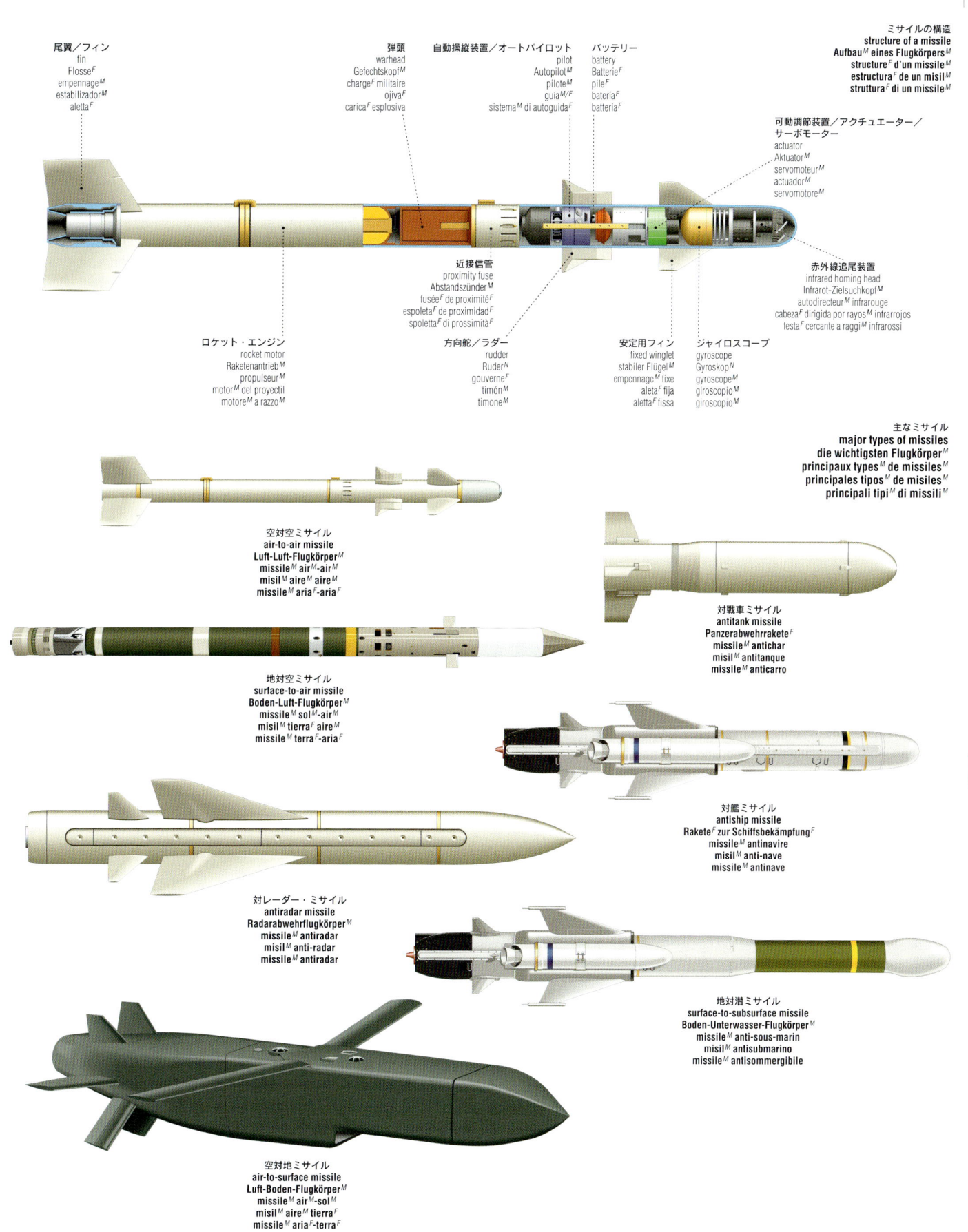

ミサイルの構造
structure of a missile
Aufbau[M] eines Flugkörpers[M]
structure[F] d'un missile[M]
estructura[F] de un misil[M]
struttura[F] di un missile[M]

尾翼／フィン — fin / Flosse[F] / empennage[M] / estabilizador[M] / aletta[F]

弾頭 — warhead / Gefechtskopf[M] / charge[F] militaire / ojiva[F] / carica[F] esplosiva

自動操縦装置／オートパイロット — pilot / Autopilot[M] / pilote[M] / guía[M/F] / sistema[M] di autoguida[F]

バッテリー — battery / Batterie[F] / pile[F] / batería[F] / batteria[F]

可動調節装置／アクチュエーター／サーボモーター — actuator / Aktuator[M] / servomoteur[M] / actuador[M] / servomotore[M]

近接信管 — proximity fuse / Abstandszünder[M] / fusée[F] de proximité / espoleta[F] de proximidad / spoletta[F] di prossimità[F]

赤外線追尾装置 — infrared homing head / Infrarot-Zielsuchkopf[M] / autodirecteur[M] infrarouge / cabeza[F] dirigida por rayos[M] infrarrojos / testa[F] cercante a raggi[M] infrarossi

ロケット・エンジン — rocket motor / Raketenantrieb[M] / propulseur[M] / motor[M] del proyectil / motore[M] a razzo[M]

方向舵／ラダー — rudder / Ruder[N] / gouverne[F] / timón[M] / timone[M]

安定用フィン — fixed winglet / stabiler Flügel[M] / empennage[M] fixe / aleta[F] fija / aletta[F] fissa

ジャイロスコープ — gyroscope / Gyroskop[N] / gyroscope[M] / giroscopio[M] / giroscopio[M]

主なミサイル
major types of missiles
die wichtigsten Flugkörper[M]
principaux types[M] de missiles[M]
principales tipos[M] de misiles[M]
principali tipi[M] di missili[M]

空対空ミサイル — air-to-air missile / Luft-Luft-Flugkörper[M] / missile[M] air[M]-air[M] / misil[M] aire[M] aire[M] / missile[M] aria[F]-aria[F]

対戦車ミサイル — antitank missile / Panzerabwehrrakete[F] / missile[M] antichar / misil[M] antitanque / missile[M] anticarro

地対空ミサイル — surface-to-air missile / Boden-Luft-Flugkörper[M] / missile[M] sol[M]-air[M] / misil[M] tierra[F] aire[M] / missile[M] terra[F]-aria[F]

対艦ミサイル — antiship missile / Rakete[F] zur Schiffsbekämpfung[F] / missile[M] antinavire / misil[M] anti-nave / missile[M] antinave

対レーダー・ミサイル — antiradar missile / Radarabwehrflugkörper[M] / missile[M] antiradar / misil[M] anti-radar / missile[M] antiradar

地対潜ミサイル — surface-to-subsurface missile / Boden-Unterwasser-Flugkörper[M] / missile[M] anti-sous-marin / misil[M] antisubmarino / missile[M] antisommergibile

空対地ミサイル — air-to-surface missile / Luft-Boden-Flugkörper[M] / missile[M] air[M]-sol[M] / misil[M] aire[M] tierra[F] / missile[M] aria[F]-terra[F]

社会

759

兵器 | WEAPONS
WAFFEN | ARMES | ARMAS | ARMI

戦闘機

combat aircraft | Kampfflugzeug^N | avion^M de combat^M | avión^M de combate^M | aeroplano^M da combattimento^M

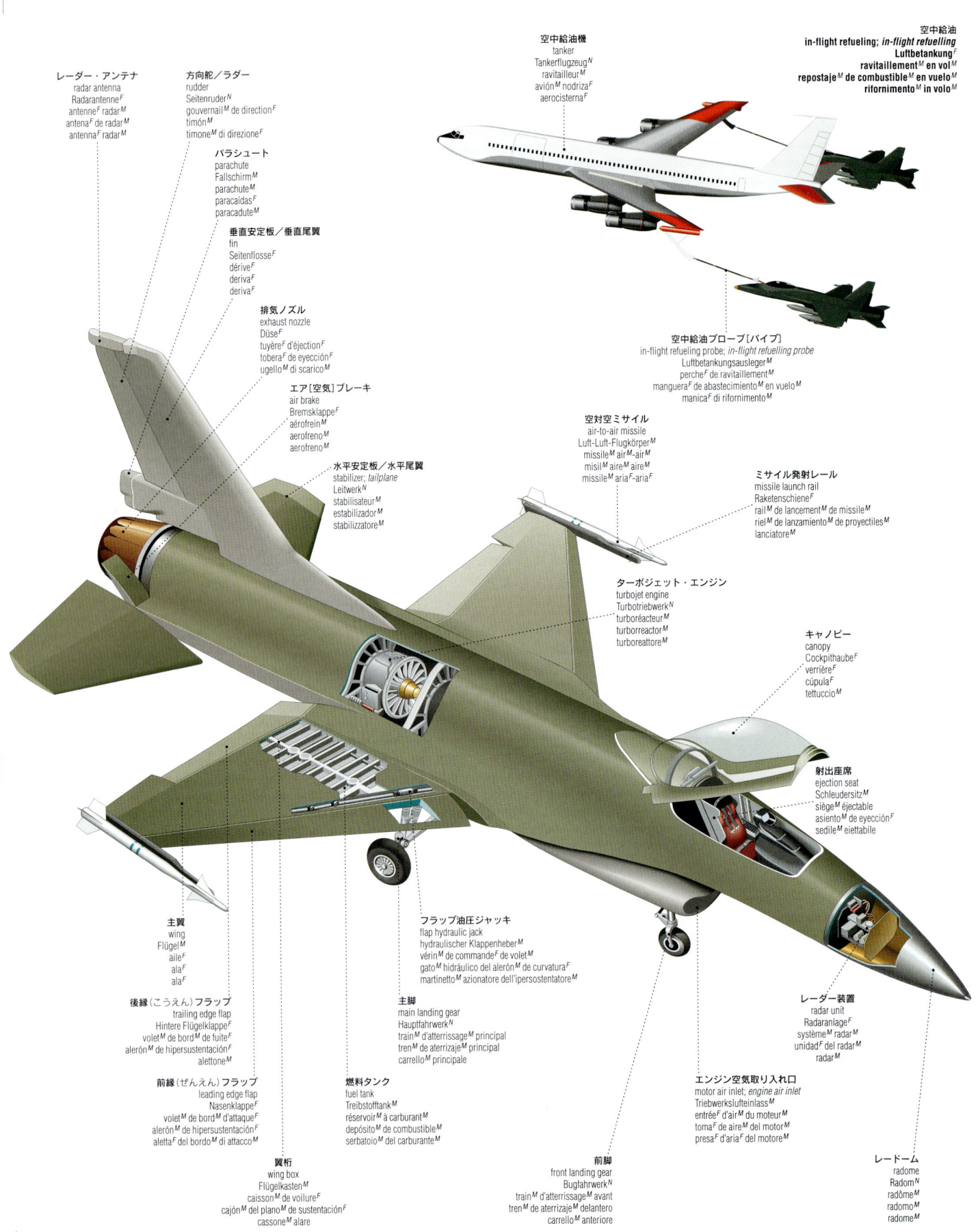

日本語 | 英語 | ドイツ語 | フランス語 | スペイン語 | イタリア語

レーダー・アンテナ
radar antenna
Radarantenne^F
antenne^F radar^M
antena^F de radar^M
antenna^F radar^M

方向舵／ラダー
rudder
Seitenruder^N
gouvernail^M de direction^F
timón^M
timone^M di direzione^F

パラシュート
parachute
Fallschirm^M
parachute^M
paracaídas^F
paracadute^M

垂直安定板／垂直尾翼
fin
Seitenflosse^F
dérive^F
deriva^F
deriva^F

排気ノズル
exhaust nozzle
Düse^F
tuyère^F d'éjection^F
tobera^F de eyección^F
ugello^M di scarico^M

エア[空気]ブレーキ
air brake
Bremsklappe^F
aérofrein^M
aerofreno^M
aerofreno^M

水平安定板／水平尾翼
stabilizer; *tailplane*
Leitwerk^N
stabilisateur^M
estabilizador^M
stabilizzatore^M

空中給油機
tanker
Tankerflugzeug^N
ravitailleur^M
avión^M nodriza^F
aerocisterna^F

空中給油
in-flight refueling; *in-flight refuelling*
Luftbetankung^F
ravitaillement^M en vol^M
repostaje^M de combustible^M en vuelo^M
rifornimento^M in volo^M

空中給油プローブ[パイプ]
in-flight refueling probe; *in-flight refuelling probe*
Luftbetankungsausleger^M
perche^F de ravitaillement^M
manguera^F de abastecimiento^M en vuelo^M
manica^F di rifornimento^M

空対空ミサイル
air-to-air missile
Luft-Luft-Flugkörper^M
missile^M air^M-air^M
misil^M aire^M aire^M
missile^M aria^F-aria^F

ミサイル発射レール
missile launch rail
Raketenschiene^F
rail^M de lancement^M de missile^M
riel^M de lanzamiento^M de proyectiles^M
lanciatore^M

ターボジェット・エンジン
turbojet engine
Turbotriebwerk^N
turboréacteur^M
turboreactor^M
turboreattore^M

キャノピー
canopy
Cockpithaube^F
verrière^F
cúpula^F
tettuccio^M

射出座席
ejection seat
Schleudersitz^M
siège^M éjectable
asiento^M de eyección^F
sedile^M eiettabile

主翼
wing
Flügel^M
aile^F
ala^F
ala^F

後縁（こうえん）フラップ
trailing edge flap
Hintere Flügelklappe^F
volet^M de bord^M de fuite^F
alerón^M de hipersustentación^F
alettone^M

前縁（ぜんえん）フラップ
leading edge flap
Nasenklappe^F
volet^M de bord^M d'attaque^F
alerón^M de hipersustentación^F
aletta^F del bordo^M di attacco^M

フラップ油圧ジャッキ
flap hydraulic jack
hydraulischer Klappenheber^M
vérin^M de commande^F de volet^M
gato^M hidráulico del alerón^M de curvatura^F
martinetto^M azionatore dell'ipersostentatore^M

主脚
main landing gear
Hauptfahrwerk^N
train^M d'atterrissage^M principal
tren^M de aterrizaje^M principal
carrello^M principale

燃料タンク
fuel tank
Treibstofftank^M
réservoir^M à carburant^M
depósito^M de combustible^M
serbatoio^M del carburante^M

翼桁
wing box
Flügelkasten^M
caisson^M de voilure^F
cajón^M del plano^M de sustentación^F
cassone^M alare

前脚
front landing gear
Bugfahrwerk^N
train^M d'atterrissage^M avant
tren^M de aterrizaje^M delantero
carrello^M anteriore

エンジン空気取り入れ口
motor air inlet; *engine air inlet*
Triebwerkslufteinlass^M
entrée^F d'air^M du moteur^M
toma^F de aire^M del motor^M
presa^F d'aria^F del motore^M

レーダー装置
radar unit
Radaranlage^F
système^M radar^M
unidad^F del radar^M
radar^M

レードーム
radome
Radom^N
radôme^M
radomo^M
radome^M

兵器 | WEAPONS
WAFFEN | ARMES | ARMAS | ARMI

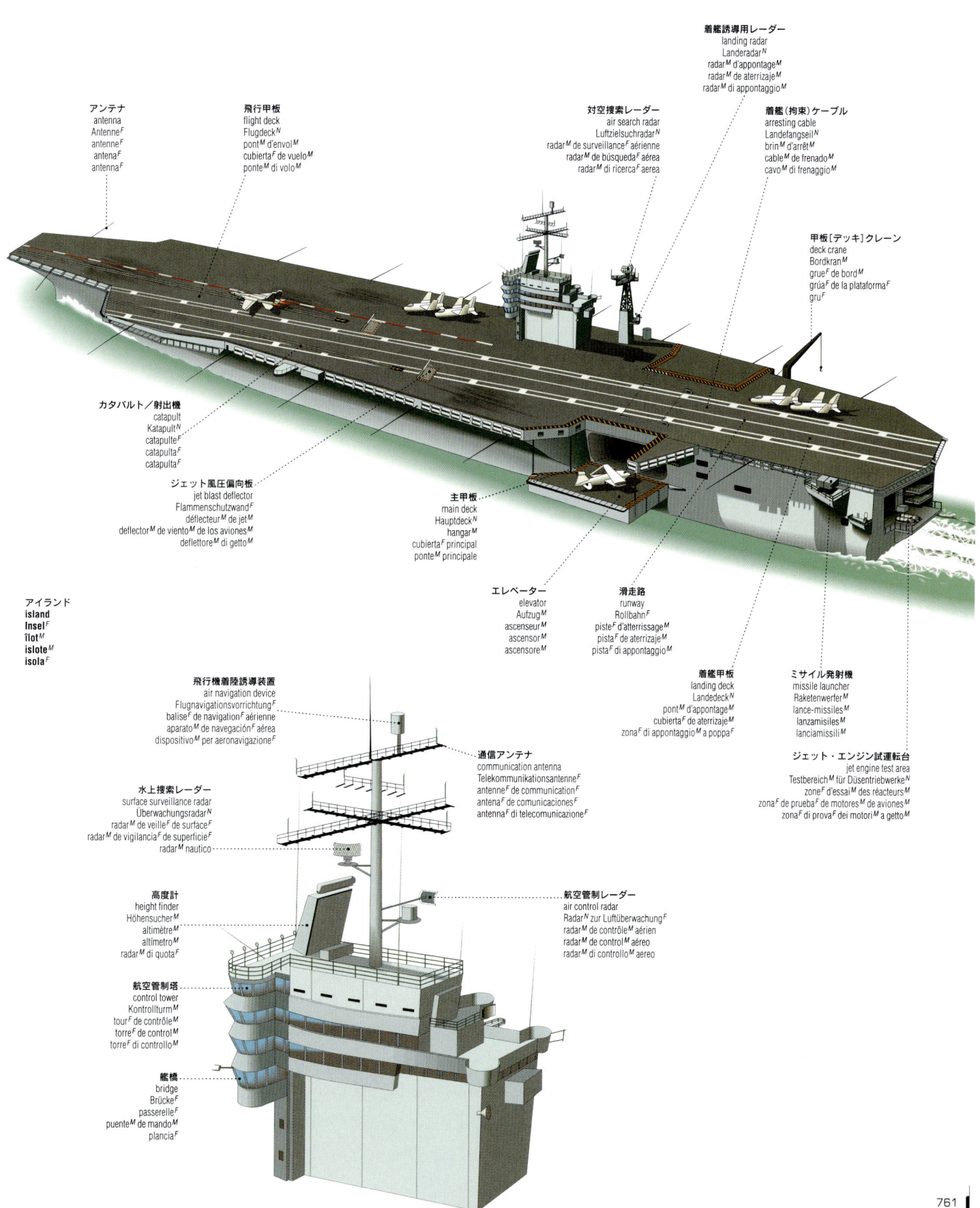

航空母艦／空母

aircraft carrier | Flugzeugträgerᴹ | porte-avionsᴹ | portaavionesᴹ | portaereiꜰ

着艦誘導用レーダー
landing radar
Landeradarᴺ
radarᴹ d'appontageᴹ
radarᴹ de aterrizajeᴹ
radarᴹ di appontaggioᴹ

アンテナ
antenna
Antenneꜰ
antenneꜰ
antenaꜰ
antennaꜰ

飛行甲板
flight deck
Flugdeckᴺ
pontᴹ d'envolᴹ
cubiertaꜰ de vueloᴹ
ponteᴹ di voloᴹ

対空捜索レーダー
air search radar
Luftzielsuchradarᴺ
radarᴹ de surveillanceꜰ aérienne
radarᴹ de búsquedaꜰ aérea
radarᴹ di ricercaꜰ aerea

着艦(拘束)ケーブル
arresting cable
Landefangseilᴺ
brinᴹ d'arrêtᴹ
cableᴹ de frenadoᴹ
cavoᴹ di frenaggioᴹ

甲板[デッキ]クレーン
deck crane
Bordkranᴹ
grueꜰ de bordᴹ
grúaꜰ de la plataformaꜰ
gruꜰ

カタパルト／射出機
catapult
Katapultᴺ
catapulteꜰ
catapultaꜰ
catapultaꜰ

ジェット風圧偏向板
jet blast deflector
Flammenschutzwandꜰ
déflecteurᴹ de jetᴹ
deflectorᴹ de vientoᴹ de los avionesᴹ
deflettoreᴹ di gettoᴹ

主甲板
main deck
Hauptdeckᴺ
hangarᴹ
cubiertaꜰ principal
ponteᴹ principale

アイランド
island
Inselꜰ
îlotᴹ
isloteᴹ
isolaꜰ

エレベーター
elevator
Aufzugᴹ
ascenseurᴹ
ascensorᴹ
ascensoreᴹ

滑走路
runway
Rollbahnꜰ
pisteꜰ d'atterrissageᴹ
pistaꜰ de aterrizajeᴹ
pistaꜰ di appontaggioᴹ

着艦甲板
landing deck
Landedeckᴺ
pontᴹ d'appontageᴹ
cubiertaꜰ de aterrizajeᴹ
zonaꜰ di appontaggioᴹ a poppaꜰ

ミサイル発射機
missile launcher
Raketenwerferᴹ
lance-missilesᴹ
lanzamisilesᴹ
lanciamissiliᴹ

飛行機着陸誘導装置
air navigation device
Flugnavigationsvorrichtungꜰ
baliseꜰ de navigationꜰ aérienne
aparatoᴹ de navegaciónꜰ aérea
dispositivoᴹ per aeronavigazioneꜰ

通信アンテナ
communication antenna
Telekommunikationsantenneꜰ
antenneꜰ de communicationꜰ
antenaꜰ de comunicacionesꜰ
antennaꜰ di telecomunicazioneꜰ

ジェット・エンジン試運転台
jet engine test area
Testbereichᴹ für Düsentriebwerkeᴺ
zoneꜰ d'essaiᴹ des réacteursᴹ
zonaꜰ de pruebaꜰ de motoresᴹ de avionesᴹ
zonaꜰ di provaꜰ dei motoriᴹ a gettoᴹ

水上捜索レーダー
surface surveillance radar
Überwachungsradarᴺ
radarᴹ de veilleꜰ de surfaceꜰ
radarᴹ de vigilanciaꜰ de superficieꜰ
radarᴹ nautico

高度計
height finder
Höhensucherᴹ
altimètreᴹ
altímetroᴹ
radarᴹ di quotaꜰ

航空管制レーダー
air control radar
Radarᴺ zur Luftüberwachungꜰ
radarᴹ de contrôleᴹ aérien
radarᴹ de controlᴹ aéreo
radarᴹ di controlloᴹ aereo

航空管制塔
control tower
Kontrollturmᴹ
tourꜰ de contrôleꜰ
torreꜰ de controlᴹ
torreꜰ di controlloᴹ

艦橋
bridge
Brückeꜰ
passerelleꜰ
puenteᴹ de mandoᴹ
planciaꜰ

社会

兵器 | WEAPONS
WAFFEN | ARMES | ARMAS | ARMI

フリゲート艦

frigate | Fregatte^F | frégate^F | fragata^F | fregata^F

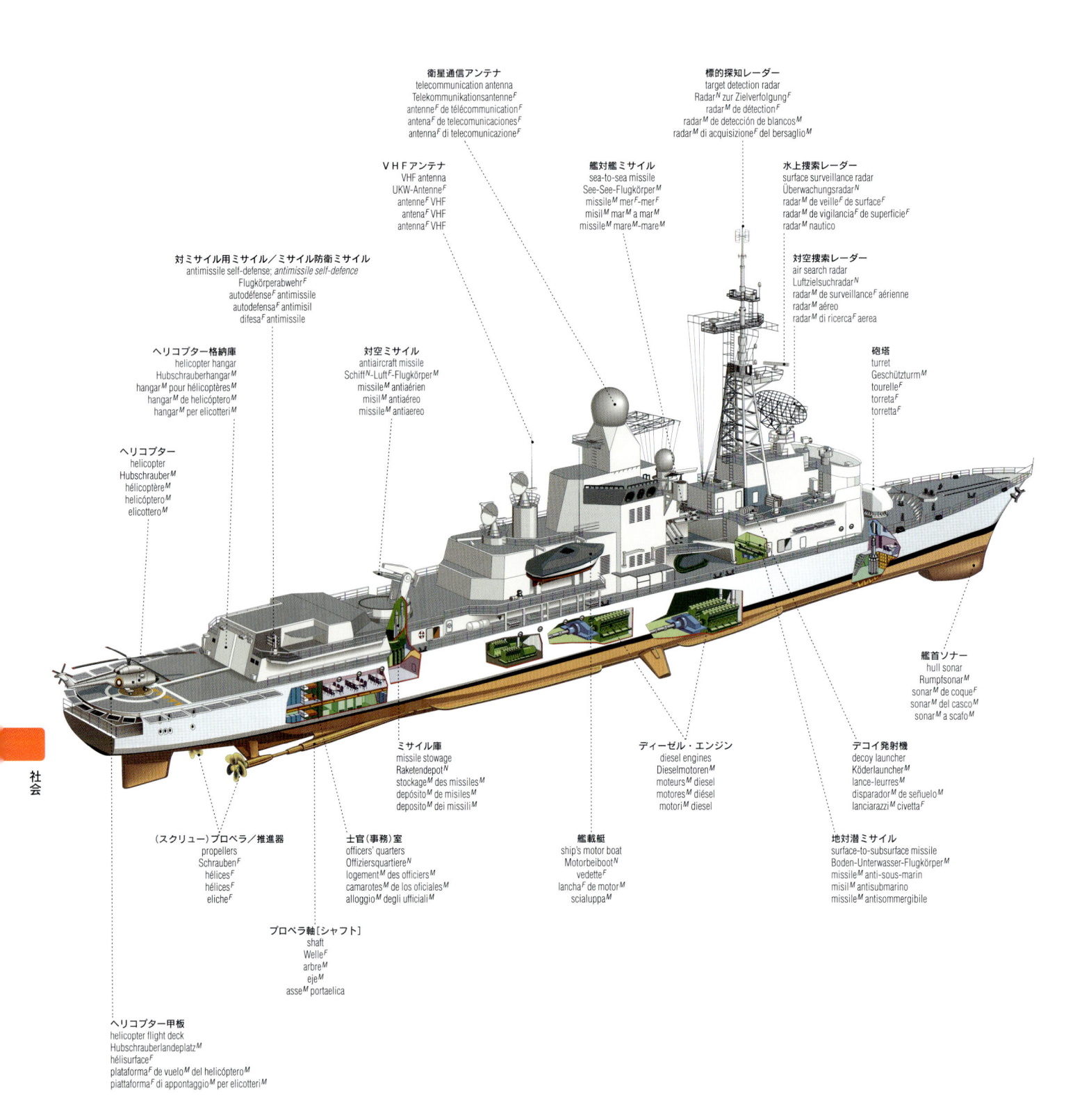

日本語 | 英語 | ドイツ語 | フランス語 | スペイン語 | イタリア語

衛星通信アンテナ
telecommunication antenna
Telekommunikationsantenne^F
antenne^F de télécommunication^F
antena^F de telecomunicaciones^F
antenna^F di telecomunicazione^F

標的探知レーダー
target detection radar
Radar^N zur Zielverfolgung^F
radar^M de détection^F
radar^M de detección de blancos^M
radar^M di acquisizione^F del bersaglio^M

ＶＨＦアンテナ
VHF antenna
UKW-Antenne^F
antenne^F VHF
antena^F VHF
antenna^F VHF

艦対艦ミサイル
sea-to-sea missile
See-See-Flugkörper^M
missile^M mer^F-mer^F
misil^M mar^M a mar^M
missile^M mare^M-mare^M

水上捜索レーダー
surface surveillance radar
Überwachungsradar^N
radar^M de veille^F de surface^F
radar^M de vigilancia^F de superficie^F
radar^M nautico

対ミサイル用ミサイル／ミサイル防衛ミサイル
antimissile self-defense; antimissile self-defence
Flugkörperabwehr^F
autodéfense^F antimissile
autodefensa^F antimisil
difesa^F antimissile

対空捜索レーダー
air search radar
Luftzielsuchradar^N
radar^M de surveillance^F aérienne
radar^M aéreo
radar^M di ricerca^F aerea

ヘリコプター格納庫
helicopter hangar
Hubschrauberhangar^M
hangar^M pour hélicoptères^M
hangar^M de helicóptero^M
hangar^M per elicotteri^M

対空ミサイル
antiaircraft missile
Schiff^N-Luft^F-Flugkörper^M
missile^M antiaérien
misil^M antiaéreo
missile^M antiaereo

砲塔
turret
Geschützturm^M
tourelle^F
torreta^F
torretta^F

ヘリコプター
helicopter
Hubschrauber^M
hélicoptère^M
helicóptero^M
elicottero^M

ミサイル庫
missile stowage
Raketendepot^N
stockage^M des missiles^M
depósito^M de misiles^M
depósito^M dei missili^M

ディーゼル・エンジン
diesel engines
Dieselmotoren^M
moteurs^M diesel
motores^M diésel
motori^M diesel

デコイ発射機
decoy launcher
Köderlauncher^M
lance-leurres^M
disparador^M de señuelo^M
lanciarazzi^M civetta^F

艦首ソナー
hull sonar
Rumpfsonar^M
sonar^M de coque^F
sonar^M del casco^M
sonar^M a scafo^M

（スクリュー）プロペラ／推進器
propellers
Schrauben^F
hélices^F
hélices^F
eliche^F

士官（事務）室
officers' quarters
Offiziersquartiere^N
logement^M des officiers^M
camarotes^M de los oficiales^M
alloggio^M degli ufficiali^M

艦載艇
ship's motor boat
Motorbeiboot^N
vedette^F
lancha^F de motor^M
scialuppa^M

地対潜ミサイル
surface-to-subsurface missile
Boden-Unterwasser-Flugkörper^M
missile^M anti-sous-marin
misil^M antisubmarino
missile^M antisommergibile

プロペラ軸[シャフト]
shaft
Welle^F
arbre^M
eje^M
asse^M portaelica

ヘリコプター甲板
helicopter flight deck
Hubschrauberlandeplatz^M
hélisurface^F
plataforma^F de vuelo^M del helicóptero^M
piattaforma^F di appontaggio^M per elicotteri^M

社会

兵器 | WEAPONS
WAFFEN | ARMES | ARMAS | ARMI

原子力潜水艦

nuclear submarine | Atom[N]-Unterseeboot[N] | sous-marin[M] nucléaire | submarino[M] nuclear | sottomarino[M] nucleare

(スクリュー)プロペラ／推進器
propeller
Schraube[F]
hélice[F]
hélice[F]
elica[F]

縦舵
upper rudder
oberes Ruder[N]
gouvernail[M] de direction[F]
timón[M] de dirección[F]
timone[M] di direzione[F]

緊急用電動機
emergency electric motor
Notstromaggregat[N]
moteur[M] électrique auxiliaire
motor[M] eléctrico de emergencia[F]
motore[M] elettrico d'emergenza[F]

エアロック／気閘(きこう)
airlock
Luftschleuse[F]
sas[M] d'accès[M] arrière
esclusa[F] de aire[M]
camera[F] di equilibrio[M]

推進装置制御室
propulsion machinery control room
Kontrollraum[M] für Antriebswerke[N]
poste[M] de conduite[F] de la propulsion[F]
sala[F] de control[M] de máquinas[F] de propulsión[F]
sala[F] di comando[M] dell'apparato[M] propulsore[M]

タービン交流発電機
turbo-alternator
Turbogenerator[M]
turbo-alternateur[M]
alternador[M] de turbina[F]
turboalternatore[M]

蒸気発生器
steam generator
Dampfgenerator[M]
générateur[M] de vapeur[F]
generador[M] de vapor[M]
generatore[M] di vapore[M]

司令塔／艦橋(セール)
conning tower
Kommandoturm[M]
kiosque[M]
torreta[F] de mando[M]
torretta[F]

潜舵／横舵
sail plane
Tiefenruder[N] des Kommandoturms[M]
gouvernail[M] de plongée[F] avant
timón[M] de inmersión[F]
timone[M] orizzontale

魚雷室
torpedo room
Torpedoraum[M]
chambre[F] des torpilles[F]
sala[F] de torpedos[M]
camera[F] di lancio[M]

主電動機
main electric motor
Hauptelektromotor[M]
moteur[M] électrique principal
motor[M] eléctrico principal
motore[M] elettrico principale

機関室
engine room
Maschinenraum[M]
chambre[F] des machines[F]
sala[F] de máquinas[F]
locale[M] macchine[F]

潜舵／横舵
diving plane
Tiefenruder[N]
barre[F] de plongée[F]
timón[M] de profundidad[F]
timone[M] di profondità[F]

発電室
electricity production room
Stromerzeugungsbereich[M]
compartiment[M] de la production[F] d'électricité[F]
sala[F] de producción[F] de electricidad[F]
locale[M] dei generatori[M] elettrici

原子炉
reactor
Reaktor[M]
réacteur[M]
reactor[M] nuclear
reattore[M] nucleare

原子炉室
nuclear boiler room
Kernreaktorraum[M]
compartiment[M] du réacteur[M]
sala[F] del reactor[M] nuclear
locale[M] del reattore[M] nucleare

魚雷
torpedo
Torpedo[M]
torpille[F]
torpedo[M]
siluro[M]

発射管
firing tube
Torpedorohr[N]
tube[M] lance-torpilles[M]
tubo[M] lanzatorpedos[M]
lanciasiluri[M]

司令塔／艦橋(セール)
conning tower
Kommandoturm[M]
kiosque[M]
torreta[F]
torretta[F]

レーダー・アンテナ
radar antenna
Radarantenne[F]
antenne[F] radar[M]
antena[F] de radar[M]
antenna[F] radar[M]

攻撃用潜望鏡
attack periscope
Angriffsperiskop[N]
périscope[M] d'attaque[F]
periscopio[M] de ataque[M]
periscopio[M] di attacco[M]

無線アンテナ
radio antenna
Funkantenne[F]
antenne[F] radio[F]
antena[F] de radio[F]
antenna[F] radio[F]

多目的アンテナ
multipurpose antenna
Multifunktionsantenne[F]
antenne[F] multifonction
antena[F] múltiple
antenna[F] multifunzione

航海用潜望鏡
navigation periscope
Navigationsperiskop[N]
périscope[M] de veille[F]
periscopio[M] de navegación[F]
periscopio[M] di esplorazione[F]

士官(事務)室
officers' quarters
Offiziersquartiere[N]
logement[M] des officiers[M]
camarotes[M] de los oficiales[M]
alloggio[M] degli ufficiali[M]

発令所
operation control room
Operationszentrale[F]
poste[M] de commandement[M]
sala[F] de control[M] de operaciones[F]
camera[F] di manovra[F]

コンピューター室
computer room
Computerraum[M]
salle[F] des ordinateurs[M]
sala[F] de ordenadores[M]
sala[F] dei computer[M]

食堂
dining room
Messe[F], Speiseraum[M]
salle[F] à manger
comedor[M]
mensa[F]

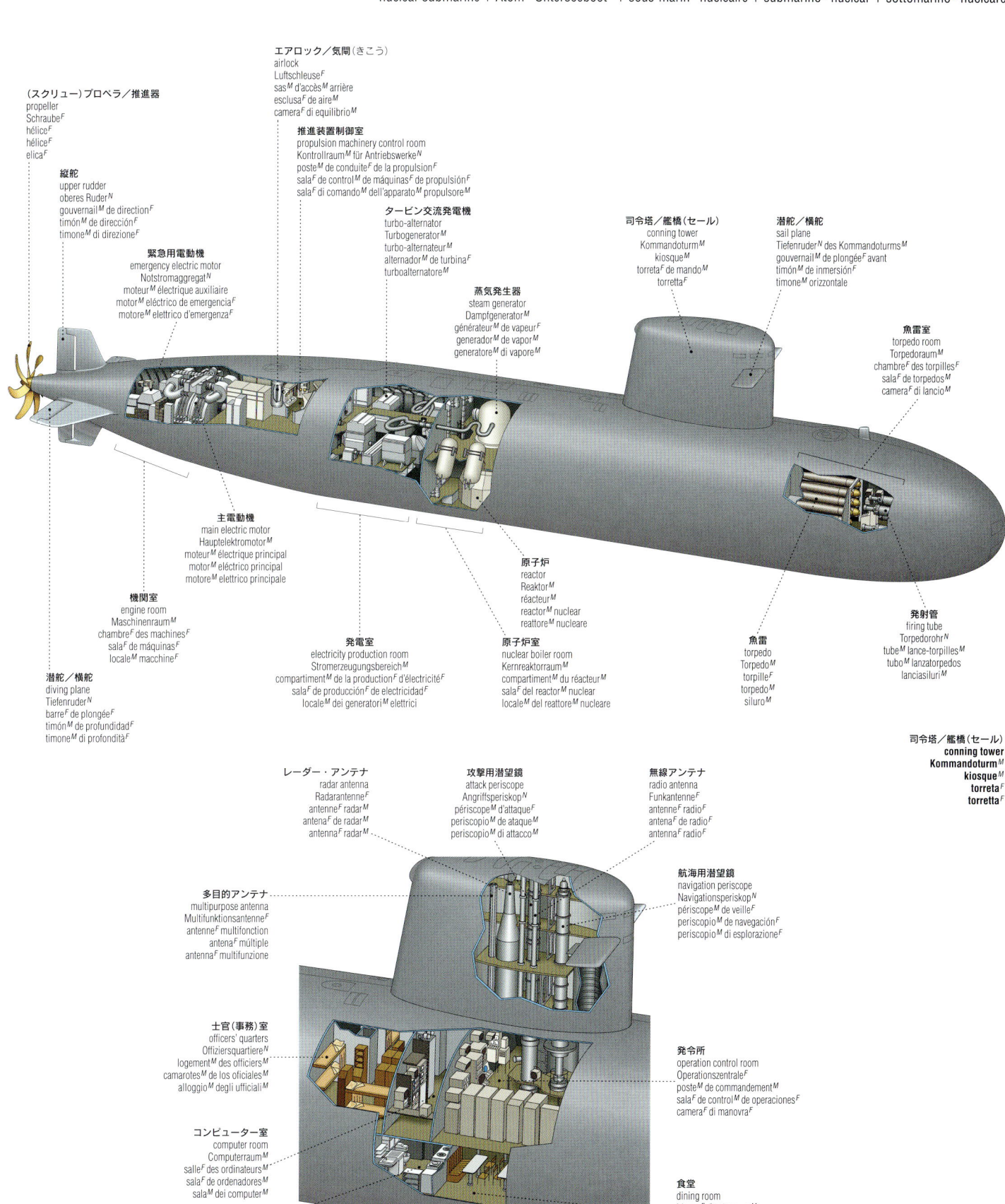

調理場／厨房(ちゅうぼう)
kitchen
Kombüse[F]
cuisine[F]
cocina[F]
cambusa[F]

安全 | SAFETY
SICHERHEIT | SÉCURITÉ | SEGURIDAD | SICUREZZA

火災予防

日本語 | 英語 | ドイツ語 | フランス語 | スペイン語 | イタリア語

fire prevention | Brandbekämpfung^F | prévention^F des incendies^M | prevención^F de incendios^M | prevenzione^F degli incendi^M

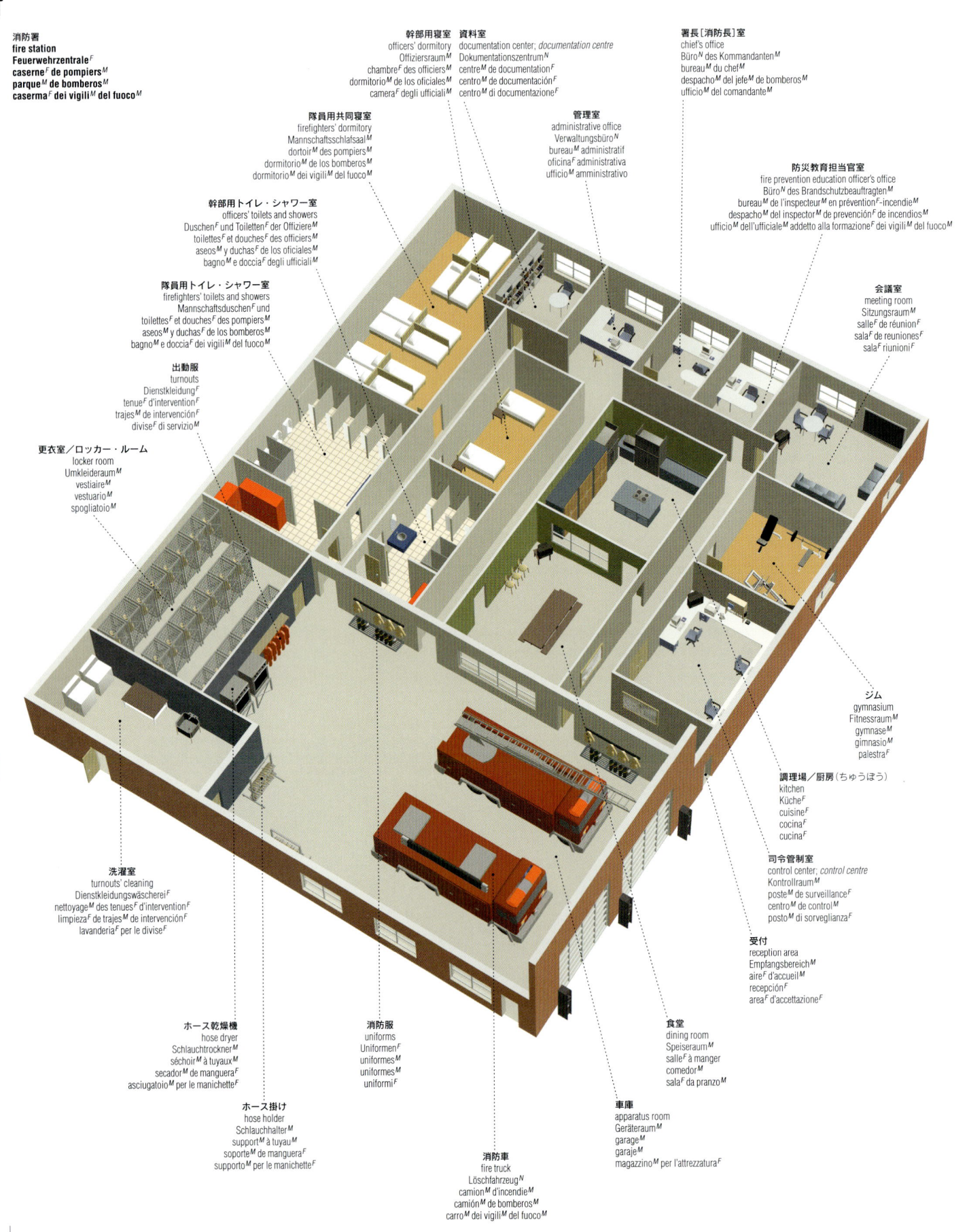

消防署
fire station
Feuerwehrzentrale^F
caserne^F de pompiers^M
parque^M de bomberos^M
caserma^F dei vigili^M del fuoco^M

幹部用寝室
officers' dormitory
Offiziersraum^M
chambre^F des officiers^M
dormitorio^M de los oficiales^M
camera^F degli ufficiali^M

資料室
documentation center; *documentation centre*
Dokumentationszentrum^N
centre^M de documentation^M
centro^M de documentación^F
centro^M di documentazione^F

署長［消防長］室
chief's office
Büro^N des Kommandanten^M
bureau^M du chef^M
despacho^M del jefe^M de bomberos^M
ufficio^M del comandante^M

隊員用共同寝室
firefighters' dormitory
Mannschaftsschlafsaal^M
dortoir^M des pompiers^M
dormitorio^M de los bomberos^M
dormitorio^M dei vigili^M del fuoco^M

管理室
administrative office
Verwaltungsbüro^N
bureau^M administratif
oficina^F administrativa
ufficio^M amministrativo

防災教育担当官室
fire prevention education officer's office
Büro^N des Brandschutzbeauftragten^M
bureau^M de l'inspecteur^M en prévention^F-incendie^M
despacho^M del inspector^M de prevención^F de incendios^M
ufficio^M dell'ufficiale addetto alla formazione^F dei vigili^M del fuoco^M

幹部用トイレ・シャワー室
officers' toilets and showers
Duschen^F und Toiletten^F der Offiziere^M
toilettes^F et douches^F des officiers^M
aseos^M y duchas^F de los oficiales^M
bagno^M e doccia^F degli ufficiali^M

隊員用トイレ・シャワー室
firefighters' toilets and showers
Mannschaftsduschen^F und
toilettes^F et douches^F des pompiers^M
aseos^M y duchas^F de los bomberos^M
bagno^M e doccia^F dei vigili^M del fuoco^M

会議室
meeting room
Sitzungsraum^M
salle^F de réunion^F
sala^F de reuniones^F
sala^F riunioni^F

出動服
turnouts
Dienstkleidung^F
tenue^F d'intervention^F
trajes^M de intervención^F
divise^F di servizio^M

更衣室／ロッカー・ルーム
locker room
Umkleideraum^M
vestiaire^M
vestuario^M
spogliatoio^M

ジム
gymnasium
Fitnessraum^M
gymnase^M
gimnasio^M
palestra^F

調理場／厨房（ちゅうぼう）
kitchen
Küche^F
cuisine^F
cocina^F
cucina^F

司令管制室
control center; *control centre*
Kontrollraum^M
poste^M de surveillance^F
centro^M de control^M
posto^M di sorveglianza^F

受付
reception area
Empfangsbereich^M
aire^F d'accueil^M
recepción^F
area^F d'accettazione^F

洗濯室
turnouts' cleaning
Dienstkleidungswäscherei^F
nettoyage^M des tenues^F d'intervention^F
limpieza^F de trajes^M de intervención^F
lavanderia^F per le divise^F

ホース乾燥機
hose dryer
Schlauchtrockner^M
séchoir^M à tuyaux^M
secador^M de manguera^F
asciugatoio^M per le manichette^F

消防服
uniforms
Uniformen^F
uniformes^M
uniformes^M
uniformi^F

食堂
dining room
Speiseraum^M
salle^F à manger
comedor^M
sala^F da pranzo^M

ホース掛け
hose holder
Schlauchhalter^M
support^M à tuyau^M
soporte^M de manguera^F
supporto^M per le manichette^F

消防車
fire truck
Löschfahrzeug^N
camion^M d'incendie^M
camión^M de bomberos^M
carro^M dei vigili^M del fuoco^M

車庫
apparatus room
Geräteraum^M
garage^M
garaje^M
magazzino^M per l'attrezzatura^F

社会

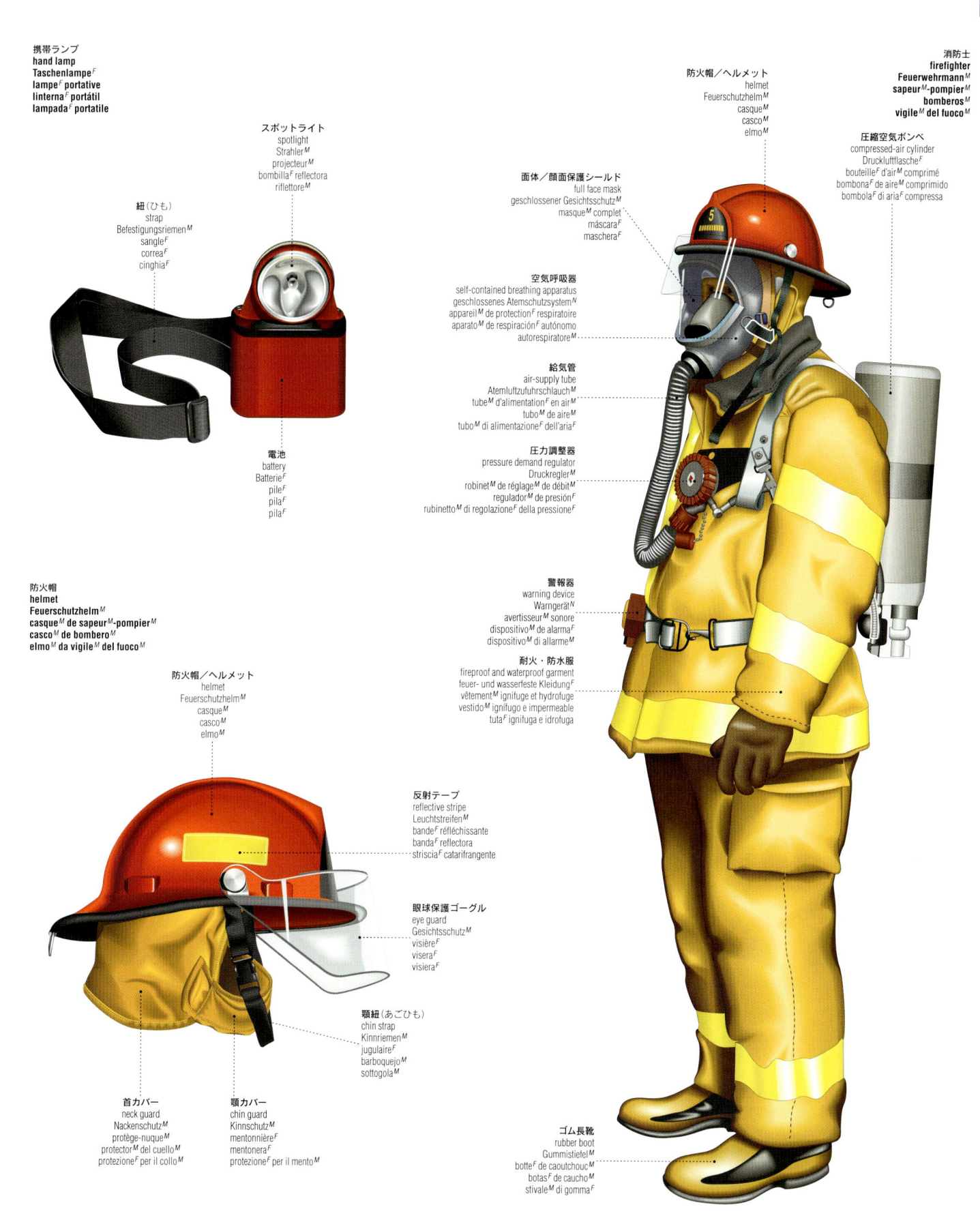

安全 | SAFETY
SICHERHEIT | SÉCURITÉ | SEGURIDAD | SICUREZZA

火災予防

携帯ランプ
hand lamp
Taschenlampe^F
lampe^F portative
linterna^F portátil
lampada^F portatile

スポットライト
spotlight
Strahler^M
projecteur^M
bombilla^F reflectora
riflettore^M

防火帽／ヘルメット
helmet
Feuerschutzhelm^M
casque^M
casco^M
elmo^M

消防士
firefighter
Feuerwehrmann^M
sapeur^M-pompier^M
bomberos^M
vigile^M del fuoco^M

紐（ひも）
strap
Befestigungsriemen^M
sangle^F
correa^F
cinghia^F

面体／顔面保護シールド
full face mask
geschlossener Gesichtsschutz^M
masque^M complet
máscara^F
maschera^F

圧縮空気ボンベ
compressed-air cylinder
Druckluftflasche^F
bouteille^F d'air^M comprimé
bombona^F de aire^M comprimido
bombola^F di aria^F compressa

空気呼吸器
self-contained breathing apparatus
geschlossenes Atemschutzsystem^N
appareil^M de protection^F respiratoire
aparato^M de respiración^F autónomo
autorespiratore^M

給気管
air-supply tube
Atemluftzufuhrschlauch^M
tube^M d'alimentation^F en air^M
tubo^M de aire^M
tubo^M di alimentazione^F dell'aria^F

電池
battery
Batterie^F
pile^F
pila^F
pila^F

圧力調整器
pressure demand regulator
Druckregler^M
robinet^M de réglage^M de débit^M
regulador^M de presión^F
rubinetto^M di regolazione^F della pressione^F

警報器
warning device
Warngerät^N
avertisseur^M sonore
dispositivo^M de alarma^F
dispositivo^M di allarme^M

防火帽
helmet
Feuerschutzhelm^M
casque^M de sapeur^M-pompier^M
casco^M de bombero^M
elmo^M da vigile^M del fuoco^M

耐火・防水服
fireproof and waterproof garment
feuer- und wasserfeste Kleidung^F
vêtement^M ignifuge et hydrofuge
vestido^M ignifugo e impermeable
tuta^F ignifuga e idrofuga

防火帽／ヘルメット
helmet
Feuerschutzhelm^M
casque^M
casco^M
elmo^M

反射テープ
reflective stripe
Leuchtstreifen^M
bande^F réfléchissante
banda^F reflectora
striscia^F catarifrangente

眼球保護ゴーグル
eye guard
Gesichtsschutz^M
visière^F
visera^F
visiera^F

顎紐（あごひも）
chin strap
Kinnriemen^M
jugulaire^F
barboquejo^M
sottogola^M

首カバー
neck guard
Nackenschutz^M
protège-nuque^M
protector^M del cuello^M
protezione^F per il collo^M

顎カバー
chin guard
Kinnschutz^M
mentonnière^F
mentonera^F
protezione^F per il mento^M

ゴム長靴
rubber boot
Gummistiefel^M
botte^F de caoutchouc^M
botas^F de caucho^M
stivale^M di gomma^F

社会

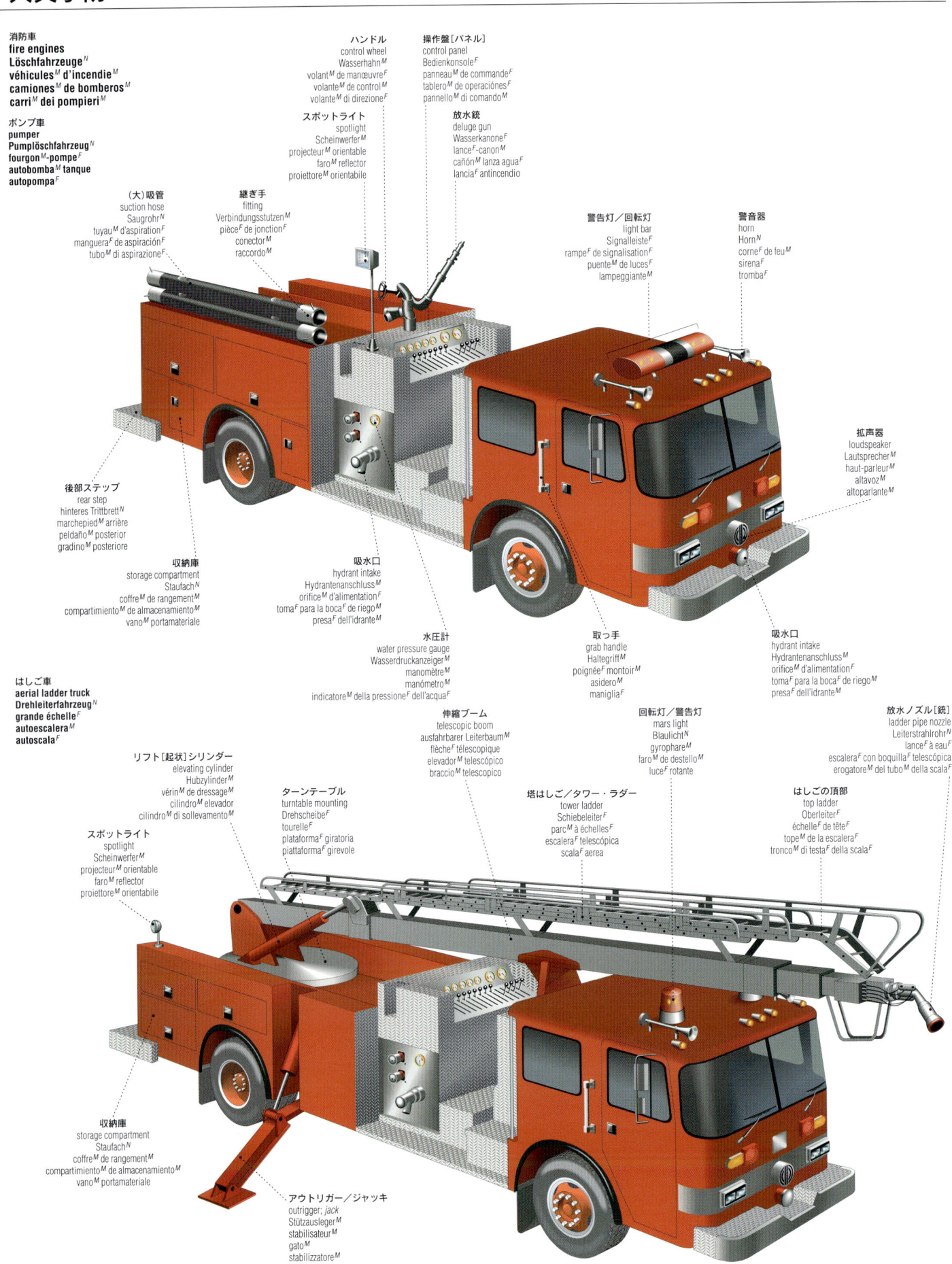

安全 | SAFETY
SICHERHEIT | SÉCURITÉ | SEGURIDAD | SICUREZZA

火災予防

日本語 | 英語 | ドイツ語 | フランス語 | スペイン語 | イタリア語

消防車
fire engines
Löschfahrzeuge^N
véhicules^M d'incendie^M
camiones^M de bomberos^M
carri^M dei pompieri^M

ポンプ車
pumper
Pumplöschfahrzeug^N
fourgon^M-pompe^F
autobomba^M tanque
autopompa^F

(大)吸管
suction hose
Saugrohr^N
tuyau^M d'aspiration^F
manguera^F de aspiración^F
tubo^M di aspirazione^F

継ぎ手
fitting
Verbindungsstutzen^M
pièce^F de jonction^F
conector^M
raccordo^M

ハンドル
control wheel
Wasserhahn^M
volant^M de manœuvre^F
volante^M de control^M
volante^M di direzione^F

スポットライト
spotlight
Scheinwerfer^M
projecteur^M orientable
faro^M reflector
proiettore^M orientabile

操作盤[パネル]
control panel
Bedienkonsole^F
panneau^M de commande^F
tablero^M de operaciones^F
pannello^M di comando^M

放水銃
deluge gun
Wasserkanone^F
lance^F-canon^M
cañón^M lanza agua^F
lancia^F antincendio

警告灯/回転灯
light bar
Signalleiste^F
rampe^F de signalisation^F
puente^F de luces^F
lampeggiante^M

警音器
horn
Horn^N
corne^F de feu^M
sirena^F
tromba^F

拡声器
loudspeaker
Lautsprecher^M
haut-parleur^M
altavoz^M
altoparlante^M

後部ステップ
rear step
hinteres Trittbrett^N
marchepied^M arrière
peldaño^M posterior
gradino^M posteriore

収納庫
storage compartment
Staufach^N
coffre^M de rangement^M
compartimiento^M de almacenamiento^M
vano^M portamateriale

吸水口
hydrant intake
Hydrantenanschluss^M
orifice^M d'alimentation^F
toma^F para la boca^F de riego^M
presa^F dell'idrante^M

水圧計
water pressure gauge
Wasserdruckanzeiger^M
manomètre^M
manómetro^M
indicatore^M della pressione^F dell'acqua^F

取っ手
grab handle
Haltegriff^M
poignée^F montoir^M
asidero^M
maniglia^F

吸水口
hydrant intake
Hydrantenanschluss^M
orifice^M d'alimentation^F
toma^F para la boca^F de riego^M
presa^F dell'idrante^M

はしご車
aerial ladder truck
Drehleiterfahrzeug^N
grande échelle^F
autoescalera^M
autoscala^F

伸縮ブーム
telescopic boom
ausfahrbarer Leiterbaum^M
flèche^F télescopique
elevador^M telescópico
braccio^M telescopico

回転灯/警告灯
mars light
Blaulicht^N
gyrophare^M
faro^M de destello^M
luce^F rotante

放水ノズル[銃]
ladder pipe nozzle
Leiterstrahlrohr^N
lance^F à eau^F
escalera^F con boquilla^F telescópica
erogatore^M del tubo^M della scala^F

リフト[起状]シリンダー
elevating cylinder
Hubzylinder^M
vérin^M de dressage^M
cilindro^M elevador
cilindro^M di sollevamento^M

ターンテーブル
turntable mounting
Drehscheibe^F
tourelle^F
plataforma^F giratoria
piattaforma^F girevole

塔はしご/タワー・ラダー
tower ladder
Schiebeleiter^F
parc^M à échelles^F
escalera^F telescópica
scala^F aerea

はしごの頂部
top ladder
Oberleiter^F
échelle^F de tête^F
tope^M de la escalera^F
tronco^M di testa^F della scala^F

スポットライト
spotlight
Scheinwerfer^M
projecteur^M orientable
faro^M reflector
proiettore^M orientabile

収納庫
storage compartment
Staufach^N
coffre^M de rangement^M
compartimiento^M de almacenamiento^M
vano^M portamateriale

アウトリガー/ジャッキ
outrigger; jack
Stützausleger^M
stabilisateur^M
gato^M
stabilizzatore^M

社会

安全 | SAFETY
SICHERHEIT | SÉCURITÉ | SEGURIDAD | SICUREZZA

火災予防

消火栓
fire hydrant
Überflurhydrant^M
borne^F d'incendie^M
boca^F de riego^F
idrante^M a colonna^F

覆い
cover
Abdeckung^F
couvercle^M
tapa^F
coperchio^M

底部
base
Unterteil^N
base^F
base^F
base^F

テスト・ボタン
test button
Testknopf^M
bouton^M d'essai^M
botón^M de ensayo^M
pulsante^M di prova^F

作動ランプ
indicator light
Kontrollleuchte^F
témoin^M lumineux
testigo^M luminoso
spia^F luminosa

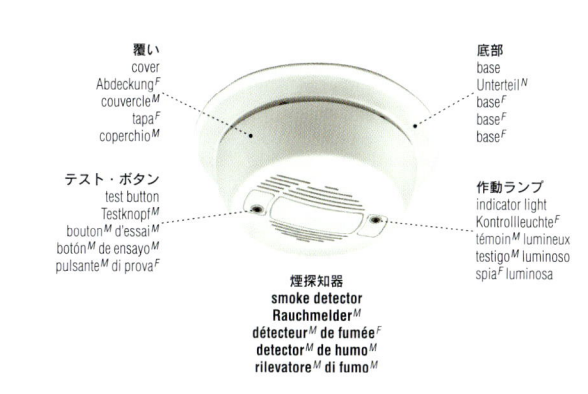

煙探知器
smoke detector
Rauchmelder^M
détecteur^M de fumée^F
detector^M de humo^M
rilevatore^M di fumo^M

安全ピン
pin
Sicherungsstift^M
goupille^F
clavija^F
copiglia^F

操作レバー
trigger
Abzug^M
gâchette^F
disparador^M
grilletto^M

消火用器材
fire-fighting material
Brandbekämpfungsmaterial^N
matériel^M de lutte^F contre les incendies^M
material^M de lucha^F contra los incendios^M
materiale^M antincendio

ノズル
nozzle
Strahlrohr^N
lance^F
boquilla^F
erogatore^M

ホース
hose
Schlauch^M
tuyau^M
manguera^F
tubo^M flessibile

はしご・ホース（止め）ストラップ
ladder and hose strap
Hakengurt^M für Leiter^F und Schlauch^M
attache^F pour tuyaux^M et échelles^F
correa^F para escalera^F y manguera^F
cinghia^F per tubi^M e scale^F

タンク
tank
Löschmittelbehälter^M
réservoir^M
tanque^M
bombola^F

携帯用消火器
portable fire extinguisher
Handfeuerlöscher^M
extincteur^M
extintor^M portátil
estintore^M portatile

分岐管
dividing breeching
Y-Verbindungsstück^N
pièce^F d'embranchement^M
conector^M de boca^F de riego^F
raccordo^M a due vie^F

消火栓開口用レンチ
fire hydrant wrench
Hydrantenschlüssel^M
clé^F de barrage^M
llave^F de boca^F de riego^M
chiave^F per idrante^M

消火（用）ホース
fire hose
Schlauchleitung^F
tuyau^M de refoulement^M
manguera^F de incendios^M
manichetta^F antincendio

パーカッション・バー
percussion bar
Brecheisen^N
clé^F à percussion^F
barra^F de percusión^F
barra^F di percussione^F

手斧（ておの／ちょうな）
hatchet
Beil^N
hache^F
hacha^F
piccozza^F

鉤竿／鉤棒／鳶口（とびぐち）
pike pole
Einreißhaken^M
gaffe^F
pica^F
rampone^M

掛けはしご
hook ladder
Hakenleiter^F
échelle^F à crochets^M
escalera^F de ganchos^M
scala^F con ganci^M

社会

安全 | SAFETY
SICHERHEIT | SÉCURITÉ | SEGURIDAD | SICUREZZA

犯罪防止

日本語 | 英語 | ドイツ語 | フランス語 | スペイン語 | イタリア語

crime prevention | vorbeugende Verbrechensbekämpfung^F | prévention^F de la criminalité^F | prevención^F de la criminalidad^F | prevenzione^F del crimine^M

警察署
police station
Polizeirevier^F
poste^M de police^F
estación^F de policía^F
stazione^F di polizia^F

未成年者房
juvenile cell
Minderjährigenzelle^F
cellule^F pour mineurs^M
celda^F de menores^M
cella^F per i minori^M

取調室／聴取室
interrogation room
Verhörraum^M
salle^F d'interrogatoire^M
sala^F de interrogatorios^M
stanza^F per gli interrogatori^M

男子房
men's cell
Männerzelle^F
cellule^F pour hommes^M
celda^F de hombres^M
cella^F per gli uomini^M

女子房
women's cell
Frauenzelle^F
cellule^F pour femmes^F
celda^F de mujeres^M
cella^F per le donne^F

収容者用シャワー室
prisoners' shower
Häftlingsdusche^F
douche^F des détenus^M
duchas^F de los presos^M
doccia^F dei detenuti^M

鑑識課
identification section
Erkennungsdienstbereich^M
section^F de l'identité^F
sección^F de identificación^F
sezione^F di riconoscimento^M

司令管制室
control room
Kontrollraum^M
poste^M de contrôle^M
sala^F de control^M
posto^M di controllo^M

署員用トイレ
staff toilet
Personaltoiletten^F
w.-c.^M du personnel^M
aseo^M del personal^M
bagno^M del personale^M

署員休憩室
staff lounge
Personalraum^M
salon^M du personnel^M
sala^F del personal^M
sala^F del personale^M

署員用クローク[ロッカー・ルーム]
staff cloakroom
Personalumkleideraum^M
vestiaire^M du personnel^M
guardarropa^M del personal^M
spogliatoio^M del personale^M

署長室
chief officer's office
Büro^N des Dienststellenleiters^M
bureau^M de l'officier^M supérieur
despacho^M del oficial^M superior
ufficio^M del comandante^M

署員入り口
staff entrance
Personaleingang^M
entrée^F du personnel^M
entrada^F del personal^M
ingresso^M del personale^M

報告書作成室
report writing room
Protokollraum^M
salle^F de rédaction^F des rapports^M
sala^F de redacción^M de informes^M
stanza^F per stilare i rapporti^M

苦情相談窓口
complaints office
Anzeigenaufnahme^F
bureau^M des plaintes^F
oficina^F de quejas^F
ufficio^M per le denunce^F

副署長室
junior officer's office
Büro^N des stellvertretenden Dienststellenleiters^M
bureau^M de l'officier^M subalterne
despacho^M del oficial^M subalterno
ufficio^M del vicecomandante^M

待合室
waiting room
Warteraum^M
salle^F d'attente^F
sala^F de espera^F
sala^F d'attesa^F

正面入り口
main entrance
Haupteingang^M
entrée^F principale
entrada^F principal
ingresso^M principale

社会

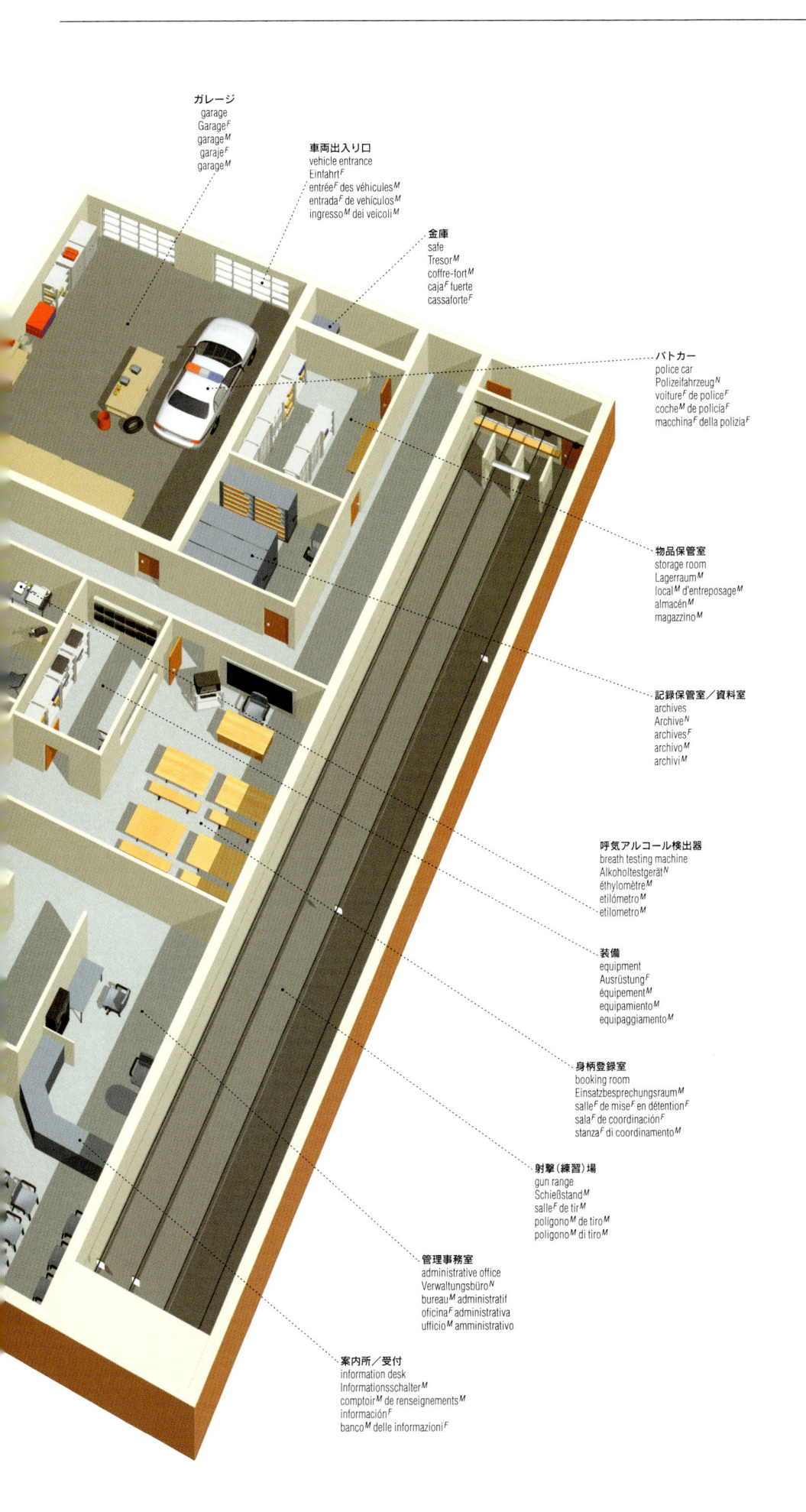

安全 | SAFETY
SICHERHEIT | SÉCURITÉ | SEGURIDAD | SICUREZZA

犯罪防止

ガレージ
garage
Garage[F]
garage[M]
garaje[F]
garage[M]

車両出入り口
vehicle entrance
Einfahrt[F]
entrée[F] des véhicules[M]
entrada[F] de vehículos[M]
ingresso[M] dei veicoli[M]

金庫
safe
Tresor[M]
coffre-fort[M]
caja[F] fuerte
cassaforte[F]

パトカー
police car
Polizeifahrzeug[N]
voiture[F] de police[F]
coche[M] de policía[F]
macchina[F] della polizia[F]

物品保管室
storage room
Lagerraum[M]
local[M] d'entreposage[M]
almacén[M]
magazzino[M]

記録保管室／資料室
archives
Archive[N]
archives[F]
archivo[M]
archivi[M]

呼気アルコール検出器
breath testing machine
Alkoholtestgerät[N]
éthylomètre[M]
etilómetro[M]
etilometro[M]

装備
equipment
Ausrüstung[F]
équipement[M]
equipamiento[M]
equipaggiamento[M]

身柄登録室
booking room
Einsatzbesprechungsraum[M]
salle[F] de mise[F] en détention[F]
sala[F] de coordinación[F]
stanza[F] di coordinamento[M]

射撃（練習）場
gun range
Schießstand[M]
salle[F] de tir[M]
polígono[M] de tiro[M]
poligono[M] di tiro[M]

管理事務室
administrative office
Verwaltungsbüro[N]
bureau[M] administratif
oficina[F] administrativa
ufficio[M] amministrativo

案内所／受付
information desk
Informationsschalter[M]
comptoir[M] de renseignements[M]
información[F]
banco[M] delle informazioni[F]

社会

769

犯罪防止

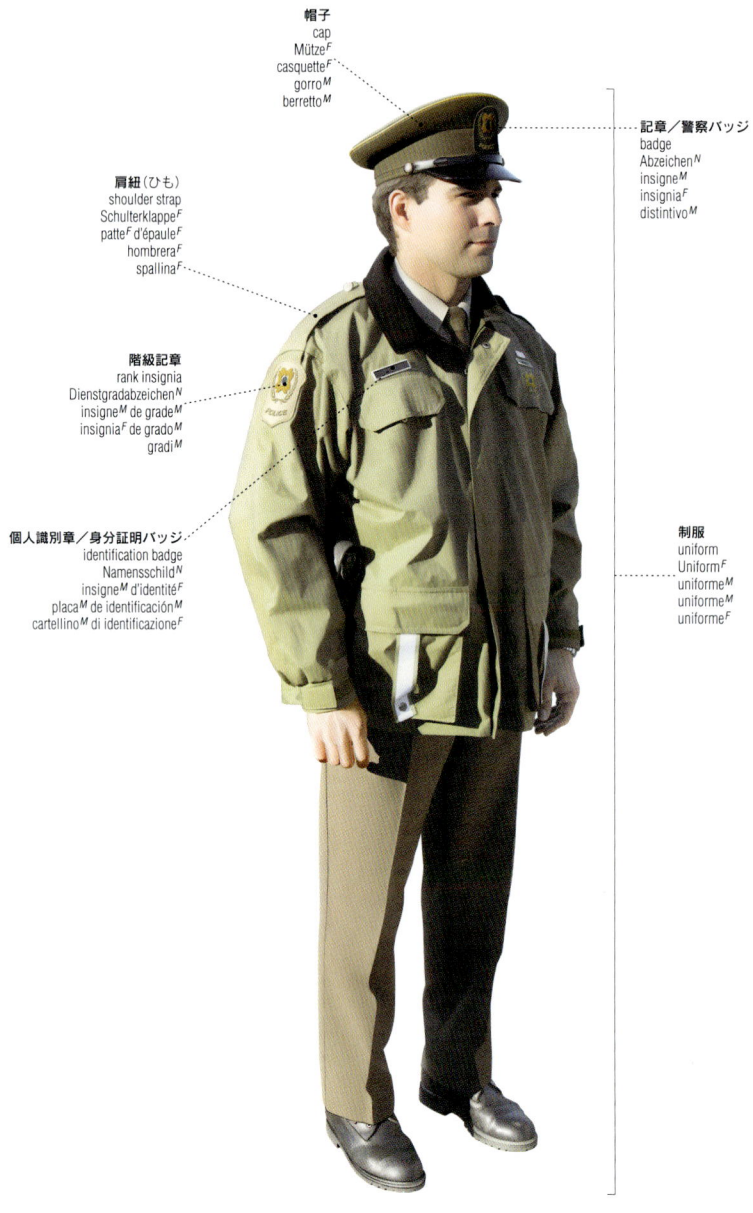

安全 | SAFETY
SICHERHEIT | SÉCURITÉ | SEGURIDAD | SICUREZZA

日本語 | 英語 | ドイツ語 | フランス語 | スペイン語 | イタリア語

警察官
police officer
Polizeibeamter^M
agent^M de police^F
agente^M de policía^F
agente^M di polizia^F

帽子
cap
Mütze^F
casquette^F
gorro^M
berretto^M

肩紐（ひも）
shoulder strap
Schulterklappe^F
patte^F d'épaule^F
hombrera^F
spallina^F

記章／警察バッジ
badge
Abzeichen^N
insigne^M
insignia^F
distintivo^M

階級記章
rank insignia
Dienstgradabzeichen^N
insigne^M de grade^M
insignia^F de grado^M
gradi^M

個人識別章／身分証明バッジ
identification badge
Namensschild^N
insigne^M d'identité^F
placa^M de identificación^M
cartellino^M di identificazione^F

制服
uniform
Uniform^F
uniforme^M
uniforme^M
uniforme^F

ガン[万能]ベルト
duty belt
Dienstgürtel^M
ceinturon^M de service^M
cinturón^M de servicio^M
cintura^F di servizio^M

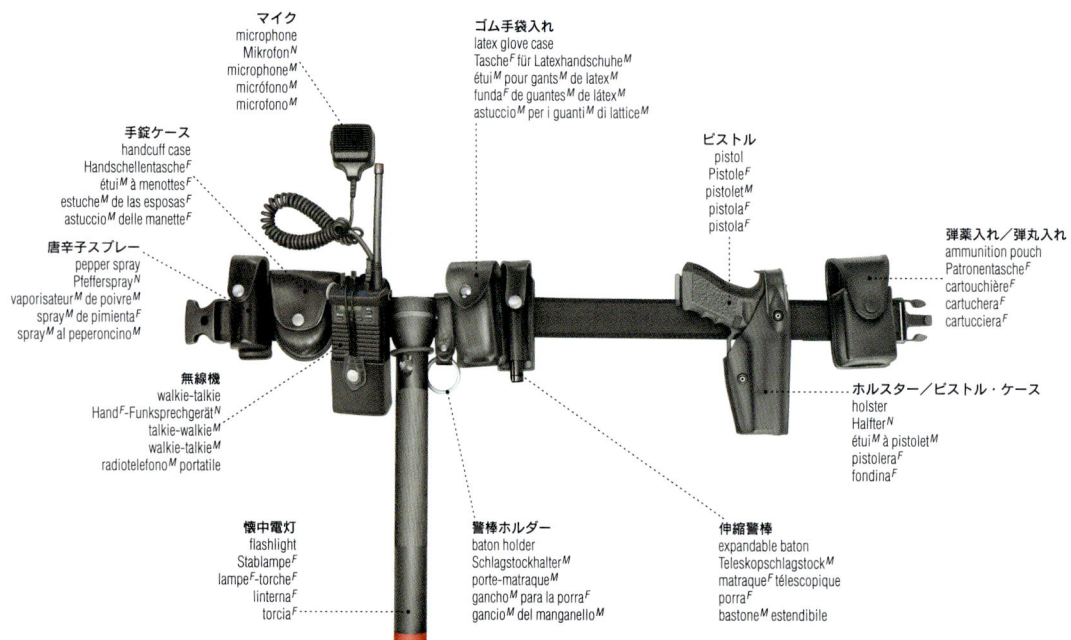

マイク
microphone
Mikrofon^N
microphone^M
micrófono^M
microfono^M

ゴム手袋入れ
latex glove case
Tasche^F für Latexhandschuhe^M
étui^M pour gants^M de latex^M
funda^F de guantes^M de látex^M
astuccio^M per i guanti^M di lattice^M

手錠ケース
handcuff case
Handschellentasche^F
étui^M à menottes^F
estuche^M de las esposas^F
astuccio^M delle manette^F

ピストル
pistol
Pistole^F
pistolet^M
pistola^F
pistola^F

唐辛子スプレー
pepper spray
Pfefferspray^N
vaporisateur^M de poivre^M
spray^M de pimienta^F
spray^M al peperoncino^M

弾薬入れ／弾丸入れ
ammunition pouch
Patronentasche^F
cartouchière^F
cartuchera^F
cartucciera^F

無線機
walkie-talkie
Hand^F-Funksprechgerät^N
talkie-walkie^M
walkie-talkie^M
radiotelefono^M portatile

ホルスター／ピストル・ケース
holster
Halfter^N
étui^M à pistolet^M
pistolera^F
fondina^F

懐中電灯
flashlight
Stablampe^F
lampe^F-torche^F
linterna^F
torcia^F

警棒ホルダー
baton holder
Schlagstockhalter^M
porte-matraque^M
gancho^M para la porra^F
gancio^M del manganello^M

伸縮警棒
expandable baton
Teleskopschlagstock^M
matraque^F télescopique
porra^F
bastone^M estendibile

安全 | SAFETY
SICHERHEIT | SÉCURITÉ | SEGURIDAD | SICUREZZA

犯罪防止

ダッシュボード[計器盤]の機器
dashboard equipment
Armaturenbrettausrüstung^F
équipement^M du tableau^M de bord^M
equipamiento^M del salpicadero^M
equipaggiamento^M del cruscotto^M

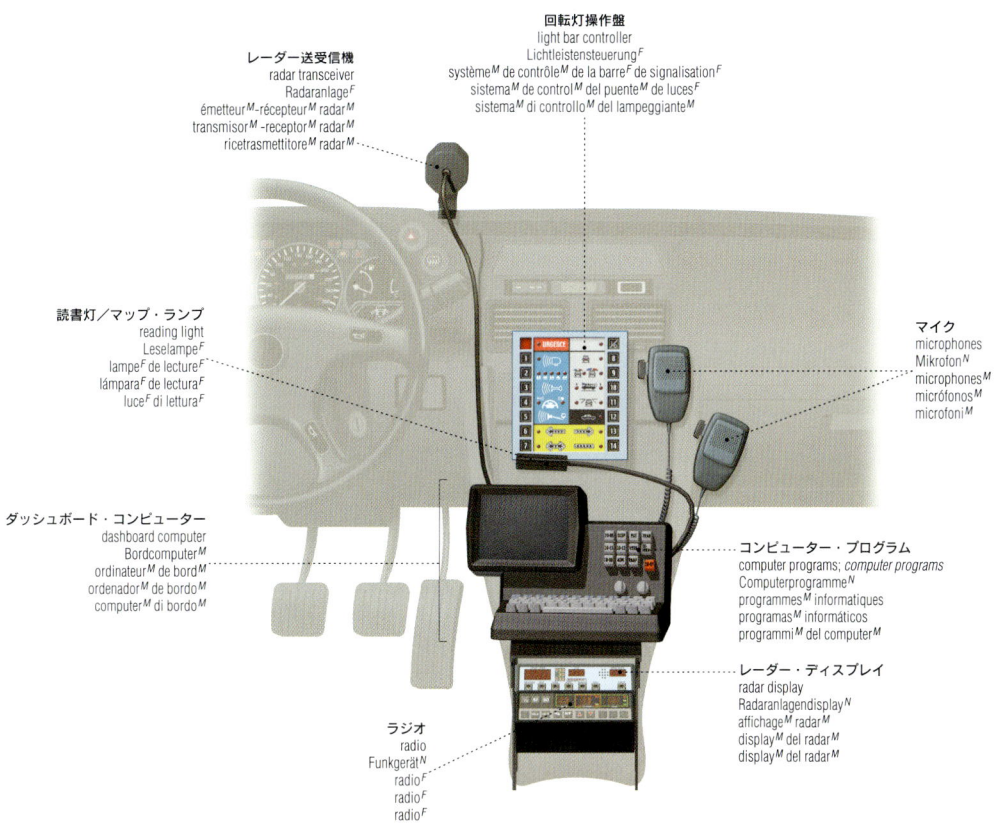

レーダー送受信機
radar transceiver
Radaranlage^F
émetteur^M-récepteur^M radar^M
transmisor^M-receptor^M radar^M
ricetrasmettitore^M radar^M

回転灯操作盤
light bar controller
Lichtleistensteuerung^F
système^M de contrôle^M de la barre^F de signalisation^F
sistema^M de control^M del puente^M de luces^F
sistema^M di controllo^M del lampeggiante^M

読書灯／マップ・ランプ
reading light
Leselampe^F
lampe^F de lecture^F
lámpara^F de lectura^F
luce^F di lettura^F

マイク
microphones
Mikrofon^N
microphones^M
micrófonos^M
microfoni^M

ダッシュボード・コンピューター
dashboard computer
Bordcomputer^M
ordinateur^M de bord^M
ordenador^M de bordo^M
computer^M di bordo^M

コンピューター・プログラム
computer programs; *computer programs*
Computerprogramme^N
programmes^M informatiques
programas^M informáticos
programmi^M del computer^M

レーダー・ディスプレイ
radar display
Radaranlagendisplay^N
affichage^M radar^M
display^M del radar^M
display^M del radar^M

ラジオ
radio
Funkgerät^F
radio^F
radio^F
radio^F

警告灯／回転灯
light bar
Lichtleiste^F
rampe^F de signalisation^F
puente^M de luces^F
lampeggiante^M

アンテナ
antenna
Antenne^F
antenne^F
antena^F
antenna^F

安全灯
safety lighting
Sicherheitsleuchte^F
éclairage^M de sécurité^F
luces^F de seguridad^F
luce^F di sicurezza^F

パトカー
police car
Polizeifahrzeug^N
voiture^F de police^F
coche^M de policía^F
macchina^F della polizia^F

消火器
fire extinguisher
Feuerlöscher^M
extincteur^M
extintor^M
estintore^M

バリケード・テープ
barrier barricade tape
Absperrband^N
ruban^M de bouclage^M
cinta^F de acordonamiento^M
nastro^M di delimitazione^F

照明弾
road flare
Leuchtrakete^F
fusée^F éclairante
faro^M de carretera^F
razzo^M illuminante

仕切り（壁）
partition
Trennwand^F
cloison^F
divisorio^M
divisorio^M

救命ブイ[浮き輪]
life buoy
Rettungsring^M
bouée^F de sauvetage^M
flotador^M
salvagente^M

救急箱
first aid kit
Erste-Hilfe^F-Kasten^M
trousse^F de secours^M
botiquín^M de urgencias^F
cassetta^F di pronto soccorso^M

使用済み注射器入れ
used syringe box
Behälter^M für gebrauchte Spritzen^F
boîte^F pour seringues^F usagées
caja^F de jeringuillas^F usadas
contenitore^M delle siringhe^F usate

社会

771

安全 | SAFETY
SICHERHEIT | SÉCURITÉ | SEGURIDAD | SICUREZZA

耳の保護具

日本語 | 英語 | ドイツ語 | フランス語 | スペイン語 | イタリア語

ear protection | Gehörschutz^M | protection^F de l'ouïe^F | protección^F para los oídos^M | protezione^F per le orecchie^F

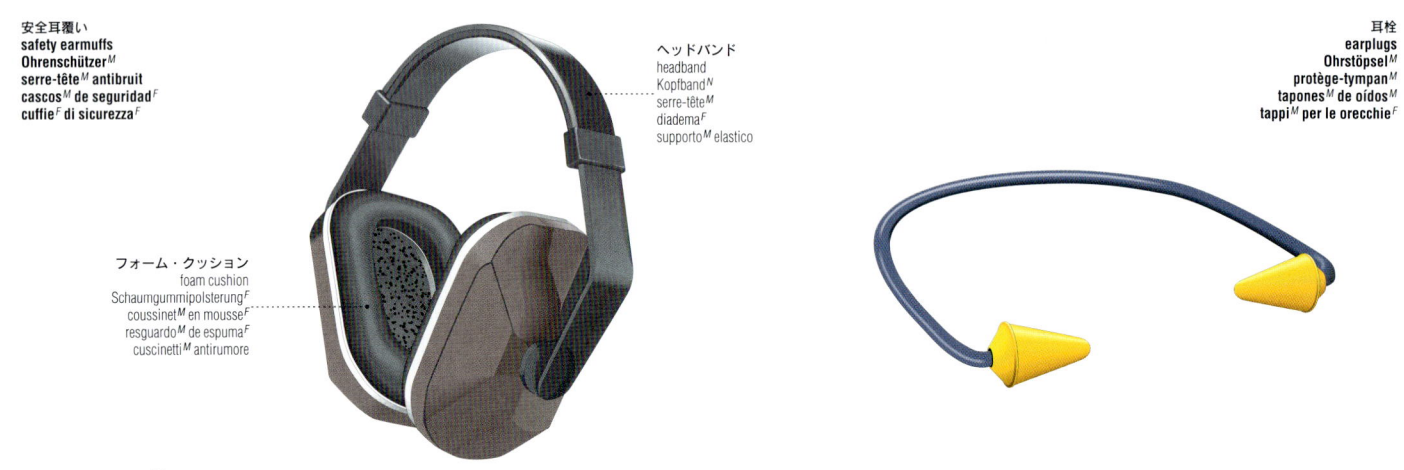

安全耳覆い
safety earmuffs
Ohrenschützer^M
serre-tête^M antibruit
cascos^M de seguridad^F
cuffie^F di sicurezza^F

ヘッドバンド
headband
Kopfband^N
serre-tête^M
diadema^F
supporto^M elastico

耳栓
earplugs
Ohrstöpsel^M
protège-tympan^M
tapones^M de oídos^M
tappi^M per le orecchie^F

フォーム・クッション
foam cushion
Schaumgummipolsterung^F
coussinet^M en mousse^F
resguardo^M de espuma^F
cuscinetti^M antirumore

目の保護具

eye protection | Augenschutz^M | protection^F des yeux^M | protección^F para los ojos^M | protezione^F per gli occhi^M

安全眼鏡
safety glasses
Schutzbrille^F
lunettes^F de sécurité^F
gafas^F de seguridad^F
occhiali^M di protezione^F con ripari^M laterali

安全ゴーグル
safety goggles
Schutzmaske^F
lunettes^F de protection^F
gafas^F protectores
occhiali^M di protezione^F panoramici

頭部の保護具

head protection | Kopfschutz^M | protection^F de la tête^F | protección^F para la cabeza^F | protezione^F per la testa^F

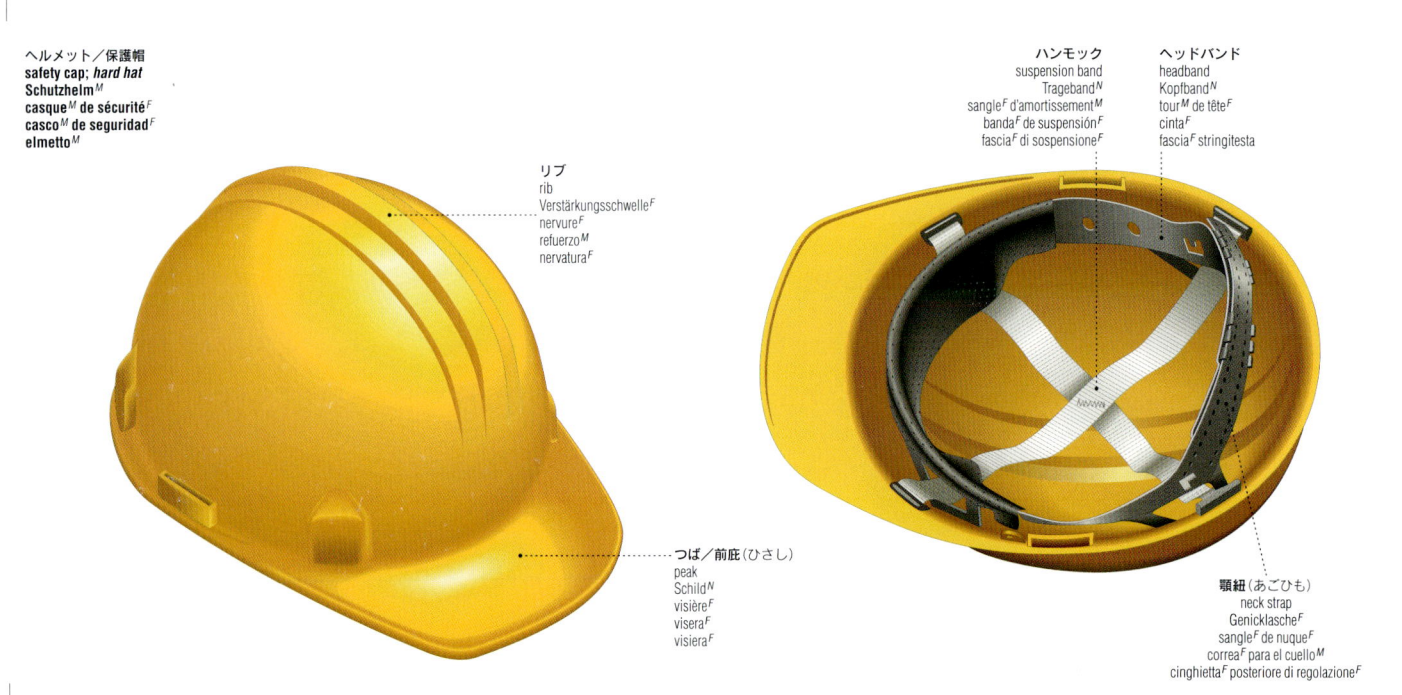

ヘルメット／保護帽
safety cap; *hard hat*
Schutzhelm^M
casque^M de sécurité^F
casco^M de seguridad^F
elmetto^M

ハンモック
suspension band
Trageband^N
sangle^F d'amortissement^M
banda^F de suspensión^F
fascia^F di sospensione^F

ヘッドバンド
headband
Kopfband^N
tour^M de tête^F
cinta^F
fascia^F stringitesta

リブ
rib
Verstärkungsschwelle^F
nervure^F
refuerzo^M
nervatura^F

つば／前庇（ひさし）
peak
Schild^N
visière^F
visera^F
visiera^F

顎紐（あごひも）
neck strap
Genicklasche^F
sangle^F de nuque^F
correa^F para el cuello^M
cinghietta^F posteriore di regolazione^F

安全 | SAFETY
SICHERHEIT | SÉCURITÉ | SEGURIDAD | SICUREZZA

呼吸器系の保護具

respiratory system protection | Atemschutz[M] | protection[F] des voies[F] respiratoires | protección[F] para el sistema[M] respiratorio[M] | protezione[F] per le vie[F] respiratorie

防毒マスク
respirator
Gasmaske[F]
masque[M] respiratoire
máscara[F] antigás[M]
maschera[F] a pieno facciale[M] bifiltro

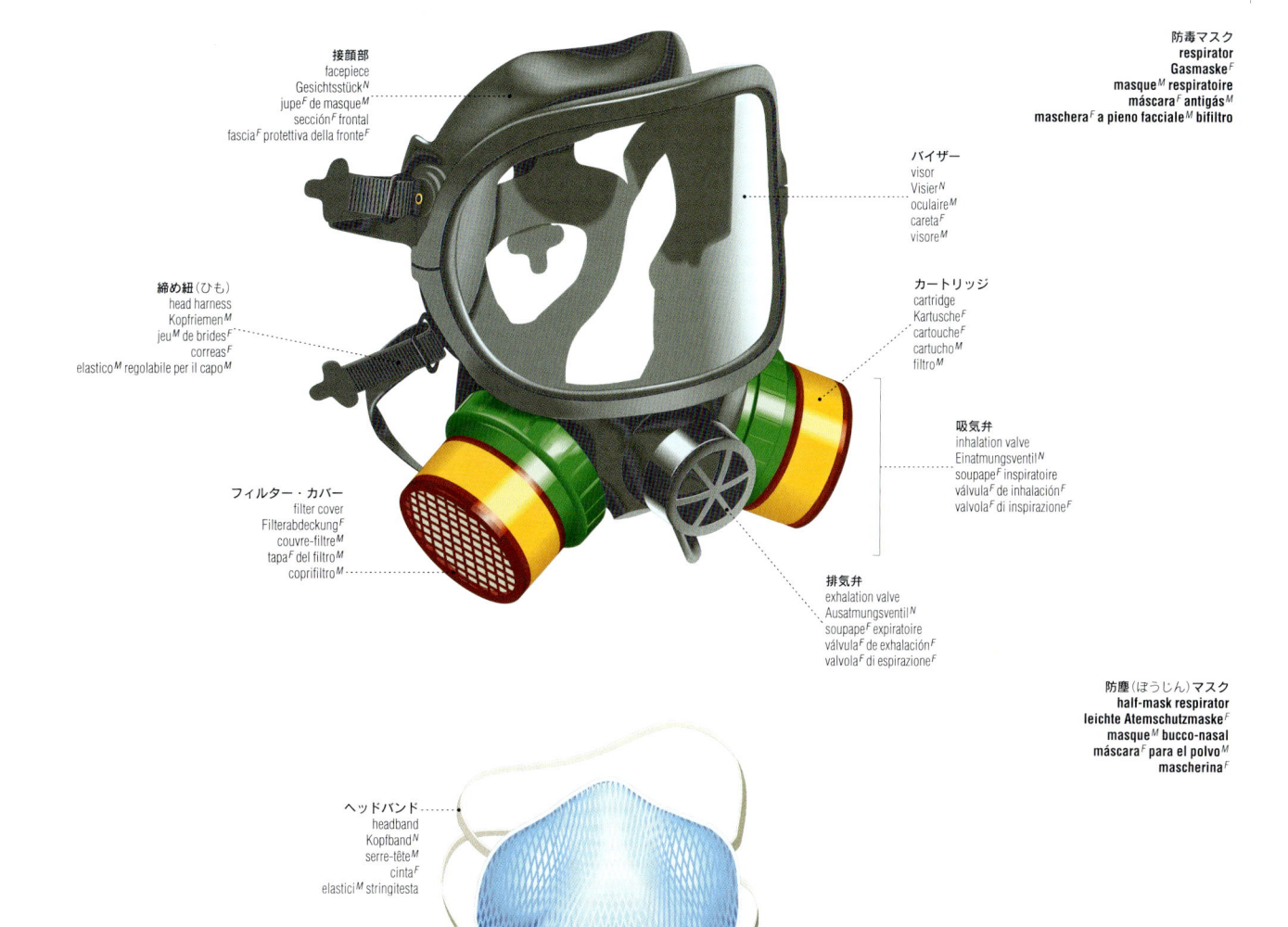

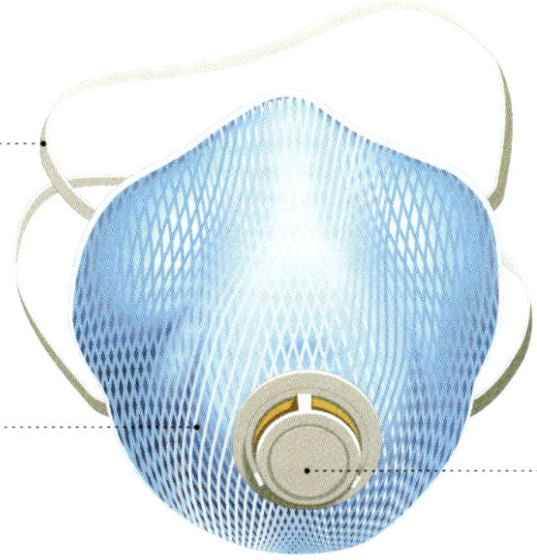

接顔部
facepiece
Gesichtsstück[N]
jupe[F] de masque[M]
sección[F] frontal
fascia[F] protettiva della fronte[F]

バイザー
visor
Visier[N]
oculaire[M]
careta[F]
visore[M]

締め紐（ひも）
head harness
Kopfriemen[M]
jeu[M] de brides[F]
correas[F]
elastico[M] regolabile per il capo[M]

カートリッジ
cartridge
Kartusche[F]
cartouche[F]
cartucho[M]
filtro[M]

吸気弁
inhalation valve
Einatmungsventil[N]
soupape[F] inspiratoire
válvula[F] de inhalación[F]
valvola[F] di inspirazione[F]

フィルター・カバー
filter cover
Filterabdeckung[F]
couvre-filtre[M]
tapa[F] del filtro[M]
coprifiltro[M]

排気弁
exhalation valve
Ausatmungsventil[N]
soupape[F] expiratoire
válvula[F] de exhalación[F]
valvola[F] di espirazione[F]

防塵（ほうじん）マスク
half-mask respirator
leichte Atemschutzmaske[F]
masque[M] bucco-nasal
máscara[F] para el polvo[M]
mascherina[F]

ヘッドバンド
headband
Kopfband[N]
serre-tête[M]
cinta[F]
elastici[M] stringitesta

防塵カップ
cup gasket
Maskendichtung[F]
coupelle[F] d'étanchéité[F]
mascarilla[F]
calotta[F] filtrante

排気弁
exhalation valve
Ausatmungsventil[N]
soupape[F] expiratoire
válvula[F] de exhalación[F]
valvola[F] di espirazione[F]

足の保護具

foot protection | Fußschutz[M] | protection[F] des pieds[M] | refuerzo[F] para los pies[M] | protezione[F] per i piedi[M]

安全靴
safety boot
Sicherheitsschuh[M]
brodequin[M] de sécurité[F]
bota[F] de seguridad[F]
scarponcino[M] di sicurezza[F]

スチール・キャップ
reinforced toe
Stahlkappe[F]
embout[M] de protection[F]
tope[M]
puntale[M] rinforzato

爪先保護
toe guard
Zehenschützer[M]
protège-orteils[M]
puntera[F] protectora
puntale[M] di protezione[F]

安全 | SAFETY
SICHERHEIT | SÉCURITÉ | SEGURIDAD | SICUREZZA

安全標識

日本語 | 英語 | ドイツ語 | フランス語 | スペイン語 | イタリア語

safety symbols | Warn- und Gebotszeichen^N | symboles^M de sécurité^F | símbolos^M de seguridad^F | simboli^M di sicurezza^F

危険物の表示
dangerous materials
gefährliche Substanzen^F
matières^F dangereuses
materiales^M peligrosos
materiali^M pericolosi

腐食性物質
corrosive
ätzend
matières^F corrosives
corrosivo
materiale^M corrosivo

感電の危険あり
electrical hazard
elektrische Spannung^F
danger^M électrique
alto voltaje^M
alta tensione^F

爆発性物質
explosive
explosionsgefährlich
matières^F explosives
explosivo
materiale^M esplosivo

可燃性物質
flammable
leicht entzündlich
matières^F inflammables
inflamable
materiale^M infiammabile

放射性物質
radioactive
radioaktiv
matières^F radioactives
radioactivo
materiale^M radioattivo

有毒性物質
poison
Gift^N
matières^F toxiques
veneno^M
materiale^M tossico

保護具着用の表示
protection
Schutzmaßnahmen^F
protection^F
protección^F
misure^F di protezione^F obbligatorie

保護眼鏡着用
eye protection
Augenschutz^M tragen
protection^F obligatoire de la vue^F
protección^F de los ojos^M
protezione^F per gli occhi^M

耳栓着用
ear protection
Gehörschutz^M tragen
protection^F obligatoire de l'ouïe^F
protección^F de los oidos^M
protezione^F per le orecchie^F

保護帽着用
head protection
Schutzhelm^M tragen
protection^F obligatoire de la tête^F
protección^F de la cabeza^F
protezione^F per la testa^F

手袋着用
hand protection
Schutzhandschuhe^M tragen
protection^F obligatoire des mains^F
protección^F de las manos^F
protezione^F per le mani^F

長靴着用
foot protection
Schutzschuhe^M tragen
protection^F obligatoire des pieds^M
protección^F de los pies^M
protezione^F per i piedi^M

防塵[防毒]マスク着用
respiratory system protection
Atemschutz^M tragen
protection^F obligatoire des voies^F respiratoires
protección^F del sistema^M respiratorio
protezione^F per le vie^F respiratorie

社会

健康 | HEALTH
GESUNDHEIT | SANTÉ | SALUD | SALUTE

救急車

ambulance | Rettungswagen^M | ambulance^F | ambulancia^F | ambulanza^F

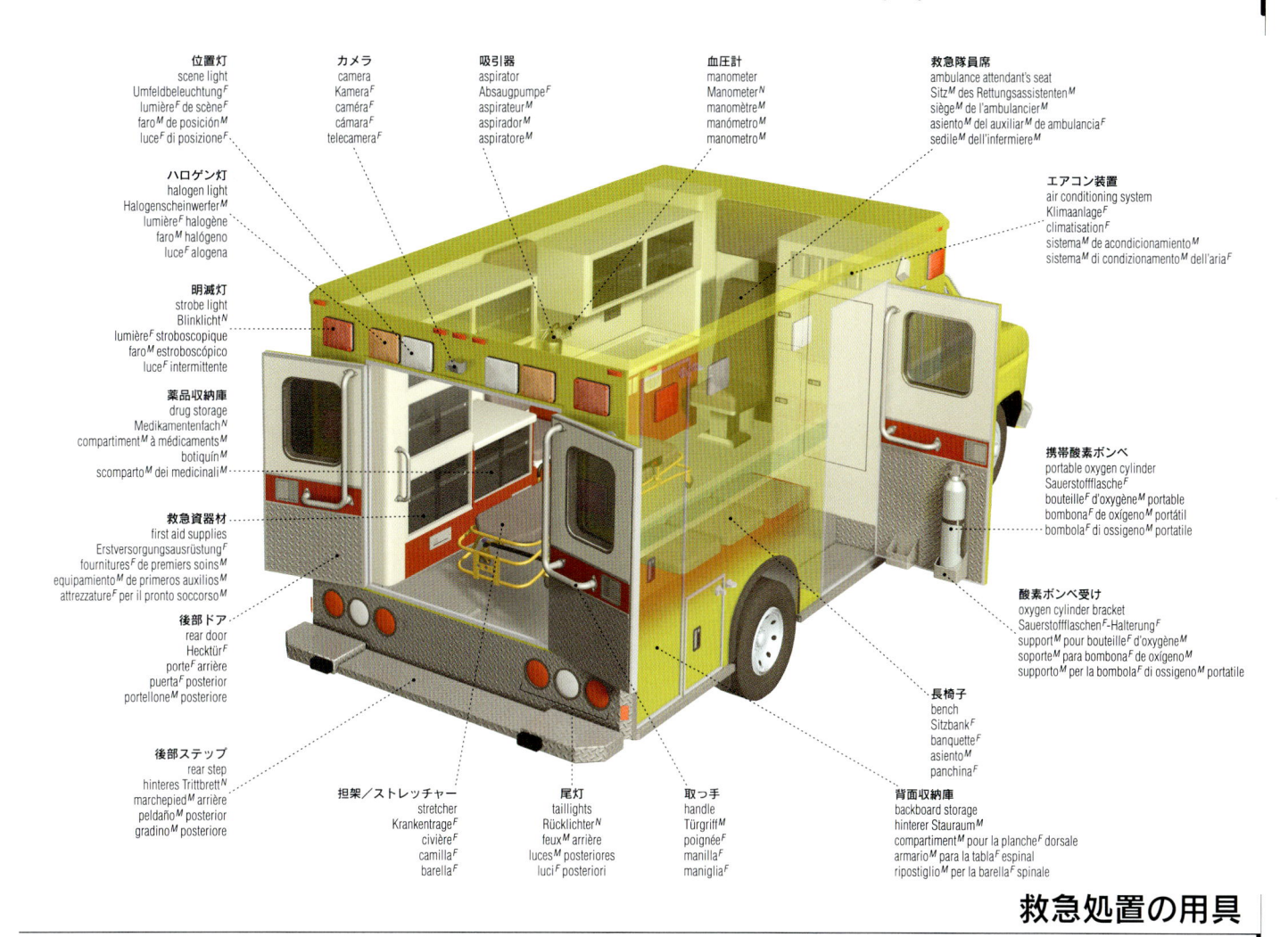

位置灯
scene light
Umfeldbeleuchtung^F
lumière^F de scène^F
faro^M de posición^F
luce^F di posizione^F

カメラ
camera
Kamera^F
caméra^F
cámara^F
telecamera^F

吸引器
aspirator
Absaugpumpe^F
aspirateur^M
aspirador^M
aspiratore^M

血圧計
manometer
Manometer^N
manomètre^M
manómetro^M
manometro^M

救急隊員席
ambulance attendant's seat
Sitz^M des Rettungsassistenten^M
siège^M de l'ambulancier^M
asiento^M del auxiliar^M de ambulancia^F
sedile^M dell'infermiere^F

ハロゲン灯
halogen light
Halogenscheinwerfer^M
lumière^F halogène
faro^M halógeno
luce^F alogena

エアコン装置
air conditioning system
Klimaanlage^F
climatisation^F
sistema^M de acondicionamiento^M
sistema^M di condizionamento^M dell'aria^F

明滅灯
strobe light
Blinklicht^N
lumière^F stroboscopique
faro^M estroboscópico
luce^F intermittente

薬品収納庫
drug storage
Medikamentenfach^N
compartiment^M à médicaments^M
botiquín^M
scomparto^M dei medicinali^M

携帯酸素ボンベ
portable oxygen cylinder
Sauerstoffflasche^F
bouteille^F d'oxygène^M portable
bombona^F de oxígeno^M portátil
bombola^F di ossigeno^M portatile

救急資器材
first aid supplies
Erstversorgungsausrüstung^F
fournitures^F de premiers soins^M
equipamiento^M de primeros auxilios^M
attrezzature^F per il pronto soccorso^M

酸素ボンベ受け
oxygen cylinder bracket
Sauerstoffflaschen^F-Halterung^F
support^M pour bouteille^F d'oxygène^M
soporte^M para bombona^F de oxígeno^M
supporto^M per la bombola^F di ossigeno^M portatile

後部ドア
rear door
Hecktür^F
porte^F arrière
puerta^F posterior
portellone^M posteriore

長椅子
bench
Sitzbank^F
banquette^F
asiento^M
panchina^F

後部ステップ
rear step
hinteres Trittbrett^N
marchepied^M arrière
peldaño^M posterior
gradino^M posteriore

担架／ストレッチャー
stretcher
Krankentrage^F
civière^F
camilla^F
barella^F

尾灯
taillights
Rücklichter^N
feux^M arrière
luces^M posteriores
luci^F posteriori

取っ手
handle
Türgriff^M
poignée^F
manilla^F
maniglia^F

背面収納庫
backboard storage
hinterer Stauraum^M
compartiment^M pour la planche dorsale
armario^M para la tabla^F espinal
ripostiglio^M per la barella^F spinale

救急処置の用具

first aid equipment | Notfallausrüstung^F | matériel^M de secours^M | equipo^M de primeros auxilios^M | strumenti^M per il pronto soccorso^M

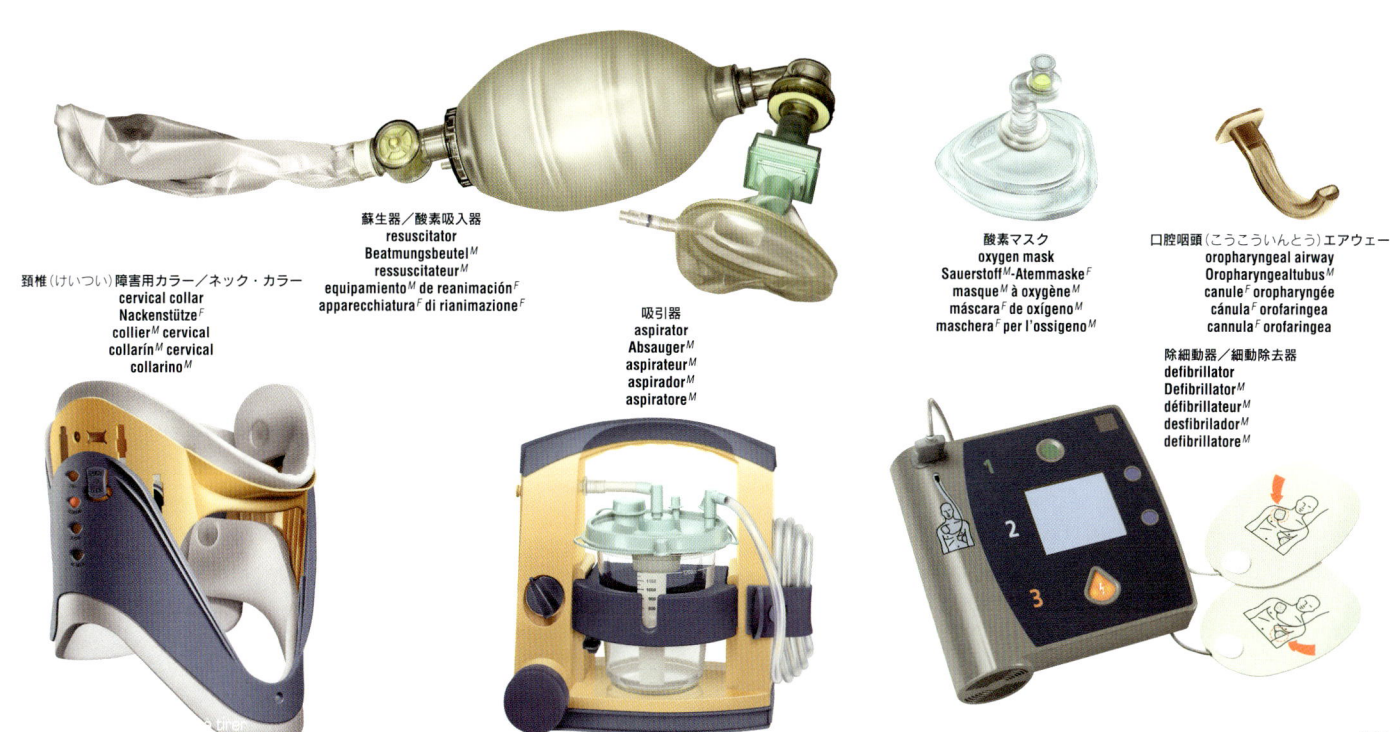

蘇生器／酸素吸入器
resuscitator
Beatmungsbeutel^M
ressuscitateur^M
equipamiento^M de reanimación^F
apparecchiatura^F di rianimazione^F

酸素マスク
oxygen mask
Sauerstoff^M-Atemmaske^F
masque^M à oxygène^M
máscara^F de oxígeno^M
maschera^F per l'ossigeno^M

口腔咽頭（こうこういんとう）エアウェー
oropharyngeal airway
Oropharyngealtubus^M
canule^F oropharyngée
cánula^F orofaringea
cannula^F orofaringea

頚椎（けいつい）障害用カラー／ネック・カラー
cervical collar
Nackenstütze^F
collier^M cervical
collarín^M cervical
collarino^M

吸引器
aspirator
Absauger^M
aspirateur^M
aspirador^M
aspiratore^M

除細動器／細動除去器
defibrillator
Defibrillator^M
défibrillateur^M
desfibrilador^M
defibrillatore^M

健康 | HEALTH
GESUNDHEIT | SANTÉ | SALUD | SALUTE

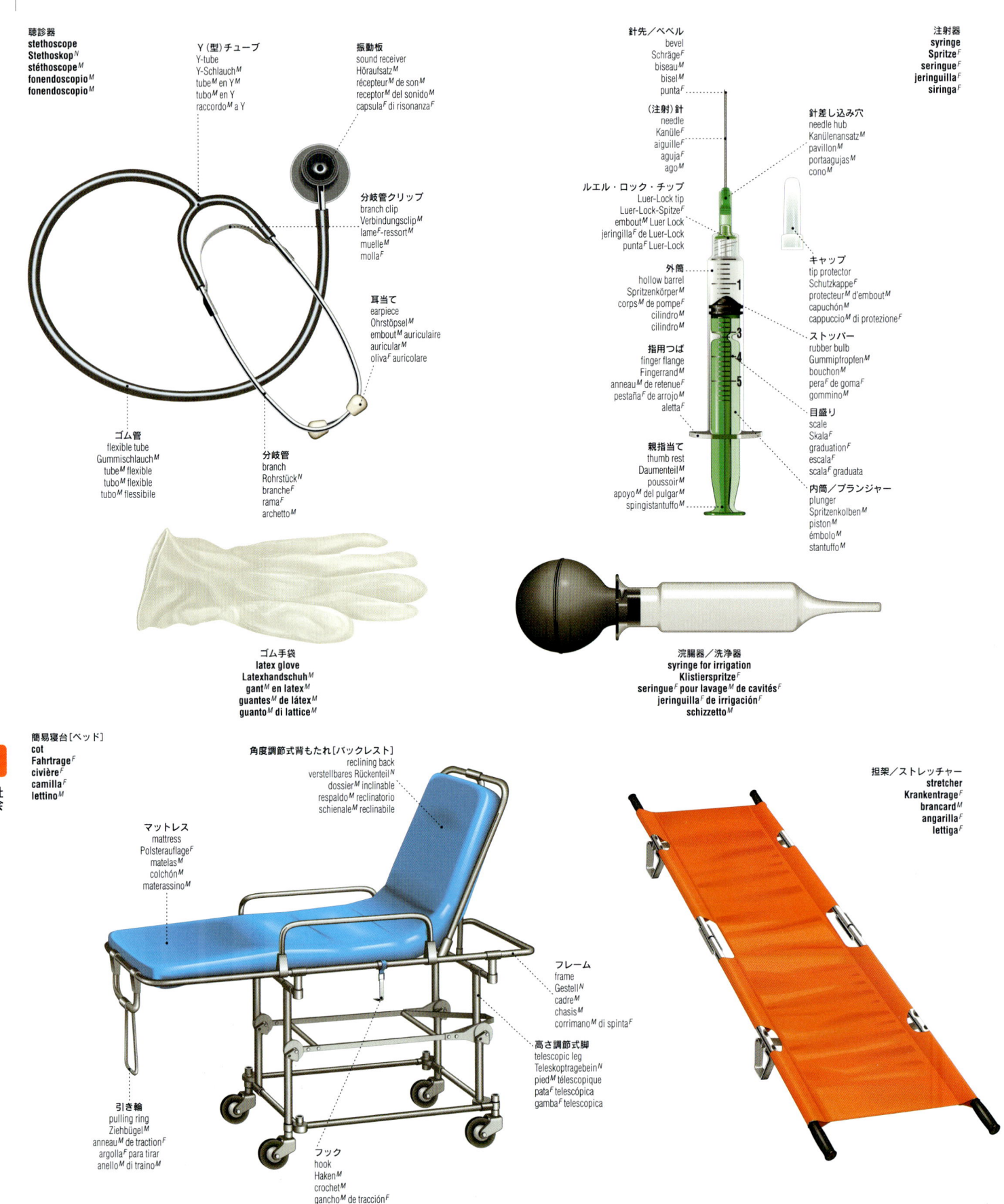

救急処置の用具

日本語 | 英語 | ドイツ語 | フランス語 | スペイン語 | イタリア語

聴診器
stethoscope
Stethoskop^N
stéthoscope^M
fonendoscopio^M
fonendoscopio^M

Y (型) チューブ
Y-tube
Y-Schlauch^M
tube^M en Y^M
tubo^M en Y
raccordo^M a Y

振動板
sound receiver
Höraufsatz^M
récepteur^M de son^M
receptor^M del sonido^M
capsula^F di risonanza^F

針先／ベベル
bevel
Schräge^F
biseau^M
bisel^M
punta^F

(注射) 針
needle
Kanüle^F
aiguille^F
aguja^F
ago^M

針差し込み穴
needle hub
Kanülenansatz^M
pavillon^M
portaagujas^M
cono^M

注射器
syringe
Spritze^F
seringue^F
jeringuilla^F
siringa^F

ルエル・ロック・チップ
Luer-Lock tip
Luer-Lock-Spitze^F
embout^M Luer Lock
jeringilla^F de Luer-Lock
punta^F Luer-Lock

分岐管クリップ
branch clip
Verbindungsclip^M
lame^F-ressort^M
muelle^M
molla^F

耳当て
earpiece
Ohrstöpsel^M
embout^M auriculaire
auricular^M
oliva^F auricolare

外筒
hollow barrel
Spritzenkörper^M
corps^M de pompe^F
cilindro^M
cilindro^M

キャップ
tip protector
Schutzkappe^F
protecteur^M d'embout^M
capuchón^M
cappuccio^M di protezione^F

ゴム管
flexible tube
Gummischlauch^M
tube^M flexible
tubo^M flexible
tubo^M flessibile

分岐管
branch
Rohrstück^N
branche^F
rama^F
archetto^M

指用つば
finger flange
Fingerrand^M
anneau^M de retenue^F
pestaña^F de arrojo^M
aletta^F

ストッパー
rubber bulb
Gummipfropfen^M
bouchon^M
pera^F de goma^F
gommino^M

目盛り
scale
Skala^F
graduation^F
escala^F
scala^F graduata

親指当て
thumb rest
Daumenteil^M
poussoir^M
apoyo^M del pulgar^M
spingistantuffo^M

内筒／プランジャー
plunger
Spritzenkolben^M
piston^M
émbolo^M
stantuffo^M

ゴム手袋
latex glove
Latexhandschuh^M
gant^M en latex^M
guantes^M de látex^M
guanto^M di lattice^M

浣腸器／洗浄器
syringe for irrigation
Klistierspritze^F
seringue^F pour lavage^M de cavités^F
jeringuilla^F de irrigación^F
schizzetto^M

簡易寝台 [ベッド]
cot
Fahrtrage^F
civière^F
camilla^F
lettino^M

角度調節式背もたれ [バックレスト]
reclining back
verstellbares Rückenteil^N
dossier^M inclinable
respaldo^M reclinatorio
schienale^M reclinabile

マットレス
mattress
Polsterauflage^F
matelas^M
colchón^M
materassino^M

担架／ストレッチャー
stretcher
Krankentrage^F
brancard^M
angarilla^F
lettiga^F

フレーム
frame
Gestell^N
cadre^M
chasis^M
corrimano^M di spinta^F

高さ調節式脚
telescopic leg
Teleskoptragebein^N
pied^M télescopique
pata^F telescópica
gamba^F telescopica

引き輪
pulling ring
Ziehbügel^M
anneau^M de traction^F
argolla^F para tirar
anello^M di traino^M

フック
hook
Haken^M
crochet^M
gancho^M de tracción^F
gancio^M

社会

776

健康 | HEALTH
GESUNDHEIT | SANTÉ | SALUD | SALUTE

救急箱

first aid kit | Erste-Hilfe-Kasten^M | trousse^F de secours^M | botiquín^M de primeros auxilios^M | cassetta^F di pronto soccorso^M

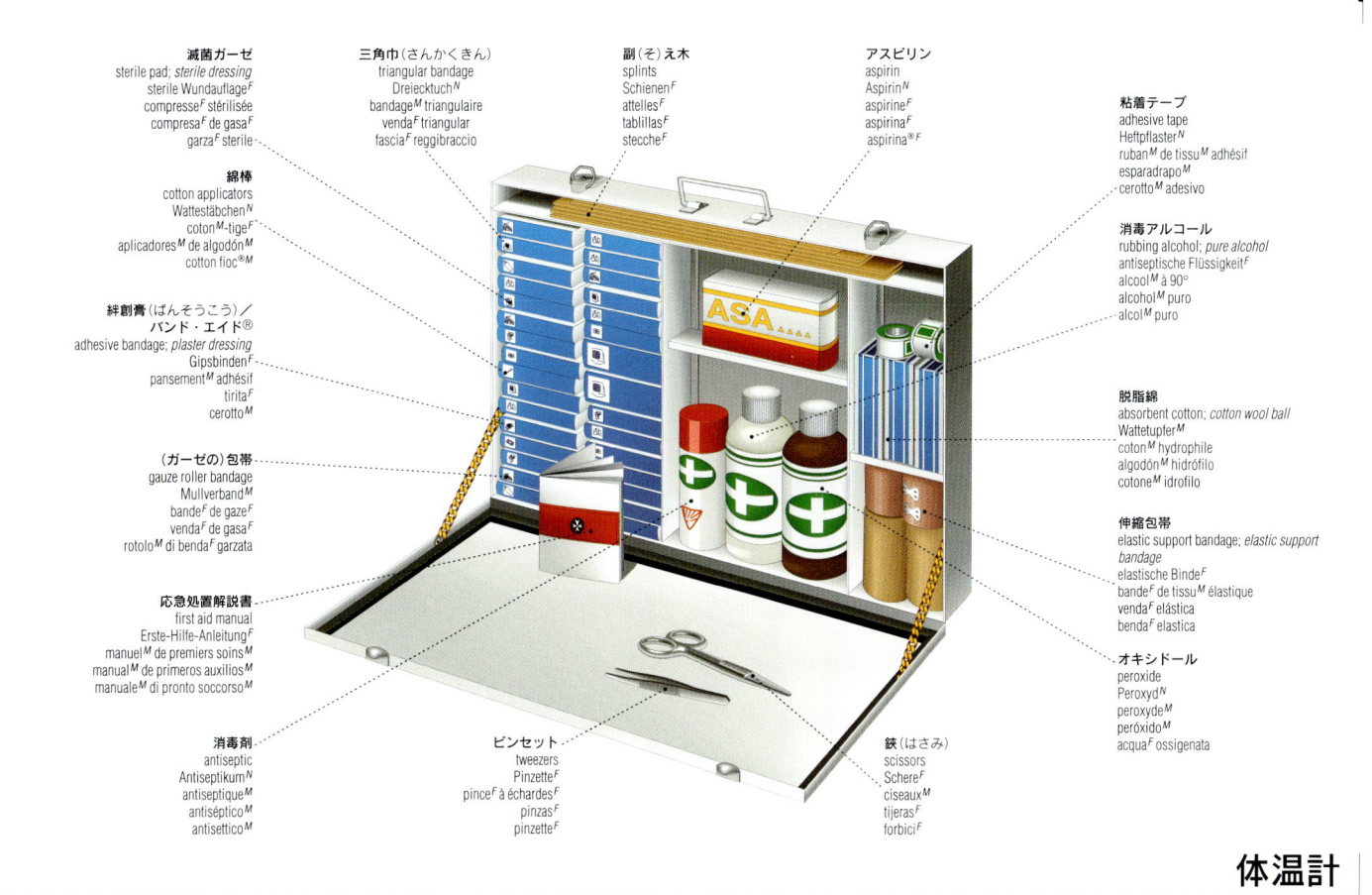

滅菌ガーゼ
sterile pad; *sterile dressing*
sterile Wundauflage^F
compresse^F stérilisée
compresa^F de gasa^F
garza^F sterile

三角巾（さんかくきん）
triangular bandage
Dreiecktuch^N
bandage^M triangulaire
venda^F triangular
fascia^F reggibraccio

副（そ）え木
splints
Schienen^F
attelles^F
tablillas^F
stecche^F

アスピリン
aspirin
Aspirin^N
aspirine^F
aspirina^F
aspirina®^F

粘着テープ
adhesive tape
Heftpflaster^N
ruban^M de tissu^M adhésif
esparadrapo^M
cerotto^M adesivo

綿棒
cotton applicators
Wattestäbchen^N
coton^M-tige^F
aplicadores^M de algodón^M
cotton fioc®^M

消毒アルコール
rubbing alcohol; *pure alcohol*
antiseptische Flüssigkeit^F
alcool^M à 90°
alcohol^M puro
alcol^M puro

絆創膏（ばんそうこう）／バンド・エイド®
adhesive bandage; *plaster dressing*
Gipsbinden^F
pansement^M adhésif
tirita^F
cerotto^M

脱脂綿
absorbent cotton; *cotton wool ball*
Wattetupfer^M
coton^M hydrophile
algodón^M hidrófilo
cotone^M idrofilo

（ガーゼの）包帯
gauze roller bandage
Mullverband^M
bande^F de gaze^F
venda^F de gasa^F
rotolo^M di benda^F garzata

伸縮包帯
elastic support bandage; *elastic support bandage*
elastische Binde^F
bande^F de tissu^M élastique
venda^F elástica
benda^F elastica

応急処置解説書
first aid manual
Erste-Hilfe-Anleitung^F
manuel^M de premiers soins^M
manual^M de primeros auxilios^M
manuale^M di pronto soccorso^M

オキシドール
peroxide
Peroxyd^N
peroxyde^M
peróxido^M
acqua^F ossigenata

消毒剤
antiseptic
Antiseptikum^N
antiseptique^M
antiséptico^M
antisettico^M

ピンセット
tweezers
Pinzette^F
pince^F à échardes^F
pinzas^F
pinzette^F

鋏（はさみ）
scissors
Schere^F
ciseaux^M
tijeras^F
forbici^F

体温計

clinical thermometers | Fieberthermometer^N | thermomètres^M médicaux | termómetros^M clínicos | termometri^M clinici

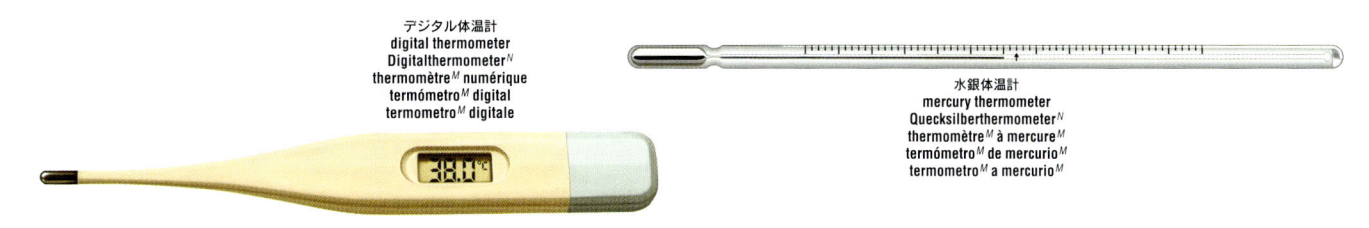

デジタル体温計
digital thermometer
Digitalthermometer^N
thermomètre^M numérique
termómetro^M digital
termometro^M digitale

水銀体温計
mercury thermometer
Quecksilberthermometer^N
thermomètre^M à mercure^M
termómetro^M de mercurio^M
termometro^M a mercurio^M

血圧計

blood pressure monitor | Blutdruckmessgerät^N | tensiomètre^M | tensiómetro^M | monitor^M della pressione^F sanguigna

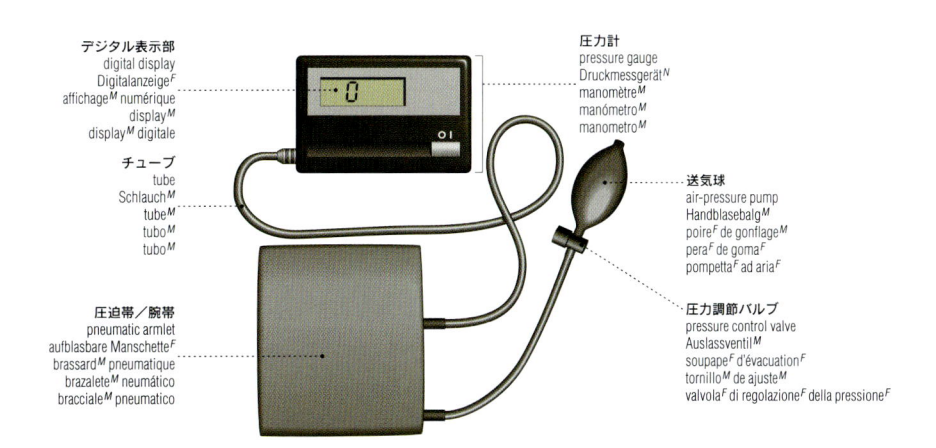

デジタル表示部
digital display
Digitalanzeige^F
affichage^M numérique
display^M
display^M digitale

圧力計
pressure gauge
Druckmessgerät^N
manomètre^M
manómetro^M
manometro^M

チューブ
tube
Schlauch^M
tube^M
tubo^M
tubo^M

送気球
air-pressure pump
Handblasebalg^M
poire^F de gonflage^M
pera^F de goma^F
pompetta^F ad aria^F

圧迫帯／腕帯
pneumatic armlet
aufblasbare Manschette^F
brassard^M pneumatique
brazalete^M neumático
bracciale^M pneumatico

圧力調節バルブ
pressure control valve
Auslassventil^M
soupape^F d'évacuation^F
tornillo^M de ajuste^M
valvola^F di regolazione^F della pressione^F

社会

777

健康 | HEALTH
GESUNDHEIT | SANTÉ | SALUD | SALUTE

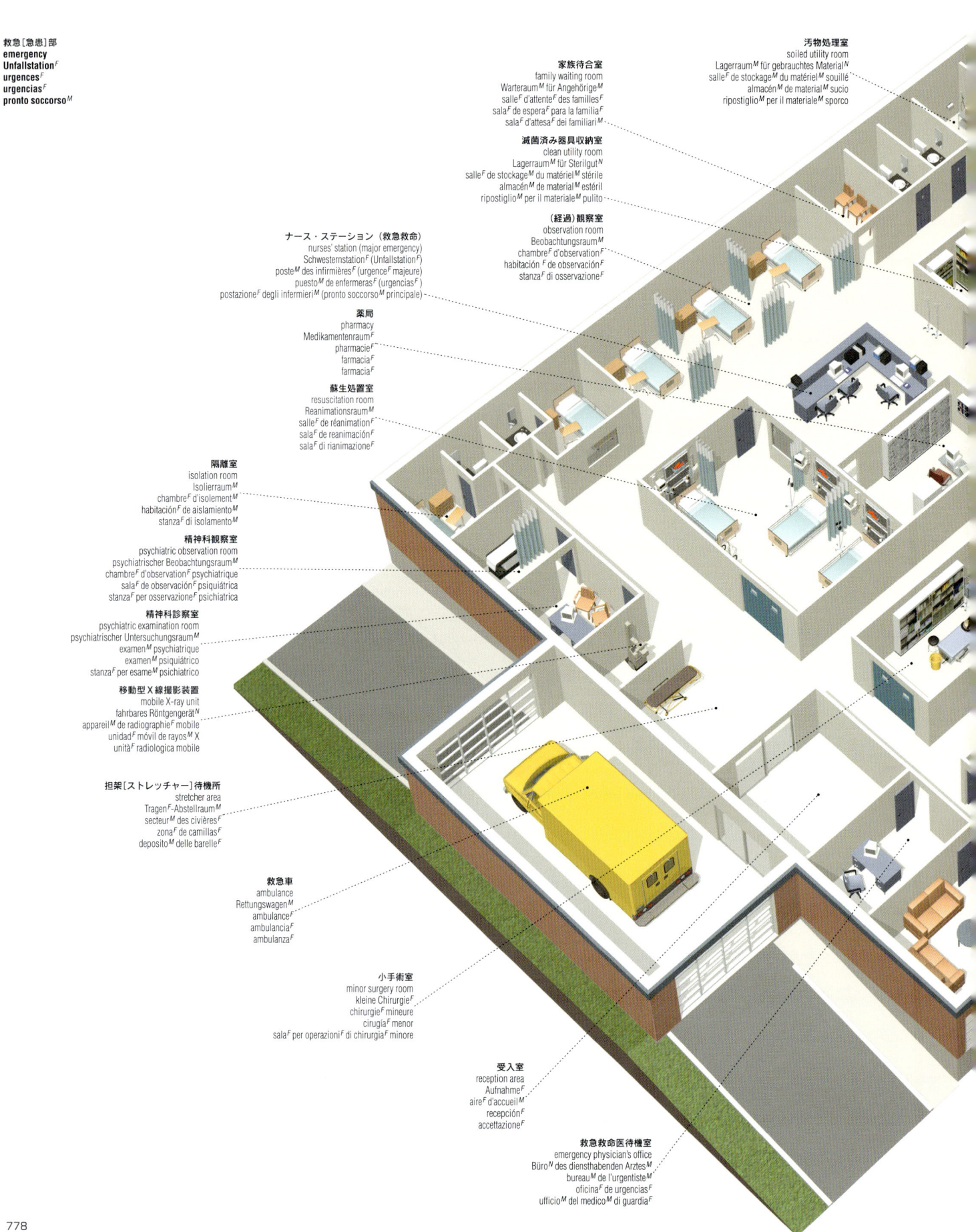

病院

hospital | Krankenhaus[N] | hôpital[M] | hospital[M] | ospedale[M]

日本語 | 英語 | ドイツ語 | フランス語 | スペイン語 | イタリア語

救急[急患]部
emergency
Unfallstation[F]
urgences[F]
urgencias[F]
pronto soccorso[M]

家族待合室
family waiting room
Warteraum[M] für Angehörige[M]
salle[F] d'attente des familles[F]
sala[F] de espera[F] para la familia
sala[F] d'attesa[F] dei familiari[M]

汚物処理室
soiled utility room
Lagerraum[M] für gebrauchtes Material[N]
salle[F] de stockage du matériel[M] souillé
almacén[M] de material[M] sucio
ripostiglio[M] per il materiale[M] sporco

滅菌済み器具収納室
clean utility room
Lagerraum[M] für Sterilgut[N]
salle[F] de stockage[F] du matériel[M] stérile
almacén[M] de material[M] estéril
ripostiglio[M] per il materiale[M] pulito

(経過)観察室
observation room
Beobachtungsraum[M]
chambre[F] d'observation[F]
habitación[F] de observación[F]
stanza[F] di osservazione[F]

ナース・ステーション(救急救命)
nurses' station (major emergency)
Schwesternstation[F] (Unfallstation[F])
poste[M] des infirmières[F] (urgence[F] majeure)
puesto[M] de enfermeras[F] (urgencias[F])
postazione[F] degli infermieri[M] (pronto soccorso[M] principale)

薬局
pharmacy
Medikamentenraum[M]
pharmacie[F]
farmacia[F]
farmacia[F]

蘇生処置室
resuscitation room
Reanimationsraum[M]
salle[F] de réanimation[F]
sala[F] de reanimación[F]
sala[F] di rianimazione[F]

隔離室
isolation room
Isolierraum[M]
chambre[F] d'isolement[M]
habitación[F] de aislamiento[M]
stanza[F] di isolamento[M]

精神科観察室
psychiatric observation room
psychiatrischer Beobachtungsraum[M]
chambre[F] d'observation[F] psychiatrique
sala[F] de observación[F] psiquiátrica
stanza[F] per osservazione[F] psichiatrica

精神科診察室
psychiatric examination room
psychiatrischer Untersuchungsraum[M]
examen[M] psychiatrique
examen[M] psiquiátrico
stanza[F] per esame[M] psichiatrico

移動型X線撮影装置
mobile X-ray unit
fahrbares Röntgengerät[N]
appareil[M] de radiographie[F] mobile
unidad[F] móvil de rayos[M] X
unità[F] radiologica mobile

担架[ストレッチャー]待機所
stretcher area
Tragen[F]-Abstellraum[M]
secteur[M] des civières[F]
zona[F] de camillas[F]
deposito[M] delle barelle[F]

救急車
ambulance
Rettungswagen[M]
ambulance[F]
ambulancia[F]
ambulanza[F]

小手術室
minor surgery room
kleine Chirurgie[F]
chirurgie[F] mineure
cirugía[F] menor
sala[F] per operazioni[F] di chirurgia[F] minore

受入室
reception area
Aufnahme[F]
aire[F] d'accueil
recepción[F]
accettazione[F]

救急救命医待機室
emergency physician's office
Büro[N] des diensthabenden Arztes[M]
bureau[M] de l'urgentiste[M]
oficina[F] de urgencias[F]
ufficio[M] del medico[M] di guardia[F]

健康 | HEALTH
GESUNDHEIT | SANTÉ | SALUD | SALUTE

病院

眼科・耳鼻咽喉（じびいんこう）科診察室
ophthalmology and ENT (ear, nose and throat) room
Augen^N- und HNO(Hals^M-Nasen^F-Ohren^N)- Behandlungsraum^M
salle^F d'ophtalmologie^F et d'oto-rhino-laryngologie^F
oftalmología^F y otorrinolaringología^F
sala^F di oftalmologia^F e otorinolaringoiatria^F

ギプス処置室
plaster room
Gipsraum^M
salle^F de plâtre^M
sala^F de enyesado^M
sala^F gessi^M

ソーシャル[ケース]ワーカー室／社会福祉相談員室
social worker's office
Sozialarbeiterbüro^N
bureau^M du travailleur^M social
despacho^M del asistente^M social
ufficio^M dell'assistente$^{M/F}$ sociale

婦人科診察室
gynecological examination room
gynäkologischer Untersuchungsraum^M
salle^F d'examen^M gynécologique
consultorio^M ginecológico
stanza^F per visite^F ginecologiche

診察処置室
examination and treatment room
Untersuchungs- und Behandlungsraum^M
salle^F d'examen^M et de soins^M
consultorio^M
stanza^F per le visite^F mediche e le terapie^F

トイレ／手洗い
toilets
Toiletten^F
w.-c.^{M}
aseos^F
toilette^F

飲み物自動販売機
beverage dispenser
Getränkeautomat^M
distributeur^M de boissons^F
distribuidor^M de bebidas^F
distributore^M di bibite^F

公衆電話
pay phone
Münzfernsprecher^M
téléphone^M public
teléfono^M público
telefono^M pubblico

ナース・ステーション（救急外来）
nurses' station (ambulatory emergency)
Schwesternstation^F (ambulante Unfallstation^F)
poste^M des infirmières^F (urgence^F ambulatoire)
puesto^M de enfermeras^F (ambulatorio^M de urgencias^F)
postazione^F degli infermieri^M (pronto soccorso^M ambulatoriale)

待合室
waiting room
Warteraum^M
salle^F d'attente^F
sala^F de espera^F
sala^F d'attesa^F

警備員席
security guard's work station
Sicherheitsdienst^M
poste^M de l'agent^M de sécurité^F
puesto^M de la guardia^M de seguridad^F
postazione^F dell'agente^M di sicurezza^F

トリアージ室／緊急[重症]度区分室
triage room
Triageraum^M
salle^F de triage^M
sala^F de clasificación^F
stanza^F del triage^M

案内所／受付
information desk
Informationsschalter^F
comptoir^M de renseignements^M
información^F
banco^M delle informazioni^F

婦長室
head nurse's office
Büro^N der Oberschwester^F
bureau^M de l'infirmière^F en chef^M
despacho^M de la enfermera^F jefe
ufficio^M del caposala^M

職員休憩室
staff lounge
Personalraum^M
salon^M du personnel^M
sala^F del personal^F
stanza^F del personale^M

社会

健康 | HEALTH
GESUNDHEIT | SANTÉ | SALUD | SALUTE

病院

日本語 | 英語 | ドイツ語 | フランス語 | スペイン語 | イタリア語

病室
patient room
Krankenzimmer^N
chambre^F d'hôpital^M
habitación^F de un paciente^M
stanza^F di degenza^F

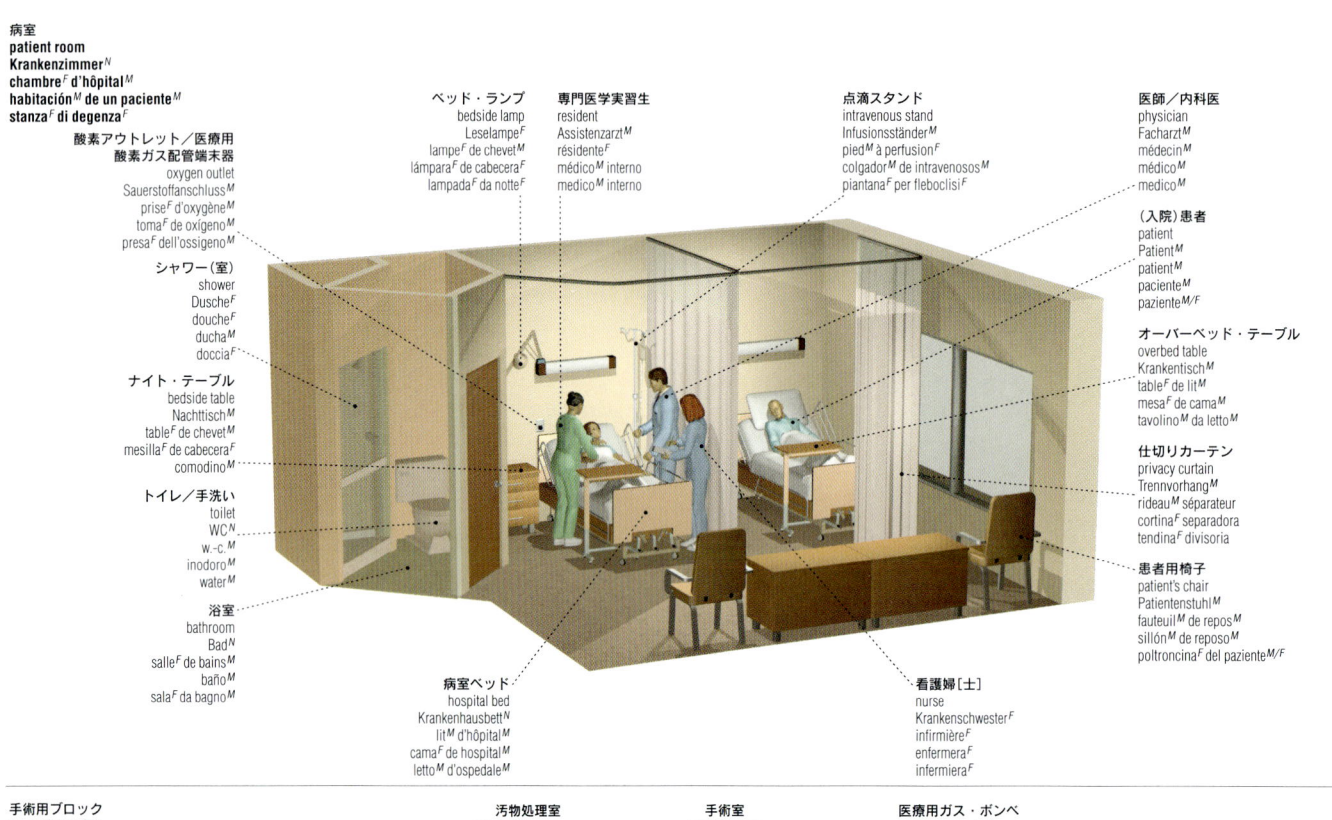

酸素アウトレット／医療用酸素ガス配管端末器
oxygen outlet
Sauerstoffanschluss^M
prise^F d'oxygène^M
toma^F de oxígeno^M
presa^F dell'ossigeno^M

シャワー（室）
shower
Dusche^F
douche^F
ducha^F
doccia^F

ナイト・テーブル
bedside table
Nachttisch^M
table^F de chevet^M
mesilla^F de cabecera^F
comodino^M

トイレ／手洗い
toilet
WC^N
w.-c.^M
inodoro^M
water^M

浴室
bathroom
Bad^N
salle^F de bains^F
baño^M
sala^F da bagno^M

ベッド・ランプ
bedside lamp
Leselampe^F
lampe^F de chevet^M
lámpara^F de cabecera^F
lampada^F da notte^F

専門医学実習生
resident
Assistenzarzt^M
résidente^F
médico^M interno
medico^M interno

病室ベッド
hospital bed
Krankenhausbett^N
lit^M d'hôpital^M
cama^F de hospital^M
letto^M d'ospedale^M

点滴スタンド
intravenous stand
Infusionsständer^M
pied^M à perfusion^F
colgador^M de intravenosos^M
piantana^F per fleboclisi^F

看護婦［士］
nurse
Krankenschwester^F
infirmière^F
enfermera^F
infermiera^F

医師／内科医
physician
Facharzt^M
médecin^M
médico^M
medico^M

（入院）患者
patient
Patient^M
patient^M
paciente^M
paziente^M/F

オーバーベッド・テーブル
overbed table
Krankentisch^M
table^F de lit^M
mesa^F de cama^F
tavolino^M da letto^M

仕切りカーテン
privacy curtain
Trennvorhang^M
rideau^M séparateur
cortina^F separadora
tendina^F divisoria

患者用椅子
patient's chair
Patientenstuhl^M
fauteuil^M de repos^M
sillón^M de reposo^M
poltroncina^F del paziente^M/F

手術用ブロック
operating suite
Operationsabteilung^F
bloc^M opératoire
bloque^M de cirugía^F
blocco^M operatorio

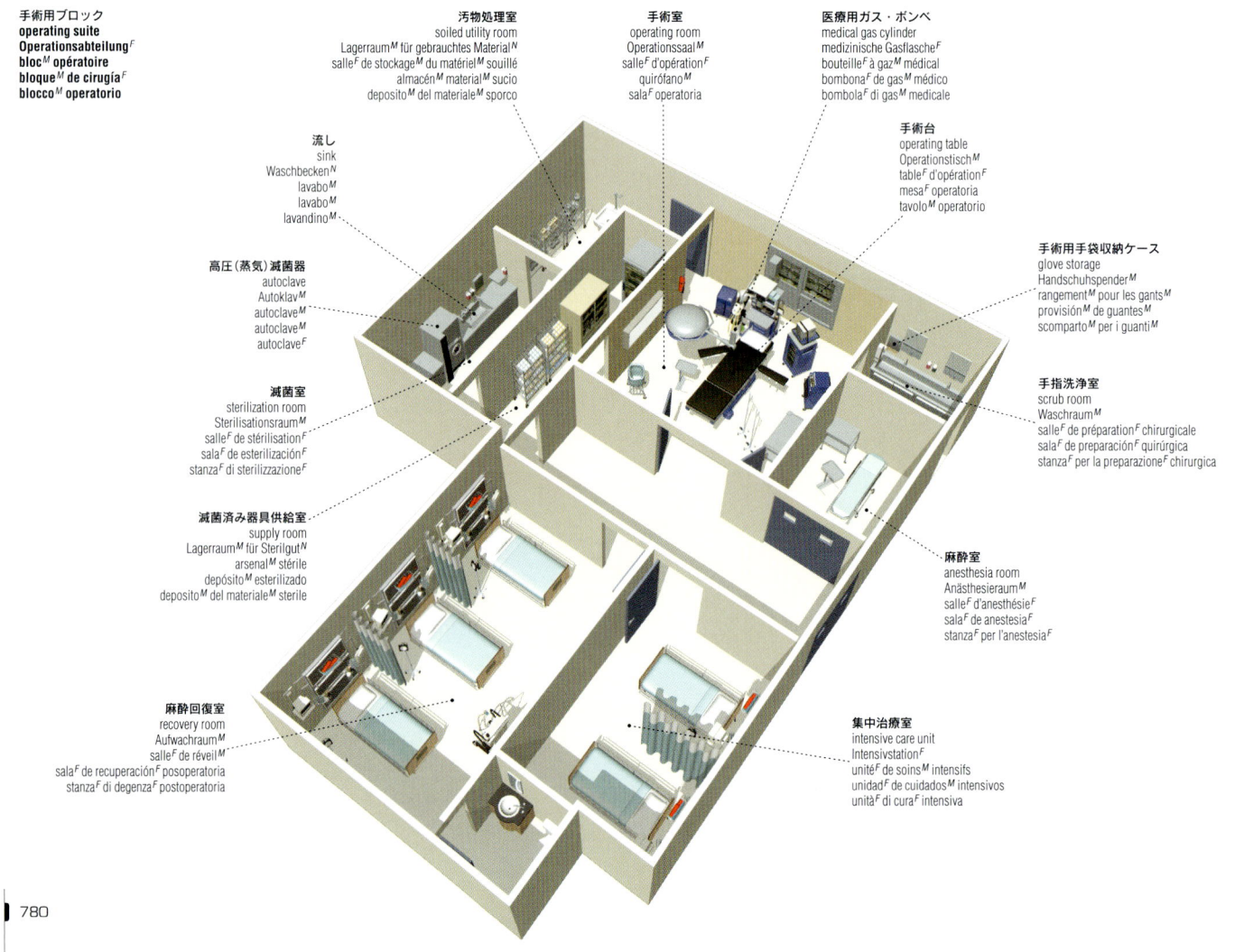

流し
sink
Waschbecken^N
lavabo^M
lavabo^M
lavandino^M

高圧(蒸気)滅菌器
autoclave
Autoklav^M
autoclave
autoclave
autoclave^F

滅菌室
sterilization room
Sterilisationsraum^M
salle^F de stérilisation^F
sala^F de esterilización^F
stanza^F di sterilizzazione^F

滅菌済み器具供給室
supply room
Lagerraum^M für Sterilgut^N
arsenal^M stérile
depósito^M esterilizado
deposito^M del materiale^M sterile

麻酔回復室
recovery room
Aufwachraum^M
salle^F de réveil^M
sala^F de recuperación^F posoperatoria
stanza^F di degenza^F postoperatoria

汚物処理室
soiled utility room
Lagerraum^M für gebrauchtes Material^N
salle^F de stockage^M du matériel^M souillé
almacén^M material^M sucio
deposito^M del materiale^M sporco

手術室
operating room
Operationssaal^M
salle^F d'opération^F
quirófano^M
sala^F operatoria

集中治療室
intensive care unit
Intensivstation^F
unité^F de soins^M intensifs
unidad^F de cuidados^M intensivos
unità^F di cura^F intensiva

医療用ガス・ボンベ
medical gas cylinder
medizinische Gasflasche^F
bouteille^F à gaz^M médical
bombona^F de gas^M médico
bombola^F di gas^M medicale

手術台
operating table
Operationstisch^M
table^F d'opération^F
mesa^F operatoria
tavolo^M operatorio

手術用手袋収納ケース
glove storage
Handschuhspender^M
rangement^M pour les gants^M
provisión^F de guantes^M
scomparto^M per i guanti^M

手指洗浄室
scrub room
Waschraum^M
salle^F de préparation^F chirurgicale
sala^F de preparación^F quirúrgica
stanza^F per la preparazione^F chirurgica

麻酔室
anesthesia room
Anästhesieraum^M
salle^F d'anesthésie^F
sala^F de anestesia^F
stanza^F per l'anestesia^F

健康 | HEALTH
GESUNDHEIT | SANTÉ | SALUD | SALUTE

病院

外来治療用ブロック
ambulatory care unit
Poliklinik^F
unité^F de soins^M ambulatoires
ambulatorio^M
poliambulatorio^M

標本採取待機室
specimen collection center waiting room; specimen collection centre waiting room
Wartebereich^M für den Entnahmeraum^M
salle^F d'attente^F du centre de prélèvements^M
sala^F de espera^F del centro^M de extracción^F de sangre^F
sala^F d'attesa^F del centro^M prelievi^M

外科用流し
surgeon's sink
Chirurgen^M-Waschraum^M
lavabo^M du chirurgien^M
lavabo^M de cirujano^M
lavandino^M del chirurgo^M

病理検査室
pathology laboratory
pathologisches Labor^N
laboratoire^M de pathologie^F
laboratorio^M patológico^M
laboratorio^M di anatomia^F patologica

滅菌室
sterilization room
Sterilisationsraum^M
salle^F de stérilisation^F
sala^F de esterilización^F
sala^F di sterilizzazione^F

手術室
operating room
Operationssaal^M
salle^F d'opération^F
quirófano^M
sala^F operatoria

脱衣所
undressing booth
Entkleidungsraum^M
cabine^F de déshabillage^M
cabina^F para desvestirse
spogliatoio^M

(経過)観察室
observation room
Beobachtungsraum^M
chambre^F d'observation^F
consultorio^M
stanza^F di osservazione^F

第2待合室
secondary waiting room
zweiter Warteraum^M
salle^F d'attente^F secondaire
sala^F de espera^F
sala^F d'attesa^F secondaria

トイレ／手洗い
toilets
Toiletten^F
w.-c.^M
aseos
toilette^F

医療福祉相談室
social services
Sozialdiensträume^M
services^M sociaux
servicios^M sociales
servizi^M sociali

職員ロッカー
staff cloakroom
Personalumkleideraum^M
vestiaire^F du personnel^M
guardarropa^M del personal^M
spogliatoio^M del personale^M

看護婦[士]休憩室
nurses' lounge
Schwesternzimmer^N
salle^F de repos^M des infirmières^F
sala^F de reposo^M de enfermeras^F
sala^F degli infermieri^{M/F}

標本採取室／採血室
specimen collection room
Entnahmeraum^M
salle^F de prélèvements^M
sala^F de extracciones^F
sala^F dei prelievi^M

治療室／処置室
treatment room
Behandlungsraum^M
salle^F de soins^M
sala^F de curas^F
stanza^F per le terapie^F

正面入り口
main entrance
Haupteingang^M
entrée^F principale
entrada^F principal
ingresso^M principale

受付
reception area
Aufnahme^F
aire^F d'accueil^M
recepción^F
accettazione^F

カルテ
medical records
Krankenakten^F
archives^F médicales
archivo^M médico
archivio^M delle cartelle cliniche

総合[第1]待合室
main waiting room
Hauptwarteraum^M
salle^F d'attente^F principale
sala^F de espera^F principal
sala^F d'attesa^F principale

医療機器保管室
medical equipment storage room
Lagerraum^M für medizinische Geräte^N
salle^F de rangement^M du matériel^M médical
botiquín^M
deposito^M del materiale^M medico

聴力検査室
audiometric examination room
Audiometrie^F- Untersuchungsraum^M
salle^F d'examen^M audiométrique
sala^F de examen^M de audiometría
stanza^F per l'esame^F audiometrico

診察室
examination room
Untersuchungsraum^M
salle^F d'examen^M
sala^F de reconocimiento^M
stanza^F per le visite^F mediche

薬局
pharmacy
Medikamentenraum^M
pharmacie^F
farmacia^F
farmacia^F

社会

健康 | HEALTH
GESUNDHEIT | SANTÉ | SALUD | SALUTE

歩行補助具

walking aids | Gehhilfen^F | aides^F à la marche^F | auxiliares^M ortopédicos para caminar | supporti^M per camminare

前腕用安全杖
forearm crutch
Gehkrücke^F
béquille^F d'avant-bras^M
muleta^F de antebrazo^M
stampella^F canadese

松葉杖
underarm crutch
Achselkrücke^F
béquille^F commune
muleta^F de sobaco^M
gruccia^F

前腕支え
forearm support
Unterarmstütze^F
embrasse^F
soporte^M para el antebrazo^M
supporto^M per il braccio^M

脇[腋]当て
underarm rest
Achselstütze^F
crosse^F
soporte^M para el sobaco^M
supporto^M sottoascellare

握り
handgrip
Griff^M
poignée^F
empuñadura^F
impugnatura^F

横木
crosspiece
Querstück^N
traverse^F
travesaño^M
appoggiamano^M

支柱
upright
Holm^M
montant^M
montante^M
telaio^M

長さ調節部
adjuster
Längenverstellung^F
réglage^M
tubo ajustable^M
regolatore^M

杖先ゴム
rubber tip; *rubber ferrule*
Gummikappe^F
embout^M de caoutchouc^M
contera^F de caucho^M
puntale^M

T字ステッキ
English cane; *English stick*
englischer Stock^M
canne^F en T^M
bastón^M inglés
bastone^M inglese

歩行器
walker; *walking frame*
Gehgestell^N
cadre^M de marche^F
andador^M
deambulatore^M

四脚ステッキ／四点杖
quad cane; *quadruped stick*
vierfüßiger Stock^M
canne^F avec quadripode^M
bastón^M cuadrangular
quadripode^M

オルソ・ステッキ
ortho-cane; *ortho-stick*
orthopädischer Stock^M
canne^F avec poignée^F orthopédique
bastón^M ortopédico
bastone^M con manico^M anatomico

散歩用ステッキ
walking stick
Spazierstock^M
canne^F en C^M
bastón^M para caminar
bastone^M da passeggio^M

社会

健康 | HEALTH
GESUNDHEIT | SANTÉ | SALUD | SALUTE

車椅子

wheelchair | RollstuhlM | fauteuilM roulant | sillaF de ruedasF | sediaF a rotelleF

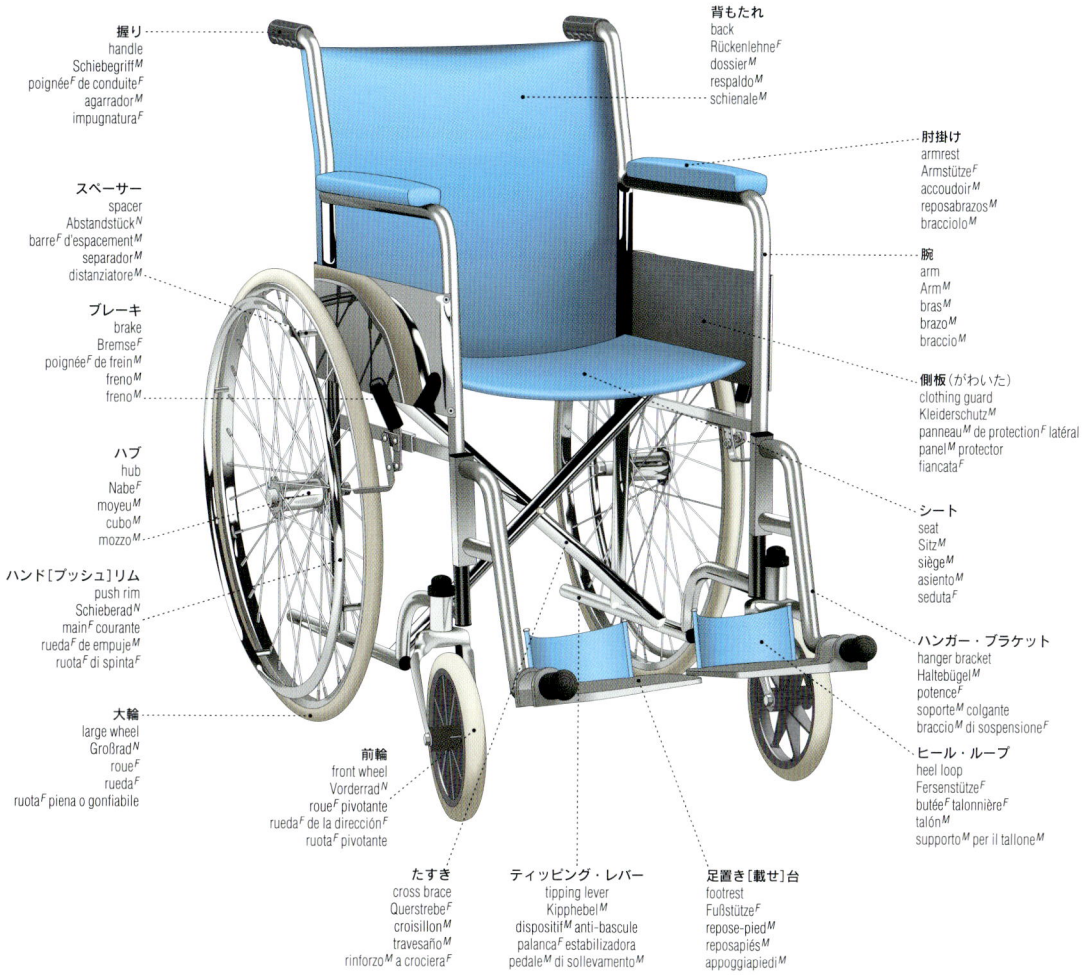

握り
handle
SchiebegriffM
poignéeF de conduiteF
agarradorM
impugnaturaF

背もたれ
back
RückenlehneF
dossierM
respaldoM
schienaleM

肘掛け
armrest
ArmstützeF
accoudoirM
reposabrazosM
braccioloM

スペーサー
spacer
AbstandstückN
barreF d'espacementM
separadorM
distanziatoreM

腕
arm
ArmM
brasM
brazoM
braccioM

ブレーキ
brake
BremseF
poignéeF de freinM
frenoM
frenoM

側板（がわいた）
clothing guard
KleiderschutzM
panneauM de protectionF latéral
panelM protector
fiancataF

ハブ
hub
NabeF
moyeuM
cuboM
mozzoM

シート
seat
SitzM
siègeM
asientoM
sedutaF

ハンド［プッシュ］リム
push rim
SchieberadN
mainF courante
ruedaF de empujeM
ruotaF di spintaF

ハンガー・ブラケット
hanger bracket
HaltebügelM
potenceF
soporteM colgante
braccioM di sospensioneF

大輪
large wheel
GroßradN
roueF
ruedaF
ruotaF piena o gonfiabile

ヒール・ループ
heel loop
FersenstützeF
butéeF talonnièreF
talónM
supportoM per il talloneM

前輪
front wheel
VorderradN
roueF pivotante
ruedaF de la direcciónF
ruotaF pivotante

たすき
cross brace
QuerstrebeF
croisillonM
travesañoM
rinforzoM a crocieraF

ティッピング・レバー
tipping lever
KipphebelM
dispositifM anti-bascule
palancaF estabilizadora
pedaleM di sollevamentoM

足置き［載せ］台
footrest
FußstützeF
repose-piedM
reposapiésM
appoggiapiediM

薬の様々な形態

forms of medications | ArzneimittelN-DarreichungsformenF | formesF pharmaceutiques des médicamentsM | formasF farmacêuticas de medicamentosM | confezioniF farmaceutiche di medicinaliM

咳止めシロップ
cough syrup
HustensirupM
siropM antitussif
jarabeM para la tosF
flaconeM

吸い口／口金
mouthpiece
MundstückN
emboutM buccal
boquillaF
boccaglioM

キャップ
cap
SchutzkappeF
capuchonM
capuchónM
cappuccioM

定量吸入器
metered dose inhaler
Dosier-AerosolN
inhalateurM-doseurM
inhaladorM-dosificadorM
inalatoreM dosimetrico

カプセル
capsule
KapselF
capsuleF
cápsulaF
capsulaF

ゼラチン・カプセル
gelatin capsule
GelatinekapselF
géluleF
cápsulaF de gelatinaF
capsulaF di gelatinaF

錠剤
tablet
TabletteF
compriméM
pastillaF
pastigliaF

アンプル
vial
AmpulleF
ampouleF
ampollaF
fialaF

社会

783

親族 | FAMILY
FAMILIE | FAMILLE | FAMILIA | FAMIGLIA

家族関係

family relationships | Verwandtschaftsbeziehungen^F | liens^M de parenté^F | vínculos^M familiares | vincoli^M di parentela^F

日本語 | 英語 | ドイツ語 | フランス語 | スペイン語 | イタリア語

曽孫息子
great-grandson
Urenkel^M
arrière-petit-fils^M
biznieto^M
pronipote^M

曽孫（ひ（い）まご）
great-grandchildren
Urenkel^M
arrière-petits-enfants^M
biznietos^M
pronipoti^M

曽孫娘
great-granddaughter
Urenkelin^F
arrière-petite-fille^F
bizniestos^F
pronipote^F

曽（そう）祖父母
great-grandparents
Urgroßeltern^{M/N}
arrière-grands-parents^M
bisabuelos^M
bisnonni^M

曽祖父
great-grandfather
Urgroßvater^M
arrière-grand-père^M
bisabuelo^M
bisnonno^M

曽祖母
great-grandmother
Urgroßmutter^F
arrière-grand-mère^F
bisabuela^F
bisnonna^F

息子
son
Sohn^M
fils^M
hijo^M
figlio^M

娘
daughter
Tochter^F
fille^F
hija^F
figlia^F

母
mother
Mutter^F
mère^F
madre^F
madre^F

父
father
Vater^M
père^M
padre^M
padre^M

孫息子
grandson
Enkel^M
petit-fils^M
nieto^M
nipote^M

孫
grandchildren
Enkelkinder^N
petits-enfants^M
nietos^M
nipoti^M

孫娘
granddaughter
Enkelin^F
petite-fille^F
nieta^F
nipote^F

息子
son
Sohn^M
fils^M
hijo^M
figlio^M

娘
daughter
Tochter^F
fille^F
hija^F
figlia^F

義理の息子／娘の夫／女婿（じょせい）
son-in-law
Schwiegersohn^M
beau-fils^M
yerno^M
genero^M

息子の妻／嫁／義理の娘
daughter-in-law
Schwiegertochter^F
belle-fille^F
nuera^F
nuora^F

祖父
grandfather
Großvater^M
grand-père^M
abuelo^M
nonno^M

祖父母
grandparents
Großeltern^{M/N}
grands-parents^M
abuelos^M
nonni^M

祖母
grandmother
Großmutter^F
grand-mère^F
abuela^F
nonna^F

(両)親
parents
Eltern^{M/N}
parents^M
padres^M
genitori^M

義父／舅（しゅうと）
father-in-law
Schwiegervater^M
beau-père^M
suegro^M
suocero^M

(両)親
parents
Eltern^{M/N}
parents^M
padres^M
genitori^M

義理の(両)親
parents-in-law
Schwiegereltern^{M/N}
beaux-parents^M
suegros^M
suoceri^M

娘
daughter
Tochter^F
fille^F
hija^F
figlia^F

義母／姑（しゅうとめ）
mother-in-law
Schwiegermutter^F
belle-mère^F
suegra^F
suocera^F

社会

784

親族 | FAMILY
FAMILIE | FAMILLE | FAMILIA | FAMIGLIA

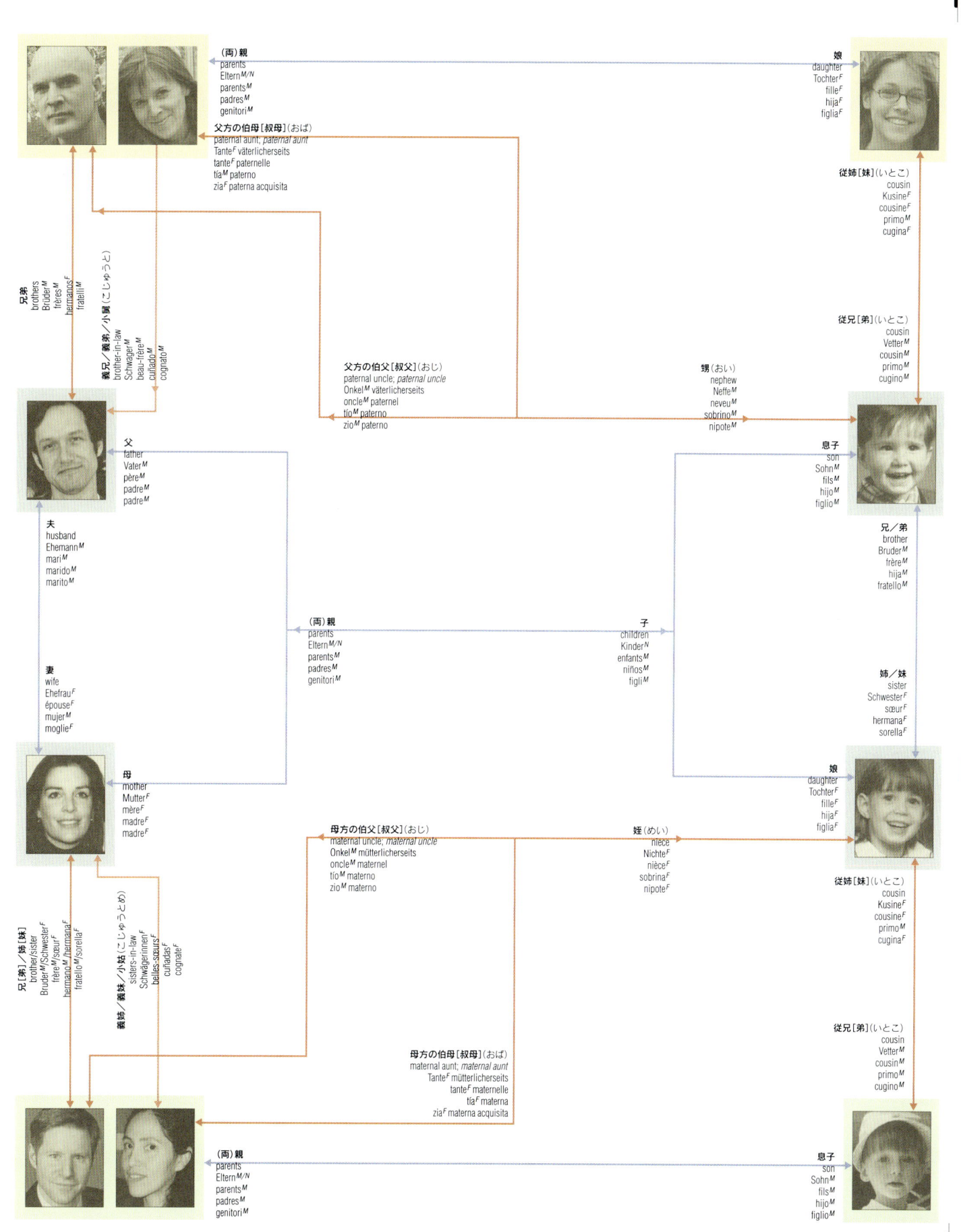

家族関係

(両)親
parents
ElternM/N
parentsM
padresM
genitoriM

娘
daughter
TochterF
filleF
hijaF
figliaF

父方の伯母[叔母](おば)
paternal aunt; *paternal aunt*
TanteF väterlicherseits
tanteF paternelle
tíaF paterno
ziaF paterna acquisita

従姉[妹](いとこ)
cousin
KusineF
cousineF
primoM
cuginaF

兄弟
brothers
BrüderM
frèresF
hermanosF
fratelliM

義兄/義弟/小舅(こじゅうと)
brother-in-law
SchwagerM
beau-frèreM
cuñadoM
cognatoM

父方の伯父[叔父](おじ)
paternal uncle; *paternal uncle*
OnkelM väterlicherseits
oncleM paternel
tíoM paterno
zioM paterno

甥(おい)
nephew
NeffeM
neveuM
sobrinoM
nipoteM

従兄[弟](いとこ)
cousin
VetterM
cousinM
primoM
cuginoM

父
father
VaterM
pèreM
padreM
padreM

息子
son
SohnM
filsM
hijoM
figlioM

夫
husband
EhemannM
mariM
maridoM
maritoM

兄/弟
brother
BruderM
frèreM
hijaM
fratelloM

(両)親
parents
ElternM/N
parentsM
padresM
genitoriM

子
children
KinderN
enfantsM
niñosM
figliM

妻
wife
EhefrauF
épouseF
mujerM
moglieF

姉/妹
sister
SchwesterF
sœurF
hermanaF
sorellaF

母
mother
MutterF
mèreF
madreF
madreF

娘
daughter
TochterF
filleF
hijaF
figliaF

母方の伯父[叔父](おじ)
maternal uncle; *maternal uncle*
OnkelM mütterlicherseits
oncleM maternel
tíoM materno
zioM materno

姪(めい)
niece
NichteF
nièceF
sobrinaF
nipoteF

従姉[妹](いとこ)
cousin
KusineF
cousineF
primoM
cuginaF

兄[弟]/姉[妹]
brother/sister
BruderM/SchwesterF
frèreM/sœurF
hermanoM/hermanaF
fratelloM/sorellaF

義姉/義妹/小姑(こじゅうとめ)
sisters-in-law
SchwägerinnenF
belles-sœursF
cuñadasF
cognateF

母方の伯母[叔母](おば)
maternal aunt; *maternal aunt*
TanteF mütterlicherseits
tanteF maternelle
tíaF materna
ziaF materna acquisita

従兄[弟](いとこ)
cousin
VetterM
cousinM
primoM
cuginoM

(両)親
parents
ElternM/N
parentsM
padresM
genitoriM

息子
son
SohnM
filsM
hijoM
figlioM

社会

788 スポーツ施設
- 788 スポーツ総合競技場
- 789 得点掲示板／スコアボード
- 789 試合／競技会

790 陸上競技
- 790 競技場／アリーナ
- 792 跳躍／ジャンプ
- 793 投てき

794 球技
- 794 野球
- 797 ソフトボール
- 798 クリケット
- 800 （フィールド）ホッケー
- 802 サッカー
- 804 ラグビー
- 806 アメリカン・フットボール
- 809 カナディアン・フットボール
- 809 ネットボール
- 810 バスケットボール
- 812 バレーボール
- 814 ハンドボール

815 ラケット・スポーツ
- 815 卓球
- 816 バドミントン
- 818 ラケットボール
- 819 スカッシュ
- 820 テニス

823 体操競技
- 823 新体操
- 823 トランポリン
- 824 体操

827 水上・水中スポーツと海上スポーツ
- 827 水球
- 828 飛び込み
- 830 水泳
- 833 セーリング
- 836 ウインドサーフィン
- 837 カヌー・カヤック：激流
- 838 ローイング［漕ぐこと］とスカーリング［幅寄せ］
- 838 カヌー・カヤック：静水競漕
- 840 水上スキー
- 840 サーフィン
- 841 スキューバ・ダイビング

842 格闘技
- 842 ボクシング
- 843 レスリング
- 844 柔道
- 845 空手
- 846 カンフー
- 846 柔術
- 846 合気道
- 847 剣道
- 847 相撲
- 848 フェンシング

850 筋力スポーツ
- 850 ウエイトリフティング
- 850 トレーニング用器具

852 乗馬スポーツ
- 852 障害飛越（ひえつ）競技
- 854 乗馬
- 855 馬場馬術
- 856 競馬：競馬場
- 857 競馬：繋駕速歩（けいがはやあし）競走
- 858 ポロ

# スポーツとゲーム

SPORTS AND GAMES | SPORT UND SPIELE | SPORTS ET JEUX | DEPORTES Y JUEGOS | SPORT E GIOCHI

859 正確さを競うスポーツ
- 859 アーチェリー
- 860 クレー射撃
- 861 ライフル射撃
- 861 ピストル射撃
- 862 ビリヤード／撞球（どうきゅう）／玉突き
- 864 ローン・ボウリング／ローン・ボウルズ
- 864 ペタンク
- 865 ボウリング
- 866 ゴルフ

870 自転車競技
- 870 ロード・レース
- 870 マウンテン・バイキング
- 871 トラック・レース
- 871 バイシクル・モトクロス

872 モーター・スポーツ
- 872 カー[自動車]レース
- 874 オートバイ・レース
- 876 水上オートバイ／ジェット・スキー
- 876 スノーモービル

877 ウインター・スポーツ
- 877 カーリング
- 878 アイス・ホッケー
- 881 フィギュア・スケート
- 882 スピード・スケート
- 884 ボブスレー
- 884 リュージュ
- 885 スケルトン
- 885 コース
- 886 スキー場
- 887 スノーボーディング
- 888 アルペン・スキー
- 890 フリースタイル・スキー
- 891 ジャンプ
- 891 スピード・スキー
- 892 クロス・カントリー・スキー
- 893 バイアスロン
- 893 スノーシュー／かんじき

894 ローラー・スポーツ
- 894 スケートボーディング
- 895 イン・ライン・スケーティング

896 空中スポーツ
- 896 スカイ・ダイビング
- 897 パラグライディング
- 897 ハング・グライディング
- 898 グライダー
- 899 気球乗り

900 マウンテン・スポーツ
- 900 登山／岩登り

902 アウトドア・レジャー
- 902 キャンプ
- 908 ロープワーク／結び
- 909 釣り
- 912 ハンティング／狩猟

914 ゲーム
- 914 さいころ[ダイス]とドミノ牌（はい）
- 914 トランプ／カード
- 915 ボード・ゲーム
- 917 ジグソー・パズル
- 917 麻雀
- 918 ビデオ・ゲーム
- 918 ダーツ
- 919 ルーレット・テーブル
- 920 スロット・マシン
- 920 サッカー・テーブル

스포츠施設 | SPORTS FACILITIES
SPORTEINRICHTUNGEN | INSTALLATIONS SPORTIVES | INSTALACIONES DEPORTIVAS | ATTREZZATURE SPORTIVE

スポーツ総合競技場

sports complex | Sportanlagen^F | complexe^M sportif | polideportivo^M | complesso^M sportivo

日本語 | 英語 | ドイツ語 | フランス語 | スペイン語 | イタリア語

水泳用プール
swimming pool
Schwimmbecken^N
piscine^F
piscina^F
piscina^F

競輪場
velodrome
Radrennbahn^F
vélodrome^M
velódromo^M
velodromo^M

アリーナ
arena
Arena^F
aréna^M
pista^F
stadio^M

トレーニング・フィールド
training area
Trainingsbereich^M
aire^F d'entraînement^M
zona^F de entrenamiento^M
zona^F di allenamento^M

射撃場
shooting range
Schießstand^M
stand^M de tir^M
campo^M de tiro^M al blanco^M
campo^M di tiro^M a segno^M

ダイビング用プール
diving well
Tauchbecken^N
bassin^M de plongeon^M
piscina^F de inmersión^F
vasca^F per tuffi^M

射場
archery range
Bogenschießanlage^F
stand^M de tir^M à l'arc^M
campo^M de tiro^M al arco^M
campo^M di tiro^M con l'arco^M

水泳競技場
swimming stadium
Schwimmstadion^N
stade^M nautique
estadio^M de natación^F
stadio^M per il nuoto^M

テニス・コート
tennis courts
Tennisplätze^M
courts^M de tennis^M
campos^M de tenis^M
campi^M da tennis^M

馬術場
equestrian sports ring
Sprungreitplatz^M
parcours^M de sports^M équestres
pista^F hípica
campo^M per sport^M equestri

ゴルフ・コース
golf course
Golfplatz^M
terrain^M de golf^M
campo^M de golf^M
campo^M da golf^M

野球場
baseball stadium
Baseballstadion^N
stade^M de baseball^M
estadio^M de baloncesto^M
stadio^M di baseball^M

観客席／スタンド
stands
Zuschauertribünen^F
tribuna^F
tribuna^F
tribune^F

体育館／屋内体操場
gymnasium
Turnhalle^F
gymnase^M
gimnasio^M
palestra^F

屋内競技場／体育館
sports hall
Sporthalle^F
palais^M des sports^M
palacio^M de los deportes^M
palazzetto^M dello sport^M

スタジアム
stadium
Stadion^N
stade^M
estadio^M
stadio^M

陸上競技用フィールド
throwing area
Wurfbereich^M
aire^F de lancer^M
zona^F de lanzamiento^M
area^F di lancio^M

係船地／マリーナ
marina
Yachthafen^M
port^M de plaisance^F
puerto^M deportivo
porticciolo^M

コース
lane
Bahn^F
couloir^M
calle^F
corsia^F

陸上競技用トラック
athletic track
Leichtathletikbahn^F
piste^F d'athlétisme^M
pista^F de atletismo^M
pista^F di atletica^F

（陸上）ホッケー
field hockey field
Feldhockeyplatz^M
terrain^M de hockey^M sur gazon^M
campo^M de hockey^M sobre hierba^F
campo^M da hockey^M su prato^M

サッカー場
football field
Fußballplatz^M
terrain^M de football^M
campo^M de fútbol^M
campo^M di calcio^M

競泳(用)プール
competition course basin
Wettkampfbecken^N
bassin^M de compétition^F
canal^M de competición^F
bacino^M per competizioni^F

スポーツとゲーム

788

スポーツ施設 | SPORTS FACILITIES
SPORTEINRICHTUNGEN | INSTALLATIONS SPORTIVES | INSTALACIONES DEPORTIVAS | ATTREZZATURE SPORTIVE

得点掲示板／スコアボード

scoreboard | AnzeigetafelF | tableauM indicateur | marcadorM | tabelloneM segnapunti

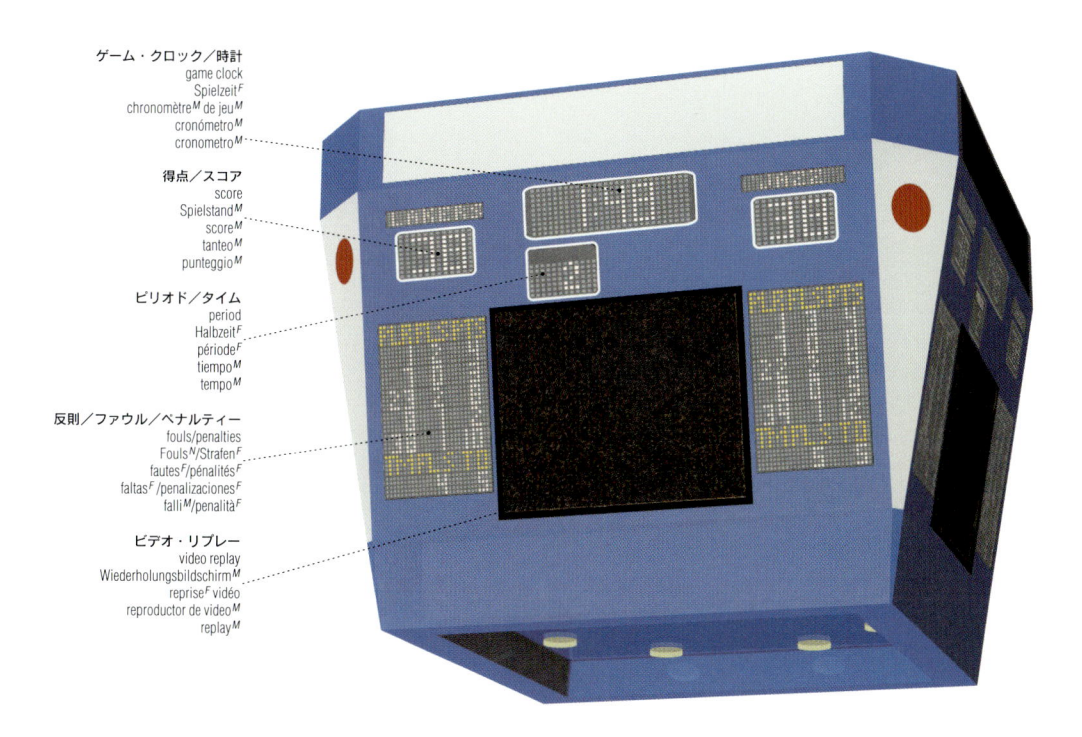

ゲーム・クロック／時計
game clock
SpielzeitF
chronomètreM de jeuM
cronómetroM
cronometroM

得点／スコア
score
SpielstandM
scoreM
tanteoM
punteggioM

ピリオド／タイム
period
HalbzeitF
périodeF
tiempoM
tempoM

反則／ファウル／ペナルティー
fouls/penalties
FoulsN/StrafenF
fautesF/pénalitésF
faltasF/penalizacionesF
falliM/penalitàF

ビデオ・リプレー
video replay
WiederholungsbildschirmM
repriseF vidéo
reproductor de videoM
replayM

試合／競技会

competition | WettkampfM | compétitionF | competiciónF | competizioneF

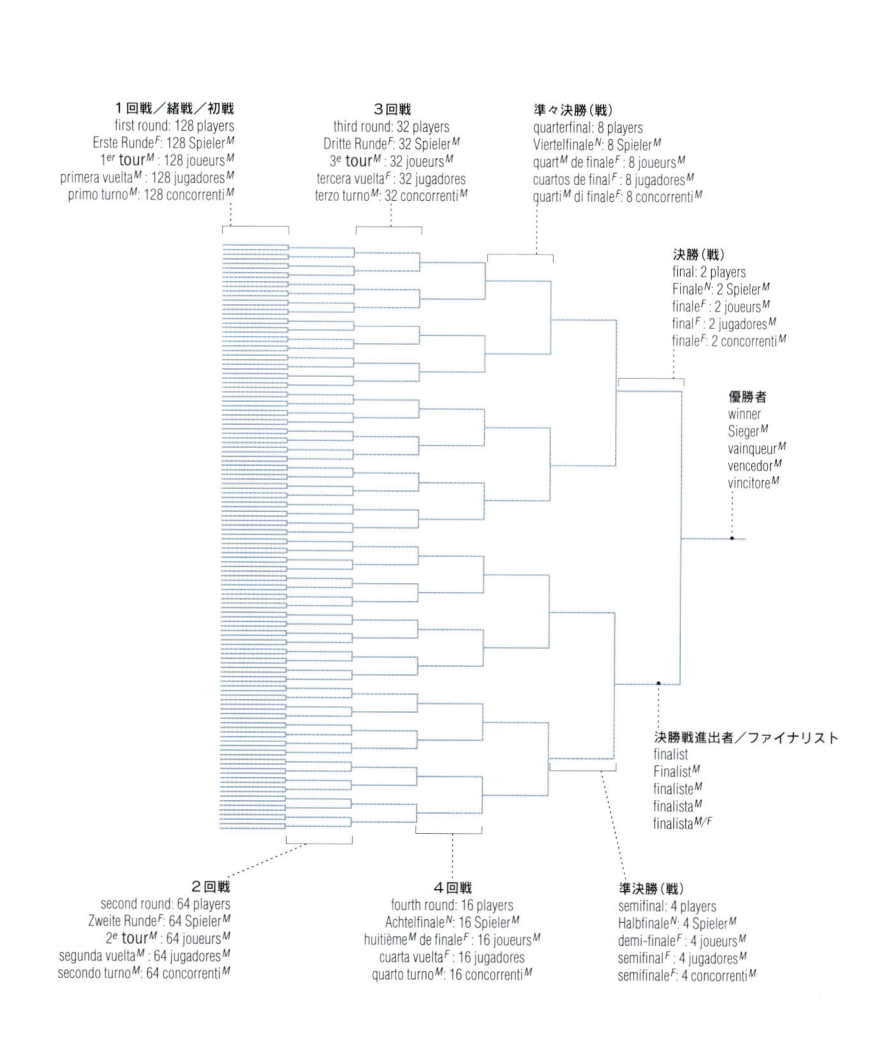

1回戦／緒戦／初戦
first round: 128 players
Erste RundeF: 128 SpielerM
1er tourF: 128 joueursM
primera vueltaM: 128 jugadoresM
primo turnoM: 128 concorrentiM

3回戦
third round: 32 players
Dritte RundeF: 32 SpielerM
3e tourF: 32 joueursM
tercera vueltaF: 32 jugadores
terzo turnoM: 32 concorrentiM

準々決勝（戦）
quarterfinal: 8 players
ViertelfinaleN: 8 SpielerM
quartM de finaleF: 8 joueursM
cuartos de finalF: 8 jugadoresM
quartiM di finaleF: 8 concorrentiM

決勝（戦）
final: 2 players
FinaleN: 2 SpielerM
finaleF: 2 joueursM
finalF: 2 jugadoresM
finaleF: 2 concorrentiM

トーナメント表／ドロー表
draw
K.O.-SystemN
tableauM de tournoiM
empateM
elencoM dei concorrentiM

優勝者
winner
SiegerM
vainqueurM
vencedorM
vincitoreM

決勝戦進出者／ファイナリスト
finalist
FinalistM
finalisteM
finalistaM
finalistaM/F

2回戦
second round: 64 players
Zweite RundeF: 64 SpielerM
2e tourF: 64 joueursM
segunda vueltaF: 64 jugadoresM
secondo turnoM: 64 concorrentiM

4回戦
fourth round: 16 players
AchtelfinaleN: 16 SpielerM
huitièmeM de finaleF: 16 joueursM
cuarta vuelta: 16 jugadores
quarto turnoM: 16 concorrentiM

準決勝（戦）
semifinal: 4 players
HalbfinaleN: 4 SpielerM
demi-finaleF: 4 joueursM
semifinalF: 4 jugadoresM
semifinaleF: 4 concorrentiM

スポーツとゲーム

陸上競技 | TRACK AND FIELD
LEICHTATHLETIK | ATHLÉTISME | ATLETISMO | ATLETICA LEGGERA

競技場／アリーナ

arena | Stadion[N] | stade[M] | estadio[M] | stadio[M]

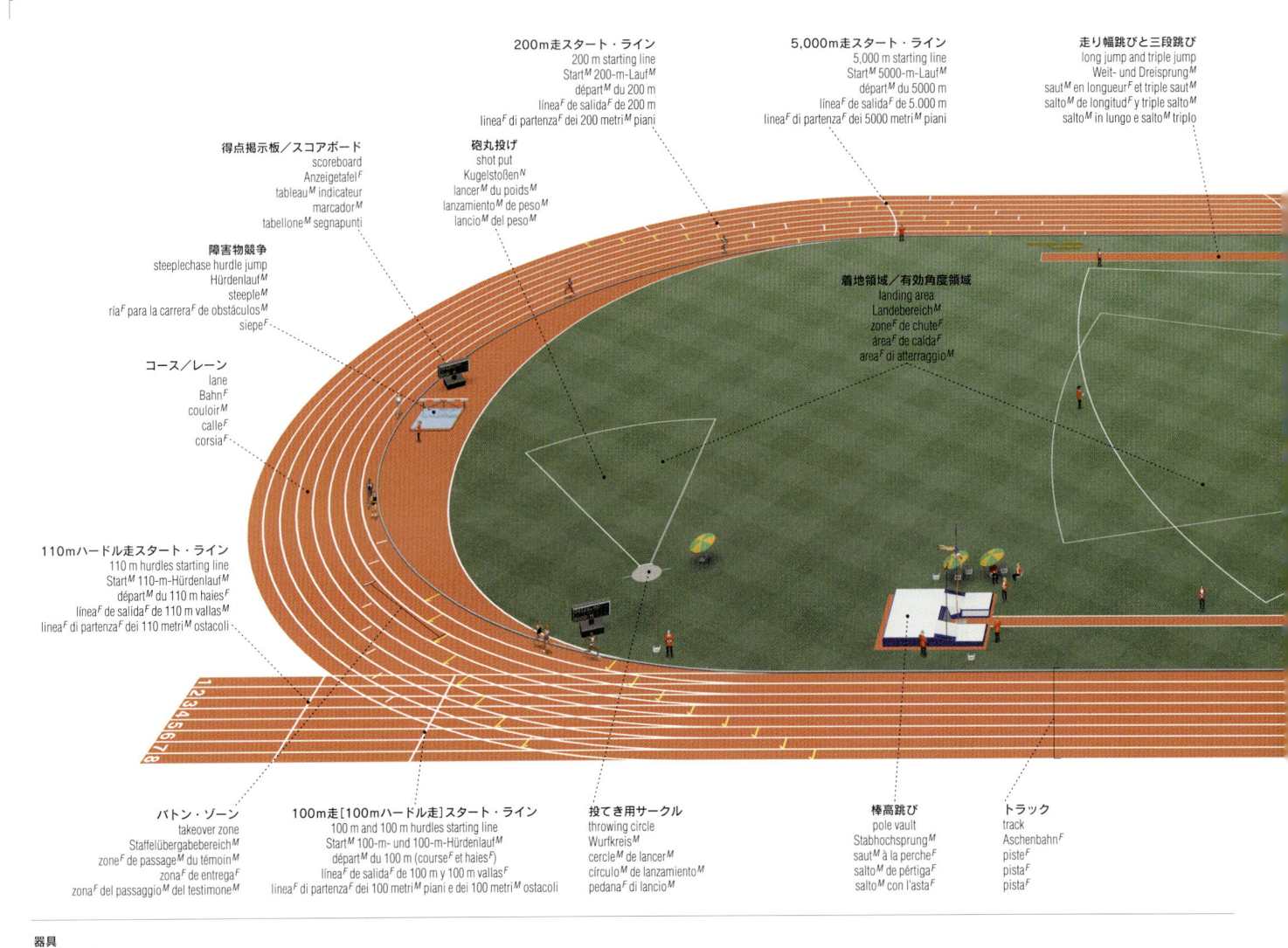

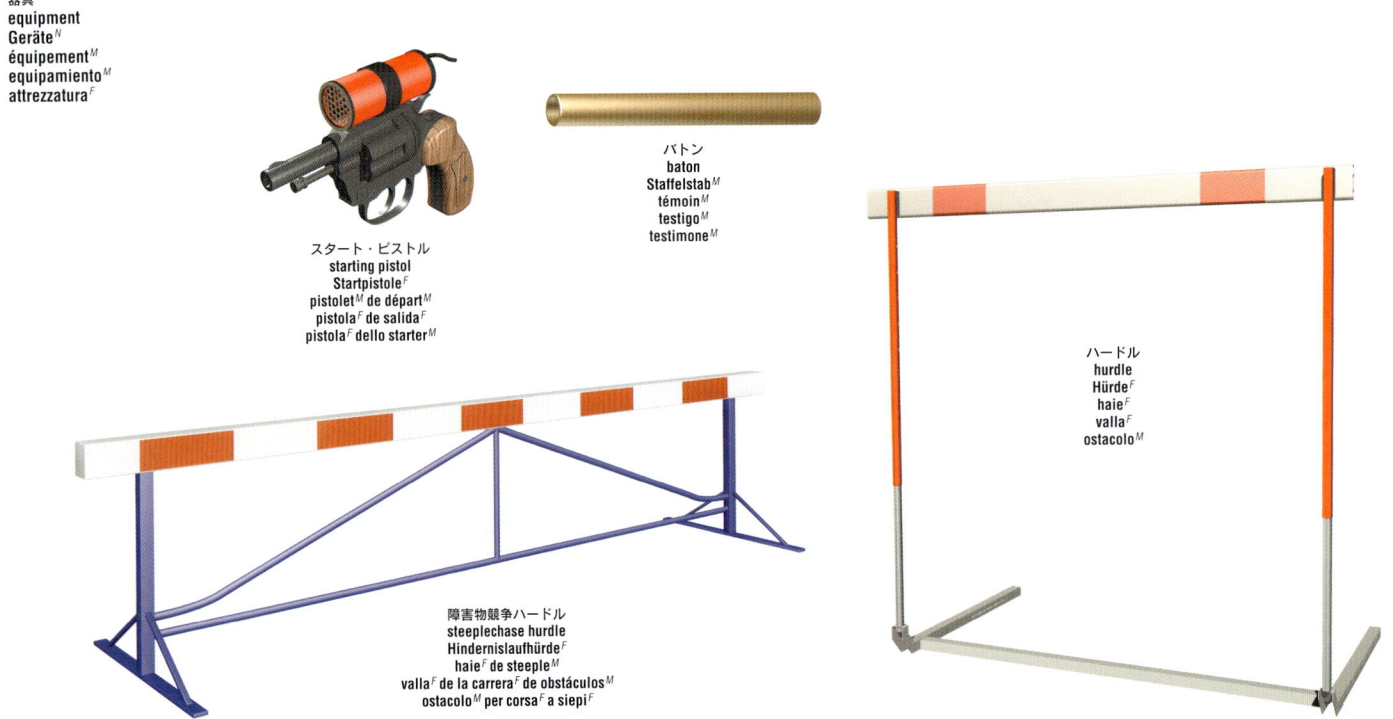

日本語 | 英語 | ドイツ語 | フランス語 | スペイン語 | イタリア語

200m走スタート・ライン
200 m starting line
Start[M] 200-m-Lauf[M]
départ[M] du 200 m
línea[F] de salida de 200 m
linea[F] di partenza dei 200 metri[M] piani

5,000m走スタート・ライン
5,000 m starting line
Start[M] 5000-m-Lauf[M]
départ[M] du 5000 m
línea[F] de salida de 5.000 m
linea[F] di partenza dei 5000 metri[M] piani

走り幅跳びと三段跳び
long jump and triple jump
Weit- und Dreisprung[M]
saut[M] en longueur[F] et triple saut[M]
salto[M] de longitud[F] y triple salto[M]
salto[M] in lungo e salto[M] triplo

得点掲示板／スコアボード
scoreboard
Anzeigetafel[F]
tableau[M] indicateur
marcador[M]
tabellone[M] segnapunti

砲丸投げ
shot put
Kugelstoßen[N]
lancer[M] du poids[M]
lanzamiento[M] de peso[M]
lancio[M] del peso[M]

着地領域／有効角度領域
landing area
Landebereich[M]
zone[F] de chute[F]
área[F] de caída[F]
area[F] di atterraggio[M]

障害物競争
steeplechase hurdle jump
Hürdenlauf[M]
steeple[M]
ría[F] para la carrera[F] de obstáculos[M]
siepe[F]

コース／レーン
lane
Bahn[F]
couloir[M]
calle[F]
corsia[F]

110mハードル走スタート・ライン
110 m hurdles starting line
Start[M] 110-m-Hürdenlauf[M]
départ[M] du 110 m haies[F]
línea[F] de salida de 110 m vallas[M]
linea[F] di partenza dei 110 metri[M] ostacoli

バトン・ゾーン
takeover zone
Staffelübergabebereich[M]
zone[F] de passage[M] du témoin[M]
zona[F] de entrega[F]
zona[F] del passaggio[M] del testimone[M]

100m走[100mハードル走]スタート・ライン
100 m and 100 m hurdles starting line
Start[M] 100-m- und 100-m-Hürdenlauf[M]
départ[M] du 100 m (course[F] et haies[F])
línea[F] de salida de 100 m y 100 m vallas[M]
linea[F] di partenza dei 100 metri[M] piani e dei 100 metri[M] ostacoli

投てき用サークル
throwing circle
Wurfkreis[M]
cercle[M] de lancer[M]
círculo[M] de lanzamiento[M]
pedana[F] di lancio[M]

棒高跳び
pole vault
Stabhochsprung[M]
saut[M] à la perche[F]
salto[M] de pértiga[F]
salto[M] con l'asta[F]

トラック
track
Aschenbahn[F]
piste[F]
pista[F]
pista[F]

器具
equipment
Geräte[N]
équipement[M]
equipamiento[M]
attrezzatura[F]

スタート・ピストル
starting pistol
Startpistole[F]
pistolet[M] de départ[M]
pistola[F] de salida[F]
pistola[F] dello starter[M]

バトン
baton
Staffelstab[M]
témoin[M]
testigo[M]
testimone[M]

ハードル
hurdle
Hürde[F]
haie[F]
valla[F]
ostacolo[M]

障害物競争ハードル
steeplechase hurdle
Hindernislaufhürde[F]
haie[F] de steeple[M]
valla[F] de la carrera[F] de obstáculos[M]
ostacolo[M] per corsa[F] a siepi[F]

スポーツとゲーム

陸上競技 | TRACK AND FIELD
LEICHTATHLETIK | ATHLÉTISME | ATLETISMO | ATLETICA LEGGERA

競技場／アリーナ

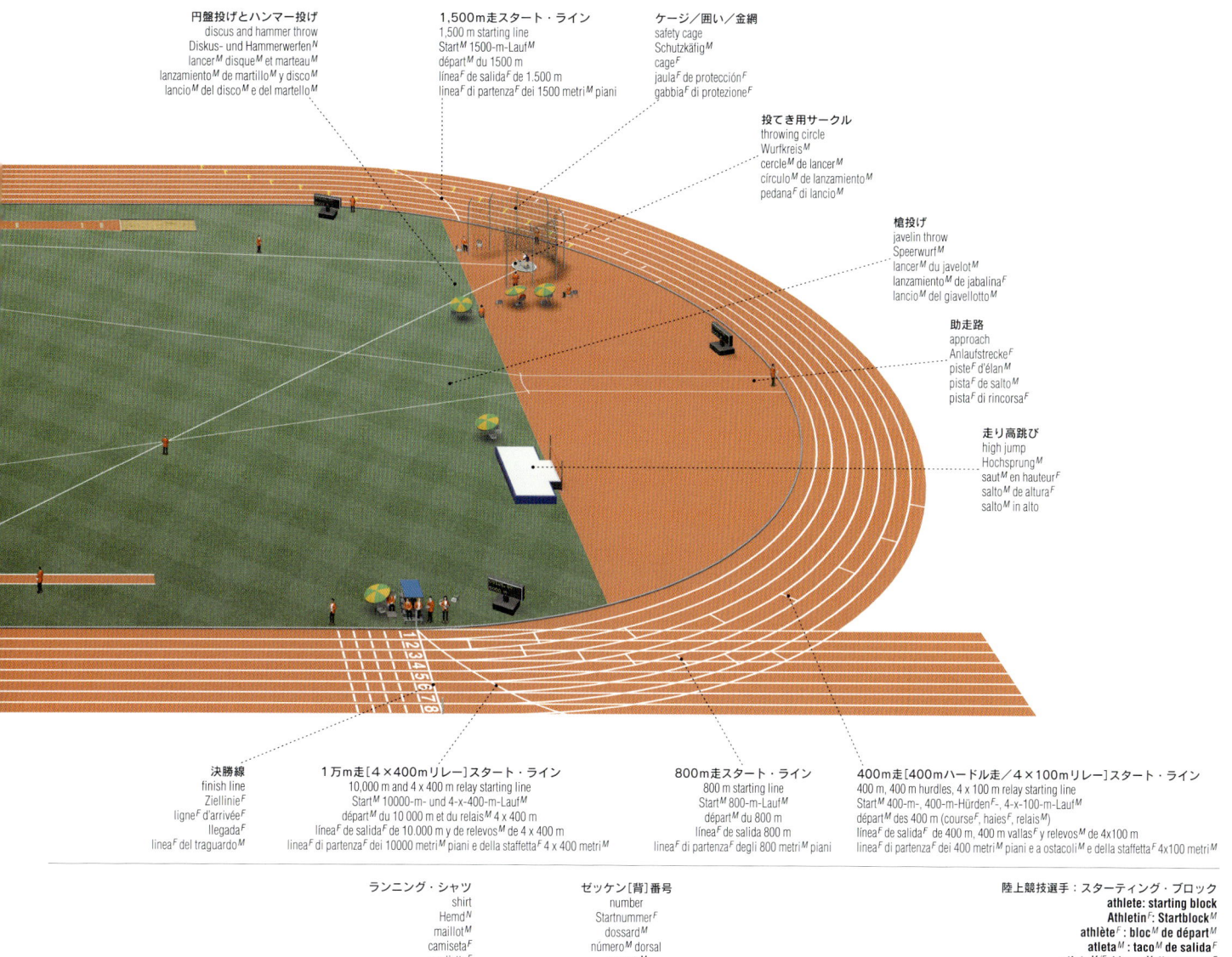

円盤投げとハンマー投げ
discus and hammer throw
Diskus- und HammerwerfenN
lancerM disqueM et marteauM
lanzamientoM de martilloM y discoM
lancioM del discoM e del martelloM

1,500m走スタート・ライン
1,500 m starting line
StartM 1500-m-LaufM
départM du 1500 m
líneaF de salidaF de 1.500 m
lineaF di partenzaF dei 1500 metriM piani

ケージ／囲い／金網
safety cage
SchutzkäfigM
cageF
jaulaF de protecciónF
gabbiaF di protezioneF

投てき用サークル
throwing circle
WurfkreisM
cercleM de lancerM
círculoM de lanzamientoM
pedanaF di lancioM

槍投げ
javelin throw
SpeerwurfM
lancerM du javelotM
lanzamientoM de jabalinaF
lancioM del giavellottoM

助走路
approach
AnlaufstreckeF
pisteF d'élanM
pistaF de saltoM
pistaF di rincorsaF

走り高跳び
high jump
HochsprungM
sautM en hauteurF
saltoM de alturaF
saltoM in alto

決勝線
finish line
ZiellinieF
ligneF d'arrivéeF
llegadaF
lineaF del traguardoM

1万m走[4×400mリレー]スタート・ライン
10,000 m and 4 x 400 m relay starting line
StartM 10000-m- und 4-x-400-m-LaufM
départM du 10 000 m et du relaisM 4 x 400 m
líneaF de salidaF de 10.000 m y de relevosM de 4 x 400 m
lineaF di partenzaF dei 10000 metriM piani e della staffettaF 4 x 400 metriM

800m走スタート・ライン
800 m starting line
StartM 800-m-LaufM
départM du 800 m
líneaF de salidaF 800 m
lineaF di partenzaF degli 800 metriM piani

400m走[400mハードル走／4×100mリレー]スタート・ライン
400 m, 400 m hurdles, 4 x 100 m relay starting line
StartM 400-m-, 400-m-HürdenF-, 4-x-100-m-LaufM
départM des 400 m (courseF, haiesF, relaisM)
líneaF de salidaF de 400 m, 400 m vallasF y relevosM de 4x100 m
lineaF di partenzaF dei 400 metriM piani e a ostacoliM e della staffettaF 4x100 metriM

ランニング・シャツ
shirt
HemdN
maillotM
camisetaF
magliettaF

ゼッケン[背]番号
number
StartnummerF
dossardM
númeroM dorsal
numeroM

陸上競技選手：スターティング・ブロック
athlete: starting block
AthletinF: StartblockM
athlèteF : blocM de départM
atletaM : tacoM de salidaF
atletaM/F: bloccoM di partenzaF

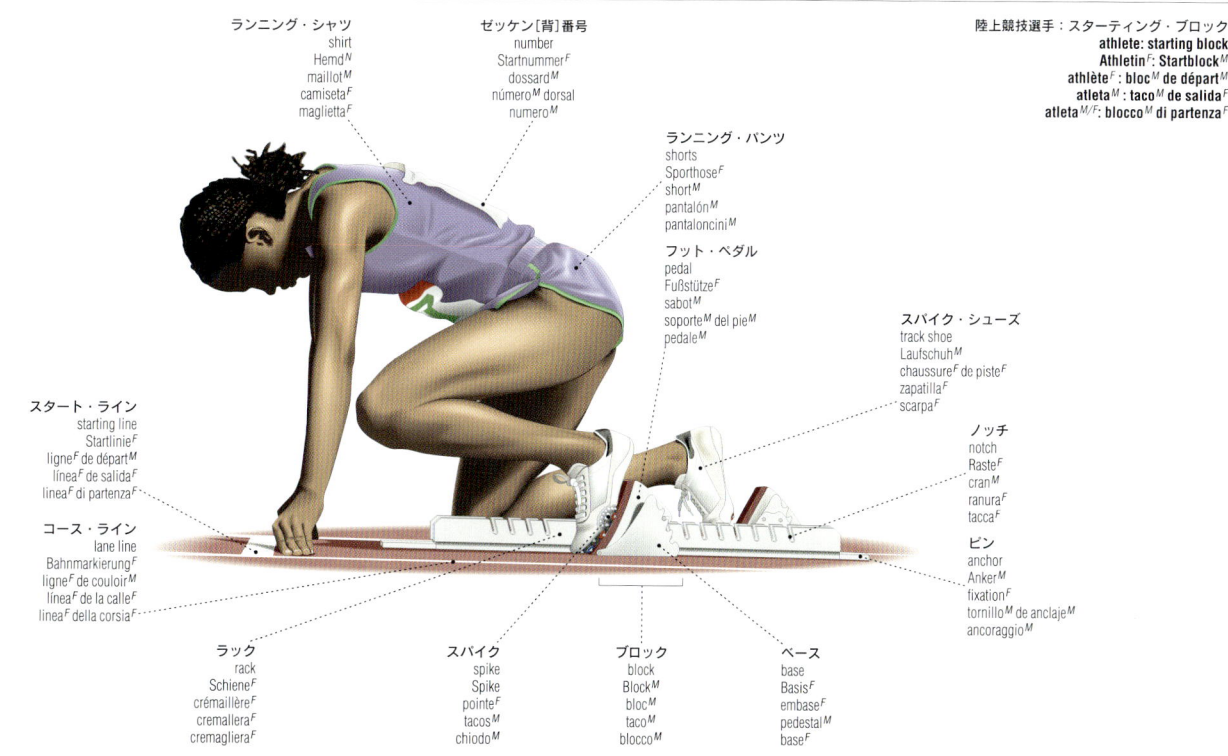

ランニング・パンツ
shorts
SporthoseF
shortM
pantalónM
pantalonciniM

フット・ペダル
pedal
FußstützeF
sabotM
soporteM del pieM
pedaleM

スパイク・シューズ
track shoe
LaufschuhM
chaussureF de pisteF
zapatillaF
scarpaF

ノッチ
notch
RasteF
cranM
ranuraF
taccaF

スタート・ライン
starting line
StartlinieF
ligneF de départM
líneaF de salidaF
lineaF di partenzaF

コース・ライン
lane line
BahnmarkierungF
ligneF de couloirM
líneaF de la calleF
lineaF della corsiaF

ピン
anchor
AnkerM
fixationF
tornilloM de anclajeM
ancoraggioM

ラック
rack
SchieneF
crémaillèreF
cremalleraF
cremaglieraF

スパイク
spike
SpikeM
pointeF
tacosM
chiodoM

ブロック
block
BlockM
blocM
tacoM
bloccoM

ベース
base
BasisF
embaseF
pedestalM
baseF

スポーツとゲーム

791

陸上競技 | TRACK AND FIELD
LEICHTATHLETIK | ATHLÉTISME | ATLETISMO | ATLETICA LEGGERA

跳躍／ジャンプ

日本語 | 英語 | ドイツ語 | フランス語 | スペイン語 | イタリア語

jumping | Sprungwettbewerbe^M | sauts^M | saltos^M | salti^M

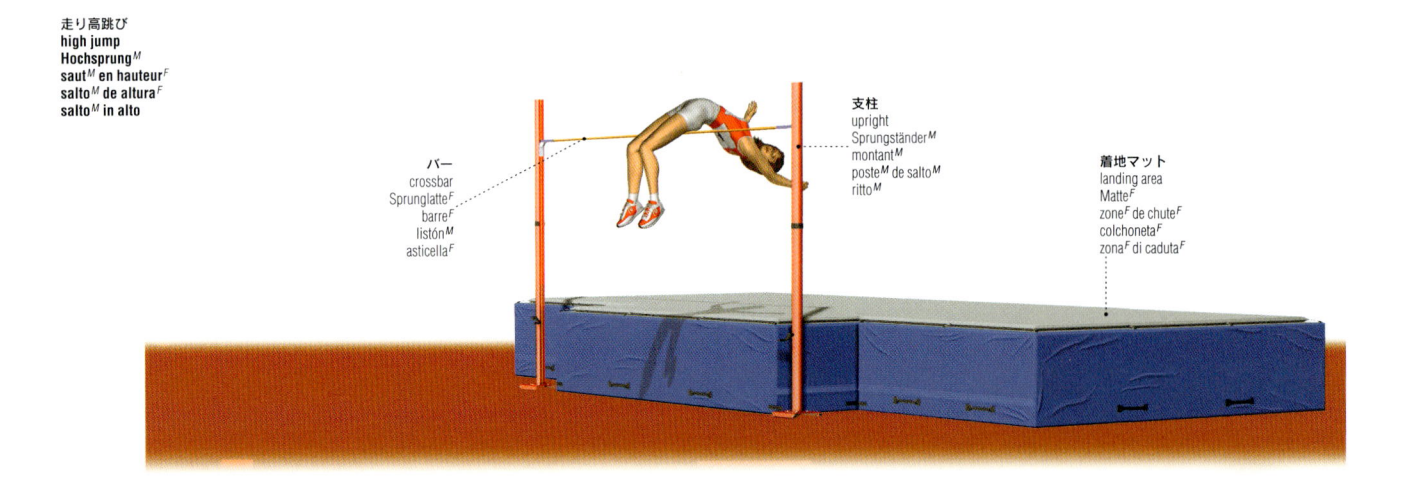

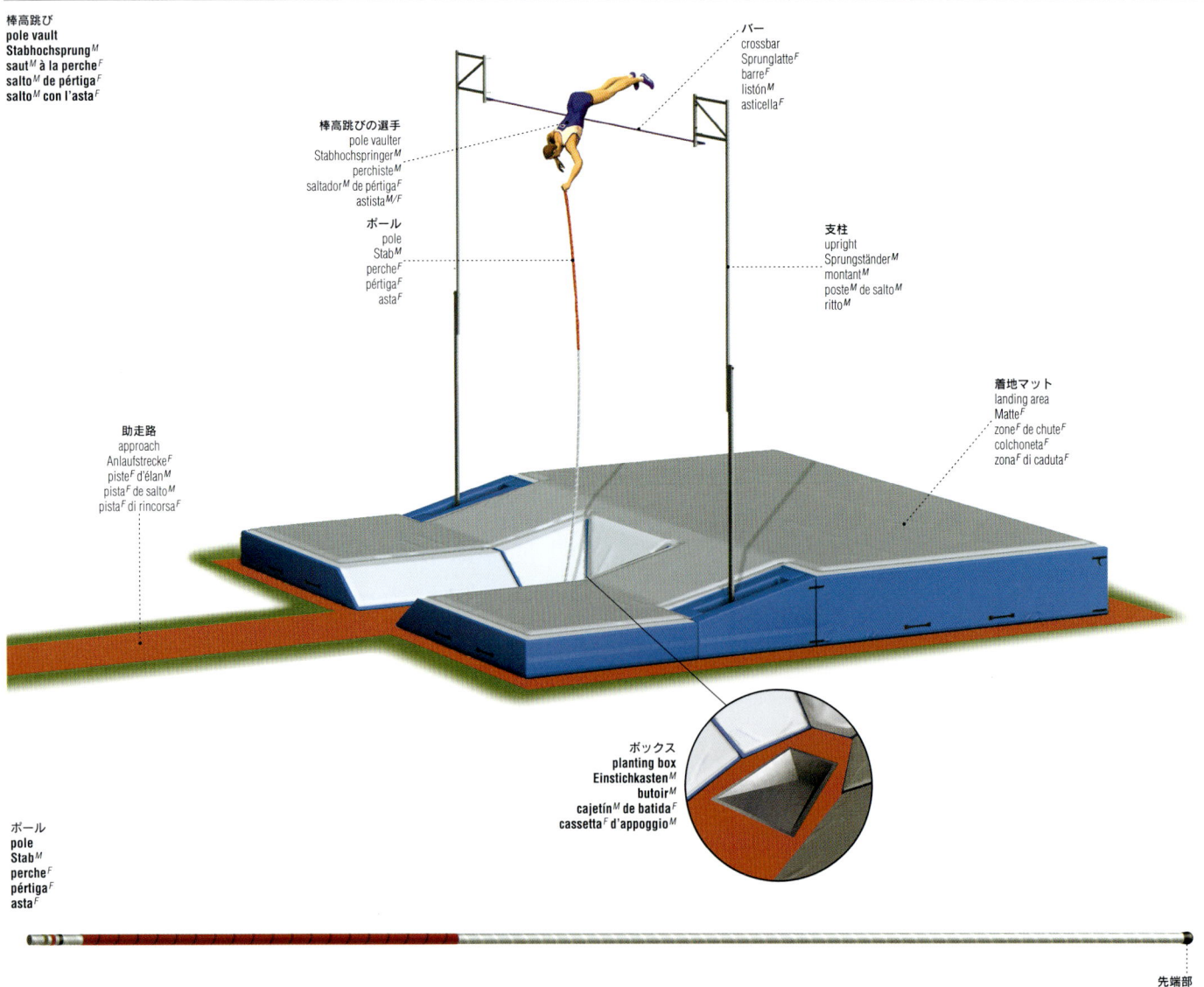

走り高跳び
high jump
Hochsprung^M
saut^M en hauteur^F
salto^M de altura^F
salto^M in alto

バー
crossbar
Sprunglatte^F
barre^F
listón^M
asticella^F

支柱
upright
Sprungständer^M
montant^M
poste^M de salto^M
ritto^M

着地マット
landing area
Matte^F
zone^F de chute^F
colchoneta^F
zona^F di caduta^F

棒高跳び
pole vault
Stabhochsprung^M
saut^M à la perche^F
salto^M de pértiga^F
salto^M con l'asta^F

バー
crossbar
Sprunglatte^F
barre^F
listón^M
asticella^F

棒高跳びの選手
pole vaulter
Stabhochspringer^M
perchiste^M
saltador^M de pértiga^F
astista^{M/F}

ポール
pole
Stab^M
perche^F
pértiga^F
asta^F

支柱
upright
Sprungständer^M
montant^M
poste^M de salto^M
ritto^M

着地マット
landing area
Matte^F
zone^F de chute^F
colchoneta^F
zona^F di caduta^F

助走路
approach
Anlaufstrecke^F
piste^F d'élan^M
pista^F de salto^M
pista^F di rincorsa^F

ボックス
planting box
Einstichkasten^M
butoir^M
cajetín^M de batida^F
cassetta^F d'appoggio^M

ポール
pole
Stab^M
perche^F
pértiga^F
asta^F

先端部
tip
Spitze^F
embout^M
punta^F
punta^F

スポーツとゲーム

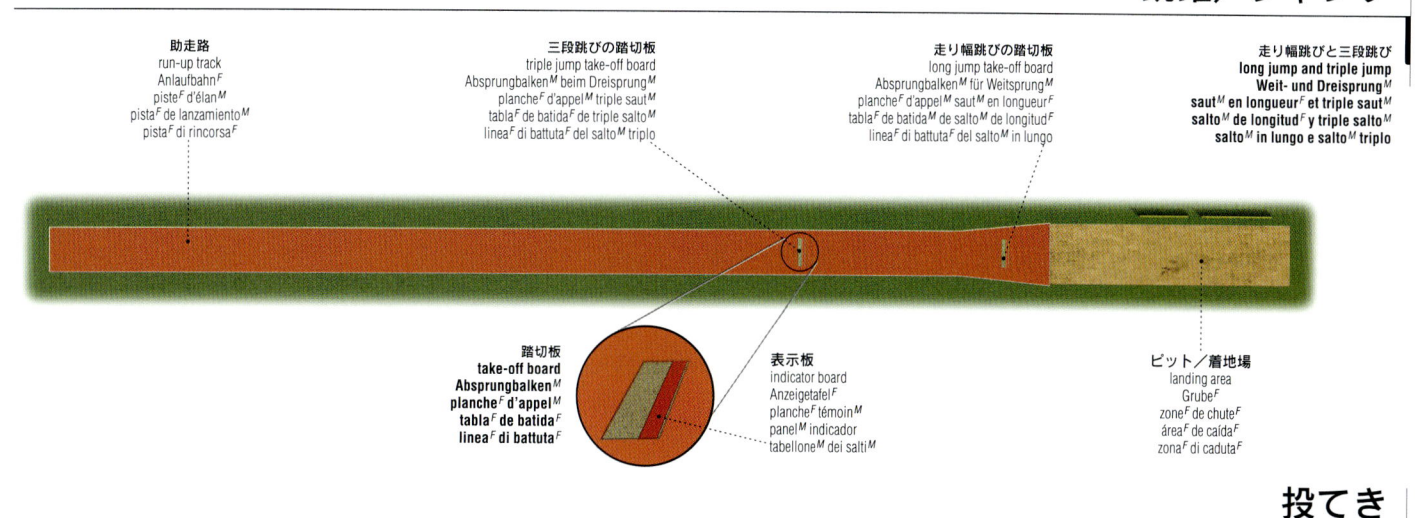

陸上競技 | TRACK AND FIELD
LEICHTATHLETIK | ATHLÉTISME | ATLETISMO | ATLETICA LEGGERA

跳躍／ジャンプ

助走路
run-up track
Anlaufbahn^F
piste^F d'élan^M
pista^F de lanzamiento^M
pista^F di rincorsa^F

三段跳びの踏切板
triple jump take-off board
Absprungbalken^M beim Dreisprung
planche^F d'appel^M triple saut^M
tabla^F de batida^F de triple salto^M
linea^F di battuta^F del salto^M triplo

走り幅跳びの踏切板
long jump take-off board
Absprungbalken^M für Weitsprung
planche^F d'appel^M saut^M en longueur^F
tabla^F de batida^F de salto^M de longitud^F
linea^F di battuta^F del salto^M in lungo

走り幅跳びと三段跳び
long jump and triple jump
Weit- und Dreisprung^M
saut^M **en longueur**^F **et triple saut**^M
salto^M **de longitud**^F **y triple salto**^M
salto^M **in lungo e salto**^M **triplo**

踏切板
take-off board
Absprungbalken^M
planche^F **d'appel**^M
tabla^F **de batida**^F
linea^F **di battuta**^F

表示板
indicator board
Anzeigetafel^F
planche^F témoin^M
panel^M indicador
tabellone^M dei salti^M

ピット／着地場
landing area
Grube^F
zone^F de chute^F
área^F de caída^F
zona^F di caduta^F

投てき

throwing | Wurfgeräte^N | lancers^M | lanzamientos^M | attrezzi^M di lancio^M

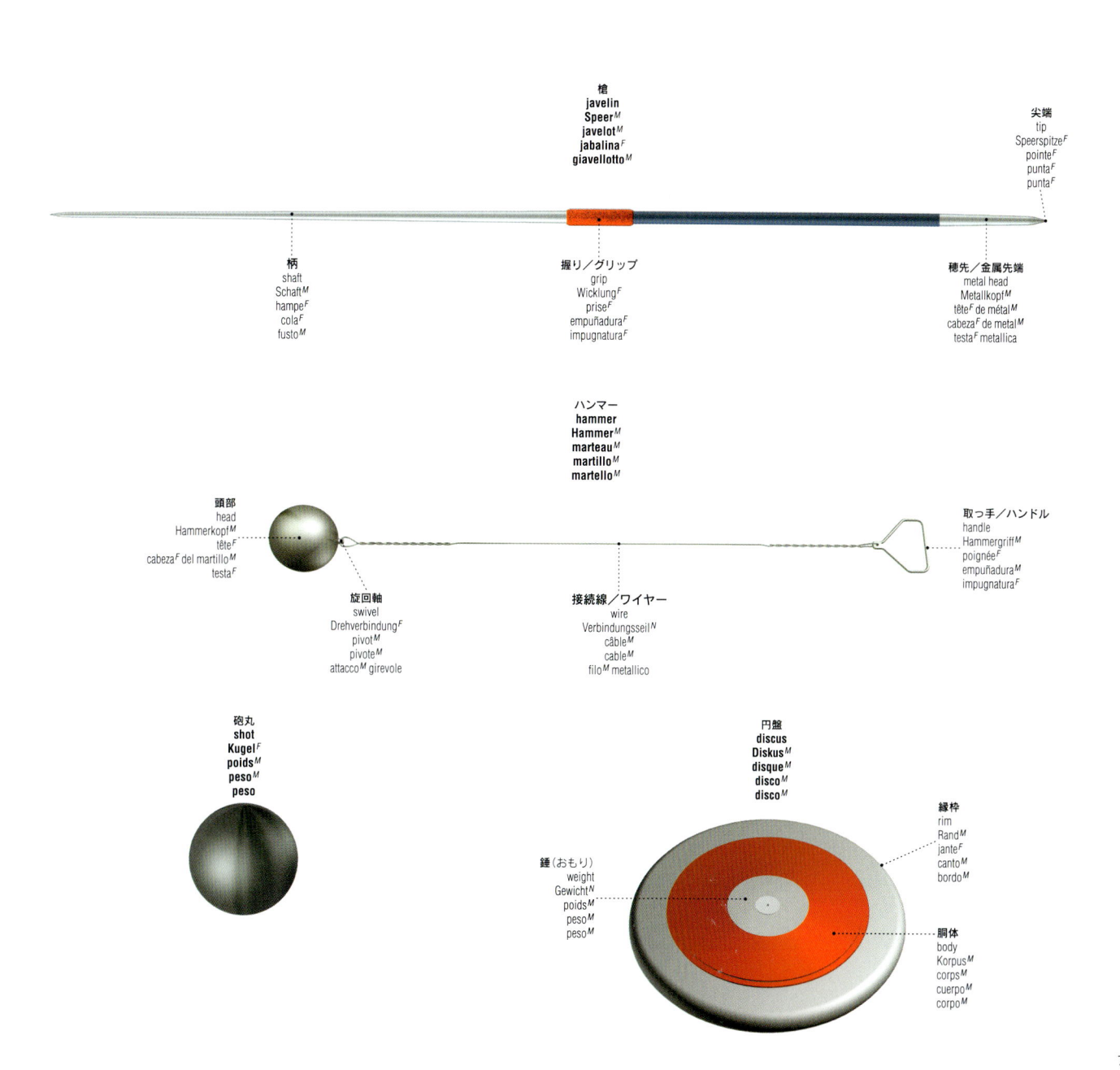

槍
javelin
Speer^M
javelot^M
jabalina^F
giavellotto^M

尖端
tip
Speerspitze^F
pointe^F
punta^F
punta^F

柄
shaft
Schaft^M
hampe^F
cola^F
fusto^M

握り／グリップ
grip
Wicklung^F
prise^F
empuñadura^F
impugnatura^F

穂先／金属先端
metal head
Metallkopf^M
tête^F de métal^M
cabeza^F de metal^M
testa^F metallica

ハンマー
hammer
Hammer^M
marteau^M
martillo^M
martello^M

頭部
head
Hammerkopf^M
tête^F
cabeza^F del martillo^M
testa^F

取っ手／ハンドル
handle
Hammergriff^M
poignée^F
empuñadura^M
impugnatura^F

旋回軸
swivel
Drehverbindung^F
pivot^M
pivote^M
attacco^M girevole

接続線／ワイヤー
wire
Verbindungsseil^N
câble^M
cable^M
filo^M metallico

砲丸
shot
Kugel^F
poids^M
peso^M
peso

円盤
discus
Diskus^M
disque^M
disco^M
disco^M

錘（おもり）
weight
Gewicht^N
poids^M
peso^M
peso^M

縁枠
rim
Rand^M
jante^F
canto^M
bordo^M

胴体
body
Korpus^M
corps^M
cuerpo^M
corpo^M

スポーツとゲーム

球技 | BALL SPORTS
BALLSPORTARTEN | SPORTS DE BALLE ET DE BALLON | DEPORTES DE PELOTA Y DE BALÓN | SPORT CON LA PALLA

野球

日本語 | 英語 | ドイツ語 | フランス語 | スペイン語 | イタリア語

baseball | Baseball^M | baseball^M | béisbol^M | baseball^M

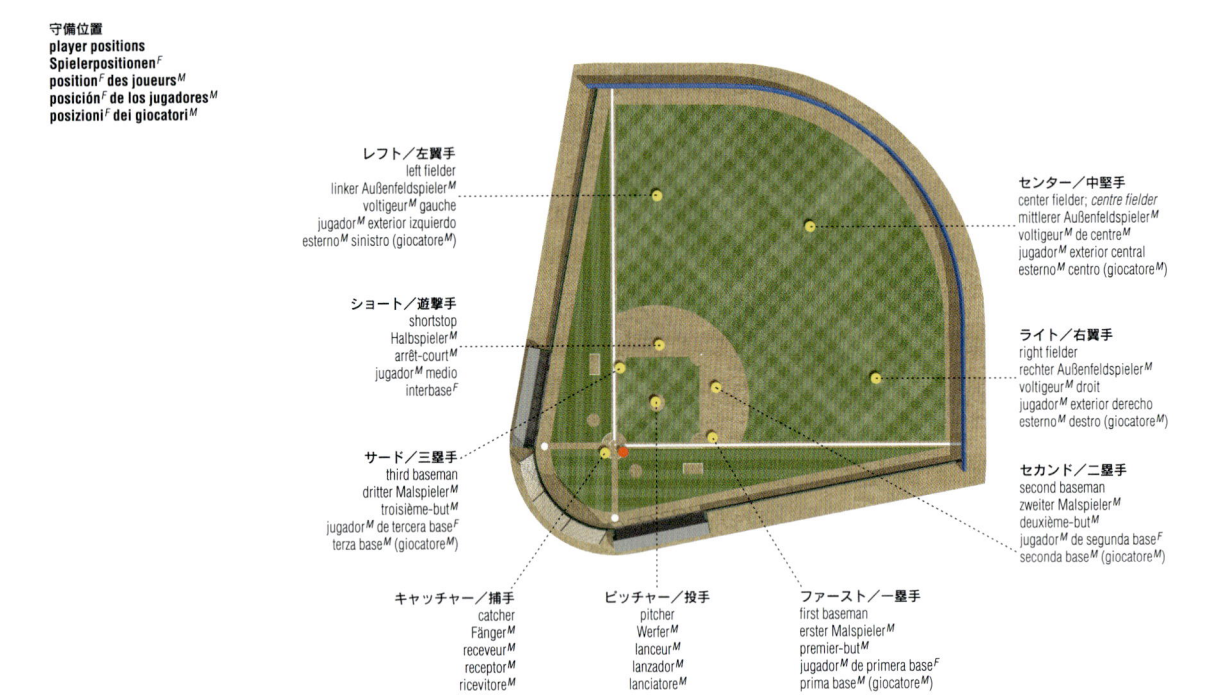

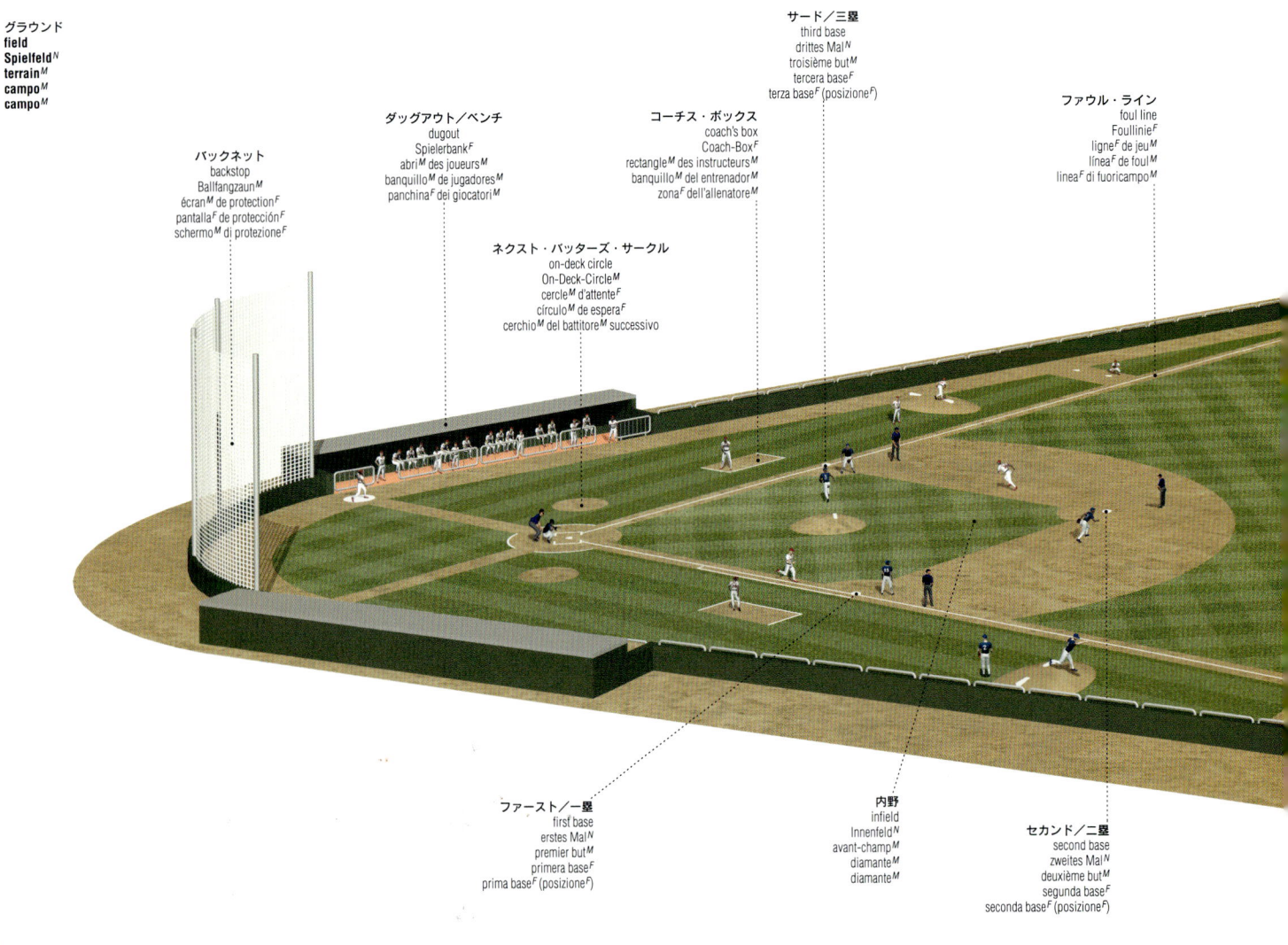

守備位置
player positions
Spielerpositionen^F
position^F des joueurs^M
posición^F de los jugadores^M
posizioni^F dei giocatori^M

レフト／左翼手
left fielder
linker Außenfeldspieler^M
voltigeur^M gauche
jugador^M exterior izquierdo
esterno^M sinistro (giocatore^M)

センター／中堅手
center fielder; centre fielder
mittlerer Außenfeldspieler^M
voltigeur^M de centre^M
jugador^M exterior central
esterno^M centro (giocatore^M)

ショート／遊撃手
shortstop
Halbspieler^M
arrêt-court^M
jugador^M medio
interbase^F

ライト／右翼手
right fielder
rechter Außenfeldspieler^M
voltigeur^M droit
jugador^M exterior derecho
esterno^M destro (giocatore^M)

サード／三塁手
third baseman
dritter Malspieler^M
troisième-but^M
jugador^M de tercera base^F
terza base^F (giocatore^M)

セカンド／二塁手
second baseman
zweiter Malspieler^M
deuxième-but^M
jugador^M de segunda base^F
seconda base^F (giocatore^M)

キャッチャー／捕手
catcher
Fänger^M
receveur^M
receptor^M
ricevitore^M

ピッチャー／投手
pitcher
Werfer^M
lanceur^M
lanzador^M
lanciatore^M

ファースト／一塁手
first baseman
erster Malspieler^M
premier-but^M
jugador^M de primera base^F
prima base^M (giocatore^M)

グラウンド
field
Spielfeld^N
terrain^M
campo^M
campo^M

サード／三塁
third base
drittes Mal^N
troisième but^M
tercera base^F
terza base^F (posizione^F)

ファウル・ライン
foul line
Foullinie^F
ligne^F de jeu^M
línea^F de foul^M
linea^F di fuoricampo^M

バックネット
backstop
Ballfangzaun^M
écran^M de protection^F
pantalla^F de protección^F
schermo^M di protezione^F

ダッグアウト／ベンチ
dugout
Spielerbank^F
abri^M des joueurs^M
banquillo^M de jugadores^M
panchina^F dei giocatori^M

コーチス・ボックス
coach's box
Coach-Box^F
rectangle^M des instructeurs^M
banquillo^M del entrenador^M
zona^F dell'allenatore^M

ネクスト・バッターズ・サークル
on-deck circle
On-Deck-Circle^M
cercle^M d'attente^F
círculo^M de espera^F
cerchio^M del battitore^M successivo

ファースト／一塁
first base
erstes Mal^N
premier but^M
primera base^F
prima base^F (posizione^F)

内野
infield
Innenfeld^N
avant-champ^M
diamante^M
diamante^M

セカンド／二塁
second base
zweites Mal^N
deuxième but^M
segunda base^F
seconda base^F (posizione^F)

球技 | BALL SPORTS
BALLSPORTARTEN | SPORTS DE BALLE ET DE BALLON | DEPORTES DE PELOTA Y DE BALÓN | SPORT CON LA PALLA

野球

投球
pitch
Wurf^M
lancer^M
lanzamiento^M
lancio^M

球審
home-plate umpire
Hauptschiedsrichter^M
arbitre^M en chef^M
árbitro^M de base^F meta^F
arbitro^M capo^M

バッター／打者
batter
Schlagmann^M
frappeur^M
bateador^M
battitore^M

ピッチャー／投手
pitcher
Werfer^M
lanceur^M
lanzador^M
lanciatore^M

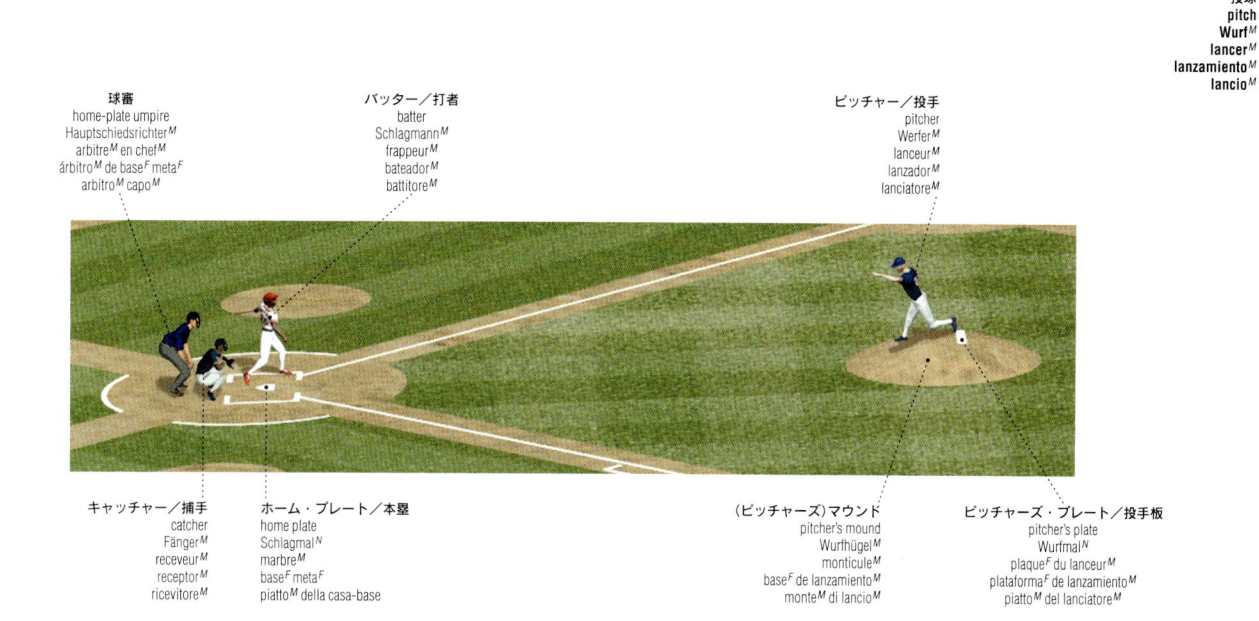

キャッチャー／捕手
catcher
Fänger^M
receveur^M
receptor^M
ricevitore^M

ホーム・プレート／本塁
home plate
Schlagmal^N
marbre^M
base^F meta^F
piatto^M della casa-base

(ピッチャーズ)マウンド
pitcher's mound
Wurthügel^M
monticule^M
base^F de lanzamiento^M
monte^M di lancio^M

ピッチャーズ・プレート／投手板
pitcher's plate
Wurfmal^N
plaque^F du lanceur^M
plataforma^F de lanzamiento^M
piatto^M del lanciatore^M

フェンス／塀
outfield fence
Outfieldzaun^M
clôture^F du champ^M extérieur
vallado^M del campo^M
recinzione^F

レフト／左翼
left field
linkes Feld^N
champ^M gauche
exterior^M izquierdo
esterno^M sinistro (posizione^F)

センター／中堅
center field; centre field
Mittelfeld^N
champ^M centre
exterior^M
esterno^M centro (posizione^F)

ライト／右翼
right field
rechtes Feld^N
champ^M droit
exterior^M derecho
esterno^M destro (posizione^F)

ファウル・ボール
foul line post
Foullinienpfosten^M
poteau^M de ligne^F de jeu^M
poste^M de foul^M
palo^M della linea^F di fuoricampo^M

警告(表示地)帯
warning track
Zuschauergrenze^F
piste^F d'avertissement^M
zona^F de atención^F
limite^M del campo^M

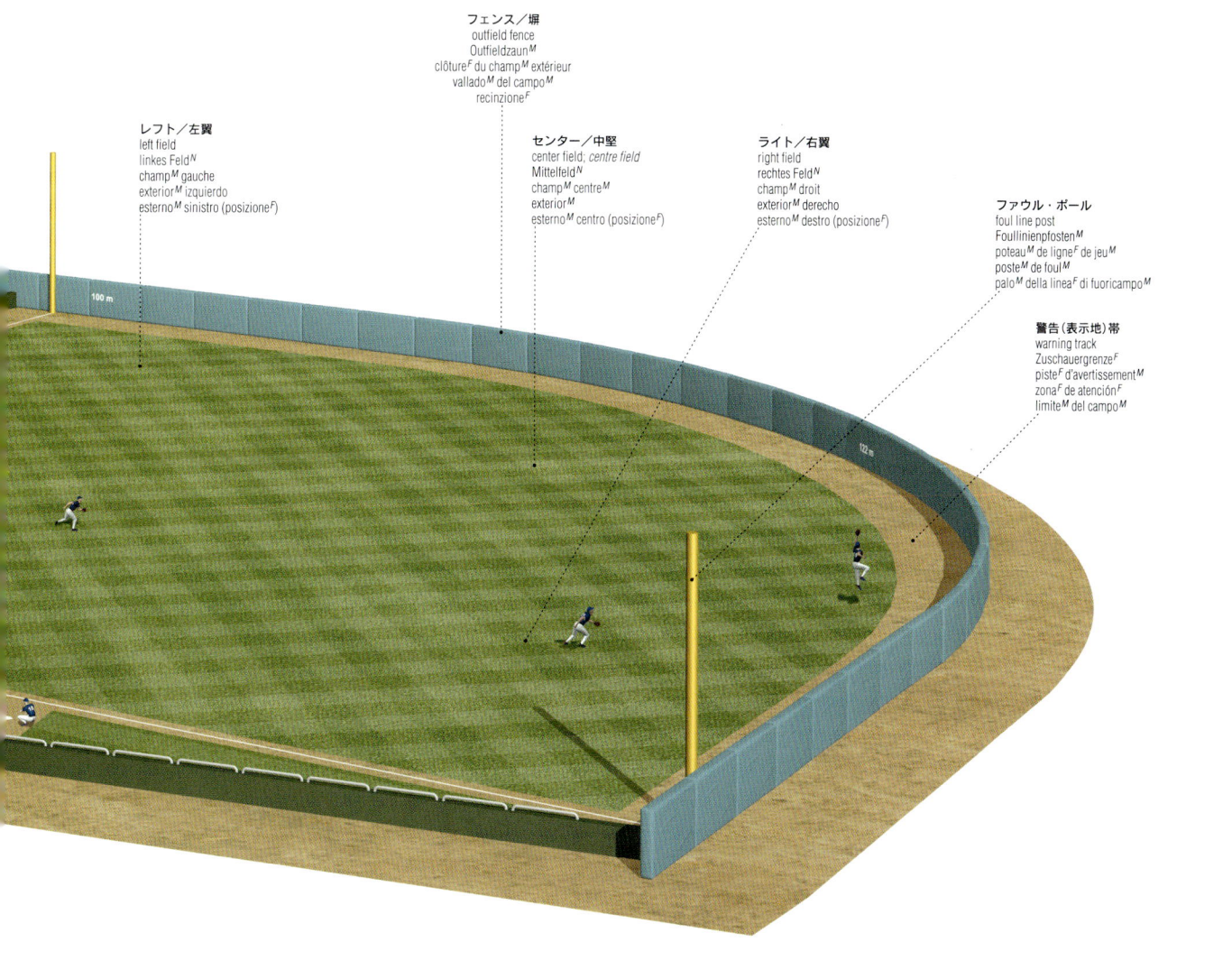

スポーツとゲーム

795

球技 | BALL SPORTS
BALLSPORTARTEN | SPORTS DE BALLE ET DE BALLON | DEPORTES DE PELOTA Y DE BALÓN | SPORT CON LA PALLA

野球

日本語 | 英語 | ドイツ語 | フランス語 | スペイン語 | イタリア語

野球ボール
baseball
Baseball^M
balle^F de baseball^M
béisbol^M
palla^F

バット
bat
Schläger^M
bâton^M
bate^M
mazza^F

打撃用ヘルメット
batter's helmet
Helm^M
casque de frappeur^M
casco^M del bateador^M
casco^M

バッター／打者
batter
Schlagmann^M
frappeur^M
bateador^M
battitore^M

キャッチャー／捕手
catcher
Fänger^M
receveur^M
receptor^M
ricevitore^M

喉のプロテクター
throat protector
Halsschutz^M
protège-gorge^M
protector^M de la garganta^F
paragola^F

マスク
mask
Maske^F
masque^M
máscara^F
maschera^F

ユニフォーム／
チーム・シャツ[ジャージー]
team shirt
Mannschaftstrikot^N
maillot^M d'équipe^F
camiseta^F
maglia^F della squadra^F

フレーム
frame
Visiergestell^N
grille^F
armazón^M de la máscara^F
griglia^F per casco^M

胸のプロテクター
chest protector
Brustschutz^M
plastron^M
peto^M
pettorina^F di protezione^F

（キャッチャー）ミット
catcher's glove
Fanghandschuh^M
gant^M de receveur^M
guante^M del receptor^M
guanto^M

アンダーシャツ
undershirt
Unterhemd^N
maillot^M de corps^M
camiseta^F interior
prima maglia^F

バッティング・グラブ／打撃用手袋
batting glove
Schlaghandschuh^M
gant^M de frappeur^M
guante^M de bateo^M
guanto^M

ズボン
pants; *trousers*
Hose^F
pantalon^M
pantalón^M
pantaloni^M

ストッキング／
スターラップ・ソックス
stirrup sock
Stutzen^M
chaussette^F-étrier^M
calcetín^M con tirante^M
calza^F con reggicalze^M

スパイク・シューズ［靴］
spiked shoe
Stollenschuh^M
chaussure^F à crampons^M
zapatilla^F con tacos^M
scarpa^F con tacchetti^M

爪先当て
toe guard
Zehenschützer^M
protège-orteils^M
protector^M del pie^M
parapunta^F

脚当て
leg guard
Beinschutz^M
jambière^F
espinillera^F
schiniere^M

膝当て
knee pad
Knieschützer^M
genouillère^F
rodillera^F
ginocchiera^F

踝（くるぶし）当て
ankle guard
Knöchelschutz^M
protège-cheville^M
tobillera^F
parastinchi^M

スポーツとゲーム

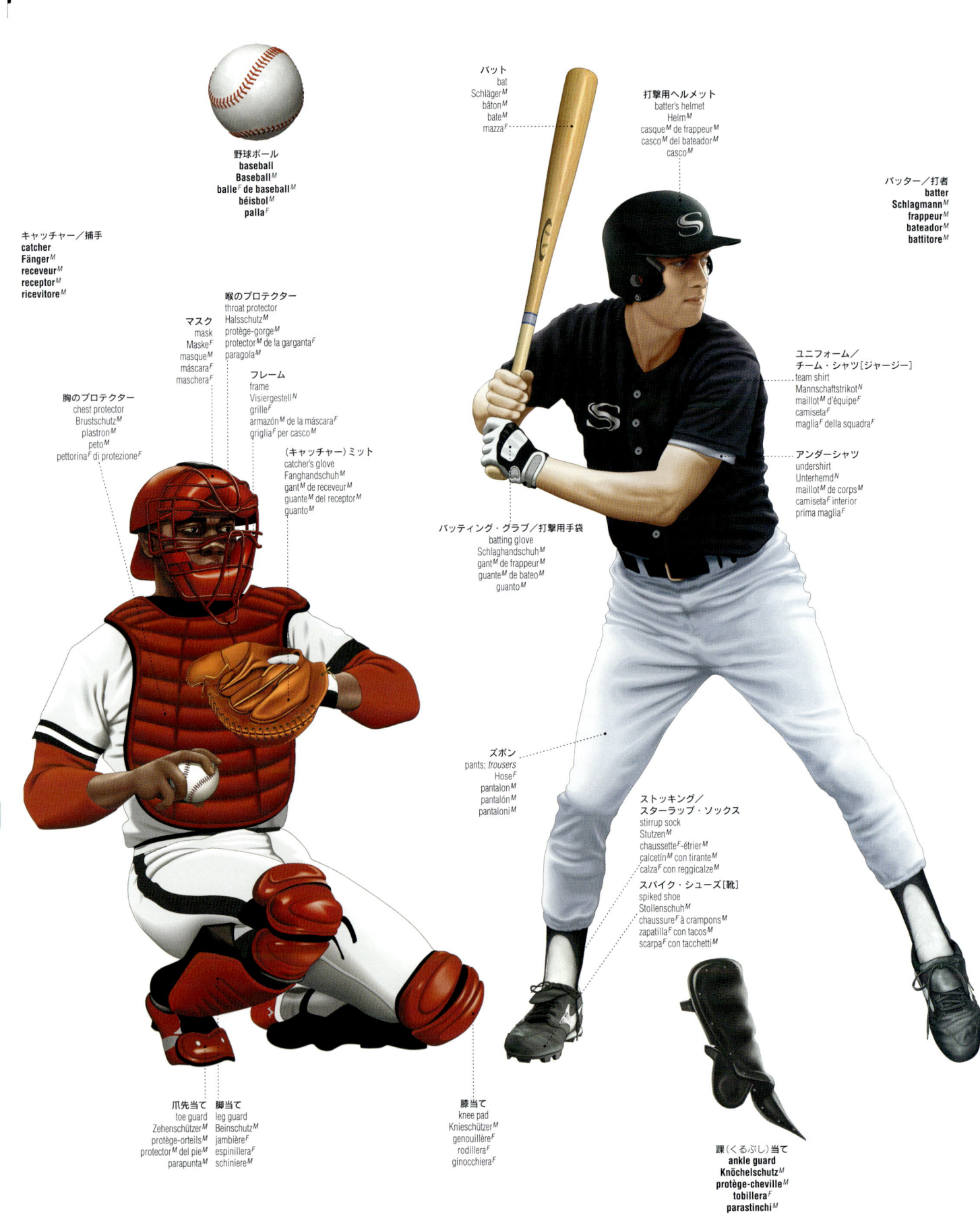

球技 | BALL SPORTS
BALLSPORTARTEN | SPORTS DE BALLE ET DE BALLON | DEPORTES DE PELOTA Y DE BALÓN | SPORT CON LA PALLA

野球

グリップ・エンド
knob
Knauf(M)
pommeau(M)
puño(M)
pomo(M)

グリップ／握り
handle
Griff(M)
manche(M)
empuñadura(F)
impugnatura(F)

ラベル
crest
Wappen(N)
écusson(M)
emblema(M)
stemma(M)

打球面
hitting area
Schlagbereich(M)
surface(F) de frappe(F)
cuadro(M) de bateo(M)
zona(F) di battuta(F)

バット
bat
Schläger(M)
bâton(M)
bate(M)
mazza(F)

野球ボールの断面図
cross section of a baseball
Baseball(M) im Querschnitt(M)
coupe(F) de la balle(F)
corte(M) de la pelota(F) de softball(M)
sezione(F) di una palla(F)

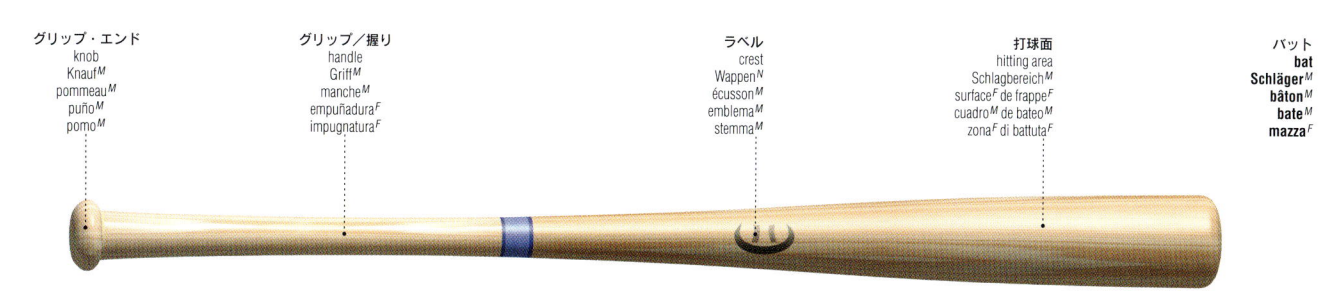

コルク芯
cork ball
Korkball(M)
balle(F) de liège(M)
bola(F) de corcho(M)
palla(F) di sughero(M)

糸芯
yarn ball
Garnball(M)
balle(F) de fil(M)
bola(F) de hilo(M)
palla(F) di filo(M)

網
web
Netz(N)
panier(M)
canasta(F)
finestra(F)

野手用グローブ
fielder's glove
Handschuh(M)
gant(M)
guante(M) de recogida(F)
guanto(M) del difensore(M)

ストラップ
strap
Riemen(M)
patte(F)
trabilla(F)
cinturino(M)

親指
thumb
Daumen(M)
pouce(M)
pulgar(M)
pollice(M)

指
finger
Finger(M)
doigt(M)
dedo(M)
dito(M)

手のひら
palm
Handfläche(F)
paume(F)
palma(F)
sacco(M)

踵
heel
Handwurzel(F)
talon(M)
talón(M)
tallone(M)

紐（ひも）
lace
Schnürband(N)
lacet(M)
cordón(M)
stringa(F)

カバー／表皮
cover
Außenschicht(F)
enveloppe(F)
forro(M)
rivestimento(M) esterno

縫い目
stitches
Nähte(F)
couture(F)
costura(F)
cucitura(F)

ソフトボール

softball | Softball(M) | softball(M) | softball(M) | softball(M)

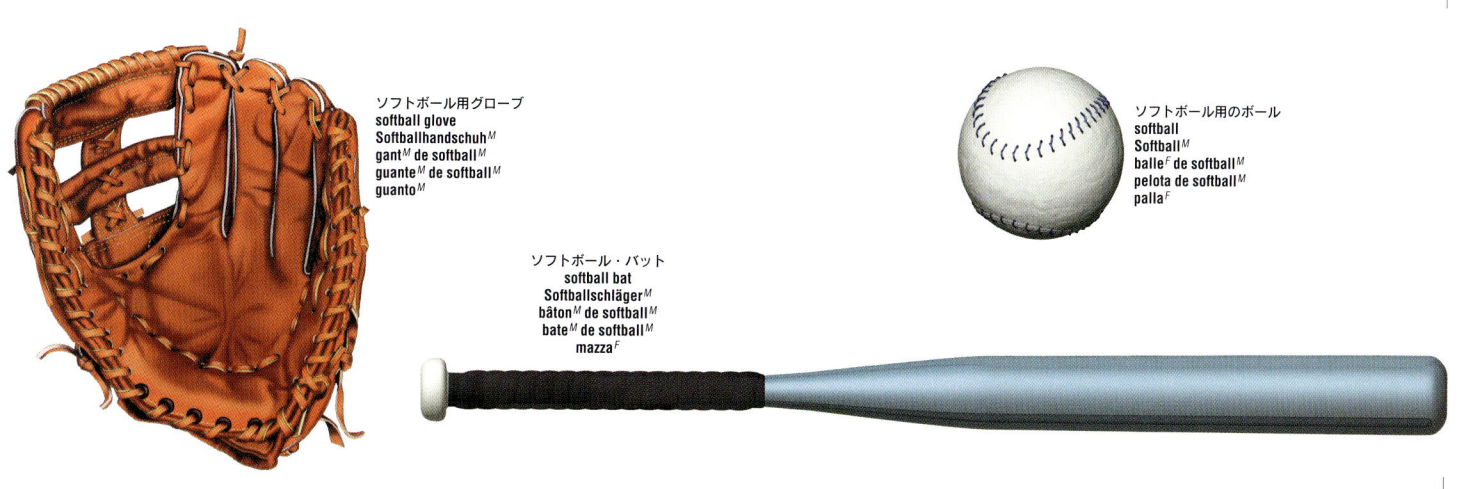

ソフトボール用グローブ
softball glove
Softballhandschuh(M)
gant(M) de softball(M)
guante(M) de softball(M)
guanto(M)

ソフトボール・バット
softball bat
Softballschläger(M)
bâton(M) de softball(M)
bate(M) de softball(M)
mazza(F)

ソフトボール用のボール
softball
Softball(M)
balle(F) de softball(M)
pelota de softball(M)
palla(F)

スポーツとゲーム

球技 | BALL SPORTS
BALLSPORTARTEN | SPORTS DE BALLE ET DE BALLON | DEPORTES DE PELOTA Y DE BALÓN | SPORT CON LA PALLA

クリケット

cricket | Cricket[N] | cricket[M] | cricket[M] | cricket[M]

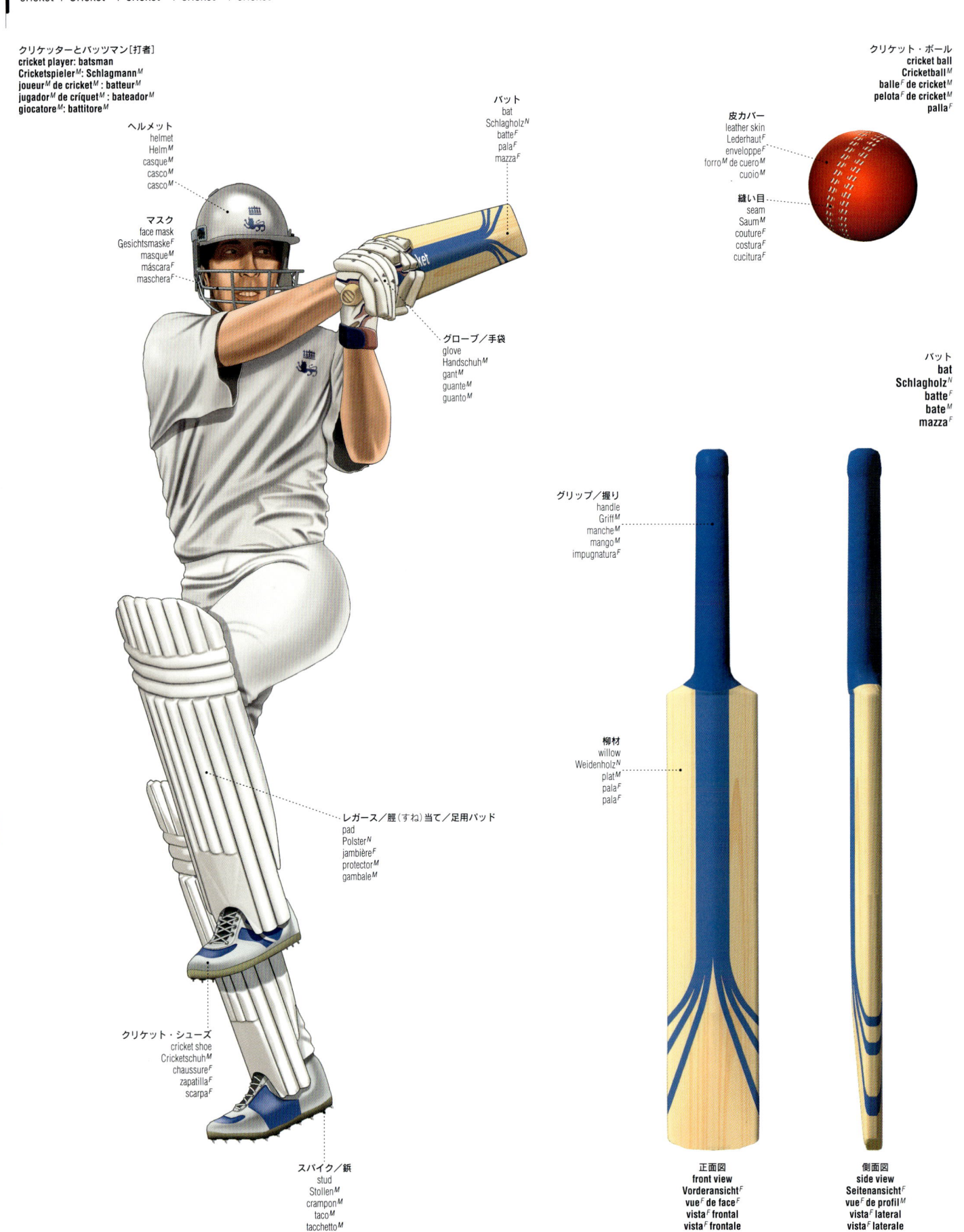

日本語 | 英語 | ドイツ語 | フランス語 | スペイン語 | イタリア語

クリケッターとバッツマン[打者]
cricket player: batsman
Cricketspieler[M]: Schlagmann[M]
joueur[M] de cricket[M] : batteur[M]
jugador[M] de críquet[M] : bateador[M]
giocatore[M]: battitore[M]

ヘルメット
helmet
Helm[M]
casque[M]
casco[M]
casco[M]

マスク
face mask
Gesichtsmaske[F]
masque[M]
máscara[F]
maschera[F]

バット
bat
Schlagholz[N]
batte[F]
pala[F]
mazza[F]

グローブ／手袋
glove
Handschuh[M]
gant[M]
guante[M]
guanto[M]

レガース／脛(すね)当て／足用パッド
pad
Polster[N]
jambière[F]
protector[M]
gambale[M]

クリケット・シューズ
cricket shoe
Cricketschuh[M]
chaussure[F]
zapatilla[F]
scarpa[F]

スパイク／鋲
stud
Stollen[M]
crampon[M]
taco[M]
tacchetto[M]

クリケット・ボール
cricket ball
Cricketball[M]
balle[F] de cricket[M]
pelota[F] de cricket[M]
palla[F]

皮カバー
leather skin
Lederhaut[F]
enveloppe[F]
forro[M] de cuero[M]
cuoio[M]

縫い目
seam
Saum[M]
couture[F]
costura[F]
cucitura[F]

バット
bat
Schlagholz[N]
batte[F]
bate[M]
mazza[F]

グリップ／握り
handle
Griff[M]
manche[M]
mango[M]
impugnatura[F]

柳材
willow
Weidenholz[N]
plat[M]
pala[F]
pala[F]

正面図
front view
Vorderansicht[F]
vue[F] de face[F]
vista[F] frontal
vista[F] frontale

側面図
side view
Seitenansicht[F]
vue[F] de profil[M]
vista[F] lateral
vista[F] laterale

スポーツとゲーム

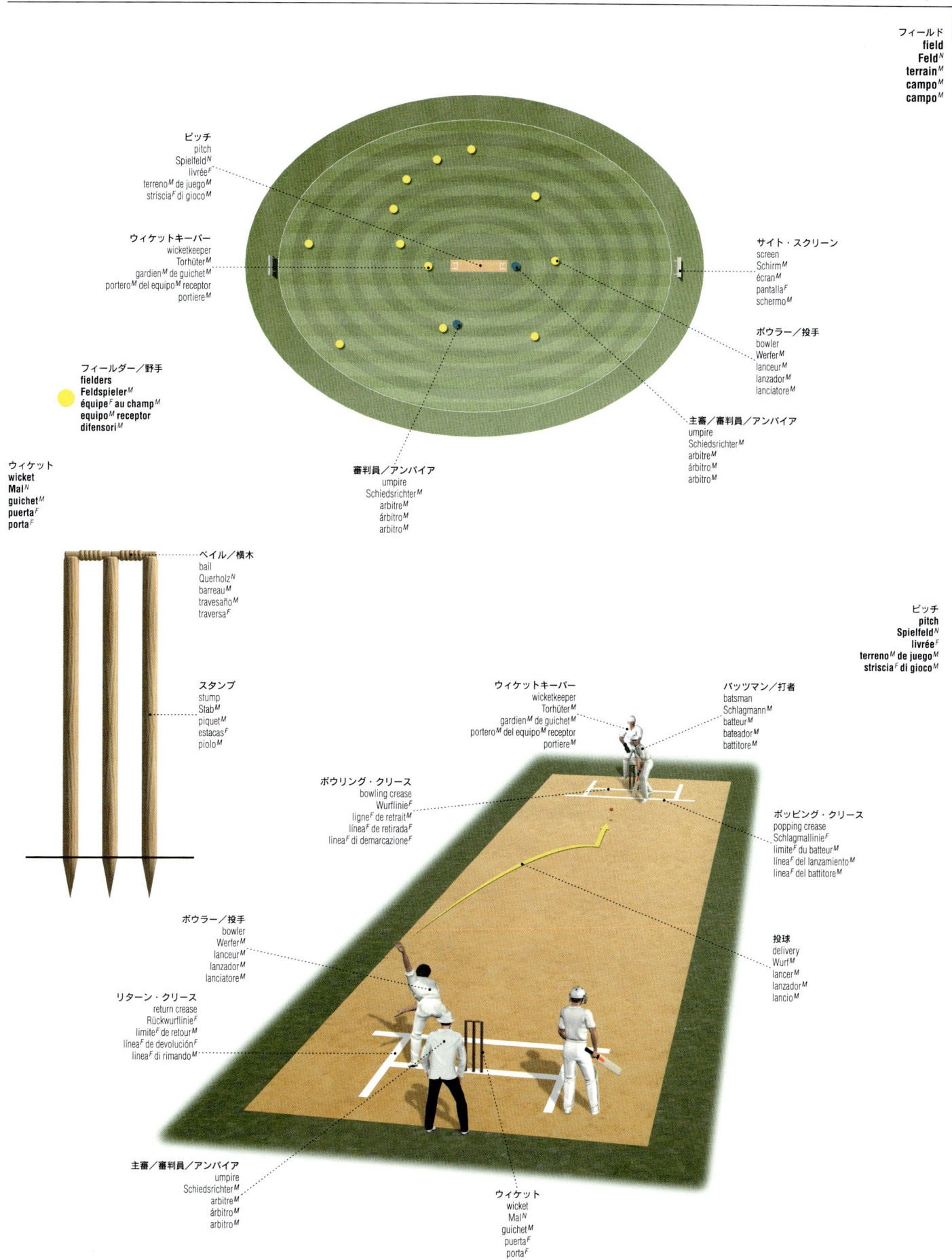

球技 | BALL SPORTS
BALLSPORTARTEN | SPORTS DE BALLE ET DE BALLON | DEPORTES DE PELOTA Y DE BALÓN | SPORT CON LA PALLA

クリケット

フィールド
field
Feld^N
terrain^M
campo^M
campo^M

ピッチ
pitch
Spielfeld^N
livrée^F
terreno^M de juego
striscia^F di gioco^M

ウィケットキーパー
wicketkeeper
Torhüter^M
gardien^M de guichet^M
portero^M del equipo^M receptor
portiere^M

サイト・スクリーン
screen
Schirm^M
écran^F
pantalla^F
schermo^M

ボウラー／投手
bowler
Werfer^M
lanceur^M
lanzador^M
lanciatore^M

主審／審判員／アンパイア
umpire
Schiedsrichter^M
arbitre^M
árbitro^M
arbitro^M

フィールダー／野手
fielders
Feldspieler^M
équipe^F au champ^M
equipo^M receptor
difensori^M

審判員／アンパイア
umpire
Schiedsrichter^M
arbitre^M
árbitro^M
arbitro^M

ウィケット
wicket
Mal^N
guichet^M
puerta^F
porta^F

ベイル／横木
bail
Querholz^N
barreau^M
travesaño^M
traversa^F

スタンプ
stump
Stab^M
piquet^M
estacas^F
piolo^M

ウィケットキーパー
wicketkeeper
Torhüter^M
gardien^M de guichet^M
portero^M del equipo^M receptor
portiere^M

バッツマン／打者
batsman
Schlagmann^M
batteur^M
bateador^M
battitore^M

ボウリング・クリース
bowling crease
Wurflinie^F
ligne^F de retrait^M
línea^F de retirada^F
linea^F di demarcazione^F

ポッピング・クリース
popping crease
Schlagmallinie^F
limite^F du batteur^M
línea^F del lanzamiento^M
linea^F del battitore^M

ピッチ
pitch
Spielfeld^N
livrée^F
terreno^M de juego^M
striscia^F di gioco^M

ボウラー／投手
bowler
Werfer^M
lanceur^M
lanzador^M
lanciatore^M

投球
delivery
Wurf^M
lancer^M
lanzador^M
lancio^M

リターン・クリース
return crease
Rückwurflinie^F
limite^F de retour^M
línea^F de devolución^F
linea^F di rimando^M

主審／審判員／アンパイア
umpire
Schiedsrichter^M
arbitre^M
árbitro^M
arbitro^M

ウィケット
wicket
Mal^N
guichet^M
puerta^F
porta^F

スポーツとゲーム

799

球技 | BALL SPORTS
BALLSPORTARTEN | SPORTS DE BALLE ET DE BALLON | DEPORTES DE PELOTA Y DE BALÓN | SPORT CON LA PALLA

（フィールド）ホッケー

日本語 | 英語 | ドイツ語 | フランス語 | スペイン語 | イタリア語

field hockey | Hockey^N | hockey^M sur gazon^M | hockey^M sobre hierba^F | hockey^M su prato^M

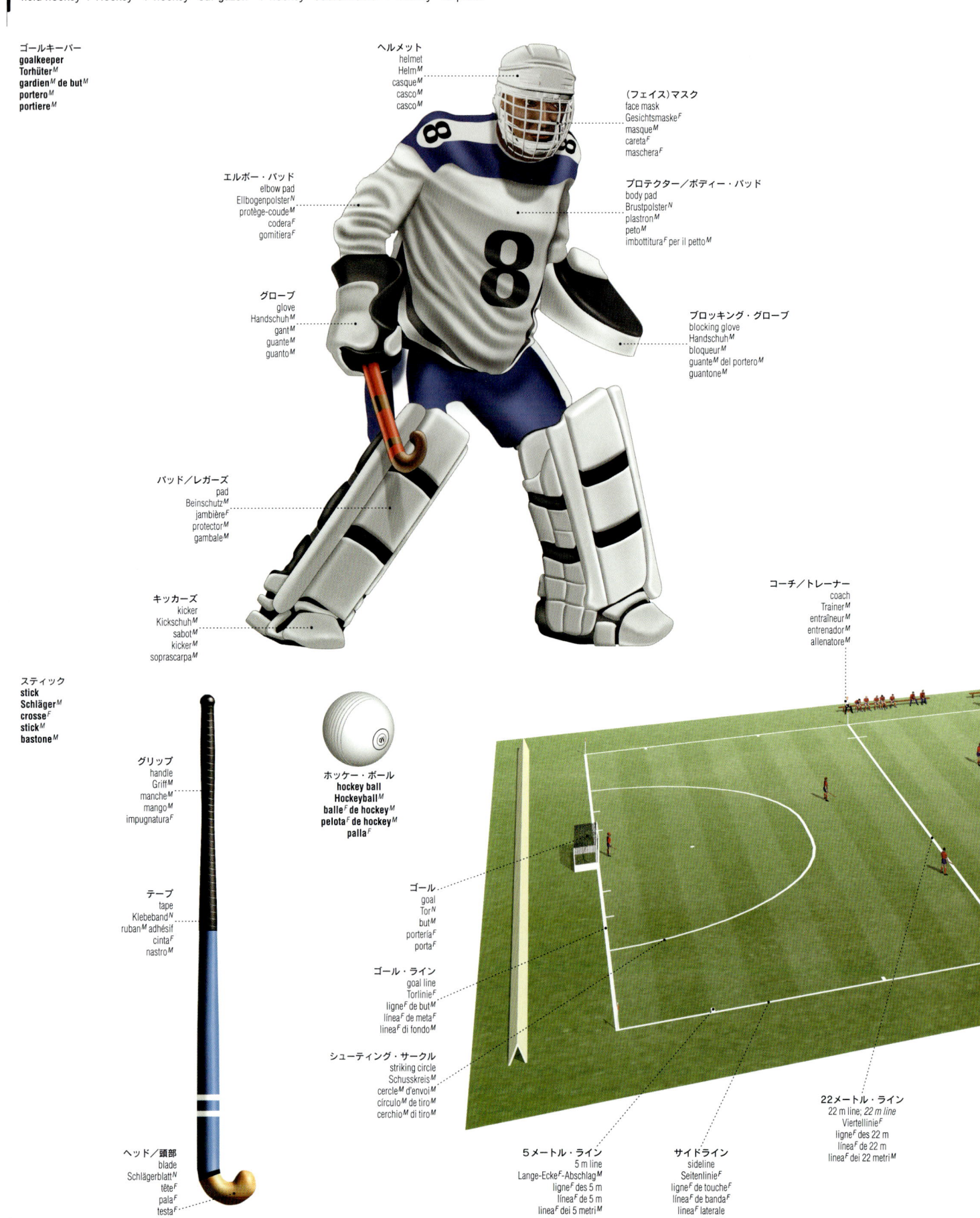

ゴールキーパー
goalkeeper
Torhüter^M
gardien^M de but^M
portero^M
portiere^M

ヘルメット
helmet
Helm^M
casque^M
casco^M
casco^M

（フェイス）マスク
face mask
Gesichtsmaske^F
masque^F
careta^F
maschera^F

エルボー・パッド
elbow pad
Ellbogenpolster^N
protège-coude^M
codera^F
gomitiera^F

プロテクター／ボディー・パッド
body pad
Brustpolster^N
plastron^M
peto^M
imbottitura^F per il petto^M

グローブ
glove
Handschuh^M
gant^M
guante^M
guanto^M

ブロッキング・グローブ
blocking glove
Handschuh^M
bloqueur^M
guante^M del portero^M
guantone^M

パッド／レガーズ
pad
Beinschutz^M
jambière^F
protector^M
gambale^M

キッカーズ
kicker
Kickschuh^M
sabot^M
kicker^M
soprascarpa^F

コーチ／トレーナー
coach
Trainer^M
entraîneur^M
entrenador^M
allenatore^M

スティック
stick
Schläger^M
crosse^F
stick^M
bastone^M

グリップ
handle
Griff^M
manche^M
mango^M
impugnatura^F

ホッケー・ボール
hockey ball
Hockeyball^M
balle^F de hockey^M
pelota^F de hockey^M
palla^F

テープ
tape
Klebeband^N
ruban^M adhésif
cinta^F
nastro^M

ゴール
goal
Tor^N
but^M
portería^F
porta^F

ゴール・ライン
goal line
Torlinie^F
ligne^F de but^M
línea^F de meta^F
linea^F di fondo^M

シューティング・サークル
striking circle
Schusskreis^M
cercle^M d'envoi^M
círculo^M de tiro^M
cerchio^M di tiro^M

ヘッド／頭部
blade
Schlägerblatt^N
tête^F
pala^F
testa^F

5メートル・ライン
5 m line
Lange-Ecke^F-Abschlag^M
ligne^F des 5 m
línea^F de 5 m
linea^F dei 5 metri^M

サイドライン
sideline
Seitenlinie^F
ligne^F de touche^F
línea^F de banda^F
linea^F laterale

22メートル・ライン
22 m line; *22 m line*
Viertellinie^F
ligne^F des 22 m
línea^F de 22 m
linea^F dei 22 metri^M

スポーツとゲーム

800

球技 | BALL SPORTS
BALLSPORTARTEN | SPORTS DE BALLE ET DE BALLON | DEPORTES DE PELOTA Y DE BALÓN | SPORT CON LA PALLA

（フィールド）ホッケー

フィールド・プレーヤー
field player
Feldspieler^M
hockeyeur^M
jugador^M de hockey
giocatore^M

ユニフォーム／チーム・シャツ
team shirt
Mannschaftstrikot^N
maillot^M d'équipe^F
camiseta^F del equipo^M
maglia^F della squadra^F

スティック
stick
Schläger^M/Stock^M
crosse^F
stick^M
bastone^M

ショート・パンツ
shorts
kurze Hose^F
short^M
pantalones^M cortos
pantaloncini^M

脛（すね）当て／シン・ガード
shin guard
Schienbeinschützer^M
protège-tibia^M
espinillera^F
parastinchi^M

ホッケー・シューズ
shoe
Schuh^M
chaussure^F
zapatilla^F
scarpa^F

競技委員
officials
Funktionäre^M
officiels^M
mesa^M de jueces^M
ufficiali^M di gara^F

ライト・ウィング
right wing
rechter Flügelspieler^M
ailier^M droit
ala^F derecha
ala^F destra

ライト・インサイド（フォワード）
right inside forward
halbrechter Läufer^M
avant^M droit
interior^M derecho
interno^M destro

選手用ベンチ
players' bench
Spielerbank^F
banc^M des joueurs^M
banquillo^M de los jugadores^M
panchina^F dei giocatori^M

センター・ハーフ
center half; *centre half*
Mittelfeldspieler^M
demi^M centre
medio^M central
centromediano^M

ライト・ハーフ
right half
rechter Mittelfeldspieler^M
demi^M droit
medio^M izquierdo
mediano^M destro

ライト・バック
right back
rechter Verteidiger^M
arrière^M droit
defensa^M derecho
terzino^M destro

ゴールキーパー
goalkeeper
Torwart^M
gardien^M de but^M
portero^M
portiere^M

コーナー・フラッグ
corner flag
Eckfahne^F
drapeau^M de coin^M
banderín^M de esquina^F
bandierina^F del calcio^M d'angolo^M

グラウンド
playing field
Spielfeld^N
terrain^M
campo^M de juego^M
campo^M

レフト・バック
left back
linker Verteidiger^M
arrière^M gauche
defensa^M izquierdo
terzino^M sinistro

審判員／主審／レフ（ェ）リー
referee
Schiedsrichter^M
arbitre^M
árbitro^M
arbitro^M

レフト・ハーフ
left half
linker Mittelfeldspieler^M
demi^M gauche
medio^M izquierdo
mediano^M sinistro

センター・フォワード
center forward; *centre forward*
Mittelstürmer^M
avant^M centre
centro^M delantero
centravanti^M

レフト・インサイド（フォワード）
left inside forward
linker Innenfeldspieler^M
avant^M gauche
interior^M izquierdo
interno^M sinistro

レフト・ウィング
left wing
linker Flügelspieler^M
ailier^M gauche
ala^F izquierda
ala^F sinistra

センター・ライン
center line; *centre line*
Mittellinie^F
ligne^F de centre^M
línea^F central
linea^F di centrocampo^M

スポーツとゲーム

801

球技 | BALL SPORTS
BALLSPORTARTEN | SPORTS DE BALLE ET DE BALLON | DEPORTES DE PELOTA Y DE BALÓN | SPORT CON LA PALLA

サッカー

soccer | Fußball[M] | football[M] | fútbol[M] | calcio[M]

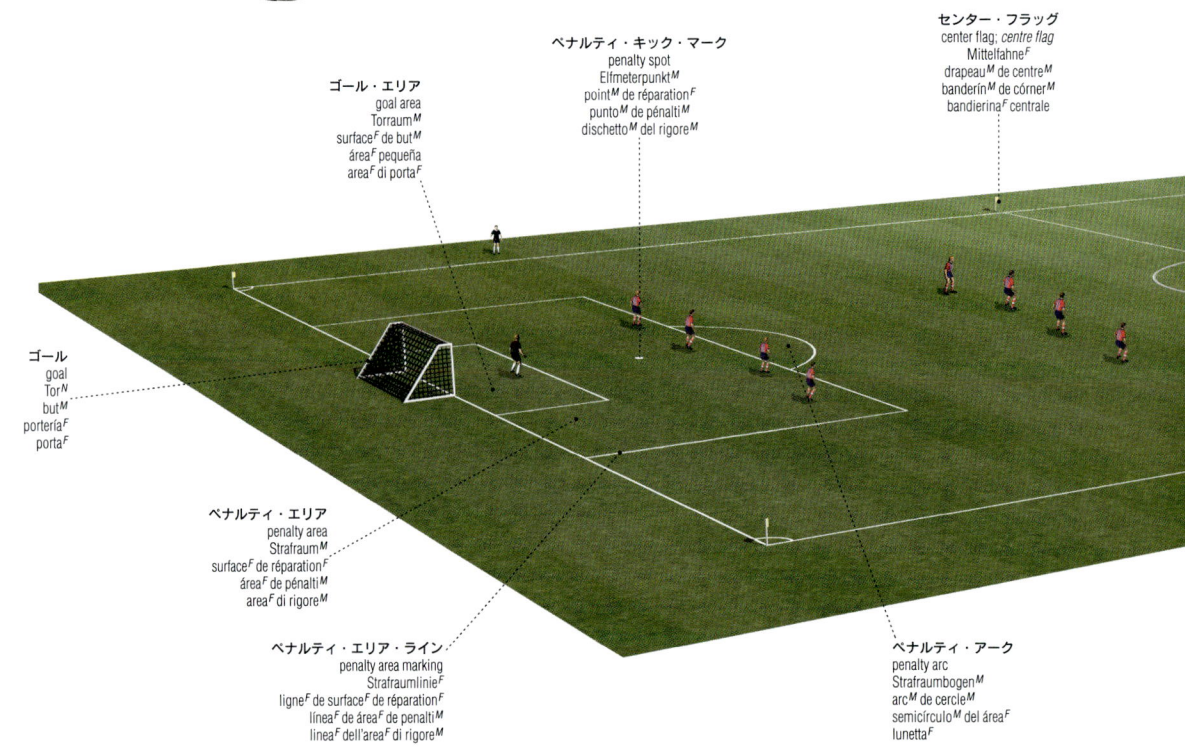

日本語 | 英語 | ドイツ語 | フランス語 | スペイン語 | イタリア語

サッカー・プレーヤー
soccer player
Fußballspieler[M]
footballeur[M]
futbolista[M/F]
calciatore[M]

ユニフォーム／チーム・シャツ
team shirt
Mannschaftstrikot[N]
maillot[M] d'équipe[F]
camiseta[F] del equipo[M]
maglia[F] della squadra[F]

ゴールキーパー・グローブ
goalkeeper's gloves
Torwarthandschuhe[M]
gants[M] de gardien[M] de but[M]
guantes[M] del portero[M]
guanti[M] del portiere[M]

ショーツ
shorts
Hose[F]
short[M]
pantalones[M]
pantaloncini[M]

取り替え式スパイク
interchangeable studs
Schraubstollen[M]
crampons[M] interchangeables
tacos[M] de rosca[F]
tacchetti[M] intercambiabili

サッカー・シューズ
soccer shoe
Fußballschuh[M]
chaussure[F] **de football**[M]
bota[F] **de fútbol**[M]
scarpa[F]

脛（すね）当て
shin guard
Schienbeinschützer[M]
protège-tibia[M]
espinillera[F]
parastinchi[M]

ストッキング
sock
Stulpen[F]
chaussette[F]
calcetín[M]
calzettone[M]

サッカー・ボール
soccer ball
Fußball[M]
ballon[M] de football[M]
balón[M] de fútbol[M]
pallone[M]

グラウンド
playing field
Spielfeld[N]
terrain[M]
campo[M]
campo[M] **di gioco**[M]

ゴール・エリア
goal area
Torraum[M]
surface[F] de but[M]
área[F] pequeña
area[F] di porta[F]

ペナルティ・キック・マーク
penalty spot
Elfmeterpunkt[M]
point[M] de réparation[F]
punto[M] de pénalti[M]
dischetto[M] del rigore[M]

センター・フラッグ
center flag; *centre flag*
Mittelfahne[F]
drapeau[M] de centre[M]
banderín[M] de córner[M]
bandierina[F] centrale

ゴール
goal
Tor[N]
but[M]
portería[F]
porta[F]

ペナルティ・エリア
penalty area
Strafraum[M]
surface[F] de réparation[F]
área[F] de pénalti[M]
area[F] di rigore[M]

ペナルティ・エリア・ライン
penalty area marking
Strafraumlinie[F]
ligne[F] de surface[F] de réparation[F]
línea[F] de área[F] de penalti[M]
linea[F] dell'area[F] di rigore[M]

ペナルティ・アーク
penalty arc
Strafraumbogen[M]
arc[M] de cercle[M]
semicírculo[M] del área[F]
lunetta[F]

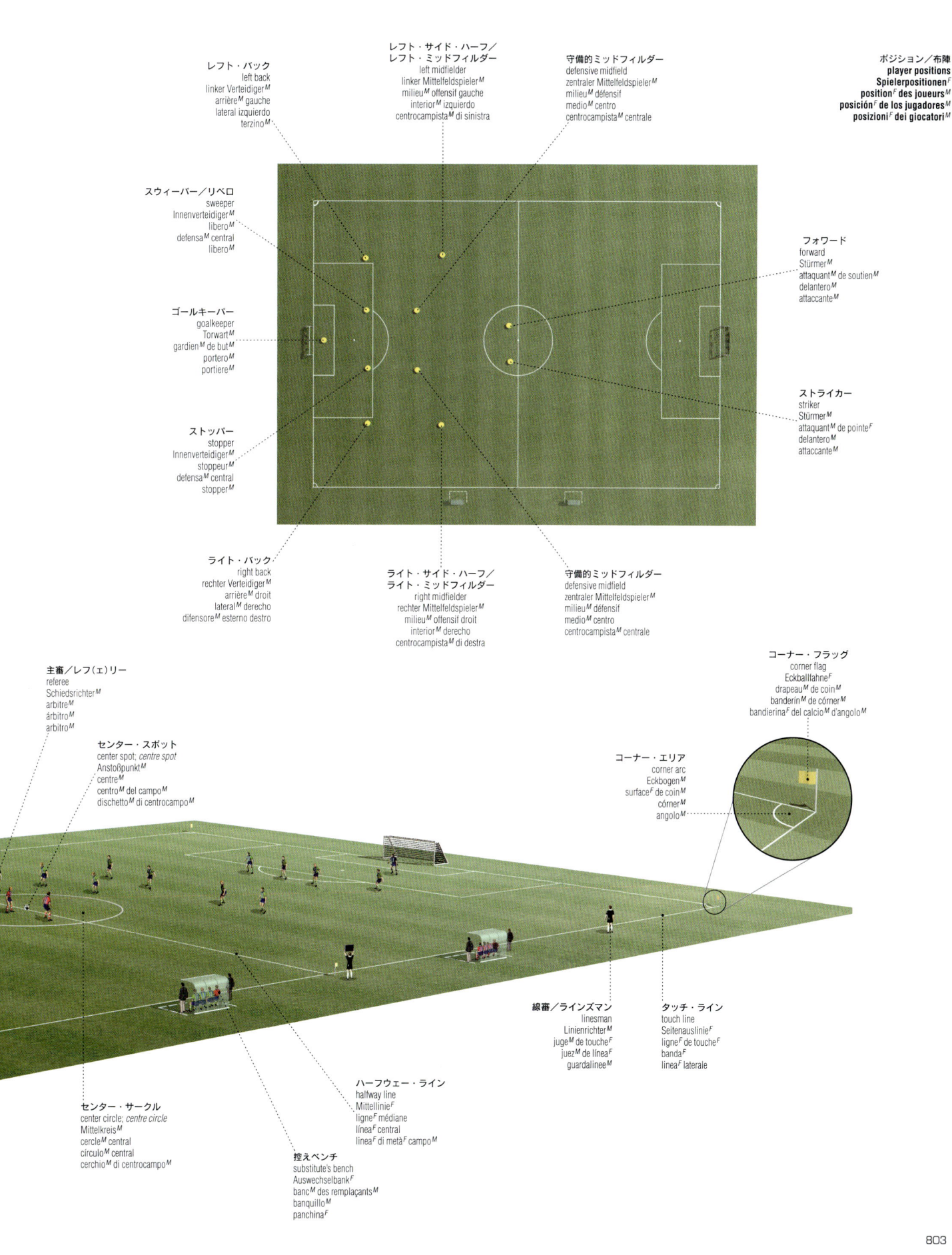

球技 | BALL SPORTS
BALLSPORTARTEN | SPORTS DE BALLE ET DE BALLON | DEPORTES DE PELOTA Y DE BALÓN | SPORT CON LA PALLA

サッカー

ポジション／布陣
player positions
Spielerpositionen^F
position^F des joueurs^M
posición^F de los jugadores^M
posizioni^F dei giocatori^M

レフト・バック / left back / linker Verteidiger^M / arrière^M gauche / lateral izquierdo / terzino^M

レフト・サイド・ハーフ／レフト・ミッドフィルダー / left midfielder / linker Mittelfeldspieler^M / milieu^M offensif gauche / interior^M izquierdo / centrocampista^M di sinistra

守備的ミッドフィルダー / defensive midfield / zentraler Mittelfeldspieler^M / milieu^M défensif / medio^M centro / centrocampista^M centrale

スウィーパー／リベロ / sweeper / Innenverteidiger^M / libero / defensa^M central / libero^M

フォワード / forward / Stürmer^M / attaquant^M de soutien^M / delantero^M / attaccante^M

ゴールキーパー / goalkeeper / Torwart^M / gardien^M de but^M / portero^M / portiere^M

ストライカー / striker / Stürmer^M / attaquant^M de pointe^F / delantero^M / attaccante^M

ストッパー / stopper / Innenverteidiger^M / stoppeur^M / defensa^M central / stopper^M

ライト・バック / right back / rechter Verteidiger^M / arrière^M droit / lateral^M derecho / difensore^M esterno destro

ライト・サイド・ハーフ／ライト・ミッドフィルダー / right midfielder / rechter Mittelfeldspieler^M / milieu^M offensif droit / interior^M derecho / centrocampista^M di destra

守備的ミッドフィルダー / defensive midfield / zentraler Mittelfeldspieler^M / milieu^M défensif / medio^M centro / centrocampista^M centrale

主審／レフ（ェ）リー / referee / Schiedsrichter^M / arbitre^M / árbitro^M / arbitro^M

センター・スポット / center spot; centre spot / Anstoßpunkt^M / centre^M / centro^M del campo^M / dischetto^M di centrocampo^M

コーナー・フラッグ / corner flag / Eckballfahne^F / drapeau^M de coin^M / banderín^M de córner^M / bandierina^F del calcio^M d'angolo^M

コーナー・エリア / corner arc / Eckbogen^M / surface^F de coin^M / córner^M / angolo^M

線審／ラインズマン / linesman / Linienrichter^M / juge^M de touche^F / juez^M de línea^F / guardalinee^M

タッチ・ライン / touch line / Seitenauslinie^F / ligne^F de touche^F / banda^F / linea^F laterale

センター・サークル / center circle; centre circle / Mittelkreis^M / cercle^F central / círculo^M central / cerchio^M di centrocampo^M

ハーフウェー・ライン / halfway line / Mittellinie^F / ligne^F médiane / línea^F central / linea^F di metà^F campo^M

控えベンチ / substitute's bench / Auswechselbank^F / banc^M des remplaçants^M / banquillo^M / panchina^F

スポーツとゲーム

803

球技 | BALL SPORTS
BALLSPORTARTEN | SPORTS DE BALLE ET DE BALLON | DEPORTES DE PELOTA Y DE BALÓN | SPORT CON LA PALLA

ラグビー

日本語 | 英語 | ドイツ語 | フランス語 | スペイン語 | イタリア語

rugby | Rugby[N] | rugby[M] | rugby[M] | rugby[M]

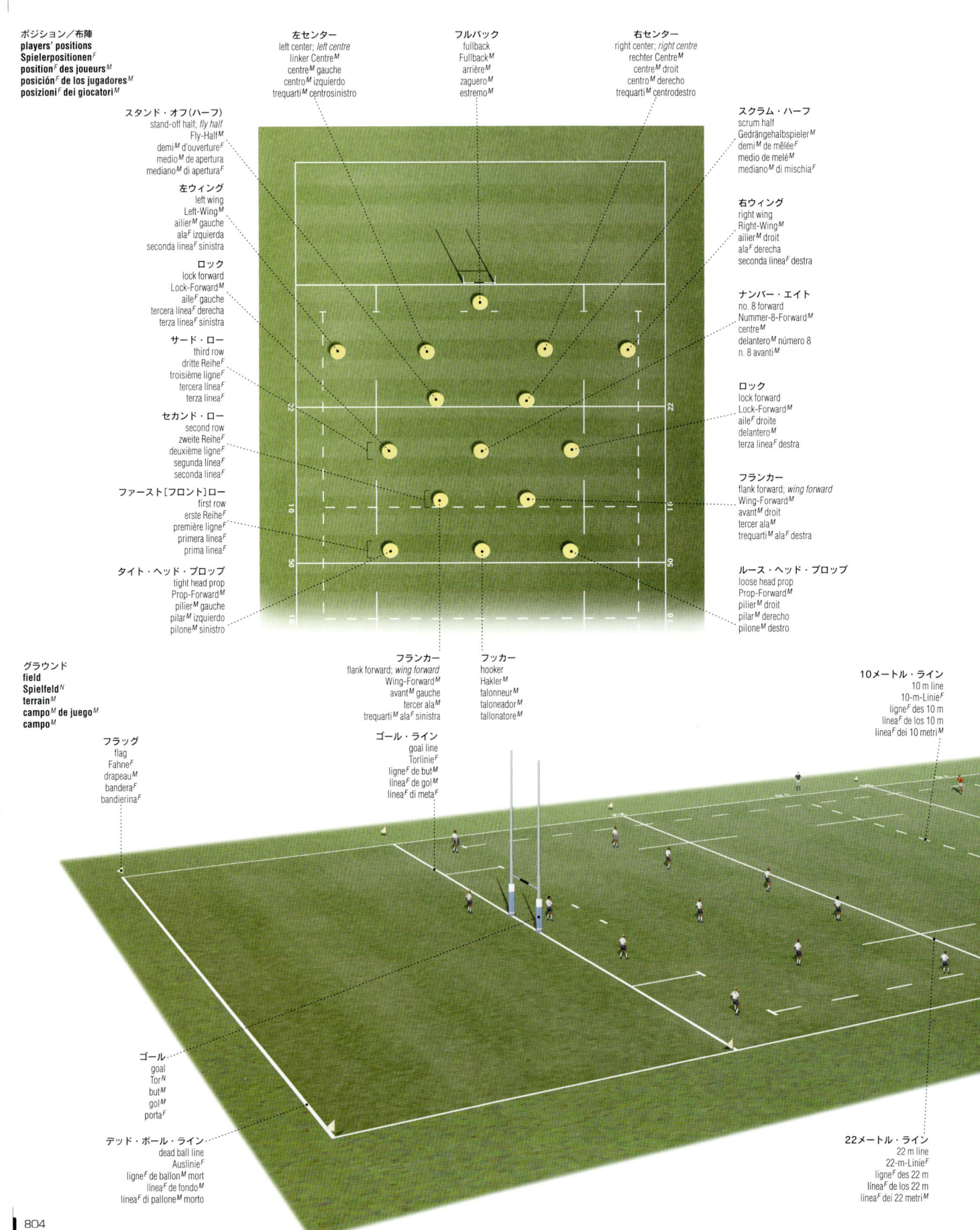

ポジション／布陣
players' positions
Spielerpositionen[F]
position[F] des joueurs[M]
posición[F] de los jugadores[M]
posizioni[F] dei giocatori[M]

左センター
left center; *left centre*
linker Centre[M]
centre[M] gauche
centro[M] izquierdo
trequarti[M] centrosinistro

フルバック
fullback
Fullback[M]
arrière[M]
zaguero[M]
estremo[M]

右センター
right center; *right centre*
rechter Centre[M]
centre[M] droit
centro[M] derecho
trequarti[M] centrodestro

スタンド・オフ（ハーフ）
stand-off half; *fly half*
Fly-Half[M]
demi[M] d'ouverture[F]
medio[M] de apertura
mediano[M] di apertura[F]

スクラム・ハーフ
scrum half
Gedrängehalbspieler[M]
demi[M] de mêlée[F]
medio de melé[F]
mediano[M] di mischia[F]

左ウィング
left wing
Left-Wing[M]
ailier[M] gauche
ala[F] izquierda
seconda linea[F] sinistra

右ウィング
right wing
Right-Wing[M]
ailier[M] droit
ala[F] derecha
seconda linea[F] destra

ロック
lock forward
Lock-Forward[M]
aile[F] gauche
tercera línea[F] derecha
terza linea[F] sinistra

ナンバー・エイト
no. 8 forward
Nummer-8-Forward[M]
centre[M]
delantero[M] número 8
n. 8 avanti[M]

サード・ロー
third row
dritte Reihe[F]
troisième ligne[F]
tercera línea[F]
terza linea[F]

ロック
lock forward
Lock-Forward[M]
aile[F] droite
delantero[M]
terza linea[F] destra

セカンド・ロー
second row
zweite Reihe[F]
deuxième ligne[F]
segunda línea[F]
seconda linea[F]

フランカー
flank forward; *wing forward*
Wing-Forward[M]
avant[M] droit
tercer ala[M]
trequarti[M] ala[F] destra

ファースト［フロント］ロー
first row
erste Reihe[F]
première ligne[F]
primera línea[F]
prima linea[F]

タイト・ヘッド・プロップ
tight head prop
Prop-Forward[M]
pilier[M] gauche
pilar[M] izquierdo
pilone[M] sinistro

ルース・ヘッド・プロップ
loose head prop
Prop-Forward[M]
pilier[M] droit
pilar[M] derecho
pilone[M] destro

グラウンド
field
Spielfeld[N]
terrain[M]
campo[M] de juego[M]
campo[M]

フランカー
flank forward; *wing forward*
Wing-Forward[M]
avant[M] gauche
tercer ala[M]
trequarti[M] ala[F] sinistra

フッカー
hooker
Hakler[M]
talonneur[M]
taloneador[M]
tallonatore[M]

10メートル・ライン
10 m line
10-m-Linie[F]
ligne[F] des 10 m
línea[F] de los 10 m
linea[F] dei 10 metri[M]

フラッグ
flag
Fahne[F]
drapeau[M]
bandera[F]
bandierina[F]

ゴール・ライン
goal line
Torlinie[F]
ligne[F] de but[M]
línea[F] de gol[M]
linea[F] di meta[F]

ゴール
goal
Tor[N]
but[M]
gol[M]
porta[F]

デッド・ボール・ライン
dead ball line
Auslinie[F]
ligne[F] de ballon[M] mort
línea[F] de fondo[M]
linea[F] di pallone[M] morto

22メートル・ライン
22 m line
22-m-Linie[F]
ligne[F] des 22 m
línea[F] de los 22 m
linea[F] dei 22 metri[M]

804

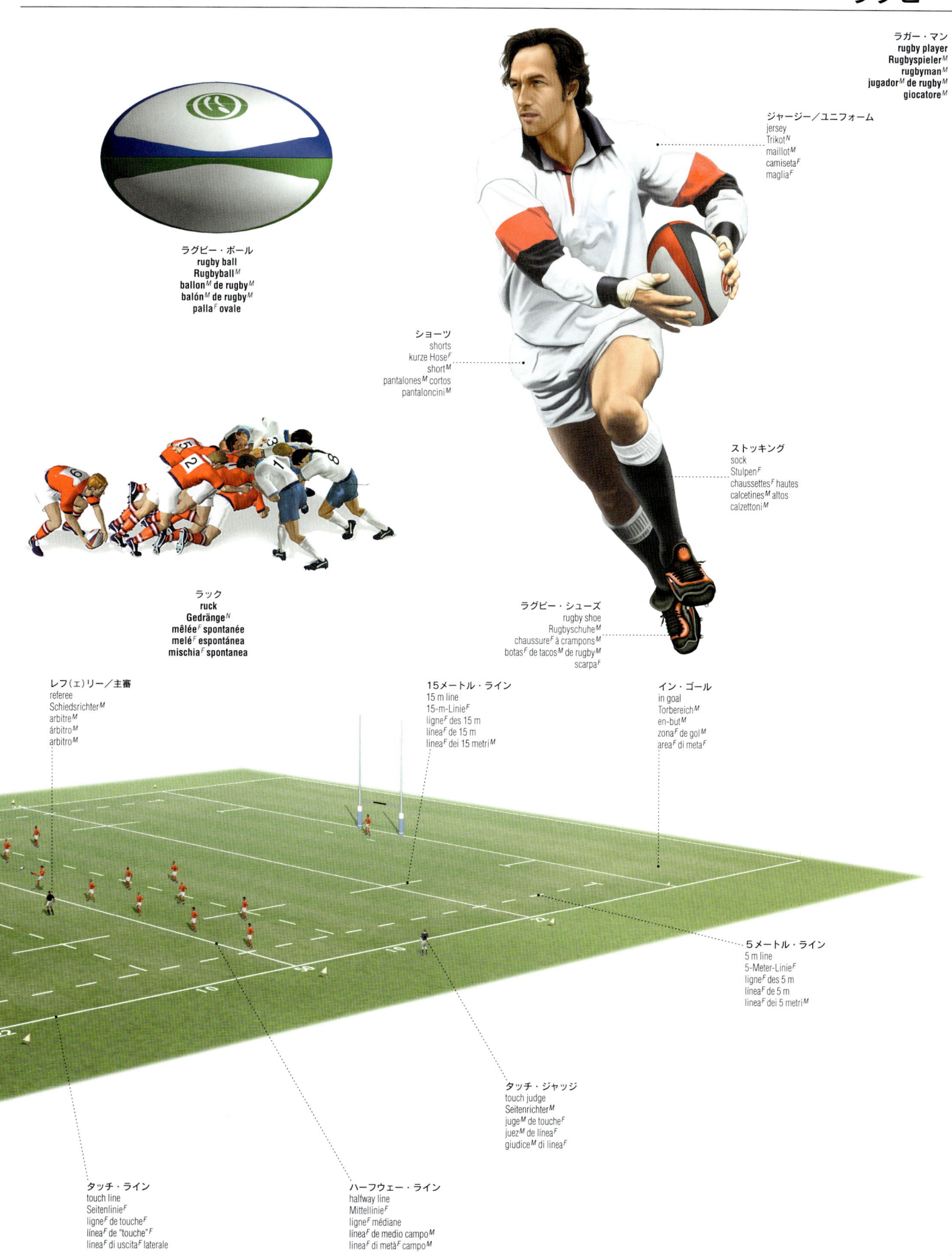

球技 | BALL SPORTS
BALLSPORTARTEN | SPORTS DE BALLE ET DE BALLON | DEPORTES DE PELOTA Y DE BALÓN | SPORT CON LA PALLA

ラグビー

ラガー・マン
rugby player
Rugbyspieler^M
rugbyman^M
jugador^M de rugby^M
giocatore^M

ジャージー／ユニフォーム
jersey
Trikot^N
maillot^M
camiseta^F
maglia^F

ラグビー・ボール
rugby ball
Rugbyball^M
ballon^M de rugby^M
balón^M de rugby^M
palla^F ovale

ショーツ
shorts
kurze Hose^F
short^M
pantalones^M cortos
pantaloncini^M

ストッキング
sock
Stulpen^F
chaussettes^F hautes
calcetines^M altos
calzettoni^M

ラック
ruck
Gedränge^N
mêlée^F spontanée
melé^F espontánea
mischia^F spontanea

ラグビー・シューズ
rugby shoe
Rugbyschuhe^M
chaussure^F à crampons^M
botas^F de tacos^M de rugby^M
scarpa^F

レフ(ェ)リー／主審
referee
Schiedsrichter^M
arbitre^M
árbitro^M
arbitro^M

15メートル・ライン
15 m line
15-m-Linie^F
ligne^F des 15 m
línea^F de 15 m
linea^F dei 15 metri^M

イン・ゴール
in goal
Torbereich^M
en-but^M
zona^F de gol^M
area^F di meta^F

5メートル・ライン
5 m line
5-Meter-Linie^F
ligne^F des 5 m
línea^F de 5 m
linea^F dei 5 metri^M

タッチ・ジャッジ
touch judge
Seitenrichter^M
juge^M de touche^F
juez^M de línea^F
giudice^M di linea^F

タッチ・ライン
touch line
Seitenlinie^F
ligne^F de touche^F
linea^F de "touche"^{F}
linea^F di uscita^F laterale

ハーフウェー・ライン
halfway line
Mittellinie^F
ligne^F médiane
línea^F de medio campo^M
linea^F di metà^F campo^M

スポーツとゲーム

805

球技 | BALL SPORTS
BALLSPORTARTEN | SPORTS DE BALLE ET DE BALLON | DEPORTES DE PELOTA Y DE BALÓN | SPORT CON LA PALLA

アメリカン・フットボール

日本語 | 英語 | ドイツ語 | フランス語 | スペイン語 | イタリア語

American football; *American football* | American Football[M] | football[M] américain | fútbol[M] americano | football[M] americano

スクリメージ：ディフェンス／守備側
scrimmage: defense
Gedränge[N]: Verteidigung[F]
mêlée[F] : défense[F]
melé[M] : defensa[F]
mischia[F]: difesa[F]

ライト・ディフェンス・エンド
right defensive end
rechter Defensive End[M]
ailier[M] défensif droit
ala[M] defensivo derecho
difensore[M] ala[F] destra

ライト・コーナーバック
right cornerback
rechter Corner Back[M]
demi[M] de coin[M] droit
esquinero[M] derecho
terzino[M] di destra

ライト・ディフェンス・タックル
right defensive tackle
rechter Defensive Tackle[M]
plaqueur[M] droit
tackle[M] defensivo derecho
placcatore[M] destro

アウトサイド・ラインバッカー
outside linebacker
äußerer Linebacker[M]
secondeur[M] extérieur droit
apoyador[M] exterior
linebacker[M] esterno

レフト・ディフェンス・タックル
left defensive tackle
linker Defensive Tackle[M]
plaqueur[M] gauche
tackle[M] defensivo izquierdo
placcatore[M] sinistro

ライト・セーフティ
right safety
rechter Safety[M]
demi[M] de sûreté[F] droit
safety[M] débil
estremo[M] di destra

ミドル・ラインバッカー
middle linebacker
mittlerer Linebacker[M]
secondeur[M] intérieur
apoyador[M]
linebacker[M] centrale

インサイド・ラインバッカー
inside linebacker
Middle Linebacker[M]
secondeur[M] extérieur gauche
apoyador[M] interior
linebacker[M] interno

レフト・ディフェンス・エンド
left defensive end
linker Defensive End[M]
ailier[M] défensif gauche
ala[M] defensivo izquierdo
difensore[M] ala[F] sinistra

ニュートラル・ゾーン
neutral zone
neutrale Zone[F]
zone[F] neutre
zona[F] neutral
zona[F] neutra

レフト・コーナーバック
left cornerback
linker Corner Back[M]
demi[M] de coin[M] gauche
esquinero[M] izquierdo
terzino[M] di sinistra

レフト・セーフティ
left safety
linker Safety[M]
demi[M] de sûreté[F] gauche
safety[M] fuerte
estremo[M] di sinistra

フィールド
playing field for American football
Spielfeld[N] für American Football[M]
terrain[M] de football[M] américain
campo[M] de juego[M] de fútbol[M] americano
campo[M]

インバウンズ・ライン
inbounds line
Inbound-Linie[F]
trait[M] de mise[F] au jeu[M]
línea[F] límite[M] de inicio[M] de jugada[F]
linea[F] di messa[F] in gioco[M]

ゴール・ライン
goal line
Torlinie[F]
ligne[F] de but[M]
línea[F] de gol[M]
linea[F] di meta[F]

50ヤード・ライン
fifty-yard line; centre line
Mittellinie[F]
ligne[F] de centre[M]
línea[F] media
linea[F] di centrocampo[M]

エンド・ゾーン
end zone
Endzone[F]
zone[F] de but[M]
zona[F] de anotación[F]
area[F] di meta[F]

エンド・ライン
end line
Endlinie[F]
ligne[F] de fond[M]
línea[F] de fondo[M]
linea[F] di fondo[M]

ヤード・ライン
yard line
Yardlinie[F]
ligne[F] des verges[F]
línea[F] yardas[F]
linea[F] delle yards[F]

サイドライン
sideline
Seitenlinie[F]
ligne[F] de touche[F]
banda[F]
linea[F] laterale

スポーツとゲーム

806

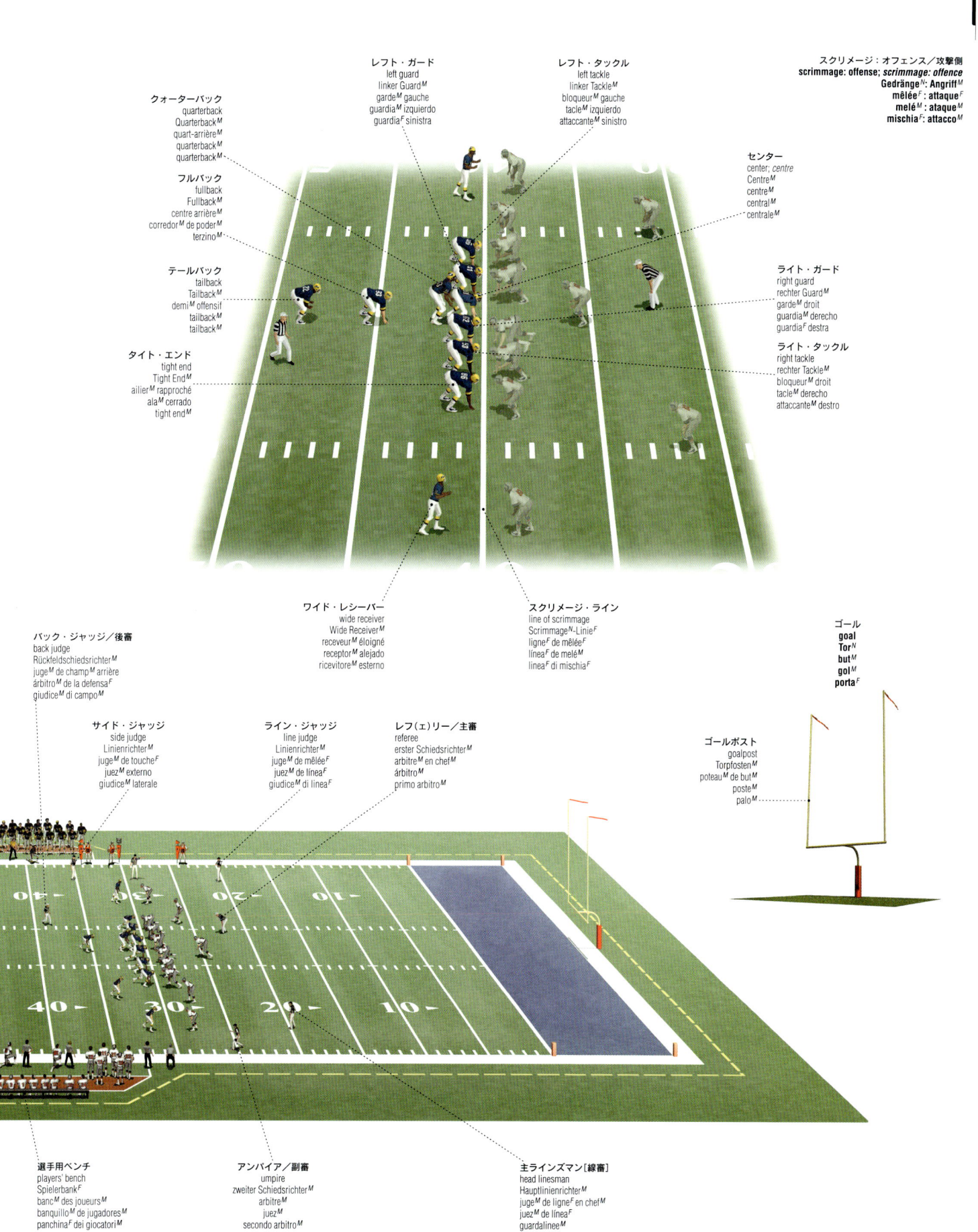

球技 | BALL SPORTS
BALLSPORTARTEN | SPORTS DE BALLE ET DE BALLON | DEPORTES DE PELOTA Y DE BALÓN | SPORT CON LA PALLA

アメリカン・フットボール

スクリメージ：オフェンス／攻撃側
scrimmage: offense; *scrimmage: offence*
Gedränge^N: **Angriff**
mêlée : **attaque**^{F}
melé^M : **ataque**^{M}
mischia^F: **attacco**^{M}

レフト・ガード
left guard
linker Guard^M
garde^M gauche
guardia^M izquierdo
guardia^F sinistra

レフト・タックル
left tackle
linker Tackle^M
bloqueur^M gauche
tacle^M izquierdo
attaccante^M sinistro

クォーターバック
quarterback
Quarterback^M
quart-arrière^M
quarterback^M
quarterback^M

センター
center; *centre*
Centre^M
centre^M
central^M
centrale^M

フルバック
fullback
Fullback^M
centre arrière^M
corredor^M de poder
terzino^M

ライト・ガード
right guard
rechter Guard^M
garde^M droit
guardia^M derecho
guardia^F destra

テールバック
tailback
Tailback^M
demi^M offensif
tailback^M
tailback^M

ライト・タックル
right tackle
rechter Tackle^M
bloqueur^M droit
tacle^M derecho
attaccante^M destro

タイト・エンド
tight end
Tight End^M
ailier^M rapproché
ala^M cerrado
tight end^M

ワイド・レシーバー
wide receiver
Wide Receiver^M
receveur^M éloigné
receptor^M alejado
ricevitore^M esterno

スクリメージ・ライン
line of scrimmage
Scrimmage^N-Linie^F
ligne^F de mêlée^F
línea^F de melé^M
linea^F di mischia^F

ゴール
goal
Tor^N
but^M
gol^M
porta^F

バック・ジャッジ／後審
back judge
Rückfeldschiedsrichter^M
juge^M de champ^M arrière
árbitro^M de la defensa^F
giudice^M di campo^M

サイド・ジャッジ
side judge
Linienrichter^M
juge^M de touche^F
juez^M externo
giudice^M laterale

ライン・ジャッジ
line judge
Linienrichter^M
juge^M de mêlée^F
juez^M de línea^F
giudice^M di linea^F

レフ(ェ)リー／主審
referee
erster Schiedsrichter^M
arbitre^M en chef^M
árbitro^M
primo arbitro^M

ゴールポスト
goalpost
Torpfosten^M
poteau^M de but^M
poste^M
palo^M

選手用ベンチ
players' bench
Spielerbank^F
banc^M des joueurs^M
banquillo^M de jugadores^M
panchina^F dei giocatori^M

アンパイア／副審
umpire
zweiter Schiedsrichter^M
arbitre^M
juez^M
secondo arbitro^M

主ラインズマン［線審］
head linesman
Hauptlinienrichter^M
juge^M de ligne^F en chef^M
juez^M de línea^F
guardalinee^M

スポーツとゲーム

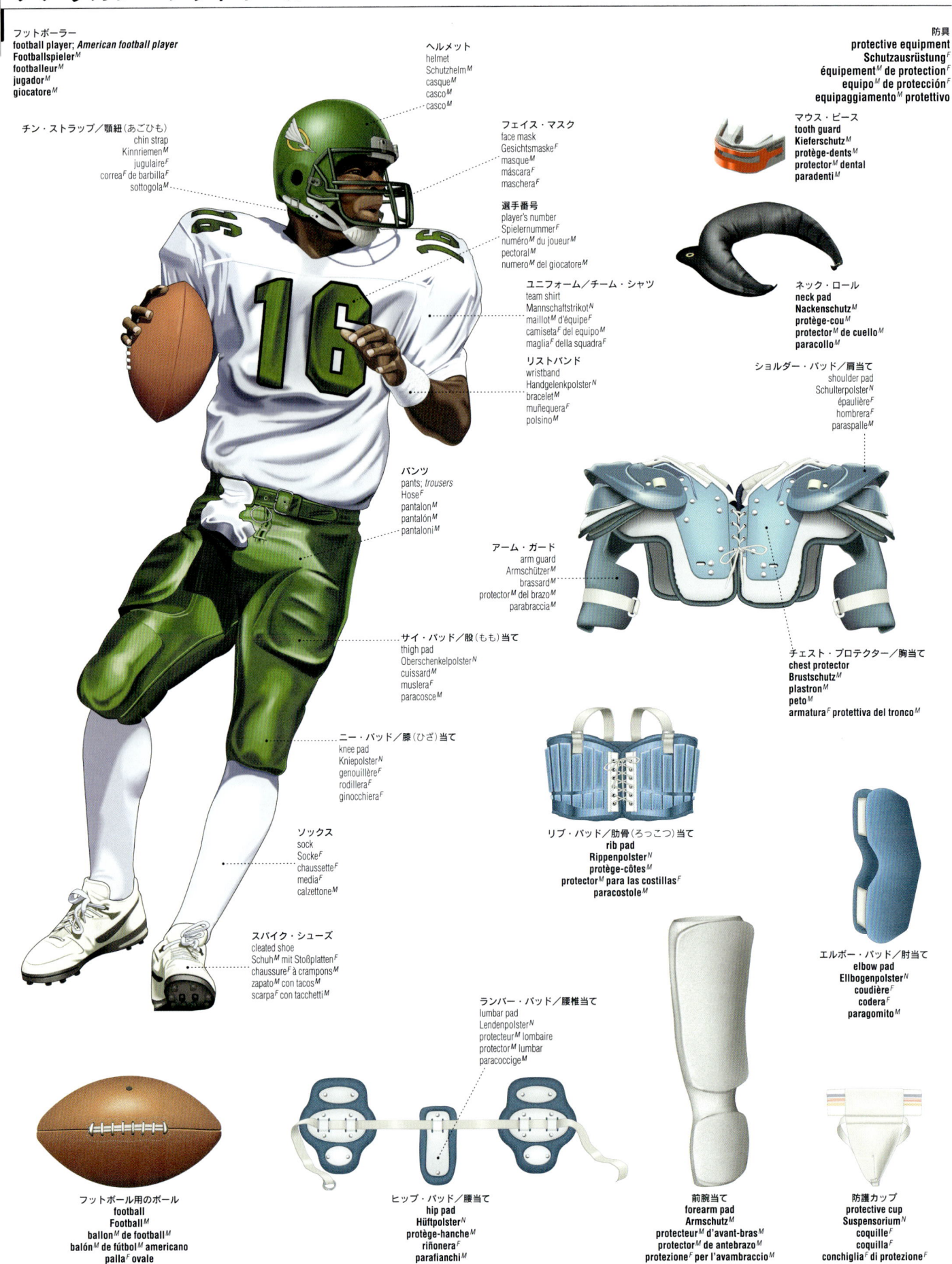

球技 | BALL SPORTS
BALLSPORTARTEN | SPORTS DE BALLE ET DE BALLON | DEPORTES DE PELOTA Y DE BALÓN | SPORT CON LA PALLA

アメリカン・フットボール

日本語 | 英語 | ドイツ語 | フランス語 | スペイン語 | イタリア語

フットボーラー
football player; American football player
Footballspieler^M
footballeur^M
jugador^M
giocatore^M

チン・ストラップ／頤紐（あごひも）
chin strap
Kinnriemen^M
jugulaire^F
correa^F de barbilla^F
sottogola^M

ヘルメット
helmet
Schutzhelm^M
casque^M
casco^M
casco^M

フェイス・マスク
face mask
Gesichtsmaske^F
masque^M
máscara^F
maschera^F

選手番号
player's number
Spielernummer^F
numéro^M du joueur^M
pectoral^M
numero^M del giocatore^M

ユニフォーム／チーム・シャツ
team shirt
Mannschaftstrikot^N
maillot^M d'équipe^F
camiseta^F del equipo^M
maglia^F della squadra^F

リストバンド
wristband
Handgelenkpolster^N
bracelet^M
muñequera^F
polsino^M

パンツ
pants; trousers
Hose^F
pantalon^M
pantalón^M
pantaloni^M

アーム・ガード
arm guard
Armschützer^M
brassard^M
protector^M del brazo^M
parabraccia^F

サイ・パッド／股（もも）当て
thigh pad
Oberschenkelpolster^N
cuissard^M
muslera^F
paracosce^M

ニー・パッド／膝（ひざ）当て
knee pad
Kniepolster^N
genouillère^F
rodillera^F
ginocchiera^F

ソックス
sock
Socke^F
chaussette^F
media^F
calzettone^M

スパイク・シューズ
cleated shoe
Schuh^M mit Stoßplatten^F
chaussure^F à crampons^M
zapato^M con tacos^M
scarpa^F con tacchetti^M

防具
protective equipment
Schutzausrüstung^F
équipement^M de protection^F
equipo^M de protección^F
equipaggiamento^M protettivo

マウス・ピース
tooth guard
Kieferschutz^M
protège-dents^M
protector^M dental
paradenti^M

ネック・ロール
neck pad
Nackenschutz^M
protège-cou^M
protector^M de cuello^M
paracollo^M

ショルダー・パッド／肩当て
shoulder pad
Schulterpolster^N
épaulière^F
hombrera^F
paraspalle^M

チェスト・プロテクター／胸当て
chest protector
Brustschutz^M
plastron^M
peto^M
armatura^F protettiva del tronco^M

リブ・パッド／肋骨（ろっこつ）当て
rib pad
Rippenpolster^N
protège-côtes^M
protector^M para las costillas^F
paracostole^M

エルボー・パッド／肘当て
elbow pad
Ellbogenpolster^N
coudière^F
codera^F
paragomito^M

ランバー・パッド／腰椎当て
lumbar pad
Lendenpolster^N
protecteur^M lombaire
protector^M lumbar
paracoccige^M

フットボール用のボール
football
Football^M
ballon^M de football^M
balón^M de fútbol^M americano
palla^F ovale

ヒップ・パッド／腰当て
hip pad
Hüftpolster^N
protège-hanche^M
riñonera^F
parafianchi^M

前腕当て
forearm pad
Armschutz^M
protecteur^M d'avant-bras^M
protector^M de antebrazo^M
protezione^F per l'avambraccio^M

防護カップ
protective cup
Suspensorium^N
coquille^F
coquilla^F
conchiglia^F di protezione^F

球技 | BALL SPORTS
BALLSPORTARTEN | SPORTS DE BALLE ET DE BALLON | DEPORTES DE PELOTA Y DE BALÓN | SPORT CON LA PALLA

カナディアン・フットボール

Canadian football | kanadischer Football^M | football^M canadien | fútbol^M canadiense | football^M canadese

フィールド
playing field for Canadian football
Spielfeld^N für kanadischen Football^M
terrain^M de football^M canadien
campo^M de juego^M de fútbol^M canadiense
campo^M

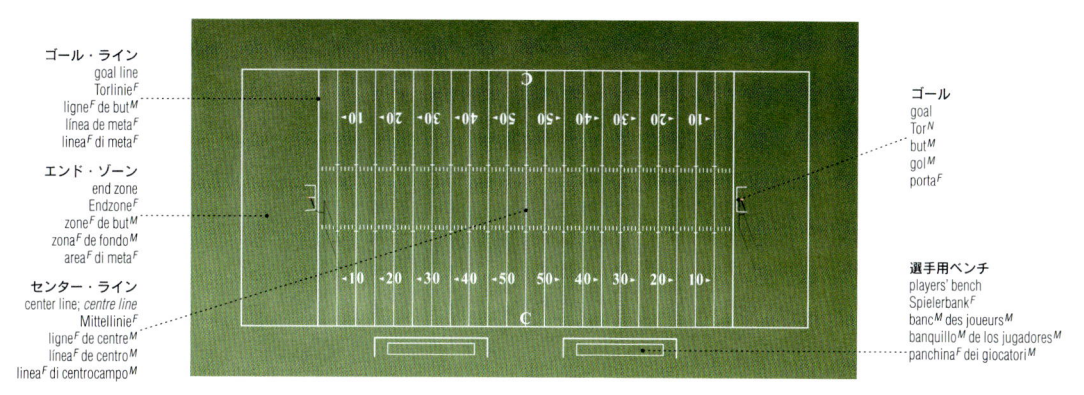

ゴール・ライン
goal line
Torlinie^F
ligne^F de but^M
línea^F de meta^F
linea^F di meta^F

エンド・ゾーン
end zone
Endzone^F
zone^F de but^M
zona^F de fondo^M
area^F di meta^F

センター・ライン
center line; centre line
Mittellinie^F
ligne^F de centre^M
línea^F de centro^M
linea^F di centrocampo^M

ゴール
goal
Tor^N
but^M
gol^M
porta^F

選手用ベンチ
players' bench
Spielerbank^F
banc^M des joueurs^M
banquillo^M de los jugadores^M
panchina^F dei giocatori^M

ネットボール

netball | Korbball^M | netball^M | netball^M | netball^M

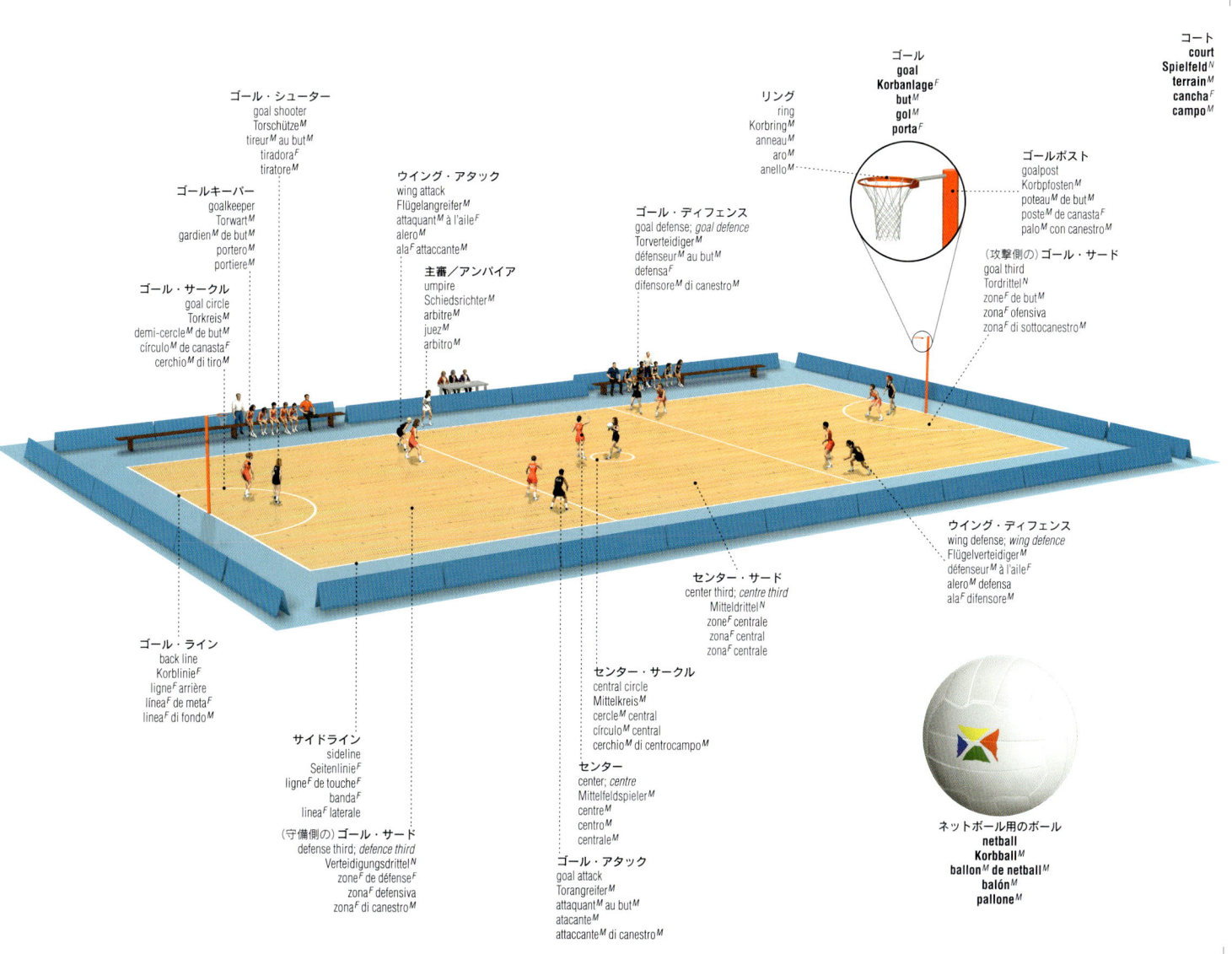

ゴール・シューター
goal shooter
Torschütze^M
tireur^M au but^M
tiradora^F
tiratore^M

ゴールキーパー
goalkeeper
Torwart^M
gardien^M de but^M
portero^M
portiere^M

ゴール・サークル
goal circle
Torkreis^M
demi-cercle^M de but^M
círculo^M de canasta^F
cerchio^M di tiro^M

ウィング・アタック
wing attack
Flügelangreifer^M
attaquant^M à l'aile^F
alero^M
ala^F attaccante^M

主審／アンパイア
umpire
Schiedsrichter^M
arbitre^M
juez^M
arbitro^M

ゴール
goal
Korbanlage^F
but^M
gol^M
porta^F

リング
ring
Korbring^M
anneau^M
aro^M
anello^M

ゴール・ディフェンス
goal defense; goal defence
Torverteidiger^M
défenseur^M au but^M
defensa^F
difensore^M di canestro^M

コート
court
Spielfeld^N
terrain^M
cancha^F
campo^M

ゴールポスト
goalpost
Korbpfosten^M
poteau^M de but^M
poste^M de canasta^F
palo^M con canestro^M

（攻撃側の）ゴール・サード
goal third
Tordrittel^N
zone^F de but^M
zona^F ofensiva
zona^F di sottocanestro^M

ゴール・ライン
back line
Korblinie^F
ligne^F arrière
línea^F de meta^F
linea^F di fondo^M

サイドライン
sideline
Seitenlinie^F
ligne^F de touche^F
banda^F
linea^F laterale

（守備側の）ゴール・サード
defense third; defence third
Verteidigungsdrittel^N
zone^F de défense^F
zona^F defensiva
zona^F di canestro^M

センター・サード
center third; centre third
Mitteldrittel^N
zone^F centrale
zona^F central
zona^F centrale

センター・サークル
central circle
Mittelkreis^M
cercle^M central
círculo^M central
cerchio^M di centrocampo^M

センター
center; centre
Mittelfeldspieler^M
centre^M
centro^M
centrale^M

ゴール・アタック
goal attack
Torangreifer^M
attaquant^M au but^M
atacante^M
attaccante^M di canestro^M

ウイング・ディフェンス
wing defense; wing defence
Flügelverteidiger^M
défenseur^M à l'aile^F
alero^M defensa
ala^F difensore^M

ネットボール用のボール
netball
Korbball^M
ballon^M de netball^M
balón^M
pallone^M

球技 | BALL SPORTS
BALLSPORTARTEN | SPORTS DE BALLE ET DE BALLON | DEPORTES DE PELOTA Y DE BALÓN | SPORT CON LA PALLA

バスケットボール

日本語 | 英語 | ドイツ語 | フランス語 | スペイン語 | イタリア語

basketball | Basketballspiel^N | basketball^M | baloncesto^M | pallacanestro^F

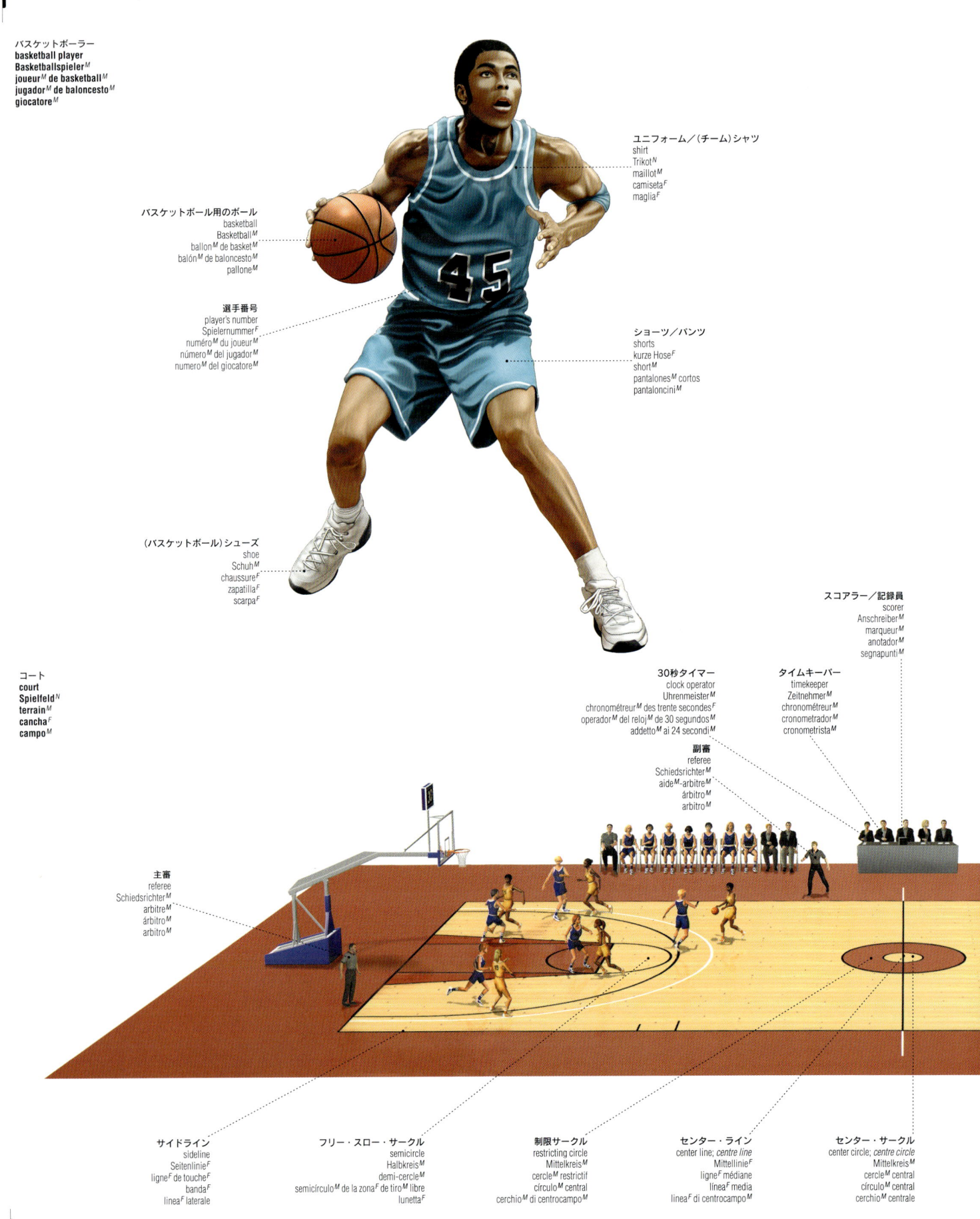

バスケットボーラー
basketball player
Basketballspieler^M
joueur^M de basketball^M
jugador^M de baloncesto^M
giocatore^M

ユニフォーム／(チーム)シャツ
shirt
Trikot^N
maillot^M
camiseta^F
maglia^F

バスケットボール用のボール
basketball
Basketball^M
ballon^M de basket^M
balón^M de baloncesto^M
pallone^M

選手番号
player's number
Spielernummer^F
numéro^M du joueur^M
número^M del jugador^M
numero^M del giocatore^M

ショーツ／パンツ
shorts
kurze Hose^F
short^M
pantalones^M cortos
pantaloncini^M

(バスケットボール)シューズ
shoe
Schuh^M
chaussure^F
zapatilla^F
scarpa^F

スコアラー／記録員
scorer
Anschreiber^M
marqueur^M
anotador^M
segnapunti^M

30秒タイマー
clock operator
Uhrenmeister^M
chronométreur^M des trente secondes^F
operador^M del reloj^M de 30 segundos^M
addetto^M ai 24 secondi^M

タイムキーパー
timekeeper
Zeitnehmer^M
chronométreur^M
cronometrador^M
cronometrista^M

コート
court
Spielfeld^N
terrain^M
cancha^F
campo^M

副審
referee
Schiedsrichter^M
aide^M-arbitre^M
árbitro^M
arbitro^M

主審
referee
Schiedsrichter^M
arbitre^M
árbitro^M
arbitro^M

サイドライン
sideline
Seitenlinie^F
ligne^F de touche^F
banda^F
linea^F laterale

フリー・スロー・サークル
semicircle
Halbkreis^M
demi-cercle^M
semicírculo^M de la zona^F de tiro^M libre
lunetta^F

制限サークル
restricting circle
Mittelkreis^M
cercle^M restrictif
círculo^M central
cerchio^M di centrocampo^M

センター・ライン
center line; *centre line*
Mittellinie^F
ligne^F médiane
línea^F media
linea^F di centrocampo^M

センター・サークル
center circle; *centre circle*
Mittelkreis^M
cercle^M central
círculo^M central
cerchio^M centrale

スポーツとゲーム

810

球技 | BALL SPORTS
BALLSPORTARTEN | SPORTS DE BALLE ET DE BALLON | DEPORTES DE PELOTA Y DE BALÓN | SPORT CON LA PALLA

バスケットボール

ポジション
player positions
Spielerpositionen^F
position^F des joueurs^M
posiciones^M de los jugadores^M
posizioni^F dei giocatori^M

ポイント・ガード
point guard
rechter Aufbauspieler^M
meneur^M de jeu^M
base^M
playmaker^M

センター
center; centre
mittlerer Angriffsspieler^M
pivot^M
pívot^M
pivot^M

ガード
guard
linker Aufbauspieler^M
arrière^M
escolta^F
guardia^F

ライト・フォワード
right forward
rechter Angriffsspieler^M
ailier^M droit
alero^M derecho
ala^F destra

レフト・フォワード
left forward
linker Angriffsspieler^M
ailier^M gauche
alero^M izquierdo
ala^F sinistra

バックボード
backboard
Korbbrett^N
panneau^M
tablero^M
tabellone^M

バックストップ
backstop
Korbanlage^F
but^M
canasta^F
canestro^M

リング
rim
Korbring^M
anneau^M
aro^M
anello^M

ネット
net
Netz^N
filet^M
red^F
retina^F

コーチ／監督
coach
Trainer^M
entraîneur^M
entrenador^M
allenatore^M

アシスタント・コーチ
assistant coach
Trainerassistent^M
entraîneur^M adjoint
entrenador^M adjunto
viceallenatore^M

トレーナー
trainer
Physiotherapeut^M
soigneur^M
preparador^M
massaggiatore^M

支柱
backboard support
Korbbretthalter^M
support^M de panneau^M
soporte^M del tablero^M
supporto^M del tabellone^M

バスケット
basket
Korb^M
panier^M
canasta^F
canestro^M

パッド付き支柱
padded upright
gepolsterte Korbstütze^F
montant^M rembourré
poste^M con protecciones^M
montante^M imbottito

パッド付き土台
padded base
gepolsterter Sockel^M
socle^M rembourré
base^F con protecciones^F
basamento^M imbottito

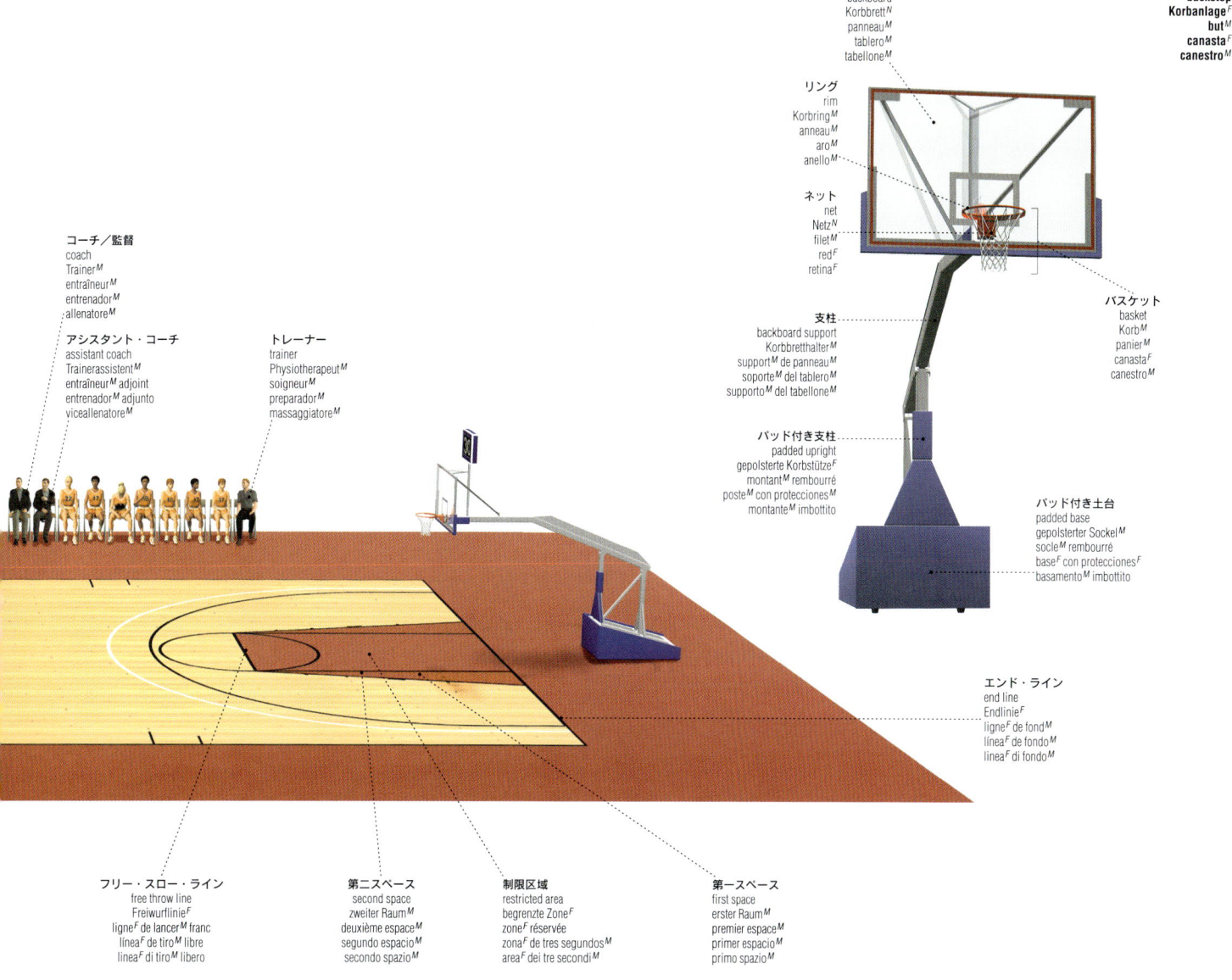

エンド・ライン
end line
Endlinie^F
ligne^F de fond^M
línea^F de fondo^M
linea^F di fondo^M

フリー・スロー・ライン
free throw line
Freiwurflinie^F
ligne^F de lancer^M franc
línea^F de tiro^M libre
linea^F di tiro^M libero

第二スペース
second space
zweiter Raum^M
deuxième espace^M
segundo espacio^M
secondo spazio^M

制限区域
restricted area
begrenzte Zone^F
zone^F réservée
zona^F de tres segundos^M
area^F dei tre secondi^M

第一スペース
first space
erster Raum^M
premier espace^M
primer espacio^M
primo spazio^M

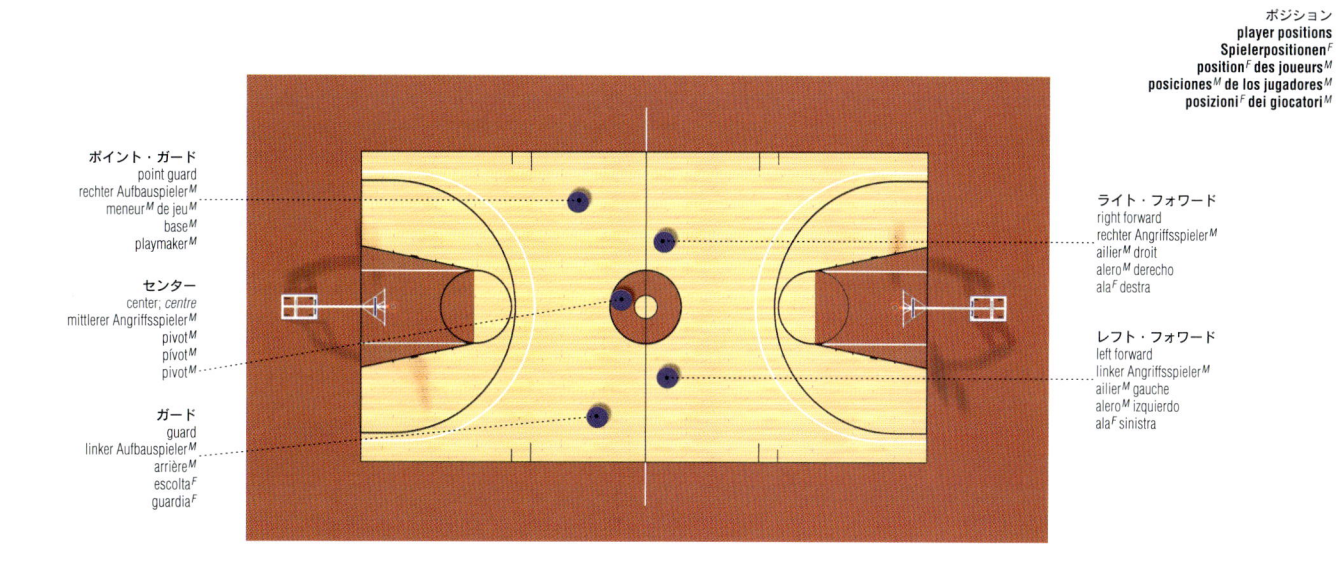

スポーツとゲーム

811

球技 | BALL SPORTS
BALLSPORTARTEN | SPORTS DE BALLE ET DE BALLON | DEPORTES DE PELOTA Y DE BALÓN | SPORT CON LA PALLA

バレーボール

日本語 | 英語 | ドイツ語 | フランス語 | スペイン語 | イタリア語

volleyball | Volleyballspiel^N | volleyball^M | voleibol^M | pallavolo^F

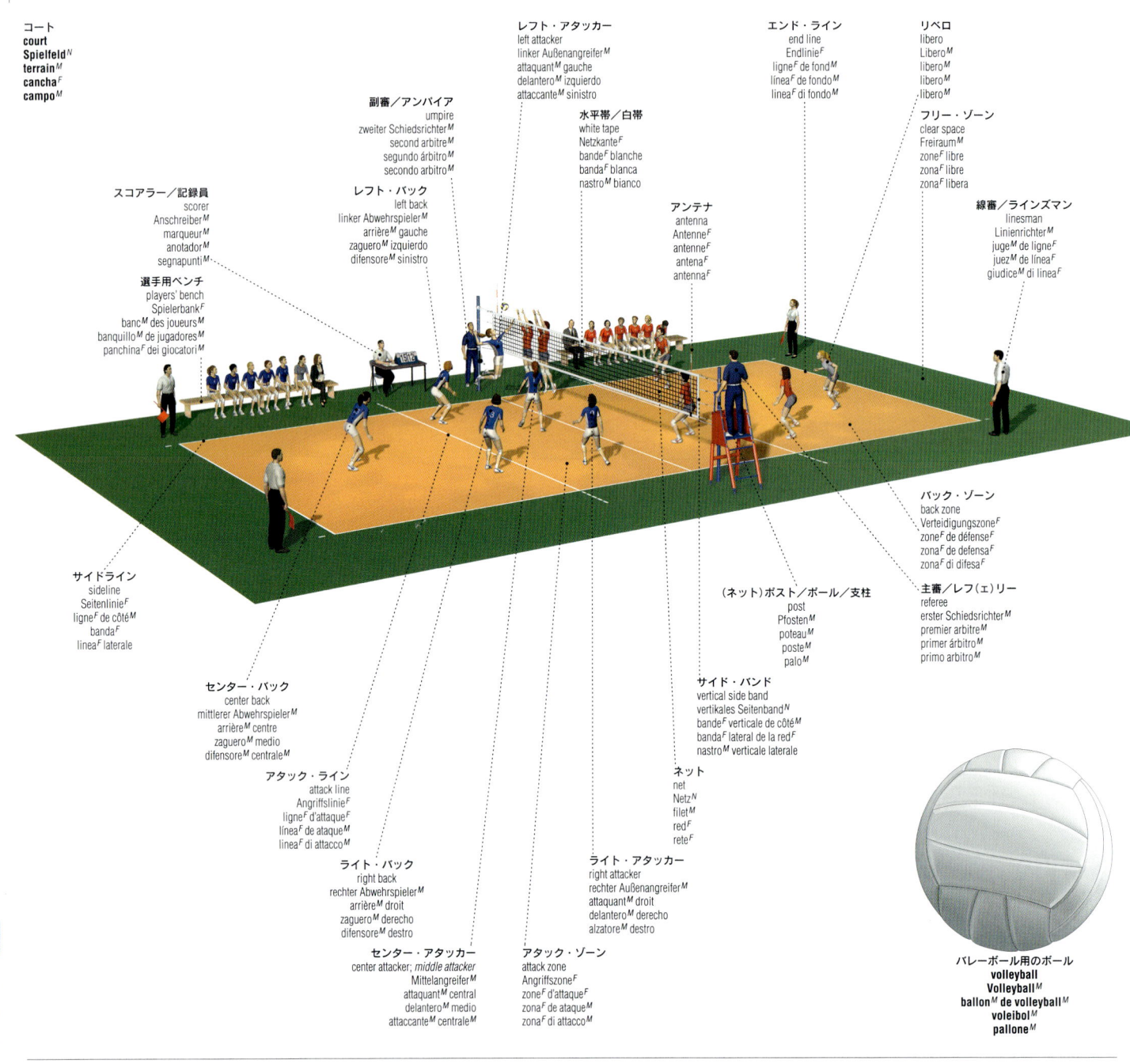

コート
court
Spielfeld^N
terrain^M
cancha^F
campo^M

レフト・アタッカー
left attacker
linker Außenangreifer^M
attaquant^M gauche
delantero^M izquierdo
attaccante^M sinistro

エンド・ライン
end line
Endlinie^F
ligne^F de fond^M
línea^F de fondo^M
linea^F di fondo^M

リベロ
libero
Libero^M
libero^M
líbero^M
libero^M

副審／アンパイア
umpire
zweiter Schiedsrichter^M
second arbitre^M
segundo árbitro^M
secondo arbitro^M

水平帯／白帯
white tape
Netzkante^F
bande^F blanche
banda^F blanca
nastro^M bianco

フリー・ゾーン
clear space
Freiraum^M
zone^F libre
zona^F libre
zona^F libera

スコアラー／記録員
scorer
Anschreiber^M
marqueur^M
anotador^M
segnapunti^M

レフト・バック
left back
linker Abwehrspieler^M
arrière^M gauche
zaguero^M izquierdo
difensore^M sinistro

アンテナ
antenna
Antenne^F
antenne^F
antena^F
antenna^F

線審／ラインズマン
linesman
Linienrichter^M
juge^M de ligne^F
juez^M de línea^F
giudice^M di linea^F

選手用ベンチ
players' bench
Spielerbank^F
banc^M des joueurs^M
banquillo^M de jugadores^M
panchina^F dei giocatori^M

バック・ゾーン
back zone
Verteidigungszone^F
zone^F de défense^F
zona^F de defensa^F
zona^F di difesa^F

サイドライン
sideline
Seitenlinie^F
ligne^F de côté^M
banda^F
linea^F laterale

（ネット）ポスト／ポール／支柱
post
Pfosten^M
poteau^M
poste^M
palo^M

主審／レフ(ェ)リー
referee
erster Schiedsrichter^M
premier arbitre^M
primer árbitro^M
primo arbitro^M

センター・バック
center back
mittlerer Abwehrspieler^M
arrière^M centre
zaguero^M medio
difensore^M centrale

サイド・バンド
vertical side band
vertikales Seitenband^N
bande^F verticale de côté^M
banda^F lateral de la red^F
nastro^M verticale laterale

アタック・ライン
attack line
Angriffslinie^F
ligne^F d'attaque^F
línea^F de ataque^M
linea^F di attacco^M

ネット
net
Netz^N
filet^M
red^F
rete^F

ライト・バック
right back
rechter Abwehrspieler^M
arrière^M droit
zaguero^M derecho
difensore^M destro

ライト・アタッカー
right attacker
rechter Außenangreifer^M
attaquant^M droit
delantero^M derecho
alzatore^M destro

センター・アタッカー
center attacker; middle attacker
Mittelangreifer^M
attaquant^M central
delantero^M medio
attaccante^M centrale

アタック・ゾーン
attack zone
Angriffszone^F
zone^F d'attaque^F
zona^F de ataque^M
zona^F di attacco^M

バレーボール用のボール
volleyball
Volleyball^M
ballon^M de volleyball^M
voleibol^M
pallone^M

テクニック
techniques
Techniken^F
techniques^F
técnicas^F
tecniche^F

ダイビング・レシーブ
dig
Hechtabwehr^F
récupération^F
plancha^F
tuffo^M

レシーブ
bump
baggern
manchette^F
rebote^M
bagher^M

サーブ
serve
Aufschlag^M
service^M
saque^M
servizio^M

球技 | BALL SPORTS
BALLSPORTARTEN | SPORTS DE BALLE ET DE BALLON | DEPORTES DE PELOTA Y DE BALÓN | SPORT CON LA PALLA

バレーボール

ビーチ・バレー（ボール）
beach volleyball
Beachvolleyball^M
volleyball^M de plage^F
voley^M playa^M
beach volley^M

スコアラー／記録員
scorer
Anschreiber^M
marqueur^M
anotador^M
segnapunti^M

副審
second referee
zweiter Schiedsrichter^M
second arbitre^M
segundo árbitro^M
secondo arbitro^M

フリー・ゾーン
free zone
Freiraum^M
zone^F libre
zona^F libre
zona^F libera

コート
court
Spielfeld^N
terrain^M
cancha^F
campo^M

選手用椅子
players' chairs
Spielerstühle^M
chaises^F des joueurs^M
sillas^F de los jugadores^M
sedie^F dei giocatori^M

線審
line judge
Linienrichter^M
juge^M de ligne^F
juez^M de línea^F
giudice^M di linea^F

主審
first referee
erster Schiedsrichter^M
premier arbitre^M
primer árbitro^M
primo arbitro^M

砂
sand
Sand^M
sable^M
arena^F
sabbia^F

ライン
line
Linie^F
ligne^F
línea^F
linea^F

ネット
net
Netz^N
filet^M
red^F
rete^F

ビーチ・バレー用のボール
beach volleyball
Beachvolleyball^M
ballon^M de volleyball^M de plage^F
voley^M playa^M
pallone^M

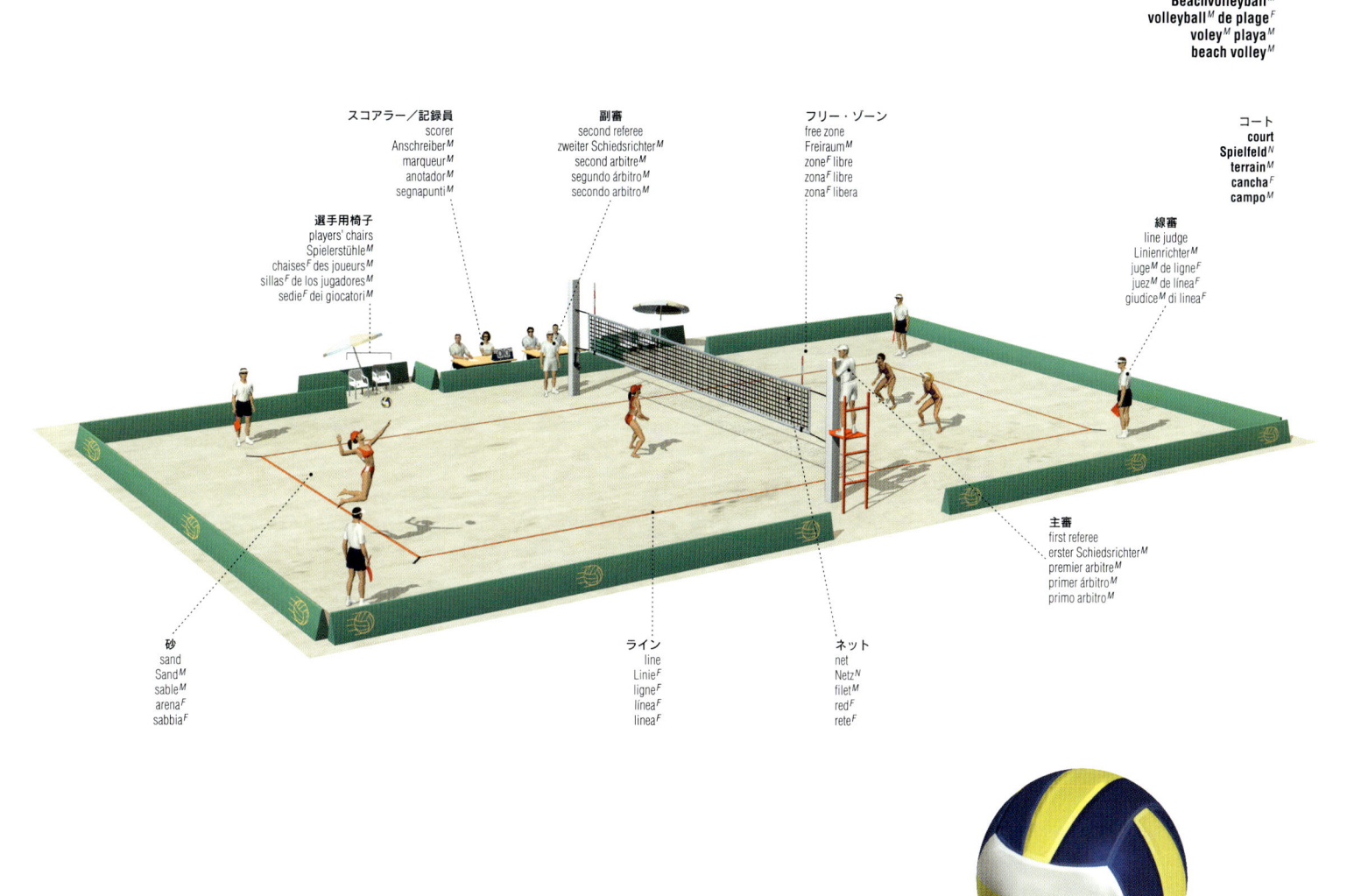

トス
tip
pritschen
touche^F
toque^M
palleggio^M

スパイク
spike
Schmetterball^M
smash^M
remate^M
schiacciata^F

ブロック
block
blocken
contre^M
tapón^M
muro^M

スポーツとゲーム

球技 | BALL SPORTS
BALLSPORTARTEN | SPORTS DE BALLE ET DE BALLON | DEPORTES DE PELOTA Y DE BALÓN | SPORT CON LA PALLA

ハンドボール

handball | Handball^M | handball^M | balonmano^M | pallamano^F

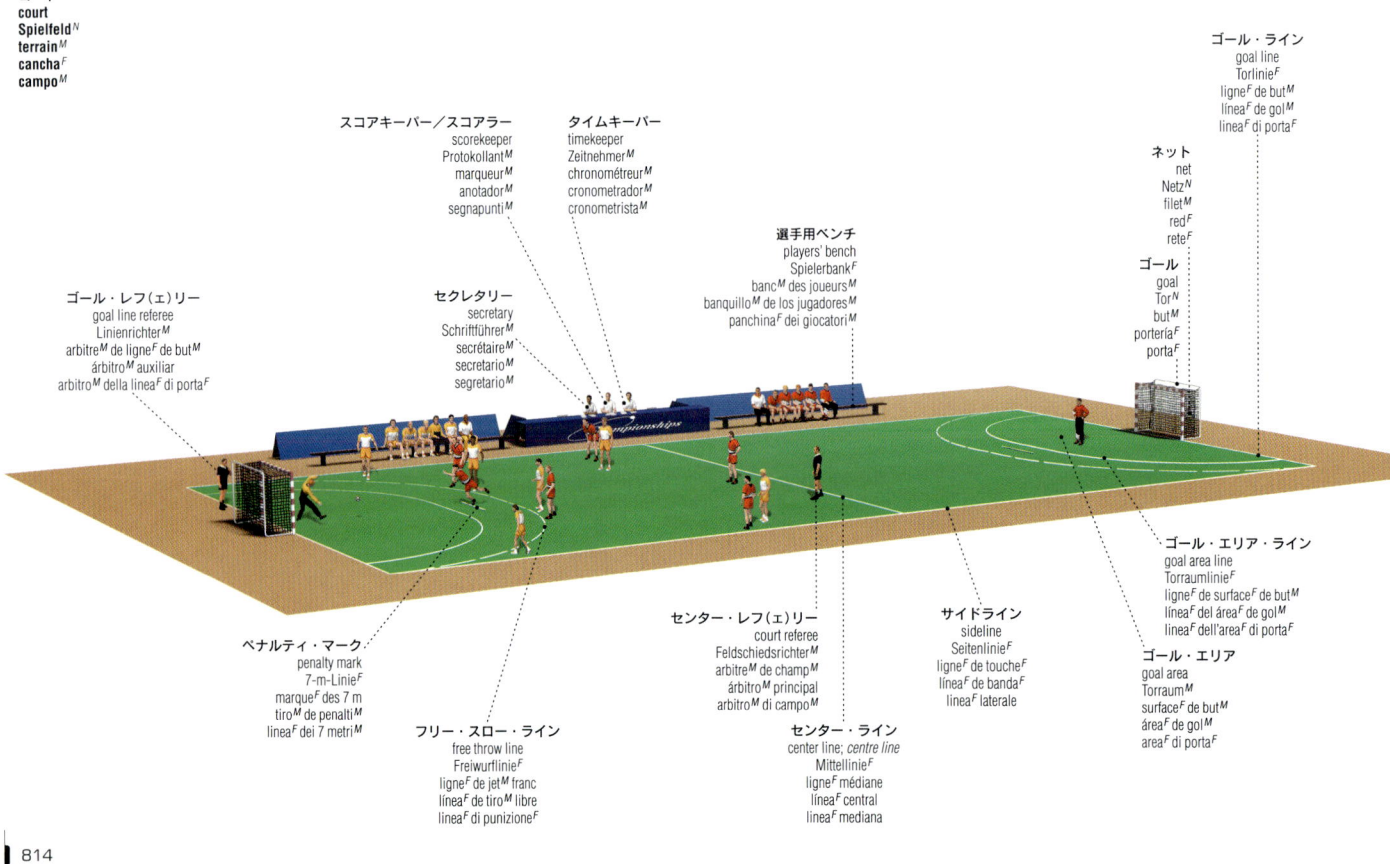

日本語 | 英語 | ドイツ語 | フランス語 | スペイン語 | イタリア語

ポジション
player positions
Spielerpositionen^F
position^F des joueurs^M
posición^F de los jugadores^F
posizioni^F dei giocatori^M

センター・フォワード
center forward; centre forward
Mittelfeldangriffsspieler^M
avant-centre^M
pivote^M
centravanti^M

ライト・ウイング
right winger
rechter Angriffsfeldspieler^M
ailier^M droit
extremo^M derecho
ala^F destra

レフト・ウイング
left winger
linker Angriffsfeldspieler^M
ailier^M gauche
extremo^M izquierdo
ala^F sinistra

ライト・バック
right back
zurückgezogener rechter Feldspieler^M
arrière^M droit
interior^M derecho
difensore^M destro

レフト・バック
left back
zurückgezogener linker Feldspieler^M
arrière^M gauche
interior^M izquierdo
difensore^M sinistro

センター・バック
center back; centre back
zurückgezogener Mittelfeldspieler^M
demi-centre^M
central^M
difensore^M centrale

ゴールキーパー
goalkeeper
Torhüter^M
gardien^M de but^M
portero^M
portiere^M

ハンドボール用のボール
handball
Handball^M
ballon^M de handball^M
balón^M de balonmano^M
pallone^M

コート
court
Spielfeld^N
terrain^M
cancha^F
campo^M

スコアキーパー/スコアラー
scorekeeper
Protokollant^M
marqueur^M
anotador^M
segnapunti^M

タイムキーパー
timekeeper
Zeitnehmer^M
chronométreur^M
cronometrador^M
cronometrista^M

ゴール・ライン
goal line
Torlinie^F
ligne^F de but^M
línea^F de gol^M
linea^F di porta^F

ネット
net
Netz^N
filet^M
red^F
rete^F

選手用ベンチ
players' bench
Spielerbank^F
banc^M des joueurs^M
banquillo^M de los jugadores^M
panchina^F dei giocatori^M

ゴール
goal
Tor^N
but^M
portería^F
porta^F

ゴール・レフ(ェ)リー
goal line referee
Linienrichter^M
arbitre^M de ligne^F de but^M
árbitro^M auxiliar
arbitro^M della linea^F di porta^F

セクレタリー
secretary
Schriftführer^M
secrétaire^M
secretario^M
segretario^M

ゴール・エリア・ライン
goal area line
Torraumlinie^F
ligne^F de surface^F de but^M
línea^F del área^F de gol^M
linea^F dell'area^F di porta^F

ペナルティ・マーク
penalty mark
7-m-Linie^F
marque^F des 7 m
tiro^M de penalti^M
linea^F dei 7 metri^M

センター・レフ(ェ)リー
court referee
Feldschiedsrichter^M
arbitre^M de champ^M
árbitro^M principal
arbitro^M di campo^M

サイドライン
sideline
Seitenlinie^F
ligne^F de touche^F
línea^F de banda^F
linea^F laterale

ゴール・エリア
goal area
Torraum^M
surface^F de but^M
área^F de gol^M
area^F di porta^F

フリー・スロー・ライン
free throw line
Freiwurflinie^F
ligne^F de jet^M franc
línea^F de tiro^M libre
linea^F di punizione^F

センター・ライン
center line; centre line
Mittellinie^F
ligne^F médiane
línea^F central
linea^F mediana

スポーツとゲーム

814

ラケット・スポーツ | RACKET SPORTS
SPIELE MIT SCHLÄGERN | SPORTS DE RAQUETTE | DEPORTES DE RAQUETA | GIOCHI CON LA RACCHETTA

卓球

table tennis | TischtennisN | tennisM de tableF | tenisM de mesaF | tennisM da tavoloM

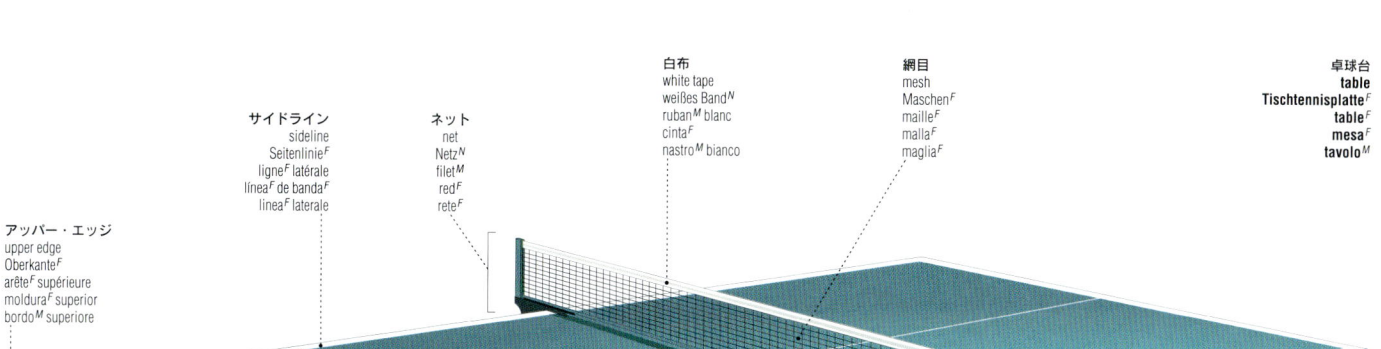

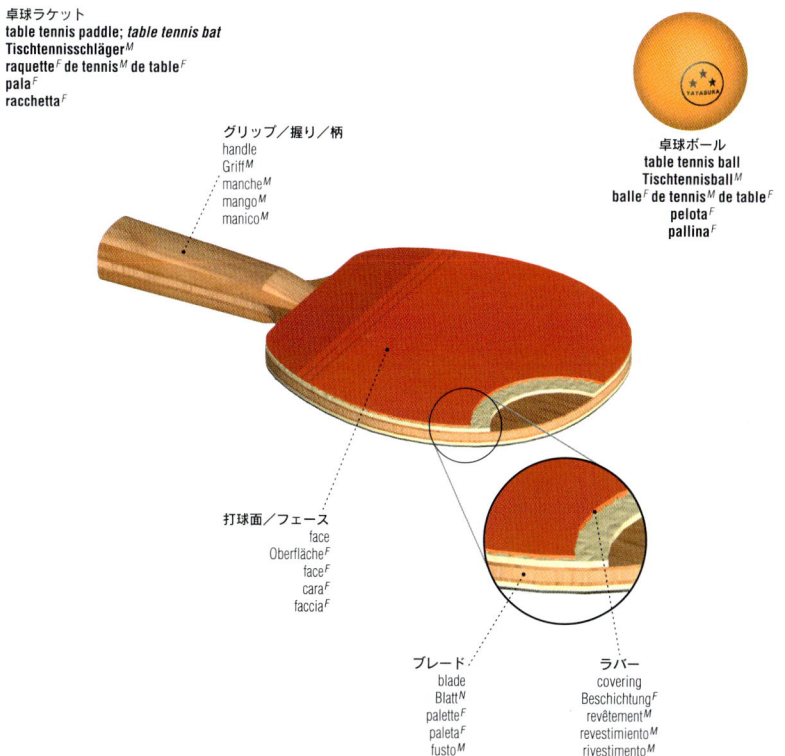

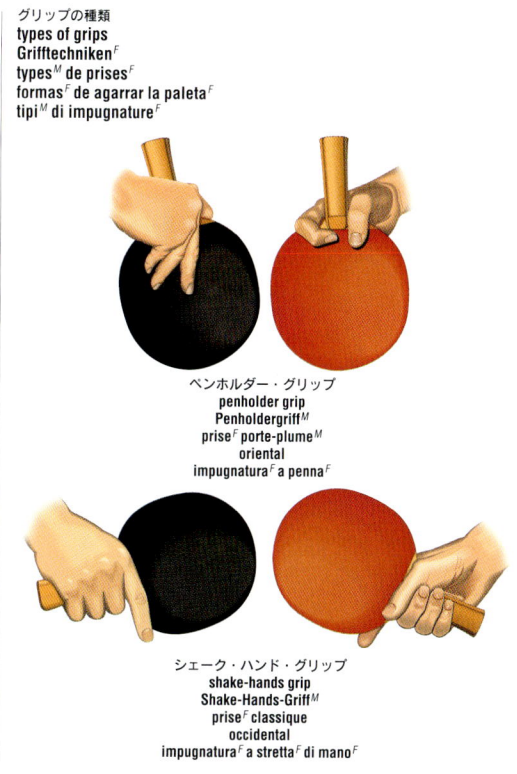

白布
white tape
weißes BandN
rubanM blanc
cintaF
nastroM bianco

網目
mesh
MaschenF
mailleF
mallaF
magliaF

卓球台
table
TischtennisplatteF
tableF
mesaF
tavoloM

サイドライン
sideline
SeitenlinieF
ligneF latérale
líneaF de bandaF
lineaF laterale

ネット
net
NetzN
filetM
redF
reteF

アッパー・エッジ
upper edge
OberkanteF
arêteF supérieure
molduraF superior
bordoM superiore

センター・ライン
center line; centre line
MittellinieF
ligneF centrale
líneaF divisoria central
lineaF centrale

(ネット)サポート／支柱
net support
NetzhalterM
supportM
soporteM de la redF
supportoM della reteF

脚
leg
BeinN
piedM
pataF de la mesaF
gambaF

テーブル／台
playing surface
SpielflächeF
surfaceF de jeuM
superficieF de juegoM
superficieF di giocoM

エンド・ライン
end line
EndlinieF
ligneF de fondM
líneaF de fondoM
lineaF di fondoM

卓球ラケット
table tennis paddle; table tennis bat
TischtennisschlägerM
raquetteF de tennisM de tableF
palaF
racchettaF

グリップ／握り／柄
handle
GriffM
mancheM
mangoM
manicoM

卓球ボール
table tennis ball
TischtennisballM
balleF de tennisM de tableF
pelotaF
pallinaF

グリップの種類
types of grips
GrifftechnikenF
typesM de prisesF
formasF de agarrar la paletaF
tipiM di impugnatureF

打球面／フェース
face
OberflächeF
faceF
caraF
facciaF

ペンホルダー・グリップ
penholder grip
PenholdergriffM
priseF porte-plumeM
oriental
impugnaturaF a pennaF

ブレード
blade
BlattN
paletteF
paletaF
fustoM

ラバー
covering
BeschichtungF
revêtementM
revestimientoM
rivestimentoM

シェーク・ハンド・グリップ
shake-hands grip
Shake-Hands-GriffM
priseF classique
occidental
impugnaturaF a strettaF di manoM

スポーツとゲーム

815

ラケット・スポーツ | RACKET SPORTS
SPIELE MIT SCHLÄGERN | SPORTS DE RAQUETTE | DEPORTES DE RAQUETA | GIOCHI CON LA RACCHETTA

バドミントン

badminton | Badminton[N] | badminton[M] | bádminton[M] | gioco[M] del volano[M]

日本語 | 英語 | ドイツ語 | フランス語 | スペイン語 | イタリア語

コート
court
Badmintonplatz[M]
terrain[M]
cancha[F]
campo[M]

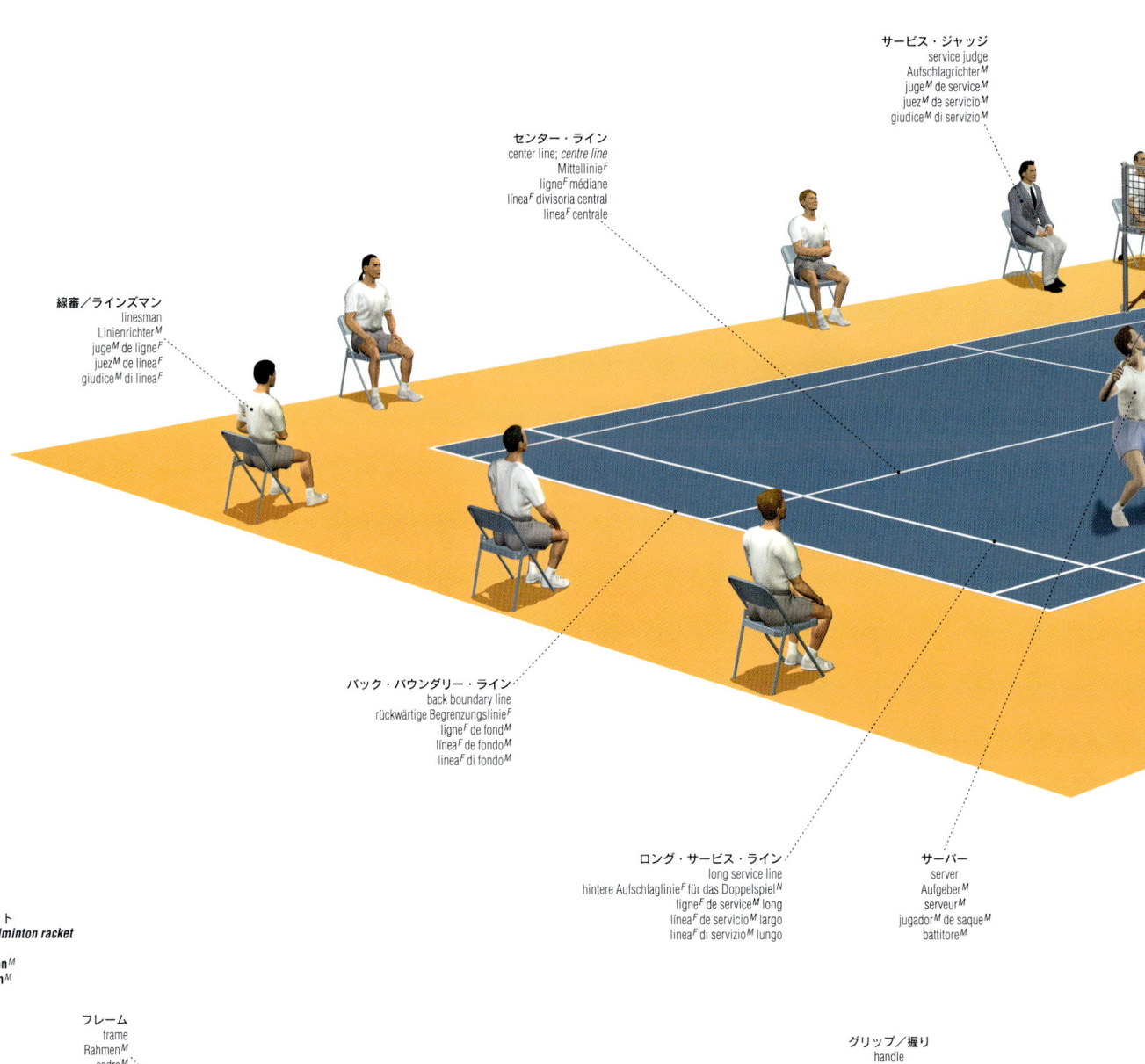

サービス・ジャッジ
service judge
Aufschlagrichter[M]
juge[M] de service[M]
juez[M] de servicio[M]
giudice[M] di servizio[M]

センター・ライン
center line; *centre line*
Mittellinie[F]
ligne[F] médiane
línea[F] divisoria central
linea[F] centrale

線審／ラインズマン
linesman
Linienrichter[M]
juge[M] de ligne[F]
juez[M] de línea[F]
giudice[M] di linea[F]

バック・バウンダリー・ライン
back boundary line
rückwärtige Begrenzungslinie[F]
ligne[F] de fond[M]
línea[F] de fondo[M]
linea[F] di fondo[M]

ロング・サービス・ライン
long service line
hintere Aufschaglinie[F] für das Doppelspiel[N]
ligne[F] de service[M] long
línea[F] de servicio[M] largo
linea[F] di servizio[M] lungo

サーバー
server
Aufgeber[M]
serveur[M]
jugador[M] de saque[M]
battitore[M]

バドミントン・ラケット
badminton racket; *badminton racket*
Badmintonschläger[M]
raquette[F] de badminton[M]
raqueta[F] de bádminton[M]
racchetta[F]

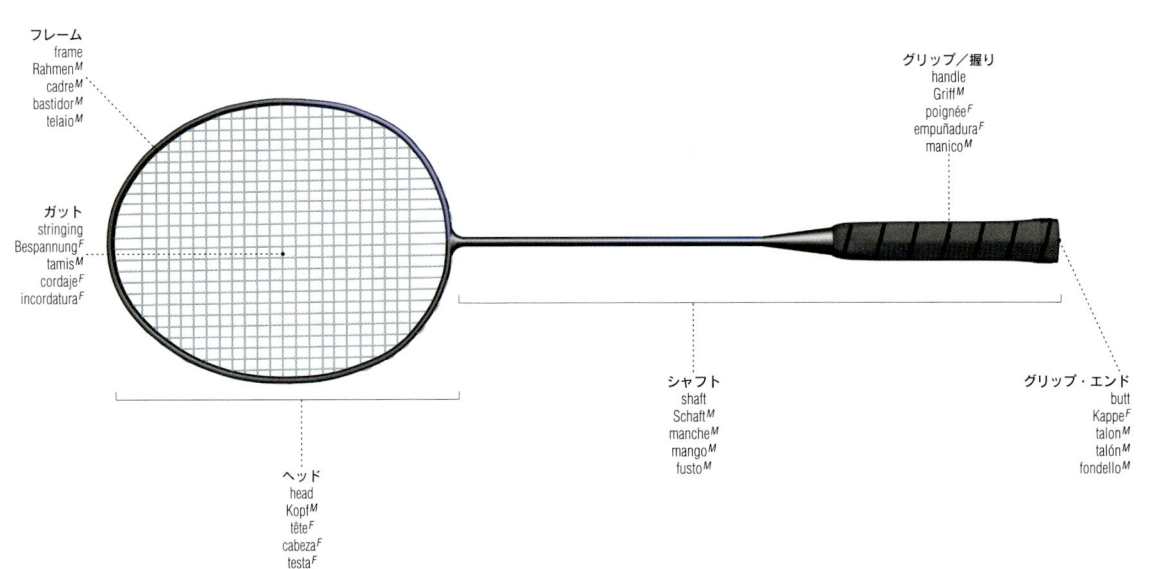

フレーム
frame
Rahmen[M]
cadre[M]
bastidor[M]
telaio[M]

グリップ／握り
handle
Griff[M]
poignée[F]
empuñadura[F]
manico[M]

ガット
stringing
Bespannung[F]
tamis[M]
cordaje[F]
incordatura[F]

シャフト
shaft
Schaft[M]
manche[M]
mango[M]
fusto[M]

グリップ・エンド
butt
Kappe[F]
talon[M]
talón[M]
fondello[M]

ヘッド
head
Kopf[M]
tête[F]
cabeza[F]
testa[F]

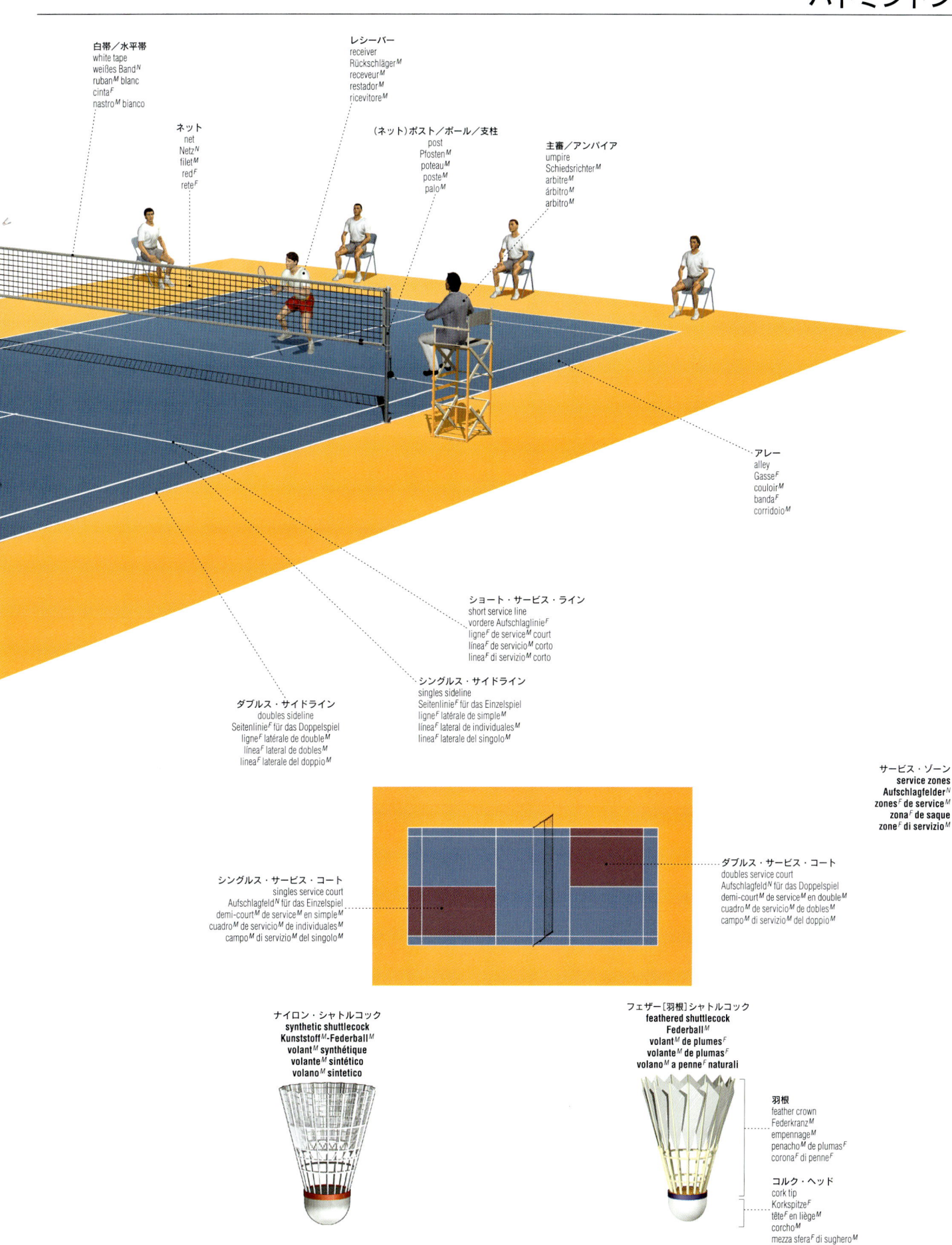

ラケット・スポーツ | RACKET SPORTS
SPIELE MIT SCHLÄGERN | SPORTS DE RAQUETTE | DEPORTES DE RAQUETA | GIOCHI CON LA RACCHETTA

バドミントン

白帯／水平帯
white tape
weißes Band^N
ruban^M blanc
cinta^F
nastro^M bianco

レシーバー
receiver
Rückschläger^M
receveur^M
restador^M
ricevitore^M

ネット
net
Netz^N
filet^M
red^F
rete^F

（ネット）ポスト／ポール／支柱
post
Pfosten^M
poteau^M
poste^M
palo^M

主審／アンパイア
umpire
Schiedsrichter^M
arbitre^M
árbitro^M
arbitro^M

アレー
alley
Gasse^F
couloir^M
banda^F
corridoio^M

ショート・サービス・ライン
short service line
vordere Aufschlaglinie^F
ligne^F de service^M court
línea^F de servicio^M corto
linea^F di servizio^M corto

シングルス・サイドライン
singles sideline
Seitenlinie^F für das Einzelspiel
ligne^F latérale de simple^M
línea^F lateral de individuales^M
linea^F laterale del singolo^M

ダブルス・サイドライン
doubles sideline
Seitenlinie^F für das Doppelspiel
ligne^F latérale de double^M
línea^F lateral de dobles^M
linea^F laterale del doppio^M

サービス・ゾーン
service zones
Aufschlagfelder^N
zones^F de service^M
zona^F de saque
zone^F di servizio^M

シングルス・サービス・コート
singles service court
Aufschlagfeld^N für das Einzelspiel
demi-court^M de service^M en simple^M
cuadro^M de servicio^M de individuales^M
campo^M di servizio^M del singolo^M

ダブルス・サービス・コート
doubles service court
Aufschlagfeld^M für das Doppelspiel
demi-court^M de service^M en double^M
cuadro^M de servicio^M de dobles^M
campo^M di servizio^M del doppio^M

ナイロン・シャトルコック
synthetic shuttlecock
Kunststoff^M-Federball^M
volant^M synthétique
volante^M sintético
volano^M sintetico

フェザー[羽根]シャトルコック
feathered shuttlecock
Federball^M
volant^M de plumes^F
volante^M de plumas^F
volano^M a penne^F naturali

羽根
feather crown
Federkranz^M
empennage^M
penacho^M de plumas^F
corona^F di penne^F

コルク・ヘッド
cork tip
Korkspitze^F
tête^F en liège^M
corcho^M
mezza sfera^F di sughero^M

スポーツとゲーム

817

ラケット・スポーツ | RACKET SPORTS
SPIELE MIT SCHLÄGERN | SPORTS DE RAQUETTE | DEPORTES DE RAQUETA | GIOCHI CON LA RACCHETTA

ラケットボール

日本語 | 英語 | ドイツ語 | フランス語 | スペイン語 | イタリア語

racquetball | Racquetballspiel^N | racquetball^M | racquetball^M | racquetball^M

コート
court
Spielfeld^N
court^M
cancha^F
campo^M

レフ(ェ)リー／主審
referee
Schiedsrichter^M
arbitre^M
árbitro^M
arbitro^M

バック・ウォール／後ろの壁／後壁
back wall
Hinterwand^F
mur^M arrière
pared^F trasera
parete^F posteriore

センター・コート
center court; centre court
Mittelfeld^N
centre^M du court^M
centro^M de la cancha^F
zona^F centrale

天井
ceiling
Decke^F
plafond^M
techo^M
soffitto^M

サイド・ウォール／横の壁／側壁
sidewall
Seitenwand^F
mur^M latéral
pared^F lateral
parete^F laterale

フロント・ウォール／正面の壁／前壁
front wall
Vorderwand^F
mur^M avant
frontis^M
parete^F anteriore

サービス・ライン
service line
Aufschlaglinie^F
ligne^F de service^M
línea^F de servicio^M
linea^F di servizio^M

サービス・ゾーン
service zone
Aufschlagbereich^M
zone^F de service^M
área^F de servicio^M
zona^F di servizio^M

フロントコート
frontcourt
Vorderfeld^N
avant^M du court^M
cancha^F delantera
zona^F d'attacco^M

サービス・ボックス・ライン
service box line
Aufschlagkastenlinie^F
ligne^F de boîte^F de service^M
línea^F de cuadro^M de servicio^M
linea^F del quadrato^M di servizio^M

サービス・ボックス
service box
Aufschlagkasten^M
boîte^F de service^M
cuadro^M de servicio^M
quadrato^M di servizio^M

ショート・ライン
short line
kurze Linie^F
ligne^F de service^M court
línea^F corta
linea^F di metà^F campo^M

ドア
door
Tür^F
porte^F
puerta^F
porta^F

ライン・ジャッジ／線審
line judge
Linienrichter^M
juge^M de ligne^F
juez^M de línea^F
giudice^M di linea^F

バックコート
backcourt
Hinterfeld^N
arrière^M du court^M
cancha^F del fondo^M
zona^F di difesa^F

床
floor
Boden^M
plancher^M
piso^M
pavimento^M

レシービング・ライン
receiving line
Empfangslinie^F
ligne^F de réception^F de service^M
línea^F de recepción^F
linea^F di ricezione^F

ラケットボール・ラケット
racquetball racket; *racquetball racket*
Racquetballschläger^M
raquette^F de racquetball^M
raqueta^F de raquetball^M
racchetta^F

バンパー・ガード
bumper guard
Schlagschutz^M
pare-chocs^M
marco^M
paracolpi^M

リスト・コード
safety thong
Sicherheitsriemen^M
courroie^F de sécurité^F
correa^F de seguridad^F
cinghia^F

I.R.F

ラケットボール用のボール
racquetball
Racquetball^M
balle^F de racquetball^M
pelota^F de raquetball^M
palla^F

アイ・ガード
protective goggles
Schutzbrille^F
lunettes^F de protection^F
gafas^F de protección^F
occhiali^M di protezione^F

スポーツとゲーム

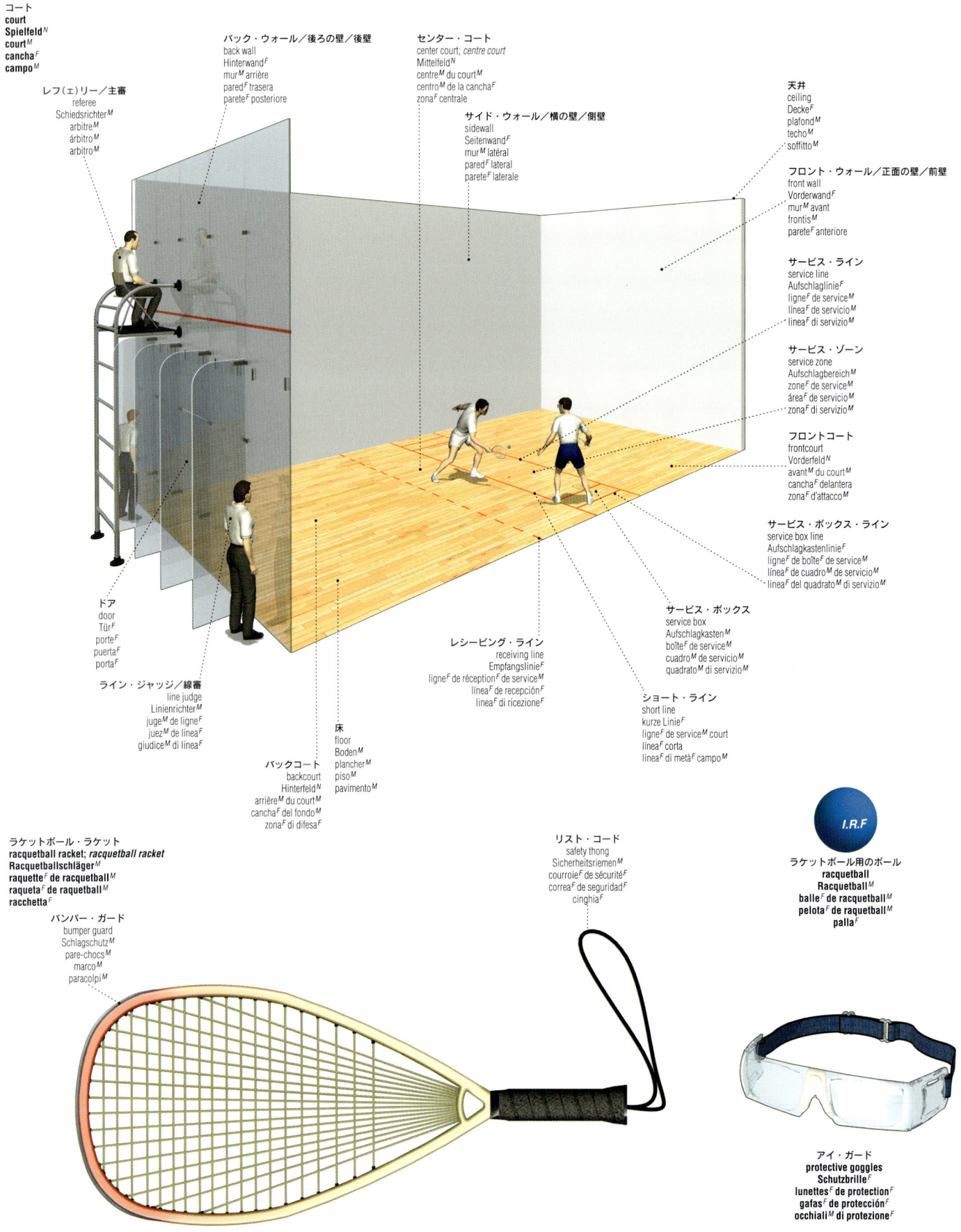

ラケット・スポーツ | RACKET SPORTS
SPIELE MIT SCHLÄGERN | SPORTS DE RAQUETTE | DEPORTES DE RAQUETA | GIOCHI CON LA RACCHETTA

スカッシュ
squash | Squash^N | squash^M | squash^M | squash^M

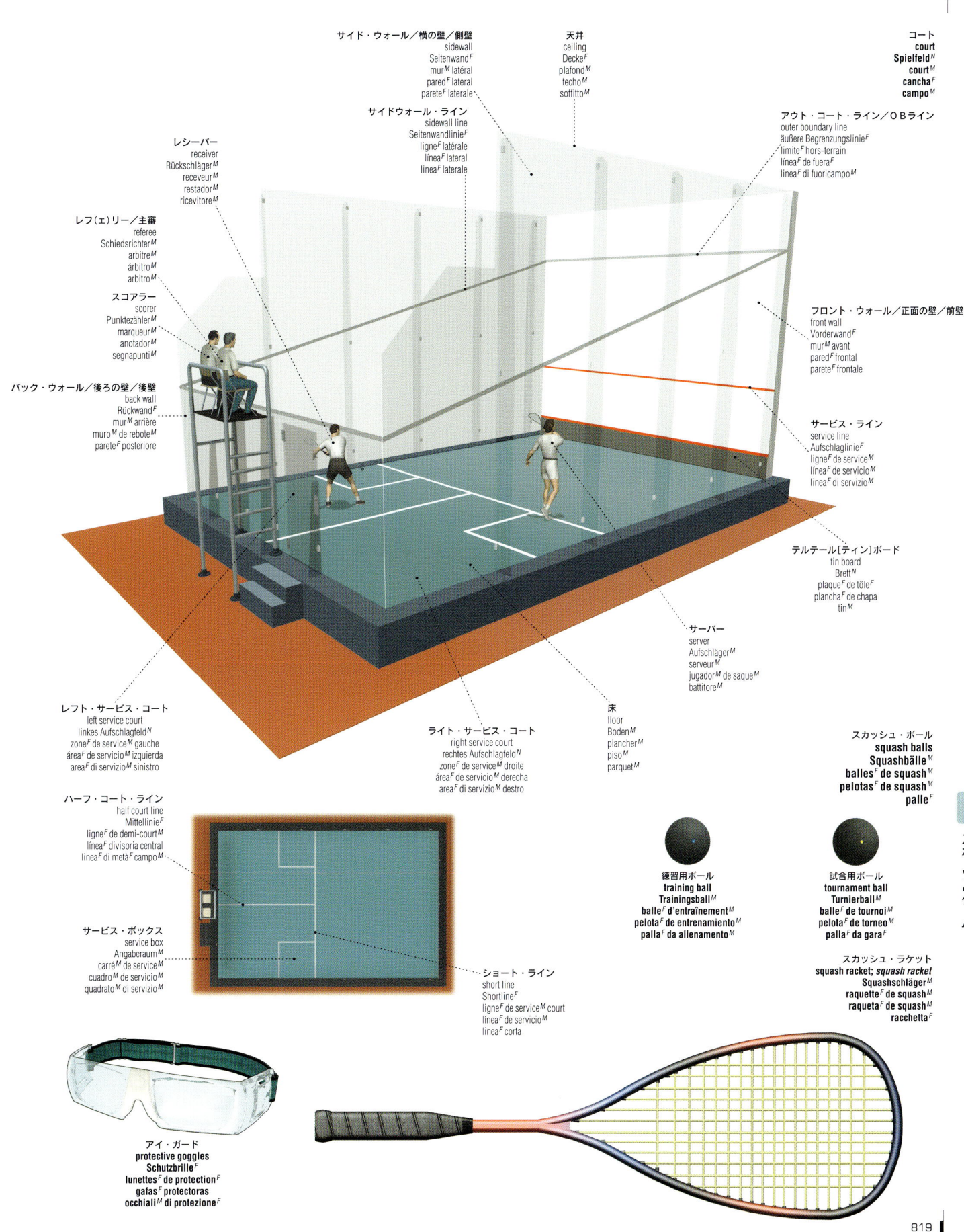

サイド・ウォール／横の壁／側壁
sidewall
Seitenwand^F
mur^M latéral
pared^F lateral
parete^F laterale

天井
ceiling
Decke^F
plafond^M
techo^M
soffitto^M

コート
court
Spielfeld^N
court^M
cancha^F
campo^M

サイドウォール・ライン
sidewall line
Seitenwandlinie^F
ligne^F latérale
línea^F lateral
linea^F laterale

アウト・コート・ライン／ＯＢライン
outer boundary line
äußere Begrenzungslinie^F
limite^F hors-terrain
línea^F de fuera
linea^F di fuoricampo^M

レシーバー
receiver
Rückschläger^M
receveur^M
restador^M
ricevitore^M

レフ(ェ)リー／主審
referee
Schiedsrichter^M
arbitre^M
árbitro^M
arbitro^M

スコアラー
scorer
Punktezähler^M
marqueur^M
anotador^M
segnapunti^M

フロント・ウォール／正面の壁／前壁
front wall
Vorderwand^F
mur^M avant
pared^F frontal
parete^F frontale

バック・ウォール／後ろの壁／後壁
back wall
Rückwand^F
mur^M arrière
muro^M de rebote^M
parete^F posteriore

サービス・ライン
service line
Aufschlaglinie^F
ligne^F de service
línea^F de servicio^M
linea^F di servizio^M

テルテール[ティン]ボード
tin board
Brett^N
plaque^F de tôle^F
plancha^F de chapa
tin^M

サーバー
server
Aufschläger^M
serveur^M
jugador^M de saque^M
battitore^M

レフト・サービス・コート
left service court
linkes Aufschlagfeld^N
zone^F de service^M gauche
área^F de servicio^M izquierda
area^F di servizio^M sinistro

床
floor
Boden^M
plancher^M
piso^M
parquet^M

ライト・サービス・コート
right service court
rechtes Aufschlagfeld^N
zone^F de service^M droite
área^F de servicio^M derecha
area^F di servizio^M destro

スカッシュ・ボール
squash balls
Squashbälle^M
balles^F de squash^M
pelotas^F de squash^M
palle^F

ハーフ・コート・ライン
half court line
Mittellinie^F
ligne^F de demi-court^M
línea^F divisoria central
linea^F di metà^F campo^M

練習用ボール
training ball
Trainingsball^M
balle^F d'entraînement^M
pelota^F de entrenamiento^M
palla^F da allenamento^M

試合用ボール
tournament ball
Turnierball^M
balle^F de tournoi^M
pelota^F de torneo^M
palla^F da gara^F

サービス・ボックス
service box
Angaberaum^M
carré^M de service^M
cuadro^M de servicio^M
quadrato^M di servizio^M

ショート・ライン
short line
Shortline^F
ligne^F de service^M court
línea^F de servicio^M
linea^F corta

スカッシュ・ラケット
squash racket; *squash racket*
Squashschläger^M
raquette^F de squash^M
raqueta^F de squash^M
racchetta^F

アイ・ガード
protective goggles
Schutzbrille^F
lunettes^F de protection^F
gafas^F protectoras
occhiali^M di protezione^F

スポーツとゲーム

819

ラケット・スポーツ | RACKET SPORTS
SPIELE MIT SCHLÄGERN | SPORTS DE RAQUETTE | DEPORTES DE RAQUETA | GIOCHI CON LA RACCHETTA

テニス

日本語 | 英語 | ドイツ語 | フランス語 | スペイン語 | イタリア語

tennis | Tennis^N | tennis^M | tenis^M | tennis^M

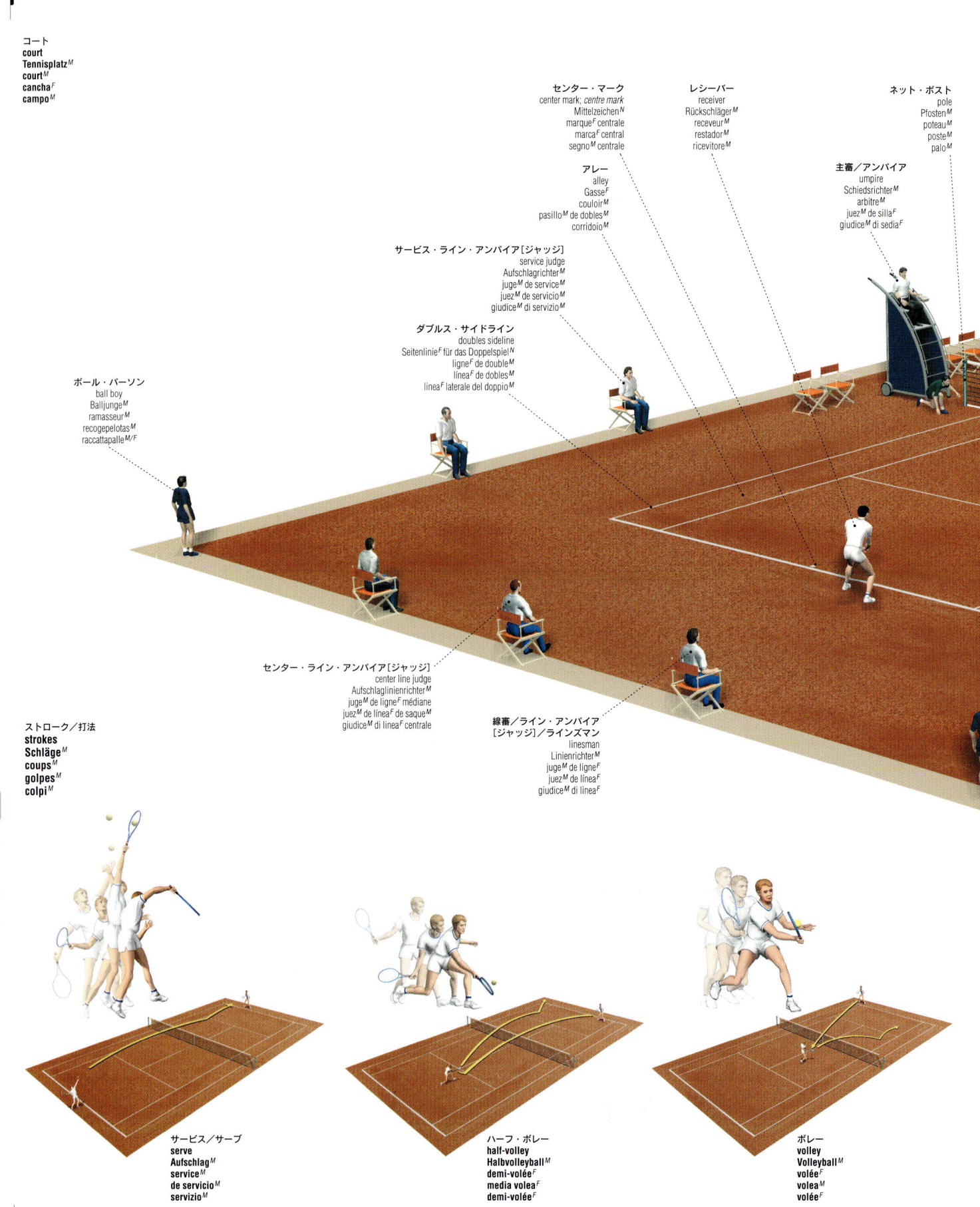

コート
court
Tennisplatz^M
court^F
cancha^F
campo^M

センター・マーク
center mark; centre mark
Mittelzeichen^N
marque^F centrale
marca^F central
segno^M centrale

レシーバー
receiver
Rückschläger^M
receveur^M
restador^M
ricevitore^M

ネット・ポスト
pole
Pfosten^M
poteau^M
poste^M
palo^M

アレー
alley
Gasse^F
couloir^M
pasillo^M de dobles^M
corridoio^M

主審／アンパイア
umpire
Schiedsrichter^M
arbitre^M
juez^M de silla^F
giudice^M di sedia^F

サービス・ライン・アンパイア［ジャッジ］
service judge
Aufschlagrichter^M
juge^M de service^M
juez^M de servicio^M
giudice^M di servizio^M

ダブルス・サイドライン
doubles sideline
Seitenlinie^F für das Doppelspiel^N
ligne^F de double^M
línea^F de dobles^M
linea^F laterale del doppio^M

ボール・パーソン
ball boy
Balljunge^M
ramasseur^M
recogepelotas^M
raccattapalle^{M/F}

センター・ライン・アンパイア［ジャッジ］
center line judge
Aufschlaglinienrichter^M
juge^M de ligne^F médiane
juez^M de línea^F de saque^M
giudice^M di linea^F centrale

線審／ライン・アンパイア
［ジャッジ］／ラインズマン
linesman
Linienrichter^M
juge^M de ligne^F
juez^M de línea^F
giudice^M di linea^F

ストローク／打法
strokes
Schläge^M
coups^M
golpes^M
colpi^M

サービス／サーブ
serve
Aufschlag^M
service^M
de servicio^M
servizio^M

ハーフ・ボレー
half-volley
Halbvolleyball^M
demi-volée^F
media volea^F
demi-volée^F

ボレー
volley
Volleyball^M
volée^F
volea^F
volée^F

スポーツとゲーム

820

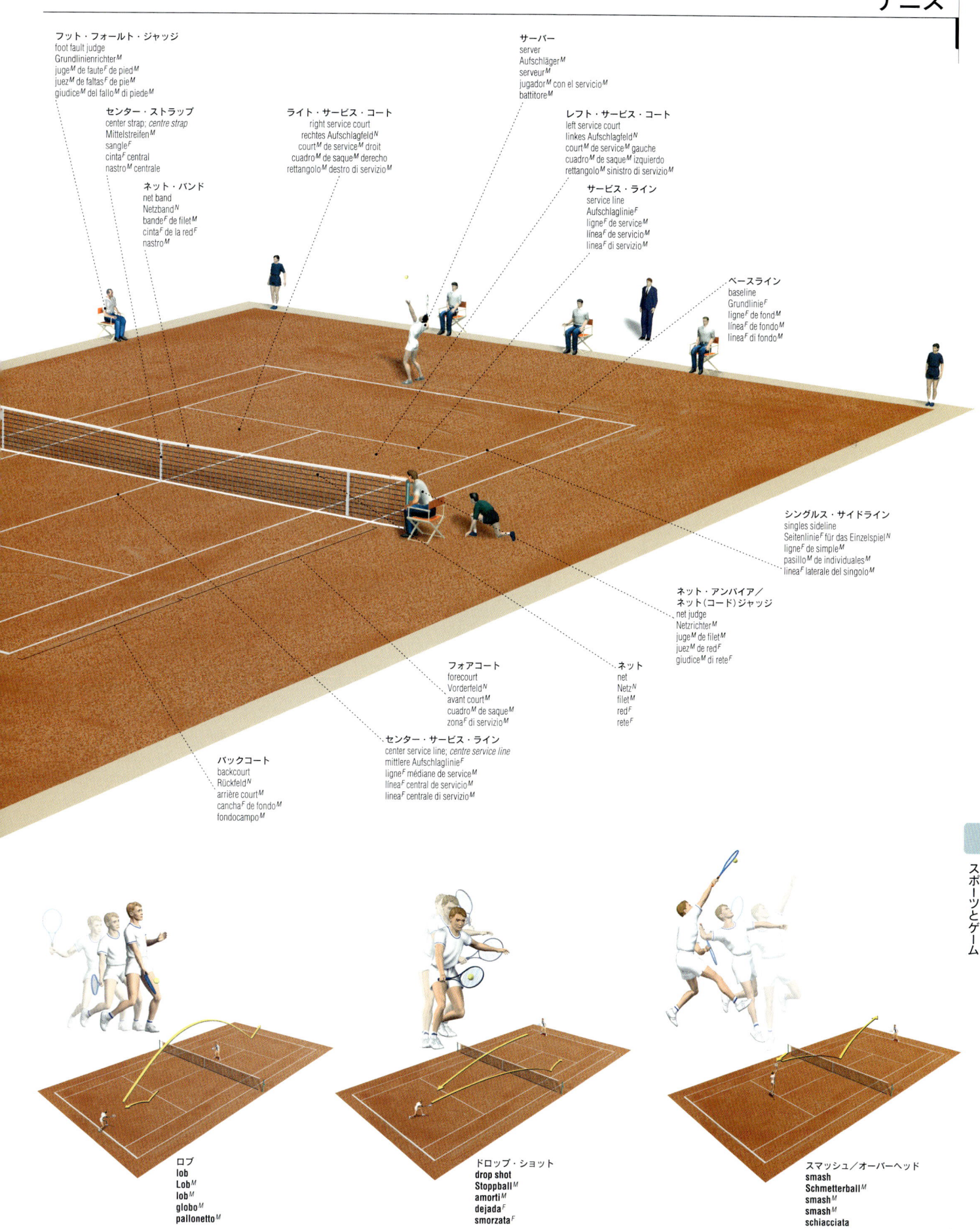

ラケット・スポーツ | RACKET SPORTS
SPIELE MIT SCHLÄGERN | SPORTS DE RAQUETTE | DEPORTES DE RAQUETA | GIOCHI CON LA RACCHETTA

テニス

フット・フォールト・ジャッジ
foot fault judge
Grundlinienrichter^M
juge^M de faute^F de pied^M
juez^M de faltas^F de pie^M
giudice^M del fallo^M di piede^M

センター・ストラップ
center strap; *centre strap*
Mittelstreifen^M
sangle^F
cinta^F central
nastro^M centrale

ネット・バンド
net band
Netzband^N
bande^F de filet^M
cinta^F de la red^F
nastro^M

ライト・サービス・コート
right service court
rechtes Aufschlagfeld^N
court^M de service^M droit
cuadro^M de saque^M derecho
rettangolo^M destro di servizio^M

サーバー
server
Aufschläger^M
serveur^M
jugador^M con el servicio^M
battitore^M

レフト・サービス・コート
left service court
linkes Aufschlagfeld^N
court^M de service^M gauche
cuadro^M de saque^M izquierdo
rettangolo^M sinistro di servizio^M

サービス・ライン
service line
Aufschlaglinie^F
ligne^F de service^M
línea^F de servicio^M
linea^F di servizio^M

ベースライン
baseline
Grundlinie^F
ligne^F de fond^M
línea^F de fondo^M
linea^F di fondo^M

シングルス・サイドライン
singles sideline
Seitenlinie^F für das Einzelspiel^N
ligne^F de simple^M
pasillo^M de individuales^M
linea^F laterale del singolo^M

ネット・アンパイア／
ネット（コード）ジャッジ
net judge
Netzrichter^M
juge^M de filet^M
juez^M de red^F
giudice^M di rete^F

フォアコート
forecourt
Vorderfeld^N
avant court^M
cuadro^M de saque^M
zona^F di servizio^M

ネット
net
Netz^N
filet^M
red^F
rete^F

バックコート
backcourt
Rückfeld^N
arrière court^M
cancha^F de fondo^M
fondocampo^M

センター・サービス・ライン
center service line; *centre service line*
mittlere Aufschlaglinie^F
ligne^F médiane de service^M
línea^F central de servicio^M
linea^F centrale di servizio^M

ロブ
lob
Lob^M
lob^M
globo^M
pallonetto^M

ドロップ・ショット
drop shot
Stoppball^M
amorti^M
dejada^F
smorzata^F

スマッシュ／オーバーヘッド
smash
Schmetterball^M
smash^M
smash^M
schiacciata

スポーツとゲーム

821

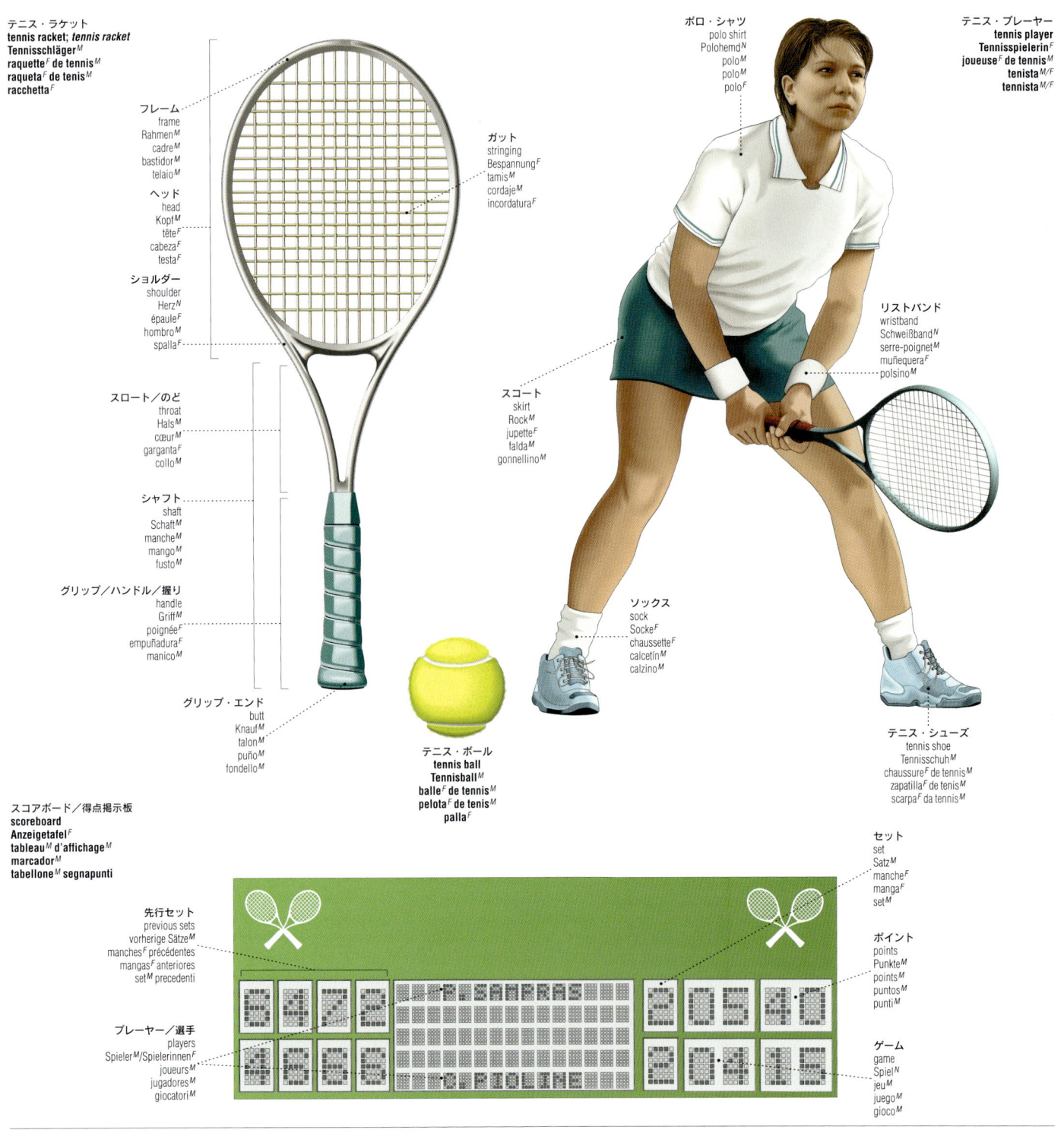

ラケット・スポーツ | RACKET SPORTS
SPIELE MIT SCHLÄGERN | SPORTS DE RAQUETTE | DEPORTES DE RAQUETA | GIOCHI CON LA RACCHETTA

テニス

日本語 | 英語 | ドイツ語 | フランス語 | スペイン語 | イタリア語

テニス・ラケット
tennis racket; *tennis racket*
Tennisschläger^M
raquette^F de tennis^M
raqueta^F de tenis^M
racchetta^F

フレーム
frame
Rahmen^M
cadre^M
bastidor^M
telaio^M

ヘッド
head
Kopf^M
tête^F
cabeza^F
testa^F

ショルダー
shoulder
Herz^N
épaule^F
hombro^M
spalla^F

スロート／のど
throat
Hals^M
cœur^M
garganta^F
collo^M

シャフト
shaft
Schaft^M
manche^M
mango^M
fusto^M

グリップ／ハンドル／握り
handle
Griff^M
poignée^F
empuñadura^F
manico^M

グリップ・エンド
butt
Knauf^M
talon^M
puño^M
fondello^M

ガット
stringing
Bespannung^F
tamis^M
cordaje^M
incordatura^F

ポロ・シャツ
polo shirt
Polohemd^N
polo^M
polo^M
polo^F

スコート
skirt
Rock^M
jupette^F
falda^F
gonnellino^M

リストバンド
wristband
Schweißband^N
serre-poignet^M
muñequera^F
polsino^M

ソックス
sock
Socke^F
chaussette^F
calcetín^M
calzino^M

テニス・ボール
tennis ball
Tennisball^M
balle^F de tennis^M
pelota^F de tenis^M
palla^F

テニス・プレーヤー
tennis player
Tennisspielerin^F
joueuse^F de tennis^M
tenista$^{M/F}$
tennista$^{M/F}$

テニス・シューズ
tennis shoe
Tennisschuh^M
chaussure^F de tennis^M
zapatilla^F de tenis^M
scarpa^F da tennis^M

スコアボード／得点掲示板
scoreboard
Anzeigetafel^F
tableau^M d'affichage^M
marcador^M
tabellone^M segnapunti

先行セット
previous sets
vorherige Sätze^M
manches^F précédentes
mangas^F anteriores
set^M precedenti

プレーヤー／選手
players
Spieler^M/Spielerinnen^F
joueurs^M
jugadores^M
giocatori^M

セット
set
Satz^M
manche^F
manga^F
set^M

ポイント
points
Punkte^M
points^M
puntos^M
punti^M

ゲーム
game
Spiel^N
jeu^M
juego^M
gioco^M

コート・サーフェス
playing surfaces
Spielfeldbeläge^M
surfaces^F de jeu^M
superficies^F de juego^M
superfici^F di gioco^M

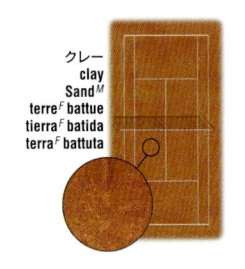

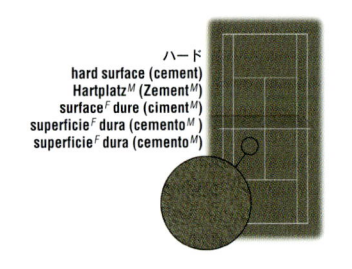

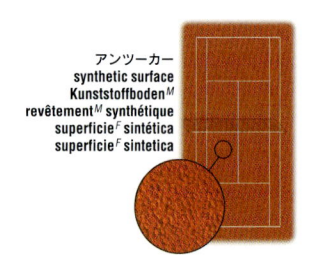

グラス／ローン／芝
grass
Rasen^M
gazon^M
hierba^F
erba^F

クレー
clay
Sand^M
terre^F battue
tierra^F batida
terra^F battuta

ハード
hard surface (cement)
Hartplatz^M (Zement^M)
surface^F dure (ciment^M)
superficie^F dura (cemento^M)
superficie^F dura (cemento^M)

アンツーカー
synthetic surface
Kunststoffboden^M
revêtement^M synthétique
superficie^F sintética
superficie^F sintetica

体操競技 | GYMNASTICS
KUNSTTURNEN | SPORTS GYMNIQUES | GIMNASIA | GINNASTICA

新体操

rhythmic gymnastics | rhythmische Sportgymnastik F | gymnastique F rythmique | gimnasia F rítmica | ginnastica F ritmica

マット
exercise area
Wettkampffläche F
praticable M
practicable M
area F di esercizio M

主任審判員
chief judge
Oberkampfrichter M
juge M en chef
juez M responsable
capogiuria M

審判員
judge coordinator
Kontrollkampfrichter M
juge M coordonnateur
juez M coordinador
giudice M di controllo M

芸術価値審判員
artistic value judges
Kampfrichter M für den künstlerischen Ausdruck M
juges M de valeur F artistique
jueces M de valor M artístico
giudici M per la valutazione F della composizione F

技術価値審判員
difficulty judges
Schwierigkeitskampfrichter M
juges M de difficultés F
juez M de dificultades F
giudici M per la valutazione F della difficoltà F

実施審判員
execution judges
Kampfrichter M für die technische Ausführung F
juges M d'exécution F
jueces M de ejecución F
giudici M per la valutazione F dell'esecuzione F

手具／道具
apparatus
Handgeräte N
engins M
aparatos M
attrezzi M

クラブ／棍棒（こんぼう）
clubs
Keulen F
massues F
mazas F
clavette F

ロープ／縄
rope
Seil N
corde F
aro M
funicella F

ボール
ball
Ball M
ballon M
pelota F
palla F

フープ／輪
hoop
Reifen M
cerceau M
aro M
cerchio M

リボン
ribbon
Band N
ruban M
cinta F
nastro M

トランポリン

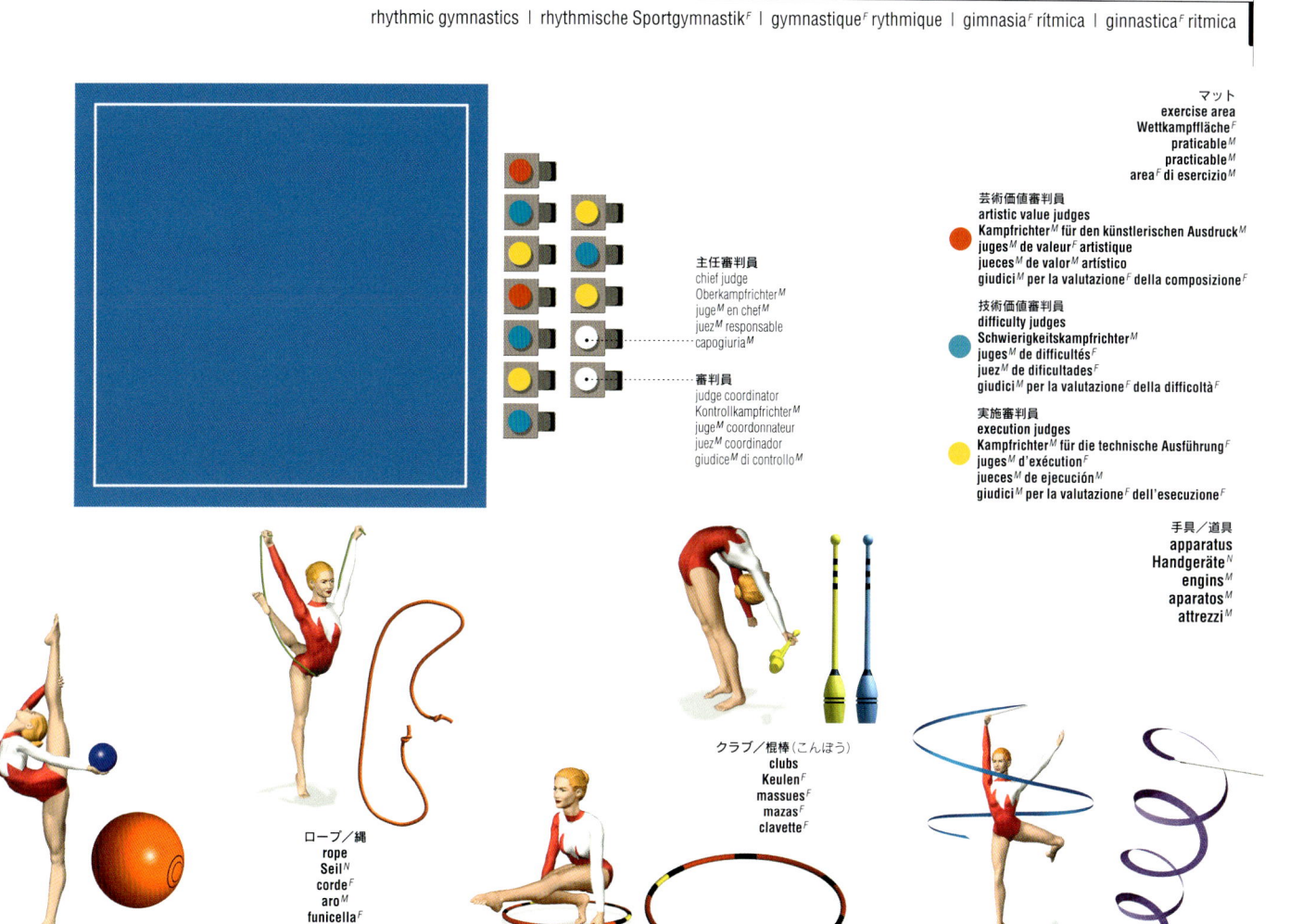

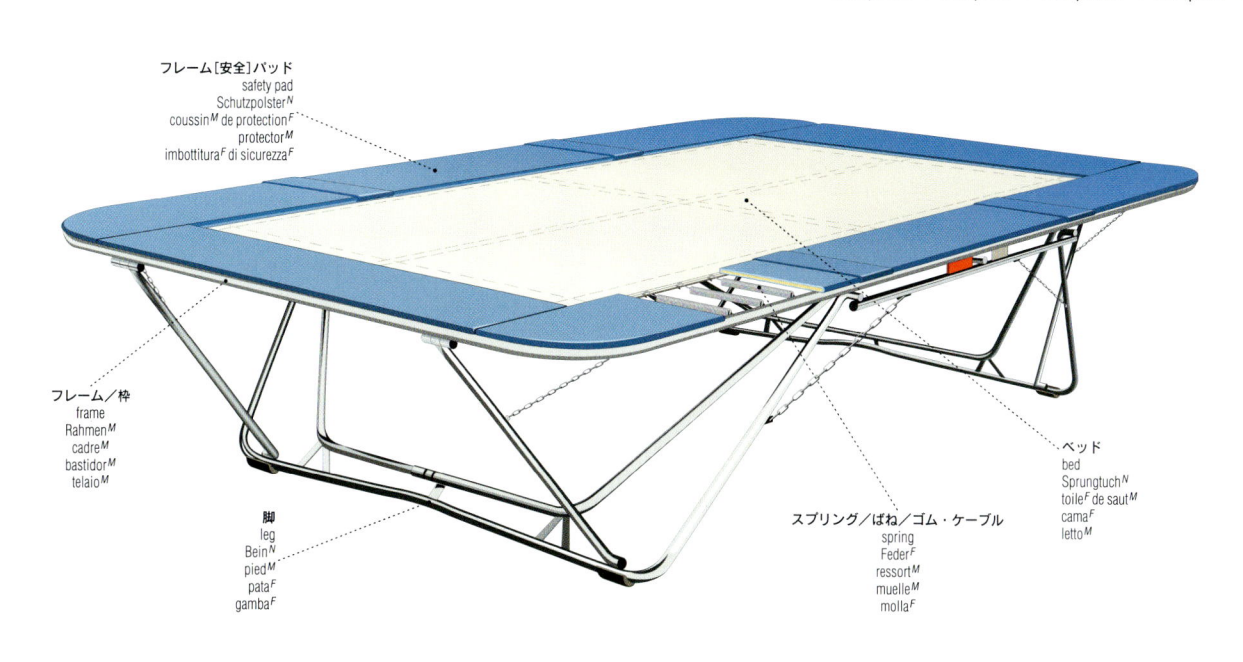

trampoline | Trampolin N | trampoline M | trampolín M | trampolino M

フレーム[安全]パッド
safety pad
Schutzpolster N
coussin M de protection F
protector M
imbottitura F di sicurezza F

フレーム／枠
frame
Rahmen M
cadre M
bastidor M
telaio M

脚
leg
Bein N
pied M
pata F
gamba F

スプリング／ばね／ゴム・ケーブル
spring
Feder F
ressort M
muelle M
molla M

ベッド
bed
Sprungtuch N
toile F de saut M
cama F
letto M

823

体操競技 | GYMNASTICS
KUNSTTURNEN | SPORTS GYMNIQUES | GIMNASIA | GINNASTICA

体操

gymnastics | Geräteturnen[N] | gymnastique[F] | gimnasia[F] | ginnastica[F]

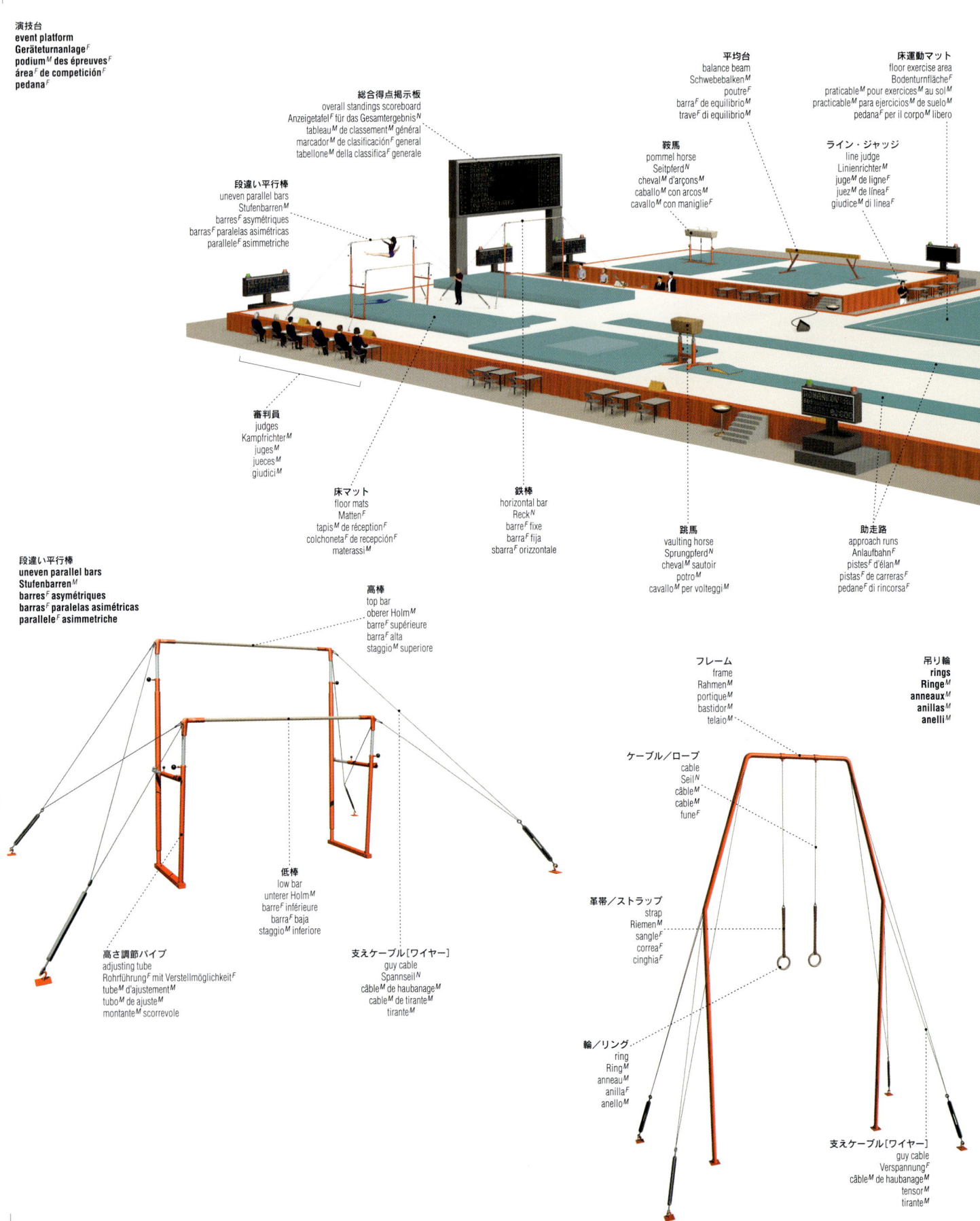

日本語 | 英語 | ドイツ語 | フランス語 | スペイン語 | イタリア語

演技台
event platform
Geräteturnanlage[F]
podium[M] des épreuves[F]
área[F] de competición[F]
pedana[F]

総合得点掲示板
overall standings scoreboard
Anzeigetafel[F] für das Gesamtergebnis[N]
tableau[M] de classement[M] général
marcador[M] de clasificación[F] general
tabellone[M] della classifica[F] generale

平均台
balance beam
Schwebebalken[M]
poutre[F]
barra[F] de equilibrio[M]
trave[F] di equilibrio[M]

床運動マット
floor exercise area
Bodenturnfläche[F]
praticable[M] pour exercices[M] au sol[M]
practicable[M] para ejercicios[M] de suelo[M]
pedana[F] per il corpo[M] libero

段違い平行棒
uneven parallel bars
Stufenbarren[M]
barres[F] asymétriques
barras[F] paralelas asimétricas
parallele[F] asimmetriche

鞍馬
pommel horse
Seitpferd[N]
cheval[M] d'arçons[M]
caballo[M] con arcos[M]
cavallo[M] con maniglie[F]

ライン・ジャッジ
line judge
Linienrichter[M]
juge[M] de ligne[F]
juez[M] de línea[F]
giudice[M] di linea[F]

審判員
judges
Kampfrichter[M]
juges[M]
jueces[M]
giudici[M]

床マット
floor mats
Matten[F]
tapis[M] de réception[F]
colchoneta[F] de recepción[F]
materassi[M]

鉄棒
horizontal bar
Reck[N]
barre[F] fixe
barra[F] fija
sbarra[F] orizzontale

跳馬
vaulting horse
Sprungpferd[N]
cheval[M] sautoir
potro[M]
cavallo[M] per volteggi[M]

助走路
approach runs
Anlaufbahn[F]
pistes[F] d'élan[M]
pistas[F] de carreras[F]
pedane[F] di rincorsa[F]

段違い平行棒
uneven parallel bars
Stufenbarren[M]
barres[F] asymétriques
barras[F] paralelas asimétricas
parallele[F] asimmetriche

高棒
top bar
oberer Holm[M]
barre[F] supérieure
barra[F] alta
staggio[M] superiore

低棒
low bar
unterer Holm[M]
barre[F] inférieure
barra[F] baja
staggio[M] inferiore

高さ調節パイプ
adjusting tube
Rohrführung[F] mit Verstellmöglichkeit[F]
tube[M] d'ajustement[M]
tubo[M] de ajuste[M]
montante[M] scorrevole

支えケーブル［ワイヤー］
guy cable
Spannseil[N]
câble[M] de haubanage[M]
cable[M] de tirante[M]
tirante[M]

フレーム
frame
Rahmen[M]
portique[M]
bastidor[M]
telaio[M]

吊り輪
rings
Ringe[M]
anneaux[M]
anillas[M]
anelli[M]

ケーブル／ロープ
cable
Seil[N]
câble[M]
cable[M]
fune[F]

革帯／ストラップ
strap
Riemen[M]
sangle[F]
correa[F]
cinghia[F]

輪／リング
ring
Ring[M]
anneau[M]
anilla[F]
anello[M]

支えケーブル［ワイヤー］
guy cable
Verspannung[F]
câble[M] de haubanage[M]
tensor[M]
tirante[M]

体操競技 | GYMNASTICS
KUNSTTURNEN | SPORTS GYMNIQUES | GIMNASIA | GINNASTICA

体操

得点掲示板／スコアボード
scoreboard
Anzeigetafel^F
tableau^M de pointage^M
marcador^M
tabellone^M segnapunti

体操選手名
gymnast's name
Name^M des Turners^M/der Turnerin^F
nom^M du gymnaste^M
nombre^M del gimnasta^M
nome^M del ginnasta^M

種目別得点掲示板
current event scoreboard
Anzeigetafel^F für die Einzeldisziplin^F
pointage^M de l'épreuve en cours^M
marcador^M del evento^M e curso^M
tabellone^M della prova^F in corso

国籍
nationality
Nationalität^F
nationalité^F
nacionalidad^F
nazionalità^F

審判員
judges
Kampfrichter^M
juges^M
jueces^M
giudici

跳馬
vaulting horse
Sprungpferd^N
cheval^M sautoir
potro^M
cavallo^M per volteggi^M

吊り輪
rings
Ringe^M
anneaux^M
anillas^M
anelli^M

平行棒
parallel bars
Barren^M
barres^F parallèles
barras^F paralelas
parallele^F

得点／スコア
score
Note^F
note^F
jueces^M
punteggio^M

滑り止め
magnesium powder
Magnesia^F
magnésie^F
polvo^M de magnesio
polvere^F di magnesia^F

審判員
judges
Kampfrichter^M
juges^M
jueces^M
giudici

鉄棒／バー
steel bar
Reckstange^F
barre^F d'acier^M
barra^F de acero^M
sbarra^F di acciaio^M

鉄棒
horizontal bar
Reck^N
barre^F fixe
barra^F fija
sbarra^F orizzontale

支えケーブル［ワイヤー］
guy cable
Verspannung^F
câble^M de haubanage^M
tensor^M
tirante

支柱
upright
Recksäule^F
montant^M
soporte^M
ritto^M

平行棒
parallel bars
Barren^M
barres^F parallèles
barras^F paralelas
parallele^F

木製バー
wooden bar
hölzerner Barrenholm^M
barre^F de bois^M
barra^F de madera^F
staggio^M

高さ調節パイプ
adjusting tube
Rohrführung^F mit Verstellmöglichkeit^F
tube^M d'ajustement^M
tubo^M de ajuste^M
montante^M scorrevole

台
base
Sockel^M
base^F
base^F
basamento^M

スポーツとゲーム

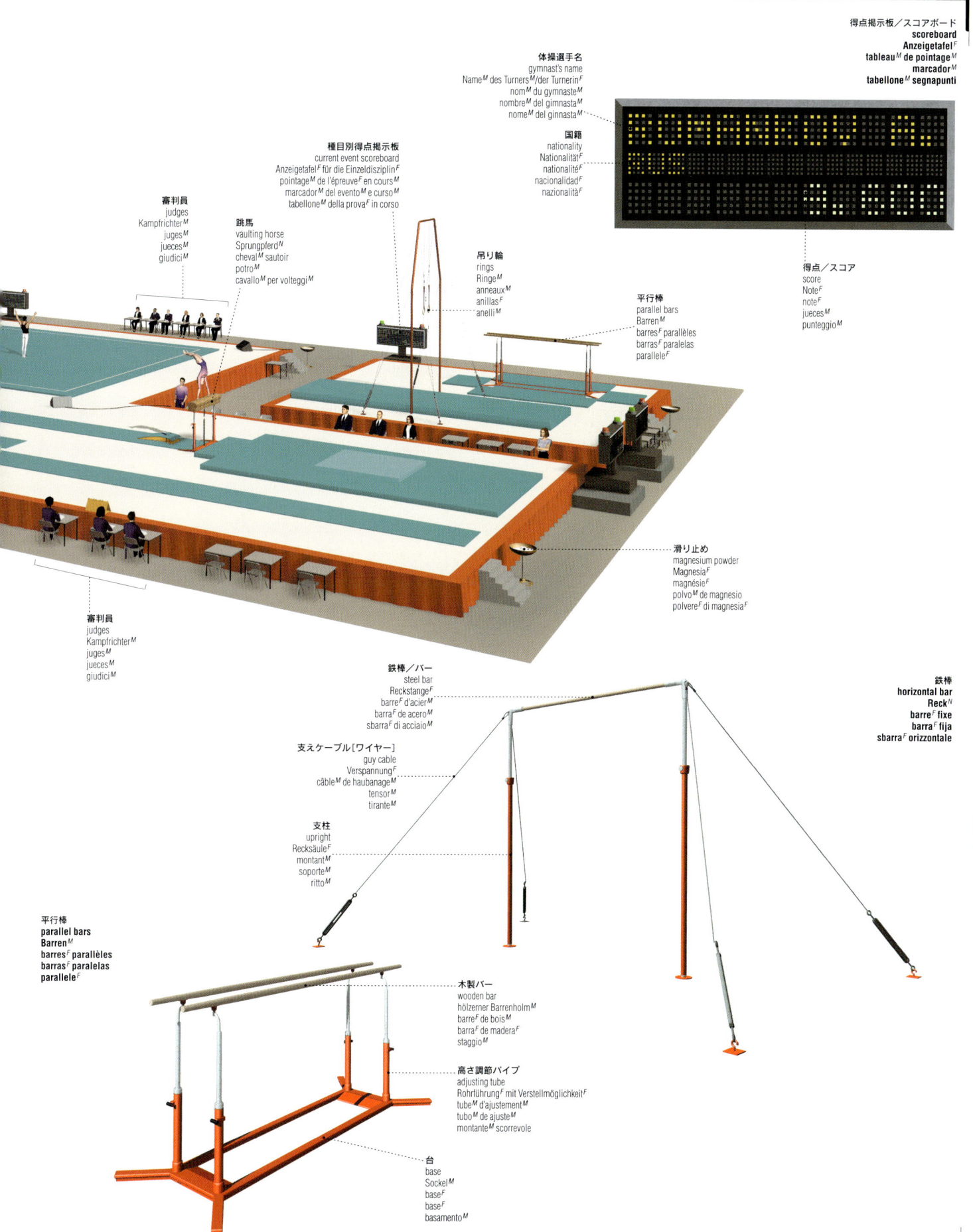

体操競技 | GYMNASTICS
KUNSTTURNEN | SPORTS GYMNIQUES | GIMNASIA | GINNASTICA

体操

日本語 | 英語 | ドイツ語 | フランス語 | スペイン語 | イタリア語

鞍馬
pommel horse
Seitpferd^N
cheval^M d'arçons^M
caballo^M con aros^M
cavallo^M con maniglie^F

鞍部
saddle
Sattel^M
selle^F
silla^F
sella^F

取っ手
pommel
Pausche^F
arçon^M
arzón^M
maniglia^F

首部／馬首
neck
Hals^M
cou^M
cabeza^F
testa^F

尾部／馬尾
croup
Kruppe^F
croupe^F
grupa^F
groppa^F

馬体
horse
Pferd^N
cheval^M
caballo^M
cavallo^M

締め具
tightener
Spanner^M
tendeur^M
tensor^M
tenditore^M rapido

台
base
Sockel^M
piètement^M
base^F
base^F

高さ調節つまみ
height adjustment
Höhenverstellung^F
réglage^M de la hauteur^F
regulador^M de altura^F
sistema^M di regolazione^F dell'altezza^F

支柱
upright
Stütze^F
montant^M
soporte^M
montante^M

鎖／チェーン
chain
Kette^F
chaîne^F
cadena^F
catena^F

滑り止めパッド［台］
antislip shoe
rutschfester Sockel^M
patin^M antidérapant
zapata^F antideslizante
piede^M antisdrucciolo

平均台
balance beam
Schwebebalken^M
poutre^F d'équilibre^M
barra^F de equilibrio^M
trave^F di equilibrio^M

高さ調節ハンドル
height adjustment
Höhenverstellung^F
réglage^M de la hauteur^F
regulador^M de altura^F
sistema^M di regolazione^F dell'altezza^F

台／ビーム
beam
Balken^M
poutre^F
barra^F
trave^F

支柱
upright
Ständer^M
montant^M
montante^M
montante^M

跳馬
vaulting horse
Sprungpferd^N
cheval^M-sautoir^M
potro^M
cavallo^M per volteggi

踏切板
springboard
Sprungbrett^N
tremplin^M
plancha^F de muelles^M
pedana^F elastica

スポーツとゲーム

826

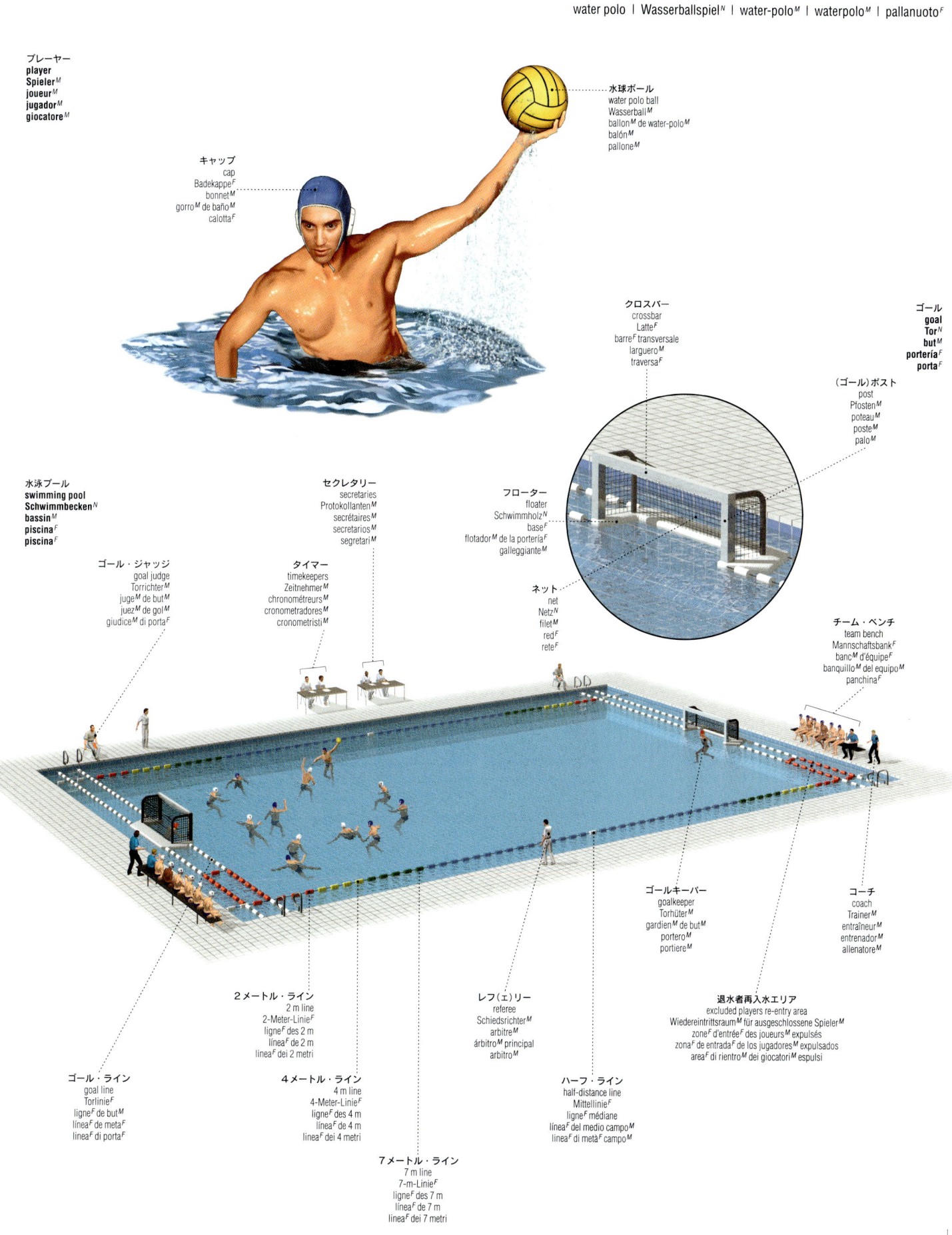

水上・水中スポーツと海上スポーツ | AQUATIC AND NAUTICAL SPORTS
WASSERSPORT | SPORTS AQUATIQUES ET NAUTIQUES | DEPORTES ACUÁTICOS Y NÁUTICOS | SPORT ACQUATICI E NAUTICI

水球

water polo | Wasserballspiel(N) | water-polo(M) | waterpolo(M) | pallanuoto(F)

プレーヤー
player
Spieler(M)
joueur(M)
jugador(M)
giocatore(M)

キャップ
cap
Badekappe(F)
bonnet(M)
gorro(M) de baño(M)
calotta(F)

水球ボール
water polo ball
Wasserball(M)
ballon(M) de water-polo(M)
balón(M)
pallone(M)

クロスバー
crossbar
Latte(F)
barre(F) transversale
larguero(M)
traversa(F)

ゴール
goal
Tor(N)
but(M)
portería(F)
porta(F)

（ゴール）ポスト
post
Pfosten(M)
poteau(M)
poste(M)
palo(M)

水泳プール
swimming pool
Schwimmbecken(N)
bassin(M)
piscina(F)
piscina(F)

セクレタリー
secretaries
Protokollanten(M)
secrétaires(M)
secretarios(M)
segretari(M)

フローター
floater
Schwimmholz(N)
base(F)
flotador(M) de la portería(F)
galleggiante(M)

ゴール・ジャッジ
goal judge
Torrichter(M)
juge(M) de but(M)
juez(M) de gol(M)
giudice(M) di porta(F)

タイマー
timekeepers
Zeitnehmer(M)
chronométreurs(M)
cronometradores(M)
cronometristi(M)

ネット
net
Netz(N)
filet(M)
red(F)
rete(F)

チーム・ベンチ
team bench
Mannschaftsbank(F)
banc(M) d'équipe(F)
banquillo(M) del equipo(M)
panchina(F)

ゴールキーパー
goalkeeper
Torhüter(M)
gardien(M) de but(M)
portero(M)
portiere(M)

コーチ
coach
Trainer(M)
entraîneur(M)
entrenador(M)
allenatore(M)

2メートル・ライン
2 m line
2-Meter-Linie(F)
ligne(F) des 2 m
línea(F) de 2 m
linea(F) dei 2 metri

レフ（ェ）リー
referee
Schiedsrichter(M)
arbitre(M)
árbitro(M) principal
arbitro(M)

退水者再入水エリア
excluded players re-entry area
Wiedereintrittsraum(M) für ausgeschlossene Spieler(M)
zone(F) d'entrée des joueurs(M) expulsés
zona(F) de entrada de los jugadores(M) expulsados
area(F) di rientro dei giocatori(M) espulsi

ゴール・ライン
goal line
Torlinie(F)
ligne(F) de but(M)
línea(F) de meta(F)
linea(F) di porta(F)

4メートル・ライン
4 m line
4-Meter-Linie(F)
ligne(F) des 4 m
línea(F) de 4 m
linea(F) dei 4 metri

ハーフ・ライン
half-distance line
Mittellinie(F)
ligne(F) médiane
línea(F) del medio campo(M)
linea(F) di metà campo(M)

7メートル・ライン
7 m line
7-m-Linie(F)
ligne(F) des 7 m
línea(F) de 7 m
linea(F) dei 7 metri

827

水上・水中スポーツと海上スポーツ | AQUATIC AND NAUTICAL SPORTS
WASSERSPORT | SPORTS AQUATIQUES ET NAUTIQUES | DEPORTES ACUÁTICOS Y NÁUTICOS | SPORT ACQUATICI E NAUTICI

飛び込み

日本語 | 英語 | ドイツ語 | フランス語 | スペイン語 | イタリア語

diving | Kunstspringen^N | plongeon^M | saltos^M | tuffi^M

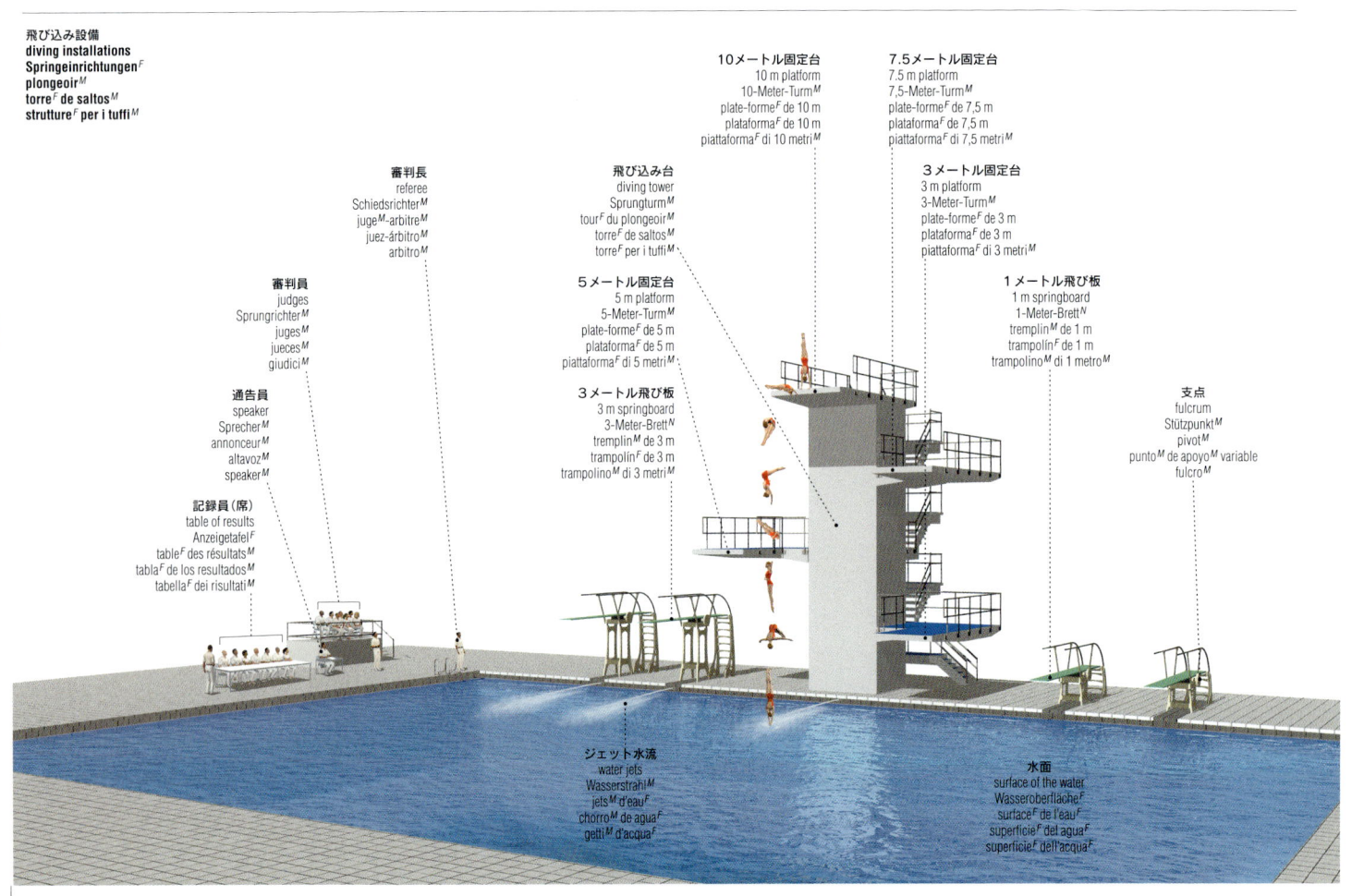

踏み切り姿勢
starting positions
Startpositionen^F
positions^F de départ^M
posiciones^F de salto^M
posizioni^F di partenza^F

前逆飛び込み
reverse
auswärts
renversé
salto^M inverso
rovesciata^F

後ろ踏み切り前飛び込み
inward
einwärts
retourné
salto^M interior
ritornata^F

後ろ飛び込み
backward
rückwärts
arrière
salto^M de espalda^F
all'indietro

前飛び込み
forward
vorwärts
avant
salto^M frontal
in avanti

逆立ち飛び込み
armstand
Handstand^M
en équilibre
salto^M en equilibrio^M
verticale^F sulle braccia^F

空中の姿勢
flights
Sprungfiguren^F
vols^M
saltos^M
voli^M

抱え型
tuck position
Saltostellung^F
position^F groupée
posición^F C - cuerpo^M encogido
posizione^F raggruppata

伸び型
straight position
Bohrerstellung^F
position^F droite
posición^F A - en plancha^F
posizione^F tesa

蝦（えび）型
pike position
Hechtsprungstellung^F
position^F carpée
posición^F B - hacer la carpa^F
posizione^F carpiata

飛び込み設備
diving installations
Springeinrichtungen^F
plongeoir^M
torre^F de saltos^M
strutture^F per i tuffi^M

審判長
referee
Schiedsrichter^M
juge^M-arbitre^M
juez-árbitro^M
arbitro^M

審判員
judges
Sprungrichter^M
juges^M
jueces^M
giudici^M

通告員
speaker
Sprecher^M
annonceur^M
altavoz^M
speaker^M

記録員（席）
table of results
Anzeigetafel^F
table^F des résultats^M
tabla^F de los resultados^M
tabella^F dei risultati^M

10メートル固定台
10 m platform
10-Meter-Turm^M
plate-forme^F de 10 m
plataforma^F de 10 m
piattaforma^F di 10 metri^M

飛び込み台
diving tower
Sprungturm^M
tour^F du plongeoir^M
torre^F de saltos^M
torre^F per i tuffi^M

5メートル固定台
5 m platform
5-Meter-Turm^M
plate-forme^F de 5 m
plataforma^F de 5 m
piattaforma^F di 5 metri^M

3メートル飛び板
3 m springboard
3-Meter-Brett^N
tremplin^M de 3 m
trampolín^M de 3 m
trampolino^M di 3 metri^M

7.5メートル固定台
7.5 m platform
7,5-Meter-Turm^M
plate-forme^F de 7,5 m
plataforma^F de 7,5 m
piattaforma^F di 7,5 metri^M

3メートル固定台
3 m platform
3-Meter-Turm^M
plate-forme^F de 3 m
plataforma^F de 3 m
piattaforma^F di 3 metri^M

1メートル飛び板
1 m springboard
1-Meter-Brett^N
tremplin^M de 1 m
trampolín^M de 1 m
trampolino^M di 1 metro^M

支点
fulcrum
Stützpunkt^M
pivot^M
punto de apoyo^M variable
fulcro^M

ジェット水流
water jets
Wasserstrahl^M
jets^M d'eau^F
chorro^M de agua^F
getti^M d'acqua^F

水面
surface of the water
Wasseroberfläche^F
surface^F de l'eau^F
superficie^F del agua^F
superficie^F dell'acqua^F

スポーツとゲーム

水上・水中スポーツと海上スポーツ | AQUATIC AND NAUTICAL SPORTS
WASSERSPORT | SPORTS AQUATIQUES ET NAUTIQUES | DEPORTES ACUÁTICOS Y NÁUTICOS | SPORT ACQUATICI E NAUTICI

飛び込み

飛び込み演技の例
examples of dives
Beispiele^N für Sprünge^M
exemples^M de plongeons^M
ejemplos^M de saltos^M
esempi^M di tuffi^M

入水の姿勢
entries
Eintauchstellungen^F
entrées^F dans l'eau^F
entradas^F al agua^F
entrate^F

足からの入水
feet-first entry
Füße^M voraus
entrée^F pieds^M premiers
entrada^F de pie^M
entrata^F di piedi^M

頭からの入水
head-first entry
Kopf^M voraus
entrée^F tête^F première
entrada^F de cabeza^F
entrata^F di testa^F

シンクロナイズド・ダイビング[飛び込み]
synchronized diving
Synchronspringen^N
plongeon^M synchronisé
salto^M sincronizado
tuffo^M sincronizzato

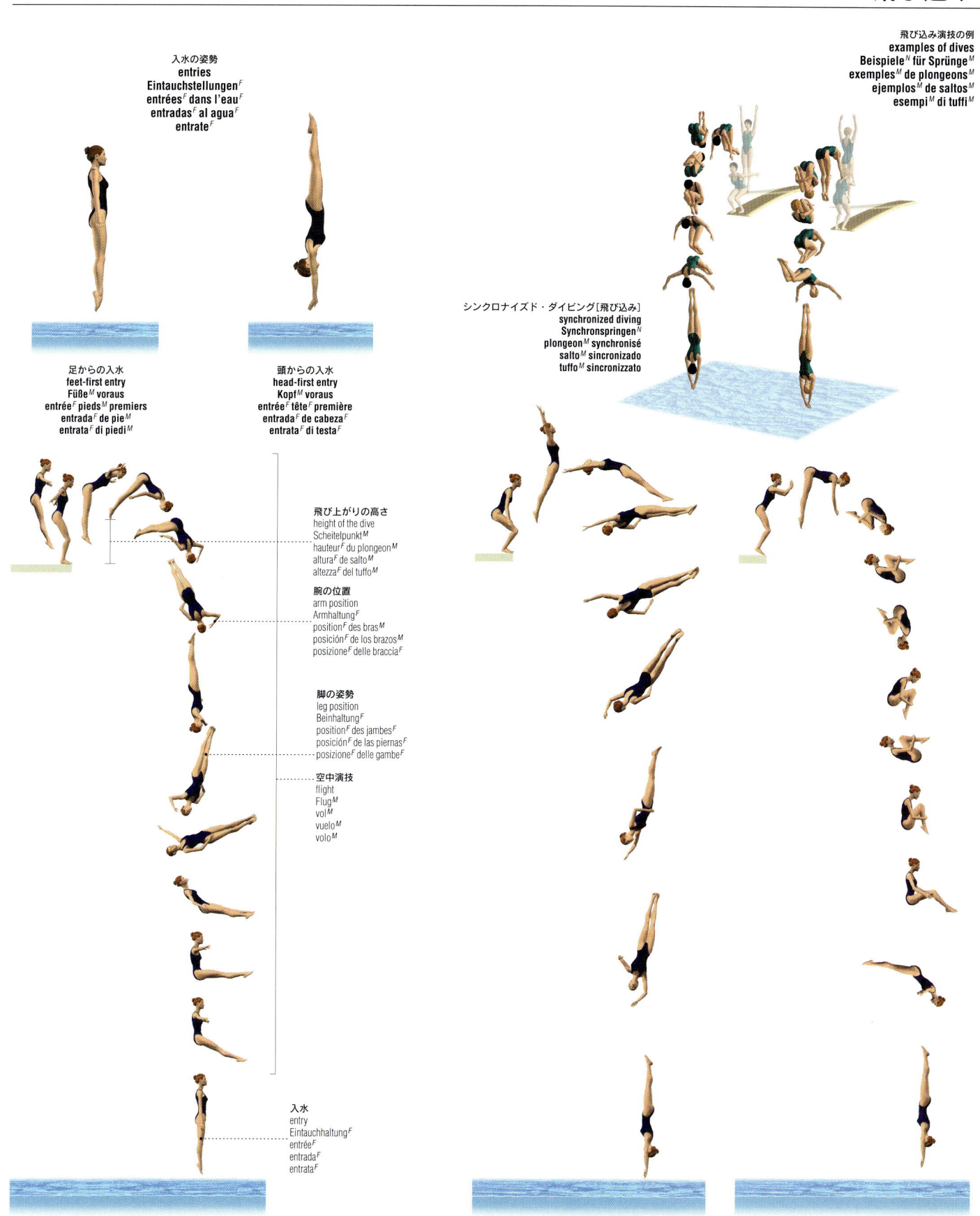

飛び上がりの高さ
height of the dive
Scheitelpunkt^M
hauteur^F du plongeon^M
altura^F de salto^M
altezza^F del tuffo^M

腕の位置
arm position
Armhaltung^F
position^F des bras^M
posición^F de los brazos^M
posizione^F delle braccia^F

脚の姿勢
leg position
Beinhaltung^F
position^F des jambes^F
posición^F de las piernas^F
posizione^F delle gambe^F

空中演技
flight
Flug^M
vol^M
vuelo^M
volo^M

入水
entry
Eintauchhaltung^F
entrée^F
entrada^F
entrata^F

前宙返り1回・1回捻り
forward somersault with a twist
Salto^M vorwärts gestreckt mit einer Schraube^F
saut^M périlleux avant avec tire-bouchon^M
salto^M frontal con tirabuzón^M
tuffo^M in avanti con avvitamento^M

前逆飛び・1回捻り
reverse dive with a twist
Auerbachkopfsprung^M gestreckt mit einer Schraube^F
plongeon^M renversé avec tire-bouchon^M
salto^M inverso con tirabuzón^M
tuffo^M rovesciato con avvitamento^M

前宙返り3回半・抱え型
forward three-and-a-half somersault tuck
dreieinhalbfacher Salto^M vorwärts gebückt
triple saut^M périlleux et demi avant groupé
triple salto^M mortal y medio hacia delante encogido
triplo salto^M mortale e mezzo in avanti raggruppato

スポーツとゲーム

829

水上・水中スポーツと海上スポーツ｜AQUATIC AND NAUTICAL SPORTS
WASSERSPORT｜SPORTS AQUATIQUES ET NAUTIQUES｜DEPORTES ACUÁTICOS Y NÁUTICOS｜SPORT ACQUATICI E NAUTICI

水泳

日本語｜英語｜ドイツ語｜フランス語｜スペイン語｜イタリア語

swimming｜Schwimmen^N｜natation^F｜natación^F｜nuoto^M

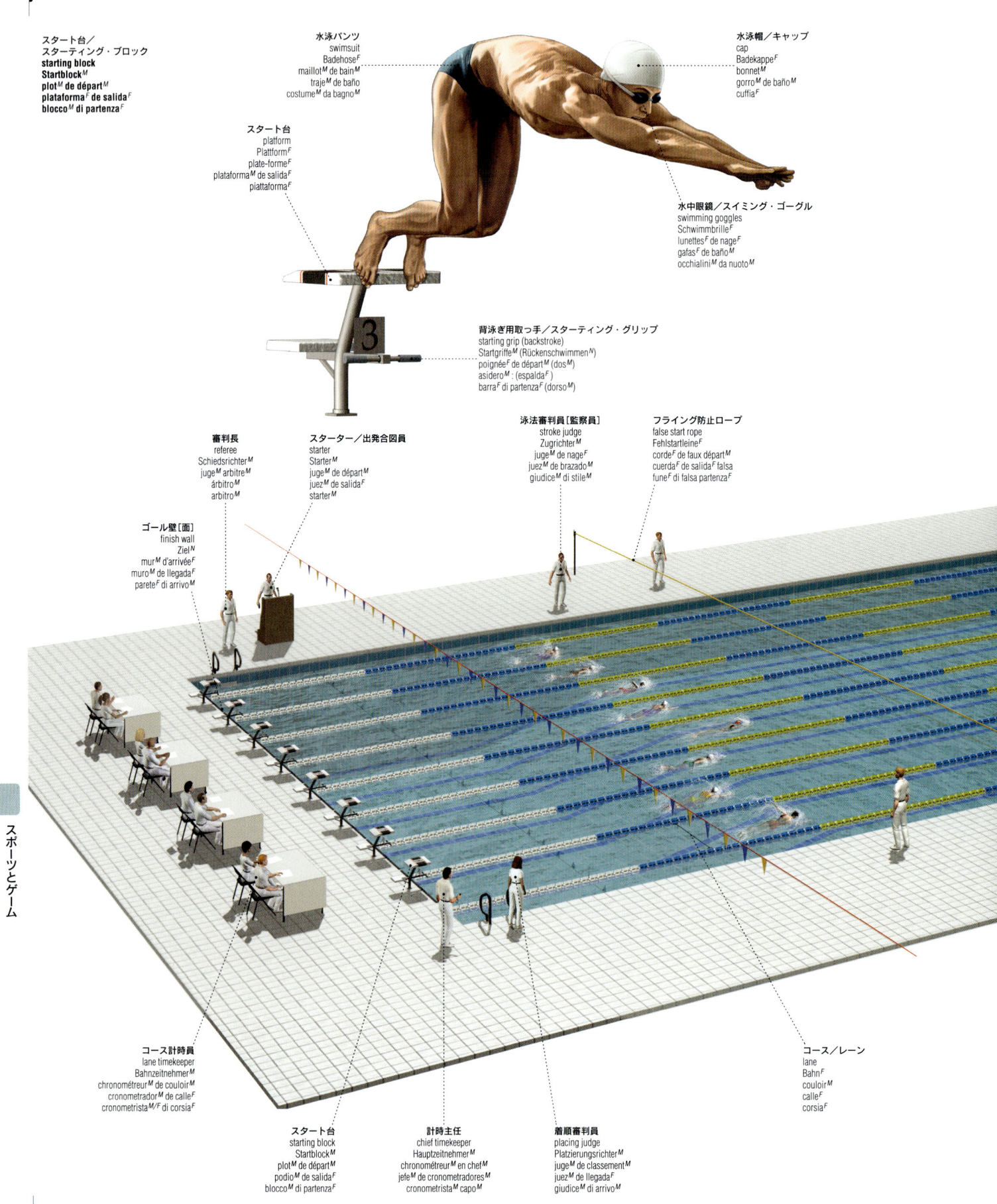

スタート台／
スターティング・ブロック
starting block
Startblock^M
plot^M de départ^M
plataforma^F de salida^F
blocco^M di partenza^F

水泳パンツ
swimsuit
Badehose^F
maillot^M de bain^M
traje^M de baño^M
costume^M da bagno^M

水泳帽／キャップ
cap
Badekappe^F
bonnet^M
gorro^M de baño^M
cuffia^F

スタート台
platform
Plattform^F
plate-forme^F
plataforma^F de salida^F
piattaforma^F

水中眼鏡／スイミング・ゴーグル
swimming goggles
Schwimmbrille^F
lunettes^F de nage^F
gafas^F de baño^M
occhialini^M da nuoto^M

背泳ぎ用取っ手／スターティング・グリップ
starting grip (backstroke)
Startgriffe^M (Rückenschwimmen^N)
poignée^F de départ^M (dos^M)
asidero^M : (espalda^F)
barra^F di partenza^F (dorso^M)

審判長
referee
Schiedsrichter^M
juge^M arbitre^M
árbitro^M
arbitro^M

スターター／出発合図員
starter
Starter^M
juge^M de départ^M
juez^M de salida^F
starter^M

泳法審判員[監察員]
stroke judge
Zugrichter^M
juge^M de nage^F
juez^M de brazado^M
giudice^M di stile^M

フライング防止ロープ
false start rope
Fehlstartleine^F
corde^F de faux départ^M
cuerda^F de salida^F falsa
fune^F di falsa partenza^F

ゴール壁[面]
finish wall
Ziel^N
mur^M d'arrivée^F
muro^M de llegada^F
parete^F di arrivo^M

コース計時員
lane timekeeper
Bahnzeitnehmer^M
chronométreur^M de couloir^M
cronometrador^M de calle^F
cronometrista$^{M/F}$ di corsia^F

コース／レーン
lane
Bahn^F
couloir^M
calle^F
corsia^F

スタート台
starting block
Startblock^M
plot^M de départ^M
podio^M de salida^F
blocco^M di partenza^F

計時主任
chief timekeeper
Hauptzeitnehmer^M
chronométreur^M en chef^M
jefe^M de cronometradores^M
cronometrista^M capo^M

着順審判員
placing judge
Platzierungsrichter^M
juge^M de classement^M
juez^M de llegada^F
giudice^M di arrivo^M

スポーツとゲーム

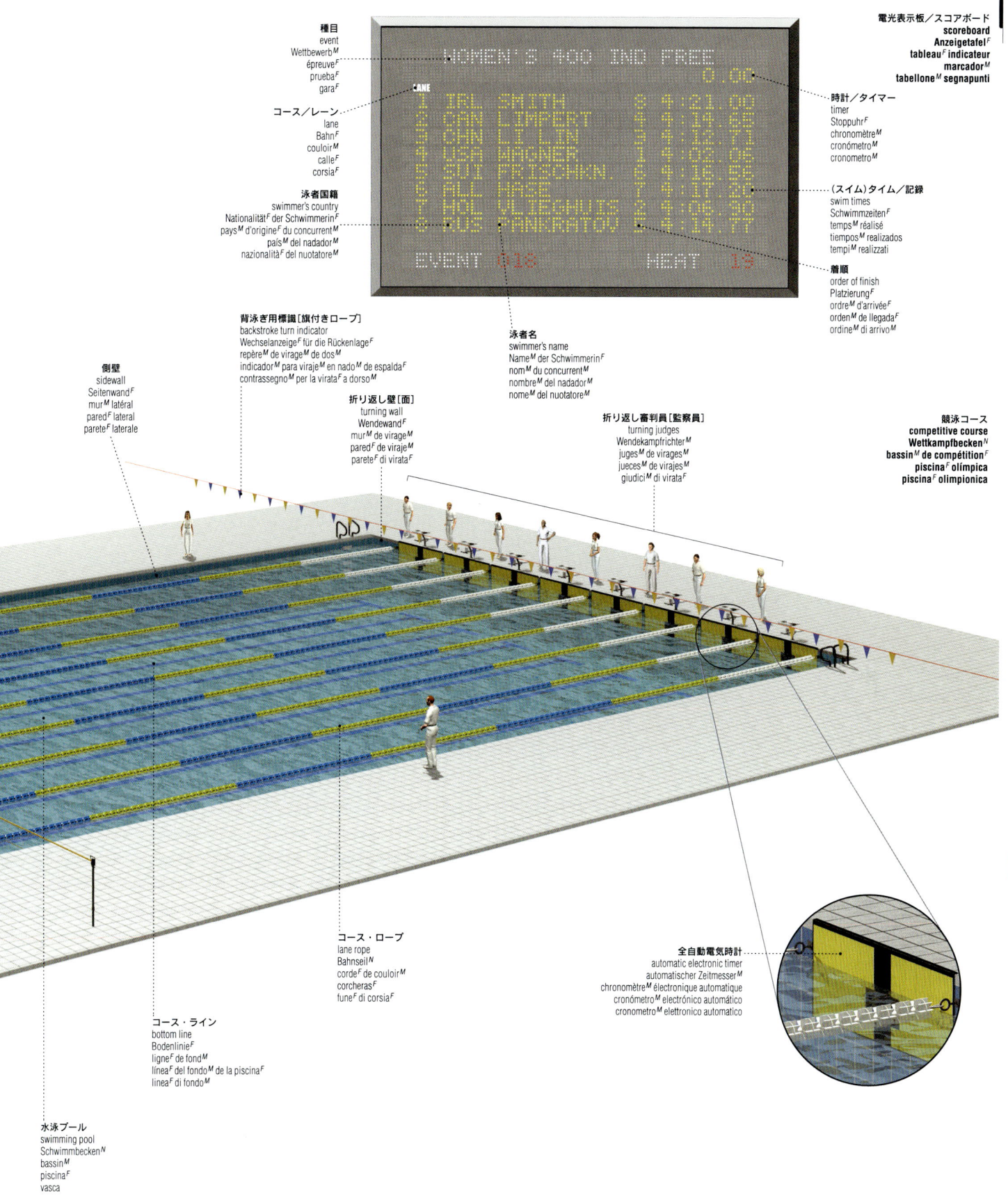

水上・水中スポーツと海上スポーツ | AQUATIC AND NAUTICAL SPORTS
WASSERSPORT | SPORTS AQUATIQUES ET NAUTIQUES | DEPORTES ACUÁTICOS Y NÁUTICOS | SPORT ACQUATICI E NAUTICI

水泳

種目
event
Wettbewerb^M
épreuve^F
prueba^F
gara^F

コース／レーン
lane
Bahn^F
couloir^M
calle^F
corsia^F

泳者国籍
swimmer's country
Nationalität^F der Schwimmerin^F
pays^M d'origine^F du concurrent^M
país^M del nadador^M
nazionalità^F del nuotatore^M

電光表示板／スコアボード
scoreboard
Anzeigetafel^F
tableau^F indicateur
marcador^M
tabellone^M segnapunti

時計／タイマー
timer
Stoppuhr^F
chronomètre^M
cronómetro^M
cronometro^M

（スイム）タイム／記録
swim times
Schwimmzeiten^F
temps^M réalisé
tiempos^M realizados
tempi^M realizzati

着順
order of finish
Platzierung^F
ordre^M d'arrivée^F
orden^M de llegada^F
ordine^M di arrivo^M

背泳ぎ用標識［旗付きロープ］
backstroke turn indicator
Wechselanzeige^F für die Rückenlage^F
repère^F de virage^M de dos^M
indicador^M para viraje en nado^M de espalda^F
contrassegno^M per la virata^F a dorso^M

側壁
sidewall
Seitenwand^F
mur^M latéral
pared^F lateral
parete^F laterale

折り返し壁［面］
turning wall
Wendewand^F
mur^M de virage^M
pared^F de viraje^M
parete^F di virata^F

泳者名
swimmer's name
Name^M der Schwimmerin^F
nom^M du concurrent^M
nombre^M del nadador^M
nome^M del nuotatore^M

折り返し審判員［監察員］
turning judges
Wendekampfrichter^M
juges^M de virages^M
jueces^M de virajes^M
giudici^M di virata^F

競泳コース
competitive course
Wettkampfbecken^N
bassin^M de compétition^F
piscina^F olímpica
piscina^F olimpionica

コース・ロープ
lane rope
Bahnseil^N
corde^F de couloir^M
corcheras^F
fune^F di corsia^F

コース・ライン
bottom line
Bodenlinie^F
ligne^F de fond^M
línea^F del fondo^M de la piscina^F
linea^F di fondo^M

全自動電気時計
automatic electronic timer
automatischer Zeitmesser^M
chronomètre^M électronique automatique
cronómetro^M electrónico automático
cronometro^M elettronico automatico

水泳プール
swimming pool
Schwimmbecken^N
bassin^M
piscine^F
vasca

スポーツとゲーム

831

水上・水中スポーツと海上スポーツ | AQUATIC AND NAUTICAL SPORTS
WASSERSPORT | SPORTS AQUATIQUES ET NAUTIQUES | DEPORTES ACUÁTICOS Y NÁUTICOS | SPORT ACQUATICI E NAUTICI

水泳

日本語 | 英語 | ドイツ語 | フランス語 | スペイン語 | イタリア語

泳法[ストローク]の種類
types of strokes
verschiedene Schwimmstile^M
types^M de nages^F
estilos^M de natación^F
stili^M di nuoto^M

クロール
front crawl stroke
Kraulen^N
crawl^M
crol^M
stile^M libero o crawl^M

吸気
breathing in
Einatmen^N
inspiration^F
inhalación^F
inspirazione^F

スタート飛び込み
starting dive
Startsprung^M
plongeon^M de départ^M
salto^M de salida^M
tuffo^M di partenza^F

呼気
breathing out
Ausatmen^N
expiration^F
exhalación^F
espirazione^F

折り返し壁[面]
turning wall
Wendewand^F
mur^M de virage^M
pared^F de viraje^M
parete^F di virata^F

クロールのキック
crawl kick
Beinarbeit^F beim Kraulen^N
coup^M de pied^M de crawl^M
patada^F de crol^M
colpo^M di gamba^F a crawl^M

クイック[フリップ]ターン
flip turn
Wende^F
virage^M-culbute^F
vuelta^F de campana^F
virata^F a capriola^F

平泳ぎ
breaststroke
Brustschwimmen^N
brasse^F
braza^F
rana^F

平泳ぎのキック
breaststroke kick
Beinarbeit^F beim Brustschwimmen^N
coup^M de pied^M de brasse^F
patada^F de rana^F
colpo^M di gamba^F a rana^F

タッチ[水平]ターン
breaststroke turn
Wende^F beim Brustschwimmen^N
virage^M de brasse^F
toque^M con dos manos^F
virata^F a rana^F

バタフライ
butterfly stroke
Schmetterlingsstil^M
papillon^M
mariposa
farfalla^F

バタフライのキック
butterfly kick
Beinarbeit^F beim Schmetterlingsstil^M
coup^M de pied^M de papillon^M
patada^F de mariposa^F
colpo^M di gamba^F a farfalla^F

タッチ[水平]ターン
butterfly turn
Wende^F beim Schmetterlingsstil^M
virage^M de papillon^M
viraje^M de mariposa^F
virata^F a farfalla

背泳ぎ
backstroke
Rückenschwimmen^N
nage^F sur le dos^M
espalda
dorso^M

背泳ぎのスタート
backstroke start
Start^M beim Rückenschwimmen^N
départ^M de dos^M
posición^F de salida^F de espalda^F
partenza^F a dorso^M

クイック[フリップ]ターン
flip turn
Wende^F
virage^M-culbute^F
vuelta^F de campana^F
virata^F a capriola^F

AQUATIC AND NAUTICAL SPORTS
WASSERSPORT | SPORTS AQUATIQUES ET NAUTIQUES | DEPORTES ACUÁTICOS Y NÁUTICOS | SPORT ACQUATICI E NAUTICI

セーリング

sailing | Segelsport[M] | voile[F] | vela[F] | vela[F]

風向
wind
Wind[M]
vent[M]
viento[M]
vento[M]

風に対する帆走方向
points of sailing
Kurse[M]
allures[F]
disposiciones[F] de las velas[F]
andature[F] delle imbarcazioni[F] a vela[F]

詰め開きで
on the wind
am Wind[M]
près[M]
viento[M] contrario
di bolina[F]

詰め開きで
on the wind
am Wind[M]
près[M]
vela[F] flameante
di bolina[F]

ビーム・リーチ
beam reach
Wind[M] querab
largue[M]
orzada[F]
al lasco[M]

ビーム・リーチ
beam reach
Wind[M] querab
largue[M]
orzada[F]
al lasco[M]

全帆いっぱいに風をはらみ詰め開きで
full and by
voll und bei
près[M] bon plein[M]
a buen viento[M]
di bolina[F]

ビーム・リーチ
beam reach
Wind[M] querab
largue[M]
por lo ancho[M]
al lasco[M]

詰め開きで
on the wind
am Wind[M]
près[M]
vela[F] flameante
di bolina[F] stretta

風上
headwind
Boot[N] ohne Fahrt[F]
vent[M] debout
viento[M] en proa[F]
prua[F] al vento[M]

クローズ・リーチ
close reach
Segeln[N] mit halbem Wind[M]
petit largue[M]
ciñendo el viento[M]
di bolina[F] larga

ブロード・リーチ
broad reach
raumer Wind[M]
grand largue[M]
a un largo[M]
al gran lasco[M]

クローズ・ホールド
close hauled
hart am Wind[M]
près[M] serré
bolina[F]
di bolina[F] molto stretta

ランニング
down wind
mit dem Wind[M]
vent[M] arrière
viento[M] en popa[F]
in poppa[F]

ウインド・アビーム
wind abeam
halber Wind[M]
vent[M] de travers[M]
viento[M] de través[M]
al traverso[M]

コース
course
Kurs[M]
parcours[M]
carrera[F]
percorso[M]

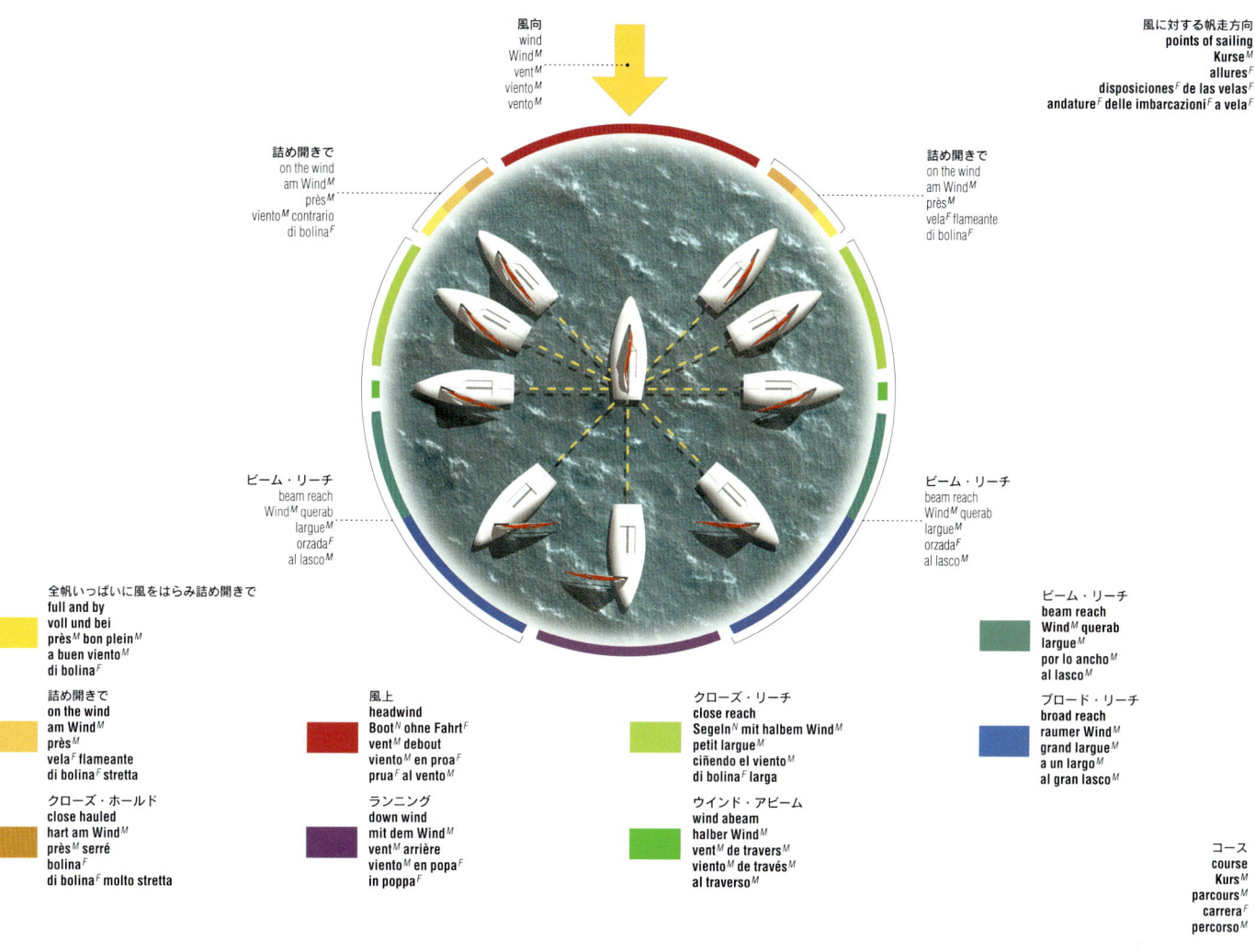

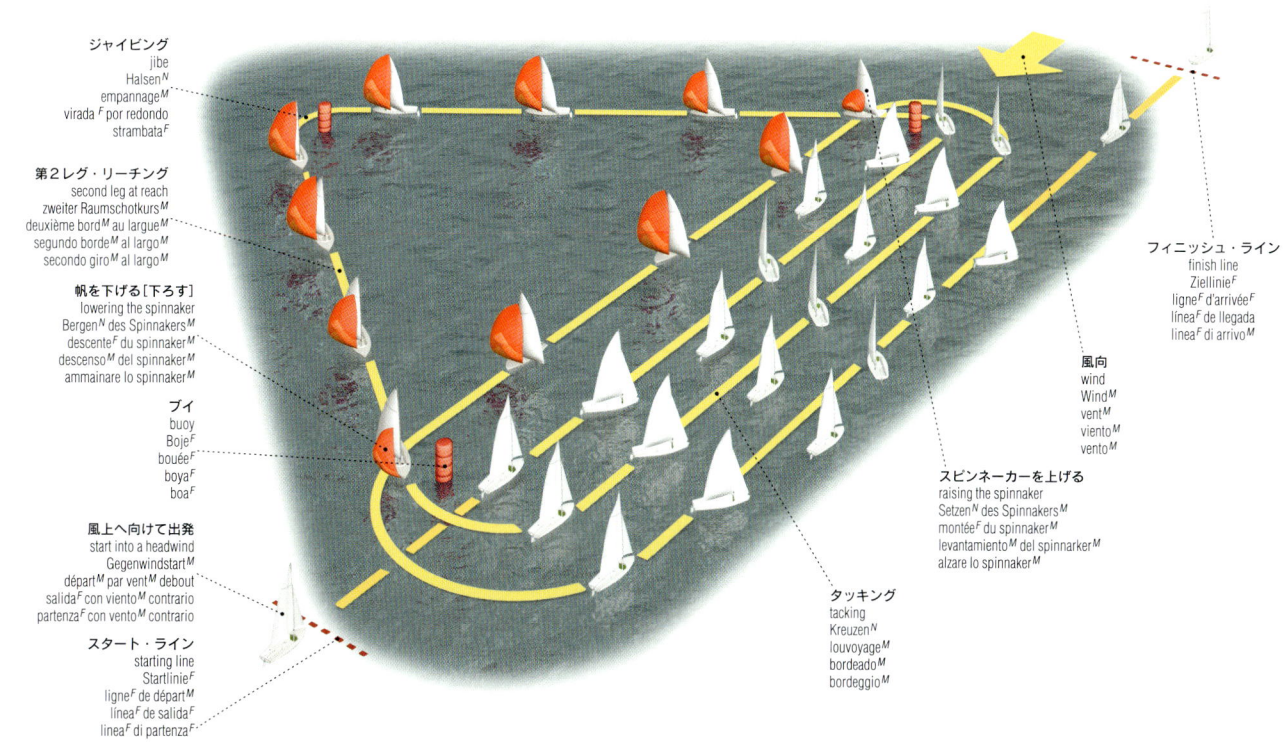

ジャイビング
jibe
Halsen[N]
empannage[M]
virada[F] por redondo
strambata[F]

第2レグ・リーチング
second leg at reach
zweiter Raumschotkurs[M]
deuxième bord[M] au largue[M]
segundo borde[M] al largo[M]
secondo giro[M] al largo[M]

帆を下げる[下ろす]
lowering the spinnaker
Bergen[N] des Spinnakers[M]
descente[F] du spinnaker[M]
descenso[M] del spinnaker[M]
ammainare lo spinnaker[M]

ブイ
buoy
Boje[F]
bouée[F]
boya[F]
boa[F]

風上へ向けて出発
start into a headwind
Gegenwindstart[M]
départ[M] par vent[M] debout
salida[F] con viento[M] contrario
partenza[F] con vento[M] contrario

スタート・ライン
starting line
Startlinie[F]
ligne[F] de départ[M]
línea[F] de salida[F]
linea[F] di partenza[F]

フィニッシュ・ライン
finish line
Ziellinie[F]
ligne[F] d'arrivée[F]
línea[F] de llegada
linea[F] di arrivo[M]

風向
wind
Wind[M]
vent[M]
viento[M]
vento[M]

スピンネーカーを上げる
raising the spinnaker
Setzen[N] des Spinnakers[M]
montée[F] du spinnaker[M]
levantamiento[M] del spinnaker[M]
alzare lo spinnaker[M]

タッキング
tacking
Kreuzen[N]
louvoyage[M]
bordeado[M]
bordeggio[M]

スポーツとゲーム

833

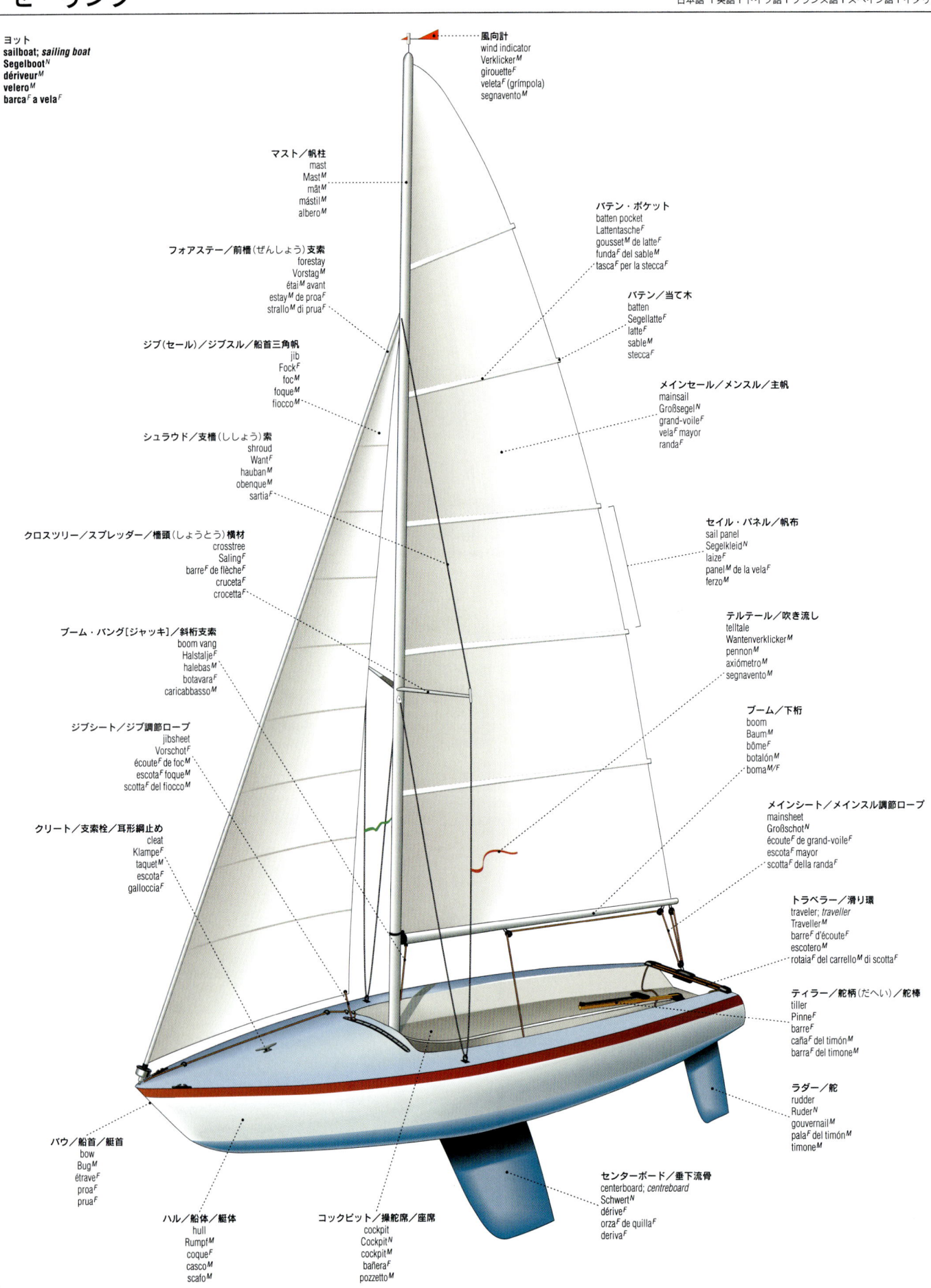

水上・水中スポーツと海上スポーツ | AQUATIC AND NAUTICAL SPORTS
WASSERSPORT | SPORTS AQUATIQUES ET NAUTIQUES | DEPORTES ACUÁTICOS Y NÁUTICOS | SPORT ACQUATICI E NAUTICI

セーリング

日本語 | 英語 | ドイツ語 | フランス語 | スペイン語 | イタリア語

ヨット
sailboat; *sailing boat*
Segelboot[N]
dériveur[M]
velero[M]
barca[F] **a vela**[F]

風向計
wind indicator
Verklicker[M]
girouette[F]
veleta[F] (grímpola)
segnavento[M]

マスト／帆柱
mast
Mast[M]
mât[M]
mástil[M]
albero[M]

バテン・ポケット
batten pocket
Lattentasche[F]
gousset[M] de latte[F]
funda[F] del sable
tasca[F] per la stecca[F]

フォアステー／前檣（ぜんしょう）支索
forestay
Vorstag[M]
étai[M] avant
estay[M] de proa[F]
strallo[M] di prua[F]

バテン／当て木
batten
Segellatte[F]
latte[F]
sable[M]
stecca[F]

ジブ（セール）／ジブスル／船首三角帆
jib
Fock[F]
foc[M]
foque[M]
fiocco[M]

メインセール／メンスル／主帆
mainsail
Großsegel[N]
grand-voile[F]
vela[F] mayor
randa[F]

シュラウド／支檣（ししょう）索
shroud
Want[F]
hauban[M]
obenque[M]
sartia[F]

セイル・パネル／帆布
sail panel
Segelkleid[N]
laize[F]
panel[M] de la vela[F]
ferzo[M]

クロスツリー／スプレッダー／檣頭（しょうとう）横材
crosstree
Saling[F]
barre[F] de flèche[F]
cruceta[F]
crocetta[F]

テルテール／吹き流し
telltale
Wantenverklicker[M]
pennon[M]
axiómetro[M]
segnavento[M]

ブーム・バング[ジャッキ]／斜桁支索
boom vang
Halstalje[F]
halebas[M]
botavara[F]
caricabbasso[M]

ブーム／下桁
boom
Baum[M]
bôme[F]
botalón[M]
boma[M/F]

ジブシート／ジブ調節ロープ
jibsheet
Vorschot[F]
écoute[F] de foc[M]
escota[F] foque[M]
scotta[F] del fiocco[M]

メインシート／メインスル調節ロープ
mainsheet
Großschot[N]
écoute[F] de grand-voile[F]
escota[F] mayor
scotta[F] della randa[F]

クリート／支索栓／耳形綱止め
cleat
Klampe[F]
taquet[M]
escota[F]
galloccia[F]

トラベラー／滑り環
traveler; *traveller*
Traveller
barre[F] d'écoute[F]
escotero[M]
rotaia[F] del carrello[M] di scotta[F]

ティラー／舵柄（だへい）／舵棒
tiller
Pinne[F]
barre[F]
caña[F] del timón[M]
barra[F] del timone[M]

ラダー／舵
rudder
Ruder[N]
gouvernail[M]
pala[F] del timón[M]
timone[M]

バウ／船首／艇首
bow
Bug[M]
étrave[F]
proa[F]
prua[F]

センターボード／垂下流骨
centerboard; *centreboard*
Schwert[N]
dérive[F]
orza[F] de quilla[F]
deriva[F]

ハル／船体／艇体
hull
Rumpf[M]
coque[F]
casco[M]
scafo[M]

コックピット／操舵席／座席
cockpit
Cockpit[N]
cockpit[M]
bañera[F]
pozzetto[M]

スポーツとゲーム

834

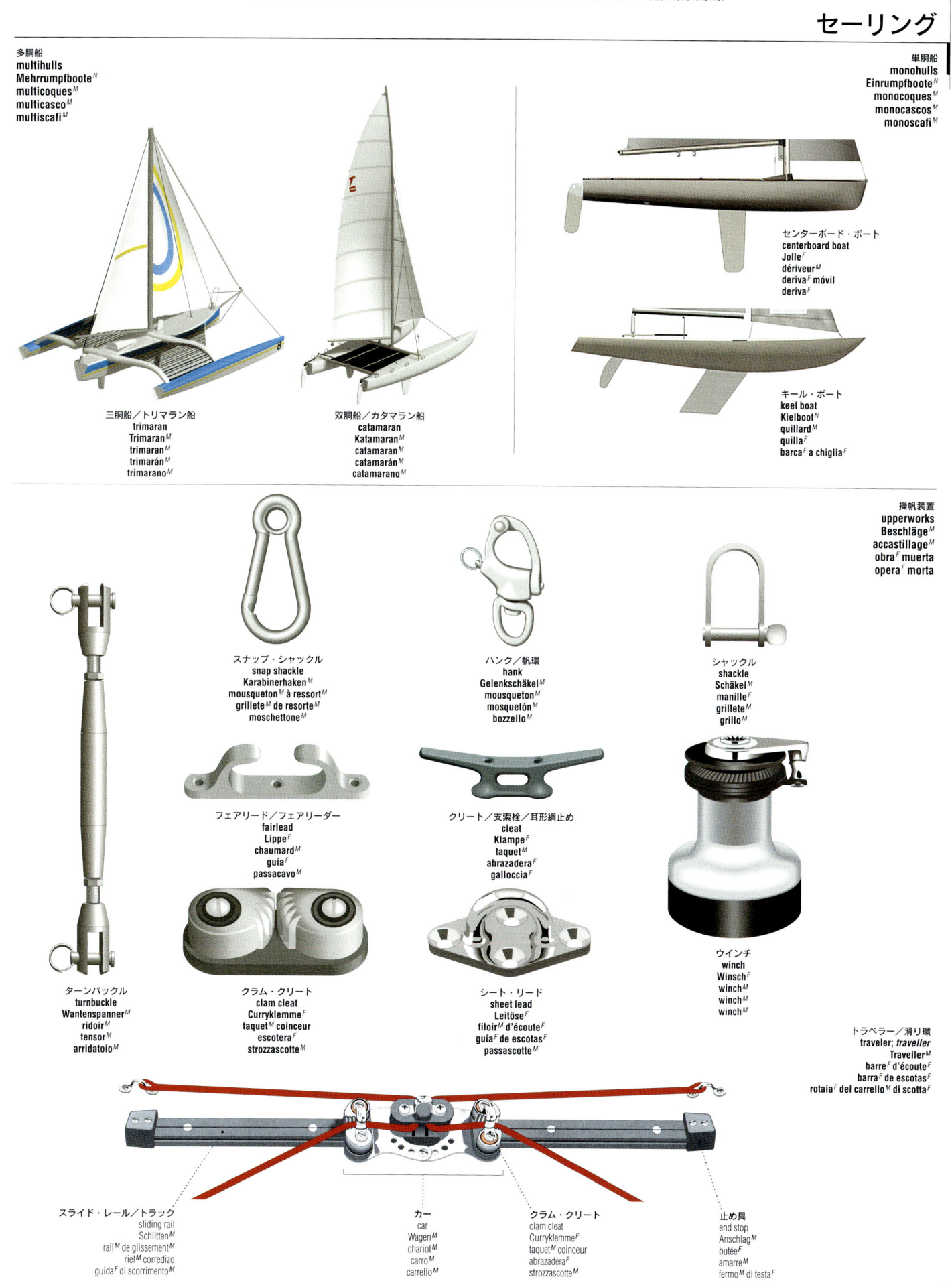

水上・水中スポーツと海上スポーツ | AQUATIC AND NAUTICAL SPORTS
WASSERSPORT | SPORTS AQUATIQUES ET NAUTIQUES | DEPORTES ACUÁTICOS Y NÁUTICOS | SPORT ACQUATICI E NAUTICI

セーリング

多胴船
multihulls
Mehrrumpfboote[N]
multicoques[M]
multicasco[M]
multiscafi[M]

単胴船
monohulls
Einrumpfboote[N]
monocoques[M]
monocascos[M]
monoscafi[M]

センターボード・ボート
centerboard boat
Jolle[F]
dériveur[M]
deriva[F] móvil
deriva[F]

三胴船／トリマラン船
trimaran
Trimaran[M]
trimaran[M]
trimarán[M]
trimarano[M]

双胴船／カタマラン船
catamaran
Katamaran[M]
catamaran[M]
catamarán[M]
catamarano[M]

キール・ボート
keel boat
Kielboot[N]
quillard[M]
quilla[F]
barca[F] a chiglia[F]

操帆装置
upperworks
Beschläge[M]
accastillage[M]
obra[F] muerta
opera[F] morta

スナップ・シャックル
snap shackle
Karabinerhaken[M]
mousqueton[M] à ressort[M]
grillete[M] de resorte[M]
moschettone[M]

ハンク／帆環
hank
Gelenkschäkel[M]
mousqueton[M]
mosquetón[M]
bozzello[M]

シャックル
shackle
Schäkel[M]
manille[F]
grillete[M]
grillo[M]

フェアリード／フェアリーダー
fairlead
Lippe[F]
chaumard[M]
guía[F]
passacavo[M]

クリート／支索栓／耳形綱止め
cleat
Klampe[F]
taquet[M]
abrazadera[F]
galloccia[F]

ターンバックル
turnbuckle
Wantenspanner[M]
ridoir[M]
tensor[M]
arridatoio[M]

クラム・クリート
clam cleat
Curryklemme[F]
taquet[M] coinceur
escotera[F]
strozzascotte[M]

シート・リード
sheet lead
Leitöse[F]
filoir[M] d'écoute[F]
guía[F] de escotas[F]
passascotte[M]

ウインチ
winch
Winsch[F]
winch[M]
winch[M]
winch[M]

トラベラー／滑り環
traveler; *traveller*
Traveller[M]
barre[F] d'écoute[F]
barra[F] de escotas[F]
rotaia[F] del carrello[M] di scotta[F]

スライド・レール／トラック
sliding rail
Schlitten[M]
rail[M] de glissement[M]
riel[M] corredizo
guida[F] di scorrimento[M]

カー
car
Wagen[M]
chariot[M]
carro[M]
carrello[M]

クラム・クリート
clam cleat
Curryklemme[F]
taquet[M] coinceur
abrazadera[F]
strozzascotte[M]

止め具
end stop
Anschlag[M]
butée[F]
amarre[M]
fermo[M] di testa[F]

水上・水中スポーツと海上スポーツ | AQUATIC AND NAUTICAL SPORTS
WASSERSPORT | SPORTS AQUATIQUES ET NAUTIQUES | DEPORTES ACUÁTICOS Y NÁUTICOS | SPORT ACQUATICI E NAUTICI

ウインドサーフィン

日本語 | 英語 | ドイツ語 | フランス語 | スペイン語 | イタリア語

sailboard | Surfbrett[N] | planche[F] à voile[F] | windsurf | windsurf[M]

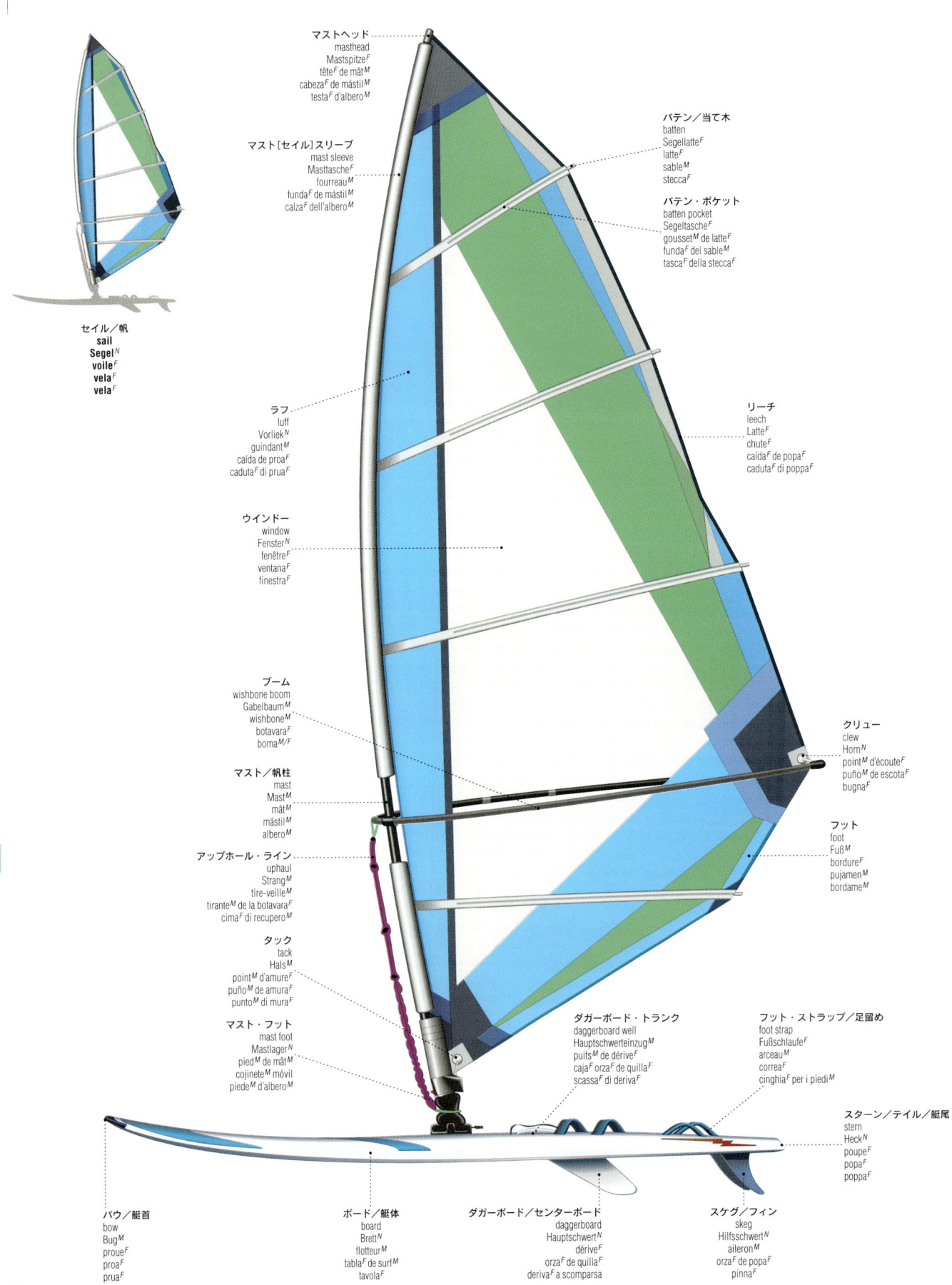

セイル／帆
sail
Segel[N]
voile[F]
vela[F]
vela[F]

マストヘッド
masthead
Mastspitze[F]
tête[F] de mât[M]
cabeza[F] de mástil[M]
testa[F] d'albero[M]

マスト[セイル]スリーブ
mast sleeve
Masttasche[F]
fourreau[M]
funda[F] de mástil[M]
calza[F] dell'albero[M]

バテン／当て木
batten
Segellatte[F]
latte[F]
sable[M]
stecca[F]

バテン・ポケット
batten pocket
Segeltasche[F]
gousset[M] de latte[F]
funda[F] del sable[M]
tasca[F] della stecca[F]

ラフ
luff
Vorliek[N]
guindant[M]
caída de proa[F]
caduta[F] di prua[F]

リーチ
leech
Latte[F]
chute[F]
caída[F] de popa[F]
caduta[F] di poppa[F]

ウインドー
window
Fenster[N]
fenêtre[F]
ventana[F]
finestra[F]

ブーム
wishbone boom
Gabelbaum[M]
wishbone[M]
botavara[F]
boma[M/F]

クリュー
clew
Horn[N]
point[M] d'écoute[F]
puño[M] de escota[F]
bugna[F]

マスト／帆柱
mast
Mast[M]
mât[M]
mástil[M]
albero[M]

フット
foot
Fuß[M]
bordure[F]
pujamen[M]
bordame[M]

アップホール・ライン
uphaul
Strang[M]
tire-veille[F]
tirante[M] de la botavara[F]
cima[F] di recupero[M]

タック
tack
Hals[M]
point[M] d'amure[F]
puño[M] de amura[F]
punto[M] di mura[F]

マスト・フット
mast foot
Mastlager[N]
pied[M] de mât[M]
cojinete[M] móvil
piede[M] d'albero[M]

ダガーボード・トランク
daggerboard well
Hauptschwerteinzug[M]
puits[M] de dérive[F]
caja[F] orza[F] de quilla[F]
scassa[F] di deriva[F]

フット・ストラップ／足留め
foot strap
Fußschlaufe[F]
arceau[M]
correa[F]
cinghia[F] per i piedi[M]

スターン／テイル／艇尾
stern
Heck[N]
poupe[F]
popa[F]
poppa[F]

バウ／艇首
bow
Bug[M]
proue[F]
proa[F]
prua[F]

ボード／艇体
board
Brett[N]
flotteur[M]
tabla[F] de surf[M]
tavola[F]

ダガーボード／センターボード
daggerboard
Hauptschwert[N]
dérive[F]
orza[F] de quilla[F]
deriva[F] a scomparsa

スケグ／フィン
skeg
Hilfsschwert[N]
aileron[M]
orza[F] de popa[F]
pinna[F]

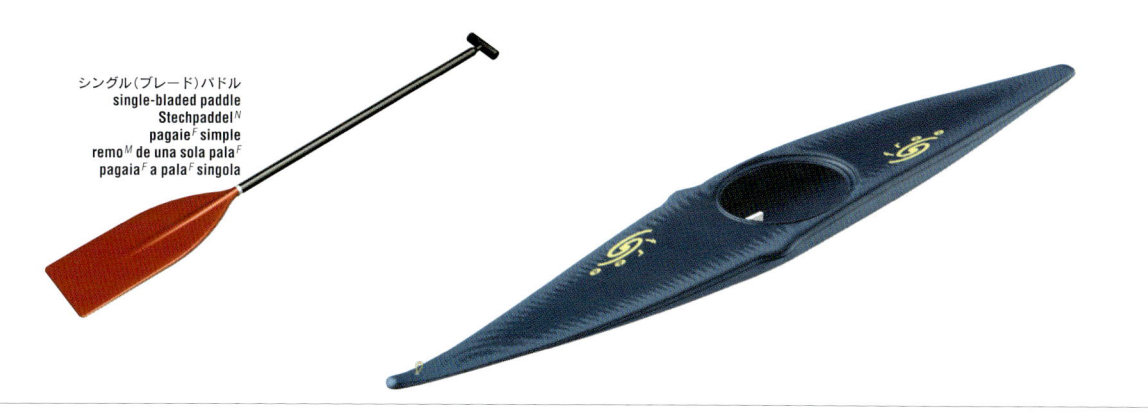

水上・水中スポーツと海上スポーツ | AQUATIC AND NAUTICAL SPORTS
WASSERSPORT | SPORTS AQUATIQUES ET NAUTIQUES | DEPORTES ACUÁTICOS Y NÁUTICOS | SPORT ACQUATICI E NAUTICI

カヌー・カヤック：激流

canoe-kayak: whitewater | Kanu[N]-Kajak[M/N]: Wildwasser[N] | canoë[M]-kayak[M]: eaux[F] vives | canoa[F]-kayak[M]: aguas[F] bravas | canoa[F] e kayak[M]: rapide[F]

カヌー
canoe
Kanu[N]
canoë[M]
canoa[F]
canoa[F]

シングル（ブレード）パドル
single-bladed paddle
Stechpaddel[N]
pagaie[F] simple
remo[M] de una sola pala[F]
pagaia[F] a pala[F] singola

カヤック
kayak
Kajak[M/N]
kayak[M]
kayak[M]
kayak[M]

ダブル（ブレード）パドル
double-bladed paddle
Doppelpaddel[N]
pagaie[F] double
remo[M] de dos palas[F]
pagaia[F] a doppia pala[F]

スプレー・スカート
spray skirt
Spritzschutz[M]
jupe[F]
cubrebañeras[M]
paraspruzzi[M]

上流ゲート
upstream gate
Aufwärtstor[N]
porte[F] en remontée[F]
puerta[F] de ascenso[M]
porta[F] in risalita[F]

ゲート審判員
gate judge
Streckenschiedsrichter[M]
juge[M] de porte[F]
juez[M] de puerta[M]
giudice[M] di partenza[F]

激流
whitewater
Wildwasser[N]
eaux[F] vives
aguas[F] bravas
rapide[F]

主審
chief judge
Hauptschiedsrichter[M]
juge[M] en chef[M]
árbitro[M] principal
giudice[M] principale

コース・ゲート
course gate
Richtungstor[N]
porte[F] du parcours[M]
puerta[F] de recorrido[M]
porta[F]

下流ゲート
downstream gate
Abwärtstor[N]
porte[F] en descente[F]
puerta[F] de descenso[M]
porta[F] in discesa[F]

安全監察員
safety officer
Rettungswart[M]
responsable[F] de la sécurité[F]
personal[M] de la seguridad[F]
responsabile[M] della sicurezza[F]

837

水上・水中スポーツと海上スポーツ | AQUATIC AND NAUTICAL SPORTS
WASSERSPORT | SPORTS AQUATIQUES ET NAUTIQUES | DEPORTES ACUÁTICOS Y NÁUTICOS | SPORT ACQUATICI E NAUTICI

ローイング［漕ぐこと］とスカーリング［幅寄せ］

日本語｜英語｜ドイツ語｜フランス語｜スペイン語｜イタリア語

rowing and sculling | Rudern^N und Skullen^N | aviron^M | remo^M | canottaggio^M con uno e due remi^M

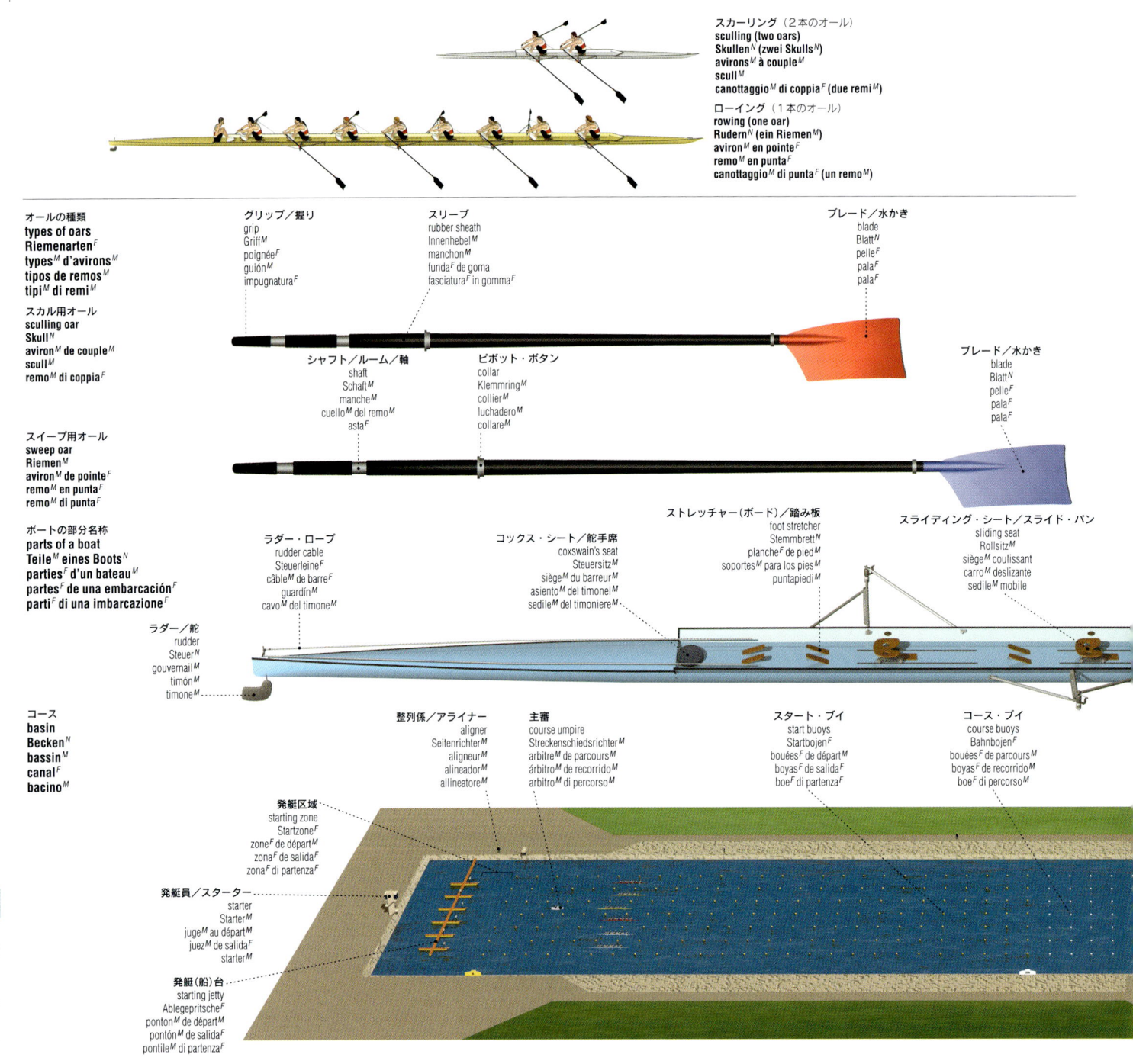

スカーリング（2本のオール）
sculling (two oars)
Skullen^N (zwei Skulls^N)
avirons^M à couple^M
scull^M
canottaggio^M di coppia^F (due remi^M)

ローイング（1本のオール）
rowing (one oar)
Rudern^N (ein Riemen^M)
aviron^M en pointe^F
remo^M en punta^F
canottaggio^M di punta^F (un remo^M)

オールの種類
types of oars
Riemenarten^F
types^M d'avirons^M
tipos de remos^M
tipi^M di remi^M

グリップ／握り
grip
Griff^M
poignée^F
guión^M
impugnatura^F

スリーブ
rubber sheath
Innenhebel^M
manchon^M
funda^F de goma
fasciatura^F in gomma^F

ブレード／水かき
blade
Blatt^N
pelle^F
pala^F
pala^F

スカル用オール
sculling oar
Skull^N
aviron^M de couple^M
scull^M
remo^M di coppia^F

シャフト／ルーム／軸
shaft
Schaft^M
manche^M
cuello^M del remo^M
asta^F

ピボット・ボタン
collar
Klemmring^M
collier^M
luchadero^M
collare^M

ブレード／水かき
blade
Blatt^N
pelle^F
pala^F
pala^F

スイープ用オール
sweep oar
Riemen^M
aviron^M de pointe^F
remo^M en punta^F
remo^M di punta^F

ボートの部分名称
parts of a boat
Teile^M eines Boots^N
parties^F d'un bateau^M
partes^F de una embarcación^F
parti^F di una imbarcazione^F

ラダー・ロープ
rudder cable
Steuerleine^F
câble^M de barre^F
guardín^M
cavo^M del timone^M

コックス・シート／舵手席
coxswain's seat
Steuersitz^M
siège^M du barreur^M
asiento^M del timonel^M
sedile^M del timoniere^M

ストレッチャー（ボード）／踏み板
foot stretcher
Stemmbrett^N
planche^F de pied^M
soportes^F para los pies^M
puntapiedi^M

スライディング・シート／スライド・パン
sliding seat
Rollsitz^M
siège^M coulissant
carro^M deslizante
sedile^M mobile

ラダー／舵
rudder
Steuer^N
gouvernail^M
timón^M
timone^M

コース
basin
Becken^N
bassin^M
canal^F
bacino^M

整列係／アライナー
aligner
Seitenrichter^M
aligneur^M
alineador^M
allineatore^M

主審
course umpire
Streckenschiedsrichter^M
arbitre^M de parcours^M
árbitro^M de recorrido^M
arbitro^M di percorso^M

スタート・ブイ
start buoys
Startbojen^F
bouées^F de départ^M
boyas^F de salida^F
boe^F di partenza^F

コース・ブイ
course buoys
Bahnbojen^F
bouées^F de parcours^M
boyas^F de recorrido^M
boe^F di percorso^F

発艇区域
starting zone
Startzone^F
zone^F de départ^M
zona^F de salida^F
zona^F di partenza^F

発艇員／スターター
starter
Starter^M
juge^M au départ^M
juez^M de salida^F
starter^M

発艇（船）台
starting jetty
Ablegpritsche^F
ponton^M de départ^M
pontón^M de salida^F
pontile^M di partenza^F

カヌー・カヤック：静水競漕

canoe-kayak: flatwater racing | Kanu^N-Kajak$^{M/N}$: Flachwasserrennen^N | canoë^M-kayak^M : course^F en ligne^F | canoa^F-kayak^M : regata^F | canoa^F e kayak^M: regate^F fluviali

一人乗りカヌー
C1 canoe
Einerkanadier^M (C1)
canoë^M monoplace (C1)
canoa^F C1
canoa^F monoposto (C1)

デッキ／甲板
deck
Deck^N
pontage^M
cubierta^F
capote^F

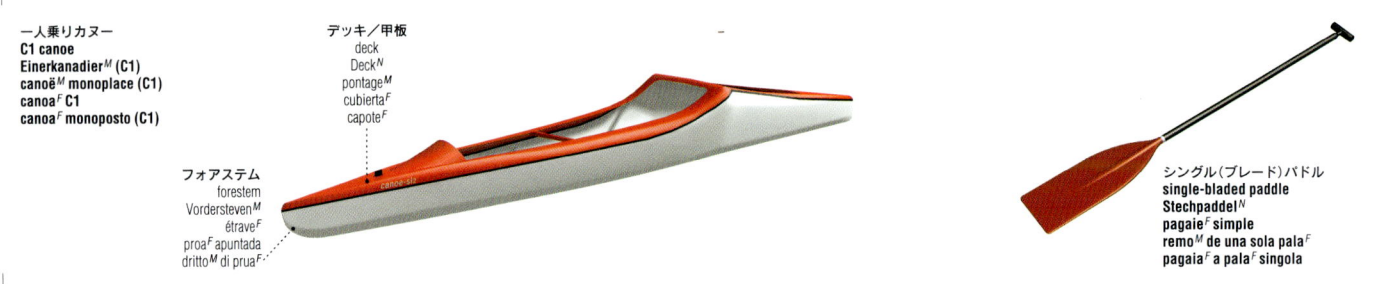

フォアステム
forestem
Vordersteven^M
étrave^F
proa^F apuntada^F
dritto^M di prua^F

シングル（ブレード）パドル
single-bladed paddle
Stechpaddel^N
pagaie^F simple
remo^M de una sola pala^F
pagaia^F a pala^F singola

水上・水中スポーツと海上スポーツ | AQUATIC AND NAUTICAL SPORTS
WASSERSPORT | SPORTS AQUATIQUES ET NAUTIQUES | DEPORTES ACUÁTICOS Y NÁUTICOS | SPORT ACQUATICI E NAUTICI

ローイング[漕ぐこと]とスカーリング[幅寄せ]

スカル・ボート
sculling boats
Ruderboote^N
bateaux^M de couple^M
skiff^M
imbarcazioni^F di coppia^F

シングル・スカル
single scull
Einer^M
skiff^M
skiff^M
singolo

ダブル・スカル
coxless double
Zweier^M ohne Steuermann^M
double-scull^M sans barreur^M
doble scull sin timonel^M
due senza^M

ローイング[スイープ]ボート
sweep boats
Riemenboot^N
bateaux^M de pointe^F
embarcaciones^F de punta^M
imbarcazioni^F di punta^F

舵手[コックス]付きペア
coxed pair
Zweier^M mit Steuermann^M
deux avec barreur^M
el dos con timonel^M
due^M con

舵手[コックス]なしペア
coxless pair
Zweier^M ohne Steuermann^M
deux sans barreur^M
el dos
due^M senza

エイト
coxed eight
Achter^M
huit avec barreur^M
ocho con timonel^M
otto^M con

舵手[コックス]付きフォア
coxed four
Vierer^M mit Steuermann^M
quatre avec barreur^M
el cuatro con timonel^M
quattro^M con

舵手[コックス]なしフォア
coxless four
Vierer^M ohne Steuermann^M
quatre sans barreur^M
el cuatro
quattro senza

オール・ロック
oarlock
Dolle^F
dame^F de nage^F
chumacera^F giratoria
scalmo^M

アウトリガー
outrigger
Ausleger^M
portant^M
arbotante^M
fuoriscalmo^M

バウ・ボール
bow ball
Bugball^M
boule^F de protection^F
bola^F de proa^F
palla^F di protezione^F

フィニッシュ・ブイ
finish buoys
Zielbojen^F
bouées^F d'arrivée^F
boyas^F de llegada^F
boe^F di arrivo^M

決勝審判員
finish line judge
Zielrichter^M
juge^M à l'arrivée^F
juez^M de llegada^F
giudice^M di arrivo^M

フィニッシュ・ライン／決勝線
finish line
Ziellinie^F
ligne^F d'arrivée^F
línea^F de llegada^F
linea^F di arrivo^M

浮きドック
floating dock
Anlegepritsche^F
ponton^M
pontón^M
pontile^M galleggiante

スコアボード／着順掲示板
scoreboard
Anzeigetafel^F
tableau^M indicateur
marcador^M
tabellone^M segnapunti

カヌー・カヤック：静水競漕

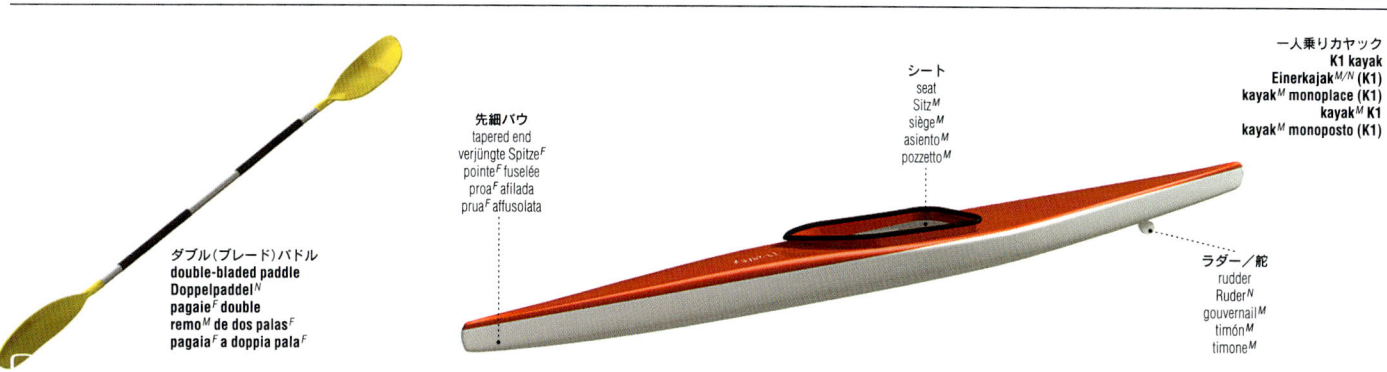

一人乗りカヤック
K1 kayak
Einerkajak^{M/N} (K1)
kayak^M monoplace (K1)
kayak^M K1
kayak^M monoposto (K1)

シート
seat
Sitz^M
siège^M
asiento^M
pozzetto^M

先細バウ
tapered end
verjüngte Spitze^F
pointe^F fuselée
proa^F afilada
prua^F affusolata

ダブル(ブレード)パドル
double-bladed paddle
Doppelpaddel^N
pagaie^F double
remo^M de dos palas^F
pagaia^F a doppia pala^F

ラダー／舵
rudder
Ruder^N
gouvernail^M
timón^M
timone^M

水上・水中スポーツと海上スポーツ ｜ AQUATIC AND NAUTICAL SPORTS
WASSERSPORT ｜ SPORTS AQUATIQUES ET NAUTIQUES ｜ DEPORTES ACUÁTICOS Y NÁUTICOS ｜ SPORT ACQUATICI E NAUTICI

水上スキー

water skiing ｜ Wasserski^N ｜ ski^M nautique ｜ esquí^M acuático ｜ sci^M nautico

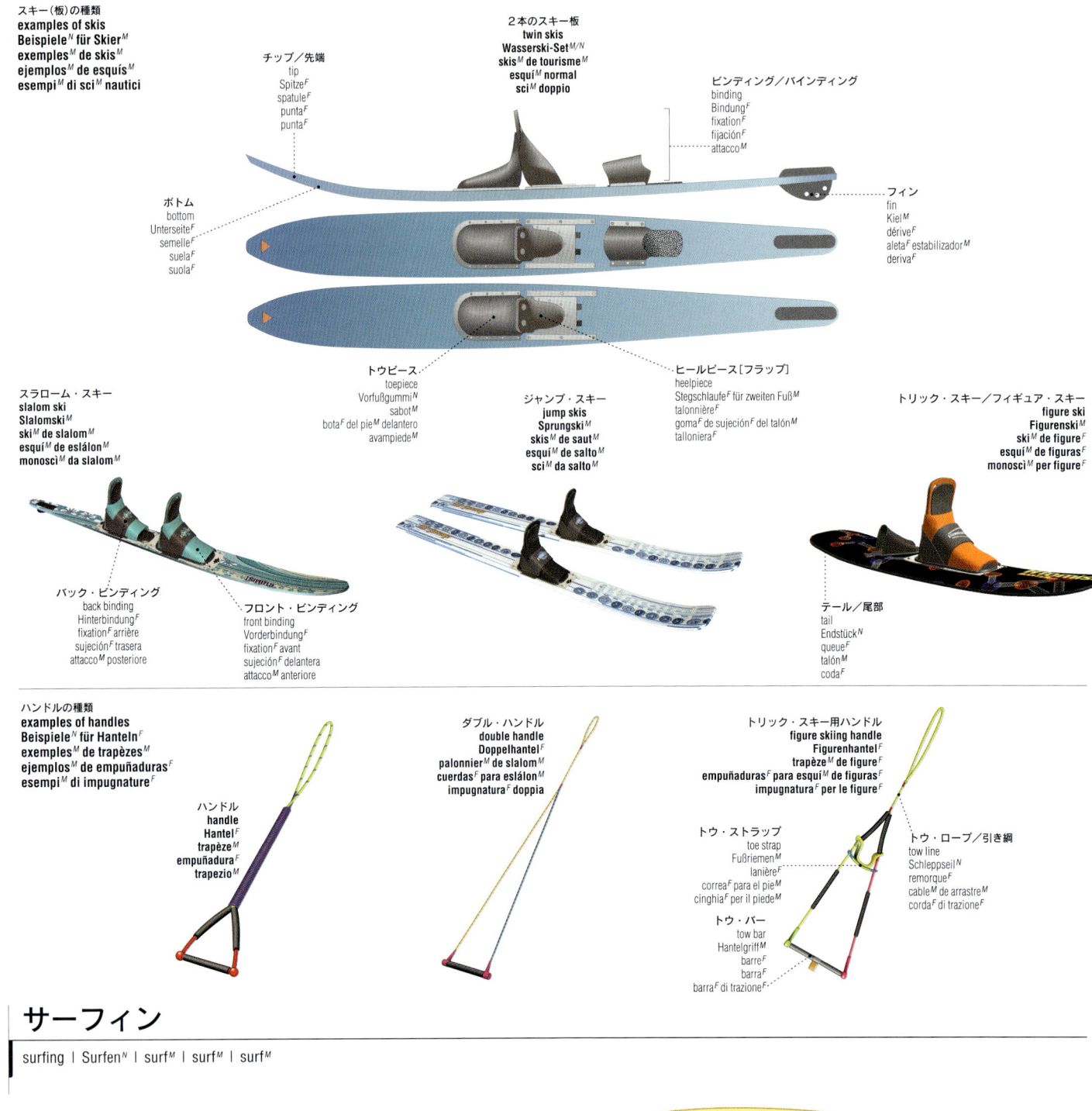

日本語 ｜ 英語 ｜ ドイツ語 ｜ フランス語 ｜ スペイン語 ｜ イタリア語

スキー（板）の種類
examples of skis
Beispiele^N für Skier^M
exemples^M de skis^M
ejemplos^M de esquís^M
esempi^M di sci^M nautici

チップ／先端
tip
Spitze^F
spatule^F
punta^F
punta^F

2本のスキー板
twin skis
Wasserski-Set$^{M/N}$
skis^M de tourisme^M
esquí^M normal
sci^M doppio

ビンディング／バインディング
binding
Bindung^F
fixation^F
fijación^F
attacco^M

ボトム
bottom
Unterseite^F
semelle^F
suela^F
suola^F

フィン
fin
Kiel^M
dérive^F
aleta^F estabilizador^M
deriva^F

トウピース
toepiece
Vorfußgummi^N
sabot^M
bota^F del pie^M delantero
avampiede^M

ヒールピース［フラップ］
heelpiece
Stegschlaufe^F für zweiten Fuß^M
talonnière^F
goma^F de sujeción^F del talón^M
talloniera^F

スラローム・スキー
slalom ski
Slalomski^M
ski^M de slalom^M
esquí^M de eslálon^M
monosci^M da slalom

ジャンプ・スキー
jump skis
Sprungski^M
skis^M de saut^M
esquí^M de salto^M
sci^M da salto^M

トリック・スキー／フィギュア・スキー
figure ski
Figurenski^M
ski^M de figure^F
esquí^M de figuras^F
monoscì^M per figure^F

バック・ビンディング
back binding
Hinterbindung^F
fixation^F arrière
sujeción^F trasera
attacco^M posteriore

フロント・ビンディング
front binding
Vorderbindung^F
fixation^F avant
sujeción^F delantera
attacco^M anteriore

テール／尾部
tail
Endstück^N
queue^F
talón^M
coda^F

ハンドルの種類
examples of handles
Beispiele^N für Hanteln^F
exemples^M de trapèzes^M
ejemplos^M de empuñaduras^F
esempi^M di impugnature^F

ダブル・ハンドル
double handle
Doppelhantel^F
palonnier^M de slalom^M
cuerdas^F para eslálon^M
impugnatura^F doppia

トリック・スキー用ハンドル
figure skiing handle
Figurenhantel^F
trapèze^M de figure^F
empuñaduras^F para esquí^M de figuras^F
impugnatura^F per le figure^F

ハンドル
handle
Hantel^F
trapèze^M
empuñadura^F
trapezio^M

トウ・ストラップ
toe strap
Fußriemen^M
lanière^F
correa^F para el pie^M
cinghia^F per il piede^M

トウ・バー
tow bar
Hantelgriff^M
barre^F
barra^F
barra^F di trazione^F

トウ・ロープ／引き綱
tow line
Schleppseil^N
remorque^F
cable^M de arrastre^M
corda^F di trazione^F

サーフィン

surfing ｜ Surfen^N ｜ surf^M ｜ surf^M ｜ surf^M

サーフボード
surfboard
Surfboard^N
planche^F de surf^M
tabla^F de surf^M
tavola^F da surf^M

サーファー
surfer
Surfer^M
surfeur^M
surfista^M
surfista$^{M/F}$

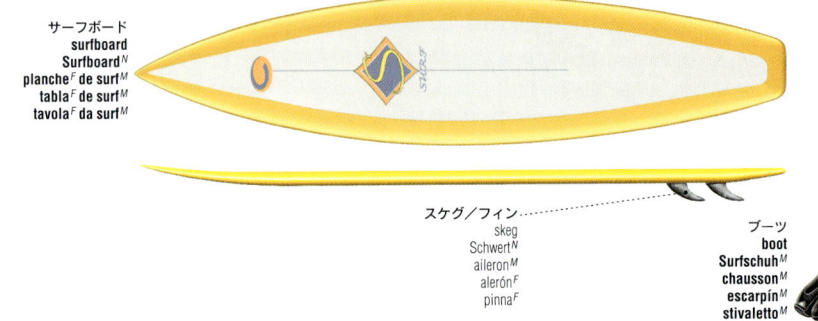

スケグ／フィン
skeg
Schwert^N
aileron^M
alerón^F
pinna^F

ブーツ
boot
Surfschuh^M
chausson^M
escarpín^M
stivaletto^M

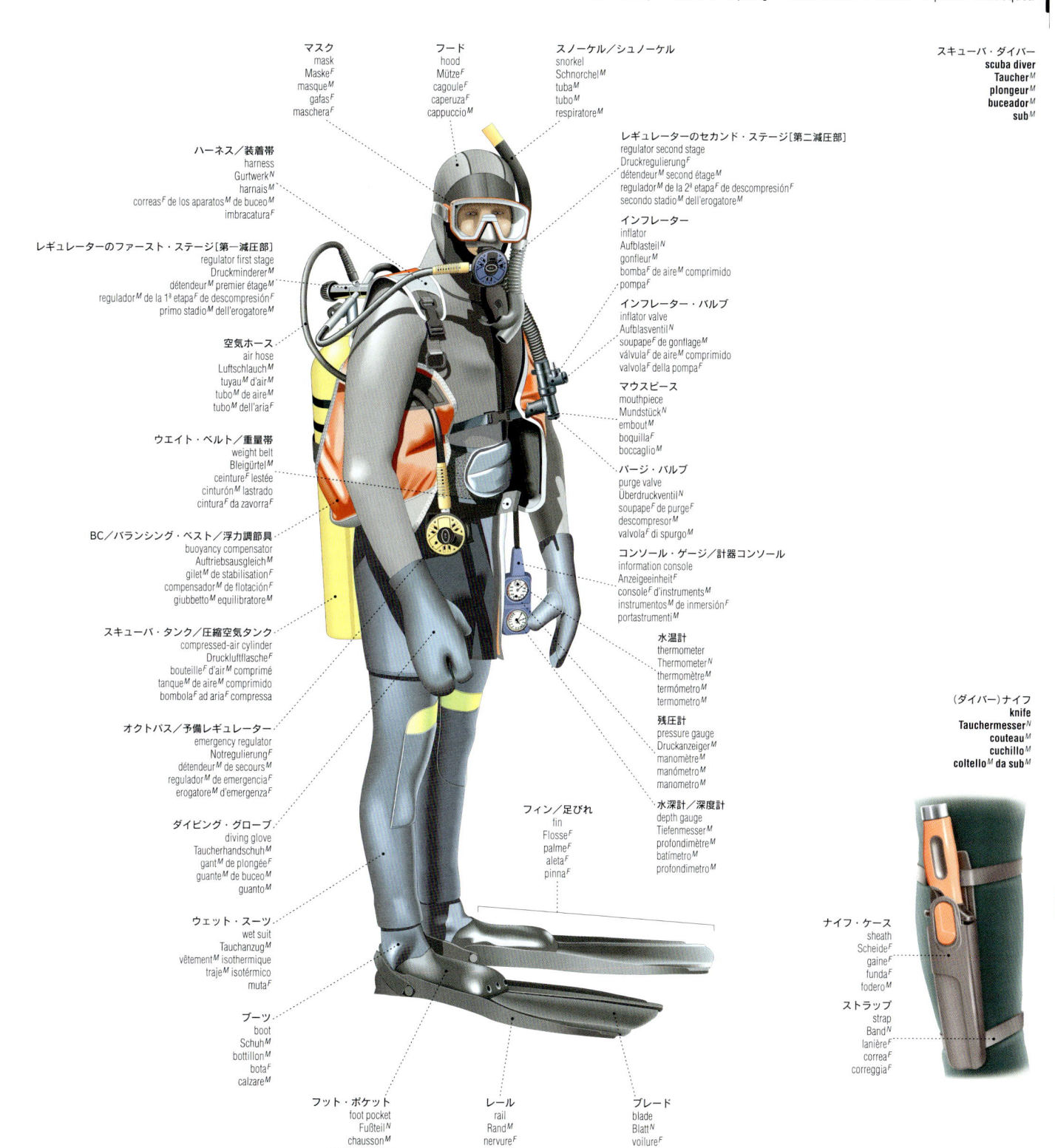

水上・水中スポーツと海上スポーツ | AQUATIC AND NAUTICAL SPORTS
WASSERSPORT | SPORTS AQUATIQUES ET NAUTIQUES | DEPORTES ACUÁTICOS Y NÁUTICOS | SPORT ACQUATICI E NAUTICI

スキューバ・ダイビング

scuba diving | Tauchen[N] | plongée[F] sous-marine | buceo[M] | pesca[F] subacquea

マスク
mask
Maske[F]
masque[M]
gafas[F]
maschera[F]

フード
hood
Mütze[F]
cagoule[F]
caperuza[F]
cappuccio[M]

スノーケル/シュノーケル
snorkel
Schnorchel[M]
tuba[M]
tubo[M]
respiratore[M]

スキューバ・ダイバー
scuba diver
Taucher[M]
plongeur[M]
buceador[M]
sub[M]

ハーネス/装着帯
harness
Gurtwerk[N]
harnais[M]
correas[F] de los aparatos[M] de buceo[M]
imbracatura[F]

レギュレーターのセカンド・ステージ[第二減圧部]
regulator second stage
Druckregulierung[F]
détendeur[M] second étage[M]
regulador de la 2ª etapa[F] de descompresión[F]
secondo stadio[M] dell'erogatore[F]

レギュレーターのファースト・ステージ[第一減圧部]
regulator first stage
Druckminderer[M]
détendeur[M] premier étage[M]
regulador[M] de la 1ª etapa[F] de descompresión[F]
primo stadio[M] dell'erogatore[F]

インフレーター
inflator
Aufblasteil[N]
gonfleur[M]
bomba[F] de aire[M] comprimido
pompa[F]

空気ホース
air hose
Luftschlauch[M]
tuyau[M] d'air[M]
tubo[M] de aire[M]
tubo[M] dell'aria[F]

インフレーター・バルブ
inflator valve
Aufblasventil[N]
soupape[F] de gonflage[M]
válvula[F] de aire[M] comprimido
valvola[F] della pompa[F]

マウスピース
mouthpiece
Mundstück[N]
embout[M]
boquilla[F]
boccaglio[M]

ウエイト・ベルト/重量帯
weight belt
Bleigürtel[M]
ceinture[F] lestée
cinturón[M] lastrado
cintura[F] da zavorra[F]

パージ・バルブ
purge valve
Überdruckventil[N]
soupape[F] de purge[F]
descompresor[M]
valvola[F] di spurgo[M]

BC/バランシング・ベスト/浮力調節具
buoyancy compensator
Auftriebsausgleich[M]
gilet de stabilisation[F]
compensador[M] de flotación[F]
giubbetto[M] equilibratore[M]

コンソール・ゲージ/計器コンソール
information console
Anzeigeeinheit[F]
console[F] d'instruments[M]
instrumentos[M] de inmersión[F]
portastrumenti[M]

スキューバ・タンク/圧縮空気タンク
compressed-air cylinder
Druckluftflasche[F]
bouteille[F] d'air[M] comprimé
tanque[M] de aire[M] comprimido
bombola[F] ad aria[F] compressa

水温計
thermometer
Thermometer[M]
thermomètre[M]
termómetro[M]
termometro[M]

オクトパス/予備レギュレーター
emergency regulator
Notregulierung[F]
détendeur[M] de secours[M]
regulador[M] de emergencia[F]
erogatore[M] d'emergenza[F]

残圧計
pressure gauge
Druckanzeiger[M]
manomètre[M]
manómetro[M]
manometro[M]

(ダイバー)ナイフ
knife
Tauchermesser[N]
couteau[M]
cuchillo[M]
coltello[M] da sub[M]

ダイビング・グローブ
diving glove
Taucherhandschuh[M]
gant[M] de plongée[F]
guante[M] de buceo[M]
guanto[M]

水深計/深度計
depth gauge
Tiefenmesser[M]
profondimètre[M]
batímetro[M]
profondimetro[M]

フィン/足びれ
fin
Flosse[F]
palme[F]
aleta[F]
pinna[F]

ウェット・スーツ
wet suit
Tauchanzug[M]
vêtement[M] isothermique
traje[M] isotérmico
muta[F]

ナイフ・ケース
sheath
Scheide[F]
gaine[F]
funda[F]
fodero[M]

ブーツ
boot
Schuh[M]
bottillon[M]
bota[F]
calzare[M]

ストラップ
strap
Band[N]
lanière[F]
correa[F]
correggia[F]

フット・ポケット
foot pocket
Fußteil[N]
chausson[M]
bota[F] de la aleta[F]
scarpetta[F]

レール
rail
Rand[M]
nervure[F]
borde[M]
costolatura[F]

ブレード
blade
Blatt[N]
voilure[F]
palma[F]
pala[F]

スポーツとゲーム

水中銃
speargun
Harpune[F]
fusil[M] à air[M] comprimé
arpón[M] submarino
fucile[M] subacqueo

841

格闘技 | COMBAT SPORTS
KAMPFSPORTARTEN | SPORTS DE COMBAT | DEPORTES DE COMBATE | SPORT DI COMBATTIMENTO

ボクシング

boxing | BoxenN | boxeF | boxeoM | pugilatoM

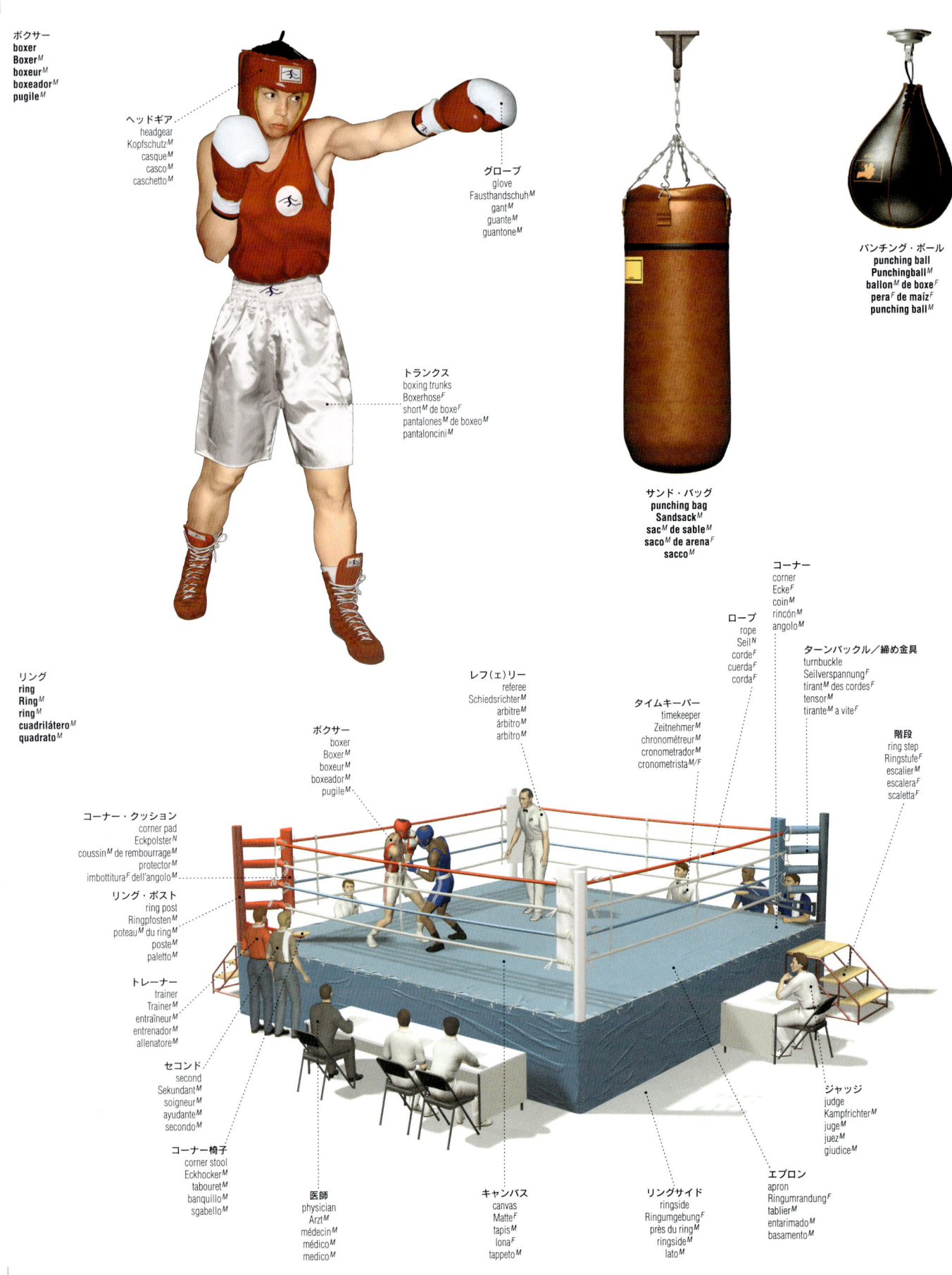

日本語 | 英語 | ドイツ語 | フランス語 | スペイン語 | イタリア語

ボクサー
boxer
BoxerM
boxeurM
boxeadorM
pugileM

ヘッドギア
headgear
KopfschutzM
casqueM
cascoM
caschettoM

グローブ
glove
FausthandschuhM
gantM
guanteM
guantoneM

トランクス
boxing trunks
BoxerhoseF
shortM de boxeF
pantalonesM de boxeoM
pantalonciniM

パンチング・ボール
punching ball
PunchingballM
ballonM de boxeF
peraF de maízF
punching ballM

サンド・バッグ
punching bag
SandsackM
sacM de sableM
sacoM de arenaF
saccoM

コーナー
corner
EckeF
coinM
rincónM
angoloM

ロープ
rope
SeilN
cordeF
cuerdaF
cordaF

ターンバックル／締め金具
turnbuckle
SeilverspannungF
tirantM des cordesF
tensorM
tiranteM a viteF

階段
ring step
RingstufeF
escalierM
escaleraF
scalettaF

リング
ring
RingM
ringM
cuadriláteroM
quadratoM

ボクサー
boxer
BoxerM
boxeurM
boxeadorM
pugileM

レフ(ェ)リー
referee
SchiedsrichterM
arbitreM
árbitroM
arbitroM

タイムキーパー
timekeeper
ZeitnehmerM
chronométreurM
cronometradorM
cronometristaM/F

コーナー・クッション
corner pad
EckpolsterN
coussinM de rembourrageF
protectorM
imbottituraF dell'angoloM

リング・ポスト
ring post
RingpfostenM
poteauM du ringM
posteM
palettoM

トレーナー
trainer
TrainerM
entraîneurM
entrenadorM
allenatoreM

セコンド
second
SekundantM
soigneurM
ayudanteM
secondoM

ジャッジ
judge
KampfrichterM
jugeM
juezM
giudiceM

コーナー椅子
corner stool
EckhockerM
tabouretM
banquilloM
sgabelloM

医師
physician
ArztM
médecinM
médicoM
medicoM

キャンバス
canvas
MatteF
tapisM
lonaF
tappetoM

リングサイド
ringside
RingumgebungF
près du ringM
ringside
latoM

エプロン
apron
RingumrandungF
tablierM
entarimadoM
basamentoM

スポーツとゲーム

842

格闘技 | COMBAT SPORTS
KAMPFSPORTARTEN | SPORTS DE COMBAT | DEPORTES DE COMBATE | SPORT DI COMBATTIMENTO

ボクシング

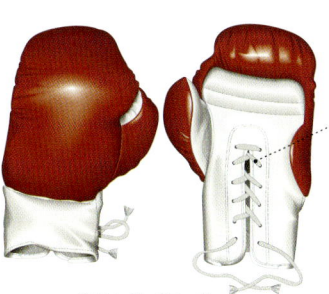

締め紐（ひも）
lace
Schnürsenkel ^{M}
lacet ^{M}
cordones ^{M}
stringa ^{F}

ボクシング・グローブ
boxing gloves
Boxhandschuhe ^{M}
gants ^{F} de boxe ^{F}
guantes ^{M} de boxeo ^{M}
guantoni ^{M}

バンデージ
bandage
Bandage ^{F}
bandage ^{M}
vendaje ^{M}
bendaggio ^{M}

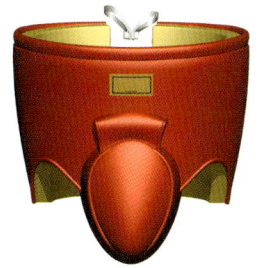

カップ・プロテクター／ノー・ファウル・カップ
protective cup
Suspensorium ^{N}
coquille ^{F} de protection ^{F}
coquilla ^{F}
conchiglia ^{F} di protezione ^{F}

マウスピース
mouthpiece
Mundschutz ^{M}
protège-dents ^{M}
protector ^{M} bucal
paradenti ^{M}

レスリング

wrestling | Ringen ^{N} | lutte ^{F} | lucha ^{F} | lotta ^{F}

開始の姿勢
starting positions
Startpositionen ^{F}
positions ^{F} de départ ^{M}
posiciones ^{M} iniciales
posizioni ^{F} di partenza ^{F}

クラウチング・ポジション（フリースタイル）
crouching position (freestyle wrestling)
gebückter Stand ^{M} (Freistil ^{M})
garde ^{F} basse (lutte ^{F} libre)
posición ^{F} en guardia ^{F} : (lucha ^{F} libre)
guardia ^{F} bassa (lotta ^{F} libera)

スタンディング・ポジション（グレコ・ローマン・スタイル）
standing position (Greco-Roman wrestling)
aufrechter Stand ^{M} (griechisch-römischer Stil ^{M})
garde ^{F} haute (lutte ^{F} gréco-romaine)
posición ^{F} vertical: (lucha ^{F} greco-romana)
guardia ^{F} in piedi ^{M} (lotta ^{F} greco-romana)

レスラー
wrestler
Ringer ^{M}
lutteur ^{M}
luchador ^{M}
lottatore ^{M}

シングレット／レスリング・タイツ
singlet
Trikot ^{N}
maillot ^{M}
camiseta ^{F}
costume ^{M}

レスリング・シューズ
wrestling shoe
Ringerschuh ^{M}
chaussure ^{F} de lutte ^{F}
botas ^{F} de lucha ^{F}
scarpa ^{F}

パッシビティー・ゾーン／消極地帯
passivity zone
Passivitätszone ^{F}
zone ^{F} de passivité ^{F}
zona ^{F} de pasividad ^{F}
zona ^{F} di passività ^{F}

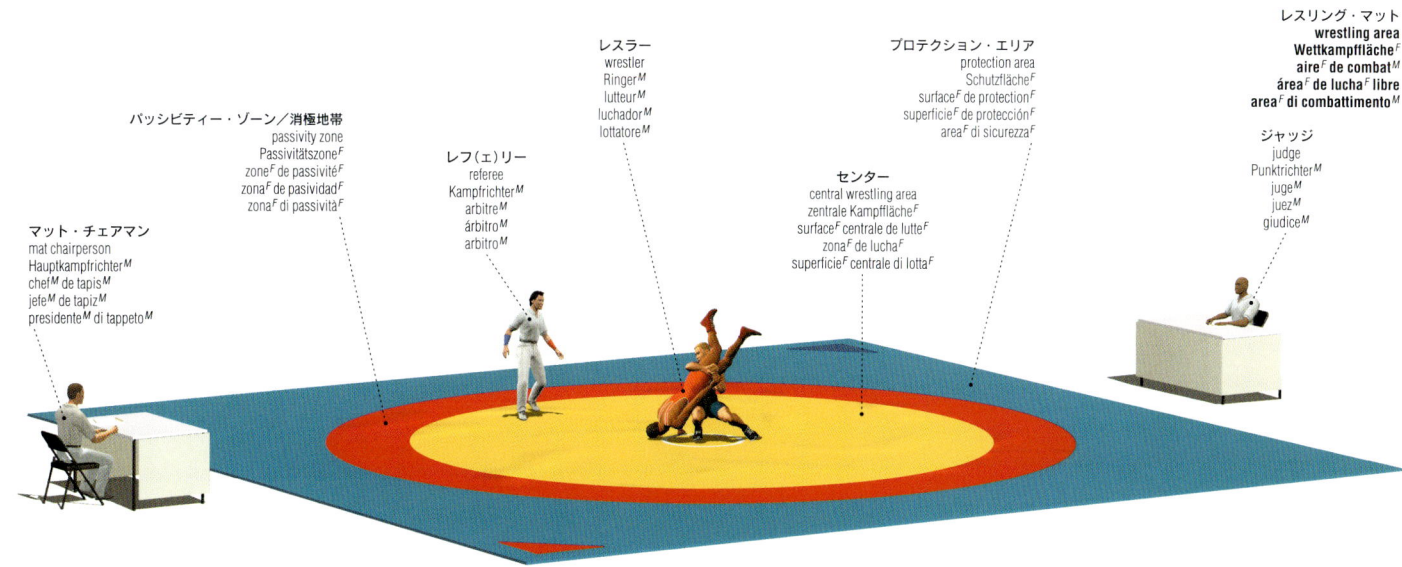

マット・チェアマン
mat chairperson
Hauptkampfrichter ^{M}
chef ^{M} de tapis ^{M}
jefe ^{M} de tapiz ^{M}
presidente ^{M} di tappeto ^{M}

レフ（ェ）リー
referee
Kampfrichter ^{M}
arbitre ^{M}
árbitro ^{M}
arbitro ^{M}

レスラー
wrestler
Ringer ^{M}
lutteur ^{M}
luchador ^{M}
lottatore ^{M}

センター
central wrestling area
zentrale Kampffläche ^{F}
surface ^{F} centrale de lutte ^{F}
zona ^{F} de lucha ^{F}
superficie ^{F} centrale di lotta ^{F}

プロテクション・エリア
protection area
Schutzfläche ^{F}
surface ^{F} de protection ^{F}
superficie ^{F} de protección ^{F}
area ^{F} di sicurezza ^{F}

レスリング・マット
wrestling area
Wettkampffläche ^{F}
aire ^{F} de combat ^{M}
área ^{F} de lucha ^{F} libre
area ^{F} di combattimento ^{M}

ジャッジ
judge
Punktrichter ^{M}
juge ^{M}
juez ^{M}
giudice ^{M}

843

格闘技 | COMBAT SPORTS
KAMPFSPORTARTEN | SPORTS DE COMBAT | DEPORTES DE COMBATE | SPORT DI COMBATTIMENTO

柔道

日本語 | 英語 | ドイツ語 | フランス語 | スペイン語 | イタリア語

judo | Judo[N] | judo[M] | judo[M] | judo[M]

畳
mat
Matte[F]
tapis[M]
tatami[M]
tappeto[M]

記録係と計時係
scorers and timekeepers
Registratoren[M] und Zeitnehmer[M]
marqueurs[M] et chronométreurs[M]
anotadores[M] y cronometradores[M]
segnapunti[M] e cronometristi[M]

得点掲示板
scoreboard
Anzeigetafel[F]
tableau[M] d'affichage[M]
marcador[M]
tabellone[M] segnapunti

医療班
medical team
Ärzteteam[N]
équipe[F] médicale
equipo[M] médico
staff[M] medico

競技者／試合者
contestant
Judokämpfer[M] Wettkampfteilnehmer[M]
combattant[M]
uke (defensor[M])
lottatore[M]

安全区域［地帯］／場外
safety area
Sicherheitsbereich[M]
surface[F] de sécurité[F]
zona[F] de seguridad[F]
area[F] di sicurezza[F]

試合場
contest area
Kampfbereich[M]
surface[F] de combat[M]
zona[F] de combate[M]
area[F] di combattimento[M]

危険区域［地帯］
danger area
Gefahrenbereich[M]
zone[F] de danger[M]
área[F] de peligro[M]
zona[F] di pericolo[M]

主審
referee
Schiedsrichter[M]
arbitre[M]
judoka[M] neutral
arbitro[M]

副審
judge
Kampfrichter[M]
juge[M]
juez[M]
giudice[M]

柔道衣／柔道着
judogi
Judogi[M]
judogi[M]
traje[M] de judo: judoji[M]
judogi[M]

上衣／上着
jacket
Jacke[F]
veste[F]
kimono[M]
giacca[F]

固め技と投げ技の例
examples of holds and throws
Griff- und Wurfbeispiele[N]
exemples[M] de prises[F]
ejemplos[M] de llaves[F]
esempi[M] di prese[F]

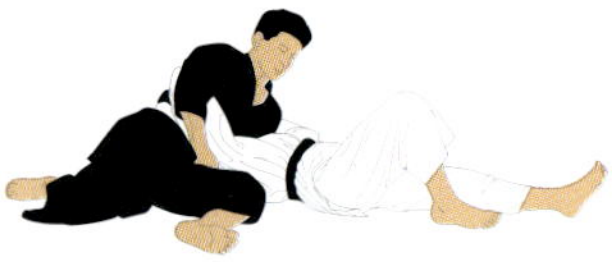

巴（ともえ）投げ
stomach throw
Kopfwurf[M]
projection[F] en cercle[M]
proyección[F] en círculo[M]
rovesciata[F] all'indietro

押さえ込み
holding
Haltegriffe[M]
immobilisation[F]
inmovilización[M]
presa[F] a terra[F]

払い腰
sweeping hip throw
Hüftwurf[M]
hanche[F] ailée
proyección[F] primera de cadera[F]
spazzata[F] d'anca[F]

大外刈り
major outer reaping throw
Große Außensichel[F]
grand fauchage[M] extérieur
osoto-gari (gran siega[F]) exterior
grande falciata[F] esterna

大内刈り
major inner reaping throw
Große Innensichel[F]
grand fauchage[M] intérieur
gran siega[F] interior
grande falciata[F] interna

裸締め
naked strangle
Halsumklammerung[F]
étranglement[M]
estrangulación[F]
presa[F] di strangolamento[M]

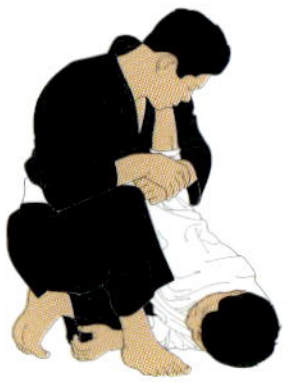

ズボン／下穿（ば）き／股下
trousers
Hose[F]
pantalon[M]
pantalón[M]
pantaloni[M]

帯
belt
Gürtel[M]
ceinture[F]
cinturón[M]
cintura[F]

腕固め
arm lock
Armhebel[M]
clé[F] de bras[M]
inmovilización[F] de brazo[M]
presa[F] a croce[F]

一本背負い投げ
one-arm shoulder throw
einarmiger Schulterwurf[M]
projection[F] d'épaule[F] par un côté[M]
proyección[F]) por encima del hombro[M] con una mano[F]
proiezione[F] di spalla[F] e braccio[M]

格闘技 | COMBAT SPORTS
KAMPFSPORTARTEN | SPORTS DE COMBAT | DEPORTES DE COMBATE | SPORT DI COMBATTIMENTO

空手

karate | Karate[N] | karaté[M] | karate[M] | karatè[M]

空手家
karateka
Karateka[M]
karatéka[F]
karateka[M]
karateka[M/F]

空手着／空手衣
karate-gi
Karategi[M]
karatégi[M]
karategi[M]
karategi[M]

競技場／コート
contest area
Wettkampfbereich[M]
surface[F] de combat[M]
zona[F] de combate[M]
area[F] di combattimento[M]

帯
obi
Obi[M]
obi[F]
obi[M]
obi[M]

主審ライン[所定線]
referee's line
Hauptkampfrichterlinie[F]
ligne[F] de l'arbitre[M]
línea[F] de árbitro[M]
linea[F] dell'arbitro[M]

開始線
competitors' line
Kämpferlinie[F]
ligne[F] des compétiteurs[M]
línea de los competidores[M]
linea[F] dei karateka[M]

試合場
competition area
Wettkampffläche[F]
aire[F] de compétition[F]
zona[F] de competición[F]
area[F] di gara[F]

監査役
arbitration committee
Kampfgericht[N]
comité[M] d'arbitrage[M]
comité[M] de arbitraje[M]
collegio[M] arbitrale

副審
corner judge
Seitenkampfrichter[M]
juge[M] de coin[M]
juez[M] de ángulo[M]
giudice[M] d'angolo[M]

記録係
scorekeeper
Listenführer[M]
marqueur[M]
anotador[M]
segnapunti[M]

計時係
timekeeper
Zeitnehmer[M]
chronométreur[M]
cronometrador[M]
cronometrista[M/F]

主審
referee
Hauptkampfrichter[M]
arbitre[M]
árbitro[M]
arbitro[M]

空手家
karateka
Karateka[M]
karatéka[M]
karateka[M]
karateka[M]

スポーツとゲーム

845

格闘技 | COMBAT SPORTS
KAMPFSPORTARTEN | SPORTS DE COMBAT | DEPORTES DE COMBATE | SPORT DI COMBATTIMENTO

カンフー

kung fu | Kung-Fu N | kung-fu M | kung fu M | kung fu M

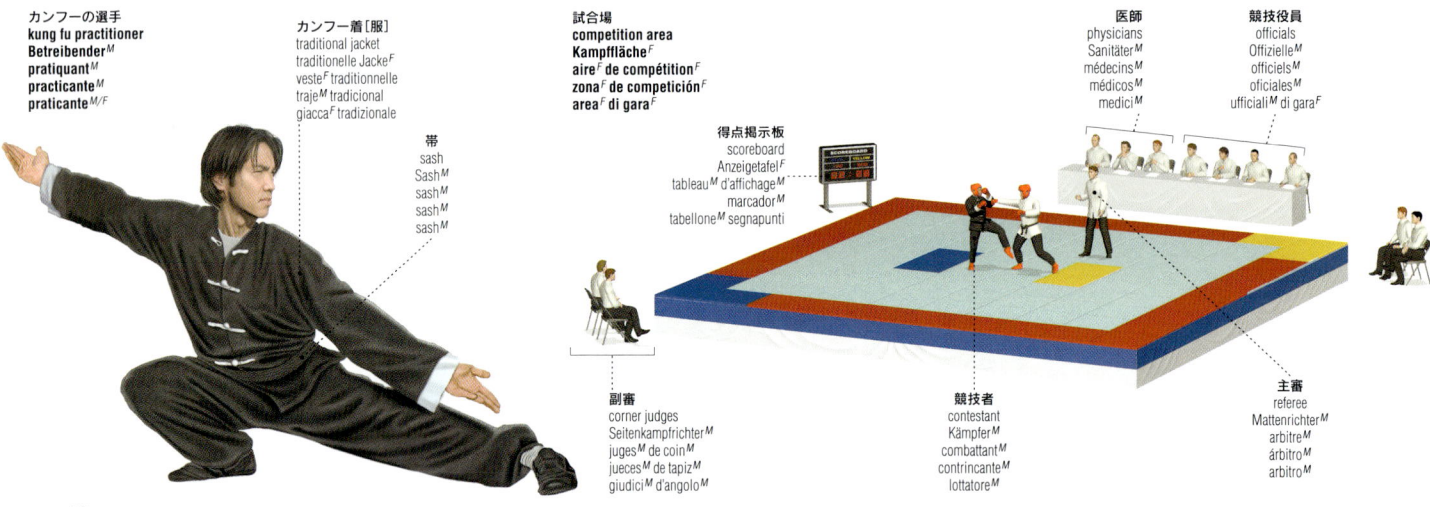

日本語 | 英語 | ドイツ語 | フランス語 | スペイン語 | イタリア語

カンフーの選手
kung fu practitioner
Betreibender M
pratiquant M
practicante M
praticante M/F

カンフー着[服]
traditional jacket
traditionelle Jacke F
veste F traditionnelle
traje M tradicional
giacca F tradizionale

帯
sash
Sash M
sash M
sash M
sash M

試合場
competition area
Kampffläche F
aire F de compétition
zona F de competición
area F di gara

得点掲示板
scoreboard
Anzeigetafel F
tableau M d'affichage
marcador M
tabellone M segnapunti

医師
physicians
Sanitäter M
médecins M
médicos M
medici M

競技役員
officials
Offizielle M
officiels M
oficiales M
ufficiali M di gara

副審
corner judges
Seitenkampfrichter M
juges M de coin
jueces M de tapiz
giudici M d'angolo

競技者
contestant
Kämpfer M
combattant M
contrincante M
lottatore M

主審
referee
Mattenrichter M
arbitre M
árbitro M
arbitro M

柔術

jujitsu | Jujutsu N | ju-jitsu M | ju-jitsu M | jujutsu M

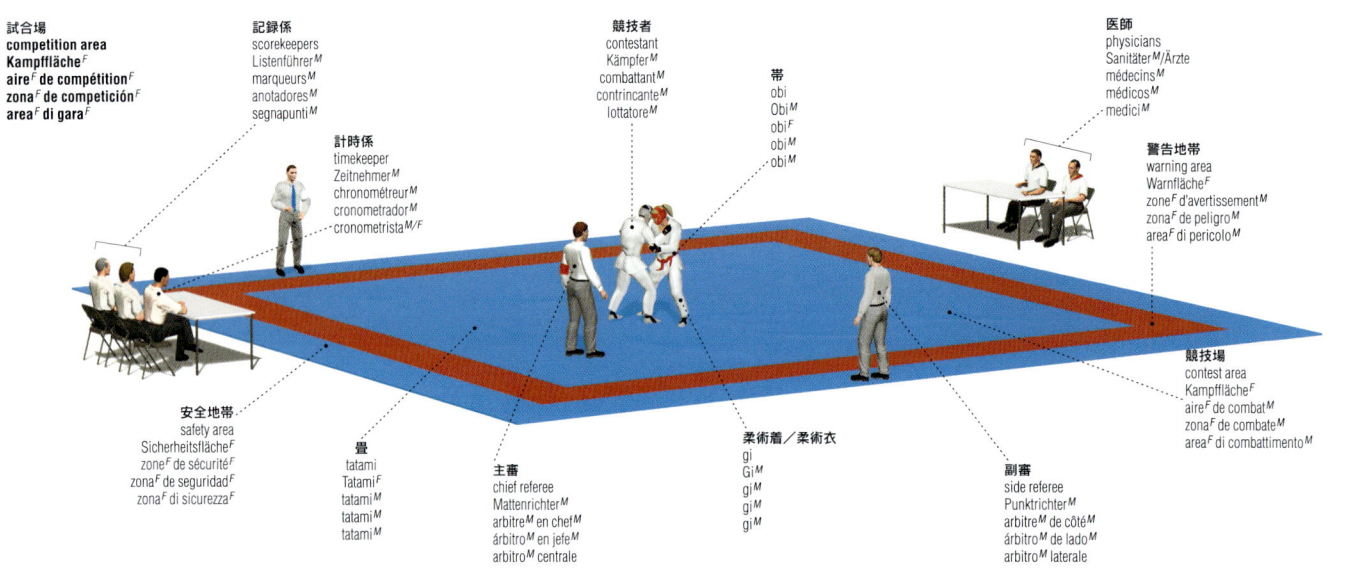

試合場
competition area
Kampffläche F
aire F de compétition
zona F de competición
area F di gara

記録係
scorekeepers
Listenführer M
marqueurs M
anotadores M
segnapunti M

競技者
contestant
Kämpfer M
combattant M
contrincante M
lottatore M

帯
obi
Obi F
obi M
obi M

医師
physicians
Sanitäter M/Ärzte
médecins M
médicos M
medici M

計時係
timekeeper
Zeitnehmer M
chronométreur M
cronometrador M
cronometrista M/F

警告地帯
warning area
Warnfläche F
zone F d'avertissement
zona F de peligro
area F di pericolo

安全地帯
safety area
Sicherheitsfläche F
zone F de sécurité
zona F de seguridad
zona F di sicurezza

畳
tatami
Tatami F
tatami M
tatami M
tatami M

主審
chief referee
Mattenrichter M
arbitre M en chef
árbitro M en jefe
arbitro M centrale

柔術着／柔術衣
gi
Gi M
gi M
gi M
gi M

副審
side referee
Punktrichter M
arbitre M de côté
árbitro M de lado
arbitro M laterale

競技場
contest area
Kampffläche F
aire F de combat
zona F de combate
area F di combattimento

合気道

aikido | Aikido N | aïkido M | aikido M | aikido M

合気道家
aikidoka
Aikidoka M
aïkidoka M
aikidoka M
aikidoka M/F

帯
obi
Obi M
obi M
obi M
obi M

合気道着
aikidogi
Aikidogi M
aïkidogi M
aikidogi M
aikidogi M

袴（はかま）
hakama
Hakama M
hakama M
hakama M
hakama M

杖
jo
Jo M
bâton M
bastón M
bastone M

木剣
bokken
Bokken M
bokken M
bokken M
bokken M

格闘技 | COMBAT SPORTS
KAMPFSPORTARTEN | SPORTS DE COMBAT | DEPORTES DE COMBATE | SPORT DI COMBATTIMENTO

剣道
kendo | Kendo[N] | kendo[M] | kendo[M] | kendo[M]

剣道家
kendoka
Kendoka[M]
kendoka[M]
kendoka[M]
kendoka[M/F]

面
men
Men[M]
men[M]
men[M]
men[M]

試合場
competition area
Kampffläche[F]
aire[F] de compétition[F]
área[F] de competición[F]
area[F] di gara[F]

竹刀（しない）
shinai
Shinai[M]
shinai[M]
shinai[M]
shinai[M]

胴
do
Do[M]
do[M]
do[M]
do[M]

中央線
center; centre
Mitte[F]
centre[M]
centro[M]
centro[M]

小手
kote
Kote
kote[M]
kote[M]
kote[M]

危険区域［地帯］
danger zone
Gefahrenzone[F]
zone[F] de danger[M]
zona[F] de peligro
zona[F] di pericolo

垂れ
tare
Tare[M]
tare[M]
tare[M]
tare[M]

開始線
competitors' line
Kämpferlinie[F]
ligne[F] des compétiteurs[M]
línea[F] de competición[F]
linea[F] dei kendoka[M]

副審
assistant referee
Schiedsrichter[M]
arbitre[M] auxiliaire
árbitro[M] auxiliar
arbitro[M] ausiliario

記録係
scorekeepers
Listenführer[M]
marqueurs[M]
marcadores[M]
segnapunti[M]

計時係
timekeeper
Zeitnehmer[M]
chronométreur[M]
cronometrador[M]
cronometrista[M/F]

主審
chief referee
Hauptschiedsrichter[M]
arbitre[M] en chef[M]
árbitro[M] en jefe[M]
arbitro[M]

袴（はかま）
hakama
Hakama[M]
hakama[M]
hakama[M]
hakama[M]

相撲
sumo | Sumo[N] | sumo[M] | sumo[M] | sumo[M]

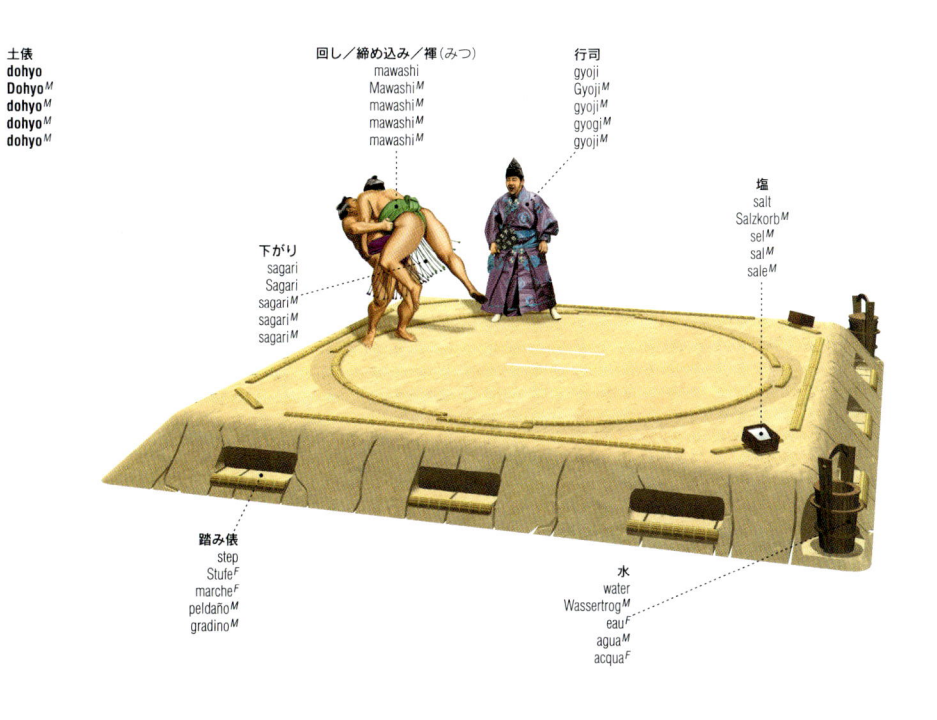

土俵
dohyo
Dohyo[M]
dohyo[M]
dohyo[M]
dohyo[M]

回し／締め込み／褌（みつ）
mawashi
Mawashi[M]
mawashi[M]
mawashi[M]
mawashi[M]

行司
gyoji
Gyoji[M]
gyoji[M]
gyogi[M]
gyoji[M]

髷（まげ）
mage
Mage[M]
mage[M]
mage[M]
mage[M]

相撲取り／力士
sumotori
Sumoringer[M]
sumotori[M]
sumotori[M]
sumotori[M]

下がり
sagari
Sagari
sagari[M]
sagari[M]
sagari[M]

塩
salt
Salzkorb[M]
sel[M]
sal[M]
sale[M]

踏み俵
step
Stufe[F]
marche[F]
peldaño[M]
gradino[M]

水
water
Wassertrog[M]
eau[F]
agua[M]
acqua[F]

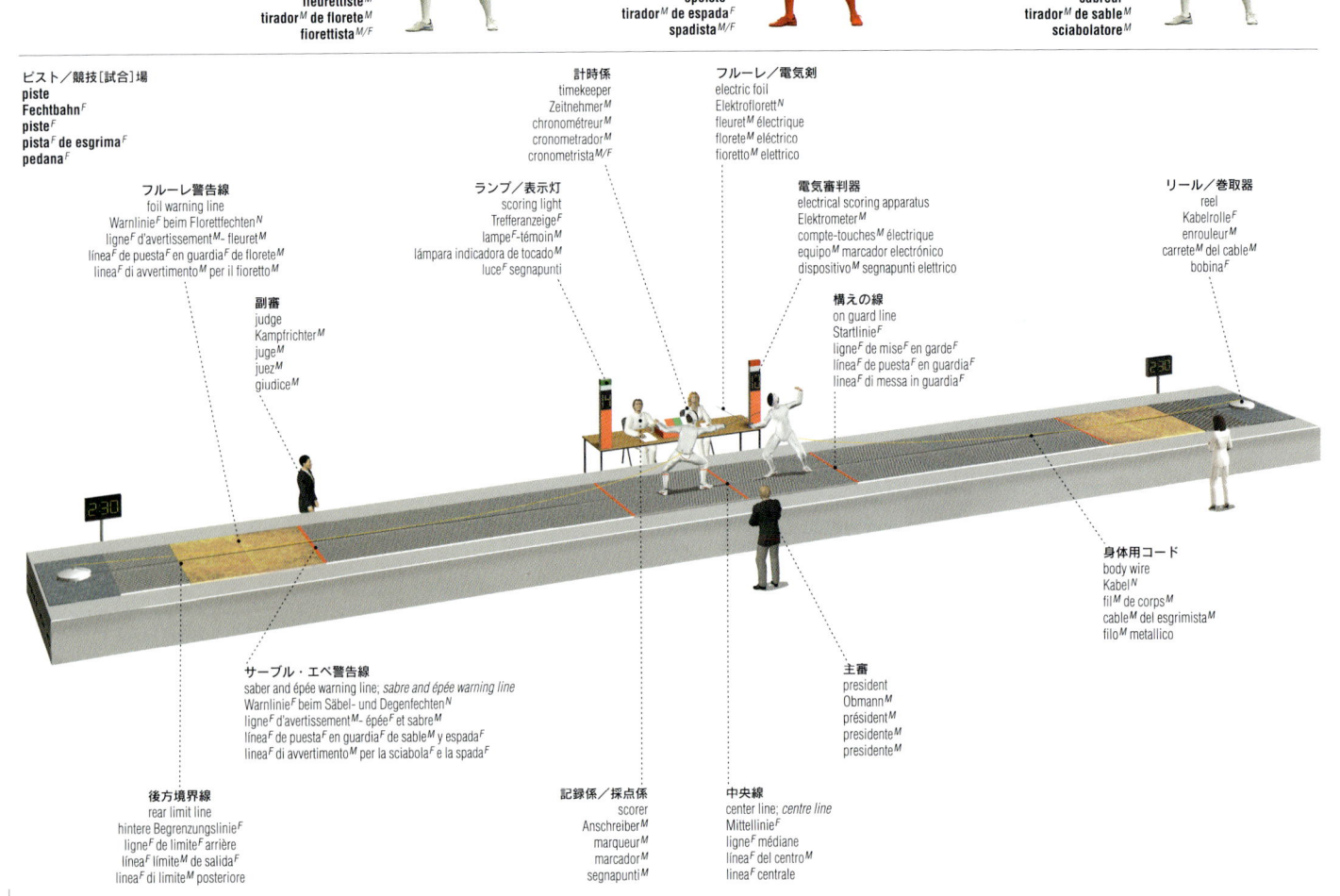

格闘技 | COMBAT SPORTS
KAMPFSPORTARTEN | SPORTS DE COMBAT | DEPORTES DE COMBATE | SPORT DI COMBATTIMENTO

フェンシング

fencing | Fechtsport^M | escrime^F | esgrima^F | scherma^F

日本語 | 英語 | ドイツ語 | フランス語 | スペイン語 | イタリア語

フェンサー
fencer
Fechter^M
escrimeur^M
esgrimista^M
schermidore^M

マスク
mask
Fechtmaske^F
masque^M
careta^F de esgrima^F
maschera^F

ビブ／喉当て
bib
Latz^M
bavette^F
gola^F
gorgiera^F

ジャケット
jacket
Fechtjacke^F
veste^F
chaqueta^F blanca de esgrima^F
giubbotto^M

グローブ／手袋
glove
Fechthandschuh^M
gant^M
guante^M de esgrima^F
guanto^M

金属(製)胴衣[ジャケット]／フルーレ用胸当て
metallic plastron
Elektroweste^F
plastron^M métallique
peto^M metálico
coprigiubbotto^M metallico

スリーブ／袖口
sleeve
Ärmelaufschlag^M
crispin^M
manga^F
manica^F

ストッキング／ソックス
stocking
Kniestrumpf^M
chaussette^F
media^F
calzettone^M

ニッカーズ
breeches
Fechthose^F
culotte^F
calzón^M
calzoni^M

フェンシング・シューズ
fencing shoe
Fechtschuh^M
chaussure^F d'escrime^F
zapatillas^F de esgrima^F
scarpetta^F

有効(命中)面
target areas
Trefflächen^F
cibles^F
áreas^F válidas de tocado^M
aree^F di bersaglio^M

フルーレ
foilist
Florettfechter^M
fleurettiste^M
tirador^M de florete^M
fiorettista^M/F

エペ
épéeist
Degenfechter^M
épéiste
tirador^M de espada^F
spadista^M/F

サーブル
sabreur
Säbelfechter^M
sabreur^M
tirador^M de sable^M
sciabolatore^M

ピスト／競技[試合]場
piste
Fechtbahn^F
piste^F
pista^F de esgrima^F
pedana^F

計時係
timekeeper
Zeitnehmer^M
chronométreur^M
cronometrador^M
cronometrista^M/F

フルーレ／電気剣
electric foil
Elektroflorett^N
fleuret^M électrique
florete^M eléctrico
fioretto^M elettrico

フルーレ警告線
foil warning line
Warnlinie^F beim Florettfechten^N
ligne^F d'avertissement^M- fleuret^M
línea^F de puesta^F en guardia^F de florete^M
linea^F di avvertimento^M per il fioretto^M

ランプ／表示灯
scoring light
Trefferanzeige^F
lampe^F-témoin^M
lámpara indicadora de tocado^M
luce^F segnapunti

電気審判器
electrical scoring apparatus
Elektrometer^M
compte-touches^M électrique
equipo^M marcador electrónico
dispositivo^M segnapunti elettrico

リール／巻取器
reel
Kabelrolle^F
enrouleur^M
carrete^M del cable^M
bobina^F

副審
judge
Kampfrichter^M
juge^M
juez^M
giudice^M

構えの線
on guard line
Startlinie^F
ligne^F de mise^F en garde^F
línea^F de puesta^F en guardia^F
linea^F di messa^F in guardia^F

身体用コード
body wire
Kabel^N
fil^M de corps^M
cable^M del esgrimista^M
filo^M metallico

サーブル・エペ警告線
saber and épée warning line; *sabre and épée warning line*
Warnlinie^F beim Säbel- und Degenfechten^N
ligne^F d'avertissement^M- épée^F et sabre^M
línea^F de puesta^F en guardia^F de sable^M y espada^F
linea^F di avvertimento^M per la sciabola^F e la spada^F

主審
president
Obmann^M
président^M
presidente^M
presidente^M

後方境界線
rear limit line
hintere Begrenzungslinie^F
ligne^F de limite^F arrière
línea^F límite^M de salida^F
linea^F di limite^M posteriore

記録係／採点係
scorer
Anschreiber^M
marqueur^M
marcador^M
segnapunti^M

中央線
center line; *centre line*
Mittellinie^F
ligne^F médiane
línea^F del centro^M
linea^F centrale

スポーツとゲーム

848

格闘技 | COMBAT SPORTS
KAMPFSPORTARTEN | SPORTS DE COMBAT | DEPORTES DE COMBATE | SPORT DI COMBATTIMENTO

フェンシング

構え
positions
Einladungen^F
positions
posiciones
posizioni^F

キント／第5の構え
quinte
Blöße^F bei der Quint-Einladung^F
quinte^F
quinta^F
quinta

ティアース／第3の構え
tierce
Blöße^F bei der Terz-Einladung^F
tierce^F
tercera^F
terza

シックスト／第6の構え
sixte
Blöße^F bei der Sixt-Einladung^F
sixte^F
sexta^F
sesta

カルト／第4の構え
quarte
Blöße^F bei der Quart-Einladung^F
quarte^F
cuarta^F
quarta

プリム／第1の構え
prime
Blöße^F bei der Prim-Einladung^F
prime^F
primera^F
prima

セコンド／第2の構え
seconde
Blöße^F bei der Second-Einladung^F
seconde^F
segunda^F
seconda

セプティム／第7の構え
septime
Blöße^F bei der Septim-Einladung^F
septime^F
séptima^F
settima

オクタブ／第8の構え
octave
Blöße^F bei der Oktav-Einladung^F
octave^F
octava^F
ottava

剣
fencing weapons
Fechtwaffen^F
armes^F
armas^F
armi^M della scherma^F

フルーレ
foil
Florett^N
fleuret^M
florete^M
fioretto^M

エペ
épée
Degen^M
épée^F
espada^F
spada^F

サーブル
saber; sabre
Säbel^M
sabre^M
sable^M
sciabola^F

剣の部分名称
parts of the weapon
Teile$^{M/N}$ der Waffe^F
parties^F de l'arme^F
partes^F del arma^F
parti^F dell'arma^F

ポンメル／ポムモウ／留めねじ
pommel
Knauf^M
pommeau^M
pomo^M
pomo^M

握り部分
mounting
Handteil^N
monture^F
empuñadura^F
guardia^F

ブレード／フェル／剣身
blade
Klinge^F
lame^F
cuerpo^M
lama^F

ポイント／ボアン・ダレ／剣先
button
Spitzenkopf^M
bouton^M
botón^M
bottone^M

グリップ／ヒルト／柄
handle
Griff^M
poignée^F
puño^M
manico^M

ガード／コキル／鍔（つば）
guard
Glocke^F
coquille^F
cazoleta^F
coccia^F

フォルト／フォール
forte
Klingenstärke^F
moyen^M
zona^F fuerte de la hoja^F
forte^F

ミドル
medium
Klingenmitte^F
moyen^M
zona^F media
media^F

フォイブル／フィーブル／フェーブル
foible
Klingenschwäche^F
faible^F
zona^F débil de la hoja^F
debole^M

スポーツとゲーム

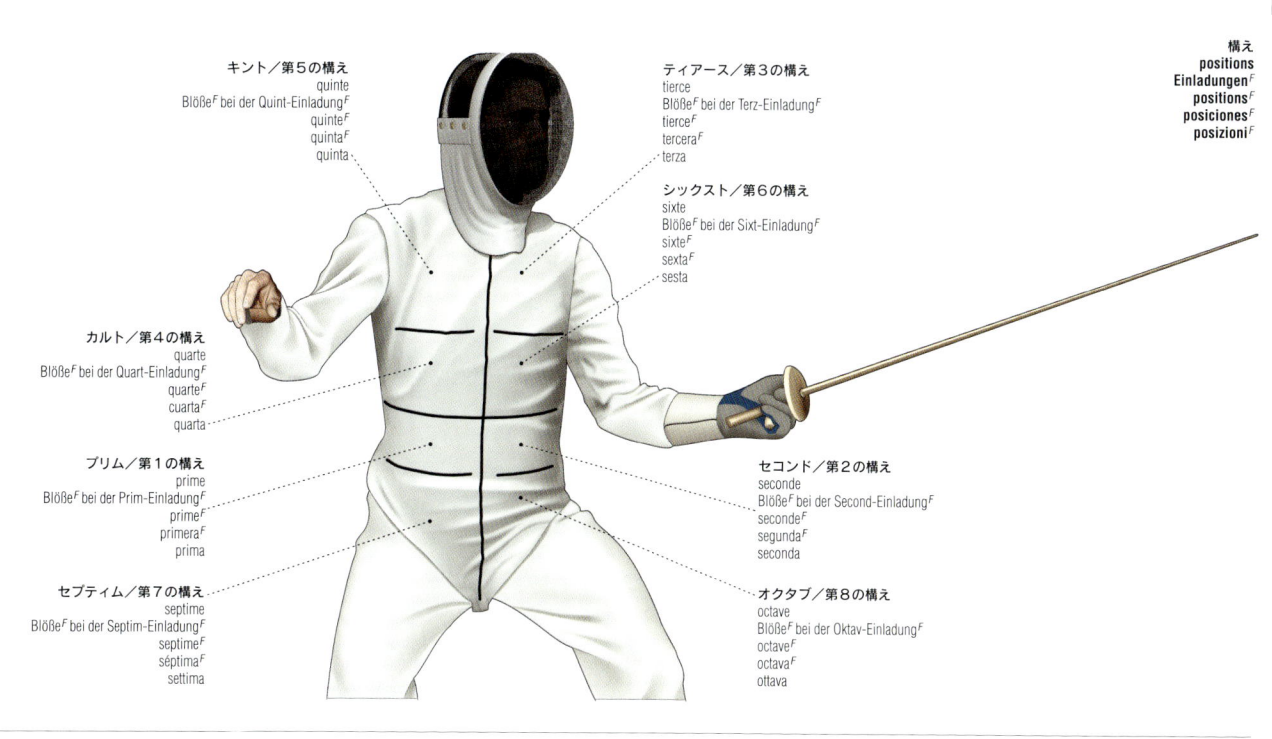

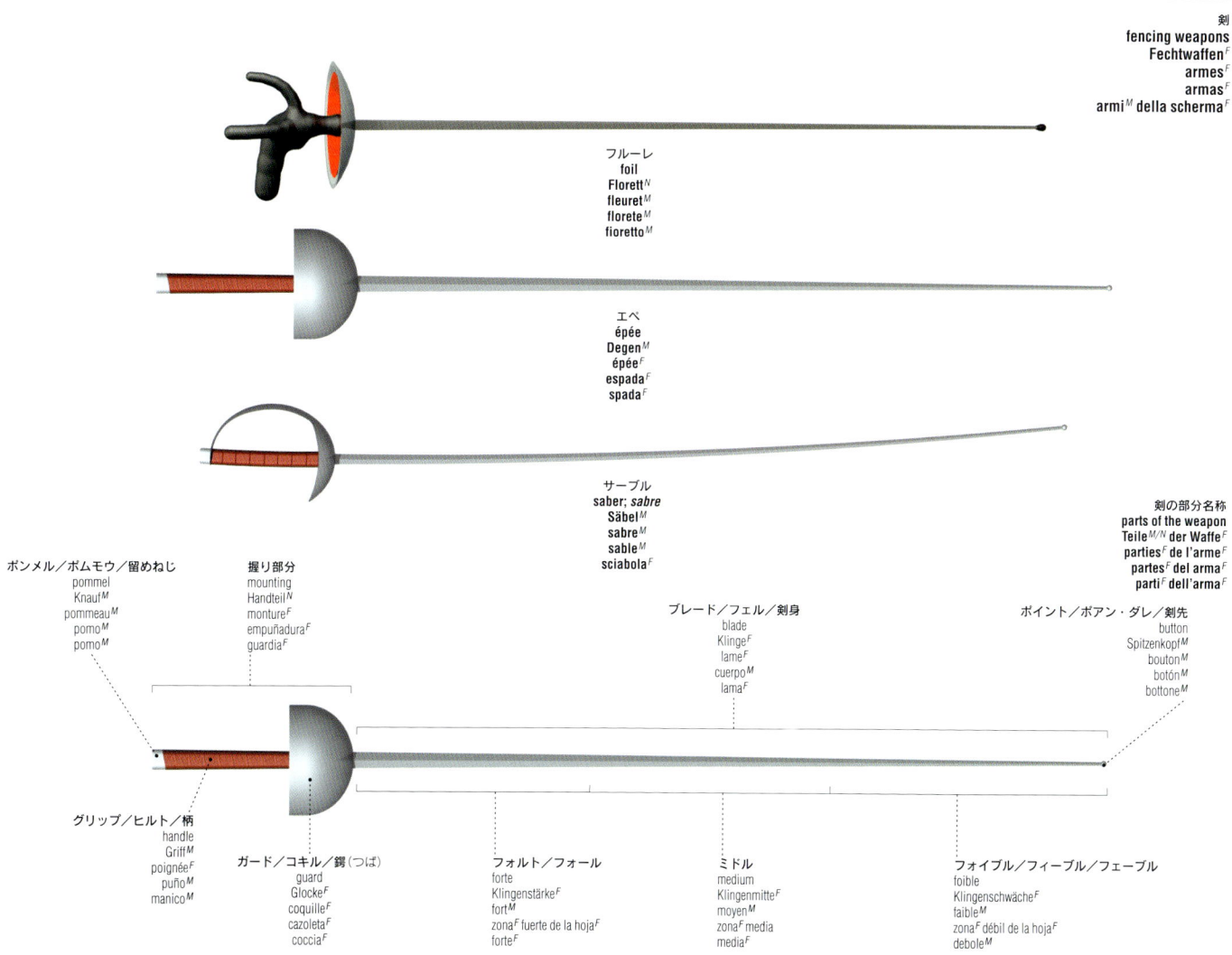

849

筋力スポーツ | STRENGTH SPORTS
KRAFTSPORT | SPORTS DE FORCE | DEPORTES DE FUERZA | SPORT DI FORZA

ウエイトリフティング

weightlifting | Gewichtheben[N] | haltérophilie[F] | halterofilia[F] | sollevamento[M] pesi[M]

バーベル
barbell
Scheibenhantel[F]
haltère[M] long
barra[F] con pesas[F]
bilanciere[M]

リストバンド／バンデージ
wristband
Handgelenksbandage[F]
poignet[M] de force[F]
muñequera[F]
polsino[M]

ウエイトリフティング・ベルト
weightlifting belt
Gewichthebergürtel[M]
ceinture[F] d'haltérophilie[F]
cinturón[M]
cintura[F] da sollevamento[M] pesi[M]

ランニング・シャツ／ユニフォーム
sleeveless jersey; *singlet*
ärmelloses Sporthemd[N]
maillot[M] de corps[M]
camiseta[F] sin mangas[F]
canottiera[F]

トランクス
trunks
Hose[F]
culotte[F]
pantalón[M]
pantaloncini[M]

膝当て／サポーター／バンデージ
knee wrap
Kniebandage[F]
genouillère[F]
rodillera[F]
ginocchiera[F]

ストラップ
strap
Riemen[M]
lanière[F]
correa[F]
cinturino[M]

ウエイトリフティング・シューズ
weightlifting shoe
Gewichtheberschuh[M]
chaussure[F] d'haltérophilie[F]
zapatilla[F]
scarpa[F]

（クリーン・アンド）ジャーク
clean and jerk
Stoßen[N]
épaulé[M]-jeté[M]
envión[M]
slancio[M]

スナッチ
snatch
Reißen[N]
arraché[M]
arranque[M]
strappo[M]

トレーニング用器具

fitness equipment | Fitnessgeräte[N] | appareils[M] de conditionnement[M] physique | aparatos[M] de ejercicios[M] | attrezzi[M] ginnici

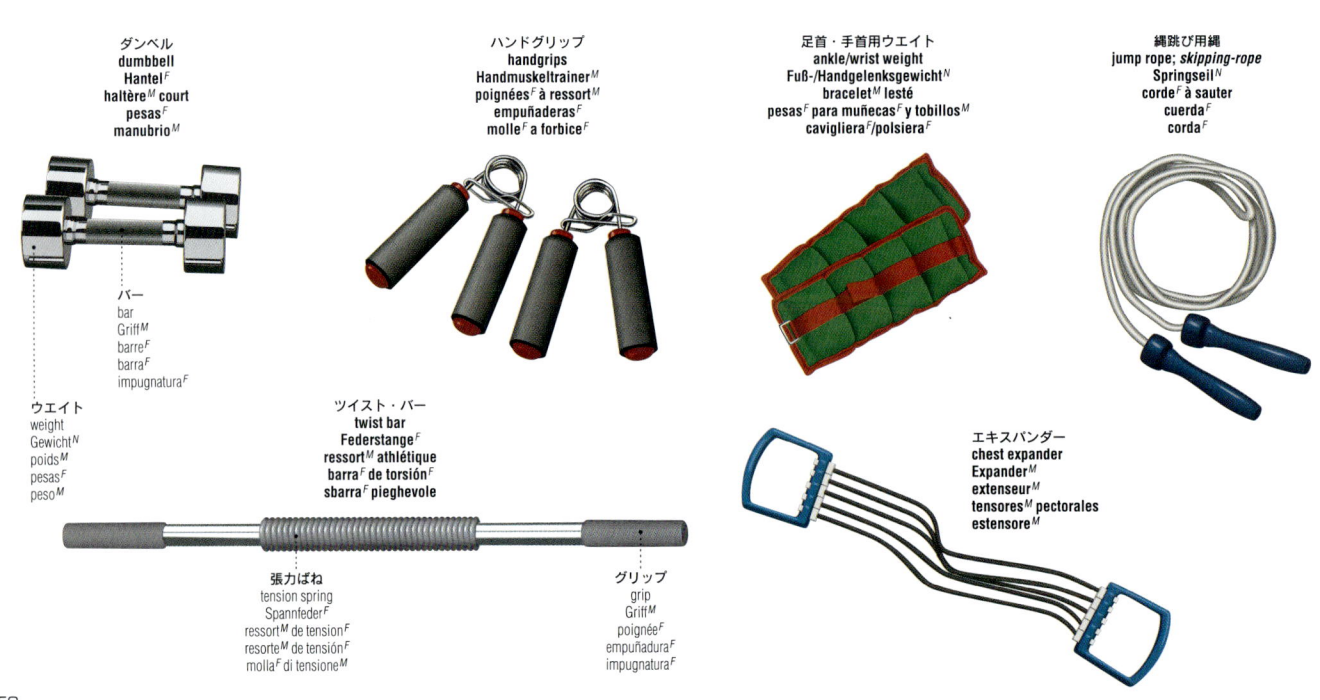

ダンベル
dumbbell
Hantel[F]
haltère[M] court
pesas[F]
manubrio[M]

ハンドグリップ
handgrips
Handmuskeltrainer[M]
poignées[F] à ressort[M]
empuñaderas[F]
molle[F] a forbice[F]

足首・手首用ウエイト
ankle/wrist weight
Fuß-/Handgelenksgewicht[N]
bracelet[M] lesté
pesas[F] para muñecas[F] y tobillos[M]
cavigliera[F]/polsiera[F]

縄跳び用縄
jump rope; *skipping-rope*
Springseil[N]
corde[F] à sauter
cuerda[F]
corda[F]

バー
bar
Griff[M]
barre[F]
barra[F]
impugnatura[F]

ウエイト
weight
Gewicht[N]
poids[M]
pesas[F]
peso[M]

ツイスト・バー
twist bar
Federstange[F]
ressort[M] athlétique
barra[F] de torsión[F]
sbarra[F] pieghevole

エキスパンダー
chest expander
Expander[M]
extenseur[M]
tensores[M] pectorales
estensore[M]

張力ばね
tension spring
Spannfeder[F]
ressort[M] de tension[F]
resorte[M] de tensión[F]
molla[F] di tensione[M]

グリップ
grip
Griff[M]
poignée[F]
empuñadura[F]
impugnatura[F]

850

筋力スポーツ | STRENGTH SPORTS
KRAFTSPORT | SPORTS DE FORCE | DEPORTES DE FUERZA | SPORT DI FORZA

トレーニング用器具

バーベル
barbell
Hantel F
haltère M long
haltera F
bilanciere M

カラー／留め金
collar
Manschette F
collier M de serrage
collarín M
anello M fermadisco M

サイクリング・マシーン
stationary bicycle
Heimtrainer M
vélo M d'exercice
bicicleta F estática
cyclette F

ディスク／プレート
disk; disc
Scheibe F
disque M
disco M
disco M

抵抗調節器
resistance adjustment
Widerstandseinstellung F
réglage M de la résistance F
ajuste M de resistencia F
regolatore M dello sforzo M

ハンドルバー
handlebar
Lenkstange F
guidon M
manillar M
manubrio M

シート
seat
Sitz M
selle F
asiento M
sella F

タイマー
timer
Timer M
minuteur M
reloj M
timer M

バー／シャフト
bar
Stange F
barre F
barra F
sbarra F

スリーブ
sleeve
Hantelstange F
manchon M
barra F
impugnatura F

高さ調節つまみ
height adjustment
Höhenverstellung F
réglage M de la hauteur F
ajuste M de altura F
regolatore M dell'altezza F

スピードメーター
speedometer
Tachometer N
indicateur M de vitesse F
velocímetro M
tachimetro M

ウエイト・マシーン
weight machine
Multitrainer M
banc M de musculation F
unidad F de pesas F
attrezzo M multiuso

ケーブル
cable
Draht M
câble M
cable M
cavo M

フットストラップ
footstrap
Fußriemen M
sangle F
trabilla F para el pie M
fermapiedi M

ブレーキ
brake
Bremse F
frein M
freno M
freno M

ペクトラル・デッキ
pectoral deck
Butterfly M
presse F à pectoraux M
pectoral M
piastra F per i pettorali M

ラテラル・バー
lateral bar
Latissimuszug M
barre F à dorsaux M
barra F lateral
barra F per i dorsali M

ペダル
pedal
Pedal N
pédale F
pedal M
pedale M

フライホイール／はずみ車
flywheel
Schwungrad N
volant M d'inertie F
rueda F
volano M

プレス・バー
press bar
Drückstange F
barre F à pectoraux M
presión F
barra F per i pettorali M

（クランチ）ベンチ
bench
Bank F
planche F
banco M
panca F

ステア・クライマー
stair climber
Climber M
simulateur M d'escalier M
escalera F
stepper M

レッグ・カール・バー
leg curl bar
Beincurler M
balancier M de traction F
barra F de flexión F de piernas F
rullo M per i bicipiti M femorali

レッグ・エクステンション・バー
leg extension bar
Beinstreckerzug M
balancier M d'extension F
barra F de extensión F de piernas F
rullo M per i quadricipiti M

トライセップ・バー
triceps bar
Trizepszug M
barre F à triceps M
barra F de triceps M
barra F per i tricipiti M

ウエイト／錘（おもり）
weights
Gewichte N
poids M
pesas F
pesi M

ローイング・マシーン
rowing machine
Rudergerät N
rameur M
remo M
vogatore M

オール
oar
Ruder N
rame F
remo M
remo M

プッシュ・アップ・スタンド
push-up stand
Pushup-Griff M
poignée F d'appui M
anillas F para flexiones F
ganci M di fissaggio M

水圧抵抗器
hydraulic resistance
hydraulischer Widerstand M
résistance F hydraulique
resorte M hidráulico
resistenza F idraulica

フット・サポート
foot support
Fußstütze F
cale-pied M
soporte M del pie M
appoggiapiedi M

スライディング・シート
sliding seat
freilaufender Sitz M
siège M coulissant
asiento M de corredera F
sedile M scorrevole

スポーツとゲーム

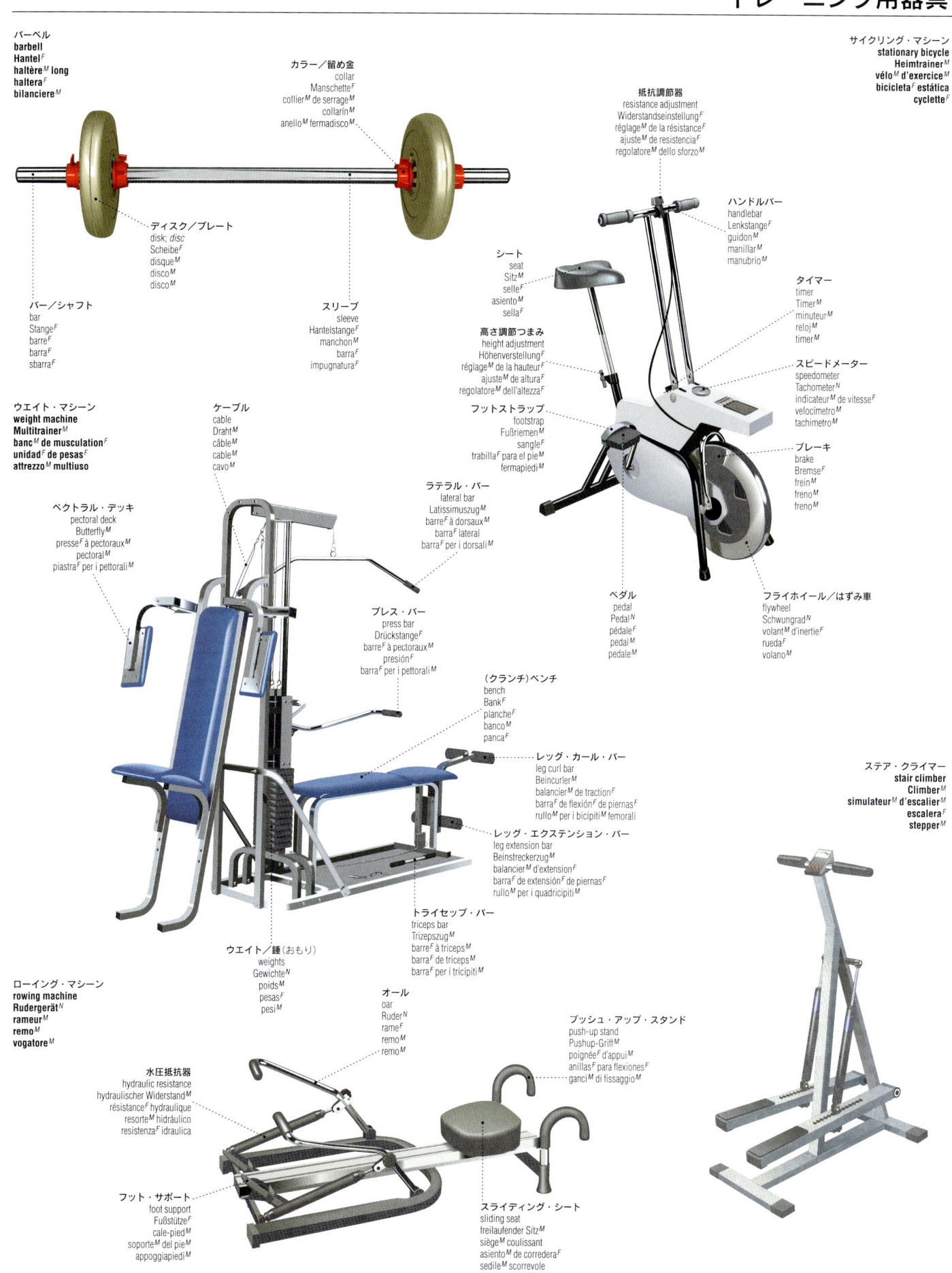

851

乗馬スポーツ | EQUESTRIAN SPORTS
REITSPORT | SPORTS ÉQUESTRES | DEPORTES ECUESTRES | SPORT EQUESTRI

障害飛越(ひえつ)競技

日本語 | 英語 | ドイツ語 | フランス語 | スペイン語 | イタリア語

show-jumping | Springreiten[N] | saut[M] d'obstacle[M] | salto[M] de obstáculos[M] | salto[M] ostacoli[M]

障害物
obstacles
Hürden[F]
obstacles[M]
obstáculos[M]
ostacoli[M]

木柵
gate
Gatter[N]
barrière[F]
barrera[F]
cancello[M]

土壁横木(おうぼく)
wall and rails
Mauer[F] mit Stangen[F]
mur[M] barré
valla[F] sobre muro[M]
muro[M] con barriere[F]

生け垣横木
brush and rails
Bürste[F] mit Stangen[F]
haie[F] barrée
valla[F] sobre seto[M]
siepe[F] con barriere[F]

垂直板
post and plank
Pfosten[M] mit Latte[F]
palanque[M]
palancas[F]
tavole[F]

三段横木
triple bars
Dreifachbalken[M]
barres[F] de Spa
triple de barras[F]
triplice[M]

垂直横木
post and rail
Pfosten[M] mit Stange[F]
stationata[F]
vertical[M] de barras[F]
barriere[F]

水濠
water ditch
Wassergraben[M]
haie[F] rivière[F]
ría[F]
riviera[F]

土壁
wall
Mauer[F]
mur[M]
muro[M]
muro[M]

平行横木/オクサー
double oxer
Doppeloxer[M]
oxer[M]
óxer[M] de barras[F]
oxer[M]

競技場／コース
competition ring
Sprungreitparcours[M]
parcours[M] d'obstacles[M]
pista[F] para salto[M] de obstáculos[M]
campo[M] di gara[F]

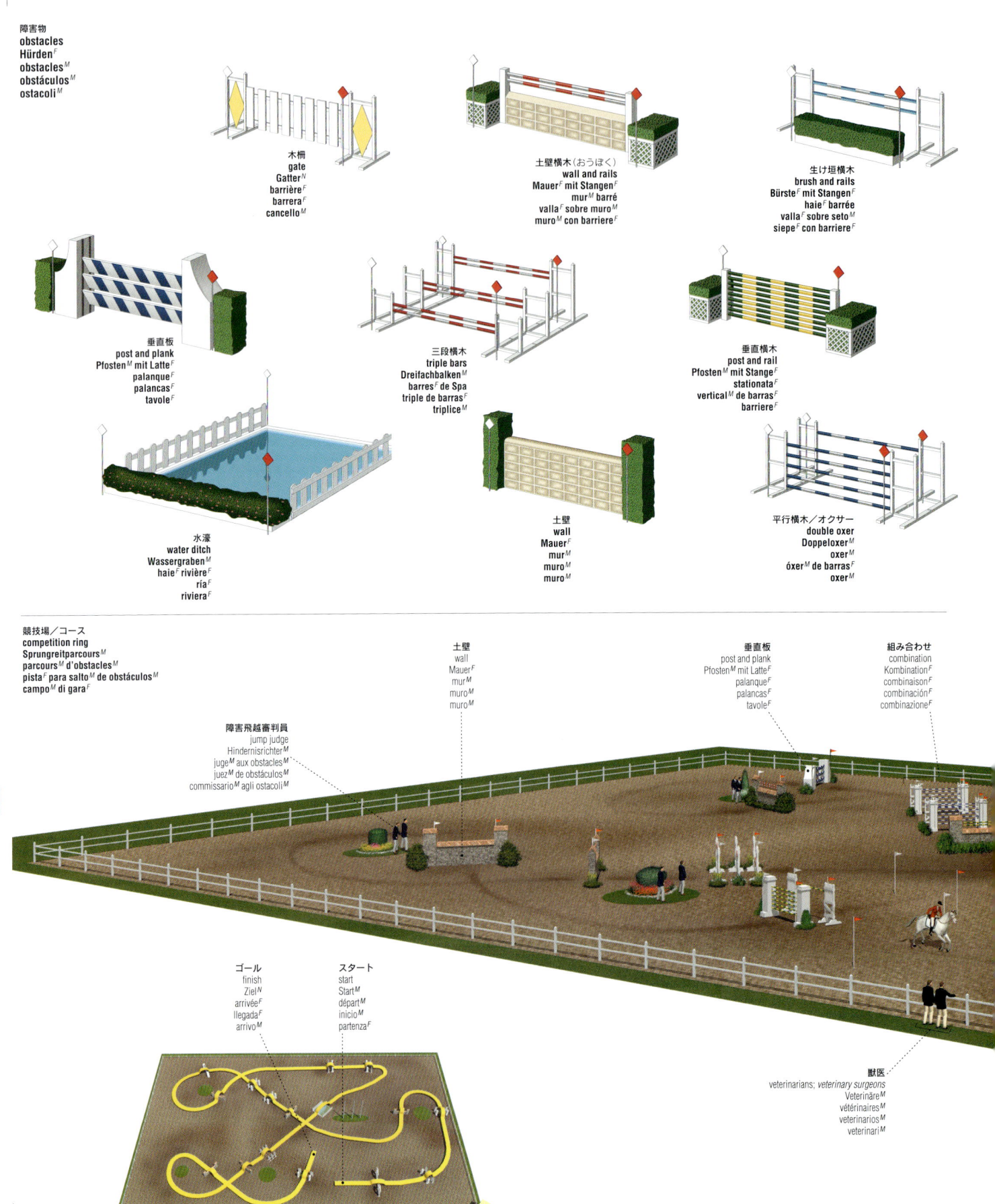

土壁
wall
Mauer[F]
mur[M]
muro[M]
muro[M]

垂直板
post and plank
Pfosten[M] mit Latte[F]
palanque[M]
palancas[F]
tavole[F]

組み合わせ
combination
Kombination[F]
combinaison[F]
combinación[F]
combinazione[F]

障害飛越審判員
jump judge
Hindernisrichter[M]
juge[M] aux obstacles[M]
juez[M] de obstáculos[M]
commissario[M] agli ostacoli[M]

ゴール
finish
Ziel[N]
arrivée[F]
llegada[F]
arrivo[M]

スタート
start
Start[M]
départ[M]
inicio[M]
partenza[F]

獣医
veterinarians; *veterinary surgeons*
Veterinäre[M]
vétérinaires[M]
veterinarios[M]
veterinari[M]

乗馬スポーツ | EQUESTRIAN SPORTS
REITSPORT | SPORTS ÉQUESTRES | DEPORTES ECUESTRES | SPORT EQUESTRI

障害飛越(ひえつ)競技

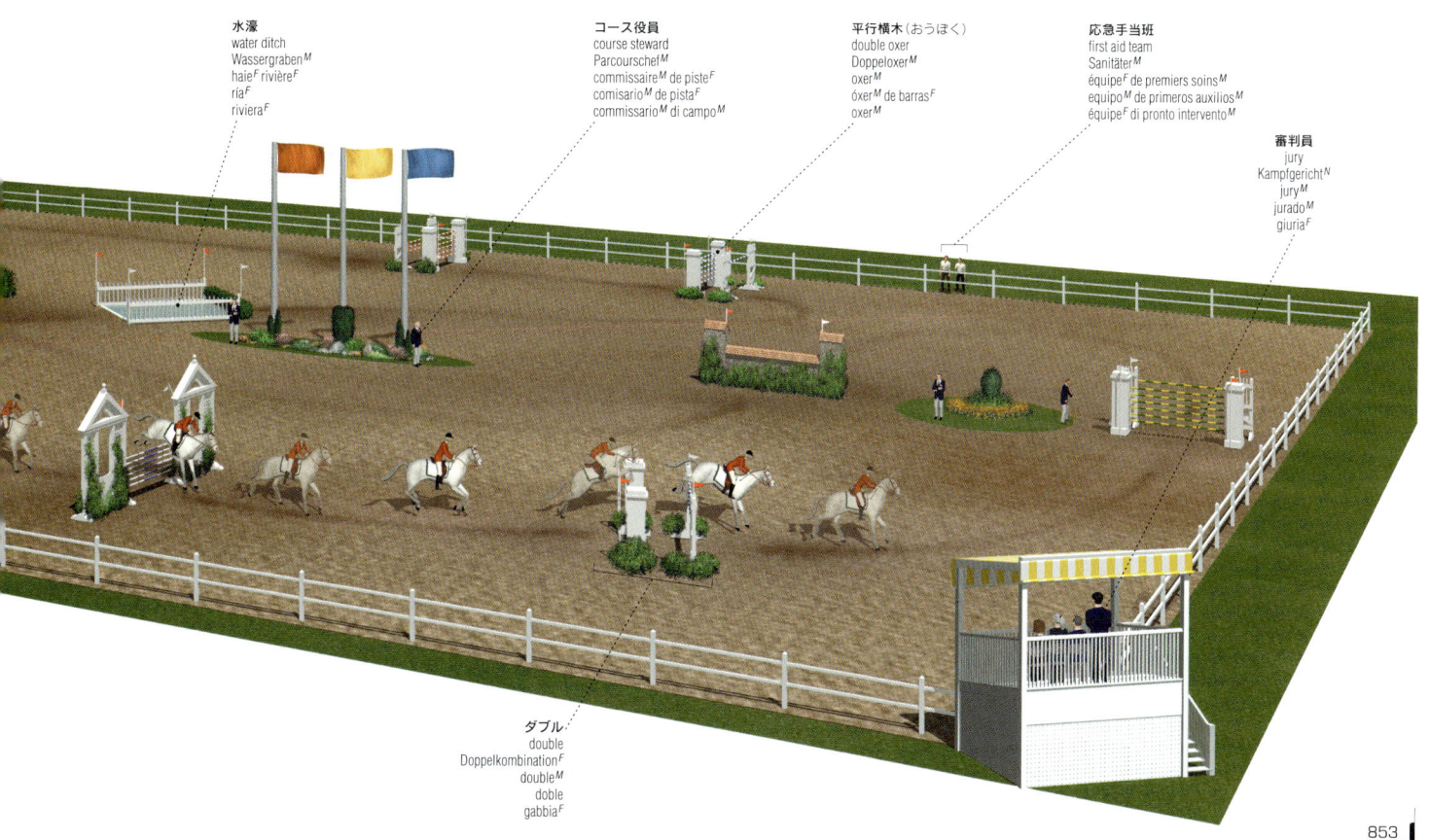

上着／上衣／乗馬服
riding jacket
Reitjacke^F
jaquette^F
chaqueta^F de montar
giacca^F da cavallo^M

猟騎帽
riding cap
Reithelm^M
bombe^F
casco^M
cap^M

乗馬ズボン／ジョッパーズ
jodhpurs
Reithose^F
jodhpurs
pantalones^M de montar
pantaloni^M da cavallo^M

鞍／鞍座
saddle
Sattel^M
selle^F
silla^F
sella^F

騎手
rider
Reiter^M
cavalier^M
jinete^M
cavaliere^M

手袋
riding glove
Reithandschuh^M
gant^M
guante^M
guanto^M

鞍覆い
saddlecloth
Woilach^M
tapis^M de selle
manta^F de la silla
copertina^F

鞭
riding crop
Reitgerte^F
cravache^F
fusta^F
frustino^M

鐙(あぶみ)
stirrup iron
Steigbügel^M
étrier^M
estribo^M
staffa^F

胸当て／胸繋(むながい)
breastplate
Brustplatte^F
bricole^F
petral^M
pettorale^M

肢(あし)巻き／防護革
shin boot
Bandage^F
botte^F de tendon
vendaje^M
stivaletto^M

腹帯(はらおび)
surcingle
Bauchgurt^M
sous-ventrière^F
sobrecincha^F
sottopancia^M

蹄(ひづめ)覆い／追突予防帯
coronet boot
Hufglocke^F
botte^F de couronne
bota^F de la corona^F del casco^M
paranocche^M

水濠
water ditch
Wassergraben^M
haie^F rivière^F
ría^F
riviera^F

コース役員
course steward
Parcourschef
commissaire^M de piste
comisario^M de pista^F
commissario^M di campo^M

平行横木(おうぼく)
double oxer
Doppeloxer^M
oxer^M
óxer^M de barras^F
oxer^M

応急手当班
first aid team
Sanitäter^M
équipe^F de premiers soins^M
equipo^M de primeros auxilios^M
équipe^F di pronto intervento^M

審判員
jury
Kampfgericht^N
jury^M
jurado^M
giuria^F

ダブル
double
Doppelkombination^F
double^M
doble
gabbia^F

スポーツとゲーム

853

乗馬スポーツ | EQUESTRIAN SPORTS
REITSPORT | SPORTS ÉQUESTRES | DEPORTES ECUESTRES | SPORT EQUESTRI

乗馬

日本語 | 英語 | ドイツ語 | フランス語 | スペイン語 | イタリア語

riding | ReitenN | équitationF | equitaciónF | equitazioneF

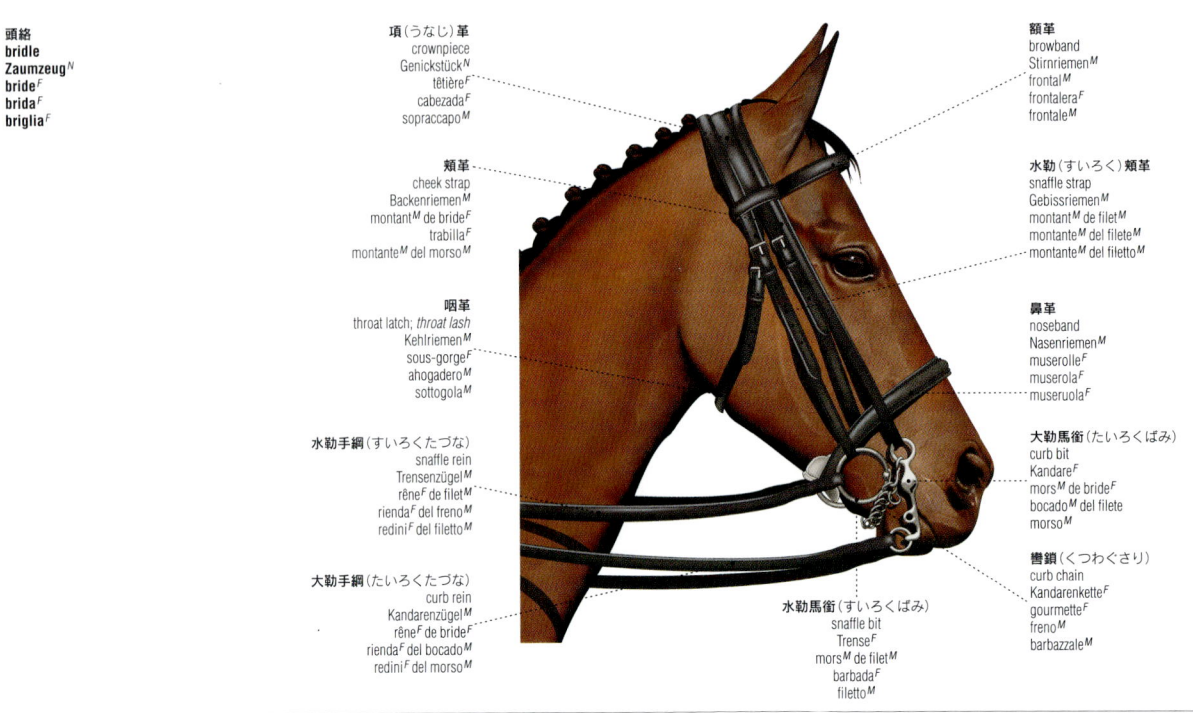

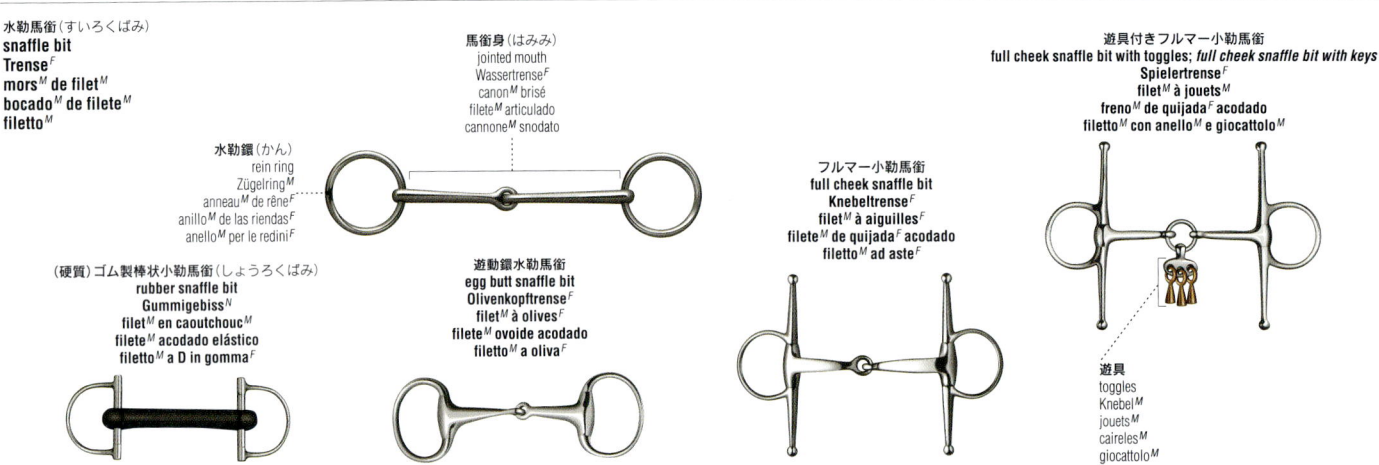

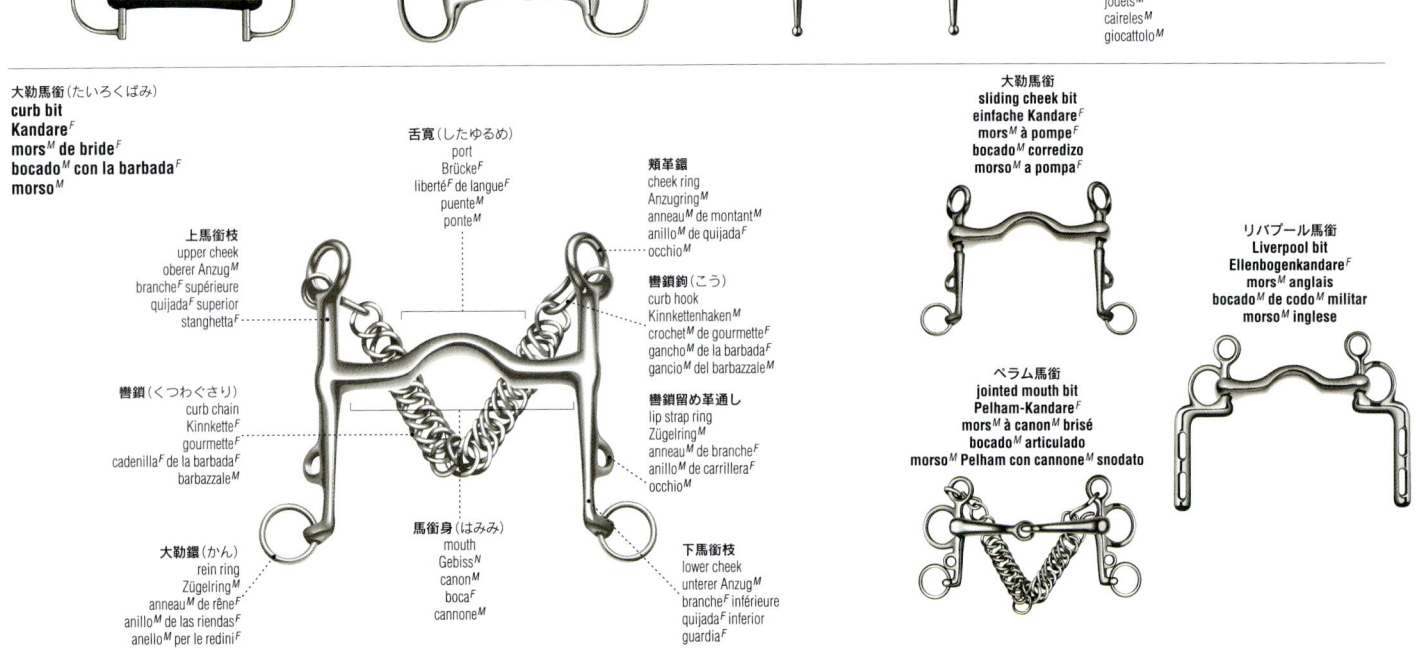

頭絡
bridle
ZaumzeugN
brideF
bridaF
brigliaF

項(うなじ)革
crownpiece
GenickstückN
têtièreF
cabezadaF
sopraccapoM

額革
browband
StirnriemenM
frontalM
frontaleraF
frontaleM

頬革
cheek strap
BackenriemenM
montantM de brideF
trabillaF
montanteM del morsoM

水勒(すいろく)頬革
snaffle strap
GebissriemenM
montantM de filetM
montanteF del fileteM
montanteM del filettoM

咽革
throat latch; *throat lash*
KehlriemenM
sous-gorgeF
ahogaderoM
sottogolaM

鼻革
noseband
NasenriemenM
muserolleF
muserolaF
museruolaF

水勒手綱(すいろくたづな)
snaffle rein
TrensenzügelM
rêneF de filetM
riendaF del frenoM
rediniF del filettoM

大勒馬銜(たいろくくばみ)
curb bit
KandareF
morsM de brideF
bocadoM del filete
morsoM

大勒手綱(たいろくたづな)
curb rein
KandarenzügelM
rêneF de brideF
riendaF del bocadoM
rediniF del morsoM

水勒馬銜(すいろくくばみ)
snaffle bit
TrenseF
morsM de filetM
barbadaF
filettoM

轡鎖(くつわぐさり)
curb chain
KandarenketteF
gourmetteF
frenoM
barbazzaleM

水勒馬銜(すいろくくばみ)
snaffle bit
TrenseF
morsM de filetM
bocadoM de fileteM
filettoM

馬銜身(はみみ)
jointed mouth
WassertrenseF
canonM brisé
fileteM articulado
cannoneM snodato

遊具付きフルマー小勒馬銜
full cheek snaffle bit with toggles; *full cheek snaffle bit with keys*
SpielertrenseF
filetM à jouetsM
frenoM de quijadaF acodado
filettoM con anelloM e giocattoloM

水勒鐶(かん)
rein ring
ZügelringM
anneauM de rêneF
anilloM de las riendasF
anelloM per le rediniF

フルマー小勒馬銜
full cheek snaffle bit
KnebeltrenseF
filetM à aiguillesF
fileteM de quijadaF acodado
filettoM ad asteF

(硬質)ゴム製棒状小勒馬銜(しょうろくくばみ)
rubber snaffle bit
GummigebissN
filetM en caoutchoucM
fileteM acodado elástico
filettoM a D in gommaF

遊鐶水勒馬銜
egg butt snaffle bit
OlivenkopftrenseF
filetM à olivesF
fileteM ovoide acodado
filettoM a olivaF

遊具
toggles
KnebelM
jouetsM
cairelesM
giocattoloM

大勒馬銜(たいろくくばみ)
curb bit
KandareF
morsM de brideF
bocadoM con la barbadaF
morsoM

舌寛(したゆるめ)
port
BrückeF
libertéF de langueF
puenteM
ponteM

頬革鐶
cheek ring
AnzugringM
anneauM de montantM
anilloM de quijadaF
occhioM

大勒馬銜
sliding cheek bit
einfache KandareF
morsM à pompeF
bocadoM corredizo
morsoM a pompaF

上馬銜枝
upper cheek
oberer AnzugM
brancheF supérieure
quijadaF superior
stanghettaF

轡鎖鉤(こう)
curb hook
KinnkettenhakenM
crochetM de gourmetteF
ganchoM de la barbadaF
gancioM del barbazzaleM

リバプール馬銜
Liverpool bit
EllenbogenkandareF
morsM anglais
bocadoM de codoM militar
morsoM inglese

轡鎖(くつわぐさり)
curb chain
KinnketteF
gourmetteF
cadenillaF de la barbadaF
barbazzaleM

轡鎖留め革通し
lip strap ring
ZügelringM
anneauM de brancheF
anilloM de carrilleraF
occhioM

ペラム馬銜
jointed mouth bit
Pelham-KandareF
morsM à canonM brisé
bocadoM articulado
morsoM Pelham con cannoneM snodato

大勒鐶(かん)
rein ring
ZügelringM
anneauM de rêneF
anilloM de las riendasF
anelloM per le rediniF

馬銜身(はみみ)
mouth
GebissN
canonM
bocaF
cannoneM

下馬銜枝
lower cheek
unterer AnzugM
brancheF inférieure
quijadaF inferior
guardiaF

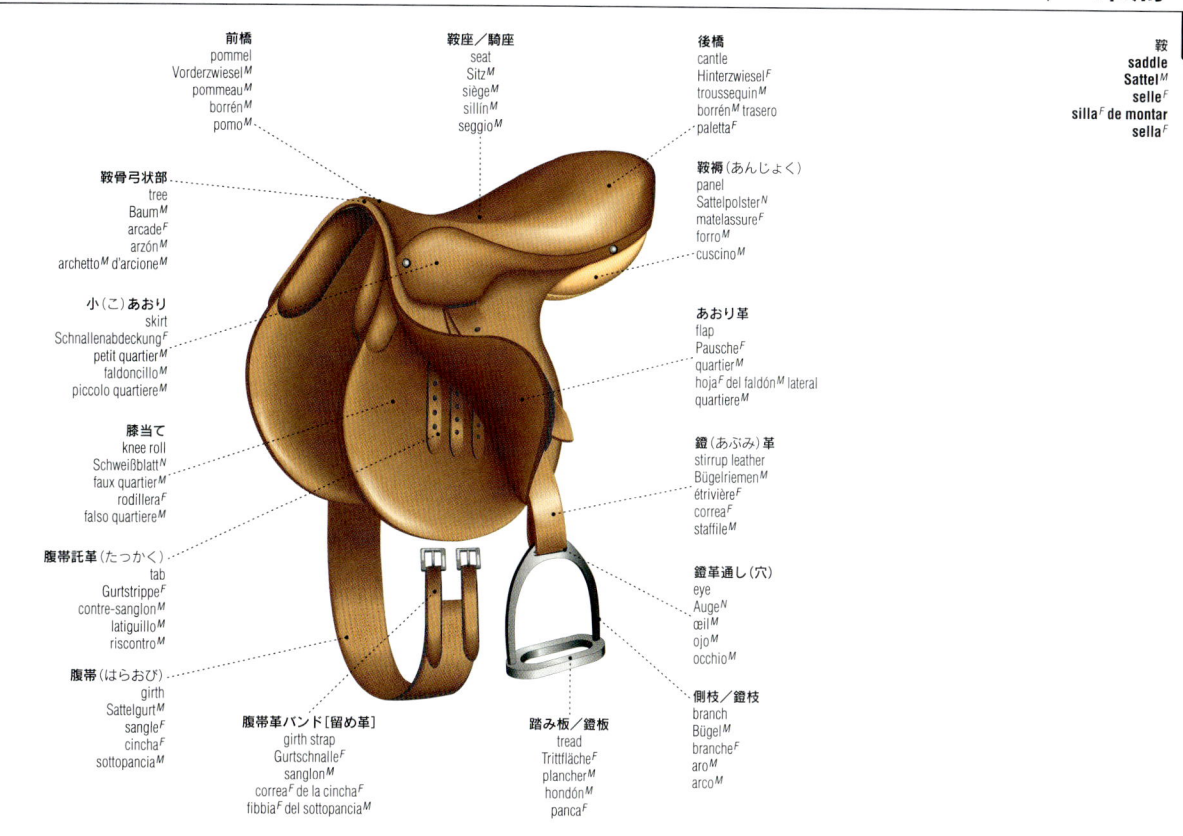

乗馬スポーツ | EQUESTRIAN SPORTS
REITSPORT | SPORTS ÉQUESTRES | DEPORTES ECUESTRES | SPORT EQUESTRI

乗馬
saddle
Sattel^M
selle^F
silla^F de montar
sella^F

前橋
pommel
Vorderzwiesel^M
pommeau^M
borrén^M
pomo^M

鞍座／騎座
seat
Sitz^M
siège^M
sillín^M
seggio^M

後橋
cantle
Hinterzwiesel^M
troussequin^M
borrén^M trasero
paletta^F

鞍骨弓状部
tree
Baum^M
arcade^F
arzón^M
archetto^M d'arcione^M

鞍褥（あんじょく）
panel
Sattelpolster^N
matelassure^F
forro^M
cuscino^M

小（こ）あおり
skirt
Schnallenabdeckung^F
petit quartier^M
faldoncillo^M
piccolo quartiere^M

あおり革
flap
Pausche^F
quartier^M
hoja^F del faldón^M lateral
quartiere^M

膝当て
knee roll
Schweißblatt^N
faux quartier^M
rodillera^F
falso quartiere^M

鐙（あぶみ）革
stirrup leather
Bügelriemen^M
étrivière^F
correa^F
staffile^M

腹帯託革（たっかく）
tab
Gurtstrippe^F
contre-sanglon^M
latiguillo^M
riscontro^M

鐙革通し（穴）
eye
Auge^N
œil^M
ojo^M
occhio^M

腹帯（はらおび）
girth
Sattelgurt^M
sangle^F
cincha^F
sottopancia^F

腹帯革バンド［留め革］
girth strap
Gurtschnalle^F
sanglon^M
correa^F de la cincha^F
fibbia^F del sottopancia^M

踏み板／鐙板
tread
Trittfläche^F
plancher^M
hondón^M
panca^F

側枝／鐙枝
branch
Bügel^M
branche^F
aro^M
arco^M

馬場馬術
dressage | Dressurreiten^N | dressage^M | doma^F | dressage^M

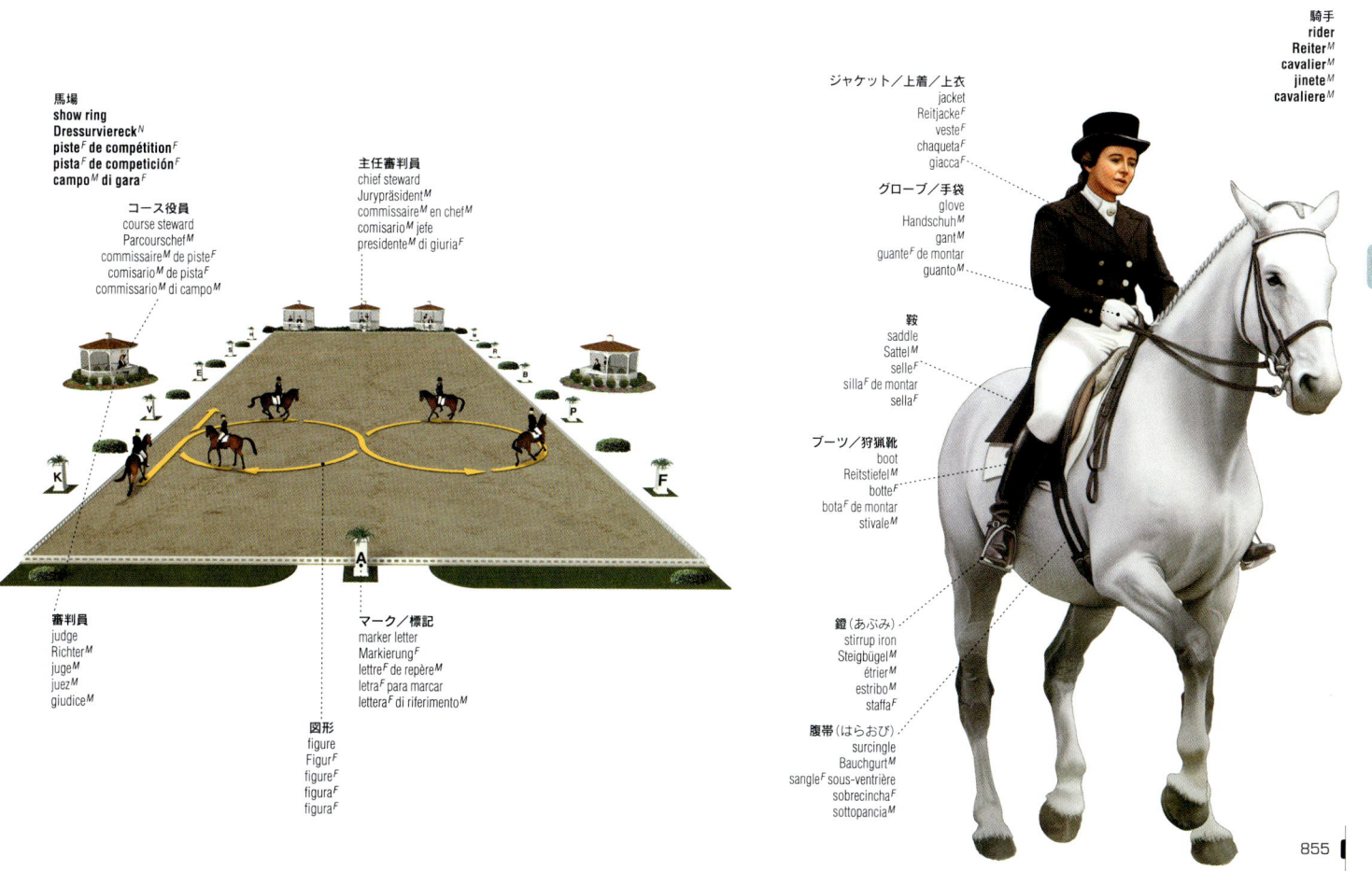

馬場
show ring
Dressurviereck^N
piste^F de compétition^F
pista^F de competición^F
campo^M di gara^F

コース役員
course steward
Parcourschef^M
commissaire^M de piste^F
comisario^M de pista^F
commissario^M di campo^M

主任審判員
chief steward
Jurypräsident^M
commissaire^M en chef^M
comisario^M jefe
presidente^M di giuria^F

騎手
rider
Reiter^M
cavalier^M
jinete^M
cavaliere^M

ジャケット／上着／上衣
jacket
Reitjacke^F
veste^F
chaqueta^F
giacca^F

グローブ／手袋
glove
Handschuh^M
gant^M
guante^M de montar
guanto^M

鞍
saddle
Sattel^M
selle^F
silla^F de montar
sella^F

ブーツ／狩猟靴
boot
Reitstiefel^M
botte^F
bota^F de montar
stivale^M

審判員
judge
Richter^M
juge^M
juez^M
giudice^M

マーク／標記
marker letter
Markierung^F
lettre^F de repère^M
letra^F para marcar
lettera^F di riferimento^M

図形
figure
Figur^F
figure^F
figura^F
figura^F

鐙（あぶみ）
stirrup iron
Steigbügel^M
étrier^M
estribo^M
staffa^F

腹帯（はらおび）
surcingle
Bauchgurt^M
sangle^F sous-ventrière^F
sobrecincha^F
sottopancia^M

855

乗馬スポーツ | EQUESTRIAN SPORTS
REITSPORT | SPORTS ÉQUESTRES | DEPORTES ECUESTRES | SPORT EQUESTRI

競馬：競馬場

日本語 | 英語 | ドイツ語 | フランス語 | スペイン語 | イタリア語

horse racing: turf | Pferderennen^N: Galopprennen^N | course^F de chevaux^M: turf^M | carrera^F de caballos^M: turf^M | corse^F dei cavalli: galoppo^M

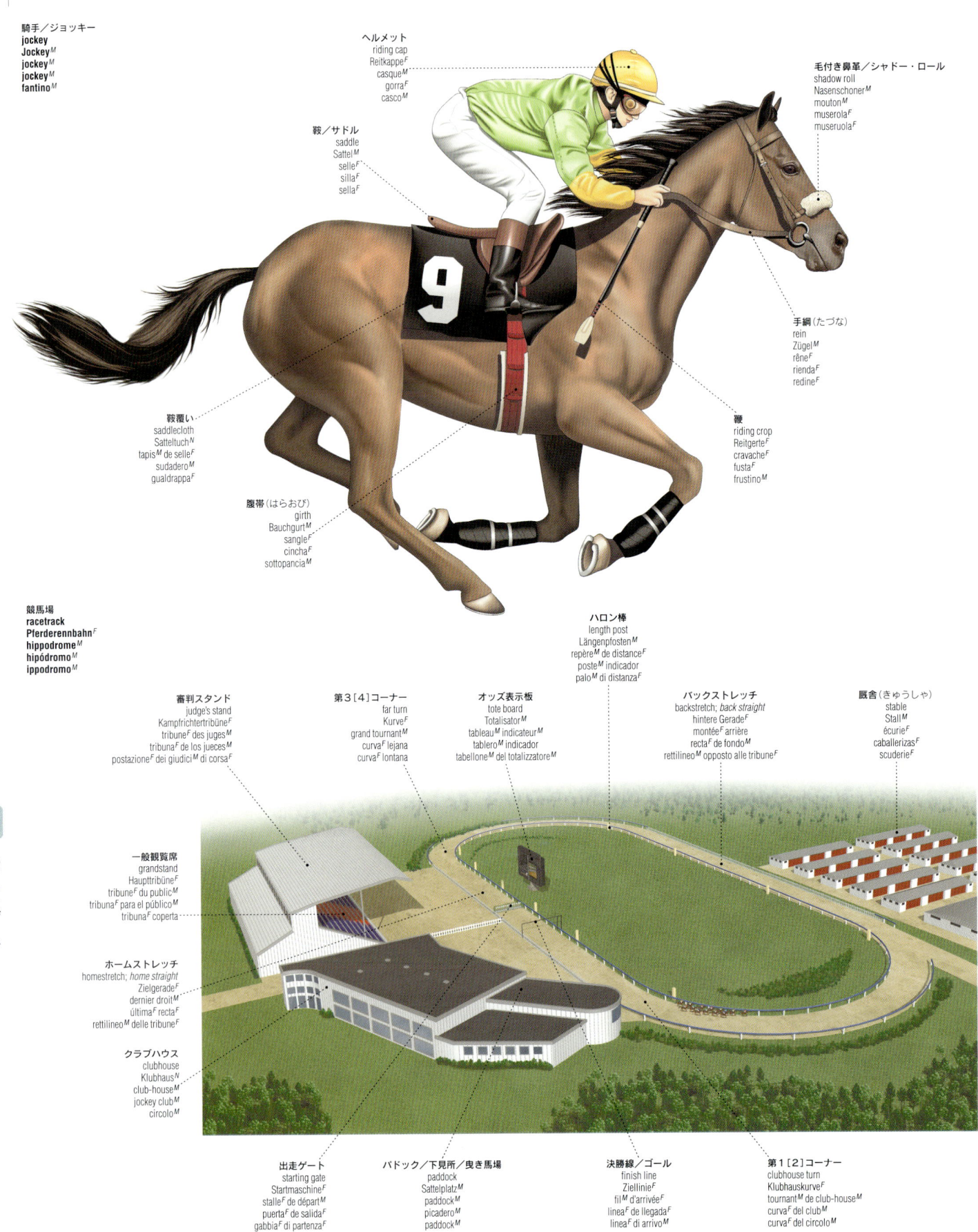

騎手／ジョッキー
jockey
Jockey^M
jockey^M
jockey^M
fantino^M

ヘルメット
riding cap
Reitkappe^F
casque^M
gorra^F
casco^M

毛付き鼻革／シャドー・ロール
shadow roll
Nasenschoner^M
mouton^M
muserola^F
museruola^F

鞍／サドル
saddle
Sattel^M
selle^F
silla^F
sella^F

手綱（たづな）
rein
Zügel^M
rêne^F
rienda^F
redine^F

鞍覆い
saddlecloth
Satteltuch^N
tapis^M de selle^F
sudadero^M
gualdrappa^F

鞭
riding crop
Reitgerte^F
cravache^F
fusta^F
frustino^M

腹帯（はらおび）
girth
Bauchgurt^M
sangle^F
cincha^F
sottopancia^M

競馬場
racetrack
Pferderennbahn^F
hippodrome^M
hipódromo^M
ippodromo^M

ハロン棒
length post
Längenpfosten^M
repère^M de distance^F
poste^M indicador
palo^M di distanza^F

審判スタンド
judge's stand
Kampfrichtertribüne^F
tribune^F des juges^M
tribuna^F de los jueces^M
postazione^F dei giudici di corsa^F

第3[4]コーナー
far turn
Kurve^F
grand tournant^M
curva^F lejana
curva^F lontana

オッズ表示板
tote board
Totalisator^M
tableau^M indicateur
tablero^M indicador
tabellone^M del totalizzatore^F

バックストレッチ
backstretch; back straight
hintere Gerade^F
montée^F arrière
recta^F de fondo^M
rettilineo^M opposto alle tribune^F

厩舎（きゅうしゃ）
stable
Stall^M
écurie^F
caballerizas^F
scuderie^F

一般観覧席
grandstand
Haupttribüne^F
tribune^F du public^M
tribuna^F para el público^M
tribuna^F coperta

ホームストレッチ
homestretch; home straight
Zielgerade^F
dernier droit^M
última^F recta^F
rettilineo^M delle tribune^F

クラブハウス
clubhouse
Klubhaus^N
club-house^M
jockey club
circolo^M

出走ゲート
starting gate
Startmaschine^F
stalle^F de départ^M
puerta^F de salida^F
gabbia^F di partenza^F

パドック／下見所／曳き馬場
paddock
Sattelplatz^M
paddock^M
picadero^M
paddock^M

決勝線／ゴール
finish line
Ziellinie^F
fil^M d'arrivée^F
linea^F de llegada^F
linea^F di arrivo^M

第1[2]コーナー
clubhouse turn
Klubhauskurve^F
tournant^M de club-house^M
curva^F del club
curva^F del circolo^M

スポーツとゲーム

856

乗馬スポーツ | EQUESTRIAN SPORTS
REITSPORT | SPORTS ÉQUESTRES | DEPORTES ECUESTRES | SPORT EQUESTRI

競馬：繋駕速歩（けいがはやあし）競走

horse racing: harness racing | Pferderennen^N: Trabrennen^N | course^F de chevaux^M: course^F attelée | carrera^F de caballos^M: carreras^F con arneses^M | corse^F dei cavalli: trotto^M e ambio^M

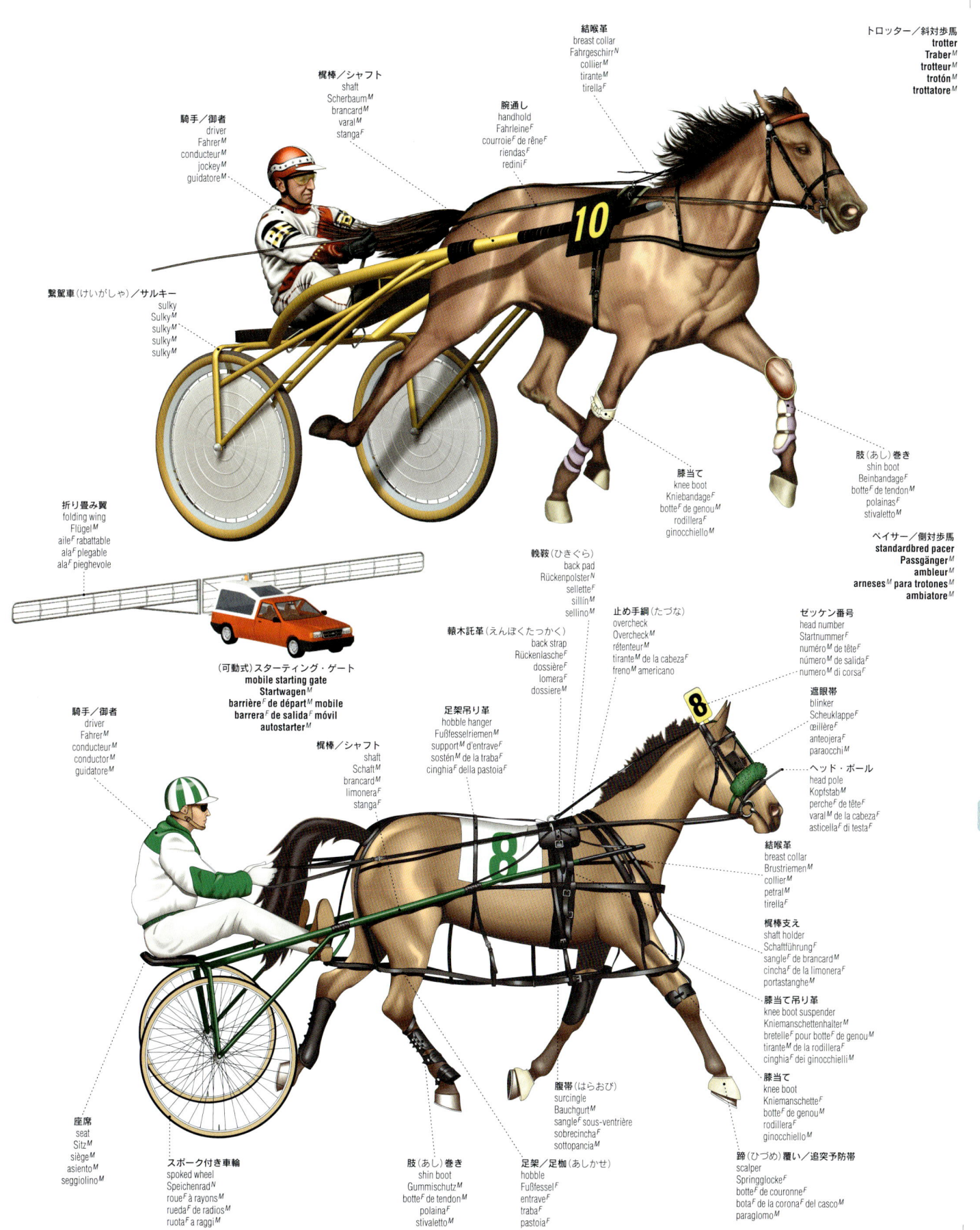

トロッター／斜対歩馬
trotter
Traber^M
trotteur^M
trotón^M
trottatore^M

結喉革
breast collar
Fahrgeschirr^N
collier^M
tirante^M
tirella^F

梶棒／シャフト
shaft
Scherbaum^M
brancard^M
varal^M
stanga^F

腕通し
handhold
Fahrleine^N
courroie^F de rêne^F
riendas^F
redini^F

騎手／御者
driver
Fahrer^M
conducteur^M
jockey^M
guidatore^M

繋駕車（けいがしゃ）／サルキー
sulky
Sulky^M
sulky^M
sulky^M
sulky^M

肢（あし）巻き
shin boot
Beinbandage^F
botte^F de tendon^M
polainas^F
stivaletto^M

膝当て
knee boot
Kniebandage^F
botte^F de genou^M
rodillera^F
ginocchiello^M

折り畳み翼
folding wing
Flügel^M
aile^F rabattable
ala^F plegable
ala^F pieghevole

ペイサー／側対歩馬
standardbred pacer
Passgänger^M
ambleur^M
arneses^M para trotones
ambiatore^M

鞍鞍（ひきぐら）
back pad
Rückenpolster^N
sellette^F
sillín^M
sellino^M

止め手綱（たづな）
overcheck
Overcheck^M
rétenteur^M
tirante^M de la cabeza^F
freno^M americano

ゼッケン番号
head number
Startnummer^F
numéro^M de tête^F
número^M de salida^F
numero^M di corsa^F

轅木託革（えんぼくたっかく）
back strap
Rückenlasche^F
dossière^F
lomera^F
dossiera^F

（可動式）スターティング・ゲート
mobile starting gate
Startwagen^M
barrière^F de départ^M mobile
barrera^F de salida^F móvil
autostarter^M

足架吊り革
hobble hanger
Fußfesselriemen^M
support^M d'entrave^F
sostén^M de la traba^F
cinghia^F della pastoia^F

遮眼帯
blinker
Scheuklappe^F
œillère^F
anteojera^F
paraocchi^M

ヘッド・ポール
head pole
Kopfstab^M
perche^F de tête^F
varal^M de la cabeza^F
asticella^F di testa^F

騎手／御者
driver
Fahrer^M
conducteur^M
conductor^M
guidatore^M

梶棒／シャフト
shaft
Schaft^M
brancard^M
limonera^F
stanga^F

結喉革
breast collar
Brustriemen^M
collier^M
petral^M
tirella^F

梶棒支え
shaft holder
Schaftführung^F
sangle^F de brancard^M
cincha^F de la limonera^F
portastanghe^M

膝当て吊り革
knee boot suspender
Kniemanschettenhalter^M
bretelle^F pour botte^F de genou^M
tirante^M de la rodillera^F
cinghia^F dei ginocchielli^M

膝当て
knee boot
Kniemanschette^F
botte^F de genou^M
rodillera^F
ginocchiello^M

腹帯（はらおび）
surcingle
Bauchgurt^M
sangle^F sous-ventrière
sobrecincha^F
sottopancia^M

蹄（ひづめ）覆い／追突予防帯
scalper
Springglocke^F
botte^F de couronne^F
bota^F de la corona^F del casco^M
paraglomo^M

座席
seat
Sitz^M
siège^M
asiento^M
seggiolino^M

スポーク付き車輪
spoked wheel
Speichenrad^N
roue^F à rayons^M
rueda^F de radios^M
ruota^F a raggi^M

肢（あし）巻き
shin boot
Gummischutz^M
botte^F de tendon^M
polaina^F
stivaletto^M

足架／足枷（あしかせ）
hobble
Fußfessel^F
entrave^F
traba^F
pastoia^F

スポーツとゲーム

857

乗馬スポーツ | EQUESTRIAN SPORTS
REITSPORT | SPORTS ÉQUESTRES | DEPORTES ECUESTRES | SPORT EQUESTRI

ポロ
polo | Polo[N] | polo[M] | polo[M] | polo[M]

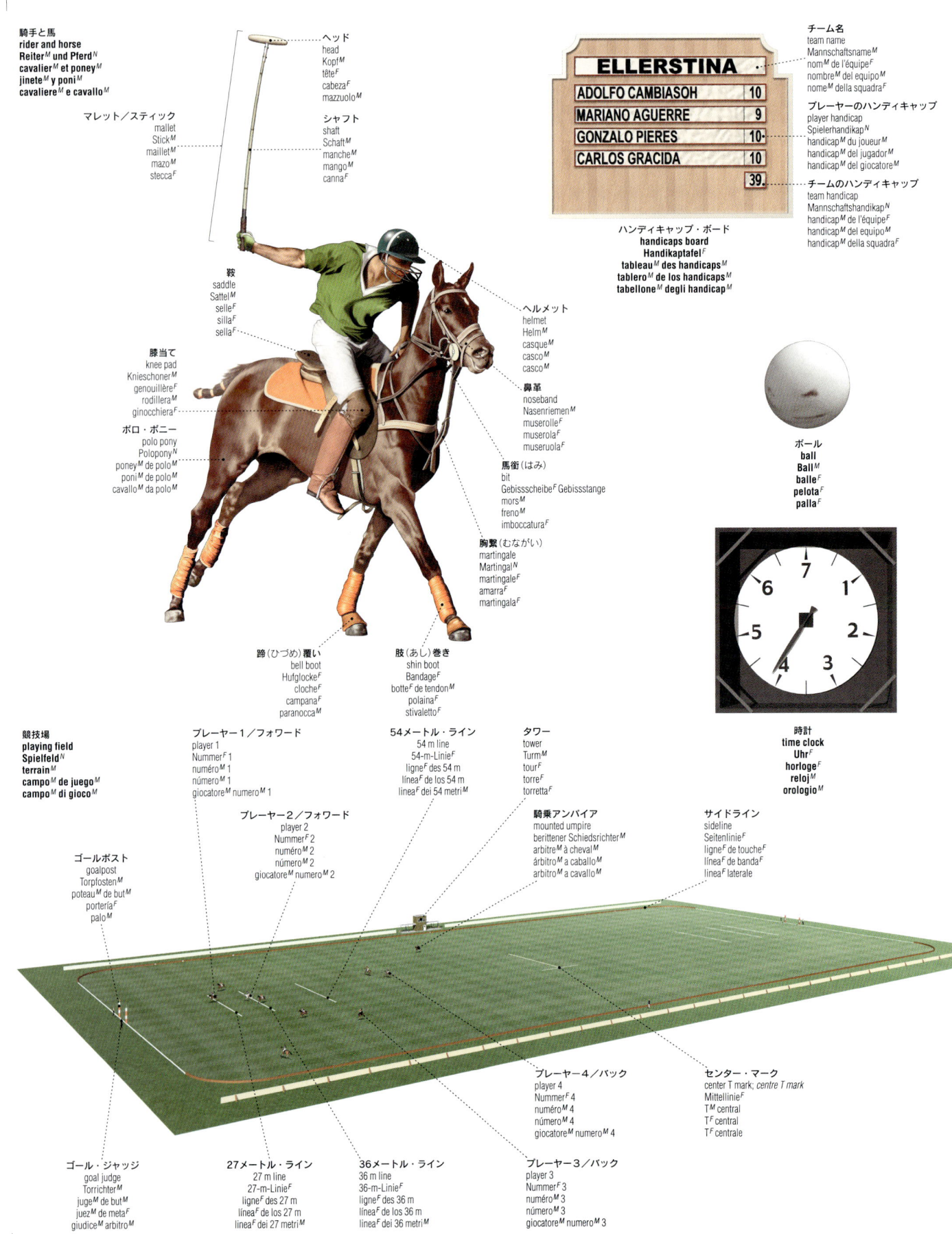

騎手と馬
rider and horse
Reiter und Pferd[N]
cavalier[M] et poney[M]
jinete[M] y poni[M]
cavaliere[M] e cavallo[M]

マレット／スティック
mallet
Stick[M]
maillet[M]
mazo[M]
stecca[F]

ヘッド
head
Kopf[M]
tête[F]
cabeza[F]
mazzuolo[M]

シャフト
shaft
Schaft[M]
manche[M]
mango[M]
canna[F]

鞍
saddle
Sattel[M]
selle[F]
silla[F]
sella[F]

膝当て
knee pad
Knieschoner[M]
genouillère[F]
rodillera[F]
ginocchiera[F]

ポロ・ポニー
polo pony
Polopony[N]
poney[M] de polo[M]
poni[M] de polo[M]
cavallo[M] da polo[M]

ヘルメット
helmet
Helm[M]
casque[M]
casco[M]
casco[M]

鼻革
noseband
Nasenriemen[M]
muserolle[F]
muserola[F]
museruola[F]

馬銜（はみ）
bit
Gebissscheibe[F] Gebissstange[F]
mors[M]
freno[M]
imboccatura[F]

胸繋（むながい）
martingale
Martingal[N]
martingale[F]
amarra[F]
martingala[F]

蹄（ひづめ）覆い
bell boot
Hufglocke[F]
cloche[F]
campana[F]
paranocca[F]

肢（あし）巻き
shin boot
Bandage[F]
botte[F] de tendon[M]
polaina[F]
stivaletto[F]

チーム名
team name
Mannschaftsname[M]
nom[M] de l'équipe[F]
nombre[M] del equipo[M]
nome[M] della squadra[F]

プレーヤーのハンディキャップ
player handicap
Spielerhandikap[N]
handicap[M] du joueur[M]
handicap[M] del jugador[M]
handicap[M] del giocatore[M]

チームのハンディキャップ
team handicap
Mannschaftshandikap[N]
handicap[M] de l'équipe[F]
handicap[M] del equipo[M]
handicap[M] della squadra[F]

ELLERSTINA
ADOLFO CAMBIASOH 10
MARIANO AGUERRE 9
GONZALO PIERES 10
CARLOS GRACIDA 10
39

ハンディキャップ・ボード
handicaps board
Handikaptafel[F]
tableau[M] des handicaps[M]
tablero[M] de los handicaps[M]
tabellone[M] degli handicap[M]

ボール
ball
Ball[M]
balle[F]
pelota[F]
palla[F]

時計
time clock
Uhr[F]
horloge[F]
reloj[M]
orologio[M]

競技場
playing field
Spielfeld[N]
terrain[M]
campo[M] de juego[M]
campo[M] di gioco[M]

ゴールポスト
goalpost
Torpfosten[M]
poteau[M] de but[M]
portería[F]
palo[M]

ゴール・ジャッジ
goal judge
Torrichter[M]
juge[M] de but[M]
juez[M] de meta[F]
giudice[M] arbitro[M]

プレーヤー１／フォワード
player 1
Nummer[F] 1
numéro[M] 1
número[M] 1
giocatore[M] numero[M] 1

プレーヤー２／フォワード
player 2
Nummer[F] 2
numéro[M] 2
número[M] 2
giocatore[M] numero[M] 2

27メートル・ライン
27 m line
27-m-Linie[F]
ligne[F] des 27 m
línea[F] de los 27 m
linea[F] dei 27 metri[M]

36メートル・ライン
36 m line
36-m-Linie[F]
ligne[F] des 36 m
línea[F] de los 36 m
linea[F] dei 36 metri[M]

54メートル・ライン
54 m line
54-m-Linie[F]
ligne[F] des 54 m
línea[F] de los 54 m
linea[F] dei 54 metri[M]

タワー
tower
Turm[M]
tour[F]
torre[F]
torretta[F]

騎乗アンパイア
mounted umpire
berittener Schiedsrichter[M]
arbitre[M] à cheval[M]
árbitro[M] a caballo[M]
arbitro[M] a cavallo[M]

プレーヤー３／バック
player 3
Nummer[F] 3
numéro[M] 3
número[M] 3
giocatore[M] numero[M] 3

プレーヤー４／バック
player 4
Nummer[F] 4
numéro[M] 4
número[M] 4
giocatore[M] numero[M] 4

サイドライン
sideline
Seitenlinie[F]
ligne[F] de touche[F]
línea[F] de banda[F]
linea[F] laterale

センター・マーク
center T mark; centre T mark
Mittellinie[F]
T[M] central
T[F] central
T[F] centrale

858

スポーツとゲーム

日本語 | 英語 | ドイツ語 | フランス語 | スペイン語 | イタリア語

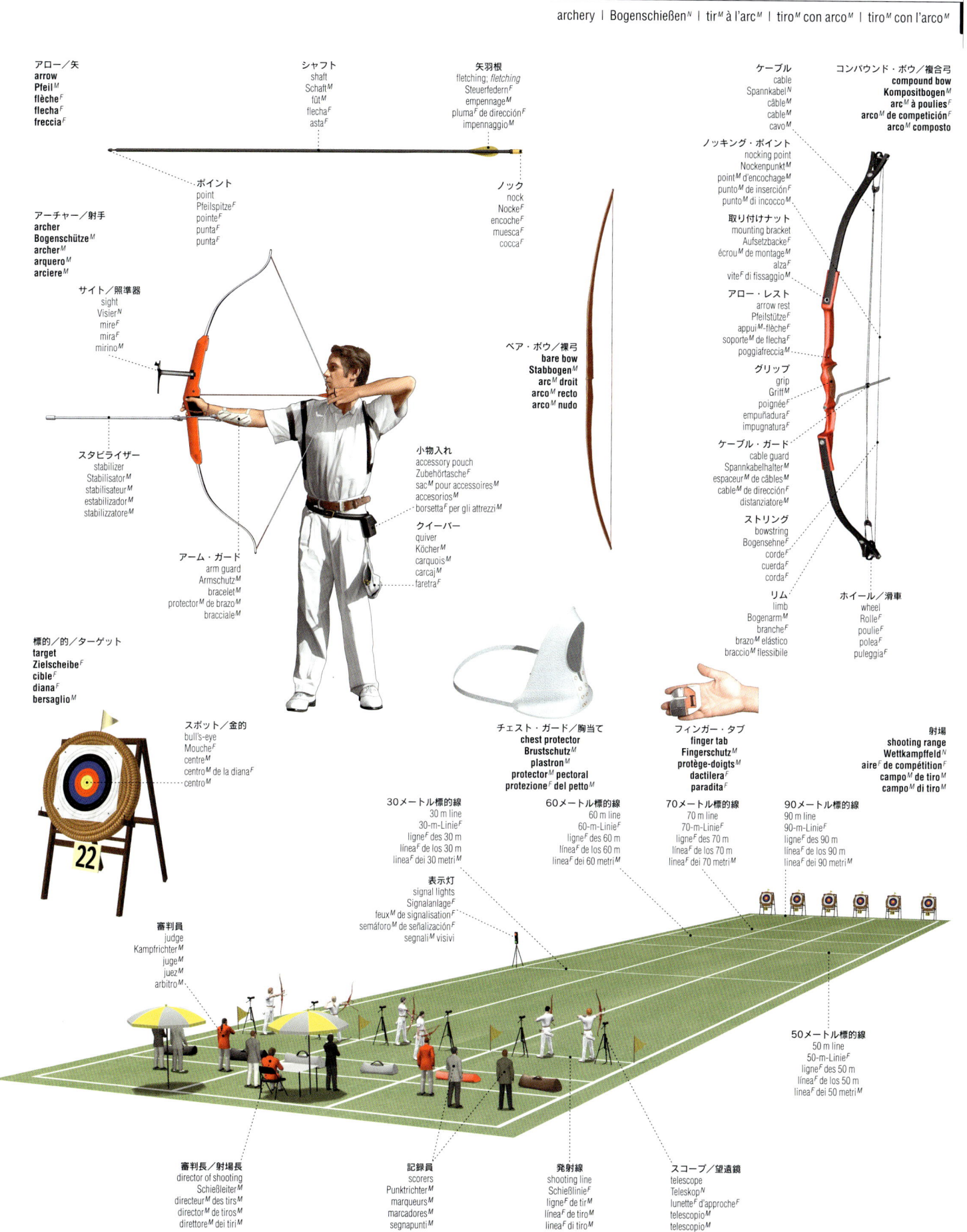

正確さを競うスポーツ | PRECISION AND ACCURACY SPORTS
PRÄZISIONSSPORT | SPORTS DE PRÉCISION | DEPORTES DE PRECISIÓN Y PUNTERÍA | SPORT DI PRECISIONE

アーチェリー

archery | Bogenschießen^N | tir^M à l'arc^M | tiro^M con arco^M | tiro^M con l'arco^M

アロー／矢
arrow
Pfeil^M
flèche^F
flecha^F
freccia^F

シャフト
shaft
Schaft^M
fût^M
flecha^F
asta^F

矢羽根
fletching; *fletching*
Steuerfedern^F
empennage^F
pluma^F de dirección^F
impennaggio^M

ケーブル
cable
Spannkabel^N
câble^M
cable^M
cavo^M

コンパウンド・ボウ／複合弓
compound bow
Kompositbogen^M
arc^M à poulies^F
arco^M de competición^F
arco^M composto

ポイント
point
Pfeilspitze^F
pointe^F
punta^F
punta^F

ノック
nock
Nocke^F
encoche^F
muesca^F
cocca^F

ノッキング・ポイント
nocking point
Nockenpunkt^M
point^M d'encochage^M
punto^M de inserción^F
punto^M di incocco^M

アーチャー／射手
archer
Bogenschütze^M
archer^M
arquero^M
arciere^M

取り付けナット
mounting bracket
Aufsetzbacke^F
écrou^M de montage^M
alza^F
vite^F di fissaggio^M

サイト／照準器
sight
Visier^N
mire^F
mira^F
mirino^M

ベア・ボウ／裸弓
bare bow
Stabbogen^M
arc^M droit
arco^M recto
arco^M nudo

アロー・レスト
arrow rest
Pfeilstütze^F
appui^M-flèche^F
soporte^M de flecha^F
poggiafreccia^M

グリップ
grip
Griff^M
poignée^F
empuñadura^F
impugnatura^F

スタビライザー
stabilizer
Stabilisator^M
stabilisateur^M
estabilizador^M
stabilizzatore^M

小物入れ
accessory pouch
Zubehörtasche^F
sac^M pour accessoires^M
accesorios^M
borsetta^F per gli attrezzi^M

ケーブル・ガード
cable guard
Spannkabelhalter^M
espaceur^M de câbles^M
cable^F de dirección^F
distanziatore^M

ストリング
bowstring
Bogensehne^F
corde^F
cuerda^F
corda^F

クイーバー
quiver
Köcher^M
carquois^M
carcaj^M
faretra^F

アーム・ガード
arm guard
Armschutz^M
bracelet^M
protector^M de brazo^M
bracciale^M

リム
limb
Bogenarm^M
branche^F
brazo^M elástico
braccio^M flessibile

ホイール／滑車
wheel
Rolle^F
poulie^F
polea^F
puleggia^F

標的／的／ターゲット
target
Zielscheibe^F
cible^F
diana^F
bersaglio^M

チェスト・ガード／胸当て
chest protector
Brustschutz^M
plastron^M
protector^M pectoral
protezione^F del petto^M

フィンガー・タブ
finger tab
Fingerschutz^M
protège-doigts^M
dactilera^F
paradita^F

射場
shooting range
Wettkampffeld^N
aire^F de compétition^F
campo^M de tiro^M
campo^M di tiro^M

スポット／金的
bull's-eye
Mouche^F
centre^M
centro^M de la diana^F
centro^M

30メートル標的線
30 m line
30-m-Linie^F
ligne^F des 30 m
línea^F de los 30 m
linea^F dei 30 metri^M

60メートル標的線
60 m line
60-m-Linie^F
ligne^F des 60 m
línea^F de los 60 m
linea^F dei 60 metri^M

70メートル標的線
70 m line
70-m-Linie^F
ligne^F des 70 m
línea^F de los 70 m
linea^F dei 70 metri^M

90メートル標的線
90 m line
90-m-Linie^F
ligne^F des 90 m
línea^F de los 90 m
linea^F dei 90 metri^M

表示灯
signal lights
Signalanlage^F
feux^M de signalisation^F
semáforo^M de señalización^F
segnali^M visivi

審判員
judge
Kampfrichter^M
juge^M
juez^M
arbitro^M

50メートル標的線
50 m line
50-m-Linie^F
ligne^F des 50 m
línea^F de los 50 m
linea^F dei 50 metri^M

審判長／射場長
director of shooting
Schießleiter^M
directeur^M des tirs^M
director^M de tiros^M
direttore^M dei tiri^M

記録員
scorers
Punktrichter^M
marqueurs^M
marcadores^M
segnapunti^M

発射線
shooting line
Schießlinie^F
ligne^F de tir^M
línea^F de tiro^M
linea^F di tiro^M

スコープ／望遠鏡
telescope
Teleskop^N
lunette^F d'approche^F
telescopio^M
telescopio^M

スポーツとゲーム

正確さを競うスポーツ | PRECISION AND ACCURACY SPORTS
PRÄZISIONSSPORT | SPORTS DE PRÉCISION | DEPORTES DE PRECISIÓN Y PUNTERÍA | SPORT DI PRECISIONE

クレー射撃

shotgun shooting | WurftaubenschießenN | tirM au fusilM | tiroM al platoM | tiroM con fucileM

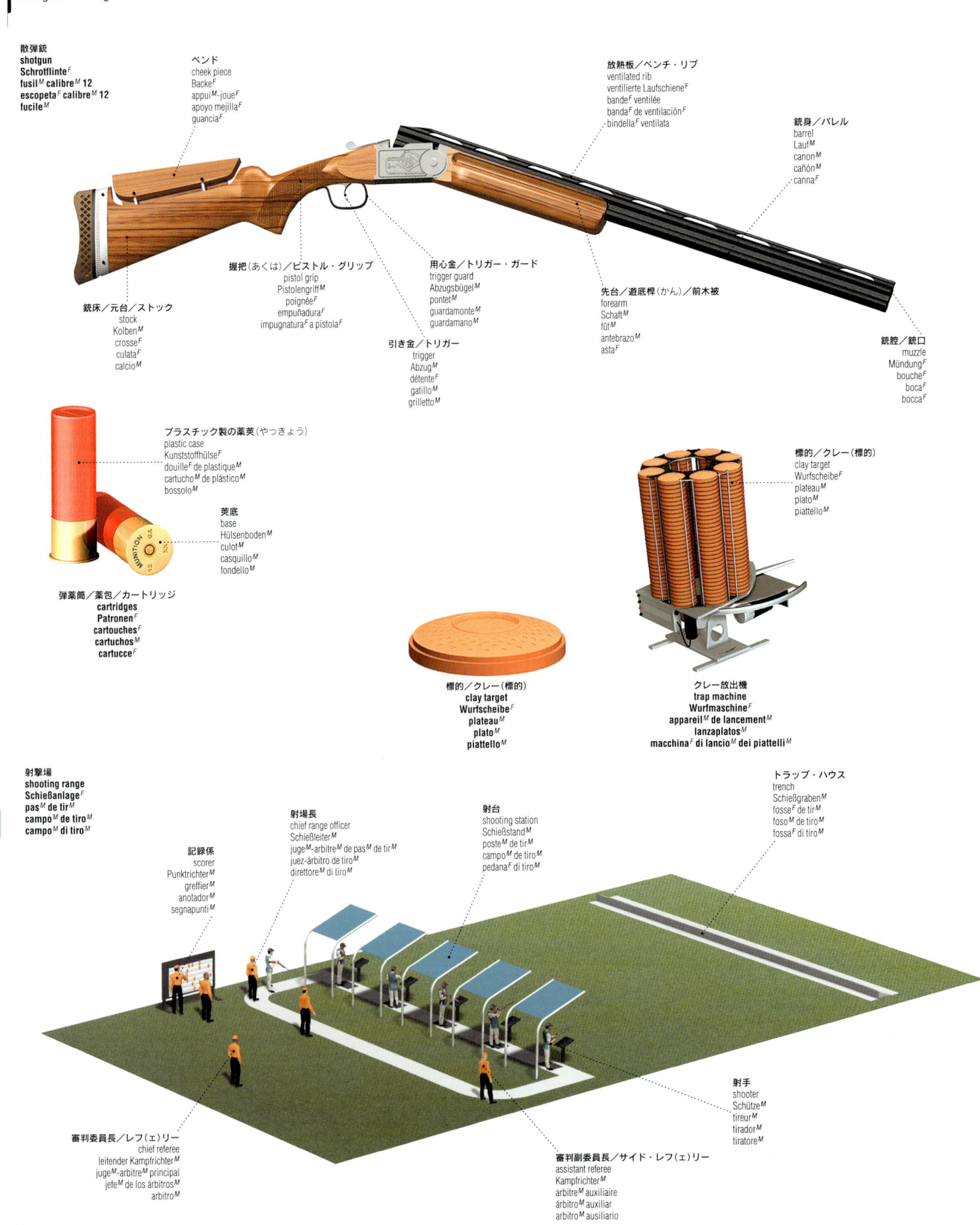

日本語 | 英語 | ドイツ語 | フランス語 | スペイン語 | イタリア語

散弾銃
shotgun
SchrotflinteF
fusilM calibreM 12
escopetaF calibreM 12
fucileM

ベンド
cheek piece
BackeF
appuiM-jouéF
apoyo mejillaF
guanciaF

放熱板／ベンチ・リブ
ventilated rib
ventilierte LaufschieneF
bandeF ventiléeF
bandaF de ventilaciónF
bindellaF ventilata

銃身／バレル
barrel
LaufM
canonM
cañónM
cannaF

銃床／元台／ストック
stock
KolbenM
crosseF
culataF
calcioM

握把（あくは）／ピストル・グリップ
pistol grip
PistolengriffM
poignéeF
empuñaduraF
impugnaturaF a pistolaF

用心金／トリガー・ガード
trigger guard
AbzugsbügelM
pontetM
guardamonteM
guardamanoM

先台／遊底桿（かん）／前木被
forearm
SchaftM
fûtM
antebrazoM
astaF

銃腔／銃口
muzzle
MündungF
boucheF
bocaF
boccaF

引き金／トリガー
trigger
AbzugM
détenteF
gatilloM
grillettoM

プラスチック製の薬莢（やっきょう）
plastic case
KunststoffhülseF
douilleF de plastiqueM
cartuchoM de plásticoM
bossoloM

莢底
base
HülsenbodenM
culotM
casquilloM
fondelloM

標的／クレー（標的）
clay target
WurfscheibeF
plateauM
platoM
piattelloM

弾薬筒／薬包／カートリッジ
cartridges
PatronenF
cartouchesF
cartuchosM
cartucceF

標的／クレー（標的）
clay target
WurfscheibeF
plateauM
platoM
piattelloM

クレー放出機
trap machine
WurfmaschineF
appareilM de lancementM
lanzaplatosM
macchinaF di lancioM dei piattelliM

射撃場
shooting range
SchießanlageF
pasM de tirM
campoM de tiroM
campoM di tiroM

射場長
chief range officer
SchießleiterM
jugeM-arbitreM de pasM de tirM
juez-árbitroM de tiroM
direttoreM di tiroM

射台
shooting station
SchießstandM
posteM de tirM
campoM de tiroM
pedanaF di tiroM

トラップ・ハウス
trench
SchießgrabenM
fosseF de tirM
fosoM de tiroM
fossaF di tiroM

記録係
scorer
PunktrichterM
greffierM
anotadorM
segnapuntiM

射手
shooter
SchützeM
tireurM
tiradorM
tiratoreM

審判委員長／レフ(ェ)リー
chief referee
leitender KampfrichterM
jugeM-arbitreM principal
jefeM de los árbitrosM
arbitroM

審判副委員長／サイド・レフ(ェ)リー
assistant referee
KampfrichterM
arbitreM auxiliaire
árbitroM auxiliar
arbitroM ausiliario

正確さを競うスポーツ | PRECISION AND ACCURACY SPORTS
PRÄZISIONSSPORT | SPORTS DE PRÉCISION | DEPORTES DE PRECISIÓN Y PUNTERÍA | SPORT DI PRECISIONE

ライフル射撃

rifle shooting | Gewehrschießen[N] | tir[M] à la carabine[F] | tiro al blanco[M] | tiro[M] con carabina[F]

ベンド
cheek piece
Backe[F]
appui[M]-joue[F]
apoyo[M] mejilla[F]
guancia[F]

照門
rear sight
Kimme[F]
hausse[F]
percusor[M]
tacca di mira[F]

22口径ライフル
.22-caliber rifle
Kleinkalibergewehr[N]
carabine[F] 22
carabina[F] 22
carabina[F] calibro[M] 22

照星
front sight
Korn[N]
guidon[M]
punto[M] de mira[F]
mirino[M]

フック
hook
Haken[M]
crochet[M]
gancho[M]
sperone[M]

用心金／トリガー・ガード
trigger guard
Abzugsbügel[M]
pontet[M]
guardamonte[M]
guardamano[M]

引き金／トリガー
trigger
Abzug[M]
détente[F]
gatillo[M]
grilletto[M]

パーム・レスト
palm rest
Handstütze[F]
pommeau[M]
empuñadura[F]
pomo[M]

射撃姿勢
shooting positions
Schießpositionen[F]
positions[F] de tir[M]
posiciones[M] de tiro[M]
posizioni[F] di tiro[M]

弾薬筒／薬包／カートリッジ
cartridges
Patronen[F]
cartouches[F]
cartuchos[M]
cartucce[F]

立射姿勢
standing position
stehender Anschlag[M]
position[F] debout
posición[F] de pie[M]
posizione[F] in piedi[M]

膝射（しっしゃ）姿勢
kneeling position
kniender Anschlag[M]
position[F] à genoux[M]
posición[F] de rodillas[F]
posizione[F] in ginocchio[M]

伏射姿勢
prone position
liegender Anschlag[M]
position[F] couchée
posición[F] supina
posizione[F] a terra[F]

標的
target
Zielscheibe[F]
cible[F]
blanco[M]
bersaglio[M]

ピストル射撃

pistol shooting | Pistolenschießen[N] | tir[M] au pistolet[M] | tiro[M] de pistola[F] | tiro[M] con pistola[F]

エア・ピストル
air pistol
Luftpistole[F]
pistolet[M] à air[M] comprimé
pistola[F] de aire[M] comprimido
pistola[F] ad aria[F] compressa

撃鉄
hammer
Hahn[M]
chien[M]
percusor[M]
cane[M]

8ミリ口径ピストル
8-mm pistol
8-mm-Pistole[F]
pistolet[M] 8 mm
pistola[F] de 8 mm
pistola[F] 8 mm[M]

耳覆い／イア・プロテクター
ear muffs
Ohrenschützer[M]
casque[M] anti-bruit
cascos[M] antirruido
paraorecchie[M]

引き金／トリガー
trigger
Abzug[M]
détente[F]
gatillo[M]
grilletto[M]

(射撃用)眼鏡／保護眼鏡
eyeglasses
Schutzbrille[F]
lunettes[F]
gafas[F] de protección[F]
occhiali[M] protettivi

銃床／ストック
stock
Schaft[M]
crosse[F]
culata[F]
calcio[M]

861

正確さを競うスポーツ | PRECISION AND ACCURACY SPORTS
PRÄZISIONSSPORT | SPORTS DE PRÉCISION | DEPORTES DE PRECISIÓN Y PUNTERÍA | SPORT DI PRECISIONE

ビリヤード／撞球（どうきゅう）／玉突き

日本語 | 英語 | ドイツ語 | フランス語 | スペイン語 | イタリア語

billiards | Billard^N | billard^M | billar^M | biliardo^M

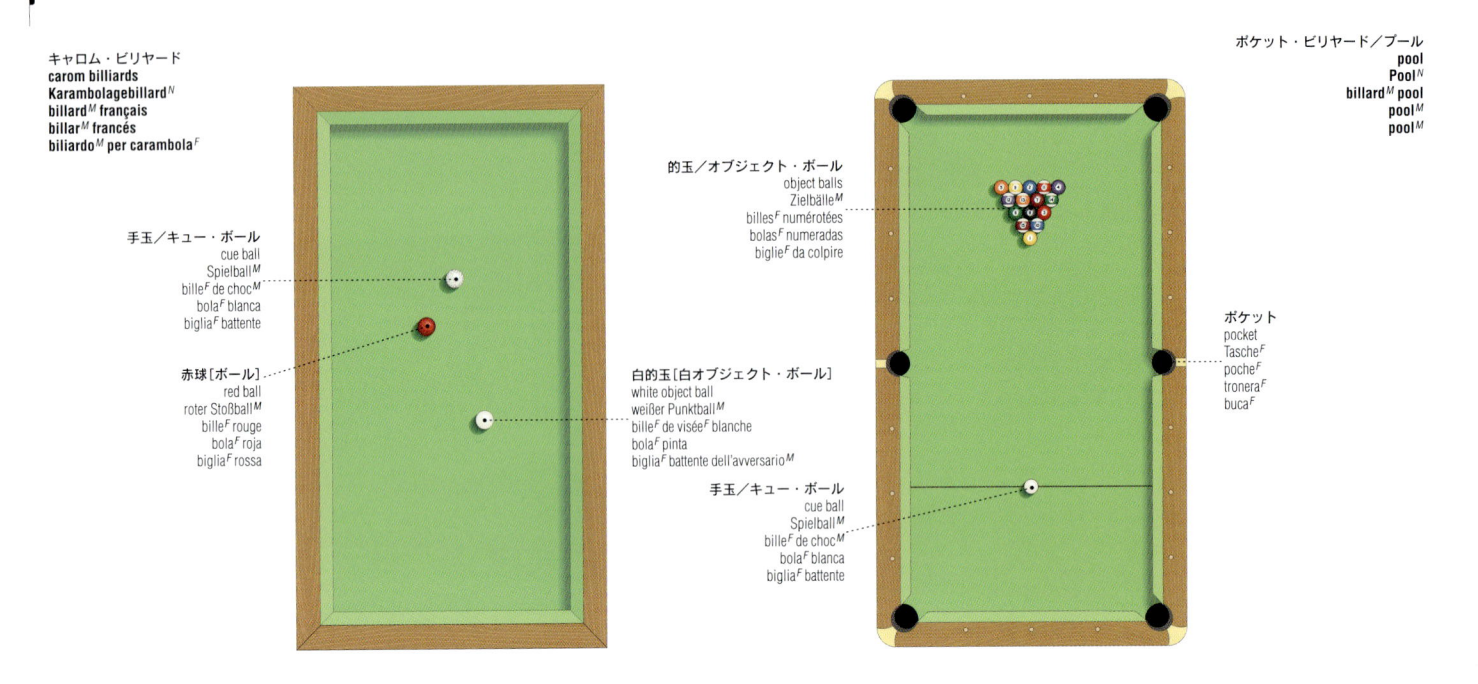

キャロム・ビリヤード
carom billiards
Karambolagebillard^N
billard^M français
billar^M francés
biliardo^M per carambola^F

手玉／キュー・ボール
cue ball
Spielball^M
bille^F de choc^M
bola^F blanca
biglia^F battente

赤球［ボール］
red ball
roter Stoßball^M
bille^F rouge
bola^F roja
biglia^F rossa

白的玉［白オブジェクト・ボール］
white object ball
weißer Punktball^M
bille^F de visée^F blanche
bola^F pinta
biglia^F battente dell'avversario^M

ポケット・ビリヤード／プール
pool
Pool^N
billard^M pool
pool^M
pool^M

的玉／オブジェクト・ボール
object balls
Zielbälle^M
billes^F numérotées
bolas^F numeradas
biglie^F da colpire

ポケット
pocket
Tasche^F
poche^F
tronera^F
buca^F

手玉／キュー・ボール
cue ball
Spielball^M
bille^F de choc^M
bola^F blanca
biglia^F battente

（ビリヤード）テーブル／
撞球台／玉突き台
table
Billardtisch^M
table^F
mesa^F
tavolo^M

Dゾーン
"D"
D^N
«D»^{M}
D^F
zona^F di inizio^M partita^F

ボーク・ライン・スポット
balk line spot
Anstoßpunkt^M
mouche^F de ligne^F de cadre^M
mosca^F de la línea^F de cuadro^M
acchito^M della linea^F di battuta^F

ピラミッド・スポット
pyramid spot
Aufstellpunkt^M
mouche^F supérieure
mosca^F superior
acchito^M superiore

ベーズ
baize
Bespannung^F
tapis^M
tapete^F
panno^M

ボーク・ゾーン
balk area
Anstoßraum^M
cadre^M
cuadro^M
rettangolo^M di battuta^F

ボトム・ポケット
bottom pocket
untere Tasche^F
poche^F inférieure
bolsillo^M
buca^F inferiore

センター・スポット
center spot; centre spot
Mittelpunkt^M
mouche^F centrale
mosca^F central
acchito^M centrale

トップ・ポケット
top pocket
obere Tasche^F
poche^F supérieure
tronera^F
buca^F superiore

ヘッド・クッション
head cushion
Endbande^F
coussin^M de tête^F
banda^F de goma^F
sponda^F inferiore

ボーク・ライン
balk line
Anstoßlinie^F
ligne^F de cadre^M
línea^F de cuadro^M
linea^F d'acchito^M

センター・ポケット
center pocket; centre pocket
Mitteltasche^F
poche^F centrale
tronera^F central
buca^F centrale

フック
hook
Haken^M
crochet^M
vástago^M
gancio^M

レール
rail
Rahmen^M
bande^F
baranda^F
soprasponda^F

ビリヤード・スポット
billiard spot
Aufstellpunkt^M
mouche^F
mosca^F
acchito^M

フット・クッション
foot cushion
Stirnbande^F
coussin^M arrière
banda^F de la cabecera^F
sponda^F superiore

正確さを競うスポーツ | PRECISION AND ACCURACY SPORTS
PRÄZISIONSSPORT | SPORTS DE PRÉCISION | DEPORTES DE PRECISIÓN Y PUNTERÍA | SPORT DI PRECISIONE

ビリヤード／撞球（どうきゅう）／玉突き

スヌーカー
snooker
Snooker^N
snooker^M
snooker^M
snooker^M

イングリッシュ・ビリヤード
English billiards
Lochbillard^N
billard^M anglais
billar^M inglés
biliardo^M inglese

手玉／キュー・ボール
cue ball
Spielball^M
bille^F de choc^M
bola^F blanca
biglia^F battente

手玉／キュー・ボール
cue ball
weißer Spielball^M
bille^F blanche
bola^F blanca
biglia^F bianca battente

緑球［ボール］
green ball
grüner Ball^M
bille^F verte
bola^F verde
biglia^F verde

黄球［ボール］
yellow ball
gelber Ball^M
bille^F jaune
bola^F amarilla
biglia^F gialla

白的玉［白オブジェクト・ボール］
white object ball
weißer Punktball^M
bille^F blanche mouchetée
bola^F pinta
biglia^F battente dell'avversario^M

茶球［ボール］
brown ball
brauner Ball^M
bille^F brune
bola^F marrón
biglia^F marrone

青球［ボール］
blue ball
blauer Ball^M
bille^F bleue
bola^F azul
biglia^F blu

赤球［ボール］
red ball
roter Ball^M
bille^F rouge
bola^F roja
biglia^F rossa

ピンク球［ボール］
pink ball
rosa Ball^M
bille^F rose
bola^F rosa
biglia^F rosa

赤球［ボール］
red balls
rote Bälle^M
billes^F rouges
bolas^F rojas
biglie^F rosse

黒球［ボール］
black ball
schwarzer Ball^M
bille^F noire
bola^F negra
biglia^F nera

ラック／トライアングル
rack
Dreieck^N
triangle^M
triángulo^M
triangolo^M

チョーク
chalk
Kreide^F
craie^F
tiza^F
gessetto^M

ビリヤード・キュー
billiard cue
Billardqueue$^{N/M}$
queue^F de billard
taco^M de billar
stecca^F

先角（さきつの）
ferrule
Kuppenring^M
virole^F
casquillo^M
girello^M

ジョイント／中輪
joint
Gewinde^N
tourillon^M
articulación^F
giunto^M

タップ／（キュー）チップ
tip
Kuppe^F
procédé^M
suela^F
cuoio^M

キュー先／シャフト
shaft
Schaft^M
flèche^F
mango^M
asta^F

キュー元（もと）／バット
butt
Griffteil^N
talon^M
virola^F
calcio^M

ブリッジ／レスト
bridge
Steg^M
râteau^M
burra^F
strega^F

ノッチ
notch
Kerbe^F
dent^F
muesca^F
dente^M

ブリッジ／レスト
endpiece
Endstück^N
tête^F
cabeza^F
testa^F

シャフト
shaft
Stiel^M
manche^M
mango^M
asta^F

スポーツとゲーム

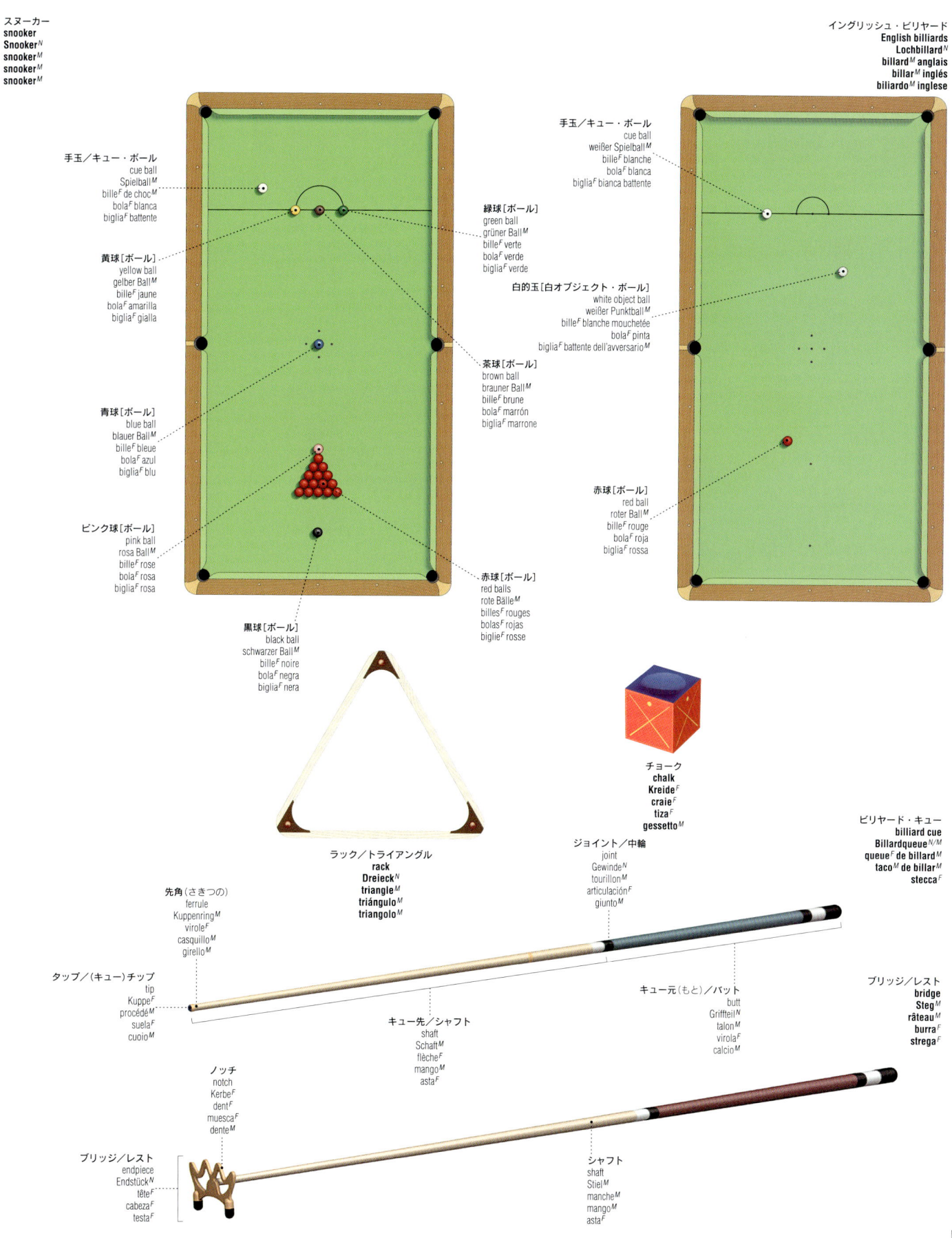

863

正確さを競うスポーツ | PRECISION AND ACCURACY SPORTS
PRÄZISIONSSPORT | SPORTS DE PRÉCISION | DEPORTES DE PRECISIÓN Y PUNTERÍA | SPORT DI PRECISIONE

ローン・ボウリング／ローン・ボウルズ

lawn bowling | Boule^N | boulingrin^M | bolos^M sobre hierba^F | bowling^M su prato^M

日本語｜英語｜ドイツ語｜フランス語｜スペイン語｜イタリア語

投球
bowling technique
Schießen^N
technique^F du lancer^M
lanzamiento^M
lancio^M

ボール／木球
bowls
Kugeln^F
boules^F
bolos^M
bocce^F

ジャック／目的球／的球
jack
Zielkugel^F
cochonnet^M
boliche^M
pallino^M

フォワード・スウィング
forward swing
Schwungholen^N
élan^M
impulso^M de lanzamiento^M
slancio^M in avanti

投球
delivery
Aufsetzen^N
lancer^M
lanzamiento^M
lancio^M

フォロー・スルー
follow-through
Abwurf^M
accompagnement^M
seguimiento^M de la bola^F
accompagnamento^M

グリーン
green
Grün^N
pelouse^F
bolera^F
campo^M

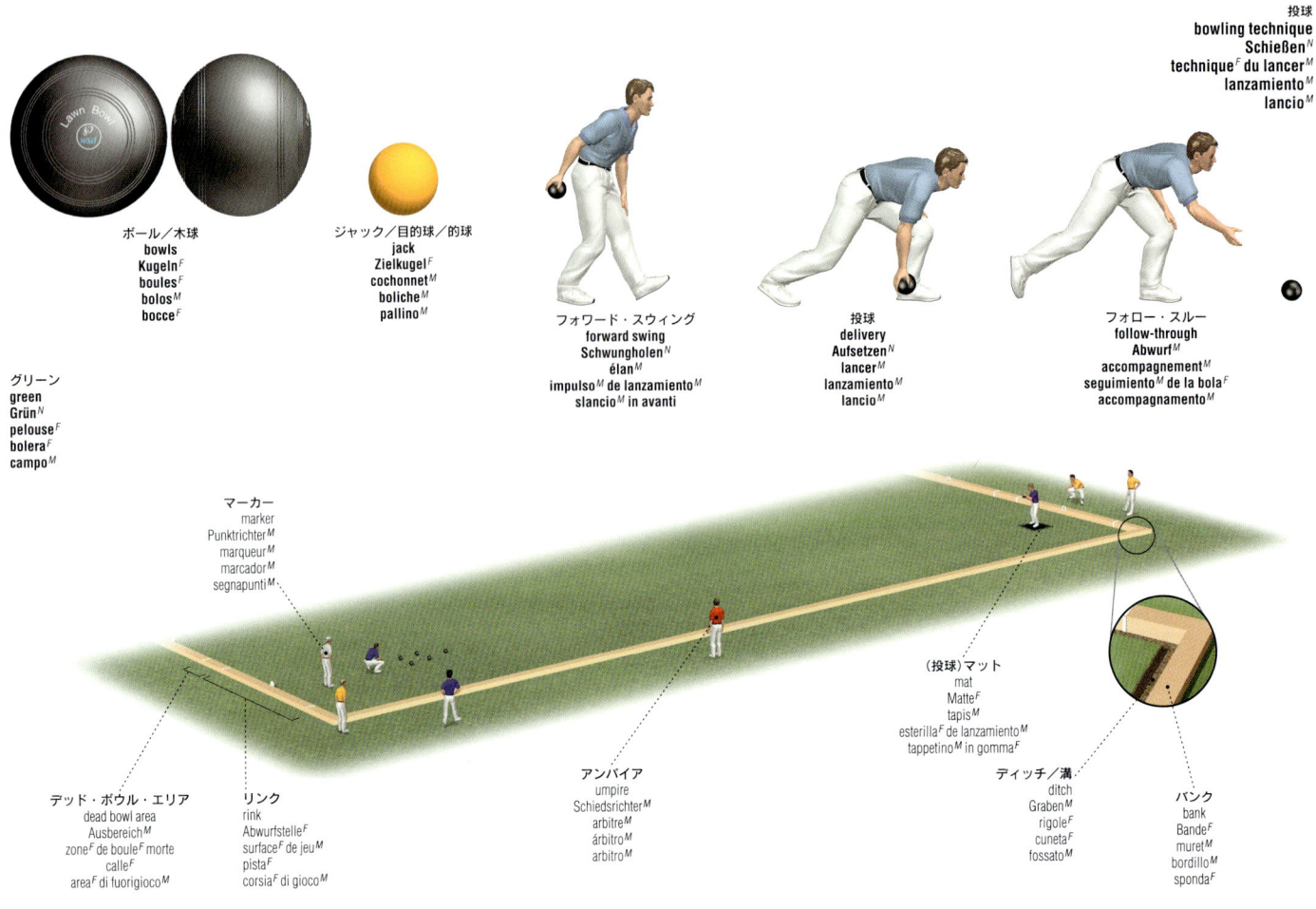

マーカー
marker
Punktrichter^M
marqueur^M
marcador^M
segnapunti^M

（投球）マット
mat
Matte^F
tapis^M
esterilla^F de lanzamiento^M
tappetino^M in gomma^F

デッド・ボウル・エリア
dead bowl area
Ausbereich^M
zone^F de boule^F morte
calle^F
area^F di fuorigioco^M

リンク
rink
Abwurfstelle^F
surface^F de jeu^M
pista^F
corsia^F di gioco^M

アンパイア
umpire
Schiedsrichter^M
arbitre^M
árbitro^M
arbitro^M

ディッチ／溝
ditch
Graben^M
rigole^F
cuneta^F
fossato^M

バンク
bank
Bande^F
muret^M
bordillo^M
sponda^F

ペタンク

petanque | Petanque^N | pétanque^F | petanca^F | petanque^M

テラン
playing field
Spielfeld^N
terrain^M
pista^F de juego^M
campo^M di gioco^M

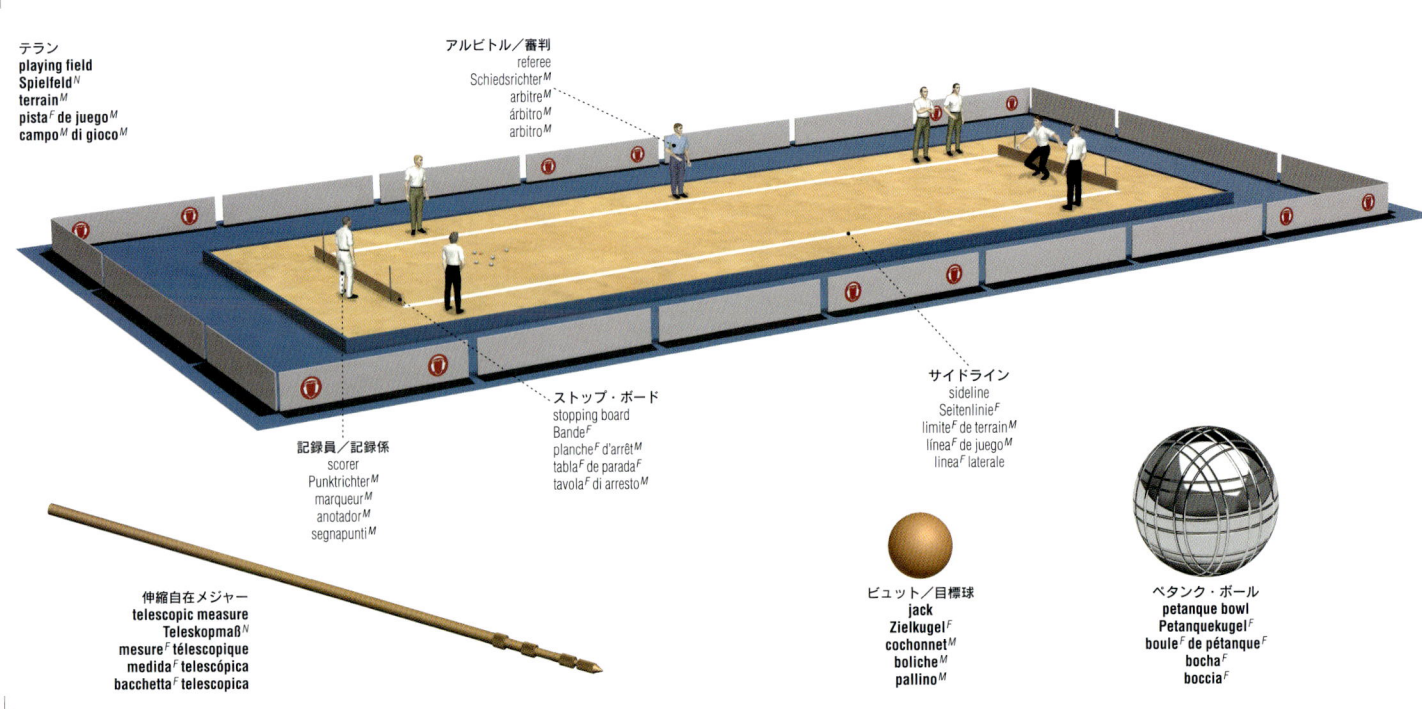

アルビトル／審判
referee
Schiedsrichter^M
arbitre^M
árbitro^M
arbitro^M

ストップ・ボード
stopping board
Bande^F
planche^F d'arrêt^M
tabla^F de parada^F
tavola^F di arresto^M

サイドライン
sideline
Seitenlinie^F
limite^F de terrain^M
linea^F de juego^M
linea^F laterale

記録員／記録係
scorer
Punktrichter^M
marqueur^M
anotador^M
segnapunti^M

伸縮自在メジャー
telescopic measure
Teleskopmaß^N
mesure^F télescopique
medida^F telescópica
bacchetta^F telescopica

ビュット／目標球
jack
Zielkugel^F
cochonnet^M
boliche^M
pallino^M

ペタンク・ボール
petanque bowl
Petanquekugel^F
boule^F de pétanque^F
bocha^F
boccia^F

スポーツとゲーム

864

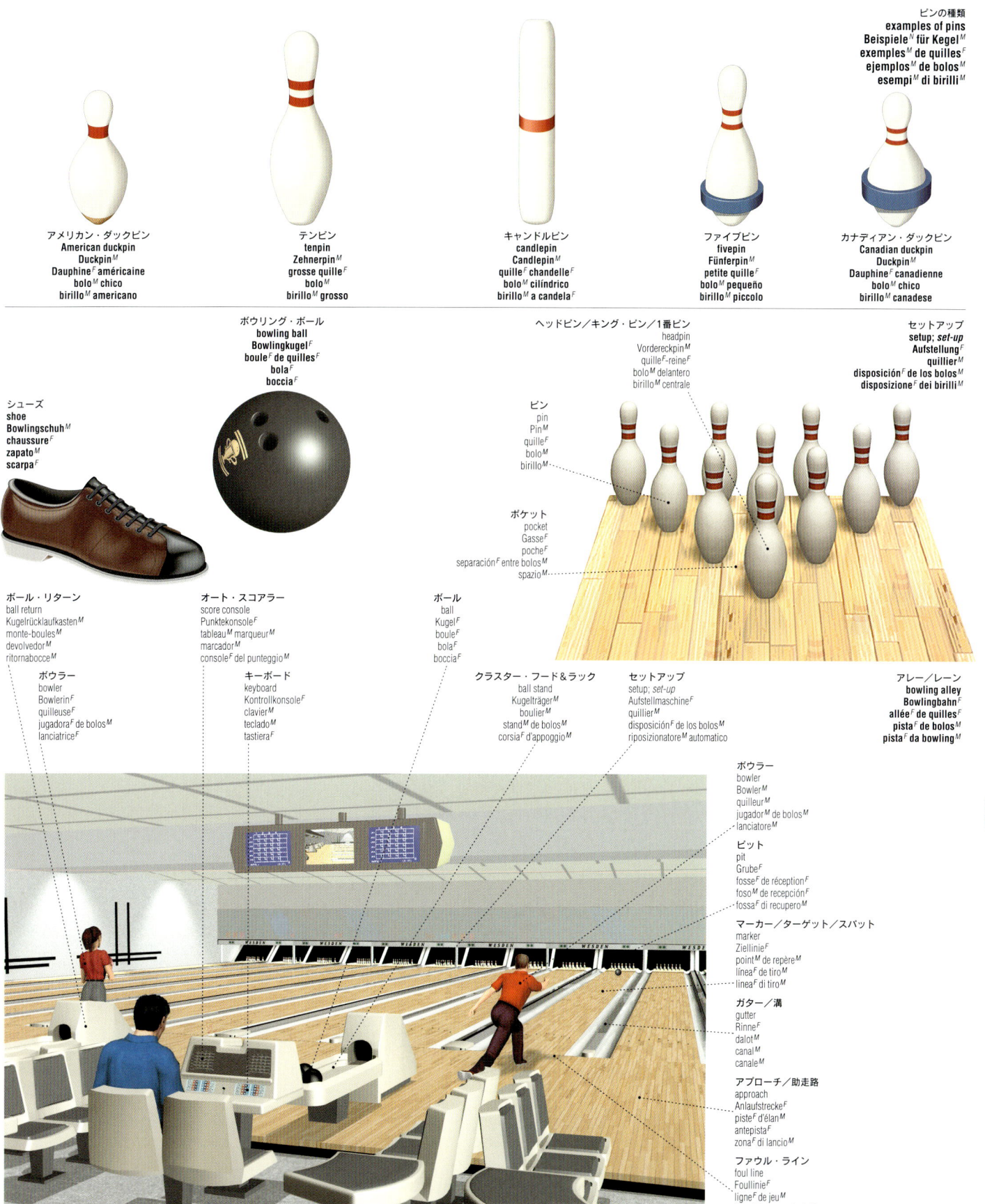

正確さを競うスポーツ | PRECISION AND ACCURACY SPORTS
PRÄZISIONSSPORT | SPORTS DE PRÉCISION | DEPORTES DE PRECISIÓN Y PUNTERÍA | SPORT DI PRECISIONE

ボウリング

bowling | Bowling^N | jeu^M de quilles^F | juego^M de bolos^M | bowling^M

ピンの種類
examples of pins
Beispiele^N für Kegel^M
exemples^M de quilles^F
ejemplos^M de bolos^M
esempi^M di birilli^M

アメリカン・ダックピン
American duckpin
Duckpin^M
Dauphine^F américaine
bolo^M chico
birillo^M americano

テンピン
tenpin
Zehnerpin^M
grosse quille^F
bolo^M
birillo^M grosso

キャンドルピン
candlepin
Candlepin^M
quille^F chandelle^F
bolo^M cilíndrico
birillo^M a candela^F

ファイブピン
fivepin
Fünferpin^M
petite quille^F
bolo^M pequeño
birillo^M piccolo

カナディアン・ダックピン
Canadian duckpin
Duckpin^M
Dauphine^F canadienne
bolo^M chico
birillo^M canadese

ボウリング・ボール
bowling ball
Bowlingkugel^F
boule^F de quilles^F
bola^F
boccia^F

ヘッドピン／キング・ピン／1番ピン
headpin
Vordereckpin^M
quille^F-reine^F
bolo^M delantero
birillo^M centrale

セットアップ
setup; *set-up*
Aufstellung^F
quillier^M
disposición^F de los bolos^M
disposizione^F dei birilli^M

シューズ
shoe
Bowlingschuh^M
chaussure^F
zapato^M
scarpa^F

ピン
pin
Pin^M
quille^F
bolo^M
birillo^M

ポケット
pocket
Gasse^F
poche^F
separación^F entre bolos^M
spazio^M

ボール
ball
Kugel^F
boule^F
bola^F
boccia^F

ボール・リターン
ball return
Kugelrücklaufkasten^M
monte-boules^M
devolvedor^M
ritornabocce^M

オート・スコアラー
score console
Punktekonsole^F
tableau^M marqueur^M
marcador^M
console^F del punteggio^M

ボウラー
bowler
Bowlerin^F
quilleuse^F
jugadora^F de bolos^M
lanciatrice^F

キーボード
keyboard
Kontrollkonsole^F
clavier^M
teclado^M
tastiera^F

クラスター・フード＆ラック
ball stand
Kugelträger^M
boulier^M
stand^M de bolos^M
corsia^F d'appoggio^M

セットアップ
setup; *set-up*
Aufstellmaschine^F
quillier^M
disposición^F de los bolos^M
riposizionatore^M automatico

アレー／レーン
bowling alley
Bowlingbahn^F
allée^F de quilles^F
pista^F de bolos^M
pista^F da bowling^M

ボウラー
bowler
Bowler^M
quilleur^M
jugador^M de bolos^M
lanciatore^M

ピット
pit
Grube^F
fosse^F de réception^F
foso^M de recepción^F
fossa^F di recupero^M

マーカー／ターゲット／スパット
marker
Ziellinie^F
point^M de repère^M
línea^F de tiro^M
linea^F di tiro^M

ガター／溝
gutter
Rinne^F
dalot^M
canal^M
canale^M

アプローチ／助走路
approach
Anlaufstrecke^F
piste^F d'élan^M
antepista^F
zona^F di lancio^M

ファウル・ライン
foul line
Foullinie^F
ligne^F de jeu^M
línea^F de lanzamiento^M
linea^F di fallo^M

スポーツとゲーム

正確さを競うスポーツ | PRECISION AND ACCURACY SPORTS
PRÄZISIONSSPORT | SPORTS DE PRÉCISION | DEPORTES DE PRECISIÓN Y PUNTERÍA | SPORT DI PRECISIONE

ゴルフ

日本語 | 英語 | ドイツ語 | フランス語 | スペイン語 | イタリア語

golf | Golfspiel^N | golf^M | accesorios^M de golf^M | golf^M

コース
course
Golfplatz^M
parcours^M
campo^M de golf^M
percorso^M

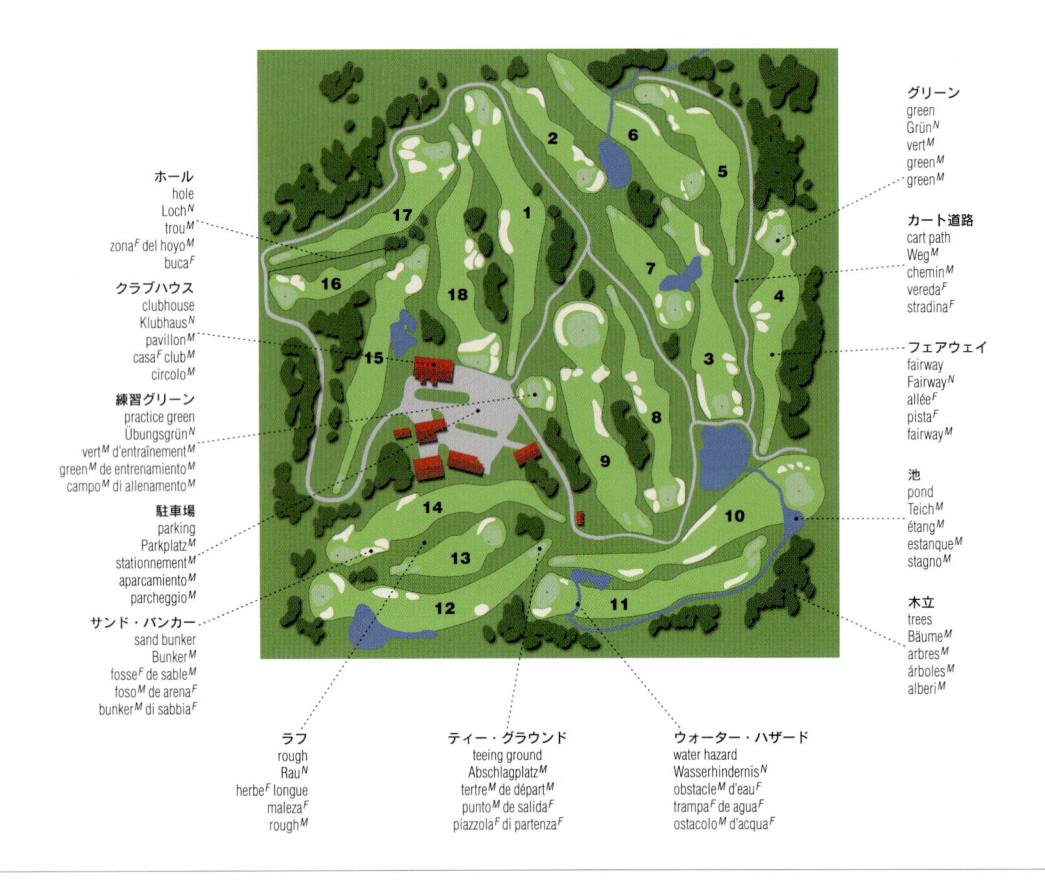

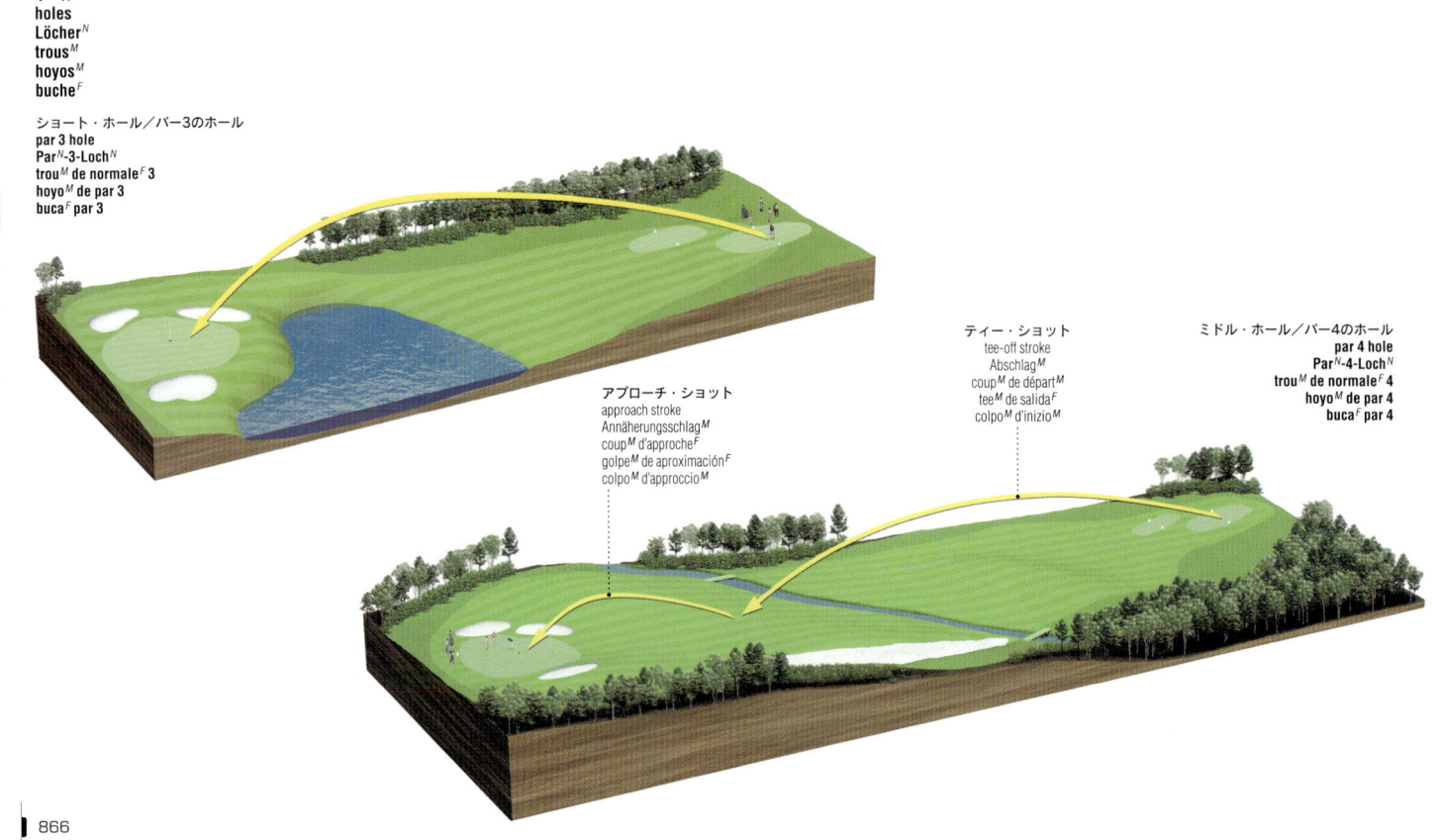

グリーン
green
Grün^N
vert
green^M
green^M

ホール
hole
Loch^N
trou^M
zona^F del hoyo^M
buca^F

カート道路
cart path
Weg^M
chemin^M
vereda^F
stradina^F

クラブハウス
clubhouse
Klubhaus^N
pavillon^M
casa^F club^M
circolo^M

フェアウェイ
fairway
Fairway^N
allée^F
pista^F
fairway^M

練習グリーン
practice green
Übungsgrün^N
vert^M d'entraînement^M
green^M de entrenamiento^M
campo^M di allenamento^M

池
pond
Teich^M
étang^M
estanque^M
stagno^M

駐車場
parking
Parkplatz^M
stationnement^M
aparcamiento^M
parcheggio^M

木立
trees
Bäume^M
arbres^M
árboles^M
alberi^M

サンド・バンカー
sand bunker
Bunker^M
fosse^F de sable^M
foso^M de arena^F
bunker^M di sabbia^F

ラフ
rough
Rau^N
herbe^F longue
maleza^F
rough^M

ティー・グラウンド
teeing ground
Abschlagplatz^M
tertre^M de départ^M
punto^M de salida^F
piazzola^F di partenza^F

ウォーター・ハザード
water hazard
Wasserhindernis^N
obstacle^M d'eau^F
trampa^F de agua^F
ostacolo^M d'acqua^F

ホール
holes
Löcher^N
trous^M
hoyos^M
buche^F

ショート・ホール／パー3のホール
par 3 hole
Par^N-3-Loch^N
trou^M de normale^F 3
hoyo^M de par 3
buca^F par 3

ティー・ショット
tee-off stroke
Abschlag^M
coup^M de départ^M
tee^M de salida^F
colpo^M d'inizio^M

アプローチ・ショット
approach stroke
Annäherungsschlag^M
coup^M d'approche^F
golpe^M de aproximación^F
colpo^M d'approccio^M

ミドル・ホール／パー4のホール
par 4 hole
Par^N-4-Loch^N
trou^M de normale^F 4
hoyo^M de par 4
buca^F par 4

スポーツとゲーム

866

正確さを競うスポーツ | PRECISION AND ACCURACY SPORTS
PRÄZISIONSSPORT | SPORTS DE PRÉCISION | DEPORTES DE PRECISIÓN Y PUNTERÍA | SPORT DI PRECISIONE

ゴルフ

ゴルフ・クラブの種類
types of golf clubs
Arten^F von Golfschläger^M
types^M de bâtons^M de golf^M
bastones^M
tipi^M di mazze^F

グリップ
grip
Griff^M
poignée^F
empuñadura^F
impugnatura^M

シャフト
shaft
Schaft^M
manche^M
mango^M
asta^F

フェース
face
Schlagfläche^F
face^F
cara^F
faccia^F

ヘッド
head
Kopf^M
tête^F
cabeza^F
testa^F

パター
putter
Putter^M
fer^M droit
putter^M
putter^M

アイアン
iron
Eisenschläger^M
fer^M
iron^M
ferro^M

ウッド
wood
Holzschläger^M
bois^M
madera^F
legno^M

ゴルフ・ボール
golf ball
Golfball^M
balle^F de golf^M
pelota^F de golf^M
palla^F

カバー
cover
Hülle^F
enveloppe^F
revestimiento^M
copertura^F

ディンプル
dimple
Delle^F
alvéole^F
hoyuelo^M
fossetta^F

ティー
tee
Tee^N
té^M
tee^M
tee^M

ゴルフボールの断面図
cross section of a golf ball
Golfball^M im Querschnitt^M
coupe^F d'une balle^F de golf^M
corte^M de una pelota^F de golf^M
sezione^F di una palla^F

カバー
cover
Hülle^F
enveloppe^F
revestimiento^M
copertura^F

ゴム糸
rubber thread
Gummieinsatz^M
ruban^M de caoutchouc^M
núcleo^M
filo^M elastico

芯
core
Kern^M
noyau^M
caucho^M central
nucleo^M

ロング・ホール／パー5のホール
par 5 hole
Par^N-5-Loch^N
trou^M de normale^F 5
hoyo^M de par 5
buca^F par 5

グリーン
green
Grün^N
vert^M
green^M
green^M

ウォーター・ハザード
water hazard
Wasserhindernis^N
obstacle^M d'eau^F
fosa^F de agua
ostacolo^M d'acqua^F

フェアウェイ
fairway
Fairway^N
allée^F
fairway^M
fairway^M

ティー・グラウンド
teeing ground
Abschlagsbereich^M
tertre^M de départ
colina^F de salida^F
piazzola^F di partenza^F

自然環境
natural environment
naturbelassene Umgebung^F
environnement^M naturel
ambiente^M natural
ambiente^M naturale

サンド・バンカー
sand bunker
Bunker^M
fosse^F de sable^M
trampas^F de arena^F
bunker^M di sabbia^F

ラフ
rough
Rau^N
herbe^F longue
rough^M
rough^M

ホール
hole
Loch^N
trou^M
hoyo^M
buca^F

ピン
removable flag pole
umsetzbare Flagge^F
drapeau^M amovible
banderín^M móvil
bandiera^F rimovibile

スポーツとゲーム

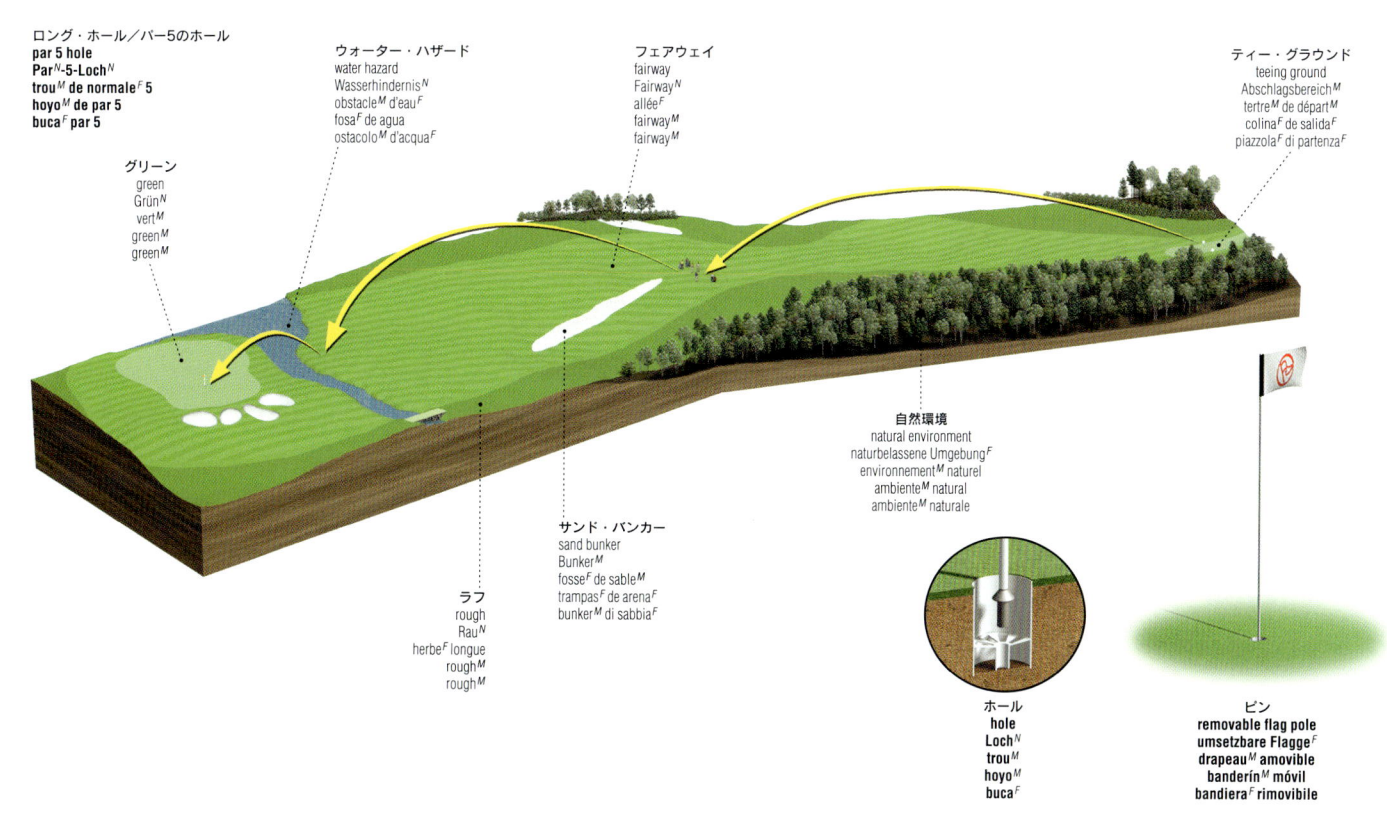

867

正確さを競うスポーツ | PRECISION AND ACCURACY SPORTS
PRÄZISIONSSPORT | SPORTS DE PRÉCISION | DEPORTES DE PRECISIÓN Y PUNTERÍA | SPORT DI PRECISIONE

ゴルフ

日本語 | 英語 | ドイツ語 | フランス語 | スペイン語 | イタリア語

ウッド
wood
Holz[N]
bois[M]
palo[M]
legno[M]

アイアン
iron
Eisen[N]
fer[M]
hierro[M]
ferro[M]

ホイッピング
whipping
Whipping[N]
bandage[M]
refuerzo[M] embobinado
collarino[M]

トウ
toe
Spitze[F]
pointe[F]
toe[M]
punta[F]

ネック
neck
Hals[M]
col[M]
pescuezo[M]
collo[M]

ホーゼル
ferrule
Verbindungshülse[F]
bague[F]
contera[F]
rinforzo[M] di plastica[F]

ネック
neck
Hals[M]
col[M]
cuello[M]
collo[M]

トウ
toe
Spitze[F]
pointe[F]
punta[F]
punta[F]

ヒール
heel
Lage[F]
talon[M]
talón[M]
tacco[M]

溝
groove
Rille[F]
rainure[F]
surco[M]
scanalatura[F]

ソール
sole
Sohle[F]
semelle[F]
zapata[F]
suola[F]

溝
groove
Rille[F]
rainure[F]
superficie[F] acanalada
scanalatura[F]

ソール
sole
Sohle[F]
semelle[F]
zapata[F]
suola[F]

ヒール
heel
Lage[F]
talon[M]
talón[M]
tacco[M]

ドライバー／1番ウッド
driver; no. 1 wood
Holz[N] 1
bois[M] nº 1
madera[F] nº 1
legno[M] 1

スプーン／3番ウッド
3-wood
Holz[N] 3
bois[M] nº 3
madera[F] nº 3
legno[M] 3

クリーク／5番ウッド
5-wood
Holz[N] 5
bois[M] nº 5
madera[F] nº 5
legno[M] 5

パター
putter
Putter[M]
fer[M] droit
putter[M]
putter[M]

3番アイアン
3-iron
Eisen[N] 3
fer[M] nº 3
hierro[M] nº 3
ferro[M] 3

4番アイアン
4-iron
Eisen[N] 4
fer[M] nº 4
hierro[M] nº 4
ferro[M] 4

5番アイアン
5-iron
Eisen[N] 5
fer[M] nº 5
hierro[M] nº 5
ferro[M] 5

6番アイアン
6-iron
Eisen[N] 6
fer[M] nº 6
hierro[M] nº 6
ferro[M] 6

7番アイアン
7-iron
Eisen[N] 7
fer[M] nº 7
hierro[M] nº 7
ferro[M] 7

8番アイアン
8-iron
Eisen[N] 8
fer[M] nº 8
hierro[M] nº 8
ferro[M] 8

9番アイアン
9-iron
Eisen[N] 9
fer[M] nº 9
hierro[M] nº 9
ferro[M] 9

ピッチング・ウェッジ
pitching wedge
Pitching-Wedge[N]
cocheur[M] d'allée
wedge[M] para rough
pitching wedge[M]

ロブ・ウェッジ
lob wedge
Lob Wedge[N]
cocheur[M]
lob wedge[M]
lob wedge[M]

サンド・ウェッジ
sand wedge
Sand-Wedge[N]
cocheur[M] de sable
wedge[M] para arena[F]
sand wedge[M]

スポーツとゲーム

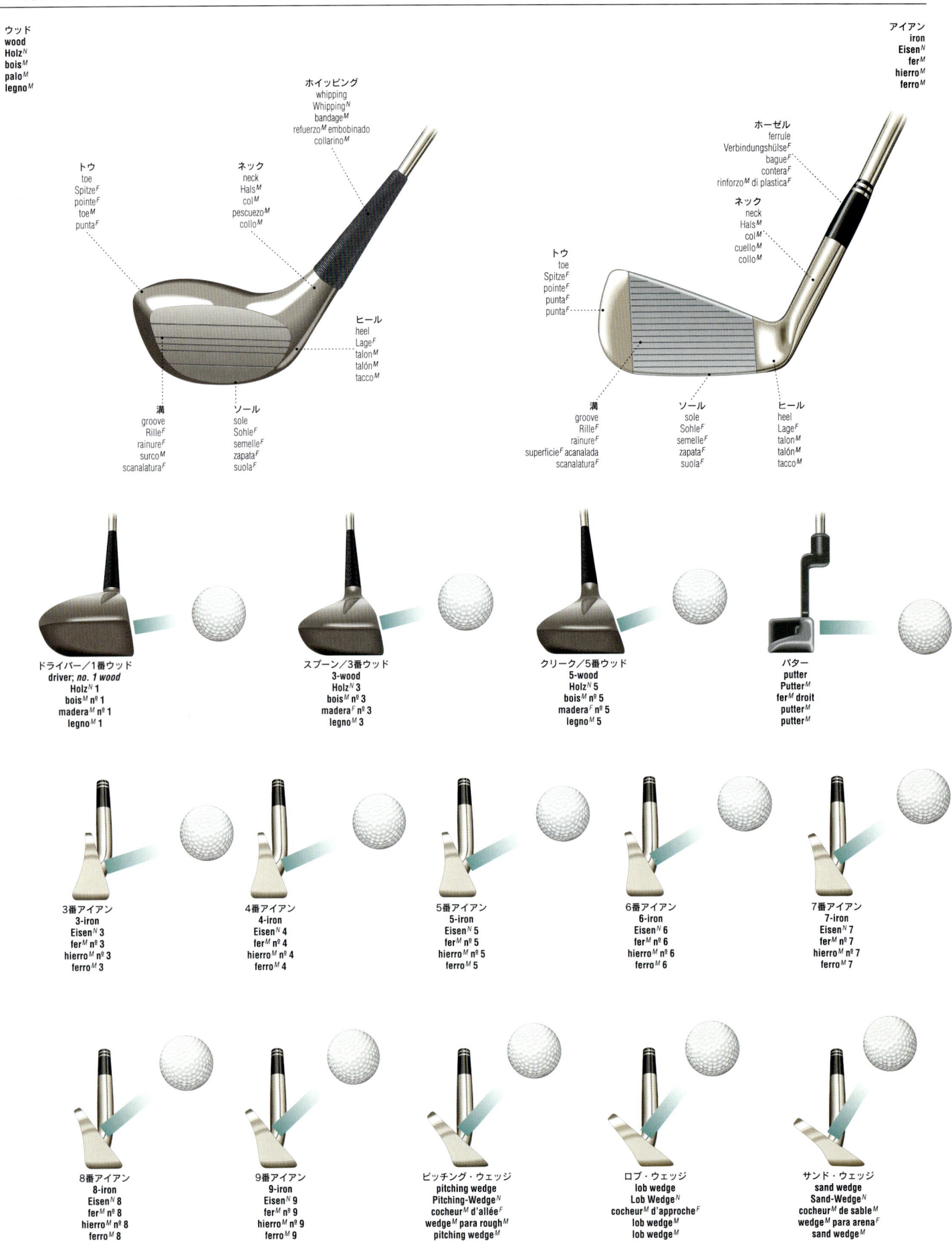

正確さを競うスポーツ | PRECISION AND ACCURACY SPORTS
PRÄZISIONSSPORT | SPORTS DE PRÉCISION | DEPORTES DE PRECISIÓN Y PUNTERÍA | SPORT DI PRECISIONE

ゴルフ

ショルダー・ストラップ
shoulder strap
Schultergurt^M
sangle^F
correa^F
tracolla^F

ゴルフ・カート
golf cart; *golf trolley*
Golfwagen^M
chariot^M
carrito^M de golf^M
carrello^M

ポケット
pocket
Seitentasche^F
poche^F
bolsillo^M
tasca^F

バッグ立て
bag well
Taschenträger^M
porte-sac^M
portabolsa^F
portasacca^M

ゴルフ[キャディー]バッグ
golf bag
Golftasche^F
sac^M de golf^M
bolsa^F de golf^M
sacca^F

ヘッド・カバー
head cover
Schlägerabdeckung^F
capuchon^M
capuchón^M de bastones^M
coprilegno^M

ゴルフ・グローブ[手袋]
golf glove
Golfhandschuh^M
gant^M de golf^M
guante^M de golf^M
guanto^M

ゴルフ・シューズ
golf shoes
Golfschuhe^M
chaussures^F de golf^M
zapatos^M de golf^M
scarpe^F

電動ゴルフ・カート
electric golf cart
elektrischer Golfwagen^M
voiturette^F de golf^M électrique
carro^M de golf^M eléctrico
vettura^F da golf^M

スポーツとゲーム

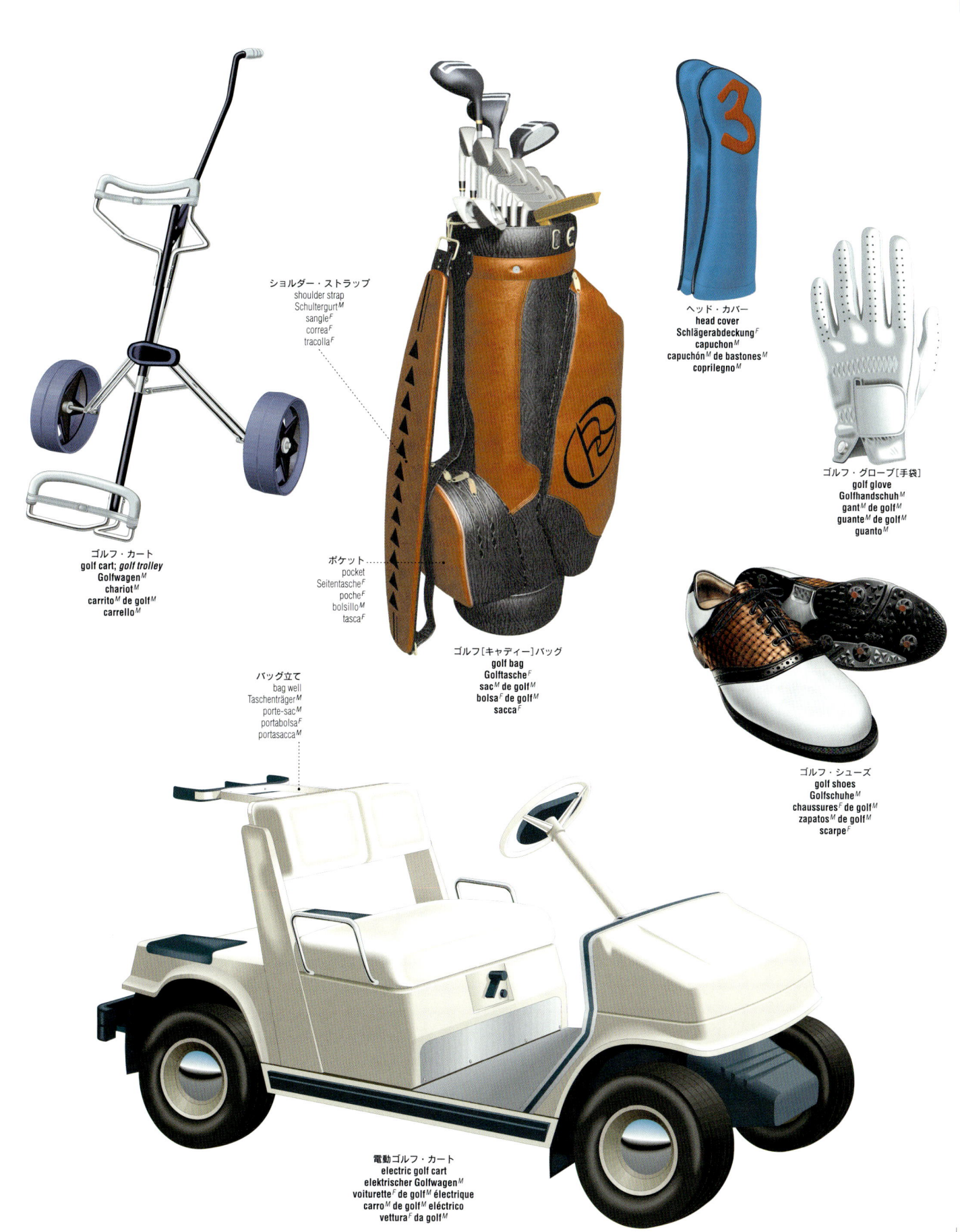

869

自転車競技 | CYCLING
RADSPORT | CYCLISME | CICLISMO | CICLISMO

ロード・レース

road racing | Straßenradsport^M | cyclisme^M sur route^F | ciclismo^M por carretera^F | ciclismo^M su strada^F

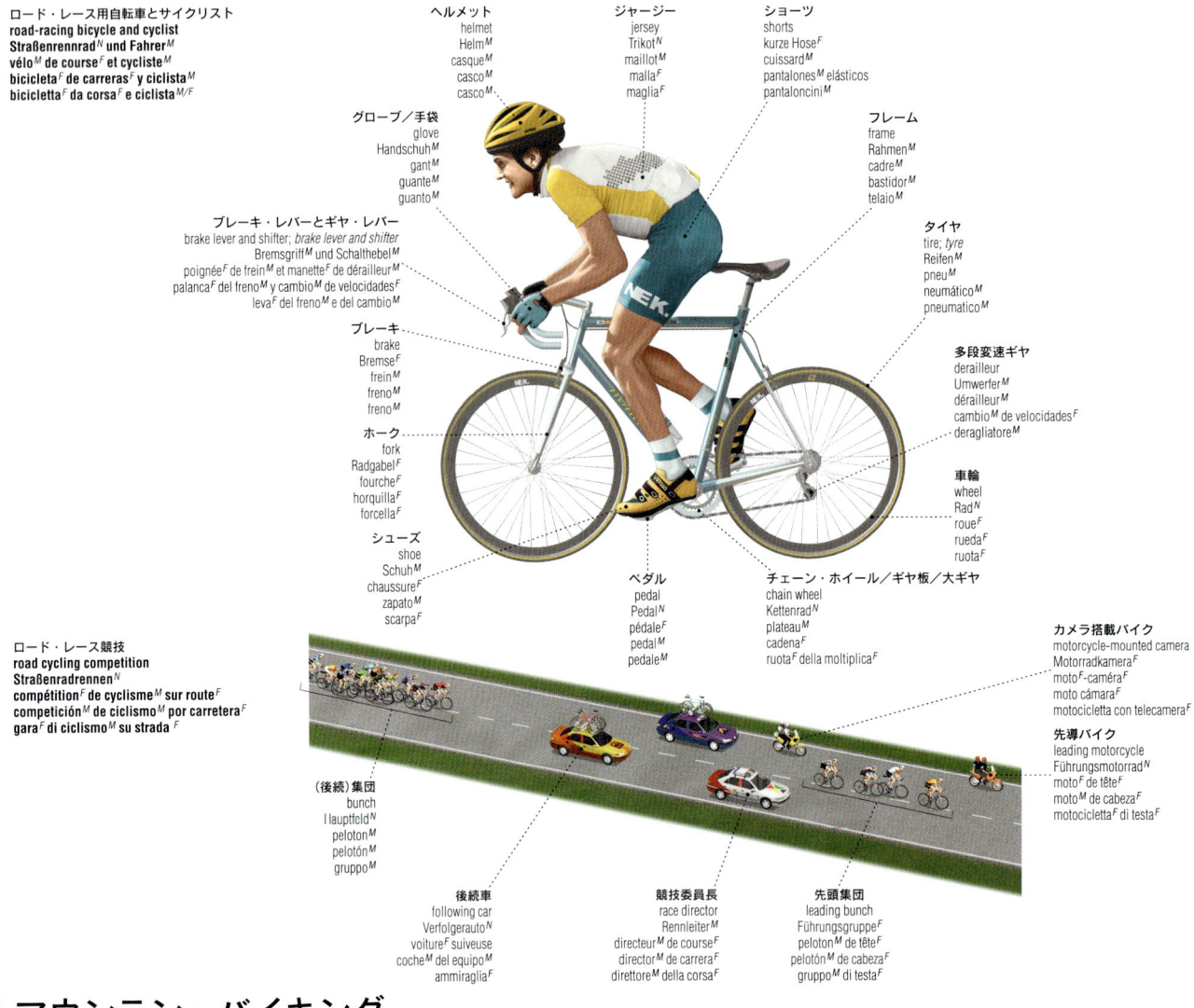

ロード・レース用自転車とサイクリスト
road-racing bicycle and cyclist
Straßenrennrad^N und Fahrer^M
vélo^M de course^F et cycliste^M
bicicleta^F de carreras^F y ciclista^M
bicicletta^F da corsa^F e ciclista^{M/F}

ヘルメット
helmet
Helm^M
casque^M
casco^M
casco^M

ジャージー
jersey
Trikot^N
maillot^M
malla^F
maglia^F

ショーツ
shorts
kurze Hose^F
cuissard^M
pantalones^M elásticos
pantaloncini^M

グローブ／手袋
glove
Handschuh^M
gant^M
guante^M
guanto^M

フレーム
frame
Rahmen^M
cadre^M
bastidor^M
telaio^M

ブレーキ・レバーとギヤ・レバー
brake lever and shifter; brake lever and shifter
Bremsgriff^M und Schalthebel^M
poignée^F de frein^M et manette^F de dérailleur^M
palanca^F del freno^M y cambio^M de velocidades^F
leva^F del freno^M e del cambio^M

タイヤ
tire; tyre
Reifen^M
pneu^M
neumático^M
pneumatico^M

ブレーキ
brake
Bremse^F
frein^M
freno^M
freno^M

多段変速ギヤ
derailleur
Umwerfer^M
dérailleur^M
cambio^M de velocidades^F
deragliatore^M

ホーク
fork
Radgabel^F
fourche^F
horquilla^F
forcella^F

車輪
wheel
Rad^N
roue^F
rueda^F
ruota^F

シューズ
shoe
Schuh^M
chaussure^F
zapato^M
scarpa^F

ペダル
pedal
Pedal^N
pédale^F
pedal^M
pedale^M

チェーン・ホイール／ギヤ板／大ギヤ
chain wheel
Kettenrad^N
plateau^M
cadena^F
ruota^F della moltiplica^F

ロード・レース競技
road cycling competition
Straßenradrennen^N
compétition^F de cyclisme^M sur route^F
competición^F de ciclismo^M por carretera^F
gara^F di ciclismo^M su strada^F

カメラ搭載バイク
motorcycle-mounted camera
Motorradkamera^F
moto^F-caméra^F
moto cámara^F
motocicletta con telecamera^F

先導バイク
leading motorcycle
Führungsmotorrad^N
moto^F de tête^F
moto^M de cabeza^F
motocicletta^F di testa^F

（後続）集団
bunch
Hauptfeld^N
peloton^M
pelotón^M
gruppo^M

後続車
following car
Verfolgerauto^N
voiture^F suiveuse
coche^M del equipo^M
ammiraglia^F

競技委員長
race director
Rennleiter^M
directeur^M de course^F
director^M de carrera^F
direttore^M della corsa^F

先頭集団
leading bunch
Führungsgruppe^F
peloton^M de tête^F
pelotón^M de cabeza^F
gruppo^M di testa^F

マウンテン・バイキング

mountain biking | Mountainbike^N | vélo^M de montagne^F | ciclismo^M de montaña^F | mountain bike^F

クロス・カントリー用自転車とサイクリスト
cross-country bicycle and cyclist
Querfeldeinrad^N und Fahrer^M
vélo^M de cross-country^M et cycliste^M
bicicleta^F de cross^M
bicicletta^F da cross-country^M e ciclista^{M/F}

ゴーグル／防護眼鏡
protective goggles
Schutzbrille^F
lunettes^F de protection^F
gafas^F protectoras
occhiali^M protettivi

ダウンヒル用自転車とサイクリスト
downhill bicycle and cyclist
Downhillrad^N und Fahrer^M
vélo^M de descente^F et cycliste^M
bicicleta^F de descenso^M y ciclista^F
bicicletta^F da downhill^M e ciclista^{M/F}

バック・サスペンション
back suspension
Stoßdämpfer^M hinten
suspension^F arrière
suspensión^F trasera
sospensione^F posteriore

ゴーグル
goggles
Brille^F
lunettes^F
gafas^F
occhiali^M

顎紐（あごひも）
chin strap
Kinnschutz^M
mentonnière^F
mentonera^F
sottogola^M

前ホーク
front fork
Radgabel^F
fourche^F avant
horquilla^F frontal
forcella^F anteriore

幅広ペダル
pedal with wide platform
Plattformpedal^N
pédale^F avec cale^F élargie
pedal^M plano
pedale^M ad ampio appoggio^M

持ち上げハンドルバー
raised handlebar
angehobener Lenkerbügel^M
guidon^M surélevé
manillar^M
manubrio^M rialzato

クリップレス[ビンディング]ペダル
clipless pedal
Klickpedal^N
pédale^F automatique
pedal^M automático
pedale^M senza fermapiedi^M

油圧式ディスク・ブレーキ
hydraulic disc brake
hydraulische Scheibenbremse^F
frein^M hydraulique à disque^M
freno^M de disco^M hidráulico
freno^M a disco^M idraulico

自転車競技 | CYCLING
RADSPORT | CYCLISME | CICLISMO | CICLISMO

トラック・レース

track cycling | BahnradsportM | cyclismeM sur pisteF | ciclismoM en pista | ciclismoM su pistaF

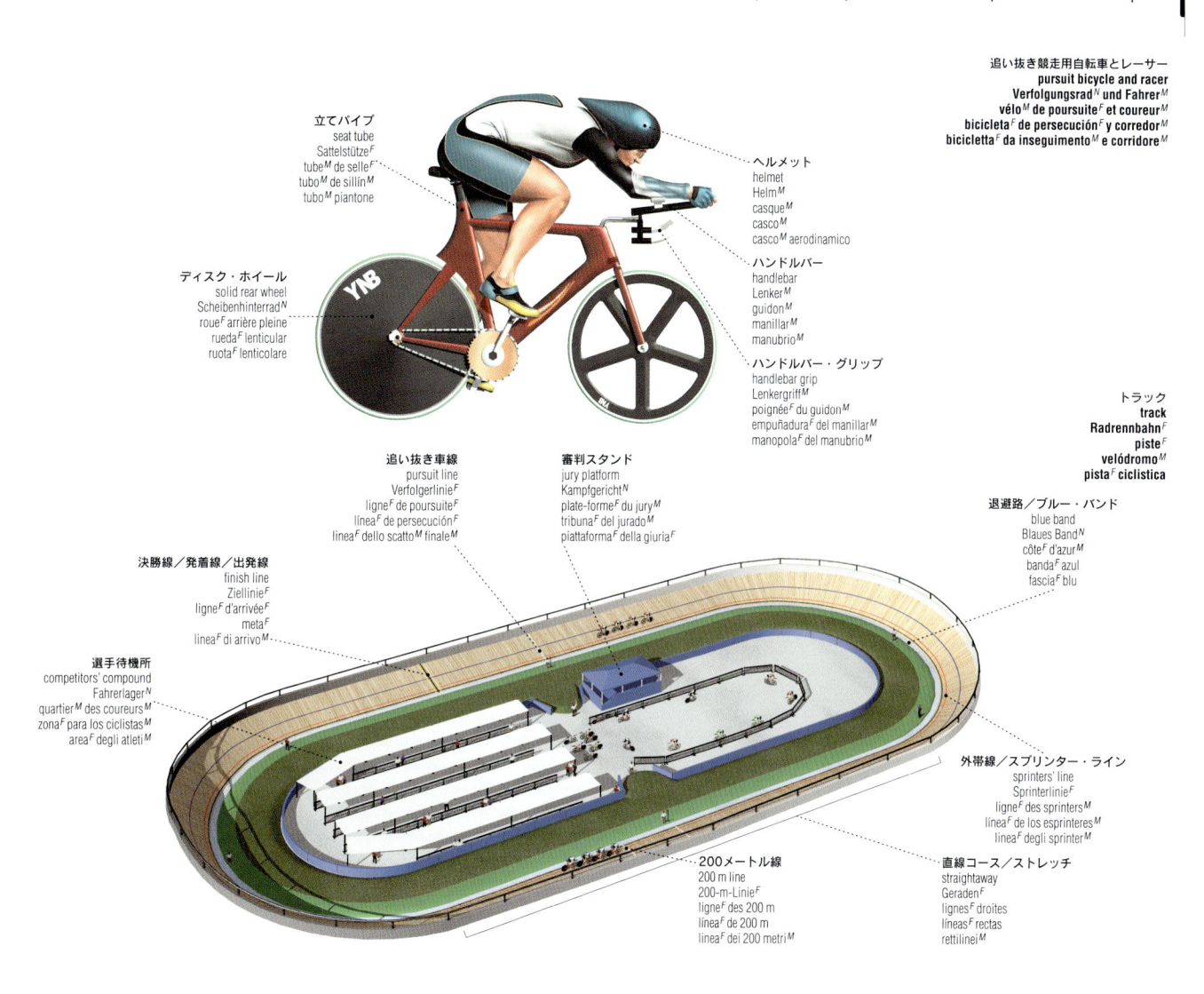

追い抜き競走用自転車とレーサー
pursuit bicycle and racer
VerfolgungsradN und FahrerM
véloM de poursuiteF et coureurM
bicicletaF de persecuciónF y corredorM
biciclettaF da inseguimentoM e corridoreM

立てパイプ
seat tube
SattelstützeF
tubeM de selleF
tuboM de sillínM
tuboM piantone

ヘルメット
helmet
HelmM
casqueM
cascoM
cascoM aerodinamico

ディスク・ホイール
solid rear wheel
ScheibenhinterradN
roueF arrière pleine
ruedaF lenticular
ruotaF lenticolare

ハンドルバー
handlebar
LenkerM
guidonM
manillarM
manubrioM

ハンドルバー・グリップ
handlebar grip
LenkergriffM
poignéeF du guidonM
empuñaduraF del manillarM
manopolaF del manubrioM

トラック
track
RadrennbahnF
pisteF
velódromoM
pistaF ciclistica

追い抜き車線
pursuit line
VerfolgerlinieF
ligneF de poursuiteF
líneaF de persecuciónF
lineaF dello scattoM finaleM

審判スタンド
jury platform
KampfgerichtN
plate-formeF du juryM
tribunaF del juradoM
piattaformaF della giuriaF

退避路／ブルー・バンド
blue band
Blaues BandN
côteF d'azurM
bandaF azul
fasciaF blu

決勝線／発着線／出発線
finish line
ZiellinieF
ligneF d'arrivéeF
metaF
lineaF di arrivoM

選手待機所
competitors' compound
FahrerlagerN
quartierM des coureursM
zonaF para los ciclistasM
areaF degli atletiM

外帯線／スプリンター・ライン
sprinters' line
SprinterlinieF
ligneF des sprintersM
líneaF de los esprinteresM
lineaF degli sprinterM

200メートル線
200 m line
200-m-LinieF
ligneF des 200 m
líneaF de 200 m
lineaF dei 200 metriM

直線コース／ストレッチ
straightaway
GeradenF
lignesF droites
líneasF rectas
rettilineiM

バイシクル・モトクロス

BMX | BMXN | bicrossM | ciclocrossM | mountain bikeF da cross

ヘルメット
helmet
HelmM
casqueM
cascoM
cascoM

ハーフ・パイプ
half-pipe
HalfpipeF
rampeF
halfpipeM
rampaF

グローブ／手袋
glove
HandschuhM
gantM
guanteM
guantoM

ハンドルバー
handlebars
LenkerbügelM
guidonM
manillarM
manubrioM

シングル・チェーン・ホイール
single chain wheel
Einfach-KettenradN
plateauM simple
ruedaF posterior lenticular
ruotaF ad una sola moltiplicaF

ステップ
foot pegs
FußstützenF
repose-piedsM
reposapiésM
pedaneF

シングル・スプロケット／小ギヤ
single sprocket
Einfach-RitzelN
pignonM simple
piñónM simple
pignoneM semplice

871

モーター・スポーツ | MOTOR SPORTS
MOTORSPORT | SPORTS MOTORISÉS | DEPORTES DE MOTOR | SPORT A MOTORE

カー[自動車]レース

car racing | Autorennen^N | course^F automobile | carreras^F de coches^M | automobilismo^M

日本語 | 英語 | ドイツ語 | フランス語 | スペイン語 | イタリア語

ドライバー
driver
Rennfahrer^M
pilote
piloto^M
pilota^M

バラクラバ帽
balaclava
Thermoschutzhaube^F
cagoule^F
pasamontañas^M
sottocasco^M

アンダーガーメント
undergarment
Unterwäsche^F
sous-vêtement^M
ropa^F interior
sottotuta^F

耐火レーシング・スーツ
flame-resistant driving suit
feuerfester Rennanzug^M
combinaison^F résistante au feu^M
traje^M ignífugo
tuta^F ignifuga

耳栓
ear plugs/earbuds
Ohrenstöpsel^M/Ohrhörer^F
bouchons^M d'oreilles^F/oreillettes^F
tapones^M para los oídos^M
tappi^M per le orecchie^F/auricolari^M

レイン・タイヤ
wet-weather tire
Regenreifen^M
pneu^M pluie^F
neumático^M de seco^M
gomma^F da bagnato

グローブ／手袋
gloves
Handschuhe^M
gants^M
guantes^M
guanti^M

スリック・タイヤ
dry-weather tire
Trockenreifen^M
pneu^M pour temps^M sec
neumático^M de lluvia^F
gomma^F da asciutto

クラッシュ・ヘルメット
crash helmet
Helm^M
casque^M
casco^M
casco^M

シューズ
shoe
Schuh^M
chaussure^F
zapato^F
scarpa^F

スターティング・グリッド
starting grid
Startaufstellung^F
grille^F de départ^M
parrilla^F de salida
griglia^F di partenza^F

チェッカー・フラッグ
checkered flag
Zielflagge^F
drapeau^M à damier^M
bandera^F de cuadros^M
bandiera^F a scacchi^M

トラック
track
Strecke^F
piste^F
pista^F
pista^F

ポール・ポジション
pole position
Poleposition^F
pole position^F
pole position^F
pole position^F

サーキット
circuit
Kurs^M
circuit^M
circuito^M
circuito^M

シケイン
chicane
Schikane^F
chicane^F
chicana^F
variante^F

スタート・ライン
starting line
Startlinie^F
ligne^F de départ^M
línea^F de salida^F
linea^F di partenza^F

ピット
pits
Boxen^F
stands^M
boxes^M
box^M

グラベル
gravel bed
Kiesbett^N
bac^M à gravier^M
gravilla^F
via^F di fuga^F

ピット・レーン
pit lane
Boxengasse^F
voie^F des stands^M
entrada^F a boxes^M
corsia^F dei box^M

カーブ
curb
Abweiser^M
bordure^F
chino^M
cordolo^M

タイヤ・バリア
tire barrier
Reifenstapel^M
barrière^F de pneus^M
barrera^F de contención^F
barriera^F di pneumatici^M

モーター・スポーツ | MOTOR SPORTS
MOTORSPORT | SPORTS MOTORISÉS | DEPORTES DE MOTOR | SPORT A MOTORE

カー[自動車]レース

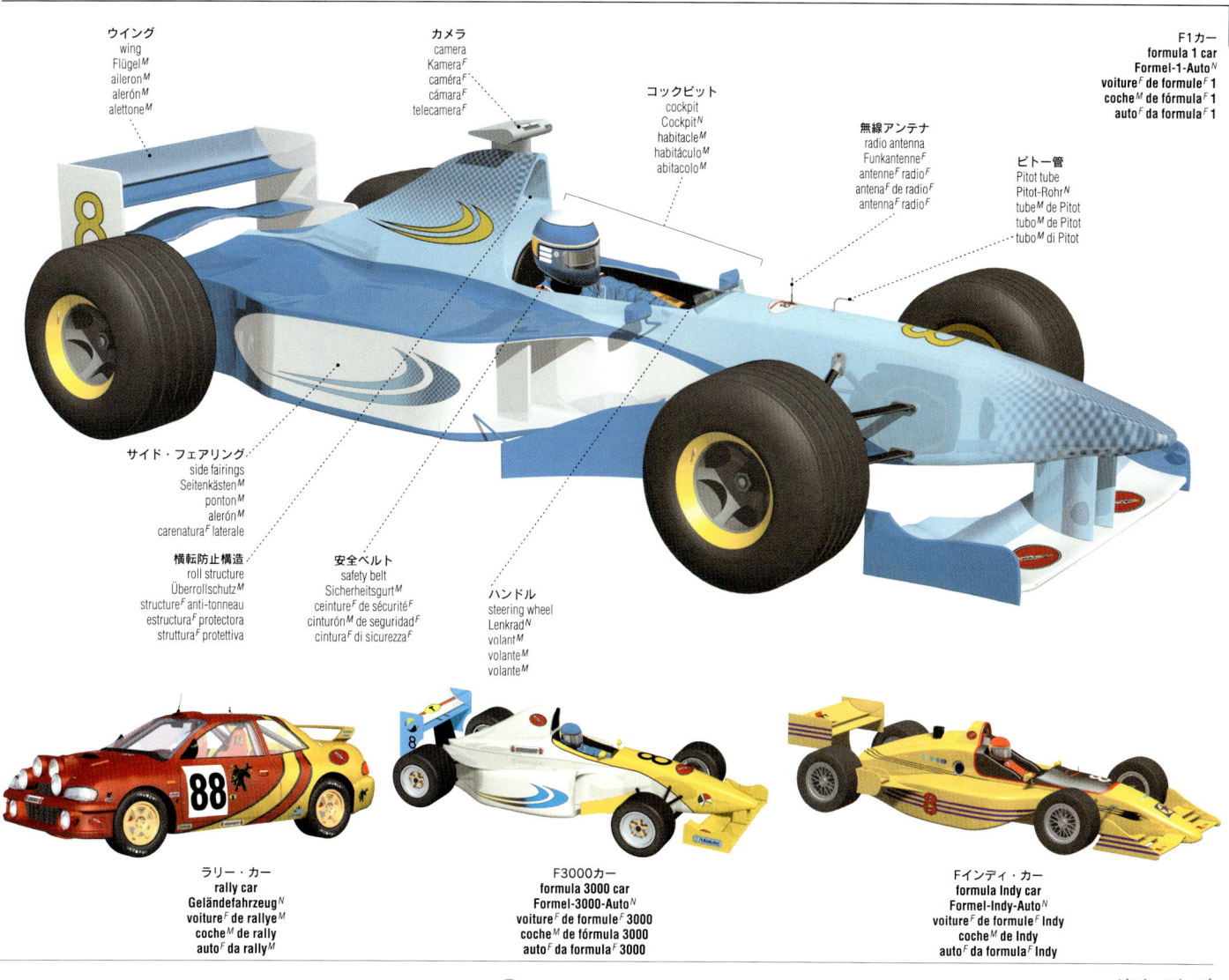

ウイング
wing
Flügel^M
aileron^M
alerón^M
alettone^M

カメラ
camera
Kamera^F
caméra^F
cámara^F
telecamera^F

コックピット
cockpit
Cockpit^N
habitacle^M
habitáculo^M
abitacolo^M

無線アンテナ
radio antenna
Funkantenne^F
antenne^F radio^F
antena^F de radio^F
antenna^F radio^F

F1カー
formula 1 car
Formel-1-Auto^N
voiture^F de formule^F 1
coche^M de fórmula^F 1
auto^F da formula^F 1

ピトー管
Pitot tube
Pitot-Rohr^N
tube^M de Pitot
tubo^M de Pitot
tubo^M di Pitot

サイド・フェアリング
side fairings
Seitenkästen^M
ponton^M
alerón^M
carenatura^F laterale

横転防止構造
roll structure
Überrollschutz^M
structure^F anti-tonneau
estructura^F protectora
struttura^F protettiva

安全ベルト
safety belt
Sicherheitsgurt^M
ceinture^F de sécurité^F
cinturón^M de seguridad^F
cintura^F di sicurezza^F

ハンドル
steering wheel
Lenkrad^N
volant^M
volante^M
volante^M

ラリー・カー
rally car
Geländefahrzeug^N
voiture^F de rallye^M
coche^M de rally
auto^F da rally^M

F3000カー
formula 3000 car
Formel-3000-Auto^N
voiture^F de formule^F 3000
coche^M de fórmula^F 3000
auto^F da formula^F 3000

Fインディ・カー
formula Indy car
Formel-Indy-Auto^N
voiture^F de formule^F Indy
coche^M de Indy
auto^F da formula^F Indy

給油装置
refueling device
Tankanlage^F
dispositif^M de ravitaillement^M
tanque^M para repostar
serbatoio^M per il rifornimento^M

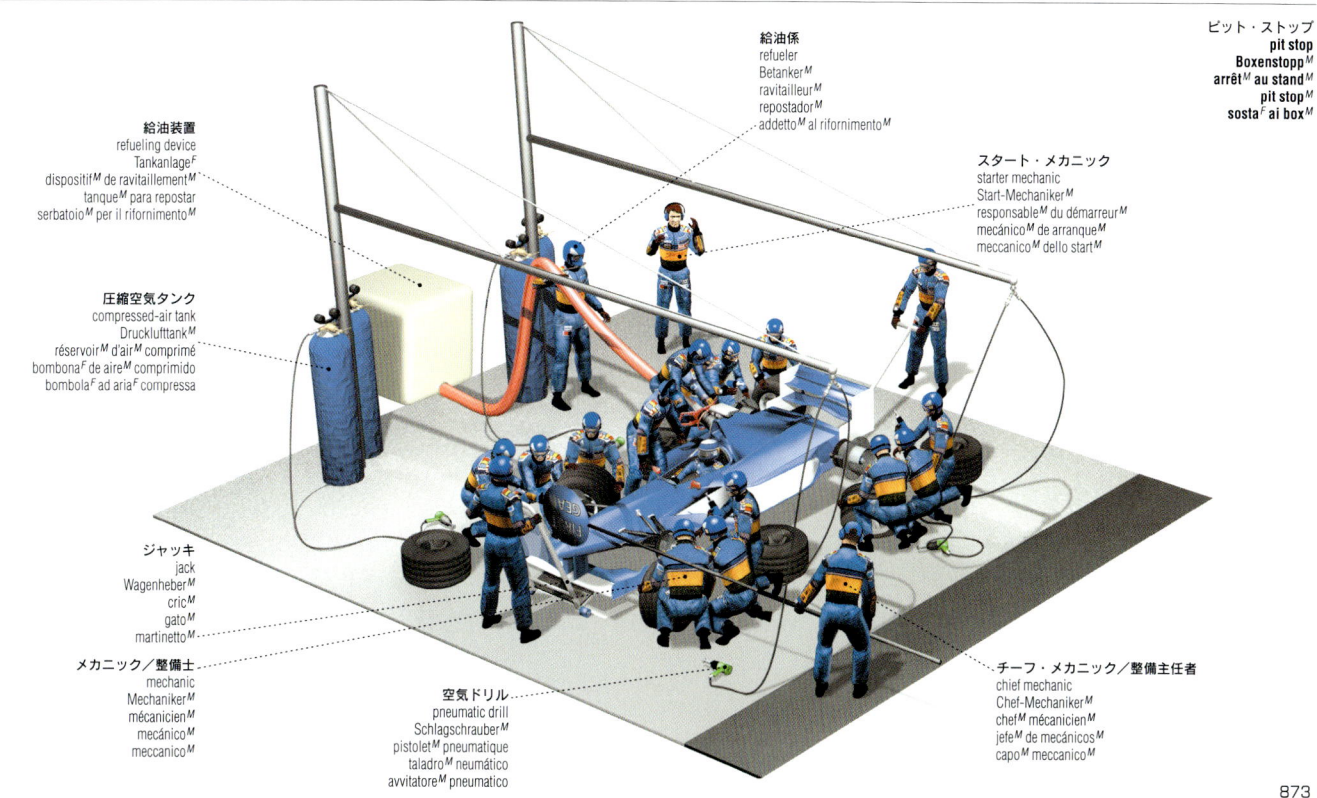

給油係
refueler
Betanker^M
ravitailleur^M
repostador^M
addetto^M al rifornimento^M

スタート・メカニック
starter mechanic
Start-Mechaniker^M
responsable^M du démarreur^M
mecánico^M de arranque^M
meccanico^M dello start^M

ピット・ストップ
pit stop
Boxenstopp^M
arrêt^M au stand^M
pit stop^M
sosta^F ai box^M

圧縮空気タンク
compressed-air tank
Drucklufttank^M
réservoir^M d'air^M comprimé
bombona^F de aire^M comprimido
bombola^F ad aria^F compressa

ジャッキ
jack
Wagenheber^M
cric^M
gato^M
martinetto^M

メカニック/整備士
mechanic
Mechaniker^M
mécanicien^M
mecánico^M
meccanico^M

空気ドリル
pneumatic drill
Schlagschrauber^M
pistolet^M pneumatique
taladro^M neumático
avvitatore^M pneumatico

チーフ・メカニック/整備主任者
chief mechanic
Chef-Mechaniker^M
chef^M mécanicien^M
jefe^M de mecánicos^M
capo^M meccanico^M

スポーツとゲーム

873

モーター・スポーツ | MOTOR SPORTS
MOTORSPORT | SPORTS MOTORISÉS | DEPORTES DE MOTOR | SPORT A MOTORE

オートバイ・レース

日本語 | 英語 | ドイツ語 | フランス語 | スペイン語 | イタリア語

motorcycling | Motorradsport^M | motocyclisme^M | motocicleta^F | motociclismo^M

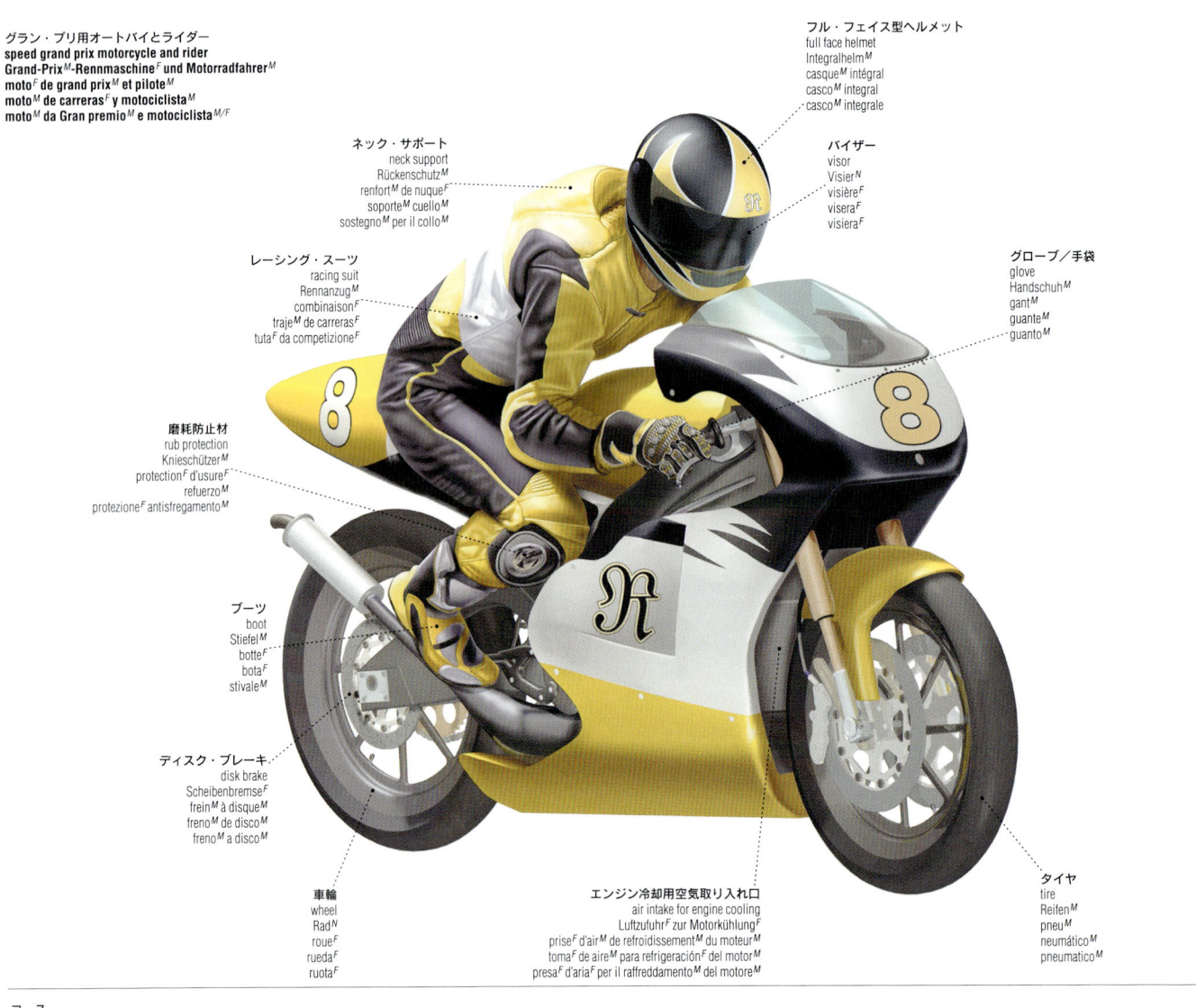

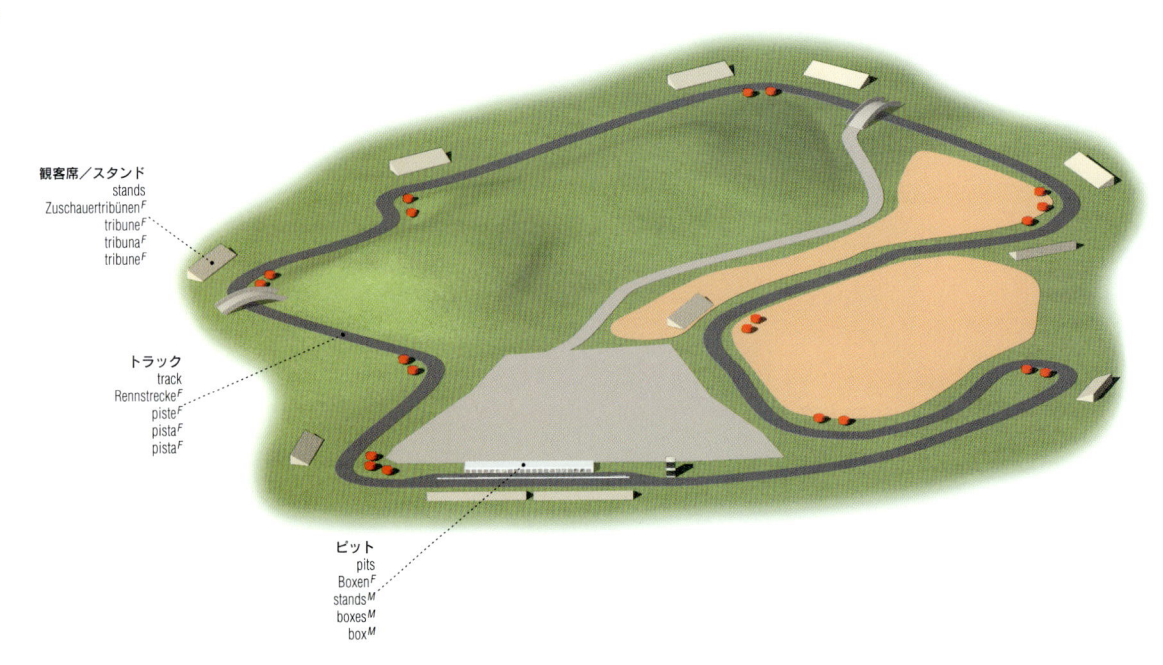

グラン・プリ用オートバイとライダー
speed grand prix motorcycle and rider
Grand-Prix^M-Rennmaschine^F und Motorradfahrer^M
moto^F de grand prix et pilote^M
moto^M de carreras^F y motociclista^M
moto^M da Gran premio^M e motociclista$^{M/F}$

ネック・サポート
neck support
Rückenschutz^M
renfort^M de nuque^F
soporte^M cuello^M
sostegno^M per il collo^M

フル・フェイス型ヘルメット
full face helmet
Integralhelm^M
casque^M intégral
casco^M integral
casco^M integrale

バイザー
visor
Visier^N
visière^F
visera^F
visiera^F

レーシング・スーツ
racing suit
Rennanzug^M
combinaison^F
traje^M de carreras^F
tuta^F da competizione^F

グローブ／手袋
glove
Handschuh^M
gant^M
guante^M
guanto^M

磨耗防止材
rub protection
Knieschützer^M
protection^F d'usure^F
refuerzo^M
protezione^F antisfregamento^M

ブーツ
boot
Stiefel^M
botte^F
bota^F
stivale^M

ディスク・ブレーキ
disk brake
Scheibenbremse^F
frein^M à disque^M
freno^M de disco^M
freno^M a disco^M

車輪
wheel
Rad^N
roue^F
rueda^F
ruota^F

エンジン冷却用空気取り入れ口
air intake for engine cooling
Luftzufuhr^F zur Motorkühlung^F
prise^F d'air^M de refroidissement^M du moteur^M
toma^F de aire^M para refrigeración^F del motor^M
presa^F d'aria^F per il raffreddamento^M del motore^M

タイヤ
tire
Reifen^M
pneu^M
neumático^M
pneumatico^M

コース
course
Rennstrecke^F
circuit^M
circuito^M
circuito^M

観客席／スタンド
stands
Zuschauertribünen^F
tribune^F
tribuna^F
tribune^F

トラック
track
Rennstrecke^F
piste^F
pista^F
pista^F

ピット
pits
Boxen^F
stands^M
boxes^M
box^M

スポーツとゲーム

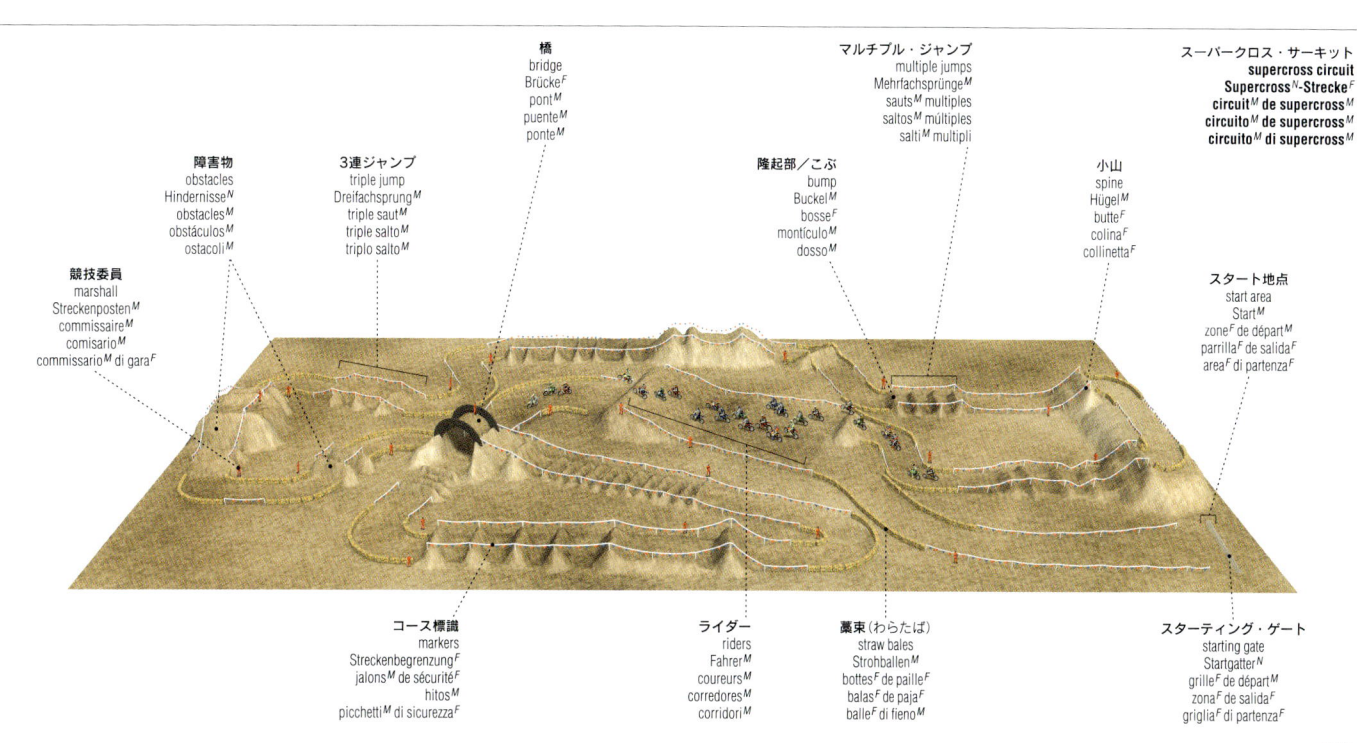

モーター・スポーツ | MOTOR SPORTS
MOTORSPORT | SPORTS MOTORISÉS | DEPORTES DE MOTOR | SPORT A MOTORE

オートバイ・レース

モトクロス・スーパークロス用のオートバイ
motocross and supercross motorcycle
Motocross^N- und Supercross^N-Motorrad^N
moto^F de motocross^M et supercross^M
moto^M de motocross^M y supercross^M
motocicletta^F da motocross^M e supercross^M

トライアル用オートバイ
trial motorcycle
Trial^N-Motorrad^N
moto^F de trial^M
moto^F de trial^M
motocicletta^F da trial^M

ラリー用オートバイ
rally motorcycle
Rallye^F-Motorrad^N
moto^F de rallye^M
moto^M de rally^M
motocicletta^F da rally^M

防護服
protective suit
Schutzanzug^M
combinaison^F de protection^F
traje^M de protección^F
tuta^F protettiva

グローブ／手袋
glove
Handschuh^M
gant^M
guante^M
guanto^M

ズボン
pants
Hose^F
pantalon^M
pantalones^M
pantaloni^M

ヘルメット
helmet
Helm^M
casque^M
casco^M
casco^M per cross

ゴーグル／防護眼鏡
protective goggles
Schutzbrille^F
lunettes^F de protection^F
guantes^M protectores
occhiali^M protettivi

ハンド・ガード
hand protector
Handschutz^M
protège-main^M
protector^M de mano^F
paramano^M

ナンバー・プレート
number plate
Startnummer^F
plaque^F-numéro^M
placa^F de número^M
numero^M di gara^F

フォーク
fork
Gabel^F
fourche^F
horquilla^F
forcella^F

モトクロス・タイヤ
nubby tire
Stollenreifen^M
pneu^M à crampons^M
neumático^M de tacos^M
pneumatico^M scolpito

ブーツ
boot
Stiefel^M
botte^F
bota^F
stivale^M

防護板
protective plate
Schutzplatte^F
plaque^F de protection^F
placa^F protectora
piastra^F di protezione^F

橋
bridge
Brücke^F
pont^M
puente^M
ponte^M

マルチプル・ジャンプ
multiple jumps
Mehrfachsprünge^M
sauts^M multiples
saltos^M múltiples
salti^M multipli

スーパークロス・サーキット
supercross circuit
Supercross^N-Strecke^F
circuit^M de supercross^M
circuito^M de supercross^M
circuito^M di supercross^M

障害物
obstacles
Hindernisse^N
obstacles^M
obstáculos^M
ostacoli^M

3連ジャンプ
triple jump
Dreifachsprung^M
triple saut^M
triple salto^M
triplo salto^M

隆起部／こぶ
bump
Buckel^M
bosse^F
montículo^M
dosso^M

小山
spine
Hügel^M
butte^F
colina^F
collinetta^F

競技委員
marshall
Streckenposten^M
commissaire^M
comisario^M
commissario^M di gara^F

スタート地点
start area
Start^M
zone^F de départ^M
parrilla^F de salida^F
area^F di partenza^F

コース標識
markers
Streckenbegrenzung^F
jalons^M de sécurité^F
hitos^M
picchetti^M di sicurezza^F

ライダー
riders
Fahrer^M
coureurs^M
corredores^M
corridori^M

藁束（わらたば）
straw bales
Strohballen^M
bottes^F de paille^F
balas^F de paja^F
balle^F di fieno^M

スターティング・ゲート
starting gate
Startgatter^N
grille^F de départ^M
zona^F de salida^F
griglia^F di partenza^F

スポーツとゲーム

875

モーター・スポーツ | MOTOR SPORTS
MOTORSPORT | SPORTS MOTORISÉS | DEPORTES DE MOTOR | SPORT A MOTORE

水上オートバイ／ジェット・スキー

日本語 | 英語 | ドイツ語 | フランス語 | スペイン語 | イタリア語

personal watercraft | **Jetski**^{M} | **scooter**^{M} **de mer**^{F} | **moto**^{F} **acuática** | **acquascooter**^{M}

ハンドルバー
handlebar
Lenker^M
guidon^M
manillar^M
manubrio^M

ミラー／鏡
mirror
Rückspiegel^M
rétroviseur^M
espejo^M
specchietto^M

シート／座席
seat
Sitz^M
selle^F
asiento^M
sella^F

スポンソン／水びれ
sponson
Stabilisator^M
stabilisateur^M
estabilizador^M
stabilizzatore^M

船体
hull
Rumpf^M
coque^F
casco^M
scafo^M

スノーモービル

snowmobile | **Schneemobil**^{N} | **motoneige**^{F} | **moto**^{M} **nieve** | **gatto**^{M} **delle nevi**^{F}

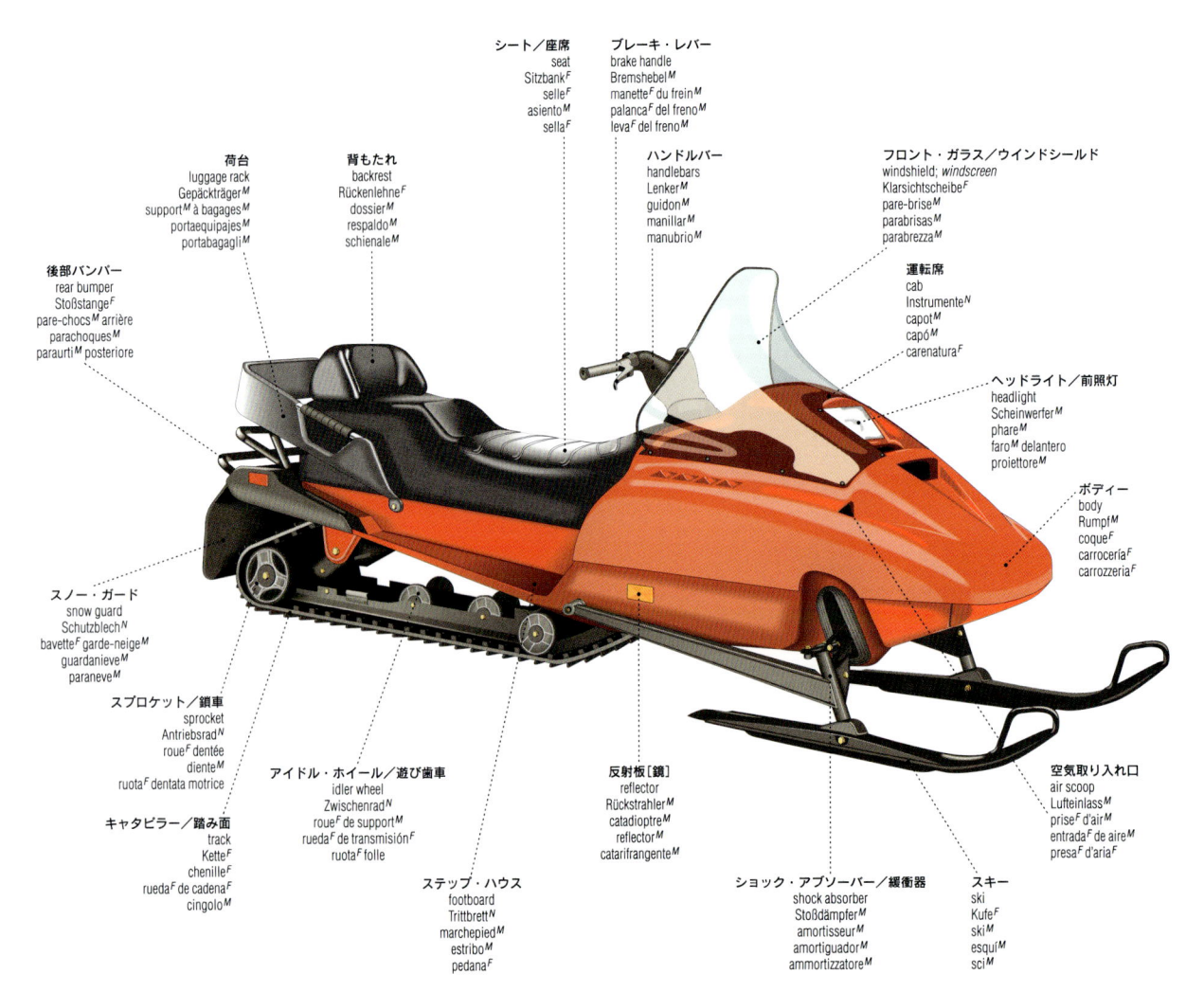

シート／座席
seat
Sitzbank^F
selle^F
asiento^M
sella^F

ブレーキ・レバー
brake handle
Bremshebel^M
manette^F du frein^M
palanca^F del freno^M
leva^F del freno^M

荷台
luggage rack
Gepäckträger^M
support^M à bagages
portaequipajes^M
portabagagli^M

背もたれ
backrest
Rückenlehne^F
dossier^M
respaldo^M
schienale^M

ハンドルバー
handlebars
Lenker^M
guidon^M
manillar^M
manubrio^M

フロント・ガラス／ウインドシールド
windshield; windscreen
Klarsichtscheibe^F
pare-brise^M
parabrisas^M
parabrezza^F

運転席
cab
Instrumente^N
capot^N
capó^M
carenatura^F

後部バンパー
rear bumper
Stoßstange^F
pare-chocs^M arrière
parachoques^M
paraurti^M posteriore

ヘッドライト／前照灯
headlight
Scheinwerfer^M
phare^M
faro^M delantero
proiettore^M

ボディー
body
Rumpf^M
coque^F
carrocería^F
carrozzeria^F

スノー・ガード
snow guard
Schutzblech^N
bavette^F garde-neige^M
guardanieve^M
paraneve^M

スプロケット／鎖車
sprocket
Antriebsrad^N
roue^F dentée
diente^M
ruota^F dentata motrice

アイドル・ホイール／遊び歯車
idler wheel
Zwischenrad^N
roue^F de support^M
rueda^F de transmisión^F
ruota^F folle

反射板［鏡］
reflector
Rückstrahler^M
catadioptre^M
reflector^M
catarifrangente^M

ショック・アブソーバー／緩衝器
shock absorber
Stoßdämpfer^M
amortisseur^M
amortiguador^M
ammortizzatore^M

空気取り入れ口
air scoop
Lufteinlass^M
prise^F d'air^M
entrada^F de aire^M
presa^F d'aria^F

スキー
ski
Kufe^F
ski^M
esquí^M
sci^M

キャタピラー／踏み面
track
Kette^F
chenille^F
rueda^F de cadena^F
cingolo^M

ステップ・ハウス
footboard
Trittbrett^N
marchepied^M
estribo^M
pedana^F

ウインター・スポーツ | WINTER SPORTS
WINTERSPORT | SPORTS D'HIVER | DEPORTES DE INVIERNO | SPORT INVERNALI

カーリング

curling | Curling^N | curling^M | curling^M | curling^M

カーリング・ストーン
curling stone
Curlingstein^M
pierre^F de curling^M
piedra^F de curling^M
pietra^F da curling^M

取っ手／ハンドル
handle
Griff^M
poignée^F
mango^M
impugnatura^F

カーリング・ブラシ
curling brush
Curlingbesen^M
brosse^F de curling^M
cepillo^M de curling^M
scopa^F da curling^M

センター・ライン
center line; *centre line*
Mittellinie^F
ligne^F de centre^M
línea^F central
linea^F di centro^M

リンク
rink
Bahn^F
piste^F
área^F de juego^M
campo^M

セカンド
second
Second^M
deuxième joueur^M
segundo jugador^M
secondo giocatore^M al lancio^M

バイス・スキップ／副主将／サード
vice-skip
Allrounder^M
vice-capitaine^M
tercero^M
vicecapitano^M

リード
lead
Lead^M
premier joueur^M
líder^M
primo giocatore^M al lancio^M

アンパイア／審判員
umpire
Schiedsrichter^M
arbitre^M
árbitro^M
giudice^M di linea^F

シート
sheet
Eisfläche^F
surface^F de la glace^F
área^F de juego^M
campo^M di gioco^M

サイド・ライン
lateral line
Seitenlinie^F
ligne^F latérale
línea^F de banda^F
linea^F laterale

スキップ／主将
skip
Skip^M
capitaine^M
capitán^M
capitano^M

バック・ライン
back line
Backline^F
ligne^F arrière
línea^F trasera
linea^F di fondo^M

ホッグ・ライン
hog line
Hoglinie^F
ligne^F de jeu^M
línea^F de juego^M
linea^F di fallo^M

ティー・ライン
tee line
Teelinie^F
ligne^F de balayage^M
línea^F de tee^M
linea^F del bersaglio^M

内円／インナー・サークル
inner circle
Innenkreis^M
cercle^M intérieur
círculo^M central
anello^M interno

カーラー
curler
Curlingstein^M
curleuse^F
primer jugador^M
giocatore^M

ハック
hack
Hack^M
appui^M-pied^M
percha^F
staffa^F di lancio^M

外円／アウター・サークル
outer circle
Außenkreis^M
cercle^M extérieur
círculo^M exterior
anello^M esterno

ティー
tee
Tee^N
centre^M
tee^M
centro^M

ハウス
house
Haus^N
maison^F
casa^F
casa^F

フリー・ガード・ゾーン
free guard zone
Free Guard Zone^F
zone^F de garde^F protégée
zona^F de defensa^F protegida
zona^F protetta

スポーツとゲーム

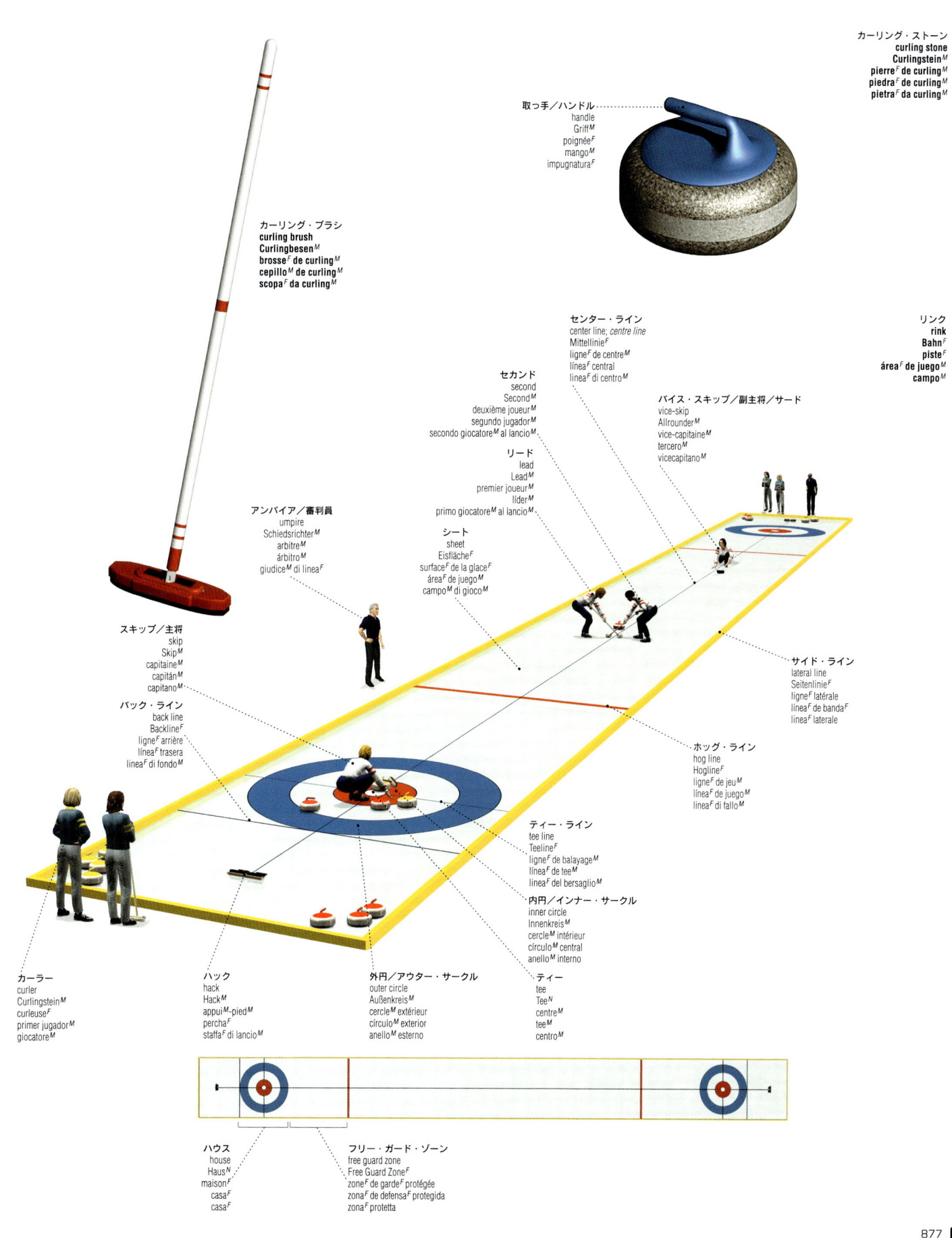

877

ウインター・スポーツ | WINTER SPORTS
WINTERSPORT | SPORTS D'HIVER | DEPORTES DE INVIERNO | SPORT INVERNALI

アイス・ホッケー

日本語 | 英語 | ドイツ語 | フランス語 | スペイン語 | イタリア語

ice hockey | Eishockey^N | hockey^M sur glace^F | hockey^M sobre hielo^M | hockey^M su ghiaccio^M

アイス・ホッケー・プレーヤー
ice hockey player
Eishockeyspieler^M
hockeyeur^M
jugador^M
giocatore^M

バイザー
visor
Gesichtsschutz^M
visière^F
visera^F
visiera^F

ヘルメット／ヘッドギア
helmet
Schutzhelm^M
casque^M
casco^M
casco^M

チーム・エンブレム
team's emblem
Mannschaftsabzeichen^N
emblème^M d'équipe^F
emblema^M del equipo^M
simbolo^M della squadra^F

ゼッケン番号
player's number
Spielernummer^F
numéro^M du joueur^M
número^M del jugador^M
numero^M del giocatore^M

グローブ
glove
Handschuh^M
gant^M
guante^M
guanto^M

ズボン
pants; *trousers*
Hose^F
culotte^F
pantalón^M
pantaloni^M

ストッキング
stocking
Stutzen^M
bas^M
calcetines^M
calzettone^M

スケート
skate
Schlittschuh^M
patin^M
bota^F
pattino^M

ブレード
blade
Kufe^F
lame^F
cuchilla^F
lama^F

リンク
rink
Eisfläche^F
patinoire^F
pista^F
campo^M

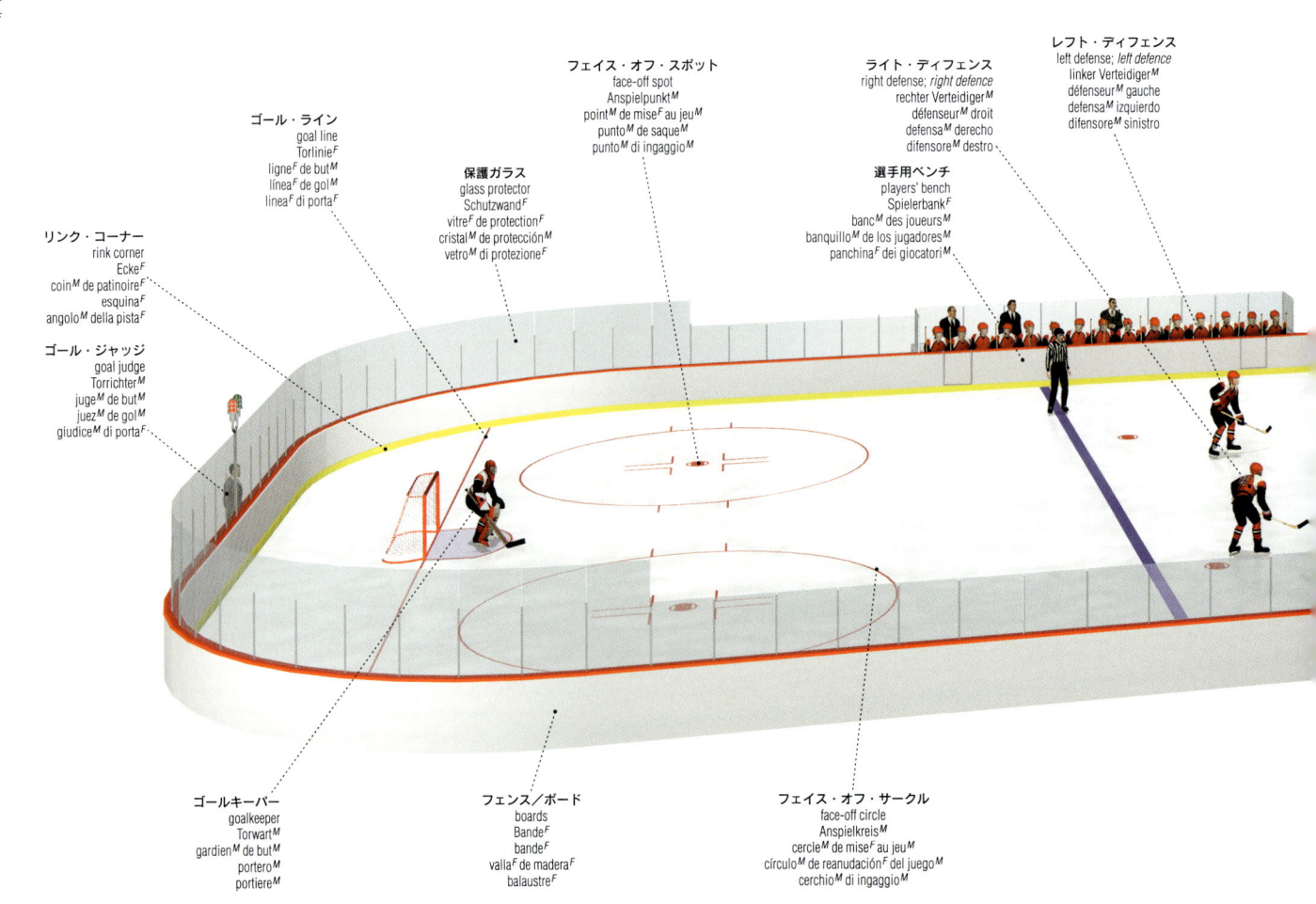

フェイス・オフ・スポット
face-off spot
Anspielpunkt^M
point^M de mise^F au jeu^M
punto^M de saque^M
punto^M di ingaggio^M

ライト・ディフェンス
right defense; *right defence*
rechter Verteidiger^M
défenseur^M droit
defensa^M derecho
difensore^M destro

レフト・ディフェンス
left defense; *left defence*
linker Verteidiger^M
défenseur^M gauche
defensa^M izquierdo
difensore^M sinistro

ゴール・ライン
goal line
Torlinie^F
ligne^F de but^M
línea^F de gol^M
linea^F di porta^F

保護ガラス
glass protector
Schutzwand^F
vitre^F de protection^F
cristal^M de protección^M
vetro^M di protezione^F

選手用ベンチ
players' bench
Spielerbank^F
banc^M des joueurs^M
banquillo^M de los jugadores^M
panchina^F dei giocatori^M

リンク・コーナー
rink corner
Ecke^F
coin^M de patinoire^F
esquina^F
angolo^M della pista^F

ゴール・ジャッジ
goal judge
Torrichter^M
juge^M de but^M
juez^M de gol^M
giudice^M di porta^F

ゴールキーパー
goalkeeper
Torwart^M
gardien^M de but^M
portero^M
portiere^M

フェンス／ボード
boards
Bande^F
bande^F
valla^F de madera^F
balaustre^F

フェイス・オフ・サークル
face-off circle
Anspielkreis^M
cercle^M de mise^F au jeu^M
círculo^M de reanudación^F del juego^M
cerchio^M di ingaggio^M

スポーツとゲーム

ウインター・スポーツ | WINTER SPORTS
WINTERSPORT | SPORTS D'HIVER | DEPORTES DE INVIERNO | SPORT INVERNALI

アイス・ホッケー

ゴールキーパー
goalkeeper
Torwart^M
gardien^M de but^M
portero^M
portiere^M

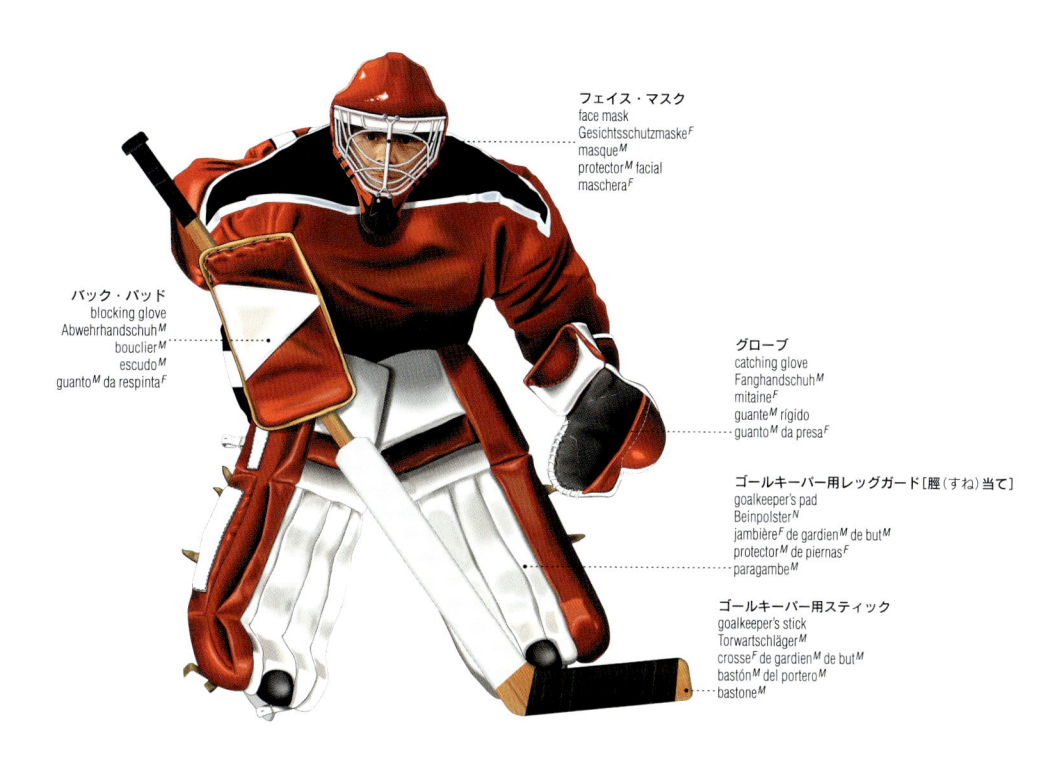

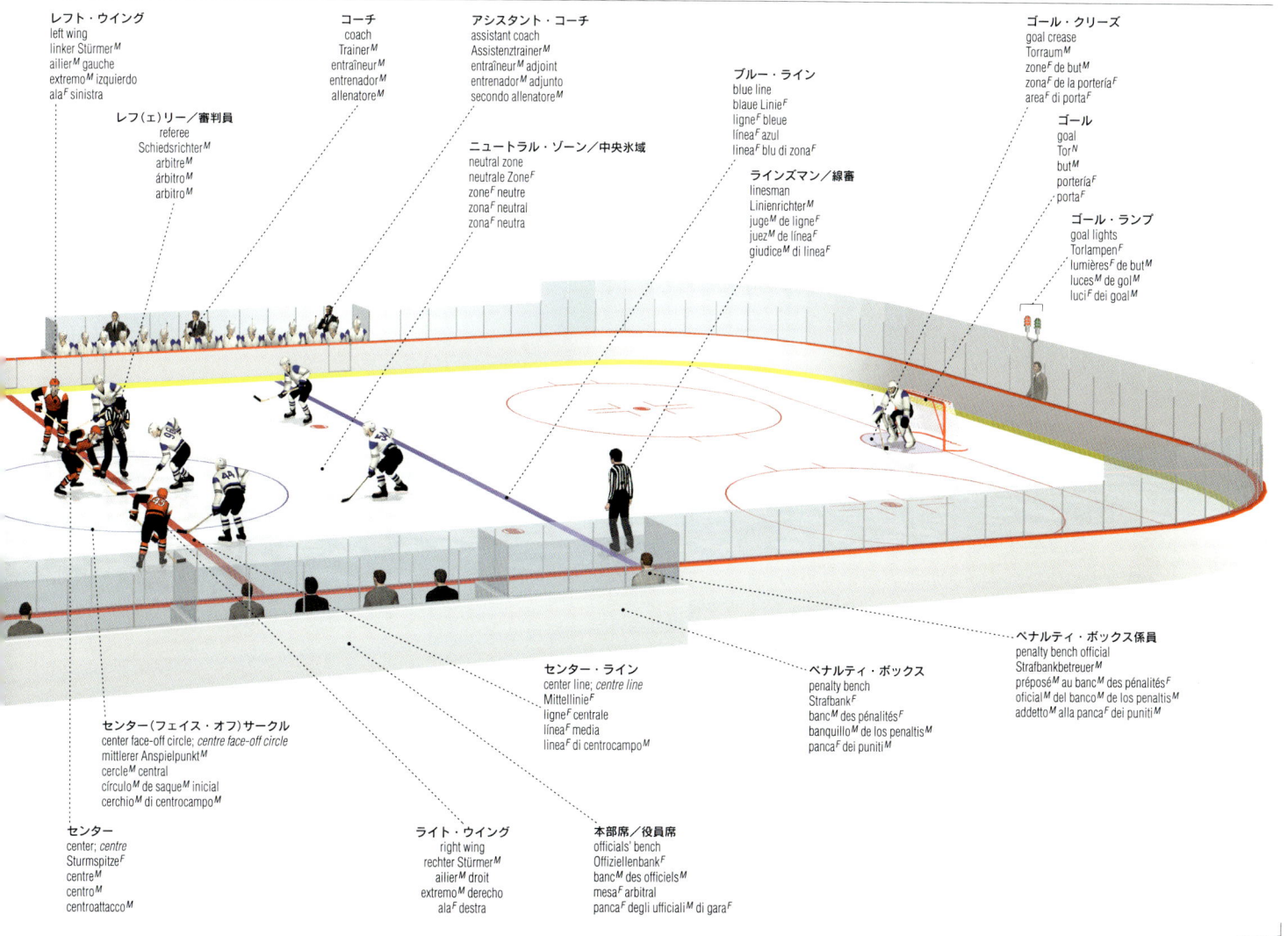

フェイス・マスク
face mask
Gesichtsschutzmaske^F
masque^M
protector^M facial
maschera^F

バック・パッド
blocking glove
Abwehrhandschuh^M
bouclier^M
escudo^M
guanto^M da respinta^F

グローブ
catching glove
Fanghandschuh^M
mitaine^F
guante^M rígido
guanto^M da presa^F

ゴールキーパー用レッグガード[脛（すね）当て]
goalkeeper's pad
Beinpolster^N
jambière^F de gardien^M de but^M
protector^M de piernas^F
paragambe^M

ゴールキーパー用スティック
goalkeeper's stick
Torwartschläger^M
crosse^F de gardien^M de but^M
bastón^M del portero^M
bastone^M

レフト・ウイング
left wing
linker Stürmer^M
ailier^M gauche
extremo^M izquierdo
ala^F sinistra

コーチ
coach
Trainer^M
entraîneur^M
entrenador^M
allenatore^M

アシスタント・コーチ
assistant coach
Assistenztrainer^M
entraîneur^M adjoint
entrenador^M adjunto
secondo allenatore^M

ゴール・クリーズ
goal crease
Torraum^M
zone^F de but^M
zona^F de la portería^F
area^F di porta^F

レフ(ェ)リー／審判員
referee
Schiedsrichter^M
arbitre^M
árbitro^M
arbitro^M

ニュートラル・ゾーン／中央氷域
neutral zone
neutrale Zone^F
zone^F neutre
zona^F neutral
zona^F neutra

ブルー・ライン
blue line
blaue Linie^F
ligne^F bleue
línea^F azul
linea^F blu di zona^F

ゴール
goal
Tor^N
but^M
portería^F
porta^F

ラインズマン／線審
linesman
Linienrichter^M
juge^M de ligne^F
juez^M de línea^F
giudice^M di linea^F

ゴール・ランプ
goal lights
Torlampen^F
lumières^F de but^M
luces^M de gol^M
luci^F dei goal^M

ペナルティ・ボックス係員
penalty bench official
Strafbankbetreuer^M
préposé^M au banc^M des pénalités^F
oficial^M del banco^M de los penaltis^M
addetto^M alla panca^F dei puniti^M

センター・ライン
center line; centre line
Mittellinie^F
ligne^F centrale
línea^F media
linea^F di centrocampo^M

ペナルティ・ボックス
penalty bench
Strafbank^F
banc^M des pénalités^F
banquillo^M de los penaltis^M
panca^F dei puniti^M

センター（フェイス・オフ）サークル
center face-off circle; centre face-off circle
mittlerer Anspielpunkt^M
cercle^M central
círculo^M de saque^M inicial
cerchio^M di centrocampo^M

センター
center; centre
Sturmspitze^F
centre^M
centro^M
centroattacco^M

ライト・ウイング
right wing
rechter Stürmer^M
ailier^M droit
extremo^M derecho
ala^F destra

本部席／役員席
officials' bench
Offiziellenbank^F
banc^M des officiels^M
mesa^F arbitral
panca^F degli ufficiali^M di gara^F

スポーツとゲーム

879

ウインター・スポーツ | WINTER SPORTS
WINTERSPORT | SPORTS D'HIVER | DEPORTES DE INVIERNO | SPORT INVERNALI

アイス・ホッケー

日本語 | 英語 | ドイツ語 | フランス語 | スペイン語 | イタリア語

プレーヤー用スティック
player's stick
Eishockeyschläger^M
crosse^F de joueur^M
palo^M del jugador^M
bastone^M del giocatore^M

バット・エンド
butt end
Knauf^M
embout^M
pomo^M
pomolo^M del bastone^M

シャフト
shaft
Schaft^M
manche^M
mango^M
asta^F

ヒール
heel
Unterkante^F
talon^M
talón^M
tallone^M

ブレード
blade
Blatt^N
lame^F
pala^F del stick^M
pala^F

喉当て
throat protector
Halsschutz^M
protège-gorge^M
protector^M de cuello^M
paracollo^M

カフ／袖当て
cuff
Manschette^F
manchette^F
muñequera^F
copripolso^M

肘当て
elbow pads
Ellbogenpolster^N
protège-coude^M
codera^F
paragomiti^M

肩当て
shoulder pads
Schulterpolster^N
épaulière^F
hombrera^F
paraspalle^M

パック
puck
Puck^M
palet^M
disco^M
dischetto^M

喉当て
throat protector
Halsschutz^M
protège-gorge^M
protector^M del cuello^M
paragola^M

防護カップ
protective cup
Suspensorium^N
coquille^F
coquilla^F
conchiglia^F di protezione^F

ゴールキーパー用スティック
goalkeeper's stick
Torwartschläger^M
crosse^F de gardien^M de but^M
palo^M del portero^M
bastone^M del portiere^M

腕当て
arm pad
Armpolster^N
brassard^M
protector^M del brazo^M
parabraccia^M

膝当て
knee pad
Kniepolster^N
genouillère^F
rodillera^F
ginocchiera^F

プレーヤー用スケート靴
player's skate
Schlittschuh^M
patin^M
patín^M
pattino^M

アキレス腱ガード
tendon guard
Sehnenschützer^M
protège-tendon^M
protector^M del tendón^M
proteggitendine^M

ゴールキーパー用胸当て［プロテクター］
goalkeeper's chest pad
Torwartbrustschutz^M
plastron^M de gardien^M de but^M
peto^M del portero^M
pettorina^F del portiere^M

トゥ・ボックス
toe box
Kappe^F
renfort^M de pointe^F
puntera^F reforzada
rinforzo^M di cuoio^M

ブーツ
boot
Stiefel^M
chaussure^F
bota^F
scarpa^F

ブレード／刃
blade
Kufe^F
lame^F
hoja^F de cuchilla^F
lama^F

ポイント
point
Spitze^F
pointe^F
puntera^F
punta^F

ゴールキーパー用スケート靴
goalkeeper's skate
Torwartschlittschuh^M
patin^M de gardien^M de but^M
patín^M del portero^M
pattino^M del portiere^M

パッド
pads
Schienbeinschützer^M
jambières^F
tobillera^F
paragambe^M

スポーツとゲーム

ウインター・スポーツ | WINTER SPORTS
WINTERSPORT | SPORTS D'HIVER | DEPORTES DE INVIERNO | SPORT INVERNALI

フィギュア・スケート

figure skating | Eiskunstlauf(M) | patinage(M) artistique | patinaje(M) artístico | pattinaggio(M) artistico

裏当て
lining
Futter(N)
doublure(F)
forro(M)
fodera(F)

舌革／ベロ
tongue
Zunge(F)
languette(F)
lengüeta(F)
linguetta(F)

フィギュア・スケート靴
figure skate
Eiskunstlaufstiefel(M)
patin(M) de figure(F)
patín(M) para figuras(F)
pattino(M) per pattinaggio(M) artistico

ホック
hook
Schnürhaken(M)
crochet(M)
corchete(M)
gancio(M)

バックステー
backstay
Rückenverstärkung(F)
tige(F)
contrafuerte(M)
rinforzo(M) posteriore

紐（ひも）
lace
Schnürsenkel(M)
lacet(M)
cordón(M)
stringa(F)

ダンス・ブレード
dance blade
Eistanzkufe(F)
lame(F) de danse(F) sur glace(F)
cuchilla(F) de baile(M)
lama(F) per danza(F)

ブーツ
boot
Stiefel(M)
chaussure(F)
bota(F)
scarpa(F)

紐穴
eyelet
Schnüröse(F)
œillet(M)
ojal(M)
occhiello(M)

ヒール
heel
Absatz(M)
talon(M)
tacón(M)
tacco(M)

ソール／底
sole
Sohle(F)
semelle(F)
suela(F)
suola(F)

フィギュア・ブレード
free skating blade
Eiskunstlaufkufe(F)
lame(F) pour programme(M) libre
cuchilla(F) de patinaje(M) artístico
lama(F) per pattinaggio(M) libero

スタンション／支柱
stanchion
Träger(M)
montant(M)
montante(M)
sostegno(M)

エッジ
edge
Schneide(F)
carre(F)
canto(M)
lamina(F)

ブレード／刃
blade
Kufe(F)
lame(F)
hoja(F) de cuchilla(F)
lama(F)

トウ・ピックス
toe pick
Abstoßsäge(F)
dent(F)
dientes(M)
punta(F) dentellata

アクセル
axel
Axel(M)
axel(M)
axel(M)
axel(M)

サルコウ／サルコー
salchow
Salchow(M)
salchow(M)
salchow(M)
salchow(M)

ジャンプの例
examples of jumps
Beispiele(N) für Sprünge(M)
exemples(M) de sauts(M)
ejemplos(M) de piruetas(F)
esempi(M) di salti(M)

トウ・ループ
toe loop
Toeloop(M)
boucle(F) piquée
loop(M) de puntera(F)
loop(M) di punta(F)

フリップ
flip
Flip(M)
flip(M)
flip(M)
flip(M)

ルッツ
lutz
Lutz(M)
lutz(M)
lutz(M)
lutz(M)

計時員
timekeeper
Zeitnehmer(M)
chronométreur(M)
cronometrador(M)
cronometrista(M/F)

審判長／レフ(ェ)リー
referee
Oberschiedsrichter(M)
arbitre(M)
presidente(M) de jurado(M)
presidente(M) di giuria(F)

審判補佐
assistant referee
Assistenzschiedsrichter(M)
arbitre(M) adjoint
asistente(M) de presidente(M) del jurado(M)
assistente(M) del presidente(M) di giuria(F)

技術運営審判団
technical delegates
technische Delegierte(M)
délégués(M) techniques
delegados(M) técnicos
referenti(M) tecnici

リンク
rink
Eisfläche(F)
patinoire(F)
pista(F) de patinaje(M) sobre hielo(M)
pista(F) di pattinaggio(M)

審査員／審判員／ジャッジ
judges
Kampfrichter(M)
juges(M)
jueces(M)
giudici(M)

審査員／審判員／ジャッジ
judges
Kampfrichter(M)
juges(M)
jueces(M)
giudici(M)

ペア
pair
Paar(N)
couple(M)
pareja(F)
coppia(F)

コーチ
coaches
Trainer(M)
entraîneurs(M)
entrenadores(M)
allenatori(M)

スポーツとゲーム

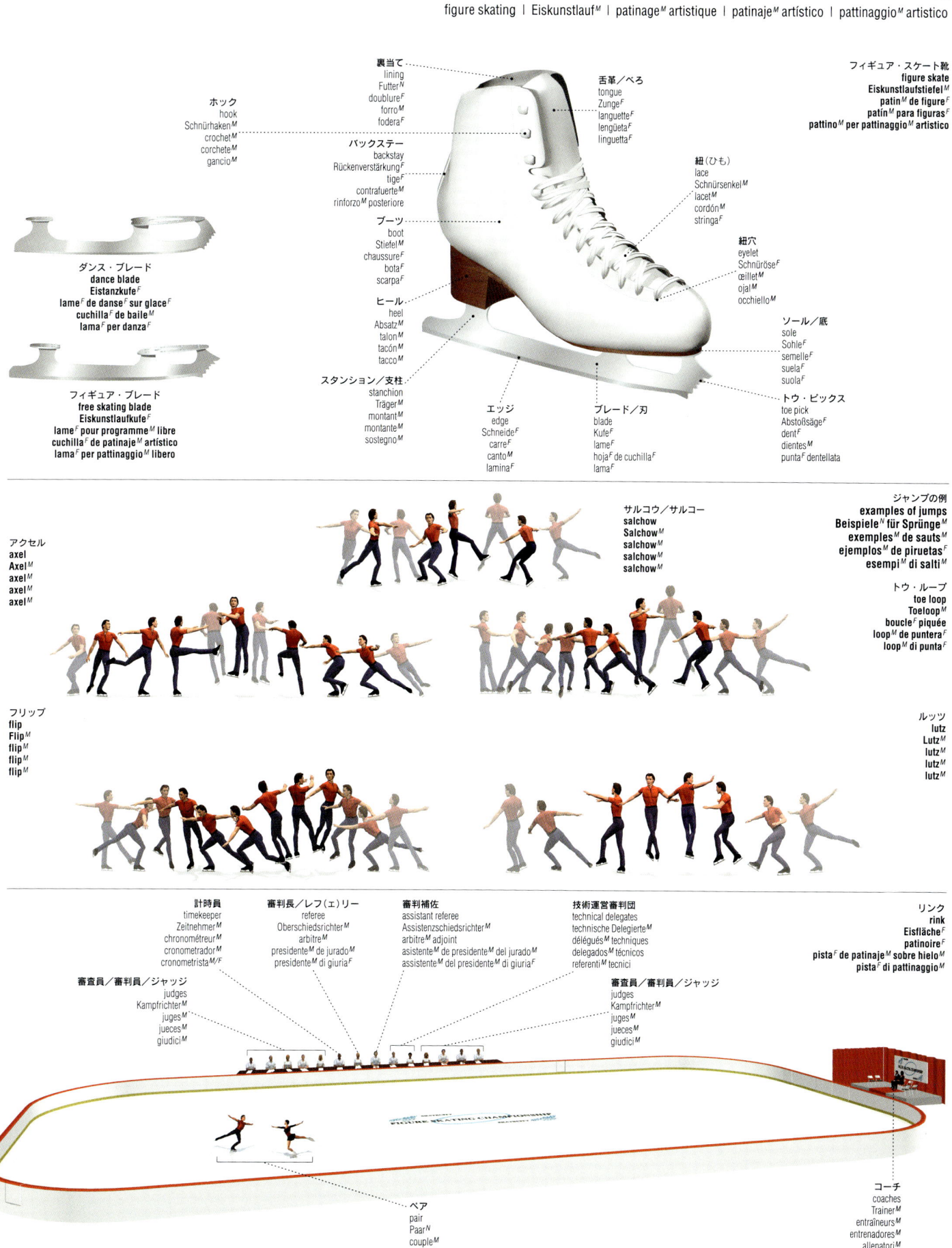

881

ウインター・スポーツ | WINTER SPORTS
WINTERSPORT | SPORTS D'HIVER | DEPORTES DE INVIERNO | SPORT INVERNALI

スピード・スケート

日本語 | 英語 | ドイツ語 | フランス語 | スペイン語 | イタリア語

speed skating | Eisschnelllauf^M | patinage^M de vitesse^F | patinaje^M de velocidad^F | pattinaggio^M di velocità^F

スケーター：ロング・トラック／長距離
skater: long track
Eisschnellläufer^M: Langstrecke^F
patineur^M : longue piste^F
patinador^M : pista^F larga
pattinatore^M : pista^F lunga

フード
hood
Kapuze^F
capuchon^M
capuchón^M
cappuccio^M

レーシング・スーツ
racing suit
Rennanzug^M
combinaison^F de course^F
traje^M de carrera^F
tuta^F

スケーター：ショート・トラック／短距離
skater: short track
Eisschnellläufer^M: Kurzstrecke^F
patineur^M : courte piste^F
patinador^M : pista^F corta
pattinatore^M : short track^M

ヘルメット
helmet
Helm^M
casque^M
casco^M
casco^M

グローブ
glove
Handschuh^M
gant^M
guante^M
guanto^M

喉（のど）当て
throat protector
Halsschutz^M
protège-gorge^M
protector^M de garganta^F
paracollo^M

脛（すね）当て
shin guard
Schienbeinschutz^M
protège-tibia^M
espinillera^F
parastinchi^M

膝当て
knee pad
Knieschützer^M
genouillère^F
rodillera^F
ginocchiera^F

ロング・トラック
long track
Eisschnelllaufbahn^F
longue piste^F
pista^F larga
pista^F lunga

スノー・ライン
marker
Kegel^M
cône^M
pivote^M
blocchetto^M

ウォーム・アップ・レーン
warm-up lane
Aufwärmbahn^F
couloir^M d'échauffement^M
calle^M de calentamiento^M
corsia^F di riscaldamento^M

レフ(ェ)リー
referee
Schiedsrichter^M
arbitre^M
árbitro^M
arbitro^M

コース／レーン
lane
Laufbahn^F
couloir^M
calle^F
corsia^F

500メートル・スタート・ライン
500 m start line
500-m-Startlinie^F
ligne^F de départ^M du 500 m
línea^F de salida^F de 500 m
linea^F di partenza^F dei 500 metri^M

スタート・ジャッジ
start judges
Starter^M
juges^M au départ^M
jueces^M de salida^F
giudici^M di partenza^F

アシスタント・レフ(ェ)リー
assistant referee
Assistenzschiedsrichter^M
arbitre^M assistant^M
árbitro^M adjunto
arbitro^M ausiliario

スポーツとゲーム

882

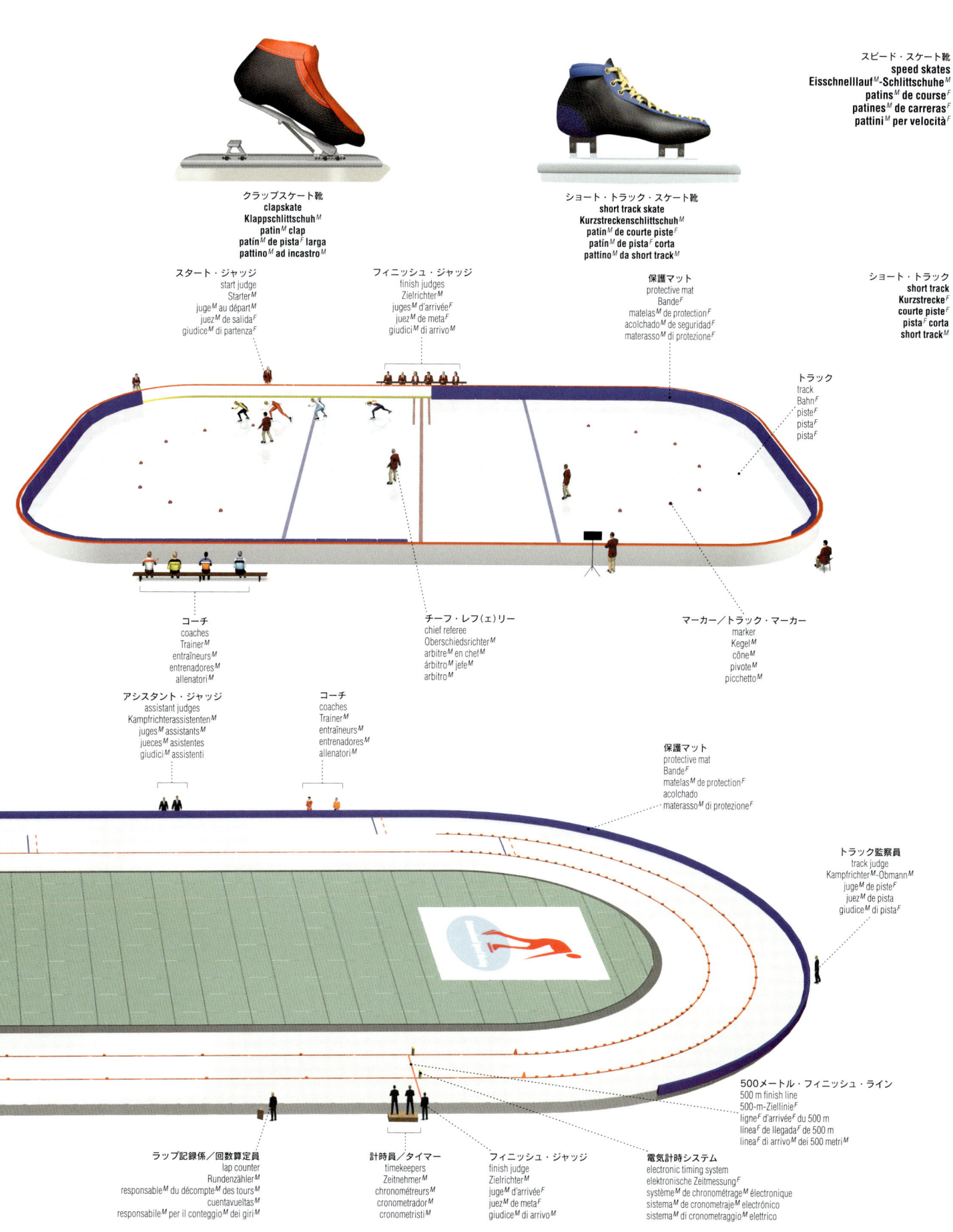

ウインター・スポーツ | WINTER SPORTS
WINTERSPORT | SPORTS D'HIVER | DEPORTES DE INVIERNO | SPORT INVERNALI

スピード・スケート

スピード・スケート靴
speed skates
Eisschnelllauf^M-Schlittschuhe^M
patins^M de course^F
patines^M de carreras^F
pattini^M per velocità^F

クラップスケート靴
clapskate
Klappschlittschuh^M
patín^M clap
patín^M de pista^F larga
pattino^M ad incastro^M

ショート・トラック・スケート靴
short track skate
Kurzstreckenschlittschuh^M
patin^M de courte piste^F
patín^M de pista^F corta
pattino^M da short track

スタート・ジャッジ
start judge
Starter^M
juge^M au départ^M
juez^M de salida^F
giudice^M di partenza^F

フィニッシュ・ジャッジ
finish judges
Zielrichter^M
juges^M d'arrivée^F
juez^M de meta^F
giudici^M di arrivo^M

保護マット
protective mat
Bande^F
matelas^M de protection^F
acolchado^M de seguridad^F
materasso^M di protezione^F

ショート・トラック
short track
Kurzstrecke^F
courte piste^F
pista^F corta
short track^M

トラック
track
Bahn^F
piste^F
pista^F
pista^F

コーチ
coaches
Trainer^M
entraîneurs^M
entrenadores^M
allenatori^M

チーフ・レフ(ェ)リー
chief referee
Oberschiedsrichter^M
arbitre^M en chef^M
árbitro^M jefe^M
arbitro^M

マーカー／トラック・マーカー
marker
Kegel^M
cône^M
pivote^M
picchetto^M

アシスタント・ジャッジ
assistant judges
Kampfrichterassistenten^M
juges^M assistants^M
jueces^M asistentes
giudici^M assistenti

コーチ
coaches
Trainer^M
entraîneurs^M
entrenadores^M
allenatori^M

保護マット
protective mat
Bande^F
matelas^M de protection^F
acolchado
materasso^M di protezione^F

トラック監察員
track judge
Kampfrichter^M-Obmann^M
juge^M de piste^F
juez^M de pista^F
giudice^M di pista^F

500メートル・フィニッシュ・ライン
500 m finish line
500-m-Ziellinie^F
ligne^F d'arrivée^F du 500 m
línea^F de llegada^F de 500 m
linea^F di arrivo^F dei 500 metri^M

ラップ記録係／回数算定員
lap counter
Rundenzähler^M
responsable^M du décompte^M des tours^M
cuentavueltas^M
responsabile^M per il conteggio^M dei giri^M

計時員／タイマー
timekeepers
Zeitnehmer^M
chronométreurs^M
cronometrador^M
cronometristi^M

フィニッシュ・ジャッジ
finish judge
Zielrichter^M
juge^M d'arrivée^F
juez^M de meta^F
giudice^M di arrivo^M

電気計時システム
electronic timing system
elektronische Zeitmessung^F
système^M de chronométrage^M électronique
sistema^M de cronometraje^M electrónico
sistema^M di cronometraggio^M elettrico

スポーツとゲーム

ウインター・スポーツ | WINTER SPORTS
WINTERSPORT | SPORTS D'HIVER | DEPORTES DE INVIERNO | SPORT INVERNALI

ボブスレー

bobsled; *bobsleigh* | Bobschlitten^M | bobsleigh^M | bobsleigh^M | bob^M

日本語 | 英語 | ドイツ語 | フランス語 | スペイン語 | イタリア語

4人乗りボブスレー
four-person bobsled
Viererbob^M
bobsleigh^M à quatre
bobsleigh^M a cuatro
bob^M a quattro

ブレーキマン／ブレーカー
brakeman
Bremser^M
freineur^M
guardafrenos^M
frenatore^M

パイロット／ドライバー／操縦者
captain
Steuermann^M
capitaine^M
capitán^M
capitano^M

ハンドル
handle
Griff^M
poignée^F
asa^F
maniglia^F

ボディー／車体
shell
Gehäuse^N
coque^F
bob^M
carena^F

2人乗りボブスレー
two-person bobsled
Zweierbob^M
bobsleigh^M à deux
bosbsleigh^M de dos
bob^M a due

後部ランナー［滑走部］
rear runner
hintere Kufe^F
patin^M arrière
patín^M trasero
pattino^M posteriore

前部ランナー［滑走部］
front runner
vordere Kufe^F
patin^M avant
patín^M delantero
pattino^M anteriore

リュージュ

luge | Rennrodel^M | luge^F | luge^M | slittino^M

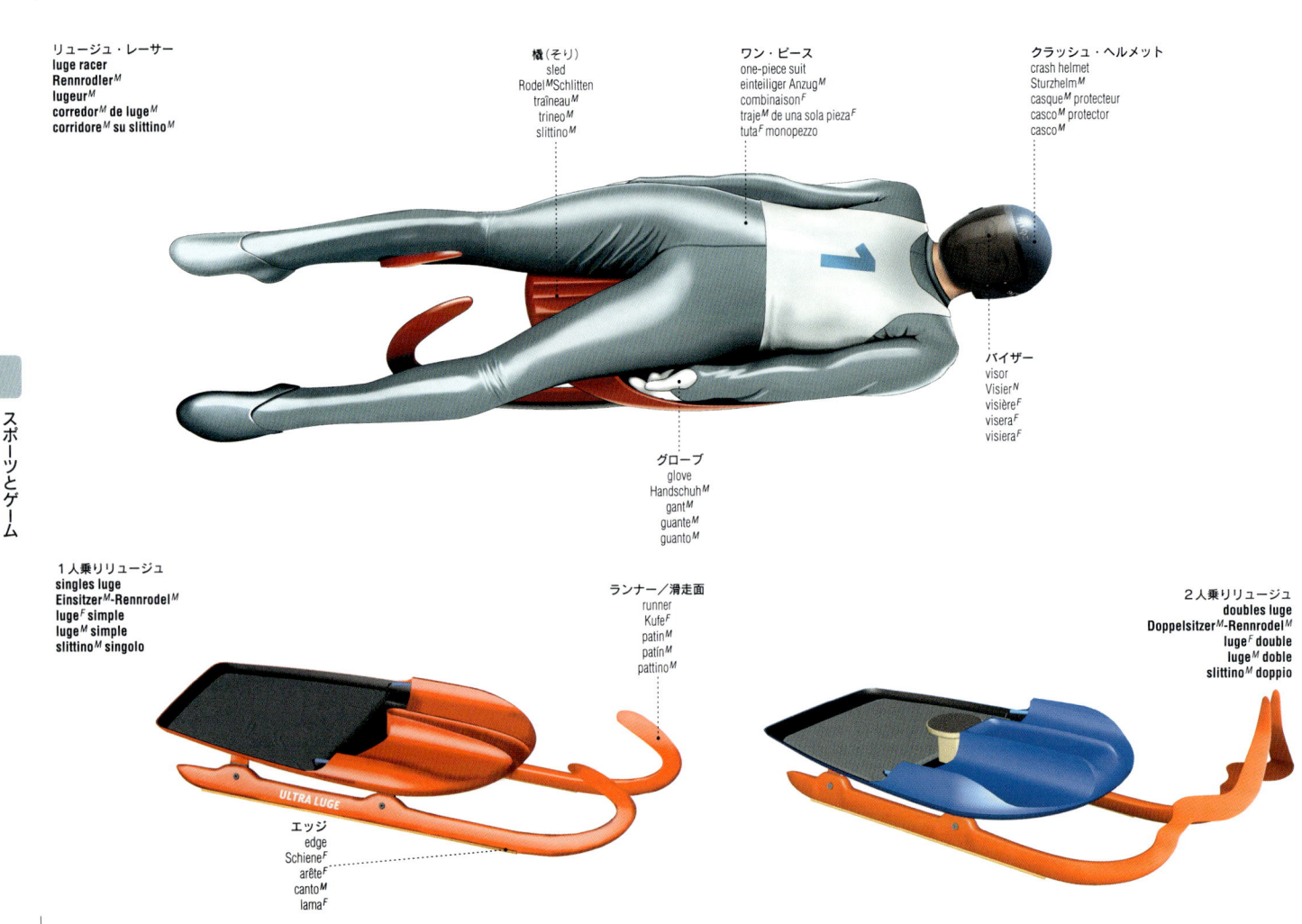

リュージュ・レーサー
luge racer
Rennrodler^M
lugeur^M
corredor^M de luge^M
corridore^M su slittino^M

橇（そり）
sled
Rodel^M Schlitten^M
traîneau^M
trineo^M
slittino^M

ワン・ピース
one-piece suit
einteiliger Anzug^M
combinaison^F
traje^M de una sola pieza^F
tuta^F monopezzo

クラッシュ・ヘルメット
crash helmet
Sturzhelm^M
casque^M protecteur
casco^M protector
casco^M

バイザー
visor
Visier^N
visière^F
visera^F
visiera^F

グローブ
glove
Handschuh^M
gant^M
guante^M
guanto^M

1人乗りリュージュ
singles luge
Einsitzer^M-Rennrodel^M
luge^F simple
luge^M simple
slittino^M singolo

ランナー／滑走面
runner
Kufe^F
patin^M
patín^M
pattino^M

2人乗りリュージュ
doubles luge
Doppelsitzer^M-Rennrodel^M
luge^F double
luge^M doble
slittino^M doppio

エッジ
edge
Schiene^F
arête^F
canto^M
lama^F

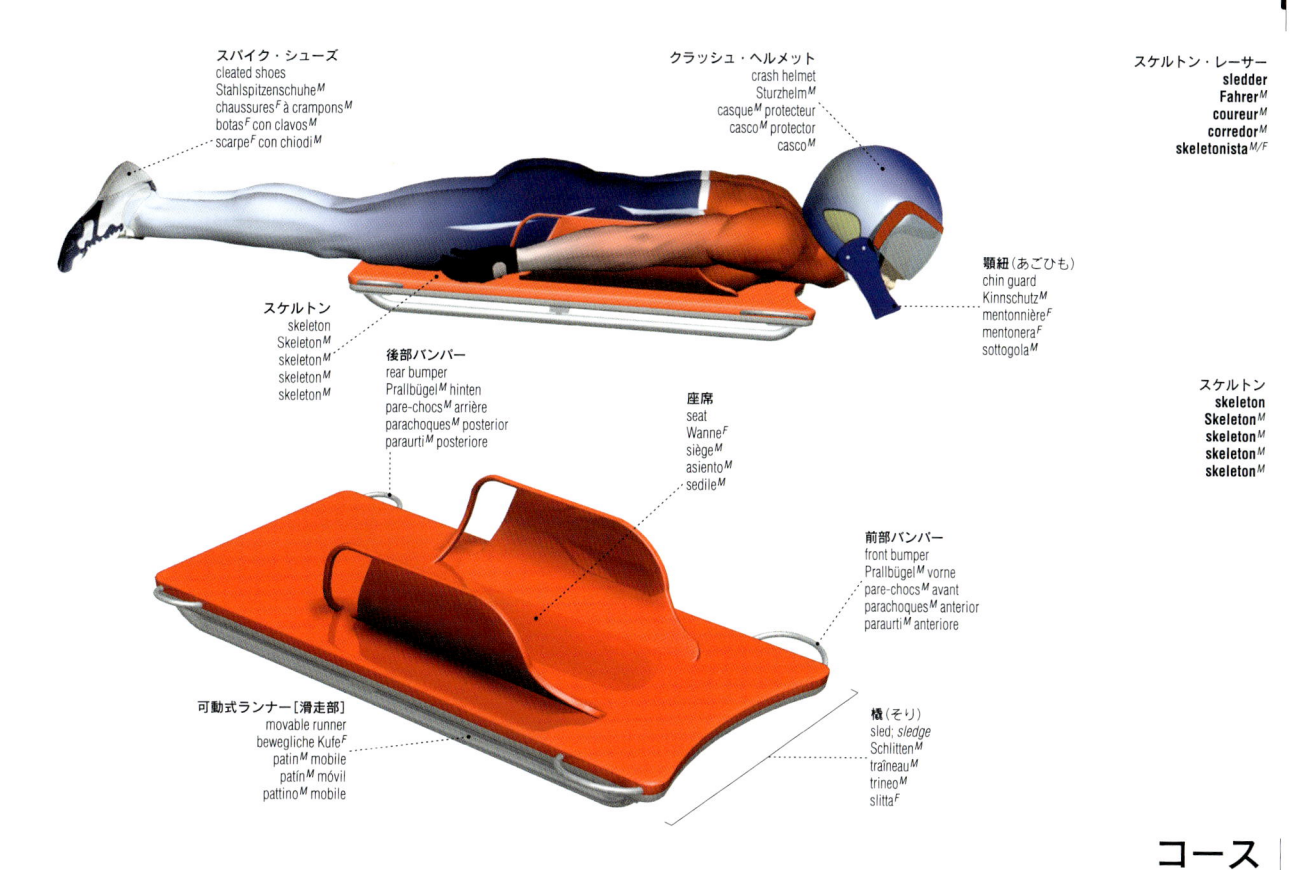

ウインター・スポーツ | WINTER SPORTS
WINTERSPORT | SPORTS D'HIVER | DEPORTES DE INVIERNO | SPORT INVERNALI

スケルトン
skeleton | Skeleton^M | skeleton^M | skeleton^M | skeleton^M

スパイク・シューズ
cleated shoes
Stahlspitzenschuhe^M
chaussures^F à crampons^M
botas^F con clavos^M
scarpe^F con chiodi^M

クラッシュ・ヘルメット
crash helmet
Sturzhelm^M
casque^M protecteur
casco^M protector
casco^M

スケルトン・レーサー
sledder
Fahrer^M
coureur^M
corredor^M
skeletonista^{M/F}

スケルトン
skeleton
Skeleton^M
skeleton^M
skeleton^M
skeleton^M

後部バンパー
rear bumper
Prallbügel^M hinten
pare-chocs^M arrière
parachoques^M posterior
paraurti^M posteriore

座席
seat
Wanne^F
siège^M
asiento^M
sedile^M

顎紐（あごひも）
chin guard
Kinnschutz^M
mentonnière^F
mentonera^F
sottogola^M

スケルトン
skeleton
Skeleton^M
skeleton^M
skeleton^M
skeleton^M

前部バンパー
front bumper
Prallbügel^M vorne
pare-chocs^M avant
parachoques^M anterior
paraurti^M anteriore

可動式ランナー［滑走部］
movable runner
bewegliche Kufe^F
patin^M mobile
patín^M móvil
pattino^M mobile

橇（そり）
sled; sledge
Schlitten^M
traîneau^M
trineo^M
slitta^F

コース
track | Bahn^F | piste^F | pista^F | pista^F

男子1人乗りリュージュのスタート地点
start: men's singles luge
Start^M: Rodeln^N Einsitzer^M Männer^M
départ^M: luge^F simple hommes^M
salida^F: luge^M simple masculino
partenza^F: slittino^M singolo maschile

ボブスレーとスケルトンのスタート地点
start: bobsled and skeleton
Start^M: Bob^M und Skeleton^N
départ^M: bobsleigh^M et skeleton^M
salida^F: bobsleigh^M y skeleton^M
partenza^F: bob^M e skeleton^M

女子1人乗り・男子2人乗りリュージュのスタート地点
start: women's and doubles luge
Start^M: Rodeln^N Frauen^F und Doppelsitzer^M Männer^M
départ^M: luge^F dames^F et luge^F double
salida^F: luge^M doble femenino
partenza^F: slittino^M doppio femminile

減速直線コース
deceleration stretch
Auslauf^M
piste^F de décélération^F
pista^F de deceleración^M
zona^F di decelerazione^F

ゴール地点
finish area
Ziel^N
aire^F d'arrivée^F
área^F de llegada^F
arrivo^M

180度カーブ
180-degree curve
180-Grad^M-Kurve^F
virage^M à 180 degrés^M
curva^F de 180 grados^M
curva^F a 180 gradi^M

迷路／ラビリンス
labyrinth
Labyrinth^N
labyrinthe^M
laberinto^M
labirinto^M

スポーツとゲーム

885

ウインター・スポーツ | WINTER SPORTS
WINTERSPORT | SPORTS D'HIVER | DEPORTES DE INVIERNO | SPORT INVERNALI

スキー場

ski resort | Skigebiet^N | station^F de ski^M | estación^F de esquí | stazione^F sciistica

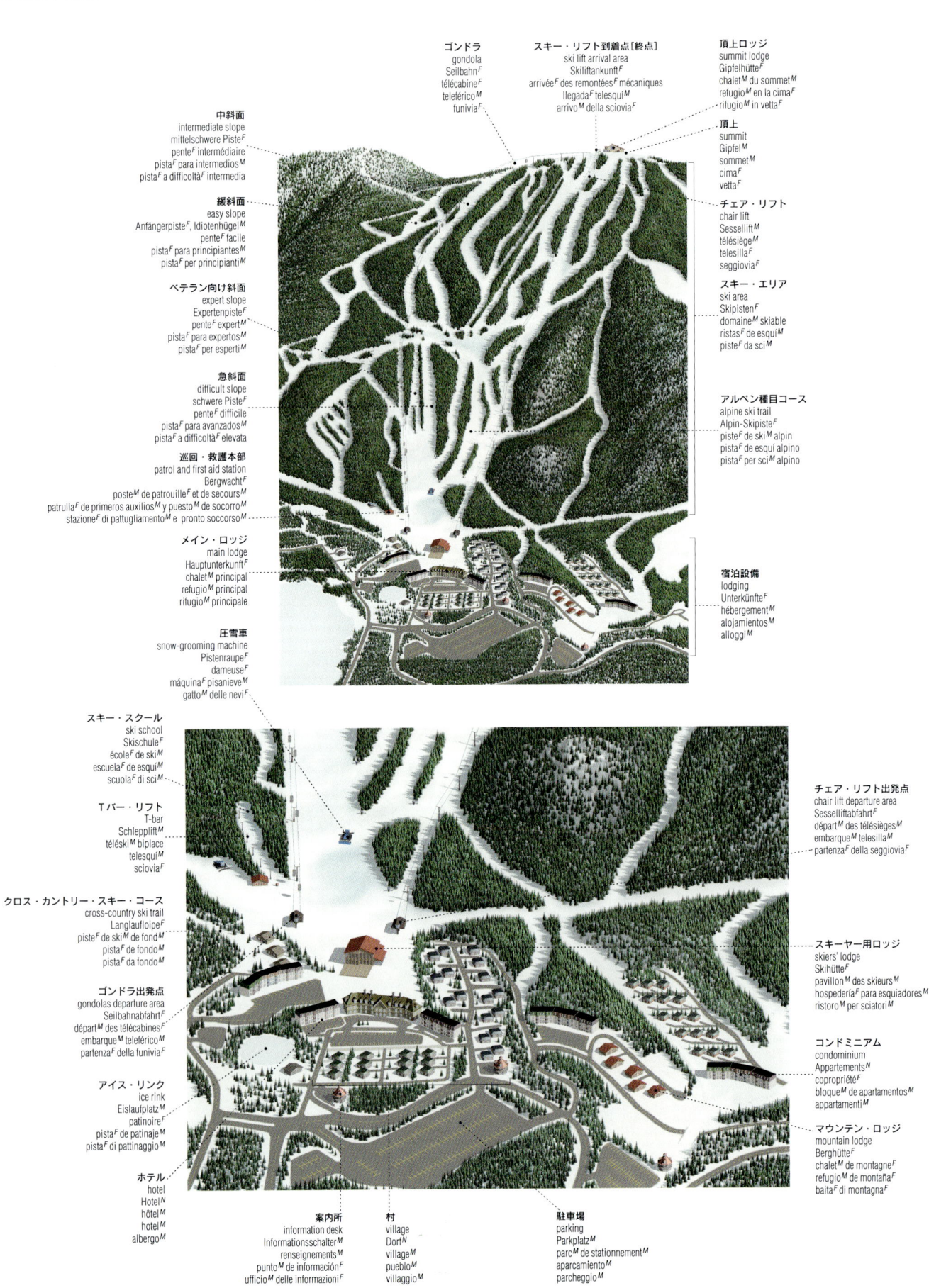

ゴンドラ
gondola
Seilbahn^F
télécabine^F
teleférico^M
funivia^F

スキー・リフト到着点[終点]
ski lift arrival area
Skiliftankunft^F
arrivée^F des remontées^F mécaniques
llegada^F telesquí^M
arrivo^M della sciovia^F

頂上ロッジ
summit lodge
Gipfelhütte^F
chalet^M du sommet^M
refugio^M en la cima^F
rifugio^M in vetta^F

中斜面
intermediate slope
mittelschwere Piste^F
pente^F intermédiaire
pista^F para intermedios^M
pista^F a difficoltà^F intermedia

頂上
summit
Gipfel^M
sommet^M
cima^F
vetta^F

緩斜面
easy slope
Anfängerpiste^F, Idiotenhügel^M
pente^F facile
pista^F para principiantes^M
pista^F per principianti^M

チェア・リフト
chair lift
Sessellift^M
télésiège^M
telesilla^F
seggiovia^F

ベテラン向け斜面
expert slope
Expertenpiste^F
pente^F expert
pista^F para expertos^M
pista^F per esperti^M

スキー・エリア
ski area
Skipisten^F
domaine^M skiable
ristas^F de esquí^M
piste^F da sci^M

急斜面
difficult slope
schwere Piste^F
pente^F difficile
pista^F para avanzados^M
pista^F a difficoltà^F elevata

アルペン種目コース
alpine ski trail
Alpin-Skipiste^F
piste^F de ski^M alpin
pista^F de esquí^M alpino
pista^F per sci^M alpino

巡回・救護本部
patrol and first aid station
Bergwacht^F
poste^M de patrouille^F et de secours^M
patrulla^F de primeros auxilios^M y puesto^M de socorro^M
stazione^F di pattugliamento^M e pronto soccorso^M

メイン・ロッジ
main lodge
Hauptunterkunft^F
chalet^M principal
refugio^M principal
rifugio^M principale

宿泊設備
lodging
Unterkünfte^F
hébergement^M
alojamientos^M
alloggi^M

圧雪車
snow-grooming machine
Pistenraupe^F
dameuse^F
máquina^F pisanieve
gatto^M delle nevi^F

スキー・スクール
ski school
Skischule^F
école^F de ski^M
escuela^F de esquí^M
scuola^F di sci^M

チェア・リフト出発点
chair lift departure area
Sesselliftabfahrt^F
départ^M des télésièges^M
embarque^M telesilla^F
partenza^F della seggiovia^F

Tバー・リフト
T-bar
Schlepplift^M
téléski^M biplace
telesquí^M
sciovia^F

クロス・カントリー・スキー・コース
cross-country ski trail
Langlaufloipe^F
piste^F de ski^M de fond^M
pista^F de fondo^M
pista^F da fondo^M

スキーヤー用ロッジ
skiers' lodge
Skihütte^F
pavillon^M des skieurs^M
hospedería^F para esquiadores^M
ristoro^M per sciatori^M

ゴンドラ出発点
gondolas departure area
Seilbahnabfahrt^F
départ^M des télécabines^F
embarque^M teleférico^M
partenza^F della funivia^F

コンドミニアム
condominium
Appartements^N
copropriété^F
bloque^M de apartamentos^M
appartamenti^M

アイス・リンク
ice rink
Eislautplatz^M
patinoire^F
pista^F de patinaje^M
pista^F di pattinaggio^M

マウンテン・ロッジ
mountain lodge
Berghütte^F
chalet^M de montagne^F
refugio^M de montaña^F
baita^F di montagna^F

ホテル
hotel
Hotel^N
hôtel^M
hotel^M
albergo^M

案内所
information desk
Informationsschalter^M
renseignements^M
punto^M de información^F
ufficio^M delle informazioni^F

村
village
Dorf^N
village^M
pueblo^M
villaggio^M

駐車場
parking
Parkplatz^M
parc^M de stationnement^M
aparcamiento^M
parcheggio^M

ウインター・スポーツ | WINTER SPORTS
WINTERSPORT | SPORTS D'HIVER | DEPORTES DE INVIERNO | SPORT INVERNALI

スノーボーディング

snowboarding | SnowboardenN | surfM des neigesF | snowboardM | snowboardM

ヘルメット
helmet
HelmM
casqueM
cascoM
cascoM

オーバーオール
coveralls
SkianzugM
combinaisonF
trajeM de esquíM
tutaF

ゴーグル
goggles
SkibrilleF
lunettesF
gafasF de esquíM
occhialiM

スノーボーダー
snowboarder
SnowboarderM
surfeurM
snowboarderM
snowboardistaM/F

脛(すね)当て
shin guard
SchienbeinschützerM
protège-tibiaM
tobilleraF
parastinchiM

スノーボード
snowboard
SnowboardN
surfM des neigesF
snowboardM
snowboardM

グローブ
glove
HandschuhM
gantM
guanteM
guantoM

ハード・ブーツ
hard boot
HardbootsM
botteF rigide
botaF rígida
scarponeM rigido

ソフト・ブーツ
flexible boot
SoftbootsM
botteF souple
botaF blanda
scarponeM morbido

フリースタイル系スノーボード
freestyle snowboard
FreestyleboardN
surfM acrobatique
tablaF de freestyle
snowboardM per freestyleM

ソフト・ブーツ用ビンディング
soft binding
SoftbindungF
fixationF à coqueF
fijacionesM blandas
attaccoM morbido

ハード・ブーツ用ビンディング
plate binding
PlattenbindungF
fixationF à plaqueF
fijacionesF
attaccoM

ヒップ／テール
tail
BrettendeN
talonM
colaF
codaF

アルペン系スノーボード
alpine snowboard
AlpinboardN
surfM alpin
tablaF alpina
snowboardM per sciM alpino

ノーズ／トップ
nose
BrettspitzeF
spatuleF
cabezaF
puntaF

エッジ
edge
KanteF
carreF
bordeM
bordoM

ハーフ・パイプの競技場
competition site: half-pipe
WettkampfplatzM: HalfpipeF
aireF de compétitionF: demi-luneF
pistaF de competiciónF: half-pipeM
pistaF di garaF: half-pipeM

審判台
judges' stand
WettkampfgerichtN
cabineF des jugesM
posiciónF del juradoM
postazioneF dei giudiciM di garaF

スタート地点
start
StartM
départM
salidaF
partenzaF

ハーフ・パイプ
half-pipe
HalfpipeF
demi-luneF
half-pipeF
half-pipeM

ゴール地点
finish area
ZielbereichM
aireF d'arrivéeF
metaF
arrivoM

ウインター・スポーツ | WINTER SPORTS
WINTERSPORT | SPORTS D'HIVER | DEPORTES DE INVIERNO | SPORT INVERNALI

アルペン・スキー

日本語 | 英語 | ドイツ語 | フランス語 | スペイン語 | イタリア語

alpine skiing | alpines Skilaufen^N | ski^M alpin | esquí^M alpino | sci^M alpino

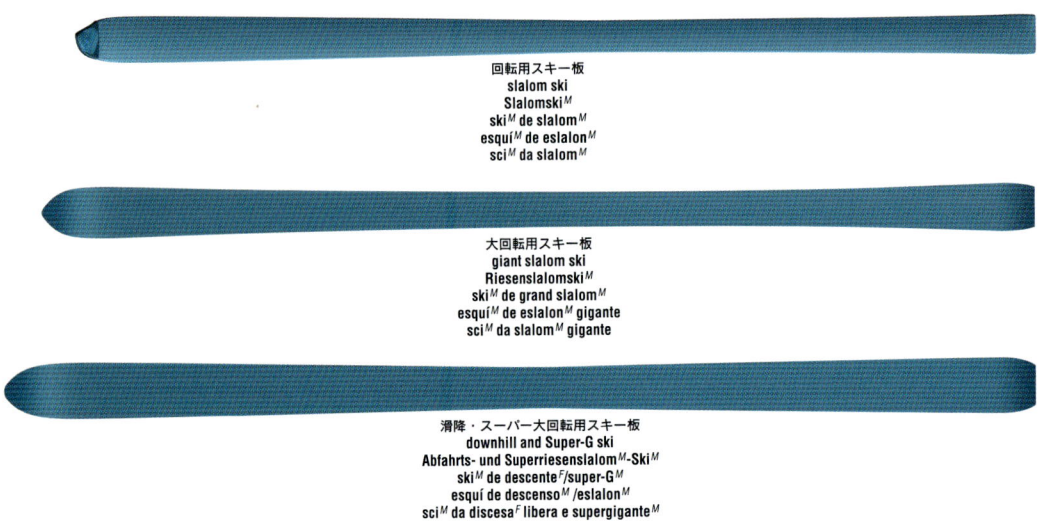

アルペン・スキーヤー
alpine skier
alpiner Skiläufer^M
skieur^M alpin
esquiador^M alpino
sciatore^M

ゴーグル
ski goggles
Skibrille^F
lunettes^F de ski^M
gafas^F de esquí^M
occhiali^M

スキー・ウエア
ski suit
Skianzug^M
combinaison^F de ski^M
traje^M de esquí^M
tuta^F

ストック・リング
basket
Stockteller^M
rondelle^F
arandela^F
rotella^F

ヘルメット
helmet
Sturzhelm^M
casque^M
casco^M
casco^M

スキー手袋[グローブ]
ski glove
Skihandschuhe^M
gant^M de ski^M
guante^M de esquí^M
guanto^M

ストック
ski pole
Skistock^M
bâton^M de ski^M
bastón^M de esquí^M
racchetta^F

スキー靴[ブーツ]
ski boot
Skistiefel^M
chaussure^F de ski^M
bota^F
scarpone^M

リスト・ストラップ
wrist strap
Handschlaufe^F
dragonne^F
correa^F para la mano^F
cappio^M

溝
groove
Führungsrille^F
rainure^F
ranura^F guía^F
scanalatura^F

グリップ
handle
Griff^M
poignée^F
empuñadura^F
impugnatura^F

スキー板
ski
Ski^M
ski^M
esquí^M
sci^M

ソール／滑走面／底
bottom
Laufsohle^F
semelle^F
superficie^F de deslizamiento^M
suola^F

(セーフティー)ビンディング／締め具／金具
safety binding
Sicherheitsbindung^F
fixation^F de sécurité^F
fijaciones^F
attacco^M di sicurezza^F

トップ
tip
Spitze^F
pointe^F
punta^F
punta^F

テール
tail
Ende^N
talon^M
cola^F
coda^F

ショベル／トップ・ベンド
shovel
Schaufel^F
spatule^F
pala^F
spatola^F

エッジ
edge
Stahlkante^F
carre^F
canto^M
lamina^F

スキー板
ski
Ski^M
ski^M
esquí^M
sci^M

スキー板の例
examples of skis
Beispiele^N für Skier^M
exemples^M de skis^M
ejemplos^M de esquís^M
esempi^M di sci^M

回転用スキー板
slalom ski
Slalomski^M
ski^M de slalom^M
esquí^M de eslalon^M
sci^M da slalom^M

大回転用スキー板
giant slalom ski
Riesenslalomski^M
ski^M de grand slalom^M
esquí^M de eslalon^M gigante
sci^M da slalom^M gigante

滑降・スーパー大回転用スキー板
downhill and Super-G ski
Abfahrts- und Superriesenslalom^M-Ski^M
ski^M de descente^F/super-G^M
esquí^M de descenso^M/eslalon^M
sci^M da discesa^F libera e supergigante^M

ウインター・スポーツ | WINTER SPORTS
WINTERSPORT | SPORTS D'HIVER | DEPORTES DE INVIERNO | SPORT INVERNALI

アルペン・スキー

競技
technical events
Disziplinen^F
épreuves^F
pruebas^F
specialità^F

スキー靴
ski boot
Skistiefel^M
chaussure^F de ski^M
botas^F para esquiar
scarpone^M

インナー・ブーツ
inner boot
Innenstiefel^M
chausson^M intérieur
botín^M interior
scarpetta^F interna

アッパー・カフ
upper cuff
obere Manschette^F
collier^M
guarnición^F
bordo^M della scarpetta^F

舌革／べろ
tongue
Zunge^F
languette^F
lengüeta^F
linguettone^M

アッパー
upper
Rücklagenstütze^F
tige^F
alto^M de caña^F
appoggio^M del polpaccio^M

アッパー・シェル
upper shell
obere Schale^F
coque^F supérieure
bota^F externa
gambale^M

アッパー・ストラップ
upper strap
oberes Verschlussband^N
courroie^F de tige^F
correa^F de ajuste^M
fascia^F di chiusura^F

バックル
buckle
Verschluss^M
boucle^F
hebilla^F
gancio^M

甲締め具／バックル
adjusting catch
Einstellkerbe^F
cran^M de réglage^M
ajustador^M de la bota^F
dispositivo^M di regolazione^F

ソール／底
sole
Sohle^F
semelle^F
suela^F rígida
suola^F

ヒンジ
hinge
Gelenk^N
charnière^F
pivote^M
snodo^M

滑降／ダウンヒル
downhill
Abfahrtslauf^M
descente^F
descenso^M
discesa^M libera

ロア・シェル
lower shell
untere Schale^F
coque^F inférieure
contrafuerte^M
scafo^M

スーパー大回転／スーパーG
super giant (super-G) slalom
Superriesenslalom^M
super-géant^M
eslalon^M supergigante
slalom^M supergigante

（セーフティー）ビンディング／締め具／金具
safety binding
Sicherheitsbindung^F
fixation^F de sécurité^F
fijación^F de seguridad^F del esquí^M
attacco^M di sicurezza^F

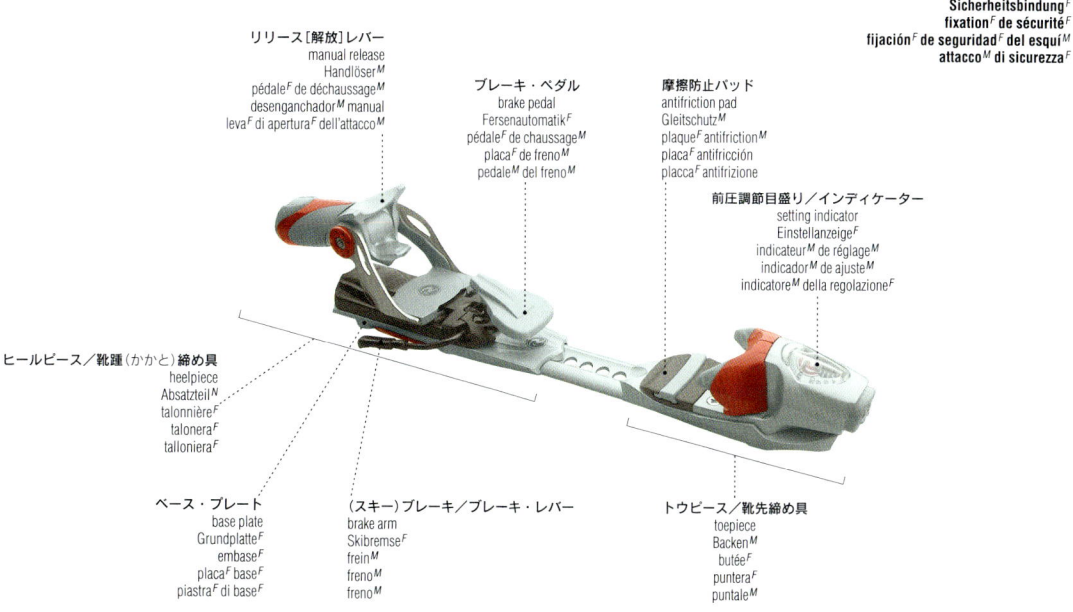

リリース［解放］レバー
manual release
Handlöser^M
pédale^F de déchaussage^M
desenganchador^M manual
leva^F di apertura^F dell'attacco^M

ブレーキ・ペダル
brake pedal
Fersenautomatik^F
pédale^F de chaussage^M
placa^F de freno^M
pedale^M del freno^M

摩擦防止パッド
antifriction pad
Gleitschutz^M
plaque^F antifriction^F
placa^F antifricción
placca^F antifrizione

前圧調節目盛り／インディケーター
setting indicator
Einstellanzeige^F
indicateur^M de réglage^M
indicador^M de ajuste^M
indicatore^M della regolazione^F

大回転／ジャイアント［リーゼン］
スラローム
giant slalom
Riesenslalom^M
slalom^M géant
eslalon^M gigante
slalom^M gigante

ヒールピース／靴踵（かかと）締め具
heelpiece
Absatzteil^N
talonnière^F
talonera^F
talloniera^F

ベース・プレート
base plate
Grundplatte^F
embase^F
placa^F base^F
piastra^F di base^F

（スキー）ブレーキ／ブレーキ・レバー
brake arm
Skibremse^F
frein^M
freno^M
freno^M

トウピース／靴先締め具
toepiece
Backen^M
butée^F
puntera^F
puntale^M

回転
special slalom
Spezialslalom^M
slalom^M spécial
eslalon^M especial
slalom^M speciale

スポーツとゲーム

889

ウインター・スポーツ | WINTER SPORTS
WINTERSPORT | SPORTS D'HIVER | DEPORTES DE INVIERNO | SPORT INVERNALI

フリースタイル・スキー

日本語 | 英語 | ドイツ語 | フランス語 | スペイン語 | イタリア語

freestyle skiing | Freestyle[N] | ski[M] acrobatique | esquí[M] artístico | freestyle[M]

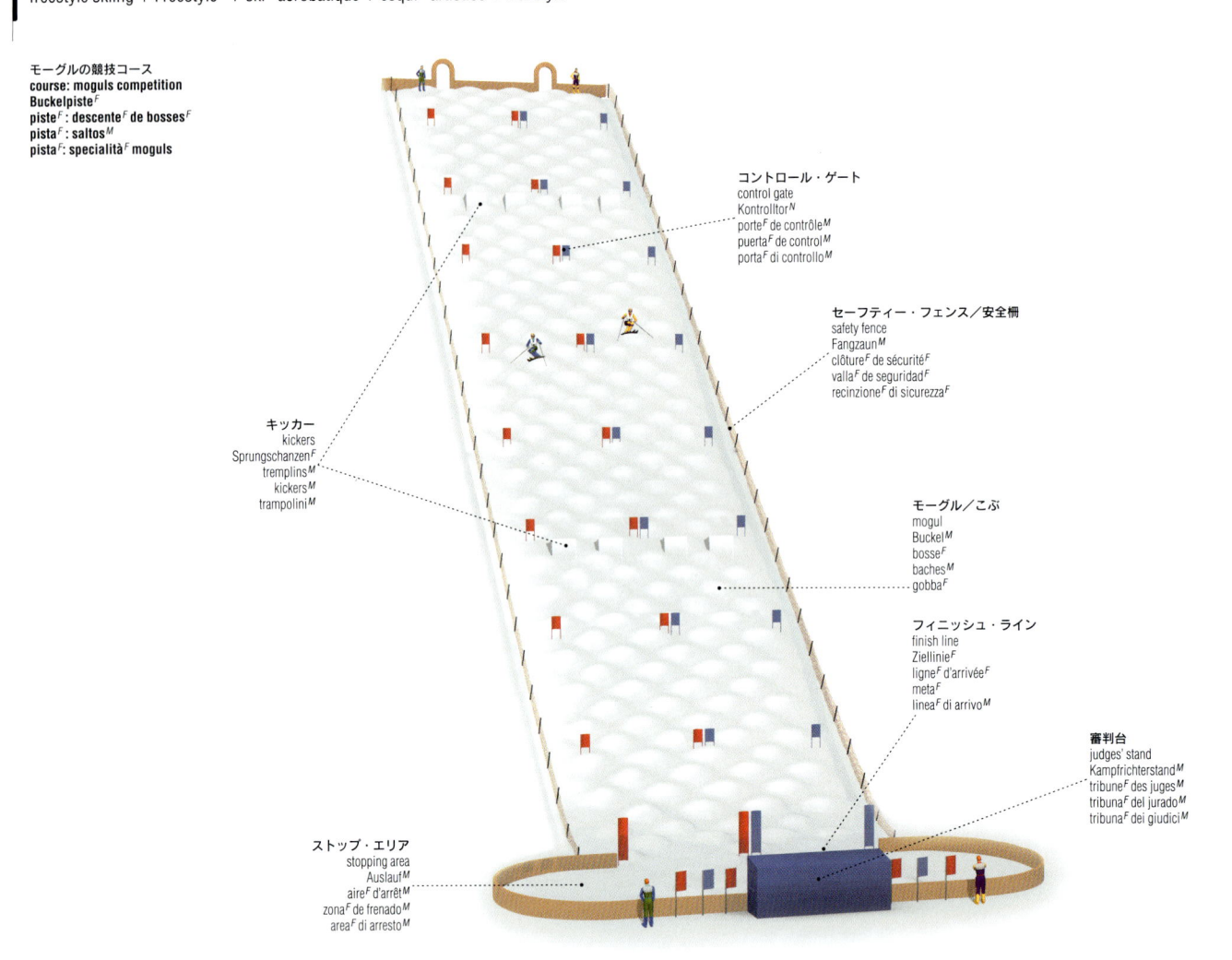

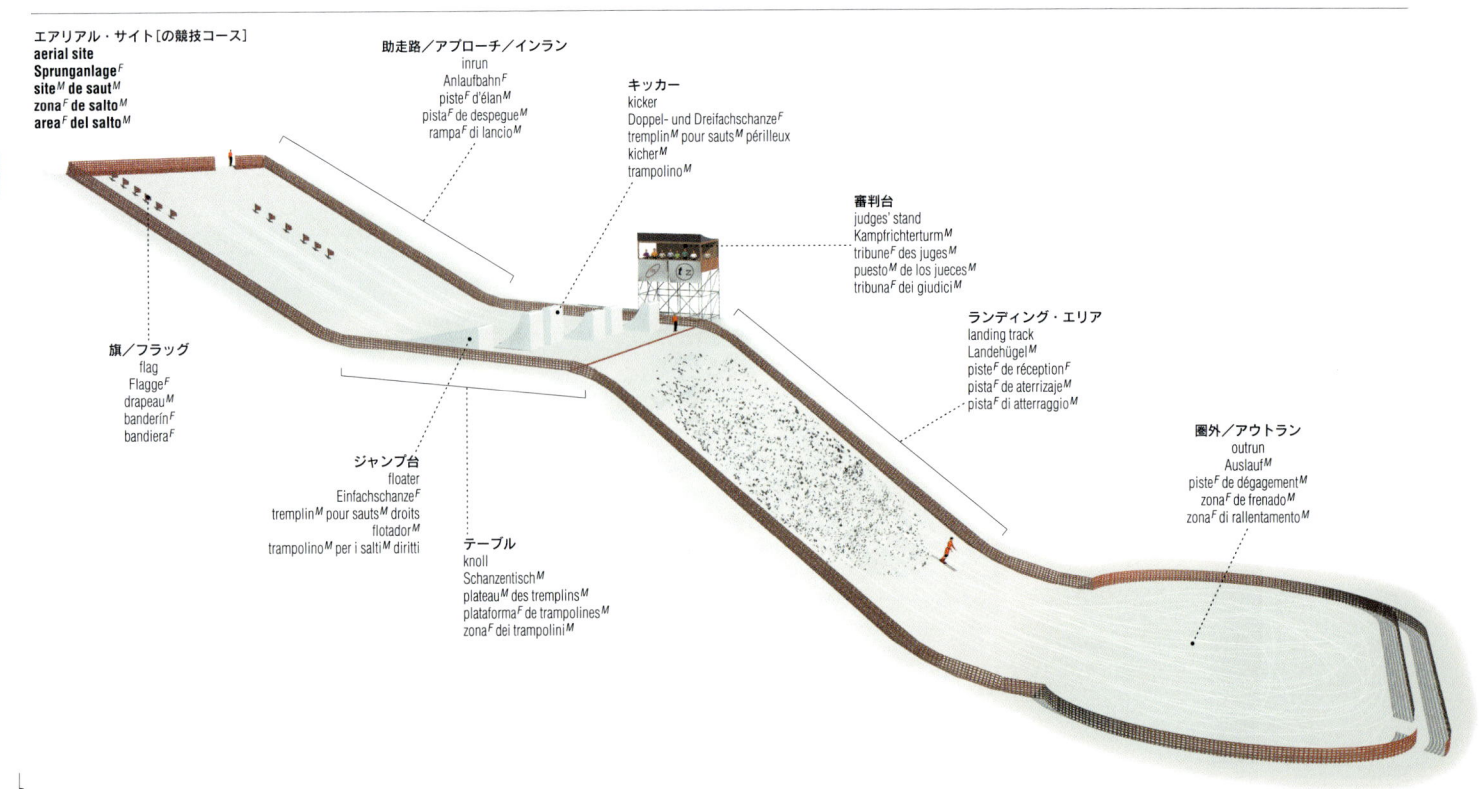

モーグルの競技コース
course: moguls competition
Buckelpiste[F]
piste[F]: descente[F] de bosses[F]
pista[F]: saltos[M]
pista[F]: specialità[F] moguls

コントロール・ゲート
control gate
Kontrolltor[N]
porte[F] de contrôle[M]
puerta[F] de control[M]
porta[F] di controllo[M]

セーフティー・フェンス／安全柵
safety fence
Fangzaun[M]
clôture[F] de sécurité[F]
valla[F] de seguridad[F]
recinzione[F] di sicurezza[F]

キッカー
kickers
Sprungschanzen[F]
tremplins[M]
kickers[M]
trampolini[M]

モーグル／こぶ
mogul
Buckel[M]
bosse[F]
baches[M]
gobba[F]

フィニッシュ・ライン
finish line
Ziellinie[F]
ligne[F] d'arrivée[F]
meta[F]
linea[F] di arrivo[M]

審判台
judges' stand
Kampfrichterstand[M]
tribune[F] des juges[M]
tribuna[F] del jurado[M]
tribuna[F] dei giudici[M]

ストップ・エリア
stopping area
Auslauf[M]
aire[F] d'arrêt[M]
zona[F] de frenado[M]
area[F] di arresto[M]

エアリアル・サイト［の競技コース］
aerial site
Sprunganlage[F]
site[M] de saut[M]
zona[F] de salto[M]
area[F] del salto[M]

助走路／アプローチ／インラン
inrun
Anlaufbahn[F]
piste[F] d'élan[M]
pista[F] de despegue[M]
rampa[F] di lancio[M]

キッカー
kicker
Doppel- und Dreifachschanze[F]
tremplin[M] pour sauts[M] périlleux
kicher[M]
trampolino[M]

審判台
judges' stand
Kampfrichterturm[M]
tribune[F] des juges[M]
puesto[M] de los jueces[M]
tribuna[F] dei giudici[M]

ランディング・エリア
landing track
Landehügel[M]
piste[F] de réception[F]
pista[F] de aterrizaje[M]
pista[F] di atterraggio[M]

圏外／アウトラン
outrun
Auslauf[M]
piste[F] de dégagement[M]
zona[F] de frenado[M]
zona[F] di rallentamento[M]

旗／フラッグ
flag
Flagge[F]
drapeau[M]
banderín[F]
bandiera[F]

ジャンプ台
floater
Einfachschanze[F]
tremplin[M] pour sauts[M] droits
flotador[M]
trampolino[M] per i salti diritti

テーブル
knoll
Schanzentisch[M]
plateau[M] des tremplins[M]
plataforma[F] de trampolines[M]
zona[F] dei trampolini[M]

スポーツとゲーム

ウインター・スポーツ | WINTER SPORTS
WINTERSPORT | SPORTS D'HIVER | DEPORTES DE INVIERNO | SPORT INVERNALI

ジャンプ

ski jumping | Skispringen^N | saut^M à ski | técnica^F de salto^M | salto^M con gli sci

ジャンプの技
jumping technique
Sprungtechnik^F
technique^F de saut^M
salto^M de esquí^M
tecnica^F di salto^M

助走
inrun
Anlauf^M
élan^M
lanzamiento^M
scivolamento^M

踏み切り
take-off
Absprung^M
envol^M
despegue^M
stacco^M

飛行
flight
Flug^M
vol^M
vuelo^M
volo^M

着地
landing
Landung^F
atterrissage^M
aterrizaje^M
atterraggio^M

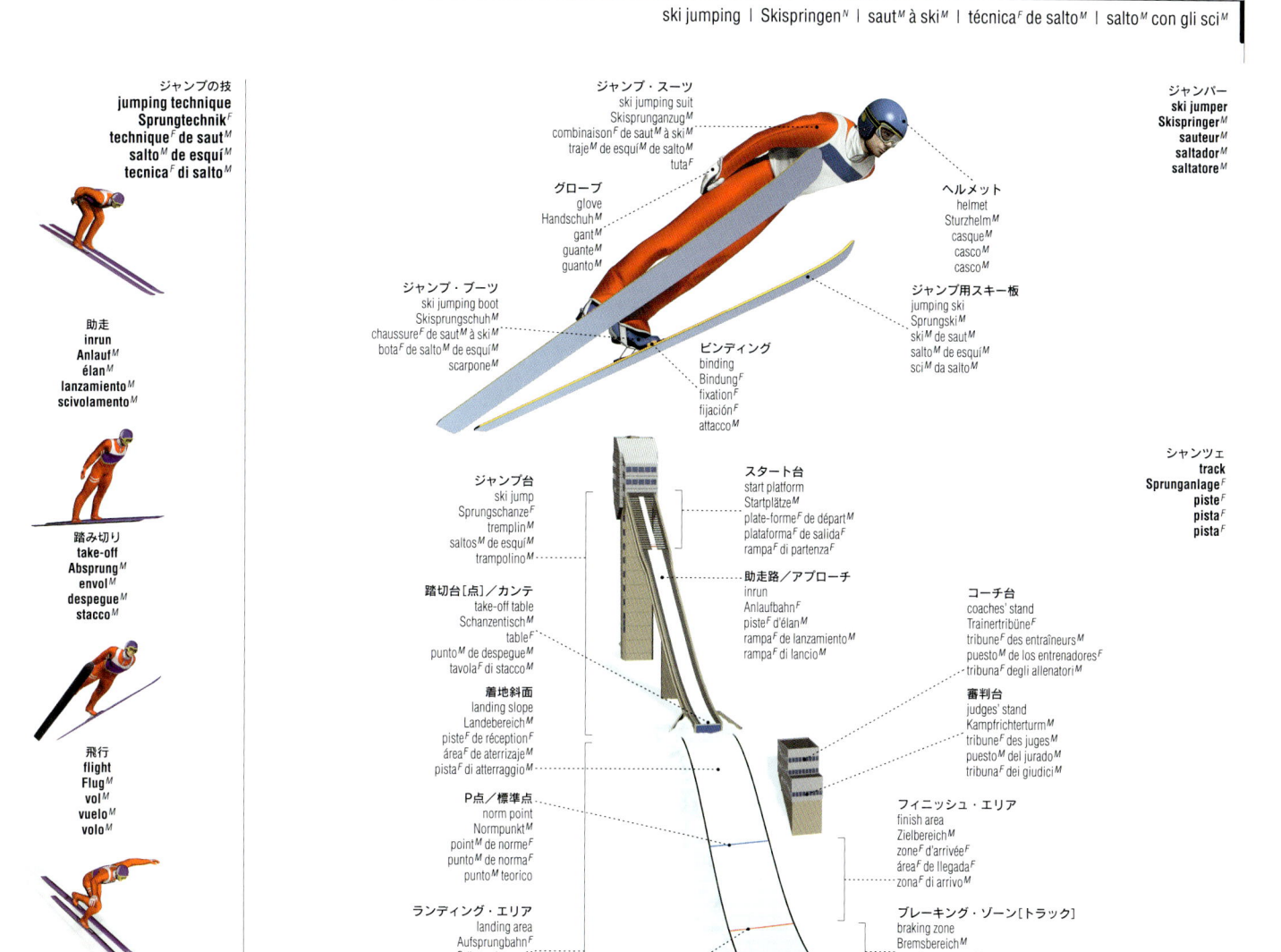

ジャンプ・スーツ
ski jumping suit
Skisprunganzug^M
combinaison^F de saut^M à ski^M
traje^M de esquí^M de salto^M
tuta^F

グローブ
glove
Handschuh^M
gant^M
guante^M
guanto^M

ジャンプ・ブーツ
ski jumping boot
Skisprungschuh^M
chaussure^F de saut^M à ski^M
bota^F de salto^M de esquí^M
scarpone^M

ビンディング
binding
Bindung^F
fixation^F
fijación^F
attacco^M

ジャンプ台
ski jump
Sprungschanze^F
tremplin^M
saltos^M de esquí^M
trampolino^M

踏切台[点]／カンテ
take-off table
Schanzentisch^M
table^F
punto^M de despegue^M
tavola^F di stacco^M

着地斜面
landing slope
Landebereich^M
piste^F de réception^F
área^F de aterrizaje^M
pista^F di atterraggio^M

P点／標準点
norm point
Normpunkt^M
point^M de norme^F
punto^M de norma^F
punto^M teorico

ランディング・エリア
landing area
Aufsprungbahn^F
zone^F d'atterrissage^M
zona^F de aterrizaje^M
zona^F di atterraggio^M

K点／極限点
critical point
Kalkulationspunkt^M
point^M critique
punto^M crítico
punto^M K

スタート台
start platform
Startplätze^M
plate-forme^F de départ^M
plataforma^F de salida^F
rampa^F di partenza^F

助走路／アプローチ
inrun
Anlaufbahn^F
piste^F d'élan^M
rampa^F de lanzamiento^M
rampa^F di lancio^M

コーチ台
coaches' stand
Trainertribüne^F
tribune^F des entraîneurs^M
puesto^M de los entrenadores^F
tribuna^F degli allenatori^M

審判台
judges' stand
Kampfrichterturm^M
tribune^F des juges^M
puesto^M del jurado^M
tribuna^F dei giudici^M

フィニッシュ・エリア
finish area
Zielbereich^M
zone^F d'arrivée^F
área^F de llegada^F
zona^F di arrivo^M

ブレーキング・ゾーン[トラック]
braking zone
Bremsbereich^M
zone^F de freinage^M
zona^F de frenado^M
zona^F di frenata^F

圏外
outrun
Auslauf^M
piste^F de dégagement^M
zona^F de frenado^M
zona^F di rallentamento^M

ジャンパー
ski jumper
Skispringer^M
sauteur^M
saltador^M
saltatore^M

ヘルメット
helmet
Sturzhelm^M
casque^M
casco^M
casco^M

ジャンプ用スキー板
jumping ski
Sprungski^M
ski^M de saut^M
salto^M de esquí^M
sci^M da salto^M

シャンツェ
track
Sprunganlage^F
piste^F
pista^F
pista^F

スピード・スキー

speed skiing | Speedski^M | ski^M de vitesse^F | esquí^M de velocidad^F | chilometro^M lanciato

スピード・トラック
speed track
Speedskistrecke^F
piste^F de vitesse^F
pista^F de velocidad^F
pista^F

スタート・トラック
starting track
Startbereich^M
piste^F d'élan^M
pista^F de salida^F
pista^F di lancio^M

計時エリア
timing area
Topspeed^F-Bereich^M
zone^F de chronométrage^M
zona^F de cronometraje^M
area^F di cronometraggio^M

減速ブレーキ・ゾーン
deceleration and braking zone
Auslauf^M- und Bremsbereich^M
piste^F de décélération^F et de freinage^M
pista^F de deceleración^F y de frenado^M
area^F di decelerazione^F e di frenata^F

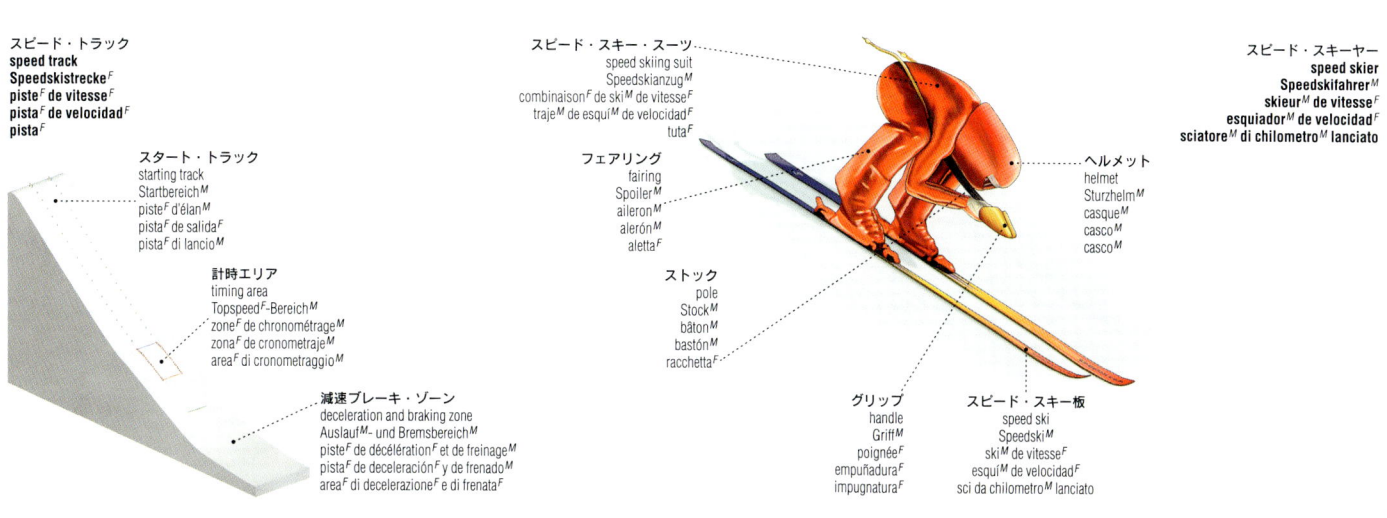

スピード・スキー・スーツ
speed skiing suit
Speedskianzug^M
combinaison^F de ski^M de vitesse^F
traje^M de esquí^M de velocidad^F
tuta^F

フェアリング
fairing
Spoiler^M
aileron^M
alerón^M
aletta^F

ストック
pole
Stock^M
bâton^M
bastón^M
racchetta^F

グリップ
handle
Griff^M
poignée^F
empuñadura^F
impugnatura^F

スピード・スキーヤー
speed skier
Speedskifahrer^M
skieur^M de vitesse^F
esquiador^M de velocidad^F
sciatore^M di chilometro^M lanciato

ヘルメット
helmet
Sturzhelm^M
casque^M
casco^M
casco^M

スピード・スキー板
speed ski
Speedski^M
ski^M de vitesse^F
esquí^M de velocidad^F
sci^M da chilometro^M lanciato

ウインター・スポーツ | WINTER SPORTS
WINTERSPORT | SPORTS D'HIVER | DEPORTES DE INVIERNO | SPORT INVERNALI

クロス・カントリー・スキー

cross-country skiing | SkilanglaufM | skiM de fondM | esquíM de fondoM | sciM da fondoM

クロス・カントリー・スキーヤー
cross-country skier
LangläuferM
skieurM de fondM
fondistaM
fondistaM/F

タートルネック
turtleneck
RollkragenM
colM roulé
jerseyM de cuelloM de cisneM
colloM alto

スキー帽
ski hat
SkimützeF
bonnetM
gorroM
berrettoM

ワックス道具一式
waxing kit
WachsausrüstungF
trousseF de fartageM
estucheM de enceradoM
accessoriM per la sciolinaturaF

グリップ
pole grip
StockgriffM
poignéeF
puñoM
impugnaturaF

コルク
cork
KorkM
liègeM
corchoM
sugheroM

シャフト
pole shaft
StockschaftM
tigeF
fusteM del bastónM
astaF

スキー・ウエア
ski suit
SkianzugM
combinaisonF de skiM
trajeM de esquíM
tutaF

リスト・ストラップ
wrist strap
HandschlaufeF
dragonneF
correaF para la manoF
cappioM

ストック
ski pole
SkistockM
bâtonM
bastónM de esquíM
racchettaF

ワックス
wax
WachsN
fartM
ceraF
sciolinaF

クロス・カントリー用スキー板
cross-country ski
LanglaufskiM
skiM de fondM
esquíM de fondoM
sciM da fondoM

スクレーパー
scraper
AbziehklingeF
racloirM
rasquetaF
raschiettoM metallico

グローブ
glove
HandschuhM
gantM
guanteM
guantoM

ツアー[距離]用スキー靴
boot
SkistiefelM
chaussureF
botaF
scarponeM

ビンディング/バインディング
binding
Langlauf-RattenfallbindungF
fixationF
fijadorM
attaccoM

ショベル/トップ・ベンド
shovel
SchaufelF
spatuleF
puntaF
spatolaF

クロス・カントリー用スキー板
cross-country ski
LanglaufskiM
skiM de fondM
esquíM de fondoM
sciM da fondoM

トップ
ski tip
SkispitzeF
pointeF de skiM
puntaF del esquíM
puntaF dello sciM

トウ・ビンディング
toe binding
VorfußbindungF
fixationF à butéeF avant
fijaciónF para el pieM
attaccoM

テール
tail
EndeN
talonM
colaF
codaF

ショベル/トップ・ベンド
shovel
SchaufelF
spatuleF
puntaF
spatolaF

締め具
clamp
BackenM
fourchetteF
ratoneraF
morsettoM anteriore

トウプレート
toeplate
VorfußplatteF
étrierM
apoyoM para el pieM
staffaF

ヒールプレート
heelplate
AbsatzplatteF
talonnièreF
piezaF de talónM
tallonieraF

ダイアゴナル[クラシカル]走法
diagonal step
diagonaler SchlittschuhschrittM
pasM alternatif
pasoM alternativo
passoM alternato

スケーティング走法
skating step
SchlittschuhschrittM
pasM de patineurM
pasoM de patinadorM
passoM pattinato

スケーティング(キック)/蹴り放し
skating kick
DoppelstockschubM
coupM de patinM
golpeM de patínM
colpoM di pattinoM

滑走
gliding phase
GleitphaseF
phaseF de glisseF
faseF de impulsiónF
faseF di scivolamentoM

突き放し
pushing phase
SchubphaseF
phaseF de pousséeF
faseF de impulsiónF
faseF di spintaF

滑走
gliding phase
GleitphaseF
phaseF de glisseF
faseF de deslizamientoM
faseF di scivolamentoM

突き放し
pushing phase
SchubphaseF
phaseF de pousséeF
faseF de impulsoF
faseF di spintaF

ウインター・スポーツ | WINTER SPORTS
WINTERSPORT | SPORTS D'HIVER | DEPORTES DE INVIERNO | SPORT INVERNALI

バイアスロン

biathlon | Biathlon[N] | biathlon[M] | biathlon[M] | biathlon[M]

射撃姿勢
shooting positions
Schießpositionen[F]
positions[F] de tir[M]
posiciones[M] de tiro[M]
posizioni[F] di tiro[M]

伏射
prone position
liegender Anschlag[M]
position[F] couchée
posición[M] supina
posizione[F] prona

立射
standing position
stehender Anschlag[M]
position[F] debout
posición[F] en pie[M]
posizione[F] in piedi

照門
rear sight
Kimme[F]
hausse[F]
alza[F]
tacca[F] di mira[F]

弾倉
magazine
Magazin[N]
chargeur[M]
cargador[M]
caricatore[M]

ライフル
rifle
Kleinkalibergewehr[N]
carabine[F]
carabina[F]
carabina[F]

照星
front sight
Korn[N]
guidon[M]
punto[M] de mira[F]
mirino[M]

吊り革
shooting slip
Gewehrriemen[M]
bretelle[F] de tir[M]
correa[F] de tiro[M]
cinghia[F]

滑り止めマット
nonslip mat
rutschfeste Matte[F]
tapis[M] antidérapant
tapete[M] antideslizante
tappeto[M] di sicurezza[F]

レーン番号
lane number
Bahnnummer[F]
numéro[M] de couloir[M]
número[M] de calle[F]
numero[M] di corsia[F]

審判員
referee
Kampfrichter[M]
juge[M]
juez[M]
arbitro[M]

標的
target
Zielscheibe[F]
cible[F]
blanco[M]
bersaglio[M]

射撃場
shooting range
Schießanlage[F]
champ[M] de tir[M]
puesto[M] de tiro[M]
campo[M] di tiro[M]

風向旗
wind flag
Windfähnchen[N]
fanion[M]-girouette[F]
mangas[F] de viento[M]
bandiera[F] segnavento

バイアスリート
biathlete
Biathlet[M]
biathlonien[M]
atleta[F] de biathlón[M]
biathleta[M/F]

射座
shooting place
Schießstand[M]
emplacement[M] de tir[M]
campo[M] de tiro[M]
linea[F] di tiro[M]

スノーシュー／かんじき

snowshoes | Schneeschuh[M] | raquettes[F] | raqueta[F] | racchetta[F] da neve[F]

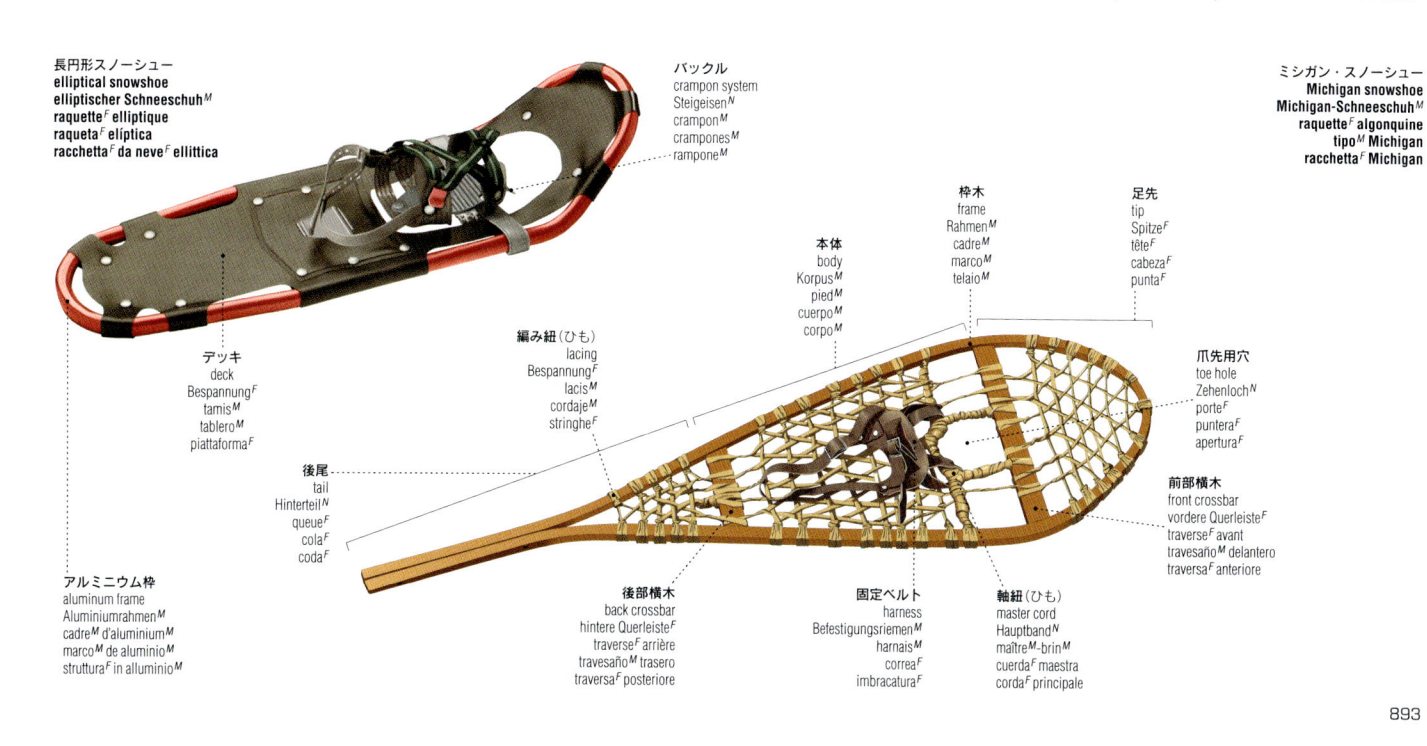

長円形スノーシュー
elliptical snowshoe
elliptischer Schneeschuh[M]
raquette[F] elliptique
raqueta[F] elíptica
racchetta[F] da neve[F] ellittica

バックル
crampon system
Steigeisen[N]
crampon[M]
crampones[M]
rampone[M]

ミシガン・スノーシュー
Michigan snowshoe
Michigan-Schneeschuh[M]
raquette[F] algonquine
tipo[M] Michigan
racchetta[F] Michigan

デッキ
deck
Bespannung[F]
tamis[M]
tablero[M]
piattaforma[F]

編み紐（ひも）
lacing
Bespannung[F]
lacis[M]
cordaje[M]
stringhe[F]

枠木
frame
Rahmen[M]
cadre[M]
marco[M]
telaio[M]

足先
tip
Spitze[F]
tête[F]
cabeza[F]
punta[F]

本体
body
Korpus[M]
pied[M]
cuerpo[M]
corpo[M]

爪先用穴
toe hole
Zehenloch[N]
porte[N]
puntera[F]
apertura[F]

後尾
tail
Hinterteil[N]
queue[F]
cola[F]
coda[F]

前部横木
front crossbar
vordere Querleiste[F]
traverse[F] avant
travesaño[M] delantero
traversa[F] anteriore

アルミニウム枠
aluminum frame
Aluminiumrahmen[M]
cadre[M] d'aluminium[M]
marco[M] de aluminio[M]
struttura[F] in alluminio[M]

後部横木
back crossbar
hintere Querleiste[F]
traverse[F] arrière
travesaño[M] trasero
traversa[F] posteriore

固定ベルト
harness
Befestigungsriemen[M]
harnais[M]
correa[F]
imbracatura[F]

軸紐（ひも）
master cord
Hauptband[N]
maître[M]-brin[M]
cuerda[F] maestra
corda[F] principale

ローラー・スポーツ | SPORTS ON WHEELS
ROLLSPORT | SPORTS À ROULETTES | DEPORTES SOBRE RUEDAS | SPORT SU ROTELLE

スケートボーディング

skateboarding | Skateboarding^N | planche^F à roulettes^F | skateboard^M | skateboard^M

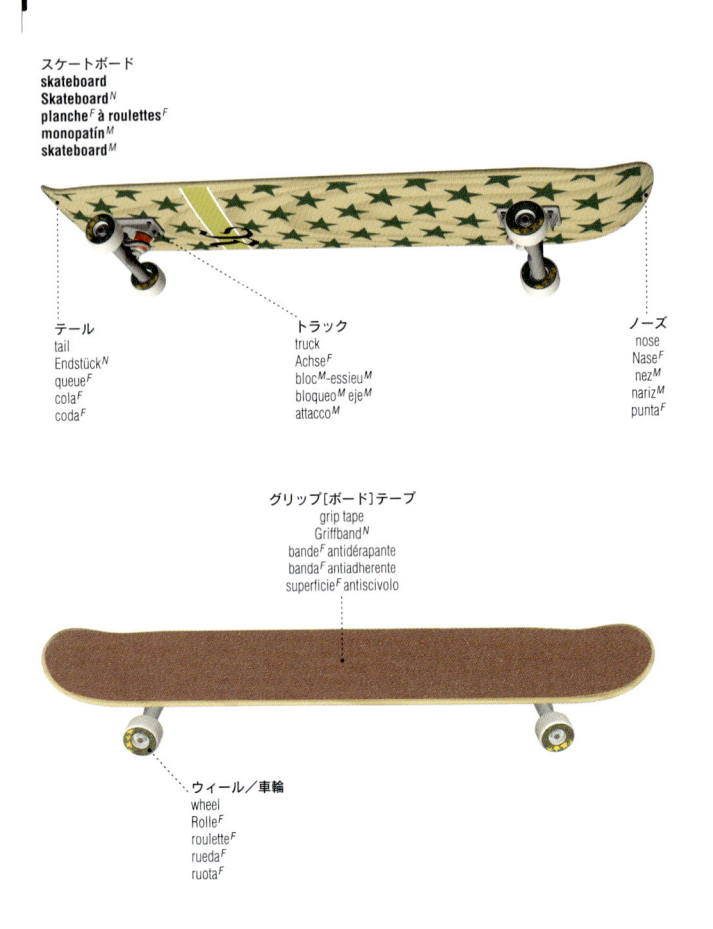

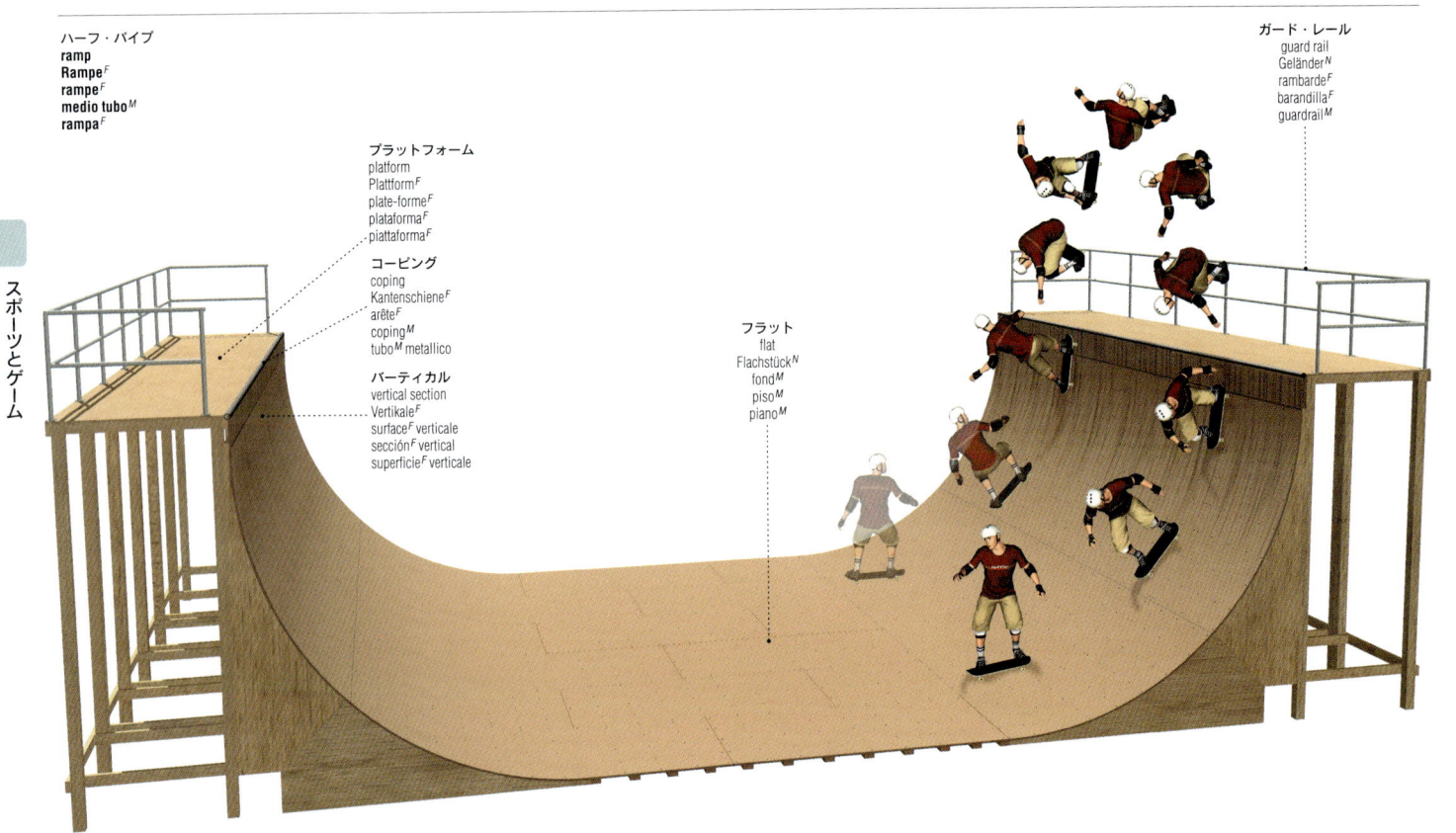

日本語 | 英語 | ドイツ語 | フランス語 | スペイン語 | イタリア語

スケートボード
skateboard
Skateboard^N
planche^F à roulettes^F
monopatín^M
skateboard^M

テール
tail
Endstück^N
queue^F
cola^F
coda^F

トラック
truck
Achse^F
bloc^M-essieu^M
bloqueo^M eje^M
attacco^M

ノーズ
nose
Nase^F
nez^M
nariz^M
punta^F

グリップ[ボード]テープ
grip tape
Griffband^N
bande^F antidérapante
banda^F antiadherente
superficie^F antiscivolo

ウィール／車輪
wheel
Rolle^F
roulette^F
rueda^F
ruota^F

膝当て
knee pad
Knieschützer^M
genouillère^F
rodillera^F
ginocchiera^F

スケートボーダー
skateboarder
Skateboarder^M
planchiste^M
monopatín^M
skater^{M/F}

肘当て
elbow pad
Ellbogenschützer^M
protège-coude^M
codera^F
gomitiera^F

ヘルメット
helmet
Helm^M
casque^M
casco^M
casco^M

コーピング
coping
Kantenschiene^F
arête^F
coping^M
tubo^M metallico

ハーフ・パイプ
ramp
Rampe^F
rampe^F
medio tubo^M
rampa^F

プラットフォーム
platform
Plattform^F
plate-forme^F
plataforma^F
piattaforma^F

コーピング
coping
Kantenschiene^F
arête^F
coping^M
tubo^M metallico

バーティカル
vertical section
Vertikale^F
surface^F verticale
sección^F vertical
superficie^F verticale

ガード・レール
guard rail
Geländer^N
rambarde^F
barandilla^F
guardrail^M

フラット
flat
Flachstück^N
fond^M
piso^M
piano^M

スポーツとゲーム

ローラー・スポーツ | SPORTS ON WHEELS
ROLLSPORT | SPORTS À ROULETTES | DEPORTES SOBRE RUEDAS | SPORT SU ROTELLE

イン・ライン・スケーティング

in-line skating | Inlineskating^N | patin^M à roues^F alignées | patinaje^M en línea^F | pattinaggio^M in linea^F

アクロバット・スケート靴
acrobatic skate
Stuntskate^M
patin^M acrobatique
patinaje^M acrobático
pattino^M acrobatico

インナー・ブーツ
inner boot
Innenstiefel^M
chausson^M intérieur
botín^M interior
scarpetta interna

アッパー・シェル
upper shell
Schalenschuh^M
coque^F supérieure
bota^F externa
gambale^M

スケーター
skater
Skaterin^F
patineuse^F
patinador^M
pattinatore^M

ヘルメット
helmet
Helm^M
casque^M
casco^M
casco^M

フレーム
frame
Schiene^F
platine^F
bastidor^M
telaio^M

ウィール／車輪
wheel
Rolle^F
roue^F
rueda^F
rotella^F

肘当て
elbow pad
Ellbogenschützer^M
coudière^F
codera^F
gomitiera^F

膝当て
knee pad
Knieschützer^M
genouillère^F
rodillera^F
ginocchiera^F

イン・ライン・スピード・スケート靴
in-line speed skate
Speedskate^M
patin^M de vitesse^F
patín^M en línea^F
pattino^M da velocità^F

リスト・ガード
wrist guard
Handgelenkschützer^M
protège-poignet^M
muñequera^F
polsiera^F

イン・ライン・スケート靴／
ローラーブレード・
in-line skate
Rollschuh^M
patin^M à roues^F alignées
patín^M en línea^F
pattino^M a rotelle^F

アッパー・シェル
upper shell
Oberschale^F
coque^F supérieure
bota^F externa
gambale^M

インナー・ブーツ
inner boot
Innenstiefel^M
chausson^M intérieur
botín^M interior
scarpetta interna

イン・ライン・ホッケー・スケート靴
in-line hockey skate
Hockeyskate^M
patin^M de hockey^M
patín^M en línea^F de hockey^M
pattino^M da hockey^M

バックル
adjusting buckle
Einstellspanner^M
boucle^F de réglage^M
hebilla^F de ajuste^M
dispositivo^M di regolazione^F

ブーツ
boot
Stiefel^M
chaussure^F
bota^F
scarpa^F

シャフト／心棒／車軸
axle
Achse^F
essieu^M
eje^M
assale^M

ヒール・ストップ
heel stop
Absatzstopper^M
frein^M de talon^M
freno^M trasero
freno^M a tampone^M

ウィール／車輪
wheel
Rolle^F
roue^F
rueda^F
ruota^F

トラック
truck
Wagen^M
bloc^M-essieu^M
bogie^M
carrello^M

スポーツとゲーム

895

空中スポーツ | AERIAL SPORTS
LUFTSPORT | SPORTS AÉRIENS | DEPORTES AÉREOS | SPORT AEREI

スカイ・ダイビング

日本語 | 英語 | ドイツ語 | フランス語 | スペイン語 | イタリア語

sky diving | Fallschirmspringen^N | chute^F libre | paracaidismo^M en caída^F libre | paracadutismo^M in caduta^F libera

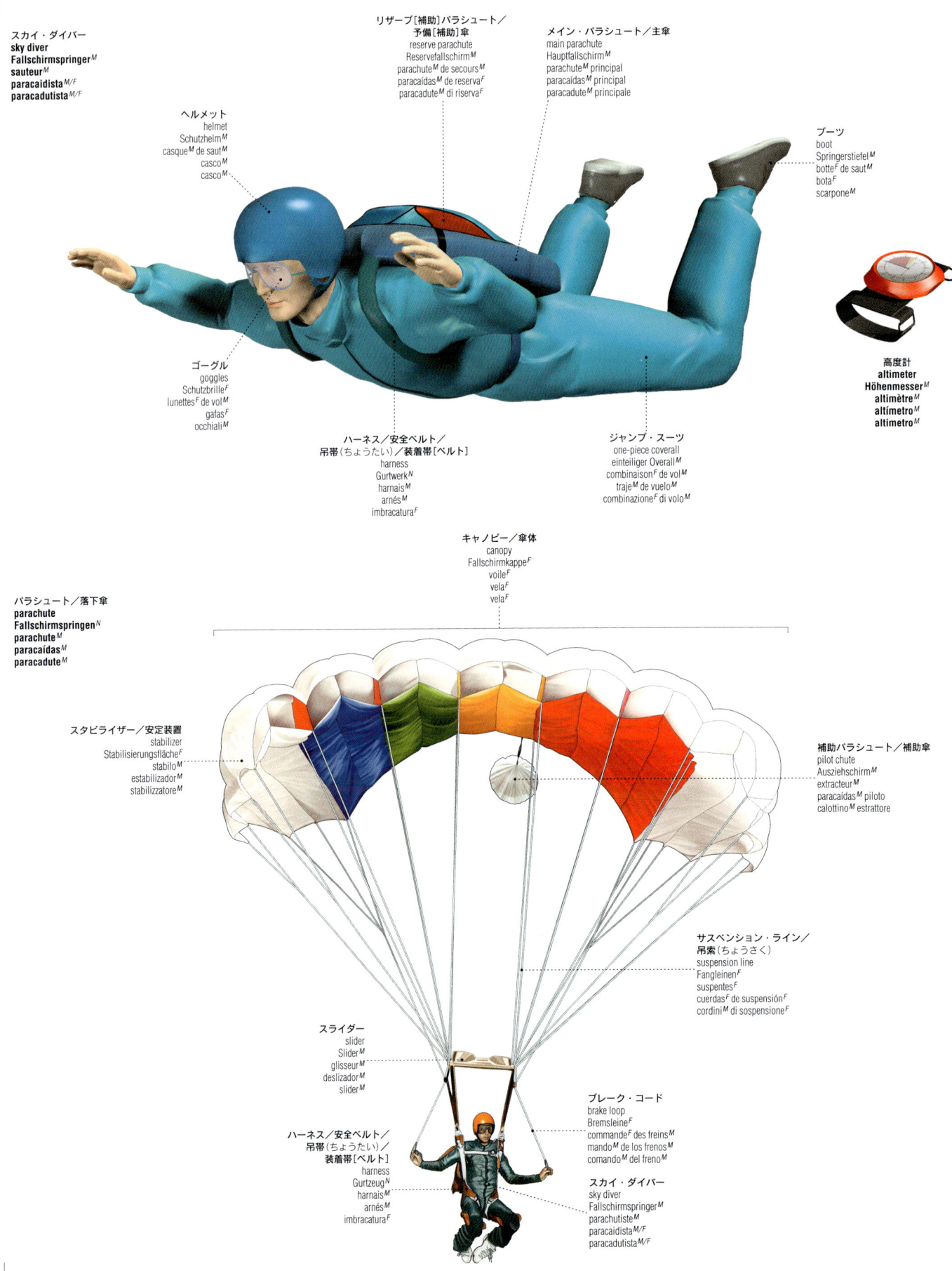

スカイ・ダイバー
sky diver
Fallschirmspringer^M
sauteur^M
paracaidista^{M/F}
paracadutista^{M/F}

ヘルメット
helmet
Schutzhelm^M
casque^M de saut^M
casco^M
casco^M

リザーブ［補助］パラシュート／
予備［補助］傘
reserve parachute
Reservefallschirm^M
parachute^M de secours^M
paracaídas^M de reserva^F
paracadute^M di riserva^F

メイン・パラシュート／主傘
main parachute
Hauptfallschirm^M
parachute^M principal
paracaídas^M principal
paracadute^M principale

ブーツ
boot
Springerstiefel^M
botte^F de saut^M
bota^F
scarpone^M

ゴーグル
goggles
Schutzbrille^F
lunettes^F de vol^M
gafas^F
occhiali^M

ハーネス／安全ベルト／
吊帯（ちょうたい）／装着帯［ベルト］
harness
Gurtwerk^N
harnais^M
arnés^M
imbracatura^F

ジャンプ・スーツ
one-piece coverall
einteiliger Overall^M
combinaison^F de vol^M
traje^M de vuelo^M
combinazione^F di volo^M

高度計
altimeter
Höhenmesser^M
altimètre^M
altímetro^M
altimetro^M

キャノピー／傘体
canopy
Fallschirmkappe^F
voile^F
vela^F
vela^F

パラシュート／落下傘
parachute
Fallschirmspringen^N
parachute^M
paracaídas^M
paracadute^M

スタビライザー／安定装置
stabilizer
Stabilisierungsfläche^F
stabilo^M
estabilizador^M
stabilizzatore^M

補助パラシュート／補助傘
pilot chute
Ausziehschirm^M
extracteur^M
paracaídas^M piloto
calottino^M estrattore

サスペンション・ライン／
吊索（ちょうさく）
suspension line
Fangleinen^F
suspentes^F
cuerdas^F de suspensión^F
cordini^M di sospensione^F

スライダー
slider
Slider^M
glisseur^M
deslizador^M
slider^M

ハーネス／安全ベルト／
吊帯（ちょうたい）／装着帯［ベルト］
harness
Gurtzeug^N
harnais^M
arnés^M
imbracatura^F

ブレーク・コード
brake loop
Bremsleine^F
commande^F des freins^M
mando^M de los frenos^M
comando^M del freno^M

スカイ・ダイバー
sky diver
Fallschirmspringer^N
parachutiste^M
paracaidista^{M/F}
paracadutista^{M/F}

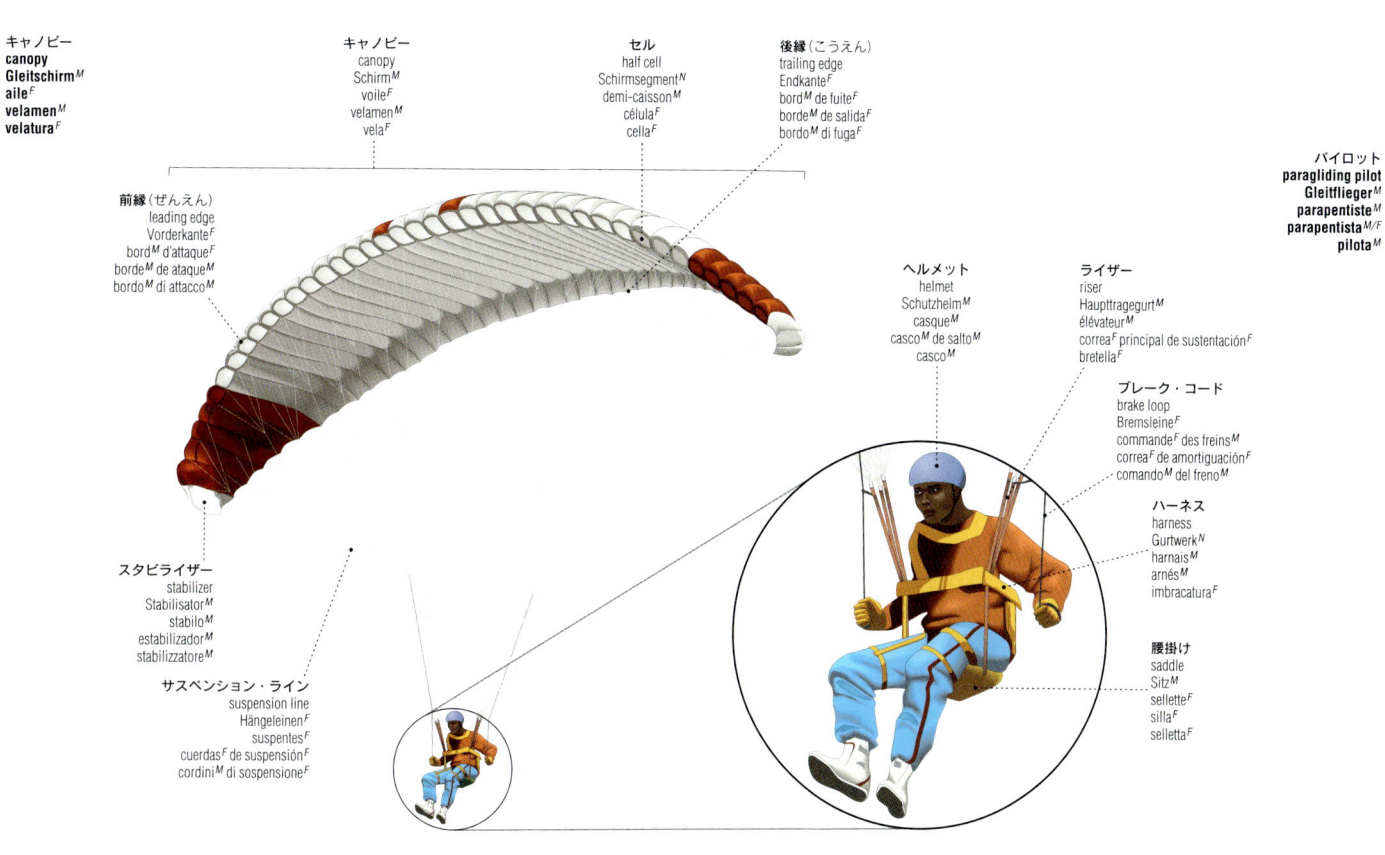

空中スポーツ | AERIAL SPORTS
LUFTSPORT | SPORTS AÉRIENS | DEPORTES AÉREOS | SPORT AEREI

パラグライディング

paragliding | Gleitschirmfliegen[N] | parapente[M] | parapente[M] | parapendio[M]

キャノピー
canopy
Gleitschirm[M]
aile[F]
velamen[M]
velatura[F]

キャノピー
canopy
Schirm[M]
voile[F]
velamen[M]
vela[F]

セル
half cell
Schirmsegment[N]
demi-caisson[M]
célula[F]
cella[F]

後縁(こうえん)
trailing edge
Endkante[F]
bord[M] de fuite[F]
borde[M] de salida[F]
bordo[M] di fuga[F]

前縁(ぜんえん)
leading edge
Vorderkante[F]
bord[M] d'attaque[F]
borde[M] de ataque[M]
bordo[M] di attacco[M]

パイロット
paragliding pilot
Gleitflieger[M]
parapentiste[M]
parapentista[M/F]
pilota[M]

ヘルメット
helmet
Schutzhelm[M]
casque[M]
casco[M] de salto[M]
casco[M]

ライザー
riser
Haupttragegurt[M]
élévateur[M]
correa[F] principal de sustentación[F]
bretella[F]

ブレーク・コード
brake loop
Bremsleine[F]
commande[F] des freins[M]
correa[F] de amortiguación
comando[M] del freno[M]

ハーネス
harness
Gurtwerk[N]
harnais[M]
arnés[M]
imbracatura[F]

スタビライザー
stabilizer
Stabilisator[M]
stabilo[M]
estabilizador[M]
stabilizzatore[M]

腰掛け
saddle
Sitz[M]
sellette[F]
silla[F]
selletta[F]

サスペンション・ライン
suspension line
Hängeleinen[F]
suspentes[F]
cuerdas[F] de suspensión[F]
cordini[M] di sospensione[F]

ハング・グライディング

hang gliding | Drachenfliegen[N] | vol[M] libre | vuelo[M] libre | deltaplano[M]

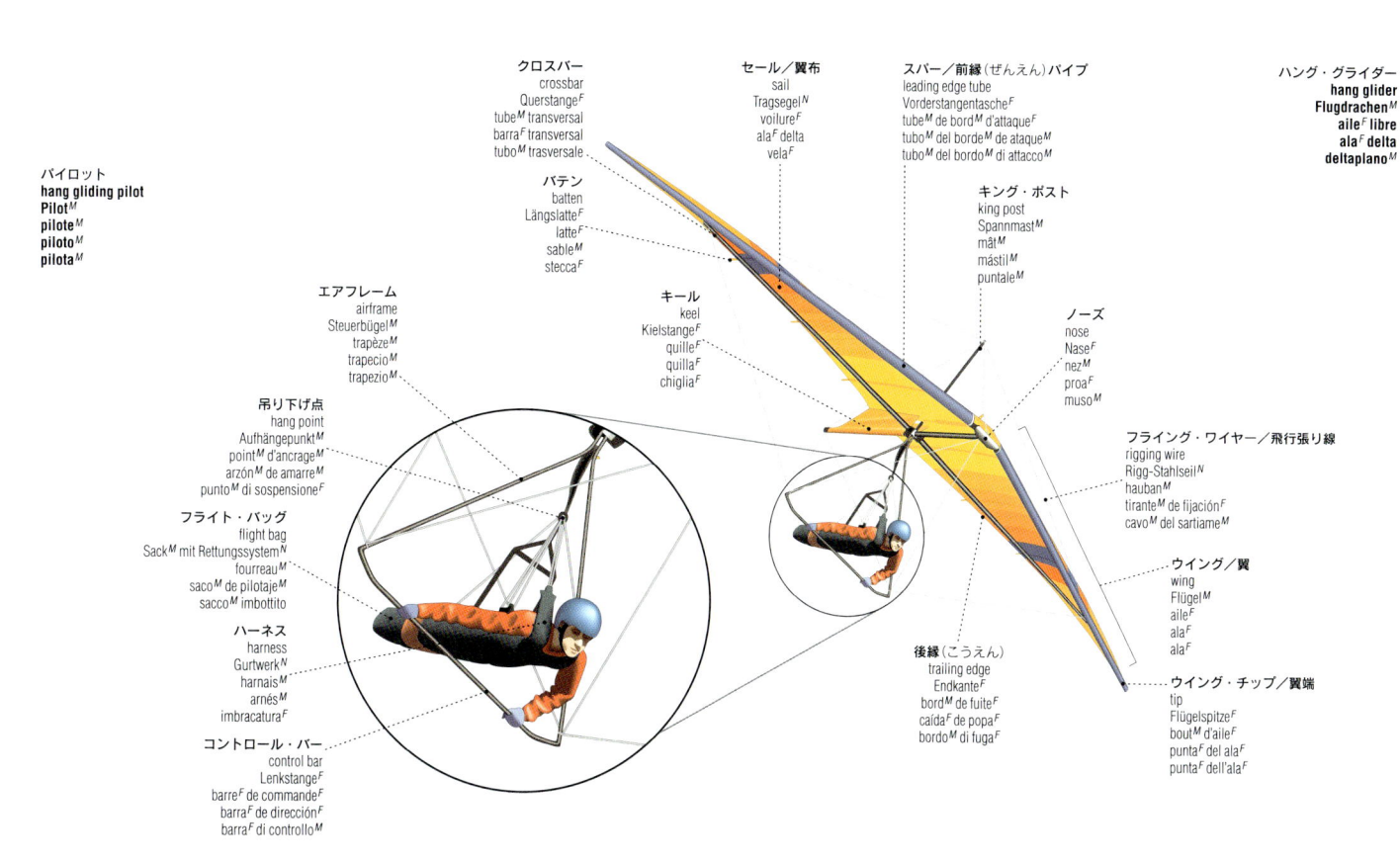

クロスバー
crossbar
Querstange[F]
tube[M] transversal
barra[F] transversal
tubo[M] trasversale

セール／翼布
sail
Tragsegel[N]
voilure[F]
ala[F] delta
vela[F]

スパー／前縁(ぜんえん)パイプ
leading edge tube
Vorderstangentasche[F]
tube[M] de bord[M] d'attaque[F]
tubo[M] del borde[M] de ataque[M]
tubo[M] del bordo[M] di attacco[M]

ハング・グライダー
hang glider
Flugdrachen[M]
aile[F] libre
ala[F] delta
deltaplano[M]

パイロット
hang gliding pilot
Pilot[M]
pilote[M]
piloto[M]
pilota[M]

バテン
batten
Längslatte[F]
latte[F]
sable[M]
stecca[F]

キング・ポスト
king post
Spannmast[M]
mât[M]
mástil[M]
puntale[M]

エアフレーム
airframe
Steuerbügel[M]
trapèze[M]
trapecio[M]
trapezio[M]

キール
keel
Kielstange[F]
quille[F]
quilla[F]
chiglia[F]

ノーズ
nose
Nase[F]
nez[M]
proa[F]
muso[M]

吊り下げ点
hang point
Aufhängepunkt[M]
point[M] d'ancrage[M]
arzón[M] de amarre[M]
punto[M] di sospensione[F]

フライング・ワイヤー／飛行張り線
rigging wire
Rigg-Stahlseil[N]
hauban[M]
tirante[F] de fijación[F]
cavo[M] del sartiame[M]

フライト・バッグ
flight bag
Sack[M] mit Rettungssystem[N]
fourreau[M]
saco[M] de pilotaje[M]
sacco[M] imbottito

ウイング／翼
wing
Flügel[M]
aile[F]
ala[F]
ala[F]

ハーネス
harness
Gurtwerk[N]
harnais[M]
arnés[M]
imbracatura[F]

後縁(こうえん)
trailing edge
Endkante[F]
bord[M] de fuite[F]
caída[F] de popa[F]
bordo[M] di fuga[F]

ウイング・チップ／翼端
tip
Flügelspitze[F]
bout[M] d'aile[F]
punta[F] del ala[F]
punta[F] dell'ala[F]

コントロール・バー
control bar
Lenkstange[F]
barre[F] de commande[F]
barra[F] de dirección[F]
barra[F] di controllo[M]

スポーツとゲーム

897

空中スポーツ | AERIAL SPORTS
LUFTSPORT | SPORTS AÉRIENS | DEPORTES AÉREOS | SPORT AEREI

グライダー

glider | Segelflugzeug[N] | planeur[M] | planeador[M] | aliante[M]

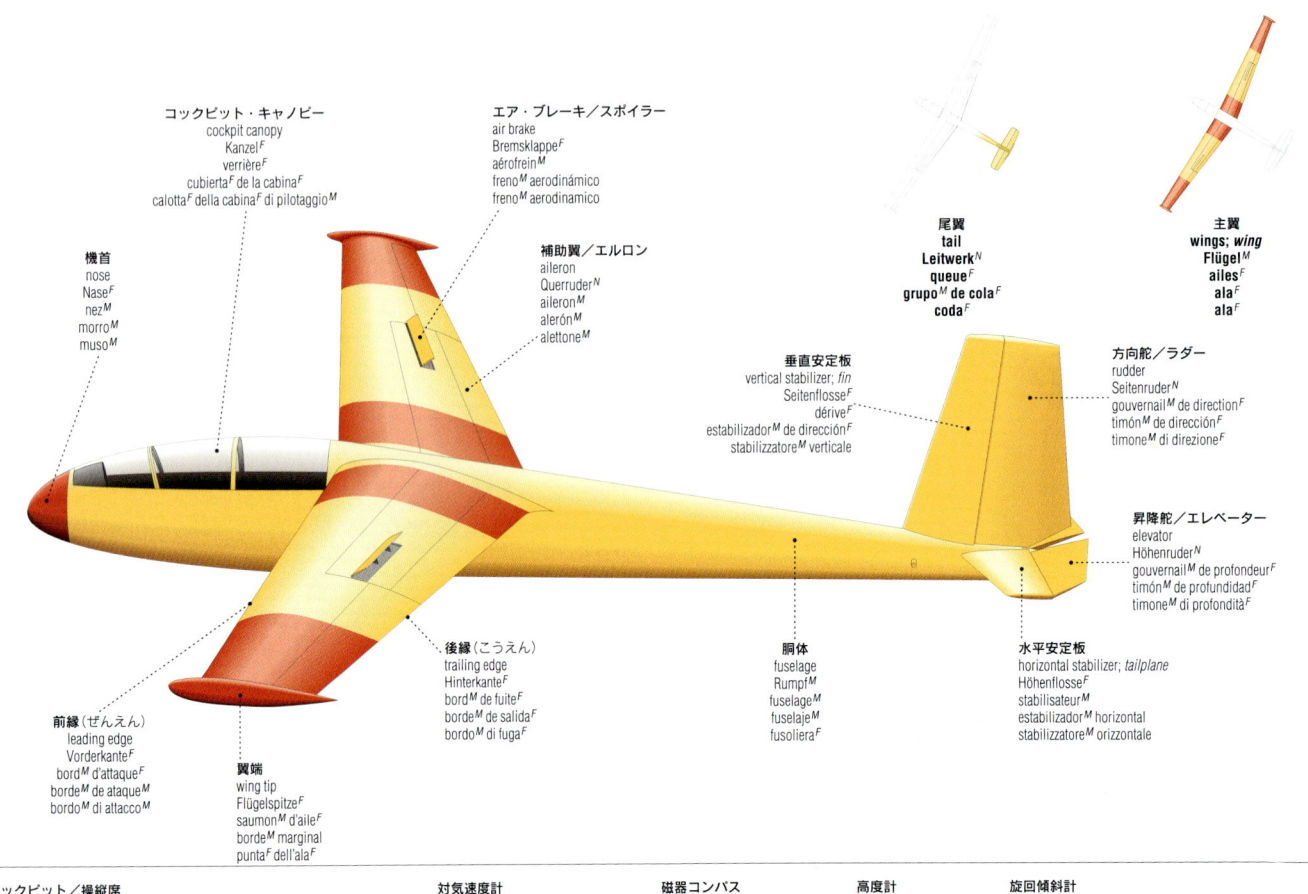

日本語 | 英語 | ドイツ語 | フランス語 | スペイン語 | イタリア語

コックピット・キャノピー
cockpit canopy
Kanzel[F]
verrière[F]
cubierta[F] de la cabina[F]
calotta[F] della cabina[F] di pilotaggio[M]

エア・ブレーキ／スポイラー
air brake
Bremsklappe[F]
aérofrein[M]
freno[M] aerodinámico
freno[M] aerodinamico

尾翼
tail
Leitwerk[N]
queue[F]
grupo[M] de cola[F]
coda[F]

主翼
wings; wing
Flügel[M]
ailes[F]
ala[F]
ala[F]

機首
nose
Nase[F]
nez[M]
morro[M]
muso[M]

補助翼／エルロン
aileron
Querruder[N]
aileron[M]
alerón[M]
alettone[M]

垂直安定板
vertical stabilizer; fin
Seitenflosse[F]
dérive[F]
estabilizador[M] de dirección[F]
stabilizzatore[M] verticale

方向舵／ラダー
rudder
Seitenruder[N]
gouvernail[M] de direction[F]
timón[M] de dirección[F]
timone[M] di direzione[F]

昇降舵／エレベーター
elevator
Höhenruder[N]
gouvernail[M] de profondeur[F]
timón[M] de profundidad[F]
timone[M] di profondità[F]

後縁（こうえん）
trailing edge
Hinterkante[F]
bord[M] de fuite[F]
borde[M] de salida[F]
bordo[M] di fuga[F]

胴体
fuselage
Rumpf[M]
fuselage[M]
fuselaje[M]
fusoliera[F]

水平安定板
horizontal stabilizer; tailplane
Höhenflosse[F]
stabilisateur[M]
estabilizador[M] horizontal
stabilizzatore[M] orizzontale

前縁（ぜんえん）
leading edge
Vorderkante[F]
bord[M] d'attaque[F]
borde[M] de ataque[M]
bordo[M] di attacco[M]

翼端
wing tip
Flügelspitze[F]
saumon[M] d'aile[F]
borde[M] marginal
punta[F] dell'ala[F]

コックピット／操縦席
cockpit
Cockpit[N]
cabine[F] de pilotage[M]
cabina[F] del piloto[M]
cabina[F] di pilotaggio[M]

対気速度計
airspeed indicator
Geschwindigkeitsanzeige[F]
anémomètre[M]
anemómetro[M]
anemometro[M]

磁器コンパス
compass
Kompass[M]
compas[M]
brújula[F]
bussola[F]

高度計
altimeter
Höhenmesser[M]
altimètre[M]
altímetro[M]
altimetro[M]

旋回傾斜計
turn and slip indicator; turn and bank indicator
Wendezeiger[M]
indicateur[M] de virage[M] et d'inclinaison[F] latérale
indicador[M] de viraje[M] y de inclinación[F]
indicatore[M] di virata[F] e di inclinazione[F]

電気式昇降計
electric variometer
Elektrovariometer[N]
variomètre[M] électrique
variómetro[M] eléctrico
variometro[M] elettrico

コックピット換気口
cockpit ventilation
Frischluftzufuhr[F]
ventilation[F] de la cabine[F]
ventilador[M] de cabina[F]
manopola[F] per l'aerazione[F] della cabina[F]

（機械式）昇降計
mechanical variometer
mechanisches Variometer[N]
variomètre[M] mécanique
variómetro[M] mecánico
variometro[M] meccanico

酸素供給調節装置
oxygen feeding control
Sauerstoffzufuhranzeige[F]
contrôle[M] d'alimentation[F] en oxygène[M]
control[M] de alimentador[M] de oxígeno[M]
indicatore[M] dell'alimentazione[F] di ossigeno[M]

曳航索（えいこうさく）切り離しノブ
tow release knob
Ausklinkhebel[M]
commande[F] de largage[M] de câble[M]
liberador[M] del cable[M] de remolque[M]
manopola[F] di sgancio[M] del cavo[M] di traino[M]

酸素供給ノブ
oxygen feeding knob
Sauerstoffzufuhrregler[M]
commande[F] d'alimentation[F] en oxygène[M]
palanca[F] de alimentador[M] de oxígeno[M]
regolatore[M] dell'alimentazione[F] di ossigeno[M]

方向舵ペダル
rudder pedal
Seitenruderpedal[N]
pédale[F] de palonnier[M]
pedal[M] del timón[M] de mando[M]
pedale[M] del timone[M]

マイクロホン
microphone
Mikrofon[N]
microphone[M]
micrófono[M]
microfono[M]

エア・ブレーキ・ハンドル
air brake handle
Bremsklappenhebel[M]
commande[F] d'aérofrein[M]
mando[M] del freno[M] aerodinámico
comando[M] del freno[M] aerodinamico

キャノピー放出ノブ
canopy release knob
Kanzellösehebel[M]
commande[F] de largage[M] de la verrière[F]
eyector[M] de la cubierta[F] de cabina[F]
manopola[F] per l'apertura[F] della calotta[F]

飛行姿勢調節ノブ
turn and slip knob; turn and bank knob
Wendehebel[M]
commande[F] de virage[M] et d'inclinaison[F] latérale
palanca[F] de viraje[M] y de inclinación[F]
comando[M] di virata[F] e di inclinazione[F]

操縦桿（かん）
control stick
Steuerknüppel[M]
manche[M] à balai[M]
palanca[F] de mando[M]
cloche[F]

無線機
radio
Funkgerät[N]
radio[F]
radio[M]
radio[F]

操縦席
seat
Sitz[M]
siège[M]
asiento[M]
sedile[M]

空中スポーツ | AERIAL SPORTS
LUFTSPORT | SPORTS AÉRIENS | DEPORTES AÉREOS | SPORT AEREI

気球乗り

ballooning | Freiballonsport^M | montgolfière^F | vuelo^M en globo^M | mongolfiera^F

排気弁／パラシュート・バルブ
parachute valve
Ventil^N
panneau^M-parachute^M
válvula^F paracaídas^M
valvola^F del paracadute^M

気球
balloon
Heißluftballon^M
ballon^M
globo^M
pallone^M aerostatico

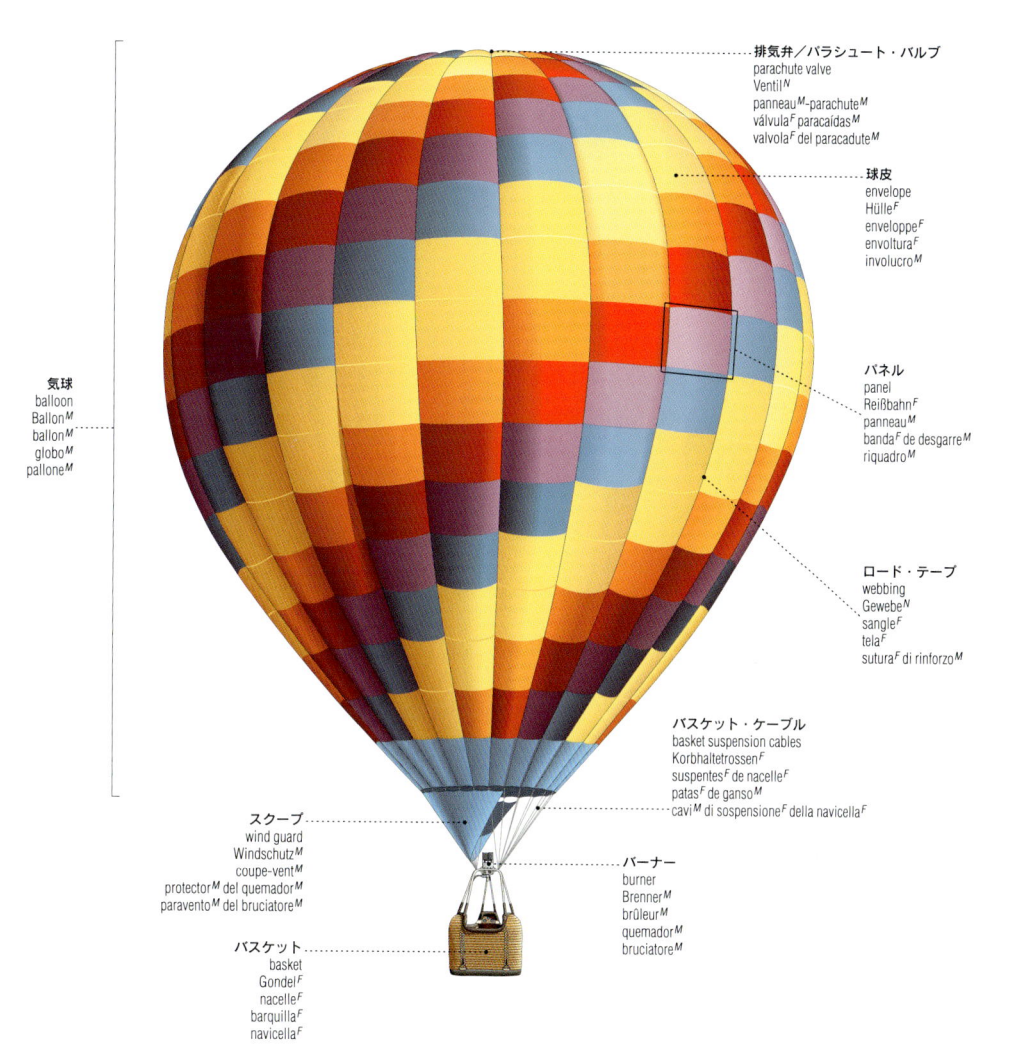

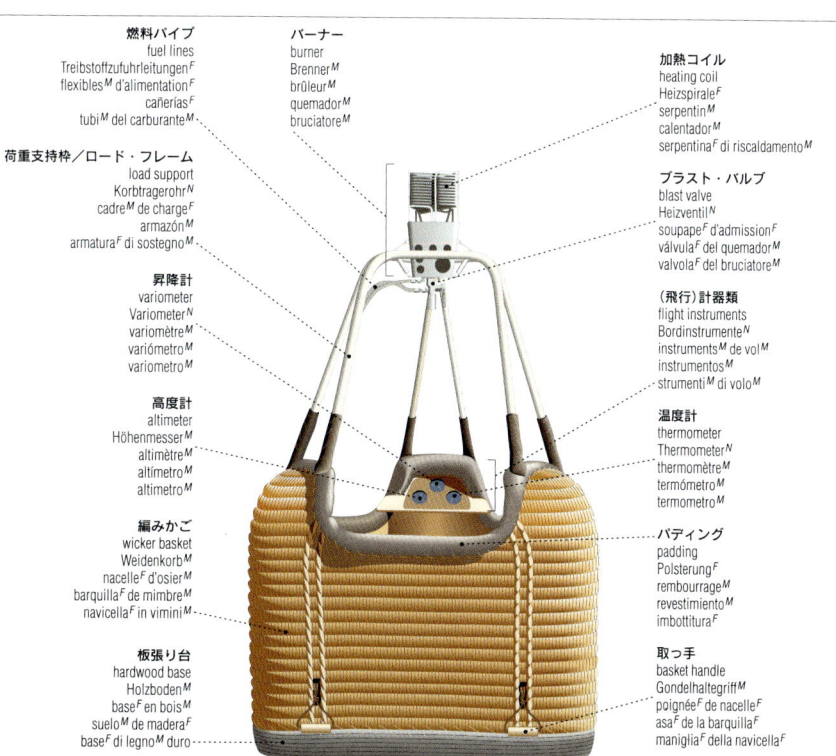

球皮
envelope
Hülle^F
enveloppe^F
envoltura^F
involucro^M

気球
balloon
Ballon^M
ballon^M
globo^M
pallone^M

パネル
panel
Reißbahn^F
panneau^M
banda^F de desgarre^M
riquadro^M

ロード・テープ
webbing
Gewebe^N
sangle^F
tela^F
sutura^F di rinforzo^M

バスケット・ケーブル
basket suspension cables
Korbhaltetrossen^F
suspentes^F de nacelle^F
patas^F de ganso^M
cavi^M di sospensione^F della navicella^F

スクープ
wind guard
Windschutz^M
coupe-vent^M
protector^M del quemador^M
paravento^M del bruciatore^M

バーナー
burner
Brenner^M
brûleur^M
quemador^M
bruciatore^M

バスケット
basket
Gondel^F
nacelle^F
barquilla^F
navicella^F

燃料パイプ
fuel lines
Treibstoffzufuhrleitungen^F
flexibles^M d'alimentation^F
cañerías^F
tubi^M del carburante^M

バーナー
burner
Brenner^M
brûleur^M
quemador^M
bruciatore^M

加熱コイル
heating coil
Heizspirale^F
serpentin^M
calentador^M
serpentina^F di riscaldamento^M

バスケット／ゴンドラ
basket
Gondel^F
nacelle^F
barquilla^F
navicella^F

荷重支持枠／ロード・フレーム
load support
Korbtragerohr^N
cadre^M de charge^F
armazón^M
armatura^F di sostegno^M

ブラスト・バルブ
blast valve
Heizventil^N
soupape^F d'admission^F
válvula^F del quemador^M
valvola^F del bruciatore^M

昇降計
variometer
Variometer^N
variomètre^M
variómetro^M
variometro^M

（飛行）計器類
flight instruments
Bordinstrumente^N
instruments^M de vol^M
instrumentos^M
strumenti^M di volo^M

高度計
altimeter
Höhenmesser^M
altimètre^M
altímetro^M
altimetro^M

温度計
thermometer
Thermometer^N
thermomètre^M
termómetro^M
termometro^M

編みかご
wicker basket
Weidenkorb^M
nacelle^F d'osier^M
barquilla^F de mimbre^M
navicella^F in vimini^M

パディング
padding
Polsterung^F
rembourrage^M
revestimiento^M
imbottitura^F

取っ手
basket handle
Gondelhaltegriff^M
poignée^F de nacelle^F
asa^F de la barquilla^F
maniglia^F della navicella^F

板張り台
hardwood base
Holzboden^M
base^F en bois^M
suelo^M de madera^F
base^F di legno^M duro

スポーツとゲーム

899

マウンテン・スポーツ | MOUNTAIN SPORTS
KLETTERSPORT | SPORTS DE MONTAGNE | DEPORTES DE MONTAÑA | SPORT ALPINI

登山／岩登り

climbing | Sportklettern^N | escalade^F | escalada^F | arrampicata^F

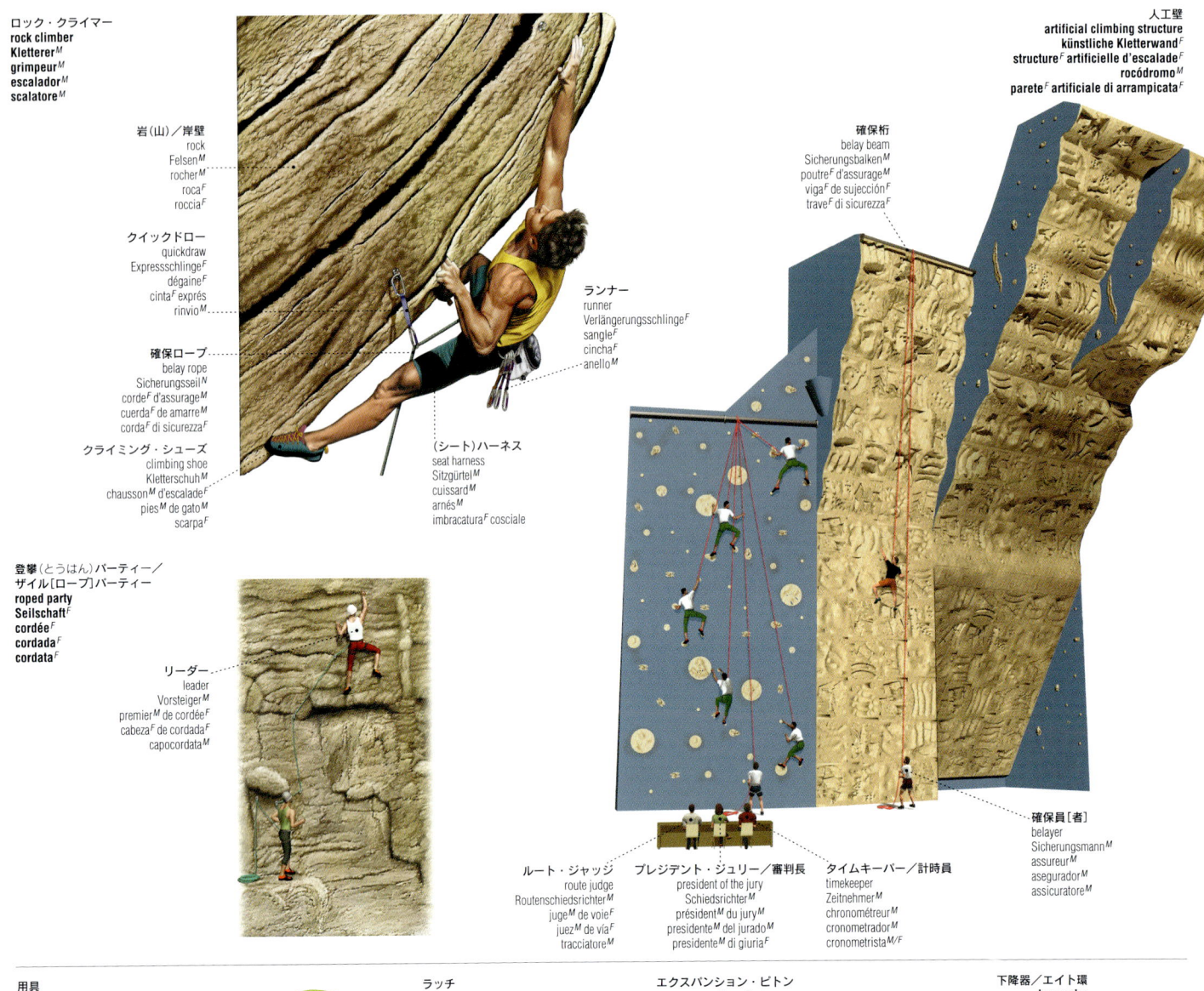

日本語 | 英語 | ドイツ語 | フランス語 | スペイン語 | イタリア語

ロック・クライマー
rock climber
Kletterer^M
grimpeur^M
escalador^M
scalatore^M

岩(山)／岸壁
rock
Felsen^M
rocher^M
roca^F
roccia^F

クイックドロー
quickdraw
Expressschlinge^F
dégaine^F
cinta^F exprés
rinvio^M

確保ロープ
belay rope
Sicherungsseil^N
corde^F d'assurage^F
cuerda^F de amarre^M
corda^F di sicurezza^F

クライミング・シューズ
climbing shoe
Kletterschuh^M
chausson^M d'escalade^F
pies^M de gato^F
scarpa^F

ランナー
runner
Verlängerungsschlinge^F
sangle^F
cincha^F
anello^M

(シート)ハーネス
seat harness
Sitzgürtel^M
cuissard^M
arnés^M
imbracatura^F cosciale

人工壁
artificial climbing structure
künstliche Kletterwand^F
structure^F artificielle d'escalade^F
rocódromo^M
parete^F artificiale di arrampicata^F

確保桁
belay beam
Sicherungsbalken^M
poutre^F d'assurage^M
viga^F de sujeción^F
trave^F di sicurezza^F

登攀(とうはん)パーティー／ザイル[ロープ]パーティー
roped party
Seilschaft^F
cordée^F
cordada^F
cordata^F

リーダー
leader
Vorsteiger^M
premier^M de cordée^F
cabeza^F de cordada^F
capocordata^M

ルート・ジャッジ
route judge
Routenschiedsrichter^M
juge^M de voie^F
juez^M de vía^F
tracciatore^M

プレジデント・ジュリー／審判長
president of the jury
Schiedsrichter^M
président^M du jury^M
presidente^M del jurado^M
presidente^M di giuria^F

タイムキーパー／計時員
timekeeper
Zeitnehmer^M
chronométreur^M
cronometrador^M
cronometrista$^{M/F}$

確保員[者]
belayer
Sicherungsmann^M
assureur^M
asegurador^M
assicuratore^M

用具
equipment
Ausrüstung^F
équipement^M
equipo^M
attrezzatura^F

スクリュースリーブ
screwsleeve
Manschette^F
bague^F filetée
cierre^M de rosca^F
ghiera^F di bloccaggio^M

ラッチ
latch
Haken^M
bec^M
traba^F
tenone^M

ゲート
gate
Schraubfeder^F
doigt^M
dedo^M
dito^M

エクスパンション・ピトン
expansion piton
Expansionsbohrhaken^M
piton^M à expansion^F
pitón^M de expansión^F
chiodo^M a espansione^F

チョック／ナット
chock
Klemmschlaufe^F
coinceur^M
cuña^F
blocco^M da incastro^M

下降器／エイト環
descender
Abseilhaken^M
descendeur^M
descensor^M de ocho^M
discensore^M

安全環付きカラビナ
locking carabiner; locking karabiner
Schraubkarabiner^M
mousqueton^M à vis^F
mosquetón^M de bloqueo^M
moschettone^M a ghiera^F

ピトン／ハーケン
piton
Kletterhaken^M
piton^M
pitón^M
chiodo^M da roccia^F

ワイヤー・スリング
wire sling
Drahtschlinge^F
câble^M d'acier^M
cable^M de acero^M
cavo^M di acciaio^M

D型カラビナ
D carabiner
D-Karabiner^M
mousqueton^M en D^M
mosquetón^M curvo
moschettone^M a D

ザイル／登山用ロープ
rope
Seil^N
corde^F
cuerda^F
corda^F

刃
blade
Spitze^F
lame^F
pata^F
lama^F

通し穴
eye
Auge^N
œil^M
ojo^M
occhiello^M

(シート)ハーネス
seat harness
Sitzgürtel^M
cuissard^M
arnés^M
imbracatura^F cosciale

スポーツとゲーム

900

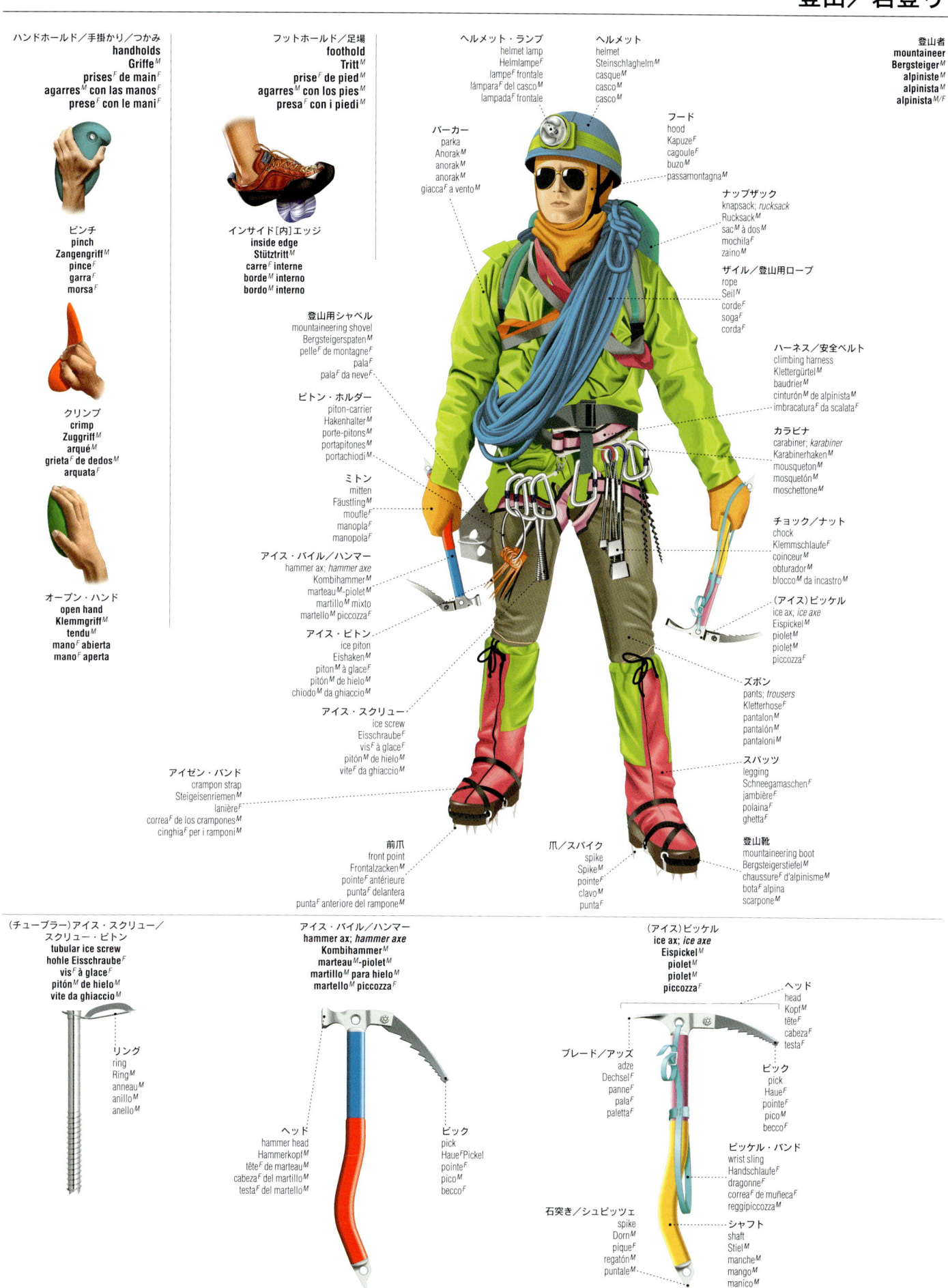

マウンテン・スポーツ｜MOUNTAIN SPORTS
KLETTERSPORT｜SPORTS DE MONTAGNE｜DEPORTES DE MONTAÑA｜SPORT ALPINI

登山／岩登り

ハンドホールド／手掛かり／つかみ
handholds
Griffe M
prises F de main
agarres M con las manos F
prese F con le mani F

ピンチ
pinch
Zangengriff M
pince F
garra F
morsa F

クリンプ
crimp
Zuggriff M
arqué M
grieta F de dedos M
arquata F

オープン・ハンド
open hand
Klemmgriff M
tendu M
mano F abierta
mano F aperta

フットホールド／足場
foothold
Tritt M
prise F de pied
agarres M con los pies F
presa F con i piedi M

インサイド[内]エッジ
inside edge
Stütztritt M
carre F interne
borde M interno
bordo M interno

ヘルメット・ランプ
helmet lamp
Helmlampe F
lampe F frontale
lámpara F del casco M
lampada F frontale

ヘルメット
helmet
Steinschlaghelm M
casque M
casco M
casco M

パーカー
parka
Anorak M
anorak M
anorak M
giacca F a vento M

登山用シャベル
mountaineering shovel
Bergsteigerspaten M
pelle F de montagne F
pala F
pala F da neve F

ピトン・ホルダー
piton-carrier
Hakenhalter M
porte-pitons M
portapitones M
portachiodi M

ミトン
mitten
Fäustling M
moufle F
manopla F
manopola F

アイス・バイル／ハンマー
hammer ax; hammer axe
Kombihammer M
marteau M-piolet M
martillo M mixto
martello F piccozza M

アイス・ピトン
ice piton
Eishaken M
piton M à glace F
pitón M de hielo M
chiodo M da ghiaccio M

アイス・スクリュー
ice screw
Eisschraube F
vis F à glace F
pitón M de hielo M
vite F da ghiaccio M

アイゼン・バンド
crampon strap
Steigeisenriemen M
lanière F
correa F de los crampones M
cinghia F per i ramponi M

前爪
front point
Frontalzacken M
pointe F antérieure
punta F delantera
punta F anteriore del rampone M

フード
hood
Kapuze F
cagoule F
buzo M
passamontagna M

ナップザック
knapsack; rucksack
Rucksack M
sac M à dos M
mochila F
zaino M

ザイル／登山用ロープ
rope
Seil N
corde F
soga F
corda F

ハーネス／安全ベルト
climbing harness
Klettergürtel M
baudrier M
cinturón M de alpinista M
imbracatura F da scalata F

カラビナ
carabiner; karabiner
Karabinerhaken M
mousqueton M
mosquetón M
moschettone M

チョック／ナット
chock
Klemmschlaufe F
coinceur M
obturador M
blocco M da incastro M

(アイス)ピッケル
ice ax; ice axe
Eispickel M
piolet M
piolet M
piccozza F

ズボン
pants; trousers
Kletterhose F
pantalon M
pantalón M
pantaloni M

スパッツ
legging
Schneegamaschen F
jambière F
polaina F
ghetta F

登山靴
mountaineering boot
Bergsteigerstiefel M
chaussure F d'alpinisme M
bota F alpina
scarpone M

爪／スパイク
spike
Spike M
pointe F
clavo M
punta F

登山者
mountaineer
Bergsteiger M
alpiniste M
alpinista M
alpinista M/F

(チューブラー)アイス・スクリュー／スクリュー・ピトン
tubular ice screw
hohle Eisschraube F
vis F à glace F
pitón M de hielo M
vite F da ghiaccio M

リング
ring
Ring M
anneau M
anillo M
anello M

アイス・バイル／ハンマー
hammer ax; hammer axe
Kombihammer M
marteau M-piolet M
martillo M para hielo M
martello M piccozza F

ヘッド
hammer head
Hammerkopf M
tête F de marteau M
cabeza F del martillo M
testa F del martello M

ピック
pick
Haue F Pickel
pointe F
pico M
becco F

(アイス)ピッケル
ice ax; ice axe
Eispickel M
piolet M
piolet M
piccozza F

ヘッド
head
Kopf M
tête F
cabeza F
testa F

ブレード／アッズ
adze
Dechsel M
panne F
pala F
paletta F

ピック
pick
Haue F
pointe F
pico M
becco F

ピッケル・バンド
wrist sling
Handschlaufe F
dragonne F
correa F de muñeca F
reggipiccozza M

石突き／シュピッツェ
spike
Dorn M
pique F
regatón M
puntale M

シャフト
shaft
Stiel M
manche M
mango M
manico M

スポーツとゲーム

アウトドア・レジャー | OUTDOOR LEISURE
FREIZEIT IN DER NATUR | LOISIRS DE PLEIN AIR | OCIO AL AIRE LIBRE | TEMPO LIBERO ALL'ARIA APERTA

キャンプ

日本語 | 英語 | ドイツ語 | フランス語 | スペイン語 | イタリア語

camping | Camping[N] | camping[M] | camping[M] | campeggio[M]

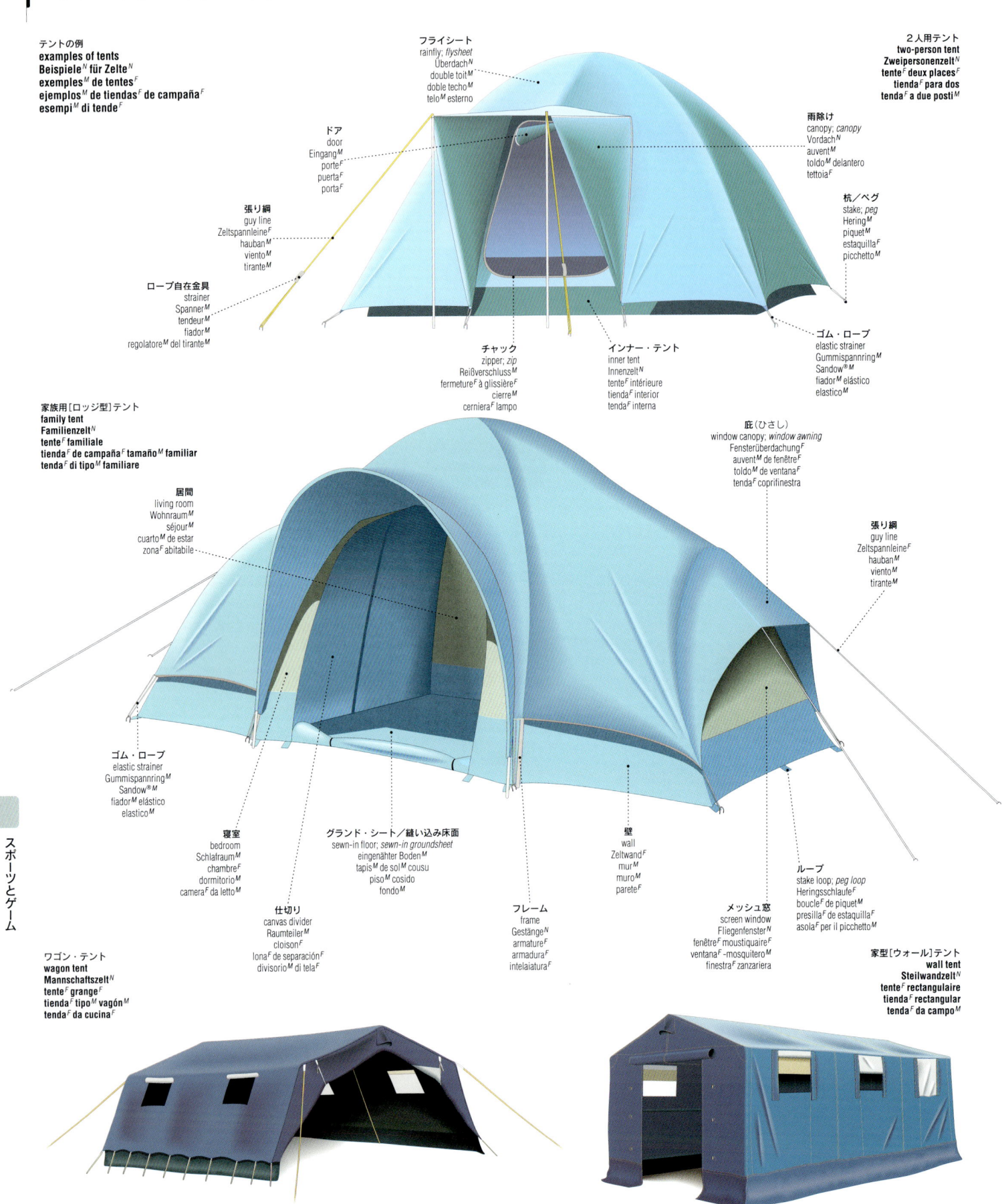

テントの例
examples of tents
Beispiele[N] für Zelte[N]
exemples[M] de tentes[F]
ejemplos[M] de tiendas[F] de campaña[F]
esempi[M] di tende[F]

フライシート
rainfly; flysheet
Überdach[N]
double toit[M]
doble techo[M]
telo[M] esterno

2人用テント
two-person tent
Zweipersonenzelt[N]
tente[F] deux places[F]
tienda[F] para dos
tenda[F] a due posti[M]

ドア
door
Eingang[M]
porte[F]
puerta[F]
porta[F]

雨除け
canopy; canopy
Vordach[N]
auvent[M]
toldo[M] delantero
tettoia[F]

張り綱
guy line
Zeltspannleine[F]
hauban[M]
viento[M]
tirante[M]

杭／ペグ
stake; peg
Hering[M]
piquet[M]
estaquilla[F]
picchetto[M]

ロープ自在金具
strainer
Spanner[M]
tendeur[M]
fiador[M]
regolatore[M] del tirante[M]

ゴム・ロープ
elastic strainer
Gummispannring[M]
Sandow®[M]
fiador[M] elástico
elastico[M]

チャック
zipper; zip
Reißverschluss[M]
fermeture[F] à glissière[F]
cierre[M]
cerniera[F] lampo

インナー・テント
inner tent
Innenzelt[N]
tente[F] intérieure
tienda[F] interior
tenda[F] interna

家族用［ロッジ型］テント
family tent
Familienzelt[N]
tente[F] familiale
tienda[F] de campaña[F] tamaño[M] familiar
tenda[F] di tipo[M] familiare

庇（ひさし）
window canopy; window awning
Fensterüberdachung[F]
auvent[M] de fenêtre[F]
toldo[M] de ventana[F]
tenda[F] coprifinestra

居間
living room
Wohnraum[M]
séjour[M]
cuarto[M] de estar
zona[F] abitabile

張り綱
guy line
Zeltspannleine[F]
hauban[M]
viento[M]
tirante[M]

ゴム・ロープ
elastic strainer
Gummispannring[M]
Sandow®[M]
fiador[M] elástico
elastico[M]

寝室
bedroom
Schlafraum[M]
chambre[F]
dormitorio[M]
camera[F] da letto[M]

グランド・シート／縫い込み床面
sewn-in floor; sewn-in groundsheet
eingenähter Boden[M]
tapis[M] de sol[M] cousu
piso[M] cosido
fondo[M]

壁
wall
Zeltwand[F]
mur[M]
muro[M]
parete[F]

ループ
stake loop; peg loop
Heringsschlaufe[F]
boucle[F] de piquet[M]
presilla[F] de estaquilla[F]
asola[F] per il picchetto[M]

仕切り
canvas divider
Raumteiler[M]
cloison[F]
lona[F] de separación[F]
divisorio[M] di tela[F]

フレーム
frame
Gestänge[N]
armature[F]
armadura[F]
intelaiatura[F]

メッシュ窓
screen window
Fliegenfenster[N]
fenêtre[F] moustiquaire
ventana[F] -mosquitero[M]
finestra[F] zanzariera

ワゴン・テント
wagon tent
Mannschaftszelt[N]
tente[F] grange[F]
tienda[F] tipo[M] vagón[M]
tenda[F] da cucina[F]

家型［ウォール］テント
wall tent
Steilwandzelt[N]
tente[F] rectangulaire
tienda[F] rectangular
tenda[F] da campo[M]

スポーツとゲーム

アウトドア・レジャー | OUTDOOR LEISURE
FREIZEIT IN DER NATUR | LOISIRS DE PLEIN AIR | OCIO AL AIRE LIBRE | TEMPO LIBERO ALL'ARIA APERTA

キャンプ

バップ[楔(くさび)形]テント
pup tent; *ridge tent*
Hauszelt^N
tente^F canadienne
tienda^F de campaña^F clásica
tenda^F canadese

フライシート
rainfly; *flysheet*
Überdach^N
double toit^M
doble toldo^M
telo^M esterno

ルーフ・ポール
roof pole
Zeltstange^F
mât^M de toit^M
palo^M de la tienda^F
palo^M frontale

ゴム・ロープ
elastic strainer
Gummispannring^M
Sandow®^{M}
fiador^M elástico
elastico^M

インナー・テント
inner tent
Innenzelt^N
tente^F intérieure
tienda^F interior
tenda^F interna

ドア
door
Eingang^M
porte^F
puerta^F
porta^F

ループ
stake loop; *peg loop*
Heringsschlaufe^F
boucle^F de piquet^M
presilla^F de estaquilla^F
asola^F per il picchetto^M

グランド・シート／縫い込み床面
sewn-in floor; *sewn-in groundsheet*
eingenähter Boden^M
tapis^M de sol^M cousu
piso^M cosido
fondo^M

杭／ペグ
stake; *peg*
Hering^M
piquet^M
estaquilla^F
picchetto^M

1人用テント
one-person tent
Einpersonenzelt^N
tente^F individuelle
tienda^F unipersonal
tenda^F a un posto^M

ドーム型テント
dome tent
Kuppelzelt^N
tente^F dôme^M
tienda^F tipo^M domo^M
tenda^F a cupola^F

ポップ・アップ・テント
pop-up tent
Igluzelt^N
tente^F igloo^M
tienda^F tipo^M iglú^M
tenda^F a igloo^M

ランタン
lantern
Lampe^F
lanterne^F
linterna^F
lanterna^F

バーナー・フレーム
burner frame
Brennsockel^M
bâti^M du brûleur^M
armazón^M del quemador^M
telaio^M del bruciatore^M

プロパン器具またはブタン器具
propane or butane accessories
Propan- oder Butangas-Geräte^N
accessoires^M au propane^M ou au butane^M
equipos^M de gas^M
accessori^M a propano^M o butano^M

火屋（ほや）
globe
Glas^N
globe^M
globo^M
globo^M di vetro^M

圧力調節つまみ
pressure regulator
Gasstromregulierung^F
régulateur^M de pression^F
regulador^M de presión^F
regolatore^M di luminosità^F

ヒーター
heater
Heizstrahler^M
chaufferette^F
calentador^M
stufa^F a gas^M

ポンプ（ノブ）
pump
Pumpe^F
pompe^F
bomba^F
pompa^F

燃料キャップ／密封栓
leakproof cap
Dichtverschluss^M
bouchon^M antifuite
tapón^M hermético
capsula^F ermetica

燃料タンク／油壺
tank
Gasbehälter^M
réservoir^M
tanque^M
bombola^F

ツー・バーナーのキャンプ用コンロ
double-burner camp stove
zweiflammiger Gasbrenner^M
réchaud^M à deux feux^M
cocina^F de campo^M
fornello^M da campo^M a due fuochi^M

バーナー
burner
Brenner^M
brûleur^M
quemador^M
bruciatore^M

燃料タンク
tank
Gasbehälter^M
réservoir^M
bombona^F de gas^M
bombola^F

火格子／焼き網
wire support
Metallaufsatz^M
grille^F stabilisatrice
parrilla^F estabilizadora
griglia^F

シングル・バーナーのキャンプ用コンロ
single-burner camp stove
einflammiger Gasbrenner^M
réchaud^M à un feu^M
camping^F gas^M
fornello^M da campo^M con un bruciatore^M

火力調節バルブ
control valve
Reglerventil^N
robinet^M relais^M
válvula^F de control^M
manopola^F di regolazione^F del gas^M

スポーツとゲーム

アウトドア・レジャー | OUTDOOR LEISURE
FREIZEIT IN DER NATUR | LOISIRS DE PLEIN AIR | OCIO AL AIRE LIBRE | TEMPO LIBERO ALL'ARIA APERTA

キャンプ

日本語 | 英語 | ドイツ語 | フランス語 | スペイン語 | イタリア語

寝袋[シュラ(ー)フ／スリーピング・バッグ]の種類
examples of sleeping bags
Beispiele^N für Schlafsäcke^M
exemples^M de sacs^M de couchage^M
ejemplos^M de sacos^M de dormir
esempi^M di sacchi^M a pelo^M

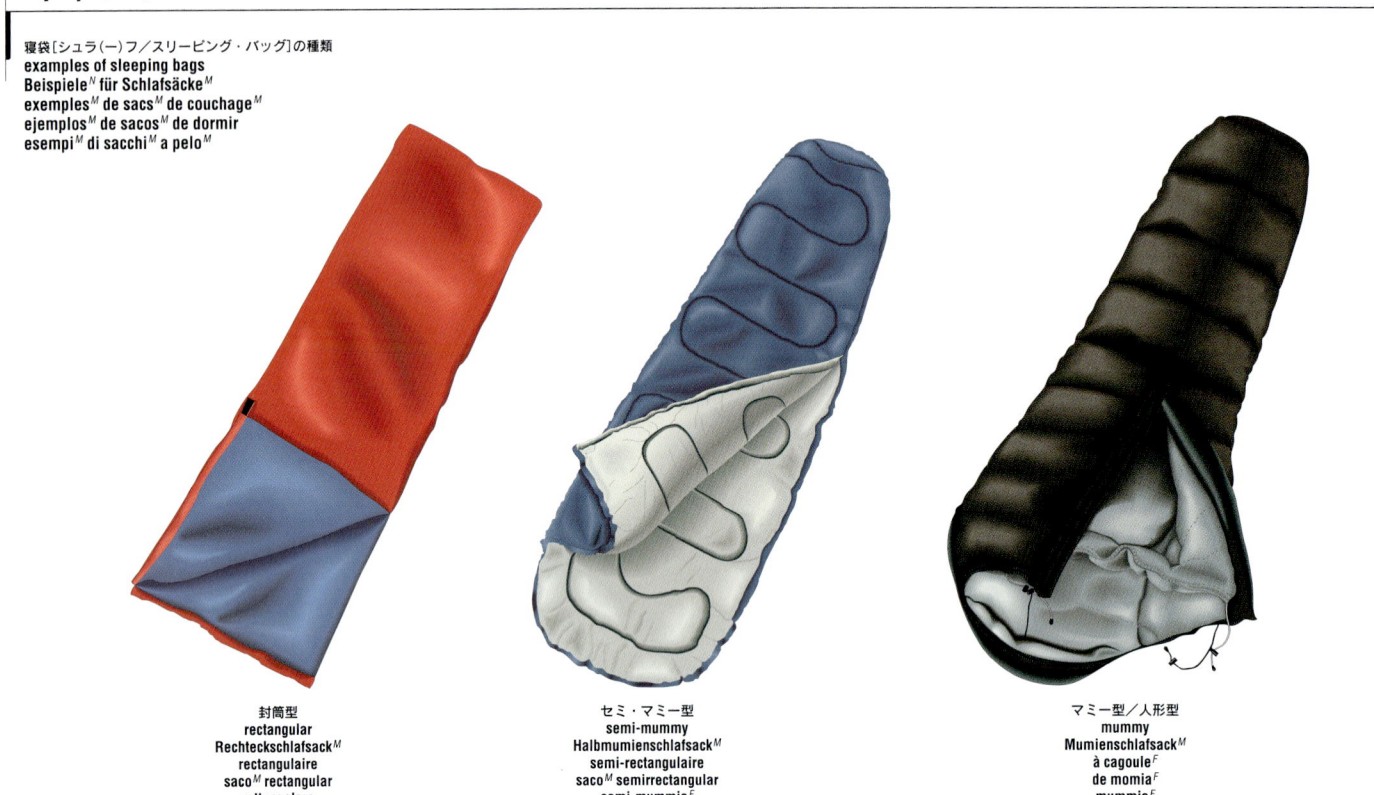

封筒型
rectangular
Rechteckschlafsack^M
rectangulaire
saco^M rectangular
rettangolare

セミ・マミー型
semi-mummy
Halbmumienschlafsack^M
semi-rectangulaire
saco^M semirrectangular
semi-mummia^F

マミー型／人形型
mummy
Mumienschlafsack^M
à cagoule^F
de momia^F
mummia^F

ベッドとマット(レス)
bed and mattress
Bett^N mit Matratze^F
lit^M et matelas^M
camas^F y colchonetas^F
branda^F e materassino^M

簡易携帯用ベッド
folding cot; *camp bed*
Feldbett^N
lit^M de camp^M pliant
catre^M desmontable
brandina^F smontabile

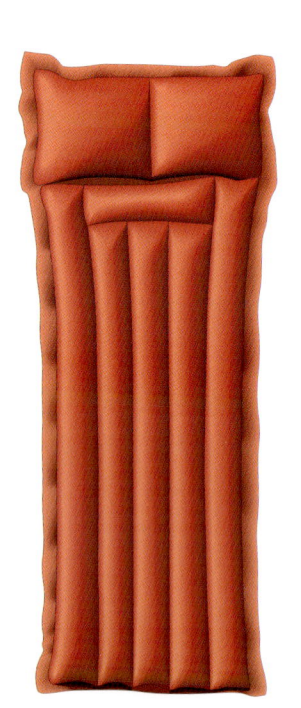

エア・マット(レス)
air mattress
Luftmatratze^F
matelas^M pneumatique
colchoneta^F de aire^M
materassino^M pneumatico

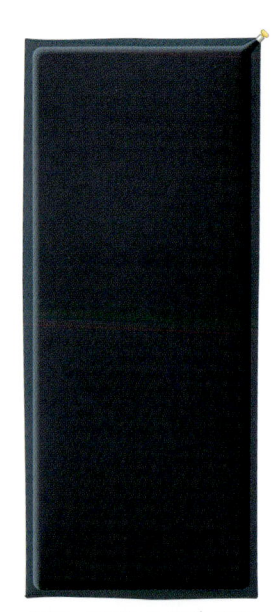

セルフ・インフレーティング・マット
self-inflating mattress
selbstaufblasbare Luftmatratze^F
matelas^M autogonflant
colchoneta^F aislante
materassino^M autogonfiante

フォーム・パッド[マット(レス)]
foam pad
Schaumgummimatratze^F
matelas^M mousse
colcheta^F de espuma^F
materassino^M isolante

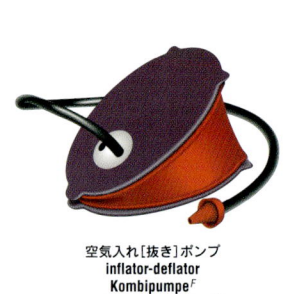

空気入れ[抜き]ポンプ
inflator-deflator
Kombipumpe^F
gonfleur^M-dégonfleur^M
muelle^M para inflar y desinflar
gonfiatore^M a soffietto^M

空気(入れ)ポンプ
inflator
Blasebalg^M
gonfleur^M
inflador^M
gonfiatore^M

スポーツとゲーム

904

アウトドア・レジャー | OUTDOOR LEISURE
FREIZEIT IN DER NATUR | LOISIRS DE PLEIN AIR | OCIO AL AIRE LIBRE | TEMPO LIBERO ALL'ARIA APERTA

キャンプ

食器類
cutlery set
Essbesteck^N
ustensiles^M de campeur^M
cubertería^F
posate^F

炊事用具
cooking set
Kochgeschirr^N
popote^F
utensilios^M de cocina^F
set^M per cucinare

スプーン
spoon
Löffel^M
cuiller^F
cuchara^F
cucchiaio^M

ベルト・ループ
belt loop
Gürtelschlaufe^F
ganse^F
presilla^F
asola^F

皿
plate
Teller^M
assiette^F plate
plato^M
piatto^M

フォーク
fork
Gabel^F
fourchette^F
tenedor^M
forchetta^F

入れ物／袋
sheath
Hülle^F
étui^M
funda^F
fodero^M

ナイフ
knife
Messer^N
couteau^M
cuchillo^M
coltello^M

コッヘル／ソースパン
saucepan
Kochtopf^M
faitout^M
cazuela^F
tegame^M

柄／取っ手
handle
Griff^M
queue^F
mango^M
manico^M

フライ・パン
frying pan
Bratpfanne^F
poêle^F
sartén^F
padella^F

コーヒー・ポット
coffee pot
Kaffeekanne^F
cafetière^F
cafetera^F
caffettiera^F

カップ
cup
Tasse^F
tasse^F
taza^F
tazza^F

鋏（はさみ）
scissors
Schere^F
ciseaux^M
tijeras^F
forbici^F

魚のうろこ落とし
fish scaler
Fischschupper^M
écailleur^M
descamador^M
desquamatore^M

定規
ruler
Lineal^N
règle^F graduée
regla^F
righello^M

キャンプ用品
camping equipment
Campingausrüstung^F
matériel^M de camping
equipamiento^M para acampar
attrezzature^F da campeggio^M

やすり
file
Feile^F
lime^F
lima^F
lima^F

スイス・アーミー・ナイフ
Swiss Army knife
schweizer Offiziersmesser^N
couteau^M suisse
navaja^F multiusos suiza
temperino^M multiuso

虫眼鏡
magnifier
Lupe^F
loupe^F
lupa^F
lente^F

スモール・ブレード
pen blade; small blade
kleine Klinge^F
petite lame^F
hoja^F corta
lama^F piccola

プラスねじ回し
cross-tip screwdriver
Kreuzschlitzschraubenzieher^M
tournevis^M cruciforme
destornillador^M en cruz^M
cacciavite^M con punta^F a croce^F

栓抜き
bottle opener
Flaschenöffner^M
décapsuleur^M
abrebotellas^M
apribottiglie^M

ねじ回し
screwdriver
Schraubenzieher^M
tournevis^M
destornillador^M
cacciavite^M

ねじ回し
screwdriver
Schraubenzieher^M
tournevis^M
destornillador^M
cacciavite^M

ラージ・ブレード
large blade
große Klinge^F
grande lame^F
hoja^F larga
lama^F grande

爪欠け
nail nick
Nagelzieher^M
onglet^M
muesca^F de apertura^F
unghia^F per apertura^F

缶切り
can opener; tin opener
Dosenöffner^M
ouvre-boîtes^M
abrelatas^M
apriscatole^M

錐（きり）／穴空け具
awl
Ahle^F
poinçon^M
punzón^M
punteruolo^M

コルク栓抜き
corkscrew
Korkenzieher^M
tire-bouchon^M
sacacorchos^M
cavatappi^M

アウトドア・レジャー｜OUTDOOR LEISURE
FREIZEIT IN DER NATUR｜LOISIRS DE PLEIN AIR｜OCIO AL AIRE LIBRE｜TEMPO LIBERO ALL'ARIA APERTA

キャンプ

日本語｜英語｜ドイツ語｜フランス語｜スペイン語｜イタリア語

バックパック
backpack
Rucksack^M
sac^M à dos^M
mochila^F
zaino^M

ショルダー・ベルト［ストラップ］／
負い紐（ひも）
shoulder strap
Schultergurt^M
bretelle^F
espaldera^F
spallaccio^M

サイド・コンプレッション・ベルト
side compression strap
seitlicher Kompressionsgurt^M
sangle^F de compression^F
correa^F de compresión^F
cinghia^F di compressione^F laterale

ウエスト・ベルト
waist belt
Hüftgurt^M
ceinture^F
cinturón^M
cintura^F a vita^F

雨蓋（あまぶた）
top flap
Deckeltasche^F
rabat^M
solapa^F
patta^F di chiusura^F

バックル／留め金
tightening buckle
Schließe^F
boucle^F de réglage^M
hebilla^F de regulación^F
fibbia^F di regolazione^F

フロント・コンプレッション・ベルト
front compression strap
vorderer Straffergurt^M
sangle^F de fermeture^F
correa^F de cierre^F
cinghia^F di compressione^F frontale

ストラップ・ループ
strap loop
Riemenschlaufe^F
passe-sangle^M
pasador^M
passacinghia^M

折り畳み式シャベル
folding shovel
Klappspaten^M
pelle^F-pioche^F pliante
pala^F plegable
badile^M pieghevole

ハリケーン・ランプ
hurricane lamp
Sturmlampe^F
lampe^F-tempête^F
lámpara^F de petróleo^M
lampada^F a petrolio^M

魔法瓶
vacuum bottle; *vacuum flask*
Thermosflasche^F
bouteille^F isolante
termo^M
thermos^M

カップ
cup
Becher^M
tasse^F
taza^F
bicchiere^M

ボトル
bottle
Flasche^F
bouteille^F
botella^F del termo^M
bottiglia^F

ストッパー
stopper
Verschluss^M
bouchon^M
tapón^M
tappo^M

水筒
canteen
Feldflasche^F
gourde^F
cantimplora^F
borraccia^F

クーラー・ボックス
cooler
Kühlbox^F
glacière^F
nevera^F
frigo^M portatile

水タンク
water carrier
Wasserkanister^M
cruche^F
termo^M con llave^F de servicio^M
contenitore^M termico

アウトドア・レジャー | OUTDOOR LEISURE
FREIZEIT IN DER NATUR | LOISIRS DE PLEIN AIR | OCIO AL AIRE LIBRE | TEMPO LIBERO ALL'ARIA APERTA

キャンプ

弓鋸（ゆみのこ）
bow saw
Bogensäge^F
scie^F de camping^M
sierra^F de campo^M
sega^F a mano^F

ナイフ
knife
Messer^N
couteau^M
cuchillo^M
coltello^M

革製鞘
leather sheath
Lederschutz^M
étui^M de cuir^M
funda^F de cuero^M
fodero^M di pelle^F

鞘（さや）
sheath
Scheide^F
gaine^F
funda^F
fodero^M

折り畳み式グリル
folding grill
Faltgrill^M
gril^M pliant
parrilla^F plegable
grill^M pieghevole

手斧
hatchet
Beil^N
hachette^F
hacha^F
accetta^F

磁気コンパス
magnetic compass
Magnetkompass^M
boussole^F magnétique
brújula^F magnética
bussola^F magnetica

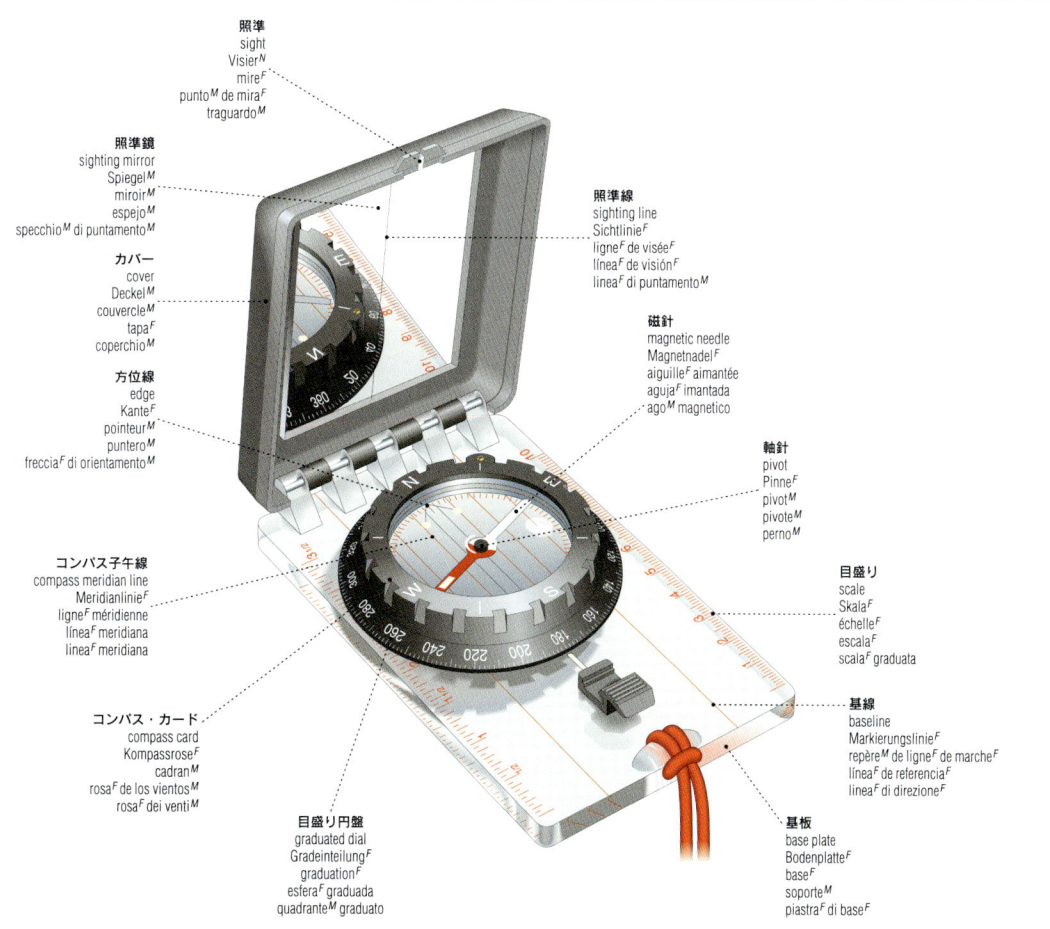

照準
sight
Visier^N
mire^F
punto^M de mira^F
traguardo^M

照準鏡
sighting mirror
Spiegel^M
miroir^M
espejo^M
specchio^M di puntamento^M

カバー
cover
Deckel^M
couvercle^M
tapa^F
coperchio^M

方位線
edge
Kante^F
pointeur^M
puntero^M
freccia^F di orientamento^M

照準線
sighting line
Sichtlinie^F
ligne^F de visée^F
línea^F de visión^F
linea^F di puntamento^M

磁針
magnetic needle
Magnetnadel^F
aiguille^F aimantée
aguja^F imantada
ago^M magnetico

軸針
pivot
Pinne^F
pivot^M
pivote^M
perno^M

目盛り
scale
Skala^F
échelle^F
escala^F
scala^F graduata

コンパス子午線
compass meridian line
Meridianlinie^F
ligne^F méridienne
línea^F meridiana
linea^F meridiana

コンパス・カード
compass card
Kompassrose^F
cadran^M
rosa^F de los vientos^M
rosa^F dei venti^M

目盛り円盤
graduated dial
Gradeinteilung^F
graduation^F
esfera^F graduada
quadrante^M graduato

基線
baseline
Markierungslinie^F
repère^M de ligne^F de marche^F
línea^F de referencia^F
linea^F di direzione^F

基板
base plate
Bodenplatte^F
base^F
soporte^M
piastra^F di base^F

スポーツとゲーム

907

アウトドア・レジャー | OUTDOOR LEISURE
FREIZEIT IN DER NATUR | LOISIRS DE PLEIN AIR | OCIO AL AIRE LIBRE | TEMPO LIBERO ALL'ARIA APERTA

ロープワーク／結び

日本語 | 英語 | ドイツ語 | フランス語 | スペイン語 | イタリア語

knots | Knoten^M | nœuds^M | nudos^M | nodi^M

本[片]結び
square knot
Kreuzknoten^M
nœud^M plat
nudo^M de rizo^M
nodo^M piano

一重(ひとえ)[止め]結び
overhand knot
Hausfrauenknoten^M
nœud^M simple
nudo^M llano
nodo^M semplice

輪奈結び
running bowline
laufender Pahlstek^M
nœud^M coulant
balso^M
nodo^M scorsoio

一重(ひとえ)つなぎ[継ぎ]／はた結び
sheet bend
einfacher Schotstek^M
nœud^M d'écoute^F simple
vuelta^F de escota^F
nodo^M di scotta^F semplice

二重(ふたえ)つなぎ[継ぎ]
double sheet bend
doppelter Schotstek^M
nœud^M d'écoute^F double
vuelta^F de escota^F doble
nodo^M di scotta^F doppio

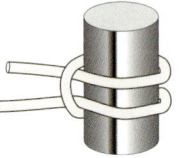

縦[逆さ]結び
granny knot
Altweiberknoten^M
nœud^M de vache^F
nudo^M de tejedor^M
nodo^M vaccaio

縮め[締め]結び
sheepshank
Verkürzungsstek^M
nœud^M de jambe^F de chien^M
margarita^F
nodo^M a margherita^F

ひばり結び
cow hitch
Kuhstek^M
demi-clé^F renversée
vuelta^F de cabo^M
nodo^M bocca^F di lupo^M

巻き結び
clove hitch
Slipstek^M
nœud^M de cabestan^M
nudo^M de dos cotes^M
nodo^M parlato semplice

てぐす結び
fisherman's knot
Fischerknoten^M
nœud^M de pêcheur^M
nudo^M de pescador^M
nodo^M del pescatore^M

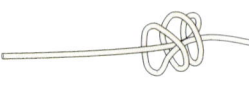

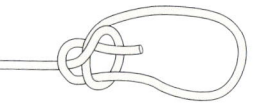

控え綱結び
heaving line knot
Wurflinienknoten^M
nœud^M de Franciscain^M
nudo^M de guía^F
nodo^M parlato doppio

8の字結び
figure-eight knot
Achtknoten^M
nœud^M d'arrêt^M
lasca^F doble
nodo^M Savoia

絡み止め
common whipping
einfacher Takling^M
surliure^F
sobrenudo^M
impalmatura^F normale

舫(もや)い結び
bowline
Pahlstek^M
nœud^M de chaise^F simple
as^M de guía^F
gassa^F d'amante^M

二重(ふたえ)舫い結び
bowline on a bight
doppelter Pahlstek^M
nœud^M de chaise^F double
as^M de guía^F de eslinga^F doble
gassa^F d'amante^M doppia

綯(よ)り継ぎ
short splice
Spleiß^M
épissure^F courte
empalmadura^F
impiombatura^F corta

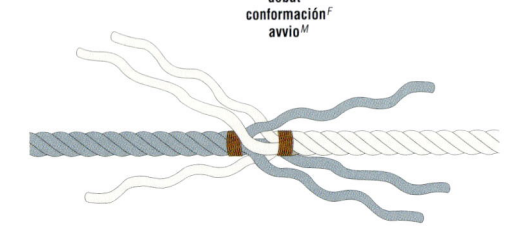

綯り始め
forming
Flechten^N
début^M
conformación^F
avvio^M

綯り終わり
completion
fertige Verbindung^F
fin^F
acabado^M
completamento^M

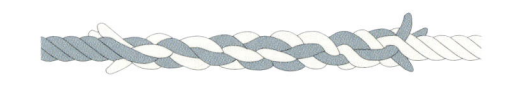

ケーブル
cable
Tauwerk^N
câble^M
cable^M
cavo^M

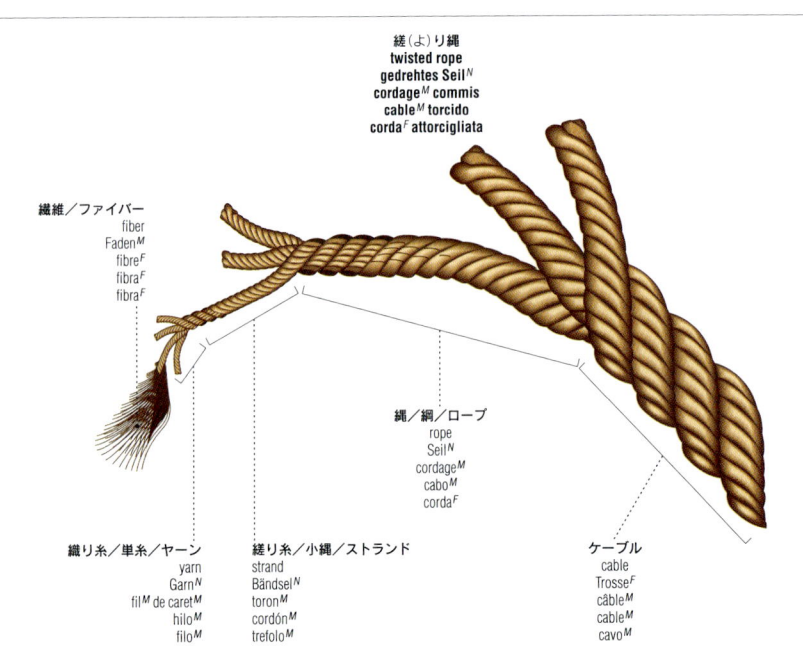

綯(よ)り縄
twisted rope
gedrehtes Seil^N
cordage^M commis
cable^M torcido
corda^F attorcigliata

編み縄
braided rope
geflochtenes Seil^N
cordage^M tressé
cable^M trenzado
corda^F intrecciata

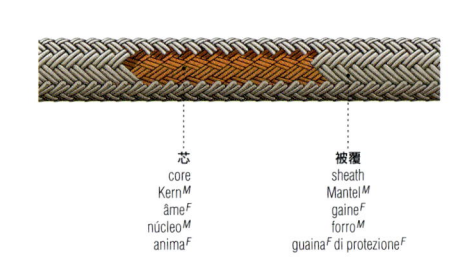

繊維／ファイバー
fiber
Faden^M
fibre^F
fibra^F
fibra^F

縄／綱／ロープ
rope
Seil^N
cordage^M
cabo^M
corda^F

芯
core
Kern^M
âme^F
núcleo^M
anima^F

被覆
sheath
Mantel^M
gaine^F
forro^M
guaina^F di protezione^F

織り糸／単糸／ヤーン
yarn
Garn^N
fil^M de caret^M
hilo^M
filo^M

綯り糸／小縄／ストランド
strand
Bändsel^N
toron^M
cordón^M
trefolo^M

ケーブル
cable
Trosse^F
câble^M
cable^M
cavo^M

アウトドア・レジャー | OUTDOOR LEISURE
FREIZEIT IN DER NATUR | LOISIRS DE PLEIN AIR | OCIO AL AIRE LIBRE | TEMPO LIBERO ALL'ARIA APERTA

釣り

fishing | Sportfischerei^F | pêche^F | pesca^F | pesca^F

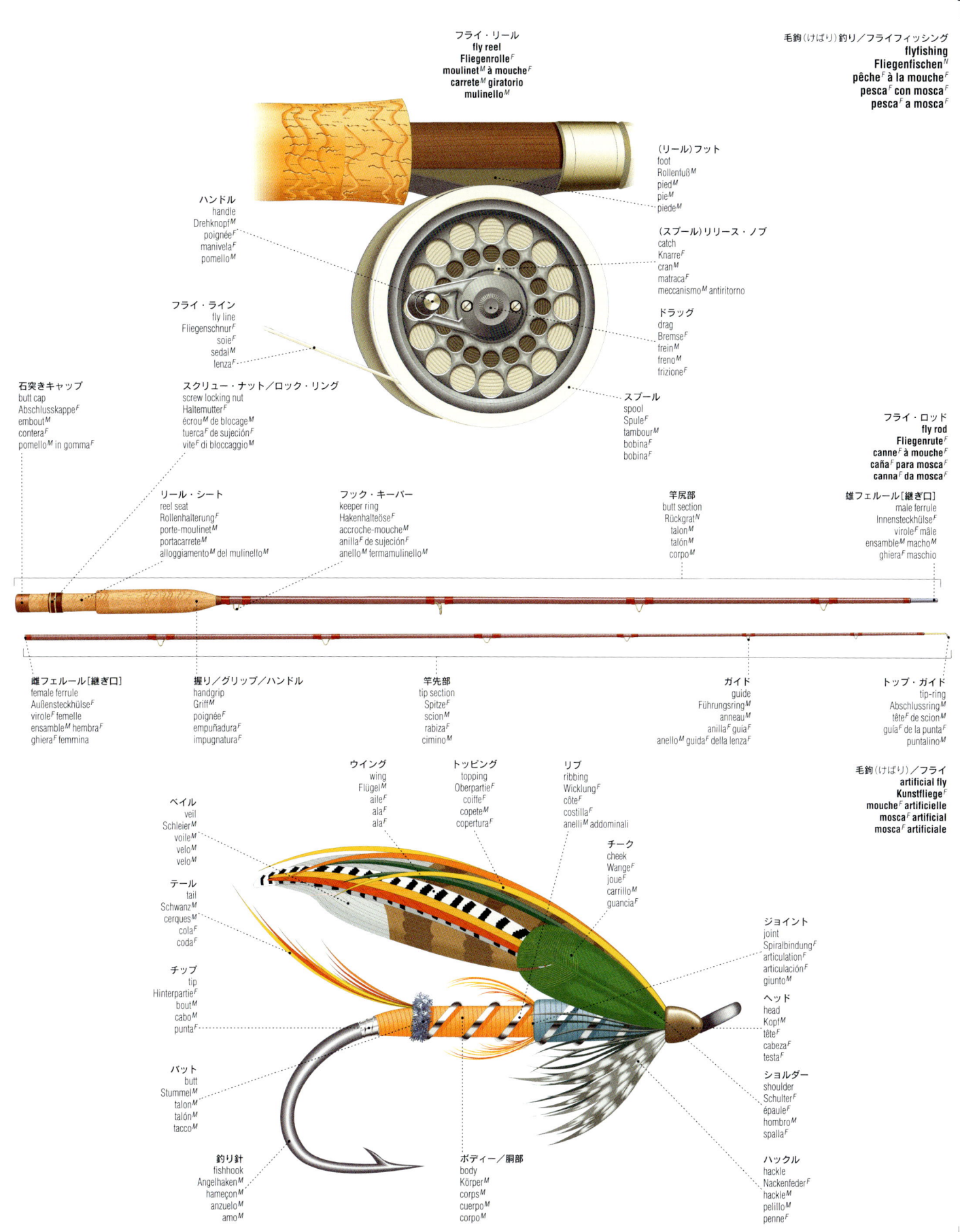

フライ・リール
fly reel
Fliegenrolle^F
moulinet^M à mouche^F
carrete^M giratorio
mulinello^M

毛鉤（けばり）釣り／フライフィッシング
flyfishing
Fliegenfischen^N
pêche^F à la mouche^F
pesca^F con mosca^F
pesca^F a mosca^F

（リール）フット
foot
Rollenfuß^M
pied^M
pie^M
piede^M

ハンドル
handle
Drehknopf^F
poignée^F
manivela^F
pomello^M

（スプール）リリース・ノブ
catch
Knarre^F
cran^M
matraca^F
meccanismo^M antiritorno

フライ・ライン
fly line
Fliegenschnur^F
soie^F
sedal^M
lenza^F

ドラッグ
drag
Bremse^F
frein^M
freno^M
frizione^F

石突きキャップ
butt cap
Abschlusskappe^F
embout^M
contera^F
pomello^M in gomma^F

スクリュー・ナット／ロック・リング
screw locking nut
Haltemutter^F
écrou^M de blocage^M
tuerca^F de sujeción^F
vite^F di bloccaggio^M

スプール
spool
Spule^F
tambour^M
bobina^F
bobina^F

フライ・ロッド
fly rod
Fliegenrute^F
canne^F à mouche^F
caña^F para mosca^F
canna^F da mosca^F

リール・シート
reel seat
Rollenhalterung^F
porte-moulinet^M
portacarrete^M
alloggiamento^M del mulinello^M

フック・キーパー
keeper ring
Hakenhalteöse^F
accroche-mouche^F
anilla^F de sujeción^F
anello^M fermamulinello^M

竿尻部
butt section
Rückgrat^N
talon^M
talón^M
corpo^M

雄フェルール［継ぎ口］
male ferrule
Innensteckhülse^F
virole^F mâle
ensamble^M macho^M
ghiera^F maschio

雌フェルール［継ぎ口］
female ferrule
Außensteckhülse^F
virole^F femelle
ensamble^M hembra^M
ghiera^F femmina

握り／グリップ／ハンドル
handgrip
Griff^M
poignée^F
empuñadura^F
impugnatura^F

竿先部
tip section
Spitze^F
scion^M
rabiza^F
cimino^M

ガイド
guide
Führungsring^M
anneau^M
anilla^F guía
anello^M guida della lenza^F

トップ・ガイド
tip-ring
Abschlussring^M
tête^F de scion^M
guía^F de la punta^F
puntalino^M

ウイング
wing
Flügel^M
aile^F
ala^F
ala^F

トッピング
topping
Oberpartie^F
coiffe^F
copete^M
copertura^F

リブ
ribbing
Wicklung^F
côte^F
costilla^F
anelli addominali

毛鉤（けばり）／フライ
artificial fly
Kunstfliege^F
mouche^F artificielle
mosca^F artificial
mosca^F artificiale

ベイル
veil
Schleier^M
voile^F
velo^M
velo^M

チーク
cheek
Wange^F
joue^F
carrillo^M
guancia^F

テール
tail
Schwanz^M
cerques^M
cola^F
coda^F

ジョイント
joint
Spiralbindung^F
articulation^F
articulación^F
giunto^M

チップ
tip
Hinterpartie^F
bout^M
cabo^M
punta^F

ヘッド
head
Kopf^M
tête^F
cabeza^F
testa^F

バット
butt
Stummel^M
talon^M
talón^M
tacco^M

ショルダー
shoulder
Schulter^F
épaule^F
hombro^M
spalla^F

釣り針
fishhook
Angelhaken^M
hameçon^M
anzuelo^M
amo^M

ボディー／胴部
body
Körper^M
corps^M
cuerpo^M
corpo^M

ハックル
hackle
Nackenfeder^F
hackle^M
pelillo^M
penne^F

スポーツとゲーム

909

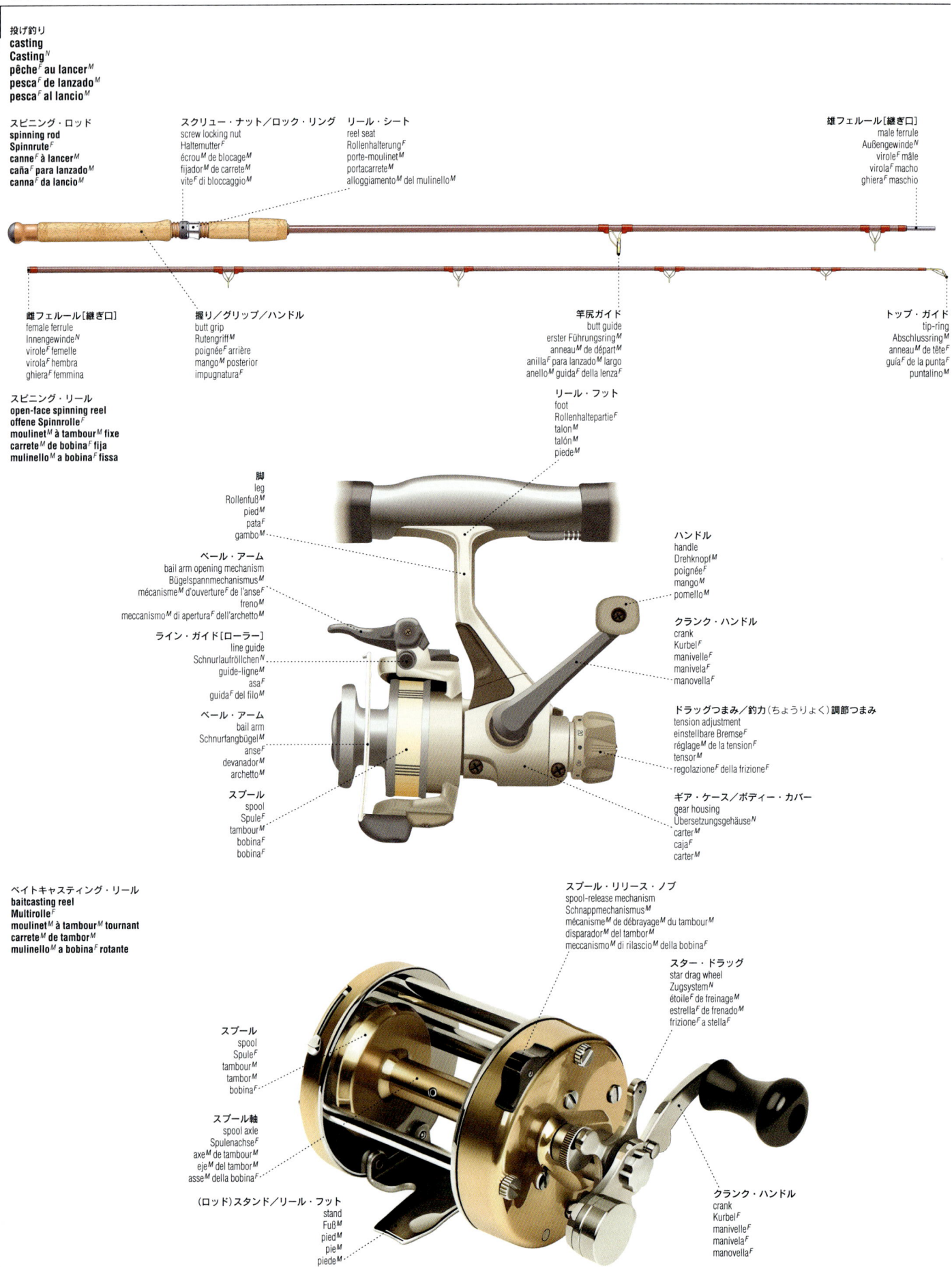

アウトドア・レジャー | OUTDOOR LEISURE
FREIZEIT IN DER NATUR | LOISIRS DE PLEIN AIR | OCIO AL AIRE LIBRE | TEMPO LIBERO ALL'ARIA APERTA

釣り

日本語 | 英語 | ドイツ語 | フランス語 | スペイン語 | イタリア語

投げ釣り
casting
Casting[N]
pêche[F] au lancer[M]
pesca[F] de lanzado[M]
pesca[F] al lancio[M]

スピニング・ロッド
spinning rod
Spinnrute[F]
canne[F] à lancer[M]
caña[F] para lanzado[M]
canna[F] da lancio[M]

スクリュー・ナット／ロック・リング
screw locking nut
Haltemutter[F]
écrou de blocage[M]
fijador[M] de carrete[M]
vite[F] di bloccaggio[M]

リール・シート
reel seat
Rollenhalterung[F]
porte-moulinet[M]
portacarrete[M]
alloggiamento[M] del mulinello[M]

雄フェルール[継ぎ口]
male ferrule
Außengewinde[N]
virole[F] mâle
virola[F] macho
ghiera[F] maschio

雌フェルール[継ぎ口]
female ferrule
Innengewinde[N]
virole[F] femelle
virola[F] hembra
ghiera[F] femmina

握り／グリップ／ハンドル
butt grip
Rutengriff[M]
poignée[F] arrière
mango[M] posterior
impugnatura[F]

竿尻ガイド
butt guide
erster Führungsring[M]
anneau de départ[M]
anilla[F] para lanzado[M] largo
anello[M] guida[F] della lenza[F]

トップ・ガイド
tip-ring
Abschlussring[M]
anneau de tête[F]
guía[F] de la punta[F]
puntalino[M]

スピニング・リール
open-face spinning reel
offene Spinnrolle[F]
moulinet[M] à tambour[M] fixe
carrete[M] de bobina[F] fija
mulinello[M] a bobina[F] fissa

リール・フット
foot
Rollenhaltepartie[F]
talon[M]
talón[M]
piede[M]

脚
leg
Rollenfuß[M]
pied[M]
pata[F]
gambo[M]

ベール・アーム
bail arm opening mechanism
Bügelspannmechanismus[M]
mécanisme[M] d'ouverture[F] de l'anse[F]
freno[M]
meccanismo[M] di apertura[F] dell'archetto[M]

ライン・ガイド[ローラー]
line guide
Schnurlaufröllchen[N]
guide-ligne[M]
asa[F]
guida[F] del filo[M]

ベール・アーム
bail arm
Schnurfangbügel[M]
anse[F]
devanador[M]
archetto[M]

スプール
spool
Spule[F]
tambour[M]
bobina[F]
bobina[F]

ハンドル
handle
Drehknopf[M]
poignée[F]
mango[M]
pomello[M]

クランク・ハンドル
crank
Kurbel[F]
manivelle[F]
manivela[F]
manovella[F]

ドラッグつまみ／釣力（ちょうりょく）調節つまみ
tension adjustment
einstellbare Bremse[F]
réglage[M] de la tension[F]
tensor[M]
regolazione[F] della frizione[F]

ギア・ケース／ボディー・カバー
gear housing
Übersetzungsgehäuse[N]
carter[M]
caja[F]
carter[M]

ベイトキャスティング・リール
baitcasting reel
Multirolle[F]
moulinet[M] à tambour[M] tournant
carrete[M] de tambor[M]
mulinello[M] a bobina[F] rotante

スプール・リリース・ノブ
spool-release mechanism
Schnappmechanismus[M]
mécanisme[M] de débrayage[M] du tambour[M]
disparador[M] del tambor[M]
meccanismo[M] di rilascio[M] della bobina[F]

スター・ドラッグ
star drag wheel
Zugsystem[N]
étoile[F] de freinage[M]
estrella[F] de frenado[M]
frizione[F] a stella[F]

スプール
spool
Spule[F]
tambour[M]
tambor[M]
bobina[F]

スプール軸
spool axle
Spulenachse[F]
axe de tambour[M]
eje[M] del tambor[M]
asse[M] della bobina[F]

(ロッド)スタンド／リール・フット
stand
Fuß[M]
pied[M]
pie[M]
piede[M]

クランク・ハンドル
crank
Kurbel[F]
manivelle[F]
manivela[F]
manovella[F]

アウトドア・レジャー | OUTDOOR LEISURE
FREIZEIT IN DER NATUR | LOISIRS DE PLEIN AIR | OCIO AL AIRE LIBRE | TEMPO LIBERO ALL'ARIA APERTA

釣り

釣り針
fishhook
Angelhaken^M
hameçon^M
anzuelo^M
amo^M

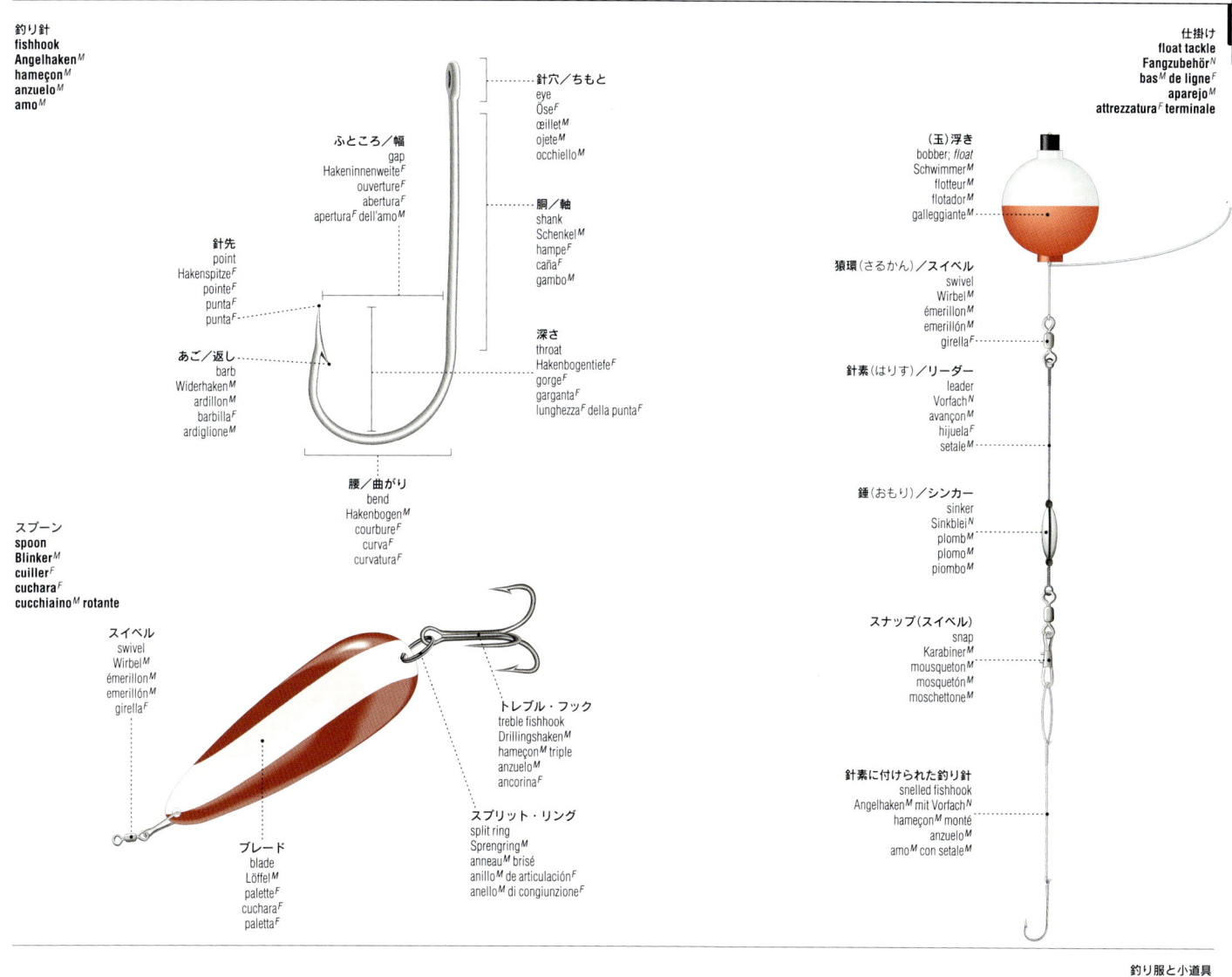

針穴／ちもと
eye
Öse^F
œillet^M
ojete^M
occhiello^M

ふところ／幅
gap
Hakeninnenweite^F
ouverture^F
abertura^F
apertura^F dell'amo^M

胴／軸
shank
Schenkel^M
hampe^F
caña^F
gambo^M

針先
point
Hakenspitze^F
pointe^F
punta^F
punta^F

深さ
throat
Hakenbogentiefe^F
gorge^F
garganta^F
lunghezza^F della punta

あご／返し
barb
Widerhaken^M
ardillon^M
barbilla^F
ardiglione^M

腰／曲がり
bend
Hakenbogen^M
courbure^F
curva^F
curvatura^F

スプーン
spoon
Blinker^M
cuiller^F
cuchara^F
cucchiaino^M rotante

スイベル
swivel
Wirbel^M
émerillon^M
emerillón^M
girella^F

トレブル・フック
treble fishhook
Drillingshaken^M
hameçon^M triple
anzuelo^M
ancorina^F

スプリット・リング
split ring
Sprengring^M
anneau^M brisé
anillo^M de articulación^F
anello^M di congiunzione^F

ブレード
blade
Löffel^M
palette^F
cuchara^F
paletta^F

仕掛け
float tackle
Fangzubehör^N
bas^M de ligne^F
aparejo^M
attrezzatura^F terminale

（玉）浮き
bobber; float
Schwimmer^M
flotteur^M
flotador^M
galleggiante^M

猿環（さるかん）／スイベル
swivel
Wirbel^M
émerillon^M
emerillón^M
girella^F

針素（はりす）／リーダー
leader
Vorfach^N
avançon^M
hijuela^F
setale^M

錘（おもり）／シンカー
sinker
Sinkblei^N
plomb^M
plomo^M
piombo^M

スナップ（スイベル）
snap
Karabiner^M
mousqueton^M
mosquetón^M
moschettone^M

針素に付けられた釣り針
snelled fishhook
Angelhaken^M mit Vorfach^N
hameçon^M monté
anzuelo^M
amo^M con setale^M

釣り服と小道具
clothing and accessories
Kleidung^F und Zubehör^N
vêtements^M et accessoires^M
ropa^F y accesorios^M
abbigliamento^M e accessori^M

タックル・ボックス
tackle box
Spinnerschachtel^F
boîte^F à leurres^M
caja^F de pesca^F
scatola^F portaesche^F

魚籠（びく）
creel
Fischkorb^M
panier^M
cesta^F de pescador^M
cestino^M

（フィッシング）ベスト
fishing vest; *fishing jacket*
Anglerweste^F
veste^F de pêche^F
chaleco^M de pescador^M
giubbotto^M da pescatore^M

ウェーダー
waders
Watstiefel^M
cuissardes^F
botas^F altas
stivaloni^M impermeabili

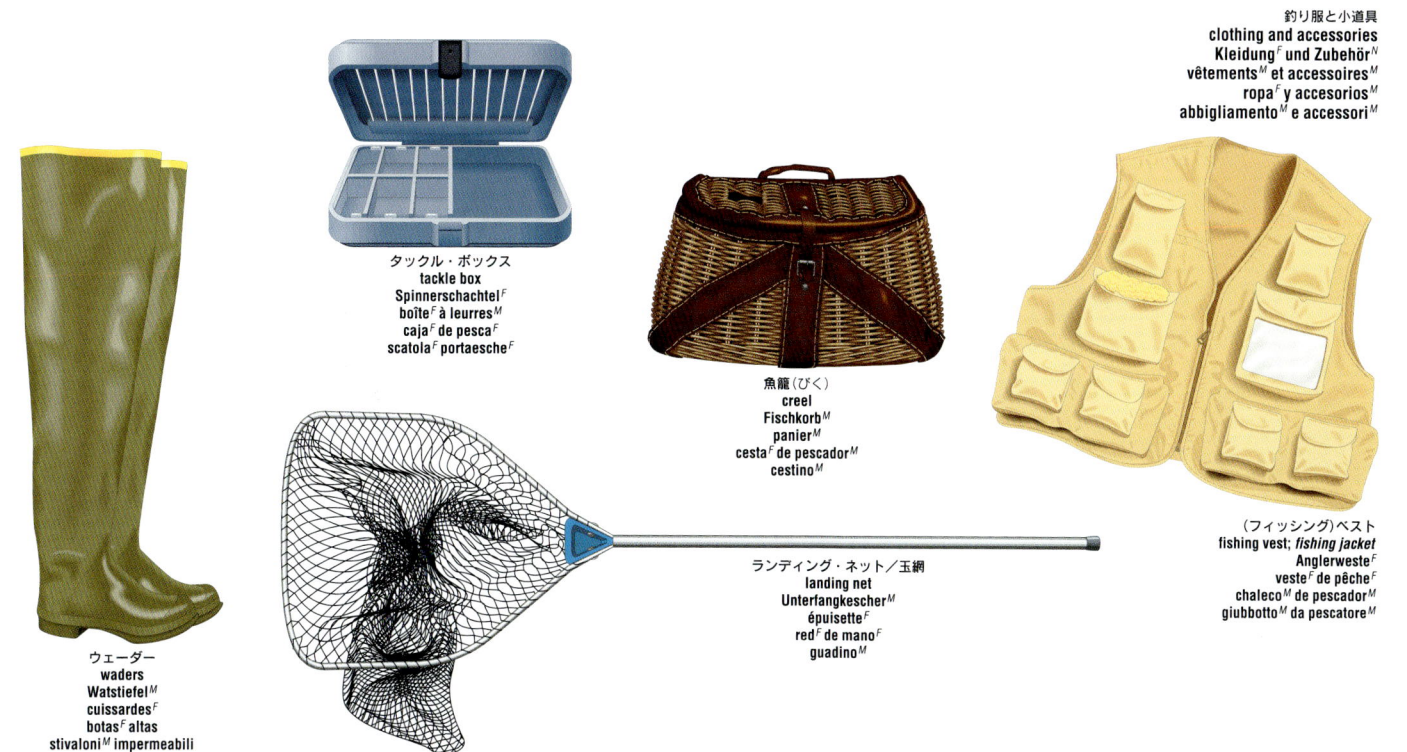

ランディング・ネット／玉網
landing net
Unterfangkescher^M
épuisette^F
red^F de mano^F
guadino^M

スポーツとゲーム

アウトドア・レジャー ｜ OUTDOOR LEISURE
FREIZEIT IN DER NATUR ｜ LOISIRS DE PLEIN AIR ｜ OCIO AL AIRE LIBRE ｜ TEMPO LIBERO ALL'ARIA APERTA

ハンティング／狩猟

日本語 ｜ 英語 ｜ ドイツ語 ｜ フランス語 ｜ スペイン語 ｜ イタリア語

hunting ｜ Jagen^N ｜ chasse^F ｜ caza^F ｜ caccia^F

ライフル銃／小銃（銃腔に旋条がある）
rifle (rifled bore)
Gewehr^N (gezogener Lauf^M)
carabine^F (canon^M rayé)
rifle^M
fucile^M a canna^F rigata

遊底 breechblock / Verschlussstück^N / bloc^M de culasse^F / bloque^M de cierre^M de la recámara^F / blocco^M della culatta^F

銃腔／銃口 muzzle / Mündung^F / bouche^F / boca^F / bocca^F

握把（あくは）／グリップ pistol grip / Kolbenhals^M / poignée^F / empuñadura^F / impugnatura^F a pistola^F

撃鉄 hammer / Hahn^M / chien^M / percutor^M / cane^M

照準眼鏡 telescopic sight / Zielfernrohr^N / lunette^F de visée^F / mira^F telescópica / mirino^M a cannocchiale^F

照門 rear sight / Kimme^F / hausse^F / alza^F / tacca^F di mira^F

照星 front sight / Korn^N / guidon^M / punto^M de mira^F / mirino^M

床尾板 butt plate / Rückschlaghinderer^M / plaque^F de couche^F / cantonera^F / calciolo^M

用心金／トリガー・ガード trigger guard / Abzugbügel^M / pontet^M / guardamonte^M / paragrilletto^M

銃身／バレル barrel / Rohr^N / canon^M / cañón^M / canna^F

銃床／元台／ストック stock / Schäftung^F / crosse^F / culata^F / calcio^M

レバー lever / Bügelhebel^M / levier^M / palanca^F / leva^F

引き金／トリガー trigger / Abzug^M / détente^F / gatillo^M / grilletto^M

銃腔／銃口 muzzle / Mündung^F / bouche^F / boca^F / bocca^F

散弾銃／ショットガン（銃腔が滑らか）
shotgun (smooth-bore)
Schrotflinte^F (glatter Lauf^M)
fusil^M (canon^M lisse)
escopeta^F
fucile^M a canna^F liscia

床尾板 butt plate / Rückschlaghinderer^M / plaque^F de couche^F / cantonera^F / calciolo^M

握把（あくは）／グリップ pistol grip / Pistolengriff^M / poignée^F / empuñadura^F / impugnatura^F a pistola^F

撃鉄 hammer / Hahn^M / chien^M / percutor^M / cane^M

放熱板 ventilated rib / Laufschiene^F / bande^F ventilée / banda^F de ventilación^F / bindella^F ventilata

照星 front sight / Korn^N / guidon^M / punto^M de mira^F / mirino^M

銃床／元台／ストック stock / Schäftung^F / crosse^F / culata^F / calcio^M

遊底 breechblock / Verschlussstück^N / bloc^M de culasse^F / bloque^M de cierre^M de recámara^F / blocco^M della culatta^F

先台／遊底桿（かん）／前木被 forearm / Vorderschaft^M / fût^M / caña^F / asta^F

銃身／バレル barrel / Rohr^N / canon^M / cañón^M / canna^F

用心金／トリガー・ガード trigger guard / Abzugbügel^M / pontet^M / guardamonte^M / paragrilletto^M

引き金／トリガー trigger / Abzug^M / détente^F / gatillo^M / grilletto^M

弾薬筒／薬包／カートリッジ（散弾銃用）
cartridge (shotgun)
Patrone^F (Schrotflinte^F)
cartouche^F (fusil^M)
cartucho^M de escopeta^F
cartuccia^F per fucile^M a canna^F liscia

クリンプ crimping / Faltverschluss^M / sertissage^M / doblez^M hacia el interior / orlatura^F a stella^F

散弾粒 pellets / Schrot^M / plombs^M / carga^F de perdigones^M / pallini^M

プラスチック製の薬莢（やっきょう） plastic case / Plastikhülse^F / douille^F de plastique^M / revestimiento^M / bossolo^M di plastica^F

莢底（きょうてい） base / Boden^M / culot^M / culote^M / fondello^M metallico

送り wad / Pfropf^M / bourre^F / taco^M / borra^F

装薬 charge / Ladung^F / poudre^F / explosivo^M / carica^F di lancio^M

雷管／プライマー primer / Zündhütchen^N / amorce^F / fulminante^M / innesco^M

弾薬筒／薬包／カートリッジ（ライフル銃用）
cartridge (rifle)
Patrone^F (Gewehr^N)
cartouche^F (carabine^F)
cartucho^M de rifle^M
cartuccia^F per fucile^M a canna^F rigata

先端／ノーズ nose / Spitze^F / pointe^F / nariz^F / punta^F

弾芯 core / Kern^M / noyau^M / núcleo^M / nucleo^M

弾頭 bullet / Kugel^F / balle^F / bala^F / pallottola^F

薬莢（やっきょう） case / Hülse^F / douille^F / casquillo^M / bossolo^M

被甲 jacket / Mantel^M / chemise^F / revestimiento^M / incamiciatura^F

発射（火）薬 propellant / Treibladung^F / poudre^F / explosivo^M / carica^F di lancio^M

雷管／プライマー primer / Zündhütchen^N / amorce^F / fulminante^M / innesco^M

莢底（きょうてい） cup / Amboss^M / culot^M / culote^M / fondello^M

スポーツとゲーム

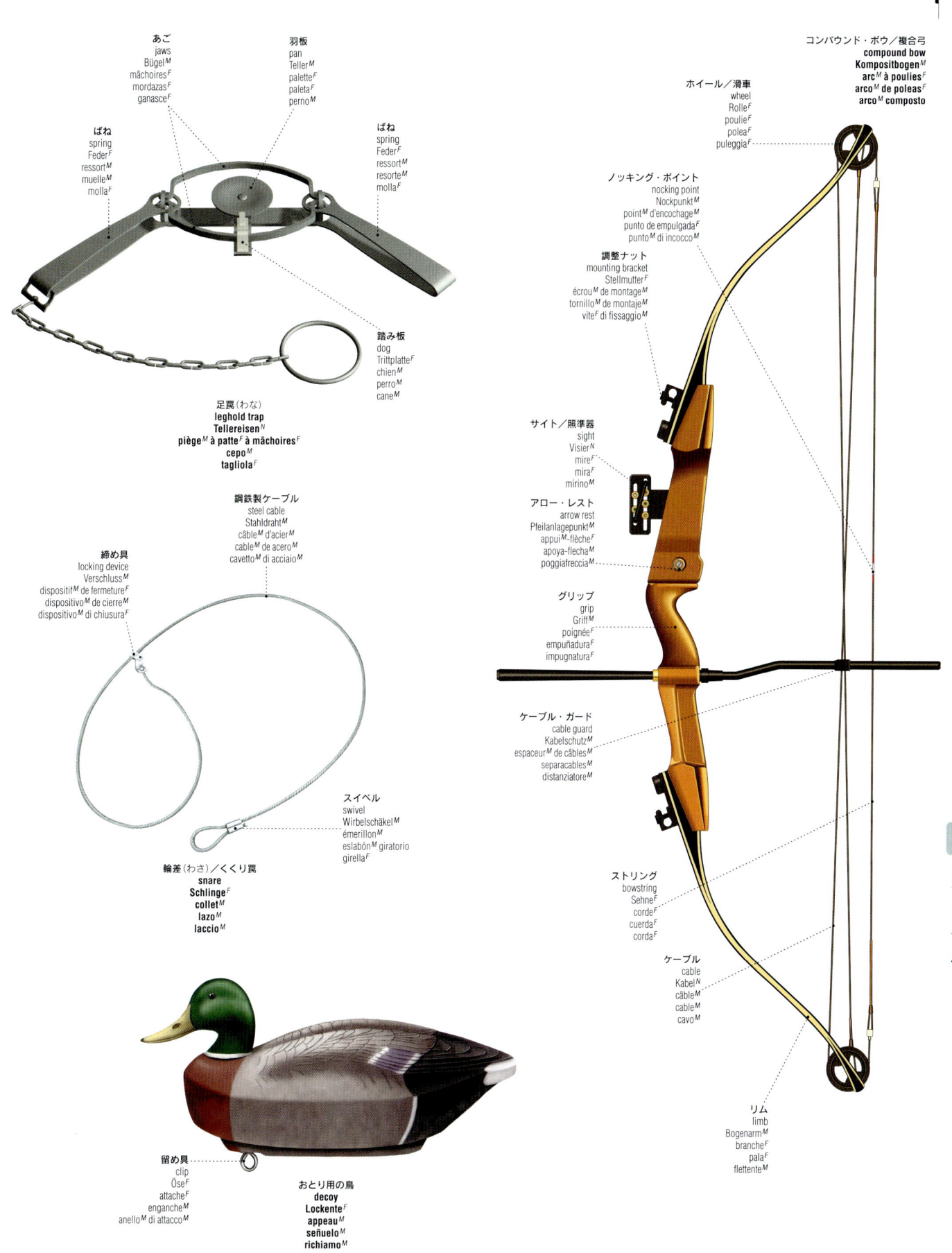

アウトドア・レジャー | OUTDOOR LEISURE
FREIZEIT IN DER NATUR | LOISIRS DE PLEIN AIR | OCIO AL AIRE LIBRE | TEMPO LIBERO ALL'ARIA APERTA

ハンティング／狩猟

あご
jaws
Bügel^M
mâchoires^F
mordazas^F
ganasce^F

羽板
pan
Teller^M
palette^F
paleta^F
perno^M

ばね
spring
Feder^F
ressort^M
muelle^M
molla^F

ばね
spring
Feder^F
ressort^M
resorte^M
molla^F

踏み板
dog
Trittplatte^F
chien^M
perro^M
cane^M

足罠（わな）
leghold trap
Tellereisen^N
piège^M **à patte**^{F} **à mâchoires**^{F}
cepo^M
tagliola^F

鋼鉄製ケーブル
steel cable
Stahldraht^M
câble^M d'acier^M
cable^M de acero^M
cavetto^M di acciaio^M

締め具
locking device
Verschluss^M
dispositif^M de fermeture^F
dispositivo^M de cierre^F
dispositivo^M di chiusura^F

スイベル
swivel
Wirbelschäkel^M
émerillon^M
eslabón^M giratorio
girella^F

輪差（わさ）／くくり罠
snare
Schlinge^F
collet^M
lazo^M
laccio^M

留め具
clip
Öse^F
attache^F
enganche^M
anello^M di attacco^M

おとり用の鳥
decoy
Lockente^F
appeau^M
señuelo^M
richiamo^M

コンパウンド・ボウ／複合弓
compound bow
Kompositbogen^M
arc^M **à poulies**^{F}
arco^M **de poleas**^{F}
arco^M **composto**

ホイール／滑車
wheel
Rolle^F
poulie^F
polea^F
puleggia^F

ノッキング・ポイント
nocking point
Nockpunkt^M
point^M d'encochage^M
punto de empulgada^M
punto^M di incocco^M

調整ナット
mounting bracket
Stellmutter^F
écrou^M de montage^M
tornillo^M de montaje^M
vite^F di fissaggio^M

サイト／照準器
sight
Visier^N
mire^F
mira^F
mirino^M

アロー・レスト
arrow rest
Pfeilanlagepunkt^M
appui^M-flèche^F
apoya-flecha^F
poggiafreccia^M

グリップ
grip
Griff^M
poignée^F
empuñadura^F
impugnatura^F

ケーブル・ガード
cable guard
Kabelschutz^M
espaceur^M de câbles^M
separacables^M
distanziatore^M

ストリング
bowstring
Sehne^F
corde^F
cuerda^F
corda^F

ケーブル
cable
Kabel^N
câble^M
cable^M
cavo^M

リム
limb
Bogenarm^M
branche^F
pala^F
flettente^M

スポーツとゲーム

ゲーム | GAMES
SPIELE | JEUX | JUEGOS | GIOCHI

さいころ[ダイス]とドミノ牌（はい）

dice and dominoes | Würfel^M und Dominosteine^M | dés et dominos^M | dados^M y dominós^M | dadi^M e domino^M

日本語 | 英語 | ドイツ語 | フランス語 | スペイン語 | イタリア語

ふつうのさいころ
ordinary die
gewöhnlicher Würfel^M
dé^M régulier
dado^M común
dado^M comune

ポーカー・ダイス
poker die
Pokerwürfel^M
dé^M à poker
dado^M de póquer
dado^M da poker^M

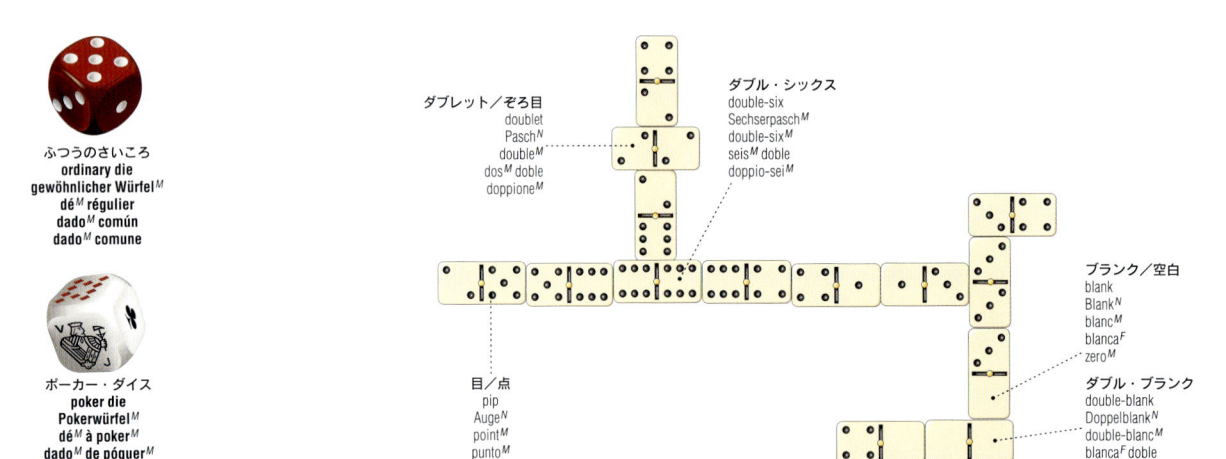

ダブレット／ぞろ目
doublet
Pasch^N
double^M
dos^M doble
doppione^M

ダブル・シックス
double-six
Sechserpasch^M
double-six^M
seis^M doble
doppio-sei^M

目／点
pip
Auge^N
point^M
punto^M
punto^M

ブランク／空白
blank
Blank^N
blanc^M
blanca^F
zero^M

ダブル・ブランク
double-blank
Doppelblank^N
double-blanc^M
blanca^F doble
doppio-zero^M

トランプ／カード

cards | Kartenspiele^N | cartes^F | baraja^F | giochi^M di carte^F

シンボル（マーク）
symbols
Farben^F
symboles^M
símbolos^M
simboli^M

ハート
heart
Herz^N
cœur^M
corazón^M
cuori^M

ダイヤ（モンド）
diamond
Karo^N
carreau^M
diamante^M
quadri^M

クラブ
club
Kreuz^N
trèfle^M
trébol^M
fiori^M

スペード
spade
Pik^N
pique^M
espada^F
picche^M

ジョーカー
joker
Joker^M
Joker^M
comodín^M
jolly^M

エース
ace
Ass^N
As^M
as^M
asso^M

キング
king
König^M
Roi^M
rey^M
re^M

クイーン
queen
Dame^F
Dame^F
reina^F
donna^F

ジャック
jack
Bube^M
Valet^M
jota^F
fante^M

標準的なポーカーの手
standard poker hands
normale Pokerblätter^N
combinaisons^F au poker^M
manos^F de póquer^M
combinazioni^F del poker^M

ハイ・カード
high card
höchste Karte^F
carte^F isolée
cartas^F altas
carta^F più alta

ワン・ペア
one pair
ein Pärchen^N
paire^F
un par^M
coppia^F

ツー・ペア
two pairs
zwei Pärchen^N
double paire^F
dos pares^M
doppia coppia^F

スリー・カード／スリー・オブ・ア・カインド
three-of-a-kind
Drilling^M
brelan^M
trío^M
tris^M

ストレート
straight
Straße^F
séquence^F
escalera^F
scala^F

フラッシュ
flush
Flush^M
couleur^F
color^M
colore^M

フル・ハウス
full house
Full House^N
main^F pleine
full^M
full^M

フォー・カード／フォー・オブ・ア・カインド
four-of-a-kind
Vierling^M
carré^M
póquer^M
poker^M

ストレート・フラッシュ
straight flush
Straight Flush^M
quinte^F
escalera^F de color^M
scala^F reale

ロイヤル・フラッシュ
royal flush
Royal Flush^M
quinte^F royale
escalera^F real
scala^F reale massima

ゲーム | GAMES
SPIELE | JEUX | JUEGOS | GIOCHI

ボード・ゲーム

board games | Brettspiel[N] | jeux[M] de plateau[M] | juegos[M] de mesa[F] | giochi[M] da tavola[F]

バックギャモン／西洋双六
backgammon
Backgammon[N]
jacquet[M]
backgammon[M]
backgammon[M]

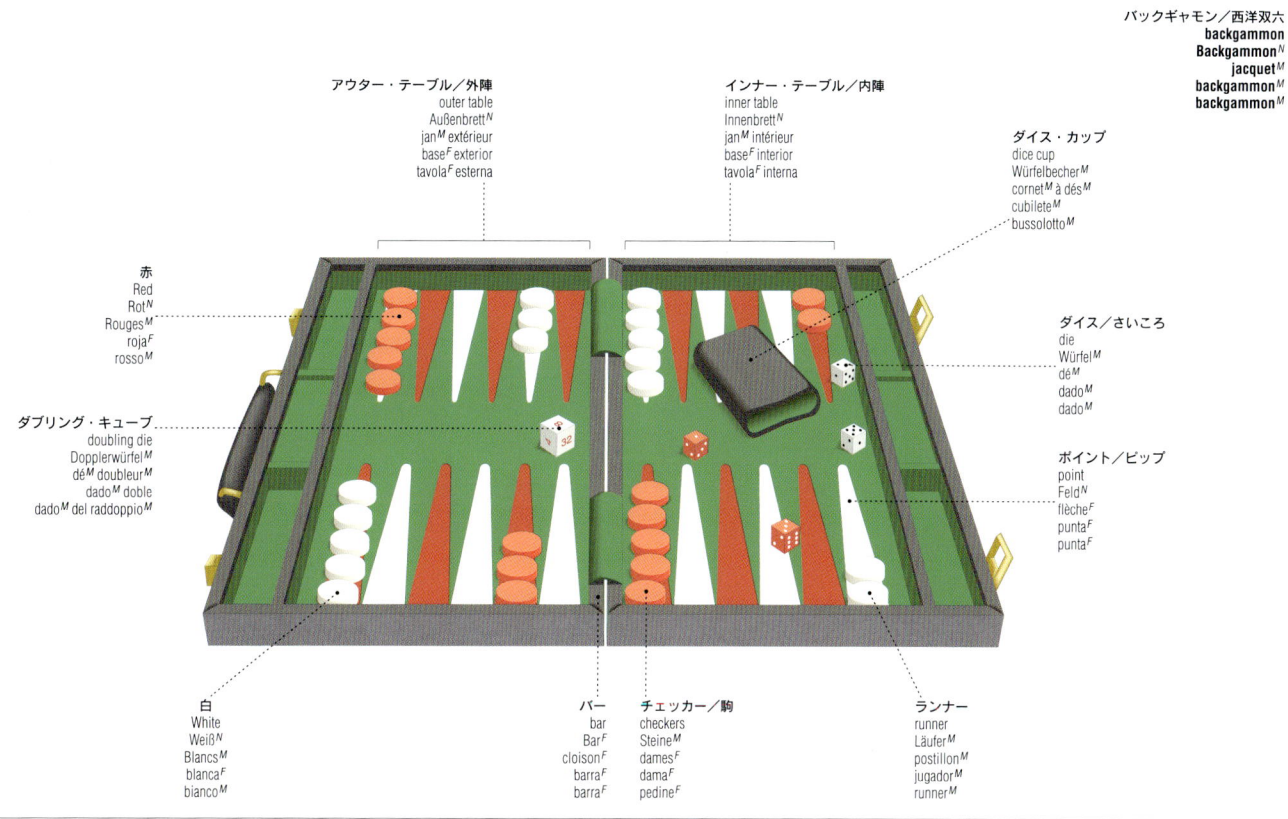

アウター・テーブル／外陣
outer table
Außenbrett[N]
jan[M] extérieur
base[F] exterior
tavola[F] esterna

インナー・テーブル／内陣
inner table
Innenbrett[N]
jan[M] intérieur
base[F] interior
tavola[F] interna

ダイス・カップ
dice cup
Würfelbecher[M]
cornet[M] à dés[M]
cubilete[M]
bussolotto[M]

赤
Red
Rot[N]
Rouges[M]
roja[F]
rosso[M]

ダイス／さいころ
die
Würfel[M]
dé[M]
dado[M]
dado[M]

ダブリング・キューブ
doubling die
Dopplerwürfel[M]
dé[M] doubleur
dado[M] doble
dado[M] del raddoppio[M]

ポイント／ピップ
point
Feld[N]
flèche[F]
punta[F]
punta[F]

白
White
Weiß[N]
Blancs[M]
blanca[F]
bianco[M]

バー
bar
Bar[M]
cloison[F]
barra[F]
barra[F]

チェッカー／駒
checkers
Steine[M]
dames[F]
dama[F]
pedine[F]

ランナー
runner
Läufer[M]
postillon[M]
jugador[M]
runner[M]

紙幣／金券
bank note
Spielgeld[N]
billet[M] de banque[F]
billetes[M] de banco[M]
banconota[F]

銀行
bank
Bank[F]
banque[F]
banco[M]
banca[F]

モノポリー®
Monopoly®
Monopoly®[N]
Monopoly®[M]
Monopoly®[M]
Monopoli®[M]

チャンス・カード
Chance card
Ereigniskarte[F]
carte[F] Chance[F]
carta[F] de Suerte[F]
carta[F] delle probabilità[F]

駒／トークン
token
Spielfigur[F]
pion[M]
ficha[F]
segnalino[M]

家
house
Haus[N]
maison[F]
casa[F]
casa[F]

ダイス／さいころ
die
Würfel[M]
dé[M]
dado[M]
dado[M]

升目
space
Spielfeld[N]
case[F]
casilla[F]
casella[F]

刑務所
jail
Gefängnis[N]
prison[F]
cárcel[F]
prigione[F]

カード
card
Karte[F]
carte[F]
carta[F]
carta[F]

ゲーム盤
game board
Spielbrett[N]
plateau[M] de jeux[M]
tablero[M] de juego[M]
tavola[F]

ホテル
hotel
Hotel[N]
hôtel[M]
hotel[M]
albergo[M]

権利書
title deed
Besitzkarte[F]
titre[M] de propriété[F]
título[M] de propiedad[F]
contratto[M]

共同募金カード
Community Chest card
Gemeinschaftskarte[F]
carte[F] Caisse[F] de communauté[F]
carta[F] Caja[F] de Comunidad[F]
carta[F] degli imprevisti[M]

スタート（地点）
go
Start[M]
départ[M]
salida[F]
via[F]

スポーツとゲーム

915

ゲーム | GAMES
SPIELE | JEUX | JUEGOS | GIOCHI

ボード・ゲーム

日本語 | 英語 | ドイツ語 | フランス語 | スペイン語 | イタリア語

チェス
chess
Schach[N]
échecs[M]
ajedrez[M]
scacchi[M]

チェス盤
chessboard
Schachbrett[N]
échiquier[M]
tablero de ajedrez[M]
scacchiera[F]

クイーン・サイド
queen's side
Damenflanke[F]
aile[F] Dame[F]
lado[M] de la reina[F]
lato[M] della regina[F]

キング・サイド
king's side
Königsflanke[F]
aile[F] Roi[M]
lado[M] del rey[M]
lato[M] del re[M]

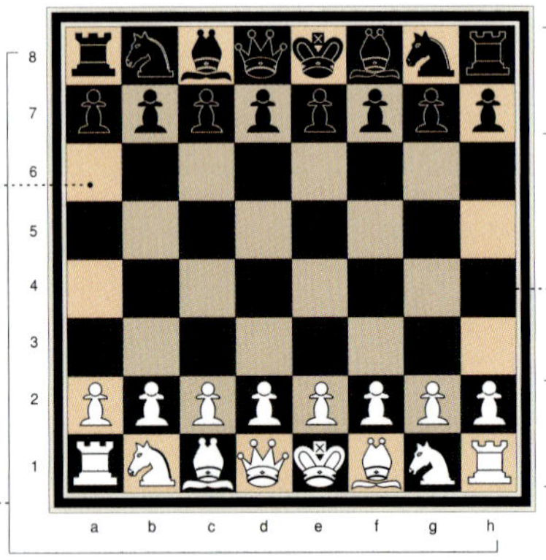

黒駒
Black
Schwarz[N]
Noirs[M]
negras[F]
neri[M]

白升
white square
weißes Feld[N]
case[F] blanche
escaque[M] blanco
casella[F] bianca

黒升
black square
schwarzes Feld[N]
case[F] noire
escaque[M] negro
casella[F] nera

チェスの座標式表記法
chess notation
Notation[F]
notation[F] algébrique
notación[F] del ajedrez[M]
notazione[F] degli scacchi[M]

白駒
White
Weiß[N]
Blancs[M]
blancas[F]
bianchi[M]

駒
chess pieces
Schachfiguren[F]
pièces[F]
piezas[F]
pezzi[M]

ポーン／歩兵
pawn
Bauer[M]
Pion[M]
peón[M]
pedone[M]

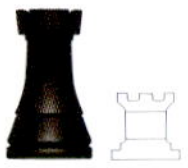

ルーク／城
rook; Castle
Turm[M]
Tour[F]
torre[F]
torre[F]

ビショップ／僧正
bishop
Läufer[M]
Fou[M]
alfil[M]
alfiere[M]

ナイト／騎士
knight
Springer[M]
Cavalier[M]
caballo[M]
cavallo[M]

動き方の種類
types of movements
Zugarten[F]
types[M] de déplacements[M]
tipos[M] de movimientos[M]
tipi[M] di movimenti[M]

斜めの動き
diagonal movement
diagonaler Zug[M]
déplacement[M] diagonal
movimiento[M] diagonal
movimento[M] diagonale

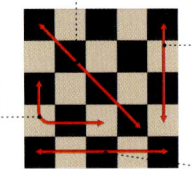

縦の動き
vertical movement
vertikaler Zug[M]
déplacement[M] vertical
movimiento[M] vertical
movimento[M] verticale

直角の動き
square movement
Rösselsprung[M]
déplacement[M] en équerre[F]
movimiento[M] en ángulo[M]
movimento[M] a L

横の動き
horizontal movement
horizontaler Zug[M]
déplacement[M] horizontal
movimiento[M] horizontal
movimento[M] orizzontale

キング／王
king
König[M]
Roi[M]
rey[M]
re[M]

クイーン／女王
queen
Dame[F]
Dame[F]
reina[F]
regina[F]

碁
go
Go[N]
go[M]
go(sun-tse)[M]
go[M]

碁盤
board
Spielbrett[N]
terrain[M]
tablero[M]
scacchiera[F]

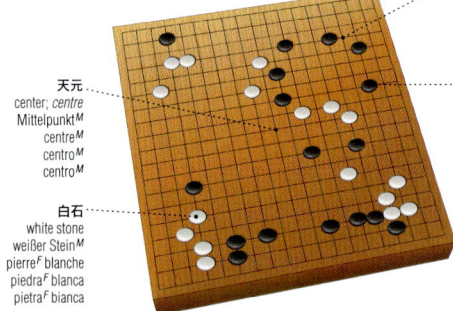

星
handicap spot
schwacher Punkt[M]
point[M] de handicap[M]
obstáculo[M]
punto[M] di handicap[M]

天元
center; centre
Mittelpunkt[M]
centre[M]
centro[M]
centro[M]

黒石
black stone
schwarzer Stein[M]
pierre[F] noire
piedra[F] negra
pietra[F] nera

白石
white stone
weißer Stein[M]
pierre[F] blanche
piedra[F] blanca
pietra[F] bianca

主な石の動き
major motions
Hauptspielzüge[M]
principaux mouvements[M]
principales movimientos[M]
mosse[F] principali

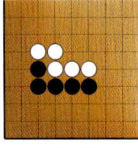

ツギ／連絡
connection
Verbindung[F]
connexion[F]
conexión[F]
gruppo[M]

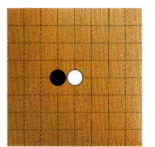

ツケ
contact
Berührung[F]
contact[M]
contacto[M]
contatto[M]

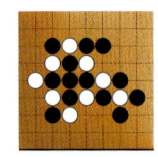

捕獲
capture
Fangen[N]
capture[F]
captura[F]
cattura[F]

チェッカー／西洋将棋
checkers
Dame[F]
jeu[M] de dames[F]
damas[F]
dama[F]

駒
checker
Spielstein[M]
Dame[F]
dama[F]
dama[F]

チェッカー盤
checkerboard
Spielbrett[N]
damier[M]
tablero[M] de damas[F]
scacchiera[F]

916

ゲーム | GAMES
SPIELE | JEUX | JUEGOS | GIOCHI

ジグソー・パズル

jigsaw puzzle | Puzzle^N | puzzle^M | puzle^M | puzzle^M

ピース
piece
Puzzleteil^N
pièce^F
pieza^F
tessera^F

絵（柄）
picture
Bild^N
image^F
imagen^F
immagine^F

ボード
board
Unterlage^F
plateau^M
tablero^M
tavola^F

麻雀

mah-jongg | Mah-Jongg^N | mah-jong^M | mah-jongg^M | mah-jongg^M

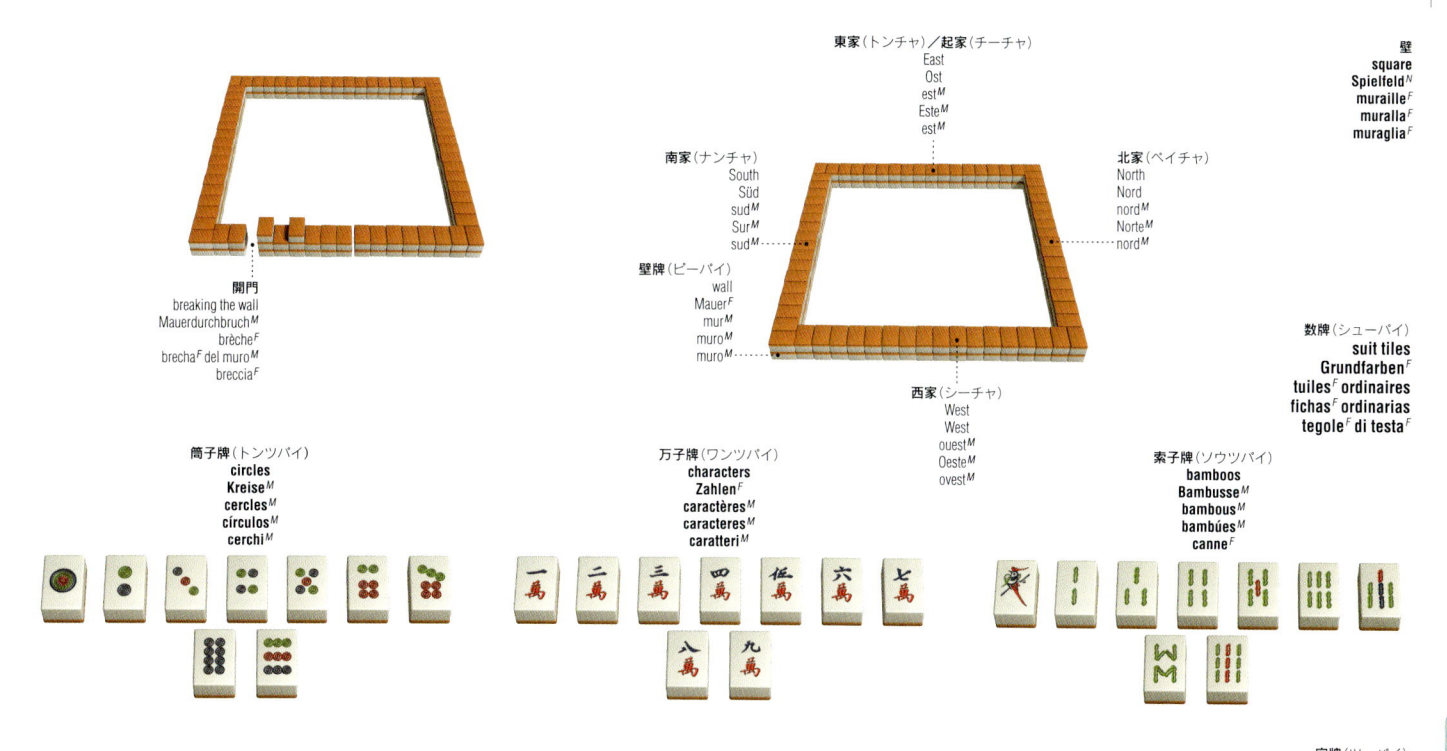

東家（トンチャ）／起家（チーチャ）
East
Ost
est^M
Este^M
est^M

南家（ナンチャ）
South
Süd
sud^M
Sur^M
sud^M

北家（ペイチャ）
North
Nord
nord^M
Norte^M
nord^M

壁
square
Spielfeld^N
muraille^F
muralla^F
muraglia^F

開門
breaking the wall
Mauerdurchbruch^M
brèche^F
brecha^F del muro^M
breccia^F

壁牌（ピーパイ）
wall
Mauer^F
mur^M
muro^M
muro^M

西家（シーチャ）
West
West
ouest^M
Oeste^M
ovest^M

数牌（シューパイ）
suit tiles
Grundfarben^F
tuiles^F ordinaires
fichas^F ordinarias
tegole^F di testa^F

筒子牌（トンツパイ）
circles
Kreise^M
cercles^M
círculos^M
cerchi^M

万子牌（ワンツパイ）
characters
Zahlen^F
caractères^M
caracteres^M
caratteri^M

索子牌（ソウツパイ）
bamboos
Bambusse^M
bambous^M
bambúes^M
canne^F

字牌（ツーパイ）
honor tiles; *honour tiles*
Trumpffarben^F
honneurs^M
fichas^F de honor^M
onori^M supremi

四風牌（スーフォンパイ）
winds
Winde^M
vents^M
vientos^M
venti^M

三元牌（サンゲンパイ）
dragons
Drachen^M
dragons^M
dragones^M
dragoni^M

付加価値牌（パイ）／花牌（ホワパイ）
bonus tiles
Hasardsteine^M
tuiles^F de bonification^F
fichas^F de beneficio^M
tegole^F bonus

花牌（ホワパイ）
flower tiles
Blumenziegel^M
fleurs^F
fichas^F de flores^F
fiori^M

四季牌（パイ）
season tiles
Jahreszeitenziegel^M
saisons^F
fichas^F de estaciones^F
stagioni^F

スポーツとゲーム

917

ゲーム｜GAMES
SPIELE｜JEUX｜JUEGOS｜GIOCHI

ビデオ・ゲーム

video entertainment system｜Videospielsystem^N｜système^M de jeux^M vidéo｜videojuego^M｜videogioco^M

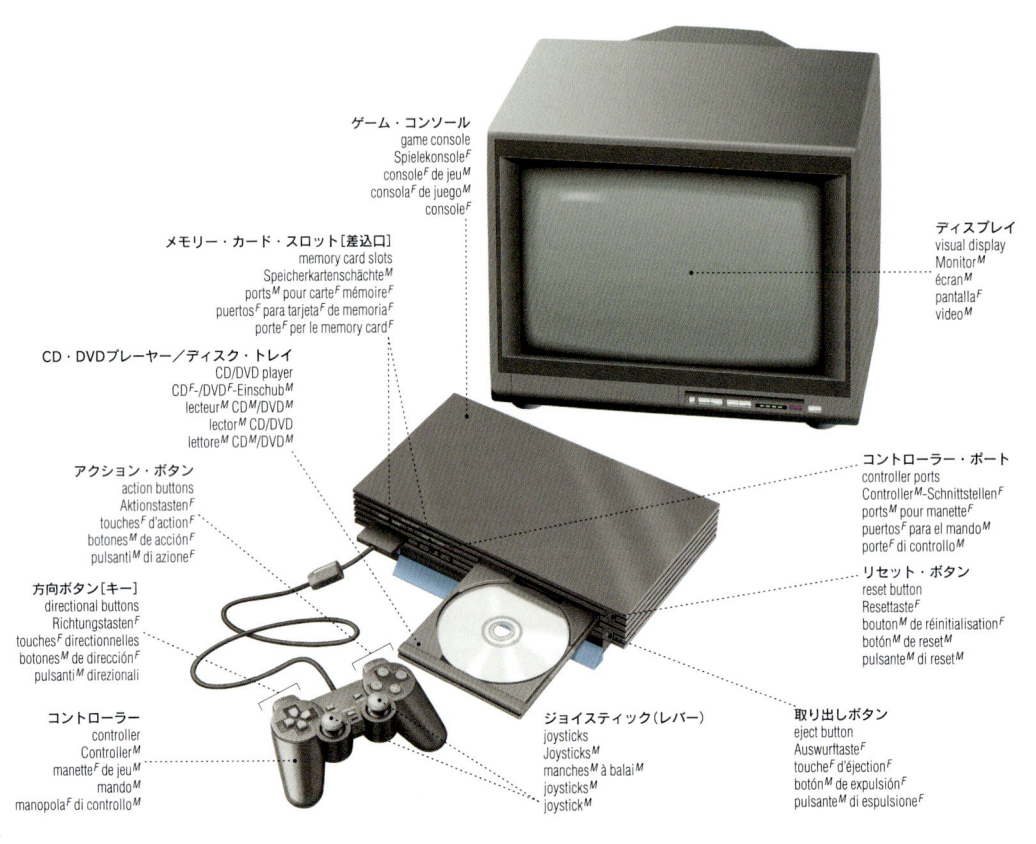

日本語｜英語｜ドイツ語｜フランス語｜スペイン語｜イタリア語

ゲーム・コンソール
game console
Spielekonsole^F
console^F de jeu^M
consola^F de juego^M
console^F

メモリー・カード・スロット［差込口］
memory card slots
Speicherkartenschächte^M
ports^M pour carte^F mémoire^F
puertos^F para tarjeta^F de memoria^F
porte^F per le memory card^F

CD・DVDプレーヤー／ディスク・トレイ
CD/DVD player
CD^F-/DVD^F-Einschub^M
lecteur^M CD^M/DVD^M
lector^M CD/DVD
lettore^M CD^M/DVD^M

アクション・ボタン
action buttons
Aktionstasten^F
touches^F d'action^F
botones^M de acción^F
pulsanti^M di azione^F

方向ボタン［キー］
directional buttons
Richtungstasten^F
touches^F directionnelles
botones^M de dirección^F
pulsanti^M direzionali

コントローラー
controller
Controller^M
manette^F de jeu^M
mando^M
manopola^F di controllo^M

ディスプレイ
visual display
Monitor^M
écran^M
pantalla^F
video^M

コントローラー・ポート
controller ports
Controller^M-Schnittstellen^F
ports^M pour manette^F
puertos^F para el mando^M
porte^F di controllo^M

リセット・ボタン
reset button
Resettaste^F
bouton^M de réinitialisation^F
botón^M de reset^M
pulsante^M di reset^M

取り出しボタン
eject button
Auswurftaste^F
touche^F d'éjection^F
botón^M de expulsión^F
pulsante^M di espulsione^F

ジョイスティック（レバー）
joysticks
Joysticks^M
manches^M à balai^M
joysticks
joystick^M

ダーツ

darts｜Dartspiel^N｜jeu^M de fléchettes^F｜juego^M de dardos^M｜freccette^F

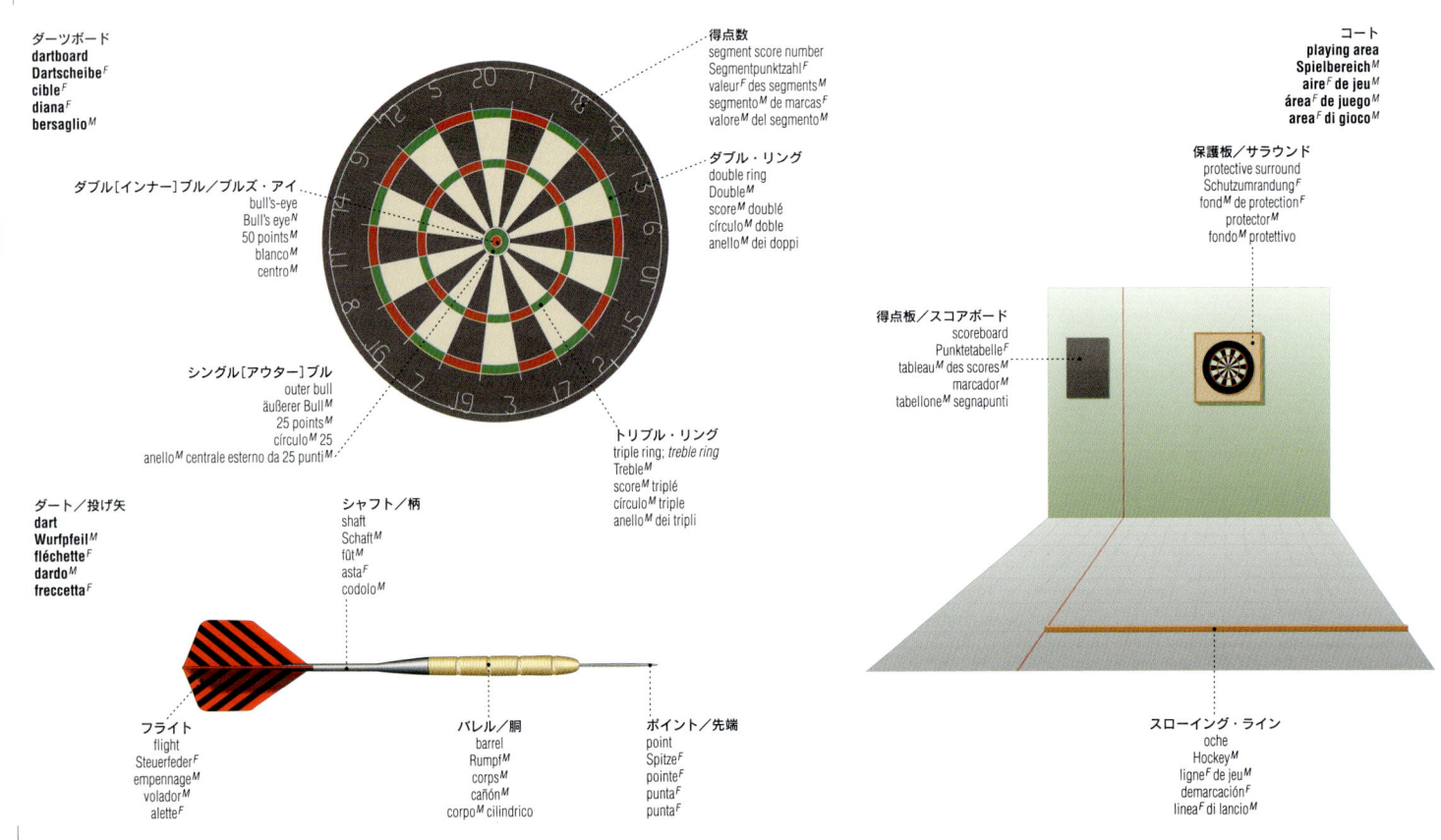

ダーツボード
dartboard
Dartscheibe^F
cible^F
diana^F
bersaglio^M

ダブル［インナー］ブル／ブルズ・アイ
bull's-eye
Bull's eye^N
50 points^M
blanco^M
centro^M

シングル［アウター］ブル
outer bull
äußerer Bull^M
25 points^M
círculo^M 25
anello^M centrale esterno da 25 punti^M

得点数
segment score number
Segmentpunktzahl^F
valeur^F des segments^M
segmento^M de marcas^F
valore^M del segmento^M

ダブル・リング
double ring
Double^M
score^M doublé
círculo^M doble
anello^M dei doppi

トリプル・リング
triple ring; treble ring
Treble^M
score^M triplé
círculo^M triple
anello^M dei tripli

コート
playing area
Spielbereich^M
aire^F de jeu^M
área^F de juego^M
area^F di gioco^M

保護板／サラウンド
protective surround
Schutzumrandung^F
fond^M de protection^F
protector^M
fondo^M protettivo

得点板／スコアボード
scoreboard
Punktetabelle^F
tableau^M des scores^M
marcador^M
tabellone^M segnapunti

ダート／投げ矢
dart
Wurfpfeil^M
fléchette^F
dardo^M
freccetta^F

シャフト／柄
shaft
Schaft^M
fût^M
asta^F
codolo^M

フライト
flight
Steuerfeder^F
empennage^M
volador^M
alette^F

バレル／胴
barrel
Rumpf^M
corps^M
cañón^M
corpo^M cilindrico

ポイント／先端
point
Spitze^F
pointe^F
punta^F
punta^F

スローイング・ライン
oche
Hockey^M
ligne^F de jeu^M
demarcación^F
linea^F di lancio^M

ゲーム | GAMES
SPIELE | JEUX | JUEGOS | GIOCHI

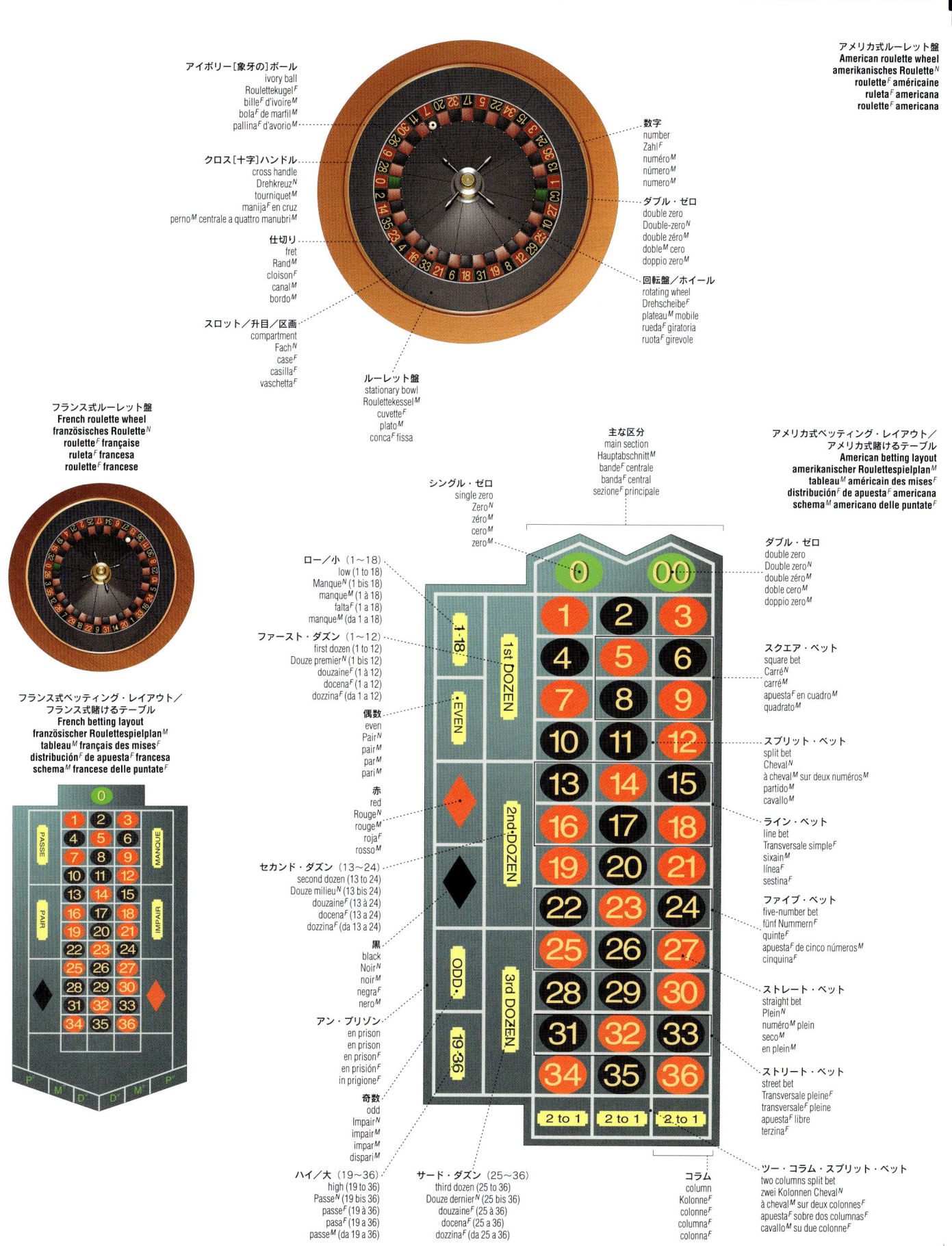

ルーレット・テーブル
roulette table | Roulettespieltischᴹ | tableᶠ de roulette | mesaᶠ de la ruletaᶠ | tavoloᴹ da rouletteᶠ

アメリカ式ルーレット盤
American roulette wheel
amerikanisches Rouletteᴺ
rouletteᶠ américaine
ruletaᶠ americana
rouletteᶠ americana

アイボリー[象牙の]ボール
ivory ball
Roulettekugelᶠ
billeᶠ d'ivoireᴹ
bolaᶠ de marfil
pallinaᶠ d'avorioᴹ

数字
number
Zahlᶠ
numéroᴹ
númeroᴹ
numeroᴹ

クロス[十字]ハンドル
cross handle
Drehkreuzᴺ
tourniquetᴹ
manijaᶠ en cruz
pernoᴹ centrale a quattro manubriᴹ

ダブル・ゼロ
double zero
Double-zeroᴺ
double zéroᴹ
dobleᴹ cero
doppio zeroᴹ

仕切り
fret
Randᴹ
cloisonᶠ
canalᴹ
bordoᴹ

回転盤／ホイール
rotating wheel
Drehscheibeᶠ
plateauᴹ mobile
ruedaᶠ giratoria
ruotaᶠ girevole

スロット／升目／区画
compartment
Fachᴺ
caseᶠ
casillaᶠ
vaschettaᶠ

ルーレット盤
stationary bowl
Roulettekesselᴹ
cuvetteᶠ
platoᴹ
concaᶠ fissa

フランス式ルーレット盤
French roulette wheel
französisches Rouletteᴺ
rouletteᶠ française
ruletaᶠ francesa
rouletteᶠ francese

主な区分
main section
Hauptabschnittᴹ
bandeᶠ centrale
bandaᶠ central
sezioneᶠ principale

アメリカ式ベッティング・レイアウト／アメリカ式賭けるテーブル
American betting layout
amerikanischer Roulettespielplanᴹ
tableauᴹ américain des misesᶠ
distribuciónᶠ de apuestaᶠ americana
schemaᴹ americano delle puntateᶠ

シングル・ゼロ
single zero
Zeroᴺ
zéroᴹ
ceroᴹ
zeroᴹ

ダブル・ゼロ
double zero
Double zeroᴺ
double zéroᴹ
doble ceroᴹ
doppio zeroᴹ

ロー／小 (1〜18)
low (1 to 18)
Manqueᴺ (1 bis 18)
manqueᴹ (1 à 18)
faltaᶠ (1 a 18)
manqueᴹ (da 1 a 18)

スクエア・ベット
square bet
Carréᴺ
carréᴹ
apuestaᶠ en cuadroᴹ
quadratoᴹ

ファースト・ダズン (1〜12)
first dozen (1 to 12)
Douze premierᴺ (1 bis 12)
douzaineᶠ (1 à 12)
docenaᶠ (1 a 12)
dozzinaᶠ (da 1 a 12)

スプリット・ベット
split bet
Chevalᴺ
à chevalᴹ sur deux numérosᴹ
partidoᴹ
cavalloᴹ

偶数
even
Pairᴺ
pairᴹ
parᴹ
pariᴹ

赤
red
Rougeᴺ
rougeᴹ
rojaᶠ
rossoᴹ

ライン・ベット
line bet
Transversale simpleᶠ
sixainᴹ
líneaᶠ
sestinaᶠ

セカンド・ダズン (13〜24)
second dozen (13 to 24)
Douze milieuᴺ (13 bis 24)
douzaineᶠ (13 à 24)
docenaᶠ (13 a 24)
dozzinaᶠ (da 13 a 24)

ファイブ・ベット
five-number bet
fünf Nummernᶠ
quinteᶠ
apuestaᶠ de cinco númerosᴹ
cinquinaᶠ

黒
black
Noirᴺ
noirᴹ
negraᶠ
neroᴹ

フランス式ベッティング・レイアウト／フランス式賭けるテーブル
French betting layout
französischer Roulettespielplanᴹ
tableauᴹ français des misesᶠ
distribuciónᶠ de apuestaᶠ francesa
schemaᴹ francese delle puntateᶠ

ストレート・ベット
straight bet
Pleinᴺ
numéroᴹ plein
secoᴹ
en pleinᴹ

アン・プリゾン
en prison
en prison
en prisonᶠ
en prisiónᶠ
in prigioneᶠ

奇数
odd
Impairᴺ
impairᴹ
imparᴹ
dispariᴹ

ストリート・ベット
street bet
Transversale pleineᶠ
transversaleᶠ pleine
apuestaᶠ libre
terzinaᶠ

ハイ／大 (19〜36)
high (19 to 36)
Passeᴺ (19 bis 36)
passeᶠ (19 à 36)
pasaᶠ (19 a 36)
passeᴹ (da 19 a 36)

サード・ダズン (25〜36)
third dozen (25 to 36)
Douze dernierᴺ (25 bis 36)
douzaineᶠ (25 à 36)
docenaᶠ (25 a 36)
dozzinaᶠ (da 25 a 36)

コラム
column
Kolonneᶠ
colonneᶠ
columnaᶠ
colonnaᶠ

ツー・コラム・スプリット・ベット
two columns split bet
zwei Kolonnen Chevalᴺ
à chevalᴹ sur deux colonnesᶠ
apuestaᶠ sobre dos columnasᶠ
cavalloᴹ su due colonneᶠ

スポーツとゲーム

919

ゲーム | GAMES
SPIELE | JEUX | JUEGOS | GIOCHI

スロット・マシン

日本語 | 英語 | ドイツ語 | フランス語 | スペイン語 | イタリア語

slot machine; *fruit machine* | einarmiger Bandit[M] | machine[F] à sous[M] | máquina[F] tragaperras | slot-machine[F]

断面図
cross section
Querschnitt
coupe[F]
corte[M] transversal
sezione[F] trasversale

ケース／枠
casing
Gehäuse[N]
boîtier[M]
caja[F]
cassa[F]

コイン投入口／（コイン）スロット
coin slot
Münzeinwurf[M]
fente[F] à monnaie[F]
ranura[F] para monedas[F]
fessura[F] per l'introduzione[F] delle monete[F]

リール／回転ウィール
reel
Glücksrad[N]
rouleau[M]
tambor[M]
rullo[M]

リール・プレート
reel plate
Drehkranz[M]
plaque[F] de rouleau[M]
engranaje[M]
piastra[F] del rullo[M]

コイン返却口
coin reject slot
Münzrückgabe[F]
réceptacle[M] pour les pièces[F] refusées
devolución[F] de monedas[F] rechazadas
fessura[F] per la restituzione[F] delle monete[F]

引き金
payout trigger
Auszahlungshebel[M]
déclencheur[M] de paiement[M]
disparador[M] de pago[M]
levetta[F] di erogazione[F] della vincita[F]

図柄／絵柄
symbol
Symbol[N]
symbole[M]
símbolo[M]
simbolo[M]

レバー／ハンドル
lever
Hebel[M]
bras[M]
palanca[F]
leva[F]

ジャックポット・フィード
jackpot feed
Jackpot-Leitung[F]
alimentation[F] jackpot[M]
selector[M] del premio[M]
alimentazione[F] del premio[M]

ばね連結器
spring linkage
Federverbindung[F]
levier[M] à ressort[M]
resorte[M] del sistema[M] articulado
collegamento[M] a molla[F]

配当金額表
winning line
Gewinnkombination[F]
combinaison[F] gagnante
combinación[F] ganadora
combinazione[F] vincente

コイン・シュート
coin chute
Münzleitung[F]
conduite[F] des pièces[F]
conducto[M] de monedas[F]
slitta[F] delle monete[F]

強化箱
strongbox
Gehäuseverstärkung[F]
caisse[F] blindée
caja[F] fuerte
cassa[F]

コイン受け皿
payout tray
Auszahlungsschale[F]
plateau[M] réceptacle[M] de paiement[M]
bandeja[F] de pago[M]
vassoio[M] delle vincite[F]

ジャックポット箱
jackpot box
Jackpot-Kasten[M]
boîte[F] jackpot[M]
casilla[F] del dinero[M]
scatola[F] del premio[M]

電気支払い制御装置
electrical payout linkage
elektrisches Auszahlungselement[N]
commande[F] électrique de paiement[M]
control[M] eléctrico de pago[M]
comando[M] elettrico di erogazione[F] della vincita[F]

サッカー・テーブル

soccer table | Tischfußball[M] | baby-foot[M] | futbolín[M] | calcio[M] balilla

スコア・カウンター
score counter
Toranzeige[F]
boulier[M]-compteur[M]
anotador[M]
segnapunti[M]

ゴム製バンパー
rubber bumper
Stoßfänger[M]
amortisseur[M] en caoutchouc[M]
amortiguador[M] de caucho[M]
paracolpi[M] di gomma[F]

プレーヤー
player
Spieler[M]
joueur[M]
jugador[M]
giocatore[M]

ゴール
goal
Tor[N]
but[M]
gol[M]
porta[F]

伸縮自在棒
telescopic rod
Teleskopstangen[F]
barre[F] télescopique
barra[F] telescópica
asta[F] telescopica

グラウンド
playing field
Spielfeld[N]
terrain[M] de jeu[M]
campo[M] de juego[M]
campo[M] di gioco[M]

ボール
ball
Ball[M]
balle[F]
bola[F]
pallina[F]

ハンドル
handle
Griff[M]
poignée[F]
empuñadura[F]
manopola[F]

日本語索引

あ

アーカイブ　394
アーキトレーブ　403, 405
アーク溶接　318
アーク溶接機　318
アーケード　407, 410
アース　272, 655
アース・クランプ　318
アースされたコンセント　263
アース接続　272
アース線　272, 273
アース端子　274, 497
アース・バス・バー　272
アース・ボンド　272
アース・リード　318
アーチ　322, 540
アーチェリー　859
アーチ橋　540
アーチ剖げ形　411
アーチ橋の例　541
アーチ・ダム　661
アーチ・ダムの断面図　661
アーチの例　413, 541
アーチボード　533
アーチャー　859
アーティチョーク　187
アーミン　741
アーム　286, 329, 452, 610, 638, 693
アーム・ガード　808, 859
アーム・シリンダー　638
アーム・スリット　355
アーム・ライト　286
アーム・ランプ　286
アーム・リフター　500
アーム・レスト　500, 554, 555
アーモンド　193
Rh陰性　702
Rhプラス　702
Rhマイナス　702
Rh陽性　702
アイ　453
アイアン　867, 868
藍色細菌　92
ISP　525
アイ・ガード　818, 819
アイ・カーラー　378
アイカップ　496
合気道　846
合気道家　846
合気道着　846
ISA拡張コネクター　513
合い決り　249
アイシャドー　378
合い印　455
アイスクリームすくい　233
アイスクリーム・スクープ　233
アイスクリーム製造機　240
アイス・スクリュー　901, 901
アイスバーグ・レタス　186
アイス・パイル　901
アイス・ピッケル　901
アイス・ピトン　901
アイス・ホッケー　878
アイス・ホッケー・プレーヤー　878
アイスランド　32, 744
アイスランド語　469
アイス・リンク　886
アイゼン　345
アイゼン・バンド　901
アイタケ　183
アイドル・ホイール　876
相乗りペイロード構造　24

アイピース　14, 15
アイブロウ・ブラシとアイ・ラッシュ・コーム　378
アイブロウ・ペンシル　378
アイボリー・ボール　919
アイマラ語　469
アイランド　224, 761
アイランド式カウンター　224
アイリッシュ海　32
アイリッシュ・ブレッド　205
アイ・リング　115
アイルランド　743
アイルランド語　469
アイレット　371
アイレット・タブ　342
アイロン掛け　347
アイロン禁止　347
アインスタイニウム　684
アウター・サークル　877
アウター・ジブ　603
アウター・ステーター　627
アウター・テーブル　915
アウター・ブル　918
アウトウォッシュ・プレーン　46
アウト・コート・ライン　819
アウトサイド・ラインバッカー　806
アウトソール　347
アウトドア・レジャー　902
アウトラン　890
アウトリガー　633, 634, 638, 766, 839
アウトリガー・フォーク　633
亜鉛　683
亜鉛缶　689
青　400, 690, 741
アオサ　183
青信号　712
青球　863
青の電子ビーム　494
青ボール　863
青緑　400
青緑色細菌　92
青紫　400
あおり革　855
赤　400, 690, 741, 915, 919
赤パプリカ　188
赤キャベツ　186
赤クランプ　558
アカグモモ　192
赤砂糖　209
赤信号　712
赤橙　400
赤球　862, 863
赤タマネギ　184
赤チコリ　186
アカトウガラシ　199
赤の電子ビーム　494
赤フィルター　485
赤ボール　862, 863
赤紫　400
アカモミタケ　183
明かり取り　186
アカンサスの葉飾り　405
アカンサス葉飾り　276
亜寒帯気候　61
亜寒帯林　66
秋　54
アギ　199
空き地　408
アキュムレーター　559
アキレス腱ガード　880
アクアマリン　375
アクサン・グラーブ　473
アクサン・シルコンフレックス　473

アクサンテギュ　473
アクション・ボタン　918
アクスル軸　553
アクスル・シャフト　553
アクセサリー　558, 580
アクセサリー・シュー　476
アクセス・ウインドー　521
アクセス・サーバー　525
アクセス・パネル　258, 266
アクセル　881
アクセル・ケーブル　332
アクセル・コントロール　331
アクセル・ペダル　556
アクセント記号　435
アクチニウム　684
アクチノイド元素　684
アクチュエーター　759
アクティブ・トラッキング・スイッチ　498
踵　124
握把　754, 755, 860, 912
アクロテリウム　403, 404
アクロバット・スケート靴　895
上げ下げ窓　415
揚げ網　739
揚げ物用ざる　231
開ける　230
顎　115, 148
あご　302, 306, 307, 310, 312, 317, 911, 913
アコースティック・ギター　440
アコーディオン　432
アコーディオン式書類入れ　386
アコーディオン・ドア　416
アコーディオン・バッグ　388
アコーディオン・プリーツ　357
アコーディオン窓　415
顎ガード　575
顎カバー　765
顎紐　765, 772, 808, 870, 885
朝顔　446, 447
浅型両手鍋　233
ASA・TIMEキー　479
浅丸曲型　401
アザラシ　137
脚　113, 139, 147, 149, 156, 277, 278, 280, 281, 323, 351, 440, 448, 815, 823, 910
足　104, 105, 139, 140, 143, 146, 147, 148, 149, 155, 368, 425, 444
趾　130
アジア　28, 33, 50, 746
脚当て　796
アジアの麺類　207
足板　280
足置き　281
足置き台　783
アシカ　137
足掛け　587
足枷　857
足からの入水　829
足首　156
足首・手首用ウエイト　850
足鍵　444
足鍵盤　444
足先　893
アジサシ　118
アジサイ　118
アシスタント・コーチ　811, 879
アシスタント・ジャッジ　883
アシスタント・レフェリー　881, 882
アシスタント・レフリー　881, 882
アシスト・グリップ　554

足台　277, 312
足留め　836
足並み　124
足肉　215
脚の姿勢　829
足載せ台　277, 464, 575, 576, 783
足の保護具　773
足の例　117
足場　901
足付きはしご　321
足びれ　841
葦ペン　470
肢巻き　853, 857, 858
味見スプーン　233
味見用スプーン　233
アジャスター　436
足指　117, 143, 146, 148
趾　117
足指用爪切り鋏　377
足用パッド　798
アジョワン　199
足裏　913
当て　439, 749
アチェート・バルサミコ　201
厚紙　400
圧砕ローラー　642
圧縮　71, 564, 565, 627
圧縮機タービン　627
圧縮・吸気　565
圧縮空気タンク　586, 841, 873
圧縮空気ボンベ　765
圧縮室　642
圧縮タービン　564
圧縮継ぎ手　269, 627
圧縮リンク　640
アッズ　901

アイピース　14, 15
圧雪車　886
圧着板　476
アッパー　889
アッパー・エッジ　815
アッパー・ガードル・ファセット　374
アッパー・カフ　889
アッパー・シェル　889, 895
アッパー・ストラップ　889
アッパー・デッキ　624
アッパー・リム　750
圧迫帯　777
アップ・クオーク　680
厚縁　459
アップホール・ライン　836
アップライト・ピアノ　442
アップライト・ピアノのアクション　443
アップライト・ピアノの打弦機構　443
アッポジャトゥーラ　435
厚み測定　700
圧力管　667
圧力計　654, 655, 777
圧力検知板　758
圧力調整器　319, 765
圧力調整器　421, 423
圧力調節器　234
圧力調節つまみ　903
圧力調節バルブ　777
圧力鍋　234
圧力逃がし弁　259, 266, 267
圧力の掛かった水　662
圧力の単位　702
圧力抑制プール　671
当て板　424
当て木　600, 834, 836
当て布　389
アデン湾　33, 34
後糸案内　457
アドビ・ハウス　418
アトモス・バルブ　655
アトラス山脈　34
アトリ　118
アドリア海　32
アトリウム　406
穴　423
孔　346
穴空き煉瓦　298
穴空け具　905
穴空け深さ固定装置　307
アナウサギ　123, 212
アナグマ　134
穴付き頭　302
穴ボタン　453
穴掘り器　324
アナログ時計　696
穴を空ける道具　306
兄　785
アニク　487
アニス　202
アニュレット　404
姉　785
亜熱帯気候　61
亜熱帯多雨気候　61
アノラック　371
アパート　711
アバクス　404
アパラチア山脈　30
肋肉　214, 215
アビシニアン　133
アブ　101
アフガニスタン　746
アブス　411

天文学 > 2-25;　地球 > 26-71;　植物 > 72-89;　動物 > 90-143;　人間 > 144-177;　食べ物と台所 > 178-241;　家屋 > 242-295;　日曜大工・園芸 > 296-333;　衣服 > 334-371;
装身具類と日用品 > 372-391;　芸術と建築 > 392-465;　情報伝達とオフィス・オートメーション > 466-535;　交通と機械 > 536-643;　エネルギー > 644-677;　科学 > 678-705;
社会 > 706-785;　スポーツとゲーム > 786-920

アフター・シェーブ・ローション 383	アラビア半島 33	安全ライン 593	椅子 277, 723, 734	イブニング・グラブ 346	命綱 20
鎧 853, 855	アラブ首長国連邦 746	アンダーガーメント 872	椅子の例 277	イベリア半島 32	
鎧板 855	アンダーシャツ 796	イズバ 418	居間 250, 902		
鎧枝 855	粗[荒]彫り 401	アンダースカート 337	イズモ 418	医務室 726	
鎧金 750	アラム語 468	アンダーウェア 540	イスラエル 746	妹 785, 785	
鎧革 855	アラメ 183	アンダーワイヤー 367	イスラム教 736	イモリ 111	
鎧革通し 855	アラル海 33	アンチ・スケーティングつまみ 500	イセエビ 218	イモ類 184	
鎧革通し穴 855	霰 64	アンチョビー 219	緯線 36	イヤーパッド 506	
鎧骨 174	アリ 101	アンチモン 682	移送管 565	イヤーホン 502	
油受け 239, 331, 566	アリアン5 24	アンチロック・ブレーキ・システム 559	位相導体 273	イヤホン 503	
油絵の具 397	アリアン4 24		板 300	イヤホン・ジャック 513	
油差し 648	アリーナ 788, 790	アンツーカー 822	板石 298, 322	イヤリング 374	
油壺 398, 903	アリエル 5	アンティグア・バーブーダ 743	イタチ 134	イラク 746	
油壺付きパレット 398	アリゲーター 114	安定ジャケット 567	板張り台 899	イラクサ 187	
油砥石 422	アリス 404	安定板 25	板目木版用版木 421	イラン 744	
アブラハム 736	アリダード 701	安定装置 896	イタヤガイ 217	入り口 427, 539, 717, 719, 724, 728, 730, 738
脂身刺し込み針 233	亜硫酸ガスの放出 70	安定用フィン 759	イタリア 744		
アフリカ 28, 34, 50, 745	アリューシャン海溝 50	アンデス山脈 31	イタリア語 469	イリジウム 683	
アフリカ・プレート 43	アリューシャン列島 30	アンテナ 17, 60, 504, 505, 506, 551, 577, 611, 624, 631, 758, 761, 771, 812	イタリック体 472	医療機関 525	
アプリケーション起動ボタン 527	アルカリ乾電池 689		1 703	医療機器保管室 781	
アプリコット 192	アルカリ金属 682		1ガロン当たりの単価表示窓 548	一眼レフ・カメラ 476, 480	医療班 844
溢れ口 264	アルカリ土類金属 682	アンテナ端子 497	1行空き 472	衣料品店 714	
溢れ防止管 265, 266, 267	アルカリマンガン乾電池 689	アンテフィックス 403	イチゴ 192	医療福祉相談室 781	
溢れ防止スイッチ 294	アルコール球 695	アンテロープ 128	イチゴの断面図 83	医療用ガス・ボンベ 780	
アフロ・アジア語族 468	アルコール柱 695	アンドウイエット 216	イチゴの仲間 83	医療用酸素ガス配管端末器 780	
アプローチ 865, 890, 891	アルゴン 684	アンドラ 743	一次演算キー 529	イルカ 136, 137	
アプローチ・ショット 866	アルザス・グラス 225	アンドロメダ座 12	一次昇圧 677	いるか座 12	
アプローチ部 540	アルジェリア 745	案内カウンター 620	一次焦点 17	イルカの形態図 136	
アフロ・ピック 380	アルゼンチン 742	案内軌条 595	一次焦点観測室 17	イルカの骨格図 136	
アベニュー 711	アルト 514	案内所 715, 719, 725, 733, 769, 779, 886	一次仕分け 474	入れ物 905	
アベレージ露光キー 479	アルト・キー 514		一時停止ボタン 495, 499	いろいろな器具 323	
アホウドリ 119	アルト：レベル3 514	案内塔 659	1天文単位 5	色鉛筆 396	
アボカド 188	アルトロブレウラ 92	案内ねじ 306	1度 434	色鉛筆画法 396	
アポクリン汗腺 172	アルバニア 744	案内羽根 659	位置灯 631, 775	色の合成 690	
アポストロフィー 473	アルバニア語 469	案内板 582	1番ウッド 868	色表示窓 456	
亜北極気候 61	アルビトレ 864	案内盤 424	一番車 696, 697	色フィルター 478	
アポロ 19	アルファベット 472	案内窓口 730	1番ピン 865	色見本 398	
雨 115, 257	アルファベット・キー 530	鞍馬 824, 826	1万m走スタート・ライン 791	岩 434	
雨覆い 247, 249, 257	アルファルファ 190	アンバーサンド 473	1メートル飛び板 828	岩小島 51	
雨押さえ板 247, 249	アルプス山脈 32	アンパイア 799, 807, 809, 812, 817, 820, 864, 877	一葉式跳開橋 542	イワシ 219	
アマガエル 111	アルベッジョ 435		一塁 794	岩滑り 47	
雨傘 391	アルペン系スノーボード 887	アンビル 700	1リットル当たりの単価表示窓 548	岩登り 900	
アマゾン川 31	アルペン種目コース 886	鞍部 826		岩山 900	
アマツバメ 118	アルペン・スキー 888	アンプ・チューナー 497, 503	一塁手 794	陰核 689	
雨垂れ 473	アルペン・スキーヤー 888	アン・プリゾン 919	一階 250	印画紙乾燥棚 485	
雨戸 249	アルミニウム 682	アンプル 783	1回戦 789	印画紙水洗器 485	
天の川 9	アルミニウムのリサイクル容器 71	アンペア 702	一階と地下 713	インカム親機 491	
雨蓋 906	アルミニウム枠 893		一階部分 713	陰極 689	
雨除け 902	アルミホイル 222	**い**	一角獣座 11	陰極端子 562, 687, 689	
アマランサス 203	アルメニア 746	胃 95, 103, 104, 105, 106, 109, 110, 112, 113, 125, 161, 164, 212	イッテルビウム 684	陰極帽 672	
アマランス 203	アルメニア語 469		1．5行空き 472	陰極板ストラップ 562	
網 797	アレー 817, 820, 865		イットリウム 683	インク 397, 421, 470	
編みかご 899	アロー 859		一般家庭のユーザー 525	インク画法 396	
アミガサタケ 183	アロー・レスト 859, 913	イア・プロテクター 861	一般観覧席 856	インクジェット・プリンター 519	
編み方 458	アワ 85, 203	イアペトゥス 5	一般的な案内標識 725	イングリッシュ・ビリヤード 863	
編み機 456	泡 749	Eコマース 525	一般的なカエル 111	イングリッシュ・ホルン 437, 446	
アミキリ 220	合わせ目 362	イーサネット・ポート 526	一般的なスギゴケ 75	イングリッシュ・マスタード 200	
編み地押さえ 456	泡立て器 232	イーゼル 399, 484	一般的なヒキガエル 111	インク・ローラー 421	
編み地押さえつまみ 456	アワビ 217	イエス・キリスト 736	一般的なカエル 111	陰茎 104, 146, 169	
網杓子 233	暗 617	イエメン 746	一般 81, 82, 83	陰茎亀頭 169	
編み図 458	アンカー 274	硫黄 683	Eメール 525	インゲン 191	
網戸 567	アンカー・ピン 559	倚音 435	Eメール・キー 514	インゲンマメ 190, 191	
編み直しキー 456	アンカー・ブロック 540	イオニア式 404	Eメール・ソフトウェア 524	イン・ゴール 805	
編み縄 908	アンカー・ワイヤー 652	イオニア式の付け柱 407	家 915	インサート 709	
鞍節 156	アンクル 697	イオの尾 8	家型テント 902	インサート・キー 515	
編み針 456	アングル・グラインダー 308	イカ 217	移動遠隔作業船 21	インサイド・エッジ 901	
編み紐 893	アングル竿 697	イガイ 217	移動型X線撮影装置 778	インサイド・ラインバッカー 806	
編み棒 457	アンクル・ブーツ 343	錨 610	移動漁車 651	印刷 420	
網目 815	アンクレット 365	錨収納部 605, 609	移動中継車 486, 489	印刷イメージ 420	
編み目ダイヤル 456	アンコウ 220	錨の例 610	移動爪 313	印刷ヘッド 528	
編み物 457	鞍骨弓状部 855	囲碁羽 115	移動展示室 395	インジウム 682	
編み物用物差し 457	鞍座 855	行き過ぎ制限スイッチ 417	糸かがり台 424	インジェクター 383	
アム語 468	暗室 484	息抜き 749	糸受け 439, 440, 441	インジケーター・ライト 515	
雨 64, 65	暗証番号入力パッド 731	イギリス海峡 32	糸掛け 453, 457	印字ヘッド 528	
アメーバ 94	鞍褥 855	イギリス・パン 205	糸切り 453	インスタレーション 395	
アメシスト 375	アンズ 192	イグアナ 114	糸屑フィルター 292, 293	インスタント食品 181	
雨の形態 64	アンズタケ 183	育児嚢 143	糸口 456	隕石 8	
アメリー棚氷 29	安全 764	イクチオサウルス 93	糸倉 439	インターチェンジ 709	
アメリカアカガエル 111	安全横断確認ミラー 568	イクチオステガ 92	糸蔵 439	インターチェンジの例 538	
アメリカインディアン語族 469	安全カバー 304, 305	イグニッション・キー 332, 333	従兄[弟] 785	インターネット 523, 524	
アメリカ型のプラグ 274	安全監察員 837	イグニッション・スイッチ 556, 576	従姉[妹] 785	インターネット・キー 514	
アメリカキンメフクロウ 118	安全環付きカラビナ 900		糸芯 797	インターネット・サービス・プロバイダー 523	
アメリカ合衆国 742	安全キャップ 757	イグニッション・ボックス 627	イトスギの鱗片葉 89		
アメリカクロマ 135	安全区域 844	育児 100	糸立て棒 452	インターネットの利用 525	
アメリカ式賭けるテーブル 919	安全ケース 332	イグルー 418	糸調節皿 453	インターネット・ユーザー 524	
アメリカ式ベッティング・レイアウト 919	安全光 484	生け垣 245, 322	糸調節ダイヤル 452, 453	インターロック 463	
アメリカ式ルーレット盤 919	安全ゴーグル 772	生け垣植木 852	糸調節ばね 453	インタビュー記事 471	
アメリカで用いられている表示 347	安全サーモスタット 293	胃口部 94	糸通し 454, 457	陰端子 687, 689	
アメリカボウフウ 189	安全柵 890	囲口部 94	糸通し穴 461	インディアン座 10	
アメリカワシミミズク 119	安全水域 616	イコール 703	糸綴じ 424	インディケーター 889	
アメリカン・コーン・ブレッド 205	安全水域標識 617	イコール・キー 529	糸取りアーム 457	インテグラル 703	
アメリカン・ショートヘア 132	安全線 729	医師 780, 842, 846	糸取り装置 457	隕鉄 8	
アメリカン・ダックピン 865	安全タンク 670	石 298, 376	糸取りばね 457	インデックス・カード 532	
アメリカン・フットボール 806	安全地帯 844, 846	石落とし 408	糸取り棒 457	インデックス・カード・キャビネット 533	
アメリカン・ベーコン 216	安全灯 771	石畳 298	糸鋸 303		
アメリカン・マスタード 200	安全トリガー 331	石突き 391, 901	糸巻き 439, 440, 441, 452, 453, 458	インデックス・カード引き出し 533	
アメリシウム 684	安全鉄 377	石突きキャップ 909	糸巻き軸 452	インデックス・拡大ボタン 477	
アメンボ 102	安全パッド 823	石引き金 408	糸巻き棒 458	インテルサット衛星 487	
綾織り 463	安全ハンドル 332	石弓 750	糸巻き箱 439	陰電荷 684	
綾棒 461	安全標識 774	衣装 428	糸巻きつまみ 440	インデント 528	
綜目 461	安全ベルト 281, 873, 896, 896, 901	衣装係 428	糸枕 439, 440, 441	インド 747	
アラーム閾値設定つまみ 613	安全弁 234, 665	衣装戸棚 251, 279	田舎パン 205	インド・イラン諸語 469	
アラーム閾値表示窓 613	安全マッチ 391	衣装部屋 251	イナゴ 102	咽頭 99, 163, 164	
アライグマ 134	安全耳覆い 772	移植鏝 325	稲妻 65	インド・オーストラリア・プレート 43	
粗石 298	安全眼鏡 772		稲光 65		
洗い済み食器台 721			イヌ 137	インドネシア 33, 747	
アライナー 838			犬釘 590	インドネシア語 469	
荒毛 320			イヌクテイトット語 469	インド洋 28, 29, 33, 34	
粗塩 201			イヌの形態図 130	インド洋中央海嶺 50	
アラスカ湾 30			イヌの骨格図 131	インド・ヨーロッパ語族 469	
粗[荒]取り 401			イヌの前節 130	インナー・サークル 877	
アラビア海 33			イヌの品種 130	インナー・シート 603	
アラビア語 468			犬走り 660	インナー・ステーター 627	
			イノシシ 128	インナー・テーブル 915	

天文学 > 2-25; 地球 > 26-71; 植物 > 72-89; 動物 > 90-143; 人間 > 144-177; 食べ物と台所 > 178-241; 家屋 > 242-295; 日曜大工・園芸 > 296-333; 衣服 > 334-371;
装身具類と日用品 > 372-391; 芸術と建築 > 392-465; 情報伝達とオフィス・オートメーション > 466-535; 交通と機械 > 536-643; エネルギー > 644-677; 科学 > 678-705;
社会 > 706-785; スポーツとゲーム > 786-920

インナー・テント 902, 903
インナー・ブーツ 889, 895
インナー・ブル 918
インナー・ミラー 556
インナー・ライナー 561
陰嚢 146, 169
インバーテッド・プリーツ 357
インバート溝 595
インバウンズ・ライン 806
インプット選択ボタン 497
インプット・ライト 497
インプルビウム 406
インフレーター 841
インフレーター・バルブ 841
陰門 148
引用符 473
イン・ライン・スケーティング 895
イン・ライン・スケート靴 895
イン・ライン・スピード・スケート靴 895
イン・ライン・ホッケー・スケート靴 895
インラン 890
飲料 180
飲料缶 223
飲料自動販売機 548
飲料配給器 723
飲料販売機 723
引力 687

う

ウィール 894, 895
ウイキョウ 185
ウィグワム 418
ウィケット 799, 799
ウィケットキーパー 799
ウィツィロポチトリ神殿 412
ウィペン 443
ウィルクス・ランド 29
ウインカー 554, 571, 576
ウイング 416, 873, 897, 909
ウイング・アタック 809
ウイング・チップ 897
ウイング・ディフェンス 809
ウイングレット 625, 628
ウインター・スポーツ 877
ウインター・タイヤ 560
ウインチ 573, 835
ウインチ操作ハンドル 573
ウインド・アビーム 833
ウインドー 554, 836
ウインドー・ガラス 551
ウインドー・タブ 532
ウインドサーフィン 836
ウインドシールド 550, 574, 577, 607, 876
ウインド・シンセサイザー・コントローラー 451
ウインドスクリーン 488, 550
ウインド・チェスト 445
ウインドブレーカー 353
ウーシャンフェン 199
ウースター・ソース 200
ウーロン茶 208
ウエイト 850, 851
ウエイト・ベルト 841
ウエイト・マシーン 851
ウエイトリフティング 850
ウエイトリフティング・シューズ 850
ウエイトリフティング・ベルト 850
ウエーター 721
ウェーダー 911
ウェーハ・ボード 300
ウェブ・クリップ 380
ウェールズ語 469
上カーソル 515
植木鉢 330
植木鉢 322
植え込み 413
ウエストゴム 351
ウエスト・スナップ 368
ウエストバンド 350, 353
ウエストバンド留め 350
ウエスト・スーツ 841
ウエスト・ベルト 906
ウェッジ 753
ウェッジ・レバー 309
ウェッデル海 29
上パイプ 578
上馬衛枝 854
ウェブカム 517
ウェブカメラ 517
ウェブ・フレーム 607
上巻葉 390
ウェルト 342
ウォーキー・トーキー 505
ウォーター・キー 447
ウォーター・ゴブレット 225
ウォーター・ハザード 866, 867
ウォーター・ポンプ・プライヤー 310
ウォーム 462, 573
ウォーム・アップ・レーン 882
ウォーム軸 686
ウォーム歯車 686
ウォー・テント 902
魚座 12
魚皿 226
ウォッシャー・ノズル 550
ウォッチ・タワー 94
ウォロフ語 468
迂回誘導路 618

ウガンダ 745
浮き 263, 615, 911
浮き石棒 911
浮き留め金 263
浮きクレーン 596
浮き玉 265
浮きドック 839
浮き橋 542
浮き網 109
浮き輪 611
ウクライナ 744
ウクライナ語 469
受け 453
受け板 445
受入室 778
受け皿 249
受け座 249
受付 509, 715, 719, 730, 733, 764, 769, 779, 781
受付デスク 730
受け皿 391
右舷 609, 616, 617
烏口骨 111, 116
動き方の種類 916
動く上顎 112
ウコン 198
ウサギ 123
兎座 11
牛飼い座 13
後ろ足 143
後ろディレーラー 578, 580
後ろ飛び込み 828
後ろの壁 818, 819
後ろの垂れ 349
後ろ踏み切り前飛び込み 828
後ろブレーキ 578
後ろブレーキ・ペダル 576
後身 348
後身頃 348
右心室 161, 162
右心房 161, 162
雨水管渠 712
渦形足 276
薄地モスリン 422
渦状の雲の帯 63
薄のみ 401
ウズベキスタン 746
渦巻 404, 405, 439
渦巻きケーシング 658, 659
渦巻き状の糸 103
渦巻き装飾 404, 405
渦巻きの腕 9
渦巻き模様 276
ウズラ 120, 212
ウズラの卵 212
ウソ 118
歌 444, 446, 447
打ち上げロケット 24
打ち上げロケットの断面図 24, 25
打ち上げロケットの例 24
内エッジ 901
内隠し 360
打ち金 752
内側エッジ 127
内側ノブ 248
内側ハンドル 554
内側ロック・ボタン 554
内筒 249
内苞 291
内歯付き座金 310
内歯ワッシャー 310
内ポケット 360, 389
宇宙物理学 18
宇宙実験室 23
宇宙探査機 18, 53
宇宙探査機の例 19
宇宙服 20
内輪 613
ウチワサボテン 197
ウッド 867, 868
腕 95, 139, 147, 149, 610, 783
腕当て 880
腕枝 399
腕固め 844
腕木 399, 433, 599, 843
腕木式信号機 583
腕支え 399
腕通し 857
腕の位置 829
うどん 207
ウナギ 219
項 147, 149
項革 853
ウニ 95
畝立てプラウ 641
右肺 161, 163
右肺静脈 162
ウプランド 338
羽柄 115
羽片 76
羽弁 115
右方屈曲あり 544, 547
ウマ 124, 129
うま 257
ウマの解剖図 125
ウマの形態図 124
ウマの骨格図 126
海 7, 38, 48, 664
海側 664
海蛇座 11, 13

ウムラウト 473
埋め立て 71
羽毛の掛け布団 280
右翼 795
右翼手 794
裏 351
裏当て 342, 370, 881
裏打ち 386
裏地 348, 349, 455
裏地と芯地 455
裏布 455
裏表紙 426
ウラル山脈 29
ウラル・アルタイ語族 469
ウラン 684
ウラン燃料が核分裂を起こす 665
売上票 699
雨量記録計 58, 59
雨量計 58
雨量升 59
雨量を測定する器具 59
ウルグアイ 742
ウルドゥー語 469
鱗 108, 112, 113
上糸掛け 452
上襟 362
上飾り 282, 282
上框 247, 249, 278
上側シーツ 280
上着 348, 844, 853, 855
上駒 439, 440, 441
上皿天秤 698
上皿 231
上付き 472
上蓋 465
上蓋支え 465
上瞼 110, 132, 177
上枠 249
ウンウンウニウム 683
ウンウンニリウム 683
ウンウンビウム 683
永年牧草地 182
衛兵所 408, 409
泳法の河床 597
泳法監察員 830
泳法審判員 830
泳法の種類 832
エウロパ 4
エーゲ海 32
AGP拡張コネクター 513
エース 914
ATM 730
AV機器 716
絵柄 917, 920
液柄 655
液化 680
液果 82, 83, 192
腋窩 146, 148
腋芽 77
液化窒素タンク 694
腋窩静脈 160
腋窩神経 166
液化窒素タンク 160
駅舎 583
液晶画面 496
液晶ディスプレイ 696
液晶表示パネル 479
液晶モニター 477
エキステンド 472
エキスパンダー 850
エキスパンド 472
液体 680, 681
液体・気体隔離板 562
液体コンパス 612
液体酸素タンク 24, 25
液体酸素タンク隔壁 25
液体水素タンク 24, 25
液体比重計 562
エキヌス 404
液胞 74, 94
駅名 592
エクアドル 742
エクササイズ・ウエア 371
エクスクラメーション・マーク 473
エクストラ・ボールド 472
エクストラ・ライト 472
エクスパンション・ピトン 900
エクスパンション・ボルト 302
エクスパンダー 450
エグゼクティブ・デスク 511
エクリン汗腺 172
エコー 40, 41
エコ 464
エジェクター 638
エジプト 745
エシャロット 184
エスカルゴ 217
エスカルゴ皿 233
エスカルゴ用トング 233
エスカレーター 417, 427, 592, 713
S極 687
エスケープ 514
エスケープ・キー 514
S状結腸 164
エストニア 744
エスパドリール 344
Sバンド・アンテナ 60
S バンド高利得アンテナ 60
Sビデオ出力 526
エスプレッソ・コーヒー・メーカー 241
エスプレッソ・マシーン 241
エゾネギ 184
エゾバイ 217
枝 87, 87, 89, 185
枝束 253

映画館 427, 608, 710, 714
鋭角 704, 704
映画のセット 428
映画名と上映時間 427
嬰記号 435
英語 469
曳航索切り離しノブ 898
エイコーン・スクウォッシュ 189
英国国教会 736
エイコンドライト 8
映写機 427
映写機室 10
泳者国籍 831
映写幕 395, 427
映写スクリーン 483
泳者 831
英数キーパッド 506
英数キーボード 507, 548, 730, 731
英数字キーパッド 506, 514
英数字キーボード 507, 548, 730, 731
衛星 24, 486
衛星遠隔計測 41
衛星航法装置 613
衛星地上局 525
衛星中継 486
衛星通信 487
衛星通信アンテナ 608, 609, 762
衛星の軌道 60
映像スクリーン 494, 494
映像接続パネル 489
映像調整室 489
映像調整装置 489, 490
映像調整担当 489, 490
映像モニター・セレクター 491
HDD 521
エイト 839
エイト・カット 375
エイト環 900
永年牧草地 182
衛兵所 408, 409
泳法の河床 597
泳法監察員 830
泳法審判員 830
泳法の種類 832
エウロパ 4
エーゲ海 32
AGP拡張コネクター 513
エース 914
ATM 730
AV機器 716
絵柄 917, 920
液柄 655
液化 680
液果 82, 83, 192
腋窩 146, 148
腋芽 77
液化窒素タンク 694
腋窩静脈 160
腋窩神経 166
液化窒素タンク 160
駅舎 583
液晶画面 496
液晶ディスプレイ 696
液晶表示パネル 479
液晶モニター 477
エキステンド 472
エキスパンダー 850
エキスパンド 472
液体 680, 681
液体・気体隔離板 562
液体コンパス 612
液体酸素タンク 24, 25
液体酸素タンク隔壁 25
液体水素タンク 24, 25
液体比重計 562
エキヌス 404
液胞 74, 94
駅名 592

枝に止まる鳥 117
枝リブ 410
エチオピア 745
X線 690
Xバンド・アンテナ 40
エッグ・タイマー 231
エッグ・ポーチャー 235
エッジ 881, 884, 887, 888
エッチング・プレス機 421
閲兵場 409
閲覧室 733
エナメル質 159
エナン 339
n型層 687
N極 687
n電極 672, 673
エネルギー源 41
エネルギーの単位 702
エネルギー放出 681
エノキタケ 183
エバ・ミルク 210
エビ 204
蝦蛄 828
えび万力 462
Fインディ・カー 873
FMモード選択ボタン 497
F3000カー 873
F1エンジン 25
F1カー 873
f字孔 439
FD 521
エプロン 577, 618, 842
エベ 848, 849
エベレスト山 53
エポーレット・スリーブ 360
エポレット 352
MPS 384
エメラルド 375
エメラルド・カット 375
エメリー板 377
エメンタール 211
腰 115
鰓 105, 106, 109
鰓蓋 108, 111
襟 348, 349, 352, 362
襟ぐり 351
襟腰 362
襟細胞 95
襟元 349, 362
襟芯 349
エリダヌス座 10
エリトリア 745
襟の例 362
L型差し金 313
Lキャリッジ 456
エルサルバドル 742
エルビウム 684
エルボ 206, 258
エルボー・パッド 800, 808
エルボ継手 269
エルロン 624, 898
エレキ・ギター 441
エレクトロニクス 689
エレベーター 16, 417, 482, 509, 625, 650, 666, 713, 724, 761, 898
エレベーター・クランク 482
エレベーター・ロック・レバー 482
エレボン 23
円 728
遺骨骨壷 155
円盤 612
円回内筋 150
円花飾り 411
遠隔計測 40
遠隔指令アンテナ 40
遠隔操作式転轍器 590
遠隔測定制御アンテナ 60
遠隔探査 40
円花窓 411
沿岸州 51
円環面 705
演技台 824
円鏡面状 79
遠近両用レンズ 385
円形 79
円柱 322
円形気泡管 701
円形建物 713
円形の胴 432
円形パノラマ 492
園芸 322
園芸用手袋 325
園芸用ホース 328
円型枠 459
縁甲板 113
遠視 691
円周 704
遠視用 385
エンジン 574, 643, 651, 758
遠心圧縮機 627
エンジン回転計 557
エンジン吸気口 568
エンジン空気取り入れ口 760
エンジン支柱 625
エンジン始動車 626
エンジン収納部 632, 639, 640
エンジン・乗員警告表示装置 626
エンジン・スイッチ 556, 576
エンジン・ストップ・スイッチ 576
エンジン燃料計 564
エンジンの種類 564
エンジン・ハウジング 331
エンジン・フード 550, 570

エンジン・ブロック 566	王の間 402	オオムギ 85, 203	オフィス家具 510	音質調節つまみ 441
エンジン・ルーム 568	横帆 601	大文字 472	オフィス・タワー 713	音場調整器 497
エンジン冷却用空気取り入れ口 874	黄斑 167	大物車 588	オフィス・チェアー 511	温水管 266, 270, 271
円錐 705	凹版印刷 420	オオヤマネコ 134	オフィス・ビル 710, 713	温水供給管 266, 270, 271
延髄 167	凹版印刷方式 422	腎 750	オブジェクト・ボール 862	温水循環 271
円錐花序 85	王妃の間 402	オール 598, 600, 851	オフセット継ぎ手 269	温水立て管 262
円錐形尖塔屋根 415	オウム 118	オール・シーズン・タイヤ 560	オフ・タートルネック 363	温水吹かさ 675
円錐形ブイ 615, 617	凹メニスカス・レンズ 691	オールスパイス 198	オプティカル・マウス 516	温水排出口 259, 267
円錐形浮標 615, 617	横列砂丘 52	オートの雲 4	オフ・ロード車 549	音声アラーム 613
塩水湖 52	凹レンズ 691	オールの種類 838	オフ・ロード・バイク 577	音声ガイド 394
円錐図法 36	大顎 97, 99	オール・ロック 839	オペラ・グラス 385	音声・映像入出力 497
延声記号 435	大雨覆い 115	丘 45	オペラ劇場 710	音声再生装置 497
縁石 582, 593, 712	大雨覆い羽 115	オカピ 128	オペラ・レングス・ネックレス 374	音声調整卓 488, 489
塩素 683	大雨 63, 64	小川 4	オペレーティング・ロッド 755	音声編集ボタン 450
沿層坑道 650	覆い 767	オキシドール 777	オペロン 5	音声モニター 488, 489, 490, 491
演奏台 444	大犬座 11	お客様用入り口 720	オマーン 746	音声録音ボタン 527
演奏用付属品 436	OHP 535	お客様用クローク 720	オマーン湾 33	音栓 444, 445
塩素系漂白剤の使用禁止 347	おえずり 404, 405	お客様用トイレ 720	緒巻き 460	温帯気候 61
塩素系漂白剤の使用不可 347	オオエゾデンダ 76	屋外装置 260	おむつ 368	温帯林 66
エンター・キー 515	大枝 87	オクサー 852	重さ 699	音程 434
掩体道 408	オーガー・ビット 323	オクターブ 434	おもちゃ 717	温度 53
エンダイブ 187	大型衣装だんす 278	オクターブ・レバー 446	おもちゃ屋 714	温度切り替えスイッチ 382
エンタプラチュア 403, 405	大型家電製品 716	オクタブ 849	表板 439	温度切り替えランプ 292, 293
演壇 734	大型貨物自動車等通行止め 545, 546	奥付 471	表地 455	温度計 655, 695, 899
円柱 403, 405, 705	大型ジェット機 624	オクトパス 841	表底 342, 371	温度自動調節器 267
円柱ブイ 617	大型スクリーン・テレビ 493	屋内競技場 788	表表紙 260	温度測定 695
円柱浮標 617	大型バス・タオル 379	屋内装置 260	主な石の動き 916	温度センサー 18, 238, 561
延長記号 435	O型リング 268	屋内体操場 788	主な技法 396	温度調節サーモスタット 239
延長パイプ 289	オオハマダラ 101	屋内用電気グリル 239	主な区分 919	温度調節スイッチ 267, 291
延長はしご 321	大釜 452	屋内用排水管 271	主な国際道路標識 544	温度調節ダイヤル 261
園丁ナイフ 330	大鎌 330	送り 460	主な静脈と動脈 160	温度調節つまみ 238, 288, 465
エンド 515	オオカミ 134	送り錘 698	主な部屋 250	温度調節蓋 256
エンドウ 84	狼座 423	送り車 453	主な刃の種類 401	温度表示器 381
煙道 390	狼爪 130	送り歯 453	主なミサイル 759	雄鶏 122
円筒形ブイ 615	扇形拡張ケーブル 541	送り溝 263	母屋 182	温度を測定する器具 59
円筒形浮標 615	扇形座 397	送り調節ダイヤル 452	錘 16, 43, 542, 615, 697, 793, 851, 911	女 148
円筒図法 36	大ギヤ 870	贈り物品 717	親 784, 785	音板 449
エンドウマメ 84, 190	オーク 88	おくるみ 368	親知らず 159	音符 434
エンド・キー 506, 515	大熊座 13	歳 460	親柱 312, 381	温風器 260
エンド・キャップ 284, 667	大皿 226	押さえ 312, 381	親杭 255	温風排気口 564
エンド・サーチ・ボタン 496	オオシモフリエダシャク 101	押さえ圧調節ダイヤル 452	親骨 391	温風吹き出し口 594
エンド・ストップ 284, 303	オーストラリア 28, 50, 747	押さえ板 424	親指 141, 156, 173, 346, 797	音部記号 434
エンド・ゾーン 806, 809	オーストラリア先住民の諸言語 469	押さえ金 452, 453	親指当て 776	オン・ボード・コンピューター 556
煙突 245, 257, 259, 599, 604, 608, 646	オーストリア 744	押さえ込み 844	親指掛け 446, 447	オンライン・ゲーム 525
煙突陶冠 245	大太鼓 437	押さえ棒 453	親指押しボタン 444	オンライン目録 733
煙突連結部 256	大玉縁 404	押さえレバー 381	オランウータン 139	音量指示計 488, 491
エンド・ブラケット 284	オオツチグモ 102	歳 460	オランダ 743	音量調節つまみ 441, 451, 497, 504, 505, 508, 513
エンド・プレート 667	オーガナイザー 530	歳框 460	オランダ語 469	音量調節ボタン 495, 503, 507
エンド・ライン 806, 811, 812, 815	大道具係 461	歳柄横木 460	檻 407	音量つまみ 497, 504, 505, 508, 513
エントランス・ホール 509	オーディオ・コンソール 488, 489, 490	筬通し 461	織り糸 908	音量ボタン 495, 503, 507
エンドレス 500	オーディオ・システム 556	押しアーム 636	オリーブ 188	温料理台 721
円の部分 704	オーディオ・ジャック 513	押し圧チューブ 470	オリーブ油 209	
円盤 423, 464, 641, 793	オーディオ入出力 527	押し誤り訂正キー 529	オリエンタル・コーチング・ステッチ 459	**か**
円盤間隔調節レバー 643	大通具係 461	オジー・アーチ 413	オリオン座 11, 12	
円盤投げとハンマー投げ 791	大通り 39, 711	押し切り 470	折り返し 348, 391	カ 101
円盤部 9	オオトカゲ 114	押出し装置 470	折り返し監察員 831	カー 835
円板ブレーキ 559, 574	オート・スコアラー 865	雄しべ 80, 82	折り返し審判員 831	カー・カバー 558
燕尾形扉 739	オート・ダイヤル一覧表 506	押し棒 416	折り返し面 831, 832	ガーキン 188
鉛筆 470	オート・トワレ 379	押しボタン 248, 294, 470	折り返し面 831, 832	カー・コート 355
鉛筆削り 534	オートバイ 574, 576	オジロジカ 128	織り台 458	カーゴ・ベイ 22
輓木託車 857	オートバイの計器盤 576	雄 702	折り畳み椅子 277	カーゴ・ベイのドア 23
煙霧 57	オートバイの例 577	汚水処理車 622	折り畳み式 391	ガーゼの包帯 777
園路 322	オートバイ・レース 874	汚水処理槽 70	折り畳み式グリル 907	カーソル移動キー 515, 529
	オートパイロット 759	汚水溜め 263	折り畳み式シャベル 906	ガーター 367
お	オート・フォーカス・スイッチ 483	雄継ぎ口 909, 910	折り畳み式テーブル 278	ガーター編み 458
	オードブル皿 226	雄バチ 99	折り畳み式やすり 377	ガーターヘビ 114
尾 107, 112, 113, 121, 122, 124, 130, 133, 136, 140, 143, 425	オードブルと冷たい料理 722	雄フェルール 909, 910	折り畳み式ランプ 608	ガーター・ベルト 367
尾脚 97	オート・マニュアル切り替えスイッチ 316	オセアニア 28, 29	折り畳みドア 416	加圧器 670, 671
オアシス 48, 52	オート麦 85, 203	オセアニア諸語 469	折り畳み翼 857	加圧重水 670
甥 785	オート麦粉 204	オセアニア・ポリネシア 747	折り丁 426	加圧水型炉 671
追い越し禁止 544, 546	オートマチック・ドライバー 302	汚染ガスの放出 69	織りの原理 463	加圧器 625
追い越し車線 539	オート・リバース・ボタン 504	汚染物質の浸透 69	オリノコ川 31	カーディガン 354, 359
オイスター・フォーク 228	オートミール 217	オゾン層 53	オリフラム 739	カーテン 282, 492
追い抜き競走用自転車とレーサー 871	オオノガイ 101	オタマジャクシ 111	折りべら 426	カーテン地 285
追い抜き車線 871	オーバーオール 358, 368, 887	尾垂木 412	折り目 350, 362	カーテンの例 283
負い紐 906	オーバー・カーテン 282	落ち込み穴 47	折り山 455	カーテン・ヘッドの例 283
オイル・ドレーン・プラグ 566	オーバーコート 352, 355	落ちこみ穴 47	オルガン 444	カーテン・ボール 284
オイル・パステル 396	オーバー・スライド式車庫扉 416	オックスフォード・シューズ 342	オルガンの構造 445	ガーデン・ライン 324
オイル・パステル画法 396	オーバーバス 540	オッズ表示板 856	オルケストラ 402	カーテン・レール 284
オイル・パン 566	オーバー・ブラウス 359	夫 785	オルソ・ステッキ 782	カード 914, 915
オイル・パン・ガスケット 566	オーバーフロー 264	オットマン 785	オルタネーター 552, 566, 586	ガード 229, 316, 811, 849
オイル・ヒーター 260	オーバーフロー管 265, 266, 267, 485	オットマン・チェア 277	オルト 514	カートウィール 341
王 916	オーバーヘッド 821	弟 785	オルト・キー 514	カード挿し 386
凹角 704	オーバーヘッド・テーブル 780	男 146	オルトケラス 92	カートゥーン 471
横隔壁 606	オーバーヘッド・プロジェクター 535	落とし穴 279	オルドビス紀 92	カード挿し付き札入れ 386
凹角堡 409	オーバーラップ・キャリアー 284	落とし卵用鍋 235	オルト・レベル3 514	カード道路 866
横隔膜 163	オオハシ 119	落とし戸 407	オレガノ 202	カード番号 729, 731
扇形 704	大羽 115	音の出る仕組み 445	オレンジ 194	カード保有者のサイン 729
応急処置解説書 777	大梁 252	緒締め 433, 439	オレンジ 400	カード保有者名 729
応急手当班 853	オーバル・カット 375	緒締め板 433, 439	オレンジの断面図 82	カード読み取り口 730, 731
甌穴 47	OBライン 819	オドメーター 557	下ろす 230	カード読み取りスロット 548
横行結腸 164	オービター 18, 22, 23	緒止め掛け 439	オン・エア・ランプ 488	カード読み取り装置 493, 507
横材 632, 632	踊り場 251, 255	音楽 432	音階 434	カード・リーダー 548
雄牛 129	おとり用の鳥 913	音楽アドバイザー 490	音楽 432	カートリッジ 268, 315, 470, 500, 754, 773, 860, 861, 912
牡牛座 12	鬼目やすり 309, 401	音楽室 734	カートリッジ受け 268	
欧州実験モジュール 21	尾根 45	音響・映像プレビュー装置 491	カートリッジ軸 268	
欧州連合旗 729	オパール 375	音響技師 429	カートリッジ式水栓 268	
横幢 409	雄花 89	音響信号 436	カートリッジ・テープ・レコーダー 488	
凹状の曲面 420	尾羽 115	音響測深機[器] 613	カートリッジ止め輪 268	
応接間 738	帯 844, 845, 846	音響測深機[器]送受波器 613	カートリッジ・ヒューズ 272	
横舵 763, 763	帯桟 247	音響担当 489, 490	カートリッジ・フィルム 481	
横帯 740	オピストドモス 403	音響調整室 489, 490	ガードル 367, 374	
王台 100	牡羊座 12	音響天井 431	ガード・レール 291, 894	
横断アーチ 410	尾ひれ 108, 136	音響発生器 488	ガードレール 590	
横断歩道 545, 547, 712	オヒョウ 221	音響モニター・セレクター 491	カートン 390	
横転防止構造 873	温室効果 68	音叉 436	ガーナ 745	
応答メッセージ録音カセット 508	温室効果ガス 68	温室 182	カーネーション 80	
応答メッセージ録音ボタン 508	温室効果ガスの濃縮 68	尾びれ 108, 136	ガーネット 375	
横突起 157, 168	大包丁 229	温室効果の上昇 68	カービング・ナイフ 229	
	オーボエ 437, 446	オフィス 509		
	オーム 702	オフィス・オートメーション 509		

天文学 > 2-25; 地球 > 26-71; 植物 > 72-89; 動物 > 90-143; 人間 > 144-177; 食べ物と台所 > 178-241; 家屋 > 242-295; 日曜大工・園芸 > 296-333; 衣服 > 334-371; 装身具類と日用品 > 372-391; 芸術と建築 > 392-465; 情報伝達とオフィス・オートメーション > 466-535; 交通と機械 > 536-643; エネルギー > 644-677; 科学 > 678-705; 社会 > 706-785; スポーツとゲーム > 786-920

カービング・フォーク 229
カーブ 872
カーペット 254
カーペンタリア湾 29
カーボベルデ 745
ガーメント・バッグ 389
カーラー 877
カーラー・ピン 380
ガーリック・プレス 230
カーリング 877
カーリング・ストーン 877
カーリング・ブラシ 877
カール 7, 206
カール・アイロン 381
カー・レース 872
ガイアナ 742
外陰部 171
海塩 201
外円 877
外縁 729
外縁堆積原 46
カイエンヌ 199
海王星 4, 5
回音 435
開花 86
絵画 395, 395
外核 42
絵画と線画 396
外果皮 81, 82, 83
貝殻 105
海岸 49
概観 248
碍管 657, 658, 663
海岸線の例 51
海岸断崖 51
海岸の地形 51
外気圏 53
会議室 394, 509, 718, 724, 735, 764
会議場 718
皆既食 6, 7
会議ホール 718
階級 99
外球 275
階級型 99
階級記章 770
海峡 38
開襟 362
会計士事務室 509
外頸静脈 160
海溝 49
開口絞り 694
開口絞り調節つまみ 694
海溝と海嶺 50
開口部扉 17
外鰓 111
開催中の展示会の案内垂れ幕 394
改札係 582
改札係ブース 592
海山 49
界磁 688
外趾 115
碍子 663
外耳 174
開始線 845, 847
外耳道 158, 173, 174
開始ボタン 512
開始の姿勢 843
界磁巻き線 688
外車 599
回収車体 573
会衆席 737
階乗 703
海上交通 596
海上の物理探鉱 653
海上浮標式 616
海上輸送 649
海食崖 51
外唇 105
外陣 915
外靭帯 105
海水パンツ 371
回数算定員 883
階数表示盤 417
海図室 604
海棲哺乳動物 136
海棲哺乳動物の例 137
解説 395
海鮮醤 200
海草 183
外槽 292
外装 689
外装コード 507
外槽底 292
外側楔状骨 155
外側広筋 150, 151
外側大腿皮神経 166
外側半月軟骨 175
外帯線 871
階段 245, 253, 255, 412, 417, 427, 431, 543, 592, 655, 724, 842
階段座席 402, 407
階段の段 255
階段の天窓 251
階段幅 255
階段吹き抜け 251
懐中電灯 770
回腸 764
海面 42
海底掘削原 604
海底ケーブル 524
海底ケーブル伝送 487
海底湖 49
海底パイプライン 654

海底油井 654
海底油田掘削 653
海底油田掘削船 653
回転 889
回転ウィール 920
回転運動をローターへ伝送する 662
回転柄 307
回転円板 273
回転改札入り口 592
回転改札出口 592
回転乾燥不可 347
回転掘削機 647
回転鍬 641
回転コード 381
回転子 659
回転式壁灯 287
回転式拳銃 754
回転式スプリンクラー 329
回転式チーズ下ろし器 230
回転式連発銃 754
回転軸 237, 436, 676, 697
回転速度切り替えボタン 500
回転速度計 576
回転台 542
回転弾倉 754
回転テーブル 651
回転灯 766, 766, 771
回転灯操作盤 771
回転ドーム 17
回転ドラム 43, 43
回転ノズル 294
回転刃 332
回転はしご 321
回転盤 919
回転用スキー板 888
回転盤とアーム 445
回転ハンドル 307
回転ブラシ 380
回転棒 421
回転枕 458
回転翼 292, 676
回転翼頂部 631
回転翼羽根 631
回転翼ハブ 631
ガイド 238, 303, 304, 909
外套 105, 106
外筒 776
街灯 287, 712
外套筋 106
外套腔 634
ガイド・チューブ 652
ガイド・バー 331
ガイド・ハンドル 308
ガイド・ローラー 499
カイパー帯 4
カイパー・ベルト 4
灰白質 167, 168
外半規管 174
外皮 655
外被 689
外鼻 175
外鼻道 110
開封テープ 390
外腹斜筋 150, 151
外部固定子 627
外部テラス 609
外部推進剤タンク 22
外部電源入力端子 504
開閉ハンドル 320
解剖学 150
解放こて 587
解放レバー 889
カイマン 114
海綿 379
海面 49, 53
海面気圧 55
海綿腔 95
海綿骨 154
海綿体 169
海綿動物 95
海綿動物の解剖図 95
開門 917
海洋 67
海洋気象観測船 54
海洋性気候 61
海洋性熱帯気団 55
海洋性北極気団 55
海洋底 49
海洋地殻 42
外翼幅 112
外来治療用盲人ブロック 781
殻斗 84
外輪 413, 599, 640
外輪砂 599
街路 711, 713
外廊 411, 614, 676
回路遮断器 260
回路遮断機 658
海路標識 614
外惑星 4
カウパー腺 169
カウル 550
カウルネック 363
カウル・パネル 550
カウンター 424, 370, 722
カウンターウェイト 500
カウンタージブ 634
カウンタージブ・バラスト 634
カウンターフープ 448
カウンター・リセット・ボタン 499
返し 911

返し縫いボタン 452
カエデ 88
カエル 110
カエルの一生 111
カエルの形態図 110
カエルの骨格図 111
顔 139, 146
家屋の外観 244
家屋の構成要素 247
家屋の構造 250
顔のメーキャップ 378
画架 399
下階の床板 417
抱え型 828
下顎 108, 124
化学 680
科学機器 17, 23
化学記号 684
家屋 402, 428, 431
科学記号 702
化学結合 680
化学元素 682
下顎骨 111, 112, 116, 121, 122, 123, 126, 131, 136, 138, 141, 142, 152, 158
化学処理 656
化学肥料の使用 69
画架座 11
踵 147, 149, 342, 351, 370, 641, 797
鏡 264, 389, 724, 876
下弦 540
下弦の月 7
火管 267
花冠 80
カキ 197, 217
鍵 249
鉤 457, 698, 699
鍵穴 249
鉤穴 291
欠き首 404, 405
書き込み禁止タブ 521
鍵座 248
鉤足 767
鉤爪 115, 117, 121, 122, 130, 133, 140, 143
牡蠣ナイフ 229
鉤針 457
牡蠣フォーク 228
鉤棒 767
鍵ホック 453
鍵溝 249
鍵屋 715
書き物机 279
書菜類 188
花菜類 187
可逆反応 684
蝸牛 174
蝸牛神経 174
核 6, 8, 掘10, 74, 94, 94, 170
萼 80, 83, 84
角穴車 697
架空送電線 663
架空地線 663
架空電線 663
角布 473
核エネルギー 665
核エネルギー発電 665
角形ドーム屋根 414
角括弧 473
角切り肉 214, 215
学芸員室 394
殻口 105
角氷ディスペンサー 224
角鑿 315
拡散板 479
殻軸 105
角質 172
角質の口 113
隠し縫い 349
隠しポケット 386
学習障害児用教室 734
学術名 81, 82, 83
萼状総苞 83
核小体 74, 94, 168, 170
殻頂 117
核心 84
角笛 275
拡声器 766
学生休憩室 735
学生室 735
学生食堂 735
隔測 40
拡大鏡 693
殻皮 104, 105
貸し金庫 731
可視光線 690
貸し出しデスク 733
果実 81
加湿器 261
力氏度 695
華氏度 695
舵 600, 834, 838, 839
舵板 606
舵取リオール 598, 598
舵取リ車軸 633
舵取リハンドル 607
舵取リレバー 633
梶棒 857
梶棒支え 857
郭内 408
確認キー 731
格納式ステップ 567
格納式の取っ手 386
格納式の握り 386
格納容器建屋 667
家具ノズル 289
荷重支持枠 636
下襦 602
花床 80, 83
顆状関節 156

各部 276, 277, 280
楽譜記号 434
額縁 249, 395
花序の種類 81
核分裂 681
核分裂性原子核 681
隔壁 82, 84, 571
萼片 80, 82, 83
確保員 900
確保桁 900
確保者 900
確保ロープ 900
核膜 74, 94
角膜 177, 691
隔膜 84
額面金箔 729, 729
家屋 402, 428, 431
隔離室 778
隔離板 562, 689
影 696
跛歩 125
渦形室 658, 659
渦形室足 276
掛け金 238, 294, 389
カケス 118
欠けていく月 7
掛けはしご 767
掛ける 703
下弦 540
下弦の月 7
かご 294
囲い 416, 791
囲い地 182
河口 38, 51
火口 44
下降エンジン 18
花崗岩層 42
下降 900
下行結腸 164
下行大動脈 161
下降通廊 402
仮根 75
傘 76
下腿 115
画材 396
火災止め 252
火災予防 764
果菜類 188
花菜類 187
カサガイ 217
傘形屋根 415
風上 833
笠木 277
カササギ 118
傘立て 391
傘とステッキ 391
傘 391
重ねテーブル 278
カサバ 195
傘歯車 307, 686
カサバ・メロン 746
カザフスタン 746
飾り穴 342, 371
飾り板 290, 432
飾りカーテン 282
飾りテープ 368
飾り房 282
飾り縁 439, 440
飾り持ち送り 405
火山 42, 44
加算・イコール・キー 529
加算キー 529
火山弾 44
火山島 49
火山の例 44
火山灰層 44
火山灰の噴煙 44
河岸 664
下肢 161
下層 115
花糸 80
舵 600, 834, 838, 839
舵板 606
舵取リオール 598, 598
舵取リ車軸 633
舵取リハンドル 607
舵取リレバー 633
梶棒 857
梶棒支え 857
郭内 408
カシオペア座 12
かじ座 11
貸し金庫 731
可視光線 690
貸し出しデスク 733
果実 81
加湿器 261
力氏度目盛り 695
華氏度目盛り 695
貨車 583, 587
貨車の例 588
果樹 473
果樹園 182
果樹園用はしご 321
下樹 602
花床 80, 83
顆状関節 156

家事用品 295
加色混合 690
花序の種類 81
下歯列弓 174
下唇 177, 444
下唇鬚 96, 99
ガス 275, 651, 656
ガス圧入モジュール 652
ガス油 656
下垂体 167
ガスケット 269, 294, 562
ガス充填装置 611
ガス・シリンダー 755
ガス栓 267
ガス筒 755
ガス・バーナー 267, 685
カスピ海 28, 33
ガス本管 712
ガス湯沸かし装置 267
ガス・ライター 391
ガス・レンジ 290, 721
風 56, 69, 70
火星 4, 5
火成岩 42
縦掛け 462
化石燃料 68, 70
カセグレン焦点 17
カセット 521
カセット・コンパートメント 496
カセット挿入口 495
カセット・テープ 499, 504
カセット・テープ・デッキ 499
カセット・デッキ 488, 499
カセット・ドライブ 521
カセット取り出しボタン 495, 499
カセット・プレーヤー 504, 504
カセット・プレーヤー操作ボタン 504
カセット・ホルダー 499
風に対する帆走方向 833
風の作用 67
風箱 445
風箱板 445
加線 434
架線 585
河川 39
下層 62
下層雲 55
画像再生ボタン 477
画像調節ボタン 496
下層土 78
仮足 94
家族関係 784
加速車線 539
家族待合室 778
家族用テント 902
下側製片 86
下側陥欠 86
ガソリン 656, 656
ガソリン・エンジン 553, 563, 566
ガソリン・スタンド 548, 711, 725
ガソリン・タンク 553, 574, 577
ガソリンの種類 548
ガソリン・ポンプ 548
ガソリン・ライン 553
肩 124, 130, 146, 148, 156, 311
ガター 865
肩当て 757, 808, 880
カタール 746
下大静脈 160, 161, 162, 165
肩飾り 352
型紙 455, 458
花托 80
カタクチイワシ 219
片口スパナ 311
片梳き用梳き狭 382
肩付き 472
カタツムリ 104
カタツムリの解剖図 104
カタツムリの形態図 104
肩吊り紐 367
片流れ屋根 414
肩羽 118
カタパルト 761
肩紐 367, 388, 391, 527, 770
肩紐クロス式オーバーオール 369
カタマラン船 835
片結び 908
片眼鏡 385
固め技と投げ技の例 844
片持ち桁 540
偏指れ 630
カタロニア語 469
花壇 245, 322
下段 24
家畜移送車用低床セミトレーラー 572
家畜車 588
花柱 80, 81, 82, 83, 84
ガチョウ 120, 213
ガチョウの卵 213
下腸間膜動脈 165
下直筋 177
カチンコ 429
楽器編成の例 438
括弧 473
滑降 889
学校 734
学校用 545, 547
滑降・スーパー大回転用スキー板 888
滑合の例 269
カッサバ 184
カッシーニ 19

天文学 > 2-25; 地球 > 26-71; 植物 > 72-89; 動物 > 90-143; 人間 > 144-177; 食べ物と台所 > 178-241; 家屋 > 242-295; 日曜大工・園芸 > 296-333; 衣服 > 334-371;
装身具類と日用品 > 372-391; 芸術と建築 > 392-465; 情報伝達とオフィス・オートメーション > 466-535; 交通と機械 > 536-643; エネルギー > 644-677; 科学 > 678-705;
社会 > 706-785; スポーツとゲーム > 786-920

活字幅 472	下部安全カバー 304	カヤック 837	革の端 350	艦対艦ミサイル 762
滑車 284, 321, 686, 750, 859, 913	下部安全カバー格納レバー 304	下葉 163	革バンド 696	寒帯気候 61
滑車装置 750	カフェ・カーテン 282	画溶液 400	カワマス 221	カンタループ 195
合掌 253	下部加圧層 646	画用ペン 397	皮むき器 229	カンタループ・メロン 195
合掌式ゲート収納部 597	下部ガラス球締め金 58	下翼 628	瓦 299, 403, 406, 412	感嘆符 473
褐色矮星 8	下部側梁 635	殻 84, 85, 104, 105, 106	瓦端飾り 403	浣腸器 776
活栓 329	下部緩衝梁 635	下顎 370, 851	管 445	館長室 394, 732
活線コネクター 663	カプカンラン 189	カラー 370, 851	缶 611	環椎 111, 122, 126, 131, 153, 157
滑走 892	下部サーモスタット 266	カラー・サークル 400	間 434	管継ぎ手 269
褐藻 75	下部支持ねじ 58	カラー・シフティング・インク 729	ガン 315	缶詰缶 223
滑走関節 156	カフス 349	カラー・スティック 378	簡易携帯用ベッド 904	缶詰食品 181
滑走面 884, 888	カフス・ボタン 361	カラー・スプレー 398	簡易寝台 776	カンテ 891
滑走路 620, 761	ガフ・スル 601	カラー・チャート 398	簡易ベッド 776	カンデラ 702
滑走路縁標識 620	被せ 387	カラー・テレビ・カメラ 20	感温筒 695	寒天 183
滑走路指示標識 620	カプセル 783	カラー調節ボタン 512	乾果 84, 193	眼点 95
滑走路着地点地帯標識 621	カフタン 339	カラー・バー 376	眼窩 112, 116, 131, 136, 138, 142	乾電池 669
滑走路中心線標識 620	兜 748, 749	カラー・フィルター 478, 494	間ճ 617	感電の危険あり 774
滑走路末端標識 621	兜飾り 748	カラー付録ページ 471	感覚器官 172	羊頭 739
カッター 317, 484, 534	ガフ・トップスル 603	カラーレット 339, 363	感覚受容器 168	管胴 444
カッター・デッキ 333	兜屋根 415	ガラガラヘビ 114	感覚ニューロン 168	監督 429, 811
カッター・デッキ・リフト・レバー 333	下部トルソ 20	絡げ針 233	眼科・耳鼻咽喉科診察室 779	監督椅子 276, 429
カッター・ヘッド 535	下部発熱体 266	カラザ 117	感覚のインパルス 168	監督助手 490
甲冑 749	カフ・ボックス 488	カラシ 84	管楽器 446	監督用コントロール・モニター 428
勝手口 720	カブラー 444	空締めボルト 248	カンガルー 142, 143	乾ドック 394
ガット 816, 822	下部ラジエーター・ホース 561	カラス 118	カンガルーの形態図 143	鉋 464
滑動部 756	カプラン水車 659	ガラス 672, 673	カンガルーの骨格図 142	館内売店 394
活版印刷 472	冠板 404	ガラス・カーテン 282	汗管 172	貫入岩 42
カップ 223, 226, 367, 905, 906	カブリオレ 276	ガラス・カバー 291	カンカン帽 340	貫入岩床 44
カップ台 367	カフ・リンク 361	ガラス器 225	ガンギエイ 218	管ねじ切り 314
カップ・プロテクター 843	下部ローラー 421	ガラス球 58, 275	雁木車 696, 697	カンバス 400
カップリング・ボルト 659	花粉かご 98	ガラス球支持台 58	換気口 261, 289, 402, 594, 675	岩盤 43, 78
滑膜性の連結の種類 156	花粉挟み 98	ガラス・ケース 699	換気扇 586	甲板クレーン 761
家庭から出るごみ 69, 70	花粉ブラシ 98	烏座 11	柑橘果物 82, 194	甲板昇降型プラットフォーム 653
家庭における汚染 69	花粉房 100	ガラス球 274	換気フード 614	岩盤滑り 47
家庭用アンテナ 486	壁 7, 246, 902, 917	ガラス戸棚 279	観客席 10, 431, 788, 874	岩盤通路 607
家庭用グランド 443	壁版 252, 253	ガラスの収集箱 71	観客の出入り口 402	ガンビア 745
家庭用品 180	貨幣と支払い形態 729	ガラスの分別 71	眼球 110, 177	カンフー 846
家庭用リンネル 716	壁キャビネット 224	ガラスのリサイクル容器 71	眼球保護ゴーグル 765	カンフーの選手 846
家庭用リンネル製品 716	壁通気口 244	ガラス瓶 223	環境 66	カンフー着 846
カテージ・チーズ 210	壁付きアーチ 410	ガラス麦 85	艦 761, 763	カンフー服 846
カテナリー 595	壁付け灯 287	ガラス窓用カーテン 282	艦橋セール 763, 763	幹部用寝室 764
過電圧保護コンセント 520	壁灯 287	ガラス屋根 250, 582, 713	眼鏡照準器 692	幹部用トイレ・シャワー室 764
過電圧保護電話ジャック 520	壁ブラケット 284	空手 845	換気用フード 721	ガン・フラップ 352
家電製品 236, 288	壁間柱 253	空手衣 845	缶切り 230, 240, 905	カンブリア紀 92
可動あご 311, 312	壁用調節装置 258	空手家 845	管切り 269	眼柄 104
可動橋 542	花弁 80	空手着 845	玩具 717	岸壁 900
可動コイル 488	可変後退翼 630	カラハリ砂漠 34	玩具店 714	岸壁クレーン 596
可動式滑走部 885	可変排気ノズル 629	カラビナ 901	雁首 390	ガン・ベルト 770
可動式スターティング・ゲート 857	加法混色 690	カラベル船 599	間欠泉 44	監房 727
可動式スタンド 734	カボション・カット 375	カラフ 241	岩圏 66	眼房水 177
可動式搭乗橋 619	カボチャ 189	カラマツ 89	管弦楽団 437	潅木地帯 66
可動式ランナー 885	ガボン 745	絡み止め 908	汗孔 172	カンボジア 747
可動仕切り壁 509, 510	窯 465	カラム 198	管口 444	カンマ 473
可動照明器具 287	構え 849	ガラム・マサラ 199	韓国語 469	ガンマ線 690
可動装置 591	構えの線 848	擽め手 408, 409	看護士 780	岩脈 44
移動ダム 664	カマキリ 102	空薬莢排出口 755	看護士休憩室 781	冠刻形 404
可動調節装置 759	釜残 656	カランドリア 669	寛骨 153	顔面保護シールド 765
可動パーティション 509, 510	がま口 387	カランボーラ 197	看護婦 780	管理室 764
可動パラボラ反射鏡 16	釜状凹地 45	ガリア人の戦士 748	看護婦休憩室 781	管理事務室 718, 769
可動板 756	鎌状種子骨 121	ガリウム 682	艦載艇 762	管理事務所 596
可動フレーム 303	カマンベール 211	ガリウム 682	観察室 778, 781	管理センター 394
移動フロア 664	紙 400, 420	ガリオン船 599	監査役 845	管理人室 724, 735
可動砲尾 756	紙送りキー 529	刈り込み鋏 330	監視カメラ 395	管理ビル 664
可動ライト 399	紙おむつ 368	カリス 737	鑑識課 768	岩流圏 42
角革 426	紙屑入れ 535	カリスト 4	かんじき 893	眼輪筋 150
カドミウム 683	紙断裁機 535	刈り取り脱殻機 643	監視室 727	寒冷紗 422
カトラリー・バスケット 294	上手 431	刈り刃 643	乾湿計 59	甘露メロン 195
カトリシズム 736	髪の毛座 13	カリパー 423	監視人デスク 732	
ガドリニウム 684	紙の収集箱 71	カリフォルニア・ミラー 569, 570	監視窓 727	**き**
金網 791	紙のリサイクル容器 71	カリフォルニア湾 30	患者 780	
金具 888, 889	紙パック 223	カリブ 28, 30	緩斜面 886	黄 400, 690
カナダ 742	紙・ボール紙の分別 71	カリブ海諸島 742	患者用椅子 780	ギア 462
金槌 301, 317	紙・ボール紙の分離 71	カリブ・プレート 43	間充組織 95	ギア・ケース 910
カナディアン・ダックピン 865	紙巻きタバコ 390	カリフラワー 187	完熟 86	ギアシフト・レバー 556, 575, 576, 577
カナディアン・フットボール 809	紙巻きタバコのパッケージ 390	カリホルニウム 684	艦首ソナー 762	ギアチェンジ・ペダル 575, 576, 577
カナディアン・ベーコン 216	紙マッチ 391	下流ゲート 597, 837	環礁 44	気圧 55
要石 410, 413	仮眠室 570	下流水位 597	岩漿 44	気圧の谷 55
カナリア・メロン 195	カム軸 566	下流底 660	緩衝器 417, 553, 583, 876	気圧水管 95
カニ 218	カムシャフト 566	下流面遮水壁 661	管状支柱 615	気圧変化傾向 55
果肉 81, 82, 83	カムチャツカ半島 33	下流面補強壁 660	環状水路 95	気圧変化量 55
カニグモ 102	カム・ボタン 456	火力調節バルブ 903	緩衝装置 18, 553, 594	気圧を測定する器具 59
蟹座 13	冠板 404	ガリレオ 19	樺状体 177	ギアボックス 423, 552
ガニメデ 4	カム・リング 307	カルシウム 682	環状燃焼室 627	ギア・レバー 579, 580
加入者通信 487	カメ 113	カルダモン 198	環状道路 39	ギア・ワイヤー 580
カヌー 600, 837	カメの解剖図 113	カルテ 781	環状刃 652	キー 432, 442, 443, 445, 446, 451
カヌー・カヤック 837, 838	カメの形態図 113	カルテット 438	管状ヒーター 656	ギー 210
曲尺 313	カメムシ 101	カルト 849	冠状縫合 158	キーウィ 196
加熱ハム 216	カメラ 18, 428, 490, 492, 775, 873	カルドン 185	肝静脈 161	キーウィ・フルーツ 196
加熱コイル 899	カメラ・オペレーター 428	カルバート山脈 32	観賞用樹木 244	キー・ガード 446
鹿の子編み 458	カメラ室 694	カルパティア山脈 32	灌水タンク 665, 669	キー・グリップ 428
可燃性物質 774	カメラ支持台 492	カルビニズム 736	灌水バルブ 669	キー・ステム 387
カバ 129	カメラ台 482	カレイ 221	関数電卓 529	キーストーン 410, 413
カバー 240, 261, 273, 274, 391, 477, 512, 757, 797, 867, 907	カメラ台ロック・レバー 482	過冷 680	完成 86	キーボード 450, 507, 526, 865
カバーオール 369, 369	カメラ搭載バイク 870	カレー粉 198	岩石圏 42	キーボード天板 511
カバー・グリル 259	カメラ取り付けネジ 482	ガレージ 244, 769	岩石砂漠 47	キーボードと絵文字 514
カバノキ 88	カメラ・ボディー 476	ガレー船 599	岩石庭園 322	キーボードとピクトグラム 514
鞄 717	カメラ用ビューファインダー 492	下路アーチ橋 541	関節軟骨 154	キーボード・ポート 513
可搬式ベルト・コンベヤー 646, 647	カメルーン 745	仮助 153	幹線道路 39, 539	キール 897
果皮 82, 84	カメレオン 114	カロン 5	幹線道路番号 39	キールバーサ 216
架尾 756	カメレオン座 11	皮 81, 82, 83	乾燥 347	キール・ボート 835
架尾鋼 756	画面 494, 494	側板 439, 440, 753, 783	肝臓 109, 110, 112, 113, 116, 125, 161, 164	キーレス・チャック 306
下鼻甲介 175	下面デッキカバー 632	カワウソ 134	乾燥機 293	キー・レバー 446
下尾筒 115	カモ 120, 213	革帯 824	乾燥気候 61	キー・ロック 386
画鉄 534	貨物駅 583	皮カバー 798	乾草梱包機 642	黄色のパプリカ 188
カフ 342, 350, 880	貨物機 629	カワカマス 220	乾燥した空洞 47	キオスク 593
カブ 189	貨物室 625	桁析 255	乾燥したチリ 199	キー 55
下部 446, 750	貨物輸送機 475	革製鞘 907	乾燥タイマー 293	気化 680
ガフ 602	カモの卵 213	革製品 386	管足 95	機械小屋 182
画布 400	カモミール 208	革製品店 714	観測室 17	機械式昇降式 898
	火門 753	カワセミ 118	観測窓 23	機械式時計 696
	火薬入れ 752	カワラニワ 220	観測地天気記号記入様式 55	
	火薬掃い棒 752	側根太 252, 253		

天文学 > 2-25; 地球 > 26-71; 植物 > 72-89; 動物 > 90-143; 人間 > 144-177; 食べ物と台所 > 178-241; 家屋 > 242-295; 日曜大工・園芸 > 296-333; 衣服 > 334-371; 装身具類と日用品 > 372-391; 芸術と建築 > 392-465; 情報伝達とオフィス・オートメーション > 466-535; 交通と機械 > 536-643; エネルギー > 644-677; 科学 > 678-705; 社会 > 706-785; スポーツとゲーム > 786-920

機械式マウス 516	キッチン・タオル 295	キャリー・オン・バッグ 388	旧約聖書 736	巨嘴鳥座 10
機械室 657, 658	キッチン用品 716	キャリッジ 632	給湯器 873	御者 857
機械船 19, 25	キツツキ 118	キャリッジ・リターン・キー 528	給湯管 266	馭者座 12
機械継ぎ手 269	切手 474	キャリパー 559	給湯器 259	居住室 650
幾何学 704	切手湿らし器 531	キャリヤー 284	給湯口 267	居眼 53
幾何学的な形 704	キツネ 134	ギャレー 624	ギャレー 624	去勢雄鶏 213
気化器 261, 574	キツネザル 139	キャロット 340	給油口 259, 553	極光 53
気化グリル 261	義弟 785	キャロム・ビリヤード 862	給油口蓋 551	魚雷 763
希ガス 684	基底材 400	キャンセル・ボタン 519	給油車 622	魚雷艇 763
気管 116, 125, 163, 163	基底層 172	キャンディー類 717	給油装置 586, 873	距離測定 700
汽缶 586	汽笛 586	キャンドルピン 865	給油艇 588	距離標識 621
希望 646	軌道 582, 595	キャンバス 842	給油ノズル 548	距離目盛り 478
基幹回線 523	軌道修正エンジン 23	キャンピング・カー 567	給油ホース 548	魚竜 93
機関室 606, 608, 763, 585	軌道修正用エンジン 23	キャンプ 902	キュウリ 188	距離用スキー靴 892
機関車線 589	軌道船 18, 22, 23	キャンプ可 725	キュウリウオ 219	魚類 108
機関銃 758	起動輪 636, 758	キャンプ禁止 725	球状隕石 8	錐 905
機器材ラック 489, 490	輝度調節つまみ 518	キャンプ用品 905	穹窖 404	霧 57, 65
機器収納部 585	希土類元素 684	球 705	穹窿前 404	切りレット 298
機器プラットフォーム 60	キトン 336	吸引器 775	キューレット 374	切り糸 464
気球 899	機内食搭載トラック 623	球果 89	キュリウム 684	切先 348
気球乗り 899	ギニア 745	球海綿体筋 169	キュロット 357	切り替えスイッチ 523
企業 525	ギニアビサウ 745	球顆隕石 8	教育 732	切り替え線 348
器具 421, 422, 423, 790	ギニア湾 34	旧顎亜綱 92	教育機関 525	切り替えつまみ 316
器具庫 734	キニャルワンダ語 468	嗅覚と味覚 174	教育施設 711	切り株 87
キクイムシ 101	キヌザル 139	競泳コース 831	頬嚢 112	切り屑排出口 304
木釘 278, 462	砧骨 174	競泳プール 788	教会 711, 737	切り込み 455
キクゴボウ 189	記念建造物 39	競泳用プール 788	境界層 471	切り込み角度固定ノブ 304
キクチシャ 186	記念銘板 738	頬骨 112	胸郭 146, 148	切り込み角度調整レバー 309
キクラゲ 183	キノア 203	球関節 156	鋏角 103	切り込み角度調整装置 304, 305
義兄 785	気嚢 75	休閑地 182	強化箱 920	切り込み用レバー 307
危険区域 844, 847	機能キー 507, 508, 514, 699	急患部 182	行間 472	錐先 307
危険地帯 844, 847	機能選択ダイヤル 476	吸気 725	競技 889	霧雨 64
危険物の表示 774	機能選択つまみ 261	吸気管 765	競技委員 801, 875	ギリシャ 744
き甲 124, 130	機能選択ボタン 506	給気管 765	競技委員長 870	ギリシャ劇場 402
生コーヒー豆 208	機能表示画面 450	吸気口 568, 605	競技会 789	ギリシャ語 469
騎座 855	機能表示窓 450	球技 794	競技者 844, 846	ギリシャ神殿 403
きさげ 320	キノコ 76, 183	吸気弁 564, 566, 773	競技役員 846	キリスト教 736
刻み付きナット 320	茸状乳頭 176	吸気マニホールド 564, 565, 566	競技場 790, 845, 846, 848, 852, 858	キリスト十字架像 737
騎士 916	キノコの構造 76	吸気マニホールド 564, 565, 566		キリスト磔刑像 737
キジ 120, 212	牙 103	救急 725	橋脚 540, 540	切り出しナイフ 401
記事 471, 471	木箱 222	嗅球 109, 175	胸脚 107	切妻 411
義姉 785	キバナスズシロ 187	救急救命医待機室 778	鏡脚 693	切妻壁 244
機軸 692	基板 907	救急資器材 775	競技役員 846	切妻壁の間柱 252
基指骨 133	基盤 500	救急室 725	供給管 643	切妻屋根 414
基趾骨 126	基盤岩 46	救急車 775, 778	供給皿 643	義理の親 784
記事索引 471	基部 78, 663	救急処置の用具 775	供給ダクト 260	義理の息子 784
気笛 117	義父 784	救急隊員席 775	供給ヘッダー 669	義理の娘 784
生地の構造 455	起伏シリンダー 573, 634, 766	救急箱 771, 777	凝結 67, 680	義理の両親 784
キジの卵 213	ギプス処置室 779	救急部 778	凝固 693	切り羽 236, 240, 382, 382, 454
機首 624, 898	基小節 107	救急ヘリコプター 631	胸甲 749	切羽 647, 650
騎手 853, 855, 856, 857	ギフト・ショップ 714	球形ビーン 301	響孔 439	キリバス 747
基種子骨 126	キプラ 738	キュウケツコウモリ 141	峡谷 48	気流 399
技術運営審判団 881	キプラ壁 738	急勾配 545, 547	胸骨 111, 116, 121, 126, 131, 141, 142, 152	キリン 129
技術価値審判員 823	キプロス 744	球根 185		きりん座 12
技術機器収納庫 489	基母 784	球根植え 324	頬骨 152, 158	切る 237
技術室 543	気泡水準器 701	球根の断面図 78	胸骨動脈 107	キルギス 746
技術文書サービス 732	喜望峰 34	キュー先 863	胸鎖乳突筋 150	キルト・スカート 357
騎手と馬 858	黄ボール 863	嗅盲 175	教師 734	キルンディ語 468
基準音 436	木彫 401	給仕長 720	行司 847	記録 831
気象 53	基本演算キー 529	給仕テーブル 584	教室 727, 734, 735	記録員 810, 812, 813, 859, 864, 828
記章 739, 770	義妹 785	給紙トレイ 512, 519	凝縮 680	
騎乗アンパイア 858	黄緑 400	給紙表示ランプ 519	凝縮器コイル 261	記録員席 828
気象衛星 54, 60	着物 856	給紙ボタン 519, 731	凝縮器ファン 261	記録係 845, 846, 847, 860, 864
気象観測機器 58	キモノ［着物］スリーブ 361	厩舎 182	橋床 540	
気象観測航空機 54	気門 96, 97	牛舎 182	教師用机 734	記録紙と計時係 844
気象観測所 54, 58	疑問符 473	急斜面 886	行政区画図 37	記録紙受け台 58
気象観測ブイ 54	ギヤ板 870	95度以下の湯で、通常の洗濯機洗い可 347	強制送水システム 259	記録装置 832
気象予報 54	脚 756		強制送風システム 258	記録保管室 394, 769
気象レーダー 54, 624	逆回転スイッチ 302, 306	吸収された日射 68	鏡体 692, 692	記録用 831
規月 313	客車 605, 608, 609, 625, 631	90度 704	橋台 540	キログラム 702
黄信号 712	客車の種類 584	90メートル標的線 859	兄弟 856	際剃り刃 383
気水分離器 646	客車 584, 585, 594	吸収面 675	胸椎 122, 126, 131, 138, 142, 153, 157	キワノ 196
奇数 919	脚飾 103	球状星団 9		金 683, 741
奇数羽状 79	客船 608	弓状動脈 160	共通集合 703	銀 683, 741
着せ替えテーブル 281	逆止め弁 263, 319	弓身 439	共通部分 703	近位骨端 155
貴足 375, 652	逆ひだ 283	球審 795	英底 860, 862	銀河 9, 13
基部 96, 98	ギャザー 359	嗅神経 109, 175	鏡筒 14, 15, 477, 692, 693	鏡筒 477
季節 54	ギャザー・カーテン 282	給水管 262, 270, 670, 671	共同住宅 419	金眼 691
基部骨 126, 133, 154, 154, 155	ギャザー・フレアー・スカート 357	吸水口 766, 766	鏡筒スリーブ 693	金管楽器の仲間 437
基部腺 103	キャスケット 340	給水塔 589	鏡筒バンド 14, 15	金環食 6
キセノン 684	キャスター 281, 289, 389, 448, 633	給水トラック 622	共同募金カード 915	銀器 227
基板 907		給水ホース 294, 485	響胴 433	銀器とナプキン 722
基礎 252, 253, 412, 660, 661	キャスター付き肘掛け椅子 511	給水本管 675	響板 432, 433, 439, 440, 442	緊急帰還艇 21
基壇 905	キャスター付きファイリング・ユニット 510	球節 124	胸部 124	緊急支援船 653
偽造防止糸 729		休憩用ソファー 276	休息用ソファー 276	緊急車両 543
基礎建材 298	脚立 321	球体 705	胸膜 433	緊急ステーション 543
基礎ブロック 660	キャタピラー 636, 758, 876	球体平面図 28	胸腹腔 163	緊急遮断 543
北 37, 616	キャッサバ 184	キュー・チップ 863	胸峰 116	緊急脱出システム 25
北アメリカ 28, 30, 50	キャッチャー 443, 794, 795, 796	キューティクル・シザー 377	強膜 177	緊急区分室 779
北アメリカの主な道路標識 546	キャッチャー・ミット 796	キューティクル・トリマー 377	業務用出入り口 732	緊急ブレーキ 594
北アメリカ・プレート 43	キャップ 275, 398, 470, 484, 676, 776, 783, 827, 830	キューティクル・ニッパー 377	共鳴箱 444, 449	緊急用電動機 763
気体 680		キューティクル・プッシャー 377	共鳴胴 440	キング 914, 916
基台 403, 404	キャップ・アイアン 309	給電点 273	共鳴板 433	キング・サイド 916
黄橙 400	キャップ・スリーブ 337, 360	弓頭 439	共鳴板 432, 433, 440, 442	キングピン 571, 865
キタオポッサム 143	キャップス・ロック・キー 514	救難ビーコン 611	鏡墓 693	キング・ポスト 253, 897
北回帰線 34, 35, 36	キャップ継ぎ手 269	牛肉 214	ギョー 49	金券 741
北の冠座 13	キャップ・ナット 268	牛乳加工所 182	魚介類 181	金庫 731, 769
北半球 35	キャディー・バッグ 869	嗅粘膜 175	魚眼レンズ 478	銀行 710, 715, 730, 915
北半球の星座 12	キャニスター 222	吸盤 106, 111	棘下筋 151	近郊通勤鉄道 583
黄球 863	キャノピー 416, 567, 611, 639, 760, 896, 897	9番アイアン 868	極気候 61	金庫室 731
黄壇 403, 405, 412		キュー 899	極軌道 60	菌糸 76
気団の種類 55	キャノピー放出ノブ 898	休符 435	極軌道衛星 60	近視 691
機長席 626	キャピタル 405	臼砲 753	棘魚類 92	菌糸体 76
喫煙具 390	キャビネット 291, 494	キュー・ボール 862, 863	極限点 891	金星 4, 5
キッカー 471, 890	キャビン 631	救命いかだ 605, 611	極軸 17	筋節 109
キッカーズ 800	キャプション 471	救命浮き輪 611, 771	極軸クランプ 14, 15	近接信管 759
キックサイド・スタンド 575	キャプスタン 443	救命ゴム・ボート 605	極軸微動ハンドル 14, 15	筋線維 168
キックスタンド 575, 577	キャプス・ロック 514	救命艇 604, 608, 652	棘突起 108	金銭出納機 535
キック・プリーツ 357	キャプレター 574	救命胴衣 611	曲折アクセント 473	金属外装 689
切っ先 227, 229	キャベツ 186	救命ボート 602, 604, 608, 652	極超短波 690	金属ジャケット 848
喫茶店 710, 715, 725	カミソール 366	救命用浮き袋 609	極低温主ステージ 24	金属色の例 741
木槌 301, 401, 421	キャラウェー 198	救命用具 611	棘皮動物 95	金属製ジャケット 848
キッチン・タイマー 231	キャラコ地のジャケット 337	キュー元 863	距骨 153, 155	金属製胴衣 848
	キャリア 389, 578		鋸歯状 79	金属先端 793
	キャリア・バッグ 388			

天文学 > 2-25; 地球 > 26-71; 植物 > 72-89; 動物 > 90-143; 人間 > 144-177; 食べ物と台所 > 178-241; 家屋 > 242-295; 日曜大工・園芸 > 296-333; 衣服 > 334-371;
装身具類と日用品 > 372-391; 芸術と建築 > 392-465; 情報伝達とオフィス・オートメーション > 466-535; 交通と機械 > 536-643; エネルギー > 644-677; 科学 > 678-705;
社会 > 706-785; スポーツとゲーム > 786-920

金属端子 672	釘穴 127	グライダー 898	車椅子 584, 783	群島 38
金属胴衣 848	釘先 301	クライミング・シューズ 900	車椅子乗り入れ可能 725	群葉 87
金属の分別 71	釘締め 301	クラウチング・ポジション 843	車椅子乗り入れ禁止 725	
金属ペン 470	茎状突起 158	クラウン 340, 341, 374, 610	車椅子用ランプ 394	**け**
金属レール 533	釘抜き 301, 301	グラウンド 794, 801, 802, 804, 920	車椅子用リフト 569	
緊締環 756	釘抜きハンマー 301		車止め 583	毛 85, 139, 172, 295, 383, 384
金的 859	供犠の石 412	クラウン・ブロック 651	クルミ 193	蹴上げ 255
キント 849	釘の例 301	鞍覆い 853, 856	クルミノキ 88	経緯儀 59, 701
キントキマメ 191	茎 470	クラシカル走法 892	クルミの断面図 84	経営管理室 718
ギンナン 193	茎野菜類 185	クラシック・ブラウス 359	クルス割り器 230	警音器 556, 766
筋肉 150	釘を打つ道具 301	グラス 723, 822	クレ 822, 860	警音器ボタン 576
菌包 76	くくり罠 913	グラス洗い機 723	クレー射撃 860	経過観察室 778, 781
金融サービス部門 730	草摺 876	クラスター・フード&ラック 865	クレーター 7, 647	繋駕車 857
筋力スポーツ 850	草取り 325	グラス・ライニング製タンク 267	グレーダー 639	繋駕速歩競走 857
	楔形センサー 903	クラス・リング 376	クレーターの線条 7	景観建築 39
く	楔材 753	クラッシュ・センサー	グレート・オーストラリア湾 29	計器 273
	鎖 697, 826	クラッシュ・ヘルメット 872, 884, 885	グレート・サンディー砂漠 29	軽機関銃 755
グアテマラ 742	鎖帷子 749		グレート・デーン 131	計器コンソール 841
グアバ 197	鎖車 876	クラッチ 552	グレート・ディバイディング山脈 29	計器板 556
杭 902, 903	鎖パイプ・レンチ 315	クラッチ・ハウジング 576	グレート・バリア・リーフ 29	計器盤 557, 574
クイーバー 859	クサリヘビ 114	クラッチ・バッグ式の折り鞄 387	グレート・ビクトリア砂漠 29	計器盤の機器 771
クイーン 914, 916	櫛 380	クラッチ・ペダル 556	グレートブリテンおよび北部アイルランド連合王国 743	計器ユニット 25
クイーン・サイド 916	櫛状突起 98	クラッチ・レバー 327, 574, 576		計器類 899
クイーン・モード・ランド 29	くし 417	クラップスケート靴 883	グレーハウンド 131	頸甲 749
食い違い継手 269	櫛の歯状羽状中裂 79	グラニュー糖 209	計標的 860	蛍光管 275
クイック・ターン 832	クジャク 10	クラブ 823, 914	クレープ・パン 235	蛍光管固定クリップ 275
クイックドロー 900	孔雀座 10	グラフィック・アート 420	グレープフルーツ 194	蛍光灯 275
クイック・レリーズ機構 482	具象図形の例 741	グラフィック・イコライザー 498	グレープフルーツ・ナイフ 229	蛍光塗料 275
クイル・ブラシ 380	苦情相談窓口 768	クラブサン 443	クレー放出機 860	警告帯 795
クインテット 438	鯨座 10, 12	クラブ・チェア 276	クレーン 634, 650	警告地帯 846
クウェート 746	屑入れ 535	クラブハウス 856, 866	クレーン・ガーダー 634	警告灯 557, 591, 766, 771
クウォーター 342	クスクス 204	グラベル 872	クレーン桁 634	警告表示地帯 795
クーガー 134	クスクス鍋 235	クラミス 336	クレジット・カード 729	脛骨 116, 122, 126, 131, 138, 140, 141, 142, 152, 155, 156
空気 565	グズベリー 192	クラリネット 437, 446	クレジット・ライン 471	
空気孔 575	薬の様々な形態 783	クランク 230, 307, 312, 580, 750	クレソン 187	脛骨神経 166
空気圧縮機 320, 586	薬指 173		クレッシェンド・ペダル 444	経済と金融 728
空気圧縮装置 585	管 241, 445	クランクケース 565	グレナダ 743	警察 725
空気孔 470	砕け波 49	クランク軸 566, 580	クレバス 46	警察官 770
空気移送装置 643	管巻き 461	クランクシャフト 564, 566	クレビス 403, 405	警察署 711, 768
空気管 578	果物 192	クランク・ハンドル 313, 423, 910, 910	クレビドーマ 403, 405	警察バッジ 770
空気入れポンプ 904	果物とデザート 723		黒 690, 741, 919	計算器 386
空気警音器 570	果物ナイフ 229	クランチ・ベンチ 851	クロアチア 744	計算盤 479
空気呼吸器 765	口 95, 104, 105, 107, 110, 136, 148, 174	グランド・キャニオン 30	黒石 916	計時員 881, 883, 900
空気室 271		グランド・シート 902, 903	クロイチゴ 192	計時エリア 891
空気清浄器 261	口絵写真 471	グラン・プリ用オートバイとライダー 874	クロー 425	計時主任 830
空気溜め 445	口金 274, 275, 783		クロック 394, 719, 723, 726, 731	計時板 845, 846, 847, 848
空気タンク 320	口ゴム 351	クリア・エントリー・キー 529		掲揚板 535, 734
空気調整ねじ 320	嘴 106, 115	クリア・キー 529	クローシュ 341	掲揚面 535
空気調節 261	嘴の例 117	クリーク 868	クローズ・アップ・レンズ 478	鶏舎 213
空気調節弁 445	唇 132, 124	グリーク・ブレッド 204	クローズ・ホールド 833	傾斜角 13
空気と燃料の混合 564	唇のメーキャップ 378	クリー語 469	クローズ・リーチ 833	傾斜路 608
空気取り入れ口 631, 876	口紅 378	グリース 656	クローゼット 724	傾斜路 407, 647
空気取り入れ調節器 256	靴 342	クリート 834, 835	クローバー型インターチェンジ 538, 539	芸術価値審判員 823
空気ドリル 873	靴踵締め具 889	クリーニング店 715		警鐘 591
空気逃がし弁 607	靴型 345	クリーニング・ブラシ 383	グローブ 198	軽食カウンター 427
空気抜きポンプ 904	クッキー型 232	クリップ 47	グローブ 798, 800, 842, 848, 855, 870, 871, 872, 874, 875, 878, 879, 881, 882, 884, 887, 891, 892	軽氷 671
空気ハンマー 649	クッキー用天板 232	クリーマー 226		形成層 87
空気袋 432	クック海峡 29	クリーム 210		形成中の食胞 94
空気フィルター 636	クックソニア 92	クリーム入れ 226		脛節 96, 98
空気ブレーキ 760	靴クリーム 345	クリーム・カップ 223	グローブ・ボックス 556	脛節節 98
空気弁 320, 398	靴先締め具 889	クリーム・チーズ 210	クロー・ボール形回転子 688	経線 36
空気ホース 648, 841	掘削糟 604	グリーン 864, 866, 867	クローラー・トラクター 636	罫線 891
空気ボタン 432	クッサン 458	グリーン・アンド・ジャック 850	クロール 832	係船ウインチ 607
空気ポンプ 548, 904	靴下 351, 365	グリーン・ペッパー 198	クロールのキック 832	係船地 788
空気冷却装置 564	クッション 280	グリーンランド 28	クロガラシ 198	ケイ素 682
空気濾過器 331	クッション封筒 531	グリーンランド海 28	黒クランプ 558	計測機器 695
空隙 675	屈折望遠鏡 14	繰り返し記号 434	クロコショウ 198	携帯酸素ボンベ 775
空港 39, 618, 708	屈折望遠鏡の断面図 14	クリケッターと打者 798	クロコダイル 114	携帯電話機 506
空港地上支援機材 622	屈折望遠鏡 14	クリケッターとバッツマン 798	黒駒 916	携帯用消火器 767
空港特殊車両 622	靴店 715	クリケット 798	クロス 740	携帯ランプ 765
空港内バス道路 618	靴の各部名称 342	クリケット・シューズ 798	クロスオーバー・カーテン 283	径違い継手 269
空集合 703	靴紐 342, 370	クリケット・ボール 798	クロス・カントリー・スキー 892	係柱 607
偶数 919	靴ブラシ 345	繰子錐 307	クロス・カントリー・スキー・コース 886	頸椎 116, 122, 126, 131, 138, 141, 142, 153, 157
偶数羽状 79	靴底 345	クリスタル・ボタン 287		
グース・ネック 255, 638	靴べら 345	クリスマス・ツリー 652, 654	クロス・カントリー・スキーヤー 892	頚椎障害用カラー 775
空対空ミサイル 759, 760	靴磨きセット 345	繰り出し筒 693		競馬 856, 857
空対地ミサイル 759	轡 854	繰り出しはしご 321	クロス・カントリー用自転車とサイクリスト 870	競馬場 856, 856
空中演技 829	轡鎖鈴 854	句読点 473		桂皮 198
空中給油 760	轡鎖留め革通し 854	グリッド 494	クロス・カントリー用スキー板 892	警備員席 779
空中給油パイプ 760	駆動軸 553, 605	グリッド法 36	クロスグリ 192	軽飛行機 628
空中給油プローブ 760	駆動タービン 564	クリップ 284, 506, 700	クロス・ステッチ 459	脛腓骨 111
空中ケーブル伝送 486	駆動チェーン 643	グリップ 320, 381, 428, 750, 793, 797, 798, 800, 815, 816, 822, 838, 849, 850, 859, 867, 888, 891, 892, 909, 910, 912, 913	クロスツリー 834	警備通路 728
空中スポーツ 896	句読執行 473		クロスバー 827, 897	頸部 169
空中の姿勢 828	駆動歯車 240		クロス・ハンドル 189	軽荷重調整ねじ 273
空調 164	駆動用バッテリー 563, 563		クロス・ベルト 389	警報器 765
空調システム 68	駆動輪 462, 639, 640		クロゼット 250, 279	警棒ホルダー 770
空調設備 608, 261, 489, 556	国 37	グリップ・エンド 797, 816, 822	クロディロン 189	刑務所 726, 915
空洞煉瓦 298	首 113, 124, 147, 148, 149, 227, 309, 315, 425	クリップ式イヤリング 374	黒球 863	刑務所長室 726
空白 914		クリップ式スポットライト 286	クロタン・ド・シャビニョール 210	契約の聖櫃 738
空母 761	頭 115	グリップの種類 815	クロッカス 80	軽油 656
クーポン・ブース 731	首カバー 765	クリップ・ボード 533	クロッシング・アーム 568	鶏卵 213
クーラー・ボックス 906	首枕 280	クリップレス・ペダル 870	黒ボール 863	係留器 615
クーラント 674	くびれ 439	クリトリス 170	黒米 916	係留チェーン 615
空力ブレーキ 676	区分表示符 473	クリノリンの入ったドレス 337	クロマチン 94	係留フック 597
クーリング・ファン 552, 561, 563, 566	区別的発音符 473	クリプトン 684	クロム 683	頭領 77
	窪み 227	グリュイエール 211	クロメマメ 190	計量カップ 231
クール・チップ 381	窪み付きパレット 398	クリュー 836	黒ライ麦パン 204	計量皿 698, 699
クーロミエ 211	熊手 327, 333	グリル 261, 290, 432, 550, 561	クロワッサン 204	計量スプーン 231
クーロン 702	組み合わせ 852	グリル・プレート 239	鍬 327	計量ビーカー 231
クエスション・マーク 473	組み鎖 437, 449	グリン・ピース 190	クワイア鍵盤 444	競輪場 788
クォーター 370	組子 249	クリンプ 901, 912	加えた力 686	ケーキ型 232
クォーター・ウインドー 551	組み物 412	クルーズ・コントロール 556	くわえる 306, 307	ケージ 791
クォーターバック 807	クミン 198	クルー・ソックス 351	加える 703	ケージ 424
クォータリー 740	雲 53, 56, 62, 65	クルー・カット 368	くわっしゅ画法 396	ケージャン・スパイス 199
クォーテーション・マーク 473	クモ 103	クルー・ネック・セーター 354, 359	グワッシュ・ケーキ・カラー 397	ケーシング 260, 261, 267, 332, 697
区画 416, 650, 663, 919	雲と高度 62			
区間距離計 557	雲による吸収 68	グルコース 78	グワッシュ・チューブ入り絵の具 397	ケーシング・ファースト・ストリング 654
茎 75, 76, 77, 78, 185	クモの形態図 103	グルジア 746		
釘 127, 129	雲の果 103	クルック 446	グワラニ語 469	ケース 259, 261, 275, 313, 313, 316, 345, 377, 389, 436, 499, 529, 613, 614, 695, 696, 700, 920
釘頭 301	雲の水分 70	クルック・キー 446	燻煙器 422	
	蜘蛛膜 167	踝 146, 148	軍事通信 487	
	クモ形 102	踝当て 796	軍団の兵士 748	ケース・ファン 513
	鞍 853, 855, 856, 858			ケース・ワーカー室 779

天文学 >2-25;　地球 >26-71;　植物 >72-89;　動物 >90-143;　人間 >144-177;　食べ物と台所 >178-241;　家屋 >242-295;　日曜大工・園芸 >296-333;　衣服 >334-371;
装身具類と日用品 >372-391;　芸術と建築 >392-465;　情報伝達とオフィス・オートメーション >466-535;　交通と機械 >536-643;　エネルギー >644-677;　科学 >678-705;
社会 >706-785;　スポーツとゲーム >786-920

ケータリング車 623
K点 891
ゲート 596, 900
ゲートウェイ 523
ゲート審判員 837
ゲートル 339
ゲート・レッグ 278
ゲート・レッグ・テーブル 278
ケープ 338, 355
ケーブル 492, 516, 517, 523, 558, 573, 824, 851, 859, 908, 913
ケーブル・ガード 859, 913
ケーブル回線 525
ケーブル・スリーブ 306
ケーブル・テレビ局 486
ケーブルトップ 223
ケーブル・ドラム収納車 489
ケーブル抜き 317
ケーブル・モデム 515
ケーブル・レリーズ 482
ゲーム 14, 822
ゲーム・クロック 789
ゲーム・コンソール 918
ゲーム盤 915
ゲーム・MIDIポート 513
ケール 186
外科用流し 781
毛皮 139
毛皮模様の例 741
劇場 430, 710, 711
撃針 757
撃鉄 752, 754, 861, 912
撃発装置 757
激流 837
蹴込み 255
蹴込み板 255
ケシ 80, 84
夏至 54
消印のある郵便物 474
消印のない郵便物 474
消しゴム 534
ケシの実 199
化粧鏡 556
化粧鞄 389
化粧石鹸 379
化粧品 717
化粧ポーチ 388
化粧用トレイ 389
化粧用品 378
下水道 712
下水道本管 712
毛梳き用レザー 381
削りべら 464
桁 632, 663
桁橋 540
桁橋の例 541
ケチャップ 201
ケチュア語 469
血圧計 775, 777
血液因子陰性 702
血液因子陽性 702
血液循環 160
血液循環の図式 161
血液の組成 162
結果表示ライン 529
血管 140, 154, 162, 172
毛付き鼻革 856
ゲッケイジュ 202
結喉革 857
結合組織 172
結合板 641
欠刻状 79
結婚指輪 376
結実 86
決勝 789
血漿 162
月状骨 154, 156
決勝審判員 839
決勝戦 789
決勝線 791, 839, 856, 871
決勝戦進出者 789
血小板 162
月食 7
齧歯類 122
齧歯類とウサギ目の動物 122
齧歯類とウサギ目の動物の顎 123
齧歯類動物 122
齧歯類の例 123
齧歯類の顎 123
血清用ピペット 685
月相 7
結束機 642
ケッチ 601
結膜 97, 113, 125
結膜 177
距 98
蹴爪 124, 140, 141
蹴爪毛 124
ケツルアズキ 191
月齢盤 697
毛止め 439
ケトル 45, 448
ケトル・ドラム 448
ケニア 745
毛革 439
毛鉤 909
毛鉤釣り 909
ゲビエール 367
ケフェウス座 12
毛縁 79
煙 65
煙探知器 767
煙調節蓋 256

ケリー 651
蹴り返し 892
ケルト諸語 469
ケルビン 702
ケルマデック・トンガ海溝 50
ゲルマニウム 682
ゲルマン諸語 469
ケルラ 403
ケロシン・タンク 25
剣 748, 849
鍵 432, 442, 443, 445, 451
腱 133
弦 433, 439, 440, 442, 443
減圧蒸留 656
減圧変圧器 646
牽引装置 573
牽引トラクター 622
牽引棒 642, 756
牽引棒止め具 756
巻雲 56, 62
弦押さえ 442
圏外 890, 891
舷外浮材 599
舷外浮材の付いたカヌー 599
圏界面 53, 68
原殻 105
懸架系 553
顕花植物 93
弦楽器 439
玄関 250, 406, 724
玄関広間 250
玄関ホール 250, 394
研究室 16, 17
研究論文コーナー 732
減極合剤 689
現金自動預入支払機 730, 731
現金自動支払機 715, 730
現金装填 731
原形質膜 94, 94
原形質連絡 74
肩甲 749
健康 775
原鉱 647
肩甲棘 153
肩甲骨 111, 116, 121, 122, 126, 131, 136, 138, 141, 142, 147, 149, 152, 153, 156
減光スイッチ 576
原稿ガイド 508
原稿カバー 512
原稿セット部 512
原稿挿入口 508
健康美容グッズ 181
圏谷 7
圏谷氷河 46
言語表示ボタン 507
現在天気 55, 57
剣先 849
検索 525
研削砥石 308
検察官席 728
減算キー 529
犬歯 121, 159
原子 680
原子核 680
絹糸腺 103
原子番号 682
検湿庫 589
検出器 694
舷橋 602
原色 400
減色混合 690
原子力潜水艦 763
原子力発電所 668
減じる 703
原子炉 665, 666, 667, 669, 763
原子炉圧力容器 671
原子炉建屋 667, 669
原子炉建屋エアロック 668
原子炉容器 667, 669, 671
剣身 849
懸垂碍子 663
懸垂氷河 46
巻層雲 56, 62
舷窓 608
巻層雲 56, 62
現像液 485
現像処理液 485
現像タンク 484
現像用リール 484
元素記号 682
舷側 602
減速材 665, 670, 671
減速材タンク 670
減速車線 539
減速直線コース 885
舷側板 602
減速ブレーキ・ゾーン 891
原組織 463
現貨の追撃砲 756
現代の弓 750
現代の榴弾砲 756
ケンタウルス座 11
建築 402
建築の要素 413
建築様式 404
間丁 460
堅鉄弾 752
検査ドライバー 316
検電ランプ 316
剣道 847
剣道家 847
剣の部分名称 849

鍵盤 442, 450
原版 483
鍵盤楽器 442
鍵盤楽器の例 443
鍵盤台 442
顕微鏡 693
顕微鏡座 10
玄武岩層 42
肩峰 153
減法混色 690
剣ぼろ 349, 361
玄米 207
研磨剤入れ 454
研磨用金盤 423
舷門 606
原油 656
原油・ガス分離器 652
原油パイプライン 654
権利書 915

こ

弧 704
子 785
5 703
昌 916
小あおり 855
ゴアー・スカート 357
ゴアード・スカート 357
コア・ボックス・ビット 308
小雨覆い 115
小雨覆い羽 115
コアラ 143
コイ 220
小犬座 13
恋矢嚢 104
コイル 688
コイルばね 285, 553
コイン受け皿 920
コイン・シュート 920
コイン・スロット 920
コイン投入口 920
コイン返却口 920
溝 176
甲 351
鋼 298
降圧 662, 677
高圧蒸気吸入管 668
高圧蒸気滅菌器 780
高圧送電 646
高圧テスター 662
高圧電気を送電する 662
高圧部 63
高圧滅菌器 780
後胃 107
広域ネットワーク 523
更衣室 428, 509, 734, 764
甲板 278
後羽 115
光遮蔽 17
耕耘機 327
後縁 624, 897, 898
後歯 624
公園 39, 711
後縁フラップ 624, 760
高温アイロン 347
高温域用鍵盤 432
高音域用スピーカー 10, 502
高音用鍵盤 432
高音用スピーカー 10, 502
高温錐 464
高温遮断装置 266
高音調整つまみ 503, 497
高音用鍵盤 432
高音レジスター 432
硬貨 729
紅海 28, 33, 34
郊外 39, 709
航海計器 612
口蓋骨 112, 123
口蓋垂 174, 175
口蓋舌弓 174
航海船庫 604, 608, 609
航海灯 605
口蓋扁桃 176
航海用潜望鏡 763
高架雲 541
後角 167
口角 174
光学 690
光学式照準眼鏡 692
光学式スキャナー 517
紅藻 75
光学式マウス 516
光学式読み取り装置 474
光学式読み取りセンサー 516
光学的走査機 181
広角ミラー 568, 569
甲殻類 107, 218
広角レンズ 478
高架交差路 539
硬貨ブレーキ 507
硬貨投入口 507
硬貨返却口 507
甲革 371, 342
高速道路 539, 709
高速誘導路 618
高速列車 585
交感神経節 167
口器 98
高気圧の中心 55
後脚 96, 98, 277
光球 6
後橋 855
後胸 97
口峡 174
工業汚染 69
交響楽団 437

公共建物 39
工業地区 709
公共庭園 713
口琴 433
咬筋 150
工具一式 580
航空管制室 618
航空管制塔 618, 761
航空管制レーダー 761
航空交通 618
航空通信 487
航空バッグ 388
航空母艦 761
航空郵便 475
坑口 650
工具綱 20
工具箱 313
工具ベルト 313
工芸 452
攻撃用潜望鏡 763
高原 38, 45
高原気候 61
口腔 163, 164
口腔咽頭エアウェー 775
硬口蓋 174, 175
光合成 78
航行灯 625
広告 471
広告パネル 592
広告板 594, 595
硬貨魚 108, 219
後根 168
虹彩 97
工作台 307
工作台固定クランプ 307
口座識別キー 731
交差点につき一時停止 544, 546
交差部 410, 411
交差廊 411
交差廊尖塔 410
交差渡り線 583
高山気候 61
鉱山労働者更衣室 649
格子 403
後肢 110, 111, 121, 143
後翅 96
後趾 115, 117
光子 692
孔子 736
子牛 128
後支索 602
閘室 597
恒湿計 261
子牛の肉 214
硬質ゴム製棒状小勒馬銜 854
恒湿度計 261
格子窓 727
甲締め具 889
後写鏡 569, 570
公衆電話 427, 715, 720, 723, 725, 779
公衆電話機 507
高周波アンテナ・ケーブル 628
光受容器 177
後槽 600, 602
工場 708
高焦点水面ブイ 615
高焦点水面浮標 615
高所剪定鋏 330
後審 807
後陣 411
交信音量調節装置 20
香辛料 198
降水 64, 67
降水地域 55
降水量を測定する器具 59
光線 691
光線による分別 71
構造 249
高層アパート 419
高層雲 56, 62
構造湖 48
高層大気の探測 59
構造プレート 43
高速回転軸 677
後続車 870
後続集団 870
高速道路 539, 709
高速誘導路 618
高速列車 585
後大腿皮神経 166
後退ペダル 333
後端 105
講壇 738
高地 7
紅茶 208
鉱柱 650
校長室 735
交通枝 168
交通島 539

交通信号 712
工程 401
校庭 735
高低照準装置 756
坑内操作口 648
鋼製ケーブル 913
荒天 65
高電圧を送電する 677
光電セル 482
光電池モジュール 21
高度 53
喉頭 163
鉱筒 650
黄道 13
講堂 394, 718, 732
坑道入り口周辺 648
喉頭蓋 163, 176
後頭筋 151
後頭骨 131, 153, 158
合同である 703
合同ではない 703
高度回転トラック 16
高度計 761, 896, 898, 899
光度の単位 702
鋼とプラスチック 269
構内入り口 592
口内洗浄液 384
口内洗浄器 384
口内洗浄剤 384
坑内掘り炭鉱 650
公認のごみ埋立地 69
コウノトリ 119
広背筋 151
勾配屋根 414
香篆車 696
甲板 838
合板 300
後半規管 174
後尾 893
交尾嚢 97, 104
交尾嚢の開口部 97
交尾矢嚢 104
後部 569
後部ウインカー 575, 576
後部滑走部 884
後部緩衝器 575
後部座席 555, 577
後部シールド 17
後部支柱 676
後部ショック・アブソーバー 575
後部水中翼 609
後部ステップ 766, 775
後部バンパー 876
後部デッキ 608
後部ドア 775
後部荷台 577
後部バケット 637
後部はしご 587
後部バンパー 885
後部プロペラ 606
後部方向指示灯 575, 576
後部横木 893
後部ランナー 884
口吻 96
後閉殻筋 105
後壁 818, 819
香箱屋 737
後房 7
高棒 824
後方境界線 848
後方支索 602
硬膜 167, 168
硬膜外腔 168
硬膜上腔 168
小馬座 12
剛毛 320
コウモリ 140
コウモリの形態図 140
コウモリの骨格図 141
コウモリの例 141
肛門 95, 97, 103, 104, 105, 106, 107, 109, 113, 164, 169, 170
肛門括約筋 164
閘門給水孔 597
閘門給水用バルブ 597
閘門給排水孔 597
閘門給排水システム 597
閘門排水システム 597
コウヤマキ 89
広葉樹の例 88
広葉樹林 66
高翼 628
高利得アンテナ 18
合流交通あり 544, 547
合流注意 544, 547
合流点 48
交流電源コード 526
交流発電機 552, 566, 586, 677, 688
抗力 630
後輪 333
後輪ブレーキ 578
後輪ブレーキ・ペダル 576
小枝 77, 87
コエビ 218
コエロフシス 93
コーキング・ガン 315
ゴーグル 318, 870, 875, 887, 888, 896
コース 788, 790, 830, 831, 833, 838, 852, 866, 874, 882, 885
コース計時員 830
コース・ゲート 837

コース標識 875	小切手帳 386	コップ座 11	5メートル固定台 828	コンドライト 8
コース・ブイ 838	小切手帳入れ 386	コッヘル 905	5メートル・ライン 800, 805	ゴンドラ出発点 886
コース役員 853, 855	小切手帳カバー 387	骨膜 154	こめかみ 146	コントラスト調節つまみ 518
コース・ライン 791, 831	小狐座 13	小手 847	米酢 201	コントラスト調節ボタン 512
コースレット 366	顧客 487	籠手 752	込め矢 752	ゴンドラ付き高所作業車 622
コーチ 800, 811, 827, 879, 881, 883	顧客サービス 731	小手先 749	鼓面 433	コントラバス 437, 439
コーチ・ボックス 794	呼吸器系 163	小手当て 749	鼓面の皮 433	コントラ・バスーン 437
コーチ台 891	呼吸器系の保護具 773	固定アーチ 541, 311, 312	小文字 472	コントラ・ファゴット 437
コーチング・ステッチ 459	呼吸弁 655	固定蓋式貯蔵タンク 655	小物 345, 454	コンドル 119
コート 352, 355, 809, 810, 812, 813, 814, 816, 818, 819, 820, 845, 918	コキル 849	固定型プラットフォーム 653	小物入れ 294, 399, 556, 859	コントローラー 918
	黒鉛 300	固定橋 540	コモロ 746	コントローラー・ボート 918
	黒鉛鉛筆 470	固定子 659	小山 875	コントロール 514
	漕ぐことと幅寄せ 838	固定ジャッキ 567	小指 173	コントロール・キー 514
コード 285, 288, 289, 316, 332, 488, 504, 505	国営放送ネットワーク 486	固定鎚 436	小指掛け 447	コントロール：グループ・セレクト 514
	国際宇宙ステーション 21	固定装置 321, 649	コヨルシャウキの石板 412	
コート置き棚 510	国際式天気図記号 56	鑿板 315	コラード 186	コントロール・ゲート 890
コート掛け 510	国際単位系 702	固定台 613	娯楽室 727	コントロール・ケーブル 323
コード・キー 528	国際郵便 475	固定台座 312	コラ半島 32	コントロール・コンソール 626
コート・サーフェス 822	谷柵 46	固定点 103	コラム 259, 403, 405, 471, 919	コントロール・バー 897
コートジボワール 745	国籍 825	固定ナット 58	コラム・ラジエーター 259	コントロール・パネル 238, 239, 261, 290, 292, 293, 294, 508, 512, 518
コート・スタンド 510	小口 426	固定刃 424	コリアンダー 202	
コード・スリーブ 308, 318	木口 300	固定バンド 59	孤立丘 481	
コード止め 285	木口木版用版木 421	固定ピン 458	孤立した諸言語 469	コントロール表示ランプ 519, 520
コート・ドレス	黒点 6	固定ベルト 52	孤立障害標識 617	コントロール・ボタン 516
コート・ハンガー 510	黒板 734	固定弁 893	ゴリラ 138	コントロール・ボックス 267
コート・フック 510	穀粉 204	固定リング 302	ゴリラの形態図 139	コントロール・ルーム 488
コード補強材 288	小熊座 12	鑿り 315	ゴリラの骨格図 138	コンバーチブル 549
コート・ラック 510	穀物 13	5度 434	護輪軌条 590	コンパートメント 416
コードレス電話機 507	穀物食品 204	小道具 401, 464	コリント式 405	コンバイン 643
コードレス・マウス 516	穀物ターミナル 596	小道具係 429	コリント式の片蓋柱 407	コンバイン・ハーベスター 643
コーナー 842	国立公園 39	琴座 13	コリント式の付け柱 407	コンパウンド・ボウ 859, 913
コーナー椅子 842	穀粒 85	子供用 581	コルク 892	コンパクト 378
コーナー・エリア 803	穀粒昇降機 643	子供靴 717	コルク芯 797	コンパクト・ディスク 501, 504
コーナー・キャップ 587	穀粒タンク 643	子供服 717	コルク栓抜き 905	コンパクト・ディスク・リライタブル 521
コーナー・クッション 842	穀粒排出管 643	子供用三輪車 581	コルク・ヘッド 817	
コーナー・フラッグ 801, 803	穀類 85, 203	子供用スポーツウエア 717	コルゲーション 562	コンパクト・ディスク・リライタブル・レコーダー 521
コーナー用食器棚 279	固形パウダー 378	粉振り器 232	ゴルゴンゾラ 211	
コーニス 403, 404	固形マスカラ 378	粉篩 232	ゴルゴンゾラ・チーズ 211	コンパクト・フラッシュ・メモリー・カード 481
コーネル 426	コケモモ 192	粉ミルク 210	ゴルジ装置 74, 94	
コーヒー 208	こけら板 299	小縄 908	ゴルフ 866	コンパクト・メモリー・カード 477
コーヒー・ショップ 725	ココア	小荷物受付所 582	ゴルフ・カート 869	コンパス・カード 37, 612, 907
コーヒー・スプーン 228	五光星 741	コネクター 272	ゴルフ・クラブの種類 867	コンパス座 11
コーヒーと茶 208	後甲板 520	コネクター・パネル 518	ゴルフ・グローブ 869	コンパス子午線 907
コーヒー・プレス 241	ココス・プレート 43	捏ね刃 236	ゴルフ・コース 708, 788	コンパニオン 390
コーヒー・ポット 241, 905	ココナッツ 193	木端 300	ゴルフ・シューズ 869	コンビネーション 351
コーヒー・マグ 226	小雨 64	小鈎 696, 697	ゴルフ手袋 869	コンビネーション・ボタン 444
コーヒー・メーカー 241	コバルト 683	小旗 739	ゴルフ・バッグ 869	コンピューター 734
コーピング 894	腰 115, 124, 147, 147, 149, 439, 663, 911	碁盤 916	ゴルフ・ボール 867	コンピューター・インターフェース・ポート 520
コーブ・ビット 308		5番アイアン 868	ゴルフ・ボールの断面図 867	
コーム 417, 461	腰当て 749, 808	5番ウッド 868	コレクター 659	コンピューター画面明度調節装置 20
コーム・バインダー 533	腰掛け 464, 897	コピー機 512, 730, 733	コレクター・ヘッド 18	コンピューター・コネクター 518
コーラ 433	腰革 370, 342	コピー室 509	コレット 308	コンピューター・コンパートメント 527
コーラ・ナッツ 193	腰革前部 342, 370	コピー出力モード 512	500 703	
コーラン 736	漉し器 231	コピー枚数ボタン 512	500メートル・スタート・ライン 882	コンピューター・サイエンス室 734
コーラングレ 437, 446	ゴシキヒワ 118	コピー・モード設定パネル 512		コンピューター室 763
氷 67	小獅子座 13	ゴビ砂漠 33	500メートル・フィニッシュ・ライン 883	コンピューター・テーブル 511
氷霰 64	個室 728	こぶ 875, 890		コンピューター・デスク 511
氷砂糖 209	漉し布 231	コフキコガネ 101	五重奏 438	コンピューター・ネットワーク 523
氷自動販売機 548	腰布 339	ゴブ・ハット 341	50天文単位 4	コンピューター・プログラム 771
ゴール 800, 802, 804, 807, 809, 814, 827, 852, 856, 879, 920	腰ベルト 281	コブラ 114	小鼻 189	昆布 183
	腰巻壁 408	個別フォルダー 532	ゴボウ 189	コンファロン 739
ゴール・アタック 803	越屋根 414	ゴング 437, 449	コマ 8	コンプルビウム 406
ゴール・エリア 802, 814	50 703	コンクリート 298	駒 433, 439, 440, 915, 916	コンプレッサー 260
ゴール・エリア・ライン 814	五重奏 438	コンクリート遮蔽体 670, 671	こま 268	コンプレッサー・タービン 627
ゴールキーパー 800, 801, 803, 809, 814, 827, 878, 879	小姑 785	コンクリート遮蔽壁 670, 671	ゴマ油 209	コンベヤー 646, 647, 649
	50メートル標的線 859	コンクリート・ドレン 655	コマドリ 118	コンベンション・センター 711, 718
ゴールキーパー・グローブ 802	50ヤード・ライン 806	コンクリート・ブロック 298	こまナット 268	根棒 823
ゴールキーパー用スケート靴 880	54メートル・ライン 858	コンクリート壁 675	コマンド・ナイフ 751	梱包 71
	胡椒入れ 226		ごみ受け 288	コンマ 473
ゴールキーパー用スティック 880	鼓状結晶 64	コンクリート・ミキサー・トラック 573	ごみ埋立地 709	根毛 77
	コショウソウ 187		ごみの分別 71	根毛部 87
ゴールキーパー用プロテクター 880	弧状列島 49	根系 77, 86	ごみ廃棄場 709	婚約指輪 376
	個人識別章 770	根茎 76	ごみ袋部 289	根用セロリ 189
ゴールキーパー用胸当て 880	漉す 231	コンゴ 745	ごみ箱 295, 723	こんろ 290
ゴールキーパー用レッグガード 879	梢 87	コンゴウインコ 118	ごみブラシ 289	こんろの火力調節つまみ 290
	コスタリカ 742	金剛砂袋 454	コミュニケーション・プロトコル 524	
ゴール・クリーズ 879	小銭入れ 387, 387	混合室 319		**さ**
ゴール・サークル 809	跨線橋 539	混交樹林 66	ゴム編み 458	
ゴール・サード 809	5,000m走スタート・ライン 790	コンゴ川 34	ゴム編みカフス 354, 369	叉 274
ゴール・ジャッジ 827, 858, 878	固体 680, 681	コンゴ共和国 745	ゴム糸 867	座 276, 277, 281
ゴール・シューター 809	小太鼓 437, 448	コンゴ民主共和国 745	ゴム入りウエストバンド 353	サーキット 872
ゴール人の戦士 748	五大湖 30	コンサート・グランド 443	ゴム入りの脚履き口 351	サーコート 337
ゴーラー 641, 643	固体ブースター・ステージ 24	根菜類 184, 189	ゴム印 531	サード 794, 877
ゴール地点 885, 887	古代ローマの円形闘技場 407	根尖 159	ゴム管 776	サード・ダズン 919
ゴール・ディフェンス 809	古代ローマの住宅 406	根尖孔 159	ゴムギ 203	サード・ロー 804
ゴール壁 830	固体ロケット・ブースター 22, 24	コンセント 274, 316, 567	小麦 85	サーバー 522, 523, 524, 525, 816, 819, 821
ゴールポスト 807, 809, 827, 858	木立 866	コンセント・テスター 316	小麦の断面図 85	
ゴール・ボタン 505	コダチトマト 196	コンソール 444	ゴム・キャップ 321	サービス 820
ゴール面 830	小タマネギ 184	コンソール・ゲージ 841	ゴム・ケーブル 823	サービス・エリア 39, 619
ゴール・ライン 800, 804, 806, 809, 809, 814, 827, 878	コタルディ 337	コンタクト・プリンター 484	ゴム・シート 500	サービス・ジャッジ 816
	固着地衣 74	コンタクト・レバー 287	ゴム・ストッパー 321	サービス・ゾーン 817, 818
ゴール・ランプ 879	固着部 75	コンタクト・レンズ 384	ゴム製オーバー・シューズ 342	サービス・ボックス 821
コールラビ 185	黒海 28, 32, 33	コンチネンタル・ライズ 49	ゴム製バンパー 920	サービス・ボックス・ライン 818
コーン・シロップ 209	コーン・サラダ 187	昆虫とクモ類 96	ゴム製棒状小勒馬銜 854	サービス・モジュール 486
ゴーントリット 346	告解場 737	昆虫の例 101	ゴム底草履 344	サービス・ライン 818, 819, 821
コーン部 494	骨格 152	コンテ担当 429	ゴム・タイヤ 633	サービス・ライン・アンパイア 820
固化 680	骨幹 155	コンテナ 605, 635, 635	ゴム手袋 605	サービス・ライン・ジャッジ 820
庫外排水栓 291	骨幹端 155	コンテナー 236	ゴム手袋入れ 770	サービス・ワゴン 278
小型園芸用具 325	国境 37	コンテナ緊締装置 572	ゴム長靴 765	サーブ 812, 820
小型家電製品 717	コックス・シート 838	コンテナ・クレーン 596	ゴムの吊り紐 350	サーファー 840
小型紙パック 223	コックス付きフォア 839	コンテナ車 588	ゴム・バンド 280, 389	サーフィン 840
小型草かき 325	コックス付きペア 839	コンテナ・セミトレーラー 572	ゴム・ホース 271	サーフボード 840
小型クッション 280	コックスなしフォア 839	コンテナ船 596, 604	ゴム・マット 500	サーブル 848, 849
小型スーツケース 389	コックスなしペア 839	コンテナ船倉 605	ゴム・ロープ 902, 903	サーブル・エペ警告線 848
小型ソースパン 235	コック長 721	コンテナ・ターミナル 596, 708	米 85, 203, 207	サーベル 751
小型バス 569	コック付きビュレット 685	コンテナ・パレット・ドーリー 623		サーボモーター 759
小型モーターボート 607	コックピット 631, 834, 873, 898	コンデンサー 646, 693, 694		サーマル・ルーバー 60
小形ライマメ 191	コックピット換気口 898	コンデンサー上下動ハンドル 693		サーモスタット 238, 260, 261, 267, 291
コガネグモ 102	コックピット・キャノピー 898	コンデンサー調節ハンドル 693		サイ 129
股間膜 140	骨髄 154	コンデンス 472		菜園 182, 244
呼気 832	骨髄腔 154	コンドミニアム 886		最下デッキ 655
呼気アルコール検出器 769	コッター・ピン 249	ゴンドラ 542, 600, 886, 899		最下段 650
小切手 729	骨単位 154			在監者出入り口 726
	骨盤 121, 126, 138, 141, 142			

天文学 > 2-25; 　地球 > 26-71; 　植物 > 72-89; 　動物 > 90-143; 　人間 > 144-177; 　食べ物と台所 > 178-241; 　家屋 > 242-295; 　日曜大工・園芸 > 296-333; 　衣服 > 334-371;
装身具類と日用品 > 372-391; 　芸術と建築 > 392-465; 　情報伝達とオフィス・オートメーション > 466-535; 　交通と機械 > 536-643; 　エネルギー > 644-677; 　科学 > 678-705;
社会 > 706-785; 　スポーツとゲーム > 786-920

再帰性反射テープ 611
サイクリング・マシーン 851
サイクル・キャリア 558
サイクロン 63
採血室 781
細孔 74
鰓孔 108
最高温度計 59
さいころ 915
さいころとドミノ牌 914
砦柵 408
祭司の席 738
再循環ポンプ 671
最上デッキ 5
再生・一時停止ボタン 501
再生ヘッド用窓 499
再生ボタン 495, 499, 504, 508
彩層 6
大腿骨 122
細断 71
裁断 424
祭壇画 737
裁断機 424
祭壇座 10
祭壇十字架 737
祭壇の正面掛け布 737
祭壇の前飾り 737
裁断線 455
裁断刃 424
最低温度計 59
採点係 848
採点器 423
サイト 859, 913
サイド 431, 632
サイド・ウォール 560, 561, 818, 819
サイドウォール・ライン 819
細動除去器 775
サイド・キャビネット 510
サイド・コンプレッション・ベルト 906
サイド・ジャッジ 807
サイド・スクリーン 799
サイド・ステップ 586
サイド・ストライプ 551
サイド・チェスト 510
サイド・ドア 594
サイド・バッグ 580
サイド・ハッチ 22
サイド・バンド 812
サイド・ハンドル 307, 308, 331
サイド・フェアリング 873
サイド・ブラシ 573
サイドブレーキ 552
サイド・ベンツ 348
サイドボード 279
サイド・マーカー・ライト 554
サイド・マーカー・ランプ 554
サイド・ミラー 381, 568, 569, 570
サイドライン 800, 806, 809, 810, 812, 814, 815, 858, 864, 877
サイド・レール 571
サイド・レフェリー 860
サイド・レフリー 860
サイナス 336
再熱器 668
サイ・パッド 808
裁判官席 728
裁判官控え室 728
裁判所 710, 728
砕氷船 606
サイ・ブーツ 343
サイフォン 241
載物台 14, 693
載物台前後動ハンドル 693
裁縫 452
細胞咽頭 94
細胞口 94
細胞肛門 94
細胞質 74, 94, 170
細胞体 168
細胞壁 74
細胞膜 74, 94
サイマ 404
再利用できないごみ 71
ザイル 900, 901
ザイル・パーティー 900
鰓裂 108
サイロ 596
ザイロフォーン 437
ザイロフォン 449
サウスウエスター 341
サウジアラビア 746
サウスウエスター 341
サウンド・フィールド調整つまみ 497
サウンド・モード選択つまみ 497
サウンド・モード・ライト 497
サウンド・ライブラリー 733
竿 698
棹 438, 439, 440, 441, 698
竿先部 909
竿尻ガイド 910
竿尻部 909
竿秤 698
棹秤 698
逆さ結び 908
逆立ち飛び込み 828
魚のうろこ落とし 905
魚用ナイフ 228
魚用鍋 234
魚用フォーク 228
座金 227, 229, 268, 310, 689
座金押さえ 268

座金止め輪 268
下がり 847
鎖環 331
左官用鏝 315
先 185, 227, 350, 425, 457
サギ 119
先台 860, 912
先角 863
先細balance 839
砂丘 51
砂丘の例 52
作業区域 10
作業台 305, 401
作業台と万力 312
作業場 726
作業面 312
作業用家具 511
柵 182, 244, 281, 322, 712
さく 75
さく果の断面図 84
削岩具 649
さく軸 75
削除 725
削除キー 515
サクソフォーン 446
サクソルン 447
搾乳場 182
さく片 84
炸薬 653, 757
炸薬充填孔 757
サクランボ 192
ザクロ 196
左舷 609, 616, 617
砂鉱床 48
砂鉱 48
鎖骨 111, 116, 122, 141, 142, 152
座骨 111, 116, 122, 153
鎖骨下静脈 160
鎖骨下動脈 160
座骨神経 166
支え 632
支えケーブル 824, 824, 825
支え線 676
支えの糸 103
支えワイヤー 824, 825
ササゲ 190
舵柄 255
差込口 274, 316, 632
差込口金 275
差込式温度調節つまみ 239
砂じょう 82
砂塵嵐 57
左心室 161, 162
左心房 161, 162
砂州 49, 51
サスペンション 594
サスペンション・アーム 553
サスペンション・ライン 896, 897
サスペンダー 350, 540
サスペンダー・クリップ 350
座席 333, 427, 431, 834, 857, 876, 885
サソリ 102
蠍座 10
サターン5 24, 25
札入れ 386, 387
撮影監督 429
撮影主任 428
撮影助手 428
撮影用アクセサリー 482
撮影レンズ 478
サッカー 802
サッカー・シューズ 802
サッカー場 788
サッカー・テーブル 920
サッカー・プレーヤー 802
サッカー・ボール 802
殺菌器 69
雑穀パン 205
雑誌 471
雑誌架 510
雑誌室 733
雑誌棚 510, 733
サッシ窓 415
サッチェル・バッグ 387
殺虫剤 69, 70
サツマイモ 184
サテライト・ターミナル 619
サトイモ 189
砂糖 209
散水管 573
散水口 328
酸性雨 69, 70
酸性雪 70
サン・セリフ書体 472
三尖弁 162
酸素 683
酸素アウトレット 780
酸素アセチレン溶接 319
酸素圧制御装置 20
酸素が取り除かれた血液 162
酸素吸入器 775
酸素供給調節装置 898
酸素供給ノブ 898
酸素の放出 78
酸素ボンベ 319
酸素ボンベ受け 775
酸素マスク 319
酸素調整ハンドル 319
酸素バルブ 319
酸素を含む血液 162
傘骨 896
サンダル 343, 344, 748
三段横木 852

サボイ・キャベツ 186
サポーター 850
サポート 815
サポジラ 197
残柱 194
サマリウム 684
サム・グリップ 439
サム・ピストン 444
サメの形態図 108
サモア 747
サモア語 469
鞘 907
莢 84
サヤインゲン 191
鞘をむいたエンドウ 190
左右調節つまみ 692
左翼 795
左翼手 794
皿 698, 699, 905
皿頭 302
皿洗い係 721
皿洗い機 224, 271, 721, 723
サラウンド 918
サラウンド・スピーカー 493
サラダ 722
サラダ皿 226
サラダナ 186
サラダ・フォーク 228
サラダ・ボウル 226
サラダ盛り皿 226
サラダ用水切り器 231
皿頭ブッシュ継ぎ手 269
サラン・ラップ 222
ザリガニ 218
ザルガイ 218
芥貝模様 276
猿環 911
ザルケー 857
サルコウ 881
サルロー 881
サロペット 368
サロン 381
サワー・クリーム 210
触り弦 448
桟 249
残圧計 319, 841
3回戦 789
三角窩 173
三角形 401
三角形 705
三角形の胴 433
三角旗 739
三角巾 777
三角筋 150
三角骨 154
三角小間 403, 404, 411, 413
三角座 12
三角州 48, 51
三角州上の分流 48
三角のみ 421
三角破風 403, 405
三角板 14
三角帽 339
三角翼 629, 630
散気筒 627
三脚 14, 436, 448, 482, 483, 489
山脚 45
三脚足 483
産業通信 487
産業廃棄物 69, 70
サングラス 385
散形花序 81
三元牌 917
散光器 428
参考図書 732
珊瑚海 29
サンゴヘビ 114
35mm静止カメラ 20
三重奏 438
32分音符 435
32分休符 435
三出 79
サンショウオ 111
散水 573
散水口 328
酸性雨 69, 70
酸性雪 70
サン・セリフ書体 472
三尖弁 162
酸素 683
酸素アウトレット 780
酸素アセチレン溶接 319

散弾銃 860, 912
散弾粒 835
山地 38
残弾 194
三中心アーチ 413
山頂 45
三跳 127
サンディング・ディスク 308
サンディング・パッド 308
サンデー・スプーン 228
サン・デッキ 607, 609
3点リーダー 473
3度 434
サンド・ウェッジ 868
三胴船 598
三橈漕船 598
サンド・バンカー 866, 867
サンド・バッグ 842
サンド・ペーパー 308
サントメ・プリンシペ 745
サンドレス 356
サン・バイザー 556, 558, 567
桟橋 653
サンパル・オレック 201
3番アイアン 868
3番ウッド 868
三番車 696, 697
ザンビア 746
360度 704
サンプラー 450
三弁アーチ 413
山腹 45
散歩用ステッキ 391, 782
3枚垂直尾翼 629
3枚羽根プロペラ 628
サンマリノ 744
山脈 7, 38, 42
3メートル固定台 828
3メートル飛び板 828
三面鏡 381
三葉形アーチ 413
三葉虫 92
残留物 656
三塁 794
三塁手 794
サン・ルーフ 551
3列風切り 115
3列風切り羽 115
3ヒンジ・アーチ 541
3連ジャンプ 875

し

シ 434
死 702
試合 789
試合者 844
試合場 844, 845, 846, 847, 848
試合用ボール 819
仕上がり線 455
仕上げ 401
仕上げ釘 301
シアノバクテリア 92
シアン 690
シーア派 736
シー・アンカー 610
C型クランプ 312
シーケンサー 450
シーケンサー・コントロール 450
シース・ドレス 356
シイタケ 183
西家 917
CD 501, 504
CD-RWレコーダー 521
CD・DVDプレーヤー 918
CDの読み取り 501
CDプレーヤー 488, 501, 503, 504
CDプレーヤー操作ボタン 504
CDレコーダー 503
CD・レコード店 714
CD-ROMイジェクト・ボタン 513
CD-ROMドライブ 513, 526
CD-ROMプレーヤー 517
シート 426, 555, 577, 578, 603, 783, 839, 851, 876, 877
シート・ステー 578
シート・ハーネス 900
シート・フィルム 481
シート・ベルト 555
シートベルト警告灯 557
シート・ポスト 578
シート・リード 835
シー・バッグ 388
GPS受信アンテナ 613
CB無線 505
C部 307
シーボーギウム 683
シーム 503
シーム・ゲージ 454
シーム・ポケット 355, 360
シーリング・ライト 286
シーリング・リング 655
ジーンズ 358
耳羽 115
J2エンジン 25
シェーク・ハンド・グリップ 815
シェード 286, 286
シェービング・カップ 383
シェービング・ブラシ 383
ジェット・エンジン試運転台 761

ジェット水流 828
ジェット・スキー 876
ジェット・チップ 384
ジェット燃料 656
ジェット風圧偏向板 761
ジェノバ・サラミ 216
シェブロン 740
シェブロン・ステッチ 459
シエラレオネ 745
シェル 206, 448
ジェンベ 433
塩 847
塩入れ 226
シガー・カッター 390
歯冠 159
歯杯 327, 642, 643
耳管 174
耳管咽頭口 175
時間管理用品 530
士官室 762, 763
士官事務室 762, 763
時間測定 696
磁気 687
敷居 247
敷石 322
自記気圧計 59
磁器コンデンサー 689
磁気コンパス 898, 907
色彩円 400
自記湿度計 59
磁気制動装置 698
色相環 400
指揮台 437
磁気帯 729
敷地 244
敷地境界 244
敷地平面図 245
磁気テープ 495
色灯 591
色灯板 591
四季牌 917
敷物 254
子宮 170, 171
指球 130, 133
趾球 130
子宮頸部 170
子宮広間膜 171
仕切り 386, 533, 771, 902, 919
仕切りカーテン 780
仕切りカード 532
仕切り壁 771
仕切りタイル 298
仕切り箱 279
軸 302, 306, 390, 425, 454, 457, 470, 648, 686, 688, 838, 911
軸受け 307
軸木 391
軸索 168
軸索小丘 168
ジグザグ幅選択つまみ 452
軸針 612, 907
ジグ・ソー 305
ジグソー・パズル 917
軸椎 122, 153, 157
軸頭 391
シグネット・リング 376
軸箱 586
軸ひだ 105
軸紐 893
軸部 301, 302
シグマ 703
軸流圧縮機の羽根車 627
シクロラマ 492
歯頸 159
シケイン 872
歯隙 123
試験管 685
試験管挟み 685
耳甲介 173
視交叉 167
時刻表 582
時刻表示ボタン 496
指骨 111, 116, 122, 136, 138, 141, 142, 154
歯骨 112
趾骨 111, 116, 122, 131, 138, 141, 142, 155
篩骨篩板 175
歯根 159
歯根部 159
歯根尖 159

歯根尖孔　159
歯根膜　159
シザーズ・カット　375
支材　652
自在鉤　291
自在スパナ　311
自在継ぎ手　641, 642
自在挟み　685
自在ホース　649
自在ホース取り付け部　649
自在連結部　569
自在レンチ　311
支索　598, 602
支索栓　834, 835
支持金具　284
指示換算目盛り　479
支持脚　461
支軸　382, 383, 436, 454, 686
支持構造　16, 40
獅子座　13
支持線　274
支持体　400
翅室　96
支持部　627, 641
時事風刺漫画　471
指示目盛り　479
磁石　454, 488, 534, 687
磁石による分離　71
耳珠　140, 173
刺繍　459
四重奏　438
耳小骨　174
支檣索　834
糸状乳頭　176
耳状部　98
司書室　732
指針　479, 695, 698, 699
時針　697
磁針　907
地震　43
地震記録　43
地震記録計　651, 653
指伸筋　151
指神経　166
視神経　177
地震計　43
視神経交叉　167
視神経乳頭　177
地震波　43
歯茎　159
耳垂　173
歯髄腔　159
止水スイッチ　263
止水栓　262, 265, 270, 271
止水層　660
止水壁　660, 661
滴状飾り　404
滴除け　567
システム・サポート室　509
システム・ディスプレイ　626
システム・ボタン　450
シストルム　449
ジスプロシウム　684
地滑り　47
沈み込み帯　43
姿勢制御スラスター　18, 22
耳舌　109
歯舌　104
自然環境　867
自然な温室効果　68
自然放射線　41
歯槽　159
歯槽骨　159
始祖鳥　93
舌　109, 110, 164, 174, 175, 433, 444
シダ　76, 92
下顎　108, 124
字体　472
次体層　105
下絵　401
下襟　348
下カーソル　515
下框　247, 278
舌革　370, 342, 881, 889
下側シーツ　280
下着　351, 366
下桁　834
下敷き　254
下付き　472
舌付き燕尾形旗　739
下止め　453
下のキャビネット　224
シダの構造　76
舌の鞘　112
シダの例　76
下パイプ　579
下穿き　844
下弾き　391
下馬衛枝　854
下張り床　252, 253, 254
シタビラメ　221
下縁索　602
下瞼　110, 132, 177
下見所　856
舌寛　854
シダレヤナギ　88
下ろくろ　391
下枠　249
七分コート　352
七分袖　360
シチメンチョウ　120, 213
試着室　716
指柱　696

支柱　43, 59, 246, 252, 307, 321, 322, 324, 424, 425, 440, 445, 448, 485, 493, 591, 594, 609, 629, 663, 685, 782, 792, 811, 812, 815, 817, 825, 826, 826, 881
支柱目盛り　485
支柱用穴　571
市庁舎　710
試聴ブース　733
室　82
室温　261
膝蓋　122, 124, 126, 131
十戒　738
膝蓋骨　122, 126, 131, 138, 152
シックスト　849
実験器具　685
実際濃度　261
湿式セル　671
膝射姿勢　861
湿潤大陸性気候　61
実施審判員　823
湿度　261
湿度計　261
湿度を測定する器具　59
室内サーモスタット　261
室内シャッター　282
ジッパー　377, 389
湿分分離器　668
質量の単位　702
シティ・サイクル　581
指定方向外進行禁止　544, 546
シデムシ　101
支点　454, 686, 828
自転車　578
自転車競技　870
自転車通行止め　545, 546
自転車の部品　578
自転車の例　581
自転車バッグ　731
自転車用チャイルド・シート　580
支店長室　731
自動応答表示ランプ　508
自動改札ドア　620
児童コーナー　732
自動式引き戸　416
自動車　549
自動車システム　553
自動車システムの主な部品　552
自動車ディーラー　711
自動車による汚染　69
自動車レース　872
自動小銃　755
自動食器洗い機　294
自動仕分けトレイ　512
指頭髄　172
自動水温調節装置　259
自動選別・取り揃え・押印機　474
自動操縦装置　626, 759
自動速度制御装置　556
自動測量計　655
自動ドア　416
児童図書　732
自動二輪車通行止め　545, 546
始動ハンドル　331
視度調節環　693
視度補正環　693
シトロン　194
市内バス　568
シナゴーグ　738
シナ・チベット語族　468
シナノキ　208
シナプス　168
シナモン　198
地均し機　639
歯肉　159, 174
蛇口　264, 268
蛇口アダプター　485
蛇口連結部　328
シニスター・チーフ　740
シニスター・フランク　740
シニスター・ベース　740
シネ・スケール　479
シネ目盛り　479
子嚢盤　74
芝　822
磁場　494, 687
支配人室　509
芝庫　726, 764
斜桁　602
斜桁支索　834
遮光板　558, 591
しゃこ万力　462
射座　893
斜材　663
車軸　895
車軸関節　156
指板　432, 439, 441
地盤　538
歯板と歯車　686
指標桿　612
指標表示ボタン　496
師部　87
ジブ　634, 635, 834
4分音符　435
4分休符　435
ジブシート　834
ジブ支持索　634
ジブスル　834
ジブ・セール　834
ジブター　579, 580
ジブチ　745
ジブ調節ロープ　834
シフト・キー　514, 528
シフト：レベル2セレクト　514
シフト・ロック・キー　528
ジブラルタル海峡　32

四分円　704
紙幣　729, 915
紙幣受取口　730
磁壁　687
四辺形　705
司法　726
子房　80
死亡　702
指方位　59, 701
死亡記事　471
四方切妻屋根　415
脂肪組織　171, 172
脂肪滴　74
絞らずに吊り乾燥　347
絞らずに吊り干し　347
絞り　477
絞り器　237
絞り紐　387
絞り紐付きフード　369
絞り袋と口金　232
絞り弁　649
絞り目盛り　478, 479
搾る　230, 237
島　38
シマウマ　128
シマオオタニワタリ　76
シマリス　123
翅脈　96
ジム　764
事務室　394, 509, 548, 582, 724, 726, 738
事務所　720
締め　425
紙名　471
締め板　425
締め金具　274, 842
締め金　446
締め機　425
締め具　284, 462, 826, 888, 889, 892, 913
締め込み　847
締め付けし　312
湿し水部　420
締め紐　282, 773, 843
締めボルト　448
締め結び　908
締める道具　310
締め枠　448
霜　65
耳毛　115
下手　431
ジャック　850
ジャージー　805, 870
シャープ　829
シャープ・ペンシル　470
ジャーマン・サラミ　216
ジャーマン・シェパード　130
ジャーマン・マスタード　200
ジャーマン・ライ麦パン　205
シャーリング　283
シャーレ　685
ジャイアント・スラローム　889
ジャイビング　833
ジャイロスコープ　759
社員食堂　509
車運車　588
ジャガー　135
ジャガイモ　184
ジャガ芋つぶし器　233
釈迦牟尼　736
遮眼帯　857
弱音器　447
弱音ペダル　442
尺側手根屈筋　151, 150
尺側手根伸筋　151
尺側皮静脈　160
斜裂　163
シャロット　184
シャワー　251, 726, 780
シャワー室　264, 780
シャワーと浴槽設備　262
シャワー・ヘッド　264
ジャワ海溝　50
車枠　641
ジャン・カルバン　736
シャンク　390, 610
ジャンクション・ボックス　272
シャンク・ボタン　453
シャンツェ　891
シャンティイ寄せ木張り　254
シャンデリア　287
ジャンパー　891
ジャンパー・スカート　356
ジャンパー・ドレス　356
シャンパン・グラス　225
ジャンプ　792, 891
ジャンプー　379
ジャンプスーツ　358, 368, 369, 891, 896
ジャンプ・スキー　840
ジャンプ台　890, 891
ジャンプの技　881
ジャンプの例　881
ジャンプ・ブーツ　891
ジャンプ用スキー板　891
ジャンベ　433
ジャズ・バンド　438
写真　476
写真館　714
写真提供者番　471
写真屋　714
社説　471
斜線　471
車線　539
斜体　472

車体　550, 567, 567, 884
射台　860
車体の例　549
車体梁　639
斜対歩馬　857
遮断器　260
遮断機　591
遮断機支持腕　591
社長室　509
車長席　758
社長秘書室　509
シャツ　349, 368, 810
シャツウエスト・ドレス　356
ジャッキ　558, 634, 638, 766, 873
ジャック・スプリング　443
ジャックフルーツ　196
ジャック形　740
ジャックポット箱　920
ジャックポット・フィード　920
シャックル　835
ジャックレッグ・ドリル　648
尺骨　116, 121, 122, 126, 131, 136, 138, 141, 142, 152, 154, 156
尺骨神経　166
ジャッジ　842, 843, 881
シャツ・スリーブ　360
シャッター　521, 675
シャッター・スピード設定キー　479
シャッター・レリーズ・ボタン　476
シャツ・ブラウス　359
斜堤　409
シャド基準露光キー　479
シャドー・バンド　58
シャドー・ロール　856
シャトル列車　620
車内表示板　587
遮熱板　274
蛇腹　432, 485, 569
蛇腹バンド　432
シャプカ　340
車輪灯　554, 570, 571
シャフト　405, 436, 462, 464, 676, 688, 692, 828, 851, 857, 858, 859, 863, 867, 880, 892, 895, 901, 918
シャベル　257, 326
ジャボ　362
ジャボチカバ　197
ジャマイカ　742
シャム・ネコ　133
斜面　244, 411, 538, 674
斜面出入口　403
斜文織り　463
車票　676
砂利　253, 263
車両運搬セミトレーラー　572
車両境界破線　539
車両甲板　608
車両進入禁止　544, 546
車両出入り口　769
車両待機所　543
車両転回禁止　544, 546
車輪　323, 570, 753, 870, 874, 894, 895
車輪昇降レバー　626
車輪速センサー　559
車輪速度センサー　559
車輪止め　622
シャルロット型　232
斜裂　163
シャロット　184
シャワー　251, 726, 780
シャワー室　264, 780
シャワーと浴槽設備　262
シャワー・ヘッド　264
ジャワ海溝　50
車枠　641
ジャン・カルバン　736
シャンク　390, 610
ジャンクション・ボックス　272
シャンク・ボタン　453
シャンツェ　891
シャンティイ寄せ木張り　254
シャンデリア　287
ジャンパー　891
ジャンパー・スカート　356
ジャンパー・ドレス　356
シャンパン・グラス　225
ジャンプ　792, 891
ジャンプー　379
ジャンプスーツ　358, 368, 369, 891, 896
ジャンプ・スキー　840
ジャンプ台　890, 891
ジャンプの技　881
ジャンプの例　881
ジャンプ・ブーツ　891
ジャンプ用スキー板　891
ジャンベ　433
シュー　571
州　37
10　703
銃　815
獣医　852
重罰記号　435
自由縁　172
シュヴェンケル付き旗　739

州界　37
縦隔壁　606
銃眼　409
周期　617
重機関　636
周期表　682
宗教　736
従業員用クローク　720
従業員用ラウンジ　731
宗教改革　736
宗教年表　736
シュー・クリーム　345
銃口　754, 860, 912
銃腔　753, 754, 860, 912
銃腔差し込み式の銃剣　751
集光レンズ　693
銃固定式の銃剣　751
15メートル・ライン　805
ジューサー　240
終糸　167
十字頭　302
十字穴付き頭　302
十字形　740
十字型尾翼　629
終糸の軟膜外　167
十字ハンドル　919
私有車道　245
収集トラック　573
収縮胞　94, 94
柔術　846
柔術衣　846
柔術着　846
銃床　860, 861, 912
重症度区分室　779
銃身　754, 755, 860, 912
囚人受入室　726
銃身覆い　755
囚人護送車　726
銃身挿入式の銃剣　751
銃身被筒　755
囚人房　727
シューズ　810, 865, 870, 872
重水　670
集水坑　650
重水再濃縮　669
重水再濃縮器　669
重水炉　670
ジューズ・ハープ　433
シューズ・ラック　345
修正液　534
中性子星　8
修正テープ　534
集積回路　689
集積回路パッケージ　689
縦線　434
臭素　683
集草器　332
従属栄養生物　67
従属栄養体　67
収束型境界　43
収束型プレート境界　43
収束レンズ　691
集束レンズ　694
縦舵　763
縦帯　740
住宅地域　709
集団　870
絨毯　254
終端器　522
絨毯床用ブラシ　289
集中治療室　780
縦張肋　105
シューティング・サークル　800
集電環　688
充電器　306
充電警告灯　527
充電残量表示ランプ　383
充電式ドライバー　302
充電式ドリル・ドライバー　306
充電台　288
充填断熱材　299
充電池　306
充電プラグ　563
集電棒　689
充電用バッテリー・パック　496
翼　784
シュート　650
柔道　844
柔道衣　844
柔道着　844
姑　784
17世紀の大砲と臼砲　752
十二指腸　116, 164
集熱パイプ　672
収納家具　278
収納庫　567, 570, 766
収納スペース　584
収納棚　723
収納ボックス　483
数牌　917
集配局　474
周波数スライダー　498
周波数帯　498
周波数ディスプレイ　498
周波数の単位　702
周波数表示画面　503
周波数表示窓　503
銃尾覆い　755
秋分　54
10分の1秒針　696
重変記号　435
周波継ぎ目　661
シュー・ポリッシャー　345
周歩廊　411

932

天文学 > 2-25；　地球 > 26-71；　植物 > 72-89；　動物 > 90-143；　人間 > 144-177；　食べ物と台所 > 178-241；　家屋 > 242-295；　日曜大工・園芸 > 296-333；　衣服 > 334-371；
装身具類と日用品 > 372-391；　芸術と建築 > 392-465；　情報伝達とオフィス・オートメーション > 466-535；　交通と機械 > 536-643；　エネルギー > 644-677；　科学 > 678-705；
社会 > 706-785；　スポーツとゲーム > 786-920

終末細気管支　163
終末分枝　168
１０メートル固定台　828
１０メートル・ライン　804
柔毛　133
重役付き秘書室　509
重役机　511
集約的畜産　68, 69
集約的農業　68, 70
集約的牧畜　68, 69
重油　656
収容者用シャワー室　768
修理場　548
重量測定　698
重量帯　841
終了ボタン　527
重力　630
重力拡散の部屋　402
重力式ダム　661
重力式ダムの断面図　661
重力バンド　610
ジュール　702
縦列砂丘　52
ジュウロクササゲ　190
１６分音符　435
１６分休符　435
守衛室　731, 733
主エンジン　656
珠芽　78
シュガー・ポット　226
主開閉器　273
主火道　44
主花柄　86
主管　447
樹冠　87
珠間切痕　173
主甲板　761
主気管支　163
主脚　625, 760
主鏡　15, 17
儒教　736
手具　823
縮充機　642
縮小・拡大ボタン　512
宿泊設備　886
縮帆帯　603
主系列星　8
主甲板　761
主根　77, 87
手根関節部　130
手根球　130
手根骨　116, 122, 126, 131, 136, 138, 141, 142, 154
手根の肉趾　130
主催者控え室　719
主祭壇　737
主索　417
主傘　896
種子　77, 81, 82, 83, 84
主軸　659
種子箱　643
主車輪　625
手術室　780, 781
手術台　780
手術用手袋収納ケース　780
手術用ブロック　780
主将　877
主楯　600, 602
主浄化栓　262
主蒸気管　669
主蒸気ヘッダー　669
樹状突起　168
主審　799, 801, 803, 805, 807, 809, 810, 813, 817, 818, 819, 820, 837, 838, 844, 845, 846, 847, 848
樹心　87
受信　16, 493
主寝室とカテドラル型天井　251
主審所定線　845
受信トレイ　508
主審ライン　845
受水器　59
取水口　658
受水漏斗　59
朱子織り　463
ジャストコール　338
受精嚢　97, 103
主線香　807
主ダクト　258
主柱　407
主通気坑　648
出国審査場　621
出札所のあるホール　582
出糸突起　103
出水孔　95
出水管　590
出走ゲート　856
出動服　764
出発点　589, 871
出力装置　518
出力端子　441
出力モニター　489, 491
主電源ケーブル　272
主電動機　763
首部　37
主塔　540
主動滑車　688
主塔基礎　540
手動式ウインドー・レギュレーター　554
手動式回転ドア　416, 719
手動式芝刈り機　332
手動式転轍器　590
手動・自動切り替えスイッチ　465

手動焦点調節ノブ　483
手動スライド・チェンジャー　483
受動センサー　41
主取り入れ口　655
シュナウツァー　130
シュノーケル　841
種の起源と進化　92
主排水口　246
主帆　834
縮帆索　603
種皮　81, 85
樹皮　87
守備位置　794
守備車　333
シュピッツェ　901
首部　826
シュブレ　210
シュベ　411
珠柄　83, 84
主変圧器　585
種目　831
樹木　87
種目別得点掲示板　825
樹木の構造　87
需要家番号　273
需要家引き込み口　273
受容器　666
受容室　666
主要な語族　468
主翼　23, 625, 760, 898
主翼形状の例　630
シュラーフの種類　904
主ラインズマン　807
シュラウド　834
ジュラ紀　93
シュラフの種類　904
手榴弾　757
狩猟　912
狩猟靴　855
狩猟帽　340
シュリンプ　218
酒類　180
種類別収集　71
シュロ林　52
受話音量調節パネル　506
受話器　506
受話器コード　506
受話口　506
シュワン鞘　168
巡回・救護本部　886
潤滑点眼液　384
潤滑油　656
潤滑油精製工場　656
循環ポンプ　259, 675
準貴石　375
準決勝　789
準決勝戦　789
準々決勝　789
準々決勝戦　789
巡視路　408, 409
春分　54
春分点　13
準宝石　375
瞬膜　132
盾面　105
ジョイスティック　516, 918
ジョイスティック・レバー　918
署員入り口　768
署員休憩室　768
ジョイント　317, 470, 863, 909
署員用クローク　768
署員用トイレ　768
署員用ロッカー・ルーム　768
小　919
省　37
錠　247, 248, 248, 278, 389
子葉　77
小顎　99
昇圧　662
昇圧変圧器　646, 646
使用圧力計　319
上衣　844, 853, 855
小陰唇　170, 171
上映室　427
省エネ電球　275
消炎器　755
小円筋　151
消音器　553, 577, 649
消音ペダル　442
昇温　680
ショウガ　199
上顎　153
省界　37
場外　844
小会議室　730
昇開橋　542
昇開スパン　542
障害飛越競技　852
障害飛越審判員　852
障害物競走　790
障害物　616, 852, 875
障害物競争ハードル　790
消火器　725, 771
消化器系　164
小核　94
衝角　598
小核果　83
上顎　108
上顎骨　111, 112, 116, 121, 122, 123, 131, 136, 138, 152, 158, 159, 175
消火活動　103, 104, 105, 106, 107
消火栓　712, 767

消火栓開口用レンチ　767
浄化槽　263
松果体　167
消火タンク　631
小果柄　82, 81, 83, 83, 83, 86
小花柄　80
消化泡モニター　607
消火ホース　767
消火用器材　767
消火用ホース　767
蒸気　681
定規　399, 424, 700, 905
定規車　333
定規座　10
蒸気の圧力でタービンを回転させる　665
蒸気排出管　668
蒸気排出口　670, 671
蒸気発生器　669, 670, 671, 674, 763
蒸気発生器室冷却器　669
蒸気ボイラー　646
蒸気放出管　669
小ギヤ　871
焼却　71
掌球　130, 133
小臼歯　121, 123, 159
小峡谷　47, 48
商業地区　709
消極地帯　843
消去ボタン　477, 508
蒸気を凝縮して水に戻す　665
渉禽　117
上空の温暖前線　56
上空の寒冷前線　56
衝撃波　651, 653
小月面　105
上下動ヘッド　236
小剣　349
上弦　540
小剣通し　349
上弦の月　7
礁湖　51
小鼻甲介　175
昇尾筒　115
床尾板　912, 754
商標　390
仕様表示　560
商品受取所　716
商品コード　699
商品陳列棚　181
商品搬入口　713
商品箱　222
上部　750
上部安全カバー　304
上部加圧管　646
上部緩衝梁　635
上部研究室　16
上部構造　615
上部デッキ　624
上部発熱体　266
上部サーモスタット　266
上部緑飾り　278
上部マントル　42
上部ローラー　421
消防士　765
消防車　764, 766
消防長室　764
消防署　711, 764
消防飛行艇　628
情報伝達　468
消防服　764
消防ヘリコプター　631
錠前　248
上膊　115
硝酸の放出　70
上肢　161
上唇　115
上趾　130
上趾球　130
硝子体　177
小室　82
上部の肉趾　130
小質量星　8
小銃　912
小手術室　778
晶出　680
照準　907
照準眼鏡　692, 912
照準器　701, 756, 859, 913
照準鏡　907
照準線　907
掌状　79
ショウジョウコウカンチョウ　118
上昇廊　402
上側列弓　115
上唇　99, 174, 444
上心半円アーチ　413
上水槽　657
渉水鳥　117
小数桁数キー　529
小数点キー　529
使用済み注射器入れ　771
使用済み燃料貯蔵室　666, 667, 669
使用済み燃料廃棄室　668
使用済み燃料ポート　666
焼成　465
照星　754, 757, 861, 893, 912
照星覆い　755
晶帯　680
小節線　434
常設展示室　395
常設歩廊　430
小尖塔　408, 410
小泉門　158
肖像　729

肖像画　729
上側裂片　86
上側湾欠　86
消火栓　167
消火タンク　631
上段部　24
上段ろくろ　460
小チェーン・ホイール　580
蒸着層　501
小腸　110, 113, 116, 125, 164
上腸間膜静脈　160
上腸間膜動脈　160, 165
上直筋　177
錠面　248, 249
小デカンタ　225
商店　710
焦点　674, 691
商店街　710, 713
焦点板　477
小刀　421
小塔　408
鐘塔　411, 737
樵楼横材　834
消毒アルコール　777
消毒剤　777
衝突防止灯　624
商取引　525
鍾乳石　47
証人台　728
小脳　167, 167
消防飛行艇　628
消防服　764
小刃　382
乗馬　854
乗馬スポーツ　852
乗馬ズボン　853
蒸発　67, 680
蒸発器　261
蒸発コイル　261
蒸発グリル　261
蒸発送風機　261
乗馬服　853
床板　590
定盤　304, 424, 425
床尾　755
上鼻甲介　175
消費者へ送電する　662, 677
上尾筒　115
床尾板　912, 754
商標　390
仕様表示　560
商品受取所　716
商品コード　699
商品陳列棚　181
商品搬入口　713
商品箱　222
上部　750
上部安全カバー　304
上部加圧管　646
上部緩衝梁　635
上部研究室　16
上部構造　615
上部デッキ　624
上部発熱体　266
上部サーモスタット　266
上部緑飾り　278
上部マントル　42
上部ローラー　421
消防士　765
消防車　764, 766
消防長室　764
消防署　711, 764
消防飛行艇　628
情報処理室　734
消防服　764
消防ヘリコプター　631
錠前　248
上膊　115
硝酸の放出　70
上肢　161
上唇　115
上趾　130
上趾球　130
硝子体　177
小室　82
上部の肉趾　130
小質量星　8
小銃　912
小手術室　778
晶出　680
照準　907
照準眼鏡　692, 912
照準器　701, 756, 859, 913
照準鏡　907
照準線　907
掌状　79
ショウジョウコウカンチョウ　118
上昇廊　402
上側列弓　115
上唇　99, 174, 444
上心半円アーチ　413
上水槽　657
渉水鳥　117
小数桁数キー　529
小数点キー　529
使用済み注射器入れ　771
使用済み燃料貯蔵室　666, 667, 669
使用済み燃料廃棄室　668
使用済み燃料ポート　666
焼成　465
照星　754, 757, 861, 893, 912
照星覆い　755
晶帯　680
小節線　434
常設展示室　395
常設歩廊　430
小尖塔　408, 410
小泉門　158
肖像　729
上層雲　55
上層雲形　55

上流水位　597
上流底　660
上流面遮水壁　661
上流面補強壁　660
小菱形骨　154
じょうろ　328
上路アーチ橋　541
鐘楼　410, 411
檣楼　602
小枠広告　471
小惑星帯　5
上腕　150
上腕甲　749
上腕骨　111, 116, 121, 122, 126, 131, 136, 138, 141, 142, 152, 156
上腕骨頭　153
上腕三頭筋　151
上腕筋　150
上腕二頭筋　150
女王　916
女王バチ　99
女王バチ隔離板　100
ジョーカー　914
ショーツ　802, 805, 810, 870
ショーティ　344
ショート　794
ショート・サービス・ライン　817
ショート・ソックス　365
ショート・トラック　882, 883
ショート・トラック・スケート靴　883
ショートニング　209
ショート・パンツ　358, 801
ショート・ブーツ　342
ショート・ホール　866
ショート・ライン　818, 819
ショール　337
ショール・カラー　362
助監督　429
書記官席　728
書記官控え室　728
職員休憩室　779
職員室　726
職員出入り管理室　726
職員出入り口　726
職員出入り口　735
職員ロッカー　781
飾冠　749
職業訓練室　730
食事コーナー　224, 250
植生と生物圏　66
植生の垂直分布　66
植生の平面分布　66
食卓塩　201
食虫性の鳥　117
食虫哺乳動物　121
食虫哺乳動物の例　121
食堂　250, 406, 608, 720, 723, 724, 727, 763, 764
食道　95, 97, 99, 103, 104, 109, 110, 112, 113, 116, 125, 163, 164
食堂　584
食堂車　584
食肉　71
食の種類　6, 7
触媒コンバーター　553
食品温度計　231
食品トレー　222
植物　77
植物細胞　74
植物の構造　77
食胞　94
触毛　132
食物連鎖　67
食物連鎖における生産者　67
食用イグチタケ　183
食用芽　185
食料貯蔵戸棚　724
食料品庫　224
食料品袋　181
触腕　106
蹠骨　111, 122, 126, 131, 138, 141, 142, 155
書斎　251
除細動器　775
除算キー　529
除湿器　261
女子トイレ　427, 509, 725
女子1人乗り・男子2人乗りリュージュのスタート地点　885
女子房　768
書状作成用　531
女性　148
女婿　784
女性生殖器　170
女性バーテンダー　720
女性用衣類　355
初戦　789
緒戦　789
助走　891
除草器　325
除草鎌　326
除草耕転機　641
除草剤　69
助走路　791, 792, 793, 824, 865, 890, 891
書簡　734
初段　255
処置室　781
署員užo　764, 768
触覚　172
触角掃除器　98

天文学 >2-25;　地球 >26-71;　植物 >72-89;　動物 >90-143;　人間 >144-177;　食べ物と台所 >178-241;　家屋 >242-295;　日曜大工・園芸 >296-333;　衣服 >334-371;
装身具類と日用品 >372-391;　芸術と建築 >392-465;　情報伝達とオフィス・オートメーション >466-535;　交通と機械 >536-643;　エネルギー >644-677;　科学 >678-705;
社会 >706-785;　スポーツとゲーム >786-920

食器 226	ジングル 449	神道 736	水上捜索レーダー 761, 762	スーパークロス・サーキット 875
食器洗い機 294	シングル・クォーテーション・マーク 473	震動記録 43	水晶体 177, 691	スーパーG 889
ジョッキー 856	シングル・ジャケット 348	振動式スプリンクラー 329	水上竜巻 63	スーパー大回転 889
ジョッキー・プーリー 580	シングル・スカル 839	振動数の単位 702	垂唇 130	スーパーマーケット 180, 711, 715
食器片付け係 721	シングルス・サービス・コート 817	振動板 488, 502, 776	推進剤タンク 18	スープ 722
食器棚 720	シングルス・サイドライン 817, 821	腎動脈 160, 165	水深計 841	四風牌 917
食器とガラス器と銀器 717	シングル・スプロケット 871	深度計 841	推進器 762, 763	スープ皿 226
食器類 905	シングル・ゼロ 919	信徒席 737	推進装置 20, 40	スープ・スプーン 228
ショック・アブソーバー 553, 876	シングル・チェーン・ホイール 871	心内膜 162	推進装置制御室 763	ズーム・ダイヤル 496
ショットガン 912	シングルのカーテン・レール 284	進入口 540	推進プロペラ 605	ズーム・ボタン 496
ジョッパーズ 853	シングル・バーナーのキャンプ用コンロ 903	進入通路 658	推進モジュール 486	ズーム・レンズ 478, 492, 496
ショッピング・カート 181	シングル・パドル 837, 838	腎乳頭 165	水深目盛り 613	ズールー語 468
ショッピング・センター 709, 714	ジンバブエ 746	進入路 618	スイス 744	末 303
ショッピング・バッグ 388	シンバル 437, 448, 449	芯抜き器 233	スイス・アーミー・ナイフ 905	据え置き式プール 246
書店 714	審判 864	腎杯 165	水星 4, 5	スカート 355, 417
書肺 103	腎盤 165	真皮 172	彗星 8	スカートの例 357
ショベル 888, 892	審判委員長 860	ジンベエ 433	水線 615	スカート・フィンガー 605
署名帳 531	審判員 799, 801, 823, 824, 825, 828, 853, 855, 859, 877, 879, 881, 893	審判 864	水洗ラック 485	スカート・マーカー 454
女優 429	吸い出し管 638, 658, 659	水素 682	スカーリング 838
書類整理用 532	審判スタンド 856, 871	深排骨神経 166	吸い出し管カバー 659	水槽 261, 264, 384	頭蓋 106
書類整理用家具 510	審判台 887, 890, 891	腎皮質 165	水中カメラ 480	膵臓 110, 116, 164	頭蓋骨 116, 121, 126, 136, 138, 141, 142, 146
書類フォルダー 532	審判長 828, 830, 859, 881, 900	振幅 471	水中眼鏡 830	水槽の蓋 265	スカイ・ダイバー 896
書類保管室 509	審判副委員長 860	シンブル 700	水中翼船 609	吸い出し管 638, 658, 659	スカイ・ダイビング 896
ショルダー 822, 909	審判補佐 881	新月 7	水中ライト 246	吸い出し管カバー 659	頭蓋の側面図 158
ショルダー・ストラップ 367, 869, 906	心形 79	新聞 471	垂直安定板 625, 631, 760, 898	水中カメラ 480	透かし 729
ショルダー・バッグ 388	神経 172	新聞スタンド 715	垂直回転窓 415	水中眼鏡 830	透かし模様 729
ショルダー・パッド 808	腎形 79	ジンベ 433	垂直材 461	水中翼船 609	スカッシュ 819
ショルダーベルト 555, 906	神経棘 109	シンボル 914	垂直軸型風力タービン 676	水中ライト 246	スカッシュ・ボール 819
ショルダー・ボルト 311	神経系 166	シンボル・マーク 914	垂直地震計 43	垂直安定板 625, 631, 760, 898	スカッシュ・ラケット 819
初列雨覆い 115	神経索 166	心膜 163	垂直立て坑 650	垂直回転窓 415	図柄 920
初列雨覆い羽 115	神経終末 172	新芽 87	垂直調節つまみ 518	垂直材 461	スカルキャップ 340
初列風切り 115	神経繊維 172	震毛 122	垂直である 704	垂直軸型風力タービン 676	スカル・ボート 839
初列風切り羽 115	神経叢 159	進物 717	垂直の瞳孔 112	垂直地震計 43	スカル用オール 838
初列中雨覆い 115	新月 7	腎門 165	垂直目盛り盤調整ねじ 701	垂直立て坑 650	スカンク 134
初列中雨覆い羽 115	震源 43	新約聖書 736	垂直板 852	垂直調節つまみ 518	スカンジウム 683
シラミ 101	震源の深さ 43	針葉樹 89	垂直尾翼 631, 760	垂直である 704	スカンジナビア・クラッカー 205
尻 124, 147, 149	人工衛星 53	針葉樹の例 89	垂直方向の地震動 43	垂直の瞳孔 112	スカンジナビア半島 32
シリア・アラブ共和国 746	唇弁 81	針葉樹林 66	垂直目盛り盤調整ねじ 701	垂直横木 852	スキー 87, 888
シリアル食品 204	信号あり 545, 547	人力散布装置 324	垂直横木 852	垂直目盛り盤調整ねじ 701	スキー板 888
シリアル・ボート 513	信号橋 583	森林火災 69	垂直離着陸機 628	垂直板 852	スキー板の種類 840
腎びれ 108	人工湖 48	森林伐採 69	スイッチ 274, 291, 305, 307, 308, 320, 523, 687	垂直尾翼 631, 760	スキー板の例 888
支流 48	針広混交樹林 66	森 45	スイッチ板 274	垂直方向の地震動 43	スキー・ウエア 888, 892
試料室 694, 694	信号所 583	身廊 411, 738	スイッチ連動コンセント 497	垂直目盛り盤調整ねじ 701	スキー・エリア 886
資料室 764, 769	深紅色 690		スイッチ・ロック 306	垂直離着陸機 628	スキー靴 888, 889
試料ステージ 694	人工壁 900	## す	水田 69	スイッチ 274, 291, 305, 307, 308, 320, 523, 687	スキー・グローブ 888
試料微動装置 694	人工放射線 41		水筒 579, 906	スイッチ板 274	スキー場 886
飼料用トウモロコシ 182	唇部 174	素 212	水道 262	スイッチ連動コンセント 497	スキー・スクール 886
磁力計 60	心材 87	水圧管 657, 658, 664	水道本管 675, 712	スイッチ・ロック 306	スキーの種類 840
磁力線 687	審査員 881	水圧計 766	吸い取り紙 531	水田 69	スキー・パンツ 358
指輪 454	診察室 781	水圧調節スイッチ 384	スイバ 187	水筒 579, 906	スキー・ブーツ 888
耳輪 173	診察処置室 779	水圧抵抗器 851	燃発銃 752	水道 262	スキー・ブレーキ 889
耳輪脚 173	伸子 461	水位 241, 261	水平安定板 625, 631, 760, 898	水道本管 675, 712	スキー帽 892
新シェケル 728	芯地 455	水位切り替えボタン 292	水平回転固定ねじ 701	吸い取り紙 531	スキーヤー用ロッジ 886
シリンダー 249, 268, 564, 754	紳士靴 342, 716	スイートハート・ネックライン 363	水平回転窓 415	スイバ 187	スキー・ラック 558
シリンダー・ケース 249	紳士コート 717	スイート・ピー 190	水平回転用レール 16	燃発銃 752	スキー・リフト終点 886
シリンダー・タイプの電気掃除機 289	紳士下着 716	スイートブレッド 212	水平回転用レバー 482	水平安定板 625, 631, 760, 898	スキー・リフト到達点 886
シリンダー・ブロック 566	紳士シャツ 716	水位表示器 239, 288	水平飾り 247	水平回転固定ねじ 701	スキップ 650, 877
シリンダー・ヘッド・カバー 552, 566	紳士スーツ 716	スイープ・ボート 839	水平鏡 612	水平回転窓 415	梳き刃 382
耳輪尾 173	紳士ズボン 716	スイープ用オール 838	水平鏡用遮光板 612	水平回転用レール 16	塾へら 641
汁受け皿 290	紳士セーター 717	水泳 830	水平坑道 650	水平回転用レバー 482	スキマー 246
シルク・ハット 340	寝室 251, 406, 902	水泳競技場 788	水平材 632	水平飾り 247	隙間用ノズル 289
ジルコニウム 683	神室 403	水泳パンツ 830	水平軸型風力タービン 677	水平鏡 612	隙間用ノズル 289
シルル紀 92	紳士手袋 346	水泳帽 830	水平地震計 43	水平鏡用遮光板 612	スキャナー 517
司令管制室 764, 768	紳士帽 340	水泳用プール 788	水平ターン 832	水平坑道 650	スキューバ・ダイバー 841
司令船 19, 25	紳士トイレ 724	水温計 557, 841	水平帯 812, 817	水平材 632	スキューバ・ダイビング 841
司令塔 763	信者席 737	スイカ 195	水平調節脚 483, 292, 293, 294	水平軸型風力タービン 677	スキューバ・タンク 841
次列風切り 115	伸縮脚 482	水解小体 94	水平調節つまみ 518	水平地震計 43	スクーター 577
次列風切り羽 115	伸縮カーテン・レール 284	吸い殻 391	水平調節ねじ 58, 699	水平ターン 832	スクーナ 601
白 690, 915	伸縮警棒 770	垂下流串 834	水平尾翼 631, 760	水平帯 812, 817	スクープ 390, 899
城 408, 916	伸縮式アーム 18	吹管 314, 319	水平方向の地震動 43	水平調節脚 483, 292, 293, 294	スクール・ゾーン 545, 547
枝路 687	伸縮式アンテナ 503	吹管 106	水平目盛り盤調整ねじ 701	水平調節つまみ 518	スクール・バス 568
シロアリ 101	伸縮自在はしご 321	水管 105	スイベル 515, 911, 913	水平調節ねじ 58, 699	スクエア・ネック 363
白骨 916	伸縮自在棒 920	水球 827	スイミング・ゴーグル 830	水平尾翼 631, 760	スクエア・ベット 919
シロイルカ 137	伸縮自在ホース 289	水泳帽 830	スイム・タイム 831	水平方向の地震動 43	スクラム・ハーフ 804
白帯 812	伸縮自在メジャー 864	水泳用プール 788	水面 828	水平目盛り盤調整ねじ 701	スグリ 192
白オブジェクト・ボール 862, 863	伸縮テーブル 278	水泳パンツ 608, 827, 831	水面貫通翼 609	スイベル 515, 911, 913	スクリーン 383, 427, 483, 658, 724
シロガラス 198	伸縮ブーム 634, 766	水泳尾翼 631, 760	水門 658, 664	スイミング・ゴーグル 830	スクリーン・ケース 483
シロキャベツ 186	伸縮包帯 777	水泳帽 830	水門操作環 659	スイム・タイム 831	スクリーン・プリント 368, 369
シロクジラ 137	紳士用アクセサリー 716	水泳用プール 788	水容器 241	水面 828	スクリプター 429
シロコショウ 198	紳士用カジュアル・ウエア 717	水温計 557, 841	水流 48, 70, 95	水面貫通翼 609	スクリメージ：オフェンス 807
シロ駒 916	針状結晶 64	スイカ 195	水量計 262	水門 658, 664	スクリメージ：攻撃側 807
シロタマゴテングタケ 76	紳士用スポーツウェア 717	水解小体 94	推力 630	水門操作環 659	スクリメージ：守備側 806
シロタマネギ 184	紳士用寝巻き 717	吸い殻 391	水力電気 657	水容器 241	スクリメージ：ディフェンス 806
白パン 205	腎静脈 160, 165	垂下流串 834	水力発電所 657	水流 48, 70, 95	スクリメージ・ライン 807
シロフォーン 437	腎随質 165	吹管 314, 319	水力発電所の断面図 658	水量計 262	スクリュー釘 301
シロフォン 449	新星 8	吹管 106	推力偏向ノズル 628	推力 630	スクリュー・コンベヤー 642, 643
白升 916	シンセサイザー 450	水管 105	水勒鋼 854	水力電気 657	スクリュースリーブ 900
白的玉 862, 863	新鮮燃料貯蔵室 666	水球 827	水勒手綱 854	水力発電所 657	スクリュードライバー・ビット 306
白ワイン・グラス 225	心 97, 99, 103, 104, 105, 106, 107, 109, 110, 112, 116, 125, 162, 163	スイギュウ 128	水勒馬銜 854	水力発電所の断面図 658	スクリュー・ナット 909, 910
仕分け機 475	腎臓 104, 105, 106, 109, 110, 112, 116, 125, 161, 212	水球ボール 827	水勒頰革 854	推力偏向ノズル 628	スクリュー・ピトン 901
仕分け[仕訳]場 589	心臓形 79	水銀 275, 683	吸い口 390, 783	水勒鋼 854	スクリュー・プロペラ 606, 608, 609, 762, 763
芯 81, 82, 867, 908	腎臓形 79	水銀気圧計 59	水圏 66	水勒手綱 854	スクレーパー 422, 423, 638, 892
仁 74, 84, 94	神像の位置 403	水銀柱 695	水源 48	水勒馬銜 854	スクレーパー装置 423
人員専用通路 650	親族 784	水銀槽 695	水瀑 852, 853	水勒頰革 854	スクローリング 515
腎盂 165	寝台 584	水銀体温計 777	吸い込み穴 47	スウィーパー 803	スクロール・ホイール 506, 516
震央 43	人体 146	水銀柱 695	吸い込み口グリル 382	スウェーデン 744	スクロール・ボタン 505
シンガー 911	靱帯 105	吸い口 390, 783	水彩 396	スウェーデンカブ 189	スクロール・ロック・キー 515
シン・ガード 801	人台 454	水圏 66	水彩ケーキ・カラー 397	スウェーデン語 469	スクワッシュ・パティバン 189
深海海丘 49	寝台客室 584	水源 48	水彩チューブ入り絵の具 397	スウェット・パーカー 370	図形 855
深海底 42	寝台車 584	水瀑 852, 853	水彩 396	スウェット・パンツ 370	スケーター 882, 895
深海平原 49	新体操 823	吸い込み穴 47	穂軸 85, 85	スウェル鍵盤 444	スケーティング 892
シンガポール 747	身体用コード 848	吸い込み口グリル 382	水質汚染 70	スウェル・ペダル 444	スケーティング・キック 892
信管 757	新着図書棚 733	水彩 396	水準 650	数学 703, 472, 919	スケーティング走法 892
信管カバー 757	人中 175	水彩ケーキ・カラー 397	水準器 313	数字キー 507, 508, 515, 529, 530	スケート 878
信管部分 757	伸長作業台 305	水彩チューブ入り絵の具 397	髄鞘 168	数字キーパッド 699	スケートボーダー 894
芯切り器 233	伸長式テーブル 278	穂状花序 81, 85	水準オートバイ 876	数字キーボード 699	スケートボーディング 894
心筋層 162	伸長部 278	水蒸気 646	穂状花序 81, 85	枢軸 571	スケートボード 894
真空室 694	真束 253	炊事用具 905	水蒸気 646	スーダン 745	スケグ 836, 840
真空蒸留 656	伸展はしご 321	水上・水中スポーツと海上スポーツ 827	炊事用具 905	スーツ 355	スケジュール帳 530
真空ポンプ 694	浸透 67	水上スキー 840	水上・水中スポーツと海上スポーツ 827	スーツ携帯用衣装バッグ 389	スケルトン 885
真空マニホールド 694			水上スキー 840	スーツケース 389	スケルトン・レーサー 885
寝具置き場 584				スーパー・ウーファー 493	スコア 789, 825
シングル 299					

天文学 > 2-25;　地球 > 26-71;　植物 >72-89;　動物 >90-143;　人間 > 144-177;　食べ物と台所 > 178-241;　家屋 > 242-295;　日曜大工・園芸 > 296-333;　衣服 > 334-371;
装身具類と日用品 > 372-391;　芸術と建築 > 392-465;　情報伝達とオフィス・オートメーション > 466-535;　交通と機械 > 536-643;　エネルギー > 644-677;　科学 > 678-705;
社会 > 706-785;　スポーツとゲーム > 786-920;

スコア・カウンター 920
スコアキーパー 814
スコアボード 789, 790, 822, 825, 831, 839, 918
スコアラー 810, 812, 813, 814, 819
スコート 822
スコープ 859
スコール 57
スコシア・プレート 43
スコットランド語 469
スコップ 326
筋交い 252
筋引き包丁 229
錫 682
スズキ 220
スズキの解剖図 109
スズキの形態図 108
すずき水注入口 294
鈴玉 753
スズメ 118
スズメバチ 101
雀類 117
スズラン 80
裾 349, 359
裾折り返し 350
裾線 455
スター型ネットワーク 522
スターター 327, 332, 830, 838
スターダスト 19
スターティング・グリッド 872
スターティング・グリップ 830
スターティング・ゲート 857, 875
スターティング・ケーブル 323
スターティング・ブロック 791, 830
スタート 852, 915
スタート・キー 508, 514
スタート・ジャッジ 882, 883
スタート台 830, 891
スタート地点 875, 887, 915
スタート飛び込み 832
スタート・トラック 790
スタート・ピストル 790
スタート・ブイ 838
スタート・ボタン 293, 512, 696
スタート・メカニック 873
スタート・ライン 791, 833, 872
スター・トラッカー 18
スター・ドラッグ 910
スター・ファセット 374
スターラップ・ソックス 796
スターン 836
スタイラス 517, 527
スタイラス・ペン 517, 527
スタイラス・ホルダー 517
スタイロベート 403, 404
スタジアム 709, 788
スタジオ 488
スタジオとコントロール・ルーム 488, 490
スタジオ・フロア 490, 492
スタッキング・チェア 277
スタッド 371
スタビライザー 859, 896, 897
スタンション 881
スタンダップ・カラー 363
スタンディング・ポジション 843
スタンド 234, 236, 362, 381, 389, 448, 577, 641, 685, 788, 874, 910
スタンド・オフ 804
スタンド・オフ・ハーフ 804
スタンバイ高度計 626
スタンバイ姿勢指示計 626
スタンバイ対気速度計 626
スタンプ 799
スタンプ台 531
スタンプ・ラック 531
スチーム・アイロン 288
スチーム調節つまみ 241, 288
スチーム・ノズル 241
スチーム噴出口 288
スチーム・ボタン 288
スチール・カメラマン 429
スチール・キャップ 773
スチール・ペン 470
スチル・カメラ 480
スチル・ビデオ・フィルム・ディスク 481
スツール 224, 722
ズッキーニ 188
ステア・クライマー 851
ステアリング・アクスル 633
ステアリング・コラム 552
ステアリング・シリンダー 638
ステアリング・レバー 633
スティール・ベルテッド・ラジアル・タイヤ 561
スティック 449, 800, 801, 858
スティック・タイプの電気掃除機 289
スティック糊 534
スティックピン 376
スティミュレーター・チップ 384
スティル 464
スティルトン 211
スティルトン・チーズ 211
スティレット 751
ステー 602
ステーキ・ナイフ 228
ステーキ肉 214
ステージ 431, 693
ステージ・ハウス 430
ステーション・ワゴン 549

ステースル・ステー 602
ステーター 659
ステープラー 534
ステー・ベーン・ブレード 659
ステー・リング 659
ステッチ 342, 346, 370
ステッチ・パターン・メモリー・キー 456
ステップ 246, 321, 417, 570, 640, 871
ステップ・カット 375
ステップ気候 61
ステップ・チェア 277
ステップ・ハウス 876
ステム 390, 456
ステム管 274
ステルス機 629
ステレオ位相モニター 491
ステレオ・カメラ 481
ステレオ・コンポ 503
ステレオ・モノ切り替えつまみ 504
ステンド・グラス 431
ステンド・グラス窓 737
ストーブ・オイル 656
ストッキング 365, 367, 796, 802, 805, 848, 878
ストッキング・キャップ 341
ストック 432, 610, 676, 860, 861, 888, 891, 892, 912
ストック・アンカー 610
ストック・リング 888
ストックレス・アンカー 610
ストッパー 482, 676, 803, 906
ストッパーのジョウ 700
ストップ 130
ストップウォッチ 488, 696
ストップ・エリア 890
ストップ・ノブ 444, 445
ストップ・ボタン 512, 696
ストップ・ロッド 445
ストマッカー 337
ストラ 336
ストライカー 803
ストラップ 377, 797, 824, 841, 850
ストラップ取り付け部 476, 477
ストラップ・バンプス 343
ストラップ・ピン 441
ストラップ・ボード 864
ストラップ・ループ 906
ストラップレス・ブラジャー 367
ストラップ・レンチ 315
ストランド 908
ストリート・ベット 919
ストリップ 416
ストリップ・ドア 416
ストリップ・ライト 287
ストリング 859, 913
ストレート 914
ストレート・アイロン 381
ストレート・フラッシュ 914
ストレート・ベット 919
ストレーナー 448
ストレッチ 871
ストレッチャー 775, 776, 838
ストレッチャー待機所 778
ストレッチャー・ボード 838
ストロー 223
ストロー管 820
ストロボ 482
ストロークの種類 832
ストロボスコープ 611
ストロボ接点 476
ストロマトライト 92
ストロンチウム 682
砂 660, 813
砂砂漠 52
砂島 51
スナッチ 850
スナッピー 448
スナップ 353, 911
スナップ・シャックル 835
スナップ・スイベル 911
スナップ付き前立て 353
スナップ付き前身頃 369
スナップ付き前身頃 369
スナップ・ボタン 346, 453
砂箱 586
スニーカー 344
ヌーカー 863
脛 124
脛当て 749, 798, 801, 802, 879, 882, 887
ネア・ドラム 437, 448
ネア・ヘッド 448
ネック・ワイヤー 314
脛肉 214, 215
スノー・ガード 876
スノーケル 841
スノーシュー 893
スノースーツ 369
スノー・ブラシ 558
スノーボーダー 887
スノーボーディング 887
スノーボード 887
スノーモビル 876
スノー・ライン 882
スパー 897
スパーク・プラグ 565, 566
スパーク・プラグ・ケーブル 552
スパークリング・ワイン・グラス 225
スパイク 640, 791, 798, 813, 901

スパイク靴 796
スパイク・シューズ 791, 796, 808, 885
スパイク・タイヤ 560
スパイダー・ナット 448
スパイラル・ノート 533
スパゲッティ 206
スパゲッティーニ 206
スパゲッティ用トング 233
巣箱本体 100
スパチュラ 397
スパッツ 371, 901
スパット 865
スパンカー 603
スパンカー・ブーム 602
スパンドレル 413
スピーカー 427, 496, 502, 503, 504, 505, 508, 513, 526, 626
スピーカー・グリル 502
スピーカー・システム選択ボタン 497
スピーカー端子 497
スピード・スキー 891
スピード・スキー板 891
スピード・スキー・スーツ 891
スピード・スキーヤー 891
スピード・スケート 892
スピード・スケート靴 883
スピード調節つまみ 236, 237
スピード調節ペダル 452
スピード調節ボタン 236
スピード・トラック 892
スピードブレーキ・レバー 626
スピードメーター 557, 576, 851
スピキュール 6
スピニング・リール 910
スピニング・ロッド 910
スピルリナ 183
スピンドル 248, 268, 500, 700
スピンドル・モーター 521
スピンドル・ロック・ボタン 308
スピンネーカーを上げる 833
スプール 458, 909, 910
スプール軸 910
スプール・ラック 462
スプール・リリース・ノブ 909, 910
スプーン 227, 390, 868, 905, 911
スプーンの例 228
スプラッシュ・プレート 655
スプリッスル 601
スプリット・ベット 919
スプリット・リング 910
スプリング 249, 268, 292, 470, 586, 823
スプリング・ウイング 302
スプリング・ノート 533
スプリンクラー 665
スプリンクラー・ホース 328
スプリング・ワッシャー 310
スプリンター・ライン 871
スプレー・アーム 294
スプレー管 655
スプレー・スカート 837
スプレー・ノズル 329, 655
スプレー・ヘッド 270
スプレー・ホース 264, 270
スフレ型 232
スプレッダー 834
スプレッド・カラー 349
スプロケット 876
スペア・タイヤ 567
スペアリブ 215
スペイン 743
スペイン語 469
スペーサー 667, 783
スペース 514
スペース・シャトル 22, 53
スペース・バー 514, 528
スペースラブ 23
スペード 914
巣枠 100
スペード・ビット 306
滑り板 452, 453
滑り金具 453
滑り支点 310
滑り止め 825
滑り止め台 826
滑り止め付き石突き 321
滑り止め付きシュー 321
滑り止めパッド 826
滑り止めマット 893
滑り嵌めの例 269
滑り防止加工の足袋 369
滑り溝 587
滑りやすし 545, 547
滑りレール 587
滑り環 834, 835
製菓用具 232
製菓用刷毛 232
精管 169
税関 596
税関検査証 621
製菓用皮革 621
製菓用刷毛 232
税関検査証 621
正九角形 705
正教会 736
制御エンジン 23
正極 689
正極活物質二酸化マンガン 689
正極合剤 689
制御室 657, 669
制御卓 10, 626
制御盤 261
制御棒 670, 671
制御用エンジン 23

スポット・メーター 479
スポットライト 287, 428, 431, 492, 765, 766
スポット露出計 479
ズボン 350, 371, 748, 796, 844, 875, 878, 901
ズボン下 351
スポンジ・チップ 378
スポンソン 876
ズボン吊り 350
スマック 199
スマッシュ 821
墨絵筆 397
隅金具 389, 635
隅切り 411
隅金 389
隅構造物 635
隅塔 408
スミレ 80
菫色 400
スミロドン 93
相撲 847
相撲取り 847
スモーク・ハム 215
スモール・キャピタル 472
スモール・ブレード 905
スモック 359
スモッグ 69
スモモ 193
スライダー 445, 453, 896
スライダーのジョウ 700
スライディング・シート 838, 851
スライディング・ブロック 595
スライド 294, 445, 483, 754
スライド映写機 483
スライド・ガラス 693
スライド後進ボタン 483
スライド式カバー 506, 612
スライド前進ボタン 483
スライド・トレイ 483
スライド・バー 456
スライド・パン 838
スライド板 445
スライド・マウント 483
スライド用枠 483
スライド・レール 555, 835
スライド・レバー 555
スラスター 40
スラスト軸受け 659
スラッシュ 473
スラット 285, 459
スラブ諸語 469
スラローム・スキー 840
スリー・オブ・ア・カインド 914
スリー・カード 914
スリーパー・キャブ 570
スリーピング・バッグの種類 904
スリーブ 838, 848, 851
スリック・タイヤ 872
スリット 386, 463
スリップ 366
スリップ・ジョイント 310
スリップ・ジョイント・プライヤー 310
スリップ注意 545, 547
スリップ・リング 688
スリナム 742
擦り鉢穴 47
スリランカ 747
スレッド刷毛車 456
スレッド・レバー 456
スローイング・ライン 918
スロー 919, 920
スローモーション・ボタン 495
スロート 312, 610, 822
スロット 312, 610, 822
スロット・グリップ 576
スロット・マシン 920
スロットル・グリップ 576
スロットル・コントロール 516
スロットル・レバー 626
スロバキア 744
スロバキア語 469
スロベニア 744
スロベニア語 469
巣枠 100
スワジランド 746
スワヒリ語 468
スンニ派 736

せ

背 115, 124, 130, 227, 277, 281, 295, 300, 425, 426, 750
正 703
生 703
セイウチ 137
静脈 56
青果 180
正確さを競うスポーツ 859
製菓用具 232
製菓用刷毛 232
精管 169
税関 596
税関検査証 621
正九角形 705
正教会 736
制御エンジン 23
正極 689
正極活物質二酸化マンガン 689
正極合剤 689
制御室 657, 669
制御卓 10, 626
制御盤 261
制御棒 670, 671
制御用エンジン 23

聖具室 737
西経 36
成形する道具 308
整経台 462
成形断熱材 299
制限区域 811
制限サークル 810
正五角形 705
制作アドバイザー 490
制作調整室 489, 490, 491
制作デスク 491
制作ビデオ・スイッチャー 491
制作補助員 490
生産企業 525
精銅所 181
生産プラットフォーム 652, 654
生産・輸送立ち管システム 652
正視 691
精子 169
政治 739
静止衛星 60
セイシェル 746
正式署名 729
静止軌道 60
正七角形 705
整備工場 648
正十一角形 705
整備工 648
正十角形 705
成熟 86
正十角形 705
整準台 701
整準台着脱レバー 701
整準ねじ 701
星状結晶 64
正常視 691
生殖器系 75
生殖口 95, 104
生殖巣 95, 105, 106
聖書台 737
聖書朗読台 737
精神科観察室 778
精神科診察室 778
静水位 49
静水競艇 838
聖水盤 737
製図台 399
製図板 399
精製 107, 110, 169
成層圏 53
成層圏界面 53
精製上体 169
製造番号 729
清掃用具 721
背板 276, 300
声帯 163
精油 169
正中神経 166
生長過程 86
成長線 104, 105
整地ローラー 333
生徒 734
制動係 884
制動系 553
制動手 884
制動スイッチ 304, 305, 306, 308
制動装置 331
制動灯 554
制動トリガー 331
生徒用机 734
生徒用ロッカー 735
西南西 37
精嚢 169
聖杯 737
正八角形 705
正八面体 705
整髪 380
整備格納庫 619
整備士 873
整備主任者 873
整備場 548
聖櫃 737
整備トラック 622
製氷機 721
製氷皿 291
政府機関 525
制服 770
セイフ砂丘 52
生物学 702
生物圏の構造 66
生物分解されない汚染物質 69
聖ペテロ 736
正方形 705
正方形の旗 739
西北西 37
聖母礼拝堂 410, 411
製本 424
製本用皮革 425
精密ガイド・センサー 17
生命維持装置 20
生命維持装置制御ユニット 20
生命科学実験施設 21
生命の進化 92
正門 735
声門 112
精油区画 652
精油所 654, 709
精油製品 656
セイヨウカボチャ 189
セイヨウかみそり 383
西洋鋸 309
西洋将棋 916
西洋双六 915

西洋だんす 279	石器時代の武器 748	セルフ・タイマー・インジケーター 476	前側頭泉門 158	前方優先道路 544, 546	
セイヨウナシ 193	説教壇 737, 738	セルフ・タイマー・ランプ 476	潜舵 763	ゼンマイ 185	
セイヨウニラネギ 184	赤経 13	セルフ・クロアチア語 469	センター 431, 794, 795, 807, 809, 811, 843, 879	洗面入れ 388	
正立レンズ 692	赤経目盛り環 14, 15	セルリアク 189		洗面所 250, 251	
整流子 688	赤血球 162	セレニウム 682	センター・アタッカー 812	前面図 146, 148, 150, 152	
整板 570	石鹸皿 264	セレン 682	センター・コート 818	洗面台 262, 724	
青緑色 690	接血室 728	セロリ 185	センター・コンソール 556	全面反射鏡 692	
青緑色細胞 92	ゼッケン番号 791, 857, 878	1,000 703	センター・サークル 803, 809, 810, 879	前面保護ガラス 494	
セイル 836	接合鉋 309	栓 379		繊毛 94	
セイル・スリーブ 836	石膏タイル 299	線 434	センター・サード 809	前木被 860, 912	
セイル・パネル 834	石膏板 464	前圧調節目盛り 889	センター・サービス・ライン 821	専門医実習生 780	
整列係 838	接合部 440	繊維 272	センター・ストラップ 821	旋律弦 432	
正六面体 705	石膏ボード 299	前胃 107, 116	センター・スピーカー 493	前立腺 169	
正六角形 705	石工用釘 301	遷移金属 683	センター・スポット 803, 862	全粒小麦粉 204	
セイロンニッケイ 198	石工用の工具 315	遷移元素 683	センター・チーフ 740	全粒粉パン 205	
セージ 202	舌根 176	繊維製品取り扱い表示 347	センター・ハーフ 801	前輪 333, 624, 639, 640, 783	
セーター 354	切削刃 331	繊維製品取り扱いマーク 347	センター・バック 812, 814	前輪ブレーキ 579	
セーフィング・センサー 556	切歯 121, 123, 159	全雲量 55, 56	センター・ピラー 551	前輪ブレーキ・レバー 576	
セーフティー・ビンディング 888, 889	摂氏目盛り 695, 702	前縁 625, 897, 898	センター・フェイス・オブ・サークル 879	蘚類 75	
セーフティー・フェンス 890	摂氏目盛り 695	全縁 79		蘚類の構造 75	
セーム革 345, 377	接写用中間リング 478	前縁パイプ 897	センター・フォワード 801, 814	蘚類の例 75	
セーラー・カラー 362	接写用レンズ 478	前縁フラップ 625, 760	センター・フラッグ 802	洗礼盤 737	
セーラー・ブラウス 359	接触改質工場 656	顎音 435	センター・ベース 897	線路 582, 592, 649	
セーリング 833	接触部 274	全音符 435	センター・ベンツ 348	前廊 737	
セール 897	舌正中溝 176	船外機 607	センター・ポイント 740	線路番号札 591	
背泳ぎ 832	舌尖 176	旋回軸 793	センターボード 834, 836	前腕 124, 130, 147, 149	
背泳ぎのスタート 832	接続管 432	旋回橋 542	センターボード・ボート 835	前腕当て 808	
背泳ぎ用取っ手 830	接続ケーブル 465	旋開橋 542	センター・ポケット 862	前腕支え 782	
背泳ぎ用旗付きロープ 831	接続コード 502	旋回傾斜計 898	センター・マーク 820, 858	前腕用安全杖 782	
背泳ぎ用標識 831	接続装置 793	旋回式スプリンクラー 329	センター・ライン 801, 809, 810, 814, 815, 816, 877, 879		
世界の気候 61	接続端子 452	旋回軸 793			
世界の言語 468	接続点 273, 687	旋回台座 312	センター・ライン・アンパイア 820	**そ**	
背固め 425	接続箱 272, 591	旋回台座ロック 312	センター・ライン・ジャッジ 820		
セカンダリー・ハード・ディスク・ドライブ 513	接続ピン 689	旋回塔 638	センター・レフェリー 814	ソ 434	
セカンド 794, 877	接続部 488	旋回ハンドル 756	センター・レフリー 814	層 300	
セカンド・アシスタント・カメラマン 428	接続ボックス 490	旋回ヘッド 312	船体 599, 834, 876	像 737	
	舌体 176	前角 167	船柱 652	ゾウ 129	
セカンド・ダズン 919	切断トーチ 319	前打音 435	前打音 435	層雲 56, 62	
セカンド・レベル・ドメイン 524	切断火口 319	洗濯機 262, 271, 292	洗濯機 262, 271, 292	痩果 83, 84	
セカンド・ロー 804	接地 51	洗濯室 250, 724, 726, 764	選択キー 506	装荷域 666	
赤緯 13	接岩 51	洗濯室 250, 724, 726, 764	選択十字方向ボタン 477	総数 699	
赤緯クランプ 14, 15	接地クランプ 318	洗顔タオル 379		葱花屋根 414	
赤緯微動ハンドル 14, 15	接地接続 272	先カンブリア期 92	洗濯槽 292	掃桿 752	
赤緯目盛り環 14, 15	接地線 272, 273	先カンブリア時代 92	洗濯タイマー 292	双眼顕微鏡 693	
積雲 56, 62	接地電極 562	先カンブリア代 92	選択ボタン 261, 505	掃気 565	
石果 81, 192	接地用線 272	前脚 96, 98, 277, 760	センタリング・キー 528	送受球 777	
赤外線 68, 690	接地ボンド 272	船客ターミナル 596	センタリング調節つまみ 518	送気ダクト 543	
赤外線感知装置 518	接着剤 293	全休符 435	先端 288, 318, 840, 912, 918	双極ブレーカー 272	
赤外線検知器 60	接着式フラップ 531	船渠 596	尖端 227, 306, 793	送迎デッキ 621	
赤外線追尾装置 759	接着テープ 254	前橋 855	前端 107	総頸動脈 160	
赤外線熱也図作成装置 18	設定温度 261	前胸 97	尖端軌条 590	象牙質 159	
赤外線ポート 526, 527	設定キー 528	線形 79	先端コーン 627	象牙のボール 919	
石質隕石 8	設定表示ボタン 477	前脛骨筋 150	先端部 494, 792	草原 66	
積集合 703	接点 274	前脛骨動脈 160	船室乗 609	草原気候 61	
石筍 47	節点 663	扇形トレリス 322	仙椎 111, 122, 126, 131, 142	倉庫 708, 716, 734	
赤色巨星 8	接点突起 382	閃光管 482, 692	泉亭 738	綜絖 460, 461	
脊髄 109, 110, 167, 168	セット 429, 822	選鉱工場 649	前庭 174	装甲 758	
脊髄神経 167, 168	セットアップ 865	先行セット 822	前庭神経 174	走行距離計 557	
脊髄神経節 167, 168	セット・イン・スリーブ 349	前後チルト・ロック・レバー 482	剪定鋏 330	走行クレーン 658	
脊髄の構造 167	Z式ファイル 532	仙骨 138, 141, 152, 153, 157	剪定鉄 330	装甲鋼板 758	
石灰塗き場 650	セット・デザイナー 428	仙骨神経叢 166	剪定用具 330	装甲車運搬用低床セミトレーラー 572	
石炭火力発電所 646	セット・ドレッサー 429	1,500m走スタート・ライン 791	セント 728		
石炭紀 92	舌背 176	浅根 87	尖塔 411, 738	走行車 539	
石柱 47	舌扁桃 176	前根 168	前頭 115	走行台枠 638	
脊柱 109, 121, 152, 157, 167	説明文 471	センサー 58, 416	戦闘機 760	綜絖綜糸 461	
脊椎骨 112	舌盲孔 176	センサー回路 559	前頭筋 150	総合得点掲示板 824	
石鉄隕石 8	雪温計 58, 59	センサー・プラグ 238	前頭骨 112, 131, 152, 158	装甲門 758	
赤道 13, 31, 34, 35, 36, 63	背 147, 149	前肢 110, 111, 121, 143	先頭集団 870	走行変速レバー 327	
赤道ギニア 745	背中洗い用ボディー・ブラシ 379	前翅 96	前頭頭頂骨 111	綜絖棒 461	
咳止めシロップ 783	セネガル 745	船室 608	前頭頭頂骨 111	総合待合室 781	
石版石 423	セネガル川 34	前室 403	前頭部 175	走行輪 594, 595	
積分 703	背柱 277	剪枝鋏 330	尖頭等辺アーチ 413	走行レール 595, 635	
石油 651, 651	セパレーター 562, 646, 689	全自動電気時計 831	先導バイク 870	走行路 595	
石油汚染 70	背番号 791	戦車 758	セントクリストファー・ネイビス 743	綜絖枠 460	
石油化学産業 656	背比べ 136	前車軸 639		爪根 172	
石油化学製品 656	セプティム 849	洗車場 548, 589	セント・バーナード 131	総菜 181	
石油基地 596	ゼブラ 128	戦車砲 758	セントビンセントおよびグレナディーン諸島 743	操作解説書 548	
石油鉱業 651, 653	セボリー 202	船 598, 606, 609, 834		操作画像表示部 694	
石油貯蔵基地 654	セミ 101	選手 822	セントリフュージ 21	操作キー 507, 730, 731	
石油貯蔵ターミナル 654	セミクジラ 137	船尾甲板 605, 609	セントリフュージ・モジュール 21	操作コード 284	
石油貯蔵タンク防壁 655	セミコロン 473	船首 602	セント・ルシア 743	操作パネル 508, 512, 518, 766	
石油バーナー 259	セミタイト・スカート 357	船首三角帆 834	セント・ローレンス川 30	操作盤 292, 293, 294, 417, 465, 694, 766	
石油備蓄基地 654	セミトレーラー 570, 571	選手待機所 871	栓抜き 230, 905		
石油ヒーター 260	セミトレーラーの例 572	戦術輸送ヘリコプター 631	線の太さ 472	操作表示ランプ 519, 520	
石油ポンプ 259	セミ・ボールド 472	船首ドア 605	船舶通信 487	操作ペダル 452	
セキュリティー・サービス 719	セミ・マミー型 904	選手番号 808, 810	船舶用ディーゼル油 656	操作ホイール 527	
石油湧出 70	ゼム・クリップ 534	船首プロペラ 606	前半規管 174	走査放射計 60	
積乱雲 56, 62	ゼム・クリップ・ホルダー 534	選手用椅子 813, 801, 807, 809, 812, 814, 878	前鼻棘 174	操作レバー 327, 643, 767	
斥力 687	セメント質 159	船首横押しプロペラ 609	船尾 598, 608	巣室 100	
セクステット 438	セメント・スクリード 254	船首 605, 609	船尾甲板 608	掃除ブラシ 383	
セクレタリー 814, 827	セメント・スクリードを用いた寄せ木張り 254	前上顎骨 108, 122, 123	船尾楼 602	掃除機 318, 752	
セクレタリー・デスク 511		洗浄器 776	浅肋骨神経 166	操車場 589, 708	
セカンド 842, 849	背もたれ 281, 555, 577, 783, 876	舟状骨 154, 155, 156	尖筆 470	操車用丘状地 589	
セシウム 682	背もたれ椅子 277	前檣支索 834	船尾楼 602	操縦桿 626, 631, 898	
セ氏 695, 702	セモリーナ 204	洗浄塔 294	洗瓶 685	操縦士 758	
セ氏目盛り 695	セラ 403	前照灯 550, 554, 570, 574, 576, 585, 586, 640, 758, 876	前部 569	操縦室 22, 624, 626, 631	
ゼスター 229	ゼラチン・カプセル 783		前部握把 757	操縦者 884	
節 77	セラック 46	洗浄ハンドル 265	前部ウインカー 574, 576	操縦手 758	
絶縁器 663	迫り 430	洗浄瓶 685	全負荷調整ねじ 273	操縦席 898, 898	
絶縁グリップ 316, 317	迫石 413	染色質 94	前部滑走部 884	操縦ハンドル 626	
絶縁材 254	セリウム 684	煎 753	前部緩衝器 577	送受信アンテナ 486	
絶縁スリーブ 275	セリフ書体 472	迫台 410, 413	前部ショック・アブソーバー 577	送受信パラボラ・アンテナ 486	
絶縁体 562	迫元石 413	セル 563, 897	前部水中翼 609	爪床 172	
絶縁取っ手 239	迫元 540	セルシウス温度の単位 702	前部バンパー 885	僧正 916	
絶縁刃 316	迫石 413	セルタス 186	前部方向指示灯 574, 576	総状花序 81, 85	
石灰海綿 95	迫元石 413	セルフ・インフレーティング・マット 904	前部マスト 607	装飾音 435	
石灰華プール 47			前部横木 893	装飾器 753	
節間 77		セルフ・サービス式レストラン 722	前部ランナー 884	装飾帯 278	
接眼鏡 692		セルフ・サービス用陳列ケース 722	前閉殻筋 105	草食動物 67	
接続部 773			前壁 571, 818, 819	装飾用品店 715	
接眼レンズ 14, 15, 477, 479, 496, 692, 693		前装式砲身 753	全帆いっぱいに風をはらみ詰め開きで 833	送信アンテナ 486	
		前装式砲身の断面図 753	旋棒 268	装身具類 374	
接眼レンズ・アダプター 14		船側 607	前房 177	送信塔 486	
			潜望鏡 758	送信トレイ 508	
			前方道路工事中 545, 547	層積雲 56, 62	

936

天文学 > 2-25; 地球 > 26-71; 植物 > 72-89; 動物 > 90-143; 人間 > 144-177; 食べ物と台所 > 178-241; 家屋 > 242-295; 日曜大工・園芸 > 296-333; 衣服 > 334-371; 装身具類と日用品 > 372-391; 芸術と建築 > 392-465; 情報伝達とオフィス・オートメーション > 466-535; 交通と機械 > 536-643; エネルギー > 644-677; 科学 > 678-705; 社会 > 706-785; スポーツとゲーム > 786-920

増速歯車箱 677	ソケット 275, 453	タービン軸が回転して発電機を回転させる 665	第三趾 115	台風の目の壁 63
曾祖父 784	ソケット・コンタクト 274	タービン建屋 668	第三次消費者 67	大伏在静脈 160
曾祖父母 784	ソケット・シェル 275	タービン止め弁 668	第三色 400	対物鏡 692
曾祖母 784	ソケット・セット 311	タービン発電機 674	第三大臼歯 159	対物転換器 693
藻本 75	ソケットの各部分 275	タービン・ランナー 664	第3段 25	対物レンズ 14, 476, 478, 479, 483, 501, 692, 693
操舵系 553	底 240, 351, 881, 888, 889	ターボジェット・エンジン 625, 760	第3抜き差し管 447	太平洋 28, 29, 33
操舵室 605, 606, 607	底板 288, 309, 689	ターボ・チャージド・エンジン 564	第3の構え 849	太平洋南極海嶺 50
操舵席 834	底板取り外し式スポンジ型 232	ターボファン・エンジン 627	大質量星 8	太平洋プレート 43
操舵輪 607	底敷き 345	ターミネーター 522	台車 586, 633, 634	タイポグラフィー 472
装置エアロック 666	蘇生器 775	ターメリック 198	台車枠 586	タイマー 238, 239, 290, 294, 484, 827, 831, 851, 883
装着帯 841, 896	蘇生処置室 778	タールタン 422	対珠 173	タイマー調整つまみ 465
装着ベルト 896	礎石 403, 404	タール紙 299	体温計 699	タイマー付きラジオ 503
総腸骨静脈 165	注ぎ口 240, 241, 295	ターン 435	大樋 600, 602	タイマー予約設定ボタン 495
総腸骨動脈 160, 165	注ぎ口付き容器 237	ターンテーブル 236, 488, 500, 638, 639, 766	対象物 691	対ミサイル用ミサイル 762
索子牌 917	粗調整棹 698	ターンバックル 835, 842	帯状面 404	タイミング・ベルト 566
装丁本 426	ソックス 365, 808, 822, 848	タイ 219, 435, 747	大触角 107	タイム 202, 789, 831
送泥ポンプ 651	足穴 444	台 43, 236, 239, 273, 286, 304, 321, 329, 381, 424, 448, 516, 517, 685, 739, 815, 825, 826	台尻 309, 755	タイム・カード 530
送電 663	測候所 54, 58	大 919	対人地雷 758	タイムキーパー 810, 814, 842, 900
送電する 665	足根骨 111, 122, 126, 131, 138, 141, 142, 152	ダイアゴナル走法 892	ダイス 915	タイム・コード 429
送電線 646	袖 337, 348, 430	台足 202	ダイズ 191	タイム・レコーダー 530
送電鉄塔 663	袖当て 880	台頭 309	ダイス・カップ 915	対面通行 544, 546
送電塔 663	ソテー・パン 235	耐圧避難所 543	ダイスとドミノ牌 914	タイヤ 551, 560, 570, 579, 870, 874
送電ボックス 273	袖口 349, 848	体育館 727, 734, 788	大聖堂 410	ダイヤ 914
送電網 674	袖口カバー 338	体育館事務室 734	大西洋 28, 29, 32, 34	タイヤの例 560
送電網にエネルギーを統合する 662, 677	袖ぐり 351	第一楔状骨 155, 156	腿節 96, 98	タイヤ・バリア 872
双胴船 835	袖の例 360	第一コーナー 856	対戦車ミサイル 759	タイヤ・バルブ 579
相導体 273	袖バンド 352	第一次消費者 67	対戦車ロケット弾 757	タイヤ・ポンプ 579
挿入 515	袖バンド通し 352	第一小臼歯 159	大泉門 158	ダイヤモンド 375, 914
挿入キー 515	袖見出し 471	第一焦点室 16	体操 824	ダイヤモンド型インターチェンジ 538
装入バスケット 650	素電池 687	第一触角 107	体操競技 823	ダイヤモンド形ラス 299
藻の構造 75	粗動ハンドル 693	第1仕分け[仕訳]線 589	大草原 38	ダイヤモンド・ポイント彫り 278
総排出腔 113	外側エッジ 127	第一推薦航路 617	体操選手名 825	ダイヤル式表示盤 613
総排泄腔 110, 116	外側カウンター 342	第一水平坑道 650	大腿 130, 147, 169, 170	ダイヤル・ロック 386
爪板 172	外側ノブ 248	第一スペース 811	大腿筋膜張筋 150	太陽 4, 6, 7, 54
操帆索 603	外底 342, 371	第一背びれ 108, 109	大腿骨 111, 116, 126, 131, 138, 141, 142, 152	大洋 7, 38
操帆装置 835	外付けハード・ディスク 521	第一大臼歯 159	大腿骨外側顆 153	太陽エネルギー 78, 672
装備 769	外付けハード・ディスク・ドライブ 521	第1段 25	大腿骨頸部 153	太陽エネルギー発電 674
総腓骨神経 166	外付けフロッピー・ディスク・ドライブ 521	第1抜き差し管 447	大腿骨頭 153	太陽系 4
送風 347	外付けフロッピー・ドライブ 521	第1の構え 849	大腿骨内側顆 153	太陽光反射板 486
送風管 258, 445, 643	外筒 249	第一バイオリン 437	大腿四頭筋 150	太陽集熱器 675
送風機 258, 260, 445, 670	外ドア 247	第一補強部 753	大腿神経 166	太陽センサー 40, 60
送風ダクト 445	外箱 292, 293, 697	第1待合室 781	大腿静脈 160	大洋中央海嶺 49
送風ファン内蔵式 382	外歯付き座金 310	第一面 471	大腿直筋 150	太陽電池 529, 672, 673
送風モーター 258, 261	外歯ワッシャー 310	第1面掲載写真 471	大腿動脈 160	太陽電池の仕組み 673
僧帽筋 150, 151	外ポケット 386, 388	第一薬覆い 753	大腿二頭筋 151	太陽電池パネル 17, 21, 40, 60, 486, 673
双方向端末 395	外濠外壁 409	第一葉 77	大腿部 143	太陽電池パネル駆動装置 60
僧帽弁 162	外濠内壁 409	第一指 140, 141	タイタン 5	太陽電池板 18
爪帽筋 172	外巻き葉 390	第一趾 115	タイタン4 24	太陽熱集熱器 675
総務部 735	外輪 413	大陰唇 170, 171	大チェーン・ホイール 580	太陽の構造 6
素麺 207	外枠 389, 688	隊員用共同寝室 764	大腸 110, 164	太陽熱 672, 673, 674, 675
ソウメンカボチャ 189	ソナー 41	隊員用トイレ・シャワー室 764	大円筋 151	太陽炉 674
臓物 212	嚢 97, 99, 104, 106, 116	大円筋 151	大臀筋 151	第四紀 93
巣穴 100	その他の織り方 463	ダイウ 185	大転子 153	第4コーナー 856
巣門スライド 100	その他の家電製品 240	ダイオード 673	体動脈 162, 163	第四指 140
装薬 912	その他の記号 435	体温計 695, 777	大動脈弓 160, 161, 162	第四趾 115
草履 344	その他の金属 682	体温調節装置 20	大動脈弁 162	第4の構え 849
ゾウリムシ 94	その他の道具 313	袋果 84	タイト・エンド 807	大陸 49
相輪 412	その他の符号 435	大河 38, 48	台所 222, 224, 250, 406	大陸縁辺部 49
藻類 75	その他の用具 233, 534	大会議室 730	台所用スポンジ 295	大陸斜面 49
藻類の構造 75	ソバ 85, 203	大会議場 718	台所用品 229, 716	大陸氷北極気団 55
藻類の例 75	蕎麦 207	大回転 889	タイト・スカート 357	大陸棚 49
総和 703	礎盤 405	大回転用スキー板 888	タイト・ヘッド・プロップ 804	大陸地殻 42
送話器 506	礎盤部 252, 253	大回廊 402	タイトル表示ボタン 496	大陸の配置 28
送話口 506	祖父 784	胎殻 105	大内転筋 151	対流 681
副え木 777	ソファ 276	大核 94	大学 710	対流圏 53
添え索 615	ソファー・ベッド 280	大学 710	対角線リブ 410	対流圏界面 53, 68
ソーシャル・ワーカー室 779	ソフト・コンタクト・レンズ 384	退化した骨盤 136	大括弧 473	対流式暖房器 260
ソースパン 235, 905	ソフト・パステル 396	大括弧 473	袋果の断面図 84	対流式電気暖房器 260
ソーダ・ファウンテン 723	ソフト・ブーツ 887	耐火・防水服 765	耐火煉瓦 256, 298, 465	対流セル 63
ソーラー・ハウス 675	ソフト・ブーツ用ビンディング 887	耐火レーシング・スーツ 872	耐火煉瓦の背壁 256	対流層 6
ソール 868, 881, 888, 889	ソフト・ペダル 442, 451	対艦ミサイル 759	大韓民国 747	対流の流れ 681
足架 857	ソフトボール 797	大気 70	大ギア 580	大菱形骨 154, 156
側車用車船 599	ソフトボール・バット 797	大ギア 580	待機域標識 620	対輪 173
足架吊り革 857	ソフトボール用グローブ 797	大気圏 69	大気汚染 69	大輪 783
側径間 540	ソフトボール用のボール 797	大気汚染物質 69	対レーダー・ミサイル 759
属さない 703	祖父母 784	大気圏 66	ダイレクト選局ボタン 498
側枝 168, 855	祖母 784	大気圏断面図 53	大勒筋 854
側スパン 540	ソマリア 745	対気速度計 898	大勒手綱 854
属する 703	ソムリエ 720	大気井 655	第6の構え 849
側切歯 159	ソムリエ・ナイフ 230	大吸器 766	大勒馬銜 854
側腺 108, 583	反らせ板 260	大臼歯 121, 123, 159	台輪 276, 277, 278, 403, 405, 413
足腺 104	ソラマメ 190	大臼歯断面 159	台輪蛇腹 403, 405
側堆石 46	橇 631, 884, 885	大胸筋 150	タイン 327
側対歩 125	剃り角度設定つまみ 383	対空捜索レーダー 761, 762	ダウン・クオーク 680
側対歩馬 857	ソリッド・ブリック 298	対空ミサイル 762	ダウンヒル 889
足底筋 151	ソリテール・リング 376	大工ハンマー 301, 317	ダウンヒル用自転車とサイクリスト 870
足底骨間筋 150	橇の鈴 449	台形 705	唾液管 99
測定して印を付ける道具 313	ソルダリング・ガン 318	大剣 349	唾液腺 97, 99, 104, 164, 176
測定端子 316	ぞろ目 914	タイ語 468	楕円銀河 9
測定値ロック・スイッチ 479	ソロモン諸島 747	大孔 95	タオル掛け 264
足底の肉趾 133		第五趾 115	タカ 119
測定ボタン 479	**た**	第5の構え 849	ダガー 751
測定モード・キー 479		第5輪 570	ダガーボード 836
側頭骨 152, 158	ターゲット 859, 865	ダイコン 189	ダガーボード・トランク 836
速度切り替えスイッチ 305, 306	ダーツ 455, 918	台座 58, 256, 268, 270, 307, 308, 370, 440, 698, 698	高さ制限 545, 547
速度制御レバー 333	ダーツボード 918	大祭壇 737	高さ調節式脚 776
速度調整つまみ 332	ダート 918	台座板 58	高さ調節装置 641
速度目盛り 436	タートルネック 354, 363, 892	ダイ語 468	高さ調節つまみ 289, 692, 826, 851
足背動脈 160	ターニング・ハンドル 307	大孔 95	高さ調節パイプ 824, 825
側板 417	ターバン 339, 341	第五趾 115	高さ調節ハンドル 642, 826
測微ねじ 612	ダービー・シューズ 342	台板 445, 485	打楽器 437, 448
側部調整レバー 309	ダービー・ハット 340	堆肥散布機 641	多角形 705
側壁 127, 571, 597, 632, 635, 818, 819, 831	タービン 646, 659, 668	堆肥散布爪 641	たがね 421
側壁換気口 567	タービンが回転する 662	堆肥台 641	たがねと図案 401
側壁 409	タービン・カバー 659	堆肥貯蔵容器 323	タガメ 101
側面 301, 374	タービン交流発電機 646, 763	堆肥用熊手 323	
側面はしご 587	タービン・コンプレッサー・シャフト 627	大鼻翼軟骨 175	
側面図 798		退避線 620	
側面標識 617		タイピン 376	
側薬帯 391		ダイビング・グローブ 841	
側薬 411		ダイビング用プール 788	
鼠径部 146, 148		ダイビング・レシーブ 812	
		台風 63	
		台風の目 63	
		第三指 140	

天文学 > 2-25; 地球 > 26-71; 植物 > 72-89; 動物 > 90-143; 人間 > 144-177; 食べ物と台所 > 178-241; 家屋 > 242-295; 日曜大工・園芸 > 296-333; 衣服 > 334-371; 装身具類と日用品 > 372-391; 芸術と建築 > 392-465; 情報伝達とオフィス・オートメーション > 466-535; 交通と機械 > 536-643; エネルギー > 644-677; 科学 > 678-705; 社会 > 706-785; スポーツとゲーム > 786-920

高床式住居 418
高床住居 418
タガログ語 469
滝 47, 48
抱ග 247
抱き石 256
多機能キー 529
打撃面 797, 815
タグ 342, 370
卓越風 63
タクシー乗り場 725
託児所 715
タグ車 623
卓上ミキサー 236
タグボート 606
托葉 443
ダグラス窩 170
打撃用手袋 796
打撃用ヘルメット 796
竹の子 185
タゲリ 118
タコ 106, 217
蛇行 48
多孔管 263
多孔体 95
多孔板 95
タコの解剖図 106
タコの形態図 106
タコメーター 557, 576
タジキスタン 746
打者 795, 796, 799
多汁葉 78
多重露出モード・ボタン 476
舵手席 838
舵手付きフォア 839
舵手付きペア 839
舵手なしフォア 839
舵手なしペア 839
タジン鍋 234
足す 703
たすき 783
ダスト・カバー 500
ダスト・バッグ 308
タスマニア 29
タスマニア・デビル 143
タスマン海 29
畳 844, 846
たたら作り 465
多段変速ギヤ 870
ダチョウ 119
ダチョウの卵 213
脱衣所 781
卓球 815
卓球台 815
卓球ボール 815
卓球ラケット 815
タッキング 833
タック 390, 836
ダグアウト 794
タック・プリーツ 350
タック・ラベル 532
タックル・ボックス 911
脱脂綿 777
ダッシュ 473
脱臭剤 379
ダッシュボード 556, 574
ダッシュボード・コンピューター 771
ダッシュボードの機器 771
脱進機 436
タッセル 282, 285
タッチ・ジャッジ 805
タッチ・スクリーン 527
タッチ・ターン 832
タッチ・バイク 581
タッチ・パッド 526
タッチ・パッド・ボタン 526
タッチ・ライン 803, 805
手綱 856
タップ 863
ダッフル・コート 353
ダッフル・バッグ 388
竜巻き 57, 63
樽 748
竪穴 402
立て坑 650
経糸 460, 461, 463
経糸巻き 460
立て入れ坑道 650
盾形 79
縦型電気掃除機 289
竪型ピアノ 442
楯形紋章の区分 740
縦框 247, 249
たてがみ 124
立て管 271
立て坑口 649
盾座 10
縦樋 244
縦二分割 740
縦布目 455
縦の動き 916
立てパイプ 578, 871
竪機 461
縦溝 404, 405
縦結び 908
桶状の区分 740
縦揺れ 630
縦レール 399
縦枠 461
多胴船 835
棚 279, 291, 321
棚板 291
掌 610
棚脇の陳列台 181

谷 45, 48, 690
ダニ 102
種 81, 82, 83
種なしキュウリ 188
種抜き器 233
種播き・植え付け用具 324
種播き器 324
束 185
ダバー 422
タバコの葉 390
タバコ・ポーチ 390
タバ屋 714
タバスコ 200
タヒチ語 469
タヒビット 606
タビット 602
ダビデ 736
ダビデの星 738
タヒニ 200
タブ 294, 352, 386, 528, 532
タブ・キー 514
タブ設定キー 528
ダブリヌム 406
ダブリング・キューブ 915
ダブル 853
ダブル編み 458
ダブル・カセット・デッキ 503
ダブル・クォーテーション・マーク 473
ダブル・クリップ 534
ダブル・シックス 914
ダブル・シャープ 435
ダブル・ジャケット 348
ダブル・スカル 484
ダブルス・サービス・コート 817
ダブルス・サイドライン 817, 820
ダブル・スラッシュ 524
ダブル・ゼロ 919
ダブル・ゼロ・キー 529
ダブルのカーテン・レール 284
ダブル・パドル 837, 839
ダブル・ハンドル 840
ダブル・フラット 435
ダブル・ブランク 914
ダブル・ブル 918
ダブル・ブレード・パドル 837, 839
ダブル・ベース 437, 439
ダブル・ベッド 724
ダブル・ベル 352
ダブル・リード 446
ダブル・リード918
ダブル・ルーム 724
タブレター 528
タブレット 517
タブレット 338, 914
タブロイド紙 471
舵柄 834
タペストリー・ボビン 461
食べ物 180
タボ 390
タボ穴 390
打棒 449
舵棒 834
玉 462
弾 752
玉網 911
玉浮き 911
卵 100, 109, 111, 117, 213
卵形 79
卵立て器 232
タマゴタケ 183
卵立て 291
卵パック 222
卵雜 207
玉杓子 233
玉突き 862
玉突き台 862
タマネギ 184
玉 253, 348, 405
玉縁 253
玉縁材 253
玉縁ポケット 354, 360
玉巻き機 462
タマリン 139
タマリンド・ペースト 200
ダム 657
タム・タム 448
ダムの地盤 660
ダムの頂上 657, 660, 661, 664
ダムの例 660
溜め池 657, 658, 660, 661
試し編み 458
打面 301, 425, 448, 449
多目的アンテナ 763
多目的室 490, 727
タラ 202
タラゴン 202
タリウム 682
垂木 252
ダルス 183
タルト型 232
ダルマシアン 131
ダルムード 736
ダルメシアン 131
垂れ 847
垂れ板 278
垂れ飾り 287
垂れ布 280, 282
タロイモ 184
タワー 674, 858
タワー・クレーン 634
タワー・ケース 513
タワー・サイロ 182

タワー・マスト 634
タワー・ラダー 766
たわみ継ぎ手 677
タン 212
段 255
段板 255
単価 699
担架 775, 776
タンカー 596, 606
断崖 45, 51
担架待機所 778
タンガニーカ湖 34
単眼 97, 99
弾丸 752
弾丸入れ 770
弾機 443
短機関銃 754
段丘 647
段丘の高さ 647
単極ブレーカー 272
短距離 882
タンク 23, 263, 266, 391, 484, 485, 607, 655, 767
タング 350
タンク車 573, 588
タンク車体 572, 573
タングステン 683
タングステン・フィラメント 274
タンク・スプレー 328
タンク・トップ 369, 371
タンク・トラック 573
タンク・トレーラー 572
タンクのハッチ 607
タンク・ボール 265
タンク・ローリー 573
短剣 751
弾庫 758
炭鉱 647
短骨 157
単語訂正キー 528
短駒 442
単細胞動物 94
段差解消機 569
探査救出アンテナ 60
探査幅 40
炭酸ガス 670
炭酸ガス冷却材 670
炭酸ガス炉 670
単糸 908
端子 272, 274, 290, 562, 663
短指伸筋 150
端子ボックス 673
単出集散花序 81
単純な生き物と棘皮動物 94
単純桁橋 541
誕生 702
短掌筋 150
男女兼用の靴 344
男女兼用の帽子 341
弾芯 752
短信欄 471
段数計 456
段数表示窓 456
ダンス・ブレード 881
ダンス・ホール 609
男性 146
弾性靱帯 133
男性生殖器 169
弾性帯 350
男性用衣類 348
端栓 667
炭素 683
弾倉 754, 755, 893
断層 43
弾倉着脱ボタン 754
弾倉底板 754
弾倉止め 754
探測気球 54, 59
炭素棒 689
タンタル 683
段違い平行棒 824
炭柱 650
単蹄 127
弾底栓 757
タンデム・シート 575
タンデム自転車 581
タンデム・ディスク・ハロー 641
タンデム・トレーラー 570
短刀 751
弾頭 759, 912
単胴船 835
短横側手根伸筋 151
段抜き大見出し 471
断熱材 22, 253, 259, 266, 267, 294, 299, 672
断熱タイル 22
胆嚢 110, 112, 164
タンパー 241, 390
ダンパー 258, 443, 465
ダンパー・ペダル 442, 451
ダンパー・レール 443
ダンパー・レバー 443
蛋白腺 104
タンバリン 449
単板 300
短腓骨筋 151
段鼻 255
段平 751

ダンプ・カー 573
ダンプ車体 572, 573
ダンプ・セミトレーラー 572
端部扉 635
ダンプ・トラック 573, 639
タンブラー・グラス 225
タンブル乾燥不可 347
段ベッド 584
ダンベル 850
端片 169
暖房 256
暖房燃料 656
暖房用燃料タンク 563
暖房炉 258
タンポポ 187
タンポン 422
淡明層 172
単面形パレット 632
断面図 920
単面パレット 632
弾薬入れ 770
弾薬筒 754, 860, 861, 912
短矢羽板 79
単葉 79
断裂ホモロサイン図法 36
暖炉 250, 256
談話室 718

ち

地 426
智 385
地域郵便 475
チーク 753, 909
チーク・ブラシ 378
チーズ 228
チーズ売り場 181
チーズ下ろし器 230
チーズ箱 223
チーター 135
起家 917
地衣の構造 74
チーフ 740
チーフ・メカニック 873
チーフ・レフェリー 883
チーフ・レフリー 883
チーム・エンブレム 878
チーム・ジャージー 796
チーム・シャツ 796, 801, 802, 808, 810
チームのハンディキャップ 858
チーム・ベンチ 827
チーム名 858
地衣類 74
地衣類の構造 74
地衣類の例 74
チェア・リフト 886
チェア・リフト出発点 886
チェーン 578, 580, 826
チェーン・ガイド 580
チェーン駆動部 641
チェーン・ステー 578
チェーン・ステッチ 459
チェーン・ソー 331
チェーン・ホイール 870
チェコ共和国 744
チェコ語 469
チェス 916
チェスターフィールド 276
チェスト・ガード 859
チェスト・フリーザー 291
チェスト・プロテクター 808
チェスの座標式表記法 916
チェス盤 916
チェッカー 915, 916
チェッカー盤 916
チェッカー・フラッグ 872
チェリー・トマト 188
チェリモヤ 196
チェロ 437, 439
チェンジ・レバー 556
チェンバロ 443
地衣 407
地階 250
地殼 42, 43
知覚根 168
知覚神経根 167
地殼断面図 43
地殼プレート 43
地下茎 78
地下ケーブル伝送 487
地下水面 47, 70
地下水流 47
地下鉄 592, 713
地下鉄駅 592, 710
地下鉄車両 592, 594
地下鉄路線図 593, 594
地下道 583
地下トンネル 592
地下の玄室 402
地下窓 245
地下流出 67
力の単位 702
地球 4, 5, 6, 7, 13
恥丘 170
地球温暖化 68
地球型惑星 5
地球儀 734
地球座標 35
地球センサー 40, 60
地球の軌道 6, 7
地球の構造 5
地球放射スキャナー 60
地球放射センサー 60

ダンプ・カー 573
地峡 38
地区 39
畜圧器 559
蓄電池 562, 673
蓄糞 70
チケット売り場 394, 427, 719
チケット・カウンター 620
チケット係 394, 427
チケット自動販売機 427
チケット販売機 427
チケット・ポケット 348
恥骨 116, 122, 146, 148
恥骨結合 169, 170
チゴリ 187
智歯 159
地質 42
千島海溝 50
千島・カムチャツカ海溝 50
チシャ 186
地上の温暖前線 56
地上の寒冷前線 56
地上パイプライン 654
地上標識 592
地図 734
地図作成法 35
地図室 732
地図投影法 36
地勢図 38
地線櫓 663
地層 538
チター 432
地対空ミサイル 759
地対潜ミサイル 759, 762
地卓 52
チタニア 5
チタン 683
父 784, 785
チチカカ湖 34
父方の伯父［叔父］ 785
父方の伯母［叔母］ 785
締め結び 908
地中海 28, 32, 34
地中海性亜熱帯性気候 61
膣 103, 104, 170, 171
窒素 683
窒素酸化物の放出 70
チップ 840, 863, 909
チップ・カバー 305
チップセット 513
チップ・セミトレーラー 572
地点円 55
地熱・化石エネルギー 646
地熱帯 646
地熱発電 646
地表 647
地表における吸収 68
乳房 146, 148, 171
チベット語 468
地方局 486
地方郵便 475
地方郵便集配局 475
チポラータ・ソーセージ 216
千巻き 460
緻密質 154
ちもと 911
茶 208
チャージの例 741
チャージ・プラグ 383
チャージ・ライト 383
チャーピル 202
チャーム 376
チャーム・ブレスレット 376
チャイルド・シート 558
チャウ・チャウ 130
着順 831
着順掲示板 839
着順審判員 830
着信表示ランプ 508
着脱式の車体 573
着地 891
着地斜面 891
着地場 793
着地台 100
着地マット 792
着地領域 790
着氷性の雨 57, 64
チャク・モル 412
着陸船 18
着陸橋 631
着陸灯 631
茶漉し 233
茶漉し球 233
茶筒 863
チャッカー・ブーツ 342
着艦甲板 761
着艦ケーブル 761
着艦拘束ケーブル 761
着艦誘導レーダー 761
チャック 302, 306, 307, 649, 902
チャック・キー 306
チャット・ルーム 525
チャド 745
チャド湖 34
チャパティ 205
茶ボール 863
チャンス・カード 915
チャンター 432
チャンネル送りボタン 495
チャンネル・セレクター 505
チャンネル選局ボタン 495
中圧配電線 273, 663
注意書き 306
中央アフリカ共和国 745
中央アフリカ部族 468

938

天文学 >2-25; 地球 >26-71; 植物 >72-89; 動物 >90-143; 人間 >144-177; 食べ物と台所 >178-241; 家屋 >242-295; 日曜大工・園芸 >296-333; 衣服 >334-371; 装身具類と日用品 >372-391; 芸術と建築 >392-465; 情報伝達とオフィス・オートメーション >466-535; 交通と機械 >536-643; エネルギー >644-677; 科学 >678-705; 社会 >706-785; スポーツとゲーム >786-920

中央アメリカ 28, 30
中央キルソン 607
中央径間 540
中央ケルソン 607
中央祭壇 737
中央スパン 540
中央線 847, 848
中央通路 584
中央土質心壁 660
中央柱 676
中央氷域 879
中央分離帯 539, 712
中央ポンピング・ステーション 654
中温アイロン 347
中音域スピーカー 10, 502
中音域用スピーカー 10, 502
中温で回転乾燥可 347
中温でタンブル乾燥可 347
中華人民共和国 747
中華鍋 234
中華鍋セット 234
中果皮 81, 82, 83
中間楔状骨 155, 156
中間圏 53
中間圏界面 53
中間昇圧所 654
中冠帯 404
中間帯 403
駐機場 619
中脚 96, 98
柱脚 405
中胸 97
肘筋 151
中空軸 307
中継器 487
中継軸 487
中継基地 486
中堅 795
中堅手 794
中膠 95
中国語 468
中国ブロッコリ 187
中砕石 46
中趾 115
中耳 174
中指骨 133
中趾骨 126
注射器 776
駐車場 583, 596, 620, 708, 713, 735, 866, 886
注射針 776
中斜面 896
中手骨 111, 116, 122, 126, 131, 133, 136, 138, 142, 154, 156
抽出井 646
駐鋤 756
柱状結晶 64
抽象図形の例 740
中心 103, 704
柱身 405, 750
中心窩 177
中心街 709, 710
中心孔 500
中心軸 692
中心小体 94
中心電極 562
中心盤 95
虫星 164
注水口 288
中枢神経系 167
中性子 680
中性線 272, 273
中性引き込み線 272
中舌 99
中節骨 126, 133, 154, 155, 172
中切歯 159
柱頭 405
中層雲 62
中層雲形 55
鋳造所 729
中足骨 155, 111, 122, 126, 131, 138, 141, 142
チューダー風アーチ 413
柱体 405
中堆石 46
抽弾棒 752
中腸 99
柱塔 583, 80, 84, 403, 405, 440
肘頭 126, 153
チューナー 498, 504
中二階 250, 251, 592
中二階への階段 251
注入井 646
チューニング切り替えスイッチ 498
チューニング・ゲージ 448
チューニング・スライド 447
チューニングつまみ 498, 503, 504
チューニング・ピン 440, 442
チューニング・ボタン 494, 497
チューニング・ボルト 448
チューバ 437, 447
中鼻甲介 175
昼標 615, 617
中部 169
チューブ 223, 777
チューブ・カッター 314
チューブ・ベル 437, 449
チューブラー・アイス・スクリュー 901
チューブラー錠 248
中片 169
中片部 169
厨房 584, 719, 721, 723, 724, 726, 735, 763, 764
中脈 84

注油器 649
中葉 163
チューリップ 80
チューリン 226
駐輪場 735
柱列 403, 406
柱列廊 403, 406
中路アーチ橋 541
中廊 738
柱廊 403, 406, 738
中肋 75, 79
チュニカ 748
チュニジア 745
チュニック・シャツ 359
チュニック・ドレス 356
チョウ 96
腸 95, 97, 103, 104, 105, 107, 109, 112, 161
丁合い 426
長方形スノーシュー 893
超音速ジェット機 53
超音速ジェット旅客機 629
超音波放射 41
頂芽 77, 77
聴覚 173
長角果の断面図 84
吊架線 595
頂冠帯 403, 404
超巨星 8
長距離 882
長距離ジェット機 624
長距離バス 568
蝶形骨 158
蝶形骨洞 175
調号 435
超広角レンズ 478
調光室 490
調光スイッチ 274
超小型車 549
彫刻 395, 401
彫刻が施された触先 598
彫刻具座 10, 11
彫刻具の例 401
腸骨 111, 116, 122, 152
長骨 157
腸骨下腹神経 166
腸骨鼠径神経 166
長骨の各部位 155
長骨の構造 154
長駒 442
長座 248
吊索 895
チョウザメ 218
丁子 198
長指伸筋 150
聴取室 768
頂上 886
長掌筋 150
頂上ロッジ 886
頂飾 749
聴診器 776
超新星 8
調整式スパッド・レンチ 315
調整室 431, 718
調整食品 180, 216
調整つまみ 317
調整ナット 317
調整ねじ 309, 310, 311, 312, 319
調整溝 310
潮汐発電所 664
調節可能な肩紐 368
調節クランプ 286
調節式座席 584
調節スライド 350
調節装置の種類 258
調節つまみ 238, 290, 294, 457
調節ねじ 436, 439
調節バンド 141
調節ペダル 399
調節弁 259
調節ボタン 443
調節用ウエスト・タブ 348
朝鮮語 469
朝鮮半島 33
朝鮮民主主義人民共和国 747
調速機 417
調速機ロープ張り車 417
長体 472
吊柄 896, 896
超短波スキャナー 60
ちょうちんばな 280
蝶番 238, 247, 249, 278, 294, 386, 389, 465, 500, 692
蝶番関節 156
蝶番ピン 638
長橈側手根伸筋 151
手斧 401, 767, 907
長内転筋 150
蝶ナット 311
チョウの形態図 96
跳馬 824, 825, 826
丁番 385
長板 404
長方形の旗 739
調味料 200, 723
調理皿 239

調理室 624
調理台 224, 721, 722
調理ピン 444
調理リング 433
調理場 584, 719, 721, 723, 724, 726, 735, 763, 764
調理室 233
調理鋏 233
調理板 722
調理盆 239
調理用具一式 233
聴力検査室 781
釣り調節つまみ 910
潮力発電所 664
張力ばねの銃剣 850
鳥類 115
頂裂片 86
チョーカー 374
チョーク 863
直接受信 486
直線コース 871
直線翼 383
直腸 97, 99, 113, 116, 125, 164, 169, 170
直腸子宮窩 170
直腸盲嚢 95
チョコレート 208
著作権 473
貯水器 59
貯水槽 59
貯水槽側 664
貯水タンク 675
貯水池 657, 658, 660, 661
貯精嚢 104
貯蔵可能推進剤上段ステージ 24
貯蔵室 720, 722
貯蔵タンク 656
貯蔵トレイ 666
貯炭室 646
貯炭式ストーブ 256
直角 704
直角の動き 916
チョップ 214, 215
チョリソ 216
チョロギ 184
ちり 426
チリ 742
地理 28
塵粒の尾 8
ちり取り 295
チリ・パウダー 199
治療室 781
チルド・ケース 291
鎮圧輪 643
チンゲンサイ 186
チン・ストラップ 808
チンパンジー 139
陳列準備区域 180
陳列材 180
陳列用冷凍庫 180

つ

ツアー用スキー靴 892
椎用板 157
椎用孔 157
椎甲板 113
椎骨 111, 136
ツイスト 206
ツイスト・バー 850
ツイスト・ハンドル 516
ツイスト・ペア・ケーブル 523
椎体 157, 168
追突予防帯 853, 857
通貨回転子 688
通貨省記号の例 728
通貨の名称 729
通気管 259
通気口 259, 402, 631
通気孔 294, 320
通気循環 262
通気縦主管 262
通気扉 571
通勤列車 583
通告員 828
ツー・コラム・スプリット・ベット 919
2サイクル・エンジンの周期 565
通常型尾翼 629
通常の渦巻き銀河 9
通信アンテナ 761
通信衛星 486, 525
通信設備 594
通信装置 522
通信端末 507
通信パネル 626
通信モジュール 486
2ストローク・サイクル・エンジンの周期 565
通帳記入口 730
ツー・ドア・セダン 549
ツー・バーナーのキャンプ用コンロ 903
字牌 917
通風口 705
通風調節装置 258
ツー・ペア 914
ツーリング・タイヤ 560
ツーリング・バイク 577, 581

ツール・ホルダー 308
通路 180, 714
通話キー 506
通話スイッチ 505
杖 846
杖先ゴム 782
ツェツェバエ 101
ツオブフ 205
柄 849
使い捨てかみそり 383
使い捨てカメラ 480
使い捨てコンタクト・レンズ 384
使い捨て燃料ボンベ 314, 319
柄付きの銃剣 751
つかみ 901
つかみ棒 594
つかむ道具 310
つかむのに適した指 139
月 4, 6, 7
ツギ 916
継ぎ環 383
接ぎ木用ナイフ 330
突き刺しレバー 240
月着陸船 19, 25
継ぎ手 269, 557, 766
継ぎ手の例 269
継ぎ手ボルト 659
月の軌道 6, 7
月の地形 7
突き放し 892
継ぎ目板 590
継ぎ目板ボルト 590
継ぎ輪 257
机 724
繋ぎ 124
繋ぎ梁 253
常に等しい 703
角形チャーム 376
ツノメロン 196
鐔 849
つば 76, 340, 341, 772
唾抜き 447
ツバメ 118
ツバル 747
粒辛子 200
つぶしたチリ 199
つぶす 230
粒マスタード 200
つぼ 76
妻 785
爪 96, 98, 107, 113, 121, 173, 313, 376, 460, 610, 611, 901
詰め替え芯 470
爪欠け 905
爪形回転子 688
爪車 460
爪切り 377
爪切り鋏 377
爪削り 377
詰め込み管 643
爪竿 611
冷たい降気流 63
冷たい空気 64, 675
詰め込み 464
詰め開きで 833
爪磨き 377
爪やすり 377
爪を出した状態 133
爪を引っ込めた状態 133
つやぺら 422
露 65
露点 391
強い断続性の雨 57
強い断続性の霧雨 57
強い断続性の雪 57
強い雷雨 57
強い雷電 57
強い連続性の雨 57
強い連続性の霧雨 57
強い連続性の雪 57
釣り 909
釣り合い錘 417, 500, 638, 639, 640
釣り合い錘のガイド・レール 417
吊り上げ装置 635
ツリウム 684
吊りカーテン 282
吊り金具 476, 477

釣り鐘状の鈴 449
吊り革 893
吊り鎖 602
吊りケーブル 540
吊り桁 540
吊り香炉 737
吊り下げ点 897
吊り下げ灯 286
吊り束 253
吊り綱 540, 602
吊り橋 540
吊り皿 697
釣り針 909, 911
釣り服と小道具 911
吊りフック 651
吊り棒 592
吊り干し 347
吊り元框 247, 278
吊り物 430, 431
吊り輪 824, 825
弦 750
蔓 322
ツルコケモモ 192
鶴座 10
蔓棚 322
つるはし 327
ツンドラ 66
ツンドラ気候 61

て

手 139, 147, 149, 154, 173
手洗い 584, 715, 719, 723, 724, 728, 731, 733, 735, 779, 780, 781
ティアース 849
ティアード・スカート 357
低アクセント 473
低圧蒸気吸入管 668
低圧配電線 273, 663
低圧部 63
ディアブル 235
ティー 867, 877
D型カラビナ 900
T形尾翼 629
ティー・グラウンド 866, 867
Tコネクター 522
ティーザー・コーム 380
T字ステッキ 782
Tシャツ・ドレス 369
ティー・ショット 866
Tストラップ・ハイヒール 343
ティースプーン 228
ティーゼル油 656
ディーゼル・エンジン 586, 762
ディーゼル・エンジン収納部 636, 637, 638, 639
ディーゼル・エンジン通風機 586
ディーゼル・エンジンの周期 565
ディーゼル機関車修繕工場 583
ディーゼル推進装置 605
ディーゼル電気機関車 586
ディーゼル浮上エンジン 605
Dゾーン 862
T継ぎ手 257, 269, 271
Tバー・リフト 886
ティー・バッグ 208
DVD 494
DVDプレーヤー 494
DVDレコーダー 521
つまみ 274, 275, 278, 448, 612
積み換え上屋 596
積み込み口 573
積み込み口開閉部 608
積み込み設備 648
積み荷ターミナル 596
DVD-ROMイジェクト・ボタン 513
DVD-ROMドライブ 513, 526
ティーポット 226
ティー・ライン 877
低アイロン 347
低音域スピーカー 10, 502
低音域用指盤 432
低音域用ボタン 432
低音域用スピーカー 10, 502
低音域用ボタン部 432
低音調整つまみ 503, 497
低温で回転乾燥可 347
低温でタンブル乾燥可 347
低音トラップ 490
低音用指盤 432
低音用ボタン 432
低音用ボタン部 432
低音レジスター 432
定滑車と動滑車の組み合わせ 686
蹄冠 124, 127
低気圧の中心 55
定期航空機 53
抵抗器 689
抵抗調節器 851
蹄叉 127
蹄叉側溝 127
蹄叉中溝 127
蹄支 127
停止液 485
停止・解除ボタン 501
停止スイッチ 331
停止ボタン 495, 499, 508, 512
艇首 834, 836
蹄踵 127
ディジョン・マスタード 200
提靼帯 177
泥水噴射ホース 651
泥水分離器 651
ディス・キャップ 566
ディスク 521, 559, 560, 851
ディスク・アーム 641
ディスク・イジェクト・ボタン 521
ディスク・カッター 237

ディスク・カメラ 481
ディスク式水栓 268
ディスク・ドライブ 450
ディスク取り出しボタン 501, 521
ディスク・トレイ 494, 501, 521, 918
ディスク・ブレーキ 552, 559, 574, 874
ディスク・ホイール 871
ディストリビューター・キャップ 552, 566
ディスプレイ 507, 518, 526, 528, 530, 730, 731, 918
ディスプレイ開閉ボタン 526
蹄尖 127
蹄側 127
低速回転軸 677
低速車線 539
ディアトリ 206
艇体 834, 836
底堆石 46
停滞前線 56
定置式電動鋸 305
定着液 485
ディッシュ 489, 493
ディッシュ・アンテナ 493
ディッチ 864
ディッパー・アーム 637
ディッパー・アーム・シリンダー 637
ディッパー・バケット 638
ティッピング・レバー 783
蹄底 127
蹄鉄 127
蹄鉄形チャーム 376
蹄鉄の打ち付け面 127
ディナー皿 226
ディナー・ナイフ 228
ディナー・フォーク 228
ディバイダー 643
底板 756
底盤 701
艇尾 836
ティピー 418
底部 531, 591, 767
ディフューザー 428
ディフレクター 260, 329, 332, 333
蹄壁 127
低棒 824
低木 322
低木状地衣 74
低木地帯 66
ディメトロドン 92
底面 288, 374
デイモス 4
ティラー 834
ティラノサウルス 93
出入り口 624
出入り台 584
低利得アンテナ 18
泥流 47
定量吸入器 783
テイル 836
テイル 202
テイル・ストップ 312
テイルデ 473
ディレクター・チェア 276
ディレクトリー 524
ティンパナム 411
ティンパニ 437, 448
ティンパヌム 403, 404
ティンプル 867
ティン・ボード 819
データ・エントリー用スライダー 450
データ記憶スイッチ 316
データ記憶装置 521
データ記録 41
データ記録装置 694
データ受信 41
データ処理 41, 54
データ送信 41
データ表示画面 495
データ表示窓 495, 508
データベース 525
データ・ロガー 58
テーパー翼 630
テープ 313, 453, 459, 757, 800
テープ・ガイド 499, 534
テープ・カウンター 499
テープ・セレクター 499
テープ・ディスペンサー 534
テープ・ホルダー 534
テープ・ライター 533
テーブル 278, 374, 723, 815, 862, 890
テーブル・カット 375
テーブル山座 10
テーブルの例 278
テーブルスプーン 228
テーブル・ランプ 286
テープ・レコーダー選択ボタン 497
テープ・ロック 313
テーラード・カラー 355, 362
テーラード・スリーブ 361
テール 840, 887, 888, 892, 894, 909
テール・コーム 380
テール・パイプ 553
テールバック 807
テールピース 270
テール・ブーム 631
テールライト 554, 571, 575, 576, 578, 640

テールランプ 554, 571, 575, 576, 640
手押し車 323, 582
手押し鋤 326
手押し式芝刈り機 332
手押し台車 633
手押し荷物運搬車 633
デオドラント 379
手斧 401, 767, 907
手掛かり 901
手紙 474
手紙秤 531
デカンタ 225, 241
デキスター 740
テキスト・キー 528
デクスター・チーフ 740
デクスター・フランク 740
デクスター・ベース 740
てぐす結び 908
出口 100, 539
出口誘導路 621
テクニカルIDナンバー 501
テクニカル・ディレクター 490
テクニカル・プロデューサー 489
テクニカル・プロデューサー用モニター 491
テクニック 812
テクネチウム 683
手首 130, 140, 147, 149, 156, 173
手首丈グラブ 346
手鍵盤 444, 445
てこ 686
デコイ発射機 762
デコルテ・ブラジャー 367
先栓 247
手作業による分別 71
手差し給紙スロット 519
デジタル映像効果モニター 491
デジタル映像特殊効果装置 491
デジタル・オーディオ・テープ・レコーダー 488
デジタル・カムコーダー 517
デジタル・カメラ 481, 517
デジタル体温計 777
デジタル多用途ディスク 494
デジタル時計 696
デジタル表示部 316, 699, 777
デジタル・ボイス・レコーダー 534
デジタル・レフレックス・カメラ 477
デシマル・タブ 528
手順チェックリスト 20
手錠ケース 770
デスクトップ・コンピューター 522, 523, 524
デスクトップ・ビデオ装置 520
デスク・トレイ 531
デスク・マット 511
デスク・ランプ 286
テスト・パターン 492
テスト棒 316
テスト・ボタン 767
手すり 250, 251, 255, 281, 417, 569, 570, 587, 607
手すり子 255
手すり綱 542
手すりの水平材 417
手玉 862, 863
鉄 683
デッキ 584, 838, 893
デッキ・クレーン 761
デッキ・チェア 277
デッキ・ドア 584
デッキ連結部 584
鉄筋コンクリート 298
鉄靴 749
鉄靴 727
鉄骨 442
鉄骨架構 582
轍叉 590
鉄唇 127
鉄側 127
鉄塔 583
鉄鎬 127
鉄道 39
鉄道駅 39, 583, 708, 710
鉄道線路 590, 591, 709, 710
鉄道引き込み線 596
鉄道輸送 582
デッド・ボウル・エリア 864
デッド・ボール・ライン 804
デッド・ボルト 248, 249
鉄尾 127
鉄棒 824, 825
テディー 366
テテュス 5
デテント 423
テナー・ドラム 448
テナガザル 139
テニス 820
テニス・コート 788
テニス・シューズ 822
テニス・プレーヤー 822
テニス・ボール 822
テニス・ラケット 822
デニッシュ・ブルー 211
デニッシュ・ライ麦パン 205
手荷物一時預かり所 582
手荷物受取所 620

手荷物検査場 621
手荷物ロッカー 582
手の甲 173
手のひら 173, 797
掌 121
デパート 715, 716
手挽き鋸 303
手挽きマイター・ソー 303
デビット・カード 731
手袋 20, 346, 798, 848, 853, 855, 870, 871, 872, 874, 875
手袋形洗顔タオル 379
手袋形浴用タオル 379
手袋着用 774
手袋の甲側 346
手袋の手のひら側 346
テフロン・テープ 314
デボン紀 92
手回しハンドル 328, 750
デマタス 226
手万力 422
手元 391
デュアル・イン・ライン・パッケージ 689
デュオ 438
手指消浄室 780
テラス 244, 322
テラス・ドア 224, 250
テラン 864
デリート 515
デリート・キー 515
デリーヌ 234
デリック 604, 607
デリック・ポスト 607
デルタ 48
デルタ2 24
デルタ翼 629, 630
テルテール 834
テルテール・ボード 819
テルビウム 684
テルル 682
テレスコピック・フロント・フォーク 574, 577
テレビ 489, 724, 734
テレビ受像機 494
テレビ電源ボタン 495
テレビ番組欄 471
テレビ・ビデオ切り替えボタン 495
テレビ・モード 495
テレビ欄 471
テレピン油 400
テレプロンプター 492
テレポート 487
テレホン・インデックス 531
テン 134
天 426
点 914
電圧降下 662, 677
電圧上昇 662
電圧の単位 702
電圧を上げる 665
電位差の単位 702
電位秤 702
田園 709
天蓋 611, 639
電解コンデンサー 689
点火装置 627
電荷の単位 702
点火プラグ 332, 562, 565, 566
点火プラグ・コード 566
点火用変圧器 259
転換器 523
電気 272
天井扇風機 261
電気オーブン 721
電気回路 274
電気学と磁気学 687
電気窯 465
電気かみそり 383
電気乾燥機 258
電気計時システム 883
電気系統 553
電気ケーブル 306, 556, 563
電気コード 237, 316, 331, 382
電気コネクター 571
電気鎚 381
電子 688
電気式昇降台 898
電気子鉄心 688
電気自動車 563
電気支払い制御装置 920
電磁子巻き線 596
電気審判器 848
電気炊飯器 239
電気洗濯機 292
電気抵抗の単位 702
電池蓋 689
天頂 10
天頂プリズム 14
点滴スタンド 780
転轍機 590
転轍器 583
転轍信号 590
転轍てこ 590
転轍機 590
伝導 681
伝統楽器 432
電動機 563
電動ゴルフ・カート 869
伝統的な衣装 339
伝統的な家屋 418
伝統的な船 599
電動鋸 331

電気レンジ 290
電気炉 258
天元 916
天空不明 56
電源 687
電源アダプター 526
電源アダプター・ポート 526
電源・音量つまみ 504
電源・機能スイッチ 496
点検台 25
電源コード 305, 308, 381, 383, 497, 513
電源コネクター 513
電車 622
電源スイッチ 237, 241, 286, 288, 289, 318, 381, 382, 383, 384, 451, 476, 477, 483, 488, 497, 498, 518, 526, 613
電源スイッチ・ボタン 240
電源テスト・ボタン 520
電源・バックライト・ボタン 527
電源表示灯 381
電源表示ランプ 508, 518, 519
電源ポイント 663
電源ボタン 494, 495, 498, 501, 504, 505, 506, 508, 513, 519
電源・用紙感知ライト 731
電源・ライト・スイッチ 452
電源ランプ 506
電源冷却ファン 513
電光 57
転向車線 539
電光表示板 831
電工ベンチ 317
伝言録音カセット 508
電子 687
電子安定器 275
展示案内版 394
展示架 510
展示会場 719
電子楽器 450
電子顕微鏡の横断面 694
電子顕微鏡の構成部品 694
電子工学 689
電子支払い端末 731
電子銃 494, 694
電磁スペクトル 690
電子制御装置 559
電子制御ボックス 563
電子制御ユニット 559
電子線 694
電子タイプライター 528
電子ドラム・パッド 451
電子の流れの方向 687, 689
電子秤 423
電子ピアノ 451
電子ビーム 494, 694
電子ビーム軸合わせ部 694
電子ビューファインダー 496
電子ブック 527
電子メトロノーム 436
電車ホーム 620
填料室 390
天井 257, 417, 818, 819
天井型扇風機 261
天井スイッチ・パネル 626
天井付け灯 286
天井灯 286
天井梁太 252
天井梁 252
天井ブラケット 284
天井用調節装置 258
テンション・スプリング 557
テンション・ボルト 448
テンション・ロッド 448
電卓 224, 238, 723
臀神経 166
転節 96, 98
電設工具 316
電線 712
伝送ケーブル 613
テンダーロイン・ロース 214
テンダーロイン・ロースト 214
天体 4
天体観測 10
電卓 529
デンタル・フロス 384
デンタル・フロス・ホルダー 384
電池 302, 482, 563, 687, 765
電池蓋 689
天頂 10
天頂プリズム 14
点滴スタンド 780
転轍機 590
転轍器 583
転轍信号 590
転轍てこ 590
転轍棒 590
伝導 681
伝統楽器 432
電動機 563
電動ゴルフ・カート 869
伝統的な衣装 339
伝統的な家屋 418
伝統的な船 599
電動鋸 331

電動歯ブラシ 384
電動マイター・ソー 304
テントウムシ 101
電動モーター 332
テント・トレーラー 567
テントの例 902
天然橋 51
天然ウラン 670
天然水 671
天王星 4, 5
天の子午線 13
天の赤道 13
天の南極 13
天の北極 13
電波 16, 690
電波送信 486
電波望遠鏡 16
天板 321, 445
天盤 647
伝票 721
伝票差し 534
伝票発行口 548
天秤 452, 698
テンピン 865
天秤座 13
臀部 147, 149, 169, 170
テンプル 385, 424, 461
澱粉 85
澱粉核 74
店舗 406
展望室 584
テンポ調節つまみ 451
デンポ 744
デンマーク語 469
天幕 407
天窓 245
点滅灯 568
天台 17
天文台の断面図 17
電流の単位 702
電力の単位 702
電力メーター 273
臀裂 147, 149
電話 491, 506, 724
電話機 506, 507
電話機の例 507
電話・ケーブル・衛星ライン 523
電話交換器 507
電話設備 489
電話線 524, 712
電話ネットワーク 487
電話番号一覧表 506
電話ボックス 725

と
ド 434
度 704
ドア 290, 417, 551, 554, 567, 699, 724, 818, 902, 903
ドア当たり 587
ドア・インナー・パネル 554
ドア内側ハンドル 554
ドア内側ロック・ボタン 554
ドア・ガスケット 291
ドア・コード 293
ドア・ストッパー 291
ドアの取っ手 247
ドアの握り 247
ドアの例 416
ドアノブ 248
ドア・ハンドル 551
ドア・ヒンジ 554
ドア・ポケット 554
ドア・ミラー 550
ドア・ロック 551
砥石 229
砥石盤 308
砥石車 308
ドイツ 744
ドイツ語 469
ドイツ・シェパード 130
トイレ 251, 395, 584, 715, 719, 723, 724, 728, 731, 733, 735, 779, 780, 781
トイレット・ペーパー・ホルダー 264
トウ 868
塔 410, 634, 635, 676, 677
胴 110, 147, 149, 240, 268, 301, 302, 303, 440, 441, 448, 847, 911, 918
銅 683
等圧線 55
糖衣注入器 232
同一である 703
同一ではない 703
凍雨 57
トゥールーズ・ソーセージ 216
投影ドーム 10
豆果 190
頭蓋 106
頭蓋骨 116, 121, 126, 136, 138, 141, 142, 146
頭蓋の側面図 158
頭蓋帽 340
灯火窓ガラス 614
塔形クレーン 634
塔形風車 676
塔形風車 676
豆果の断面図 84
糖菓用温度計 231
トウガラシ 188

940

天文学 > 2-25; 　地球 > 26-71; 　植物 > 72-89; 　動物 > 90-143; 　人間 > 144-177; 　食べ物と台所 > 178-241; 　家屋 > 242-295; 　日曜大工・園芸 > 296-333; 　衣服 > 334-371; 装身具類と日用品 > 372-391; 　芸術と建築 > 392-465; 　情報伝達とオフィス・オートメーション > 466-535; 　交通と機械 > 536-643; 　エネルギー > 644-677; 　科学 > 678-705; 社会 > 706-785; 　スポーツとゲーム > 786-920

唐辛子スプレー　770	導流壁　597	塗装用スプレー・ガン　320	トラックボール　517	ドレープト・ネック　363
套管　657, 658	動力式アース・オーガー　323	土台　253, 591, 676	トラック・マーカー　883	ドレープト・ネックライン　363
トウガン　188	動力式穴掘り機　323	土台下枠　252, 253	トラック・レース　871	トレーラー客車　594
灯器　614	動力式芝刈り機　332	トチャカ　183	トラップ　262, 265	トレーラー・ハウス　567
胴着　338	動力車　594	徒長枝　86	トラップ継ぎ手　269, 270	ドレーン　660
同期ケーブル　527	動力転轍機　590	凸角　409	トラップ・ハウス　860	トレス海峡　29
闘技場　399	動力取り出し装置　640	独居房　727	ドラフター　399	トレサリー　411
同期発電機　688	導輪　333	ドッキング・クレードル　527	ドラフト・アーム　638	ドレスの例　356
塔脚　663	トウ・ループ　881	ドック　596	ドラフト・チューブ　638	ドレッサー　279
投球　795, 799, 864	道路　39, 708	ドッグ・イヤー・カラー　362	トラベラー　834, 835	トレッド　561
撞球　862	トウ・ロープ　840	凸状の曲線　420	トラベラーズ・チェック　729	トレッド・デザイン　560, 561
撞球台　862	登録商標　473	取っ手　230, 236, 237, 238, 239, 240, 248, 256, 268, 270, 280, 289, 290, 291, 295, 309, 316, 328, 381, 382, 386, 387, 388, 389, 433, 503, 504, 534, 567, 584, 611, 755, 766, 775, 793, 826, 877, 890, 899, 905	トラベリング・ブロック　651	トレブル調節つまみ　441
投球マット　864	道路工事中　545, 547		ドラム　230, 285, 292, 293, 404, 448, 559, 697	トレブル・ピックアップ　441
動鏡　612	道路交通　538			トレブル・フック　911
頭胸甲　107	道路清掃車　573		ドラム・ブレーキ　559	トレブル・レジスター　432
頭胸部　103, 107	道路地図　39		ドラムリン　45	トレモロ・アーム　441
動鏡用遮光板　612	道路通信　487		トラロク神殿　412	トレンチ　647
等距離標識　621	道路トンネル　543		トランク　389, 551	トレンチコート　352
道具　823	道路の断面図　538	取っ手カバー　268	トランクス　351, 842, 850	ドレン弁　266, 267, 655
洞窟　51	道路番号　39	ドット・プリンター　520	トランク・ホース　338	泥受け　651
トウ・クリップ　578, 580	道路標識　544	凸版印刷　909	トランス　663	ドローストリング・バッグ　387, 388
峠　336	道路網　538	凸版印刷方式　421	トランスファー・カナル　666	
東経　36	道路輸送車　596	トッピング　909	トランスミッション　292, 563	ドロー表　789
陶芸　464	等和色　400	トッピング・リフト　602	トランスミッション系　553	トロール船　606
洞穴　47	トーガ　336	トップ　602, 887, 888, 892	トランプ　914	ドローワークス　651
刀剣　751	トーキング・ドラム　433	トップ・ガイド　909, 910	トランペット　437, 447	ドローン　432
島弧　49	トーク　341	トップ・カバー　528	トランペット型インターチェンジ　538	ドローン管　432
灯光　615, 617	トークバック・ボックス　488	トップ・コート　355		トロッター　857
瞳孔　132, 177	トークン　915	トップ・ステッチ・プリーツ　357	トランポリン　823	ドロップ・ショット　821
等号キー　529	トーゴ　745	トップ・ハイ・ハット　448	トリアージ室　779	ドロップ・イヤリング　374
頭頸　109	通し穴　900	トップ・ベンド　888, 892	ドリアン　197	ドロップト・トルソー・ドレス　356
横骨　116, 121, 122, 126, 131, 136, 138, 140, 141, 142, 152, 154, 156	通し針　461	トップ・ポケット　862	ドリー　428	ドロップ・ライト　316
	トースター　238	トップ・ボックス　577	ドリー・トラック　428	トロピカル・フルーツ　196
	トーチ　341	トップマーク　615, 616	ドリーネ　47	泥除け　551, 570, 571, 574, 578, 640
橈骨神経　166	トーチ・ランプ　314, 319	トップ・リフト　342	鳥打ち帽　340	
搭載機器ベイ　24	トート・バッグ　388	凸メニスカス・レンズ　691	トリウム　684	トロリー　542, 634
東西教会の分裂　736	トーナメント表　789	凸レンズ　691	トリオ　438	トロリー滑車　634
冬至　21	ドーム外板　17	土手　538	トリガー　331, 516, 750, 754, 755, 757, 860, 861, 912	トロンプ壁　675
トウシキミ　84	ドーム型テント　903	トナー・カートリッジ　519		トロンボーン　437, 447
同軸ケーブル　523	ドーム・シャッター　17	ドナウ川　32		トンガ　747
同時通訳室　718	ドーム内板　17	トナカイ　128	トリガー・ガード　754, 860, 861, 912	鈍角　704
橈尺骨　111	ドーム屋根　415	ドニエプル川　32		トング　233
投手　794, 795, 799	ドーラーの巻き物　738	トパーズ　375	トリガー・スイッチ　320	豚舎　182
導出溝　500	トーラス　404, 405, 705	飛び上がりの高さ　829	取り替え式スパイク　802	東家　917
投手板　795	通り　711, 713	飛魚座　11	トリクイグモ　102	蚊帳　430, 431
道床　591	ドーリス式　404	鳶口　767	トリグリフ　404	筒升牌　917
搭乗員帰還機　21	ドーリス式の付け柱　407	飛び込み　828	トリグリュフォス　404	トンネル　23
頭状花序　81	トーリック・レンズ　691	飛び込み演技の例　829	取調室　768	トンボ　102
豆状骨　154	通り抜け式金属探知器　726	飛び込み設備　828	取り出しボタン　477, 918	トンボロ　51
同乗者用フットレスト　575, 576	トーン・アーム　500	飛び込み台　246, 828	トリック・スキー　840	
搭乗手続きカウンター　620	音記号　434	飛び込み用の窪み　246	トリック・スキー用ハンドル　840	**な**
搭乗控え室　621	トーン調節つまみ　441	トビネズミ　123		
塔状氷塊　46	トカゲ　114	土俵　847	取り付け脚　482	ナース・ステーション　778, 779
投書欄　789	とかげ座　12	扉　238, 278, 293, 416, 699	取り付けシーツ　280	ナース・ステーション救急外来　779
同心円層板　154	尖り岩　52	扉パッキン　291	取り付け台　275, 423	ナース・ステーション救急救命　778
等震度線　43	トガリネズミ　121	扉パネル　278	取り付けナット　859	内円　877
導水壁　657	尖り屋根　411	ドブニウム　683	取り付け部　692	内科医　780
導水路　657, 658	ドキュメント・ファイル　533	トマト　188	ドリップ・ガード　551	内核　42
トウ・ストラップ　840	毒牙　112	トマト・クーリ　200	ドリップ式コーヒー・メーカー　241	内郭　409
導線　689	毒管　112	トマト・ペースト　200	ドリップ・トレイ　241	内果皮　81, 82
塔足　663	毒キノコ　76	ドミニカ　743	ドリップ・メーター　557	内頸静脈　160
橈側皮静脈　160	特集文芸欄　471	ドミニカ共和国　743	ドリップ・モールディング　551	内趾　115
灯台　596, 614	特殊演算キー　529	ドミニカ国　743	ドリップ・レバー　329	内耳　174
導体　663	特殊効果選択ダイヤル　496	止め板　280	トリトン　5	ナイジェリア　745
胴体　444, 625, 663, 793, 898	特殊効果ボタン　496	ドメイン・ネーム　524	鳥肉　213	内歯　910
灯台部　695	特殊標識　617	止め飾り　282	鳥の解剖図　116	内陣　410, 411, 915
同値である　703	読書室　732	止め金具　389	鳥の形態図　115	内陣燈　737
到着線　589	読書灯　771	止め金具　321	鳥の形態図　115	内臓神経節　105
灯柱　287	読書用　385	止め金　750	鳥の骨格　116	内装パネル　554
頭頂　115	読書用眼鏡　385	留め金具　284, 350, 386, 387, 446, 851, 906	鳥の例　118	内蔵モデム・ポート　513, 526
頭頂骨　112, 122, 131, 153, 158	毒腺　103, 106, 112		取り外し可能ハード・ディスク　521	内側模状骨　155, 156
導通テスター　316	毒腺の導管　112	留め木　739	取り外し可能ハード・ディスク・ドライブ　521	内側広筋　153
投てき　793	得点　789, 825	止め具　282, 835		内側上顆　153
投てき用サークル　790, 791	得点係　789, 790, 822, 825, 844, 846	留め具　453, 913	取り外し可能パネル　719	内側板　417
灯塔　614		止め台　700	取り外し式バーム・レスト　514	内腸骨静脈　161
銅と銅　269	得点板　918	止め手網　857	取り外し屋根付き無蓋車　588	内腸骨動脈　160, 161, 165
銅とプラスチック　269	得点板　918	止めナット　700	取引明細書　731	ナイチンゲール　118
東南東　37	毒素　99	止めねじ　700	取引明細書受取口　730	ナイト　916
導入線　274, 275	毒針　98	留めねじ　229, 849	トリプル・リング　918	内筒　776
導入溝　500	毒ヘビの解剖図　112	止め針　336	トリマー　383	ナイトウエア　364
トウ・バー　567, 622, 840	毒ヘビの形態図　112	止め具　282	トリマラン船　835	ナイトガウン　364
導波管　489	毒ヘビの骨格　112	留めピン　350	トリム・タブ　60	ナイト・テーブル　724, 780
塔はしご　766	独立栄養生物　67	止め結び　908	トリュフ　183	ナイトドレス　364
頭髪　147, 149	独立栄養体　67	鱧　598, 608	塗料カップ　398	内胚葉　95
銅板　422	棘　95	巴投げ　844	鳥居　11	内皮　84
頭半棘筋　151	時計　238, 290, 488, 489, 491, 734, 789, 831, 858	幡座　11	鳥山鉄　233	ナイフ　227, 841, 905, 907
登攀パーティー　900		トラ　135	塗料調整ねじ　320	ナイフ・ケース　841
トウヒ　89	時計座　10	どら　437, 449	ドリリング・リグ　651	内部固定子　627
トウピース　840, 889	時計と宝飾品　717	トライアル用オートバイ　875	ドリル　435	ナイフの例　228
トウ・ピストン　444	とげのあるミズゴケ　75	トライアングル　437, 449, 863	ドリル・カラー　651	ナイフ・プリーツ　357
トウ・ピックス　881	登山　900	ドライバー　302, 868, 872, 884	ドリル・パイプ　651	内部炉床　256
頭標　615, 616	登山靴　901	ドライ・パステル描法　396	ドリル・ロッド　648	内野　728
トウ・ビンディング　892	登山者　901	ドライブ・シャフト　553, 605, 631	ドル　746	ナイル川　34
頭部　8, 96, 97, 99, 112, 115, 161, 169, 440, 441, 591, 663, 793, 800	登山用シャベル　901	ドライブ・ホイール　307	ドループ・スヌート　629	ナイロン・シャトルコック　817
	登山用ロープ　900, 901	ドライブ・リンク　331	トルクコンバーター　292	ナイロン製フリル・タイツ　368
胴部　381, 909	都市　37, 708	ドライポイント　422, 423	トルク調整カラー　306	ナイロン・ヤーン　332
動物細胞　94	都市圏　708	トラクター　640	トルクメニスタン　746	内惑星　5
頭部の保護具　772	都市の住宅　419	トラクター・エンジン収納部　638	トルコ　746	ナウル　747
トウプレート　892	土砂崩れ　47	トラザメ　218	トルコ語　469	ナオス　403
東方位標識　617	土砂流　47	トラス・アーチ　540	トルコ石　375	中雨覆い　115
東北東　37	吐出口　315	トラス構造　21	トルコ帽　339	中雨覆い羽　115
トウ・ボックス　880	土壌　70, 661	トライセップ・バー　851	トルティージャ　205	長椅子　276, 775
糖蜜　209	土壌汚染　69	トラッカー　445, 790, 835, 871, 872, 874, 883, 894, 895	トルティーヤ　205	鞅　642
透明帯　170	土壌断面　78		トルテッリーニ　206	長柄ボディ・ブラシ　379
透明中隔　167	土壌の肥沃化　69	ドラッグ　909	トルネード　63	長傘　391
トウポケット　386	図書館　711, 732	トラック運送　570	トルマリン　375	長釜　452
トウモロコシ　85, 203	図書館分室　732	トラック監督員　883	トレイ　261, 279, 281, 313, 320, 323, 389, 722	長靴着用　774
トウモロコシ粉　204	図書室　395, 732, 734	ドラッグ式集草レーキ　642		中子　227, 229, 309, 315
トウモロコシ油　209	図書返却デスク　733	トラックつまみ　910		長さ測定　700
灯油　656	トス　813	トラック・トラクター　570	トレーサー　454	長さ調節ボー　782
トウヨウゴキブリ　101	土星　4, 5	トラック・トレーラー　570	トレーニング・スーツ　370	長さの単位　702
頭絡　854	土石流　47	トラック番号　501	トレーニング・フィールド　788	流し　224, 264, 270, 780
	塗装　320	トラックの例　573	トレーニング用器具　850	中敷き　345
			ドレープ　283	中仕切り　389

天文学 > 2-25;　地球 > 26-71;　植物 > 72-89;　動物 > 90-143;　人間 > 144-177;　食べ物と台所 > 178-241;　家屋 > 242-295;　日曜大工・園芸 > 296-333;　衣服 > 334-371;
装身具類と日用品 > 372-391;　芸術と建築 > 392-465;　情報伝達とオフィス・オートメーション > 466-535;　交通と機械 > 536-643;　エネルギー > 644-677;　科学 > 678-705;
社会 > 706-785;　スポーツとゲーム > 786-920

流し台 722
流し旗 739
中玉縁 405
長手袋 318
中庭 182, 408, 727, 738
中パネル 247
中棒 391
中方立て 249, 278
長枕 280
長持ち 279
長物車 588
中指 173
流れ 597
中輪 863
中枠 249, 278
ナキウサギ 123
投げ釣り 910
投げ矢 918
投げ槍 748
ナシ状果 82, 193
ナス 188
ナスカ・プレート 43
ナセル 677
ナセルの断面図 677
ナタウリ 189
鉈鎌 330
ナチュラル 435
夏 54
ナックル 587
ナックル・ピン 587
ナット 248, 269, 310, 311, 439, 440, 441, 590, 750, 900, 901
ナップザック 901
ナツメ 197
ナツメグ 198
ナツメグ下ろし器 230
ナツメヤシ 192
ナトリウム 682
七枝の燭台 738
7〜17号の男の子用子供服 717
7〜17号の女の子用子供服 717
斜子織り模様 254
70メートル標的線 859
7.5メートル固定台 828
7度 434
7番アイアン 868
7メートル・ライン 827
斜めの動き 916
斜めのコーニス 403
斜め分割 740
ナバホ語 469
ナビゲーション・ディスプレイ 626
ナビゲーション・ライト 625
名札 389
鍋頭 302
鍋用流し台 721
ナポリタン・コーヒー・メーカー 241
生ごみ処理機 270
生ごみ処理機組み込み流し台 270
生チーズ 210
鉛 682
鉛玉 757
波 49, 690
常歩 124
並木 64
波形やすり 401
並木大通り 39
波の谷間 49
並の断続性の雨 57
並の断続性の雪 57
並の連続性の雨 57
並の連続性の雪 57
ナミビア 746
ナミブ砂漠 34
波目やすり 401
ナムロック 515
ナムロック・キー 515
納屋 182
奈落 430
ナロー 472
縄 823, 908
縄編み 458
縄跳び用縄 850
ナワトル語 469
縄ばしご 321
ナン 205
南極 29, 35
南極横断山脈 29
南極圏 29, 35, 36
南極大陸 28, 29
南極半島 29
南極プレート 43
軟口蓋 174, 175
軟骨魚 108, 218
軟条 108
南西 37, 616
南西インド洋海嶺 50
南西諸島海溝 50
軟体動物 104, 217
軟家 917
納戸 509
南東 573
南東 37, 616
南東インド洋海嶺 50
南南西 37
南南東 37
ナンバー・エイト 804
ナンバー・プレート 875
ナンバー・プレート・ライト 554
ナンバー・プレート・ランプ 554
ナンバリング 531
南方位標識 617
南北アメリカ 742

軟膜 167

に

荷 686
ニア 19
荷揚げ場 713
ニードル 398
ニードル・アセンブリー 398
ニードル・キャップ 398
ニー・パッド 808
ニオブ 683
荷下ろし場 395, 715, 716, 719, 724
2階 250, 251, 569
二階席 431, 624, 738
2回戦 789
二階建て住宅 419
二階建てバス 569
ニガウリ 188
二角帽 339
ニカラグア 742
2〜6号の男の子用子供服 717
2〜6号の女の子用子供服 717
二眼レフ・カメラ 480
荷脚 742
二級道路 39
2行空き 472
握り 304, 307, 310, 313, 386, 387, 388, 389, 424, 754, 782, 783, 793, 797, 798, 815, 816, 822, 838, 909, 910
握り索 542
握り部 750
握り部分 849
握り棒 587
肉売り場 180
肉食動物 67
肉食哺乳動物 130
肉食哺乳動物の例 134
肉汁受け皿 234, 239
肉穂花序 81
肉挽き器 230
肉用温度計 231
肉太 472
肉細 472
入浴槽 264
入力キー 515
入力切り替えつまみ 497
入力コンセント 520
入力装置 514
入力表示ライン 529
入力モニター 491
乳 171
西 37, 616
虹 65
西インド諸島 30
ニジェール 745
ニジェール川 34
二次演算キー 529
二次演算切り替えキー 529
ニシキヘビ 114
二次構造体 651
二次厚圧 677
二次取り入れ口 655
西半球 35
西方位標識 617
二重イン・ライン・パッケージ 689
二重ガラス 675
二重ギュメ 473
二重歯状冠 79
二重三角旗 739
二重奏 435
27メートル・ライン 858
22口径ライフル 861
22メートル・ライン 800, 804
二重ねじり錐 306
二重山形 473
二重枠 252
二出張散花序 81
二畳紀 92
ニシン 219
ニス・ローラー 422
偽ポケット 355
二槽流し台 262
荷台 542, 571, 577, 578, 639, 876
日曜大工 298
日曜大工店 714
日用品 383
ニッカーズ 848
ニッカボッカーズ 358
肉桂皮 198
ニッケル 683
日射 67, 68
日射計 58
日射量を測定する器器 58
日照記録紙 58
日照計 58
日照時間を観測する器器 58
日食 6
ニット・アンサンブル 359
ニット・ベスト 354
ニップル継手 269
二蹄 127
2度 434
荷棚 573
二番車 696, 697
200メートル線 871
200m走スタート・ライン 790
240度 704
240ボルト給電ケーブル 272
240ボルト用回線 272
2ヒンジ・アーチ 541
2分音符 435
2分休符 435
2分の2拍子 434
二方向交通 544, 546

日本 33, 747
日本海 33
日本海溝 50
日本語 469
日本実験モジュール 21
2本のスキー板 840
二枚貝 105
二枚貝の解剖図 105
二枚貝の形態図 105
2枚羽根プロペラ 628
2メートル・ライン 827
荷物預かりカウンター 620
荷物入れ 577
荷物受取所 621
荷物置き場 605
荷物室 568, 585, 631
荷物台 567, 577, 578
荷物棚 584
荷物発送所 621
荷物トレーラー 623
荷役マスト 607
入院患者 780
ニューカレドニア 29
乳管 171
ニュージーランド 29, 747
入射光測定用拡散板 479
入射中性子 681
入水 829
入水孔 95
入水の姿勢 829
乳製品 180, 210
乳製品室 291
乳製品搬入区域 180
乳腺 171
乳頭 146, 148, 171
乳頭筋 162
ニュートラル・ゾーン 806, 879
ニュートラル表示灯 576
ニュートン 702
ニューファンドランド島 30
乳房 146, 148, 171
乳棒 230
乳突起 158
入力キー 515
入力切り替えつまみ 497
ニューロン結合 168
尿管 165
二葉式跳開橋 542
尿道 165, 169, 170
尿道口 169
ニョッキ 206
二塁 794
二塁手 794
2列風切り 115
2列風切り羽 115
庭 322, 406
ニワトリ 213
庭の通路 244
人形型 904
ニンジン 189
ニンニク 184
にんにく搾り器 230

ぬ

縫い込み床面 902, 903
縫い代 455
縫い付け穴 453
縫い目 346, 348, 797, 798
縫い目線 455
縫い模様選択ダイヤル 452
貫 277, 278
抜け道 408, 409
布地 459
布地別温度表示板 288
布巻き 460
ぬるま湯で手洗い 347

ね

根 78
ネイル・エナメル 377
ネイル・ケア 377
ネイル・バッファー 377
ネイル・ホワイト・ペンシル 377
粘着テープ 777
粘土の塊 464
燃料 665, 670, 671
燃料油 656
燃料移送パイプ 25
燃料インジェクター 565, 566
燃料キャップ 903
燃料供給系 353
燃料残量警告灯 557
燃料集合体 670
燃料装荷機 666, 669, 670
燃料タンク 25, 331, 553, 563, 570, 574, 577, 586, 631, 758, 760, 903
燃料タンク・キャップ 576
燃料注入機 669, 670
燃料注入キャップ 332
燃料調整器 627
燃料計 557
燃料取り扱いの流れ 666
燃料パイプ 563, 899

ネコの品種 132
ねじ 302, 439
ねじ頭 302
ねじ頭の溝 302
ねじ頭の例 302
ねじ切り 268
ねじ切りキャップ継ぎ手 269
ねじ釘 590
ねじ込み口金 275
ねじ式イヤリング 374
ねじ筋 302
ねじの溝 302
ねじ蓋 223
ねじ回し 302, 905
ねじ山 302, 311
ねじれ 306
ねじれ錐 306
ねじを締める道具 302
ネズの実 198
ネズミ 123
ネズミイルカ 137
ネズミの形態図 122
ネズミの骨格図 122
根太 254
根引掛け 252
寝棚 584
熱エネルギー 68, 646
熱エネルギー発電 646
熱が発生する 665
熱吸収板 672
ネック 440, 441, 868
ネック・エンド 349
ネック・カラー 775
ネック・サポート 874
ネック部 494
ネックライン 363
ネックレス 374
ネック・ロール 808
熱圏 53
熱圏界面 53
熱交換器 259, 670, 675
熱シールド 22
熱遮蔽板 22
熱制御パネル 21
熱せられた冷却液 665, 674
熱損失 68
熱帯雨林 61
熱帯雨林気候 61
熱帯気候 61
熱帯果物 196
熱帯サバナ気候 61
熱帯サバンナ気候 61
熱帯性低気圧 63
熱帯性低気圧の名称 63
熱帯暴風 57
熱帯林 66
熱調節装置 259
熱伝達 681
ネット 222, 811, 812, 813, 814, 815, 817, 821, 827
ネット・アンパイア 821
熱湯 671
ネット・コード・ジャッジ 821
ネット・サポート 815
ネット・ジャッジ 821
ネット・バンド 821
ネットボール 809
ネットボール用のボール 809
ネット・ポスト 812, 817, 820
ネットワーク・アクセス・ポイント・トランシーバー 522
ネットワーク・インターフェース・カード 522
ネットワーク・カード 522
ネットワーク接続 273
ネットワークの例 522
ネットワーク・ポート 513
熱風ダクト 293
熱風調節装置 258
熱風排気口 564
熱風吹き出し口 256, 258
熱ポンプ 260, 669
熱力学温度の単位 702
熱を水に伝える 665
ネパール 747
臥床 584
寝袋の種類 904
ネプツニウム 684
根元 227
練り歯磨き 384
練り盤 421
燃焼 564, 565, 627
燃焼ガス 564
燃焼室 564, 566

燃料噴射器 565, 566
燃料ペレット 667
燃料棒 667
燃料ポート 561, 570
燃料補給口 561, 570
燃料補給車 622
年輪 87

の

脳 99, 103, 106, 107, 109, 110, 212
脳下垂体 167
脳弓体 167
脳橋 167
農業汚染 69
農業機械 641
濃縮ウラン 671
ノウサギ 123, 212
農場 182
脳神経 166
脳脊髄液 168
脳脊髄膜 167
脳側神経節 105
能動的センサー 41
濃度調節ボタン 512
脳梁 167
ノーズ 887, 894, 897, 912
ノーズ・コーン 627
ノー・ファウル・カップ 843
ノーベリウム 684
ノーマル 472
ノーマル・ソックス 351
軒 412
芒 85
軒蛇腹 245, 247
軒樋 244
軒持ち送り 404
鋸 424
鋸屋根 414
鋸歯 303
鋸刃 303, 304, 305
鋸刃固定ボルト 304
鋸身 303, 304, 305
伸し棒 232
ノズル 22, 24, 25, 259, 268, 270, 294, 315, 319, 320, 329, 398, 767
ノズル・キャップ 319
載せ台 699
覗き穴 591, 749
覗き窓 238, 239, 290
ノッキング・ポイント 859, 913
ノック 750, 859
ノックアウト 272
ノッチ 346, 362, 698, 791, 863
ノッチ・ラベル 352
ノット 463
ノット・ステッチ 459
のど 312, 822
咽 115
喉 115
喉当て 749, 848, 880, 882
咽頭 854
喉のプロテクター 796
喉座 174
喉仏 146
ノネズミ 123
伸び型 828
ノブ 278, 285, 304, 309
伸べぞり 464
幟 739
登り 255
のみ 309
ノミ 101
飲み物自動販売機 779
海苔 183
乗組員居住区 604
乗り込み用はしご 611
乗り継ぎ券売機 593
ノルウェー 744
ノルウェー海 32
ノルウェー語 469
ノンブレーキング・スペース 514

は

歯 108, 112, 159, 227, 304, 331, 382, 636, 638, 641, 642, 686
刃 227, 229, 237, 240, 302, 303, 304, 305, 309, 320, 327, 331, 332, 377, 383, 390, 880, 881, 900
葉 75, 76, 77, 78, 79, 185
バー 431, 710, 714, 719, 720, 792, 792, 825, 850, 851, 915
パーカー 353, 901
バー・カウンター 720
パーカッション・バー 767
バーガンディ・グラス 225
バークリウム 684
ハーケン 900
バー・コード・リーダー 517
パーゴラ 322
パーコレーター 241, 723
バーサ・カラー 363
バージ・バルブ 841
バー・スツール 277, 720
バースニップ 189
バー3のホール 866

バー先端　331
パーセント　703
パーセント・キー　529
パーソナル・コンピューター　513
パーチ　220
パーチメント紙　222
バーティカル　894
バーティカル・ポケット　337
バーティクル・ボード　300
ハート　914
ハード　822
ハード・コンタクト・レンズ　384
ハード・ディスク・ドライブ　521
ハード・ブーツ　887
ハード・ブーツ用ビンディング　887
ハード・ボード　300
ハードル　790
バートロー・チャート　571
バーナー　234, 259, 290, 899, 903
バーナー・フレーム　903
バーニア　612
バーニヤ　700
バーニヤ目盛り　700
ハーネス　841, 896, 897, 900, 901
バーバー・コーム　380
ハーブ　202
ハープ　437, 440
パー5のホール　867
ハーフウェー・ライン　803, 805
バー・フェス　740
パー4のホール　866
ハープ型斜張ケーブル　541
ハーフ・グラス　385
ハーフ・コート・ライン　819
ハーフ・サイド　632
ハープシコード　443
ハーフ・スリップ　366
ハーフ・ティー　208
ハーフ・パイプ　871, 887, 894
ハーフ・パイプの競技場　887
ハーフ・ボレー　820
ハーフ・ライン　827
バー・ベイル　740
バーベナ　208
バーベル　851, 850
バー・ベンド　911
バーボイルド米　207
バーム　610
バーム・レスト　861
バーモニカ　432
バール　301
バーレーン　746
バーレン　473
灰　391
肺　104, 110, 112, 116, 125, 163
胚　85
ハイ　919
パイ　704
バイアス　455
バイアス・タイヤ　561
バイアス・テープ　368
バイアス・プライ・タイヤ　561
バイアスリート　893
バイアスロン　893
ハイイロマングース　134
ハイエナ　134
排煙器　758
パイオニア　19
バイオリン　439
バイオリンの仲間　437, 439
バイオレット　400
胚芽　85
ハイ・カード　914
パイ型　232
パイ・カッター　232
バイカル湖　33
配管　262, 654
配管工具　654
配管工具　314
配管システム　262
配管バルブ　654
配管用レンチ　315
排気　564, 565, 627
排気案内羽根　627
排気ガス取り入れ口　564
排気管　274, 275, 552, 553, 564, 565, 575, 576
排気系　553
排気口　649
排気ダクト　543, 627
排気筒　570, 631, 636, 639, 640
排気ノズル　760
廃棄物の層　69
廃棄物の分別　71
排気弁　259, 564, 566, 773, 899
排気マニホールド　552, 564, 565, 566
排気マニホルド　552, 564, 565, 566
肺胸膜　163
バイキング　18
バイキング船　598
ハイキング・ブーツ　344
背景幕　430
背甲　113
バイザー　20, 575, 773, 874, 878, 884
バイザー・ヒンジ　575
灰皿　391
バイシクル・モトクロス　871
排紙トレイ　512, 519
背斜　651

胚珠　80
排出孔　104
排出口　418
排出筒　642
排障器　585, 586
肺静脈　160
廃水　70
排水　662
排水管　262, 263, 265
排水管T継ぎ手　271
排水口　246, 262
排水溝　538
排水質　167, 168
排水循環　262
排水層　660
排水縦主管　262
排水溜め　263
排水陶管　253
排水ハンドル　265
排水弁　266, 267
排水ホース　271, 292, 294, 485
排水横枝管　262
排水横主管　262, 263
排水路　265
排水路　657
バイス・スキップ　877
バイス・プライヤー　310
配膳コーナー　509
焙煎コーヒー豆　208
配膳室　250
配線接続箱　272
配膳台　720
背側血管　97
ハイ・ソックス　351, 365
バイソン　128
羽板　913
刃板　641
背大動物　99
ハイチ　742
排泥ポンプ　651
売店　548, 593
配電パネル　489
配電盤　272, 273, 489
配電引き込み線　273
配当金額表　920
肺動脈　160, 163
肺動脈幹　162
肺動脈弁　162
排土板　636
ハイドロメーター　562
パイナップル　196
ハイパーリンク　524
バイパス・ダクト　627
ハイ・ハット・シンバル　448
胚盤　117
ハイ・ビーム　554
ハイ・ビーム警告灯　576
ハイビーム表示灯　577
パイプ　289, 312, 390, 445
パイプA　269
パイプ・カッター　314
パイプ・クランプ　312
パイプ・クリーナー　390
パイプ群　445
パイプ・ツール　390
パイプ・ディフューザー　627
パイプの断面図　390
パイプB　269
パイプ被覆用断熱材　299
パイプ部分　257
パイプライン　654
パイプ・ラック　390
ハイブリッド自動車　563
ハイブリッド兼用椅子　277
パイプ・レンチ　315
ハイボール・グラス　225
ハイ・マウント・ストップ・ライト　554
ハイ・マウント・ストップ・ランプ　554
バイメタル温度計　695
背面　391
背面収納庫　775
背面図　147, 149, 151, 153, 171
俳優　428
俳優の椅子　428
培養皿　685
ハイライト基準露光キー　479
パイル　254
パイル織物　458
パイロット　884, 897
パイロン　625
バインダー・クリップ　534
バインディング　840, 892
パウ　834, 836
ハウサ語　468
ハウジング　306, 308, 316, 318, 383, 488, 507, 614
ハウス　297
ハウス・ドレス　356
ハウスプリット　602
ハウスボート　607
バウ・スラスター　609
パウダー　378
パウダー・パフ　378
パウダー・ブラシ　378
パウチ袋　222
バウ・ドア　605
パウ・ボール　839
ハエ　101
蠅座　11
パオ　418
葉書　474

歯飾り　404, 405
刃型カートリッジ・ヒューズ　272
袴　846, 847
秤台　699
計る　231
胚珠　80
白亜紀　93
白楽　596
白菜　186
白質　167, 168
白色体　74
白色矮星　8
白線　127
白亜　127
白鳥座　12
白灯　616
白熱電球　274, 614, 673
バグパイプ　432
爆発　564
爆発性の火山　44
爆発性物質　774
白斑　6
白布　815
博物館　711
白墨線　313
白米　207
歯車　462, 686
歯車装置　686
刷毛　320, 422
バケツ　295
バケツ台　321
バケット　637, 659
バゲット　204
バケット・カット　375
バケット・シリンダー　637, 638
バケット・ヒンジ・ピン　637
バケットの切れ刃　637
バケット・ピン　659
バケット・レバー　637
ハゲワシ　119
波高　49
刃高調節計　304
刃高調節ノブ　305
箱形サイド・ポケット　352, 355, 356
箱形ポケット　348
箱形胸ポケット　348
箱錠　249
箱接着テープ・ディスペンサー　534
箱接着テープ・ホルダー　534
パゴダ・スリーブ　361
箱びな　283
ハゴロモカンラン　186
破砕機　759
歯先　304, 641
刃先　227, 229, 302, 303, 307, 454, 648
刃先の例　302
狭間　409
挟間飾り　411
狭間胸壁　408, 409
鋏　454, 777, 905
はさみ　107
挟み金具　350
橋　39, 875
橋形クレーン　635
橋形走行クレーン　596, 657, 658
はしご　246, 418, 567, 597, 615, 639, 655
はしご兼用椅子　277
はしご車　766
はしご脚立　225
はしごとストラップ　767
はしごの頂部　766
はしごホースストラップ　767
はしごホース止ストラップ　767
端縫い　350
端根　252, 253
ハシバミの実　193
ハシバミの実の断面図　194
端プレート　667
パジャマ　364, 369
把会　756
馬皿　826
播種管　643
播種機　643
馬術場　788
柱　410, 412, 413, 424, 452, 540, 676, 677
走り高跳び　791, 792
走り幅跳びと三段跳び　793, 790
走り幅跳びの踏切板　793
バジル　202
バシロサウルス　93
バス　220, 513, 522, 568, 713
バズーカ砲　757
バス海峡　29
バスカル　702
バス・クラリネット　437
バスケット　291, 292, 811, 899
バスケット編み　458
バスケット・ケーブル　899
バスケットボーラー　810
バスケットボール　810
バスケットボール・シューズ　810
バスケットボール用のボール　810
パスタ　206
バス・ターミナル　710
バス・タオル　379

バスタブ　251
バスタ・マシーン　230
バス停　712
バス・トイレ用品　717
バス・ドラム　437, 448
パスファインダー　19
バス・ブラシ　379
バスポート・ケース　387
バス待合所　712
バスマティ米　207
弾み車　452, 464, 566, 851
バス・モジュール　40
バスルーム　251, 264
バス・レジスター　432
バスローブ　364
パセリ　202
破線　538, 539
パソコン　513
破損燃料室　666
破損燃料被覆加工　666
旗　56, 742, 890
バター　210
バター　867, 868
バター・カーラー　229
バター・カップ　223
バター皿　226
バター室　291
バター・ナイフ　228
バターヘッド・レタス　186
バターミルク　210
馬体　826
裸締め　844
裸弓　859
パタゴニア　31
旗竿　739
旗の各部名称　739
旗の形　739
バタフライ　832
バタフライ・スリーブ　361
バタフライのキック　832
はた結び　908
働きバチ　99
働きバチの形態図　98
鉢　749
枹　433
ばち　449
パチカン市国　744
8度　434
ハチドリ　118
パチニ小体　172
8の字結び　908
蜂の巣　100
8番アイアン　868
8分音符　435
8分休符　435
八分儀座　10
8ミリ径ピストル　861
爬虫類　112
爬虫類の例　114
波長　49, 690
ハツ　212
発煙弾発射機　758
発音器　112
発芽　77
発火石　318
八角屋根　415
ハツカダイコン　189
白金　162
薄筋　151
パッキン　265, 268
パッキン押さえ　268, 445
バッキング　425
パッキング・ハンマー　425
パッキング・プレート　559
パッキング・ボード　425
ハック　877
バック　858
バッグ　880
バッグ　432
バックアップ記憶装置　523
バックアップ・ライト　554
バックアップ・ランプ　554
バック・ウォール　818, 819
バックギャモン　915
バックコート　818, 821
バック・サスペンション　870
バック・ジャッジ　807
バックステー　602, 881
バックストップ　811
バックストレッチ　856
バックスペース　515
バックスペース・キー　515, 528
バック済み肉売り場　180
バック・ゾーン　812
バック立て　869
バック・チェック　443
バックネット　794
バック・バウンダリー・ライン　816
バックポケット　906
バック・パッド　879
バック・ビンディング　840
バック・フィルム　481
バックホー　637
バックホー操縦装置　637
バックボード　811
バック・ポケット　350
バック・ミラー　550, 568
バック・ミラー・スイッチ　554
バック・ライン　877
バックリップ　214
ハックル　909

バックル　350, 388, 555, 611, 889, 893, 895, 906
バックレス　343
バックレスト　555
バックレス・パンプス　343
白血球　162
発行銀行名の頭文字　729
発行人欄　471
発光ランプ　436
発散プレート境界　43
発散レンズ　691
ハッシウム　683
パッシビティー・ゾーン　843
発射火薬　912
発射筒　763
発射桿　756
発車時刻案内板　582
発射時のスペース・シャトル　22
発射線　859
発射薬　912
パッション・フルーツ　196
発信パルス　40
バッスル　337
バッスルの入ったドレス　337
パッセンジャー・ステップ　623
パッセンジャー・ステップ車　623
パッタ　101, 102
バッター　795, 796
ハッチ　23, 758
パッチ盤　488
パッチ・ポケット　348, 353, 360, 368
発着案内板　621
発着線　871
ハッチング　463
バッツマン　799
発艇員　838
発艇区域　838
発艇船台　838
発艇台　838
バッティング・グラブ　796
バッテリー　513, 552, 562, 563, 586, 687, 759
バッテリー・カバー　562
バッテリー警告灯　557
バッテリー・ケース　562
バッテリー・チャージ・モジュール　563
バッテリー・バックアップ過電圧保護コンセント　520
バッテリー・ボックス　571
バッテリー・モジュール　60
バッテン　600
発電器　578
発電機　563, 646, 659, 668
発電機から電気が発生する　665
発電機により電気が発生する　662
発電機の電圧の高さでエネルギーを伝達する　662
発電室　763
発電所　657, 664
発電所建屋　666
発電装置　658, 659
発電所の断面図　664
発電ブレーキ　586
バット　425, 456, 796, 797, 798, 863, 909
パッド　385, 800, 880
パッド・アーム　385
パッドウイング・スリーブ　361
パット・エンド　880
ハット・スイッチ　516
パッド付き支柱　811
パッド付き土台　811
撥土板　641
ハットバンド　340
パッド・プレート　385
ヘッド・ランプ　579
バットレス　660
バットレス・ダム　660
バットレス・ダムの断面図　660
発熱体　258, 259, 293, 294, 318, 465
800m走スタート・ライン　791
バッファー・タンク　654
バッファロー　128
バッフィン島　30
バップ・テント　903
ハッブル宇宙望遠鏡　17, 53
ハッブル分類　9
発泡断熱材　299
発砲用附属品　752
発令所　763
パティオ　244, 322
馬蹄形アーチ　413
馬蹄型マウント　17
バティパン　189
馬蹄マウント　17
バティング　899
バテラ模様　276
バテン　834, 836, 897
バテン・ポケット　834, 836
ハト　120, 212
波頭　49
バトカー　769, 771
鳩座　11
ハドソン湾　30
ハドック　856
バドミントン　816
バドミントン・ラケット　816
鳩目　284, 342, 371, 387
歯止め　307
バトレス　410

日本語索引

パトローネ室 476	腹帯 853, 855, 856, 857	半円筒ボールト 407	ハンド・ミキサー 236	火打ち石銃 752
バトン 285, 430, 790	腹帯革 855	ハンガー 483, 540	ハンド・リング 783	火打ち石でできたナイフ 748
バトン・ゾーン 790	腹帯託革 855	ハンガー・サイロ 182	バンド・リング 376	火打ち石でできた矢尻 748
花 77, 80	腹帯留め革 855	ハンガー・フォルダー 532	ハンドル 268, 288, 304, 305, 307, 308, 309, 312, 320, 323, 331, 332, 333, 383, 421, 425, 456, 460, 552, 556, 558, 574, 577, 579, 607, 640, 649, 750, 766, 793, 822, 840, 873, 877, 884, 909, 910, 920	ビオラ 437, 439
鼻 121, 122, 124, 130, 132, 143, 148	ばら形装飾 405	ハンガー・ブラケット 783		控え壁 410
バナー 471	パラグライディング 897	ハンガー・ループ 354		控え網結び 908
鼻当て 385, 749	バラクラバ帽 341, 872	パン・菓子屋 715		控えベンチ 803
花飾り模様 440	パラシュウム 683	パン型 239		控え棒 590
鼻革 854, 858	パラシュート 760, 896	パン型トラック 572		火掻き棒 257
花布 426	パラシュート・バルブ 899	ハンガリー 744		皮革製品店 714
鼻先 110, 255	バラス 591	帆環 835	反トルク尾部回転翼 631	非加算・小計キー 529
バナジウム 683	ばら積み貨物船 604	半球 35, 705	反トルク尾部ローター 631	東 37, 616
鼻面 130, 132, 143	腹びれ 9	パン切りナイフ 229	ハンドル・ステム 579	東シナ海 33
バナナ 196	バラペーニョ 199	パン切り包丁 229	ハンドルの種類 840	東太平洋海嶺 50
花の構造 80	パラボラ・アンテナ 489, 493	ハンキング・スリーブ 338	ハンドルバー 327, 579, 851, 871, 876	東半球 35
花の例 80	パラボラ鏡 674	ハンキング・バスケット 322		皮下組織 172
花屋 715	パラボラ反射鏡 16, 489, 493	ハンキング・フォルダー 532	ハンドルバー・グリップ 871	光 14, 15, 17
離れ岩 51	ばら窓 411	半金属 682	ハンド・レスト 516	光屈折環 614
パニエの入ったドレス 337	パラモンジン 189	ハンク 835	搬入エリア 395	光センサー 477
バニッシャー 422	パララデシュ 747	ハング 567, 864	搬入区域 180	光電池電球 615
バニティー・キャビネット 264	パラレル・ボート 513	ハング・グライダー 897	万能圧着工具 317	光ファイバー・ケーブル 523
バニティー・ミラー 556	パランサー 441, 591	ハング・グライディング 897	反応の方向 684	尾管 270
バニラ・エキス 200	パランシング・ベスト 841	バングラデシュ 747	万能ベルト 770	引き上げリンク 640
バヌアツ 747	バランス 282	バングル 376	パンの笛 433	引き上げリング 610
翅 97, 98	バランス・ウエイト 14, 634	半径 704	バンパー 289, 550, 570, 571, 577	ピギーバック車 588
羽根 261, 285, 659, 676, 677, 817	バランス調節つまみ 497	半月 172, 173		引き金 750, 752, 754, 755, 757, 860, 861, 912, 920
	バランス・レール 443	半月板 409	バンパー・ガード 818	
ばね 43, 286, 292, 310, 445, 470, 757, 823, 913	針 453, 454, 776, 464	半鍵様筋 151	バンパイプ 433	鞍装 857
	針穴 453, 454, 911	バンケット 277	バンバラ語 468	引き鋏 326
跳ね上げリンク 416	針松 67	番傘灯 554	反発式スプリンクラー 329	引き込みばしご 321
跳ね上げ戸 407	針位置選択つまみ 452	犯罪防止 768	バンバラ語 468	引き締め紐 353
羽根板 281, 285	バリウム 682	パン皿 226	ハンプ 589	引き出し 224, 278, 279, 281, 290
羽根飾り 748	反射 41	バンプ 342, 371		
羽根車 688	反射鏡 571, 578, 693, 876		ハンプ仕分け[仕訳]室 589	引き違い窓 415
ばね座金 310	張り滑車 284	反射された日射 68	バンプス 343	引き網 756, 840
羽根シャトルコック 817	針切り 317	反射式望遠鏡 15	ハンプ引き上げ線 589	引き手 453
ばね収納部 284	バリカン 381	反射式望遠鏡の断面図 15	パンフレット棚 730	引き戸 264, 416
ハネジュー・メロン 195	針棒 320	反射した太陽光線 674	ハンマー 442, 443, 793, 901	ビキニ 367
刎ね出し狭間 408	バリケード・テープ 771	反射シリンダー 692	ハンマー掛け 443	ビキニ・ブリーフ 351
ばね秤 699	ハリケーン 57, 63	反射テープ 765	ハンマー・シャンク 443	挽き肉 214, 215
跳ね橋 408	ハリケーン・ランプ 906	反射板 316, 571, 578, 876	ハンマー・ドリル 648	引き伸ばし機 485
羽ペン 470	針先 453, 776, 911	反射望遠鏡 15	ハンマー・バット 443	引き伸ばし機タイマー 485
パネル 247, 350, 367, 400, 511, 899	針刺し 454	反射防止膜 672	ハンマー・フェルト 443	引き伸ばしレンズ 485
	針差し込み穴 776	反射面 674	ハンマーヘッド 443	曳き馬場 856
ばね連結器 920	針素 911	板状結晶 64	ハンマー・レール 442, 443	引き綱 389
歯のあるあご 310	針素に付けられた釣り針 911	板状結晶 151	半膜様筋 151	引き紐 433
葉の構造 79	張り出し櫓 408, 409	バンジョー 432	半丸頭 302	引き船 606
パノラマ雲台 482	張り付け材 252, 253	パン・セミトレーラー 572	版面 420	尾脚 107
パノラマ窓 713	ハリッサ 201	半潜水焼プラットフォーム 653	版面台 421, 423	鼻鏡 132
葉の例 89	張り綱 902	搬送 632	ハンモック 772	引き輪 776
幅 699	針止め 453	伴奏弦 432	パン焼き器 239	非常капリ 683
母 784, 785	針止めねじ 453	絆創膏 777	汎用小麦粉 204	引く 703
馬場 855	張り縄 433	搬送装置 632	泥濫原 48	魚籠 911
ハバース管 154	ハリネズミ 121	帆装の例 601		鼻腔 163
ハバヤード 902	針坊主 776	反則 789		杓口棒 461
パパイヤ 197	針棒 453	半側壁 632	**ひ**	ビクトリア湖 34
母方の伯父[叔父] 785	針目 459	はんだ 318		ピクニック禁止 725
母方の伯母[叔母] 785	ハル 834	パンタグラフ 585, 595	杓 461	ピクニック地域 725
幅木 253, 255	バルーン・カーテン 283	パンタグラフ付きフラッドライト 492	尾 625	ピケ 458
はば挟み 533	バルカン半島 32		ピア 411, 413	ひげぜんまい 696
幅木用調節装置 258	バルクヘッド 571	はんだ鏝 318	ピアス・イヤリング 374	髭剃り 383
馬場馬術 855	バルコニー 251, 431	はんだ銃 318	ピアノ 437	被甲 912
幅広ペダル 870	バルコニー窓 251	はんだ銃・溶接工具 318	ビア・マグ 225	飛行 891
バハマ 742	バルサー 8	パンチ 390	被圧帯水層 646	尾鉤 97
馬尾 826	バルジ 9	パンチ 685	pn 接合部 672	鼻孔 108, 112, 115, 124, 175
パビリオン 374, 710	バルス・ルビー・レーザー 692	パンチ穴 350	BMX自転車 581	鼻腔 257
パビリオン・ファセット 374	春タマネギ 184	パンチェッタ 216	ビーカー 685	飛行甲板 761
破風 403, 405, 411	バルト海 32	パンチング・ボール 842	ピーク・ラベル 348	飛行管理コンピューター 626
ハブ 522, 523, 534, 579, 659, 677, 783	バルバドス 743	パンツ 808, 810	ピーク・レベル・メーター 499	飛行機着陸誘導装置 761
	バルブ 391, 426, 500	パンツの例 358	肥育鶏 213	飛行機搭載レーダー 40
パブア諸語 469	バルブ・ケース 447	パンティー・ガードル 367	ピー・ジャケット 355	飛行機に作用する力 630
パブアニューギニア 29, 747	バルブ・シート 268	パンティー・コルセット 366	BC 841	飛行機の動き 630
ハブ・カバー 659	バルブ・スプリング 566	パンティー・ストッキング 365	PCI 拡張カード 513	飛行機の部分 628
バフ・スリーブ 360	バルブ・ボタン 447	ハンディキャップ・ボード 858	PCI 拡張コネクター 513	飛行計器類 899
バフ・ペースト 205	バルブ・ユニット 664	ハンティング 912	PCカード・スロット 526	飛行姿勢調節ノブ 898
ハフニウム 683	バルメザン 211	ハンティング・キャップ 340	ピース 917	飛行張り線 897
ハブボルト 559	バルメザン・チーズ 211	バンデージ 843, 850	ヒーター 290, 903	飛行表示装置
歯ブラシ 384	バルメット模様 276	バンド 391, 426, 500	ヒーター 448, 449	鼻口部 124, 130, 132, 143
歯ブラシ立て 384	バレー楽団 812	半ドア警告灯 557	ヒーター・ファン・カラー 362	飛行哺乳動物 140
歯ブラシ取り付け軸 384	バレーボール用のボール 812	半島 38	ひいたコショウ 199	被告席 728
パブリカ 199	バレッタ 812	ハンドウォーマー・ポケット 353, 355	ビーチ・バレー 813	腓骨 122, 126, 131, 138, 141, 142, 152, 155, 156
バブル・バス 379	バレット 445, 632, 697		ビーチ・バレーボール 813	
破片 63	バレット・スプリング 445	反動エンジン部 60	ビーチ・バレー用のボール 813	尾骨 152, 157
葉巻 390	バレット台車 633	反動推進エンジン 18	P点 891	鼻骨 158, 175
ハマグリ 217	バレット・ナイフ 397	バン投入口 238	p電極 672, 673	鼻根 175
ハマナ 186	バレリーナ・シューズ 343	バンド・エイド 777	ビート 189	膝 124, 130, 146, 148
刃身 229	バレル 381, 753, 754, 755, 756, 860, 912, 918	ハンド・ガード 331, 755, 875	ビード 560	膝当て 796, 808, 850, 855, 857, 858, 880, 882, 894, 895
馬銜 858		バンド型リング 376	ヒート・ガン 320	
歯磨き 384	バレン 421	バンド切り替えスイッチ 498	ヒート・シールしたフィルム 223	
歯磨身 854	バレンツ海 32	ハンド・クリーナー 288	ヒート・シンク 513	膝当て吊り革 857
バミューダ・パンツ 358	波浪作用限界深度 49	ハンドグリップ 574, 577, 850	ビード・ワイヤー 561	膝上ストッキング 365
バミューダ帆 601	ハロー 9	ハンド・シールド 318	ピーナッツ 190	膝覆い 749
ハムスター 123	ハロゲン・デスク・ランプ 286	ハンド・スプレー 327	ピーバー 123	庇 416, 632, 902
ハム・ナイフ 229	ハロゲン電球 274, 275	バンド選択ボタン 497	壁牌 917	火皿 390, 752
はめ込み台 376	ハロゲン灯 775	パンとチーズ 722	ピーフン 207	ヒシ 184
刃元 229	ハロン棒 856	ハンド・トラック 633	ピーマン 188	肘 124, 130, 140, 147, 149, 156
速歩 124	パワー・コントロール・モジュール 563	ハンド・ドリル 307	ビーム 641, 826	
早送り・早戻しボタン 501		ハンド・バイス 422	ビーム径の絞り込み部 694	肘当て 749, 808, 880, 894, 895
早送りボタン 495, 499, 504, 508	パワー・ショベル 647	ハンドバッグ 387	ビーム・リーチ 833	肘掛け 276, 281, 554, 555, 783
ハヤトウリ 189	パワー・タービン 627	ハンド・パレット・リフト 633	ヒール 303, 440, 868, 880, 881	肘掛け机 276, 734
早戻しボタン 495, 499, 504, 508	パワー・トレイン 580	ハンド・フォーク 325	ヒール・グリップ 342	肘掛け椅子の例 276
バヨネット・マウント 478	パワー・ユニット 585	ハンド・ブレーキ・ギアボックス 587	ヒール・シューズ 339	肘掛け支柱 276
腹 115, 124, 146, 148, 227, 300	ハワイ語 469		ヒール・ストップ 895	菱形 389
	パン 204	ハンド・ブレーキ・ホイール 587	ヒール・ピース 840, 889	ヒジキ 183
バラ 80	パン売り場 181	ハンド・ブレーキ巻き上げレバー 587	ヒール・フラップ 840	皮脂腺 172
バラ 336	半影 6, 7		ヒール・ループ 783	ビジネス街 708, 710
腹脚 97	半円 704	ハンド・ブレーキ・レバー 556	ヒール・レスト 236, 288	ビジネス機 628
払い腰 844	半円アーチ 413	ハンド・ブレンダー 236	鼻咽頭 175	肘部 302
パラオ 747		ハンド・プロテクター 331	ビーン・バッグ 277	被写界深度確認ボタン 476
		ハンドボール 814	ビーン・バッグ・チェア 277	被写界深度目盛り 478
		ハンドボール用のボール 814	火打ち石 752	美術 394
		ハンドホールド 901		美術館 257
				美術監督 428
				美術室 734
				非常階段 509
				微小管 94

天文学 > 2-25; 地球 > 26-71; 植物 > 72-89; 動物 > 90-143; 人間 > 144-177; 食べ物と台所 > 178-241; 家屋 > 242-295; 日曜大工・園芸 > 296-333; 衣服 > 334-371; 装身具類と日用品 > 372-391; 芸術と建築 > 392-465; 情報伝達とオフィス・オートメーション > 466-535; 交通と機械 > 536-643; エネルギー > 644-677; 科学 > 678-705; 社会 > 706-785; スポーツとゲーム > 786-920

非晶質固体　680
微小繊維　94
秘書室　731, 735
ビショップ　916
ビショップ・スリーブ　361
披針形　79
ピスタチオ　193
ビスト　848
ビストゥラ川　32
ピストル　754, 770
ピストル型グリップ　306, 318
ピストル・グリップ　754, 755, 860
ピストル・ケース　770
ピストル射撃　861
ピストル・ノズル　329
ピストン　447, 559, 564, 566
ピストン・スカート　566
ピストン・リリース　315
ピストン・リング　566
ピストン・レバー　315
ビスマス　682
ビスワ川　32
飛節　124, 130
尾節　107
鼻尖　175
ヒ素　682
脾臓　109, 110, 113, 125, 161
ヒソップ　202
尾橈　631
ひだ　76, 336
ビタ　205
ビター・チョコレート　208
額　146
額革　854
ひだ襟　339
ひだ飾り　282, 337
ひだの例　83
左ウイング　804
左カーソル　515
左側　384
左側の　740
左腎臓　165
左センター　804
左揃えタブ　514
左チャンネル　502
左肺　161, 163
左肩向屈折あり　544, 547
左肺静脈　162
尾端骨　111, 116
鼻中隔　175
微調整棒　698
櫃　279
尾椎　122, 126, 131, 138, 141, 142
筆記用具　470
ピック　390, 433, 901
ピックアップ　441
ピックアップ・セレクター　441
ピックアップ・トラック　549
ピックガード　441
日付印　531
日付釘　590
日付表示ボタン　496
ピッケル　901
ピッケル・バンド　901
ピッコロ　437, 446
ヒツジ　128
羊革ジャケット　353
羊小屋　182
ピッチ　630, 799
ピッチ・ピン　442
ピッチフォーク・コーム　380
ピッチ・ホイール　450
ピッチ・ボール　558
ピッチャー　794, 795
ピッチャーズ・プレート　795
ピッチャーズ・マウンド　795
ピッチング・ウェッジ　868
ビット　302, 390, 607, 648, 651
ビット　501, 793, 865, 872, 874
ビット・ストップ　873
ビットとドリルの例　306
ビットの例　308
ビット・レーン　872
引っ張りねじ　534
引っ張りリンク　640
引っ張る力　686
ヒップ　887
ヒップ　915
ヒップ・パッド　808
VIP用ラウンジ　718
火壺　256, 259
蹄　124, 127
蹄覆い　853, 857, 858
蹄の例　127
ビデ　264
ビデオカセット　495
ビデオカセット・アダプター　496
ビデオカセット・レコーダー　495
ビデオ・カメラ　496
ビデオ・ゲーム　918
ビデオ・スイッチャー　489, 490
ビデオテープ操作ボタン　496
ビデオ・デジタル端子　477
ビデオ電源ボタン　495
ビデオ・ポート　513, 526
ビデオ・モード　495
ビデオ・ライブラリー　789
ビデオ・リプレー　789
ビデオ・レコーダー　495
ヒト　93
尾灯　554, 571, 575, 576, 578, 640, 775
微動載物台　693

微動調整送りねじ　700
微動ハンドル　693
尾筒部補助装置　755
一重継ぎ　908
一重つなぎ　908
一重結び　908
ピト一管　873
日時計　696
ヒトコブラクダ　129
人差し指　173
等しい　703
等しくない　703
ヒトデの解剖図　95
ヒトデの形態図　95
人の歯列　159
1人掛けシート　594
一人乗りカヌー　838
一人乗りカヤック　839
1人乗りリリュージュ　884
1人用テント　903
ピトン　900
ピトン・ホルダー　901
避難所　543
避難路　543
ビニール断熱材　299
ピニオン　697
ピニオン・ギア　307
泌尿器系　165
泌尿生殖口　109
火の粉止めの衝立　257
鼻背　175
火袋　257
火鉢　412
火花　564
火花キャップ　562
火花隙間　562
脾腹　124
ひばり結び　908
眉斑　115
ヒヒ　139
響き線　448
響き線スイッチ　448
皮膚　168, 172
ビブ　848
尾部　169, 625, 826, 840
被覆　418
腓腹筋　150, 151
被覆材　299
被覆神経　166
被覆破損燃料　666
被覆破損燃料　666
尾部支材　631
尾部支え三脚　623
火蓋　752
ビブ・ネックレス　374
皮膚の表面　172
微粉砕所　646
ピボット　317, 398
ピボット・ボタン　838
飛膜　140
曾孫　784
曾孫息子　784
曾孫娘　784
ヒマラヤ山脈　33
ヒマワリ　80
ヒマワリ油　209
拎道棒　461
ヒメジ　219
日めくりカレンダー　530
日めくり式卓上カレンダー　530
平座金　310
ヒラタケ　183
平土間　431
平鍋　239
平のみ　421
平歯車　686
平縁　404, 405
平筆　397
平干し　347
ピラミッド　402
ピラミッド・スポット　862
ピラミッドの入り口　402
ヒラメ　221
ひらめ筋　150
平目打鏨　315
フィッシング・ベスト　911
平野　310
平屋住宅　419
平ワッシャー　310
ビリオッド　473, 789
ビリヤード　862
ビリヤード・キュー　863
ビリヤード・スポット　862
ビリヤード・テーブル　862
飛梁　410, 411
ビル　610
ヒルト　849
ピル　610
ビルボックス　341
ビルマ語　468
ヒレ肉　214
ピレネー山脈　32
ピロー　458
広場　408
火を通す　238
瓶　379, 685
ピン　275, 376, 791, 865, 867
ピン板　442
ピンキング鋏　454
ピン球　863
ピンク・ペッパー　198
ピンク・ボール　863
ヒンジ　385, 889
ヒンジ・ピン　638
ピンセット　777
ピンチ　901
ヒンディー語　469
ビンディング　840, 888, 889, 891, 892
ビンディング・ペダル　870
ピント合わせリング　478

標識灯　585, 625, 631
標識板　591
病室　780
表紙作り　425
病室ベッド　780
表示灯　238, 239, 240, 241, 288, 290, 294, 465, 848, 859
表示に従い、塩素系漂白剤の使用可　347
表示パネル　476, 496
表示板　261, 730, 731, 793
表示部　529, 613, 699
表示窓　494, 497, 501, 503, 505, 506, 507, 530, 548
表示窓設定ボタン　506
標準的なポーカーの手　914
標準点　891
標準レンズ　478
苗条　77
氷晶雨　64
表示ランプ　494
秒針　696
氷雪気候　61
表層　538
氷堆丘　45
錨頂　610
標的　40, 41, 859, 860, 861, 893
標的探知レーダー　762
表土　78, 647
漂白禁止　347
表皮　172, 797
標本押さえ　693
標本クリップ　693
標本採取室　781
標本採取機室　781
表面遮水壁型ダム　660
表面遮水壁型ダムの断面図　660
表面流去　67
表面流出　67
病理検査室　781
尾翼　625, 676, 759, 898
鼻翼　175
尾翼形状の例　629
比翼式打ち合い　355, 369
比翼式打ち合わせ　355, 369
火除け　257
日除け　556, 567, 575
日除けコード　285
日除けチューブ　285
日除け板　556
日除けロッド　285
ヒヨコ　120
ヒヨコマメ　190
ひら　346
避雷針　663
避雷計　245, 658, 677
平エンド・ピン　285
平泳ぎ　832
平泳ぎのキック　832
平織り　463
平型　401

ヒンドゥー教　736
ピント調節ハンドル　14, 15
ピントつまみ　692
ピント・リング　692
ピント・ルーペ　485
瓶嚢　95
ピンの種類　865

ふ

負　703
ファ　434
ファースト　794
ファースト・アシスタント・カメラマン　428
ファースト・クラス客室　624
ファースト・ダズン　919
ファースト・フード店　715
ファースト・ロー　804
ファイナリスト　789
ファイバー　908
ファイビン　865
ファイブ・ベット　919
ファイヤウォール　523
ファイヤワイヤー・ポート　526
ファイル　524
ファイル・サーバー　523
ファイル・フォーマット　524
ファイル・ボックス　533
ファインダー　14, 15, 476, 477
ファインダー支持脚　15
ファインダー内液晶表示照明ボタン　479
ファイン・データ・エントリー・コントロール　450
ファウル　789
ファウル・ボール　795
ファウル・ライン　794, 865
ファクシミリ　508
ファゴット　437, 446
ファシェット　346
ファスキア　404
ファスナー　353, 369, 453
ファスナー隠し　350
ファスナー式ファイル　532
ファスナー線　455
ファセット　629
ファローピウス管　170, 171
ファン　259, 260, 293, 627, 643
ファンクション・キー　507, 508, 514
ファン内蔵部　382
ファンデーション・スリップ　366
ファン・ヒーター　260
ファン・ブラシ　378
ファン・ベルト　552, 566
ファン・モーター　261
ブイ　833
フィード・チューブ　237, 240
フィードホン　493
フィーブル　849
フィールダー　799
フィールド　799, 806, 809
フィールド・プレーヤー　800
フィールド・ホッケー　800
VHFアンテナ　762
Vカット　348
フィギュア・スキー　840
フィギュア・スケート　881
フィギュア・スケート靴　881
フィギュア・ブレード　881
フィクサチーフ　400
ふいご　445
フィジー　747
フィジー諸島　29
フィッシュ・ナイフ　228
フィッシュ・フォーク　228
フィッシュボーン・ステッチ　459
フィッシュ・ワイヤー　317
フィニッシュ・エリア　891
フィニッシュ・ジャッジ　883
フィニッシュ・ブイ　839
フィニッシュ・ライン　833, 839, 890
Vネック　348, 354, 363
Vネック・カーディガン　354
Vベルト　292
VU計　488, 491
VUメーター　488, 491
フィヨルド　51
フィラー　390
フィラー・キャップ　561, 570
フィラー・プレート　513
フィラメント　274
フィラメント支持線　274
フィリピン　747
フィリピン海溝　50
フィリピン海プレート　43
フィリピン諸島　33
フィルター　238, 246, 258, 290, 390, 675
フィルター・カバー　773
フィルター・バスケット　241
フィルター・ホルダー　241
フィルヒナー棚氷　29
フィルム・ガイド・レール　476
フィルム・ガイド・ローラー　476
フィルム乾燥キャビネット　484
フィルム感度　479
フィルム感度設定ボタン　476
フィルム・スプロケット　476

フィルム・スライド室　733
フィルム先端インジケーター　476
フィルム・ディスク　481
フィルムとデジタル記憶装置　481
フィルム・パック　481
フィルム包装　223
フィルム巻き上げモード・ボタン　476
フィルム巻き戻し軸　476
フィルム巻き戻しボタン　476
フィルム・レコーダー　520
フィルン　55
フィロの生地　205
フィン　260, 759, 836, 840, 841
フィンガー・タブ　859
フィンガーボード　441
フィン・スタビライザー　608
フィンチ　118
フィンランド　744
封　390
風　55, 833
風向旗　893
風向計　58, 59, 677, 834
封口剤　689
風向軸　56
封口物管　689
風向板　260, 261
風向と風速　55
風向を測定する器具　59
風車　676
風車軸　676
封書　390
ブースター・ケーブル　558
ブースター・コード　558
ブースター・シート　281
ブースター用パラシュート　22
風速　55
風速計　58, 59, 677
風袋　56
ブータン　747
風鳥座　10
フーチン　252, 253
フーチング　252, 253
ブーツ　343, 551, 840, 841, 855, 874, 875, 880, 881, 895, 896
ブーツ・ジャック　345
ブーティー　342
フード　14, 256, 289, 333, 353, 368, 382, 550, 570, 721, 841, 857
フード・プロセッサー　237
フード・ミル　230
プードル　130
フートン　280
ブーブー　339
ブーブ　823
フープ・イヤリング　374
ブーブー　339
風防ガラス　574, 577, 607, 624, 626
ブーム　573, 637, 638, 834, 836
ブーム係　429
ブーム・ジャッキ　834
ブーム・シリンダー　637, 638
ブーム・バング　834
プーリー　452, 566, 750
プーリー・ブロック　750
風量調節スイッチ　382
風量調節つまみ　261
風力エネルギー　676
風力エネルギー発電　677
風力計　58, 59, 677
風力タービンと発電　676
風力発電　677
風力を測定する器具　59
プール　246, 664, 675, 862
プレーヌ　339
フェアウェイ　866, 867
フェアリーダー　835
フェアリード　835
フェアリング　24, 574, 891
フェイジョア　197
フェイス・オフ・サークル　878
フェイス・オフ・スポット　878
フェイスプレート　248, 249
フェイス・マスク　800, 808, 879
フェーブル　815, 867
フェーブル　815, 867
フェゴ島　31
フェザー・シャトルコック　817
フェザー・ステッチ　459
フェズ　339
フェットチーネ　206
フェネック　134
フェラッカ船　600
フェリー　608
フェリーポート　596
フェル　849
フェルト　421
フェルト・ペン　397
フェルト・ペン画法　396
フェルト帽　340, 341
フェルトリコ海溝　50
フェルマータ　435
フェルミウム　684
フェンサー　848
フェンシング　848
フェンシング・シューズ　848
フェンス　182, 244, 795, 878
フェンダー　550, 570, 640
フォア・アッパー・トゲルン・スル　603
フォア・アッパー・トップスル　603
フォア・グラ　216

フォアコート 821	復水器冷却水出口 669	仏陀 736	プラスチックの分別 71	フリル・パンツ 368
フォアステー 834	複数分割 740	フット 836, 909	プラスチック・フィルム・コンデンサ 689	プリンセス・シーム 366
フォアステム 838	副操縦士席 626	仏塔 412		プリンセス・ドレス 356
フォアスル 603	副題 471	沸騰水型炉 671	プラスチック・ラミネート・チップボード 300	プリンター 523, 529
フォア・トゲルン・マスト 602	腹大動脈 109, 160, 165	フット・クッション 862		プリンター・テーブル 511
フォア・トップ・マスト 602	腹直筋 150	フット・サポート 851	プラスチック・ラミネート・パーティクル・ボード 300	プリンター電卓 529
フォア・ロイヤル・スル 600, 602	覆幅 409	フットスツール 277		プリント・ウォッシャー 485
フォア・ロイヤル・マスト 602	覆土輪 643	フットストラップ 358, 836, 851	プラスねじ回し 905	プリント・カートリッジ表示ランプ 519
フォア・ロワー・トゲルン・スル 603	腹背動脈 107	フット・フォールト・ジャッジ 821	プラスの電極 672, 673	
	腹板 112	フットボーラー 808	プラス・マイナス 703	プリント回路 689
フォア・ロワー・トップスル 603	副反射鏡 16	フットホールド 901	プラスモデカス 74	プリント回路基盤 689
フォイブル 849	腹部 96, 97, 98, 103, 107, 591	フットボール用のボール 808	フラッグ 804, 890	プリント・スクリーン 515
フォー 207	腹膜 169, 170	フット・ポケット 841	ブラック 472	プリント・スクリーン・キー 515
フォー・オブ・ア・カインド 914	複葉 79	フットレスト 575, 576	ブラック・チョコレート 208	飾り 231
フォー・カード 914	複葉機 628	フットロープ 602	ブラック・ビーン 191	フルーク 610
フォーカス・キー 496	袋 82, 905	物標 40, 41	ブラック・ホール 8	ブルー・チーズ 211
フォーカス・スコープ 485	袋詰め係 181	物品保管室 769	フラッシュ 914	フルーティング 404, 405
フォーカス・モード切り換えボタン 476	袋ナット 311	物理 686	フラッシュ・キューブ 482	フルート 437, 446
	筆 337	筆 470	フラッシュチューブ 482	フルー・パイプ 444
フォーカル・プレーン・シャッター 476, 477	不定根 76		フラッシュ・ブラシ 378	フルー・バンド 871
	フクロネズミ 143	ブドウ 86, 192	フラッシュ・ランプ 482	ブルーベリー 192
フォーク 14, 227, 632, 633, 875, 905	符号変換キー 529	不透水性岩石 651	ブラッチャー 342	ブルー・ライン 879
	ふ 337	ぶどう弾 752	フラット 435, 894	フルーレ 848, 849
フォーク・アーム 632	房縁 337	ブドウの株 86	フラット・スクリーン・モニター 518	フルーレ警告線 848
フォーク支柱 632, 633	フジッリ 206	ブドウの断面図 83		フルーレ用胸当て 848
フォークの例 228	フジマメ 190	ブドウの葉 86, 186	フラット・ステッチ 459	ブルガリア 744
フォーク・ポケット 635	ふ節 115	ブドウの房 86	ブラッド・ソーセージ 216	ブルガリア語 469
フォークランド諸島 31	浮上ファン 605	埠頭ランプ 596	フラット・バック・ブラシ 380	ブルキナファノ 745
フォークリフト 632	浮上用空気取り入れ口 605	浮動肋骨 152	フラップ 348, 387	フル・キャップ 551
4サイクル・エンジン 564	腐食性物質 774	ふところ 911	フラップ・ポケット 348, 352, 360	フルズ・アイ 918
4ストローク・サイクル・エンジン 564	腐植土 78	太矢 750	フラップ油圧ジャッキ 760	ブルゾン 353
	ふ蹠骨 116	布団 280	フラップ・レバー 626	プル・タブ 223, 453
フォースル 603	布陣 803, 804	舟形略帽 340	プラテオサウルス 93	フルテロニ 401
フォー・ドア・セダン 549	婦人科診察室 779	船荷用横梁 607	プラテン 528	ブルドーザー 636, 647
フォーム・クッション 772	婦人靴 343, 716	ブナノキ 88	プラニ語 468	ブルドッグ 130
フォーム・パッド 904	婦人コート 716	ブナの実 193	浮標式地域 616	プルトニウム 684
フォーム・マット 904	婦人スーツ 716	船 41	部品箱 456	ブルトン語 469
フォーム・マットレス 904	婦人手袋 346	船の錨 610	部分集合である 703	ブルネイダルサラーム 747
フォーム・ラバー断熱材 299	婦人セーター 716	譜表 434	部分 6, 7	ブルネイダルサラーム国 747
フォーメ 410	婦人トイレ 724	浮標 456	部分反射鏡 692	プルバード 711
フォール 849	婦人帽 341	扶壁 660	プラネタリウム 10	フル・ハウス 914
フォクスル 605, 609	婦人用アクセサリー 717	扶壁ダム 660	プラネタリウム投影機 10	フルマー小勒馬帯 854
フォーレージ・ブロワー 643	婦人用カジュアル・ウエア 716	踏み板 255, 838, 855, 913	フラミンゴ 119	ブルワーク 602
フォッグ・ホーン 611		踏み木 460	プラム 192	ブレンジ 745
フォッグ・ライト 554, 570	婦人用スポーツウエア 716	踏み木紐 460	プラム・ソース 201	フレア 6
フォッグ・ランプ 554	婦人用寝巻き 716	踏み切り 891	フランカー 804	フレア形管接合工具 314
フォトン 692	付随車 594	踏切 583, 591	フランク 914	フレア継手 269
フォボス 4	付属ノズル 289	踏切あり 545, 547	フランクフルト・ソーセージ 216	フレア・ナット・スパナ 311
フォルクマン管 154	付属品 289, 399, 454, 462, 558, 580	踏み切り姿勢 828	ブランケット断熱材 299	プレイベン 281
フォルト 849		踏切台 891	フランジ 595	プレー 338
フォロー・スルー 864	付属品収納部 289	踏切点 891	フランシウム 684	ブレーカー 260, 884
フォワード 803, 858	付属礼拝堂 410	踏切板 793, 826	フランシス水車 659	ブレーキ 559, 783, 851, 870, 889
フォワード・スウィング 864	蓋 234, 236, 237, 238, 239, 240, 241, 290, 291, 292, 295, 313, 391, 535, 689	踏み木レバー 460	プランジャー 314, 776	
フォンデュ・セット 234		踏み台 321	プランジング・ネックライン 363	ブレーキ回路 552, 559
フォンデュ鍋 234		踏み俵 847	フランス 743	ブレーキ・キャリパー 574
フォンデュ・フォーク 228	ブタ 128	踏み段 321, 417, 676	フランス語 469	ブレーキ・シュー 559
フォントのタイプ 472	舞台 402, 430	踏み段付き椅子 321	フランス式賭けるテーブル 919	ブレーキ・パッド 559
深揚げ鍋 238	舞台芸術 427	踏み面 321, 876	フランス式ベッティング・レイアウト 919	ブレーキ・ブースター 552, 559
浮蓋 655	舞台後方壁 430, 431	踏み輪 750		ブレーキ・ペダル 333, 552, 556, 559, 889
深い揚げ鍋 721	舞台左 430	譜面台 436, 444, 451	フランス式ルーレット盤 919	
浮蓋式貯蔵タンク 655	二重継ぎ 908	譜面立て 436, 451	フランス・パン 204	ブレーキ・ホース 559
深いトレッドのタイヤ 577	二重つなぎ 908	冬 54	フランス窓 415	ブレーキマン 884
深型両手鍋 235	二重舫い結び 908	フタプラクダ 129	プランター 322	ブレーキ・モジュレーター 559
付加価値牌 917	蓋がされた巣房 100	豚肉 215	ブランデー・グラス 225	ブレーキ・ライニング 559
深さ 911	双子座 13	二叉旗 739	プランテーン 196	ブレーキ・ランプ 554
深さ調節装置 308	不活性ガス 692	二股の舌 112	ブリー 211	ブレーキ・リザーバー・タンク 559
不活性ガス 692	吹き口 446, 447	二又フレーム 663	フリー・ガード・ゾーン 877	ブレーキ・レバー 559, 876, 889
吹き込み管 432, 446, 447	吹き出し口 551	2人掛けシート 594	フリーザー・バッグ 222	ブレーキ・レバーとギア・レバー 870
不規則銀河Ⅰ型 9	吹き出し口グリル 260, 382	2人掛けソファー 724	フリーザー容器 240	
不規則銀河Ⅱ型 9	吹き流し 739, 834	2人乗リシート 575	フリーズ 403, 404	ブレーキ・ワイヤー 579
不規則結晶 64	俯仰装置 756	2人乗リボブスレー 884	フリースタイル 843	ブレーキング・ゾーン 891
不規則骨 157	俯仰ハンドル 756	2人乗リリュージュ 884	フリースタイル系スノーボード 887	ブレーキング・トラック 891
吹き出し口 551	負極 689	2人用テント 902	フリースタイル・スキー 890	ブレーク 515
吹き出しロゴグリル 260, 382	負極活物質亜鉛 689	蓋を持ち上げる磁石 240	フリー・スロー・サークル 810	ブレーク・コード 896, 897
吹き流し 739, 834	幅員減少 544, 547	フダンソウ 185	フリー・スロー・ライン 811, 814	ブレーズ 339
俯仰装置 756	複郭 409	緑 385, 729	フリー・ゾーン 812, 813	ブレード 274, 302, 636, 639, 659, 815, 838, 841, 849, 878, 880, 881, 901, 911
俯仰ハンドル 756	複眼 96, 98, 99	プチインゲン 191	フリー棚 291	
負極 689	副鏡 15, 17	プチ・オニオン 184	プリーチ 446	
負極活物質亜鉛 689	副刑務所長室 726	縁飾り 282, 337	プリーチ・ガード 446	ブレード 238, 381, 482, 851
幅員減少 544, 547	腹甲 113	縁金具 386	ブリーチズ 338	ブレード吊り上げ装置 639
複郭 409	腹腔 169, 170	縁刈り機 332	プリーツ 351	ブレード・リフト・シリンダー 636, 639
複眼 96, 98, 99	複合弓 859, 913	縁甲板張り 254	プリーツの例 283, 357	
副鏡 15, 17	複合砂丘 52	縁付きスープ皿 226	ブリーフ 351	ブレード・ローテーション・シリンダー 639
副刑務所長室 726	複合仙稚 116	縁取り 340	ブリーフケース 386	
腹甲 113	腹腔動脈 161, 165	縁取り花壇 244	フリーホイール 580	ブレーヌ 749
腹腔 169, 170	伏在神経 166	婦長室 779	ブリオレット・カット 375	フレーム 256, 280, 303, 312, 321, 327, 352, 385, 386, 389, 423, 449, 575, 612, 632, 633, 638, 639, 641, 642, 672, 673, 676, 688, 700, 776, 796, 816, 822, 823, 824, 870, 895, 902
複合弓 859, 913	副座壇 737	縁縁 793	ブリガティン 601	
複合砂丘 52	復座管先端部 756	ふつうのさいころ 914	振れ子 436, 697	
複合仙稚 116	復座管 756	普通煉瓦 298	振香炉 737	
腹腔動脈 161, 165	伏射 893	フッカー 804	振れ子式箱型大時計 697	
伏在神経 166	副尺 612, 700	仏教 736	振れ子時計の仕組み 697	
副座壇 737	副尺付きノギス 700	仏像の例 359	ブリザー・バルブ 655	
復座管先端部 756	副尺目盛り 700	フック 249, 284, 313, 316, 382, 453, 456, 457, 573, 611, 634, 698, 699, 776, 861, 862	振竿 697	
復座管 756	輻射式暖房器 260		プリズム双眼鏡 692	フレーム・パッド 823
伏射 893	伏射姿勢 861		プラウ・アンカー 610	プレーヤー 822, 827, 920
副尺 612, 700	輻射層 6	フック・エンド 535	ブラウザー 524	プレーヤー3 858
副尺付きノギス 700	副主将 877	フック・キーパー 909	ブラウス・スリーブ 361	プレーヤー2 858
副尺目盛り 700	服飾用品 716	フック付きはしご 321	ブラウスの例 359	プレーヤーのハンディキャップ 858
輻射式暖房器 260	副署長室 768	ブックマッチ 391	ブラウン管 494	プレーヤー4 858
伏射姿勢 861	副審 807, 810, 812, 813, 844, 845, 846, 847, 848	物質 680	プラグ 306, 408, 502, 613	プレーヤー用スケート靴 880
輻射層 6		物質の状態 680	プラグ・アダプター 274, 383	プレーヤー用スティック 880
副主将 877	副腎 165	物質量の単位 702	プラグ継ぎ手 269	プレーヤー1 858
服飾用品 716	腹神経索 107	プッシャー 230, 237, 240	プラグ・ヒューズ 272	プレーリー 38
副署長室 768	復水器 668, 674	プッシュアップ・ブラジャー 367	ブラケット 285, 287, 473	フレール式草刈り機 642
副審 807, 810, 812, 813, 844, 845, 846, 847, 848	復水器逆洗水入り口 669	プッシュ・ボタン 248, 391, 506, 507	ブラケット灯 287	フレキシブル・スカート 605
	復水器逆洗水出口 669	プッシュ・ボタン電話機 507	ブラシ 289, 295, 384, 688	ブレザー 358
副腎 165	復水器冷却水入り口 669	プッシュ・リム 783	ブラシラー 601	プレジデント・ジュリー 900
腹神経索 107	復水器冷却水出口 669	弗素 683	ブラジャー 367	プレス 425
復水器 668, 674			ブラジル 742	プレス機 425
			プラス 302, 703	フレスコ画 406
			＋端子 687, 689	プレストレスト・コンクリート 298
			浮力チューブ 611	プレス・チーズ 211
			浮力調節具 841	プレス 851
			ブリリアント・カットのカット面 374	プレス・ボタン 453
			ブリリアント・フル・カット 375	

天文学 > 2-25;　地球 > 26-71;　植物 > 72-89;　動物 > 90-143;　人間 > 144-177;　食べ物と台所 > 178-241;　家屋 > 242-295;　日曜大工・園芸 > 296-333;　衣服 > 334-371; 装身具類と日用品 > 372-391;　芸術と建築 > 392-465;　情報伝達とオフィス・オートメーション > 466-535;　交通と機械 > 536-643;　エネルギー > 644-677;　科学 > 678-705; 社会 > 706-785;　スポーツとゲーム > 786-920

ブレスレット 376
ブレッサー 390
フレット 440, 441
プラテン・ノブ 528
プレナム 258
フレネル・レンズ 614
プレビューモニター 489, 491
プレビュー用モニター 489, 491
ブレンダー 232, 236
フレンチ・カット 375
フレンチ・カフス 361
フレンチ・ノット・ステッチ 459
フレンチ・プレス 241
フレンチ・ホルン 437, 447
風呂 724
フロア・スタンド 286
フロア・タム 448
フロア・マット 558
フロア・ランプ 286
ブロウ・ブラシとアイ・ラッシュ・コーム 378
フローター 827
ブローチ 376
フローティング・スリーブ 337
フローティング・ヘッド 383
フロート 628
フロート水上機 628
ブロードスウォード 751
ブロード・リーチ 833
ブロー・パイプ 432
ブロー・ランプ 314, 319
フログ 590
プログラマブル・ボタン 516
プログラム式サーモスタット 261
プログラム・セレクター 450
プログラム・ボタン 261
プロコンスル 93
プロシウット 216
プロジェクター 518
プロジェクター・ステージ 535
プロジェクター・ヘッド 535
プロセッサー 513
プロダクション・マネージャー室 509
ブロッキング・グローブ 800
フロッグ 353, 439, 590
ブロック 632, 791, 813
ブロック・コート 338
ブロック・ハンマー 315
浮肋骨 138
ブロッコリ 187
ブロッコリカブ 187
ブロッター 520
フロッピー・イジェクト・ボタン 513
フロッピー・ディスク 521
フロッピー・ディスク・イジェクト・ボタン 513
フロッピー・ディスク・ドライブ 513
フロッピー・ドライブ 513
プロテクション・エリア 843
プロテクター 800
プロテスタンティズム 736
プロデューサー 429, 489, 490
プロトアクチニウム 684
プロトニューロン 168
プロナオス 403
プロパン・ガス・ボンベ 567
プロパン器具またはブタン器具 903
プロペラ 606, 608, 609, 762, 763
プロペラ軸 609, 762
プロペラ・シャフト 609, 762
プロペラ・ダクト 605
プロミネンス 6
プロムナード・デッキ 608
プロメネ 684
フロント・ウォール 818, 819
フロント・エンド・ローダー 637
フロント・カバー 519
フロントガラス 550, 570, 574, 577, 876
フロント・グリル 261
フロントコート 818
フロント・コンプレッション・ベルト 906
フロント・スポイラー 550
フロント・ディレーラー 578, 580
フロント・デスク 724
フロント・ノブ 307
フロント板 248, 249
フロント・ビーム 698
フロント・ビンディング 840
フロント・フェンダー 574
フロント・ロー 804
分 704
吻 121
分界溝 176
分解者 67
文化機関 525
噴火中の火山 44
分割図形の例 740
分岐 687
分岐管 767, 776
分岐管クリップ 776
分岐管の例 270
噴気孔 44, 136
分岐帯 687
分岐ダクト 258
分光計 694
分光放射計 60
粉砕機 71
分子 680
分枝 86

噴射式除雪車 573
噴射装置 573
噴射・爆発 565
ベース調節つまみ 441
噴射瓶 685
噴出性の火山 44
文書コンパートメント 527
分針 696, 697
分水槽 263
分数 703
分析用天秤 699
粉糖 209
分銅 698
分度器 701
糞尿 103
文房具 528, 717
文房具キャビネット 510
粉末辛子 200
粉末マスタード 200
分離器 668
分離器 606
分流 48
分留器 656
分裂生成物 681
分裂生成物放射性原子核 681
分路 687

へ

ベア 741
ベア 881
ヘア・カーラー 380
ヘアカラー 379
ヘア・クリップ 380
ヘア・コンディショナー 379
ヘア・シェイブ・カット 375
ヘア・スタイリスト 428
ヘア・ドライヤー 382
ヘアピン 380
ヘアブラシ 380
ベア・ボウ 859
ベアリング・パッド 667
塀 795
平凹レンズ 691
兵舎 748
平均位置 690
平均台 824, 826
平行移動型境界 43
平行移動型プレート境界 43
平行ガイド 304, 305
平行ガイド・ヘッド 305
平行ガイド溝 305
平行ガイド目盛り 305
平行ガイド・ロック 305
平衡機 756
平行四辺形 705
平衡錘 634
平行である 704
平行でない 704
平行棒 825
平行横木 852, 853
平行六面体 705
米国居住モジュール 21
米国実験モジュール 21
ベイサー 857
閉鎖機 756
閉鎖機操作桿 756
閉鎖孔 122
閉鎖神経 166
兵舎 409
平床式トレーラー 571
平床トレーラー 571
閉塞前線 56
平体 472
北家 917
平頂山山 49
ベイトキャスティング・リール 910
平凸レンズ 691
餅盤 17
平版印刷 420
平版印刷方式 423
平板型太陽熱器 672
平板型太陽集熱器 672
ベイ・フィラー・パネル 513
平方根 703
平方根キー 529
米麺 217
米面 472
平面鏡 17
平面状の画線 420
平面図 411
平面図法 36
平野 38, 48
ベイリー橋 542
ベイル 799, 909
ベイル 17
並列電気回路 687
ペイロード 24, 25
ペイロード・アダプター 24
ペイロード・モジュール 40
ペインティング・ナイフ 397
ベークライト弾丸 757
ベーグル 204
ページ・アップ 515
ページ・アップ・キー 527
ページ送りボタン 527
ページ・ダウン 515
ページ・ダウン・キー 515
ページめくりボタン 527
ページ戻しボタン 527
ベージャー 505
ベース 305, 405, 440, 448, 516, 517, 531, 740, 791

ベース 862
ベース・ギター 441
ベース・ピックアップ 441
ベース・プレート 500, 889
ベースライン 821
ヘーゼルナッツ 193
ペーパー・ガイド 508, 519
ペーパー・シュレッダー 535
ペーパー・ナイフ 531
ペーパー・ベイル 528
ペーパー・ベイル・リリース・レバー 528
ペーパー・リリース・レバー 528
ベーリング海 28
ベーリング海峡 30
へら 233, 421
へら 456
へら形 79
ヘラクレス座 13
ヘラコウモリ 141
ヘラジカ 129
ベラム馬衛 854
ベラルーシ 744
縁 285
ヘリ 322
ベリーズ 742
ベリー・タンク 631
ヘリウム 684
ヘリウム気蓄器 25
ヘリカル状バイメタル 695
ペリカン 119
ベリクレル 702
ベゴニア 80
触先の装飾 600
ベスト 338, 348, 359, 911
ベゼル 376
ベゼル・ファセット 374
ペソ 728
ペソ 146, 148
ペダル 440, 444, 448, 578, 580, 851, 870
ペダル鍵盤 444
ペダル・プッシャー・パンツ 358
ペダル・レール 442
ベタンク 864
ベタンク・ボール 864
ペちまスポンジ 379
ヘチマカボチャ 189
ベッカーリ 128
ヘッジ・トリマー 331
ヘッダー 643
ヘッド 301, 308, 311, 383, 384, 390, 440, 441, 448, 449, 458, 516, 800, 822, 858, 867, 901, 909, 816
ベッド 280, 823
ヘッド・アーム 521
ヘッド・アーム駆動用モーター 521
ヘッド・ガード 632
ヘッド・カバー 869
ヘッドギア 842, 878
ヘッドキャップ 426
ヘッド・クッション 862
ヘッド・シェル 500
ペット・ショップ 714
ヘッドセット 506
ヘッド・チューブ 579
ベッドとマット 904
ベッドとマットレス 904
ヘッド・パイプ 579
ヘッドバンド 502, 504, 772, 773
ヘッドピン 865
ペット・フードとペット用品 181
ヘッド・プレート 421, 423
ヘッド・ボックス 285
ヘッド・ポール 857
ヘッドホン 502, 504
ヘッドホン端子 450, 451, 497, 504
ヘッドホン・プラグ 504
ヘッドライト 333, 550, 554, 570, 574, 576, 585, 586, 640, 758, 876
ヘッドライト・方向指示レバー 556
ヘッド・ランプ 286, 780
ヘッド・レール 285
ヘッドレスト 555
ペティコート 366
ペディメント 403, 405
ベテラン向け斜面 886
ペトリ皿 685
ヘドル 460, 461
ベトナム 747
ベトナム語 468
ペナルティ・アーク 802
ペナルティ・エリア 802
ペナルティ・エリア・ライン 802
ペナルティ・キック・マーク 802
ペナルティ・ボックス 879
ペナルティ・ボックス係員 879
ペナルティ・マーク 814
ペナント 745
ペナント 739
紅殻チョーク 423
ベニシングタケ 76
ベニバナインゲン 191
ベニヤ板 300
ベニヤ合板 300
ベネシエラ 742
ベネチアン・ブラインド 285
ベネラ 19
ペパローニ 216
ヘビ 112
ベビー・グランド 443
ベビーグロウ 368

ベビー・サークル 281
ベビー・チェア 281
ベビー・デューティー・ブーツ 342
ベビー・ドール 364
ベビーノ 197
ベビー・フード・タオル 368
ベビー服 368, 717
ベビー・ベッド 281
蛇座 11, 13
蛇遣い座 11, 13
ヘブライ語 468
ヘブロス 336
ベベル 776
ベベル・ギア 686
ベポカボチャ 188
部屋番号 724
へら 233, 421
へら 456
へら形 79
ヘ音記号 434
ヘラクレス座 13
ヘラコウモリ 141
ヘラジカ 129
ベラム馬衛 854
ベラルーシ 744
縁 285
ヘリ 322
ベリーズ 742
ベリー・タンク 631
ヘリウム 684
ヘリウム気蓄器 25
ヘリオスタット群 674
ヘリカル状バイメタル 695
ペリカン 119
ヘリコプター 631, 762
ヘリコプター格納庫 762
ヘリコプター甲板 762
ヘリコプターの例 631
ベリスコープ 758
ヘリポート 652
ベリリウム 682
ヘリンボーン・ステッチ 459
ベル 446, 447
ベルー 742
ベルー・チリ海溝 50
ベルオキシソーム 94
ベルガモット 194
ベルギー 743
ベルクシュルント 46
ベルサイユ寄せ木張り 254
ベルジェール 276
ペルシャ語 469
ペルシャ・ネコ 132
ペルシャ湾 33
ペルセウス座 12
ベルソー 422
ヘルツ 702
ベルト 313, 350, 352, 561, 611
ベルト・カバー 307
ベルト・クリップ 505
ベルト通し 350, 352
ベルト・ドライブ 605
ベルト・扉 416
ベルト・ループ 905
ベルト・ローダー 646, 647
ベルト・ローダー車 623
ベルトン水車 659
ベルの留め金 446
ベルベット・チョーカー 374
ベルベル語体 468
ベル・ボトム 358
ヘルマス 676
ヘルメット 20, 748, 749, 765, 772, 798, 800, 808, 856, 858, 870, 871, 875, 878, 882, 887, 888, 891, 894, 895, 896, 897, 901
ヘルメット接続リング 20
ヘルメット・ランプ 901
ベル屋根 415
ベルリーヌ 355
ベレー帽 341
べろ 342, 370, 386, 881, 889
ペン 43
変圧器 287, 658, 663, 668, 674
変位 690
ベンガル湾 33
変換器 613
便器 264, 265
変換器尾翼 676
変記号 435
返却ワゴン 733
ペンギン 119
偏光フィルター 478
弁護士補佐 728
弁護人席 728
便座 264, 265
便座カバー 265
ペン先 470
弁座軸 265
弁座レンチ 314
便所 406
鞭状器 104
ペンシル・プリーツ 283
変成岩 42
弁足 117
変速機 563
変速装置 292
変速てこ 649
変速レバー 552, 575, 576, 577, 579, 580
弁台座軸 265
弁台座レンチ 314
ペンタプリズム 477

ペンダント 286, 374
ベンチ 277, 593, 715, 794, 851
ベンチ・シート 555
ベンチ・スクリュー 401
ベンチュリ管 757
ベンチュリ管固定レバー 757
ベンチ・リブ 860
変電所 664
ベンド 385, 860, 861
扁桃 174
扁平骨 157
扁平細胞 95
ペン・ホルダー 386
ペンホルダー・グリップ 815
ヘンリー8世 736

ほ

帆 603, 676, 836
穂 302
ボア 114
ボアン・ダレ 849
ホイール 320, 323, 516, 560, 570, 753, 859, 913, 919
ホイール・カバー 551
ホイール・キャップ 551
ホイール・シリンダー 559
ホイール・トラクター 637
ホイール・マウス 516
ホイール・ローダー 637
ボイジャー 19
ホイスト 739
ホイスト・ロープ 417
ホイッパー 232
ホイッピング 868
ホイップ・クリーム 210
ホイヘンス 19
ボイラー 259, 262, 266, 674
ポインター 261, 698, 699
ポイント 822, 849, 859, 880, 915, 918
ポイント・ガード 811
ポイント部 590
ポイント・ワイヤー 590
砲 758
房 407
棒 667, 686
方位線 907
方位微調整ナット 58
方位標識 616
棒渦巻き銀河 9
望遠鏡 17, 612, 701, 859
望遠鏡座 10
望遠鏡土台 17
望遠レンズ 478
鳳凰座 10
砲架 753, 756
防火扉 416
防火帽 765
防火幕 430
ボウ・カラー 362
砲丸 793
砲丸投げ 790
箒 257, 295
防具 808
棒グラフ型ピーク・メーター 488
方形骨 112
方形屋根 415
奉献物 737
防乾ミラー 556
砲口 753, 756
縫合 84, 105
膀胱 109, 110, 113, 165, 169, 170
方向キー 918
縫工筋 150
膀胱子宮窩 170
方向指示計 557
方向指示灯 554, 571, 576
縫合線 84
方向舵 23, 605, 606, 608, 625, 759, 760, 898
方向舵尾翼 676
方向舵ペダル 898
砲口凸縁 753
砲口凸状剥形 753
砲口凸状装飾剥形 753
方向ボタン 918
防護カップ 808, 880
防護革 853
報告書作成室 768
防護装備 318
防護板 875
防護服 875
防護ヘルメット 575, 580
防護眼鏡 870, 875
防災教育担当官室 764
胞子 76
砲台 753
帽子 340, 770
蜂児室 100
帽子スタンド 510
胞子嚢群 76
帽子のバンド 340
放射 681
放射口 170
放射管 95
放射計 95
放射状の糸 103

天文学 > 2-25; 地球 > 26-71; 植物 >72-89; 動物 > 90-143; 人間 > 144-177; 食べ物と台所 > 178-241; 家屋 > 242-295; 日曜大工・園芸 > 296-333; 衣服 > 334-371;
装身具類と日用品 > 372-391; 芸術と建築 > 392-465; 情報伝達とオフィス・オートメーション > 466-535; 交通と機械 > 536-643; エネルギー > 644-677; 科学 > 678-705;
社会 > 706-785; スポーツとゲーム > 786-920

放射水管 95	ボートと船の例 604	補助傘 896	ホムス 200	マイクロホン 488, 492, 496, 505, 506, 508, 516, 517, 527, 898
放射性同位体熱電発電機 18	ボート・ネック 363	補助水管 265	ボムモウ 849	マイクロホン・アーム 490
放射性廃棄物 70	ボートの部分名称 838	補助タンク 571	ホモ牛乳 210	マイクロホン・ブーム 492
放射性物質 774	ボート・フック 611	補助暖房 260	ホモ・サピエンス 93	マイクロホン端子 505
放射層 6	ホーバン式要塞 409	補助テーブル 452	火屋 903	マイクロホン・ブーム・スタンド 492
放射暖房器 260	ホー・フォーク 326	補助電源装置 520, 523	ポラロイド・カメラ 480	マイクロメーター 700
放射能の単位 702	ポーフォート海 30	補助投影機 10	濠 408, 409	マイクロメーター調節ねじ 701
放射リブ 410	頬紅 378	補助バッテリー 563	掘り起こし用熊手 326	マイクロメーターねじ 612, 700
防臭装置 270	ホーボー・バッグ 388	補助パラシュート 896	掘り管 651	マイスネル小体 172
防臭トラップ 270	ホーム 515	補助ハンドル 306, 307, 309, 331	掘り下がり 650	埋設式プール 246
防臭弁 262	ホーム・キー 515	補助目盛り 698	ボリビア 742	マイター・ゲージ 305
砲手用照準器 758	ホーム・シアター 493	補助翼 624, 898	ボリューム・コントローラー 450	マイター・ゲージ移動溝 305
堡障 409	ホームストレッチ 856	補助輪 595	ボリューム調節つまみ 441	マイター・ゲート収納部 597
棒状弾 752	ホーム・プレート 795	補水管 265	ボルガ川 32	マイター・スケール 303, 304
紡織 460	ホーム屋根 583	歩数計 700	ホルスター 770	マイター・ボックス 303
宝飾店 714	ポーランド 744	ポスター 427	ホルダー 685	マイター・ラッチ 303, 304
宝飾品 374	ポーランド語 469	ポスト 453, 460, 474, 812, 817, 827	ボルト 248, 310, 311, 312, 702	マイター・ロック・ハンドル 304
砲身 753, 756, 757	ポーリウム 683	ポスト・バインダー 532	ボルドー・グラス 225	巻いている若葉 76
防塵カップ 773	ポーリング場 714	ボスニア・ヘルツェゴビナ 744	ポルトガル 743	マイトネリウム 683
防塵マスク 773	ホール 608, 866, 867	ポスニア湾 32	ポルトガル語 469	マイナス 302, 703
防塵マスク着用 774	ボール 227, 248, 453, 516, 823, 858, 864, 865, 920	補正線 455	ホルミウム 684	一定値 687, 689
法人窓口 731	ポール 284, 602, 792, 812, 817	墓石地形 47	ホレー 820	マイナス端子 562
防水カバー 368	ボール紙 400	母線 658	ボレロ 358	マイナスの電極 672, 673
放水銃 766	ボール式水栓 268	細革 342	ボロ 858	枚葉 426
放水庭 657, 658, 661	ボール・タップ弁 265	保存修復作業室 395	歩廊 411	マウスパイプ 447
放水ノズル 766	ボール・ナット 410	ホタテガイ 217	ホロ・カラー 363	マウス・パッド 516
放水路 658	ボール・ペル 472	ほた山 647, 648	ホロ・シャツ 354, 359, 822	マウスピース 446, 447, 451, 808, 841, 843
宝石のカット 375	ボール・パーソン 820	ホタルジャコ 220	ホロ・ドレス 356	マウスピース・レシーバー 447
ホウ素 682	ボール盤 307	ボタン 236, 274, 349, 354, 398, 432, 753	ホロニウム 682	マウス・ボート 513, 518
包装 222	ボール・フロート弁 265	ボタン穴 350	ホロ・プリズム 692	マウンテン・スポーツ 900
包帯 777	ボール・ベアリング 470, 677	ボタン・ストラップ 369	ボロ・ポニー 858	マウンテン・バイキング 870
帽体 575	ボール・ペン 470	ボタンダウン・カラー 349	ホロホロチョウ 120, 212	マウンテン・バイク 581
棒高跳び 790, 792	ボール・ポジション 872	ボタン付き前開き 354, 349	ホワイエ 431	マウンテン・ロッジ 886
棒高跳びの選手 792	ボール・マウント 558	ボタン留め 350	ホワイティング 221	マウンド 795
砲弾 752, 753	ボール・ライト 287	ボタンホール 352	ホワイト・チョコレート 208	前足 143
砲弾詰め材 753	ボール・リターン 865	墓地 39, 711	花牌 917	前髪 124
包丁 229	ホーン 556	本影 6, 7	ボワロン 239	前逆さ飛び・1回捻り 829
膨張室 695	ポーン 916	北海 28, 32	帆を下ろす 833	前逆さ飛び込み 828
膨張タンク 259, 675	保温板 241	北極 35	帆を下げる 833	前立て 350, 351, 368, 748
傍聴人 728	ホーン・ナイフ 229	北極海 28	本位記号 435	前宙返り1回・1回捻り 829
包丁の例 229	ホーン・ボタン 576	北極星 13	本影 6, 7	前宙返り3回半・抱え型 829
方杖橋 541	ホーン岬 31	ホック 353, 881	ボンゴ 449	前爪 901
法廷 728	捕獲 916	ホッキョクグマ 135	本締めボルト 248, 249	前ディレーラー 578, 580
放電室 666	ほかの指に対置できる親指 139	北極圏 28, 35, 36	本尺目盛り 700	前飛び込み 828
砲塔 758, 762	保管庫 394	北極星 13	ホンジュラス 742	前の垂れ 349
防毒マスク 773	保管用家具 510	ホック 353, 881	本初子午線 36	前肢 341, 772
防毒マスク着用 774	ボギー台車 585	ボックス 792	本線 539, 583	前フォーク 579
放熱器 552, 561, 586	ボギー台車と線路 595	ボックス・スプリング 280	本底 342, 371	前舞台 430
放熱器格子 570	補機駆動歯車装置 627	ボックス席 431, 720	本体 288, 306, 382, 442, 446, 893	前縁 625
放熱パネル 23	歩脚 103	ボックス・バッグ 388	ポンチョ 355	前ブレーキ 579
放熱板 860, 912	補給口 655	ボックス・パレット 632	ポンツーン 542, 652	前ブレーキ・レバー 576
奉納物 737	補給紙 512	ホッケー 788, 800	ボンド 728	前ホーク 870
奉納絵馬 737	補強材 676	ホッケー・シューズ 801	本通り 711	前ポケット 350, 387
防波堤 660	補強壁 738	ホッケー・ボール 800	ボンネット 268, 550, 570	前身 348, 349, 352
防犯用鉄格子 730	ボクサー 842	木剣 846	本の背 425	前身頃 348, 349, 352
包皮 169	ボクサー・ショーツ 371	ホチキス 534	ホンビノスガイ 217	マオリ語 469
砲尾環 753	墨汁嚢 106	ホット・シュー接点 476	ポンピング・ステーション 654	マカク 139
砲尾取っ手 753	ボクシング 842	ホット・バス・バー 272	ポンプ 246, 292, 294, 320, 670, 671, 674, 903	マガジン 754, 755
砲尾把手 753	ボクシング・グローブ 843	ホット・プレート 239, 721	ポンプ座 11	マカダミア・ナッツ 193
砲尾輪帯 753	北西 37, 616	ポットホール 47	ポンプ施設 654	曲がり 911
暴風雨帽 341	牧草地 182	ホッパー 573, 643	ポンプ室 606	曲がり脚 276
放射線型砂丘 52	蹼足 117	ホッパー車 588	ポンプ車 766	マカロニ 401
放射線状砂丘 52	火口 234, 290	ポッピング・クリース 799	本部席 879	マキ 66
ホウ素 219	火口格子 290	ポップ・アップ・テント 903	ポンプで水を再び蒸気発生器へ送る 665	巻き上げ機 417
泡沫器 268	北東 37	ポツワナ 746	ポンプ・ノブ 903	巻き上げ機室 417
宝物殿 403	北北東 37	ボディ 423, 440, 441, 442, 446, 454, 562, 876, 884, 909	ポンプ番号 548	巻き上げ式ブラインド 285
棒やすり 229	北北西 37	ボディー・カバー 910	ポンプ・モーター 263	巻き上げシリンダー 642
苞葉 84	捕鯨ボート 601	ボディー・ケア 379	ポンプ・モーター・ユニット 559	巻き上げ装置 285, 696, 697
ボウラー 799, 865	帆桁 602	ボディー・クリース 799	本丸 408	巻き上げ塔 649, 650
ボウリング 865	ポケット 313, 386, 862, 865, 869	ボディー・シャツ 359	本結び 908	巻き上げハンドル 460
ボウリング・クリース 799	ポケット・カメラ 480	ボディー・スーツ 366	ポンメル 849	巻き上げ用ロープ 634
ボウリング・ボール 865	ポケット・クリップ 470	ボディー・パッド 800	本屋 714	巻き上げロープ 321
ボウル 232, 236, 390, 638	ポケット・コンピューター 527	ボディー・フラップ 23	本塁 795	巻き貝 105
ホウレンソウ 187	ポケット・チーフ 348	ボディー・サイド・モールディング 551	ボンレベック 211	巻き貝の形態図 105
ホウレンソウのタリアテッレ 206	ポケットの例 360	ホテル 710, 724, 886, 915		巻き紙 390
ホエール・ボート 601	ポケット・ビリヤード 862	ホテルの客室 724	**ま**	巻き尺 313, 454
頬 115, 148	ポケット・ベル 505	ホテル予約カウンター 620		巻きスカート 357
ほお 130	保険業務部門 730	ホテル予約デスク 620	マーカー 470, 864, 865, 883	巻き綱 688
ボー 340	歩行器 782	歩道 245, 712	マーカー・ペン 397	薪投入扉 256
ポーカー・ダイス 914	歩行距離 700	歩道橋 408, 583, 593	マーカー・ライト 570, 571	巻線器 848
頬革 854	歩行姿勢のライオン 741	ボトム 840	マーカー・ランプ 570, 571	巻き取りスプール 476
頬革鋼 854	歩行者信号 712	ボトム・ハイ・ハット 448	マーガリン 209	巻き取りリール 499
ホーク 870	歩行者通行止め 545, 546	ボトム・ポケット 862	マーキーズ・カット 375	巻きねじ 436
ポーク・ゾーン 862	歩行者用押しボタン 712	ボトム・リング 659	マーク 855	薪燃料 256
ポーク・ライン 862	歩行補助具 782	ボトム・レール 285	マーシャル諸島 747	薪載台 257
ポーク・ライン・スポット 862	矛形 79	ボトル 579, 685, 906	麻雀 917	薪箱 256
ポーズ 289, 319, 767	保護ガラス 494, 878	ボトル・カート 319	マージン設定キー 528	薪運び台 257
ポーズ 515	保護キャップ 692	ボトル・ケージ 579	マージン・リリース 528	巻きひげ 86
ホース掛け 764	保護具着用の表示 774	ほどき等しい 703	マーズ・オデッセイ 19	巻き結び 908
ホース乾燥機 764	保護層 501	ボニアード 751	マーモセット 139	幕 430, 431
ホオズキ 192	帆骨 676	帆布 676, 834	マーモット 123	まぐさ 247, 252, 256, 411
ホース・ノズル 328	保護板 918	骨 391	マールスティック 399	まぐさ運搬車 642
ホース・ブレーキ・キー 515	保護帽 772	骨受け 391	麻雀 917	まぐさ台 642
ホース・リール 329	保護帽着用 774	骨切り包丁 229	マグネシウム 682	マグネット 534
ホーゼル 868	保護マット 883, 883	骨の種類 157	マイク 488, 492, 496, 505, 506, 508, 516, 517, 527, 770, 771	幕壁 408
ポーター 340	保護眼鏡 861	炎 652, 857	マイク係 429	マグマ 44, 49
ポー・タイ 349	保護眼鏡着用 774	炎調整つまみ 391	マイク端子 505	マグマ溜り 44, 646
ポータブル音響装置 503	帆座 11	帆の例 601	マイク付きヘッドホン 506	幕面 404
ポータブルCDプレーヤー 503	穂先 302, 307, 793	ホバークラフト 605	マイク・ブーム 492	枕 280, 555
ポータブルCDラジカセ 504	星 8, 916	帆柱 834, 836	マイク・ブーム・スタンド 492	枕カバー 280
ポータブル・シャワー・ヘッド 264	干し草置き場 182	帆柱と索具 602	マイクロ・アーム 490	枕木 591
ポータブル・デジタル・オーディオ・プレーヤー 503	干し草小屋 182	歩幅設定 700	マイクロウェーブ送信機 489	枕ばね 594
ポータブル・ラジオ 503	干し草用熊手 326	ホピー・ピン 380	マイクロ・コンパクト・カー 549	枕元ランプ 724
ポータブル・ラジカセ 504	ホシザメ 218	ボビン 452, 453, 458	マイクロ波 690	マクロ・レンズ 478
ポーチ 245, 411, 738	ポジション 803, 804, 811, 814	ボビン・ケース 452	マイクロバス 569	鬣 847
ポーチ・ドーム 738	ポジション・マーク 440, 441	ボビン巻き機 462	マイクロ波中継局 524	マケドニア旧ユーゴースラビア共和国 744
ボード 836, 878, 917	星印 473	ボビン・ケース 458	マイクロフィルム室 732	孫 784
ボート掛け 602	捕手 794, 795, 796	ポプラ 88	マイクロフィルム・リーダー 732	孫息子 784
ボート・グラス 225	補助映像スイッチャー 491	歩兵 916		
ボート・レース 915	補助脚 567			
ボード断熱材 299	補助基部 538			
ボード吊り柱 602	補助ハンドル 571			
ボード・テープ 894	補助コンセント 290			

天文学 > 2-25; 地球 > 26-71; 植物 > 72-89; 動物 > 90-143; 人間 > 144-177; 食べ物と台所 > 178-241; 家屋 > 242-295; 日曜大工・園芸 > 296-333; 衣服 > 334-371; 装身具類と日用品 > 372-391; 芸術と建築 > 392-465; 情報伝達とオフィス・オートメーション > 466-535; 交通と機械 > 536-643; エネルギー > 644-677; 科学 > 678-705; 社会 > 706-785; スポーツとゲーム > 786-920

孫娘 784	丸頭 302	水瓶座 10	味蕾 176	メイン・ロワー・トップスル 603	
マコモ 203	丸頭ワンウェイ 302	水着 371, 716	ミランダ 5	雌牛 128	
マザーボード 513	丸エンド・ピン 285	水切り 231	ミルク 210	メーキャップ係 428	
鉞 330	丸括弧 473	水切り用ざる 231	ミルク・カップ 223	メーソンリー・ドリル 306	
摩擦ストリップ 318	丸木舟 599	水切り用スプーン 233	ミルク・チョコレート 208	メーター 702	
摩擦防止綱 560, 561	丸鋸 401	ミズグモ 102	民間放送ネットワーク 486	メープル・シロップ 209	
摩擦防止パッド 889	丸釘 301	水気を切る 231	ミンク 134	メカジキ 219	
マジック・テープ 368	マルコーニ・カッター 601	水差し 226	民族楽器 432	メカニカル・マウス 516	
マス 221	丸座 248	水・蒸気混合物 646	ミント 202	メカニック 873	
麻酔回復室 780	丸皿頭 302	水タンク 241, 586, 628, 906		眼鏡 385, 861	
麻酔室 780	丸底フラスコ 685	水鳥 117	**む**	メガネウラ 92	
マスカラ・ブラシ 378	マルタ 744	水取り入れ口 268		眼鏡ケース 387	
マスク 796, 798, 800, 841, 848	丸太 847	水抜き栓 270	ムールガイ 217	眼鏡スパナ 311	
マスクメロン 195	丸太の断面図 300	水抜きホース 292	無蓋車 588	眼鏡店 715	
マスター・キャリアー 284	マルチ・イメージ・ジャンプ・ボタン 477	水の供給源 662	無顎動物 92	眼鏡の各部名称 385	
マスター・シリンダー 559	マルチパーパス・ソリューション 384	水の循環 67	昔の衣装 336	眼鏡の例 385	
マスト 493, 600, 632, 633, 834, 836	マルチパック 223	水の落差 662	昔の船 598	眼鏡レンズ 385	
マスト・スリーブ 836	マルチプル・ジャンプ 875	水びれ 876	無機栄養生物 67	メキシコ 742	
マスト操作レバー 632, 633	マルチメーター 316	水分離器 648	無機栄養体 67	メキシコ湾 30	
マスト灯 605	マルティン・ルター 736	水蛇座 10	無機物 67	メキャベツ 186	
マストと索具 602	丸頭 301	水撒き用具 328	無球顆粒体 8	メサ 52	
マスト・フット 836	丸頭ハンマー 301	水戻り顆粒管 259	無球粒顆体 8	目先 115	
マストヘッド 602, 836	丸鍬 304	水戻り本管 259	ムクドリ 118	目地鏝 315	
升目 915, 919	丸鍬刃 304	ミズン・スル 603	無限軌道 758	雌しべ 80	
マゼラン 19	丸のみ 401, 421	ミズン・トゲルン・ステースル 603	無限大 703	雌 702	
混ぜる 236	マルハナバチ 101	ミズン・トップマスト・ステースル 603	無酵母パン 205	メス・シリンダー 685	
マゼンタ 690	マルビーギ管 97, 99	ミズンマスト 600, 602	務歯 453	雌のクモの解剖図 103	
股 351	マルメロ 193	ミズン・ロイヤル・ステースル 603	蒸し器 235, 722	雌継ぎ口 909, 910	
股当て 359	丸筆 397	ミズン・ロイヤル・ブレース 603	蒸し器用かご 235	雌のチョウの解剖図 97	
マダガスカル 34, 746	マレーシア 747	店 710	虫眼鏡 693, 905	雌フェルール 909, 910	
股鍬 327	マレー・ポリネシア語族 469	未成年者房 784	息子 784, 785	メソサウルス 92	
股下 844	マレット 449, 858	溝 227, 229, 424, 453, 647, 864, 865, 868, 888	息子の妻 784	メタル・アーム 329	
股下スナップ・ボタン 368, 369	回し 847	溝板 456	結び 282, 908	メタロイド 682	
股紐 611	回しハンドル式台所用蛇口 270	溝板とキャリッジ 456	娘 784, 785	メッカの方向 738	
襠 386, 388	回し挽き銀 303	溝彫 308	娘の夫 784	滅菌ガーゼ 777	
待合室 509, 768, 779	マンガン 683	溝切り 268	無線アンテナ 604, 606, 608, 609, 652, 763, 873	滅菌室 780, 781	
待合所 730	マンガン乾電池 689	溝付きボール 284	無線機 770, 898	滅菌済み器具供給室 780	
マチェーテ 751	マンゴー 197	溝なしボール 284	無線通信 505	滅菌済み器具収納室 778	
襠付きの折り鞄 386	マンゴー・チャツネ 201	溝彫り 404, 405	無線ネットワーク・インターフェース・カード 522	メッシュ 281	
襠付きポケット 359, 360	マンゴスチン 196	霧 64	無線ネットワーク・カード 522	メッシュ窓 902	
マチネ・レングス・ネックレス 374	マンサード屋根 414	見出し 471	無停電電源装置 520, 523	メッセージ表示部 512	
待ち針 454	まんじゅう剣形 404	満ちていく月 7	霧笛 611	メトープ 404	
待ち列 731	マンダリン 194	道の断面図 712	霧灯 554, 570	メトロノーム 436	
マッキンジー川 30	マンダリン・カラー 363	道火桿 752	無頭釘 301	メニュー 217	
マッコウクジラ 137	マンドリーヌ 230	褌 847	ムトゥルス 404	メニュー・ボタン 477, 505	
未指骨 133	マンドリン 433	蜜入 100	胸受け 307	目の高さ以下の弱か並の地吹雪 57	
末趾骨 126	マントルピース 256	ミット 346, 796	胸繋 853, 858	目の高さ以上の弱か並の地吹雪 57	
末種子骨 126	万年筆 470	ミッドソール 370	胸ひれ 108, 136	目の保護具 721	
マッシュルーム 183	万年雪 45, 46	三つ葉飾り 411	胸 115, 124	メノラー 738	
マッシュルーム・アンカー 610	マンホール 655, 712	ミツバチ 98	胸当て 368, 369, 749, 808, 853, 859	雌花 89	
末梢神経系 166	万力 312	ミツバチの解剖図 99	胸ダーツ 352	メバル 221	
末節骨 126, 133, 154, 155, 172		ミツバチの巣の断面図 100	胸のプロテクター 796	目引き 424	
末端堆石 46	**み**	ミツバチの巣箱 100, 182	ムナジロテン 134	目引き穴 424	
マッチ箱 391		密封剤 689	胸びれ 460	目元のメーキャップ 378	
マット 823, 864	ミ 434	密封栓 903	棟木 252	メモ・パッド 530	
マッド・スクリーン 651	未洗い食器台 721	密封物質 689	胸脚 97	目盛り 313, 436, 695, 698, 699, 700, 776, 907	
マット・チェアマン 843	ミエリン鞘 168	蜜房 100	胸当て 368, 369, 749, 808, 853, 859	メモリー・カード 477	
マッド・ピット 651	身卸し包丁 229	ミディアム 472	胸ポケット 349, 352	メモリー・カード差込口 918	
マッド・ポンプ 651	見盛り 426	MIDIケーブル 451	棟割り住宅 419	メモリー・カード・スロット 918	
マットレス 280, 281, 776	ミカエル・ケルラリオス 736	ミトコンドリア 74, 94	無反動ライフル 757	メモリー・キー 479	
マットレス・カバー 282	磨かれた石の握斧 748	緑 400, 690, 741	ムハンマド 736	メモリー・クリヤ・キー 479	
マットレスとボックス・スプリング 716	磨かれた石の手斧 748	見取り図 403	霧終 65	メモリー取り消しキー 529	
マツの針葉 89	ミドル 472	緑球 863	無漂白の小麦粉 204	メモリー・プラス・キー 529	
マツの実 89, 193	ミドル・ジブ 603	緑ボール 863	ムフロン 128	メモリー・ボタン 497, 498, 501, 506	
マツ葉 89	ミドル・ピックアップ 441	ミトン 318, 346, 901	村 708, 886	メモリー・マイナス・キー 529	
松葉杖 782	ミドル・ホール 866	港 596, 709	紫 400, 741	メモリー呼び出しキー 529	
マップ・ランプ 771	ミドル・ラインバッカー 806	南 37, 616	紫の縁飾り 336	目盛り円盤 907	
マテガイ 217	ミトン 318, 346, 901	右ウイング 804	ムラサキウマゴヤシ 190	目盛り尺 612	
的 859	三日月 7, 741	南アフリカ 746	柴 400, 886	目盛り穴 695	
窓 249, 251, 290, 485, 554, 567, 594, 624, 663	三日月湖 48	南アメリカ 28, 31, 50	ムンステール 211	目盛り盤 698	
マトウダイ 221	三日月状砂丘 52	南アメリカ・プレート 43		メラネシア 29	
窓ガラス 249, 551, 554	幹 76, 86, 87, 453	南回帰線 34, 35, 36	**め**	メラネシア諸語 469	
窓ガラス開閉調節ハンドル 554	右ウイング 804	南シナ海 29		メリディエンヌ 276	
窓台 731	右カーソル 515	南十字座 11	芽 78	メリヤス編み 458	
窓石 205	右側 740	南の魚座 11	目 103, 104, 106, 107, 112, 113, 121, 133, 136, 148, 177, 309, 914	メルゲーズ 216	
的球 864	右側の 740	南の冠座 10	明 617	メロンくりぬき器 233	
的の玉 862	ミキサー 236	南の三角座 10	銘 729	メロン類 195	
窓の例 415	右腎臓 165	南半球 35, 35	姫 785	面 847	
窓付属品 282	右センター 804	南半球の星座 10	冥王星 4, 5	面板 452	
窓枠 249	右揃えタブ 514	ミナレット 738	名所 39	面会室 726	
俎 229	右チャンネル 502	ミニバン 549	銘板 273, 306	面会者受付 726	
マニキュア・セット 377	幹の断面 87	峰 45, 227, 229, 749	明滅灯 591, 775	面会者出入口 726	
マニホールド 652	右肺 161, 163	ミフラーブ 738	迷路 885	面会者待合室 726	
マニュアル 444, 445	右背向屈折あり 544, 547	ミフラーブ・ドーム 738	メイン・アッパー・トゲルン・スル 603	メンズ・バッグ 388	
招木 460	右肺静脈 162	身分証明バッジ 770	メイン・アッパー・トップスル 603	メンスル 834	
間柱 252	ミクロネシア 747	ミマス 5	メイン・キャリッジ 456	免税店 621	
眉庇 749	ミサイル 759	耳 133, 140, 146, 277, 426, 455	メイン・クーン 132	面体 847	
マフ 388	ミサイル庫 762	耳当て 385, 776	メインシート 834	メンテナンス室 489	
瞼 113	ミサイルの構造 759	耳覆い 340, 861	メイン・スイッチ 273	メンテレビウム 684	
マフィン型 232	ミサイル発射機 760	耳隠し 340	メイン・スタンド 575	雌鳥 120	
マフ・ポケット 360	ミサイル発射レール 760	耳形網止め 834, 835	メイン・スピーカー 493	面取りリベット 308	
マフラー 553, 577	ミサイル防衛ミサイル 762	耳栓 772, 872	メイン・スル 603	綿棒 308	
マフラー・フェルト 442	岬 38, 51	耳栓着用 774	メイン・デッキ 607		
魔法瓶 906	ミシガン・スノーシュー 893	耳染 173	メイン・パラシュート 896	**も**	
マホメット 736	ミシシッピ川 30	耳の構造 174	メイン・ブラシ 573		
マミー型 904	ミシン 452	耳の保護具 772	メイン・プレビュー・モニター 491	毛衣 121, 122, 143	
マメヨヤシ 191	ミシン・ステッチ 368	脈絡膜 177	メイン・プレビュー用モニター 491	毛幹 172	
摩耗防止材 874	ミシン針 452, 453	ミヤコドリ 118	メイン・ブレーカー 272	猛禽 117	
マヤ語 469	水 646, 847	ミャンマー 747	メインマスト 600, 602	毛根 172	
眉毛抜き 377	水洗い 347	ミュージアム・ショップ 394	メイン・ミラー 477	毛細管 695	
マラウイ 746	水洗い禁止 347	ミュート 447	メイン・ロイヤル・スル 603	毛細血管 172	
マラウイ湖 34	水洗い不可 347	ミュート・ペダル 442	メイン・ロッジ 886	盲点 103, 106, 116, 125, 164	
マラガシ語 469	水受け 261	ミュール 344	メイン・ロワー・トゲルン・スル 603	猛毒キノコ 76	
マランガ 189	湖 7, 38, 45, 48	ミュチュール 404		毛乳頭 172	
マリ 745	湖の酸化 70	ミラー 535, 574, 576, 577, 876		毛茎 172	
マリアナ海溝 50	水かき 110, 117, 838			毛布 280	
マリーナ 788	水かきのある足 110			毛包 172	
マリナー 19	水が蒸気になる 665			網膜 177, 691	
マリ・バード・ランド 29					
マリネ・スパイス 199					

天文学 > 2-25; 地球 > 26-71; 植物 > 72-89; 動物 > 90-143; 人間 > 144-177; 食べ物と台所 > 178-241; 家屋 > 242-295; 日曜大工・園芸 > 296-333; 衣服 > 334-371;
装身具類と日用品 > 372-391; 芸術と建築 > 392-465; 情報伝達とオフィス・オートメーション > 466-535; 交通と機械 > 536-643; エネルギー > 644-677; 科学 > 678-705;
社会 > 706-785; スポーツとゲーム > 786-920

網膜錐状体　177
網膜錐体　177
毛様体　177
モーグル　890
モーグルの競技コース　890
モーゼ　736
モーター　261, 292, 293, 294, 304, 307, 308, 320, 323, 327, 332, 563, 643
モーター・コントロール・モジュール　563
モーター軸　631
モーター・スポーツ　872
モーター台車　585
モーター付きボギー台車　595
モーター内蔵部　236, 237, 240, 288, 384
モーター・ホーム　567
モーター・ユニット　585
モーター・ヨット　607
モード・キー　528
モード切り替えスイッチ　504, 498
モーベッド　577
モーリシャス　746
モーリタニア　745
モカシン　344
木構造上の寄せ木張り　254
木材　300, 403, 406
木材チップ輸送車　588
木材を切る道具　303
木桶　852
木星　4
木生シダ　76
木製バー　825
木造胸壁　408
木炭　397
木炭画法　396
目的球　864
目標　40, 41
目標球　864
木部放射組織　87
木目　300
木目方向　300
モグラ　121
モグラの形態図　121
モグラの骨格図　121
モケット　254
モザイク　406
モザイク寄せ木張り　254
モザンビーク　746
モザンビーク海峡　34
文字　472
文字位置　472
文字訂正キー　528
文字盤　696, 697
文字ピッチ・スケール　528
モジュレーション・ホイール　450
モスク　738
持ち上げハンドルバー　870
持ち送り　256, 408, 661
持ち送り台　278
持ち手　377, 383, 384, 454, 458
持ち手穴　535
持ち手穴付き段ボール箱　535
モツァレラ　210
モツァレラ・チーズ　210
木管楽器の仲間　437
木球　864
木琴　437, 449
木工　301
モップ　295
モディリオン　405
モデム　522, 523, 524
モデル人形　398
元　303
モトクロス・スーパークロス用のオートバイ　875
モトクロス・タイヤ　875
元栓　654
元台　860, 912
元である　703
元でない　703
戻り空気ダクト　258
戻り空気ダクト　258
モナコ　744
モニター　518, 694
モニター・ウォール　489, 490, 491
モニター壁　490
モニター・ボタン　505
物置　244, 509
物置小屋　322
モノクル　385
モノポリー　915
モホロビチッチ不連続面　42
モミ　89
モミの針葉　89
目盛り板　273
モモ　192
腿　115, 124
股当て　808
腿当て　749
モモの断面図　81
靄　57, 65
筋い結び　908
模様始めキー　456
模様変化キー　456
盛り土　538
モリブデン　683
モル　702
モルタデッラ　216
モルタル　298
モルディブ　747
モルドバ共和国　744
モルト・ビネガー　201

モルモット　123
モロコシ　85
モロッコ　745
門型ポスト　607
モンゴル語　469
モンゴル国　747
門歯　121, 123
紋章　739
モンスズメバチ　101
モンタニェ語　469
モンツキダラ　221
門脈　161

や

矢　750, 859
ヤード　602
ヤード・ライン　806
ヤールスバーグ　211
ヤーン　240
夜間金庫　731
夜間録画スイッチ　496
ヤギ　128
やかん　240
焼き網　290, 903
焼き色調節つまみ　238
山羊座　10
ヤギチーズ　210
ヤギ乳　210
野球　794
野球場　788
野球ボール　796
野球ボールの断面図　797
薬　80
ヤク　129
役員席　879
薬室　753, 754, 755
役者の出入り口　402
薬品収納庫　775
薬包　754, 860, 861, 912
櫓形ブイ　614, 617
櫓形浮標　614, 617
野渓　45
矢羽　12
野菜　184
野菜ブラシ　233
野菜ボウル　226
野菜保存室　291
ヤシ　88
野手　799
野手用グローブ　797
矢状切断　169, 170
矢状断　169, 170
矢印キー　261
やすり　309, 391, 905
やすり棒　229
薬莢　912
薬缶　714, 725, 778, 781
ヤツメウナギ　219
柳材　798
薬包　714, 299
屋根　100, 245, 257, 412, 567, 635
屋根飾り　403, 404
屋根換気口　567
屋根通気口　262
屋根のトラス　253
屋根の例　414
屋根窓　244
屋根窓型熱制御装置　60
矢筈模様　254
矢筈寄せ木張り　254
矢羽根　56, 859
夜標の周期　617
ヤベトゥス　5
山　45, 690
ヤマアラシ　123
山形　740
山刀　751
山高帽　340
山付きファイル　532
山津波　47
山猫座　12
山ひだ　283
矢溝　750
ヤムイモ　184
矢来　408
槍　748, 793
槍投げ　791

ゆ

油圧警告灯　557, 576
油圧式ジャッキ　567
油圧式ショベル　638
油圧式ディスク・ブレーキ　870
油圧式パレット・トラック　633
油圧式連結器　640
油圧シリンダー　633, 640
油圧装置　632
油圧ホース　641, 642
URL [ユー・アール・エル] アドレス　524
UHFアンテナ　18, 60
USBポート　513, 526
融解　680
有蓋車　587, 588
有機栄養生物　67
有機乳頭　176
遊間　590
遊技場　608

有棘層　172
遊具　854
遊具付きフルマー小勒馬銜　854
遊撃手　794
有効角度領域　790
有効期限　729
有鉤骨　154
有孔ボード　300
有効命中面　848
有効面　848
有罪　154
ユーゴスラビア　744
有人移動ユニット　20
遊園　436
Uターン禁止　544, 546
有袋動物の例　143
有袋哺乳動物　142
有袋哺乳動物の例　142
U継ぎ手　269
遊底　754, 912
遊底桿　860, 912
有蹄哺乳動物　124
有蹄哺乳動物の例　128
ユーテルサット衛星　486
遊鉤鏡水勒馬銜　854
有頭骨　154
誘導ライン　619
誘動輪　636
誘導輪　758
誘導路　618
有毒性物質　774
融氷水　46
UPS　523
郵便為替　475
郵便局　474, 475, 711, 715
郵便小包　475
郵便室　509
郵便自動車　474, 475
郵便車　474, 475
郵便トーチ　474, 475
郵便配達人　475
郵便箱　474
郵便ネットワーク　474
郵便網　474
郵便物載せ皿　531
郵便料金印字器　531
郵便料金当て　808
郵便料金計器　531
遊歩デッキ　608
幽門垂　109
幽門盲嚢　95
ユーラシア大陸　28
ユーラシア・プレート　43
ユーロ　728
ユーロピウム　684
床　257, 417, 676, 818, 819
床板　254, 577
床板張り　253
床運動マット　824
床ばり　299
ユカタン半島　30
床根太　252, 253
床排水　262
床部　676
床マット　824
雪　64
雪霰　64
行き先　582
行き先表示板　587, 593
雪の結晶　64
油彩　396
油脂類　209
輸精管　104
ユーロッパバイ　217
油性パステル　396
油井フロー・ライン　652
油井櫓　651, 652, 654
預金投入口　730
ユダヤ教　736
ユニオン・スーツ　351
ユニオン継ぎ手　269
ユニオン・ナット　269
ユニフォーム　796, 801, 802, 805, 808, 810, 850
輸尿管　104, 116
弓筈　750
指　110, 122, 172, 346, 797
指当て　446, 457
指貫き　278
指時計　696
指なしアーム・ロング　346
指笛　346
指の肉趾　130, 133
趾の肉趾　130
指の褥　346
指輪　432, 439, 441
指掛けリング　447
指輪の各部　376
弓　439, 750
弓足　439
弓先　439
弓と石弓　750
弓鋸　303, 314, 907
弓　439
輸卵管　97, 103, 113
ユリ　80
ユリシーズ　19
百合の花　741

ユルト　418
湯沸かし装置　262, 266

よ

与圧結合アダプター　21
葉腋　79
葉縁　79
揚音アクセント　473
揺架　756
溶岩層　44
溶岩流　44
容器　236, 237, 240, 320
葉気管支　163
陽極　689
陽極端子　562, 687, 689
陽極板　562
陽極板ストラップ　562
陽極棒　266
用具　900
用具庫　734
幼児　77, 87
葉菜類　186
陽子　680
用紙受け　511, 528
用紙送り口　511
用紙トレイ　511, 512
幼児の頭蓋　158
葉鞘　79
幼児用家具　281
葉状体　74, 75
葉状地衣　74
葉状乳頭　176
葉身　76, 79
用心金　754, 860, 861, 912
腰神経叢　166
溶接カーテン　318
溶接トーチ　319
溶接棒　318
ヨウ素　683
溶脱　70
陽端子　687, 689
幼虫　97, 100
葉頂　79
腰椎　122, 126, 131, 138, 141, 142, 153, 157, 168
腰椎当て　808
陽電荷　684
ヨウトウ　197
溶媒抽出プラント　656
揚錨架　606
用布　459
腰帯　147, 149
洋服だんす　279
葉柄　76, 79
葉柄の塊　185
葉柄湾欠　86
葉脈　79
揚力　630
葉緑体　74
葉肋　185
ヨー　630
ヨーク　349, 353, 359
ヨーク・スカート　357
ヨーグルト　210
ヨーロッパ　28, 32, 50, 743
ヨーロッパ型のコンセント　274
ヨーロッパ型の差込口　274
ヨーロッパ型のプラグ　274
ヨーロッパ・タマキビガイ　217
ヨーロッパで用いられている表示　347
ヨーロッパバイ　217
ヨーロッパヤマウズラ　118
抑音アクセント　473
翼形　338
翼形パレット　632
翼桁　760, 624
翼　628, 897
翼後小骨　624
翼支柱　628
浴室　251, 264, 780
浴室の天窓　251
翼小骨　624
翼状骨　112
浴槽　251, 262, 264
浴槽とシャワー　724
弓筈　750
翼端　897, 898
翼端小翼　625, 628
翼布　897
翼部　676
浴用タオル　379
横板　477, 439, 440
横桟　277, 278, 424, 433, 460, 461, 663, 676, 782, 799
横材　278
横桟　321
横水栓　268
横静索　602
横手すり　594
横二分割　740
横梁　663
横揺れ　630
汚れ除け　290, 292, 293
余水路　657
余水路ゲート　657
余水路の頂上　657

ユルト　418
湯沸かし装置　262, 266

寄せ木張り　254
寄せ木張りの配列　254
寄棟屋根　414
よだれ掛け　368
四つ爪アンカー　610
ヨット　834
ヨングニサン　102
4人乗りボブスレー　884
四番車　696
予備洗い流し台　721
呼び子　240
予備傘　896
呼び出し音量調節パネル　506
呼び出しボタン　505
呼びボタン　417
予備レギュレーター　841
読み出し面　501
読み取り・書き込みヘッド　521
嫁　784
予約設定ボタン　495
縒り糸　908
より大きい　703
より大きいか等しい　703
より小さい　703
より小さいか等しい　703
縒り継ぎ　908
縒り終わり　908
縒り縄　908
縒り始め　908
ヨルダン　746
ヨルバ語　468
鎧　748, 749
鎧板　411
鎧兜　875
鎧戸　249
鎧窓　415
弱い驟雨　57
弱い驟雨性の雪　57
弱い驟雪　57
弱い断続性の雨　57
弱い断続性の霧雨　57
弱い断続性の雪　57
弱い連続性の雨　57
弱い連続性の霧雨　57
弱い連続性の雪　57
4回戦　789
4×100mリレー・スタート・ライン　791
4×400mリレー・スタート・ライン　791
四脚ステッキ　782
4行程エンジン　564
45度　704
45度エルボ継ぎ手　269
四重奏　438
4番アイアン　868
4番車　875
400mスタート・ライン　791
400mハードル走スタート・ライン　791
4分の3拍子　434
4分の4拍子　434
4本マスト・バーク　602
4本マスト・バーク型帆船　602
四枚刃　236
4メートル・ライン　827
四輪駆動の全地形型車両　577

ら

ラ　434
ラージ・ブレード　905
ラード　209
ライオン　135
雷管　757, 912
ライコムギ　203
ライザー　897
ライス・ペーパー　207
ライダー　875
ライチ　197
ライティング・ケース　387
ライティング・レール　287
雷電　57
ライト　472, 615, 617, 794, 795
ライト・アタッカー　812
ライト・インサイド　801
ライト・インサイド・フォワード　801
ライト・ウイング　801, 814, 879
ライト・ガード　805
ライト・コーナーバック　806
ライト・サービス・コート　819, 821
ライト・サイド・ハーフ　803
ライト・セーフティ　806
ライト・タックル　807
ライト・ディフェンス　878
ライト・ディフェンス・エンド　806
ライト・ディフェンス・タックル　806
ライト・ハーフ　801
ライト・バック　801, 803, 812, 814
ライト・フォワード　811
ライト・ボタン　505
ライトボックス　484, 535
ライト・ミッドフィルダー　803
ライフル　893
ライフル射撃　861
ライフル銃　912

ライマメ 191
ライム 194
ライ麦 85, 203
ライ麦クラッカー 205
ライン 813
ライン・アンパイア 820
ライン・ガイド 910
ライン・ジャッジ 807, 818, 820, 824
ラインズマン 803, 812, 816, 820, 879
ライン・ベット 919
ライン・ローラー 910
ラウンジ 608, 724
ラウンド・ネック 363
ラオス人民民主共和国 747
ラガー・マン 805
ラギング 655
ラグ 448
ラグ・ スル 601
落石注意 545, 547
落石の恐れあり 545, 547
落盤 47
ラグビー 804
ラグビー・シューズ 805
ラグビー・ボール 805
ラグラン 355
ラグラン・コート 355
ラグラン・スリーブ 361, 369
ラグラン袖 352, 355
ラクレット 211
ラクレット・グリル 239
ラグ・レンチ 558
ラケット・スポーツ 815
ラケットボール 818
ラケットボール用のボール 818
ラケットボール・ラケット 818
ラコリス 44
ラザーニャ 206
ラザフォルジウム 683
ラジアル・タイヤ 561
ラジアル・プライ 561
ラジウム 682
ラジエーター 21, 23, 259, 552, 561, 586
ラジエーター・キャップ 561
ラジエーター・グリル 570
ラジオ 488, 771
ラジオゾンデ 59
ラジオ・ベンチ 317
羅針箱 612
ラス・エル・ハヌート 199
ラズベリー 192
ラズベリーの断面図 83
螺旋 302, 705
螺旋階段 655
螺旋形溝 306
螺旋錐 306
螺旋状刃 236
螺旋状発熱体 290
螺層 104
ラダー 625, 759, 760, 834, 838, 839, 898
ラダー・ロープ 838
ラチェット 302, 307, 460
ラチェット切り替え装置 307
ラチェット・ストップ 700
ラチェット・ハンドル 311
ラチェット・リング・スパナ 311
落下傘 896
落下式甲板 279
落花生油 209
ラック 234, 294, 791, 805, 863
ラックとピニオン 686
ラックボード 445
ラッチ 900
ラッチ・ボルト 248
ラッパ 611
ラッパー 390
ラッパズイセン 80
ラップアラウンド・ドレス 356
ラップ記録係 883
ラップ・スカート 357
ラップトップ型コンピューター 526
ラップトップ型コンピューターのブリーフケース 527
ラップトップ・コンピューター 523, 526
ラップトップ・コンピューターのブリーフケース 527
ラップ・ブラウス 359
ラテラル・バー 851
ラテラル・ファイリング・キャビネット 510
ラドガ湖 32
ラトビア 744
ラドン 684
ラバ 128
ラバー 815
ラバー・ガスケット 270
羅牌 37
ラビオリ 206
陸上競技 790
ラピス・ラズリ 375
ラビッジ 202
ラビリンス 885
ラビング・ストリップ 560, 561
ラフ 836, 866, 867
ラブ・シート 724
ラブ・チェア 276
ラベット・ビット 308
ラベル 500, 797
ラベル 348, 362
ラベル入れ 533
ラベル・ライター 533
ラマ 128

ラミン・ボード 300
ラム 215
ラムカン皿 226
RAMコネクター 513
ラムダ状縫合 158
ラムダ縫合 158
ラリー・カー 873
ラリー用オートバイ 875
螺肋 105
卵 170
欄 471
ラン 80
卵黄 117
卵黄膜 117
卵核 170
卵殻 117
卵殻膜 117
卵管 170, 171
欄干 255, 540
卵管采 171
卵管峡部 171
卵管膨大部 171
乱視 691
卵子 170
ランジェリー・ショップ 714
乱視矯正用レンズ 691
卵精嚢 104
ランセット・アーチ 413
卵巣 97, 103, 170, 171
乱層雲 56, 62
ランタナイド元素 684
ランタノイド元素 684
ランダム・アクセス・メモリ 513
ランダム・オービット・サンダー 308
ランタン 684, 903
乱継ぎ張り 254
ランディング・ウインドー 631
ランディング・エリア 890, 891
ランディング・ギア補助脚 571
ランディング・ネット 911
ランド 306
ランナー 659, 884, 900, 915
ランナー・ブレード 659, 664
ランニング 833
ランニング・シャツ 351, 791, 850
ランニング・シューズ 370, 716
ランニング・パンツ 791
ランバー・パッド 808
卵胞 170
ランピエ絞輪 168
ランプ 539, 693, 848
ランプウェー 608
ランプータン 197
ランプ底部 614
ランプハウス 485
ランプハウス持ち上げレバー 485

り

リア・シート 555
リア・シート・ベルト 555
リアス式海岸 35
リア・ディレーラー 578, 580
リア・ビーム 698
リア・フェンダー 577
リーキ 184
リーゼン・スラローム 889
リーダー 900, 911
リーチ 836
リーディング・ミラー 20
リード 444, 446, 471, 877
リード・イン 501
リード受け 444
リード押さえ 444
リード・パイプ 445
リード・ピックアップ 441
リード・ボタン 505
リード・レール 590
リーフ 483, 493, 495
リーフ・バンド 603
リーフ・ポイント 603
リーフ・ポケット 386
リール 328, 484, 495, 848, 920
リール・シート 909, 910
リール・フット 909, 910
リール・プレート 920
リエット 216
理科室 734
リガチャー 446
リガトーニ 206
力学 686
力学的エネルギーを電気に変換する 662
力士 847
リキッド・アイライナー 378
リキッド・ファンデーション 378
リキッド・マスカラ 378
リキュール・グラス 225
陸繋島 51
陸上競技 790
陸上競技場 791
陸上競技用トラック 788
陸上競技用フィールド 788
陸上ホッケー 788
陸上の物理探査 651
リクライニング・ハンドル 555
リコール・メモリー・キー 479
リコッタ 210
リコッタ・チーズ 210
リザーブ・パラシュート 896
リサイクリング 71
リサイクル容器 71
リサイクル用の大箱 71
犂先軸 641

リス 123
リスト・ガード 895
リスト・コード 818
リスト・ストラップ 888, 892
リストバンド 808, 822, 850
リズム設定ボタン 451
リズム・ピックアップ 441
リセット・キー 508
リセット・ボタン 267, 495, 512, 513, 519, 696, 700, 918
リソスフェア 42
リソゾーム 94
リターン 515
リターン・クリース 799
リターン・スプリング 559
履帯 636, 758
履帯フレーム 636
リチウム 682
犂柱 641
陸橋 541
立射 893
立射姿勢 861
立体 705
立体樹状結晶 64
立体駅 582
立体コピー・パネル 512
立体使用形パレット 632
立方骨 155
立方体 705
立面図 250
立毛筋 172
リッパー 682
リッパー・シリンダー 636
リッパー歯 636
リッパー歯先端部 636
リッパー歯プロテクター 636
リップブラシ 378
リップライナー 378
立方骨 229
利得調節つまみ 613
リトアニア 744
リト・インク 423
リトグラフ・プレス機 423
リト・クレヨン 423
リト・ペンシル 423
リネン室 724
リネン類 280
理髪鉄 382
リバブール馬衛 854
履板 758
リビア 745
リピート・ボタン 501
リヒテンシュタイン 744
リブ 639, 772, 909
リブ編み 458
利札ブース 731
リフト 602
リフト・アーム 637, 640
リフト・アーム・シリンダー 637
リフト・シリンダー 573, 634, 766
リフト・チェーン 265, 632
リフト・ドア 569
リフト・パッド 808
リフト・ワイヤ 265
リブ・ロース 214
リブ・ロースト 214
リベット 229
リベリア 745
リボ核 803, 812
リボソーム 74, 94
リボルバー 754
リボン 823
リム 385, 560, 574, 579, 640, 859, 913
リムーバー 534
リム・フランジ 560
リムジン 549
リモート・センサー 518
リモート・センシング 40
リモート・マニピュレーター・システム 21, 22
リモコン 483, 493, 495
リモコン受光部 494, 501
リモコン受信部 494, 501
リモコン装置 493
リモコン端子 477
リモコン端末 476
リュウガン 196
旒旗 739
隆起部 875
琉球海溝 50
竜骨 108, 116
竜骨座 11
竜座 13
硫酸紙 222
硫散弾 752
硫酸の放出 70
竜巻 696
流星 53
流体変速装置 292
榴弾 752
流通倉庫 596
留点 695
流入溝 95
流木路 657
流量調節ノズル 654
梁 418
稜 404
両凹レンズ 691
両替所 725
猟騎帽 853
料金表示メーター 548
料金別納郵便 475

両口スパナ 311
猟犬座 13
猟獣肉 212
両親 784, 785
両梳き用目梳き鋏 382
両性管 104
両生類 110
両生類の例 111
両袖事務机 511
猟鳥肉 212
両凸レンズ 691
両刃 383
両刃かみそり 383
量表示メーター 548
両開きドア 568
両開き窓 415
稜堡 409
両面コピー・パネル 512
両面使用形パレット 632
両面パレット 632
料理長 721
料理人 721
料理包丁 229
旅客連絡橋 621, 623
旅客駅 582
旅客ターミナル 619, 620
旅客通路 619
旅客用プラットホーム 582
旅客列車 582
緑藻 107
緑茶 75
緑茶 208
リョクトウ 191
緑豆春雨 207
旅行鞄 389
旅行者用小切手 729
旅行代理店 714
旅行用鞄 388
リラ 433
リト・インク 423
利札ブース 731
利礼 731
リリース・ノブ 909
リリース・レバー 310, 889
リレー・接続ボックス 563
燐 683
リンガラ語 468
リンク 864, 877, 878, 881
リング 249, 284, 290, 390, 522, 610, 629, 696, 699, 809, 811, 824, 842, 901
リンク・コーナー 878
リングサイド 842
リング・ナット 269
リング・バインダー 532
リング・ハンドル 390
リング・ファイル 532
リング・ポスト 842
リンゴ 193
りんご酢 201
リンゴの断面図 82
リンシード・オイル 400
臨時記号 435
輪状平緩 404
鱗状体 158
林地 39
鱗翅類 280
鱗片 117
鱗片葉 78

る

涙管 177
涙丘 177
涙腺 177
塁道 409
塁壁 408, 409
ルーク 916
ルーシュ 368
ルース・カーテン 283
ルース・ヘッド・プロップ 804
ルーズリーフ・バインダー 532
ルーズリーフ・ファイル 532
ルーター 308, 523, 524
ルート 703
ルート・キー 529
ルート・ジャッジ 900
ルーバー 261
ルーフ 551, 567
ループ 539, 902, 903
ループ・ステッチ 459
ルーフ・ボール 903
ルーフ・ラック 567
ルーペ 693
ルーペと顕微鏡 693
ルーマニア 884
ルーマニア語 469
ルーマニアン・コーチング・ステッチ 459
ルーム 838
ルーム・エアコン 261
ルーム・ミラー 556
ルーレット 422, 454
ルーレット・テーブル 919
ルーレット盤 919
ルエル・ロック・チップ 776
ルクセンブルグ 743
ルター派 736
留守番電話機 508
ルツァー 881
ルテチウム 684
ルテニウム 683
ルビー 375
ルビー 728
ルビー・シリンダー 692

ルビジウム 682
ルピナス 190
ルフィニ小体 172
ルリヂシャ 202
ルワンダ 745

れ

レ 434
レア 5
冷温帯気候 61
冷却液 674
冷却 656
冷却液入り口 672
冷却液出口 672
冷却管 260
冷却系 553
冷却剤 674
冷却材 665, 670, 671
冷却剤入り口 672
冷却剤出口 672
冷却車 670
冷却シリンダー 692
冷却塔 646
冷却ファン 497, 552, 561, 563, 566
冷却用通風孔 526
冷水管 265, 266, 267, 270, 271
冷水供給管 265, 266, 267, 270, 271
冷水循環 262
冷水立て管 262
冷蔵庫 224, 291, 720, 722
冷蔵室 180, 181, 291, 722
冷蔵室ドア 291
冷蔵車 588
冷蔵倉庫 596
冷蔵陳列ケース 720
冷帯気候 61
冷暖房車 622
霊長類 138
霊長類の動物の例 139
O度 704
冷凍庫 224, 720
冷凍室 291
冷凍室ドア 291
冷凍食品 181
冷凍食品保存庫 181
冷凍セミトレーラー 572
冷凍ユニット 571
礼拝所 726
礼拝堂 408, 738
レイピアー 751
レイヨウ 128
レインコート 352
レイン・タイヤ 872
レーキ 327, 643
レーキ・コーム 380
レーキ棒 642
レーザー光線 501, 692
レーザー・プリンター 519
レーシング・スーツ 874, 882
レースのカーテン 282
レーダー 40, 604, 605, 608, 609
レーダー・アンテナ 40, 760, 763
レーダー機 629
レーダー吸収材料 629
レーダー光線 40
レーダーサット衛星 40
レーダー送受信機 771
レーダー装置 760
レーダー・ディスプレイ 771
レーダー反射器 615
レーダー・ビーム 40
レーダー・マスト 606
レードーム 760
レドル 233
レベル 500
レール 284, 456, 571, 591, 841, 862
レール・チェア 590
レールの接続 590
レールの断面図 591
レール路面 590
レーン 790, 830, 831, 865, 882
レーン番号 893
レオタード 371
レガース 798
レガーズ 800
レカミエ 371
レギオンの兵士 748
レギュレーターのセカンド・ステージ 841
レギュレーターの第一減圧部 841
レギュレーターの第二減圧部 841
レギュレーターのファースト・ステージ 841
レコード 500
レコード・プレーヤー 500
レジ 181, 716, 717, 723
レシーバー 506, 817, 819, 820
レシービング・ライン 818
レシーブ 812
レジ係 181
レジスター 181
レスト 863
レスト・エリア 39
レストラン 710, 713, 714, 719, 720, 725
レストラン紹介欄 471
レスラー 843
レスリング 843
レスリング・シューズ 843
レスリング・タイツ 843

レスリング・マット 843
レソト 746
レター・スケール 531
レタス 186
レチクル 692
レチクル座 10
列 384, 431, 731
レッカー車 573
レッグ 323
レッグ・ウォーマー 371
レッグ・エクステンション・バー 851
レッグ・オブ・マトン・スリーブ 361
レッグ・カール・バー 851
列車時刻表 582
列島 38
レッド・ペッパー 199
裂片状 79
レニウム 683
レバー 212, 238, 268, 270, 310, 377, 423, 424, 686, 912, 920
レバー・キャップ 309
レバー式コルク抜き 230
レバー・ファイル 532
レバノン 746
レバノンスギ 89
レフェリー 801, 803, 805, 807, 812, 818, 819, 827, 842, 843, 860, 879, 881, 882
レフト 794, 795
レフト・アタッカー 812
レフト・インサイド 801
レフト・インサイド・フォワード 801
レフト・ウイング 801, 814, 879
レフト・ガード 807
レフト・コーナーバック 806
レフト・サービス・コート 819, 821
レフト・サイド・ハーフ 803
レフト・セーフティ 806
レフト・タックル 807
レフト・ディフェンス 878
レフト・ディフェンス・エンド 806
レフト・ディフェンス・タックル 806
レフト・ハーフ 801
レフト・バック 801, 803, 812, 814
レフト・フォワード 811
レフト・ミッドフィルダー 803
レフリー 801, 803, 805, 807, 812, 818, 819, 827, 842, 843, 860, 879, 881, 882
レフレックス・カメラ 477
レベル 313, 650
レボルバー 693
レモン 194
レモン搾り器 230, 237
レモン・バーム 202
漣音 435
煉瓦 298
煉瓦壁 253
煉瓦ハンマー 315
煉瓦壁 298
連結器 444, 567, 585, 640
連結器ヘッド 586, 587, 640, 641, 642
連結バス 569
連結棒 567
連鎖反応 681
レンジ 722
レンジ上面 290
レンジ上面の縁 290
レンジの上面 224
レンジファインダー・カメラ 480
レンジ・フード 224, 290, 722
練習グリーン 866
練習用ボール 819
レンズ 476, 477, 478, 479, 483, 517, 518, 535, 691

レンズ・アクセサリー 478
レンズ・キャップ 478
レンズ系 692
レンズ・ケース 384
レンズ状銀河 9
レンズ付きフィルム 480
レンズ取り外しボタン 476
レンズ・フード 478, 612
レンズ・マウント 477
レンズマメ 190
連節バス 569
連続棒 564, 566
連続桁 540
連続桁橋 541
レンチ 311, 315
連棟住宅 419
連動装置 444
連絡 916
連絡壕 541
連絡通路 23, 543, 709
連絡ランプ 539
連絡路 539
連廊 584

ろ

炉 465, 674
ロア・シェル 889
炉圧調整つまみ 465
ロイヤル・フラッシュ 914
ロイン・チョップ 215
ろう面 287
ろうそく 737
漏電遮断機 272
漏斗 231, 241
漏斗雲 63
蝋引き灯芯 422
ロー 919
ローイング 838
ローイングとスカーリング 838
ローイング・ボート 839
ローイング・マシーン 851
ローズ・カット 375
ロースト鍋 234
ロース肉 214, 215
ローズマリー 202
ローゼット 405
ロータ 565, 659, 676
ローター・ハブ 631
ローター・ブレード 631
ローター・ヘッド 631
ローター・マスト 631
ロータリー 39
ロータリー・エンジンの周期 565
ロータリー型インターチェンジ 538
ロータリー式カード・ファイル 531
ロータリー式掘削 651
ロータリー・テーブル 651
ロード・テープ 899
ロード・バイク 581
ロード・フレーム 899
ロード・レース 870
ロード・レース競技 870
ロード・レース用自転車とサイクリスト 870
ローネット 385
ロー・ビーム 554
ロゼット 440
ローファー 344
ロープ自在金具 902
ロープ 611, 686, 823, 824, 842, 908
ロープ・ネックレス 374
ロープ・パーティー 900
ロープワーク 908
ローマ時代の武器 748
ローマ・シェード 285
ローマ数字 703
ローマン・ビーン 191
ローラー 284, 285, 380, 423, 454, 516, 528, 633

ローラー・カバー 320
ローラー・シェード 558
ローラー・スポーツ 894
ローラー・ノブ 528
ローラー刷毛 320
ローラーブレード 895
ローラー・フレーム 320
ローラー・ボードとアーム 445
ローリング・タワー 321
ロール 630
ロールアップ・ブラインド 285
ロール・スクリーン 285
ロール・フィルム 481
ローレル 202
ローレンシウム 684
ローン 822
ローン・ボウリング 864
ローン・ボウルズ 864
濾過器 237, 240
濾過器継手 270
濾過器本体 270
路肩 538
録音装置 429
録音テープ 499
録音入力レベル調整つまみ 499
録音ボタン 499
録音ミューティング・ボタン 499
録音用竿持ち 808
録音レベル調整つまみ 499
録画開始／停止ボタン 496
録画編集ボタン 496
録画ボタン 495
64分音符 435
64分休符 435
六重奏 438
60度以下の湯で、弱水流による洗濯機洗い可 347
60度以下の湯で、通常の洗濯機洗い可 347
60メートル標的線 859
肋軟骨 122
陸染 253
陸軍 375
6度 434
6番アイアン 868
六分儀 612
六分儀座 11
陸屋根 414
ろくろ 464
ろくろ成形 464
ろくろ面 464
ロケット 374
ロケット・エンジン 24, 759
ロシア黒パン 205
ロシア語 469
ロシア・モジュール 21
ロシア連邦 744
ロシアン・プンパーニッケル 205
ロジウム 683
露出 479
露出時間目盛り 479
露出値 479
露出補正ボタン 476
露出モード・ボタン 476
路床 538
濾床 263
炉心 670, 671
ロス棚氷 29
ロゼット 440
路線系統図 593, 594
路線図 592
路線表示板 568, 569, 595
炉棚 256
ロタンダ 713
ロッカー 422, 510
ロッカー・アーム 565
ロッカー・ルーム 764
六角頭ブッシュ継手 269
六角ナット 311, 562
肋間神経 166
ロッキー山脈 30

ロッキング・チェア 276, 277
ロッキング・プライヤー 310
ロッキング・レバー 312, 587
ロック 387, 389, 554, 580, 804
ロック・ガーデン 322
ロック・クライマー 900
ロック装置 289
ロック・ダイヤル 516
ロックナット 270
ロックフォール 211
ロックフォール・チーズ 211
ロック・ボタン 288, 305, 308, 505
ロック・リング 302, 483, 909, 910
肋甲板 113
肋骨 112, 116, 121, 122, 126, 131, 136, 138, 141, 142, 152
肋骨当て 808
ロッジ型テント 902
ロッド 261
ロッド・スタンド 910
露点温度 55
露天掘り 647
露天掘り鉱山 647
露天掘り炭鉱 647
炉筒 267
炉筒フード 267
ロトドーム 629
ロトンダ 713
ロバ 128
炉箱 256
路盤 538
露盤 403, 404
ロビー 620, 713, 717, 719, 724, 728, 730
ロビー階 724
ロビン 118
ロブ 741
ロブ・ウェッジ 868
ロブスターの解剖図 107
ロブスターの形態図 107
炉辺用鉄器具 257
ロボット・アーム 22
ロマーノ 211
ロマンス諸語 469
路面 538
路面凹凸あり 545, 547
路面電車 595
櫓門 408
ロシア黒パン 205
ロワー・ガードル・ファセット 374
ロワー・マスト 602
ロワー・リム 750
ロング・アンド・ショート・ステッチ 459
ロング・サービス・ライン 816
ロング・トラック 882
ロング・ホール 867
ロンパース 369

わ

環 699
輪 699, 823, 824
ワークステーション 509
Y型チューブ 776
Yチューブ 776
Y継ぎ手 269
ワイド 472
ワイド・レシーバー 807
ワイパー 550, 557
ワイパー・アーム 557
ワイパー・ウォッシャー・スイッチ 556
ワイパー・シャフト 557
ワイパー・スイッチ 556
ワイパー・ブレード 557
ワイパー・ブレード・ゴム 557
ワイヤー 367, 793

ワイヤー・カッター 317
ワイヤー・ストリッパー 317
ワイヤー・スリング 900
ワイヤー・ナット 317
ワイヤー・ブラシ 449
ワイヤー・レリーズ 482
ワイヤレス・ネットワーク・インターフェース・カード 522
ワイヤレス・ネットワーク・カード 522
ワイン貯蔵庫 720
ワイン・ビネガー 201
ワイン・リスト 721
和音 435
若枝 86
ワカメ 183
脇当て 782
腋当て 782
脇祭壇 737
脇机 510, 511
脇腹 115, 425
湧き水 47
脇見出し 471
枠 249, 278, 284, 433, 449, 459, 460, 612, 672, 673, 823, 920
枠框 278
枠木 893
枠組み 252
惑星状星雲 8
惑星と衛星 4
ワゴン車 549
ワゴン・テント 902
輪差 913
山葵 201
ワサビダイコン 189
鷲 119
ワシ 52
鷲座 10, 12
和集合 703
ワシリー・チェア 276
山 385
渡り線 583
ワックス 892
ワックス・クレヨン 396
ワックス・クレヨン画法 396
ワックス道具一式 892
ワックス・ペーパー 222
ワッシャー 268, 310, 689
ワット 702
ワッフル焼き器 238
輪奈結び 908
ワニス 400
輪針 457
ワピチ 128
環縁 404
わら散布装置 643
藁束 875
ワラビー 143
わら葺き小屋 418
割り栗石 298
割り座 265
割り鋲 534
割る 7, 38
湾 7, 38
腕甲 749
腕骨 116, 122, 126, 131, 136, 138, 141, 142, 154
腕神経叢 166
腕足動物 92
腕帯 777
ワンタンの皮 207
万子牌 917
腕焼骨筋 150, 151
ワン・ピース 884
ワン・ペア 914

English Index

«D» 862
.22-caliber rifle 861
1 astronomical unit 5
1,500 m starting line 791
1.5 spacing 472
1/10th second hand 696
10 m line 804
10,000 m relay starting line 791
100 m hurdles starting line 790
100 m starting line 790
110 m hurdles starting line 790
120-volt circuit 272
15 m line 805
180-degree curve 885
1st cuneiform 156
2 m line 827
200 m line 871
200 m starting line 790
22 m line 800, 804
240-volt circuit 272
240-volt feeder cable 272
27 m line 858
3-iron 868
3-wood 868
30 m line 859
35 mm still camera 20
36 m line 858
4 m line 827
4 x 400 m relay starting line 791
4-iron 868
45° elbow 269
5 m line 800, 805
5,000 m starting line 790
5-iron 868
5-wood 868
50 astronomical units 4
50 m line 859
50,000 astronomical units 4
500 m finish line 883
500 m start line 882
54 m line 858
6-iron 868
60 m line 859
7 m line 827
7-iron 868
70 m line 859
8-iron 868
8-mm pistol 861
800 m starting line 791
9-iron 868
90 m line 859

A

A 434
abacus 404
abalone 217
abdomen 96, 97, 98, 103, 107, 115, 146, 148
abdominal aorta 160, 165
abdominal cavity 169, 170
abdominal rectus 150
abdominal segment 97
ablutions fountain 738
above ground swimming pool 246
aboveground pipeline 654
Abraham 736
abruptly pinnate 79
ABS 559
absorbed solar radiation 68
absorbent cotton 777
absorbing plate 672

absorbing surface 675
absorption by clouds 68
absorption by Earth surface 68
absorption of water and mineral salts 78
abutment 410, 540
abyssal hill 49
abyssal plain 49
Abyssinian 133
acanthodian 92
acanthus leaf 276, 405
acceleration lane 539
accelerator cable 332
accelerator control 331
accelerator pedal 556
accent mark 435
accept machine 666
access gallery 658
access panel 258, 266
access road 618
access server 525
access shaft 664
access to the second level of operations 529
access window 521
accessories 401, 558, 580
accessory box 456
accessory gear box 627
accessory pocket 554
accessory pouch 859
accessory shoe 476
accidentals 435
accordion 432
accordion bag 388
accordion pleat 357
account book 535
account identification 731
accountant's office 509
accumulator 559
accuracy sports 859
ace 914
acetylene cylinder 319
acetylene valve 319
achene 83, 84
achondrite 8
acid rain 69, 70
acid snow 70
acorn nut 311
acorn squash 189
acoustic ceiling 431
acoustic guitar 440
acoustic meatus 173, 174
acquisition rack 733
acrobatic skate 895
acromion 153
acroterion 403, 404
actinides 684
actinium 684
action buttons 918
action lever 443
action of wind 67
active sensor 41
active tracking 498
actor 428
actors' seats 428
actress 429
actual temperature 261
actuator 759
actuator arm 521
actuator arm motor 521
acute accent 473
acute angle 704
Adam's apple 146
adaptor 485

add in memory 529
add key 529
add/equals key 529
additional production personnel 490
additive color synthesis 690
Aden, Gulf 33, 34
adhesive bandage 777
adhesive disc 111
adhesive disk 111
adhesive tape 777
adipose tissue 171, 172
adjustable channel 310
adjustable clamp 286
adjustable frame 303
adjustable lamp 286, 399
adjustable platen 511
adjustable seat 584
adjustable shelf 511
adjustable spanner 311
adjustable spud wrench 315
adjustable strap 368
adjustable thermostat 239
adjustable waist tab 348
adjuster 782
adjusting band 502
adjusting buckle 895
adjusting catch 889
adjusting lever 436
adjusting screw 310, 312, 319
adjusting tube 824, 825
adjustment for horizontal-circle image 701
adjustment for vertical-circle image 701
adjustment knob 555
adjustment pedal 399
adjustment slide 350
adjustment wheel 317
administration 394, 735
administrative building 664
administrative office 764, 769
administrative offices 718
adobe house 418
adrenal gland 165
Adriatic Sea 32
adventitious roots 76
advertisement 471
advertising panel 592
advertising sign 594, 595
adze 401, 901
adzuki bean 191
Aegean Sea 32
aerator 268
aerial 504, 551
aerial cable network 486
aerial ladder truck 766
aerial site 890
aerial sports 896
aerocyst 75
aerodynamic brake 676
affluent 48
Afghanistan 746
Africa 28, 34, 50, 745
African Plate 43
Afro pick 380
Afro-Asiatic languages 468
aft shroud 17
after shave 383
afterbay 657, 658, 661
afterfeather 115
agar-agar 183
agglomeration 708
agitator 292
agnathan 92

AGP expansion connector 513
agricultural machinery 641
agricultural pollution 69
aikido 846
aikidogi 846
aikidoka 846
aileron 624, 898
air 565
air bag 556
air bag restraint system 556
air bladder 109
air brake 760, 898
air brake handle 898
air bubbles 531
air bulb shutter release 482
air cap 320
air chamber 271
air communications 487
air compression unit 585
air compressor 320, 586
air concentrator 382
air conditioner 567
air conditioner compressor 566
air conditioning 261
air conditioning appliances 261
air conditioning equipment 608
air conditioning system 68, 775
air conditioning unit 489
air control radar 761
air data computer 626
air filter 261, 331, 552, 586
air flow 398
air gap 675
air hole 390, 470
air horn 570
air hose 398, 648, 841
air hose connection 320
air inlet 575, 631
air inlet control 256
air intake 568, 605
air intake for engine cooling 874
air leg 648
air mail 475
air mass, type 55
air mattress 904
air navigation device 761
air pistol 861
air pollutants 69
air pollution 69
air pre-cleaner filter 636
air pressure, measure 59
Air Pump 11
air pump 548
air purifier 261
air relief valve 607
air return 258
air scoop 876
air sealing gland 445
air search radar 761, 762
air shaft 402
air space 117
air start unit 622
air tank 320
air temperature 55
air transport 618
air tube 259
air unit 370
air valve 320, 398
air vent 294
air-inlet grille 382
air-outlet grille 382
air-pressure pump 777

air-supply tube 765
air-to-air missile 759, 760
air-to-surface missile 759
air/fuel mixture 564
airborne radar 40
airbrush 398
airbrush, cross section 398
aircraft carrier 761
aircraft maintenance truck 622
aircraft weather station 54
airframe 897
airliner 53
airlock 763
airplane, forces 630
airplane, movements 630
airport 39, 618, 708
airspeed indicator 898
aisle 180, 411
ajowan 199
ala 175
alarm threshold display button 613
alarm threshold setting 613
alarm/charge indicator light 527
Alaska, Gulf 30
Albania 744
Albanian 469
albatross 119
albumen 117
albumin gland 104
alcohol bulb 695
alcohol column 695
Aleutian Islands 30
Aleutian Trench 50
alfalfa 190
alga 75
alga, structure 75
algae, examples 75
Algeria 745
alidade 59, 701
alidade level 701
alighting board 100
aligner 838
alkali metals 682
alkaline earth metals 682
alkaline manganese-zinc cell 689
alkekengi 192
all-purpose flour 204
all-season tire 560
all-season tyre 560
all-terrain vehicle 549, 577
alley 817, 820
alligator 114
allspice 198
alluvial deposits 48
almond 81, 193
alphabetical keypad 530
alphanumeric keyboard 507, 548, 730, 731
alphanumeric keypad 506, 514
alpine ski trail 886
alpine skier 888
alpine skiing 888
alpine snowboard 887
Alps 32
Alsace glass 225
Altar 10
altar cross 737
altarpiece 737
alteration line 455
alternate 514
alternate: level 3 select 514
alternating-current power cord 526
alternative key 514

ASTRONOMY > 2-25; EARTH > 26-71; VEGETABLE KINGDOM >72-89; ANIMAL KINGDOM > 90-143; HUMAN BEING > 144-177; FOOD AND KITCHEN > 178-241; HOUSE > 242-295;
DO-IT-YOURSELF AND GARDENING > 296-333; CLOTHING > 334-371; PERSONAL ADORNMENT AND ARTICLES > 372-391; ARTS AND ARCHITECTURE > 392-465; COMMUNICATIONS AND
OFFICE AUTOMATION > 466-535; TRANSPORT AND MACHINERY > 536-643; ENERGY > 644-677; SCIENCE > 678-705; SOCIETY > 706-785; SPORTS AND GAMES > 786-920

alternator 552, 566, 586, 677, 688
alternator warning light 557
altimeter 896, 898, 899
altitude clamp 14, 15
altitude fine adjustment 14, 15
altitude scale 53
altocumulus 56, 62
altostratus 56, 62
alula 115
aluminium 682
aluminum 682
aluminum foil 222
aluminum frame 893
aluminum layer 501
aluminum recycling container 71
alveolar bone 159
amaranth 203
Amazon River 31
ambulance 775, 778
ambulance attendant's seat 775
ambulance helicopter 631
ambulatory 411
ambulatory care unit 781
American bacon 216
American betting layout 919
American corn bread 205
American duckpin 865
American football 806
American football player 808
American football, playing field 806
American mustard 200
American plug 274
American roulette wheel 919
American shorthair 132
Americas 742
americium 684
Amerindian languages 469
Amery Ice Shelf 29
amethyst 375
Amharic 468
ammunition pouch 770
ammunition stowage 758
amoeba 94
amorphous solid 680
amount of substance, measurement 702
ampere 702
ampersand 473
amphibians 110
amphibians, examples 111
amphibious firefighting aircraft 628
amphitheater, Roman 407
ampli-tuner 497, 503
amplitude 690
ampulla 95
ampulla of fallopian tube 171
anal clasper 97
anal fin 108
analog camcorder 496
analog watch 696
analogue watch 696
analytical balance 699
anatomy 150
anatomy of a bird 116
anatomy of a bivalve shell 105
anatomy of a female butterfly 97
anatomy of a female spider 103
anatomy of a honeybee 99
anatomy of a horse 125
anatomy of a lobster 107
anatomy of a male frog 110
anatomy of a perch 109
anatomy of a snail 104
anatomy of a sponge 95
anatomy of a starfish 95
anatomy of a turtle 113
anatomy of a venomous snake 112
anatomy of an octopus 106
anatomy, human being 150
anchor 610, 791
anchor pin 559
anchor point 103
anchor wires 652
anchor-windlass room 605, 609
anchorage block 540
anchors, examples 610
anchovy 219
ancient costume, elements 336
ancient ships 598
anconeus 151
Andes Cordillera 31
andirons 257
Andorra 743
andouillette 216
anemometer 58, 59, 677
anesthesia room 780
angle grinder 308
angles, examples 704
angles, measure 701
Anglicanism 736
Angola 746
Anik 487
animal cell 94
animal dung 70
animal kingdom 92
anise 202
ankle 146, 148
ankle boot 343
ankle guard 796
ankle length 351
ankle sock 365
ankle-strap 343

ankle/wrist weight 850
anklet 365
announcer turret 488
annual ring 87
annular combustion chamber 627
annular eclipse 6
annulet 404
anode 689
anode rod 266
anorak 371
ant 101
Antarctic Circle 29, 35, 36
Antarctic Peninsula 29
Antarctic Plate 43
Antarctic Ridge 50
Antarctica 28, 29
antefix 403
antelope 128
antenna 17, 60, 96, 97, 98, 99, 107, 504, 505, 506, 551, 577, 611, 624, 631, 758, 761, 771, 812
antenna terminals 497
antennae cleaner 98
antennule 107
anterior adductor muscle 105
anterior chamber 177
anterior end 105
anterior fontanelle 158
anterior horn 167
anterior nasal spine 158
anterior notch 173
anterior root 168
anterior tibial 150
anterior tibial artery 160
anterior view 146, 148, 150
anther 80
anti-skating device 500
anti-torque tail rotor 631
antiaircraft missile 762
anticline 651
anticollision light 624
anticyclone 55
antifriction pad 889
Antigua and Barbuda 743
antihelix 173
antilock braking system 559
antimissile self-defence 762
antimissile self-defense 762
antimony 682
antipersonnel mine 758
antiradar missile 759
antireflection coating 672
antiseptic 777
antiship missile 759
antislip shoe 321, 826
antitank missile 759
antitank rocket 757
antitragus 173
antivibration handle 331
anus 95, 97, 103, 104, 105, 106, 107, 109, 113, 164, 169, 170
anvil 700
aorta 162, 163
aorta, arch 160, 161, 162
aortic valve 162
apartment building 711
aperture 105
aperture changer 694
aperture diaphragm 694
aperture door 17
aperture scale 479
aperture/exposure value display 479
apex 104, 105, 159, 176
apical foramen 159
Apollo 19
apostrophe 473
apothecium 74
Appalachian Mountains 30
apparatus 823
apparatus room 764
apple 193
apple cider vinegar 201
apple corer 233
apple, section 82
application launch buttons 527
appoggiatura 435
appointment book 530
approach 791, 792, 865
approach ramp 540
approach runs 824
approach stroke 866
approach wall 597
apricot 192
apron 276, 277, 278, 577, 618, 842
apse 411
apsidiole 410, 411
aquamarine 375
aquastat 259
aquatic bird 117
aquatic sports 827
aqueous humor 177
aqueous humour 177
Arab Jamahiriya 745
Arabian Peninsula 33
Arabian Sea 33
Arabic 468
arachnids 96
arachnids, examples 102
arachnoid 167
Aral Sea 33

Aramaic 468
arame 183
arbitration committee 845
arbor 322
arc 704
arc welding 318
arc welding machine 318
arcade 407, 410
archaeognatha 92
archaeopteryx 93
archboard 533
Archer 10
archer 859
archery 859
archery range 788
arches, examples 413, 541
archipelago 38
architectural styles 404
architecture 402
architecture, elements 413
architrave 403, 405
archives 394, 769
Arctic 28
Arctic Circle 35, 36
Arctic Ocean 28
area, parking 708, 735
arena 407, 788, 790
Arenberg parquet 254
areola 171
argent 741
Argentina 742
argon 684
Ariane IV 24
Ariane V 24
Ariel 5
ark 738
arm 95, 139, 147, 149, 276, 286, 329, 433, 452, 456, 610, 638, 693, 783
arm cylinder 638
arm elevator 500
arm guard 808, 859
arm lock 844
arm nut 456
arm pad 880
arm position 829
arm rest 500
arm slit 355
arm stump 276
arm zone 812
armature 688
armature core 688
armature winding 688
armchair 276, 734
armchairs, examples 276
Armenia 746
Armenian 469
armet 749
armhole 351
armless chair 734
armoire 278
armor 749, 758
armored cord 507
armored plate 758
armoured cord 507
armoured flex 507
armoured plate 758
armour 749, 758
armpit 146, 148
armrest 281, 554, 555, 783
armstand 828
arpeggio 435
arquebus 752
arrector pili muscle 172
arresting cable 761
arris 404
Arrow 12
arrow 750, 859
arrow key 261
arrow rest 859, 913
arsenic 682
art director 428
art room 734
arteries 160
arthropleura 92
artichoke 187
article 471
articular cartilage 154
articulated bus 569
articulated joint 569
articulated lorry with trailer 570
articulated mannequin 398
articulation 557
artificial climbing structure 900
artificial fly 909
artificial lake 48
artificial radiation 41
artificial satellite 53
artistic value judges 823
arts and architecture 394
arugula 187
asafetida 199
ascending aorta 161
ascending colon 164
ascending passage 402
ascot tie 349
ash 391

ash layer 44
ashtray 391
Asia 28, 33, 50, 746
Asian noodles 207
Asian pear 197
asparagus 185
asphalt 656
asphalt shingle 299
asphalt still 656
aspirator 775
aspirin 777
ass 128
assist grip 554
assistant camera operator 428
assistant coach 811, 879
assistant director 429
assistant governor's office 726
assistant judges 883
assistant property man 429
assistant referee 847, 860, 881, 882
astatine 683
asterisk 473
asteroid belt 5
asthenosphere 42
astigmatism 691
astragal 405, 753
astrakhan cap 340
astronautics 18
astronomical observation 10
astronomical observatory 17
astronomical observatory, cross section 17
astronomical unit 5
astronomy 4
Atacama Desert 31
athlete 791
athletic shirt 351
athletic track 788
Atlantic cod 221
Atlantic Ocean 28, 29, 32, 34
Atlantic salmon 221
atlas 111, 122, 126, 131, 153, 157
atlas moth 102
Atlas Mountains 34
ATM 730, 731
atmosphere 66, 70
atoll 51
atom 680
atomic number 682
atoms 680
atrium 406
attaché case 386
attached curtain 283
attack line 812
attack periscope 763
attack zone 812
attacker, middle 812
attendant's desk 732
attitude control thruster 18
attitude control thrusters 22
attraction 687
aubergine 188
audience 728
audio console 488, 489, 490
audio control room 489, 490
audio input/output jack 527
audio jack 513
audio monitor 488, 489, 490, 491
audio monitoring selector 491
audio system 556
audio technician 489, 490
audio volume unit meters 491
audio/video preview unit 491
audioguide 394
audiometric examination room 781
audiovisual equipment 716
auditorium 10, 394, 718, 732
auditory meatus, external 158
auditory ossicles 174
auger bit 323
auger bit, solid center 306
aunt, maternal 785
aunt, paternal 785
auricle 98, 174
auricle, ear 173
auriculars 115
Australia 28, 50, 747
Australian aboriginal languages 469
Australian-Indian Plate 43
Austria 744
authorized landfill site 69
auto answer indicator 508
auto-reverse button 504
auto/manual range 316
autoclave 780
autofocus on-off switch 483
automatic dialer index 506
automatic drip coffee maker 241
automatic electronic timer 831
automatic filter coffee maker 241
automatic rifle 755
automatic sliding door 416
automatic sorting trays 512
automatic tank gauge 655
automatic teller machine 731
automatic teller machine (ATM) 730
automatically-controlled door 620
automobile 549
automobile car 588
automobile systems 552, 553
automobile transport semitrailer 572
autopilot controls 626

autotrophs 67
autumn 54
autumn squash 189
autumnal equinox 54
auxiliary battery 563
auxiliary facilities room 490
auxiliary handle 306
auxiliary heating 260
auxiliary projector 10
auxiliary tank 571
auxiliary video switcher 491
avenue 39, 711
average key 479
avocado 188
awl 905
awning channel 567
axe 330
axel 881
axial compressor blade 627
axial rib 105
axillary artery 160
axillary bud 77
axillary nerve 166
axillary vein 160
axis 122, 153, 157
axle 586, 895
axle shaft 553
axon 168
axon hillock 168
Aymara 469
Azerbaijan 746
azimuth clamp 14, 15
azimuth fine adjustment 14, 15
Aztec temple 412
azure 741

B

B 434
baboon 139
baby doll 364
baby grand 443
baby wear 717
babygro 368
back 115, 124, 130, 147, 149, 173, 227, 229, 277, 281, 300, 303, 348, 391, 750, 783
back beam 460
back binding 840
back board 426
back boundary line 816
back brush 379
back check 443
back crossbar 893
back judge 807
back line 809, 877
back of a glove 346
back pad 857
back pocket 350
back ribs 214
back straight 856
back strap 857
back suspension 870
back waiter 721
back wall 818, 819
back zone 812
backboard 811
backboard storage 775
backboard support 811
backbone 523
backcourt 818, 821
backdrop 430
backgammon 915
backguard 290, 292, 293
backhoe 637
backhoe controls 637
backing 425
backing board 425
backing hammer 425
backing plate 559
backing press 425
backpack 906
backrest 555, 577, 876
backspace 515
backspace key 515
backstay 602, 881
backstop 794, 811
backstretch 856
backstroke 832
backstroke start 832
backstroke turn indicator 831
backup storage unit 523
backward 828
backward bucket 637
bacon 216
bactrian camel 129
badge 770
badger 134
badminton 816
badminton racket 816
Baffin Island 30
bag compartment 289
bag well 869
bagel 204
baggage cart 582
baggage check-in counter 620
baggage claim area 620
baggage compartment 568, 585, 631
baggage conveyor 623
baggage lockers 582

954

ENGLISH INDEX

ASTRONOMY > 2-25; EARTH > 26-71; VEGETABLE KINGDOM >72-89; ANIMAL KINGDOM > 90-143; HUMAN BEING > 144-177; FOOD AND KITCHEN > 178-241; HOUSE > 242-295;
DO-IT-YOURSELF AND GARDENING > 296-333; CLOTHING > 334-371; PERSONAL ADORNMENT AND ARTICLES > 372-391; ARTS AND ARCHITECTURE > 392-465; COMMUNICATIONS AND
OFFICE AUTOMATION > 466-535; TRANSPORT AND MACHINERY > 536-643; ENERGY > 644-677; SCIENCE > 678-705; SOCIETY > 706-785; SPORTS AND GAMES > 786-920

baggage racks 605
baggage room 582
baggage trailer 623
bagger 181
bagpipes 432
baguette 204
baguette cut 375
Bahamas 742
Bahrain 746
Baikal, Lake 33
bail 799
bail arm 910
bail arm opening mechanism 910
bailey 408
Bailey bridge 542
baitcasting reel 910
baize 862
Bakelite body 757
bakery 181
baking sheet 232
balaclava 341, 872
balalaika 433
balance beam 824, 826
balance control 497
balance rail 443
balancer 441
balcony 251, 431, 738
balcony window 251
baling 71
balk area 862
balk line 862
balk line spot 862
Balkan Peninsula 32
ball 453, 462, 516, 752, 823, 858, 865, 920
ball assembly 268
ball bearing 470, 677
ball boy 820
ball mount 558
ball of clay 464
ball peen 301
ball return 865
ball sports 794
ball stand 865
ball winder 462
ball-and-socket joint 156
ball-cock supply valve 265
ball-peen hammer 301
ball-type faucet 268
ball-type mixer tap 268
ballast 591
ballerina 343
balloon 899
balloon curtain 283
ballooning 899
ballpoint pen 470
ballroom 609
balsamic vinegar 201
Baltic Sea 32
baluster 255
balustrade 412, 417
Bambara 468
bamboo shoot 185
bamboos 917
banana 196
band 500
band ring 376
band select button 497
band selector 498
bandage 843
banding wheel 464
Bangladesh 747
bangle 376
banister 250, 251, 255
banjo 432
bank 538, 664, 710, 715, 730, 864, 915
bank note 915
bank of heliostats 674
banknote 729
banknote, back 729
banknote, front 729
banner 471
banner for the coming exhibition 394
banner for the current exhibition 394
banquette 277
Bantu languages 468
baptismal font 737
bar 127, 385, 431, 449, 686, 710, 714, 719, 720, 850, 851, 915
bar code reader 517
bar counter 720
bar frame 287
bar line 434
bar nose 331
bar shot 752
bar stool 277, 720
barb 56, 115, 911
Barbados 743
barbell 850, 851
barber comb 380
barbican 408
Barbuda 743
bare bow 859
baren 421
Barents Sea 32
bargraph-type peak meter 488
barium 682
bark 87
barley 85, 203
barley: spike 85
barmaid 720

barn 182
barograph 59
barometric pressure 55
barometric tendency 55
barrack buildings 409
barred spiral galaxy 9
barred window 727
barrel 381, 382, 470, 696, 753, 754, 755, 756, 757, 860, 912, 918
barrel jacket 755
barrel vault 407
barrette 380
barrier 281, 712
barrier barricade tape 771
barrier beach 51
barrow 633
bartizan 408, 409
basaltic layer 42
base 78, 239, 240, 256, 273, 274, 275, 286, 305, 307, 308, 381, 405, 412, 425, 494, 500, 516, 517, 531, 538, 591, 676, 685, 693, 698, 739, 740, 767, 791, 825, 826, 860, 912
base cabinet 224
base course 538
base of splat 276
base plate 58, 304, 500, 701, 756, 889, 907
base plug 757
base ring 753
base width 663
baseball 794, 796
baseball stadium 788
baseball, cross section 797
baseboard 253, 255, 485
baseboard register 258
baseline 821, 907
basement 250, 713
basement window 245
basic building materials 298
basic operations 529
basic source of food 67
basic weaves 463
basil 202
basilic vein 160
basilosaur 93
basin 664, 838
basin side 664
basin wrench 315
basket 238, 241, 281, 291, 292, 811, 888, 899
basket handle 413, 899
basket stitch 458
basket suspension cables 899
basket weave pattern 254
basketball 810
basketball player 810
basmati rice 207
bass 220
bass bridge 442
bass clarinet 437
bass drum 437, 448
bass guitar 441
bass keyboard 432
bass pickup 441
bass register 432
Bass Strait 29
bass tone control 441, 497, 503
bass trap 490
bassoon 446
bassoons 437
baster 233
bastion 409
bat 140, 643, 796, 797, 798
bat, morphology 140
bateau neck 363
bath 251, 262, 264, 724
bath and shower mixer 262
bath brush 379
bath sheet 379
bath towel 379
bathing wrap 368
bathrobe 364
bathroom 251, 264, 724, 780
bathroom articles 717
bathroom scale 699
bathroom skylight 251
bathtub 251, 264
baton 790
baton holder 770
bats, examples 141
batsman 798, 799
bergamot 194
bergère 276
bergschrund 46
Bering Sea 28
Bering Strait 30
berkelium 684
berm 660
Bermuda sail 601
Bermuda shorts 358
berries 192
berry fruit 83
berth 584
bertha collar 363
beryllium 682
bevel 776
bevel gear 686
bevel square 313, 701
beverage can 223
beverage dispenser 779
bezel 376
bezel facet 374
batten 285, 430, 600, 834, 836, 897
batten pocket 834, 836
batter 795, 796
batter head 448
batter skin 433
batter's helmet 796
battery 302, 482, 513, 552, 562, 563, 586, 673, 687, 759, 765
battery backup receptacles 520
battery box 571
battery case 562
battery condition module 563
battery cover 562
battery modules 60
battery pack 306
battery warning light 557
batting glove 796
battlement 408, 409
batwing sleeve 361
bay 7, 38

bay filler panel 513
Bay of Bengal 33
bayonet base 275
bayonet mount 478
bazooka 757
beach 51
beach volleyball 813
bead 560
bead wire 561
beak 106
beaker 231, 685
beam 412, 418, 641, 698, 826
beam balance 698
beam bridge 540
beam bridges, examples 541
beam diameter reduction 694
beam gantry 663
beam reach 833
bean bag chair 277
bean thread cellophane noodles 207
beans 190, 191
bearer 445
bearing pad 667
beater 236, 460, 641
beater ejector 236
beater handtree 460
beater sley 460
beaters 236
Beaufort Sea 30
beauty care 181
beaver 123, 749
becquerel 702
bed 280, 424, 538, 823, 904
bed chamber 406
bed lamp 286
bedrock 43, 78
bedroom 251, 902
bedside lamp 724, 780
bedside table 724, 780
beech 88
beechnut 193
beef cubes 214
beef, cuts 214
beer 180
beer mug 225
beet 189
beetle 101
beetroot 189
begonia 80
Belarus 744
belay beam 900
belay rope 900
belayer 900
Belgian endive 187
Belgium 743
Belize 742
bell 446, 447
bell boot 858
bell bottoms 358
bell brace 446
bell roof 415
bell tower 411, 737
bellow 445
bellows 432, 485
bellows strap 432
bells 449
belly 124
belly scale 112
belly tank 631
below-stage 430
belt 313, 350, 352, 561, 611, 844
belt clip 505
belt drive 605
belt highway 39
belt loader 646, 647
belt loop 350, 352, 905
belted radial tyre 561
beluga whale 137
bench 277, 593, 647, 715, 775, 851
bench height 647
bench seat 555
bench, defence counsel's 728
bend 385, 911
Bengal, Bay 33
Benin 745
bent blade 401
Berber 468
Berenice's Hair 13
beret 341

Bhutan 747
bias 455
bias-ply tire 561
biathlete 893
biathlon 893
bib 368, 369, 848
bib necklace 374
bib tap 268
biceps of arm 150
biceps of thigh 151
biconcave lens 691
biconvex lens 691
bicorne 339
bicycle 578
bicycle bag 580
bicycle parking 735
bicycle, accessories 580
bicycle, parts 578
bicycles, examples 581
bidet 264
bifocal lens 385
Big Dog 11
bike carrier 558
bikini 367
bikini briefs 351
bilberry 192
bill 115, 610
bill compartment 386
bill presenter 730
bill-file 534
billfold 387
billhook 330
billiard cue 863
billiard spot 862
billiards 862
billiards, carom 862
billiards, English 863
bills, examples 117
bimah 738
bimetallic helix 695
bimetallic thermometer 695
bin, rubbish 723
binder 642
binding 340, 840, 891, 892
binocular microscope 693
biology 702
biosphere 66
biosphere, structure 66
biparous cyme 81
biplane 628
bipod 755, 756
birch 88
bird 115
Bird of Paradise 10
bird of prey 117
bird's eye chile 199
bird's nest fern 76
bird, anatomy 116
bird, morphology 115
bird, skeleton 116
birds 115
birds, examples 118
birth 702
biscuit cutters 232
bishop 916
bishop sleeve 361
bismuth 682
bison 128
bit 302, 390, 648, 651, 858
bits 306
bits, examples 308
bitt 607
bitter melon 188
bivalve shell 105
bivalve shell, anatomy 105
bivalve shell, morphology 105
Black 916
black 472, 690, 919
black ball 863
black bean 191
black bear 135
black clamp 558
black currant 192
black dwarf 8
black flying fox 141
black gram 191
black hole 8
black mustard 198
black pepper 198
black pollock 221
black radish 189
black rye bread 204
black salsify 189
Black Sea 28, 32, 33
black square 916
black stone 916
black tea 208
black-eyed pea 190
blackberry 192
blackboard 734
blackcurrant 192
bladder 113
blade 76, 79, 227, 229, 237, 240, 261, 274, 302, 303, 304, 305, 309, 315, 320, 331, 332, 382, 383, 390, 453, 454, 636, 639, 659, 676, 677, 800, 815, 838, 841, 849, 878, 880, 881, 900, 911
blade close stop 382
blade guard 304, 305
blade height adjustment 305

blade injector 383
blade lever 424
blade lift cylinder 636, 639
blade lift fan 605
blade locking bolt 304
blade rotation cylinder 639
blade shifting mechanism 639
blade tilting lock 304
blade tilting mechanism 304, 305
blade with two beveled edges 401
blade with two bevelled edges 401
blades, major types 401
blank 914
blanket 280, 421
blanket insulation 299
blanket sleepers 369
blanket sleepsuit 369
blast valve 899
blasting charge 653
blastodisc 117
blazer 358
bleeder valve 259
blender 236
blending attachment 236
blind cloth 285
blind spot mirror 568, 569
blinds 285
blinker 857
blinking lights 568
block 295, 444, 632, 791, 813
block bracket 284
block cutter 401, 421
blockboard 300
blocking glove 800, 879
blood circulation 160
blood circulation, schema 161
blood factor negative 702
blood factor positive 702
blood pressure monitor 777
blood sausage 216
blood vessel 154, 162, 172
blood vessels 140
blood, composition 162
blotting paper 531
blouses, examples 359
blow pipe 432
blower 258, 445, 670
blower motor 258, 261
blowhole 136
blowtorch 314, 319
blucher oxford 342
blue 400, 690
blue ball 863
blue band 871
blue beam 494
blue line 879
blue mussel 217
blue-green 400
blue-veined cheeses 211
blueberry 192
bluefish 220
blusher brush 378
BMX 871
BMX bike 581
boa 114
board 300, 836, 916, 917
board cutter 424
board games 915
board insulation 299
board, bulletin 734
boarding ladder 611
boarding room 621
boarding step 631
boarding walkway 619
boards 878
boat hook 611
boater 340
boats 604
boats, sculling 839
bobber 911
bobbin 452, 453, 458, 461
bobbin case 452
bobbin lace 458
bobbin winder 452, 462
bobby pin 380
bobeche 287
bobsled 884
bobsleigh 884
bobstay 602
bodies, examples 549
body 176, 240, 268, 288, 306, 440, 441, 444, 446, 550, 567, 692, 697, 793, 876, 893, 909
body care 379
body flap 23
body of fornix 167
body of nail 172
body pad 800
body shirt 359
body side molding 551
body side moulding 551
body suit 366
body temperature control unit 20
body tube 693
body wire 848
bogie 586, 595
bogie and track 595
bogie frame 586
bogie goods truck 588
bogie goods van 588
bogie tank wagon 588

bogie van 587
bohrium 683
boiler 259, 674
boiling-water reactor 671
bokken 846
bold 472
bole 87
bolero 358
Bolivia 742
bolster 227, 229, 280
bolt 248, 310, 311, 312, 750
bolt assist mechanism 755
bolts 311
bonding jumper 272
bone folder 426
bone marrow 154
bone, parts 155
bone, structure 154
bones, types 157
bongos 449
boning knife 229
bonnet 268, 550, 570
bonus tiles 917
bony fish 108
bony fishes 219
book ends 535
book lung 103
book return desk 733
book truck 733
bookbinding leather 425
bookcase 734
booking hall 582
booking room 769
bookstore 714
boom 573, 637, 638, 834
boom cylinder 637, 638
boom operator 429
boom truck 622
boom vang 834
booster parachute 22
booster seat 281
boot 343, 551, 840, 841, 855, 874, 875, 880, 881, 892, 895, 896
boot jack 345
bootee 342
booth 720
borage 202
bordeaux glass 225
border 244, 431
borders 430
bore 753
boreal forest 66
boron 682
Bosnia and Herzegovina 744
Bothnia, Gulf 32
Botswana 746
bottle 379, 685, 906
bottle cart 319
bottle opener 230, 905
bottom 840, 888
bottom bracket axle 580
bottom cap 689
bottom cylinder 421
bottom deck 655
bottom deckboard 632
bottom face 374
bottom line 831
bottom pocket 862
bottom rail 247, 278, 285
bottom ring 659
bottom road 650
bottom side rail 635
bottom-end transverse member 635
bottom-fold portfolio 386
bottomboard 445
boubou 339
boudoir grand 443
boulevard 39, 711
bound book 426
bow 340, 439, 609, 750, 834, 836
bow ball 839
bow collar 362
bow door 605
bow loading door 608
bow saw 907
bow thruster 609
bow tie 349
bow-winged grasshopper 102
bowl 227, 237, 240, 390, 612, 638
bowl with serving spout 237
bowler 340, 799, 865
bowline 908
bowline on a bight 908
bowling 865
bowling alley 714, 865
bowling ball 865
bowling crease 799
bowling technique 864
bowls 864
bows 750
bowsprit 602
bowstring 750, 859, 913
box 256, 259, 431, 641
box bag 388
box car 587, 588
box end wrench 311
box office 427
box pallet 632
box pleat 283
box sealing tape dispenser 534
box spring 280

box springs 716
boxer 842
boxer shorts 351, 371
boxing 842
boxing gloves 843
boxing trunks 842
boys' wear (size 2 to 6) 717
boys' wear (size 7 to 17) 717
bra 367
brace 252, 307, 321, 663
brace clip 350
bracelets 376
braces 350
brachial 150
brachial artery 160
brachial plexus 166
brachiopoli 92
brachioradialis 150, 151
bracket 285, 412, 613
bracket base 278
bract 84
braided rope 908
braies 338
brain 99, 103, 106, 107, 109, 110
brains 212
brake 783, 851, 870
brake arm 889
brake booster 552, 559
brake cable 579
brake caliper 574
brake fluid reservoir 559
brake handle 876
brake lever 579, 870
brake lever and shifter 870
brake light 554
brake line 559
brake lining 559
brake loop 896, 897
brake pad 559
brake pedal 333, 552, 556, 559, 889
brake pressure modulator 559
brake shoe 559
brake van 588
brake, disc 552, 559
brakeman 884
brakes 559
braking circuit 552, 559
braking system 553
braking zone 891
branch 86, 87, 89, 127, 185, 262, 687, 776, 855
branch clip 776
branch duct 258
branch return pipe 259
branch supply pipe 259
branches 87
branching, examples 270
brandy snifter 225
brass family 437
brattice 408
brayer 421
brazier 412
Brazil 742
Brazil nut 193
bread 204, 722
bread and butter plate 226
bread guide 238
bread knife 229
bread machine 239
break 515
break line 362
break-out room 718
breaker 49
breaking the wall 917
breast 115, 146, 148, 171
breast beam 460
breast collar 857
breast dart 352
breast pocket 349, 352
breast welt pocket 348
breastplate 749, 853
breaststroke 832
breaststroke kick 832
breaststroke turn 832
breath testing machine 769
breather valve 655
breathing in 832
breathing out 832
breech 446
breech guard 446
breechblock 756, 912
breechblock operating lever assembly 756
breeches 338, 748, 848
Breton 469
brick 298
brick carton 223
brick wall 253, 298
bricklayer's hammer 315
bridge 39, 284, 385, 433, 439, 440, 441, 523, 596, 692, 761, 863, 875
bridge assembly 441
bridge of nose 175
bridging 252
bridle 854
bridle assembly 615
bridle tape 443
Brie 211
briefcase 386
briefs 351, 367
brig 601
brigantine 601

brightness control 518
brilliant cut facets 374
brilliant full cut 375
brim 340, 341
briolette cut 375
bristle 383, 384
bristles 320
broad beans 190
broad ligament of uterus 171
broad reach 833
broad welt side pocket 352, 355, 360
broadcast satellite communication 486
broadest of back 151
broadleaved trees, examples 88
broadsword 751
broccoli 187
broccoli rabe 187
brochure rack 730
broken line 538, 539
bromine 683
brooch 376
brood chamber 100
brook 48
brook trout 221
broom 257, 295
brother 785
brother-in-law 785
brother/sister 785
brothers 785
brow brush and lash comb 378
brow reinforce 749
browband 854
brown alga 75
brown ball 863
brown dwarf 8
brown rice 207
brown sugar 209
browser 524
Brunei Darussalam 747
brush 85, 289, 295, 320, 384, 397, 422, 688
brush and rails 852
brushes 688
Brussels sprouts 186
bubble 575
bubble bath 379
buccal cavity 116
bucket 261, 637, 659
bucket cylinder 637, 638
bucket hinge pin 637
bucket lever 637
bucket ring 659
bucket seat 555
bucket wheel excavator 647
buckle 350, 388, 555, 611, 889
buckwheat 85, 203
buckwheat: raceme 85
bud 78
Buddha 736
Buddhism 736
buffalo 128
buffer 417
buffer tank 654
buffers 583
buffet 279, 720, 725
bug 101
bugle 447
building sewer 262, 263
bulb 127, 185, 274, 275, 316, 607, 687
bulb dibber 324
bulb dibble 324
bulb unit 664
bulb vegetables 184
bulb, section 78
bulbil 78
bulbocavernous muscle 169
Bulgaria 744
Bulgarian 469
bulge 9
bulk carrier 604
bulk mail letter 475
bulk terminal 596
bulkhead 571
bulkhead flat car 588
bulkhead flat truck 588
Bull 12
bull's-eye 859
bulldog 130
bulldozer 636, 647
bullet 912
bulletin board 535, 734
bullfinch 118
bullion stitch 459
bulwark 602
bumblebee 101
bump 812, 875
bumper 289, 570, 571, 577, 583
bumper guard 818
bumper molding 550
bumper, rear 577
bumps 545, 547
bun tin 232
bunch 390, 870
bunch of grapes 86
bund wall 655
bundle 185, 663
bunk 567
bunker oil 656
bunker silo 182
bunting 739
bunting bag 368

buoy 833
buoy weather station 54
buoyage regions 616
buoyancy compensator 841
buoyancy tube 611
burdock 189
bureau 279
burgee 739
burgundy glass 225
burial 71
Burkina Faso 745
Burmese 468
burned gases 564
burner 234, 259, 290, 899, 903
burner control knobs 290
burner frame 903
burner ring 234
burnisher 422
bursting charge 757
Burundi 745
bus 513, 522, 568, 713
bus module 40
bus network 522
bus shelter 712
bus station 710
bus stop 712
busbar 658
bush 322
bush-cricket 101
bushing 657, 658, 663
business aircraft 628
business district 708, 710
business transactions 525
business wicket 731
bustle 337
butane accessories 903
butane tank 391
butt 391, 425, 456, 754, 755, 816, 822, 863, 909
butt cap 909
butt end 880
butt grip 910
butt guide 910
butt plate 754, 912
butt section 909
butt-strap 385
butte 52
butter 210
butter compartment 291
butter cup 223
butter curler 229
butter dish 226
butter knife 228
butterfly 96
butterfly kick 832
butterfly stroke 832
butterfly turn 832
butterfly, anatomy 97
butterfly, hind leg 96
butterfly, morphology 96
butterhead lettuce 186
buttermilk 210
buttock 147, 149, 169, 170
button 274, 349, 354, 432, 753, 849
button loop 350
button strap 369
button-through smock 359
buttondown collar 349
buttoned placket 349, 354
buttonhole 352
buttress 410, 660
buttress dam 660
buttress dam, cross section 660
by-pass taxiway 618
bypass duct 627
bypass feeder 512

C

C 434
C clef 434
C-clamp 312
C1 canoe 838
cab 636, 637, 638, 639, 640, 643, 876
cabbage 186
cabin 608, 631
cabinet 224, 291, 292, 293, 494
cable 306, 488, 504, 516, 517, 558, 573, 824, 851, 859, 908, 913
cable distributor 486
cable drum compartment 489
cable guard 859, 913
cable line 525
cable modem 525
cable ripper 317
cable shutter release 482
cable sleeve 306
cable stay anchorage 541
cable stitch 458
cable, spark plug 552
cable-stayed bridges 541
cables 492, 523
cabochon cut 375
caboose 588
cabriole leg 276
cabriolet 276
cadmium 683
caecum 164
café curtain 282
cafeteria 735

caftan 339
cage 407
caiman 114
cajun spice seasoning 199
cake mascara 378
cake pan 232
cake tin 232
calamus 115
calandria 669
calcaneus 126, 153, 155
calcar 140, 141
calcareous sponge 95
calcium 682
calculator 386
calculator dial 479
calculator, pocket 529
calculator, printing 529
calculator/cheque book holder 386
calendar pad 530
calf 128, 147, 149
California, Gulf 30
californium 684
caliper 423, 559
call button 417, 505
call director telephone 507
Callisto 4
calls indicator 508
calm 56
Calvin 736
calyx 80, 83, 84, 165
cam ring 307
cambium 87
Cambodia 747
Cambrian 92
camcorder, digital 517
camel 129
Camembert 211
camera 18, 428, 490, 492, 775, 873
camera body 476
camera control area 489
camera control technician 489, 490
camera control unit 489, 490
camera operator 428
camera pedestal 492
camera platform 482
camera platform lock 482
camera screw 482
camera viewfinder 492
camera, digital 517
Cameroon 745
camisole 366
camp bed 904
camp stove 903
camper 567
camping 902
camping (caravan and tent) 725
camping (caravan) 725
camping (tent) 725
camping (trailer and tent) 725
camping (trailer) 725
camping equipment 905
camping prohibited 725
camshaft 566
can opener 230, 240, 905
Canada 742
Canadian bacon 216
Canadian duckpin 865
Canadian elk 128
Canadian football 809
Canadian football, playing field 809
canal bed 597
canal lock 596, 597
canary melon 195
cancel button 519
canceled stamped mail 474
candela 702
candies 717
candle 737
candlepin 865
candy thermometer 231
cane pen 470
canine 121, 159
canister 611
canisters 222
canned failed fuel 666
canned goods 181
cannelloni 206
cannon 124, 758
cannon and mortar, seventeenth-century 752
canoe 600, 837
canoe, C1 838
canoe-kayak 837, 838
canopy 391, 416, 567, 611, 628, 639, 760, 896, 897, 902
canopy release knob 898
cantaloupe 195
canteen 906
cantilever 661
cantilever bridge 540
cantilever span 540
cantle 855
canvas 400, 842
canvas divider 902
cap 76, 236, 255, 269, 275, 340, 398, 470, 484, 676, 770, 783, 827, 830
cap iron 309
cap sleeve 360
capacitor 689
cape 38, 338, 355
Cape Horn 31
Cape of Good Hope 34

Cape Verde 745
capillary blood vessel 172
capillary bore 695
capital 37, 405
capitals lock 514
capitals lock key 514
capitate 154
capitulum 81
capon 213
caponiere 409
capped column 64
capped tee 257
capstan 421
capstan button 443
capsule 75, 783
capsule, section 84
captain 884
captain's quarters 609
captain's seat 626
caption 471
capture 916
car 587, 835
car ceiling 417
car cleaning yard 589
car coat 355
car cover 558
car dealer 711
car deck 608
car floor 417
car guide rail 417
car racing 872
car repair shop 589
car safety 417
car systems : main parts 552
car wash 548
car, electric 563
car, hybrid 563
carabiner 901
carabiner, D 900
carabiner, locking 900
caraco jacket 337
carafe 241
carambola 197
carapace 107, 113
caravan 567
caravel 599
caraway 198
carbon 683
carbon dioxide absorption 78
carbon dioxide gas coolant 670
carbon dioxide reactor 670
carbon rod 689
carbon-zinc cell 689
Carboniferous 92
carburetor 574
carburettor 574
card 915
card case 386
card number 729, 731
card reader 493, 507
card reader slot 548, 730, 731
card support 58
cardamom 198
cardboard 400
cardholder's name 729
cardholder's signature 729
cardiac stomach 107
cardigan 354, 359
cardinal 118
cardinal marks 616
cardoon 185
cards 914
cargo aircraft 475, 629
cargo bay 22
cargo bay door 23
cargo dispatch 621
cargo hold 625
cargo reception 621
Caribbean Islands 742
Caribbean Plate 43
Caribbean Sea 28, 30
caribou 128
carina 108
carnation 80
carnivores 67
carnivorous mammals 130
carnivorous mammals, examples 134
carom billiards 862
carp 220
carpal pad 130
Carpathian Mountains 32
Carpentaria, Gulf 29
carpenter's hammer 301
Carpenter's Square 10
carpentry material 313
carpentry: drilling tools 306
carpentry: nailing tools 301
carpentry: sawing tools 303
carpentry: screwing tools 302
carpentry: shaping tools 308
carpet 254
carpus 116, 122, 126, 131, 136, 138, 141, 142, 154
carriage 632, 753, 756
carriage control dial 456
carriage handle 456
carriage return 528
carriages 456
carrier 284, 577, 578
carrier bag 388
carrot 189

carry-on bag 388
carrying handle 755
cart path 866
cartilaginous fish 108
cartilaginous fishes 218
cartography 35
carton 223, 390
cartoon 471
cartridge 268, 315, 470, 500, 754, 773
cartridge (rifle) 912
cartridge (shotgun) 912
cartridge faucet 268
cartridge film 481
cartridge fuse 272
cartridge mixer 268
cartridge stem 268
cartridge tape recorder 488
cartridges 860, 861
cartwheel hat 341
carved prow 598
carver's bench screw 401
carving 401
carving fork 229
carving knife 229
casaba melon 195
case 313, 345, 377, 436, 442, 695, 696, 700, 912
case fan 513
casement 249
casement window 415
cash dispenser 715, 730
cash register 181
cash supply 731
cashew 193
cashier 181
casing 249, 260, 261, 332, 920
casing first string 654
Caspian Sea 28, 33
cassava 184
Cassegrain focus 17
cassette 499, 504, 521
cassette compartment 495, 496
cassette deck 488
cassette drive 521
cassette eject switch 495
cassette holder 499
cassette player 504
cassette player controls 504
cassette tape deck 499
Cassini 19
cast-on stitches 457
castanets 437, 449
caster 281, 289, 448
castes 99
casting 910
Castle 916
castle 408
casual shoe 343
cat 132
cat breeds 132
cat's head 132
cat, morphology 133
Catalan 469
catalytic converter 553
catalytic reforming plant 656
catamaran 835
catapult 761
catch 909
catcher 443, 794, 795, 796
catcher's glove 796
catching glove 879
catenary 585, 595
catering vehicle 623
caterpillar 97
cathedral 410
cathedral ceiling 251
cathedral roof 251
cathedral, plan 411
cathode 689
Catholicism 736
catwalk 430
caudal fin 108, 136
caudal vertebrae 122, 126, 131, 138, 141, 142
cauliflower 187
caulking gun 315
cave 47, 51
cavernous body 169
cayenne chile 199
CB radio 505
CD radio cassette recorder, portable 504
CD/DVD player 918
CD/DVD-ROM drive 513, 526
CD/DVD-ROM eject button 513
CD/ROM player 517
cecum 103, 106, 116, 125, 164
cedar of Lebanon 89
cedilla 473
ceiling 257, 818, 819
ceiling bracket 284
ceiling collar 257
ceiling fan 261
ceiling fitting 286
ceiling joist 252
ceiling outlet 258
ceiling projector 59
ceiling register 258
celeriac 189
celery 185
celestial bodies 4
celestial coordinate system 13

celestial equator 13
celestial meridian 13
celestial sphere 13
celiac trunk 161, 165
cell 96, 100, 407, 563, 727
cell body 168
cell membrane 74, 94
cell wall 74
cello 439
cellos 437
cells 687, 728
cellular telephone, portable 506
Celsius 702
Celsius scale 695
Celsius temperature, measurement 702
Celtic languages 469
celtuce 186
cement 822
cement screed 254
cementum 159
cemetery 39, 711
censer 737
cent 728
Centaur 11
center 431, 704, 807, 809, 811, 847, 879, 916
center aisle 584
center attacker 812
center back 812, 814
center back vent 348
center base 740
center chief 740
center circle 803, 810
center console 556
center court 818
center divider strip 712
center drive 641, 643
center electrode 562
center face-off circle 879
center field 795
center fielder 794
center flag 802
center forward 801, 814
center half 801
center hole 500
center keelson 607
center line 801, 809, 810, 814, 815, 816, 848, 877, 879
center line judge 820
center loudspeaker 493
center mark 820
center pocket 862
center point 740
center post 278, 551
center service line 821
center span 540
center spot 803, 862
center strap 821
center T mark 858
center third 809
center wheel 696, 697
centerboard 834
centerboard boat 835
centering 528
centering control 518
Central African languages 468
Central African Republic 745
Central America 28, 30
central brush 573
central circle 809
central column 676
central disk 95
central focusing wheel 692
central incisor 159
central nave 738
central nervous system 167
central pumping station 654
central reservation 539, 712
central screw 425
central wrestling area 843
centre 704, 807, 809, 811, 847, 879, 916
centre back 814
centre back vent 348
centre base 740
centre chief 740
centre circle 803, 810
centre console 556
centre court 818
centre electrode 562
centre face-off circle 879
centre field 795
centre fielder 794
centre flag 802
centre forward 801, 814
centre half 801
centre hole 500
centre Keelson 607
centre line 801, 806, 809, 810, 814, 815, 816, 848, 877, 879
centre mark 820
centre pocket 862
centre point 740
centre post 278
centre service line 821
centre span 540
centre spot 803, 862
centre strap 821
centre T mark 858
centre third 809
centre wheel 696, 697
centre, city 709, 710
centre, control 727, 764

centre, convention 711, 718
centre, day-care 715
centre, documentation 764
centre, exhibition 708
centre, shopping 709, 714
centre-aisle 584
centreboard 834
centrifugal compressor 627
centrifuge module 21
centring 528
centring control 518
centriole 94
cephalic vein 160
cephalothorax 103, 107
ceramic capacitor 689
cereal 203
cereal products 204
cereals 85
cerebellum 167
cerebropleural ganglion 105
cerebrospinal fluid 168
cerebrum 167
cerium 684
cervical collar 775
cervical vertebra 153, 157
cervical vertebrae 116, 122, 126, 131, 138, 141, 142
cervix of uterus 170
cesium 682
cesspit emptier 573
Chac-Mool 412
Chad 745
Chad, Lake 34
chain 580, 697, 826
chain brake 331
chain drive 641, 643
chain guide 580
chain mail 749
chain of dunes 52
chain of neurons 168
chain pipe wrench 315
chain reaction 681
chain stay 578
chain stitch 459
chain wheel 870
chain wheel A 580
chain wheel B 580
chainsaw 331
chainsaw chain 331
chair 723
chair lift 886
chair lift departure area 886
chairs, examples 277
chaise longue 277
chalaza 117
chalice 737
chalk 863
chalk line 313
Chameleon 11
chameleon 114
chamfer bit 308
chamois leather 345, 377
chamomile 208
champagne flute 225
Chance card 915
chandelier 287
change sign key 529
changing room 734
changing table 281
changing table 281
channel scan button 495
channel scan buttons 495
channel selector 505
channel selector controls 495
chanter 432
chanterelle 183
Chantilly parquet 254
chapati bread 205
chapel 408, 726
character 472
character correction 528
characters 917
characters of a font 472
charcoal 397
charcoal drawing 396
chard 185
charge 912
charge air cooler 564
charge indicator 383
charger 306
charges, examples 741
charging handle 755
charging light 383
charging plug 383, 563
Charioteer 12
charlotte mold 232
charm bracelet 376
charms 376
Charon 5
chart room 604
chase 753
chat room 525
chayote 189
check 721
check nut 58
check valve 263, 319
check-rail 590
checkbook 386, 387
checkbook/secretary clutch 386
checker 916
checkerboard 916

checkered flag 872
checkers 915, 916
checkout 181, 723
checkouts 181, 716, 717
checks 729
cheek 124, 130, 148, 301, 753, 909
cheek piece 860, 861
cheek ring 854
cheek strap 854
cheese 722
cheese box 223
cheese counter 181
cheese grater, rotary 230
cheese knife 228
cheeses, blue-veined 211
cheeses, fresh 210
cheeses, goat's-milk 210
cheeses, soft 211
cheetah 135
chef 721
chemical bond 680
chemical elements 682
chemical treatment 656
chemise 408
chemist's shop 725
chemistry 680
chemistry symbols 684
cheque book 386
cheque book cover 387
cherimoya 196
cherry 192
chervil 202
chess 916
chess notation 916
chess pieces 916
chessboard 916
chest 124
chest expander 850
chest freezer 291
chest protector 796, 808, 859
chesterfield 276
chestnut 193
chevet 411
Chèvre cheese 210
chevron 740
chevron stitch 459
chicane 872
chick 120
chick peas 190
chicken 213
chief 740
chief executive officer's office 509
chief judge 823, 837
chief mechanic 873
chief officer's office 768
chief range officer 860
chief referee 846, 847, 860, 883
chief steward 855
chief timekeeper 830
chief's office 764
chiffonier 279
child carrier 580
child safety seat 558
child's skull 158
child's tricycle 581
children 785
children's books 732
children's clothing 369
children's furniture 281
children's section 732
children's shoes 717
children's sportswear 717
Chile 742
chile 199
Chile Trench 50
chili powder 199
chilli 188
chimney 245, 257, 259
chimney connection 256
chimney pot 245
chimpanzee 139
chin 115, 148
chin guard 765, 885
chin protector 575
chin rest 439
chin strap 765, 808, 870
China 747
China Sea, East 33
China Sea, South 33
Chinese 468
chinois 231
chip cover 305
chip van 572
chipboard 300
chipmunk 123
chipolata sausage 216
chipset 513
Chisel 11
chisel 421
chiton 336
chive 184
chlamys 336
chlorine 683
chloroplast 74
choanocyte 95
chock 900, 901
chocolate 208
choir 410, 411
choir organ manual 444
choker 374
chondrite 8

choosing key 261
chop 214, 215
chord 435
chorizo 216
choroid 177
chow chow 130
Christianity 736
Christmas tree 652, 654
chromatin 94
chromium 683
chromosphere 6
chronology of religions 736
chrysalis 97
chuck 302, 306, 307, 649
chuck key 306
chuck, keyless 306
chukka 342
church 711, 737
chute 650
cicada 101
cigar 390
cigar band 390
cigar cutter 390
cigarette 390
cigarette pack 390
cigarette papers 390
ciliary body 177
ciliate 79
cilium 94
cine scale 479
cinema 608, 710, 714
cinnamon 198
circle, parts 704
circles 917
circuit 872
circuit breaker 260, 658
circuit vent 262
circular body 432
circular needle 457
circular route 39
circular saw 304
circular saw blade 304
circular track 16
circulating pump 259, 675
circulation desk 733
circumference 704
circumflex accent 473
circumvallate papilla 176
cirque 7
cirque, glacial 46
cirrocumulus 56, 62
cirrostratus 56, 62
cirrus 56, 62
cistern 264
cistern ball 265
cistern lid 265
citron 194
citrus fruit 82
citrus fruits 194
citrus juicer 230, 237
city 37, 708
city bicycle 581
city bus 568
city centre 709, 710
city hall 710
city houses 419
clam 217
clam cleat 835
clamp 274, 303, 381, 424, 462, 892
clamp binder 532
clamp lever 381
clamp spotlight 286
clamp/holder 685
clamping block 700
clamping screw 312
clamping screws 700
clapper/the slate 429
clapskate 883
clarinet 446
clarinets 437
clasp 386, 387
class ring 376
classic blouse 359
classification yard 589
classified advertisements 471
classroom 727, 734, 735
classroom for students with learning disabilities 734
clavicle 111, 116, 122, 141, 142, 152
claw 96, 98, 107, 113, 115, 121, 122, 130, 133, 140, 143, 301, 376, 425
claw hammer 301
claw, extended 133
claw, retracted 133
claw-pole rotor 688
clay 822
clay core 660
clay target 860
clean and jerk 850
clean dish table 721
clean utility room 778
cleaner height adjustment knob 289
cleaning brush 383
cleaning eye 270
cleaning supplies 721
cleaning tools 289
cleanout 270
clear key 529
clear sky 56
clear space 812
clear-entry key 529

cleat 834, 835
cleated shoe 808
cleated shoes 885
cleaver 229
clefs 434
clerks' desk 728
clerks' office 728
clew 836
click 696, 697
cliff 7, 45, 51
climate control 556
climates of the world 61
climbing 900
climbing harness 901
climbing iron 345
climbing plant 322
climbing shoe 900
climbing structure, artificial 900
clinical thermometer 695
clinical thermometers 777
clip 284, 470, 506, 534, 700, 913
clip earrings 374
clipboard 533
clipless pedal 870
clippers 381
clitoris 170
cloaca 103, 110, 113, 116
cloakroom 394, 719, 723, 731
cloche 341
Clock 10
clock 488, 489, 491, 734
clock mechanism 697
clock operator 810
clock radio 503
clock timer 238, 290
clog 344
close hauled 833
close reach 833
close-up lens 478
closed stringer 255
closed to bicycles 545, 546
closed to motorcycles 545, 546
closed to pedestrians 545, 546
closed to trucks 545, 546
closeness setting 383
closet 250, 279
closure rail 590
cloth roller 460
clothing 336
clothing guard 783
clothing store 714
cloud 53, 65
cloud amount 56
cloud ceiling, measure 59
cloud of volcanic ash 44
cloudless sky 56
clouds 56, 62
clouds of vertical development 62
cloudwater 70
cloudy sky 56
clove 198
clove hitch 908
cloverleaf 538, 539
club 914
club chair 276
clubhouse 856, 866
clubhouse turn 856
clubs 823
clump of flowers 322
clutch 552
clutch housing 576
clutch lever 327, 574, 576
clutch pedal 556
coach 568, 800, 811, 827, 879
coach car 584
coach's box 794
coaches 881, 883
coaches' stand 891
coal mine 647
coal storage yard 646
coal-fired thermal power plant 646
coarse adjustment knob 693
coarse salt 201
coastal features 51
coat dress 356
coat hook 510
coat rack 510
coat tree 510
coatroom 726
coats 352, 355
coaxial cable 523
cob 85
cobalt 683
cobra 114
coccyx 152, 157
cochlea 174
cochlear nerve 174
cock 752
cockatoo 118
cockchafer 101
cocking lever 757
cockle 217
cockleshell 276
cockpit 834, 873, 898
cockpit canopy 898
cockpit ventilation 898
cockroach 101
cocktail cabinet 279
cocktail glass 225
cocktail lounge 724

cocoa 208
coconut 193
Cocos Plate 43
code 528
coeliac trunk 161, 165
coelophysis 93
coffee 208
coffee beans 208
coffee makers 241
coffee mill 240
coffee mug 226
coffee pot 905
coffee shop 710, 715, 725
coffee spoon 228
coil 688
coil spring 285, 553
coiling 465
coin 729
coin chute 920
coin purse 387
coin reject slot 920
coin return bucket 507
coin slot 507, 920
coin, reverse 729
coin: obverse 729
cola nut 193
colander 231
cold air 64, 675
cold coolant 665, 674
cold food 722
cold heavy water 670
cold room 722
cold shed 596
cold storage chamber 180, 181
cold temperate climates 61
cold-water circuit 262
cold-water line 266
cold-water riser 262
cold-water supply line 265, 267, 270, 271
collar 77, 348, 349, 352, 362, 370, 383, 838, 851
collar bar 376
collar point 349, 362
collar stay 349
collards 186
collaret 339, 363
collars, examples 362
collateral 168
collecting funnel 59
collecting vessel 59
collection body 573
collection truck 573
collector 659
collector head 18
collector rings 688
collet 308, 482
collie 130
Colombia 742
colon 97, 113, 125, 473
color chart 398
color circle 400
color control 512
color display 456
color filter 478
color selection filter 494
color shifting ink 729
color spray 398
color supplement 471
color synthesis 690
color television camera 20
colored pencil drawing 396
colored pencils 396
colors 400
colors, examples 741
colour chart 398
colour control 512
colour display 456
colour filter 478
colour selection filter 494
colour supplement 471
colour television camera 20
colouring pencils 396
colours, examples 741
colter 641, 643
colter's shaft 641
columella 105
columella fold 105
column 47, 64, 259, 287, 307, 403, 405, 452, 471, 482, 485, 540, 919
column crank 482
column lock 482
column of mercury 695
column radiator 259
coma 8
comb 417, 461, 749
comb binding 533
combat aircraft 760
combat sports 842
combination 852
combination box and open end wrench 311
combination lock 386
combination pliers 317
combination spanner 311
combinations 351
combine harvester 643
combs 380
combustion 564, 565, 627
combustion chamber 564, 566
comet 8
comforter 280

comma 473
command control dial 476
command module 19, 25
commander's seat 758
commando knife 751
commercial area 713
commercial concern 525
commercial zone 709
commissure of lips of mouth 174
common carotid artery 160
common coastal features 51
common extensor of fingers 151
common frog 111
common hair cap moss 75
common iliac artery 160, 165
common iliac vein 165
common nail 301
common periwinkle 217
common peroneal nerve 166
common plaice 221
common polypody 76
common symbols 725
common toad 111
common whipping 908
communicating ramus 168
communication antenna 761
communication by telephone 506
communication devices 522
communication module 486
communication panels 626
communication protocol 524
communication set 594
communication tunnel 23
communications 468
communications volume controls 20
communion rail 737
Community Chest card 915
commutator 688
commuter train 583
Comoros 746
compact 378
compact bone 154
compact disc 501, 504
compact disc player 488, 501, 503, 504
compact disc player controls 504
compact disc player, portable 503
compact disc reading 501
compact disc recorder 503
compact disc rewritable 521
compact disc rewritable recorder 521
compact flash memory card 481
compact memory card 477
compact videocassette adapter 496
compacting 71
compartment 416, 919
Compass 11
compass 898
compass bridge 604, 608, 609
compass card 37, 612, 907
compass meridian line 907
compass saw 303
competition 789
competition area 845, 846, 847
competition course basin 788
competition ring 852
competition site: half-pipe 887
competitive course 831
competitors' compound 871
competitors' line 845, 847
complaints office 768
complex dune 52
complexus 151
compluvium 406
composition of the blood 162
compost bin 323
compound bow 859, 913
compound eye 96, 98, 99
compound leaves 79
compressed air reservoir 586
compressed-air cylinder 765, 841
compressed-air tank 873
compression 564, 565, 627
compression coupling 270
compression fitting 269
compression link 640
compression/intake 565
compressor 260, 533
compressor turbine 627
computer 734
computer compartment 527
computer connector 518
computer interface port 520
computer network 523
computer programs 771
computer room 763
computer science room 734
computer screen intensity controls 20
computer table 511
concave lens 691
concave primary mirror 15
concentric lamellae 154
concert grand 443
concha 173
conchiglie 206
concrete 298
concrete block 298
concrete drain 655
concrete mixer truck 573
concrete shielding 670, 671
concrete wall 675

condensation 67, 680
condensation of steam into water 665
condensation pool 671
condensed 472
condenser 646, 668, 674, 693, 694
condenser adjustment knob 693
condenser backwash inlet 669
condenser backwash outlet 669
condenser coil 261
condenser cooling water inlet 669
condenser cooling water outlet 669
condenser fan 261
condenser height adjustment 693
condiments 200, 723
condominium 886
condominiums 419
condor 119
conduction 681
conductor's podium 437
conduit, fuel 553, 563
condyloid joint 156
cone 89, 177, 705
conference room 509, 718, 730
confessionals 737
configuration of the continents 28
confined aquifer 646
confirmation key 731
confluent 48
Confucianism 736
Confucius 736
Congo 745
Congo River 34
conic projection 36
conical broach roof 415
conical buoy 615, 617
conical washer 265
conifer 89
coniferous forest 66
conifers, examples 89
conjunctiva 177
connecting cable 465, 502
connecting gallery 543
connecting rod 564, 566
connecting terminal 452
connection 916
connection box 490
connection pin 689
connection point 273
connective tissue 172
connector 269, 272, 488
connector panel 518
conning tower 763
conservation laboratory 395
constellations of the northern hemisphere 12
constellations of the southern hemisphere 10
constriction 695
consumer 487
consumer number 273
contact 274, 916
contact devices 274
contact lenses 384
contact lever 287
contact printer 484
container 59, 236, 320, 605, 635
container car 588
container hold 605
container semitrailer 572
container ship 596, 604
container terminal 596, 708
container truck 588
container-loading bridge 596
container/pallet loader 623
containers 635
containment building 665, 667
contest area 844, 845, 846
contestant 844, 846
continent 49
continental crust 42
continental margin 49
continental rise 49
continental shelf 49
continental slope 49
continents, configuration 28
continuity person 429
continuity tester 316
continuous beam 540
contour feather 115
contrabassoons 437
contractile vacuole 94
contrast control 512, 518
control 514
control bar 897
control box 267
control button 516
control cable 323, 580
control center 394, 727, 764
control centre 727, 764
control column 626
control console 10, 626
control deck 605
control gate 890
control key 514
control keys 508
control knob 290, 292, 293, 294
control lever 649
control lights 519, 520
control of staff entries and exits 726
control panel 238, 239, 261, 290, 292, 293, 294, 476, 512, 518, 694, 766
control rod 670, 671

control room 10, 431, 488, 657, 669, 718, 768
control room, radio 488
control rooms, television 490
control stand 586
control stick 631, 898
control tower 618, 761
control tower cab 618
control valve 903
control visual display 694
control wheel 626, 766
control: group select 514
controller 918
controller ports 918
convection 681
convection current 681
convection zone 6
convective cell 63
convector 260
convenience food 181
convenience outlet 316
convention center 711, 718
convention centre 711, 718
convention hall 718
conventional door 416
convergent plate boundaries 43
converging lenses 691
convertible 549
convex lens 691
conveyor 646, 647, 649
conveyor belt 71, 620
Cook Strait 29
cook's knife 229
cooked ham 216
cookie cutters 232
cooking area 722
cooking dishes 239
cooking plate 239, 722
cooking set 905
cooking surface 239
cooking utensils 234, 722
cooksonia 92
cooktop 224, 290
cooktop edge 290
cool tip 381
coolant 665, 674
coolant inlet 672
coolant outlet 672
coolant: boiling water 671
coolant: carbon dioxide 670
coolant: pressurized heavy water 670
coolant: pressurized water 671
cooler 906
cooling 656
cooling cylinder 692
cooling fan 497, 552, 561, 563, 566
cooling system 553
cooling tower 646
cooling vent 526
coping 894
coping saw 303
copper 683
copper plate 422
copper to plastic 269
copper to steel 269
copperplate 422
copulatory bursa 97, 104
copy output mode 512
copy quantity 512
copyright 473
cor anglais 446
coracoid 111, 116
Coral Sea 29
coral snake 114
corbel 408
corbel piece 256
cord 285, 288, 289, 316, 331, 332, 424, 505
cord sleeve 308, 318
cord tieback 282
cordate 79
cordless drill-driver 306
cordless mouse 516
cordless screwdriver 302
cordless telephone 507
core 6, 82, 867, 908, 912
core box bit 308
coriander 202
Corinthian column 407
Corinthian order 405
Corinthian pilaster 407
cork 892
cork ball 797
cork tip 817
corkscrew 230, 905
corn 85, 203
corn bread 205
corn flour 204
corn oil 209
corn salad 187
corn syrup 209
corn: cob 85
cornea 177, 691
corner 426, 842
corner arc 803
corner cap 587
corner cupboard 279
corner fitting 635
corner flag 801, 803
corner judge 845

corner judges 846
corner pad 842
corner stool 839
corner structure 635
corner stud 251
corner tower 408
cornerpiece 389
cornet 437, 447
cornice 245, 247, 278, 282, 403, 404
corolla 80
corona 6
corona radiata 170
coronal suture 158
coronet 124, 127
coronet boot 853
corpus callosum 167
corpus cavernosum 169
correction fluid 534
correction key 456
correction paper 534
corridor connection 584
corrosive 774
cors anglais 437
corselette 366
corset 337, 367
cortex 165
corymb 81
cos lettuce 186
cosmetic tray 389
cosmetics 717
Costa Rica 742
costal cartilage 122
costal shield 113
costume 428
cot 776
Côte d'Ivoire 745
cotehardie 337
cottage cheese 210
cottage curtain 282
cotter pin 249
cotton applicators 777
cotton wool ball 777
cotyledon 77
couched stitches 459
coudé focus 17
cougar 134
cough syrup 783
coulomb 702
Coulommiers 211
coulter 641, 643
coulter shaft 641
counsels' assistants 728
counter 370, 722
counter reset button 499
counterguard 409
counterjib 634
counterjib ballast 634
counterscarp 409
countersunk head 302
countertop 224
counterweight 14, 16, 417, 500, 542, 591, 634, 638, 639, 640
counterweight guide rail 417
country 37, 709
coupé 549
coupler head 586, 587, 640, 641
coupler knuckle 587
coupler knuckle pin 587
coupler-tilt tablet 444
coupling bolt 659
coupling guide device 585
coupon booth 731
courgette 188
course 833, 866, 874, 890
course buoys 838
course gate 837
course steward 853, 855
course umpire 838
court 343, 728, 809, 810, 812, 813, 814, 816, 818, 819, 820
court referee 814
courthouse 710
courtroom 728
courtyard 727, 735, 738
cousin 785
couter 749
cove bit 308
cover 240, 261, 273, 274, 391, 477, 512, 755, 757, 767, 797, 867, 907
coveralls 887
covered bogie truck 588
covered parapet walk 408
covered way 409
covering 425, 815
covering disc 643
covering disk 643
covering grille 259
covering materials 299
cow 128
cow hitch 908
cowl 550
cowl neck 363
Cowper's gland 169
cowshed 182
coxa 96, 98
coxal gland 103
coxed eight 839
coxed four 839

coxed pair 839
coxless double 839
coxless four 839
coxless pair 839
coxswain's seat 838
Coyolxauhqui stone 412
Crab 13
crab 218
crab spider 102
cracked bread 205
cracked rye bread 205
cradle 14, 15, 485, 756
crafts 452
crakow 339
crampon strap 901
crampon system 893
cranberry 192
Crane 10
crane 652
crane runway 634
cranes 634
cranial nerves 166
crank 230, 307, 312, 580, 750, 910
crank handle 313, 423
crankcase 565
crankshaft 564, 566
crash helmet 872, 884, 885
crate 222
crater 7, 44, 647
crater ray 7
cravat 349
crawl kick 832
crawler tractor 636
crayfish 218
cream 210
cream cheese 210
cream cup 223
cream jug 226
creamer 226
crease 350
credenza 510
credit card 729
credit card wallet 386
Cree 469
creel 911
creep 47
cremaster 97
crenate 79
crenel 741
crescendo pedal 444
crescent 741
crescent wrench 311
crescentic dune 52
crest 45, 49, 690, 748, 797
crest of spillway 657
Cretaceous 93
crevasse 46
crevice tool 289
crew neck 368
crew neck sweater 354, 359
crew quarters 604
crew return vehicle 21
crew's locker 584
crib 281
cribriform plate of ethmoid 175
cricket 798
cricket ball 798
cricket player 798
cricket shoe 798
crime prevention 768
crimp 901
crimping 912
crisper 291
crisscross curtains 283
critical point 891
Croatia 744
crochet hook 457
crocodile 114
crocus 80
croissant 204
crook 446
crook key 446
crookneck squash 189
crop 97, 99, 104, 106, 116
crosne 184
cross 740
cross brace 783
cross cut 650
cross handle 919
cross head 302
cross rail 277
cross section 920
cross section of a baseball 797
cross section of a buttress dam 660
cross section of a golf ball 867
cross section of a gravity dam 661
cross section of a hydroelectric power plant 658
cross section of a molar 159
cross section of a muzzle loading 753
cross section of a pipe 390
cross section of a power plant 664
cross section of a reflecting telescope 15
cross section of a reflex camera 477
cross section of a refracting telescope 14
cross section of a road 538
cross section of a street 712
cross section of an airbrush 398
cross section of an arch dam 661

cross section of an astronomical observatory 17
cross section of an electron microscope 694
cross section of an embankment dam 660
cross stitches 459
cross-country bicycle 870
cross-country cyclist 870
cross-country ski 892
cross-country ski trail 886
cross-country skier 892
cross-country skiing 892
cross-headed tip 302
cross-ply tyre 561
cross-tip screwdriver 905
crossarm 663
crossbar 424, 433, 461, 578, 792, 827, 897
crossbeam 460
crossbow 750
crossbuck sign 591
crosshead 632
crossing 410, 411
crossing arm 568
crossing gate mechanism 591
crossover 583
crossover back straps overalls 369
crossover cargo deck line 607
crossover mirror 568
crosspiece 278, 460, 782
crosstree 834
crosswise grain 455
crotch 351
crotch piece 359
crotchet 435
crotchet rest 435
Crottin de Chavignol 210
crouching position (freestyle wrestling) 843
croup 124, 826
Crow 11
crown 87, 115, 159, 340, 341, 374, 398, 440, 448, 610, 696
crown block 651
crownpiece 854
crucifix 737
crude oil 656
crude-oil pipeline 654
cruise control 556
cruise control lever 333
cruiseliner 608
crus of helix 173
crushed chiles 199
crusher 71, 646
crushing roll 642
crustaceans 107, 218
crustose lichen 74
crutch 782
crystal button 287
crystal drop 287
crystallization 680
Cuba 742
cube 705
cuboid 155
cucumber 188
cue ball 862, 863
cuff 338, 342, 349, 350, 880
cuff link 361
cuirass 748
cuisse 749
culet 374
culler-facer-canceler 474
cultivated mushroom 183
cultivator 641
cultural organization 525
cumin 198
cumulonimbus 56, 62
cumulus 56, 62
cuneiform, 1st 155
cuneiform, 2nd 155, 156
Cup 11
cup 223, 226, 367, 905, 906, 912
cup gasket 773
cupola 614
cupped Pacific oyster 217
cupule 84
curator's office 394
curb 712, 872
curb bit 854
curb chain 854
curb hook 854
curb rein 854
curium 684
curled endive 187
curled kale 186
curler 877
curling 877
curling brush 877
curling iron 381
curling stone 877
curly endive 187
curly kale 186
currant 192
currant tomato 188
currency abbreviations, examples 728
currency exchange 725
currency, name 729
current event scoreboard 825
curry 198
cursor down 515
cursor left 515

cursor movement keys 515, 529
cursor right 515
cursor up 515
curtain 282, 389, 492
curtain pole 284
curtain track 284
curtain wall 408
curtains, examples 283
curved jaw 310
customer service 731
customer's service entrance 273
customers' cloakroom 720
customers' entrance 720
customers' toilets 720
customs control 621
customs house 596
cut for gemstones 375
cut nail 301
cut stone 298
cut-off trench 660, 661
cut-throat razor 383
cuticle nippers 377
cuticle pusher 377
cuticle scissors 377
cuticle trimmer 377
cutlery basket 294
cutlery set 905
cuts of beef 214
cuts of lamb 215
cuts of pork 215
cuts of veal 214
cutter 317
cutter bar 642, 643
cutter link 331
cutting blade 236, 240, 424, 534
cutting board 229
cutting cylinder 332
cutting edge 227, 229, 382, 636, 637, 638
cutting guide 424
cutting head 535
cutting line 455
cutting nozzle 319
cutting oxygen handle 319
cutting tip 319
cutting tools 330
cutting torch 319
cutting weapons 751
cutting wire 464
cuttlefish 217
cyan 690
cyanobacteria 92
cycling 870
cyclone 63
cyclone names 63
cyclorama 492
cylinder 249, 268, 564, 705, 754
cylinder case 249
cylinder head cover 552, 566
cylinder pressure gauge 319
cylinder vacuum cleaner 289
cylindrical buoy 615
cylindrical projection 36
cymbal 448
cymbals 437, 449
cypress scalelike leaves 89
Cyprus 744
cytopharynx 94
cytoplasm 74, 94, 170
cytoproct 94
cytostome 94
Czech 469
Czech Republic 744

D

D 434
D carabiner 900
d quark 680
dabber 422
daffodil 80
dagger 751
daggerboard 836
daggerboard well 836
daikon 189
dairy 182
dairy compartment 291
dairy products 180, 210
dairy products receiving area 180
dalmatian 131
dam 657
damper 258, 443, 465
damper lever 443
damper pedal 442, 451
damper rail 443
dance blade 881
dandelion 187
danger 616
danger area 844
danger zone 847
dangerous materials 774
Danish 469
Danish Blue 211
Danish rye bread 205
Danube River 32
dark chocolate 208
darkness 617
darkroom 484
dart 455, 918
dart sac 104
dartboard 918

darts 918
dash 473
dashboard 556, 574
dashboard computer 771
dashboard equipment 771
data display 479, 495, 508
data display illumination button 479
data hold 316
data logger 58
data processing 41, 54
data reception 41
data record system 694
data recording 41
data storage devices 521
data transmission 41
database 525
date 192, 729
date display/recording button 496
dater 531
dating nail 590
daughter 784, 785
daughter-in-law 784
David 736
davit 602, 606
day-care center 715
day-care centre 715
daymark 615
daymarks 617
dayroom 727
dead ball line 804
dead bolt 248, 249
dead bowl area 864
deadly poisonous mushroom 76
death 702
debit card 731
debris 63
decagon 705
decanter 225
deceleration and braking zone 891
deceleration lane 539
deceleration stretch 885
deciduous forest 66
decimal key 529
decimal tab 528
deck 471, 540, 571, 650, 838, 893
deck arch bridge 541
deck crane 761
declination 13
declination setting scale 14, 15
décolleté bra 367
decomposers 67
decorative accessories 716
decorative articles store 715
decorative braid 368
decoy 913
decoy launcher 762
dedicated line 523, 524
deep fryer 238, 721
deep peroneal nerve 166
deep-sea floor 42
deer crossing 545, 547
defence counsel's bench 728
defence third 809
defense counsels' bench 728
defense third 809
defensive midfield 803
deferent duct 169
defibrillator 775
deflector 260, 329, 332, 333
deforestation 69
defrost drain 291
degree 704
degree Celsius 702
dehumidifier 261
Deimos 4
delete 515
delete key 515
delicatessen 180, 216
delicious lactarius 183
delivery 799, 864
delivery entrance 713
delta 48, 51
delta distributary 48
Delta II 24
delta wing 629, 630
deltoid 150
deluge gun 766
demilune 409
demisemiquaver 435
demisemiquaver rest 435
demitasse 226
Democratic People's Republic of Korea 747
Democratic Republic of the Congo 745
dendrite 168
Denmark 744
denomination 729
dental alveolus 159
dental care 384
dental floss 384
dental floss holder 384
dentary 112
dentate 79
dentil 404, 405
dentin 159
deodorant 379
deoxygenated blood 162
department store 715, 716
departure time indicator 582
depolarizing mix 689
deposit slot 730

depressed-center flat car 588
depression 55
depth adjustment 308
depth gauge 841
depth of focus 43
depth scale 613
depth stop 307
depth-of-cut adjustment knob 309
depth-of-field preview button 476
depth-of-field scale 478
derailleur 578, 580, 870
derby 340
dermis 172
derrick 604, 607, 651, 652, 654
derrick mast 607
descender 900
descending aorta 161
descending colon 164
descending passage 402
desert 52, 61, 66
desired temperature 261
desk 724
desk lamp 286
desk mat 511
desk pad 511
desk tray 531
desktop computer 522, 523, 524
desktop video unit 520
dessert fork 228
dessert knife 228
dessert spoon 228
desserts 723
destination 582
destroying angel 76
detachable body 573
detachable control 239
detachable palm rest 514
detergent dispenser 294
detonator 757
deuterium oxide upgrading 669
developer bath 485
developing baths 485
developing tank 484
Devonian 92
dew 65
dew pad 130
dew shield 14
dewclaw 130
dexter 740
dexter base 740
dexter chief 740
dexter flank 740
diable 235
diacritic symbols 473
diagonal 663
diagonal buttress 410
diagonal movement 916
diagonal step 892
dial 273, 695, 696, 697, 698
dial-type display 613
dial/action button 527
diameter 704
diamond 375, 914
diamond interchange 538
diamond mesh metal lath 299
diamond point 278
diaper 368
diaphragm 163, 477, 488, 502
diaphysis 155
diastema 123
dibber 324
dibble 324
dice 914
dice cup 915
die 915
diesel engine 586
diesel engine compartment 637, 638, 639
diesel engine cycle 565
diesel engine ventilator 586
diesel engines 762
diesel lift engine 605
diesel motor compartment 636
diesel oil 656
diesel propulsion engine 605
diesel shop 583
diesel-electric locomotive 586
differential 553
difficult slope 886
difficulty judges 823
diffuser 428, 479
diffuser pin 329
dig 812
digestive gland 104, 105, 106, 107
digestive epiphysis 103
digestive system 164
digging fork 326
digit 110, 122, 143
digital audio player, portable 503
digital audio tape recorder 488
digital camcorder 517
digital camera 481, 517
digital display 316, 699, 777
digital frequency display 498
digital nerve 166
digital pad 130, 133
digital pulp 172
digital reflex camera 477
digital storage 481
digital thermometer 777
digital versatile disc 494

digital video effects monitor 491
digital video special effects 491
digital voice recorder 534
digital watch 696
digitizing pad 517
digits 116
Dijon mustard 200
dike 44
dill 202
dimetrodon 92
dimmer room 490
dimmer switch 274
dimple 867
dinette 224, 250
dining car 584
dining room 250, 406, 608, 720, 723, 724, 727, 763, 764
dining section 584
dinner fork 228
dinner knife 228
dinner plate 226
dinnerware 226
dinnerware, glassware and silverware 717
dinnerware, glassware, and silverware 717
diode 673
dioptric ring 614
dip switch 576
dipped beam headlight 554
dipper 398
dipper arm 637
dipper arm cylinder 637
dipper bucket 638
dipping/indicator stalk 556
direct home reception 486
direct-current power cord 526
direct-reading rain gauge 58, 59
direction of electron flow 687, 689
direction of Mecca 738
direction to be followed 544, 546
directional buttons 918
directional sign 593
director 429
director of photography 429
director of shooting 859
director's chair 276
director's control monitors 428
director's office 731, 732
director's seat 429
directory 524
dirty dish table 721
disc 273, 423, 559, 560, 641, 851
disc arm 641
disc brake 552, 559, 574, 874
disc camera 481
disc compartment 501
disc compartment control 501
disc drive 450
disc faucet 268
disc mixer 268
disc spacing lever 643
disc tray 494, 521
discharge bay 666
discharge line 263
discharge outlet 246
discs 237
discus 793
discus throw 791
dish 239, 493
dish antenna 493
dishwasher 224, 271, 294, 721, 723
disk 9, 273, 423, 521, 560, 851
disk camera 481
disk drive 450
disk eject button 521
disk motor 521
disk spacing lever 643
diskette 521
disks 237
displacement 690
display 261, 494, 497, 503, 505, 506, 507, 526, 529, 530, 548, 613, 699, 730, 731
display cabinet 279, 510
display panel 496
display preparation area 180
display release button 526
display setting 506
disposable camera 480
disposable contact lens 384
disposable diaper 368
disposable fuel cylinder 314, 319
disposable razor 383
distal epiphysis 155
distal phalange 154, 155
distal phalanx 126, 133, 172
distal sesamoid 126
distance 385
distance scale 478
distance traveled 700
distance travelled 700
distance, measure 700
distress beacon 611
distributary, delta 48
distribution box 263
distribution by aerial cable network 486
distribution by submarine cable 487
distribution by underground cable network 487
distribution center 474

distribution panel 272, 273
distributor cap 552, 566
distributor service loop 273
district 39
ditali 206
ditch 538, 864
divergent plate boundaries 43
diverging lenses 691
diversion canal 657
divide key 529
divided by 703
divider 386, 389, 643
dividers 532
dividing breeching 767
diving 828
diving board 246
diving glove 841
diving installations 828
diving plane 763
diving tower 828
diving well 246, 788
djembe 433
Djibouti 745
Dnieper River 32
do 847
do not iron 347
do not tumble dry 347
do not use chlorine bleach 347
do not wash 347
do-it-yourself 298
do-it-yourself shop 714
dock 596
docking cradle 527
document compartment 527
document folder 532
document handler 512
document-to-be-sent position 508
documentation center 764
documentation centre 764
dodecagon 705
dog 130, 913
dog breeds 130
dog ear collar 362
dog's forepaw 130
dog, morphology 130
dog, skeleton 131
dohyo 847
dolichos beans 190
dollar 728
dolly 428
dolly tracks 428
Dolphin 12
dolphin 136, 137
dolphin, morphology 136
dolphin, skeleton 136
domain name 524
dome roof 415
dome shutter 17
dome tent 903
domestic appliances 236, 240, 288
domestic appliances, major 716
domestic appliances, small 717
domestic pollution 69
Dominica 743
Dominican Republic 743
dominoes 914
door 238, 278, 290, 293, 417, 551, 554, 567, 624, 724, 738, 818, 902, 903
door access 699
door handle 247, 248, 551
door lock 551
door open warning light 557
door panel 278
door pillar 551
door shelf 291
door stop 291, 587
door switch 293
doorknob 247, 248
doors, examples 416
Doric column 407
Doric order 404
dormer window 244
dorsal abdominal artery 107
dorsal aorta 99
dorsal blood vessel 97
dorsal fin 136
dorsal mantle cavity 106
dorsalis pedis artery 160
dorsum of nose 175
dorsum of tongue 176
dose inhaler 783
dot matrix printer 520
double 853
double bass 439
double basses 437
double bed 724
double bend 544, 547
double boiler 235
double curtain rod 284
double drop lowbed semitrailer 572
double flat 435
double glazing 675
double handle 840
double kitchen sink 262
double oxer 852, 853
double pennant 739
double plate 252
double pole breaker 272
double pulley system 686

double reed 446
double ring 918
double room 724
double seat 594
double sharp 435
double sheet bend 908
double slash 524
double spacing 472
double virgule 524
double zero 919
double zero key 529
double-bladed paddle 837, 839
double-blank 914
double-breasted buttoning 352
double-breasted jacket 348
double-burner camp stove 903
double-deck bus 569
double-decked pallet 632
double-edged blade 383
double-edged razor 383
double-leaf bascule bridge 542
double-six 914
double-twist auger bit 306
doubles luge 884
doubles service court 817
doubles sideline 817, 820
doublet 338, 914
doubling die 915
doubly dentate 79
dough hook 236
Douglas, pouch 170
dousing water tank 665, 669
dousing water valve 669
Dove 11
dovetail 692
dovetail bit 308
down tube 579
down wind 833
downhill 889
downhill bicycle 870
downhill cyclist 870
downhill ski 888
downspout 244
downstream face 661
downstream gate 837
downstream shoulder 660
downstream toe 660
downtown 709, 710
draft arm 638
draft hole 259
draft link 640
draft tube 638, 658, 659
draft tube liner 659
drafting machine 399
drafting table 399
drag 630, 909
Dragon 13
dragonfly 102
dragons 917
drain 262
drain hose 271, 292, 294
drain tile 253
drain valve 266, 267, 655
drainage blanket 660
drainage layer 660
draining circuit 262
draining spoon 233
Drake Passage 29, 31
draped neck 363
draped neckline 363
draped swag 283
draught arm 638
draught tube 638, 658, 659
draught tube liner 659
draw 789
draw bar hitch 641
draw bar hitch head 642
draw curtain 282
draw drapery 282
draw hoe 326
draw tube 693
drawbar 756
drawbar lock 756
drawbridge 408
drawer 224, 278, 279, 281, 290
drawers 351
drawing 396, 401
drawing board 399
drawing pins 534
drawing, accessories 399
drawing, equipment 396
drawstring 353, 387
drawstring bag 387, 388
drawstring hood 369
dredger 232
dress with bustle 337
dress with crinoline 337
dress with panniers 337
dressage 855
dresser 279, 428
dresses, examples 356
dressing room 428, 431, 509, 734
dressing table 279
dressmaker's model 454
dried chiles 199
drift 650
drifting snow high 57
drifting snow low 57
drill 307
drill collar 651

drill pipe 651
drill press 307
drill rod 648
drill ship 604, 653
drilling drawworks 651
drilling rig 651
drilling tools 306
drills 306
drink box 223
drinks 180
drip bowl 290
drip dry 347
drip molding 551
drip moulding 551
drip pan 239
drip tray 241
dripping pan 234
drive belt 292
drive chain 578
drive pulley 688
drive shaft 553, 605, 631
drive wheel 240, 307
drive wheels 639
driven compressor wheel 564
driver 857, 868, 872
driver seat 577
driver's cab 585, 586
driver's seat 758
driveway 245
driving glove 346
driving turbine wheel 564
driving wheel 462, 640
drizzle 64
dromedary camel 129
drone 99
drone pipe 432
droop nose 629
drop earrings 374
drop light 316
drop shot 821
drop waist dress 356
drop-leaf 278
drug storage 775
drum 230, 285, 292, 293, 404, 448, 559, 612, 697
drum brake 559
drumlin 45
drums 448
drumstick 433
drupelet 83
dry cells 689
dry cleaner 715
dry climates 61
dry dock 596
dry flat 347
dry fruits 84, 193
dry gallery 47
dry pastel drawing 396
dry well 671
dry-point 423
dry-weather tire 872
drying 347
drypoint 422, 423
dual cassette deck 503
dual launch structure 24
dual seat 575
dual swivel mirror 381
dual-in-line package 689
dubnium 683
duck 120, 213
duck egg 213
duffel bag 388
duffle coat 353
dugout 794
dugout canoe 599
dulse 183
dumbbell 850
dump 647, 648
dump body 572, 573, 639
dump semitrailer 572
dump truck 573, 639
dune 51
dunes, examples 52
dungarees 358
dungarees with crossover back straps 369
duo 438
duodenum 116, 164
dura mater 167, 168
durian 197
dust canister 308
dust cover 500
dust receiver 288
dust spout 304
dust storm 57
dust tail 8
dusting brush 289
dustpan 295
Dutch 469
Dutch bicycle 581
Dutch oven 235
duty belt 770
duty-free shop 621
DVD 494
DVD player 494
DVD recorder 521
dynamic brake 586
dynamic microphone 488
dynamics propeller 605
dynamo 578, 688
dysprosium 684

E

E 434
e-commerce 525
e-mail 525
e-mail key 514
e-mail software 524
Eagle 10, 12
eagle 119, 741
ear 133, 140, 146, 277
ear drum 174
ear flap 340
ear loaf 204
ear muffs 861
ear plugs 872
ear protection 772, 774
ear, auricle 173
ear, structure 174
earbud 506
earbuds 872
earphone 502
earphone jack 513
earphones 503
earpiece 385, 776
earplugs 772
earrings 374
Earth 0, 4, 5, 6, 7, 28
earth auger, motorized 323
earth clamp 318
earth connection 272
Earth coordinate system 35
earth foundation 538
Earth radiation scanner 60
Earth radiation sensor 60
earth terminal 274
earth wire 272, 273
Earth's atmosphere, profile 53
Earth's crust 42, 43
Earth's crust, section 42
Earth's orbit 6, 7
Earth, structure 42
earth-wire peak 663
earthflow 47
earthing pin 274
earthquake 43
easel 399, 484
East 37, 616, 917
East cardinal mark 617
East China Sea 33
East Pacific Rise 50
East-Northeast 37
East-Southeast 37
Eastern hemisphere 35
Eastern meridian 36
easy slope 886
eau de parfum 379
eau de toilette 379
eave 412
eccrine sweat gland 172
echinoderms 94, 95
echinus 404
echo 40, 41
echo sounder 613
echo sounder probe 613
eclipses, types 6, 7
ecliptic 13
economy and finance 728
ectoderm 95
ectopterygoid 112
Ecuador 742
edge 300, 454, 729, 881, 884, 887, 888, 907
edger 332
edging 322
edible boletus 183
edit search button 496
editorial 471
education 732
educational institution 525, 711
eel 219
effluent 48
effort 686
effusive volcano 44
egg 100, 117, 170
egg beater 232
egg butt snaffle bit 854
egg carton 222
egg noodles 207
egg poacher 235
egg slicer 233
egg timer 231
egg tray 291
eggplant 188
eggs 109, 111, 213
Egypt 745
Egyptian reed pen 470
eiderdown 280
eight cut 375
eighth note 435
eighth rest 435
einsteinium 684
ejaculatory duct 169
eject button 477, 499, 918
ejection port 755
ejection seat 760
ejector 638
El Salvador 742
elastic 280
elastic ligament 133
elastic strainer 902, 903
elastic support bandage 777
elastic waistband 353
elastic webbing 350
elasticized leg opening 351
elbow 124, 130, 140, 147, 149, 156, 258, 269
elbow pad 800, 808, 894, 895
elbow pads 880
elbow, 45° 269
elbows 206
electric automobile 563
electric baseboard radiator 260
electric cable 563
electric car 563
electric charge, measurement 702
electric circuit 274
electric connection 258, 260
electric cooker 290
electric current, measurement 702
electric drill 306
electric dryer 293
electric fan motor 561
electric foil 848
electric furnace 258
electric golf cart 869
electric grill, indoor 239
electric guitar 441
electric kiln 465
electric knife 237
electric miter saw 304
electric motor 259, 331, 332, 563
electric potential difference, measurement 702
electric range 290, 721
electric razor 383
electric resistance, measurement 702
electric steamer 239
electric supply 266
electric toothbrush 384
electric variometer 898
electric water-heater tank 266
electrical box 274
electrical cable 556
electrical circuit, parallel 687
electrical connection 571
electrical connection panel 489
electrical hazard 774
electrical inlet 465
electrical payout linkage 920
electrical power unit 622
electrical scoring apparatus 848
electrical system 553
electricity 272, 687
electricity meter 273
electricity production room 763
electricity tools 316
electricity transmission 663, 665
electricity transmission network 674
electrode 275, 318
electrode assembly 259
electrode holder 318
electrode lead 318
electrolytic capacitors 689
electrolytic separator 689
electromagnetic spectrum 690
electron 680
electron beam 494, 694
electron beam positioning 694
electron collector 689
electron flow, direction 687, 689
electron gun 494, 694
electron microscope elements 694
electron microscope, cross section 694
electronic ballast 275
electronic book 527
electronic control box 563
electronic control unit 559
electronic drum pad 451
electronic flash 482
electronic instruments 450
electronic payment terminal 181, 731
electronic piano 451
electronic scale 699
electronic timing system 883
electronic typewriter 528
electronic viewfinder 496
electronics 689
electronics store 714
elements of a house 247
elements of architecture 413
elements, table 682
elephant 129
elevating arc 756
elevating cylinder 573, 634, 766
elevating hand-wheel 756
elevating handle 756
elevation 250
elevation adjustment 692
elevation zones 66
elevator 16, 407, 417, 509, 625, 650, 666, 713, 724, 761, 898
elevator car 417
elevon 23
elk 129
ellipses 473
ellipsis 473
elliptical galaxy 9
elliptical snowshoe 893
embankment 538
embankment dam 660
embankment dam, cross section 660
emblem 739
embrasure 409
embroidered fabric 459
embroidery 459
emerald 375
emerald cut 375
emergency 778
emergency brake 594
emergency electric motor 763
emergency physician's office 778
emergency regulator 841
emergency station 543
emergency support vessel 653
emergency switch 576
emergency truck 543
emery boards 377
emery pack 454
Emmenthal 211
employee lunchroom 509
empty set 703
emptying hose 292
en prison 919
enamel 159
enclosure 182, 416
end 515
end aisle display 181
end bracket 284
end button 439
end cap 284, 667
end door 635
end grain 300
end joist 252, 253
end key 506, 515
end ladder 587
end line 806, 811, 812, 815
end moraine 46
end piece 169
end plate 667
end search button 496
end stop 284, 303, 835
end zone 806, 809
endocardium 162
endocarp 81, 82
endoderm 95
endoplasmic reticulum 74, 94
endpaper 426
endpiece 385, 863
energy 646
energy integration to the transmission network 662, 677
energy release 681
energy saving bulb 275
energy source 41
energy transmission at the generator voltage 662
energy, measurement 702
engaged Corinthian column 407
engaged Doric column 407
engaged Ionic column 407
engagement ring 376
engine 574, 643, 651, 758
engine air inlet 23
engine air intake 568
engine block 566
engine and crew alarm display 626
engine compartment 568, 632, 639, 640
engine control route 543
engine fuel valves 626
engine housing 331
engine mounting pylon 625
engine room 608, 763
engine, outboard 607
engine, petrol 553, 563
engines, types 564
English 469
English billiards 863
English cane 782
English Channel 32
English horn 446
English horns 437
English loaf 205
English mustard 200
English stick 782
enhanced greenhouse effect 68
enlarger 485
enlarger timer 485
enlarging lens 485
enoki mushroom 183
ensiling tube 643
ENT room 779
entablature 247, 403, 405
enter key 515
enterprise 525
entire 79
entrance 100, 539, 719
entrance door 568, 569
entrance doors 427
entrance for the public 402
entrance hall 250, 394, 509
entrance slide 100
entrance to the pyramid 402
entrance turnstile 592
entrances for the actors 402
entries 829
entries line 529
entry 632, 829
envelope 899
environment 66
epaulet 352
epaulet sleeve 360
épée 849
épéeist 848
epicalyx 83
epicenter 43
epicentre 43
epicondyle 153
epidermis 172
epididymis 169
epidural space 168
epiglottis 163, 176
epitrochlea 153
equalizing buckle 285
equals 703
equals key 529
Equator 31, 34, 35, 36, 63
equator 13
Equatorial Guinea 745
equestrian sports 852
equestrian sports ring 788
equilateral 413
equilibrator 756
equipment 421, 422, 423, 769, 790, 900
equipment compartment 585
equipment lock 666
equipment rack 489, 490
equipment storage room 734
erase button 477, 508
eraser 534
erbium 684
erecting lenses 692
Eritrea 745
Erlenmeyer flask 685
ermine 741
escalator 417, 427, 592, 713
escape 514
escape key 514
escape wheel 696, 697
escapement mechanism 436
escarole 186
escutcheon 105, 248, 268, 270
escutcheon plate 274
esophagus 95, 97, 99, 103, 104, 109, 110, 112, 113, 116, 125, 163, 164
espadrille 344
espresso coffee maker 241
espresso machine 241
estate car 549
Estonia 744
etching press 421
eternal light 738
Ethernet port 526
Ethiopia 745
ethmoid, cribriform plate 175
Eurasia 28
Eurasian Plate 43
euro 728
Europa 4
Europe 28, 32, 50, 743
European experiment module 21
European outlet 274
European plug 274
European robin 118
European Union, flag 729
europium 684
Eustachian tube 174, 175
Eutelsat 486
euthynteria 403, 404
evacuation route 543
evaporated milk 210
evaporation 67, 680
evaporator blower 261
evaporator coil 261
even 919
evening glove 346
event 831
event platform 824
evolution of life 92
ex-voto 737
examination room 779, 781
examples of airplanes 628
examples of algae 75
examples of amphibians 111
examples of anchors 610
examples of angles 704
examples of arachnids 102
examples of arch bridges 541
examples of arches 413, 541
examples of armchairs 276
examples of bats 141
examples of beam bridges 541
examples of bicycles 581
examples of bills 117
examples of birds 118
examples of bits 308
examples of blouses 359
examples of bodies 549
examples of branching 270
examples of broadleaved trees 88
examples of carnivorous mammals 134
examples of chairs 277
examples of charges 741
examples of collars 362
examples of colors 741
examples of colours 741
examples of conifers 89
examples of currency abbreviations 728
examples of curtains 283
examples of dams 660
examples of dives 829
examples of doors 416

examples of dresses 356
examples of dunes 52
examples of eyeglasses 385
examples of feet 117
examples of ferns 76
examples of fittings 269
examples of flowers 80
examples of forks 228
examples of freight cars 588
examples of freight wagons 588
examples of furs 741
examples of fuses 272
examples of handles 840
examples of headings 283
examples of heads 302
examples of helicopters 631
examples of holds and throws 844
examples of hoofs 127
examples of insectivorous mammals 121
examples of insects 101
examples of instrumental groups 438
examples of interchanges 538
examples of jumps 881
examples of keyboard instruments 443
examples of kitchen knives 229
examples of knives 228
examples of lagomorphs 123
examples of leaves 89
examples of lichens 74
examples of marine mammals 137
examples of marsupials 143
examples of metals 741
examples of mosses 75
examples of motorcycles 577
examples of nails 301
examples of networks 522
examples of ordinaries 740
examples of pants 358
examples of partitions 740
examples of pins 865
examples of pleats 283, 357
examples of pockets 360
examples of primates 139
examples of reptiles 114
examples of rigs 601
examples of rodents 123
examples of roofs 414
examples of sails 601
examples of semitrailers 572
examples of shorelines 51
examples of skirts 357
examples of skis 840, 888
examples of sleeping bags 904
examples of sleeves 360
examples of space launchers 24
examples of space probes 19
examples of spoons 228
examples of tables 278
examples of tail shapes 629
examples of telephones 507
examples of tents 902
examples of tips 302
examples of tires 560
examples of tools 401
examples of transition fittings 269
examples of trousers 358
examples of trucks 573
examples of ungulate mammals 128
examples of volcanoes 44
examples of windows 415
examples of wing shapes 630
exclamation mark 473
exclamation point 473
excluded players re-entry area 827
excretory pore 104
execution judges 823
executive desk 511
executive length 351
executive secretary 509
exercise area 823
exercise wear 371
exhalation valve 773
exhaust 564, 565, 627
exhaust air duct 543
exhaust duct 627
exhaust gas admission 564
exhaust guide vanes 627
exhaust manifold 552, 564, 565, 566
exhaust nozzle 760
exhaust pipe 552, 553, 564, 575, 576, 631
exhaust pipe stack 636
exhaust port 565, 649
exhaust stack 570, 639, 640
exhaust system 553
exhaust tube 274, 275
exhaust valve 564, 566
exhaust/scavaging 565
exhibit hall 719
exhibition billboard 394
exhibition center 708
exhibition centre 708
exhibition rooms 395
exhibition stand 719
exit 539
exit button 527
exit cone 150
exit taxiway 621
exit turnstile 592
exocarp 81, 82, 83
exosphere 53
expandable baton 770

expandable file pouch 386
expander 450
expanding file 533
expansion bolt 302
expansion chamber 695
expansion piton 900
expansion space 590
expansion tank 259, 675
expert slope 886
expiration date 729
explosion 564
explosive 774
explosive volcano 44
export pipeline 652
exposure adjustment knob 476
exposure meter 479
exposure mode 476
exposure value 479
exposure-time scale 479
extended 472
extended claw 133
extension 278
extension ladder 321
extension pipe 289
extension table 278
exterior dome shell 17
exterior door 247
exterior of a house 244
exterior pocket 386, 388
exterior sign 592
external auditory meatus 158
external ear 174
external floppy disk drive 521
external fuel tank 22
external gills 111
external jugular vein 160
external nose 175
external oblique 150, 151
external socket 567
external tooth lock washer 310
extra-bold 472
extra-light 472
extractor hood 290
extrados 413
eye 63, 103, 104, 106, 107, 112, 113, 121, 133, 136, 148, 177, 301, 453, 454, 461, 855, 900, 911
eye guard 765
eye make-up 378
eye makeup 378
eye protection 772, 774
eye ring 115
eye wall 63
eyeball 110, 177
eyebrow pencil 378
eyebrow stripe 115
eyebrow tweezers 377
eyecup 496
eyeglasses 385, 861
eyeglasses case 387
eyeglasses parts 385
eyeglasses, examples 385
eyelash 177
eyelash curler 378
eyelashes 132
eyelet 284, 342, 371, 387, 457, 881
eyelet tab 342
eyelid 113
eyepiece 14, 15, 477, 479, 496, 692, 693
eyepiece holder 14
eyeshadow 378
eyespot 95
eyestalk 104
Eyre, Lake 29

F

F 434
F clef 434
F-1 engine 25
fabric care symbols 347
fabric guide 288
fabric structure 455
façade 411
face 139, 146, 301, 409, 425, 647, 650, 815, 867
face mask 798, 800, 808, 879
face shield 318
face side 300
face-off circle 878
face-off spot 878
facepiece 773
faceplate 248, 249
facet 629
facial makeup 378
facsimile machine 508
factorial 703
factory 708
faculae 6
Fahrenheit scale 695
failed fuel bay 666
failed fuel canning 666
fairing 24, 574, 891
fairlead 835
fairway 866, 867
falcatus 92
falciform sesamoid bone 121
falcon 119
Falkland Islands 31
fall 362

fall front 279
falling rocks 545, 547
fallopian tube 170
fallopian tubes 171
fallow 182
false rib 153
false start rope 830
false tuck 368
family 784
family relationships 784
family tent 902
family waiting room 778
fan 259, 260, 293, 627, 643
fan belt 552, 566
fan brush 378, 397
fan cable stays 541
fan control 261
fan heater 260
fan housing 382
fan motor 261
fan trellis 322
fan wheel 688
fan's tube 643
fang 103, 112
fanion 739
fantail 676
far turn 856
farmhouse 182
farmhouse bread 205
farmstead 182
farmyard 182
fascia 404
fast data entry control 450
fast operation buttons 501
fast-food restaurants 715
fast-forward button 495, 499, 504, 508
fastener binder 532
fasteners 453
fastening device 284
father 784, 785
father-in-law 784
fats and oils 209
faucet 264
faucets 268
fault 43
feather crown 817
feather stitch 459
feathered shuttlecock 817
feed deck 531
feed dog 453
feed lever 307
feed table 643
feed tube 237, 240
feeder header 669
feeder lane 539
feeder output tray 512
feedhorn 493
feeding tube 643
feedwater 670, 671
feet, examples 117
feet-first entry 829
feijoa 197
felt 421
felt hat 340, 341
felt tip pen 397
felt tip pen drawing 396
felucca 600
female 702
female cone 89
female ferrule 909, 910
female reproductive organs 170
femoral artery 160
femoral nerve 166
femoral vein 160
femur 96, 98, 111, 116, 122, 126, 131, 138, 141, 142, 152
fence 182, 244, 303, 304
fencer 848
fencing 848
fencing shoe 848
fencing weapons 849
fender 550, 570, 578, 640
fennec 134
fennel 185
fenugreek 198
fermium 684
fern 76
fern, structure 76
ferns 92
ferns, examples 76
ferrule 320, 391, 863, 868
ferry 608
ferryboat 596
fertilizer application 69
fetlock 124
fetlock joint 124
fettling knife 464
fettucine 206
fez 339
fiber 908
fiber optic cable 523
fibers 295
fibula 122, 126, 131, 138, 141, 142, 152, 155, 156, 336
fiddlehead 76
fiddlehead fern 185
field 190, 794, 799, 804
field electromagnet 688
field hockey 800
field hockey field 788
field lens 692

field lens adjustment 693
field line 687
field mouse 123
field player 801
field winding 688
field, field hockey 788
fielder's glove 797
fielders 799
fifth 434
fifth wheel 570
fifty 703
fifty-yard line 806
fig 197
figure 855
figure skate 881
figure skating 881
figure ski 840
figure skiing handle 840
figure-eight knot 908
figures 472
Fiji 747
Fiji Islands 29
filament 80, 274
filament support 274
Filchner Ice Shelf 29
file 309, 524, 905
file format 524
file guides 532
file room 509
file server 523
filing box 533
filing furniture 510
fill opening 288
filler 390
filler cap 332, 561, 570
filler neck 553
filler plate 513
filler tube 265
fillet 404, 405
filleting knife 229
filling hole 757
filling inlet 655
film 477, 481
film advance mode 476
film cartridge chamber 476
film disc 481
film disk 481
film drying cabinet 484
film guide rail 476
film guide roller 476
film leader indicator 476
film pack 481
film recorder 520
film rewind knob 476
film rewind system 476
film speed 476, 479
film sprocket 476
filter 238, 246, 258, 290, 390, 675
filter cover 773
filter holder 241
filter tip 390
fin 260, 625, 631, 759, 760, 840, 841, 898
fin-mounted tail unit 629
final drive 636
final: 2 players 789
finalist 789
financial services 730
finch 118
finderscope 14, 15
fine adjustment knob 693
fine adjustment wheel 700
fine arts 394
fine bookbinding 424
fine data entry control 450
fine guidance system 17
finely threaded screw 700
finger 172, 797
finger button 447
finger flange 776
finger tab 859
finger tip 531
fingerboard 432, 439, 441
fingerless mitt 346
fingernail 173
finial 412, 739
finish 852
finish area 885, 887, 891
finish buoys 839
finish judge 883
finish judges 883
finish line 791, 833, 839, 856, 871, 890
finish line judge 839
finish wall 830
finishing 401
finishing nail 301
Finland 744
Finnish 469
fir 89
fir needles 89
fire box 256
fire door 416
fire engines 766
fire escape stairs 509
fire extinguisher 725, 771
fire extinguisher, portable 767
fire hose 767
fire hydrant 712, 767
fire hydrant wrench 767
fire irons 257
fire pot 259

fire prevention 764
fire prevention education officer's office 764
fire station 711, 764
fire truck 764
fire-fighting material 767
firebrick 256, 298
firebrick back 256
firefighter 765
firefighters' dormitory 764
firefighters' toilets and showers 764
fireplace 250, 256
fireplace screen 257
fireproof and waterproof garment 765
firestopping 252
firewall 523
FireWire port 526
firing 465
firing accessories 752
firing chamber 465
firing lanyard 756
firing mechanism 757
firing shaft 756
firing tube 763
firing, wood 256
firmer chisel 401
firn 46
first aid 725
first aid equipment 775
first aid kit 771, 777
first aid manual 777
first aid station 886
first aid supplies 775
first aid team 853
first assistant camera operator 428
first base 794
first baseman 794
first classification track 589
first dorsal fin 108, 109
first dozen (1 to 12) 919
first floor 250, 251
first focal room 16
first leaves 77
first level of operations 529
first molar 159
first officer's seat 626
first premolar 159
first quarter 7
first referee 813
first reinforce 753
first round: 128 players 789
first row 804
first space 811
first stage 25
first valve slide 447
first violins 437
first voltage increase 677
first-class cabin 624
fish fork 228
fish kettle 234
fish knife 228
fish platter 226
fish poacher 234
fish scaler 905
fish wire 317
fishbone stitch 459
fisherman's knot 908
Fishes 12
fishes 108
fishes, bony 219
fishes, cartilaginous 218
fisheye lens 478
fishhook 909, 911
fishing 909
fishing jacket 911
fishing vest 911
fishnet stocking 365
fishplate 590
fishplate bolt 590
fission of uranium fuel 665
fission products 681
fissionable nucleus 681
fitness equipment 850
fitted sheet 280
fitting 766
fitting room 716
fittings 269, 389
fittings, examples 269
five 703
five hundred 703
five spice powder 199
five-number bet 919
fivepin 865
fixative 400
fixed arch 541
fixed base 312
fixed blade 424
fixed bridges 540
fixed distance marking 621
fixed jaw 311, 312, 700
fixed platform 653
fixed weight 436
fixed winglet 759
fixed-roof tank 655
fixing bath 485
fixture drain 262
fjords 51
flag 804, 890
flag of the European Union 729
flag shapes 739
flag with Schwenkel 739
flag, parts 739

flagellum 104
flageolet 191
flags 742
flagstone 298, 322
flail mower 642
flame 681
flame adjustment wheel 391
flame spreader tip 319
flame-resistant driving suit 872
flamingo 119
flammable 774
flank 115, 124, 409, 425
flank forward 804
flanking tower 408
flap 348, 387, 535, 855
flap hydraulic jack 760
flap lever 626
flap pocket 348, 352, 360
flap, fuel tank 551
flare 6, 652
flare joint 269
flare nut spanner 311
flare nut wrench 311
flash hider 755
flash lamp 482
flash tube 692
flashcube 482
flashing 257
flashing light 591
flashlight 770
flashtube 482
flask, vacuum 906
flat 435, 894
flat bone 157
flat brush 397
flat car 588
flat end pin 285
flat head 302
flat mirror 17
flat oyster 217
flat part 457
flat roof 414
flat screen monitor 518
flat sheet 280
flat shuttle 461
flat stitches 459
flat tip 302
flat truck 588
flat washer 310
flat-back brush 380
flat-bed 452
flat-plate solar collector 672
flatbed pushcart 633
flatbed semi-trailer 571
flatwater racing, canoe-kayak 838
flea 101
flesh 81, 82, 83
fleshy fruit 82, 83
fleshy leaf 78
fletching 859
fleur-de-lis 741
flews 130
flex 288, 289, 316, 331, 332, 382, 383
flex sleeve 308, 318
flex support 288
flexible boot 887
flexible coupling 677
flexible hose 289, 649
flexible hose connection 649
flexible rubber hose 271
flexible skirt 605
flexible tube 776
flies 430
flight 829, 891, 918
flight bag 388, 897
flight deck 22, 624, 626, 631, 761
flight information board 621
flight instruments 899
flight management computer 626
flight of stairs 255
flights 828
flint 318, 752
flint arrowhead 748
flint knife 748
flintlock 752
flip 881
flip turn 832
flip-flop 344
float 263, 628, 756, 911
float ball 265
float clamp 263
float seaplane 628
float tackle 911
floater 827, 890
floating bridge 542
floating crane 596
floating dock 839
floating head 383
floating rib 138, 152
floating roof 655
floating sleeve 337
floating-roof tank 655
floodlight 492
floodlight on pantograph 492
floodplain 48
floor 257, 676, 818, 819
floor brush 289
floor coverings, textile 254
floor drain 262
floor exercise area 824

floor joist 252, 253
floor lamp 286
floor mat 558
floor mats 824
floor tile 299
floor-level electric convector 260
floorboard 254, 577
floppy disk drive 513
floppy disk eject button 513
florist 715
flotation section 615
flour 204
flow 597
flow bean 654
flow tube 672
flower 77, 80
flower bed 245, 322
flower bud 77
flower tiles 917
flower, inflorescences 81
flower, structure 80
flowering 86
flowering plants 93
flowers, examples 80
flue 267, 444
flue hat 267
flue pipe 444
fluff trap 293
fluid adjustment screw 320
fluid cup 398
fluke 610
fluorescent tube 275
fluorine 683
flush 914
flush bushing 269
flush handle 265
flute 306, 404, 405
fluted land 306
fluted pole 284
fluted shaft 557
fluteroni 401
flutes 437
Fly 11
fly 101, 350, 351, 368, 739
fly agaric 76
fly front closing 355, 369
fly half 804
fly line 909
fly reel 909
fly rod 909
flyfishing 909
flying buttress 410, 411
Flying Fish 11
Flying Horse 12
flying jib 603
flying mammal 140
flyleaf 426
flyover 539, 540
flysheet 902, 903
flywheel 421, 464, 566, 851
FM mode select button 497
foam 49
foam cushion 772
foam insulation 299
foam monitor 607
foam pad 904
foam-rubber insulation 299
focal plane shutter 476, 477
focus 43, 691
focus mode selector 476
focus selector 496
focus setting ring 478
focusing knob 14, 15
focusing lenses 694
focusing magnifier 485
focusing ring 692
focusing screen 477
fodder corn 182
fog 57, 65
fog horn 611
fog lamp 554
fog light 554, 570
foible 849
foie gras 216
foil 849
foil warning line 848
foil, aluminum 222
foilist 848
fold 336
fold line 455
foldaway ladder 321
folder 532
folding chair 277
folding cot 904
folding door 416
folding grill 907
folding nail file 377
folding ramp 608
folding shovel 906
folding wing 857
foliage 87
foliate papilla 176
foliose lichen 74
follicle 84
follicle, section 84
follow-through 864
following car 870
fondue fork 228
fondue pot 234
fondue set 234

fontanelle 158
food 180
food and kitchen 180
food can 223
food chain 67
food mill 230
food processor 237
food reserves 724
food tray 222
food vacuole 94
food, basic source 67
foot 104, 105, 139, 140, 143, 146, 147, 148, 149, 155, 278, 368, 425, 440, 444, 448, 836, 909, 910
foot control 452
foot cushion 862
foot fault judge 821
foot hole 444
foot pegs 871
foot pocket 841
foot protection 773, 774
foot strap 836
foot stretcher 838
foot support 851
football 808
football field 788
football player 808
football, American 806
football, Canadian 809
footboard 280, 876
footbridge 408, 583, 593
foothold 901
footing 252, 253
footless tights 371
footrest 281, 312, 464, 783
footrope 602
footstool 224, 277
footstrap 358, 851
for filing 532
for opening 230
forage blower 643
forage harvester 642
foramen caecum 176
foramen cecum 176
force, measurement 702
forced hot-water system 259
forced warm-air system 258
forces acting on an airplane 630
fore and aft passage 607
fore edge 426
fore royal sail 603
fore-royal mast 602
fore-topgallant mast 602
fore-topmast 602
forearm 124, 130, 147, 149, 860, 912
forearm crutch 782
forearm pad 808
forearm support 782
forecastle 605, 609
forecourt 548, 821
forehead 115, 146
foreleg 96, 98
foreleg, honeybee 98
forelimb 110, 111, 121, 143
forelock 124
foremast 600, 602, 607
foresail 603
forest 45
forest fire 69
forestay 834
forestem 838
forewing 96
fork 14, 227, 579, 632, 697, 870, 875, 905
fork pocket 635
forked tongue 112
forklift truck 632
forks 632, 633
forks, examples 228
Former Yugoslav Republic of Macedonia 744
formeret 410
forming food vacuole 94
forms of medications 783
formula 1 car 873
formula 3000 car 873
formula Indy car 873
forte 849
fortification 409
fortified wall 738
forward 803, 828
forward slide change 483
forward somersault with a twist 829
forward swing 864
forward three-and-a-half somersault tuck 829
forward travel pedal 333
forward/reverse 327
fossil fuel 68, 70
foul line 794, 865
foul line post 795
fouls/penalties 789
foundation 252, 253, 660
foundation blockage 660
foundation of dam 660
foundation of tower 540
foundation slip 366
foundations 253
fountain pen 470
four blade beater 236
four-door saloon 549
four-door sedan 549
four-four time 434

four-masted bark 602
four-of-a-kind 914
four-person bobsled 884
four-stroke-cycle engine 564
four-toed hoof 127
four-way lug wrench 558
four-way selector 477
fourchette 346
fourth 434
fourth round: 16 players 789
fourth wheel 696
fovea 177
Fox 13
fox 134
foyers 431
fraction 703
fractionating tower 656
fraise 339
frame 100, 252, 256, 278, 280, 303, 312, 321, 327, 350, 352, 386, 389, 395, 423, 433, 449, 460, 575, 612, 632, 633, 638, 639, 641, 642, 672, 673, 676, 688, 700, 776, 796, 816, 822, 823, 824, 870, 893, 895, 902
frame stile 278
frame, embroidery 459
frames 385
framing square 313
France 743
Francis runner 659
francium 682
frankfurter 216
free guard zone 877
free margin 172
free skating blade 881
free throw line 811, 814
free zone 813
freestyle skiing 890
freestyle snowboard 887
freestyle wrestling 843
freeway 539, 709
freewheel 580
freezer 224, 291, 720
freezer bag 222
freezer bucket 240
freezer compartment 291
freezer door 291
freezing 680
freezing rain 57, 64
freight car 583
freight cars, examples 588
freight expedition 621
freight hold 625
freight reception 621
freight station 583
freight wagon 583
freight wagons, examples of 588
French 469
French betting layout 919
French bread 204
French cuff 361
French cut 375
French horn 447
French horns 437
French knot stitch 459
French roulette wheel 919
French window 415
frequency bands 498
frequency display 503
frequency setting slide control 498
frequency, measurement 702
fresco 406
fresh air duct 543
fresh cheeses 210
fresh meat counter 180
fret 440, 441, 919
friction strip 318, 391
frieze 278, 403, 404
frigate 762
frilly nylon tights 368
frilly pants 368
fringe 337
frock coat 338
frog 110, 127, 353, 439, 590, 641
frog, anatomy 110
frog, life cycle 111
frog, morphology 110
frog, skeleton 111
frog-adjustment screw 309
frond 76
front 348, 349
front apron 349
front axle 639
front beam 698
front binding 840
front board 426
front brake 579
front brake lever 576
front bumper 885
front compression strap 906
front cover 519
front crawl stroke 832
front crossbar 893
front derailleur 578, 580
front desk 724
front fascia 550
front fender 574
front flap 391
front foil 609
front footrest 575, 576

front fork 870
front grille 261
front grip 757
front indicator 574, 576
front knob 307
front landing gear 760
front leg 277
front lights 554
front mudguard 574
front office, visitors' 726
front page 471
front picture 471
front pocket 387
front point 901
front rigid section 569
front runner 884
front shock absorber 577
front sight 754, 757, 861, 893, 912
front sight housing 755
front tip 288
front top pocket 350
front view 798
front wall 818, 819
front wheel 333, 639, 640, 783
front-end loader 637
frontal 112, 150, 737
frontal bone 131, 152, 158
frontal sinus 175
frontcourt 818
frontoparietal 111
fronts 56
frontwall 571
frost 65
frozen food storage 181
frozen foods 181
fruit branch 86
fruit machine 920
fruit tree 182
fruit vegetables 188
fruit-picking ladder 321
fruition 86
fruits 81, 180, 192, 723
fruits, tropical 196
fruticose lichen 74
fry basket 231
frying pan 235, 905
fuel 665, 670
fuel bundle 667
fuel conduit 553, 563
fuel control 627
fuel handling sequence 666
fuel indicator 557
fuel injector 565, 566
fuel lines 899
fuel oil 656
fuel pellet 667
fuel supply system 553
fuel tank 331, 553, 563, 570, 577, 586, 631, 758, 760
fuel tank flap 551
fuel transfer pipe 25
fuel: enriched uranium 671
fuel: natural uranium 670
fueling machine 666, 669, 670
fuelling machine 666, 669, 670
fuelport 666
Fulani 468
fulcrum 686, 828
full and by 833
full cheek snaffle bit 854
full cheek snaffle bit with keys 854
full cheek snaffle bit with toogles 854
full face helmet 874
full face mask 765
full house 914
full moon 7
full stop 473
full-load adjustment screw 273
fullback 804, 807
fully reflecting mirror 692
fumarole 44
fume extractor 758
function display 450
function keys 507, 508, 514, 699
function selector 261
function selectors 506
fungicide 69
fungiform papilla 176
funiculus 83, 84
funnel 231, 494, 599, 604, 608
funnel cloud 63
fur 121, 122, 133, 139, 143
furcula 116
furlable boom 18
Furnace 10
furnace 258, 674
furniture beetle 101
furrow 176
furs, examples 741
fuse 273, 663, 673
fuse body 757
fuse cutout 663
fuse holder 663
fuse puller 317
fuselage 625, 898
fuselage mounted tail unit 629
fuses, examples 272
fusilli 206
futon 280

ASTRONOMY > 2-25;   EARTH > 26-71;   VEGETABLE KINGDOM >72-89;   ANIMAL KINGDOM > 90-143;   HUMAN BEING > 144-177;   FOOD AND KITCHEN > 178-241;   HOUSE > 242-295;
DO-IT-YOURSELF AND GARDENING > 296-333;   CLOTHING > 334-371;   PERSONAL ADORNMENT AND ARTICLES > 372-391;   ARTS AND ARCHITECTURE > 392-465;   COMMUNICATIONS AND
OFFICE AUTOMATION > 466-535;   TRANSPORT AND MACHINERY > 536-643;   ENERGY > 644-677;   SCIENCE > 678-705;   SOCIETY > 706-785;   SPORTS AND GAMES > 786-920

ENGLISH INDEX

G

G 434
G clef 434
gable 244, 411
gable roof 414
gable stud 252
gable vent 244
gabletop 223
Gabon 745
gadolinium 684
gaff 602
gaff sail 601
gaff sail boom 602
gaff topsail 603
gaffer 429
Gai-lohn 187
gain control 613
gaiter 339
gaits, horse 124
galaxy 9
galaxy, classification 9
Galileo 19
gall-bladder 164
gallbladder 110, 112, 164
galleon 599
gallery 411, 614, 676
galley 598, 624
Gallic warrior 748
gallium 682
gallop 125
galosh 342
Gambia 745
game 212, 822
game board 915
game clock 789
game console 918
game port 513
games 788, 914
gamma rays 690
gangway 606
gantry crane 635, 657, 658
Ganymede 4
gap 911
garage 244, 726, 769
garage door 416
garam masala 199
garbage can 723
garbage disposal sink 270
garbage disposal unit 270
garden 406
garden cress 187
garden hose 328
garden line 324
garden path 244
garden sorrel 187
garden spider 102
garden, pleasure 322
garden, public 713
garden, vegetable 182
gardening 298, 322
gardening gloves 325
garlic 184
garlic press 230
garment bag 389
garment fabric 455
garment strap 389
garnet 375
garrison cap 340
garter 367
garter belt 367
garter snake 114
garter stitch 458
gas 275, 651, 656, 680
gas burner 267, 685
gas cock 267
gas conduit 563
gas cylinder 755
gas lift module 652
gas lighter 391
gas line 553
gas main 712
gas pedal 556
gas range 290, 721
gas supply system 553
gas tank 553, 563, 574, 577
gas tank cap 558
gas tank door 551
gas water-heater tank 267
gases, noble 684
gasket 269, 294
gaskin 124
gasoline 656
gasoline engine 553, 563, 566
gasoline pump 548
gasoline pump hose 548
gastrocnemius 150, 151
gate 596, 658, 664, 852, 900
gate arm 591
gate arm lamp 591
gate arm support 591
gate judge 837
gate operating ring 659
gate-leg 278
gate-leg table 278
gateway 523
gather 359
gather skirt 357
gathering 426
gauge 424

gauge wheel 333
gauntlet 318, 346, 749
gauze roller bandage 777
gear 462
gear cable 580
gear housing 910
gear lever 552, 579, 580
gear shift 576
gear tooth 686
gearbox 423, 552
gearchange lever 556
gearchange pedal 575, 576
gearing systems 686
gearshift lever 552, 556, 575, 577
gelatin capsule 783
gemstones, cut 375
generator 563, 637, 646, 659, 668
generator unit 658, 659
generators 688
Genoa salami 216
gentlemen's toilet 427
gentlemen's toilet 509, 724
geographical map 734
geography 28
geology 42
geometrical shapes 704
geometry 704
Georgia 746
geostationary orbit 60
geostationary satellite 60
geothermal and fossil energy 646
geothermal energy 646
geothermal field 646
germ 85
German 469
German mustard 200
German rye bread 205
German salami 216
German shepherd 130
Germanic languages 469
germanium 682
germination 77
Germany 744
geyser 44, 267
Ghana 745
ghee 210
gherkin 188
gi 846
giant slalom 889
giant slalom ski 888
giant water bug 101
gibbon 139
Gibraltar, Strait 32
gift store 714
gifts 717
gill 76, 106
gill slits 108
gills 105, 109
ginger 199
ginkgo nut 193
Giraffe 12
giraffe 129
girder 252
girdle 367, 374
girls' wear (size 2 to 6) 717
girls' wear (size 7 to 17) 717
girth 855, 856
girth strap 855
give way 544, 546
gizzard 116
glacial cirque 46
glacial lake 48
glacier 46, 48, 66
glacier tongue 46
glacis 409
gladius 748
glans penis 169
glass 672, 673
glass bottle 223
glass case 699
glass collection unit 71
glass cover 291
glass curtain 282
glass dome 612
glass lens 385
glass protector 878
glass recycling container 71
glass slide 693
glass sorting 71
glass sphere 58
glass washer 723
glass-fronted display cabinet 279
glass-lined tank 267
glassed roof 250, 582, 713
glasses 723
glassware 225
glazed frost 65
glider 898
gliding joint 156
gliding phase 892
global warming 68
globe 734, 903
globular cluster 9
glottis 112

glove 20, 798, 800, 842, 848, 855, 870, 871, 874, 875, 878, 882, 884, 887, 891, 892
glove compartment 556
glove finger 346
glove storage 780
glove, back 346

glove, palm 346
gloves 346, 872
glucose 78
glue 254
glue stick 534
gluteal nerve 166
gluteus maximus 151
gnocchi 206
gnomon 696
go 915, 916
goal 800, 802, 804, 807, 809, 814, 827, 879, 920
goal area 802, 814
goal area line 814
goal attack 809
goal circle 809
goal crease 879
goal defence 809
goal defense 809
goal judge 827, 858, 878
goal lights 879
goal line 800, 804, 806, 809, 814, 827, 878
goal line referee 814
goal shooter 809
goal third 809
goalkeeper 800, 801, 803, 809, 814, 827, 878, 879
goalkeeper's chest pad 880
goalkeeper's gloves 802
goalkeeper's pad 879
goalkeeper's skate 880
goalkeeper's stick 879, 880
goalpost 807, 809, 858
goat 128
goat's milk 210
goat's-milk cheeses 210
goatfish 219
gob hat 341
Gobi Desert 33
goggles 318, 870, 887, 896
gold 683
goldfinch 118
golf 866
golf bag 869
golf ball 867
golf ball, cross section 867
golf cart 869
golf cart, electric 869
golf clubs, types 867
golf course 708, 788
golf glove 869
golf shoes 869
golf trolley 869
Golgi apparatus 74, 94
gonad 95, 105, 106
gondola 181, 600, 886
gondola car 588
gondolas departure area 886
gonfalon 739
gong 437, 449
gonopore 95, 104
goods station 583
goods van 587
goose 120, 213
goose egg 213
goose-neck 255
gooseberry 192
gooseneck 638
gored skirt 357
gorge 47, 48
gorget 749
Gorgonzola 211
gorilla 138
gorilla, morphology 139
gorilla, skeleton 138
Gothic cathedral 410
gouache 396
gouache cakes 397
gouache tube 397
gouge 401
gour 47
government organization 525
governor tension sheave 417
governor's office 726
GPS receiver-antenna 613
grab handle 567, 570, 584, 766
gracile 151
grade slope 244
grader 639
graduated arc 612
graduated cylinder 685
graduated dial 907
graduated scale 698, 699
grafting knife 330
grain 300
grain elevator 643
grain of wheat, section 85
grain tank 643
grain terminal 596
grain tube 643
Grand Canyon 30
grand gallery 402
grandchildren 784
granddaughter 784
grandfather 784
grandfather clock 697
grandmother 784
grandparents 784
grandson 784
grandstand 856

granitic layer 42
granivorous bird 117
granny knot 908
granulated sugar 209
granulation 6
grape 86, 192
grape leaf 86, 186
grape, section 83
grapefruit 194
grapefruit knife 229
grapeshot 752
graphic arts 420
graphic equalizer 498
grapnel 610
grass 822
grassbox 332
grasshopper 102
grassland 66
grate 290
grater 230
grave accent 473
gravel 253, 263
gravel bed 872
gravity band 610
gravity dam 661
gravity dam, cross section 661
gravy boat 226
gray matter 167, 168
grease well 239
greases 656
great adductor 151
Great Australian Bight 29
Great Barrier Reef 29
Great Bear 13
Great Britain 743
Great Dane 131
Great Dividing Range 29
great green bush-cricket 101
great horned owl 119
Great Lakes 30
great organ manual 444
great saphenous vein 160
Great Sandy Desert 29
great scallop 217
Great Schism 736
Great Victoria Desert 29
great-grandchildren 784
great-granddaughter 784
great-grandfather 784
great-grandmother 784
great-grandparents 784
great-grandson 784
greater alar cartilage 175
greater covert 115
greater pectoral 150
greater trochanter 153
greatest gluteal 151
greave 749
Greco-Roman wrestling 843
Greece 744
Greek 469
Greek bread 204
Greek temple 403
Greek temple, plan 403
Greek theater 402
green 400, 690, 864, 866, 867
green alga 75
green ball 863
green beam 494
green bean 191
green cabbage 186
green coffee beans 208
green gland 107
green light 712
green onion 184
green peas 190
green pepper 198
green russula 183
green sweet pepper 188
green tea 208
green walnut 84
greenhouse 182
greenhouse effect 68
greenhouse effect, enhanced 68
greenhouse effect, natural 68
greenhouse gas 68
greenhouse gas concentration 68
Greenland 30
Greenland Sea 28
Grenada 743
grenade 757
Grenadines 743
grey matter 168
greyhound 131
grid 494
grid system 36
griddle 239
grille 261, 403, 432, 550, 561, 727
grinding wheel 308
grip 428, 793, 838, 850, 859, 867, 913
grip handle 303
grip tape 894
gripping tools 310
grocery bags 181
groin 146, 148
groove 229, 424, 453, 750, 868, 888
ground 272, 655
ground air conditioner 622
ground airport equipment 622
ground beef 214
ground bond 272

ground clamp 318
ground connection 272
ground electrode 562
ground fault circuit interrupter 272
ground floor 250
ground lamb 215
ground moraine 46
ground pepper 199
ground pork 215
ground sill 409
ground surface 647
ground terminal 497
ground veal 214
ground wire 272, 273
ground-wire peak 663
ground/neutral bus bar 272
grounded receptacle 263
groundhog 123
grounding prong 274
grow sleepers 368
growth line 104, 105
Gruyère 211
Guarani 469
guard 229, 255, 316, 811, 849
guard rail 291, 894
guardhouse 408, 409
Guatemala 742
guava 197
guide 909
guide bar 331
guide handle 308
guide roller 499
guiding and current bar 595
guiding tower 542
guillotine trimmer 484
Guinea 745
Guinea fowl 120, 212
guinea pig 123
Guinea, Gulf 34
Guinea-Bissau 745
guitar 440, 441
gules 741
gulf 38
Gulf of Aden 33, 34
Gulf of Alaska 30
Gulf of Bothnia 32
Gulf of California 30
Gulf of Carpentaria 29
Gulf of Guinea 34
Gulf of Mexico 30
Gulf of Oman 33
Gulf of Panama 31
gum 159, 174
gun 315, 758
gun body 320
gun flap 352
gun range 769
gunner's sight 758
gurnard 219
gusset 386, 388
gusset pocket 359, 360
Gutenberg discontinuity 42
gutta 404
gutter 244, 865
guy cable 824, 825
guy line 902
guy wire 676
Guyana 742
guyot 49
gymnase office 734
gymnasium 608, 727, 734, 764, 788
gymnast's name 825
gymnastics 823, 824
gynecological examination room 779
gyoji 847
gypsum board 299
gypsum tile 299
gyroscope 759

H

hack 877
hackle 909
hacksaw 303, 314
haddock 221
hafnium 683
hail 64
hail shower 57
hair 147, 149, 172, 439
hair bulb 172
hair clip 380
hair conditioner 379
hair dryer 382
hair follicle 172
hair grip 380
hair roller 380
hair roller pin 380
hair shaft 172
hair slide 380
hair stylist 428
hairbrushes 380
haircolor 379
haircutting scissors 382
hairdressing 380
hairdressing salon 714
hairpin 380
hairspring 696
Haiti 742
hakama 846, 847
half barb 56

half cell 897
half court line 819
half handle 229
half indexing 528
half note 435
half rest 435
half-distance line 827
half-glasses 385
half-mask respirator 773
half-pipe 871, 887
half-pipe, competition site 887
half-side 632
half-slip 366
half-through arch bridge 541
halfway line 803, 805
halibut 221
hall 250, 608, 719, 724
hallah 205
halo 9
halogen desk lamp 286
halogen light 775
halyard 603, 739
ham knife 229
hamate 154
hammer 317, 442, 443, 754, 793, 861, 912
hammer ax 901
hammer axe 901
hammer butt 443
hammer drill 648
hammer felt 443
hammer head 901
hammer loop 313
hammer rail 442, 443
hammer shank 443
hammer throw 791
hamster 123
hand 139, 147, 149, 154, 173
hand blender 236
hand brake 552
hand brake gear housing 587
hand brake wheel 587
hand brake winding lever 587
hand cultivator 325
hand drill 307
hand fork 325
hand grenade 757
hand hole 535
hand lamp 765
hand miter saw 303
hand mixer 236
hand mower 332
hand post 433
hand protection 774
hand protector 331, 875
hand rest 516
hand shield 318
hand tools 325
hand truck 633
hand vacuum cleaner 288
hand vice 422
hand wash in lukewarm water 347
hand wheel 452
hand-warmer pocket 353, 355
hand-warmer pouch 360
hand-wheel 425
handbags 387
handball 814
handbrake lever 556
handcuff case 770
handgrip 574, 577, 782, 909
handgrips 850
handguard 755
handheld computer 527
handhold 857
handholds 901
handicap spot 916
handicaps board 858
handle 227, 230, 236, 237, 238, 239, 240, 256, 268, 280, 288, 289, 290, 291, 295, 301, 302, 303, 304, 305, 307, 308, 309, 310, 311, 312, 313, 315, 316, 319, 320, 323, 328, 331, 332, 381, 382, 383, 384, 386, 387, 388, 389, 391, 425, 439, 454, 458, 460, 503, 504, 534, 558, 611, 649, 750, 775, 783, 793, 797, 798, 800, 815, 816, 822, 840, 849, 877, 884, 888, 891, 905, 909, 910, 920
handlebar 327, 851, 871, 876
handlebar grip 871
handlebars 579, 871, 876
handles, examples 840
handling 632
handrail 255, 417, 569, 594, 607
handsaw 303
handset 506, 507
handset cord 506
handset flex 506
hang glider 897
hang gliding 897
hang gliding pilot 897
hang point 897
hang to dry 347
hang-up ring 382
hanger 483
hanger bracket 783
hanger loop 354
hanging basket 322
hanging cupboard 279

hanging file 532
hanging glacier 46
hanging pendant 286
hanging sleeve 338
hanging stile 247, 249, 278
hank 835
hapteron 75
harbor 596
harbour 596
hard boot 887
hard contact lens 384
hard disk drive 521
hard disk drive, secondary 513
hard hat 772
hard palate 174, 175
hard surface 822
hard top gondola 588
hard-shell clam 217
hardboard 300
hardwood base 899
Hare 11
hare 123, 212
harissa 201
harmonica 432
harness 460, 841, 893, 896, 897
harness racing 857
harnesses 460
harp 440
harp cable stays 541
harps 437
harpsichord 443
harquebus 752
hasp 389
hassium 683
hastate 79
hat stand 510
hat switch 516
hatband 340
hatch 23, 758
hatchback 549
hatchet 767, 907
hatching 463
haulage road 647
Hausa 468
Haversian canal 154
Hawaiian 469
hawk 315
hay baler 642
hayloft 182
haze 57
hazelnut 193
hazelnut, section 84
head 8, 96, 97, 99, 104, 115, 140, 147, 149, 161, 169, 185, 301, 302, 308, 311, 383, 384, 390, 391, 425, 439, 440, 441, 449, 452, 457, 458, 516, 591, 793, 816, 822, 858, 867, 901, 909
head cover 869
head cushion 862
head harness 773
head light 579
head linesman 807
head number 857
head nurse's office 779
head of femur 153
head of frame 249
head of humerus 153
head of water 662
head pole 857
head protection 772, 774
head roller 460
head tube 319, 579
head, bat 140
head, bird 115
head-first entry 829
headband 426, 502, 504, 772, 773
headbay 657
headboard 280, 281
headcap 426
header 247, 252, 643
headframe 650
headgear 340, 341, 842
heading 471
headings, examples 283
headland 51
headlight 333, 550, 570, 574, 576, 585, 586, 640, 758, 876
headlight/turn signal 556
headlights 554
headline 471
headphone jack 450, 451, 497, 504
headphone plug 504
headphones 502, 504
headpin 865
headrail 285
headrest 555
heads, examples 302
headset kit 506
headwind 833
headwind, start 833
health 775
health and beauty care 181
health organization 525
hearing 173
heart 97, 99, 103, 104, 105, 106, 107, 109, 110, 112, 116, 125, 162, 163, 212, 914
Herzegovina 744
heartwood 87
heat control 259
heat deflecting disc 274

heat energy 68
heat exchanger 259, 670, 675
heat gun 320
heat loss 68
heat production 665
heat ready indicator 381
heat selector switch 382
heat shield 22
heat sink 513
heat transfer 681
heat transport pump 669
heat-sealed film 223
heater 903
heating 256
heating coil 899
heating duct 293
heating element 258, 259, 293, 294, 318, 465
heating equipment 608
heating fuel tank 563
heating grille 594
heating oil 656
heating, forced hot-water system 259
heating, forced warm-air system 258
heaving line knot 908
heavy continuous rain 57
heavy continuous snow 57
heavy duty boot 342
heavy gasoline 656
heavy intermittent rain 57
heavy intermittent snow 57
heavy machinery 636
heavy petroleum 656
heavy rainfall 63
heavy thunderstorm 57
heavy-water reactor 670
Hebrew 468
heddle rod 461
heddles 460, 461
hedge 245, 322
hedge shears 330
hedge trimmer 331
hedgehog 121
heel 127, 147, 149, 229, 303, 309, 342, 351, 370, 439, 440, 641, 797, 868, 880, 881
heel grip 342
heel loop 783
heel rest 236, 288
heel stop 895
heeled shoe 339
heelpiece 840, 889
heelplate 892
height adjustment 641, 642, 826, 851
height adjustment foot 483
height adjustment scale 304
height control 485
height finder 761
height of the dive 829
height scale 485
helicopter 631, 762
helicopter flight deck 762
helicopter hangar 762
helicopters, examples 631
heliostats 674
helipad 652
helium 684
helium sphere 25
helix 173, 705
helm roof 415
helmet 20, 748, 765, 798, 800, 808, 858, 870, 871, 875, 878, 882, 887, 888, 891, 894, 895, 896, 897, 901
helmet lamp 901
helmet ring 20
hem 285
hemidemisemiquaver 435
hemidemisemiquaver rest 435
hemisphere 705
hemispheres 35
hemlath 676
hemline 455
hen 120
hen egg 213
hen house 182
hendecagon 705
hennin 339
Henry VIII 736
hepatic vein 161
heptagon 705
heraldry 739
herbal teas 208
herbicide 69
herbivores 67
herbs 202
Herdsman 13
hermaphroditic duct 104
Hero 12
heron 119
herring 219
herringbone parquet 254
herringbone pattern 254
herringbone stitch 459
hertz 702
Hertzian wave transmission 486
Herzegovina 744
heterotrophs 67
hex nut 562
hexagon bushing 269
hexagon nut 311

hidden pocket 386
high (19 to 36) 919
high altar 737
high beam 554
high beam indicator light 557
high beam warning indicator 576
high card 914
high chair 281
high cloud, type 55
high clouds 62
high focal plane buoy 615
high frequency antenna cable 628
high gain antenna 18
high jump 791, 792
high pressure area 63
high pressure center 55
high warp loom 461
high wing 628
high-back dungarees 368
high-back overalls 368
high-hat cymbal 448
high-pressure steam inlet 668
high-rise apartment 419
high-rise block 419
high-speed exit taxiway 618
high-speed shaft 677
high-speed train 585
high-temperature cutoff 266
high-tension electricity transmission 646, 662, 677
high-voltage tester 316
highball glass 225
highland 7, 61
highland climates 61
highlight key 479
highway 39, 539
highway crossing 591
highway crossing bell 591
highway number 39
hijiki 183
hiking boot 344
hill 45, 674
hilted bayonet 751
Himalayas 33
hind leg 96
hind leg, butterfly 96
hind leg, honeybee 98
hind limb 110, 111, 121, 143
hind toe 115, 117
hind wing 96
Hindi 469
Hinduism 736
hinge 238, 247, 249, 278, 294, 386, 389, 465, 500, 554, 692, 889
hinge joint 156
hinge pin 638
hinged presser foot 452, 453
hip 147, 149
hip pad 808
hip roof 414
hip-and-valley roof 415
hippopotamus 129
hitch ball 558
hitch pin 442
hitting area 797
hive 100, 182
hive body 100
hobble 857
hobble hanger 857
hobo bag 388
hock 124, 130, 215
hockey ball 800
hockey skate, in-line 895
hoe 327
hoe-fork 326
hog line 877
hoisin sauce 200
hoist 739
hoist room 649
hoisting block 634
hoisting rig 610
hoisting rope 321, 417, 634
hoisting system 635
holdback 282
holder 685
holding 844
holding area marking 620
holds, examples 844
hole 423, 866, 867
holes 866
hollow barrel 776
hollow brick 298
hollow shot 752
holmium 684
hologram foil strip 729
holster 770
holy water font 737
home 515
home antenna 486
home key 515
home plate 795
home straight 856
home theater 493
home theatre 493
home user 525
home-plate umpire 795
homestretch 856
homo sapiens 93
homogenized milk 210
Honduras 742
honey 209

honey cell 100
honeybee 98
honeybee, anatomy 99
honeybee, foreleg 98
honeybee, hind leg 98
honeybee, middle leg 98
honeybee, morphology 98
honeycomb 100
honeycomb section 100
honeydew melon 195
honor tiles 917
honour tiles 917
hood 256, 289, 333, 353, 368, 550, 570, 721, 841, 882, 901
hood, range 722
hooded sweat shirt 370
hooded towelling robe 368
hoof 124, 127
hoof, plantar surface 127
hoofs, types 127
hook 249, 284, 313, 316, 327, 452, 453, 456, 457, 573, 611, 634, 699, 776, 861, 862, 881
hook and eyes 453
hook ladder 321, 767
hooker 804
hoop 459, 823
hoop earrings 374
hopper 643
hopper car 588
hopper ore car 588
hopper ore wagon 588
hopper tank wagon 588
horizon mirror 612
horizon shade 612
horizontal bar 824, 825
horizontal clamp 701
horizontal control 518
horizontal end handhold 587
horizontal ground movement 43
horizontal member 663
horizontal motion lock 482
horizontal movement 916
horizontal pivoting window 415
horizontal seismograph 43
horizontal stabilizer 625, 631, 898
horizontal-axis wind turbine 677
horn 376, 556, 576, 586, 766
horned melon 196
hornet 101
horny beak 113
hors d'oeuvre dish 226
hors d'oeuvres 722
horse 124, 129, 826, 858
horse racing 856, 857
horse, anatomy 125
horse, gaits 124
horse, morphology 124
horse, skeleton 126
horsefly 101
horseradish 189
horseshoe 127, 376, 413
horseshoe mount 17
hose 289, 319, 365, 367, 767
hose connector 328, 329
hose dryer 764
hose holder 764
hose nozzle 328
hose trolley 328
hospital 711, 725, 778
hospital bed 780
hot bus bar 272
hot coolant 665, 674
hot food 722
hot food table 721
hot line connector 663
hot pepper 188
hot plate 721
hot-air outflow 258
hot-air outlet 256
hot-air register 258
hot-shoe contact 476
hot-water circuit 262
hot-water heater 262
hot-water line 266
hot-water outlet 259, 267
hot-water riser 262
hot-water supply line 270, 271
hotel 710, 724, 886, 915
hotel reservation desk 620
hotel rooms 724
houppelande 338
hour angle gear 17
hour hand 697
house 244, 431, 877, 915
house drain 271
house dress 356
house furniture 276
house, elements 247
house, elevation 250
house, exterior 244
house, foundations 253
house, frame 252
house, structure 250
houseboat 607
household equipment 295
household linen 716
household products 180
household waste 69, 70
houses, city 419
houses, traditional 418

housing 261, 275, 306, 308, 316, 318, 383, 488, 499, 507, 613, 614
hovercraft 605
howitzer 756
hub 103, 522, 523, 534, 579, 659, 677, 783
hub cover 659
Hubble space telescope 17, 53
Hubble's classification 9
Hudson Bay 30
Huitzilopochtli, Temple 412
hull 84, 599, 834, 876
hull column 652
hull sonar 762
human being 146
human body 146
human denture 159
humerus 111, 116, 121, 122, 126, 131, 136, 138, 141, 142, 152, 156
humid continental - hot summer 61
humid continental - warm summer 61
humid subtropical 61
humidifier 261
humidistat 261
humidity 261
humidity, measure 59
hummingbird 118
hummus 200
hump 589
hump lead 589
hump office 589
humpback whale 137
Hungarian 469
Hungary 744
Hunter 11, 12
hunting 912
hunting cap 340
Hunting Dogs 13
hurdle 790
hurdle, steeplechase 790
hurricane 57, 63
hurricane lamp 906
husband 785
husk 84, 85
hut 418
Huygens 19
hybrid automobile 563
hybrid car 563
hydrant intake 766
hydraulic coupler 640
hydraulic cylinder 633, 640
hydraulic disc brake 870
hydraulic hose 641, 642
hydraulic jack 567
hydraulic pallet truck 633
hydraulic resistance 851
hydraulic shovel 638
hydraulic system 632
hydroelectric complex 657
hydroelectric power plant, cross section 658
hydroelectricity 657
hydrofoil boat 609
hydrogen 682
hydrologic cycle 67
hydrometer 562
hydrosphere 66
hyena 134
hygrograph 59
hygrometer 261
hyperlinks 524
hyperopia 691
hypha 76
hyracotherium 93
hyssop 202

I

Iapetus 5
Iberian Peninsula 32
ice 67
ice ax 901
ice axe 901
ice breaker 606
ice cream freezer 240
ice cream scoop 233
ice cube dispenser 224
ice cube tray 211
ice dispenser 548
ice hockey 878
ice hockey player 878
ice machine 721
ice piton 901
ice rink 886
ice screw 901
iceberg lettuce 186
Iceland 32, 744
Icelandic 469
ichthyosaur 93
ichthyostega 92
icing syringe 232
identification badge 770
identification bracelet 376
identification section 768
identification tag 389
identity tag 389
idler wheel 876
igloo 418
igneous rocks 42
ignition box 627
ignition key 332, 333
ignition lead 566
ignition switch 556, 576
ignition transformer 259
iguana 114
ileum 164
iliohypogastric nerve 166
ilioinguinal nerve 166
ilium 111, 116, 122, 152
illumination mirror 701
image adjustment buttons 496
image review button 477
imager 60
imperial roof 414
impervious rock 651
impluvium 406
impost 413
impulse sprinkler 329
in goal 805
in-flight refueling 760
in-flight refueling probe 760
in-flight refuelling 760
in-flight refuelling probe 760
in-ground swimming pool 246
in-line hockey skate 895
in-line skate 895
in-line skating 895
in-line speed skate 895
inactive dike 664
inbounds line 806
incandescent lamp 274, 614, 673
incident neutron 681
incineration 71
incised figure 420
incisor 121, 123
incisors 159
inclination 13
incoming message cassette 508
incurrent pore 95
incus 174
indent 528
Index 0
index 471
index arm 612
index card cabinet 533
index card drawer 533
index cards 532
index finger 173
index mirror 612
index shade 612
index/enlarge button 477
India 747
Indian 10
Indian chapati bread 205
Indian naan bread 205
Indian Ocean 28, 29, 33, 34
indicator 554, 571
indicator board 582, 793
indicator light 767
indicator lights 515
indicator needle 479
indicator telltale 557, 576
indicators 494, 501
indicators display button 496
indium 682
Indo-European languages 469
Indo-Iranian languages 469
Indonesia 33, 747
Indonesian 469
indoor activity area 727
indoor electric grill 239
indoor shutters 282
indoor unit 260
industrial area 709
industrial communications 487
industrial pollution 69
industrial waste 69, 70
industry 525
inert gas 274
inferior 472
inferior cymbal 448
inferior dental arch 174
inferior mesenteric artery 165
inferior nasal concha 175
inferior rectus muscle 177
inferior umbilicus 115
inferior vena cava 160, 161, 162, 165
infield 794
infiltration 67
infinity 703
infirmary 726
inflated carrying tire 594, 595
inflated carrying tyre 594
inflated guiding tire 594, 595
inflated guiding tyre 594
inflation system 611
inflator 841, 904
inflator valve 841
inflator-deflator 904
inflorescences, types 81
inflorescent vegetables 187
information 725
information booth 715
information console 841
information counter 620
information desk 719, 730, 733, 769, 779, 886
information spreading 525
infrared homing head 759
infrared port 526, 527
infrared radiation 68, 690
infrared sounder 60

infrared thermal mapper 18
infraspinatus 151
infraspinous 151
infundibulum of fallopian tube 171
infusions 208
inhalation valve 773
initials of the issuing bank 729
injection well 646
injection/combustion 565
ink 397, 421, 470
ink drawing 396
ink roller 421
ink sac 106
inked surface 420
inking slab 421
inkjet printer 519
inlaid parquet 254
inlet hose 485
inlet valve 566
inmates' admission office 726
inmates' entrance 726
inner boot 889, 895
inner circle 877
inner core 42
inner door shell 554
inner edge 127
inner hearth 256
inner jib 603
inner lining 561
inner lip 105
inner planets 5
inner stators 627
inner table 915
inner tent 902, 903
inner toe 115
inorganic matter 67
input devices 514
input lights 497
input monitors 491
input receptacle 520
input select button 497
input selector 497
input terminal 316
input tray 519
input/output audio/video jacks 497
inrun 890, 891
insectivorous bird 117
insectivorous mammals 121
insectivorous mammals, examples 121
insects 96
insects, examples 101
insert 515
insert key 515
inset pocket 360
inside 227
inside edge 901
inside knob 248
inside linebacker 806
inside-leg snap-fastening 368, 369
insole 345
installation work 395
instant-read thermometer 231
instep 351
instrument panel 557
instrument platform 60
instrument shelter 58
instrument unit 25
instrumental groups, examples 438
insulated blade 316
insulated handle 239, 316, 317
insulating material 253, 254, 294
insulating materials 299
insulating sleeve 275
insulation 259, 266, 267, 672
insulator 562, 663
insurance services 730
intaglio printing 420
intaglio printing process 422
intaglio printing process, equipment 422
intake 564, 565
intake manifold 564, 565, 566
intake port 565
intake valve 564
integral 703
integral bayonet 751
integrated circuit 689
Intelsat 487
intensive care unit 780
intensive farming 68, 70
intensive husbandry 68, 69
interactive terminals 395
interchange 709
interchangeable studs 802
interchanges, examples 538
intercom microphone 491
intercom station 491
intercostal nerve 166
interface card, network 522
interface card, wireless network 522
interfacing 455
interfemoral membrane 140
interior dome shell 17
interior door handle 554
interior door lock button 554
interior pocket 389
interlining 455
interlock 463
intermediate booster station 654
intermediate slope 886
internal boundary 37
internal ear 174

internal filum terminale 167
internal iliac artery 160, 161, 165
internal iliac vein 161
internal jugular vein 160
internal modem port 513, 526
internal tooth lock washer 310
international boundary 37
international mail 475
international road signs 544
international space station 21
international system of units 702
international weather symbols 56
Internet 523, 524
Internet keys 514
Internet service provider 525
Internet user 524
Internet uses 525
internode 77
interrogation room 768
interrupted projection 36
intersection of two sets 703
intertragic notch 173
interval 617
intervals 434
interventricular septum 162
intervertebral disk 157
intervertebral foramen 157
interview rooms 728
intestine 95, 97, 103, 104, 105, 107, 109, 112, 161
intrados 413
intravenous stand 780
intrusive filtration 69
intrusive rocks 42
Inuktitut 469
invert 595
inverted pleat 283, 357
inward 828
Io 4
iodine 683
ion tail 8
Ionic column 407
Ionic order 404
Iran 746
Iraq 746
Ireland 743
iridium 683
iris 177
Irish 469
Irish bread 205
Irish moss 183
Irish Sea 32
iron 683, 867, 868
iron at high setting 347
iron at low setting 347
iron at medium setting 347
iron curtain 430
iron meteorite 8
ironing 347
irregular bone 157
irregular crystal 64
is an element of 703
is approximately equal to 703
is equivalent to 703
is greater than 703
is greater than or equal to 703
is identical with 703
is included in/is a subset of 703
is less than 703
is less than or equal to 703
is not an element of 703
is not equal to 703
is not identical with 703
is not parallel to 704
is parallel to 704
ISA expansion connector 513
isba 418
ischium 111, 116, 122, 153
Islam 736
island 38, 224, 539, 761
island arc 49
isobar 55
isolated danger mark 617
isolated languages 469
isolation cell 727
isolation room 778
isoseismal line 43
Israel 746
ISS 21
issuing bank, initials 729
isthmus 38
isthmus of fallopian tube 171
isthmus of fauces 174
Isthmus of Panama 30
Italian 469
italic 472
Italy 744
ivory ball 919

J

J-2 engine 25
jabot 362
jaboticaba 197
jack 443, 558, 634, 638, 766, 864, 873, 914
jack field 488
jack spring 443
jack stand 641
jack-up platform 653

jacket 338, 353, 355, 521, 689, 844, 848, 855, 912
jackets 348, 358
jackfruit 196
jackleg drill 648
jackpot box 920
jackpot feed 920
jaguar 135
jail 915
jalapeño chile 199
jalousie 249
Jamaica 742
jamb 247, 256
janitor's closet 724, 731
Japan 33, 747
Japan Trench 50
Japan, Sea 33
Japanese 469
Japanese experiment module 21
Japanese persimmon 197
Japanese plum 193
Jarlsberg 211
Java Trench 50
javelin 748, 793
javelin throw 791
jaw 302, 306, 307, 312, 317, 377
jaw, rabbit 123
jaw, rat 123
jaw, rodent's 123
jaws 312, 913
jay 118
jazz band 438
jeans 358
jejunum 164
jerboa 123
jersey 805, 870
Jerusalem artichoke 184
Jesus Christ 736
jet blast deflector 761
jet engine test area 761
jet fuel 656
jet refueler 622
jet tip 384
Jew's harp 433
jewel 696
jewellery 374
jewellery shop 714
jewellery, watches and 717
jewelry 374
jewelry store 714
Jewish challah 205
Jewish hallah 205
jib 634, 635, 834
jib tie 634
jibe 833
jibsheet 834
jicama 184
jig saw 305
jigger topgallant staysail 603
jigger topmast staysail 603
jiggermast 602
jigsaw puzzle 917
jingle 449
jo 846
jockey 856
jockey rollers 580
jodhpurs 853
jogging pants 370
John Calvin 736
John dory 221
joint 426, 470, 863, 909
joint filler 315
jointed mouth 854
jointed mouth bit 854
jointer plane 309
joist 254
joker 914
Jordan 746
joule 702
journal box 586
joystick 516
joysticks 918
Judaism 736
judge 842, 843, 844, 848, 855, 859
judge coordinator 823
judge's stand 856
judges 824, 825, 828, 881
judges' bench 728
judges' office 728
judges' stand 887, 890, 891
judo 844
judogi 844
jug 241
juice extractor 240
juice sac 82
juicer 240
jujitsu 846
jujube 197
jump judge 852
jump rope 850
jump skis 840
jump, steeplechase hurdle 790
jumper 356
jumper cables 558
jumping 792
jumping ski 891
jumping technique 891
jumps, examples 881
jumpsuit 358, 368, 369
junction box 591
junior officer's office 768

966

ASTRONOMY > 2-25; EARTH > 26-71; VEGETABLE KINGDOM >72-89; ANIMAL KINGDOM > 90-143; HUMAN BEING > 144-177; FOOD AND KITCHEN > 178-241; HOUSE > 242-295;
DO-IT-YOURSELF AND GARDENING > 296-333; CLOTHING > 334-371; PERSONAL ADORNMENT AND ARTICLES > 372-391; ARTS AND ARCHITECTURE > 392-465; COMMUNICATIONS AND
OFFICE AUTOMATION > 466-535; TRANSPORT AND MACHINERY > 536-643; ENERGY > 644-677; SCIENCE > 678-705; SOCIETY > 706-785; SPORTS AND GAMES > 786-920

juniper berry 198
junk 600
Jupiter 4
Jurassic 93
jurors' room 728
jury 853
jury box 728
jury platform 871
justaucorps 338
justice 726
juvenile cell 768

K

K-frame 663
K1 kayak 839
Kalahari Desert 34
kale 186
Kamchatka Peninsula 33
kangaroo 142, 143
kangaroo, morphology 143
kangaroo, skeleton 142
Kaplan runner 659
karabiner 901
karabiner, locking 900
karate 845
karate-gi 845
karateka 845
kayak 837
kayak, K1 839
Kazakhstan 746
keel 116, 897
keel boat 835
keep 408
keeper ring 909
kelly 651
kelvin 702
kendo 847
kendoka 847
Kenya 745
kerb 712
Kermadec-Tonga Trench 50
kernel 85
kerosene 656
kerosene tank 25
Keroularios 736
ketch 601
ketchup 201
kettle 45, 240
kettledrum 448
key 249, 432, 436, 442, 443, 445, 446
key case 387
key cutting shop 715
key finger button 446
key grip 428
key guard 446
key lever 446
key lock 386
key signature 435
keybed 442
keyboard 442, 450, 507, 514, 526, 865
keyboard instruments 442
keyboard port 513
keyless chuck 306
keys 451
keystone 410, 413
keyway 249
kick pleat 357
kicker 471, 800, 890
kickers 890
kickstand 575, 577
kidney 104, 105, 106, 109, 110, 112, 116, 125, 161, 212
kielbasa sausage 216
killer whale 137
kilogram 702
kilt 357
kimono 364
kimono sleeve 361
King 12
king 914, 916
king post 253, 897
king's side 916
king's chamber 402
kingfisher 118
kingpin 571
Kinyarwanda 468
kiosk 548, 593
Kiribati 747
Kirundi 468
kitchen 222, 224, 250, 406, 584, 719, 721, 723, 724, 726, 735, 763, 764
kitchen articles 716
kitchen facilities 509
kitchen knife 229
kitchen knives, examples 229
kitchen scale 231
kitchen shears 233
kitchen timer 231
kitchen towel 295
kitchen utensils 229
kiwi 196
knapsack 901
knee 124, 130, 146, 148
knee boot 857
knee boot suspender 857
knee pad 796, 808, 858, 880, 882, 894, 895
knee roll 855
knee wrap 850

knee-high sock 365
knee-length sock 351
kneeling position 861
knickerbockers 358
knickers 358
knife 227, 401, 421, 841, 905, 907
knife pleat 350, 357
knife-blade cartridge fuse 272
knight 916
knit shirt 354
knitting 457
knitting machine 456
knitting measure 457
knitting needle 457
knives, examples 228
knob 278, 309, 797
knob handle 304
knobby tread tire 577
knockout 272
knoll 890
knot 463
knot stitches 459
knots 908
knurled bolt 320
koala 143
kohlrabi 185
Kola Peninsula 32
kombu 183
kora 433
Koran 736
Korea 747
Korean 469
Korean Peninsula 33
kote 847
krypton 684
Kuiper belt 4
kumquat 194
kung fu 846
kung fu practitioner 846
Kuril Trench 50
Kuwait 746
Kyrgyzstan 746

L

label 500
label holder 533
label maker 533
labial palp 96, 99, 105
labium majus 170, 171
labium minus 170, 171
lablab bean 190
laboratory 16, 17
laboratory equipment 685
labyrinth 885
laccolith 44
lace 797, 843, 881
lace carriage 456
lace needle 456
lace-up 342
lacing 893
lachrymal canal 177
lachrymal duct 177
lachrymal gland 177
lacing 893
lactiferous duct 171
ladder 246, 418, 567, 597, 615, 639, 655
ladder and hose strap 767
ladder pipe nozzle 766
ladder scaffold 321
ladders 321
ladies' toilet 427
ladies' toilet 509, 724
ladle 233, 752
Ladoga, Lake 32
Lady chapel 410, 411
ladybird 101
ladybird beetle 101
lagging 655
lagomorph's jaw 123
lagomorph's jaw: rabbit 123
lagomorphs 122
lagomorphs, examples 123
lagoon 51
lake 7, 38, 45, 48
lake acidification 70
Lake Baikal 33
Lake Chad 34
Lake Eyre 29
Lake Ladoga 32
Lake Malawi 34
Lake Tanganyika 34
Lake Titicaca 31
Lake Victoria 34
lakes 48
lam 460
lamb cubes 215
lamb, cuts 215
lambdoid suture 158
lamina 75
laminboard 300
lamp 693
lamp base 614
lamp socket 275
lamp socket, parts 275
lamphouse elevation control 485
lamphouse head 485
lamprey 219
lanceolate 79
lancet 413
land 306
land pollution 69

land station 54
lander (Viking) 18
landfill 709
landfill site 69
landing 251, 255, 650, 891
landing area 790, 792, 793, 891
landing deck 761
landing gear 567, 571
landing gear crank 571
landing gear lever 626
landing light 631
landing net 911
landing radar 761
landing slope 891
landing track 890
landing window 631
landslides 47
lane 711, 788, 790, 830, 831, 882
lane line 791
lane number 893
lane rope 831
lane timekeeper 830
language display button 507
language families 468
languages of the world 468
languid 444
lantern 322, 614, 903
lantern pane 614
lanthanides 684
lanthanum 684
Lao People's Democratic Republic 747
lap counter 883
lapel 348, 362
lapiaz 47
lapis lazuli 375
laptop computer 523, 526
laptop computer briefcase 527
laptop computer: front view 526
laptop computer: rear view 526
lapwing 118
larch 89
lard 209
larding needle 233
large blade 905
large intestine 110, 164
large wheel 783
large-screen television set 493
larger round 151
larger spotted dogfish 218
larva 100
larynx 163
lasagna 206
laser beam 501, 692
laser printer 519
last quarter 7
latch 238, 294, 389, 456, 900
latch bolt 248
latch lever 452
latch needle 456
lateen sail 601
lateen yard 600
lateral bar 851
lateral brush 573
lateral condyle of femur 153
lateral cuneiform 155
lateral cutaneous femoral nerve 166
lateral cutaneous nerve of thigh 166
lateral filing cabinet 510
lateral great 150, 151
lateral groove 127
lateral incisor 159
lateral line 108, 877
lateral mark 617
lateral moraine 46
lateral semicircular canal 174
lateral view of skull 158
lateral-adjustment lever 309
latex glove 776
latex glove case 770
lath 285
lath tilt device 285
latissimus dorsi 151
latrines 406
Latvia 744
launch escape system 25
laundry 724, 726
laundry room 250
lava flow 44
lava layer 44
lavatory truck 622
lawn 245, 322
lawn aerator 333
lawn bowling 864
lawn care 332
lawn edger 326
lawn rake 333
lawn tractor 333
lawrencium 684
leach field 263
leaching 70
lead 471, 682, 877
lead ball 757
lead pencil 470
lead screw 306
lead-in wire 274, 275
leader 900, 911
leading 472
leading bunch 870
leading edge 362, 625, 897, 898
leading edge flap 760
leading edge tube 897

leading motorcycle 870
leaf 75, 77, 78, 79, 185
leaf axil 79
leaf margin 79
leaf node 77
leaf vegetables 186
leaf, structure 79
leakproof cap 903
lean-to roof 414
leash rod 461
leather end 350
leather goods 386
leather goods shop 714
leather sheath 907
leather skin 798
Lebanon 746
lectern 737
ledger 252
ledger line 434
leech 836
leek 184
left atrium 161, 162
left attacker 812
left back 801, 803, 812, 814
left center 804
left centre 804
left channel 502
left cornerback 806
left defence 878
left defense 878
left defensive end 806
left defensive tackle 806
left field 795
left fielder 794
left forward 811
left guard 807
left half 801
left inside forward 801
left kidney 165
left lung 161, 163
left midfielder 803
left pulmonary vein 162
left safety 806
left service court 819, 821
left side 384
left tackle 807
left ventricle 161, 162
left wing 801, 804, 879
left winger 814
left-luggage office 582
leg 113, 139, 147, 149, 156, 278, 280, 281, 323, 351, 448, 641, 815, 823, 910
leg curl bar 851
leg extension bar 851
leg guard 796
leg position 829
leg strap 611
leg-of-mutton sleeve 361
leg-warmer 371
legging 901
leghold trap 913
legionary 748
legume, section 84
legumes 190
lemon 194
lemon balm 202
lemon squeezer 230, 237
lemur 139
length post 856
length, measure 700
length, measurement 702
lengthways bulkhead 606
lengthwise bulkhead 606
lengthwise grain 455
lens 177, 477, 478, 517, 518, 691
lens accessories 478
lens aperture scale 478
lens cap 478
lens case 384
lens hood 478, 612
lens mount 477
lens release button 476
lens system 692
lenses 478, 691
lenticular galaxy 9
lentils 190
leopard 135
leotard 371
Lesotho 746
lesser covert 115
letter 474
letter opener 531
letter scale 531
letters 472
letters to the editor 471
lettuce 186
leucoplast 74
level 650
level crossing 545, 547, 583, 591
level crossing bell 591
level crossing sign 591
leveling foot 292, 293, 294
leveling head 701
leveling head level 701
leveling head locking knob 701
leveling screw 58, 699, 701
leveling-adjustment foot 483
levelling foot 292, 293, 294

levelling head 701
levelling head level 701
levelling head locking knob 701
levelling screw 58, 699, 701
lever 234, 268, 270, 310, 377, 423, 686, 912, 920
lever cap 309
lever corkscrew 230
lever cover 268
lever kitchen-tap 270
lever, gear 552
levigator 423
Liberia 745
libero 812
librarian's office 732
library 395, 711, 726, 732, 734
Libyan Arab Jamahiriya 745
license plate light 554
lichen 74
lichen, structure 74
lichens, examples 74
lid 234, 237, 238, 239, 240, 241, 290, 291, 292, 295, 313, 465, 484, 689
lid brace 465
Liechtenstein 744
lierne 410
life buoy 609, 611, 771
life cycle of the frog 111
life jacket 611
life raft 605, 611
life support system 20
life support system controls 20
life, evolution 92
life-saving equipment 611
lifeboat 602, 604, 608, 652
lift 16, 407, 509, 602, 630, 650, 713, 724
lift arm 637
lift bridge 542
lift chain 265
lift cord 285
lift cord lock 285
lift door 569
lift span 542
lift-arm cylinder 637
lift-fan air inlet 605
lifting chain 632
lifting handle 756
lifting hook 651
lifting link 640
ligament 175
ligature 446
light 14, 15, 17, 472, 594, 615, 617
light aircraft 628
light bar 766, 771
light bar controller 771
light button 505
light continuous drizzle 57
light continuous rain 57
light continuous snow 57
light intermittent drizzle 57
light intermittent rain 57
light intermittent snow 57
light machine gun 755
light rain 64
light ray 691
light sensor 477
light shield 17
light signal 436
light-load adjustment screw 273
light-reading scale 479
lightbox 484, 535
lighted mirror 381
lighthouse 596, 614
lighthouse lantern 614
lighting 274, 381, 626
lighting board 490
lighting board operator 490
lighting cable 567
lighting grid 429, 492
lighting grid access 490
lighting technician 429, 490
lighting/camera control area 490
lightning 57, 65
lightning arrester 658, 663
lightning rod 245, 677
lights 286, 431
lily 80
lily of the valley 80
Lima bean 191
limb 313, 434, 731, 813, 919
limb 87, 859, 913
limb top 693
lime 194
limit switch 417
limousine 549
limpet 217
linden 208
line 313, 434, 731, 813, 919
line guide 910
line hook 597
line judge 807, 813, 818, 824
line map 592
line of scrimmage 807
line, 22 m 800
line, centre 809
linear 79
lineman's pliers 317
linen 280, 584
linen chest 279
linen room 724
lines of latitude 36
lines of longitude 36

linesman 803, 812, 816, 820, 879
Lingala 468
lingerie 716
lingerie shop 714
lingual papilla 176
lingual tonsil 176
lining 342, 348, 349, 370, 386, 455, 881
linseed oil 400
linstock 752
lint filter 292
lint trap 293
lintel 256, 411
Lion 13
lion 135
lion passant 741
lip 124, 132
lip make-up 378
lip makeup 378
lip strap ring 854
lipbrush 378
lipid droplet 74
lipliner 378
lipstick 378
liqueur glass 225
liquid 680, 681
liquid compass 612
liquid crystal display 477, 496
liquid eyeliner 378
liquid foundation 378
liquid hydrogen tank 24, 25
liquid mascara 378
liquid nitrogen tank 694
liquid oxygen tank 24, 25
liquid oxygen tank baffle 25
liquid-crystal display 696
liquid/gas separator 562
listen button 508
listening posts 733
lists 408
litchi 197
literary supplement 471
lithium 682
litho crayon 423
litho pencil 423
lithographic press 423
lithographic printing 420
lithographic stone 423
lithographic tusche 423
lithography 423
lithography, equipment 423
lithosphere 42, 66
Lithuania 744
Little Bear 12
Little Dog 13
little finger 173
little finger hook 447
Little Horse 12
Little Lion 13
liver 109, 110, 112, 113, 116, 125, 161, 164, 212
Liverpool bit 854
livestock car 588
livestock van 588
living room 250, 902
Lizard 12
lizard 114
llama 128
load 686
load support 899
loading area 666
loading bunker 648
loading dock 713
loading door 256
loading hopper 573
loaf pan 239
loafer 344
loan services 730
lob 821
lob wedge 868
lobate 79
lobate toe 117
lobby 620, 713, 717, 724, 728, 730
lobe 117
lobe bronchus 163
lobster 107, 218
lobster, anatomy 107
lobster, morphology 107
lobule 173
local mail 475
local station 486
location 244
location of the statue 403
lock 247, 248, 278, 291, 387, 389, 554, 580, 664
lock button 505
lock dial 516
lock emptying system 597
lock filling and emptying opening 597
lock filling and emptying system 597
lock filling intake 597
lock filling opening 597
lock forward 804
lock nut 58, 700
lock rail 247
lock ring 483
lock switch 479
lock washer 310
lock-chamber 597
lock-on button 305, 308
locked groove 500
locker 510

locker room 764
locket 374
locking button 288
locking carabiner 900
locking device 289, 321, 913
locking karabiner 900
locking lever 312, 587
locking pliers 310
locking ring 302, 756
locknut 270
locomotive track 589
locomotive, diesel-electric 586
loculus 82
lodging 886
log 300
log carrier 257
log chute 657
log semitrailer 572
log tongs 257
log, section 300
loin 124, 147, 149
loin chop 215
loincloth 339
long adductor 150
long and short stitch 459
long bone 157
long extensor of toes 150
long johns 351
long jump 790, 793
long jump take-off board 793
long palmar 150
long peroneal 150
long radial extensor of wrist 151
long residue 656
long service line 816
long track 882
long-range jet 624
longan 196
longitudinal dunes 52
longship 598
loop 349, 539
loop stitches 459
loose curtain 283
loose fill insulation 299
loose head prop 804
loose powder 378
loose powder brush 378
lopping shears 330
lore 115
lorgnette 385
lost and found articles 725
lost property 725
loudspeaker 503, 766
loudspeaker system select buttons 497
loudspeaker terminals 497
loudspeakers 502
lounge 608, 724
louse 101
louver 261
louver-board 411
louvered window 415
louvre 261
louvre-board 411
louvred window 415
lovage 202
love seat 276, 724
low (1 to 18) 919
low bar 824
low beam 554
low cloud, type 55
low clouds 62
low fuel warning light 557
low gain antenna 18
low pressure area 63
low pressure center 55
low warp loom 460
low-mass stars 8
low-pressure steam inlet 668
low-speed shaft 677
low-tension distribution line 273, 663
lower blade guard 304
lower bowl 241
lower cheek 854
lower chord 540
lower confining bed 646
lower eyelid 110, 132, 177
lower fore topgallant sail 603
lower fore topsail 603
lower gate 597
lower girdle facet 374
lower guard retracting lever 304
lower heating element 266
lower landing 417
lower lateral lobe 86
lower lateral sinus 86
lower level 597
lower limb 750
lower lip 174, 444
lower lobe 163
lower mandible 115
lower mantle 42
lower mast 602
lower radiator hose 561
lower section 24
lower shell 889
lower sphere clamp 58
lower support screw 58
lower thermostat 266
lower wing 628
lowercase 472
lowering the spinnaker 833

lubricant eye drops 384
lubricants plant 656
lubricating oils 656
lubricating system 586
lubricator 649
Luer-Lock tip 776
luff 836
lug 448, 559
lug sail 601
lug wrench 558
luge 884
luge racer 884
luggage 388, 717
luggage carrier 389
luggage compartment 585, 631
luggage elastic 389
luggage lockers 582
luggage rack 567, 577, 584, 876
luggage racks 605
luggage trolley 389, 582
lumbar pad 808
lumbar plexus 166
lumbar vertebra 153, 157, 168
lumbar vertebrae 122, 126, 131, 138, 141, 142
luminous intensity, measurement 702
lunar eclipse 7
lunar features 7
lunar module 19, 25
lunate 154, 156
lung 104, 110, 112, 116, 125
lungs 163
lunula 172, 173
lunule 105
lupine 190
lutetium 684
Luther 736
Lutheranism 736
lutz 881
Luxembourg 743
Lynx 12
lynx 134
Lyre 13
lyre 433
lysosome 94

M

macadamia nut 193
macaque 139
macaroni 401
macaw 118
Macedonia 744
machete 751
machicolation 408
machine gun 755, 758
machine hall 657, 658
machine wash in hot water at a normal setting 347
machine wash in lukewarm water at a gentle setting/reduced agitation 347
machine wash in warm water at a gentle setting/reduced agitation 347
machine wash in warm water at a normal setting 347
machinery shed 182
machinery, agricultural 641
Mackenzie River 30
mackerel 219
macro lens 478
macronucleus 94
macula 177
Madagascar 746
madreporite 95
magazine 471, 754, 755, 893
magazine base 754
magazine catch 754
mage 847
Magellan 19
magenta 690
magma 44, 49
magma chamber 44, 646
magnesium 682
magnesium powder 825
magnet 454, 488, 534, 687
magnetic compass 907
magnetic damping system 698
magnetic field 494, 687
magnetic gasket 291
magnetic lid holder 240
magnetic needle 907
magnetic separation 71
magnetic stripe 729
magnetic tape 495
magnetism 687
magnetometer 60
magnifier 905
magnifying glass 693
magpie 118
mah-jongg 917
mail 474
mail box 474
mail carrier 475
mail processing room 509
main beam headlight 554
main beam indicator light 557
main beam warning light 576
main breaker 272
main bronchus 163
main carriage 456

main circuit vent 262
main cleanout 262
main cryogenic stage 24
main deck 607, 761
main drain 246
main duct 258
main electric motor 763
main engine 23
main entrance 250, 713, 733, 735, 768, 781
main fan 648
main handle 307
main inlet 655
main landing gear 625, 760
main lanes 539
main leg 663
main lever 398
main line 583
main lodge 886
main loudspeaker 493
main lower topgallant sail 603
main lower topsail 603
main parachute 896
main power cable 272
main preview monitor 491
main reflex mirror 477
main return pipe 259
main road 539
main rooms 250
main royal sail 603
main sail 603
main scale 700
main scope tube 692
main section 919
main sewer 712
main stalk 86
main stand 575
main steam header 669
main steam pipes 669
main supply pipe 259
main switch 273
main transformer 585
main tube 14, 15
main upper topgallant sail 603
main upper topsail 603
main vent 44
main waiting room 781
main wheel 697
main-sequence star 8
Maine coon 132
mainmast 600, 602
mainsail 834
mainsheet 834
maintenance 548
maintenance area 489
maintenance hangar 619
maintenance shop 648
maitre d'hôtel 720
major domestic appliances 716
major inner reaping throw 844
major international road signs 544
major language families 468
major motions 916
major North American road signs 546
major outer reaping throw 844
major types of blades 401
major types of missiles 759
make-up 378
makeup 378
makeup artist 428
Malagasy 469
malanga 189
malar region 115
Malawi 746
Malawi, Lake 34
Malayo-Polynesian languages 469
Malaysia 747
Maldives 747
male 702
male cone 89
male ferrule 909, 910
male reproductive organs 169
male urethra 169
Mali 745
mallet 301, 401, 421, 448, 858
mallets 449
malleus 174
Malpighian tubule 99
Malpighian tubules 97
malt vinegar 201
Malta 744
mammary gland 171
mammoth 93
man 146
management office 718
mandarin 194
mandarin collar 363
mandible 97, 99, 108, 111, 112, 116, 121, 122, 123, 126, 131, 136, 138, 141, 142, 152, 158
mandolin 433
mandoline 230
mane 124
maneuvering bar 643
maneuvering engine 23
manganese 683
manganese mix 689
mangetout 190
mango 197
mango chutney 201
mangosteen 196

manhole 655, 712
manicure set 377
manifold 652
manned maneuvering unit 20
manned manœuvring unit 20
manometer 655, 775
manœuvring bar 643
manœuvring engine 23
manrope 542
mansard roof 414
mantel 256
mantel shelf 256
mantid 102
mantle 105, 106
mantle muscles 106
manual 445
manual feed slot 519
manual focusing knob 483
manual release 889
manual revolving door 416
manual revolving doors 719
manual sorting 71
manual/automatic mode 465
manually-operated points 590
manually-operated switch 590
manuals 444
manure spreader 641
manway 650
Manx 133
Maori 469
map library 732
map projections 36
map, physical 38
map, political 37
map, road 39
map, urban 39
map, weather 55
maple 88
maple syrup 209
maquis 66
Marconi cutter 601
margarine 209
margin 79
margin control 528
margin release 528
marginal shield 113
Mariana Trench 50
Marie Byrd Land 29
marina 788
marinade spices 199
marine 61
marine diesel 656
marine mammals 136
marine mammals, examples 137
Mariner 19
maritime buoyage system 616
maritime communications 487
maritime signals 614
maritime transport 596, 649
marker 470, 864, 865, 882, 883
marker letter 855
marker light 570, 571
marker pen 397
markers 875
marking dot 455
marking tools 313
marks by night, rhythm 617
marmoset 139
marrow 188, 212
Mars 4, 5
mars light 766
Mars Odyssey 19
marshall 875
Marshall Islands 747
marshalling yard 589
marsupial mammals 142
marsupials, examples 143
marten 134
martingale 858
mascara brush 378
mask 796, 841, 848
mason's trowel 315
masonry drill 306
masonry nail 301
masonry tools 315
mass 43
mass, measurement 702
massage glove 379
masseter 150
massive stars 8
mast 407, 583, 591, 600, 631, 632, 633, 834, 836
mast control lever 633
mast foot 836
mast operating lever 632
mast sleeve 836
master bedroom 251
master carrier 284
master cord 893
master cylinder 559
master gate valve 654
masthead 471, 602, 836
masthead light 605
masting 602
mastoid fontanelle 158
mastoid process 158
masts 602
mat 844, 864
mat chairperson 843
matchbook 391
matchbox 391

matchstick 391
material handling 632
maternal aunt 785
maternal uncle 785
mathematics 703
matinee-length necklace 374
mating adaptor 21
matter 680
mattress 280, 281, 776, 904
mattress cover 280
mattresses 716
mattresses and box springs 716
maturing steps 86
maulstick 399
Mauritania 745
Mauritius 746
mawashi 847
maxilla 99, 108, 111, 112, 116, 121, 122, 123, 131, 136, 138, 152, 158, 175
maxillary bone 159
maximum thermometer 59
Maya 469
meadow 182
mean position 690
meander 48
measure of air pressure 59
measure of angles 701
measure of cloud ceiling 59
measure of distance 700
measure of humidity 59
measure of length 700
measure of rainfall 59
measure of sky radiation 58
measure of snowfall 59
measure of sunshine 58
measure of temperature 59, 695
measure of thickness 700
measure of time 696
measure of weight 698
measure of wind direction 59
measure of wind strength 59
measurement of amount of substance 702
measurement of Celsius temperature 702
measurement of electric charge 702
measurement of electric current 702
measurement of electric potential difference 702
measurement of electric resistance 702
measurement of energy 702
measurement of force 702
measurement of frequency 702
measurement of length 702
measurement of luminous intensity 702
measurement of mass 702
measurement of power 702
measurement of pressure 702
measurement of radioactivity 702
measurement of thermodynamic temperature 702
measurement of time 702
measuring beaker 231
measuring button 479
measuring cup 231
measuring cups 231
measuring devices 695
measuring spoons 231
measuring tools 313
measuring tube 59
meat 214
meat grinder 230
meat keeper 291
meat thermometer 231
Mecca, direction 738
mechanic 873
mechanical connectors 269
mechanical mouse 516
mechanical pencil 470
mechanical shovel 647
mechanical stage 693
mechanical stage control 693
mechanical variometer 898
mechanical watch 696
mechanics 548, 686
mechanism of the organ 445
medial condyle of femur 153
medial great 150
medial moraine 46
median 539
median groove 127
median lingual sulcus 176
median nerve 166
medical equipment storage room 781
medical gas cylinder 780
medical records 781
medical team 844
medications, forms 783
Mediterranean Sea 28, 32, 34
Mediterranean subtropical 61
medium 472, 849
medium format SLR (6 x 6) 481
medium-tension distribution line 273, 663
medulla 165
medulla oblongata 167
medullary cavity 154
meeting room 394, 724, 730, 735, 764
meeting rooms 718
meganeura 92
megazostrodon 93
Meissner's corpuscle 172
meitnerium 683
Melanesia 29

Melanesian 469
melody strings 432
melon 195
melon baller 233
melons 195
melting 680
meltwater 46
memo pad 530
memorial board 738
memory button 497, 498, 501, 506
memory cancel 479, 529
memory card 481
memory card slots 918
memory key 479
memory recall 529
memory recall key 479
men 497
men's accessories 716
men's bag 388
men's casual wear 717
men's cell 768
men's clothing 348
men's coats 717
men's gloves 346
men's headgear 340
men's nightwear 717
men's pants 716
men's rest room 725
men's shirts 716
men's shoes 342, 716
men's sportswear 717
men's suits 716
men's sweaters 717
men's toilet 725
men's underwear 716
mendelevium 684
meninges 167
menorah 738
menu 721
menu button 477, 505
Mercury 4, 5
mercury 275, 683
mercury barometer 59
mercury bulb 695
mercury thermometer 777
merging traffic 547
merguez sausage 216
méridienne 276
mesa 52
mesh 281, 815
mesh bag 222
mesh strainer 231
mesocarp 81, 82, 83
mesohyl 95
mesopause 53
mesosaur 92
mesosphere 53
mesothorax 97
message display 512
metacarpal 154, 156
metacarpal, 2nd 140
metacarpal, 3rd 140
metacarpal, 4th 140
metacarpal, 5th 140
metacarpus 111, 116, 122, 126, 131, 133, 136, 138, 142, 154
metal arm 329
metal counterhoop 448
metal detector, walk-through 726
metal frame 442
metal head 793
metal rail 533
metal rod 449
metal sorting 71
metal structure 582
metallic contact grid 672
metallic plastron 848
metalloids 682
metals, alkali 682
metals, alkaline earth 682
metals, examples 741
metals, transition 683
metamorphic rocks 42
metaphysis 155
metatarsal 155
metatarsus 98, 111, 122, 126, 131, 138, 141, 142, 155
metathorax 97
meteorite 8
meteorological forecast 54
meteorological measuring instruments 58
meteorological station 58
meteorology 53
meteorology, measuring instruments 58
meteorology, station model 55
meter 702
metered dose inhaler 783
metope 404
metre 702
metronome 436
Mexico 742
Mexico, Gulf 30
mezzanine 431, 592
mezzanine floor 250, 251
mezzanine stairs 251
Michigan snowshoe 893
micro compact car 549
microfilament 94
microfilm reader 732
microfilm room 732
micrometer caliper 700

micrometer screw 612, 701
Micronesia 747
micronucleus 94
microphone 488, 492, 496, 505, 506, 508, 516, 517, 527, 770, 898
microphone boom 490, 492
microphone boom tripod 492
microphone jack 505
microphones 771
Microscope 10
microscope 693
microscope, binocular 693
microscopes 693
microtubule 94
microwave dish 489
microwave oven 224, 238
microwave ovens 723
microwave relay station 524
microwave scanner 60
microwave transmitter 489
microwaves 690
Mid-Atlantic Ridge 50
mid-calf length 351
mid-calf length sock 351
Mid-Indian Ridge 50
mid-ocean ridge 49
middle attacker 812
middle cloud, type 55
middle clouds 62
middle covert 115
middle ear 174
middle finger 173
middle jib 603
middle leg 96
middle leg, honeybee 98
middle linebacker 806
middle lobe 163
middle nasal concha 175
middle panel 247
middle phalange 154, 155
middle phalanx 126, 133, 172
middle piece 169
middle primary covert 115
middle sole 370
middle toe 115
middle torus 405
middy 359
midgut 99
MIDI cable 451
MIDI port 513
midrange 10, 502
midrange pickup 441
midrib 75, 79, 84
midriff band 367
Mihrab 738
Mihrab dome 738
mileometer 557
military communications 487
milk 210
milk chocolate 208
milk cup 223
Milky Way 9, 13
millet 85, 203
millet: spike 85
Mimas 5
minaret 738
Minbar 738
mincer 230
miners' changing-room 649
mini shirtdress 359
mini stereo sound system 503
minibus 549, 569
minim 435
minim rest 435
minimum thermometer 59
minivan 549
mink 134
minor sciatic nerve 166
minor surgery room 778
mint 202
minus/negative 703
minute 704
minute hand 696, 697
Miranda 5
mirror 264, 389, 535, 574, 576, 577, 693, 724, 876
mirror, outside 568
mirror, West Coast 569
miscellaneous articles 534
miscellaneous symbols 473
missile launch rail 760
missile launcher 761
missile stowage 762
missile, structure 759
missiles 759
missiles, major types 759
Mississippi River 30
mist 57, 65
miter box 303
miter gate recess 597
miter gauge 305
miter gauge slot 305
miter latch 303, 304
miter lock handle 304
miter saw, electric 304
miter saw, hand 303
miter scale 303, 304
mitral valve 162
mitre gate recess 597
mitre gauge 305

mitre gauge slot 305
mitt 346
mitten 318, 346, 901
mixed forest 66
mixing bowl 236
mixing bowls 232
mixing chamber 319
mizzen royal brace 603
mizzen royal staysail 603
mizzen sail 603
mizzen topgallant staysail 603
mizzen topmast staysail 603
mizzenmast 600, 602
moat 408, 409
mobile drawer unit 510
mobile filing unit 510
mobile passenger stairs 623
mobile remote servicer 21
mobile starting gate 857
mobile unit 486, 489
mobile X-ray unit 778
moccasin 344
mock pocket 355
mode 528
mode selector 498
mode selectors 504
modem 522, 523, 524
moderate continuous drizzle 57
moderate continuous rain 57
moderate continuous snow 57
moderate intermittent drizzle 57
moderate intermittent rain 57
moderate intermittent snow 57
moderate rain 64
moderator 665
moderator tank 670
moderator: graphite 670
moderator: heavy water 670
moderator: natural water 671
modern bow 750
modern howitzer 756
modern mortar 756
modes of payment 729
modillion 405
modulation wheel 450
mogul 890
moguls competition 890
Mohorovicic discontinuity 42
moist surface 420
moistener 531
molar 121, 123
molar, cross section 159
molars 159
molasses 209
moldboard 641
molded insulation 299
molding 253
Moldova 744
mole 121, 702
mole, morphology 121
mole, skeleton 121
molecule 680
molluscs 217
mollusks 104, 217
molybdenum 683
Monaco 744
monarch butterfly 101
money 729
Mongolia 747
Mongolian 469
mongoose 134
monitor button 505
monitor lizard 114
monitor roof 414
monitor speaker 488
monitor wall 489, 490, 491
monkfish 220
monocle 385
monograph section 732
monohulls 835
Monopoly 915
mons pubis 170
Montagnais 469
monument 39
Moon 4, 6, 7
Moon dial 697
Moon's orbit 6, 7
Moon, phases 7
moons 4
mooring chain 615
mooring winch 607
moose 129
mop 295
moped 577
moraine 46
mordent 435
morel 183
Morocco 745
morphology of a bat 140
morphology of a bird 115
morphology of a bivalve shell 105
morphology of a butterfly 96
morphology of a cat 133
morphology of a dog 130
morphology of a dolphin 136
morphology of a frog 110
morphology of a gorilla 139
morphology of a honeybee: worker 98
morphology of a horse 124
morphology of a kangaroo 143
morphology of a lobster 107

morphology of a mole 121
morphology of a perch 108
morphology of a rat 122
morphology of a shark 108
morphology of a snail 104
morphology of a spider 103
morphology of a starfish 95
morphology of a turtle 113
morphology of a univalve shell 105
morphology of a venomous snake: head 112
morphology of an octopus 106
mortadella 216
mortar 230, 298, 753
mortar, modern 756
mortise 390
mortise lock 249
mosaic 406
Moses 736
mosque 738
mosquito 101
moss 75
moss stitch 458
moss, structure 75
mosses, examples 75
moth 101
mother 784, 785
mother-in-law 784
motherboard 513
motion detector 416
motocross motorcycle 875
motor 261, 292, 293, 294, 304, 307, 308, 320, 323, 327, 332, 643
motor air inlet 760
motor bogie 585, 595
motor car 594
motor control module 563
motor end plate 168
motor home 567
motor neuron 168
motor root 167, 168
motor scooter 577
motor sports 872
motor truck 585
motor unit 236, 237, 240, 288, 384, 585
motor vehicle pollution 69
motor yacht 607
motorcycle 574, 576
motorcycle dashboard 576
motorcycle-mounted camera 870
motorcycles, examples 577
motorcycling 874
motorized earth auger 323
motorway 39, 539, 709
motorway number 39
motto 729
mouflon 128
moulded insulation 299
moulding 253
mount frame binder 483
mountain 45
mountain bike 581
mountain biking 870
mountain lodge 886
mountain mass 38
mountain range 7, 38, 42
mountain slope 45
mountain sports 900
mountain torrent 45
mountaineer 901
mountaineering boot 901
mountaineering shovel 901
mounted umpire 858
mounting 849
mounting bracket 859, 913
mounting foot 482
mounting plate 275
mounting point 627
mouse pad 516
mouse port 513, 518
mouse, mechanical 516
mouth 95, 104, 105, 107, 110, 136, 148, 174, 444, 854
mouthparts 98
mouthpiece 446, 447, 451, 783, 841, 843
mouthpiece receiver 447
mouthpipe 447
mouthwash 384
movable bridges 542
movable jaw 311, 312
movable maxillary 112
movable panel 510, 719
movable runner 885
movable stands 734
moveable panel 509
movements of an airplane 630
movie set 428
movie theater 427, 608, 710, 714
movies' titles and schedules 427
moving coil 488
mower deck 333
mower deck lift lever 333
Mozambique 746
Mozambique Channel 34
mozzarella 210
Mt Everest 53
mud flap 551, 570, 571
mud injection hose 651
mud pit 651
mud pump 651
mudflow 47
mudguard 578

ASTRONOMY > 2-25;   EARTH > 26-71;   VEGETABLE KINGDOM >72-89;   ANIMAL KINGDOM > 90-143;   HUMAN BEING > 144-177;   FOOD AND KITCHEN > 178-241;   HOUSE > 242-295;
DO-IT-YOURSELF AND GARDENING > 296-333;   CLOTHING > 334-371;   PERSONAL ADORNMENT AND ARTICLES > 372-391;   ARTS AND ARCHITECTURE > 392-465;   COMMUNICATIONS AND OFFICE AUTOMATION > 466-535;   TRANSPORT AND MACHINERY > 536-643;   ENERGY > 644-677;   SCIENCE > 678-705;   SOCIETY > 706-785;   SPORTS AND GAMES > 786-920;

muff 388
muffin pan 232
muffler 553, 577
muffler felt 442
muffler pedal 442
Muhammad 736
mule 128, 344
mullet 220, 741
multi-image jump button 477
multi-ply plywood 300
multigrain bread 205
multihulls 835
multimeter 316
multipack 223
multiple exposure mode 476
multiple jumps 875
multiple use key 529
multiple-span beam bridge 541
multiplied by 703
multiply key 529
multipurpose antenna 763
multipurpose ladder 321
multipurpose room 727
multipurpose solution 384
multipurpose tool 317
mummy 904
mung bean 191
Munster 211
muntin 247, 249
muscle fiber 168
muscle fibre 168
muscle segment 109
muscles 150
museum 394, 711
museum shop 394
mushroom 76
mushroom anchor 610
mushroom, structure 76
mushrooms 183
music 432
music rest 436
music room 734
music stand 436, 444, 451
music store 714
musical accessories 436
musical advisers 490
musical instrument digital interface cable 451
musical instruments, traditional 432
musical notation 434
muskmelon 195
muslin 231
mussel 217
mustard 200
mute 447
mutule 404
muzzle 124, 130, 132, 753, 754, 756, 860, 912
muzzle loading 753
muzzle loading, cross section 753
Myanmar 747
mycelium 76
myelin sheath 168
myocardium 162
myopia 691

N

naan bread 205
nacelle 677
nacelle, cross-section 677
Nahuatl 469
nail 127, 301
nail bed 172
nail buffer 377
nail care 377
nail cleaner 377
nail clippers 377
nail enamel 377
nail file 377
nail hole 127
nail matrix 172
nail nick 905
nail scissors 377
nail set 301
nail shaper 377
nail whitener pencil 377
nailing tools 301
nails, examples 301
naked strangle 844
name of the currency 729
name plate 273, 306
nameplate 376, 471
Namib Desert 34
Namibia 746
naos 403
nape 115, 147, 149
napkins 722
nappy 368
naris 175
narrow 472
narwhal 137
nasal bone 158, 175
nasal cavity 163
nasal fossae 175
nasopharynx 175
national broadcasting network 486
national park 39
nationality 825
natural 435

natural arch 51
natural environment 867
natural greenhouse effect 68
natural radiation 41
natural sponge 379
Nauru 747
nautical sports 827
Navajo 469
nave 411
navel 146, 148
navette cut 375
navicular 155, 156
navigation devices 612
navigation display 626
navigation light 605, 625
navigation periscope 763
Nazca Plate 43
Neapolitan coffee maker 241
NEAR 19
near/far dial 496
neck 113, 124, 147, 148, 149, 159, 169, 227, 425, 433, 439, 440, 441, 494, 826, 868
neck end 349
neck guard 765
neck of femur 153
neck pad 808
neck strap 772
neck support 874
neckhole 351
necklaces 374
necklines 363
neckroll 280
necks 363
neckstrap eyelet 476
necktie 349
neckties 716
nectarine 192
needle 52, 64, 398, 452, 453, 454, 776
needle assembly 398
needle bar 453
needle bed 456
needle bed groove 456
needle clamp 453
needle clamp screw 453
needle hub 776
needle plate 452
needle position selector 452
needle threader 454
needle tool 464
needle-nose pliers 317
negative 485
negative carrier 485
negative charge 684
negative contact 672, 673
negative meniscus 691
negative plate 562
negative plate strap 562
negative region 672
negative terminal 562, 687, 689
negligee 364
neodymium 684
neon 684
neon lamp 316
neon tester 316
Nepal 747
nephew 785
Neptune 4, 5
neptunium 684
nerve 172
nerve cord 99
nerve fiber 172
nerve fibre 172
nerve termination 172
nerve, olfactory 175
nervous system 166
nervous system, central 167
nervous system, peripheral 166
nest of tables 278
Net 10
net 811, 812, 813, 814, 815, 817, 821, 827
net band 821
net judge 821
net stocking 365
net support 815
netball 809
Netherlands 743
nettle 187
network access point transceiver 522
network connection 273
network interface card 522
network port 513
networks, examples 522
neural spine 109
neurons 168
neutral conductor 273
neutral indicator 576
neutral line 687
neutral service wire 272
neutral wire 272
neutral zone 806, 879
neutron 680
neutron star 8
Nevis 743
New Caledonia 29
new crescent 7
new fuel storage room 666
New Guinea 29, 747
new moon 7
new shekel 728

New Testament 736
New Zealand 29, 747
newborn children's clothing 368
newel 417
newel post 255
Newfoundland Island 30
news items 471
newspaper 471
newspaper shop 715
newt 111
newton 702
next call 507
nib 470
Nicaragua 742
nickel 683
nictitating membrane 132
niece 785
Niger 745
Niger River 34
Nigeria 745
night deposit box 731
nightgown 364
nightingale 118
nightshot switch 496
nightwear 364
Nile 34
nimbostratus 56, 62
niobium 683
nipple 146, 148, 171, 269
nitric acid emission 70
nitrogen 683
nitrogen oxide emission 70
no entry 544, 546
no U-turn 544, 546
no wheelchair access 725
no. 1 wood 868
no. 8 forward 804
nobelium 684
noble gases 684
nock 750, 859
nocking point 859, 913
node 663, 687
node of Ranvier 168
non-add/subtotal 529
non-biodegradable pollutants 69
non-metals 683
non-reusable residue waste 71
nonagon 705
nonbreaking space 514
nonslip mat 893
noodles 207
nori 183
norm point 891
normal 472
normal spiral galaxy 9
normal vision 691
North 37, 616, 917
North America 28, 30, 50
North American Plate 43
North American road signs 546
North celestial pole 13
North Pole 35
north pole 687
North Sea 28, 32
North Star 13
North-Northeast 37
North-Northwest 37
Northeast 37, 616
Northern Crown 13
Northern hemisphere 35
Northern leopard frog 111
northern right whale 137
northern saw-whet owl 118
Northwest 37, 616
Norway 744
Norwegian 469
Norwegian Sea 32
nose 122, 124, 148, 175, 624, 749, 887, 894, 897, 898, 912
nose cone 627
nose landing gear 624
nose leaf 140
nose leather 132
nose of the quarter 342, 370
nose pad 385
noseband 854, 858
nosing 255
nostril 108, 110, 112, 115, 124
notation, musical 434
notch 348, 362, 455, 698, 791, 863
notched double-edged thinning scissors 382
notched edge 382
notched lapel 352
notched single-edged thinning scissors 382
note symbols 435
nothosaur 93
nova 8
nozzle 22, 24, 25, 259, 315, 319, 320, 329, 398, 767
nubby tire 875
nuclear boiler room 763
nuclear energy 665
nuclear energy, production of electricity 665
nuclear envelope 74, 94
nuclear fission 681
nuclear fuel handling sequence 666
nuclear generating station 668
nuclear membrane 74, 94
nuclear power station 668
nuclear reactor 667
nuclear submarine 763

nuclear waste 70
nuclear whorl 105
nucleolus 74, 94, 170
nucleus 8, 9, 74, 94, 168, 170, 680
nucleus splitting 681
number 791, 919
number key 508, 529
number of decimals 529
number of tracks sign 591
number plate 875
number plate light 554
numbering machine 531
numeric keyboard 507, 699
numeric keypad 515, 530
numeric lock 515
numeric lock key 515
numeric pager 505
nurse 780
nurses' lounge 781
nurses' station (ambulatory emergency) 779
nurses' station (major emergency) 778
nut 193, 248, 269, 310, 311, 439, 440, 441, 590, 750
nutcracker 230
nutmeg 198
nutmeg grater 230
nuts 311
nylon rumba tights 368
nylon yarn 332

O

O-ring 268
oak 88
oar 598, 600, 851
oarlock 839
oars, types 838
oasis 48, 52
oat flour 204
oats 85, 203
oats: panicle 85
Oberon 5
obi 845, 846
obituaries 471
object 691
object balls 862
objective 693
objective lens 14, 476, 478, 479, 483, 501, 692
oblique fissure 163
oboe 446
oboes 437
obscured sky 56
observation deck 621
observation post 17
observation room 778, 781
observation window 23
observatory 17
obstacles 852, 875
obturator foramen 122
obturator nerve 166
obtuse angle 704
occipital 151
occipital bone 131, 153, 158
occluded front 56
ocean 7, 38, 67
ocean floor 49
ocean ridges 50
ocean trenches 50
ocean weather station 54
Oceania 28, 29
Oceania and Polynesia 747
Oceanian languages 469
oceanic crust 42
oche 918
octave 434, 849
octave mechanism 446
octopus 106, 217
octopus, anatomy 106
octopus, morphology 106
odd 919
odd pinnate 79
odometer 557
oesophagus 109, 112, 163, 164
off-road motorcycle 577
office 509, 548, 582, 720, 724, 726
office automation 468, 509
office building 596, 710, 713
office furniture 510
office tower 713
officers' dormitory 764
officers' quarters 762, 763
officers' toilets and showers 764
official signature 729
officials 801, 846
officials' bench 879
offset 269
offshore drilling 653
offshore prospecting 653
offshore well 654
ogee 413
ogee roof 414
Ogen melon 195
ohm 702
oil 651
oil burner 259
oil drain plug 566
oil paint 397
oil painting 396

oil pan 331, 566
oil pan gasket 566
oil pastel 396
oil pastel drawing 396
oil pollution 70
oil pressure warning indicator 576
oil processing area 652
oil pump 259
oil spill 70
oil supply inlet 259
oil supply line 259
oil tank 331
oil terminal 596
oil warning light 557
oil-filled heater 260
oil-filled radiator 260
oil/gas separator 652
oiler 648
oilstone 422
okapi 128
okra 188
old crescent 7
Old Testament 736
old-fashioned glass 225
olecranon 126, 153
olfactory bulb 109, 175
olfactory mucosa 175
olfactory nerve 109, 175
olfactory tract 175
olive 188
olive oil 209
Oman 746
Oman, Gulf 33
on guard line 848
on the wind 833
on-air warning light 488
on-board computer 556
on-deck circle 794
on-off button 240, 504
on-off indicator 381
on-off light 506
on-off switch 237, 241, 263, 286, 288, 289, 318, 381, 382, 383, 384, 476, 483, 488, 613
on-off/volume 504
on/off switch 289
on/off/test button 520
on/play button 508
one 703
one hundred 703
one pair 914
one thousand 703
one-arm shoulder throw 844
one-bar shoe 343
one-person tent 903
one-piece coverall 896
one-piece suit 884
one-storey house 419
one-toe hoof 127
one-way head 302
one-way traffic 544, 546
onion 184
online catalogue 733
online game 525
oolong tea 208
Oort cloud 4
Op-Ed article 471
opal 375
open crate 222
open end wrench 311
open hand 901
open stringer 255
open strings 432
open-air terrace 609
open-ended spanner 311
open-face spinning reel 910
open-pit mine 647
opening 346
opening of copulatory bursa 97
opening, utensils 230
opera glasses 385
opera house 710
opera-length necklace 374
operating cord 284
operating dam 664
operating floor 664
operating instructions 548
operating panel 417
operating rod 755
operating room 780, 781
operating suite 780
operating table 780
operation control room 763
operation keys 507, 730, 731
operator's cab 634
operator's cab 634
operculum 108, 111
ophthalmology room 779
opisthodomos 403
opossum 143
opposable thumb 139
opposite prompt side 431
optic chiasm 167
optic nerve 177
optical character reader 474
optical lens 535
optical mouse 516
optical scanner 181, 517
optical sensor 516
optical sight 701
optical sorting 71

970

ASTRONOMY > 2-25; EARTH > 26-71; VEGETABLE KINGDOM >72-89; ANIMAL KINGDOM > 90-143; HUMAN BEING > 144-177; FOOD AND KITCHEN > 178-241; HOUSE > 242-295; DO-IT-YOURSELF AND GARDENING > 296-333; CLOTHING > 334-371; PERSONAL ADORNMENT AND ARTICLES > 372-391; ARTS AND ARCHITECTURE > 392-465; COMMUNICATIONS AND OFFICE AUTOMATION > 466-535; TRANSPORT AND MACHINERY > 536-643; ENERGY > 644-677; SCIENCE > 678-705; SOCIETY > 706-785; SPORTS AND GAMES > 786-920

optical stage 535
optician 715
optics 690
or 741
oral cavity 163, 164
oral hygiene center 384
oral irrigator 384
orange 194, 400
orange, section 82
orange-red 400
orange-yellow 400
orangutan 139
orbicular of eye 150
orbicularis oculi 150
orbiculate 79
orbit 112, 116, 131, 136, 138, 142
orbit of the satellites 60
orbital-action selector 305
orbiter 22, 23
orbiter (Viking) 18
orchard 182
orchestra 402, 437
orchestra pit 430
orchid 80
order 411
order of finish 831
ordinaries, examples 740
ordinary die 914
Ordovician 92
ore 647
ore pass 650
oregano 202
organ 444
organ console 444
organ, mechanism 445
organ, production of sound 445
organizer 530
organizers' offices 719
oriental cockroach 101
Oriental couching stitch 459
oriflamme 739
origin and evolution of species 92
original overlay 512
Orinoco River 31
ornamental kale 186
ornamental tree 182, 244, 322
ornaments 435
oropharyngeal airway 775
ortho-cane 782
ortho-stick 782
orthoceras 92
Orthodox Church 736
oscillating sprinkler 329
osculum 95
osmium 683
osteon 154
ostrich 119
ostrich egg 213
otolith 109
ottoman 277
outboard engine 607
outbound track 589
outdoor leisure 902
outdoor unit 260
outer boundary line 819
outer bull 918
outer circle 877
outer core 42
outer edge 127
outer jacket 267
outer jib 603
outer lip 105
outer planets 4
outer ring 729
outer shell 275
outer stators 627
outer table 915
outer toe 115
outfield fence 795
outgoing announcement cassette 508
outlet 274, 567
outlet grille 260
outlet hose 485
outlets, types of 258
output devices 518
output jack 441
output monitor 489, 491
output tray 519
outrigger 599, 634, 638, 766, 839
outrigger boom 599
outrigger canoe 599
outrun 890, 891
outside counter 342
outside knob 248
outside linebacker 806
outside mirror 550, 568
outside mirror control 554
outside ticket pocket 348
outsole 342, 371
outwash plain 46
oval 881
oval cut 375
oval head 302
ovary 80, 97, 103, 170, 171
ovate 79
oven 224, 290, 721, 722
oven control knob 290
oven thermometer 231
over curtain 282
over-blouse 359
overall standings scoreboard 824
overalls 358

overbed table 780
overburden 647
overcast sky 56
overcheck 857
overcoat 352, 355
overdrapery 282
overflow 262, 264
overflow pipe 266, 267
overflow protection switch 294
overflow tube 265, 485
overhand knot 908
overhead clearance 545, 547
overhead connection 663
overhead earth wire 663
overhead frame 639
overhead ground wire 663
overhead guard 632
overhead projector 535
overhead switch panel 626
overlap carrier 284
overlay flooring 254
overpass 539, 540
overshirt 359
overtaking lane 539
oviduct 97, 103, 113
ovotestis 104
ovule 80
owl 118, 119
ox 129
oxbow 48
oxbow lake 48
oxford shoe 342
oxyacetylene welding 319
oxygen 683
oxygen cylinder 319
oxygen cylinder bracket 775
oxygen cylinder, portable 775
oxygen feeding control 898
oxygen feeding knob 898
oxygen mask 775
oxygen outlet 780
oxygen pressure actuator 20
oxygen valve 319
oxygenated blood 162
oyster 217
oyster fork 228
oyster knife 229
oyster mushroom 183
oystercatcher 118
ozone layer 53

P

pace 125
Pacific Ocean 28, 29, 33
Pacific Plate 43
Pacific salmon 221
Pacific-Antarctic Ridge 50
Pacinian corpuscle 172
package 223
packaged integrated circuit 689
packaging 222
packaging products 180
packer body 573
packing 268
packing nut 268
packing retainer ring 268
pad 798, 800
pad arm 385
pad plate 385
padded base 811
padded envelope 531
padded upright 811
padding 899
paddle wheel 599
paddle, double-bladed 837
paddle, double-bladed 839
paddle, single-bladed 837, 838
paddock 856
paddy field 69
pads 880
page backward button 527
page down 515
page down key 515
page forward button 527
page up 515
page up key 515
pagoda 412
pagoda sleeve 361
pail 295
paint roller 320
paint spray 398
Painter's Easel 11
painting 395, 396
painting knife 397
painting upkeep 320
painting, accessories 399
painting, equipment 396
pair 881
Pair of Compasses 11
pajama 369
pajamas 364
pak-choi 186
Pakistan 746
palatine 112, 123
palatine tonsil 176
palatoglossal arch 174
Palau 747
pale 740
palette with dipper 398

palette with hollows 398
paling fence 322
palla 336
palladium 683
pallet 445, 632, 697
pallet spring 445
pallet truck 633
pallets 632
palm 121, 173, 346, 610, 797
palm grove 52
palm of a glove 346
palm rest 861
palm tree 88
palmar pad 130
palmate 79
palmette 276
pan 698, 699, 752, 913
pan cover 752
pan hook 698
Panama 742
panama 340
Panama, Gulf 31
Panama, Isthmus 30
pancake pan 235
pancetta 216
pancreas 110, 116, 164
pane 249
panel 247, 350, 367, 400, 511, 650, 663, 855, 899
pannier bag 580
panoramic head 482
panoramic window 584, 713
panpipe 433
pantograph 585, 595
pantry 224, 250
pants 350, 371, 796, 808, 875, 878, 901
pants, examples 358
panty corselette 366
panty girdle 367
panty hose 365
papaya 197
paper 390, 400, 420
paper bail 528
paper bail release lever 528
paper catcher 511
paper clip holder 534
paper clips 534
paper collection unit 71
paper cutter 535
paper fasteners 534
paper feed button 519, 731
paper feed channel 511
paper feed key 529
paper feed light 519
paper guide 508, 519
paper in reserve 512
paper punch 533
paper recycling container 71
paper release lever 528
paper separation 71
paper shredder 535
paper sorting 71
paper support 528
paper tray 511
paper trays 512
paperboard separation 71
paperboard sorting 71
papilla 172, 177
papillary muscle 162
paprika 199
Papua New Guinea 29, 747
Papuan languages 469
par 3 hole 866
par 4 hole 866
par 5 hole 867
parabolic antenna 489
parabolic dune 52
parabolic mirror 674
parabolic reflector 16
parachute 760, 896
parachute valve 899
parade ground 409
paraffin 656
paraffins 656
paragliding 897
paragliding pilot 897
Paraguay 742
parallel 36
parallel bars 825
parallel electrical circuit 687
parallel port 513
parallelepiped 705
parallelogram 705
paramecium 94
Paraná River 31
parapet 540
parapet walk 408, 409
parboiled rice 207
parcels office 582
parchment paper 222
parentheses 473
parents 784, 785
parents-in-law 784
parietal 112, 122
parietal bone 131, 153, 158
parietal pleura 163
paring knife 229
park 39, 711
parka 353, 901
parking 583, 713, 866, 886
parking area 619, 708, 735

parking brake lever 556
parking lot 596, 620
Parmesan 211
parsley 202
parsnip 189
parterre 431
partial eclipse 6, 7
partially reflecting mirror 692
particle board 300
partition 84, 771
partition tile 298
partitions, examples 740
partlow chart 571
partridge 118
parts 276, 277, 280
parts of a bicycle 578
parts of a boat 838
parts of a circle 704
parts of a flag 739
parts of a lamp socket 275
parts of a long bone 155
parts of a ring 376
parts of a shoe 342
parts of the weapon 849
party 740
pascal 702
pass 45
passbook update slot 730
passenger cabin 605, 608, 609, 625
passenger car 585, 594
passenger cars, types 584
passenger liner 608
passenger platform 582
passenger seat 577
passenger station 582, 583
passenger terminal 596, 619, 620
passenger train 582
passenger transfer vehicle 621, 623
passing lane 539
passing prohibited 544, 546
passion fruit 196
passive sensor 41
passivity zone 843
passport case 387
passport control 621
pasta 206
pasta maker 230
pastern 124
pastry bag and nozzles 232
pastry blender 232
pastry brush 232
pastry cutting wheel 232
pastry shop 715
Patagonia 31
patch pocket 348, 353, 360, 368
patella 122, 126, 131, 138, 152
patera 276
paternal aunt 785
paternal uncle 785
path 322
Pathfinder 19
pathology laboratory 781
patient 780
patient room 780
patient's chair 780
patio 244, 322
patio door 224, 250
patrol and first aid station 886
patrol wagon 726
pattern 401, 455, 458
pattern start key 456
pattypan squash 189
pauldron 749
pause 435, 515
pause button 499
pause/break key 515
pause/still button 495
pavement 712
pavilion 374, 710
pavilion facet 374
pavilion roof 415
pawl 307
pawn 916
pay phone 427, 507, 715, 720, 723, 779
payload 24, 25
payload adaptor 24
payload module 40
payout tray 920
payout trigger 920
PC card slot 526
PCI expansion card 513
PCI expansion connector 513
pe-tsai 186
pea 84
pea jacket 355
peach 192
peach, section 81
Peacock 10
peacock 119
peak 45, 340, 341, 772
peak level meter 499
peaked lapel 348
peanut 190
peanut oil 209
pear 193
pear-shaped body 433
pear-shaped cut 375
peas 190
pecan nut 193
peccary 128

pecten 98
pectoral deck 851
pectoral fin 108, 136
pectoral limb 161
pedal 440, 448, 578, 580, 791, 851, 870
pedal gland 104
pedal key 444
pedal keyboard 444
pedal pushers 358
pedal rod 442
pedal with wide platform 870
pedestal 440
pedestal-type sump pump 263
pedestrian call button 712
pedestrian crossing 545, 547, 712
pedestrian lights 712
pedicel 80, 81, 82, 83, 86
pediment 403, 405, 697
pedipalp 103
pedometer 700
peeled veneer 300
peeler 229
peep hole 591
peg 278, 312, 390, 439, 440, 459, 462, 902, 903
peg box 439
peg loop 902, 903
pelerine 355
pelican 119
pellets 912
peltate 79
Pelton runner 659
pelvic fin 108
pelvic limb 161
pelvis 121, 126, 138, 141, 142
pen 43
pen blade 905
pen holder 386
penalty arc 802
penalty area 802
penalty area marking 802
penalty bench 879
penalty bench official 879
penalty mark 814
penalty spot 802
pencil 470, 667
pencil pleat heading 283
pencil point tip 314, 319
pencil sharpener 534
pendant 374
pendulum 697
pendulum bar 436
pendulum rod 697
penguin 119
penholder grip 815
peninsula 38
penis 104, 146, 169
pennant 56, 739
penne 206
penstock 657, 658, 664
pentagon 705
pentaprism 477
penumbra shadow 6, 7
pepino 197
peplos 336
pepper shaker 226
pepper spray 770
peppered moth 101
pepperoni 216
pepperpot 226
per bend 740
per fess 740
per pale 740
percent 703
percent key 529
perch 220
perch, anatomy 109
perch, morphology 108
perching bird 117
percolator 241
percolators 723
percussion bar 767
percussion instruments 437, 448
perforated brick 298
perforated hardboard 300
perforated pipe 263
perforated toe cap 342
perforation 346
performance tire 560
performance tyre 560
performing arts 427
perfume 717
perfume shop 714
pergola 322
pericardium 163
pericarp 82, 84
period 473, 617, 789
periodicals rack 733
periodicals room 733
periodontal ligament 159
periosteum 154
peripheral 709
peripheral joint 661
peripheral nervous system 166
periscopic sight 758
peristome 94
peristyle 403, 406
peritoneum 169, 170
periwinkle 217
permanent exhibition rooms 395
permanent pasture 182

ASTRONOMY > 2-25;   EARTH > 26-71;   VEGETABLE KINGDOM >72-89;   ANIMAL KINGDOM > 90-143;   HUMAN BEING > 144-177;   FOOD AND KITCHEN > 178-241;   HOUSE > 242-295;
DO-IT-YOURSELF AND GARDENING > 296-333;   CLOTHING > 334-371;   PERSONAL ADORNMENT AND ARTICLES > 372-391;   ARTS AND ARCHITECTURE > 392-465;   COMMUNICATIONS AND
OFFICE AUTOMATION > 466-535;   TRANSPORT AND MACHINERY > 536-643;   ENERGY > 644-677;   SCIENCE > 678-705;   SOCIETY > 706-785;   SPORTS AND GAMES > 786-920;

Permian 92
peroxide 777
peroxisome 94
perpendicular 704
perpetual snows 45
Persian 132, 469
Persian Gulf 33
personal adornment 374
personal articles 374, 383
personal communications 487
personal computer 513
personal identification number pad 731
personal radio cassette player 504
personal watercraft 876
Peru 742
Peru-Chile Trench 50
peso 728
pesticide 69, 70
pestle 230
pet food 181
pet shop 714
petal 80
petanque 864
petanque bowl 864
Peter Pan collar 362
petiolar sinus 86
petiole 76, 79
Petri dish 685
petrochemical industry 656
petrochemicals 656
petrol 656
petrol engine 553, 563, 566
petrol pump 548
petrol pump hose 548
petrol station 725
petrol tank cap 576
petroleum 656
petroleum trap 651, 653
pew 737
phalanges 111, 122, 131, 136, 138, 141, 142, 154, 155
pharmacy 714, 725, 778, 781
pharynx 99, 163, 164
phase conductor 273
phases of the Moon 7
pheasant 120, 212
pheasant egg 213
Philippine Plate 43
Philippine Trench 50
Philippines 33, 747
philtrum 175
phloem 87
Phobos 4
Phoenix 10
phosphorescent coating 275
phosphorus 683
photo booth 715
photo credit line 471
photocopier 512, 730, 733
photocopy control 512
photocopy room 509
photoelectric cell 482
photographer 714
photographic accessories 482
photographic chamber 694
photographic picture 483
photography 476
photography, director of 429
photon 692
photoreceptors 177
photosphere 6
photosynthesis 78
photovoltaic arrays 21
photovoltaic panel 615
phyllo dough 205
physical map 38
physician 780, 842
physicians 846
physics 690
pi 704
pia mater 167
piano 437, 442
piccolo 437, 446
pick 327, 390, 901
pickguard 441
pickling onion 184
pickup cylinder 642
pickup reel 642, 643
pickup selector 441
pickup truck 549
pickups 441
picnic area 725
picnics prohibited 725
pictograms 514
picture 917
picture tube 494
picture window 727
pie pan 232
pie tin 232
piece 917
pier 411, 413, 540, 653
pierce lever 240
pierced earrings 374
pig 128
pigeon 120, 212
piggyback car 588
piggyback flat truck 588
pigsty 182
pika 123
pike 220
pike perch 220

pike pole 767
pike position 828
pile 254
pile carpet 254
pile dwelling 418
pillar 43, 410, 412, 440, 650
pillar buoy 614, 617
pillbox hat 341
pillion footrest 575, 576
pillow 280, 458
pillow protector 280
pillowcase 280
pilot 585, 586, 759
pilot chute 896
pilot house 607
pin 274, 275, 454, 767, 865
pin base 275
pin block 442
pin cushion 454
PIN pad 731
pinacocyte 95
pinafore 356
pince-nez 385
pinch 274, 275, 901
pinch pleat 283
pine needles 89
pine nut 193
pine seed 89
pineal body 167
pineapple 196
pinion 307, 697
pink ball 863
pink pepper 198
pinking shears 454
pinna 76, 122, 143
pinnacle 408, 410
pinnatifid 79
pins 310
pins, examples 865
pinto bean 191
Pioneer 19
pip 82, 83, 914
pipe 289, 312, 390, 445
pipe clamp 312
pipe cleaners 390
pipe coupling 269
pipe diffuser 627
pipe rack 390
pipe section 257
pipe threader 314
pipe tools 390
pipe wrench 315
pipe, cross section 390
pipe-wrapping insulation 299
pipeline 654
pipework 445
pisiform 154
pistachio nut 193
piste 848
pistil 80
pistol 754, 770
pistol grip 754, 755, 860, 912
pistol grip handle 306, 318
pistol nozzle 329
pistol shooting 861
pistol, 8-mm 861
piston 559, 564, 566
piston release 315
piston lever 315
piston ring 566
piston skirt 566
pit 112, 501, 865
pit lane 872
pit stop 873
pita bread 205
pitch 630, 795, 799
pitch scale 528
pitch wheel 450
pitched roof 414
pitcher 794, 795
pitcher's mound 795
pitcher's plate 795
pitchfork comb 380
pitching 660
pitching wedge 868
pith 87
pithead 648, 650
piton 900
piton-carrier 901
Pitot tube 873
pits 872, 874
pitta bread 205
pituitary gland 167
pivot 317, 382, 383, 398, 436, 454, 612, 686, 907
pivot cab 638
pivot joint 156
pivot spindle 557
placard board 587
placing judge 830
plaice 221
plain 38, 48
plain pole 284
plain weave 463
plan 403, 411
plane 309
plane figure 420
plane projection 36
plane surfaces 704
planetarium 10
planetarium projector 10

planetary nebula 8
planets 4
planets, inner 5
planets, outer 4
planisphere 28
plano-concave lens 691
plano-convex lens 691
plant 77
plant cell 74
plant kingdom 74
plant litter 78
plant, structure 77
plantain 196
plantar 151
plantar interosseous 150
plantar pad 133
plantar surface of the hoof 127
planting box 792
planting tools 324
plasma 162
plasma membrane 94
plasmodesma 74
plaster bat 464
plaster dressing 777
plaster room 779
plastic case 860, 912
plastic film 222
plastic film capacitor 689
plastic insulator 272
plastic-coated chipboard 300
plastic-laminated particle board 300
plastics sorting 71
plastron 113
plate 238, 381, 482, 905
plate binding 887
plate crystal 64
plate grid 562
plateau 38, 45
plateosaur 93
platelet 162
platen 425, 528
platform 321, 542, 569, 593, 620, 699, 830, 894
platform edge 582, 593
platform entrance 582
platform ladder 321
platform number 582
platform pallet truck 633
platform shelter 583
platform trolley 633
platform, 10 m 828
platform, 3 m 828
platform, 5 m 828
platform, 7.5 m 828
platinum 683
platter 226
play button 495, 499, 504
play/pause button 501
player 827, 920
player 1 858
player 2 858
player 3 858
player 4 858
player handicap 858
player positions 794, 803, 811, 814
player's number 808, 810, 878
player's skate 880
player's stick 880
players 822
players' bench 801, 807, 809, 812, 878
players' bench 814
players' chairs 813
players' positions 804
playing area 608, 918
playing field 801, 802, 858, 864, 920
playing surface 815
playing surfaces 822
playing window 499
playpen 281
pleasure garden 322
pleated heading 283
pleats, examples 283, 357
plectrum 433
plenum 258
pleural cavity 163
plexus of nerves 159
pliers 310
plimsoll 344
plinth 697
plotter 520
plow anchor 610
plug 274, 306, 488, 502, 613
plug adapter 274, 383
plug bayonet 751
plug fuse 272
plum 192
plum sauce 201
plumber's snake 314
plumbing 262
plumbing system 262
plumbing tools 314
plumbing wrench 315
plunger 241, 314, 776
plungerhead 642
plunging neckline 363
plus or minus 703
plus/positive 703
Pluto 4, 5
plutonium 684
ply 300
pneumatic armlet 777

pneumatic drill 873
pneumatic hammer 649
pneumatic-tyred guide wheel 595
pneumatic-tyred running wheel 595
pocket 313, 386, 862, 865, 869
pocket calculator 529
pocket camera 480
pocket handkerchief 348
pockets, examples 360
podium 412, 713, 734
point 227, 229, 439, 453, 457, 470, 859, 880, 911, 915, 918
point guard 811
point of interest 39
point wire 590
pointed tab end 349, 361
pointer 261, 695, 698, 699
points 583, 822
points lever 590
points of sailing 833
points signal 590
poison 774
poison gland 103, 106
poisonous mushroom 76
poker 257
poker die 914
Poland 744
polar axis 17
polar bear 135
polar climates 61
polar ice cap 61
polar lights 53
polar orbit 60
polar tundra 61
polar-orbiting satellite 60
polarizing filter 478
Polaroid® camera 480
pole 284, 493, 602, 792, 820, 891
pole grip 892
pole position 872
pole shaft 892
pole vault 790, 792
pole vaulter 792
poles 284
poleyn 749
police 725
police car 769, 771
police officer 770
police station 711, 768
Polish 469
polished stone hand axe 748
political map 37
politics 739
pollen basket 98
pollen brush 98
pollen cell 100
pollen packer 98
pollen press 98
pollutants, non-biodegradable 69
polluting gas emission 69
pollution, agricultural 69
pollution, air 69
pollution, domestic 69
pollution, industrial 69
pollution, land 69
pollution, motor vehicle 69
pollution, oil 70
polo 858
polo collar 363
polo dress 356
polo pony 858
polo shirt 359, 822
polonium 682
polygons 705
Polynesia 747
pome fleshy fruit 82
pome fruits 193
pomegranate 196
pomelo 194
pommel 826, 849, 855
pommel horse 824, 826
poncho 355
pond 322, 866
poniard 751
pons Varolii 167
Pont-l'Évêque 211
pontoon 542, 652
poodle 130
pool 246, 675, 862
poop 602
pop-up tent 903
poplar 88
popping crease 799
poppy 80
poppy seeds 199
porch 245, 411, 738
porch dome 738
porcupine 123
pore 74, 84, 172
pork, cuts 215
porpoise 137
Porro prism 692
port 709, 854
port glass 225
port hand 609, 616, 617

portable radio 503
portable shower head 264
portable sound systems 503
portal 411
portal bridge 541
portal frame 540
portal vein 161
porthole 608
portrait 729
Portugal 743
Portuguese 469
position indicator 417
position light 585, 631
position marker 440, 441
position of a character 472
positions 849
positive charge 684
positive contact 672, 673
positive meniscus 691
positive plate 562
positive plate strap 562
positive region 672
positive terminal 562, 687, 689
positive/negative junction 672
possum-belly body semitrailer 572
post 460, 676, 812, 817, 827
post and plank 852
post and rail 852
post binder 532
post lantern 287
post mill 677
post office 474, 475, 711, 715
postage meter 531
postage stamp 474
postal order 475
postal parcel 475
postal van 474, 475
postbox 474
postcard 474
poster 427
posterior adductor muscle 105
posterior chamber 177
posterior cutaneous nerve of thigh 166
posterior end 105
posterior fontanelle 158
posterior horn 167
posterior root 168
posterior rugae 147, 149
posterior semicircular canal 174
posterior view 147, 149, 151
postern 408, 409
posting surface 535
postmarking module 531
pot-and-pan sink 721
potable water truck 622
potassium 682
potato 184
potato masher 233
pothole 47
pottery 464
pottery, tools 464
pouch 143, 222
pouch of Douglas 170
poulaine 749
poultry 213
poultry shears 233
pound 728
pouring spout 295
powder blusher 378
powder chamber 753
powder flask 752
powder puff 378
powdered milk 210
powdered mustard 200
powdered sugar 209
power 565
power adapter 526
power adapter port 526
power and backlight button 527
power button 494, 495, 497, 498, 501, 505, 506, 513, 519, 526
power cable 513
power cable plug 513
power car 585
power control module 563
power cord 237, 305, 308, 381, 383, 497
power indicator 518
power light 519
power mower 332
power plant 657
power plant, cross section 664
power plug 504, 527
power socket 504
power source 687
power station 664
power supply cord 382
power supply fan 513
power supply unit 513
power switch 451, 477, 518
power switch machine 590
power takeoff 640
power train 580
power turbine 627
power zoom button 496
power, measurement 702
power-off/slide-select bar 483
power-on button 508
power-on light 508
power-on/paper-detect light 731
power-takeoff shaft 641, 642
power/functions switch 496

972

ASTRONOMY > 2-25; EARTH > 26-71; VEGETABLE KINGDOM >72-89; ANIMAL KINGDOM > 90-143; HUMAN BEING > 144-177; FOOD AND KITCHEN > 178-241; HOUSE > 242-295; DO-IT-YOURSELF AND GARDENING > 296-333; CLOTHING > 334-371; PERSONAL ADORNMENT AND ARTICLES > 372-391; ARTS AND ARCHITECTURE > 392-465; COMMUNICATIONS AND OFFICE AUTOMATION > 466-535; TRANSPORT AND MACHINERY > 536-643; ENERGY > 644-677; SCIENCE > 678-705; SOCIETY > 706-785; SPORTS AND GAMES > 786-920

power/light switch 452
practice green 866
practitioner, kung fu 846
prairie 38
praseodymium 684
prawn 218
prayer hall 738
Precambrian 92
precious stones 375
precipitation 67
precipitation area 55
precipitations 64
precision sports 859
preferred channel 617
prehensile digit 139
premaxilla 108, 122, 123
premolar 121, 123
premolars 159
prepared foods 181
prepuce 169
prerinse sink 721
present state of weather 55
present weather 57
preset buttons 495
preset tuning button 497, 498
president 848
president of the jury 900
president's office 509
president's secretary 509
press bar 851
press bed 421, 423
press chamber 642
press wheel 643
pressed area 501
pressed cheeses 211
pressed powder 378
presser bar 453
presser foot 453
pressing 425
pressing board 425
pressure bar 442
pressure change 55
pressure control 384
pressure control valve 777
pressure cooker 234
pressure demand regulator 765
pressure dial 452
pressure gauge 654, 777, 841
pressure plate 476, 758
pressure regulator 234, 319, 903
pressure relief valve 259, 266
pressure screw 421, 423
pressure tube 667
pressure, measurement 702
pressure-relief valve 267
pressurized heavy water 670
pressurized refuge 543
pressurized-water reactor 671
pressurizer 670, 671
prestressed concrete 298
prevailing wind 63
preview monitor 489
preview monitors 491
previous sets 822
price per gallon/liter 548
price per gallon/litre 548
pricker 458
prickly pear 197
prickly sphagnum 75
primaries 115
primary colors 400
primary consumers 67
primary covert 115
primary crash sensor 556
primary flight display 626
primary hard disk drive 513
primary marshalling track 589
primary mirror 17
primary root 77
primary sorting 474
primate mammals 138
primates, examples 139
prime 849
prime focus 17
prime focus observing capsule 17
prime meridian 36
primer 757, 912
Princess 12
princess dress 356
princess seaming 366
principal rafter 253
principal's office 735
Principe 745
print cartridge light 519
print drying rack 485
print screen 515
print screen/system request key 515
print washer 485
printed circuit 689
printed circuit board 689
printed image 420
printer 523, 529
printer table 511
printer, ink jet 519
printing 420
printing calculator 529
printing unit 528
printout 699
priority intersection 544
prism binoculars 692
prison 726

prisoner's dock 728
prisoners' shower 768
privacy curtain 780
private broadcasting network 486
private dressing room 428
probe 316
probe receptacle 238
proboscis 96
procedure checklist 20
processor 513
proconsul 93
producer 429, 489, 490
producer turret 488
product code 699
production adviser 490
production control room 489, 490, 491
production designer 428
production desk 491
production manager 509
production of electricity by the generator 662, 665
production of electricity from geothermal energy 646
production of electricity from nuclear energy 665
production of electricity from solar energy 674
production of electricity from thermal energy 646
production of electricity from wind energy 677
production of electricity, steps 662
production of sound 445
production platform 652, 654
production video switcher 491
production well 646
production/export riser system 652
professional training office 730
profile of the Earth's atmosphere 53
program selector 450
programmable buttons 516
programmable function keys 731
programmable thermostat 261
programming control 261
programs, computer 771
projectiles 752
projection booth 427
projection device 573
projection dome 10
projection head 535
projection room 395, 427
projection screen 427, 483
projector 427, 518
proleg 97
promenade deck 608
promethium 684
prominence 6
prompt side 431
pronaos 403
prone position 861, 893
propane accessories 903
propane gas cylinder 567
propellant 912
propellant tank 18
propeller 606, 608, 609, 763
propeller duct 605
propeller shaft 609
propellers 762
property line 244
property man 429
propulsion machinery control room 763
propulsion module 486
proscenium 430
prosciutto 216
prosecution counsels' bench 728
prostate 169
protactinium 684
protect tab 521
protection 774
protection area 843
protection layer 20
protective clothing 318
protective cup 808, 843, 880
protective equipment 808
protective goggles 818, 819, 870, 875
protective helmet 575, 580
protective mat 883
protective plate 875
protective suit 875
protective surround 918
protective window 494
Protestantism 736
prothorax 97
proton 680
protoneuron 168
protractor 701
proventriculus 116
province 37
prow ornament 600
proximal epiphysis 155
proximal phalange 154, 155
proximal phalanx 126, 133
proximal sesamoid 126
proximity fuse 759
pruning knife 330
pruning saw 330
pruning shears 330
pruning tools 330
pry bar 301
pseudopod 94
psychiatric examination room 778

psychiatric observation room 778
psychrometer 59
pterygoid 112
pubis 116, 122, 146, 148
public building 39
public garden 713
public postal network 474
puck 880
Puerto Rico Trench 50
puff sleeve 360
pull rod 590
pull strap 389
pull tab 223
pulley 284, 321, 566, 686, 750
pulley block 750
pulley safety guard 307
pulling ring 776
Pullman case 389
pulmonary artery 160, 163
pulmonary trunk 162
pulmonary valve 162
pulmonary vein 160
pulp 82, 159
pulp chamber 159
pulpit 737, 738
pulsar 8
pulsed ruby laser 692
pulverizer 646
pulvino 661
pumice correcting pencil 423
pump 246, 292, 294, 320, 343, 670, 671, 674, 903
pump and motor assembly 559
pump island 548
pump motor 263
pump nozzle 548
pump number 548
pump room 606
pumper 766
pumpernickel 205
pumping station 654
pumpkin 189
punch 401
punch hole 342, 350, 371
punching bag 842
punching ball 842
punctuation marks 473
pup tent 903
pupa 100
pupil 132, 177
pure alcohol 777
purfling 439, 440
purge valve 841
purple border 336
purpure 741
purse 387
purslane 187
pursuit bicycle 871
pursuit line 871
pursuit racer 871
push bar 416
push button 236, 294, 391, 507
push buttons 506
push frame 636
push rim 783
push-button 248, 470
push-button telephone 507
push-to-talk switch 505
push-up bra 367
push-up stand 851
pusher 230, 237, 240
pushing phase 892
putter 867, 868
pygal shield 113
pygostyle 116
pyjamas 364
pylon 663
pylon body 663
pylon foot 663
pylon top 663
pylon window 663
pyloric caecum 109
pyloric cecum 95, 109
pyloric stomach 107
pyramid 402, 705
pyramid spot 862
pyramid, entrance 402
pyranometer 58
Pyrenees 32
pyrometric cone 464
python 114

Q

Qatar 746
Qibla wall 738
quad cane 782
quadrant 704
quadrate 112
quadrilateral 705
quadruped stick 782
quail 120, 212
quail egg 213
quark 680
quarte 849
quarter 127, 342, 370
quarter note 435
quarter rest 435
quarter window 551
quarter-deck 608

quarterback 807
quarterfinal: 8 players 789
quarterly 740
quartet 438
quartz metronome 436
Quaternary 93
quaver 435
quaver rest 435
quay 596, 708
quay ramp 596
quayside crane 596
quayside railway 596
Quechua 469
Queen 12
queen 99, 914, 916
queen cell 100
queen excluder 100
Queen Maud Land 29
queen's chamber 402
queen's side 916
question mark 473
quiche plate 232
quiche tin 232
quick release system 482
quick ticket system 427
quickdraw 900
quill 307, 470
quill brush 380
quince 193
quinoa 203
quinte 849
quintet 438
quiver 859
quotation marks 473
quotation marks (French) 473

R

rabbet bit 308
rabbi's seat 738
rabbit 123, 212
raccoon 134
race director 870
raceme 81
racetrack 856
rachis 115
racing suit 874, 882
rack 234, 238, 290, 294, 791, 863
rack and pinion gear 686
rackboard 445
rackboard support 445
racket sports 815
Raclette 211
raclette with grill 239
racquetball 818
racquetball racket 818
radar 40, 604, 605, 608, 609
radar aircraft 629
radar antenna 40, 760, 763
radar beam 40
radar display 771
radar mast 606
radar reflector 615
radar transceiver 771
radar unit 760
radar-absorbent material 629
Radarsat satellite 40
radial artery 160
radial nerve 166
radial passenger loading area 619
radial ply 561
radial thread 103
radial tire 561
radial tyre 561
radiant heater 260
radiation 681
radiation zone 6
radiator 259, 552, 561, 586
radiator grille 570
radiator panel 23
radiators 21
radicchio 186
radicle 77, 87
radio 771, 898
radio antenna 604, 606, 608, 609, 763, 873
radio mast 652
radio telescope 16
radio wave 16
radio waves 690
radio-ulna 111
radioactive 774
radioactive nuclei 681
radioactivity, measurement 702
radioisotope thermoelectric generator 18
radiometer 60
radiosonde 59
radish 189
radium 682
radius 116, 121, 122, 126, 131, 136, 138, 140, 141, 142, 152, 154, 156, 704
radome 760
radon 684
radula 104
rafter 252
raglan 355
raglan sleeve 352, 355, 361, 369
rail 278, 456, 591, 841, 862
rail joint 590
rail section 591

rail track 649
rail transport 582
railing 251
railroad crossing 545, 547
railroad line 39
railroad station 39, 583, 708, 710
railroad track 590, 591, 710
railway 39
railway shuttle service 620
railway station 39, 583, 708, 710
railway track 590, 591
railyard 708
rain 64, 65
rain cap 257
rain forms 64
rain gauge recorder 58, 59
rain shower 57
raincoat 352
rainbow 65
rainfall, measure 59
rainfly 902, 903
raised band 426
raised figure 420
raised handlebar 870
raised head 302
raising the spinnaker 833
rake 327, 642
rake bar 642
rake comb 380
rally car 873
rally motorcycle 875
Ram 12
ram 598
RAM connector 513
RAM module 513
rambutan 197
ramekin 226
rammer 752
ramp 403, 407, 539, 647, 894
rampart 408, 409
random access memory module 513
random orbit sander 308
range 722
range hood 224, 290, 722
range, electric 721
range, gas 721
rangefinder 480
rank insignia 770
Ranvier, node 168
rapier 751
rare earth 684
ras el hanout 199
rasp 309, 401
raspberry 192
raspberry, section 83
rat 123
rat, morphology 122
rat, skeleton 122
ratchet 302, 307, 460
ratchet box end wrench 311
ratchet knob 700
ratchet ring spanner 311
ratchet socket wrench 311
ratchet wheel 460, 696, 697
rattle 112
rattlesnake 114
raven 118
ravioli 206
razor clam 217
reach-in freezer 180
reaction direction 684
reaction engine assembly 60
reactor 665, 666, 669, 763
reactor building 667, 669
reactor building airlock 668
reactor core 670, 671
reactor tank 671
reactor vessel 667
reactor, carbon dioxide 670
reactor, heavy-water 670
read button 505
read/write head 521
reading 385
reading light 771
reading mirror 20
reading room 732
reading start 501
reamer 237
rear apron 349
rear beam 698
rear brake 578
rear brake pedal 576
rear bumper 577, 876, 885
rear cargo rack 577
rear derailleur 578, 580
rear door 775
rear fender 577
rear foil 609
rear indicator 575, 576
rear leg 277
rear light 554, 571, 575, 576, 578
rear lights 554
rear limit line 848
rear propeller 606
rear rigid section 569
rear runner 884
rear seat 302
rear shock absorber 575
rear sight 754, 755, 757, 861, 893, 912
rear step 766, 775
rear wheel 333

ASTRONOMY > 2-25;   EARTH > 26-71;   VEGETABLE KINGDOM >72-89;   ANIMAL KINGDOM > 90-143;   HUMAN BEING > 144-177;   FOOD AND KITCHEN > 178-241;   HOUSE > 242-295;
DO-IT-YOURSELF AND GARDENING > 296-333;   CLOTHING > 334-371;   PERSONAL ADORNMENT AND ARTICLES > 372-391;   ARTS AND ARCHITECTURE > 392-465;   COMMUNICATIONS AND OFFICE AUTOMATION > 466-535;   TRANSPORT AND MACHINERY > 536-643;   ENERGY > 644-677;   SCIENCE > 678-705;   SOCIETY > 706-785;   SPORTS AND GAMES > 786-920

rearview mirror 556
récamier 276
receiver 16, 493, 506, 754, 755, 817, 819, 820
receiver volume control 506
receiving area 180, 395, 716
receiving line 818
receiving tray 508
receiving yard 589
receptacle 75, 80, 83
receptacle analyzer 316
reception 509
reception area 764, 778, 781
reception bay 666
reception desk 730
reception hall 738
reception level 727
rechargeable battery pack 496
recharging base 288
reclining back 776
recoil sleigh 756
recoilless rifle 757
record 500
record announcement button 508
record button 495, 499
record muting button 499
record player 500
recording level control 499
recording start/stop button 496
recording tape 499
recording unit 59
recovery room 780
rectal cecum 95
rectangle 705
rectangular 904
rectangular flag 739
rectum 97, 99, 113, 116, 125, 164, 169, 170
rectus femoris 150
recuperator cylinder 756
recuperator cylinder front head 756
recycling 71
recycling bin 71
recycling containers 71
Red 915
red 400, 690, 919
red alga 75
red ball 862, 863
red balls 863
red beam 494
red blood cell 162
red cabbage 186
red clamp 558
red giant 8
red kidney bean 191
red light 712
red ocher pencil 423
red ochre pencil 423
red onion 184
red safelight filter 485
Red Sea 28, 33, 34
red sweet pepper 188
red whortleberry 192
red-kneed tarantula 102
red-violet 400
redcurrant 192
redfish 221
reduce/enlarge 512
reducing coupling 269
reed 446, 460
reed hooks 461
reed pipe 444
reel band 603
reel point 603
reel 328, 484, 495, 848, 920
reel plate 920
reel seat 909, 910
reentrant angle 704
referee 801, 803, 805, 807, 810, 812, 818, 819, 827, 828, 830, 842, 843, 844, 845, 846, 864, 879, 881, 882, 893
referee's line 845
reference books 732
reference room 733
refill 470
refill tube 265
refinery 654, 709
refinery products 656
reflected solar radiation 68
reflecting cylinder 692
reflecting surface 674
reflecting telescope 15
reflecting telescope, cross section 15
reflection 41
reflective stripe 765
reflector 316, 571, 578, 876
reflex camera, cross section 477
Reformation 736
refracting telescope 14
refracting telescope, cross section 14
refractory brick 465
refrigerant tubing 260
refrigerated display case 720
refrigerated semitrailer 572
refrigeration unit 571
refrigerator 224, 291, 720, 722
refrigerator car 588
refrigerator compartment 291
refrigerator van 588
refrigerators 720
refueler 873

refueling device 873
refuse container 295
regional distribution center 475
regional mail 475
register 273
registered trademark 473
registers, types 258
regular decagon 705
regular dodecagon 705
regular hendecagon 705
regular heptagon 705
regular hexagon 705
regular nonagon 705
regular octagon 705
regular octahedron 705
regular pentagon 705
regulating button 443
regulating valve 259
regulator first stage 841
regulator second stage 841
reheater 668
rein 856
rein ring 854
reindeer 128
reinforced concrete 298
reinforced toe 773
relationships, family 784
relay starting line 791
relay station 486
relay/interconnection box 563
release lever 310
release of oxygen 78
release treadle 460
relief printing 420
relief printing process 421
relief printing process, equipment 421
relieving chamber 402
religion 736
religions, chronology 736
relocation 528
remote command antenna 40
remote control 483, 493, 495
remote control sensor 494, 501
remote control terminal 476, 477
remote manipulator system 21, 22
remote sensing 40
remote sensor 518
remote-controlled points 590
remote-controlled switch 590
removable flag pole 867
removable hard disk 521
removable hard disk drive 521
removable-bottomed pan 232
removable-bottomed tin 232
renal artery 160, 165
renal hilus 165
renal papilla 165
renal pelvis 165
renal vein 160, 165
reniform 79
repair shop 548
repeat buttons 501
repeat mark 434
repeater 487
report writing room 768
reproductive organs, female 170
reproductive organs, male 169
reptiles 112
reptiles, examples 113
Republic of Korea 747
Republic of Moldova 744
repulsion 687
rerebrace 749
reserve parachute 896
reservoir 241, 445, 657, 658, 660, 661
reservoir-nib pen 397
reset 512
reset button 267, 495, 513, 519, 696, 700, 918
reset key 508
resident 780
residential district 709
residue waste, non-reusable 71
resin surface 501
resistance adjustment 851
resistors 689
resonator 444, 449, 502
respirator 773
respiratory system 163
respiratory system protection 773, 774
rest area 39
rest symbols 435
restaurant 608, 710, 713, 714, 719, 720, 725
restaurant car 584
restaurant review 471
restaurant, fast-food 715
restaurant, self-service 722
restricted area 811
restricting circle 810
result line 529
resurgence 47
resuscitation room 778
resuscitator 775
retainer 649
retaining ring 268
reticle 692
retina 177, 691
retractable handle 386
retractable step 567
retracted claw 133

retrenchment 409
retro-reflective tape 611
return 511, 515
return crease 799
return spring 559
reverse 828
reverse dive with a twist 829
reverse light 554
reverse slide change 483
reverse stitch button 452
reverse travel pedal 333
reversible reaction 684
reversing light 554
reversing switch 302, 306
revolver 754
revolving cylinder 458
revolving nosepiece 693
revolving sprinkler 329
rewind button 495, 499, 504, 508
Rhea 5
rhenium 683
rhinoceros 129
rhizoid 75
rhizome 76
rhodium 683
rhombus 705
rhubarb 185
rhythm of marks by night 617
rhythm selector 451
rhythmic gymnastics 823
rias 51
rib 112, 116, 121, 122, 126, 131, 136, 138, 141, 142, 185, 391, 439, 440, 639, 772
rib joint pliers 310
rib pad 808
rib roast 214
rib stitch 458
ribbing 354, 369, 909
ribbing plough 641
ribbing plow 641
ribbon 823
ribosome 74, 94
ribs 152, 464
rice 85, 203, 207
rice noodles 207
rice papers 207
rice vermicelli 207
rice vinegar 201
rice: spike 85
ricotta 210
rider 853, 855, 858
riders 875
ridge 45
ridge beam 253
ridge board 252
ridge tent 903
riding 854
riding cap 853, 856
riding coat 355
riding crop 853, 856
riding glove 853
riding jacket 853
riegel 46
riffler 401
rifle 893
rifle (rifled bore) 912
rifle shooting 861
rigatoni 206
rigging 602
rigging wire 897
right angle 704
right ascension 13
right ascension setting scale 14, 15
right atrium 161, 162
right attacker 812
right back 801, 803, 812, 814
right bend 544, 547
right center 804
right centre 804
right channel 502
right cornerback 806
right defence 878
right defense 878
right defensive end 806
right defensive tackle 806
right field 795
right fielder 794
right forward 811
right guard 807
right half 801
right inside forward 801
right kidney 165
right lung 161, 163
right midfielder 803
right pulmonary vein 162
right safety 806
right service court 819, 821
right side 384
right tackle 807
right ventricle 161, 162
right wing 801, 804, 879
right winger 814
rigs, examples 601
rillettes 216
rim 385, 560, 574, 579, 640, 793, 811
rim flange 560
rim soup bowl 226
rime 65
rinceau 276
rind 82

ring 76, 249, 284, 391, 447, 453, 522, 610, 611, 659, 696, 699, 809, 824, 842, 901
ring binder 532
ring canal 95
ring handle 390
ring network 522
ring nut 269
ring post 842
ring road 39
ring spanner 311
ring step 842
ring, equestrian sports 788
ring, parts 376
ringhandle 382
ringing volume control 506
rings 376, 824, 825
ringside 842
rink 864, 877, 878, 881
rink corner 878
rinse-aid dispenser 294
rip fence 304, 305
rip fence guide 305
rip fence lock 305
rip fence rule 305
rip fence slot 305
ripeness 86
ripening 86
ripper 636
ripper cylinder 636
ripper shank 636
ripper tip tooth 636
rise 255
riser 255, 897
rising warm air 63
River 10
river 38, 39, 48
river estuary 38, 51
river otter 134
rivet 229, 310
road 39, 708
road bicycle 581
road communications 487
road cycling competition 870
road flare 771
road map 39
road number 39
road racing 870
road signs 544
road system 538
road transport 538, 596
road tunnel 543
road works ahead 545, 547
road, cross section 538
road-racing bicycle 870
road-racing cyclist 870
roadway 538, 543, 712
roadway narrows 544, 547
roast 214, 215
roasted coffee beans 208
roasting pans 234
Roberval's balance 698
robin 118
rock 900
rock basin 46
rock candy 209
rock climber 900
rock garden 322
rock shaft lift arm 640
rocker arm 566
rocket engine 24
rocket motor 759
rocking chair 276, 277
rocking tool 422
rockslide 47
rocky desert 52
rocky islet 51
Rocky Mountains 30
rod 177, 261, 436, 461, 685
rodent 122
rodent's jaw 123
rodents 122
rodents, examples 123
roll 362, 630
roll film 481
roll structure 873
roll-up blind 285
roller 284, 285, 333, 380, 423, 516, 633
roller blind 285
roller board and arms 445
roller cover 320
roller frame 320
roller shade 285, 558
rolling ladder 321
rolling pin 232
rolling stock cleaning yard 589
rolling stock repair shop 589
romaine lettuce 186
Roman amphitheater 407
roman bean 191
Roman house 406
Roman legionary 748
Roman metal pen 470
Roman numerals 703
roman shade 285
Romance languages 469
Romania 744
Romanian 469
Romanian couching stitch 459
Romano 211

rompers 368, 369
roof 100, 245, 257, 412, 551, 567, 635, 647
roof pole 903
roof truss 253
roof vent 262, 567
roofing felt 299
roofs, examples 414
rook 916
room 650
room air conditioner 261
room number 724
room thermostat 261
room, changing 734
rooms, main 250
rooster 120
root 78, 159, 176, 227
root canal 159
root cap 77
root hairs 77
root of nail 172
root of nose 175
root rib 624
root system 77, 86
root vegetables 189
root-hair zone 87
rope 374, 611, 686, 823, 842, 900, 901, 908
rope ladder 321
roped party 900
Roquefort 211
rose 80, 248, 328, 440
rose cut 375
rose window 411
rosemary 202
rosette 405
Ross Ice Shelf 29
rotary cheese grater 230
rotary engine cycle 565
rotary file 531
rotary hoe 641
rotary system 651
rotary table 651
rotating auger 642, 643
rotating dome 17
rotating drum 43
rotating track 16
rotating wheel 919
rotation of the turbine 662
Rotavator 327
rotini 206
rotodome 629
rotor 249, 565, 659, 676
rotor blade 631
rotor head 631
rotor hub 631
rotunda 713
rotunda roof 415
rough 866, 867
roughing out 401
roulette 422
roulette table 919
round brush 380
round end pin 285
round eye 453
round head 302
round neck 363
round pronator 150
round-bottom flask 685
roundabout 39
rounding-over bit 308
route judge 900
route sign 568, 569, 595
router 308, 524
routers 523
routing cardboard 587
row 384, 431
row counter 456
row number display 456
rowboat, parts 838
rowing 838
rowing (one oar) 838
rowing machine 851
royal agaric 183
royal flush 914
RTG 18
rub protection 874
rub rail 571
rubber 342
rubber boot 765
rubber bulb 776
rubber bumper 920
rubber ferrule 782
rubber gasket 270
rubber mat 500
rubber sheath 838
rubber snaffle bit 854
rubber stamp 531
rubber stopper 321
rubber thread 867
rubber tip 321, 782
rubber wall 560, 561
rubbing alcohol 777
rubbing strip 560, 561
rubbish bin 723
rubble 298
rubidium 682
ruby 375
ruby cylinder 692
ruching 368
ruck 805

rucksack 901
rudder 23, 600, 605, 606, 608, 625, 759, 760, 834, 838, 839, 898
rudder blade 606
rudder cable 838
rudder pedal 898
Ruffini's corpuscle 172
ruffle 282, 337
ruffled rumba pants 368
ruffled skirt 357
rug 254
rug and floor brush 289
rugby 804
rugby ball 805
rugby player 805
rugby shoe 805
rule 471
ruler 399, 424, 700, 905
rump 115
run 255
run-up track 793
runabout 607
rung 321
runner 659, 884, 900, 915
runner blade 659, 664
runners 659
running bowline 908
running rail 595
running shoe 370
running shoes 716
running surface 590
running track 635
runway 595, 620, 761
runway center line markings 620
runway centre line markings 620
runway designation marking 620
runway side stripe markings 620
runway threshold markings 621
runway touchdown zone marking 621
rupee 728
Russian 469
Russian Federation 744
Russian module 21
Russian pumpernickel 205
rutabaga 189
ruthenium 683
rutherfordium 683
Rwanda 745
rye 85, 203
rye bread 204
rye crispbread 205
rye: spike 85
Ryukyu Trench 50

S

S-band antenna 60
S-band high gain antenna 60
S-Video output 526
sabaton 749
saber 751, 849
saber and épée warning line 848
sable 741
sabre 751, 849
sabre and épée warning line 848
sabreur 848
sacral plexus 166
sacral vertebra 111
sacral vertebrae 122, 126, 131, 142
sacristy 737
sacrum 138, 141, 152, 153, 157
saddle 483, 826, 853, 855, 856, 858, 897
saddle joint 156
saddlebag 577
saddlecloth 853, 856
safari jacket 359
safe 731, 769
safe deposit box 731
safe water mark 617
safelight 484
safest water 616
safety 755, 764
safety area 844, 846
safety belt 873
safety binding 888, 889
safety boot 773
safety cage 791
safety cap 757, 772
safety earmuffs 772
safety fence 890
safety glasses 772
safety goggles 772
safety handle 332
safety lighting 771
safety line 593
safety match 391
safety niche 543
safety officer 837
safety pad 823
safety pin 453
safety rail 321, 586
safety scissors 377
safety symbols 774
safety tank 670
safety tether 20
safety thermostat 293
safety thong 818
safety valve 234, 665
saffron 198
safing sensor 556

sagari 847
sage 202
sagittal section 169, 170
Sahara Desert 34
sail 676, 836, 897
sail cloth 676
sail panel 834
sail plane 763
sailbar 676
sailboard 836
sailboat 834
sailing 833
sailing boat 834
sailing, points 833
sailor collar 362
sailor tunic 359
sails 603
sails, examples 601
Saint Bernard 131
Saint Kitts and Nevis 743
Saint Lawrence River 30
Saint Lucia 743
Saint Peter 736
Saint Vincent and the Grenadines 743
salad bowl 226
salad dish 226
salad fork 228
salad plate 226
salad spinner 231
salads 722
salamander 111
salami 216
salchow 881
salient angle 409
saline lake 52
salivary duct 99
salivary gland 97, 99, 104, 176
salivary glands 164
salmon, Atlantic 221
salmon, Pacific 221
salsify 189
salt 201, 847
salt shaker 226
saltcellar 226
samarium 684
sambal oelek 201
Samoa 747
Samoan 469
sample 458
sampler 450
San Marino 744
sanctuary lamp 737
sand 660, 813
sand bar 49
sand bunker 866, 867
sand island 51
sand paper 308
sand shoe 571
sand wedge 868
sandal 343, 344, 748
sandbox 586
sanding disc 308
sanding pad 308
sandstorm 57
sandy desert 52
sans serif type 472
Sao Tome and Principe 745
saphenous nerve 166
sapodilla 197
sapphire 375
sapwood 87
sardine 219
sarong 357
sartorius 150
sash 846
sash frame 249
sash window 415
satchel bag 387
satellite 24, 486
satellite earth station 525
satellite navigation system 613
satellite remote sensing 41
satellites, orbit 60
satin weave 463
Saturn 4, 5
Saturn V 24, 25
saucepan 235, 905
Saudi Arabia 746
sausage 216
sauté pan 235
savanna 66
savanna climate 61
savory 202
savoy cabbage 186
sawing tools 303
sawing-in 424
sawtooth roof 414
saxhorn 447
saxophone 446
scale 108, 112, 113, 117, 313, 434, 695, 700, 776, 907
scale leaf 78
Scales 11
scallion 184
scallop 217
scalper 857
scampi 218
Scandinavian cracked bread 205
Scandinavian crispbread 205
Scandinavian Peninsula 32
scandium 683

scaphoid 154, 156
scapula 111, 116, 121, 122, 126, 131, 136, 138, 141, 142, 152, 153, 156
scapular 115
scarlet runner bean 191
scarp 409
scatter cushion 280
scene 402
scene light 775
scenic route 39
schedules 582
schema of circulation 161
Schism, Great 736
schnauzer 130
school 734
school bus 568
school zone 545, 547
schooner 601
Schwann, sheath 168
sciatic nerve 166
science room 734
scientific air lock 23
scientific calculator 529
scientific instruments 17, 23
scientific symbols 702
scissors 454, 777, 905
scissors crossing 583
scissors cut 375
scissors-glasses 385
sclera 177
sconce 287
scoop 390
score 789, 825
score console 865
score counter 920
scoreboard 789, 790, 822, 825, 831, 839, 844, 846, 918
scoreboard, current event 825
scoreboard, overall standings 824
scorekeeper 814, 845
scorekeepers 846, 847
scorer 810, 812, 813, 819, 848, 860, 864
scorers 844, 859
scoring light 848
Scorpion 10
scorpion 102
scotia 404, 405
Scotia Plate 43
Scottish 469
scouring pad 295
scraper 320, 422, 423, 638, 892
scraper bar holder 423
screen 383, 483, 494, 658, 724, 799
screen case 483
screen door 567
screen print 368, 369
screen window 902
screw 302, 439
screw base 275
screw cap 223
screw earrings 374
screw locking nut 909, 910
screwdriver 302, 905
screwdriver bit 306
screwdriver, cordless 302
screwing tools 302
screwsleeve 900
scrimmage: defense 806
scrimmage: offence 807
scrimmage: offense 807
script assistant 490
scroll 439
scroll button 505
scroll case 658
scroll foot 276
scroll wheel 506, 516
scrolling 515
scrolling lock key 515
scrotum 146, 169
scrub room 780
scrum half 804
scuba diver 841
scuba diving 841
scuffle hoe 326
sculling 838
sculling (two oars) 838
sculling boats 839
sculling oar 838
Sculptor's Tools 10
sculpture 395
scuttle panel 550
scythe 330
sea 7, 38, 48, 664
sea anchor 610
sea bag 388
sea bass 220
sea bream 219
Sea Goat 10
sea kale 186
sea lettuce 183
sea level 42, 49, 53
sea lion 137
Sea of Japan 33
sea salt 201
Sea Serpent 10
sea side 664
sea urchin 95
sea-level pressure 55
sea-to-sea missile 762
seabed 683
seafood 181

seal 137, 268
sealed cell 100
sealing material 689
sealing plug 689
sealing ring 655
seam 346, 348, 390, 798
seam allowance 455
seam gauge 454
seam line 455
seam pocket 355, 360
seamount 49
search 525
search-and-rescue antennas 60
season tiles 917
seasons of the year 54
seat 264, 265, 276, 277, 281, 333, 427, 431, 464, 555, 577, 578, 783, 839, 851, 855, 857, 876, 885, 898
seat belt 555
seat cover 265
seat harness 900
seat post 578
seat stay 578
seat tube 578, 871
seat-belt warning light 557
seats 277
seaweed 183
sebaceous gland 172
secateurs 330
second 434, 702, 704, 842, 877
second assistant camera operator 428
second base 794
second baseman 794
second classification track 589
second dorsal fin 108, 109
second dozen (13 to 24) 919
second floor 250, 251
second focal room 16
second hand 696
second leg at reach 833
second level of operations 529
second molar 159
second premolar 159
second referee 813
second reinforce 753
second round: 64 players 789
second row 804
second space 811
second stage 25
second valve slide 447
second violins 437
second voltage increase 677
second-level domain 524
secondaries 115
secondary altar 737
secondary channel 617
secondary colors 400
secondary consumers 67
secondary hard disk drive 513
secondary inlet 655
secondary marshalling track 589
secondary mirror 15, 17, 477
secondary reflector 16
secondary road 39
secondary root 77
secondary waiting room 781
seconde 849
secretarial desk 511
secretaries 827
secretaries' office 735
secretary 279, 814
secretary's office 731
section 471
section of a bulb 78
section of a capsule: poppy 84
section of a follicle: star anise 84
section of a grape 83
section of a hazelnut 84
section of a legume: pea 84
section of a log 300
section of a peach 81
section of a raspberry 83
section of a silique: mustard 84
section of a strawberry 83
section of a walnut 84
section of an apple 82
section of an orange 82
section of the Earth's crust 42
sectional garage door 416
sector 704
security casing 332
security check 621
security grille 730
security guard's office 733
security guard's work station 779
security service 719
security thread 729
security trigger 331
security vestibule 728
sedimentary rocks 42
seed 77, 81, 82, 83, 84
seed coat 81, 85
seed drill 643
seed leaf 77
seeder 324
seeding tools 324
seedless cucumber 188
segment 82
segment score number 918
seismic wave 43
seismogram 43

seismograph, vertical 43
seismographic recording 651, 653
seismographs 43
select button 505
selection key 506
selective sorting of waste 71
selector switch 316
selenium 682
self-adhesive labels 532
self-contained breathing apparatus 765
self-inflating mattress 904
self-sealing flap 531
self-service display case 722
self-service meat counter 180
self-service restaurant 722
self-timer indicator 476
selvage 455
semaphore 583
semi-bold 472
semi-detached cottage 419
semi-fisheye lens 478
semi-metals 682
semi-mummy 904
semibreve 435
semibreve rest 435
semicircle 704, 810
semicircular arch 413
semicircular canal, lateral 174
semicircular canal, posterior 174
semicircular canal, superior 174
semicolon 473
semifinal: 4 players 789
semimembranosus 151
semimembranous 151
seminal receptacle 97, 103
seminal vesicle 169
semiprecious stones 375
semiquaver 435
semiquaver rest 435
semisubmersible platform 653
semitendinosus 151
semitendinous 151
semitrailer 570, 571
semitrailers, examples 572
semolina 204
Senegal 745
Senegal River 34
sense organs 172
sense receptor 168
sensitive root 167
sensor 58
sensor probe 238
sensor swath 40
sensor wiring circuit 559
sensory impulse 168
sensory neuron 168
sensory receptor 168
sensory root 168
sent document tray 508
sepal 80, 82, 83
separate collection 71
separator 562, 600, 646, 668, 689
separator steam release 668
septal cartilage of nose 175
septic tank 70, 263
septime 849
septum 84, 175
septum pellucidum 167
sequencer 450
sequencer control 450
serac 46
Serbo-Croatian 469
serial number 729
serial port 513
serif type 472
serological pipette 685
Serpent 11, 13
Serpent Bearer 11, 13
serve 812, 820
server 522, 523, 524, 525, 816, 819, 821
service area 39, 619
service bay 548
service box 273, 818, 819
service box line 818
service building 666
service entrance 732
service judge 816, 820
service line 818, 819, 821
service main 712
service module 19, 25, 486
service provider, Internet 525
service road 618
service room 738
service station 548, 711, 725
service table 720
service zone 818
service zones 817
serving cart 278
serving trolley 278
sesame oil 209
set 429, 528, 822
set dresser 429
set of bells 449
set of utensils 233
set width 472
set-in sleeve 349
set-up 865
setting 376
setting indicator 889
settings display button 477
setup 865

seventeenth century cannon 752
seventeenth century mortar 752
seventeenth-century cannon and mortar 752
seventh 434
sew-through buttons 453
sewer 712
sewing 424, 452
sewing frame 424
sewing machine 452
sewing, accessories 454
sewn-in floor 902, 903
sewn-in groundsheet 902, 903
Sextant 11
sextant 612
sextet 438
sexton beetle 101
Seychelles 746
shackle 835
shad 220
shade 286
shade cloth 285
shadow 696
shadow band 58
shadow key 479
shadow roll 856
shady arcades 738
shaft 56, 402, 405, 462, 464, 659, 686, 688, 695, 762, 793, 816, 822, 838, 857, 858, 859, 863, 867, 880, 901, 918
shaft head 649
shaft holder 857
shake-hands grip 815
shallot 184, 444
shallow root 87
sham 280
shampoo 379
shank 214, 215, 301, 302, 306, 382, 390, 391, 453, 454, 456, 457, 610, 911
shank button 453
shank protector 636
shape of characters 472
shaping tools 308
shapka 340
shark, morphology 108
sharp 435
sharpening steel 229
sharpening stone 229
shaving 383
shaving brush 383
shaving foam 383
shaving mug 383
shawl 337
shawl collar 362
shear 641
sheath 79, 841, 905, 907, 908
sheath dress 356
sheath of Schwann 168
sheath skirt 357
sheathing 252, 253
shed 244, 322
shed stick 461
sheep 128
sheep shelter 182
sheepshank 908
sheepskin jacket 353
sheer curtain 282
sheet 426, 603, 877
sheet bend 908
sheet film 481
sheet lead 835
sheet, baking 232
shekel, new 728
shelf 279, 291, 321
shelf channel 291
shell 84, 104, 105, 106, 117, 389, 448, 655, 884
shell membrane 117
shelter 543
Shield 10
shield 748
shield bug 101
shield divisions 740
shift key 514, 528
shift lock key 528
shift: level 2 select 514
shifter 579, 580
Shiism 736
shiitake mushroom 183
shin boot 853, 857, 858
shin guard 801, 802, 882, 887
shinai 847
shingle 299
Shinto 736
ship 41
ship's anchor 610
Ship's Keel 11
ship's motor boat 762
Ship's Sails 11
Ship's Stern 11
ships 604
ships, ancient 598
ships, traditional 599
shirred heading 283
shirt 349, 368, 791, 810
shirt collar 362
shirt sleeve 361
shirttail 349, 359
shirtwaist dress 356
shock absorber 18, 553, 876
shock wave 651, 653

shoe 483, 801, 810, 865, 870, 872
shoe polish 345
shoe polisher 345
shoe rack 345
shoe store 715
shoe, parts 342
shoebrush 345
shoehorn 345
shoelace 342, 370
shoes 342
shoes, accessories 345
shoeshine kit 345
shoetree 345
shoot 77, 87
shooter 860
shooting line 859
shooting place 893
shooting positions 861, 893
shooting range 788, 859, 860, 893
shooting slip 893
shooting star 53
shooting station 860
shop 406
shop, jewellery 714
shopping bag 388
shopping carts 181
shopping center 709, 714
shopping centre 709, 714
shopping street 710
shore 49
shore cliff 51
shorelines, examples 51
short bone 157
short extensor of toes 150
short glove 346
short line 818, 819
short palmar 150
short peroneal 151
short radial extensor of wrist 151
short service line 817
short sleeve 337
short sock 365
short splice 908
short track 883
short track skate 883
shortening 209
shorts 358, 369, 471, 791, 801, 802, 805, 810, 870
shortstop 794
shot 753, 793
shot put 790
shotgun 860
shotgun (smooth-bore) 912
shotgun shooting 860
shoulder 124, 130, 146, 148, 156, 311, 440, 538, 822, 909
shoulder bag 388
shoulder belt 555
shoulder blade 147, 149
shoulder bolt 311
shoulder pad 808
shoulder pads 880
shoulder rest 757
shoulder strap 367, 388, 391, 527, 770, 869, 906
shovel 257, 326, 888, 892
show ring 855
show-jumping 852
shower 251, 724, 726, 780
shower and tub fixture 262
shower head 264
shower stall 264
shredding 71
shrew 121
shrimp 218
shroud 602, 834
shunt 687
shutoff switch 263
shutoff valve 262, 265, 270, 271
shutter 249, 521, 675
shutter release button 476
shutter speed setting 479
shutting stile 247
shuttle 461
shuttlecock, synthetic 817
Siamese 133
sickle 330
side 227, 431, 602, 632
side back vent 348
side chair 277
side chapel 410
side compression strap 906
side door 594
side fairings 873
side footboard 586
side handle 307, 308
side handrail 594
side hatch 22
side judge 807
side ladder 587
side lane 539
side marker light 554, 570, 571
side mirror 381
side panel 352
side post 253
side rail 321, 571
side referee 846
side span 540
side vent 44, 567
side view 798
side wall 127, 597, 635

side-marker light 554
side-tilt lock 482
side-wheeler 599
sideboard 279
sideline 800, 806, 809, 810, 812, 814, 815, 858, 864
sidewalk 245, 712
sidewall 571, 818, 819, 831
sidewall line 819
Sierra Leone 745
sieve 231
sifter 232
sight 177, 756, 859, 907, 913
sighting line 907
sighting mirror 907
sigmoid colon 164
signal ahead 545, 547
signal background plate 591
signal box 583
signal gantry 583
signal lamp 238, 239, 240, 241, 288, 290, 294, 465
signal lights 859
signature 426
signature book 531
signet ring 376
silencer 553, 649
silicon 682
silique, section 84
silk 85
silk glands 103
sill 44, 253
sill of frame 249
sill plate 252, 253
sill step 587
silos 596
Silurian 92
silver 683
silverware 227, 717, 722
sima 404
simple eye 97, 99
simple leaves 79
simple organisms 94
simple spacing 472
simple-span beam bridge 541
simultaneous interpretation booth 718
Singapore 747
single bed 724
single chain wheel 871
single curtain rod 284
single pole breaker 272
single quotation marks 473
single reed 446
single room 724
single scull 839
single seat 594
single sprocket 871
single zero 919
single-bladed paddle 837, 838
single-breasted jacket 348
single-burner camp stove 903
single-decked pallet 632
single-handle kitchen faucet 270
single-leaf bascule bridge 542
single-lens reflex (SLR) camera 480
single-lens reflex camera 476
singles luge 884
singles service court 817
singles sideline 817, 821
singlet 843, 850
sinister 740
sinister base 740
sinister chief 740
sinister flank 740
sink 224, 262, 264, 270, 722, 724, 780
sink with waste disposal unit 270
sinker 615, 911
sinkhole 47
Sino-Tibetan languages 468
sinus 336
siphon 267
siphonal canal 105
sister 785
sisters-in-law 785
sistrum 449
site plan 245
sitting room 250
sixte 849
sixteenth note 435
sixteenth rest 435
sixth 434
sixty-fourth note 435
sixty-fourth rest 435
skate 218, 878
skateboard 894
skateboarder 894
skateboarding 894
skater 895
skater: long track 882
skater: short track 882
skating kick 892
skating step 892
skeg 836, 840
skeleton 152, 885
skeleton of a bat 141
skeleton of a bird 116
skeleton of a dog 131
skeleton of a dolphin 136
skeleton of a frog 111
skeleton of a gorilla 138
skeleton of a kangaroo 142

skeleton of a mole 121
skeleton of a rat 122
skeleton of a venomous snake: head 112
skeleton, horse 126
skerry 51
ski 876, 888
ski area 886
ski boot 888, 889
ski glove 888
ski goggles 888
ski hat 892
ski jump 891
ski jumper 891
ski jumping 891
ski jumping boot 891
ski jumping suit 891
ski lift arrival area 886
ski pants 358
ski pole 888, 892
ski rack 558
ski resort 886
ski school 886
ski suit 888, 892
ski tip 892
ski, giant slalom 888
ski, jumping 891
skid 631
skiers' lodge 886
skimmer 233, 246
skin 81, 82, 83, 168, 172
skin surface 172
skip 650, 877
skipping-rope 850
skirt 355, 417, 749, 822, 855
skirt finger 605
skirt marker 454
skirting outlet 258
skirts, examples 357
skis, examples 840, 888
skull 106, 109, 116, 121, 126, 136, 138, 141, 142, 146, 749
skull, lateral view 158
skullcap 340
skunk 134
sky coverage 55, 56
sky diver 896
sky diving 896
sky radiation, measure 58
skylight 245, 251
slab 300
slab building 465
slalom ski 840, 888
slash 473
slash, double 524
slat 281, 285, 459
slat tilt device 285
Slavic languages 469
sled 329, 884, 885
sledder 885
sledge 885
sleeper 591
sleeper-cab 570
sleepers 369
sleeping bags, examples 904
sleeping car 584
sleeping compartment 584
sleepsuit 369
sleet 57, 64
sleeve 337, 348, 848, 851
sleeve strap 352
sleeve strap loop 352
sleeveless jersey 850
sleeves, examples 360
sleigh bells 449
slender 151
slide 294, 453, 483, 754
slide chair 590
slide mount 483
slide plate 452, 453
slide projector 483
slide tray 483
slide-bar 456
slider 445, 896
sliding block 595
sliding breech 756
sliding channel 587
sliding cheek bit 854
sliding cover 506, 612
sliding door 264, 416
sliding folding door 416
sliding folding window 415
sliding jaw 700
sliding lever 555
sliding rail 555, 835
sliding seat 838, 851
sliding sunroof 551
sliding weight 436, 698
sliding window 415
slightly covered sky 56
sling back shoe 343
slip 366
slip joint 310
slip joint pliers 310
slip presenter 548
slip-on 344
slip-on pyjamas 369
slip-stitched seam 349
slipover 354
slippery road 545, 547
slit 463
slope 538

sloped turret 415
sloping cornice 403
slot 227, 238, 302, 386, 424
slot machine 920
slotted box 535
Slovak 469
Slovakia 744
Slovene 469
Slovenia 744
slow-burning stove 256
slow-motion button 495
slower traffic 539
SLR camera 476
small blade 905
small capital 472
small carton 223
small crate 222
small decanter 225
small domestic appliances 717
small hand cultivator 325
small intestine 110, 113, 116, 125, 164
small open crate 222
small saucepan 235
smaller round 151
smash 821
smell 174
smelt 219
smilodon 93
smock 359
smog 69
smoke 57
smoke baffle 256
smoke bomb discharger 758
smoke detector 767
smoke shop 714
smoked ham 215
smoking accessories 390
smoking candle 422
smoking-apparatus 422
smooth hound 218
snack bar 427
snaffle bit 854
snaffle rein 854
snaffle strap 854
snail 104, 217
snail dish 233
snail tongs 233
snail, anatomy 104
snail, morphology 104
snake 112
snap 453, 911
snap fastener 346, 353
snap shackle 835
snap-fastening front 369
snap-fastening tab 353
snap-fastening waist 368
snare 448, 913
snare drum 437, 448
snare head 433, 448
snare strainer 448
snatch 850
snelled fishhook 911
snooker 863
snorkel 841
snout 108, 110, 121, 143
snow 64
snow brush 558
snow crystals 64
snow gauge 58, 59
snow guard 876
snow pellet 64
snow shower 57
snow-grooming machine 886
snowblower 573
snowboard 887
snowboard, alpine 887
snowboard, freestyle 887
snowboarder 887
snowboarding 887
snowfall, measure 59
snowmobile 876
snowshoe 893
snowshoe, elliptical 893
snowshoes 893
snowsuit 369
soap dish 264
soba noodles 207
soccer 802
soccer ball 802
soccer player 802
soccer shoe 802
soccer table 920
social services 781
social worker's office 779
society 708
sock 365, 802, 805, 808, 822
socket 275, 453
socket bayonet 751
socket head 302
socket set 311
socket tester 316
socket-contact 274
socks 351
soda fountain 723
sodium 682
sofa 276
sofa bed 280
soft binding 887
soft cheeses 211
soft contact lens 384
soft palate 174, 175

976

ENGLISH INDEX

ASTRONOMY > 2-25; EARTH > 26-71; VEGETABLE KINGDOM >72-89; ANIMAL KINGDOM > 90-143; HUMAN BEING > 144-177; FOOD AND KITCHEN > 178-241; HOUSE > 242-295; DO-IT-YOURSELF AND GARDENING > 296-333; CLOTHING > 334-371; PERSONAL ADORNMENT AND ARTICLES > 372-391; ARTS AND ARCHITECTURE > 392-465; COMMUNICATIONS AND OFFICE AUTOMATION > 466-535; TRANSPORT AND MACHINERY > 536-643; ENERGY > 644-677; SCIENCE > 678-705; SOCIETY > 706-785; SPORTS AND GAMES > 786-920

soft pastel 396
soft pedal 442, 451
soft ray 108
soft shell clam 217
soft-drink dispenser 548
softball 797
softball bat 797
softball glove 797
soil 70, 661
soil fertilization 69
soil profile 78
soiled utility room 778, 780
solar array 40, 60, 486
solar array drive 60
solar cell 529, 672, 673
solar collector 672, 675
solar eclipse 6
solar energy 78, 672
solar energy, production of electricity 674
solar furnace 674
solar house 675
solar panel 17, 18
solar radiation 67, 68, 672, 673, 674, 675
solar ray reflected 674
solar reflectors 486
solar shield 20
solar system 4
solar-cell panel 673
solar-cell system 673
solder 318
soldering gun 318
soldering iron 318
soldering tools 318
soldering torch 314, 319
sole 127, 221, 309, 351, 868, 881, 889
soleplate 288, 590
soleus 150
solid 680, 681
solid booster stage 24
solid brick 298
solid center auger bit 306
solid line 538
solid rear wheel 871
solid rocket booster 22, 24
solid rubber tire 633
solid rubber tyre 633
solid shot 752
solids 705
solitaire ring 376
Solomon Islands 747
solvent extraction unit 656
Somalia 745
somen noodles 207
son 784, 785
son-in-law 784
sonar 41
sorghum 85
sorghum: panicle 85
sorting machine 475
sorting plant 71
sorus 76
sou'wester 341
soufflé dish 232
sound alarm 613
sound box 433, 440
sound console 488, 489
sound control room 489, 490
sound desk 490
sound engineer 429
sound field control 497
sound hole 439
sound library 733
sound mode lights 497
sound mode selector 497
sound monitor 489, 490, 491
sound monitoring selector 491
sound receiver 776
sound recording equipment 429
sound reproducing system 497
sound signal 436
sound system 556
sound systems, portable 503
sound technician 489, 490
sound/video preview unit 491
soundboard 432, 433, 439, 440, 442
sounder 60
sounding balloon 54, 59
soup 722
soup bowl 226
soup spoon 228
soup tureen 226
sour cream 210
South 37, 616, 917
South Africa 746
South America 28, 31, 50
South American Plate 43
South cardinal mark 617
South celestial pole 13
South China Sea 28, 33
South Pole 35
south pole 687
South Pole 29
South-Southeast 37
South-Southwest 37
Southeast 37, 616
Southeast Indian Ridge 50
Southern Cross 11
Southern Crown 10
Southern Fish 10
Southern hemisphere 35
Southern Triangle 10

Southwest 37, 616
Southwest Indian Ridge 50
southwester 341
soy sauce 200
soybean sprouts 191
soybeans 191
space 434, 514, 915
space bar 514, 528
space launcher 24, 25
space launchers, examples 24
space probe 18, 53
space probes, examples 19
space shuttle 22, 53
space shuttle at takeoff 22
space telescope 17, 53
spacelab 23
spacer 667, 783
spacesuit 20
spacing 472
spade 326, 756, 914
spade bit 306
spading fork 326
spadix 81
spaghetti 206
spaghetti squash 189
spaghetti tongs 233
spaghettini 206
Spain 743
spandrel 413
Spanish 469
spanker 603
spar 624
spar buoy 617
spare tire 567
spareribs 215
spark 564
spark plug 332, 562, 565, 566
spark plug body 562
spark plug cable 552, 566
spark plug gap 562
spark plug gasket 562
spark plug seat 562
spark plug terminal 562
sparking plug 332
sparkling wine glass 225
sparrow 118
spatial dendrite 64
spatula 233, 397, 421
spatulate 79
speaker 427, 496, 504, 505, 508, 513, 526, 626, 828
speaker cover 502
spear 185, 748
spear-nosed bat 141
speargun 841
special effects buttons 496
special effects selection dial 496
special mark 617
special slalom 889
species, origin and evolution 92
specific operations 529
specimen chamber 694
specimen collection center waiting room 781
specimen collection centre waiting room 781
specimen collection room 781
specimen positioning control 694
spectrometer 694
speed control 236, 332
speed controller 452
speed governor 417
speed grand prix motorcycle 874
speed grand prix rider 874
speed selector 236, 237, 500
speed selector switch 305, 306, 382
speed skate, in-line 895
speed skates 883
speed skating 882
speed ski 891
speed skier 891
speed skiing 891
speed skiing suit 891
speed track 891
speed-increasing gearbox 677
speedbrake lever 626
speedometer 557, 576, 851
spelling corrector 528
spelt wheat 203
spencer 358
spent fuel discharge bay 668
spent fuel port 666
spent fuel storage bay 666, 667, 669
sperm whale 137
spermatheca 104
spermatozoon 169
spermoviduct 104
sphenoid bone 158
sphenoidal fontanelle 158
sphenoidal sinus 175
sphere 705
sphere support 58
sphincter muscle of anus 164
spices 198
spicules 6
spider 103
spider web 103
spider, anatomy 103
spider, morphology 103
spike 81, 590, 791, 813, 901
spike file 534
spiked shoe 796
spillway 657

spillway chute 657
spillway gate 657
spinach 187
spinach tagliatelle 206
spinal column 109, 152, 167
spinal cord 109, 110, 167, 168
spinal cord, structure 167
spinal ganglion 167, 168
spinal nerve 167, 168
spindle 237, 248, 268, 277, 500, 697, 700
spindle lock button 308
spine 95, 121, 426, 875
spine of scapula 153
spine of the book 425
spinnaker, lowering 833
spinnaker, raising 833
spinner 911
spinneret 103
spinning rod 910
spinous process 168
spiny lobster 218
spiny ray 108
spiracle 96, 97
spiral 302, 500
spiral arm 9
spiral beater 236
spiral binder 533
spiral case 659
spiral cloud band 63
spiral nail 301
spiral rib 105
spiral screwdriver 302
spiral staircase 655
spiral thread 103
spiral-in groove 500
spire 411
spirit level 313
spirulina 183
spit 51
splash plate 655
splat 276
splay 411
spleen 109, 110, 113, 125, 161
splenius muscle of head 151
spline 562
splints 777
split bet 919
split link 911
split peas 190
spoiler 574, 624
spoke 579
spoked wheel 857
sponge 95, 752
sponge, anatomy 95
sponge-tipped applicator 378
spongocoel 95
spongy bone 154
sponson 876
spool 458, 909, 910
spool axle 910
spool pin 452
spool rack 462
spool-release mechanism 910
spoon 227, 905
spoon blade 401
spoons, examples 228
spores 76
sport-utility vehicle 549
sporting goods store 715
sports 788
sports car 549
sports complex 709, 788
sports facilities 788
sports hall 788
sports on wheels 894
sports, combat 842
sports, equestrian 852
sportswear 370
spot 287
spotlight 428, 492, 765, 766
spotlights 431
spotmeter 479
spout 240, 241, 268, 642
spout assembly 270
spray 288
spray arm 294
spray button 288
spray control 288
spray head 270
spray hose 264, 270
spray nozzle 329, 655
spray paint gun 320
spray skirt 837
sprayer 329
spread collar 349
spreader 324, 391
spreader adjustment screw 320
spring 43, 48, 54, 249, 268, 286, 292, 310, 470, 586, 757, 823, 913
spring balance 699
spring binder 532
spring housing 284
spring linkage 920
spring onion 184
spring washer 310
spring wing 302
spring-metal insulation 299
springboard 826
springboard, 1 m 828
springboard, 3 m 828
springer 413

sprinkler hose 328
sprinklers 665
sprinters' line 871
spritsail 601
sprocket 876
sprocket wheel 758
spruce 89
spur 45, 98, 306, 448
spur gear 686
squall 57
squamous suture 158
square 426, 705, 917
square bet 919
square brackets 473
square flag 739
square head plug 269
square knot 908
square movement 916
square neck 363
square root key 529
square root of 703
square sail 601
square trowel 315
square-headed tip 302
squash 188, 819
squash balls 819
squash racket 819
squid 217
squirrel 123
Sri Lanka 747
stabilizer 760, 859, 896, 897
stabilizer fin 608
stabilizer jack 567
stabilizing fin 25
stabilizing shaft 633
stable 856
stack 51, 604, 646
stacking chairs 277
stadium 709, 788
staff 434, 739
staff cloakroom 720, 768, 781
staff entrance 720, 726, 735, 768
staff lounge 731, 768, 779
staff toilet 768
stage 402, 430, 431, 693, 694
stage clip 693
stage curtain 430, 431
stage-house 430
stained glass 411
stained glass window 737
stair climber 851
stairs 250, 255, 412, 427, 431, 543, 592, 655, 724
stairways 412
stairwell 251
stairwell skylight 251
stake 322, 324, 902, 903
stake loop 902, 903
stake pocket 571
stalactite 47
stalagmite 47
stalk 75, 81, 82, 83, 185
stalk vegetables 185
stamen 80, 82
stamp 390
stamp pad 531
stamp rack 531
stanchion 881
stand 43, 234, 236, 286, 362, 381, 389, 401, 448, 685, 910
stand-off half 804
stand-up collar 363
standard A 436
standard lamp 286
standard lens 478
standard poker hands 914
standardbred pacer 857
standby airspeed indicator 626
standby altimeter 626
standby attitude indicator 626
standing position 861, 893
standing position (Greco-Roman wrestling) 843
standing press 425
standpipe 271
stands 788, 874
stapes 174
staple remover 534
stapler 534
staples 534
star 8
star diagonal 14
star drag wheel 910
star facet 374
star network 522
Star of David 738
star tracker 18
star, main-sequence 8
starboard hand 609, 616, 617
starch 85
starch granule 74
Stardust 19
starfish, anatomy 95
starfish, morphology 95
starling 118
stars, low-mass 8
stars, massive 8
start 512, 852, 887
start area 875
start buoys 838
start button 696

start into a headwind 833
start judge 883
start judges 882
start key 508, 514
start platform 891
start switch 293
start: bobsled and skeleton 885
start: men's singles luge 885
start: women's and doubles luge 885
starter 327, 332, 830, 838
starter button 576
starter handle 331
starter mechanic 873
starting block 791, 830
starting cable 323
starting dive 832
starting gate 856, 875
starting gate, mobile 857
starting grid 872
starting grip (backstroke) 830
starting jetty 838
starting line 791, 833, 872
starting pistol 790
starting positions 828, 843
starting step 255
starting track 891
starting zone 838
state 37
states of matter 680
station chef 721
station circle 55
station entrance 592
station model 55
station name 592
station platform 583
station wagon 549
station, railway 708, 710
station, service 711
station, underground railway 710
stationary bicycle 851
stationary bowl 919
stationary front 56
stationery 528, 717
stationery cabinet 510
stator 249, 659
statue 737
stay 598, 602
stay ring 659
stay vane blade 659
stays 541
staysail-stay 602
steak 214
steak knife 228
stealth aircraft 629
steam 646
steam control knob 241
steam generator 646, 669, 670, 671, 674, 763
steam generator room cooler 669
steam iron 288
steam nozzle 241
steam outlet 670, 671
steam pressure drives turbine 665
steam release pipes 669
steamer 235, 722
steamer basket 235
steel 298, 367, 752
steel bar 825
steel belted radial tire 561
steel cable 913
steel casing 689
steel pen 470
steel safety wheel 595
steel spring 752
steel to plastic 269
steelyard 698
steep hill 545, 547
steeplechase hurdle 790
steeplechase hurdle jump 790
steerable parabolic reflector 16
steering axle 633
steering column 552
steering cylinder 638
steering lever 633
steering oar 598
steering system 553
steering wheel 333, 552, 556, 607, 640, 873
stellar crystal 64
stem 75, 76, 77, 78, 241, 274, 390, 579, 602, 606, 695
stem bulb 609
stem faucet 268
stem holder 268
stem propeller 606
stem washer 268
stempost 598
steno book 531
step 255, 321, 417, 570, 640, 847
step chair 277
step cut 375
step groove 255
step setting 700
step stool 321
stepladder 321
stepladders 321
steppe 61
steps 245, 246, 250, 401, 676
steps in production of electricity 662
stereo camera 481
stereo control 504

ASTRONOMY > 2-25;   EARTH > 26-71;   VEGETABLE KINGDOM >72-89;   ANIMAL KINGDOM > 90-143;   HUMAN BEING > 144-177;   FOOD AND KITCHEN > 178-241;   HOUSE > 242-295;
DO-IT-YOURSELF AND GARDENING > 296-333;   CLOTHING > 334-371;   PERSONAL ADORNMENT AND ARTICLES > 372-391;   ARTS AND ARCHITECTURE > 392-465;   COMMUNICATIONS AND
OFFICE AUTOMATION > 466-535;   TRANSPORT AND MACHINERY > 536-643;   ENERGY > 644-677;   SCIENCE > 678-705;   SOCIETY > 706-785;   SPORTS AND GAMES > 786-920

stereo phase monitor 491
sterile dressing 777
sterile pad 777
sterilization room 780, 781
stern 598, 608, 836
sternal artery 107
sternocleidomastoid 150
sternum 111, 116, 121, 122, 126, 131, 141, 142, 152
stethoscope 776
steward's desk 584
stick 391, 439, 800, 801
stick umbrella 391
stickpin 376
sticks 449
stifle 124
stigma 80, 84
stile 277
stile groove of sash 249
stile tongue of sash 249
stiletto 751
still cameras 480
still video film disc 481
still video film disk 481
still water level 49
stills photographer 429
stilt 464
stilted 413
Stilton 211
stimulator tip 384
sting 98
stipule 79
stirrup 750
stirrup iron 853, 855
stirrup leather 855
stirrup sock 796
stitch 342, 370
stitch control buttons 456
stitch length regulator 452
stitch pattern memory 456
stitch patterns 458
stitch selector 452
stitch width selector 452
stitches 797
stitches, embroidery 459
stitching 346
stock 432, 610, 676, 860, 861, 912
stock pot 235
stockade 408
stocked anchor 610
stocking 365, 367, 848, 878
stocking cap 341
stocking stitch 458
stockless anchor 610
stockroom 716
stola 336
stomach 95, 103, 104, 105, 106, 109, 110, 112, 113, 125, 161, 164
stomach throw 844
stomacher 337
stone 81, 298, 376
Stone Age weapons 748
stone fleshy fruit 81
stone for sacrifice 412
stone fruits 192
stone marten 134
stone wall 298
stone, curling 877
stoner 233
stony meteorites 8
stony-iron meteorite 8
stool 722
stop 130, 453, 458, 512
stop at intersection 544, 546
stop bath 485
stop button 331, 495, 499, 508, 696
stop knob 444, 445
stop rod 445
stop watch 488
stop/clear button 501
stopper 379, 803, 906
stopping area 890
stopping board 864
stopwatch 696
storable propellant upper stage 24
storage 394
storage compartment 483, 567, 570, 766
storage door 291
storage furniture 278, 510
storage rack 723
storage room 769
storage space 584
storage tank 656, 675
storage tray 399, 666
store 710
store room 720, 722
storeroom 509, 734
stork 119
storm collar 257
storm sewer 712
stormy sky 65
stove oil 656
straight 914
straight bet 919
straight blade 401
straight eye 453
straight flush 914
straight jaw 310
straight ladder 321
straight muscle of thigh 150

straight position 828
straight razor 383
straight skirt 357
straight stopcock burette 685
straight wing 630
straight-up ribbed top 351
straightaway 871
straightening iron 381
straightneck squash 189
strainer 237, 240, 902
strainer body 270
strainer coupling 270
strait 38
Strait of Gibraltar 32
strand 908
strap 377, 696, 765, 797, 824, 841, 850
strap eyelet 477
strap loop 906
strap system 441
strap wrench 315
strapless bra 367
stratocumulus 56, 62
stratopause 53
stratosphere 53
stratum basale 172
stratum corneum 172
stratum granulosum 172
stratum lucidum 172
stratum spinosum 172
stratus 56, 62
straw 223
straw bales 875
straw spreader 643
strawberry 192
strawberry, section 83
streamer 739
street 39, 711, 713
street bet 919
street light 712
street sweeper 573
streetcar 595
strength sports 850
stretch-limousine 549
stretcher 278, 775, 776
stretcher area 778
strike plate 249
striker 318, 757, 803
striker wheel 391
striking circle 800
string 439, 440, 443
stringed instruments 439
stringer 632
stringing 816, 822
strings 433, 442
strip 416
strip door 416
strip flooring with alternate joints 254
strip light 287
strip mine 647
strobe 611
strobe light 775
stroke judge 830
strokes 820
strokes, types 832
stromatolite 92
Strong Man 13
strongbox 920
strontium 682
structure 249
structure of a fern 76
structure of a flower 80
structure of a house 250
structure of a leaf 79
structure of a lichen 74
structure of a long bone 154
structure of a missile 759
structure of a moss 75
structure of a mushroom 76
structure of a plant 77
structure of a tree 87
structure of an alga 75
structure of the biosphere 66
structure of the ear 174
structure of the Earth 42
structure of the spinal cord 167
structure of the Sun 6
strut 253, 448, 609, 629, 676
stud 252, 371, 798
studded tire 560
studded tyre 560
student 734
student's desk 734
students' lockers 735
students' room 735
studio 488
studio floor 490, 492
studio, radio 488
studio, television 490, 492
study 251
stummel 390
stump 87, 799
sturgeon 218
style 80, 81, 82, 83, 84
stylobate 403, 404
styloid process 158
stylus 470, 517, 527
stylus cartridge 500
stylus holder 517
sub-base 58
subarctic 61

subbase 538
subclavian artery 160
subclavian vein 160
subcutaneous tissue 172
subduction 43
subfloor 252, 253, 254
subgrade 538
subhead 471
sublimation 680
submachine gun 754
submarine cable 487
submarine canyon 49
submarine line 524
submarine pipeline 654
submarine, nuclear 763
subsidiary track 583
subsiding cold air 63
subsoil 78
substation 664
substitute's bench 803
substructure 651
subterranean stream 47
subtract from memory 529
subtract key 529
subtractive color synthesis 690
suburb 709
suburban commuter railroad 583
suburban commuter railway 583
suburbs 39
subway 583, 592, 713
subway map 593, 594
subway station 592, 710
subway train 592, 594
subwoofers 493
sucker 86, 106
suction hose 766
Sudan 745
sudoriferous duct 172
sugar 209
sugar bowl 226
suit 355
suit tiles 917
suitcase 389
sulcus terminalis 176
sulfur 683
sulfur dioxide emission 70
sulfuric acid emission 70
sulky 857
sum 703
sumac 199
sumi-e brush 397
summer 54
summer solstice 54
summer squash 188
summit 45, 886
summit lodge 886
sumo 847
sumotori 847
sump 263, 566, 650
sump gasket 566
Sun 4, 6, 7, 54
sun deck 607
sun roof 551
sun sensor 40
sun sensor 60
sun visor 556, 558, 567
Sun, structure 6
sundae spoon 228
sundeck 609
sundial 696
sundress 356
sunflower 80
sunflower-seed oil 209
sunglasses 385
Sunnism 736
sunshine card 58
sunshine recorder 58
sunshine, measure 58
sunspot 6
super 100
super giant slalom 889
Super-G ski 888
super-G slalom 889
supercooling 680
supercross circuit 875
supercross motorcycle 875
superficial peroneal nerve 166
supergiant 8
superintendent's office 394
superior 472
superior cymbal 448
superior dental arch 174
superior mesenteric artery 160, 165
superior mesenteric vein 160
superior nasal concha 175
superior rectus muscle 177
superior semicircular canal 174
superior umbilicus 115
superior vena cava 160, 161, 162
supermarket 180, 711, 715
supernova 8
supersonic jet 53
supersonic jetliner 629
superstructure 615
supervisor's office 735
supplement, colour 471
supply duct 260
supply line 262
supply of water 662
supply point 273, 663

supply room 780
supply tube 270
support 15, 59, 274, 277, 284, 461
support structure 16, 40
support thread 103
supports 400
suprarenal gland 165
sural nerve 166
surcingle 853, 855, 857
surcoat 337
surface cold front 56
surface course 538
surface element 290
surface insulation 22
surface of the water 828
surface pipe 652
surface prospecting 651
surface runoff 67
surface surveillance radar 761, 762
surface warm front 56
surface water drain 712
surface-piercing foils 609
surface-to-air missile 759
surface-to-subsurface missile 759, 762
surfboard 840
surfer 840
surfing 840
surge protection receptacle 520
surge protection receptacles 520
surgeon's sink 781
surgeons, veterinary 852
Suriname 742
surround loudspeaker 493
surveillance camera 395
suspended span 540
suspender 367, 540
suspender belt 367
suspender clip 350
suspenders 350
suspension 594
suspension arm 292, 553
suspension band 772
suspension bogie 585
suspension bridge 540
suspension cable 540
suspension file 532
suspension insulator string 663
suspension line 896, 897
suspension spring 697
suspension system 553
suspension truck 585
suspensory ligament 177
suture 84, 105
Swahili 468
swallow 118
swallow hole 47
swallowtail 739
swallowtail and tongue 739
Swan 12
Swaziland 746
sweat pants 370
sweat shirt 370
sweater vest 354
sweaters 354, 358
swede 189
Sweden 744
Swedish 469
sweep boats 839
sweep oar 838
sweeper 803
sweeper, street 573
sweeping hip throw 844
sweet bay 202
sweet peas 190
sweet pepper 188
sweet potato 184
sweetbreads 212
sweetcorn 85
sweetheart neckline 363
swell organ manual 444
swell pedals 444
swept-back wing 630
swift 118, 462
swim times 831
swimmer's country 831
swimmer's name 831
swimming 830
swimming goggles 830
swimming pool 608, 788, 827, 831
swimming pool, above ground 246
swimming pool, in-ground 246
swimming stadium 788
swimming trunks 371
swimsuit 371, 830
swimsuits 716
swing bridge 542
Swiss Army knife 905
Swiss chard 185
switch 274, 291, 305, 307, 308, 320, 523, 583, 687
switch lock 306
switch plate 274
switch point 590
switch rod 590
switch signal 590
switch stand 590
switch tower 583
switched outlet 497
Switzerland 744
swivel 651, 793, 911, 913

swivel base 312
swivel cord 381
swivel flex 381
swivel head 312
swivel lock 312
swivel wall lamp 287
swivel-tilter armchair 511
swiveling nozzle 628
Swordfish 11
swordfish 219
symbol 682, 920
symbols 914
symbols, common 725
symbols, dangerous materials 774
symbols, fabric care 347
symbols, protection 774
sympathetic ganglion 167
symphony orchestra 437
symphysis pubis 169, 170
synagogue 738
synapse 168
sync cable 527
synchronized diving 829
synovial joints, types 156
synsacrum 116
synthesizer 450
synthetic shuttlecock 817
synthetic sponge 378
synthetic surface 822
Syrian Arab Republic 746
syringe 776
syringe for irrigation 776
system buttons 450
system of units 702
system support 509
system, fuel supply 553
systems display 626

T

T-bar 886
T-connector 522
T-shirt dress 369
T-strap shoe 343
T-tail unit 629
tab 352, 386, 391, 453, 532, 855
tab setting 528
Tabasco® sauce 200
tabernacle 737
table 278, 304, 305, 307, 374, 424, 723, 815, 862
table cut 375
table extension 305
table lamp 286
table mixer 236
Table Mountain 10
table of elements 682
table of results 828
table salt 201
table saw 305
table tennis 815
table tennis ball 815
table tennis bat 815
table tennis paddle 815
table-locking clamp 307
tables, examples 278
tablespoon 228
tablet 783
tablinum 406
tabloid 471
tabulation key 514
tabulation left 514
tabulation right 514
tabulator 528
tachometer 557, 576
tack 301, 836
tacking 833
tackle box 911
tackless strip 254
tactical transport helicopter 631
tadpole 111
tag 342, 370
Tagalog 469
tagliatelle 206
tahini 200
Tahitian 469
tail 107, 112, 113, 121, 122, 124, 130, 133, 136, 140, 143, 169, 425, 625, 840, 887, 888, 892, 893, 894, 898, 909
tail assembly 625
tail boom 631
tail comb 380
tail edge 426
tail feather 115
tail of helix 173
tail pipe 553
tail pole 676
tail shapes, examples 629
tail skid 631
tail stop 312
tail-out groove 500
tailback 807
taillight 554, 571, 575, 576, 640
taillights 554, 775
tailored collar 355, 362
tailored sleeve 361
tailpiece 270, 433, 439
tailplane 625, 631, 760, 898
tailrace 658

ASTRONOMY > 2-25; EARTH > 26-71; VEGETABLE KINGDOM >72-89; ANIMAL KINGDOM > 90-143; HUMAN BEING > 144-177; FOOD AND KITCHEN > 178-241; HOUSE > 242-295; DO-IT-YOURSELF AND GARDENING > 296-333; CLOTHING > 334-371; PERSONAL ADORNMENT AND ARTICLES > 372-391; ARTS AND ARCHITECTURE > 392-465; COMMUNICATIONS AND OFFICE AUTOMATION > 466-535; TRANSPORT AND MACHINERY > 536-643; ENERGY > 644-677; SCIENCE > 678-705; SOCIETY > 706-785; SPORTS AND GAMES > 786-920

Tajikistan 746
tajine 234
take-off 891
take-off board 793
take-off table 891
take-up handle 460
take-up reel 499
take-up spool 476
takeover zone 790
talk key 506
talking drum 433
tall tumbler 225
Talmud 736
talon 117
talus 153, 155
tamarillo 196
tamarin 139
tamarind paste 200
tambourine 449
tamper 241, 390
tandem bicycle 581
tandem disc harrow 641
tandem tractor trailer 570
tang 227, 229, 309, 315
Tanganyika, Lake 34
tank 23, 263, 266, 484, 485, 607, 758, 767, 903
tank ball 265
tank body 572, 573
tank car 588
tank farm 654
tank gauge float 655
tank hatch 607
tank lid 265
tank sprayer 328
tank top 369, 371
tank trailer 572
tank truck 573
tank, fuel 553, 563, 577
tanker 596, 606, 760
tanks 655
tantalum 683
Tanzania 745
tap 264
tap connector 328
tape 313, 453, 459, 757, 800
tape counter 499
tape dispenser 534
tape guide 534
tape lock 313
tape measure 313, 454
tape recorder select button 497
tape selector 499
tape-guide 499
taper 422
tapered end 839
tapered wing 630
tapestry bobbin 461
taproot 87
tar paper 299
tarantula 102
tare 847
target 40, 41, 859, 861, 893
target area 674
target areas 848
target detection radar 762
tarlatan 422
taro 184
tarragon 202
tarsometatarsus 116
tarsus 96, 98, 111, 115, 122, 126, 131, 138, 141, 142, 155, 156
Tasman Sea 29
Tasmania 29
Tasmanian devil 143
tassel 282, 285
tasset 749
taste 174
taste bud 176
taste receptors 176
tasting spoon 233
tatami 846
taxi rank 725
taxi transportation 725
taxiway 618
taxiway line 619
tea 208
tea bag 208
tea ball 233
tea infuser 233
teacher 734
teacher's desk 734
teachers' room 735
team bench 827
team handicap 858
team name 858
team shirt 796, 801, 802, 808
team's emblem 878
teapot 226
tear tape 390
tear-off calendar 530
teaser comb 380
teaspoon 228
technetium 683
technical delegates 881
technical equipment compartment 489
technical events 889
technical identification band 501
technical producer 489, 490
technical producer monitor 491

technical room 543
technical services 732
technical specifications 560
techniques 812
tectonic lake 48
tectonic plates 43
teddy 366
tee 269, 271, 867, 877
tee line 877
tee-off stroke 866
teeing ground 866, 867
teeth 159, 309
Teflon tape 314
tele-converter 478
telecommunication antenna 608, 609, 762
telecommunication satellite 525
telecommunication satellites 486
telecommunication terminal 507
telecommunications by satellite 487
telemetry and command antenna 60
telephone 491, 724, 725
telephone answering machine 508
telephone cable 712
telephone index 506, 531
telephone line 524
telephone network 487
telephone set 489, 506
telephone surge protection jacks 520
telephone, communication 506
telephone/cable/satellite line 523
telephones, examples 507
telephoto lens 478
teleport 487
teleprompter 492
Telescope 10
telescope 17, 612, 701, 859
telescope base 17
telescopic boom 634, 766
telescopic corridor 619
telescopic front fork 574, 577
telescopic leg 776
telescopic measure 864
telescopic rod 920
telescopic sight 692, 912
telescopic umbrella 391
telescoping antenna 503
telescoping leg 482
telescoping uncoupling rod 587
television 489
television program schedule 471
television set 494, 724, 734
telltale 834
tellurium 682
telson 107
temperate forest 66
temperature 261
temperature control 238, 261, 267, 288, 291
temperature control knob 465
temperature indicator 557
temperature of dew point 55
temperature scale 53
temperature selector 238, 292, 293
temperature sensor 18, 561
temperature, measure 59, 695
temple 146, 385, 424, 461
Temple of Huitzilopochtli 412
Temple of Tlaloc 412
tempo control 451
tempo scale 436
temporal bone 152, 158
temporary exhibition rooms 395
ten 703
Ten Commandments 738
tenaille 409
tenderloin roast 214
tendon 133
tendon guard 880
tendril 86
tennis 820
tennis ball 822
tennis courts 788
tennis player 822
tennis racket 822
tennis shoe 344, 822
tenon saw 424
tenor drum 448
tenpin 865
tension adjusting screw 534
tension adjustment 910
tension block 452, 453, 457
tension dial 453, 456, 457
tension disc 453, 457
tension disk 453, 457
tension guide 457
tension pulley wheel 284
tension rod 448
tension rope 433
tension screw 448
tension spring 453, 457, 557, 850
tensor of fascia lata 150
tent trailer 567
tentacle 104, 106
tents, examples 902
tepee 418
terbium 684
teres major 151
teres minor 151
terminal 272, 274, 290, 654, 663
terminal arborization 168

terminal box 673
terminal bronchiole 163
terminal bud 77
terminal descent engine 18
terminal filament 167
terminal lobe 86
terminal moraine 46
terminator 522
tern 118
terreplein 409
terrestrial sphere 13
terrine 234
tertial 115
Tertiary 93
tertiary colors 400
tertiary consumers 67
test button 767
test pattern 492
test tube 685
Test US 999
test-lamp 316
tester screwdriver 316
testicle 169
testis 107, 110
Tethys 5
text 528
text display 528
textile floor coverings 254
Thai 468
Thailand 747
thallium 682
thallus 74, 75
theater 430, 710, 711
theater, Greek 402
theatre 430, 710, 711
theatre, home 493
theodolite 59, 701
thermal energy 646
thermal louver 60
thermal louvre 60
thermodynamic temperature, measurement 702
thermometer 655, 695, 841, 899
thermopause 53
thermosphere 53
thermostat 238, 260, 261, 267
thermostat control 291
thick continuous drizzle 57
thick intermittent drizzle 57
thickness, measure 700
thigh 115, 124, 130, 143, 147, 149, 169, 170
thigh pad 808
thigh-boot 343
thigh-high stocking 365
thimble 454, 700
thinning razor 381
thinning scissors 382
third 434
third base 794
third baseman 794
third dozen (25 to 36) 919
third finger 173
third round: 32 players 789
third row 804
third stage 25
third valve slide 447
third wheel 696, 697
thirty-second note 435
thirty-second rest 435
thong 344
thoracic legs 107
thoracic vertebra 153, 157
thoracic vertebrae 122, 126, 131, 138, 142
thorax 96, 97, 98, 146, 148
thorium 684
thread 268, 302
thread guide 452, 453
thread take-up lever 452
thread trimmer 453
threaded cap 269
threaded rod 311
three-blade propeller 628
three-four time 434
three-hinged arch 541
three-of-a-kind 914
three-pin socket 274
three-quarter coat 352
three-quarter sleeve 360
three-tier car carrier 588
three-toed hoof 127
threshold 247
throat 115, 312, 610, 822, 911
throat lash 854
throat latch 854
throat protector 796, 880, 882
throttle control 516
throttle valve 649
throttles 626
through arch bridge 541
throwing 793
throwing area 788
throwing circle 790, 791
thrust 540, 630
thrust bearing 659
thrust device 470
thrust tube 470
thruster 20, 40
thruster engine 18

thrusting weapons 751
thulium 684
thumb 140, 141, 156, 173, 346, 797
thumb hook 447
thumb piston 444
thumb rest 446, 776
thumb tacks 534
thumbscrew 311
thunderstorm 57
thyme 202
Tibetan 468
tibia 96, 98, 122, 126, 131, 138, 140, 141, 142, 152, 155, 156
tibial nerve 166
tibiofibula 111
tibiotarsus 116
tick 102
ticket clerk 394, 427
ticket collecting booth 592
ticket collector 582
ticket counter 620
ticket office 394, 719
tidal power plant 664
tie 391, 435, 591
tie bar 376
tie closure 391
tie plate 590
tie rod 448
tieback 282
tiepin 376
tier 407
tierce 849
tierceron 410
Tierra del Fuego 31
tiers 402
tiger 135
tight end 807
tight head prop 804
tightener 826
tightening band 59
tightening buckle 906
tightening tools 310
tights 365
tilde 473
tile 22, 299, 403, 406, 412
tiles, honour 917
tiller 327, 750, 834
tilt tube 285
tilt-back head 236
timber 403, 406
time card 530
time clock 530, 858
time code 429
time display/recording button 496
time signatures 434
time, measurement 702
timed outlet 290
timekeeper 810, 814, 842, 845, 846, 847, 848, 881, 900
timekeepers 827, 844, 883
timer 238, 239, 465, 484, 831, 851
timing area 891
timing belt 566
timpani 437
tin 682
tin board 819
tin opener 230, 240, 905
tine 227, 327, 641
tip 79, 185, 227, 301, 302, 304, 315, 318, 319, 350, 391, 792, 793, 813, 840, 863, 888, 893, 897, 909
tip cleaners 318
tip of nose 175
tip protector 776
tip section 909
tip-ring 909, 910
tipper truck 573, 639
tipping lever 783
tips, examples 302
tire 551, 560, 570, 579, 870, 874
tire barrier 872
tire pump 578
tire valve 579
tires, examples 560
tissue holder 264
Titan 5
Titan IV 24
Titania 5
titanium 683
Titicaca, Lake 31
title deed 915
title display button 496
Tlaloc, Temple 412
toad 111
toaster 238
tobacco 390
tobacco hole 390
tobacco pouch 390
Tobago 743
toe 117, 127, 130, 146, 148, 303, 309, 351, 868
toe binding 892
toe box 880
toe clip 127, 578, 580
toe guard 773, 796
toe hole 893
toe loop 881
toe pick 881
toe piston 444
toe strap 840

toe-strap 344
toenail scissors 377
toepiece 840, 889
toeplate 892
toga 336
toggle 739
toggle bolt 302
toggle fastening 353
toggles 854
Togo 745
toilet 250, 251, 262, 264, 265, 584, 724, 728, 731, 735, 780
toilet bowl 265
toilet soap 379
toilet tank 264
toilet truck 622
toilets 395, 715, 719, 723, 733, 779, 781
token 915
tom-tom 448
tomatillo 188
tomato 188
tomato coulis 200
tomato paste 200
tombolo 51
tone arm 500
tone control 441
tone leader generator 488
toner cartridge 519
Tonga 747
Tonga Trench 50
tongs 233
tongue 99, 109, 110, 164, 174, 175, 212, 342, 350, 370, 433, 444, 881, 889
tongue sheath 112
tongue, dorsum 176
tonsil 174
tool 649
tool belt 313
tool box 313
tool holder 308
tool kit 580
tool shelf 321
tool storage area 289
tool tether 20
tools 289
tools for loosening the earth 326
tools, electricity 317
tools, wood carving 401
tooth 108, 112, 303, 304, 331, 382, 453, 636, 638, 642, 643
tooth guard 808
toothbrush 384
toothbrush shaft 384
toothbrush well 384
toothed jaw 310
toothed wheel 686
toothpaste 384
top 87, 278, 321, 602
top bar 824
top box 577
top cap 689
top coat 355
top cylinder 421
top deck 655
top deckboard 632
top edge 426
top face 374
top flap 906
top hat 340
top ladder 766
top lift 342
top of dam 657, 660, 661, 664
top plate 528
top pocket 862
top rail 247, 277, 278, 281
top rail of sash 249
top road 650
top stitched pleat 357
top stitching 350, 368
top-end transverse member 635
top-level domain 524
topaz 375
topmark 615, 616
topping 909
topping lift 602
topsoil 78
toque 341
Torah scrolls 738
toric lens 691
tornado 57, 63
torpedo 763
torpedo room 763
torque adjustment collar 306
torque converter 292
Torres Strait 29
tortellini 206
tortilla 205
torus 404, 405, 705
total 699
total eclipse 6, 7
total sale display 548
tote bag 388
tote board 856
Toucan 11
toucan 119
touch 172
touch judge 805
touch line 803, 805
touch pad 526
touch pad button 526

touch screen 527
Toulouse sausage 216
touring bicycle 581
touring motorcycle 577
touring tire 560
touring tyre 560
tourmaline 375
tournament ball 819
tow bar 567, 622, 642, 840
tow line 840
tow release knob 898
tow safety chain 567
tow tractor 622, 623
tow truck 573
towel bar 264
towel rail 264
tower 410, 540, 614, 635, 674, 676, 677, 858
tower case 513
tower crane 634
tower ladder 766
tower mast 634
tower mill 676
tower silo 182
towing device 573
towing eye 756
towing hitch 567, 640
town houses 419
toy store 714
toys 717
tracery 411
trachea 116, 125, 163
tracing wheel 454
track 284, 399, 582, 592, 595, 636, 709, 790, 871, 872, 874, 876, 883, 885, 891
track cycling 871
track idler 636
track judge 883
track lighting 287
track link 758
track number 501
track roller frame 636
track search buttons 501
track shoe 758, 791
trackball 517
tracker 445
traction batteries 563
tractor 640
tractor engine compartment 638
tractor unit 570
trade name 390
traditional clothing 339
traditional houses 418
traditional jacket 846
traditional musical instruments 432
traditional ships 599
traffic circle 39, 538
traffic lane 539
traffic lights 712
tragus 140, 173
trail 756
trail-view mirror 570
trailer 567
trailer car 594
trailer caravan 567
trailing edge 624, 897, 898
trailing edge flap 624, 760
train indicator 582
trainer 811, 842
training area 788
training ball 819
training set 369
training suit 370
training wall 657
trampoline 823
transaction receipt 731
transaction record slot 730
Transantarctic Mountains 29
transceiver, network access point 522
transceiving dish 486
transceiving parabolic antenna 486
transducer 613
transept 411
transept spire 410
transfer canal 666
transfer dispensing machine 593
transfer of heat to water 665
transfer port 565
transfer ramp 539
transfer scale 479
transform plate boundaries 43
transformation of mechanical work into electricity 662
transformer 287, 658, 663, 668, 674
transit shed 596
transition fittings, examples 269
transition metals 683
transmission 292, 563
transmission cable 613
transmission dish 486
transmission of the rotative movement to the rotor 662
transmission system 553
transmission to consumers 646, 662, 677
transmitted pulse 40
transmitter 506
transmitting tower 486
transparency slide 483
transpiration 67

transport and machinery 538
transport, air 618
transport, maritime 596
transporter bridge 542
transverse bulkhead 606
transverse colon 164
transverse dunes 52
transverse process 157, 168
tranverse 404
tranverse flute 446
trap 262, 265, 269, 270, 430
trap coupling 270
trap machine 860
trapdoor 407
trapeze dress 356
trapezium 154, 156
trapezius 150, 151
trapezoid 154, 705
travel agency 714
travel bag 388
traveler 834, 835
traveler's check 729
traveling block 651
traveling crane 658
traveller 834, 835
travelling block 651
travelling crane 658
traverse arch 410
traverse rod 284
traversing handle 756
trawler 606
tray 261, 279, 281, 313, 320, 323, 389
trays 722
tread 255, 561, 855
tread bar 640
tread design 560, 561
treadle 460
treadle cord 460
treatment plant 649
treatment room 779, 781
treble bridge 442
treble fishhook 911
treble keyboard 432
treble pickup 441
treble register 432
treble ring 918
treble tone control 441, 497, 503
tree 87, 855
tree fern 76
tree frog 111
tree pruner 330
tree, structure 87
tree, trunk 87
trees 866
trefoil 411, 413
trench 49, 647, 860
trench coat 352
triage room 779
trial motorcycle 875
Triangle 12
triangle 437, 449, 705
triangular bandage 777
triangular body 433
triangular fossa 173
Triassic 93
triceps bar 851
triceps of arm 151
triceratops 93
tricorne 339
tricuspid valve 162
trifoliolate 79
trigger 320, 331, 516, 750, 752, 754, 755, 757, 767, 860, 861, 912
trigger guard 754, 860, 861, 912
trigger switch 304, 305, 306, 308
triglyph 404
trilby 340, 341
trill 435
trilobite 92
trim 389
trim panel 554
trim ring 290
trim tab 60
trimaran 835
trimmer 383
trimming 386, 424
trimming tool 464
Trinidad and Tobago 743
trio 438
trip lever 265, 329
trip mileometer 557
trip odometer 557
tripe 212
triple bars 852
triple jump 790, 793, 875
triple jump take-off board 793
triple ring 918
triple tail unit 629
tripod 14, 436, 482, 483, 489
tripod accessories shelf 14
tripod stand 448
tripod tail support 623
triquetral 154
trireme 598
triticale 203
Triton 5
trochanter 96, 98
trolley 542, 634
trolley crank 328
trolley pulley 634

Trombe wall 675
trombone 447
trombones 437
Tropic of Cancer 34, 35, 36
Tropic of Capricorn 34, 35, 36
tropical climates 61
tropical cyclone 63
tropical cyclone names 63
tropical forest 66
tropical fruits 196
tropical rain forest 61, 66
tropical storm 57
tropical wet-and-dry (savanna) 61
tropopause 53, 68
troposphere 53
trot 124
trotter 857
trough 49, 55, 690
trousers 350, 371, 716, 796, 808, 844, 878, 901
trousers, examples of 358
trout 221
trowel 325
truck 586, 595, 894, 895
truck crane 634
truck frame 586
truck tractor 570
truck trailer 570
truck, collection 573
truck, tow 573
trucking 570
trucks, examples 573
truffle 183
trumpet 447, 611
trumpet interchange 538
trumpets 437
trunk 76, 86, 87, 110, 147, 149, 389, 551
trunk hose 338
trunk, cross section 87
trunks 850
trunnion 753
truss structure 21
trussed arch 540
trussing needle 233
tsetse fly 101
tub 292, 294, 322
tub platform 264
tub rim 292
tuba 437, 447
tubas 437
tube 223, 756, 757, 777
tube cutter 314
tube end 269
tube flaring tool 314
tube foot 95
tube retention clip 275
tuber vegetables 184
tubing 654
tubing head 654
tubing valve 654
tubular bells 437, 449
tubular element 290
tubular heater 656
tubular ice screw 901
tubular lock 248
tubular member 652
tubular structure 615
tuck 390
tuck position 828
Tudor 413
tug 606
tulip 80
tumble dry at low temperature 347
tumble dry at medium temperature 347
tuna 220
tundra 66
tuner 498, 504
tungsten 683
tungsten filament 274
tungsten-halogen lamp 274, 275
tunic 359, 748
tunic dress 356
tuning buttons 497
tuning control 498, 503, 504
tuning controls 494
tuning dial 504
tuning fork 436
tuning gauge 448
tuning mode 498
tuning peg 440, 441
tuning pin 442
tuning ring 433
tuning slide 447
tuning wire 444
Tunisia 745
tunnel 592
turban 339, 341
turbine 646, 659, 668
turbine building 668
turbine headcover 659
turbine runner 664
turbine shaft turns generator 665
turbine stop valve 668
turbine-compressor shaft 627
turbined water draining 662
turbo-alternator 674, 763
turbo-alternator unit 646
turbo-charged engine 564
turbo-compressor engine 564
turbofan engine 627
turbojet engine 625, 760

turbot 221
turf 856
Turkey 746
turkey 120, 213
Turkish 469
Turkmenistan 746
turmeric 198
turn 435
turn and bank indicator 898
turn and bank knob 898
turn and slip indicator 898
turn and slip knob 898
turn signal 554, 571, 574, 575, 576
turn signal indicator 557, 576
turn-up 350
turnbuckle 835, 842
turner 233
turning 464
turning handle 307
turning judges 831
turning wall 831, 832
turning wheel 464
turnip 189
turnouts 764
turnouts' cleaning 764
turnstile 592
turntable 236, 488, 500, 542, 638, 639
turntable mounting 766
turpentine 400
turquoise 375
turret 408, 758, 762
turret cap 692
turtle 113
turtle, anatomy 113
turtle, morphology 113
turtleneck 354, 363, 892
Tuvalu 747
TV mode 495
TV power button 495
TV/video button 495
tweeter 10, 502
tweezers 777
twig 77, 87
twill weave 463
twin skis 840
twin-lens reflex camera 480
twin-set 359
Twins 13
twist 306
twist bar 850
twist bit 306
twist drill 306
twist grip throttle 576
twist handle 516
twist lock 572
twisted rope 908
twisted-pair cable 523
two columns split bet 919
two pairs 914
two-blade propeller 628
two-door sedan 549
two-hinged arch 541
two-leaf door 568
two-person bobsled 884
two-person tent 902
two-seater settee 276
two-sided copies 512
two-storey house 419
two-stroke-cycle engine cycle 565
two-toed hoof 127
two-two time 434
two-way collar 352
two-way traffic 544, 546
tympanum 110, 403, 404, 411
type I irregular galaxy 9
type II irregular galaxy 9
type of fuel 548
type of high cloud 55
type of low cloud 55
type of middle cloud 55
type of the air mass 55
type, sans serif 472
type, serif 472
types of bones 157
types of eclipses 6, 7
types of engines 564
types of golf clubs 867
types of movements 916
types of oars 838
types of outlets 258
types of passenger cars 584
types of passenger coach 584
types of registers 258
types of strokes 832
types of synovial joints 156
typewriter 528
typhoon 63
typist's chair 511
typography 472
tyrannosaurus 93
tyre 560, 570, 579, 870
tyre inflator 548
tyre pump 578
tyre valve 579
tyre, all-season 560
tyre, performance 560
tyre, studded 560
tyre, touring 560
tyre, winter 560

U

u quark 680
U-bend 269
U-shaped gouge 421
U.S. habitation module 21
U.S. laboratory 21
udon noodles 207
Uganda 745
UHF antenna 18, 60
Ukraine 744
Ukrainian 469
ulna 116, 121, 122, 126, 131, 136, 138, 141, 142, 152, 154, 156
ulnar extensor of wrist 151
ulnar flexor of wrist 150, 151
ulnar nerve 166
ultrasound waves emission 41
ultraviolet radiation 690
ultraviolet spectrometer 60
Ulysses 19
umbel 81
umbo 105
umbra shadow 6, 7
umbrella 391
umbrella pine 89
umbrella stand 391
Umbriel 5
umlaut 473
umpire 799, 807, 809, 812, 817, 820, 864, 877
unbleached flour 204
uncanceled stamped mail 474
uncle, maternal 785
uncle, paternal 785
under tail covert 115
underarm crutch 782
underarm portfolio 387
underarm rest 782
undergarment 872
underground 407, 713
underground cable network 487
underground chamber 402
underground flow 67
underground map 593, 594
underground mine 650
underground passage 583
underground railway 592
underground railway station 710
underground station 592
underground stem 78
underground train 592, 594
underlay 254
underlining 455
underlying fabrics 455
underpass 540
undershirt 796
underskirt 337
underwater camera 480
underwater light 246
underwear 351, 366
underwire 367
undressing booth 781
uneven parallel bars 824
ungulate mammals 124
ungulate mammals, examples of 128
unicellulars 94
Unicorn 11
uniform 770
uniform resource locator 524
uniforms 764
uninterruptible power supply 520, 523
union 269
union nut 269
union of two sets 703
union suit 351
uniparous cyme 81
unisex headgear 341
unisex shoes 344
unison 434
unit price 699
United Arab Emirates 746
United Kingdom of Great Britain and Northern Ireland 743
United Republic of Tanzania 745
United States of America 742
univalve shell 105
univalve shell, morphology 105
universal step 623
university 710
unleavened bread 205
unloading dock 395, 715, 719, 724
unloading docks 716
unloading tube 643
ununbium 683
ununnilium 683
unununium 683
up and over garage door 416
uphaul 836
upholstery nozzle 289
upper 889
upper blade guard 304
upper bowl 241
upper cheek 854
upper chord 540
upper cold front 56
upper confining bed 646
upper cuff 889
upper deck 569, 624

upper edge 815
upper eyelid 110, 132, 177
upper fore topgallant sail 603
upper fore topsail 603
upper gate 597
upper girdle facet 374
upper heating element 266
upper laboratory 16
upper landing 417
upper lateral lobe 86
upper lateral sinus 86
upper level 597
upper limb 750
upper lip 99, 174, 444
upper lobe 163
upper mandible 115
upper mantle 42
upper rudder 763
upper section 24
upper shell 889, 895
upper strap 889
upper tail covert 115
upper thermostat 266
upper warm front 56
upper wing 628
upper-air sounding 59
upperboard 445
uppercase 472
upperworks 835
upright 246, 424, 425, 460, 461, 782, 792, 825, 826
upright piano 442
upright piano action 443
upright vacuum cleaner 289
UPS 520, 523
upstage 430, 431
upstream blanket 660
upstream face 661
upstream gate 837
upstream shoulder 660
upstream toe 660
Ural Mountains 32
Ural-Altaic languages 469
uranium 684
Uranus 4, 5
urban map 39
Urdu 469
ureter 104, 116, 165
urethra 165, 170
urinary bladder 109, 110, 165, 169, 170
urinary meatus 169
urinary system 165
URL 524
urogenital aperture 109
uropod 107
urostyle 111
Uruguay 742
USB port 513, 526
use chlorine bleach as directed 347
used syringe box 771
usual terms 82, 83
utensils, cooking 722
utensils, kitchen 229
utensils, set 233
uterovesical pouch 170
uterus 170, 171
utility case 388
utility liquids 400
uvula 174, 175
Uzbekistan 746

V

V-neck 348, 354
V-neck cardigan 354
V-shaped gouge 421
V-shaped neck 363
vacuole 74, 94
vacuum bottle 906
vacuum chamber 694
vacuum cleaner, cylinder 289
vacuum cleaner, hand 288
vacuum cleaner, upright 289
vacuum coffee maker 241
vacuum diaphragm 566
vacuum distillation 656
vacuum flask 906
vacuum manifold 694
vacuum system console 694
vagina 103, 104, 170, 171
vair 741
valance 280, 282
valley 45, 48
valve 84, 105, 447
valve casing 447
valve seat 268
valve seat shaft 265
valve seat wrench 314
valve spring 566
vambrace 749
vamp 342, 371
vampire bat 141
van body semitrailer 572
van straight truck 573
vanadium 683
vane 115, 293
vanilla extract 200
vanity cabinet 264
vanity case 389

vanity mirror 556
Vanuatu 747
vapor 681
vaporizer 261
vaporizing grille 261
variable ejector nozzle 629
variable geometry wing 630
variable spacer 528
variation keys 456
variety meat 212
variometer 899
varnish 400
varnish-roller 422
vastus lateralis 150, 151
vastus medialis 150
Vatican City State 744
Vauban fortification 409
vault 410, 731
vaulting horse 824, 825, 826
VCR controls 495
VCR mode 495
VCR power button 495
vector/waveform monitor 491
vegetable bowl 226
vegetable brush 233
vegetable garden 182, 244
vegetable kingdom 74
vegetable sponge 379
vegetables 180, 184
vegetables, bulb 184
vegetables, fruit 188
vegetables, inflorescent 187
vegetables, leaf 186
vegetables, root 189
vegetables, stalk 185
vegetables, tuber 184
vegetation 66
vegetation regions 66
vehicle entrance 769
vehicle equipment bay 24
vehicle rest area 543
veil 909
vein 79
veins 160
velarium 407
Velcro® closure 368
velodrome 788
velum 98
velvet-band choker 374
Venera 19
Venetian blind 285
Venezuela 742
venom canal 112
venom gland 112
venom sac 99
venom-conducting tube 112
venomous snake, anatomy 112
venomous snake, morphology 112
venomous snake, skeleton 112
vent 261, 556, 753
vent brush 380
vent door 571
vent hole 320
vent-tail 749
ventilated rib 860, 912
ventilating circuit 262
ventilating fan 586
ventilating grille 289
ventilation 675
ventilation hood 614
ventilator 594
ventral abdominal artery 107
ventral aorta 109
ventral nerve cord 107
venturi 757
venturi fastening lever 757
Venus 4, 5
verbena 208
vermicelli 207
vermiform appendix 164
vernal equinox 13, 54
vernier 698, 700
vernier caliper 700
vernier scale 612, 700
Versailles parquet 254
vert 741
vertebra 112, 136
vertebrae 111
vertebral body 157, 168
vertebral column 109, 152, 157, 167
vertebral shield 113
vertical control 518
vertical cord lift 288
vertical frame 461
vertical ground movement 43
vertical movement 916
vertical pivoting window 415
vertical pocket 337
vertical pupil 112
vertical section 894
vertical seismograph 43
vertical shaft 650
vertical side band 812
vertical stabilizer 898
vertical take-off and landing aircraft 628
vertical-axis wind turbine 676
very cloudy sky 56
vest 338, 348, 351, 359

vestibular nerve 174
vestibule 174, 406, 584
vestibule door 584
vestigial pelvis 136
veterinarians 852
veterinary surgeons 852
VHF antenna 762
viaduct 541
vial 783
vibrating mudscreen 651
vibrato arm 441
vibrissa 122
vice 312
vice-skip 877
Victoria, Lake 34
video and digital terminals 477
video connection panel 489
video entertainment system 918
video monitor 518
video monitoring selector 491
video port 513, 526
video replay 789
video switcher technician 489, 490
videocassette 495
videocassette recorder 495
videotape library 733
videotape operation controls 496
Viet Nam 747
Vietnamese 468
view camera 480
viewfinder 476, 477
viewing room 733
Viking 18
village 708, 886
vine leaf 86, 186
vine shoot 86
vine stock 86
vine, maturing steps 86
vinyl grip sole 369
vinyl insulation 299
viola 439
violas 437
violet 80, 400
violet-blue 400
violin 439
violin family 437, 439
VIP lounge 718
viper 114
Virgin 11, 13
virgule 473
visceral ganglion 105
visceral pleura 163
vise 312
visible light 690
vision 691
vision defects 691
vision device 765
vision slit 749
visiting room 726
visitors' entrance 726
visitors' front office 726
visitors' front office 726
visitors' waiting room 726
visor 575, 591, 749, 773, 874, 878, 884
visor hinge 575
Vistula River 32
visual display 918
visual display unit 507
visual transmission 694
vitelline membrane 117
vitreous body 177
vocal cord 163
vocal sac 111
voice edit buttons 450
voice recorder button 527
voice selector 451
volcanic bomb 44
volcanic island 49
volcanic lake 48
volcano 42, 44
volcano during eruption 44
volcanoes, examples 44
Volga River 32
volley 820
volleyball 812
volleyball, beach 813
volt 702
voltage decrease 646, 662, 677
voltage increase 646, 662, 665
voltage tester 316
volume control 441, 450, 451, 495, 497, 503, 504, 505, 507, 508, 513
volume display 548
volume unit meters 488
volute 276, 404, 405
volva 76
voussoir 413
Voyager 19
VU meters 491
vulture 119
vulva 148, 171

W

wad 753, 912
waders 911
wadi 52
wading bird 117
waferboard 300
waffle iron 238

wagon 642
wagon tent 902
waist 147, 149, 342, 439, 663
waist belt 281, 906
waistband 350, 351, 353
waistband extension 350
waistcoat 338, 348, 359
waistcoats and jackets 358
waiter 721
waiting area 730
waiting room 509, 768, 779
wakame 183
walk 124
walk-in closet 251
walk-in wardrobe 251
walk-through metal detector 726
walker 782
walkie-talkie 505, 770
walking aids 782
walking frame 782
walking leg 97, 103
walking stick 391, 782
walkway 714
wall 7, 82, 127, 246, 852, 902, 917
wall and rails 852
wall bracket 284
wall cabinet 224
wall cloud 63
wall fitting 287
wall grille 258
wall lantern 287
wall register 258
wall side 607
wall stack section 258
wall stud 253
wall tent 902
wallaby 143
wallet 387, 529
wallet section 386
walnut 88, 193
walnut, section 84
walrus 137
waning gibbous 7
wapiti 128
wardrobe 251, 279, 724
warehouse 708
warhead 759
warm air 64, 675
warm air outlet 564
warm temperate climates 61
warm-air baffle 256
warm-air outlet 258
warm-up lane 882
warming plate 241
warning area 846
warning device 765
warning lights 557
warning plate 306
warning track 795
warp 460, 461
warp roller 460
warp threads 463
warping frame 462
wasabi 201
wash bottle 685
wash tower 294
washcloth 379
washer 262, 268, 271, 292, 689
washer nozzle 550
washers 310
washing 347
washing machine 271
wasp-waisted corset 367
Wassily chair 276
waste basket 535
waste disposal unit 270
waste layers 69
waste pipe 262, 265, 271
waste stack 262
waste tee 271
waste water 70
waste, selective sorting 71
watches and jewellery 717
watches and jewelry 717
water 646, 847
Water Bearer 10
water bomber helicopter 631
water bottle 579
water bottle clip 579
water carrier 906
water chestnut 184
water cools the used steam 665
water ditch 852, 853
water flow 95
water goblet 225
water hazard 866, 867
water hose 294, 648
water inlet 268
water intake 658
water is pumped back into the steam generator 665
water jets 828
water jug 226
water key 447
water level 241, 261
water level indicator 239
water main 675, 712
water meter 262
Water Monster 11, 13

water pitcher 226
water pollution 70
water polo 827
water polo ball 827
water pressure gauge 766
water separator 648
water service pipe 262
water skiing 840
water spider 102
water strider 102
water table 47, 70
water tank 241, 261, 384, 586
water tower 589
water turns into steam 665
water under pressure 662
water-heater tank 266, 675
water-heater tank, electric 266
water-level selector 292
water-level tube 288
water-steam mix 646
water-tank area 628
watercolor 396
watercolor cakes 397
watercolor tube 397
watercourse 48, 70
watercress 187
waterfall 47, 48
watering can 328
watering tools 328
watering tube 573
waterline 615
watermark 729
watermelon 195
waterproof pants 368
waterproofed electricity supply 263
waterspout 63
watt 702
wave 49, 690
wave base 49
wave clip 380
wave guide 489
wave height 49
wave length 49
wave wall 660
wavelength 690
wax 892
wax bean 191
wax crayon drawing 396
wax crayons 396
wax gourd 188
wax seal 265
waxed paper 222
waxing gibbous 7
waxing kit 892
weapon, parts 849
weapons 748
weapons in the age of the Romans 748
weapons in the Stone Age 748
weasel 134
weather map 54, 55
weather radar 54, 624
weather satellite 54
weather satellites 60
weather symbols, international 56
weatherboard 247, 249
weaving 460
weaving pattern brush 456
weaving pattern lever 456
weaving principle, diagram 463
weaving, accessories 462
web 110, 117, 591, 797
web frame 607
webbed foot 110
webbed toe 117
webbing 459, 555, 899
Webcam 517
Weddell Sea 29
wedding ring 376
wedge 444, 753
wedge lever 309
weeder 325
weeding hoe 326
weekend case 389
weekender 389
weeping willow 88
weft 460, 461
weft thread 463
weighing platform 699
weight 472, 630, 697, 698, 699, 793, 850
weight belt 841
weight machine 851
weight, measure 698
weight-driven clock mechanism 697
weightlifting 850
weightlifting belt 850
weightlifting shoe 850
weights 851
welding curtain 318
welding tools 318
welding torch 319
well flow line 652
well wagon 588
Welsh 469
welt 342, 348
welt pocket 348, 354, 360
West 37, 616, 917
West cardinal mark 617
West Coast mirror 569, 570
West Indies 30

ASTRONOMY > 2-25;   EARTH > 26-71;   VEGETABLE KINGDOM >72-89;   ANIMAL KINGDOM > 90-143;   HUMAN BEING > 144-177;   FOOD AND KITCHEN > 178-241;   HOUSE > 242-295;
DO-IT-YOURSELF AND GARDENING > 296-333;   CLOTHING > 334-371;   PERSONAL ADORNMENT AND ARTICLES > 372-391;   ARTS AND ARCHITECTURE > 392-465;   COMMUNICATIONS AND
OFFICE AUTOMATION > 466-535;   TRANSPORT AND MACHINERY > 536-643;   ENERGY > 644-677;   SCIENCE > 678-705;   SOCIETY > 706-785;   SPORTS AND GAMES > 786-920

West-Northwest 37
West-Southwest 37
Western hemisphere 35
Western meridian 36
wet suit 841
wet well 671
wet-weather tire 872
Whale 10, 12
whale 137
whale boat 601
wheat 85, 203
wheat, grain 85
wheat: spike 85
wheel 320, 323, 389, 423, 454, 560, 570, 753, 758, 859, 870, 874, 894, 895, 913
wheel chock 622
wheel cover 551
wheel cylinder 559
wheel guard 308
wheel head 464
wheel loader 637
wheel mouse 516
wheel speed sensor 559
wheel tractor 637
wheelbarrow 323
wheelchair 584, 783
wheelchair access 725
wheelchair lift 569
wheelchair ramp 394
wheelhouse 606
whelk 217
whipping 868
whipping cream 210
whisk 232
whiskers 132
whisky tumbler 225
whistle 240
White 915, 916
white 690
white blood cell 162
white bread 205
white cabbage 186
white chocolate 208
white dwarf 8
white light 616
white line 127
white matter 167, 168
white mustard 198
white object ball 862, 863
white onion 184
white pepper 198
white rice 207
white square 916
white stone 916
white tape 812, 815, 817
white wine glass 225
white-tailed deer 128
whitewater 837
whitewater, canoe-kayak 837
whiting 221
whole note 435
whole rest 435
whole-wheat flour 204
wholegrain mustard 200
wholemeal bread 205
whorl 104, 105
wicker basket 899

wicket 731, 799
wicket gate 659
wicketkeeper 799
wide 472
wide area network 523
wide receiver 807
wide-angle lens 478
wife 785
wigwam 418
wild boar 128
wild rice 203
Wilkes Land 29
willow 798
winch 417, 573, 835
winch controls 573
wind 56, 69, 70, 833
wind abeam 833
wind arrow 56
wind chest 445
wind chest table 445
wind deflector 570
wind direction 55
wind direction, measure 59
wind duct 445
wind energy 676
wind flag 893
wind guard 899
wind indicator 834
wind instruments 446
wind sock 739
wind speed 55
wind strength, measure 59
wind supply 445
wind synthesizer controller 451
wind trunk 445
wind turbine, horizontal-axis 677
wind turbines 676
wind vane 58, 59, 677
windbag 432
windbreaker 353
windcheater 353
winder 696
winder house 649
winding adjustment 692
winding mechanism 285, 697
winding shaft 650
winding tower 649
windmill 676
window 238, 239, 249, 251, 290, 386, 485, 551, 554, 567, 594, 624, 836
window accessories 282
window awning 902
window canopy 902
window regulator handle 554
window sill 252
window tab 532
window winder handle 554
windows 386
windows, examples 415
winds 917
windscreen 488, 550, 570, 574, 624, 626, 876
windscreen wiper 550, 557
windscreen wiper blade 557
windshaft 676
windshield 550, 570, 574, 577, 607, 624, 626, 876
windshield wiper 550, 557

windshield wiper blade 557
wine 180
wine cellar 720
wine list 721
wine steward 720
wine vinegar 201
wine waiter corkscrew 230
wing 23, 97, 98, 115, 338, 416, 550, 570, 625, 760, 873, 897, 898, 909
wing attack 809
wing box 760
wing covert 115
wing defence 809
wing defense 809
wing forward 804
wing membrane 140
wing nut 311
wing pallet 632
wing rib 624
wing shapes, examples 630
wing slat 625
wing strut 628
wing tip 898
wing vein 96
wing, bird 115
winglet 625, 628
wings 140, 430, 628, 898
wings, bat 140
winner 789
winning line 920
winter 54
winter precipitations 64
winter solstice 54
winter sports 877
winter tire 560
winter tyre 560
winze 650
wiper 557
wiper arm 557
wiper blade rubber 557
wiper switch 556
wire 689, 793
wire beater 236
wire brush 449
wire cutter 317
wire nut 317
wire sling 900
wire stripper 317
wire support 903
wireless communication 505
wireless network interface card 522
wisdom tooth 159
wishbone boom 836
withers 124, 130
witness stand 728
wok 234
wok set 234
Wolf 11
wolf 134
Wolof 468
woman 148
women's accessories 717
women's casual wear 716
women's cell 768
women's clothing 355
women's coats 716
women's gloves 346
women's headgear 341

women's nightwear 716
women's rest room 725
women's shoes 343, 716
women's sportswear 716
women's suits 716
women's sweaters 716
women's toilet 725
won ton skins 207
wood 300, 867, 868
wood carving 401
wood chip car 588
wood chip wagon 588
wood chisel 309
wood ear 183
wood engraving 421
wood firing 256
wood flooring 253, 254
wood flooring arrangements 254
wood flooring on cement screed 254
wood flooring on wooden structure 254
wood frog 111
wood ray 87
wood-based materials 300
woodbox 256
woodcut 421
woodpecker 118
woods 39
woodwind family 437
woofer 10, 502
Worcestershire sauce 200
word correction 528
work bench and vise 312
work furniture 511
work lead 318
work sheet 395
work top 721, 722
worker 99
working area 10
working pressure gauge 319
working surface 312
workshop 726
workstation 509
worm 462, 573, 752
worm gear 686
wraparound dress 356
wraparound skirt 357
wrapover dress 356
wrapover skirt 357
wrapover top 359
wrapper 390
wrenches 311, 315
wrestler 843
wrestling 843
wrestling area 843
wrestling shoe 843
wrist 130, 140, 147, 149, 156, 173
wrist guard 895
wrist sling 901
wrist strap 888, 892
wrist-length glove 346
wristband 808, 822, 850
writing brush 470
writing case 387
writing instruments 470

X

X-band antenna 40
X-ray unit, mobile 778
X-rays 690
xenon 684
xylophone 437, 449

Y

Y-branch 269
Y-tube 776
yak 129
yam 184
yard 589, 602
yard line 806
yard-long bean 190
yarn 908
yarn ball 797
yarn clip 457
yarn feeder 456
yarn rod 457
yarn tension unit 457
yaw 630
yellow 400, 690
yellow ball 863
yellow light 712
yellow onion 184
yellow sweet pepper 188
yellow-green 400
yellowjacket 101
Yemen 746
yen 728
Yiddish 469
yield 544, 546
yogurt 210
yoke 284, 349, 353, 359
yoke skirt 357
yolk 117
Yoruba 468
ytterbium 684
yttrium 683
Yucatan Peninsula 30
Yugoslavia 744
yurt 418

Z

Zambia 746
zebra 128
zenith 10
zest 82
zester 229
Zimbabwe 746
zinc 683
zinc can 689
zinc-electrolyte mix 689
zip 369, 377, 389, 902
zip fastener 453
zip line 455
zipper 353, 369, 377, 389, 453, 902
zipper line 455
zirconium 683
zither 432
zona pellucida 170
zoom lens 478, 492, 496
zucchini 188
Zulu 468
zygomatic bone 152, 158

Deutsches Register

1-Meter-Brett 828
10-m-Linie 804
10-Meter-Turm 828
100-m- und 100-m-Hürdenlauf, Start 790
10000-m- und 4-x-400-m-Lauf, Start 791
110-m-Hürdenlauf, Start 790
120 V Stromkreis 272
15-m-Linie 805
1500-m-Lauf, Start 791
180-Grad-Kurve 885
2-Meter-Linie 827
2. Finger 140
200-m-Lauf, Start 790
200-m-Linie 871
22-m-Linie 804
240 V Speisekabel 272
240 V Stromkreis 272
27-m-Linie 858
3-Meter-Brett 828
3-Meter-Turm 828
3. Finger 140
30-m-Linie 859
35mm-Fotoapparat 20
36-m-Linie 858
4-Meter-Linie 827
4. Finger 140
400-m-, 400-m-Hürden-, 4-x-100-m-Lauf, Start 791
4x4-Geländemotorrad 577
5-Meter-Linie 805
5-Meter-Turm 828
5. Finger 140
50-m-Linie 859
500-m-Startlinie 882
500-m-Ziellinie 883
5000-m-Lauf, Start 790
54-m-Linie 858
60-m-Linie 859
7,5-Meter-Turm 828
7-m-Linie 814, 827
70-m-Linie 859
8-mm-Pistole 861
800-m-Lauf, Start 791
90-m-Linie 859

A

A 434
Aal 219
Abakus 404
Abbaufront 650
Abbaupfeiler 650
Abblendlicht 554
Abblendschalter 576
Abbruch 514
Abbruchtaste 519, 527
Abdampfleitung 668
Abdampfleitungen 669
Abdeckhaube 500
Abdeckkappe 391
Abdeckscheibe 689
Abdeckung 259, 261, 266, 273, 290, 477, 502, 512, 611, 767
Abdichtungsgraben 660
Abdomenarterie 107
Abendhandschuh, langer 346
Abessinierkatze 133
Abfackelung 652
Abfahrt, Seilbahn 886
Abfahrt, Sessellift 886
Abfahrtslauf 889

Abfahrtsski 888
Abfahrtzeiten 582
Abfall, radioaktiver 70
Abfalleimer 295, 723
abfallendes Revers 352
Abflugwartehalle 621
Abfluss 48, 262
Abfluss, oberirdischer 67
Abfluss, unterirdischer 67
Abfluss-T-Stück 271
Abflusskreislauf 262
Abflussrohr 271
Abflussschlauch 271
Abflusssieb 270
Abgabe von Sauerstoff 78
Abgabeöffnung für verbrauchte Brennstäbe 666
Abgas 267, 627
Abgase 564
Abgaseintritt 564
Abgasleitschaufeln 627
Abgasleitung 631
Abgasrohr 259, 564
Abgasturbolader 564
abgedecktes Gebiet 40
abgesenkte Nase 629
abgesteppte Falte 357
Abhalter 580
Abhörlautsprecher 488, 489
Abisolierzange 317
Abklingbecken 666, 667, 669
Abkoppelvorrichtung 587
Abladegebläse 643
Ablage 321, 532
Ablage für sauberes Geschirr 721
Ablage für schmutziges Geschirr 721
Ablagebrett 399
Ablassventil 655
Ablauf, Boden 246
Ablaufberg 589
Ablaufrohr 265
Ablaufschlauch 271, 292, 294
Ablaufstellwerk 589
Ablegepritsche 838
Ablenkkanal 657
Abluftleitung 543
Abnäher 455
abnehmbare Handballenauflage 514
abnehmender Mond 7
Abraham 736
Abreißkalender 530
Abrollbahn 621
Absatz 342, 370, 881
Absatz, oberer 417
Absatz, unterer 417
Absatzoberflecken 342
Absatzplatte 892
Absatzschuh 339
Absatzstopper 895
Absatzteil 889
Absauger 775
Absaugpumpe 775
Abscheider 606
Abschlag 866
Abschlag, Lange Ecke 800
Abschlagplatz 866
Abschlagsbereich 867
Abschleppkran 573
Abschleppstange 622
Abschleppwagen 573
Abschluss, oberer 281

Abschlusskappe 909
Abschlusskappe, obere 689
Abschlusskappe, untere 689
Abschlussknopf 284
Abschlussplatte 667
Abschlussprofil 285
Abschlussring 909, 910
Abseihkelle 233
Abseihlöffel 233
Abseilhaken 900
absinkende kalte Luft 63
Absorber 672
absorbierte Sonneneinstrahlung 68
Absorption der Erdoberfläche 68
Abspannseile 541
Absperrarm 568
Absperrband 771
Absperrgitter 100
Absperrventil 262, 265, 270, 271, 319
Abspieltaste 495
Absprung 891
Absprungbalken 793
Absprungbalken beim Dreisprung 793
Absprungbalken für Weitsprung 793
Abstandstück 783
Abstandszünder 759
absteigende Aorta 161
absteigender Dickdarm 164
absteigender Gang 402
Abstellfläche 543
Abstellplatz 619
Abstellraum 509
Abstellrost 291
Abstoßsäge 881
Abstoßung 687
Abstrakte 445
Abtastradiometer 60
Abteilklammer 380
Abteilung 181
Abwärtstor 837
Abwasser 70
Abwasserkanal 712
Abwehrhandschuh 879
Abwehrspieler, mittlerer 812
Abwehrspieler, rechter 812
Abweiser 872
Abwurf 864
Abwurfstelle 864
Abzeichen 770
abziehbarer Temperaturregler 239
Abziehklinge 892
Abzug 750, 752, 754, 755, 757, 767, 860, 861, 912
Abzugbügel 754, 912
Abzüge, verschiedene 258
Abzugsbügel 860, 861
Abzugsleine 756
Abzugstange 750
Abzweig 687
Abzweig 45° 269
Abzweigkanal 258
Abzweigleitung 262
Acanthodier 92
Accent aigu 473
Accent grave 473
Accessoires, Damen 717
Accessoires, Herren 716
Acetylflasche 319
Acetylventil 319
Achondrit 8
Achse 384, 894, 895

Achselarterie 160
Achselhöhle 146, 148
Achselknospe 77
Achselkrücke 782
Achselnerv 166
Achselstück 338
Achselstütze 782
Achselvene 160
Achsgetriebe 586
Achswelle 553
Achteck, regelmäßiges 705
Achtelfinale 789
Achtelnote 435
Achtelpause 435
Achter 839
Achterschiff 11
Achtersteven 598
Achtkantschliff 375
Achtknoten 908
Actinium 684
Actinoide (Seltenerdmetalle) 684
Adamsapfel 146
Adapter 274, 383, 485, 526
Adapterschnittstelle 526
Addiertaste 529
Addition 703
Additionstaste 529
additive Farbmischung 690
Aden, Golf 33, 34
Aderhaut 177
Adler 10, 12, 119, 741
Adria 32
aerodynamische Bremse 676
Afghanistan 746
Afrika 28, 34, 50, 745
Afrikanische Platte 43
afroasiatische Sprachen 468
After 95, 97, 103, 104, 105, 106, 107, 109, 113, 164, 169, 170
Afterfeder 115
Afterflosse 108
Afterfurche 147
Afterklaue 141
Afterkralle 130
Afterkrallenballen 130
Afterschließmuskel 164
Ägäis 32
Agar-Agar 183
Aggregat, irreguläres 64
Aggregatzustände 680
AGP-Erweiterungsport 513
Ägypten 745
Ahle 905
Ahorn 88
Ahornsirup 209
Ährchen 85
Ähre 81, 85
Ährenbrot 204
Ährenrispe 85
Aikido 846
Aikidogi 846
Aikidoka 846
Aimara 469
Airbag 556
Airbag-Rückhaltesystem 556
Ajowan 199
Akanthusblatt 276, 405
Akkord 435
Akkordeon 432
Akku 306, 496, 513

Akku-Bohrschrauber 306
Akku-Mini-Staubsauger 288
Akkumulator 559
Akromion 153
Akroterion 403, 404
Akrylharz, transparentes 501
Aktenablage, fahrbare 510
Aktenbox 533
Aktenkoffer 386
Aktenmappe 532
Aktenordner 532
Aktenschrank 510
Aktentasche 386, 387
Aktenvernichter 535
Aktionstasten 918
aktiver Sensor 41
Aktuator 759
Akustikdecke 431
akustische Gitarre 440
akustisches Signal 436
Alarm, Kontrollleuchte 527
Alarmschwellenwert-Anzeige 613
Alarmschwellenwert-Einstellung 613
Alaska, Golf 30
Albanien 744
Albanisch 469
Albatros 119
Aleuten 30
Aleutengraben 50
Alge 75
Alge, Aufbau 75
Algen, Beispiele 75
Algerien 745
Alhidade 59, 612, 701
Alhidadenebene 701
Alkalimetalle 682
alkalische Zink-Mangan-Zelle 689
Alkoholkolben 695
Alkoholsäule 695
Alkoholtestgerät 769
Allee 39
allgemeine Zeichen 725
allgemeiner Geräteraum 490
Alligator 114
Alluvion 48
Alpen 32
alphabetische Tastatur 530
alphanumerische Tastatur 506, 507, 514, 548, 730, 731
Alpin-Skipiste 886
Alpinboard 887
alpiner Skiläufer 888
alpines Skilaufen 888
Alse 220
Alt-Taste 514
altaische Sprachen 469
Altar 10
Altarbild 737
Altarkreuz 737
Altarm 48
Alternative 514
Altes Testament 736
Altglas-Container 71
Altglas-Sammelbehälter 71
Altokumulus 56, 62
Altostratus 56, 62
Altpapier-Container 71
Altpapier-Sammelbehälter 71
Altschlüssel 434
Altweiberknoten 908

ASTRONOMIE > 2-25;   ERDE > 26-71;   PFLANZENREICH >72-89;   TIERREICH > 90-143;   MENSCH > 144-177;   NAHRUNGSMITTEL UND KÜCHE > 178-241;   HAUS > 242-295;
HEIMWERKEN UND GARTENARBEIT > 296-333;   KLEIDUNG > 334-371;   PERSÖNLICHE AUSSTATTUNG > 372-391;   KUNST UND ARCHITEKTUR > 392-465;   KOMMUNIKATION UND BÜROTECHNIK > 466-535;
TRANSPORT UND FAHRZEUGE > 536-643;   ENERGIE > 644-677;   WISSENSCHAFT > 678-705;   GESELLSCHAFT > 706-785;   SPORT UND SPIELE > 786-920

Aluminium 682
Aluminiumfolie 222
Aluminiumrahmen 893
Aluminiumschicht, reflektierende 501
Alveolarknochen 159
am Wind 833
Amarant 203
Amazonas 31
Amboss 174, 912
Ambulakralfüßchen 95
ambulante Unfallstation 779
Ameise 101
American Football 806
Americium 684
Amerika 742
Amerika, Vereinigte Staaten 742
amerikanische Faltschachtel 535
Amerikanische Kurzhaarkatze 132
amerikanischer Bacon 216
amerikanischer Roulettespielplan 919
amerikanischer Senf 200
amerikanisches Labor 21
amerikanisches Maisbrot 205
amerikanisches Roulette 919
amerikanisches Wohnmodul 21
Amery-Eisschelf 29
Amethyst 375
Amharisch 468
Amöbe 94
amorpher Festkörper 680
Ampel 322
Ampelanlage 545, 547
Ampere 702
Amphibien 110
Amphibien, Beispiele 111
Amphibien-Löschflugzeug 628
Amphitheater, römisches 407
Amplitude 690
Amplituner: Rückansicht 497
Ampulle 95, 783
amtliche Unterschrift 729
An-/Aus-Kontrolllampe 506
Analfuß 97
Analog-Camcorder: Rückansicht 496
Analog-Camcorder: Vorderansicht 496
Analoguhr 696
Ananas 196
Ananasguave 197
Anästhesieraum 780
Anatomie 150
Anatomie einer Giftschlange 112
Anatomie einer Honigbiene 99
Anatomie einer Schildkröte 113
Anatomie einer Schnecke 104
Anatomie einer weiblichen Spinne 103
Anatomie einer zweischaligen Muschel 105
Anatomie eines Flußbarschs 109
Anatomie eines männlichen Froschs 110
Anatomie eines Hummers 107
Anatomie eines Pferdes 125
Anatomie eines Schwamms 95
Anatomie eines Seesterns 95
Anatomie eines Tintenfischs 106
Anatomie eines Vogels 115
Anatomie eines weiblichen Schmetterlings 97
Anden 31
Änderungslinie 455
Andorra 743
Andromeda 12
Andruckplatte 476
Anemometer 59, 677
Anemometer, Windgeschwindigkeitsmesser 58
Anfänger 413
Anführungszeichen 473
Anführungszeichen (französisch) 473
Anführungszeichen, halbe 473
Angaberaum 819
angehobener Lenkerbügel 870
Angehörige, Warteraum 778
Angel 227, 229, 315
Angelhaken 909, 911
Angelhaken mit Vorfach 911
Angelwurzel 229
angeschnittener Ärmel 360
Angerweste 911
Anglikanismus 736
Angola 746
Angriff 807
Angriffsfeldspieler, linker 814
Angriffsfeldspieler, rechter 814
Angriffslinie 812
Angriffsperiskop 763
Angriffszone 812
anhaltend dichter Sprühregen 57
anhaltend leichter Regen 57
anhaltend leichter Schneefall 57
anhaltend leichter Sprühregen 57
anhaltend mäßiger Regen 57
anhaltend mäßiger Schneefall 57
anhaltend mäßiger Sprühregen 57
anhaltend starker Regen 57
anhaltend starker Schneefall 57
Anhängemähwerk 642
Anhängemaul 641
Anhänger 374, 376, 570
Anhängerkupplung 558, 567
Anhöhe 674
Anik 487

Anis 202
Anker 610, 688, 791
Anker, Beispiele 610
Ankerbolzen 559
Ankerhand 610
Ankerkern 688
Ankerkette 615
Ankerketten 652
Ankerklüsen 605, 609
Ankerrad 696
Ankerspitze 610
Ankerwicklung 688
Anklagebank 728
Ankleidekabine 716
Ankleideraum 251, 428
Ankleideraum, privater 428
Anlage 244, 641
Anlage für Außenaufstellung 260
Anlage für Innenaufstellung 260
Anlage zur Formattrennung, Ausrichtung und Stempelung 474
Anlage, elektrische 553
Anlagen, unterirdische 407
Anlassbatterie 586
Anlasser 327, 332
Anlauf 891
Anlaufbahn 793, 824, 890, 891
Anlaufhülse 308
Anlaufstrecke 791, 792, 865
Anlaufzapfen 308
Anlegeeinrichtung 424
Anlegeleiter 321
Anlegepritsche 839
annähernd gleich 703
Annäherungsschlag 866
Annahmebereich 395
Annahmemaschine 666
Anode 266, 689
Anordnung von Sonnenspiegeln 674
anorganische Substanzen 67
Anpressknauf 307
Anrufbeantworter 508
Ansagekassette 508
Ansatz 311
Ansatzrohr 289
Ansatzsäge 424
Ansauggitter 382
Ansaugkanal 565
Ansaugkrümmer 564
Ansaugung 564, 565
Anschlag 303, 304, 700, 835
Anschlag, knieender 861
Anschlag, liegender 861, 893
Anschlag, stehender 861, 893
Anschlagfläche 535
Anschlagführung 305
Anschlagrahmen 278
Anschlagtafel der Ausstellungen 394
Anschluss 284, 290
Anschluss für Hochspannungsleitung 663
Anschluss für Schlauchleitung 649
Anschluss für Zündkabel 562
Anschluss, Schlauchleitung 649
Anschlussbuchse 441
Anschlussbuchsen für Video- und Digitalübertragung 477
Anschlüsse, Beispiele 270
Anschlussfeld 518
Anschlusskabel 305, 502
Anschlusskasten 673
Anschlussklemme 274
Anschlussleitung 262
Anschlussstelle 709
Anschlussstellen, Beispiele 538
Anschlussstifte 286
Anschlusstafel 488
Anschreiber 810, 812, 813, 848
Anschriftentafel 587
Ansicht 250
Ansichtsraum 733
Anspielkreis 878
Anspielpunkt 878
Anstecknadeln 376
Anstoßlinie 862
Anstoßpunkt 803, 862
Anstoßraum 862
Anstreichen 320
Antarktis 28, 29
Antarktische Halbinsel 29
Antarktische Platte 43
Antenne 17, 60, 96, 97, 98, 99, 107, 504, 505, 506, 551, 577, 611, 624, 631, 758, 761, 771, 812
Antenne für die Linienzugbeeinflussung 585
Antenne, hoch verstärkende 18
Antenne, schwach verstärkende 18
Antennenbuchsen 497
Antennula 107
Antependium 737
anthropogener Treibhauseffekt 68
Anti-Reflex-Beschichtung 672
Antiblockiersystem (ABS) 559
Antigua und Barbuda 743
Antiklinale 51
Antilope 128
Antimon 682
Antipersonenmine 758
Antiseptikum 777

antiseptische Flüssigkeit 777
Antiskating-Vorrichtung 500
Antrieb 591, 643
Antriebsbatterien 563
Antriebslagerschild 688
Antriebsmodul 486
Antriebsrad 636, 640, 876
Antriebsräder 639
Antriebsriemen 566
Antriebssystem 553
Antriebswalze 421
Antriebswelle 237
Antriebswerk 651, 696, 697
Antriebswerke 763
Antrittspfosten 255
Antrittsstufe 255
Anwendungsstarttasten 527
Anzahl der Gleise 591
Anzahl der Kommastellen 529
Anzeige 471, 529, 548, 698, 699
Anzeige «Sicherheitsgurte anlegen» 557
Anzeige für Blende 479
Anzeigeeinheit 841
Anzeigenadel 479
Anzeigenaufnahme 768
Anzeigeskala 613, 695, 699
Anzeigetafel 789, 790, 793, 822, 825, 828, 831, 839, 844, 846
Anzeigetafel für das Gesamtergebnis 824
Anzeigetafel für die Einzeldisziplin 825
Anzeigetaste 496
Anziehung 687
Anzugring 854
Anzünder 318
Aorta 162, 163
Aorta, absteigende 161
Aorta, aufsteigende 161
Aorta, ventrale 109
Aortenbogen 160, 161, 162
Aortenklappe 162
Aperturblende 694
Apex 104, 105
Apfel 193
Apfel im Querschnitt 82
Apfelessig 201
Apfelfrucht, fleischige 82
Apfelfrüchte 193
apokrine Schweißdrüse 172
Apollo 19
Apostroph 473
Apotheke 714, 725
Appalachen 30
Appartements 886
Aprikose 192
Aquamarin 375
Aquarell 396
Aquarellfarbe/Gouachefarbe, Näpfchen 397
Aquarellfarbe/Gouachefarbe, Tube 397
Äquator 13, 31, 34, 35, 36, 63
Äquatorialguinea 745
Ara 118
Arabisch 468
Arabische Halbinsel 33
Arabisches Meer 33
Arachnoidea 167
Aralsee 33
Aramäisch 468
Arame 183
Arbeiterin 99
Arbeitsbrett 321
Arbeitsdruckmesser 319
Arbeitskittel 359
Arbeitslampe 399
Arbeitsleuchte 286
Arbeitsmöbel 511
Arbeitsplatte 224, 312, 721, 722
Arbeitsplatz 509, 511
Arbeitsprozess des Dieselmotors 565
Arbeitsprozess des Kreiskolbenmotors 565
Arbeitsprozess des Zweitaktmotors 565
Arbeitsstiefel 342
Arbeitstisch 305
Arbeitszimmer 251
Archaeognatha 92
Archaeopteryx 93
Archipel 38
Architektur 394, 402
Architekturelemente 413
Architrav 403, 405
Archiv 394, 509
Archive 769
Archivmöbel 510
Archivolte 411
Arena 407, 788
Arenberg-Parkett 254
Argentinien 742
Argon 684
Ariane IV 24
Ariel 5
Arkade 407, 410
Arkaden 738
Arkebuse 752
Arktis 28
Arm 95, 124, 139, 147, 149, 286, 452, 610, 783
Armaturen 268
Armaturenbrett 556

Armaturenbrettausrüstung 771
Armausschnitt 351
Armband 376
Armbänder 376
Armbeuger 150
Armbrust 750
Armdecken, große 115
Armdecken, kleine 115
Armdecken, mittlere 115
Ärmel 337, 348
Ärmel, angeschnittener 360
Ärmel, Beispiele 360
Ärmel, eingesetzter 349
Ärmelaufschlag 848
Ärmelkanal 32
Ärmellasche 352
ärmelloses Sporthemd 850
Ärmelpuff 337
Ärmelschlitz 349, 361
Armenien 746
Armenisch 469
Armgeflecht 166
Armhaltung 829
Armhebel 844
Armkachel 749
Armlehne 276, 281
Armlehnstuhl 276
Armpolster 880
Armreif 376
Armschutz 808, 859
Armschützer 808
Armschwingen 115
Armstrecker, dreiköpfiger 151
Armstrecker, zweiköpfiger 150
Armstuhl 734
Armstühle, Beispiele 276
Armstütze 276, 554, 555, 783
Arpeggio 435
Arretierhebel 304, 309, 312
Arretierknopf 308
Arsen 682
Art der hohen Wolken 55
Art der mittelhohen Wolken 55
Art der tiefen Wolken 55
Arten von Blütenständen 81
Arten von echten Gelenken 156
Arten von Golfschläger 867
Arten, Entstehung und Entwicklung 92
Arterien 160
Arthropleura 92
Artikel 473
Artischocke 187
Arzneimittel-Darreichungsformen 783
Arzt 842
Ärzteteam 844
Asche 391
Asche, vulkanische 44
Aschenbahn 790
Aschenbecher 391
Ascheschicht 44
Aserbeidschan 746
Asche 87
asiatische Birne 197
asiatische Eiernudeln 207
asiatische Teigwaren 207
Asien 28, 33, 50, 746
Asphalt 656
Asphalt-Destillationsanlage 656
Asphaltschindel 299
Aspirin 777
Ass 914
Assistenzarzt 780
Assistenzschiedsrichter 881, 882
Assistenztrainer 879
Ast 87, 89, 115
Astat 683
Asteroidengürtel 5
Asthenosphäre 42
Astigmatismus 691
Astragal 405
Astronomie 4
astronomische Einheit 4, 5
Astschere 330
Asukibohne 191
Atacama-Wüste 31
Atemluftzufuhrschlauch 765
Atemschutz 773, 774
Atemschutz tragen 774
Atemschutzmaske, leichte 773
Atemschutzsystem, geschlossenes 765
Äthiopien 745
Athletin 791
Atlantik 28
atlantischer Kabeljau 221
atlantischer Lachs 221
Atlantischer Ozean 29, 32, 34
Atlas 111, 122, 126, 131, 153, 157
Atlasbindung 463
Atlasgebirge 34
Atlasspinner 102
Atmosphäre 66, 70
Atoll 51
Atom 680
Atom-Unterseeboot 763
Atome 680
Atomkern 680
Atrium 406
ätzend 774
Aubergine 188

Audio-Ausgänge 527
Audio-Eingänge 527
Audiobedarf 716
Audiobuchse 513
Audioführer 394
Audiometrie- Untersuchungsraum 781
Auerbachkopfsprung gestreckt mit einer Schraube 829
Aufbau 567
Aufbau der Biosphäre 66
Aufbau der Sonne 6
Aufbau des Ohres 174
Aufbau des Rückenmarks 167
Aufbau einer Alge 75
Aufbau einer Blume 80
Aufbau einer Flechte 74
Aufbau einer Pflanze 77
Aufbau eines Baumes 87
Aufbau eines Blatts 79
Aufbau eines Farns 76
Aufbau eines Flugkörpers 759
Aufbau eines langen Knochens 154
Aufbau eines Mooses 75
Aufbau eines Pilzes 76
Aufbauspieler, linker 811
Aufbauspieler, rechter 811
Aufbereitungsanlage 649
Aufbewahrung schadhafter Brennstäbe 666
Aufbewahrungsfach 483
Aufbewahrungsmöbel 278, 510
aufblasbare Manschette 777
Aufblassystem 611
Aufblasteil 841
Aufblasventil 841
Aufdruck 368
Aufenthaltsraum 724
Auffahrgleis 589
Auffahrt 539, 540
Auffanggefäß 59
Auffangschale 241
Auffangschüssel 290
Aufgeber 816
aufgepflanztes Bajonett 751
aufgesatteler Kippanhänger 572
aufgesetzte Tasche 348, 353, 360, 368
aufgeständerte Bogenbrücke 541
aufgewirbelter Staub 63
Aufhängeband 177
Aufhängefeder 697
Aufhängeöse 382
Aufhängepunkt 897
Aufhänger 354, 483
Aufhängung 284, 448, 553, 627
Aufheizer 668
Aufladen, Kontrollleuchte 527
Auflage 280
Auflagehumus 78
Auflagetisch 424
Auflaufförmchen 226
Auflieger 570, 571
Auflösungszeichen 435
Aufnahme 778, 781
Aufnahme von Kohlendioxid 78
Aufnahme von Wasser und Mineralstoffen 78
Aufnahme-Starttaste 496
Aufnahme-Stopptaste 496
Aufnahme-Taste 499
Aufnahme-Ziffer 429
Aufnahmebecken 666
Aufnahmebühne 428
Aufnahmefläche 675
Aufnahmekammer 694
Aufnahmelicht 488
Aufnahmetaste 495
Aufnahmezeitanzeige 488
Aufreißband 390
Aufreißer 8
Aufreißerspitze 636
Aufreißerzylinder 636
Aufsatz 234
Aufsatzstück 432
Aufschaumdüse 241
Aufschlag 338, 350, 812, 820
Aufschlagbereich 818
Aufschläger 819, 821
Aufschlagfeld für das Doppelspiel 817
Aufschlagfeld für das Einzelspiel 817
Aufschlagfelder 817
Aufschlagkasten 818
Aufschlagkastenlinie 818
Aufschlaglinie 818, 819, 821
Aufschlaglinienrichter 820
Aufschlagrichter 816, 820
Aufschnitt 444
Aufsetzbacke 859
Aufsetzen 864
Aufsetzzonenmarkierungen 621
Aufsichtsingenieur 489, 490, 491
Aufsichtsperson, Tisch 732
Aufsitzmäher 333
aufspringender Winkel 409
Aufsprungbahn 891
Aufsteckbürste 384
Aufsteckdüse 384
Aufsteckschuh 482
aufsteigende Aorta 161
aufsteigende warme Luft 63
aufsteigender Dickdarm 164

aufsteigender Gang 402
Aufstellmaschine 865
Aufstellpunkt 862
Aufstellung 865
Aufstieg 640
Auftrieb 630
Auftriebsausgleich 841
Aufwachraum 780
Aufwärmbahn 882
Aufwärtstor 13
Aufwickelkern 499
Aufzeichnung, seismologische 651, 653
Aufzeichnungsgerät 59
Aufzeichnungskassette 508
Aufzeichnungstaste 508
Aufziehbrett 315
Aufzug 16, 407, 417, 509, 650, 666, 713, 724, 761
Aufzugseil 634
Aufzugsmechanismus 697
Aufzugsrad 696
Augapfel 110, 177
Auge 63, 103, 104, 106, 107, 112, 113, 121, 133, 136, 148, 177, 301, 382, 756, 855, 900, 914
Auge, einfaches 95
Augen-Make-up 378
Augenbehandlungsraum 779
Augenbrauenpinzette 377
Augenbrauenstift 378
Augengläser, Beispiele 385
Augenhöhle 112, 116, 131, 136, 138, 142
Augenkammer, hintere 177
Augenkammer, vordere 177
Augenlid 113
Augenlid, oberes 110, 132
Augenlid, unteres 110, 132
Augenmuschel 612
Augenmuskel, unterer gerader 177
Augenring 115
Augenringmuskel 150
Augenschutz 772, 774
Augenschutz tragen 774
Augenstreif 115
Augenträger 104
Augenwand 63
Ausatmen 832
Ausatmungsventil 773
Ausbeinmesser 229
Ausbereich 864
ausbrechbare Kabeldurchführung 272
Ausbruchtätigkeit, Vulkan 44
Ausdehnungsgefäß 259
Ausdehnungskammer 695
ausfahrbarer Baum 634
ausfahrbarer Leiterbaum 766
Ausfahrtgleis 589
Ausfahrt 539
Ausfahrtspur 539
Ausfallpforte 409
Ausflugloch 100
Ausführungsgang, Schweißdrüse 172
Ausgabebank, Kürzel 729
Ausgabegeräte 518
Ausgangsmonitor 490, 491
Ausgangssperre 592
Ausgangstür, zweiflügelige 568
ausgeschlossene Spieler, Wiedereintrittsraum 827
ausgestreckte Kralle 133
Ausgleichsbecken 657, 658, 661
Ausguss 295
Ausgussreiniger 314
Ausklapparretierung 321
ausklappbare Stützvorrichtung 571
Ausklinkhebel 898
Auskragung 661
Auskratzer 390
Auslasskanal 565
Auslassschlitz 649
Auslassventil 564, 566, 777
Auslauf 182, 268, 885, 890, 891
Auslaufbereich 891
Auslaufgarnitur 270
Auslaufleitung 263
Auslaufrille 500
Auslaufrohr 643, 658
Auslaufschütz 597
Ausleger 599, 634, 635, 637, 638, 839
Ausleger, beweglicher 622
Ausleger, einfahrbarer 18
Auslegerboot 799
Auslegerbrücke 540
Auslegerseil 634
Auslegerstange 599
Auslegerzylinder 637, 638
Ausleihe 733
Auslenkungsrichtung 690
Auslinie 804
Auslöseknopf 391
Auslösepuppe 443
Auslöser 476
Auslöser, pneumatischer 482
Auspuff 640
Auspuffanlage 553
Auspuffendrohr 553
Auspuffkanal 565
Auspuffkrümmer 552, 564, 566
Auspuffrohr 570, 575, 576, 577, 636, 639

Auspuffrohr, hinteres 553
Auspuffrohr, vorderes 552
Ausrichtkopf 701
Ausrichtkopfblockierung 701
Ausrichtkopfebene 701
Ausrichtschraube 699, 701
Ausrufezeichen 473
Ausrüstung 769, 900
Ausrüstung, technische 489
Ausrüstungsspind 489, 490
Aussägen 401
Ausschalter 331
Ausschaltrille 500
Ausschnitt 455
Ausschnitt, drapierter 363
Ausschnitt, halsnaher 354, 359, 368
Ausschnitt, runder 363
Ausschnitt, viereckiger 363
Ausschnitte 363
Aussendung von Ultraschall 41
Aussparung für Magnetköpfe 499
Ausstatter 428
Ausstattung 396, 421, 422, 423
Ausstattung, persönliche 374
Ausstechformen 232
Ausstellung, Banner 394
Ausstellungen, Anschlagtafel 394
Ausstellungsraum 719
Ausstellungsregal 510
Ausstellungsstand 719
Aussteuerung, manuelle 499
Ausstoß 564, 565
Ausstreichmesser 464
Ausströmmantel 659
Auster 217
Austernfischer 118
Austerngabel 228
Austernmesser 229
Austernseitling 183
Australien 28, 50, 747
Australische Kordilleren 29
australische Sprachen 469
Austrittsdüse 627
Austrittskante 624
auswärts 828
Auswaschung 70
Auswechselbank 803
Auswerfer 638
Auswurf, Staub 304
Auswurf-Taste 499
Auswurfrohr 642
Auswurftaste 236, 477, 918
Auswurftaste für das 501
Auszahlungshebel 920
Auszahlungsschale 920
ausziehbare Fluggastbrücke 619
ausziehbarer Griff 386
Ausziehbein 278
Ausziehleiter 321
Ausziehschirm 896
Ausziehtisch 278
Auszug 278, 290
Außenangreifer, linker 812
Außenangreifer, rechter 812
Außenansicht eines Hauses 244
Außenbordmotor 607
Außenbrett 915
Außenfeldspieler, linker 794
Außenfeldspieler, mittlerer 794
Außenfeldspieler, rechter 794
Außengewinde 910
außengezahnte Fächerscheibe 310
Außenkelch 83
Außenklüver 603
Außenknauf 248
Außenkreis 877
Außenlippe 105
Außenring 729
Außenrohr, druckfestes 667
Außenschicht 797
Außenspiegel 568, 569
Außensteckhülse 909
Außensteg 426
Außentank 22
Außentanks 386, 388
äußere Begrenzungslinie 819
äußere Drosselvene 160
äußere Hülse 275
äußere Kappe 275
äußere Kappe 342
äußere Kiemen 111
äußere Kuppelhülle 17
äußere Leitschaufeln 627
äußere Merkmale einer einschaligen Muschel 105
äußere Merkmale einer Fledermaus 140
äußere Merkmale einer Giftschlange: Kopf 112
äußere Merkmale einer Honigbiene: Arbeiterin 98
äußere Merkmale einer Katze 133
äußere Merkmale einer Ratte 122
äußere Merkmale einer Schildkröte 113
äußere Merkmale einer Schnecke 104
äußere Merkmale einer Spinne 103
äußere Merkmale einer zweischaligen Muschel 105
äußere Merkmale eines Delphins 136
äußere Merkmale eines Flußbarschs 108
äußere Merkmale eines Froschs 110

äußere Merkmale eines Gorillas 139
äußere Merkmale eines Hais 108
äußere Merkmale eines Hummers 107
äußere Merkmale eines Hundes 130
äußere Merkmale eines Kängurus 143
äußere Merkmale eines Maulwurfs 121
äußere Merkmale eines Pferdes 124
äußere Merkmale eines Schmetterlings 96
äußere Merkmale eines Seesterns 95
äußere Merkmale eines Tintenfischs 106
äußere Merkmale eines Vogels 115
äußere Nase 175
äußere Oberschenkelkondyle 153
äußere Planeten 4
äußere Verkleidung 267
äußerer Bull 918
äußerer Gehörgang 158
äußerer Hausflur 406
äußerer Kern 42
äußerer Linebacker 806
äußerer Ohrmuschelrand 173
äußerer Rand 127
äußerer Schenkelmuskel 150
äußerer schräger Bauchmuskel 150, 151
äußerer Schneidezahn 159
äußeres Keilbein 155, 156
äußeres Ohr 174
Auto 549
Auto-Manualumschalter 316
Autobahn 39, 539, 709
Autobahnnummer 39
Autocoat 355
Autofocus-Schalter 483
Autofocus-Umschalter 476
Autogenschweißen 319
Autohandschuh 346
Autohaus 711
Autoklav 780
Automat für Umsteigekarten 593
automatische Füllanzeige 655
automatische Schiebetür 416
automatische Sortierablagen 512
automatische Tür 620
automatischer Bankschalter 730, 731
automatischer Sendersuchlauf 498
automatischer Zeitmesser 831
automatisches Gewehr 755
Autopilot 759
Autoplane 558
Autorennen 872
Autoreverse-Taste 504
Autotransporter 572
Autotransportwagen 588
autotrophe Organismen 67
Autowaschanlage 548
Avocado 188
Axel 881
Axialrippe 105
Axialverdichterschaufel 627
Axis 122
Axon 168
Axt 330
Azimutalprojektion 36
Azimutfeineinstellung 14, 15
Azimutfesteller 14
Azimutfeststeller 15
aztekischer Tempel 412

B

B 435
Baby-Doll 364
Babybekleidung 368, 717
Bach 48
Bachsaibling 221
Back 605, 609
Backblech 232
Backbone 523
Backbordseite 609, 616, 617
Backe 130, 307, 385, 860, 861
Backe, bewegliche 311, 312
Backe, feste 311, 312
Backen 302, 306, 307, 312, 317, 889, 892
Backenhörnchen 123
Backenriemen 854
Backenzahn 121, 123
Backenzahn im Längsschnitt 159
Backenzahn, erster 159
Backenzahn, erster vorderer 159
Backenzahn, zweiter 159
Backenzahn, zweiter vorderer 159
Backenzähne, vordere 159
Bäckerei 715
Backfett 209
Backform 239
Backgammon 915
Backline 877
Backofen 224, 290, 721, 722
Backofenfolie 222
Backofenschalter 290
Backofenthermometer 231
Backofentür 290
Backrost 290
Backsteinhaus 418
Backup-Speichereinheit 523
Backwaren 181
Bacon, amerikanischer 216

Bacon, kanadischer 216
Bad 251, 724, 780
Badartikel 717
Badeanzug 371
Badebürste 379
Badehose 371, 830
Badekappe 827, 830
Badeleiter 246
Bademantel 364
Bademoden 716
Badetuch 379
Badetuch mit Kapuze 368
Badewanne 251, 262, 264, 724
Badezimmer-Oberlicht 251
Badminton 816
Badmintonplatz 816
Badmintonschläger 816
Baffinland 30
Baggerlöffel 638
baggern 812
Baggerstiel 638
Baggerstielzylinder 638
Baguette 204
Baguetteform 375
Bahamas 742
Bahn 301, 788, 790, 830, 831, 877, 883, 885
Bahnbojen 838
Bahnende 831, 832
Bahnenplissee 357
Bahnenrock 357
Bahngleise 649
Bahnhof 39, 582, 583, 708, 710
Bahnhofshalle 582
Bahnmarkierung 791
Bahnnummer 893
Bahnradsport 871
Bahnseil 831
Bahnsteig 582, 583, 593, 620
Bahnsteigkante 582, 593
Bahnsteigüberdachung 583
Bahnübergang 545, 547, 583
Bahnübergang, schienengleicher, gesicherter 591
Bahnzeitnehmer 830
Bahrain 746
Baikalsee 33
Bailey-Brücke 542
Bajonett, aufgepflanztes 751
Bajonettanschluss 478
Bajonettfassung 275
Bakelit-Splitterkörper 757
Balalaika 433
Balancegewicht 500
Balanceregler 497
Balg 432, 445
Balg, Schnitt 84
Balgen 485
Balgenverschluss 432
Balkanhalbinsel 32
Balken 167, 403, 406, 412, 418, 698, 826
Balken, hinterer 698
Balken, vorderer 698
Balkenbrücke 540
Balkenbrücken, Beispiele 541
Balkenspiralgalaxie 9
Balkenwaage 698
Balkon 251
Balkontür 251
Ball 823, 858, 920
Balleisen, gerades 401
Ballen 127
Ballerinaschuh 343
Ballfangzaun 794
Balljunge 820
Ballon 899
Ballonsonde 54, 59
Ballsportarten 794
Ballungsgebiet 708
Balsamessig 201
Balustrade 412, 417
Bambara 468
Bambusse 917
Bambussprosse 185
Banane 196
Band 453, 459, 753, 757, 823, 841
Band, Blaues 871
Band, erhabenes 426
Band, reflektierendes 611
Bandage 843, 853, 858
Bändchen 443
Bande 864, 878, 883
Banderole 390
Bandführung 499, 534
Bandring 376
Bandscheibe 157
Bandschlüssel 315
Bändsel 908
Bandsortenschalter 499
Bandsperre 313
Bandwahltaste 497
Banglaesh 747
Banjo 432
Bank 277, 647, 710, 715, 730, 851, 915
Bankett 538
Bankhöhe 647
Banknote: Rückseite 729
Banknote: Vorderseite 729
Bankschalter, automatischer 730, 731

Banner der derzeitigen Ausstellung 394
Banner der kommenden Ausstellung 394
Bantusprachen 468
Bar 431, 710, 719, 720, 915
Barbados 743
Barbakane 408
Bardame 720
Baren 421
Bärenhüter 13
Barentssee 32
Bargeldbestückung 731
Barhocker 277, 720
Barium 682
Bärlatsch 749
Barograph 59
Baronstange 440
Barren 825
Barriereriff, Großes 29
Barsch 220
Bart 85
Bartregion 115
Basalschicht 172
Basaltschicht 42
Baseball 794, 796
Baseball im Querschnitt 797
Baseballstadion 788
Basilikum 202
Basilosaurus 93
Basis 405, 494, 791
Basis der Rückenlehne 276
Basisstation für Funknetzwerk 522
Baskenmütze 341
Basketball 810
Basketballspiel 810
Basketballspieler 810
Basmatireis 207
Bass-Straße 29
Bass-Tonabnehmer 441
Bassfalle 490
Bassgitarre 441
Bassklarinette 437
Basslautsprecher 10
Bassregister 432
Bassregler 497, 503
Bassschlüssel 434
Basssteg 442
Bassstatur 432
Basstrommel 437, 448
Bast 87
Bateau-Kragen 363
Batterie 302, 482, 552, 562, 563, 673, 687, 759, 765
Batterie-Schraubendreher 302
Batteriegehäuse 562
Batteriekasten 571
Batterieladekontrollleuchte 557
Batteriemodule 60
Bauch 115, 124, 146, 148
Bauchaorta 160, 165
Baucharterie 107
Bauchfell 169, 170
Bauchflosse 108
Bauchfuß 97
Bauchgurt 853, 855, 856, 857
Bauchhöhle 169, 170
Bauchmuskel, äußerer Schräger 150
Bauchmuskel, äußerer schräger 151
Bauchmuskel, gerader 150
Bauchpanzer 113
Bauchreifen 749
Bauchschuppe 112
Bauchspeck 216
Bauchspeicheldrüse 164
Bauchtank 631
Bauer 916
Bauernbrot 205
Bauernhof 182
Baum 87, 834, 855
Baum, Aufbau 87
Baum, ausfahrbarer 634
Baumaterialien 298
Bäume 866
Baumfarn 76
Baumhippe 330
Baumsäge 330
Baumschere 330
Baumstamm 300
Baumstamm im Querschnitt 87, 300
Baumstammtransport, Sattelanhänger 572
Baumstütze 324
Baumtomate 196
Baumvogel 117
Bauplatte, Gipskarton 299
Bauschärmel 361
Bauschaumisolierung 299
Bauschmuskel 151
Baustelle 545, 547
Baustile 404
Bautischlerei 301, 302, 303, 306, 308, 310, 313
Beachvolleyball 813
Beatmungsbeutel 775
Beaufortsee 30
Becher 11, 223, 226, 906
Becherglas 685
Becken 121, 138, 141, 142, 246, 263, 437, 448, 449, 664, 788, 838
Becken, oberes 448
Becken, rudimentäres 136

Becken, unteres 448
Beckengurt 555
Beckenseite 664
Becquerel 702
bedeckte Säule 64
bedeckter Himmel 56
Bedeckungsgrad 56
Bedienblende 238
Bedienfeld 518
Bedienkonsole 766
Bedienleiste 290, 292, 293, 294
Bedienpult 694
Bedientasten 494
Bedienungsanleitung 548
Bedienungsfeld 239
Bedienungshebel 643
Bedienungshebel für Verschlussblock 756
Bedienungskonsole 512
Bedienungsschnur 284
Bedienungstafel 417
Bedienungstasten 507, 508
Beere 83
Beeren 192
Beet 245
Beete, rote 189
Beetpflug 641
befestigte Umfassungsmauer 738
Befestigungshebel 287
Befestigungsriemen 765, 893
Befestigungsschiene 692
Befeuchter 531
befeuchtete Oberfläche 420
Befruchtungstasche 104
Begattungskammer, Öffnung 97
Begattungstasche 97
begehbarer Kleiderschrank 251
Begleitkarte 395
Begonie 80
begrenzte Zone 811
Begrenzungseinsatz 533
Begrenzungsleuchte 554
Behaarung 121, 122, 139, 143
Behälter 59, 236, 240, 320, 643
Behälter für gebrauchte Spritzen 771
Behälter mit flüssigem Stickstoff 694
Behälter mit Gießer 237
Behandlung, chemische 656
Behandlungsraum 779, 781
Behindertenrampe 394
Beichtstuhl 737
beidhändiges Schwert 751
beidseitiges Kopieren 512
Beifahrer-Fußraste 576
Beifahrerfußraste 575
Beil 767, 907
Beilage, farbige 471
Beilagen 723
Bein 113, 139, 147, 149, 156, 278, 351, 448, 815, 823
Beinarbeit beim Brustschwimmen 832
Beinarbeit beim Kraulen 832
Beinarbeit beim Schmetterlingsstil 832
Beinausschnitt, elastischer 351
Beinbandage 857
Beincurler 851
Beingurt 611
Beinhaltung 829
Beininnenseite 368, 369
Beinklemme 482
Beinlinge 338
Beinpolster 879
Beinröhre 749
Beinschutz 796, 800
Beinstreckerzug 851
Beispiele für Algen 75
Beispiele für Amphibien 111
Beispiele für Anker 610
Beispiele für Anschlussstellen 538
Beispiele für Ärmel 360
Beispiele für Armstühle 276
Beispiele für Augengläser 385
Beispiele für Balkenbrücken 541
Beispiele für Beuteltiere 143
Beispiele für Bits und Bohrer 306
Beispiele für Blumen 80
Beispiele für Blusen und Hemden 359
Beispiele für Bögen 413, 541
Beispiele für Bogenbrücken 541
Beispiele für Boote und Schiffe 604
Beispiele für Fahrräder 581
Beispiele für Falten 357
Beispiele für Farne 76
Beispiele für Fenster 415
Beispiele für Fittings 269
Beispiele für Flechten 74
Beispiele für Fledertiere 141
Beispiele für Flugzeuge 628
Beispiele für Fräser 308
Beispiele für Gabeln 228
Beispiele für Hanteln 840
Beispiele für Hasentiere 123
Beispiele für Heroldsbilder 740
Beispiele für Hosen 358
Beispiele für Hubschrauber 631
Beispiele für Hufe 127
Beispiele für Huftiere 128
Beispiele für Insekten 101
Beispiele für Insektenfresser 121

Beispiele für Instrumentalgruppierungen 438
Beispiele für Karosserien 549
Beispiele für Kegel 865
Beispiele für Kleider 356
Beispiele für Kragen 362
Beispiele für Kräuselfalten 283
Beispiele für Küchenmesser 229
Beispiele für Lastkraftwagen 573
Beispiele für Laubhölzer 88
Beispiele für Leitwerke 629
Beispiele für Löffel 228
Beispiele für Meeressäugetiere 137
Beispiele für Messer 228
Beispiele für Metall 741
Beispiele für Moose 75
Beispiele für Motorräder 577
Beispiele für Nadelblätter 89
Beispiele für Nadelhölzer 89
Beispiele für Nägel 301
Beispiele für Nagetiere 123
Beispiele für Netzwerke 522
Beispiele für Pelzwerk 741
Beispiele für Primaten 139
Beispiele für Raubtiere 134
Beispiele für Raumsonden 19
Beispiele für Reptilien 114
Beispiele für Riggs 601
Beispiele für Röcke 357
Beispiele für Sattelkraftfahrzeuge 572
Beispiele für Schlafsäcke 904
Beispiele für Segel 601
Beispiele für Sicherungen 272
Beispiele für Skier 840, 888
Beispiele für Spinnentiere 102
Beispiele für Sprünge 829, 881
Beispiele für Staudämme 660
Beispiele für Stühle 277
Beispiele für Taschen 360
Beispiele für Tasteninstrumente 443
Beispiele für Telefone 507
Beispiele für Tische 278
Beispiele für Trägerraketen 24
Beispiele für Türen 416
Beispiele für Übergangsfittings 269
Beispiele für Vogelfüße 117
Beispiele für Vogelschnäbel 117
Beispiele für Vorhänge 283
Beispiele für Vorhangköpfe 283
Beispiele für Währungsabkürzungen 728
Beispiele für Wappenzeichen 741
Beispiele für Werkzeuge 401
Beispiele für Winkel 704
Beispiele für Zelte 902
Beitel 421
Beitrag, redaktioneller 471
Beiwagen 594
Bekleidungsgeschäft 714
Belegausgabe 548
Beleuchterbrücke 430
beleuchteter Spiegel 381
Beleuchtung 274, 381, 490, 626
Beleuchtungsanlage 490, 492
Beleuchtungsgitter 429
Beleuchtungskopf 485
Beleuchtungsschiene 287
Beleuchtungsspiegel 701
Beleuchtungstechniker 490
Belgien 743
Belichtungs-Schaltuhr 485
Belichtungseinstellung 476
Belichtungskorrekturknopf 476
Belichtungsmesser 476, 479
Belichtungswert 479
Belichtungszeitskala 479
Belize 742
Belüftungsfenster 244
Belüftungsschlitz 294
bemannte Manövriereinheit 20
Bengalen, Golf 33
Benin 745
Benzin 656
Benzinmotor 553, 563
Benzintank 563
Benzintankverschluss 576
Beobachtung des Weltraums 10
Beobachtungsposten 17
Beobachtungsraum 778, 781
Beobachtungsraum, psychiatrischer 778
Berbersprache 468
Bereich der Bildkontrolle 489
Bereichsumschalter 316
Bereitschaftsanzeige 381, 508
Berg 45
Bergamotte 194
Bergen des Spinnakers 833
Bergère 276
Bergfried 408
Berghang 45
Berghütte 886
Bergkette 7
Bergschrund 46
Bergsteiger 901
Bergsteigerspaten 901
Bergsteigerstiefel 901
Bergwacht 886
Beringsee 28
Beringstraße 30
berittener Schiedsrichter 858
Berkelium 684

Berme 538, 660
Bermudashorts 358
Bernhardiner 131
Berthe 363
Berührung 916
Beryllium 682
Besan 603
Besan-Bramstagsegel 603
Besan-Stengestagsegel 603
Besanbaum 602
Besanmast 600, 602
Besantoppsegel 603
Besatzungsunterkünfte 604
Beschichtung 815
Beschickungsbereich 666
Beschickungsmaschine 666, 669, 670
Beschläge 835
Beschleunigungsspur 539
Besen 257, 295
Besitzkarte 915
Bespannung 816, 822, 862, 893
Besprechungszimmer 718, 728
Besteck 722
Besteckkorb 294
bestickter Stoff 459
Bestückung 304
Besucher, Empfangsraum 726
Besucher, Warteraum 726
Besucherterrasse 621
Besuchereingang 726
Beton 298
Betonauslauf 655
Betonblock 298
Betonmantel 670, 671
Betonmauer 675
Betonnte Fahrwasser 616
Betonnungssystem 616
Betreibender 846
Betriebs- und Versorgungseinheit 19
Betriebsanzeigen 494
Betriebsbremse 586
Betriebsebene 664
Betriebseinstellung 504
Betriebsraum 738
Betriebsschalter 527
Bett 280, 567
Bett mit Matratze 904
Betttuch 280
Bettwäsche 280, 584
Beutel 143, 222
Beutelfach 289
Beutelklammern 534
Beuteltasche 387
Beuteltasche, kleine 388
Beuteltiere 142
Beuteltiere, Beispiele 143
Beweger 292
bewegliche Backe 311, 312
bewegliche Brücken 542
bewegliche Fluggasttreppe 623
bewegliche Kufe 885
bewegliche Trennwand 509
bewegliche Tribünen 734
beweglicher Oberkiefer 112
Bewegungen eines Flugzeugs 630
Bewegungsenergie 662
Bewegungsmelder 416
bewölkter Himmel 56
Bezahnung 112
Bezeichnungen tropischer Wirbelstürme 63
Bezugsstoff 391
BH 367
Bhutan 747
Biathlet 893
Biathlon 893
Biber 123
Bibliothek 395, 711, 726, 732, 734
Bibliothekar, Büro 732
Bidet 264
Bienenstock 100, 182
Bier 180
Bierkrug 225
bikonkave Linse 691
bikonvexe Linse 691
Bild 917
Bildanzeige 477
Bildeinstelltasten 496
bildende Künste 394
Bilderwascher 485
Bildhauer 17
Bildkontrolle 489, 490
Bildregie 490
Bildröhre 494
Bildschirm 494, 507, 518, 613
Bildschirminhalt drucken 515
Bildschirmverriegelung 526
Bildsucher 476, 492
Bildtechniker 489, 490
Bildträger 400
Bildung 732
Bildungseinrichtung 525, 711
Bildunterschrift 471
Bildvorlauf 477
Billard 862
Billardqueue 863
Billardtisch 862
Billettasche 348
Bimah 738

Bimetall-Thermometer 695
Bimetallspirale 695
Bimsstein-Korrekturstift 423
Binde, elastische 777
Bindebogen 435
Bindegewebe 172
Bindehaut 177
Bindeteil 349
Bindung 840, 887, 891
Bindung, chemische 680
Binnenklüver 603
Binnenraum 409
Binokularmikroskop 693
Binsenstängel 470
Bioabfallbehälter 71
Biologie 702
biologisch nicht abbaubare Schadstoffe 69
Biosphäre 66
Biosphäre, Aufbau 66
Birke 88
Birkenspanner 101
Birmanisch 468
Birne 193
Birne, asiatische 197
birnenförmiger Korpus 433
Birnenmelone 197
Bison 128
Biss 390
Bit 302
Bits und Bohrer, Beispiele 306
Bittermelone 188
Bitterschokolade 208
Blank 914
Blase 75
Blasebalg 904
Blasebalgtasche 359, 360
Blasinstrumente 446
Blaspfeife 432
Blassynthesizer 451
Blatt 77, 78, 79, 185, 261, 303, 304, 315, 320, 382, 454, 659, 815, 838, 841, 880
Blatt, Aufbau 79
Blatt, Säge 303, 304, 305
Blattachsel 79
Blattader 79
Blattansatz 79
Blättchen 75
Blätter, einfache 79
Blätter, zusammengesetzte 79
Blätterpapille 176
Blätterteig 205
Blattgemüse 186
Blattgrund 77
Blattrand 79
Blattscheide 79
Blattschraube 446
Blattspindel 76
Blattstecher 461
Blattstiel 79
Blattstieleinschnitt 86
Blau 400, 690
blau 741
blaue Linie 879
blaue Luzerne 190
blauer Ball 863
Blaues Band 871
blaues Schildhaupt in Silber 740
Blaufisch 220
Blaugrün 400
Blaulicht 766
Blaustrahl 494
Blauviolett 400
Blazer 355, 358
Blechbläser 437
Blechverkleidung 256
Blei 682
Bleigürtel 841
Bleikopf 444
Bleikugel 757
Bleistift 470
Bleistiftspitzer 534
Bleistiftfaltenband 283
Blende 290, 292, 293, 389, 477
Blendeneinstellung 694
Blendenöffnung 17
Blendenskala 478, 479
Blendglätter 612
Blendrahmen 249
Blendrahmen oben 249
Blinddarm 103, 106, 125, 164
blinde Tasche 355
blinder Enddarm 95
blinder Fleck 177
Blindsack 116
Blindschacht 650
Blinker 571, 911
Blinkerhebel 556
Blinkerkontrollleuchte 576
Blinkleuchte 554, 574, 575, 576
Blinklicht 591, 775
Blinklichter 568
Blinklichtkontrolle 557
Blitz 57, 65
Blitzableiter 245, 658, 663, 677
Blitzbirne 482
Blitzkontakt 476
Blitzröhre 482, 692
Blitzwürfel 482

Block 791
Block, numerischer 515
Blockdeckel 562
blocken 813
Blöße bei der Oktav-Einladung 849
Blöße bei der Prim-Einladung 849
Blöße bei der Quart-Einladung 849
Blöße bei der Quint-Einladung 849
Blöße bei der Second-Einladung 849
Blöße bei der Septim-Einladung 849
Blöße bei der Sixt-Einladung 849
Blöße bei der Terz-Einladung 849
Blouson 353
Blume, Aufbau 80
Blumen, Beispiele 80
Blumenbeet 322
Blumenkohl 187
Blumenkrone 80
Blumenladen 715
Blumenrabatte 322
Blumenziegel 917
Bluse, klassische 359
Blusen und Hemden, Beispiele 359
Blut, sauerstoffarmes 162
Blut, sauerstoffreiches 162
Blutbestandteile 162
Blutdruckmessgerät 777
Blüte 77, 80, 86
Blütenblatt 80
Blütenboden 80, 83
Blütengemüse 187
Blütenkelch 80
Blütenknospe 77
Blütenpflanzen 93
Blütenständen, Arten 81
Blütenstandstiel 78
Blütenstiel 80, 86
Blutgefäß 154, 162, 172
Blutgefäß, dorsales 97
Blutgefäße 140
Blutkörperchen, rotes 162
Blutkörperchen, weißes 162
Blutkreislauf 160
Blutkreislauf, Schema 161
Blutplasma 162
Blutwurst 216
BMX 871
BMX-Rad, Mountainbike 581
Bö 57
Boa 114
Bobschlitten 884
Bock 401
Böckchen 448
Bockkäfer 101
Bockkran 657, 658
Bockmühle 676
Bocksfuß 276
Bockshornkleesamen 198
Boden 70, 240, 614, 818, 819, 912
Boden, gewachsener 538
Boden-Luft-Flugkörper 759
Boden-Unterwasser-Flugkörper 759, 762
Bodenablauf 246, 262
Bodenanlassgerät 622
Bodenausrüstung 622
Bodenbalken 252, 256
Bodenbeläge, textile 254
Bodenbewegung, horizontale 43
Bodenbewegung, vertikale 43
Bodenbewegungen 47
Bodendiele 254
Bodendüngung 69
Bodendüse 289
Bodenentleererwagen 588
Bodengesims 753
Bodenkriechen 47
Bodenlinie 831
Bodenplättchen 440
Bodenplatte 448, 907
Bodenprofil 78
Bodenstaubsauger 289
Bodenstöpsel 757
Bodenstromgerät 622
Bodenturnfläche 824
Bodenverschmutzung 69
Bodyshirt 359
Bodysuit 366
Bogen 258, 426, 439, 446, 540, 704, 750
Bögen, Beispiele 413, 541
Bogen, gelenkloser 541
Bogen, gestelzter 413
Bogen, moderner 750
Bogenansatz 439
Bogenarm 859, 913
Bogenbrücke 540
Bogenbrücke, aufgeständerte 541
Bogenbrücken, Beispiele 541
Bogenfeld 411
Bogengang, äußerer knöcherner 174
Bogengang, hinterer knöcherner 174
Bogengang, oberer knöcherner 174
Bogenminute 704
Bogensäge 907
Bogenschießanlage 788
Bogenschießen 859
Bogenschütze 859
Bogenschutz 446
Bogensehne 750, 859
Bogensekunde 704

Bogenstaudamm 661
Bogenstaudamm im Querschnitt 661
Bohne, Flageolet 191
Bohne, grüne 191
Bohne, römische 191
Bohne, schwarzäugige 190
Bohne, schwarze 191
Bohnen 190, 191
Bohnen, dicke 190
Bohnenkraut 202
Bohranlage 651
Bohrer 307
Bohrerstellung 828
Bohrfutter 302, 306, 307
Bohrfutterschlüssel 306
Bohrgestänge 651
Bohrhammer 648
Bohrium 683
Bohrkopf 648, 651
Bohrkörper 306
Bohrkragen 651
Bohrmaschine, elektrische 306
Bohrschiff 604, 653
Bohrschnecke 323
Bohrstange 648
Bohrtisch 307
Bohrturm 651, 652, 654
Bohrungsdurchmesser 753
Bohrwerkzeuge 306
Bohrwinde 307
Boje 833
Bokken 846
Bolero 358
Bolivien 742
Bollwerk 409
Bolzen 310, 312, 382, 383, 750
Bolzenmutter 590
Bombe, vulkanische 44
Bongos 449
Boot 342
Boot ohne Fahrt 833
Boot, Teile 838
Boote und Schiffe, Beispiele 604
Boote, traditionelle 599
Bootshaken 611
Bor 682
Bordcomputer 556, 771
Bordeauxglas 225
Bördelgerät 314
Bördelverbindung 269
Bordinstrumente 899
Bordkran 761
Bordküche 624
Bordstein 712
Bordunpfeife 432
borealer Wald 66
Boretsch 202
Borke 87
Borste 383, 384
Borsten 295, 320
Böschung 244
Böschung im Auftrag 538
Bosnien und Herzegowina 744
Botswana 746
Bottich 294
Bottichrand 292
Bottnischer Meerbusen 32
Boubou 339
Boule 864
Boulevard 39, 711
Boulevardblatt 471
Bowler 865
Bowlerin 865
Bowling 865
Bowlingbahn 714, 865
Bowlingkugel 865
Bowlingschuh 865
Box 384, 873
Box für die Aufsteckbürsten 384
Boxen 842, 872, 874
Boxengasse 872
Boxenstopp 873
Boxer 842
Boxerhose 842
Boxershorts 351
Boxhandschuhe 843
Boxtasche 388
Brachacker 182
Brachiopode 92
Bramstenge 602
Brandbekämpfung 764
Brandbekämpfungsmaterial 767
Brandschutzbeauftragte, Büro 764
Brandungspfeiler 51
Brandungstor 51
Brasilien 742
Braten 215
Bratenthermometer, digitales 231
Bratentopf, flacher 235
Bräter 234
Bratpfanne 235, 905
Bratsche 439
Bratschen 437
Bratwurst 216
Brauchdampf 665
Brauenbürstchen 378
Braunalge 75
brauner Ball 863
brauner Zucker 209

Brauner Zwerg 8
Braunreis 207
Brause 328
Brausegarnitur 262
Brausenkopf 264, 270
Brauseschlauch 264, 270
Brecheisen 767
Brecher 49
Breiapfel 197
breit 472
Breitbild-Fernseher 493
Breitengrade 36
Breitenkreis 36
breiter Rückenmuskel 151
breites Mutterband 171
Breitfußgeschoß 713
Breithalter 461
Bremsanlage 553
Bremsbacke 559
Bremsbelag 559
Bremsbereich 891
Bremse 101, 783, 851, 870, 874, 909
Bremsen 559
Bremser 884
Bremsflüssigkeitsbehälter 559
Bremsgriff 579, 870
Bremshebel 876
Bremsklappe 760, 898
Bremsklappenhebel 898
Bremsklotz 622
Bremskraftregler 559
Bremskraftverstärker 552, 559
Bremskreis 559
Bremsleine 896, 897
Bremsleitung 552
Bremsleuchte 554
Bremspedal 333, 552, 556, 559, 576
Bremssattel 559, 574
Bremsscheibe 559
Bremsschlauch 559
Bremsträger 559
Bremstrommel 559
Bremswagen 588
Bremszug 579
Bremszylinder 559
Brennelemente, Becken für schadhafte 666
Brennelemente, Tonnen mit schadhaften 666
Brennen 465
Brenner 234, 259, 290, 899, 903
Brennerhebel 319
Brennholzstauraum 256
Brennofen, elektrischer 465
Brennpunkt 691
Brennraum 256, 259, 465
Brennsockel 903
Brennspiritus 656
Brennstab 667
Brennstabbeschickung 666
Brennstabbündel 667
Brennstäbe, Abgabeöffnung 666
Brennstäbe, Aufbewahrung 666
Brennstäbe, Becken 666
Brennstäbe, Füllöffnung 666
Brennstäbe, Lagerraum 666
Brennstäbe, Tonnen 666
Brennstoff 665, 670, 671
Brennstoff, fossiler 70
Brennstoffregelung 627
Brennstofftablette 667
Brennstoffventile 626
Bretonisch 469
Brett 300, 819, 836
Brett, schwarzes 734
Brettende 887
Brettspiel 915
Brettspitze 887
Bridge 523
Brie 211
Brief 474
Briefkasten 474
Briefmarke 474
Brieföffner 531
Brieftasche 387
Briefträger 475
Briefwaage 531
Brigantine 601
Brigg 601
Brillantschliff 374
Brille 385, 870, 887
Brille, Teile 385
Brillenetui 387
Briolettschliff 375
Broccoli 187
Brom 683
Brombeere 192
Brosche 376
Brot 204, 722
Brotbackautomat 239
Brothalter 238
Brotmesser 229
Browser 524
Bruch 703
Bruchstein 298
Brücke 39, 167, 284, 385, 692, 761, 854, 875
Brücke mit untenliegender Fahrbahn 541
Brücken, bewegliche 542
Brücken, starre 540
Brückenlift 596

Bruder 785
Brüder 785
Bruder/Schwester 785
Brunei 747
Brunnen für rituelle Waschungen 738
Brunnenkresse 187
Brust 115, 124, 146, 148, 171
Brustbaum 460
Brustbein 116, 121, 122, 126, 131, 141, 142, 152
Brustbeine 107
Brustdrüse 171
Brustflosse 108, 136
Brustkorb 146, 148
Brustleistentasche 348
Brustmuskel, großer 150
Brustplatte 853
Brustpolster 800
Brustriemen 857
Brustschutz 796, 808, 859
Brustschwimmen 832
Bruststück 749
Brusttasche 349, 352
Brüstungsriegel 252
Brustwarze 146, 148, 171
Brustwehr 409
Brustwirbel 122, 126, 131, 138, 142, 153, 157
Brutraum 100
Brutzwiebel 468
Bube 914
Bubikragen 362
Buch, elektronisches 527
Buch, gebundenes 426
Buche 87
Buchecker 193
Bücherregal 734
Bücherrückgabe 733
Bücherstütze 535
Bücherwagen 733
Buchhaltung 509
Buchhandlung 714
Buchrücken 425
Buchrückenbearbeitung 425
Buchrückenpresse 425
Buchsenhalter 274
Büchsenöffner 230
Buchstaben 472
Bucht 7, 38
Bucht, Große Australische 29
Buchweizen 85, 203
Buckel 875, 890
Buckelpiste 890
Buckelwal 137
Buddha 736
Buddhismus 736
Büfett 279
Büffel 128
Buffet 720
Bug 606, 609, 624, 834, 836
Bug, geschnitzter 598
Bugball 839
Bügel 303, 385, 439, 502, 750, 855, 913
Bügel, verstellbarer 303
Bügelanschlag 385
Bügelende 385
Bügelfalte 350
Bügelhebel 912
Bügelheck 288
Bügelhorn 447
Bügeln 347
bügeln 347
Bügelriemen 855
Bügelrundung 385
Bügelsäge 303, 314
Bügelsohle 288
Bügelspannmechanismus 910
Bügeltritt 587
Bugfahrwerk 624, 760
Bugladeklappe 608
Bugpropeller 606
Bugspriet 602
Bugstrahler 107
Bugtür 605
Bugverzierung 600
Bugwulst 607, 609
Bühne 402, 430, 431
Bühnenhaus 402, 430
Bühnenhintergrund 430
Bulbospongiosus 169
Bulgarien 744
Bulgarisch 469
Bullauge 608
Bulldogge 130
Bulldozer 647
Bund 185, 353, 440, 441
Bund mit Druckknöpfen 368
Bund, elastischer 353
Bündchen 351
Bündel 663
Bundesstaat 37
Bundmarkierung 441
Bundverlängerung 350
Bunker 866, 867
Bunkeröl 656
Bunsenbrenner 685
Buntstifte 396
Buntstiftzeichnung 396
Bürette 685

Burg 408
Bürgersteig 712
Burggraben 408
Burghof 408
Burkina Faso 745
Büro 509, 582, 720, 724, 726
Büro der Geschäftsleitung 718
Büro der Oberschwester 779
Büro der Schulaufsicht 735
Büro des Bibliothekars 732
Büro des Brandschutzbeauftragten 764
Büro des dienstthabenden Arztes 778
Büro des Dienststellenleiters 768
Büro des Direktors 394, 726, 731, 732
Büro des Geschäftsführers 509
Büro des Kommandanten 764
Büro des Konservators 394
Büro des Richters 728
Büro des Schulleiters 735
Büro des stellvertretenden Dienststellenleiters 768
Büro des stellvertretenden Direktors 726
Büro des Wachpersonals 733
Büroautomation 509
Bürodrehstuhl 511
Bürogebäude 596, 710, 713
Büroklammerhalter 534
Büroklammern 534
Büromöbel 510
Bürotechnik 468
Büroturm 713
Bürstchen für Webeffekt 456
Bürste 289, 295, 384, 688
Bürste mit Stangen 852
Bürsten 688
Bürstenkörper 295
Burundi 745
Bürzel 115
Bus 513, 522, 568, 713
Busbahnhof 710
Bushaltestelle 712
Busmodul 40
Busnetzwerk 522
Büstenhalter, trägerloser 367
Büstenschale 367
Butangastank 391
Butter 210
Butterdose 223, 226
Butterfach 291
Butterfly 851
Buttermesser 228
Buttermilch 210
Butterroller 229
Button-Down-Kragen 349

C

C 434
Cabanjacke 355
Cabochonschliff 375
Cadmium 683
Café 710, 715
Cafeteria 725, 735
Cajun-Gewürzmischung 199
Californium 684
Callisto 4
Calvinismus 736
Camcorder 496, 517
Camembert 211
Camisol 366
Camping 902
Camping für Wohnwagen 725
Camping für Zelte und Wohnwagen 725
Campingausrüstung 905
Candela 702
Candlepin 865
Cannelloni 206
Cañon, unterseeischer 49
Cape 355
Caprihose 358
Caraco 337
Carapax 107
Cardigan 359
Carina 108
Carpentariagolf 29
Carpus 116
Carré 919
Casabamelone 195
Cashewkern 193
Cäsium 682
Cassegrain-Fokus 17
Cassini 19
Casting 910
Cayennepfeffer 199
CB-Funkanlage 505
CD 501, 504
CD, wiederbeschreibbare 521
CD-/DVD-Auswurftaste 513
CD-/DVD-Laufwerk 513, 526
CD-Einschub 918
CD-Fach 501
CD-Lade 521
CD-Rekorder 503
CD-ROM-Laufwerk 517
CD-Spieler 488, 501, 503, 504
CD-Spieler, tragbarer 503
CD-Tasten 504
Cedille 473

Celli 437
Cello 439
Celsius-Temperatur, Maßeinheit 702
Celsiusskala 695
Cembalo 443
Cent 728
Centerlautsprecher 493
Centre 807
Cephalica 160
Cephalothorax 103
Cer 684
Chac-Mool 412
Chaiselongue 276
Chamäleon 11, 114
Chantilly-Parkett 254
Charlestonmaschine 448
Charlottenform 232
Charon 5
Chaton 376
Chatroom 525
Chayote 189
Check-in-Schalter 620
Checkliste 20
Chef-Kameramann 429
Chef-Mechaniker 873
Chefmaschinist 428
Chefschreibtisch 511
Chefsekretärin 509
Chefzimmer 509
Chemie 680
chemische Behandlung 656
chemische Bindung 680
chemische Elemente 682
chemische Reinigung 715
chemische Symbole 684
Chesterfieldsofa 276
Cheval 919
Chicorée 187
Chiffonière 279
Chile 742
Chili, Jalapeño 199
Chilipulver 199
Chilis, getrocknete 199
Chilis, zerstoßene 199
China 747
China-Broccoli 187
Chinakohl 186
Chinesenkragen 363
Chinesisch 468
chinesische Dattel 197
Chipset 513
Chirimoya 197
Chirurgen-Waschraum 781
Chirurgie, kleine 778
Chiton 336
Chlamys 336
Chlor 683
Chlorbleiche möglich 347
Chlorbleiche nicht möglich 347
chloren 347
Chloroplast 74
Choanocyte 95
Chokerkette 374
Chondrit 8
Chor 410, 411
Chorhaupt 411
Chorizo-Wurst 216
Chorlampe 737
Chorscheitelkapelle 410, 411
Chorumgang 411
Chow-Chow 130
Christentum 736
Chrom 683
Chromatin 94
Chromosphäre 6
Chronologie der Religionen 736
Chutney 201
Cine-Skala 479
Circumflex 473
Climber 851
Clip 470, 506
Cliphalterung 275
Clubsessel 276
Coach-Box 794
Cockpit 22, 624, 626, 834, 873, 898
Cockpithaube 760
Cocktailbar 279, 724
Cocktailglas 225
Cocos-Platte 43
Code-Taste 528
Coelophysis 93
Coeur-Dekolleté 363
Collegering 376
Collie 130
Compact Discs, Lesen 501
Compact-Flash-Speicherkarte 481
Compluvium 406
Computer 734
Computer-Schnittstellenport 520
Computeranschlussbuchse 518
Computerbildschirm 20
Computerfach 527
Computerprogramme 771
Computerraum 734, 763
Computertisch 511
Conchiglie 206
Container 605, 635
Containerauflieger 572
Containerbrücke 596

Containerflachwagen 588
Containerlaschsystem 605
Containerschiff 596, 604
Containerterminal 596, 708
Containmentvolumen, freies 671
Controller 918
Controller-Schnittstellen 918
Cooksonia 92
Cookstraße 29
Copyright 473
Costa Rica 742
Costalschild 113
Cotardie 337
Coudé-Fokus 17
Coulomb 702
Coulommiers 211
Coupé 549
Couscous 204
Couscoustopf 235
Cowper-Drüse 169
Coxaldrüse 103
Coyolxauhqui-Stein 412
Cree 469
Crêpe-Pfanne 235
Cricket 798
Cricketball 798
Cricketschuh 798
Cricketspieler 798
Crochetwinkel 348, 362
Croissant 204
Crottin de Chavignol 210
Cubiculum 406
Curium 684
Curling 877
Curlingbesen 877
Curlingstein 877
Curry 198
Curryklemme 835
Cursor an Zeilenanfang 515
Cursor an Zeilenende 515
Cursor nach links 515
Cursor nach oben 515
Cursor nach rechts 515
Cursor nach unten 515
Cursortasten 529
Cyanobakterium 92

D

D 434, 862
D-Karabiner 900
Dach 100, 245, 257, 412, 551, 567, 635, 647
Dach mit Firstlaterne 414
Dachbinder 253
Dachbodenleiter 321
Dächer 414
Dachfenster 245
Dachkranz, vorkragender 412
Dachluke 567
Dachrinne 244
Dachs 134
Dachziegel 299, 412
Dackelohrkragen 362
Dalmatiner 131
Dame 914, 916
Damen-Accessoires 717
Damen-Freizeitbekleidung 716
Damen-Nachtwäsche 716
Damen-Sportbekleidung 716
Damenflanke 916
Damenhandschuhe 346
Damenjacken 716
Damenkleidung 355
Damenkopfbedeckungen 341
Damenkostüme 716
Damenmäntel 716
Damenpullover 716
Damenschuhe 343, 716
Damentoilette 427, 509, 724
Damm 445, 657
Dammbrust 660
Dammkrone 657, 660, 661
Dammsockel 660
Dampf 646, 665, 681
Dampfauslass 670, 671
Dampfbügeleisen 288
Dampfdruck 665
Dampfdüse 288
Dämpfeinsatz 235
Dämpfer 443, 447
Dämpferarm 443
Dämpferpralleiste 443
Dampferzeuger 646
Dampfgenerator 665, 669, 670, 671, 674, 763
Dampfgeneratorraum, Kühler 669
Dampfkocher 722
Dampfkochtopf 235
Dampfregler 241
Dampfstärkeregler 288
Dämpfung, magnetische 698
Dänemark 744
Dänisch 469
Dänische Dogge 131
dänisches Roggenbrot 205
Danish Blue 211

Darm 97, 104, 105, 107, 109, 112, 161
Darmbein 122, 126, 152
Darmblindsack 95
Darmblindschlauch 95
Darreichungsformen, Arzneimittel 783
darstellende Künste 427
Dartscheibe 918
Dartspiel 918
Datei 524
Dateiformat 524
Datenanfang 501
Datenaufzeichnung 41
Datenauswertung 41, 54
Datenbank 525
Datendisplay 508
Dateneingabe, Feinregler 450
Dateneingabe, Grobregler 450
Datenempfang 41
Datenspeicherung 694
Datentechnik 509
Datenübertragung 41
Datierungsnagel 590
Dattel 192
Dattel, chinesische 197
Datumaufnahmetaste 496
Datumeinblendetaste 496
Datumstempel 531
Dauerausstellungsräume 395
Dauerbrand 256
Daumen 140, 141, 156, 173, 346, 797
Daumen, opponierbarer 139
Daumenauflage 446
Daumenfittich 115
Daumenring 447
Daumenteil 776
Daunendecke 280
David 736
Davidstern 738
Davitgürtel 770
Davit 602
Dechsel 401, 901
Deck 838
Deckblatt 84, 390
Decke 257, 280, 538, 818, 819
Deckel 234, 237, 238, 239, 240, 241, 268, 291, 292, 295, 313, 391, 398, 465, 484, 755, 907
Deckelbügel 465
Deckelhalter, magnetischer 240
Deckelknopf 236
Deckeltasche 906
Deckenbalken 252, 254
Deckendurchführung 257
Deckendurchlass 258
Deckenleuchte 286
Deckenträger 284
Deckenventilator 261
Deckfeder 115
Deckleiste 249
Defibrillator 775
Deflektor 260
Degen 849
Degenfechter 848
Dehnungsfuge 590
Deichkrone 664
Deimos 4
Deklination 13
Deklinationsachse 14, 15
Dekolletés 363
Dekorateur 429
Dekorationen 282
Dekorationsartikel 716
Dekorationsgeschäft 715
Delegierte, technische 881
Delle 867
Delphin 12, 136, 137
Delphin, äußere Merkmale 136
Delphin, Skelett 136
Delta 48, 51
Delta II 24
Delta-Arm 48
Deltaflügel 629, 630
Deltamuskel 150
Dendrit 168
Dendrit, räumlicher 64
Denkmal 39
Deodorant 379
Depolarisationsgemisch 689
Derrickkran 604
Dessertgabel 228
Dessertlöffel 228
Dessertmesser 228
Desserts 723
Detektorkopf 18
Deutsch 469
Deutscher Schäferhund 130
deutscher Senf 200
deutsches Roggenbrot 205
Deutschland 744
Devon 92
Dezimal-Tabuliertaste 528
Dia 483
diagonaler Schlittschuhschritt 892
diagonaler Zug 916
Diagonalreifen 561
Diagonalstrebe 663
diakritische Zeichen 473
Diamagazin 483
Diamant 375

Diaphyse 155
Diapositiv 483
Diaprojektor 483
Diarähmchen 483
Diastema 123
Diawahl, manuelle 483
Diawechsel 483
Diawechsel, rückwärts 483
Diawechsel, vorwärts 483
Dichtemesser 562
dichtes Windelhöschen 368
Dichtring 655
Dichtung 268, 269
Dichtung, magnetische 291
Dichtungsmutter 268
Dichtungsring 294
Dichtungsschleier 661
Dichtverschluss 903
Dickdarm 110, 164
Dickdarm, absteigender 164
Dickdarm, aufsteigender 164
Dickdarm, quer verlaufender 164
dicke Bohnen 190
Dickemessung 700
Dickte 472
die wichtigsten Baumaterialien 298
die wichtigsten Flugkörper 759
die wichtigsten internationalen Verkehrszeichen 544
die wichtigsten nordamerikanischen Verkehrszeichen 546
die wichtigsten Schnitzeisen 401
Diechling 749
Diele 250, 254
Dienst, technischer 732
Diensteingang 732, 735
Dienstgradabzeichen 770
Dienstgürtel 770
diensthabender Arzt, Büro 778
Dienstkleidung 764
Dienstkleidungswäscherei 764
Dienststellenleiter, Büro 768
Dieselkraftstoff 656
Dieselmotor 586, 605
Dieselmotor, Arbeitsprozess 565
Dieselmotoren 762
Dieselmotorlüfter 586
Dieselmotorraum 636, 637, 638, 639
Dieseltriebwerk 605
Differenzial 553
Diffusionskalotte 479
Diffusorrohr 627
Digital-Camcorder 517
Digitalanzeige 316, 699, 777
digitale Frequenzanzeige 498
digitale Pegelanzeige 488
digitale Spiegelreflexkamera: Rückansicht 477
digitales Bratenthermometer 231
digitales Tonbandgerät 488
Digitalisierungsunterlage 517
Digitalkamera 481, 517
Digitalthermometer 777
Digitaluhr 696
Digiti 116
Digitus 122, 143
Dijon-Senf 200
Diktiergerät 534
Dill 202
Dimetrodon 92
Dimmerraum 490
Dimmerschalter 274
Dinkel 203
Diode 476, 673
Dione 5
dioptrischer Ring 614
direkte Ablesung, Regenmesser 58
Direktor, Büro 394, 726, 731, 732
Dirigent(in) 437
Dirigentenpult 437
Dirndl-BH 367
Disc-Kamera 481
Diskantregister 432
Diskantsteg 442
Diskanttastatur 432
Diskette 513
Disketten-Auswurftaste 513
Diskettenauswurftaste 513
Diskettenlaufwerk 450, 513
Diskettenlaufwerk, externes 521
Diskus 793
Diskus- und Hammerwerfen 791
Display 261, 476, 479, 494, 495, 497, 503, 505, 506, 507, 526, 530, 730, 731
Display-Panel 496
Displayanzeige 626
Displaybeleuchtungstaste 479
Displayeinstellung 506
distale Epiphyse 155
Distanzstück 667
Disziplinen 889
Ditali 206
divergierende Plattengrenzen 43
Division 703
Divisionstaste 529
Djembe 433
Dnjepr 32

Do 847
Dock 596
Docking-Station 527
Dogge, Dänische 131
Dohyo 847
Dokumentationszentrum 764
Dokumente 508
Dokumentenablage 531
Dokumentenfach 527
Dokumentenmappe 532
Dolch 751
Dolch, langer 751
Dolde 81
Doldenrispe 85
Doldentraube 81
Doline 47
Dollar 728
Dolle 839
Dolly 428
Dollyschienen 428
Dom 410
Dom, gotischer 410
Dom, Grundriss 411
Domain zweiten Grades 524
Domain, Toplevel 524
Domainname 524
Dominica 743
Dominikanische Republik 743
Dominosteine 914
Donau 32
Doppel- und Dreifachschanze 890
Doppel-B 435
Doppel-Kassettendeck 503
Doppel-Null-Taste 529
Doppelbett 724
Doppelblank 914
Doppelblatt 446
Doppelbogen 269
Doppeldeck-Flachpalette 632
Doppeldecker 628
Doppeldeckerbus 569
doppelfett 472
Doppelhantel 840
Doppelhaus 419
Doppelklappbrücke 542
Doppelkombination 853
Doppelkreuz 435
Doppelkurve 544, 547
Doppelmanschette 361
Doppelmaulschlüssel 311
Doppeloxer 852, 853
Doppelpaddel 837, 839
Doppelpunkt 473
Doppelriegel 252
Doppelringschlüssel 311
Doppelringschlüssel, offener 311
Doppelschlag 435
Doppelschrägstrich 524
Doppelsitz 594
Doppelsitzer-Rennrodel 884
Doppelspiel 820
Doppelspüle 262
Doppelständer 739
Doppelständer mit Zunge 739
Doppelstockschub 892
Doppelvergiasung 675
Doppelwimpel 739
Doppelzimmer 724
Dopplerwürfel 915
Dorf 708, 886
dorische Halbsäule 407
dorische Säulenordnung 404
Dorn 350, 390, 461, 462, 901
Dornablage 534
Dornfortsatz 168
dorsales Blutgefäß 97
Dose 223, 484, 611
Dose, Konserven 223
Dosen-Aerosol 783
Dosenöffner 223, 240, 905
Dosierteller 643
Dotterhaut 117
Double 918
Double zero 919
Double-zero 919
Douglasscher Raum 170
Douze dernier (25 bis 36) 919
Douze milieu (13 bis 24) 919
Douze premier (1 bis 12) 919
Down-Quark 680
Downhillrad 870
Drache 13
Drachen 917
Drachenfliegen 897
Draggen 610
Draht 689, 851
Drahtauslöser 482
Drahtbesen 236
Drahtbürste 380
drahtlose Kommunikation 505
Drahtschlinge 900
Drahtschneider 317
Drahtschneidezange 317
Drahtzug 590

Drainage-Decke 660
Drainage-Schicht 660
Drakestraße 29, 31
drapierter Ausschnitt 363
drapierter Kragen 363
Dreh- und Verriegelungsmechanik 248
drehbare Walze 458
Drehbohrverfahren 651
Drehbrücke 542
Drehdüse 329
Drehen 464
Drehfeststeller 572
Drehflügel nach außen 415
Drehflügel nach innen 415
Drehflügeltür 416
Drehführung 16
Drehgehäuse 416
Drehgelenk 156
Drehgeschwindigkeitssensor, Räder 559
Drehgestell 585, 586, 595
Drehgestell-Rahmen 586
Drehgestellflachwagen 588
Drehgestellkastenwagen 587
Drehgestellwaggon 588
Drehgriff 516
Drehjustierung 692
Drehkartei 531
Drehknopf 909, 910
Drehkranz 542, 638, 920
Drehkreuz 421, 919
Drehkuppel 17
Drehleiterfahrzeug 766
Drehmoment-Einstellring 306
Drehmomentwandler 292
Drehpunkt 686
Drehscheibe 236, 273, 464, 766, 919
Drehschiene 464
Drehschwengel 750
Drehsessel 511
Drehspiegel 381
Drehstromgenerator 674
Drehteller 464
Drehtisch 651
Drehtür 416
Drehtüren 719
Drehverbindung 793
Drehwalze 43
Drehzahl-Einstellung 500
Drehzahlgeber 563
Drehzahlmesser 557, 576
Drehzahlschalter 306
Drehzapfen 317
Drei-Zehenhuf 127
Dreieck 12, 705, 863
Dreieckchen 154
Dreieckfenster 551
dreieckiger Korpus 433
Dreiecksgruppe 173
Dreiecktuch 777
dreieinhalbfacher Salto vorwärts gebückt 829
Dreifachbalken 852
Dreifachnetwerk 629
Dreifachsprung 875
dreiflügeliger Propeller 628
Dreifuß 436
Dreifußständer 448
Dreigelenkbogen 541
dreiköpfiger Armstrecker 151
Dreipass 172
dreipolige Steckdose 274
dreipoliger, amerikanischer Stecker 274
Dreipunktbocke 641
Dreirad 581
Dreispitz 339
Dreisprung 790, 793
dreitürige Kombilimousine 549
Dreiviertelarm 360
Dreiviertellange Jacke 352
Dreivierteltakt 434
dreizählig 79
Dressiernadel 233
Dressurreiten 855
Dressurviereck 855
Drilling 914
Drillingshaken 911
Drillmaschine 643
Drillschraubenzieher 302
Drittbelegung 514
dritte Reihe 804
Dritte Runde 789
dritte Stufe 25
dritte Zehe 115
dritter Malspieler 794
dritter Ventilzug 447
drittes Mal 794
Drohne 99
Dromedar 129
Drosselvene, äußere 160
Drosselvene, innere 160
Drosselventil 649
Druck, Maßeinheit 702
Druckabzug 320
Druckanzeiger 841
Druckbehälter 671
Druckbild 420
Druckbleistift 470
Druckbogen 421
Druckeinsteller 452

988

DEUTSCHES REGISTER

ASTRONOMIE > 2-25; ERDE > 26-71; PFLANZENREICH > 72-89; TIERREICH > 90-143; MENSCH > 144-177; NAHRUNGSMITTEL UND KÜCHE > 178-241; HAUS > 242-295;
HEIMWERKEN UND GARTENARBEIT > 296-333; KLEIDUNG > 334-371; PERSÖNLICHE AUSSTATTUNG > 372-391; KUNST UND ARCHITEKTUR > 392-465; KOMMUNIKATION UND BÜROTECHNIK > 466-535;
TRANSPORT UND FAHRZEUGE > 536-643; ENERGIE > 644-677; WISSENSCHAFT > 678-705; GESELLSCHAFT > 706-785; SPORT UND SPIELE > 786-920

Drucken 420
Drucker 523
Drücker 447
Drückerbügel 315
Druckerteil 529
Druckertisch 511
Druckerzeuger 670
druckfestes Außenrohr 667
Druckgasförderanlage 652
Druckkammer 543, 671
Druckknopf 248, 346, 353, 444, 453, 470
Druckknopfleiste 353, 369
Druckknopfleiste an der Beininnenseite 368, 369
Drucklager 659
Druckluft 548
Druckluft-Bohrknecht 648
Druckluftanschluss 320
Druckluftbehälter 320
Druckluftflasche 765, 841
Drucklufttank 873
Druckmechanik 470
Druckmesser 654
Druckmessgerät 777
Druckminderer 319, 841
Druckmotiv 369
Druckregler 384, 765
Druckregulierung 841
Druckrohr 470
Druckrolle 643
Druckschalter 304, 305, 306, 308, 331
Drückstange 851
Drucksteg 442
Drucktaste 236, 294
Drucktendenz 55
Drucktisch 421, 423
Druckverschluss 386
Druckverstärkerpumpanlage 654
Druckwasser 662, 671
Druckwasserreaktor 671
Druckwelle 651, 653
Druckzahnrädchen 240
Druckzünder 758
Drumlin 45
Drüsenmagen 116
Dschibuti 745
Dschunke 600
Dual-in-line-Gehäuse 689
Dubnium 683
Duckpin 865
Dudelsack 432
Dufflecoat 353
Dulse 183
Düne 51
Düne, komplexe 52
Dünenformen 52
Dünenzug 52
Dung 70
Düngemitteln, Einsatz 69
Düngerstreuer 324
Dungstreuer 641
Dunkelkammer 484
dunkles Roggenbrot 204
Dünndarm 110, 113, 116, 125, 164
dünne Wachskerze 422
Dunst 57, 65
Dunstabzugshaube 224, 290, 721, 722
Dunstrohrabzug 262
Duo 438
Duodenum 116
Durchflussrohr 672
Durchführung 657, 658, 663
Durchgangsmetalldetektor 726
Durchgangsprüfer 316
Durchgangstülle 272
durchgehende Linie 538
Durchgrifftasche 355
Durchladegriff 755
Durchlaufträger 540
Durchmesser 704
Durchschnitt, Erdatmosphäre 53
Durchschuss 472
durchsichtiger Reiter 532
Durchziehschnur 353
Durchzug 283
Durchzugsöffnung 259
Durianfrucht 197
Dusche 251, 724, 726, 780
Duschen und Toiletten der Offiziere 764
Duschkabine 264
Düse 22, 24, 25, 259, 315, 319, 320, 329, 398, 760
Düsenflugzeugbenzin 656
Düsenkappe 398
Düsenreiniger 318
Düsentriebwerke 761
Duty-free-Shop 621
DVD 494
DVD-Einschub 918
DVD-Lade 494
DVD-Rekorder 521
DVD-Spieler 494
Dynamo 578, 688
Dysprosium 684

E

E 434
E-Commerce 525
E-Mail-Software 524
E-Mail-Taste 514
Eau de parfum 379
Eau de toilette 379
Ebene 38
ebene Flächen 704
ebener Spiegel 17
ebenes Gelenk 156
Echinodermen 94, 95
Echinus 404
Echo 40, 41
Echolot 613
echte Teilmenge von 703
echter Reizker 183
Eckballfahne 803
Eckbeschlag 587, 635
Eckbogen 803
Ecke 426, 842, 878
Eckfahne 801
Eckhocker 842
eckige Klammern 473
Eckpfosten 252
Eckpolster 842
Ecksäule 635
Eckschrank 279
Eckstrebe 127
Eckstück 389
Eckturm 408
Eckzahn 121, 159
Ecuador 742
Edelgas 274
Edelgase 684
Edelpilzkäse 211
Edelsteine 375
Editier-Such-Taste 496
Effiliermesser 381
Effilierschere, einseitig gezahnte 382
Effilierschere, zweiseitig gezahnte 382
effusiver Vulkan 44
Ehefrau 785
Ehemann 785
Ehering 376
Ehrensessel, steinerner 738
Ei 100, 117
Eiche 88
Eichel 169
Eichelhäher 118
Eichelkürbis 189
Eichhörnchen 123
Eidechse 12, 114
Eier 109, 111, 213
Eier, Karton 222
Eierfach 291
Eierkarton 222
Eiernudeln, asiatische 207
Eierschneider 233
Eierstock 170, 171
Eieruhr 231
eiförmig 79
Eigelb 117
Eigentumswohnungen 419
Eileiter 97, 170, 171
Eileiterampulle 171
Eileiterenge 171
Eileitertrichter 171
Eimer 295
Eimer, Abfall 295
ein Pärchen 914
Ein- und Auslaufschütz 597
Ein- und Ausschalter 237, 240, 241
Ein-/Ausschalter 263, 286, 288, 289, 318, 476, 479, 483, 488, 494, 498, 505, 506, 513, 518, 519, 520, 526, 613
Ein-Zehenhuf 127
Ein/Aus 504
Ein/Aus/Lautstärke 504
einarmiger Bandit 920
einarmiger Schulterwurf 844
Einatmen 832
Einatmungsventil 773
einäugige Spiegelreflexkamera 480
Einbahnstraße 544, 546
Einbandleder 425
Einbaum 599
Einbauwaschtisch 264
Einbinden 425
Einblicklupe 694
Einbuchtung, vordere 173
Einer 839
Einerkajak (K1) 839
Einerkanadier (C1) 838
Einfach-Kettenrad 871
Einfach-Ritzel 871
Einfachdeck-Flachpalette 632
einfache Blätter 79
einfache Falte 350, 357
einfache Kandare 854
einfache Organismen 94
einfache Stange 284
einfacher Flaschenzug 686
einfacher Schotstek 908
einfacher Takling 908
einfacher Zeilenabstand 472
einfaches Auge 95
Einfachschanze 890
Einfädler 454
einfahrbarer Ausleger 18
Einfahrgleis 589
Einfahröffnung 632
Einfahrt 539, 769
einfallendes Neutron 681
Einfassband 340
Einfassung 322, 342
Einfassung, seitliche 256
Einfeldbrücke 541
einflammiger Gasbrenner 903
Einflugloch 100
Einfügen 515
Einfügetaste 515
Einfüllöffnung 288
Einfüllschacht 237, 240
Einfüllstutzen 332, 553, 655
Eingabe 515
Eingabe-Löschtaste 529
Eingabegerät für persönliche Identifikationsnummer (PIN) 731
Eingabegeräte 514
Eingabetaste 515, 731
Eingabezeile 529
Eingang 402, 592, 719, 738, 902, 903
Eingangsbereich 489, 717
Eingangsbuchse 316, 520
Eingangshalle 250, 394, 509, 620, 713
Eingangsmonitore 491
Eingangsschalter 497
Eingangssperre 592
Eingangstüren 427
eingebautes Schwimmbecken 246
eingefärbte Oberfläche 420
eingehängte Spannweite 540
eingelegte Falte 283
eingenähter Boden 902, 903
eingerollter junger Wedel 76
eingeschlossenes Grundwasser 646
eingeschnittenes Satteldach 415
eingesetzte Tasche 360
eingesetzter Ärmel 349
eingetragenes Warenzeichen 473
Eingeweideganglion 105
eingezogene Kralle 133
eingliedrige Trugdolde 81
Einhand-Mischbatterie 270
Einhand-Rohrzange 315
Einhängeleiter 321
Einheit, mobile 486
Einheitensystem, internationales 702
Einhorn 11
Einkaufsstraße 710
Einkaufstasche 388
Einkaufstasche, große 388
Einkaufstüten 181
Einkaufswagen 181
Einkaufszentrum 709, 714
Einladungen 849
Einlage 313, 390, 439, 440, 455
Einlasskanal 565
Einlassventil 564, 566
einläufige Gardinenstange 284
Einlaufkanal 597
Einlaufrille 500
Einlegegurke 188
Einlegesohle 345
Einmachthermometer 231
Einmündung 544, 547
Einpackhilfe 181
Einpersonenzelt 903
einpoliger Schalter 272
Einreiher 348
Einreißhaken 767
Einrumpfboote 835
Eins 703
Einsägen 424
Einsatz 389, 649
Einsatz für Imbusschrauben 302
Einsatz für Kreuzschlitzschrauben 302
Einsatz für Schlitzschrauben 302
Einsatz von Düngemitteln 69
Einsatzbesprechungsraum 769
Einsätze 239
einschalige Muschel 105
einschalige Muschel, äußere Merkmale 105
Einschalter 293
Einschalttaste 508
Einschnitt, oberer seitlicher 86
Einschnitt, unterer seitlicher 86
einseitig gezahnte Effilierschere 382
Einsitzer Männer, Start 885
Einsitzer-Rennrodel 884
Einspangenschuh 343
Einspeisung in das Elektrizitätsnetz 662
Einspeisung in das Leitungsnetz 677
Einspritzdüse 565, 566
Einspritzung 565
Einstechhebel 240
Einsteckschloss mit Dreh- und Verriegelungsmechanik 248
Einstecktuch 348
Einsteiggriff 594
Einsteigestation, radiale 619
Einsteigetreppe 631
Einsteinium 684
Einstellanzeige 889
einstellbare Bremse 910
Einstellhebel 643
Einstellkerbe 889
Einstellrad 555
Einstellspanner 895
Einstellung 502
Einstellung der Deklinationsachse 14, 15
Einstellung der Rektaszensionsachse 14, 15
Einstellung, horizontale 518
Einstellung, Pendelhub 305
Einstellung, vertikale 518
Einstellungen löschen 512
Einstellungsanzeige 477
Einstellventil für die Flüssigkeitsmenge 320
Einstellventil für die Strahlbreite 320
Einstichkasten 792
Einstiegschacht 650
Einstiegsloch 47
Einstiegsluke 23, 655
Einstiegstür 568, 569, 584, 594
einstöckiges Haus 419
Eintauchhaltung 829
Eintauchstellungen 829
einteilige Klappbrücke 542
einteiliger Anzug 884
einteiliger Overall 896
Einteilung 386
Eintrittskante 625
Eintrittskartenautomat 427
einwärts 828
Einwärtsdreher, runder 150
Einweg-Brennstoffflasche 314, 319
Einwegkamera 480
Einwegkontaktlinse 384
Einwegrasierer 383
Einzahlungsschlitz 730
Einzelbett 724
Einzelblatteinzug 519
Einzeldisziplin, Anzeigetafel 825
Einzelgefahrenzeichen 617
Einzeller 94
Einzelschritte bei der Elektrizitätserzeugung 662
Einzelsitz 594
Einzelspiel 821
Einzelzimmer 724
Einziehdraht 317
Einzugsablage 531
Einzugsschnecke 643
Einzugswalze 642
Einzugtaste 528
Eipochierer 235
Eis 67
Eisautomat 548
Eisbär 135
Eisbehälter 240
Eisbein 215
Eisbergsalat 186
Eisbrecher 606
Eisen 683, 868
Eisen 3 868
Eisen 4 868
Eisen 5 868
Eisen 6 868
Eisen 7 868
Eisen 8 868
Eisen 9 868
Eisen mit zwei schrägen Seiten 401
Eisen, gebogenes 401
Eisen, gerades 401
Eisenbahn 39
Eisenbahn-Oberbau 590
Eisenbahnstrecke 709
Eisenmeteorit 8
Eisenschläger 867
Eisenträger 582
eiserner Vorhang 430
Eisfläche 877, 878, 881
Eishaken 901
Eishockey 878
Eishockeyschläger 880
Eishockeyspieler 878
Eishutfeh 741
Eiskappe 61
Eiskörnchen 64
Eiskratzer 558
Eiskunstlauf 881
Eiskunstlaufkufe 881
Eiskunstlaufstiefel 881
Eislaufplatz 886
Eismaschine 240, 721
Eispickel 901
Eisportionierer 233
Eisregen 57
Eisschelf, Amery 29
Eisschnelllauf 882
Eisschnelllauf-Schlittschuhe 883
Eisschnelllaufbahn 882
Eisschnellläufer: Kurzstrecke 882
Eisschnellläufer: Langstrecke 882
Eisschraube 901
Eistanzkufe 881
Eisvogel 118
Eiswürfelschale 291
Eiswürfelspender 224
Eiweiß 117
Eiweißdrüse 104
Eizelle 170
Ejakulationsgang 169
ekkrine Schweißdrüse 172
Ekliptik 13
Ektoderm 95
Ektopterygoid 112
El Salvador 742
elastische Binde 777
elastische Kupplung 677
elastische Schürze 605
elastischer Beinausschnitt 351
elastischer Bund 353
elastischer Fingerhut 531
elastisches Ligament 133
Elch 129
Elefant 129
elektrische Anlage 553
elektrische Bohrmaschine 306
elektrische Gehrungssäge 304
elektrische Gitarre 441
elektrische Heckenschere 331
elektrische Schiebetür 569
elektrische Schreibmaschine 528
elektrische Spannung 774
elektrische Steuereinheit 559
elektrische Stichsäge 305
elektrische Stromstärke, Maßeinheit 702
elektrische Zahnbürste 384
elektrischer Brennofen 465
elektrischer Golfwagen 869
elektrischer Heißwasserbereiter 266
elektrischer Heizkessel 258
elektrischer Kreislauf 274
elektrischer Schnellkocher 239
Elektrischer Tischgrill 239
elektrischer Widerstand, Maßeinheit 702
elektrisches Auszahlungselement 920
elektrisches Potential, Maßeinheit 702
elektrisches Spulgerät 462
Elektrizität 272, 662
Elektrizität aus Wasserkraft 657
Elektrizität und Magnetismus 687
Elektrizitätserzeugung 662, 674, 676
Elektrizitätserzeugung aus geothermischer Energie 646
Elektrizitätserzeugung aus Kernenergie 665
Elektrizitätserzeugung aus Wärmeenergie 646
Elektrizitätserzeugung aus Windenergie 677
Elektrizitätserzeugung durch den Generator 665
Elektrizitätsmenge, Maßeinheit 702
Elektrizitätsnetz, 662
Elektrizitätsverteilung 663
Elektrode 275, 318
Elektrodenhalter 318
Elektrodenkabel 318
elektrodynamisches Mikrofon 488
Elektroelement 465
Elektrofahrzeug 563
Elektroflorett 848
Elektrohaushaltsgeräte, große 716
Elektrohaushaltsgeräte, kleine 717
Elektroherd 290, 721
Elektroinstallateurwerkzeuge 316
Elektrokabel 556, 563
Elektrokonvektor 260
Elektrolytkondensatoren 689
Elektrolytseparator 689
elektromagnetisches Spektrum 690
Elektromesser 237
Elektrometer 848
Elektromotor 259, 331, 332, 561, 563
Elektron 680
Elektronenblitz 482
Elektronenflussrichtung 687, 689
Elektronenkanone 494, 694
Elektronenkollektor 689
Elektronenmikroskop 694
Elektronenmikroskop im Querschnitt 694
elektronenoptische Linsen 694
Elektronenstrahl 494, 694
Elektronenstrahljustierung 694
Elektronik 689
Elektronikgeschäft 714
elektronische Instrumente 450
elektronische Post 525
elektronische Steuerung 563
elektronische Waage 699
elektronische Zeitmessung 883
elektronischer Sucher 496
elektronisches Buch 527
elektronisches Piano 451
elektronisches Schlagpolster 451
elektronisches Vorschaltgerät 275
elektronisches Zahlungsterminal 181, 731
Elektropumpe 559
Elektrorasierer 383
Elektroschweißen 318
Elektrovariometer 898
Elektroweste 848
Element 703
Element von 703
Elemente historischer Kostüme 336
Elemente, chemische 682
Elfeck, regelmäßiges 705
Elfenbeinküste 745
Elfmeterpunkt 802
Ellbogen 124, 130, 140, 147, 149, 156
Ellbogenfortsatz 153
Ellbogenhöcker 126
Ellbogenpolster 800, 808, 880
Ellbogenschützer 894, 895
Elle 116, 121, 122, 126, 131, 136, 138, 141, 142, 152, 154, 156
Ellenbogenkandare 854
Ellennerv 166
Ellenseite, Handbeuger 150, 151
Ellenseite, Handstrecker 151
Ellipsoidgelenk 156
elliptische Galaxie 9

ASTRONOMIE > 2-25; ERDE > 26-71; PFLANZENREICH >72-89; TIERREICH > 90-143; MENSCH > 144-177; NAHRUNGSMITTEL UND KÜCHE > 178-241; HAUS > 242-295; HEIMWERKEN UND GARTENARBEIT > 296-333; KLEIDUNG > 334-371; PERSÖNLICHE AUSSTATTUNG > 372-391; KUNST UND ARCHITEKTUR > 392-465; KOMMUNIKATION UND BÜROTECHNIK > 466-535; TRANSPORT UND FAHRZEUGE > 536-643; ENERGIE > 644-677; WISSENSCHAFT > 678-705; GESELLSCHAFT > 706-785; SPORT UND SPIELE > 786-920

989

elliptischer Schneeschuh 893
Elsassglas 225
Elster 118
Eltern 784, 785
emaillierter Stahlbehälter 267
Emblem 739
Embryonalgewinde 105
Emeraldcut 375
Emission schädlicher Gase 69
Emission von Salpetersäure 70
Emission von Schwefeldioxid 70
Emission von Schwefelsäure 70
Emission von Stickoxiden 70
Emmentaler 211
Empfang 509, 724, 730
Empfang von Dokumenten 508
Empfänger 16
Empfangsantenne 486
Empfangsantenne, GPS 613
Empfangsbereich 764
Empfangsebene 724
Empfangsgleise 589
Empfangshalle 724, 738
Empfangslinie 818
Empfangsraum für Besucher 726
Empfangsteil 504
en prison 919
End-Suchtaste 496
Endableitung 663
Endanschlag 303
Endbande 862
Enddarm, blinder 95
Ende 309, 888, 892
Ende, hinteres 105, 303, 309
Ende, vorderes 105
Endfaden 167
Endivie, krause 187
Endkante 897
Endklammer 453
Endknospe 77
Endlagerung 71
Endlappen 86
Endlinie 806, 811, 812, 815
Endlosperlenkette 374
Endmoräne 46
Endokarp 81, 82
endoplasmatisches Retikulum 74, 94
Endplatte, motorische 168
Endschalter 417
Endstück 169, 390, 667, 840, 863, 894
Endteil 349
Endträger 284
Endverzweigung 168
Endzone 806, 809
Energie 646
Energie, fossile 646
Energie, geothermische 646
Energie, Maßeinheit 702
Energiefreisetzung 681
Energiequelle 41
Energiesparlampe 275
Englisch 469
englischer Senf 200
englischer Stock 782
englisches Weißbrot 205
Englischhorn 446
Englischhörner 437
Enkel 784
Enkelin 784
Enkelkinder 784
Enoki 183
Ente 120, 213
Entenei 213
Entfernungsmessung 700
Entfernungsskala 478
Entklammerer 534
Entkleidungsraum 781
Entladerampe 395, 715, 719, 724
Entladerampen 716
Entladungsröhre 274, 275
Entlastungsraum 402
Entleerungsschlauch 292
Entleerungsventil 266, 267
Entlüfter 261, 271
Entlüftung 320
Entlüftungskreis 262
Entlüftungskreislauf 262
Entlüftungsventil 259, 607, 655
Entnahmeraum 781
Entnahmeraum, Wartebereich 781
Entodem 95
Entriegelungstaste 288
Entsafter 240
Entschärfer 758
Entsorgungsbecken 666, 668
Entstehung und Entwicklung der Arten 92
Entsteiner 233
Entwaldung 69
Entwässerungsrinne 538
Entwickler 485
Entwicklung des Lebens 92
Entwicklungsbäder 485
Entwicklungstrommel 484
Epiduralraum 168
Epiphyse, distale 155
Epiphyse, proximale 155
Epizentrum 43
EPS-Oberstufe 24
Equalizer 498
Erbium 684
Erbse 84

Erbsen 190
Erbsen, gespaltene 190
Erbsen, grüne 190
Erbsenbein 154
Erdalkalimetalle 682
Erdanschluss 272
Erdatmosphäre im Querschnitt 53
Erdaufbau 42
Erdaufschüttung 538
Erdbahn 6, 7
Erdbeben 43
Erdbeere 192
Erdbeere im Querschnitt 83
Erdbewegung, Geräte 326
Erdbohrer 323
Erde 0, 4, 5, 6, 7, 28
Erdeaufbau 42
Erdefunkstelle 525
Erdgas 651
Erdgeschoß 250
Erdkröte, gemeine 111
Erdkruste 42, 43
Erdkruste im Querschnitt 42
Erdkugel 13
Erdkugel, Koordinatensystem 35
Erdleitung 272, 273
Erdnuss 190
Erdnuss 190
Erdnussöl 209
Erdoberfläche 28, 647
Erdoberfläche, Absorption 68
Erdöl 651, 656
Erdöleruptionskreuz 652, 654
Erdölterminal 654
Erdölvorkommen 651, 653
Erdreich 661
Erdrutsch 12
Erdsatellit, künstlicher 53
Erdsensor 40, 60
Erdstrahlungsscanner 60
Erdstrahlungssensor 60
Erdung 655
Erdungsdraht 272
Erdungskabel 663
Erdungskabelhalterung 663
Erdungsklemme 274
Erdungsstift 274
Ereigniskarte 915
Ergebniszeile 529
erhabenes Band 426
Erhebung 453
Eridanus 10
Eritrea 745
Erkennungsdienstbereich 768
Erlenmeyer-Kolben 685
Erstarren 680
erste Funktionsebene 529
Erste Hilfe 725
erste Holzlage 252, 253
erste Laubblätter 77
erste Reihe 804
erste Rückenflosse 108, 109
Erste Runde 789
erste Spannungserhöhung 677
erste Stufe 25
erste Violinen 437
Erste-Hilfe-Anleitung 777
Erste-Hilfe-Kasten 771, 777
erster Backenzahn 159
erster Führungsring 910
erster Kamera-Assistent 428
erster Malspieler 794
erster Rang 431
erster Raum 811
erster Ring 753
erster Schiedsrichter 807, 812, 813
erster Stock 250, 251
erster Ventilzug 447
erster vorderer Backenzahn 159
erstes Mal 794
Erstversorgungsausrüstung 775
Eruptionsdüse 654
Eruptivgesteine 42
Erwärmung, globale 68
Erweiterungskarte, PCI 513
Erweiterungskartei 533
Erweiterungsport, AGP 513
Erweiterungsport, ISA 513
Erweiterungsport, PCI 513
Erythrozyt 162
Erz 647
Erzgang 650
Escapetaste 514
Esel 128
Eskariol 186
Espadrille 344
Espresso-Maschine 241
Espressomaschine 241
Essbesteck 905
Essecke 224
Essig 201
Esskastanie 193
Esslöffel 228
Esstablett 281
Esszimmer 250
Estland 744
Estragon 202
Et-Zeichen 473
Etagenbogen 269
Ethernet-Schnittstelle 526
Etikettenfenster 533
Etui 377, 529

Etui für Taschenrechner und Scheckheft 386
Etuirock 357
Eurasiatische Platte 43
Eurasien 28
Euro 728
Europa 4, 28, 32, 50, 743
Europäische Union, Flagge 729
europäisches Experimentiermodul 21
Europium 684
Eutelsat 486
Euthynterie 403, 404
Evakuierungskapsel 21
ewiger Schnee 45
Ewiges Licht 738
Exokarp 81, 82, 83
Exosphäre 53
Expander 450, 850
Expansionsbohrrhaken 900
Expansionsgefäß 675
Experimentiermodul, europäisches 21
Experimentiermodul, japanisches 21
Expertenpiste 886
explosionsgefährlich 774
explosiver Vulkan 44
Exportpipeline 652
Exportsteigsystem 652
Expressschlinge 900
externes Diskettenlaufwerk 521
externes Festplattenlaufwerk 521
extra breit 472
extra fett 472
extra mager 472
extra schmal 472
Extrakt, Vanille 200
Exzenterschleifer 308
Eyeliner, flüssiger 378
Eyresee 29

F

F 434
F-1-Triebwerk 25
Fabrik 708
Facette 629
Facetten 374
Facettenauge 96, 98, 99
Fach 279, 386, 919
Fach für Kabeltrommel 489
Fach für Molkereiprodukte 291
Fach für technische Ausrüstung 489
Facharzt 780
Fächerkorb 485
Fächerlunge 103
Fächerpinsel 378, 397
Fächerscheibe, außengezahnte 310
Fächerscheibe, innengezahnte 310
Fachwerkbogen 540
Fackeln 6
Faden 908
Fadenabschneider 453
Fadenauge 461
fadenförmige Papille 176
Fadenführung 457
Fadenhebel 452
Fadenkreuz 692
Fadenleitöse 452, 453
Fagott 446
Fagotte 437
Fagottroller 320
Fahne 115, 739, 804
Fahne mit Schwenkel 739
Fahne, rechteckige 739
Fahne, viereckige 739
Fahnenband 739
Fahnenformen 739
Fahrbahn 538, 540, 543, 712
Fahrbahn, unebene 545, 547
Fahrbahn, verengte 544, 547
Fahrbalken 595
fahrbare Aktenablage 510
fahrbares Röntgengerät 778
fahrbares Schubladenelement 510
Fährbrücke 542
Fähre 542, 608
Fahrenheitskala 695
Fahrer 857, 870, 871, 875, 885
Fahrerlager 871
Fahrersitz 577
Fahrerstand 758
Fahrgastanlage 596
Fahrgeschirr 857
Fahrgestell 753, 756
Fahrkartenkontrolleur 582
Fahrkartenschalter 592
Fahrkorb 417
Fahrkorb-Fangvorrichtung 417
Fahrkorb-Führungsschiene 417
Fahrkorbboden 417
Fahrkorbdecke 417
Fahrkran 634
Fahrleine 857
Fahrmotor 585
Fahrplan 582
Fahrrad 578
Fahrrad, Teile 578
Fahrräder, Beispiele 581
Fahrradhelm 580
Fahrradständer 735
Fahrradträger 578
Fahrtrage 776

Fahrtregler 333
Fahrtreppe 427
Fahrtrichtung, vorgeschriebene 544, 546
Fahrtrichtungsanzeige 593
Fahrwassermitte 617
Fahrwerkhebel 626
Fahrzeuge 538
Fairway 866, 867
Fakultät 703
Falcatus 92
Falke 119
Falkland-Inseln 31
Fall 362, 598, 603
Falle 248
Fallleitung 657, 658, 664
Fallrohr 643
Fallschirm 760
Fallschirm für die Feststoffrakete 22
Fallschirmkappe 896
Fallschirmspringen 896
Fallschirmspringer 896
Fallstrang 262
Falltür 407
falsche Rippe 138
Falte, abgesteppte 357
Falte, einfache 357
Falte, eingelegte 283
Falten, Beispiele 357
Faltfenster 415
Faltgrill 907
Faltkegeldach 415
Falttür 416
Faltverschluss 912
Falz 249, 426
Falzbein 426
Falzfräser 308
Familie 784
Familie der Blechbläser 437
Familie der Holzblasinstrumente 437
Familienzelt 902
Fanfare 570
Fangen 916
Fänger 443, 794, 795, 796
Fanghandschuh 796, 879
Fangleinen 896
Fangmütze 340
Fangvorrichtung, Fahrkorb 417
Fangzaun 890
Fangzubehör 911
Fanion 739
Farbabbrennervorsatz 319
Farbanzeige 456
Farbbehälter 398
Farbbeispiele 741
Farbe 421
Farbeinstellung 512
Farben 914
Farben dritter Ordnung 400
Farben erster Ordnung 400
Farben zweiter Ordnung 400
Farbfernsehkamera 20
Farbfilter 478, 494
farbige Beilage 471
Farbkreis 400
Farbmasse 470
Farbmischung 690
Farbmischung, additive 690
Farbmischung, subtraktive 690
Farbroller 320
Farbspray 398
Farbstein 421
Farbtafel 398
Farbwalze 421
Farn 76
Farn, Aufbau 76
Farne 92
Farne, Beispiele 76
Farnspitze 185
Fasan 120, 212
Fasanenei 213
Fase 92
Faserfräser 308
Faserwurzel 77, 87
Fassade 411
Fassonübertritt 362
Fassung 275, 376
Fassungen 385
Fastfood-Restaurant 715
Faszie 404
Faulbecken 70
Fausthandschuh 318, 842
Fäustling 346, 901
Fechtbecken 848
Fechter 848
Fechthandschuh 848
Fechthose 848
Fechtjacke 848
Fechtmaske 848
Fechtschuh 848
Fechtwaffen 849
Feder 43, 249, 268, 286, 292, 310, 391, 470, 757, 823, 913
Federball 817
Federball, Kunststoff 817
Federflügel 302
Federgehäuse 284
Federhaus 696
Federkiel 470
Federkranz 817
Federring 310

Federstange 850
Federung 594
Federverbindung 920
Federwaage 699
Fehlerstromschutzschalter 272
Fehlstartleine 830
Feige 197
Feile 905
feine Salami 216
Feineinstellung 693, 698, 700
Feinkost 180
Feinmahlanlage 646
Feinnachführungssystem 17
Feinregler für Dateneingabe 450
Feintrieb 693
Feld 799, 915
Feld im Abbau 650
Feld, Abbau 650
Feld, geothermisches 646
Feld, langes 753
Feld, magnetisches 494, 687
Feldbett 904
Feldelektromagnet 688
Feldflasche 906
Feldhäcksler 642
Feldhockeyplatz 788
Feldlinie 687
Feldlinse 692
Feldlinseneinstellung 693
Feldmaus 123
Feldsalat 187
Feldschiedsrichter 814
Feldspieler 799, 801
Feldspieler, zurückgezogener linker 814
Feldspieler, zurückgezogener rechter 814
Feldstärkeregler 497
Feldwicklung 688
Felge 560, 574, 579, 640
Felgenbremse, hintere 578
Felgenbremse, vordere 579
Felgenhorn 560
Fell 133, 449
Fellmütze 340
Felsen 7, 900
Felsenbecken 46
Felseninselchen 51
Felssäule 51
Feluke 600
Fenchel 185
Fenster 249, 251, 554, 567, 594, 624, 836
Fenster des Scheinwerferraumes 614
Fenster, Beispiele 415
Fensterbrett 249
Fenstergardine 282
Fensterheber 554
Fensterladen 249
Fensterüberdachung 902
Fermium 684
fernbediente Weiche 590
Fernbedienung 483, 493, 495
Fernbedienungssensor 501
Fernerkundung 40
Fernerkundung, Satelliten 41
ferngesteuerte Kommandoantenne 40
ferngesteuertes Servicemodul 21
Fernlicht 554
Fernlichtanzeige 557
Fernlichthebel 556
Fernlichtkontrollleuchte 576
Fernmeldeantenne 608
Fernmeldesatelliten 486
Fernmeldeturm 486
Fernrohr 10, 612, 701
Fernsehapparat 494
Fernsehen 489
Fernsehgerät 724, 734
Fernseher 147, 149, 351
Fernsehprogramm 471
Fernsprecher, öffentlicher 507
Fernsteuerungsanschlussbuchse 477
Fernteil 385
Ferse 147, 149, 351
Fersenautomatik 889
Fersenbein 153, 155
Fersenbeinhöcker 126
Fersenhalter 342
Fersenrand 370
Fersenriemen 343
Fersenstütze 783
Fertiggerichte 181
Fes 339
Fessel 124
Fesselbein 126, 133
Festabstandmarkierung 621
Festdachtank 655
feste Backe 311, 312
fester Sockel 312
festes Wehr 664
festgestelltes Messer 424
Festkörper 680, 681
Festkörper, amorpher 680
Festplatte, herausnehmbare 521
Festplattenlaufwerk 521
Festplattenlaufwerk, externes 521
Festplattenlaufwerk, zusätzliches 513
Festplattform 653
feststehender Messschnabel 700
feststehendes Gewicht 436
Feststeller 284
Feststeller für Säule 482
Feststellgriff für Hochkantstellung 482
Feststellgriff für Kameraplattform 482

Feststellgriff für Panoramadrehung 482
Feststellhebel für Venturidüse 757
Feststellknopf 305, 306
Feststellring 302
Feststellschraube 534, 700
Feststellschraube für das Blatt 304
Feststellschraube für Schrägstellung 304
Feststellschrauben 700
Feststellspitze 448
Feststelltaste 505
Feststelltaste, Scrollen 515
Feststellvorrichtung 284
Feststoff-Booster 22, 24
Feststoffrakete, Fallschirm 22
Festtreibstoffstufe 24
Festung 409
Festungswall 409
fett 472
Fett-Tröpfchen 74
Fettauffangschale 239
Fette 209, 656
Fettgewebe 171, 172
Fettgießer 233
Fettpfanne 234, 239
Fettuccine 206
feucht-kontinental - heißer Sommer 61
feucht-kontinental - warmer Sommer 61
feuchte Subtropen 61
feuer- und wasserfeste Kleidung 765
Feuerbecken 412
Feuerbock 257
Feuerbohne 191
Feuerdämpfer 755
feuerfester Rennanzug 872
feuerfester Ziegel 298
feuerfester Ziegelstein 465
feuerhemmendes Element 252
Feuerland 31
Feuerlöscher 725, 771
Feuerschutzhelm 765
Feuerschutztür 416
Feuerstein 318, 748, 752
Feuerstätte 256
Feuertaste 516
Feuertreppe 509
Feuerwache 711
Feuerwehrmann 765
Feuerwehrzentrale 764
Feuerzange 257
Fiale 408, 410
Fibel 336
Fibula 111
Fichte 89
Fidschi 747
Fidschiinseln 29
Fieberthermometer 695, 777
Fieder 76
fiederteilig 79
Figur 855
Figurenhantel 840
Figurenski 840
Filchner-Schelfeis 29
Fileserver 523
Filiermesser 229
Filigrangewinde 700
Film 477
Filmanfang, Markierung 476
Filmaufnahmegerät 520
Filmaufrollspule 476
Filmdiskette 481
Filme und digitale Speicher 481
Filmempfindlichkeit 476, 479
Filmkamera 428
Filmkassette 481
Filmrückspulung 476
Filmset 429
Filmtitel 427
Filmtransporteinstellung 476
Filter 238, 246, 258, 290, 390, 675
Filterabdeckung 773
Filterhalter 241
Filterspitze 390
filum terminale 167
Filzhut 340, 341
Filzstift 397
Filzstiftzeichnung 396
Finale 789
Finalist 789
Finanzabteilung 730
Finanzwesen 728
Finger 110, 172, 346, 797
Finger, kleiner 173
Fingerbeere 172
Fingerendglied 154, 172
Fingerglieder 154
Fingergrundglied 154
Fingerhut 454
Fingerhut, elastischer 531
fingerloser Spitzenhandschuh 346
Fingermittelglied 154, 172
Fingernagel 173
Fingernerv 166
Fingerrand 776
Fingerschutz 859
Fingerstrecker, gemeinsamer 151
Fink 118
Finne 425
Finnland 744
Finsternis, partielle 6, 7
Finsternis, ringförmige 6
Finsternis, totale 6, 7

Finsternisarten 6, 7
Firewall 523
FireWire-Schnittstelle 526
Firmenkundenschalter 731
Firn 46
Firnis 400
Firstpfette 252
Fisch 181
Fischauge 478
Fische 12, 108
Fischerknoten 908
Fischgabel 228
Fischgrätmuster 254
Fischgrätparkett 254
Fischkochtopf 234
Fischkorb 911
Fischmesser 228
Fischmutter 311
Fischplatte 226
Fischschupper 905
Fitnessgeräte 850
Fitnessraum 764
Fittings 269
Fittings, Beispiele 269
Fixativ 400
Fixierbad 485
Fixiertaste 528
Fjordküste 51
Flachbett 452
Flachbildschirm 518
Flachbogen 413
Flachdach 414
flache Frisierbürste 380
flache Kuchenform 232
Flächen, ebene 704
Flächenleuchte 492
flacher Bratentopf 235
flacher Teil 457
flacher Teller 226
Flachfeile 309
Flachform 420
Flachfräsbohrer 306
Flachkollektor 672
Flachland 48
Flachpalettenwagen 633
Flachpinsel 397
Flachsilo 182
Flachstück 894
Flachwasserrennen, Kanu-Kajak 838
Flachwebstuhl 460
Flachwurzel 87
Flagellum 104
Flagge 890
Flagge der Europäischen Union 729
Flagge, umsetzbare 867
Flaggen 742
Flamingo 119
Flamme 681
Flammenregulierung 391
Flammenschutzwand 761
Flanke 115, 124, 409
Flanke, linke 740
Flanke, rechte 740
Flare 6
Flasche 379, 685, 906
Flasche, Glas 223
Flaschendruckmesser 319
Flaschenöffner 230, 905
Flaschenwagen 319
Flaschenzug, einfacher 686
Flechte 74
Flechte, Aufbau 74
Flechten, Beispiele 74
Fleck, blinder 177
Fleck, gelber 177
Fledermaus 140
Fledermaus, äußere Merkmale 140
Fledermaus, Skelett 141
Fledermausärmel 361
Fledertiere 140
Fledertiere, Beispiele 141
Fleisch 214
Fleisch- und Wurstfach 291
Fleisch-Selbstbedienungstheke 180
Fleischfresser 67
fleischige Apfelfrucht 82
fleischige Frucht 82, 83
fleischige Steinfrucht 81
Fleischtheke 180
Fleischthermometer 231
Fleischwolf 230
flexible Trennwand 510
flexibler Schlauch 289
Fliege 11, 101, 349
Fliegender Fisch 11
Fliegenfenster 902
Fliegengittertür 567
Fliegenpilz 76
Fliegenrolle 909
Fliegenrute 909
Fliegenschnur 909
Flieger 603
Fliese 299
Flip 881
Floh 101
Florett 849
Florettfechter 848
Flosse 628, 759, 841
Flossenlenkwerk 629
Flossenstrahl 108

Flug 829, 891
Flugbremshebel 626
Flugbrettchen 100
Flugdaten 626
Flugdeck 761
Flugdrachen 897
Flügel 97, 98, 115, 140, 249, 416, 437, 628, 676, 760, 857, 873, 897, 898, 909
Flügel, oberer 628
Flügel, stabiler 759
Flügel, unterer 628
Flügelader 96
Flügelangreifer 809
Flügelkasten 760
Flügelklappe, hintere 760
Flügelmutter 311
Flügelrahmen 249
Flügelspitze 897, 898
Flügelstrebe 628
Flügeltasche 350
Flügelverteidiger 809
Flügelwurzel 624
Flugfuchs 141
Fluggastbrücke 619
Fluggastbrücke, ausziehbare 619
Fluggasttreppe, bewegliche 623
Flughafen 39, 618, 708
Flughaut 140
Fluginformationsanzeige 621
Flugkörper 759
Flugkörper, Aufbau 759
Flugkörper, wichtigste 759
Flugkörperabwehr 762
Fluglochschieber 100
Flugnavigationsvorrichtung 761
Flugradar 40
Flugrechner 626
Flugseite 739
Flugtasche 388
Flugzeug, Bewegungen 630
Flugzeuge, Beispiele 628
Flugzeuge, wirkende Kräfte 630
Flugzeugträger 761
Flugzeugwartungshalle 619
Flunder 221
Flunke 610
Fluor 683
Flusensieb 292
Flush 914
Fluss 38, 39, 48
Flussbarsch 220
Flusskrebs 218
Flusslandschaft 48
Flussmündung 38, 51
Flußbarsch, Anatomie 109
Flußbarsch, äußere Merkmale 108
Fluten 597
Fly-Half 804
Fock 603, 834
Fockmast 600, 602
Fokussiersteuerung 496
Folie 223
Folie, Aluminium 222
Fön 382
Fondue-Set 234
Fonduegabel 228
Fondutopf 234
Föngehäuse 382
Fontanelle, hintere 158
Football 808
Football, American 806
Football, kanadischer 809
Footballspieler 808
Foramen caecum 176
Foramen Obturator 122
Förderanlage 646, 647, 649
Förderband 71, 620
Fördergebäude 649
Förderkübel 650
Förderplattform 652, 654
Förderschacht 650
Fördersteigsystem 652
Förderstockwerk 650
Förderturm 649
Förderwagen 582
Forelle 221
Form, hochstehende 420
Form, ovale 375
Form, tiefliegende 420
Formel 1 873
Formel 3000 873
Formel Indy 873
Formel-1-Auto 873
Formel-3000-Auto 873
Formel-Indy-Auto 873
Formen, geometrische 704
Formwerkzeuge 308
Fortbildungsbüro 730
Fortkörper 74
Fortepedal 442, 451

Fortführungspunkte 473
fossiler Brennstoff 68, 70
Fotoapparate 480
Fotograf 714
Fotografie 476
fotografisches Zubehör 482
Fotokopierer 512
Fotokopiergerät 730, 733
Fotozelle 482
Fotozellenspiegel 615
Foullinie 794, 865
Foullinienpfosten 795
Fouls 789
Foyers 431
Frachtempfang 621
Frachtflugzeug 475, 629
Frachtraum 625
Frachtschiff 604
Frachtversand 621
Fragezeichen 473
Fraktionierturm 656
Francisturbine 659
Frankfurter Würstchen 216
Frankiermaschine 531
Frankiermodul 531
Frankreich 743
Franse 337
Franzium 682
Französisch 469
französischer Knötchenstich 459
französischer Roulettespielplan 919
französisches Roulette 919
französisches Weißbrot 204
Fräser, Beispiele 308
Frau 148
Frauenzelle 768
Free Guard Zone 877
Freestyle 890
Freestyleboard 887
Fregatte 762
frei endende Rippe 152
Freiballonsport 899
freie Rippe 153
freier Nagelrand 172
freies Containmentvolumen 671
Freihand-Dekoration 283
Freilauf 580
freilaufender Sitz 851
Freileitung 663
Freileitungen, Verteilung 486
Freiluftterrasse 609
Freiraum 812, 813
Freisaiten 432
Freisprechanlage 506
Freistil 843
Freiwange 255
Freiwurflinie 811, 814
Freizeit in der Natur 902
Freizeitbekleidung, Damen 716
Freizeitbekleidung, Herren 717
Frenchcut 375
Frequenz, Maßeinheit 702
Frequenzanzeige 503
Frequenzanzeige, digitale 498
Frequenzbänder 498
Frequenzregler 498
Frequenzwähler 503
Fresko 406
Friedhof 39, 711
Fries 278, 403, 404
Frischhaltefolie 222
Frischkäse 210
Frischluftzufuhr 898
Frischwasserwagen 622
Friseesalat 186
Friseur 428, 714
Frisierbürste, flache 380
Fritteuse 238, 721
Frittierkorb 231, 238
Front, stationäre 56
Frontabdeckung 519
Frontale 112
Frontalzacken 901
Frontblech 577
Fronten 56
Frontgewicht 640
Frontgitter 261
Frontoparietale 111
Frontscheibe 290
Frontscheinwerfer 554
Frontstoßdämpfer 577
Frontstoßfänger 550
Frosch 110, 439
Frosch, Anatomie 110
Frosch, äußere Merkmale 110
Frosch, Lebenszyklus 111
Frosch, Skelett 111
Fruchtbecher 84
Fruchtbildung 86
Fruchtblatt 84
Früchte 81
Fruchtfach 82
Fruchtfleisch 81, 82, 83
Fruchtgemüse 188
Fruchtholz 86
Fruchtkapsel 84
Fruchtknoten 80
Fruchtknotenfach 82
Fruchtwand 82, 84

Frühling 54
Frühlingsäquinoktium 13, 54
Frühlingszwiebel 184
Fuchs 134
Füchslein 13
Fuchsschwanz 303
Fugendüse 289
Fugenkelle 315
Fühlerputzer 98
Führerhaus 639
Führerkabine 634, 636, 637, 638, 639
Führerpult 586
Führerraum 631
Führerstand 585, 586
Fuhrmann 12
Führung 12
Führungsgriff 304, 308
Führungsgruppe 870
Führungshebel 307
Führungsmotorrad 870
Führungsnut 305
Führungsrille 888
Führungsring 909
Führungsrolle 499
Führungsschiene 456, 533, 555, 595
Führungsschiene, Fahrkorb 417
Führungsschienenantrieb 521
Führungsständer 632, 633
Führungsturm 542
Ful 468
Full House 914
Füllanzeige, automatische 655
Füllanzeigeschwimmer 655
Fullback 804, 807
Füllen 12
Füllfederhalter 470
Fülliloch 275
Füllmengenanzeige 548
Füllöffnung für neue Brennstäbe 666
Füllrohr 265
Fülltür 256
Füllung 247
Fumarole 44
Fundament 252, 253, 660
Fundamentklotz 660
Fundamentstreifen 252, 253
Fundamenttafel 445
Fundbüro 725
Fünf 703
fünf Nummern 919
Fünf-Kräuter-Gewürz 199
Fünfeck, regelmäßiges 705
Fünferpin 865
fünffingriger Schweißerhandschuh 318
Fünfhundert 703
Fünfzig 703
Fungizid 69
Funkantenne 604, 606, 608, 609, 628, 763, 873
Funken 564
Funkenstrecke 562
Funkgerät 771, 898
Funkmast 652
Funkmaus 516
Funknetzwerk, Basisstation 522
Funknetzwerkkarte, wireless-LAN-Karte 522
Funktionäre 801
Funktionsanzeige 450
Funktionsdisplay 450
Funktionsebene, erste 529
Funktionsebene, zweite 529
Funktionsschalter 496
Funktionstasten 507, 508, 514, 699, 730, 731
Funktionstasten, programmierbare 731
Funktionswähler 261
Funktionswahltaste 506
Funkübertragungssystem 20
Furche 176
Fusilli 206
Fusselfilter 293
Fuß 96, 98, 104, 105, 139, 140, 143, 146, 147, 148, 149, 278, 280, 286, 307, 308, 329, 351, 368, 425, 440, 444, 461, 483, 516, 517, 685, 693, 739, 836, 910
Fuß, geschwungener 278
Fuß-/Handgelenksgewicht 850
Fußball 802
Fußballplatz 788
Fußballschuh 802
Fußballspieler 802
Fußboden 257
Fußbohrung 444
Fußbrüse 104
Füße voraus 829
Fußende 280
Fußfessel 857
Fußfesselriemen 857
Fußgänger 545, 546
Fußgängerampel 712
Fußgängerbrücke 583, 593
Fußgängerknopf 712
Fußgängerüberweg 545, 547, 712
Fußgelenk 130
Fußgestell 277
Fußgewölbearterie 160
Fußholz 247
Fußknochen 155
Fußnagelschere 377
Fußpferd 602
Fußplatte 305

Fußraste, vordere 575, 576
Fußraummatte 558
Fußriemen 840, 851
Fußrückenarterie 160
Fußschlaufe 836
Fußschutz 773
Fußsteg 426
Fußstelle 740
Fußstrecke 650
Fußstück 425
Fußstütze 281, 312, 464, 577, 783, 791, 851
Fußstützen 871
Fußteil 841
Fußtritt 444
Fußweg 714
Fußwurzel 122, 126, 131, 138, 141, 142, 155, 156
Futter 342, 348, 349, 370, 386, 455, 881
Futteral 391
Futtergetreide 182
Futterstoffe 455

G

G 434
Gabel 14, 227, 632, 697, 875, 905
Gabelbaum 836
Gabelbein 116
Gabeln 632, 633
Gabeln, Beispiele 228
Gabelstapler 632
Gabelstaplertasche 635
Gabun 745
Gadolinium 684
Gaffel 602
Gaffelsegel 601
Galaxie 9
Galaxie, elliptische 9
Galaxie, irreguläre 9
Galaxie, linsenförmige 9
Galeere 598
Galeone 599
Galerie 411, 430, 614, 676, 738
Galerie, Große 402
Galileo 19
Gallenblase 110, 112, 164
gallischer Krieger 748
Gallium 682
Galopp 125
Galopprennen 856
Gamasche 339
Gambia 745
Gammastrahlen 690
Ganasche 124
Gang 44, 180, 402
Gang, absteigender 402
Gang, aufsteigender 402
Gangarten 124
Ganglion, sympathisches 167
Gangway 606
Gans 120, 213
Gänseei 213
Ganymed 4
ganze Note 435
ganze Pause 435
ganzer Querstrich 56
Ganzjahresreifen 560
ganzrandig 79
Garage 244, 726, 769
Garam Masala 199
Garderobe 250, 394, 431, 510, 719, 723, 726, 731
Garderobenständer 510
Garderobier 428
Gardinenschiene 284
Gardinenstange 284
Gardinenstange, einläufige 284
Gardinenstange, zweiläufige 284
Gardinenstangen 284
Garn 908
Garnball 797
Garnele 218
Garnführer 456
Garnhalter 457
Garnierspritze 232
Garnrollenstift 452
Garnspannungseinheit 457
Garnstange 457
Garten 406
Garten-Sauerampfer 187
Gartenarbeit 298, 322
Gartenfräse 327
Gartenhandschuhe 325
Gartenkresse 187
Gartenkreuzspinne 102
Gartenkürbis 188
Gartenschlauch 328
Gartenspritze 328
Gartenteich 322
Gartenweg 244, 322
Gas 275, 656, 680
Gasabscheider 652
Gasbehälter 903
Gasbrenner 267
Gasfeuerzeug 391
Gasflasche, medizinische 780
Gashebel 331, 576, 626
Gasherd 290, 721
Gaskolben 755

Gasleitung 712
Gasmaske 773
Gasöl 656
Gaspedal 556
Gasse 711, 817, 820, 865
Gasstromregulierung 903
Gästeeingang 720
Gästegarderobe 720
Gästetoiletten 720
Gaststätte 714
Gasventil 267
Gaswarmwasserbereiter 267
Gaszug 323, 332
Gateway 523
Gatter 852
Gaumen, harter 174, 175
Gaumen, weicher 174, 175
Gaumenbein 112, 123
Gaumenbogen, vorderer 174
Gaumenmandel 176
Gebälk 247, 403, 405
Gebärmutter 170, 171
Gebärmutterhals 170
Gebäude, öffentliches 39
Gebetshalle 738
Gebiet, abgedecktes 40
Gebirge, Transantarktisches 29
Gebirgsbach 45
Gebirgskette 38, 42
Gebirgsmassiv 38
Gebiss 854
Gebiss, menschliches 159
Gebissriemen 854
Gebissscheibe Gebissstange 858
Gebläse 258, 259, 293, 445, 643, 670
Gebläsemotor 258
Gebläserohr 643
gebogenes Eisen 401
gebogenes Hohleisen 401
geboren 702
gebräuchliche Bezeichnungen 82, 83
gebrauchte Spritzen, Behälter 771
gebrauchtes Material, Lagerraum 778, 780
gebuchtet 79
gebundenes Buch 426
Gedankenstrich 473
gedeckter Weg 409
gedeckter Wehrgang 408
Gedenktafel 738
Gedränge 805, 806, 807
Gedrängehalbspieler 804
gedrehtes Seil 908
gedruckte Schaltung 689
Gefahrenbereich 844
Gefahrenstelle 616
Gefahrenzone 847
gefährliche Substanzen 774
Gefälle 545, 547
Gefangenentransporter 726
Gefängnis 915
Gefechtskopf 759
geflochtenes Seil 908
Geflügel 213
Geflügelschere 233
Gefrierbeutel 222
Gefrierfach 291
gefrierender Regen 64
Gefrierschrank 180, 224, 720
Gefriertruhe 291
Gegenausleger 634
Gegenauslegerballast 634
Gegenfänger 443
Gegengewicht 14, 16, 417, 542, 591, 634, 638, 639
Gegengewichtsführung 417
Gegenleiste 173
Gegenlichtblende 478
Gegenmutter 58
Gegensprechanlage 594
Gegenverkehr 544, 546
gegenwärtige Wetterlage 55
Gegenwindstart 833
Gehäuse 100, 104, 240, 260, 261, 275, 288, 292, 293, 306, 308, 313, 316, 318, 332, 383, 442, 488, 494, 499, 507, 613, 614, 688, 695, 696, 700, 884, 920
Gehäuse, hinteres 17
Gehäuseabdeckung 528
Gehäusedach 416
Gehäuselüfter 513
Gehäuseverstärkung 920
Gehfalte 357
Gehgestell 782
Gehhilfen 782
Gehirn 99, 103, 106, 107, 109, 110
Gehirn-Rückenmark-Flüssigkeit 168
Gehkrücke 782
Gehörgang 173, 174
Gehörgang, äußerer 158
Gehörknöchelchen 174
Gehörschutz 772, 774
Gehörschutz tragen 774
Gehrmaß 303, 304
Gehrungsanschlag 305
Gehrungssäge 303
Gehrungssäge, elektrische 304
Gehrungsschneidlade 303
Gehweg 245
Geier 119
Geigenfamilie 437

Geißfuß 421
gekerbt 79
gekerbtes Scherenblatt 382
gekochter Schinken 216
Gekröse 212
gekrümmte Greifbacke 310
Geländefahrzeug 873
Geländegarderobe 577
Geländemotorrad 577
Geländemotorrad, 4x4 577
Geländer 250, 251, 255, 540, 894
Geländerstab 255
Geländewagen 549
Gelatinekapsel 783
Gelb 400, 690
gelbe Zucchini 189
gelber Ball 863
gelber Fleck 177
gelber Paprika 188
gelbes Licht 712
Gelbgrün 400
Gelborange 400
Geld 729
Geldausgabeautomat 715, 730
Geldbeleg 387
Geldbeutel 387
Geldbeutel für Münzen 387
Gelddrückgabefach 507
Geldscheinausgabe 730
Geldscheinfach 386
Geldwechsel 725
Gelenk 342, 557, 569, 638, 889
Gelenk, ebenes 156
Gelenkbus 569
Gelenkhöcker 153
gelenkloser Bogen 541
Gelenkknorpel 154
Gelenke, echte 156
Gelenkschäkel 835
gelochte Hartfaserplatte 300
gelochte Knöpfe 453
geschlossene Traube 81
geschlossener Gesichtsschutz 765
geschlossenes Atemschutzsystem 765
gemahlener Pfeffer 199
Gemälde 395
gemäßigter Wald 66
gemeine Erdkröte 111
Gemeiner 472
gemeiner Tüpfelfarn 76
gemeines Widertonmoos 75
gemeinsame Hüftarterie 160, 165
gemeinsame Hüftvene 165
gemeinsamer Fingerstrecker 151
gemeinsamer Wadenbeinnerv 166
Gemeinschaftskarte 915
Gemüse 180, 184
Gemüsebürste 233
Gemüsegarten 182, 244
Gemüseterrine 226
Gemüsezwiebel 184
Generator 563, 586, 646, 659, 662, 665, 668, 677
Generator, Elektrizitätserzeugung 665
Generatoreinheit 658
Generatoren 688
Genicklasche 772
Genickstück 854
Genitalöffnung 104
Genitalporus 95
Geographie 28
Geologie 42
geometrische Formen 704
Geometrie 704
Georgien 746
geostationäre Umlaufbahn 60
geostationärer Satellit 60
geothermische Energie, Elektrizitätserzeugung 646
geothermisches Feld 646
Gepäck 388
Gepäckablage 584
Gepäckanhänger 389, 623
Gepäckaufbewahrung 582
Gepäckausgabe 620
Gepäckcontainer 605
Gepäckförderer 623
Gepäckraum 568, 584, 585, 631
Gepäckroller 389
Gepäckschließfächer 582
Gepäckschnur 389
Gepäckträger 567, 577, 578, 876
gepolsterte Korbstütze 811
gepolsterter Sockel 811
gerade Greifbacke 310
gerade Öse 453
Geraden 871
gerader Bauchmuskel 150
gerader Rock 357
gerader Schenkelmuskel 150
gerades Balleisen 401
gerades Eisen 401
gerades Hohleisen 401, 421
gerades Rippenbündchen 351
Geradseite 607
Geräte 790
Geräte zur Erdbewegung 326
Geräteanschluss 383
Gerätefach 585
Geräteraum 734, 764
Gerätemast, allgemeiner 490
Geräteschrank 489
Geräteschuppen 182
Geräteumanlage 824
Geräteturnen 824

geräumige Tasche 388
Gericht 728
Gerichtsgebäude 710
Gerichtskanzlei 728
Gerichtssaal 728
Gerichtsschreiber, Tisch 728
germanische Sprachen 469
Germanium 682
geröstete Kaffeebohnen 208
Gerste 85, 203
Gerstenkornmuster 458
Geruchssinn 174
Geruchsverschluss 262, 265, 270
Gerüstprofil 417
Gerüstträger 663
gesägt 79
Gesamtergebnis, Anzeigetafel 824
Gesäß 147, 149, 169, 170
Gesäßmuskel, großer 151
Gesäßnerv 166
Gesäßspalte 149
Gesäßtasche 350
Geschäft 710
Geschäftsbeleg 731
Geschäftsbuch, Journal 535
Geschäftsführers, Büro 509
Geschäftsviertel 708, 710
geschaltete Steckdose 497
Geschenkartikel 717
Geschenkwarenladen 714
Geschirr 226, 460
Geschirr, Glaswaren und Silberwaren 717
Geschirrspüler 224, 721, 723
Geschirrspülmaschine 271, 294
Geschirrtuch 295
Geschlechtsorgane, männliche 169
Geschlechtsorgane, weibliche 170
Geschmacksknospe 176
Geschmacksrezeptoren 176
Geschmackssinn 174
geschnitzter Bug 598
Geschoss 753
Geschosszubehör 752
Geschütz, rückstoßfreies 757
Geschützrohr 758
geschütztes Leerzeichen 514
Geschützturm 762
Geschwindigkeitsanzeige 898
Geschwindigkeitsregelung 236, 237, 452
Geschwindigkeitsregler 332, 417
Geschwindigkeitswähler 236
Geschworenenbank 728
Geschworenenraum 728
geschwungener Fuß 276
Gesellschaft 708
Gesicht 139, 146
Gesichtsmaske 798, 800, 808
Gesichtsschutz 318, 765, 878
Gesichtsschutz, geschlossener 765
Gesichtsschutzmaske 879
Gesichtsstück 773
Gesims 245, 247
gespalten 740
gespaltene Erbsen 190
gespaltene Zunge 112
gespreizter Kragen 349
Gestänge 902
gestanztes Loch 342, 350, 371
Gestein, undurchlässiges 651
Gestell 281, 321, 391, 776
gestelzter Bogen 413
gestempelte Post 474
gestorben 702
Gesundheit 775
Gesundheitsorganisation 525
Getränke 180
Getränkeautomat 548, 779
Getränkedose 223
Getränkekarton 223
Getränkekarton, kleiner 223
Getränkespender 723
Getreide 85, 203
Getreideprodukte 204
Getreidesilo 596
getrennte Sammlung 71
Getriebe 292, 552, 563
getrocknete Chilis 199
gewachsener Boden 538
Gewände 411
Gewebe 899
Gewebe-Einstellskala 288
Gewebestruktur 455
Gewehr (gezogener Lauf) 912
Gewehr, automatisches 755
Gewehrriemen 893
Gewehrschießen 861
Gewerbegebiet 709
Gewicht 630, 697, 698, 699, 793, 850
Gewicht, feststehendes 436
Gewichte 851
Gewichtheben 850
Gewichthebergürtel 850
Gewichtheberschuh 850
Gewichtsantrieb 697
Gewichtsausgleicher 756
Gewichtsstaudamm 661

gewimpert 79
Gewinde 268, 302, 863
Gewindegang 306
Gewindehülse 248
Gewindekappe 269
Gewindeschaft 311
Gewindeschneider 314
Gewinnkombination 920
Gewitter 57
Gewitter, starkes 57
Gewitterwolken 63
gewöhnlicher Nagel 301
gewöhnlicher Würfel 914
Gewölbe 410
Gewölbekörper 167
gewölbter Zentralbereich 9
Gewürz, Fünf-Kräuter 199
Gewürze 198
Gewürzmischung, Cajun 199
Gewürznelke 198
Geysir 44
gezahnte Greifbacke 310
Gezeitenkraftwerk 664
Ghana 745
Ghee 210
Gi 846
Gibbon 139
Gibraltar, Straße 32
Giebel 223, 244
Giebeldach 251
Giebeldecke 251
Giebeldreieck 403, 405, 697
Giebelständer 252
Gierbewegung 630
Gießbrause 329
Gießgerät 328
Gießkanne 328
Gießpistole 329
Gift 774
Gift-Leitfurche 112
Giftdrüse 99, 103, 106, 112
Giftkanal 112
Giftklaue 103
Giftpilz 76
Giftschlange, Anatomie 112
Giftschlange, äußere Merkmale 112
Giftschlange, Skelett 112
Giftzahn 112
Gimpel 118
Ginkgonuss 193
Gipfel 45, 886
Gipfel, Hütte 886
Gipfelhütte 886
Gipsbinden 777
Gipskarton-Bauplatte 299
Gipskartonplatte 299
Gipsraum 779
Gipsschlinge 464
Giraffe 12, 129
Gitarre, akustische 440
Gitarre, elektrische 441
Gitter 361, 403, 432, 494, 727
Gitterbett 281
Gitterboxpalette 632
Gittereinsatz 234
Gitterfenster 727
Glacis 493
Glanzschicht 172
Glas 385, 903
Glas, Sortierung 71
Glasabdeckung 672, 673
Glasdach 250, 713
Gläser 225, 723
Gläserspülmaschine 723
Glasflasche 223
Glasgehäuse 699
Glashaube 612
Glaskolben, oberer 241
Glaskolben, unterer 241
Glaskörper 177
Glaskugel 58
Glasmalerei 411
Glasnudeln 207
Glasplatte 291, 535
Glasscheibe 693
Glasüberdachung 582
Glattstrick 458
gleich 703
gleich oder größer als 703
gleich oder kleiner als 703
Gleichgewichtslage 690
Gleichstrom-Netzkabel 526
Gleichtaste 529
Gleis 582, 592, 595, 710
Gleise 591
Gleiskette 636
Gleiskettenschlepper 636
Gleiskreuzung 583
Gleisnummer 582
Gleitflieger 897
Gleitfuge 310
Gleitphase 892
Gleitschirm 897
Gleitschirmfliegen 897
Gleitschuh 301
Gleitschutz 889
Gleitstuhl 590
Gletscher 46, 48, 66
Gletschersee 48
Gletscherspalte 46
Gletscherzunge 46

Gliederpuppe 398
Gliedmaßen, obere 161
Gliedmaßen, untere 161
Glimmlampe 316
globale Erwärmung 68
Globus 734
Glocke 849
Glockenband 449
Glockendach 415
Glockendichtung 265
Glockenstube 410, 411
Glockenturm 411, 737
Glottis 112
Glücksrad 920
Glühbirne 316, 673
Glühfaden 274
Glühlampe 274, 614, 687
Glukose 78
Gnocchi 206
Gnomon 696
Go 916
Gobelinbindung 463
Gold 683, 741
Goldbrasse 219
Golf 38
Golf von Aden 33, 34
Golf von Alaska 30
Golf von Bengalen 33
Golf von Guinea 34
Golf von Kalifornien 30
Golf von Mexiko 30
Golf von Oman 33
Golf von Panama 31
Golf, Persischer 33
Golfball 867
Golfball im Querschnitt 867
Golfhandschuh 869
Golfplatz 708, 788, 866
Golfschuhe 869
Golftasche 869
Golfspiel 866
Golfwagen 869
Golgi-Apparat 74, 94
Gonade 95, 105, 106
Gondel 600, 899
Gondelhaltegriff 899
Gonfalon 739
Gong 437, 449
Gorgonzola 211
Gorilla 138
Gorilla, äußere Merkmale 139
Gorilla, Skelett 138
gotischer Dom 410
Gottesanbeterin 102
Gouache 396
GPS-Empfangsantenne 613
Graben 409, 647, 864
Graben, Kermadec-Tonga 50
Graben, Peru-Chile 50
Graben, Puerto-Rico 50
Grabenböschung, innere 409
Grabgabel 326
Grabkammer der Königin 402
Grabkammer des Königs 402
Grabschaufel 326
Grabstichel 11
Grad 704
Grad Celsius 702
Gradbogen 612
Gradeinteilung 907
Gradnetz 36
grafische Künste 420
Granat 375
Granatapfel 196
Granatwerfer 756
Grand Canyon 30
Grand-Prix-Rennmaschine 874
Granitschicht 42
Granne 85
Granulation 6
Grapefruit 194
Grapefruitmesser 229
Graphit 670
Graphitstift 470
Graphosfeder 397
Grasfang 332
grasgrüner Täubling 183
Grasland 66
Grat 45, 404
graue Substanz 167, 168
Graviernadel 423
Gravurplatte 376
Greif- und Spannwerkzeuge 310
Greifbacke, gekrümmte 310
Greifbacke, gerade 310
Greifer 452
Greiffinger 139
Greifleine 611
Greifzirkel 423
Grenada 743
Griechenland 744
Griechisch 469
griechisch-römischer Stil 843
griechischer Tempel 403
griechischer Tempel, Grundriss 403
griechisches Brot 204
griechisches Theater 402
Griessäule 641
Grieß 204

Griff 227, 230, 236, 237, 238, 239, 240, 256, 280, 288, 290, 291, 295, 303, 304, 305, 308, 309, 310, 311, 313, 315, 316, 319, 320, 323, 328, 331, 332, 381, 382, 383, 384, 386, 387, 388, 389, 391, 425, 439, 453, 454, 458, 460, 534, 564, 649, 782, 797, 798, 800, 815, 816, 822, 838, 849, 850, 859, 867, 877, 884, 888, 891, 905, 909, 913, 920
Griff, ausziehbarer 386
Griff, isolierter 316, 317
Griff, wärmeisolierter 239
Griff, zusätzlicher 306
Griff- und Wurfbeispiele 844
Griffband 894
Griffbrett 432, 439, 441
Griffe 901
Griffel 80, 81, 82, 84
Griffelbein 126
Griffelfortsatz 158
Griffhebel für S-Bogen 446
Griffkamm 380
Griffloch 535
Griffteil 863
Grill, Raclette 239
Grillfläche 239
Grillplatte 239
Grillrost 290
Grindel 641
Gripzange 310
grobe Salami 216
Grobeinstellung 693
grobes Salz 201
Grobregler für Dateneingabe 450
Grobspanplatte 300
Grobtrieb 693
Grönland 30
Grönlandsee 28
groß gefleckter Katzenhai 218
Groß-Oberbramsegel 603
Groß-Obermarssegel 603
Groß-Royalsegel 603
Groß-Unterbramsegel 603
Groß-Untermarssegel 603
große Armdecken 115
Große Australische Bucht 29
große Außensichel 844
große Einkaufstasche 388
große Elektrohaushaltsgeräte 716
Große Galerie 402
große Handdecken 115
Große Innensichel 844
große Klinge 905
große Nackenrolle 280
große Rosenvene 160
Große Sandwüste 29
große Schamlippe 170, 171
Große Seen 30
Große Victoriawüste 29
Großeltern 784
größer als 703
Großer Bär 13
großer Brustmuskel 150
großer Gesäßmuskel 151
Großer Hund 11
großer Nasenflügelknorpel 175
großer Oberschenkelanzieher 151
großer Rundmuskel 151
großes Kettenblatt 580
großes Vieleckbein 154, 156
Großformatkamera 480
Großhirn 167
Großmast 600, 602
Großmutter 784
Großrad 783
Großraumwagen 584
Großschot 834
Großschriftfeststellung 514
Großschriftfeststellungstaste 514
Großschriftumschaltung 514
Großsegel 603, 834
Großtonne 615
Großvater 784
Groteskschrift 472
Grubber 641
Grube 650, 793, 865
Grube, offene 647
Grubenorgan 112
Grün 400, 690, 864, 866, 867
grün 741
Grünalge 75
Grünanlage 713
Grundbindungen 463
Grundfarben 917
Grundgestein 43
Grundierung, flüssige 378
Grundlinie 821
Grundlinienrichter 821
Grundmoräne 46
Grundplatte 58, 273, 485, 500, 756, 889
Grundrechenarten 529
Grundring 659
Grundriss 403, 411
Grundstücksgrenze 244
Grundwasser, eingeschlossenes 646
Grundwasserspiegel 47, 70
grüne Bohne 191
grüne Erbsen 190
grüne Tagliatelle 206

grüner Ball 863
grüner Paprika 188
grüner Pfeffer 198
grüner Tee 208
grünes Licht 712
Grünkohl 186
Grünstrahl 494
Gruppenwahl 514
Gruyèrekäse 211
Guaraní 469
Guatemala 742
Guave 197
Guckloch 591
Guidon 739
Guinea 745
Guinea, Golf 34
Guinea-Bissau 745
Gummiband 280, 350
Gummieinsatz 867
Gummigebiss 854
Gummihöschen 368
Gummikappe 782
Gummimatte 500
Gummipfropfen 776
Gummiring 270
Gummischlauch 271, 776
Gummischutz 857
Gummispannring 902, 903
Gummistiefel 765
Gummistöpsel 321
Gurke 188
Gurt 281, 611
Gurtbefestigung 441
Gurtbogen 410
Gürtel 350, 352, 844
Gürtelband 350
Gürtelclip 505
Gürtellage 561
Gürtelschatten 6, 7
Gürtelschlaufe 350, 352, 905
Gürtelschnalle 350
Gürtelspitze 350
Gurtschließe 555
Gurtschnalle 350
Gurtstrippe 855
Gurtwerk 841, 896, 897
Gurtzeug 896
Gusserker 408
Gutenberg-Diskontinuität 42
Güterbahnhof 583, 708
Güterwagen 583
Güterwagen, Beispiele 588
Güterwagen, offener 588
Gutta 404
Guyana 742
Guyot 49
gynäkologischer Untersuchungsraum 779
Gyoji 847
Gyroskop 759

H

H 434
Haar 147, 149, 172, 439
Haar der Berenike 13
Haaraufrichter 172
Haarbalg 172
Haarbürsten 380
Haarclip 380
Haarfärbemittel 379
Haarglätter 381
Haarklemme 380
Haarliftkamm 380
Haarpflege 380
Haarschaft 172
Haarschneidekamm 380
Haarschneider 381
Haarschneideschere 382
Haarspange 380
Haarspülung 379
Haarstecker 380
Haarzwiebel 172
Hachse 214, 215
Hack 877
Hafen 596, 709
Hafenbahn 596
Hafenfähre 596
Hafenzollamt 596
Hafer 85, 203
Hafermehl 204
Haferwurz 189
Hafnium 683
Haftgurtband 368
Häftlingsdusche 768
Haftorgan 75
Haftscheibe 111
Hagel 64
Hagelschauer 57
Hagelschnur 117
Hahn 120, 752, 754, 861, 912
Hai, äußere Merkmale 108
Haiti 742
Hakama 846, 847
Häkelnadel 457
Haken 284, 313, 316, 453, 456, 457, 573, 611, 634, 699, 776, 861, 862, 900
Hakenbein 154
Hakenbogen 911
Hakenbogentiefe 911
Hakengurt 767
Hakengurt für Leiter und Schlauch 767

Hakenhalteöse 909
Hakenhalter 901
Hakeninnenweite 911
Hakenleiter 767
Hakenspitze 911
Hakenverriegelung 249
Hakler 804
Halbbrille 385
halbe Anführungszeichen 473
halbe Note 435
halbe Pause 435
Halbedelsteine 375
halber Querstrich 56
halber Wind 833
halbes Heft 229
halbfett 472
Halbfinale 789
Halbinsel 38
Halbinsel, Antarktische 29
Halbinsel, Arabische 33
Halbinsel, Iberische 32
Halbinsel, Kamtschatka 33
Halbinsel, Kola 32
Halbinsel, Skandinavische 32
Halbinsel, Yucatan 30
Halbkreis 704, 810
Halbkugel 705
Halbmetalle (Metalloide) 682
Halbmond 409
Halbmond (erstes Viertel) 7
Halbmond (letztes Viertel) 7
Halbmumienschlafsack 904
halbrechter Läufer 801
Halbsäule, dorische 407
Halbsäule, ionische 407
Halbsäule, korinthische 407
Halbschale 367
Halbschatten 6, 7
Halbsehnenmuskel 151
Halbseite 632
Halbspieler 794
Halbstiefel 342
Halbtaucher 653
Halbtrogbrücke 541
Halbvolleyball 820
Halbzeit 789
Halfpipe 871, 887
Halfter 770
Halle 719
Halm 382, 454
Halmteiler 643
Halo 9
Halogen-Tischleuchte 286
Halogenscheinwerfer 775
Hals 77, 113, 124, 147, 148, 149, 159, 169, 227, 425, 433, 439, 440, 441, 458, 494, 610, 822, 826, 836, 868
Halsausschnitt 351
Halsberge 749
Halsen 833
Halskette in Matineelänge 374
Halskette in Opernlänge 374
Halskette, mehrreihige 374
Halsketten 374
Halskrause 339, 363
halsnaher Ausschnitt 368
Halsring 404
Halsschlagader 160
Halsschutz 796, 880, 882
Halstalje 834
Halsumklammerung 844
Halswirbel 116, 122, 126, 131, 138, 141, 142, 153, 157
Halt! Vorfahrt gewähren 544, 546
Haltebügel 783
Haltegriff 567, 569, 766
Haltegriff, vorderer 757
Haltegriffe 844
Haltemutter 909, 910
Halter 274
Halterung 15, 285, 579, 649, 699
Halterung für die Registrierkarten 58
Halterung, schwenkbare 613
Halterungen 40
Halterungsschraube, untere 58
Haltestange 570
Hammer 174, 301, 317, 329, 442, 443, 793
Hammer mit runder Bahn 301
Hammer zum Rundklopfen 425
Hammerbahn 425
Hammerfilz 443
Hammergriff 793
Hammerhalter 313
Hammerkopf 793, 901
Hammerleiste 442
Hammernuss 443
Hammerruheleiste 443
Hammerstiel 443
Hamster 123
Hand 139, 147, 149, 173
Hand-Funksprechgerät 770
Hand-Gehrungssäge 303
Handauflage 516
Handball 814
Handballenauflage, abnehmbare 514
handbediente Weiche 590
Handbeuger der Ellenseite 150, 151
Handblasebalg 777
Handbohrer 307
Handbrause 264

Handbremse 552
Handbremse, Schutzkasten 587
Handbremshebel 556, 587
Handbremsrad 587
Handbuchbinderei 424
Handdecken, große 115
Handdecken, mittlere 115
Handelsunternehmen 525
Handfeuerlöscher 767
Handfläche 121, 173, 797
handförmig 79
Handgabel 325
Handgelenk 140, 147, 149, 156, 173
Handgelenkpolster 808
Handgelenksbandage 850
Handgelenkschützer 895
Handgeräte 823
Handgranate 757
Handgriff 309, 416, 433, 750
Handhabung 632
Handheld-Computer 527
Handikaptafel 858
Handknochen 154
Handkreissäge 304
Handkultivator 326
Handkurbel 313, 423
Handlampe 316
Handlauf 255, 417
Handlöser 889
Handmuskeltrainer 850
Handrad 452
Handrasenmäher 332
Handrücken 173
Handrührgerät 236
Handschellentasche 770
Handschild 318
Handschlaufe 888, 892, 901
Handschuh 20, 145, 779, 800, 855, 870, 871, 874, 875, 878, 882, 884, 887, 891, 892
Handschuh-Außenseite 346
Handschuh-Innenseite 346
Handschuhe 346, 872
Handschuhfach 556
Handschuhspender 780
Handschutz 331, 755, 875
Handschwingen 115
Handspulgerät 462
Handstand 828
Handstange 587, 594
Handstaubsauger 289
Handstrecker der Ellenseite 151
Handstrecker, kurzer 151
Handstrecker, langer 151
Handstütze 861
Handtaschen 387
Handteil 849
Handtuch 379
Handtuchhalter 264
Handwaage 698
Handwagen 633
Handwäsche 347
Handwerkzeuge 325
Handwurzel 122, 131, 136, 138, 141, 142, 154, 797
Handy 506
Hängeärmel 337, 338
Hängebank 650
Hängebrücke 540
Hängegletscher 46
Hängeisolator 663
Hängekartei 510
Hängeleinen 897
Hängeleuchte 286
Hängemappe 532
Hanger 602
Hänger 540
Hantel 840, 850, 851
Hantelgriff 840
Hanteln, Beispiele 840
Hantelstange 851
Hardboots 887
Harfe 440
Harfen 437
Harissasoße 201
Harmonikatür 416
Harnapparat 165
Harnblase 109, 110, 113, 165, 169, 170
Harnleiter 165
Harnleitermündung 104
Harnröhre 165, 169, 170
Harnröhrengang 169
Harpune 875
hart am Wind 833
harte Kontaktlinse 384
harte Rückenmarkshaut 167, 168
harter Gaumen 174, 175
Hartfaserplatte 300
Hartfaserplatte, gelochte 300
Hartfaserplatte, kunststoffbeschichtete 300
Hartkäse 211
Hartplatz (Zement) 822
Hasardsteine 917
Hase 11, 123, 212
Haselnuss 193
Haselnuss, Längsschnitt 84
Hasentiere 122
Hasentiere, Beispiele 123
Hasentierkiefer 123
Hasentierkiefer: Kaninchen 123
Haspel 642, 643

DEUTSCHES REGISTER

993

Haspelrohr 643
Hassium 683
Hat-Switch 516
Häubchen 426
Haube 289
Haubitze, moderne 756
Haue 901
HauePickel 901
Hauptabschnitt 919
Hauptanschluss 273
Hauptanzeige 626
Hauptapsis 411
Hauptband 893
Hauptbolzen 587
Hauptbronchus 163
Hauptdampfleitungen 669
Hauptdampfverteiler 669
Hauptdeck 607, 761
Haupteinfüllstutzen 655
Haupteingang 250, 713, 733, 735, 768, 781
Hauptelektromotor 763
Hauptentlüftungssteigrohr 262
Hauptfahrwasser 617
Hauptfahrwerk 625, 760
Hauptfallschirm 896
Hauptfeld 870
Hauptfestplattenlaufwerk 513
Hauptgleis 583
Hauptgriff 307
Hauptkampfrichter 843, 845
Hauptkampfrichterlinie 845
Hauptlautsprecher 493
Hauptlinienrichter 807
Hauptluftbehälter 586
Hauptlüfter 648
Hauptmaßstab 700
Hauptrad 697
Hauptrand 740
Haupträume 250
Haupttreihenstern 8
Hauptschalter 272, 273, 477, 496
Hauptschieberventil 654
Hauptschiedsrichter 795, 837, 847
Hauptschlitten 456
Hauptschlot 44
Hauptschwert 836
Hauptschwerteinzug 836
Hauptspiegel 15, 17
Hauptspielzüge 916
Hauptspuren 539
Hauptstadt 37
Hauptständbein 663
Hauptständer 575
Hauptstiel 86, 253
Hauptstufe, kryogene 24
Haupttragegurt 897
Haupttransformator 585
Haupttreibachse 595
Haupttribüne 856
Haupttriebwerk 23
Hauptunterkunft 886
Hauptverteilleitung 258
Hauptvorhang 430, 431
Hauptvorschaumonitor 491
Hauptwarteraum 781
Hauptwurzel 77
Hauptzeitnehmer 830
Hauptzylinder 559
Haus 244, 877, 915
Haus, einstöckiges 419
Haus, Teile 247
Haus, zweistöckiges 419
Hausa 468
Hausanschluss 273
Hausantenne 486
Hausboot 607
Hauseinrichtung 276
Häuserformen in der Stadt 419
Hausflur, äußerer 406
Hausfrauenknoten 908
Haushaltsartikel 180
Haushaltsgegenstände 295
Haushaltsgeräte 236, 288
Haushaltsgeräte, verschiedene 240
Haushaltsmehl 204
Haushaltswaren 716
Haushaltswäsche 716
Hauskleid 356
Hausmeisterraum 731
Hausmüll 69, 70
Haustein 298
Haustür 247
Hauszelt 903
Haut 81, 83, 168, 172
Hautnerv, seitlicher 166
Hautoberfläche 172
Haversche Lamellen 154
Haverscher Kanal 154
Hawaiianisch 469
Hebeglied 443
Hebegriff 756
Hebel 238, 268, 270, 310, 377, 398, 423, 576, 686, 920
Hebel für den Klemmbügel 381
Hebel-Korkenzieher 230
Hebeleisen 301
Hebeleiste der unteren Schutzhaube 304
Hebelstützpunkt 686
Heber 638
Hebestück 651

Hebewerk 651
Hebräisch 468
Hecht 220
Hechtabwehr 812
Hechtsprungstellung 828
Heck 236, 608, 625, 836
Hecke 245, 322
Heckenschere 330
Heckleuchten 554
Heckpropeller 606
Heckrotor 631
Hecksporn 631
Hecktür 775
Heft 302
Heft, halbes 229
Heften 424
Hefter 532, 534
heftige Regenfälle 63
Heftklammern 534
Heftlade 424
Heftpflaster 777
Heidelbeere 192
Heilbutt 221
Heiliger Petrus 736
Heimkino 493
Heimtierbedarf 181
Heimtrainer 851
Heimwerken 298
Heimwerkerladen 714
HiFi-System 503
Heinrich VIII 736
heißes Kühlmittel 674
Heißluftaustritt 256
Heißluftballon 899
Heißluftpistole 320
Heißring 610
heißversiegelte Folie 223
heiterer Himmel 56
Heizelement 258, 259, 293, 294, 318, 465
Heizer 674
Heizkessel 258, 259
Heizkessel, elektrischer 258
Heizkörper 259
Heizlüfter 260
Heizöl 656
Heizplatte 721
Heizspirale 290, 899
Heizstab, oberer 266
Heizstab, unterer 266
Heizstrahler 260, 903
Heizung 256, 608
Heizungsgitter 594
Heizventil 899
Helium 684
Heliumsphäre 25
Helix 705
Helixende 173
Helligkeitsregelung 20
Helligkeitsregler 14
Helligkeitstaste 505
Helm 20, 748, 749, 796, 798, 858, 870, 871, 872, 874, 875, 882, 887, 894, 895
Helmbohne 190
Helmbusch 748
Helmdach 415
Helmglocke 749
Helmlampe 901
Hemd 349, 791
Hemdblusenärmel 361
Hemdblusenkleid 356
Hemdblusenkragen 362
Hemdchen 368
Hemden 716
Hemdhose 351
Hemisphäre, nördliche 35
Hemisphäre, östliche 35
Hemisphäre, südliche 35
Hemisphäre, westliche 35
Hemisphären 35
Hemmungslappen 697
Hemmungsrad 696, 697
Henkel 295
Hennin 339
Heraldik 739
heranwachsende Nahrungsvakuole 94
Herausarbeiten 401
herausklappbare Schreibplatte 279
herausnehmbare Festplatte 521
Herbizid 69
Herbst 54
Herbstäquinoktium 54
Herd 43, 722
Herdkante 290
Herdtiefe 43
Hering 219, 902, 903
Heringskönig 221
Heringsschlaufe 902, 903
Herkules 13
Hermelin 741
Heroldsbilder 740
Herren-Accessoires 716
Herren-Freizeitbekleidung 717
Herren-Nachtwäsche 717
Herren-Sportbekleidung 717
Herrenanzüge 716
Herrenhalbschuh 342
Herrenhandschuhe 346
Herrenjacken 717

Herrenkleidung 348
Herrenkopfbedeckungen 340
Herrenmäntel 717
Herrenpullover 717
Herrenring 376
Herrenschuhe 342, 716
Herrentasche 388
Herrentoilette 427, 509, 724
Herrenunterwäsche 716
Hertz 702
Heruntertransformation der Spannung 646, 662, 677
Herz 97, 99, 103, 104, 105, 106, 107, 109, 110, 112, 116, 125, 162, 163, 212, 822, 914
Herzbeutel 163
Herzförmig 79
Herzkammer, linke 161, 162
Herzkammer, rechte 161, 162
Herzmuschel 217
Herzmuskel 162
Herzstelle 740
Herzstück 587, 590
Herzwandschicht 162
heterotrophe Organismen 67
Heuboden 182
Hexenstich 459
Hiebwaffen 751
Hilfe 181
Hilfsbatterie 563
Hilfslinie 434
Hilfsmittel 400
Hilfsprojektor 10
Hilfsschiff 653
Hilfsschwert 836
Himalaja 33
Himbeere 192
Himbeere im Querschnitt 83
Himmel, bedeckter 56
Himmel, bewölkter 56
Himmel, heiterer 56
Himmel, klarer 56
Himmel, stark bewölkter 56
Himmel, stürmischer 65
Himmel, wolkenloser 56
Himmelsäquator 13
Himmelsbedeckung 55
Himmelskörper 4
Himmelskugel 13
Himmelskugel, Koordinatensystem 13
Himmelsmeridian 13
Himmelsnordpol 13
Himmelsstrahlung, Messung 58
Himmelssüdpol 13
Hindernislaufhürde 790
Hindernisrichter 852
Hindernisse 875
Hindi 469
Hinduismus 736
Hinterbein 96, 98, 110, 111, 277
Hinterbein (Innenseite) 98
Hinterbindung 840
Hinterbühne 431
Hinterdeckel 426
hintere Aufschlaglinie für das Doppelspiel 816
hintere Augenkammer 177
hintere Begrenzungslinie 848
hintere Felgenbremse 578
Hintere Flügelklappe 760
hintere Fontanelle 158
hintere Gerade 856
hintere Klappe 23
hintere Kufe 884
hintere Nervenwurzel 167, 168
hintere Querleiste 893
hintere Schaufel 637
hintere Seitenfontanelle 158
hinterer Balken 698
hinterer knöcherner Bogengang 174
hinterer Schließmuskel 105
hinterer Stauraum 775
hinterer Stoßdämpfer 575
hinterer Streben 578
hinterer Tragflügel 609
hinterer Umwerfer 578, 580
hinteres Ende 105, 303, 309
hinteres Gehäuse 17
hinteres Trittbrett 766, 775
Hinterextremität 121, 143
Hinterfeld 818
Hinterflügel 96
Hintergrundbeleuchtung 527
Hinterhauptbein 131, 158
Hinterhauptmuskel 151
Hinterhauptsbein 153, 158
Hinterhorn 167
Hinterkante 898
Hinterkappe 370
Hinterleib 96, 97, 98, 103, 107
Hinterleibssegment 97
Hinterpartie 909
Hinterrad 333
Hinterteil 893
Hinterwand 818
Hinterzehe 115, 117

Hinterzwiesel 855
Hippe 330
Hirn 212
Hirnanhangdrüse 167
Himholzende 300
Himnerven 166
Hirse 85, 203
historische Schiffe 598
Hitzeschild 22
HNO(Hals-Nasen-Ohren)-Behandlungsraum 779
Hobel 309
Hobeleisen 309
Hobeleisen-Stellschraube 309
Hobelschar 639
Hobelzahn 331
Hochaltar 737
Hochdruck 420
Hochdruckdampfeinlass 668
Hochdruckgebiet 55, 63
Hochdruckpresse 642
Hochdruckturbine 627
Hochdruckverfahren 421
Hochebene 45
Hochgebirge 61
Hochgeschwindigkeitszug 585
hochgestellt 472
Hochland 7
Hochlandklimate 61
Hochschrank 224
Hochsilo 182
Hochspannungsleitung 646, 662, 677
Hochspannungsleitung, Anschluss 663
Hochspannungsmast 663
Hochspannungsprüfer 316
Hochsprung 791, 792
höchste Karte 914
hochstehende Form 420
Hochstuhl 281
Hochtöner 502
Hochtonlautsprecher 10
Hochtransformation der Spannung 646, 662, 665
hochverstärkende S-Band-Antenne 60
Hochwasserentlastungswehr 657
Hochwasserentlastungswehr, Verschluss 657
Hochwebstuhl 461
Hocker 224, 277, 722
Hockey 800, 918
Hockeyball 800
Hockeyskate 895
Hoden 107, 110, 169
Hodensack 146, 169
Hof 182, 727
Hogline 877
hohe Rippe 214
hohe Wolken 62
Höhen-Tonabnehmer 441
Höheneinstellung 692
Höheneinstellhebel 756
Höhenfeineinstellung 14, 15
Höhenfeintrieb 701
Höhenfeststellers 14, 15
Höhenflosse 625, 631, 898
Höhenkaltfront 56
Höhenkontrolle 485
Höhenlagen, Vegetationsbild 66
Höhenmesser 896, 898, 899
Höhenregler 441, 497, 503
Höhenrichtwerk 7
Höhenruder 625, 898
Höhenskala 13, 485
Höhensucher 761
Höhenverstellfuß 483
Höhenverstellskala 304
Höhenverstellung 289, 826, 851
Höhenwarmfront 56
höherer Wasserstand 597
Hohlbeitel 401
Höhle 47, 51
hohle Eisschraube 901
Hohleisen, gebogenes 401
Hohleisen, gerades 401, 421
Höhlenraum, trocken liegender 47
Hohlhandmuskel, kurzer 150
Hohlhandmuskel, langer 150
Hohlkehlfräser 308
Hohlkehlfräser mit Anlaufzapfen 308
Hohlladungsgeschoss 772
Hohlvene, obere 160, 161, 162
Hohlvene, untere 160, 161, 162, 165
Hohlziegel 298
Hoisinsoße 200
Hollandrad 581
Holm 321, 390, 624, 782
Holmium 684
Hologramm, metallisiertes 729
Holz 300, 868
Holz 1 868
Holz 3 868
Holz 5 868
Holzbeheizung 256
Holzblasinstrumente 437
Holzboden 899
Holzhammer 301
Holzkiste 222
Holzleibung 249

Holzohr 183
Holzschläger 867
Holzschnitt 421
Holzschnitzerei 401
Holzstock 421
Holzträger 257
Holzunterbau 254
Holzwerkstoffe 300
Homo sapiens 93
homogenisierte Milch 210
Honduras 742
Honig 209
Honigbiene 98
Honigbiene, Anatomie 99
Honigbiene, äußere Merkmale 98
Honigmelone 195
Honigraum 100
Honigzelle 100
Höraufsatz 776
Hörer 506, 507
horizontale Bodenbewegung 43
horizontale Einstellung 518
horizontaler Zug 916
horizontales Schiebefenster 415
Horizontalseismograph 43
Horizontspiegel 612
Hörmuschel 506
Horn 376, 766, 836
Hörnchennudeln 206
Hörnerv 174
Hornhaut 177, 691
Hornisse 101
Hornschicht 172
Hornschnabel 113
Hornschuppe 117
Hornsohle 127
Hornstrahl 127
Hornwand 127
Hörplätze 733
Hors-d'Oeuvre-Schale 226
Hörsaal 394, 718, 732
Hose 124, 350, 371, 748, 796, 802, 808, 844, 850, 875, 878
Hose, kurze 369, 801, 805, 810
Hosen 716
Hosen, Beispiele 358
Hosenbluse 359
Hosenbund 350
Hosenrock 357
Hosenschlitz 350
Hosenträger 350
Hotel 710, 724, 886, 915
Hotelreservierungsschalter 620
Hotelzimmer 724
Houppelande 338
Hub 522, 523
Hubarm 637, 640
Hubarmzylinder 637
Hubble-Weltraumteleskop 17, 53
Hubblesche Klassifikation 9
Hubbrücke 542
Hubel 464
Hubgebläse 605
Hubkette 632
Hubplattform 653
Hubschrauber 631, 762
Hubschrauber, Beispiele 631
Hubschrauberhangar 762
Hubschrauberlandeplatz 652, 762
Hubstreben 640
Hubvorrichtung 635
Hubwerk 641
Hubwinde 634
Hubzahlvorwahl 305
Hubzylinder 573, 634, 766
Hudson Bay 30
Huf 124, 127
Huf, Unterseite 127
Hufbein 126
Hufe, Beispiele 127
Hufeisen 127, 376
Hufeisenbogen 413
Hufeisenmontierung 17
Hufglocke 853, 858
Hüft-Becken-Nerv 166
Hüft-Leisten-Nerv 166
Hüftarterie, gemeinsame 160, 165
Hüftarterie, innere 160, 161, 165
Hüftbein 122
Hüfte 96, 98, 147, 149
Hüftgurt 906
Huftiere 124
Huftiere, Beispiele 128
Hüftlochnerv 166
Hüftpolster 808
Hüftvene, gemeinsame 165
Hüftvene, innere 161
Hüftwurf 844
Hügel 45, 875
Huhn 120, 213
Hühnerei 213
Hühnerstall 182
Huitzilopochtli-Tempel 412
Hülle 84, 521, 867, 899, 905
Hüllen, Wan-tan 207
Hülse 85, 307, 912
Hülse, äußere 275
Hülse, Schnitt 84
Hülsenauswurf 755
Hülsenboden 860

Hülsenfrüchte 190
Humeruskopf 153
Hummel 101
Hummer 107, 218
Hummer, Anatomie 107
Hummer, äußere Merkmale 107
Hummus 200
Hund 130
Hund, äußere Merkmale 130
Hund, Skelett 131
Hund, Vorderpfote 130
Hunderassen 130
Hundert 703
Hundshai 218
Hupe 556, 576
Hürde 790
Hürden 852
Hürdenlauf 790
Hurrikan 63
Hustensirup 783
Hut 76
Hutband 340
Hutmutter 311
Hüttenkäse 210
Huygens 19
Hyäne 134
Hybridfahrzeug 563
Hydrant 712
Hydrantenanschluss 766
Hydrantenschlüssel 767
Hydraulik 632
Hydraulik-Heber 567
Hydraulik-Hochlöffelbagger 638
Hydraulikanschluss 642
Hydraulikkupplung 640
Hydraulikschlauch 641
Hydraulikzylinder 633, 640
hydraulische Scheibenbremse 870
hydraulischer Klappenheber 760
hydraulischer Palettenhubwagen 633
hydraulischer Widerstand 851
Hydrosphäre 66
Hygrograph 59
Hygrometer 261
Hygrostat 261
Hyperlinks 524
Hyracotherium 93

I

Iapetus 5
Iberische Halbinsel 32
Ichthyosaurus 93
Ichthyostega 92
Identifikationsnummer, technische 501
identisch 703
Identitätsband 376
Idiotenhügel 886
Igel 121
Iglu 418
Igluzelt 903
Ileum 164
Ilium 111, 116
Imbusschrauben 302
Impair 919
Impluvium 406
Impressum 471
Impulslaser, Rubin 692
Impulsregner 329
Inbound-Linie 806
Incisura intertragica 173
Inder 10
Indexanzeigeregler 477
Indexspiegel 612
Indianersprachen 469
Indien 747
Indisch-Antarktischer Rücken 50
Indisch-Australische Platte 43
Indischer Ozean 28, 29, 33, 34
indisches Fladenbrot 205
indisches Naanbrot 205
Indium 682
indoarische Sprachen 469
indoeuropäische Sprachen 469
Indonesien 33, 747
Indonesisch 469
Induktionsspule 488
Industrie 525
Industrie, petrochemische 656
Industrieabfälle 69, 70
Industriegebiet 709
industrielle Telekommunikation 487
industrielle Verschmutzung 69
Infiltration 67, 69
Information 725
Informationsdisplay 512
Informationsschalter 620, 719, 730, 733, 769, 779, 886
Informationsstand 715
Informationsverbreitung 525
Infrarot-Scanner 18
Infrarot-Zielsuchkopf 759
Infrarotschnittstelle 526, 527
Infrarotsensor 60, 518
Infrarotstrahlung 68, 690
Infusionsständer 780
Ingwer 199
Inhaber, Name 729
Inhaber, Unterschrift 729

Inhalt 471
Injektionsbohrung 646
Inklination 13
Inlineskating 895
Innenbehälter 266
Innenbeleuchtung 594
Innenbrett 915
Innenfeld 794
Innenfläche 346
Innengewinde 910
innengezahnte Fächerscheibe 310
Innenhebel 838
Innenhof 738
Inneninsolierung 561
Innenknauf 248
Innenkreis 877
Innenläden 282
Innenlippe 105
Innenohr 174
Innenohrvorhof 174
Innenstadt 709, 710
Innensteckhülse 909
Innenstiefel 889, 895
Innentasche 389
Innentür 291
Innenverteidiger 803
Innenzelt 902, 903
innere Drosselvene 160
innere Grabenböschung 409
innere Hüftarterie 160, 161, 165
innere Hüftvene 161
innere Kuppelhülle 17
innere Leitschaufeln 627
innere Oberschenkelkondyle 153
innere Planeten 5
Innereien 212
innerer Kern 42
innerer Oberarmgelenkhöcker 153
innerer Rand 127
innerer Schenkelmuskel 150
inneres Keilbein 155
Insassenaufnahme 726
Insasseneingang 726
Insekten 96
Insekten, Beispiele 101
Insektenfresser 117, 121
Insektenfresser, Beispiele 121
Insel 38, 539, 761
Inselkette 49
Installation 395
Instrumentalgruppierungen, Beispiele 438
Instrumente 17, 876
Instrumente, elektronische 450
Instrumente, wissenschaftliche 23
Instrumenteneinheit 25
Instrumentenplattform 60
Instrumententafel 557, 574, 576
Instrumentenring 24
Intelsat 487
intensive Kultur 68, 69
intensive Landwirtschaft 68, 70
Intensivstation 780
interaktive Terminals 395
Interlobärspalt, schräger 163
internationale Post 475
internationale Raumstation 21
internationale Wettersymbole 56
internationales Einheitensystem 702
interne Modemschnittstelle 513, 526
Internet 523, 524
Internet-Nutzer 524
Internet-Nutzungen 525
Internet-Provider 525
Internet-Tasten 514
Intervalle 434
Interview 471
Intrusivgesteine 42
Inuktikut 469
Io 4
Ionenschweif, Plasmaschweif 8
ionische Halbsäule 407
ionische Säulenordnung 404
Irak 746
Iran 746
Iridium 683
Iris 177
Irisch 469
Irisch Moos 183
Irische See 32
irisches Brot 205
Irland 743
irreguläre Galaxie Typ I 9
irreguläre Galaxie Typ II 9
irreguläres Aggregat 64
ISA-Erweiterungsport 513
Isba 418
Ischiasnerv 166
Ischiasnerv, kleiner 166
Ischium 111, 116
Islam 736
Island 32, 744
Isländisch 469
Isobare 55
Isolationszelle 727
Isolator 562, 663
Isolierhülse 275

Isoliermaterial 294, 655
Isoliermaterialien 299
Isolierraum 778
Isolierstoff 254
isolierte Klinge 316
isolierte Sprachen 469
isolierter Griff 316, 317
Isolierung 253, 267, 672
Isoseiste 43
Israel 746
ist annähernd gleich 703
ist äquivalent mit 703
ist gleich 703
ist gleich oder größer als 703
ist gleich oder kleiner als 703
ist größer als 703
ist identisch mit 703
ist kleiner als 703
ist nicht identisch mit 703
ist nicht parallel zu 704
ist parallel zu 704
ist senkrecht zu 704
ist ungleich 703
Italien 744
Italienisch 469

J

J-2-Triebwerk 25
Jabot 362
Jaboticaba 197
Jacke 338, 355, 844
Jacke, dreiviertellange 352
Jacke, traditionelle 846
Jacken 352, 355, 358
Jackett 348
Jackfrucht 196
Jackpot-Kasten 920
Jackpot-Leitung 920
Jagdhunde 13
Jagdkappe 340
Jagen 912
Jaguar 135
Jahresring 87
Jahreszahl 729
Jahreszeiten 54
Jahreszeitenziegel 917
Jakobsmuschel 217
Jalapeño-Chili 199
Jalousie 249, 285
Jalousiefenster 415
Jalousieschweller 444
Jalousieverschluss 261
Jamaika 742
Jamaikapfeffer 198
Japan 33, 747
Japangraben 50
Japanisch 469
japanischer Rettich 189
japanisches Experimentiermodul 21
Japanisches Meer 33
Japanpinsel 397
Jarlsberg 211
Javagraben 50
Jazzband 438
Jazzbesen 449
Jeans 358
Jemen 746
Jesus Christus 736
Jetski 876
Jicama 184
Jiddisch 469
Jo 846
Jocharm 433
Jochbein 152, 158
Jochweite 540
Jockey 856
Jod 683
Joggingschuh 370
Joghurt 210
Johann Calvin 736
Johannesbeere 192
Johannisbeere, schwarze 192
Joker 914
Jolle 835
Jordanien 746
Joule 702
Joystick 516
Joysticks 918
Judaism 736
jüdisches Weißbrot 205
Judo 844
Judogi 844
Judokämpfer Wettkampfteilnehmer 844
Jugoslawien 744
Jujutsu 846
Jungfrau 11, 13
Jupiter 4
Jura 93
Jurte 418
Jurypräsident 855
Justaucorps 338
Justierring 383
Justiz 726
Justizvollzugsanstalt 726
Juweliergeschäft 714

K

K-Gerüst 663
K.O.-System 789
Kabel 289, 306, 316, 331, 332, 488, 492, 504, 505, 516, 517, 523, 558, 573, 848, 913
Kabel der Schnittstelle für digitale Musikinstrumente (MIDI) 451
Kabel, Anschluss 305
Kabelabisolierer 317
Kabeldurchführung, ausbrechbare 272
Kabeljau, atlantischer 221
Kabelleitung 525
Kabelmantel 308, 318
Kabelmodem 525
Kabelmuffe 306
Kabelrolle 848
Kabelschutz 913
Kabeltrommel 489
Kabeltülle 317
Kabelversteifung 288
Kabelverteiler 486
Kabine 608, 640, 643, 731
Kabriolett 549
Kachel 22
Kaffee 208
Kaffee-Filterkanne 241
Kaffeebohnen, geröstete 208
Kaffeehausgardine 282
Kaffeekanne 905
Kaffeeküche 509
Kaffeelöffel 228
Kaffeemaschine 241
Kaffeemaschinen 241, 723
Kaffeemühle 240
Kaffeepresser 241
Käfig 407
Kaftan 339
Kahnbein 154, 155, 156
Kai 596
Kaianlage 708
Kaiman 114
Kairampe 596
Kaiserdach 414
Kaiserling 183
Kajak 837
Kakadu 118
Kakao 208
Kaki 197
Kaktusfeige 197
Kalahari 34
Kalandriagefäß 669
Kalb 128
Kalbfleisch 214
Kalbfleischwürfel 214
Kalbshackfleisch 214
Kaldaune 212
Kalifornien, Golf 30
Kalium 682
Kalkschwamm 95
Kalkulationspunkt 891
Kalmar 217
kalte Gerichte 722
kalte Luft 64, 675
Kältemittelleitung 260
kaltes Kühlmittel 665, 674
kaltes Schwerwasser 670
Kaltfront am Boden 56
kaltgemäßigte Klimate 61
Kaltnadel 422
Kaltwasserkreislauf 262
Kaltwassersteigleitung 262
Kaltwasserzulauf 265, 266, 267, 270, 271
Kalzium 682
Kambium 87
Kambodscha 747
Kambrium 92
Kamel 129
Kamera 18, 490, 492, 775, 873
Kamera-Assistent, erster 428
Kamera-Assistent, zweiter 428
Kamera-Dolly 492
Kamera-Steckfeld 490
Kameragehäuse 476
Kameramann 428
Kameraplattform 482
Kameraschraube 482
Kamerun 745
Kamille 208
Kamin 250, 256, 257
Kaminabdeckung 257
Kaminabdichtung 257
Kaminanschluss 256
Kaminaufsatz 245
Kaminbesteck 257
Kamineinfassung 256, 257
Kamingitter 257
Kaminsims 256
Kamm 45, 417, 461
Kämme 380
Kammer 650
Kammer, unterirdische 402
Kammerseptum 162
Kammerton A 436
Kammerwasser 177
Kammlade 460
Kammmuschel 217
Kampfbereich 844
Kämpfer 413, 846

Kämpferlinie 845, 847
Kampffläche 846, 847
Kampffläche, zentrale 843
Kampfflugzeug 760
Kampfgericht 845, 853, 871
Kampfmesser 751
Kampfrichter 824, 825, 842, 843, 844, 848, 859, 860, 881, 893
Kampfrichter für den künstlerischen Ausdruck 823
Kampfrichter für die technische Ausführung 823
Kampfrichter, leitender 860
Kampfrichter-Obmann 883
Kampfrichterassistenten 883
Kampfrichterstand 890
Kampfrichterturm 890, 891
Kampfrichtertribüne 856
Kampfsportarten 842
Kamtschatka-Halbinsel 33
Kanada 742
kanadischer Bacon 216
kanadischer Football 809
Kanal, Haverscher 154
Kanal, linker 502
Kanal, rechter 502
Kanalabschnitt 258
Kanäle, Volkmannsche 154
Kanaleinstiegsschacht 712
Kanalisation 262, 263
Kanalschleuse 596, 597
Kanalsohle 709
Kanalsuchtasten 495
Kanalwahlschalter 505
Kanalwahltasten für Lautsprecher 497
Kanapee 276
kanarische Melone 195
Kandare 854
Kandarenkette 854
Kandarenzügel 854
Kandiszucker 209
Känguru 142, 143
Känguru, äußere Merkmale 143
Känguru, Skelett 142
Kaninchen 123, 212
Kanne 241
Kannelüre 404, 405
Kanone aus dem 17. Jahrhundert 752
Kante 887, 907
Kantenfläche 300
Kantenschiene 894
Kantenstecher 326
Kantholz 460
Kanu 600, 837
Kanu-Kajak: Flachwasserrennen 838
Kanu-Kajak: Wildwasser 837
Kanüle 776
Kanülenansatz 776
Kanzel 737, 738, 898
Kanzellösehebel 898
Kap 38
Kap der Guten Hoffnung 34
Kap Horn 31
Kap Verde 745
Kapaun 213
Kapelle 408, 726
Kapillargefäß 172
Kapillarröhrchen 695
Kapitalband 426
Kapitälchen 472
Kapitänssitz 626
Kapitell 405
Kaplanturbine 659
Käppchen 340
Kappe 269, 274, 275, 470, 484, 816, 880
Kappe, äußere 342
Kapsel 75, 783
Kapsel, Schnitt 84
Kapselfinger 452
Kapuze 353, 368, 882, 901
Kapuze mit Zugband 369
Kapuzenmuskel 150, 151
Kapuzenmütze 341
Kar 7, 46
Karabiner 911
Karabinerhaken 835, 901
Karaffe 225
Karaffe, kleine 225
Karambolagebillard 862
Karate 845
Kategeri 845
Karateka 845
Karavelle 599
Karbon 92
Kardamom 198
Kardinal 118
Kardinalseezeichen 616
Kardinalseezeichen, östliches 617
Kardinalseezeichen, südliches 617
Kardinalseezeichen, westliches 617
Kardone 185
Karibik 28, 30
Karibische Inseln 742
Karibische Platte 43
Karikatur 471
Karo 914
Karosserie 550, 567
Karosserien, Beispiele 549
Karotte 189
Karpalballen 130
Karpaten 32

Karpfen 220
Kartätsche 752
Karte 915
Karte, politische 37
Karteikarten 532
Karteikasten 533
Karteiregister 532
Karteischubfach 533
Kartendarstellungen 36
Kartenkontrolleur 394, 427
Kartenlesegerät 730, 731
Kartenleser 493
Kartenleserschlitz 548
Kartennummer 729, 731
Kartenraum 604, 732
Kartenschacht, PC 526
Kartenschlitz 507
Kartenspiele 914
Kartoffel 184
Kartoffelstampfer 233
Kartographie 35
Karton 223
Kartusche 268, 315, 773
Kartuschendichtung 268
Kartuschenkolben 268
Kartuschenpistole 315
Kasachstan 746
Käse 722
Käsemesser 228
Käsereibe 230
Kaserne 409
Käseschachtel 223
Käsetheke 181
Kaspisches Meer 28, 33
Kasse 181, 394, 427, 548, 719, 723
Kassen 181, 716, 717
Kassette 499, 504, 521
Kassettenauswurfschalter 495
Kassettenband 499
Kassettendeck 488, 499, 503
Kassettendecktasten 504
Kassettenfach 499
Kassettenfilm 481
Kassettenlaufwerk 521
Kassettenrekorder-Wahltaste 497
Kassettenschacht 495
Kassettenteil 504
Kassiererin 181
Kassiopeia 12
Kastagnetten 437, 449
Kasten 99, 436
Kasteneisen 401
Kastenwagen, langer 588
Katalanisch 469
Katalysator 553
katalytische Umwandlungsanlage 656
Katamaran 835
Katapult 761
Katar 746
Kathode 689
Katholizismus 736
Katze 132, 409
Katze, äußere Merkmale 133
Katze, Kopf 132
Katzenhai, groß gefleckter 218
Katzenrassen 132
Kaufhaus 715, 716
Kaulquappe 111
Kaumuskel 150
Kegel 237, 705, 882, 883
Kegel, Beispiele 865
Kegeldach 415
Kegelprojektion 36
Kegelradgetriebe 686
Kehldeckel 163, 176
Kehle 115, 444
Kehlkopf 163
Kehlriemen 854
Kehrschaufel 295
Keil 346, 386, 388, 444, 753
Keilbein 158
Keilbein, äußeres 155, 156
Keilbein, inneres 155
Keilbein, mittleres 155, 156
Keilbeinhöhle 175
Keilhebel 309
Keilriemen 292, 552, 566
Keilstein 413
Keim 85
Keimblatt 77
Keimblatt, verwelkendes 77
Keimscheibe 117
Keimung 77
Keimwurzel 77
Kelch 83, 84, 737
Kelchblatt 80, 83
Kelimbindung mit wechselnden Wenden 463
Kelimbindung, senkrechte 463
Keller 250
Kellerfalte 357
Kellerfenster 245
Kellner 721
Kellnerbesteck 230
keltische Sprachen 469
Kelvin 702
Kendo 847
Kendoka 847
Kenia 745
Kennplakette 273
Kennzeichnung 560
Kepheus 12

Keramikdichtung 268
Keramikkondensator 689
Kerbe 698, 863
Kerbel 202
Kermadec-Tonga-Graben 50
Kern 8, 9, 81, 82, 83, 85, 444, 867, 908, 912
Kern, äußerer 42
Kern, innerer 42
Kern, spaltbarer 681
Kernenergie 665
Kernenergie, Elektrizitätserzeugung 665
Kerngehäuse 82
Kerngehäuseausstecher 233
Kernholz 87
Kernkörperchen 74, 170
Kernkraftwerk 668
kernlose Salatgurke 188
Kernreaktor 667
Kernreaktorraum 763
Kernschatten 6, 7
Kernspalte 444
Kernspaltung 681
Kernspaltung des Uranbrennstoffs 665
Kerosin 656
Kerosintank 433
Kerze 737
Kessel 45, 448, 612
Kesselpauke 448
Kesselwagen 588
Ketchup 201
Ketsch 601
Ketschua 469
Kettbaum 460
Kette 265, 460, 461, 578, 580, 697, 826, 876
Kettenantrieb 641
Kettenblatt, großes 580
Kettenblatt, kleines 580
Kettenblattumwerfer 578, 580
Kettenblende 758
Kettenbremse 331
Kettenfäden 463
Kettenführung 580
Kettenlaufwerkrahmen 636
Kettenplatte 758
Kettenrad 758, 870
Kettenreaktion 681
Kettenrohrzange 315
Kettensäge 331
Kettenschuh 758
Kettensicht 459
Kettenstrebe 578
Keule 130
Keulen 823
Keulenärmel 361
Kibla 738
Kichererbsen 190
Kickschuh 800
Kidneybohne, rote 191
Kiebitz 118
Kiefer 106
Kiefernnadeln 89
Kieferschutz 808
Kiefertaster 103
Kiel 840
Kielbasa-Wurst 216
Kielbein 116
Kielbogen 413
Kielboot 835
Kieldach 414
Kielstange 897
Kieme 106
Kiemen 105, 109
Kiemen, äußere 111
Kiemendeckel 108, 111
Kiemenspalten 108
Kies 253, 263
Kiesbett 872
Kilogramm 702
Kilometerzähler 557
Kilowattstundenzähler 273
Kimme 754, 755, 757, 861, 893, 912
Kimono 364
Kimonoärmel 361
Kinder 545, 785
Kinderabteilung 732
Kinderbekleidung 369
Kinderbetreuung 715
Kinderbücher 732
Kindermöbel 281
Kinderschuhe 717
Kindersessel 281
Kindersitz 558, 580
Kinn 115, 148
Kinnkette 854
Kinnkettenhaken 854
Kinnreff 749
Kinnriemen 765, 808
Kinnschutz 575, 765, 870, 885
Kinnstütze 439
Kino 427, 608, 710, 714
Kinoleinwand 427
Kinosaal 427
Kinyarwanda 468
Kiosk 548, 593
Kippanhänger, aufgesatelter 572
Kippe 647
Kipper 573

Kippermulde 639
Kipphebel 783
Kipplader 572
Kipppritsche 573
Kirche 711, 737
Kirchenbank 737
Kirchenfenster 737
Kirgisistan 746
Kiribati 747
Kirschband 283
Kirsche 192
Kirschtomate 188
Kirsorfalte 283
Kirundi 468
Kissen 458
Kissen, kleines 280
Kiste 222
Kittelbluse 359
Kiwano 196
Kiwi 196
Klaffmuschel 217
Klammer 284
Klammern, eckige 473
Klammern, runde 473
Klampe 834, 835
Klangfarbenregler 441
Klangfell 433
Klangwahlanzeige 497
Klangwahlschalter 497
klappbare Laderampe 608
klappbare Nagelfeile 377
Klappbrücke, einteilige 542
Klappe 105, 278, 309, 348, 429, 446, 535
Klappe, hintere 23
Klappendrücker 446
Klappenhebel 626
Klappenheber, hydraulischer 760
Klappenschutz 446
Klappenstiel 446
Klappentasche 348, 352, 360
Klapperschlange 114
Klappschlittschuh 883
Klappspaten 906
Klappspiegel 477
Klappstufe 567
Klappstuhl 277
Klapptisch 278
klarer Himmel 56
Klarinette 446
Klarinetten 437
Klarsichtfenster 386
Klarsichthüllen 386
Klarsichtscheibe 876
Klarspülmittelbehälter 294
Klassenzimmer 727, 734, 735
Klassenzimmer für Schüler mit Lernschwierigkeiten 734
klassische Bluse 359
Klaue 96, 98, 107, 121, 122, 140, 143, 301
Klauenpolrad 688
Klaviaturboden 442
Klavier 442
Klaviermechanik 443
Klavikula 111
Klebeband 254, 800
Klebebandabroller 534
Klebefilmspender 534
Klebestift 534
Klebfaden 103
Klebstoff 254
Kleeblatt 538, 539
Kleeblattbogen 413
Kleid in Trapez-Form 356
Kleid mit angesetztem Schoß 356
Kleid mit flachem Reifrock 337
Kleid mit Krinolinenrock 337
Kleid mit Turnüre 337
Kleid, mit angesetztem Schoß 356
Kleider, Beispiele 356
Kleiderhaken 510
Kleidersack 389
Kleiderschrank 251, 278, 279, 510, 724
Kleiderschutz 783
Kleiderstoff 455
Kleidung 338
Kleidung, feuer- und wasserfeste 765
Kleidung, traditionelle 339
Kleinanzeigen 471
Kleinbus 569
kleine Armdecken 115
kleine Beuteltasche 388
kleine Chirurgie 777
kleine Elektrohaushaltsgeräte 717
kleine Karaffe 225
kleine Klinge 905
kleine Schamlippe 170, 171
kleine Sterne 8
kleine Trommel 437, 448
Kleine Wasserschlange 10
kleiner als 703
Kleiner Bär 12
kleiner Finger 173
Kleiner Getränkekarton 223
Kleiner Hund 13
kleiner Ischiasnerv 166
kleiner Kragen 339
kleiner Lehnstuhl 276
Kleiner Löwe 13
kleiner Rundmuskel 151
kleiner Teller 226

kleiner Tentakel 104
kleines Kettenblatt 580
kleines Kissen 280
kleines Vieleckbein 154
Kleinfingerhaken 447
Kleinflügel 443
Kleinhirn 167
Kleinkalibergewehr 861, 893
Kleinwagen 549
Klemmbacke 377
Klemmbrett 533
Klemmbügel 381
Klemmbügel, Hebel 381
Klemme 700
Klemme, rote 558
Klemme, schwarze 558
Klemme, verstellbare 286
Klemmgriff 901
Klemmhalter 685
Klemmhefter 532
Klemmring 838
Klemmschlaufe 900, 901
Klemmschraube, untere 58
Klemmspot 286
Klemmverschraubung 270
Klemmvorrichtung 700
Klempnerwerkzeuge 314
Klettenwurzel 189
Kletterer 900
Klettergürtel 901
Kletterhaken 900
Kletterhose 901
Kletterpflanze 322
Kletterschuh 900
Klettersport 900
Kletterwand, künstliche 900
Klickpedal 870
Kliff, Klippe 51
Klimaanlage 68, 489, 567, 608, 775
Klimagerät 622
Klimageräte 261
Klimate der Welt 61
Klimate, kaltgemäßigte 61
Klimate, tropische 61
Klimate, warmgemäßigte 61
Klinge 227, 229, 237, 302, 383, 390, 849
Klinge, isolierte 316
Klinge, zweischneidige 383
Klingenarten 302
Klingendose 383
Klingenmitte 849
Klingenschwäche 849
Klingenstärke 849
Klingenstopper 382
Klinke 460
Klinkenstecker 488
Klips 350, 374
Klistierspritze 776
Klitoris 170
Kloake 103, 110, 113, 116
Klöppel 458
Klöppelbrief 458
Klöppelkissen 458
Klöppelspitze 458
Klosettbecken 265
Klosettdeckel 265
Klotz 632
Klubhaus 856, 866
Klubhauskurve 856
Knabenbekleidung 2 bis 6 Jahre 717
Knabenbekleidung 7 bis 17 Jahre 717
Knarre 307, 311, 909
Knäuel 462
Knauf 277, 278, 797, 822, 849, 880
Knebel 312, 739, 854
Knebelbolzen 302
Knebeltrense 854
Knebelverschluss 353
Kneifer 385
Knethaken 236
Knickschutztülle 381
Knie 124, 130, 146, 148
Kniebandage 850, 857
Kniebuckel 749
Kniebundhose 358
Kniehose 338
Kniemanschette 857
Kniemanschettenhalter 857
kniender Anschlag 861
Kniepolster 800, 880
Kniescheibe 122, 124, 126, 131, 138, 152
Knieschoner 858
Knieschützer 796, 874, 882, 894, 895
Kniestrumpf 351, 365, 848
Knoblauch 184
Knoblauchpresse 230
Knöchel 146, 148
knöchelhohe Stiefelette 343
Knöchelschutz 796
Knöchelsocke 351
Knochen, kurzer 157
Knochen, langer 157
Knochen, platter 157
Knochen, unregelmäßiger 157
Knochenfisch 108
Knochenfische 219
Knochenhaut 154
Knochenmark 154
Knolle 185
Knollenblätterpilz 76

Knollengemüse 184
Knollensellerie 189
Knollenziest 184
Knopf 274, 285, 305, 349, 354, 432, 753
Knopf für Alarmschwellenwert-Anzeige 613
Knöpfe, gelochte 453
Knopfflasche 350
Knopfleiste 349, 354
Knopfleiste, verdeckte 355, 369
Knopfloch 352
Knorpelfisch 108
Knorpelfische 218
Knorrenmuskel 151
Knospe 78
Knötchenstich, französischer 459
Knötchenstiche 459
Knoten 463, 663, 687, 908
Knoter 642
Knurrhahn 219
Koala 143
Koaxialkabel 523
Kobalt 683
Kobra 114
Koch 721
Kochbereich 722
Kochecke 509
Köcher 859
Kochfeld 239
Kochgeräte 234
Kochgeschirr 722, 905
Kochmesser 228
Kochmulde 224, 290
Kochplatte 290, 722
Kochtopf 905
Köderlauncher 762
Koffer 389, 717
Kofferauflieger 572
Kofferradio 503
Kofferraum 551
Kognakschwenker 225
Kohl 186
Kohle 397
Kohle-Zink-Zelle 689
Kohlebergwerk 647
Kohlekraftwerk 646
Kohlendioxid 670
Kohlendioxid, Aufnahme 78
Kohlendioxidkühlgas 670
Kohlendioxidreaktor 670
Kohlenhalde 646
Kohlenschaufel 257
Kohlenstoff 683
Kohlestab (Kathode) 689
Kohlezeichnung 396
Kohlrabi 185
Kohlrübe 189
Kokosnuss 193
Kola-Halbinsel 32
Kolanuss 193
Kolben 81, 85, 274, 275, 453, 559, 564, 565, 566, 754, 860
Kolbenantrieb 642
Kolbenhals 912
Kolbenring 566
Kolbenschaft 566
Kolibri 118
Kolk 47
Kollaterale 168
Kollegmappe 386
Kollegmappe mit Griff 386
Kollektor 659
Koller 352
Kolon 97, 113, 125
Kolonne 919
Kolumbien 742
Koma 8
Kombi 549
Kombi-Pflegelösung 384
Kombibacke 326
Kombihammer 901
Kombilimousine, dreitürige 549
Kombination 852
Kombipumpe 904
Kombizange 310, 317
Kombu 183
Kombüse 763
Komet 8
Komma 473
Kommandant, Büro 764
Kommandantenstand 758
Kommandoantenne, ferngesteuerte 40
Kommandobrücke 605
Kommandoeinheit 19
Kommandokapsel 25
Kommandoturm 763
Kommataste 529
Kommode 279
Kommunikation 468
Kommunikation, drahtlose 505
Kommunikationsmodul 486
Kommunikationsprotokoll 524
Kommunikationsschaltbrett 626
Kommunikationsterminal 507
Kommunionbank 737
Kommutator 688
Komoren 746
Kompakta 154
Kompaktpuder 378
Kompaktspeisesystem 493
Kompass 11, 898
Kompassrose 612, 907

komplexe Düne 52
Kompositbogen 859, 913
Kompostkiste 323
Kompressionsgurt, seitlicher 906
Kompressor 260, 320
Kompressor für Klimaanlage 566
Kondensatauslass 669
Kondensateinlass 669
Kondensation 67
Kondensationskammer 646, 668
Kondensationskühlwasserbecken 671
Kondensatorventilator 261
Kondensieren 680
Kondensmilch 210
Kondensor 646, 668, 674, 693, 694
Kondensoreinstellung 693
Kondensorhöhenverstellung 693
Kondensorkühlwasserauslass 669
Kondensorkühlwassereinlass 669
Kondenssammler 261
Konditionierer 642
Konditorei 715
Kondor 119
Konferenzraum 509, 718, 730, 735
Konfuzianismus 736
Konfuzius 736
Kongo 34, 745
Kongresssaal 718
Kongresszentrum 711, 718
König 914, 916
König, Grabkammer 402
Königin 99
Königin, Grabkammer 402
Königin-Maud-Land 29
königliche Vene 160
Königsbaum 676
Königsflanke 916
konkave Linse 691
konkavkonvexe Linse 691
Konservator, Büro 394
Konserven 181
Konservendose 223
Konservierungslabor 395
Konsole 412
Konstruktion 249
Konstruktion eines Hauses 250
Konsument 487
Kontakt 274
Kontaktelemente 274
Kontaktkopiergerät 484
Kontaktlinse, harte 384
Kontaktlinse, weiche 384
Kontaktlinsen 384
Kontaktlinsenbehälter 384
Kontergarde 409
Kontermutter 270
Kontinent 49
kontinentale Kruste 42
Kontinentalfuß 49
Kontinentalhang 49
Kontinentalrand 49
Kontinentalschelf 49
Kontinente, Lage 28
Kontoidentifikation 731
Kontrabass 439
Kontrabasse 437
Kontrafagotte 437
Kontrasteinstellung 512
Kontrastregler 518
Kontreskarpe 409
Kontrollbildschirm 694
Kontrollkampfrichter 823
Kontrollkonsole 865
Kontrolllampe 381
Kontrollleuchte 238, 239, 240, 241, 288, 290, 294, 465, 731, 767
Kontrollleuchte Netzspannung 731
Kontrollleuchte Papiereinzug 519
Kontrollleuchte, Tintenpatrone 519
Kontrollleuchten 515, 519, 520
Kontrollleuchten für Tonsignalquellen 497
Kontrollmonitor des Aufsichtsingenieurs 491
Kontrollmonitore 489, 490, 491
Kontrollmonitore, Regie 428
Kontrollmutter 58
Kontrollraum 618, 718, 763, 764, 768
Kontrolltaste 505
Kontrolltor 890
Kontrolltower 618
Kontrollturm 761
Kontrolluhr 489, 491
Konturfeder 115
Konvektion 681
Konvektionsströmung 681
Konvektionszelle 63
Konvektionszone 6
Konvektor 259, 260
konvergierende Plattengrenzen 43
konvexe Linse 691
konvexkonkave Linse 691
Konzertflügel 443
Koordinatensystem der Erdkugel 35
Koordinatensystem der Himmelskugel 13
Köperbindung 463
Kopf 8, 96, 97, 99, 104, 115, 140, 147, 149, 161, 169, 301, 302, 308, 311, 383, 384, 391, 425, 439, 441, 452, 457, 458, 516, 816, 822, 858, 867, 901, 909
Kopf der Katze 132
Kopf voraus 829

Kopfarten 302
Kopfband 772, 773
Kopfbedeckungen 340, 341
Kopfbein 154
Kopfbruststück 107
Kopfbügel 504
Kopfende 280
Kopfganglion 105
Kopfhörer 502, 503, 504
Kopfhöreranschlussbuchse 450, 451, 513
Kopfhörerbuchse 497, 504
Kopfhörerstecker 504
Kopfkissen 280
Kopfkissenbezug 280
Kopfkissenschonbezug 280
Kopfnicker 150
Kopfprofil 285
Kopfregal 181
Kopfriegel 247
Kopfriemen 773
Kopfsalat 186
Kopfschiene 284
Kopfschutz 772, 842
Kopfstab 857
Kopfsteg 426
Kopfstrecke 650
Kopfstütze 555
Kopfteil 255, 281, 340, 341
Kopfwurf 844
Kopienablage 512
Kopienanzahl 512
Kopienausgabemodus 512
Kopieren, beidseitiges 512
Kopierkontrolle 512
Kopierrad 454
Kopierraum 509
Kopilotensitz 626
Koppel-Kipptaste 444
Koppelungsmodul 21
Koppen 287
Kora 433
Korakoid 111, 116
Korallenmeer 29
Korallennatter 114
Koran 736
Korb 291, 294, 811
Korbanlage 809, 811
Korbball 809
Korbbrett 811
Korbbretthalter 811
Körbchen 81
Korbhaltetrossen 899
Korblinie 809
Korbpfosten 811
Korbring 809, 811
Korbstütze, gepolsterte 811
Korbtragerohr 899
Kordel 282
Kordilleren, Australische 29
Korea 33
Koreanisch 469
Koriander 202
korinthische Halbsäule 407
korinthische Säulenordnung 405
korinthischer Pilaster 407
Kork 892
Korkball 797
Korkenzieher 905
Korkspitze 817
Korn 754, 757, 861, 893, 912
Kornelevator 643
Körner 301
Körnerfresser 117
Körnerschicht 172
Kornett 437, 447
Kornhalter mit Korn 755
Korntank 643
Korona 6
Körper 176, 444, 705, 909
Körper, menschlicher 146
Körperchen, Ruffinisches 172
Körperchen, Vater-Pacinisches 172
Körperpflege 181, 379
Körpertemperaturregelung 20
Korpus 440, 441, 446, 793, 893
Korpus, birnenförmiger 433
Korpus, dreieckiger 433
Korpus, massiver 441
Korpus, runder 432
Korrekturflüssigkeit 534
Korrekturstreifen 534
Korrekturtaste 456
Korselett 366
Korsett 337, 367
Kosakenmütze 340
Kosmetikartikel 717
Kosmetikeinsatz 389
Kosmetikkoffer 389
Kostüm 355, 428
Kostüme, historische 336
Kote 847
Köte 124
Kotelett 214, 215
Kötengelenk 124
Kotflügel 550, 570
Kotflügel, hinterer 577
Krabbe 218
Krabbenspinne 102
Kraft 686
Kraft, Maßeinheit 702
Kraftfahrzeuganlagen 553

Kraftfahrzeuge: Hauptbauteile 552
Krafträder 545, 546
Kraftsport 850
Kraftstoff-Luft-Gemisch 564
Kraftstoffanlage 553
Kraftstoffanzeige 557
Kraftstoffleitung 553, 563
Kraftstoffreserveanzeige 557
Kraftstoffschlauch 25
Kraftstofftank 331, 553, 570, 574, 577, 586
Kraftübertragung 580
Kraftwerk 664
Kraftwerk im Querschnitt 664
Kraftwerksgebäude 666
Kragen 348, 349, 352, 362, 440, 441
Kragen, Beispiele 362
Kragen, drapierter 363
Kragen, gespreizter 349
Kragen, kleiner 339
Kragenecke 362
Kragenklammer 376
Kragenspitze 349
Kragenstäbchen 349
Kragenflechte 74
Kragensteg 362
Kragstein 256, 408
Kragträger 540
Krähenfußstich 459
Krail 327
Krake 217
Kralle 113, 115, 117, 130, 133, 325
Kralle, ausgestreckte 133
Kralle, eingezogene 133
Krallenbein 133
Kran 652
Kranbahn 634
Kräne 634
Kranführerkabine 634
Kranich 10
Krankenakten 781
Krankenhaus 711, 725, 778
Krankenhausbett 780
Krankenreibe 230
Krankenschwester 780
Krankenstation 726
Krankentisch 780
Krankentrage 775, 776
Krankenzimmer 780
Kranzgesims 403, 404
Kranznaht 158
Kranzprofil 278
Krappe 376
Krater 7, 44, 647
Kraterstrahlen 7
Kraterwall 7
Kraulen 832
krause Endivie 187
Kräuselfalte 359
Kräuselfalten, Beispiele 283
Kräuselrock 357
Krausstrick 458
Kräuter 202
Kräutertees 208
Krawatte 349
Krawatten 716
Krawattenklemme 376
Krawattennadel 376
Krawattenschal 349
Krebs 13
Krebs, Wendekreis 34, 35, 36
Krebse 107
Krebstiere 218
Kreditabteilung 730
Kreditkarte 729
Kreditkartenetui 386
Kreditkartenfach 386
Kreide 93, 863
Kreis, Teile 917
Kreise 917
Kreiskolbenmotor, Arbeitsprozess 565
Kreislauf, elektrischer 274
Kreisregner 329
Kreissägeblatt 304
Kreisverkehr 39
Kremaster 97
Krempe 340, 341
Kreolen 374
Krepis 403, 405
Kreuz 435, 610, 740, 914
Kreuz des Südens 11
Kreuz-Bramstagsegel 603
Kreuz-Royalbrasse 603
Kreuz-Royalstagsegel 603
Kreuz-Stengestagsegel 603
Kreuzaussteifung 252
Kreuzbein 138, 141, 152, 153, 157
Kreuzbeinwirbel 122, 126, 131, 142
Kreuzen 833
Kreuzgeflecht 166
Kreuzhacke 327
Kreuzknoten 908
Kreuzkopf 632
Kreuzkümmel 198
Kreuzmast 602
Kreuzmuster-Teppichmuschel 217
Kreuzrippe 410
Kreuzschlitzschrauben 302
Kreuzschlitzschraubenzieher 905
Kreuzschlüssel 558
Kreuzsegel 603
Kreuzstiche 459
Kreuztisch 693
Kreuztischeinstellung 693

Kriechstrombarriere 562
Krieger, gallischer 748
Kringel 204
Krinolinenrock 337
Kristallisation 680
Kristalltropfen 287
Kristallzucker 209
Kroatien 744
Krokodil 114
Krokus 80
Krone 87, 124, 159, 227, 229, 374, 412, 440, 696
Kronenabschnitt der Pulpahöhle 159
Kronleuchter 287
Kropf 97, 99, 104, 106, 116
Krummhalskürbis 189
Kruppe 124, 826
Kruste, kontinentale 42
Kruste, ozeanische 42
Krustenflechte 74
Kruzifix 737
kryogene Hauptstufe 24
Krypton 684
Kuba 742
Kübel 322
Küche 180, 222, 224, 250, 406, 719, 721, 723, 724, 726, 735, 764
Küchenbeil 229
Küchenchef 721
Kuchenform 232
Kuchenform, flache 232
Küchenhilfe 721
Kücheninsel 224
Küchenmaschine 237
Küchenmesser 229
Küchenmesser, Beispiele 229
Kuchenpinsel 232
Kuchenrad 232
Küchenreibe 230
Küchenschere 233
Küchenset 233
Küchenuhr 231
Küchenutensilien 229
Küchenwaage 231
Küchenwagen 623
Kufe 631, 876, 878, 880, 881, 884
Kufe, bewegliche 885
Kugel 470, 516, 705, 752, 793, 865, 912
Kugel-Sternhaufen 9
Kugelaggregat 268
Kugeldichtung 268
Kugelgelenk 156
Kugelhalterung 58, 516
Kugellager 677
Kugelmass 516
Kugeln 864
Kugelrücklaufkasten 865
Kugelschreiber 470
Kugelstoßen 790
Kugelträger 865
Kuh 128
Kühlabteilung 180, 181
Kühlaggregat 571
Kühlauflieger 572
Kühlbox 906
Kühler 552, 561, 674
Kühler für Dampfgeneratorraum 669
Kühleranlage 553
Kühleranschluss, unterer 561
Kühlerblock 561
Kühlergrill 550, 570
Kühlergruppe 586
Kühlerhaube 570
Kühlerverschlussdeckel 561
Kühlfach 291
Kühlhaus 596
Kühlmantel 755
Kühlmittel 665, 670, 671
Kühlmittel, erwärmtes 665
Kühlmittel, heißes 674
Kühlmittel, kaltes 665, 674
Kühlmittelauslass 672
Kühlmitteleinlass 672
Kühlraum 181, 722
Kühlschrank 224, 291, 720, 722
Kühlschränke 720
Kühlturm 646
Kühlung 656
Kühlvitrine 720
Kühlwagen 588
Kühlwassertank 665, 669
Kühlwasserventil 669
Kühlwasserventilator 586
Kühlzylinder 692
Kuhstall 182
Kuhstek 908
Kuiper-Gürtel 4
Küken 120
Kulette 374
Kulissen 430
Kultbild, Standort 403
Kultur, intensive 68, 69
Kulturbeutel 388
Kulturorganisation 525
Kümmel 198
Kumquat 194
Kumulonimbus 56, 62
Kumulus 56, 62
Kundenbetreuung 731

Kung-Fu 846
Kunst 394
Künste, bildende 394
Künste, darstellende 427
Künste, grafische 420
Kunstfliege 909
Kunstgewerbe 452
künstlerischer Ausdruck, Kampfrichter 823
künstlicher Leiter 428
künstliche Kletterwand 900
künstliche Strahlung 41
künstlicher Erdsatellit 53
künstlicher See 48
Kunstraum 734
Kunstschwamm 378
Kunstspringen 828
Kunststoff 269
Kunststoff, Sortierung 71
Kunststoff-Federball 817
kunststoffbeschichtete Hartfaserplatte 300
Kunststoffboden 822
Kunststoffhülse 860
Kunststoffisolator 272
Kunststoffkondensator 689
kunststoffummantelter Stoßfänger 550
Kunsttürmen 823
Kupfer 269, 683
Kupferplatte 422
Kuppe 863
Kuppel 614, 628
Kuppel des Mihrab 738
Kuppeldach 415
Kuppelhülle, äußere 17
Kuppelhülle, innere 17
Kuppelspaltabdeckung 17
Kuppelzelt 903
Kuppenring 863
Kupplung 576
Kupplung, elastische 677
Kupplungsbolzen 659
Kupplungsbügel 586
Kupplungshebel 327, 574, 576
Kupplungsgehäuse 576
Kupplungskopf 587, 640
Kupplungspedal 556
Kürass 748
Kurbel 230, 307, 312, 328, 558, 580, 910
Kurbel der Stützvorrichtung 571
Kurbel für Säule 482
Kurbelgehäuse 565
Kurbelgriff 307
Kurbelwelle 564, 566
Kürbis 189
Kurilengraben 50
Kurkuma 198
Kurs 833, 872
Kursbuchtafeln 582
Kurse 833
kursiv 472
Kurtine 408
Kurve 856
kurze Hose 369, 801, 805, 810, 870
kurze Linie 818
Kürzel der Ausgabebank 729
kurzer Hohlhandmuskel 151
kurzer Knochen 157
kurzer Wadenbeinmuskel 151
kurzer Zehenstrecker 150
Kurzhaarkatze, Amerikanische 132
Kurzhandschuh 346
Kurzmeldungen 471
Kurzschwert 748
Kurzsichtigkeit 691
Kurzsocke 365
Kurzstrecke 882, 883
Kurzstreckenschlittschuh 883
Kusine 785
Küste 49
Küstenformen 51
Küstenformen, typische 51
Kuttelwurst 216
Kuttenkragen 363
Kuwait 746

L

Label 500
Labor 17
Labor, amerikanisches 21
Labor, pathologisches 781
Laboratorium 16
Laborgeräte 685
Laborleuchte 484
Laboruhr 484
Labyrinth 885
Lachs, atlantischer 221
Lachs, pazifischer 221
Lackieren 320
Lade-Anschlussbuchse 288
Ladeanzeige 383
Ladebagger 646
Ladebaum 606, 607
Ladefläche 571, 641
Ladegerät 306, 623
Ladekontrolleinheit 563
Ladekontrolllampe 383
Lademast 607
Laden 123, 406
Ladenbahn 460
Ladenpassage 713

Laderampe 713
Laderampe, klappbare 608
Ladeschaufel 752
Ladestock 752
Ladevorrichtung 573
Ladogasee 32
Ladung 912
Ladung, negative 684
Ladung, positive 684
Lafettenwand 753
Laffe 227
Lage 868
Lage der Kontinente 28
Lageplan 245
Lager 716
Lagergang 44
Lagergestell 666
Lagerhaus 708
Lagerholz 252
Lagerraster 667
Lagerraum 394, 720, 722, 769
Lagerraum für gebrauchtes Material 778, 780
Lagerraum für medizinische Geräte 781
Lagerraum für neue Brennstäbe 666
Lagerraum für Sterilgut 778, 780
Lagertank 656
Lagerzapfen 753
Lagune 51
Laibung 413
Lakkolith 44
Lama 128
Lambdanaht 158
Lamelle 76, 285
Lamellen, Haversche 154
Lammfelljacke 353
Lammfleisch 215
Lammfleischwürfel 215
Lammhackfleisch 215
Lampe 591, 693, 903
Lampen 286
Lampenfassung 275
Lampenfassung, Teile 275
Lampenreihe 287
Land 37, 709
Landebereich 790, 891
Landedeck 761
Landefangseil 761
Landefenster 631
Landehügel 890
Landeklappe 624
Landemodul (Viking) 18
Landemotor 18
Landenge 38
Landenge von Panama 30
Landeradar 751
Landescheinwerfer 631
Landfeste 540
Landhausgardine 282
Landkarte 734
landschaftlich schöne Strecke 39
Landspitze 51
Landung 891
Landwirtschaft, intensive 68, 70
landwirtschaftliche Maschinen 641
landwirtschaftliche Nutzleiter 321
landwirtschaftliche Verschmutzung 69
Landzunge 51
lange Unterhose 351
Länge, Maßeinheit 702
Lange-Ecke-Abschlag 800
Längengrade 36
Längenmessung 700
Längenposten 856
Längenverstellung 782
langer Abendhandschuh 346
langer Dolch 751
langer Hohlhandmuskel 150
langer Kastenwagen 588
langer Knochen 157
langer Knochen, Aufbau 154
langer Knochen, Teile 155
langer Oberschenkelanzieher 150
langer Wadenbeinmuskel 150
langer Zehenstrecker 150
langes Feld 753
Langhaarschneider 383
Langhandschuh 346
Langhobel 309
Langlauf-Rattenfallbindung 892
Langläufer 892
Langlaufloipe 886
Langlaufski 892
langsam drehende Welle 677
Längsdünen 52
Längsfaden 455
Längslatte 897
Längslenkerachse 553
Längsschnitt durch ein Weizenkorn 85
Längsschnitt durch eine Haselnuss 84
Längsschnitt durch eine Walnuss 84
Längsschnitt, Backenzahn 159
Längsschott 606
Längsträger, unterer 635
Langstrecke 882
Langstrecken-Düsenflugzeug 624
Languste 218
Langustine 218
Lanthan 684
Lanthanoide (Seltenerdmetalle) 684
Lanze 748
Lanzettbogen 413

lanzettförmig 79
Laos 747
Lapislazuli 375
Lappen 117
Lappen, oberer seitlicher 86
Lappen, unterer seitlicher 86
Lappenbronchus 163
Laptop 523, 526
Laptop-Tasche 527
Laptop: Rückansicht 526
Laptop: Vorderansicht 526
Lärche 89
Larve 100
Lasagne 206
Lasche 353, 386
Lasche, selbstklebende 531
Laschenbolzen 590
Laserdrucker 519
Laserstrahl 501, 692
Last 686
Lastenfortbewegung 632
Lastkraftfahrzeuge 570
Lastkraftwagen, Beispiele 573
Lateinersegel 601
Laterne 322, 614, 615
Latexhandschuh 776
Latissimuszug 851
Latrinen 406
Latte 459, 827, 836
Lattenzaun 834
Lattenzaun 322
Latz 848
Lätzchen 368, 369
Latzenstab 461
Latzhose 358
Latzhose mit gekreuzten Rückenträgern 369
Latzhose mit hohem Rückenteil 368
Laub 87
Laubblatt 78
Laubblätter, erste 77
Laubflechte 74
Laubfrosch 111
Laubheuschrecke 101
Laubhölzer, Beispiele 88
Laubsäge 303
Laubwald 66
Laubwerk 276
Lauch 184
Lauf 115, 755, 860
Laufbahn 882
Laufbein 97, 103
Laufbrett 586
Laufbrücke 607
laufender Pahlstek 908
Läufer 915, 916
Läuferblatt 659, 664
Lauffläche 561, 590
Laufgewicht 436, 698
Laufkatze 542, 634
Laufkatzenrolle 634
Laufkran 635, 658
Laufrad 423, 659
Laufrad, pneubereiftes 594, 595
Laufräder 659
Laufrolle 281, 516, 758
Laufschiene 399, 635, 912
Laufschiene, ventilierte 860
Laufschuh 791
Laufsohle 342, 371, 888
Laufwagen 284
Laufwerksantrieb 521
Laugenbottich 292
Laus 101
Lautsprecher 427, 490, 491, 493, 496, 503, 504, 505, 506, 508, 513, 526, 613, 626, 766
Lautsprecher, Kanalwahltasten 497
Lautsprecherbox 502
Lautsprecherbuchsen 497
Lautstärkeregler 20, 441, 450, 451, 495, 497, 503, 504, 505, 507, 508, 513
Lautstärkeregler für den Hörer 506
Lautstärkeregler für den Rufton 506
Lavaschicht 44
Lavastrom 41
Lawrencium 684
LCD-Anzeige 696
Lead 877
Leben, Entwicklung 92
Lebenserhaltungssystem 20
Lebenserhaltungssystem, Steuerung 20
Lebenszyklus des Frosches 111
Leber 109, 110, 112, 113, 116, 125, 161, 164, 212
Lebervene 161
LED-Pegelanzeige 499
Lederhaut 172, 177, 798
Lederschutz 907
Lederstrippe 350
Ledertuch 345
Lederwalze 422
Lederwaren 386
Lederwarengeschäft 714
Leerdarm 164
leere Menge 703
Leerlaufanzeige 576
Leertaste 514, 528
Leerzeichen 514
Leerzeichen, geschütztes 514
Left-Wing 804

Lefzen 130
Leggins 371
Legionär, römischer 748
Leguan 114
Legwarmer 371
Lehmhütte 418
Lehmkern 660
Lehnstuhl, kleiner 276
Lehrbücher 732
Lehrbuchsaal 733
Lehrer/Lehrerin 734
Lehrerpult 734
Lehrerzimmer 735
leicht entzündlich 774
Leichtathletik 790
Leichtathletikbahn 788
Leichtbelastungsstellschraube 273
leichter Regen 64
leichter Maschinengewehr 755
leichtes Sonnenkleid 356
Leichtflugzeug 628
Leier 13
Leine 739
Leinöl 400
Leinwand 400, 483, 724
Leinwandbehälter 483
Leinwandbindung 463
Leiste 146, 148, 424
Leistentasche 348
Leistung, Maßeinheit 702
Leistungsabgabe mit Generatorspannung 662
Leistungskabel 272
leitender Kampfrichter 860
Leiter 246, 418, 567, 597, 611, 615, 639, 655
Leiter, künstlerischer 428
Leiterbaum, ausfahrbarer 766
Leitergerüst 321
Leiterkordel 285
Leiterplatte 689
Leitern 321
Leiterstrahlrohr 766
Leitöse 835
Leitrad, pneubereiftes 594
Leitrohr 652
Leitschaufel 659
Leitschaufeln, äußere 627
Leitschaufeln, innere 627
Leitspruch 729
Leitungsnetz, Einspeisung 677
Leitwerk 625, 657, 760, 898
Leitwerke, Beispiele 629
Leitwerksträger 631
Leitwerkstütze 623
Lemure 139
Lende 124, 147, 149
Lendengeflecht 166
Lendenpolster 808
Lendenwirbel 122, 126, 131, 138, 141, 142, 153, 157, 168
Lenkachse 633
Lenkanlage 553
Lenker 871, 876
Lenkerbügel 871
Lenkerbügel, angehobener 870
Lenkergriff 574, 577, 871
Lenkhebel 633
Lenkholm 323, 327
Lenkkopf 579
Lenkrad 333, 552, 556, 607, 640, 873
Lenkrolle 289
Lenksäule 552
Lenkstange 851, 897
Lenkzylinder 638
Leopard 135
Leopardfrosch 111
Leselampe 771, 780
Leseleuchte 286
Lesen von Compact Discs 501
Leserbriefe 471
Lesesaal 732
Lesetaste 505
Lesotho 746
Lettland 744
Leuchtanzeige 518
Leuchtfeder 617
Leuchtfeuerkennung 617
Leuchtkasten 535
Leuchtpult 484
Leuchtrakete 771
Leuchtröhre 275
Leuchtstreifen 765
Leuchtstoffröhre 275
Leuchtturm 596, 614
Leuchtturmlampe 614
Leukoplast 74
Leukozyt 162
Libanon 746
Libanonzeder 89
Libelle 102
Liberia 745
Libero 812
Libyen 746
Licht 14, 15, 17
Licht, Ewiges 738
Licht, gelbes 712
Licht, grünes 712
Licht, rotes 712
Licht, sichtbares 690
Lichterscheinung 617

Lichtleiste 771
Lichtleistensteuerung 771
Lichtleitkabel 523
Lichtmaschine 552, 566
Lichtregelanlage 490
Lichtrezeptoren 177
Lichtschutzschirm 17
Lichtsensor 477
Lichtstärke, Maßeinheit 702
Lichtstrahl 691
Lichttechniker 429
Lichtwertskala 479
Lidschatten 378
Liebstöckel 202
Liechtenstein 744
Lieferanteneinfahrt 713
liegender Anschlag 861, 893
Liegestuhl 277
Ligament, elastisches 133
Likörglas 225
Lilie 80, 741
Limabohne 191
Limette 194
Limonadenlöffel 228
Limousine, viertürige 549
Linde 208
Lineal 399, 424, 700, 905
linealisch 79
Lingala 468
Linie 813
Linie, durchgehende 538
Linie, neutrale 687
Linie, unterbrochene 538, 539
Linienanzeige 568, 569, 595
Linienbus 568
Linienrichter 803, 807, 812, 813, 814, 816, 818, 820, 824, 879
Liniensystem 434
linke Flanke 740
linke Herzkammer 161, 162
linke Lunge 161, 163
linke Lungenvene 162
linke Mittelstelle 740
linke Niere 165
linke Seite 300, 384
linker Abwehrspieler 812
linker Angriffsfeldspieler 814
linker Angriffsspieler 811
linker Aufbauspieler 811
linker Außenangreifer 812
linker Außenfeldspieler 794
linker Centre 804
linker Corner Back 806
linker Defensive End 806
linker Defensive Tackle 806
linker Flügelspieler 801
linker Guard 807
linker Innenfeldspieler 801
linker Kanal 502
linker Mittelfeldspieler 801, 803
linker Safety 807
linker Stürmer 879
linker Tackle 807
linker Verteidiger 801, 803, 878
linker Vorhof 161, 162
linkes Aufschlagfeld 819, 821
linkes Feld 795
linkes Obereck 740
linkes Untereck 740
links 431
Linse 177, 477, 478, 691
Linse, bikonkave 691
Linse, bikonvexe 691
Linse, konkave 691
Linse, konkavkonvexe 691
Linse, konvexe 691
Linse, konvexkonkave 691
Linse, plankonkave 691
Linse, plankonvexe 691
Linsen 190, 691
Linsen, elektronenoptische 694
Linsenfernrohr 14
Linsenfernrohr im Querschnitt 14
linsenförmige Galaxie 9
Linsenkopf mit Schlitz 302
Linsensystem 692
Lippe 124, 132, 835
Lippen-Make-up 378
Lippenkonturenstift 378
Lippenpfeife 444
Lippenpinsel 378
Lippenstift 378
Lippentaster 96, 99, 105
Listenführer 845, 846, 847
Litauen 744
Litchi 197
Literaturbeilage 471
Lithium 682
Lithografie 420, 423
Lithografiestein 423
lithografische Tusche 423
Lithokreide 423
Lithosphäre 42, 66
Lithostift 423
Litze 391
Litzen 460, 461
Litzenstab 461
Lob 821
Lob Wedge 868
Loch 423, 866, 867
Loch, gestanztes 342, 350

Loch, Par-3 866
Loch, Par-4 866
Loch, Par-5 867
Lochbillard 863
Locher 533
Löcher 866
Lochrohr 263
Lochschlitten 456
Lochziegel 298
Lock-Forward 804
Lockennadel 380
Lockenstab 381
Lockente 913
Lockenwickler 380
Löffel 227, 905, 911
Löffel, Beispiele 228
Löffeleisen 401
Löffelstiel 637
Löffelstielzylinder 637
Loge 431
Lokale Station 486
Lokomotive 585
Lokomotive, dieselelektrische 586
Lokschuppen 583
Lokverkehrsgleis 589
Longanfrucht 196
Longdrinkglas 225
Lorbeer 202
Lorgnette 385
Löschen 515
löschender Rückschritt 515
Löschfahrzeug 764
Löschfahrzeuge 766
Löschflugzeug 628
Löschhubschrauber 631
Löschmittelbehälter 767
Löschpapier 531
Löschtaste 477, 501, 508, 515, 529
loser Puder 378
loser Vorhang 283
Löshebel 310
Lötkolben 318
Lötlampe 314, 319
Lötpistole 318
Lötspitze 318
Lötwerkzeuge 318
Lötzinn 318
Lounge 608
Löwe 13, 135
Löwe, schreitender 741
Löwenzahn 187
Luchs 12, 134
Luer-Lock-Spitze 776
Luffaschwamm 379
Luft 565
Luft, absinkende kalte 63
Luft, aufsteigende warme 63
Luft, kalte 64, 675
Luft, warme 64, 675
Luft-Boden-Flugkörper 759
Luft-Luft-Flugkörper 759, 760
Luftansaugrohr 605
Luftaufbereitung 261
Luftaustrittsöffnung 260, 382
Luftaustrittsschlitz 289
Luftbefeuchter 261
Luftbetankung 760
Luftbetankungsausleger 760
Luftdatenrechner 626
Luftdruck 55
Luftdruck in Meereshöhe 55
Luftdruck, Messung 59
Luftdruckänderung 55
Luftdüse 556
Lufteinlass 320, 567, 568, 575, 605, 876
Lufteinlauf 631
Luftentfeuchter 261
Lüfter 497, 526, 552, 561, 563, 566
Lüfterkopf 614
Luftfahrt 487
Luftfeuchtigkeit 261
Luftfeuchtigkeit, Messung 59
Luftfilter 261, 331, 552, 586, 636
Luftkammer 117
Luftkissenfahrzeug 605
Luftklappe 571
Luftkompressor 585, 586
Luftkühler 564
Luftloch 390, 470
Luftlöcher 749
Luftmasse 55
Luftmatratze 904
Luftmatratze, selbstaufblasbare 904
Luftpistole 861
Luftpolster 370, 531
Luftpolsterumschlag 531
Luftpost 475
Luftpropeller 605
Luftpumpe 11, 578
Luftreiniger 261
Luftröhre 116, 125, 163
Luftschacht 402
Luftschadstoffe 69
Luftschlauch 398, 648, 841
Luftschleuse 23, 763
Luftschleuse des Reaktorgebäudes 668
Luftspalt 675
Luftsport 896
Luftsprudler 268
Luftstrom 398
Luftstromrichtdüse 382

Luftstromschalter 382
Lufttemperatur 55
Lüftung 594, 675
Lüftungsgitter 258
Lüftungsschlitz 261
Luftventil 320, 398
Luftverkehr 618
Luftverschmutzung 69
Luftwege 163
Luftwiderstand 630
Luftzielsuchradar 761, 762
Luftzufuhr 874
Luftzufuhrregler 256
Luggersegel 601
Luke 758
Lunge 104, 110, 112, 116, 125
Lunge, linke 161, 163
Lunge, rechte 161, 163
Lungen 163
Lungenarterie 160, 163
Lungenarterienstamm 162
Lungenfell 163
Lungenmittellappen 163
Lungenoberlappen 163
Lungenunterlappen 163
Lungenvene 160
Lungenvene, linke 162
Lungenvene, rechte 162
Luntenstock 752
Lunula 105
Lupe 693, 905
Lupine 190
Lutetium 684
Luthertum 736
Lutz 881
Luxemburg 743
Luzerne, blaue 190
Lyra 433
Lysosom 94

M

Mäander 48
Macadamianuss 193
Macchie 66
Machete 751
Mackenzie 30
Madagaskar 34, 746
Mädchenbekleidung 2 bis 6 Jahre 717
Mädchenbekleidung 7 bis 17 Jahre 717
Madreporenplatte 95
Magazin 754, 755, 893
Magazinbalg 445
Magazinboden 754
Magazinhalter 754
Mage 847
Magellan 19
Magen 95, 104, 105, 106, 109, 110, 112, 113, 125, 161, 164
Magenmund 107
Magenpförtner 107
Magenstütze 367
Magenta 690
mager 472
Magma 44, 49
Magmakammer 44, 646
Magnesia 825
Magnesium 682
Magnet 454, 488, 534, 687
Magnetband 495
Magnetbandmaschine 488
magnetische Dämpfung 698
magnetische Dichtung 291
magnetische Trennung 71
magnetischer Deckelhalter 240
magnetisches Feld 494, 687
Magnetismus 687
Magnetkompass 907
Magnetnadel 907
Magnetometer 60
Magnetstreifen 729
Mah-Jongg 917
Mähdrescher 643
Mähne 124
Mähwerk 333
Mähwerkaushebung 333
Maiglöckchen 80
Maikäfer 101
Maine Coon 132
Mais 85, 203
Maismehl 204
Maisöl 209
Maissirup 209
Majuskel 472
Makak 139
Make-up 378
Makrele 219
Makronukleus 94
Makroobjektiv 478
Mal 799
Mal, drittes 794
Mal, zweites 794
Malagasy 469
malaiopolynesische Sprachen 469
Malawi 746
Malawisee 34
Malaysia 747
Malediven 747
Malen 396
Malerpinsel 320

Malerstaffelei 11
Mali 745
Malpappe 400
Malpighi-Gefäß 99
Malpighi-Gefäße 97
Malspachtel 397
Malspieler, dritter 794
Malspieler, erster 794
Malspieler, zweiter 794
Malstock 399
Malta 744
Malzessig 201
Mammut 93
Mandarine 194
Mandel 174, 193
Mandoline 433
Mangan 683
Manganmischung (Kathode) 689
Mango 197
Mangochutney 201
Mangold 185
Mangostane 196
Maniküre 377
Maniok 184
Mann 146
Männerzelle 768
männlich 702
männliche Blütenstände 89
männliche Geschlechtsorgane 169
Mannschaftsabzeichen 878
Mannschaftsbank 827
Mannschaftsduschen 764
Mannschaftshandikap 858
Mannschaftsname 858
Mannschaftsschlafsaal 764
Mannschaftstrikot 796, 801, 802, 808
Mannschaftszelt 902
Manometer 655, 775
Manövriereinheit, bemannte 20
Manque (1 bis 18) 919
Mansardendach 414
Mansardenfenster 244
Manschette 349, 851, 880, 900
Manschette, aufblasbare 777
Manschettenknopf 361
Mantel 105, 106, 352, 355, 689, 757, 908, 912
Mäntel 352, 355
Mantel, oberer 42
Mantel, unterer 42
Mantelblech 655
Mantelhöhle 95
Mantelkleid 356
Mantelmauer 408
Mantelmuskeln 106
Mantelstromführung 627
Manual 445
Manual für das Hauptwerk 444
Manual für das Oberwerk 444
Manual für das Rückpositiv 444
Manuale 444
Manuell-/Automatikeinstellung 465
manuelle Aussteuerung 499
manuelle Diawahl 483
manuelle Scharfeinstellung 483
Manxkatze 133
Maori 469
Marcato-Zeichen 435
Marconikutter 601
Marder 134
Margarine 209
Marginalschild 113
Marianengraben 50
Marie-Byrd-Land 29
Marienkäfer 101
Marine-Dieselkraftstoff 656
Mariner 19
Mariniergewürze 199
maritim 61
Mark 87, 165, 200, 212
Mark, verlängertes 167
Markenname 390
Marker 397, 470
Markhöhle 154
Markierschnur 313
Markierung 855
Markierung für Filmanfang 476
Markierungslinie 907
Markierungspunkt 455
Markscheide 168
Markstrahlen 87
Marokko 745
Mars 4, 5
Mars Odyssey 19
Marshallinseln 747
Marsstenge 602
Martin Luther 736
Martingal 858
Mascara, flüssiges 378
Mascarabürstchen 378
Mascarastein 378
Maschen 815
Maschenanschlag 457
Maschenprobe 458
Maschinen, landwirtschaftliche 641
Maschinengewehr 758
Maschinengewehr, leichtes 755
Maschinenhalle 657, 658
Maschinenhaus 648
Maschinenpistole 754
Maschinenraum 606, 608, 763

Maschinenwäsche 347
Maschinist 428
Maserung 300
Maske 796, 841
Maskenbildner 428
Maskendichtung 773
Massagebürste 379
Massagehandschuh 379
Massagespitze 384
Masse 43, 272
Masse, Maßeinheit 702
Masseelektrode 562
Massekabel 318
Massekontakt 497
Massengut-Terminal 596
Massenversand 475
massereiche Sterne 8
Massezange 318
massiver Korpus 441
Mast 591, 600, 834, 836
Mastdarm 164, 169, 170
Mastfenster 663
Masthalterung 493
Mastkörper 663
Mastlager 836
Mastobertteil 663
Mastspitze 836
Maststeuerhebel 632, 633
Masttasche 836
Masttraverse 663
Maß 231
Maßband 313, 454
Maßeinheit der Celsius-Temperatur 702
Maßeinheit der elektrischen Ladung 702
Maßeinheit der elektrischen Spannung 702
Maßeinheit der elektrischen Stromstärke 702
Maßeinheit der Energie 702
Maßeinheit der Frequenz 702
Maßeinheit der Kraft 702
Maßeinheit der Länge 702
Maßeinheit der Leistung 702
Maßeinheit der Lichtstärke 702
Maßeinheit der Masse 702
Maßeinheit der Radioaktivität 702
Maßeinheit der Stoffmenge 702
Maßeinheit der thermodynamischen Temperatur 702
Maßeinheit der Zeit 702
Maßeinheit des Drucks 702
Maßeinheit des elektrischen Widerstands 702
mäßiger Regen 64
Maßwerk 411
Matchbeutel 388
Material, radarabsorbierendes 629
Materialraum 734
Materialschleuse 666
Materie 680
Mathematik 703
Matratze 280, 281
Matratzenauflage 280
Matratzenrahmen 716
Matrosenbluse 359
Matrosenkragen 362
Matte 792, 842, 844, 864
Matte, rutschfeste 893
Matten 824
Mattenisolierung 299
Mattenrichter 846
Mattscheibe 477
Mauer 852, 917
Mauer mit Stangen 852
Mauerdurchbruch 917
Mauernagel 301
Mauersegler 118
Mauerturm 408
Mauertürmchen 408
Mauerwerk 253
Maul 108, 124, 136
Maul-Ringschlüssel 311
Maultier 128
Maultrommel 433
Maulwurf 121
Maulwurf, äußere Merkmale 121
Maulwurf, Skelett 121
Maurerhammer 315
Maurerkelle 315
Maurerwerkzeuge 315
Mauretanien 745
Mauritius 746
Maus, mechanische 516
Maus, optische 516
Mauspad 516
Mausschnittstelle 513, 518
Mausschnittstelle 517
Mawashi 847
Maximumthermometer 59
Maya 469
Mazedonien 744
Mazerationskörper 744
Mechanik 686
Mechaniker 873
mechanische Maus 516
mechanische Uhr 696
mechanische Verbindungen 269
mechanisches Variometer 898
Medaillon 374
mediane Zungenfurche 176
Medikamentenfach 775
Medikamentenraum 778, 781
mediterrane Subtropen 61

medizinische Gasflasche 780
medizinische Geräte, Lagerraum 781
Meer 38, 664
Meer, Arabisches 33
Meer, Japanisches 33
Meer, Kaspisches 33
Meer, Mare 7
Meer, Ostchinesisches 33
Meer, Rotes 33, 34
Meer, Schwarzes 32, 33
Meer, Südchinesisches 33
Meerasche 220
Meerbarbe, rote 219
Meerbusen, Bottnischer 32
Meerenge 38
Meeresalgen 183
Meeresboden 49
Meeressäugetiere 136
Meeressäugetiere, Beispiele 137
Meeresseite 664
Meeresspiegel 42, 49, 53
Meerkohl 186
Meerneunauge 219
Meerohr 217
Meerrettich 189
Meersalat 183
Meersalz 201
Meerschweinchen 123
Meganeura 92
Megazostrodon 93
Mehl 204
Mehl, ungebleichtes 204
Mehlsieb 231, 232
Mehrfachsprünge 875
Mehrfachstartstruktur 24
Mehrfeldbrücke 541
Mehrkornbrot 205
mehrreihige Halskette 374
Mehrrumpfboote 835
Mehrschichtsperrholz 300
Mehrzweckleiter 321
Mehrzweckraum 727
Mehrzweckzange 717
Meissnersches Tast-Körperchen 172
Meitnerium 683
Melanesien 29
Melanesisch 469
Melasse 209
Melodiepfeife 432
Melodiesaiten 432
Melone 340
Melone, kanarische 195
Melonen 195
Melonenlöffel 233
Membran 502
Membrane 488
Men 847
Mendelevium 684
Mengenschnitt 703
Mengenvereinigung 703
Menora 738
Mensch 146
menschlicher Körper 146
menschliches Gebiss 159
Menügabel 228
Menümesser 228
Menütaste 477, 505
Merguez-Wurst 216
Meridian, östlicher 36
Meridian, westlicher 36
Meridianlinie 907
Merkur 4, 5
Mesenterialarterie, obere 160, 165
Mesenterialarterie, untere 165
Mesenterialvene, obere 160
Mesogloea 95
Mesokarp 81, 82, 83
Mesopause 53
Mesosaurus 92
Mesosphäre 53
Mesothorax 97
Mess- und Markierinstrumente 313
Messband 313
Messbecher 231
Messbügel 700
Messdatenspeicher 316
Messe, Speiseraum 763
Messer 227, 240, 317, 331, 332, 401, 421, 534, 905, 907
Messer aus Feuerstein 748
Messer, Beispiele 228
Messer, feststelltes 424
Messerbajonett 751
Messerbalken 642, 643
Messermuschel 217
Messerschutz 236
Messersicherung 272
Messerwalze 332
Messezentrum 708
Messingkörper 268, 270
Messinstrumente 695
Messinstrumente, meteorologische 58
Messkabel 316
Messkabine 16
Messlöffel 231
Messrohr 59
Messschnabel, feststehender 700
Messschnabel, verschiebbarer 700
Messspindel 700
Messspitze 316
Messtaste 479

Messtrommel 700
Messung der Himmelsstrahlung 58
Messung der Luftfeuchtigkeit 59
Messung der Regenmenge 59
Messung der Sonneneinstrahlung 58
Messung der Temperatur 59
Messung der Windrichtung 59
Messung der Windstärke 59
Messung der Wolkenhöhe 59
Messung des Luftdrucks 59
Messung des Schneefalls 59
Messung in der oberen Atmosphäre 59
Messwandler 613
Messwertsammler 58
Messzylinder 685
Metacarpus 111, 116
Metall 741
Metall, Sortierung 71
Metallaufsatz 903
Metallbandisolierung 299
Metallfeder, römische 470
metallische Tinte 729
metallisiertes Hologramm 729
Metallkontaktgitter 672
Metallkopf 793
Metalloide 682
Metallrahmen 442
Metallspannreifen 448
Metallwinkel 313
metamorphe Gesteine 42
Metaphyse 155
Metatarsus 111
Metathorax 97
Meteorit 8
Meteorologie 53
meteorologische Messinstrumente 58
Meter 702
Metope 404
Metronom 436
Mexikanische Rotknievogelspinne 102
Mexiko 742
Mexiko, Golf 30
Michael Kyrillos 736
Michigan-Schneeschuh 893
Middle Linebacker 806
MIDI (Schnittstelle für digitale Musikinstrumente), Kabel 451
MIDI-Schnittstelle 513
Mieder 337, 367
Miederhose 367
Miesmuschel 217
Mihrab 738
Mikrofichelesegerät 732
Mikroficheraum 732
Mikrofilament 94
Mikrofon 488, 492, 496, 505, 506, 508, 516, 517, 527, 770, 771, 897, 898
Mikrofon zum Studio 491
Mikrofon, elektrodynamisches 488
Mikrofon-Fahrspinne 492
Mikrofonanschlussbuchse 505
Mikrofonausleger 490, 492
Mikrometerknopf 701
Mikrometerschraube 612, 700
Mikronesien 747
Mikronukleus 94
Mikroskop 10, 693
Mikroskope 693
Mikroskopokular 701
Mikrotubulus 94
Mikrowellen 690
Mikrowellen-Relaisstation 524
Mikrowellengerät 238
Mikrowellengeräte 723
Mikrowellenherd 224
Mikrowellenscanner 60
Mikrowellenschüssel 489
Mikrowellensender 489
Milch 210
Milch, homogenisierte 210
Milchbecher 223
Milchgang 171
Milchkammer 182
Milchkännchen 226
Milchprodukte 180, 210
Milchprodukte, Wareneingang 180
Milchpulver 210
Milchschokolade 208
Milchstraße 9, 13
Milchstraße (Ansicht von oben) 9
Milchstraße (Seitenansicht) 9
militärische Telekommunikation 487
Milz 109, 110, 113, 125, 161
Mimas 5
Minarett 738
Minbar 738
Minderjährigenzelle 768
Mine 470
Mini-HiFi-System 503
Minibus 549
Minimumthermometer 59
Minislip 351
Minusbereich 672
Minusglas 691
Minuskel 472
Minuskontakt 672, 673
Minusplatte 562
Minuspol 562, 689
Minuspolbrücke 562
Minutenzeiger 696, 697
Minze 202

Miranda 5
Mischbatterie 268
Mischkammer 258, 319
Mischpult 488
Mischwald 66
Mischwasserkanal 712
Mispel 193
Mississippi 30
mit dem Wind 833
Mitarbeiter der Rechtsanwälte 728
Mithörtaste 508
Mitnehmerrippe 293
Mitnehmerstange 651
Mitochondrium 74, 94
Mitralklappe 162
Mitte 431, 847
Mittelamerika 28, 30
Mittelangreifer 812
Mittelarmnerv 166
Mittelatlantischer Rücken 50
Mittelbein 96, 98
Mittelbein (Außenseite) 98
Mitteldarm 99, 103
Mitteldarmdrüse 104, 105, 106, 107
Mitteldarmdrüsen, zentraler 803
Mitteldrittel 809
Mittelelektrode 562
Mittelfahne 802
Mittelfeld 795, 818
Mittelfeldangriffsspieler 814
Mittelfeldspieler 801, 809
Mittelfeldspieler, linker 803
Mittelfeldspieler, rechter 803
Mittelfeldspieler, zentraler 803
Mittelfinger 173
Mittelformatkamera SLR (6 x 6) 481
Mittelfuß 98, 122, 124, 131, 138, 141, 142, 155
Mittelfußknochen 126, 155
Mittelgang 584
Mittelglied 133
Mittelhand 122, 131, 136, 138, 142, 154
Mittelhandknochen 154, 156
mittelhohe Wolken 62
Mittelkielschwein 607
Mittelkonsole 556
Mittelkreis 803, 809, 810
Mittellage-Tonabnehmer 441
Mittellinie 801, 803, 805, 806, 809, 810, 814, 815, 816, 819, 827, 848, 858, 877, 879
Mittelloch 500
Mittelmeer 28, 32, 34
Mittelmoräne 46
Mittelohr 174
Mittelpaneele 247
Mittelpunkt 704, 862, 916
Mittelrippe 75, 79, 84
Mittelsäule 287, 551, 676
Mittelschiff 411, 738
mittelschwere Piste 886
Mittelspannungsleitung 273, 663
Mittelspur 539
Mittelsteg 367
Mittelstelle, linke 740
Mittelstelle, rechte 740
Mittelstreifen 539, 712, 821
Mittelstück 169, 390
Mittelstürmer 801
Mitteltasche 862
Mittelteil 663
Mitteltöner 502
Mitteltonlautsprecher 10
Mitteltorus 405
Mittelwagen 585, 594
Mittelzeichen 820
mittlere Armdecken 115
mittlere Aufschlaglinie 821
mittlere Handdecken 115
mittlere Nasenmuschel 175
mittlere Strahlgrube 127
mittlerer Abwehrspieler 812
mittlerer Angriffsspieler 811
mittlerer Anspielpunkt 879
mittlerer Außenfeldspieler 794
mittlerer Linebacker 806
mittlerer Schneidezahn 159
mittleres Keilbein 155, 156
Mixer 236
mobile Einheit 486
Mode-Taste 528
Modellierhölzer 464
Modellierscheibe 464
Modem 522, 523, 524
Modemschnittstelle, interne 513, 526
Moderator 665, 670, 671
Moderatorfilz 442
Moderatorpedal 442
Moderatortank 670
moderne Haubitze 756
moderner Bogen 750
Modillon 405
Modul, russisches 21
Modulationsrad 450
Modus-Taste 498
Mofa 577
Mohammed 736
Mohn 80, 84
Mohnsamen 199
Mohorovicic-Diskontinuität 42
Mohrenhirse 85

Mokassin 344
Mokkatasse 226
Mol 702
Molar 123
Molch 111
Moldawien 744
Molekül 680
Mollusken 217
Molybdän 683
Monaco 744
Monarchfalter 101
Mond 4, 6, 7
Mond, Oberflächenformationen 7
Mondbahn 6, 7
Mondbein 154, 156
Monde 4
Mondfinsternis 7
Mondkapsel 19
Mondlandeeinheit 25
Mondphasen 7
Mondphasenanzeiger 697
Mondsichel 741
Mondsichel (abnehmender Mond) 7
Mondsichel (zunehmender Mond) 7
Mongolei 747
Mongolisch 469
Monitor 918
Mono-Stereo-Taste 498
Monographiebereich 732
Monokel 385
Monopoly® 915
Montagnais 469
Moos 75
Moos, Aufbau 75
Moose, Beispiele 75
Mop 295
Mordent 435
Morchel 183
Morgenländisches Schisma 736
Mörser 230, 753
Mörser aus dem 17. Jahrhundert 752
Mortadella 216
Mörtel 298
Mosaik 406
Mosaikparkett 254
Mosambik 746
Moschee 738
Moses 736
Moskito 101
Motherboard 513
Motocross-Motorrad 875
Motor 18, 261, 292, 293, 294, 304, 307, 308, 320, 323, 327, 332, 564, 574, 640, 643, 651, 758
Motorbeiboot 762
Motorblock 236, 237, 240, 288, 384, 566
Motorboot 607
Motorgehäuse 331
Motorhaube 333, 550
motorische Endplatte 168
motorisches Neuron 168
Motorjacht 607
Motorkühlung 874
Motorlufteinlass 568
Motorrad 574
Motorrad, Rallye 875
Motorrad, Touring 577
Motorrad, Trial 875
Motorrad: Draufsicht 576
Motorräder, Beispiele 577
Motorradfahrer 874
Motorradkamera 870
Motorradsport 874
Motorrasenmäher 332
Motorraum 568, 632, 638, 639
Motorroller 577
Motorsport 872
Motorsteuerung 563
Motortypen 564
Mouche 859
Mount Everest 53
Mountain Bike 581
Mountainbike 870
Mozambique, Straße 34
Mozzarella 210
MP3-Spieler 503
Muffe 269
Muffinform 232
Mufftasche 353, 355, 360, 388
Mufflon 128
Mulde 323
Muldenkipper 639
Müllabfuhrwagen 573
Mülldeponie 69, 709
Müllschichten 69
Müllschlucker 270
Mülltrennung 71
Mullverband 777
Multifunktionsantenne 763
Multifunktionstaste 529
Multimeter 316
Multipack 223
Multiplikation 703
Multiplikationstaste 529
Multirolle 910
Multitrainer 851
Mumienschlafsack 904
Mund 104, 107, 110, 148, 174
Munddusche 384
Mundharmonika 432
Mundhöhle 116, 163, 164

Mundöffnung 95, 105
Mundrohr 447
Mundschutz 843
Mundspeicheldrüse 164
Mundstück 446, 447, 451, 783, 841
Mundstückaufnahme 447
Mündung 105, 753, 754, 756, 860, 912
Mundwasser 384
Mundwerkzeuge 98
Mundwinkel 174
Mungo 134
Mungobohne 191
Mungobohne, schwarze 191
Munitionsbehälter 758
Munster 211
Münze: Rückseite 729
Münze: Vorderseite 729
Münzeinwurf 507, 920
Münzfernsprecher 427, 715, 720, 723, 779
Münzleitung 920
Münzrückgabe 920
Muschel 276
Muschel, einschalige 105
Muschel, zweischalige 105
Museum 394, 711
Museumsshop 394
Musik 432
Musikinstrumente, traditionelle 432
Musiknotation 434
Musikraum 734
Musikregie 490
Musikzubehör 436
Muskatnuss 198
Muskatnussreibe 230
Muskel, oberer gerader 177
Muskelblock 109
Muskelfaser 168
Muskelmagen 116
Muskeln 150
Musselin 231
Muster 401
Mutter 269, 310, 311, 784, 785
Mutterband, breites 171
Muttergestein 78
Muttern 311
Mutulus 404
Mütze 770, 841
Mützenschirm 340, 341
Myanmar 747
Myzel 76

N

Nabe 103, 534, 579, 659, 677, 783
Nabel 146, 148
Nabel, oberer 115
Nabel, unterer 115
Nabelschwein 128
Nabelstrang 83, 84
Nabenabdeckung 659
Nabenführungseinheit 18
Nachfüllmine 470
Nachfüllrohr 265
Nachläufer, steifer 569
Nachrichten 471
Nachrichtenanzeige 508
Nachrichtensatellit 487
Nachsortierung von Hand 71
nächste Seite 515
nächster Ruf 507
Nachtaufnahmeschalter 496
Nachthemd 364
Nachtigall 118
Nachtigall-Grashüpfer 102
Nachtschalter 731
Nachttisch 724, 780
Nachttischlampe 724
Nachtwäsche 364
Nachtwäsche, Damen 716
Nachtwäsche, Herren 717
Nacken 115, 147, 149
Nackenfeder 909
Nackenrolle 280
Nackenrolle, große 280
Nackenschutz 765, 808
Nackenstütze 775
Nadel 52, 64, 398, 452, 453, 454
Nadelbaum 89
Nadelbett 456
Nadelbettrille 456
Nadelblätter, Beispiele 89
Nadeldrucker 520
Nadelfuß 456
Nadelhalter 453
Nadelhalterschraube 453
Nadelhölzer, Beispiele 89
Nadelkissen 454
Nadelklemmschraube 398
Nadelpositionswähler 452
Nadelstange 453
Nadelwald 66
Nadelwerkzeug 464
Nagel 127, 301
Nägel, Beispiele 301
Nagel, geschnittener 301
Nagel, gewöhnlicher 301
Nagelbett 172
Nagelbettepitel 172
Nagelfeile 377
Nagelfeile, klappbare 377

Nagelhalbmond 172, 173
Nagelhautentferner 377
Nagelhautschaber 377
Nagelhautschere 377
Nagelhautschieber 377
Nagelknipser 377
Nagelkörper 172
Nagellack 377
Nagelloch 127
Nagelnecessaire 377
Nagelrand, freier 172
Nagelreiniger 377
Nagelschere 377
Nagelweißstift 377
Nagelwerkzeuge 301
Nagelwurzel 172
Nagelzange 377
Nagelzieher 905
Nagetier 122
Nagetiere 122
Nagetiere, Beispiele 123
Nagetierkiefer 123
Nagetierkiefer: Ratte 123
Nagezahn 123
Nähen 452
Nähmaschine 452
Nährichtungseinsteller 452
Nahrungskette 67
Nahrungsmittel 180
Nahrungsmittelquelle, primäre 67
Nahrungsvakuole 94
Nahrungsvakuole, heranwachsende 94
Naht 84, 105, 342, 346, 370, 390
Nähte 797
Nahtlinse 478
Nahtlinie 455
Nahttasche 355, 360
Nahtzugabe 455
Nahuatl 469
Nahverkehrszug 583
Name der Schwimmerin 831
Name der Station 592
Name des Inhabers 729
Name des Turners/der Turnerin 825
Namensschild 770
Namib 34
Namibia 746
Naos 403
Näpfchen mit Aquarellfarbe/Gouachefarbe 397
Napfschnecke 217
Narbe 80, 84
Narwal 137
Narzisse 80
Nase 108, 122, 124, 148, 749, 894, 897, 898
Nase, abgesenkte 629
Nase, äußere 175
Nasen-Bartschere 377
Nasenbein 158, 175
Nasenblatt 140
Nasenflügel 175
Nasenflügelknorpel, großer 175
Nasenhöhle 163, 175
Nasenklappe 760
Nasenloch 110, 112, 115, 175
Nasenmuschel, mittlere 175
Nasenmuschel, obere 175
Nasenmuschel, untere 175
Nasenöffnung 108
Nasenrachenraum 175
Nasenriemen 854, 858
Nasenrücken 175
Nasenschoner 856
Nasenspiegel 132
Nasenspitze 175
Nasenstachel 158
Nasenwurzel 175
Nashorn 129
Nationalität 825
Nationalität der Schwimmerin 831
Nationalpark 39
Natrium 682
Natur, Freizeit 902
naturbelassene Umgebung 867
natürliche Strahlung 41
natürlicher Treibhauseffekt 68
Naturschwamm 379
Natururan 670
Nauru 747
Navajo 469
Navette 375
Navigationsanzeige 626
Navigationsinstrumente 612
Navigationsperiskop 763
Nazca-Platte 43
Neapolitanische Tropfkanne 241
NEAR 19
Nebel 57, 65
Nebel, planetarischer 8
Nebelhorn 611
Nebelleuchte 554
Nebelscheinwerfer 570
Nebenaltar 737
Nebeneinfüllstutzen 655
Nebenfahrwasser 617
Nebengleis 583
Nebenhoden 169
Nebenniere 165

Nebenschluss 687
Nebenstraße 39
Neffe 785
Negativ 485
negativ geladen 684
negativer Pol 687
Negativhalter 485
Negligé 364
Nehrung 51
Neigung 660
Nektarine 192
Nelke 80
Neodym 684
Neon 684
Nepal 747
Nephridium 107
Neptun 4, 5
Neptunium 684
Nerv 172
Nervenendung 172
Nervenfaser 172
Nervengeflecht 159
Nervenimpuls 168
Nervenstrang, ventraler 107
Nervensystem 99, 166
Nervensystem, peripheres 166
Nervensystem, zentrales 166
Nervenwurzel, hintere 167, 168
Nervenwurzel, vordere 167, 168
Nerz 134
Nessel 187
Nestfarn 76
Netz 10, 222, 281, 797, 811, 812, 813, 814, 815, 817, 821, 827
Netz-/Lichtschalter 452
Netzabschlusswiderstand 522
Netzanschluss 504
Netzanschlussbuchse 513
Netzband 821
Netzhalter 815
Netzhaut 177, 691
Netzhautgrube 177
Netzkabel 237, 288, 308, 381, 382, 383, 497, 513
Netzkabel, Gleichstrom 526
Netzkabel, Wechselstrom 526
Netzkante 812
Netzkontrolllampe 508
Netzkontrollleuchte 519
Netzplan 592
Netzrichter 815
Netzschalter 451, 494, 495, 497, 498, 501, 508, 518
Netzstecker 527
Netzstrumpf 365
Netzteil 513
Netzteillüfter 513
Netzwerke, Beispiele 522
Netzwerkkabel 523
Netzwerkkarte, LAN-Karte 522
Netzwerkschnittstelle 513
neuer Schekel 728
Neues Testament 736
Neufundland 30
Neukaledonien 29
Neumond 7
Neuneck, regelmäßiges 705
Neuralfortsatz 109
Neuron, motorisches 168
Neuron, peripher-sensorisches 168
Neuron, sensibles 168
Neuronenkette 168
Neuseeland 29, 747
neutrale Linie 687
neutrale Zone 806, 879
Neutron 680
Neutron, einfallendes 681
Neutronenstern 8
Neuzugänge, Regal 733
Newton 702
Nicaragua 742
nicht angebbar (da nicht erkennbar) 56
nicht bügeln 347
nicht Element von 703
nicht gestempelte Post 474
nicht identisch 703
Nicht in die Trockenmaschine geben 347
nicht wärmeleitende Spitze 381
nicht waschen 347
nicht wieder verwertbarer Restmüll 71
Nichte 785
Nichtmetalle 683
Nickbewegung 630
Nickel 683
Nickhaut 132
Niederdruckdampfzuleitung 668
Niederdruckverdichtung 627
Niederlande 743
Niederländisch 469
Niederschlag 67
Niederschläge 57, 64
Niederschlagsgebiet 55
Niederschlagsschreiber 59
Niederspannungsleitung 273
niedriger Wasserstand 597
Niedrigspannungsleitung 663
Niere 104, 105, 106, 109, 110, 112, 116, 125, 161, 212
Niere, linke 165
Niere, rechte 165

1000

ASTRONOMIE > 2-25; ERDE > 26-71; PFLANZENREICH >72-89; TIERREICH > 90-143; MENSCH > 144-177; NAHRUNGSMITTEL UND KÜCHE > 178-241; HAUS > 242-295;
HEIMWERKEN UND GARTENARBEIT > 296-333; KLEIDUNG > 334-371; PERSÖNLICHE AUSSTATTUNG > 372-391; KUNST UND ARCHITEKTUR > 392-465; KOMMUNIKATION UND BÜROTECHNIK > 466-535;
TRANSPORT UND FAHRZEUGE > 536-643; ENERGIE > 644-677; WISSENSCHAFT > 678-705; GESELLSCHAFT > 706-785; SPORT UND SPIELE > 786-920

Nierenarterie 160, 165
Nierenbecken 165
nierenförmig 79
Nierenhilus 165
Nierenkelch 165
Nierenpapille 165
Nierenvene 160, 165
Niete 229, 310
Niger 34, 745
Nigeria 745
Nil 34
Nilpferd 129
Nimbostratus 56, 62
Niob 683
Nippel 269
Nivellierfuß 292, 293, 294
Nivellierschraube 58
Nobelium 684
Nocke 750, 859
Nockenpunkt 859
Nockenring 307
Nockenwelle 566
Nockpunkt 913
Noir 919
Nonius 612, 700
Nord 37, 917
Nord-Korea 747
Nord-Nordost 37
Nord-Nordwest 37
Nordamerika 28, 30, 50
Nordamerikanische Platte 43
Norden 616
nördliche Halbkugel 35
nördliche Halbkugel, Sternbilder 12
nördliche Hemisphäre 35
Nördliche Krone 13
Nördliche Wasserschlange 13
nördlicher Polarkreis 35, 36
Nordmeer 32
Nordost 37
Nordosten 616
Nordpol 35, 687
Nordpolarmeer 28
Nordsee 28, 32
Nordwest 37
Nordwesten 616
Nori 183
normal 472
normale Pokerblätter 914
normale Spiralgalaxie 9
Normalsichtigkeit 691
Normalwaschgang 347
Normpunkt 891
Norwegen 744
Norwegisch 469
Notation 916
Notbremse 594
Note 825
Note, ganze 435
Note, halbe 435
Notenablage 436, 444, 451
Notenlinie 434
Notenschlüssel 434
Notenständer 436
Notenwerte 435
Notfallausrüstung 775
Nothosaurus 93
Notizblock 530
Notlaufschiene 595
Notregulierung 841
Notrufnische 543
Notschalter 576
Notstromaggregat 763
Nova 8
Nudelholz 232
Nudelmaschine 230
Nukleolus 94
Nullleiter 272, 273
Nullleitersammelschiene 272
Nullleiterverbinder 272
Nullmeridian 36
numerische Tastatur 507, 530
numerischer Block 515
numerisches Tastenfeld 515, 699
Nummer 1 858
Nummer 2 858
Nummer 3 858
Nummer 4 858
Nummer-8-Forward 804
Nummerierstempel 531
Nummernschildbeleuchtung 554
Nummerntasten 508
Nuss 750
Nussknacker 230
Nüster 124
Nut 255
Nutzer, Internet 524
Nutzer, privater 525
Nutzlast 24, 25
Nutzlastadapter 24
Nutzlastmodul 40
Nutzlastraum 22
Nutzlastraum, Tür 23
Nutzlastverkleidung 24
Nutzleiter, landwirtschaftliche 321
Nylonschnur 332

O

O-Ring 268
Oase 48, 52
oben liegender Rahmen 639
Oberarmarterie 160
Oberarmbein 126
Obergelenkhöcker, innerer 153
Oberarmknochen 111, 116, 121, 122, 131, 136, 138, 141, 142, 152, 156
Oberarmschiene 749
Oberarmspeichenmuskel 150, 151
Oberbau 591
Oberbeleuchter 429
Oberbeleuchtungstechniker 490
Oberboden 78
Oberdeck 569, 624, 655
obere Abschlusskappe 689
obere Atmosphäre, Messung 59
obere Gliedmaßen 161
obere Hohlvene 160, 161, 162
obere Manschette 889
obere Mesenterialarterie 160, 165
obere Mesenterialvene 160
obere Nasenmuschel 175
obere Querleiste 278
obere Rolle 460
obere Rondistenfacette 374
obere Schale 889
obere Schutzhaube 304
obere Sektion 24
obere Sohlschicht 646
obere Sprosse 277
obere Tasche 862
obere Tragschicht 538
obere Vertäfelung 632
obere Zahnreihe 174
Obereck, linkes 740
Obereck, rechtes 740
oberer Absatz 417
oberer Abschluss 281
oberer Anzug 854
oberer Flügel 628
oberer gerader Muskel 177
oberer Glaskolben 241
oberer Heizstab 266
oberer Holm 824
oberer knöcherner Bogengang 174
oberer Mantel 42
oberer Nabel 115
oberer Querträger 635
oberer seitlicher Einschnitt 86
oberer seitlicher Lappen 86
oberer Thermostat 266
oberer Wurfarm 750
oberes Augenlid 110, 132
oberes Becken 448
oberes Ruder 763
oberes Schleusentor 597
oberes Verschlussband 889
Oberfläche 815
Oberfläche, befeuchtete 420
Oberfläche, eingefärbte 420
Oberflächenerkundung 651
Oberflächenformationen des Mondes 7
Oberflächenisolierung 22
Oberfräse 308
Obergestein 647
Obergurt 253, 540
Oberhaut 172
oberirdischer Abfluss 67
Oberkampfrichter 823
Oberkante 815
Oberkellner 720
Oberkiefer 99, 108, 111, 112, 116, 121, 122, 123, 131, 136, 138, 152, 175
Oberkiefer, beweglicher 112
Oberkiefer, vorderer 108
Oberkieferknochen 158, 159
Oberleiter 766
Oberleitung 585, 595
Oberlenker 640
Oberlicht, Badezimmer 251
Oberlicht, Treppenhaus 251
Oberlid 177
Oberlippe 99, 174, 444
Oberlippenrinne 175
Obermaschinerie 430
Obermesser 424
Obermesserhebel 424
Oberon 5
Oberpartie 909
Oberrohr 578
Oberschale 575, 895
Oberschenkel 111, 126, 143, 147, 149, 249
Oberschenkelanzieher, großer 151
Oberschenkelanzieher, langer 150
Oberschenkelarterie 160
Oberschenkelbereich 170
Oberschenkelknochen 116, 122, 131, 138, 141, 142, 152
Oberschenkelkopf 153
Oberschenkelnerv 166
Oberschenkelpolster 808
Oberschenkelregion 169
Oberschenkelvene 160
Oberschiedsrichter 881, 883
Oberschnabel 115

Oberschrank 224
Oberschwanzdecken 115
Oberschwester, Büro 779
Oberstützmauer 660
Oberteilhauptfacette 374
Obertor 597
Oberwalze 421
Oberwasser 657
Oberwasserdecke 660
Oberwassermauer 661
Obi 845, 846
Objekt 691
Objektiv 14, 476, 478, 479, 483, 517, 518, 535, 692, 693
Objektivanschluss 477
Objektivauswurf 476
Objektive 478
Objektivlinse 501
Objektivrevolver 693
Objektivschutzdeckel 478
Objektivzubehör 478
Objektklammer 693
Objekttisch 693, 694
Obmann 848
Obmann, Kampfrichter 883
Oboe 446
Oboen 437
Obst 180, 192, 723
Obstbaum 182
Obstgarten 182
Obst- und Gemüseschale 291
Ochse 129
Ockerstift, roter 423
Ofen 10, 256, 674
offene Grube 647
offene Spinnrolle 910
offener Doppelringschlüssel 311
offener Güterwagen 588
offenes Fernsprecher 507
öffentliche Wasserversorgung 675
öffentliches Postnetz 474
öffentliches Gebäude 39
öffentliches Übertragungsnetz 486
Offizielle 846
Offiziellenbank 879
Offiziere, Duschen und Toiletten 764
Offizierskabine 609
Offiziersquartiere 762, 763
Offiziersraum 764
Öffnen 230
Öffner 346
Öffner, Dosen 223
Öffnung 346
Öffnung der Begattungskammer 97
Öffnung für die Papierzufuhr 511
Öffnung zum Fluten und Leeren der Schleusenkammer 597
Offshore-Bohrung 653
Offshore-Erkundung 653
Ogenmelone 195
Ohm 702
Ohr 133, 140, 146
Öhr 453, 454
Ohr, Aufbau 174
Ohr, äußeres 174
Ohrdecken 115
Ohrenschützer 340, 772, 861
Ohrenstöpsel 872
Ohrgehänge 374
Ohrhörer 872
Ohrklappe 140
Ohrläppchen 173
Ohrlautsprecher 506
Ohrmuschel 122, 143, 173, 174, 502
Ohrmuschelhöcker 173
Ohrmuschelhöhlung 173
Ohrmuschelrand, äußerer 173
Ohrmuschelwindung 173
Ohrringe 374
Ohrringe mit Schraubverschluss 374
Ohrstecker 374
Ohrstöpsel 772, 776
Ohrtrompete 174, 175
Okapi 128
Okklusion 56
Okraschote 188
Oktaeder, regelmäßiges 705
Oktant 10
Oktave 434
Oktavmechanik 446
Okular 14, 15, 692, 693
Okularhalterung 14
Okulartubus 693
Ölablassschraube 566
Ölabscheider 652
Ölausfluss 70
Ölbrenner 259
Öldruckkontrollleuchte 576
Öldruckwarnleuchte 557
Öle 209
Öler 648
Ölfarbe 397
ölgefüllter Heizkörper 260
Olive 188
Olivenkopftrense 854
Olivenöl 209
Öllöschbrücke 596
Ölmalerei 396
Ölpastell 396
Ölpalme 396
Ölpumpe 259
Ölstein 422
Ölsumpf 331
Ölverarbeitungsbereich 652

Ölverschmutzung 70
Ölwanne 566
Ölwannendichtung 566
Ölzufuhr 259
Oman 746
Oman, Golf 33
On-Deck-Circle 794
Onkel mütterlicherseits 785
Onkel väterlicherseits 785
Online-Katalog 733
Online-Spiel 525
Oolong-Tee 208
Oortsche Wolke 4
Opal 375
Operationen, spezifische 529
Operationsabteilung 780
Operationssaal 780, 781
Operationstisch 780
Operationszentrale 763
Opernglas 385
Opernhaus 710
Opferstein 412
Opisthodomos 403
Opossum 143
opponierbarer Daumen 139
Optik 690
Optiker 715
optische Maus 516
optische Sortierung 71
optischer Sensor 516
optischer Zeichenleser 474
optisches Signal 436
Orang-Utan 139
Orange 194, 400
Orange im Querschnitt 82
Orbiter 22
Orbiter (Viking) 18
Orchester 402
Orchestergraben 430
Orchidee 80
Ordner, Verzeichnis 524
Ordnungsgleis 589
Ordnungszahl 682
Ordovizium 92
Orgel 444
Orgelmechanik 445
Orgelspieltisch 444
orientalische Schabe 101
orientalischer Überfangstich 459
Orientierungsseinlage 440, 441
Oriflamme 739
Origano 202
Originaleinzug 508
Originalrückführung 508
Orinoko 31
Orion 11, 12
Orkan 57
Oropharyngealtubus 775
Ort 740
Orthoceras 92
Orthodoxe Kirche 736
orthopädischer Stock 782
Ortspost 475
Osculum 95
Öse 284, 371, 387, 457, 911, 913
Öse für Schulterriemen 476
Öse für Tragriemen 477
Öse, gerade 453
Öse, runde 453
Ösen 453
Ösenknopf 453
Ösler 453
Osmium 683
Ösophagus 95, 97, 99, 103, 104, 110, 113, 116, 125
Ost 37, 917
Ost-Nordost 37
Ost-Südost 37
Ostchinesisches Meer 33
Osten 616
Osteon 154
Österreich 744
östliche Hemisphäre 35
Östlicher Indischer Rücken 50
östlicher Kardinalseezeichen 617
östlicher Meridian 36
Ostpazifischer Rücken 50
Ostsee 32
Oszillograph-/Oszilloskopmonitor 491
Otolith 109
Ottomotor 566
Outfieldzaun 795
Overall 358, 369
Overcheck 857
Overknee-Strumpf 365
Oviduct 103, 113
Ozean 7, 38, 67
Ozean, Atlantischer 29, 32, 34
Ozean, Indischer 29, 33, 34
Ozean, Pazifischer 29, 33
Ozeane 28, 29, 747
ozeanische Gräben 50
ozeanische Kruste 42
ozeanische Rücken 50
ozeanische Sprachen 469
ozeanischer Rücken 49
Ozonschicht 53

P

Paar 881
paarig gefiedert 79
Packlage 538
Packriemen 389
Packung 223, 268
Pager 505
Pagode 412
Pagodenärmel 361
Pahlstek 908
Pair 919
Pak-Choi 186
Paketannahme 582
Pakistan 746
Palau 747
Palette 233, 632
Palette mit Palettstecker 398
Palette mit Vertiefungen 398
Paletten 632
Paletten und Container 623
Palettenhubwagen 633
Palettenhubwagen, hydraulischer 633
Palettmesser 397
Palettstecker 398
Palisade 408
Palla 336
Palladium 683
Palme 88
Palmenhain 52
Palmette 276
Pampelmuse 194
Panama 742
Panama, Golf 31
Panama, Landenge 30
Panamahut 340
Panflöte 433
Pankreas 110, 116
Panoramafenster 584, 713, 727
Panoramakopf 482
Pantoffel 344
Pantolette 344
Panty-Korselett 366
Panzer 758
Panzerabwehrgeschoss 757
Panzerabwehrrakete 759
Panzerfahrzeugen, Transport 572
Panzerfaust 757
Panzerhandschuh 749
Panzerschnur 507
Panzerschurz 749
Panzerturm 758
Papaya 197
Papier 390, 400, 420
Papier/Pappe, Sortierung 71
Papierablage 511
Papierablagen 512
Papieraufnehmer 511
Papierausgabe 519
Papierclip 534
Papiereinschubfach 512
Papiereinzugstaste 731
Papiereinzug, Kontrollleuchte 519
Papiereinzugtaste 519
Papierfreigabehebel 528
Papierführung 508, 519
Papierhalter 528
Papierkassette 519
Papierkorb 535
Papierlösehebel 528
Papierschneider 535
Papierstütze 528
Papiervorschubtaste 529
Papierzufuhr 511
Papillarmuskel 162
Papille 172
Papille, fadenförmige 176
Pappel 88
Pappschere 424
Paprika 199
Paprika, gelber 188
Paprika, grüner 188
Paprika, roter 188
Papua-Neuguinea 29, 747
Papuasprachen 469
Par-3-Loch 866
Par-4-Loch 867
Par-5-Loch 867
Parabeldüne 52
Parabolantenne 16, 486, 489, 493
Parabolantenne, schwenkbare 16
Parabolspiegel 674
Paradiesvogel 10
Paraffine 656
Paraguay 742
parallel 704
Parallelanschlag 304, 305
parallele Zügelgurte 541
Parallelepiped 705
Parallelogramm 705
Parallelschaltung 687
Parallelschnittstelle 513
Paramecium 94
Paraná 31
Paranuss 193
Parboiled Reis 207
Parcourschef 853, 855
Pardune 602
Parfümerie 714, 717
Parietale 112, 122

Park 39, 711
Parka 353
Parkdeck 713
Parkettboden 253, 254
Parkettmuster 254
Parkplatz 583, 596, 620, 708, 735, 866, 886
Parmesan 211
Parterre 431
partielle Finsternis 6, 7
Partlow-Schreiber 571
Pascal 702
Pasch 914
Paspel 368
Paspeltasche 354, 360
Pass 45
Passagierdampfer 608
Passagierkabine 605, 608, 609
Passagierraum 625, 631
Passagierraum 1. Klasse 624
Passagierterminal 619, 620
Passagiertransferfahrzeug 621, 623
Passbildautomat 715
Passe (19 bis 36) 919
Passgänger 857
Passiergerät 230
Passiersieb 231
Passierte Tomaten 200
Passionsfrucht 196
passiver Sensor 41
Passivitätszone 843
Passkontrolle 621
Paste 201
Pastell 396
Pastinake 189
Paßgang 125
Patagonien 31
Patent-Strickbündchen 354
Patentanker 610
Patera 276
Pathfinder 19
pathologisches Labor 781
Patient 780
Patientenstuhl 780
Patisson 189
Patisson-Kürbis 189
Patrone 754
Patrone (Gewehr) 912
Patrone (Schrotflinte) 912
Patronen 860, 861
Patronenkammer 476, 754, 755
Patronensicherung 272
Patronentasche 770
Patte 348
Pattentasche, schräge 352, 355, 360
Pauken 437
Pausche 826, 855
Pause 435, 515
Pause, ganze 435
Pause, halbe 435
Pause-Taste 499
Pausenraum 735
Pausenzeichen 435
Pausetaste 495
Pavian 139
Pavillon 710
Pavillondach 445
Pazifik 28
Pazifische Platte 43
pazifischer Lachs 221
Pazifischer Ozean 29, 33
PC 513
PC-Kartenschacht 526
PCI-Erweiterungskarte 513
PCI-Erweiterungsport 513
Pecannuss 193
Pechnase 408
Pecorino Romano 211
Pedal 440, 448, 578, 580, 851, 870
Pedal zur Verstellung 399
Pedalhaken 578, 580
Pedalklaviatur 444
Pedalstange 442
Pedaltaste 444
Pegasus 12
Pegelanzeige, digitale 488
Pegeltongenerator 488
Peildeck 604, 608, 609
Peilstableuchte 570, 571
Pelerine 355
Pelham-Kandare 854
Pelikan 119
Peltonturbine 659
Pelzwerk 741
Pendel 436, 697
Pendelaufhängung 43
Pendelhub-Einstellung 305
Pendeloque-Schliff 375
Pendelstab 697
Penduluhr 10
Pendelzug 620
Penholdergriff 815
Penis 104, 146, 169
Penne 206
Pentaprisma 477
Peplos 336
Pepperoniwurst 216
perforierte Vorderkappe 342
Perforierung 346
Pergola 322
Perikarp 82

Periodensystem 682
peripher-sensorisches Neuron 168
peripheres Nervensystem 166
Peristom 94
Peristyl 403, 406
Perlhuhn 120, 212
Perlrippen 458
Perlzwiebel 184
Perm 92
Peroxyd 777
Peroxysom 94
Perserkatze 132
Perseus 12
Persisch 469
Persischer Golf 33
Personalausgangskontrolle 726
Personalcomputer 513
Personaleingang 720, 726, 768
Personaleingangskontrolle 726
Personalgarderobe 720
Personalraum 731, 768, 779
Personaltoiletten 768
Personalumkleideraum 768, 781
Personenbahnhof 583
Personenwaage 699
Personenzüge 584
Persönliche Artikel 383
persönliche Ausstattung 374
persönliche Identifikationsnummer (PIN), Eingabegerät 731
Peru 742
Peru-Chile-Graben 50
Peso 728
Pestizid 69, 70
Petanque 864
Petanquekugel 864
Petersilie 202
Petri-Schale 685
Petrochemikalien 656
petrochemische Industrie 656
Petroleum 656
Pfahl 740
Pfahlbau 418
Pfahlwurzel 87
Pfännchen 239
Pfanndeckel 752
Pfanne 235, 752
Pfannenwender 233
Pfau 10, 119
Pfeffer, gemahlener 199
Pfeffer, grüner 198
Pfeffer, rosa 198
Pfeffer, schwarzer 198
Pfeffer, weißer 198
Pfefferschote 188
Pfefferspray 770
Pfefferstreuer 226
Pfeife 240, 390, 445
Pfeife im Querschnitt 390
Pfeifenbesteck 390
Pfeifenkopf 390
Pfeifenmundstück 390
Pfeifenputzer 390
Pfeifenrastbrett 445
Pfeifenrastbretter, Stützen 445
Pfeifenständer 390
Pfeifenstock 445
Pfeifenstummel 390
Pfeifenwerk 445
Pfeifhase 123
Pfeil 12, 56, 750, 859
Pfeilanlagepunkt 913
Pfeiler 407, 410, 411, 412, 540, 583
Pfeilerfundament 540
Pfeilflügel 630
Pfeilförmig 79
Pfeilsack 104
Pfeilspitze 748, 859
Pfeilstütze 859
Pfeiltaste 261
Pferd 124, 129, 826, 858
Pferd, Anatomie 125
Pferd, äußere Merkmale 124
Pferd, Skelett 126
Pferderennbahn 856
Pferderennen 856, 857
Pfifferling 183
Pfirsich 192
Pfirsich im Querschnitt 81
Pflanze 77
Pflanze, Aufbau 77
Pflanzenfresser 67
Pflanzenreich 74
Pflanzenzelle 74
Pflanzholz 324
Pflanzkelle 325
Pflanzlochstecher 324
Pflanzschnur 324
Pflanzwerkzeuge 324
Pflasterstein 298, 322
Pflaume 192
Pflaumensoße 201
Pflegelösung 384
Pfluganker 610
Pflugrahmen 641
Pfortader 161
Pfosten 252, 460, 812, 817, 820, 827
Pfosten mit Latte 852
Pfosten mit Stange 852
Pfropf 753, 912
Pfund 728

Phalangen 111, 122, 136, 138, 141, 142
Pharynx 99
Phase 273
Philippinen 33, 747
Philippinen-Platte 43
Philippinengraben 50
Phobos 4
Phönix 10
Phonothek 733
Phosphor 683
Phosphorschicht 275
Photon 692
Photosphäre 6
Photosynthese 78
Physalis 192
Physik 686, 687, 690
Physiotherapeut 811
physische Karte 38
Pi 704
Pia Mater 167
Piano, elektronisches 451
Pianopedal 442, 451
Picknick verboten 725
Pickup 549, 642
Pier 653
Pik 914
Pikkoloflöte 437, 446
Piktogramme 514
Pilaster, korinthischer 407
Pillbox 341
Pilot 897
Pilote 443
Pilz 76
Pilz, Aufbau 76
Pilz, tödlich giftiger 76
Pilzanker 610
Pilze 183
Pilzfaden 76
Pilzpapille 176
Pin 865
Pinakocyte 95
Pinguin 119
Pinie 89
Pinienkern 89, 193
Pinne 398, 436, 612, 834, 907
Pinnwand 535
Pinsel 397, 422
Pinseläffchen 139
Pintobohne 191
Pinzette 777
Pioneer 19
Pipeline 654
Pipeline, überirdische 654
Pipette 685
Pistazie 193
Piste, Anfänger 886
Piste, Experte 886
Piste, mittelschwere 886
Piste, schwere 886
Pisten-Mittellinienmarkierungen 620
Pistenbezeichnungsmarkierung 620
Pistenrandmarkierungen 620
Pistenraupe 886
Pistole 315, 754, 770
Pistolengriff 306, 318, 320, 754, 755, 860, 912
Pistolenschießen 861
Pit 501
Pitching-Wedge 868
Pitot-Rohr 873
Pittabrot 205
Plakat 427
Planenwagen 588
planetarischer Nebel 8
Planetarium 10
Planetariumsprojektor 10
Planeten 4
Planeten, äußere 4
Planeten, innere 5
Planfilm 481
Planierraupe 636
Planierschaufel 636
Planierschild 636
plankonkave Linse 691
plankonvexe Linse 691
Plantainbanane 196
Planum 538
Plasmabrücke 74
Plasmamembran 94
Plastikhülse 912
Plateau, Hochebene 38
Plateosaurier 93
Platin 683
Plättchen 64
Platte 238, 381, 400, 449, 482, 521
Platte, Afrikanische 43
Platte, Antarktische 43
Platte, Cocos 43
Platte, Eurasiatische 43
Platte, Indisch-Australische 43
Platte, Karibische 43
Platte, Nazca 43
Platte, Nordamerikanische 43
Platte, Pazifische 43
Platte, Philippinen 43
Platte, Scotia 43
Platte, Südamerikanische 43
Platten ausrollen 465
Platten, tektonische 43
Plattenbindung 887
Plattengitter 562

Plattengrenzen, divergierende 43
Plattengrenzen, konvergierende 43
Plattenhalter 422
Plattenheizkörper 259
Plattenisolierung 299
Plattenspieler 488, 500
Plattenstift 442, 500
Plattenteller 500
platter Knochen 157
Plattform 321, 569, 830, 894
Plattformpedal 870
Plattsehnenmuskel 151
Plattstiche 459
Platzierung 831
Platzierungsrichter 830
Play-Taste 499
Plein 919
Plektron 433
Pleuelstange 564, 566
Pleurahöhle 163
Plinthe 697
Plotter 520
Pluderhose 338
plus oder minus 703
Plusbereich 672
Plusglas 691
Pluskontakt 672, 673
Plusplatte 562
Pluspol 562, 689
Pluspolbrücke 562
Pluto 4, 5
Plutonium 684
PN-Übergang 672
pneubereiftes Laufrad 594, 595
pneubereiftes Leitrad 594, 595
pneumatischer Auslöser 482
Pocket-Instamatic-Kamera 480
Podest 17, 255, 264, 321
Podium 412, 734
Pokerwürfel 914
Pol, negativer 687
Pol, positiver 687
Polachse 17
polar umlaufender Satellit 60
polare Umlaufbahn 60
Polarisationsfilter 478
Polarklimate 61
Polarkreis, nördlicher 36
Polarkreis, südlicher 29, 36
Polarlicht 53
Polarstern 13
Polartundra 61
Polen 744
Poleposition 872
Polierstahl 422
polierter Steinfaustkeil 748
Poliklinik 781
Politik 739
politische Karte 37
Polizei 725
Polizeibeamter 770
Polizeifahrzeug 769, 771
Polizeirevier 711, 768
Pollenbürste 98
Pollenkamm 98
Pollenkörbchen 98
Pollenschieber 98
Pollenzange 98
Pollenzelle 100
Poller 607
Polnisch 469
Polo 858
Polohemd 359, 822
Polokleid 356
Polokragen 363
Polonium 682
Polopony 858
Poloschläger 858
Poloshirt 354
Polster 798
Polsterauflage 776
Polsterdüse 289
Polsterung 899
Polynesien 747
Pont-l'Évêque 211
Ponton 542
Ponton, Schwimmkörper 652
Pontonbrücke 542
Pool 862
Poop 602
Pore 74, 84, 172
Porenzelle 95
Porro-Prisma 692
Portal 411, 738
Portalbrücke 541
Portalkuppel 738
Portalrahmen 540
Portierszimmer 724
Porträt 729
Portugal 743
Portugiesisch 469
Portulak 187
Portweinglas 225
Posaune 447
Posaunen 437
Positionskontrolle der Probe 694
Positionsleuchte 585
Positionslicht 605, 625, 631
positiv geladen 684
positiver Pol 687

Post 474
Post, elektronische 525
Post, gestempelte 474
Post, internationale 475
Post, nicht gestempelte 474
Post, regionale 475
Postamt 474, 475, 711, 715
Postanweisung 475
Postauto 474, 475
Postkarte 474
Postnetz, öffentliches 474
Postpaket 475
Poststelle 509
Postwertzeichen 474
Poterne 408
Pottwal 137
Präger 533
Prägung 401
Präkambrium 92
Prallbügel hinten 885
Prallbügel vorne 885
Prämaxilla 122, 123
Prämolar 123
Prärie 38
Praseodym 684
Präzisionssport 859
Präzisionswaage 699
Preis pro Einheit 699
Preis pro Liter/Gallone 548
Preiselbeere 192
Prellbock 583
Pressbalken 424, 425
Pressen 425
Pressfilterkanne 241
Presshebel 230, 315
Presskammer 642
Pressluftbohrer 649
Pressplatte 425
Pressspindel 421, 423
primäre Nahrungsmittelquelle 67
Primärfokus 17
Primärfokuskabine 16, 17
Primärkonsumenten 67
Primärspiegel 17
Primärwurzel 77
Primaten 138
Primaten, Beispiele 139
Prime 434
Prinzesskleid 356
Prinzessnaht 366
Prismenfernglas 692
pritschen 813
private Telekommunikation 487
privater Ankleideraum 428
privater Nutzer 525
privates Rundfunknetz 486
Privatflugzeug 628
Probenkammer 694
Probierlöffel 233
Proconsul 93
Produktionsbohrung 646, 652
Produktionsleitung 509
Produzent 429
Profil 560, 561
Programmbereich 501
programmierbare Funktionstasten 731
programmierbare Tasten 516
programmierbarer Thermostat 261
Programmiertasten 495
Programmsteuerung 261
Programmwähler 292, 293, 294
Programmwahlscheibe 476
Programmwahlschalter 450
Programmwahltasten 495
Projektile 752
Projektionskopf 535
Projektionskuppel 10
Projektionsraum 395
Projektionswand 483
Projektor 427, 518
Promenadendeck 608
Promethium 684
Pronaos 403
Prop-Forward 804
Propan- oder Butangas-Geräte 903
Propanflasche 567
Propeller, dreiflügeliger 628
Propeller, zweiflügeliger 628
Propellerummantelung 605
Prospektständer 730
Prospektzug 430
Prostata 169
Protactinium 684
Protestantismus 736
Prothorax 97
Protokollant 814
Protokollanten 827
Protokollraum 768
Proton 680
Protuberanz 6
Provider, Internet 525
Provinz 37
Provinzgrenze 37
proximale Epiphyse 155
Prozent 703
Prozenttaste 529
Prozessor 513
Prüflampe 316
Pseudopodium 94
psychiatrischer Beobachtungsraum 778
psychiatrischer Untersuchungsraum 778

Psychrometer 59
Pterygoid 112
Pubis 116
Publikumseingang 402
Puck 880
Pudel 130
Pudelmütze 341
Puder, loser 378
Puderdose 378
Puderkissen 378
Puderpinsel 378
Puderrouge 378
Puderzucker 209
Puerto-Rico-Graben 50
Puff 277
Puffärmel 360
Puffer 417
Puffertank 654
Pullman Limousine 549
Pullover 354, 359
Pullunder 354
Pulmonalklappe 162
Pulpa 159
Pulpahöhle, Kronenabschnitt 159
Pulpete 445
Pulsar 8
pulsierende Vakuole 94
Pult 737
Pultdach 414
Pulver 200
Pulverhorn 752
Pulverkammer 753
Pulvino 67
Puma 134
Pumpe 246, 292, 294, 320, 670, 671, 674, 903
Pumpenmotor 263
Pumpenraum 606
Pumpensumpf 263
Pumplöschfahrzeug 766
Pumps 343
Pumpstation 654
Pumpstation, zentrale 654
Punchingball 842
Punkt 473
Punktauge 97, 99
Punktbrenner 314, 319
Punkte 822
Punktekonsole 865
Punktetabelle 918
Punktezähler 819
Punktrichter 843, 846, 859, 860, 864
Pupille 132, 177
Pupille, senkrechte 112
Puppe 97, 100
purpurn 741
Purpursaum 336
Pushup-Griff 851
Puter 213
Putter 867, 868
Putzkelle 315
Putzmittel 721
Putzschwamm 295
Putzsporn 98
Puzzle 917
Puzzleteil 917
Pygalschild 113
Pygostyl 116
Pylon 540
Pylon zur Aufhängung des Triebwerks 625
pylorische Blindsäcke 109
Pyramide 402, 705
Pyramidendach 415
Pyranometer 58
Pyrenäen 32
Python 114

Q

Quadrant 704
Quadrat 705
Quadratbein 112
Quadratwurzel 703
Quadratwurzel aus 703
Quadratwurzeltaste 529
Quark 680
Quartär 93
Quarte 434
Quarterback 807
Quarterdeck 608
Quartett 438
Quartier 342, 370
Quarzmetronom 436
Quecksilber 275, 683
Quecksilberbarometer 59
Quecksilberkolben 695
Quecksilbersäule 695
Quecksilberthermometer 777
Quelle 48
Quellenangabe 471
Quellwolken 62
quer verlaufender Dickdarm 164
Querbalken 461
Querbehang 282
Querdünen 52
Querfaden 455
Querfeldeinrad 870
Querflöte 446
Querflöten 437
Querfortsatz 157, 168

Querholz 277, 460, 799
Querjoch 433
Querleiste 278, 424
Querleiste, obere 278
Querleiste, untere 278
Querriegel 247
Querrippe 214
Querruder 23, 624, 898
Querschiff 411
Querschlag 650
Querschnitt 920
Querschnitt durch eine Sternwarte 17
Querschnitt durch eine Trägerrakete (Ariane V) 24
Querschnitt durch eine Trägerrakete (Saturn V) 25
Querschnitt, Apfel 82
Querschnitt, Baseball 797
Querschnitt, Baumstamm 87, 300
Querschnitt, Bogenstaudamm 661
Querschnitt, Elektronenmikroskop 694
Querschnitt, Erdbeere 83
Querschnitt, Erdkruste 42
Querschnitt, Golfball 867
Querschnitt, Himbeere 83
Querschnitt, Kraftwerk 664
Querschnitt, Linsenfernrohr 14
Querschnitt, Orange 82
Querschnitt, Pfeife 390
Querschnitt, Pfirsich 81
Querschnitt, Rotorgondel 677
Querschnitt, Schiene 591
Querschnitt, Schwergewichtsstaudamm 661
Querschnitt, Spiegelreflexkamera 477
Querschnitt, Spiegelteleskop 15
Querschnitt, Spritzpistole 398
Querschnitt, Straße 538, 712
Querschnitt, Stützpfeilerstaudamm 660
Querschnitt, Uferdamm 660
Querschnitt, Vorderlade-Geschütz 753
Querschnitt, Wasserkraftwerk 658
Querschnitt, Weintraube 83
Querschnitt, Zwiebel 78
Querschott 606
Querstange 897
Querstraße, Allee 711
Querstrebe 663, 783
Querstrich, ganzer 56
Querstrich, halber 56
Querstück 278, 782
Querträger, oberer 635
Querträger, unterer 635
Quetschfuß 274, 275
Quetschverschraubung 269, 270
Quicheform 232
Quinte 434
Quintett 438
Quitte 193
Quittungsausgabe 730

R

Rabatte 244
Rabe 11, 118
Rachen 163, 164
Rachenenge 174
Raclette 211
Raclette-Grill 239
Racquetball 818
Racquetballschläger 818
Racquetballspiel 818
Rad 320, 323, 423, 560, 570, 753, 870, 874
Rad-Schneeschläger 232
Radar 40, 604, 605, 608, 609
Radar zur Luftüberwachung 761
Radar zur Zielverfolgung 762
radarabsorbierendes Material 629
Radarabwehrflugkörper 759
Radaranlage 760, 771
Radaranlagendisplay 771
Radarantenne 40, 760, 763
Radarflugzeug 629
Radarmast 606
Radarreflektor 615
Radarsat 40
Radarstrahl 40
Rädchen 454
Rädelung 311
Räder-Drehgeschwindigkeitssensor 559
Radfahrer 545, 546
Radgabel 870
radiale Einsteigestation 619
Radialgürtelreifen 561
Radialkapelle 410, 411
Radialkarkasse 561
Radialreifen 561
Radiärkanal 95
Radicchio 186
Radieschen 189
Radio-/Kassettengerät 556
Radio-Wellen 486
radioaktiv 774
radioaktive Kerne 681
radioaktiver Abfall 70

Radioaktivität, Maßeinheit 702
Radioisotopengenerator, thermoelektrischer 18
Radiometer 60
Radiorecorder mit CD-Spieler 504
Radiosonde 59
Radioteleskop 16
Radiowelle 16
Radiowellen 690
Radium 682
Radius 704
Radius-Ulna 111
Radkappe 551
Radlader 637
Radlenker 590
Radom 760
Radon 684
Radrennbahn 788, 871
Radsatzgetriebe 586
Radschüssel 560
Radsport 870
Radtraktor 637
Radula 104
Raffgardine 283
Raffhalter 282
Raffinerie 654, 709
Raffinerieerzeugnisse 656
Raffrollo 285
Raglanärmel 352, 355, 361, 369
Raglanmantel 355
Rah 602
Rahe 600
Rähmchen 100
Rahmen 252, 256, 278, 280, 312, 327, 342, 386, 389, 395, 423, 433, 449, 459, 460, 575, 612, 632, 633, 638, 639, 641, 642, 672, 673, 676, 816, 822, 823, 824, 862, 870, 893
Rahmen, oben liegender 639
Rahmen, senkrechter 461
Rahmenleiste 278
Rahmenspant 607
Rahsegel 601
Rakete zur Schiffsbekämpfung 759
Raketenantrieb 759
Raketendepot 762
Raketenschiene 760
Raketentriebwerk 24
Raketenwerfer 761
Rallye-Motorrad 875
RAM 513
RAM-Anschluss 513
Rambutan 197
Rammschutzleiste 571
Rammsporn 598
Rampe 403, 407, 539, 647, 894
Rampenlicht 431
Rand 385, 729, 793, 841, 919
Rand, äußerer 127
Rand, innerer 127
Rändelbolzen 320
Randkontrolltaste 528
Randlösetaste 528
Rang, erster 431
Range 402, 407
Rangierbahnhof 589
Ranviersche Schnürringe 168
Rapier 751
Ras-El-Hanout 199
Rasen 245, 322, 822
Rasenbesen 333
Rasenpflege 332
Rasentrimmer 332
Rasierer, zweischneidiger 383
Rasiermesser 383
Rasierpinsel 383
Rasierschaum 383
Rasierwasser 383
Raspel 309, 401
Rassel 112
Raste 791
Rasterleiste 291
Rasthebel 331
Rastplatz 39, 725
Raststätte 39
Raststütze 577
Rasur 383
Ratsche 302
Ratschenringschlüssel 311
Ratte 123
Ratte, äußere Merkmale 122
Ratte, Skelett 122
Rau 866, 867
Raubtiere 130
Raubtiere, Beispiele 134
Raubvogel 117
Rauch 57
Rauchabsauger 758
Rauchbombe 758
Räucherapparat 422
Räucherschinken 215
Rauchklappe 256
Rauchmantel 256
Rauchmelder 767
Rauke 187
Raum 584

Raum, Douglasscher 170
Raum, Douglasscher, vorderer 170
Raumanzug 20
raumer Wind 833
Raumfähre 22, 23, 53
Raumfähre beim Start 22
Raumfahrt 18
Raumklimaanlage 261
Raumlaboratorium 23
räumlicher Dendrit 64
Raumschotkurs, zweiter 833
Raumsonde 18, 53
Raumsonden, Beispiele 19
Raumstation, internationale 21
Raumteiler 902
Raumthermostat 261
Raupe 97
Raupenschere mit Teleskopstiel 330
Raureif 65
Raute 538
Rautenspitze 278
Ravioli 206
Reagenzglas 685
Reaktion, reversible 684
Reaktionsrichtung 684
Reaktionstriebwerk 60
Reaktor 665, 666, 669, 763
Reaktorgebäude 667, 669
Reaktorgebäude, Luftschleuse 668
Reaktorkern 670, 671
Reaktorkessel 667
Reaktortank 671
Reanimationsraum 778
Rebe 86
Rebhuhn 118
Rebstock 86
Receiver 493, 503
Receiver: Vorderansicht 497
Rechen 327, 658, 664
Rechenbalken 642
Rechenscheibe 479
Rechnernetzwerk 523
Rechnung 721
rechte Flanke 740
rechte Herzkammer 161, 162
rechte Lunge 161, 163
rechte Lungenvene 162
rechte Mittelstelle 740
rechte Niere 165
rechte Seite 300, 384
rechte Spur 539
Rechteck 705
rechteckige Fahne 739
Rechteckflügel 630
Rechteckschlafsack 904
rechter Abwehrspieler 812
rechter Angriffsfeldspieler 814
rechter Angriffsspieler 811
rechter Aufbauspieler 811
rechter Außenangreifer 812
rechter Außenfeldspieler 794
rechter Centre 823
rechter Corner Back 806
rechter Defensive End 806
rechter Defensive Tackle 806
rechter Flügelspieler 801
rechter Guard 807
rechter Kanal 502
rechter Mittelfeldspieler 801, 803
rechter Safety 806
rechter Stürmer 879
rechter Tackle 807
rechter Verteidiger 801, 803, 878
rechter Vorhof 161, 162
rechter Winkel 704
rechtes Aufschlagfeld 819, 821
rechtes Feld 795
rechtes Obereck 740
rechtes Untereck 740
rechts 431
Rechtsanwälte, Mitarbeiter 728
Rechtschreibkorrekturtaste 528
Rechtskurve 544, 547
Reck 824, 825
Recksäule 825
Reckstange 825
Recycling 71
redaktioneller Beitrag 471
Redaktionsteil 471
Redingote 355
Reduziermuffennippel 269
Reffband 603
Reffbänsel 603
reflektierende Aluminiumschicht 501
reflektierendes Band 611
reflektierte Sonneneinstrahlung 68
reflektierte Sonnenstrahlen 674
Reflektor 316, 493
Reflexion 41
Reformation 736
Regal 181, 723
Regal der Neuzugänge 733
regelbarer Thermostat 239
Regelgerät 267
regelmäßiges Achteck 705
regelmäßiges Elfeck 705
regelmäßiges Fünfeck 705
regelmäßiges Neuneck 705

regelmäßiges Oktaeder 705
regelmäßiges Sechseck 705
regelmäßiges Siebeneck 705
regelmäßiges Zehneck 705
regelmäßiges Zwölfeck 705
Regelschalter 290
Regen 64, 65
Regen, anhaltend leichter 57
Regen, anhaltend mäßiger 57
Regen, anhaltend starker 57
Regen, gefrierender 64
Regen, leichter 64
Regen, mäßiger 64
Regen, saurer 69, 70
Regen, zeitweise leichter 57
Regen, zeitweise mäßiger 57
Regen, zeitweise starker 57
Regenarten 64
Regenbogen 65
Regenfälle, heftige 63
Regenhut 341
Regenleiste 551
Regenmantel 352
Regenmenge, Messung 59
Regenmesser mit direkter Ablesung 58
Regenmesser, selbst schreibender 59
Regenreifen 872
Regenrohr 244
Regenschauer 57
Regenschreiber 58
Regenwald, tropischer 61, 66
Regenwasserabfluss 712
Regie-Kontrollmonitore 428
Regieassistent 429, 490
Regiepult 488, 491
Regieraum 431, 488, 489, 490, 491
Regierungsorganisation 525
Regiestuhl 276, 429
Regisseur 429
Register 0
Registerleiste 445
Registerschleife 445
Registerzug 444, 445
Registratoren 844
Registriereinheit 273
Registriereinlagen 532
Registrierkarten, Halterung 58
Registrierkasse 181
Registrierstreifen 58
Registriertrommel 43
Regler 238
Reglerspanngewicht 417
Reglerventil 903
Regnerschlauch 328
Regulierklappe 258
Regulierventil 259
Reh 128
Reibe 230
Reibefläche 318, 391
Reiber 423
Reibergehäuse 423
Reif 65
Reif- und Frostgraupel 64
Reife, Stufen 86
Reifen 551, 560, 570, 579, 823, 870, 874
Reifenarten 560
Reifenflanke 560
Reifenstapel 872
Reifeprozess 86
Reifrock, flacher 337
Reihe 384, 431
Reihe, dritte 804
Reihe, erste 804
Reihe, zweite 804
Reihenanzeige 456
Reihenhaus 419
Reihenzähler 456
Reiher 119
Reinigung, chemische 715
Reinigungsbürste 383
Reinigungsmittelbehälter 294
Reinigungsöffnung 262, 270
Reinigungswelle 314
Reis 85, 203, 207
Reis, weißer 207
Reisebett mit Wickelauflage 281
Reisebüro 714
Reisebus 568
Reisessig 201
Reisetasche 388
Reisetaschen 717
Reisezug 582
Reisfadennudeln 207
Reisfeld 69
Reismelde 203
Reisnudeln 207
Reispapier 207
Reißbahn 899
Reißbrett 399
Reißen 850
Reißnägel 534
Reißschenkelschutz 636
Reißverschluss 353, 369, 377, 389, 453, 902
Reißverschlusslinie 455
Reiten 854

ASTRONOMIE > 2-25; ERDE > 26-71; PFLANZENREICH >72-89; TIERREICH > 90-143; MENSCH > 144-177; NAHRUNGSMITTEL UND KÜCHE > 178-241; HAUS > 242-295;
HEIMWERKEN UND GARTENARBEIT > 296-333; KLEIDUNG > 334-371; PERSÖNLICHE AUSSTATTUNG > 372-391; KUNST UND ARCHITEKTUR > 392-465; KOMMUNIKATION UND BÜROTECHNIK > 466-535;
TRANSPORT UND FAHRZEUGE > 536-643; ENERGIE > 644-677; WISSENSCHAFT > 678-705; GESELLSCHAFT > 706-785; SPORT UND SPIELE > 786-920

Reiter 532, 853, 855, 858
Reiter, durchsichtiger 532
Reitgerte 853, 856
Reithandschuh 853
Reithelm 853
Reithose 853
Reitjacke 853, 855
Reitkappe 856
Reitsport 852
Reitstiefel 855
Rektaszension 13
Rektaszensionsachse 14, 15
Rektum 97, 99, 113, 116, 125
Relaiskasten 563
Relaisstation 486
Relaisstation, Mikrowellen 524
Relaisstelle 487
Religion 736
Religionen, Chronologie 736
Reling 607
Rennanzug 874, 882
Rennanzug, feuerfester 872
Rennbügel 579
Rennfahrer 872
Rennleiter 870
Rennrad 581
Rennrodel 884
Rennrodel, Doppelsitzer 884
Rennrodel, Einsitzer 884
Rennrodler 884
Rennstrecke 874
Rentier 128
Reparaturwerkstatt 548
Reportage 471
Reptilien 112
Reptilien, Beispiele 114
Republik Kongo 745
Requisiteur 429
Requisiteurassistent 429
Reserve-Fahrtmesser 626
Reserve-Fluglageanzeige 626
Reserve-Höhenmesser 626
Reservefallschirm 896
Reservepapier 512
Reserverad 567
Resettaste 513, 519, 918
Resonanzboden 442
Resonanzdecke 432, 433, 439, 440
Resonanzfell 448
Resonanzkörper 433, 440
Resonanzröhren 449
Ressourcenzugriff, vereinheitlichter 524
Restaurant 608, 710, 713, 714, 719, 720, 725
Restaurantkritik 471
Restmüll, nicht wieder verwertbarer 71
Retikulum, endoplasmatisches 74, 94
Rettich 189
Rettich, japanischer 189
Rettungsassistent 611
Rettungsboje 611
Rettungsboot 602, 604, 608, 652
Rettungsfloß 605
Rettungsgeräte 611
Rettungshubschrauber 631
Rettungsinsel 611
Rettungsring 609, 611, 771
Rettungsschacht 543
Rettungsschiff 653
Rettungsstation 543
Rettungsturm für die Startphase 25
Rettungswagen 543, 775, 778
Rettungswart 837
Rettungsweste 611
Revers 348, 362
Revers, abfallendes 352
Revers, steigendes 348
reversible Reaktion 684
Revisionsöffnung 257
Revisionstür 258
Revolver 754
Rewritable-Rekorder 521
Rezeptakel 75
Rezeptor, sensorischer 168
Rhabarber 185
Rhea 5
Rhenium 683
Rhesusfaktor negativ 702
Rhesusfaktor positiv 702
Rhizoid 75
Rhizom 76
Rhodium 683
Rhombus 705
rhythmische Sportgymnastik 823
Rhythmuswahlschalter 451
Riasküste 51
Ribosom 74, 94
Richtaufsatz 756
Richter 855
Richter, Büro 728
Richterkurbel 756
Richtertisch 728
Richtschacht 650
Richtschütze, Stand 758
Richtung Mekka 738
Richtungsgleis 589
Richtungstasten 515, 918
Richtungstor 837

Ricotta 210
Riechbahn 175
Riechkapsel 109
Riechkolben 175
Riechnerv 109, 175
Riechschleimhaut 175
Riegel 46, 238, 248, 249, 294, 352, 389
Riemen 313, 797, 824, 838, 850
Riemenantrieb 605
Riemenarten 838
Riemenboot 839
Riemenmuskel 151
Riemenscheibe 566
Riemenschlaufe 906
Riementriebabdeckung 307
Riese, Roter 8
Riesenkohl 186
Riesenslalom 889
Riesenslalomski 888
Riesenwasserwanze 101
Riet 460
Riffelfeile 401
Riffküste 51
Rigatoni 206
Rigg-Stahlseil 897
Riggs, Beispiele 601
Right-Wing 804
Rille 424, 868
Rillettes 216
Rinde 265
Rinderfilet 214
Rinderhackfleisch 214
Rindfleisch 214
Rindfleischwürfel 214
Ring 76, 284, 383, 390, 447, 453, 610, 611, 659, 696, 824, 842, 901
Ring, dioptrischer 614
Ring, erster 753
Ring, Teile 376
Ring, zweiter 753
Ringablage 533
Ringbrennkammer 627
Ringbuch 532
Ringbuchkalender 530
Ringe 376, 824, 825
Ringelnatter 114
Ringen 843
Ringer 843
Ringerschuh 843
Ringfinger 173
ringförmige Finsternis 6
Ringkanal 95
Ringmutter 269
Ringnetzwerk 522
Ringpfosten 842
Ringschütz 659
Ringstufe 842
Ringumgebung 842
Ringumrandung 842
Ringverschluss 20
Rinne 453, 750, 865
Rippe 112, 116, 121, 122, 126, 131, 136, 138, 141, 142, 185, 260
Rippe, falsche 138
Rippe, frei endende 152
Rippe, freie 153
Rippe, hohe 214
Rippen 152
Rippenbündchen 369
Rippenbündchen, gerades 351
Rippenfell 163
Rippenknorpel 122
Rippenpolster 808
Rispe 85
Ritzel 307, 697
Roberval-Waage 698
Roboterarm 21, 22
Robotersystem 21
Rochen 218
Rock 355, 822
Rock, gerader 357
Rockabrunder 454
Röcke, Beispiele 357
Rocky Mountains 30
Rodehacke 327
RodelSchlitten 884
Roggen 85, 203
Roggenknäckebrot 205
roher Schinken 216
Rohkaffee 208
Rohöl 656
Rohölpipeline 654
Rohr 270, 312, 753, 754, 755, 756, 757, 912
Rohrabschneider 314
Rohrabschnitt 257
Röhrbein 126
Rohrblatt 446
Röhre 241, 697
Rohrende 269
Röhrenfassung 275
Röhrenglocken 437, 449
Röhrenkessel 656
Rohrfahrteingang 654
Rohrfeder 470
Rohrführung mit Verstellmöglichkeit 824, 825
Rohrquerstrebe 652
Rohrrücklauf 756

Rohrschraubstock 312
Rohrstück 776
Rohrstütze 615
Rohrturbine 664
Rohrummantelung 299
Rohrummantelung, vorgeformte 299
Rohrverschraubung 269
Rohrverteilerstück 652
Rohrzangen 315
Rollbahn 618, 761
Rollbahnmarkierung 619
Rollbewegung 630
Rollbraten 214
Rolle 284, 389, 423, 448, 633, 859, 894, 895, 913
Rolle, obere 460
Rollenfuß 909, 910
Rollenhaltepartie 910
Rollenhalterung 909, 910
Rollenleiter 321
Rollfilm 481
Rollgabelschlüssel 311
Rollgabelschlüssel für Vierkant 315
Rollkloben 750
Rollkragen 363, 892
Rollkragenpullover 354
Rollkugel 517
Rollmechanismus 285
Rollo 285
Rollo-Fallasche 285
Rollostoff 285
Rollring 265
Rollschuh 895
Rollschweller 444
Rollsitz 838
Rollsport 894
Rollstuhl 584, 783
Rollstuhllift 569
Rolltreppe 417, 592, 713
Romagna-Salat 186
romanische Sprachen 469
Römerpantolette 344
Römertopf 235
römische Bohne 191
römische Metallfeder 470
römische Ziffern 703
römischer Legionär 748
römisches Amphitheater 407
römisches Wohnhaus 406
Rondiste 374
Rondistenfacette, obere 374
Rondistenfacette, untere 374
Röntgengerät, fahrbares 778
Röntgenstrahlen 690
Roquefort 211
rosa Ball 863
rosa Pfeffer 198
Rose 80
Rosenkohl 186
Rosennerv 166
Rosenschliff 375
Rosenvene, große 160
Rosette 248, 249, 268, 405, 411
Rosmarin 202
Ross-Schelfeis 29
Rösselsprung 916
Rost 290
Rotalge 75
Rotbarsch 221
rote Bälle 863
rote Beete 189
rote Heidelbeere 192
rote Kidneybohne 191
rote Klemme 558
rote Meerbarbe 219
rote Zwiebel 184
roter Ball 863
roter Ockerstift 423
roter Paprika 188
Roter Riese 8
roter Sicherheitsfilter 485
roter Stoßball 862
rotes Licht 712
Rotes Meer 28, 33, 34
Rotini 206
Rotkehlchen 118
Rotkniespinne, Mexikanische 102
Rotkohl 186
Rotodom 629
Rotor 249, 659, 662, 676
Rotorange 400
Rotorblatt 631, 676, 677
Rotorgondel im Querschnitt 677
Rotorkopf 631
Rotormast 631
Rotornabe 631
Rotstrahl 494
Rotunde 713
Rotviolett 400
Rotweinglas 225
Rouge 919
Rougepinsel 378
Roulette 422
Roulettekessel 919
Roulettekugel 919

Roulettespieltisch 919
Routenschiedsrichter 900
Router 523, 524
Royal Flush 914
Royalstenge 602
Ruanda 745
Rübe 189
Rübenhacke 326
Rübenspross 187
Rubidium 682
Rubin 375
Rubin-Impulslaser 692
Rubinzylinder 692
Rückansicht 151
Rückbank 555
Rücken 115, 124, 130, 147, 149, 227, 229, 303, 306, 348, 391, 413, 426
Rücken, Indisch-Antarktischer 50
Rücken, Mittelatlantischer 50
Rücken, Östlicher Indischer 50
Rücken, Ostpazifischer 50
Rücken, ozeanischer 49
Rücken, Westlicher Indischer 50
Rücken, Zentralindischer 50
Rückenansicht 147, 149
Rückenflosse 136
Rückenflosse, erste 108, 109
Rückenflosse, zweite 108, 109
Rückengefäß 99
Rückenlasche 857
Rückenlehne 276, 277, 281, 555, 577, 783, 876
Rückenlehne, Basis 276
Rückenmark 109, 110, 167, 168
Rückenmark, Aufbau 167
Rückenmarkshaut 167
Rückenmarkshaut, harte 167, 168
Rückenmarksnerv 167, 168
Rückenmittelschlitz 348
Rückenmuskel, breiter 151
Rückenpanzer 113
Rückenpolster 857
Rückenschlitz, seitlicher 348
Rückenschutz 874
Rückenschwimmen 832
Rückenschwimmen, Startgriffe 830
Rückenspange 348
Rückenteil 368
Rückenteil, verstellbares 776
Rückenträger, gekreuzt 369
Rückenverstärkung 881
Rückfahrscheinwerfer 554
Rückfeld 821
Rückfeldschiedsrichter 807
Rückgrat 909
Rückhaltesystem, Airbag 556
Rückholfeder 559
Rücklagenstütze 889
Rücklauf 259, 501
Rücklauf-Taste 499
Rücklauftaste 504, 508
Rücklaufverschraubung 259
Rücklicht 571, 578
Rücklichter 775
Rückruftaste 479
Rucksack 901, 906
Rückschläger 817, 819, 820
Rückschlaghinderer 754, 912
Rückschlagventil 263
Rückschritt, löschender 515
Rückseite 374
Rückspiegel 556, 574, 876
Rücksprungpalette 632
Rückspulknopf 476
Rückspultaste 495
Rückstellknopf 696, 700
Rückstelltaste 495, 499, 508
rückstoßfreies Geschütz 757
Rückstoßtriebwerk, vorderes 22
Rückstrahler 571, 578, 876
Rückwand 819
rückwärtige Begrenzungslinie 816
rückwärts 828
Rückwärtsantrieb 333
Rückwurflinie 799
Ruder 23, 598, 600, 605, 606, 608, 759, 834, 839, 851
Ruder, oberes 763
Ruderblatt 606
Ruderboote 839
Rudergerät 851
Ruderhaus 606
Rudern (ein Riemen) 838
Rudern und Skullen 838
rudimentäres Becken 136
Ruf, nächster 507
Ruf-beenden-Taste 506
Ruffinisches Körperchen 172
Rufnummernregister 506
Rufnummernregister für automatische Wahl 506
Ruftaste 417, 505, 506
Rugby 804
Rugbyball 805
Rugbyschuhe 805
Rugbyspieler 805
Rührbesen 236
Rührschüssel 236

Rührschüsseln 232
Rumänien 744
Rumänisch 469
rumänischer Überfangstich 459
Rumpf 110, 147, 149, 625, 834, 876, 898, 918
Rumpfleitwerk 629
Rumpfsonar 762
rund 79
Rundblickperiskop 758
Rundbogen 413
Rundbürste 380
runde Bahn 301
runde Klammern 473
runde Öse 453
Rundeisen 421
Rundenzähler 883
runder Ausschnitt 363
runder Einwärtsdreher 150
runder Korpus 432
runder Stickrahmen 459
runder Träger 284
Rundfunk: Sprecherraum und Regieraum 488
Rundfunkempfänger 498
Rundfunknetz, privates 486
Rundkolben 685
Rundkopf mit Schlitz 302
Rundmuskel, großer 151
Rundmuskel, kleiner 151
Rundstricknadel 457
Rungentasche 571
Rupie 728
Rüschen 368
Rüschenhöschen 368
Rüschenstrumpfhose 368
Rüssel 96
Russisch 469
russischer Pumpernickel 205
russisches Modul 21
Russland 744
Rüstung 749
Rutengriff 910
Rutenschwellkörper 169
Ruthenium 683
Rutherfordium 683
Rutsche 650
rutschfeste Matte 893
rutschfester Fuß 321
rutschfester Sockel 826
Ryukyugraben 50

S

S-Bahn-Strecke 583
S-Band Antenne 60
S-Bogen 446
S-Bogen, Griffhebel 446
S-Video-Ausgang 526
Saal 608
Saatgutbehälter 643
Säbel 751, 849
Säbelfechten 848
Sack mit Rettungssystem 897
Sackkarren 633
Safarijacke 359
Safran 198
Saftrinne 229
Sagari 847
Sägeblatt 303, 304, 305
Sägeblatthöhenverstellung 305
Sägekauz 118
Sägekette 331
Sägewerkzeuge 303
Sagittalschnitt 169, 170
Sahara 34
Sahne 210
Sahne, saure 210
Sahnebecher 223
Saint Kitts und Nevis 743
Saint Vincent und die Grenadinen 743
Saite 439, 440, 443
Saiten 433
Saitenaufhängung 441
Saitenbezug 442
Saitenhalter 439
Saitenhalterung 433
Saiteninstrumente 439
Säkelle 324
Sakralwirbel 111
Sakristei 737
Salamander 111
Salami, feine 216
Salami, grobe 216
Salate 722
Salatgabel 228
Salatgurke, kernlose 188
Salatschale 226
Salatschleuder 231
Salatschüssel 226
Salatteller 226
Salbei 202
Salchow 881
Saling 602, 834
Salomoninseln 747
Salonflügel 443
Salpetersäure, Emission 70
Salto vorwärts gebückt, dreieinhalbfacher 829

Salto vorwärts gestreckt mit einer Schraube 829
Saltostellung 828
Salz, grobes 201
Salzkorb 847
Salzsee 52
Salzstreuer 226
Samarium 684
Sambal Oelek 201
Sambia 746
Samen 77, 81, 82, 83, 84
Samenanlage 80
Samenbläschen 169
Samenleiter 104, 169
Samenmantel 81
Samenschale 85
Sammelbehälter 573
Sammelrohr 643
Sammelschiene 658
Sammeltrichter 59
Sammlung, getrennte 71
Samoa 747
Samoanisch 469
Sampler 450
Samtkopfband 374
San Marino 744
Sand 660, 813, 822
Sand- oder Staubsturm 57
Sand-Wedge 868
Sandale 344, 748
Sandale mit Zehenriemchen 344
Sandalette 343
Sandbank 49
Sandblattfeilen 377
Sandinsel 51
Sandkasten 586
Sandsack 842
Sandwüste 52
Sandwiche, Große 29
Sanitärinstallation 262, 264, 270
Sanitärinstallationssystem 262
Sanitäter 846, 853
Sanitäter/Ärzte 846
Sankt-Lorenz-Strom 30
São Tomé und Príncipe 745
Saphir 375
Sardelle 219
Sardine 219
Sarong 357
Sash 846
Satellit 24, 486
Satellit, geostationärer 60
Satellit, polar umlaufender 60
Satelliten, Umlaufbahn 60
Satelliten-Direktempfang 486
Satelliten-Fernerkundung 41
Satelliten-Navigationssystem 613
Satellitenübertragungstechnik 486
Sattel 349, 353, 359, 439, 440, 441, 483, 578, 826, 853, 855, 856, 858
Sattelanhänger für den Baumstammtransport 572
Sattelanhänger für den Spantransport 572
Satteldach 414
Satteldach, eingeschnittenes 415
Satteldach, steiles 414
Sattelgelenk 156
Sattelgurt 855
Sattelkraftfahrzeuge, Beispiele 572
Sattelkupplung 570
Sattelplatz 856
Sattelpolster 855
Sattelpritschenanhänger 571
Sattelrock 357
Sattelschlepper 570
Sattelstütze 578, 871
Satteltasche 580
Satteltiefladeanhänger 572
Satteltiefladeanhänger für den Tiertransport 572
Satteltuch 856
Sattelzug 570
Saturn 4, 5
Saturn V 24
Satz 822
Sätze, vorherige 822
Satztische 278
Satzzeichen 473
sauberes Geschirr, Ablage 721
Sauciere 226
Saudi-Arabien 746
Sauerstoff 683
Sauerstoff, Abgabe 78
Sauerstoff-Atemmaske 775
Sauerstoffanschluss 780
sauerstoffarmes Blut 162
Sauerstoffdruck-Stelleinrichtung 20
Sauerstoffflasche 319, 775
Sauerstoffflaschen-Halterung 775
sauerstoffreiches Blut 162
Sauerstoffventil 319
Sauerstoffzufuhranzeige 898
Sauerstoffzufuhrregler 898
Saugarm 638
Saugbürste 289
Saugfahrzeug 573
Saugmagen 103

Saugnapf 106
Saugrohr 289, 566, 638, 658, 659, 766
Saugzubehör 289
Säule 47, 64, 403, 405, 424, 425, 460, 461, 482, 485, 540
Säule, bedeckte 64
Säulenordnung, dorische 404
Säulenordnung, ionische 404
Säulenordnung, korinthische 405
Saum 285, 455, 798
Saumlatte 676
Saummaß 454
Saumrand 127
saure Sahne 210
saurer Regen 69, 70
saurer Schnee 70
Savanne 61, 66
Säwerkzeuge 324
Saxhorn 447
Saxophon 446
Scandium 683
Scanner 181, 517
Schabe, orientalische 101
Schaber 320, 422
Schabracke 282
Schach 916
Schachbrett 916
Schachfiguren 916
Schacht 650
Schachtel, Käse 223
Schachtelfalte 283
Schachtgerüst 650
Schachtgerüsteingang 649
Schachtsumpf 650
Schädel 106, 109, 116, 121, 126, 136, 138, 141, 142, 146, 158
Schädel eines Kleinkindes 158
Schädel, Seitenansicht 158
schädliche Gase, Emission 69
Schadstoffe, biologisch nicht abbaubare 69
Schaf 128
Schäferhund, Deutscher 130
Schaffnertisch 584
Schafstall 182
Schaft 115, 301, 302, 306, 309, 405, 453, 456, 457, 460, 610, 793, 816, 822, 838, 857, 858, 859, 860, 861, 863, 867, 880, 918
Schaftführung 857
Schaftstiefel 343
Schäftung 912
Schäkel 835
Schäkelband 610
Schal 337
Schale 82, 84, 105, 106, 117, 222, 389
Schalenhaut 117
Schalenschuh 895
Schalensitz: Seitenansicht 555
Schalensitz: Vorderansicht 555
Schäler 229
Schälfurnier 300
Schalkragen 362
Schallbecher 444
Schallbecherstütze 446
Schallbrett 411
Schalldämpfer 553, 649
Schalloch 439
Schallplatte 500
Schallplattenladen 714
Schallrille 500
Schallrose 440
Schälmesser 229
Schalotte 184
Schalter 274, 290, 291, 305, 307, 308, 320, 381, 382, 383, 384, 687, 731
Schalter für Belüftung 556
Schalter für Heizung 556
Schalter, einpoliger 272
Schalter, zweipoliger 272
Schalterabdeckplatte 274
Schalthebel 552, 556, 577, 579, 580, 870
Schaltpedal 575, 576
Schaltraum 10
Schalttafel 261
Schaltuhr 290
Schaltung, gedruckte 689
Schaltung, integrierte 689
Schaltzug 580
Scham 148, 171
Schambein 122, 146, 148
Schamhügel 170
Schamlippe, große 170, 171
Schamlippe, kleine 170, 171
Schamotteplatte 256
Schamottestein 256
Schanzentisch 890, 891
Schanzkleid 602
Schar 641
Schärbaum 462
Schardrehkranz 639
Schardrehzylinder 639
Scharfeinsteller 485
Scharfeinstellung 14, 15
Scharfeinstellung, manuelle 483
Schärfentiefenknopf 476
Schärfentiefenskala 478
Scharfsteller 485
Scharfstellrad, zentrales 692

Scharfstellring 478, 692
Scharhubzylinder 639
Scharnier 238, 247, 249, 278, 294, 386, 389, 465, 500, 554, 575, 692
Scharniergelenk 156
Scharrknochen 121
Scharverstellvorrichtung 639
Scharwachturm 408, 409
Schatten 696
Schattenring 58
Schaubild für das Webprinzip 463
Schaufel 637, 888, 892
Schaufel, hintere 637
Schaufelarm 637
Schaufelblatt 659
Schaufelbolzengelenk 637
Schaufellader 637
Schaufelrad 599
Schaufelradbagger 647
Schaufelraddampfer 599
Schaufelzahn 638
Schaufelzylinder 637, 638
Schaukelstuhl 276, 277
Schaum 49
Schaumanzeiger 607
Schaumbad 379
Schaumgummiisolierung 299
Schaumgummimatratze 904
Schaumgummipolsterung 772
Schauspieler 428
Schauspielereingang 402
Schauspielerin 429
Schauspielerstühle 428
Scheckheft 386
Scheckhülle 387
Scheckkarte 731
Schecks 729
Scheibe 9, 249, 423, 641, 851
Scheiben 237
Scheibenarm 641
Scheibenbremse 552, 559, 574, 874
Scheibenbremse, hydraulische 870
Scheibenhantel 850
Scheibenhinterrad 871
Scheibenkopf 464
Scheibensech 641
Scheibensechshalter 641
Scheibenschraube 606
Scheibenwaschdüse 550
Scheibenwischer 550, 557
Scheibenwischerhebel 556
Scheide 76, 170, 171, 307, 841, 907
Scheide, Schwannsche 168
Scheidewand 82, 84, 175
Scheidewandknorpel 175
Scheider 562
Scheinwerfer 333, 428, 431, 550, 570, 574, 576, 579, 585, 586, 640, 758, 766, 876
Scheinwerferraum 614
Scheitel 115
Scheitelbein 131, 153, 158
Scheitelpunkt 829
Scheitelrippe 410
Scheitelstück 749
Schekel, neuer 728
Schelfeis, Filchner 29
Schelfeis, Ross 29
Schelle 59, 449
Schellen 449
Schellfisch 221
Schema des Blutkreislaufs 161
Schenkel 96, 98, 115, 124, 127, 911
Schenkelbein 153
Schenkelbindenspanner 150
Schenkelhals 153
Schenkelmuskel, äußerer 150, 151
Schenkelmuskel, gerader 150
Schenkelmuskel, innerer 150
Schenkelmuskel, zweiköpfiger 151
Schenkelring 96, 98
Scherbaum 857
Schere 107, 454, 777, 905
Scherenaufhängung 492
Scherenblatt, gekerbtes 382
Scherenbrille 385
Scherenleuchte 287
Scherenschliff 375
Scherenstromabnehmer 585, 595
Scherkopf 383
Scherkopfhalter 383
Scheuerleiste 560
Scheuerrippe 561
Scheuklappe 857
Scheune 182
Schichten, überlagernde 647
Schiebebach 551
Schiebedeckel 612
Schiebefenster, horizontales 415
Schiebefenster, vertikales 415
Schiebegriff 456, 783
Schiebeleiter 766
Schiebeöffnung 699
Schiebeplatte 452, 453
Schieber 391, 453, 465, 700, 754
Schieberad 783
Schiebetür 264, 416
Schiebetür, automatische 416
Schiebetür, elektrische 569

Schieblehre, Messschieber 700
Schiedsrichter 799, 801, 803, 805, 809, 810, 817, 818, 819, 820, 827, 828, 830, 842, 844, 847, 864, 877, 879, 882, 900
Schiedsrichter, berittener 858
Schiedsrichter, erster 813
Schiedsrichter, zweiter 813
Schienbein 122, 131, 138, 141, 142, 152, 155, 156
Schienbeinarterie, vordere 160
Schienbeinmuskel, vorderer 150
Schienbeinnerv 166
Schienbeinschutz 882
Schienbeinschützer 801, 802, 880, 887
Schiene 96, 98, 284, 287, 294, 456, 591, 791, 884, 895
Schiene im Querschnitt 591
Schienen 777
Schienenfuß 591
schienengleicher, gesicherter Bahnübergang 591
Schienenkopf 591
Schienenlasche 590
Schienenräumer 585, 586
Schienensteg 591
Schienenstoß 590
Schienenverkehr 582
Schießanlage 860, 893
Schießen 864
Schießgraben 860
Schießgrube 429
Schießleiter 859, 860
Schießlinie 859
Schießpositionen 861, 893
Schießscharte 409
Schießstand 769, 788, 860, 893
Schiff 41
Schiff-Luft-Flugkörper 762
Schiffe, historische 598
Schifffahrt 596
Schiffsanker 610
Schiffsbekämpfung, Rakete 759
Schiffsbodenverband 254
Schiffskiel 11
Schiffskörper 599
Schiffsschraube 606
Schiffssegel 11
Schiffstransport 649
Schiismus 736
Schiitakepilz 183
Schikane 872
Schild 10, 229, 425, 748, 772
Schildbogen 410
Schildchen 105
schildförmig 79
Schildfuß 740
Schildhaupt 740
Schildhubzylinder 636
Schildkröte 113
Schildkröte, Anatomie 113
Schildkröte, äußere Merkmale 113
Schildplätze 740
Schildwanze 101
Schimpanse 139
Schindel 299
Schinken, gekochter 216
Schinken, roher 216
Schinkenmesser 229
Schintoismus 736
Schirm 286, 391, 591, 799, 897
Schirmfeder 115
Schirmmütze 340
Schirmsegment 897
Schirmständer 391
Schirmwinde 462
Schisma, Morgenländisches 736
Schlackenhalde 648
Schlafanzug 364, 369
Schlafanzug in Schlupfform 369
Schlafanzug, zweiteilig 368
Schlafcouch 276
Schläfe 146
Schläfenbein 152, 158
Schlafkabine 570
Schlafplatz 584
Schlafraum 902
Schlafsäcke, Beispiele 904
Schlafwagen 584
Schlafwagenabteil 584
Schlafzimmer 251
Schlafzimmer, großes 251
Schlagbereich 797
Schlagbohrer 648
Schlagbolzen 755, 757
Schlagbolzenmechanismus 755
Schlagbolzenschutz 756
Schläge 820
Schläger 796, 797, 800, 801
Schlägerabdeckung 869
Schlägerblatt 800
Schlagfläche 867
Schlaghandschuh 796
Schlaghebel 791
Schlagholz 798
Schlaginstrumente 437, 448
Schlagmal 795

Schlagmallinie 799
Schlagmann 795, 796, 798, 799
Schlagpolster, elektronisches 451
Schlagrad 425
Schlagsahne 210
Schlagschrauber 873
Schlagschutz 441, 818
Schlagstockhalter 770
Schlagzeile 471
Schlammfles 47
Schlammgrube 651
Schlammpumpe 651
Schlammpumpenschlauch 651
Schlange 11, 13, 112
Schlangenträger 11, 13
Schlangenbohrer mit doppeltem Gewindegang 306
Schlankmuskel 151
Schlauch 289, 319, 767, 777
Schlauch für Wasserablauf 485
Schlauch für Wasserzufluss 485
Schlauch, flexibler 289
Schlauchdüse 328
Schlauchhalter 764
Schlauchkleid 356
Schlauchkupplung 328, 329
Schlauchleitung 649, 767
Schlauchtrockner 764
Schlauchwagen 328
Schlaufe 349, 377, 539
Schlechtwetterraum 727
Schlegel 401, 421, 448, 449
Schleier 909
Schleifblatt 308
Schleife 340
Schleifenkragen 362
Schleifpapier 308
Schleiffringe 688
Schleifscheibe 308, 423
Schleifteller 308
Schlepper 606, 622, 623
Schlepplift 886
Schleppseil 840
Schleppstange 756
Schleppvorrichtung 573
Schleuder 573
Schleudergefahr 545, 547
Schleudersitz 760
Schleuse 664
Schleuse: Seitenansicht 597
Schleusenkammer 597
Schleusentor, oberes 597
Schleusentor, unteres 597
Schleusenwand 597
Schließblech 249
Schließe 906
Schließfach 731
Schließfrucht 84
Schließklappe 675
Schließmuskel, hinterer 105
Schließmuskel, vorderer 105
Schließzylinder 249
Schliffformen 375
Schlinge 913
Schlingerwand 25
Schlingstiche 459
Schlitten 249, 835, 885
Schlitteneinstellung 456
Schlittschuh 878, 880
Schlittschuhe, Eisschnelllauf 883
Schlittschuhschritt 892
Schlittschuhs, diagonaler 892
Schlitz 227, 238, 302, 351, 368, 424
Schlitzschrauben 302
Schlitzverschluss 476, 477
Schloss 248, 278, 291, 387, 389, 454, 580
Schlossbrett 247
Schloßband 105
Schlucht 47, 48
Schluckloch 47
Schlupfform 369
Schlüssel 249, 311, 436
Schlüsselbein 116, 122, 141, 142, 152
Schlüsselbeinarterie 160
Schlüsselbeinvene 160
Schlüsseldienst 715
Schlüsseletui 387
Schlüsselloch 249
Schlüsselschild 387
Schlüsselschloss 386
Schlussleuchte 554, 575, 576, 640
Schlussstein 410, 413
schmal 472
Schmelz 159
Schmelzen 680
Schmelzwasser 46
Schmetterball 813, 821
Schmetterling 96
Schmetterling, Anatomie 97
Schmetterling, äußere Merkmale 96
Schmetterlingsstil 832
Schmierknopf 649
Schmiermittelraffinerie 656
Schmieröle 656
Schmiersystem 586
Schmirgelsäckchen 454
Schmorpfanne 235

Schmuck 374, 717
Schmuck und Schönheitspflege 374
Schmutzfänger 551, 570, 571
schmutziges Geschirr, Ablage 721
Schmutzwasserhebeanlage 263
Schnabel 115, 749
Schnabelschuh 339
Schnalle 350, 352, 388, 611
Schnallenabdeckung 855
Schnappmechanismus 910
Schnappschloss 386
Schnappverschluss 387
Schnarrsaite 448
Schnarrsaitenspanner 448
Schnauze 110, 121, 130, 132, 143
Schnauzer 130
Schnecke 104, 174, 217, 439, 573
Schnecke, Anatomie 104
Schnecke, äußere Merkmale 104
Schneckenbohrer 306
Schneckengetriebe 686
Schneckenpfännchen 233
Schneckenzange 233
Schnee 64
Schnee, ewiger 45
Schnee, saurer 70
Schneeanzug 369
Schneebesen 232
Schneefall, anhaltend leichter 57
Schneefall, anhaltend mäßiger 57
Schneefall, anhaltend starker 57
Schneefall, Messung 59
Schneefall, zeitweise leichter 57
Schneefall, zeitweise mäßiger 57
Schneefall, zeitweise starker 57
Schneefegen 57
Schneefeger 558
Schneefräse 573
Schneegamaschen 901
Schneekristalle 64
Schneemesser 58, 59
Schneemobil 876
Schneeregen 57, 64
Schneesack 368
Schneeschauer 57
Schneeschuh 893
Schneeschuh, elliptischer 893
Schneetreiben 57
Schneidbrett 229
Schneiddüse 319
Schneide 227, 229, 302, 382, 454, 881
Schneidedraht 464
Schneideeinsatz 319
Schneidegerät 484
Schneiden 309, 424
Schneiderärmel 361
Schneiderbüste 454
Schneiderkragen 355, 362
Schneidermuskel 150
Schneidezahn 121, 123
Schneidezahn, äußerer 159
Schneidezahn, mittlerer 159
Schneidezähne 159
Schneidkante 636, 637, 638
Schneidklinge 240
Schneidkopf 535
Schneidlade, Gehrung 303
Schneidmesser 236, 237
Schneidwerk 643
Schneidwerkzeuge 330
schnell drehende Welle 677
Schnellabrollbahn 618
Schnellhefter 532
Schnellkocher, elektrischer 239
Schnellkochtopf 234
Schnellkupplungssystem 482
Schnellspannbohrfutter 306
Schnellstraße 539
Schnellvorlauf-Taste 499
Schnellvorlauftaste 504
Schnittfläche 331
Schnittführung 424
Schnitthöhenverstellung 333
Schnittlauch 184
Schnittlinie 455
Schnittmuster 455
Schnittstelle, Ethernet 526
Schnittstelle, FireWire 526
Schnittstelle, serielle 513
Schnittstelle, USB 513, 526
Schnittstellen, Controller 918
Schnittstellenport, Computer 520
Schnitzbankschraube 401
Schnitzeisen, wichtigste 401
Schnitzel 214
Schnitzen 401
Schnorchel 841
Schnur 313, 424, 506
Schnur am Tritt 460
Schnürband 797
Schnurfangbügel 910
Schnurfeststeller 285
Schnurhaken 881
Schnurlaufröllchen 910
Schnürloch 342
Schnürlochteil 342
schnurloses Telefon 507
Schnüröse 881

Schnurrhaare 132
Schnürringe, Ranviersche 168
Schnürschuh 342
Schnürsenkel 342, 370, 843, 881
Schnürsenkelende 342, 370
Schnurspanner 284
Schnurversteller 285
Schnurwelle 284
Schokolade 208
Schokolade, weiße 208
Scholle 221
Schollenmuskel 150
Schoner 601
Schonwaschgang 347
Schöpflöffel 233
Schöpfteil 227
Schornstein 245, 599, 604, 608, 646
Schössling 77, 87
Schoß 349, 359
Schoßrock 338
Schot 603
Schote 84
Schote, Schnitt 84
Schottenrock 357
Schotter 591
Schotterfläche 46
Schottisch-Gälisch 469
schräg geteilt 740
schräg zum Fadenlauf 455
Schräge 776
schräge Pattentasche 352, 355, 360
schräger Interlobärspalt 163
Schrägförderer 643
Schräggeison 403
Schrägmaß 313
Schrägseilbrücke 541
Schrägseilverankerung 541
Schrägstellungsvorrichtung 304
Schrägstrich 473
Schrank 510
Schranke 591
Schrankteil 279
Schrapper 638
Schratten 47
Schraube 248, 302, 439, 606, 608, 609, 763
Schrauben 311, 762
Schraubenbolzen 311
Schraubenbolzen mit Ansatz 311
Schraubendreher 302
Schraubenfeder 553, 586
Schraubenkarabiner 900
Schraubenwelle 605, 609
Schraubenzieher 302, 905
Schraubfassung 275
Schraubfeder 900
Schraubfläche 843
Schraubklemme 272
Schraubstock 312
Schraubstollen 802
Schraubverschluss 223
Schraubwerkzeuge 302
Schreib-/Lesekopf 521
Schreiber 2
Schreibgeräte 470
Schreibkopf 528
Schreibmappe 387
Schreibmaschine, elektrische 528
Schreibpinsel 470
Schreibplatte, herausklappbare 279
Schreibschutz 521
Schreibspitze 43
Schreibtisch 724
Schreibtisch-Videogerät 520
Schreibtischleuchte 286
Schreibunterlage 511
Schreibwaren 528, 717
schreitender Löwe 741
Schriftarten 472
Schriftführer 814
Schriftgrößenskala 528
Schriftstärke 472
Schritt 124, 351, 359
Schritte 435
Schrittlängeneinstellung 700
Schrittzähler, Pedometer 700
Schrot 912
Schrotflinte 860
Schrotflinte (glatter Lauf) 912
Schubdüse 20
Schubfach 279
Schubkarre 323
Schubkasten 281
Schubkontrolle 516
Schubkurbelverschluss 756
Schublade 224, 278, 279
Schubladenelement, fahrbares 510
Schubphase 892
Schubrahmen 636
Schubrechwender 642
Schuh 342, 801, 810, 841, 870, 872
Schuh mit Stoßplatten 808
Schuhbürste 345
Schuhcreme 345
Schuhe 342
Schuhgeschäft 715
Schuhlöffel 345

Schuhputzzeug 345
Schuhspanner 345
Schuhständer 345
Schukosteckdose 274
Schukostecker 274
Schulaufsicht, Büro 735
Schulbank 734
Schulbus 568
Schule 547, 734
Schüler mit Lernschwierigkeiten, Klassenzimmer 734
Schüler/Schülerin 734
Schülerspinde 735
Schulhof 735
Schulleiter, Büro 735
Schulter 124, 130, 146, 148, 156, 440, 909
Schulterblatt 111, 116, 121, 122, 126, 131, 136, 138, 141, 142, 147, 149, 152, 153, 156
Schulterblattgräte 153
Schulterfeder 115
Schultergurt 555, 869, 906
Schulterklappe 352, 770
Schulterpolster 808, 880
Schulterriemen 388, 391, 527
Schulterriemen, Öse 476
Schulterstütze 755, 757
Schultertasche 388
Schuppe 108, 112, 113
Schuppen 244, 322
Schuppenblatt 78
Schuppennaht 158
Schürhaken 257
Schürkübel 638
Schürze, elastische 605
Schürzenfinger 605
Schuss 460, 461
Schüssel 237
Schussfaden 463
Schusskreis 800
Schüttelsieb 651
Schüttgutwagen 588
Schüttungsisolierung 299
Schutz 305
Schutzanzug 875
Schutzausrüstung 808
Schutzbezug 280
Schutzblech 578, 876
Schutzblech, vorderes 574
Schutzbrille 318, 772, 818, 819, 861, 870, 875, 896
Schutzdach 632
Schutzdeckel 513
Schütze 10, 860
Schützer, Schienbein 887
Schutzfläche 843
Schutzgehäuse 332
Schutzgeländer 586
Schutzgitter 281, 316, 730
Schutzglas 494
Schutzhandschuhe 774
Schutzhandschuhe tragen 774
Schutzhaube 304, 305, 308
Schutzhaube, obere 304
Schutzhaube, untere 304
Schutzhelm 575, 772, 774, 808, 878, 896, 897
Schutzhelm tragen 774
Schutzkäfig 791
Schutzkante 389
Schutzkappe 692, 776, 783
Schutzkasten für Handbremse 587
Schutzkleidung 318
Schutzkontaktbügel 274
Schutzmaske 772
Schutzmaßnahmen 774
Schutzpolster 823
Schutzplatte 875
Schutzraum 543
Schutzring 290
Schutzschicht 20
Schutzschirm 318
Schutzschuhe 774
Schutzschuhe tragen 774
Schutzumrandung 918
Schutzwand 878
schwach verstärkende Antenne 18
schwacher Punkt 916
Schwadenblech 332, 333
Schwager 785
Schwägerinnen 785
Schwalbe 118
Schwamm 95, 295, 752
Schwamm, Anatomie 95
Schwammstäbchen 378
Schwan 12
Schwanenhals 638
Schwannsche Scheide 168
Schwanz 107, 112, 113, 121, 122, 124, 130, 133, 136, 140, 143, 169, 425, 909
Schwanzfächer 107
Schwanzfeder 115
Schwanzflosse 108, 136
Schwanzflughaut 140
Schwanzwirbel 122, 126, 131, 138, 141, 142

Schwarte 300
Schwarz 690, 916
schwarz 741
schwarzäugige Bohne 190
Schwarzbär 135
schwarze Bohne 191
schwarze Johannisbeere 192
schwarze Klemme 558
schwarze Mungobohne 191
schwarze Senfkörner 198
schwarzer Ball 863
schwarzer Pfeffer 198
schwarzer Stein 916
schwarzer Tee 208
Schwarzer Zwerg 8
schwarzes Brett 734
schwarzes Feld 916
Schwarzes Loch 8
Schwarzes Meer 28, 32, 33
Schwarzrettich 189
Schwarzwurzel 189
Schwebebalken 824, 826
Schweden 744
Schwedisch 469
Schwefel 683
Schwefeldioxid, Emission 70
Schwefelsäure, Emission 70
Schwein 128
Schweinefleisch 215
Schweinehackfleisch 215
Schweinespeck 209
Schweinestall 182
Schweißband 822
Schweißblatt 855
Schweißbrenner 319
Schweißdrüse, apokrine 172
Schweißdrüse, Ausführungsgang 172
Schweißdrüse, ekkrine 172
Schweißeinsatz 319
Schweißerhandschuh, fünffingriger 318
Schweißtransformator 318
Schweißwerkzeuge 318
Schweiz 744
schweizer Offiziersmesser 905
Schwelle 247, 253, 591
Schwellenmarkierungen 621
Schwellenschraube 590
Schwenkarm 236
schwenkbare Halterung 613
schwenkbare Parabolantenne 16
Schwenkbrückenstand 638
Schwenkdüse 628
Schwenkflügel 630
Schwenkkopf 312
Schwenklade 460
Schwenksockel 312
Schwenkverschluss 312
Schwenkverstellung für das Sägeblatt 305
schwere Piste 886
Schwerfahrzeugen, Transport 588
Schwergewichtsstaudamm im Querschnitt 661
Schwerkraftmodul 21
Schwermaschinen 636
Schweröl 656
Schwert 331, 834, 840
Schwert, beidhändiges 751
Schwertfisch 11, 219
Schwertwal 137
Schwerwasser 670
Schwerwasser unter Druck 670
Schwerwasser, kaltes 670
Schwerwasseranreicherung 669
Schwerwasserreaktor 670
Schwester 785
Schwesternstation 778, 779
Schwesternzimmer 781
Schwiegereltern 784
Schwiegermutter 784
Schwiegersohn 784
Schwiegertochter 784
Schwiegervater 784
Schwierigkeitskampfrichter 823
Schwimmbecken 246, 675, 788, 827, 831
Schwimmbecken, eingebautes 246
Schwimmblase 109
Schwimmbrille 830
Schwimmdach 655
Schwimmdachtank 655
Schwimmen 830
Schwimmer 263, 265, 756, 911
Schwimmerin, Name 831
Schwimmerin, Nationalität 831
Schwimmerstange 263
Schwimmerventil 265
Schwimmfuß 110
Schwimmhaut 110, 117
Schwimmhautzeh 117
Schwimmholz 827
Schwimmkörper 615, 628
Schwimmkran 596
Schwimmlappenzeh 117
Schwimmstadion 788
Schwimmzeiten 831
Schwinger 613
Schwingflügel 551
Schwinggaragentor 416
Schwinghebel 566

schwingungsdämpfender Bügelgriff 331
Schwingungsdämpfer 292
Schwungholen 864
Schwungrad 464, 566, 851
Scotia-Platte 43
Scrimmage-Linie 807
Scriptgirl 429
Scrollen 515
Scrollen-Feststelltaste 515
Scrollrad 506, 516
Scrolltaste 505
Seaborgium 683
Sech 643
Sechseck, regelmäßiges 705
Sechserpasch 914
Sechskantmutter 311, 562
Sechskantreduzierhülse 269
Sechzehntelnote 435
Sechzehntelpause 435
Second 877
Sedimentgesteine 42
See 7, 38, 45, 48
See, Irische 32
See, künstlicher 48
See, tektonischer 48
See, vulkanischer 48
See-See-Flugkörper 762
Seebarsch 220
Seehund 137
Seeigel 95
Seelachs 221
Seelöwe 137
Seen 48
Seen, Große 30
Seenversauerung 70
Seeotter 134
Seestern, Anatomie 95
Seestern, äußere Merkmale 95
Seeteufel 220
Seezeichen 614
Segel 603, 836
Segel, Beispiele 601
Segelboot 834
Segelflugzeug 898
Segelkleid 834
Segellatte 600, 834, 836
Segeln mit halbem Wind 833
Segelsport 833
Segelstange 676
Segeltasche 836
Segeltuchbespannung 676
Segerkegel 464
Segmentpunktzahl 918
Sehen 691
Sehenswürdigkeit 39
Sehfehler 691
Sehne 133, 913
Sehnenschützer 880
Sehnerv 177
Sehnervenkreuzung 167
Sehschlitz 749
Seifenbecher 383
Seifenschale 264
Seiher 231
Seil 321, 542, 686, 823, 824, 842, 900, 901, 908
Seilbahn 886
Seilbahnabfahrt 886
Seilschaft 900
Seilverspannung 842
Seilzug 321
seismische Welle 43
Seismogramm 43
Seismographen 43
seismologische Aufzeichnung 651, 653
Seite 227, 425, 431, 602
Seite, linke 300, 384
Seite, nächste 515
Seite, rechte 300, 384
Seite, vorherige 515
Seitenansicht 798
Seitenansicht eines Schädels 158
Seitenauslinie 803
Seitenband, vertikales 812
Seitenfach 554
Seitenfeintrieb 701
Seitenfenster 551
Seitenflosse 625, 631, 760, 898
Seitenfontanelle, hintere 158
Seitenfontanelle, vordere 158
Seitengriff 307, 554
Seitenkampfrichter 845, 846
Seitenkapelle 410
Seitenkästen 873
Seitenklemme 701
Seitenkoffer 577
Seitenlinie 108, 800, 805, 806, 809, 810, 812, 814, 815, 858, 864, 877
Seitenlinie für das Doppelspiel 817, 820
Seitenlinie für das Einzelspiel 817, 821
Seitenluke 22
Seitenmoräne 46
Seitenöffnung 540
Seitenrad 676
Seitenrichter 805, 838
Seitenruder 625, 760, 898
Seitenruderpedal 898

Seitenschiff 411
Seitenschlot 44
Seitenschwinge 460
Seitenspiegel 381, 550, 570, 576
Seitenspiegelverstellhebel 554
Seitensprossen 587
Seitenspur 539
Seitenständer 575
Seitensteg 385
Seitenstollen 650
Seitenstück 277
Seitentasche 869
Seitenteil 352, 632
Seitenverkleidung 551
Seitenverstellhebel 309
Seitenwand 127, 561, 571, 635, 818, 819, 831
Seitenwandlinie 819
Seitenwurzel 77
seitliche Einfassung 256
seitliche Strahlgrube 127
seitlicher Hautnerv des Oberschenkels 166
seitlicher knöcherner Bogengang 174
seitlicher Kompressionsgurt 906
seitlicher Rückenschlitz 348
Seitpferd 824, 826
Sekretär 279
Sekretariat 731, 735
Sekretärin 509
Sektion, obere 24
Sektion, untere 24
Sektionalgaragentor 416
Sektkelch 225
Sektor 704
Sektschale 225
Sekundant 842
Sekundärfokuskabine 16
Sekundärkonsumenten 67
Sekundärspiegel 15, 16, 17, 477
Sekunde 434, 702
Sekundenzeiger 696, 697
selbst schreibender Regenmesser 59
selbstaufblasbare Luftmatratze 904
Selbstauslöser 476
Selbstauslöser-Lichtsignal 476
Selbstbedienungsrestaurant 722
Selbstbedienungstheke 180, 722
Selbstklebeetiketten 532
selbstklebende Lasche 531
Selen 682
Seltenerdmetalle 684
Sendeantenne 486
Sendeimpuls 40
Sendeleiter 489, 490
Sendereinstellung 498, 504
Sendersuchlauf, automatischer 498
Sendersuchlauftasten 497
Sendung mit Radio-Wellen 486
Senegal 34, 745
Senf 84, 200
Senf, amerikanischer 200
Senf, deutscher 200
Senf, englischer 200
Senfkörner 200
Senfkörner, schwarze 198
Senfkörner, weiße 198
Senfpulver 200
Senkkopf mit Imbus 302
Senkkopf mit Kreuzschlitz 302
Senkkopf mit Schlitz 302
senkrechte Kelimbindung 463
senkrechte Pupille 112
senkrechte Tasche 337
senkrechter Rahmen 461
Senkrechtstartflugzeug 628
Sense 330
sensibles Neuron 168
Sensor 58, 238
Sensor für Fernbedienung 494
Sensor, aktiver 41
Sensor, optischer 516
Sensor, passiver 41
Sensorhülse 238
sensorischer Rezeptor 168
Sensorkreis 559
Sepalum 82
Separator 689
Septime 434
Septum pellucidum 167
Sequencer 450
Sequenzerregler 450
Serac 46
Serbokroatisch 469
serielle Schnittstelle 513
Seriennummer 729
Serifenschrift 472
Server 522, 523, 524, 525
Service-Bereich 548
Servicemodul, ferngesteuertes 21
Servierplatte 226
Serviertisch 720
Servierwagen 278
Servietten 722
Sesambein 126
Sesamöl 209
Sessellift 886
Sessselliftabfahrt 886
Setzen des Spinnakers 833

Setzholz 278
Setzstufe 255
Sextant 11, 612
Sexte 434
Sextett 438
Seychellen 746
Shake-Hands-Griff 815
Shampoo 379
Sheddach 414
Shinai 847
Shortline 819
Shorts 358, 371
Siamkatze 133
Sichel 330
Scheldüne 52
Sicherheit 764
Sicherheitsbereich 844
Sicherheitsbindung 888, 889
Sicherheitsdienst 719, 779
Sicherheitsfaden 729
Sicherheitsfilter, roter 485
Sicherheitsfläche 846
Sicherheitsgriff 332
Sicherheitsgurt 555, 873
Sicherheitshinweisschild 306
Sicherheitsholm 321
Sicherheitshülle 665, 667
Sicherheitskette 567
Sicherheitskontrolle 621
Sicherheitsleiste 291
Sicherheitsleuchte 771
Sicherheitsnadel 453
Sicherheitsraum 728
Sicherheitsriemen 20, 818
Sicherheitsschuh 773
Sicherheitssensor 556
Sicherheitsspiegel 568
Sicherheitsstreichholz 391
Sicherheitsstreifen 593
Sicherheitstank 670
Sicherheitsthermostat 293
Sicherheitsventil 234, 259, 267, 665
sicherstes Wasser 616
Sicherung 273, 663, 673, 755
Sicherungen, Beispiele 272
Sicherungsabschnitt 663
Sicherungsautomat 260, 658
Sicherungsbalken 900
Sicherungskappe 757
Sicherungsknopf 554
Sicherungskopf 302
Sicherungsmann 900
Sicherungsseil 900
Sicherungsstift 767
Sicherungsträger 663
Sicherungszieher 317
sichtbares Licht 690
Sichtfenster 23, 238, 239, 290, 485
Sichtlinie 907
Sickeranlage 263
Sickerrohr 253
Sieb 237, 240
Siebbeinplatte 175
Siebeneck, regelmäßiges 705
Siedewasser 671
Siedewasserreaktor 671
Sieger 789
Sierra Leone 745
Sigmoid 164
Signal 583
Signal, akustisches 436
Signal, optisches 436
Signalanlage 859
Signalbrücke 583
Signalhorn 586
Signalleiste 766
Signalschirm 591
Signatur 426
Silber 683, 741
Silberbesteck 227
Silizium 682
Silos 596
Silur 92
Sima 404
Simbabwe 746
Simultandolmetscherkabine 718
Sinfonieorchester 437
Singapur 747
Sinkblei 911
Sinnesorgane 172, 173, 177
sinotibetische Sprachen 468
Sinus 336
Sinushaar 122
Siphonalkanal 105
Siphonwinkel 269
Sirene 611
Sistrum 449
Sitz 264, 265, 276, 277, 281, 333, 464, 555, 577, 783, 839, 851, 855, 857, 876, 897, 898
Sitz des Rettungsassistenten 775
Sitz, verstellbarer 584
Sitzbank 277, 555, 575, 593, 775, 876
Sitzbein 153
Sitzgürtel 900
Sitzmöbel 277
Sitzplatz 427
Sitzplätze 431

Sitzrohr 578
Sitzsack 277
Sitzungsraum 730, 764
Sitzungsräume 718
Sitzungssaal 394, 724
Sitzverstellung 555
Skala 305, 313, 695, 698, 700, 776, 907
Skateboard 894
Skateboarder 894
Skateboarding 894
Skaterin 895
Skeleton 885
Skelett 152
Skelett einer Fledermaus 141
Skelett einer Giftschlange 112
Skelett einer Ratte 122
Skelett eines Froschs 111
Skelett eines Delphins 136
Skelett eines Gorillas 138
Skelett eines Hunds 131
Skelett eines Kängurus 142
Skelett eines Maulwurfs 121
Skelett eines Pferdes 126
Skelett eines Vogels 116
Skelettbürste 380
Ski 888
Skianzug 887, 888, 892
Skibremse 889
Skibrille 887, 888
Skier, Beispiele 840, 888
Skigebiet 886
Skihandschuhe 888
Skihütte 886
Skilanglauf 892
Skiliftankunft 886
Skimmer 246
Skimütze 892
Skip 877
Skipiste 886
Skipisten 886
Skischule 886
Skispitze 892
Skispringen 891
Skispringer 891
Skisprunganzug 891
Skisprungschuh 891
Skistiefel 888, 889, 892
Skistock 888, 892
Skiträger 558
Skorpion 10, 102
Skript-Assistent 490
Skull 838
Skullen (zwei Skulls) 838
Skulptur 395
Slalomski 840, 888
slawische Sprachen 469
Slider 896
Slingpumps 343
Slip 351, 367
Slipper 344
Slipstek 908
Slowakisch 469
Slowakische Republik 744
Slowenien 744
Slowenisch 469
SLR-Kamera 476
Smaragd 375
Smilodon 93
Smog 69
Smokstich 459
Snackbar 427
Snooker 863
Snowboard 887
Snowboarden 887
Snowboarder 887
Sobanudeln 207
Socke 365, 808, 822
Sockel 58, 256, 274, 275, 286, 381, 412, 440, 500, 591, 676, 698, 825, 826
Sockel, fester 312
Sockel, gepolsterter 811
Sockelbreite 663
Sockelgeschoß 676
Sockelleiste 253, 255, 417
Sockelplatte 701
Sockelprofil 278
Socken 351
Sofa 276
Sofa, zweisitziges 724
Soffitte 431
Soffitten 430
Sofortbildkamera 480
Softball 797
Softballhandschuh 797
Softballschläger 797
Softbindung 887
Softboots 887
Software, E-Mail 524
Sohle 309, 351, 650, 868, 881, 889
Sohlenballen 130, 133
Sohlenspanner 151
Sohlschicht, obere 646
Sohlschicht, untere 646
Sohn 784, 785
Sojabohnen 191

Sojasoße 200
Sojasprossen 191
Solarhaus 675
Solarreflektoren 486
Solarzelle 529, 672, 673
Solarzellenfläche 60
Solarzellenfläche, Steuerung 60
Solarzellengenerator 21
Solarzellensystem 673
Solitärring 376
Solltemperatur 261
Solvent-Extraktionsanlage 656
Somalia 745
Somennudeln 207
Sommer 31
Sommersonnenwende 54
Sonar 41
Sonde 18
Sonderfunktionstasten 456
Sonderzeichen 617
Sonne 4, 6, 7, 54
Sonne, Aufbau 6
Sonnenblende 14, 556, 567
Sonnenblume 80
Sonnenblumenöl 209
Sonnenbrille 385
Sonnendeck 607, 609
Sonneneinstrahlung 68
Sonneneinstrahlung, absorbierte 68
Sonneneinstrahlung, Messung 58
Sonneneinstrahlung, reflektierte 68
Sonnenenergie 78, 672, 674
Sonnenfinsternis 6
Sonnenfleck 6
Sonnenkleid, leichtes 356
Sonnenkollektor 675
Sonnenofen 674
Sonnenrollo 558
Sonnenscheinautograph 58
Sonnenschutz, Windschutzscheiben 558
Sonnenschutzblende 496
Sonnenschutzschicht 20
Sonnensegel 17, 18, 60
Sonnensensor 40, 60
Sonnenspiegel 674
Sonnenstrahl, reflektierter 674
Sonnenstrahlen 67
Sonnenstrahlung 672, 673, 674, 675
Sonnensystem 4
Sonnenuhr 696
Sonnenzellenausleger 40, 486
Sonnenzellenkollektor 673
Sortierablagen, automatische 512
Sortieranlage 71
Sortiermaschine 475
Sortierung von Glas 71
Sortierung von Kunststoff 71
Sortierung von Metall 71
Sortierung von Papier/Pappe 71
Sortierung, optische 71
Sortierzentrum 474
Sorus 76
Soufléform 232
Sozialarbeiterbüro 779
Sozialdiensträume 781
Soziussitz 577
Spachtel 421
Spaghetti 206
Spaghettikürbis 189
Spaghettini 206
Spaghettizange 233
Spalier 322
Spalierbogen 322
Spalt 82
spaltbarer Kern 681
Spalte 471
Spaltprodukte (radioaktive Kerne) 681
Späneschutz 305
Spangang 306
Spange 352
Spanien 743
Spanisch 469
Spannbeton 298
Spannbetttuch 280
Spanneinrichtung 452, 453, 457
Spanner 283, 826, 902
Spanner, Werkstück 303
Spannfeder 453, 457, 850
Spannfutter 649
Spanngriff 312
Spannhandgriff 460
Spannhebel 305, 757
Spannkabel 676, 859
Spannkabelhalter 859
Spannmast 897
Spannpratze 312
Spannrad 636, 696, 697
Spannscheibe 453, 457
Spannschnur 433
Spannschraube 309, 312, 448
Spannseil 824
Spannstich, kurzer 459
Spannstich, langer 459
Spannung, elektrische 774
Spannungseinsteller 453, 456, 457
Spannungserhöhung, erste 677
Spannungserhöhung, zweite 677
Spannungsprüfer 316

Spannungssammelschiene 272
Spannungsstift 274
Spannweite 312
Spannweite, eingehängte 540
Spanplatte 300
Spantransport, Sattelanhänger 572
Sparbuchnachtrag 730
Spareribs/Schälrippchen 215
Spargel 185
Spargelbohne 190
Spargelsalat 186
Sparren 252, 740
sparriges Torfmoos 75
spatelförmig 79
Spaten 326, 756
Spazierstock 391, 782
Specht 118
Speedskate 895
Speedski 891
Speedskianzug 891
Speedskifahrer 891
Speedskistrecke 891
Speer 748, 793
Speerspitze 793
Speerwurf 791
Speiche 103, 116, 121, 122, 126, 131, 136, 138, 141, 142, 152, 154, 156, 579
Speicheldrüse 97, 99, 104, 176
Speichelkanal 99
Speichennerv 166
Speichenrad 857
Speichenseite, Handstrecker 151
Speicheradditionstaste 529
Speicheranzeigetaste 529
Speichereinheit, Backup 523
Speichergeräte 521
Speicherkarte 477
Speicherkartenschächte 918
Speicherkraftwerk 657
Speicherlöschtaste 479, 529
Speichersubtraktionstaste 529
Speichertaste 479, 497, 498, 501, 506
Speisekabel 272
Speisekammer 250
Speisekarte 721
Speisekopf 669
Speisen, warme 722
Speiseraum 584, 727, 764
Speiseröhre 109, 112, 163, 164
Speisesaal 608, 720, 723, 724
Speisewagen 584
Speisewasser 670, 671
Spektrometer 694
Spektroradiometer 60
Spektrum, elektromagnetisches 690
Spenzer 358
Sperling 118
Spermatheka 97, 103, 104
Spermium 169
Sperrdrehknopf 700
Sperre 712
Sperrengeschoss 592
Sperrholzschichten 300
Sperrklinke 307
Sperrrad 460, 697
Sperrstift 696, 697
Spezialflachwagen 588
Spezialitäten 216
Spezialslalom 889
spezifische Operationen 529
Spicknadel 233
Spiegel 20, 264, 389, 535, 556, 577, 693, 724, 907
Spiegel, beleuchteter 381
Spiegel, ebener 17
Spiegel, teilreflektierender 692
Spiegel, vollreflektierender 692
Spiegelreflexkamera im Querschnitt 477
Spiegelreflexkamera, digitale 477
Spiegelreflexkamera, einäugige 476, 480
Spiegelreflexkamera, zweiäugige 480
Spiegelteleskop 15
Spiegelteleskop im Querschnitt 15
Spiegelzylinder 692
Spiel 822
Spielanzug 369
Spielball 862, 863
Spielbereich 918
Spielbrett 915, 916
Spiele 788, 914
Spiele mit Schlägern 815
Spielekonsole 918
Spieler 789, 822, 827, 920
Spielerbank 794, 801, 807, 809, 812, 814, 878
Spielerhandikap 858
Spielerinnen 822
Spielernummer 808, 810, 878
Spielerpositionen 794, 803, 804, 811, 814
Spielerstühle 813
Spielertrense 854
Spieleschnittstelle 513
Spielfeld 794, 799, 801, 802, 804, 809, 810, 812, 813, 814, 818, 819, 858, 864, 915, 917, 920
Spielfeld für American Football 806
Spielfeld für kanadischen Football 809

ASTRONOMIE > 2-25;   ERDE > 26-71;   PFLANZENREICH >72-89;   TIERREICH > 90-143;   MENSCH > 144-177;   NAHRUNGSMITTEL UND KÜCHE > 178-241;   HAUS > 242-295;
HEIMWERKEN UND GARTENARBEIT > 296-333;   KLEIDUNG > 334-371;   PERSÖNLICHE AUSSTATTUNG > 372-391;   KUNST UND ARCHITEKTUR > 392-465;   KOMMUNIKATION UND BÜROTECHNIK > 466-535;
TRANSPORT UND FAHRZEUGE > 536-643;   ENERGIE > 644-677;   WISSENSCHAFT > 678-705;   GESELLSCHAFT > 706-785;   SPORT UND SPIELE > 786-920

Spielfeldbeläge 822
Spielfigur 915
Spielfläche 815
Spielgeld 915
Spielstand 789
Spielstein 916
Spielventil 445
Spielwaren 717
Spielwarengeschäft 714
Spielzeit 789
Spierentonne 614, 617
Spießblattnase 141
Spike 791, 901
Spikereifen 560
Spikulen 6
Spinalganglion 167, 168
Spinat 187
Spindel 105, 248, 268, 425, 462, 697
Spindelarretierknopf 308
Spindelfalte 105
Spinnaker, Bergen 833
Spinnaker, Setzen 833
Spinndrüsen 103
Spinne 103
Spinne, Anatomie 103
Spinne, äußere Merkmale 103
Spinnennetz 103
Spinnentiere 96
Spinnentiere, Beispiele 102
Spinnerschachtel 911
Spinnrute 910
Spinnwarze 103
Spiralarm 9
Spiralbindung 909
Spiralbohrer 306
Spirale 306, 484, 752
Spiralfeder 696
spiralförmiges Wolkenband 63
Spiralgalaxie, normale 9
Spiralgehäuse 659
Spiralheftung 533
Spiralkneter 236
Spiralnagel 301
Spiralringbuch 533
Spiralskulptur 105
Spiralspindel 302
Spiralwülste rollen 465
Spirulina 183
Spitzbogen 413
Spitze 45, 79, 159, 185, 227, 229, 288, 301, 302, 303, 315, 351, 390, 391, 439, 453, 457, 470, 602, 627, 739, 792, 840, 868, 880, 882, 893, 900, 909, 912, 918
Spitze, nicht wärmeleitend 381
Spitze, verjüngte 839
Spitzenhandschuh, fingerloser 346
Spitzenkopf 849
Spitzenvolant 337
spitzer Winkel 704
spitzes Dekolleté 363
Spitzmaus 121
Spitzsegel 601
Spitzsieb 231
Spitztonne 615, 617
Spitzzange 317
Spleiß 908
Splint 249
Splintholz 87
Splitterkörper, Bakelit 757
Spoiler 574, 891
Spongiosa 154
Spongoöl 95
Sporen 76
Sporn 98, 140
Sport 788
Sportanlagen 709, 788
Sportartikelgeschäft 715
Sportbekleidung, Damen 716
Sportbekleidung, Herren 717
Sportbekleidung, Kinder 717
Sporteinrichtungen 788
Sportfischerei 909
Sportgymnastik, rhythmische 823
Sporthalle 608, 727, 788
Sporthose 791
Sportkleidung 370, 371
Sportklettern 900
Sportplatz 608
Sportreifen 560
Sportschuhe 716
Sportset 369
Sportwagen 549
Spot 287
Spotlight 492
Spotmeter 479
Sprachanzeigetaste 507
Sprachaufnahmetaste 527
Sprachen der Erde 468
Sprachen, afroasiatische 468
Sprachen, altaische 469
Sprachen, australische 469
Sprachen, germanische 469
Sprachen, indoarische 469
Sprachen, indoeuropäische 469
Sprachen, isolierte 469
Sprachen, keltische 469
Sprachen, malaiopolynesische 469

Sprachen, ozeanische 469
Sprachen, romanische 469
Sprachen, sinotibetische 468
Sprachen, slawische 469
Sprachen, zentralafrikanische 468
Sprachgruppen, wichtigste 468
Sprecher 828
Sprecher- und Regieräume 490
Sprecherpult 488
Sprecherraum 488
Sprechmuschel 506
Sprechtrommel 433
Sprechzimmer 726
Spreite 75, 76, 79
Spreizdübel 302
Sprengkapsel 757
Sprengladung 653, 757
Sprengring 911
Sprietsegel 601
Springeinrichtungen 828
Springer 916
Springerstiefel 896
Springform 232
Springglocke 857
Springreiten 852
Springseil 850
Sprinkler 665
Sprinterlinie 871
Spritzbeutel 232
Spritzblech 655
Spritze 776
Spritzenkolben 776
Spritzenkörper 776
Spritzflasche 685
Spritzlappen 571
Spritzloch 136
Spritzpistole 320, 398
Spritzpistole im Querschnitt 398
Spritzschutz 640, 837
Spross 78
Sprosse 247, 249, 281, 321
Sprosse, obere 277
Sprossenarretierung 321
Sprossengemüse 185
sproßbürtige Wurzeln 76
Sprüharm 294
Sprühflasche 329
Sprühknopf 288
Sprühregen 64
Sprühregen, anhaltend dichter 57
Sprühregen, anhaltend leichter 57
Sprühregen, anhaltend mäßiger 57
Sprühregen, zeitweise dichter 57
Sprühregen, zeitweise leichter 57
Sprühregen, zeitweise mäßiger 57
Sprunganlage 890, 891
Sprungbein 153, 155
Sprungbrett 246, 826
Sprünge, Beispiele 829, 881
Sprungfeder 285
Sprungfederrahmen 280
Sprungfiguren 828
Sprunggelenk 124, 130
Sprunglatte 792
Sprungpferd 824, 825, 826
Sprungreitparcours 852
Sprungreitplatz 788
Sprungrichter 828
Sprungschanze 891
Sprungschanzen 890
Sprungski 840, 891
Sprungständer 792
Sprungtechnik 891
Sprungtuch 823
Sprungturm 828
Sprungwettbewerbe 792
Spülarm 265
Spülbecken 722
Spülbecken für Töpfe und Pfannen 721
Spule 115, 452, 453, 461, 495, 688, 909, 910
Spüle 224, 270
Spulenachse 910
Spulengestell 462
Spulenkapsel 452
Spuler 452
Spüler 721
Spulgerät, elektrisches 462
Spülhebel 265
Spülkasten 264
Spülkastendeckel 265
Spülkopf 651
Spulrad 462
Spundbajonett 751
Spur, rechte 539
Spurkranzrad 595
Spurstange 590
Squash 819
Squashbälle 819
Squashschläger 819
Sri Lanka 747
St. Lucia 743
Staatsanwaltschaft, Tisch 728
Staatsgrenze 37
Stab 274, 322, 367, 436, 792, 799
Stabbogen 859
Stäbchen 177
Stäbchenplatte 300

Stabhochspringer 792
Stabhochsprung 790, 792
stabiler Flügel 759
Stabilisator 633, 859, 876, 897
Stabilisierungsfläche 896
Stabilisierungsflosse 25, 608
Stabkranz 170
Stablampe 770
Stabmixer 236
Stabparkett 254
Stabplatte 300
Stachel 95, 98
Stachelbeere 192
Stachelschwein 123
Stachelzellenschicht 172
Stadion 709, 788, 790
Stadt 37, 708
Stadtplan 39
Stadtrad 581
Stadtteil 39
Staffelei 399
Staffelstab 790
Staffelübergabebereich 790
Stag 602
Stagsegel-Stag 602
Stahl 269, 298, 752
Stahlbehälter, emaillierter 267
Stahlbeton 298
Stahlbreite 320
Stahldraht 913
Stahlfeder 752
Stahlkante 888
Stahlkappe 773
Stahlmantel 689
Stahlschreibfeder 470
Stahlspitze 391
Stahlspitzenschuhe 885
Stahlstab 449
Stalagmit 47
Stalaktit 47
Stall 856
Stamm 76, 86, 87
Stämmchen 75
Stampfstag 602
Stand 362, 789
Stand des Richtschützen 758
Stand, aufrechter 843
Stand, gebückter 843
Standardobjektiv 478
Standbagger 647
Ständer 59, 234, 236, 307, 381, 389, 448, 452, 464, 826
Ständerbohrmaschine 307
Standfotograf 429
Standhahn-Mutternschlüssel 315
Standheizungstank 563
Standleitung 523, 524
Standleuchte 286
Standort des Kultbildes 403
Standortanzeiger 417
Standrohr 271
Standsockel 321
Standtom 448
Standuhr 697
Stange 185, 261, 284, 390, 391, 439, 611, 686, 739, 851
Stange, einfache 284
Stangenkugel 752
Stangensellerie 185
Stapelstühle 277
Star 118
Stardust 19
stark bewölkter Himmel 56
Stärke 85
Stärkekörnchen 74
starkes Gewitter 57
starre Brücken 540
Start 852, 875, 887, 915
Start 100-m- und 100-m-Hürdenlauf 790
Start 10000-m- und 4-x-400-m-Lauf 791
Start 110-m-Hürdenlauf 790
Start 1500-m-Lauf 791
Start 200-m-Lauf 790
Start 400-m-, 400-m-Hürden-, 4-x-100-m-Lauf 791
Start 5000-m-Lauf 790
Start 800-m-Lauf 791
Start beim Rückenschwimmen 832
Start- und Landebahn 620
Start-Mechaniker 873
Start-Taste 512
Start/Pause 501
Start: Bob 885
Start: Doppelsitzer Männer 885
Start: Rodeln 885
Start: Rodeln Frauen 885
Start: Skeleton 885
Startaufstellung 872
Startbereich 891
Startblock 791, 830
Startbojen 838
Starter 830, 838, 882, 883
Startergriff 331
Starterzug 323
Startgatter 875
Startgriffe (Rückenschwimmen) 830
Starthilfekabel 558
Startknopf 696

Startlinie 791, 833, 848, 872
Startlinie, 500-m 882
Startmaschine 856
Startmenütaste 514
Startnummer 791, 857, 875
Startpistole 790
Startplätze 891
Startpositionen 828, 843
Startsprung 832
Starttaste 508
Starttaste für Strickmuster 456
Startwagen 857
Startzone 838
stationäre Front 56
Stationskreis 55
Stationsmodell 55
Stationsspeichertaste 498
Stativ 14, 482, 483, 489, 685, 693
Stativablage 14
Stativklemme 685
Stativstange 685
Stator 249, 659
Statue 737
Staub, aufgewirbelter 63
Staubauswurf 304
Staubbehälter 288, 308
Staubbeutel 80
Staubblatt 80, 82
Staubfaden 80
Staubschweif 73
Staudämme, Beispiele 660
Staufach 766
Staumoräne 46
Stauraum 567, 570
Stausee 657, 658, 660, 661
Steak 214
Steakmesser 228
Stecher 458
Stechpaddel 837, 838
Steckbuchse 274
Steckdose 563, 567
Steckdose für Überspannungsschutz 520
Steckdose, dreipolige 274
Steckdose, geschaltete 497
Steckdosen für Notversorgung ab Batterie 520
Steckdosen für Überspannungsschutz 520
Steckdosenprüfer 316
Stecker 306, 502, 613
Stecker, dreipoliger, amerikanischer 274
Stecknadel 454
Steckschlüsselsatz 311
Steg 277, 358, 385, 404, 405, 408, 433, 439, 440, 441, 863
Steghose 358
Stegplättchen 385
Stegschlaufe für zweiten Fuß 840
Stegspangenschuh 343
Stegstütze 385
Stehbundkragen 363
stehender Anschlag 861, 893
Stehleiter 321
Stehleitern 321
steifer Nachläufer 569
steifes Vorderteil 569
Steigbügel 174, 750, 853, 855
Steigeisen 345, 893
Steigeisenriemen 901
steigendes Revers 348
Steigleitung 262
Steigleitung Rücklauf 259
Steigleitung Vorlauf 259
Steigradmechanismus 436
Steigrohr 654
Steigrohrkopf 654
Steigrohrventil 654
Steigung 255
Steigungseinstellung 631
steiles Satteldach 414
Steilhang 45
Steilküste 51
Steilwandzelt 902
Stein 81, 298, 376, 696
Steinbock 10
Steinbock, Wendekreis 34, 35, 36
Steinbohrer 306
Steinbutt 221
Steindruckpresse 423
Steine 81
Steineisenmeteorit 8
steinerner Ehrensessel 738
Steinfaustkeil, polierter 748
Steinfrucht, fleischige 81
Steinfrüchtchen 83
Steinfrüchte 192
Steingarten 322
Steinmarder 134
Steinmauer 298
Steinmeteoriten 8
Steinpilz 183
Steinschlag 47, 545, 547
Steinschlaghelm 901
Steinschloss 752
Steinwüste 52
Steinzeitwaffen 748
Steißbein 152, 157
Stellhebel 590
Stellmutter 913

Stellring 329
Stellschraube 312, 317, 319, 448
Stellstange 590
stellvertretender Dienststellenleiter, Büro 768
stellvertretender Direktor, Büro 726
Stellwerk 583
Stemmbrett 838
Stemmeisen 309
Stemmtornische 597
Stempel 80, 531
Stempelkarte 530
Stempelkissen 531
Stempelrad 531
Stempeluhr 530
Stengel 77
Stengelgemüse 185
Stengelglied 77
Stenografieblock 531
Steppe 61
Stereokamera 481
Stereotaste 504
sterile Wundauflage 777
Sterilgut, Lagerraum 778, 780
Sterilisationsraum 780, 781
Stern 8, 64, 741
Sternalarterie 107
Sternanis 84
Sternbilder der nördlichen Halbkugel 12
Sternbilder der südlichen Halbkugel 10
Sternchen 73
Sterne, kleine 8
Sterne, massereiche 8
Sternfrucht 197
Sternnetzwerk 522
Sternscheibe 641
Sternschnuppe 53
Sternum 111
Sternwarte 17
Sternwarte, Querschnitt 17
Stert 676
Stethoskop 776
Steuer 838
Steuer 918
Steueranlage für den Autopiloten 626
Steuerantenne 60
Steuerantrieb 40
Steuerbordseite 609, 616, 617
Steuerbügel 897
Steuereinheit, elektrische 559
Steuerfeder 918
Steuerfedern 859
Steuerhaus 607
Steuerhebel 649
Steuerknüppel 626, 631, 898
Steuerleine 838
Steuermann 884
Steuermarke 390
Steuerpult 10, 626
Steuerrad 626
Steuerruder 598
Steuersitz 838
Steuerstab 670, 671
Steuertaste 516
Steuertriebwerk 23
Steuerung 514
Steuerung der Solarzellenfläche 60
Steuerung des Lebenserhaltungssystems 20
Steuerung, elektronische 563
Steuerungstaste 514
Steuerzentrale 657, 669
Steven 602
Stichbreitenwähler 452
Stichlängenwähler 452
Stichplatte 452
Stichsäge 303
Stichsäge, elektrische 305
Stichwaffen 751
Stichwähler 452
Stick 858
Sticker 376
Stickerei 459
Stickoxiden, Emission 70
Stickrahmen, runder 459
Stickstiche 459
Stickstoff 683
Stickstoff, flüssiger 694
Stiefel 343, 444, 874, 875, 880, 881, 895
Stiefelette, knöchelhohe 343
Stiefelknecht 345
Stieglitz 118
Stiel 75, 76, 78, 81, 82, 83, 185, 227, 253, 295, 301, 863, 901
Stielgrund 185
Stielkamm 380
Stielkasserolle 235
Stier 12
Stift 274, 275, 517, 527
Stift mit rundem Ende 285
Stifthalter 386, 517
Stiftsockel 275
Stigma 96, 97
Stilett 751
Stillwasserspiegel 49
Stilton 211
Stilus 470
Stimmanzeiger 448
Stimmband 163
Stimmeinrichtung 448
Stimmenwahlschalter 450, 451

1008

ASTRONOMIE > 2-25; ERDE > 26-71; PFLANZENREICH > 72-89; TIERREICH > 90-143; MENSCH > 144-177; NAHRUNGSMITTEL UND KÜCHE > 178-241; HAUS > 242-295;
HEIMWERKEN UND GARTENARBEIT > 296-333; KLEIDUNG > 334-371; PERSÖNLICHE AUSSTATTUNG > 372-391; KUNST UND ARCHITEKTUR > 392-465; KOMMUNIKATION UND BÜROTECHNIK > 466-535;
TRANSPORT UND FAHRZEUGE > 536-643; ENERGIE > 644-677; WISSENSCHAFT > 678-705; GESELLSCHAFT > 706-785; SPORT UND SPIELE > 786-920

Stimmgabel 436
Stimmkrücke 444
Stimmnagel 442
Stimmring 433
Stimmstock 442
Stimmwirbel 440, 441
Stimmzug 447
Stinktier 134
Stint 219
Stirn 115, 146, 150, 309, 749
Stirnbalken 252, 253
Stirnbande 862
Stirnbein 131, 152, 158
Stirnfontanelle 158
Stirnhöhle 175
Stirnradgetriebe 686
Stirnriemen 854
Stirnschopf 124
Stirntür 635
Stirnwand 571, 639
Stirnwandflachwagen 588
Stirnwandleiter 587
Stirnzahnrad 307
Stirnziegel 403
Stock 320, 391, 610, 801, 891
Stock, orthopädischer 782
Stock, vierfüßiger 782
Stockanker 610
Stöcke 449
Stockgriff 892
Stockpresse 425
Stockschaft 892
Stockschirm 391
Stockseite 739
Stockteller 888
Stoff, bestickter 459
Stoffbruch 455
Stoffdrücker 452, 453
Stoffdrückerstange 453
Stoffmenge, Maßeinheit 702
Stoffstreifen 459
Stola 336
Stollen 371, 640, 798
Stollenreifen 577, 875
Stollenschuh 796
Stop 130, 458
Stopfen 379
Stopfer 237, 240, 390
Stopfleber 216
Stopp-Taste 499, 512
Stoppbad 485
Stoppball 821
Stoppknopf 696
Stopptaste 495, 501, 508
Stoppuhr 696, 831
Stöpselsicherung 272
Stör 218
Storch 119
Store 282
Störklappe 624
Stoßdämpfer 18, 553, 876
Stoßdämpfer hinten 870
Stoßdämpfer, hinterer 575
Stößel 230
Stoßen 850
Stoßfänger 570, 577, 920
Stoßfänger, kunststoffummantelter 550
Stoßleiste 289
Stoßspannungsunterdrückung 520
Stoßstange 876
Stoßzunge 443
Stoßzungenschraubenfeder 443
Strafbank 879
Strafbankbetreuer 879
Strafen 789
Straffergurt, vorderer 906
Strafraum 802
Strafraumbogen 802
Strafraumlinie 802
Strahlbein 126
Strahldurchmesser, Verminderung 694
Strahlenkörper 177
Strahlgrube, mittlere 127
Strahlgrube, seitliche 127
Strahlrohr 767
Strahlstörer 329
Strahler 246, 765
Strahlung 681
Strahlung, künstliche 41
Strahlung, natürliche 41
Strahlung, ultraviolette 690
Strahlungszone 6
Strähnenkamm 380
Straight Flush 914
Strampelhöschen 368
Strand 51
Strandschnecke 217
Strang 836
Straße 39, 708, 711, 713, 914
Straße im Querschnitt 538, 712
Straße von Gibraltar 32
Straße von Mozambique 34
Straße, Bass 29
Straßenbahn 595
Straßenbau 538
Straßenhobel 639
Straßenkarte 573

Straßenkehrmaschine 573
Straßenlaterne 287, 712
Straßennummer 39
Straßenradrennen 870
Straßenradsport 870
Straßenrennrad 870
Straßenschuh 343
Straßentunnel 543
Straßenverkehr 487, 538
Stratokumulus 56, 62
Stratopause 53
Stratosphäre 53
Stratus 56, 62
Strauch 322
Strauchflechte 74
Strauß 119
Straußenei 213
Strebe 252, 253, 448
Strebebogen 410, 411
Streben, hinterer 578
Strebepfeiler 410
Strecke 872, 874
Strecke, landschaftlich schöne 39
Strecke, Supercross 875
Strecke, zurückgelegte 700
Streckenbegrenzung 875
Streckenposten 875
Streckenschiedsrichter 837, 838
Streckmetall-Unterlage 299
Streichbaum 460
Streichblech 641
Streichholz 391
Streichholzheftchen 391
Streichholzschachtel 391
Streichkäse 210
Streifen 416
Streifenvorhang 416
Streuer 232
Streuscheibe 428
Streuwerk 641
Strichcodeleser 517
Strichpunkt 473
Strickabstreifer 456
Strickabstreiferknopf 456
Strickarttasten 456
Stricken 457
Strickjacke 354
Strickjacke mit V-Ausschnitt 354
Strickleiter 321
Strickmaschine 456
Strickmaß 457
Strickmuster 458
Strickmusterspeicherung 456
Stricknadel 457
Stroboskop 611
Strohballen 875
Strohhalm 223
Strohhut 340
Strohhütte 418
Strohverteiler 643
Stromabgabe an Verbraucher 662
Stromabnehmer 595
Stromanschluss 258, 260, 571
Stromanschluss, wasserdichter 263
Stromanschlusskabel 567
Stromanschlusspunkt 273, 663
Stromatolith 92
Stromerzeugungsabschnitt 664
Stromerzeugungsbereich 763
Stromfortleitung 665
Stromgenerator 659
Stromkreis 272
Stromleitung an die Verbraucher 677
Stromleitung zu den Verbrauchern 646
Stromnetz 674
Stromquelle 687
Stromschiene 595
Strömung 597
Strömungs-T 269
Strömungssicherung 267
Stromverbrauchernummer 273
Stromversorgung, unterbrechungsfreie 520, 523
Stromversorgungskabel 712
Stromverteiler 489
Stromzuleitung 266
Stromzähler 273
Strontium 682
Stroße 647
Strumpf 365, 367
Strümpfe 365
Strumpfhalter 367
Strumpfhaltergürtel 367
Strumpfhose 365
Studio-Kommandoanlage 491
Studioebene 490, 492
Studiopersonal, zusätzliches 490
Stufe 255, 321, 847
Stufe, dritte 25
Stufe, erste 25
Stufe, zweite 25
Stufen 246, 412
Stufenbarren 824
Stufenrock 357
Stuhl 277, 723, 734
Stühle, Beispiele 277
Stulp 248, 249

Stulpe 346
Stulpen 802, 805
Stulpenhandschuh 346
Stummaufnahme-Taste 499
Stummel 391, 909
Stumpf 87
stumpfer Winkel 704
Stumpftonne 615, 617
Stundenwinkelantrieb 17
Stundenzeiger 697
Stuntskate 895
Stürmer 803
stürmischer Himmel 65
Sturmlampe 906
Sturmspitze 879
Sturm, tropischer 57
Sturz 247, 252, 256
Sturzhelm 884, 885, 888, 891
Stützarm 634
Stützausleger 766
Stütze 246, 323, 567, 591, 609, 629, 663, 826
Stutzen 796, 878
Stützen der Pfeifenrastbretter 445
Stützfuß 567, 571, 641
Stützpfeiler 660
Stützpfeilerstaudamm 660
Stützpfeilerstaudamm im Querschnitt 660
Stützpunkt 828
Stützring 16, 659
Stütztritt 901
Stützvorrichtung, ausklappbare 571
Stützvorrichtung, Kurbel 571
Stylobat 403, 404
Stylus 83
Suaheli 468
subarktisch 61
Subduktionszone 43
Sublimation 680
Substanz, graue 167, 168
Substanz, weiße 167, 168
Substanzen, anorganische 67
Substanzen, gefährliche 774
Subtraktion 703
Subtraktionstaste 529
Subtropen, feuchte 61
Subtropen, mediterrane 61
Subwoofer 493
Such- und Rettungsantennen 60
Sucharm 521
Suche 525
Sucher 477, 479, 496
Sucher, elektronischer 496
Sucherkamera 480
Sucherokular 477
Suchfernrohr 14, 15
Süd 37, 917
Süd-Korea 747
Süd-Südost 37
Süd-Südwest 37
Südafrika 746
Südamerika 28, 31, 50
Südamerikanische Platte 43
Sudan 745
Südchinesisches Meer 28, 33
Süden 616
Südfrüchte 196
südliche Halbkugel 35
südliche Halbkugel, Sternbilder 10
südliche Hemisphäre 35
Südliche Krone 10
Südliche Wasserschlange 11
Südlicher Fisch 10
südlicher Polarkreis 29, 35, 36
Südliches Dreieck 10
südliches Kardinalseezeichen 617
Südost 37
Südosten 616
Südpol 29, 35, 687
Südwest 37
Südwesten 616
Südwester 341
Sulcus terminalis 176
Sulky 857
Sumach 199
Summe 699, 703
Sumo 847
Sumoringer 847
Sunnismus 736
Super-G 889
Super-Weitwinkelobjektiv 478
Supercross-Motorrad 875
Supercross-Strecke 875
Supermarkt 180, 711, 715
Supernova 8
Superriesenslalom 889
Superriesenslalom-Ski 888
Suppe 722
Suppenlöffel 228
Suppenschale 226
Suppenteller 226
Suppenterrine 226
Suppentopf 235
Surfboard 840
Surfbrett 836
Surfen 840
Surfer 840

Surfschuh 840
Surinam 742
Surround-Lautsprecher 493
Suspensorium 808, 843, 880
Süßkartoffel 184
Süßwaren 717
Swasiland 746
Sweatshirt 370
Sweatshirt mit Kapuze 370
Swimmingpool 608
Symbol 682, 920
Symbole 473
Symbole, chemische 684
Symbole, wissenschaftliche 702
symphatisches Ganglion 167
Symphyse 169, 170
Synagoge 738
Synapse 168
Synchronisationskabel 527
Synchronspringen 829
Synsakrum 116
Synthesizer 450
Syrien 746
Systemschalter 450

T

T-Leitwerk 629
T-Shirt Kleid 369
T-Stück 271
T-Verbinder 522
Tabak 390
Tabakkammer 390
Tabaksbeutel 390
Tabakwarengeschäft 714
Tablette 783
Tabletts 722
Tablinum 406
Tabulator nach links 514
Tabulator nach rechts 514
Tabulatoreinstelltaste 528
Tabulatorsetztaste 528
Tabulatortaste 514, 528
Tachometer 557, 576, 851
Tadschikistan 746
Tafel 374, 734
Tafelberg 10, 52
Tafelfacette 374
Tafelsalz 201
Tafelschliff 375
Tagalog 469
Tagebau 647
Tageskilometerzähler 557
Tageslichtprojektor 535
Tagesraum 727
Tagliatelle, grüne 206
Tagzeichen 615
Tagzeichen (Region B) 617
Tahinisoße 200
Tahitianisch 469
Taifun 63
Tailback 807
Taille 147, 149
Taillenabnäher 352
Tajine 234
Takelage 602
Taktarten 434
Taktischer Transporthubschrauber 631
Taktkennung 617
Taktstrich 434
Tal 45, 48
Talgdrüse 172
Talmud 736
Tamarin 139
Tamarindenmark 200
Tambour 404
Tamburin 449
Tampon 422
Tandem 581
Tandemscheibenegge 641
Tanganjikasee 34
Tank 23, 261, 573, 607
Tankanlage 654, 873
Tankauflieger 572
Tankdeckel 551, 570
Tanker 596, 606
Tankerflugzeug 760
Tanklastzug 572
Tankluke 607
Tanks 655
Tankstelle 548, 711, 725
Tankwagen 573, 622
Tankwall 655
Tanne 89
Tannennadeln 89
Tansania 745
Tante mütterlicherseits 785
Tante väterlicherseits 785
Tanzsaal 609
Tare 847
Tarlatan 422
Tarnkappenbomber 629
Taro 184
Tarsometatarsus 116
Tarsus 111

Tasche 313, 345, 386, 862
Tasche für Latexhandschuhe 770
Tasche, aufgesetzte 348, 353, 360, 368
Tasche, blinde 355
Tasche, eingesetzte 360
Tasche, geräumige 388
Tasche, senkrechte 337
Taschen, Beispiele 360
Taschenlampe 765
Taschenrechner 386, 529
Taschenrechner, wissenschaftlicher 529
Taschenschirm 391
Taschenträger 869
Tasmanien 29
Tasmanischer Teufel 143
Tasmansee 29
Tasse 226, 905
Tast-Körperchen, Meissnersches 172
Tastatur 442, 450, 507, 514, 526
Tastatur, alphabetische 530
Tastatur, alphanumerische 506, 507, 514, 548, 730, 731
Tastatur, numerische 507, 530
Tastaturablage, verstellbare 511
Tastaturschnittstelle 513
Tastaturschutz, verschiebbarer 506
Taste 432, 442, 443, 445, 507
Taste Cursor an Zeilenanfang 515
Taste Druck 515
Taste Ende 515
Taste für helles Licht 479
Taste für Normallicht 479
Taste für schattiges Licht 479
Taste löschender Rückschritt 515
Taste nächste Seite 515, 527
Taste numerischer Block 515
Taste Pause 515
Taste Systemabfrage 515
Taste Unterbrechung 515
Taste vorherige Seite 515, 527
Tasten 451, 506
Tasten für Absenken 479
Tasten für Erhöhen 479
Tasten, programmierbare 516
Tastenfeld, numerisches 515, 699
Tasteninstrumente 442
Tasteninstrumente, Beispiele 443
Tastentelefon 507
Tatami 846
tatsächliche Temperatur 261
Tau 65
Taube 11, 120, 212
Taubesfestigung 597
Täubling, grasgrüner 183
Tauchanzug 841
Tauchbecken 788
Tauchen 841
Taucher 841
Taucherhandschuh 841
Tauchermesser 841
Taufbecken 737
Taupunkttemperatur 55
Tausend 703
Tauwasserablauf 291
Tauwerk 908
Taxi 725
Technetium 683
Techniken 812
technische Ausführung, Kampfrichter 823
technische Delegierte 881
technische Identifikationsnummer 501
technischer Dienst 732
Teddy 366
Tee 208, 867, 877
Tee, grüner 208
Tee, Oolong 208
Tee, schwarzer 208
Tee-Ei 233
Teebeutel 208
Teekanne 226
Teeline 877
Teelöffel 228
Teerpappe 299
Teflonband 314
Teich 866
Teigmischer 232
Teigwaren 206
Teigwaren, asiatische 207
Teil über Wasser 615
Teil, flacher 457
Teile 276, 277, 280
Teile der Brille 385
Teile der Waffe 849
Teile des Elektronenmikroskops 694
Teile des Schuhs 342
Teile einer Fahne 739
Teile einer Lampenfassung 275
Teile eines Boots 838
Teile eines Fahrrads 578
Teile eines Hauses 247
Teile eines Kreises 704
Teile eines langen Knochens 155
Teile eines Rings 376
teilgetauchter Tragflügel 609
Teilmenge, echte 703
teilreflektierender Spiegel 692
Teilungsbeispiele 740
Teilungsnaht 348

tektonische Platten 43
tektonischer See 48
Telefaxgerät 508
Telefon 491, 724, 725
Telefon, schnurloses 507
Telefon-/Kabel-/Satellitenleitung 523
Telefonapparat 489, 506
Telefone, Beispiele 507
Telefonieren 506
Telefonkabel 712
Telefonleitung 524
Telefonnetz 487
Telefonnummernverzeichnis 531
Telefonsteckdose 520
Telefonzentrale 507
Telekommunikation 487
Telekommunikation für die Schifffahrt 487
Telekommunikation, industrielle 487
Telekommunikation, militärische 487
Telekommunikation, private 487
Telekommunikation, Schifffahrt 487
Telekommunikationsantenne 609, 761, 762
Telekommunikationssatellit 525
Telekonverter 478
Telemetrie-Antenne 60
Teleobjektiv 478
Teleport 487
Teleskop 17, 859
Teleskopantenne 503
Teleskopbein 482
Teleskopgabel 574, 577
Teleskopmaß 864
Teleskopschlagstock 770
Teleskopstangen 920
Teleskoptragebein 776
Teller 287, 905, 913
Teller, flacher 226
Teller, kleiner 226
Tellerbürste 573
Tellereisen 913
Tellur 682
Telson 107
Tempel, aztekischer 412
Tempel, griechischer 403
Tempel, Huitzilopochtli 412
Tempel, Tlaloc 412
Temperatur 261
Temperatur, Messung 59
Temperaturanzeige 557
Temperatureinsteller 465
Temperaturfühler 18, 561
Temperaturmessung 695
Temperaturregler 238, 259, 261, 267, 288, 291
Temperaturregler, abziehbarer 239
Temperaturschalter 382
Temperaturskala 53
Temperaturwähler 238, 292, 293
Tempomat 556
Temporegler 451
Temposkala 436
Tennis 820
Tennisball 822
Tennisplatz 820
Tennisplätze 788
Tennisschläger 822
Tennisschuh 344, 822
Tennisspielerin 822
Tentakel 106
Tentakel, kleiner 104
Teppich 254
Teppichboden 254
Teppichmuschel, Kreuzmuster 217
Teppichschiffchen 461
Terbium 684
Terminalbronchiole 163
Terminals, interaktive 395
Terminkalender 530
Termite 101
Terpentin 400
Terrasse 244, 322
Terrassentür 250
Terrine 234
Tertiär 93
Tertiärkonsumenten 67
Terz 434
Test-Schalter 520
Testbereich für Düsentriebwerke 761
Testbild 492
Testknopf 767
Teufel, Tasmanischer 143
Teufelsdreck 199
Textablesetafel 492
Textanzeige 528
textile Bodenbeläge 254
Texttaste 528
Thai 468
Thailand 747
Thallium 682
Thallus 74, 75
Theater 430, 710, 711
Theater, griechisches 402
Theke 720, 722
Theodolit 59, 701
thermodynamische Temperatur, Maßeinheit 702
thermoelektrischer Radioisotopengenerator 18

Thermometer 259, 655, 695, 841, 899
Thermopause 53
Thermoschutzhaube 872
Thermosflasche 906
Thermosphäre 53
Thermostat 238, 260, 261, 267
Thermostat, oberer 266
Thermostat, programmierbarer 261
Thermostat, regelbarer 239
Thermostat, unterer 266
Thetys 5
Third 877
Thorarollen 738
Thoraschrein 738
Thorax 96, 97, 98
Thorium 684
Thrombozyt 162
Thulium 684
Thunfisch 220
Thymian 202
Tibetisch 468
Tibia 111
Tibiotarsus 116
Ticketschalter 620
Tiefdruck 420
Tiefdruckgebiet 55, 63
Tiefdruckverfahren 422
tiefe Wolken 62
Tiefenanschlag 307
Tiefeneinstellung 308
Tiefenmesser 841
Tiefenregler 441
Tiefenruder 763
Tiefenskala in m 613
tiefer Wadenbeinnerv 166
tiefgestellt 472
Tiefkühlprodukte 181
Tiefladewagen 588
tiefliegende Form 420
Tieflöffel 637
Tieflöffelsteuerung 637
Tiefsee-Ebene 49
Tiefseeberg 49
Tiefseeboden 42
Tiefseegraben 49
Tiefseehügel 49
Tiefseekabel 524
Tiefseekabel, Verteilung 487
Tieftöner 502
Tierceron 410
Tierhandlung 714
tierische Zelle 94
Tierreich 92
Tiertransport, Satteltiefladeanhänger 572
Tiger 135
Tight End 807
Tilde 473
Timer 851
Tinte 397
Tinte, metallische 729
Tintenbeutel 106
Tintenfisch 106, 217
Tintenfisch, Anatomie 106
Tintenfisch, äußere Merkmale 106
Tintenpatronen-Kontrollleuchte 519
Tintenraum 470
Tintenstrahldrucker 519
Tipi 418
Tisch 278, 304, 424, 720, 723
Tisch der Aufsichtsperson 732
Tisch der Staatsanwaltschaft 728
Tisch der Verteidigung 728
Tisch des Gerichtsschreibers 728
Tischcomputer 522, 523, 524
Tische, Beispiele 278
Tischfeststellschraube 307
Tischfußball 920
Tischklammer 693
Tischkreissäge 305
Tischleuchte 286
Tischleuchte, Halogen 286
Tischplatte 278
Tischrechner mit Druckerteil 529
Tischrührgerät 236
Tischtennis 815
Tischtennisball 815
Tischtennisplatte 815
Tischtennisschläger 815
Tischverlängerung 305
Titan 5, 683
Titan IV 24
Titania 5
Titeleinblendetaste 496
Titelfoto 471
Titelnummer 501
Titelseite 471
Titelsuchtasten 501
Titelzeile 471
Titicacasee 31
TL-Triebwerk 625
Tlaloc-Tempel 412
Toaster 238
Tochter 784, 785
Todesanzeigen 471
tödlich giftiger Pilz 76
Toeloop 881
Toga 336
Togo 745

Toilette 262, 264, 265, 395, 584, 719, 735
Toiletten 715, 723, 728, 731, 733, 779, 781
Toiletten (Damen) 725
Toiletten (Herren) 725
Toilettenpapierhalter 264
Toilettenseife 379
Toilettenwagen 622
Tomate 188
Tomatenmark 200
Tomatillo 188
Tomtom 448
Ton-/Bild-Vorschaueinheit 491
Tonabnehmer 441, 500
Tonabnehmer-Wahlschalter 441
Tonabnehmerregler 441
Tonabnehmersystem 500
Tonarm 500
Tonarmheber 500
Tonarmstütze 500
Tonartvorzeichen 435
Tonassistent 429
Tonaufnahmegeräte 429
Tonbandgerät, digitales 488
Tonerpatrone 519
Tonerzeugung 445
Tonga 747
Tonhöhenrad 450
Tonhohlplatte 298
Tonleiter 434
Tonmeister 429
Tonnengewölbe 407
Tonnenstein 615
Tonregiepult 489, 490
Tonregieraum 489, 490
Tonsignalquellen, Kontrollleuchten 497
Tonsignalquellen-Wahltaster 497
Tontechniker 489, 490
Tonvormischung 491
Tonwiedergabesystem 497
Tonwiedergabesysteme, tragbare 503
Topas 375
Topcase 577
Töpfe und Pfannen, Spülbecken 721
Töpferei 464
Topfhut 341
Topinambur 184
Toplevel-Domain 524
Toplicht 605
Toppnant 602
Toppzeichen 615, 616
Toprückstand 656
Topspeed-Bereich 891
Toque 341
Tor 596, 800, 802, 804, 807, 809, 814, 827, 879, 920
Torangreifer 809
Toranzeige 920
Torbereich 805
Tordrittel 809
Torfmoos, sparriges 75
Torhüter 799, 800, 814, 827
Torkreis 809
Torlampen 879
Torlinie 800, 804, 806, 809, 814, 827, 878
Tornado 57, 63
Torpedo 763
Torpedoraum 763
Torpedorohr 763
Torpfosten 807, 858
Torraum 802, 814, 879
Torraumlinie 814
Torresstraße 29
Torrichter 827, 858, 878
Torschütze 809
Torselett 367
Tortellini 206
Tortilla 205
Torus 404, 405, 705
Torverteidiger 809
Torwart 801, 803, 809, 878, 879
Torwartbrustschutz 880
Torwarthandschuhe 802
Torwartschläger 879, 880
Torwartschlittschuh 880
totale Finsternis 6, 7
Totalisator 856
Totengräber 101
Touchpad 526
Touchpad-Taste 526
Touchscreen 527
Toulouser Wurst 216
Toupierkamm 380
Tourenrad 581
Touring-Motorrad 577
Touringreifen 560
Towergehäuse: Innenansicht 513
Towergehäuse: Rückansicht 513
Towergehäuse: Vorderansicht 513
Trab 124
Traber 857
Trabrennen 857
Trachte 127
Trachtenwand 127
Track 500
traditionelle Boote 599
traditionelle Jacke 846
traditionelle Kleidung 339

traditionelle Musikinstrumente 432
traditionelle Wohnhäuser 418
tragbare Tonwiedergabesysteme 503
tragbarer CD-Spieler 503
Trageband 772
Tragebügel 503, 504
Tragegriff 289, 755
Tragen-Abstellraum 778
Träger 252, 367, 632, 663, 881
Träger mit Knopf 369
Träger, runder 284
Träger, verstellbarer 368
Trägerhemd 351, 371
Trägerhemdchen 369
trägerloser Büstenhalter 367
Trägerrakete 24
Trägerrakete(Ariane V), Querschnitt 24
Trägerrakete(Saturn V), Querschnitt 25
Trägerraketen, Beispiele 24
Trägerrock 356
Trägerstruktur 21
Tragfaden 103
Tragflügel 23, 625, 628
Tragflügel, hinterer 609
Tragflügel, teilgetauchter 609
Tragflügel, vorderer 609
Tragflügelformen 630
Tragflügelschiff 609
Tragkabel 540
Tragriemen, Öse 477
Tragsäule 652
Tragschicht, obere 538
Tragschicht, untere 538
Tragsegel 897
Tragseil 77
Tragus 173
Trainer 800, 811, 827, 842, 879, 881, 883
Trainerassistent 811
Trainertribüne 891
Training 788
Trainingsanzug 370
Trainingsball 819
Trainingsbereich 788
Trainingshose 370
Traktor 640
Traktor: Hinteransicht 640
Traktor: Vorderansicht 640
Trampolin 823
Tranchiergabel 229
Tranchiermesser 229
Tränendrüse 177
Tränengang 177
Transantarktisches Gebirge 29
Transformator 287, 658, 663, 668, 674
Transformstörungen 43
Transitlagerschuppen 596
transparentes Akrylharz 501
Transpiration 67
Transport 538
Transportbandanlage 647
Transporter 573
Transporteur 453
Transporthubschrauber, taktischer 631
Transportmischer 573
Transporträdchen 476
Transportschiene 476
Transportstrecke 647
Transportwalze 476
Transversale pleine 919
Transversale simple 919
Trapezflügel 630
Traube, geschlossene 81
Traubenhenkel 86
Trauerweide 88
Traveller 834, 835
Travellerscheck 729
Traverse 278, 409, 663
Trawler 606
Treble 918
Trefferanzeige 848
Trefflächen 848
Treibanker 610
Treibhaus 182
Treibhauseffekt 68
Treibhauseffekt, anthropogener 68
Treibhauseffekt, natürlicher 68
Treibhausgase 68
Treibhausgaskonzentration 68
Treibladung 912
Treibscheibe 417
Treibstoffart 548
Treibstofftank 18, 631, 758, 760
Treibstoffzufuhrleitungen 899
Trenchcoat 352
Trennklappe 389
Trennlinie 471
Trennstab 461
Trennvorhang 780
Trennwand 771
Trennwand, bewegliche 509
Trennwand, flexible 510
Trennwand, versetzbare 719
Trense 854
Trensenzügel 854
Treppe 250, 251, 255, 412, 427, 431, 543, 592, 676, 724
Treppenabsatz 251
Treppenaufgang 655

Treppenhaus 251
Treppenhaus-Oberlicht 251
Treppenlauf 255
Treppenschliff 375
Treppenstufe 255
Treppenvorbau 245
Tresor 731, 769
Tresorraum 731
Tressenstich 459
Tretlager 580
Tretplatte 452
Triageraum 779
Trial-Motorrad 875
Triangel 437, 449
Trias 93
Tribünen, bewegliche 734
Triceratops 93
Trichter 106, 231, 446, 447, 494
Trickeffektetasten 496
Trickeffektewähler 496
Trickmischer 491
Trieb 86
Triebdrehgestell 585
Triebwagen 594
Triebwerk 18, 625
Triebwerksluftteinlass 760
Trift 657
Triglyphe 404
Triklinium 406
Triller 435
Trilobit 92
Trimaran 835
Trimmruder 60
Trinidad und Tobago 743
Trinkflasche 579
Trinkpackung 223
Trinkwasserleitung 712
Trio 438
Trireme 598
Triticale 203
Triton 5
Tritt 321, 460, 901
Trittbrett 876
Trittbrett, hinteres 766, 775
Trittfläche 855
Tritthocker 277, 321
Trittleiter 321
Trittlöser 460
Trittplatte 913
Trittstufe 255, 417, 570
Trizepszug 851
Trochilus 404, 405
trocken liegender Höhlenraum 47
Trockendock 596
Trockenelemente 689
Trockenfrüchte 84, 193
Trockenklimate 61
Trockenpastell 396
Trockenreifen 872
Trockenschrank 484
Trockenseite 660
Trockenständer 485
Trocknen 347
Troddel 282
Trog 55
Trombe-Wand 675
Trommel 230, 285, 292, 293, 328, 612, 697, 754
Trommel, kleine 437, 448
Trommelbremse 559
Trommelfell 110, 174, 433, 448
Trommeln 448
Trommelschlegel 433
Trompete 447, 538
Trompeten 437
Tropenwald 66
Tropfen für trockene Augen 384
tropfnass hängen 347
tropische Klimate 61
tropisch feucht und trocken 61
tropische Wirbelstürme, Bezeichnungen 63
tropischer Regenwald 61, 66
tropischer Sturm 57
tropischer Wirbelsturm 63
Tropopause 53, 68
Troposphäre 53
Trosse 908
Trüffel 183
Trugdolde, eingliedrige 81
Trugdolde, zweigliedrige 81
Truhe 279
Truhenkörper 291
Trumpffarben 917
Truncus coeliacus 161, 165
Truthahn 120
Tschad 745
Tschadsee 34
Tschechisch 469
Tschechische Republik 744
Tsetsefliege 101
Tuba 437, 447
Tube 223
Tube mit Aquarellfarbe/Gouachefarbe 397
Tubus 14, 15, 692, 693
Tubusträger 693
Tuch, Geschirr 295

Tudorbogen 413
Tukan 10, 119
Tülle 240, 241
Tüllen 232
Tüllenbajonett 751
Tulpe 80
Tümmler 137
Tundra 66
Tunesien 745
Tunika 359, 748
Tunikakleid 356
Tunnel 592
Tunnelsohle 595
Tüpfelfarn, gemeiner 76
Tür 238, 278, 291, 293, 417, 551, 567, 624, 724, 818
Tür zum Nutzlastraum 23
Tür, automatische 620
Turban 339, 341
Turbine 646, 659, 665, 668
Turbinenabschaltventil 668
Turbinendrehung 662
Turbinengebläse 668
Turbinengebäude 668
Turbinengenerator 646
Turbinenlaufrad 664
Turbinenmantelung 659
Turbinenrad 564
Turbinenummantelung 659
Turbinenwasserabfluss 662
Turbinenwelle 665
Turbogenerator 763
Turbotriebwerk 760
Turboverdichter 627
Turboverdichterwelle 627
Türen, Beispiele 416
Türfach 291
Türführungsschiene 587
Türfüllung 278
Türgriff 248, 551, 775
Türinnenverschalung 554
Türkei 746
Türkis 375
Türkisch 469
Turkmenistan 746
Türknopf 247
Turm 410, 614, 635, 674, 676, 677, 858, 916
Turmalin 375
Turmkran 634
Turmmast 634
Turmrollen 651
Turmspitze 411
Turmwindmühle 676
Turners/Turnerin, Name 825
Turnhalle 734, 788
Turnhallenbüro 734
Turnierball 819
Turnüre 337
Türöffnungshebel 554
Türpfosten 247
Türsäule 587
Türschloss 247, 293, 551, 554
Türstopper 291
Türsturz 411
Türverkleidung 554
Türzapfen 247
Tusche, lithografische 423
Tuschezeichnung 396
Tuvalu 747
TV-Einstellung 495
TV-Netzschalter 495
TV/Video-Taste 495
Twinset 359
Tympanon 403, 404
Typenschild 306
typische Küstenformen 51
Typografie 472
Tyrannosaurus 93

U

U-Bahn 592, 713
U-Bahn-Netzplan 593, 594
U-Bahn-Schild 592
U-Bahn-Station 592, 710
U-Bahn-Zug 592, 594
Überbau 542
Überdach 902, 903
Überdruckventil 234, 266, 841
Überfallrinne 657
Überfallschloss 389
Überfangstich, orientalischer 459
Überfangstich, rumänischer 459
Überfangstiche 459
Überflurhydrant 767
Überführung 539, 540
Übergangsfittings, Beispiele 269
Übergangsmetalle 683
Übergardine 282
Überholrollbahn 618
Überholspur 539
Überholverbot 544, 546
überirdische Pipeline 654
Überkleid 337
Überkopfschaltbrett 626
überlagernde Schichten 647
Überlappanzeige 512
Überlauf 246, 262, 264, 265, 267
Überlaufkrone 657

Überlaufrohr 266
Überlaufschutz 294
Überlaufstutzen 485
Überleitungstunnel 666
Überriese 8
Überrollschutz 873
Überschallflugzeug 53, 629
Überschlag 387
Überschwemmungsebene 48
Überseekoffer 389
Übersetzungsgehäuse 910
Übersetzungsgetriebe 677
Überspannungsschutz, Steckdose 520
Überstand 255
Überströmkanal 565
überstumpfer Winkel 704
Übertageanlage 648, 650
Übertemperatursicherung 266
Übertragung der Drehbewegung auf den Rotor 662
Übertragungsgeräte 522
Übertragungskabel 613
Übertragungsnetz, öffentliches 486
Übertragungswagen 489
Überwachungskamera 395
Überwachungsradar 761, 762
Überwachungsraum 394, 543, 727
Überwurfmutter 270
Überziehschuh 342
Übungsgrün 866
Übungsplatz 409
Udonnudeln 207
Ufer 664
Uferdamm 660
Uferdamm im Querschnitt 660
Uganda 745
Uhr 488, 734, 858
Uhr, mechanische 696
Uhrband 696
Uhren 717
Uhrenmeister 810
Uhrenradio 503
Uhrkasten 697
Uhrwerk 697
Uhu 119
Ukraine 744
Ukrainisch 469
UKW-Antenne 18, 60, 762
UKW-Wahltaste 497
Ultrakurzwelle, Antenne 18
Ultraschall, Aussendung 41
Ultraviolett-Spektrometer 60
ultraviolette Strahlung 690
Ulysses 19
Umbriel 5
Umfang 704
Umfangsverbindung 661
Umfeldbeleuchtung 775
Umgebung, naturbelassene 867
Umgehungsstraße 39, 709
Umhang 338
Umhängetasche mit Dehnfalte 388
Umhängetasche mit Reißverschluss 388
Umkehrlinsen 692
Umkleideraum 509, 649, 734, 764
Umladeabschnitt 607
Umlaufbahn, geostationäre 60
Umlaufbahn, polare 60
Umlaufkammer 658
Umlaut 473
Umlenkrolle 686
Umlenkstern 331
Umluft 258
Umrechnungsskala 479
Umschalter 302, 306, 523
Umschaltfeststelltaste 528
Umschalttaste 528
Umschalttasten 514
Umschlag 336, 362
umsetzbare Flagge 867
Umspannwerk 664
Umwälzpumpe 259, 675
Umwandlungsanlage, katalytische 656
Umwelt 66
Umwerfer 870
Umwerfer, hinterer 578, 580
undurchlässiges Gestein 651
unebene Fahrbahn 545, 547
unendlich 703
Unfallstation 778
Ungarn 744
ungebleichtes Mehl 204
ungesäuertes Brot 205
ungleich 703
Uniform 770
Uniformen 764
Unisex-Kopfbedeckungen 341
Unisex-Schuhe 344
Universaltreppe 623
Universität 710
Unkrautstecher 325
unpaarig gefiedert 79
unregelmäßiger Knochen 157
unregelmäßiges Trapez 705
Unterarm 130, 140, 147, 149
Unterarmmappe 387
Unterarmschiene 749
Unterarmstütze 782

Unterbau 651
Unterblock des Flaschenzuges 651
Unterboden 78, 252, 253, 254
Unterbrechung 515, 617
unterbrechungsfreie Stromversorgung 523
unterbrechungsfreie Stromversorgung (USV) 520
Unterbrett 445
unterbrochene Linie 538, 539
Unterbruststäbchen 367
Unterbühne 430
Unterdeck 655
untere Abschlusskappe 689
untere Gliedmaßen 161
untere Halterungsschraube 58
untere Hohlvene 160, 161, 162, 165
untere Klemmschraube 58
untere Mesenterialarterie 165
untere Nasenmuschel 175
untere Querleiste 278
untere Rondistenfacette 374
untere Schale 889
untere Schutzhaube 304
untere Sektion 24
untere Sohlschicht 646
untere Tasche 862
untere Tragschicht 538
untere Vertäfelung 632
untere Zahnreihe 174
Untereck, linkes 740
Untereck, rechtes 740
unterer Absatz 417
unterer Anzug 854
unterer Flügel 628
unterer gerader Augenmuskel 177
unterer Glaskolben 241
unterer Heizstab 266
unterer Holm 824
unterer Kühleranschluss 561
unterer Längsträger 635
unterer Mantel 42
unterer Nabel 115
unterer Querträger 635
unterer seitlicher Einschnitt 86
unterer seitlicher Lappen 86
unterer Thermostat 266
unterer Wurfarm 750
unteres Augenlid 110, 132
unteres Becken 448
unteres Schleusentor 597
Unterfach 386
Unterfahrschutz 571
Unterfangantenne 18
Unterfangkescher 911
Unterfutter 455
Untergeschoß 713
Untergrätenmuskel 151
Untergrund 538
Untergurt 253, 540
Unterhautbindegewebe 172
Unterhemd 796
Unterhose, lange 351
unterirdische Anlagen 407
unterirdische Kammer 402
unterirdischer Abfluss 67
unterirdisches Gerinne 47
unterirdisches Kabelnetz, Verteilung 487
Unterkante 880
Unterkiefer 97, 99, 108, 111, 112, 116, 121, 122, 123, 126, 131, 136, 138, 141, 142, 152
Unterkieferknochen 158
Unterkleid 366
Unterkühlen 680
Unterkunft 886
Unterkünfte 886
Unterlage 254, 917
Unterlage, dritter 447
Unterlage, Streckmetall 299
Unterlagsplatte 590
Unterlagsscheibe 268, 310
Unterlegscheiben 310
Unterlenker 640
Unterlid 177
Unterlippe 174, 444
Untermast 602
Unternehmen 525
Unterrock 337, 366
Unterrohr 579
Untersattel 439
Unterschenkel 126, 140
unterschiedliche Vogeltypen 118
Unterschnabel 115
Unterschrank 224
Unterschrift des Inhabers 729
Unterschrift, amtliche 729
Unterschriftenmappe 531
Unterschwanzdecken 115
unterseeischer Cañon 49
Unterseite 840
Unterseite des Hufs 127
Unterstock 391
Unterstützmauer 660
Untersuchungsraum 779, 781
Untersuchungsraum, Audiometrie 781
Untersuchungsraum, gynäkologischer 779
Untersuchungsraum, psychiatrischer 778
Unterteil 239, 374, 531, 558, 767
Unterteilhauptfacette 374

Untertitel 471
Untertor 597
Unterwäsche 351, 366, 716, 872
Unterwäschegeschäft 714
Unterwasser-Strahler 246
Unterwasserbohrung 654
Unterwasserkamera 480
Unterwassermauer 661
Unterwasserpipeline 654
Ununbium 683
Ununnilium 683
Unununium 683
Up-Quark 680
Ural 32
Uran 684
Uran, angereichertes 671
Uranbrennstoff, Kernspaltung 665
Uranus 4, 5
Urdu 469
Urenkel 784
Urenkelin 784
Ureter 104, 116
Urgroßeltern 784
Urgroßmutter 784
Urgroßvater 784
URL-Adresse 524
Urogenital-Öffnung 109
Urostyl 111
Ursprungskegel 168
Uruguay 742
USB-Schnittstelle 513, 526
Usbekistan 746

V

V-Ausschnitt 348, 354, 363
Vagina 103, 104
Vakuole 74, 94
Vakuole, pulsierende 94
Vakuum-Kaffeemaschine 241
Vakuumdestillation 656
Vakuumkammer 694
Vakuumpumpe 694
Vakuumrohr 694
Vampir 141
Vanadium 683
Vanille-Extrakt 200
Vanuatu 747
Variometer 899
Vater 784, 785
Vater-Pacinisches Körperchen 172
Vatikanstaat 744
VCR-Einstellung 495
VCR-Netzschalter 495
VCR-Tasten 495
Vegetation 66
Vegetationsbild nach Höhenlagen 66
Vegetationspunkt 77
Vegetationszonen 66
Veilchen 80
Velarium 407
Velours 254
Vene, königliche 160
Venen 160
Venera 19
Venezuela 742
Ventil 265, 447, 579, 899
Ventilator 260, 688
Ventilatormotor 261
Ventilatorregler 261
Ventilbüchse 447
Ventilfeder 445, 566
ventilierte Laufschiene 860
Ventilsitz 265, 268
Ventilsitzzange 314
Ventilteller 268
Ventilzug, dritter 447
Ventilzug, erster 447
Ventilzug, zweiter 447
ventrale Aorta 109
ventraler Nervenstrang 107
Venturidüse 757
Venus 4, 5
Venusmuschel 217
Verandatür 224
Verankerung 540
Verankerungspunkt 103
Veranstalterbüros 719
Verbene 208
Verbindung 470, 916
Verbindungen, mechanische 269
Verbindungsast 168
Verbindungsclip 776
Verbindungsdraht 272
Verbindungsgang 543
Verbindungshülse 868
Verbindungskabel 452, 465, 516
Verbindungskasten 563
Verbindungspunkt 273
Verbindungsseil 793
Verbindungsstück 488
Verbindungsstutzen 766
Verbindungstunnel 23
Verblendung 511
Verbot der Einfahrt 544, 546
Verbot für Fahrzeuge mit mehr als der angegebenen Höhe 545, 547
Verbot für Fußgänger 545, 546

Verbot für Krafträder 545, 546
Verbot für Lkws über einem zulässigen Gesamtgewicht 545, 546
Verbot für Radfahrer 545, 546
Verbot für Rollstuhlfahrer 725
Verbraucher, Stromleitung 646, 677
Verbrechensbekämpfung, vorbeugende 768
Verbrennen 71
Verbrennung 564, 565, 627
Verbrennungsraum 564, 566
Verdampfen 680
Verdampfer 261
Verdampfergebläse 261
Verdampferspirale 261
Verdampfungsgitter 261
Verdauungsapparat 164
verdeckelte Zelle 100
verdeckte Knopfleiste 355
Verdichten 565
Verdichter 573
Verdichterrad 564
Verdichtertrubine 627
Verdichtung 71, 564, 565, 627
Verdunkelung 617
Verdunstung 67
Veredelungsmesser 330
Vereinigte Arabische Emirate 746
Vereinigte Staaten von Amerika 742
Vereinigtes Königreich von Großbritannien und Nordirland 743
verengte Fahrbahn 544, 547
Verengung 695
Verfallsdatum 729
Verfolgerauto 870
Verfolgerlinie 871
Verfolgungsrad 871
Vergaser 574
Vergrößerer 485
Vergrößerungsobjektiv 485
Vergrößerungsrahmen 484
Verhol-Winde 607
Verhörraum 768
verjüngte Spitze 839
Verkehrsampel 712
Verkehrsflugzeug 53
Verkehrszeichen 544
Verkehrszeichen, internationale 544
Verkehrszeichen, nordamerikanische 546
Verkleidung 252, 253, 259, 574
Verkleidung, äußere 267
Verkleidungsmaterialien 299
Verkleinern/Vergrößern 512
Verklicker 834
Verkürzungstek 908
Verladebunker 648
verlängertes Mark 167
Verlängerungsschlinge 900
Verlobungsring 376
Verminderung des Strahldurchmessers 694
Verpackung 71
Verpackungen 222
Verpackungsmaterial 180
Verpackungsraum 180
Versailles-Parkett 254
Versalie 472
verschiebbarer Messschnabel 700
verschiebbarer Tastaturschutz 506
verschiedene Abzüge 258
verschiedene Haushaltsgeräte 240
verschiedene Schwimmstile 832
Verschiedenes 534
verschiedenes Zubehör 313
Verschlagwagen 588
Verschluss 223, 289, 303, 304, 369, 521, 889, 906, 913
Verschluss des Hochwasserentlastungswehrs 657
Verschlussblock 756
Verschlussdeckel 689
Verschlüsse 453
Verschlusshebel 587
Verschlussmaterial 689
Verschlussring 483, 756
Verschlussstopfen 689
Verschlussstück 912
Verschmutzung 69
Verschmutzung durch Autoabgase 69
Verschmutzung durch Haushalte 69
Verschmutzung, industrielle 69
Verschmutzung, landwirtschaftliche 69
Verschraubung 269
Verschraubungsmutter 269
Versenkknagel 301
Versenkpodium 430
versetzbare Trennwand 719
Versetzungszeichen 435
Versicherungsabteilung 730
Versitzgrube 263
Versorgungsbereich 619
Versorgungskapsel 25
Versorgungsmodul 486
Versorgungsstraße 618
Verspannung 824, 825
Verstärkerregler 613
Verstärkungsrippe 639
Verstärkungsschwelle 772
Versteifungsrippe 624
verstellbare Klemme 286

verstellbare Tastaturablage 511
verstellbarer Bügel 303
verstellbarer Sitz 584
verstellbarer Träger 368
verstellbares Rückenteil 776
Verstelldüse 629
Versteller 350
Verstellnut 310
Verstellschraube 436
Verstellspindel 642
Verstellung 310
Verstrebung 676
Vertäfelung, obere 632
Vertäfelung, untere 632
Vertebralschild 113
Verteidiger, rechter 803
Verteidigung 806
Verteidigungsdrittel 809
Verteidigungszone 812
Verteiler 538
Verteilerdose 591
Verteilerkasten 272, 273
Verteilerschleife 273
Verteilung über Freileitungen 486
Verteilung über Tiefseekabel 487
Verteilung über unterirdisches Kabelnetz 487
Verteilzentrum, regionales 475
Vertiefung 453
Vertikale 894
vertikale Bodenbewegung 43
vertikale Einstellung 518
vertikaler Zug 916
vertikales Schiebefenster 415
vertikales Seitenband 812
Vertikalseismograph 43
Vertikutierer 333
Verwaltung 394, 735
Verwaltungsbüro 764, 769
Verwaltungsbüros 718
Verwaltungsgebäude 664
Verwandtschaftsbeziehungen 784
verwelkendes Keimblatt 77
Verwerfung 43
Verziehnaht 349
Verzierungen 435
Vestibularnerv 174
Veterinäre 852
Vetter 785
Viadukt 541
Vibratohebel 441
Victoriasee 34
Victoriawüste, Große 29
Video- und Digitalübertragung, Anschlussbuchsen 477
Video-Ausgänge 497
Video-Eingänge 497
Video-Kreuzschiene 491
Video-Switch-Techniker 490
Video-Switcher 489, 491
Video-Switcher, zusätzlicher 491
Videobandsteuerungen 496
Videobedarf 716
Videofilmdiskette 481
Videokassette 495
Videokassettenadapter 496
Videokassettenschacht 496
Videorecorder 495
Videoschalttafel 489
Videoschnittstelle 513, 526
Videospielsystem 918
Videothek 733
Vieleckbein, großes 154, 156
Vieleckbein, kleines 154
Vielecke 705
Vier-Zehenhuf 127
Viereck 426, 705
viereckige Fahne 789
vierfüßiger Stock 782
Vierer mit Steuermann 839
Vierer ohne Steuermann 839
Viererbob 884
viereckiger Ausschnitt 363
Viereckregner 329
Vierkantstift 285
Vierkantstopfen 269
Vierling 914
Viermastbark 602
Viertaktmotor 564
vierte Zehe 115
Viertelfinale 789
Viertellinie 800
Viertelnote 435
Viertelpause 435
Viertelstab 253
Viertelstabfräser 308
viertürige Limousine 549
Vierundsechzigstelnote 435
Vierundsechzigstelpause 435
Vierung 410, 411
Vierungsturm 410
Vierviertel 434
Vierwegeregler 477
Vietnam 747
Vietnamesisch 468
Vinyl-Laufsohle 369
Vinylisolierung 299
Violett 400
Violine 439

Violinen, erste 437
Violinen, zweite 437
Violinfamilie 439
Violinschlüssel 434
VIP-Bereich 718
Viper 114
Visier 575, 749, 773, 859, 874, 884, 907, 913
Visiergestell 796
Vitrine 279
Vitrinenschrank 279
Vizeskip 877
Vogel 115
Vögel 115
Vogel, Anatomie 116
Vogel, äußere Merkmale 115
Vogel, Skelett 116
Vogelaugenchili 199
Vogelfüße, Beispiele 117
Vogelschnäbel, Beispiele 117
Vogeltypen, unterschiedliche 118
Volant 280, 282
Volkmannsche Kanäle 154
voll und bei 833
Vollachsel-Unterkleid 366
Vollbelastungsstellschraube 273
Vollbrillantschliff 375
Volleyball 812, 820
Volleyballspiel 812
Vollgeschoss 752
Vollgummirad 633
Vollkornbrot 205
Vollkornmehl 204
Vollmessingstange 284
Vollmond 7
vollreflektierender Spiegel 692
Vollreife 86
Vollziegel 298
Volt 702
Volute 276, 404, 405
Vor-Oberbramsegel 603
Vor-Obermarssegel 603
Vor-Royalsegel 603
Vor-Unterbramsegel 603
Vor-Untermarssegel 603
Vorbackenzahn 121, 123
Vorbau 245, 579
vorbeugende Verbrechensbekämpfung 768
Vorbramsaling 602
Vorbühne 430
Vordach 567, 902
Vordachrille 567
Vorderachse 639
Vorderansicht 146, 148, 150, 798
Vorderbein 96, 98, 110, 111, 277
Vorderbein (Außenseite) 98
Vorderbindung 840
Vorderblatt 342, 371
Vorderbremse 576
Vorderdeckel 426
vordere Aufschlaglinie 817
vordere Augenkammer 177
vordere Backenzähne 159
vordere Druckknopfleiste 369
vordere Einbuchtung 173
vordere Felgenbremse 579
vordere Fußraste 575, 576
vordere Kufe 884
vordere Nervenwurzel 167, 168
vordere Querleiste 893
vordere Schienbeinarterie 160
vordere Seitenfontanelle 158
vorderer Balken 698
vorderer Douglasscher Raum 170
vorderer Gaumenbogen 174
vorderer Haltegriff 757
vorderer Oberkiefer 108
vorderer Schienbeinmuskel 150
vorderer Schließmuskel 105
vorderer Straffergurt 906
vorderer Tragflügel 609
vorderes Auspuffrohr 552
vorderes Ruckstoßtriebwerk 22
vorderes Schutzblech 574
Vorderextremität 121, 143
Vorderfeld 818, 821
Vorderfläche 391
Vorderflug 749
Vorderflügel 96
Vorderfußwurzel 126
Vordergabel 579
Vorderhorn 167
Vorderkante 897, 898
Vorderkappe, perforierte 342
Vorderlade-Geschütz 753
Vorderlade-Geschütz im Querschnitt 753
Vordermast 607
Vorderpfote des Hundes 130
Vorderrad 333, 639, 640, 783
Vorderschaft 912
Vorderschürze 749
Vorderseite 348, 349, 374, 409
Vorderstangentasche 897
Vordersteven 598, 838
Vorderteil 342, 349, 370
Vorderteil, steifes 569

Vorderwand 818, 819
Vorderzwiesel 855
Vorfach 911
Vorfahrt 544, 546, 547
Vorfahrt an nächster Einmündung 544
Vorfahrt gewähren 544, 546
Vorfeld 618
Vorflügel 625
Vorführraum 427
Vorführzeiten 427
Vorfußbindung 892
Vorfußgummi 840
Vorfußplatte 892
vorgeformte Rohrummantelung 299
vorgeschriebene Fahrtrichtung 544, 546
Vorhafenwand 597
Vorhalle 724, 728, 730
Vorhang 282, 492
Vorhang, eiserner 430
Vorhang, loser 283
Vorhänge, Beispiele 283
Vorhangköpfe, Beispiele 283
Vorhaut 169
vorherige Sätze 822
vorherige Seite 515
vorherrschender Wind 63
Vorhof 548
Vorhof, linker 161, 162
Vorhof, rechter 161, 162
Vorholer 756
Vorholervorderteil 756
Vorkommen 651, 653
vorkragender Dachkranz 412
Vorlageneinzug 512
Vorlauf 259, 501
Vorlauftaste 508
Vorläutewerk 591
Vorliek 836
Vororte 39
Vorratsdosen 222
Vorratsschrank 724
Vorraum 584
Vorsatzblatt 426
Vorschaltgerät, elektronisches 275
Vorschaumonitor 489
Vorschaumonitore 491
Vorschlag 435
Vorschneider 306
Vorschot 834
Vorsortierung 474
Vorspeisen 722
Vorsprung 45
Vorspülbecken 721
Vorspultaste 495
Vorstadt 709
Vorstag 834
Vorsteiger 900
Vorstenge-Stagsegel 603
Vortasche 387
Vortitel 471
Vortrieb 630
Vorwahlsender-Wahltaste 497
vorwärts 828
vorwärts/rückwärts 327
Vorwärtsantrieb 333
Vorzeichentaste 529
Voyager 19
VU-Meter 488, 491
Vulkan 42, 44
Vulkan mit Ausbruchstätigkeit 44
Vulkan, effusiver 44
Vulkan, explosiver 44
vulkanische Asche 44
vulkanische Bombe 44
vulkanische Insel 49
vulkanischer See 48
Vulkantypen 44

W

Waage 11
Waage, elektronische 699
Waagebalken 443
Waagschale 698, 699
Waagschalenhaken 698
Wabe 100
Wabenausschnitt 100
Wabenstrick 458
Wache 408
Wachhäuschen 409
Wacholderbeere 198
Wachpersonal, Büro 733
Wachs 892
Wachsausrüstung 892
Wachsbohne 191
Wachsfarbstifte 396
Wachskerze, dünne 422
Wachskürbis 188
Wachsmalerei 396
Wachspapier 222
Wachtel 120, 212
Wachtelei 213
Wade 147, 149
Wadenbein 122, 131, 138, 141, 142, 152, 155, 156
Wadenbeinmuskel, kurzer 151
Wadenbeinmuskel, langer 150
Wadenbeinnerv, gemeinsamer 166

Wadenbeinnerv, oberflächlicher 166
Wadenbeinnerv, tiefer 166
Wadennerv 166
Wadenstrumpf 351
Wadi 52
Waffeleisen 238
Waffen 748
Waffen in der Römerzeit 748
Wagen 181, 642, 835, 895
Wagenanzug 369
Wagenausbesserungshalle 589
Wagendeck 608
Wagenheber 558, 873
Wagenlaufschild 587
Wagenradhut 341
Wagenrücklauftaste 528
Wagentür 554
Wagentypen 584
Wagenübergang 584
Waggon 587
Wahlrad 527
Wahltaste 261, 505, 506
Währungsangabe 729
Wakame 183
Wal 137
Walboot 601
Wald 39, 45
Wald, borealer 66
Wald, gemäßigter 66
Waldbrand 69
Waldfrosch 111
Waldhorn 447
Waldhörner 437
Waldmurmeltier 123
Walfisch 10, 12
Walisisch 469
Walkie-Talkie 505
Walkman® mit Radioteil 504
Wallaby 143
Wallpapille 176
Walmdach 414
Walnuss 88, 193
Walnuss, Längsschnitt 84
Walross 137
Walze 320, 333, 528
Walze, drehbare 458
Walzenbefestigung 320
Walzenbürste 573
Walzendrehknopf 528
Wams 338
Wan-tan-Teigblätter 207
Wand 246
Wand-Untergurt 571
Wandauslaufventil 268
Wanderausstellungsräume 395
Wanderschuh 344
Wandgitter 258
Wandlaterne 287
Wandleuchte 287
Wandpfosten 253
Wandträger 284
Wandwange 255
Wange 148, 301, 909
Wanne 320, 885
Wannengarnitur 262
Wantenspanner 835
Wantenverklicker 834
Wapitihirsch 128
Wappen 797
Wappenzeichen 741
Waran 114
Warenannahmebereich 716
Warenbaum 460
Warencode 699
Wareneingang 180
Wareneingang für Milchprodukte 180
Warengeschäfte 525
Warenzeichen, eingetragenes 473
warme Luft 64, 675
warme Speisen 722
Wärmeabgabe an Wasser 665
Wärmedämmung 259
Wärmedeflektorscheibe 274
Wärmeenergie 68, 646
Wärmeenergie, Elektrizitätserzeugung 646
Wärmeerzeugung 665
wärmeisolierter Griff 239
Wärmejalousie 60
Wärmeleitung 681
Wärmepumpe 260, 669
Wärmesenke 513
Wärmetauscher 259, 261, 670, 675
Wärmeübertragung 681
Wärmeverlust 68
Warmfront am Boden 56
warmgemäßigte Klimate 61
Warmhalteplatte 241, 721
Warmluftauslass 564
Warmluftaustritt 258
Warmluftklappe 257
Warmluftsystem mit Zwangsumlauf 258
Warmluftzufuhr 293
Warmwasseraustritt 267
Warmwasserbereiter 262
Warmwasserheizung mit Zwangsumlauf 259
Warmwasserkreislauf 262

Warmwasserleitung 266
Warmwassersteigleitung 262
Warmwasserzulauf 270, 271
Warn- und Gebotszeichen 774
Warnanzeige Besatzung 626
Warnanzeige Triebwerke 626
Warnblinklicht 624
Warnfläche 846
Warngerät 765
Warnkreuz 591
Warnleuchte «Tür offen» 557
Warnleuchten 557
Warnlinie beim Florettfechten 848
Warnlinie beim Säbel- und Degenfechten 848
Wartebereich 731
Wartebereich für den Entnahmeraum 781
Wartebereichmarkierung 620
Wartehäuschen 712
Warteraum 509, 768, 779
Warteraum für Angehörige 778
Warteraum für Besucher 726
Warteraum, zweiter 781
Warteschlange 731
Wartungsfahrzeug 622
Wartungskasten 273
Wartungsschacht 10
Warzenfortsatz 158
Warzenhof 171
Wasabipaste 201
Wasch- und Pflegesymbole 347
Waschbär 134
Waschbecken 262, 264, 780
Wäschekammer 724
Waschen 347
Wascherarm 294
Wäscherei 724, 726
Wäschetrockner 293, 347
Waschhandschuh 379
Waschküche 250
Waschlappen 379
Waschmaschine 262, 271, 292
Waschplatte 589
Waschraum 780
Waschtisch 724
Wasser 646, 665
Wasser verdampft 665
Wasser, leichtes 671
Wasser, schweres 670
Wasser, sicherstes 616
Wasser, Wärmeabgabe 665
Wasser-Dampf-Gemisch 646
Wasserablauf, Schlauch 485
Wasserabscheider 648
Wasserbadtopf 235
Wasserball 827
Wasserballspiel 827
Wasserbehälter 241, 261, 384, 586
wasserdichter Stromanschluss 263
Wasserdruckanzeiger 766
Wassereinlass 658
Wasserfall 47, 48
Wasserflugzeug 628
Wasserfluß 95
Wasserfrosch 111
Wasserglas 226
Wassergraben 852, 853
Wasserhahn 264, 766
Wasserheizkessel 266
Wasserhindernis 866, 867
Wasserhose 63
Wasserkanister 906
Wasserkanone 766
Wasserkessel 240
Wasserklappe 447
Wasserkraftwerk 657
Wasserkraftwerk im Querschnitt 658
Wasserkreislauf 67
Wasserkrug 226
Wasserlauf 70
Wasserläufer 102
Wasserlinie 615
Wassermann 10
Wassermelone 195
Wassernuss 184
Wasseroberfläche 828
Wasserpumpen-Zange 310
Wasserschlauch 294, 648
Wasserski 840
Wasserski-Set 840
Wasserspinne 102
Wassersport 827
Wassersprühdüse 573
Wasserstand 241, 261, 662
Wasserstand, höherer 597
Wasserstand, niedrigerer 597
Wasserstandsanzeige 288
Wasserstandsanzeige 239
Wasserstandsregler 292
Wasserstoff 682
Wasserstrahl 828
Wassertank 241, 611, 628
Wasserterrasse 854
Wassertrog 847
Wasserturm 589
Wässerungswanne 485
Wasserverschmutzung 70
Wasserversorgung, öffentliche 675
Wasservogel 117

Wasservorrat 662
Wasservorratstank 675
Wasserwaage 313
Wasserzähler 262
Wasserzeichen 729
Wasserzufluss, Schlauch 485
Wasserzulauf 268
Wassily-Stuhl 276
Watstiefel 911
Watt 702
Wattestäbchen 777
Wattetupfer 777
Watvogel 117
WC 250, 251, 724, 780
Webcam 517
Weben 460
Webkante 455
Webmustereinstellung 456
Webnadel 461
Webprinzip, Schaubild 463
Webschütz 461
Wechselanzeige für die Rückenlage 831
Wechselaufbau 573
Wechselsprechschalter 505
Wechselstrom-Netzkabel 526
Wechselstromgenerator 688
Weddellmeer 29
Wedel 76
Wedel, eingerollter junger 76
Weg 866
Wehr, festes 664
Wehrgang 408, 409
Wehrgang, gedeckter 408
Wehrmauer 408
weiblich 702
weibliche Blütenstände 89
weibliche Geschlechtsorgane 170
Weiche 583
weiche Kontaktlinse 384
Weiche, fernbediente 590
Weiche, handbediente 590
Weichenantrieb 590
Weichensignal 590
Weichenzunge 590
weicher Gaumen 174, 175
Weichkäse 211
Weichsel 32
Weichstrahl 108
Weichtiere 104
Weideland 831
Weidenholz 798
Weidenkorb 899
Weihgabe 737
Weihrauchkessel 737
Weihwasserbecken 737
Wein 180
Weinblatt 86, 186
Weinessig 201
Weinkarte 721
Weinkeller 720
Weinkellner, Sommelier 720
Weinranke 86
Weintraube 86, 192
Weintraube im Querschnitt 83
Weiselwiege 100
Weisheitszahn 159
Weiß 690, 915, 916
Weißbrot 205
weiße Linie 127
weiße Schokolade 208
weiße Senfkörner 198
weiße Substanz 167, 168
weiße Zwiebel 184
weißer Pfeffer 198
weißer Punktkball 862, 863
weißer Reis 207
weißer Spielball 863
weißer Stein 916
Weißer Zwerg 8
weißes Band 815, 817
Weißes Feuer 616
weißes Feld 916
Weißfisch 221
Weißkohl 186
Weißrussland 744
Weißwal 137
Weißweinglas 225
Weitere Symbole 473
Weitsichtigkeit 691
Weitsprung 790, 793
Weitverkehrsnetzwerk 523
Weitwinkelobjektiv 478
Weitwinkelspiegel 568, 569
Weizen 85, 203
Weizenkorn, Längsschnitt 85
Wellärmchen 445
Wellbrett 445
Welle 49, 285, 464, 659, 676, 686, 688, 690, 695, 762
Welle, langsam drehende 677
Welle, schnell drehende 677
Wellenbasis 49
Wellenbereichseinstellung 498
Wellenberg 690
Wellenhöhe 49
Wellenkamm 49
Wellenlänge 49, 690
Wellenleiter 489

Wellenmauer 660
Wellental 49, 690
Wellhornschnecke 217
Weltraum, Beobachtung 10
Weltraumteleskop, Hubble 53
Wende 832
Wende beim Brustschwimmen 832
Wende beim Schmetterlingsstil 832
Wendeflügel 415
Wendehebel 898
Wendekampfrichter 831
Wendekragen 352
Wendekreis des Krebses 34, 35, 36
Wendekreis des Steinbocks 34, 35, 36
Wendelhalter 274
Wendeltreppe 655
Wenden 546
Wenden verboten 544, 546
Wenderohr 285
Wendestab 285
Wendewand 831, 832
Wendezeiger 898
Werbeplakat 595
Werbetafel 592, 594
Werfer 794, 795, 799
Werftkran 596
Werkbank 312
Werkstatt 731
Werkstückspanner 303
Werkzeug 464
Werkzeuge, Beispiele 401
Werkzeugfutter 308
Werkzeuggürtel 313
Werkzeughalter 20
Werkzeugkasten 313
Werkzeugsatz 580
Wertangabe 729
Wertstoff-Sammelbehälter 71
Wespe 101
West 37, 917
West-Nordwest 37
West-Südwest 37
Weste 338, 348, 359
Westen 358, 616
Westindien 30
westliche Hemisphäre 35
Westlicher Indischer Rücken 50
westlicher Meridian 36
westliches Kardinalseezeichen 617
Wettbewerb 61
Wetterboje 54
Wetterflugzeug 54
Wetterhütte 58
Wetterkarte 54, 55
Wetterlage, gegenwärtige 55
Wetterradar 54, 624
Wettersatellit 54, 60
Wetterschenkel 247, 249
Wetterschiff 54
Wetterstation 54, 58
Wettersymbole, internationale 56
Wettervorhersage 54
Wettkampf 789
Wettkampfbecken 788, 831
Wettkampfbereich 845
Wettkampffeld 859
Wettkampffläche 823, 843, 845
Wettkampfgericht 887
Wettkampfplatz 887
Wetzstahl 229
Wetzstein 229
Whipping 868
Whiskyglas 225
wichtigste Sprachgruppen 468
Wickelauflage 281
Wickelbluse 359
Wickelkleid 356
Wickelkommode 281
Wickelrock 339, 357
Wickler 380
Wicklung 793, 909
Widder 12
Wide Receiver 807
Widerhaken 911
Widerlager 410, 413, 540
Widerrist 124, 130
Widerstände 689
Widerstandseinstellung 851
Widertonmoos, gemeines 75
Wiederaustritt 47
wiederbeschreibbare CD 521
Wiedereintrittsraum für ausgeschlossene Spieler 827
Wiedergabetasten 495, 504, 508
Wiederholungsbildschirm 789
Wiederholungstasten 501
Wiederholungszeichen 434
Wiege 14, 15, 756
Wiegeetikett 699
Wiegefläche 699
Wiegen 698
Wiegestahl 422
Wiese 182
Wiesel 134
Wigwam 418
Wikingerschiff 598
Wild 212
Wildleder 377

Wildreis 203
Wildschwein 128
Wildwasser 837
Wildwasser, Kanu-Kajak 837
Wildwechsel 545, 547
Wilkesland 29
Wimpel 739
Wimpelgirlande 739
Wimper 94, 177
Wimperg 411
Wimpern 132
Wimpernkämmchen 378
Wimpernzange 378
Wind 56, 69, 70, 833
Wind querab 833
Wind, vorherrschender 63
Wind, Wirkung 67
Windabweiser 570
Winde 573, 750, 917
Windel 368
Windelhöschen, dichtes 368
Windenergie 676
Windenergie, Elektrizitätserzeugung 677
Windensteuerung 573
Windfähnchen 893
Windfahne 58, 59, 677
Windgeschwindigkeit 55
Windhund 131
Windjacke 353
Windkanal 445
Windkraftwerk mit horizontaler Achse 677
Windkraftwerk mit vertikaler Achse 676
Windkraftwerke 676
Windlade 445
Windlaufquerteil 550
Windmühle 676
Windmühlenhaube 676
Windrichtung 55
Windrichtung, Messung 59
Windrose 37
Windrute 676
Windsack 432, 739
Windschutz 488, 899
Windschutzscheibe 550, 570, 574, 577, 607, 624, 626
Windschutzscheiben-Sonnenschutz 558
Windstärke, Messung 59
Windstärkefähnchen 56
Windstille 56
Windung 104, 105
Windzuleitung 445
Wing-Forward 804
Winglet 625
Winkel 269
Winkel 45° 269
Winkel, Beispiele 704
Winkel, rechter 704
Winkel, spitzer 704
Winkel, stumpfer 704
Winkel, überstumpfer 704
Winkelmaß 10
Winkelmesser 701
Winkelmessung 701
Winkelschleifer 308
Winkeltisch 511
Winsch 835
Winter 54
Winterniederschläge 64
Winterreifen 560
Wintersonnenwende 54
Wintersport 877
Wipfel 87
Wirbel 105, 111, 112, 136, 439, 440, 911
Wirbelkasten 439
Wirbelkörper 157, 168
Wirbelsäule 109, 121, 152, 157, 167
Wirbelschäkel 913
Wirbelschraube 441
Wirbelsturm 63
Wirbelsturm, tropischer 63
Wirkung des Windes 67
Wirsing 186
Wirtschaft 728
Wischblatt 557
Wischeraches 557
Wischerarm 557
Wischgummi 557
Wismut 682
wissenschaftliche Instrumente 23
wissenschaftliche Symbole 702
wissenschaftlicher Taschenrechner 529
Wissenschaftsraum 734
Wochenendkoffer 389
Wohnblock 419, 500, 508
Wohnen 470, 711
Wohngebiet 709
Wohnhaus 182
Wohnhaus, römisches 406
Wohnhäuser, traditionelle 418
Wohnküche 250
Wohnmobil 567
Wohnmodul, amerikanisches 21
Wohnraum 902
Wohnwagen 567
Wohnzimmer 250
Woilach 853
Wok 234
Wok-Set 234
Wolf 11, 134

Wolfram 683
Wolfram-Halogenlampe 274, 275
Wolframwendel 274
Wolga 32
Wolke 53, 65
Wolke, Oortsche 4
Wolken 56, 62
Wolken, hohe 55, 62
Wolken, mittelhohe 55, 62
Wolken, tiefe 55, 62
Wolkenabsorption 68
Wolkenband, spiralförmiges 63
Wolkenhöhe, Messung 59
Wolkenhöhenmesser 59
wolkenloser Himmel 56
Wolkenstore 283
Wolkentrichter 63
Wolkenwasser 70
Wolof 468
Worcestershire-Soße 200
Wortkorrekturtaste 528
Wulst 560
Wulstkern 561
Wundauflage, sterile 777
Wurf 795, 799
Wurfarm, oberer 750
Wurfarm, unterer 750
Wurfbereich 788
Würfel 705, 914, 915
Würfelbecher 915
Würfelbein 155
Würfelmusterparkett 254
Wurfgeräte 793
Wurfhügel 795
Wurfkreis 790, 791
Wurflinie 799
Wurflinienknoten 908
Wurfmal 795
Wurfmaschine 860
Wurfpfeil 918
Wurfscheibe 860
Wurftaubenschießen 860
Wurmfortsatz 164
Wurst, Chorizo 216
Wurst, Kielbasa 216
Wurst, Merguez 216
Wurst, Toulouser 216
Würstchen, Frankfurter 216
Wurzel 78, 159, 227
Wurzelgemüse 189
Wurzelhaare 77
Wurzelhaarzone 87
Wurzelhaube 77
Wurzelhaut 159
Wurzelkanal 159
Wurzeln, sproßbürtige 76
Wurzelspitzenöffnung 159
Wurzelsystem 77, 86
Würzen 200
Wüste 52, 61, 66
Wüste Gobi 33
Wüste, Atacama 31
Wüstenfuchs 134
Wüstenspringmaus 123

X

X-Band-Antenne 40
Xenon 684
Xylophon 437, 449

Y

Y-Schlauch 776
Y-Verbindungsstück 767
Yachthafen 788
Yak 129
Yardlinie 806
Yen 728
Yoruba 468
Ysop 202
Ytterbium 684
Yttrium 683
Yucatan-Halbinsel 30

Z

Zahl 919
Zahlen 917
Zahlenschloss 386
Zahlungsbetragsanzeige 548
Zahlungsmodalitäten 729
Zahlungsterminal, elektronisches 181, 731
Zählwerk 499
Zahn 108, 112, 303, 304, 382, 636, 686
Zahnbein 159
Zahnbogen 756
Zahnbürste 384
Zahnbürste, elektrische 384
Zähne 159, 453
Zahnfach 159
Zahnfleisch 159, 174
Zahnpasta 384
Zahnpflege 384
Zahnrad 462, 686
Zahnrädchen 391
Zahnradgetriebe 686

Zahnreihe, obere 174
Zahnreihe, untere 174
Zahnschritt 404, 405
Zahnseide 384
Zahnseidenhalter 384
Zahnstangengetriebe 686
Zander 220
Zange 233
Zangen 310
Zangengriff 901
Zangenwerk 409
Zäpfchen 174, 175
Zapfen 89, 177, 278, 390, 459, 462
Zapfenloch 390
Zapfhahn 548
Zapfsäule 548
Zapfsäulennummer 548
Zapfschlauch 548
Zapfwelle 641, 642
Zapfwellenstummel 640
Zarge 276, 277, 278, 439, 440
Zaumzeug 854
Zaun 182, 244
Zebra 128
Zecke 102
Zeh 127, 130, 146, 148
Zehe 117
Zehe, dritte 115
Zehe, vierte 115
Zehe, zweite 115
Zehen 155
Zehenaufzug 127
Zehenballen 130, 133
Zehenendglied 155
Zehenglieder 131
Zehengrundglied 155
Zehenloch 893
Zehenmittelglied 155
Zehenriemchen 344
Zehenschützer 773, 796
Zehenstrecker, kurzer 150
Zehenstrecker, langer 150
Zehenwand 127
Zehn 703
Zehn Gebote 738
Zehneck, regelmäßiges 705
Zehnerpin 865
Zehntelsekundenzeiger 696
Zeichen, diakritische 473
Zeichenform 472
Zeichenkorrekturtaste 528
Zeichenleser, optischer 474
Zeichenmaschine 399
Zeichenstellung 472
Zeichnen 396, 401
Zeigefinger 173
Zeiger 261, 695, 698, 699
Zeilenabstand 1,5 Zeilen 472
Zeilenabstand, doppelter 472
Zeilenabstand, einfacher 472
Zeit, Maßeinheit 702
Zeitaufnahmetaste 496
Zeiteinblendetaste 496
Zeitlupe 495
Zeitmesser, automatischer 831
Zeitmessung 696
Zeitmessung, elektronische 883
Zeitnehmer 810, 814, 827, 842, 844, 845, 846, 847, 848, 881, 883, 900
Zeitschalter 238
Zeitschaltuhr 239
Zeitschrift 471
Zeitschriftenladen 715
Zeitschriftensaal 733
Zeitschriftenständer 733
Zeituhr 238, 465
Zeitung 471
Zeitungskopf 471
Zeitungsname 471
zeitweise dichter Sprühregen 57
zeitweise leichter Regen 57
zeitweise leichter Schneefall 57
zeitweise leichter Sprühregen 57
zeitweise mäßiger Regen 57
zeitweise mäßiger Schneefall 57
zeitweise mäßiger Sprühregen 57
zeitweise starker Schneefall 57
zeitweise starker Schneefall 57
Zellafter 94
Zelle 96, 100, 407, 416, 563, 659, 677, 727
Zelle, tierische 94
Zelle, verdeckelte 100
Zellen 687, 728
Zellenring 659
Zellkern 74, 94, 168, 170
Zellkörper 168
Zellwand 74
Zelte, Beispiele 902
Zelten verboten 725
Zeltplatz 725
Zeltspannleine 902
Zeltstange 903
Zeltwagen 567
Zeltwand 902
Zement 159
Zement, Hartplatz 822
Zementestrich 254

Zenit 10
Zenitprisma 14
Zentaurus 11
Zentralafrikanische Republik 745
zentralafrikanische Sprachen 468
Zentralbereich 6
Zentralbereich, gewölbter 9
zentrale Kampffläche 843
zentrale Pumpstation 654
zentraler Mittelfeldspieler 803
zentrales Scharfstellrad 692
Zentralindischer Rücken 50
Zentralnervensystem 167
Zentralscheibe 95
Zentriereinstellung 518
Zentrierspitze 306
Zentriertaste 528
Zentriol 94
Zerkleinerer 71
Zerkleinerung 71
Zerkleinerungswerk 646
zerlappte Projektion 36
Zero 919
zersetzende Organismen 67
Zerstäuber 655
Zerstäuberstift 329
zerstoßene Chilis 199
Zerstreuungslinsen 691
Zeugenberg 52
Zeugenstand 728
Zickzackschere 454
Ziege 128
Ziegel 403, 406
Ziegel, feuerfester 298
Ziegelmauer 298
Ziegelstein 298
Ziegelstein, feuerfester 465
Ziegenfrischkäse 210
Ziegenkäse 210
Ziegenmilch 210
Ziehbügel 776
Ziehhacke 326
Ziehharmonikafach 386
Ziel 40, 41, 830, 852, 885
Zielbahnhof 582
Zielbälle 862
Zielbereich 887, 891
Zielbojen 839
Zielfernrohr 692, 912
Zielflagge 872
Zielgebiet 674
Zielgerade 856
Zielkugel 864
Ziellinie 791, 833, 839, 856, 865, 871, 890
Ziellinie, 500-m 883
Zielrichter 839, 883
Zielscheibe 859, 861, 893
Zier-Steppnaht 350, 368
Zierbaum 182, 244, 322
Zierborte 368
Ziergarten 322
Zierkohl 186
Ziernaht 346
Zifferblatt 696, 697
Ziffern 472
Ziffern, römische 703
Ziffernblatt 273

Zifferntaste 529
Zigarette 390
Zigarettenpapier 390
Zigarettenschachtel 390
Zigarre 390
Zigarrenschneider 390
Zikade 101
Zimmermannshammer 301
Zimmernummer 724
Zimtstangen 198
Zink 683
Zink-Elektrolytmischung (Anode) 689
Zink-Mangan-Zelle, alkalische 689
Zinke 227, 641, 642, 643
Zinken 327
Zinkenfräser 308
Zinkzylinder (Anode) 689
Zinn 682
Zinnenkranz 408
Zirbeldrüse 167
Zirkel 11
Zirkonium 683
Zirrokumulus 56, 62
Zirrostratus 56, 62
Zirrus 56, 62
Zither 432
Zitronatzitrone 194
Zitrone 194
Zitronenmelisse 202
Zitronenpresse 230
Zitronenschaber 229
Zitrusfrucht 82
Zitrusfrüchte 194
Zitruspresse 237
Zollkontrolle 621
Zona pellucida 170
Zoomer 496
Zoomobjektiv 478, 492, 496
Zoomregler 477
Zoomwippe 496
Zopfmuster 458
Zopfstich 459
Zubehör 289, 345, 399, 401, 454, 462, 558, 580
Zubehör, fotografisches 482
Zubehörfach 289, 456
Zubehörschuh 476
Zubehörtasche 859
Zubringer 709
Zucchini 188
Zucchini, gelbe 189
Zuchtchampignon 183
Zucker 209
Zucker, brauner 209
Zuckerdose 226
Zuckererbsen 190
Zuckermelone 195
Zufahrtsstraße 618
Zufahrtsweg 245
Zufluss 48
Zugang 658
Zugang für Behinderte 725
Zugang zum Gleis 582
Zugang zur Beleuchtungsanlage 490
Zugang zur zweiten Funktionsebene 529
Zugangsschacht 664
Zugangsserver 525

Zugarten 916
Zugbrücke 408
Zügel 115, 856
Zügelgurte 541
Zügelgurte, parallele 541
Zügelring 854
Zugentlastungsklemme 274
Zugfeder 557
Zugküche 584
Zuggriff 901
Zugmaschine 570
Zugpendel 640
Zugpersonal 584
Zugrichter 830
Zugriemen 389
Zugriffsöffnung 521
Zugrohr 642
Zugrollo 285
Zugsattelzapfen 571
Zugschnur 285, 387
Zugstange 756
Zugstangenverschluss 756
Zugsystem 910
Zugvorhang 282
Zugwagen 284
Zulauf 270
Zulaufverteiler 263
Zuleitungsdraht 274, 275
Zulu 468
Zuluft 259
Zuluftkanal 260
Zuluftleitung 543
zum Trocknen hängen 347
zum Trocknen legen 347
Zündanlage 627
Zündelektrode 259
Zündergehäuse 757
Zündhütchen 912
Zündkabel 566
Zündkabel, Anschluss 562
Zündkerze 332, 562, 565, 566
Zündkerzendichtring 562
Zündkerzengehäuse 562
Zündkerzenkabel 552
Zündknopf 267
Zündladung 757
Zündloch 753
Zündmechanismus 757
Zündschalter 576
Zündschloss 556
Zündschlüssel 332, 333
Zündtransformator 259
Zündung 564
Zündverteiler 566
Zündverteiler 552, 566
zunehmender Mond 7
Zunge 99, 109, 110, 164, 174, 175, 212, 342, 370, 433, 444, 456, 739, 881, 889
Zunge, gespaltene 112
Zungenmandel 176
Zungennadel 456
Zungenpapille 176
Zungenpfeife 444
Zungenraglan 360
Zungenrücken 176
Zungenscheide 112

Zungenspitze 176
Zungenwurzel 176
zurückgelegte Strecke 700
zurückgezogener linker Feldspieler 814
zurückgezogener Mittelfeldspieler 814
zurückgezogener rechter Feldspieler 814
Zusammenfassung 471
Zusammenfluss 48
zusammengesetzte Blätter 79
Zusammentragen 426
Zusatzgetriebegehäuse 627
Zusatzgriff 308
Zusatzheizung 260
zusätzlicher Griff 306
zusätzlicher Video-Switcher 491
zusätzliches Festplattenlaufwerk 513
zusätzliches Studiopersonal 490
Zusatzsteckdose 316
Zusatzstecker 290
Zusatztank 571
Zuschauer 728
Zuschauergrenze 795
Zuschauerraum 10, 431
Zuschauertribünen 788, 874
Zustreicher 643
Zuwachsstreifen 104, 105
Zwangsumlauf 258, 259
Zwecke 301
zwei Kolonnen Cheval 919
zwei Pärchen 914
Zwei-Zehenhuf 127
Zweiäugige Spiegelreflexkamera 480
Zweibein 755, 756
Zweier mit Steuermann 839
Zweier ohne Steuermann 839
Zweierbob 884
zweiflammiger Gasbrenner 903
zweiflügelige Ausgangstür 568
zweiflügeliger Propeller 628
Zweig 77, 87
Zweigelenkbogen 541
zweigliedrige Trugdolde 81
Zweihalbetakt 434
Zweikanalton 491
zweiköpfiger Armstrecker 150
zweiköpfiger Schenkelmuskel 151
zweiläufige Gardinenstange 284
Zweipersonenzelt 902
zweipoliger Schalter 272
Zweireiher 348
zweireihig 352
zweischalige Muschel 105
zweischalige Muschel, Anatomie 105
zweischalige Muschel, äußere Merkmale 105
zweischneidige Klinge 383
zweischneidiger Rasierer 383
zweiseitig gezahnte Effilierschere 382
Zweisitzer 276
zweisitziges Sofa 724
Zweispitz 339
Zweistärkenglas 385
zweistöckiges Haus 419
Zweistromtriebwerk 627
Zweitaktmotor, Arbeitsprozess 565
Zweitbelegung 514
zweite Funktionsebene 529
zweite Funktionsebene, Zugang 529

zweite Reihe 804
zweite Rückenflosse 108, 109
Zweite Runde 789
zweite Spannungserhöhung 677
zweite Stufe 25
zweite Violinen 437
zweite Zehe 115
zweiteiliger Schlafanzug 368
zweiter Backenzahn 159
zweiter Halswirbel 153, 157
zweiter Kamera-Assistent 428
zweiter Malspieler 794
zweiter Raum 811
zweiter Raumschotkurs 833
zweiter Ring 753
zweiter Schiedsrichter 807, 812, 813
zweiter Ventilzug 447
zweiter vorderer Backenzahn 159
zweiter Warteraum 781
zweites Mal 794
Zweiunddreißigstelnote 435
Zweiunddreißigstelpause 435
Zwerchfell 163
Zwerg, Brauner 8
Zwerg, Weißer 8
Zwickel 413, 615
Zwiebel im Querschnitt 78
Zwiebel, rote 184
Zwiebel, weiße 184
Zwiebelgemüse 184
Zwillinge 13
Zwillingswadenmuskel 150, 151
Zwinge 312, 462
Zwinger 408
Zwischenfutter 455
Zwischengeschoß 250, 251
Zwischenknochenmuskel 150
Zwischenrad 876
Zwischenraum 434
Zwischenrippennerv 166
Zwischenschiene 590
Zwischensohle 370
Zwischensummentaste 529
Zwischentitel 471
Zwischenwirbelloch 157
Zwitterdrüse 104
Zwittergang 104
Zwölfeck, regelmäßiges 705
Zwölffingerdarm 164
Zyan 690
Zyclorama 492
Zylinder 268, 340, 381, 382, 564, 705
Zylinderdruckpresse 421
Zylindergehäuse 249
Zylinderglas 691
Zylinderkopfabdeckung 552
Zylinderkopfdeckel 566
Zylinderprojektion 36
Zylinderschloss 249
Zypern 744
Zypressennadeln 89
Zytopharynx 492
Zytoplasma 74, 94, 170
Zytoplasmamembran 74, 94
Zytostom 94

Index français

1er cunéiforme 155, 156
2e cunéiforme 155, 156
2e métacarpien 140
25 points 918
3e cunéiforme 155
3e métacarpien 140
4e métacarpien 140
5e métacarpien 140
50 000 unités astronomiques 4
50 unités astronomiques 4

A

à cheval sur deux colonnes 919
à cheval sur deux numéros 919
abaissement de la tension 646, 662, 677
abaque 404
abat-jour 286
abat-son 411
abats 212
abattant 264, 265, 278, 279
abdomen 96, 97, 98, 103, 107, 115
abeille 98
abeille : ouvrière, morphologie 98
abeille, anatomie 99
about 270
Abraham 736
abrégé 445
abri 543, 583
abri des joueurs 794
abri météorologique 58
abribus 712
abricot 192
abside 411
absidiole 410, 411
absorption d'eau 78
absorption de dioxyde de carbone 78
absorption de sels minéraux 78
absorption par le sol 68
absorption par les nuages 68
abyssin 133
acanthodien 92
accastillage 835
accent 435
accent aigu 473
accent circonflexe 473
accent grave 473
accès à la grille d'éclairage 490
accès au réservoir à essence 551
accès au second niveau d'opérations 529
accès aux quais 582
accès interdit 544, 546
accès interdit aux bicyclettes 545, 546
accès interdit aux camions 545, 546
accès interdit aux motocycles 545, 546
accès interdit aux piétons 545, 546
accès pour handicapés physiques 725
accessoires 289, 345, 401, 436, 454, 462, 558, 580
accessoires au butane 903
accessoires au propane 903
accessoires d'hommes 716
accessoires de décoration 716
accessoires de femmes 717
accessoires de foyer 257
accessoires de l'objectif 478
accessoires de mise à feu 752
accessoires photographiques 482
accessoires, automobile 558

accessoiriste 429
accompagnement 864
accord 435
accordéon 432
accotement 538
accotoir 276
accoudoir 281, 783
accouplement électrique 571
accouplement flexible 677
accroche-mouche 909
accueil 730
accumulateur 559
achondrite 8
acidification des lacs 70
acier 298
acromion 153
acrotère 403, 404
acteur 428
actinides 684
actinium 684
action du vent 67
actrice 429
adaptateur de cassette vidéo compacte 496
adaptateur de charge utile 24
adaptateur de courant 526
adaptateur de fiche 274, 383
adaptateurs 269
addition 529, 703, 721
addition en mémoire 529
administration 394, 735
admission 564, 565
admission d'air refroidi 564
adresse URL 524
adresse URL (localisateur universel de ressources) 524
aérateur 268
aérateur à gazon 333
aérateur de toit 567
aérateur latéral 567
aérocyste 75
aérofrein 676, 760, 898
aérogare 620
aérogare de passagers 619
aérogare satellite 619
aéroglisseur 605
aérographe 398
aérographe, coupe 398
aéroport 39, 618, 708
affichage 529
affichage de l'heure de départ 582
affichage de la couleur 456
affichage des données 495, 529
affichage des fonctions 450
affichage des stations 503
affichage du numéro de rang 456
affichage du résultat 529
affichage du texte 528
affichage indice d'exposition 479
affichage numérique 699, 777
affichage numérique des stations 498
affichage ouverture 479
affichage radar 771
affiche 427
affiche publicitaire 594, 595
afficher 261, 494, 497, 503, 505, 506, 699
afficher numérique 316
afficher prix 548
afficher totaliseur 548

afficheur volume 548
affluent 48
affût 753, 756
Afghanistan 746
Afrique 28, 34, 50, 745
Afrique du Sud 746
agar-agar 183
age 641
agence de voyages 714
agenda 530
agent de police 770
agglomération 708
agitateur 292
agnathe 92
agneau haché 215
agrafe 284, 470, 700
agrafes 453, 534
agrafeuse 534
agrandisseur 485
agriculture intensive 68, 70
agrumes 82, 194
aide de caisse 181
aide-arbitre 810
aide-mémoire des procédures 20
aides à la marche 782
Aigle 10, 12
aigle 119, 123
aigue-marine 375
aiguillage 583
aiguillage manœuvré à distance 590
aiguillage manœuvré à pied d'œuvre 590
aiguille 51, 52, 64, 261, 398, 452, 453, 454, 479, 590, 695, 698, 776
aiguille à brider 233
aiguille à clapet 456
aiguille à piquer 233
aiguille à tricoter 457
aiguille aimantée 907
aiguille circulaire 457
aiguille des dixièmes de seconde 696
aiguille des heures 697
aiguille des minutes 696, 697
aiguilles de nettoyage 318
aiguilles de pin 89
aiguilles de sapin 89
aiguilleur vidéo de production 491
aiguillon 98
aikido 846
aikidogi 846
aïkidoka 846
ail 184
aile 23, 97, 98, 115, 550, 570, 625, 676, 760, 897, 909
aile à géométrie variable 630
aile antérieure 96
aile arrière 609
aile avant 609
aile Dame 916
aile de quartier 342, 370
aile droite 804
aile du nez 175
aile gauche 804
aile haute 628
aile inférieure 628
aile libre 897
aile postérieure 96
aile rabattable 857
aile Roi 916
aile supérieure 628

aile, oiseau 115
aile, parapente 897
aileron 338, 624, 836, 840, 873, 891, 898
ailes 140, 898
ailes en V 609
ailes, chauve-souris 140
ailette 260, 293, 625, 628
ailette à ressort 302
ailier défensif droit 806
ailier défensif gauche 806
ailier droit 801, 804, 811, 814, 879
ailier gauche 801, 804, 811, 814, 879
ailier rapproché 807
aimant 454, 488, 534, 687
aimant de retenue 240
aine 146, 148
air 565
air calme 56
air chaud 64, 675
air chaud ascendant 63
air frais 675
air froid 64
air froid subsident 63
aire d'accueil 764, 778, 781
aire d'arrêt 890
aire d'arrivée 885, 887
aire d'attente 730
aire d'entraînement 788
aire de combat 843, 846
aire de compétition 845, 846, 847, 859
aire de compétition : demi-lune 887
aire de jeu 918
aire de jeux 608
aire de lancer 788
aire de manœuvre 618
aire de préparation de l'étalage 180
aire de ravitaillement 548
aire de réception 180, 395, 716
aire de réception des produits laitiers 180
aire de repos 39
aire de service 39, 619
aire de stationnement 619
aire de trafic 618
airelle 192
ais 425
ais ferré 425
aisselle 146, 148
ajowan 199
ajustement de l'image du cercle horizontal 701
ajustement de l'image du cercle vertical 701
ajustement de la hauteur 641, 642
akène 83, 84
alarme sonore 613
albanais 469
Albanie 744
albatros 119
albumen 117
albumen farineux 85
alcool à 90° 777
Algérie 745
algue 75
algue brune 75
algue rouge 75
algue verte 75
algue, structure 75
algues 183
alidade 59, 612, 701
alignement du faisceau dans l'axe 694

aligneur 838
alimentation 180
alimentation en air 445
alimentation en eau 670, 671
alimentation jackpot 920
alimentation solaire 529
alimentation sur secteur 504
aliments congelés 181
aliments prêts-à-servir 181
alkékenge 192
allée 180, 322, 866, 867
allée de jardin 244
allée de quilles 865
Allemagne 744
allemand 469
alliance 376
alligator 114
allumage manuel 267
allumette de sûreté 391
allumeur 552, 566
allures, cheval 124
allures, voile 833
alluvions 48
alose 220
Alpes 32
alpiniste 901
altérations 435
alternateur 552, 566, 586, 646, 659, 668, 677, 688
alternative 514
alternative : sélection du niveau 3 514
altimètre 761, 896, 898, 899
altimètre de secours 626
alto 439
alto-cumulus 56, 62
alto-stratus 56, 62
altos 437
alule 115
aluminium 682
alvéole 100, 274, 867
alvéole à miel 100
alvéole à pollen 100
alvéole de plaque 562
alvéole dentaire 159
alvéole operculée 100
amande 81, 193
amanite vireuse 76
amarante 203
amas globulaire 9
amble 125
ambleur 857
ambulance 775, 778
âme 591, 753, 908
américain à poil court 132
américium 684
Amérique centrale 28, 30
Amérique du Nord 28, 30, 50
Amérique du Sud 28, 31, 50
Amériques 742
améthyste 375
ameublement de la maison 276
amharique 468
amibe 94
amidon, grain 74
amorce 757, 912
amorti 821
amortisseur 18, 382, 417, 553, 876
amortisseur arrière 575

ASTRONOMIE > 2-25; TERRE > 26-71; RÈGNE VÉGÉTAL >72-89; RÈGNE ANIMAL > 90-143; ÊTRE HUMAIN > 144-177; ALIMENTATION ET CUISINE > 178-241; MAISON > 242-295;
BRICOLAGE ET JARDINAGE > 296-333; VÊTEMENTS > 334-371; PARURE ET OBJETS PERSONNELS > 372-391; ARTS ET ARCHITECTURE > 392-465; COMMUNICATIONS ET BUREAUTIQUE > 466-535;
TRANSPORT ET MACHINERIE > 536-643; ÉNERGIES > 644-677; SCIENCE > 678-705; SOCIÉTÉ > 706-785; SPORTS ET JEUX > 786-920

amortisseur avant 577
amortisseur en caoutchouc 920
amortisseur magnétique 698
ampère 702
amphibiens 110
amphithéâtre romain 407
ampli-syntoniseur 503
ampli-syntoniseur : vue arrière 497
ampli-syntoniseur : vue avant 497
amplitude 690
ampoule 95, 274, 275, 687, 783
ampoule de la trompe utérine 171
amygdale 174
amygdale linguale 176
amygdale palatine 176
ananas 196
anatomie 150
anatomie de l'abeille 99
anatomie de l'araignée femelle 103
anatomie de l'éponge 95
anatomie de l'escargot 104
anatomie de l'étoile de mer 95
anatomie de l'oiseau 116
anatomie de la grenouille mâle 110
anatomie de la perche 109
anatomie de la pieuvre 106
anatomie de la tortue 113
anatomie du cheval 125
anatomie du coquillage bivalve 105
anatomie du homard 107
anatomie du papillon femelle 97
anatomie du serpent venimeux 112
anche 444, 446
anche double 446
anche simple 446
anchois 219
Ancien Testament 736
anconé 151
ancrage des haubans 541
ancre 610, 697
ancre à champignon 610
ancre à jas 610
ancre charrue 610
ancre de marine 610
ancre flottante 610
ancre sans jas 610
ancres, exemples 610
Andorre 743
andouillette 216
Andromède 12
âne 128
anémomètre 58, 59, 677, 898
anémomètre de secours 626
aneth 202
anglais 469
angle aigu 704
angle droit 704
angle obtus 704
angle rentrant 704
angles, mesure 701
anglicanisme : Henri VIII 736
Angola 746
anguille 219
Anik 487
animalerie 714
anis 202
anneau 76, 249, 284, 290, 382, 383, 390, 454, 522, 611, 696, 699, 809, 811, 824, 901, 909
anneau brisé 911
anneau d'étanchéité 268
anneau d'étanchéité en cire 265
anneau de branche 854
anneau de départ 910
anneau de montant 854
anneau de rêne 854
anneau de retenue 776
anneau de suspension 382
anneau de tête 910
anneau de traction 776
anneau dioptrique 614
anneau du cliquet 307
anneau oculaire 115
anneaux 374, 824, 825
annelet 404
annonce publicitaire 471
annonceur 828
annulaire 173
anode 266, 689
anorak 371, 901
anse 295, 328, 910
Antarctique 28, 50, 747
antéfixe 403
antenne 17, 60, 96, 97, 98, 99, 107, 504, 505, 506, 551, 577, 600, 611, 624, 631, 758, 761, 771, 812
antenne à faible gain 18
antenne à haut gain 18
antenne d'émission 60, 486
antenne d'émission à haut gain 60
antenne d'émission/réception 486
antenne de communication 761
antenne de télécommande 40, 60
antenne de télécommunication 608, 609, 762
antenne de télémesure 60

antenne domestique 486
antenne en bande X 40
antenne multifonction 763
antenne parabolique 489, 493
antenne parabolique d'émission/réception 486
antenne radar 40, 760, 763
antenne radio 604, 606, 608, 609, 652, 763, 873
antenne télescopique 503
antenne UHF 18, 60
antenne VHF 762
antenne-récepteur GPS 613
antennule 107
anthélix 173
anthère 80
anticlinal 651
anticyclone 55
Antigua-et-Barbuda 743
Antilles 30, 742
antilope 128
antimoine 682
antiseptique 777
antitragus 173
anus 95, 97, 103, 104, 105, 106, 107, 109, 113, 164, 169, 170
aorte 162, 163
aorte abdominale 160, 165
aorte ascendante 161
aorte descendante 161
aorte dorsale 99
aorte ventrale 109
apex 104, 105, 159, 176
Apollo 19
apophyse épineuse 168
apophyse mastoïde 158
apophyse styloïde 158
apophyse transverse 157, 168
apostrophe 473
apothécie 74
Appalaches 30
appareil à dessiner 399
appareil à télémètre couplé 480
appareil à visée reflex mono-objectif 480
appareil à visée reflex mono-objectif : dos 476
appareil à visée reflex mono-objectif : vue avant 476
appareil à visée reflex numérique : dos 477
appareil de cartographie thermique 18
appareil de forage 651
appareil de Golgi 74, 94
appareil de lancement 860
appareil de levage 635
appareil de plongée 480
appareil de pointage 756
appareil de prise de son et d'enregistrement 429
appareil de protection respiratoire 765
appareil de radiographie mobile 778
appareil digestif 164
appareil enregistreur 59
appareil jetable 480
appareil numérique 481, 517
appareil petit-format 480
appareil photographique 35 mm 20
appareil pour photodisque 481
appareil reflex 6 X 6 mono-objectif 481
appareil reflex à deux objectifs 480
appareil reflex, coupe 477
appareil respiratoire 163
appareil stéréoscopique 481
appareil urinaire 165
appareils de conditionnement de l'air 261
appareils de conditionnement physique 850
appareils de mesure 695
appareils de navigation 612
appareils de son portatifs 503
appareils électroménagers 236, 288, 716, 717
appareils électroménagers divers 240
appareils photographiques 480
appareils scientifiques 17
appartement du commandant 609
appartements en copropriété 419
appartenance 703
appeau 913
appel suivant 507
appendice nasal 140
appendice vermiculaire 164
applicateur-mousse 378
applique 287
applique du robinet 268, 270
applique orientable 287
appoggiature 435
approvisionnement en numéraire 731
appui de fenêtre 252
appui-bras 554, 555
appui-flèche 859, 913
appui-joue 860, 861
appui-main 399
appui-pied 464, 877
appui-pieds 312
appui-tête 555
après-rasage 383
aquarelle 396

aquastat 259
aqueduc de remplissage 597
aqueduc de vidange 597
aquifère captif 646
ara 118
arabe 468
Arabie saoudite 746
arachide 190
arachnides 96
arachnoïde 167
araignée 103
araignée femelle, anatomie 103
araignée, morphologie 103
araignée-crabe 102
aramé 183
araméen 468
arbalète 750
arbalétrier 253
arbitre 799, 801, 803, 805, 807, 809, 810, 817, 818, 819, 820, 827, 842, 843, 844, 845, 846, 864, 877, 879, 881, 882
arbitre à cheval 858
arbitre adjoint 881
arbitre assistant 882
arbitre auxiliaire 847, 860
arbitre de côté 846
arbitre de champ 814
arbitre de ligne de but 814
arbitre de parcours 838
arbitre en chef 795, 807, 846, 847, 883
arborisation terminale 168
arbre 87, 237, 659, 676, 686, 688, 695, 697, 762
arbre à cames 566
arbre cannelé 557
arbre centre 812
arbre d'ornement 182, 322
arbre d'ornement 244
arbre de l'hélice 609
arbre de mise à feu 756
arbre de Noël 652, 654
arbre de roue 553
arbre de transmission 605
arbre de transmission longitudinal 553
arbre fruitier 182
arbre lent 677
arbre moteur 631
arbre rapide 677
arbre turbine-compresseur 627
arbre, structure 87
arbres 866
arbres feuillus, exemples 88
arbrier 750
arbuste 322
arc 704, 750
arc à deux articulations 541
arc à poulies 859, 913
arc à trois articulations 541
arc de cercle 802
arc de l'aorte 160, 161, 162
arc diagonal 410
arc droit 859
arc en plein cintre 413
arc encastré 541
arc insulaire 49
arc métallique à treillis 540
arc moderne 750
arc-boutant 410, 411
arc-doubleau 410
arc-en-ciel 65
arc-formeret 410
arcade 407, 410, 855
arcade dentaire inférieure 174
arcade dentaire supérieure 174
arceau 322, 836
archaeognatha 92
arche 540, 738
arche naturelle 51
archéoptéryx 93
archer 859
archet 439
archipel 38
architecture 394, 402
architecture, styles 404
architrave 403, 405
archives 394, 509, 769
archives médicales 781
arçon 826
arcs 750
arcs, exemples 413, 541
Arctique 28
ardillon 350, 911
arène 407
aréole 171
arête 45, 884, 894
arête neurale 109
arête plate 404, 405
arête supérieure 815
arête vive 404
argent 683, 741
Argentine 742
argon 684
argyronète 102
Ariane IV 24
Ariel 11
armature 320, 367, 389, 902

armature de la clé 435
Arménie 746
arménien 469
armes 748
armes blanches 751
armes de l'âge de pierre 748
armes de l'époque romaine 748
armes, escrime 849
armet 749
armoire 278
armoire à papeterie 510
armoire de séchage 484
armoire inférieure 224
armoire réfrigérée 180
armoire supérieure 224
armoire-penderie 279, 724
armoire-vestiaire 510
armure 749
armures de base 463
arpège 435
arqué 901
arquebuse 752
arraché 850
arrache-bottes 345
arrache-clou 301
arrangements des parquets 254
arrêt 495, 499, 508
arrêt à l'intersection 544, 546
arrêt au stand 873
arrêt d'autobus 712
arrêt d'impression 512
arrêt-court 794
arrêt/effacement de mémoire 501
arrêtoir de chargeur 754
arrière 804, 811, 828
arrière centre 812
arrière court 821
arrière droit 801, 803, 812, 814
arrière du court 818
arrière gauche 801, 803, 812, 814
arrière-grand-mère 784
arrière-grand-père 784
arrière-grands-parents 784
arrière-petit-fils 784
arrière-petite-fille 784
arrière-petits-enfants 784
arrivée 852
arrivée des remontées mécaniques 886
arrivée du mazout 259
arrondi 79
arrondissement 39
arrondisseur 454
arroseur canon 329
arroseur oscillant 329
arroseur rotatif 329
arrosoir 328
arsenal stérile 780
arsenic 682
artère abdominale dorsale 107
artère arquée 160
artère axillaire 160
artère brachiale 160
artère carotide primitive 160
artère dorsale du pied 160
artère fémorale 160
artère iliaque 160
artère iliaque commune 160, 165
artère iliaque interne 160, 165
artère mésentérique inférieure 165
artère mésentérique supérieure 160, 165
artère pulmonaire 160, 162, 163
artère rénale 160, 165
artère sous-clavière 160
artère sternale 107
artère tibiale antérieure 160
artère ventrale 107
artères 160
arthropleura 92
artichaut 187
article 471
articles de bureau 528
articles de cuisine 716
articles de fumeur 390
articles de maroquinerie 386
articles de salle de bains 717
articles divers, bureau 534
articles ménagers 295
articles perdus et retrouvés 725
articulation 557, 909
articulation à glissement 156
articulation charnière 156
articulation de la pelleteuse 637
articulation ellipsoïdale 156
articulation en selle 156
articulation pivot 156
articulation sphérique 156
articulations synoviales, types 156
artisanat 452
arts 394
arts de la scène 427
arts graphiques 420
artisanat 452
As 914
asa-fœtida 199
ascenseur 16, 407, 417, 509, 650, 713, 724, 761
ascension droite 13

Asie 28, 33, 50, 746
asperge 185
aspérité 501
asphalte 656
aspirateur 658, 659, 775
aspirateur à main 288
aspirateur-balai 289
aspirateur-traîneau 289
aspirine 777
assaisonnement au chili 199
assiette à dessert 226
assiette à salade 226
assiette creuse 226
assiette plate 226, 905
assistance 728
assistant à la réalisation 490
assistant accessoiriste 429
assistant réalisateur 429
assistants des avocats 728
assureur 900
astate 683
astérisque 473
astéroïdes, ceinture 5
asthénosphère 42
astigmatisme 691
astragale 153, 155, 405, 753
astronautique 18
astronomie 4
atelier 726
atelier d'entretien 648
atelier de mécanique 548
atelier de réparation des wagons 589
atelier diesel 583
Atelier du Sculpteur 10
athlète : bloc de départ 791
athlétisme 790
Atlas 34
atlas 102, 111, 122, 126, 131, 153, 157
atmosphère 66, 70
atmosphère terrestre, coupe 53
atoll 51
atome 680
atomes 680
âtre 256
atrium 406
attache 391, 448, 913
attache d'accordage 433
attache de pavillon 446
attache de sécurité 20
attache du tube 275
attache pour outils 20
attache pour tuyaux et échelles 767
attaches 453
attaches parisiennes 534
attaquant à l'aile 809
attaquant au but 809
attaquant central 812
attaquant de pointe 803
attaquant de soutien 803
attaquant droit 812
attaquant gauche 812
attaque 807
attelles 777
atterrissage 891
atterrisseur (Viking) 18
attraction 687
attrape 443
aubage directeur de sortie 627
aube 659
aube avant-directrice 659
aube de roue 659
aube directrice 659
aube du compresseur axial 627
aubergine 188
aubier 87
audioguide 394
auditorium 394, 718, 732
auge 659
augmentation de l'effet de serre 68
auriculaire 173
aurore polaire 53
Australie 28, 50, 747
Autel 10
autel secondaire 737
auto-caravane 567
auto-inversion 504
autobus 568, 713
autobus à impériale 569
autobus articulé 569
autobus scolaire 568
autocar 568
autoclave 780
autocuiseur 234
autodéfense antimissile 762
autodirecteur infrarouge 759
automne 54
automobile 549
automobile électrique 563
automobile hybride 563
automobile, organes des systèmes 552
autoroute 39, 539, 709
autoroute de ceinture 39
autotrophes 67
Autriche 744
autruche 119
auvent 550, 567, 639, 902

1016

ASTRONOMIE > 2-25; **TERRE** > 26-71; **RÈGNE VÉGÉTAL** >72-89; **RÈGNE ANIMAL** > 90-143; **ÊTRE HUMAIN** > 144-177; **ALIMENTATION ET CUISINE** > 178-241; **MAISON** > 242-295;
BRICOLAGE ET JARDINAGE > 296-333; **VÊTEMENTS** > 334-371; **PARURE ET OBJETS PERSONNELS** > 372-391; **ARTS ET ARCHITECTURE** > 392-465; **COMMUNICATIONS ET BUREAUTIQUE** > 466-535;
TRANSPORT ET MACHINERIE > 536-643; **ÉNERGIES** > 644-677; **SCIENCE** > 678-705; **SOCIÉTÉ** > 706-785; **SPORTS ET JEUX** > 786-920.

auvent de fenêtre 902
avance 504
avance rapide 495, 499, 504, 508
avançon 911
avant 828
avant court 821
avant droit 801, 804
avant du court 818
avant gauche 801, 804
avant-bec 635
avant-bras 130, 147, 149
avant-centre 801, 814
avant-champ 794
avant-distributeur 659
avant-scène 430
avant-toit 412
aven 47
avenue 39, 711
averse de grêle 57
averse de neige 57
averse de pluie 57
avertisseur 556, 576, 586
avertisseur de brume 611
avertisseur pneumatique 570
avertisseur sonore 765
avion à décollage et atterrissage verticaux 628
avion d'affaires 628
avion de combat 760
avion de ligne 53
avion de ligne supersonique 629
avion furtif 629
avion léger 628
avion long-courrier 624
avion radar 629
avion supersonique 53
avion, forces agissant sur un 630
avion, mouvements 630
avion-cargo 475, 629
avion-citerne amphibie 628
avions, exemples 628
aviron 598, 600, 838
aviron de couple 838
aviron de pointe 838
aviron de queue 598
aviron en pointe 838
avirons, types 838
avocat 188
avoine 85, 203
avoine : panicule 85
axe 248, 454, 464, 500
axe central 676
axe d'attelage 587
axe de tambour 910
axe du pédalier 580
axe horaire 17
axe principal 86
axel 881
axis 122, 153, 157
axone 168
aymara 469
Azerbaïdjan 746
azimut 15
azote 683
azur 741

B

babeurre 210
babines 130
bâbord 609, 616, 617
babouin 139
baby-foot 920
bac 320
bac à boue 651
bac à compost 323
bac à glaçons 291
bac à gravier 872
bac à légumes 291
bac à plante 322
bac à viande 291
bac d'alimentation 519
bac de ramassage 332
bac de recyclage 71
bac de sortie 519
bac ramasse-jus 239
bâche spirale 658, 659
bacon américain 216
bacon canadien 216
badminton 816
bagages 388, 717
bagel 204
bague 390, 447, 868
bague de blocage 302, 700
bague de correction dioptrique 692
bague de fiançailles 376
bague de finissant 376
bague de fond 268
bague de mise au point 478
bague de réglage 329
bague de réglage du couple de serrage 306
bague de serrage 268, 446, 482
bague filetée 900
bague inférieure de blocage de la sphère 58
bague solitaire 376
bagues 376
bagues collectrices 688
baguette 346, 439
baguette d'écartement 461
baguette d'encroix 461
baguette de flanc 551
baguette épi 204
baguette parisienne 204
baguettes 449
Bahamas 742
Bahreïn 746
bahut 510
baie 7, 38, 83
Baie d'Hudson 30
baie de contrôle 489, 490, 491
baie de genièvre 198
baie de jacks 488
baie vitrée 727
baies 192
baignoire 251, 262, 264, 724
bain d'arrêt 485
bain de fixation 485
bain de révélateur 485
bain moussant 379
bain-marie 235
bains de développement 485
baïonnette à douille 751
baïonnette à manche 751
baïonnette à poignée 751
baïonnette incorporée 751
bajoyer 597
baladeur 504
baladeur numérique 503
baladeur pour disque compact 503
baladeuse 316
balai 257, 295, 688
balai à feuilles 333
balai à franges 295
balai à neige à gratter 558
balai d'essuie-glace 557
balai métallique 449
balais 688
balalaïka 433
Balance 11
balance à fléau 698
balance de cuisine 231
balance de précision 699
balance de Roberval 698
balance électronique 699
balance romaine 698
balancier 329, 599
balancier d'extension 851
balancier de traction 851
balancine 602
balayage automatique des stations 498
balayeuse 573
balcon 251, 431, 738
balcon de veille 614
balconnet 291
Baleine 10, 12
baleine 137, 367, 391
baleine de col 349
baleinière 601
balisage maritime, système 616
balise de détresse 611
balise de navigation aérienne 761
ballast 591
ballast électronique 275
balle 752, 858, 912, 920
balle d'entraînement 819
balle de baseball 796
balle de baseball, coupe 797
balle de cricket 798
balle de fil 797
balle de golf 867
balle de golf, coupe 867
balle de hockey 800
balle de liège 797
balle de racquetball 818
balle de softball 797
balle de tennis 822
balle de tennis de table 815
balle de tournoi 819
ballerine 343
balles de squash 819
ballon 241, 823, 899
ballon à fond rond 685
ballon de basket 810
ballon de football 802, 808
ballon de handball 814
ballon de netball 809
ballon de rugby 805
ballon de volleyball 812
ballon de volleyball de plage 813
ballon de water-polo 827
ballon, montgolfière 899
ballon-sonde 54, 59
balluchon 388
balustrade 412, 417
bambara 468
bambous 917
banane 196
banane plantain 196
banc 277, 593, 715, 737

banc d'équipe 827
banc de musculation 851
banc de sable 49
banc des accusés 728
banc des avocats de l'accusation 728
banc des avocats de la défense 728
banc des joueurs 801, 807, 809, 812, 814, 878
banc des juges 728
banc des officiels 879
banc des pénalités 879
banc des remplaçants 803
banc des témoins 728
banc du jury 728
bandage 843, 868
bandage de roue caoutchoutée 633
bandage triangulaire 777
bande 862, 878
bande antidérapante 894
bande blanche 812
bande centrale 919
bande d'ancrage 254
bande d'identification technique 501
bande de filet 821
bande de gaze 777
bande de pourpre 336
bande de ris 603
bande de roulement 561
bande de tissu élastique 777
bande élastique 350
bande magnétique 495, 499, 729
bande métallisée holographique 729
bande nuageuse spirale 63
bande pare-soleil 58
bande réfléchissante 765
bande rétro-réfléchissante 611
bande transporteuse 71
bande ventilée 860, 912
bande verticale de côté 812
bandeau 282
bandelette d'arrachage 390
banderole 739
banderole d'exposition à venir 394
banderole d'exposition en cours 394
bandes de fréquences 498
bandoulière 388, 391, 527
Bangladesh 747
banjo 432
banlieue 39, 709
banque 710, 715, 730, 915
banque de données 525
banquette 264, 277, 555, 775
banquette arrière 555
Banquise d'Amery 29
Banquise de Filchner 29
Banquise de Ross 29
bar 279, 431, 608, 710, 714, 719, 720
bar commun 220
bar-salon 724
barbacane 408
Barbade 743
barbe 85, 115
barboteuse 369
barbotin 636, 758
barbule 56
bardane 189
bardeau 299
bardeau d'asphalte 299
baren 421
barge de service d'urgence 653
barillet 249, 754
barmaid 720
baromètre à mercure 59
baromètre enregistreur 59
barquette 222
barrage 657
barrage à contreforts 660
barrage à contreforts, coupe 660
barrage en remblai 660
barrage en remblai, coupe 660
barrage mobile 664
barrage-poids 661
barrage-poids, coupe 661
barrage-voûte 661
barrage-voûte, coupe 661
barrages, exemples 660
barre 123, 127, 284, 385, 686, 792, 834, 840, 850, 851
barre à aiguille 453
barre à dorsaux 851
barre à lisses 461
barre à pectoraux 851
barre à triceps 851
barre blindée 658
barre cannelée 284
barre collectrice 272
barre collectrice neutre 272
barre d'acier 825
barre d'attelage 756
barre d'écoute 834, 835
barre d'espacement 514, 528, 783
barre d'étouffoir 443
barre de bois 825
barre de commande 897
barre de contrôle 670, 671
barre de coupe 642, 643
barre de flèche 834

barre de guidage et de prise de courant 595
barre de maintien 569
barre de manœuvre 643
barre de mesure 434
barre de pied presseur 453
barre de plongée 763
barre de poussée 416
barre de pression 442
barre de repos des marteaux 442, 443
barre de reprise 434
barre de retenue 291
barre de tractage 622
barre de témoins 728
barre fixe 824, 825
barre inférieure 285, 824
barre lisse 284
barre oblique 473
barre supérieure 824
barre télescopique 920
barre transversale 827
barreau 255, 277, 281, 799
barres asymétriques 824
barres de Spa 852
barres parallèles 825
barrette 380
barrette de mémoire vive (RAM) 513
barrette négative 562
barrette positive 562
barrière 281, 712, 852
barrière de départ mobile 857
barrière de pneus 872
baryum 682
bas 365, 367, 878
bas de casse 472
bas de ligne 911
bas résille 365
bas-cuissarde 365
bas-mât 602
base 17, 58, 176, 308, 381, 405, 531, 578, 591, 739, 767, 825, 827, 907
base de dormant 249
base de la vague 49
base en bois 899
baseball 794
baseball, lancer 795
baseball, position des joueurs 794
basilaire 713
basilic 202
basilosaure 93
basketball 810
basque 367
bassin 121, 126, 138, 141, 142, 322, 596, 664, 827, 831, 838
bassin de compétition 788, 831
bassin de plongeon 788
bassin de radoub 596
bassinet 165, 752
basson 446
bassons 437
bastion 409
bateau à vapeur à roues latérales 599
bateaux de couple 839
bateaux de pointe 839
bateaux et embarcations, exemples 604
bâti 298, 423, 460, 612
bâti d'équipement 489, 490
bâti de la pompe à vide 694
bâti du brûleur 903
bâtiment administratif 596, 664
bâtiment de la turbine 668
bâtiment des services 666
bâtiment du réacteur 667, 669
bâton 796, 797, 846, 891, 892
bâton de craie 423
bâton de ski 888
bâton de softball 797
bâtonnet 177
bâtonnet de colle 534
bâtons de golf, types 867
battant 249, 449, 460, 739
batte 643, 798
batterie 302, 306, 448, 563, 586, 687, 752
batterie auxiliaire 563
batterie d'accumulateurs 562, 673
batterie d'accumulateurs 552
batterie de cuisine 234, 722
batteries 60
batteries de traction 563
batteur 798, 799
batteur à main 236
batteur à œufs 232
batteur sur socle 236
baudrier 555, 901
baudroie 220
bavette 368, 369, 848
bavette garde-boue 551, 570, 571
bavette garde-neige 876
bavoir 368
bavolet 352
bazooka 757
beau-fils 784
beau-frère 785
beau-père 784
beaux-arts 394
beaux-parents 784

bec 106, 115, 227, 268, 270, 315, 446, 451, 457, 610, 900
bec corné 113
bec de bord d'attaque 625
bec fixe 700
bec mobile 700
bec verseur 240, 241, 295
bec-de-cane 248
bécarre 435
bêche 326, 756
bécher 685
becquerel 702
becs, exemples 117
bégonia 80
Bélarus 744
belette 134
Belgique 743
Bélier 12
Belize 742
belle-fille 784
belle-mère 784
belles-sœurs 785
béluga 137
bémol 435
Bénin 745
bénitier 737
benne 638
benne à ordures 573
benne basculante 572, 573, 639
benne tasseuse 573
béquet 574
béquille 389, 571, 609, 631
béquille centrale 575
béquille commune 782
béquille d'appoint 567
béquille d'appui 567, 641
béquille d'avant-bras 782
béquille latérale 575, 577
berbère 468
berceau 422, 756
berceuse 276
béret 341
bergamote 194
berge 538
berger allemand 130
bergère 276
bergerie 182
berkélium 684
berline 549
berlingot 223
bermuda 358
béryllium 682
bésicles à pont élastique 385
béton 298
béton armé 298
béton précontraint 298
bette à carde 185
betterave 189
beurre 210
beurrier 226
bezel (8) 374
Bhoutan 747
biais 368, 455
biathlon 893
biathlonien 893
bibliothèque 395, 711, 726, 732, 734
bibliothèque enfantine 732
biceps brachial 150
biceps crural 151
bicorne 339
bicross 871
bicyclette 578
bicyclette de course 581
bicyclette de tourisme 581
bicyclette de ville 581
bicyclette hollandaise 581
bicyclette tout-terrain 581
bicyclette, accessoires 580
bicyclettes, exemples 581
bidet 264
bidon 579
bief aval 661
bief d'amont 657
bief d'aval 657, 658
bielle 564, 566
bielle de compression 640
bière 180
bifteck 214
bigorneau 217
bigoudi 380
bijouterie 374, 714
bijoux 717
billard 862
billard anglais 863
billard français 862
billard pool 862
bille 300, 470, 516
bille blanche 863
bille blanche mouchetée 863
bille bleue 863
bille brune 863
bille creuse 268
bille d'ivoire 919
bille de choc 862, 863
bille de plomb 757
bille de visée blanche 862

bille jaune 863
bille noire 863
bille rose 863
bille rouge 862, 863
bille verte 863
bille, coupe 300
billes numérotées 862
billes rouges 863
billet de banque 729, 915
billetterie 394, 427, 719
billetterie express 427
bimah 738
binette 326
binocle 385
biologie 702
biosphère 66
biosphère, structure 66
bipied 755, 756
biplan 628
birman 468
biseau 444, 776
bismuth 682
bison 128
bitte 607
blague à tabac 390
blaireau 134, 383
blanc 690, 914
blanche 435
Blancs 915, 916
blatte orientale 101
blazer 358
blé 85, 203
blé : épi 85
bleu 400, 690
bleu danois 211
bleu vert 400
bleu violet 400
bleuet 192
blindage 758
blindage d'aspirateur 659
bloc 791
bloc aiguille 398
bloc convertisseur 493
bloc d'alimentation 513
bloc d'arrêt 309
bloc d'arrêt 309
bloc d'équipement 25
bloc de béton 298
bloc de commande des caméras 489, 490
bloc de culasse 912
bloc de départ 791
bloc de pression 700
bloc opératoire 780
bloc pneumatique 585
bloc-cylindres 566
bloc-éphéméride 530
bloc-essieu 894, 895
bloc-moteur 236, 237, 240, 288, 384, 585
bloc-notes 530
bloc-sténo 531
bloc-tension 452, 453, 457
blocage 660
blocage de l'inclinaison 304
blocage de l'interrupteur 306
blocage de la colonne 482
blocage de la plate-forme 482
blocage de profondeur 307
blocage du cordon de tirage 285
blocage du guide 305
blocage du pivot 312
blocage du pivotement 701
blocage horizontal 482
blocage vertical 482
bloqueur 800
bloqueur droit 807
bloqueur gauche 807
blouson court 353
blouson long 353
blousons 352
boa 114
bob 341
bobinage 688
bobine 458, 462, 495
bobine mobile 488
bobine réceptrice 476, 499
bobineur 452
bobinoir 462
bobsleigh 884
bobsleigh à deux 884
bobsleigh à quatre 884
bocal 446
body 366
bogie 586, 595
bogie moteur 585, 595
bogie porteur 585
bohrium 683
bois 39, 300, 867, 868
bois de bout 300
bois de cœur 87
bois n° 1 868
bois n° 3 868
bois n° 5 868
bois, dérivés 300
bois, famille 437

boisseau d'embouchure 447
boissons 180
boîte à canette 452
boîte à courrier 531
boîte à fromage 223
boîte à gants 556
boîte à leurres 911
boîte à lumière 485
boîte à lumière, ouverture de la 485
boîte à onglet 303
boîte à outils 313
boîte à œufs 222
boîte à poussière 308
boîte aux lettres 474
boîte d'accessoires 456
boîte d'allumage 627
boîte d'allumettes 391
boîte d'encastrement 274
boîte d'engrenage multiplicateur 677
boîte d'essieu 586
boîte de cirage 345
boîte de conserve 223
boîte de contrôle 267
boîte de culasse 754, 755
boîte de jonction 591
boîte de Pétri 685
boîte de raccordement 490
boîte de service 818
boîte de vitesses 552
boîte électrique 673
boîte en zinc (anode) 689
boîte jackpot 920
boîte pour seringues usagées 771
boîte-classeur 533
boîtes alimentaires 222
boîtier 261, 275, 285, 306, 308, 313, 316, 318, 383, 436, 476, 488, 499, 507, 613, 614, 695, 696, 700, 920
boîtier à double rangée de connexions 689
boîtier de batterie 562, 571
boîtier de relais/d'interconnexion 563
boîtier du moteur 331
boîtier du ventilateur 382
boîtier électronique de commande 563
boîtier tour : vue arrière 513
boîtier tour : vue avant 513
boîtier tour : vue intérieure 513
bokken 846
bol 226, 236, 237
bol à raser 383
bol à salade 226
bol verseur 237
boléro 358
Bolivie 742
bols à mélanger 232
bols de cuisson 239
bombe 853
bombe volcanique 44
bôme 834
bonbout 342
bonde 270
bonde de fond 246
bongo 449
bonnet 367, 827, 830, 892
bonnet pompon 341
bord 79, 340, 341, 602
bord antérieur 105
bord d'attaque 625, 897, 898
bord d'une feuille 79
bord de fuite 624, 897, 898
bord de pli 362
bord externe 105
bord interne 105
bord libre 172
bord postérieur 105
bord tranchant 636
bord-côte 351, 354, 369
bordure 244, 281, 836, 872
bordure d'allée 322
bordure de quai 582, 593
bordure de trottoir 712
bore 682
borne 272, 274, 290, 562, 663
borne d'entrée 316
borne d'incendie 712
borne d'incendie 767
borne de gonflage 548
borne de mise à la terre 497
borne négative 562, 687, 689
borne positive 562, 687, 689
bornes de raccordement des antennes 497
bornes de raccordement des enceintes 497
bornes interactives 395
Bosnie-Herzégovine 744
bosse 875, 890
bossoir 602, 606
Botswana 746
botte 185, 343, 855, 874, 875
botte de caoutchouc 765
botte de couronne 853, 857
botte de genou 857
botte de saut 896
botte de tendon 853, 857, 858
botte rigide 887

botte souple 887
bottes de paille 875
bottillon 342, 841
bottine 343
boubou 339
bouche 95, 104, 105, 107, 110, 136, 148, 174, 444, 753, 754, 756, 860, 912
bouche à feu 753
bouche à feu, coupe 753
bouche à induction 258
bouche d'air 556
bouche d'extraction 258
bouche de soufflage 258
boucherie 180
bouchon 236, 379, 667, 776, 906
bouchon antifuite 903
bouchon d'air 320
bouchon de chargement 757
bouchon de dégorgement 270
bouchon de fermeture 757
bouchon de remplissage 332, 561, 576
bouchon de scellement 689
bouchon de vidange 262, 291
bouchon de vidange d'huile 566
bouchon du réservoir 570
bouchon femelle 269
bouchon femelle à visser 269
bouchon mâle sans bourrelet 269
bouchons d'oreilles/oreillettes 871
boucle 350, 388, 453, 539, 555, 611, 889
boucle de ceinture 350, 352
boucle de piquet 902, 903
boucle de réglage 285, 895, 906
boucle piquée 881
boucles d'oreille 374
boucles d'oreille à pince 374
boucles d'oreille à tige 374
boucles d'oreille à vis 374
bouclier 331, 748, 879
bouclier annulaire 16
bouclier arrière 17
bouclier thermique 22
Bouddha 736
bouddhisme : Bouddha 736
boudin 216
bouée 833
bouée à plan focal élevé 615
bouée charpente 614, 617
bouée conique 615, 617
bouée cylindrique 615
bouée de sauvetage 609, 611, 771
bouée espar 617
bouées d'arrivée 839
bouées de départ 838
bouées de parcours 838
bougie 332
bougie d'allumage 562, 565, 566
bouilloire 240
boulangerie 181
boulangerie-pâtisserie 715
boule 517, 865
boule à thé 233
boule d'attelage 558
boule de pétanque 864
boule de protection 839
boule de quilles 865
bouleau 88
bouledogue 130
boules 864
boulet 124, 752, 753
boulet creux 752
boulet ramé 752
boulevard 39, 711
boulevard périphérique 39
boulier 865
boulier-compteur 920
boulingrin 864
boulon 248, 310, 311, 312
boulon à ailettes 302
boulon à épaulement 311
boulon à gaine d'expansion 302
boulon d'accouplement 659
boulon d'éclisse 590
boulons 311
bourdalou 340
bourdon 101, 432
bourgeon 78
bourgeon axillaire 77
bourgeon gustatif 176
bourgeon terminal 77
bourrache 202
bourre 753, 912
bourre-pipe 390
bourrelet 127, 560, 561
bourriquet 423
bourse à monnaie 387
bourse copulatrice 97
boursette 445
Boussole 11
boussole magnétique 907
bout 227, 909
bout d'aile 897
bout du nez 124
bout fleuri 342

bout-filtre 390
boutefeu 752
bouteille 685, 906
bouteille à gaz médical 780
bouteille d'acétylène 319
bouteille d'air comprimé 765, 841
bouteille d'oxygène 319
bouteille d'oxygène portable 775
bouteille en verre 223
bouteille isolante 906
bouteur 636, 647
boutique 406
boutique du musée 394
boutique hors taxe 621
bouton 274, 278, 349, 354, 432, 439, 849
bouton à friction 700
bouton à tige 453
bouton alimentation papier 519
bouton champignon 516
bouton d'alimentation papier 731
bouton d'appel 417
bouton d'appel pour piétons 712
bouton d'arrêt 331
bouton d'assemblage 456
bouton d'échappement 443
bouton d'éjection 499
bouton d'éjection 477
bouton d'éjection de la disquette 513
bouton d'éjection du CD/DVD-ROM 513
bouton d'éjection du disque 521
bouton d'enregistreur vocal 527
bouton d'essai 767
bouton d'interligne variable 528
bouton de blocage 308, 313
bouton de blocage de l'arbre 308
bouton de clé 446
bouton de combinaisons 444
bouton de commande 290
bouton de contrôle 516
bouton de culasse 753
bouton de démarrage 513, 526
bouton de démarrage et de rétroéclairage 527
bouton de démarreur 576
bouton de déverrouillage de l'écran 526
bouton de manchette 361
bouton de mise au point 14, 15
bouton de mise au point manuelle 483
bouton de mise en circuit 479, 508
bouton de piston 447
bouton de point arrière 452
bouton de registre 444, 445
bouton de réglage du micromètre optique 701
bouton de réinitialisation 513, 918
bouton de remise à zéro 499, 700
bouton de sortie 527
bouton de tension 457
bouton de vaporisation 288
bouton de verrouillage 554
bouton de verrouillage de l'embase 701
bouton de verrouillage de l'interrupteur 305
bouton du pavé tactile 526
bouton extérieur 248
bouton fixe-courroie 441
bouton floral 77
bouton intérieur 248
bouton marche/arrêt 240, 519
bouton marche/arrêt/test 520
bouton moleté 320
bouton-guide 304
bouton-poussoir 236, 294, 470
bouton-pression 346, 353, 453
boutonnage sous patte 355
boutonnière 350, 352
boutons à trous 453
boutons de contrôle du point 456
boutons de lancement d'applications 527
boutons de réglage 494
boutons programmables 516
Bouvier 13
bouvreuil 118
box 720
boxe 842
boxeur 842
bœuf 129
bœuf haché 214
bracelet 696, 808, 859
bracelet lesté 850
bracelet tubulaire 376
bracelets 376
brachial antérieur 150
brachiopode 92
bractée 84
braconnière 749
brancard 323, 638, 776, 857
braies 338, 748
braguette 350, 351, 368
branche 127, 185, 310, 382, 385, 454, 687, 776, 855, 859, 913
branche à fruits 86
branche d'embouchure 447
branche inférieure 750, 854
branche maîtresse 87

branche supérieure 750, 854
branche télescopique 482
branchement aérien 663
branchement au réseau 273
branchement de l'abonné 273
branchement du distributeur 273
branchement pluvial 712
branchement, exemples 270
branchie 106
branchies 105, 109
branchies externes 111
brandebourg 353
bras 95, 124, 139, 147, 149, 286, 329, 452, 610, 637, 638, 641, 676, 783, 920
bras d'éloignement 568
bras d'essuie-glace 557
bras de balancier 599
bras de coutre 641
bras de delta 48
bras de fourche 632
bras de grand cacatois arrière 603
bras de lecture 500
bras de levage 637
bras de plaquette 385
bras de relevage 640
bras de suspension 292, 553
bras de traction 640
bras du longeron 636
bras gicleur 294
bras mort 48
bras spiral 9
bras télescopique 18
brasero 412
brassard 749, 808, 880
brassard pneumatique 777
brasse 832
brassière 368
break 549
brèche 917
bréchet 116
brelan 914
breloques 376
Brésil 742
bretèche 408
bretelle 367, 539, 583, 618, 906
bretelle boutonnée 369
bretelle de raccordement 539
bretelle de tir 893
bretelle pour botte de genou 857
bretelle réglable 368
bretelles 350
breton 469
brèves 471
brick 601
bricolage 298
bricole 853
bride 377, 453, 854
bride de corps-mort 615
bride de fixation 14, 15
bride de raccord 284
bride de suspension 354
brie 211
brigantin 601
brigantine 603
brin d'arrêt 761
brique 223, 298
brique creuse 298
brique perforée 298
brique plâtrière 298
brique pleine 298
brique réfractaire 256, 298, 465
briquet 318
briquet à gaz 391
briquette 223
brise-glace 606
brise-jet 329
broche 274, 275, 376, 461
broche de connexion 689
broche épingle 376
broche porte-bobine 452
brochet 220
brocoli 187
brocoli italien 187
brodequin de randonnée 344
brodequin de sécurité 773
brodequin de travail 342
broderie 459
brome 683
bronche lobaire 163
bronche principale 163
bronchiole terminale 163
brosse 85, 289, 295, 384, 397
brosse à chaussure 345
brosse à dents 384
brosse à épousseter 289
brosse à légumes 233
brosse à mascara 378
brosse à planchers 289
brosse à pollen 98
brosse anglaise 380
brosse centrale 573
brosse d'antennes 98
brosse de curling 877
brosse de nettoyage 383
brosse de tissage 456

1018

brosse éventail 397
brosse latérale 573
brosse pneumatique 380
brosse pour le bain 379
brosse pour le dos 379
brosse ronde 380
brosse-araignée 380
brosse-peigne pour cils et sourcils 378
brosses à cheveux 380
brou 84
brouette 323
brouillard 57, 65
broyeur 71, 270, 646
bruine 64
bruine continue faible 57
bruine continue forte 57
bruine continue modérée 57
bruine intermittente faible 57
bruine intermittente forte 57
bruine intermittente modérée 57
brûleur 259, 267, 290, 899, 903
brûleur à gaz 685
brûleur à mazout 259
brûleur bec plat 319
brûleur flamme crayon 314, 319
brume 57, 65
brume sèche 57
Brunéi Darussalam 747
brunissoir 422
buanderie 250, 724, 726
buccin 217
bûcher 256
bûchette 353
buffet 279, 720
buffet-vaisselier 279
buffle 128
buisson 63
bulbe 9, 172, 185
bulbe d'étrave 607, 609
bulbe olfactif 109, 175
bulbe rachidien 167
bulbe, coupe 78
bulgare 469
Bulgarie 744
bulles d'air 531
bureau 251, 509, 548, 720, 724, 726
bureau administratif 764, 769
bureau d'accueil des visiteurs 726
bureau d'admission des détenus 726
bureau de l'agent de sécurité 733
bureau de direction 511
bureau de formation professionnelle 730
bureau de l'élève 734
bureau de l'enseignant 734
bureau de l'infirmière en chef 779
bureau de l'inspecteur en prévention-incendie 764
bureau de l'officier subalterne 768
bureau de l'officier supérieur 768
bureau de l'urgentiste 778
bureau de la direction 718
bureau de poste 474, 475, 711, 715
bureau de réservation de chambres d'hôtel 620
bureau des douanes 596
bureau des greffiers 728
bureau des plaintes 768
bureau des surveillants 735
bureau du bibliothécaire 732
bureau du chef 764
bureau du conservateur 394
bureau du directeur 394, 726, 731, 732, 735
bureau du directeur adjoint 726
bureau du directeur général 509
bureau du gymnase 734
bureau du président 509
bureau du surveillant 732
bureau du travailleur social 779
bureau secrétaire 511
bureautique 468, 509
bureaux administratifs 718
bureaux des organisateurs 719
burette à robinet droit 685
Burin 11
burin 401, 421
Burkina Faso 745
Burundi 745
bus 513, 522
buse 315, 319, 320, 329, 382, 384, 398
buse à fluide 320
buse d'aspiration 304
buse de refoulement 246
buse vapeur 241
bustier 367
but 800, 802, 804, 807, 809, 811, 814, 827, 879, 920
butée 453, 540, 835, 889
butée 303
butée de porte 291, 587
butée talonnière 783
butoir 284, 583, 792
butte 52, 875
butte de débranchement 589

C

caban 355
cabas 388
cabillot 739
cabine 608, 631, 636, 637, 638, 639
cabine d'ascenseur 417
cabine d'essayage 716
cabine d'interprétation simultanée 718
cabine de commande 634
cabine de conduite 585, 586, 640, 643
cabine de déshabillage 781
cabine de douche 264
cabine de pilotage 605, 607, 898
cabine de projection 427
cabine des juges 887
cabine des passagers 605, 608, 609
cabine focale 16
cabine photographique 715
cabinet des juges 728
câble 306, 516, 517, 558, 573, 793, 824, 851, 859, 908, 913
câble à fibres optiques 523
câble à paire torsadée 523
câble coaxial 523
câble d'accélération 332
câble d'acier 900
câble d'acier 913
câble d'alimentation 513
câble d'alimentation de 240 V 272
câble d'alimentation de l'électrode 318
câble de barre 838
câble de bougie 552, 566
câble de commande 323, 580
câble de frein 579
câble de garde 663
câble de haubanage 824, 825
câble de levage 417, 634
câble de l'antenne haute fréquence 628
câble de masse 318
câble de raccordement 465, 502, 516
câble de synchronisation 527
câble de traction 317
câble de transmission 613
câble du démarreur 323
câble électrique 266, 556, 563, 712
câble porteur 540
câble pour interface numérique d'instruments de musique (MIDI) 451
câble téléphonique 712
câbles 492, 523
câbles de démarrage 558
câblodistributeur 486
cabriolet 276, 549
cacao 208
cacatoès 118
cachalot 137
cache-cœur 359
cache-flammes 755
cache-oreilles abattant 340
cæcum 103, 106, 116, 125, 164
cæcum pylorique 95, 109
cæcum rectal 95
cadeaux 717
cadenas 580
cadence images/seconde 479
cadmium 683
cadran 273, 695, 696, 697, 698, 907
cadran de tension 456
cadran des phases de la Lune 697
cadran solaire 696
cadre 100, 280, 386, 389, 395, 433, 575, 676, 776, 816, 822, 823, 862, 870, 893
cadre d'aluminium 893
cadre de charge 899
cadre de marche 782
cadre métallique 442
cadre porte-épreuves 485
cadre-cache 483
cadreur 428
café 208, 710, 715
café et infusions 208
café torréfié, grains 208
café verts, grains 208
cafetan 339
cafétéria 509, 735
cafetière 905
cafetière à infusion 241
cafetière à piston 241
cafetière espresso 241
cafetière filtre 241
cafetière napolitaine 241
cafetières 241
cage 407, 791
cage d'escalier 251
cage de scène 430
cage vitrée 699
cageot 222
cahier 426, 471
caïeu 78
caille 120, 212
caïman 114
caisse 181, 323, 440, 441, 442, 697, 723

caisse américaine 535
caisse blindée 920
caisse bombée 433
caisse circulaire 432
caisse claire 437, 448
caisse de batterie électronique 451
caisse de résonance 432, 433, 440
caisse enregistreuse 181
caisse roulante 448
caisse triangulaire 433
caisses 181, 716, 717
caissette 222
caissière 181
caisson 256, 259, 510
caisson de porte 554
caisson de voiture 760
calame 470
calamus 115
calandre 550, 570, 667
calcanéum 126, 153, 155
calcium 682
calculatrice à imprimante 529
calculatrice scientifique 529
calculette 386, 529
cale 312, 622, 753
cale à conteneurs 605
cale de couvercle 465
cale-pied 578, 580, 851
caleçon 351
caleçon long 351
calendrier-mémorandum 530
calice 80, 83, 84, 165, 737
calicule 83
californium 684
Callisto 4
calmar 217
caloporteur 665
caloporteur : eau bouillante 671
caloporteur : eau lourde sous pression 670
caloporteur : eau sous pression 671
caloporteur : gaz carbonique 670
caloporteur refroidi 665, 674
calot 340
calotte 115, 340, 341, 676
calotte glaciaire 61
calvinisme : Jean Calvin 736
cambium 87
Cambodge 747
cambre 385
Cambrien 92
cambrure 342
Caméléon 11
caméléon 114
camembert 211
caméra 18, 428, 490, 492, 775, 873
caméra de surveillance 395
caméra de télévision couleur 20
Cameroun 745
caméscope analogique 496
caméscope numérique 517
camion 338, 355, 390
camion avitailleur 622
camion commissariat 623
camion d'incendie 764
camion de vidange 573
camion porteur fourgon 573
camion vide-toilette 622
camion-benne 573, 639
camion-citerne 573
camion-citerne d'eau potable 622
camion-toupie 573
camionnage 570
camionnette 549
camions, exemples 573
camomille 208
campagne 709
camping 725, 902
camping interdit 725
Canada 742
canadienne 353
canal à venin 112
canal annulaire 95
canal d'admission 565
canal d'échappement 565
canal d'écoulement 655
canal de dérivation 627, 657
canal de fuite 658
canal de Havers 154
canal de projection 573
canal de transfert 565, 666
canal déférent 169
canal droit 502
Canal du Mozambique 34
canal éjaculateur 169
canal gauche 502
canal hermaphrodite 104
canal lacrymal 177
canal médullaire 154
canal radiaire 95
canal radiculaire 159
canal salivaire 99
canal semi-circulaire antérieur 174
canal semi-circulaire externe 174
canal semi-circulaire postérieur 174
canal siphonal 105
canal sudoripare 172

canalisation 559
canalisation d'alimentation 259
canalisation d'arrosage 573
canalisation de branchement 262
canalisation de pompage 694
canalisation de refoulement 263
canalisation de retour 259
canaux de Volkmann 154
canard 120, 213
Cancer 13
candela 702
canetière 462
canette 452, 453, 461
caniche 130
canif 421
canine 121, 159
canne 391
canne à lancer 910
canne à mouche 909
canne avec poignée orthopédique 782
canne avec quadripode 782
canne en C 782
canne en T 782
canneberge 192
cannelle 198
cannelloni 206
cannelure 404, 405, 562
cannette 223
canoë 600, 837
canoë monoplace (C1) 838
canoë-kayak : course en ligne 838
canoë-kayak : eaux vives 837
canon 124, 754, 755, 756, 758, 854, 860, 912
canon à électrons 494, 694
canon à mousse 607
canon brisé 854
canon d'avant-bras 749
canon du XVIIe siècle 752
canon sans recul 757
canot automobile 607
canot de sauvetage 602, 652
canot pneumatique de sauvetage 605
canotier 340
cantaloup 195
canton dextre de la pointe 740
canton dextre du chef 740
canton senestre de la pointe 740
canton senestre du chef 740
cantonnière 282, 389
cantonnière drapée 283
cantre 462
canule oropharyngée 775
canyon sous-marin 49
cap 38
Cap de Bonne-Espérance 34
Cap Horn 31
Cap-Vert 745
cape 338, 355, 390
cape de bain 368
capeline 341
capitaine 877, 884
capitale 37, 472
capitule 81
caponnière 409
capot 288, 289, 333, 519, 528, 550, 570, 689, 876
Capricorne 10
capsule 75, 783
capsule à membrane 566
capsule à vis 223
capsule, coupe 84
capteur 58
capteur actif 41
capteur de radiations terrestres 60
capteur de signaux de détresse 60
capteur de télécommande 494, 501
capteur de température 18
capteur de vitesse de roue 559
capteur infrarouge 518
capteur optique 516
capteur passif 41
capteur solaire 675
capteur solaire plan 672
capture 916
capuche 368
capuche coulissée 369
capuchon 275, 353, 470, 484, 783, 869, 882
capuchon d'objectif 478
capuchon de connexion 317
capuchon de protection 692
capuchon de sûreté 757
capuchon de ventilation 614
capuchon du levier 268
capucin 350
caquelon 234
car de reportage 486, 489
carabine 893
carabine (canon rayé) 912
carabine 22 861
caraco 337, 366
caractère avec empattements 472

caractère sans empattement 472
caractère, position 472
caractères 917
caractères d'une police 472
caractères, forme 472
carafe 225
carafon 225
carambole 197
carapace 107
caravane 567
caravane flottante 607
caravane tractée 567
caravaning 725
caravelle 599
carbone 683
Carbonifère 92
carburant diesel 656
carburateur 574
carburéacteur 656
carcasse 688
cardamome 198
cardan 641, 642
carde 185
cardigan 354, 359
cardinal 118
cardon 185
carénage 574
carénage avant 550
Carène 11
carène 108
caricature 471
carillon tubulaire 437, 449
carlingue centrale 607
carnivores 67
caroncule lacrymale 177
carotte 189
Carpates 32
carpe 116, 122, 126, 131, 136, 138, 141, 142, 154, 220
carquois 859
carré 881, 887, 888
carré 112, 705, 914, 919
carré de service 819
carre interne 901
carreau 249, 299, 458, 914
carreau d'arbalète 750
carreau de mine 648
carreau de plâtre 299
carrefour giratoire 538
carrière en entonnoir 647
carrière exploitée en chassant 647
carrosserie 292, 293, 550
carrosserie amovible 573
carrosseries, exemples 549
carte 915
carte Caisse de communauté 915
carte Chance 915
carte d'extension PCI 513
carte d'insolation 58
carte de circuit imprimé 689
carte de crédit 729
carte de débit 731
carte de ligne 592
carte de mémoire 477
carte de mémoire flash compacte 481
carte de pointage 530
carte de réseau 593, 594
carte des vins 721
carte géographique 734
carte isolée 914
carte mère 513
carte météorologique 54, 55
carte physique 38
carte politique 37
carte postale 474
carte réseau 522
carte réseau sans fil 522
carte routière 39
carter 260, 332, 483, 565, 566, 910
carter d'embrayage 576
carter d'engrenage de frein à main 587
carter de meule 308
carter de sécurité 332
cartes 914
cartes, symboles 914
cartilage articulaire 154
cartilage costal 122
cartilage de l'aile du nez 175
cartilage de la cloison 175
cartographie 35
carton 223, 400
cartothèque 732
cartouche 268, 315, 390, 470, 500, 611, 754, 773
cartouche (carabine) 912
cartouche (fusil) 912
cartouche d'encre en poudre 519
cartouche jetable 314, 319
cartouches 860, 861
cartouchière 770
carvi 198
casaque 359
case 418, 915, 919
case à bagages 584
case à équipements 24
case blanche 916

case noire 916
caserne de pompiers 711, 764
casernement 409
casier 279
casier à beurre 291
casier à munitions 758
casier laitier 291
casiers des élèves 735
casque 20, 318, 748, 765, 798, 800, 808, 842, 856, 858, 870, 871, 872, 875, 878, 882, 887, 888, 891, 894, 895, 897, 901
casque anti-bruit 861
casque d'écoute 502, 504
casque de frappeur 796
casque de protection 575, 580
casque de sapeur-pompier 765
casque de saut 896
casque de sécurité 772
casque intégral 874
casque protecteur 884, 885
casquette 340, 770
casquette norvégienne 340
casse-croûte 725
casse-noix 230
Cassegrain, foyer 17
casserole 235
cassette 499, 504, 521
cassette annonce 508
cassette de pellicule 481
cassette messages 508
cassette vidéo 495
cassette vidéo compacte, adaptateur 496
Cassini 19
Cassiopée 12
cassis 192
cassonade 209
cassure 362
castagnettes 437, 449
castes 99
castor 123
catadioptre 578, 876
catalan 469
catalogue informatisé 733
catamaran 835
catapulte 761
catégories de points 459
caténaire 585, 595
cathédrale 410
cathédrale gothique 410
cathédrale, plan 411
cathode 689
catholicisme 736
causeuse 276, 724
Cavalier 916
cavalier 409, 853, 855, 858
cave à vins 720
cavité abdominale 169, 170
cavité buccale 165, 163, 164
cavité gastrale 95
cavité nasale 163
cavité palléale 106
cavité pleurale 163
cédez le passage 544, 546
cédille 473
cédrat 194
cèdre du Liban 89
ceinture 276, 277, 278, 313, 350, 352, 561, 611, 844, 906
ceinture d'astéroïdes 5
ceinture d'haltérophilie 850
ceinture de Kuiper 4
ceinture de sécurité 555, 873
ceinture élastique 351, 353
ceinture lestée 841
ceinture montée 350, 353
ceinture porte-outils 313
ceinture ventrale 281
ceinturon de service 770
céleri 185
céleri-rave 189
cellule 96, 407, 727
cellule animale 94
cellule convective 63
cellule d'isolement 727
cellule photoélectrique 482
cellule pour femmes 768
cellule pour hommes 768
cellule pour mineurs 768
cellule royale 100
cellule végétale 74
cellules 728
cément 159
cendre 391
cendrier 391
cent 703, 728
Centaure 11
centrage 528
centrale 657
centrale hydroélectrique, coupe 658
centrale nucléaire 668
centrale thermique au charbon 646
centre 431, 704, 740, 803, 804, 807, 809, 847, 859, 877, 879, 916
centre arrière 807
centre commercial 709, 714

centre de cuisson 722
centre de documentation 764
centre de gravité 610
centre de tri 71, 474
centre de tri régional 475
centre droit 804
centre du court 818
centre gauche 804
centre-ville 709, 710
centrifugeuse 21, 240
centriole 94
cep de vigne 86
cèpe 183
céphalothorax 103, 107
Céphée 12
cerceau 823
cercle 385
cercle central 803, 809, 810, 879
cercle d'ascension droite 14, 15
cercle d'attente 794
cercle d'envoi 800
cercle de déclinaison 14, 15
cercle de la station 55
cercle de lancer 790, 791
cercle de mise au jeu 878
cercle de serrage 448
cercle de vannage 659
cercle de verrouillage 756
cercle des couleurs 400
cercle extérieur 877
cercle intérieur 877
cercle polaire antarctique 29, 35, 36
cercle polaire arctique 35, 36
cercle porte-lame 639
cercle restrictif 810
cercles 917
céréales 85, 203
cerf de Virginie 128
cerf du Canada 128
cerfeuil 202
cerise 192
cérium 684
cerne annuel 87
cerneau 84
cerques 909
cerveau 99, 103, 106, 107, 109, 110, 167
cervelet 167
cervelle 212
césium 682
Chac-Mool 412
chaîne 455, 460, 461, 578, 580, 697, 826
chaîne alimentaire 67
chaîne coupante 331
chaîne d'entraînement 643
chaîne de levage 632
chaîne de montagnes 7, 38, 42
chaîne de mouillage 615
chaîne de neurones 168
chaîne de sûreté 567
chaîne de suspension 663
chaîne nerveuse 99
chaîne nerveuse ventrale 107
chaîne stéréo 497
chaînes d'ancrage 652
chaînette de levage 265
chaire 737
chaise 277, 723, 734
chaise berçante 277
chaise dactylo 511
chaise haute 281
chaise longue 277
chaise pliante 277
chaise-escabeau 277
chaises des joueurs 813
chaises empilables 277
chaises, exemples 277
chalaze 117
châle 337
chalet de montagne 886
chalet du sommet 886
chalet principal 886
chaloupe de sauvetage 604, 608
chalumeau 319, 432
chalumeau coupeur 319
chalumeau soudeur 319
chalutier 606
chambranle 247, 249
chambre 251, 584, 650, 902
chambre à air 117
chambre à poudre 753
chambre à vide 694
chambre antérieure 177
chambre d'expansion 695
chambre d'hôpital 780
chambre d'isolement 778
chambre d'observation 694
chambre d'observation 778, 781
chambre d'observation psychiatrique 778
chambre de combustion 256, 259, 564, 566
chambre de combustion annulaire 627
chambre de cuisson 465
chambre de décharge 402
chambre de la reine 402
chambre de mélange 319
chambre des machines 763
chambre des vantail 597

chambre des officiers 764
chambre des pompes 606
chambre des torpilles 763
chambre double 724
chambre du roi 402
chambre forte 731
chambre froide 180, 181, 722
chambre noire 484
chambre photographique 480, 694
chambre postérieure 177
chambre principale, plafond cathédrale 251
chambre principale, toit cathédrale 251
chambre pulpaire 159
chambre simple 724
chambre souterraine 402
chambres d'hôtel 724
chameau 129
champ centre 795
champ d'épandage 263
champ d'héliostats 674
champ de tir 893
champ droit 795
champ gauche 795
champ géothermique 646
champ magnétique 494, 687
champignon 76, 591
champignon de couche 183
champignon mortel 76
champignon vénéneux 76
champignon, structure 76
champignons 183
chandelle de relevage 640
chanterelle commune 183
chape 254, 284, 445
changement de piste 501
chanfrein 124
change 725
Charon 5
charpente 252, 403, 406
charpente verticale 461
charrue à soc 641
chas 453, 454
chasse 426, 472, 912
chasse-neige à soufflerie 573
chasse-neige basse 57
chasse-neige haute 57
chasse-pierres 585, 586
chasse-clou 301
châssis 327, 448, 449, 632, 633, 638, 639, 641, 642
châssis de bogie 586
châssis-presse 484
chasuble 356
chat 132
chat de l'île de Man 133
chat, morphologie 133
chat, tête 132
châtaigne d'eau 184
château d'eau 589
château fort 408
chaton 376
chats, races 132
chaudière 259, 674
chauffage 256
chauffage à air chaud pulsé 258

chauffage à eau chaude 259
chauffage au bois 256
chauffage d'appoint 260
chauffage, bouches 258
chauffe-eau 262, 266, 675
chauffe-eau au gaz 267
chauffe-eau électrique 266
chaufferette 903
chaumard 835
chausse-pied 345
chaussée 538, 543, 712
chaussée cahoteuse 545, 547
chaussée glissante 545, 547
chaussée rétrécie 544, 547
chaussette 351, 365, 802, 808, 822, 848
chaussette-étrier 796
chaussettes 351
chaussettes hautes 805
chausson 840, 841
chausson d'escalade 900
chausson intérieur 889, 895
chaussure 798, 801, 810, 865, 870, 872, 880, 881, 892, 895
chaussure à crampons 796, 805, 808
chaussure d'alpinisme 901
chaussure d'escrime 848
chaussure d'haltérophilie 850
chaussure de football 802
chaussure de lutte 843
chaussure de piste 791
chaussure de saut à ski 892
chaussure de ski 888, 889
chaussure de sport 370
chaussure de tennis 822
chaussure, parties 342
chaussures 342
chaussures à crampons 885
chaussures d'enfants 717
chaussures d'homme 342
chaussures d'hommes 716
chaussures de femme 343
chaussures de femmes 716
chaussures de golf 869
chaussures de sport 716
chaussures unisexes 344
chaussures, accessoires 345
chauve-souris 140
chauve-souris fer de lance 141
chauve-souris, morphologie 140
chauve-souris, squelette 141
chauves-souris, exemples 141
chayote 189
chef 740
chef de cuisine 721
chef de partie 721
chef de tapis 843
chef décorateur 428
chef électricien 429
chef machiniste 428
chef mécanicien 873
chef opérateur du son 429
chemin 866
chemin couvert 409
chemin d'évacuation 543
chemin de fer 39
chemin de fer métropolitain 592
chemin de ronde 408, 409
chemin de ronde couvert 408
chemin de roulement 634
cheminée 44, 245, 250, 257, 259, 267, 599, 604, 646, 650
cheminée à foyer ouvert 256
cheminée à minerai 650
cheminée antisuie 608
cheminée d'échappement 570, 639, 640
chemise 349, 532, 912
chemise de nuit 364
chemise du donjon 408
chemise en acier 689
chemises d'hommes 716
chemisier classique 359
chemisiers, exemples 359
chenal principal 617
chenal secondaire 617
chêne 88
chenets 257
chenille 97, 636, 758, 876
chèque de voyage 729
chèques 729
chéquier 386
chercheur 14, 15
chérimole 196
chevalement 650
chevalet 399, 433, 439, 440, 441, 443
chevalet de câble de garde 663
chevalet des aigus 442
chevalet des basses 442
Chevalet du Peintre 11
chevalière 376

chevelu 87
Chevelure de Bérénice 13
chevet 411
cheveux 147, 149
cheville 146, 148, 278, 439, 440, 459, 462
cheville d'accord 442
chevillier 439
chèvre 128
chèvre frais 210
chevron 252, 740
chiasma optique 167
chicane 872
chicorée de Trévise 186
chicorée frisée 187
chien 130, 752, 754, 861, 912, 913
chien, morphologie 130
chien, squelette 131
Chiens de Chasse 13
chiens, races 130
chiffonnier 279
chiffres 472
chiffres romains 703
chignole 307
chiisme 736
Chili 742
chimie 680
chimie, symboles 684
chimpanzé 139
Chine 747
chinois 231, 468
chipolata 216
chirurgie mineure 778
chiton 336
chlamyde 336
chlore 683
chloroplaste 74
choanocyte 95
chocolat 208
chocolat au lait 208
chocolat blanc 208
chocolat noir 208
chondrite 8
chope à bière 225
chope à café 226
chorizo 216
choroïde 177
chou cavalier 186
chou de Milan 186
chou frisé 186
chou laitue 186
chou marin 186
chou pommé blanc 186
chou pommé rouge 186
chou pommé vert 186
chou-fleur 187
chou-rave 185
choux de Bruxelles 186
chow-chow 130
chœur 410, 411
christianisme : le Nouveau Testament 736
chromatine 94
chrome 683
chromosphère 6
chronique 471
chronologie des religions 736
chronomètre 488, 696, 831
chronomètre de jeu 789
chronomètre électronique automatique 831
chronométreur 810, 814, 842, 845, 846, 847, 848, 881, 900
chronométreur de couloir 830
chronométreur des trente secondes 810
chronométreur en chef 830
chronométreurs 827, 844, 883
chrysalide 97
chukka 342
chute 47, 362, 836
chute d'eau 48
chute de neige, mesure 59
chute libre 896
chutes de pierres 545, 547
chutney à la mangue 201
Chypre 744
cible 40, 41, 859, 861, 893, 918
cibles 848
ciboule 184
ciboulette 184
cierge 737
cigale 101
cigare 390
cigarette 390
cigogne 119
cil 94, 177
cilié 79
cils 132
cimaise 404
cime 87
cimetière 39, 711

cimier 748
cimier mobile 17
cinéma 427, 608, 710, 714
cinéma maison 493
cinq 703
cinq cents 703
cinq-épices chinois 199
cinquante 703
cintres 430
circonférence 704
circuit capteurs 559
circuit d'eau chaude 262
circuit d'eau froide 262
circuit d'évacuation 262
circuit de 120 V 272
circuit de 240 V 272
circuit de freinage 552, 559
circuit de photopiles 673
circuit de plomberie 262
circuit de supercross 875
circuit de ventilation 262
circuit électrique 274
circuit électrique en parallèle 687
circuit imprimé 689
circuit intégré 689
circuit intégré en boîtier 689
circuit, course automobile 872
circuit, motocyclisme 874
circulation dans les deux sens 544, 546
circulation de l'eau 95
circulation sanguine 160
circulation sanguine, schéma 161
cireur 345
cirque 7
cirque glaciaire 46
cirro-cumulus 56, 62
cirro-stratus 56, 62
cirrus 56, 62
cisaille 424, 484, 535
cisaille à haies 330
cisaille à volaille 233
ciseau 421
ciseau à bois 309
ciseaux 454, 777, 905
ciseaux à cuticules 377
ciseaux à denteler 454
ciseaux à effiler 382
ciseaux à ongles 377
ciseaux de coiffeur 382
ciseaux de cuisine 233
ciseaux de pédicure 377
ciseaux de sûreté 377
ciseaux sculpteurs 382
citerne 572, 573, 607
cithare 432
citron 194
citrouille 189
civière 775, 776
clairon 447
clapet 265, 268, 456, 506
clapet de non-retour 319
clapet de retenue 263
claque 342, 371
claquette 429
clarinette 446
clarinette basse 437
clarinettes 437
classeur 532
classeur à clapets 510
classeur à soufflets 386
classeur mobile 510
classification de Hubble 9
clavardage 525
claveau 413
clavecin 443
clavette 249
clavicule 111, 116, 122, 141, 142, 152
clavier 442, 450, 506, 507, 514, 526, 865
clavier à pédales 444
clavier accompagnement 432
clavier alphanumérique 506, 507, 548, 730, 731
clavier chant 432
clavier d'identification personnelle 731
clavier de grand orgue 444
clavier de positif 444
clavier de récit 444
clavier manuel 445
clavier numérique 507, 699
claviers manuels 444
clayette 291
clé 249, 446
clé à chaîne 315
clé à crémaillère 315
clé à douille à cliquet 311
clé à fourches 311
clé à molette 311
clé à percussion 767
clé à sangle 315
clé à tuyau 315
clé coudée à tuyau 315
clé d'ut 434
clé de barrage 767
clé de bocal 446
clé de bras 844
clé de contact 332, 333
clé de fa 434
clé de mandrin 306
clé de sol 434
clé de voûte 410, 413
clé en croix 558
clé mixte 311
clé polygonale 311
clé polygonale à cliquet 311
clé polygonale à têtes fendues 311
clés 311, 315, 434, 451
client 487
clignotant 571
clignotant arrière 575
climatisation 775
climatiseur 567
climatiseur de fenêtre 261
climats arides 61
climats de montagne 61
climats du monde 61
climats polaires 61
climats tempérés chauds 61
climats tempérés froids 61
climats tropicaux 61
clinfoc 603
cliquet 302, 307, 460, 696, 697
clitoris 170
cloaque 103, 110, 113, 116
cloche 341, 858
clocher 411, 737
clocheton 408, 410, 411
clochettes 449
cloison 82, 175, 771, 902, 915, 919
cloison longitudinale 606
cloison mobile 509, 510, 719
cloison transversale 606
clôture 182, 244
clôture de sécurité 890
clôture du champ extérieur 795
clôture en lattis 322
clou 127, 301
clou à maçonnerie 301
clou à tête homme 301
clou à tige spiralée 301
clou commun 301
clou coupé 301
clou de girofle 198
clou millésimé 590
clous, exemples 301
club-house 856
coach 549
cobalt 683
cobaye 123
cobra 114
coccinelle 101
coccyx 152, 157
Cocher 12
cocheur d'allée 868
cocheur d'approche 868
cocheur de sable 868
cochlée 174
cochonnet 864
cockpit 834
code 528
code des produits 699
code temporel 429
coelophysis 93
coffre 279, 551, 577, 672, 673
coffre à bagages 567
coffre d'appareillage 585
coffre de rangement 570, 766
coffre-fort 731, 769
coffret 494
coffret de branchement 273
coffret de sûreté 731
coiffe 24, 77, 426, 909
coiffeur 428
coiffeuse 264
coiffure 340, 380
coiffures d'homme 340
coiffures de femme 341
coiffures unisexes 341
coin 426, 444, 842
coin cuisine 509
coin de patinoire 878
coin-repas 224, 250
coinceur 900, 901
coing 193
col 45, 348, 349, 352, 362, 370, 494, 868
col banane 362
col berthe 363
col cagoule 363
col châle 362
col chemisier 362
col chinois 363
col Claudine 362
col cravate 362
col de l'utérus 170
col du fémur 153
col italien 349
col marin 362
col officier 363
col pointes boutonnées 349
col polo 363
col roulé 354, 363, 892
col tailleur 355, 362
col transformable 352
col-de-cygne 255, 638
colette 374
colibri 118
colis postal 475
collant 365
collant fantaisie 368
collant sans pied 371
collatéral 411
collatérale 168
colle 254
collecte sélective 71
collecteur 659, 688
collecteur d'appareil 262
collecteur d'échappement 552, 564, 566
collecteur d'électrons 689
collecteur d'évacuation 262
collecteur de graisse 239
collecteur de vapeur primaire 669
collecteur du réacteur 669
collecteur principal 262, 263
collerette 339, 363
collet 77, 159, 227, 257, 308, 425, 610, 913
collet de l'axone 168
collet repoussé 269
colley 130
collier 234, 838, 857, 889
collier cervical 775
collier coupe-feu 257
collier de perles, longueur matinée 374
collier de serrage 59, 851
collier de serrage du casque 20
collier de soirée 374
collier-de-chien 374
colliers 374
colline 45
colline abyssale 49
collybie à pied velouté 183
Colombe 11
Colombie 742
colombin 465
côlon 97, 113, 125
côlon ascendant 164
côlon descendant 164
côlon pelvien 164
côlon transverse 164
colonne 47, 64, 307, 403, 405, 425, 440, 452, 471, 482, 485, 594, 919
colonne ascendante 259
colonne avec capuchon 64
colonne corinthienne engagée 407
colonne d'air 271
colonne d'alcool 695
colonne de collecte du papier 71
colonne de collecte du verre 71
colonne de direction 552
colonne de mercure 695
colonne de production 654
colonne de radiateur 259
colonne de stabilisation 652
colonne de ventilation 262
colonne de ventilation principale 262
colonne descendante 259
colonne dorique engagée 407
colonne ionique engagée 407
colonne montante d'eau chaude 262
colonne montante d'eau froide 262
colonne vertébrale 109, 121, 152, 167
colorant capillaire 379
cols, exemples 362
columelle 105
coma 8
combattant 844, 846
combinaison 351, 369, 852, 874, 884, 887
combinaison de course 882
combinaison de nuit 369
combinaison de protection 875
combinaison de saut à ski 891
combinaison de ski 888, 892
combinaison de ski de vitesse 891
combinaison de vol 896
combinaison gagnante 920
combinaison résistante au feu 872
combinaison-jupon 366
combinaison-pantalon 358
combinaisons au poker 914
combiné 366, 506, 507
combiné 2 dans 1 380
combiné bucco-dentaire 384
combiné-culotte 366
combustible 665, 670
combustible : uranium enrichi 671
combustible : uranium naturel 670
combustible défectueux sous gaine 666
combustible fossile 68, 70
combustible nucléaire, manipulation 666
combustion 564, 565, 627
comète 8
comité d'arbitrage 845
commande amovible 239
commande au pied 452
commande d'accélération 331
commande d'aérofrein 898
commande d'alimentation en oxygène 898
commande d'arrêt 495
commande d'avance rapide 495
commande d'éjection de la cassette 495
commande d'enregistrement 495
commande d'essuie-glace 556
commande d'inclinaison latérale 898
commande d'insertion du papier 529
commande de barrières 591
commande de chauffage 556
commande de dossier 555
commande de largage de câble 898
commande de largage de la verrière 898
commande de lecture 495
commande de marche arrière 483
commande de marche avant 483
commande de marge 528
commande de mémoire 479
commande de panneau solaire 60
commande de positionnement du spécimen 694
commande de rebobinage 495
commande de remise à zéro 495
commande de sélection de l'ouverture 694
commande de sélection manuelle 483
commande de température 291
commande de ventilateur 261
commande de virage 898
commande de vitesse 236
commande de volume 508
commande de volume de la sonnerie 506
commande de volume du récepteur 506
commande des freins 896, 897
commande du chariot 456, 693
commande du rétroviseur 554
commande électrique de paiement 920
commande électrique du zoom 496
commande mémoire 506
commandes de la bande vidéo 496
commandes de préréglage 495
commandes du magnétoscope 495
commandes du pilote automatique 626
commandes du treuil 573
commencement du patron 456
commerce électronique 525
commis débarrasseur 721
commissaire 875
commissaire de piste 853, 855
commissaire en chef 855
commissure labiale 174
commode 279
communication par téléphone 506
communication sans fil 505
communications 468
communications aériennes 487
communications individuelles 487
communications industrielles 487
communications maritimes 487
communications militaires 487
communications routières 487
commutateur 316, 483, 523
commutateur alimentation/fonctions 496
commutateur d'alimentation 477
commutateur d'allumage 556
commutateur de prise de vues nocturne 496
commutateur marche/arrêt 476
commutateur mono/stéréo 498
Comores 746
compactage 71
compartiment 416
compartiment à fret 625
compartiment à médicaments 775
compartiment bagages 585
compartiment d'accessoires 289
compartiment de la production d'électricité 763
compartiment de première classe 624
compartiment de réservoir d'eau 628
compartiment de sac 289
compartiment des instruments 60
compartiment des voitures 608
compartiment du réacteur 763
compartiment moteur 568
compartiment pour documents 527
compartiment pour la planche dorsale 775
compartiment pour ordinateur 527
compartiment touriste 625
compartiment voyageurs 585
compartiment-couchette 570
Compas 11
compas 898
compas d'épaisseur 423
compas magnétique liquide 612
compensateur de poussée latérale 500
compétition 789
compétition de cyclisme sur route 870
complexe hydroélectrique 657
complexe sportif 709, 788
compluvium 406
composantes d'un microscope électronique 694
composite inférieur 24
composite supérieur 24
composition du sang 162
compresse stérilisée 777
compresseur 260, 533
compresseur centrifuge 627
compresseur d'air 586
compresseur d'air 320
compresseur du climatiseur 566
compression 564, 565, 627
compression/admission 565
comprimé 783
comptabilité 509
compte-pose 485
compte-rangs 456
compte-touches électrique 848
compte-tours 557
compteur 262, 499
compteur d'électricité 273
compteur kilométrique 557
comptoir 722
comptoir d'enregistrement 620
comptoir de prêt 733
comptoir de renseignements 620, 719, 730, 733, 769, 779
comptoir de retour des livres 733
comptoir de vente de friandises 427
comptoir de vente des billets 620
comptoir des fromages 181
comptoir des viandes libre-service 180
comptoir du bar 720
comptoir libre-service 722
concentrateur 522, 523
concentration des gaz à effet de serre 68
concentration du faisceau 694
concentré de tomate 200
concessionnaire d'automobiles 711
conchiglie 206
concombre 188
concombre sans pépins 188
condensateur à film plastique 689
condensateur céramique 689
condensateurs électrolytiques 689
condensation 67, 680
condensation de la vapeur 665
condenseur 646, 668, 674, 693, 694
condiments 200, 723
conditionnement d'air 608
conditionnement de l'air 261
conditionnement de l'air, appareils 261
condor 119
conducteur 857
conducteur de phase 273
conducteur de terre 273
conducteur dérivé 687
conducteur en faisceau 663
conducteur neutre 273
conduction 681
conduit 445
conduit auditif 174
conduit auditif externe 158
conduit d'aération 402
conduit d'essence 553, 563
conduit de chauffage 293
conduit de distribution vertical 258
conduit de la glande 112
conduit de raccordement 256
conduit hydraulique 641, 642
conduit lactifère 171
conduite à la terre 655
conduite d'admission principale 655
conduite d'admission secondaire 655
conduite d'alimentation 262
conduite d'eau 294
conduite d'eau chaude 270, 271
conduite d'eau froide 270, 271
conduite d'eau potable 712
conduite de gaz 712
conduite de transfert de carburant 25
conduite des pièces 920
conduite forcée 657, 658, 664
conduite principale 265
condyle externe 153
condyle interne 153
cône 89, 177, 494, 705, 882, 883
cône adventif 44
cône d'entrée 627
cône d'ombre 6, 7
cône de pénombre 6, 7
cône femelle 89
cône mâle 89
confessionnal 737
configuration des continents 28
configuration du littoral 51
confiserie 717
confluent 48
confucianisme : Confucius 736
Confucius 736
congélateur 224, 291, 720
congélateur coffre 291
Congo 34, 745
conifère 89
conifères, exemples 89
conjonctive 177
connecteur 272, 488
connecteur à serrage mécanique 663
connecteur d'extension AGP 513
connecteur d'extension ISA 513
connecteur d'extension PCI 513
connecteur de liaison 272
connecteur de mémoire vive 513
connecteur en T 522
connexion 916
conque 173

INDEX FRANÇAIS

ASTRONOMIE > 2-25; **TERRE** > 26-71; **RÈGNE VÉGÉTAL** >72-89; **RÈGNE ANIMAL** > 90-143; **ÊTRE HUMAIN** > 144-177; **ALIMENTATION ET CUISINE** > 178-241; **MAISON** > 242-295; **BRICOLAGE ET JARDINAGE** > 296-333; **VÊTEMENTS** > 334-371; **PARURE ET OBJETS PERSONNELS** > 372-391; **ARTS ET ARCHITECTURE** > 392-465; **COMMUNICATIONS ET BUREAUTIQUE** > 466-535; **TRANSPORT ET MACHINERIE** > 536-643; **ÉNERGIES** > 644-677; **SCIENCE** > 678-705; **SOCIÉTÉ** > 706-785; **SPORTS ET JEUX** > 786-920

1021

conseiller de production 490
conseillers musicaux 490
conserves 181
consigne automatique 582
console 412, 440, 661, 663
console centrale 556
console d'accotoir 276
console d'instruments 841
console d'orgue 444
console de jeu 918
consolette de l'annonceur 488
consolette du réalisateur 488
consommateurs primaires 67
consommateurs secondaires 67
consommateurs tertiaires 67
constellations de l'hémisphère austral 10
constellations de l'hémisphère boréal 12
contact 916
contact de terre 274
contact électrique 476
contact négatif 672, 673
contact positif 672, 673
contacteur 263
conteneur 605, 635
conteneur à boîtes métalliques 71
conteneur à papier 71
conteneur à verre 71
conteneurs 635
conteneurs de collecte sélective 71
continent 7, 49
continental humide, à été chaud 61
continental humide, à été frais 61
continents, configuration 28
contre 813
contre-attrape 443
contre-fer 309
contre-fiche 253
contre-flèche 634
contre-garde 409
contre-platine 500
contre-rail 590
contre-sanglon 855
contrebasse 439
contrebasses 437
contrebassons 437
contrefiche 663
contrefort 45, 370, 410, 660
contremarche 255, 460
contreparement 300
contreplaqué multiplis 300
contrepoids 14, 16, 417, 500, 542, 591, 634, 638, 639, 640
contrescarpe 409
contrevent 249
contrôle 514
contrôle : sélection de groupe 514
contrôle d'alimentation en oxygène 898
contrôle de la couleur 512
contrôle de la photocopie 512
contrôle de la stéréophonie 504
contrôle de la température 267
contrôle de la température du corps 20
contrôle de la vapeur 288
contrôle de la vitesse 452
contrôle de programmation 261
contrôle de sécurité 621
contrôle de tabulation 528
contrôle de température 465
contrôle de tonalité des aigus 441, 497, 503
contrôle de tonalité des graves 441, 497, 503
contrôle des entrées et sorties du personnel 726
contrôle des passeports 621
contrôle douanier 621
contrôle du champ sonore 497
contrôle du contraste 512
contrôle du gain 613
contrôle du plateau 501
contrôle du séquenceur 450
contrôle du volume 450, 507
contrôle thermique 259
contrôles de l'équipement de survie 20
contrôles du lecteur de cassette 504
contrôles du lecteur laser 504
contrôleur 582
contrôleur à vent de synthétiseur 451
contrôleur d'images 489, 490
convecteur 260
convection 681
conversion du travail mécanique en électricité 662
convertisseur catalytique 553
convertisseur de couple 292
convoyeur 646, 647, 649
convoyeur à bagages 623
cooksonia 92
coordonnées célestes 13
coordonnées terrestres 35
copie recto/verso 512
copropriété 886
copyright 473
coq 120
coque 84, 217, 389, 567, 575, 599, 834, 876, 884
coque inférieure 889

coque supérieure 889, 895
coquelicot 80
coquillage bivalve 105
coquillage bivalve, anatomie 105
coquillage bivalve, morphologie 105
coquillage univalve 105
coquillage univalve, morphologie 105
coquille 104, 105, 106, 117, 276, 808, 849, 880
coquille de protection 843
coquille Saint-Jacques 217
coquilleur à beurre 229
cor anglais 446
cor d'harmonie 447
coracoïde 111, 116
Coran 736
Corbeau 11
corbeau 118, 256, 408
corbeille 431
corbeille à papier 535
corbeille à pollen 98
corbeille suspendue 322
cordage 908
cordage commis 908
cordage tressé 908
corde 439, 440, 443, 686, 750, 823, 842, 859, 900, 901, 913
corde à sauter 850
corde d'accrochage 460
corde d'assurage 900
corde de couloir 831
corde de faux départ 830
corde de tension 433
corde de tirage 321
corde vocale 163
cordeau 313, 324
cordeau à tracer 313
cordée 79, 900
cordelière 282
cordes 433, 442
cordes d'accompagnement 432
cordes de mélodie 432
cordes de timbre 448
cordier 433, 439
Cordillère australienne 29
Cordillère des Andes 31
cordon 285, 288, 289, 316, 331, 332, 488, 504, 505
cordon à gaine métallique 507
cordon coulissant 353
cordon d'alimentation 382, 383
cordon d'alimentation 237, 305, 308, 381, 497
cordon d'alimentation en courant continu 526
cordon d'alimentation pivotant 381
cordon d'alimentation secteur 526
cordon de combiné 506
cordon de dunes 52
cordon de tirage 284, 285
cordon littoral 51
cordon tire-feu 756
coréen 469
coriandre 202
corme 376, 602
corne antérieure 167
corne de feu 766
corne de guidage de l'attelage 585
corne postérieure 167
cornée 177, 691
cornemuse 432
cornet à dés 915
cornet à pistons 437, 447
cornet inférieur 175
cornet moyen 175
cornet supérieur 175
corniche 245, 247, 278, 403, 404, 697
cornichon 188
corolle 80
corona radiata 170
corps 176, 240, 268, 306, 382, 390, 444, 446, 470, 693, 700, 793, 909, 918
corps calleux 167
corps caverneux 169
corps célestes 4
corps cellulaire 168
corps ciliaire 177
corps de garde 408, 409
corps de la fusée 757
corps de l'ongle 172
corps de pompe 776
corps de piston 447
corps de ruche 100
corps du fornix 167
corps du pistolet 320
corps en bakélite® 757
corps humain 146
corps vertébral 157, 168
corps vitré 177
corps-mort 615
corpuscule de Meissner 172
corpuscule de Pacini 172
corpuscule de Ruffini 172
correcteur liquide 534
correcteur orthographique 528
correction d'exposition 476

correction de caractères 528
correction de mots 528
cors anglais 437
cors d'harmonie 437
corsage-culotte 359
corsaire 358
corset 337, 367, 663
corymbe 81
cosmétiques 717
cosse 84
Costa Rica 742
costume 428
costume ancien, éléments 336
costumes 716
cotardie 337
côte 49, 112, 116, 121, 122, 126, 131, 136, 138, 141, 142, 214, 215, 909
côté 431
côte axiale 105
côte bassin 664
côté cour 431
côte d'azur 871
Côte d'Ivoire 745
côté femelle 453
côte flottante 138
côte flottante (2) 152
côté jardin 431
côté mâle 453
côté mer 664
côte spiralée 105
côtelette 215
côtes 152
côtes levées de dos 214
côtes, exemples 51
coton hydrophile 777
coton-tige 777
cotre Marconi 601
cotret 676
cottage 210
cotte de mailles 749
cotylédon 77
cou 113, 147, 148, 149, 169, 826
couche 368
couche antireflet 672
couche arable 78
couche basale 172
couche claire 172
couche cornée 172
couche d'aluminium 501
couche d'ozone 53
couche de base 538
couche de cendres 44
couche de fondation 538
couche de laves 44
couche de Malpighi 172
couche de surface 538
couche drainante 660
couche fluorescente 275
couche granuleuse 172
couche imperméable 651
couche-culotte 368
couches de déchets 69
couchette 584
coude 124, 130, 140, 147, 149, 156, 258, 269, 385
coude à 180° 269
coude à 45° 269
coude de renvoi 269
coudes 206
coudière 808, 895
coulant 391
coulée de boue 47
coulée de lave 44
couleur 914
couleur à l'huile 397
couleurs primaires 400
couleurs secondaires 400
couleurs tertiaires 400
couleurs, exemples 741
couleurs, synthèse 690
couleuvre rayée 114
coulis de tomate 200
coulisse 350
coulisse d'accord 447
coulisse d'entrée 100
coulisse du deuxième piston 447
coulisse du premier piston 447
coulisse du troisième piston 447
coulisses 430
couloir 788, 790, 817, 820, 830, 831, 882
couloir ascendant 402
couloir central 584
couloir d'échauffement 882
couloir d'intercommunication 584
couloir de sécurité 728
couloir descendant 402
coulomb 702
coulommiers 211
coup d'approche 866
coup de départ 866
coup de patin 892
coup de pied de brasse 832
coup de pied de crawl 832
coup de pied de papillon 832
Coupe 11
coupe 920

coupé 740
coupe à mousseux 225
coupe d'un aérographe 398
coupe d'un appareil reflex 477
coupe d'un barrage à contreforts 660
coupe d'un barrage en remblai 660
coupe d'un barrage-poids 661
coupe d'un barrage-voûte 661
coupe d'un bulbe 78
coupe d'un follicule : anis étoilé 84
coupe d'un grain de blé 85
coupe d'un lanceur spatial (Ariane V) 24
coupe d'un lanceur spatial (Saturn V) 25
coupe d'un microscope électronique 694
coupe d'un observatoire astronomique 17
coupe d'un raisin 83
coupe d'un rayon de miel 100
coupe d'un télescope 15
coupe d'une balle de golf 867
coupe d'une bille 300
coupe d'une bouche à feu 753
coupe d'une capsule : pavot 84
coupe d'une centrale hydroélectrique 658
coupe d'une fraise 83
coupe d'une framboise 83
coupe d'une gousse : pois 84
coupe d'une lunette astronomique 14
coupe d'une molaire 159
coupe d'une noisette 84
coupe d'une noix 84
coupe d'une orange 82
coupe d'une pêche 81
coupe d'une pipe 390
coupe d'une pomme 82
coupe d'une route 538
coupe d'une rue 712
coupe d'une silique : moutarde 84
coupe de l'atmosphère terrestre 53
coupe de l'usine 664
coupe de la croûte terrestre 42
coupe de la nacelle 677
coupe sagittale 169, 170
coupe transversale du tronc 87
coupe-bordures 326
coupe-cigare 390
coupe-circuit 663
coupe-circuit d'urgence 576
coupe-circuit limiteur de température 266
coupe-cuticules 377
coupe-feu 252
coupe-fil 317, 453
coupe-ongles 377
coupe-œuf 233
coupe-papier 531
coupe-tube 314
coupe-vent 899
coupée 606
coupelle 287
coupelle d'étanchéité 773
couperet 229
couple 881
coupleur hydraulique 640
coupole 614
coupole du mihrab 738
coupole du porche 738
coupole rotative 17
coups 820
cour 182, 408, 727, 738
cour de récréation 735
courant 597
courant de convection 681
courant électrique, mesure 702
courant, adaptateur 526
courbure 911
coureur, skeleton 885
coureurs 875
courge 188
courge à cou droit 189
courge à cou tors 189
courge spaghetti 189
courgeron 189
courgette 188
couronne 6, 124, 159, 398, 416, 448, 696, 729
Couronne australe 10
Couronne boréale 13
couronne d'aubage 659
couronne d'orientation 638
couronne de table 374
couronnement 255, 661
couronnement du barrage 664
courrier 474
courrier des lecteurs 471
courrier électronique 525
courrier international 475
courrier local 475
courrier non oblitéré 474
courrier oblitéré 474
courrier régional 475
courroie d'attache 391
courroie d'entraînement 292
courroie de distribution 566
courroie de rêne 857
courroie de sécurité 818
courroie de tige 605
courroie de transmission 605

courroie de ventilateur 552, 566
cours d'eau 48, 70
course automobile 872
course de chevaux : course attelée 857
course de chevaux : turf 856
coursier d'évacuateur 657
court 818, 819, 820
court de service droit 821
court de service gauche 821
court péronier latéral 151
courte piste 883
courtine 408
courts de tennis 788
couscous 204
couscoussier 235
cousin 785
cousine 785
cousoir 424
coussin 458
coussin arrière 862
coussin carré 280
coussin d'air 370
coussin de protection 823
coussin de rembourrage 842
coussin de tête 862
coussinet carpien 130
coussinet d'émeri 454
coussinet de glissement 590
coussinet de l'ergot 130
coussinet digité 130, 133
coussinet en mousse 772
coussinet palmaire 130
coussinet plantaire 133
couteau 217, 227, 236, 237, 240, 401, 841, 905, 907
couteau à beurre 228
couteau à bifteck 229
couteau à découper 229
couteau à désosser 229
couteau à dessert 228
couteau à filets de sole 229
couteau à fromage 228
couteau à huîtres 229
couteau à jambon 229
couteau à pain 229
couteau à pamplemousse 229
couteau à peindre 397
couteau à poisson 228
couteau à zester 229
couteau d'électricien 317
couteau d'office 229
couteau de chef 229
couteau de combat 751
couteau de cuisine 229
couteau de potier 464
couteau de table 228
couteau électrique 237
couteau en silex 748
couteau suisse 905
couteaux de cuisine, exemples 229
couteaux, exemples 228
coutisse 459
coutre 641, 643
couture 390, 424, 452, 797, 798
couture d'assemblage 346
couture médiane 349
couture, accessoires 454
couturier 150
couvercle 234, 237, 238, 239, 240, 241, 261, 265, 273, 274, 291, 292, 295, 313, 391, 398, 465, 477, 483, 484, 500, 512, 767, 907
couvercle coulissant 612
couvercle de batterie 562
couvercle de culasse 552, 566
couvercle de la turbine 659
couvercle de propreté 290
couvercle de réservoir 265
couvercle inférieur 689
couvercle supérieur 689
couvert 227
couverts 722
couverture 280
couvre-bassinet 752
couvre-culasse 755
couvre-filtre 773
couvre-oreillet 280
couvre-plateau 500
couvrure 425
Cowper, glande 169
cœur 82, 97, 99, 103, 104, 105, 106, 107, 109, 110, 112, 116, 125, 162, 163, 212, 256, 822, 914
cœur de croisement 590
cœur du réacteur 670, 671
crabe 218
cracker de seigle 205
cracker scandinave 205
craie 863
crampon 345, 371, 590, 798, 893
crampon de fermeture 265
crampons interchangeables 802
cran 348, 350, 362, 455, 698, 791, 909
cran de mire 754
cran de réglage 310, 889

crâne 106, 109, 116, 121, 126, 136, 138, 141, 142, 146
crâne d'enfant 158
crâne, vue latérale 158
crapaud commun 111
cratère 7, 44, 647
cravache 853, 856
cravate 349
cravates 716
crawl 832
crayon 470, 667
crayon à sourcils 378
crayon blanchisseur d'ongles 377
crayon contour des lèvres 378
crayon de pierre ponce 423
crayon en plomb 470
crayon lithographique 423
crayons de cire 396
crayons de couleur 396
crédit photographique 471
crémaillère 238, 255, 291, 791
crémaillère de pointage 756
crème 210
crème aigre 210
crème épaisse 210
crémier 226
crénelé 79
crépis 403, 405
cresson alénois 187
cresson de fontaine 187
Crétacé 93
crête 45, 49, 657, 660, 690, 749
crêtemètre graphique 488
creux 49, 227, 690
creux barométrique 55
crevasse 46
crevette 218
cri 469
cric 558, 873
cricket 798
crinière 124
criquet mélodieux 102
crispin 848
cristallin 177, 691
cristallisation 680
cristaux de neige 64
cristaux irréguliers 64
cristaux liquides 696
critique gastronomique 471
Croatie 744
croc à défricher 327
croche 435
crochet 103, 105, 112, 249, 313, 316, 452, 453, 456, 457, 483, 573, 611, 634, 699, 776, 861, 862, 881
crochet à venin 112
crochet d'attelage 640
crochet de gourmette 854
crochet de levage 651
crochet de petit doigt 447
crochet de pouce 447
crochet du plateau 698
crochet pétrisseur 236
crochets 473
crocodile 114
crocus 80
croisée 410
croisée du transept 411
croisement 463
croisillon 783
croissant 7, 204, 741
croix 740
croix d'autel 737
croix de Saint-André 252, 591
Croix du Sud 11
crosne 184
crosse 76, 417, 440, 754, 755, 756, 800, 801, 860, 861, 912
crosse de fougère 185
crosse de gardien de but 879, 880
crosse de joueur 880
crottin de Chavignol 210
croupe 124, 826
croupion 115
croupon 425
croûte basaltique 42
croûte continentale 42
croûte de cuir 350
croûte granitique 42
croûte océanique 42
croûte terrestre 42, 43
croûte terrestre, coupe 42
cruche 906
crucifix 737
crustacés 107, 218
Cuba 742
cube 705
cubes d'agneau 215
cubes de bœuf 214
cubes de veau 214
cubiculum 406
cubital antérieur 150, 151
cubital postérieur 151

cubitière 749
cubitus 111, 116, 121, 122, 126, 131, 136, 138, 141, 142, 152, 154, 156
cuboïde 155
cuiller 227, 905, 911
cuiller à café 228
cuiller à dessert 228
cuiller à égoutter 233
cuiller à glace 233
cuiller à goûter 233
cuiller à soda 228
cuiller à soupe 228
cuiller à thé 228
cuiller de table 228
cuiller parisienne 233
cuilleron 227
cuillers doseuses 231
cuillers, exemples 228
cuirasse 748
cuiseur-vapeur 722
cuisine 180, 222, 224, 250, 406, 584, 719, 721, 723, 724, 726, 735, 763, 764
cuisinière 722
cuisinière à gaz 290, 721
cuisinière électrique 290, 721
cuissard 749, 808, 870, 900
cuissarde 343
cuissardes 911
cuisse 124, 130, 143, 147, 149, 169, 170
cuisson 465
cuit-vapeur 235
cuit-vapeur électrique 239
cuivre 683
cuivre et acier 269
cuivres, famille 437
cul-de-sac de Douglas 170
cul-de-sac dural 167
cul-de-sac vésico-utérin 170
culasse 374, 446, 756
culbuteur 566
culée 410, 540
culot 274, 275, 494, 562, 614, 860, 912
culot à baïonnette 275
culot à broches 275
culot à vis 275
culotte 269, 338, 367, 848, 850, 878
culotte à ruchés 368
cultivateur 641
cumin 198
cumulo-nimbus 56, 62
cumulus 56, 62
cupule 84
curcuma 198
cure-ongles 377
curette 390
curiosité 39
curium 684
curleuse 877
curling 877
curry 198
curseur 453, 698
curseur de réglage de la fréquence 498
curseur vers la droite 515
curseur vers la gauche 515
curseur vers le bas 515
curseur vers le haut 515
cuve 266, 291, 292, 294, 484
cuve de développement 484
cuve du modérateur 670
cuve du réacteur 669, 671
cuve vitrifiée 267
cuvette 265, 290, 440, 612, 919
cuvette porte-clapet 268
cuvette ramasse-gouttes 241
cyan 690
cyanobactéries 92
cycle d'un moteur à deux temps 565
cycle d'un moteur diesel 565
cycle d'un moteur rotatif 565
cycle de l'eau 67
cycle des saisons 54
cyclisme 870
cyclisme sur piste 871
cyclisme sur route 870
cyclomoteur 577
cyclone 63
cyclone tropical 63
cyclorama 492
Cygne 12
cylindre 268, 528, 564, 705
cylindre de coupe 332
cylindre de roue 559
cylindre de rubis 692
cylindre des gaz 755
cylindre enregistreur 43
cylindre guide-film 476
cylindre inférieur 421
cylindre récupérateur 756
cylindre réflecteur 692
cylindre rotatif 458
cylindre supérieur 421
cymbale charleston 448
cymbale inférieure 448
cymbale supérieure 448

cymbale suspendue 448
cymbales 437, 449
cymbalette 449
cyme bipare 81
cyme unipare 81
cytopharynx 94
cytoplasme 74, 94, 170
cytoprocte 94
cytostome 94

D

D 862
dague 751
dalle 322
dalle de pierre 298
dalmatien 131
dalot 865
Dame 914, 916
dame de nage 839
dameuse 886
damier 916
Danemark 744
danger 616
danger électrique 774
danois 131, 469
Danube 32
date d'expiration 729
datte 192
Dauphin 12
dauphin 136, 137
dauphin, morphologie 136
dauphin, squelette 136
Dauphine américaine 865
Dauphine canadienne 865
David 736
dé 454, 915
dé à poker 914
dé doubleur 915
dé régulier 914
déambulatoire 411
débarbouillette 379
débarcadère 620
débardeur 354, 369, 371
débarras 509
débit de tabac 714
déblocage instantané 482
débouchure 272
début 515
début de lecture 501
décagone régulier 705
décapeur thermique 320
décapeuse 638
décapsuleur 230, 905
décharge 709
déchets industriels 69
déchets nucléaires 70
déchiquetage 71
déclencheur 476
déclencheur de paiement 920
déclencheur pneumatique 482
déclencheur souple 482
déclinaison 13
déclivité du terrain 244
décolleté carré 363
décolleté drapé 363
décolleté en cœur 363
décolleté en V 363
décolleté plongeant 363
décolletés 363
décomposeurs 67
décor 429
décorateur 429
découpe 348
découpe princesse 366
découpes d'agneau 215
découpes de bœuf 214
découpes de porc 215
découpes de veau 214
défauts de la vision 691
défense 806
défenseur à l'aile 809
défenseur au but 809
défenseur droit 878
défenseur gauche 878
défibrillateur 775
défilement 515
déflecteur d'air chaud 256
déflecteur de chaleur 274
déflecteur de copeaux 305
déflecteur de fumée 256
déflecteur de jet 761
déflecteur de réservoir d'oxygène liquide 25
défonceuse 308, 636
déforestation 69
dégagement d'air des citernes 607
dégagement du margeur 528
dégagement du piston 315
dégageur de fumée 758
dégaine 900
dégrafeuse 534
degré 704

degré Celsius 702
dégrossissage 401
Deimos 4
déjections animales 70
délégués techniques 881
delta 48, 51
Delta II 24
deltoïde 150
démarreur électrique 576
démarreur manuel 327, 332
démêloir 380
demeure seigneuriale 408
demi centre 801
demi d'ouverture 804
demi de coin droit 806
demi de coin gauche 806
demi de mêlée 804
demi de sûreté droit 806
demi de sûreté gauche 806
demi droit 801
demi gauche 801
demi offensif 807
demi-barbule 56
demi-caisson 897
demi-centre 814
demi-cercle 704, 810
demi-cercle de but 809
demi-clé renversée 908
demi-court de service en double 817
demi-court de service en simple 817
demi-finale : 4 joueurs 789
demi-gras 472
demi-lune 385, 409, 887
demi-manche 229
demi-membraneux 151
demi-panneau 632
demi-pause 435
demi-soupir 435
demi-tendineux 151
demi-volée 820
dendrite 168
dendrite spatiale 64
dénominations des cyclones tropicaux 63
dénoyauteur 233
dent 108, 112, 227, 303, 304, 327, 331, 382, 453, 636, 638, 641, 642, 643, 686, 863, 881
dent de défonceuse 636
dent de godet 637
dent de sagesse 159
dentaire 112
denté 79
dentelle aux fuseaux 458
denticule 404, 405
dentifrice 384
dents 159, 309
denture humaine 159
dénude-fil 317
dénudeur de fil 317
déodorant 379
dépanneuse 573
départ 852, 887, 915
départ : bobsleigh et skeleton 885
départ : luge dames et luge double 885
départ : luge simple hommes 885
départ de dos 832
départ des 400 m (course, haies, relais) 791
départ des télécabines 886
départ des télésièges 886
départ du 10 000 m et du relais 4 x 400 m 791
départ du 100 m (course et haies) 790
départ du 110 m haies 790
départ du 1500 m 791
départ du 200 m 790
départ du 5000 m 791
départ du 800 m 791
départ par vent debout 833
déplacement 690
déplacement des électrons, sens 687, 689
déplacement diagonal 916
déplacement en équerre 916
déplacement horizontal 916
déplacement vertical 916
déplacements, échecs 916
déporteur 624
dépression 55
dérailleur 870
dérailleur arrière 578, 580
dérailleur avant 578, 580
derby 342
dérive 625, 631, 760, 834, 836, 840, 898
dérive aérienne 605
dérivés du bois 300
dériveur 834, 835
dériveur de tirage 267
derme 172
dernier croissant 7
dernier droit 856
dernier quartier 7
dés 914
descenderie 650
descendeur 900
descente 889

descente dangereuse 545, 547
descente de gouttière 244
descente du spinnaker 833
désert 52, 61, 66
Désert d'Atacama 31
Désert de Gobi 33
désert de pierres 52
désert de sable 52
Désert du Kalahari 34
Désert du Namib 34
Désert du Sahara 34
déshabillé 364
déshumidificateur 261
desserte 278, 584
dessin 396
dessin à l'encre 396
dessin au crayon de cire 396
dessin au crayon de couleur 396
dessin au feutre 396
dessin au fusain 396
dessin au pastel gras 396
dessin au pastel sec 396
dessin, accessoires 399
dessous 430
destination 582
destructeur de documents 535
détecteur à infrarouge 60
détecteur d'horizon terrestre 40
détecteur d'impact primaire 556
détecteur de fumée 767
détecteur de mouvement 416
détecteur de sécurité 556
détecteur solaire 40, 60
détecteur terrestre 60
détendeur de secours 841
détendeur premier étage 841
détendeur second étage 841
détente 750, 752, 754, 755, 757, 860, 861, 912
détonateur 757
détroit 38
Détroit de Bass 29
Détroit de Béring 30
Détroit de Cook 29
Détroit de Drake 29, 31
Détroit de Gibraltar 32
Détroit de Torres 29
deux avec barreur 839
deux sans barreur 839
deux-points 473
deuxième bord au largue 833
deuxième but 794
deuxième espace 811
deuxième étage 25
deuxième joueur 877
deuxième ligne 804
deuxième molaire 159
deuxième phalange 126
deuxième prémolaire 159
deuxième radial externe 151
deuxième tour : 64 joueurs 789
deuxième-but 794
devant 348, 349
devant d'autel 737
déverrouillage de l'objectif 476
déversement d'hydrocarbures 70
déversoir 657
dévidoir 328, 462
dévidoir de ruban adhésif 534
dévidoir pistolet 534
dévidoir sur roues 328
devise 729
dextre 740
Dévonien 92
diable 235, 633
diable de Tasmanie 143
diagonale 663
diamant 375, 610
diamant, taille 374
diamètre 704
diapason 436
diaphragme 163, 477
diaphragme d'ouverture 694
diaphyse 155
diapositive 483
diastème 123
dièse 435
diesel-navire 656
différence de potentiel électrique, mesure 702
différentiel 553
diffuseur 428
diffuseur tubulaire 627
diffusion d'information 525
digue morte 664
dimétrodon 92
dinde 213
dindon 120
diode 673
Dioné 5
directeur artistique 428
directeur de course 870
directeur de la photographie 429
directeur de production 509

directeur des tirs 859
directeur technique 489, 490
direction d'une réaction 684
direction de la Mecque 738
direction du vent 55
direction et force du vent 55
direction obligatoire 544, 546
discontinuité de Gutenberg 42
discontinuité de Mohorovicic 42
disjoncteur 260, 658
disjoncteur bipolaire 272
disjoncteur de fuite de terre 272
disjoncteur principal 272
disjoncteur unipolaire 272
dispositif anti-bascule 783
dispositif antidébordement 294
dispositif de blocage 321
dispositif de fermeture 913
dispositif de gonflement 611
dispositif de poussée 470
dispositif de ravitaillement 873
dispositif de remorquage 573
dispositifs de contact 274
disposition des informations d'une station 55
disquaire 714
disque 9, 273, 423, 454, 500, 521, 559, 641, 793, 851
disque abrasif 308
disque central 95
disque compact 501, 504
disque compact réinscriptible 521
disque d'enterrage 643
disque de papier-diagramme 571
disque de réglage 479
disque de tension 453, 457
disque dur amovible 521
disque intervertébral 157
disque numérique polyvalent (DVD) 494
disque vidéophoto 481
disques 237
disquette 521
dissipateur thermique 513
distance parcourue 700
distance, mesure 700
distillation sous vide 656
distributeur 263
distributeur d'essence 548
distributeur de billets 715, 730
distributeur de boissons 548, 779
distributeur de correspondances 593
distributeur de détergent 294
distributeur de glaçons 224, 548
distributeur de lames 383
distributeur de produit de rinçage 294
distributeur de trombones 534
distribution de la végétation 66
ditali 206
diviseur 643
division 529, 703
division du noyau 681
division territoriale 37
divisions cartographiques 36
divisions de l'écu 740
dix 703
Dix commandements 738
djembé 433
Djibouti 745
Dniepr 32
do 434, 847
dodécagone régulier 705
dohyo 847
doigt 110, 117, 122, 143, 172, 346, 797, 900
doigt de jupe 605
doigt externe 115
doigt interne 115
doigt lobé 117
doigt médian 115
doigt palmé 110, 117
doigt postérieur 115
doigt préhensile 139
doigtier 531
doigts 116
doline 47
dolique à œil noir 190
dolique asperge 190
dolique d'Égypte 190
doliques 190
dollar 728
domaine de premier niveau 524
domaine de second niveau 524
domaine skiable 886
Dominique 743
domino d'accouplement 444
dominos 914
donjon 408
Dorade 11
dorade 219
dormant 249, 278
dormeuse de croissance 368
dormeuse-couverture 369
dorsale 523
dorsale du Pacifique est 50
dorsale médio-atlantique 50

dorsale médio-indienne 50
dorsale médio-océanique 49
dorsale Pacifique-Antarctique 50
dorsale sud-est-indienne 50
dorsale sud-ouest-indienne 50
dorsales océaniques 50
dortoir des pompiers 764
dos 115, 124, 130, 147, 149, 173, 227, 229, 303, 348, 391, 426, 750
dos d'un gant 346
dos de la langue 176
dos du livre 425
dos du nez 175
dossard 791
dosse 300
dosseret 290, 292, 293
dossier 277, 281, 555, 577, 783, 876
dossier inclinable 776
dossier suspendu 532
dossière 113, 857
double 853, 914
double barre oblique 524
double bémol 435
double boutonnage 352
double croche 435
double dièse 435
double paire 914
double platine cassette 503
double rideau 282
double toit 902, 903
double virage 544, 547
double vitrage 675
double zéro 919
double-blanc 914
double-scull sans barreur 839
double-six 914
doublement denté 79
doublure 342, 348, 349, 370, 386, 455, 881
douche 251, 724, 726, 780
douche des détenus 768
douches des officiers 764
douches des pompiers 764
douchette 264, 270
Douglas, cul-de-sac 170
douille 275, 912
douille de lampe 275
douille de lampe, éléments 275
douille de plastique 860, 912
douilles, jeu 311
douve 408
douzaine (1 à 12) 919
douzaine (13 à 24) 919
douzaine (25 à 36) 919
Dragon 13
dragonne 389, 888, 892, 901
dragons 917
draille 602
drain 253, 263
drakkar 598
drap 280
drap de bain 379
drap-housse 280
drapeau 804, 890
drapeau à damier 872
drapeau à Schwenkel 739
drapeau amovible 867
drapeau carré 739
drapeau de centre 802
drapeau de coin 801, 803
drapeau de l'Union Européenne 729
drapeau rectangulaire 739
drapeau, éléments 739
drapeaux 742
drapeaux, formes 739
dressage 855
drisse 603, 739
droit antérieur de la cuisse 150
droit fil 455
droit interne 151
dromadaire 129
drumlin 45
drupéole 83
duffle-coat 353
dune 51
dune complexe 52
dune en croissant 52
dune parabolique 52
dunes longitudinales 52
dunes transversales 52
dunes, exemples 52
dunette 602
duo 438
duodénum 116, 164
dure-mère 167, 168
durian 197
durite de radiateur 561
duse 734
duvet 115
dyke 44
dynamo 578, 688
dysprosium 684

E

eau 646, 847
eau de fonte 46
eau de parfum 379
eau de toilette 379
eau de ville 675
eau dentifrice 384
eau des nuages 70
eau lourde froide 670
eau lourde sous pression 670
eau sous pression 662
eau usées 791
eaux sécuritaires 616
eaux usées 70
eaux vives 837
ébarbage 424
éboir 422
ébauchoirs 464
éboulement 47
ébrancheur 330
ébrasement 411
écaille 78, 108, 112, 113, 117
écaille ventrale 112
écailles de cyprès 89
écailleur 905
écartelé 740
écartement des électrodes 562
échalote 184
échancrure 439
échancrure de la conque 173
échangeur 709
échangeur de chaleur 259, 670
échangeur en losange 538
échangeur en trèfle 538, 539
échangeur en trompette 538
échangeur thermique 675
échangeurs, exemples 538
échantillon 458
échantillonneur 450
échappement 514, 564, 565, 627
échauguette 408, 409
échecs 916
échecs, mouvements 916
échelle 246, 418, 567, 597, 615, 639, 655, 907
échelle à crochets 321, 767
échelle Celsius 695
échelle coulissante 321
échelle d'accès 611
échelle d'échafaudage 321
échelle d'espacement 528
échelle d'onglet 303, 304
échelle d'ouverture 479
échelle d'ouverture de diaphragme 478
échelle de bout 587
échelle de corde 321
échelle de hauteur 485
échelle de lecture de la luminosité 479
échelle de profondeur 304, 613
échelle de profondeur de champ 478
échelle de tête 766
échelle des altitudes 53
échelle des distances 478
échelle des mouvements 436
échelle des températures 53
échelle des temps d'exposition 479
échelle droite 321
échelle escamotable 321
échelle Fahrenheit 695
échelle fruitière 321
échelle graduée 698, 699
échelle latérale 587
échelle roulante 321
échelle transformable 321
échelles 321
échelon 321
échenilloir-élagueur 330
échine 404
échinodermes 94, 95
échiquier 916
écho 40, 41
éclair 57, 65
éclairage 274, 381, 594, 626
éclairage de l'écran d'affichage 479
éclairage de sécurité 771
éclairage inactinique 484
éclairage/clignotant 556
éclairagiste 490
éclaircie 6
éclipse annulaire 6
éclipse de Lune 7
éclipse de Soleil 6
éclipse partielle 6, 7
éclipse totale 6, 7
éclipses de Lune, types 7
éclipses de Soleil, types 6
écliptique 13
éclisse 439, 440, 590
écluse 596, 597, 664
écluse : vue latérale 597
écoinçon 413
école de ski 886
économie 728
écorce 82, 87
écossais 469

écoulement souterrain 67
écoute 508, 603
écoute de foc 834
écoute de grand-voile 834
écouteur 502
écouteurs 503
écoutille 23, 758
écoutille d'accès 22
écouvillon 752
écran 494, 507, 518, 526, 530, 548, 613, 724, 730, 731, 799, 918
écran à cristaux liquides 477, 496
écran à main 318
écran d'affichage 479, 508
écran d'affichage 512
écran de contrôle 476, 694
écran de précontrôle 489
écran de projection 427, 483
écran de protection 794
écran de sortie 489, 491
écran de soudeur 318
écran de visibilité 591
écran du directeur technique 491
écran du truqueur numérique 491
écran plat 518
écran principal de précontrôle 491
écran protecteur 17
écran tactile 527
écrans d'entrée 491
écrans de précontrôle 491
écrevisse 218
écritoire 387
écriture, instruments 470
écrou 248, 269, 310, 311, 590
écrou à cabestan 58
écrou à collet 270
écrou à oreilles 311
écrou borgne 311
écrou de blocage 909, 910
écrou de bonde 270
écrou de contrôle 58
écrou de fixation 270
écrou de la lame 304
écrou de montage 859, 913
écrou de serrage 269
écrou du presse-étoupe 268
écrou hexagonal 311, 562
écrous 311
ectoderme 95
ectoptérygoïde 112
Écu 10
écu, divisions 740
écubier 605, 609
écueil 51
écume 49
écumoire 233
écureuil 123
écurie 856
écusson 105, 248, 797
édicule 592
édifice à bureaux 710, 713
édifice public 39
éditorial 471
édredon 280
éducation 732
effacement 508
effacement arrière : effacement 515
effacement de mémoire 479, 529
effacement partiel 529
effacement total 529
effet de serre 68
effet de serre naturel 68
effigie 729
effluent 48
effort 686
égal ou plus grand que 703
égal ou plus petit que 703
égale 703
égale à peu près 703
égalisateur graphique 498
églefin 221
église 711, 737
église orthodoxe : Michel Keroularios 736
égout 712
égout collecteur 712
Égypte 745
einsteinium 684
éjecteur 638
éjecteur de fouets 236
El Salvador 742
élan 129, 864, 891
élastique 280
électricien 429
électricité 272
électricité : outils 316
électrode 275, 318
électrode centrale 562
électrode d'allumage 259
électrode de masse 562
électron 680
électronique 689
élément 465
élément bimétallique hélicoïdal 695
élément chauffant 293, 318
élément chauffant inférieur 266
élément chauffant supérieur 266

élément de chauffe 258, 259
élément tubulaire 290
éléments chimiques 682
éléments d'architecture 413
éléments d'un drapeau 739
éléments d'une douille de lampe 275
éléments de la maison 247
éléments du costume ancien 336
éléphant 129
élevage intensif 68, 69
élévateur 666, 897
élévateur à grain 643
élévateur pour fauteuils roulants 569
élévation 250
élévation de la tension 646, 662, 665, 677
élève 734
élevon 23
émail 159
emballage 222
embarcations anciennes 598
embarcations traditionnelles 599
embase 482, 701, 791, 889
embase de plat de dos 276
embauchoir 345
emblème 739
emblème d'équipe 878
embouchure 447
embout 284, 302, 321, 391, 483, 792, 841, 880, 909
embout auriculaire 776
embout buccal 783
embout de baleine 391
embout de caoutchouc 782
embout de protection 773
embout de vissage 306
embout isolant 381
embout Luer Lock 776
embrasse 282, 782
embrasure 409
embrayage 552
émeraude 79
émerillon 911, 913
émetteur micro-ondes 489
émetteur-récepteur d'accès réseau 522
émetteur-récepteur radar 771
émetteur/récepteur 613
Émirats arabes unis 746
émission d'acide nitrique 70
émission d'acide sulfurique 70
émission d'oxyde d'azote 70
émission d'ultrasons 41
émission de dioxyde de soufre 70
émission de gaz polluants 69
émissole 218
emmanchure 351
emmarchement 255
emmenthal 211
empannage 833
empattement 663
empennage 625, 759, 817, 859, 918
empennage bas 629
empennage de stabilisation 25
empennage en T 629
empennage fixe 759
empennage surélevé 629
empennages, exemples 629
empiècement 349, 353, 359
emplacement 244
emplacement de la statue 403
emplacement de tir 893
emporte-pièces 232
en accolade 413
en équilibre 828
en fer à cheval 413
en lancette 413
en ogive 413
en prison 919
en-but 805
encadrement 256
enceinte acoustique 502, 503
enceinte ambiophonique 493
enceinte centrale 493
enceinte de confinement 665, 667
enceinte en béton 670, 671
enceinte humide 671
enceinte principale 493
enceinte sèche 671
enceintes d'extrêmes graves 493
encensoir 737
enclos 182
enclume 174
encoche 750, 859
encoignure 279
encolure 124, 351
encolure bateau 363
encolure drapée 363
encolure en V 354
encolure ras-de-cou 363, 368
encolures 363
encre 397, 421, 470
encre à couleur changeante 729
encre lithographique 423
endive 187
endocarde 162
endocarpe 81, 82
endoderme 95

ASTRONOMIE > 2-25; TERRE > 26-71; RÈGNE VÉGÉTAL >72-89; RÈGNE ANIMAL > 90-143; ÊTRE HUMAIN > 144-177; ALIMENTATION ET CUISINE > 178-241; MAISON > 242-295;
BRICOLAGE ET JARDINAGE > 296-333; VÊTEMENTS > 334-371; PARURE ET OBJETS PERSONNELS > 372-391; ARTS ET ARCHITECTURE > 392-465; COMMUNICATIONS ET BUREAUTIQUE > 466-535;
TRANSPORT ET MACHINERIE > 536-643; ÉNERGIES > 644-677; SCIENCE > 678-705; SOCIÉTÉ > 706-785; SPORTS ET JEUX > 786-920

endossure 425
énergie calorifique 68
énergie éolienne 676, 677
énergie fossile 646
énergie géothermique 646
énergie nucléaire 665
énergie solaire 78, 672, 674
énergie thermique 646
énergie, mesure 702
énergies 646
enfants 785
enfile-aiguille 454
enfouissement 71
enfourchure 351
enfumoir 422
engageante 337
engins 823
engrenage à pignon et crémaillère 686
engrenage à vis sans fin 686
engrenage conique 686
engrenage cylindrique à denture droite 686
engrenage horaire 17
engrenages 686
engreneur 643
enjoliveur 268, 551
ennéagone régulier 705
enregistrement 495, 499, 508
enregistrement des bagages 582
enregistrement des données 41
enregistrement sismographique 651, 653
enregistreur de données 58
enregistreur de film 520
enregistreur numérique 534
enroulement d'induit 688
enroulement inducteur 688
enrouleur 848
enseignant 734
enseigne directionnelle 593
enseigne extérieure 592
ensemble du chevalet 441
ensemble oreillette/microphone 506
ensemble vide 703
ensoleillement, mesure 58
ensouple de chaîne 460
ensouple de tissu 460
entablement 247, 403, 405
entier 79
entoilage 455
entonnoir 106, 231, 237, 240
entonnoir collecteur 59
entraînement de la chaîne 641
entraînement de la turbine par la vapeur 665
entraînement du rotor de l'alternateur 665
entraîneur 800, 811, 827, 842, 879
entraîneur adjoint 811, 879
entraîneurs 881, 883
entrait 253
entrave 857
entre-nœud 77
entredent 227
entredoublure 455
entrée 100, 539, 632, 719, 829
entrée d'air 631
entrée d'air du moteur 760
entrée d'air du ventilateur 605
entrée d'eau 268
entrée d'électricité 465
entrée de clé 249
entrée de courant 274, 275
entrée de garage 245
entrée de l'eau de refroidissement du condenseur 669
entrée de la pyramide 402
entrée de la vapeur à haute pression 668
entrée de service 732
entrée des clients 720
entrée des détenus 726
entrée des gaz d'échappement 564
entrée des marchandises 713
entrée des originaux 508
entrée des véhicules 769
entrée des visiteurs 726
entrée du caloporteur 672
entrée du personnel 720, 726, 735, 768
entrée du public 402
entrée du reflux du condenseur 669
entrée électrique 258
entrée informatique 518
entrée pieds premiers 829
entrée principale 250, 713, 733, 735, 768, 781
entrée tête première 829
entrées dans l'eau 829
entrées des acteurs 402
entrejambe 278
entrejambe pressionné 368, 369
entreposage des produits congelés 181
entrepôt 708
entrepôt frigorifique 596
entreprise 525
entreprise de distribution/vente 525
entretoise 321, 460, 632, 676
enveloppe 275, 521, 797, 798, 867, 899
enveloppe extérieure 17, 267
enveloppe intérieure 17
enveloppe matelassée 531

environnement 66
environnement naturel 867
envoi en nombre 475
envol 891
éolienne à axe horizontal 677
éolienne à axe vertical 676
éoliennes et production d'électricité 676
épaisseur, mesure 700
épandage d'engrais 69
épandeur 324
épandeur de fumier 641
éparpilleur 641
éparpilleur de paille 643
épaule 124, 130, 146, 148, 156, 822, 909
épaulé-jeté 850
épaulement 229, 311
épaulière 749, 757, 808, 880
épeautre 203
épée 849
épée à deux mains 751
épeire 102
épéiste 848
éperlan 219
éperon 98, 448, 598
éperon calcanéen 140, 141
épi 81, 85
épi, blé 85
épi, maïs 85
épi, millet 85
épi, orge 85
épi, riz 85
épi, seigle 85
épicarpe 81, 82, 83
épicéa 89
épicentre 43
épicerie fine 180
épices 198
épices à marinade 199
épicondyle 153
épididyme 169
épiderme 172
épididyme 169
épiglotte 163, 176
épinard 187
épine de l'omoplate 153
épine nasale antérieure 158
épingle 454
épingle à bigoudi 380
épingle à cheveux 380
épingle à cravate 376
épingle de sûreté 453
épingles 376
épiphyse 167
épiphyse distale 155
épiphyse proximale 155
épiscope du tireur 758
épissure courte 908
épitrochlée 153
éplucheur 229
éponge 95, 127
éponge à récurer 295
éponge calcaire 95
éponge de mer 379
éponge synthétique 378
éponge végétale 379
éponge, anatomie 95
épouse 785
épreuve 831
épreuves, ski alpin 889
éprouvette graduée 59, 685
épuisette 911
Équateur 742
équateur 13, 31, 34, 35, 36, 63
équateur céleste 13
équerre 313
équilibrage des haut-parleurs 497
équilibreur 756
équinoxe d'automne 54
équinoxe de printemps 54
équipe au champ 799
équipe de premiers soins 853
équipe médicale 844
équipement 769, 790, 900
équipement de protection 318
équipement de sauvetage 611
équipement de survie 20
équipement de survie, contrôles 20
équipement du tableau de bord 771
équipements aéroportuaires 622
équitation 854
équivalent à 703
érable 88
erbium 684
ergot 130
Éridan 10
erlenmeyer 685
éruption 6
Érythrée 745
escabeau 321
escabeaux 321
escalade 900
escalade, équipement 900
escalier 246, 250, 255, 412, 427, 431, 543, 592, 655, 676, 724, 842
escalier automoteur 623
escalier d'accès 623
escalier de la mezzanine 251

escalier de secours 509
escalier en spirale 655
escalier mécanique 417, 427, 592, 713
escaliers 412
escargot 104, 217
escargot, anatomie 104
escargot, morphologie 104
escarpe 409
escarpin 343
escarpin-sandale 343
escrime 848
escrimeur 848
espace 514
espace d'activités intérieures 727
espace épidural 168
espace insécable 514
espaceur de câbles 859, 913
espadon 219
espadrille 344
Espagne 743
espagnol 469
esperluette 473
esquimau 369
essence 656
essence lourde 656
essieu 586, 895
essieu à roue 647
essieu avant 639
essieu directeur 633
essoreuse à salade 231
essuie-glace 550, 557
Est 37
est 616, 917
est identique à 703
Est Nord-Est 37
Est Sud-Est 37
estacade de guidage 597
estèques 464
estomac 95, 103, 104, 105, 106, 109, 110, 112, 113, 125, 161, 164
estomac cardiaque 107
estomac pylorique 107
Estonie 744
estrade 412, 734
estragon 202
esturgeon 218
étable 182
établi étau 312
établissement d'enseignement 525
établissement scolaire 711
étage 250, 251, 650, 676
étage à propergol stockable 24
étage d'accélération à poudre 24
étage d'exploitation 664
étage principal cryotechnique 24
étagère de rangement 723
étai 252, 598, 602
étai avant 834
étain 682
étamine 80, 82
étampure 127
étançon 641
étang 866
étapes de maturation 86
étapes de production de l'électricité 662
État 37
État de la cité du Vatican 744
état présent du temps 55
états de la matière 680
États-Unis d'Amérique 742
étau 312, 422
étau à endosser 425
été 54
étendu 472
Éthiopie 745
éthylomètre 769
étincelle 564
étiquette 500, 699
étiquettes autocollantes 532
étoile 8, 64, 741
étoile (8) 374
étoile à neutrons 8
étoile de David 738
étoile de freinage 910
étoile de la séquence principale 8
étoile de mer, anatomie 95
étoile de mer, morphologie 95
étoile filante 53
Étoile Polaire 13
étoiles de faible masse 8
étoiles massives 8
étouffoir 443
étranglement 695, 844
étrave 598, 602, 606, 834, 838
être humain 146
étrier 174, 274, 559, 574, 750, 853, 855, 892
étrier de fixation 613
étrier du flotteur 263
étrivière 855
étroit 472
étui 345, 377, 529, 905
étui à lentilles 384
étui à lunettes 387
étui à menottes 770

étui à pistolet 770
étui de cuir 907
étui pour gants de latex 770
Eurasie 28
euro 728
Europe 4, 28, 32, 50, 743
europium 684
Eutelsat 486
euthynterie 403, 404
évacuation de l'eau turbinée 662
évaporation 67
évaseur 314
évent 136, 465, 470
évent de pignon 244
évent latéral 261
évier 224, 270, 722
évier à batterie de cuisine 721
évier de prérinçage 721
évier double 262
évier-broyeur 270
évolution de la pression 55
évolution de la vie 92
Ex-République yougoslave de Macédoine 744
ex-voto 737
examen psychiatrique 778
excavatrice à roue 647
exemples d'adaptateurs 269
exemples d'algues 75
exemples d'amphibiens 111
exemples d'ancres 610
exemples d'angles 704
exemples d'arachnides 102
exemples d'arbres feuillus 88
exemples d'arcs 413
exemples d'arcs 541
exemples d'avions 628
exemples d'échangeurs 538
exemples d'empennages 629
exemples d'hélicoptères 631
exemples d'insectes 101
exemples d'instruments à clavier 443
exemples d'oiseaux 118
exemples d'unités monétaires 728
exemples de barrages 660
exemples de bateaux et d'embarcations 604
exemples de becs 117
exemples de bicyclettes 581
exemples de branchement 270
exemples de camions 573
exemples de carrosseries 549
exemples de chaises 277
exemples de chauves-souris 141
exemples de chemisiers 359
exemples de clous 301
exemples de cols 362
exemples de conifères 89
exemples de côtes 51
exemples de couleurs 741
exemples de couteaux 228
exemples de couteaux de cuisine 229
exemples de cuillers 228
exemples de dunes 52
exemples de fauteuils 276
exemples de fenêtres 415
exemples de feuilles 89
exemples de fleurs 80
exemples de fougères 76
exemples de fourchettes 228
exemples de fourrures 741
exemples de fraises 308
exemples de fusibles 272
exemples de gréements 601
exemples de groupes instrumentaux 438
exemples de jupes 357
exemples de lanceurs spatiaux 24
exemples de lichens 74
exemples de lunettes 385
exemples de mammifères carnivores 134
exemples de mammifères insectivores 121
exemples de mammifères lagomorphes 123
exemples de mammifères marins 137
exemples de mammifères ongulés 128
exemples de mammifères primates 139
exemples de mammifères rongeurs 123
exemples de manches 360
exemples de marsupiaux 143
exemples de mèches et de forets 306
exemples de métaux 741
exemples de meubles 741
exemples de motos 577
exemples de mousses 75
exemples de pantalons 358
exemples de partitions 740
exemples de pattes 117
exemples de pièces honorables 740
exemples de plis 283, 357
exemples de plongeons 829
exemples de pneus 560
exemples de poches 360
exemples de pointes 302
exemples de ponts à poutre 541
exemples de ponts en arc 541
exemples de portes 416
exemples de postes téléphoniques 507
exemples de prises 844
exemples de quilles 865

exemples de raccords 269
exemples de reptiles 114
exemples de réseaux 522
exemples de rideaux 283
exemples de robes 356
exemples de sabots 127
exemples de sacs de couchage 904
exemples de sauts 881
exemples de semi-remorques 572
exemples de skis 840, 888
exemples de sondes spatiales 19
exemples de tables 278
exemples de tentes 902
exemples de têtes 283, 302
exemples de toits 414
exemples de trapèzes 840
exemples de voiles 601
exemples de voitures 630
exemples de volcans 44
exemples de wagons 588
exosphère 53
expandeur 450
expédition du fret 621
expiration 832
explosion 564
exposant 472
extenseur 850
extenseur commun des doigts 151
extenseur commun des orteils 150
extérieur d'une maison 244
extincteur 767, 771
extincteur d'incendie 725
extra-gras 472
extra-maigre 472
extracteur 896
extrados 413
extrait de vanille 200
eye-liner liquide 378

F

fa 434
façade 411
face 139, 227, 409, 815, 867
face antérieure 146, 148, 150
face inférieure 374
face plantaire du sabot 127
face postérieure 147, 149, 151
face supérieure 374
face-à-main 385
facette 629
facteur 475
facteur Rhésus négatif 702
facteur Rhésus positif 702
factorielle 703
facule 6
faible 849
faille 43
faîne 193
faisan 120, 212
faisceau bleu 494
faisceau d'électrons 494, 694
faisceau laser 501, 692
faisceau radar 40
faisceau rouge 494
faisceau vert 494
faîtage 252
faîteau 412
faitout 235, 905
faits divers 471
falaise 7, 45, 51
falaise côtière 51
falcatus 92
Fallope, trompe 170
famille 784
famille des bois 437
famille des cuivres 437
famille du violon 437, 439
familles de langues 468
fanion 56, 739
fanion-girouette 893
fanon 124
fard à joues en poudre 378
farine d'avoine 204
farine de blé complet 204
farine de maïs 204
farine et semoule 204
farine non blanchie 204
farine tout usage 204
fart 892
fasce 404
fauchée 40
faucheuse-conditionneuse 642
faucille 330
faucon 119
fausse côte (3) 153
fausse oronge 76
fausse poche 355
fausse-équerre 313, 701
fautes/pénalités 789
fauteuil 276, 427, 431, 734
fauteuil club 276
fauteuil de repos 780
fauteuil du réalisateur 429
fauteuil metteur en scène 276

fauteuil pivotant à bascule 511
fauteuil roulant 584, 783
fauteuil Wassily 276
fauteuil-sac 277
fauteuils des acteurs 428
fauteuils, exemples 276
faux 330
faux bourdon 99
faux foc 603
faux quartier 855
faux registre 445
faux sommier 445
Fédération de Russie 744
feijoa 197
felouque 600
femelle 702
femme 148
fémur 96, 98, 111, 116, 122, 126, 131, 138, 141, 142, 152
fenêtre 249, 251, 346, 485, 567, 594, 663, 836
fenêtre à barreaux 727
fenêtre à guillotine 415
fenêtre à jalousies 415
fenêtre à l'anglaise 415
fenêtre à la française 415
fenêtre basculante 415
fenêtre coulissante 415
fenêtre d'éjection 755
fenêtre de lecture 499, 521
fenêtre de sous-sol 245
fenêtre en accordéon 415
fenêtre moustiquaire 902
fenêtre panoramique 584, 713
fenêtre pivotante 415
fenêtres, exemples 415
fenil 182
fennec 134
fenouil 185
fente 238, 302, 386, 424, 463
fente à monnaie 507, 920
fente d'alimentation 511
fente d'alimentation manuelle 519
fente de dépôt 730
fente de mise à jour du livret bancaire 730
fente de relevé d'opération 730
fente de vision 749
fente du lecteur de carte 548, 730, 731
fente latérale 348
fente médiane 348
fente pour carte PC 526
fentes branchiales 108
fentes d'aération 526
fenugrec 198
fer 127, 309, 683, 867, 868
fer à cheval 127, 376
fer à friser 381
fer à souder 318
fer à vapeur 288
fer droit 867, 868
fer n° 3 868
fer n° 4 868
fer n° 5 868
fer n° 6 868
fer n° 7 868
fer n° 8 868
fer n° 9 868
ferme 182
ferme de toit 253
fermeture à glissière 353, 369, 377, 389, 453, 902
fermeture du soufflet 432
fermeture sous patte 369
fermeture Velcro® 368
fermium 684
fermoir 386, 387, 401
ferret 342, 370, 391
ferrure 389
ferrure d'attelage 558
fertilisation des sols 69
fesse 147, 149, 169, 170
fettucine 206
feu 615, 617
feu antibrouillard 554, 570
feu anticollision 624
feu arrière 575, 576, 578
feu blanc 616
feu clignotant 554, 591
feu clignotant arrière 576
feu clignotant avant 574, 576
feu de circulation 712
feu de croisement 554
feu de gabarit 554, 570, 571
feu de lisse 591
feu de navigation 605, 625
feu de plaque 554
feu de position 585, 631
feu de recul 554
feu de route 554
feu de tête de mât 605
feu jaune 712
feu pour piétons 712
feu rouge 712
feu rouge arrière 554, 571
feu stop 554
feu vert 712

feuillage 87
feuille 75, 77, 78, 79, 85, 185
feuille d'acanthe 276, 405
feuille de vigne 86, 186
feuille, bord 79
feuille, structure 79
feuilles composées 79
feuilles simples 79
feuilles, exemples 89
feuillet 426
feuillets 386
feuillets intercalaires 532
feutre 341, 397, 443
feutre d'étouffoir 442
feux arrière 554, 775
feux avant 554
feux de signalisation 859
feux intermittents 568
fèves 190
fez 339
fibre 908
fibre musculaire 168
fibre nerveuse 172
fibres 295
fibule 336
ficelle 424
fiche 306, 316, 613
fiche américaine 274
fiche d'alimentation 527
fiche européenne 274
fiche pour jack 488, 502
fiche technique 395
fiche, adaptateur 274, 383
fiches 532
fichier 524, 533
fichier rotatif 531
Fidji 747
figue 197
figue de Barbarie 197
figure 855
fil 300, 689
fil à couper la pâte 464
fil d'arrivée 856
fil d'attache 103
fil de caret 908
fil de corps 848
fil de liaison 272
fil de nylon 332
fil de phase 272
fil de sécurité 729
fil de service neutre 272
fil de terre 272
fil de trame 463
fil dentaire 384
fil neutre 272
filament 274
filament de tungstène 274
file d'attente 731
filet 80, 281, 302, 405, 439, 440, 471, 811, 812, 813, 814, 815, 817, 821, 827
filet à aiguilles 854
filet à jouets 854
filet à olives 854
filet de bœuf 214
filet en caoutchouc 854
filetage 268
filière 103, 314
filigrane 729
filin 611
fille 784, 785
film 477
film-disque 481
film-pack 481
filoir d'écoute 835
fils 784, 785
fils de chaîne 463
filtre 238, 246, 290, 675
filtre à air 258, 261, 331, 552, 586, 636
filtre à charpie 292, 293
filtre coloré 612
filtre de couleur 478
filtre de polarisation 478
filtre rouge inactinique 485
filum terminal 167
fin 515
finale : 2 joueurs 789
finaliste 789
finance 728
fines herbes 202
finition 401
Finlande 744
finnois 469
fission de l'uranium 665
fission nucléaire 681
fixatif 400
fixation 284, 791, 840, 891, 892
fixation à butée avant 892
fixation à coque 887
fixation à plaque 887
fixation arrière 840
fixation avant 840
fixation de sécurité 888, 889
fixe-lecture 479
fjords 51
flacon 379

flagelle 104
flageolet 191
flamant 119
flamme 681
flanc 115, 124, 409, 425, 560, 561
flanc dextre 740
flanc senestre 740
flash électronique 482
flash-cube 482
flasque 659, 753
flasque inférieur 659
fléau 698
fléau arrière 698
fléau avant 698
Flèche 12
flèche 411, 634, 637, 638, 750, 859, 863, 915
flèche de transept 410
flèche du vent 56
flèche littorale 51
flèche télescopique 634, 766
fléchette 918
flétan 221
fleur 77, 80
fleur de lis 741
fleur, structure 80
fleuret 648, 849
fleuret électrique 848
fleurettiste 848
fleuriste 715
fleurs 917
fleurs, exemples 80
fleuve 38, 39, 48
flexible 264, 270
flexible d'air 398, 648
flexible d'eau 648
flexible d'injection de boue 651
flexible de branchement 485
flexible de distribution 548
flexibles d'alimentation 899
flip 881
floraison 86
flotteur 263, 265, 611, 615, 628, 655, 756, 836, 911
fluide caloporteur 674
fluor 683
flûte à champagne 225
flûte de Pan 433
flûte à bécher 326
flûte traversière 446
fluteroni 401
flûtes 437
foc 834
foie 109, 110, 112, 113, 116, 125, 161, 164, 212
foie gras 216
follicule 84, 172
follicule, coupe 84
fonctions système 450
fond 401, 894
fond d'yeux 227
fond de l'océan 42
fond de l'océan 49
fond de protection 918
fond de robe 366
fond de teint liquide 378
fond de tour 656
fondation 660
fondation de pylône 540
fondations 253
fongicide 69
fontaine à soda 723
fontaine des ablutions 738
fontanelle antérieure 158
fontanelle mastoïdienne 158
fontanelle postérieure 158
fontanelle sphénoïdale 158
fonts baptismaux 737
fonture 456
football 802
football américain 806
football américain, protection 808
football canadien 809
footballeur 802, 808
forage en mer 653
foramen apical 159
foramen cæcum 176
force du vent 55
force, mesure 702
forces agissant sur un avion 630
foret 307
forêt 45
forêt boréale 66
forêt de conifères 66
forêt de feuillus 66
foret hélicoïdal 306
foret de maçonnerie 306
forêt mixte 66
forêt tempérée 66
forêt tropicale 66
forêt tropicale humide 66
format du fichier 524
formation de jazz 438
forme des caractères 472
formes de drapeaux 739
formes de pluie 64
formes géométriques 704

formes pharmaceutiques des médicaments 783
fort 849
forte pluie 63
fortification à la Vauban 409
fossé 409, 538
fosse à plonger 246
fosse abyssale 49
fosse d'orchestre 430
fosse de Java 50
fosse de Porto Rico 50
fosse de réception 865
fosse de sable 866, 867
fosse de tir 860
fosse des Aléoutiennes 50
fosse des Kouriles 50
fosse des Mariannes 50
fosse des Philippines 50
fosse des Ryukyu 50
fosse des Tonga-Kermadec 50
fosse du Japon 50
fosse Pérou-Chili 50
fosse septique 70, 263
fosses nasales 175
fosses océaniques 50
fossette 112
fossette de l'anthélix 173
Fou 916
fouet 232, 236
fouet à fil 236
fouet en spirale 236
fouet quatre pales 236
fouets 236
fougère 76
fougère arborescente 76
fougère nid d'oiseau 76
fougère, structure 76
fougères 92
fougères, exemples 76
fouine 134
foulon 642
four 224, 290, 674, 721, 722
four à micro-ondes 224, 238
four électrique 465
four solaire 674
four tubulaire 656
fourche 14, 579, 663, 870, 875
fourche à bêcher 326
fourche à fleurs 325
fourche avant 870
fourche télescopique 577
fourche télescopique hydraulique 574
fourches 632, 633
fourchette 116, 127, 227, 346, 697, 892, 905
fourchette à découper 229
fourchette à dessert 228
fourchette à fondue 228
fourchette à huîtres 228
fourchette à poisson 228
fourchette à salade 228
fourchette de table 228
fourchettes, exemples 228
fourgon postal 474, 475
fourgon-pompe 766
fourgonnette 549
fourmi 101
Fourneau 10
fourneau 390
fournisseur de services Internet 525
fournitures de premiers soins 775
fourragère 642
fourreau 307, 391, 836, 897
fourreau de la langue 112
fourrure 121, 133
fourrures, exemples 741
fours à micro-ondes 723
fovéa 177
foyer 43, 674, 691
foyer Cassegrain 17
foyer coudé 17
foyer des élèves 735
foyer primaire 17
foyer, accessoires 257
foyers 431
frac 338
fraction 703
fraise 192, 339
fraise à chanfrein 308
fraise à congé 308
fraise à feuillure 308
fraise à gorge 308
fraise à quart de rond 308
fraise à queue d'aronde 308
fraise, coupe 83
fraises, exemples 308
framboise 192
framboise, coupe 83
français 469
France 743
Francis, roue 659
francium 682
frange 337
frappeur 795, 796
frégate 762
frein 458, 851, 870, 889, 909

frein à disque 552, 559, 574, 874
frein à main 552
frein à tambour 559
frein arrière 578
frein avant 579
frein d'urgence 594
frein de chaîne 331
frein de talon 895
frein direct 586
frein hydraulique à disque 870
freineur 884
freins 559
frelon 101
fréquence, mesure 702
frère 785
frère/sœur 785
frères 785
fresque 406
frette 440, 441
frise 247, 278, 403, 404, 431
frises 430
friteuse 238, 721
fromage 722
fromage à la crème 210
fromages à pâte molle 211
fromages à pâte persillée 211
fromages à pâte pressée 211
fromages de chèvre 210
fromages frais 210
françage tuyauté 283
fronce 359
fronde 75, 76
front 115, 146, 647
front chaud en altitude 56
front chaud en surface 56
front de taille 647, 650
front froid en altitude 56
front froid en surface 56
front occlus 56
front stationnaire 56
frontal 112, 131, 150, 152, 158, 749, 854
frontière 37
fronto-pariétal 111
fronton 403, 405
fronts 56
frottoir 595
frottoir 318, 391
fruit charnu 83
fruit charnu à noyau 81
fruit charnu à pépins 82
fruit de la Passion 196
fruits 81, 180, 192
fruits à noyau 192
fruits à pépins 193
fruits charnus 82
fruits et desserts 723
fruits secs 84, 193
fruits tropicaux 196
fumée 57
fumerolle 44
funicule 83, 84
furet de dégorgement 314
fusain 397
fuseau 358, 458, 462
fusée 602
fusée à propergol solide 22, 24
fusée de proximité 759
fusée éclairante 771
fuselage 625, 898
fusible 273, 663, 673
fusible à culot 272
fusible-cartouche 272
fusible-cartouche à lames 272
fusibles, exemples 272
fusil 229
fusil (canon lisse) 912
fusil à air comprimé 841
fusil automatique 755
fusil calibre 12 860
fusil mitrailleur 755
fusilli 206
fusion 680
fût 87, 287, 302, 405, 448, 663, 859, 860, 912, 918
futon 280

G

gâble 411
Gabon 745
gâche 249
gâchette 320, 331, 398, 516, 767
gâchette de sécurité 331
gadolinium 684
gaffe 611, 767
Gai lon 187
gainage du combustible défectueux 666
gaine 79, 367, 689, 841, 907, 908
gaine d'air frais 543
gaine d'air vicié 543
gaine de dérivation 258
gaine de distribution 260
gaine de myéline 168
gaine de rancher 571
gaine de Schwann 168

gaine du ressort 284
gaine isolante 275
gaine principale 258
gaine-culotte 367
galaxie 9
galaxie elliptique 9
galaxie irrégulière de type I 9
galaxie irrégulière de type II 9
galaxie lenticulaire 9
galaxie spirale barrée 9
galaxie spirale normale 9
galère 598
galerie 411, 676
galerie de circulation 650
galerie de liaison 543
galerie de visite 658
galerie en direction 650
galerie marchande 713
galerie sèche 47
galet 284, 423, 499, 516
galets tendeurs 580
galettage 465
galettes de riz 207
galhauban 602
Galileo 19
galion 599
gallium 682
gallois 469
galon 340
galon d'ornement 368
galop 125
Gambie 745
gamme 434
ganache 124
ganglion cérébropleural 105
ganglion du tronc sympathique 167
ganglion spinal 167, 168
ganglion viscéral 105
ganse 905
gant 20, 797, 798, 800, 842, 848, 853, 855, 870, 871, 874, 875, 878, 882, 884, 887, 891, 892
gant à crispin 318, 346
gant court 346
gant de conduite 346
gant de crin 379
gant de frappeur 796
gant de golf 869
gant de plongée 841
gant de receveur 796
gant de ski 888
gant de softball 797
gant de toilette 379
gant en latex 776
gant long 346
gant saxe 346
gantelet 749
gants 346, 872
gants d'homme 346
gants de boxe 843
gants de femme 346
gants de gardien de but 802
gants de jardinage 325
Ganymède 4
garage 244, 543, 726, 764, 769
garam masala 199
garant 342
garcette de ris 603
garde 426
garde basse (lutte libre) 843
garde de clé 446
garde de culasse 446
garde droit 807
garde gauche 807
garde haute (lutte gréco-romaine) 843
garde volante 426
garde-boue 578, 640
garde-boue arrière 577
garde-boue avant 574
garde-corps 321, 540, 542, 586
garde-fou 251
garde-main 755
garde-manger 224, 250
garde-robe 251
gardien de but 800, 801, 803, 809, 814, 827, 878, 879
gardien de guichet 799
gare 39, 583, 708, 710
gare de marchandises 583
gare de triage 589, 708
gare de voyageurs 582, 583
gare maritime 596
gare routière 710
garniture 269, 389
garniture de frein 559
garrot 124, 130
gaufrier-gril 238
gaz 275, 651, 656, 680
gaz à effet de serre 68
gaz brûlés 564
gaz carbonique de refroidissement 670
gaz inerte 274
gaz rares 684
gazole 656
gazon 322, 822
geai 118

géante rouge 8
gélule 783
Gémeaux 13
gencive 159, 174
générateur d'air chaud 258
générateur d'air chaud électrique 258
générateur de tonalités d'amorces 488
générateur de vapeur 646, 669, 670, 671, 674, 763
générateur thermoélectrique à radio-isotopes 18
générateurs 688
genou 124, 130, 146, 148
genouillère 749, 796, 808, 850, 858, 880, 882, 894, 895
géographie 28
géologie 42
géométrie 704
Géorgie 746
géothermie 646
gerbeur 633
gerboise 123
germanium 682
germe 85, 117
germes de soja 191
germination 77
gésier 116
geyser 44
Ghana 745
ghee 210
gi 846
gibbeuse croissante 7
gibbeuse décroissante 7
gibbon 139
gibier 212
gicleur 259, 655
gicleur de lave-glace 550
gicleurs 665
gilet 338, 348, 359
gilet athlétique 351
gilet de laine 354
gilet de sauvetage 611
gilet de stabilisation 841
gingembre 199
Girafe 12
girafe 129
girelle 464
giron 255
girouette 58, 59, 677, 834
gisement de pétrole 651, 653
givre 65
glace 67, 551, 554, 612
glace de custode 551
glacier 46, 48, 66
glacier suspendu 46
glacière 906
glacis 409
glacis précontinental 49
glaive 748
gland 169, 282, 285
glande à venin 103, 106, 112
glande coxale 103
glande de Cowper 169
glande de l'albumine 104
glande digestive 104, 105, 106, 107
glande lacrymale 177
glande mammaire 171
glande pédieuse 104
glande salivaire 97, 99, 104, 176
glande sébacée 172
glande sudoripare apocrine 172
glande sudoripare eccrine 172
glande surrénale 165
glandes digestives 103
glandes salivaires 164
glandes séricigènes 103
glissement de terrain 47
glisseur 896
glissière 294, 456, 587, 754
glissière d'ajustement 502
glissière d'auvent 567
glissière de fixation 692
glissière du guide 305
glissoir 342
glissoire de recul 756
globe 903
globe oculaire 110, 177
globe terrestre 734
globule blanc 162
globule rouge 162
glome 127
glotte 112
glucose 78
gnocchi 206
go 916
godet 320, 398, 637
godet à couleur 398
godet à poussière 288
godet chargeur 638
godet de beurre 223
godet de lait/crème 223
godet rétro 637
goélette 601
golf 866
golfe 38
Golfe d'Aden 33, 34

Golfe d'Alaska 30
Golfe d'Oman 33
Golfe de Botnie 32
Golfe de Californie 30
Golfe de Carpentarie 29
Golfe de Guinée 34
Golfe de Panama 31
Golfe du Bengale 33
Golfe du Mexique 30
Golfe Persique 33
Golgi 74, 94
gombo 188
gomme 534
gonade 95, 105, 106
gond 247, 278
gondole 181, 600
gonfalon 739
gonfleur 841, 904
gonfleur-dégonfleur 904
gong 437, 449
gorge 47, 48, 115, 312, 911
gorgerin 749
gorgonzola 211
gorille 138
gorille, morphologie 139
gorille, squelette 138
gouache 396
gouffre 47
gouge 401
gouge creuse 421
gouge en V 421
goujon 559
goujure 306
goulot de remplissage 553
gourde 906
gourmand 86
gourmette 376, 854
gourmette d'identité 376
gousse, coupe 84
gousset de latte 834, 836
goût 174
goutte 404
gouttelette lipidique 74
gouttes ophtalmiques lubrifiantes 384
gouttière 244, 287, 551
gouvernail 23, 600, 606, 608, 676, 834, 838, 839
gouvernail de direction 760, 763, 898
gouvernail de plongée avant 763
gouvernail de profondeur 898
gouverne 759
gouverne de direction 625
gouverne de profondeur 625
goyave 197
grenouille 110
gradateur 274
gradin 407, 647
gradins 402
gradins mobiles 734
graduation 313, 695, 700, 776, 907
graduation de la règle 700
graduation du vernier 700
grain 57, 85
grain d'amidon 74
grain de blé, coupe 85
graine 77, 81, 82, 83, 84
graine de soja 191
graines de pavot 199
grains de café torréfiés 208
grains de café verts 208
graisse 472
graisses 656
graisseur 648
gril barbecue 239
grand adducteur 151
grand cacatoès avant 603
Grand Canyon 30
Grand Chien 11
grand complexus 151
Grand Désert de Sable 29
Grand Désert Victoria 29
grand dorsal 151
grand droit de l'abdomen 150
grand duc d'Amérique 119
grand fauchage extérieur 844
grand fauchage intérieur 844
grand fessier 151
grand foc 603
grand hunier fixe avant 603
grand hunier volant avant 603
grand largue 833
grand mât 600
grand mât arrière 602
grand mât avant 602
grand miroir 612
grand oblique de l'abdomen 150, 151
grand os 154
grand palmaire 150
grand pectoral 150
grand perroquet fixe avant 603
grand perroquet volant avant 603
grand rabat 391
grand rond 151
grand sésamoïde 126
grand tournant 856
grand trochanter 153

grand-mère 784
grand-père 784
grand-voile 834
grand-voile arrière 603
grand-voile avant 603
grand-voile d'étai arrière 603
Grande Baie australienne 29
grande échelle 766
grande galerie 402
grande lame 905
grande lèvre 170, 171
Grande Ourse 13
grande roussette 218
grande sauterelle verte 101
grande sus-alaire 115
grande ville 37
grandes familles de langues 468
grandes lignes 583
Grands Lacs 30
grands-parents 784
grange 182
granulation 6
grappe 81
grappe de combustible 667
grappe de raisin 752
grappe de raisins 86
grappe, sarrasin 85
grappin 610
gras 472
grasset 124
gratte-ongles 377
grattoir 320
graveur de disque compact 503
graveur de disque compact réinscriptible 521
graveur de DVD 521
gravier 253, 263
gravure en creux 422
gravure en relief 421
gravure sur bois de fil 421
gravure sur bois debout 421
grébiche 386
grec 469
Grèce 744
grecquage 424
grecque 424
gréement 602
gréements, exemples 601
greffier 860
greffoir 330
grêlon 64
grelots 449
Grenade 743
grenade 196
grenade à main 757
grenat 375
grenouille 110
grenouille des bois 111
grenouille léopard 111
grenouille mâle, anatomie 110
grenouille rousse 111
grenouille, métamorphose 111
grenouille, morphologie 110
grenouille, squelette 111
grenouillère 368
grève 749
griffe 96, 98, 107, 113, 115, 121, 122, 130, 133, 140, 143, 376
griffe à fleurs 325
griffe abaissée, chat 133
griffe d'entraînement 453
griffe porte-accessoires 476
griffe rétractée, chat 133
gril barbecue 239
gril électrique 239
gril pliant 907
grillage 260, 261
grillage de protection 316
grille 234, 261, 290, 383, 403, 432, 494, 561, 658, 727, 796
grille à reine 100
grille d'aération 294, 594
grille d'aspiration 382
grille d'éclairage 492
grille d'éclairage 429
grille d'entrée d'air 575
grille d'extrémité 667
grille d'habillage 259
grille de chauffage 594
grille de départ 872, 875
grille de sécurité 730
grille de sortie d'air 382
grille de vaporisation 261
grille de ventilation 289
grille des programmes de télévision 471
grille métallique conductrice 672
grille stabilisatrice 903
grille-pain 238
grimpeur 900
grondin 219
gros intestin 110, 164
gros sel 201
groseille à grappes 192
groseille à maquereau 192
grosse caisse 437, 448

grosse quille 865
grotte 47, 51
groupe bulbe 664
groupe de climatisation 622
groupe de démarrage pneumatique 622
groupe électrogène 622
groupe électropompe 559
groupe frigorifique 571
groupe turbo-alternateur 646, 658, 659
groupes instrumentaux, exemples 438
Grue 10
grue 652
grue à flèche 596
grue à tour 634
grue de bord 761
grue sur ponton 596
grue sur porteur 634
grues 634
gruppetto 435
gruyère 211
guarani 469
Guatemala 742
guépard 135
guêpe 101
guêpière 367
guerrier gaulois 748
guêtre 339
gueules 741
gui 602
guichet 731, 799
guichet automatique bancaire 730, 731
guichet commercial 731
guichet de nuit 731
guichet de vente des billets 592
guide 238, 303, 304, 424, 521
guide à onglet 305
guide d'ondes 489
guide de refend 304, 305
guide des températures 288
guide papier 519
guide-bande 499, 534
guide-chaîne 331, 580
guide-fil 452, 453, 457
guide-ligne 910
guide-papier 508
guides de classement 532
guidon 332, 579, 739, 754, 757, 851, 861, 871, 876, 893, 912
guidon surélevé 870
guillemets 473
guimbarde 433
guindant 739, 836
Guinée 745
Guinée équatoriale 745
Guinée-Bissau 745
guitare acoustique 440
guitare basse 441
guitare électrique 441
Gutenberg, discontinuité 42
Guyana 742
guyot 49
gymnase 608, 727, 734, 764, 788
gymnastique 824
gymnastique rythmique 823
gyoji 847
gyrophare 766
gyroscope 759

H

habilleur 428
habitacle 22, 873
habitation 182
hache 330, 767
hache en pierre polie 748
hachette 907
hachoir 230
hachure 463
hackle 909
hafnium 683
haie 245, 322, 790
haie barrée 852
haie de steeple 790
haie rivière 852, 853
Haïti 742
hakama 846, 847
halebas 834
halefis de culasse (16) 374
halefis de table (16) 374
hall 713, 719, 724
hall d'entrée 250, 394, 509
hall public 620
halo 9
halte-garderie 715
haltère court 850
haltère long 850, 851
haltérophilie 850
hameçon 909, 911
hameçon monté 911
hameçon triple 911
hampe 56, 739, 793, 911
hamster 123
hanche 96, 98, 147, 149
hanche ailée 844
handball 814

handicap de l'équipe 858
handicap du joueur 858
hangar 182, 619, 761
hangar de transit 596
hangar pour hélicoptères 762
hanneton 101
haoussa 468
haptère 75
hareng 219
haricot adzuki 191
haricot d'Espagne 191
haricot de Lima 191
haricot jaune 191
haricot mungo 191
haricot mungo à grain noir 191
haricot noir 191
haricot pinto 191
haricot romain 191
haricot rouge 191
haricot vert 191
haricots 191
harissa 201
harmonica 432
harnais 460, 841, 893, 896, 897
harpe 440
harpes 437
hassium 683
hastée 79
hauban 578, 602, 628, 676, 834, 897, 902
haubans 541
haubans en éventail 541
haubans en harpe 541
hausse 100, 439, 754, 755, 757, 861, 893, 912
haut-de-chausse 338
haut-de-forme 340
haut-parleur 427, 496, 504, 505, 508, 513, 526, 626, 766
haut-parleur d'aigus 502
haut-parleur d'aigus 10
haut-parleur de contrôle 488, 489, 490, 491
haut-parleur de graves 10, 502
haut-parleur de médium 502
haut-parleur de médiums 10
hautbois 437, 446
hauteur de chute 662
hauteur de la vague 49
hauteur de marche 255
hauteur du gradin 647
hauteur du plongeon 829
Havers, canal 154
hawaïen 469
hébergement 886
hébreu 468
hélice 606, 608, 609, 705, 763
hélice arrière 606
hélice bipale 628
hélice d'étrave 606
hélice de propulsion 605
hélice de ventilation 688
hélice tripale 628
hélices 762
hélicoptère 631, 762
hélicoptère bombardier d'eau 631
hélicoptère de transport tactique 631
hélicoptère-ambulance 631
hélicoptères, exemples 631
héliographe 58
hélisurface 652, 762
hélium 684
hélix 173
hémisphère 705
hémisphère austral 35
hémisphère boréal 35
hémisphère occidental 35
hémisphère oriental 35
hémisphères 35
hendécagone régulier 705
hennin 339
Henri VIII 736
héraldique 739
herbe longue 866, 867
herbicide 69
herbivores 67
Hercule 13
hérisson 121
hermine 741
herminette 401
héron 119
herse 430
hertz 702
hétérotrophes 67
hêtre 88
hexagone régulier 705
hijiki 183
hile du rein 165
Himalaya 33
hindi 469
hindouisme 736
hippodrome 856
hippopotame 129
hirondelle 118
hiver 54
hockey sur gazon 800
hockey sur glace 878

hockeyeur 801, 878
holmium 684
homard 107, 218
homard, anatomie 107
homard, morphologie 107
homme 146
homo sapiens 93
Honduras 742
Hongrie 744
hongrois 469
honneurs 917
hôpital 711, 725, 778
horizon de secours 626
Horloge 10
horloge 858
horloge de parquet 697
horloge programmatrice 238, 290
hors-d'œuvre 722
hôtel 710, 724, 886, 915
hôtel de ville 710
hotte 224, 256, 290, 721, 722
houe 327
houe rotative 641
hoummos 200
houppelande 338
houppette 378
houppier 87
housse à vêtements 389
housse d'oreiller 280
housse pour automobile 558
Hubble, classification des galaxies, 9
Hubble, télescope spatial 17, 53
hublot 238, 239, 290, 608, 624
hublot d'atterrissage 631
hublot d'observation 23
hublot de chargement 666
hublot de déchargement du combustible irradié 666
huile d'arachide 209
huile d'olive 209
huile de lin 400
huile de maïs 209
huile de sésame 209
huile de tournesol 209
huiles 209
huiles lubrifiantes 656
huit avec barreur 839
huitième de finale : 16 joueurs 789
huitième de soupir 435
huître creuse du Pacifique 217
huître plate 217
huîtrier pie 118
huméro-stylo-radial 150
humérus 111, 116, 121, 122, 126, 131, 136, 138, 141, 142, 152, 156
humeur aqueuse 177
humidificateur 261
humidité 261
humidité, mesure 59
hune 602
hutte 418
Huygens 19
hydravion à flotteurs 628
Hydre femelle 11, 13
Hydre mâle 10
hydroélectricité 657
hydrogène 682
hydromètre 562
hydroptère 609
hydrosphère 66
hyène 134
hygiène dentaire 384
hygromètre 261
hygromètre enregistreur 59
hygrostat 261
hypergone 478
hyperliens 524
hypermétropie 691
hyphe 76
hypoderme 172
hypophyse 167
hyracothérium 93
hysope 202

I

ichtyosaure 93
ichtyostéga 92
identification du compte 731
igloo 418
igname 184
iguane 114
île 38
île de sable 51
île de Terre-Neuve 30
île volcanique 49
iléon 164
Îles Aléoutiennes 30
Îles Falkland 31
Îles Fidji 29
Îles Marshall 747
Îles Salomon 747
ilion 111, 116, 122
îlot 224, 539, 761
îlot rocheux 51

image 917
image imprimée 420
immeuble résidentiel 711
immobilisation 844
impair 919
imparipennée 79
imparisseux 150
impériale 569
imperméable 352
impluvium 406
imposte 413
impressiom, modèle à plat 420
impression 420, 512
impression à plat 420
impression de l'écran 515
impression en creux 420
impression en relief 420
impression, modèle en creux 420
impression, modèle en relief 420
imprimante 523, 529
imprimante à jet d'encre 519
imprimante laser 519
imprimante matricielle 520
impulsion 40
incendie de forêt 69
incinération 71
incisive 121, 123
incisive centrale 159
incisive latérale 159
incisives 159
inclinaison 13
inclinaison de la lame 304, 305
inclusion 703
Inde 747
Index 0
index 173, 699
index de composition automatique 506
indicateur de charge 383
indicateur de ligne 568, 569, 595
indicateur de niveau 499
indicateur de niveau d'eau 239
indicateur de niveau de carburant 557
indicateur de position 417
indicateur de réglage 889
indicateur de température 557
indicateur de tension 453
indicateur de virage et d'inclinaison latérale 898
indicateur de vitesse 557, 576, 851
indice 472
indice d'exposition 479
Indien 10
indium 682
Indonésie 33, 747
indonésien 469
inducteur à électroaimant 688
induit 688
industrie 525
infiltration 67, 69
infini 703
infirmerie 726
infirmière 780
inflorescence, modes 81
influx nerveux 168
informations-navigation 626
informations-pilotage 626
informations-systèmes de bord 626
infrastructure 538
inhalateur-doseur 783
initiales de la banque émettrice 729
injecteur 565, 566
injecteur de lubrifiant 649
injection/explosion 565
insectes 96
insectes, exemples 101
insertion 515
insigne 770
insigne d'identité 770
insigne de grade 770
inspiration 832
installation 395
installation à air chaud pulsé 258
installation à eau chaude 259
installations sportives 788
instruments à clavier 442
instruments à clavier, exemples 443
instruments à cordes 439
instruments à percussion 437, 448
instruments à vent 446
instruments d'écriture 470
instruments de bord 557
instruments de mesure météorologique 58
instruments de vol 899
instruments électroniques 450
instruments scientifiques 23
instruments traditionnels 432
intégrale 703
intégration de l'électricité au réseau de transport 662
intégration de l'électricité au réseau de transport 677
Intelsat 487
intensité lumineuse, mesure 702
interdiction de dépasser 544, 546
interdiction de faire demi-tour 544, 546
interlignage 472
interligne 434

interligne 1,5 472
interligne double 472
interligne simple 472
internaute 524
Internet 523, 524
interosseux 150
interphone 491
interrupteur 237, 241, 274, 286, 288, 289, 291, 305, 307, 308, 318, 320, 381, 382, 383, 384, 488, 505, 506, 518, 613, 687
interrupteur à gâchette 304, 305, 306, 308
interrupteur d'accord 499
interrupteur d'alimentation 451, 494, 495, 497, 498, 501
interrupteur d'alimentation 494, 498, 518
interrupteur d'éclairage 381
interrupteur d'émission 505
interrupteur de démarrage 293
interrupteur de fin de course 417
interrupteur de la porte 293
interrupteur de mise au point automatique 483
interrupteur du magnétoscope 495
interrupteur du téléviseur 495
interrupteur moteur/éclairage 452
interrupteur principal 273
interruption 515
intersection 703
intersection avec priorité 544, 547
intertitre 471
intervalle 617
intervalle d'air 675
intervalles 434
interview 471
intestin 95, 97, 103, 104, 105, 107, 109, 112, 161
intestin grêle 110, 113, 116, 125, 164
intestin moyen 99
intrados 413
inuktitut 469
inverseur de marche 302, 306
inverseur de signe 529
inverseur route-croisement 576
Io 4
iode 683
Iran 746
Iraq 746
iridium 683
iris 177
irlandais 469
Irlande 743
isba 418
ischion 111, 116, 122, 153
islam : Mahomet 736
islandais 469
Islande 32, 744
isobare 55
isolant 253, 254, 259, 266, 267, 294, 672
isolant en caoutchouc-mousse 299
isolant en coquille 299
isolant en panneau 299
isolant en plastique 272
isolant en rouleau 299
isolant en ruban 299
isolant en ruban métallique 299
isolant en vinyle 299
isolant en vrac 299
isolant moussé 299
isolants 299
isolateur 562, 663
isoloir 731
Israël 746
isthme 38
isthme de la trompe utérine 171
Isthme de Panama 30
isthme du gosier 174
Italie 744
italien 469
italique 472
ivoire 159

J

jabot 97, 99, 104, 106, 116, 362
jaboticaba 197
jachère 182
jack de sortie 441
jacquet 915
jaguar 135
jalons de sécurité 875
Jamahiriya arabe libyenne 745
Jamaïque 742
jambage 256
jambe 124, 139, 147, 149, 156, 351
jambe élastique 351
jambette 253
jambier antérieur 150
jambière 371, 796, 798, 800, 901
jambière de gardien de but 879
jambières 880
jambon cuit 216
jambon fumé 215
jan extérieur 915
jan intérieur 915

jante 560, 574, 579, 640, 793
Japet 5
Japon 33, 747
japonais 469
jaque 196
jaquette 338, 853
jardin 406
jardin d'agrément 322
jardin potager 182, 244
jardin public 713
jardinage 298, 322
jarlsberg 211
jarret 124, 130, 214, 215
jarretelle 367
jas 610
jauge à aiguilles 457
jauge magnétique à lecture directe 655
jaune 117, 400, 690
jaune orangé 400
jaune vert 400
javelot 748, 793
jazz, formation 438
jean 358
Jean Calvin 736
jéjunum 164
Jésus-Christ 736
jet d'air 398
jet d'eau 247, 249
jet de couleur 398
jet dentaire 384
jetée 653
jets d'eau 828
jeu 822
jeu d'ustensiles 233
jeu de brides 773
jeu de dames 916
jeu de dilatation 590
jeu de douilles 311
jeu de fléchettes 918
jeu de petits outils 325
jeu de plateau 915
jeu de puces 513
jeu de quilles 865
jeu de rail 590
jeux 914
jeux de plateau 915
jeux en ligne 525
jicama 184
jockey 856
jodhpurs 853
joint 294, 470
joint à coulisse 310
joint d'étanchéité 270, 655
joint de bougie 562
joint de carter 566
joint de rail 590
joint magnétique 291
joint périmétral 661
joint torique 268
Joker 914
jonc 376
jonction positif/négatif 672
jonque 600
jonquille 80
Jordanie 746
joue 130, 148, 301, 909
joue de jante 560
jouets 717, 854
joueur 827, 920
joueur de basketball 810
joueur de cricket : batteur 798
joueurs 822
joueuse de tennis 822
joule 702
journal 471
ju-jitsu 846
judaïsme : l'Ancien Testament 736
judo 844
judogi 844
juge 842, 843, 844, 848, 855, 859, 893
juge à l'arrivée 839
juge arbitre 830
juge au départ 838, 883
juge aux obstacles 852
juge coordonnateur 823
juge d'arrivée 883
juge de but 827, 858, 878
juge de champ arrière 807
juge de classement 830
juge de coin 845
juge de départ 830
juge de faute de pied 821
juge de filet 821
juge de ligne 812, 813, 816, 818, 820, 824, 879
juge de ligne en chef 807
juge de ligne médiane 820
juge de mêlée 807
juge de nage 830
juge de piste 883
juge de porte 837
juge de service 816, 820
juge de touche 803, 805, 807
juge de voie 900
juge en chef 823, 837
juge-arbitre 828
juge-arbitre de pas de tir 860
juge-arbitre principal 860

juges 824, 825, 828, 881
juges assistants 883
juges au départ 882
juges d'arrivée 883
juges d'exécution 823
juges de coin 846
juges de difficultés 823
juges de valeur artistique 823
juges de virages 831
jugulaire 765, 808
jujube 197
jumeau 150, 151
jumelles à prismes 692
jupe 355, 837
jupe à empiècement 357
jupe à lés 357
jupe à volants étagés 357
jupe de masque 773
jupe de piston 566
jupe droite 357
jupe fourreau 357
jupe froncée 357
jupe portefeuille 357
jupe souple 605
jupe-culotte 357
jupes, exemples 357
jupette 822
Jupiter 4
jupon 337, 366
Jurassique 93
jury 853
justaucorps 338, 371
justice 726

K

kaki 197
kangourou 142, 143
kangourou, morphologie 143
kangourou, squelette 142
Kaplan, roue 659
karaté 845
karatégi 845
karatéka 845
kayak 837
kayak monoplace (K1) 839
Kazakhstan 746
kelvin 702
kendo 847
kendoka 847
Kenya 745
kérosène 656
ketch 601
ketchup 201
kettle 45
kilogramme 702
kilt 357
kimono 364
kinyarwanda 468
kiosque 548, 593, 763
Kirghizistan 746
Kiribati 747
kirundi 468
kiwi 196
knicker 358
koala 143
kombu 183
kora 433
kote 847
Koweït 746
krypton 684
Kuiper, ceinture 4
kumquat 194
kung-fu 846

L

la 434
la universel 436
laboratoire 16, 17
laboratoire américain 21
laboratoire de conservation 395
laboratoire de pathologie 781
laboratoire européen 21
laboratoire japonais 21
laboratoire spatial 23
laboratoire supérieur 16
labyrinthe 885
lac 7, 38, 45, 48
lac artificiel 48
Lac Baïkal 33
lac d'origine glaciaire 48
lac d'origine tectonique 48
lac d'origine volcanique 48
lac en croissant 48
Lac Eyre 29
Lac Ladoga 32
Lac Malawi 34
lac salé 52
Lac Tanganyika 34
Lac Tchad 34
Lac Titicaca 31
Lac Victoria 34
laccolite 44
lacet 342, 370, 630, 797, 843, 881

lacet de serrage 387
lacis 893
lacs 48
lactaire délicieux 183
lacune latérale 127
lacune médiane 127
lagomorphes 122
lagon 51
lagune 51
lait 210
lait concentré 210
lait de chèvre 210
lait en poudre 210
lait homogénéisé 210
laiterie 182
laitue asperge 186
laitue de mer 183
laitue frisée 186
laitue iceberg 186
laitue pommée 186
laize 834
lama 128
lambourde 252
lame 227, 229, 237, 254, 274, 285, 302, 303, 304, 305, 315, 320, 331, 332, 382, 383, 390, 433, 449, 454, 460, 534, 557, 636, 639, 849, 878, 880, 881, 900
lame à deux biseaux 401
lame à double tranchant 383
lame coudée 401
lame criblée de l'ethmoïde 175
lame d'étouffoir 443
lame de coupe 240
lame de danse sur glace 881
lame de scie circulaire 304
lame de suspension 697
lame dentée 382
lame droite 382, 401
lame en cuiller 401
lame fixe 316
lame isolée 316
lame mobile 424
lame porte-objet 693
lame pour programme libre 881
lame racleuse 638
lame-ressort 776
lamelle 76, 254
lamelles concentriques 154
lames, principales formes 401
lampadaire 286
lampe 316, 693
lampe à économie d'énergie 275
lampe à halogène 274, 275
lampe à incandescence 274, 614, 673
lampe à souder 314, 319
lampe au néon 316
lampe d'architecte 286
lampe d'architecte 399
lampe de bureau 286
lampe de bureau halogène 286
lampe de chevet 724, 780
lampe de lecture 771
lampe de sanctuaire 737
lampe de table 286
lampe frontale 901
lampe liseuse 286
lampe portative 765
lampe-éclair 482
lampe-témoin 848
lampe-tempête 906
lampe-torche 770
lampes témoins 494, 557
lamproie 219
lance 319, 748, 767
lance à eau 766
lance d'arrosage 328
lance-canon 766
lance-leurres 762
lance-missiles 761
lance-pots fumigènes 758
lancéolée 79
lancer 795, 799, 864
lancer disque 791
lancer du javelot 791
lancer du poids 790
lancer marteau 791
lancers 793
lanceur 794, 795, 799
lanceur spatial 24
lanceur spatial (Ariane V), coupe 24
lanceur spatial (Saturn V), coupe 25
lanceurs spatiaux, exemples 24
lange 421
langouste 218
langoustine 218
langue 99, 109, 110, 164, 174, 175, 212
langue bifide 112
langue d'affichage, choix 507
langue glaciaire 46
langue, dos 176
langues aborigènes d'Australie 469
langues afro-asiatiques 468
langues amérindiennes 469
langues bantoues 468
langues celtiques 469

langues d'Afrique centrale 468
langues d'Océanie 469
langues du monde 468
langues germaniques 469
langues indo-européennes 469
langues indo-iraniennes 469
langues isolées 469
langues malayo-polynésiennes 469
langues ouralo-altaïques 469
langues papoues 469
langues romanes 469
langues sino-tibétaines 468
langues slaves 469
languette 342, 370, 444, 881, 889
lanière 416, 443, 840, 841, 850, 901
lanterne 322, 614, 752, 903
lanterne de phare 614
lanterne de pied 287
lanterne murale 287
lanterneau 245
lanterneau de la cage d'escalier 251
lanterneau de la salle de bains 251
lanthane 684
lanthanides (terres rares) 684
lapiaz 47
lapin 123, 212
lard 209
large 472
largue 833
larve 100
larynx 163
lasagne 206
laser à rubis pulsé 692
latitude 14, 15, 36
latrines 406
latte 285, 459, 600, 676, 834, 836, 897
lattis métallique à losanges 299
laurier 202
lavabo 262, 264, 724, 780
lavabo du chirurgien 781
lavage 347
lavallière 349
lave-auto 548
lave-linge 262, 271, 292
lave-vaisselle 224, 271, 294, 721, 723
laver à la machine à l'eau chaude avec agitation normale 347
laver à la machine à l'eau chaude avec agitation réduite 347
laver à la machine à l'eau tiède avec agitation réduite 347
laver à la machine à l'eau très chaude avec agitation normale 347
laver à la main à l'eau tiède 347
laveuse pour épreuves 485
lawrencium 684
laye 445
lèchefrite 234
lecteur CD/DVD 918
lecteur de carte 493, 507
lecteur de cassette 504, 521
lecteur de CD/DVD-ROM 513, 526
lecteur de chevet 724, 780
lecteur de code-barres 517
lecteur de disque compact 488, 501, 503, 504, 517
lecteur de disque dur 521
lecteur de disque dur amovible 521
lecteur de disque dur primaire 513
lecteur de disque dur secondaire 513
lecteur de disquette 450, 513
lecteur de disquette externe 521
lecteur de DVD vidéo 494
lecteur de microfilm 732
lecteur optique 181
lecteur optique de caractères 474
lecture 495, 499
lecture automatique/manuelle 316
lecture du disque compact 501
lecture rapide 501
lecture/pause 501
légende 471
légionnaire romain 748
légumes 180, 184
légumes bulbes 184
légumes feuilles 186
légumes fleurs 187
légumes fruits 188
légumes racines 189
légumes tiges 185
légumes tubercules 184
légumier 226
légumineuses 190
lémurien 139
lentille 390, 477, 478, 535, 697
lentille biconcave 691
lentille biconvexe 691
lentille concave 691
lentille convexe 691
lentille cylindrique 691
lentille de champ 692
lentille de macrophotographie 478
lentille jetable 384
lentille objectif 14, 692
lentille plan-concave 691
lentille plan-convexe 691

lentille rigide 384
lentille souple 384
lentilles 190, 691
lentilles convergentes 691
lentilles de contact 384
lentilles de mise au point 694
lentilles de redressement 692
lentilles divergentes 691
léopard 135
Lesotho 746
lessivage du sol 70
lest 634
Lettonie 744
lettre 474
lettre de repère 855
lettres 472
leucoplaste 74
lève-fil 288
lève-soupape 314
levier 268, 270, 310, 377, 381, 423, 686, 912
levier à ressort 920
levier coudé 637
levier d'armement 755, 757
levier d'écartement 643
levier d'échappement 443
levier d'embrayage 327, 574, 576
levier de blocage 312
levier de commande 307, 649
levier de commande manuelle 590
levier de conduite 633
levier de déclenchement 265
levier de dégagement 310
levier de dégagement du papier 528
levier de dégagement du presse-papier 528
levier de fixation de venturi 757
levier de frein à main 556, 587
levier de frein avant 576
levier de la lame 424
levier de manœuvre de la culasse 756
levier de manœuvre du mât 632, 633
levier de perçage 240
levier de réglage 436
levier de réglage latéral 309
levier de relevage du plateau de coupe 333
levier de serrage 312
levier de tissage 456
levier de verrouillage 587
levier de vibrato 441
levier de vitesse 859
levier de vitesses 552
levier des aérofreins 626
levier des volets 626
levier du bloc 309
levier du piston 315
levier du protège-lame inférieur 304
levier du train d'atterrissage 626
levier plat 301
levier télescopique de dételage 587
lèvres 124, 132, 306
lèvre inférieure 174, 444
lèvre supérieure 99, 174, 444
lévrier 131
Lézard 12
lézard 114
liaison 435
liaison chimique 680
liaison électrique 260
liaison frigorifique 260
Liban 746
libellule 102
liber 87
libération d'énergie 681
Libéria 745
libero 803, 812
liberté de langue 854
librairie 714
lice 408
lichen 74
lichen crustacé 74
lichen foliacé 74
lichen fruticuleux 74
lichen, structure 74
lichens, exemples 74
Licorne 11
Liechtenstein 744
liège 892
liens de parenté 784
lierre 410
lieu noir 221
lieuse 642
Lièvre 11
lièvre 123, 212
ligament 105
ligament alvéolo-dentaire 159
ligament élastique 133
ligament large de l'utérus 171
ligament suspenseur 177
ligne 434, 813
ligne arrière 809, 877
ligne blanche 127
ligne bleue 879
ligne câblée 525
ligne centrale 815, 879
ligne continue 538

ligne d'arrivée 791
ligne d'arrivée 833, 839, 871, 890
ligne d'arrivée du 500 m 883
ligne d'attaque 812
ligne d'avertissement- épée et sabre 848
ligne d'avertissement- fleuret 848
ligne d'ourlet 455
ligne de balayage 877
ligne de ballon mort 804
ligne de bâti 455
ligne de boîte de service 818
ligne de but 800, 804, 806, 809, 814, 827, 878
ligne de cadre 862
ligne de centre 801, 806, 809, 877
ligne de côté 812
ligne de couloir 791
ligne de coupe 455
ligne de croissance 104, 105
ligne de demi-court 819
ligne de départ 791, 833, 872
ligne de départ du 500 m 882
ligne de distribution à basse tension 273, 663
ligne de distribution à moyenne tension 273, 663
ligne de double 820
ligne de fond 806, 811, 812, 815, 816, 821, 831
ligne de force 687
ligne de jet franc 814
ligne de jeu 794, 865, 877, 918
ligne de l'arbitre 813
ligne de lancer franc 811
ligne de limite arrière 848
ligne de mêlée 807
ligne de mise en garde 848
ligne de modification 455
ligne de piqûre de la fermeture 455
ligne de poursuite 871
ligne de réception de service 818
ligne de retrait 799
ligne de sécurité 593
ligne de service 818, 819, 821
ligne de service court 817, 818, 819
ligne de service long 816
ligne de simple 821
ligne de surface de but 814
ligne de surface de réparation 802
ligne de suture 105
ligne de tir 859
ligne de touche 800, 803, 805, 806, 809, 810, 814, 858
ligne de visée 907
ligne dédiée 523, 524
ligne des 10 m 804
ligne des 15 m 805
ligne des 2 m 827
ligne des 200 m 871
ligne des 22 m 800, 804
ligne des 27 m 858
ligne des 30 m 859
ligne des 36 m 858
ligne des 4 m 827
ligne des 5 m 800, 805
ligne des 50 m 859
ligne des 54 m 858
ligne des 60 m 859
ligne des 7 m 827
ligne des 70 m 859
ligne des 90 m 859
ligne des compétiteurs 845, 847
ligne des sprinters 871
ligne des verges 806
ligne discontinue 538, 539
ligne isosiste 43
ligne latérale 108, 815, 819, 877
ligne latérale de double 817
ligne latérale de simple 817
ligne médiane 803, 805, 810, 814, 816, 827, 848
ligne médiane de service 821
ligne méridienne 907
ligne neutre 687
ligne sous-marine 524
ligne supplémentaire 434
ligne téléphonique 524
ligne téléphonique/câblée/satellite 523
lignes droites 871
limbe 76, 79, 612
lime 194, 309, 377, 905
lime à ongles 377
limes-émeri 377
limitation de hauteur 545, 547
limite de retour 799
limite de terrain 864
limite du batteur 799
limite du terrain 244
limite hors-terrain 819
limiteur de surchauffe 293
limon 255
limousine 549
linéaire 79
lingala 468
linge de maison 716
lingerie 584, 716, 724

linteau 247, 252, 256, 411
Lion 13
lion 135
lion passant 741
liquette 359
liquide 680, 681
liquide céphalo-rachidien 168
liquides d'appoint 400
lis 80
lisière 455
lisse 253, 591
lisse d'assise 252, 253
lisses 460, 461
listel 306
lit 280, 567, 904
lit à barreaux 281
lit à deux places 724
lit à une place 724
lit d'hôpital 780
lit de camp pliant 904
lit de l'ongle 172
lit pliant 281
litchi 197
literie 280
lithium 682
lithographie 423
lithosphère 42, 66
litière 78
littoral, configuration 51
Lituanie 744
livèche 202
livre 728
livre électronique 527
livre relié 426
livrée 799
livres pour enfants 732
loafer 344
lob 821
lobe 117
lobé 79
lobe du nez 175
lobe inférieur 163
lobe latéral inférieur 86
lobe latéral supérieur 86
lobe moyen 163
lobe supérieur 163
lobe terminal 86
lobule 173
local d'entreposage 769
local d'entreposage du matériel 734
local d'entretien 724, 731, 734
local technique 543
locaux administratifs 582
locaux de l'équipage 604
locaux de service 738
locomotive diesel-électrique 586
loge 82, 431
loge d'artiste 431
loge privée 428
logement de cassette 499
logement de la bobine 476
logement de la cassette 495, 496
logement de rangement 483
logement des officiers 762, 763
logement droit 384
logement du barillet 249
logement du plateau 501
logement gauche 384
logiciel de courrier électronique 524
lointain 430, 431
loisirs de plein air 902
long péronier latéral 150
long supinateur 151
longane 196
longeron 571, 624
longeron de chenille 636
longeron latéral inférieur 635
longeron stabilisateur 633
longitude 36
longue piste 882
longueur d'onde 690
longueur de la vague 49
longueur, mesure 700, 702
loquet 238, 294
lorgnette 385
lorum 115
losange 705
louche 233
Loup 11
loup 134
loupe 693, 905
loupe de mise au point 485
loupe et microscopes 693
loutre de rivière 134
louvoyage 833
lucarne 244
Luer Lock, embout 776
luette 174, 175
luge 884
luge double 884
luge simple 884
lugeur 884
lumière 14, 15, 17, 444, 617, 753
lumière de scène 775
lumière halogène 775
lumière perpétuelle 738

lumière stroboscopique 775
lumière visible 690
lumières de but 879
luminaires 286
Lune 4, 6, 7
Lune, cadran des phases 697
Lune, éclipse 7
Lune, phases 7
Lune, relief 7
lunette 701, 756
lunette astronomique 14
lunette astronomique, coupe 14
lunette d'approche 859
lunette de visée 692, 912
lunette prismatique 612
lunettes 318, 385, 861, 870, 887
lunettes de nage 830
lunettes de protection 772, 818, 819, 870, 875
lunettes de sécurité 772
lunettes de ski 888
lunettes de soleil 385
lunettes de vol 896
lunettes, exemples 385
lunettes, parties 385
lunule 105, 172, 173
lupin 190
lustre 287
lutécium 684
lutrin 737
lutte 843
lutteur 843
lutz 881
Luxembourg 743
luzerne 190
Lynx 12
lynx 134
Lyre 13
lyre 433
lysosome 94

M

macaque 139
macaroni 401
mâche 187
machette 751
mâchicoulis 408
machine à affranchir 531
machine à combustible 669
machine à coudre 452
machine à écrire électronique 528
machine à éliminer, à redresser et à oblitérer 474
machine à espresso 241
machine à faire les pâtes 230
machine à glaçons 721
machine à laver les verres 723
machine à sous 920
machine à tricoter 456
machine à trier 475
machine de chargement 666, 670
machine de déchargement 666
Machine pneumatique 11
machinerie 538
machinerie agricole 641
machinerie lourde 636
machiniste 428
mâchoire 99, 312, 317
mâchoire d'attelage 587
mâchoire d'étau 150
mâchoire de lagomorphe : lapin 123
mâchoire de rongeur 123
mâchoire dentée 310
mâchoire droite 310
mâchoire fixe 311
mâchoire incurvée 310
mâchoire mobile 311
mâchoires 312, 913
mâchoires de lagomorphe 123
mâchoires de rongeur 123
Mackenzie 30
maçonnerie : outils 315
macronucleus 94
Madagascar 34, 746
magasin 710, 716
magasin à rayons 715, 716
magasin d'articles de sport 715
magasin d'électronique 714
magasin de bricolage 714
magasin de cadeaux 715
magasin de chaussures 715
magasin de décoration 715
magasin de jouets 714
magasin de lingerie 714
magasin de prêt-à-porter 715
magasins 512
magazine 471
mage 847
Magellan 19
magenta 690
magma 44, 49
magnésie 825
magnésium 682
magnétisme 687

magnétomètre 60
magnétophone à cartouches 488
magnétophone à cassette numérique 488
magnétoscope 495
mah-jong 917
Mahomet 736
maigre 472
mail 714
maille 815
mailles de montage 457
maillet 301, 401, 421, 858
mailloche 433, 448
mailloches 449
maillon-gouge 331
maillot 791, 805, 810, 843, 870
maillot d'équipe 796, 808
maillot d'équipe 801, 802
maillot de bain 371, 830
maillot de corps 796, 850
Maine coon 132
mains, protection 774
maïs 85, 203
maïs : épi 85
maïs fourrager 182
maison 244, 877, 915
maison à deux étages 419
maison à plain-pied 419
maison de plain-pied 419
maison en adobe 418
maison jumelée 419
maison romaine 406
maison solaire 675
maison sur pilotis 418
maison, ameublement 276
maison, charpente 252
maison, éléments 247
maison, extérieur 244
maison, fondations 253
maison, principales pièces 250
maison, structure 250
maisons de ville 419
maisons en rangée 419
maisons traditionnelles 418
maître d'hôtel 720
maître-autel 737
maître-brin 893
maître-cylindre 559
majeur 173
majuscule : sélection du niveau 2 514
malaire 152, 158
Malaisie 747
malanga 189
Malawi 746
Maldives 747
mâle 702
malgache 469
Mali 745
malle 389
mallette d'ordinateur portable 527
mallette de toilette 389
mallette porte-documents 386
Malpighi, couche 172
Malpighi, tubes 97, 99
Malte 744
mamelle 127
mamelon 146, 148, 171
mamelon double 269
mammifère volant 140
mammifères carnivores 130
mammifères carnivores, exemples 134
mammifères insectivores 121
mammifères insectivores, exemples 121
mammifères lagomorphes, exemples 123
mammifères marins 136
mammifères marins, exemples 137
mammifères marsupiaux 142
mammifères ongulés 124
mammifères ongulés, exemples 128
mammifères primates 138
mammifères primates, exemples 139
mammifères rongeurs 122
mammouth 93
Manche 32
manche 227, 295, 301, 302, 309, 311, 315, 316, 319, 320, 337, 348, 383, 384, 391, 425, 433, 439, 440, 441, 443, 454, 458, 611, 797, 798, 800, 815, 816, 822, 838, 858, 863, 867, 880, 901
manche à air 739
manche à balai 516, 631, 898
manche ballon 360
manche bouffante 361
manche chauve-souris 361
manche chemisier 361
manche de commande 626
manche flottante 337
manche gigot 361
manche isolant 317
manche isolé 316
manche kimono 361
manche marteau 360
manche montée 349
manche pagode 361

manche pendante 338
manche raglan 352, 355, 361, 369
manche rotatif 516
manche tailleur 361
manche trois-quarts 360
mancheron 323, 327, 337, 360
manches à balai 918
manches précédentes 822
manches, exemples 360
manchette 471, 812, 880
manchon 259, 269, 320, 388, 838, 851
manchon de câble 306
manchon de culasse 756
manchon de refroidissement 755
manchon du cordon 308, 318
manchon refroidisseur 692
manchot 119
mandarine 194
mandat-poste 475
mandibule 97, 99, 108, 111, 112, 115, 116, 121, 122, 123, 126, 131, 136, 138, 141, 142
mandoline 230, 433
mandrin 302, 306, 307
mandrin autoserrant 306
manette 238
manette d'admission d'air 256
manette de blocage du plateau 307
manette de chasse d'eau 265
manette de contact 287
manette de dérailleur 579, 580, 870
manette de glissement 555
manette de jeu 918
manette des gaz 516
manette du frein 876
manette vapeur 241
manettes de poussée 626
manganèse 683
mangoustan 196
mangouste 134
mangue 197
manifold 652
manille 835
manioc 184
manivelle 230, 307, 312, 328, 460, 558, 571, 580, 750, 910
manivelle d'enroulement 313
manivelle d'orientation des lames 285
manivelle de la colonne 482
manivelle de lève-glace 554
manivelle de pointage en direction 756
manivelle de pointage en hauteur 756
mannequin 454
mannequin articulé 398
manomètre 654, 655, 766, 775, 777, 841
manomètre d'accord 448
manomètre de bouteille 319
manomètre de chalumeau 319
manœuvre de la pelleteuse 637
manque (1 à 18) 919
mante religieuse 102
manteau 105, 106, 256, 355
manteau inférieur 42
manteau supérieur 42
manteaux 352, 355
manteaux d'hommes 717
manteaux de femmes 716
manucure 377
manuel de premiers soins 777
manutention 632
maori 469
maquereau 219
maquillage 378
maquillage des lèvres 378
maquillage des yeux 378
maquilleuse 428
maquis 66
marbre 421, 795
marchand de journaux 715
marche 255, 321, 417, 460, 847
marche avant/marche arrière 327
marche de départ 255
marche/arrêt 504
marche/arrêt/volume 504
marchepied 321, 570, 602, 631, 640, 876
marchepied arrière 766, 775
marchepied en étrier 587
marchepied escamotable 567
marchepied latéral 586
margarine 209
marge continentale 49
margeur 484
margose 188
mari 785
Mariner 19
marinière 359
maritime, transport 596
marmite 235
marmotte 123
Maroc 745
maroquinerie 714
marque cardinale est 617
marque cardinale ouest 617
marque cardinale sud 617
marque centrale 820
marque d'aire de prise de contact 621

marque d'axe de piste 620
marque d'eaux sécuritaires 617
marque de danger isolé 617
marque de distance constante 621
marque de jour 615
marque de point d'attente 620
marque déposée 390, 473
marque des 7 m 814
marque latérale 617
marque spéciale 617
marques cardinales 616
marques d'identification 620
marques de circulation 619
marques de jour (région B) 617
marques de nuit, rythme 617
marques de seuil de piste 621
marques latérales de piste 620
marqueur 397, 470, 810, 812, 813, 814, 819, 845, 848, 864
marqueurs 844, 846, 847, 859
marquise 603
marron 193
Mars 4, 5
Mars Odyssey 19
marsouin 137
marteau 174, 442, 443, 793
marteau à endosser 425
marteau à panne ronde 301
marteau d'électricien 317
marteau de charpentier 301
marteau de maçon 315
marteau de menuisier 301
marteau perforateur 648
marteau perforateur à poussoir pneumatique 648
marteau pneumatique 649
marteau-piolet 901
Martin Luther 736
martin-pêcheur 118
martinet 118, 602
martingale 602, 858
martre 134
mascara en pain 378
mascara liquide 378
masque 796, 798, 800, 808, 841, 848, 879
masque à oxygène 777
masque bucco-nasal 773
masque complet 765
masque de sélection des couleurs 494
masque respiratoire 773
masse 43
masse pendulaire 436
masse, mesure 698, 702
masse-tige 651
masséter 150
massette de réglage 436
massif 245
massif d'ancrage des câbles 540
massif de fleurs 322
massif de fondation 651
massif montagneux 38
massues 823
mât 407, 493, 591, 600, 632, 633, 834, 836, 897
mât avant 607
mât d'artimon 602
mât d'artimon 600
mât de beaupré 602
mât de cacatois 602
mât de charge 607
mât de hune 602
mât de misaine 600, 602
mât de perroquet 602
mât de toit 903
mât radar 606
mât rotor 631
matelas 280, 281, 776, 904
matelas autogonflant 904
matelas de protection 883
matelas et sommiers 716
matelas mousse 904
matelas pneumatique 904
matelassure 855
mâteraeu 607
matériau absorbant les ondes radars 629
matériau de scellement 689
matériaux de base 298
matériaux de revêtement 299
matériel 396, 421, 422, 423
matériel audiovisuel 716
matériel de camping 905
matériel de laboratoire 685
matériel de lutte contre les incendies 767
matériel de secours 775
mathématiques 703
matière 680
matière inorganique 67
matières corrosives 774
matières dangereuses 774
matières explosives 774
matières grasses 209
matières inflammables 774
matières radioactives 774
matières toxiques 774
matraque télescopique 770
matrice de l'ongle 172

1030

ASTRONOMIE > 2-25; TERRE > 26-71; RÈGNE VÉGÉTAL >72-89; RÈGNE ANIMAL > 90-143; ÊTRE HUMAIN > 144-177; ALIMENTATION ET CUISINE > 178-241; MAISON > 242-295; BRICOLAGE ET JARDINAGE > 296-333; VÊTEMENTS > 334-371; PARURE ET OBJETS PERSONNELS > 372-391; ARTS ET ARCHITECTURE > 392-465; COMMUNICATIONS ET BUREAUTIQUE > 466-535; TRANSPORT ET MACHINERIE > 536-643; ÉNERGIES > 644-677; SCIENCE > 678-705; SOCIÉTÉ > 706-785; SPORTS ET JEUX > 786-920

maturation, vigne 86
mâture 602
maturité 86
Maurice 746
Mauritanie 745
mawashi 847
maxillaire 108, 111, 112, 121, 122, 123, 136, 175
maxillaire basculant 112
maxillaire inférieur 152, 158
maxillaire supérieur 115, 116, 131, 138, 152, 158
maya 469
mazout domestique 656
mazout léger 656
mazout lourd 656
méandre 48
méat de l'urètre 169
mécanicien 873
mécanique 686
mécanique d'accordage 441
mécanique d'accordage 441
mécanique du piano droit 443
mécanisme à échappement 436
mécanisme d'assistance de la culasse 755
mécanisme d'engrenage 423
mécanisme d'enroulement 285
mécanisme d'octave 445
mécanisme d'ouverture de l'anse 910
mécanisme de débrayage du tambour 910
mécanisme de déplacement de la lame 639
mécanisme de l'horloge à poids 697
mécanisme de l'orgue 445
mécanisme de propulsion 580
mécanisme de rebobinage 476
mécanisme de tir 757
mèche 439
mèche à centre plat 306
mèche de tarière 323
mèche hélicoïdale 306
mèche hélicoïdale à âme centrale 306
mèche hélicoïdale à double torsade 306
médaillon 374
médecin 780, 842
médecins 846
médiator 433
médicaments, formes 783
méditerranéen 61
meganeura 92
mégazostrodon 93
mégot 391
Meissner, corpuscule 172
meitnerium 683
Mélanésie 29
mélanésien 469
mélange air/carburant 564
mélange au manganèse (cathode) 689
mélange d'épices cajun 199
mélange de zinc et d'électrolyte (anode) 689
mélange dépolarisant 689
mélange eau-vapeur 646
mélangeur 236
mélangeur à main 236
mélangeur à pâtisserie 232
mélangeur bain-douche 262
mélasse 209
mêlée : attaque 807
mêlée : défense 806
mêlée spontanée 805
mélèze 89
mélisse 202
melon 340
melon à cornes 196
melon brésilien 195
melon brodé 195
melon Casaba 195
melon d'hiver chinois 188
melon d'Ogen 195
melon miel 195
melons 195
membrane 488, 502
membrane alaire 140
membrane coquillière 117
membrane cytoplasmique 74, 94
membrane du tympan 174
membrane interfémorale 140
membrane médiane 84
membrane nucléaire 74, 94
membrane pellucide 170
membrane plasmique 94
membrane squelettique 74
membrane vitelline 117
membre inférieur 161
membre supérieur 161
membrure inférieure 540
membrure principale 663
membrure supérieure 540
mémoire des patrons 456
mémorisation des données 316
men 847
mendélévium 684
meneur de jeu 811
méninges 167
ménisque convergent 691
ménisque divergent 691
menora 738

menthe 202
menton 115, 148
mentonnière 439, 575, 749, 765, 870, 885
menu 721
menuiserie : instruments de traçage et de mesure 313
menuiserie : matériel divers 313
menuiserie : outils pour clouer 301
menuiserie : outils pour façonner 308
menuiserie : outils pour percer 306
menuiserie : outils pour scier 303
menuiserie : outils pour serrer 310
menuiserie : outils pour visser 302
méplat 457
mer 7, 38, 48, 664
Mer Adriatique 32
Mer Baltique 32
Mer Caspienne 28, 33
Mer d'Aral 33
Mer d'Irlande 32
Mer d'Oman 33
Mer de Barents 32
Mer de Beaufort 30
Mer de Béring 28
Mer de Chine méridionale 28, 33
Mer de Chine orientale 33
Mer de Corail 29
Mer de Norvège 32
Mer de Tasman 29
Mer de Weddell 29
Mer des Antilles 28, 30
Mer du Groenland 28
Mer du Japon 33
Mer du Nord 28, 32
Mer Égée 32
Mer Méditerranée 28, 32, 34
Mer Noire 28, 32, 33
Mer Rouge 28, 33, 34
Mercure 4, 5
mercure 275, 683
mère 785
merguez 216
méridien céleste 13
méridien de Greenwich 36
méridien est 36
méridien ouest 36
méridienne 276
merlan 221
merlon de protection 655
mesa 52
mésocarpe 81, 82, 83
mésoglée 95
mésopause 53
mésosaure 92
mésosphère 53
mésothorax 97
mesure à deux temps 434
mesure à quatre temps 434
mesure à trois temps 434
mesure de l'énergie 702
mesure de l'ensoleillement 58
mesure de l'épaisseur 700
mesure de l'humidité 59
mesure de l'intensité lumineuse 702
mesure de la charge électrique 702
mesure de la chute de neige 59
mesure de la différence de potentiel électrique 702
mesure de la direction du vent 59
mesure de la distance 700
mesure de la force 702
mesure de la fréquence 702
mesure de la hauteur des nuages 59
mesure de la longueur 700, 702
mesure de la masse 698, 702
mesure de la pluviosité 59
mesure de la pression 59, 702
mesure de la puissance 702
mesure de la quantité de matière 702
mesure de la radioactivité 702
mesure de la résistance électrique 702
mesure de la température 59, 695
mesure de la température Celsius 702
mesure de la température thermodynamique 702
mesure de la vitesse du vent 59
mesure des angles 701
mesure du courant électrique 702
mesure du rayonnement du ciel 58
mesure du temps 696, 702
mesure télescopique 864
mesure, appareils 695
mesures 231, 434
métacarpe 111, 116, 122, 126, 131, 133, 136, 138, 142, 154
métacarpien 154, 156
métalloïdes 682
métamorphose de la grenouille 111
métaphyse 155
métatarse 98, 111, 122, 126, 131, 138, 141, 142, 155
métatarsien 155
métathorax 97
métaux alcalino-terreux 682
métaux alcalins 682
métaux de transition 683

métaux, exemples 741
météores 57
météorite 8
météorite ferreuse 8
météorite métallo-rocheuse 8
météorites rocheuses 8
météorologie 53
météorologie, instruments de mesure 58
métier à broder 459
métier de basse lisse 460
métier de haute lisse 461
métope 404
mètre 702
mètre à ruban 313, 454
métro 713
métronome à quartz 436
métronome mécanique 436
mets chauds 722
mets froids 722
meuble 528
meubles d'enfants 281
meubles de classement 510
meubles de rangement 278, 510
meubles de travail 511
meubles, exemples 741
meule 308
meuleuse d'angle 308
Mexique 742
mezzanine 250, 251, 592
mi 434
mi-bas 351, 365
mi-chaussette 351, 365
Michel Keroularios 736
micro 441
micro de fréquences aiguës 441
micro de fréquences graves 441
micro de fréquences moyennes 441
micro-ondes 690
micro-ordinateur 513
microfilament 94
micromètre palmer 700
Micronésie 747
micronucleus 94
microphone 488, 492, 496, 505, 506, 508, 516, 517, 527, 770, 898
microphone d'interphone 491
microphone dynamique 488
microphones 771
micropropulseur de contrôle d'altitude 18
Microscope 10
microscope 693
microscope binoculaire 693
microscope électronique, composantes 694
microscope électronique, coupe 694
microtubule 94
miel 209
mihrab 738
milieu défensif 803
milieu offensif droit 803
milieu offensif gauche 803
mille 703
millésime 729
millet 85, 203
millet : épi 85
Mimas 5
minaret 738
minbar 738
mine antipersonnel 758
mine de charbon 647
mine souterraine 650
minerai 647
mini-slip 351
minibus 569
minichaîne stéréo 503
minute 704
minuterie 238, 239, 273, 465, 484
minuteur 231, 851
Miranda 5
mire 859, 907, 913
mire de réglage 492
mirette 464
miroir 264, 389, 535, 693, 724, 907
miroir à réflexion partielle 692
miroir à réflexion totale 692
miroir d'éclairage 693
miroir de courtoisie 556
miroir de lecture 20
miroir de traversée avant 568
miroir double pivotant 381
miroir latéral 381
miroir lumineux 381
miroir parabolique 674
miroir plan rétractable 17
miroir primaire 17
miroir primaire concave 15, 17
miroir principal 477
miroir secondaire 15, 17, 477
misaine 603
mise à feu, accessoires 752
mise en balles 71
mise en marche 508
mise en presse 425
missile air-air 759, 760
missile air-sol 759
missile anti-sous-marin 759, 762
missile antiaérien 762
missile antichar 759

missile antinavire 759
missile antiradar 759
missile mer-mer 762
missile sol-air 759
missile, structure 759
missiles 759
missiles, principaux types 759
Mississippi 30
mitaine 346, 879
mitigeur à bille creuse 268
mitigeur à cartouche 268
mitigeur à disque 268
mitigeur d'évier 270
mitigeurs 268
mitochondrie 74, 94
mitrailleuse 758
mitre 227, 229, 257
mitron 245
mobilier de bureau 510
mocassin 344
mode 528
mode d'emploi 548
mode d'entraînement du film 476
mode d'exposition 476
mode de mise au point 476
mode de sélection des stations 498
mode de sortie des copies 512
mode magnétoscope 495
mode manuel/automatique 465
mode télévision 495
modèle à plat, impression 420
modèle en creux, impression 420
modèle en relief, impression 420
modem 522, 523, 524
modem-câble 525
modérateur 665
modérateur : eau lourde 670
modérateur : eau naturelle 671
modérateur : graphite 670
modes d'inflorescence 81
modification fine des variables 450
modification rapide des variables 450
modillon 405
modulateur de pression de freinage 559
modulation de la hauteur du son 450
modulation du timbre du son 450
module d'affranchissement 531
module d'habitation américain 21
module d'injection de gaz 652
module de charge utile 40
module de commande 19, 25
module de commande du moteur électrique 563
module de commande électronique 559
module de communication 486
module de gestion de la puissance 563
module de photopiles 673
module de propulsion 486
module de service 19, 25, 486
module extérieur 260
module intérieur 260
module lunaire 19, 25
module régulateur de charge de la batterie 563
module russe 21
moelle 87, 212
moelle épinière 109, 110, 167, 168
moelle épinière, structure 167
moelle osseuse 154
moellon 298
Mohorovicic, discontinuité 42
moineau 118
Moïse 736
moissonneuse-batteuse 643
molaire 121, 123
molaire, coupe 159
molaires 159
mole 702
molécule 680
molette 311, 391
molette d'ajustage 700
molette d'entraînement 240
molette de mise au point 692
molette de réglage 317
molette de réglage de la flamme 391
molette de réglage de la saillie 309
molette de réglage près/loin 496
molette de sélection des effets spéciaux 496
mollet 147, 149
mollusques 104, 217
molybdène 683
Monaco 744
monarque 101
mongol 469
Mongolie 747
moniteurs de contrôle du réalisateur 428
monnaie et modes de paiement 729
monocle 385
monocoques 835
Monopoly 915
mont de Vénus 170
montagnais 469
montagne 45
Montagnes Rocheuses 30

montant 246, 252, 277, 321, 362, 424, 433, 460, 461, 782, 792, 825, 826, 881
montant d'angle 635
montant de bâti 278
montant de bride 854
montant de ferrage 247, 278
montant de filet 854
montant de la serrure 247
montant de rive 249
montant embrevé 249
montant latéral 551
montant mouton 249
montant rembourré 811
monte-boules 865
montée arrière 856
montée du spinnaker 833
montgolfière 899
monticule 795
montre 464
montre à affichage analogique 696
montre à affichage numérique 696
montre mécanique 696
montres 717
Monts Oural 32
Monts Transantarctiques 29
monture 295, 303, 312, 385, 432, 849
monture baïonnette 478
monture d'objectif 477
monture en fer à cheval 17
monture réglable 303
monument 39
moquette 254
moraillon 389
moraine de fond 46
moraine frontale 46
moraine latérale 46
moraine médiane 46
moraine terminale 46
mordache 424
mordant 435
morille 183
morphologie de l'abeille : ouvrière 98
morphologie de l'araignée 103
morphologie de l'escargot 104
morphologie de l'étoile de mer 95
morphologie de l'oiseau 115
morphologie de la chauve-souris 140
morphologie de la grenouille 110
morphologie de la perche 108
morphologie de la pieuvre 106
morphologie de la taupe 121
morphologie de la tortue 113
morphologie du chat 133
morphologie du cheval 124
morphologie du chien 130
morphologie du coquillage bivalve 105
morphologie du coquillage univalve 105
morphologie du dauphin 136
morphologie du gorille 139
morphologie du homard 107
morphologie du kangourou 143
morphologie du papillon 96
morphologie du rat 122
morphologie du requin 108
morphologie du serpent venimeux : tête 112
mors 302, 306, 307, 377, 426, 858
mors à canon brisé 854
mors à pompe 854
mors anglais 854
mors de bride 854
mors de filet 854
mors fixe 312
mors mobile 312
morse 137
mort 702
mortadelle 216
mortaise 390
mortier 230, 298, 753
mortier du XVIIe siècle 752
mortier moderne 756
morts-terrains 647
morue de l'Atlantique 221
mosaïque 406
mosquée 738
moteur 258, 261, 292, 293, 294, 304, 307, 308, 320, 323, 327, 332, 574, 632, 639, 640, 643, 651, 758
moteur à deux temps, cycle 565
moteur à essence 553, 563, 566
moteur à quatre temps 564
moteur à turbocompression 564
moteur d'aiguillage 590
moteur de descente 18
moteur de disques 521
moteur de guides 521
moteur de manœuvre 23
moteur de propulsion 18
moteur diesel 586, 636, 637, 638, 639
moteur diesel de propulsion 605
moteur diesel de sustentation 605
moteur diesel, cycle 565
moteur du ventilateur 261
moteur électrique 259, 263, 331, 332, 561, 563
moteur électrique auxiliaire 763

moteur électrique principal 763
moteur électrique/générateur 563
moteur F-1 25
moteur hors-bord 607
moteur J-2 25
moteur principal 23
moteur rotatif, cycle 565
moteur-fusée 24, 60
moteurs diesel 762
moteurs, types 564
motif 368, 369
moto 574
moto 576
moto de grand prix et pilote 874
moto de motocross et supercross 875
moto de rallye 875
moto de tête 870
moto de tourisme 577
moto de trial 875
moto tout-terrain 577
moto-caméra 870
motoculteur 327
motocyclisme 874
motoneige 876
motrice 585, 594
Mouche 11
mouche 101, 862
mouche artificielle 909
mouche centrale 862
mouche de ligne de cadre 862
mouche supérieure 862
mouche tsé-tsé 101
moufette 134
moufle 318, 346, 750, 901
moufle fixe 651
moufle mobile 651
mouflon 128
mouilleur 531
moule 217
moule à charlotte 232
moule à fond amovible 232
moule à gâteau 232
moule à muffins 232
moule à pain 239
moule à quiche 232
moule à soufflé 232
moule à tarte 232
moulin à café 240
moulin à légumes 230
moulin à vent 676
moulin pivot 676
moulin tour 676
moulinet 421
moulinet à mouche 909
moulinet à tambour fixe 910
moulinet à tambour tournant 910
moulure de pare-chocs 550
mousqueton 835, 901, 911
mousqueton à ressort 835
mousqueton à vis 900
mousqueton en D 900
mousse 75
mousse à raser 383
mousse d'Irlande 183
mousse, structure 75
mousseline 231
moustaches 132
moustique 101
moutarde à l'ancienne 200
moutarde allemande 200
moutarde américaine 200
moutarde anglaise 200
moutarde blanche 198
moutarde de Dijon 200
moutarde en poudre 200
moutarde noire 198
mouton 128, 856
mouvement horizontal du sol 43
mouvement rotatif de la turbine 662
mouvement vertical du sol 43
mouvements de l'avion 630
mouvements de terrain 47
moyen 849
moyen adducteur 150
moyenne sus-alaire 115
moyenne tectrice primaire 115
moyeu 534, 579, 659, 677, 783
moyeu rotor 631
Mozambique 746
mozzarella 210
Mt Everest 53
muguet 80
mule 344
mulet 128, 220
mulot 123
multicoques 835
multimètre 316
multiplicateur de focale 478
multiplication 529, 703
munster 211
muqueuse olfactive 175
mur 246, 852, 902, 917
mur arrière 818, 819
mur avant 818, 819

mur bajoyer 657
mur barré 852
mur d'arrivée 830
mur de batillage 660
mur de briques 253, 298
mur de fondation 252, 253
mur de l'œil 63
mur de la qibla 738
mur de nuages 63
mur de pierres 298
mur de virage 831, 832
mur en béton 675
mur fortifié 738
mur latéral 818, 819, 831
mur Trombe 675
muraille 607, 917
muret 864
musaraigne 121
muscle adducteur antérieur 105
muscle adducteur postérieur 105
muscle arrecteur 172
muscle bulbo-caverneux 169
muscle droit inférieur 177
muscle droit supérieur 177
muscle fessier 166
muscle papillaire 162
muscles 150
muscles du manteau 106
museau 108, 110, 121, 130, 132, 143
musée 394, 711
muserolle 854, 858
musique 432
musique, accessoires 436
mutule 404
Myanmar 747
mycélium 76
mye 217
mygale du Mexique 102
myocarde 162
myomère 109
myopie 691
myrtille 192

N

n'égale pas 703
n'est pas identique à 703
nacelle 542, 677, 899
nacelle d'observation 17
nacelle d'osier 899
nacelle élévatrice 622
nacelle, coupe 677
nage sur le dos 832
nageoire anale 108
nageoire caudale 107, 108, 136
nageoire dorsale 108, 109, 136
nageoire pectorale 108, 136
nageoire pelvienne 108
nages, types 832
nahuatl 469
naine blanche 8
naine brune 8
naine noire 8
naissance 702
Namibie 746
naos 403
nappe phréatique 47, 70
narine 108, 110, 112, 115, 175
narval 137
nasal 158, 749
naseau 124
natation 830
nationalité 825
Nauru 747
navaho 469
navet 189
navette 461
navette ferroviaire 620
navette spatiale 22, 53
navette spatiale au décollage 22
navigateur 524
navigation, appareils 612
navire 41
navire de forage 604, 653
navire porte-conteneurs 596, 604
ne pas laver 347
ne pas repasser 347
ne pas sécher par culbutage 347
ne pas utiliser avec un fauteuil roulant 725
ne pas utiliser de chlorure décolorant 347
NEAR 19
nébuleuse planétaire 8
nébulosité 55, 56
nécessaire à chaussures 345
nécrologie 471
nécrophore 101
nectarine 192
néerlandais 469
nef 411
nef centrale 738
nèfle du Japon 193
négatif 485, 684
négatoscope 484, 535
neige 64

neige continue faible 57
neige continue forte 57
neige continue modérée 57
neige intermittente faible 57
neige intermittente forte 57
neige intermittente modérée 57
neige roulée 64
neiges acides 70
neiges éternelles 45
néodyme 684
néon 684
Népal 747
néphridie 107
neptunium 684
nerf 172, 426
nerf circonflexe 166
nerf cochléaire 174
nerf crural 166
nerf cubital 166
nerf digital 166
nerf fémoro-cutané 166
nerf fessier 166
nerf grand abdomino-génital 166
nerf grand sciatique 166
nerf intercostal 166
nerf médian 166
nerf musculo-cutané 166
nerf obturateur 166
nerf olfactif 109, 175
nerf optique 177
nerf petit abdomino-génital 166
nerf petit sciatique 166
nerf rachidien 167, 168
nerf radial 166
nerf saphène externe 166
nerf saphène interne 166
nerf sciatique poplité externe 166
nerf sciatique poplité interne 166
nerf tibial antérieur 166
nerf vestibulaire 174
nerfs crâniens 166
nervure 6, 639, 772, 841
nervure d'aile 624
nervure d'emplanture 624
nervure médiane 75
nervure principale 79, 84
nervure secondaire 79
netball 809
nettoie-pipes 390
nettoyage des tenues d'intervention 764
neurone moteur 168
neurone sensoriel 168
neurones 168
neutron 680
neutron incident 681
névé 46
neveu 785
newton 702
nez 122, 148, 309, 624, 894, 897, 898
nez basculant 629
nez du guide 331
nez, parties externes 175
nez-de-marche 255
Nicaragua 742
niche de sécurité 543
nickel 683
nid à couvain 100
nid d'ange 368
nièce 785
Niger 34, 745
Nigeria 745
Nil 34
nimbo-stratus 56, 62
niobium 683
niveau 650
niveau à bulle 313
niveau d'eau 241, 261
niveau d'eau 261
niveau d'équilibre 49
niveau d'opérations 529
niveau de la mer 42, 49, 53
niveau de la réception 724
nuancier 398
nucléole 74, 94, 170
nuisette 364
numéro 919
numéro 1 858
numéro 2 858
numéro 3 858
numéro 4 858
numéro atomique 682
numéro d'autoroute 39
numéro de carte 729, 731
numéro de chambre 724
numéro de couloir 893
numéro de l'abonné 273
numéro de la piste 501
numéro de la pompe 548
numéro de quai 582
numéro de route 39
numéro de série 729
numéro de tête 857
numéro du joueur 808, 810, 878
numéro plein 919
numéroteur 531
nuque 115, 147, 149
nymphe 100

nom de la monnaie 729
nom de la station 592
nom du concurrent 831
nom du gymnaste 825
nom du titulaire 729
nombre de copies 512
nombre de décimales 529
nombril 146, 148
non-addition 529
non-appartenance 703
non-métaux 683
non-parallèle 704
Nord 37
nord 616, 917
Nord Est 37
Nord Nord-Est 37
Nord Nord-Ouest 37
Nord Ouest 37
nord-est 616
nord-ouest 616
nori 183
normal 472
Norvège 744
norvégien 469
notation algébrique 916
notation musicale 434
note 825
nothosaure 93
nouaison 86
nouilles asiatiques 207
nouilles aux œufs 207
nouilles de haricots mungo 207
nouilles de riz 207
nouilles soba 207
nouilles somen 207
nouilles udon 207
Nouveau Testament 736
nouvelle Lune 7
Nouvelle-Calédonie 29
Nouvelle-Zélande 29, 747
nova 8
noyau 6, 8, 74, 81, 94, 168, 170, 444, 680, 867, 912
noyau d'argile 660
noyau d'induit 688
noyau externe 42
noyau fissile 681
noyau galactique 9
noyau interne 42
noyer 88
nœud 77, 463, 663, 687
nœud coulant 908
nœud d'arrêt 908
nœud d'arrimage de l'orbiteur 21
nœud d'écoute double 908
nœud d'écoute simple 908
nœud de cabestan 908
nœud de chaise double 908
nœud de chaise simple 908
nœud de Franciscain 908
nœud de jambe de chien 908
nœud de pêcheur 908
nœud de Ranvier 168
nœud de vache 908
nœud papillon 349
nœud plat 340, 908
nœud simple 908
nœuds 908
nu-pied 344
nuage 53, 65
nuage de cendres 44
nuage de Oort 4
nuage en entonnoir 63
nuages 56, 62
nuages à développement vertical 62
nuages de basse altitude 62
nuages de haute altitude 62
nuages de moyenne altitude 62
nuages, mesure de la hauteur 59

O

oasis 48, 52
Obéron 5
obi 845, 846
objectif 476, 478, 479, 483, 501, 517, 518, 693
objectif d'agrandissement 485
objectif grand-angulaire 478
objectif macro 478
objectif normal 478
objectif super-grand-angle 478
objectif zoom 478, 496
objectif, accessoires 478
objectifs 478
objet 691
objets personnels 374, 383
obscurité 617
observation astronomique 10
observatoire 17
observatoire astronomique 17
observatoire astronomique, coupe 17
obstacle d'eau 866
obstacle d'eau 867
obstacles 875
obstacles, sports équestres 852
obturateur 513
obturateur de baie 513
obusier moderne 756
occipital 131, 151, 153, 158
océan 7, 38, 67
Océan Arctique 28
Océan Atlantique 28, 29, 32, 34
Océan Indien 28, 29, 33, 34
Océan Pacifique 28, 29, 33
océan, dorsale 49
Océanie 28, 29, 747
océanique 61
octaèdre régulier 705
Octant 10
octave 434, 849
octogone régulier 705
oculaire 14, 15, 477, 479, 496, 692, 693, 773
oculaire coudé 14
odorat 174
œuf 100, 117
œuf d'autruche 213
œuf d'oie 213
œuf de caille 213
œuf de cane 213
œuf de faisane 213
œuf de poule 213
œufrier 291
œufs 109, 111, 213
office 624
officiels 801, 846
ogive 659
ohm 702
oie 120, 213
oignon à mariner 184
oignon blanc 184
oignon jaune 184
oignon rouge 184
oignon vert 184
oiseau 115
oiseau aquatique 117
Oiseau de Paradis 10
oiseau de proie 117
oiseau échassier 117
oiseau granivore 117
oiseau insectivore 117
oiseau percheur 117
oiseau, anatomie 116
oiseau, morphologie 115
oiseau, squelette 116
oiseaux 115
oiseaux, exemples 118
okapi 128
olécrane 126
olécrâne 153
oléoduc 654
oléoduc d'évacuation 652
oléoduc sous-marin 654
oléoduc surélevé 654
olive 188
Oman 746
ombelle 81
ombilic 46
ombilic inférieur 115
ombilic supérieur 115
omble de fontaine 221
ombre 696
ombre à paupières 378
omoplate 111, 116, 121, 122, 126, 131, 136, 138, 141, 142, 147, 149, 152, 153, 156
oncle maternel 785
oncle paternel 785
onde 690
onde de choc 651, 653
onde radio 16
onde sismique 43
ondes radio 690
onduleur 520, 523

ongle 173
onglet 223, 532, 905
onglet à fenêtre 532
Oort, nuage 4
opale 375
opéra 710
opérateur de régie d'éclairage 490
opérations de base 529
opérations spécifiques 529
opercule 108, 111
opercule thermoscellé 223
Ophiuchus 11, 13
opisthodome 403
opossum 143
opticien 715
optique 690
or 683, 741
orage 57
orage fort 57
orang-outan 139
orange 194, 400
orange, coupe 82
orbiculaire des paupières 150
orbite 112, 116, 131, 136, 138, 142
orbite des satellites 60
orbite géostationnaire 60
orbite lunaire 6, 7
orbite polaire 60
orbite terrestre 6, 7
orbiteur 22, 23
orbiteur (Viking) 18
orchestre 402
orchestre symphonique 437
orchidée 80
ordinateur 734
ordinateur de bord 556, 771
ordinateur de bureau 522, 523, 524
ordinateur de gestion de vol 626
ordinateur de poche 527
ordinateur des données aérodynamiques 626
ordinateur portable 523, 526
ordinateur portable : vue arrière 526
ordinateur portable : vue avant 526
Ordovicien 92
ordre corinthien 405
ordre d'arrivée 831
ordre dorique 404
ordre ionique 404
ordures ménagères 69, 70
oreille 133, 140, 146, 277, 610
oreille externe 174
oreille interne 174
oreille moyenne 174
oreille, pavillon 173
oreille, structure 174
oreille-de-Judas 183
oreiller 280
oreillette 506
oreillette droite 161, 162
oreillette gauche 161, 162
Orénoque 31
organeau 610
organeau de hissage 610
organes des sens 172
organes génitaux féminins 170
organes génitaux masculins 169
organisation gouvernementale 525
organiseur 530
organisme culturel 525
organisme de santé 525
organismes simples 94
orge 85, 203
orge : épi 85
orgue 444
orgue, mécanisme 445
orgue, production du son 445
orifice d'aération 320
orifice d'alimentation 766
orifice d'échappement 649
orifice de la bourse copulatrice 97
orifice de remplissage 288
orifice du conduit auditif 173
orifice du pied 444
orifice excréteur 104
orifice génital 95, 104
orifice uro-génital 109
oriflamme 739
origan 202
origine et évolution des espèces 92
Orion 11, 12
ormeau 217
ornement de proue 600
ornements 435
oronge vraie 183
orque 137
orteil 130, 146, 148
orthocère 92
ortie 187
os alvéolaire 159
os compact 154
os court 157
os crochu 154
os de la colonne vertébrale 157
os iliaque 152
os irrégulier 157
os long 157

os long, structure 154
os maxillaire 159
os plat 157
os propre du nez 175
os sésamoïde falciforme 121
os spongieux 154
os, types 157
oscilloscope de phase audio 491
oscilloscope/vectoscope 491
oscule 95
oseille 187
osmium 683
osselets 174
ostéon 154
otarie 137
otolithe 109
oued 52
Ouest 37
ouest 616, 917
Ouest Nord-Ouest 37
Ouest Sud-Ouest 37
Ouganda 745
ouïe 173, 439
ouïe, protection 772, 774
ouistiti 139
ouragan 57, 63
ourdissoir 462
ourdou 469
ourlet 285
ours 471
ours noir 135
ours polaire 135
oursin 95
outil 649
outils 464
outils pour arroser 328
outils pour couper 330
outils pour remuer la terre 326
outils pour scier 303
outils pour semer et planter 324
outils pour serrer 310
outils pour visser 302
outils, électricité 316
outils, plomberie 315
outils, sculpture sur bois 401
outils, soudage 318
ouverture 105, 911
ouverture de la boîte à lumière 485
ouvrages de référence 732
ouvre-boîtes 230, 240, 905
ouvrière 99
ouvrière, abeille 99
Ouzbékistan 746
ovaire 80, 97, 103, 170, 171
oviducte 97, 103, 113
ovoïde 79
ovotestis 104
ovule 80, 170
oxer 852, 853
oxygène 683
œil 63, 103, 104, 106, 107, 112, 113, 121, 133, 136, 148, 177, 301, 461, 855, 900
œil composé 96, 98, 99
œil primitif 95
œil simple 97, 99
œil témoin 591
œillère 857
œillet 80, 284, 342, 371, 387, 457, 881, 911
œillet d'attache 476, 477
œilleton 496
œsophage 95, 97, 99, 103, 104, 109, 110, 112, 113, 116, 125, 163, 164

P

Pacini, corpuscule 172
pack 223
paddock 856
pagaie double 837, 839
pagaie simple 837, 838
page précédente 515, 527
page suivante 515, 527
pagne 339
pagode 412
paiement électronique, terminal 731
paille 223
pain 204, 722
pain azyme 205
pain blanc 205
pain chapati indien 205
pain complet 205
pain de campagne 205
pain de maïs américain 205
pain de mie 205
pain de seigle allemand 205
pain de seigle danois 205
pain de seigle noir 204
pain grec 204
pain irlandais 205
pain multicéréales 205
pain naan indien 205
pain noir russe 205
pain parisien 204

pain pita 205
pain tchallah juif 205
pair 919
paire 914
pak-choï 186
Pakistan 746
pal 740
palais de justice 710
palais des congrès 711, 718
palais des sports 788
palanque 852
Palaos 747
palatin 112, 123
pale 261, 659, 664, 676, 677
pale de rotor 631
palet 880
palette 632, 815, 911, 913
palette à ailes 632
palette à alvéoles 398
palette à double face 632
palette à simple face 632
palette avec godet 398
palette-caisse 632
palettes 632
palier 251, 255
palier de butée 659
palier inférieur 417
palier supérieur 417
palissade 408
palla 336
palladium 683
palme 841
palmée 79
palmeraie 52
palmette 276
palmier 88
palmure 110, 117
palonnier 638
palonnier de slalom 840
palourde 217
palpe 105
palpe labial 96, 99
pampille 287
pamplemousse 194
pan 349, 352, 359
pan arrière 349
pan avant 349
panais 189
Panama 742
panama 340
pancetta 216
pancréas 110, 116, 164
panicule, avoine 85
panicule, sorgho 85
panier 238, 241, 291, 294, 797, 811, 911
panier à couverts 294
panier à friture 231
panier cuit-vapeur 235
panier d'alimentation 511
panier de lavage 292
panier de projection 483
panier de réception 511
panne 318, 425, 901
panne ronde 301
panneau 247, 400, 650, 811, 899
panneau à âme lamellée 300
panneau à âme lattée 300
panneau avant 349
panneau d'accès 258
panneau d'accès 266
panneau de citerne 607
panneau de commande 261, 508, 766
panneau de connexions 518
panneau de contrôle 518
panneau de copeaux 300
panneau de disjoncteurs 626
panneau de distribution 272, 273
panneau de fibres 300
panneau de fibres perforé 300
panneau de fonctions 508
panneau de garnissage 554
panneau de l'écran 496
panneau de modestie 511
panneau de particules 300
panneau de particules lamifié 300
panneau de protection latéral 783
panneau de raccordement électrique 489
panneau de raccordement vidéo 489
panneau de refroidissement 23
panneau de séparation 389
panneau de vantail 278
panneau indicateur 582
panneau nombre de voies 591
panneau photovoltaïque 615
panneau publicitaire 592
panneau solaire 17, 18, 40, 60, 486
panneau de commandes radio 626
panneaux internationaux 544
panneaux nord-américains 546
panneaux solaires 21
pansement adhésif 777
pantalon 350, 371, 796, 808, 844, 875, 901
pantalon molleton 370

pantalon pattes d'éléphant 358
pantalons d'hommes 716
pantalons, exemples 358
pantographe 585, 595
Paon 10
paon 119
papaye 197
papeterie 717
papier 390, 400, 420
papier à cigarettes 390
papier aluminium 222
papier buvard 531
papier de verre 308
papier goudronné 299
papier paraffiné 222
papier sulfurisé 222
papille 172, 177
papille caliciforme 176
papille filiforme 176
papille foliée 176
papille fongiforme 176
papille linguale 176
papille rénale 165
papillon 96, 832
papillon femelle, anatomie 97
papillon, morphologie 96
Papouasie-Nouvelle-Guinée 29, 747
paprika 199
paquebot 608
paquet 223
paquet de cigarettes 390
parachute 22, 760, 896
parachute de cabine 417
parachute de secours 896
parachute principal 896
parachutiste 896
paraffines 656
parafoudre 658, 663
parafouille 660, 661
Paraguay 742
parallèle 36, 704
parallélépipède 705
parallélogramme 705
paramécie 94
paramètres moteurs/alarmes 626
Paraná 31
parapente 897
parapentiste 897
parapet 408, 409
parapharmacie et cosmétiques 181
parapheur 531
parapluie 391
parapluie télescopique 391
parapluie-canne 391
parasoleil 478
paratonnerre 245, 677
parc 39, 711
parc à charbon 646
parc à échelles 766
parc à vélos 735
parc de stationnement 708, 735, 886
parc de stockage 654
parc de stockage terminal 654
parc des expositions 708
parc national 39
parcours 866
parcours d'obstacles 852
parcours de sports équestres 788
parcours pittoresque 39
parcours, voile 833
pardessus 352
pare-brise 550, 570, 574, 577, 607, 624, 626, 876
pare-chocs 289, 570, 571, 577, 818
pare-chocs arrière 876, 885
pare-chocs avant 885
pare-feu 257, 523
pare-soleil 14, 556, 558, 567, 612
parement 300, 338
parement amont 661
parement aval 661
parenthèses 473
parents 784, 785
paréo 357
parfum 717
parfumerie 714
pariétal 112, 122, 131, 153, 158
paripennée 79
parka 353
parking 583, 596
parloir 726
parmesan 211
paroi 127, 128, 130
paroi avant 571
paroi de bout 571
paroi latérale 571, 635
parquet 253, 254
parquet à bâtons rompus 254
parquet à coupe de pierre 254
parquet à coupe perdue 254
parquet d'Arenberg 254
parquet en chevrons 254
parquet en vannerie 254
parquet mosaïque 254

parquet sur chape de ciment 254
parquet sur ossature de bois 254
parquet Versailles 254
parquets, arrangements 254
parterre 431
parti 710
parties 276, 277, 280
parties d'un bateau 838
parties d'un cercle 704
parties d'un os long 155
parties d'une bague 376
parties d'une bicyclette 578
parties de l'arme, escrime 849
parties des lunettes 385
parties externes du nez 175
partitions, exemples 740
parure 374
parures de fenêtre 282
pas 124
pas alternatif 892
pas de patineur 892
pas de tir 860
pascal 702
passage à niveau 545, 547, 583, 591
passage d'animaux sauvages 545, 547
passage de fourche 635
passage inférieur 540
passage pour piétons 545, 547, 712
passage souterrain 583
passage supérieur 539, 540
passant 349, 350, 352
passavant 607
passe (19 à 36) 919
passe à billes 657
passe-bras 355
passe-sangle 906
passerelle 408, 430, 523, 583, 593, 761
passerelle de navigation 604, 608, 609
passerelle télescopique 619
passettes 461
passoire 231, 237, 240
passoire fine 231
pastels gras 396
pastels secs 396
pastèque 195
pastille de combustible 667
pastilles d'aquarelle 397
pastilles de gouache 397
Patagonie 31
patate 184
pâte d'argile 464
pâte de tamarin 200
pâte phyllo 205
patelle 217
patère 276, 510
patère à embrasse 282
pâtes alimentaires 206
pâtes won-ton 207
Pathfinder 19
patient 780
patin 591, 631, 878, 880, 884
patin à roues alignées 895
patin acrobatique 895
patin antidérapant 321, 826
patin arrière 884
patin avant 884
patin clap 883
patin d'appui 667
patin d'espacement 667
patin de chenille 758
patin de courte piste 883
patin de figure 881
patin de gardien de but 880
patin de hockey 895
patin de vitesse 895
patin mobile 885
patinage artistique 881
patinage de vitesse 882
patineur : courte piste 882
patineur : longue piste 882
patineur d'eau 102
patineuse 895
patinoire 878, 881, 886
patins de course 883
pâtisson 189
patron 455, 458
patte 113, 348, 350, 352, 386, 425, 610, 797
patte à boutons-pression 353
patte ambulatoire 97
patte anale 97
patte antérieure 96, 98, 110, 111, 121, 130, 143
patte autocollante 531
patte boutonnée 350
patte capucin 349, 361
patte d'entrejambe 359
patte d'épaule 352
patte d'épaule 770
patte de boutonnage 349
patte de coq 464
patte de serrage 352
patte locomotrice 103
patte médiane 96, 98
patte médiane (face externe) 98

ASTRONOMIE > 2-25; TERRE > 26-71; RÈGNE VÉGÉTAL >72-89; RÈGNE ANIMAL > 90-143; ÊTRE HUMAIN > 144-177; ALIMENTATION ET CUISINE > 178-241; MAISON > 242-295;
BRICOLAGE ET JARDINAGE > 296-333; VÊTEMENTS > 334-371; PARURE ET OBJETS PERSONNELS > 372-391; ARTS ET ARCHITECTURE > 392-465; COMMUNICATIONS ET BUREAUTIQUE > 466-535;
TRANSPORT ET MACHINERIE > 536-643; ÉNERGIES > 644-677; SCIENCE > 678-705; SOCIÉTÉ > 706-785; SPORTS ET JEUX > 786-920

patte polo 354
patte postérieure 96, 98, 110, 111, 121, 143
patte ventouse 97
pattes thoraciques 107
pattes, exemples 117
pâturage 182
paturon 124
paume 121, 173, 346, 797
paume d'un gant 346
paumelle 249
paupière 113
paupière inférieure 110, 132, 177
paupière interne 132
paupière supérieure 110, 132, 177
pause 435, 499, 515
pause/arrêt sur l'image 495
pavé alphabétique 530
pavé alphanumérique 514
pavé numérique 515, 530
pavé tactile 526
pavillon 122, 143, 174, 444, 446, 447, 551, 710, 776, 866
pavillon (8) 374
pavillon à deux pointes 739
pavillon à deux pointes et langue 739
pavillon de la trompe utérine 171
pavillon des skieurs 886
pavillon, oreille 173
pavois 602, 739
pavot, graines 199
pays 37
pays d'origine du concurrent 831
Pays-Bas 743
paysage végétal selon l'altitude 66
pe-tsaï 186
peau 81, 82, 83, 168, 172, 425, 449
peau de batterie 433, 448
peau de chamois 345, 377
peau de timbre 433, 448
pécari 128
pêche 192, 909
pêche à la mouche 909
pêche au lancer 910
pêche, coupe 81
pêcheur 457
pédale 440, 448, 578, 580, 851, 870
pédale automatique 870
pédale avec cale élargie 870
pédale crescendo 444
pédale d'accélérateur 556
pédale d'ajustement 399
pédale de chaussage 889
pédale de combinaisons 444
pédale de débrayage 556
pédale de déchaussage 889
pédale de frein 333, 460, 552, 556, 559
pédale de frein arrière 576
pédale de marche arrière 333
pédale de marche avant 333
pédale de palonnier 898
pédale de sourdine 442
pédale douce 442, 451
pédale forte 442, 451
pédales d'expression 444
pédicelle 75
pédieux 150
pédipalpe 103
pédoncule 80, 81, 82, 83, 86
Pégase 12
peigne 417, 461, 642
peigne à crêper 380
peigne à pollen 98
peigne à tige 380
peigne afro 380
peigne de coiffeur 380
peignes 380
peignoir 364
peinture 396
peinture à l'huile 396
peinture d'entretien 320
peinture, accessoires 399
pelage 122, 139, 143
pèlerine 355
pélican 119
pelle 233, 257, 326, 838
pelle à poussière 295
pelle de montagne 901
pelle hydraulique 638
pelle mécanique 647
pelle-pioche pliante 906
pelleteuse 637
pellicule en feuille 481
pellicule plastique 222
pellicules 481
pelote 454
peloton 870
peloton de tête 870
pelouse 245, 864
peltée 79
Pelton, roue 659
pelvis vestigial 136
pendants d'oreille 374
pendeloque 287
pendentif 374
penderie 251, 279

pendule 488, 489, 491, 697, 734
pêne demi-tour 248
pêne dormant 248, 249
péninsule 38
Péninsule Antarctique 29
Péninsule d'Arabie 33
Péninsule de Corée 33
Péninsule de Kola 32
Péninsule des Balkans 32
Péninsule du Kamtchatka 33
Péninsule du Yucatan 30
Péninsule Ibérique 32
Péninsule Scandinave 32
pénis 104, 146
penne 115, 206
pennée 79
pennon 739, 834
pennon double 739
pentagone régulier 705
pente 674
pente difficile 886
pente expert 886
pente facile 886
pente intermédiaire 886
pépin 82, 83
pepino 197
péplos 336
pepperoni 216
perceuse à colonne 307
perceuse électrique 306
perceuse-visseuse sans fil 306
perche 220, 490, 492, 792
perche de ravitaillement 760
perche truitée 220
perche de tête 857
perche, anatomie 109
perche, morphologie 108
perchiste 429, 792
percolateur 241
percolateurs 723
percuteur 757
perdrix 118
père 784, 785
perforation 342, 346, 371
perforatrice 533
pergola 322
péricarde 163
péricarpe 82, 84
période 617, 789
périoste 154
périphérique 709
périphériques d'entrée 514
périphériques de communication 522
périphériques de sortie 518
périphériques de stockage 521
périscope d'attaque 763
périscope de veille 763
péristome 94
péristyle 403, 406
péritoine 169, 170
Permien 92
péroné 111, 122, 126, 131, 138, 141, 142, 152, 155, 156
Pérou 742
peroxyde 777
peroxysome 94
perpendiculaire 704
perré 660
perron 245, 250
persan 132, 469
Persée 12
persienne 249
persil 202
personnel additionnel de production 490
perte de chaleur 68
pertuis de remplissage 597
pertuis de remplissage et de vidange 597
pèse-lettres 531
pèse-personne 699
peso 728
peson 699
pesticide 69, 70
pétale 80
pétanque 864
pétiole 76, 79
petit bois 249
petit cacatois 603
Petit Cheval 12
Petit Chien 13
petit foc 603
petit hunier fixe 603
petit hunier volant 603
petit largue 833
Petit Lion 13
petit miroir 612
petit montant 247
petit palmaire 150
petit perroquet fixe 603
petit perroquet volant 603
petit quartier 855
petit rabat 391
Petit Renard 13
petit rond 151
petit sésamoïde 126
petit-fils 784
petite capitale 472

petite lame 905
petite lèvre 170, 171
petite nyctale 118
Petite Ourse 12
petite quille 865
petite sus-alaire 115
petite vrillette 101
petite-fille 784
petites annonces 471
petits outils, jeu 325
petits pois 190
petits-enfants 784
pétoncle 217
Pétri, boîte 685
pétrole 651
pétrole brut 656
pétrolier 596, 606
peul 468
peuplier 88
phalange distale 133, 154, 155, 172
phalange médiane 133, 154, 155, 172
phalange proximale 133, 154, 155
phalanges 111, 122, 131, 136, 138, 141, 142, 154, 155
phalène du bouleau 101
phare 333, 550, 570, 574, 576, 586, 596, 614, 640, 758, 876
phare arrière 640
phare central 585
phare d'atterrissage 631
pharmacie 714, 725, 778, 781
pharynx 99, 163, 164
phase de glisse 892
phase de poussée 892
phases de la Lune 7
Phénix 10
Philippines 33, 747
Phobos 4
phonothèque 733
phoque 137
phosphore 683
photocopieur 512, 733
photodiode 477
photographe 714
photographe de plateau 429
photographie 476
photographie à la une 471
photographie, accessoires 482
photon 692
photopile 672, 673
photorécepteurs 177
photosphère 6
photosynthèse 78
phototype 483
physique : électricité 687
physique : magnétisme 687
physique : mécanique 686
physique : optique 690
pi 704
piano 437
piano à queue de concert 443
piano demi-queue 443
piano droit 442
piano droit, mécanique 443
piano électronique 451
piano quart-de-queue 443
pic 45, 118
piccolo 437, 446
pichet 226, 240
pictogrammes 514
pie 118
pie-mère 167
pièce 917
pièce : avers 729
pièce : revers 729
pièce d'embranchement 767
pièce d'estomac 337
pièce de coin 635
pièce de jonction 766
pièce intermédiaire 169
pièce terminale 169
pièces 916
pièces buccales 98
pièces honorables, exemples 740

pieds, protection 773
piège à patte à mâchoires 913
pierre 298, 318, 376
pierre à affûter 229
pierre à aiguiser 422
pierre blanche 916
pierre de Coyolxauhqui 412
pierre de curling 877
pierre de taille 298
pierre lithographique 423
pierre noire 916
pierre sacrificielle 412
pierres fines 375
pierres précieuses 375
pierres, taille 375
piètement 277, 321, 826
pieuvre 106, 217
pieuvre, anatomie 106
pieuvre, morphologie 106
pige 464
pigeon 120, 212
pignon 89, 193, 223, 244, 307, 697
pignon simple 871
pika 123
pilastre 255
pilastre corinthien 407
pile 482, 513, 540, 563, 759, 765
pile alcaline manganèse-zinc 689
pile carbone-zinc 689
pile rechargeable 496
piles 687
piles sèches 689
pilier 43, 410, 412, 650
pilier droit 804
pilier du voile 174
pilier gauche 804
pilon 230, 233
pilote 443, 759, 872
pilote, vol libre 897
pilotes 445
pilotin 445
piment 188
piment de Cayenne 199
piment de la Jamaïque 198
piment Jalapeño 199
piment oiseau 199
piments broyés 199
piments séchés 199
pin parasol 89
pinacle 410
pinacocyte 95
pince 107, 127, 233, 257, 284, 350, 381, 455, 506, 901
pince à boucles de cheveux 380
pince à cheveux 380
pince à cravate 376
pince à cuticules 377
pince à défriser 381
pince à dénuder 317
pince à échardes 777
pince à épiler 377
pince à escargots 233
pince à étiqueter 533
pince à fusible 317
pince à joint coulissant 310
pince à long bec 317
pince à spaghettis 233
pince avec noix de serrage 685
pince d'électricien 317
pince de ceinture 505
pince de mise en plis 380
pince de taille 352
pince multiprise 310
pince noire 558
pince rouge 558
pince tibio-tarsienne 98
pince universelle 317
pince-aiguille 453
pince-étau 310
pince-fil 457
pince-notes 534
pinceau 320, 397, 422, 470
pinceau à lèvres 378
pinceau à pâtisserie 232
pinceau à sumie 397
pinceau éventail 378
pinceau pour fard à joues 378
pinceau pour poudre libre 378
pincement 274, 275
pinces 310
pinçon 127
pinnacle 410
pinnule 76
pinson 118
pintade 120, 212
pioche 327
piolet 901
Pion 916
pion 915
Pioneer 19
pipe 390
pipe, coupe 390
pipette sérologique 685
piquant 95
pique 901, 914
pique-nique 725
pique-nique interdit 725

pique-notes 534
piquet 799, 902, 903
piquoir 458
pirogue à balancier 599
pirogue monoxyle 599
piscine 246, 608, 675, 788
piscine de condensation 671
piscine de déchargement 666
piscine de déchargement du combustible irradié 668
piscine de réception 666
piscine de stockage du combustible irradié 666, 667, 669
piscine du combustible défectueux 666
piscine enterrée 246
piscine hors sol 246
pisiforme 154
pissenlit 187
pissette 685
pistache 193
piste 620, 790, 848, 871, 872, 874, 877, 883, 885, 891
piste : descente de bosses 890
piste d'athlétisme 788
piste d'atterrissage 761
piste d'avertissement 795
piste d'élan 791, 792, 865
piste d'élan 793, 890, 891
piste de compétition 855
piste de décélération 885
piste de décélération et de freinage 891
piste de dégagement 890, 891
piste de réception 890, 891
piste de roulement 595, 635
piste de ski alpin 886
piste de ski de fond 886
piste de vitesse 891
pistes d'élan 824
pistil 80
pistolet 315, 754, 770
pistolet 8 mm 861
pistolet à air comprimé 861
pistolet à calfeutrer 315
pistolet à peinture 320
pistolet à souder 318
pistolet arrosoir 329
pistolet d'arrosage 329
pistolet de départ 790
pistolet de distribution 548
pistolet mitrailleur 754
pistolet pneumatique 873
piston 447, 559, 564, 566, 776
piston à décorer 232
piton 900
piton à expansion 900
piton à glace 901
piton sous-marin 49
pivot 317, 382, 383, 398, 436, 454, 612, 676, 686, 793, 811, 828, 907
pivot d'attelage 571
placage déroulé 300
place d'armes 409
plaçure 426
plafond 257, 818, 819
plafond acoustique 431
plafond cathédrale 251
plafond de cabine 417
plafonnier 286
plage 51
plage arrière 608
plage avant 605, 609
plage de séparation 500
plaine 38, 48
plaine abyssale 49
plaine d'inondation 48
plaine fluvio-glaciaire 46
plan 403, 411
plan à langer 281
plan de travail 224, 721, 722
plan du terrain 245
plan urbain 39
plan, élévation 250
planche 300, 851
planche à découper 229
planche à dessin 399
planche à roulettes 894
planche à voile 836
planche d'appel 793
planche d'appel saut en longueur 793
planche d'appel triple saut 793
planche d'arrêt 864
planche de pied 838
planche de surf 840
planche de vol 100
planche témoin 793
plancher 257, 577, 818, 819, 855
plancher de cabine 417
plancher inférieur 632
plancher supérieur 632
planchette à arches 533
planchette à pince 533
planchiste 894
planétaire 10
planétarium 10
planètes 4
planètes externes 4

1034

planètes internes 5
planeur 898
planisphère 28
plantaire grêle 151
plante 77
plante grimpante 322
plante, structure 77
plantes à fleurs 93
plantoir 324
plantoir à bulbes 324
plaque 238, 381
plaque à aiguille 452
plaque à pâtisserie 232
plaque absorbante 672
plaque africaine 43
plaque antarctique 43
plaque antifriction 889
plaque chauffante 241, 721
plaque costale 113
plaque d'identité 376
plaque d'instructions 306
plaque de base 756
plaque de commutateur 274
plaque de couche 912
plaque de cuisson 722
plaque de cuivre 422
plaque de fixation 701
plaque de montage 275
plaque de plâtre 299
plaque de protection 441, 875
plaque de rouleau 920
plaque de tôle 819
plaque des Caraïbes 43
plaque des îles Cocos 43
plaque du lanceur 795
plaque eurasiatique 43
plaque indo-australienne 43
plaque madréporique 95
plaque marginale 113
plaque motrice 168
plaque Nazca 43
plaque négative 562
plaque nord-américaine 43
plaque pacifique 43
plaque philippine 43
plaque positive 562
plaque Scotia 43
plaque signalétique 273, 306
plaque sud-américaine 43
plaque supra-caudale 113
plaque tournante 542
plaque vertébrale 113
plaque-glissière 452, 453
plaque-numéro 875
plaques convergentes 43
plaques divergentes 43
plaques tectoniques 43
plaques transformantes 43
plaquette 64, 162, 385, 559
plaqueur droit 806
plaqueur gauche 806
plasma 162
plasmodesme 74
plastique 269
plastique et acier 269
plastique et cuivre 269
plastron 113, 367, 749, 796, 800, 808, 859
plastron de gardien de but 880
plastron métallique 848
plat 798
plat à escargots 233
plat à poisson 226
plat de dos 276
plat ovale 226
plat recto 426
plat verso 426
plate-bande 322
plate-bande de culasse 753
plate-forme 40, 321, 482, 569, 584, 699, 830, 894
plate-forme auto-élévatrice 653
plate-forme de 10 m 828
plate-forme de 3 m 828
plate-forme de 5 m 828
plate-forme de 7,5 m 828
plate-forme de départ 891
plate-forme de production 652, 654
plate-forme du jury 871
plate-forme élévatrice automotrice 623
plate-forme fixe 653
plate-forme semi-submersible 653
plateau 38, 45, 78, 261, 278, 281, 305, 307, 312, 313, 321, 389, 402, 424, 425, 452, 485, 490, 492, 500, 571, 698, 699, 860, 870, 917
plateau A 580
plateau B 580
plateau continental 49
plateau d'alimentation 531
plateau de chargement 494, 521
plateau de clavier 442
plateau de coupe 333
plateau de frein 559
plateau de jeu 915
plateau de ponçage 308
plateau de pression 758

plateau de rangement 399
plateau de sciage 305
plateau de sortie 519
plateau de stockage 666
plateau de tournage 428
plateau de tri automatique 512
plateau des tremplins 890
plateau mobile 919
plateau pour accessoires 14
plateau réceptacle de paiement 920
plateau récepteur 512
plateau simple 871
plateau tournant 236
plateau, télévision 490, 492
plateaux 722
platéosaure 93
platine 425, 683, 693, 895
platine à silex 752
platine cassette 488, 499
platine de projection 535
platine tourne-disque 488, 500
plats à rôtir 234
pleine Lune 7
plénum 258
pleurote en forme d'huître 183
plèvre pariétale 163
plèvre viscérale 163
plexus brachial 166
plexus lombaire 166
plexus sacré 166
pli 300, 350, 561
pli creux 283, 357
pli d'aisance 357
pli de la columelle 105
pli pincé 283
pli plat 350, 357
pli rond 283
pli surpiqué 357
plie commune 221
plinthe 253, 255, 417
plinthe chauffante électrique 260
plioir 426
plis, exemples 283, 357
plissé accordéon 357
pliure 455
plomb 682, 911
plomberie 262
plomberie : outils 314
plomberie, circuit 262
plombs 912
plongée sous-marine 841
plongeoir 828
plongeon 828
plongeon de départ 832
plongeon renversé avec tire-bouchon 829
plongeon synchronisé 829
plongeons, exemples 829
plongeur 721, 841
plot 274
plot de départ 830
pluie 64, 65
pluie continue faible 57
pluie continue forte 57
pluie continue modérée 57
pluie faible 64
pluie intermittente faible 57
pluie intermittente forte 57
pluie intermittente modérée 57
pluie modérée 64
pluie verglaçante 57, 64
pluie, formes 64
pluies acides 69, 70
plume 43, 397, 470
plume creuse de roseau 470
plume d'oie 470
plume métallique 470
plume métallique romaine 470
plus grand que 703
plus ou moins 703
plus petit que 703
Pluton 4, 5
plutonium 684
pluviomètre à lecture directe 58, 59
pluviomètre enregistreur 58, 59
pluviosité, mesure 59
pneu 551, 560, 570, 579, 870, 874
pneu à carcasse diagonale 561
pneu à carcasse radiale 561
pneu à carcasse radiale ceinturée 561
pneu à crampons 560, 577, 875
pneu autoroutier 560
pneu d'hiver 560
pneu de performance 560
pneu pluie 872
pneu pour temps sec 872
pneu toutes saisons 560
pneumatique de guidage 594, 595
pneumatique porteur 594, 595
pneus, exemples 560
poche 143, 313, 862, 865, 869
poche à douilles 232
poche à encre 106
poche à rabat 352, 360
poche à venin 99
poche américaine 386
poche cavalière 350

poche centrale 862
poche copulatrice 104
poche du dard 104
poche extérieure 386, 388
poche frontale 387
poche gilet 348
poche inférieure 862
poche intérieure 389
poche intérieure isolante 368
poche manchon 360
poche passepoilée 354, 360
poche plaquée 348, 353, 360, 368
poche poitrine 349, 352
poche prise dans une couture 355, 360
poche prise dans une découpe 360
poche raglan 352, 355, 360
poche repose-bras 353, 355
poche secrète 386
poche soufflet 359, 360
poche supérieure 862
poche tiroir 348
poche tourne-disque 488, 500
poche verticale 337
poche-revolver 350
poche-ticket 348
poches, exemples 360
pochette 348, 386
pochette d'allumettes 391
pochette d'homme 388
pochette d'information 532
pochette de classement 533
pocheuse 235
podium des épreuves 824
podomètre 700
poêle 905
poêle à combustion lente 256
poêle à crêpes 235
poêle à frire 235
poêlon 235, 239
poids 630, 697, 698, 699, 793, 850, 851
poignard 751
poignée 230, 236, 237, 238, 239, 240, 256, 268, 280, 288, 289, 290, 291, 295, 302, 303, 304, 305, 307, 308, 309, 313, 320, 331, 381, 382, 386, 387, 388, 389, 391, 439, 503, 504, 534, 574, 577, 594, 649, 750, 775, 782, 793, 816, 822, 838, 849, 850, 859, 860, 867, 877, 884, 888, 891, 892, 909, 910, 912, 913, 920
poignée antivibrations 331
poignée arrière 910
poignée auxiliaire 306
poignée avant 757
poignée d'appui 851
poignée de blocage d'onglet 304
poignée de chariot 456
poignée de conduite 783
poignée de départ (dos) 830
poignée de frein 579, 783, 870
poignée de guidage 308
poignée de la manivelle 423
poignée de maintien 554
poignée de nacelle 899
poignée de porte 247, 551
poignée de soulèvement 554
poignée de sécurité 332
poignée de transport 755
poignée découpée 535
poignée des gaz 576
poignée du démarreur 331
poignée du guidon 871
poignée intérieure 554
poignée isolante 239
poignée latérale 307, 308
poignée montoir 567, 570, 584, 766
poignée pistolet 318
poignée profilée 381
poignée rentrante 386
poignée supérieure 307
poignée-oxygène de coupe 319
poignée-pistolet 306, 754, 755
poignées à ressort 850
poignet 130, 140, 147, 149, 156, 173, 349
poignet de force 850
poignet mousquetaire 361
poil 172, 384
poils absorbants 77
poinçon 253, 401, 905
point 473, 914
point critique 891
point d'alimentation 273, 663
point d'amure 836
point d'ancrage 897
point d'appui 686
point d'arête 459
point d'articulation 638
point d'attache 79, 627
point d'attache 103
point d'écoute 836
point d'encochage 859
point d'encochage 913
point d'épine 459
point d'exclamation 473
point d'information 715
point d'interrogation 473
point d'orgue 435

point d'Orient 459
point de chaînette 459
point de chausson 459
point de chevron 459
point de côtes 458
point de damier 458
point de handicap 916
point de jersey 458
point de mise au jeu 878
point de norme 891
point de nœud 459
point de poste 459
point de raccordement 273
point de réparation 802
point de repère 455, 865
point de riz 458
point de torsades 458
point du chef 740
point fixe 559
point indicateur de température 381
point mousse 458
point passé empiétant 459
point roumain 459
point vernal 13
point vertical 459
point-virgule 473
pointage de l'épreuve en cours 825
pointe 51, 79, 185, 227, 229, 301, 302, 303, 304, 351, 362, 390, 439, 443, 453, 457, 470, 740, 791, 793, 859, 868, 880, 888, 901, 911, 912, 918
pointe antérieure 901
pointe avant 288
pointe carrée 302
pointe cruciforme 302
pointe d'attache 442
pointe de centrage 306
pointe de col 349
pointe de dent 636
pointe de diamant 278
pointe de flèche en silex 748
pointe de hampe 739
pointe fuselée 839
pointe plate 285, 302
pointe ronde 285
pointe sèche 422, 423
pointe de ski 892
pointes, exemples 302
pointeur 907
pointeuse 530
points 822
points bouclés 459
points couchés 459
points croisés 459
points de suspension 473
points de tricot 458
points noués 459
points plats 459
points, broderie 459
poire 193
poire à jus 233
poire à poudre 752
poire de gonflage 777
poireau 184
pois 84, 190
pois cassés 190
pois chiches 190
pois mange-tout 190
Poisson austral 10
poisson cartilagineux 108
poisson osseux 108
Poisson volant 11
poissonnerie 181
poissonnière 234
Poissons 12
poissons 108
poissons cartilagineux 218
poissons osseux 219
poitrail 124
poitrine 115
poitrinière 460
poivre blanc 198
poivre moulu 199
poivre noir 198
poivre rose 198
poivre vert 198
poivrière 226
poivron jaune 188
poivron rouge 188
poivron vert 188
Polaroid® 480
pôle Nord 35
pôle nord 687
pôle Nord céleste 13
pole position 872
pôle Sud 29, 35
pôle sud 687
pôle Sud céleste 13
police 725
polissoir d'ongles 377
politique 739
polluants atmosphériques 69
polluants non biodégradables 69
pollution agricole 69
pollution automobile 69
pollution de l'air 69
pollution de l'eau 70

pollution domestique 69
pollution du sol 69
pollution industrielle 69
pollution par le pétrole 70
polo 354, 359, 822, 858
polochon 280
Pologne 744
polojama 369
polonais 469
polonium 682
polygones 705
Polynésie 747
polypode commun 76
polytric commun 75
pomelo 194
pomme 193, 328
pomme d'Adam 146
pomme de douche 264
pomme de terre 184
pomme, coupe 82
pomme-poire 197
pommeau 307, 309, 797, 849, 855, 861
pompe 246, 259, 292, 294, 320, 578, 670, 671, 674, 903
pompe à boue 651
pompe à chaleur 260
pompe de caloportage 669
pompe de circulation 259, 675
pompe de puisard 263
pompe de recirculation 671
ponceuse excentrique 308
poncho 355
poney 858
poney de polo 858
pont 39, 385, 523, 692, 875
pont à béquilles 541
pont à poutre 540
pont à poutre simple 541
pont à poutres indépendantes 541
pont à tablier inférieur 541
pont à tablier intermédiaire 541
pont à tablier supérieur 541
pont Bailey 542
pont bain de soleil 609
pont basculant à double volée 542
pont basculant à simple volée 542
pont cantilever 540
pont d'appontage 761
pont d'envol 761
pont de Varole 167
pont en arc 540
pont flottant 542
pont inférieur 655
pont levant 542
pont principal 607
pont roulant 658
pont supérieur 624, 655
pont suspendu à câble porteur 540
pont tournant 542
pont transbordeur 542
pont-l'évêque 211
pont-levis 408
pont-promenade 608
pontage 838
pontet 754, 860, 861, 912
ponton 542, 652, 839, 873
ponton de départ 838
ponts à poutre, exemples 541
ponts en arc, exemples 541
ponts fixes 540
ponts mobiles 542
ponts suspendus à haubans 541
popote 905
porc 128
porc haché 215
porc-épic 123
porche 245, 411, 738
porcherie 182
pore 115, 84
pore inhalant 95
pore sudoripare 172
porque 607
Porro, prisme 692
port 709
port clavier 513
port d'interface ordinateur 520
port de plaisance 788
port Ethernet 526
port FireWire 526
port infrarouge 526, 527
port jeux/MIDI 513
port maritime 596
port modem interne 513, 526
port parallèle 513
port pour adaptateur de courant 526
port réseau 513
port série 513
port souris 513, 518
port USB 513, 526
port vidéo 513, 526
portail 411
portance 630
portant 839
porte 238, 290, 291, 293, 417, 453, 567, 596, 624, 699, 724, 738, 818, 893, 902, 903

porte à deux vantaux 568
porte à lanières 416
porte à tambour manuelle 416
porte accordéon 416
porte amont 597
porte arrière 775
porte automatique 620
porte aval 597
porte avant 605, 608
porte classique 416
porte coulissante 264, 416
porte coulissante automatique 416
porte coupe-feu 505
porte d'accès de plate-forme 584
porte d'entrée 568, 569
porte d'extrémité 635
porte de contrôle 890
porte de garage basculante 416
porte de garage sectionnelle 416
porte de l'élévateur 569
porte de la soute 23
porte du parcours 837
porte en descente 837
porte en remontée 837
porte étagère 291
porte extérieure 247
porte latérale 594
porte moustiquaire 567
porte pliante 416
porte-adresse 389
porte-avions 761
porte-bagages 389, 567, 577, 578
porte-bagages arrière 577
porte-bidon 579
porte-bûches 257
porte-cartes 58, 386
porte-chaussures 345
porte-chéquier 387
porte-clés 387
porte-coupures 387
porte-documents à soufflet 386
porte-documents plat 387
porte-électrode 318
porte-étiquette 533, 587
porte-étiquette d'acheminement 587
porte-fenêtre 224, 250, 251
porte-fil dentaire 384
porte-fils 460
porte-filtre 241
porte-foyer 256
porte-fusible 663
porte-jarretelles 367
porte-manteau 510
porte-marteau 313
porte-matraque 770
porte-mine 470
porte-monnaie 387
porte-moulinet 909, 910
porte-négatif 485
porte-outil 308, 649
porte-parapluies 391
porte-passeport 387
porte-pipes 390
porte-pitons 901
porte-râteau 423
porte-rouleau 264
porte-sac 869
porte-savon 264
porte-serviettes 264
porte-skis 558
porte-spécimen 694
porte-stylet 517
porte-stylo 386
porte-tension 457
porte-timbres 531
porte-tube 693
porte-vélos 558
porte-vent 445
portée 434
portefeuille 387
portefeuille chéquier 386
portes à tambour manuelles 719
portes d'entrée 427
portes, exemples 416
portière 551, 554
portique 540, 596, 634, 635, 657, 658, 738, 824
portique de chargement de conteneurs 596
portique de signalisation 583
portique détecteur de métal 726
ports pour carte mémoire 918
ports pour manette 918
portugais 469
Portugal 743
posemètre à visée reflex 479
posemètre photoélectrique 479
positif 684
position à genoux 861
position carpée 828
position couchée 861, 893
position d'équilibre 690
position d'un caractère 472
position debout 861, 893
position des bras 829
position des jambes 829

position des joueurs 794, 803, 804, 811, 814
position droite 828
position groupée 828
positionnement du papier 528
positionneur 452
positions de départ, lutte 843
positions de départ, plongeon 828
positions de tir 861, 893
positions, escrime 849
poste 664
poste à clavier 507
poste CB 505
poste d'aiguillage 583
poste d'observation 17
poste de carburant 725
poste de commandement 758, 763
poste de communication 594
poste de conduite de la propulsion 763
poste de contrôle 727, 768
poste de contrôle audio/vidéo 491
poste de débranchement 589
poste de l'agent de sécurité 779
poste de patrouille 886
poste de pilotage 624, 626, 631, 758
poste de police 711, 768
poste de secours 543, 886
poste de soudage 318
poste de surveillance 394, 764
poste de tir 860
poste de travail 509
poste des infirmières (urgence ambulatoire) 779
poste des infirmières (urgence majeure) 778
poste sans cordon 507
poste téléphonique 489, 491, 506
postes d'écoute 733
postes téléphoniques, exemples 507
postillon 915
pot 223
pot d'échappement 553, 575, 576
pot d'échappement 577
potassium 682
poteau 252, 540, 812, 817, 820, 827
poteau cornier 252
poteau de but 807, 809, 858
poteau de ligne de jeu 795
poteau du ring 842
poteau mural 253
potence 579, 693, 783
poterie 464
poterie, outils 464
poterne 408, 409
potiron 189
pou 101
poubelle 295, 723
pouce 117, 140, 141, 156, 173, 346, 797
pouce opposable 139
poudre 912
poudre libre 378
poudre pressée 378
poudrier 378
pouf 277
poulailler 182
poulaine 749
poule 120
poulet 213
poulie 284, 321, 566, 686, 750, 859, 913
poulie d'entraînement 688
poulie de chariot 634
poulie de tension du régulateur 417
principales formes de lames 401
principales pièces d'une maison 250
principaux organes des systèmes automobiles 552
principaux panneaux internationaux 544
principaux panneaux nord-américains 546
printemps 54
prise 793
prise antisurtension 520
prise audio 513
prise avec borne de terre 263
prise casque 450, 451, 497, 504
prise chronométrée 290
prise classique 815
prise d'air 605, 876
prise d'air 568
prise d'air de refroidissement du moteur 874
prise d'air du moteur 568
prise d'alimentation 513
prise d'eau 658
prise d'entrée 520
prise d'entrée/sortie audio 527
prise d'oxygène 780
prise de charge 383, 563
prise de courant 274, 316
prise de courant commutée 497
prise de courant européenne 274
prise de force 640
prise de la sonde thermique 238
prise de masse 318
prise de pied 901
prise de raccordement 452
prise de télécommande 476, 477
prise de terre 272
prise électrique 567
prise microphone 505
prise porte-plume 815

praticable 823
praticable pour exercices au sol 824
pratiquant, kung-fu 846
préblindage 758
Précambrien 92
précipitation 67
précipitations 64
précipitations hivernales 64
prémaxillaire 108, 122, 123
premier arbitre 812, 813
premier assistant cadreur 428
premier but 794
premier croissant 7
premier de cordée 900
premier espace 811
premier étage 25
premier joueur 877
premier quartier 7
premier radial externe 151
premier tour : 128 joueurs 789
premier-but 794
première ligne 804
première molaire 159
première phalange 126
première prémolaire 159
premières feuilles 77
premiers soins 725
premiers soins, fournitures 775
premiers violons 437
preneur de son 489, 490
préposé au banc des pénalités 879
préposé au contrôle des billets 394, 427
prépuce 169
près 833
près bon plein 833
près du ring 842
près serré 833
présentoir à revues 510
présentoir de brochures 730
présentoir des nouveautés 733
présentoir des périodiques 733
présentoir réfrigéré 720
président 848
président du jury 900
presse 642
presse à pectoraux 851
presse à percussion 425
presse à taille-douce 421
presse lithographique 423
presse-agrumes 230, 237
presse-ail 230
presse-café 241
presse-étoupe 268
presse-papier 528
presseur 476
pressing 715
pression à la taille 368
pression au niveau de la mer 55
pression barométrique 55
pression devant 369
pression, mesure 59, 702
pressuriseur 670, 671
prétoire 728
prévention de la criminalité 768
prévention des incendies 764
prévision météorologique 54
prime 849
principaux organes des systèmes automobiles 552
prosciutto 216
prospection en mer 653
prospection terrestre 651
prostate 169
protactinium 684
protecteur d'avant-bras 808
protecteur d'embout 776
protecteur lombaire 808
protection 716
protection d'usure 874
protection de l'ouïe 772, 774
protection de la tête 772, 774
protection de la vue 774
protection des mains 774
protection des pieds 773, 774
protection des voies respiratoires 773, 774
protection des yeux 772
protège-cheville 796
protège-côtes 808
protège-cou 808
protège-coude 800, 880, 894
protège-dents 808, 843
protège-doigts 859
protège-gorge 796, 880, 882
protège-guidon 755
protège-hanche 808
protège-lame 304, 305
protège-lame inférieur 304
protège-lame supérieur 304
protège-main 875
protège-matelas 280
protège-nuque 765
protège-orteils 773, 796

prise pour écouteurs 513
prises antisurtension alimentées par batterie 520
prises d'entrée/de sortie audio/vidéo 497
prises de main 901
prises téléphoniques antisurtension 520
prises vidéo et numérique 477
prises, exemples 844
prisme de Porro 692
prisme pentagonal 477
prison 726, 915
prix à l'unité 699
prix à payer 699
procédé 863
processeur 513
proconsul 93
producteur 429
production d'électricité par énergie éolienne 677
production d'électricité par énergie géothermique 646
production d'électricité par énergie nucléaire 665
production d'électricité par énergie solaire 674
production d'électricité par énergie thermique 646
production d'électricité par l'alternateur 662
production d'électricité par l'alternateur 665
production de chaleur 665
production de l'électricité, étapes 662
production du son 445
produits céréaliers 204
produits d'emballage 180
produits d'entretien 180
produits de fission (noyaux radioactifs) 681
produits de la raffinerie 656
produits de nettoyage 721
produits de traiteur 181
produits laitiers 180, 210
produits pétrochimiques 656
produits pour animaux familiers 181
profil de rail 591
profil du sol 78
profondeur du foyer 43
profondimètre 841
programmateur 292, 293, 294
programmation des voix 450
programmes informatiques 771
projecteur 427, 428, 579, 585, 765
projecteur à faisceau concentré 492
projecteur auxiliaire 10
projecteur d'ambiance 492
projecteur d'ambiance sur pantographe 492
projecteur de diapositives 483
projecteur de plafond 59
projecteur orientable 766
projecteur sous-marin 246
projecteurs 431
projectile antichar 757
projectiles 752
projection conique 36
projection cylindrique 36
projection d'épaule par un côté 844
projection en cercle 844
projection horizontale 36
projection interrompue 36
projections cartographiques 36
prométhium 684
pronaos 403
propulseur 20, 40, 759
propulseur d'étrave 609
propulseurs de commande d'orientation 22

protège-poignet 895
protège-poulie 307
protège-tendon 880
protège-tibia 801, 802, 882, 887
protège-tympan 772
protestantisme 736
prothorax 97
protocole de communication 524
proton 680
protoneurone sensitif 168
protubérance 6
proue 609, 836
proue sculptée 598
province 37
provision d'eau 662
prune 192
pseudopode 94
psychromètre 59
ptérygoïde 112
pubis 116, 122, 146, 148
puce 101
puisard 262, 263, 650
puissance, mesure 702
puits 402
puits d'accès 664
puits d'extraction 650
puits d'injection 646
puits de dérive 836
puits de production 646
puits sous-marin 654
puits vertical 650
pull à capuche 370
pull d'entraînement 370
pulls 358
pulpe 81, 82, 83, 159, 172
pulsar 8
pulvérisateur 328, 646
pulvériseur tandem 641
pulvino 661
puma 134
punaise d'eau géante 101
punaise rayée 101
punaises 534
pupille 132, 177
pupille verticale 112
pupitre 436, 444, 451
pupitre à musique 436
pupitre d'éclairage 490
pupitre de commande 626
pupitre de commandes 10
pupitre de contrôle 586
pupitre de son 488, 489, 490
pupitre dirigeur 507
pupitre du chef d'orchestre 437
purgeur 259
purificateur d'air 261
puzzle 917
pygostyle 116
pyjama 364
pylône 540, 583, 629, 663
pylône du moteur 625
pyramidal 154
pyramide 402, 705
pyranomètre 58
Pyrénées 32
python 114

Q

Qatar 746
quad 577
quadrant 704
quadrilatère 705
quadruple croche 435
quai 583, 593, 596, 708
quai d'embarquement 619
quai de chargement 713
quai de déchargement 395, 715, 719, 724
quai de gare 582
quais de déchargement 716
quantité de matière, mesure 702
quark d 680
quark u 680
quart de finale : 8 joueurs 789
quart de soupir 435
quart-arrière 807
quart-de-rond 253
quarte 434, 849
Quaternaire 93
quatre avec barreur 839
quatre sans barreur 839
quatre-mâts barque 602
quatuor 438
quechua 469
queue 81, 82, 83, 112, 113, 121, 122, 124, 130, 133, 136, 140, 143, 169, 306, 425, 625, 676, 840, 893, 894, 898, 905
queue de billard 863
queue de l'hélix 173
queue de poussières 8
queue ionique 8

INDEX FRANÇAIS

1036

ASTRONOMIE > 2-25; TERRE > 26-71; RÈGNE VÉGÉTAL >72-89; RÈGNE ANIMAL > 90-143; ÊTRE HUMAIN > 144-177; ALIMENTATION ET CUISINE > 178-241; MAISON > 242-295; BRICOLAGE ET JARDINAGE > 296-333; VÊTEMENTS > 334-371; PARURE ET OBJETS PERSONNELS > 372-391; ARTS ET ARCHITECTURE > 392-465; COMMUNICATIONS ET BUREAUTIQUE > 466-535; TRANSPORT ET MACHINERIE > 536-643; ÉNERGIES > 644-677; SCIENCE > 678-705; SOCIÉTÉ > 706-785; SPORTS ET JEUX > 786-920

queue-de-cochon 401
queusot 274, 275
quillard 835
quille 865, 897
quille chandelle 865
quille-reine 865
quilles, exemples 865
quilleur 865
quilleuse 865
quillier 865
quinoa 203
quinte 203
quinte 434, 849, 914, 919
quinte royale 914
quintette 438

R

rabat 348, 387, 535, 906
rabatteur 642, 643
rabot 309
raccord 269, 485
raccord à collet repoussé 269
raccord à compression 269, 270
raccord d'arrivée d'air 320
raccord de réduction 269
raccord de robinet 328
raccord de signalisation 567
raccord de tuyau 329
raccord femelle 269
raccord mâle 269
raccord té 271
raccord té d'égout 271
raccord union 269
raccordement du flexible 649
raccords 269
raccords mécaniques 269
races de chats 132
races de chiens 130
rachis 115
racine 78, 159
racine antérieure 168
racine carrée 529
racine carrée de 703
racine de l'hélix 173
racine de l'ongle 172
racine du nez 175
racine motrice 167, 168
racine pivotante 87
racine postérieure 168
racine principale 77
racine secondaire 77
racine sensitive 167, 168
racine traçante 87
racines adventives 76
raclette 211
raclette-gril 239
racloir 892
racquetball 818
radar 40, 604, 605, 608, 609
radar aéroporté 40
radar d'appontage 761
radar de contrôle aérien 761
radar de détection 762
radar de surveillance aérienne 761, 762
radar de veille de surface 761, 762
radar météorologique 54, 624
radeau de sauvetage 611
radiateur 259, 552, 561, 586
radiateur à colonnes 259
radiateur bain d'huile 260
radiateur rayonnant 260
radiateur soufflant 260
radiateurs 21
radicelle 77, 87
radicule 77
radier 595, 597
radio 504, 771, 898
radio portable 503
radio-réveil 503
radioactivité, mesure 702
radiocassette laser 504
radiomètre 60
radiomètre imageur 60
radiomètre sondeur 60
radiosonde 59
radiotélescope 16
radis 189
radis noir 189
radis oriental 189
radium 682
radius 111, 116, 121, 122, 126, 131, 136, 138, 140, 141, 142, 152, 154, 156
radôme 760
radon 684
radula 104
raffinerie 654, 709
raffinerie, produits 656
raglan 355
raie 218
raie des fesses 147, 149
raie sourcilière 115
raifort 189
rail 284, 456, 591
rail circulaire 16
rail d'éclairage 287

rail de glissement 555, 835
rail de guidage 16, 399, 571
rail de lancement de missile 760
rail de raccord 590
rail et retour de courant 595
rail guide-film 476
rail, profil 591
rail-guide de contrepoids 417
rail-guide de la cabine 417
rails de travelling 428
rainette 111
rainure 229, 453, 456, 750, 868, 888
rainure du guide à onglet 305
rainure du guide de refend 305
raisin 86, 192
raisin, coupe 83
ralenti 495
rallonge 278, 289
rallonge du plateau 305
ramasseur 642, 820
ramasseuse-presse 642
rambarde 894
ramboutan 197
rame 851
rame de métro 592, 594
rameau 77, 86, 87, 89
rameau communicant 168
ramequin 226
rameur 851
ramille 87
rampant 403
rampe 250, 251, 255, 403, 407, 431, 647
rampe d'accès 540, 608
rampe d'accès pour fauteuils roulants 394
rampe d'éclairage 287
rampe de quai 596
rampe de signalisation 766, 771
rampe, bicross 871
rampe, planche à roulettes 894
ramure 87
rang 384
rangée 431
rangement 584
rangement pour les gants 780
Ranvier, nœud 168
râpe 230, 309, 401
râpe à fromage cylindrique 230
râpe à muscade 230
rapière 751
rappel de mémoire 479, 529
rapporteur d'angle 713
raquette algonquine 893
raquette de badminton 816
raquette de racquetball 818
raquette de squash 819
raquette de tennis 822
raquette de tennis de table 815
raquette elliptique 893
raquette parabolique 16, 489
raquettes 893
ras-de-cou 354, 359, 374
ras-el-hanout 199
rasage 383
rasette 444
rasoir à double tranchant 383
rasoir à manche 383
rasoir effileur 381
rasoir électrique 383
rasoir jetable 383
rat 123
rat de cave 422
rat, morphologie 122
rat, squelette 122
rate 109, 110, 113, 125, 161
râteau 327, 423, 642, 863
ratissoire 326
raton laveur 134
ravier 226
ravioli 206
ravitaillement en vol 760
ravitailleur 760, 873
rayon 103, 391, 579, 704
rayon de miel 100
rayon de miel, coupe 100
rayon épineux 108
rayon lumineux 691
rayon médullaire 87
rayon mou 108
rayon solaire réfléchi 674
rayonnement 681
rayonnement artificiel 41
rayonnement du ciel, mesure 58
rayonnement infrarouge 68, 690
rayonnement naturel 41
rayonnement solaire 67, 68, 672, 673, 674, 675
rayonnement solaire absorbé 68
rayonnement solaire réfléchi 68
rayonnement ultraviolet 690
rayons gamma 690
rayons X 690
ré 434

réacteur 665, 666, 669, 763
réacteur à eau bouillante 671
réacteur à eau lourde 670
réacteur à eau sous pression 671
réacteur au gaz carbonique 670
réacteur nucléaire 667
réaction en chaîne 681
réaction réversible 684
réalisateur 429, 489, 490
rebobinage 476, 495, 499, 504, 508
rebord 290
rebord de cuve 292
rebras 346
récamier 276
réceptacle 75, 80, 83
réceptacle à déchets 573
réceptacle de brosses 384
réceptacle pour les pièces refusées 920
réceptacle séminal 97, 103
récepteur 16, 506
récepteur de son 776
récepteur sensoriel 168
récepteurs du goût 176
réception 509, 724
réception des données 41
réception des messages 508
réception directe 486
réception du fret 621
recette 650
receveur 794, 795, 796, 817, 819, 820
receveur éloigné 807
recharge 470
recharge amont 660
recharge aval 660
réchaud 234
réchaud à deux feux 903
réchaud à un feu 903
réchauffement global 68
réchauffeur 668
recherche 525
recherche des canaux 495
Récif de la Grande Barrière 29
récipient 59, 236
récipient collecteur 59
reconcentration de l'oxyde de deutérium 669
recourbe-cils 378
rectangle 705
rectangle des instructeurs 794
rectangulaire 904
rectrice 115
rectum 97, 99, 113, 116, 125, 164, 169, 170
récupération 812
recyclage 71
redingote 355
réduction mâle-femelle 269
réduction mâle-femelle hexagonale 269
réduction/agrandissement 512
réfectoire 727
réflecteur 316, 482, 493, 571
réflecteur parabolique 16, 489
réflecteur parabolique orientable 16
réflecteur radar 615
réflecteur secondaire 16
réflecteurs solaires 486
réflexion 41
Réforme 736
réformeur catalytique 656
refouloir 752
réfrigérateur 224, 291, 720, 722
réfrigérateurs 720
refroidissement 656
refroidissement de la vapeur par l'eau 665
refroidisseur d'air 564
refroidisseur de la salle des générateurs de vapeur 669
regard 259
regard de visite 712
régie 431, 488
régie de production 489, 490, 491
régie du son 489, 490
régie image 489
régie image/éclairage 490
régie technique 718
régie, radio 488
régies, télévision 490
région auriculaire 115
région malaire 115
région négative 672
région positive 672
régions de balisage 616
registre coulissant 445
registre de comptabilité 535
registre de réglage 258
registre des aigus 432
registre des basses 432
réglage 782
réglage de centrage 518
réglage de hausse 692
réglage de l'afficheur 506
réglage de l'angle 309
réglage de l'écran de l'ordinateur 20
réglage de la balance 441
réglage de la hauteur 826, 851
réglage de la luminosité 518
réglage de la pression 384
réglage de la pression d'oxygène 20
réglage de la résistance 851
réglage de la température 261
réglage de la tension 910
réglage de la tonalité 441

réglage de la vitesse d'obturation 479
réglage de largeur de point 452
réglage de niveau d'enregistrement 499
réglage de pression 452
réglage de profondeur 308
réglage de tempo 451
réglage des températures 288
réglage du contraste 518
réglage du diaphragme 693
réglage du four 290
réglage du pas 700
réglage du pointeau du fluide 320
réglage du seuil d'alarme 613
réglage du volume 441, 451, 495, 497, 503, 504, 505, 513
réglage du volume des communications 20
réglage en hauteur 483, 485
réglage en hauteur du condenseur 693
réglage horizontal 518
réglage latéral 692
réglage micrométrique (azimut) 14, 15
réglage micrométrique (latitude) 14, 15
réglage sur demi-teinte 479
réglage sur haute lumière 479
réglage sur ombre 479
réglage vertical 518
Règle 10
règle 399, 424, 700
règle d'équerrage 424
règle de couture 454
règle du guide de refend 305
règle graduée 700, 905
règle-point 452
réglette 461
règne animal 92
règne végétal 74
régulateur 267
régulateur de carburant 627
régulateur de pression 234, 319, 903
régulateur de vitesse 333, 417, 556
rehausseur 281
rein 104, 105, 106, 109, 110, 112, 116, 125, 161
rein droit 165
rein gauche 165
reine 99
reine, abeille 99
reins 124, 147, 149
rejet 87
rejet d'oxygène 78
rejets industriels 69, 70
relais d'accessoires 627
relevé de transaction 731
relève-bras 500
relèvement de la lame 305
releveur de fil 452
relief lunaire 7
religion 736
religions, chronologie 736
reliure à anneaux plastiques 533
reliure à glissière 532
reliure à pince 532
reliure à ressort 532
reliure à vis 532
reliure d'art 424
reliure spirale 533
rembourrage 899
rémige primaire 115
rémige secondaire 115
rémige tertiaire 115
remise 244, 823
remise à zéro 512
remontoir 436, 696, 697
remorque 570, 594, 641, 642, 840
remorque à bagages 623
remorqueur 606
rempart 7, 408, 409
remplage 411
remplissage 655
renard 134
rêne 856
rêne de bride 854
rêne de filet 854
renfort de culasse 753
renfort de nuque 874
renfort de pointe 880
réniforme 79
renne 128
renseignements 725, 886
rentré 455
renversé 828
renvoi 262, 271
renvoi d'eau 485
repassage 347
repasser à basse température 347
repasser à haute température 347
repasser à moyenne température 347
repère de distance 856
repère de ligne de marche 907
repère de niveau d'eau 288
repère de touche 440, 441
repère de virage de dos 831
répertoire 524
répertoire téléphonique 506, 531
répéteur 487
repli 336

répondeur téléphonique 508
report de lecture 479
repose-bras 500
repose-main 516
repose-pied 783
repose-pied du passager 575, 576
repose-pied du pilote 575, 576
repose-pieds 281, 871
repose-poignets détachable 514
repositionnement 528
repousse-chair 377
reprise 519
reprise d'air 258
reprise vidéo 789
reproduction de clés 715
reprographie 730
reptation 47
reptiles 112
République arabe syrienne 746
République centrafricaine 745
République de Corée 747
République de Moldova 744
République démocratique du Congo 745
République démocratique populaire lao 747
République dominicaine 743
République populaire démocratique de Corée 747
République tchèque 744
République-Unie de Tanzanie 745
répulsion 687
requin, morphologie 108
réseau d'oléoducs 654
réseau de transport d'électricité 674
réseau en anneau 522
réseau en bus 522
réseau en étoile 522
réseau étendu 523
réseau informatique 523
réseau national 486
réseau nerveux 159
réseau privé 486
réseau public postal 474
réseau téléphonique 487
réseaux, exemples 522
réserve 394
réserve d'eau 384
réserve de papier 512
réserves alimentaires 724
réservoir 23, 241, 261, 263, 320, 391, 445, 485, 657, 658, 660, 661, 767, 903
réservoir à carburant 570, 586, 631, 758, 760
réservoir à essence 553, 563, 574, 577
réservoir à grain 643
réservoir à toit fixe 655
réservoir à toit flottant 655
réservoir auxiliaire 571
réservoir d'air comprimé 586
réservoir d'air comprimé 873
réservoir d'alcool 695
réservoir d'arrosage 665, 669
réservoir d'azote liquide 694
réservoir d'eau 261
réservoir d'eau 241
réservoir d'essence 331
réservoir d'huile 331
réservoir d'hydrogène liquide 24, 25
réservoir d'oxygène liquide 24, 25
réservoir de brut 656
réservoir de carburant de chauffage 563
réservoir de chasse d'eau 264
réservoir de kérosène 25
réservoir de liquide de frein 559
réservoir de mercure 695
réservoir de propergol 18
réservoir de sécurité 670
réservoir de stockage 675
réservoir externe 22
réservoir magmatique 44, 646
réservoir propane 567
réservoir tampon 654
réservoir ventral 631
réservoirs 655
résidente 780
résidus non recyclables 71
résistance électrique, mesure 702
résistance hydraulique 851
résistances 689
résonateur 502
responsable de la sécurité 837
responsable du décompte des tours 883
responsable du démarreur 873
ressort 43, 249, 268, 286, 310, 470, 757, 823, 913
ressort athlétique 850
ressort compensateur de fil 453
ressort d'échappement 443
ressort de batterie 752
ressort de rappel 559
ressort de soupape 445, 566
ressort de suspension 292, 586
ressort de tension 557, 850
ressort en spirale 285
ressort hélicoïdal 553
ressuscitateur 775

restaurant 608, 710, 713, 714, 719, 720, 725
restaurant libre-service 722
restaurants-minute 715
résurgence 47
retable 737
rétenteur 857
Réticule 10
réticule 692
réticulum endoplasmique 74, 94
rétine 177, 691
retour 511, 515
retour de chariot 528
retour de courant 595
retour de l'eau au générateur de vapeur 665
retourné 828
retrait 528
rétroprojecteur 535
rétroviseur 556, 569, 570, 574, 576, 577, 876
rétroviseur extérieur 550, 568
rétroviseur grand angle 568, 569
réunion 703
réverbère 712
revers 342, 348, 350, 362
revers à cran aigu 348
revers cranté 352
revêtement 252, 253, 655, 815
revêtement de sécurité 20
revêtement intérieur 561
revêtement synthétique 822
revêtement thermique 22
revêtement, matériaux 299
revêtements de sol textiles 254
revitalisant capillaire 379
revolver 754
rez-de-chaussée 250
Rhéa 5
rhénium 683
rhino-pharynx 175
rhinocéros 129
rhizoïde 75
rhizome 76
rhodium 683
rhodyménie palmé 183
rhubarbe 185
rias 51
ribosome 74, 94
richelieu 342
ricotta 210
rideau 282, 492
rideau ballon 283
rideau bonne femme 282
rideau brise-bise 282
rideau coulissé 283
rideau d'obturateur 476, 477
rideau de fer 430
rideau de scène 430, 431
rideau de vitrage 282
rideau flottant 283
rideau séparateur 780
rideaux croisés 283
rideaux, exemples 283
ridoir 835
rifleur 401
rigatoni 206
rigole 864
rillettes 216
rimaye 46
rinceau 276
ring 842
ris 212
risberme 660
rive 300, 664
rive externe 127
rive interne 127
rivet 229, 310
rivière 38, 48
rivière souterraine 47
riz 85, 203, 207
riz : épi 85
riz basmati 207
riz blanc 207
riz complet 207
riz étuvé 207
riz sauvage 203
rizière 69
robe 655
robe à crinoline 337
robe à paniers 337
robe à tournure 337
robe bain-de-soleil 356
robe chemisier 356
robe de maison 356
robe enveloppe 356
robe fourreau 356
robe princesse 356
robe taille basse 356
robe tee-shirt 369
robe trapèze 356
robe tunique 356
robe-manteau 356
robe-polo 356
Roberval, balance 698
robes, exemples 356
robinet 264, 268

robinet d'acétylène 319
robinet d'arrêt 265, 270, 271
robinet d'arrêt général 262
robinet d'oxygène 319
robinet de réglage de débit 765
robinet de vidange 266, 267, 655
robinet flotteur à clapet 265
robinet relais 903
robinets 290
robinets de carburant 626
robot boulanger 239
robot de cuisine 237
roc 43
rocaille 322
rocher 900
roche mère 78
roches d'intrusion 42
roches ignées 42
roches métamorphiques 42
roches sédimentaires 42
rochet 307, 696, 697
rognons 212
Roi 914, 916
romaine 186
romano 211
romarin 202
rond pronateur 150
rond-point 39
ronde 435
rondeau 464
rondelle 268, 689, 888
rondelle à denture extérieure 310
rondelle à denture intérieure 310
rondelle à ressort 310
rondelle conique 265
rondelle de fibre 269
rondelle plate 310
rondelles 310
rondiste 374
rongeur 122
rongeur, mâchoire 123
roquefort 211
roquette 187
rorqual 137
ros 460
rosace 440
rose 80, 411
rose des vents 37, 612
rosée 65
rosette 248, 405
rossignol 118
rôti 214, 215
rôti de côtes 214
rotini 206
rotodôme 629
rotonde 713
rotor 249, 565, 659, 676
rotor à griffes 688
rotor anticouple 631
rotule 122, 126, 131, 138, 152, 312
roue 320, 323, 560, 570, 659, 753, 758, 783, 870, 874, 895
roue à aubes 599
roue à rayons 857
roue arrière 333
roue arrière pleine 871
roue avant 333, 639, 640
roue d'échappement 696, 697
roue d'engrenage 307, 462
roue d'entraînement 462
roue de centre 696, 697
roue de champ 696
roue de jauge 333
roue de poulie 284
roue de pression 643
roue de secours 567
roue de sécurité 595
roue de support 876
roue de turbine 664
roue dentée 460, 686, 876
roue folle 636
roue Francis 659
roue Kaplan 659
roue libre 580
roue motrice 640, 697
roue Pelton 659
roue petite moyenne 696, 697
roue pivotante 783
roues 659
roues motrices 639
rouge 400, 690, 919
rouge à lèvres 378
rouge orangé 400
rouge violet 400
rouge-gorge 118
Rouges 915
rouget barbet 219
rouleau 285, 320, 333, 380, 423, 920
rouleau à pâtisserie 232
rouleau à vernir 422
rouleau conditionneur 642
rouleau d'encrage 421
rouleau de pellicule 481
rouleau principal 460
rouleaux de la Torah 738
roulement à billes 677

roulette 281, 289, 389, 422, 448, 454, 633, 894
roulette américaine 919
roulette de commande 527
roulette de défilement 506, 516
roulette de pâtissier 232
roulette française 919
roulis 630
roumain 469
Roumanie 744
roupie 728
roussette noire 141
route 39, 539, 708
route d'accès 618
route secondaire 39
route, coupe 538
routeur 524
routeurs 523
Royaume-Uni de Grande-Bretagne et d'Irlande du Nord 743
ruban 313, 453, 757, 823
ruban adhésif 800
ruban blanc 815, 817
ruban correcteur 534
ruban de bouclage 771
ruban de caoutchouc 867
ruban de Téflon 314
ruban de tissu adhésif 777
rubidium 682
rubis 375, 696
ruche 100, 182
ruché 368
rue 39, 711, 713
rue commerçante 710
rue, coupe 712
ruelle 711
Ruffini, corpuscule 172
rugby 804
rugbyman 805
ruisseau 48
ruissellement 67
russe 469
russule verdoyante 183
rutabaga 189
ruthénium 683
rutherfordium 683
Rwanda 745
rythme des marques de nuit 617

S

sable 660, 741, 813
sablier 231
sablière 586
sablière double 252
sabot 124, 127, 312, 571, 791, 800, 840
sabot à deux doigts 127
sabot à quatre doigts 127
sabot à trois doigts 127
sabot à un doigt 127
sabot de protection 636
sabot, face plantaire 127
sabots, exemples 127
sabre 751, 849
sabreur 848
sac 432
sac à bandoulière 388
sac à dos 901, 906
sac à provisions 388
sac accordéon 388
sac besace 388
sac boîte 388
sac cartable 387
sac de congélation 222
sac de golf 869
sac de sable 842
sac de vol 388
sac fourre-tout 388
sac gonflable 556
sac marin 388
sac polochon 388
sac pour accessoires 859
sac seau 387
sac-filet 222
sachet 222
sacoche 577, 580
sacristie 737
sacrum 138, 141, 152, 153, 157
sacs à main 387
sacs à provisions 181
sacs de couchage, exemples 904
safran 198, 606
sagari 847
Sagittaire 10
saharienne 359
saillant 409
saindoux 209
saint-bernard 131
Saint-Kitts-et-Nevis 743
Saint-Laurent 30
Saint-Marin 744
Saint-Pierre 736
saint-pierre 221
Saint-Vincent-et-les Grenadines 743
Sainte-Lucie 743

saisie des données 694
saisons 917
saisons, cycle 54
salades 722
saladier 226
salamandre 111
salami allemand 216
salami de Gênes 216
salchow 881
salière 226
salle 431
salle à manger 250, 584, 608, 720, 723, 724, 763, 764
salle commune 727
salle d'anesthésie 780
salle d'arts plastiques 734
salle d'atelier 718
salle d'attente 509, 768, 779
salle d'attente des familles 778
salle d'attente des visiteurs 726
salle d'attente du centre de prélèvements 781
salle d'attente principale 781
salle d'attente secondaire 781
salle d'embarquement 621
salle d'entreposage 720, 722
salle d'examen 781
salle d'examen audiométrique 781
salle d'examen et de soins 779
salle d'examen gynécologique 779
salle d'exposition 719
salle d'habillage 428
salle d'informatique 734
salle d'interrogatoire 768
salle d'opération 780, 781
salle d'ophtalmologie et d'oto-rhino-laryngologie 779
salle de bains 251, 264, 724, 780
salle de bal 609
salle de classe 727, 734, 735
salle de classe pour élèves en difficultés d'apprentissage 734
salle de commande 657, 669
salle de conférences 509, 718, 730
salle de contrôle 10
salle de contrôle des machines 606
salle de courrier 509
salle de lecture 732
salle de mise en détention 769
salle de musique 734
salle de plâtre 779
salle de prélèvements 781
salle de préparation chirurgicale 780
salle de prière 738
salle de projection 10, 395, 427
salle de quilles 714
salle de rangement du matériel médical 781
salle de réanimation 778
salle de réception 738
salle de rédaction des rapports 768
salle de référence 733
salle de repos des infirmières 781
salle de reprographie 509
salle de réunion 394, 724, 730, 735, 764
salle de réveil 780
salle de sciences 734
salle de séjour 250
salle de soins 781
salle de spectacle 430, 710
salle de stérilisation 780, 781
salle de stockage du combustible neuf 666
salle de stockage du matériel souillé 778, 780
salle de stockage du matériel stérile 778
salle de tir 769
salle de triage 779
salle de visionnement 733
salle des cartes 604
salle des congrès 718
salle des enseignants 735
salle des gradateurs 490
salle des jurés 728
salle des machines 608, 657, 658
salle des microfilms 732
salle des ordinateurs 763
salle des pas perdus 582
salle des périodiques 733
salle du treuil 649
salle polyvalente 490, 727
salles d'entrevue 728
salles d'expositions permanentes 395
salles d'expositions temporaires 395
salles de réunion 718
salomé 343
salon 250, 608
salon d'attente 724
salon d'honneur 718
salon de coiffure 714
salon des employés 731
salon du personnel 768, 779
salopette 358
salopette à bretelles croisées 369
salopette à dos montant 368
salsifis 189
samarium 684
sambal oelek 201

Samoa 747
samoan 469
sandale 343, 748
sandalette 344
Sandow® 902, 903
sandre 220
sang désoxygéné 162
sang oxygéné 162
sang, composition 162
sangle 555, 765, 821, 824, 851, 855, 856, 869, 899, 900
sangle d'amortissement 772
sangle de brancard 857
sangle de compression 906
sangle de fermeture 906
sangle de nuque 772
sangle élastique 389
sangle serre-vêtements 389
sangle sous-cutale 611
sangle sous-ventrière 855, 857
sanglier 128
sanglon 855
sanguine 423
santé 775
São Tomé-et-Príncipe 745
sapeur-pompier 765
saphir 375
sapin 89
sapotille 197
sarcloir 326
sardine 219
sarment 86
sarrasin 85, 203
sarrasin : grappe 85
sariette 202
sas 416, 597
sas d'accès arrière 763
sas du bâtiment du réacteur 668
sas du laboratoire 23
sas pour équipement 666
sas pressurisé 543
sash 846
satellite 24, 486
satellite à défilement 60
satellite artificiel 53
satellite de télécommunications 525
satellite géostationnaire 60
satellite météorologique 54
satellite Radarsat 40
satellites 4
satellites de télécommunications 486
satellites météorologiques 60
satin 463
Saturn V 24
Saturne 4, 5
sauce aux prunes 201
sauce hoisin 200
sauce soja 200
sauce Tabasco® 200
sauce Worcestershire 200
saucière 226
saucisse de Francfort 216
saucisse de Toulouse 216
saucisson kielbasa 216
sauge 202
saule pleureur 88
saumon d'aile 898
saumon de l'Atlantique 221
saumon du Pacifique 221
saupoudreuse 232
saut à la perche 790, 792
saut à ski 891
saut d'obstacle 852
saut en hauteur 791, 792
saut en longueur 790, 793
saut périlleux avant avec tire-bouchon 829
sauterelle 646, 647
sauteur 891, 896
sauteuse 235
sautoir 374
sautoir, longueur opéra 374
sauts 792
sauts multiples 875
sauts, exemples 881
savane 61, 66
savon de toilette 379
saxhorn 447
saxophone 446
scandium 683
scanneur 517
scanneur à hyperfréquences 60
scanneur de radiations terrestres 60
scaphandre spatial 20
scaphoïde 154, 155, 156
scapulaire 115
scellement, matériau 689
scène 402, 430, 431
schéma de la circulation 161
schéma du principe du tissage 463
schisme d'Orient 736
schnauzer 130
Schwann, gaine 168
scie à chantourner 303
scie à greocer 424
scie à guichet 303

scie à métaux 303, 314
scie à onglet électrique 304
scie à onglet manuelle 303
scie circulaire 304
scie d'élagage 330
scie de camping 907
scie égoïne 303
scie sauteuse 305
scion 909
scissure oblique 163
sclérotique 177
scooter 577
scooter de mer 876
score 789
score doublé 918
score triplé 918
Scorpion 10
scorpion 102
scorsonère 189
scotie 404, 405
scripte 429
scrotum 146, 169
sculpture 395, 401, 640
sculpture sur bois 401
sculpture sur bois, étapes 401
sculptures 560, 561
seaborgium 683
seau 295
seau isotherme 240
sébaste 221
sébile de remboursement 507
sécateur 330
séchage 347
sèche-cheveux 382
sèche-linge électrique 293
sécher à plat 347
sécher par culbutage à basse température 347
sécher par culbutage à moyenne température 347
séchoir à tuyaux 764
séchoir d'épreuves 485
second arbitre 812, 813
second assistant cadreur 428
second renfort 753
seconde 434, 702, 704, 849
secondeur extérieur droit 806
secondeur extérieur gauche 806
secondeur intérieur 806
seconds violons 437
secrétaire 279, 814
secrétaire de direction 509
secrétaire du président 509
secrétaires 827
secrétariat 731, 735
secteur 704
secteur des civières 778
secteur maintenance 489
section articulée 569
section de conduit 257
section de l'identité 768
section des monographies 732
section raffinerie 652
section tubulaire 652
sécurité 764
segment 559, 566
segment abdominal 97
segment de loin 385
segment de près 385
seiche 217
seigle 85, 203
seigle : épi 85
sein 146, 148, 171
séisme 43
seizième de soupir 435
séjour 902
sel 847
sel fin 201
sel marin 201
sélecteur 261
sélecteur d'entrée 497
sélecteur d'inclinaison de la lame 305
sélecteur de bandes 499
sélecteur de canaux 505
sélecteur de contrôle audio 491
sélecteur de contrôle vidéo 491
sélecteur de coupe 383
sélecteur de fonctions 476
sélecteur de hauteur 289
sélecteur de micro 441
sélecteur de mise au point 496
sélecteur de mode sonore 497
sélecteur de niveau d'eau 292
sélecteur de points 452
sélecteur de programme 450
sélecteur de régime 332
sélecteur de rythme 451
sélecteur de stations 498, 503, 504
sélecteur de température 238, 292, 293, 382
sélecteur de vitesse 236, 237, 305, 382, 500
sélecteur de vitesse de rotation 306
sélecteur de vitesses 575, 576, 577
sélecteur de voix 451
sélecteur quadridirectionnel 477

sélecteur télé/vidéo 495
sélecteur vidéo auxiliaire 491
sélecteurs de fonctions 506
sélecteurs de mode 504
sélection des canaux 495
sélénium 682
selle 577, 578, 826, 851, 853, 855, 856, 858, 876
selle biplace 575
selle conducteur 577
selle de rail 590
selle passager 577
sellette 401, 857, 897
sellette d'attelage 570
sémaphore 583
semelle 252, 253, 288, 304, 305, 309, 345, 351, 840, 868, 881, 888, 889
semelle antidérapante 369
semelle d'usure 342, 371
semelle de chargeur 754
semelle du battant 460
semelle intercalaire 370
semelle pivotante 312
semence 301
semi-lunaire 154, 156
semi-métaux (métalloïdes) 682
semi-rectangulaire 904
semi-remorque 570, 571
semi-remorque à copeaux 572
semi-remorque à grumes 572
semi-remorque benne 572
semi-remorque bétaillère surbaissée 572
semi-remorque citerne 572
semi-remorque frigorifique 572
semi-remorque fourgon 572
semi-remorque plateau 571
semi-remorque porte-conteneur 572
semi-remorque porte-engins surbaissée 572
semi-remorque porte-véhicules 572
semoir à main 324
semoir en lignes 643
semoule 204
Sénégal 34, 745
senestre 740
sens de déplacement des électrons 687, 689
sensibilité du film 476, 479
sep 641
sépale 80, 82, 83
séparateur 562, 606, 646, 668, 689
séparateur d'eau 648
séparateur de gaz 652
séparateur électrolytique 689
séparateur liquide/gaz 562
séparation magnétique 71
séparation papier/carton 71
séparation-classeur 386
septième 434
septime 849
septum interventriculaire 162
septum lucidum 167
séquence 914
séquence de manipulation du combustible 666
séquenceur 450
sérac 46
serbo-croate 469
serfouette 326
sergé 463
seringue 776
seringue pour lavage de cavités 776
serpe 330
Serpent 11, 13
serpent 112
serpent à sonnette 114
serpent corail 114
serpent venimeux : tête, squelette 112
serpent venimeux, anatomie 112
serpent venimeux, morphologie 112
serpentin 290, 899
serpentin de l'évaporateur 261
serpentin du condenseur 261
serpette 330
serre 117, 182
serré 472
serre-joint 303, 312, 462
serre-joint à tuyau 312
serre-livres 535
serre-poignet 822
serre-tête 502, 504, 772, 773
serre-tête antibruit 772
serrure 247, 248, 278, 291, 387, 389, 554
serrure à clé 386
serrure à combinaison 386
serrure à mortaiser 249
serrure de porte 551
serrure tubulaire 248
sertissage 912
sertissure 376
serveur 522, 523, 524, 525, 721, 816, 819, 821
serveur d'accès 525
serveur de fichiers 523
service 812, 820
service à fondue 234
service à la clientèle 731
service d'entretien 548

service de colis 582
service de sécurité 719
services d'assurance 730
services de crédit 730
services financiers 730
services sociaux 781
services techniques 732
serviette 386
serviette de toilette 379
serviettes 722
servofrein 552, 559
servomoteur 759
seuil 247
seuil de déversoir 657
Sextant 11
sextant 612
sextuor 438
Seychelles 746
shampooing 379
shekel 728
shiitake 183
shinai 847
shintoïsme 736
short 358, 369, 791, 801, 802, 805, 810
short boxeur 371
short de boxe 842
si 434
siamois 133
siège 265, 268, 276, 277, 281, 333, 464, 555, 783, 839, 855, 857, 885, 898
siège coulissant 838, 851
siège de l'ambulancier 775
siège de sécurité pour enfant 558
siège double 594
siège du barreur 838
siège du commandant 626
siège du copilote 626
siège du rabbin 738
siège éjectable 760
siège réglable 584
siège simple 594
siège-baquet : vue de face 555
siège-baquet : vue de profil 555
sièges 277
Sierra Leone 745
sifflet 240
signal de position d'aiguille 590
signal lumineux 436
signal sonore 436
signalisation lumineuse 545, 547
signalisation maritime 614
signalisation routière 544
signature du titulaire 729
signature officielle 729
signes de ponctuation 473
signes diacritiques 473
silencieux 649
silex 752
silicium 682
silique, coupe 84
sill 44
sillet 439, 440, 441
sillon 176
sillon antérieur 173
sillon concentrique 500
sillon de départ 500
sillon de sortie 500
sillon médian 176
sillon naso-labial 175
sillon terminal 176
silo de chargement 648
silo-couloir 182
silo-tour 182
silos 596
Silurien 92
simulateur d'escalier 851
Singapour 747
sinople 741
sinus 336
sinus frontal 175
sinus latéral inférieur 86
sinus latéral supérieur 86
sinus pétiolaire 86
sinus sphénoïdal 175
siphon 262, 265, 269, 270
sirop antitussif 783
sirop d'érable 209
sirop de maïs 209
sismogramme 43
sismographe horizontal 43
sismographe vertical 43
sismographes 43
sistre 449
site d'enfouissement 69
site de saut 890
sixain 919
sixte 434, 849
skeleton 885
ski 876, 888
ski acrobatique 890
ski alpin 888
ski de descente/super-G 888
ski de figure 840
ski de fond 892
ski de grand slalom 888

ski de saut 891
ski de slalom 840, 888
ski de vitesse 891
ski nautique 840
skieur alpin 888
skieur de fond 892
skieur de vitesse 891
skiff 839
skimmer 246
skip 650
skis de saut 840
skis de tourisme 840
skis, exemples 840, 888
slalom géant 889
slalom spécial 889
slip 367
slip de bain 371
slip ouvert 351
slovaque 469
Slovaquie 744
slovène 469
Slovénie 744
smash 813, 821
smilodon 93
smog 69
snooker 863
soc 641
société 708
socle 43, 58, 236, 239, 240, 256, 273, 286, 307, 425, 500, 516, 517, 676, 685, 697, 698
socle fixe 312
socle rembourré 811
socle-chargeur 288
socque 344
socquette 365
sodium 682
softball 797
soie 227, 229, 309, 315, 383, 909
soies 320
soigneur 811, 842
soins de la pelouse 332
soins du corps 379
soja, germes 191
soja, graine 191
sol 70, 434, 661
sol naturel 538
solarium 607
sole 127, 221
soléaire 150
Soleil 4, 6, 7, 54
Soleil, éclipse 6
Soleil, structure 6
soleret 749
solide 680, 681
solide amorphe 680
solidification 680
solin 257
solive 254
solive de plafond 252
solive de plancher 252, 253
solive de rive 252, 253
solstice d'été 54
solstice d'hiver 54
solution multifonctions 384
Somalie 745
sommaire 471
sommation 703
sommelier 720
sommet 45, 886
sommier 413, 442, 445
sommier tapissier 280
sonar 41
sonar de coque 762
sondage en altitude 59
sonde 613
sonde spatiale 18, 53
sonde thermique 238
sondes spatiales, exemples 19
sondeur à éclats 613
sonnerie de passage à niveau 591
sonnette 112
sopranos 76
sorgho 85
sorgho : panicule 85
sortie 100, 539
sortie d'air chaud 256, 258, 564
sortie de l'eau chaude 259
sortie de l'eau de refroidissement du condenseur 669
sortie de la vapeur 670, 671
sortie de la vapeur des séparateurs 668
sortie de piste 621
sortie de piste à grande vitesse 618
sortie des billets 730
sortie des originaux 508
sortie des tickets 548
sortie du caloporteur 672
sortie du reflux du condenseur 669
sortie S-Video 526
soubassement 278, 412
souche 87
soudage : outils 318
soudage à l'arc 318
soudage oxyacétylénique 319

Soudan 745
soudure 318
soufflante 627, 670
soufflerie 445
soufflet 386, 388, 432, 445, 485
souffleuse 642
souffleuse de fourrage 643
soufre 683
soulier à la poulaine 339
soulier à talon 339
soupape 234, 445, 649
soupape à air 320
soupape à pression et dépression 655
soupape d'admission 564, 566, 899
soupape d'arrivée d'air 398
soupape d'échappement 564, 566
soupape d'évacuation 447, 777
soupape de gonflage 841
soupape de purge 841
soupape de réglage du fluide 320
soupape de sûreté 259, 266, 267, 665
soupape expiratoire 773
soupape inspiratoire 773
soupe 722
soupière 226
soupir 435
source 48
source alimentaire fondamentale 67
source d'énergie 41
source de courant 687
sourcils 132
sourdine 447
souris à roulette 516
souris mécanique 516
souris optique 516
souris sans fil 516
sous-couche 254
sous-épineux 151
sous-fondation 538
sous-gorge 854
sous-main 511
sous-marin nucléaire 763
sous-pied 358
sous-plancher 252, 253, 254
sous-sol 78, 250, 407, 713
sous-titre 471
sous-ventrière 853
sous-vêtements 872
sous-vêtements 351, 366
sous-vêtements d'hommes 716
soustraction 529, 703
soustraction en mémoire 529
soute 22
soute à bagages 568, 605, 631
soute à eau 586
soute d'équipement technique 489
soute des bobines de câbles 489
soutien informatique 509
soutien-gorge 367
soutien-gorge balconnet 367
soutien-gorge corbeille 367
sœur 785
spadice 81
spaghetti 206
spaghettini 206
spatule 233, 397, 421, 840, 887, 888, 892
spatulée 79
spécifications techniques 560
spectre électromagnétique 690
spectromètre 694
spectromètre à ultraviolet 60
spencer 358
spermathèque 104
spermatozoïde 169
spermiducte 104
sphaigne squarreuse 75
sphénoïde 158
sphère 705
sphère céleste 13
sphère d'hélium 25
sphère de verre 58
sphère terrestre 13
sphincter anal 164
spicule 6
spiral 696
spirale 103, 302, 484
spirale centrale 103
spiruline 183
spores 76
sports 788
sports à roulettes 894
sports aériens 896
sports aquatiques 827
sports d'hiver 877
sports de balle 794
sports de ballon 794
sports de combat 842
sports de force 850
sports de montagne 900
sports de précision 859
sports de raquette 815
sports équestres 852
sports gymniques 823
sports motorisés 872
sports nautiques 827

ASTRONOMIE > 2-25;   TERRE > 26-71;   RÈGNE VÉGÉTAL >72-89;   RÈGNE ANIMAL > 90-143;   ÊTRE HUMAIN > 144-177;   ALIMENTATION ET CUISINE > 178-241;   MAISON > 242-295;
BRICOLAGE ET JARDINAGE > 296-333;   VÊTEMENTS > 334-371;   PARURE ET OBJETS PERSONNELS > 372-391;   ARTS ET ARCHITECTURE > 392-465;   COMMUNICATIONS ET BUREAUTIQUE > 466-535;
TRANSPORT ET MACHINERIE > 536-643;   ÉNERGIES > 644-677;   SCIENCE > 678-705;   SOCIÉTÉ > 706-785;   SPORTS ET JEUX > 786-920

spot 287
spot à pince 286
squash 819
squelette 152
squelette de l'oiseau 116
squelette de la chauve-souris 141
squelette de la grenouille 111
squelette de la taupe 121
squelette du cheval 126
squelette du chien 131
squelette du dauphin 136
squelette du gorille 138
squelette du kangourou 142
squelette du rat 122
squelette du serpent venimeux : tête 112
Sri Lanka 747
stabilisateur 625, 631, 634, 638, 760, 766, 859, 876, 898
stabilisateur à triple plan vertical 629
stabilisateur de roulis 608
stabilo 896, 897
stade 709, 788, 790
stade d'hiver 788
stade de baseball 788
stade nautique 788
stalactite 47
stalagmite 47
stalle de départ 856
stand d'exposition 719
stand de tir 788
stand de tir à l'arc 788
stands 872, 874
Stardust 19
statif 685
station d'accueil 527
station de métro 592, 710
station de pompage 654
station de pompage intermédiaire 654
station de pompage principale 654
station de ski 886
station locale 486
station météorologique 58
station météorologique d'aéronef 54
station météorologique océanique 54
station météorologique sur bouée 54
station météorologique, disposition des informations 55
station spatiale internationale 21
station terrestre 54
station terrestre de télécommunications 525
station-relais 486
station-relais à micro-ondes 524
station-service 548, 711
stationata 852
stationnement 713, 866
stator 249, 659
stators extérieurs 627
stators intérieurs 627
statue 737
steeple 790
steppe 61
sterne 118
sterno-cléido-mastoïdien 150
sternum 111, 116, 121, 122, 126, 131, 141, 142, 152
stéthoscope 776
stigmate 80, 84, 96, 97
stilton 211
stimulateur de gencives 384
stipule 79
stockage des missiles 762
stockage numérique 481
stola 336
stop 130
stoppeur 803
store à enroulement automatique 285, 558
store à enroulement manuel 285
store bateau 285
store vénitien 285
stores 285
strato-cumulus 56, 62
stratopause 53
stratosphère 53
stratus 56, 62
stroboscope 611
stromatolite 92
strontium 682
structure 249, 538
structure anti-tonneau 873
structure artificielle d'escalade 900
structure d'un arbre 87
structure d'un champignon 76
structure d'un lichen 74
structure d'un missile 759
structure d'un os long 154
structure d'une algue 75
structure d'une feuille 79
structure d'une fleur 80
structure d'une fougère 76
structure d'une maison 250
structure d'une mousse 75
structure d'une plante 77
structure de l'oreille 174
structure de la moelle épinière 167
structure de la Terre 42

structure de lancement multiple 24
structure du Soleil 6
structure du support 40
structure du tissu 455
structure en treillis 21
structure métallique 582
structure tubulaire 615
studio 488
studio, radio 488
style 80, 81, 82, 83, 84, 696
styles d'architecture 404
stylet 470, 517, 527, 751
stylo-bille 470
stylo-plume 470
stylobate 403, 404
subarctique 61
subduction 43
sublimation 680
substance blanche 167, 168
substance corticale 165
substance grise 167, 168
substance médullaire 165
substratum imperméable 646
subtropical humide 61
sucre 209
sucre candi 209
sucre glace 209
sucre granulé 209
sucrier 226
Sud 37
sud 616, 917
Sud Est 37
Sud Ouest 37
Sud Sud-Est 37
Sud Sud-Ouest 37
sud-est 616
sud-ouest 616
Suède 744
suédois 469
Suisse 744
suiveur stellaire 18
sulky 857
sumac 199
sumo 847
sumotori 847
sunnisme 736
super-géant 889
supergéante 8
supermarché 180, 711, 715
supernova 8
superposition d'originaux 512
superstructure 615
supplément en couleurs 471
supplément littéraire 471
support 59, 234, 274, 284, 285, 381, 448, 461, 483, 632, 815
support à bagages 876
support à tuyau 764
support ajustable 511
support d'entrave 857
support d'extrémité 284
support de fixation 15, 284, 286
support de lisse 591
support de main 433
support de panneau 811
support de plafond 284
support de plaquette 385
support de pouce 446
support de sphère 58
support de tension 457
support du filament 274
support du rouleau 460
support mural 284
support pour bouteille d'oxygène 775
support-papier 528
supports 400
suppression 515
surbaissé 413
surcot 337
surf 840
surf acrobatique 887
surf alpin 887
surf des neiges 887
surface absorbante 675
surface centrale de lutte 843
surface d'affichage 535
surface de but 802, 814
surface de coin 803
surface de combat 844, 845
surface de cuisson 239, 290
surface de frappe 797
surface de jeu 815, 864
surface de l'eau 615, 828
surface de la glace 877
surface de la peau 172
surface de protection 843
surface de réparation 802
surface de résine 501
surface de sécurité 844
surface dure (ciment) 822
surface encrée 420
surface gravée 500
surface mouillée 420

surface pressée 501
surface réfléchissante 674
surface verticale 894
surfaces 704
surfaces de jeu 822
surfeur 840, 887
surfusion 680
surhaussé 413
surimpression 476
Suriname 742
surliure 908
suroît 341
surpiqûre 342, 350, 368, 370
surtitre 471
survêtement 370
suspendre pour sécher 347
suspendre pour sécher sans essorer 347
suspension 286, 594
suspension arrière 870
suspente 540
suspentes 896, 897
suspentes de nacelle 899
suture 84
suture coronale 158
suture lambdoïde 158
suture squameuse 158
swahili 468
Swaziland 746
symbole 682, 920
symboles d'entretien des tissus 347
symboles d'usage courant 725
symboles de chimie 684
symboles de sécurité 774
symboles divers 473
symboles météorologiques internationaux 56
symboles scientifiques usuels 702
symboles, cartes 914
symboles, protection 774
symphyse pubienne 169, 170
synagogue 738
synapse 168
synsacrum 116
synthèse additive 690
synthèse des couleurs 690
synthèse soustractive 690
synthétiseur 450
syntoniseur 498
système à deux poulies 686
système audio 556
système d'alimentation en essence 553
système d'échappement 553
système de balisage maritime 616
système de chronométrage électronique 883
système de climatisation 68, 489
système de contrôle de la barre de signalisation 771
système de direction 553
système de fixation 649
système de freinage 553
système de freinage antiblocage 559
système de jeux vidéo 918
système de lentilles 692
système de lubrification 586
système de pointage fin 17
système de refroidissement 553
système de remplissage et de vidange 597
système de retenue à sacs gonflables 556
système de suspension 553
système de transmission 553
système de verrouillage 289
système électrique 553
système filtre 390
système hydraulique 632
système international d'unités 702
système nerveux 166
système nerveux central 167
système nerveux périphérique 166
système racinaire 77, 86
système radar 760
système rotary 651
système routier 538
système solaire 4
systèmes automobiles 553

T

T central 858
T.G.V. 585
tabac 390
tabernacle 737
Table 10
table 278, 304, 374, 421, 423, 424, 723, 815, 862, 891
table à abattants 278
table à dessin 399
table à langer 281
table à rallonges 278
table chaude 721
table d'alimentation 643
table d'harmonie 439, 440, 442
table d'imprimante 511
table d'opération 780
table d'ordinateur 511
table de chevet 724, 780
table de communion 737

table de cuisson 224
table de lecture 738
table de lit 780
table de production 491
table de rotation 651
table de roulement 590
table de roulette 919
table de service 720
table de travail 290
table des greffiers 728
table des résultats 828
table du sommier 445
table pour la vaisselle propre 721
table pour la vaisselle sale 721
tableau 395, 734
tableau américain des mises 919
tableau d'affichage 535, 734, 822, 844, 846
tableau d'affichage des expositions 394
tableau d'affichage des vols 621
tableau de bord 556, 574, 576
tableau de classement général 824
tableau de commande 238, 239, 261, 290, 292, 293, 294, 512
tableau de commandes 694
tableau de manœuvre 417
tableau de pointage 825
tableau de tournoi 789
tableau des handicaps 858
tableau des scores 918
tableau du souvenir 738
tableau français des mises 919
tableau horaire 582
tableau indicateur 789, 790, 831, 839, 856
tableau marqueur 865
tableau périodique des éléments 682
tables gigognes 278
tables, exemples 278
tablette 256, 279, 321
tablette de verre 291
tablette graphique 517
tablette porte-outil 321
tablinum 406
tabloïd 471
tablier 540, 577, 632, 643, 842
tablier-blouse 359
tabouret 224, 277, 722, 842
tabouret de bar 720
tabouret-bar 277
tabouret-escabeau 321
tabulateur 528
tabulateur décimal 528
tabulation à droite 514
tabulation à gauche 514
tache 6
tache jaune 177
tachymètre 576
Tadjikistan 746
tagalog 469
tagliatelle aux épinards 206
tahini 200
tahitien 469
taie d'oreiller 280
taillant 648
taille 147, 149
taille baguette 375
taille brillant 375
taille cabochon 375
taille d'un diamant 374
taille des pierres 375
taille émeraude 375
taille en ciseaux 375
taille en escalier 375
taille en goutte 375
taille en poire 375
taille en rose 375
taille en table 375
taille française 375
taille huit facettes 375
taille marquise 375
taille ovale 375
taille-bordures 332
taille-crayon 534
taille-haies 331
tailleur 355
tailleurs 716
tajine 234
talkie-walkie 505, 770
Talmud 736
taloche 315
talon 127, 147, 149, 229, 303, 309, 342, 351, 370, 385, 390, 439, 440, 453, 456, 560, 641, 797, 816, 822, 863, 868, 880, 881, 887, 888, 892, 909, 910
talon d'appui 236, 288
talonnette de dessus 342
talonneur 804
talonnière 840, 889, 892
talus 538
talus continental 49
tam-tam 448
tamarillo 196
tamarin 139
tambour 230, 285, 293, 404, 459, 559, 612, 697, 700, 909, 910

tambour d'aisselle 433
tambour d'entraînement 476
tambour de basque 449
tambourin 341
tamia 123
tamis 231, 816, 822, 893
tamis à farine 232
tamis vibrant 651
tampon 422
tampon encreur 531
tandem 359, 581
tangage 630
tantale 683
tante maternelle 785
tante paternelle 785
taon 101
tapis 254, 842, 844, 862, 864
tapis amont 660
tapis antidérapant 893
tapis de plancher 558
tapis de réception 824
tapis de selle 853, 856
tapis de sol cousu 902, 903
tapis de souris 516
tapis drainant 660
tapis roulant 620
taquet 834, 835
taquet coinceur 835
taquet d'amarrage 597
taquet de verrouillage 521
tare 847
tarière motorisée 323
tarlatane 422
taro 184
tarse 96, 98, 111, 115, 122, 126, 131, 138, 141, 142, 155, 156
tarso-métatarse 116
Tasmanie 29
tasse 905, 906
tasse à café 226
tasse à mesurer 231
tasse à thé 226
tassergal 220
tassette 749
tatami 845
taupe 121
taupe, morphologie 121
taupe, squelette 121
Taureau 12
Tchad 745
tchèque 469
té 269, 867
té de base 257
technétium 683
technicien aiguilleur 489, 490
technique de saut 891
technique du lancer 864
techniques 812
tectrice primaire 115
tectrice sous-caudale 115
tectrice sus-alaire 115
tectrice sus-caudale 115
teddy 366
tégument 85
tégument de la graine 81
téléavertisseur numérique 505
télécabine 886
télécommande 483, 493, 495
télécommunications par satellite 487
télécopieur 508
télédétection 40
télédétection par satellite 41
télédiffusion par satellite 486
télémanipulateur 21, 22
téléobjectif 478
téléphone 724, 725
téléphone portable 506
téléphone public 427, 507, 715, 720, 723, 779
téléport 487
Télescope 10
télescope 15, 17
télescope spatial Hubble 17, 53
télescope, coupe 15
télésiège 886
téléski biplace 886
télésouffleur 492
téléviseur 494, 724, 734
téléviseur grand écran 493
télévision 489
tellure 682
telson 107
témoin 790
témoin d'alimentation 518
témoin d'ouverture de porte 557
témoin de bas niveau de carburant 557
témoin de ceinture de sécurité 557
témoin de charge 557
témoin de clignotants 557, 576
témoin de l'amorce du film 476
témoin de niveau d'huile 557
témoin de phare 576
témoin de position neutre 576
témoin de pression d'huile 557
témoin des feux de route 557
témoin du retardateur 476

témoin lumineux 767
tempe 146
température 261
température ambiante 261
température Celsius, mesure 702
température de l'air 55
température désirée 261
température du point de rosée 55
température thermodynamique, mesure 702
température, mesure 59, 695
tempête de sable ou de poussière 57
tempête tropicale 57
temple aztèque 412
temple de Huitzilopochtli 412
temple de Tlaloc 412
temple grec 403
temple grec, plan 403
templet 424, 461
temporal 152, 158
temps réalisé 831
temps, mesure 696, 702
tenaille 409
tendance barométrique 55
tendeur 826, 902
tendeur de timbre 448
tendon 133
tendu 901
tennis 344, 820
tennis de table 815
tenon 385, 390
tenseur du fascia lata 150
tensiomètre 777
tentacule 106
tentacule oculaire 104
tentacule tactile 104
tente 611
tente canadienne 903
tente deux places 902
tente dôme 903
tente familiale 902
tente grange 902
tente igloo 903
tente individuelle 903
tente intérieure 902, 903
tente rectangulaire 902
tente-caravane 567
tentes, exemples 902
tentoir 460
tenue d'exercice 369, 370
tenue d'intervention 764
terbium 684
térébenthine 400
termes familiers 82, 83
terminaison nerveuse 172
terminal à céréales 596
terminal à conteneurs 596, 708
terminal de paiement électronique 181, 731
terminal de télécommunication 507
terminal de vrac 596
terminal numérique 493
terminal pétrolier 596
terminateur 522
termite 101
terrain 794, 799, 801, 802, 804, 809, 810, 812, 813, 814, 816, 858, 864, 916
terrain de fondation 660
terrain de football 788
terrain de football américain 806
terrain de football canadien 809
terrain de golf 708, 788
terrain de hockey sur gazon 788
terrain de jeu 920
terrain naturel 647
terrasse 244, 322, 621
terrasse extérieure 609
terrassement 538
Terre 0, 4, 5, 6, 7, 28
terre battue 822
Terre de Baffin 31
Terre de Feu 31
Terre de la Reine-Maud 29
Terre de Wilkes 29
Terre Marie-Byrd 29
Terre, structure 42
terre-plein 409, 712
terre-plein central 539
terres rares 684
terril 647, 648
terrine 234
Tertiaire 93
tertre de départ 866, 867
Test FR 999
testicule 110, 169
testicules 107
têtard 111
tête 8, 96, 97, 99, 104, 115, 132, 140, 147, 149, 161, 169, 301, 302, 308, 311, 383, 384, 390, 391, 425, 439, 440, 441, 452, 457, 458, 516, 663, 757, 793, 800, 816, 822, 858, 863, 867, 893, 901, 909
tête à sens unique 302
tête amont 597
tête aval 597
tête avant du cylindre récupérateur 756
tête basculante 236

tête bombée 302
tête creuse 302
tête cruciforme 302
tête d'attelage 567, 586, 587, 640, 641, 642
tête d'impression 528
tête d'injection 651
tête de coupe 319, 535
tête de dormant 249
tête de frappe 301
tête de gondole 181
tête de l'humérus 153
tête de lecture 500
tête de lecture/écriture 521
tête de lit 280, 281
tête de marteau 901
tête de mât 836
tête de métal 793
tête de projection 535
tête de puits 649, 654
tête de ramassage 18
tête de rotor 631
tête de scion 909
tête diffusante 479
tête du fémur 153
tête du vérin de levage 632
tête en liège 817
tête flottante 383
tête froncée 283
tête panoramique 482
tête plate 302
tête plissée 283
tête ronde 302
tête, chauve-souris 140
tête, oiseau 115
tête, protection 772, 774
têtes, exemples 283, 302
Téthys 5
tétière 248, 249, 854
texte 528
thaï 468
Thaïlande 747
thalle 74, 75
thallium 682
thé 208
thé en sachet 208
thé noir 208
thé oolong 208
thé vert 208
théâtre 711
théâtre grec 402
théière 226
théodolite 59, 701
thermocontact 561
thermomètre 655, 695, 841, 899
thermomètre à maxima 59
thermomètre à mercure 777
thermomètre à mesure instantanée 231
thermomètre à minima 59
thermomètre à sucre 231
thermomètre à viande 231
thermomètre bimétallique 695
thermomètre de four 231
thermomètre médical 695
thermomètre numérique 777
thermomètres médicaux 777
thermopause 53
thermosphère 53
thermostat 238, 260, 261, 267, 291
thermostat d'ambiance 261
thermostat inférieur 266
thermostat programmable 261
thermostat réglable 239
thermostat supérieur 266
thon 220
thorax 96, 97, 98, 146, 148
thorium 684
thulium 684
thym 202
tibétain 468
tibia 96, 98, 111, 115, 122, 126, 131, 138, 140, 141, 142, 152, 155, 156
tibio-tarse 116
tierce 434, 849
tiercron 410
tige 75, 77, 78, 185, 241, 261, 268, 301, 302, 384, 390, 391, 436, 453, 456, 457, 461, 685, 695, 697, 881, 889, 892
tige carrée d'entraînement 651
tige de carbone (cathode) 689
tige de forage 651
tige de manœuvre 755
tige de pendule 436
tige de selle 578
tige du poil 172
tige filetée 311
tige pour col 376
tigre 135
tilde 473
tilleul 208
timbale 448
timbales 437
timbre 390, 749
timbre caoutchouc 531
timbre dateur 531

timbre-poste 474
timon 567, 642
timonerie 606
tipi 418
tique 102
tir à l'arc 859
tir à la carabine 861
tir au fusil 860
tir au pistolet 861
tirant 448, 634
tirant de registre 445
tirant de réglage 348
tirant des cordes 842
tire-bouchon 905
tire-bouchon à levier 230
tire-bouchon de sommelier 230
tire-bourre 752
tire-joint 315
tire-racine 325
tire-veille 836
tireur 860
tireur au but 809
tiroir 224, 278, 279, 281, 290
tiroir de fichier 533
tisanes 208
tisonnier 257
tissage 460
tissage, accessoires 462
tissage, schéma de principe 463
tissu adipeux 171, 172
tissu brodé 459
tissu conjonctif 172
tissu du vêtement 455
tissu, structure 455
tissus de soutien 455
Titan 5
Titan IV 24
titane 683
Titania 5
titre 471
titre de propriété 915
titre du journal 471
titres et horaires des films 427
toge 336
Togo 745
toile 285, 391, 400, 463, 483
toile d'araignée 103
toile de fond 430
toile de saut 823
toilettes 584
toilettes des officiers 764
toilettes des pompiers 764
toilettes femmes 427
toilettes hommes 427
toilettes pour dames 725
toilettes pour hommes 725
toit 100, 245, 257, 412, 567, 635
toit à deux croupes 414
toit à l'impériale 414
toit à la Mansard 414
toit à pignon 414
toit à quatre versants 415
toit à tourelle à pans 415
toit avec lanterneau 414
toit cathédrale 415
toit de la couche 647
toit de protection 632
toit en appentis 414
toit en carène 414
toit en coupole 415
toit en dôme 415
toit en flèche 415
toit en pavillon 415
toit en pente 414
toit en poivrière 415
toit en rotonde 415
toit en shed 414
toit flottant 655
toit imperméable 646
toit ouvrant 551
toit plat 414
toiture 100
tôle pare-gouttes 655
tomate 188
tomate en grappe 188
tomatille 188
tombant 362
tombolo 51
ton de mât 602
tondeuse 381, 383
tondeuse à moteur 332
tondeuse autoportée 333
tondeuse mécanique 332
tong 344
Tonga 747
topaze 375
topinambour 184
toque 341
torche 652
torchon 295
tore 404, 405, 705
tornade 57, 63
tornade marine 63
toron 908

torpille 763
torrent 45
torsade 306
tortellini 206
tortilla 205
tortue 113
tortue, anatomie 113
tortue, morphologie 113
total partiel 529
totalisateur journalier 557
Toucan 10
toucan 119
touche 432, 439, 441, 442, 443, 445, 813
touche alternative 514
touche d'affichage de titre 496
touche d'affichage des indicateurs 496
touche d'affichage des réglages 477
touche d'annulation 519
touche d'appel 505, 506
touche d'arrêt du défilement 515
touche d'échappement 514
touche d'effacement 515
touche d'effacement 477
touche d'éjection 918
touche d'enregistrement 496
touche d'impression de l'écran/d'appel système 515
touche d'index/agrandissement 477
touche d'insertion 515
touche de composition automatique 508
touche de confirmation 731
touche de contrôle 505, 514
touche de correction 456, 508
touche de courriel 514
touche de décimale 529
touche de défilement 505
touche de démarrage 514
touche de déplacement 261
touche de double zéro 529
touche de fin d'appel 506
touche de l'heure 496
touche de la date 496
touche de lecture 505
touche de luminosité 505
touche de menu 505
touche de modulation 497, 498
touche de pause/d'interruption 515
touche de pédalier 444
touche de préférence 261
touche de présélection 497, 498
touche de raccord d'enregistrement 496
touche de résultat 529
touche de retour 515
touche de saut d'images 477
touche de sélection 505, 506
touche de sélection d'entrée 497
touche de sélection des menus 477
touche de sélection du magnétophone 497
touche de sélection du mode FM 497
touche de suppression 515
touche de tabulation 514
touche de verrouillage 505
touche de verrouillage des majuscules 514
touche de verrouillage numérique 515
touche de visualisation des images 477
touche début 515
touche fin 515
touche fixe 700
touche fixe-majuscules 528
touche majuscule 514
touche mémoire 497, 498, 501
touche mobile 700
touche multifonctionnelle 529
touche numérique 529
touche page précédente 515
touche page suivante 515
touche plus-égalité 529
touche-majuscules 528
toucher 172
touches d'action 918
touches d'effets spéciaux 496
touches d'opérations 730, 731
touches de commande 507
touches de déplacement du curseur 515, 529
touches de fonction 514
touches de fonctions 507, 699
touches de fonctions programmables 731
touches de réglage de l'image 496
touches de répétition 501
touches de sélection des enceintes 497
touches de sélection des stations 497
touches de variation 456
touches directionnelles 918
touches Internet 514
toundra 61, 66
toupet 124
toupie 237
Tour 916
tour 410, 614, 634, 674, 676, 677, 858
tour à bureaux 713
tour à pied 464
tour d'angle 408
tour d'émission 486
tour d'extraction 649, 650
tour d'habitation 419

tour de contrôle 618, 761
tour de coquille 104
tour de cou 349
tour de flanquement 408
tour de forage 604, 651, 652, 654
tour de fractionnement 656
tour de guidage 542
tour de refroidissement 646
tour de sauvetage 25
tour de spire 105
tour de tête 772
tour du plongeoir 828
tour embryonnaire 105
tourelle 294, 408, 638, 762, 766
tourelle mobile 758
tourelle porte-objectifs 693
tourillon 753, 863
tourmaline 375
tournage 464
tournant de club-house 856
tournesol 80
tournette 464
tournevis 302, 905
tournevis à spirale 302
tournevis cruciforme 905
tournevis sans fil 302
tourniquet 919
tourniquet d'accès 592
tourniquet de sortie 592
tournure 337
traçage 401
traceur 520
traceur de route 613
trachée 116, 125, 163
traçoir 306
tracteur 570, 623, 637
tracteur à chenilles 636
tracteur agricole 640
tracteur agricole : vue arrière 640
tracteur agricole : vue avant 640
tracteur de piste 622
tracteur routier 570
tracteur-remorqueur 638
traction 630
tractus olfactif 175
tragus 140, 173
train 582
train à grande vitesse 585
train d'atterrissage avant 624, 760
train d'atterrissage principal 625, 760
train de banlieue 583
train routier 570
traîneau 329, 884, 885
traînée 620
traînée lumineuse 7
trait de mise au jeu 806
traitement chimique 656
traitement des données 41, 54
trame 455, 460, 461
trampoline 823
tramway 595
tranchant 227, 229, 382, 454
tranche 729
tranché 740
tranche de gouttière 426
tranche de queue 426
tranche de tête 426
tranchée 647
tranchefile 426
transactions financières 525
transbordeur 596, 608, 621, 623
transept 411
transfert de la chaleur 681
transformateur 259, 287, 658, 663, 668, 674
transformateur principal 585
transformation de l'eau en vapeur 665
transmission 292, 563
transmission de l'image 694
transmission de la chaleur à l'eau 665
transmission des données 41
transmission du mouvement au rotor 662
transmission funiculaire 590
transmission hertzienne 486
transmission par câble aérien 486
transmission par câble sous-marin 487
transmission par câble souterrain 487
transpalette manuelle 633
transpiration 67
transplantoir 325
transport 538
transport aérien 618
transport aérien du courrier 475
transport de l'électricité 663, 665
transport de l'électricité à haute tension 662
transport de l'électricité à haute tension 646, 677
transport de l'énergie à la tension de l'alternateur 662
transport ferroviaire 582
transport maritime 596, 649
transport par taxi 725
transport routier 538, 596
transport vers les usagers 646, 662, 677
transversale pleine 919
trapèze 150, 151, 154, 156, 705, 840, 897

trapèze de figure 840
trapèzes, exemples 840
trapézoïde 154
trappe 407, 430
trappe acoustique 490
travaux 545, 547
travée centrale 540
travée latérale 540
travée levante 542
travers 215
travers-banc 650
traverse 278, 409, 424, 433, 460, 461, 591, 663, 782
traverse arrière 893
traverse avant 893
traverse d'extrémité inférieure 635
traverse d'extrémité supérieure 635
traverse de chargement 607
traverse inférieure 247, 278
traverse intermédiaire 247
traverse médiane 277
traverse supérieure 247, 277, 278
traverse supérieure d'ouvrant 249
traversée 663
traversée de transformateur 657, 658
traversin 280
trèfle 411, 914
treillis 322, 502
treillis de protection 488
tréma 473
trémie 643
trémie de chargement 573
tremplin 246, 826, 891
tremplin de 1 m 828
tremplin de 3 m 828
tremplin pour sauts droits 890
tremplin pour sauts périlleux 890
tremplins 890
trench 352
trépan 651
trépied 14, 436, 448, 482, 483, 489
trépied de caméra 492
trépied de perche 492
trépointe 342
tréteau 278
treuil 417, 573
treuil d'amarrage 607
treuil de forage 651
treuil de levage 634
tri des métaux 71
tri du papier/carton 71
tri du plastique 71
tri du verre 71
tri manuel 71
tri optique 71
tri primaire 474
tri sélectif des déchets 71
Triangle 12
triangle 437, 449, 705, 863
Triangle austral 10
Trias 93
tribord 609, 616, 617
tribunal 728
tribune 471, 788, 874
tribune des entraineurs 891
tribune des juges 856, 890, 891
tribune du public 856
triceps brachial 151
tricératops 93
triclinium 406
tricorne 339
tricot 457
tricots 354
tricots d'hommes 717
tricots de femmes 716
tricycle d'enfant 581
trifoliée 79
triglyphe 404
trille 435
trilobé 413
trilobite 92
trimaran 835
tringle 561
tringle d'écartement 590
tringle de commande 590
tringle de pédale 442
tringle de tension 448
tringle double 284
tringle extensible 284
tringle métallique 533
tringle simple 284
tringle-barre 284
tringle-rail 284
tringles 284
Trinité-et-Tobago 743
trio 438
tripe 390
tripes 212
triple croche 435
triple saut 790, 793, 875
triple saut périlleux et demi avant groupé 829
triplure 455
tripode de stabilisation 623
trirème 598
triticale 203
Triton 5

triton 111
trochanter 96, 98
trois-portes 549
troisième but 794
troisième étage 25
troisième ligne 804
troisième phalange 126
troisième tour : 32 joueurs 789
troisième-but 794
trombe marine 63
trombone 447
trombones 437, 534
trompe 96, 611
trompe d'Eustache 174, 175
trompe de Fallope 170
trompe utérine, ampoule 171
trompes de Fallope 171
trompette 447
trompettes 437
tronc 76, 86, 87, 110, 147, 149
tronc cœliaque 161, 165
tronc, coupe transversale 87
tronçon 663
tronçon rigide arrière 569
tronçon rigide avant 569
tronçonneuse 331
trop-plein 262, 264, 265, 266, 267, 485
tropical humide 61
tropical humide et sec (savane) 61
tropique du Cancer 34, 35, 36
tropique du Capricorne 34, 35, 36
tropopause 53, 68
troposphère 53
trot 124
trotteur 343, 857
trotteuse 696
trottoir 245, 712
trou 423, 866, 867
trou central 500
trou d'homme 655
trou de conjugaison 157
trou de l'embout 390
trou de normale 3 866
trou de normale 4 866
trou de normale 5 867
trou noir 8
trou perforé 328
trou obturateur 122
trous 866
trousse de dépannage 580
trousse de fartage 892
trousse de manucure 377
trousse de secours 771, 777
trousse de toilette 388
troussequin 855
truelle de maçon 315
truelle de plâtrier 315
truffe 132, 183
truite 221
trumeau 411
truqueur numérique 491
tuba 437, 447, 841
tubage de production 652
tubage de production/expédition 652
tubage de surface 654
tube 14, 15, 223, 275, 381, 692, 753, 756, 757, 777
tube à éclairs 692
tube à essai 685
tube capillaire 695
tube conducteur 652
tube d'ajustement 824, 825
tube d'alimentation en air 765
tube d'aquarelle 397
tube d'arrivée 270
tube d'ensemencement 643
tube d'orientation des lames 285
tube de bord d'attaque 897
tube de circulation 672
tube de déchargement 643
tube de direction 579
tube de force 667
tube de gouache 397
tube de Pitot 873
tube de poussée 470
tube de remplissage de la cuvette 265
tube de remplissage du réservoir 265
tube de résonance 449
tube de selle 578, 871
tube droit 289
tube en Y 776
tube flexible 776
tube fluorescent 275
tube horizontal 578
tube lance-torpilles 763
tube oblique 579
tube porte-oculaire 14, 693
tube transversal 897
tube-image 494
tubes de Malpighi 97, 99
tubulure d'admission 565, 566
tubulure d'échappement 565
Tudor 413
tuile 22, 299, 403, 406, 412
tuiles de bonification 917
tuiles ordinaires 917
tulipe 80, 241

tungstène 683
tunique 78, 359, 748
Tunisie 745
tunnel 592
tunnel de communication 23
tunnel routier 543
turban 339, 341
turbine 646, 659, 668
turbine d'entraînement 564
turbine du compresseur 564, 627
turbine motrice 627
turbo-alternateur 674, 763
turboréacteur 625, 760
turboréacteur à double flux 627
turbot 221
turc 469
turf 856
turion 185
Turkménistan 746
Turquie 746
turquoise 375
tuteur 322, 324
Tuvalu 747
tuyau 312, 319, 390, 445, 767
tuyau à anche 444
tuyau à bouche 444
tuyau arrière 553
tuyau d'air 841
tuyau d'arrosage 328
tuyau d'aspiration 766
tuyau d'eau chaude 267
tuyau d'eau chaude 266
tuyau d'eau froide 267
tuyau d'eau froide 266
tuyau d'échappement 552, 553, 564, 636
tuyau d'ensilage 643
tuyau d'évacuation 271, 292
tuyau d'insufflation 432
tuyau de chute 262, 265, 271
tuyau de refoulement 767
tuyau de vidange 271, 292, 294
tuyau du ventilateur 643
tuyau flexible 289, 649
tuyau perforé 328
tuyau souple d'arrivée 271
tuyauterie 445
tuyauterie de sortie de la vapeur des séparateurs 669
tuyauterie de vapeur primaire 669
tuyère 22, 24, 25, 605, 631
tuyères à section variable 629
tuyère d'échappement 627
tuyère d'éjection 760
tuyère orientable 628
tympan 110, 403, 404, 411
type de carburant 548
type de la masse d'air 55
type de nuage bas 55
type de nuage élevé 55
type de nuage moyen 55
types d'articulations synoviales 156
types d'avirons 838
types d'éclipses 6, 7
types d'os 157
types de bâtons de golf 867
types de bouches 258
types de déplacements 916
types de missiles 759
types de moteurs 564
types de nages 832
types de voitures 584
typhon 63
typographie 472
tyrannosaure 93

U

Ukraine 744
ukrainien 469
Ulysses 19
Umbriel 5
un 703
une 471
unicellulaires 94
uniforme 770
uniformes 764
unisson 434
unité astronomique 4, 5
unité d'extraction par solvant 656
unité de sauvegarde 523
unité de soins ambulatoires 781
unité de soins intensifs 780
unité mobile d'entretien télécommandée 21
unité vidéo 520
unités monétaires, exemples 728
université 710
ununnilium 683
ununium 683
unununium 683
uranium 684
Uranus 4, 5
uretère 104, 116, 165
urètre 165, 170
urètre pénien 169
urgence ambulatoire 779

urgence majeure 778
urgences 778
uropode 107
urostyle 111
Uruguay 742
usager domestique 525
usine 664, 708
usine à asphalte 656
usine de traitement 649
usine des lubrifiants 656
usine marémotrice 664
usine marémotrice, coupe 664
usine pétrochimique 656
ustensiles de campeur 905
ustensiles de cuisine 229
ustensiles, jeu 233
utérus 170, 171
utilisations d'Internet 525
utiliser un chlorure décolorant suivant les indications 347

V

vache 128
vacuole 74, 94
vacuole contractile 94
vacuole digestive 94
vacuole digestive en formation 94
vagin 103, 104, 170, 171
vague 49
vague déferlante 49
vainqueur 789
vair 741
vaisseau capillaire 172
vaisseau sanguin 154, 162, 172
vaisseau sanguin dorsal 97
vaisseaux sanguins 140
vaisselle 226
vaisselle, verres et couverts 717
Valet 914
valet 693
valeur des notes 435
valeur des segments 918
valeur des silences 435
validation 528
valise fin de semaine 389
valise pullman 389
vallée 45, 48
valve 84, 105, 579
valve de réglage 259
valvule aortique 162
valvule mitrale 162
valvule pulmonaire 162
valvule tricuspide 162
vampire commun 141
vanadium 683
vanne 657, 658, 664
vanne d'arrêt de la turbine 668
vanne d'arrosage 669
vanne de production 654
vanne maîtresse 654
vanneau 118
vantail 278, 416
Vanuatu 747
vapeur 646, 681
vapeur à basse pression 668
vaporisateur 288, 329
vaporisateur de poivre 770
vaporisation 680
vaporiseur 261
varan 114
variomètre 899
variomètre électrique 898
variomètre mécanique 898
varlope 309
Varole, pont 167
vase d'expansion 259, 675
vaste externe du membre inférieur 150, 151
vaste interne du membre inférieur 150
vautour 119
veau 128
veau haché 214
vedette 762
végétation 66
végétation, distribution 66
véhicule de sauvetage 21
véhicule de secours 543
véhicule de service technique 622
véhicule spatial autonome 20
véhicule tout-terrain 549
véhicules d'incendie 766
veine axillaire 160
veine basilique 160
veine cave inférieure 160, 161, 162, 165
veine cave supérieure 160, 161, 162
veine céphalique 160
veine fémorale 160
veine iliaque 161
veine iliaque commune 165
veine jugulaire externe 160
veine jugulaire interne 160
veine mésentérique supérieure 160
veine porte 161
veine pulmonaire 160

veine pulmonaire droite 162
veine pulmonaire gauche 162
veine rénale 160, 165
veine saphène interne 160
veine sous-clavière 160
veine sus-hépatique 161
veines 160
velarium 407
vélo cross 581
vélo d'exercice 851
vélo de course et cycliste 870
vélo de cross-country et cycliste 870
vélo de descente et cycliste 870
vélo de montagne 870
vélo de poursuite et coureur 871
vélodrome 788
velours 254
vélum 98
Venera 19
Venezuela 742
vent 56, 69, 70, 833
vent arrière 833
vent de travers 833
vent debout 833
vent dominant 63
vent, mesure de la direction 59
vent, mesure de la vitesse 59
ventail 749
ventilateur 258, 259, 293, 497, 552, 561, 563, 566, 643
ventilateur de l'évaporateur 261
ventilateur de moteur diesel 586
ventilateur de plafond 261
ventilateur de sustentation 605
ventilateur des radiateurs 586
ventilateur du bloc d'alimentation 513
ventilateur du boîtier 513
ventilateur du condenseur 261
ventilateur hélicoïde 260
ventilateur principal 648
ventilation 675
ventilation de la cabine 898
ventouse 106, 111, 314
ventre 124, 146, 148
ventricule droit 161, 162
ventricule gauche 161, 162
ventricule succenturié 116
vents 917
venturi 757
Vénus 4, 5
véraison 86
verge 169, 610
verger 182
vergette 445
verglas 65
vergue 602
vérificateur de circuit 316
vérificateur de continuité 316
vérificateur de haute tension 316
vérificateur de prise de courant 316
vérificateur de tension 316
vérification de la profondeur de champ 476
vérin 573
vérin d'orientation de la lame 639
vérin de commande de volet 760
vérin de défonceuse 636
vérin de direction 638
vérin de dressage 634, 766
vérin de la flèche 637, 638
vérin de levage de la lame 636, 639
vérin du bras 637, 638
vérin du bras de levage 637
vérin du godet 637, 638
vérin du godet rétro 637
vérin hydraulique 567, 633, 640
vermicelles de riz 207
vernier 612, 698, 700
vernis 400
vernis à ongles 377
verre 385
verre à bordeaux 225
verre à bourgogne 225
verre à cocktail 225
verre à cognac 225
verre à eau 225
verre à gin 225
verre à liqueur 225
verre à mesurer 231
verre à porto 225
verre à vin blanc 225
verre à vin d'Alsace 225
verre à whisky 225
verre bifocal 385
verre de visée 477
verres 225, 723
verrière 250, 582, 628, 713, 760, 898
verrou 46, 452, 516
verrou d'onglet 303, 304
verrou de barre d'attelage 756
verrou de chargeur 754
verrou de sûreté 755
verrou tournant 572
verrouillage 288
verrouillage des majuscules 514
verrouillage numérique 515
versant 45

Verseau 10
verseuse 241
versoir 641
vert 400, 690, 866, 867
vert d'entraînement 866
vertèbre 112, 136
vertèbre cervicale (7) 153, 157
vertèbre dorsale (12) 153, 157
vertèbre lombaire 168
vertèbre lombaire (5) 153, 157
vertèbre sacrée 111
vertèbres 111
vertèbres cervicales 116, 122, 126, 131, 138, 141, 142
vertèbres coccygiennes 122, 126, 131, 138, 141, 142
vertèbres dorsales 122, 126, 131, 138, 142
vertèbres lombaires 122, 126, 131, 138, 141, 142
vertèbres sacrées 122, 126, 131, 142
verveine 208
vésicule biliaire 110, 112, 164
vésicule séminale 169
vessie 109, 110, 113, 165, 169, 170
vessie natatoire 109
veste 338, 355, 844, 848, 855
veste de pêche 911
veste droite 348
veste traditionnelle 846
vestes 358
vestiaire 250, 394, 509, 719, 723, 726, 731, 734, 764
vestiaire de bureau 510
vestiaire des clients 720
vestiaire des mineurs 649
vestiaire du personnel 584, 720, 768, 781
vestibule 174, 250, 406, 717, 724, 728, 730
veston croisé 348
veston et veste 348
vêtement d'exercice 371
vêtement ignifuge et hydrofuge 765
vêtement isothermique 841
vêtements 336
vêtements d'enfant 369
vêtements d'homme 348
vêtements de bain 716
vêtements de bébés 717
vêtements de femme 355
vêtements de filles de 2 à 6 ans 717
vêtements de filles de 7 à 17 ans 717
vêtements de garçons de 2 à 6 ans 717
vêtements de garçons de 7 à 17 ans 717
vêtements de nouveau-né 368
vêtements de nuit 364
vêtements de nuit d'hommes 717
vêtements de nuit de femmes 716
vêtements de sport d'enfants 717
vêtements de sport d'hommes 717
vêtements de sport de femmes 716
vêtements décontractés d'hommes 717
vêtements décontractés de femmes 716
vêtements traditionnels 339
vétérinaires 852
vexille 115
viaduc 541
viande 214
vibrisse 122
vice-capitaine 877
vide-poches 554
vide-pomme 233
vidéoprojecteur 518
vidéothèque 733
Vierge 11, 13
Viet Nam 747
vietnamien 468
vigie 618
vigne 86
Viking 18

vilebrequin 307, 564, 566
village 708, 886
ville 708
vin 180
vinaigre balsamique 201
vinaigre de cidre 201
vinaigre de malt 201
vinaigre de riz 201
vinaigre de vin 201
violet 400
violette 80
violon 439
violon, famille 437, 439
violoncelle 439
violoncelles 437
vipère 114
virage à 180 degrés 885
virage à droite 544, 547
virage de brasse 832
virage de papillon 832
virage-culbute 832
virgule 473
virole 320, 863
virole femelle 909, 910
virole mâle 909, 910
vis 302, 439
vis à glace 901
vis calante 699, 701
vis centrale 425
vis d'alimentation 642, 643
vis de blocage 700
vis de blocage (azimut) 14, 15
vis de blocage (latitude) 14, 15
vis de fixation 482
vis de nivellement 58
vis de pince-aiguille 453
vis de pression 421, 423
vis de réglage 310, 319
vis de réglage de grand débit 273
vis de réglage de petit débit 273
vis de réglage de tension 534
vis de réglage du condenseur 693
vis de serrage 312
vis de support inférieur 58
vis de tension 448
vis macrométrique 693
vis micrométrique 612, 693, 700
vis sans fin 462, 573
visage 146
viseur 476, 477, 701
viseur de caméra 492
viseur électronique 496
viseur périscopique 758
visière 340, 341, 575, 591, 749, 765, 772, 874, 878, 884
visière antisolaire 20
vision 691
vision normale 691
vision, défauts 691
vison 134
Vistule 32
visualisation du seuil d'alarme 613
vitrage 614
vitrail 411, 737
vitre 672, 673
vitre de protection 878
vitre protectrice 494
vitrine 279
voie 592, 595
voie à sens unique 544, 546
voie d'accélération 539
voie de banlieue 583
voie de butte 589
voie de circulation 539, 618
voie de circulation des locomotives 589
voie de décélération 539
voie de dépassement 539
voie de fond 650

voie de sortie 589
voie de tête 650
voie de transport 647
voie de tri primaire 589
voie de tri secondaire 589
voie des stands 872
voie ferrée 582, 590, 591, 649, 709, 710
voie ferrée bord à quai 596
Voie lactée 9, 13
voie latérale 539
voie pour véhicules lents 539
voies de circulation 539
voies respiratoires, protection 773
voilage 282
voile 560, 676, 833, 836, 896, 897, 909
voile à livarde 601
voile au tiers 601
voile aurique 601
voile bermudienne 601
voile carrée 601
voile d'étai de flèche 603
voile d'étai de grand perroquet arrière 603
voile d'étai de hune arrière 603
voile de flèche 603
voile du palais 174, 175
voile latine 601
Voiles 11
voiles, exemples 601
voilure 603, 628, 841, 897
voilure delta 629, 630
voilure droite 630
voilure en flèche 630
voilure trapézoïdale 630
voilures, exemples 630
voiture 594
voiture cellulaire 726
voiture de formule 1 873
voiture de formule 3000 873
voiture de formule Indy 873
voiture de police 769, 771
voiture de rallye 873
voiture micro-compacte 549
voiture sport 549
voiture suiveuse 870
voiture-coach 584
voiture-lit 584
voiture-restaurant 584
voitures, types 584
voiturette de golf électrique 869
vol 829, 891
vol libre 897
volaille 213
volant 280, 282, 333, 425, 452, 464, 552, 556, 566, 607, 640, 873
volant d'inertie 851
volant de frein à main 587
volant de manche 626
volant de manœuvre 766
volant de plumes 817
volant synthétique 817
volcan 42, 44
volcan effusif 44
volcan en éruption 44
volcan explosif 44
volcans, exemples 44
volée 255, 753, 820
volet 23, 521, 675
volet compensateur 60
volet d'air 571
volet de bord d'attaque 760
volet de bord de fuite 624, 760
volet de contrôle thermique 60
volet mobile 17
volet transparent 386
volets d'intérieur 282
Volga 32
Volkmann, canaux 154
volleyball 812
volleyball de plage 813

vols, plongeon 828
volt 702
voltigeur de centre 794
voltigeur droit 794
voltigeur gauche 794
volumes 705
volute 276, 404, 405, 439
volve 76
voussure 411
voûte 410
voûte de projection 10
voûte du palais 174, 175
voûte en berceau 407
Voyager 19
voyant cartouche d'impression 519
voyant chargement du papier 519
voyant conique 615, 616
voyant d'alarme/de mise en charge 527
voyant d'alimentation 519
voyant de charge 383
voyant de mise en circuit 506, 508
voyant de mise en ondes 488
voyant de mise sous tension/détection du papier 731
voyant de réception de messages 508
voyant de réponse automatique 508
voyant lumineux 238, 239, 240, 241, 288, 290, 294, 381, 465
voyants 515
voyants d'entrée 497
voyants d'indication du mode sonore 497
voyants de contrôle 501, 519, 520
vraquier 604
vrille 86
vue 177
vue de face 798
vue de profil 798
vue, protection 774
vulve 148, 171
vumètres 488
vumètres audio 491

W

w.-c. 250, 251, 262, 264, 265, 395, 715, 719, 720, 723, 724, 728, 731, 733, 735, 779, 780, 781
w.-c. du personnel 768
w.-c. femmes 509, 724
w.-c. hommes 509, 724
wagon 583, 587
wagon à bestiaux 588
wagon à copeaux 588
wagon couvert 587, 588
wagon de queue 588
wagon plat 588
wagon plat à parois de bout 588
wagon plat surbaissé 588
wagon porte-automobiles 588
wagon porte-conteneurs 588
wagon rail-route 588
wagon réfrigérant 588
wagon-citerne 588
wagon-tombereau 588
wagon-tombereau couvert 588
wagon-trémie 588
wagon-trémie à minerai 588
wagons, exemples 588
wakamé 183
wallaby 143
wasabi 201
water-polo 827
watt 702
webcaméra 517
wigwam 418
winch 835
wishbone 836
wok 234
wolof 468

X

xénon 684
xylophone 437, 449

Y

yacht à moteur 607
yack 129
yaourt 210
Yémen 746
yen 728
yeux, protection 772
yiddish 469
yoruba 468
Yougoslavie 744
yourte 418
ytterbium 684
yttrium 683

Z

Zambie 746
zèbre 128
zénith 10
zéro 919
zeste 82, 84
Zimbabwe 746
zinc 683
zirconium 683
zone centrale 809
zone commerciale 709
zone d'arrivée 891
zone d'attaque 812
zone d'atterrissage 891
zone d'avertissement 846
zone d'entrée des joueurs expulsés 827
zone d'essai des réacteurs 761
zone de basse pression 63
zone de boule morte 864
zone de but 806, 809, 879
zone de chargement 666
zone de chronométrage 891
zone de chute 790, 792, 793
zone de convection 6
zone de danger 844, 847
zone de défense 809, 812
zone de départ 838, 875
zone de freinage 891
zone de garde protégée 877
zone de haute pression 63
zone de lavage des wagons 589
zone de manœuvre 10
zone de passage du témoin 790
zone de passivité 843
zone de précipitation 55
zone de radiation 6
zone de réception 589
zone de retrait des bagages 620
zone de sécurité 846
zone de service 818
zone de service droite 819
zone de service gauche 819
zone de triage 589
zone industrielle 709
zone libre 812, 813
zone neutre 806, 879
zone réservée 811
zone résidentielle 709
zone scolaire 545, 547
zones de service 817
zoom 492
zoulou 468

Indice español

2º hueso metacarpiano 140
3er hueso metacarpiano 140
4º hueso metacarpiano 140
5º hueso metacarpiano 140

A

a buen viento 833
a un largo 833
ábaco 404
abdomen 96, 97, 98, 103, 107, 115, 146, 148
abdomen, oblicuo mayor 150, 151
abdomen, recto 150
abedul 88
abeja 98
abeja trabajadora, morfología 98
abeja, anatomía 99
abejorro 101
abertura 911
abertura con tirilla 349
abertura de llenado 597
abertura de llenado y vaciado 597
abertura del diafragma 694
abertura para el brazo 355
abertura para el cambio de gases 694
abertura para horquilla 635
abertura trasera central 348
abertura trasera lateral 348
aberturas branquiales 108
aberturas para los nudillos 346
abeto 89
abisinio 133
abocinamiento 411
abono compuesto, cajón 323
Abraham 736
abrazadera 14, 15, 274, 284, 389, 835
abrazadera inferior 58
abrebotellas 230, 905
abrecartas 531
abrelatas 230, 240, 905
abreviaciones de monedas, ejemplos 728
abrigo 352, 355
abrigo con esclavina 355
abrigo de tres cuartos 352
abrigo raglán 355
abrigo redingote 355
abrigos 352, 355
abrigos de hombre 717
abrigos de mujer 716
ábside 411
absorción de agua y sales minerales 78
absorción de dióxido de carbono 78
absorción por el suelo 68
absorción por las nubes 68
abuela 784
abuelo 784
abuelos 784
acabado 401
acampada 902
acantilado 51
acantodio 92
acceso a los andenes 582
acceso al segundo nivel de operaciones 529
acceso para minusválidos 725
accesorios 289, 345, 399, 401, 454, 462, 558, 580, 859
accesorios de decoración 716
accesorios de disparo 752

accesorios de golf 866
accesorios de hombre 716
accesorios femeninos 717
accesorios fotográficos 482
accesorios musicales 436
accesorios para cerrar 453
accesorios para el objetivo 478
accesorios para la pipa 390
accesorios para las ventanas 282
accesorios personales 374
accesorios, cajetín 289
accesorios, objetivos 478
accidentales 435
acción del viento 67
accionador de presión del oxígeno 20
acedera 187
aceite de cacahuete 209
aceite de girasol 209
aceite de linaza 400
aceite de maíz 209
aceite de oliva 209
aceite de sésamo 209
aceitera 648
aceites 209
aceites lubricantes 656
aceituna 188
acelerador 331, 576
acelga 185
acento 435
acento agudo 473
acento circunflejo 473
acento grave 473
acera 245, 712
acerico 454
acero 298
achicoria de Treviso 186
acicular 79
acidificación de los lagos 70
ácido nítrico, emisión 70
ácido sulfúrico, emisión 70
acolchado 883
acolchado de seguridad 883
acometida aérea 663
acondicionado 379
acondicionador de aire 261
acondrito 8
acoplamiento de pedal 444
acoplamiento flexible 677
acorazonada 79
acorde 435
acordeón 432
acromion 153
acrotera 403, 404
actínidos 684
actino 684
actor 428
actores, entrada 402
actriz 429
actuador 759
acuarela 396
Acuario 10
acuífero confinado 646
acumulador 559, 673
adaptador 383, 485
adaptador de acoplamiento 21
adaptador de carga útil 24
adaptador de cinta de video compacto 496
adaptador de corriente 526
adaptador de enchufes 274
adaptadores, ejemplos 269

adarve 408, 409
adarve cubierto 408, 409
Adén, golfo 33, 34
adición en la memoria 529
administración 394, 735
admisión 564, 565
admisión de los detenidos, oficina 726
adobes, casa 418
adormidera, semillas 199
adornos 435
Adriático, mar 32
aduana 596, 621
aductor del muslo 150
aductor mayor 151
aerocisto 75
aerodeslizador (hovercraft) 605
aerofreno 760
aerógrafo 398
aerógrafo, sección transversal 398
aeropuerto 39, 618, 708
aerosol de pimienta 770
afeitado 383
afeitado, loción 383
Afganistán 746
afilador 229
afinación 448
afinador 444
afluente 48
África 28, 34, 50, 745
afuste 756
agar-agar 183
agarrador 783
agavilladora 642
agencia de viajes 714
agenda 387, 530
agenda de caja 535
agenda electrónica 530
agenda telefónica 506, 531
agente de policía 770
agitador de aspas 292
agnato 92
agricultura intensiva 68, 70
agu bendita, pila 737
agua 646, 847
agua a presión 662
agua a presión, reactor 671
agua caliente a presión, sistema 259
agua de alimentación 671
agua de colonia 379
agua de deshielo 46
agua de nubes 70
agua de perfume 379
agua hirviente, reactor 671
agua hirviente, refrigerante 671
agua natural 671
agua pesada 670
agua pesada a presión 670
agua pesada de refrigeración 670
agua pesada presurizada 670
agua pesada, reactor 670
agua presurizada, refrigerante 671
agua, castaña 184
agua, corriente 48, 95
agua, depósito 241
agua, sales minerales, absorción 78
aguacate 188
aguamarina 375
aguanieve 57, 64
aguarrás 400
aguas bravas 837

aguas bravas, kayak 837
aguas residuales 70
aguas seguras 616
aguaturma 184
aguijón 98
aguijón, saco 104
Águila 10, 12
águila 119, 741
aguja 52, 64, 398, 411, 452, 453, 454, 590, 695, 776
aguja circular 457
aguja con lengüeta 456
aguja de cambio 583
aguja de control a larga distancia 590
aguja de coser 233
aguja de décimas de segundo 696
aguja de punto 457
aguja del transepto 410
aguja imantada 907
aguja indicadora 261, 479
aguja picadora 233
agujas del abeto 89
agujas del pino 89
agujero 423
agujero apical 159
agujero ciego 176, 272
agujero intervertebral 157
agujero negro 8
agujero obturado 122
ahogadero 854
ahumador 422
aikido 846
aikidogi 846
aikidoka 846
airbag 556
airbag, sistema de restricción 556
aire 565
aire acondicionado 567
aire acondicionado de tierra 622
aire cálido ascendente 63
aire caliente 64, 675
aire caliente a presión, sistema 258
aire comprimido 398
aire comprimido, bombona 873
aire frío 64, 675
aire frío subsidente 63
aire libre, ocio 902
aislador 562, 663
aislador de suspensión 663
aislamiento 259
aislante 266, 267, 294, 672
aislante a granel 299
aislante de cera 265
aislante de gomaespuma 299
aislante plástico 272
aislante premoldeado 299
aislante vinílico 299
ajedrea 202
ajedrez 916
ajo 184
ajowán 199
ajustador de la bota 889
ajuste 528
ajuste de altura 851
ajuste de elevación 692
ajuste de la altura del condensador 693
ajuste de la lente de campo 693
ajuste de la llama 391
ajuste de la velocidad del obturador 479
ajuste de profundidad 308

ajuste de resistencia 851
ajuste de tonos agudos 441
ajuste de tonos bajos 441
ajuste de volumen 505
ajuste del display 506
ajuste del tabulador 528
ajuste fino de la altura 14, 15
ajuste fino del acimut 14, 15
ajuste lateral 692
ala 23, 97, 98, 115, 340, 341, 387, 625, 760, 897, 898, 909
ala alta 628
ala cerrado 807
ala de la nariz 132
ala de popa 609
ala defensivo derecho 806
ala defensivo izquierdo 806
ala del cuarto 342, 370
ala delantera 96
ala delta 629, 897
ala derecha 801, 804
ala en delta 630
ala en flecha 630
ala izquierda 801, 804
ala plegable 857
ala recta 630
ala superior 628
ala trapezoidal 630
ala trasera 96
ala variable 630
álabe 659
alamar 353
alambre del reborde 561
alambre para cortar 464
álamo 88
alargada 472
alarma sonora 613
alas 140, 628
alas, diferentes formas 630
alas, tarima 632
Alaska, golfo 30
albahaca 202
albanés 469
Albania 744
albañilería 315
albaricoque 192
albatros 119
albornoz 364
albúmina 117
albumina, gándula 104
albura 87
alcachofa 187
alcachofa de la ducha 264
alcantarilla 712
alcantarilla principal 712
alcaravea 198
alce 129
alcohol puro 777
aldabilla 389
alemán 469
Alemania 744
alerce 89
alero 403, 412, 809
alero defensa 809
alero derecho 811
alero izquierdo 811
alerón 23, 624, 840, 873, 891, 898
alerón de hipersustentación 760
aleta 260, 293, 625, 628, 631, 841
aleta abdominal 108

ASTRONOMÍA > 2-25; TIERRA > 26-71; REINO VEGETAL > 72-89; REINO ANIMAL > 90-143; SER HUMANO > 144-177; PRODUCTOS ALIMENTARIOS Y DE COCINA > 178-241; CASA > 242-295; BRICOLAJE Y JARDINERÍA > 296-333; VESTIDO > 334-371; ACCESORIOS Y ARTÍCULOS PERSONALES > 372-391; ARTE Y ARQUITECTURA > 392-465; COMUNICACIONES Y AUTOMATIZACIÓN DE OFICINA > 466-535; TRANSPORTE Y VEHÍCULOS > 536-643; ENERGÍA > 644-677; CIENCIA > 678-705; SOCIEDAD > 706-785; DEPORTES Y JUEGOS > 786-920

aleta anal 108
aleta caudal 108, 136
aleta compensadora 60
aleta de fuselaje 23
aleta de la nariz 175
aleta de penetración superficial 609
aleta de proa 609
aleta del borde de fuga 624
aleta dorsal 136
aleta dorsal anterior 109
aleta dorsal posterior 109
aleta estabilizador 840
aleta estabilizadora 608
aleta fija 759
aleta hipersustentadora 625
aleta pectoral 108, 136
aleta pélvica 108
Aleutianas, fosa 50
Aleutianas, islas 30
alfalfa 190
alféizar 249, 252
alfil 916
alfiler 380, 454
alfiler de corbata 376
alfileres 376
alfombra 254
alfombrilla 558
alfombrilla de ratón 516
alforfón 85
alga 75
alga parda 75
alga roja 75
alga verde 75
alga, estructura 75
algas 183
algas, ejemplos 75
algodón hidrófilo 777
alheña 202
alianza 376
alicates 310
alicates de electricista 317
alicates de presión 310
alicates de punta 317
alicates para cutículas 377
alicates pico de loro 310
alidada 59, 612
alidada móvil 701
aligátor 114
alimentación de agua 670, 671
alimentación, cordón 237, 381
alimentación, fuente 687
alimentador 493, 512
alimentador de oxígeno, palanca 898
alimentos para animales 181
alimentos selectos 180
alineador 838
alitán 218
aliviadero 657
aljuba 338
alma 444, 591, 753
almacén 716, 734, 769
almacén de combustible nuevo 666
almacén de congelados 181
almacén de material estéril 778
almacén de material sucio 778
almacén material sucio 780
almacenamiento de información, unidades 521
almacenamiento digital 481
almeja 217
almena 408
almendra 81, 193
almidón 85
almidón, glóbulo 74
almirez 230
almohada 280
almohadilla carpal 130
almohadilla del espolón 130
almohadilla digital 130, 133
almohadilla palmar 130
almohadilla plantar 133
alojamiento de disco 521
alojamiento de la casete 499
alojamiento de la cinta 496
alojamiento para el disco 501
alojamiento para la cinta 495
alojamientos 886
alpargata 344
Alpes 32
alpinista 901
alquequenje 192
alta presión, área 63
alta velocidad, tren 585
Altar 10
altar lateral 737
altar mayor 737
altar, cruz 737
altavoces extremos de graves 493
altavoz 427, 496, 502, 503, 504, 505, 508, 513, 526, 626, 766, 828
altavoz central 493
altavoz de agudos 10
altavoz de comunicación 594
altavoz de control 488
altavoz de frecuencias de graves 502
altavoz de frecuenciasde medias 502
altavoz de graves 10

altavoz de medios 10
altavoz defrecuencias altas 502
altavoz principal 493
altavoz surround 493
alternado: selección de nivel 3 514
alternador 552, 566, 586, 677, 688
alternador de la turbina 674
alternador de turbina 763
alternativa 514
altímetro 761, 896, 898, 899
altímetro de emergencia 626
altitud 66
alto 546
alto de caña 889
alto voltaje 774
altocúmulo 56
altocúmulos 62
altostrato 56
altostratos 62
altramuz 190
altura 739
altura de la ola 49
altura de las nubes, medición 59
altura de salto 829
altura del agua 662
altura del banco 647
altura del peldaño 255
altura máxima 545, 547
alubias 191
álula 115
aluminio 682
alumno 734
alumno, pupitre 734
alveolo 274
alvéolo dental 159
alza 100, 439, 754, 755, 757, 859, 893, 912
alzada 362
alzado 250, 292
alzapaños 282
amanita virosa 76
amantillo 602
amantillo de botavara 602
amapola 80, 84
amaranto 203
amárico 468
amarillo 400, 690
amarillo verdoso 400
amarra 607, 858
amarre 458, 835
amarre anterior retráctil 567
amasadora 239
amatista 375
Amazonas, río 31
ambiente 66
ambiente natural 867
ambulancia 775, 778
ambulatorio 781
ameba 94
América Central 28, 30
América del Norte 28, 30, 50
América del Sur 28, 31, 50
American shorthair 132
americana 358
americano, clavija de tipo 274
Américas 742
americio 684
Amery, Plataforma de Hielo 29
ametralladora 758
amígdala 174
amígdala lingual 176
amígdala palatina 176
amoladora de ángulo 308
amortiguador 18, 417, 553, 575, 876
amortiguador de caucho 920
amortiguador de fieltro 442
amortiguador delantero 577
amperio 702
ampliación del voltaje 665
ampliadora 485
amplificador 450
amplificador /sintonizador : vista frontal 497
amplificador /sintonizador : vista posterior 497
amplificador de voltaje 662
amplificador-sintonizador 503
amplitud 690
ampolla 95, 274, 275, 783
ampolla de la trompa uterina 171
ampolla de vidrio 275
amurada 607
anacardo 193
anaquel 279, 291, 723
anatomía 150
anatomía de un árbol 87
anatomía de un bogavante 107
anatomía de un caballo 125
anatomía de un caracol 104
anatomía de un hongo 76
anatomía de un pájaro 116
anatomía de un pulpo 106
anatomía de una abeja 99
anatomía de una araña hembra 103
anatomía de una concha bivalva 105
anatomía de una esponja 95
anatomía de una estrella de mar 95
anatomía de una mariposa hembra 97

anatomía de una perca 109
anatomía de una planta 77
anatomía de una rana macho 110
anatomía de una serpiente venenosa 112
anatomía de una tortuga 113
ancha 472
ancho de barrido del radar 40
anchura de la base 663
ancla 610
ancla de arado 610
ancla de buque 610
ancla de cepo 610
ancla de hongo 610
ancla flotante 610
ancla sin cepo 610
anclaje 540
anclas, ejemplos 610
anclote 610
ancóneo 151
áncora 697
andador 782
andaduras 124
andamio sobre ruedas 321
andén 583, 593, 620
andén de pasajeros 582
Andes, cordillera 31
andouillete 216
Andrómeda 12
anémometro 58, 59, 677, 898
anemómetro de emergencia 626
anfibios 110
anfibios, ejemplos 111
anfiteatro romano 407
Anglicanismo : Enrique VIII 736
Angola 746
anguila 219
ángulo agudo 704
ángulo entrante 704
ángulo horario 17
ángulo obtuso 704
ángulo recto 704
ángulo saliente 409
ángulos, ejemplos 704
ángulos, medición 701
Anik 487
anilla 284, 696, 699, 824
anilla de la tuerca 269
anilla de sujeción 909
anilla del cordón 282
anilla guía 909
anilla para colgar 382
anilla para lanzado largo 910
anillas 824, 825
anillas para flexiones 851
anillo 76, 249, 284, 383, 390, 391, 447, 482, 522, 659, 901
anillo de ajuste 302, 320, 446
anillo de ajuste del enfoque 478
anillo de articulación 911
anillo de bloqueo 756
anillo de carrillera 854
anillo de cierre 483
anillo de compromiso 376
anillo de crecimiento 87
anillo de enfoque 692
anillo de graduación 376
anillo de gravedad 610
anillo de la leva 307
anillo de las riendas 854
anillo de quijada 854
anillo de reglaje del par de apriete 306
anillo de retención 263, 268
anillo de retención de la empaquetadura 268
anillo de unión del casco 20
anillo dióptrico 614
anillo distribuidor 659
anillo graduado de ascensión recta 14, 15
anillo graduado de declinación 15
anillo inferior 659
anillo ocular 115
anillo regulador 659
anillo sellador 655
anillo, partes 376
anillos 376
anillos colectores 688
anillos de sonido 433
anís 202
anís estrellado 84
anjova 220
ano 95, 97, 103, 104, 105, 106, 107, 109, 113, 164, 169, 170
año, estaciones 54
ánodo 266, 689
anorak 371, 901
anotador 810, 812, 813, 814, 819, 845, 860, 864, 920
anotadores 844, 846
Antártica 28, 29
Antártica, península 29
antebrazo 130, 147, 149, 860
antefija 403
antehélix 173
antena 17, 60, 96, 97, 98, 99, 107, 504, 505, 506, 551, 577, 611, 624, 631, 758, 761, 771, 832
antena de alta frecuencia, cable 628
antena de alta ganancia 18

antena de baja ganancia 18
antena de banda S 60
antena de banda S de alta ganancia 60
antena de banda X 40
antena de comunicaciones 761
antena de control remoto 40
antena de emisión 486
antena de emisión /recepción 486
antena de radar 760, 763
antena de radio 604, 606, 608, 609, 652, 763, 873
antena de telecomunicaciones 608, 609, 762
antena de telecontrol 60
antena de telemetría 60
antena del radar 40
antena doméstica 486
antena múltiple 763
antena parabólica 489, 493
antena parabólica de recepción 486
antena parabólica de transmisión 486
antena telescópica 503
antena UHF 18, 60
antena VHF 762
antena-receptor GPS 613
antenas de exploración y rescate 60
anténula 107
anteojera 857
anteojo buscador 14, 15
anteojo telescópico 612
antepista 865
antera 80
anticiclón 55
anticlinal 651
Antigua y Barbuda 743
Antillas 30
antílope 128
antimonio 682
antiséptico 777
antitrago 173
anudado 463
anulación de la memoria 529
anuncio 471
anuncios por palabras 471
anuncios, tablero 535
anzuelo 909, 911
aorta 162, 163
aorta abdominal 160, 165
aorta ascendente 161
aorta descendente 161
aorta dorsal 99
aorta ventral 109
aorta, cayado 160, 161, 162
aovada 79
apagador 443
apagallama 755
Apalaches, montes 30
aparador 279
aparador con vitrina 279
aparato de Golgi 74, 94
aparato de navegación aérea 761
aparato de respiración autónomo 765
aparato digestivo 164
aparato respiratorio 163
aparato urinario 165
aparatos 823
aparatos acondicionadores 261
aparatos de ejercicios 850
aparatos de medición 695
aparatos electrodomésticos 236, 288
aparcamiento 620, 713, 735, 866, 886
aparcamiento de bicicletas 735
aparejo 911
aparejo de juanete de estay 603
aparejo de mastelero de estay 603
aparejos 602
aparejos, ejemplos 601
apartado 720
apartamentos 886
apéndice nasal 140
apéndice vermiforme 164
apéndices bucales 98
apéndices torácicos 107
apertura terminal 105
apertura urogenital 109
ápice 104, 105, 159, 176
apilador hidráulico 633
apio 185
apio nabo 189
aplicador de esponja 378
aplicadores de algodón 777
aplique 287
apófisis espinosa 168
apófisis estiloides 158
apófisis mastoides 158
apófisis transversal 157
apófisis trasversa 168
Apollo 19
apóstrofe 473
apotecio 74
apoya-flecha 913
apoyador 806
apoyador exterior 806
apoyador interior 806
apoyatura 435
apoyo 661
apoyo de espalda 757

apoyo de la sordina 443
apoyo del macillo 442, 443
apoyo del pulgar 776
apoyo mejilla 860, 861
apoyo para el mentón 439
apoyo para el pie 892
apoyo, punto 103
apuesta de cinco números 919
apuesta en cuadro 919
apuesta libre 919
apuesta sobre dos columnas 919
apuntador electrónico 492
aquenio 83, 84
árabe 468
Arabia Saudí 746
Arabia, península 33
Arábigo, mar 33
arácnidos 96
arácnidos, ejemplos 102
aracnoides 167
arado de vertedera 641
Aral, mar 33
arame 183
arameo 468
araña 103, 287
araña cangrejo 102
araña de agua 102
araña hembra, anatomía 103
araña, morfología 103
araña, tela 103
arándano 192
arándano agrio 192
arándano negro 192
arándano rojo 192
arandela 268, 287, 290, 689, 888
arandela de presión 310
arandela de presión de dientes externos 310
arandela de presión de dientes internos 310
arandela plana 310
arandelas 310
árbitro 799, 801, 803, 805, 807, 810, 817, 818, 819, 830, 842, 843, 845, 846, 864, 877, 879, 882
árbitro a caballo 858
árbitro adjunto 882
árbitro auxiliar 814, 847, 860
árbitro de base meta 795
árbitro de la defensa 807
árbitro de lado 846
árbitro de recorrido 838
árbitro en jefe 846, 847
árbitro jefe 883
árbitro principal 814, 827, 837
árbol 87, 659, 686, 688
árbol de la hélice 609
árbol de levas 566
árbol de Navidad 652, 654
árbol de transmisión 553
árbol de transmisión longitudinal 553
árbol del turbocompresor 627
árbol frutal 182
árbol ornamental 182, 244, 322
árbol oscilante, brazo de elevación 640
árbol, anatomía 87
arboladura 602
árboles 866
árboles latifoliados, ejemplos 88
arborización terminal 168
arbotante 410, 411, 839
arbusto 182
arca 738
arcabuz 752
arcada 407, 410
arce 88
arce, jarabe 209
archaeognatha 92
archipiélago 38
archivador colgante 532
archivador de fichas 533
archivador de fuelle 533
archivador lateral 510
archivador móvil 510
archivador, gaveta 533
archivadores 510
archivar 532
archivo 509, 524, 769
archivo médico 781
archivo, formato 524
archivos 394
archivos, servidor 523
arcilla de modelar 464
arco 307, 439, 540, 704, 750
arco compuesto 913
arco de competición 859
arco de dos articulaciones 541
arco de elevación 756
arco de entramado 540
arco de medio punto 413
arco de tres articulaciones 541
arco dentario inferior 174
arco dentario superior 174
arco fijo 541
arco formero 410
arco insular 49
arco iris 65
arco moderno 750
arco natural 51

arco recto 859
arco tensor 448
arco, puente 540
arcón congelador 291
arcos y ballesta 750
arcos, ejemplos 541
ardilla 123
ardilla listada 123
área de actividades al cubierto 727
área de alta presión 63
área de aterrizaje 891
área de baja presión 63
área de caída 790, 793
área de cocina 722
área de competición 824, 847
área de control de la cámara 489
área de descanso 39
área de estacionamiento 708
área de gol 814
área de juego 877, 918
área de lixiviación 263
área de llegada 885, 891
área de lucha libre 843
área de mantenimiento 489
área de peligro 844
área de penalti 802
área de procesamiento del petróleo 652
área de recepción 395, 716
área de servicio 39, 818
área de servicio derecha 819
área de servicio izquierda 819
área grabada 501
área pequeña 802
áreas válidas de tocado 848
arena 407, 660, 813
arenera 586
arenque 219
aréola 171
arganeo 610
Argelia 745
Argentina 742
argolla de izar 610
argolla de remolque 756
argolla para tirar 776
argón 684
Ariane IV 24
Ariel 5
Aries 12
arista 404
armadura 435, 749, 902
armadura del techo 253
armario 224, 278, 724
armario alto 224
armario bajo 224, 510
armario de secado de negativos 484
armario del lavabo 264
armario para el personal 584
armario para la tabla espinal 775
armario para papelería 510
armas 748, 849
armas blancas 751
armas de la Edad de Piedra 748
armas del imperio romano 748
armazón 252, 256, 259, 278, 280, 287, 288, 292, 293, 308, 320, 321, 389, 449, 460, 676, 899
armazón de empuje 636
armazón de la máscara 796
armazón de madera 403
armazón de metal 442
armazón del quemador 903
Armenia 746
armeno 469
armiño 741
armónica 432
arnés 611, 896, 897, 900
arnés 896
arneses para trotones 857
aro 385, 459, 611, 809, 811, 823, 855
arpa 440
arpas 437
arpegio 435
arpón submarino 841
arqueópteris 93
arquero 859
arquitectura 394, 402
arquitrabe 403, 405
arquivoltas 411
arranque 327, 850
Arrecife, Gran Barrera 29
arrendajo 118
arriate 244, 322
arroyo 48
arroz 85, 203, 207
arroz : espiga 85
arroz basmati 207
arroz blanco 207
arroz integral 207
arroz silvestre 203
arroz vaporizado 207
arroz, fideos 207
arroz, galletas 207
arroz, vermicelli 207
arrozal 69
arsénico 682
arte 394
arteria arcuata 160

arteria axilar 160
arteria braquial 160
arteria carótida primitiva 160
arteria dorsal del pie 160
arteria dorsoabdominal 107
arteria esternal 107
arteria femoral 160
arteria ilíaca común 160, 165
arteria ilíaca interna 160, 161, 165
arteria mesentérica inferior 165
arteria mesentérica superior 160, 165
arteria pulmonar 160, 162, 163
arteria renal 160, 165
arteria subclavia 160
arteria tibial anterior 160
arteria ventral 107
artes escénicas 427
artes gráficas 420
Ártico 28
Ártico, océano Glacial 28
articulación 557, 863, 909
articulación artrodial 156
articulación condilar 156
articulación en bisagra 156
articulación en pivote 156
articulación en silla de montar 156
articulación esferoidea 156
articulación plana 156
articulaciones sinoviales, tipos 156
artículo 471
artículos de cocina 716
artículos de escritorio 528
artículos de fumador 390
artículos de limpieza 180, 295
artículos de marroquinería 386
artículos de tocador 717
artículos para animales 181
artículos personales 374, 383
artículos varios 534
artropleura 92
arzón 826, 855
arzón de amarre 897
as 914
as de guía 908
as de guía de eslinga doble 908
asa 236, 237, 238, 239, 240, 280, 289, 290, 295, 303, 304, 308, 313, 328, 386, 387, 388, 389, 504, 884, 910
asa aislante 239
asa de la barquilla 899
asa de levantamiento 756
asa extensible 386
asado 214
asado de cerdo 215
asadores 234
asafétida 199
ascensión recta 13
ascensor 16, 417, 509, 713, 724, 761
ascensor, cabina 417
asegurador 900
aseo 250, 719, 728, 731, 733
aseo de caballeros 509, 724
aseo de señoras 509, 724
aseo del personal 768
aseos 395, 584, 715, 723, 735, 779, 781
aseos de caballeros 427
aseos de los bomberos 764
aseos de los oficiales 764
aseos de señoras 427, 725
aseos para los clientes 720
aseoss de caballeros 725
asfalto 656
Asia 28, 33, 50, 746
asidero 554, 567, 570, 584, 766
asidero : (espalda) 830
asidero horizontal 587
asidero lateral 594
asidero vertical 594
asidero, espalda 830
asiento 264, 265, 276, 277, 281, 333, 464, 538, 555, 577, 775, 783, 839, 851, 857, 876, 885, 898
asiento : vista frontal 555
asiento : vista lateral 555
asiento ajustable 584
asiento de corredera 851
asiento de eyección 760
asiento de la válvula 268
asiento del auxiliar de ambulancia 775
asiento del capitán 626
asiento del comandante 758
asiento del copiloto 626
asiento del piloto 758
asiento del rabino 738
asiento del tapón 265
asiento del teclado 442
asiento del timonel 838
asiento doble 594
asiento individual 594
asiento trasero 555
asientos 277
asistente de presidente del jurado 881
asistente del guionista 490
asistentes de los abogados 728
asno 128
aspa 261, 676, 677
aspirador 289, 775

aspirador de aire 259
aspirador manual 288
aspiradora de fangos 573
aspirina 777
asta 739, 918
astada 79
Atacama, desierto 31
atacante 809
atacador 752
atención al cliente 731
aterrizaje 891
aterrizaje y despegue, pista 620
atizador 257
Atlántico medio, dorsal 50
Atlántico, océano 28, 29, 32, 34
atlas 111, 122, 126, 131, 153, 157
Atlas, cordillera 34
atleta : taco de salida 791
atleta de biathlón 893
atletismo 788, 790
atmósfera 66, 70
atmósfera terrestre, corte 53
atolón 51
átomo 680
átomos 680
atracción 687
atrecista 429
atril 436, 444, 451, 737
atrio 406
atún 220
audiencia 728
audio player portátil digital 503
audioguía 394
auditorio 394, 718, 732
aula 727, 735
aula de artes plásticas 734
aula de ciencias 734
aula de informática 734
aula de música 734
aula para alumnos con dificultad de aprendizaje 734
aumento de la tensión 646
aumento del efecto invernadero 68
aurícula 98
aurícula derecha 161, 162
aurícula izquierda 161, 162
auricular 502, 506, 507, 776
auricular, micrófono 506
auriculares 115, 502, 503, 504
aurora polar 53
Australia 28, 50, 747
Austria 744
autobomba tanque 766
autobús 568, 713
autobús articulado 569
autobús escolar 568
autobús urbano 568
autobuses, estación 710
autocar 568
autocar de dos pisos 569
autocaravana 567
autoclave 780
autodefensa antimisil 762
autoescalera 766
automático 453
automatización de la oficina 509
automóvil 549
automóvil eléctrico 563
automóvil híbrido 563
automóvil urbanita 549
automóviles : componentes principales 552
automóviles, contaminación 69
autopista 39, 539, 709
autoservicio, restaurante 722
autótrofos 67
auxiliares ortopédicos para caminar 782
avambrazo 749
avance rápido 495
ave 115
ave acuática 117
ave de rapiña 117
Ave del Paraíso 10
ave granívora 117
ave insectívora 117
ave zancuda 117
avefría 118
avellana 193
avellana, corte 84
avellanador de tubos 314
avena 85, 203
avena : panícula 85
avena, harina 204
avenida 39, 711
aventador de forraje 643
aves 115
aves acuáticas 117
aves de corral 213
aves de rapiña 117

aves paseriformes 117
avestruz 119
avión carga 629
avión de combate 760
avión de despegue y aterrizaje verticales 628
avión de línea 53
avión ligero 628
avión nodriza 760
avión particular 628
avión postal 475
avión radar 629
avión stealth 629
avión supersónico 629
avión turborreactor de pasajeros 624
avión, movimientos 630
aviones, ejemplos 628
avispa 101
avispón 101
axel 881
axila 146, 148
axila de la hoja 79
axiómetro 834
axis 122, 153, 157
axón 168
ayudante 181, 842
ayudante del atrecista 429
ayudante del director 429
ayuntamiento 710
azada 326
azada de doble filo 326
azadón 327
azadón rotatorio 641
azafrán 198
Azerbaiyán 746
azúcar 209
azúcar candi 209
azúcar glas 209
azúcar granulado 209
azúcar moreno 209
azúcar, termómetro 231
azucarero 226
azucena 80
azuela 326
azuela para desbastar 401
azufre 683
azul 400, 690
azul danés 211
azul verdoso 400
azul violeta 400
azur 741

B

babera 749
babero 368
babilla 124
babor 609, 616, 617
babuino 139
bacalao del Atlántico 221
baches 890
backgammon 915
bacón americano 216
bacón canadiense 216
badén 545
bádminton 816
Baffin, bahía 30
baguette 204
Bahamas 742
bahía 7, 38
bahía de Baffin 30
bahía de Bengala 33
bahía de Hudson 30
Bahrein 746
Baikal, lago 33
bailarina 343
baile, cuchilla 881
bajada de aguas 244
bajada peligrosa 545
bajada pronunciada 547
bajante 265
bajo 441
bala 752, 753, 912
bala con perdigones 752
bala de barra 752
bala de plomo 757
bala sólida 752
balalaika 433
balancín 284, 566, 599
balanza 698
balanza de astil 698
balanza de precisión 699
balanza de Roberval 698
balanza para cartas 531
balas de paja 875
balasto 591
balaustrada 412
balaustre 255
Balcanes, península 32
balcón 251, 431, 614, 738
baldosa 299, 322
baliza de socorro 611
Ballena 10, 12
ballena 137, 349
ballena blanca 137
ballenera 601
ballesta 750

ballesta, arcos 750
balón 685, 809, 827
balón de baloncesto 810
balón de balonmano 814
balón de fútbol 802
balón de fútbol americano 808
balón de rugby 805
baloncesto 788, 810
balonmano 814
balsa salvavidas 605, 611
balso 908
Báltico, mar 32
bambalina 430
Bambara 468
bambú, brote 185
bambúes 917
banana 196
bancada 304
banco 277, 593, 647, 710, 715, 730, 737, 851, 915
banco de arena 49
banco de trabajo 312
banco emisor, iniciales 729
banda 602, 803, 806, 809, 810, 812, 817
banda acolchada 502
banda antiadherente 894
banda azul 871
banda blanca 812
banda central 919
banda de ajuste 502, 504
banda de arquitrabe 404
banda de desgarre 899
banda de goma 862
banda de identificación técnica 501
banda de jazz 438
banda de la cabecera 862
banda de rodamiento 640
banda de suspensión 772
banda de tensión 59
banda de ventilación 860, 912
banda elástica 350
banda fotosensible 58
banda frontal 550
banda grabada 500
banda holográfica metalizada 729
banda lateral de la red 812
banda lateral protectora 571
banda magnética 729
banda nubosa en espiral 63
banda parasol 58
banda protectora 560, 561, 571
banda reflectante 611
banda reflectora 765
bandas de frecuencia 498
bandeja 239, 261, 281, 313, 389
bandeja de accesorios 399
bandeja de alimentación 519
bandeja de correspondencia 531
bandeja de pago 920
bandeja de pastelería 232
bandeja de pintura 320
bandeja de recepción de copias 512
bandeja de salida 519
bandeja de vidrio 291
bandeja del disco 494
bandeja para cosméticos 389
bandeja para cubitos de hielo 291
bandeja para el papel 511
bandeja para herramientas 321
bandeja para los entremeses 226
bandeja para recoger el papel 511
bandejas 722
bandejas para el papel 512
bandera 804
bandera con Schwenkel 739
bandera cuadrada 739
bandera de cuadros 872
bandera de dos puntas 739
bandera de dos puntas y lengua 739
bandera de la Unión Europea 729
bandera rectangular 739
bandera, partes 739
banderas 742
banderas, formas 739
banderín 739, 890
banderín de esquina 801
banderín de centro 802
banderín de saque de esquina 803
banderín doble 739
banderín móvil 867
banderola 739
banderola de la exposición en curso 394
banderola de la exposición futura 394
bandolera 388, 391, 527
bañera 251, 262, 264, 724, 834
Bangladesh 747
banjo 432
baño 724, 780
baño de fijación 485
baño de revelado 485
baño de stop 485
baños de revelado 485
banqueta 277
banquillo 803, 842
banquillo de jugadores 794, 807, 812
banquillo de los acusados 728

ASTRONOMÍA > 2-25; TIERRA > 26-71; REINO VEGETAL >72-89; REINO ANIMAL > 90-143; SER HUMANO > 144-177; PRODUCTOS ALIMENTARIOS Y DE COCINA > 178-241; CASA > 242-295; BRICOLAJE Y JARDINERÍA > 296-333; VESTIDO > 334-371; ACCESORIOS Y ARTÍCULOS PERSONALES > 372-391; ARTE Y ARQUITECTURA > 392-465; COMUNICACIONES Y AUTOMATIZACIÓN DE OFICINA > 466-535; TRANSPORTE Y VEHÍCULOS > 536-643; ENERGÍA > 644-677; CIENCIA > 678-705; SOCIEDAD > 706-785; DEPORTES Y JUEGOS > 786-920

banquillo de los jugadores 801, 809, 814, 878
banquillo de los penaltis 879
banquillo del entrenador 794
banquillo del equipo 827
banquisa de Ross 29
baqueta 433
baquetas 449
bar 427, 431, 710, 714, 719, 720
bar, barra 720
bar, taburete 720
baraja 914
baranda 862
barandilla 250, 251, 255, 321, 417, 542, 586, 894
barba 115, 390
barbacana 408
barbada 854
Barbados 743
barbecho 182
barbilla 115, 911
barbiquejo 602
barboquejo 765
barbote 749
barco de perforación 653
barco de vapor de ruedas 599
barco de vela de cuatro palos 602
barco perforador 604
bardana 189
Barents, mar 32
bario 682
barján 52
barniz 400
barógrafo 59
barómetro de mercurio 59
barqueta 222
barquilla 899
barquilla de mimbre 899
barra 51, 127, 284, 332, 385, 449, 578, 641, 686, 695, 722, 826, 840, 850, 851, 915
barra acanalada 284
barra alta 824
barra antivibración 331
barra baja 824
barra colectora 658
barra con pesas 850
barra de acero 825
barra de arrastre 638
barra de camareros 584
barra de combustible 667
barra de compás 434
barra de cortina 284
barra de cuchillas 643
barra de dirección 552, 897
barra de equilibrio 824, 826
barra de escotas 835
barra de extensión de piernas 851
barra de flexión de piernas 851
barra de la aguja 453
barra de madera 825
barra de maniobra 643
barra de operación 755
barra de pan 204
barra de percusión 767
barra de rastrillos 642
barra de remolque 567, 622, 642
barra de repetición 434
barra de torsión 850
barra de tracción 756
barra de tríceps 851
barra de varilla doble 284
barra de varilla simple 284
barra del bar 720
barra del prensatelas 453
barra deslizable 456
barra distanciadora 568
barra espaciadora 514, 528
barra estabilizadora 633
barra fija 824, 825
barra inferior 285
barra lateral 851
barra lisa 284
barra sujetadora 448
barra telescópica 920
barra tensora 457
barra transversal 897
barras paralelas 825
barras paralelas asimétricas 824
barredora 573
barrena 648, 649, 651
barrena de muro 306
barrera 281, 852
barrera de contención 872
barrera de salida móvil 857
barrera del paso a nivel 591
barrote 281
basamento 412
báscula de baño 699
báscula de cocina 231
báscula electrónica 699
báscula romana 698
base 58, 185, 239, 240, 273, 286, 305, 307, 308, 381, 405, 424, 425, 494, 500, 515, 517, 531, 591, 676, 685, 693, 698, 739, 767, 811, 825, 826
base con protecciones 811

base de cemento 254
base de cemento, parqué sobre 254
base de datos 525
base de la espiga 268
base de la lámpara 614
base de la ola 49
base de lanzamiento 795
base de prensado 425
base del bulbo 78
base del cargador 754
base del hogar 256
base del plato 500
base del respaldo 276
base del telescopio 17
base del tronco 87
base del tubo 275
base exterior 915
base fija 312
base giratoria 312
base impermeable 254
base interior 915
base líquida 378
base meta 795
basilosaurus 93
Bass, estrecho 29
bastidor 100, 303, 312, 386, 389, 423, 459, 575, 612, 641, 672, 673, 688, 816, 822, 823, 824, 870, 895
bastidor de coser 424
bastidor de los rodillos 636
bastidores 430
bastión 409
bastón 391, 846, 891
bastón cuadrangular 782
bastón de esquí 888, 892
bastón del portero 879
bastón inglés 782
bastón ortopédico 782
bastón para caminar 782
bastoncillo 177
bastones 391, 867
basura, cubo 295
basura, separación selectiva 71
bata 364
batán 460
batata 184
bate 796, 797, 798
bate de softball 797
bateador 795, 796, 798, 799
batería 302, 306, 448, 513, 552, 562, 563, 586, 687, 759
batería auxiliar 563
batería de cocina 722
batería electrónica 451
baterías de tracción 563
batidor 232, 641
batidor mecánico 232
batidora de mano 236
batidora de mesa 236
batidora de pie 236
batidora de vaso 236
batiente 249
batímetro 841
baúl 279, 389
bauprés 602
baya 83
bayas 192
bayas de enebro 198
bayeta de cocina 295
bayeta, cocina 295
bayoneta con empuñadura 751
bayoneta de cubo 751
bayoneta de mango 751
bayoneta integral 751
bazo 109, 110, 113, 125, 161
bazuca 757
Beaufort, estrecho 30
bebé, ropa 368
bebidas 180
becquerel 702
becuadro 435
begonia 80
béisbol 794, 796
belfo 124
belfos 130
Bélgica 743
Belice 742
bellas artes 394
bemol 435
Bengala, bahía 33
Benin 745
berberecho 217
berbiquí 307
bereber 468
berenjena 188
bergamota 194
bergantín 601
bergantín goleta 601
berilio 682
Bering, estrecho 30
Bering, mar 28
berlina 549
berma 660
bermudas 358
berquelio 684
berro 187
berros de jardín 187

berza 186
besuguera 234
betún 345
biathlon 893
biblioteca 395, 711, 726, 732, 734
bíceps braquial 150
bíceps femoral 151
bichero 611
bicicleta 578
bicicleta BMX 581
bicicleta de carreras 870
bicicleta de carretera 581
bicicleta de ciudad 581
bicicleta de cross 870
bicicleta de descenso 870
bicicleta de persecución 871
bicicleta de turismo 581
bicicleta estática 851
bicicleta holandesa 581
bicicleta todo terreno 581
bicicleta, partes 578
bicicletas, ejemplos 581
bicornio 339
bidé 264
biela 564, 566
Bielorrusia 744
bies 455
bígaro 217
bigotes 132
billar 862
billar francés 862
billar inglés 863
billete : verso 729
billete, recto 729
billete, verso 729
billete: recto 729
billetero 387
billetera 386, 387
billetes de banco 915
billetes, emisión 730
bimah 738
binóculos de tijera 385
biología 702
biombo para soldar 318
biosfera 66
biosfera, estructura 66
bióxido de carbono, reactor 670
biplano 628
bípode 755, 756
birimbao 433
birmano 468
bisabuela 784
bisabuelo 784
bisabuelos 784
bisagra 238, 247, 249, 278, 294, 386, 389, 465, 500, 554, 692
bisel 776
bismuto 682
bisonte 128
bistec 214
bita 607
bizna 84
bizniestos 784
biznieto 784
biznietos 784
blanca 435, 914, 915
blanca doble 914
blancas 916
blanco 40, 41, 690, 861, 893
blanquear con cloro, siguiendo las indicaciones 347
blastodisco 117
blindaje 758
blindaje de hormigón 670, 671
bloque 444
bloque corredizo 595
bloque de apartamentos 419, 711, 886
bloque de cierre de la recámara 756, 912
bloque de cierre de recámara 912
bloque de cirugía 780
bloque de contención 667
bloque de hormigón 298
bloque de madera grabado 421
bloque de madera para grabar 421
bloque del motor 566
bloqueo 700
bloqueo corrimiento 515
bloqueo de inclinación lateral 482
bloqueo de la columna 482
bloqueo de la plataforma 482
bloqueo de los cimientos 660
bloqueo de movimiento horizontal 482
bloqueo eje 894
bloqueo giratorio 572
bloqueo mayúsculas 514
bloqueo numérico 515
bloqueo, tornillos 700
blusa caracó 337
blusas, ejemplos 359
blusón 359
blusón con tirilla 359
BMX 871
boa 114
bob 884
bobina 495, 909, 910
bobina móvil 488
bobinado 688

bobinas 452
bobsleigh 884
bobsleigh a cuatro 884
boca 95, 104, 105, 107, 110, 136, 148, 174, 301, 312, 444, 753, 754, 756, 854, 860, 912
boca de acceso 655
boca de aspiración de aire 605
boca de llenado 553
boca de riego 712, 767
boca del depósito 332
boca para la manguera 329
bocado articulado 854
bocado con la barbada 854
bocado corredizo 854
bocado de codo militar 854
bocado de filete 854
bocado del filete 854
bocallave 249
bocamina 650
bocha 864
bocina de niebla 611
bocina neumática 570
bodega 720
bodega de carga 22
bodega de contenedores 605
bodega de equipaje 625, 631
bodega de equipos 24
body 359, 366, 371
bogabante 218
bogavante 107
bogavante, anatomía 107
bogavante, morfología 107
bogie 586, 595, 895
bogie del motor 585
bogie motor 595
bohrio 683
boina 341
bokken 846
bol 237
bol mezclador 236
bol para ensalada 226
bola 268, 301, 865, 920
bola amarilla 863
bola azul 863
bola blanca 862, 863
bola de corcho 797
bola de hilo 797
bola de marfil 919
bola de proa 839
bola de rodamiento 470
bola marrón 863
bola negra 863
bola pinta 862, 863
bola roja 862, 863
bola rosa 863
bola verde 863
bolas numeradas 862
bolas rojas 863
bolera 864
bolera 714
bolero 358
bolero con botones 358
boles para batir 232
boleto comestible 183
boliche 864
bolígrafo 470
bolillo 458
bolillos 458
bolina 833
Bolivia 742
bolo 865
bolo chico 865
bolo cilíndrico 865
bolo delantero 865
bolo pequeño 865
bolos 864
bolos sobre hierba 864
bolos, ejemplos 865
bolsa 143, 222
bolsa copuladora 97, 104
bolsa de cuero 529
bolsa de golf 869
bolsa de lona 388
bolsa de malla 222
bolsa de tinta 106
bolsa de veneno 99
bolsa para congelados 222
bolsa, cajetín 289
bolsas 181
bolsillo 313, 354, 386, 862, 869
bolsillo con cartera 348, 352
bolsillo de fuelle 359, 360
bolsillo de manguito 360
bolsillo de ojal 348, 353, 355
bolsillo de ojal con ribete 360
bolsillo de ojal de sastre 360
bolsillo de parche 348, 353, 360, 368
bolsillo de parche con cartera 360
bolsillo de ribete 348
bolsillo de ribete ancho 352, 355
bolsillo del cambio 348
bolsillo delantero 350, 386
bolsillo disimulado 355, 360
bolsillo exterior 387, 388
bolsillo lateral 554
bolsillo secreto 386

bolsillo simulado 355, 360
bolsillo superior 349, 352
bolsillo trasero 350
bolsillo vertical 337
bolsillos, ejemplos 360
bolsita de té 208
bolso clásico 388
bolso de bandolera 388
bolso de fuelle 388
bolso de hombre 388
bolso de la compra 388
bolso de vestir 388
bolso de viaje 388
bolso interior 389
bolso manguito 388
bolso saco 388
bolso tipo cubo 387
bolsos 387
bomba 246, 292, 294, 320, 670, 671, 674, 903
bomba de aire 578
bomba de aire comprimido 841
bomba de circulación 259, 675
bomba de petróleo 259
bomba para lodos 651
bomba tipo pedestal para sumidero 263
bomba transportadora de calor 669
bomba volcánica 44
bombachos 358
bombardino 447
bombero 765
bombilla 316, 687
bombilla de bajo consumo 275
bombilla de bayoneta 275
bombilla de flash 482
bombilla de rosca 275
bombilla incandescente 274
bombilla reflectora 765
bombo 437, 448
bombona de aire comprimido 765, 873
bombona de gas 314, 903
bombona de gas desechable 319
bombona de gas médico 780
bombona de oxígeno portátil 775
bongos 449
boniato 184
boquerón 219
boquilla 259, 265, 315, 319, 320, 328, 329, 390, 398, 446, 447, 451, 657, 658, 663, 767, 783, 841
boquilla de aspiración 304
boquilla de corte 319
boquilla de llenado 288
boquilla de vertido 246
boquilla del soplete 314
boquilla para concentrar la llama 319
boquilla para expandir la llama 319
boquilla para suelos y alfombras 289
boquilla para tapicería 289
boquilla pulverizadora 329
boquilla rinconera 289
boquilla rociadora 655
bordado 459
bordado plano 459
bordados planos 459
borde 79, 281, 290, 841, 887, 894
borde 894
borde de ataque 625, 897, 898
borde de fuga 624
borde de la cuba 292
borde de la punta 306
borde de salida 897, 898
borde del andén 582, 593
borde del lomo 306
borde externo 127
borde interno 127, 901
borde marginal 898
borde, hoja 79
bordeado 833
bordes, podadora 332
bordillo 322, 712, 864
borla 282, 285, 378
borne 562
borne de enlace 272
borne negativo 562, 687
borne positivo 562, 689
boro 682
borraja 202
borrar 515
borrén 855
borrén trasero 855
bosbsleigh de dos 884
Bosnia-Herzegovina 744
bosque 45
bosque de coníferas 66
bosque de hoja caduca 66
bosque mixto 66
bosque templado 66
bosque tropical 66
bosque tropical húmedo 66
bosques 39
Bostuana 746
bota 343, 841, 874, 875, 878, 880, 881, 888, 892, 895, 896
bota alpina 901
bota blanda 887
bota de fútbol 802

bota de la aleta 841
bota de la corona del casco 853, 857
bota de medio muslo 343
bota de montaña 344
bota de montar 855
bota de salto de esquí 891
bota de seguridad 773
bota de trabajo 342
bota del pie delantero 840
bota externa 889, 895
bota rígida 887
botador 301
botafuego 752
botalón 834
botas altas 911
botas con clavos 885
botas de caucho 765
botas de lucha 843
botas de tacos de rugby 805
botas para esquiar 889
botavara 602, 834, 836
botavara de cangreja 602
bote salvavidas 602, 604, 608, 652
botella 379, 579, 685
botella de vidrio 223
botella del termo 906
botella, vidrio 223
botes herméticos 222
botín 342, 343
botín interior 889, 895
botiquín 775, 781
botiquín de primeros auxilios 777
botiquín de urgencias 771
Botnia, golfo 32
botón 274, 349, 354, 432, 439, 849
botón de acoplamiento 444
botón de ajuste a cero del contador 499
botón de ajuste fino 693
botón de ajuste grueso 693
botón de alimentación del papel 519, 731
botón de apagado 331
botón de avance rápido 495, 499, 508
botón de avance/parada 519
botón de bloqueo 305, 313
botón de bloqueo de la pantalla 526
botón de bloqueo del eje 308
botón de cancelación 477
botón de cierre 288
botón de compensación de la exposición 476
botón de control 516
botón de control del alojamiento del disco 501
botón de control remoto 477
botón de desbloqueo del objetivo 476
botón de encendido 494, 497, 498, 508
botón de encendido del touch pad 526
botón de encendido TV 495
botón de encendido VCR 495
botón de encendido/apagado/test 520
botón de enclavamiento 308
botón de enfoque 14, 15
botón de enfoque manual 483
botón de ensayo 767
botón de expulsión 477, 495, 499, 918
botón de expulsión de CD/DVD-ROM 513
botón de expulsión de disquete 513
botón de expulsión del disco 521
botón de fantasía 453
botón de fijación del nivel principal 701
botón de fuerte luminosidad 479
botón de funcionamiento 504
botón de grabación 495, 508
botón de grabación silenciosa 499
botón de grabador vocal 527
botón de iluminación de la pantalla 479
botón de índice /ampliación 477
botón de inicio 527
botón de inicio de grabación 499
botón de inicio de marcha 696
botón de inicio del contador 696, 700
botón de la bandolera 441
botón de la culata 753
botón de la llave 446
botón de la memoria 501
botón de lectura 505
botón de llamada de memoria 479
botón de llamada para peatones 712
botón de luminosidad media 479
botón de madera 353
botón de mando 290
botón de medición 479
botón de memoria 479, 498, 506
botón de montaje 496
botón de nivel de grabación 499
botón de parada 696
botón de pausa 499
botón de presión 346, 353, 368, 391, 470
botón de previsionado de profundidad de campo 476
botón de puntada 452
botón de rebobinado 495, 499, 504, 508
botón de rebobinado automático 504
botón de rebobinado de la película 476
botón de rebobinado rápido 504
botón de registro 444
botón de reiniciación 513
botón de reproducción 495, 499, 508
botón de reset 918
botón de retroiluminación 527
botón de salida 527
botón de salto de imágenes 477
botón de seguridad 267
botón de selección 261, 496, 505
botón de selección de idioma 507
botón de selección del menú 477
botón de seta 516
botón de sintonización 504
botón de sombra 479
botón de stop 495, 499, 508
botón de velocidades 236
botón de visualización de ajustes 477
botón de visualización de imágenes 477
botón de visualización del nivel de alarma 613
botón del contador a cero 495
botón del horno 290
botón del menú 505
botón del seguro 554
botón del vaporizador 288
botón del zoom eléctrico 496
botón grabación fecha 496
botón grabación hora 496
botón página precedente 527
botón página siguiente 527
botón para ajustar la imágen horizontalmente 701
botón para ajustar la imágen verticalmente 701
botón para borrar 508
botón para buscar las pistas 501
botón para cancelar la memoria 479
botón para parar y borrar 501
botón selector 294
botón selector de temperatura 382
botón selector de velocidad 382
botón TV video 495
botón visualización fecha 496
botón visualización hora 496
botonadura cruzada 352
botonera de cabina 417
botones comunes 453
botones de acción 918
botones de ajuste 495
botones de ajuste de imagen 496
botones de búsqueda de canales 495
botones de dirección 918
botones de efectos especiales 496
botones de lanzamiento de las aplicaciones 527
botones de presión de la pierna 369
botones de presión delanteros 369
botones para búsqueda de canales 495
botones para editar la voz 450
botones programables 516
boubou 339
bóveda 410
bóveda de cañón 407
bóveda de proyección 10
bóveda del salpicadero 550
bóveda palatina 174, 175
bóveda, presa 661
boxeador 842
boxeo 842
boxes 872, 874
boya 54, 833
boya cilíndrica 615
boya cónica 615, 617
boya de pértiga 617
boya de plano focal elevado 615
boya torre 614, 617
boyas de llegada 839
boyas de recorrido 838
boyas de salida 838
boyas marítimas, sistema 616
boyas, regiones 616
Boyero 13
bráctea 84
brafonera 749
braga 367
braga de volantes 368
bragueta 350, 351, 368
branquia 106
branquias 105, 109
branquias externas 111
braquial anterior 150
braquiópodo 92
brasero 412
Brasil 742
braza 832
brazalete de identificación 376
brazalete neumático 777
brazalete tubular 376
brazaletes 376
brazas de sobrejuanete de mesana 603
brazo 95, 124, 139, 147, 149, 276, 286, 323, 329, 346, 382, 433, 452, 456, 557, 610, 638, 693, 783
brazo actuador 521
brazo de arrastre 638
brazo de balancín 599
brazo de disco 641
brazo de elevación 573
brazo de elevación del árbol oscilante 640
brazo de la plaqueta 385
brazo de la sierra 331
brazo de presión 312
brazo de suspensión 292, 553
brazo de tracción 640
brazo del cucharón 637
brazo del panel solar 60
brazo del raspador 423
brazo delantero 698
brazo elástico 859
brazo elevador 307, 637
brazo espiral 9
brazo extensible 465
brazo fonocaptor 500
brazo metálico 329
brazo muerto 48
brazo muerto, lago 48
brazo por control remoto 21
brazo retráctil 18
brazo telescópico 634
brazo trasero 698
brazos 281
brazos del delta 48
brecha del muro 917
brécol 187
brécol chino 187
bretón 469
brick 223
brick pequeño 223
bricolaje 298
brida 854
brida de sujeción 613
brida de unión 615
brie 211
brillante 375
brisa leve 56
broca 302, 307, 648
broca de atornillado 306
broca de pala 306
broca helicoidal 306
broca helicoidal central 306
broca salomónica de canal angosto 306
brocas, barrenas, ejemplos 306
brocha 85, 320, 378, 397
brocha aplicadora de colorete 378
brocha de afeitar 383
brocha en forma de abanico 378
broche 376, 386, 387
broche automático 386
bromo 683
bronquio lobular 163
bronquio principal 163
bronquiolo terminal 163
brote 77
brote de bambú 185
brotes de soja 191
Brújula 11
brújula 898
brújula líquida 612
brújula magnética 907
Brunei 747
bruñidor 422
bruñidor con rascador 401
bruza 422
buccino 217
buceador 841
buceo 841
buche 97, 99, 104, 106, 116
Budismo : Buda 736
Buena Esperanza, cabo 34
buey 129
búfalo 128
bufete 279
buffet 720
búho real 119
buitre 119
bujía 332, 562, 565, 566
bujías, cable 552
bulbillo 78
bulbo 9, 185, 607, 609, 664
bulbo olfativo 109
bulbo olfatorio 175
bulbo piloso 172
bulbo raquídeo 167
bulbo, base 78
bulbo, corte 78
bulbo, tallo 78
bulbos 184
buldog 130
bulevar 39, 711
Bulgaria 744
búlgaro 469
bulldozer 636
buque de carga 604
buque portacontenedores 596
buque trasatlántico 608
buque, ancla 610
burbujas de aire 531
burda 602
bureta con llave a la derecha 685
Buril 11
buril 421
Burkina Faso 745
burra 863
Burundi 745
bus 513, 522
buscapersonas 505
busco 597
búsqueda 525
búsqueda automática de canales 498
butaca 276, 427
butacas 431
butacas, ejemplos 276
Bután 747
buzo 358, 901
buzón 474
buzón de depósito nocturno 731

C

caballa 219
caballerizas 856
caballero 409
caballete 252, 399
caballete central 575
Caballete del pintor 11
caballete lateral 575
caballete portapoleas 651
caballo 124, 129, 826, 916
caballo con arcos 824
caballo con aros 826
Caballo Menor 12
caballo, anatomía 125
caballo, esqueleto 126
caballo, morfología 124
cabeceo 630
cabecera 280, 281, 411, 426, 471
cabellera 8
Cabellera de Berenice 13
cabello, tinte 379
cabestrante 573
cabeza 8, 96, 97, 99, 104, 115, 132, 140, 147, 149, 161, 169, 229, 300, 301, 302, 308, 311, 383, 390, 391, 417, 425, 439, 440, 441, 452, 457, 458, 516, 591, 816, 822, 826, 858, 863, 867, 887, 893, 901, 909
cabeza cortadora 535
cabeza de cordada 900
cabeza de empalme 586, 640, 641
cabeza de enganche 587, 641, 642
cabeza de inyección 651
cabeza de la caja de iluminación 485
cabeza de la torre 663
cabeza de la tubería 654
cabeza de lectura /escritura 521
cabeza de mástil 836
cabeza de metal 793
cabeza de proyección 535
cabeza del fémur 153
cabeza del gato elevador 632
cabeza del húmero 153
cabeza del martillo 793, 901
cabeza del mastil 602
cabeza delantera del cilindro de recuperación 756
cabeza dirigida por rayos infrarrojos 759
cabeza hexagonal 384
cabeza móvil 236
cabeza panorámica 482
cabeza; tipos 302
cabezada 426, 854
cabezal 227, 252, 280
cabezal del colector 18
cabezal flotante 383
cabezuela 81
cabina 631, 636, 637, 638, 639, 640, 643, 731
cabina armario 251
cabina de clase turista 625
cabina de control 10, 431, 634, 718
cabina de interpretación simultánea 718
cabina de la ducha 264
cabina de la torre de control 618
cabina de mando 22, 605, 624, 631, 634
cabina de pasajeros 608, 609
cabina de pilotaje 607
cabina de primera clase 624
cabina de proyección 427
cabina del ascensor 417
cabina del maquinista 585, 586
cabina del piloto 898
cabina en el foco primario 17
cabina focal 16
cabina giratoria 638
cabina para desvestirse 781
cabina para dormir 570
cabina, botonera 417
cabina, guía 417
cabina, suelo 417
cabina, techo 417
cabinas de control 490
cabio alto 247
cabio bajo 247
cable 306, 316, 331, 332, 465, 488, 504, 516, 517, 558, 573, 793, 824, 851, 859, 908, 913
cable coaxial 523
cable con funda metálica 507
cable de acero 900, 913
cable de alimentación 305, 381, 382, 383, 497, 513
cable de alimentación de 240 voltios 272
cable de alumbrado 567
cable de arranque 323
cable de arrastre 840
cable de bujía 566
cable de conexión 502, 516
cable de control 323
cable de corriente 318
cable de corriente de la aguja 590
cable de dirección 859
cable de elevación 634
cable de enlace 272
cable de fibra óptica 523
cable de frenado 761
cable de interfaz digital para instrumentos musicales (MIDI) 451
cable de la antena de alta frecuencia 628
cable de las bujías 552
cable de par 523
cable de sincronización 527
cable de tierra 272, 318
cable de tirante 824
cable de tracción 417
cable de transmisión 613
cable del acelerador 332
cable del auricular 506
cable del cambio 580
cable del esgrimista 848
cable del freno 579
cable distribuidor 486
cable eléctrico 556, 563, 712
cable neutro 272
cable portante 540
cable principal 272
cable principal neutro 272
cable torcido 908
cable trenzado 908
cables 492, 523
cables de anclaje 652
cables de baja tensión 273, 663
cables de conexión 273
cables de emergencia 558
cables de suministro 273, 663
cables de tensión mediana 273
cabo 38, 422, 432, 908, 909
cabo de Buena Esperanza 34
cabo de Hornos 31
cabo de soporte 103
cabo del macillo 443
Cabo Verde, islas(f) de 745
cabra 128
cabra, quesos 210
cabrestante 443
cabrio 252
cacahuete 190
cacahuete, aceite 209
cacao 208
cacatúa 118
cacerola 235
cacerola para baño de María 235
cacerola para fondue 234
cacerola refractaria 235
cachalote 137
cadena 331, 580, 697, 826, 870
cadena alimentaria 67
cadena de amarre 615
cadena de dunas 52
cadena de elevación 632
cadena de neuronas 168
cadena de seguridad 567
cadena de transmisión 578, 641, 643
cadena, reacción 681
cadena, sierra 331
cadena, transmisión 580
cadeneta 459
cadenilla de la barbada 854
cadenita del tapón 265
cadera 147, 149
cadmio 683
café 208
café expres, máquina 241
café, granos torrefactos 208
café, granos verdes 208
cafetera 241, 905
cafetera de émbolo 241
cafetera de filtro automática 241
cafetera de infusión 241
cafetera italiana 241
cafetera napolitana 241
cafeteras 241
cafetería 710, 715, 725, 735
caftán 339
caída 362
caída de popa 836, 897
caída de proa 836
caída de tensión 646
caimán 114
caireles 854
caja 58, 181, 222, 313, 316, 318, 323, 332, 383, 436, 440, 441, 442, 476, 488, 494, 507, 613, 614, 695, 697, 700, 723, 910, 920
caja abierta 222
caja archivo 533
caja basculante 639
caja circular 432
caja clara 437, 448
caja colectora de polvo 308
caja de accesorios 456

caja de cambios 552
caja de caracol 658
caja de cartón 535
caja de cerillas 391
caja de cinc (ánodo) 689
caja de compresión 642
caja de conexiones 274, 490
caja de control electrónico 563
caja de distribución 263
caja de doble fila de conexiones 689
caja de empalmes 591
caja de engranajes 423, 627
caja de herramientas 313
caja de ignición 627
caja de ingletes 303
caja de jeringuillas usadas 771
caja de la batería 562
caja de la pantalla 483
caja de luz 484, 535
caja de pesca 911
caja de relés 563
caja de resonancia 432, 433, 440
caja de seguridad 731
caja de servicio 273
caja de terminales 673
caja del acumulador 571
caja del aire 445
caja del cerrojo 754, 755
caja del cilindro 249
caja del motor 331
caja del ventilador 382
caja espiral 659
caja fuerte 731, 769, 920
caja media pera 433
caja neumática 445
caja orza de quilla 836
caja para la ceniza 256
caja para queso 223
caja registradora 181
caja superior 285
caja triangular 433
caja, palé 632
caja, queso 223
cajas 181, 716, 717
cajas de cartón para huevos 222
cajas de cartón, huevos 222
cajera 181
cajero automático 715, 730, 731
cajetín 249
cajetín de accesorios 289
cajetín de batida 792
cajetín portabolsa 289
cajita reguladora 267
cajo 426
cajón 224, 278, 279, 281, 641
cajón calientaplatos 290
cajón de abono compuesto 323
cajón de basura 573
cajón del plano de sustentación 760
cajón para carnes 291
cajonera móvil 510
calabacín 188
calabaza bonetera 189
calabaza bonetera amarilla 189
calabaza común 189
calabaza de China 188
calabaza de cuello largo 189
calabaza de cuello retorcido 189
calabaza romana 189
calamar 217
cálamo 115
cálamo egipcio 470
calandra 550, 570
calandria 667, 669
calapié 580
calcáneo 126, 140, 141, 153, 155
calce 753
calcetín 365, 802, 822
calcetín a media pantorrilla 351
calcetín con tirante 796
calcetín corto 351
calcetín largo 365
calcetín largo ejecutivo 351
calcetines 351, 878
calcetines altos 805
calcio 682
calculadora 386
calculadora científica 529
calculadora con impresora 529
calculadora de bolsillo 529
caldera 259, 674, 675
caldera de gas 267
calderón 435
calefacción 256
calefacción auxiliar 260
calefacción de leña 256
calefactor de aceite 260
calefactor eléctrico a infrarrojos 260
calendario 530
calendario de sobremesa 530
calentador 899, 903
calentador de agua 262
calentador de agua eléctrico 266
calentador de petróleo 259
calentador de pierna 371
calentador eléctrico 266
calibrador 423, 559
calibre de ajuste de profundidad de corte 309
calículo 83
California, golfo 30
californio 684
caliptra 77
Calisto 4
cáliz 80, 83, 84, 165, 737
calle 39, 711, 713, 788, 790, 830, 831, 864, 882
calle comercial 710
calle de calentamiento 882
callejón 711
calor, transmisión 681
Calvinismo : Juan Calvino 736
calza de descarga 659
calzada 538, 712
calzado 342
calzado unisex 344
calzador 345
calzapié 578
calzas 338
calzo de la rueda 622
calzón 848
calzoncillos 351
calzoncillos largos 351
calzones 338
cama 280, 424, 823
cama de hospital 780
cama doble 724
cama individual 724
cama, coche 584
Camaleón 11
camaleón 114
cámara 18, 428, 490, 492, 650, 775, 873
cámara acorazada 731
cámara anterior 177
cámara anular de combustión 627
cámara de aire 117, 271, 370, 675
cámara de bolsillo 480
cámara de combustión 259, 564, 566
cámara de descarga 402
cámara de disco 481
cámara de expansión 695
cámara de fotografía 694
cámara de fuelle 480
cámara de incubación 100
cámara de la esclusa 597
cámara de la pólvora 753
cámara de la reina 402
cámara de magma 44
cámara de mezcla 319
cámara de televisión en color 20
cámara de vacío 694
cámara de vigilancia 395
cámara del rey 402
cámara del timón 606
cámara desechable 480
cámara digital 481, 517
cámara estereoscópica 481
cámara fría 722
cámara frigorífica 180
cámara frigorífica 181, 596
cámara lenta 495
cámara magmática 646
cámara oscura 484
cámara para el carrete de la película 476
cámara para la muestra 694
cámara Polaroid Land 480
cámara posterior 177
cámara pulpar 159
cámara réflex con dos objetivos 480
cámara reflex de formato medio SLR (6x6) 481
cámara reflex de un solo objetivo 480
cámara réflex digital: vista posterior 477
cámara réflex monocular: vista frontal 476
cámara réflex monocular: vista posterior 476
cámara reflex, sección transversal 477
cámara rígida de 35 mm 20
cámara submarina 480
cámara subterránea 402
cámara web 517
cámaras fijas 480
camarera 720
camarero 721
camarote 608
camarote del capitán 609
camarotes de la tripulación 604
camarotes de los oficiales 762, 763
camas y colchonetas 904
cambiador 281
cambiador manual de vía 590
cambio 725
cambio automático de bandejas 512
cambio de marchas delantero 578, 580
cambio de marchas trasero 578, 580
cambio de presión 55
cambio de velocidades 870
cambium 87
Camboya 747
Cámbrico 92
cambrillón 370
camcorder digital 517
camello 129
camembert 211
camerino 428, 431
camerino privado 428
Camerún 745
camilla 775, 776
camino de arrastre 647
camino de evacuación 543
camión articulado 570
camión basculante 573
camión cisterna 572, 573
camión cisterna de agua potable 622
camión cisterna de combustible 622
camión de aprovisionamiento 623
camión de bomberos 764
camión sanitario 622
camión tractor 570
camión volquete 572
camiones 570
camiones articulados, ejemplos 572
camiones de bomberos 766
camiones, ejemplos 573
camioneta 549, 573
camioneta con canastilla telescópica 622
camioneta de mantenimiento de aviones 622
camisa 349, 359, 408
camisa de pistón 566
camisa marinera 359
camisas 716
camisera clásica 359
camiseta 351, 368, 369, 371, 791, 796, 805, 810, 843
camiseta de cuerpo entero 369
camiseta del equipo 801, 802, 808
camiseta interior 796
camiseta sin mangas 850
camisola 366
camisón 364
campana 256, 290, 721, 722, 858
campana de aviso de cruce 591
campana de cocina 224
campanario 411, 737
campanas tubulares 437, 449
campanillas 449
campo 709, 794, 799, 802
campo de fútbol 788
campo de golf 708, 788, 866
campo de hockey sobre hierba 788
campo de juego 801, 804, 858, 920
campo de juego de fútbol americano 806
campo de juego de fútbol canadiense 809
campo de tiro 859, 860, 893
campo de tiro al arco 788
campo de tiro al blanco 788
campo de visión, escala de profundidad 478
campo geotérmico 646
campo magnético 494, 687
campo, línea 687
campos de tenis 788
Can Mayor 11
Can Menor 13
caña 124, 390, 444, 470, 610, 753, 911, 912
caña del timón 834
caña para lanzado 910
caña para mosca 909
caña simple 446
Canadá 742
canal 306, 750, 838, 865, 919
canal anular 95
canal de ajuste 310
canal de arrastre del papel 511
canal de carga 664
canal de competición 788
canal de derivación 657
canal de descarga 658
canal de drenaje 655
canal de la Mancha 32
canal de Mozambique 34
canal del aliviadero 657
canal del sifón 105
canal del veneno 112
canal derecho 502
canal izquierdo 502
canal lacrimal 177
canal principal 617
canal radial 95
canal salivar 99
canal secundario 617
canal transportador 666
canal, esclusa 597
canales de Wolkman 154
canalización de vacío 694
canalón 244
canasta 797, 811
canastilla 238
Cáncer 13
Cáncer, trópico 34, 35, 36
cancha 809, 810, 812, 813, 814, 816, 818, 820
cancha de fondo 821
cancha del fondo 818
cancha delantera 818
candado para bicicleta 580
candela 702
candelabro de siete braz 738
canela 198
canelones 206
cañería 262, 270
cañería de agua fría 271
cañería de desagüe 263
cañería del desagüe 262
cañería perforada 263
cañerías 262, 899
canesú 349, 359, 366
cangreja de popa 603
cangreja mayor popel 603
cangrejo de mar 218
cangrejo de río 218
canguro 142, 143
canguro, esqueleto 142
canguro, morfología 143
caniche 130
canilla 452, 453, 461
caño 444
canoa 600, 837
canoa C1 838
canoa de balancín 599
canoa-kayak : aguas bravas 837
canoa-kayak : regata 838
cañón 390, 754, 755, 756, 757, 758, 860, 912, 918
cañón de avancarga 753
cañón de electrones 494, 694
cañón de la presión 445
cañón del siglo XVII 752
cañón expulsor de espuma 607
cañón lanza agua 766
cañón sin retroceso 757
cañón submarino 49
cañonera 409
cañonería 445
canotier 340
cantidad de copias 512
cantidad de materia, unidad de medida 702
cantilever 661
cantimplora 906
canto 300, 303, 729, 793, 881, 884, 888
canto de la cabeza 426
canto de la cara 426
canto del pie 426
cantón diestro de la punta 740
cantón diestro del jefe 740
cantón siniestro de la punta 740
cantón siniestro del jefe 740
cantonera 426, 912
cánula orofaringea 775
capa 338, 355, 390
capa basáltica 42
capa de aluminio 501
capa de arcilla 660
capa de ozono 53
capa de rodadura 538
capa del casco 561
capa drenante 660
capa granítica 42
capa protectora 20
capa superficial del suelo 78
capa superior impermeable 646
caparazón 107
capas de residuos 69
capazo 388
caperuza 257, 267, 841
caperuza de la chimenea 245
capilla 408, 726
capilla axial 410, 411
capilla lateral 410
capilla radial 410, 411
capital 37
capitán 877, 884
capitate 154
capitel 405
capó 333, 550, 570, 876
capón 213
caponera 409
Capricornio 10
Capricornio, trópico 34, 35, 36
cápsula 75, 84, 783
cápsula de gelatina 783
cápsula de Petri 685
captura 916
capucha 353
capucha con cordón 369
capucha de ventilación 614
capuchón 368, 478, 484, 776, 783, 882
capuchón de bastones 869
capuchón de plástico 317
capuchón de protección 692
capullo 77
caquí 197
cara 139, 146, 227, 300, 425, 815, 867
cara inferior 374
cara superior 374
carabela 599
carabina 893
carabina 22 861
caracol 104
caracol terrestre 217
caracol, anatomía 104
caracol, morfología 104
carácter, posición 472
caracteres 917
caracteres de una fundición 472
carambola 197
caramillo 432
caravana 567
caravana plegable 567
carbón 683
carbón, minas 647
carboncillo 397
carboncillo litográfico 423
carboncillo, dibujo 396
carbonero 221
Carbonífero 92
carburador 574
carburante de calentamiento, depósito 563
carcaj 859
carcasa 261, 521
cárcel 726, 915
carcoma 101
cardamomo 198
cardán 642
cardenal 118
cárdigan 354
cardo 185
Carena 11
carena 108
carenado 574
careta 318, 773, 800
careta de esgrima 848
careta de mano 318
carga 24, 470, 686
carga de perdigones 912
carga del reactor nuclear 667
carga eléctrica, unidad de medida 702
carga explosiva 653, 757
carga útil 25
carga y descarga 724
carga, muelle 715, 716
carga, toma 563
cargador 288, 306, 754, 755, 893
cargador de contenedores y plataformas 623
cargador de documentos 512
cargador delantero 637
cargadora, retroexcavadora 637
cargadora-retroexcavadora 637
carguero portacontenedores 604
Caribe, islas del 742
Caribe, mar 28, 30
Caribe, Placa 43
caricatura 471
carlota, molde 232
carne 214
carne de cordero troceada 215
carne de ternera troceada 214
carne de vacuno troceada 214
carne picada 214
carne picada de cerdo 215
carne picada de cordero 215
carne picada de vacuno 214
carnívoros 67
Carón 5
carpa 220
Cárpatos, montes 32
Carpentaria, golfo 29
carpeta con guardas 532
carpeta con mecanismo de presión 532
carpeta de archivo 532
carpeta de argollas 532
carpeta de broches 532
carpeta de costilla de resorte 532
carpeta de espiral 533
carpeta de tornillos 532
carpinteria 313
carpintería 301, 302, 303, 306, 308, 310, 313
carpo 116, 122, 126, 131, 136, 138, 141, 142, 154
carrera 833
carrera de caballos 856
carrera de caballos: 857
carreras con arneses 857
carreras de coches 872
carrete 328, 458
carrete de bobina fija 910
carrete de rebobinado 476
carrete de tambor 910
carrete del cable 848
carrete giratorio 909
carrete receptor de la cinta 499
carrete recogedor 642
carretera 39, 539, 543, 708
carretera de acceso 618
carretera de circunvalación 39
carretera secundaria 39, 709
carretera, sección transversal 538
carretera, túnel 543
carreteras, mapa 39
carreteras, sistema 538
carretilla 319, 323, 633
carretilla elevadora de horquilla 632
carretilla para manguera 328
carretilla transportadora 633
carril 595
carril circular 16
carril de aceleración 539
carril de adelantamiento 539
carril de desaceleración 539
carril de enlace 583
carril de tránsito 539
carril de tránsito lento 539
carril guía de la película 476
carril para el tope de ingletes 305
carriles 539

1050

ASTRONOMÍA > 2-25; TIERRA > 26-71; REINO VEGETAL >72-89; REINO ANIMAL > 90-143; SER HUMANO > 144-177; PRODUCTOS ALIMENTARIOS Y DE COCINA > 178-241; CASA > 242-295; BRICOLAJE Y JARDINERÍA > 296-333; VESTIDO > 334-371; ACCESORIOS Y ARTÍCULOS PERSONALES > 372-391; ARTE Y ARQUITECTURA > 392-465; COMUNICACIONES Y AUTOMATIZACIÓN DE OFICINA > 466-535; TRANSPORTE Y VEHÍCULOS > 536-643; ENERGÍA > 644-677; CIENCIA > 678-705; SOCIEDAD > 706-785; DEPORTES Y JUEGOS > 786-920

carrillo 909
carrito de golf 869
carrito de libros 733
carrito del supermercado 181
carrito portamaletas 389
carro 284, 542, 835
carro de combate 758
carro de encaje 456
carro de golf eléctrico 869
carro deslizante 838
carro portaequipaje 582
carro principal deslizante 456
carrocería 550, 567, 876
carrocería amovible 573
carrocerías, ejemplos 549
carrusel 483
carta 474, 915
carta Caja de Comunidad 915
carta de la Suerte 915
carta de vinos 721
cartas al editor 471
cartas altas 914
cartel 427
cartel comercial 594
cartel publicitario 595
cartelera 427
cartelera de las exposiciones 394
cárter 306, 565, 566
cárter del disco 308
cárter del embrague 576
cartera 386, 580
cartera de fondo plegable 386
cartera portadocumentos 387
carterita de cerillas 391
cartero 475
cartílago alar mayor 175
cartílago articular 154
cartílago costal 122
cartílago nasal del tabique 175
cartilla, puesta al día 730
cartografía 35
cartógrafo infrarrojo térmico 18
cartón 223, 400
cartón de cigarrillos 390
cartón pequeño 223
cartuchera 770
cartucho 268, 315, 500, 754, 773
cartucho de escopeta 912
cartucho de la cinta grabadora 488
cartucho de la película 481
cartucho de plástico 860
cartucho de rifle 912
cartucho de tóner 519
cartuchos 860, 861
casa 244, 877, 915
casa club 866
casa de adobes 418
casa de dos plantas 419
casa de una planta 419
casa flotante 607
casa romana 406
casa solar 675
casa, elementos 247
casa, estructura 250
casa, exterior 244
casaca 338, 359
casas adosadas 419
casas pareadas 419
cascabel 112, 449
cascabeles 449
cascada 48
cascanueces 230
cáscara 84, 85
cascarón 117
casco 20, 124, 127, 575, 599, 655, 748, 765, 798, 800, 808, 834, 842, 853, 858, 870, 871, 872, 875, 876, 878, 882, 887, 888, 891, 894, 895, 896, 901
casco de bombero 765
casco de salto 897
casco de seguridad 772
casco del bateador 796
casco integral 575, 874
casco protector 580, 884, 885
casco, superficie plantar del 127
cascos antirruido 861
cascos de seguridad 772
caserna 409
casete 499, 504, 521
casete con saludo 508
casete para grabar los mensajes 508
casi igual a 703
casilla 426, 915, 919
casilla del dinero 920
casillero 279
Casiopea 12
Caspio, mar 28, 33
casquete 268, 676
casquete de la palanca 268
casquete de seguridad 757
casquete del distribuidor 566
casquillo 274, 275, 860, 863, 912
Cassini 19
castaña 193
castaña de agua 184
castañuelas 437, 449

castas 99
castillete de extracción 650
castillo 408
castillo de proa 605, 609
castor 123
catalán 469
catalogo online 733
catamarán 835
catapulta 761
catarata 47
catedral 410
catedral gótica 410
catedral, plano 411
catenaria 595
cátodo 689
Catolicismo 736
catre desmontable 904
caucho central 867
cauda helicis 173
cávea 402, 407
cavidad abdominal 169, 170
cavidad bucal 116, 163, 164
cavidad gástrica 95
cavidad medular 154
cavidad nasal 112, 163
cavidad paleal 106
cavidad pleural 163
cayado de la aorta 160, 161, 162
caza 212, 912
cazadora 353
cazo 233
cazoleta 390, 752, 753, 849
cazonete 739
cazuela 905
cazuela vaporera 235
cebada 85, 203
cebada : espiga 85
cebador 752, 757
cebolla amarilla 184
cebolla blanca 184
cebolla roja 184
cebolla tierna 184
cebolleta 184
cebollino 184
cebra 128
ceda el paso 544, 546
cedilla 473
cedro del Líbano 89
cefalotórax 103, 107
Cefeo 12
ceja 442
cejilla 439, 440, 441
celada 749
celda 96, 407, 727
celda de aislamiento 727
celda de hombres 768
celda de menores 768
celda de mujeres 768
celda fotoeléctrica 482
celdas 728
celdilla 82, 100
celdilla de la miel 100
celdilla del polen 100
celdilla operculada 100
celdilla sellada 100
cellisca 64
celosía veneciana 249
célula 897
célula animal 94
célula convectiva 63
célula de Schwann 168
célula solar 529, 672, 673
célula vegetal 74
cementerio 39, 711
cemento 159
cenefa 282
cenefa drapeada 283
cenefa fruncida 283
cenefa plisada 283
cenefa plisada de canotillo 283
cenefas, ejemplos 283
cenicero 391
cenit 10
ceniza 391
Centauro 11
centavo 728
centeno 85, 203
centeno : espiga 85
central 807, 814
central eléctrica 657
central eléctrica, sección transversal 664
central hidroeléctrica, sección transversal 658
central nuclear 668
central térmica de carbón 646
centralita 507
centriolo 94
centro 431, 704, 809, 847, 879, 916
centro ciudad 709, 710
centro comercial 709, 714
centro de clasificación 474
centro de clasificación regional 475
centro de control 764
centro de documentación 764
centro de la cancha 818
centro de la diana 859
centro de la punta 740

centro de negocios 708, 710
centro del campo 803
centro del jefe 740
centro delantero 801
centro derecho 804
centro educativo 711
centro izquierdo 804
cepa de vid 86
cepillo 98, 289, 295, 309, 345, 384
cepillo aplicador de rímel 378
cepillo con base de goma 380
cepillo de baño 379
cepillo de curling 877
cepillo de dientes 384
cepillo de dientes eléctrico 384
cepillo de espalda 379
cepillo de esqueleto 380
cepillo de púas 380
cepillo de tejido 456
cepillo para cejas y pestañas 378
cepillo para suelos 289
cepillo para verduras 233
cepillo redondo 380
cepillo-plumero 289
cepillos 380
cepo 610, 913
cera 892
cera, dibujo 396
cerámica 464
cerámica, condensador 689
ceras 396
cerca 182
cercado 182
cerda 384
cerdas 295, 320, 383
cerdo 128
cerdo, asado 215
cerdo, carne picada 215
cerdo, cortes 215
cereales 85, 203, 204
cerebelo 167
cerebro 99, 103, 106, 107, 109, 110, 167
cereza 192
cerilla 391
cerillas de seguridad 391
cerio 684
cero 919
cerradura 247, 248, 278, 386, 389, 551, 554
cerradura de combinación 386
cerradura embutida 249
cerradura tubular con seguro 248
cerrajería 248, 715
cerros 741
cerveza 180
cerviz 115
césped 245, 322
cesio 682
cesta de freír 231
cesta de pescador 911
cestillo 98
cesto 291, 294
cesto de cocción al vapor 235
cesto para cubiertos 294
cesto para verdura 291
Chac-Mool 412
Chad 745
Chad, lago 34
chal 337
chalaza 117
chaleco 338, 348, 359
chaleco de pescador 911
chaleco de punto 348
chaleco salvavidas 611
chalecos 348
chalecos , jerseys y chaquetas 358
chalecos, jerseys, chaquetas 358
chalote 184
champiñón 183
champú 379
chancleta 344
chancleta playera 344
chanclo de goma 342
chapa 248
chapa de madera de desenrollo 300
chaparrón 57
chapka 340
chaqueta 355, 855
chaqueta blanca de esgrima 848
chaqueta cruzada 348, 359
chaqueta de montar 853
chaqueta de punto 354, 359
chaqueta recta 348
chaquetas 348
chaquetón 355
chaquetón de tres cuartos 355
chaquetón marinero 355
chaquetones 355
charcutería 216
charnela lateral 79
chasis 327, 632, 633, 638, 639, 641, 642, 776
chasis del bogie 586
chasis delantero 639
chateo 525
chayote 189
checo 469

chef 721
cheque de viaje 729
chequera con calculadora 386
cheques 729
chesterfield 276
cheurón 740
chicana 872
chifonier 279
Chile 742
chile 188
chile jalapeño 199
chimenea 245, 250, 256, 257, 259, 465, 599, 604, 608, 646, 650
chimenea de evacuación 650
chimenea de expulsión 573
chimenea lateral 44
chimenea principal 44
chimenea, conexión 256
chimenea, utensilios 257
chimpancé 139
China 747
China Meridional, mar 28, 33
China Oriental, mar 33
chinche acuática gigante 101
chinche de campo 101
chinchetas 534
chino 231, 468, 872
Chipre 744
chirimoya 196
chirivía 189
chispa 564
chistera 340
chocolate 208
chocolate amargo 208
chocolate blanco 208
chocolate con leche 208
chorizo 216
chorrera 362
chorrillo, sembradora 643
chorro de agua 828
chow chow 130
choza 418
choza indígena 418
Chubasco 57
chubasco de nieve 57
chuleta 214, 215
chuletón 214
chumacera giratoria 839
chutney de mango 201
chutney, mango 201
cian 690
cianobacterias 92
ciclismo 870
ciclismo de montaña 870
ciclismo en pista 871
ciclismo por carretera 870
ciclismo por carretera, competición 870
ciclista 870
ciclo de un motor de dos tiempos 565
ciclo de un motor diesel 565
ciclo de un motor rotatorio 565
ciclo hidrológico 67
ciclomotor 577
ciclón 63
ciclón tropical 63
ciclones tropicales, denominación 63
ciclorama 492
cidra cayote 189
ciego 103, 106, 116, 164
ciego pilórico 95, 109
ciego rectal 95
cielo abierto, excavación 647
cielo abierto, mina 647
cielo completamente nuboso 56
cielo despejado 56
cielo ligeramente nuboso 56
cielo medio nuboso 56
cielo muy nuboso 56
cielo no observable 56
cielo sereno 56
cielo turbulento 65
cien 703
ciere, tapa 689
cierre 291, 387, 391, 902
cierre con broche 391
cierre de polea 750
cierre de rosca 900
cierre en relieve 223
ciervo 128
ciervo de Virginia 128
cifras 472
cigala 218
cigarra 101
cigarrillo 390
cigüeña 119
cigüeñal 564, 566
cilantro 202
ciliada 79
cilindro 249, 268, 564, 611, 697, 705, 776
cilindro de corte 332
cilindro de dirección 638
cilindro de elevación de la hoja 639
cilindro de elevación del zanco 636
cilindro de freno 559
cilindro de orientación de la pala 639
cilindro de recuperación 756

cilindro de recuperación, cabeza delantera 756
cilindro de rotación 458
cilindro del brazo 638
cilindro del brazo elevador 637
cilindro del cucharón 637, 638
cilindro del elevador 637, 638
cilindro del elevador de la pala 636
cilindro del gas 755
cilindro elevador 573, 634, 766
cilindro hidráulico 633, 640
cilindro inferior 421
cilindro maestro 559
cilindro neumático 648
cilindro recogedor 642
cilindro superior 421
cilio 94
cima 45, 87, 886
cima bípara 81
cima unípara 81
cimacio 404
cimentación 253
cimiento del pilón 540
cimientos 253, 660
cimientos de una presa 660
cinc 683
cincel de rincón 421
cincha 855, 856, 900
cincha de la limonera 857
cinco 703
cinco especias chinas 199
cincuenta 703
cine 427, 710, 714
ciñendo el viento 833
cinta 313, 340, 453, 459, 757, 772, 773, 800, 815, 817, 823
cinta adhesiva 254
cinta aislante para tubería 299
cinta cargadora 646, 647
cinta central 821
cinta de acordonamiento 771
cinta de grabación 499
cinta de la red 821
cinta de teflón 314
cinta digital grabadora 488
cinta exprés 900
cinta magnética 495
cinta metálica 299
cinta métrica 313, 454
cinta transportadora 71, 620, 646, 647, 649
Cinto 736
cintura 147, 149, 663
cinturón 350, 352, 561, 611, 844, 850, 906
cinturón de alpinista 901
cinturón de asteroides 5
cinturón de herramientas 313
cinturón de hombros 555
cinturón de Kuiper 4
cinturón de seguridad 281, 555, 873
cinturón de servicio 770
cinturón lastrado 841
cinturón subabdominal 555
cinturones, neumático radial 561
circo 7
circo glaciar 46
circuito 872, 874
circuito de 120 voltios 272
circuito de 240 voltios 272
circuito de agua caliente 262
circuito de agua fría 262
circuito de desagüe 262
circuito de frenado 552, 559
circuito de supercross 875
circuito de ventilación 262
circuito eléctrico 274
circuito eléctrico de los captadores 559
circuito eléctrico en paralelo 687
circuito impreso 689
circuito impreso, placa 689
circuito integrado 689
circulación sanguínea 160
circulación, señales 544
circular 236
círculo 25 918
Círculo Antártico 29, 35, 36
círculo central 803, 809, 810, 877
círculo de canasta 809
círculo de espera 794
círculo de la estación 55
círculo de lanzamiento 790, 791
círculo de los colores 400
círculo de reanudación del juego 878
círculo de saque inicial 879
círculo de tiro 800
círculo doble 918
círculo exterior 877
círculo graduado de declinación 14
Círculo polar Ártico 35, 36
círculo triple 918
circulo, partes 704
círculos 917
circunferencia 704
circunvalación 39
cirro 56
cirrocúmulo 56
cirrocúmulos 62

ASTRONOMÍA > 2-25; TIERRA > 26-71; REINO VEGETAL >72-89; REINO ANIMAL > 90-143; SER HUMANO > 144-177; PRODUCTOS ALIMENTARIOS Y DE COCINA > 178-241; CASA > 242-295; BRICOLAJE Y JARDINERÍA > 296-333; VESTIDO > 334-371; ACCESORIOS Y ARTÍCULOS PERSONALES > 372-391; ARTE Y ARQUITECTURA > 392-465; COMUNICACIONES Y AUTOMATIZACIÓN DE OFICINA > 466-535; TRANSPORTE Y VEHÍCULOS > 536-643; ENERGÍA > 644-677; CIENCIA > 678-705; SOCIEDAD > 706-785; DEPORTES Y JUEGOS > 786-920

ÍNDICE ESPAÑOL

cirros 62
cirrostrato 56
cirrostratos 62
ciruela 192
cirugía menor 778
Cisne 12
cisterna 572, 573
cisterna del inodoro 264
cisterna, camión 572
cisura oblicua 163
cítara 432
citofaringe 94
citoplasma 74, 94, 170
citoprocto 94
citostoma 94
cítricos 82, 194
ciudad 37, 708
Ciudad del Vaticano 744
cizalla 424
cizallas para setos 330
clámide 336
claqueta 429
clarín 447
clarinete 446
clarinete bajo 437
clarinetes 437
clase 734
clasificación de Hubble 9
clasificación de plásticos 71
clasificación general, marcador 824
clasificador de fuelle 386
clasificadora, rectificadora, franqueadora 474
clasificadora-rectificadora-franqueadora 474
clave 410, 413
clave de do 434
clave de fa 434
clave de sol 434
clavecín 443
clavel 80
clavera 127
claves 434
clavícula 111, 116, 122, 141, 152
clavícula 142
clavija 439, 440, 442, 488, 502, 613, 767
clavija de acorde 441
clavija de afinación 441
clavija de alimentación 527
clavija de conexión 689
clavija de tensión 448
clavija de tipo americano 274
clavija europea 274
clavijero 439, 442
clavo 127, 198, 301, 901
clavo común 301
clavo cortado 301
clavo de albañil 301
clavo fechador 590
clavo helicoidal 301
clavo sin cabeza 301
clavos, ejemplos 301
claxon 576
cláxon 556
clientes, entrada 720
clientes, guardarropa 720
climas áridos 61
climas de alta montaña 61
climas de montaña 61
climas del mundo 61
climas polares 61
climas templados cálidos 61
climas templados fríos 61
climas tropicales 61
climatizador automático 556
clip 284, 534
clip de ajuste 275
clips, distribuidor 534
clítoris 170
cloaca 103, 110, 113, 116
cloro 683
cloroplasto 74
coanocito 95
cobalto 683
cobaya 123
cobertera inferior de la cola 115
cobertera superior de la cola 115
coberteras 115
coberteras mayores 115
coberteras medias 115
coberteras menores 115
coberteras primarias 115
coberteras primarias medias 115
cobertizo 182, 244, 322
cobertizo para ovejas 182
cobra 114
cobre 683
cocción 465
cocción al vapor, cesto 235
cocción, placa 239
cocción, platos 239
cóccix 152, 157
coche cama 584
coche celular 726
coche de fórmula 1 873
coche de fórmula 3000 873
coche de Indy 873
coche de policía 769, 771
coche de rally 873
coche de tracción 594
coche del equipo 870
coche familiar 549
Cochero 12
cocina 222, 224, 250, 406, 509, 584, 719, 721, 722, 723, 724, 726, 735, 763, 764
cocina de a bordo 624
cocina de campo 903
cocina de gas 290
cocina eléctrica 290, 721
cocina, tijeras 233
cocina, utensilios 229, 234
cóclea 174
coco 193
cocodrilo 114
Cocos, Placa 43
codal 749
codera 800, 808, 880, 894, 895
código 528
código de barras, lector 517
código del producto 699
codillo 124, 130, 215
codo 130, 140, 147, 149, 156, 258, 385
codo de 45 grados 269
codo de 90 grados 269
codo de cambio de eje 269
codorniz 120, 212
coelophysis 93
cofia 24
cofia cónica 339
cofre 577
cohete anticarro 757
cohete de combustible sólido 24
cohete espacial 24
cojín 280, 458
cojín para sellos 531
cojinete 586
cojinete de bolas 677
cojinete de empuje 659
cojinete móvil 836
col 186
col china 186
col lombarda 186
col marina 186
col ornamental 186
col rizada 186
col rizada de otoño 186
col verde 186
cola 107, 112, 113, 121, 122, 124, 130, 133, 136, 140, 143, 169, 254, 425, 625, 793, 887, 888, 892, 893, 894, 909
cola de ion 8
cola de polvo 8
colada de lava 44
colador 237, 240, 270
colador fino 231
colchón 281, 776
colchón de muelles 280
colchones 716
colchoneta 792
colchoneta aislante 904
colchoneta de aire 904
colchoneta de espuma 904
colchoneta de recepción 824
colector 652, 659
colector de admisión 565, 566
colector de electrones 689
colector de escape 552, 564, 565, 566
colector de grasa 239
colector del reactor 669
colector principal 712
colector principal de vapor 669
colector solar 675
colector solar plano 672
colegio 734
coles de Bruselas 186
colgador de intravenosos 780
colgante 287
colgar al aire libre después de escurrir 347
colibrí 118
coliflor 187
colilla 391
colina 45, 674, 875
colina abisal 49
colina de salida 867
colinabo 185
collar 320
collar cortafuego 257
collar de 5 vueltas , peto 374
collar de perforación 651
collar de una vuelta , matinée 374
collar de una vuelta , ópera 374
collares 374
collarín 257, 308, 311, 851
collarín cervical 775
collarino 404
colleja 187
collie 130
colmena 100, 182
colmillo 112, 121, 159
Colombia 742
colon 97, 113, 125
colon ascendente 164
colon descendente 164
colon sigmoideo 164
colon transverso 164
colonia, agua de 379
color 914
color pulverizado 398
colores aditivos síntesis 690
colores primarios 400
colores secundarios 400
colores sustractivos, síntesis 690
colores terciarios 400
colores, círculo 400
colores, ejemplos 741
colores, síntesis 690
colorete en polvo 378
columela 105
columna 47, 64, 287, 403, 405, 440, 452, 471, 482, 485, 540, 919
columna central 676
columna con capuchón 64
columna corintia adosada 407
columna de alcohol 695
columna de control 626
columna de estabilización 652
columna de mercurio 695
columna de tensión 453
columna dórica adosada 407
columna fraccionadora 656
columna jónica adosada 407
columna vertebral 109, 121, 152, 157, 167
colutorio 384
coma 473
comadreja 134
combinación 366, 852
combinación con sujetador 366
combinación ganadora 920
combustible 665, 670, 671
combustible defectuoso envasado 666
combustible fósil 68, 70
combustible para aviones 656
combustible para calderas 656
combustible para calefacción 656
combustión 564, 565, 627
comedor 250, 584, 608, 720, 723, 724, 727, 763, 764
comedor de los empleados 509
comedor, vagón 584
comercio electrónico 525
cometa 8
comienzo de lectura 501
comillas 473
comillas sencillas 473
comino 198
comisaría de policía 711
comisario 875
comisario de pista 853, 855
comisario jefe 855
comisura labial 174
comité de arbitraje 845
cómoda 279
comodín 914
Comoras 746
compact flash, tarjeta de memoria 481
compactadora 573
compartimento para almacenamiento 567
compartimento para equipaje 585
compartimento para los equipos 585
compartimiento 416
compartimiento de almacenamiento 766
compartimiento de documentos 527
compartimiento de pasajeros 605
compartimiento del cable de la batería 489
compartimiento del depósito del agua 628
compartimiento del equipo técnico 489
compartimiento dormitorio 584
compartimiento motor 568
compartimiento para almacenamiento 483
compartimiento para el equipaje 584
compartimiento para lácteos 291
compartimiento para mantequilla 291
compartimiento para ordenador 527
Compás 11
compás 434
compensador de flotación 841
compensador gráfico de sintonización 498
competición 789
competición de ciclismo por carretera 870
competición, canal 788
complejo hidroeléctrico 657
complexo mayor 151
compluvio 406
componentes del portalámpara 275
composición de la sangre 162
compresa de gasa 777
compresión 71, 564, 565, 627
compresor 260, 533, 670
compresor centrífugo 627
compresor de aire 320, 585, 586
compresor del aire acondicionado 566
compuerta 596, 658, 664
compuerta de la cisterna 607
compuerta de llenado 597
compuerta del aliviadero 657
compuerta inferior 597
comulgatorio 737
comunicación por teléfono 506
comunicación sin hilos 505
comunicación vía satélite 486
comunicación, unidades 522
comunicaciones 468
comunicaciones aéreas 487
comunicaciones industriales 487
comunicaciones marítimas 487
comunicaciones militares 487
comunicaciones particulares 487
comunicaciones terrestres 487
con hombrera 360
concentración de gas de efecto invernadero 68
concentrado de tomate 200
concentrado, tomate 200
concentrador 522, 523
concentrador de aire 382
concesionariode automóviles 711
concha 104, 105, 106, 173, 276, 448
concha bivalva 105
concha bivalva, anotomía 105
concha bivalva, morfología 105
concha univalva 105
concha univalva, morfología 105
conchitas 206
condensación 67, 680
condensada 472
condensador 646, 668, 674, 693, 694
condensador de cerámica 689
condensador de película plástica 689
condensadores electrolíticos 689
cóndilo externo 153
cóndilo interno 153
condimento de especias cajún 199
condimentos 200, 723
cóndor 119
condrito 8
conducción 681
conducción forzado 658
conducto de admisión 564
conducto de aire caliente 293
conducto de aire comprimido 398
conducto de aire fresco 543
conducto de aire viciado 543
conducto de desviación 627
conducto de distribución vertical 258
conducto de Havers 154
conducto de monedas 920
conducto de salida de aire 627
conducto de ventilación 402
conducto deferente 169
conducto del aire 445
conducto del veneno 112
conducto espermático 104
conducto eyaculador 169
conducto galactóforo 171
conducto hermafrodito 104
conducto lacrimal 177
conducto principal 258
conducto principal del gas 712
conducto radicular 159
conducto secundario 258
conducto semicircular lateral 174
conducto semicircular posterior 174
conducto semicircular superior 174
conducto sudorífero 172
conductor 857
conductor de fase 273
conductor neutral 273
conector 269, 272, 488, 766
conector de alimentación del adaptador 526
conector de altavoces 497
conector de boca de riego 767
conector de expansión AGP 513
conector de expansión PCI 513
conector de extensión ISA 513
conector de línea cargada 663
conector de puesta de tierra 497
conector de RAM 513
conector de salida 441
conector de tierra macho 274
conector de tierra, macho 274
conector del desagüe 262
conector del ordenador 518
conector del ratón 518
conector en T 522
conectores de antenas 497
conejo 123, 212
conexión 273, 663, 916
conexión a la red 273
conexión de la chimenea 256
conexión de tierra 273
conexión eléctrica 258, 260, 266
conexión eléctrica a tierra 655
conexión para la manguera de aire 320
conexión, clavija 689
conexión, galería 543
conexiones 269, 571
conexiones, ejemplos 270
confesionarios 737
configuración de los continentes 28
configuración del litoral 51
confirmación, tecla 731
confitería 717
confluente 48
Confucianismo 736
congelador 224, 720
congelador incorporado 291
congelados 181
Congo 745
Congo, río 34
congresos, palacio 711
congresos, sala 718
conífera 89
coníferas, ejemplos 89
conjuntiva 177
conjunto deportivo 369
conjunto vacío 703
conjuntos instrumentales, ejemplos 438
conmutador 523, 688
conmutador de alimentación 477
conmutador de corriente 497
conmutador de grabación nocturna 496
conmutador de intensidad 274
cono 177, 494, 705
cono de admisión 627
cono de penumbra 6, 7
cono de sombra 6, 7
cono femenino 89
cono masculino 89
cono pirométrico 464
conopial 413
consejero de producción 490
consejeros musicales 490
conservación, laboratorio 395
conservador, despacho 394
conservas 181
consigna 582
consola 440, 444
consola central 556
consola de control 626
consola de juego 918
consola de la unidad de vídeo 520
consola de sonido 488, 489, 490
consola del productor 488
consola para el sistema de vacío 694
constelaciones del hemisferio austral 10
constelaciones en el hemisferio boreal 12
consultorio 779, 781
consultorio ginecológico 779
consumidor 487
consumidores primarios 67
consumidores secundarios 67
consumidores terciarios 67
contabilidad 509
contacto 274, 275, 916
contacto central 476
contacto con conexión de tierra 263
contacto de conexión a tierra 274
contacto negativo 672, 673
contacto positivo 672, 673
contacto, dispositivos 274
contador 499, 700
contador de agua 262
contador de kilovatio-hora 273
contador de pasadas 456
contador eléctrico 273
contaminación agrícola 69
contaminación de automóviles 69
contaminación de petróleo 70
contaminación del agua 70
contaminación del aire 69
contaminación del suelo 69
contaminación doméstica 69
contaminación industrial 69
contaminantes del aire 69
contaminantes no biodegradables 69
contenedor 605, 635, 638
contenedor de reciclado de aluminio 71
contenedor de reciclado de papel 71
contenedor de reciclado de vidrio 71
contenedor de recogida de papel 71
contenedor de recogida de vidrio 71
contenedores de reciclaje 71
contenedores, plataformas, cargador 623
contenedores, terminal 708
contera 389, 391, 483, 868, 909
contera de caucho 782
contestador automático 508
continente 7, 49
continente húmedo 61
continentes, configuración 28
contorno del cuello 349
contrabajo 439
contrabajos 437
contrachapado 300
contrachapado multiplex 300
contraescarpa 409
contrafagots 437
contrafoque 603
contrafuerte 370, 410, 540, 660, 881, 889
contrafuerte del talón 342
contrafuertes, presa 660
contraguardia 409
contrahilo de la tela 455
contrahoja 309
contrahuella 255
contramesana 602
contrapeso 14, 16, 417, 500, 542, 591, 634, 638, 639, 640
contrapeso, guía 417
contrapiso 252, 253, 254
contrapluma 634
contraquilla 607
contratuerca 270
contraventana 249

1052

ASTRONOMÍA > 2-25; TIERRA > 26-71; REINO VEGETAL >72-89; REINO ANIMAL > 90-143; SER HUMANO > 144-177; PRODUCTOS ALIMENTARIOS Y DE COCINA > 178-241; CASA > 242-295; BRICOLAJE Y JARDINERÍA > 296-333; VESTIDO > 334-371; ACCESORIOS Y ARTÍCULOS PERSONALES > 372-391; ARTE Y ARQUITECTURA > 392-465; COMUNICACIONES Y AUTOMATIZACIÓN DE OFICINA > 466-535; TRANSPORTE Y VEHÍCULOS > 536-643; ENERGÍA > 644-677; CIENCIA > 678-705; SOCIEDAD > 706-785; DEPORTES Y JUEGOS > 786-920

contrincante 846
control 514
control : selección de grupo 514
control a larga distancia 483
control a larga distancia, aguja 590
control de agudos 497
control de alimentador de oxígeno 898
control de altura 485
control de balance 497
control de brillo 518
control de centrado 518
control de color 512
control de combustible 627
control de contraste 512, 518
control de elevación de la caja de iluminación 485
control de entrada de información fina 450
control de entrada de información rápida 450
control de entrada del personal 726
control de fotocopias 512
control de ganancia 613
control de graves 497
control de la entrada de aire 256
control de la plataforma corrediza 693
control de oxígeno 319
control de pasaportes 621
control de posición de la muestra 694
control de presión 384
control de producción, sala 491
control de salida del personal 726
control de secuencias 450
control de seguridad 621
control de sintonización 504
control de sonido 490
control de temperatura 259, 261, 267, 288, 465
control de tonos de bajos 503
control de tonos de graves 503
control de velocidad 332, 516
control de volumen 441, 450, 451, 495, 504, 507, 513
control de volumen del auricular 506
control de volumen del timbre 506
control del campo audio 497
control del espejo retrovisor exterior 554
control del margen 528
control del nivel de alarma 613
control del sintonizador 498
control del sonido 441
control del sonido estereofónico 491
control del tiempo 451
control del vaporizador 288
control del ventilador 261
control del volumen 441, 497, 508
control eléctrico de pago 920
control electrónico, caja 563
control estéreo 504
control horizontal 518
control mecánico de agujas 590
control remoto, unidad móvil de servicio 21
control vertical 518
controlador de entradas 394, 427
controlador de viento del sintetizador 451
controles de intensidad de la pantalla del ordenador 20
controles de la pletina 504
controles de sintonización 494
controles de volumen de comunicaciones 20
controles del lector de discos compactos 504
controles del piloto automático 626
controles del sistema de soporte vital 20
controles VCR 495
conurbación 708
convección 681
convención, corriente 681
conversión del agua en vapor 665
convertidor catalítico 553
convertidor de tensión 292
Cook, estrecho 29
cooksonia 92
coordenadas astronómicas, sistema 13
coordenadas terrestres, sistema 35
Copa 11
copa 87, 223, 340, 341, 367
copa de agua 225
copa de champaña 225
copa de cóctel 225
copa de flauta 225
copa para brandy 225
copa para licores 225
copa para oporto 225
copa para vino blanco 225
copa para vino de Alsacia 225
copa para vino de Borgoña 225
copa para vino de Burdeos 225
copete 124, 909
copias anverso /reverso 512
copo de nieve 64
copyright (derechos de autor) 473
coquilla 808, 843, 880
coquina 217
coracoides 111, 116
Coral, mar 29
Corán 736
corazón 82, 97, 99, 103, 104, 105, 106, 107, 109, 110, 112, 116, 125, 162, 163, 212, 740, 914
corbata 349
corbata inglesa 349
corbatas 716
corchea 435
corcheras 831
corchete 881
corchetes 453, 473
corcho 817, 892
cordada 900
cordaje 816, 822, 893
cordal 433, 439
cordero, carne picada 215
cordero, carne troceada 215
cordero, cortes 215
cordero, pierna 215
cordillera 7, 38, 42
cordillera de los Andes 31
cordillera del Atlas 34
cordón 282, 284, 285, 288, 289, 313, 342, 353, 370, 387, 505, 797, 881, 908
cordón de alimentación 237, 308, 381
cordón de alimentación de corriente alterna 526
cordón de alimentación de corriente continua 526
cordón de alimentación, corriente continua 526
cordón de trazar 313
cordón del pedal 460
cordón litoral 51
cordón nervioso 99
cordón nervioso ventral 107
cordón para espirales 465
cordoncillo 729
cordones 843
cordones de listones 285
Corea, península 33
coreano 469
corimbo 81
corintio, orden 405
córnea 177, 691
córner 803
corneta 739
cornete inferior 175
cornete medio 175
cornete superior 175
cornetín 437, 447
cornisa 245, 247, 278, 403, 404
corno francés 437, 447
corno inglés 446
cornos ingleses 437
coro 410, 411
coroides 177
corola 80
corona 6, 124, 127, 159, 374, 398, 440, 448, 696
Corona Austral 10
Corona Boreal 13
corona externa de la cadena 580
corona interna de la cadena 580
corona radiata 170
corona rotatoria 639
coronación 660
coronamiento 661, 664
corpúsculo de Meissner 172
corpúsculo de Pacini 172
corpúsculo de Ruffini 172
corral 182
corral, aves 213
correa 377, 389, 696, 765, 824, 836, 841, 850, 855, 869, 893
correa de ajuste 889
correa de amortiguación 897
correa de barbilla 808
correa de cierre 906
correa de compresión 906
correa de distribución 566
correa de la cincha 855
correa de la manga 352
correa de los crampones 901
correa de muñeca 901
correa de retención 389
correa de seguridad 20, 818
correa de tiro 893
correa de transmisión 605
correa del tambor 292
correa del ventilador 552, 566
correa elástico 389
correa para el cuello 772
correa para el pie 840
correa para escalera y manguera 767
correa para herramientas 20
correa para la mano 888, 892
correa principal de sustentación 897
correas 773
correas de los aparatos de buceo 841
corrección de caracteres 528
corrección de palabras 528
corrector de ortografía 528
corredera 284, 445, 453
corredera con enganches 284
corredera de afinamiento 447
corredera de ajuste 350
corredera de la guía 305
corredor 676, 871, 885
corredor de luge 884
corredor de poder 807
corredores 875
correo 474
correo aéreo 475
correo de masa 475
correo electrónico 525
correo electrónico, programa 524
correo internacional 475
correo no obliterado 474
correo obliterado 474
correo postal 475
correo regional 475
correos 474, 711
correos, oficina 715
corriente 597
corriente de agua 48, 70
corriente de convección 681
corriente eléctrica, unidad de medida 702
corriente subterránea 47
corrimiento 47
corrosivo 774
corsé 337
corsé de cintura de avispa 367
cortacésped 332
cortacésped con motor 332
cortacutículas 377
cortador de alambre 317
cortador de huevos duros 233
cortafuego 252, 523
cortahilos 453
cortapastas 232
cortapatillas 383
cortapuros 390
cortasetos eléctrico 331
cortatubos 314
cortaúñas 377
corte de la atmósfera terrestre 53
corte de la corteza terrestre 42
corte de la pelota de béisbol 797
corte de un bulbo 78
corte de un grano de trigo 85
corte de un melocotón 81
corte de un panal 100
corte de un rail 591
corte de un tronco 300
corte de una avellana 84
corte de una frambuesa 83
corte de una fresa 83
corte de una manzana 82
corte de una naranja 82
corte de una nuez 84
corte de una pelota de golf 867
corte de una uva 83
corte princesa 356
corte transversal 920
corte transversal de un microscopio de electrones 694
corte transversal de un molar 159
corte transversal de un tronco 87
corte transversal de una pipa 390
corte, riel 591
cortes de cerdo 215
cortes de cordero 215
cortes de ternera 214
cortes de vacuno 214
corteza 82, 87
corteza continental 42
corteza cortical 165
corteza oceánica 42
corteza terrestre 42, 43
corteza terrestre, corte 42
cortina 276, 282, 285, 492
cortina abombada 283
cortina de enrollamiento automático 558
cortina de inyecciones 660, 661
cortina de riel 284
cortina de ventana 282
cortina separadora 780
cortina suelta corrediza 283
cortina sujeta de doble barra 283
cortinas corredera 282
cortinas cruzadas 283
cortinas recogidas 282
cortinas, ejemplos 283
corvejón 124, 130
cosechadora trilladora 643
cosechera de forraje 642
coser, máquina 452
cosido 426
cosméticos 717
costa 49
Costa de Marfil 745
Costa Rica 742
costado 425, 560, 561, 632
costas, ejemplos 51
costero 300
costilla 112, 116, 121, 122, 126, 131, 136, 138, 141, 142, 909
costilla axial 105
costilla de encastre 624
costilla espiral 105
costilla falsa 153
costilla flotante 138, 152
costillar 214, 215
costillas 152
costura 342, 346, 348, 390, 452, 797, 798
costura de corte princesa 366
costura invisible 349
cota de malla 749
cotiledón 77
cotillo 301
coulommiers 211
Cowper, glándula 169
coxa 96, 98
crampones 893
cráneo 106, 109, 116, 121, 126, 136, 138, 141, 142, 146
cráneo de un niño 158
cráneo, vista lateral 158
cráter 7, 44, 647
cráter, estela luminosa 7
creciente 741
cree 469
cremallera 307, 353, 369, 377, 389, 453, 791
cremallera de fijación 692
cremáster 97
crepidoma 403, 405
cresta 45, 49, 690
cresta de la presa 657
cresta del aliviadero 657
crestón 749
Cretáceo 93
cricket 798
criminalidad, prevención 768
crin 124, 439
criptón 684
crisálida 97, 100
cristal 672, 673
cristal de protección 878
cristalería 225
cristales de nieve 64
cristales irregulares 64
cristalino 177
cristalización 680
Cristiandad : Nuevo Testamento 736
Croacia 744
croco 80
crol 832
cromatina 94
cromo 683
cromosfera 6
Cronología de las Religiones 736
cronometrador 810, 814, 842, 845, 846, 847, 848, 881, 883, 900
cronometrador de calle 830
cronometradores 827, 844
cronómetro 488, 696, 789, 831
cronómetro electrónico automático 831
crosne 184
Crottin de Chavignol 210
cruasán 204
cruce 590
cruce con preferencia 544
cruce de animales en libertad 545, 547
crucero 410, 411
cruces de carreteras, ejemplos 538
cruceta 268, 834
crucifijo 737
crudo, oleoducto 654
crus hélix 173
crustáceo 218
crustáceos 107
cruz 124, 130, 610, 740
cruz de San Andrés 591
cruz del altar 737
Cruz del Sur 11
cuaderna 607, 639
cuadernillo 426
cuaderno de taquigrafía 531
cuadrado 112, 705
cuadrante 273, 695, 696, 704
cuadrante calculador 479
cuadrilátero 705, 842
cuadro 245, 862
cuadro de bateo 797
cuadro de distribución 272
cuadro de saque 821
cuadro de saque derecho 821
cuadro de saque izquierdo 821
cuadro de servicio 818, 819
cuadro de servicio de dobles 817
cuadro de servicio de individuales 817
cuadro de temperaturas 288
cuarta 434, 849
cuarta vuelta 789
cuarteto 438
cuartilla 124
cuarto 127, 342, 370
cuarto creciente 7
cuarto de baño 251, 264
cuarto de estar 902
cuarto de la limpieza 731
cuarto menguante 7
cuartos de final 789
cuarzo, metrónomo 436
Cuaternario 93
cuatro palos, barco de vela 602
Cuba 742
cuba 291, 292
cuba de lavado 294
cubertería 227, 905
cubeta 484
cubeta colectora de gotas 241
cubeta congeladora 240
cubeta de alcohol 695
cubeta de mercurio 695
cubeta de precipitación 685
cubeta para lavar impresiones 485
cubículo 406
cubierta 240, 260, 261, 275, 425, 499, 608, 755, 757, 838
cubierta cónica 415
cubierta de aterrizaje 761
cubierta de cabina, eyector 898
cubierta de cuatro aguas 414
cubierta de cuatro aguas con canalera 415
cubierta de cúpula peraltada 415
cubierta de dos aguas 414
cubierta de la aguja 500
cubierta de la cabina 898
cubierta de linternilla 414
cubierta de pabellón 415
cubierta de popa 608
cubierta de rotonda 415
cubierta de seguridad 332
cubierta de sol 607
cubierta de tejas 403
cubierta de torrecilla 415
cubierta de vertiente simple 414
cubierta de vuelo 761
cubierta del cubo 659
cubierta del mecanismo del freno 587
cubierta deslizable 612
cubierta en artesa 414
cubierta en diente de sierra 414
cubierta en pendiente 414
cubierta exterior de la cúpula 17
cubierta frontal 426
cubierta imperial 414
cubierta inferior 655
cubierta interior de la cúpula 17
cubierta mansarda 414
cubierta para automóviles 608
cubierta piramidal 415
cubierta posterior 426
cubierta principal 607, 761
cubierta protectora 639
cubierta superior 609, 624, 655
cubierta superior de la turbina 659
cubierta térmica 22
cubiertas 414
cubiertos 722
cubilete 915
cubital anterior 150, 151
cubital posterior 151
cúbito 116, 121, 122, 126, 131, 136, 138, 141, 142, 152, 154, 156
cubitos de hielo, bandeja 291
cubo 295, 534, 659, 677, 705, 783
cubo de basura 295, 723
cubo de basura reciclable 71
cubo de flash 482
cubo del rotor 631
cuboides 155
cubre cazoleta 752
cubrebañeras 837
cucaracha oriental 101
cuchara 227, 401, 905, 911
cuchara de degustación 233
cuchara de helado 228
cuchara de mesa 228
cuchara de postre 228
cuchara de sopa 228
cuchara de té 228
cuchara para servir helado 233
cucharas dosificadoras 231
cucharas, ejemplos 228
cucharita de café 228
cucharón 637, 752
cucharón excavador 638
cucharón trasero 637
cuchilla 236, 237, 240, 303, 317, 331, 332, 382, 390, 534, 643, 878
cuchilla de baile 881
cuchilla de corte 636, 638
cuchilla de disco 641
cuchilla de patinaje artístico 881
cuchilla del cucharón 637
cuchilla fija 424
cuchilla móvil 424
cuchilla para delimitar el césped 326
cuchilla, mecanismo de desplazamiento 639
cuchillas para batir 236
cuchillas, tipos 401
cuchillo 227, 841, 905, 907
cuchillo de carne 228
cuchillo de carnicero 229
cuchillo de cocina 229
cuchillo de combate 751
cuchillo de contornear 401, 421
cuchillo de mantequilla 228
cuchillo de mesa 228
cuchillo de pan 229
cuchillo de pelar 229
cuchillo de pescado 228
cuchillo de postre 228
cuchillo de queso 228
cuchillo de sílex 748
cuchillo de trinchar 229
cuchillo eléctrico 237
cuchillo filetero 229

ASTRONOMÍA > 2-25; TIERRA > 26-71; REINO VEGETAL >72-89; REINO ANIMAL > 90-143; SER HUMANO > 144-177; PRODUCTOS ALIMENTARIOS Y DE COCINA > 178-241; CASA > 242-295; BRICOLAJE Y JARDINERÍA > 296-333; VESTIDO > 334-371; ACCESORIOS Y ARTÍCULOS PERSONALES > 372-391; ARTE Y ARQUITECTURA > 392-465; COMUNICACIONES Y AUTOMATIZACIÓN DE OFICINA > 466-535; TRANSPORTE Y VEHÍCULOS > 536-643; ENERGÍA > 644-677; CIENCIA > 678-705; SOCIEDAD > 706-785; DEPORTES Y JUEGOS > 786-920
1053

cuchillo paleta 397
cuchillo para desbastar 464
cuchillo para deshuesar 229
cuchillo para jamón 229
cuchillo para ostras 229
cuchillo para pomelos 229
cuchillos de cocina, ejemplos 229
cuchillos, ejemplos 228
cuello 77, 113, 124, 147, 148, 149, 159, 169, 227, 319, 348, 349, 351, 352, 362, 494, 868
cuello Berta 363
cuello camisero 362
cuello chino 363
cuello con botones 349
cuello de chal 362
cuello de cisne 255
cuello de doble vista 352
cuello de ganso 638
cuello de hechura de sastre 362
cuello de Holanda 339
cuello de lazo 362
cuello de pico 354
cuello de polo 363
cuello de tortuga 363
cuello de volantes 363
cuello de 180 grados 885
cuello del fémur 153
cuello del remo 838
cuello del útero 170
cuello drapeado 363
cuello en V 348
cuello hechura sastre 355
cuello italiano 349
cuello Mao 363
cuello marinero 362
cuello plano con orejas 362
cuello plano tipo Peter Pan 362
cuello redondo 363, 368
cuello redondo, jersey 359
cuello tipo cogulla 363
cuellos, ejemplos 362
cuenca oceánica 49
cuenco 227
cuenco de queso blando 226
cuenta 721
cuentakilómetros 557
cuentalitros 548
cuentavueltas 883
cuerda 324, 439, 440, 443, 611, 686, 696, 750, 842, 850, 859, 900, 913
cuerda de amarre 900
cuerda de disparo 756
cuerda de elevación 321
cuerda de salida falsa 830
cuerda de tensión 433
cuerda inferior 540
cuerda maestra 893
cuerda para el cosido 424
cuerda superior 540
cuerda vocal 163
cuerda, instrumentos 439
cuerdas 433, 442, 448
cuerdas de acompañamiento 432
cuerdas de suspensión 896, 897
cuerdas melódicas 432
cuerdas para eslálon 840
cuerno 376
cuerno anterior 167
cuerno posterior 167
cuero 350
cuerpo 240, 268, 306, 390, 446, 700, 793, 849, 893, 909
cuerpo calloso 167
cuerpo cavernoso 169
cuerpo celular 168
cuerpo ciliar 177
cuerpo de baquelita 757
cuerpo de guardia 408, 409
cuerpo de la colmena 100
cuerpo de la torre 663
cuerpo de la uña 172
cuerpo del fórnix 167
cuerpo humano 146
cuerpo metálico de la bujía 562
cuerpo sólido 441
cuerpo vertebral 157, 168
cuerpo vítreo 177
cuerpos celestes 4
cuerpos de Nissl 168
cuerpos sólidos 705
Cuervo 11
cuervo 118
cueva 51
cuidado de los tejidos 347
cuidado del césped 332
cuidado personal 379
culata 374, 446, 754, 755, 860, 861, 912
culata de los cilindros 566
culombio 702
culote 757, 912
cultivador 326, 641
cultivador de mano 325
cúmulo 56
cúmulo globular 9
cumulonimbo 56
cumulonimbos 62
cúmulos 62

cuna 281
cuña 444, 756, 900
cuna plegable 281
cuñadas 785
cuñado 785
cuneiforme lateral 155
cuneta 538, 864
cupé 549
cúpula 84, 415, 614, 760
cúpula del Mihrab 738
cúpula del pórtico 738
cúpula giratoria 17
cúrcuma 198
cureña 750, 753
curio 684
curling 877
curry 198
cursiva 472
cursor abajo 515
cursor arriba 515
cursor de ajuste de la frecuencia 498
cursor hacia la derecha 515
cursor hacia la izquierda 515
curva 539, 911
curva a la derecha 544, 547
curva de 180 grados 885
curva del club 856
curva doble 547
curva lejana 856
curvada 401
cuscús 204
cúter Marconi 601

D

D 862
dactilera 859
dado 915
dado común 914
dado de póquer 914
dado doble 915
dados 914
daga 751
dálmata 131
dama 915, 916
damas 916
damas, tablero 916
danés 469
Danubio, río 32
dardo 918
dátil 192
datos, recepción 41
datos, registro 41
datos, transmisión 41
datos, tratamiento 41, 54
David 736
David, estrella 738
de acero a plástico 269
de aspas 236
de cobre a acero 269
de cobre a plástico 269
de cuatro cuartos 434
de dos mitades 434
de gancho 236
de herradura 413
de momia 904
de ojiva lanceolada 413
de servicio 820
de tres cuartos 434
deambulatorio 411
decágono regular 705
decantador 225
declinación 13
decorador 429
decorador jefe de producción 428
dedal 454
dedalitos 206
dedil 531
dedo 110, 117, 122, 143, 172, 346, 797, 900
dedo anular 173
dedo de pata lobulada 117
dedo de pata palmípeda 117
dedo del corazón 173
dedo del pie 146, 148
dedo externo 115
dedo índice 173
dedo interno 115
dedo medio 115
dedo meñique 173
dedo palmeado 110
dedo posterior 115, 117
dedos 116
dedos del pie, extensor largo 150
dedos prensiles 139
dedos, extensor común 151
defectos de la visión 691
defensa 809
defensa central 803
defensa derecho 801, 878
defensa izquierdo 801, 878
deflector 260, 329, 332, 333
deflector de viento 570
deflector de viento de los aviones 761
deflector del tanque de oxígeno líquido 25
deforestación 69

degustación, cuchara 233
Deimos 4
dejada 821
delantero 348, 349, 803, 804
delantero derecho 812
delantero izquierdo 812
delantero medio 812
delantero número 8 804
delco 552
delegados técnicos 881
Delfín 12
delfín 136, 137
delfín, esqueleto 136
delfín, morfología 136
delineador 378
delineador de labios 378
delta 48, 51
Delta II 24
delta, brazos 48
deltoides 150
demarcación 918
dendrita 168
dendrita espacial 64
denominación de los ciclones tropicales 63
dentada 79
dentadura humana 159
dentario 112
dentículo 404, 405
dentífrico 384
dentina 159
deportes 788
deportes acuáticos 827
deportes aéreos 896
deportes de balón 794
deportes de combate 842
deportes de fuerza 850
deportes de invierno 877
deportes de montaña 900
deportes de motor 872
deportes de pelota 794
deportes de precisión 859
deportes de puntería 859
deportes de raqueta 815
deportes ecuestres 852
deportes náuticos 827
deportes sobre ruedas 894
deportivo 549
depósito 394
depósito de aceite 331
depósito de agua 241, 586
depósito de aire comprimido 586
depósito de carbón 646
depósito de carburante de calentamiento 563
depósito de combustible 586, 760
depósito de contenedores 596
depósito de de los utensilios 734
depósito de gas 391
depósito de gasolina 553, 563, 574, 577
depósito de gasolina, tapón 551
depósito de lodos 651
depósito de mercancía en tránsito 596
depósito de mercancías 708
depósito de misiles 762
depósito de municiones 758
depósito de pintura 320
depósito de polvo 288
deposito de tinta 398
depósito de tinta 398
depósito del agua 384
depósito del combustible 631, 758
depósito del grano 643
depósito del líquido de frenos 559
depósito del propulsor 18
depósito esterilizado 780
depósito externo de combustible 22
depósito nocturno, buzón 731
depósito ventral 631
depósitos aluviales 48
depresión 55
depresión barométrica 55
derecha del actor 431
derecha del espectador 431
deriva 760
deriva móvil 835
derivación 687
derivación de la toma de aire 262
derivación en T 269, 271
derivación en T del desagüe 271
derivación en U 269
derivación en Y 269
dermis 172
derrubios 47
derrumbamiento 47
desagüe 262, 264
desagüe de fondo 246
desagüe de la turbina 662
desagüe principal 262
desatascador 314
desbaste 401
descamador 905
descanso del macillo 443
descapotable 549
descarga, cámara 402
descenso 889
descenso del spinnaker 833
descensor de ocho 900

descomponedores 67
descompresor 841
descorazonador 233
descote rapeado 363
desenganchador 315
desenganchador manual 889
desértico 61
desfibrilador 775
deshuesador 233
deshumidificador 261
desierto 52, 66
desierto arenoso 52
desierto de Atacama 31
desierto de Gobi 33
desierto de Kalahari 34
desierto de Namibia 34
desierto del Sahara 34
desierto rocoso 52
deslizador 896
desmenuzamiento 71
desnivel 244
desodorante 379
despacho 251, 724
despacho de dirección 718
despacho de la enfermera jefe 779
despacho de la guardia de seguridad 733
despacho del administrador delegado 509
despacho del asistente social 779
despacho del bedel 735
despacho del bibliotecario 732
despacho del conservador 394
despacho del director 394, 726, 731, 732, 735
despacho del gimnasio 734
despacho del inspector de prevención de incendios 764
despacho del jefe de bomberos 764
despacho del juez 728
despacho del oficial subalterno 768
despacho del oficial superior 768
despacho del secretario judicial 728
despacho del subdirector 726
despegue 891
despensa 250, 720, 722, 724
desplantador 325
desplazamiento 515, 690
desplazamiento del cursor, teclas 529
despojos 212
desprendimiento 47
desprendimientos 545, 547
desprendimientos de tierras 47
destellos, tubo 692
destilador para asfalto 656
destinos 582
destornillador 302, 905
destornillador de trinquete 302
destornillador en cruz 905
destornillador inalámbrico 302
desyerbador 325
detector de alta tensión 316
detector de continuidad 316
detector de humo 767
detector de metales 726
detector de tensión 316
detonador 757
devanadera 462
devanado de inducido 688
devanado inductor 688
devanador 462, 910
devanador de bobinas 462
devolución de libros, mostrador 733
devolución de monedas 507
devolución de monedas rechazadas 920
devolvedor 865
Devónico 92
diablo de Tasmania 143
diadema 772
diáfisis 155
diafragma 163, 477, 488, 502
diafragma de vacío 566
diafragma, escala de abertura 478
diagonal 473, 663
diagrama de la circulación 161
diagramas de tejidos 463
diamante 375, 794, 914
diamante, corte 374
diámetro 704
diana 859, 918
diapasón 436, 439, 441, 697
diapositiva 483
diapositivas, proyector 483
diastema 123
dibujo 368, 369, 396, 458
dibujo a la cera 396
dibujo al carboncillo 396
dibujo de la superficie de rodadura 560, 561
dibujo de lápices de colores 396
dibujo de tinta china 396
dibujo, tablero 399
diente 108, 112, 227, 303, 304, 331, 382, 636, 638, 642, 643, 876
diente de la desterronadora 636
diente de la rueda 686
diente de león 187
dientes 159, 309, 453, 881
dientes de la leva 453

dientes rectos, rueda cilíndrica 686
dientes rotor 688
dientes, cepillo 384
diéresis 473
diésel 656
diésel para barcos 656
diez 703
diez mandamientos 738
diferencia de potencial eléctrico, unidad de medida 702
diferencial 553
diferentes formas de alas 630
difusión de información 525
difusor 428, 479
difusor tubular 627
digestivo, aparato 164
dijes 376
dimetrodon 92
Dinamarca 744
dinamo 688
dínamo 578
dinamómetro 699
dinero 729
dinero en efectivo, provisión 731
dintel 247, 256, 411
diodo 673
Dione 5
dióxido de carbono 670
dióxido de carbono, absorción 78
dióxido de sulfuro, emisión 70
dique 44, 596
dique fijo 664
dique seco 596
dirección 589, 684
dirección de flujo de electrones 689
dirección de la Meca 738
dirección del flujo de los electrones 687
dirección del viento 55
dirección del viento, medición 59
dirección obligatoria 544, 546
dirección URL 524
director 429
director artístico 428
director de carrera 870
director de fotografía 429
director de producción 509
director de tiros 859
director, despacho 394
director, monitor de control 428
directorio 524
disco 9, 237, 273, 304, 305, 423, 500, 521, 559, 560, 641, 793, 851, 880
disco abrasivo 308
disco central 95
disco compacto 501, 504, 521
disco compacto regrabable, grabador 521
disco compacto, lector 501
disco compacto, lectura 501
disco compacto, reproductor 503
disco de articulación 570
disco de caucho 500
disco de tensión 453, 457
disco desviador de calor 274
disco duro 513
disco duro extraíble 521
disco giratorio 236
disco intervertebral 157
disco tapador 643
disco versátil digital (DVD) 494
discontinuidad de Gutenberg 42
discontinuidad de Mohorovicic 42
diseño 401
disipador térmico 513
disminución de la tensión 677
disparador 329, 476, 767
disparador de cable 482
disparador de pago 920
disparador de señuelo 762
disparador del tambor 910
disparador neumático 482
disparo, accesorios 752
display 261, 497, 503, 505, 506, 548, 731, 777
display a colores 456
display de frecuencia 503
display de funciones 450
display de la información 479
display de las funciones 450
display de mensajes 512
disposición 244
disposición de los bolos 865
disposiciones de las velas 833
dispositivo antideslizante 500
dispositivo de alarma 765
dispositivo de amarre 571
dispositivo de bloqueo 321
dispositivo de cierre 913
dispositivo de inflado 611
dispositivo de protección 446
dispositivo de remolque 573
dispositivo para enmarcar 424
dispositivos de contacto 274
disprosio 684
disquete 521
disquete externo, unidad 521
disquete para vídeo fijo 481
distancia recorrida 700

1054

distancia, medición 700
distribución al consumidor 662
distribución de apuesta americana 919
distribución de apuesta francesa 919
distribución de la vegetación 66
distribución, cuadro 272
distribución, tablero 273
distribuidor de bebidas 723, 779
distribuidor de calor 259
distribuidor de clips 534
distribuidor de hielos 224
distribuidor de hojas de afeitar 383
distrito 39
divanes, ejemplos 276
división 703
divisiones de los escudos 740
divisores 532
divisorio 771
Dniéper, río 32
do 847
do(C) 434
doble 853
doble barra oblicua 524
doble bemol 435
doble caña 446
doble cero 919
doble cortina 282
doble curva 544
doble dentada 79
doble filo, tijeras para entresacar 382
doble fuelle 432
doble pletina de casete 503
doble scull sin timonel 839
doble sostenido 435
doble techo 902
doble toldo 903
doble vía 544, 546
doble vidrio 675
doblez 362, 455
doblez hacia el interior 912
docena (1 a 12) 919
docena (13 a 24) 919
docena (25 a 36) 919
dodecágono regular 705
dohyo 847
dólar 728
dolichos 190
doma 855
Dominica 743
dominio 524
dominio de primer nivel 524
dominio de segundo nivel 524
dominio, nombre 524
dominós 914
domo de vidrio 612
dorada 219
Dorado 11
dórico, orden 404
dormitorio 251, 902
dormitorio de los bomberos 764
dormitorio de los oficiales 764
dormitorio principal 251
dorsal 523
dorsal ancho 151
dorsal del Atlántico medio 50
dorsal del Índico medio 50
dorsal del Índico sureste 50
dorsal del Índico suroeste 50
dorsal del Pacífico oriental 50
dorsal del Pacífico-Antártico 50
dorsal oceánica 49
dorsales oceánicas 50
dorso 173, 176, 300, 750
dorso de la nariz 175
dorso de un guante 346
dos doble 914
dos pares 914
dos puntos 473
dosificador 783
Douglas, saco 170
dovela 413
Dragón 13
dragón vikingo 598
dragones 917
Drake, paso 29, 31
drenaje de aguas superficiales 712
driza 603, 739
dromedario 129
drumlin 45
drupa 81
drupas 192
drupéola 83
dubnio 683
ducha 251, 724, 726, 780
ducha de teléfono 264
ducha y bañera 262
ducha, bañera 262
duchas de los bomberos 764
duchas de los oficiales 764
duchas de los presos 768
duerto 788
dulse 183
duna 51
duna compleja 52
duna parabólica 52
dunas longitudinales 52
dunas transversales 52

dunas, ejemplos 52
dúo 438
duodeno 116, 164
duramadre 167, 168
duramen 87
durión 197

E

eclipse anular 6
eclipse de Luna 7
eclipse parcial 6, 7
eclipse solar 6
eclipse total 6, 7
eclipses, tipos 6, 7
eclíptica 13
eclisa 590
eco 40, 41
economía 728
ectodermo 95
ectopterigoides 112
Ecuador 36, 742
ecuador 13, 31, 34, 35, 63
ecuador celeste 13
Edad de Piedra, armas 748
edificio de hormigón 665
edificio de la administración 664
edificio de la turbina 668
edificio de oficinas 710, 713
edificio del reactor 667, 669
edificio público 39
editorial 471
edredón 280
educación 732
efecto invernadero 68
efecto invernadero natural 68
efecto invernadero, aumento 68
efecto invernadero, gas 68
efectos especiales video/digitales 491
efluente 48
Egeo, mar 32
Egipto 745
eglefino 221
einstenio 684
eje 237, 248, 383, 462, 464, 586, 697, 762, 895
eje de alta velocidad 677
eje de baja velocidad 677
eje de cuchillas 641
eje de dirección 633
eje de la rueda 579
eje de las aspas 676
eje de tiro 756
eje de toma de fuerza 641
eje del cepillo 384
eje del pedal 580
eje del tambor 910
eje delantero 639
eje horizontal, turbina de viento 677
eje polar 17
eje propulsor 605
eje vertical, turbina de viento 676
ejemplos de abreviaciones de monedas 728
ejemplos de adaptadores 269
ejemplos de algas 75
ejemplos de anclas 610
ejemplos de anfibios 111
ejemplos de ángulos 704
ejemplos de aparejos 601
ejemplos de arácnidos 102
ejemplos de arcos 413, 541
ejemplos de aviones 628
ejemplos de barcos 604
ejemplos de bicicletas 581
ejemplos de blusas 359
ejemplos de bolos 865
ejemplos de bolsillos 360
ejemplos de brocas y barrenas 306
ejemplos de camiones 573
ejemplos de camiones articulados 572
ejemplos de carrocerías 549
ejemplos de cenefas 283
ejemplos de clavos 301
ejemplos de colores 741
ejemplos de conexiones 270
ejemplos de coníferas 89
ejemplos de conjuntos instrumentales 438
ejemplos de cortinas 283
ejemplos de costas 51
ejemplos de cucharas 228
ejemplos de cuchillos 228
ejemplos de cuchillos de cocina 229
ejemplos de cuellos 362
ejemplos de dunas 52
ejemplos de embarcaciones 604
ejemplos de empenajes de cola 629
ejemplos de empuñaduras 840
ejemplos de esquís 840, 888
ejemplos de faldas 357
ejemplos de flores 80
ejemplos de forros 741
ejemplos de fruncidos 283
ejemplos de fusibles 272
ejemplos de gafas 385

ejemplos de helechos 76
ejemplos de helicópteros 631
ejemplos de hojas 89
ejemplos de insectos 101
ejemplos de instrumentos de teclado 443
ejemplos de lagomorfos 123
ejemplos de lanzadores espaciales 24
ejemplos de latifolios 88
ejemplos de líquenes 74
ejemplos de llaves 844
ejemplos de mamíferos insectívoros 121
ejemplos de mamíferos carnívoros 134
ejemplos de mamíferos marinos 137
ejemplos de mamíferos ungulados 128
ejemplos de mamíferos voladores 141
ejemplos de mangas 360
ejemplos de marsupiales 143
ejemplos de mesas 278
ejemplos de metales 741
ejemplos de motocicletas 577
ejemplos de muebles 741
ejemplos de musgos 75
ejemplos de neumáticos 560
ejemplos de pájaros 118
ejemplos de pantalones 358
ejemplos de particiones 740
ejemplos de patas 117
ejemplos de pezuñas 127
ejemplos de picos 117
ejemplos de piezas honorables 740
ejemplos de piruetas 881
ejemplos de presas 660
ejemplos de primates 139
ejemplos de puentes de vigas 541
ejemplos de puentes en arco 541
ejemplos de puertas 416
ejemplos de racores 269
ejemplos de redes 522
ejemplos de reptiles 114
ejemplos de roedores 123
ejemplos de sacos de dormir 904
ejemplos de saltos 829
ejemplos de sillas 277
ejemplos de sondas espaciales 19
ejemplos de tablas 357
ejemplos de teléfonos 507
ejemplos de tenedores 228
ejemplos de tiendas de campaña 902
ejemplos de utensilios 401
ejemplos de vagones 588
ejemplos de velas 601
ejemplos de ventanas 415
ejemplos de vestidos 356
ejemplos de volcanes 44
el agua enfría el vapor utilizado 665
el agua regresa al generador de vapor 665
el cuatro 839
el cuatro con timonel 839
el dos 839
el dos con timonel 839
el eje de la turbina hace girar el generador 665
El Gran Cisma 736
El Salvador 742
el vapor se condensa en agua 665
elástico 280
encendedor 318, 391
encendido 332
encendido/apagado 504
encendido/apagado/volumen 504
enceradora 345
enchufe 274, 290, 306, 316, 452, 465, 504
enchufe con control de tiempo 290
enchufe de recarga 383
enchufe de tipo europeo 274
enchufe del termómetro 238
enchufe para auriculares 504
enchufe y selector desmontables 239
encía 159, 174
encimera 224, 290, 721, 722
encinera, colectores 689
electrones, dirección de flujo 689
encofrado metálico 689
encuadernación a mano 424
encuadernación de anillas 533
encuadernación en rústica 424
endecágono regular 705
endivia 187
endocardio 162
endocarpio 81, 82
endodermo 95
enebro, bayas 198
eneldo 202
energía 646
energía calorífica 68
energía eólica 676
energía eólica, producción de electricidad 677
energía fósil 646
energía geotérmica 646
energía nuclear 665
energía nuclear, producción de electricidad 665
energía solar 78, 672
energía solar, producción de electricidad 674
energía térmica 646
energía, fuente 41
energía, liberación 681
energía, unidad de medida 702
enfermera 780
enfermería 726

emblema 739, 797
emblema del equipo 878
embocadura 446
embocadura del cable 288
émbolo 642, 776
embrague 552
embudo 231
embudo colector 59
emergencia, estación 543
emergencia, vehículo 543
emerillón 911
Emiratos Árabes Unidos 746
emisión de ácido nítrico 70
emisión de ácido sulfúrico 70
emisión de billetes 730
emisión de dióxido de sulfuro 70
emisión de gases contaminantes 69
emisión de ondas ultrasónicas 41
emisión de óxido de nitrógeno 70
emisor-receptor de acceso a la red 522
emmental 211
empacadora de heno 642
empalizada 322, 408
empalmadura 908
empalme de rieles 590
empalme hidráulico 640
empaque 655
empaquetadora 573
empaquetadura 268
empate 789
empate de la boquilla 447
empavesado 739
empeine 351
empella 342, 371
empenajes de cola, ejemplos 629
empresa 525
empresas distribución /venta 525
empujador 230, 237, 240
empujador neumático, perforadora 648
empuje 540, 630
empuñaderas 850
empuñadura 304, 305, 308, 309, 320, 391, 534, 750, 755, 782, 793, 797, 816, 822, 840, 849, 850, 859, 860, 861, 867, 883, 891, 909, 912, 913, 920
empuñadura de pistola 320
empuñadura del carro 456
empuñadura del dispositivo de cierre de ingletes 304
empuñadura del manillar 871
empuñadura delantera 757
empuñadura lateral 308
empuñadura recortada 535
empuñaduras para esquí de figuras 840
empuñaduras, ejemplos 840
en espiral 236
en prisión 919
en tijera 375
enaguas 337
enana blanca 8
enana negra 8
enana parda 8
encaje de bolillos 458
encañado 322

enfoque 691
enfoque de cerca 385
enfoque de lejos 385
enfranque 342
enganche 453, 555, 913
enganche de bola 558
enganche del remolque 567
enganche, cabeza 587
engaste 376
engranaje 460, 462, 920
engranaje cónico 686
engranaje de avance 240
engranaje de piñón y cremallera 686
engranaje de tornillo sin fin 686
engranaje, diente 686
engranajes, sistemas 686
engrasador 233
enhebrador 454
enjuta 413
enlace de arcén 538
enlace de diamante 538
enlace de glorieta 538
enlace de trébol 538, 539
enlace químico 680
enlomado 425
enlosado del jardín 244
enramada 322
enredadera 322
enriquecimiento del agua pesada 669
ensaladas 722
ensaladera 226
ensamblaje a espiga 424
ensamble hembra 909
ensamble macho 909
entablado 252, 253
entablamento 247, 403, 405
entarimado 253, 254, 842
entarimado sobre estructura de madera 254
entena 600
entera 79
enterramiento 71
entintado 420
entrada 100, 251, 539, 632, 719, 724, 728, 730, 829
entrada a boxes 872
entrada de actores 402
entrada de admisión de combustible 666
entrada de agua 268, 658
entrada de agua fría 267
entrada de aire 631, 876
entrada de aire caliente 258
entrada de cabeza 829
entrada de campo 488
entrada de clientes 720
entrada de corriente 274, 275
entrada de detenidos 726
entrada de la contracorriente 669
entrada de la estación 592
entrada de la pirámide 402
entrada de los visitantes 726
entrada de pie 829
entrada de público 402
entrada de servicio 732
entrada de vapor a alta presión 668
entrada de vapor a baja presión 668
entrada de vehículos 769
entrada del agua de refrigeración del condensador 669
entrada del garaje 245
entrada del personal 720, 726, 735, 768
entrada del refrigerante 672
entrada del residuo de combustible 666
entrada del suministro 274
entrada para mercancías 713
entrada principal 250, 713, 733, 735, 768, 781
entradas al agua 829
entradas, taquilla 427
entradilla 471
entrecejo 130
entrecruzado 463
entrediente 227
entrega de equipaje 620
entremeses 722
entrenador 800, 811, 827, 842, 879
entrenador adjunto 811, 879
entrenadores 881, 883
entrenamiento 788
entrenamiento, pelota 819
entrenudo 77
entrepaño 278, 321
entrepaño horizontal 247
entrepaño vertical 247
entrepierna 351, 359
entrepiso 92
entrerrosca 269
entresuelo 250, 251
entretela de abrigo 455
entretela de armado 455
entretela de refuerzo 455
entrevista 471
envasado del combustible defectuoso 666
envase 215
envases 222
envergue de rizo 603
envero 86
envión 850

1055

ÍNDICE ESPAÑOL

envoltura 899
envoltura metálica 267
epeira 102
eperlano 219
epicarpio 81, 82, 83
epicentro 43
epicóndilo 153
epidermis 172
epidídimo 169
epífisis 167
epífisis distal 155
epífisis proximal 155
epiglotis 163, 176
epitróclea 153
equilibrador 441
equilibrio, posición 690
equino 404
equinoccio de otoño 54
equinoccio de primavera 13, 54
equinodermos 94, 95
equipaje 388
equipamiento 769, 790
equipamiento de primeros auxilios 775
equipamiento de reanimación 775
equipamiento del salpicadero 771
equipamiento para acampar 905
equipo 396, 421, 422, 423, 900
equipo de alimentación, ventilador 513
equipo de alta fidelidad 497
equipo de auricular /micrófono 506
equipo de climatización 608
equipo de grabación 429
equipo de primeros auxilios 775, 853
equipo de protección 808
equipo de soldadura autógena 319
equipo de soldadura eléctrica 318
equipo de sonido 429
equipo de soporte 489
equipo de tierra 622
equipo electrobomba 559
equipo marcador electrónico 848
equipo médico 844
equipo receptor 799
equipo salvavidas 611
equipo turboalternador 646
equipo, camiseta 801
equipo, handicap 858
equipos de gas 903
equitación 854
equivalente a 703
erbio 684
Erídano 10
Eritrea 745
erizo 121
erizo de mar 95
Erlenmeyer, frasco 685
erupción 6
erupción, volcan 44
es paralelo a 704
escabel 277
escafoides 154, 156
escala 313, 434, 776, 907
escala Celsius 695
escala de abertura 479
escala de abertura del diafragma 478
escala de ajuste 528
escala de altitud 53
escala de altura 304
escala de ampliación 485
escala de distancia 478
escala de duración de la exposición 479
escala de imágenes por segundo 479
escala de inclinación 304
escala de ingletes 303, 304
escala de la regla 700
escala de lectura 479
escala de profundidad 613
escala de profundidad de campo de visión 478
escala de temperaturas 53, 695
escala de tiempo 436
escala de transferencia 479
escala Fahrenheit 695
escala graduada 698, 699, 700
escala graduada de vernier 700
escalada 900
escalador 900
escalera 246, 255, 418, 655, 676, 842, 851, 914
escalera común 321
escalera con boquilla telescópica 766
escalera de caracol 655
escalera de color 914
escalera de cuerda 321
escalera de embarque 611
escalera de gancho 321
escalera de ganchos 767
escalera de plataforma 321
escalera de recolección de fruta 321
escalera de tijera 321
escalera del entresuelo 251
escalera extensible 321
escalera extensible de buhardilla 321
escalera mecánica 417, 427, 592, 713
escalera multiuso 321
escalera real 914
escalera rodante 321
escalera telescópica 766
escalera, hueco 251
escaleras 250, 427, 431, 543, 592, 724
escaleras de incendios 509
escaleras de mano 321
escalerilla 567, 597, 615, 639, 655
escalerilla de estribo 587
escalerilla lateral 586, 587
escalerilla rodante 623
escalerilla transportable 623
escalfador de huevos 235
escalinata 245, 412
escalón 570
escalón retráctil 567
escalones 246, 412
escama 108, 112, 113, 117
escama ventral 112
escanda común 203
escandalosa 603
Escandinava, península 32
escandio 683
escáner 517
escáner óptico 181
escape 514, 564, 565, 627
escape del vapor de los separadores 668
escápula 147, 149, 152, 153, 156
escápula 111, 116, 121, 122, 138
escapulares 115
escaque blanco 916
escaque negro 916
escarabajo 101
escarabajo necróforo 101
escarcela 749
escarcha 65
escarola 186
escarola rizada 187
escarpa 409
escarpe 749
escarpia 590
escarpín 749, 840
escena, número 429
escenario 402, 430, 431
escisión del núcleo 681
esclavina 355
esclerótica 177
esclusa 664
esclusa : vista lateral 597
esclusa científica de aire 23
esclusa de aire 763
esclusa de aire del edificio del reactor 668
esclusa de canal 596, 597
esclusa de materiales 666
esclusa, vista lateral 597
esclusas de vaciado y desagüe, sistema 597
esclusas de vaciado y llenado, sistema 597
escoba 295
escoba central 573
escoba de nieve con rascador 558
escoba eléctrica 289
escoba lateral 573
escobén 605, 609
escobilla 257, 688
escobilla limpiadora 383
escobilla metálica 449
escobillas 390, 688
escobillón 752
escocés 469
escocia 404, 405
Escocia, Placa 43
escofina 309, 401
escollo 51
escolta 811
escombrera 647, 648
escopeta 912
escopeta calibre 12 860
escoplo 309, 401, 421
escoplo de acanalar 401
escoplo de macarrón 401
escoplo redondo 401
Escorpión 10
escorpión 102
escorrentía subterránea 67
escorrentía superficial 67
escorzonera 189
escota 603, 834
escota foque 834
escota mayor 834
escotadura 439
escotadura intertrágica 173
escote 362
escote bajo 363
escote cuadrado 363
escote de barco 363
escote de corazón 363
escote de pico 363
escotera 835
escotero 834
escotes 363
escotilla 22, 23, 758
escritorio 279, 724
escritorio de ejecutivo 511
escritorio de secretaria 511
escritorio del celador 732
escritorio, artículos 528
escroto 146, 169
escuadra 313
escudilla 226
Escudo 10
escudo 748, 879
escudo acuartelado 740
escudo cortado 740
escudo partido 740
escudo solar 17
escudo tronchado 740
escudos, divisiones 740
escuela de esquí 886
escultura 395
escurridera 233
escurridor 231
escúter 577
esfagno 75
esfera 516, 697, 698, 705
esfera celeste 13
esfera de helio 25
esfera de té 233
esfera de vidrio 58
esfera graduada 907
esfera lunar 697
esfera terrestre 13
esfínter anal 164
esfuerzo 686
esgrima 848
esgrimista 848
eslabón 752
eslabón de compresión 640
eslabón de corte 331
eslabón giratorio 913
eslalon especial 889
eslalon gigante 889
eslalon supergigante 889
eslovaco 469
Eslovaquia 744
Eslovenia 744
esloveno 469
esmalte 159
esmalte de uñas 377
esmeralda 375
esmeril 454
esófago 95, 97, 99, 103, 104, 109, 110, 112, 113, 116, 125, 163, 164
espacio 434, 472, 514
espacio de almacenamiento 584
espacio de expansión 590
espacio epidural 168
espacio interior 291
espacio para almacenamiento 570
espacio para la chispa 562
espacio sin pausa 514
espada 748, 849, 914
espádice 81
espadín 751
espagueti 206
espalda 124, 147, 149, 348, 832
espaldar 113
espaldarón 749
espaldera 906
España 743
español 469
esparadrapo 777
esparavel 315
esparcidor de paja 643
esparcidora de abono 324
esparcidora de estiércol 641
esparcimiento de fertilizante 69
espárrago 185
espátula 233, 397, 421
espatulada 79
espátulas de modelar 464
especias 198
especias para salmuera 199
especificaciones técnicas 560
espectro electromagnético 690
espectrómetro 694
espectrómetro de rayos ultravioletas 60
espejo 264, 389, 535, 693, 724, 876, 907
espejo cóncavo primario 15
espejo de cercanías 568
espejo de cortesía 556
espejo de lectura 20
espejo de reflexión parcial 692
espejo de reflexión total 692
espejo doble giratorio 381
espejo iluminador 701
espejo lateral 381, 550, 570
espejo luminoso 381
espejo mayor 612
espejo menor 612
espejo parabólico 674
espejo plano 17
espejo primario 17
espejo reflez principal 477
espejo retrovisor 556, 569, 574, 577
espejo retrovisor exterior 568
espejo secundario 15, 17, 477
espermateca 104
espermatozoide 169
espesor, medición 700
espículas 6
espiga 81, 227, 229, 278, 309, 315, 385, 390, 459, 462, 559
espiga de punta cuadrada 285
espiga de punta redonda 285
espiga del cartucho 268
espina 95
espina escapular 153
espina nasal anterior 158
espina neural 109
espinaca 187
espinacas, tallarines 206
espinillera 796, 801, 802, 882
espira 104
espiráculo 136
espiral 103, 105, 302, 484, 696
espiral central 103
espiral de separación 500
espiral embrionaria 105
espirulina 183
esplenio 151
espoiler 574
espoleta 116, 757
espoleta de proximidad 759
espolón 98, 124, 130, 306, 448, 598, 641
espolvoreador 232
esponja 95
esponja calcárea 95
esponja natural 379
esponja sintética 378
esponja vegetal 379
esponja, anatomía 95
esporas 76
esposa 785
esposo 785
espuma 49
espuma aislante 299
espuma de afeitar 383
espumadera 233
esqueleto 152
esqueleto de un caballo 126
esqueleto de un canguro 142
esqueleto de un delfín 136
esqueleto de un gorila 138
esqueleto de un murciélago 141
esqueleto de un pájaro 116
esqueleto de un perro 131
esqueleto de un topo 121
esqueleto de una rana 111
esqueleto de una rata 122
esqueleto de una serpiente venenosa 112
esquí 876, 888
esquí acuático 840
esquí alpino 888
esquí alpino, pista 886
esquí artístico 890
esquí de descenso 888
esquí de eslalon 888
esquí de eslálon 840
esquí de eslalon gigante 888
esquí de figuras 840
esquí de fondo 892
esquí de salto 840
esquí de velocidad 891
esquí normal 840
esquí supergigante 888
esquí, pista 886
esquí, salto 891
esquiador alpino 888
esquiador de velocidad 891
esquina 635, 878
esquinera 587
esquinero derecho 806
esquinero izquierdo 806
esquís, ejemplos 840, 888
estabilizador 25, 634, 756, 759, 760, 859, 876, 896, 897
estabilizador de dirección 898
estabilizador horizontal 631, 898
establo 182
estaca 602, 799
estación central de bombeo 654
estación de autobuses 710
estación de carga 583, 650
estación de clasificación 589
estación de emergencia 543
estación de esquí 886
estación de ferrocarril 582, 583
estación de ferrocarriles 708, 710
estación de metro 592, 710
estación de policía 768
estación de servicio 548, 711
estación del ferrocarril 39
estación espacial internacional 21
estación local 486
estación meteorológica 58
estación meteorológica aeronaval 54
estación meteorológica de boya 54
estación meteorológica oceánica 54
estación repetidora 486
estación repetidora de microondas 524
estación terrestre 54
estación terrestre de telecomunicaciones 525
estación, metro 592
estación, modelo 55
estacionamiento 583, 596
estaciones del año 54
estadio 709, 788, 790
estadio de baloncesto 788
estadio de natación 788
estado 37
estado actual del tiempo 55
estados de la materia 680
Estados Unidos de América 742
estalactita 47
estalagmita 47
estambre 80, 82
estanco 714
estaño 682
estaño de soldar 318
estanque 322, 866
estante para revistas 510
estantería de periódicos 733
estaquilla 902, 903
estator 249, 659
estatores externos 627
estatores internos 627
estatua 737
estay 602
estay de proa 834
Este 37, 917
este 616
Este Noreste 37
Este Sudeste 37
estela luminosa del cráter 7
estepario 61
esterilla de lanzamiento 864
esternocleidomastoideo 150
esternón 111, 116, 121, 122, 126, 131, 141, 142, 152
estiercol, esparcidora 641
estigma 80, 84, 96, 97
estilete 751
estilo 80, 81, 82, 83, 84, 470, 696
estilóbato 403, 404
estilos arquitectónicos 404
estilos de natación 832
estimulador de encías 384
estípula 79
estique 464
estocada, armas cortantes 751
estómago 95, 103, 104, 105, 106, 109, 110, 112, 113, 125, 161, 164
estómago cardiaco 107
estómago pilórico 107
Estonia 744
estornino 118
estrado 734
estrado de la acusación 728
estrado de los jueces 728
estrado de los secretarios judiciales 728
estrado de los testigos 728
estrado del abogado defensor 728
estrado del director 437
estragón 202
estrangulación 844
estrato 56
estrato basal 172
estrato córneo 172
estrato de cenizas 44
estrato de lava 44
estrato de Malpighi 172
estrato granuloso 172
estrato lúcido 172
estratocúmulo 56
estratocúmulos 62
estratopausa 53
estratos 62
estratosfera 53
estrave 598
estrecha 472
estrechamiento 695
estrechamiento de la calzada 544, 547
estrecho 38
estrecho de Bass 29
estrecho de Bering 30
estrecho de Cook 29
estrecho de Gibraltar 32
estrecho de Torres 29
estrella 8, 64, 741
estrella de David 738
estrella de frenado 910
estrella de mar, anatomía 95
estrella de mar, morfología 95
estrella de neutrones 8
estrella de secuencia principal 8
estrella fugaz 53
Estrella Polar 13
estrellas de alta magnitud 8
estrellas de baja magnitud 8
estría 404, 405
estribación 45
estribera 575, 576, 750
estribera del pasajero 575, 576
estribo 100, 174, 410, 464, 631, 853, 855, 876
estribor 609, 616, 617
estroboscopio 611
estromatolito 92
estroncio 682
estropajo con esponja 295
estropajo, esponja 295
estructura 249, 433
estructura de la biosfera 66
estructura de la médula espinal 167
estructura de la Tierra 42
estructura de lanzamiento doble 24
estructura de madera, entarimado sobre 254
estructura de metal 582
estructura de soporte 16, 40

INDICE ESPAÑOL
1056
ASTRONOMÍA > 2-25; TIERRA > 26-71; REINO VEGETAL >72-89; REINO ANIMAL > 90-143; SER HUMANO > 144-177; PRODUCTOS ALIMENTARIOS Y DE COCINA > 178-241; CASA > 242-295; BRICOLAJE Y JARDINERÍA > 296-333; VESTIDO > 334-371; ACCESORIOS Y ARTÍCULOS PERSONALES > 372-391; ARTE Y ARQUITECTURA > 392-465; COMUNICACIONES Y AUTOMATIZACIÓN DE OFICINA > 466-535; TRANSPORTE Y VEHÍCULOS > 536-643; ENERGÍA > 644-677; CIENCIA > 678-705; SOCIEDAD > 706-785; DEPORTES Y JUEGOS > 786-920

estructura de un alga 75
estructura de un helecho 76
estructura de un hueso largo 154
estructura de un liquen 74
estructura de un misil 759
estructura de un musgo 75
estructura de una casa 250
estructura de una flor 80
estructura de una hoja 79
estructura del ala 624
estructura del oído 174
estructura del Sol 6
estructura en K 663
estructura inferior 651
estructura interior 416
estructura protectora 873
estructura tubular 615, 652
estuario 38, 51
estuche 313, 345, 377, 696
estuche de encerado 892
estuche de hilo dental 384
estuche de las esposas 770
estuche de manicura 377
estuche portalentes 384
estudio 488, 490, 492
estudio de televisión 490
estufa de leña a fuego lento 256
esturión 218
etapa del propelente sólido 24
etapa principal criogénica 24
etapa superior del tanque de propelente 24
etapas 401
etapas de la maduración 86
etapas de la producción de electricidad 662
etilómetro 769
Etiopía 745
etiqueta 500
etiqueta de identificación 389
etiquetas adhesivas 532
etmoides, lámina cribosa 175
Eurasia 28
euro 728
Europa 4, 28, 32, 50, 743
europeo, clavija de tipo 274
europio 684
Eustaquio, trompa 174, 175
Eutelsat 486
euthynteria 403, 404
evaporación 67, 680
evaporador, serpentín 261
Everest, monte 53
evolución de la vida 92
evolución de las especies 92
examen psiquiátrico 778
excavación a cielo abierto 647
excavación vesicouterina 170
excavadora 637
excavadora de rueda de cangilones 647
excrementos de animales 70
exhalación 832
exlamación 473
exosfera 53
expedición de carga 621
expedidor de recibo 548
explanada 409
explorador de microondas 60
explorador de radiaciones terrestres 60
explosión 564
explosivo 774, 912
exposición en curso, banderola 394
exposición futura, banderola 394
exposición permanente, salas 395
exposición temporal, salas 395
exposición, cartelera 394
expositor de final de pasillo 181
expositor de folletos 730
expositor de nuevas adquisiciones 733
exprimidor 230, 237
exprimidor de cítricos 237
extensión 278
extensión de la mesa 305
extensión plegable 278
extensor 391
extensor común de los dedos 151
extensor largo de los dedos del pie 150
exterior 795
exterior de una casa 244
exterior derecho 795
exterior izquierdo 795
extintor 771
extintor de incendios 725
extintor portátil 767
extra-fina 472
extra-negrita 472
extracto de vainilla 200
extracto, vainilla 200
extractor de fusibles 317
extractor de humo 758
extremidad delantera 111
extremidad posterior 111
extremo 385
extremo abocinado 269
extremo anterior 105
extremo del brazo 331
extremo derecho 814, 879
extremo izquierdo 814, 879
extremo libre 172

extremo posterior 105
exvoto 737
eyector 638
eyector de la cubierta de cabina 898
eyector de las varillas 236
Eyre, lago 29

F

fa(F) 434
fábrica 708
faceta 629
faceta de pabellón 374
faceta estrella (8) 374
faceta fundamental exterior (8) 374
faceta inferior del contorno 374
fachada 411
factor RH negativo 702
factor RH positivo 702
factorial 703
facturación de equipaje 620
fáculas 6
fagot 446
fagotes 437
fairway 867
faisán 120, 212
faja 367
faja braga 367
faja con liguero 367
faja con sostén 366
faja corsé 366
faja de la culata 753
falange 133
falange distal 154, 155
falange media 154, 155
falange proximal 154, 155
falanges 111, 122, 131, 136, 138, 141, 142, 154, 155
falangeta 126, 133, 172
falangina 126, 133, 172
falcatus 92
falda 355, 822
falda acampanada 357
falda combinación 366
falda cruzada 357
falda de piezas 357
falda de tubo 357
falda de volantes 357
falda escocesa 357
falda fruncida 357
falda pantalón 357
falda recta 357
falda sarong 357
faldar 749
faldas, ejemplos 357
faldón 280, 359
faldón de la camisa 349
faldón delantero 349
faldón flexible 605
faldón trasero 349
faldoncillo 855
falla 43
fallas transformantes 43
Falopio, istmo de la trompa 171
Falopio, pabellón de la trompa 171
Falopio, trompa 170, 171
falsa doblez 368
falsa oronja 76
falsa escuadra 313, 701
falso almohadón 280
falso registro 445
falso secreto 445
falta (1 a 18) 919
faltas 789
falucho 600
familia 784
familia de instrumentos de madera 437
familia de los metales 437
familia de los violines 437, 439
fangos, aspiradora 573
farallón 51
faringe 99, 163, 164
farmacia 714, 725, 778, 781
faro 333, 596, 758
faro de carretera 771
faro de destello 766
faro de posición 775
faro delantero 550, 570, 574, 576, 585, 586, 640, 876
faro estroboscópico 775
faro halógeno 775
faro maritimo 614
faro reflector 766
faro, lintena 614
farol 287, 322, 712
farola 287
faros delanteros 554
faros intermitentes 568
faros traseros 640
fascia lata, tensor 150
fase de deslizamiento 892
fase de impulsión 892
fase de impulso 892
fases de la Luna 7
fauces, itsmo 174
fax 508

fecha 729
fecha de vencimiento 729
fechador 531
Federación Rusa 744
feijoa 197
femenino 702
femeninos, órganos genitales 170
fémur 96, 98, 111, 116, 122, 126, 131, 138, 141, 142, 152
fémur, cabeza 153
fémur, cuello 153
fenec 134
Fénix 10
fenogreco 198
fenómenos atmosféricos 57
fermio 684
ferrocarril del muelle 596
ferrocarril, estación 39, 582, 583
fertilización del suelo 69
fertilizante, esparcimiento 69
festoneada 79
fetuchinas 206
fez 339
fiador 902
fiador elástico 902, 903
fibra 908
fibra muscular 168
fibra nerviosa 172
fíbula 122, 152, 336
ficha 915
ficha técnica 395
fichas 532
fichas de beneficio 917
fichas de estaciones 917
fichas de flores 917
fichas de honor 917
fichas ordinarias 917
fichero giratorio 531
fideos 206
fideos asiáticos 207
fideos de arroz 207
fideos de huevo 207
fideos de judías mungo 207
fideos de soba 207
fideos de somen 207
fideos de udon 207
fiel 698, 699
fieltro 421
fieltro asfáltico 299
figura 855
fijación 840, 891
fijación de seguridad del esquí 889
fijación para el pie 892
fijaciones 887, 888
fijaciones blandas 887
fijador 400, 892
fijador de carrete 910
Fiji 747
Fiji, islas 29
fila 431, 731
filamento 80, 274
filamento de tungsteno 274
Filchner,plataforma de hielo 29
filete 404, 405, 439, 440, 471
filete acodado elástico 854
filete articulado 854
filete de quijada acodado 854
filete ovoide acodado 854
filetín 374
filigrana 729
Filipinas 33, 747
Filipinas, fosa 50
filmación, plató 428
filmadora 520
filo 227, 229, 382, 454
filo simple, tijeras para entresacar 382
filón-capa 44
filtro 238, 241, 246, 258, 268, 290, 390, 612, 675
filtro coloreado 612
filtro de aire 261, 331, 586, 636
filtro de almacenamiento de combustible agotado 666, 667, 669
filtro de color 478
filtro de focalización 477
filtro de pelusa 292, 293
filtro de polarización 478
filtro del aire 552
filtro rojo de seguridad 485
filtro selector del color 494
filum terminal 167
filum terminal interno 167
fin 515
fina 472
final 789
final de carrera 303, 417
finalista 789
finanzas 728
Finlandia 744
fiordo 51
firma del titular 729
firma oficial 729
firmas, libro 531
física : electricidad y magnetismo 687
física : mecánica 686
física : óptica 690
fisión nuclear 681
flagelo 104
flamenco 119

flanco 115, 409
flanco diestro 740
flanco siniestro 740
flash electrónico 482
flauta 446
flautas traverseras 437
Flecha 12
flecha 261, 750, 859
flecha indicadora de la dirección del viento 56
flexo 286
flexo extensible 399
flip 881
flor 77, 80, 425
flor de lis 741
flor, anatomía de una 80
floración 86
flores, ejemplos 80
florete 849
florete eléctrico 848
floristería 715
florón 412
flotador 263, 265, 611, 628, 756, 771, 890, 911
flotador de la portería 827
flotador del medidor 655
flujo de agua 95
flujo de los electrones, dirección 687
flúor 683
Fobos 4
foca 137
foco 287, 691
foco Cassegrain 17
foco coudé 17
foco primario 17
foco subacuático 246
focos 431
foroque 603
fogón 256
foie gras 216
foliador 531
folículo 84
folículo piloso 172
follaje 87, 276
fondista 892
fondo 430
fondo de la señal 591
fondo del escenario 431
fondo oceánico 49
fonendoscopio 776
fonoteca 733
fontanela anterior 158
fontanela esfenoidal 158
fontanela mastoidea 158
fontanela posterior 158
fontanería 262, 314
fontura 456
foque 603, 834
forma de los caracteres 472
formación profesional, oficina 730
formas de banderas 739
formas de lluvia 64
formas de onda, osciloscopio de control 491
formas farmacéuticas de medicamentos 783
formas geométricas 704
formato del archivo 524
formón 401
fórmula 1, coche 873
fórnix, cuerpo 167
forraje, aventador 643
forraje, cosechera 642
forro 342, 348, 349, 370, 386, 455, 797, 855, 881, 908
forro de cuero 798
forro de la lengua 112
forro y entretelas 455
forros, ejemplos 741
fortificación de Vauban 409
fosa abisal 49
fosa de agua 867
fosa de almacenamiento de combustible agotado 666, 667, 669
fosa de combustible defectuoso 666
fosa de descarga de combustible agotado 668
fosa de Japón 50
fosa de Java 50
fosa de Kermadec-Tonga 50
fosa de Kuril 50
fosa de las Aleutianas 50
fosa de las Filipinas 50
fosa de las Marianas 50
fosa de Puerto Rico 50
fosa de recepción 666
fosa de refrigeración del condensador 671
fosa de vertido de residuos de combustible 666
fosa Perú-Chile 50
fosa Ryukyu 50
fosa séptica 70, 263
fosa triangular 173
fosas 50
fosas nasales 175
fósforo 683
foso 408, 409
foso de arena 866
foso de escenario 430

foso de orquesta 430
foso de recepción 865
foso de tiro 860
foto 471
fotocopiadora 512, 730, 733
fotografía 476
fotógrafo 714
fotógrafo de plató 429
fotomatón(r) 715
fotómetro 479
fotómetro spot 479
fotón 692
fotorreceptores 177
fotosfera 6
fotosíntesis 78
fototipo 483
fóvea 177
foyer 431
fracción 703
fragata 762
frambuesa 192
frambuesa, corte 83
francés 469
Francia 743
francio 682
Francis, turbina 659
franja del faldón 605
franqueado, módulo 531
frasco Erlenmeyer 685
frasco lavador 685
frecuencia, unidad de medida 702
fregadero 224, 270, 722
fregadero con triturador de basura 270
fregadero de prelavado 721
fregadero doble 262
fregadero para las cazuelas 721
fregona 295
freidora 238, 721
freno 783, 851, 854, 858, 870, 889, 909, 910
freno aerodinámico 676, 898
freno de disco 552, 559, 574, 874
freno de disco hidráulico 870
freno de emergencia 594
freno de la cadena 331
freno de mano 552, 556
freno de quijada acodado 854
freno de tambor 559
freno delantero 579
freno dinámico 586
freno trasero 578, 895
frenos 559, 624
frente 115, 146, 409
frente cálido de superficie 56
frente cálido en las alturas 56
frente de corte 647, 650
frente estacionario 56
frente frío de superficie 56
frente frío en las alturas 56
frente ocluido 56
frentes 56
fresa 192
fresa de acanalar 308
fresa de biselar 308
fresa de caveto 308
fresa de cola de milano 308
fresa de enrasar 308
fresa de pecho de paloma 308
fresa, corte 83
fresadora 308
fresas, ejemplos 308
fresco 406
frigorífico 224, 291, 720, 722
frigoríficos 720
frijol 191
friso 278, 403, 404
fronda 76
frontal 112, 150, 737, 749
frontalera 854
frontera interna 37
frontera internacional 37
frontis 818
frontón 403, 405, 697
frontoparietal 111
frotador 318, 421
frotador de fósforo 391
fructificación 86
fruncido 359
fruncidos, ejemplos 283
fruta 180
fruta de jack 196
fruta de la pasión 196
frutas 192, 723
frutas pomo 193
frutas secas 193
frutas tropicales 196
fruto carnoso 82, 83
frutos 81
frutos secos 84
fuelle 386, 388, 445, 485
fuente 48
fuente básica de alimento 67
fuente de alimentación 687
fuente de energía 41
fuente de servicio 471
fuente de servir 226
fuente de verdura 226

ASTRONOMÍA > 2-25; TIERRA > 26-71; REINO VEGETAL >72-89; REINO ANIMAL > 90-143; SER HUMANO > 144-177; PRODUCTOS ALIMENTARIOS Y DE COCINA > 178-241; CASA > 242-295; BRICOLAJE Y JARDINERÍA > 296-333; VESTIDO > 334-371; ACCESORIOS Y ARTÍCULOS PERSONALES > 372-391; ARTE Y ARQUITECTURA > 392-465; COMUNICACIONES Y AUTOMATIZACIÓN DE OFICINA > 466-535; TRANSPORTE Y VEHÍCULOS > 536-643; ENERGÍA > 644-677; CIENCIA > 678-705; SOCIEDAD > 706-785; DEPORTES Y JUEGOS > 786-920

fuente para abluciones 738
fuente para pescado 226
fuertes lluvias 63
fuerza de sustentación 630
fuerza del viento, medición 59
fuerza, unidad de medida 702
fuerzas que actúan sobre un avión 630
fulani 468
fulcro 443, 686
full 914
fulminante 912
fumador, artículos 390
fumarola 47
funcionamiento 495
funciones programables, teclas 731
funda 391, 689, 841, 905, 907
funda de almohada 280
funda de automóvil 558
funda de colchón 280
funda de cuero 907
funda de gafas 387
funda de goma 838
funda de guantes de látex 770
funda de la almohada 280
funda de mástil 836
funda del sable 834, 836
funda telescópica 307
fundición, caracteres 472
funguicida 69
funículo 83, 84
furgón 587
furgón de cola 588
furgón postal 474, 475
fusa 435
fuselaje 625, 898
fusible 273, 663, 673
fusible de bayoneta 272
fusible de cartucho 272
fusible de rosca 272
fusible de seguridad de tierra 272
fusil ametrallador 755
fusil automático 755
fusilli 206
fusión 680
fusta 853, 856
fuste 405
fuste del bastón 892
fútbol 788, 802
fútbol americano 806
fútbol canadiense 809
futbolín 920
futbolista 802
futón 280

G

gablete 411
Gabón 745
gadolinio 684
gafa 385
gafas 385, 841, 870, 896
gafas : partes 385
gafas de baño 830
gafas de esquí 887, 888
gafas de protección 818, 861
gafas de seguridad 772
gafas de sol 385
gafas protectoras 318, 772, 819, 870
gafas, ejemplos 385
gaita 432
gajo 82
galaxia 9
galaxia elíptica 9
galaxia espiral barrada 9
galaxia espiral normal 9
galaxia irregular 9
galaxia lenticular 9
galeón 599
galera 598
galería 411
galería de acceso 650, 658
galería de arrastre 650
galería de conexión 543
galería inferior 650
galería seca 47
galería superior 650
galería transversal 650
galés 469
Galileo 19
galio 682
galleta de centeno 205
galleta escandinava 205
galletas de arroz 207
gallina 120
gallinero 182
gallineta 221
gallo 120
galope 125
gama de colores 398
gamba 218
Gambia 745
gamuza 345
ganadería intensiva 68, 69
ganchillo 457
gancho 284, 313, 316, 456, 457, 483, 573, 634, 699, 861

gancho de amarre 597
gancho de arrastre 558
gancho de la barbada 854
gancho de tracción 651, 776
gancho del meñique 447
gancho del pulgar 446, 447
gancho del remolque 640
gancho para el platillo 698
gancho para la porra 770
ganchos peinadores 461
ganchoso 154
ganglio cerebropleural 105
ganglio espinal 167, 168
ganglio pedal 104
ganglio simpático 167
ganglio visceral 105
Ganimedes 4
garabato 327
garaje 244, 543, 726, 764, 769
garaje, entrada 245
garaje, puerta basculante 416
garam masala 199
garbanzos 190
garduña 134
garfio 611
garganta 47, 48, 115, 822, 911
gargantilla 374
gargantilla de terciopelo 374
garita 408, 409
garlopa 309
garra 117, 121, 122, 130, 143, 376, 425, 901
garrafa 225
garrapata 102
garrucha montacarga 634
garza 119
gas 651, 656, 680
gas de efecto invernadero 68
gas inerte 274, 275
gas refrigerante de dióxido de carbono 670
gases contaminantes, emisión 69
gases nobles 684
gases quemados 564
gasóleo 656
gasolina 656
gasolina pesada 656
gasolina, motor 566
gasolinera 725
gatillo 315, 320, 331, 398, 516, 750, 752, 754, 755, 757, 860, 861, 912
gatillo de seguridad 331
gato 558, 766, 873
gato doméstico 132
gato estabilizador 567
gato hidráulico 567
gato hidráulico del alerón de curvatura 760
gato hidráulico, alerón de curvatura 760
gato, morfología 133
gatos mecánicos, plataforma 653
gatos, razas 132
gaveta de archivador 533
gavia inferior proel 603
gavia mayor alta 603
gavia mayor baja 603
gavia proel alta 603
géiser 44
gel de baño 379
gemelos 150, 151, 361
gemelos de teatro 385
Géminis 13
generador 563, 646, 659, 668
generador de aire caliente 258
generador de vapor 646, 669, 670, 671, 674, 763
generador eléctrico de aire caliente 258
generador principal de tono 488
generador termoeléctrico de radioisótopos 18
generadores 688
geografía 28
geología 42
geometría 704
Georgia 746
germanio 682
germen 85
germinación 77
Ghana 745
gi 846
gibón 139
Gibraltar, estrecho 32
gigante roja 8
gimnasia 823, 824
gimnasia rítmica 823
gimnasio 608, 727, 734, 764, 788
girasol 80
girasol, aceite 209
giro postal 475
giroscopio 759
glaciar 46, 48, 66
glaciar suspendido 46
glande 169
glándula coccígea 103
glándula de albúmina 104
glándula de Cowper 169
glándula de veneno 112
glándula digestiva 104, 105, 106, 107
glándula lacrimal 177
glándula mamaria 171

glándula salival 104, 176
glándula salival 97, 99
glándula sebácea 172
glándula sudorípara apocrina 172
glándula sudorípara ecrina 172
glándula suprarrenal 165
glándula venenosa 103, 106
glándulas digestivas 103
glándulas salivales 164
glándulas sericígenas 103
globo 821, 899, 903
globo ocular 110, 177
globo sonda 54, 59
globo terráqueo 734
glóbulo blanco 162
glóbulo rojo 162
glotis 112
glucosa 78
glúteo mayor 151
go (sun-tse) 916
Gobi, desierto 33
gofrera 238
gol 807, 809, 920
gola 749, 848
goleta 601
golf 788
golfo 38
golfo de Adén 33, 34
golfo de Alaska 30
golfo de Botnia 32
golfo de California 30
golfo de Carpentaria 29
golfo de Guinea 34
golfo de la plataforma 761
golfo de México 30
golfo de Omán 33
golfo de Panamá 31
golfo Pérsico 33
Golgi, aparato 74, 94
golondrina 118
golondrina de mar 118
golpe de aproximación 866
golpe de patín 892
golpes 820
goma 534
goma de sujeción del talón 840
gombo 188
gónada 95, 105, 106
góndola 181, 600, 677
góndola, sección transversal 677
gonfalón 739
gong 437, 449
gorgonzola 211
gorguera 339
gorila 138
gorila, esqueleto 138
gorila, morfología 139
gorra 340, 770, 856
gorra de cuartel 340
gorra noruega 340
gorrión 118
gorro 892
gorro de baño 827, 830
gorro de marinero 341
gorro de punto con borla 341
gorrón 753
gota 287, 404
gotas oftalmológicas lubricantes 384
grabación 495
grabación nocturna, conmutador 496
grabador de disco compacto regrabable 521
grabadora digital 534
gradas móviles 734
grado 704
grado Celsius 702
gráfico de líneas 488
grafito 670
Gran Bahía australiana 29
Gran Barrera de Arrecifes 29
Gran Cañón 30
Gran Cordillera divisoria 29
Gran Danés 131
Gran Desierto de Arena 29
Gran Desierto Victoria 29
Gran Galería 402
gran roncón 432
gran siega) interior 844
Granada 743
granada 196
granada de mano 757
granate 375
grandes almacenes 715, 716
grandes electrodomésticos 716
grandes familias lingüísticas 468
Grandes Lagos 30
grandes titulares 471
graneador 422
granero 182
granizada 57
granizo 64
granja 182
grano 85
grano de almidón 74
grano de trigo, corte 85
granos torrefactos de café 208
granos verdes de café 208
granulación 6
gránulo de lípido 74

grapadora 534
grapas 534
grasa para cocinar 209
grasa, glóbulo 74
grasas 209, 656
grasera 234, 239
grava 253, 263
gravilla 872
greba 749
Grecia 744
green 866, 867
green de entrenamiento 866
grégüescos 338
griego 469
grieta 46
grieta de dedos 901
grifo 264
grifo de bola 268
grifo de cartucho 268
grifo de cocina de tres vías 270
grifo de plato 268
grifos 268
grillete 835
grillete de resorte 835
grillo campestre 102
Groenlandia 30
Groenlandia, mar 28
grosella 192
grosella espinosa 192
grosella negra 192
grúa 607, 652
grúa de caballete 657, 658
grúa de la plataforma 761
grúa de muelle 596
grúa de pórtico 635
grúa de puente 658
grúa flotante 596
grúa móvil 634
grúa remolque 573
grúa torre 634
grúas 634
Grulla 10
grupa 124, 826
grupeto 435
grupo de cola 898
grupo electrógeno 622
grupo motor 585
grupo turboalternador 658, 659
gruta 47
gruyère 211
guacamayo 118
guache 396
guadaña 330
gualdera 753, 756
guante 20, 798, 800, 842, 853, 870, 871, 874, 875, 878, 882, 884, 887, 891, 892
guante a la muñeca 346
guante corto 346
guante de bateo 796
guante de buceo 841
guante de crin 379
guante de esgrima 848
guante de esquí 888
guante de golf 869
guante de montar 855
guante de recogida 797
guante de softball 797
guante del portero 800
guante del receptor 796
guante largo 346
guante para conducir 346
guante rígido 879
guante, dorso 346
guante, palmo 346
guantelete 749
guantera 556
guantes 318, 346, 872
guantes de boxeo 843
guantes de hombre 346
guantes de jardinería 325
guantes de látex 776
guantes de mujer 346
guantes del portero 802
guantes protectores 875
guaraní 469
guarda 229, 426
guarda del disco 304, 305
guarda fija del disco 304
guarda móvil del disco 304
guardabarros 550, 551, 570, 571, 578, 640
guardabarros delantero 574
guardafrenos 884
guardamalleta 282
guardamano 755
guardamonte 754, 860, 861, 912
guardanieve 876
guardarropa 250, 251, 279, 394, 509, 510, 719, 723, 726, 731
guardarropa de los clientes 720
guardarropa de los mineros 649
guardarropa del personal 720, 768, 781
guardería 715
guardia derecho 807
guardia izquierdo 807
guardín 838
guarnición 277, 278, 389, 889

Guatemala 742
guayaba 197
gubia 401, 421
guepardo 135
guerrero galo 748
guía 303, 304, 456, 754, 759, 835
guía corrediza 587
guía de cabina 417
guía de cinta 534
guía de corte 304, 305
guía de enganche 585
guía de escotas 835
guía de hilo 457
guía de la cadena 580
guía de la máquina de dibujar 399
guía de la onda 489
guía de la punta 909, 910
guía de tensión 457
guía del contrapeso 417
guía del hilo 452, 453
guía del papel 508
guía papel 519
guía para enmarcar 424
guía para la cinta 499
guía pasacables 317
guías de archivo 532
guías en T 629
guías normales 629
guillotina 424, 484, 535
guiñada 630
guindilla 199
guindilla molida 199
guindilla seca 199
guindilla triturada 199
Guinea 745
Guinea Ecuatorial 745
Guinea, golfo 34
Guinea-Bissau 745
guión 838
guión largo 473
guisante 84
guisantes 190
guisantes mollares 190
guisantes partidos 190
guitarra clásica 440
guitarra eléctrica 441
gules 741
gusto 174
Guyana 742
guyot 49
gyogi 847

H

habas 190
habitación de observación 778
habitación de aislamiento 778
habitación de hotel 724
habitación de un paciente 780
habitación doble 724
habitación individual 724
habitaciones principales 250
habitáculo 873
hacha 330, 767, 907
hacha de cocinero 229
hacha de piedra pulida 748
hafnio 683
Haití 742
hakama 846, 847
halcón 119
half-pipe 887
halfpipe 871
halibut 221
hall 509
hall de entrada 250
halo 9
haltera 851
halterofilia 850
hamada 52
hámster 123
handicap del equipo 858
handicap del jugador 858
handicaps, tablero 858
hangar de helicóptero 762
hangar de mantenimiento 619
hapterio 75
harina 204
harina común 204
harina de avena 204
harina de maíz 204
harina integral 204
harina sin blanquear 204
harissa 201
hassio 683
hastial 244
hausa 468
Havers, conducto 154
hawaiano 469
haya 88
hayuco 193
haz 663
haz azul 494
haz de electrones 494, 694
haz del radar 40
haz rojo 494
haz verde 494

hebilla 350, 352, 388, 611, 889
hebilla de ajuste 895
hebilla de regulación 906
hebilla niveladora 285
hebreo 468
heladera 240
helecho 76, 92
helecho arbóreo 76
helecho canela 185
helecho nido de pájaro 76
helecho, estructura 76
helechos, ejemplos 76
hélice 606, 608, 609, 705, 763
hélice bimetálica 695
hélice de dos aspas 628
hélice de proa 606
hélice de tres aspas 628
hélice de ventilación 688
hélice posterior 606
hélice propulsora 605
hélices 762
helicóptero 631, 762
helicóptero ambulancia 631
helicóptero contraincendios 631
helicóptero de transporte táctico 631
helicópteros, ejemplos 631
helio 684
heliógrafo 58
helipuerto 652
hélix 173
hembra 453
hemisferio 705
hemisferio austral, constelaciones 10
hemisferio boreal, constelaciones 12
hemisferio Norte 35
hemisferio occidental 35
hemisferio oriental 35
hemisferio Sur 35
hemisferios 35
hendidura 424
henil 182
heptágono regular 705
heráldica 739
herbicida 69
herbívoros 67
hercio 702
Hércules 13
hermana 785
hermano 785
hermanos 785
herradura 127, 376
herraje 389
herraje de la esquina 635
herramientas 314, 315, 316, 464, 580
herramientas de perfilado 308
herramientas de soldadura 318
herramientas para apretar 310
herramientas para clavar 301
herramientas para cortar 330
herramientas para plantar 324
herramientas para regar 328
herramientas para remover la tierra 326
herramientas para segar 303
herramientas para sembrar 324
herramientas percutoras 306
herramientas, caja 313
herramientas, cinturón 313
herramientaspara atornillar 302
herrete 342, 370
hervidero 45
hervidor 240
heterótrofos 67
hexagonal 562
hexágono regular 705
Hidra Hembra 11, 13
Hidra macho 10
hidroavión cisterna 628
hidroavión de flotadores 628
hidrocarburos, vertido 70
hidroelectricidad 657
hidrógeno 682
hidróptero 609
hidrosfera 66
hielo 65, 67
hielos perpetuos 61
hielos, distribuidor 224
hiena 134
hierba 822
hierbabuena 202
hierbas aromáticas 202
hierro 683, 867, 868
hierro nº 3 868
hierro nº 4 868
hierro nº 5 868
hierro nº 6 868
hierro nº 7 868
hierro nº 8 868
hierro nº 9 868
hifa 76
hígado 109, 110, 112, 113, 116, 125, 161, 164, 212
higiene dental 384
higiene personal 181
higo 197
higo chumbo 197
higrógrafo 59
higrómetro 261
higróstato 261
hija 784, 785
hijiki 183
hijo 784, 785
hijuela 911
hilera 384
hileras 103
hilio renal 165
hilo 689, 908
hilo de la tela 455
hilo de nailon 332
hilo de seguridad 729
hilo de trama 463
hilo dental 384
hilos de urdimbre 463
Himalaya 33
Hindi 469
Hinduismo 736
hinojo 185
hipermetropía 691
hipervínculos 524
hipocentro 43
hipódromo 856
hipófisis 167
hipopótamo 129
hisopo 202
hitos 875
hocico 108, 121, 130, 132, 143
hockey sobre hielo 878
hockey sobre hierba 788, 800
hogar 256
hogar, muebles 276
hoja 75, 77, 78, 79, 85, 185, 227, 229, 302, 303, 304, 305, 309, 315, 320, 382, 383, 416, 454
hoja corta 905
hoja de acanto 276, 405
hoja de afeitar 383
hoja de cuchilla 880, 881
hoja de la película 481
hoja de la vid 86
hoja de parra 186
hoja del faldón lateral 855
hoja dentada 382
hoja flexible 78
hoja larga 905
hoja, axila 79
hoja, estructura 79
hojaldre, pasta 205
hojas compuestas 79
hojas escamadas del ciprés 89
hojas simples 79
hojas, ejemplos 89
hojita enrollada 76
holandés 469
holmio 684
hombre 146
hombre, guantes 346
hombre, ropa de 348
hombre, sombreros 340
hombre, zapatos 342
hombrera 338, 352, 440, 757, 770, 808, 880
hombrillo 353
hombro 146, 148, 156, 822, 909
home theatre 493
homo sapiens 93
hondón 855
Honduras 742
hongo 76
hongo mortal 76
hongo venenoso 76
hongo, anatomía 76
hongos 183
horario de la programación televisiva 471
horarios 582
horarios de las películas 427
horca 326
horma 345
hormiga 101
hormigón 298
hormigón armado 298
hormigón pretensado 298
hormigonera 573
hornillo 290, 390, 903
Horno 10
horno 224, 290, 674, 721, 722
horno eléctrico 465
horno microondas 224, 238
horno solar 674
horno tubular 656
horno, termómetro 231
hornos microondas 723
Hornos, cabo 31
horquilla 14, 346, 380, 579, 632, 870, 875
horquilla de mano 325
horquilla de moño 380
horquilla frontal 870
horquilla telescópica 574, 577
horquilla trasera 578
horquilla, carretilla elevadora 632
horquillas 632, 633
hortalizas 185
hortalizas de fruto 188
hortalizas de tallos 185
hospedería para esquiadores 886
hospital 711, 725, 778
hotel 710, 724, 886, 915
hotel, habitación 724
hoyo 47, 867
hoyo de par 3 866
hoyo de par 4 866
hoyo de par 5 867
hoyos 866
hoyuelo 867
hoz 330
Hubble, clasificación 9
Hubble, telescopio espacial 17
Hudson, bahía 30
hueco de la escalera 251
hueco del motor 632
huecograbado 420
huella 255
huerta 182
huerto 182, 244
huesillos auditivos 174
hueso 81
hueso alveolar 159
hueso cigomático 158
hueso compacto 154
hueso corto 157
hueso cuneiforme 155, 156
hueso esfenoides 158
hueso esponjoso 154
hueso falciforme sesamoideo 121
hueso frontal 131, 152, 158
hueso ilíaco 152
hueso irregular 157
hueso largo 157
hueso largo, estructura 154
hueso largo, partes 155
hueso maxilar 159
hueso nasal 158, 175
hueso occipital 131, 158
hueso parietal 131, 158
hueso plano 157
hueso temporal 152, 158
huesos de la mano 154
huesos del pie 155
huesos, tipos 157
hueva 109
huevera 291
huevo 100, 117
huevo de avestruz 213
huevo de codorniz 213
huevo de faisán 213
huevo de gallina 213
huevo de oca 213
huevo de pato 213
huevo, fideos 207
huevos 111, 213
Huitzilopochtli, templo 412
humano, cuerpo 146
humedad del aire 261
humedad, medición 59
húmero 111, 116, 121, 122, 126, 131, 136, 138, 141, 142, 152, 156
húmero, cabeza 153
humidificador 261
hummus 200
humo 57
humor acuoso 177
humus 78
Hungría 744
huracán 57, 63
husillo 268, 425, 700
huso 462
Huygens 19
hyracotherium 93

I

Ibérica, península 32
ichthyostega 92
ictiosaurio 93
idéntico a 703
identificación de cuenta 731
iglesia 711, 737
Iglesia ortodoxa: Miguel Keroularios 736
iglú 418
igual a 703
igual o mayor que 703
igual o menor que 703
iguana 114
ijar 124
íleon 164
ilion 111, 116, 122
iluminación 274, 381
iluminación de la placa de matrícula 554
imagen 917
imagen impresa 420
imán 291, 454, 488, 534, 687
impar 919
imparipinnada 79
imperdible 453
Imperio romano, armas 748
impermeable 352
impermeables 352
impertinentes 385
impluvio 406
imposta 413
impresión 420
impresión en huecograbado 422
impresión en relieve 420, 421
impresión litográfica 420
impresión pantalla 515
impresiones, cubeta para lavar 485
impresora 523, 529
impresora de líneas 519
impresora láser 519
impresora matriz 520
impresora, calculadora 529
impresora, mesa 511
impulso de lanzamiento 864
impulso electromagnético 40
impulso nervioso 168
impulso, irrigador 329
incendio forestal 69
incensario 737
incineración 71
incisivo 121, 123
incisivo central 159
incisivo lateral 159
incisivos 159
incisura angular 173
inclinación 13
inclusión 703
India 747
indicador 532
indicador de ajuste 889
indicador de alimentación 519
indicador de carga del papel 519
indicador de emergencia de inclinación 626
indicador de encendido 518
indicador de hora de salida 582
indicador de inclinación 898
indicador de inicio de la película 476
indicador de la mitad 528
indicador de línea 568, 569, 595
indicador de llamadas 508
indicador de luz larga 576
indicador de nivel de gasolina 557
indicador de número de andén 582
indicador de posición 417
indicador de puesta en marcha de papel 731
indicador de punto muerto 576
indicador de recarga 383
indicador de respuesta automática 508
indicador de temperatura 381, 557
indicador de tiempo 476
indicador de velocidad 476
indicador de viraje 898
indicador dedetección de papel 731
indicador del cartucho 519
indicador del cuadrante 613
indicador del importe total 548
indicador del intermitente 576
indicador del nivel del agua 239
indicador del precio por litro /galón 548
indicador digital 699
indicador digital de frecuencia 498
indicador luminoso 239, 699
indicador para viraje en nado de espalda 831
indicador transparente 532
indicadores 494, 501
indicadores de control 520
indicadores de entrada 497
indicadores del modo audio 497
Indice 0
índices de exposición 479
Índico medio, dorsal 50
Índico sureste, dorsal 50
Índico suroeste, dorsal 50
Índico, océano 28, 29, 33, 34
Indio 10
indio 682
Indonesia 33, 747
indonesio 469
inducido 688
inducido, devanado 688
inducido, núcleo 688
indumentaria antigua 336
indumentaria tradicional 339
industria 525
industria petroquímica 656
infiltración 67, 69
infinito 703
inflador 904
inflamable 774
inflorescencias 187
inflorescencias, variedades 81
información 715, 725, 730, 769, 779
infraestructura 538
infraspinoso 151
infusiones 208
ingeniero de sonido 429
ingle 146, 148
inglés 469
inhalación 832
inhalador 783
iniciales del banco emisor 729
inicio 515, 852
inmersión, piscina 788
inmovilización 844
inmovilización de brazo 844
inodoro 251, 262, 264, 265, 724, 780
insectos 96
insectos, ejemplos 101
insert 515
insertar 515
insignia 770
insignia de grado 770
insolación, medición 58
instalación 395
instalaciones deportivas 788
institución educativa 525
instrucciones operativas 548
instrumentos 899
instrumentos científicos 17, 23
instrumentos de cuerda 439
instrumentos de inmersión 841
instrumentos de madera, familia 437
instrumentos de medición meteorológica 58
instrumentos de navegación 612
instrumentos de percusión 437, 448
instrumentos de teclado 442
instrumentos de teclado, ejemplos 443
instrumentos de trazado y medición 313
instrumentos de viento 446
instrumentos del salpicadero 557
instrumentos electrónicos 450
instrumentos musicales tradicionales 432
instrumentos para escribir 470
integración de energía a la red de transporte 677
integral 703
Intelsat 487
intensidad luminosa, unidad de medida 702
intercambiador de calor 670, 675
intercomunicador 491
interconexión 563
interior derecho 801, 803, 814
interior izquierdo 801, 803, 814
interlineado 472
interlineado 1.5 472
interlineado doble 472
interlineado sencillo 472
intermitente 554, 557, 571
intermitente delantero 574, 576
intermitente trasero 575, 576
internauta 524
Internet 523, 524
Internet, usos 525
interóseos del pie 150
interpretación simultánea, cabina 718
interrogación 473
interruptor 237, 240, 241, 274, 286, 287, 288, 289, 291, 293, 305, 307, 308, 318, 320, 381, 382, 383, 384, 451, 488, 495, 501, 505, 506, 518, 613, 687
interruptor alimentación 496
interruptor automático 260, 658
interruptor automático bipolar 272
interruptor automático principal 272
interruptor automático unipolar 272
interruptor de alimentación 494, 498
interruptor de arranque automático 263
interruptor de comunicación 526
interruptor de emergencia 576
interruptor de emisión 505
interruptor de encendido 513, 518, 556, 576
interruptor de encendido/apagado 476, 483
interruptor de focalización automática 483
interruptor de gatillo 304, 305, 306, 308
interruptor de la puerta 293
interruptor de ráfagas 576
interruptor de sobretemperatura 266
interruptor de transmisión 505
interruptor del limpiaparabrisas 556
interruptor funciones 496
interruptor luminoso 452
interruptor on/off 289
interruptor para el vídeo auxiliar 491
interruptor para la producción de vídeo 491
interruptor principal 273
interruptor selector de velocidad 305
intersección 703
intertítulo 471
intervalo 617
intervalos 434
intestino 95, 97, 103, 104, 105, 107, 109, 112, 161
intestino ciego 125
intestino delgado 110, 113, 116, 125, 164
intestino grueso 110, 164
intestino medio 99
intradós 413
inuktitut 469
inundación, llanura 48
invernadero 182
inversor 302, 306
invertido 595
invierno 54
inyección 565
inyector 566
inyector de combustible 565
ío 4
Irán 746
Iraq 746
iridio 683
iris 177
Irish moss 183
Irlanda 743
Irlanda, mar 32

ÍNDICE ESPAÑOL

ASTRONOMÍA > 2-25; TIERRA > 26-71; REINO VEGETAL >72-89; REINO ANIMAL > 90-143; SER HUMANO > 144-177; PRODUCTOS ALIMENTARIOS Y DE COCINA > 178-241; CASA > 242-295; BRICOLAJE Y JARDINERÍA > 296-333; VESTIDO > 334-371; ACCESORIOS Y ARTÍCULOS PERSONALES > 372-391; ARTE Y ARQUITECTURA > 392-465; COMUNICACIONES Y AUTOMATIZACIÓN DE OFICINA > 466-535; TRANSPORTE Y VEHÍCULOS > 536-643; ENERGÍA > 644-677; CIENCIA > 678-705; SOCIEDAD > 706-785; DEPORTES Y JUEGOS > 786-920

1059

irlandés 469
irrigador bucal 384
irrigador de impulso 329
irrigador giratorio 329
irrigador oscilante 329
isba 418
isla 38, 224, 539
isla de arena 51
isla de Terranova 30
isla volcánica 49
Islamismo : Mahoma 736
islandés 469
Islandia 32, 744
islas Aleutianas 30
islas de Cabo Verde 745
islas del Caribe 742
islas Fiji 29
islas Malvinas 31
Islas Marshall 747
Islas Salomón 747
islote 761
islote rocoso 51
isobara 55
isosista 43
isquion 111, 116, 122, 153
Israel 746
istmo 38
istmo de la trompa de Falopio 171
istmo de las fauces 174
istmo de Panamá 30
Italia 744
italiano 469
iterbio 684
itrio 683

J

jabalí 128
jabalina 748, 793
jabón de tocador 379
jabonera 264, 383
jaboticaba 197
jaguar 135
Jamaica 742
jamba 247, 256, 413
jamón ahumado 215
jamón de York 216
jamón serrano 216
Jápeto 5
Japón 33, 747
Japón, fosa 50
Japón, mar 33
japonés 469
jarabe de arce 209
jarabe de maíz 209
jarabe para la tos 783
jardín 322, 406
jardín de rocalla 322
jardín público 713
jardín, enlosado 244
jardinería 298, 322
jardinería, guantes 325
jareta 285
jarlsberg 211
jarra de agua 226
jarra de cerveza 225
jarra medidora 231
jarra para café 226
jarrita de leche 226
jaula 407, 650
jaula de protección 791
Java, fosa 50
jefe 740
jefe de cronometradores 830
jefe de los árbitros 860
jefe de luminotecnia 429
jefe de mecánicos 873
jefe de tapiz 843
jefe de vestuario 428
jengibre 199
jerbo 123
jeringa de decoración 232
jeringilla de Luer-Lock 776
jeringuilla 776
jeringuilla de irrigación 776
jerséis de hombre 717
jerséis de mujer 716
jersey de cuello de cisne 892
jersey de cuello de tortuga 354
jersey de cuello redondo 354, 359
jerseys 354
jerseys combinados 359
Jesucristo 736
jet supersónico 53
jicama 184
jilguero 118
jinete 853, 855, 858
jirafa 12
jirafa 129, 492
jirafa del micrófono 490
jockey 856, 857
jockey club 856
jojoba 197
jónico, orden 404
Jordania 726
jota 914

joyería 374, 714, 717
joystick 516
joysticks 918
ju-jitsu 846
juanete de mesana de estay 603
juanete de proa alto 603
juanete de proa bajo 603
juanete mayor bajo 603
juanete mayor proel alto 603
jubón 338
Judaísmo : Antiguo Testamento 736
judía adzuki 191
judía amarilla 191
judía china larga 190
judía de Egipto 190
judía de Lima 191
judía mungo 191
judía mungo negra 191
judía negra 191
judía pinta 191
judía roja 191
judía roja 191
judía romana 191
judías de ojo 190
judías mungo, fideos 207
judías verdes 191
judo 844
judoji 844
judoka neutral 844
jueces 824, 825, 828, 881
jueces asistentes 883
jueces de ejecución 823
jueces de salida 882
jueces de tapiz 846
jueces de valor artístico 823
jueces de virajes 831
juego 822
juego de bolos 865
juego de casquillos 311
juego de dardos 918
juego de mesas 278
juego de pequeñas herramientas 325
juego de utensilios 233
juego en línea 525
juego limpiabotas 345
juegos de mesa 915
juegos 788, 914
juez 807, 809, 842, 843, 844, 848, 855, 859, 893
juez coordinador 823
juez de ángulo 845
juez de brazado 830
juez de dificultades 823
juez de faltas de pie 821
juez de gol 827, 878
juez de línea 803, 805, 807, 812, 813, 816, 818, 820, 824, 879
juez de línea de saque 820
juez de llegada 830, 839
juez de meta 858, 883
juez de obstáculos 852
juez de pista 883
juez de puerta 837
juez de red 821
juez de salida 830, 838, 883
juez de servicio 816, 820
juez de silla 820
juez de vía 900
juez externo 807
juez responsable 823
juez-árbitro 828
juez-árbitro de tiro 860
jugador 808, 827, 878, 915, 920
jugador con el servicio 821
jugador de baloncesto 810
jugador de bolos 865
jugador de criquet 798
jugador de hockey 801
jugador de primera base 794
jugador de rugby 805
jugador de saque 816, 819
jugador de segunda base 794
jugador de tercera base 794
jugador exterior central 794
jugador exterior derecho 794
jugador exterior izquierdo 794
jugador medio 794
jugador, handicap 858
jugadora de bolos 865
jugadores 822
jugadores, banquillo 809
jugadores, posición 803, 804, 814
juguetería 714
juguetes 717
julio 702
junco 600
junta 268, 269, 294, 562
junta cónica 265
junta de estanquidad 268
junta de goma 270
junta del cárter 566
junta positivo/negativo 672
junta tórica 268
Júpiter 4
jurado 853
Jurásico 93
justicia 726
Justicia, Palacio 710

K

kajak, regata 838
Kalahari, desierto 34
Kamchatka, península 33
Kaplan, turbina 659
karate 845
karategi 845
karateka 845
kayak 837
kayak K1 839
Kazajistán 746
kelvin 702
kendo 847
kendoka 847
Kenia 745
Kermadec-Tonga, fosa 50
ketchup 201
kicher 890
kicker 800
kickers 890
kilogramo 702
kimono 364, 844
Kinyarwanda 468
kiosco 548, 593
Kirguizistán 746
Kiribati 747
kirundi 468
kiwano 196
kiwi 196
koala 143
Kola, península 32
kombu 183
kora 433
kote 847
Kuiper, cinturón 4
kung fu 846
Kuril, fosa 50
Kuwait 746

L

la hoja según su borde 79
la presión del vapor impulsa las turbinas 665
la(A) 434
laberinto 885
labio 124, 132
labio córneo 113
labio externo 105
labio inferior 174, 444
labio interno 105
labio mayor 170, 171
labio menor 170, 171
labio superior 99, 174, 444
laboratorio 16, 17
laboratorio alto 16
laboratorio americano 21
laboratorio de conservación 395
laboratorio espacial 23
laboratorio patológico 781
laboratorio, material 685
lacolito 44
ladera 45
ladillo 471
lado 431
lado de la reina 916
lado del mar 664
lado del rey 916
lado derecho 384
lado hacia el embalse 664
lado izquierdo 384
Ladoga, lago 32
ladrillo 298
ladrillo hueco 298
ladrillo macizo 298
ladrillo perforado 298
ladrillo refractario 256, 298, 465
ladrillo tabiquero 298
ladrillos refractarios 256
ladronera 408
Lagarto 12
lagarto 114
lago 7, 38, 45, 48
lago artificial 48
lago Baikal 33
lago Chad 34
lago de brazo muerto 48
lago Eyre 29
lago glaciar 48
lago Ladoga 32
lago Malaui 34
lago Tanganyika 34
lago tectónico 48
lago Titicaca 31
lago Victoria 34
lago volcánico 48
lagomorfos 122
lagomorfos, ejemplos 123
lagos 48
lagos, acidificación 70
laguna 51
laguna lateral 127
laguna medial 127
laguna salada 52
lama 676
lámina 75

lámina cribosa del etmoides 175
lámina de contacto de positiva 562
lámina de contacto negativa 562
láminas 300
laminillas 76
laminillas periféricas 154
lámpara 594, 693
lámpara de cabecera 286, 724, 780
lámpara de despacho halógena 286
lámpara de escritorio 286
lámpara de lectura 771
lámpara de mesa 286
lámpara de neón 316
lámpara de petróleo 906
lámpara de pie 286
lámpara de pinza 286
lámpara de prueba de neón 316
lámpara de techo 286
lámpara del casco 901
lámpara del santuario 737
lámpara halógena 274, 275
lámpara incandescente 614, 673
lámpara indicadora de tocado 848
lámpara orientable de pared 287
lámparas 286
lámparas en serie 287
lamprea 219
lana de vidrio aislante 299
lanceolada 79
lancha de motor 762
lancha pequeña 607
lancería 364, 584, 714, 716, 724
lantánidos 684
lantano 684
lanza 748
lanzadera 461
lanzadera plana 461
lanzado desigual 459
lanzador 794, 795, 799
lanzador de bombas fumígenas 758
lanzador espacial, sección transversal 24, 25
lanzadores espaciales, ejemplos 24
lanzamiento 788, 795, 799, 864, 891
lanzamiento de jabalina 791
lanzamiento de martillo y disco 791
lanzamiento de peso 790
lanzamientos 793
lanzamisiles 761
lanzaplatos 860
Laos 747
lapa 217
lapiaz 47
lápices de colores 396
lápices de colores, dibujo 396
lápida conmemorativa 738
lapislázuli 375
lápiz 470
lápiz adhesivo 534
lápiz blanco para uñas 377
lápiz corrector de piedra pómez 423
lápiz de cejas 378
lápiz de grafito 470
lápiz litográfico 423
larguerillo 632
larguero 249, 277, 321, 624, 676, 827
larguero de la bisagra 278
larguero del marco 278
larguero inferior 635
laringe 163
larva 100
lasañas 206
lasca doble 908
láser de rubí pulsado 692
lata 223
lata de conserva 223
latas 222
lateral derecho 803
lateral izquierdo 803
latiguillo 855
laurel 202
laurencio 684
lavabo 262, 264, 724, 780
lavabo de cirujano 781
lavado 347
lavado de automóviles 548
lavadora 262, 271, 292
lavandería 250, 724, 726
lavar a mano con agua tibia 347
lavar a máquina con agua caliente en el ciclo para ropa delicada 347
lavar a máquina con agua caliente, en el ciclo normal 347
lavar a máquina con agua tibia en el ciclo para ropa delicada 347
lavar en lavadora con agua muy caliente, en el ciclo normal 347
lavavajillas 224, 271, 294, 721, 723
laya 460
lazo 340, 374, 913
Lebreles 13
lebrero 131
leche 210
leche de cabra 210
leche en polvo 210
leche evaporada 210
leche homogeneizada 210
leche, suero 210

lecho 597
lecho oceánico 42
lecho ungular 172
lechuga de cogollo 186
lechuga de tallo 186
lechuga iceberg 186
lechuga marina 183
lechuga rizada 186
lechuga romana 186
lechuza norteña 118
lector CD/DVD 918
lector de casetes 504
lector de CD 450
lector de CD-ROM 517
lector de código de barras 517
lector de disco compacto 488, 501, 503
lector de discos compactos 504
lector de microfilmes 732
lector de tarjeta 493, 730, 731
lector de tarjetas 507
lector óptico de caracteres 474
lectura /pausa 501
lectura de disco compacto 501
lectura de tarjeta, ranura 548
legionario romano 748
legumbre 84
legumbres 190
lema 729
lémur 139
lencería 364, 584, 714, 716, 724
leñera 256
lengua 99, 109, 110, 164, 174, 175, 176, 212
lengua bífida 112
lengua glaciar 46
lenguado 221
lenguas afro-asiáticas 468
lenguas aisladas 469
lenguas amerindias 469
lenguas australianas aborígenes 469
lenguas bantúes 468
lenguas célticas 469
lenguas centro-africanas 468
lenguas chinotibetanas 468
lenguas del mundo 468
lenguas eslavas 469
lenguas germánicas 469
lenguas indoeuropeas 469
lenguas indoiranias 469
lenguas malayo-polinesias 469
lenguas oceánicas 469
lenguas papúas 469
lenguas romances 469
lenguas uraloaltaicas 469
lengüeta 342, 352, 370, 386, 444, 446, 452, 453, 456, 881, 889
lengüeta de cuero 350
lengüeta de la caña 433
lengüeta protectora 521
lengüeta, tubo 444
lente 385, 535, 691
lente bifocal 385
lente cóncava 691
lente convexa 691
lente convexo-plana 691
lente de 180 grados 478
lente de acercamiento 478
lente de ampliación 485
lente de campo 692
lente tórica 691
lentejas 190
lentes 691
lentes bicóncavas 691
lentes biconvexas 691
lentes cóncavas 691
lentes cóncavo-planas 691
lentes convergentes 691
lentes convexas 691
lentes de contacto 384
lentes de contacto blandas 384
lentes de contacto desechables 384
lentes de contacto duras 384
lentes de enfoque 694
lentes de imágen recta 692
lentes divergentes 691
León 13
león 135
León Menor 13
león rampante 741
leopardo 135
Lesoto 746
letra para marcar 855
letras 472
letrero de número de vías 591
Letonia 744
letrinas 406
leucoplasto 74
leva 460
levantamiento del spinnarker 833
levita 338
Líbano 746
libélula 102
liber 87
liberación de energía 681
liberador del cable de remolque 898
liberador del margen 528
liberador del seguro 310

Liberia 745
libero 812
Libia 745
Libra 11
libra 728
librería 714, 734
libreta 530
libro de firmas 531
libro electrónico 527
libro encuadernado 426
libros de consulta 732
libros para niños 732
libros, carrito 733
lichi 197
licuadora 240
líder 877
Liebre 11
liebre 123, 212
Liechtenstein 744
lienzo 400
liga 367
ligadura 435
ligamento 105
ligamento alveolo-dentario 159
ligamento ancho del útero 171
ligamento elástico 133
ligamento suspensorio 177
ligamentos textiles básicos 463
liguero 367
lija 308
lijadora excéntrica 308
lima 194, 309, 905
lima de uñas 377
limbo 76, 612
limbo de la palma 127
limitador de velocidad 417
limitador de velocidad, polea tensora 417
limón 194
limonera 857
limpiador 557
limpiador de antenas 98
limpiador de boquillas 318
limpiador de uñas 377
limpiaparabrisas 550, 557
limpieza 295
limpieza de trajes de intervención 764
limusina 549
Lince 12
lince 134
lindero 244
línea 434, 813, 919
línea azul 879
línea cableada 525
línea central 801, 814, 877
línea central de servicio 821
línea de azote 818
línea de «touche» 805
línea de 10 m 804
línea de 15 m 805
línea de 2 m 827
línea de 200 m 871
línea de 22 m 800, 804
línea de 4 m 827
línea de 5 m 800, 805
línea de 7 m 827
línea de árbitro 845
línea de área de penalti 802
línea de ataque 812
línea de banda 800, 814, 815, 858, 877
línea de caída 362
línea de campo 687
línea de centro 803, 809
línea de competición 847
línea de corte 455
línea de costura 455
línea de crecimiento 104, 105
línea de cuadro 862
línea de cuadro de servicio 818
línea de datos introducidos 529
línea de devolución 799
línea de distribución de media tensión 663
línea de dobles 820
línea de flotación 615
línea de flujo del pozo 652
línea de fondo 804, 806, 811, 812, 815, 816, 821
línea de foul 794
línea de fuera 819
línea de gol 806, 814, 878
línea de juego 864, 877
línea de la calle 791
línea de lanzamiento 799, 865
línea de llegada 856
línea de llegada 833, 839
línea de llegada de 500 m 883
línea de los 27 m 858
línea de los 30 m 859
línea de los 36 m 858
línea de los 50 m 859
línea de los 54 m 858
línea de los 60 m 859
línea de los 70 m 859
línea de los 90 m 859
línea de los competidores 845
línea de los esprinteres 871
línea de marca 804
línea de medio campo 805
línea de melé 807
línea de meta 800, 809, 827
línea de persecución 871
línea de pista 619
línea de puesta en guardia 848
línea de puesta en guardia de florete 848
línea de puesta en guardia de sable y espada 848
línea de recepción 818
línea de referencia 907
línea de retirada 799
línea de salida 791, 833, 872
línea de salida 100 m 790
línea de salida 800 m 791
línea de salida de 1.500 m 791
línea de salida de 10.000 m 791
línea de salida de 100 m vallas 790
línea de salida de 110 m vallas 790
línea de salida de 200 m 790
línea de salida de 400 m 791
línea de salida de 400 m vallas, línea de relevos de 4x100 m 791
línea de salida de 5.000 m 790
línea de salida de 500 m 882
línea de salida de relevos 4 x 400 m 791
línea de seguridad 593
línea de servicio 818, 819, 821
línea de servicio corto 817
línea de servicio largo 816
línea de tee 877
línea de tiro 859, 865
línea de tiro libre 811, 814
línea de visión 907
línea del área de gol 814
línea del centro 848
línea del dobladillo 455
línea del fondo de la piscina 831
línea del medio campo 827
línea del resultado 529
línea divisoria central 815, 816, 819
línea lateral 108, 539, 819
línea lateral de dobles 817
línea lateral de individuales 817
línea límite de inicio de jugada 806
línea límite de salida 848
línea media 806, 810, 879
línea meridiana 907
línea neutra 687
línea para modificaciones 455
línea reservada 523, 524
línea submarina 524
línea suplementaria 434
línea telefónica 524
línea telefónica/cableada/satélite 523
línea trasera 877
línea yardas 806
líneas de latitud 36
líneas de longitud 36
líneas rectas 871
lingala 468
linterna 614, 770, 903
linterna del faro 614
linterna movible 316
linterna portátil 765
liquen 74
liquen custráceo 74
liquen foliáceo 74
liquen fruticuloso 74
liquen, estructura 74
líquenes, ejemplos 74
líquido 680, 681
líquido cerebroespinal 168
líquido corrector 534
líquidos accesorios 400
Lira 13
lira 433
lisosoma 94
lista de procedimientos 20
lista superciliar 115
listón 285, 291, 792
listón de madera 459
litera 567, 584
litio 682
litografía 423
litoral, configuración 51
litosfera 42, 66
Lituania 744
lixiviación 70
liza 408
lizos 460, 461
llama 128, 461
llama perpetua 738
llana 315
llanta 560, 574, 579, 640
llanta maciza 633
llanta neumática de tracción 594, 595
llanta neumática guía 594, 595
llanura 38, 48
llanura abisal 49
llanura de inundación 48
llave 249, 436, 446, 447
llave a la derecha, bureta 685
llave ajustable 315
llave allen 314
llave combinada 311
llave de apriete 312
llave de boca de riego 767
llave de cadena 315
llave de carraca 311
llave de cincho 315
llave de embocadura 446
llave de estrella abierta 311
llave de estrella común 311
llave de estrella hexagonal 311
llave de fontanero 315
llave de gas 267
llave de inyección 333
llave de paso 262, 265, 270, 271
llave de pedernal 752
llave de tuercas española 311
llave del mandril 306
llave del libro 425
llave en cruz 558
llave inglesa 311, 315
llave para agua 447
llavero 387
llaves 311, 315
llegada 791, 852
llegada del telesquí 886
llovizna 64
llovizna fuerte continua 57
llovizna fuerte intermitente 57
llovizna ligera continua 57
llovizna ligera intermitente 57
llovizna moderada continua 57
llovizna moderada intermitente 57
lluvia 64, 65
lluvia ácida 69, 70
lluvia fuerte continua 57
lluvia helada 57, 64
lluvia intensa intermitente 57
lluvia ligera 64
lluvia ligera continua 57
lluvia ligera intermitente 57
lluvia moderada 64
lluvia moderada continua 57
lluvia moderada intermitente 57
lluvia, formas 64
lluvia, medición 59
lob wedge 868
Lobo 11
lobo 134
lobulada 79
lóbulo 117, 173, 175
lóbulo inferior 163
lóbulo lateral inferior 86
lóbulo lateral superior 86
lóbulo medio 163
lóbulo superior 163
lóbulo terminal 86
local técnico 543
loción para después del afeitado 383
locomotora 585
locomotora diésel eléctrica 586
lóculo 82
locutorio 726
lomera 857
lomo 115, 124, 130, 214, 227, 229, 295, 425, 426
lomo con canal 306
lomo del libro 425
Mackenzie, río 30
macronúcleo 94
mácula lútea 177
Madagascar 34, 746
madera 300, 867
madera nº 1 868
madera nº 3 868
madera nº 5 868
madera, pisos de 254
madre 784, 785
maduración, etapas 86
madurez 86
mage 847
Magellan 19
magenta 690
maceta 322
maceta colgante 322
machete 751
macho 453
macillo 442, 443
macillo de fieltro 443
macizo 38
macizo de flores 322
magma 44, 49
magnesio 682
magnetismo 687
magnetómetro 60
mah-jongg 917
Maine Coon 132
maître 720
maíz 85, 203
maíz : mazorca 85
maíz forrajero 182
maíz, aceite 209
maíz, harina 204
maíz, jarabe 209
maíz, pelo 85
malanga 189
Malasia 747
Malaui 746
Malaui, lago 34
Maldivas 747
maleta 577
maleta clásica 389
maleta de fin de semana 389
maletas 717
maletero 551, 568
maletín 386, 388
maletín para ordenador portátil 527
maleza 866
malgache 469
malla 815, 870
Luna menguante 7
Luna nueva 7
Luna, eclipse 7
Luna, fases 7
luneta 431
lúnula 105, 172, 173
lupa 693, 905
lupa de focalización 485
lutecio 684
Luteranismo : Martín Lutero 736
lutz 881
Luxemburgo 743
luz 14, 15, 17, 615, 617, 626
luz anticolisión 624
luz antiniebla 554, 570
luz blanca 616
luz de advertencia de emisión 488
luz de advertencia de la gasolina 557
luz de advertencia de puerta abierta 557
luz de advertencia del aceite 557
luz de advertencia del alternador 557
luz de advertencia del cinturón de seguridad 557
luz de aterrizaje 631
luz de cruce 554
luz de encendido 383, 508
luz de encendido/apagado 506
luz de freno 554
luz de la barrera 591
luz de marcha atrás 554
luz de navegación 605, 625, 631
luz de posición 554, 585
luz de seguridad 484
luz de tope 605
luz delantera 579
luz indicadora de cargado 527
luz indicadora de la presión del aceite 576
luz indicadora de luz larga 557
luz intermitente 591
luz larga 554
luz lateral 570, 571
luz piloto 381
luz roja 712
luz trasera 554, 571, 575, 576, 578
luz verde 712
luz visible 690

M

macaco 139
macarrones 206
Macedonia 744
longan 196
longitud de la ola 49
longitud de onda 690
longitud, medición 700
longitud, unidad de medida 702
loop de puntera 881
loriga 748
losa de piedra 298
loseta 22
lubina 220
lubricador 649
lucernario 245
lucernario del baño 251
lucernario del hueco de la escalera 251
lucernas del campanario 411
luces de advertencia 557
luces de controles 519
luces de estado 515
luces de gol 879
luces de seguridad 771
luces posteriores 775
luces traseras 554, 640
lucha 843
lucha greco-romana 843
lucha libre 843
luchadero 838
luchador 843
lucio 220
lucioperca 220
luge 884
luge doble 884
luge simple 884
luge simple masculino, salida 885
luge, corredor 884
lumbrera de admisión 565
lumbrera de escape 565
lumbrera de transferencia 565
luminotécnico 429
Luna 4, 6, 7
Luna creciente 7
Luna llena 7
mallas 371
mallas con volantes 368
mallas de metal expandido 299
Malpighi, estrato 172
Malpighi, tubo 99
Malta 744
Malvinas, islas 31
mamíferos voladores, ejemplos 141
mamíferos acuáticos 136
mamíferos carnívoros 130
mamíferos carnívoros, ejemplos 134
mamíferos insectívoros 121
mamíferos insectívoros, ejemplos 121
mamíferos marinos, ejemplos 137
mamíferos marsupiales 142
mamíferos primates 138
mamíferos ungulados 124
mamíferos ungulados, ejemplos 128
mamíferos voladores 140
mampara de contención 571
mamut 93
mancha ocular 95
mancha solar 6
Mancha, canal 32
mandarina 194
mandíbula 97, 99, 108, 111, 112, 116, 121, 122, 123, 131, 136, 138, 141, 142, 152, 158
mandíbula de un lagomorfo : conejo 123
mandíbula de un roedor : rata 123
mandíbula deslizante 700
mandíbula fija 700
mandíbula inferior 115, 126
mandíbula superior 115
mandíbulas de lagomorfos 123
mandíbulas de roedores 123
mandioca 184
mando 918
mando a distancia 493, 495
mando de control del carro 456
mando de los frenos 896
mando del freno aerodinámico 898
mando, puente 626
mandoble 751
mandolina 230, 433
mandos de la videocinta 496
mandos de los quemadores 290
mandos del cabestrante 573
mandril 302, 306, 307, 649
manecilla de las horas 697
manecilla de vapor 241
manejo de materiales 632
manejo del combustible, secuencia 666
maneta del embrague 574, 576
maneta del freno delantero 576
manga 337, 348, 739, 822, 848
manga camisera 361
manga colgante 338
manga común fruncida 361
manga corta 337
manga corta sencilla 360
manga de aislamiento 275
manga de distribución 260
manga de hechura sastre 361
manga de jamón 361
manga de murciélago 361
manga de pagoda 361
manga de volante 337
manga empotrada 349
manga farol 360
manga flotante 337
manga kimono 361
manga raglán 352, 355, 361, 369
manga recta de tres cuartos 360
manga y boquillas 232
manganeso 683
mangas anteriores 822
mangas de viento 893
mangas, ejemplos 360
mango 197, 227, 229, 230, 288, 301, 302, 303, 306, 307, 309, 310, 311, 312, 315, 316, 318, 319, 320, 331, 381, 382, 383, 384, 425, 439, 454, 503, 611, 649, 798, 800, 815, 816, 822, 858, 863, 867, 877, 880, 901, 905, 910
mango aislado 316
mango aislante 317
mango auxiliar 306
mango posterior 910
mangosta 134
mangostán 196
manguera 264, 270, 271, 319, 328, 767
manguera de abastecimiento en vuelo 760
manguera de agua 648
manguera de aire 648
manguera de alimentación 294
manguera de aspiración 766
manguera de conexión 649
manguera de desagüe 271, 292, 294
manguera de incendios 767
manguera de inyección de lodo 651
manguera de líquido para frenos 559
manguera de llenado 485
manguera de riego 328
manguera de servicio 548
manguera de vaciado 292, 485

ÍNDICE ESPAÑOL

1061

manguera del rebosadero 265
manguera flexible 649
manguera hidráulica 641, 642
manguera, carretilla 328
manguera, secador 764
manguito 307
manguito de enfriamiento 755
manguito inferior del radiador 561
manicura 377
manicura, estuche 377
manija en cruz 919
manilla 247, 248, 256, 291, 775
manilla de la puerta 551
manillar 323, 327, 574, 577, 579, 851, 870, 871, 876
manillar, empuñadura 871
maniobra de la excavadora 637
manipulación 632
maniquí 398, 454
manivela 230, 307, 312, 423, 460, 558, 571, 580, 750, 909, 910
manivela de dirección 756
manivela de elevación 756
manivela de enrollado 313
manivela de la columna 482
manivela de la ventanilla 554
manivela del carrete 328
mano 139, 147, 149, 173, 230
mano abierta 901
mano, huesos 154
manojo 185
manómetro 259, 654, 655, 766, 775, 777, 841
manómetro del soplete 319
manómetro del tanque 319
manopla 346, 901
manopla de baño 379
manoplas 318
manos de póquer 914
manta 280
manta de la silla 853
manteca de cerdo 209
mantenimiento 548
mantenimiento de pinturas 320
mantequera 226
mantequilla 210
mantequilla clarificada 210
mantis 102
manto 105, 106, 256
manto externo 42
manto freático 70
manto interno 42
manto, músculos 106
manual 445
manual de primeros auxilios 777
Manx 133
manzana 193
manzana, corte 82
manzanilla 208
maori 469
mapa 610
mapa de carreteras 39
mapa de la ruta 592
mapa de ruta 594
mapa de rutas 593
mapa físico 38
mapa geográfico 734
mapa meteorológico 54, 55
mapa político 37
mapa urbano 39
mapache 134
maquillador 428
maquillaje 378
maquillaje facial 378
maquillaje labial 378
maquillaje para ojos 378
máquina 417
máquina abastecedora de combustible 669
máquina cargadora de combustible 666
máquina cargadora del combustible 670
máquina de afeitar eléctrica 383
máquina de café exprés 241
máquina de clasificación 475
máquina de coser 452
máquina de descarga 666
máquina de dibujar con guía 399
máquina de dibujar, guía 399
máquina de escribir electrónica 528
máquina de hielo 721
máquina de soldar eléctrica 318
máquina expendedora de bebidas 548
máquina expendedora de billetes 593
máquina franqueadora 531
máquina lava vasos 723
máquina para hacer pasta italiana 230
máquina pisanieve 886
Máquina Pneumática 11
máquina tragaperras 920
máquina tricotar 456
maquinaria agrícola 641
maquinaria pesada 636
máquinas de propulsión, sala de control 763
máquinas de tejer 456
maquinilla de afeitar 383
maquinilla desechable 383
maquinilla para cortar el cabello 381
maquinista 428

maquinista jefe 428
maquis 66
mar 7, 38, 48
mar abierto 664
mar Adriático 32
mar Arábigo 33
mar Báltico 32
mar Caribe 28
mar Caspio 28, 33
mar de Aral 33
mar de Barents 32
mar de Beaufort 30
mar de Bering 28
mar de Caribe 30
mar de Coral 29
mar de Groenlandia 28
mar de Irlanda 32
mar de Japón 33
mar de la China Meridional 28, 33
mar de la China Oriental 33
mar de Noruega 32
mar de Tasmania 29
mar de Weddell 29
mar del Norte 28, 32
mar Egeo 32
mar Mediterráneo 28, 32, 34
mar Negro 28, 32, 33
mar Rojo 28, 33, 34
mar, erizo 95
marca central 820
marca de tope 615, 616
marca registrada 390, 473
marcador 397, 454, 470, 789, 790, 822, 825, 831, 839, 844, 846, 848, 864, 865, 918
marcador automático 506
marcador de clasificación general 824
marcador de posición 440, 441
marcador del dobladillo 454
marcador del evento en curso 825
marcadores 847, 859
marchapié 602
marco 249, 395, 460, 818, 893
marco ajustable 303
marco de aluminio 893
marco vertical 461
marcos 460
margarina 209
margarita 908
marginador 484
Marianas, fosa 50
Marie Byrd, Tierra 29
Mariner 19
mariposa 96, 832
mariposa de resorte 302
mariposa hembra, anatomía 97
mariposa monarca 101
mariposa, morfología 96
mariquita 101
marítimo 61
marmota 123
marquesa 375
marquesina 712
marquesina del andén 583
marroquinería, artículos 386
Marruecos 745
Mars Odyssey 19
marsopa 137
marsupiales, ejemplos 143
marta 134
Marte 4, 5
martillo 174, 317, 752, 793
martillo de albañil 315
martillo de bola 301
martillo de carpintero 301
martillo de encuadernador 425
martillo de uña 301
martillo mixto 901
martillo neumático 649
martillo para hielo 901
martín pescador 118
martinete 443
más o menos 703
masa 43
masa de aire 55
masa inerte 43
masa, unidad de medida 702
máscara 765, 796, 798, 808
máscara antigás 773
máscara de oxígeno 775
máscara para el polvo 773
mascarilla 773
masculino 702
masculinos, órganos genitales 169
masetero 150
mastelero 602
mastelero de juanete 602
mastelero de mesana de estay 603
mastelero de sobrejuanete 602
mástil 407, 433, 439, 440, 441, 493, 631, 632, 633, 834, 836, 897
matacán 408
matemáticas 703
materia 680
materia inorgánica 67
materia, estados 680
material aislante 253, 254

material audiovisual 716
material de cierre 689
material de laboratorio 685
material de lucha contra los incendios 767
material impermeable 368
material que absorbe las ondas radar 629
materiales aislantes 299
materiales básicos 298
materiales de revestimiento 299
materiales peligrosos 774
materiales varios 313
materiales, manejo 632
matraca 909
matriz en relieve 420
matriz plana 420
matriz tallada 420
matriz ungular 172
Mauricio 746
Mauritania 745
mawashi 847
maxilar 108, 111, 112, 116, 121, 122, 123, 131, 136, 138, 158, 175
maxilar separable 112
maxilar superior 99, 152
maya 469
mayor que 703
mayúscula 472, 514
maza 421, 449
mazas 823
mazo 301, 401, 858
mazorca 85
meandro 48
meato auditivo 173, 174
meato auditivo externo 158
meato urinario 169
mecánico 873
mecánico de arranque 873
mecanismo asistido de descarga 755
mecanismo de avance y cambio de la diapositiva 483
mecanismo de cuerda 697
mecanismo de desplazamiento de la hoja 639
mecanismo de disparo 757
mecanismo de empuje 470
mecanismo de enrollado 285
mecanismo de escape 436
mecanismo de indicación del disco 305
mecanismo de la barrera 591
mecanismo de la palanca 443
mecanismo de retroceso y cambio de la diapositiva 483
mecanismo del órgano 445
mecanismo del piano vertical 443
mecanismo del reloj de pesas 697
mecanismo elevador del disco 305
mecanismo para las octavas 446
mecedora 276, 277
mechero de gas 685
medallón 374
media 365, 472, 808, 848
media antideslizante 365
media bota 342
media de malla 365
media faceta superior 374
media luna 385
media volea 820
media vuelta prohibida 544
medialuna 409
mediana 539, 712
medias 365, 367
medicamentos, formas farmacéuticas 783
medición de ángulos 701
medición de la altura de las nubes 59
medición de la dirección del viento 59
medición de la distancia 700
medición de la fuerza del viento 59
medición de la humedad 59
medición de la insolación 58
medición de la lluvia 59
medición de la longitud 700
medición de la nieve 59
medición de la presión del aire 59
medición de la temperatura 59, 695
medición de nevadas 59
medición del espesor 700
medición del peso 698
medición del tiempo 696
medición metereológica, instrumentos 58
médico 780, 842
médico interno 780
médicos 846
medida de radiación del cielo 58
medida instantánea, termómetro 231
medida telescópica 864
medidor automático 655
medidor de agua 562
medidor de altos niveles de frecuencia 499
medio central 801
medio centro 803
medio de apertura 804
medio de melé 804
medio izquierdo 801
medio lado 632
medio punto, arco 413
medio tubo 894
Mediterráneo, mar 28, 34
Mediterráneo, mar 32

médula 87, 165, 212
médula espinal 109, 110, 167, 168
médula espinal, estructura 167
médula ósea 154
meganeura 92
megazostrodon 93
Meissner, corpúsculo 172
meitnerio 683
mejilla 148
mejillón 217
Melanesia 29
melanesia 469
melazas 209
melé espontánea 805
melé: 806, 807
melisa 202
melocotón 192
melocotón, corte 81
melón amarillo 195
melón cantalupo 195
melón de miel 195
melón de Ogen 195
melón escrito 195
melón invernal 195
melones 195
membrana 82, 110
membrana celular 74, 94
membrana de plasma 94
membrana del ala 140
membrana del cascarón 117
membrana del tímpano 174
membrana interdigital 117
membrana interfemoral 140
membrana nuclear 74, 94
membrana plásmica 94
membrana vitelina 117
membrillo 193
memoria de tipos de puntos 456
men 847
mendelevio 684
meninges 167
menisco convergente 691
menisco divergente 691
menor que 703
ménsula 256, 412
mentón 115, 148
mentonera 765, 870, 885
menú 721
menudillo 124
Mercurio 4, 5
mercurio 275, 683
meridiana 276
meridiano celeste 13
meridiano occidental 36
meridiano oriental 36
meridiano principal 36
merlán 221
Mesa 10
mesa 52, 224, 278, 305, 307, 723, 815, 862
mesa alimentadora 643
mesa arbitral 879
mesa auxiliar de escritorio 511
mesa caliente 721
mesa de cama 780
mesa de hojas abatibles 278
mesa de jueces 801
mesa de la impresora 511
mesa de la ruleta 919
mesa de producción 491
mesa de servicio 720
mesa del ordenador 511
mesa operatoria 780
mesa para la vajilla limpia 721
mesa para la vajilla sucia 721
mesa plegable 278
mesa rotatoria 651
mesas, ejemplos 278
meseta 38, 45
mesilla de cabecera 780
mesilla de noche 724
mesita de servicio 278
mesocarpio 81, 82, 83
mesoglea 95
mesopausa 53
mesosauro 92
mesosfera 53
mesotórax 97
meta 871, 887, 890
metacarpiano 154, 156
metacarpo 111, 116, 122, 126, 131, 133, 136, 138, 142, 154
metafisis 155
metáfisis 155
metal, selección 71
metales alcalinos 682
metales alcalinotérreos 682
metales de transición 683
metales, ejemplos 741
metales, familia 437
metaloides 682
metamórfosis de la rana 111
metatarsiano 155
metatarso 98, 111, 122, 126, 131, 138, 141, 142, 155
metatórax 97
meteorito 97

meteorito ferroso 8
meteorito pétreo-ferroso 8
meteoritos pétreos 8
meteorología 53
metopa 404
metralla 752
metralleta 754
metro 592, 702, 713
metrónomo 436
metrónomo de cuarzo 436
México 434
México, golfo 30
mezcla de agua y vapor 646
mezcla de aire y combustible 564
mezcla de manganeso (cátodo) 689
mezcla de zinc y electrolito (ánodo) 689
mezclador de disco 268
mezclador de pastelería 232
mezcladores 268
mezquita 738
mi(E) 434
micelio 76
microfilamento 94
micrófono 488, 492, 496, 505, 506, 508, 516, 517, 527, 770, 898
micrófono del intercomunicador 491
micrófono electrodinámico 488
micrófonos 771
micrómetro 700
Micronesia 747
micronúcleo 94
microondas 690
Microscopio 10
microscopio 693
microscopio binocular 693
microscopio de electrones, corte transversal 694
microscopio de electrones, elementos 694
microscopios 693
microtúbulo 94
miel 209
miel, celdilla 100
miembro inferior 161
miembro superior 161
migala 102
mihrab 738
mijo 85, 203
mijo : espiga 85
mil 703
Mimas 5
mimbar 738
mina a cielo abierto 647
mina subterránea 650
mina, planta exterior 648
minarete 738
minas antipersonas 758
minas de carbón 647
mineral 647
mini-cadena estéreo 503
minibús 569
miniporción de leche /nata 223
miniporción, leche/nata 223
minúscula 472
minutero 231, 239, 696, 697
minuto 704
miocardio 162
miopía 691
mira 754, 756, 859, 913
mira del tirador 758
mira periscópica 758
mira telescópica 912
mirador 621
Miranda 5
mirilla 591
misil aire aire 759, 760
misil aire tierra 759
misil anti-nave 759
misil anti-radar 759
misil antiaéreo 762
misil antisubmarino 759, 762
misil antitanque 759
misil mar a mar 762
misil tierra aire 759
misil, estructura 759
misiles, principales tipos 759
Mississippi, río 30
mitocondria 74
mitocondria 94
mitón largo 346
mízcalo 183
mobiliario para el hogar 276
mocasín 344
mochila 901, 906
modalidad 528
modalidad de avance de la película 476
modalidad de exposición 476
modalidad de exposición múltiple 476
modalidad de producción de copia 512
modalidad sintonizador 498
modalidad TV 495
modalidad VCR 495
modelo de estación 55
módem 522, 523, 524
módem cableado 525
moderador 585, 665, 670, 671
modillón 405, 408
modos de pago 729

modulador de presión de frenado 559
módulo centrífugo 21
módulo de aterrizaje (Viking) 18
módulo de células solares 673
módulo de comunicación 486
módulo de control de la potencia 563
módulo de control del motor 563
módulo de franqueado 531
módulo de habitación americano 21
módulo de inyección de gas 652
módulo de la plataforma 40
módulo de mando 19, 25
módulo de propulsión 486
módulo de servicio 19
módulo de servicio 25, 486
módulo del equipo 40
módulo lunar 19, 25
módulo orbital (Viking) 18
módulo para experimentos europeo 21
módulo para experimentos japonés 21
módulo regulador de carga de la batería 563
módulo ruso 21
módulos de batería 60
mofeta 134
mogol 469
Moisés 736
molar 121, 123
molar, corte transversal 159
molares 159
Moldavia 744
molde 464
molde acanalado 232
molde de carlota 232
molde de pan 239
molde de soufflé 232
molde para bizcocho 232
molde para magdalenas 232
molde para tartas 232
molde redondo con muelles 232
moldeador de cutículas 377
moldes de pastas 232
moldura 253, 560
moldura lateral 551
moldura superior 815
mole 702
molécula 680
molibdeno 683
molinete 643, 676
molinillo de café 240
molino de plataforma giratoria 676
molino de torre 676
molino de viento 676
molleja 116
mollejas 212
moluscos 104, 217
moneda : anverso 729
moneda, anverso 729
moneda, reverso 729
moneda: reverso 729
monedero 387
Mongolia 747
monitor 507
monitor de control del director 428
monitor de efectos video/digitales 491
monitor de la producción técnica 491
monitor de producción 489
monitor de salida 491
monitor de sonido 489, 491
monitor de vídeo 518
monitor de visualización previa 489
monitor del sonido 490
monitor principal de visualización previa 491
monitores de entrada 491
monitores de visualización previa 491
mono 369
mono de esquí con capucha 369
monocascos 835
monóculo 385
monopatín 894
monopatín 894
Monopoly® 915
monovolumen 549
montacargas 634, 650
montagnais 469
montaña 45, 886
montaña alta, climas 61
montañas Rocosas 30
montante 246, 252, 371, 424, 425, 460, 461, 628, 629, 641, 782, 826, 881
montante central 247, 249, 278, 551
montante de la bisagra 247
montante de la cerradura 247
montante del filete 854
montante del muro 253
montante embarbillado 249
montante esquinero 252
montante quicial 249
monte de Venus 170
monte Everest 53
montes Apalaches 30
montes Cárpatos 32
montes marinos 49
montes Transantárticos 29
montes Urales 32
montículo 875
montura 385
montura de bayoneta 478

montura de cartón 483
montura de la hebilla 350
montura del objetivo 477
montura en herradura 17
monumento 39
moqueta 254
moras 192
morcilla 216
morcillo 214
mordaza 302, 303, 306, 307, 308, 310, 312, 317, 377
mordaza curva 310
mordaza fija 311, 312
mordaza móvil 311, 312
mordaza recta 310
mordazas 312, 913
mordente 435
morfología de un bogavante 107
morfología de un caballo 124
morfología de un canguro 143
morfología de un caracol 104
morfología de un delfín 136
morfología de un gato 133
morfología de un gorila 139
morfología de un murciélago 140
morfología de un pájaro 115
morfología de un perro 130
morfología de un pulpo 106
morfología de un tiburón 108
morfología de un topo 121
morfología de una abeja trabajadora 98
morfología de una araña 103
morfología de una concha bivalva 105
morfología de una concha univalva 105
morfología de una estrella de mar 95
morfología de una mariposa 96
morfología de una perca 108
morfología de una rana 110
morfología de una rata 122
morfología de una serpiente venenosa: cabeza 112
morfología de una tortuga 113
morilla 183
morillos 257
morral 388
morrena central 46
morrena de fondo 46
morrena frontal 46
morrena lateral 46
morrena terminal 46
morrillo 298
morro 624, 898
morro abatible 629
morsa 137
mortadela 216
mortero 298, 612, 753
mortero del siglo XVII 752
mortero moderno 756
mosaico 406
Mosca 11
mosca 101, 862
mosca artificial 909
mosca central 862
mosca de la línea de cuadro 862
mosca superior 862
mosca tsetsé 101
mosquetón 835, 901, 911
mosquetón curvo 900
mosquetón de bloqueo 900
mosquito 101
mostaza 84
mostaza alemana 200
mostaza americana 200
mostaza blanca 198
mostaza de Dijon 200
mostaza en grano 200
mostaza en polvo 200
mostaza inglesa 200
mostaza negra 198
mostrador 620
mostrador de autoservicio 722
mostrador de carne de autoservicio 180
mostrador de carne fresca 180
mostrador de devolución de libros 733
mostrador de préstamo 733
mostrador de quesos 181
mostrador frigorífico 720
mostrador, carne 180
mostrador, quesos 181
moto acuática 876
moto cámara 870
moto de cabeza 870
moto de carreras y motociclista 874
moto de motocross 875
moto de rally 875
moto de trial 875
moto nieve 876
moto, motociclista 874
motocicleta 574, 874
motocicleta : vista desde lo alto 576
motocicleta de turismo 577
motocicleta todo terreno 577
motocicletas, ejemplos 577
motocultor 327

motor 18, 236, 237, 240, 261, 288, 292, 293, 294, 304, 307, 308, 320, 323, 327, 332, 384, 574, 639, 640, 643, 651, 758
motor a reacción 60
motor de arranque 332
motor de aterrizaje 18
motor de cuatro tiempos 564
motor de elevación diésel 605
motor de gasolina 553, 563, 566
motor de la bomba 263
motor de propulsión diésel 605
motor del brazo actuador 521
motor del cohete 24
motor del disco 521
motor del proyectil 759
motor del tractor 638
motor del ventilador 258, 261
motor diésel 586, 637, 638, 639
motor diésel 636
motor eléctrico 259, 331, 332, 561, 563
motor eléctrico de emergencia 763
motor eléctrico principal 763
motor fueraborda 607
motor principal 23
motor turbocompresor 564
motor, bogie 585
motores diésel 762
motores, tipos 564
movimiento diagonal 916
movimiento en ángulo 916
movimiento horizontal 916
movimiento horizontal del suelo 43
movimiento vertical 916
movimiento vertical del suelo 43
movimientos de un avión 630
Mozambique 746
Mozambique, canal 34
mozzarella 210
mucosa olfatoria 175
mueble bar 279
muebles contenedores 278, 510
muebles de oficina 510
muebles de trabajo 511
muebles infantiles 281
muebles, ejemplos 741
muela 308
muela del juicio 159
muelle 249, 596, 653, 708, 776, 823, 913
muelle de carga 395, 713, 715, 716, 719
muelle helicoidal 553
muelle para inflar y desinflar 904
muerte 702
muesca 348, 362, 698, 750, 859, 863
muesca de apertura 905
muescas 424
muestra 458
muestreador 450
muflón 128
muguete 80
mujer 148
mujer, guantes 346
mujer, ropa 355
mujer, sombreros 341
mujer, zapatos 343
mújol 220
mula 128
muleta de antebrazo 782
muleta de sobaco 782
multicasco 835
multipack 223
multiplicación 703
multiplicador 677
mundo, climas 61
mundo, lenguas 468
muñeca 140, 147, 149, 156, 173
muñequera 808, 822, 850, 880, 895
munster 211
muralla 408, 409, 917
murciélago 140
murciélago hoja de lanza 141
murciélago vampiro 141
murciélago, morfología 140
muro 7, 246, 852, 902, 917
muro de abordaje 597
muro de cimentación 252
muro de encauzamiento 657
muro de la Qibla 738
muro de ladrillos 253, 298
muro de llegada 830
muro de nubes 63
muro de piedras 298
muro de rebote 819
muro del ojo 63
muro fortificado 738
muro lateral 597
musaraña 121
músculo aductor anterior 105
músculo aductor posterior 105
músculo bulbocavernoso 169
músculo erector del pelo 172
músculo papilar 162
músculo recto inferior 177
músculo recto superior 177
músculos 150
músculos del manto 106
muselina 231

museo 394, 711
museo, tienda 394
muserola 854, 856, 858
musgo 75
musgo, estructura 75
musgos, ejemplos 75
música 432
muslera 808
muslo 115, 124, 130, 147, 149, 169, 170
muslo, aductor 150
muslo, recto interno 151
musola 218
mútulo 404
Myanmar 747

N

nabiza 187
nabo 189
nabo sueco 189
nacimiento 702
nacionalidad 825
nadador, país 831
nahualt 469
nalga 147, 149, 169, 170
Namibia 746
Namibia, desierto 34
naos 403
naranja 194, 400
naranja amarillento 400
naranja china 194
naranja rojizo 400
naranja, corte 82
narciso 80
narina 108, 110, 112, 115
nariz 122, 148, 175, 912
nariz, aleta 175
nariz, dorso 175
nariz, ventana 175
narval 137
nasal 749
nasofaringe 175
nata 210
nata agria 210
nata de montar 210
natación 788, 830
Nauru 747
navaja 217
navaja de barbero 383
navaja de injertar 330
navaja jardinera 330
navaja multiusos suiza 905
navaja para entresacar 381
navajo 469
nave 41, 411
nave central 738
nave espacial 53
nave lateral 411
navegación, instrumentos 612
navegador 524
navicular 155, 156
Nazca, Placa 43
NEAR 19
neblina 57, 65
nebulosa planetaria 8
neceser 388, 389
necrológico 471
nectarina 192
nefridio 107
negativo 485
negativos, armario de secado 484
negra 435, 919
negras 916
negrita 472
negro 472, 690
Negro, mar 28, 32, 33
neodimio 684
neón 684
Nepal 747
neptunio 684
Neptuno 4, 5
nervadura central 84
nervadura principal 79
nervadura secundaria 79
nervio 96, 172, 426
nervio abdominogenital mayor 166
nervio abdominogenital menor 166
nervio auditivo 174
nervio central 167
nervio ciático mayor 166
nervio ciático menor 166
nervio ciático poplíteo externo 166
nervio ciático poplíteo interno 166
nervio circunflejo 166
nervio crural 166
nervio cubital 166
nervio de vela estay 602
nervio diagonal 410
nervio digital 166
nervio espinal 167
nervio femorocutáneo 166
nervio glúteo 166
nervio intercostal 166
nervio mediano 166
nervio musculocutáneo de la pierna 166
nervio obturador 166

nervio olfativo 109
nervio olfatorio 175
nervio óptico 177
nervio radial 166
nervio raquídeo 168
nervio safeno externo 166
nervio safeno interno 166
nervio secundario 410
nervio tibial anterior 166
nervio transversal 410
nervio vestibular 174
nervios craneales 166
nervioso, sistema 166
netball 809
neumático 551, 560, 570, 579, 870, 874
neumático de capas al sesgo 561
neumático de invierno 560
neumático de lluvia 872
neumático de rendimiento 560
neumático de seco 872
neumático de tacos 560, 577, 875
neumático de todas las estaciones 560
neumático de turismo 560
neumático radial 561
neumático radial con cinturones 561
neumáticos, ejemplos 560
neurona motora 168
neurona sensorial 168
neuronas, cadena 168
neutrón 680
neutrón incidente 681
nevadas, medición 59
nevera 548, 906
neviza 46
newton 702
Nicaragua 742
nicho de seguridad 543
niebla 57, 65
nieta 784
nieto 784
nietos 784
nieve 64
nieve ácida 70
nieve fuerte continua 57
nieve fuerte intermitente 57
nieve ligera continua 57
nieve ligera intermitente 57
nieve moderada continua 57
nieve moderada intermitente 57
nieves perpetuas 45
Níger 745
Níger, río 34
Nigeria 745
Nilo 34
nimbostrato 56
nimbostratos 62
niño, cráneo 158
niños 785
niños, ropa 369
niobio 683
níquel 683
níspero 193
Nissl, cuerpos 168
nitrógeno 683
nivel 650
nivel de agua 241, 261
nivel de aire 313
nivel de equilibrio del agua 49
nivel de la recepción 724
nivel del agua 261, 268
nivel del mar 42, 49, 53
nivel del mar, presión barométrica 55
nivel el agua, indicador 239
nivel freático 47
nivel inferior 597
nivel superior 597
nivelación principal 701
nivelador 309
nivelador de la alidada 701
nivelador principal 701
niveladora 639
nivómetro 58, 59
no blanquear con cloro 347
no es idéntico a 703
no es igual a 703
no es paralelo a 704
no lavar 347
no metales 683
no pertenece a 703
no planchar 347
no secar en secadora mecánica 347
nobelio 684
nódulo 663
nódulo de Ranvier 168
nogal 88
nombre de la estación 592
nombre de la moneda 729
nombre del dominio 524
nombre del equipo 858
nombre del gimnasta 825
nombre del nadador 831
nombre del periódico 471
nombre del titular 729
nonágono regular 705
nonio 612, 698
ñoquis 206
Nor Noroeste 37

ASTRONOMÍA > 2-25;   TIERRA > 26-71;   REINO VEGETAL >72-89;   REINO ANIMAL > 90-143;   SER HUMANO > 144-177;   PRODUCTOS ALIMENTARIOS Y DE COCINA > 178-241;   CASA > 242-295;
BRICOLAJE Y JARDINERÍA > 296-333;   VESTIDO > 334-371;   ACCESORIOS Y ARTÍCULOS PERSONALES > 372-391;   ARTE Y ARQUITECTURA > 392-465;   COMUNICACIONES Y AUTOMATIZACIÓN DE
OFICINA > 466-535;   TRANSPORTE Y VEHÍCULOS > 536-643;   ENERGÍA > 644-677;   CIENCIA > 678-705;   SOCIEDAD > 706-785;   DEPORTES Y JUEGOS > 786-920;

1063

Noreste 37
noreste 616
nori 183
normal 472
Noroeste 37
noroeste 616
Norte 37, 917
norte 616
Norte Noreste 37
Norte, mar 28, 32
Noruega 744
Noruega, mar 32
noruego 469
notación del ajedrez 916
notación musical 434
notas musicales, valores 435
nothosaurus 93
noticias breves 471
nova 8
nube 53, 65
nube alta, tipo 55
nube baja, tipo 55
nube de cenizas 44
nube de Oort 4
nube en forma de embudo 63
nube media, tipo 55
nubes 56, 62
nubes altas 62
nubes bajas 62
nubes de desarrollo vertical 62
nubes medias 62
nubes, absorción 68
nubosidad 56
nuca 147, 149
núcleo 6, 8, 9, 74, 94, 168, 170, 680, 867, 908, 912
núcleo de arcilla 660
núcleo del inducido 688
núcleo del reactor 670, 671
núcleo externo 42
núcleo fisionable 681
núcleo interno 42
núcleo, escisión 681
nucléolo 74, 94, 170
núcleos radiactivos 681
nudo 77, 687
nudo de dos cotes 908
nudo de guía 908
nudo de pescador 908
nudo de rizo 908
nudo de tejedor 908
nudo llano 908
nudo viario 709
nudos 908
nuera 784
Nueva Caledonia 29
Nueva Zelanda 29, 747
nuevas adquisiciones, expositor 733
nuevo shekel 728
nuez 146, 193, 685, 750
nuez de cola 193
nuez de ginkgo 193
nuez de macadamia 193
nuez del Brasil 193
nuez moscada 198
nuez moscada, rallador 230
nuez verde 84
nuez, corte 84
nuez, pinzas 685
número 919
número 1 858
número 2 858
número 3 858
número 4 858
número atómico 682
número de calle 893
número de decimales 529
número de habitación 724
número de identificación personal (PIN), teclado 731
número de la autopista 39
número de la carretera 39
número de la escena 429
número de la tarjeta 729
número de pista 501
número de salida 857
número de serie 729
número de tarjeta 731
número del consumidor 273
número del jugador 810, 878
número del surtidor 548
número dorsal 791
números romanos 703
nutria de río 134

O

oasis 48, 52
obenque 602, 834
Oberón 5
obi 845, 846
obispillo 115
objetivo 14, 476, 477, 478, 479, 483, 501, 517, 518, 692, 693
objetivo gran angular 478
objetivo macro 478
objetivo normal 478
objetivo ojo de pez 478
objetivo zoom 478, 496
objetivos 478
objeto 691
oblicuo mayor del abdomen 150, 151
oboe 446
oboes 437
obra muerta 835
obras 545, 547
obrera 99
observación astronómica 10
observación, puesto 17
observatorio 17
observatorio astronómico 17
observatorio astronómico, sección transversal 17
obstáculo 916
obstáculos 852, 875
obturador 513, 521, 901
obturador de la cúpula 17
obturador de plano focal 476, 477
obturador para la circulación del aire 675
obús moderno 756
oca 120, 213
occidental 815
occipital 151, 153
Oceanía 28, 29, 747
océano 7, 38, 67
océano Atlántico 28, 29, 32, 34
océano Glacial Ártico 28
océano Índico 28, 29, 33, 34
océano Pacífico 28, 29, 33
ocelo 97, 99
ocho con timonel 839
ocio al aire libre 902
octaedro regular 705
octágono regular 705
Octante 10
octava 434, 849
ocular 14, 15, 477, 479, 496, 692, 693
ocular acodado 14
odómetro 557, 700
Oeste 37, 917
oeste 616
Oeste Noroeste 37
Oeste Suroeste 37
office 250
oficial del banco de los penaltis 879
oficiales 846
oficina 509, 548, 582, 720, 726
oficina administrativa 764, 769
oficina de admisión de los detenidos 726
oficina de correos 474, 475, 711, 715
oficina de formación profesional 730
oficina de los organizadores 719
oficina de objetos perdidos 725
oficina de quejas 768
oficina de recepción de visitantes 726
oficina de reservas de hotel 620
oficina de urgencias 778
oficina del gerente 509
oficina del puerto 596
oficina, muebles 510
oficinas administrativas 718
oficios 452
ofimática 468
Ofiuco 11, 13
oftalmología 779
ohm 702
ohmnio 702
oído 173, 439
oído interno 174
oído medio 174
oído, estructura 174
ojal 352, 387, 461, 881
ojera 496
ojete 284, 342, 350, 371, 911
ojete para la correa 477
ojete para la correa del cuello 476
ojiva 759
ojival 413
ojo 63, 103, 104, 106, 107, 112, 113, 121, 133, 136, 148, 177, 301, 382, 453, 454, 855, 900
ojo compuesto 96, 98, 99
ojo de buey 608
ojos, maquillaje 378
okapi 128
ola 49
olécrano 126, 153
óleo 397
óleo, pintura 396
oleoducto 654
oleoducto de exportación 652
oleoducto de superficie 654
oleoducto para crudo 654
oleoducto submarino 654
olfato 174
oliva, aceite 209
olla 235
olla a presión 234
olla para cuscús 235
Omán 746
Omán, golfo 33
ombligo 46, 146, 148
ombligo inferior 115
ombligo superior 115
omoplato 126, 131, 136, 141, 142, 147, 149, 152, 153
omóplato 116
onda 690
onda de choque 651, 653
onda radioeléctrica 16
onda sísmica 43
onda, longitud 690
ondas hertzianas, transmisión 486
ondas radio 690
ondas ultrasónicas, emisión 41
Oort, nube 4
ópalo 375
opera 710
operación rápida 501
operación, teclas 730, 731
operaciones básicas 529
operaciones específicas 529
operador de cámara 428
operador de jirafa 429
operador del reloj de 30 segundos 810
operador del tablero de luces 490
operador técnico de vídeo 489, 490
opérculo 108, 111
opilión 102
opistodomo 403
oposum 143
óptica 715
orangután 139
orbicular 79
orbicular de los párpados 150
órbita 112, 116, 131, 136, 138, 142
órbita de los satélites 60
órbita geoestacionaria 60
órbita lunar 6, 7
órbita polar 60
órbita polar, satélite 60
órbita terrestre 6, 7
orbitador 22, 23
orca 137
orden corintio 405
orden de llegada 831
orden dórico 404
orden jónico 404
ordenador 734
ordenador portátil 526
ordenador a bordo 556, 771
ordenador de bolsillo 527
ordenador de gestión de vuelo 626
ordenador de vuelo 626
ordenador personal 513
ordenador portátil 523
ordenador portátil, maletín 527
ordenador portátil: vista frontal 526
ordenador portátil: vista posterior 526
ordenador: vista frontal 513
ordenador: vista interna 513
ordenador: vista posterior 513
Ordovícico 92
orégano 202
organismo cultural 525
organismo de salud 525
organismos simples 94
organización gubernamental 525
órgano 444
órgano, mecanismo 445
órganos genitales femeninos 170
órganos genitales masculinos 169
órganos sensoriales 172
orientación de la cuchilla, cilindro 639
oriental 815
orificio 470
orificio central 500
orificio de carga 757
orificio de entrada de aire 320
orificio de escape 649
orificio de la bolsa copuladora 97
orificio del pie 444
orificio excretor 104
orificio genital 104
orificio nasal 124
oriflama 739
origen de las especies 92
orilla 664
orillo 455
Orinoco, río 31
Orión 11, 12
orla 337
orla de púrpura 336
orla decorativa 368
ornamento de proa 600
oro 683, 741
oronja 183
orquesta 402
orquesta sinfónica 437
orquídea 80
ortiga 187
ortocerátido 92
oruga 97, 636, 758
oruga de polilla 102
orza de popa 836
orza de quilla 834, 836
orzada 833
Osa Mayor 13
Osa Menor 12
oscilación 630
osciloscopio de control de las formas de onda 491
ósculo 95
oscuridad 617
osmio 683
oso negro 135
oso polar 135
osoto-gari (gran siega) exterior 844
osteón 154
ostra 217
ostrero 118
otaria 137
otolito 109
otoño 54
otorrinolaringología 779
ovario 80, 97, 103, 170, 171
oveja 128
oviducto 97, 103, 113
ovotestis 104
óvulo 80, 170
óxer de barras 852, 853
óxido de nitrógeno, emisión 70
oxígeno 683
oxígeno, producción 78

P

pabellón 374, 446, 447, 710
pabellón auricular 173, 174
pabellón de la oreja 122, 143
pabellón de la trompa de Falopio 171
pacana 193
paciente 780
Pacífico Oriental, dorsal 50
Pacífico, océano 28, 29, 33
Pacífico, Placa 43
Pacífico-Antártico, dorsal 50
Pacini, corpúsculo de 172
padre 784, 785
padres 784, 785
página adelante 515
página atrás 515
pago electrónico, terminal 731
pagoda 412
país 37
país del nadador 831
Países Bajos 743
paja, empacadora 642
pajarita 349
pájaro carpintero 118
pájaro, anatomía 116
pájaro, esqueleto 116
pájaro, morfología 115
pájaros, ejemplos 118
pajita 223
pak-choi 186
Pakistán 746
pala 257, 326, 376, 636, 639, 756, 798, 800, 815, 838, 888, 901, 913
pala de timón 606
pala del rotor 631
pala del stick 880
pala del timón 834
pala del ventilador de sustentación 605
pala hidráulica 638
pala mecánica 647
pala plegable 906
palacio de congresos 711, 718
Palacio de Justicia 710
palacio de los deportes 788
paladar, velo 175
paladio 683
palafito 418
palanca 238, 268, 270, 301, 377, 381, 446, 686, 912, 920
palanca conmutadora de puntos 456
palanca corrediza de selección de diapositivas 483
palanca de accionamiento de la recámara 756
palanca de accionamiento del freno de mano 587
palanca de aflojar el papel 528
palanca de alimentador de oxígeno 898
palanca de armar 757
palanca de arranque 331
palanca de avance /marcha atrás 327
palanca de bloqueo 309
palanca de bloqueo de la altura 14, 15
palanca de bloqueo del acimut 14, 15
palanca de cambio 552
palanca de cambio de velocidades 556, 575, 576, 577
palanca de cierre 294, 587
palanca de compensación 460
palanca de control 649
palanca de dirección 633
palanca de enclavamiento 312
palanca de espaciamiento de los discos 643
palanca de fijación del venturi 757
palanca de freno 626
palanca de inclinación 898
palanca de la cisterna 265
palanca de la cuchilla 424
palanca de la cuña 309
palanca de levantamiento del tablero de corte 333
palanca de los alerones de hipersustentación 626
palanca de luces e intermitentes 556
palanca de mando 631, 898
palanca de maniobra 632, 633
palanca de maniobra de la aguja 590
palanca de perforación 240
palanca de presión 423
palanca de regulación de altura 289
palanca de seguridad 332
palanca de vibración 441
palanca de viraje 898
palanca del apagador 443
palanca del cambio de velocidades 579, 580
palanca del cerrojo 755
palanca del cucharón 637
palanca del deslizador 555
palanca del embrague 327
palanca del freno 579, 870, 876
palanca del tapón 265
palanca del tren de aterrizaje delantero 626
palanca estabilizadora 783
palanca para graduar la altura 641, 642
palanca para liberar el sujetapapel 528
palanca retráctil de la guarda móvil 304
palanca rotativa 516
palanca tensora 452
palancas 852
palatino 112, 123
Palau 747
palco 431
palé 632
palé con alas 632
palé de caja 632
palé de plataforma doble 632
palé de plataforma sencilla 632
palés 632
paleta 214, 233, 659, 815, 913
paleta con huecos para pintura 398
paleta con tarrito 398
paleta de albañil 315
paleta de la rueda 664
paleta de la turbina 659
paleta de relleno 315
paleta del rodete 659
paletas de la turbina 659
paletas del compresor 627
paletas del escape 627
paletilla 130, 215
palillo 390, 448
palla 336
palma 121, 127, 173, 346, 797, 841
palma de un guante 346
palmar 52
palmar mayor 150
palmar menor 150
palmeada 79
palmera 88
palmeta 276
palo 295, 740, 868
palo de la tienda 903
palo de mesana 600, 602
palo de proa 607
palo de trinquete 600, 602
palo del jugador 880
palo del portero 880
palo del radar 606
palo macho 602
palo mayor 600, 602
palo, 600
Paloma 11
paloma 120
palos 804
palpo 105
palpo labial 96, 99
pamela 341
pan 204, 722
pan ácimo 205
pan alemán de centeno 205
pan americano de maíz 205
pan blanco 205
pan campesino 205
pan danés de centeno 205
pan de centeno negro 204
pan de flor 205
pan de pita 205
pan espiga 204
pan griego 204
pan indio chapati 205
pan indio naan 205
pan integral 205
pan irlandés 205
pan judío hallah 205
pan multicereales 205
pan negro ruso 205
pan, molde 239
panadería 181, 715
panal 100
pañal 368
pañal desechable 368

1064

ASTRONOMÍA > 2-25; TIERRA > 26-71; REINO VEGETAL >72-89; REINO ANIMAL > 90-143; SER HUMANO > 144-177; PRODUCTOS ALIMENTARIOS Y DE COCINA > 178-241; CASA > 242-295; BRICOLAJE Y JARDINERÍA > 296-333; VESTIDO > 334-371; ACCESORIOS Y ARTÍCULOS PERSONALES > 372-391; ARTE Y ARQUITECTURA > 392-465; COMUNICACIONES Y AUTOMATIZACIÓN DE OFICINA > 466-535; TRANSPORTE Y VEHÍCULOS > 536-643; ENERGÍA > 644-677; CIENCIA > 678-705; SOCIEDAD > 706-785; DEPORTES Y JUEGOS > 786-920

panal, corte 100
Panamá 742
panamá 340
Panamá, golfo 31
Panamá, istmo 30
panceta 216
páncreas 110, 116, 164
pandereta 449
panel 511
panel absorbente de frecuencias bajas 490
panel de acceso 258, 266
panel de cierre 513
panel de conexión 518
panel de conexión del vídeo 489
panel de conexiones eléctricas 489
panel de control 292, 293, 294, 518
panel de controles 476
panel de la puerta 554
panel de la vela 834
panel de mandos 238, 239, 290, 293
panel de monitores 490, 491
panel de publicidad 592
panel de separación 389
panel de yeso 299
panel del display 496
panel fotovoltaico 615
panel frontal 571
panel indicador 793
panel lateral 571, 635
panel protector 783
panel radiador 23
panel solar 17, 18, 40, 60, 486
paneles de comunicación 626
paneles fotovoltaicos 21
paño lateral 352
pantalla 257, 275, 286, 483, 494, 526, 528, 529, 530, 613, 724, 730, 799, 918
pantalla de alarma de motor y tripulación 626
pantalla de control 694
pantalla de cristal líquido 477
pantalla de los sistemas 626
pantalla de navegación 626
pantalla de protección 794
pantalla de proyección 427, 483
pantalla del contador de pasadas 456
pantalla del radar 771
pantalla plana 518
pantalla principal de vuelo 626
pantalla táctí 496
pantalla táctil 527
pantalla, tubo 494
pantalón 791, 796, 808, 844, 850, 878, 901
pantalón corto 358, 369
pantalón de boxeo 371
pantalón de peto 368
pantalón peto 358
pantalones 350, 371, 716, 748, 802, 875
pantalones acampanados 358
pantalones de boxeo 842
pantalones de chándal 370
pantalones de montar 853
pantalones de peto 369
pantalones de tubo 358
pantalones elásticos 870
pantalones, ejemplos 358
pantis 365
pantógrafo 585, 595
pantorrilla 147, 149
pantufla 344
pañuelo de bolsillo 348
papaya 197
papel 390, 400, 420
papel corrector 534
papel de aluminio 222
papel de celofán 222
papel de fumar 390
papel de reserva 512
papel encerado 222
papel para el horno 222
papel secante 531
papelera 535
papelería 717
papila 172
papila filiforme 176
papila foliada 176
papila fungiforme 176
papila gustativa 176
papila lingual 176
papila óptica 177
papila renal 165
papilla circunvalada 176
Papua Nueva Guinea 29, 747
paquete 223
paquete de cigarrillos 390
paquete de placas fotográficas 481
paquete postal 475
par 253, 919
parábola 493
parabrisas 550, 570, 574, 577, 607, 624, 626, 628, 876
paracaídas 417, 760, 896
paracaídas auxiliar 22
paracaídas de reserva 896

paracaídas piloto 896
paracaídas principal 896
paracaidismo en caída libre 896
paracaidista 896
parachoques 570, 571, 577, 876
parachoques anterior 885
parachoques posterior 577, 885
parada de autobús 712
parafinas 656
paraguas 391
paraguas de bastón 391
paraguas plegable 391
Paraguay 742
paragüero 391
paralelepípedo 705
paralelo 36
paralelogramo 705
paramecio 94
paramento de aguas contenidas 661
paramento de aguas corrientes 661
Paraná, río 31
parapente 897
parapentista 897
parapeto 409, 540
parapeto contra olas 660
pararrayos 245, 658, 663, 677
parasol 14, 556, 558, 567, 612
parche 449
parche inferior 448
parche superior 448
pardillo 118
pared 127, 650
pared celular 74
pared de hormigón 675
pared de Trombe 675
pared de viraje 831, 832
pared frontal 819
pared lateral 127, 607, 818, 819, 831
pared transversal de contención 606
pared trasera 818
pareja 881
paréntesis 473
pareo 339
parietal 112, 122, 153
paripinnada 79
parka 353
parmesano 211
párpado 113
párpado inferior 110, 132, 177
párpado interno 132
párpado superior 110, 132, 177
párpados, orbicular 150
parque 39, 711
parqué 254
parqué alternado a la inglesa 254
parqué Arenberg 254
parqué Chantilly 254
parque de bomberos 711, 764
parque de cestería 254
parque de estacionamiento 619
parqué de mosaico 254
parqué en punta de Hungría 254
parqué espinapez 254
parque nacional 39
parqué sobre base de cemento 254
parqué sobrepuesto 254
parqué Versailles 254
parqué, tipos 254
parrilla 238, 290
parrilla de salida 872, 875
parrilla eléctrica 239
parrilla estabilizadora 903
parrilla plegable 907
parte plana 457
parte superior 321
parteluz 249, 411
partes 276, 277, 280
partes de un anillo 376
partes de un círculo 704
partes de un hueso largo 155
partes de un zapato 342
partes de una bandera 739
partes de una bicicleta 578
partes de una embarcación 838
partes del arma 849
particiones, ejemplos 740
partido 919
pasa (19 a 36) 919
pasadizo ascendente 402
pasadizo descendente 402
pasador 248, 249, 350, 380, 906
pasahilos 456
pasaje subterráneo 583
pasajeros, avión turborreactor 624
pasajeros, terminal 620
pasajeros, vagones 584
pasamano 569, 607
pasamanos 255, 417
pasamontañas 341, 872
pasapuré 233
pasarela 408, 430, 523, 583, 606
pasarela superior 593
pasarela telescópica 619
pasaverduras 230
pascal 702
paseo 322
pasillo 180, 714

pasillo central 584
pasillo de dobles 820
pasillo de enlace 584
pasillo de individuales 821
pasillo de seguridad 728
paso 45, 124
paso a nivel 545, 547, 583, 591
paso alternativo 892
paso de Drake 29, 31
paso de la energía hacia la red de transmisión 662
paso de patinador 892
paso de peatones 545, 547, 712
paso de popa a proa 607
paso elevado 540
paso inferior 540
pasta 206
pasta de hojaldre 205
pasta won ton 207
pastel 396
pastel al óleo 396
pastel al óleo, pintura 396
pastel blando, pintura 396
pastelería 715
pastelería, bandeja 232
pastelería, mezclador atrás 333
pastilla 783
pastilla de combustible 667
pastilla de fricción 559
pastillas de acuarela 397
pastillas de guaches 397
pastor alemán 130
pata 113, 139, 143, 275, 277, 278, 280, 281, 323, 448, 461, 823, 900, 910
pata anal 97
pata anterior 121
pata curvada 276
pata de ajuste de altura 483
pata de gallo 459
pata de la mesa 815
pata de locomoción 103
pata delantera 96, 98, 110, 143, 277
pata delantera (superficie exterior) 98
pata delantera del perro 130
pata lobulada, dedo 117
pata media 96, 98
pata media (superficie exterior) 98
pata móvil 278
pata palmípeda, dedo 117
pata posterior 121, 143
pata principal 663
pata telescópica 482, 776
pata torácica 97
pata trasera 96, 98, 110, 277
pata trasera (superficie interior) 98
pata ventosa 97
patada de crol 832
patada de mariposa 832
patada de rana 832
Patagonia 31
patas de ganso 899
patas, ejemplos 117
patata 184
pátera 276
Pathfinder 19
patilla 385
patín 880, 884
patín de aterrizaje 631
patín de cola 631
patín de deslizamiento 590
patín de los accesorios 476
patín de oruga 758
patín de pista corta 883
patín de pista larga 883
patín de retroceso 756
patín del portero 880
patín delantero 884
patín en línea 895
patín en línea de hockey 895
patín en línea, 895
patín móvil 885
patín para figuras 881
patín trasero 884
patinador 882, 895
patinaje acrobático 895
patinaje artístico 895
patinaje artístico, cuchilla 881
patinaje de velocidad 882
patinaje en línea 895
patinaje sobre hielo, pista 881
patinaje, pista 886
patines de carreras 883
patio 322, 727, 735, 738
patio de armas 408, 409
patio de butacas 431
patio de tanques 654
pato 120, 213
patrón 455
patrón de prueba 492
patrulla de primeros auxilios y puesto de socorro 886
pausa 515
pausa /imagen fija 495
pauta A 436
pavimento 538
pavimento deslizante 545, 547
Pavo 10

pavo 120, 213
pavo real 119
PC 522, 523
PC 524
PC, 522
peatones, semáforo 712
pécari 128
peces 108
peces cartilaginosos 218
peces óseos 219
pecho 124, 146
pechuga 115
pecíolo 76, 79
pecorino romano 211
pectoral 808, 851
pectoral mayor 150
pedal 440, 448, 460, 578, 580, 851, 870
pedal automático 870
pedal crescendo 444
pedal de ajuste 399
pedal de expresión 444
pedal de la sordina 442
pedal de los bajos 451
pedal de los frenos 556
pedal de marcha adelante 333
pedal de marcha atrás 333
pedal de velocidad 452
pedal del acelerador 556
pedal del embrague 556
pedal del freno 333, 460, 552, 559
pedal del freno trasero 576
pedal del timón de mando 898
pedal eléctrico 452
pedal fuerte 442, 451
pedal plano 870
pedal suave 442
pedalero 444
pedalier 318, 752
pedazo 286, 307, 440, 791
pedestal de la cámara 492
pedio 150
pedipalpo 103
pedúnculo 75, 80, 81, 82, 83, 86
Pegaso 12
peinado 380
peinazo 278
peinazo de la cerradura 247
peinazo inferior 277, 278
peinazo superior 277, 278
peine 417, 460
peine afro 380
peine combinado 380
peine de cardar 380
peine de iluminación 429
peine de mango 380
peine de peluquero 380
peine de polen 98
peine de tapicería 461
peine para desenredar 380
peine y cuchilla 383
peines 380
pelacables 317
pelaje 121, 122, 133, 139, 143
pelapatatas 229
peldaño 255, 321, 417, 640, 847
peldaño de arranque 255
peldaño inferior 587
peldaño posterior 766, 775
pelele 369
pelele de dos piezas 368
peleteria 714
pelícano 119
película 477
película de disco 481
película plástica, condensador 689
película termosaldada 223
peliculas 481
peligro 616
pelillo 909
pelo 147, 149, 172, 254
pelo de maíz 85
pelos absorbentes 77
pelos absorbentes, zona 87
pelos radicales 77
pelota 815, 823, 858
pelota de béisbol, corte 797
pelota de cricket 798
pelota de entrenamiento 819
pelota de golf 867
pelota de hockey 800
pelota de raquetball 818
pelota de softball 797
pelota de tenis 822
pelota de torneo 819
pelotas de squash 819
pelotón 870
pelotón de cabeza 870
peltada 79
Pelton, turbina 659
peluquería 714
peluquero 428
peluquero, tijeras 382
pelvis 121, 126, 138, 141, 142
pelvis renal 165
pelvis vestigial 136
penacho 115, 748
penacho de plumas 817

penalizaciones 789
pendiente 374
pendientes 374
pendientes de aro 374
pendientes de clip 374
pendientes de espiga 374
pendientes de tornillo 374
pendolón 253
pendón 739
péndulo 436, 697
péndulo, reloj 697
pene 104, 146, 169
península 38
península Antártica 29
península de Arabia 33
península de Corea 33
península de Kamchatka 33
península de Kola 32
península de los Balcanes 32
península del Yucatán 30
península Escandinava 32
península Ibérica 32
pentágono regular 705
pentagrama 434
peón 916
pepinillo 188
pepino 188
pepino amargo 188
pepino dulce 197
pepino sin pepitas 188
pepita 82, 83
peplo 336
pepperoni 216
pequeños electrodomésticos 717
pera 193
pera asiática 197
pera de goma 776, 777
pera de maíz 842
peraltado 413
perca 220
perca, anatomía 109
perca, morfología 108
percha 877
perchero 510
perchero de pared 510
perchero de pie 510
percoladora 241
percoladoras 723
percusión, instrumentos 437, 448
percusor 861
percutor 754, 757, 912
pérdida de calor 68
perdiz 118
perejil 202
perfil del suelo 78
perfil, suelo 78
perforación 371
perforación marina 653
perforación, torre 651
perforaciones 342, 346
perforadora 533
perforadora con empujador neumático 648
perfumería 181, 714
perfumes 717
pérgola 322
pericardio 163
pericarpio 82, 84
perifollo 202
perilla 304, 307
perilla de registro 445
periódico 471
periódico, nombre 471
periódicos 733
periodo 617
periostio 154
periscopio de ataque 763
periscopio de navegación 763
peristilo 403, 406
peristoma 94
peritoneo 169, 170
Pérmico 92
perno 248, 310, 311, 312
perno con collarín 311
perno de acoplamiento 659
perno de articulación del cucharón 637
perno de expansión 302
perno de fijación 559
perno de la bisagra 638
perno de la eclisa 590
perno difusor 329
perno maestro 571
perno para falso plafón 302
pernos 311
peroné 126, 131, 138, 141, 142, 152, 155, 156
peroneo corto 151
peroneo largo 150
peróxido 777
perpendicular 704
perro 130, 913
perro, esqueleto 131
perro, morfología 131
perro, pata delantera 130
perros, razas 130
persa 132, 469
Perseo 12

1065

persiana enrollable 285
persiana enrollable automática 285
persiana veneciana 285
persianas enrollables 285
persianas romana 285
Pérsico, golfo 33
personal de la seguridad 837
personal suplementario de producción 490
personal, entrada 720
personal, guardarropa 720
pertenece a 703
pértiga 792
pértiga de inclinación 285
pértiga, saltador 792
Perú 742
Perú-Chile, dorsal 50
pesa 697, 698
pesa corrediza 698
pesas 850, 851
pesas para muñecas y tobillos 850
pesca 909
pesca con mosca 909
pesca de lanzado 910
pescado 181
pescante 602, 606, 634, 635
pescuezo 868
peso 630, 699, 728, 793
peso corredizo 436
peso, medición 698
pespunte 346, 350, 368, 459
pespunteada 357
pespunteado 370
pestaña 127, 177, 355, 455
pestaña de arrojo 776
pestaña de la llanta 560
pestañas 132
pesticida 69, 70
pestillo 248, 249
pestillo de ingletes 303, 304
pétalo 80
petanca 864
petición del sistema 515
petifoque 603
petirrojo 118
peto 337, 368, 369, 749, 796, 800, 808
peto del portero 880
peto metálico 848
petral 853, 857
Petri, cápsula 685
petróleo 651, 656
petróleo crudo 656
petrolero 596, 606
Pez Austral 10
pez cartilaginoso 108
pez de San Pedro 221
pez espada 219
pez óseo 108
Pez Volador 11
pezón 146, 148, 171
pezuña de cuatro pesuños 127
pezuña de dos pesuños 127
pezuña de tres pesuños 127
pezuña de un pesuño 127
pezuñas, ejemplos 127
pi 704
piamadre 167
piano 437
piano cuarto de cola 443
piano de cola de concierto 443
piano de media cola 443
piano electrónico 451
piano vertical 442
piano vertical, mecanismo 443
pica 123, 767
picadero 856
picadora de carne 230
picardía 364
piccolo 437, 446
picea 89
pichi 356
pichón 212
pickguard 441
pico 45, 106, 115, 327, 901
pico de loro 610
pico de rey 700
pico muesca 455
picos, ejemplos 117
pictogramas 514
pie 76, 104, 105, 139, 140, 143, 146, 147, 148, 149, 236, 274, 368, 440, 444, 693, 909, 910
pie ajustable 292, 293, 294
pie ambulacral 95
pie de apoyo 641
pie de foto 471
pie de la cama 280
pie de la torre 663
pie de montura 482
pie de voluta 276
pie del electrodo 275
pie del talud 660
pie derecho 252, 411
pie, arteria dorsal 160
pie, dedo 146, 148
pie, huesos 155
pie, interóseos 150
piedra 298, 376

piedra al aceite 422
piedra blanca 916
Piedra Coyolxauhqui 412
piedra de afilar 229
piedra de curling 877
piedra de sacrificio 412
piedra litográfica 423
piedra negra 916
piedra tallada 298
piedras preciosas 375
piedras preciosas, tallas 375
piedras semipreciosas 375
piel 81, 82, 83, 168, 172, 433
piel armónica 433
piel de gamuza 377
piel para encuadernar 425
pierna 124, 147, 149, 156, 351
pierna de cordero 215
pierna elástica 351
pies de gato 900
pieza 917
pieza de talón 892
piezas 916
piezas honorables, ejemplos 740
pigostilo 116
pijama 364, 369
pijama de una pieza 351
pijamas de hombre 717
pila 482, 563, 687, 765
pila alcalina de manganeso-zinc 689
pila bautismal 737
pila de agua bendita 737
pila de carbón-cinc 689
pila recargable 496
pilar 43, 410, 412, 540, 650
pilar anterior del velo del paladar 174
pilar derecho 804
pilar izquierdo 804
pilas secas 689
pilastra corintia 407
pilón 540
pilón de los tirantes 541
pilón del turborreactor 625
pilón guía 542
piloto 238, 240, 241, 288, 290, 294, 465, 872, 897
pimentero 226
pimentón, 199
pimienta blanca 198
pimienta de cayena 199
pimienta de Jamaica 198
pimienta molida 199
pimienta negra 198
pimienta rosa 198
pimienta verde 198
pimiento dulce amarillo 188
pimiento dulce rojo 188
pimiento dulce verde 188
piña 89, 196
pinacocito 95
pináculo 408, 410, 411
pinatifida 79
pincel 397, 470
pincel de repostería 232
pincel para labios 378
pincel puro 397
pinchador 534
pinche de cocina 721
pingüino 119
pinna 76
pino piñonero 89
piñón 89, 193, 307, 697
piñón la rueda de la película 476
piñón libre 580
piñón simple 871
piñón, cremallera, engranaje 686
pintada 120, 212
pintalabios 378
pintura 395, 396
pintura al óleo 396
pintura al pastel al óleo 396
pintura al pastel blando 396
pintura con rotuladores 396
pinza 96, 107, 350, 352, 381, 422, 470, 506, 534, 700
pinza de cinturón 505
pinza de conexión a tierra 318
pinza del electrodo 318
pinza del freno 574
pinza negra 558
pinza para el cabello 380
pinza para rizar 380
pinza roja 558
pinza sujetamuestras 693
pinza tibiotarsiana 98
pinzas 233, 455, 777
pinzas con nuez 685
pinzas multiuso 317
pinzas para caracoles 233
pinzas para depilar cejas 377
pinzas para espagueti 233
pinzas pelacables 317
pinzas universales 310
pinzas verticales 455
pinzón 118
piojo 101
piolet 901

Pioneer 19
pipa 390
pipa, accesorios 390
pipa, corte transversal 390
pipeta 685
piragua monóxilo 599
piramidal 154
pirámide 402, 705
pirámide, entrad 402
piranómetro 58
pirata 358
Pirineos 32
piruetas, ejemplos 881
pisacorbatas 376
piscina 246, 608, 675, 788, 827, 831
piscina de inmersión 788
piscina elevada 246
piscina enterrada 246
piscina olímpica 831
Piscis 12
pisiforme 154
piso 257, 676, 818, 819, 894
piso cosido 902, 903
piso de operaciones 664
piso superior 569
pisón 390
pisos de madera 254
pista 788, 790, 819, 864, 866, 872, 874, 878, 883, 885, 891
pista : saltos 890
pista corta 882, 883
pista de aterrizaje 761, 890
pista de aterrizaje y despegue 620
pista de atletismo 788
pista de bolos 865
pista de competición 855
pista de competición : half-pipe 887
pista de competición, half-pipe 887
pista de deceleración 885, 891
pista de despegue 890
pista de enlace 618
pista de esgrima 848
pista de esquí alpino 886
pista de estacionamiento 618
pista de fondo 886
pista de frenado 891
pista de juego 864
pista de lanzamiento 793
pista de muelles 826
pista de patinaje 886
pista de patinaje sobre hielo 881
pista de rodaje 618
pista de salida 891
pista de salto 791, 792
pista de velocidad 891
pista hípica 788
pista larga 882
pista para avanzados 886
pista para expertos 886
pista para intermedios 886
pista para principiantes 886
pista para salto de obstáculos 852
pistacho 193
pistas de carreras 824
pistas de esquí 886
pistilo 80
pistola 315, 754, 770
pistola de 8 mm 861
pistola de aire comprimido 861
pistola de calor 320
pistola de pintar 320
pistola de salida 790
pistola del surtidor 548
pistola para calafateo 315
pistola para soldar 318
pistola pulverizadora 329
pistolera 770
pistolete 754, 755
pistón 447, 559, 564, 566
pit 501
pit stop 873
pitón 114, 900
pitón de expansión 900
pitón de hielo 901
pitorro 241, 295
pivot 811
pivote 317, 382, 398, 436, 454, 500, 612, 686, 793, 814, 882, 883, 889, 907
pivote de la rótula 587
pivote móvil 310
pizarra 734
placa 224, 268, 270, 482
placa africana 43
placa antártica 43
placa antifricción 889
placa base 58, 889
placa blindada 758
placa calcárea 105
placa calientaplatos 721
placa corrediza (cubrecanilla) 453
placa corrediza de la canilla 452
placa costal 113
placa de absorción 672
placa de advertencias 306
placa de agujas 456
placa de apoyo 756
placa de asiento 590
placa de base 452

placa de circuito impreso 689
placa de cobre 422
placa de cocción 239
placa de cocina 722
placa de Cocos 43
placa de Escocia 43
placa de especificaciones 306
placa de fijación 701
placa de Filipinas 43
placa de freno 889
placa de hielo 64
placa de identificación 376, 770
placa de instalación 275
placa de la aguja 452
placa de la culata 756
placa de Nazca 43
placa de número 875
placa de presión 476
placa del Caribe 43
placa del interruptor 274
placa del Pacífico 43
placa eléctrica 290
placa espigadora 643
placa euroasiática 43
placa indicadora 273
placa indoaustraliana 43
placa madrepórica 95
placa marginal 113
placa motora 168
placa negativa 562
placa norteamericana 43
placa para fusibles 663
placa positiva 562
placa protectora 875
placa sudamericana 43
placa supracaudal 113
placa térmica 241
placa terminal 667
placa vertebral 113
placas convergentes 43
placas divergentes 43
placas tectónicas 43
plafón 286
plana 401
plancha 239, 288, 381, 812
plancha de chapa 819
plancha de entintado 421
plancha de muelles 826
plancha de pelo 381
plancha de vapor 288
plancha eléctrica 239
plancha superior 238
planchado 347
planeador 898
planetario 10
planetas 4
planetas externos 4
planetas internos 5
planicie 38
planicie fluvio-glaciar 46
planisferio 28
plano 414
plano de deriva 625
plano de la catedral 411
plano del templo griego 403
plano del terreno 245
plano focal elevado, boyas 615
plano horizontal 625
plano vertical 625
planta 77, 351
planta alta 250, 251
planta baja 250
planta de bombeo 654
planta de energía maremotriz 664
planta de lubricantes 656
planta de reforma catalítica 656
planta de separación selectiva 71
planta de tratamiento 649
planta exterior de una mina 648
planta intermedia de refuerzo 654
planta, anatomía 77
plantador 324
plantador de bulbos 324
plantar delgado 151
plantas de flor 93
plantilla 345
plantilla de desagüe 660
plaqueta 162, 385
plasma 162
plasmodesmo 74
plástico transparente 386
plásticos transparentes 386
plásticos, clasificación 71
plastrón 113
plata 683, 741
plataforma 43, 321, 482, 538, 542, 569, 571, 588, 632, 699, 894
plataforma continental 49
plataforma de 10 m 828
plataforma de 3 m 828
plataforma de 5 m 828
plataforma de 7,5 m 828
plataforma de alimentación 531
plataforma de corte 333, 642
plataforma de entrada 584
plataforma de hielo de Amery 29
plataforma de hielo de Filchner 29

plataforma de instrumentos 60
plataforma de jaula 650
plataforma de lanzamiento 795
plataforma de piso bajo 588
plataforma de producción 652, 654
plataforma de salida 830, 891
plataforma de trampolines 890
plataforma de vuelo del helicóptero 762
plataforma elevadora para silla de ruedas 569
plataforma fija 653
plataforma giratoria 766
plataforma giratoria, molino 676
plataforma inferior 632
plataforma montada en gatos mecánicos 653
plataforma móvil 633
plataforma para transportar vagones 588
plataforma petrolera semisumergida 653
plátano 196
platea 402
plateosaurus 93
platija 221
platillo 698, 699
platillo de presión 758
platillo high hat 448
platillo inferior 448
platillo superior 448
platillo suspendido 448
platillos 437, 449
platina 423, 693, 694
platina mecánica 693
platino 683
platito para el pan 226
plato 464, 500, 860, 905, 919
plato ajustable 511
plato de postre 226
plato de retroceso 559
platò de rodaje 428
plato giratorio 312, 638
plato lijador 308
plato llano 226
plato para caracoles 233
plato sopero 226
platos calientes 722
platos de cocción 239
platos fríos 722
playa 51
plegadera 426
plegador de urdimbre 460
plegador del tejido 460
plegador posterior 460
plenum 258
pletina 504
pletina de casete 488, 499
pletina de proyección 535
pleura parietal 163
pleura visceral 163
plexo braquial 166
plexo lumbar 166
plexo nervioso 159
plexo sacro 166
pliego 426
pliegue 336
pliegue anal 147, 149
pliegue de cajón 283
pliegue de cajón invertido 283
pliegue de la columela 105
pliegue de pinza 283
pliegues, ejemplos 357
plisada 357
plomo 615, 682, 911
plotter 520
pluma 43, 115, 397, 638
pluma de ave 470
pluma de caña 470
pluma de dirección 859
pluma estilográfica 470
pluma metálica 470
pluma metálica romana 470
plumas timoneras 115
plumón 115
Plutón 4, 5
plutonio 684
pluviómetro 58, 59
pluviómetro de lectura directa 58, 59
pocilga 182
podadera 330
podadera de árboles 330
podadera de bordes 332
podio 412, 713
podio de salida 830
podio y sótanos 713
podón 330
polaco 469
polaina 339, 857, 858, 901
polainas 857
pole position 872
polea 284, 321, 566, 686, 750, 859, 913
polea de tracción 688
polea de transmisión 462
polea del montacargas 634
polea tensora 284
polea tensora del limitador de velocidad 417
poleas de tensión 580
polen, celdilla 100
policía 725

polideportivo 709, 788
polígono de tiro 769
polígono industrial 709
polígonos 705
polilla de abedul 101
Polinesia 747
polipasto 651
polipodio común 76
polisón 337
política 739
polítrico 75
pollo 213
polluelo 120
polo 354, 359, 822, 858
polo negativo 689
polo Norte 35
polo norte 687
polo Norte celeste 13
polo positivo 687
polo Sur 29, 35
polo sur 687
polo Sur celeste 13
Polonia 744
polonio 682
polvera 378
polvo compacto 378
polvo de magnesio 825
polvos sueltos 378
poma 445
pomelo 194
pomo 277, 278, 307, 309, 849, 880
pomo carnoso 82
pomo exterior 248
pomo interior 248
pómulo 152
poncho 355
poni 858
poni de polo 858
Pont-l'Évêque 211
pontón 542, 652, 839
pontón de salida 838
pontones, puente 542
pool 862
Popa 11
popa 598, 602, 608, 836
póquer 914
por lo ancho 833
porcentaje 703
porche 245
poro 74, 84, 172
poro inhalante 95
porra 770
porta martillo 313
porta pasaportes 387
porta pipas 390
porta stilus 517
porta-celo 534
porta-cinta adhesiva 534
porta-esquí 558
porta-filtro 241
portaaguja 453
portaagujas 776
portaaviones 761
portabicicletas 558
portabobina 452
portabobinas 462
portabolsa 869
portabotellas 579
portabrocas de sujeción 306
portacanilla 452
portacarrete 909, 910
portaequipajes 567, 577, 578, 605, 876
portaequipajes posterior 577
portafusible 663
portahorquilla 632
portal 411, 540
portalámpara, componentes 275
portalámparas 275
portaleños 257
portaminas 470
portamonedas 387
portanegativos 485
portante 125
portaobjetivo rotatorio 693
portaobjeto 693
portaobjetos 693
portaocular 14
portapitones 901
portaplumas 386
portarrollos de papel higiénico 264
portasellos 531
portatrajes 389
portatubo 693
portaviento 432
portería 724, 800, 802, 814, 827, 858, 879
portero 799, 800, 801, 803, 809, 814, 827, 878, 879
portero del equipo receptor 799
portero, guante 800
pórtico 411, 738
pórtico de tirantes 663
pórtico detector de metales 726
Portugal 743
portugués 469
posición A - en plancha 828
posición B - hacer la carpa 828
posición C - cuerpo encogido 828
posición de equilibrio 690
posición de guardia: 843
posición de la cremallera 455
posición de lanzamiento, transbordador espacial 22
posición de las piernas 829
posición de los brazos 829
posición de los jugadores 794, 803, 804, 814
posición de pie 861
posición de rodillas 861
posición de salida de espalda 832
posición de un carácter 472
posición del documento a enviar 508
posición del haz de electrones 694
posición del jurado 887
posición en pie 893
posición supina 861, 893
posición vertical 843
posiciones 849
posiciones de los jugadores 811
posiciones de salto 828
posiciones de tiro 861, 893
posiciones iniciales 843
postal 474
poste 255, 583, 591, 807, 812, 817, 820, 827, 842
poste con protecciones 811
poste de canasta 809
poste de foul 795
poste de la grúa 607
poste de salto 792
poste del asiento 578
poste indicador 856
postigos interiores 282
postres 723
potasio 682
potencia eléctrica, unidad de medida 702
poterna 408, 409
potro 824, 825, 826
pozo 402, 671
pozo ciego 650
pozo de acceso 664
pozo de extracción 650
pozo de inyección 646
pozo de producción 646
pozo marino 654
pozo principal 649
pozo seco 671
pozo, línea de flujo 652
practicable 823
practicable para ejercicios de suelo 824
practicante 846
pradera 182
praderas 66
prado 182
praseodimio 684
Precámbico 92
precio total 699
precio unitario 699
precipitación 67
precipitación, cubeta 685
precipitaciones 64
precipitaciones invernales 64
precisión, balanza 699
precocinados 181
premaxilar 108, 122, 123
premolar 121, 123
premolares 159
prensa 424, 425
prensa de aguafuerte 421
prensa de cajos 425
prensa de contactos 484
prensa de tornillo 425
prensa en C 312
prensa litográfica 423
prensa-café 241
prensado 425
prensatelas 452, 453
preparador 811
prepucio 169
presa 657, 661
presa de bóveda 661
presa de bóveda, sección transversal 661
presa de contrafuertes 660
presa de contrafuertes, sección transversal 660
presa de tierra 660
presa de tierra, sección transversal 660
presa móvil 664
presa, sección transversal 661
presas de mano 901
presas de pie 901
presas, ejemplos 660
presidente 848
presidente de jurado 881
presidente del jurado 900
presilla 349, 350, 905
presilla de estaquilla 902, 903
presilla de la manga 352
presilla del cinturón 352
presión 851
presión barométrica 55
presión barométrica a nivel del mar 55
presión del aire, medición 59
presión, unidad de medida 702
préstamo 733
presurizador 671
pretina 350, 353
pretina con botones de presión 368
pretina elástica 351, 353
prevención de incendios 764
prevención de la criminalidad 768
previsión meteorológica 54
primates, ejemplos 139
primavera 54
primer árbitro 812, 813
primer aumento de la tensión 677
primer ayudante de cámara 428
primer espacio 811
primer jugador 877
primer molar 159
primer nivel de operaciones 529
primer pistón móvil 447
primer premolar 159
primera 849
primera aleta dorsal 108
primera base 794
primera clasificación 474
primera etapa 25
primera falange 126
primera línea 804
primera plana 471
primera plana, foto 471
primera vía de clasificación 589
primera vuelta 789
primeras hojas 77
primeros auxilios, botiquín 775
primeros auxilios, equipamiento 775
primeros auxilios, puesto de socorro 886
primeros violines 437
primo 785
Principado de Andorra 743
Principado de Mónaco 744
principales movimientos 916
principales señales de circulación internacionales 544
principales señales de circulación norteamericanas 546
principales tipos de cuchillas 401
principales tipos de misiles 759
principales venas y arterias 160
prisma 477
prisma de Porro 692
prismáticos binoculares 692
proa 606, 609, 834, 836, 897
proa afilada 839
proa apuntada 838
proa tallada 598
probador 716
probador de contactos con tierra 316
probeta graduada 59, 685
probóscide 96
procesador 513
procónsul 93
producción de calor 665
producción de electricidad por energía eólica 677
producción de electricidad por energía geotérmica 646
producción de electricidad por energía nuclear 665
producción de electricidad por energía solar 674
producción de electricidad por energía térmica 646
producción de electricidad por generador 662, 665
producción de electricidad, etapas 662
producción de oxígeno 78
producción del sonido 445
producción eléctrica 676
producción, plataforma 652
productor 429, 489, 490
productor técnico 489, 490
productos alimenticios 180
productos de cocina 180
productos de fisión 681
productos de limpieza 721
productos del refinado 656
productos en oferta 181
productos lácteos 180, 210
productos para envasar 180
productos petroquímicos 656
productos, oferta 181
profesor 734
profesor, pupitre 734
profundidad del hipocentro 43
programa de correo electrónico 524
programación televisiva, horario 471
programador 261, 292, 293, 294
programas informáticos 771
prohibido acampar 725
prohibido adelantar 544, 546
prohibido el cambio de sentido 546
prohibido el paso 544, 546
prohibido el paso de bicicletas 545, 546
prohibido el paso de camiones 545, 546
prohibido el paso de motocicletas 545, 546
prohibido el paso de peatones 545, 546
prohibido hacer comidas campestres 725
prohibido usar silla de ruedas 725
promecio 684
promontorio 51
pronador redondo 150
pronaos 403
proporción de nubes 55
propulsor 18, 20, 22, 25, 40
propulsor de maniobras 23
propulsor de proa 609
propulsor F-1 25
propulsor J-2 25
propulsor sólido 22
propulsores de control de actitud 22
proscenio 430
prospección marina 653
prospección terrestre 651
próstata 169
protactinio 684
protección 774
protección contra salpicaduras 655
protección de la cabeza 774
protección de las manos 774
protección de los oidos 774
protección de los ojos 774
protección de los pies 774
protección del sistema respiratorio 774
protección para el sistema respiratorio 773
protección para la cabeza 772
protección para los oidos 772
protección para los ojos 772
protección para los pies 773
protector 290, 331, 352, 798, 800, 823, 842, 918
protector bucal 843
protector contra virutas 305
protector de antebrazo 808
protector de brazo 859
protector de cuello 808, 880
protector de espuma 772
protector de garganta 882
protector de la barbilla 575
protector de la correa 307
protector de la culata 446
protector de la garganta 796
protector de mano 875
protector de piernas 879
protector del brazo 808, 880
protector del cable 306, 308, 318
protector del cuello 765, 880
protector del pie 796
protector del quemador 899
protector del tendón 880
protector del zanco 636
protector dental 808
protector facial 879
protector lumbar 808
protector para las costillas 808
protector pectoral 859
protector solar 20
Protestantismo 736
protocolo de comunicación 524
protón 680
protoneurona 168
protórax 97
protuberancia 6
proveedor de servicios Internet 525
proventrículo 116
provincia 37
provisión de dinero en efectivo 731
provisión de guantes 780
próxima llamada 507
proyección cilíndrica 36
proyección cónica 36
proyección en círculo 844
proyección interrumpida 36
proyección plana 36
proyección por encima del hombro con una mano 844
proyección primera de cadera 844
proyección, cabina 427
proyección, pantalla 427, 483
proyección, sala 427
proyecciones cartográficas 36
proyectiles 752, 759
proyector 427, 428, 518, 535, 585
proyector auxiliar 10
proyector de altura máxima 59
proyector de diapositivas 483
proyector de luz difusa 492
proyector para planetario 10
proyector sobre el pantógrafo 492
proyectores 431
prueba 831
pruebas 889
pseudópodo 94
psicrómetro 59
pterigoides 112
púa 433
púa de muelle 327, 641
pubis 116, 122, 146, 148
público, entrada 402
pueblo 708, 886
puente 39, 115, 284, 385, 433, 439, 440, 441, 523, 539, 596, 692, 854, 875
puente cantilever 540
puente colgante 540
puente de arco 540
puente de carga para contenedores 596
puente de ensamblaje 441
puente de la nariz 175
puente de los altos 442
puente de los bajos 442
puente de luces 766, 771
puente de luces, sistema de control 771
puente de mando 604, 608, 609, 626, 761
puente de pontones 542
puente de portal 541
puente de señales 583
puente de tablero inferior 541
puente de tablero intermedio 541
puente de tablero superior 541
puente de Varolio 167
puente de viga 540
puente de viga de un tramo 541
puente de viga de varios tramos 541
puente desmontable tipo Bailey 542
puente elevador 542
puente giratorio 542
puente levadizo 408
puente levadizo doble 542
puente levadizo sencillo 542
puente transbordador 542
puentes de arcos, ejemlos 541
puentes de tirantes 541
puentes de vigas, ejemplos 541
puentes fijos 540
puentes móviles 542
puerco espín 123
puerro 184
puerta 17, 238, 278, 290, 293, 417, 551, 554, 567, 624, 699, 724, 738, 799, 818, 902, 903
puerta automática 620
puerta basculante de garaje 416
puerta convencional 416
puerta corredera 416
puerta corredera automática 416
puerta cortafuego 416
puerta de acceso a la rejilla de las luces 490
puerta de ascenso 837
puerta de control 890
puerta de descenso 837
puerta de dos hojas 568
puerta de entrada 247, 568, 569
puerta de garaje seccional 416
puerta de la bodega de carga 23
puerta de la plataforma elevadora 569
puerta de librillo 416
puerta de proa 605, 608
puerta de recorrido 837
puerta de salida 856
puerta de tiras 416
puerta del congelador 291
puerta del entrada 584
puerta del fogón 256
puerta del refrigerador 291
puerta giratoria manual 416
puerta inferior 597
puerta lateral 594
puerta mosquitera 567
puerta plegable 264, 416
puerta posterior 775
puerta superior 597
puerta trasera 250, 635
puerta ventana 224, 251
puertas de entrada 427
puertas giratorias manuales 719
puertas, ejemplos 416
puerto 596, 709
puerto de Ethernet 526
puerto de infrarrojos 526
puerto de interfaz de ordenador 520
puerto de módem interno 513, 526
puerto de red 513
puerto de salida de S-video 526
puerto de salida de TV 526
puerto de vídeo 513
puerto deportivo 788
puerto FireWire 526
puerto infrarrojos 527
puerto juego 513
puerto MIDI 513
puerto paralelo 513
puerto ratón 513
Puerto Rico, fosa 50
puerto serial 513
puerto teclado 513
puerto USB 513, 526
puertos para el mando 918
puertos para tarjeta de memoria 918
puesta en marcha 456, 512
puesto de bombeo 548
puesto de clasificación 589
puesto de control 394, 727
puesto de enfermeras (ambulatorio de urgencias) 779
puesto de enfermeras (urgencias) 778
puesto de información 620
puesto de la guardia de seguridad 779
puesto de los entrenadores 891
puesto de los jueces 890
puesto de observación 17
puesto de socorro 725
puesto de tiro 893
puesto de trabajo 509
puesto del jurado 891
puestos de escucha 733

ASTRONOMÍA > 2-25; **TIERRA** > 26-71; **REINO VEGETAL** >72-89; **REINO ANIMAL** > 90-143; **SER HUMANO** > 144-177; **PRODUCTOS ALIMENTARIOS Y DE COCINA** > 178-241; **CASA** > 242-295; **BRICOLAJE Y JARDINERÍA** > 296-333; **VESTIDO** > 334-371; **ACCESORIOS Y ARTÍCULOS PERSONALES** > 372-391; **ARTE Y ARQUITECTURA** > 392-465; **COMUNICACIONES Y AUTOMATIZACIÓN DE OFICINA** > 466-535; **TRANSPORTE Y VEHÍCULOS** > 536-643; **ENERGÍA** > 644-677; **CIENCIA** > 678-705; **SOCIEDAD** > 706-785; **DEPORTES Y JUEGOS** > 786-920

1067

puf 277
pujamen 836
pulga 101
pulgar 140, 141, 156, 173, 346, 797
pulgar oponible 139
pulidora 423
pulmón 103, 104, 110, 112, 116, 125
pulmón derecho 161, 163
pulmón izquierdo 161, 163
pulmones 163
pulpa 81, 82, 83, 159
pulpejo 127
púlpito 737, 738
pulpo 106, 217
pulpo, anatomía 106
pulpo, morfología 106
pulsador de llamada 417
pulsar 8
pulsera de dijes 376
pulverizador 294, 328, 329, 646
pulverizador de agua 550
pulverizador tándem 641
puma 134
puñal 751
puño 338, 349, 797, 822, 849, 892
puño de amura 836
puño de escota 836
puño para gemelos 361
punta 79, 185, 227, 229, 301, 302, 303, 304, 315, 318, 350, 351, 374, 390, 391, 439, 453, 457, 470, 739, 740, 792, 793, 840, 859, 868, 888, 892, 894, 911, 915, 918
punta cruciforme 302
punta de caja cuadrada 302
punta de diamante 278
punta de flecha de sílex 748
punta de hoja plana 302
punta de la plancha 288
punta de plástico 381
punta de sujeción 442
punta del ala 897
punta del cuello 349, 362
punta del diente de la desterronadora 636
punta del esquí 892
punta delantera 901
punta seca 422, 423
puntal 253, 448, 663
puntal trasero 676
puntales de refuerzo 252
puntas; tipos 302
punteado 463
punteo 401
puntera 309, 880, 889, 893
puntera perforada 342
puntera protectora 773
puntera reforzada 880
puntero 907
punto 473, 914
punto crítico 891
punto de apoyo 103
punto de apoyo variable 828
punto de arroz 458
punto de concentración 674
punto de cruz 459
punto de despegue 891
punto de empulgada 913
punto de escapulario 459
punto de espiga 459
punto de información 715, 719, 733, 886
punto de inserción 859
punto de interés 39
punto de malla 458
punto de marcado 455
punto de mira 754, 755, 757, 861, 893, 907, 912
punto de montaje 627
punto de norma 891
punto de nudos 459
punto de ochos 458
punto de penalti 802
punto de respiguilla 458
punto de salida 866
punto de saque 878
punto del derecho 458
punto del revés 458
punto y coma 473
punto, tipos 458
puntos 822
puntos cardinales, señales 616
puntos de cruz 459
puntos de malla 459
puntos de montado 457
puntos de relleno 459
puntos de relleno sueltos 459
puntos suspensivos 473
puntos, tipos 459
puntuación, signos 473
punzón 458, 464, 905
pupila 132, 177
pupila vertical 112
pupitre del alumno 734
pupitre del profesor 734
purificador de aire 261
puro 390
púrpura 741
putter 867, 868
puzle 917

Q

Qatar 746
quad 577
quark d 680
quark u 680
quarterback 807
queche 601
quechua 469
quelícero 103
quemador 234, 259, 290, 652, 899, 903
quemador de gas 267
queroseno 656
queso 722
queso chèvre 210
queso cottage 210
queso cremoso 210
queso, rallador cilíndrico 230
quesos azules 211
quesos blandos 211
quesos de cabra 210
quesos frescos 210
quesos prensados 211
quevedos 385
quiasma óptico 167
quijada 124, 130
quijada inferior 854
quijada superior 854
quijote 749
quilla 116, 600, 835, 897
química 680
quingombó 188
quinientos 703
quinta 434, 849
quinteto 438
quinto octante 7
quinua 203
quiosco 715
quirófano 780, 781
quitagrapas 534
quitanieves 573
quitapiedras 585, 586
quitón 336

R

rábano 189
rábano blanco 189
rábano daikon 189
rábano negro 189
rabillo 81, 82, 83
rabiza 909
racimo 81
racimo de uvas 86
raclette 211
raclette-grill 239
racor abocinado 269
racor por compresión 269
racores mecánicas 269
racores, ejemplos 269
radar 40, 604, 605, 608, 609
radar aéreo 762
radar aerotransportado 40
radar de aterrizaje 761
radar de búsqueda aérea 761
radar de control aéreo 761
radar de detección de blancos 762
radar de navegación 624
radar de vigilancia de superficie 761, 762
radar meteorológico 54
Radarsat, satélite 40
radiación 681
radiación artificial 41
radiación del cielo, medida 58
radiación infrarroja 68, 690
radiación natural 41
radiación solar 67, 68, 672, 673, 674, 675
radiación solar absorbida 68
radiación solar refleja 68
radiación ultravioleta 690
radiador 259, 552, 561, 586
radiador de convexión 260
radiador eléctrico 260
radiador tubular 259
radiador, manguito 561
radiadores 21
radial externo primero 151
radial externo segundo 151
radícula 77, 87
radio 103, 116, 121, 122, 126, 131, 136, 138, 140, 141, 142, 152, 154, 156, 488, 579, 682, 704, 771, 898
radio blando 108
radio CB 505
radio despertador 503
radio espinoso 108
radio medular 87
radio portátil 503
radio y cúbito 111
radioactividad, unidad de medida 702
radioactivo 774
radiocasete con lector de disco compacto 504
radiocasete portátil personal (Walkman) 504
radioisótopos, generador 18
radiómetro 60
radiómetro de imágenes 60
radiosonda 59
radiotelescopio 16
radomo 760
radón 684
rádula 104
raíces 77, 86, 189
raíces adventicias 76
raíces superficiales 87
rail 591, 595
rail de cierre 590
rail de retención 590
rail eléctrico 595
rail guía 16
railes del travelín 428
raíz 78, 159, 176, 227
raíz anterior 168
raíz cuadrada de 703
raíz de la uña 172
raíz motora 167, 168
raíz posterior 168
raíz primaria 77, 87
raíz principal 77
raíz secundaria 77
raíz sensitiva 167, 168
rallador 229, 230
rallador cilíndrico de queso 230
rallador de nuez moscada 230
rally, coche 873
rama 77, 87, 89, 127, 776
rama comunicante 168
rama con fruto 86
rama inferior 750
rama madre 87
rama superior 750
ramaje 87
ramal de enlace 539
rambután 197
ramificación 86
ramificación colateral 168
ramilla 87
rampa 407, 539
rampa de acceso 403, 540
rampa de lanzamiento 891
rampa del muelle 596
rampa para sillas de ruedas 394
rampa plegable 608
ran, metamórfosis 111
rana 110
rana arborícola 111
rana bermeja 111
rana de bosque 111
rana leopardo 111
rana macho, anatomía 110
rana, esqueleto 111
rana, morfología 110
ranilla 127
ranita 369
ranura 229, 302, 386, 453, 562, 791
ranura de alimentación 519
ranura de corte 305
ranura de depósito 730
ranura de la tarjeta PC 526
ranura de lectura de tarjeta 548
ranura de puesta al día de la cartilla 730
ranura de registro de la transacción 730
ranura de ventilación 526
ranura de visión 749
ranura guía 888
ranura para el pan 238
ranura para monedas 507, 920
ranura para toldo 567, 571
Ranvier, nódulo 168
rape 220
raqueta 893
raqueta de bádminton 816
raqueta de raquetball 818
raqueta de squash 819
raqueta de tenis 822
raqueta elíptica 893
raquetball 818
raquis 115
ras el hanout 199
rascador 422
raspador 390, 423, 464, 638
rasqueta 320, 892
rastrillo 327, 333, 642, 643
rastrillso 430
rata 123
rata, esqueleto 122
rata, morfología 122
ratón de campo 123
ratón inalámbrico 516
ratón mecánico 516
ratón óptico 516
ratónde rueda 516
ratonera 892
raviolis 206
raya 218, 350
raya continua 538
raya discontinua 538, 539
rayo 65
rayo de luz 691
rayo láser 501, 692
rayo solar reflejado 674
rayos gamma 690
rayos X 690
razas de gatos 132
razas de perros 130
re(D) 434
Rea 5
reacción 684
reacción en cadena 681
reactor 665, 666, 669
reactor de agua a presión 671
reactor de agua hirviente 671
reactor de agua pesada 670
reactor de bióxido de carbono 670
reactor nuclear 763
reactor nuclear, carga 667
reanimación, equipamiento 775
rebajado 413
rebajo de escalón 255
rebobinado 495
rebobinador 452
reborde 431, 439, 440
rebosadero 262, 265, 657
rebote 812
rebozuelo 183
recalentador 668
recalentamiento global 68
recámara 465
recámara, palanca de accionamiento 756
recepción 509, 724, 730, 764, 778, 781
recepción de carga 621
recepción de datos 41
recepción de documentos 508
recepción directa en la casa 486
recepción, nivel 724
receptáculo 75, 80, 83
receptáculo del cepillo 384
receptáculo seminal 97, 103
receptor 16, 441, 443, 493, 506, 795, 796
receptor 794
receptor alejado 807
receptor de los bajos 441
receptor de los intermedios 441
receptor del sonido 776
receptor sensorial 168
receptor triple 441
receptores gustativos 176
recibo 699
recibo de transacción 731
reciclado 71
reciclado de aluminio, contenedor 71
reciclado de papel, contenedor 71
reciclado de vidrio, contenedor 71
reciclaje, contenedores 71
recinto ferial 708
recipiente 240, 261
recipiente con vertedor 237
recipiente de acumulación 59
recipiente de agua 261
recipiente de vertido 59
recipiente del abrillantador 294
recipiente del detergente 294
recipiente inferior 241
recipiente para almacenamiento 666
recipiente superior 241
reclamo 913
recogedor 295, 332
recogepelotas 820
recogida de papel, contenedor 71
recogida de vidrio, contenedor 71
recogida diferenciada 71
recta de fondo 856
rectángulo 705
recto 97, 99, 113, 116, 125, 164, 169, 170
recto anterior 150
recto del abdomen 150
recto entallado 356
recto interno del muslo 151
recuadro 663
recubrimiento aislante 22
recubrimiento antirreflectante 672
recubrimiento de la primera tubería 654
recuperación de aire 258
recuperación del documento enviado 508
red 281, 811, 812, 813, 814, 815, 817, 821, 827
red de área amplia 523
red de cables telefónicos 712
red de correos pública 474
red de distribución por cable aéreo 486
red de mano 911
red de transmisión de electricidad 674
red de transmisión por cable subterráneo 487
red de transmisión privada 486
red en anillo 522
red en bus 522
red en estrella 522
red informática 523
red nacional de transmisión 486
red telefónica 487
redonda 435
redondo mayor 151
redondo menor 151
reducción /ampliación 512
reducción del diámetro del haz 694
reducción/ampliación 512
reductor 269
reductor con cabeza hexagonal 269
reductor de calibre 269
reductor de entrada 100
reductor de flujo 654
reductor de voltaje 662
refinado, productos 656
refinería 654, 709
reflector 316, 571, 578, 876
reflector del radar 615
reflector orientable 492
reflector parabólico 16
reflector parabólico de microondas 489
reflector parabólico móvil 16
reflector secundario 16
reflectores solares 486
reflexión 41
reflexión parcial, espejo 692
reflexión total, espejo 692
Reforma 736
refrigeración, torre 646
refrigeración, varilla 692
refrigerador de aire 564
refrigerante 656, 665, 670, 671, 674
refrigerante caliente 665, 674
refrigerante de la cámara del generador de vapor 669
refrigerante frío 665, 674
refuerzo 367, 772, 874
refuerzo de la culata 753
refuerzo del talón 342
refuerzo embobinado 868
refugio 543
refugio de montaña 886
refugio en la cima 886
refugio meteorológico 58
refugio presurizado 543
refugio principal 886
regadera 328
regalos 717
regatón 901
región lumbar 147, 149
región malar 115
región negativa 672
región positiva 672
regiones de boyas 616
registrador de datos 58
registro 273
registro de altos 432
registro de cristal líquido 696
registro de datos 41
registro digital 316
registro sísmico 651, 653
registro, cilindro 43
registros de bajos 432
Regla 10
regla 424, 454, 905
regla de corte 305
regla de escuadra 399
regla graduada 700
regla para medir puntos 457
regla, escala 700
regleta colectora térmica 272
regleta de neutro/de tierra 272
regulador 443
regulador de altura 826
regulador de ancho de puntada 452
regulador de emergencia 841
regulador de entrada de agua 294
regulador de fluidos 320
regulador de la 1ª etapa de descompresión 841
regulador de la 2ª etapa de descompresión 841
regulador de la presión 445
regulador de largo de puntada 452
regulador de luminosidad 285
regulador de presión 234, 319, 452, 765, 903
regulador de tamaño de punto 453
regulador de temperatura 571
regulador de tensión 452, 456, 457
regulador de velocidad 333, 556
reina 99, 914, 916
Reina Maud, Tierra 29
reina, cámara 402
reiniciación 512
reino animal 92
Reino Unido de Gran Bretaña e Irlanda del Norte 743
reino vegetal 74
reja 316, 641, 727
reja de entrada al pronaos 403
reja de entrada, pronaos 403
reja de seguridad 730
reja metálica de contacto 672
rejilla 234, 238, 259, 261, 290, 291, 432, 488, 494, 561, 562, 658
rejilla de calefacción 594
rejilla de control térmico 60
rejilla de entrada de aire 382
rejilla de iluminación 492

INDICE ESPAÑOL

1068

ASTRONOMÍA > 2-25; TIERRA > 26-71; REINO VEGETAL >72-89; REINO ANIMAL > 90-143; SER HUMANO > 144-177; PRODUCTOS ALIMENTARIOS Y DE COCINA > 178-241; CASA > 242-295; BRICOLAJE Y JARDINERÍA > 296-333; VESTIDO > 334-371; ACCESORIOS Y ARTÍCULOS PERSONALES > 372-391; ARTE Y ARQUITECTURA > 392-465; COMUNICACIONES Y AUTOMATIZACIÓN DE OFICINA > 466-535; TRANSPORTE Y VEHÍCULOS > 536-643; ENERGÍA > 644-677; CIENCIA > 678-705; SOCIEDAD > 706-785; DEPORTES Y JUEGOS > 786-920

rejilla de pared 258
rejilla de piso 258
rejilla de salida 260
rejilla de salida de aire 382
rejilla de techo 258
rejilla de vaporización 261
rejilla de ventilación 261, 294
rejilla del ventilador 289
rejilla desmontable 234
rejilla frontal 261
rejilla protectora 502
rejilla regulable 258
rejilla, sistema 36
rejillas, tipos 258
relámpago 57
religión 736
religiones, cronología 736
rellano 255
rellano de la escalera 251
rellano inferior 417
rellano superior 417
relleno alternado 459
relleno exterior 647
Reloj 10
reloj 238, 290, 484, 488, 489, 491, 734, 851, 858
reloj automático 465
reloj de arena 231
reloj de la ampliadora 485
reloj de péndulo 697
reloj de pesas, mecanismo 697
reloj de pulsera 696
reloj de sol 696
reloj digital 696
reloj mecánico 696
reloj programador 238
relojes 717
remache 229, 310
remate 255, 813
remate en T 257
remeras primarias 115
remeras secundarias 115
remeras terciarias 115
remo 598, 600, 838, 851
remo de dirección 598
remo de dos palas 837, 839
remo de una sola pala 837, 838
remo en punta 838
remolacha 189
remolcador 606
remolque 567, 623
remolque rígido trasero 569
remolque tipo caja 570
renacuajo 111
reniforme 79
renio 683
reno 128
repetidor 487
repisa 256
repisa para accesorios 14
repollo 186
repollo verde 186
reposa-mano 516
reposabrazo 555
reposabrazos 783
reposacabezas 555
reposamanos 514
reposapies 281, 577
reposapiés 312, 783, 871
reposicionamiento 528
repostador 873
repostaje de combustible en vuelo 760
reproductor de CD portátil 503
reproductor de disco compacto 503
reproductor de DVD 521
reproductor de vídeo 789
reproductor DVD 494
reproductor/grabador de vídeo VCR 495
reptación 47
reptiles 112
reptiles, ejemplos 114
República Centroafricana 745
República Checa 744
República de Corea 747
República de Mali 745
República de San Marino 744
República Democrática del Congo 745
República Democrática Popular de Corea 747
República Dominicana 743
repuesto 470
repulsión 687
reseña gastronómica 471
resguardo del parachoques 550
residuos industriales 69
residuos domésticos 69, 70
residuos industriales 69, 70
residuos no reciclables 71
residuos nucleares 70
residuos primarios 656
resistencia 290, 293, 294, 318, 465
resistencia aerodinámica 630
resistencia eléctrica, unidad de medida 702
resistencia inferior 266
resistencia superior 266

resistencias 689
resonador 444, 449, 502
resonador de rayos infrarrojos 60
resorte 43, 268, 284, 286, 292, 310, 391, 470, 586, 757, 913
resorte de la válvula 566
resorte de retorno 559
resorte de suspensión 697
resorte de tensión 453, 850
resorte de válvula 445
resorte del eslabón 752
resorte del martinete 443
resorte del sistema articulado 920
resorte del tensor 457
resorte espiral 285
resorte hidráulico 851
resorte tensor 557
respaldo 276, 277, 281, 391, 555, 577, 783, 876
respaldo reclinatorio 776
respiradero 100, 244, 261, 575, 655
respiradero lateral 567
resta 703
restablecimiento 519
restador 817, 819, 820
restaurante 608, 710, 713, 714, 719, 720, 725
restaurante de autoservicio 722
restaurantes de comida rápida 715
resurgencia 47
retablo 737
retén 649
retén de la esfera 516
retén del cargador 754
retén imantado 240
retención de datos 316
retícula 692
Retículo 10
retículo endoplasmático 74, 94
retina 177, 691
retira cutículas 377
retoño 87
retorno 515
retorno a la memoria 529
retrato 729
retroceso 515
retrovisor 576
retrovisor de gran angular 568
retrovisor gran angular 569
revelado, baños 485
revelado, tanque 484
revestimiento 559, 660, 815, 867, 899, 912
revestimiento de fibra de vidrio 267
revestimiento de fósforo 275
revestimiento de la popa 17
revestimiento interior 554, 561
revestimientos textiles del suelo 254
revisor 582
revista sensacionalista 471
revólver 754
revólver portaobjetivos 693
rey 914, 916
rey, cámara 402
ría 852, 853
ría para la carrera de obstáculos 790
ría, carrera de obstáculos 790
rías 51
ribete 340, 342, 348, 370
ribosoma 74, 94
ricotta 210
riel 284, 635
riel corredizo 294, 835
riel de iluminación 287
riel de lanzamiento de proyectiles 760
riel de rodamiento 634
riel deslizador 555
riel metálico 533
riel para las rejillas 291
rieles, empalme 590
rienda 856
rienda del bocado 854
rienda del freno 854
riendas 857
rifle 912
rigatoni 206
rillettes 216
rimaya 46
rímel en pasta 378
rímel líquido 378
rincón 842
rinconera 279
ringside 842
rinoceronte 129
riñón 104, 105, 106, 109, 110, 112, 116, 125, 161
riñón derecho 165
riñón izquierdo 165
riñonera 808
riñones 124, 212
río 38, 39, 48
río Amazonas 31
río Congo 34
río Danubio 32
río Dniéper 32
río Mackenzie 30

río Mississippi 30
río Níger 34
río Orinoco 31
río Paraná 31
río San Lorenzo 30
río Senegal 34
río Vístula 32
río Volga 32
ripia 299
risco 7, 45
ritmo de las señales nocturnas 617
rizador de mantequilla 229
rizador de pestañas 378
rizoide 75
rizoma 76
róbalo 220
Roberval, balanza 698
roble 88
robot de cocina 237
roca 900
roca firme 43
roca impermeable 651
roca madre 78
rocas ígneas 42
rocas intrusivas 42
rocas metamórficas 42
rocas sedimentarias 42
rociador 270
rociadores 665
rocío 65
rocódromo 900
Rocosas, montañas 30
roda 602
rodaballo 221
rodamiento 516
rodapié 278, 417
rodete 659
rodete de la turbina 664
rodetes 659
rodilla 124, 130, 146, 148
rodillera 749, 796, 808, 850, 855, 857, 858, 880, 882, 894, 895
rodillo 232, 285, 320, 333, 423, 465, 528
rodillo de entrada 642, 643
rodillo de pintor 320
rodillo entintador 421
rodillo guía 499
rodillo guía de la película 476
rodillo para barnizar 422
rodillo para graduar el respaldo 553
rodillo triturador 642
rodio 683
rodrigón 322, 324
roedor 122
roedores 122
roedores, ejemplos 123
roja 915, 919
rojo 400, 690
rojo violeta 400
Rojo, mar 28, 33, 34
rollo de película 481
rollos de la Torá 738
rombo 705
rompehielos 606
rompiente 49
ropa de bebé 368, 717
ropa de cama 280
ropa de deporte de mujer 716
ropa de deportes de hombre 717
ropa de deportes para niños 717
ropa de hombre 348
ropa de mujer 355
ropa de niños 369
ropa de noche de mujer 716
ropa de protección 318
ropa deportiva 370
ropa informal de hombre 717
ropa informal de mujer 716
ropa interior 351, 366, 872
ropa interior de hombre 716
ropa para ejercicio 371
ropa para el hogar 716
ropa para niñas de 2 a 6 años 717
ropa para niñas de 7 a 17 años 717
ropa para niños de 2 a 6 años 717
ropa para niños de 7 a 17 años 717
ropero 279
roquefort 211
rorcual 137
rosa 80
rosa de los vientos 37, 612, 907
rosca 268, 302, 311, 700
roseta 248, 328, 405, 440
rosetón 411
rosquilla 204
Ross, banquisa 29
rotación de la turbina 662
rotodomo 629
rotonda 39, 713
rotor 249, 565, 631, 659, 676
rotor de cola 631
rotor de dientes 688
rótula 122, 126, 131, 138, 152
rótula de enganche 587
rotulador 397, 533

rotuladores, pintura 396
rough 867
router 524
routers 523
Ruanda 745
rubí 375, 696
rubí pulsado, láser 692
rubí, varilla 692
rubidio 682
rubio 219
rueda 320, 323, 423, 454, 560, 570, 633, 753, 758, 783, 851, 870, 874, 894, 895
rueda central 696, 697
rueda central de enfoque 692
rueda cilíndrica de dientes rectos 686
rueda compresora 643
rueda de alabes 659
rueda de aspas 599
rueda de cadena 876
rueda de calibrado 333
rueda de corona 697
rueda de corrimiento 506
rueda de desplazamiento 516
rueda de elevación 756
rueda de empuje 783
rueda de escape 696, 697
rueda de la dirección 783
rueda de los segundos 696
rueda de mando 527
rueda de modulación 450
rueda de radios 857
rueda de repuesto 567
rueda de transmisión 876
rueda de trinquete 696, 697
rueda de volante 464
rueda delantera 639, 640
rueda dentada 686
rueda frontal 333
rueda giratoria 281, 919
rueda guía 636
rueda humedecedora 531
rueda lenticular 871
rueda libre 566
rueda media 696
rueda metálica de seguridad 595
rueda motriz 636, 640, 697, 758
rueda para ajustar el tono 450
rueda para graduar el respaldo 553
rueda posterior lenticular 871
rueda trasera 333
ruedas de tracción 639
ruedecilla 289, 389, 422, 448
ruedecilla de la piedra 391
Ruffini, corpúsculo 172
rugby 804
rugby, botas de tacos 805
ruibarbo 185
ruiseñor 118
ruleta americana 919
ruleta de enfoque lejos/cerca 496
ruleta de selección de efectos especiales 496
ruleta francesa 919
rulo 380
rulo para el cabello 380
Rumania 744
rumano 469
rupia 728
ruqueta 187
ruso 469
rusula verde 183
ruta de servicio 618
ruta pintoresca 39
rutenio 683
rutherfodio 683
Ryukyu, fosa 50

S

sábalo 220
sabana 61, 66
sábana 280
sábana ajustable 280
sable 741, 751, 834, 836, 849, 897
sacabotas 345
sacacorchos 206, 230, 905
sacacorchos con brazos 230
sacapuntas 534
sacatrapos 752
saco de arena 842
saco de Douglas 170
saco de marinero 388
saco de piel 432
saco de pilotaje 897
saco del aguijón 104
saco portabebé 368
saco rectangular 904
saco semirrectangular 904
sacos de dormir, ejemplos 904
sacrificio, piedra 412
sacristía 737
sacro 138, 141, 152, 153, 157
safety débil 806
safety fuerte 806

sagari 847
Sagitario 10
Sahara, desierto 34
sahariana 359
Saint Kitts and Nevis 743
sal 847
sal de mesa 201
sal gorda 201
sal marina 201
sala 250, 431
sala común 727
sala de alumnos 735
sala de anestesia 780
sala de audiencias 728, 738
sala de bombeo 606
sala de ceremonias 738
sala de cine 608
sala de clasificación 779
sala de conferencias 718, 730
sala de congresos 718
sala de consulta 733
sala de control 488, 657, 669, 768
sala de control de cámara 490
sala de control de la producción 489
sala de control de luces 490
sala de control de máquinas de propulsión 763
sala de control de operaciones 763
sala de control de producción 491
sala de control de sonido 489
sala de control, estudio 488
sala de coordinación 769
sala de correos 509
sala de curas 781
sala de discusión 718
sala de enyesado 779
sala de equipajes 582
sala de espera 509, 768, 779, 781
sala de espera de embarque 621
sala de espera de visitantes 726
sala de espera del centro de extracción de sangre 781
sala de espera para la familia 778
sala de espera principal 781
sala de estar 250
sala de esterilización 780, 781
sala de examen de audiometría 781
sala de exposición 719
sala de extracciones 781
sala de instalaciones auxiliares 490
sala de interrogatorios 768
sala de lectura 732
sala de máquinas 606, 608, 657, 658, 763
sala de microfilmes 732
sala de navegación 604
sala de observación psiquiátrica 778
sala de oración 738
sala de ordenadores 763
sala de preparación quirúrgica 780
sala de producción de electricidad 763
sala de producción y control 490
sala de profesores 735
sala de proyección 10, 395, 427
sala de reanimación 778
sala de reconocimiento 768
sala de recuperación posoperatoria 780
sala de redacción de informes 768
sala de regulación de luces 490
sala de reposo de enfermeras 781
sala de reprografía 509
sala de reuniones 394, 509, 724, 730, 735, 764
sala de torpedos 763
sala de visión 733
sala del jurado 728
sala del montacargas 649
sala del personal 731, 768, 779
sala del reactor nuclear 763
sala periódicos 733
sala polivalente 727
sala VIP 718
salamandra 111
salami alemán 216
salami de Génova 216
salas de entrevistas 728
salas de exposición permanente 395
salas de exposición temporal 395
salas de reuniones 718
salchicha chipolata 216
salchicha de Frankfurt 216
salchicha de Toulouse 216
salchicha kielbasa 216
salchicha merguez 216
salchow 881
salero 226
salida 539, 887, 915
salida : luge doble femenino 885
salida : luge simple masculino 885
salida con viento contrario 833
salida de agua caliente 259, 267
salida de agua fría 270
salida de aire caliente 256, 258, 564
salida de humo 256
salida de la contracorriente 669
salida de la pista 621

ASTRONOMÍA > 2-25;   TIERRA > 26-71;   REINO VEGETAL >72-89;   REINO ANIMAL > 90-143;   SER HUMANO > 144-177;   PRODUCTOS ALIMENTARIOS Y DE COCINA > 178-241;   CASA > 242-295;
BRICOLAJE Y JARDINERÍA > 296-333;   VESTIDO > 334-371;   ACCESORIOS Y ARTÍCULOS PERSONALES > 372-391;   ARTE Y ARQUITECTURA > 392-465;   COMUNICACIONES Y AUTOMATIZACIÓN DE
OFICINA > 466-535;   TRANSPORTE Y VEHÍCULOS > 536-643;   ENERGÍA > 644-677;   CIENCIA > 678-705;   SOCIEDAD > 706-785;   DEPORTES Y JUEGOS > 786-920

salida de la pista de alta velocidad 618
salida de vapor 670, 671
salida del agua de refrigeración del condensador 669
salida del refrigerante 672
salida: bobsleigh 885
salida: skeleton 885
salmer 413
salmón del Atlántico 221
salmón del Pacífico 221
salmonete 219
salmuera, especias 199
salón 250, 724
salón bar 724
salón de baile 609
salón de pasajeros 608
salpicadero 556, 577
salpicadero, equipamiento 771
salsa de ciruelas 201
salsa de soja 200
salsa de tamarindo 200
salsa de tomate 200
salsa hoisin 200
salsa Tabasco 200
salsa Worcertershire 200
salsa, ciruelas 201
salsa, soja 200
salsa, Tabasco 200
salsa, tamarindo 200
salsa, tomate 200
salsa, Worcertershire 200
salsera 226
salsifí 189
saltador 891
saltador de pértiga 792
saltamontes verde 101
salto de altura 791, 792
salto de espalda 828
salto de esquí 891
salto de longitud 790, 793
salto de obstáculos 852
salto de pértiga 790, 792
salto de salida 832
salto en equilibrio 828
salto frontal 828
salto frontal con tirabuzón 829
salto interior 828
salto inverso 828
salto inverso con tirabuzón 829
salto sincronizado 829
saltos 792, 828
saltos de esquí 891
saltos múltiples 875
saltos, ejemplos 829
saltos, pista 890
salud 775
salvavidas 609, 611
salvelino 221
salvia 202
samario 684
sambal oelek 201
Samoa 747
samoano 469
San Bernardo 131
San Lorenzo, río 30
San Pedro 736
San Vicente y las Granadinas 743
sandalia 343, 344, 748
sandía 195
sangre desoxigenada 162
sangre oxigenada 162
sangre, composición 162
sanguina 423
Santa Lucía 743
Santo Tomé y Príncipe 745
santuario. lámpara 737
sapo común 111
saque 812
sardina 219
sarga 463
sargento 312
sarmiento 86
sartén 235, 905
sartén doble 235
sartén honda 235
sartén para crepes 235
sartén pequeña 235
sartorio 150
sash 846
satélite 24, 486
satélite artificial 53
satélite de órbita polar 60
satélite de telecomunicaciones 525
satélite geoestacionario 60
satélite meteorológico 54, 60
satélite Radarsat 40
satélite, comunicación 486
satélite, telecomunicaciones 487
satélite, teledetección 41
satélites 4
satélites de telecomunicaciones 486
satélites, órbita 60
satén 463
Saturno 4, 5
Saturno V 24
sauce llorón 88
saxofón 446
schnauzer 130
Schwann, célula 168
Schwenkel, bandera 739
scull 838
seaborgio 683
secado 347
secador de manguera 764
secador de mano 382
secadora de ensalada 231
secadora de pruebas 485
secadora de ropa 293
secar en secadora a baja temperatura 347
secar en secadora a temperatura media 347
secar extendido sobre una toalla después de escurrir 347
secar sin escurrir 347
sección 471
sección articulada 569
sección cartográfica 732
sección de avancarga, corte transversal 753
sección de carga del combustible 666
sección de flotación 615
sección de identificación 768
sección de monografías 732
sección del cañón 257
sección frontal 773
sección infantil 732
sección inferior 24
sección rígida de tracción delantera 569
sección sagital 169, 170
sección superior 24
sección transversal de la góndola 677
sección transversal de un aerógrafo 398
sección transversal de un cañón de avancarga 753
sección transversal de un lanzador espacial (Ariane V) 24
sección transversal de un lanzador espacial (Saturno V) 25
sección transversal de un observatorio astronómico 17
sección transversal de un telecopio reflector 15
sección transversal de un telescopio refractor 14
sección transversal de una cámara reflex 477
sección transversal de una carretera 538
sección transversal de una central eléctrica 664
sección transversal de una central hidroeléctrica 658
sección transversal de una presa de bóveda 661
sección transversal de una presa de contrafuerte 660
sección transversal de una presa de gravedad 661
sección transversal de una presa de tierra 660
sección vertical 894
seco 919
secretaría 731, 735
secretaría de dirección 509
secretaría de dirección 509
secretario 814
secretario/a de producción 429
secretarios 827
sector 704
secuencia en el manejo de combustible 666
secuencia principal, estrella 8
secuenciador 450
sedal 909
segadora 642
segmento 566
segmento abdominal 97
segmento de marcas 918
segmento intermedio 169
segmento muscular 109
segmento terminal 169
seguimiento de la bola 864
segunda 434, 849
segunda aleta dorsal 108
segunda base 794
segunda etapa 25
segunda línea 804
segunda vía de clasificación 589
segunda vuelta 789
segundero 696
segundo 702, 704
segundo árbitro 812, 813
segundo aumento de tensión 677
segundo ayudante de cámara 428
segundo borde al largo 833
segundo espacio 811
segundo jugador 877
segundo molar 159
segundo nivel de operaciones 529
segundo pistón móvil 447
segundo premolar 159
segundo refuerzo 753
segundos violines 437
seguridad 764
seguridad, símbolos 774
seguro 238, 248, 289, 307, 310, 479, 755
seguro de inclinación del disco 304
seguro de la barra de tracción 756
seguro de la base 312
seguro de la guía 305
seguro de la mesa 307
seguro del brazo 456
seguro del cargador 754
seguro del cordón 285
seguro del fuelle 432
seguro del interruptor 306
seis doble 914
selección auto/manual 316
selección de cartón 71
selección de metal 71
selección de nivel 2 514
selección de papel 71
selección de vidrio 71
selección manual 71
selección óptica 71
selector 238, 261, 316
selector automático/manual 465
selector cuadro-direccional 477
selector de banda 498
selector de canales 495, 505
selector de corte 383
selector de emisoras memorizadas 498
selector de enfoque 496
selector de entrada 497
selector de focalización 476
selector de la recepción 441
selector de la voz 451
selector de movimiento orbital 305
selector de nivel de agua 292
selector de posición de aguja 452
selector de programa 450, 476
selector de puntada 452
selector de sintonización 503
selector de temperatura 238, 292, 293
selector de tipo de cinta 499
selector de tostado 238
selector de velocidad 236, 306, 500
selector de velocidades 236, 237
selector de volumen 503
selector del control de vídeo 491
selector del control de volumen 491
selector del modo audio 497
selector del premio 920
selector del ritmo 451
selector mono/estéreo 498
selectores de funciones 506
selectores de modalidad 504
selenio 682
sellado, tapa 689
sello de correos 474
sello de goma 531
selva 66
semáforo 545, 547, 583, 712
semáforo de peatones 712
semáforo de señalización 859
sembradora a chorrillo 643
sembradora de mano 324
semi-negrita 472
semicírculo 704
semicírculo de la zona de tiro libre 810
semicírculo del área 802
semicorchea 435
semieje 553
semifinal 789
semifusa 435
semilla 77, 81, 82, 83, 84
semilla, tegumento 81
semillas de adormidera 199
semillas de soja 191
semilunar 154, 156
semimembranoso 151
semimetales 682
semirremolque bajo portamáquinas 572
semirremolque con lona 572
semirremolque frigorífico 572
semirremolque furgón 572
semirremolque jaula bajo para transporte ganadero 572
semirremolque para el transporte de troncos 572
semirremolque porta container 572
semirremolque tipo caja 570, 571
semirremolque tipo plataforma 571
semirremolque, caja, tipo 571
semisótano 250
semitendinoso 151
semola 204
sémola 204
señal aislada de peligro 617
señal cardinal del este 617
señal cardinal del oeste 617
señal cardinal del sur 617
señal de aguas seguras 617
señal de dirección 593
señal de distancia fija 621
señal de eje de pista 620
señal de identificación de pista 620
señal de posición de la aguja 590
señal de unión 547
señal de zona de contacto de pista 621
señal de zona de espera 620
señal del sonido 436
señal diurna 615
señal especial 617
señal exterior 592
señal lateral 617
señal luminosa 436
señales de circulación 544
señales de límite de la pista 621
señales de los puntos cardinales 616
señales diurnas (región B) 617
señales laterales de pista 620
señales marítimas 614
señales nocturnas, ritmo 617
Senegal 745
Senegal, río 34
seno 49, 148, 171, 336, 690
seno del pecíolo 86
seno esfenoidal 175
seno frontal 175
seno lateral inferior 86
seno lateral superior 86
sensibilidad de la película 479
sensor 58
sensor activo 41
sensor de colisión primario 556
sensor de luz 477
sensor de movimiento 416
sensor de radiaciones terrestres 60
sensor de seguridad 556
sensor de temperatura 18, 561
sensor de velocidad de las ruedas 559
sensor del mando a distancia 494, 501
sensor estelar 18
sensor infrarrojos 518
sensor óptico 516
sensor pasivo 41
sensor solar 40, 60
sensor terrestre 40, 60
sépalo 80, 82, 83
separacables 913
separación cartón 71
separación entre bolos 865
separación magnética 71
separación papel 71
separación selectiva de residuos 71
separador 386, 606, 643, 646, 667, 668, 689, 783
separador de agua 648
separador de gas y líquido 562
separador de petróleo y gas 652
separador de placas 562
separador de reinas 100
separador electrolítico 689
sepia 217
séptima 434, 849
septum 84
septum pellucidum 167
ser humano 146
serac 46
serbocroata 469
serie, número 729
serpentín del condensador 261
serpentín del evaporador 261
Serpiente 11, 13
serpiente 112
serpiente coral 114
serpiente de cascabel 114
serpiente de jarretera 114
serpiente venenosa, anatomía 112
serpiente venenosa, esqueleto 112
serpiente venenosa, morfología, cabeza 112
serpollo 86
serrucho 303
serrucho de punta 303
servicio de enlace ferroviario 620
servicio de mesa 226
servicio de seguridad 719
servicio de taxis 725
servicio para fondue 234
servicio, estación 548
servicios de crédito 730
servicios de seguros 730
servicios financieros 730
servicios sociales 781
servicios técnicos 732
servidor 522, 523, 524, 525
servidor de acceso 525
servidor de archivos 523
servilletas 722
servofreno 552, 559
sésamo, aceite 209
sesamoideo mayor 126
sesamoideo menor 126
sesos 212
set 429
seta enoki 183
seto 245, 322
setos, cizallas 330
sexta 434, 849
Sextante 11
sextante 612
sexteto 438
Seychelles 746
Shiísmo 736
shiitake 183
shinai 847
si(B) 434
siamés 133
sien 146
sierra circular de mano 304
sierra circular de mesa 305
sierra de cadena 331
sierra de calar 305
sierra de campo 907
sierra de ensamblar 424
sierra de ingletes 303
sierra de marquetería 303
sierra de podar 330
sierra ingletadora eléctrica 304
Sierra Leona 745
sierra para metales 303, 314
sifón 106, 262, 265, 269, 270
sifón de desagüe 271
signos de puntuación 473
signos diacríticos 473
silbato 240, 586
silenciador 553, 575, 577, 649
silencio de blanca 435
silencio de corchea 435
silencio de fusa 435
silencio de negra 435
silencio de redonda 435
silencio de semicorchea 435
silencio de semifusa 435
silencios, valores 435
silicio 682
silicua 84
silla 723, 826, 853, 856, 858, 897
silla alzadora 281
silla cabriolé 276
silla cojín 277
silla de brazos 276
silla de montar 855
silla de ruedas 394, 584, 783
silla de secretaria 511
silla de seguridad para niños 558
silla del director 429
silla escalera 277
silla plegable 277
silla plegable de lona 276
silla poltrona 276
silla porta-niño 580
silla sin brazos 277, 734
silla Wassily 276
sillas apilables 277
sillas de los actores 428
sillas de los jugadores 813
sillas, ejemplos 277
sillín 577, 578, 855, 857
sillín del conductor 577
sillín del pasajero 577
sillín doble 575
sillón 734
sillón de reposo 780
sillón giratorio 511
silo 182
silo de carga 648
silos 596
Silúrico 92
símbolo 682, 920
símbolos 914
símbolos científicos 702
símbolos de seguridad 774
símbolos de uso común 725
símbolos del cuidado de los tejidos 347
símbolos meteorológicos internacionales 56
símbolos químicos 684
sinagoga 738
sinapsis 168
sínfisis púbica 169, 170
Singapur 747
sinople 741
sinsacro 116
síntesis de los colores 690
síntesis de los colores aditivos 690
síntesis de los colores sustractivos 690
sintetizador 450
sintonizador 498, 504
sirena 766
Siria 746
sisa 351
sismógrafo 43
sismógrafo horizontal 43
sismógrafo vertical 43
sismógrafos 43
sismograma 43
sistema antibloqueo de frenos 559
sistema de acondicionamiento 775
sistema de agua caliente a presión 259
sistema de aire acondicionado 68
sistema de aire caliente a presión 258
sistema de alimentación de gasolina 553
sistema de alimentación ininterrumpida 523
sistema de alimentación ininterrumpida (SAI/UPS) 520
sistema de audio 556
sistema de bomba de calor 260
sistema de botones 450
sistema de boyas marítimas 616

sistema de carreteras 538
sistema de células solares 673
sistema de control del puente de luces 771
sistema de coordenadas astronómicas 13
sistema de coordenadas terrestres 35
sistema de cronometraje electrónico 883
sistema de dirección 553
sistema de disparo rápido 482
sistema de doble polea 686
sistema de elevación 635
sistema de escape 553
sistema de esclusas de vaciado y desagüe 597
sistema de esclusas de vaciado y llenado 597
sistema de frenado 553
sistema de lentes 692
sistema de lubricación 586
sistema de navegación por satélite 613
sistema de rebobinado de la película 476
sistema de refrigeración 553
sistema de registro de la información 694
sistema de restricción del airbag 556
sistema de retícula 36
sistema de soporte vital 20
sistema de suspensión 553
sistema de tensión 457
sistema de transmisión 553
sistema de tubería de producción /expedición 652
sistema eléctrico 553
sistema fino de guía 17
sistema hidráulico 632
sistema internacional de unidades de medida 702
sistema magnético de amortiguación 698
sistema manipulador remoto 21, 22
sistema nervioso 166
sistema nervioso central 167
sistema nervioso periférico 166
sistema rotativo 651
sistema solar 4
sistemas de engranajes 686
sistemas de sonido portátiles 503
sistemas del automóvil 553
sistro 449
skateboard 894
skeleton 885
skiff 839
skimmer 246
slip 351
smash 821
Smidolon 93
smog/niebla tóxica 69
snooker 863
snowboard 887
snowboarder 887
soba, fideos 207
sobre almohadillado 531
sobrecincha 853, 855, 857
sobrefusión 680
sobreimpresión del original 512
sobrejuanete de mesana de estay 603
sobrejuanete de proa 603
sobrejuanete mayor 603
sobrenudo 908
sobretemperatura, interruptor 266
sobreveste 337
sobrina 785
sobrino 785
sociedad 708
sodio 682
sofá 276
sofá cama 280
sofá de dos plazas 276, 724
sofá tipo imperio 276
softball 797
soga 901
Sol 4, 6, 7, 54
sol(G) 434
Sol, estructura 6
solapa 348, 362, 391, 535, 906
solapa autoadhesiva 531
solapa con ojal 352
solapa puntiaguda 348
soldador 318
soldadura, herramientas 318
sóleo 150
solera 253
solera doble 252
solera inferior 252
solera interior 253
solideo 340
solidificación 680
sólido 680, 681
sólido amorfo 680
solitario 376
solsticio de invierno 54
solsticio de verano 54
solución multipropósito 384
Somalia 745
sombra 696
sombra de ojos 378
sombrero 76
sombrero de campana 341

sombrero de fieltro 340, 341
sombrero de hongo 340
sombrero sin alas 341
sombreros 340
sombreros de hombre 340
sombreros de mujer 341
sombreros unisex 341
somen, fideos 207
somier 280
somieres 716
sonar 41, 613
sonar del casco 762
sonda 613
sonda atmosférica 60
sonda destapacaños 314
sonda espacial 18, 53
sonda térmica 238
sondas espaciales, ejemplos 19
sondeo 59
sonido, producción 445
sonido, sistemas portátiles 503
sopa 722
sopera 226
soplador 445
soplete 314, 319
soplete de corte 319
soplete de soldadura autógena 319
soporte 15, 59, 234, 274, 284, 285, 304, 329, 381, 389, 448, 464, 483, 485, 557, 577, 609, 632, 667, 685, 825, 826, 907
soporte colgante 783
soporte de acoplamiento 527
soporte de flecha 859
soporte de la barrera 591
soporte de la cadena 578
soporte de la conexión 663
soporte de la esfera 58
soporte de la mano 433
soporte de la plaqueta 385
soporte de la plataforma 676
soporte de la red 815
soporte de manguera 764
soporte de pared 284
soporte de techo 284
soporte del brazo 276, 500
soporte del falso secreto 445
soporte del juego de marcos 460
soporte del papel 528
soporte del pie 791, 851
soporte del plano fijo 638
soporte del rótulo 533
soporte del tablero 811
soporte informático 509
soporte para bombona de oxígeno 775
soporte para el antebrazo 782
soporte para el brazo 554
soporte para el cuello 874
soporte para el equipo 490
soporte para el sobaco 782
soporte plegable 436
soporte trípode de cola 623
soportes 400
soportes para los pies 838
sordina 447
sorgo 85
sorgo : panícula 85
soro 76
sortija de sello 376
sosegado 56
sostén de la traba 857
sostenido 435
soufflé, molde 232
squash 819
Sri Lanka 747
stand de bolos 865
stand de exposición 719
Stardust 19
stick 800, 801
stilton 211
stola 336
stop 512, 544
stylus 517, 527
Suazilandia 746
subártico 61
subducción 43
subestación 664
subíndice 472
sublimación 680
submarino nuclear 763
substracción de la memoria 529
subsuelo 78
subterráneo 407
subtítulo 471
subtotal /sin adición 529
subtropical húmedo 61
subtropical mediterráneo 61
sucesos 471
sudadera 370
sudadera con capucha 370
sudadero 856
Sudáfrica 746
Sudán 745
Sudeste 37
Suecia 744

sueco 469
suegra 784
suegro 784
suegros 784
suela 309, 342, 371, 840, 863, 881
suela antiderrapante 369
suela rígida 889
suelo 70, 661
suelo de cabina 417
suelo de madera 899
suelo, absorción 68
suelo, capa superficial 78
suelo, fertilización 69
suelo, movimiento horizontal 43
suelo, movimiento vertical 43
suelo, revestimientos 254
suero de la leche 210
sueste 341
Suiza 744
sujeción 284
sujeción delantera 840
sujeción trasera 840
sujetador 367, 448, 693
sujetador de aros 367
sujetador de escote bajo 367
sujetador del hilo 457
sujetador del pabellón 446
sujetador sin tirantes 367
sujetalibros 535
sujetapapel 528
sulky 857
suma 703
sumario 471
sumidero 263, 650
sumie 397
sumiller 720
suministro de agua 662, 675
sumo 847
sumotori 847
Sunnismo 736
supercross 875
superestructura 615
superficie acanalada 868
superficie de absorción 675
superficie de cocción 239
superficie de deslizamiento 888
superficie de fijación 535
superficie de juego 815
superficie de la piel 172
superficie de protección 843
superficie de resina 501
superficie de rodadura 561
superficie de rodamiento 590
superficie del agua 828
superficie del terreno 647
superficie dura (cemento) 822
superficie humedecida 420
superficie irregular 547
superficie lucha 843
superficie lunar 7
superficie plantar del casco 127
superficie reflectante 674
superficie sintética 822
superficies 704
superficies de juego 822
supergigante 8
superíndice 472
supermercado 180, 711, 715
supernova 8
supinador largo 150, 151
suplemento a color 471
suplemento literario 471
suprimir 515
Sur 37, 917
sur 616
Sur Sudeste 37
Sur Suroeste 37
surco 176, 868
surco concéntrico 500
surco de salida 500
surco en espiral 500
surco medio 176
surco nasolabial 175
surco terminal 176
surf 840
surfista 840
Surinam 742
Suroeste 37
suroeste 616
surtidor 268, 270, 642
surtidor de agua 384
surtidor de gasolina 548
surtidor principal 259
suspensión 585, 594
suspensión trasera 870
suspensión, brazo 553
sustancia blanca 167, 168
sustancia despolarizante 689
sustancia gris 167, 168
sustrato impermeable 646
sutura 84, 105
sutura coronal 158
sutura escamosa 158
sutura lambdoidea 158
swahili 468

T

T central 858
tabaco 390
tábano 101
tabaquera 390
tabernáculo 737
tabique cortafuego 655
tabique de contención longitudinal 606
tabique interventricular 162
tabique móvil 509, 510, 719
tabique nasal 175
tabique, cartílago nasal 175
tabla 300, 374, 400
tabla abierta 357
tabla alpina 887
tabla armónica 439, 440
tabla biselada 425
tabla con argollas 533
tabla con pinza 533
tabla de batida 793
tabla de batida de salto de longitud 793
tabla de batida de triple salto 793
tabla de cortar 229
tabla de freestyle 887
tabla de los resultados 828
tabla de parada 864
tabla de surf 836, 840
tabla delantera 357
tabla harmónica 442, 445
tabla periódica de los elementos 682
tablas 357
tablero 278, 312, 540, 811, 893, 916, 917
tablero alistonado 300
tablero de aglomerado 300
tablero de aglomerado plastificado 300
tablero de ajedrez 916
tablero de anuncios 535
tablero de base 485
tablero de conmutadores 626
tablero de control 261, 694
tablero de controles 512
tablero de corte, palanca de levantamiento 333
tablero de damas 916
tablero de dibujo 399
tablero de distribución 273
tablero de fibra de madera 300
tablero de fibra de madera perforada 300
tablero de información 582
tablero de instrumentos 574, 576
tablero de juego 915
tablero de llegadas y salidas 621
tablero de los handicaps 858
tablero de luces 490
tablero de mandos 10, 586
tablero de operaciones 766
tablero de partículas waferboard 300
tablero de rodillos y brazos 445
tablero de rótulo 587
tablero de yeso 299
tablero indicador 856
tablero laminado 300
tablero rígido aislante 299
tableros 300
tableta de resonancia 444
tableta digitalizada 517
tablillas 777
tablinum 406
tablón de anuncios 734
tabulación a la derecha 514
tabulación a la izquierda 514
tabulador 528
tabulador decimal 528
taburete 224, 277, 401, 722
taburete de bar 720
taburete escalera 321
tachuela 301
tachuelas para papel 534
tacita de café 226
tackle defensivo derecho 806
tackle defensivo izquierdo 806
tacle derecho 807
tacle izquierdo 807
taco 753, 791, 798, 912
taco de billar 863
taco de salida, atleta 791
tacómetro 557, 576
tacón 881
tacos 791
tacos de rosca 802
tacto 172
tafetán 463
tagalo 469
tahitiano 469
Tailandia 747
tailback 807
Tajikistán 746
tajín 200
tajina 234
taladro 323
taladro de mano 307
taladro de motor 323
taladro eléctrico 306
taladro neumático 873

taladro percutor 648
taladro percutor inalámbrico 306
taladro vertical 307
talio 682
talla 401
talla brillante de un diamante 374
talla en baguette 375
talla en briolette 375
talla en cabujón 375
talla en madera 401
talla en pera 375
talla en rosa holandesa 375
talla en tabla 375
talla escalonada 375
talla francesa 375
talla octógono 375
talla oval 375
tallarines de espinacas 206
tallas de piedras preciosas 375
talle corto 367
taller 726
Taller de Escultor 10
taller de mantenimiento 648
taller de máquinas diésel 583
taller de reparación de vagones 589
taller mecánico 548
tallo 75, 77, 78, 172, 185
tallo del bulbo 78
tallo principal 86
Talmud 736
talo 74, 75
talón 127, 147, 149, 303, 306, 309, 342, 351, 370, 439, 440, 641, 783, 797, 816, 840, 868, 880, 909, 910
talón de aguja 453
talón de apoyo 236, 288
talón de la aguja 456
talón de la hoja 229
talonario de cheques 386, 387
taloneador 804
talonera 889
talud 538, 647
talud continental 49
talud de aguas abajo 660
talud de aguas contenidas 660
tam-tam 448
tamaño 472
tamarillo 196
tamarino 139
tambor 230, 285, 292, 293, 404, 416, 559, 612, 700, 754, 910, 920
tambor distanciador 528
tambor giratorio 43
tambor hablante 433
tambor principal 460
tamboril 448
tamiz 231, 232
tamiz vibratorio para lodos 651
tampón 422
tándem 581
Tanganyika, lago 34
tanque 23, 263, 266, 485, 607, 767, 903
tanque auxiliar 571
tanque de acetileno 319
tanque de agua 589
tanque de agua de rociado 665, 669
tanque de aire 320
tanque de aire comprimido 841
tanque de almacenamiento 656, 675
tanque de expansión 259, 675
tanque de gas propano 567
tanque de hidrogeno líquido 24
tanque de hidrógeno líquido 25
tanque de keroseno 25
tanque de oxígeno 319
tanque de oxígeno líquido 25
tanque de oxígeno líquido 24
tanque de regulación de presión 654
tanque de revelado 484
tanque de seguridad 670
tanque de techo fijo 655
tanque de techo pontón 655
tanque del combustible 331, 570
tanque del nitrógeno 694
tanque del reactor 671
tanque moderador 670
tanque para repostar 873
tanques 655
tántalo 683
tanteo 789
Tanzania 745
tapa 234, 236, 237, 238, 239, 240, 241, 248, 249, 261, 273, 274, 275, 289, 290, 291, 292, 295, 313, 342, 389, 391, 398, 444, 445, 465, 470, 477, 484, 512, 528, 561, 689, 767, 907
tapa cierre 689
tapa de la batería 562
tapa de la cisterna 265
tapa de la culata 552
tapa de sellado 689
tapa del filtro 773
tapa del inodoro 265
tapa del objetivo 478
tapa del tanque 570

ASTRONOMÍA > 2-25; TIERRA > 26-71; REINO VEGETAL >72-89; REINO ANIMAL > 90-143; SER HUMANO > 144-177; PRODUCTOS ALIMENTARIOS Y DE COCINA > 178-241; CASA > 242-295; BRICOLAJE Y JARDINERÍA > 296-333; VESTIDO > 334-371; ACCESORIOS Y ARTÍCULOS PERSONALES > 372-391; ARTE Y ARQUITECTURA > 392-465; COMUNICACIONES Y AUTOMATIZACIÓN DE OFICINA > 466-535; TRANSPORTE Y VEHÍCULOS > 536-643; ENERGÍA > 644-677; CIENCIA > 678-705; SOCIEDAD > 706-785; DEPORTES Y JUEGOS > 786-920

tapa deslizante 506
tapa flotante 655
tapa frontal 519
tapa guardapolvo 500
tapa inferior 689
tapa superior 445, 689
tapa terminal 667
tapacubos 551
tapete 862
tapete antideslizante 893
tapón 265, 269, 379, 813, 906
tapón de registro 262
tapón de rosca 223
tapón de vaciado 566
tapón del depósito de gasolina 551
tapón del depósito de la gasolina 576
tapón del sifón 270
tapón hembra 269
tapón hermético 903
tapón macho 269
tapones de oídos, 872
tapones para los oídos 772
taquigrafía, cuaderno 531
taquilla 394, 427, 719
taquilla automática 427
taquilla de venta de billetes 592
taquillas de consigna automática 582
taquillas de los alumnos 735
tare 847
tarjeta de circuito impreso 689
tarjeta de crédito 729
tarjeta de débito 731
tarjeta de expansión PCI 513
tarjeta de interfaz de red 522
tarjeta de interfaz de red sin hilos 522
tarjeta de memoria 477
tarjeta de memoria compact flash 481
tarjeta de ruta 587
tarjeta madre 513
tarjeta, número 729
tarjetero 386
tarlatana 422
taro 184
tarrito para pincel 398
tarso 96, 98, 111, 115, 122, 126, 131, 138, 141, 142, 155, 156
tarso metatarso 116
Tasmania 29
Tasmania, mar 29
tatami 844, 846
Tauro 12
taza 226, 265, 905, 906
tazas medidoras 231
té 208
té negro 208
té oolong 208
té verde 208
té, bolsita 208
teatro 430, 710, 711
teatro griego 402
techo 100, 257, 551, 567, 635, 818, 819
techo a dos aguas 251
techo acústico 431
techo corredizo 551
techo de cabina 417
techo de protección 632
techo de vidiro 582
techo de vidrio 250, 713
techo fijo, tanque 655
techo ponton, tanque 655
techo, armadura del 253
tecla 432, 442, 443, 445
tecla alternativa 514
tecla bloqueo numérico 515
tecla correctora 456
tecla de adición 529
tecla de anular 519
tecla de arrastre del papel 529
tecla de bloqueo 505
tecla de bloqueo de mayúsculas 514
tecla de cambio de signo 529
tecla de centrado 528
tecla de confirmación 731
tecla de desplazamiento 505
tecla de dirección 261
tecla de división 529
tecla de doble cero 529
tecla de enter 515
tecla de fijación de pantalla 496
tecla de final de búsqueda 496
tecla de final de llamada 506
tecla de igualdad 529
tecla de impresión pantalla 515
tecla de iniciación 508
tecla de inicio/stop de grabación 496
tecla de llamada 505, 506
tecla de luminosidad 505
tecla de más/igual 529
tecla de mayúsculas 514, 528
tecla de menú 505
tecla de multiplicación 529
tecla de número 529
tecla de pedal 444
tecla de porcentaje 529
tecla de raíz cuadrada 529
tecla de regreso del carro 528
tecla de reiniciación 508
tecla de repetición 501
tecla de retroceso 515
tecla de sangrado 528
tecla de seguro para las mayúsculas 528
tecla de selección 506
tecla de selección de banda 497
tecla de selección de entrada 497
tecla de selección de modalidad FM 497
tecla de selección del grabador 497
tecla de selección sintonía 497
tecla de servicio 514
tecla de sustracción 529
tecla de utilización múltiple 529
tecla de visualización del título 496
tecla decimal 529
tecla del menú 505
tecla email 514
tecla escape 514
tecla inicio 514
tecla memoria 497
tecla para limpiar la pantalla 529
tecla para limpiar la pantalla y de acceso 529
tecla pausa 515
tecla tabulación 514
teclado 442, 450, 506, 507, 514, 526, 865
teclado alfabético 530
teclado alfanumérico 506, 507, 514, 548, 730, 731
teclado de bajos 432
teclado de funciones 699
teclado del número de identificación personal(PIN) 731
teclado del órgano de expresión 444
teclado del órgano mayor 444
teclado del órgano positivo 444
teclado numérico 507, 508, 515, 530, 699
teclado triple 432
teclado, instrumentos 442
teclados manuales 444
teclas 451
teclas conmutadoras de puntos 456
teclas de control 508
teclas de cursor 515
teclas de desplazamiento del cursor 529
teclas de función 507, 508
teclas de funciones 514
teclas de funciones programables 731
teclas de Internet 514
teclas de operación 507, 730, 731
teclas de selección 456
teclas de selección de la sintonía 497
teclas de selección de los altavoces 497
tecnecio 683
técnica de salto 891
técnicas 812
técnico de control de cámaras 490
técnico de control de la cámara 489
técnico de luces 490
técnico de sonido 489, 490
tee 867, 877
tee de salida 866
tegumento de la semilla 81
teja 299, 406, 412
teja de asfalto 299
tejado 245, 257, 412
tejido 460
tejido adiposo 171, 172
tejido conjuntivo 172
tejido de punto 457
tejido subcutáneo 172
tejidos 455
tejidos, diagramas 463
tejón 134
tela 455, 899
tela bordada 459
tela de araña 103
tela impermeable 391
telar de cuatro marcos 460
telar de tapicería 461
telares 430
telecomunicaciones vía satélite 487
telecomunicaciones, satélites 486
teleconvertidor 478
teledetección 40
teledetección por satélite 41
teleférico 886
teléfono 489, 491, 506, 724, 725
teléfono de teclado 507
teléfono inalámbrico 507
teléfono móvil 506
teléfono público 427, 507, 715, 720, 723, 779
teléfono, comunicación 506
teléfonos, ejemplos 507
telémetro 480
teleobjetivo 478
teleporte 487
Telescopio 10
telescopio 17, 701, 859
telescopio espacial Hubble 17, 53
telescopio reflector 15
telescopio reflector, sección transversal 15
telescopio refractor 14
telescopio refractor, sección transversal 14
telesilla 886
telesquí 886
televisión 489, 724
televisior 734
televisor 494
televisor de pantalla ancha 493
telón cortafuegos 430
telón de boca 430, 431
telón de fondo 430
telson 107
telurio 682
temperatura 261
temperatura ambiente 55
temperatura Celsius, unidad de medida 702
temperatura del punto de rocío 55
temperatura deseada 261
temperatura real 261
temperatura termodinámica, unidad de medida 702
temperatura, medición 695
temperatura, sensor 561
temperatura,medición 59
tempestad 56
templador 424
templazo 461
templo azteca 412
Templo de Huitzilopochtli 412
Templo de Tlaloc 412
templo griego 403
templo griego, plano 403
tenacillas 381
tenaza 409
tenazas 257
tendencia barométrica 55
tendón 133
tenedor 227, 905
tenedor de ensalada 228
tenedor de fondue 228
tenedor de mesa 228
tenedor de ostras 228
tenedor de pescado 228
tenedor de postre 228
tenedor de trinchar 229
tenedores, ejemplos 228
tenis 788, 820
tenis de mesa 815
tenista 822
tensiómetro 777
tensión, disminución 677
tensor 676, 824, 825, 826, 835, 842, 910
tensor de la fascia lata 150
tensor de las cuerdas 448
tensores pectorales 850
tentáculo 106
tentáculo ocular 104
tentáculo táctil 104
teodolito 59, 701
terbio 684
tercelete 410
tercer ala 804
tercer octante 7
tercer pistón móvil 447
tercera 434, 849
tercera base 794
tercera etapa 25
tercera línea 804
tercera línea izquierda 804
terceravuelta 789
tercero 877
Terciario 93
tercio diestro 740
tercio siniestro 740
terminación nerviosa 172
terminador 522
terminal 272, 274, 654, 663
terminal de carga 596
terminal de comunicaciones 507
terminal de contenedores 708
terminal de entrada 316
terminal de granos 596
terminal de mercancías 708
terminal de pago electrónico 181, 731
terminal de pasajeros 596, 619, 620
terminal de petróleo 596
terminal de tierra 274
terminal del control remoto 476
terminal satélite de pasajeros 619
terminales interactivos 395
términos familiares 82, 83
termita 101
termo 906
termo con llave de servicio 906
termómetro 655, 695, 841, 899
termómetro bimetálico 695
termómetro clínico 695
termómetro de azúcar 231
termómetro de horno 231
termómetro de máxima 59
termómetro de medida instantánea 231
termómetro de mercurio 777
termómetro de mínima 59
termómetro digital 777
termómetro para carne 231
termómetros clínicos 777
termopausa 53
termosfera 53
termostato 238, 260, 261, 267, 291
termostato de seguridad 293
termostato inferior 266
termostato programable 261
termostato regulable 239
termostato superior 266
ternera, carne troceada 214
ternera, cortes 214
ternero 128
terraja 314
Terranova, isla 30
terraplén 409, 538
terraplén de desenganche 589
terraplén de los helióstatos 674
terraza 244, 609
terremoto 43
terreno de juego 799
terreno de recubrimiento 647
terrina 234
terrina para mantequilla 223
terrina, mantequilla 223
testículo 169
testículos 107, 110
testigo 790
testigo luminoso 767
testuz 124
tetera 226
Tetis 5
texto 528
thai 468
tía materna 785
tía paterno 785
tibetano 468
tibia 96, 98, 122, 126, 131, 138, 140, 141, 142, 152, 155, 156
tibia tarso 116
tibia y peroné 111
tibial anterior 150
tiburón, morfología 108
tiburones 206
tiempo 789
tiempo, medición 696
tiempo, unidad de medida 702
tiempos realizados 831
tienda 406, 710
tienda de animales 714
tienda de artículos de decoración 715
tienda de bricolaje 714
tienda de campaña clásica 903
tienda de campaña tamaño familiar 902
tienda de deportes 715
tienda de discos 714
tienda de electrónica 714
tienda de regalos 714
tienda de ropa 714
tienda del museo 394
tienda interior 902, 903
tienda libre de impuestos 621
tienda para dos 902
tienda rectangular 902
tienda tipo domo 903
tienda tipo iglú 903
tienda tipo vagón 902
tienda unipersonal 903
tiendas de campaña, ejemplos 902
tiento 399
Tierra 0, 4, 5, 6, 7, 28
tierra apisonada 538
tierra batida 822
Tierra de la Reina Maud 29
Tierra de Marie Byrd 29
Tierra de Wilkes 29
Tierra del Fuego 31
tierra, equipo 622
Tierra, estructura 42
tierras raras 684
tifón 63
tigre 135
tijeras 777, 905
tijeras con doble filo para entresacar 382
tijeras con filo simple para entresacar 382
tijeras de cocina 233
tijeras de modista 454
tijeras de pedicura 377
tijeras de peluquero 382
tijeras de podar 330
tijeras de punta roma 377
tijeras de uñas 377
tijeras para aves 233
tijeras para cutículas 377
tijeras para rematar 454
tila 208
tilde 473
timbal 448
timbales 437
timbradora 530
timbre 390
timón 23, 600, 605, 606, 608, 625, 759, 760, 838, 839
timón de control 626
timón de dirección 763, 898
timón de inmersión 763
timón de mando, pedal 898
timón de profundidad 625, 763, 898
tímpano 110, 403, 404, 411, 421
tímpano, membrana 174
tinta 421, 470
tinta china 397
tinta china, dibujo 396
tinta de color cambiante 729
tinta litográfica 423
tinta, bolsa 106
tinte para el cabello 379
tintorería 715
tío materno 785
tío paterno 785
tipi 418
tipo de combustible 548
tipo de nube alta 55
tipo de nube baja 55
tipo de nube media 55
tipo Michigan 893
tipo sans serif 472
tipo serif 472
tipografía 472
tipos de articulaciones sinoviales 156
tipos de cabeza 302
tipos de eclipses 6, 7
tipos de huesos 157
tipos de motores 564
tipos de movimientos 916
tipos de parqué 254
tipos de puntas 302
tipos de punto 458
tipos de puntos 459
tipos de rejillas 258
tipos de remos 838
tipos de varillas 236
tira 416
tira de tela 459
tira para rasgar la envoltura 390
tirador 223, 290, 416, 860
tirador de espada 848
tirador de florete 848
tirador de la puerta 554
tirador de sable 848
tiradora 809
tiraje 390
tiranosaurus 93
tirante 252, 253, 321, 367, 443, 540, 857
tirante ajustable 368
tirante con botones 369
tirante de fijación 897
tirante de la botavara 836
tirante de la cabeza 857
tirante de la rodillera 857
tirante del pescante 634
tirantes 350, 541
tirantes en abanico 541
tirantes en forma de arpa 541
tirantes, puentes 541
tirilla 349, 354, 361
tirilla elástica 351, 354, 369
tirita 777
tirita Velcro® 368
tiro 390
tiro al arco 788
tiro al blanco 788, 861
tiro al plato 860
tiro con arco 859
tiro de aire caliente 256
tiro de penalti 814
tiro de pistola 861
tiro vertical 650
tisanas 208
Titán 5
Titan IV 24
Titania 5
titanio 683
tití 139
Titicaca, lago 31
titular 471
titular, firma 729
título de propiedad 915
tiza 863
toalla con capuchón 368
toalla de baño 379
toalla de lavabo 379
toalla para la cara 379
toallero 264
tobera 24
tobera de eyección 760
tobera de sección variable 629
tobera orientable 628
tobillera 365, 796, 880, 887
tobillo 146, 148
toca 341
tocadiscos 488, 500
tocón 87
toe 868
toga 336, 338
Togo 745
toldo 567, 611
toldo de ventana 902
toldo delantero 902
tolva 643
tolva de carga 573

1072

ASTRONOMÍA > 2-25; **TIERRA** > 26-71; **REINO VEGETAL** >72-89; **REINO ANIMAL** > 90-143; **SER HUMANO** > 144-177; **PRODUCTOS ALIMENTARIOS Y DE COCINA** > 178-241; **CASA** > 242-295; **BRICOLAJE Y JARDINERÍA** > 296-333; **VESTIDO** > 334-371; **ACCESORIOS Y ARTÍCULOS PERSONALES** > 372-391; **ARTE Y ARQUITECTURA** > 392-465; **COMUNICACIONES Y AUTOMATIZACIÓN DE OFICINA** > 466-535; **TRANSPORTE Y VEHÍCULOS** > 536-643; **ENERGÍA** > 644-677; **CIENCIA** > 678-705; **SOCIEDAD** > 706-785; **DEPORTES Y JUEGOS** > 786-920

toma 328
toma audio 513
toma contra sobretensión 520
toma contra sobretensión alimentadas por baterías 520
toma de aire 271, 548, 568
toma de aire del motor 568, 760
toma de aire del tejado 262
toma de aire para el ventilador de sustentación 605
toma de aire para refrigeración del motor 874
toma de aire principal 262
toma de alimentación 513
toma de auriculares 513
toma de carga 563
toma de corriente 567
toma de entrada 520
toma de entrada audio 527
toma de fuerza 640
toma de gases de combustión 564
toma de llenado 597
toma de oxígeno 780
toma de salida audio 527
toma de tierra 272
toma del micrófono 505
toma para auriculares 450, 451, 504
toma para la boca de riego 766
toma para los auriculares 497
toma principal de llenado 655
toma secundaria 655
tomarrizos 603
tomas entrada/salida video 497
tomas telefónicas contra sobretensiones 520
tomas video 477
tomate 188
tomate en rama 188
tomatillo 188
tómbolo 51
tomillo 202
Tonga 747
topacio 375
tope 284, 312, 382, 453, 583, 602, 773
tope amortiguador 289
tope de ingletes 305
tope de la escalera 766
tope de la puerta 291, 587
tope de profundidad 307
tope fijo 700
tope móvil 700
topo 121
topo, esqueleto 121
topo, mofología 121
toque 813
toque con dos manos 832
Torá, rollos 738
tórax 96, 97, 98, 146, 148
torca 47
torio 684
tormenta 57
tormenta de polvo y arena 57
tormenta eléctrica 57
tormenta tropical 57
tornado 57, 63
torneo, pelota 819
tornillo 302, 311, 320, 439, 462
tornillo cruciforme (Phillips) 302
tornillo de ajuste 286, 310, 312, 317, 319, 436, 777
tornillo de ajuste de ranilla 309
tornillo de ajuste de tensión 534
tornillo de ajuste del condensador 693
tornillo de anclaje 791
tornillo de apriete 312
tornillo de banco 401
tornillo de cabeza achaflanada 302
tornillo de cabeza avellanada 302
tornillo de cabeza redonda 302
tornillo de caja cuadrada 302
tornillo de fijación 482
tornillo de fijación horizontal 701
tornillo de la aguja 453
tornillo de montaje 913
tornillo de presión 421, 423
tornillo de regulación para carga completa 273
tornillo de regulación para carga ligera 273
tornillo de soporte inferior 58
tornillo de sujeción 304
tornillo de un solo sentido 302
tornillo guía 306
tornillo macrométrico 693
tornillo micrométrico 612, 693, 700, 701
tornillo nivelador 58, 699, 701
tornillo sin fin 573
tornillo sin fin, engranaje 686
tornillo sinfín 462
tornillos de bloqueo 700
torniquete de entrada 592
torniquete de salida 592
torno 464
torno de banco 312
torno de mesa 464
torno de perforación 651
toro 404, 405, 705
toro intermedio 405

toronja 194
torpedo 763
torre 410, 614, 634, 635, 674, 676, 677, 858, 916
torre de alta tensión 663
torre de control 618, 761
torre de escape 25
torre de extracción 649
torre de oficinas 713
torre de perforación 604, 651, 652, 654
torre de recepción 486
torre de refrigeración 646
torre de saltos 828
torre de señales 583
torre de transmisión 486
torre del homenaje 408
torre del locutor 488
torre esquinera 408
torre flanqueante 408
torre, grúa 634
torrecilla de lavado 294
torrente de montaña 45
Torres, estrecho 29
torreta 408, 762, 763
torreta de mando 763
torreta giratoria 758
torsión 306
tortellini 206
tortilla 205
tortuga 113
tortuga, anatomía 113
tortuga, morfología 113
tostador 238
touch pad 526
traba 857, 900
trabajo, muebles 511
trabilla 350, 358, 797, 854
trabilla de la pretina 350
trabilla de suspensión 354
trabilla para el pie 851
tracción, baterías 563
tracción, coche 594
tracería 411
trackball 517
tracto olfatorio 175
tractor 640
tractor : vista frontal 640
tractor : vista trasera 640
tractor cortacésped 333
tractor de orugas 636
tractor de ruedas 637
tractor nivelador 647
tractor remolcador 623
tractor remolque 622
tractor, motor 638
tragadero 47
tragaluz 244
trago 140, 173
trailer para transporte de vehículos 572
trainera 606
traje cruzado 356
traje de baño 371, 830
traje de carrera 882
traje de carreras 874
traje de chaqueta 355
traje de entrenamiento 370
traje de esquí 888
traje de esquí 887, 892
traje de esquí de salto 891
traje de esquí de velocidad 891
traje de judo 844
traje de protección 875
traje de una sola pieza 884
traje de vuelo 896
traje espacial 20
traje ignífugo 872
traje isotérmico 841
traje tradicional 846
trajes de baño 716
trajes de hombre 716
trajes de intervención 764
trajes sastre de señora 716
trama 460, 461
tramo 255
tramo central 540
tramo de elevación 542
tramo giratorio 542
tramo lateral 540
tramo suspendido 540
trampa de agua 866
trampa de petróleo 653
trampa petrolífera 651
trampas de arena 867
trampilla 407, 430
trampilla de acceso 712
trampolín 246, 823
trampolín de 1 m 828
trampolín de 3 m 828
transacción, recibo 731
transacciones financieras 525
transbordador 596, 608, 621
transbordador espacial 22
transbordador espacial en posición de lanzamiento 22
transductor 613

transepto 411
transferencia de calor al agua 665
transformación del trabajo mecánico en electricidad 662
transformador 287, 658, 663, 668, 674
transformador de ignición 259
transformador principal 585
transición, metales 683
transmisión 292, 563
transmisión de cadena 580
transmisión de calor 681
transmisión de datos 41
transmisión de electricidad 665
transmisión de energía al generador de voltaje 662
transmisión de ondas hertzianas 486
transmisión del movimiento hacia el rotor 662
transmisión longitudinal, árbol 553
transmisión por cable submarino 487
transmisión visual 694
transmisor 506
transmisor de microondas 489
transmisor-receptor radar 771
transpaleta 633
transpiración 67
transportador 701
transportador de equipaje 623
transporte 538
transporte aéreo 618
transporte de electricidad 663
transporte de electricidad de alta tensión 646, 662, 677
transporte ferroviario 582
transporte hacia los usuarios 646, 677
transporte marítimo 596, 649
transporte terrestre 538, 596
Transtárticos, montes 29
tranvía 595
trapecio 150, 151, 154, 156, 705, 897
trapezoide 154
tráquea 116
tráquea 125, 163
trasbordador 623
trasdós 413
traste 432, 440, 441
trastero 509
tratamiento de datos 41, 54
tratamiento químico 656
travelín 428
travelín, raíles 428
traversa 409, 598
travesaño 252, 277, 278, 321, 424, 433, 460, 461, 663, 676, 782, 783, 799
travesaño de apoyo 676
travesaño delantero 893
travesaño frontal 460
travesaño frontal interior 460
travesaño inferior 635
travesaño intermedio del batán 460
travesaño superior 249, 635
travesaño superior de la vidriera 249
travesaño superior del batán 460
travesaño trasero 893
traviesa 591
trébol 914
trebolado 413
tren de alta velocidad 585
tren de aterrizaje delantero 624, 760
tren de aterrizaje principal 625, 760
tren de pasajeros 582
tren subterráneo 592, 594
tren suburbano 583
trenca 353
trepadora 345
Triángulo 12
triángulo 437, 449, 705, 863
Triángulo Austral 10
Triásico 93
tribuna 788, 874
tribuna de los jueces 856
tribuna del jurado 728, 871, 890
tribuna para el público 856
tribunal 728
tríceps braquial 151
triceratops 93
triciclo 581
triclinio 406
tricornio 339
trifoliada 79
trifolio 411
triglifo 404
trigo 85, 203
trigo : espiga 85
trigo sarraceno 85, 203
trilladora, cosechadora 643
trilobites 92
trimarán 835
trincha 348
trinchera 352
trineo 884, 885
Trinidad y Tobago 743
trino 435
trinquete 302, 307, 603, 696, 697
trío 438, 914

tripa 212, 390
triple de barras 852
triple plano vertical 629
triple salto 790, 793, 875
triple salto mortal y medio hacia delante encogido 829
trípode 14, 436, 448, 482, 483, 489
trípode de la jirafa para el micrófono 492
tripulantes, vehículo de emergencia 21
trirreme 598
triticale 203
Tritón 5
tritón 111
triturador de ajos 230
triturador de basura 270
trituradora 71, 646
trituradora de documentos 535
trocánter 96, 98
trocánter mayor 153
troje 182
tromba marina 63
trombarina 63
Trombe, pared 675
trombón 447
trombones 437
trompa 110, 437, 447
trompa de Eustaquio 174, 175
trompa de Falopio 170, 171
trompa uterina, ampolla 171
trompeta 447, 538, 611
trompetas 437
trona 281
tronco 76, 86, 87, 110, 147, 149, 300
tronco celiaco 161, 165
tronco, corte 300
tronco, corte transversal 87
troncos, semirremolque 572
tronera 862
tronera central 862
tropical húmedo y seco 61
tropical lluvioso 61
trópico de Cáncer 34, 35, 36
trópico de Capricornio 34, 35, 36
tropopausa 53, 68
troposfera 53
trote 124
trotón 124
trucha 221
trufa 183
tuba 437, 447
tubérculos 184
tubería 654
tubería ascendente 259
tubería de agua caliente 262, 270, 271
tubería de agua fría 262, 265, 271
tubería de carga 657
tubería de conducción de carburante 25
tubería de escape del vapor 669
tubería de refrigeración 260
tubería de retorno 259
tubería del caudal del pozo 652
tubería descendente 259
tubería principal del vapor 669
tubo 223, 259, 267, 275, 312, 445, 447, 692, 753, 756, 757, 777, 841
tubo ajustable 782
tubo alimentador 240
tubo articulado 557
tubo binocular 693
tubo capilar 695
tubo de acuarela 397
tubo de agua caliente 266
tubo de agua fría 266
tubo de aire 259, 382, 765, 841
tubo de ajuste 824, 825
tubo de alimentación 643
tubo de aspiración 658, 659
tubo de circulación 672
tubo de cristal 695
tubo de desagüe 267
tubo de descarga 643
tubo de destellos 692
tubo de drenaje 253, 485
tubo de embocadura 444
tubo de empuje 470
tubo de ensayo 685
tubo de ensilaje 643
tubo de entrada 237
tubo de escape 274, 275, 552, 553, 564, 570, 576, 631, 636, 639, 640
tubo de extensión 289
tubo de flash 482
tubo de gasolina 553, 563
tubo de guache 397
tubo de irrigación 573
tubo de la hélice 605
tubo de lengüeta 444
tubo de Malpighi 99
tubo de pantalla 494
tubo de perforación 651
tubo de Pitot 873
tubo de presión 667
tubo de salida 263
tubo de sillín 871
tubo de subida del agua 241

tubo de suministro de agua 262, 270
tubo de suministro de petróleo 259
tubo de toma de agua 262
tubo de vapor 241
tubo de ventilación 643
tubo del asiento 578
tubo del borde de ataque 897
tubo del manillar 579
tubo del pistón 447
tubo en Y 776
tubo flexible 289, 776
tubo fluorescente 275
tubo inferior del cuadro 579
tubo lanzatorpedos 763
tubo para el grano 643
tubo portaocular 693
tubo principal 14, 15
tubo principal de observación 692
tubo rebosadero 266
tubo rígido 289
tubos de Malpighi 97
Tucán 10
tucán 119
Tudor 413
tuerca 248, 269, 310, 311, 590
tuerca cerrada 311
tuerca de ajuste 269, 270
tuerca de bloqueo 700
tuerca de fijación 58
tuerca de mariposa 311
tuerca de seguridad 58
tuerca de sujeción 909
tuerca de sujeción de la aguja 398
tuerca del prensaestopas 268
tuerca hexagonal 311
tuercas 311
tulio 684
tulipán 80
tumbona 277
tundra 61, 66
túnel 592
túnel de carretera 543
túnel de comunicación 23
túnel de embarque 619
Túnez 745
tungsteno 683
túnica 356, 748
túnica de manga larga 337
turbante 339, 341
turbina 646, 659, 668
turbina de transmisión 564
turbina de viento de eje horizontal 677
turbina de viento de eje vertical 676
turbina del compresor 564, 627
turbina Francis 659
turbina Kaplan 659
turbina motriz 627
turbina Pelton 659
turbinas de viento 676
turbo-alternador 646
turborreactor 625, 627, 760
turco 469
turf 856
turión 185
turismo de tres puertas 549
turismo, neumático 560
Turkmenistán 746
turmalina 375
turquesa 375
Turquía 746
Tuvalu 747

U

uapití 128
ubicación de la estatua 403
Ucrania 744
ucranio 469
udon, fideos 207
ued 52
Uganda 745
uke (defensor) 844
Ulisses 19
última recta 856
umbela 81
umbo 105
umbral 46, 247
Umbriel 5
un par 914
uña 98, 113, 115, 127, 130, 133, 140, 173, 301, 610
uña extendida 133
uña retraída 133
una vía 544, 546
uña, cuerpo 172
uña, raíz 172
uñas, esmalte 377
uñas, lima 377
unicelulares 94
Unicornio 11
unidad astronómica 5
unidad CD/DVD-ROM 513, 526
unidad cruciforme 629
unidad de aire 622
unidad de aire acondicionado 489

unidad de casetes 521
unidad de CD/DVD-ROM 513
unidad de control de cámaras 490
unidad de control de la cámara 489
unidad de control de la temperatura del cuerpo 20
unidad de control electrónico 559
unidad de copia de seguridad 523
unidad de cuidados intensivos 780
unidad de destilación al vacío 656
unidad de disco duro extraíble 521
unidad de disco duro primario 513
unidad de discos 450
unidad de disquete 513
unidad de disquete externo 521
unidad de disquetes 513
unidad de extracción de solventes 656
unidad de grupo de la alimentación 513
unidad de impresión 528
unidad de instrumentos 25
unidad de medición de volumen 488
unidad de medida de cantidad de materia 702
unidad de medida de carga eléctrica 702
unidad de medida de corriente eléctrica 702
unidad de medida de energía 702
unidad de medida de frecuencia 702
unidad de medida de fuerza 702
unidad de medida de intensidad luminosa 702
unidad de medida de la diferencia de potencial eléctrico 702
unidad de medida de la temperatura Celsius 702
unidad de medida de longitud 702
unidad de medida de masa 702
unidad de medida de potencia eléctrica 702
unidad de medida de presión 702
unidad de medida de radioactividad 702
unidad de medida de resistencia eléctrica 702
unidad de medida de temperatura termodinámica 702
unidad de medida de tiempo 702
unidad de memoria de acceso aleatorio (RAM) 513
unidad de pesas 851
unidad de refrigeración 571
unidad de registro 59
unidad de visualización de imagen /sonido 491
unidad del disco duro 521
unidad del radar 760
unidad exterior 260
unidad interior 260
unidad móvil 486, 489
unidad móvil de rayos X 778
unidad móvil de servicio por control remoto 21
unidad para maniobras en el espacio 20
unidad secundaria de disco duro 513
unidades astronómicas 4
unidades de almacenamiento de información 521
unidades de comunicación 522
unidades de entrada de información 514
unidades de medida, sistema internacional 702
unidades de salida de información 518
uniforme 770
uniformes 764
unión 269, 470, 703
unión de caña y brazos 610
unión periférica 661
unísono 434
universidad 710
uno 703
ununbio 683
ununnilio 683
unununio 683
Urales, montes 32
uranio 684
uranio en fisión 665
uranio enriquecido 671
uranio natural 670
Urano 4, 5
urdidor 462
urdimbre 460, 461
urdimbre, hilos 463
urdu 469
uréter 165
uretra 104, 116, 165, 169, 170
urgencias 778
urinario, aparato 165
URL localizador universal de recursos 524
urna 699
urópodo 107
urostilo 111
urraca 118
Uruguay 742
usar plancha caliente 347
usar plancha muy caliente 347
usar plancha tibia 347
uso común, símbolos 725
usos de Internet 525
usuario particular 525
utensilios de cocina 229, 234, 905
utensilios para abrir y descorchar 230
utensilios para la chimenea 257
utensilios, ejemplos 401
útero 170, 171
útero, ligamento ancho 171
uva 86, 192
uva, corte 83
uvas, racimo 86
úvula 174, 175
Uzbekistán 746

V

vaca 128
vaciador 233
vacuno, carne picada 214
vacuno, carne troceada 214
vacuno, cortes 214
vacuola 74, 94
vacuola contráctil 94
vacuola digestiva 94
vacuola digestiva en formación 94
vade 511
vagina 103, 104, 170, 171
vagón 587, 642
vagón cerrado 588
vagón cisterna 588
vagón comedor 584
vagón de carga 583
vagón de mercancías 588
vagón de pasajeros 584, 585, 594
vagón frigorífico 588
vagón máquina 594
vagón para automóviles 588
vagón para contenedores 588
vagón para ganado 588
vagón para madera 588
vagón plano con retenedores 588
vagón tolva 588
vagón tolva para minerales 588
vagones de pasajeros 584
vagones, ejemplos 588
vaina 79, 84
vaina de mielina 168
vajilla 226
vajillas , cristalerías y cuberterías 717
vajillas, cristalerías, cuberterías 717
valla 712, 790
valla de la carrera de obstáculos 790
valla de madera 878
valla de seguridad 890
valla sobre muro 852
valla sobre seto 852
vallado 244
vallado del campo 795
valle 45, 48
valor 729
valores de las notas musicales 435
valores de los silencios 435
valva 105
válvula 445, 579
válvula aórtica 162
válvula de aceleración 649
válvula de acetileno 319
válvula de admisión 564, 566
válvula de agua de rociado 669
válvula de aire 320, 398
válvula de aire comprimido 841
válvula de ajuste 320
válvula de alivio 259
válvula de control 263, 903
válvula de drenaje 266, 267, 291
válvula de entrada 265
válvula de escape 564, 566
válvula de exhalación 773
válvula de freno 319
válvula de inhalación 773
válvula de la tubería 654
válvula de liberación de aire 607
válvula de llenado 655
válvula de oxígeno 319
válvula de parada de la turbina 668
válvula de purga 259
válvula de regulación 259
válvula de seguridad 234, 266, 267, 665
válvula de vaciado 655
válvula del quemador 899
válvula maestra 654
válvula mitral 162
válvula paracaídas 899
válvula pulmonar 162
válvula tricúspide 162
válvulas de combustible del motor 626
válvulas de control de combustible 626
vanadio 683
Vanuatu 747
vapor 646, 681
vapor, tubo 241
vaporera 722
vaporera eléctrica 239
vaporizador 261, 288
vaquería 182
vaqueros 358
vara 439
varal 857
varal de la cabeza 857
varano 114
variedades de inflorescencias 81
varilla 274, 367, 391, 436, 457, 461, 685
varilla de acero 449
varilla de batir 236
varilla de calada 461
varilla de cambio 590
varilla de carbón (cátodo) 689
varilla de contacto 316
varilla de control 670, 671
varilla de empuje 590
varilla de lizos 461
varilla de refrigeración 692
varilla de registro 445
varilla de rubí 692
varilla de tensión 448
varilla del pedal 442
varilla del péndulo 436, 697
varilla reflectante 692
varilla rizadora 381
varilla telescópica de desenganche 587
varilla tensora 461
varillas 284, 445
varillas, tipos de 236
variómetro 899
variómetro eléctrico 898
variómetro mecánico 898
varios 473
varios aparatos electrodomésticos 240
Varolio, puente 167
vaso 246
vaso capilar 172
vaso corto 225
vaso largo 225
vaso medidor 231
vaso mezclador 236
vaso sanguíneo 162, 172
vaso sanguíneo dorsal 97
vasos 723
vasos sanguíneos 140, 154
vástago 301, 302, 454, 456, 579, 862
vástago aislado 316
vástago de arrastre 651
vástago de elevación 640
vástago del macillo 443
vasto externo 150
vasto interno 150, 151
vatio 702
Vauban, fortificación 409
vegetación 66
vegetación, distribución 66
vehículo de emergencia 543
vehículo de emergencia para los tripulantes 21
vehículo todo terreno 549
vehículos 538
vehículos, trailer 572
vejiga 110, 113, 165, 169, 170
vejiga natatoria 109
vejiga urinaria 109
Vela 11
vela 737, 833, 836, 896
vela al tercio 601
vela áurica 601
vela Bermuda 601
vela cuadrada 601
vela flameante 833
vela latina 601
vela mayor 834
vela mayor proel 603
vela tarquina 601
velamen 603, 897
velarium 407
velas, ejemplos 601
velero 834
veleta 58, 59, 677
veleta (grímpola) 834
velo 98, 909
velo del paladar 174, 175
velo del paladar, pilar anterior 174
velocidad de la película 479
velocidad del viento 55
velocidad, selector 236
velocímetro 557, 576, 851
velódromo 788, 871
vena axilar 160
vena basílica 160
vena cava inferior 160, 161, 162, 165
vena cava superior 160, 161, 162
vena cefálica 160
vena femoral 160
vena hepática 161
vena ilíaca 161
vena ilíaca común 165
vena mesentérica superior 160
vena porta 161
vena pulmonar 160
vena pulmonar derecha 162
vena pulmonar izquierda 162
vena renal 160, 165
vena safena interna 160
vena subclavia 160
vena yugular externa 160
vena yugular interna 160
venas y arterias, principales 160
vencedor 789
vencejo 118
venda de gasa 777
venda elástica 777
venda triangular 777
vendaje 843, 853
veneno 774
veneno, conducto 112
veneno, glándula 112
Venera 19
venera 217
Venezuela 742
venta de billetes, taquilla 592
ventalla 84
ventalle 749
ventana 238, 239, 249, 251, 485, 567, 836
ventana a la francesa 415
ventana a la inglesa 415
ventana abajo 515
ventana arriba 515
ventana basculante 415
ventana con rejas 727
ventana corredera 415
ventana de acceso 521
ventana de celosía 415
ventana de eyección 755
ventana de guillotina 415
ventana de la nariz 175
ventana de la torre 663
ventana de lectura 499
ventana de librillo 415
ventana del semisótano 245
ventana panorámica 713
ventana pivotante 415
ventana protectora 494
ventana-mosquitero 902
ventanal de control 727
ventanas, accesorios para las 282
ventanas, ejemplos 415
ventanilla 551, 554, 594, 624, 731
ventanilla comercial 731
ventanilla de aterrizaje 631
ventanilla de observación 23
ventanilla de ventilación del techo 567
ventanilla panorámica 584
ventanilla trasera 551
ventilación 556, 675
ventilación, hélice 688
ventilador 258, 259, 260, 293, 497, 552, 561, 563, 566, 571, 586, 594, 627, 643
ventilador de aire caliente 260
ventilador de cabina 898
ventilador de césped 333
ventilador de la carcasa 513
ventilador de techo 261
ventilador del condensador 261
ventilador del equipo de alimentación 513
ventilador del evaporador 261, 670
ventilador del motor diésel 586
ventilador principal 648
ventosa 106, 111
ventrículo derecho 161, 162
ventrículo izquierdo 161, 162
venturi 757
Venus 4, 5
verano 54
verano fresco 61
verano tórrido 61
verbena 208
verde 400, 690
verdolaga 187
verdura 180
verdura 184
verduras de hojas 186
vereda 866
verga 602
vermicelli de arroz 207
vernier 700
versalita 472
vértebra 112, 136
vértebra cervical 157
vértebra lumbar 157, 168
vértebra sacra 111
vértebra torácica 157
vértebras 111
vértebras caudales 126, 131, 142
vértebras cervicales 116, 122, 126, 131, 138, 141, 142, 153
vértebras coccígeas 122, 138, 141
vértebras dorsales 153
vértebras lumbares 122, 126, 131, 138, 141, 142, 153
vértebras sacrales 142
vértebras sacras 122, 126, 131
vértebras torácicas 122, 126, 131, 138, 142
vertedera 641
vertedera, arado 641
vertedero 709
vertedero autorizado 69
vertedor 240
vertical 463
vertical de barras 852
vertido de hidrocarburos 70
vesícula biliar 110, 112, 164
vesícula seminal 169
vestíbulo 174, 250, 406, 582, 608, 620, 713, 717, 719, 724
vestíbulo de entrada 394
vestido 336
vestido acampanado 356
vestido camisero 356
vestido camisero sin mangas 356
vestido con crinolina 337
vestido con miriñaque 337
vestido con polisón 337
vestido cruzado 356
vestido de camiseta 356
vestido de talle bajo 356
vestido de tirantes 356
vestido ignífugo e impermeable 765
vestidos, ejemplos 356
vestuario 428, 764
vestuarios 734
veta 300
veterinarios 852
vía 582, 592
vía de salida 589
vía de tren suburbano 583
vía férrea 39, 590, 591, 649
vía ferroviaria 709, 710
Vía Láctea 9, 13
Vía Láctea (vista desde arriba) 9
Vía Láctea (vista lateral) 9
vía locomotriz 589
vía principal 583
vía subsidiaria 583
vía, cambiador manual 590
viaducto 541
vía] 595
víbora 114
vibrisas 122
Victoria, lago 34
vid 86
vid, hoja 86
vida, evolución 92
videocámara analógica: vista frontal 496
videocámara analógica: vista posterior 496
videocinta 495
videojuego 918
videoteca 733
vidriera 614, 737
vidrio 249
vidrio, selección 71
vieira 217
viento 56, 69, 70, 833, 902
viento contrario 833
viento contrario, salida 833
viento de través 833
viento dominante 63
viento en popa 833
viento en proa 833
viento fuerte invernal alto 57
viento fuerte invernal bajo 57
viento moderado 56
viento suave 56
viento, instrumentos 446
viento, molino 676
vientos 917
vientre 124
vierteaguas 551
vierteguas 247, 249, 257
Vietnam 747
vietnamita 468
viga 406, 412, 418
viga cantilever 540
viga continua 540
viga de cola 631
viga de sujección 900
viga maestra 21, 252
viga, puente 540
vigueta 254
vigueta del piso 252, 253
vigueta del techo 252
vigueta esquinera 252, 253
vinagre balsámico 201
vinagre de arroz 201
vinagre de malta 201
vinagre de manzana 201
vinagre de vino 201
vinagre, arroz 201
vinagre, malta 201
vinagre, manzana 201
vinagre, vino 201
vínculos familiares 784
vino 180
vinos, carta 721
viola 439
violas 437
violeta 80, 400
violín 439
violines, familia 437, 439
violoncelo 439
violoncelos 437
vira 342
virada por redondo 833
viraje de mariposa 832

1074

ASTRONOMÍA > 2-25; **TIERRA** > 26-71; **REINO VEGETAL** >72-89; **REINO ANIMAL** > 90-143; **SER HUMANO** > 144-177; **PRODUCTOS ALIMENTARIOS Y DE COCINA** > 178-241; **CASA** > 242-295; **BRICOLAJE Y JARDINERÍA** > 296-333; **VESTIDO** > 334-371; **ACCESORIOS Y ARTÍCULOS PERSONALES** > 372-391; **ARTE Y ARQUITECTURA** > 392-465; **COMUNICACIONES Y AUTOMATIZACIÓN DE OFICINA** > 466-535; **TRANSPORTE Y VEHÍCULOS** > 536-643; **ENERGÍA** > 644-677; **CIENCIA** > 678-705; **SOCIEDAD** > 706-785; **DEPORTES Y JUEGOS** > 786-920

Virgo 11, 13
virola 863
virola hembra 910
virola macho 910
virotillo 253
visera 340, 341, 575, 591, 749, 765, 772, 874, 878, 884
visillo 282
visillos 282
visión 691
visión normal 691
visión, defecos 691
visitantes, oficina de recepción 726
visitantes, sala de espera 726
visón 134
visor 290, 476, 477, 492, 701
visor electrónico 496
visor telescópico 692
vista 177
vista anterior 146, 148, 150
vista frontal 798
vista lateral 798
vista lateral del cráneo 158
vista posterior 147, 149, 151
vista transversal de una calle 712
Vístula, río 32
visualización 507
visualización de datos 508
visualización de la información 495
visualización de valores de abertura 479
visualización de valores de exposición 479
vitola 390
vitrales 411
vitrina 279
vitrinas refrigeradas 180
vivienda 182
viviendas plurifamiliares 419
viviendas tradicionales 418
viviendas urbanas 419
volador 918
volante 282, 333, 425, 452, 552, 556, 607, 640, 873
volante de aspas 421
volante de control 766
volante de plumas 817
volante del freno manual 587
volante sintético 817
volantes 368
volcadora 639

volcán 42, 44
volcán efusivo 44
volcán en erupción 44
volcán explosivo 44
volcanes, ejemplo 44
volea 820
voleibol 812
voley playa 813
Volga, río 32
volquete 573
volquete basculante 572
volt 702
voltímetro 316
voltio 702
voluta 276, 404, 405, 439
volva 76
Voyager 19
vuelo 739, 829, 891
vuelo del peldaño 255
vuelo en globo 899
vuelo libre 897
vuelta 350
vuelta de cabo 908
vuelta de campana 832
vuelta de escota 908
vuelta de escota doble 908
vulva 148, 171
vúmetro 491

W

wakame 183
walaby 143
walkie-talkie 505, 770
wasabi 201
waterpolo 827
Weddel, mar 29
wedge para arena 868
wedge para rough 868
wigwam 418
Wilkes, Tierra 29
winch 835
windsurf 836
wok 234
Wolkman, canales 154
Wolof 468

X

xenón 684
xilófono 437, 449

Y

y 473
yak 129
yate de motor 607
yelmo 749
yema 78, 117, 172
yema axilar 77
yema terminal 77
yembé 433
Yemen 746
yen 728
yerno 784
yeyuno 164
Yibouti 745
yidish 469
yodo 683
yogur 210
yoruba 468
Yucatán, península 30
yugo 376
Yugoslavia 744
yunque 174
yurta 418

Z

zafiro 375
zaguero 804
zaguero derecho 812
zaguero izquierdo 812
zaguero medio 812
zamarra 353
Zambia 746
zampoña 433
zanahoria 189
zanca 255
zanca de contén 255
zanco 636
zángano 99
zanja 647
zapata 312, 559, 571, 868
zapata antideslizante 321, 826
zapata de goma 321

zapatería 715
zapatero de alambre 345
zapatilla 791, 798, 801, 810, 850
zapatilla con tacos 796
zapatilla de tenis 344, 822
zapatilla deportiva 370
zapatillas de deporte 716
zapatillas de esgrima 848
zapato 865, 870, 872
zapato a la polaca 339
zapato con cordones 343
zapato con tacos 808
zapato de cordones 342
zapato de correa 343
zapato de salón 343
zapato de tacón 339
zapato de tacón con correa 343
zapato de talón abierto 343
zapato oxford 342
zapatos de golf 869
zapatos de hombre 342, 716
zapatos de mujer 343, 716
zapatos de niños 717
zapote 197
zarcillo 86
zarpa 252, 253
Zimbabue 746
zirconio 683
zócalo 253, 255, 697
zócalo de la bañera 264
zona central 809
zona comercial 709, 713
zona de anotación 806
zona de ataque 812
zona de atención 795
zona de aterrizaje 891
zona de camillas 778
zona de clasificación 589
zona de combate 844, 845, 846
zona de comidas campestres 725
zona de competición 845, 846
zona de convección 6
zona de cronometraje 891
zona de defensa 812
zona de defensa protegida 877
zona de entrada de los jugadores expulsados 827
zona de entrega 790
zona de entrenamiento 788
zona de espera 730

zona de fondo 809
zona de frenado 890, 891
zona de la portería 879
zona de lanzamiento 788
zona de lavado de vagones 589
zona de marca 805
zona de pasividad 843
zona de pelos absorbentes 87
zona de peligro 846, 847
zona de precipitación 55
zona de preparación de productos 180
zona de prueba de motores de aviones 761
zona de radiación 6
zona de recepción 589
zona de recepción de mercancías 180
zona de recepción productos lácteos 180
zona de recreo 608
zona de salida 838, 875
zona de salto 890
zona de saque 817
zona de seguridad 844, 846
zona de servicio 619, 666
zona de trabajo 10
zona de traspaso de carga 607
zona de tres segundos 811
zona débil de la hoja 849
zona defensiva 809
zona del hoyo 866
zona escolar 545, 547
zona fuerte de la hoja 849
zona libre 812, 813
zona media 849
zona neutral 806, 879
zona ofensiva 809
zona para acampar 725
zona para acampar y para caravanas 725
zona para caravanas 725
zona para los ciclistas 871
zona pelúcida 170
zona residencial 709
zona residencial (de las afueras) 39
zona residencial de las afueras 709
zoom 492
Zorra 13
zorro 134
zorro volador 141
zulú 468
zumaque 199

Indice delle voci italiane

2° metacarpale 140
3° metacarpale 140
4° metacarpale 140
5° metacarpale 140

A

a ferro di cavallo 413
abaco 404
abat-son 411
abbaino 244
abbellimenti 435
abbigliamento 336
abbigliamento antinfortunistico 318
abbigliamento casual femminile 716
abbigliamento casual maschile 717
abbigliamento da ginnastica 371
abbigliamento femminile 355
abbigliamento maschile 348
abbigliamento per bambine dai 2 ai 6 anni 717
abbigliamento per bambini dai 2 ai 6 anni 717
abbigliamento per bebè 717
abbigliamento per ragazze dai 7 ai 17 anni 717
abbigliamento per ragazzi dai 7 ai 17 anni 717
abbigliamento sportivo 370
abbigliamento sportivo da uomo 717
abbigliamento sportivo femminile 716
abbigliamento sportivo per bambini 717
abbigliamento, negozio di 714
abbottonatura a doppiopetto 352
abbottonatura a polo 354
abbottonatura a pressione 368
abbottonatura anteriore a pressione 369
abbottonatura della cintura 350
abete 89
abete, aghi d' 89
abissino 133
abitacolo 873
abitazioni urbane 419
abiti da donna 716
abiti da uomo 716
abiti tradizionali 339
abiti, esempi di 356
abito a polo 356
abito a trapezio 356
abito a tunica 356
abito a vestaglia 356
abito a vita bassa 356
abito con crinolina 337
abito con panieri 337
abito con sellino 337
abito da casa 356
Abramo 736
ABS, sistema frenante antibloccaggio 559
abside 411
acagiù, noce di 193
acanto, foglia di 276, 405
acantodi 92
accappatoio 364
acceleratore, manopola dell' 576
acceleratore, pedale dell' 556
accelerazione, cavo di 332
accelerazione, grilletto di 331
accendino a gas 391

accensione, blocchetto di 556
accensione, candela di 332
accensione, cavo di 323
accensione, chiave dell' 332, 333
accensione, interruttore di 526
accensione, pulsante di 293
accensione/spegnimento, spia luminosa di 506
accento 435
accento acuto 473
accento circonflesso 473
accento grave 473
accesso al secondo livello di operazioni 529
accesso alla griglia di illuminazione 490
accesso non consentito alle sedie a rotelle 725
accesso per i portatori di handicap 725
accesso, pannello di 258
accesso, pista di 618
accesso, portello di 607
accesso, strada di 618
accessori 289, 345, 399, 401, 454, 462, 558, 580
accessori a propano o butano 903
accessori da donna 717
accessori da uomo 716
accessori dell'obiettivo 478
accessori di bellezza 374
accessori di pulitura 289
accessori fotografici 482
accessori musicali 436
accessori per finestre 282
accessori per fumatori 390
accessori per il tiro 752
accessori per la sciolinatura 892
accessori personali 374
accessori, espulsore degli 236
accessori, scatola degli 456
accessori, scomparto degli 289
accessori, slitta per gli 476
accessori, vano 483
accetta 330, 907
accettazione 778, 781
accettazione, area d' 764
acchito 862
acchito centrale 862
acchito della linea di battuta 862
acchito superiore 862
acciaio 298
acciaio, corpo d' 689
acciaiolo 229
acciarino 318, 752
acciarino, molla dell' 752
accidenti 435
acciuga 219
accompagnamento 864
accompagnamento, corde per l' 432
acconciatura, articoli per 380
accoppiamento flessibile 677
accoppiamento, adattatore di 21
accoppiatore idraulico 640
accordatura, anello d' 433
accordo 435
accordo, asta d' 444
accumulatore 559
acero 88
acero, sciroppo d' 209
acetilene, bombola d' 319
acetilene, valvola dell' 319
aceto balsamico 201

aceto di malto 201
aceto di mele 201
aceto di riso 201
aceto di vino 201
acetosa 187
achenio 83, 84
acidificazione dei laghi 70
acido nitrico, emissione di 70
acido solforico, emissione di 70
acino 86
acino, sezione di un 83
acondrite 8
acqua 646, 665, 847
acqua bollente 671
acqua calda, colonna montante dell' 262
acqua calda, rete di distribuzione dell' 262
acqua calda, tubo di uscita dell' 267
acqua calda, uscita dell' 259
acqua di alimentazione 670, 671
acqua di disgelo 46
acqua fredda, colonna montante dell' 262
acqua fredda, ingresso dell' 267
acqua fredda, rete di distribuzione dell' 262
acqua in pressione 662
acqua naturale 671
acqua ossigenata 777
acqua pesante 670
acqua pesante fredda 670
acqua pesante pressurizzata 670
acqua pesante, riconcentrazione dell' 669
acqua pressurizzata 671
acqua, altezza di caduta dell' 662
acqua, attacco del tubo di alimentazione dell' 328, 329
acqua, bicchiere da 225
acqua, bottiglia dell' 579
acqua, chiave dell' 447
acqua, contatore dell' 262
acqua, corso d' 48, 70
acqua, entrata dell' 268
acqua, flusso d' 95
acqua, getti d' 828
acqua, inquinamento dell' 70
acqua, livello dell' 241, 261
acqua, scarico dell' 662
acqua, serbatoio dell' 241, 261, 384, 586
acqua, superficie dell' 828
acquamarina 375
acquaragia 400
acquasantiera 737
acquascooter 876
acque reflue 70
acque sicure 616
acquedotto per il riempimento della chiusa 597
acquerello 396
acquifero artesiano 646
acromion 153
acroterio 403, 404
acuti, ponticello degli 442
acuti, registro degli 432
acuti, tastiera degli 432
Adamo, pomo d' 146
adattatore 274, 383, 485, 523
adattatore del carico utile 24
adattatore di accoppiamento 21
adattatore per oculare 496
adattatore per videocassette compatte 496
adattatori 269

adattatori, esempi di 269
addebito, carta di 731
addetto ai 24 secondi 810
addetto al controllo biglietti 394, 427
addetto al rifornimento 873
addetto alla panca dei puniti 879
addizione 703
addome 96, 97, 98, 103, 107, 115, 146, 148
adduttore lungo 150
Aden, Golfo di 33, 34
Adriatico, Mar 32
aeratore 268
aerazione, canale di 402
aerazione, comando dell' 556
aerazione, griglia di 244
aereo da ricognizione meteorologica 54
aereo di linea 53
aerociste 75
aerocisterna 760
aerofreni, leva degli 626
aerofreno 760
aerografo 398
aerografo, sezione trasversale di un 398
aeronavigazione, dispositivo per 761
aeroplani, esempi di 628
aeroplano a decollo e atterraggio verticale 628
aeroplano anfibio antincendio 628
aeroplano da carico 629
aeroplano da combattimento 760
aeroplano leggero 628
aeroplano privato 628
aeroplano radar 629
aeroplano, movimenti di un 630
aeroporto 39, 618, 708
affari, quartiere degli 708, 710
affettauova 233
affettaverdure 230
affissione, superficie di 535
affluente 48
affrancamento, modulo di 531
affrancatrice 531
affresco 406
affusto 753, 756
Afghanistan 746
afnio 683
Africa 28, 34, 50, 745
agar-agar 183
agarico delizioso 183
agenda 530
agente di polizia 770
agente di sicurezza, postazione dell' 779
agente di sicurezza, ufficio dell' 733
agenzia di viaggi 714
aggancio, pulsante di 305
aggetto, manopola di regolazione dell' 309
aggomitolatore 462
aghi d'abete 89
aghi di pino 89
aglio 184
agnato 92
agnello, tagli di 215
ago 64, 398, 452, 453, 454, 590, 776
ago a linguetta 456
ago magnetico 907
ago per legare 233
ago, barra dell' 453
ago, cappelletto dell' 398
ago, placca dell' 452

ago, selettore della posizione dell' 452
agricoltura intensiva 68, 70
agrippina 276
agrume 82
agrumi 194
aikido 846
aikidogi 846
aikidoka 846
air bag 556
air bag, sistema di ritenuta degli 556
airone 119
aiuola 245, 322
aiutante 181, 721
aiuto attrezzista 429
aiuto cuoco 721
aiuto regista 429
ajowan 199
al gran lasco 833
al lasco 833
al traverso 833
ala 23, 97, 98, 115, 175, 338, 625, 760, 897, 898, 909
ala a delta 629, 630
ala a freccia 630
ala a geometria variabile 630
ala alta 628
ala anteriore 96
ala attaccante 809
ala destra 801, 811, 814, 879
ala difensore 809
ala inferiore 628
ala pieghevole 857
ala poppiera 609
ala posteriore 96
ala prodiera 609
ala rettangolare 630
ala semiimmersa 609
ala sinistra 801, 811, 814, 879
ala superiore 628
ala trapezia 630
alamaro 353
alano 131
alari 257
Alaska, Golfo dell' 30
albanese 469
Albania 744
albatros 119
alberatura 602
albergo 710, 724, 886, 915
albergo, camera d' 724
alberi 866
albero 87, 464, 600, 659, 676, 686, 688, 695, 697, 834, 836
albero a bassa velocità 677
albero a camme 566
albero a gomiti 564, 566
albero ad alta velocità 677
albero da frutto 182
albero del coltro 641
albero del derrick 607
albero del radar 606
albero del turbocompressore 627
albero dell'elica 609
albero della vite 86
albero delle pedivelle 580
albero di contromezzana 602
albero di controvelaccino 602
albero di maestra 600, 602
albero di mezzana 600, 602
albero di Natale 652, 654

INDICE DELLE VOCI ITALIANE

ASTRONOMIA > 2-25; TERRA > 26-71; REGNO VEGETALE > 72-89; REGNO ANIMALE > 90-143; ESSERE UMANO > 144-177; GENERI ALIMENTARI E CUCINA > 178-241; CASA > 242-295;
FAI DA TE E GIARDINAGGIO > 296-333; ABBIGLIAMENTO > 334-371; ACCESSORI E ARTICOLI PERSONALI > 372-391; ARTE E ARCHITETTURA > 392-465; COMUNICAZIONI E BUROTICA > 466-535;
TRASPORTI E VEICOLI > 536-643; ENERGIA > 644-677; SCIENZA > 678-705; SOCIETÀ > 706-785; SPORT E GIOCHI > 786-920

1077

albero di parrocchetto 602
albero di trasmissione 605
albero di trasmissione longitudinale 553
albero di trinchetto 600, 602
albero di velaccino 602
albero motore 631
albero ornamentale 182, 322
albero oscillante, braccio di sollevamento dell' 640
albero prodiero 607
albero, struttura di un 87
albero, supporto dell' 307
albicocca 192
albume 117
alburno 87
alce 129
alchechengi 192
alcol puro 777
alcool, bulbo d' 695
alcool, colonna d' 695
alesatori per la pulizia degli ugelli 318
aletta 259, 348, 387, 625, 628, 759, 776, 891
aletta a molla 302
aletta autoadesiva 531
aletta del bordo di attacco 760
aletta del parafango 570
aletta di compensazione 60
aletta fissa 759
aletta frontale 391
aletta parasole 556
aletta radiante 260
aletta staccata 352
aletta, manica ad 360
aletta, tasca applicata con 349, 360
aletta, tasca interna con 348, 352, 353, 355, 360
aletta, tasca profilata con 348, 352
aletta, taschino con 348
aletta, taschino tagliato con 348
alette 918
alettone 624, 760, 873, 898
alettone del parafango 571
alettone parafango 571
Aleutine, Fossa delle 50
Aleutine, Isole 30
alfiere 916
alga 75
alga bruna 75
alga marina 183
alga rossa 75
alga verde 75
alga, struttura di un' 75
Algeria 745
alghe, esempi di 75
ali 140, 628
ali, tipi di 630
aliante 898
alidada 59, 612, 701
alidada, livella fissata all' 701
alimentatore 513, 526, 643
alimentatore automatico 512
alimentatore manuale 512
alimentatore, ventola dell' 513
alimentatore del premio 920
alimentazione dell'acqua, tubo di 294
alimentazione dell'aria 445
alimentazione dell'aria, tubo di 765
alimentazione dell'elettrodo, cavo di 318
alimentazione di ossigeno, indicatore dell' 898
alimentazione di ossigeno, regolatore dell' 898
alimentazione manuale, fessura di 519
alimentazione, acqua di 670, 671
alimentazione, cavo a 240 volt 272
alimentazione, cavo d' 237, 308
alimentazione, cavo di 305, 381, 382, 497, 513
alimentazione, collettore dell'acqua di 669
alimentazione, condotto di 260
alimentazione, cordone dell' 383
alimentazione, filo neutro di 272
alimentazione, piano di 531
alimentazione, presa di 504, 513
alimentazione, pulsante di 494
alimentazione, punto di 273, 663
alimentazione, sistema di 553
alimentazione, spia luminosa di 508
alimentazione, spina di 527
alimentazione, tubo di 270
alimenti e prodotti per animali 181
alimenti, latta per 223
alimenti, rete per 222
alimenti, vaschetta per 222
aliscafo 609
all'indietro 828
allacciamento alla rete 273
allacciamento, esempi di 270
allacciamento, punto di 273
allacciatura con bottoni a pressione 353
allargatubi 314
allarme acustico 613
allarme, dispositivo di 765
allenamento, zona di 788
allenatore 800, 811, 827, 842, 879
allenatore, zona dell' 794
allenatori 881, 883
allenatori, tribuna degli 891
allevamento intensivo 68, 69
alligatore 114
allineatore 838
alloggi 886
alloggi dell'equipaggio 604
alloggiamento 275, 416, 527, 614
alloggiamento del bocchino 447
alloggiamento del caricatore 476
alloggiamento del mulinello 909, 910
alloggiamento del ventilatore 382
alloggiamento della strumentazione 24
alloggio degli ufficiali 762, 763
alloggio del comandante 609
alloro 202
alluminio 682
alluminio, strato riflettente in 501
alone 9
alosa 220
Alpi 32
alpinista 901
alta pressione, area di 63
alta tensione 774
alta tensione, tester dell' 316
Altare 10
altare maggiore 737
altare secondario 737
altare, croce dell' 737
altare, pala dell' 737
alte frequenze, pick-up per 441
alternato 514
alternato: selezione di livello 3 514
alternatore 552, 566, 586, 646, 665, 677, 688
altezza del gradino 647
altezza del tuffo 829
altezza dell'onda 49
altezza delle nubi, proiettore per determinare l' 59
altezza di caduta dell'acqua 662
altezza, indice di regolazione dell' 304
altezza, regolazione micrometrica dell' 14, 15
altezza, scala dell' 485
alti, regolatore degli 497
altimetro 896, 898, 899
altimetro di riserva 626
altitudine 66
altitudini, scala delle 53
altocumulo 56, 62
altoparlante 496, 504, 505, 508, 513, 526, 594, 626, 766
altoparlante per alte frequenze 10
altoparlante per basse frequenze 10
altoparlante per medie frequenze 10
altoparlanti, bilanciamento degli 497
altopiano 7, 38, 45
altostrato 56, 62
alula 115
alveolo della presa 274
alveolo dentario 159
alzacristalli, manopola 554
alzare lo spinnaker 833
alzata 255, 290, 292, 293
alzatore destro 812
amanita muscaria 76
amanita virosa 76
amantiglio 602
amaranto 203
amarico 468
Amazzoni, Rio delle 31
ambiatore 857
ambiente 66
ambiente naturale 867
ambio 125
ambulanza 775, 778
ameba 94
America Centrale 28, 30
America Meridionale 28, 31, 50
America Settentrionale 28, 30, 50
America, Stati Uniti d' 742
Americhe 742
americio 684
Amery, Banchisa di 29
ametista 375
amido 85
ammainare lo spinnaker 833
ammasso globulare 9
amministrazione 394, 735
ammiraglia 870
ammiragliato britannico, ancora tipo 610
ammortizzatore 18, 417, 553, 876
ammortizzatore anteriore 577
ammortizzatore posteriore 575
amo 909, 911
amo con setale 911
amo, apertura dell' 911
ampere 702
ampiezza 690
ampiezza dei punti, selettore dell' 452
ampiezza della base 663
amplificazione, regolatore di 613
ampolla 95
ampolla della tuba di Falloppio 171
ananas 196
anatomia 150
anatomia di un astice 107
anatomia di un cavallo 125
anatomia di un persico 109
anatomia di un polpo 106
anatomia di un ragno femmina 103
anatomia di un serpente velenoso 112
anatomia di un uccello 116
anatomia di un'ape 99
anatomia di una chiocciola 104
anatomia di una conchiglia bivalve 105
anatomia di una farfalla femmina 97
anatomia di una rana maschio 110
anatomia di una spugna 95
anatomia di una stella marina 95
anatomia di una tartaruga 113
anatomia patologica, laboratorio di 781
anatra 120, 213
anatra, uovo di 213
ancia 444, 446
ancia doppia 446
ancia semplice 446
ancia, canna ad 444
anconeo 151
ancora 610, 697
ancora a fungo 610
ancora a scatto 302
ancora a vomere 610
ancora Danforth 610
ancora della nave 610
ancora galleggiante 610
ancora tipo ammiragliato britannico 610
ancoraggio 791
ancoraggio degli stralli 541
ancoraggio, sistema di 595
ancore, esempi di 610
ancorina 911
andata, tubazione di 259
andature 124
andature delle imbarcazioni a vela 833
Ande, Cordigliera delle 31
Andorra 743
Andromeda 12
anelli 376, 824, 825
anelli addominali 909
anelli collettori 688
anello 76, 249, 284, 382, 447, 453, 454, 522, 611, 659, 696, 699, 809, 811, 824, 900, 901
anello a fascia 376
anello a strappo 223
anello centrale esterno da 25 punti 918
anello con sigillo 376
anello d'accordatura 433
anello dei doppi 918
anello dei tripli 918
anello della camma 307
anello di ancoraggio 659
anello di arresto 483
anello di attacco 913
anello di bloccaggio 516
anello di chiusura 290
anello di congiunzione 911
anello di fidanzamento 376
anello di fondo 659
anello di regolazione 329
anello di regolazione della coppia di serraggio 306
anello di regolazione diottrica 692
anello di schermo 58
anello di sollevamento 610
anello di sospensione 382
anello di tenuta 268
anello di tenuta della guarnizione 268
anello di traino 776
anello diottrico 614
anello esterno 877
anello fermadisco 851
anello fermamulinello 909
anello guida della lenza 909, 910
anello interno 877
anello oculare 115
anello per le redini 854
anello studentesco 376
anello, componenti di un 376
anello, orecchini ad 374
anemometro 58, 59, 677, 898
anemometro di riserva 626
anestesia, stanza per l' 780
aneto 202
anfibi 110
anfibi, esempi di 111
anfiteatro romano 407
anfora, gonna ad 357
anglicanesimo 736
Angola 746
angolare 389
angoli, esempi di 704
angoli, lenzuolo con 280
angoli, misura degli 701
angoliera 279
angolo 426, 803, 842
angolo acuto 704
angolo concavo 704
angolo cucina 509
angolo della pista 878
angolo di elevazione, regolazione dell' 692
angolo ottuso 704
angolo retto 704
angolo, giudice d' 845
angolo, giudici d' 846
anguilla 219
anice 202
anice stellato 84
anidride carbonica 670
anidride carbonica di raffreddamento 670
anidride carbonica, assorbimento di 78
anidride solforosa, emissione di 70
Anik 487
anima 444, 753, 908
anima, canna ad 444
animali selvatici vaganti 545, 547
animali, negozio di 714
animelle 212
annaffiatoio 328
anno 729
anno, stagioni dell' 54
annodatura 349, 463
ano 95, 97, 103, 104, 105, 106, 107, 109, 113, 164, 169, 170
anodo 689
anta, pannello dell' 278
Antartide 28, 29
antefissa 403
antelice 173
antenna 17, 60, 96, 97, 98, 99, 107, 504, 505, 506, 551, 577, 600, 611, 624, 631, 758, 761, 771, 812
antenna a basso guadagno 18
antenna a frequenza ultraelevata (UHF) 18
antenna ad alta frequenza, cavo dell' 628
antenna ad alto guadagno 18
antenna ad alto guadagno in banda S 60
antenna comandata a distanza 40
antenna di captazione 585
antenna di casa 486
antenna di telecomando 60
antenna di telecomunicazione 761, 762
antenna di telemetria 60
antenna di trasmissione/ricezione 486
antenna emittente 486
antenna in banda S 60
antenna in banda X 40
antenna multifunzione 763
antenna parabolica 489, 493
antenna parabolica ricetrasmittente 486
antenna per telecomunicazioni 608, 609
antenna radar 40, 760, 763
antenna radio 604, 606, 608, 609, 652, 763, 873
antenna ricevente GPS 613
antenna telescopica 503
antenna UHF 60
antenna VHF 762
antenne per ricerca e soccorso 60
antenne, stregghia per le 98
antenne, terminali di collegamento delle 497
antennula 107
antera 80
antiallagamento, dispositivo 294
anticlinale 651
anticollisione, luce 624
Antigua e Barbuda 743
Antille, Isole delle 742
antilope 128
antimonio 682
antipasti 722
antipastiera 226
antisettico 777
antisfregamento, protezione 874
antiskating, controllo 500
antitrago 173
antivibrazione, impugnatura con sistema 331
anulare 173
aorta 162, 163
aorta addominale 160, 165
aorta ascendente 161
aorta discendente 161
aorta dorsale 99
aorta ventrale 109
aorta, arco dell' 160, 162
ape 98
ape operaia 99
ape operaia, morfologia di un' 98
ape regina 99
ape, anatomia di un' 99
apertura 105, 312, 346, 351, 893
apertura del diaframma, scala dell' 479
apertura dell'amo 911
apertura di diaframma, scala dell' 478
apertura di termoregolazione 60
apertura per il riempimento della chiusa 597
apertura per il riempimento e lo svuotamento della chiusa 597
apertura per le braccia 355
apertura, diaframma di 694
apertura, tasto per il valore di 479
apice 79, 104, 105, 159, 176, 374, 472
Apollo 19
apostrofo 473
apotecio 74
apparato del Golgi 74, 94
apparato digerente 164
apparato radicale 77, 86
apparato respiratorio 163
apparato urinario 165
apparecchi per il condizionamento dell'aria 261
apparecchiatura di rianimazione 775
apparecchio telefonico 489, 506
apparecchio telefonico a gettoni 507
appartamenti 886
appartiene a 703
appendere per asciugare 347
appendere senza strizzare 347
appendice dattilo 511
appendice vermiforme 164
applicatore a spugnetta 378
appoggiamano 399, 782
appoggiapiedi 312, 577, 783, 851
appoggiapiedi del guidatore 575, 576
appoggiapiedi del passeggero 575, 576
appoggiatura 435
appoggio 661
appoggio del mignolo 447
appoggio del pollice 446, 447
appoggio del polpaccio 889
appoggio della spalla 757
appoggio, barra d' 321
appoggio, filo d' 103
appoggio, guida di 304
appoggio, piano di 304, 632
appoggio, piastra d' 309
appoggio, piastra di 590, 756
appoggio, piede d' 461
appoggio, piede di 641
appoggio, punto d' 103
appontaggio a poppa, zona di 761
appontaggio, pista di 761
approccio, colpo d' 866
approssimativamente uguale a 703
apribottiglie 230, 905
apriscatole 230, 240, 905
aptero 75
Aquila 10, 12
aquila 119, 741
Arabia Saudita 746
Arabico, Mare 33
arabo 468
arachide 190
arachidi, olio di 209
aracnidi 96
aracnidi, esempi di 102
aracnoide 167
aragosta 218
Aral, Lago di 33
araldica 739
aramaico 468
arame 183
arancia 194
arancia, sezione di un' 82
arancio 400
aratro a vomere-versoio 641
arazzi, navetta per 461
arbitro 799, 801, 803, 805, 809, 810, 817, 818, 819, 827, 828, 830, 842, 843, 844, 845, 846, 847, 859, 860, 864, 879, 882, 883, 893
arbitro a cavallo 858
arbitro ausiliario 847, 860, 882
arbitro capo 795
arbitro centrale 846
arbitro della linea di porta 814
arbitro di campo 814
arbitro di percorso 838
arbitro laterale 846
arbitro, linea dell' 845
arborizzazione terminale 168
arca 738
arcata 407, 410
arcata dentale inferiore 174
arcata dentale superiore 174
archaeopteryx 93
archeognato 92
archetto 439, 700, 776, 910
archetto d'arcione 855
archetto, meccanismo di apertura dell' 910
archi 750
archi, esempi di 413, 541
archi, famiglia degli 437, 439
archibugio 752
architettura 394, 402
architettura, stili di 404
architrave 247, 256, 403, 405, 411
archivi 394, 769
archiviazione 532
archivio 509
archivio delle cartelle cliniche 781
archivio, scatola per 533
archivolto 411
arciere 859
arcipelago 38
arco 540, 704, 750, 855
arco a due cerniere 541
arco a ferro di cavallo 413
arco a tre cerniere 541
arco a tutto sesto 413
arco aortico 160, 161, 162
arco composto 859, 913
arco dentato di elevazione 756
arco diagonale 410
arco inflesso 413
arco insulare 49

INDICE DELLE VOCI ITALIANE

1078

ASTRONOMIA > 2-25; TERRA > 26-71; REGNO VEGETALE >72-89; REGNO ANIMALE > 90-143; ESSERE UMANO > 144-177; GENERI ALIMENTARI E CUCINA > 178-241; CASA > 242-295; FAI DA TE E GIARDINAGGIO > 296-333; ABBIGLIAMENTO > 334-371; ACCESSORI E ARTICOLI PERSONALI > 372-391; ARTE E ARCHITETTURA > 392-465; COMUNICAZIONI E BUROTICA > 466-535; TRASPORTI E VEICOLI > 536-643; ENERGIA > 644-677; SCIENZA > 678-705; SOCIETÀ > 706-785; SPORT E GIOCHI > 786-920

arco lanceolato 413
arco longitudinale 410
arco moderno 750
arco naturale 51
arco nudo 859
arco ogivale 413
arco palatoglosso 174
arco rampante 410, 411
arco reticolare 540
arco rialzato 413
arco ribassato policentrico 413
arco senza cerniere 541
arco trasversale 410
arco trilobato 413
arco Tudor 413
arco, saldatrice ad 318
arco, saldatura ad 318
arcobaleno 65
ardiglione 350, 911
area commerciale 713
area d'accettazione 764
area d'attesa 730
area degli atleti 871
area dei jack 488
area dei tre secondi 811
area del salto 890
area di alta pressione 63
area di arresto 890
area di atterraggio 790
area di bassa pressione 63
area di carico del combustibile nuovo 666
area di combattimento 843, 844, 845, 846
area di controllo delle telecamere 489
area di controllo luci/video 490
area di cronometraggio 891
area di decelerazione 891
area di esercizio 823
area di frenata 891
area di fuorigioco 864
area di gara 845, 846, 847
area di gioco 608, 918
area di lancio 788
area di lavaggio delle carrozze 589
area di lavorazione del greggio 652
area di meta 805, 806, 809
area di parcheggio 619
area di partenza 875
area di pericolo 846
area di porta 802, 814, 879
area di precipitazione 55
area di ricevimento 395
area di ricevimento delle merci 716
area di rientro dei giocatori espulsi 827
area di rifornimento 548
area di rigore 802
area di servizio 39, 489, 619
area di servizio destro 819
area di servizio sinistro 819
area di sicurezza 843, 844
area di smistamento 589
area di sosta 39
area di sosta dei veicoli 543
area operativa 10
area per campeggio e caravan 725
area per caravan 725
area per il ritiro dei bagagli 620
area per le attività interne 727
area per pic-nic 725
area registrata 501
area ricevitrice 589
aree di bersaglio 848
arena 407
areola 171
argani di perforazione 651
argani, sala degli 649
argano 417
Argentina 742
argento 683, 741
argine 538
argo 684
aria 565
aria calda 64, 675
aria calda ascendente 63
aria calda, deflettore dell' 256
aria calda, efflusso dell' 258
aria calda, uscita dell' 256
aria compressa, bombola ad 873
aria compressa, bombola di 765
aria compressa, serbatoio d' 586
aria fredda 64, 675
aria fredda discendente 63
aria, cappellotto dell' 320
aria, compressore d' 320
aria, compressore dell' 585, 586
aria, condizionamento dell' 261
aria, condotto dell' 259
aria, depuratore d' 261
aria, filtro dell' 261, 331, 586, 636
aria, flusso d' 398
aria, foro per l' 390
aria, griglia di uscita dell' 260
aria, inquinamento dell' 69
aria, misurazione della pressione dell' 59
aria, presa d' 575, 605, 631
aria, serbatoio d' 320
aria, temperatura dell' 55
aria, tipo di massa d' 55
aria, tubo flessibile per l' 398
aria, valvola dell' 320, 398
aria-aria, missile 759, 760
aria-terra, missile 759
Ariane IV 24
Ariele 5
Ariete 12
aringa 219
arma, parti dell' 849
armadietti degli studenti 735
armadietto 510
armadietto per cancelleria 510
armadio 278, 293, 724
armadio appendiabiti 279
armadio essiccatore 484
armadio frigorifero 720
armamento, leva d' 757
armatura 749
armatura di chiave 435
armatura di sostegno 899
armatura metallica 612
armatura protettiva del tronco 808
armature di base 463
Armenia 746
armeno 469
armi 748
armi al tempo dei Romani 748
armi da lancio 751
armi da taglio 751
armi dell'età della pietra 748
armi della scherma 849
armonica a bocca 432
arnia 100, 182
aromatiche, piante 202
arpa 440
arpe 437
arpeggio 435
arquata 901
arrampicata 900
arrampicata, parete artificiale di 900
arredamento per la casa 276
arresto 453
arresto della guida parallela 305
arresto, anello di 483
arresto, area di 890
arresto, bagno di 485
arresto, blocco d' 309
arresto, dente d' 460
arresto, dispositivo di 458
arresto, pulsante di 308, 696
arresto, ruota dentata d' 460
arresto, tasto di 495, 499, 508, 512
arresto, tavola di 864
arresto/cancellazione, tasto di 501
arricciaburro 229
arricciacapelli 381
arricciatura 359
arricciatura a cannoncino 283
arricciatura a pince 283
arricciature, esempi di 283
arridatoio 835
arrivo 852, 885, 887
arrivo del combustibile 259
arrivo della sciovia 886
arrivo, boe di 839
arrivo, giudice di 839
arrivo, parete di 830
arrivo, zona di 891
arrosto 215
arrotolato 214
arsenico 682
arte 394
arteria addominale dorsale 107
arteria ascellare 160
arteria brachiale 160
arteria carotide comune 160
arteria dell'arco del piede 160
arteria dorsale del piede 160
arteria femorale 160
arteria iliaca comune 160, 165
arteria iliaca interna 160, 161, 165
arteria mesenterica inferiore 165
arteria mesenterica superiore 160, 165
arteria polmonare 160, 162, 163
arteria renale 160, 165
arteria sternale 107
arteria succlavia 160
arteria tibiale anteriore 160
arteria ventrale 107
arterie 160
arti grafiche 420
arti plastiche, aula di 734
arti sceniche 427
arti toracici 107
articolazione 557
articolazione a perno 156
articolazione a sella 156
articolazione artrodiale 156
articolazione condiloidea 156
articolazione del nodello 124
articolazioni sinoviali, tipi di 156
articoli da cucina 716
articoli da regalo 717
articoli da regalo, negozio di 714
articoli di cancelleria 528
articoli di pelletteria 386
articoli per acconciatura 380
articoli per il bagno 717
articoli personali 374, 383
articoli sportivi, negozio di 715
articoli vari 534
articolo 471
articolo di spalla 471
Artide 28
artiglio 117, 121, 122, 143
arto anteriore 110, 143
arto inferiore 161
arto locomotore 103
arto locomotorio 97
arto posteriore 110, 143
arto superiore 161
artropleura 92
ascella 146, 148
ascella fogliare 79
ascensione retta 13
ascensione retta, cerchio graduato dell' 14, 15
ascensore 16, 417, 509, 650, 713, 724, 761
ascensore, cabina dell' 417
ascia 401
ascia levigata 748
asciugacapelli 382
asciugamano 379
asciugamano da bagno 379
asciugatoio per le manichette 764
asciugatrice 293
asciugatura 347
ascolto, postazioni di 733
Asia 28, 33, 50, 746
asino 128
asola 350, 905
asola per il picchetto 902, 903
asparago 185
aspirapolvere 289
aspirapolvere verticale 289
aspiratore 775
aspirazione 564, 565
aspirazione, tubo di 766
aspirina® 777
aspo 462
aspo abbattitore 643
assafetida 199
assale 895
assale anteriore 639
assalto, pugnale d' 751
asse 122, 300, 586
asse della bobina 910
asse di trasmissione del motore 237
asse orizzontale, regolazione micrometrica dell' 15
asse polare 17
asse portaelica 762
asse sterzante 633
assegni 729
assegni libretto degli 386
assicella 459
assicuratore 900
assistente alla regia 490
assistente sociale, ufficio dell' 779
assistenti degli avvocati 728
asso 914
assone 168
assorbimento attraverso la superficie terrestre 68
assorbimento attraverso le nuvole 68
assorbimento di acqua e sali minerali 78
assorbimento di anidride carbonica 78
asta 248, 268, 274, 445, 685, 695, 739, 792, 838, 859, 860, 863, 867, 880, 892, 912
asta d'accordo 444
asta del filo 457
asta del galleggiante 263
asta del martelletto 443
asta del meccanismo a scatto 470
asta del pendolo 436, 697
asta del registro 445
asta di comando per l'orientamento delle lamelle 285
asta di guida 456
asta di perforazione 651
asta di sostegno 594
asta di sparo 756
asta filettata 248
asta mobile 700
asta motrice quadra 651
asta telescopica 920
astata 79
astato 683
astenosfera 42
asterisco 473
asteroidi, fascia degli 5
astice 107, 218
astice, anatomia di un 107
astice, morfologia di un 107
asticella 461, 792
asticella di testa 857
astigmatismo 691
astista 792
astragalo 153, 155, 405, 753
astronautica 18
astronomia 4
astuccio 345, 377
astuccio delle manette 770
astuccio per i guanti di lattice 770
astuccio per occhiali 387
Atacama, Deserto di 31
atlante 111, 122, 126, 131, 153, 157
Atlante, Monti dell' 34
Atlantico, merluzzo dell' 221
Atlantico, Oceano 28, 29, 32, 34
Atlantico, salmone dell' 221
atleta 791
atleti, area degli 871
atletica leggera 790
atletica, pista di 788
atmosfera 66, 70
atmosfera terrestre, profilo dell' 53
atollo 51
atomi 680
atomizzatore 328
atomo 680
atrio 406, 582, 713, 717, 724, 728, 730
atrio destro 161, 162
atrio sinistro 161, 162
attaccante 803
attaccante centrale 812
attaccante destro 807
attaccante di canestro 809
attaccante sinistro 807, 812
attaccapanni a muro 510
attaccapanni a rastrelliera 510
attaccapanni a stelo 510
attacco 274, 275, 385, 807, 840, 887, 891, 892, 894
attacco a baionetta 275, 478
attacco a spina 275
attacco a vite 275
attacco anteriore 840
attacco degli attrezzi, snodo per l' 640
attacco del manubrio 579
attacco del tubo dell'aria 320
attacco del tubo di alimentazione dell'acqua 328, 329
attacco del tubo di scarico 256
attacco dell'obiettivo 477
attacco della barra di traino 641
attacco della campana 446
attacco di sicurezza 20, 888, 889
attacco girevole 793
attacco morbido 887
attacco per attrezzi 20
attacco posteriore 840
attacco, leva di apertura dell' 889
atterraggio 891
atterraggio, faro di 631
atterraggio, finestrino di 631
atterraggio, modulo di 18
atterraggio, motore di 18
atterraggio, pista di 891
atterraggio, zona di 891
attesa, area d' 730
attinidi 684
attinio 684
attività interne, area per le 727
attizzatoio 257
attore 428
attori, ingresso degli 402
attori, sedie degli 428
attraversamento pedonale 545, 547
attrazione 687
attrezzatura 396, 421, 422, 423, 790, 900
attrezzatura elettrica 316
attrezzatura terminale 911
attrezzatura, magazzino per l' 764
attrezzatura, ripostiglio per l' 734
attrezzature da campeggio 905
attrezzature di terra 622
attrezzature per il pronto soccorso 775
attrezzature sportive 788
attrezzature tecniche, scomparto delle 489
attrezzature, esempi di 601
attrezzi 823
attrezzi da muratore 315
attrezzi di brasatura 318
attrezzi di lancio 793
attrezzi di saldatura 318
attrezzi di serraggio 310
attrezzi domestici 295
attrezzi ginnici 850
attrezzi idraulici 314
attrezzi per annaffiare 328
attrezzi per chiodare 301
attrezzi per piccoli lavori di giardinaggio 325
attrezzi per potare e tagliare 330
attrezzi per sagomare 308
attrezzi per seminare e piantare 324
attrezzi per smuovere la terra 326
attrezzi per trapanare 306
attrezzi, cassetta degli 313
attrezzi, kit di 580
attrezzista 429
attrezzo multiuso 851
attrice 429
audio, cabina di controllo 489, 490
audio, controllo del campo 497
audio, selettore della modalità 497
audio, selettore di controllo 491
audio, sistema di registrazione 429
audio, spie della modalità 497
audiofrequenze, generatore di 488
audioguida 394
auditorium 394, 718, 732
augnatura elettrica, sega per 304
augnatura manuale, sega per 303
augnatura, cassetta ad 303
aula 727, 734, 735
aula di arti plastiche 734
aula di informatica 734
aula di musica 734
aula di scienze 734
aula di tribunale 728
aula per studenti con difficoltà d'apprendimento 734
aumento di tensione 646, 662, 665
auricolare 503, 506
auricolari 872
aurora polare 53
Australia 28, 50, 747
Australia, lingue aborigene dell' 469
Austria 744
auto da formula 1 873
auto da formula 3000 873
auto da formula Indy 873
auto da rally 873
auto-reverse, tasto dell' 504
autoarticolati, esempi di 572
autoarticolato 570
autobotte 573
autobotte di rifornimento del carburante 622
autobotte per il rifornimento dell'acqua potabile 622
autobus 568, 713
autobus a due piani 569
autobus articolato 569
autobus urbano 568
autobus, fermata dell' 712
autobus, stazione degli 710
autocaravan 567
autocarro a cassone ribaltabile 639
autocarro a pianale 571
autocarro per il trasporto dei tronchi 572
autocarro per trucioli 572
autocisterna 572
autoclave 780
autofocus, interruttore dell' 483
autogrù 573, 634
autogruista, cabina dell' 634
autoguida, sistema di 759
autolavaggio 548
automezzo con braccio mobile 622
automezzo del catering 623
automezzo per l'assistenza tecnica 622
automobile 549
automobile elettrica 563
automobile ibrida 563
automobilismo 872
automotrice 585
autopompa 766
autoradio 556
autoreggente, calza 365
autorespiratore 765
autoscala 766
autoscatto, spia luminosa dell' 476
autostarter 857
autostrada 39, 539, 709
autostrada, numero di 39
autotrofi, organismi 67
autoveicoli industriali 570
autovetture, ponte per le 608
autunno 54
autunno, equinozio d' 54
avambraccio 130, 147, 149
avambraccio, protezione per l' 808
avampiede 840
avanzamento della carta, tasto d' 731
avanzamento rapido, tasto di 495, 499, 504, 508
avena 85, 203
avena, farina di 204
avena: pannocchia 85
avenue 39, 711
aviogetto a lungo raggio 624
aviorimessa 619
avocado 188
avvertenze, targhetta delle 306
avviamento, manovella di 331
avviamento, motorino d' 327, 332
avvio, tasto di 508, 512
avvisatore acustico 586, 591
avvisatore acustico a tromba 570
avvitatore pneumatico 873
avvocati dell'accusa, banco degli 728
avvocati difensori, banco degli 728
avvocati, assistenti degli 728
avvolgimento dell'indotto 688
avvolgimento induttore 688
avvolgimento, bobina di 499
avvolgimento, manovella d' 313
avvolgimento, meccanismo di 285
avvolgitore della bobina 452
avvoltoio 119
axel 881
aymara 469
Azerbaigian 746
azienda 525
azienda commerciale 525

ASTRONOMIA > 2-25; **TERRA** > 26-71; **REGNO VEGETALE** >72-89; **REGNO ANIMALE** > 90-143; **ESSERE UMANO** > 144-177; **GENERI ALIMENTARI E CUCINA** > 178-241; **CASA** > 242-295; **FAI DA TE E GIARDINAGGIO** > 296-333; **ABBIGLIAMENTO** > 334-371; **ACCESSORI E ARTICOLI PERSONALI** > 372-391; **ARTE E ARCHITETTURA** > 392-465; **COMUNICAZIONI E BUROTICA** > 466-535; **TRASPORTI E VEICOLI** > 536-643; **ENERGIA** > 644-677; **SCIENZA** > 678-705; **SOCIETÀ** > 706-785; **SPORT E GIOCHI** > 786-920

1079

azione del vento 67
azoto 683
azoto liquido, serbatoio di 694
azzeramento, pulsante di 696, 700
azzeramento, tasto di 495, 512
azzurro 741

B

babbuino 139
baby-doll 364
bacca 83
bacca di ginepro 198
baccello 84
bacche 192
bacchetta 439
bacchetta di metallo 449
bacchetta per il passo d'ordito 461
bacchetta telescopica 864
bacchette 449
bacheca 535, 734
bachelite, involucro esterno di 757
bacinella di raccolta della condensa 261
bacinella raccogligocce 290
bacinella raccogligrasso 239
bacino 121, 138, 141, 142, 596, 597, 657, 658, 660, 661, 662, 664, 838
bacino a monte 657
bacino a valle 657, 658, 661
bacino di carenaggio 596
bacino per competizioni 788
bacino, porta del 596
backgammon 915
backspace 515
bacon americano 216
bacon canadese 216
badile 326
badile pieghevole 906
Baffin, Isola di 30
bagagli 388
bagagli, deposito 582
bagagli, nastro trasportatore dei 623
bagagli, scompartimento 585
bagagliai 605
bagagliaio 568, 625, 631
bagaglio a mano 388
bagher 812
bagni di sviluppo 485
bagno degli ufficiali 764
bagno degli uomini 427, 509
bagno dei vigili del fuoco 764
bagno del personale 768
bagno delle donne 427, 509
bagno di arresto 485
bagno di fissaggio 485
bagno di sviluppo 485
bagno, costume da 371
bagno, lucernario del 251
bagno, slip da 371
bagno, stanza da 724
bagno, vasca da 264
bagnomaria, pentola per cucinare a 235
bagnoschiuma 379
baguette 204
baguette, taglio a 375
Bahama 742
Bahrein 746
baia 7, 38
Baia di Hudson 30
Baikal, Lago 33
Bailey 542
baionetta a ghiera 751
baionetta a tappo 751
baionetta fissa ripiegabile 751
baionetta, attacco a 275
baita di montagna 886
balalaica 433
balaustra 250, 251, 412, 417
balaustra della comunione 737
balaustre 878
balaustro 255
balconata 738
balconcino, reggiseno a 367
balcone 251, 676
Balena 10, 12
balena 137
balena bianca 137
baleniera 601
balenottera 137
balestra 750
ballatoi 430
ballatoio 614
balle di fieno 875
ballerina 343
ballerino 220
ballo, sala da 609
balsamo per capelli 379
Baltico, Mar 32
balze increspate 337
balze, gonna a 357
bambara 468
bambini 545, 547
bambini, vestiti per 369
bambino, cranio di 158
banana 196
banana plantain 196
banca 710, 715, 730, 915
banca di emissione, iniziali della 729
banchina 596
banchina di scarico 395, 719
banchina di scarico delle merci 715, 724
banchina laterale 538
banchine di scarico delle merci 716
Banchisa di Amery 29
Banchisa di Filchner 29
Banchisa di Ross 29
banco 734
banco da scultore, vite di 401
banco degli avvocati dell'accusa 728
banco degli avvocati difensori 728
banco dei formaggi 181
banco dei giudici 728
banco dei testimoni 728
banco del self-service 722
banco del sorvegliante 732
banco dell'imputato 728
banco della carne fresca 180
banco della carne self-service 180
banco della giuria 728
banco della reception 730
banco delle informazioni 620, 715, 719, 730, 733, 769, 779
banco di registrazione 620
banco di sabbia 49
banco per il prestito dei libri 733
banco per la prenotazione degli hotel 620
banco per la restituzione dei libri 733
banco, sega da 305
bancomat, sportello 715, 730
bancone 722
bancone del bar 720
banconota 915
banconota: dritto 729
banconota: rovescio 729
banconote, emissione di 730
banconote, scomparto per 386
banda 416, 500, 739
banda di identificazione tecnica 501
banda magnetica 729
banda nuvolosa a spirale 63
banda olografica 729
banda, selettore di 498
banda, tasto di selezione della 497
bande di frequenza 498
bande verticali, porta a 416
bandella di rinforzo 389
banderuola 56, 58, 59, 677
bandiera 890
bandiera a scacchi 872
bandiera con Schwenkel 739
bandiera dell'Unione Europea 729
bandiera quadrata 739
bandiera rettangolare 739
bandiera rimovibile 867
bandiera segnavento 893
bandiera, parti della 739
bandiera, tipi di 739
bandiere 742
bandierina 804
bandierina centrale 802
bandierina del calcio d'angolo 801, 803
Bangladesh 747
banjo 432
bar 431, 710, 714, 719, 720
bar, bancone del 720
bar, mobile 279
bar, sgabello da 720
barattoli 222
barba 85, 115
barba, pennello da 383
barbabietola 189
barbacane 408
Barbados 743
barbaforte 189
barbazzale 854
barbazzale, gancio del 854
barbetta 56, 85, 127
barbone 130
barbozza 749
barca a chiglia 835
barca a vela 834
barcana 52
barche, esempi di 604
barchetta, scollatura a 363
bardana 189
barella 775
barella spinale, ripostiglio per la 775
barelle, deposito delle 778
Barents, Mar di 32
bariletto 696
bario 682
barista 720
barografo 59
barometro a mercurio 59
barra 127, 285, 676, 915
barra collettrice 658
barra collettrice sotto tensione 272
barra d'appoggio 321
barra d'invergatura 461
barra dei licci 461
barra dei martelletti 442
barra del martelletto 443
barra del premistoffa 453
barra del timone 834
barra dell'ago 453
barra dello smorzatore 443
barra di comando 626, 631
barra di controllo 670, 671, 897
barra di manovra 643
barra di partenza 830
barra di percussione 767
barra di pressione 442
barra di stabilizzazione 633
barra di traino 567, 622
barra di traino, attacco della 641
barra di trazione 840
barra distanziatrice 568
barra falciante 642, 643
barra inferiore 285
barra obliqua 473
barra per i dorsali 851
barra per i pettorali 851
barra per i tricipiti 851
barra spaziatrice 514, 528
barretta 385
barretta di combustibile 667
barriera 712
barriera di pneumatici 872
barriere 852
basamento 43, 305, 412, 701, 713, 825, 842
basamento del telescopio 17
basamento imbottito 811
basamento, livella del 701
baschina, gonna con 357
basco 341
base 224, 234, 236, 239, 240, 256, 268, 270, 273, 286, 307, 308, 381, 389, 405, 424, 425, 432, 448, 500, 516, 517, 531, 591, 676, 685, 693, 698, 739, 767, 791, 826
base del bulbo 78
base del tergale 276
base dell'intelaiatura 249
base della lampada 614
base di legno duro 899
base di sostegno 278
base di supporto 613
base fissa 312
base girevole 312
base inferiore 58
base, ampiezza della 663
base, piastra di 43, 304, 500
baseball 794
baseball, stadio di 788
basilico 202
basilosauro 93
Bass, Stretto di 29
bassa pressione, area di 63
bassa tensione, linea di distribuzione a 273
basse frequenze, pick-up per 441
bassi, bottoniera dei 432
bassi, pannello di assorbimento dei 490
bassi, ponticello dei 442
bassi, registro dei 432
bassi, regolatore dei 497
basso carico, vite di regolazione a 273
basso, chiave di 434
bastione 409
bastoncello 177
bastoncino di carbone (catodo) 689
bastone 284, 391, 800, 801, 846, 879
bastone con manico anatomico 782
bastone da passeggio 391, 782
bastone da tenda 284
bastone del giocatore 880
bastone estendibile 770
bastone inglese 782
bastone liscio 284
bastone scanalato 284
bastone, pomolo del 880
bastoni da tenda 284
battello a vapore a ruote laterali 599
battente 416, 587, 739
battente, cassa 460
batteria 302, 306, 448, 482, 552, 562, 563, 586, 673, 687, 759
batteria ausiliaria 563
batteria da cucina 722
batteria di eliostati 674
batteria elettronica 451
batteria ricaricabile 496
batteria, contenitore della 562
batterie 60
batterie di trazione 563
battiscopa 253
battistrada 561
battistrada, scolpitura del 560, 561, 640
battitoia 433, 448
battitore 795, 796, 798, 799, 816, 819, 821
battuta, zona di 797
baule 389
bauletto 577
bavaglino 368
bazooka 757
beach volley 813
Beaufort, Mar di 30
beauty-case 389
beccaccia di mare 118
beccatello 408
beccheggio 630
becchi lunghi, pinza a 317
becchi, esempi di 117
becco 106, 115, 901
becco Bunsen 685
becco corneo 113
beccuccio 240, 241, 295, 380
beccuccio spruzzatore 384
beccuccio, vaschetta con 237
becher 685
becquerel 702
begonia 80
Belgio 743
Belize 742
belle arti 394
bellezza, prodotti di 717
belvedere, vela di straglio di 603
bemolle 435
benda elastica 777
benda perioplica 127
bendaggio 843
Bengala, Golfo del 33
Benin 745
benna di caricamento 650
benzina auto 656
benzina avio 656
benzina leggera 656
benzina pesante 656
bequadro 435
berbero 468
berchelio 684
bergamotto 194
bergère 276
berillio 682
Bering, Mar di 28
Bering, Stretto di 30
berlina 549
berma 660
bermuda 358
berretto 340, 770, 892
berretto con pompon 341
berretto da cacciatore 340
berretto impermeabile 341
bersaglio 40, 41, 859, 861, 893, 918
bersaglio, aree di 848
bersaglio, radar di acquisizione del 762
berta 363
bertesca 408
bestiame, carro 588
betoniera 573
betulla 88
beuta di Erlenmeyer 685
Bhutan 747
biancheria da letto 280
biancheria da notte 364
biancheria da notte per donna 716
biancheria da notte per uomo 717
biancheria intima 351, 366
biancheria intima per donna 716
biancheria intima per uomo 716
biancheria intima, negozio di 714
biancheria per la casa 716
biancheria, loale per la 724
biancheria, ripostiglio per la 584
bianchi 916
bianco 690, 915
biathleta 893
biathlon 893
bibita, bicchiere da 225
bibita, cucchiaio da 228
bibite 180
bibite, distributore automatico di 723
bibite, distributore di 779
biblioteca 395, 711, 726, 732, 734
bibliotecario, ufficio del 732
bicchiere 236, 906
bicchiere da acqua 225
bicchiere da bibita 225
bicchiere da Bordeaux 225
bicchiere da Borgogna 225
bicchiere da brandy 225
bicchiere da porto 225
bicchiere da vino alsaziano 225
bicchiere da vino bianco 225
bicchieri 723
bicchieri, macchina per lavare i 723
bicchierino da liquore 225
bicicletta 578
bicicletta da corsa 581, 870
bicicletta da cross-country 870
bicicletta da downhill 870
bicicletta da inseguimento 871
bicicletta da turismo 581
bicicletta olandese 581
bicicletta, componenti di una 578
biciclette, esempi di 581
biciclette, parcheggio per le 735
bicipite brachiale 150
bicipite femorale 151
bicipiti femorali, rullo per i 851
bicorno 339
bidè 264
bidello, ufficio del 735
bidone carrellato per il riciclaggio del vetro 71
bidone carrellato per il riciclaggio dell'alluminio 71
bidone carrellato per il riciclaggio della carta 71
bidone dei rifiuti 295
biella 564, 566
Bielorussia 744
bietola da coste 185
bietta 439
biglia battente 862, 863
biglia battente dell'avversario 862, 863
biglia bianca battente 863
biglia blu 863
biglia gialla 863
biglia marrone 863
biglia nera 863
biglia rosa 863
biglia rossa 862, 863
biglia verde 863
biglie da colpire 862
biglie rosse 863
biglietteria 394, 427, 620, 719
biglietteria automatica 427
biglietti, distributore automatico di 593
biglietti, vendita dei 592
bigodino 380
Bilancia 11
bilancia 430
bilancia a molla 699
bilancia a sospensione inferiore 698
bilancia da analisi 699
bilancia da cucina 231
bilancia di precisione 698
bilancia elettronica 699
bilancia pesapersone 699
bilanciamento 441
bilanciamento degli altoparlanti 497
bilanciere 443, 566, 599, 850, 851
bilanciere, braccio del 599
bilanciere, piroga a un 599
bilanciere, placchetta a 444
biliardo 862
biliardo inglese 863
biliardo per carambola 862
bimah 738
binari del carrello 428
binario 284, 287, 399, 582, 592, 595, 709
binario da tenda 284
binario di guida 16
binario di primo smistamento 589
binario di raccordo 583
binario di rampa 589
binario di secondo smistamento 589
binario di uscita 589
binario doppio 284
binario ferroviario 649, 710
binario morto 583
binario per le locomotive 589
binario semplice 284
binario, faretto da 287
binario, numero del 582
bindella ventilata 860, 912
binocolo da teatro 385
binocolo prismatico 692
biologia 702
biosfera 66
biosfera, struttura della 66
bipiede 755, 756
biplano 628
bipolare, interruttore 272
birilli, disposizione dei 865
birilli, esempi di 865
birillo 865
birillo a candela 865
birillo americano 865
birillo canadese 865
birillo centrale 865
birillo grosso 865
birillo piccolo 865
birmano 468
birra 180
birra, boccale da 225
bisarca 572
biscaglina 321
biscroma 435
biscroma, pausa di 435
bismuto 682
bisnonna 784
bisnonni 784
bisnonno 784
bisonte 128
bistecca 214
bistecca, coltello da 228
bitta 607
bitume 656
blastodisco 117
blatta orientale 101
blazer 358
bloc-notes 530
bloccacorda 284
bloccaggio della base 312
bloccaggio, dispositivo di 289, 424
bloccaggio, ghiera di 302, 756
bloccaggio, leva di 312
bloccaggio, manicotto di 482
bloccaggio, manopola di 304
bloccaggio, pulsante di 288
bloccaggio, viti di 700
blocchetto 448, 882

INDICE DELLE VOCI ITALIANE

1080

ASTRONOMIA > 2-25; **TERRA** > 26-71; **REGNO VEGETALE** >72-89; **REGNO ANIMALE** > 90-143; **ESSERE UMANO** > 144-177; **GENERI ALIMENTARI E CUCINA** > 178-241; **CASA** > 242-295; **FAI DA TE E GIARDINAGGIO** > 296-333; **ABBIGLIAMENTO** > 334-371; **ACCESSORI E ARTICOLI PERSONALI** > 372-391; **ARTE E ARCHITETTURA** > 392-465; **COMUNICAZIONI E BUROTICA** > 466-535; **TRASPORTI E VEICOLI** > 536-643; **ENERGIA** > 644-677; **SCIENZA** > 678-705; **SOCIETÀ** > 706-785; **SPORT E GIOCHI** > 786-920

blocchetto di accensione 556
blocchetto di avviamento 576
blocchetto per stenografia 531
blocco 444, 632, 791
blocco d'arresto 309
blocco da incastro 900, 901
blocco del movimento orizzontale 482
blocco del movimento verticale 482
blocco del ponticello 441
blocco della colonna 482
blocco della culatta 912
blocco della piattaforma 482
blocco delle maiuscole 514
blocco di ancoraggio dei cavi 540
blocco di calcestruzzo 298
blocco di chiusura 700
blocco di partenza 791, 830
blocco di tensione 452, 453, 457
blocco motore 236, 237, 240, 288, 384
blocco numerico 515
blocco operatorio 780
blocco, dispositivo di 303, 304, 321
blocco, tasto di 505
blu 400, 690
blu-verde 400
blu-viola 400
boa 114, 833
boa a piano focale elevato 615
boa a pilastro cilindrico 614
boa cilindrica 615
boa conica 615
boa di ricognizione meteorologica 54
boa di salvataggio 611
bob 884, 885
bob a due 884
bob a quattro 884
bobina 452, 453, 495, 688, 848, 909, 910
bobina di avvolgimento 499
bobina mobile 488
bobina, asse della 910
bobina, meccanismo di rilascio della 910
bocca 95, 104, 105, 107, 110, 136, 148, 174, 301, 425, 444, 753, 754, 756, 860, 912
bocca da fuoco 753, 756
bocca di carico 288
bocca di erogazione 268, 270
bocca laterale 261
boccaglio 783, 841
boccale da birra 225
boccaporto 23
bocce 864
bocchetta 237, 240, 248, 249
bocchetta 248
bocchetta a soffitto 258
bocchetta del serbatoio 332
bocchetta dello scarico della polvere 304
bocchetta di estrazione 258
bocchetta di immissione 258
bocchetta di ventilazione 556
bocchetta per fessure 289
bocchetta per tappezzeria 289
bocchette 232
bocchette, tipi di 258
bocchettone di riempimento 553
bocchino 390, 446, 447, 451
boccia 864, 865
body 359, 366, 371
boe di arrivo 839
boe di partenza 838
boe di percorso 838
boe, sistema di segnalamento marittimo per mezzo di 616
bohrio 683
bokken 846
bolero 358
bolina larga, di 833
bolina molto stretta, di 833
bolina stretta, di 833
bolina, di 833
Bolivia 742
bolla, livella a 313
bolle d'aria 531
bollitore 240
bollo del monopolio 390
boma 602, 834, 836
bomba a mano 757
bomba vulcanica 44
bombetta 340
bombo 101
bombola 767, 903
bombola ad aria compressa 841, 873
bombola d'acetilene 319
bombola d'ossigeno 319
bombola del gas 314, 319
bombola di aria compressa 765
bombola di gas medicale 780
bombola di gas propano 567
bombola di ossigeno portatile 775
bombola di ossigeno portatile, supporto per la 775
bomboletta 611
bompresso 602
bompresso, briglia del 602
bongos 449
booster, paracadute del 22
Boote 13

bordame 836
Bordeaux, bicchiere da 225
bordeggio 833
bordo 281, 793, 887, 919
bordo a coste 354, 369
bordo del cerchio 560
bordo del piano di cottura 290
bordo del risvolto 362
bordo della scarpetta 889
bordo di attacco 625, 897, 898
bordo di fuga 897, 898
bordo di porpora 336
bordo di rifinitura 389
bordo di uscita 624
bordo elastico 351
bordo interno 901
bordo superiore 815
bordo, radar di 40
bordone 432
bordoniera 448
bordura 244, 322
Borgogna, bicchiere da 225
boro 682
borra 912
borraccia 906
borragine 202
borsa a manicotto 388
borsa a soffietto 388
borsa a telaio rigido 388
borsa a tracolla 388
borsa da postino 388
borsa da viaggio 388
borsa del tabacco 390
borsa della spesa 388
borsa laterale 577
borsa melaria 99
borse 387
borsellino 387
borsello 388
borsetta 445
borsetta per gli attrezzi 859
borsone da viaggio 388
boschi, rana dei 111
bosco 39
Bosnia ed Erzegovina 744
bossolo 860, 912
bossolo di plastica 912
Botnia, Golfo di 32
botola 407, 430
Botswana 746
botte igienica semovente 622
bottega 406
bottiglia 379, 685, 906
bottiglia da tavola 225
bottiglia dell'acqua 579
bottiglia di vetro 223
bottone 274, 349, 354, 432, 439, 753, 849
bottone a gambo 453
bottone a pressione 346, 353
bottone automatico 453
bottone della tracolla 441
bottone di marcia indietro 452
bottone di regolazione 443
bottoni forati 453
bottoniera dei bassi 432
boubou 339
boulevard 39, 711
bowling 714, 865
bowling su prato 864
bowling, pista da 865
box 872, 874
box doccia 264
boxer 351
bozzello 634, 835
bracci 445
braccia, apertura per le 355
bracciale 282, 859
bracciale a cordoncino 282
bracciale con ciondoli 376
bracciale con piastrina 376
bracciale pneumatico 777
bracciale tubolare 376
bracciali 376
braccio 95, 124, 139, 147, 149, 286, 329, 382, 433, 452, 456, 500, 521, 610, 634, 651, 661, 663, 676, 693, 783
braccio d'attacco dell'occhione 756
braccio del bilanciere 599
braccio del disco 641
braccio del pennone di controbelvedere 603
braccio del tergicristallo 557
braccio del tremolo 441
braccio della forca 632
braccio della pala caricatrice 637
braccio della sospensione 553
braccio della spirale 9
braccio di posizionamento 638
braccio di scavo 633
braccio di sollevamento 573, 637, 638
braccio di sollevamento dell'albero oscillante 640
braccio di sospensione 292, 783
braccio di trazione 640
braccio distanziatore 321
braccio flessibile 859
braccio inferiore 750
braccio manipolatore telecomandato 22

braccio metallico 329
braccio retraibile 18
braccio spruzzante 294
braccio superiore 750
braccio telecomandato 21
braccio telescopico 634, 766
braccio telescopico di disaccoppiamento 587
braccio, levetta per il sollevamento del 500
braccio, supporto del 500
braccio, tirante del 634
bracciolo 276, 281, 554, 555, 783
bracciolo, sostegno del 276
brache 338
brachiale 150
brachiopodo 92
brachioradiale 150, 151
braciere 412
braciola 214, 215
branca 310, 454
branca del corpo morto 615
branchia 106
branchie 105, 109
branchie esterne 111
branda 904
brandina smontabile 904
brandy, bicchiere da 225
brano, numero del 501
brano, tasti di ricerca del 501
branzino 220
Brasile 742
Brasile, noce del 193
brattea 84
breccia 917
bretella 897
bretella abbottonabile 369
bretella di raccordo 539
bretella di uscita 621
bretella di uscita della pista ad alta velocità 618
bretella regolabile 368
bretelle 350
bretone 469
bricco del latte 226
bricolage, negozio di 714
brick 223
brick a tappo 223
brie 211
brigantino 601
brigantino goletta 601
briglia 854
briglia del bompresso 602
briglia inferiore 540
briglia superiore 540
brillamento 6
brillantante, serbatoio per il 294
brillante, taglio a 375
brina 65
briolette, taglio a 375
broccolo 187
brochure, espositore di 730
brodo, cucchiaio da 228
bromo 683
bromografo 484
bronchiolo terminale 163
bronco lobare 163
bronco principale 163
browser 524
bruciatore 259, 290, 422, 899, 903
bruciatore a corona 234
bruciatore del gas 267
bruciatore per combustibile liquido 259
bruciatore, paravento del 899
bruciatore, telaio del 903
bruciatore, valvola del 899
bruco 97
brugola, chiave a 314
bruma umida 57
Brunei 747
brunitoio 422
Bruxelles, cavolini di 186
buca 862, 866, 867
buca centrale 862
buca inferiore 862
buca par 3 866
buca par 4 866
buca par 5 867
buca superiore 862
buccia 81, 82, 83
buccino 217
buche 866
buco nero 8
Budda 736
buddismo 736
bue 129
bufalo 128
buffet 720
bugna 836
bulbillo 78
bulbo 185, 274, 275, 607, 609, 664
bulbo d'alcool 695
bulbo del pelo 172
bulbo di mercurio 695
bulbo olfattivo 175
bulbo olfattorio 109
bulbo, base del 78
bulbo, fusto del 78
bulbo, sezione di un 78

Bulgaria 744
bulgaro 469
Bulino 11
bulino 401, 421
bulldog 130
bulldozer 636, 647
bulletta 301
bullone 310, 311, 312, 559
bullone a espansione 302
bullone della ganascia 590
bullone di accoppiamento 659
bullone di spallamento 311
bullone zigrinato 320
bulloni 311
bunker di sabbia 866, 867
Bunsen, becco 685
Buona Speranza, Capo di 34
bure 641
buretta con rubinetto a destra 685
Burkina Faso 745
burotica 468
burotica e forniture per l'ufficio 509
burriera 226
burro 210
burro, coltello da 228
burro, scomparto per il 291
Burundi 745
bus 513, 522
Bussola 11
bussola 898
bussola a liquido 612
bussola magnetica 907
bussole, set di 311
bussolotto 915
busta imbottita 531
busta portadocumenti 387
bustina 340
bustina di fiammiferi 391
bustina di tè 208
bustine trasparenti 386
buttafuoco 752
button-down, collo 349

C

C, morsetto a 312
cabina 608, 636, 637, 638, 639, 640, 643, 731
cabina armadio 251
cabina del fuoco primario 16
cabina del fuoco secondario 16
cabina del gruista 634
cabina dell'ascensore 417
cabina dell'autogruista 634
cabina della torre di controllo 618
cabina di classe turistica 625
cabina di controllo audio 489, 490
cabina di controllo della parigina 589
cabina di guida 585, 586
cabina di manovra 583
cabina di osservazione del fuoco primario 17
cabina di pilotaggio 22, 607, 624, 626, 631, 898
cabina di pilotaggio, calotta della 898
cabina di prima classe 624
cabina di proiezione 427
cabina di regia 431, 488, 489, 490, 491, 718
cabina passeggeri 631
cabina per l'interpretazione simultanea 718
cabina, guida della 417
cabina, manopola per l'aerazione della 898
cabina, pavimento della 417
cabina, soffitto della 417
cabine di regia 490
cabochon, taglio a 375
cabriolet 276
cacao 208
cacatua 118
caccia 912
cacciapietre 585, 586
cacciavite 302, 905
cacciavite automatico 302
cacciavite con batteria incorporata 302
cacciavite con punta a croce 905
cachi 197
caditoia 408
cadmio 683
caducifoglie, foresta di 66
caduta di poppa 836
caduta di prua 836
caduta massi 545, 547
caffè 208, 710, 715, 735
caffè, chicchi tostati di 208
caffè, chicchi verdi di 208
caffè, cucchiaino da 228
caffè, macchine da 241
caffè, macchine per il 723
caffè, tazza alta da 226
caffè, tazzina da 226
caffettano 339
caffettiera 905
caffettiera a filtro 241
caffettiera a infusione 241
caffettiera a pistone 241
caffettiera napoletana 241

caffettiera per espresso 241
caimano 114
calabrone 101
calamaro 217
calamita 454, 534
calamo 460
calamo vegetale 470
calaza 117
calcagno 126, 153, 155, 351
calcagno, rinforzo del 370
calcagno, rinforzo esterno del 342
calcagno, rinforzo interno del 342
calcare 140, 141
calcatoio 752
calcestruzzo 298
calcestruzzo precompresso 298
calcestruzzo, blocco di 298
calciatore 802
calcio 682, 755, 802, 860, 861, 863, 912
calcio balilla 920
calcio, campo di 788
calciolo 754, 755, 912
calcola 460
calcola di disinnesto 460
calcola, corda della 460
calcolatrice 386
calcolatrice da tavolo 529
calcolatrice scientifica 529
calcolatrice tascabile 529
calcolo, ghiera di 479
caldaia 259, 448, 674
calendario a fogli staccabili 530
calendario da tavolo 530
calibratura, ruota di 333
calibro 423
calibro a corsoio con nonio 700
calice 80, 83, 84, 165, 737
calice da cocktail 225
calice gustativo 176
calicetto 83
California, Golfo di 30
californio 684
Callisto 4
calma 56
calore 665, 670
calore, disco deflettore del 274
calore, dispersione di 68
calore, pompa di 260
calore, produzione di 665
calore, scambiatore di 259, 675
calore, trasferimento di 681
calotta 273, 288, 289, 340, 341, 575, 676, 827
calotta della cabina di pilotaggio 898
calotta della torretta 692
calotta di sicurezza 332
calotta filtrante 773
calotta polare, della 61
calotta, manopola per l'apertura della 898
calottino estrattore 896
calvinismo 736
calza 365, 367
calza a rete 365
calza autoreggente 365
calza con reggicalze 796
calza dell'albero 836
calzare 841
calzascarpe 345
calze 351, 365
calzerotto 351, 365
calzettone 365, 802, 808, 848, 878
calzettoni 805
calzino 365, 822
calzino corto 351
calzino lungo 351
calzoni 748, 848
calzoni a palloncino 338
Camaleonte 11
camaleonte 114
cambiaaperture 694
cambio 87, 725
cambio diapositiva avanti 483
cambio diapositiva indietro 483
cambio, cavo del 580
cambio, leva del 552, 556, 579, 580
cambio, pedale del 575, 576, 577
cambio, scatola del 552
Cambogia 747
Cambriano 92
cambusa 763
Camciatca, Penisola di 33
camembert 211
camera 650
camera a secco 671
camera a spirale 658, 659
camera a umido 671
camera a vuoto 694
camera anteriore 177
camera blindata 731
camera d'albergo 724
camera d'aria 117
camera da letto 251, 902
camera da letto principale 251
camera degli ufficiali 764
camera del re 402
camera della regina 402
camera di combustione anulare 627

camera di compressione 642
camera di cottura 465
camera di equilibrio 763
camera di equilibrio del reattore 668
camera di equilibrio delle apparecchiature 666
camera di espansione 695
camera di lancio 763
camera di manovra 763
camera di miscelazione 319
camera di pressione 258
camera di scarico 402
camera di scoppio 564, 566, 753
camera doppia 724
camera fotografica 694
camera magmatica 44, 646
camera matrimoniale 724
camera oscura 484
camera portacampioni 694
camera posteriore 177
camera pressurizzata 543
camera pulpare 159
camera sotterranea 402
camera, numero della 724
cameraman 428
cameriere 721
camerino 428, 431, 716
camerino privato 428
Camerun 745
camicetta classica 359
camicetta incrociata 359
camicette, esempi di 359
camicia 349
camicia da notte 364
camicia di scarico 659
camicia, collo a 349, 362
camicia, lembo della 349
camicie 716
camicione 359
camiciotto 359
caminiera 256
camino 245, 250, 256, 257, 259
camino principale 44
camino, ferri per il 257
camion a cassone amovibile 573
camion frigorifero 572
camion per spurghi 573
camion, esempi di 573
camma, anello della 307
cammello 129
cammino di ronda 408, 409
cammino di ronda coperto 408
camomilla 208
camoscio, pelle di 345, 377
campagna 709
campana 446, 447
campana per la raccolta del vetro 71
campana per la raccolta della carta 71
campana, attacco della 446
campane tubolari 437, 449
campanelle 449
campanile 737
campata centrale 540
campata laterale 540
campeggio 725, 902
campeggio, attrezzature da 905
campi da tennis 788
campi solcati 47
campionatore 450
campione 458
campione, manopola di posizionamento del 694
campo 794, 799, 801, 804, 806, 809, 810, 812, 813, 814, 816, 818, 819, 820, 864, 877, 878
campo da golf 708, 788
campo da hockey su prato 788
campo di allenamento 866
campo di calcio 788
campo di dispersione 263
campo di gara 852, 855
campo di gioco 802, 858, 864, 877, 920
campo di servizio del doppio 817
campo di servizio del singolo 817
campo di tiro 859, 860, 893
campo di tiro a segno 788
campo di tiro con l'arco 788
campo geotermico 646
campo magnetico 494, 687
campo per sport equestri 788
Canada 742
canale 865
canale circolare 95
canale del sifone 105
canale del vento 445
Canale della Manica 32
canale della radice 159
canale deltizio 48
canale destro 502
canale di aerazione 402
canale di derivazione 657
Canale di Drake 29, 31
canale di Havers 154
Canale di Mozambico 34
canale di scarico 658
canale di scolo 655
canale di trasporto 666
canale lacrimale 177
canale per le acque meteoriche 712
canale privilegiato 617
canale radiale 95
canale secondario 617
canale semicircolare laterale 174
canale semicircolare posteriore 174
canale semicircolare superiore 174
canale sinistro 502
canale velenifero 112
canale, chiusa di un 596, 597
canali di Volkmann 154
canali, selettore dei 505
canali, tasti di selezione dei 495
cancellazione 515
cancellazione, pulsante di 477
cancellazione, tasto di 508
cancelleria, articoli di 528
cancellieri, scrivania dei 728
cancellieri, ufficio dei 728
cancello 278, 852
Cancro 13
Cancro, Tropico del 34, 35, 36
candela 562, 565, 566, 702, 737
candela di accensione 332
candela, cavo della 552, 566
candelotto 422
cane 130, 752, 754, 861, 912, 913
Cane Maggiore 11
Cane Minore 13
cane, morfologia di un 130
cane, scheletro di un 131
cane, zampa anteriore di un 130
canestro 811
canestro, zona di 809
canguro 142, 143
canguro, morfologia di un 143
canguro, scheletro di un 142
canino 121, 159
canna 445, 578, 600, 754, 755, 858, 860, 912
canna ad ancia 444
canna ad anima 444
canna da lancio 910
canna da mosca 909
canna della melodia 432
canna di imboccatura 447
canna, zucchero di 209
canne 917
canneggio 445
cannella 198
cannello 432
cannello per saldare 319
cannello per tagliare 319
cannelloni 206
cannocchiale 14, 612, 701
cannocchiale cercatore 14, 15
cannocchiale di mira 692
cannolicchio 217
cannoncino 349
cannone 124, 283, 758, 854
cannone ad avancarica 753
cannone ad avancarica, sezione di un 753
cannone del XVII° secolo 752
cannone di antibraccio 749
cannone di braccio 749
cannone elettronico 494, 694
cannone senza rinculo 757
cannone snodato 854
cannoniera 409
cannotto reggisella 578
cannuccia 223, 390
cannula orofaringea 775
canoa 600, 837
canoa e kayak: rapide 837
canoa e kayak: regate fluviali 838
canoa monoposto (C1) 838
canottaggio con uno e due remi 838
canottaggio di coppia (due remi) 838
canottaggio di punta (un remo) 838
canottiera 351, 369, 371, 850
canovaccio 459
cantalupo 195
cantarello 183
cantina dei vini 720
cantone destro del capo 740
cantone destro della punta 740
cantone sinistro del capo 740
cantone sinistro della punta 740
canyon sottomarino 49
cap 853
capanna di fango 418
capanna di paglia 418
capannina meteorologica 58
capannoni delle merci in transito 596
capasanta 217
capelli 147, 149
capelli, pinza per 380
capelli, spazzole per 380
capezzale 280
capezzolo 146, 148, 171
capi antichi 336
capitale 37
capitano 877, 884
capitato 154
capitello 405, 426
capo 38, 96, 97, 99, 104, 115, 740
capo centrale 740
Capo di Buona Speranza 34
Capo Horn 31
capo meccanico 873
Capo Verde 745
capocchia 391
capocordata 900
capocroce 411
capocuoco 721
capodoglio 137
capogiuria 823
capolino 81
capomacchinista 428
caporali 473
caposala, ufficio del 779
caposquadra 429
capotasto 439, 440, 441
capote 838
cappa 224, 256, 290, 338, 721, 722
cappa di raccolta dei gas combusti 267
cappa di ventilazione 614
cappella 408, 726
cappella assiale 410, 411
cappella laterale 410
cappella radiale 410, 411
cappelletto 351
cappelletto dell'ago 398
cappello 76, 255, 416, 471
cappello a cono 339
cappello a falda larga 341
cappello da marinaio 341
cappello di feltro 340, 341
cappello terminale 667
cappellotto 275
cappellotto dell'aria 320
cappio 888, 892
cappone 213
capponiera 409
cappotti, esempi di 352, 355
cappotto 352, 355
cappotto alla raglan 355
cappotto con pellegrina 355
cappuccio 268, 353, 368, 470, 783, 841, 882
cappuccio con cordoncino 369
cappuccio della leva 268
cappuccio di protezione 776
cappuccio di sicurezza 757
cappuccio, collo a 363
cappuccio, felpa con 370
capra 128
capra, formaggi di 210
capra, latte di 210
capriata 253
Capricorno 10
Capricorno, Tropico del 34, 35, 36
capsula 75, 757, 783
capsula a depressione 566
capsula della bobina 452
capsula di gelatina 783
capsula di Petri 685
capsula di risonanza 776
capsula ermetica 903
capsula, sezione di una 84
captazione, antenna di 585
carabina 893
carabina calibro 22 861
caraffa 225, 226, 241
carambola 197
carapace 107, 113
carattere con grazie 472
carattere senza grazie 472
carattere, extra-nero 472
carattere, grassetto 472
carattere, medio 472
carattere, molto sottile 472
carattere, nero 472
carattere, posizione di un 472
carattere, semi-grassetto 472
carattere, sottile 472
caratteri 917
caratteri di un font 472
caratteri, forma dei 472
caratteristiche della costa 51
caratteristiche della Luna 7
caravella 599
carboncino 397
carboncino, disegno a 396
carbone, deposito di 646
Carbonifero 92
carbonio 683
carburante riscaldante, serbatoio del 563
carburante, condotto del 553, 563
carburante, serbatoio del 331, 553, 574, 577, 586, 758, 760
carburante, serbatoio per il 570
carburante, tipo di 548
carburante, tubi del 899
carburante, tubo di trasferimento del 25
carburante, valvole di controllo del flusso del 626
carburatore 574
carcassa 306, 308
carcere 726
carciofo 187
cardamomo 198
cardellino 118
cardigan 354, 359
cardigan con scollo a V 354
cardinale 118
cardine 554
cardio 217
cardo 185
Carena 11
carena 108, 884
carena dello sterno 116
carenaggio, bacino di 596
carenatura 24, 574, 876
carenatura laterale 873
cargo 475
Caribico, Mar 28, 30
carica di lancio 912
carica di scoppio 757
carica elettrica, unità di misura della 702
carica esplosiva 653, 759
carica negativa 684
carica positiva 684
carica, indicatore di 383
carica, meccanismo di 697
carica, ruota di 696
caricabatteria 306
caricabbasso 834
caricatore 481, 483, 499, 754, 755, 893
caricatore di lamette 383
caricatore, alloggiamento del 476
caricatore, fondello del 754
caricatore, vincolo del 754
carico 686
carico utile 24, 25
carico utile, adattatore del 24
carico utile, modulo del 40
carico, aeroplano da 629
carico, bocca di 288
carico, piano di 632
carico, piattaforma di 699
carico, tubo di 265
cariosside 85
carne 214
carne, cassetto per la 291
carnivori 67
Caronte 5
carota 189
carpa 220
Carpentaria, Golfo di 29
carpenteria 301, 302, 303, 306, 308, 310, 313
carpo 116, 122, 126, 131, 136, 138, 141, 142, 154
carpo, flessore ulnare del 150, 151
carré 353, 359
carreggiata 539
carrelli 181, 456
carrello 284, 328, 428, 542, 585, 586, 595, 633, 634, 754, 835, 869, 895
carrello a forca per palette di carico 633
carrello a piattaforma 633
carrello a piattaforma per palette di carico 633
carrello anteriore 585, 595, 624, 760
carrello avvolgitubo 328
carrello della guida parallela 305
carrello di sormonto 284
carrello elevatore 632
carrello idraulico per palette di carico 633
carrello per i libri 733
carrello per merletti 456
carrello portabagagli 389, 582, 623
carrello portabombole 319
carrello portavivande 278
carrello principale 284, 456, 625, 760
carrello stivatore 642
carrello tenda 567
carrello, binari del 428
carrello, leva del 626
carrello, maniglia del 456
carrello, regolatore di comando del 456
carrello, telaio del 586
carri dei pompieri 766
carri merci, esempi di 588
carriola 323
carro 642
carro a tramoggia 588
carro a tramoggia per minerali 588
carro armato 758
carro bestiame 588
carro bisarca 588
carro chiuso 587
carro chiuso con tetto apribile 588
carro cisterna 588
carro dei vigili del fuoco 764
carro frigorifero 588
carro merci 583, 587
carro merci chiuso 588
carro pianale 588
carro pianale a carrelli 588
carro pianale con stanti 588
carro pianale per il trasporto di rimorchi 588
carro pianale portacontainer 588
carro scoperto a sponde alte 588
carro scoperto a sponde basse 588
carrozza passeggeri 594
carrozze, area di lavaggio delle 589
carrozzeria 550, 567, 876
carrozzerie, esempi di 549
carrucola 284, 750
carrucola del carrello 634
carta 390, 400, 420, 915
carta assorbente 531
carta catramata 299
carta cerata 222
carta da forno 222
carta degli imprevisti 915
carta dei contintinenti 28
carta del tempo 54, 55
carta della rete metropolitana 593, 594
carta delle probabilità 915
carta di addebito 731
carta di credito 729
carta di riserva 512
carta fisica 38
carta geografica 734
carta più alta 914
carta politica 37
carta stradale 39
carta vetrata 308
carta, cestello di alimentazione della 511
carta, cestello di uscita della 511
carta, fessura di alimentazione della 511
carta, guida della 508
carta, numero della 729, 731
carta, pulsante di alimentazione della 519
carta, spia di alimentazione della 519
carta, vassoio di uscita della 512
carte di credito, portafoglio per 386
carte di credito, scomparto per 386
carte geografiche, sezione delle 732
carte, lettore di 730, 731
cartella 387
cartella con linguetta 532
cartella con pressino 532
cartella per documenti 532
cartella sospesa 532
cartelletta 532
cartellino di identificazione 770
cartellino indicatore di destinazione 587
cartellino orario 530
cartellino segnaletico 587
cartello del numero di binari 591
cartello indicatore delle stazioni della linea 592
cartello pubblicitario 592, 594, 595
carter 565, 910
carter della mola 308
cartilagine alare maggiore 175
cartilagine articolare 154
cartilagine costale 122
cartilagine del setto nasale 175
cartine per sigarette 390
cartoccio 85
cartografia 35
cartoleria 717
cartolina 474
cartoncino 400
cartone 223
cartone piccolo 223
cartonfeltro bitumato, listello di 299
cartucce 860, 861
cartuccia 268, 315, 470, 754
cartuccia del toner 519
cartuccia per fucile a canna liscia 912
cartuccia per fucile a canna rigata 912
cartuccia, fusibile a 272
cartuccia, perno della 268
cartuccia, spia della 519
cartucciera 770
carvi 198
casa 244, 877, 915
casa a due piani 419
casa a un piano 419
casa colonica 182
casa galleggiante 607
casa in mattoni cotti 418
casa romana 406
casa solare 675
casa, abito da 356
casa, arredamento per la 276
casa, elementi della 247
casa, esterno di una 244
casa, struttura di una 250
casacca 359
casalinghi 180
casatorre 419
cascata 47, 48
caschetto 842
casco 20, 796, 798, 800, 808, 856, 858, 870, 871, 872, 878, 882, 884, 885, 887, 888, 891, 894, 895, 896, 897, 901
casco aerodinamico 871
casco di protezione 575, 580
casco integrale 874
casco per cross 875
case a schiera 419
case tradizionali 418
casella 915
casella bianca 916
casella nera 916
caserma 409
caserma dei vigili del fuoco 711, 764
Caspio, Mar 28, 33

INDICE DELLE VOCI ITALIANE

1082

ASTRONOMIA > 2-25; TERRA > 26-71; REGNO VEGETALE >72-89; REGNO ANIMALE > 90-143; ESSERE UMANO > 144-177; GENERI ALIMENTARI E CUCINA > 178-241; CASA > 242-295; FAI DA TE E GIARDINAGGIO > 296-333; ABBIGLIAMENTO > 334-371; ACCESSORI E ARTICOLI PERSONALI > 372-391; ARTE E ARCHITETTURA > 392-465; COMUNICAZIONI E BUROTICA > 466-535; TRASPORTI E VEICOLI > 536-643; ENERGIA > 644-677; SCIENZA > 678-705; SOCIETÀ > 706-785; SPORT E GIOCHI > 786-920

cassa 181, 316, 318, 383, 436, 440, 441, 442, 695, 696, 697, 723, 920
cassa acustica 427, 502, 503
cassa acustica centrale 493
cassa acustica principale 493
cassa acustica surround 493
cassa armonica circolare 432
cassa armonica piriforme 433
cassa armonica triangolare 433
cassa battente 460
cassa chiara 437, 448
cassa del cilindro 249
cassa di risonanza 433, 440
cassa piena 441
cassa portabatteria 571
cassa, registratore di 181
cassaforte 731, 769
cassapanca 279
casse 181, 716, 717
casse acustiche, tasti di selezione delle 497
casse acustiche, terminali di collegamento delle 497
cassero poppiero 608
casseruola 235
cassetta 222, 499, 504, 521
cassetta ad augnatura 303
cassetta aperta 222
cassetta d'appoggio 792
cassetta degli attrezzi 313
cassetta dei messaggi in entrata 508
cassetta del messaggio registrato 508
cassetta delle lettere 474
cassetta di pronto soccorso 771, 777
cassetta di sicurezza 731
cassetta filtro 241
cassetta, coperchio della 265
cassetta, vano 495
cassetta, vano della 499
cassette di deposito per bagagli 582
cassetti della carta 512
cassetti di smistamento automatico 512
cassettiera 279
cassettiera mobile 510
cassetto 224, 278, 279, 281, 290
cassetto di schedario 533
cassetto per la carne 291
cassetto per la verdura 291
cassiera 181
Cassini 19
Cassiopea 12
cassone 323, 638, 641
cassone ribaltabile, autocarro a 639
cassone alare 760
cassone di compattazione 573
cassone di raccolta dei rifiuti 573
cassone per legna da ardere 256
cassone ribaltabile 572, 573, 639
cassonetto 285
castagna 193
castagna d'acqua 184
caste 99
castelletto di testa del pozzo 650
castello 408, 605
castello di prua 609
castello motore 625
castello per munizioni 758
castone 376
castoro 123
catalano 469
catalogo on-line 733
catamarano 835
catapulta 761
catarifrangente 571, 578, 876
catena 253, 578, 580, 697, 826
catena alimentare 67
catena di dune 52
catena di isolatori sospesi 663
catena di neuroni 168
catena di ormeggio 615
catena di sicurezza 567
catena di sollevamento 632
catena montuosa 7, 38, 42
catena trinciante 331
catena, freno della 331
catena, guida della 331, 580
catena, trasmissione a 641, 643
catering, automezzo del 623
catodo 689
cattedra 734
cattedrale 410
cattedrale gotica 410
cattedrale, pianta della 411
cattolicesimo 736
cattura 916
cavalcavia 539, 540
cavaliere 409, 853, 855, 858
cavalletta 102
cavalletta verde 101
cavalletto 399, 443, 483
cavalletto centrale 575
Cavalletto del Pittore 11
cavalletto laterale 575, 577
cavallo 124, 129, 351, 359, 826, 858, 916, 919
cavallo con maniglie 824, 826
cavallo da polo 858
cavallo per volteggi 824, 825, 826
cavallo su due colonne 919
cavallo, anatomia di un 125
cavallo, ferro di 127
cavallo, morfologia di un 124
cavallo, scheletro di un 126
Cavalluccio 12
cavastivali 345
cavastracci 752
cavatappi 905
cavatappi a leva 230
cavatappi da cameriere 230
cavatorsoli 233
cavea 402, 407
cavetto di acciaio 913
cavi 492, 523
cavi di accoppiamento 558
cavi di ancoraggio 652
cavi di sospensione della navicella 899
cavi, blocco di ancoraggio dei 540
cavi, scomparto delle bobine dei 489
cavia 123
cavicchiera 439
cavicchio 439, 440, 441
caviglia 146, 148, 440, 442, 590, 739
cavigliera 442, 850
cavità addominale 169, 170
cavità boccale 116
cavità midollare 154
cavità nasale 163
cavità orale 163, 164
cavità palleale 106
cavità pleurica 163
cavo 306, 488, 504, 505, 516, 517, 558, 573, 690, 851, 859, 908, 913
cavo a fibre ottiche 523
cavo a treccia 523
cavo armato 507
cavo coassiale 523
cavo d'alimentazione 237, 308
cavo del cambio 580
cavo del freno 579
cavo del sartiame 897
cavo del timone 838
cavo dell'antenna ad alta frequenza 628
cavo dell'elettricità 712
cavo della candela 552, 566
cavo di accelerazione 332
cavo di accensione 323
cavo di acciaio 900
cavo di alimentazione 305, 381, 382, 497, 513
cavo di alimentazione a 240 volt 272
cavo di alimentazione a corrente alternata 526
cavo di alimentazione a corrente continua 526
cavo di alimentazione dell'elettrodo 318
cavo di collegamento 502
cavo di comando 323
cavo di connessione 465
cavo di frenaggio 761
cavo di interfaccia digitale per strumenti musicali (MIDI) 451
cavo di messa a terra 273, 318
cavo di potenza 272
cavo di raccordo per luci di segnalazione 567
cavo di sincronizzazione 527
cavo di sollevamento 634
cavo di sospensione 540
cavo di traino, manopola di sgancio del 898
cavo di trasmissione 590, 613
cavo di trazione 317
cavo elettrico 556, 563
cavo per la combustione del tabacco 390
cavo telefonico 712
cavo, manicotto del 306
cavolfiore 187
cavolini di Bruxelles 186
cavolo bianco 186
cavolo marittimo 186
cavolo ornamentale 186
cavolo rapa 185
cavolo riccio 186
cavolo rosso 186
cavolo verza 186
cavolo verzotto 186
cazzuola da muratore 315
ceci 190
ceco 469
cediglia 473
cedro 194
cedro del Libano 89
cefalo 220
cefalotorace 103, 107
Cefeo 12
celata 749
cella 96, 100, 407, 727, 897
cella da miele 100
cella da polline 100
cella di isolamento 727
cella frigorifera 180, 181, 722
cella per gli uomini 768
cella per i minori 768
cella per le donne 768
cella reale 100
cella sigillata 100
cella solare 529, 672, 673
celle 728
celle solari, pannello di 673
celle solari, sistema a 673
cellula animale 94
cellula convettiva 63
cellula del succo 82
cellula fotoelettrica 482
cellula vegetale 74
cellula, membrana della 74, 94
cellula, parete della 74
cellulare 726
Celsius, grado 702
Celsius, scala 695
cemento 159
cemento armato 298
cemento, sottofondo di 254
cenere 391
ceneri vulcaniche, nube di 44
ceneri, strato di 44
cent 728
Centauro 11
centina 624
centina di radice alare 624
cento 703
Centrafricana, Repubblica 745
centrale 807, 809
centrale elettrica 657, 664
centrale elettrica mareomotrice 664
centrale elettrica, sezione trasversale di una 664
centrale elettronucleare 668
centrale idroelettrica, sezione trasversale di una 658
centrale termoelettrica a carbone 646
centralina 507
centratura, regolatore di 518
centravanti 801, 814
centrifuga 240, 292
centrifuga scolainsalata 231
centrifugare a bassa temperatura 347
centrifugare a temperatura media 347
centriolo 94
centro 431, 704, 847, 859, 877, 916
centro commerciale 709, 714
centro della città 709, 710
centro della ragnatela 103
centro di alta pressione 55
centro di bassa pressione 55
centro di documentazione 764
centro di smistamento 474
centro di smistamento regionale 475
centro prelievi, sala d'attesa del 781
centroattacco 879
centrocampista centrale 803
centrocampista di destra 803
centrocampista di sinistra 803
centromediano 801
ceppo 87, 610
cera, pastelli a 396
ceramica 464
ceramica, condensatore di 689
cercafase 316
cercapersone 505
cerchi 917
cerchia annuale 87
cerchietto 561
cerchio 560, 574, 579, 823
cerchio azimutale, regolazione dell'immagine del 701
cerchio centrale 810
cerchio dei colori 400
cerchio del battitore successivo 794
cerchio di centrocampo 803, 809, 810, 879
cerchio di ingaggio 878
cerchio di serraggio 448
cerchio di stazione 55
cerchio di tiro 800, 809
cerchio graduato dell'ascensione retta 14, 15
cerchio graduato della declinazione 14, 15
cerchio zenitale, regolazione dell'immagine del 701
cerchio, bordo del 560
cerchio, parti di un 704
cerchione 551, 640
cereali 85, 203
cerfoglio 202
cerimolia 196
cerio 684
cerniera 105, 238, 247, 249, 278, 294, 465, 500, 692
cerniera della visiera 575
cerniera lampo 377, 389, 902
cerniera regolabile 310
cerotto 777
cerotto adesivo 777
cervella 212
cervelletto 167
cervello 99, 103, 106, 107, 110, 167
cervo dalla coda bianca 128
cesio 682
cesoie 330
cesoie da giardino 330
cespo 185
cespuglio 322
cestella 98
cestello 237, 238, 240, 291, 292, 294
cestello di alimentazione della carta 511
cestello di refrigerazione 240
cestello di uscita della carta 511
cestello per friggere 231
cestello per la cottura a vapore 235
cestello per le posate 294
cestino 535, 911
cestino per i rifiuti 723
cetriolino 188
cetriolo 188
cetriolo senza semi 188
Chac-Mool 412
chanel, scarpa 343
charleston 448
charlotte, stampo per 232
châssis: dorso 513
châssis: interno 513
châssis: vista frontale 513
chat room 525
chayote 189
chela 107
chelicero 103
chemisier 356
cherosene 656
Chesterfield, divano 276
chiamata automatica, tasti di 506
chiamata successiva, tasto di 507
chiamata, pulsante di 417
chiamata, tasto di 505, 506
chiambrana 249
chiasma ottico 167
chiave 249, 413, 446
chiave a brugola 314
chiave a bussola a cricchetto 311
chiave a catena 315
chiave a croce 558
chiave a forchetta doppia 311
chiave a nastro 315
chiave a rullino 311
chiave combinata 311
chiave del chiver 446
chiave del mandrino 306
chiave dell'accensione 332, 333
chiave dell'acqua 447
chiave di basso 434
chiave di carica 436
chiave di contralto 434
chiave di violino 434
chiave di volta 410
chiave per idrante 767
chiave poligonale a cricco 311
chiave poligonale doppia 311
chiave poligonale doppia ad anello aperto 311
chiave regolabile 315
chiave regolabile da lavandino 315
chiave, leva della 446
chiave, serratura a 386
chiavi 311, 315, 434, 451
chiavi di tensione 448
chiavi, negozio per la riproduzione delle 715
chiavi, protezione delle 446
chiavistello a scatto 248
chiavistello senza scatto 248, 249
chicchi di caffè tostati 208
chicchi di caffè verdi 208
chicco di grano, sezione di un 85
chiesa 711, 737
chiesa ortodossa 736
chiglia 897
chilometro lanciato 891
chimica 680
chinois 231
chiocciola 104, 217
chiocciola per nastro adesivo 534
chiocciola, anatomia di una 104
chiocciola, morfologia di una 104
chiocciole, molle per 233
chiocciole, tegamino per 233
chiodi, esempi di 301
chiodo 127, 301, 791
chiodo a espansione 900
chiodo a spirale 301
chiodo comune 301
chiodo con data 590
chiodo da ghiaccio 901
chiodo da muratore 301
chiodo da roccia 900
chiodo di finitura 301
chiodo di garofano 198
chiodo troncato 301
chioma 8, 87
Chioma di Berenice 13
chiosco 548
chipset 513
chirurgia minore, sala per operazioni di 778
chirurgo, lavandino del 781
chitarra acustica 440
chitarra basso 441
chitarra elettrica 441
chitone 336
chiusa 664
chiusa di un canale 596, 597
chiusa di un canale: vista laterale 597
chiusa, acquedotto per il riempimento della 597
chiusa, apertura per il riempimento della 597
chiusa, apertura per il riempimento e lo svuotamento della 597
chiusa, sistema di riempimento e di svuotamento della 597
chiusa, sistema di svuotamento della 597
chiusura 386, 387
chiusura a occhiello 389
chiusura a scatto 238, 294
chiusura in rilievo 223
chiusura lampo 353, 369, 453
chiusura lampo, linea della 455
chiusura metallica a pressione 386
chiusura, anello di 290
chiusura, blocco di 700
chiusura, cordoncino di 387
chiusura, dispositivo di 913
chiusura, leva di 587
chiusura, valvola di 265
chiusure 453
chiver 446
chiver, chiave del 446
chorizo 216
chow-chow 130
chutney al mango 201
Ciad 745
Ciad, Lago 34
ciak 429
ciambella 204
ciano 690
cianobatteri 92
cibi pronti 181
cicala 101, 610
ciccioli 216
ciclismo 870
ciclismo su pista 871
ciclismo su strada 870
ciclismo su strada, gara di 870
ciclista 870
ciclo biologico della rana 111
ciclo del motore a due tempi 565
ciclo del motore diesel 565
ciclo del motore rotativo 565
ciclo idrologico 67
ciclomotore 577
ciclone 63
ciclone tropicale 63
cicloni tropicali, denominazione dei 63
ciclorama 492
cicogna 119
ciechi intestinali 103
cieco 125, 164
cieco intestinale 106, 116
cieco pilorico 95, 109
cieco rettale 95
cieletti 430
cieletto 431
cielo 647
cielo coperto 56
cielo invisibile 56
cielo limpido 56
cielo molto nuvoloso 56
cielo nuvoloso 56
cielo poco nuvoloso 56
cielo sereno 56
cielo tempestoso 65
cielo, copertura del 55
cifre 472
ciglia 94, 132
ciglio 94, 177
Cigno 12
Cile 742
ciliato 79
ciliegia 192
cilindretto 559
cilindro 249, 268, 340, 564, 705, 776
cilindro del braccio di scavo 638
cilindro del braccio di sollevamento 637, 638
cilindro del gas 755
cilindro della pala caricatrice 637, 638
cilindro dello scarificatore 636
cilindro di raffreddamento 692
cilindro di riflessione 692
cilindro di rotazione della lama 639
cilindro di rubino 692
cilindro di sollevamento 573, 634, 637, 766
cilindro di sollevamento della lama 636, 639
cilindro di taglio 332
cilindro direzionale 638
cilindro graduato 685
cilindro idraulico 633
cilindro inferiore 421
cilindro principale 559
cilindro ricuperatore 756
cilindro rotante 458
cilindro superiore 421
cilindro, cassa del 249
cima 45, 87, 321
cima bipara 81
cima di recupero 836
cima unipara 81
cimasa 278
cime di rapa 187
cimice acquatica gigante 101
cimice rigata 101
cimiero 748
ciminiera 646
cimino 909

ASTRONOMIA > 2-25; TERRA > 26-71; REGNO VEGETALE >72-89; REGNO ANIMALE > 90-143; ESSERE UMANO > 144-177; GENERI ALIMENTARI E CUCINA > 178-241; CASA > 242-295; FAI DA TE E GIARDINAGGIO > 296-333; ABBIGLIAMENTO > 334-371; ACCESSORI E ARTICOLI PERSONALI > 372-391; ARTE E ARCHITETTURA > 392-465; COMUNICAZIONI E BUROTICA > 466-535; TRASPORTI E VEICOLI > 536-643; ENERGIA > 644-677; SCIENZA > 678-705; SOCIETÀ > 706-785; SPORT E GIOCHI > 786-920

1083

cimitero 39, 711
cimosa 455
Cina 747
cinema 427, 608, 710, 714
cinescopio 494
cinese 468
Cinese Meridionale, Mar 28, 33
Cinese Orientale, Mar 33
cinghia 765, 818, 824, 893
cinghia dei ginocchielli 857
cinghia del mantice 432
cinghia del ventilatore 566
cinghia della pastoia 857
cinghia della ventola 552
cinghia di compressione frontale 906
cinghia di compressione laterale 906
cinghia di distribuzione 566
cinghia di sicurezza sottogamba 611
cinghia di tramissione 292
cinghia per i piedi 836
cinghia per i ramponi 901
cinghia per il piede 840
cinghia per tubi e scale 767
cinghiale 128
cinghietta posteriore di regolazione 772
cingolo 636, 758, 876
cingolo, maglia del 758
cingolo, piastra di protezione del 758
cinquanta 703
cinque 703
cinque spezie, miscela di 199
cinquecento 703
cinquina 919
cinta muraria 408
cintura 313, 350, 352, 374, 561, 611, 663, 844
cintura a vita 906
cintura da sollevamento pesi 850
cintura da zavorra 841
cintura di Kuiper 4
cintura di ritenuta 281
cintura di servizio 770
cintura di sicurezza 555, 873
cintura portautensili 313
cintura ventrale 555
cintura, abbottonatura della 350
cintura, gancio della 505
cintura, passante della 352
cinturino 391, 696, 797, 850
cinturino a T, scarpa con 343
cinturino della manica 352
cinturino di chiusura 391
cinturino regolabile 348
cinturino, scarpa con 343
cioccolato 208
cioccolato al latte 208
cioccolato bianco 208
cioccolato fondente 208
ciondoli 376
ciondoli, bracciale con 376
ciotola 236
ciotole per mescolare 232
cipolla 328
cipolla bianca 184
cipolla d'inverno 184
cipolla di Spagna 184
cipolla rossa 184
cipolla verde 184
cipollina 184
cipresso, foglie squamiformi del 89
cipria compatta 378
cipria in polvere 378
cipria in polvere, pennello da 378
cipria, piumino da 378
Cipro 744
circo 7
circo glaciale 46
circolazione del sangue 160
circolazione, pompa di 259
circolazione, schema della 161
circolo 856, 866
Circolo Polare Antartico 29, 35, 36
Circolo Polare Artico 35, 36
circonferenza 704
circonvallazione 39
circuito 872, 874
circuito a 120 volt 272
circuito a 240 volt 272
circuito di distribuzione 273
circuito di supercross 875
circuito elettrico 274
circuito elettrico dei sensori 559
circuito elettrico parallelo 687
circuito frenante 552, 559
circuito integrato 689
circuito integrato inscatolato 689
circuito stampato 689
circuito stampato, scheda del 689
cirro 56, 62
cirrocumulo 56, 62
cirrostrato 56, 62
cisterna 572, 573, 607
cisterna, carro 588
cisterna, nave 606
cistifellea 110, 112, 164
citofaringe 94
citopigio 94
citoplasma 74, 94, 170
citostoma 94
città 37, 708
Città del Vaticano 744
città, centro della 709, 710
città, pianta di 39
city bike 581
ciuffo 124
ciuffolotto 118
civetta acadica 118
clacson 556, 576
clamide 336
clarinetti 437
clarinetto 446
clarinetto basso 437
classifica generale, tabellone della 824
classificatore a soffietto 533
classificazione di Hubble 9
clavette 823
clavicembalo 443
clavicola 111, 116, 122, 141, 142, 152
clessidra per uova alla coque 231
climatizzazione, sistema di 68, 489
climi aridi 61
climi del mondo 61
climi di montagna 61
climi polari 61
climi temperati caldi 61
climi temperati freddi 61
climi tropicali 61
clip 506, 700
clip, orecchini a 374
clitoride 170
cloaca 103, 110, 113, 116
cloche 341, 898
cloro 683
cloroplasto 74
coanocita 95
cobalto 683
cobra 114
cocca 750, 859
Cocchiere 12
coccia 849
coccige 152, 157
coccinella 101
cocco, noce di 193
coccodrillo 114
cocktail, calice da 225
coclea 174
cocomero 195
Cocos, placca delle 43
coda 107, 112, 113, 121, 122, 124, 130, 133, 136, 140, 143, 169, 425, 625, 756, 840, 887, 888, 892, 893, 894, 898, 909
coda dell'elice 173
coda di polvere 8
coda di rondine 739
coda di rondine con una lingua 739
coda ionica 8
coda, pattino di 631
coda, supporto per la 623
coda, trave di 631
codetta 274, 275
codice del prodotto 699
codice di identificazione personale (PIN), tastierina per il 731
codice temporale 429
codolo 227, 229, 306, 309, 315, 918
codrione 115
coelophysis 93
cofano 333
cofano anteriore 550, 570
cofano posteriore 551
coffa 602
cognate 785
cognato 785
coincide con 703
cola, noce di 193
colapasta 231
colata di fango 47
colata lavica 44
colbacco 340
colibrì 118
colino 231
colla in stick 534
collana 374
collana a cinque giri 374
collana lunga 374
collana lunga alla vita 374
collane 374
collant 365
collante 254
collare 257, 308, 391, 838
collare del solaio 257
collare di chiusura del casco 20
collare tagliafuoco 257
collaretto 339, 363
collarino 269, 404, 775, 868
collarino di velluto 374
collegamenti elettrici, pannello dei 489
collegamenti ipertestuali 524
collegamenti video, pannello dei 489
collegamenti, scatola dei 490
collegamento a molla 920
collegamento elettrico 258, 260, 266, 571
collegamento, cavo di 502
collegio arbitrale 845
colletto 77, 159, 349, 383
colletto, punta del 349
collettore 652, 659, 688
collettore a vuoto 694
collettore del vapore primario 669
collettore dell'acqua di alimentazione 669
collettore di alimentazione 566
collettore di aspirazione 564, 565
collettore di elettroni 689
collettore di scarico 262, 552, 564, 565, 566
collettore principale 262, 263
collettore solare 675
collettore solare piatto 672
collettore, testa del 18
colli, esempi di 362
collibia 183
collie 130
collimatore ottico 701
collina 45, 674
collina abissale 49
collinetta 875
collo 113, 124, 147, 148, 149, 169, 227, 342, 348, 352, 362, 370, 425, 494, 610, 822, 868
collo a camicia 349, 362
collo a cappuccio 363
collo a listino 363
collo a orecchie di cane 362
collo a polo 363
collo a scialle 362
collo a uomo 355, 362
collo alla coreana 363
collo alla marinara 362
collo alla Peter Pan 362
collo alto 892
collo button-down 349
collo con sciarpa 362
collo d'oca 255, 638
collo del femore 153
collo dell'utero 170
collo, parte superiore del 362
collo, protezione per il 765
collo, punta del 362
collo, sostegno per il 874
colloquio, sale di 728
collutorio 384
Colomba 11
Colombia 742
colombino, tecnica a 465
colon 97, 113, 125
colon ascendente 164
colon discendente 164
colon sigmoideo 164
colon trasverso 164
colonna 47, 64, 287, 307, 403, 405, 440, 452, 471, 482, 485, 919
colonna centrale 676
colonna con lamelle terminali 64
colonna d'alcool 695
colonna di andata 259
colonna di frazionamento 656
colonna di mercurio 695
colonna di ritorno 259
colonna di stabilizzazione 652
colonna di superficie 654
colonna di ventilazione 262
colonna montante dell'acqua calda 262
colonna montante dell'acqua fredda 262
colonna principale di scarico 262
colonna principale di ventilazione 262
colonna vertebrale 109, 121, 152, 157, 167
colore 914
colore a olio 397
colori primari 400
colori secondari 400
colori terziari 400
colori, cerchio dei 400
colori, display dei 456
colori, esempi di 741
colori, sintesi dei 690
colori, tabella dei 398
colpi 820
colpo d'approccio 866
colpo d'inizio 866
colpo di gamba a crawl 832
colpo di gamba a farfalla 832
colpo di gamba a rana 832
colpo di pattino 892
coltelli da cucina, esempi di 229
coltelli, esempi di 228
coltello 227, 236, 317, 401, 421, 423, 905, 907
coltello baionetta 751
coltello da bistecca 228
coltello da burro 228
coltello da cucina 229
coltello da dessert 228
coltello da formaggio 228
coltello da ostriche 229
coltello da pane 229
coltello da pesce 228
coltello da pompelmo 229
coltello da prosciutto 229
coltello da sub 841
coltello da tavola 228
coltello di selce 748
coltello elettrico 237
coltello miscelatore 236
coltello per affettare 229
coltello per disossare 229
coltivatore 326, 641
coltro 641, 643
coltro, albero del 641
columella 105
columella, piega della 105
comandante, posto del 758
comandante, sedile del 626
comandante, ufficio del 764, 768
comandi del pilota automatico 626
comandi del retroescavatore 637
comandi del VCR 495
comandi del verricello 573
comandi della videocassetta 496
comandi di sintonia 494
comandi radio 626
comandi, pannello dei 261
comando a distanza, presa per il 476, 477
comando a pedale 452
comando del freno 896, 897
comando del freno aerodinamico 898
comando del pannello solare 60
comando del tavolino traslatore 693
comando del tergicristallo 556
comando del tiraggio 256
comando del ventilatore 261
comando dello zoom elettrico 496
comando di selezione manuale 483
comando elettrico di erogazione della vincita 920
comando programmabile 261
comando, cavo di 323
comando, modulo di 25
comando, pannello di 586, 694
comando, ponte di 604, 605, 608, 609
comando, quadro di 238, 239, 290, 292, 293, 294
comando, scatola di 267
combattimento, area di 843, 845, 846
combinazione 351, 852
combinazione di volo 896
combinazione vincente 920
combinazione, serratura a 386
combinazioni del poker 914
combustibile 665, 670, 671
combustibile esaurito, portello di scarico del 666
combustibile esaurito, vasca di deposito del 666, 667, 669
combustibile esaurito, vasca di scarico del 666, 668
combustibile fossile 68, 70
combustibile nuovo, area di carico del 666
combustibile nuovo, sala di stoccaggio del 666
combustibile per motori diesel 656
combustibile per motori diesel marini 656
combustibile, arrivo del 259
combustibile, barretta di 667
combustibile, condotto di alimentazione del 259
combustibile, manipolazione del 666
combustibile, pastiglia di 667
combustibile, pompa del 259
combustione 565, 627
combustione del tabacco, cavo per la 390
combustione lenta, stufa a 256
cometa 8
comignolo 245
commessura labiale 130, 174
commissario agli ostacoli 852
commissario di campo 853, 855
commissario di gara 875
commutatore 316, 523
commutatore delle luci 576
commutatore mono/stereo 498
commutatore video di regia 491
comò 279
comodino 724, 780
comodino, lampada da 724
Comore 746
compact disc 501, 504
compact disc riscrivibile 521
Compasso 11
compattatore 573
compattazione 71
compensazione dell'esposizione, pulsante di 476
compensazione, aletta di 60
competizione 789
competizioni, bacino per 788
complesso scolastico 711
complesso sportivo 709, 788
completo da ginnastica 369
compluvio 406
componenti del portalampada 275
componenti di un anello 376
componenti di una bicicletta 578
composizione del sangue 162
composta, contenitore della 323
compressione 564, 565, 627
compressore 260
compressore centrifugo 627
compressore d'aria 320
compressore del climatizzatore 566
compressore dell'aria 585, 586
compressore semovente 622
compressore, turbina del 627
computer 734
computer da tavolo 522, 523, 524
computer di bordo 556, 771
computer portatile 523, 526
computer portatile: dorso 526
computer portatile: vista frontale 526
computer tascabile 527
computer, programmi del 771
computer, sala dei 763
comunicazione senza fili 505
comunicazione via telefono 506
comunicazione, dispositivi di 522
comunicazione, modulo di 486
comunicazione, tunnel di 23
comunicazioni 468
comunicazioni aeree 487
comunicazioni industriali 487
comunicazioni marittime 487
comunicazioni militari 487
comunicazioni private 487
comunicazioni stradali 487
comunione, balaustra della 737
conca 173
conca di concrezione 47
conca fissa 919
conca nasale inferiore 175
conca nasale media 175
conca nasale superiore 175
concentrato di pomodoro 200
concentrazione di gas serra 68
concessionaria di automobili 711
conchiglia 104, 105, 106, 276
conchiglia bivalve 105
conchiglia bivalve, anatomia di una 105
conchiglia bivalve, morfologia di una 105
conchiglia di protezione 808, 843, 880
conchiglia portatestina 500
conchiglia univalve 105
conchiglia univalve, morfologia di una 105
conchiglie 206
concime organico 70
concio d'imposta 413
concorrenti 789
concorrenti, elenco dei 789
condensa, bacinella di raccolta della 261
condensatore 646, 668, 674, 693, 694
condensatore a pellicola plastica 689
condensatore di ceramica 689
condensatore, ingresso del riflusso del 669
condensatore, ingresso dell'acqua di raffreddamento del 669
condensatore, manopola di regolazione del 693
condensatore, uscita del riflusso del 669
condensatore, uscita dell'acqua di raffreddamento del 669
condensatore, ventilatore del 261
condensatori elettrolitici 689
condensazione 67, 680
condilo laterale del femore 153
condilo mediale del femore 153
condimenti 200, 723
condimento alle spezie cajun 199
condizionamento dell'aria 261
condizionamento dell'aria, sistema di 775
condizionatore 567
condizionatore d'aria da camera 261
condizionatore semovente 622
condominio 711
condor 119
condotta dell'acquedotto 712
condotta di produzione 654
condotta di produzione, testa della 654
condotta di raccolta 652
condotta fognaria 712
condotta fognaria principale 712
condotta forzata 657, 658, 664
condotto 402
condotto del carburante 553, 563
condotto del flusso freddo 627
condotto del ventilatore 643
condotto dell'aria 259
condotto dell'aria di ritorno 258
condotto dell'aria di scarico 543
condotto dell'aria pulita 543
condotto di alimentazione 260, 262
condotto di alimentazione del combustibile 259
condotto di derivazione 258
condotto di distribuzione verticale 258
condotto di insilamento 643
condotto di passaggio della miscela 565
condotto di riscaldamento 293
condotto di scarico 642
condotto di scarico dell'aria calda 564
condotto principale 258
condrite 8
conducente, posto del 758
conduttore di fase 273
conduttore di messa a terra 655
conduttore di terra 272
conduttore neutro 273

conduttori, fascio di 663
conduttura del gas 712
conduttura dell'acqua calda 270, 271
conduttura dell'acqua fredda 270, 271
conduttura dell'acquedotto 675
conduzione 681
conferma, tasto di 731
confessionale 737
confezionamento, prodotti per 180
confezione in cartone per uova 222
confezione multipla 223
confezioni 222
confezioni farmaceutiche di medicinali 783
confine di proprietà 244
confine internazionale 37
confine interno 37
confluente 48
confluenza a destra 544, 547
confucianesimo 736
Confucio 736
congegno di puntamento 756
congegno di sparo 757
congelatore 224, 720
congelatore orizzontale 291
congelatore, porta del 291
congelatore, scomparto del 291
congiuntiva 177
Congo 745
Congo, Fiume 34
Congo, Repubblica Democratica del 745
congressi, palazzo dei 711, 718
conifera 89
conifere, esempi di 89
conifere, foresta di 66
coniglio 123, 212
connessione aerea 663
connessione, cavo di 465
connessione, spinotto di 689
connessioni elettriche 465
connettore 272, 488
connettore a T 522
connettore della linea attiva 663
connettore per espansioni AGP 513
connettore per espansioni ISA 513
connettore per espansioni PCI 513
connettore RAM 513
cono 89, 177, 705, 776
cono avventizio 44
cono d'ombra 6, 7
cono di emergenza 168
cono di penombra 6, 7
cono di spremitura 237
cono di uscita 100
cono femminile 89
cono maschile 89
cono pirometrico 464
conservatore, ufficio del 394
conservazione, laboratorio di 395
console 918
console centrale 556
console del mixer audio 488, 490
console del punteggio 865
console dell'annunciatore 488
console dell'organo 444
console di anteprima audio/video 491
console di comando 626
console di regia 488, 491
console per il vuoto 694
consulenti musicali 490
consumatori primari 67
consumatori secondari 67
consumatori terziari 67
contachilometri parziale 557
contachilometri totale 557
contagiri 557, 576
container 605, 635
containers 635
containers, deposito per 708
contaminuti 231, 238, 239, 290
contanti, rifornimento di 731
contarighe 456
contasecondi 488
contatore 499
contatore dell'acqua 262
contatore di kilowattora 273
contatore elettrico 273
contatore, tasto di azzeramento del 499
contatto 274, 916
contatto caldo 476
contatto negativo 672, 673
contatto positivo 672, 673
contatto, dispositivi di 274
contatto, leva di 287
contenitore 59, 613
contenitore della batteria 562
contenitore della composta 323
contenitore delle siringhe usate 771
contenitore in calcestruzzo 665, 667
contenitore per filo interdentale 384
contenitore per il riciclaggio 71
contenitore termico 906
contenitori per la raccolta differenziata 71
contenuto in 703
continentale umido - estate calda 61
continentale umido - estate torrida 61
continente 49
continenti, carta dei 28
continuità, tester di 316
conto 721
conto, tasti di identificazione del 731
contorno 729
contrabbassi 437
contrabbasso 439
contraffisso 253
contrafforte 410, 660
contrago 590
contralto, chiave di 434
contrappeso 14, 16, 417, 500, 542, 591, 634, 638, 639, 640
contrappeso, guida del 417
contrassegno per la virata a dorso 831
contrasto, regolatore di 518
contrasto, tasto regolatore di 512
contratto 915
controbocchetta 249
controbraccio 634
controdado 58
controfagotti 437
controferro 309
controfiocco 603
controfodera 455
controguardia 409
controllo 514
controllo antiskating 500
controllo biglietti, addetto al 394, 427
controllo dei passaporti 621
controllo del campo audio 497
controllo del sequencer 450
controllo del tempo 451
controllo del volume 450, 451
controllo dell'accelerazione 516
controllo dell'entrata del personale 726
controllo dell'uscita del personale 726
controllo della copiatura 512
controllo della velocità di crociera 556
controllo di sicurezza 621
controllo fine dei dati 450
controllo veloce dei dati 450
controllo, posto di 727, 768
controllo, tasto di 505
controllo, torre di 761
controllo, vetro di 727
controllo, video di 694
controllo: selezione di gruppo 514
controllore 582
contromarce 460
contromezzana, albero di 602
controporta attrezzata 291
controporta, scomparto della 291
contropunta 700
controranda 603
controrotaia 590
controscarpa 409
controstecca 391
controtelaio 249
controvelaccino 603
controvelaccino, albero di 602
controvelaccio 603
controvelaccio, vela di straglio di 603
controvento 252, 663
conurbazione 708
conversione, scala di 479
convertitore 493
convertitore catalitico 553
convertitore di coppia 292
convettore 260
convezione 681
convezione, corrente di 681
convogliatore 646
convogliatore a coclea 642, 643
Cook, Stretto di 29
cooksonia 92
coordinamento, stanza di 769
coordinate celesti, sistema di 13
coordinate terrestri, sistema di 35
coperchio 234, 237, 238, 239, 240, 241, 274, 290, 291, 292, 295, 313, 391, 398, 441, 465, 477, 484, 500, 512, 519, 528, 562, 689, 767, 907
coperchio del sedile 265
coperchio della cassetta 265
coperchio della turbina 659
coperchio delle punterie 552, 566
coperchio di alimentazione 755
coperchio di protezione dell'obiettivo 478
coperchio inferiore 689
coperchio protettivo 521
coperchio scorrevole 506, 612
coperchio superiore 689
coperchio, sostegno del 465
coperta 280
coperta, ponte di 607
copertina 391, 853
copertura 391, 867, 909
copertura del cielo 55
copertura, sezione di 100
copia, modo di uscita della 512
copie fronte-retro 512
copiglia 249, 767
copiglia arrotondata 285
copiglia piatta 285
copilota, sedile del 626
coppa da spumante 225
coppa del reggiseno 367
coppa dell'olio 331, 566
coppa dell'olio, guarnizione della 566
coppa inferiore 241
coppa superiore 241
coppetta 287
coppetta per l'insalata 226
coppetta per latte/panna 223
coppia 881, 914
coppia di serraggio, anello di regolazione della 306
coppia, convertitore di 292
coppia, imbarcazioni di 839
coppia, remo di 838
coppo 749
copricanna 755
copricapi 340
copricapi femminili 341
copricapi maschili 340
copricapi unisex 341
copricerniera 385
coprifiltro 773
coprigiubbotto metallico 848
copriguanciale 280
coprilegno 869
coprimaterasso 280
coprimolla 284
copripolso 880
copripuleggia 307
copripunta 391
copriscodellino 752
copritrice primaria 115
copritrice primaria media 115
copritrice secondaria mediana 115
copyright 473
coracoide 111, 116
Coralli, Mar dei 29
Corano 736
corazza 758
corda 284, 285, 439, 440, 443, 611, 750, 842, 850, 859, 900, 901, 908, 913
corda attorcigliata 908
corda della calcola 460
corda di sicurezza 900
corda di sollevamento 285
corda di tensione 433
corda di trazione 840
corda intrecciata 908
corda principale 893
corda vocale 163
cordata 79, 900
corde 433, 442
corde per l'accompagnamento 432
corde per la melodia 432
corde, strumenti a 439
cordiera 433, 439, 448
Cordigliera delle Ande 31
cordini di sospensione 896, 897
cordolo 712, 872
cordoncino 353
cordoncino di chiusura 387
cordoncino, bracciale a 282
cordoncino, cappuccio con 369
cordone 288, 289, 316, 331, 332
cordone del microtelefono 506
cordone dell'alimentazione 383
cordone litorale 51
cordone nervoso 99
cordone nervoso ventrale 107
cordone, manicotto del 308, 318
cordone, supporto del 288
Corea, Repubblica Democratica Popolare di 747
Corea, Repubblica di 747
coreana, collo alla 363
coreano 469
coriandolo 202
corimbo 81
cornamusa 432
cornea 177, 691
cornetta 437, 447
corni 437
corni inglesi 437
cornice 247, 278, 395, 403, 404
cornice inclinata 403
cornicione 245
corno 376, 447
corno anteriore 167
corno inglese 446
corno posteriore 167
coro 410, 411
coroide 177
corolla 80
corona 6, 124, 159, 374, 440, 448, 542, 696, 729
Corona Australe 10
Corona Boreale 13
corona di penne 817
corona radiata 170
coronamento 657, 660, 661, 664
corpi celesti 4
corpo 176, 240, 268, 306, 382, 390, 444, 446, 470, 488, 663, 692, 793, 893, 909
corpo calloso 167
corpo cavernoso 169
corpo cellulare 168
corpo ciliare 177
corpo cilindrico 918
corpo d'acciaio 689
corpo del fornice 167
corpo dell'arnia 100
corpo dell'unghia 172
corpo della macchina fotografica 476
corpo della spoletta 757
corpo della valvola 447
corpo di guardia 408, 409
corpo isolante 562
corpo libero, pedana per il 824
corpo morto 615
corpo stradale 538
corpo umano 146
corpo vertebrale 157, 168
corpo vitreo 177
corpo, cura del 379
corpuscolo di Meissner 172
corpuscolo di Pacini 172
corpuscolo di Ruffini 172
correggia 841
corrente 597
corrente di convezione 681
corrente di fondazione 252, 253
corrente elettrica, unità di misura della 702
corrente inferiore 253
corrente orizzontale 252
corrente, doppio 252
corrente, presa di 316
corrente, presa temporizzata di 290
corrente, regolatore di 275
corrente, sorgente di 687
correttore liquido 534
correzione, tasto di 456
corridoio 817, 820
corridoio centrale 584
corridoio di discesa 402
corridoio di salita 402
corridoio di sicurezza 728
corridoio intercomunicante 584
corridoio telescopico 619
corridore 871
corridore su slittino 884
corridori 875
corrimano 255, 417, 569, 587, 607
corrimano di spinta 776
corsa, bicicletta da 581
corsa, direttore della 870
corsa, scarpa da 370
corse dei cavalli 856, 857
corsetto 337, 367
corsia 180, 712, 788, 790, 830, 831, 882
corsia d'appoggio 865
corsia dei box 872
corsia di accelerazione 539
corsia di decelerazione 539
corsia di entrata 539
corsia di gioco 864
corsia di marcia normale 539
corsia di riscaldamento 882
corsia di sorpasso 539
corsia di traffico lento 539
corsia di uscita 539
corsia laterale 539
corsia, numero di 893
corsivo 472
corso d'acqua 48, 70
corso d'acqua sotterraneo 47
corsoio 436
corteccia 87
cortile 182, 408, 727, 735, 738
cortina 408
Corvo 11
corvo 118
coscia 124, 130, 143, 147, 149, 169, 170, 753
cosciale 749
costa 49, 185, 227, 229
costa a rias 51
costa assiale 105
Costa d'Avorio 745
Costa Rica 742
costa spirale 105
costa, caratteristiche della 51
costate 214
coste, bordo a 354, 369
costellazioni dell'emisfero meridionale 10
costellazioni dell'emisfero settentrionale 12
costine 214
costola 112, 116, 121, 122, 126, 131, 136, 138, 141, 142
costola fluttuante 138
costolatura 841
costole 152
costole false 153
costole fluttuanti 152
costolette 215
costolone dorsale 410
costolone intermedio 410
costruttore, targhetta del 306
costruzione, pietra da 298
costume 428, 843
costume da bagno 371, 830
costumi da bagno 716
costumista 428
cotiledone 77
cotone idrofilo 777
cotta di maglia 749
cottage cheese 210
cottardita 337
cotton fioc® 777
cottura 465
cottura a vapore, cestello per la 235
cottura, camera di 465
cottura, piano di 224, 239, 290
cottura, piastra di 239, 721, 722
cottura, piatti di 239
cottura, zona 722
coulisse 353
coulomb 702
coulommiers 211
coupé 549
Cowper, ghiandola di 169
coxa 96, 98
Coyolxauhqui, pietra di 412
cranio 106, 109, 116, 121, 126, 136, 138, 141, 142, 146
cranio di bambino 158
cranio, vista laterale del 158
Cratere 11
cratere 7, 44, 647
cratere, scia luminosa del 7
cravatta 349
cravatte 716
credenza 279
credenza con vetrina 279
credito, carta di 729
cree 469
cremagliera 791
cremastere 97
crenato 79
crepaccio 46
crepaccio terminale 46
crêpe, padella per 235
crepidine 403, 405
crescente 741
crescione 187
crescione d'orto 187
cresta 45, 49, 690, 749
Cretaceo 93
cric 558
cricchetto 302, 696, 697
cricco 307
cricco, chiave poligonale a 311
criceto 123
cricket 798
crimine, prevenzione del 768
crinale 45
crine 439
criniera 124
crinolina, abito con 337
cripto 684
crisalide 97, 100
cristalleria 225
cristalli di neve 64
cristallino 177, 691
cristallizzazione 680
cristallo dendritico spaziale 64
cristallo di sicurezza 494
cristallo irregolare 64
cristallo lamellare 64
cristallo stellare 64
cristallo, goccia di 287
cristianesimo 736
Croazia 744
croce 740
Croce del Sud 11
croce dell'altare 737
croce di sant'Andrea 252
croce, punta a 302
croce, testa a 302
crocetta 834
crochet 452
crociera 410, 411
crociera, maniglia a 421
crocifisso 737
croco 80
croissant 204
croma 435
croma, pausa di 435
cromatina 94
cromo 683
cromosfera 6
cronologia delle religioni 736
cronometraggio elettrico, sistema di 883
cronometraggio, area di 891
cronometrista 810, 814, 842, 845, 846, 847, 848, 881, 900
cronometrista capo 830
cronometrista di corsia 830
cronometristi 827, 844, 883
cronometro 696, 789, 831
cronometro elettronico automatico 831
crosne 184
cross, motocicletta da 577
crosta continentale 42
crosta oceanica 42
crosta terrestre 42, 43
crosta terrestre, sezione della 42
crostacei 107, 218
crostata, stampo per 232
crottin de chavignol 210
cruna 453, 454, 461
cruschello di segale, pane 205

cruscotto 574, 576
cruscotto, equipaggiamento del 771
Cuba 742
cubetti di ghiaccio, vaschetta per 291
cubia 605, 609
cubicolo 406
cubitiera 749
cubo 705
cuboflash 482
cuboide 155
cuccetta 570, 584
cucchiai dosatori 231
cucchiai, esempi di 228
cucchiai, ruota dei 659
cucchiaia 752
cucchiaino 390
cucchiaino da caffè 228
cucchiaino da tè 228
cucchiaino rotante 911
cucchiaio 227, 659, 905
cucchiaio da assaggio 233
cucchiaio da bibita 228
cucchiaio da brodo 228
cucchiaio da dessert 228
cucchiaio da tavola 228
cucchiaio forato 233
cucchiaio, lama a 401
cucina 180, 222, 224, 250, 406, 584, 719, 721, 722, 723, 724, 726, 735, 764
cucina a gas 290, 721
cucina a vapore 722
cucina di bordo 624
cucina elettrica 290, 721
cucina, batteria da 722
cucina, bilancia da 231
cucina, coltello da 229
cucina, forbici da 233
cucina, robot da 237
cucina, strofinaccio da 295
cucina, utensili da 229
cucito 452
cucitrice 534
cucitura 346, 348, 424, 797, 798
cucitura a princesse 366
cucitura a sottopunto 349
cucitura, linea di 455
cucitura, misuratore di 454
cucitura, tasca inserita nella 355, 360
cucitura, telaio di 424
cuffia 426, 502, 504, 830
cuffia, presa per 450, 451, 504
cuffia, spinotto della 504
cuffie di sicurezza 772
cugina/cugina 785
cugino/cugina 785
culatta mobile 756
culatta, blocco della 912
culatta, plinto di 753
culatta, rinforzo di 753
culatta, scatola di 754, 755
culla 756
culottes 338
cumino 198
cumulo 56, 62
cumulonembo 56, 62
cuneiforme laterale 155
cuneiforme, primo 155, 156
cuneiforme, secondo 155, 156
cuneo 312, 444
cuneo di mira 753
cuoio 798, 863
cuore 97, 99, 103, 104, 105, 106, 107, 109, 110, 112, 116, 125, 162, 163, 212, 590
cuore del legno 87
cuore, scollatura a 363
cuori 914
cupola 84, 415, 614
cupola di proiezione 10
cupola di vetro 612
cupola ovoide rialzata 415
cupola rotante 17
cupola sul mihrab 738
cupola sul porticato 738
cupola, portellone della 17
cupola, volta esterna della 17
cupola, volta interna della 17
cura del corpo 379
cura del prato 332
cura intensiva, unità di 780
curapipe 390
curcuma 198
Curili, Fossa delle 50
curio 684
curling 877
curling, pietra da 877
curling, scopa da 877
curry 198
cursore 350, 453
cursore a destra 515
cursore a sinistra 515
cursore di regolazione della frequenza 498
cursore in alto 515
cursore in basso 515
curva 446
curva a 180 gradi 885
curva a destra 544, 547
curva del circolo 856
curva lontana 856
curva, rinforzo della 446
curvatura 385, 911
cuscinetti antirumore 772
cuscinetto a sfere 677
cuscinetto ad aria 370
cuscinetto assiale 659
cuscinetto carpale 130
cuscinetto dello sperone 130
cuscinetto digitale 130, 133
cuscinetto palmare 130
cuscinetto plantare 133
cuscinetto reggispinta 659
cuscinetto smerigliato 454
cuscino 280, 855
cuscino a rullo 280
cuscus 204
cuscus, pentola per 235
custodia 529
custodia a pareti di vetro 699
custodia dello schermo 483
cute 168, 172
cute, superficie della 172
cuticole, forbicine per 377
cuticole, tronchesina per 377
cyclette 851

D

dadi 311, 914
dado 310, 311, 915
dado cieco 311
dado comune 914
dado da poker 914
dado del braccio 456
dado del premistoppa 268
dado del raddoppio 915
dado di fissaggio 270
dado di serraggio 269, 270, 590
dado esagonale 311, 562
daga 751
dalmata 131
dama 916
danese 469
Danforth, ancora 610
Danimarca 744
danish blue 211
Danubio, Fiume 32
danza, lama per 881
dardo 750
dardo, sacco del 104
dare precedenza 544, 546
data base 525
data di scadenza 729
data, tasto di visualizzazione della 496
datario 531
dati tecnici 560
dati, controllo fine dei 450
dati, controllo veloce dei 450
dati, elaborazione dei 41, 54
dati, memoria 316
dati, piastrina dei 273
dati, registratore di 58
dati, registrazione dei 41
dati, ricezione dei 41
dati, sistema di registrazione dei 694
dati, trasmissione dei 41
dattero 192
davanti 348, 349
David 736
David, stella di 738
deambulatore 782
deambulatorio 411
deasfaltizzazione, impianto di 656
debole 849
decagono regolare 705
decelerazione, zona di 885
decimi di secondo, lancetta dei 696
declinazione 13
declinazione, cerchio graduato della 14, 15
décolleté, reggiseno 367
décolleté, scarpa 343
decompositori, organismi 67
decoratore scenico 429
decorazione a trifoglio 411
decorazioni, siringa per 232
defibrillatore 775
deflettore 260, 329, 332, 333
deflettore del fumo 256
deflettore dell'aria calda 256
deflettore di getto 761
deflusso superficiale 67
deforestazione 69
degenza postoperatoria, stanza di 780
degenza, stanza di 780
Deimos 4
Delfino 12
delfino 136, 137
delfino, morfologia di un 136
delfino, scheletro di un 136
delimitazione, nastro di 771
della calotta polare 61
della tundra polare 61
delta 48, 51
Delta II 24
delta, ala a 629
deltaplano 897
deltoide 150
demi-volée 820
denaro 729
dendrite 168
denominazione dei cicloni tropicali 63
densimetro 562
dentale 112, 641
dentato 79
dentatura nell'uomo 159
dente 108, 112, 303, 304, 331, 348, 362, 382, 390, 636, 638, 642, 643, 863
dente d'arresto 460
dente del giudizio 159
dente dello scarificatore 636
dente di ingranaggio 686
dente di leone 187
dente di roccia 756
dente velenifero 112
dentellare, forbici per 454
dentello 404, 405
denti 159, 309
denti, spazzolino da 384
denti, spazzolino elettrico da 384
dentifricio 384
dentina 159
dentini 453
denunce, ufficio per le 768
deodorante 379
depositi alluvionali 48
deposito 394
deposito bagagli 582
deposito dei cereali 596
deposito dei containers 596
deposito dei missili 762
deposito del materiale medico 781
deposito del materiale sporco 780
deposito del materiale sterile 780
deposito del petrolio 596
deposito delle barelle 778
deposito delle rinfuse 596
deposito di carbone 646
deposito per containers 708
deposito, fessura per il 730
depuratore d'aria 261
deragliatore 870
deragliatore anteriore 578, 580
deragliatore posteriore 578, 580
deriva 625, 631, 760, 834, 835, 840
deriva a scomparsa 836
derivazione 687
derma 172
derrick 604, 607
derrick, albero del 607
desertico 61
deserto 52, 66
Deserto dei Gobi 33
Deserto del Kalahari 34
Deserto del Namib 34
Deserto del Sahara 34
Deserto di Atacama 31
deserto roccioso 52
deserto sabbioso 52
deserto, volpe del 134
designer di produzione 428
desquamatore 905
dessert, coltello da 228
dessert, cucchiaio da 228
dessert, forchetta da 228
destinazione 582
destra 740
detenuti, doccia dei 768
detenuti, ingresso dei 726
detenuti, ufficio d'ammissione dei 726
detersivo, vaschetta per il 294
detonatore 757
detriti 63
deumidificatore 261
deviatore 269
Devoniano 92
di bolina 833
di bolina larga 833
di bolina molto stretta 833
di bolina stretta 833
di montagna 61
diafisi 155
diaframma 163, 477, 488, 502
diaframma del serbatoio dell'ossigeno liquido 25
diaframma di apertura 694
diagonale 663
diagramma di carico 571
diamante 375, 610, 794
diamante, punta di 278
diametro 704
diapason 436
diapositiva 483
diastema 123
diavolo della Tasmania 143
dicco 44
didascalia 395, 471
dieci 703
dieci comandamenti 738
dieresi 473
diesel, motore 586
diesis 435
dietro 348
difensore ala destra 806
difensore ala sinistra 806
difensore centrale 812, 814
difensore destro 812, 814, 878
difensore di canestro 809
difensore esterno destro 803
difensore sinistro 812, 814, 878
difensori 799
difesa 806
difesa antimissile 762
difetti della vista 691
differenziale 553
differenziale, interruttore 272
diffusione di informazioni 525
diffusore 428, 479
diffusore della fiamma 319
diffusore tubolare 627
diga 657
diga a contrafforti 660
diga a contrafforti, sezione trasversale di una 660
diga a gravità 661
diga a gravità, sezione trasversale di una 661
diga a volta 661
diga a volta, sezione trasversale di una 661
diga fissa 664
diga in terra 660
diga in terra, sezione trasversale di una 660
diga mobile 664
dighe, esempi di 660
digiuno 164
dimetrodonte 92
diminuzione di tensione 646, 662, 677
dinamo 578, 688
diodo 673
Dione 5
directory 524
direttore artistico 428
direttore d'orchestra, podio del 437
direttore dei tiri 859
direttore della corsa 870
direttore della fotografia 429
direttore di tiro 860
direttore tecnico 489, 490
direttore, ufficio del 394, 726, 731, 732
direzione del flusso di elettroni 687, 689
direzione del vento 55
direzione della Mecca 738
direzione della reazione 684
direzione e forza del vento 55
direzione obbligatoria a destra 546
direzione obbligatoria a sinistra 544, 546
direzione obbligatoria diritto 544, 546
direzione, tasto di 261
direzione, timone di 760
direzione, ufficio della 718
direzioni consentite diritto e a destra 546
direzioni consentite diritto e a sinistra 544
disaccoppiamento, braccio telescopico di 587
discarica 709
discarica autorizzata 69
discenderia 650
discensore 900
discesa libera 889
discesa pericolosa 545, 547
discesa, corridoio di 402
dischetto 880
dischetto del rigore 802
dischetto di centrocampo 803
dischi 237
dischi, negozio di 714
disco 9, 273, 423, 493, 500, 521, 559, 560, 641, 793, 851
disco abrasivo 308
disco abrasivo, supporto del 308
disco adesivo 111
disco centrale 95
disco deflettore del calore 274
disco del freno 574
disco di copertura 643
disco di tensione 453, 457
disco intervertebrale 157
disco per macchina fotografica digitale 481
disco versatile digitale (DVD) 494
disco, braccio del 641
disco, freno a 874
disco, vano del 501
discontinuità di Gutenberg 42
discontinuità di Mohorovicic 42
disegno 396
disegno a carboncino 396
disegno a inchiostro 396
disegno a matite colorate 396
disegno a pastelli a cera 396
disegno a pastelli a olio 396
disegno a pastelli secchi 396
disegno a pennarelli 396
disegno stampato 368, 369
disegno, piano da 399
disegno, tavolo da 399
disgelo, acqua di 46
disinnesto del pistone 315
disinnesto, calcola di 460
dispari 919
dispensa 224, 250, 724
dispersione di calore 68
display 261, 476, 494, 495, 497, 503, 505, 506, 507, 508, 526, 528, 529, 530, 548, 613, 699, 730, 731
display a cristalli liquidi 477, 496
display dei colori 456
display dei controlli di bordo 626
display dei dati 479
display dei dati, pulsante di illuminazione del 479
display dei parametri del motore e delle avarie 626
display del numero delle righe 456
display del radar 771
display delle frequenze 503
display delle funzioni 450
display di navigazione 626
display di pilotaggio 626
display digitale 699, 777
display informativo 512
display, pannello del 496
display, pulsante di apertura del 526
display, regolatore del 506
dispositivi di comunicazione 522
dispositivi di contatto 274
dispositivi di entrata 514
dispositivi di memorizzazione dei dati 521
dispositivi di uscita 518
dispositivo antiallagamento 294
dispositivo di agganciamento 586, 587
dispositivo di allarme 765
dispositivo di arresto 458
dispositivo di bloccaggio 289, 424
dispositivo di blocco 303, 304, 321
dispositivo di blocco dell'inclinazione della lama 304
dispositivo di blocco dell'interruttore 306
dispositivo di chiusura 913
dispositivo di espulsione del cestello 238
dispositivo di fissaggio 284, 649
dispositivo di fissaggio del tubo 275
dispositivo di gonfiaggio 611
dispositivo di regolazione 889, 895
dispositivo di rimorchio 573
dispositivo di serraggio 685
dispositivo di sicurezza per sovratemperatura 266
dispositivo di smorzamento magnetico 698
dispositivo per aeronavigazione 761
dispositivo segnapunti elettrico 848
disposizione 244
disposizione dei birilli 865
disprosio 684
dissipatore termico 513
distanza percorsa 700
distanza tra le puntine 562
distanza, misura della 700
distanze, scala delle 478
distanziatore 783, 859, 913
distendere per asciugare 347
distillazione sotto vuoto 656
distintivo 770
distributore 659
distributore automatico di bibite 723
distributore automatico di biglietti 593
distributore del ghiaccio 548
distributore di bibite 548, 779
distributore di ghiaccio in cubetti 224
distributore via cavo 486
distribuzione del fertilizzante 69
distribuzione della vegetazione 66
distribuzione, pannello di 272
distribuzione, quadro di 273
distruggidocumenti 535
dita 116
ditale 454
ditale in gomma 531
ditali 206
dito 110, 117, 122, 130, 143, 172, 797, 900
dito del guanto 346
dito del piede 146, 148
dito esterno 115
dito interno 115
dito lobato 117
dito medio 115
dito palmato 117
dito posteriore 115, 117
dito prensile 139
divanetto 277
divani 276
divano 276
divano a due posti 276, 724
divano Chesterfield 276
divano posteriore 555
divano-letto 280
diverso da 703
divieto di inversione di marcia 544, 546
divieto di sorpasso 544, 546
divise di servizio 764
divise, lavanderia per le 764
divisione 703
divisioni dello scudo 740
divisori 532
divisori alfabetici per schedario 532
divisorio 771
divisorio di tela 902

INDICE DELLE VOCI ITALIANE

djembè 433
Dnepr, Fiume 32
do 434, 847
doccetta 270
doccia 251, 264, 724, 726, 780
doccia a telefono 264
doccia degli ufficiali 764
doccia dei detenuti 768
doccia dei vigili del fuoco 764
doccia orale 384
doccia, box 264
documentazione, centro di 764
dodecagono regolare 705
dogana 596, 621
dohyo 847
dolcevita 363
dolcevita, maglione 354
dolci 723
dolci, miscelatore per 232
dolci, pennello per 232
dolci, stampini per 232
dolciumi 717
dolichi 190
dolina 47
dollaro 728
Dominica 743
Dominicana, Repubblica 743
dominio di livello superiore 524
dominio di secondo livello 524
dominio, nome del 524
domino 914
dondolo, sedia a 276, 277
donna 148, 914
donna, scarpe da 343
donnola 134
dopobarba 383
doppia coppia 914
doppia curva, la prima a destra 544, 547
doppia piastra di registrazione 503
doppiamente dentato 79
doppio bemolle 435
doppio corrente 252
doppio diesis 435
doppio lavello 262
doppio pennello 739
doppio senso di circolazione 544, 546
doppio slash 524
doppio zero 919
doppio-sei 914
doppio-zero 914
doppione 914
doppiopetto, abbottonatura a 352
doppiopetto, giacca a 348
Dorado 11
dormitorio dei vigili del fuoco 764
Dorsale Medio-Atlantica 50
Dorsale Medio-Indiana 50
Dorsale medio-oceanica 49
Dorsale Pacifico-Antartica 50
Dorsale Pacifico-Orientale 50
Dorsale Sud Occidentale Indiana 50
Dorsale Sud Orientale Indiana 50
dorsali oceaniche 50
dorsali, barra per i 851
dorso 115, 124, 130, 173, 227, 295, 303, 391, 426, 750, 830, 832
dorso del guanto 346
dorso del libro 425
dorso del naso 175
dorso della lingua 176
dossiere 857
dosso 875
dotto deferente 169
dotto della spermateca 104
dotto eiaculatore 169
dotto ermafrodito 104
dotto galattoforo 171
dotto lacrimale 177
dotto salivare 99
dotto sudoriparo 172
dotto velenifero 112
Douglas, tasca di 170
dozzina (da 1 a 12) 919
dozzina (da 13 a 24) 919
dozzina (da 25 a 36) 919
draglia 602
dragoncello 202
Dragone 13
dragoni 917
drakar 598
Drake, Canale di 29, 31
drenaggio, tubo del 253
drenaggio, tubo di 292, 294
drenaggio, valvola di 291
dressage 855
dritta 609, 616, 617
dritto di prua 598, 838
drittofilo 455
drive per cassette 521
drizza 603, 739
drizza di picco 602
dromedario 129
drumlin 45
drupa 81
drupe 192
drupeola 83
dubnio 683
due con 839
due metà, tempo di 434
due punti 473
due senza 839
dulse 183
duna 51
duna complessa 52
duna parabolica 52
dune longitudinali 52
dune trasversali 52
dune, catena di 52
dune, esempi di 52
duo 438
duodeno 116, 164
dura madre 167, 168
durian 197
duty free 621

E

e commerciale 473
e-commerce 525
eau de toilette 379
ebraico 468
echino 404
echinodermi 94, 95
eclissi anulare 6
eclissi di Luna 7
eclissi di Sole 6
eclissi parziale 6, 7
eclissi totale 6, 7
eclittica 13
eco 40, 41
economia 728
ecoscandaglio 613
ectoderma 95
ectopterigoideo 112
Ecuador 742
edicola 593, 715
edificio dei servizi 664
edificio del reattore 667, 669
edificio delle turbine 668
edificio per uffici 710, 713
edificio pubblico 39
editing del suono, tasti per l' 450
editoriale 471
effetti speciali video digitali 491
effetti speciali, rotella di selezione degli 496
effetti speciali, tasti degli 496
effetto serra 68
effetto serra naturale 68
effetto serra, incremento dell' 68
effigie 729
efflusso dell'aria calda 258
Egeo, Mare 32
Egitto 745
eglefino 221
eiettore 638
einsteinio 684
El Salvador 742
elaboratore dei dati aerodinamici 626
elaboratore di gestione del volo 626
elaborazione dei dati 41, 54
elastici stringitesta 773
elastico 280, 351, 902, 903
elastico ferma abiti 389
elastico regolabile per il capo 773
elefante 129
elementi architettonici 413
elementi chimici 682
elementi del microscopio elettronico 694
elementi della casa 247
elementi di combustibile difettosi incamiciati 666
elementi di combustibile difettosi, incamiciatura degli 666
elementi di combustibile difettosi, vasca degli 666
elementi, tavola periodica degli 682
elemento della canna fumaria 257
elemento di combustibile 667
elemento orizzontale 663
elemento riscaldante 258, 259, 293, 294, 318
elemento riscaldante inferiore 266
elemento riscaldante superiore 266
elemento tubolare 652
elemento verticale 663
elenco dei concorrenti 789
elettricità 272, 662, 663, 665, 677
elettricità, rete di trasmissione dell' 674
elettrodo 275, 318
elettrodo centrale 562
elettrodo di accensione 259
elettrodo di massa 562
elettrodo negativo 562
elettrodo positivo 562
elettrodomestici 236, 288
elettrodomestici vari 240
elettromagnete di campo 688
elettrone 680
elettroni, collettore di 689
elettroni, direzione del flusso di 687, 689
elettronica 689
elettronica, negozio di 714
elevatore 407, 643, 666
elevatore a nastro 646
elevatore a nastro trasportatore 647
elevatore della granella 643
elevatore per containers e palette di carico 623
elevatore per sedie a rotelle 569
elevone 23
eliambulanza 631
elica 306, 606, 608, 609, 705, 763
elica bipala 628
elica di propulsione 605
elica di prua 606
elica di ventilazione 688
elica posteriore 606
elica tripala 628
elica, albero dell' 609
elica, mantello d' 605
elice 173, 405
elice, coda dell' 173
elice, radice dell' 173
eliche 206, 762
elicotteri, esempi di 631
elicotteri, hangar per 762
elicotteri, piattaforma di appontaggio per 762
elicottero 631, 762
elicottero antincendio 631
elicottero da trasporto tattico 631
elio 684
elio, serbatoio dell' 25
eliografo 58
eliporto 652
elmetto 772
elmo 748, 749, 765
elmo da vigile del fuoco 765
ematite, matita di 423
emblema 739
emergenza, freno di 594
emergenza, veicolo di 21
Emirati Arabi Uniti 746
emisferi 35
emisfero meridionale 35
emisfero meridionale, costellazioni dell' 10
emisfero occidentale 35
emisfero orientale 35
emisfero settentrionale 35
emisfero settentrionale, costellazioni dell' 12
emissario 48
emissione dello scontrino 548
emissione di acido nitrico 70
emissione di acido solforico 70
emissione di anidride solforosa 70
emissione di banconote 730
emissione di gas inquinanti 69
emissione di onde ultrasonore 41
emissione di ossido d'azoto 70
emittenti, tasti di ricerca 495
emmental 211
en plein 919
enartrosi 156
encefalo 109
endecagono regolare 705
endocardio 162
endocarpo 81, 82
endoderma 95
energia 646
energia eolica 676
energia eolica, produzione di elettricità da 677
energia fossile 646
energia geotermica 646
energia geotermica, produzione di elettricità da 646
energia nucleare 665
energia nucleare, produzione di elettricità da 665
energia solare 78, 672
energia solare, produzione di elettricità da 674
energia termica 68, 646
energia termica, produzione di elettricità da 646
energia, fonte di 41
energia, rilascio di 681
energia, unità di misura dell' 702
enneagono regolare 705
Enrico VIII 736
enti sanitari 525
entrata 100, 719, 829
entrata del pozzo 649
entrata dell'acqua 268
entrata di piedi 829
entrata di servizio 732
entrata di testa 829
entrata principale 250
entrate 829
epeira 102
epicentro 43
epicondilo 153
epidermide 172
epididimo 169
epifisi 167
epifisi distale 155
epifisi prossimale 155
epiglottide 163, 176
epistrofeo 153, 157
epitroclea 153
equalizzatore grafico 498
Equatore 31, 34, 35, 36, 63
equatore 13
equatore celeste 13
equilibratore 756
equilibratore orizzontale 631
equilibrio, posizione d' 690
equinozio d'autunno 54
equinozio di primavera 13, 54
equipaggiamento 769
equipaggiamento del cruscotto 771
equipaggiamento di guida 25
equipaggiamento di salvataggio 611
equipaggiamento protettivo 808
equipaggio, alloggi dell' 604
équipe di pronto intervento 853
equitazione 854
equivalente a 703
erba 822
erba cipollina 184
erba medica 190
erbicida 69
erbio 684
erbivori 67
Ercole 13
Eridano 10
Eritrea 745
Erlenmeyer, beuta di 685
ermellino 741
erogatore 767
erogatore d'emergenza 841
erogatore del tubo della scala 766
erogatore, primo stadio dell' 841
erogatore, secondo stadio dell' 841
erogazione, bocca di 268, 270
erpice doppio a dischi 641
eruzione, vulcano in 44
esagono regolare 705
esame audiometrico, stanza per l' 781
esame psichiatrico, stanza per 778
escape 514
escavatore idraulico 638
escavatrice a ruota di tazze 647
escludi regina 100
esempi di abiti 356
esempi di adattatori 269
esempi di aeroplani 628
esempi di alghe 75
esempi di ancore 610
esempi di anfibi 111
esempi di angoli 704
esempi di aracnidi 102
esempi di archi 413, 541
esempi di arricciature 283
esempi di attrezzature 601
esempi di autoarticolati 572
esempi di becchi 117
esempi di biciclette 581
esempi di birilli 865
esempi di camicette 359
esempi di camion 573
esempi di carri merci 588
esempi di carrozzerie 549
esempi di chiodi 301
esempi di colli 362
esempi di colori 741
esempi di coltelli 228
esempi di coltelli da cucina 229
esempi di conifere 89
esempi di cucchiai 228
esempi di dighe 660
esempi di dune 52
esempi di elicotteri 631
esempi di felci 76
esempi di fettucce 283
esempi di figure 741
esempi di finestre 415
esempi di fiori 80
esempi di foglie 89
esempi di forchette 228
esempi di frese 308
esempi di fusibili 272
esempi di giacche e pullover 358
esempi di gonne 357
esempi di gruppi strumentali 438
esempi di impennaggi 629
esempi di impugnature 840
esempi di insetti 101
esempi di lagomorfi 123
esempi di latifoglie 88
esempi di licheni 74
esempi di linee di costa 51
esempi di mammiferi carnivori 134
esempi di mammiferi insettivori 121
esempi di mammiferi marini 137
esempi di mammiferi ungulati 128
esempi di mammiferi volanti 141
esempi di maniche 360
esempi di marsupiali 143
esempi di mecchie e punte da trapano 306
esempi di metalli 741
esempi di motociclette e ciclomotore 577
esempi di muschi 75
esempi di occhiali 385
esempi di pantaloni 358
esempi di partizioni 740
esempi di pellicce 741
esempi di pezze onorevoli 740
esempi di pieghe 357
esempi di pneumatici 560
esempi di ponti a travata 541
esempi di ponti ad arco 541
esempi di porte 416
esempi di prese 844
esempi di primati 139
esempi di raccordi 269
esempi di raccordo 538
esempi di razzi spaziali 24
esempi di reti 522
esempi di rettili 114
esempi di roditori 123
esempi di sacchi a pelo 904
esempi di salti 881
esempi di sci 888
esempi di sci nautici 840
esempi di sedie 277
esempi di simboli di valute 728
esempi di sonde spaziali 19
esempi di strumenti a tastiera 443
esempi di tasche 360
esempi di tavoli 278
esempi di telefoni 507
esempi di tende 283, 902
esempi di tuffi 829
esempi di uccelli 118
esempi di utensili 401
esempi di vele 601
esempi di vulcani 44
esempi di zampe 117
esempi di zoccoli 127
esercizio, area di 823
esocarpo 81, 82, 83
esofago 95, 97, 99, 103, 104, 109, 110, 112, 113, 116, 125, 163, 164
esosfera 53
espadrille 344
espansa 472
espansione fissa 700
espansione mobile 700
espansione, bullone a 302
espansione, camera di 695
espansione, vaso di 259
espirazione 832
esplosione 564
esposimetro 479
esposimetro spot 479
espositore 510
espositore di brochure 730
espositore di fine corsia 181
esposizione, impostazione del tempo di 479
esposizione, indice di 479
esposizione, scala dei tempi di 479
esposizione, tasto per il valore di 479
esposizioni multiple, tasto per le 476
espressione, pedali d' 444
espulsione del cestello, dispositivo di 238
espulsione, pulsante di 477
espulsione, tasto di 495, 499, 501
espulsore degli accessori 236
essere umano 146
Est 37
est 616, 917
Est Nord-Est 37
Est Sud-Est 37
estate 54
estate, solstizio d' 54
estensore 850
estensore breve delle dita 150
estensore comune delle dita 151
estensore lungo delle dita 150
estensore radiale breve del carpo 151
estensore radiale lungo del carpo 151
estensore ulnare del carpo 151
esterno centro (giocatore) 794
esterno centro (posizione) 795
esterno della miniera 648
esterno destro 794
esterno destro (posizione) 795
esterno di una casa 244
esterno sinistro 794
esterno sinistro (posizione) 795
estintore 725, 771
estintore portatile 767
estirpatore 325
Estonia 744
estradosso 413
estratto conto, fessura di aggiornamento dell' 730
estratto di vaniglia 200
estrattore dei gas combusti 758
estrazione dell'aria, tubo di 274, 275
estremità del braccio 693
estremità della guida 331
estremo 804
estremo di destra 806
estremo di sinistra 806
estuario 38, 51
età della pietra, armi dell' 748
eterotrofi, organismi 67
etichetta 500
etichetta portaindirizzo 389
etichettatrice 533
etichette autoadesive 532
etilometro 769
Etiopia 745

INDICE DELLE VOCI ITALIANE

ettagono regolare 705
Eurasia 28
euro 728
Europa 4, 28, 32, 50, 743
europio 684
Eustachio, tuba di 174, 175
Eutelsat 486
euthynteria 403, 404
evacuazione, percorso di 543
evaporazione 67, 680
evidenziatore 397, 470
evoluzione della vita 92
evoluzione delle specie 92
ex voto 737
expander 450
extra-nero 472
eye-liner 378
Eyre, Lago 29

F

fa 434
faccetta 306, 629
faccetta scanalata 306
faccia 146, 300, 409, 815, 867
faccia del padiglione (8) 374
faccia della stella (8) 374
faccia inferiore della cintura (16) 374
faccia principale della corona (8) 374
faccia superiore della cintura (16) 374
facciata 411
facole 6
faggio 88
faggiola 193
fagiano 120, 212
fagiano, uovo di 213
fagioli 191
fagiolino 191
fagiolino giallo 191
fagiolo adzuki 191
fagiolo asparagio 190
fagiolo borlotto 191
fagiolo cannellino 191
fagiolo dall'occhio nero 190
fagiolo di Lima 191
fagiolo di Spagna 191
fagiolo egiziano 190
fagiolo mungo 191
fagiolo mungo nero 191
fagiolo nero 191
fagiolo pinto 191
fagiolo romano 191
faglia 43
fagotti 437
fagotto 446
Fahrenheit, scala 695
fai da te 298
faina 134
fairway 866, 867
falange distale 133, 154, 155
falange media 154, 155
falange mediana 133
falange prossimale 133, 154, 155
falange, prima 126
falange, seconda 126, 172
falange, terza 126, 172
falangi 111, 122, 131, 136, 138, 141, 142, 154, 155
falcatus 92
falce 330
falcetto 330
falciacondizionatrice 642
falciatrice a mano 332
falco 119
falda 352, 749
falda freatica 70
falda larga, cappello a 341
falena della betulla 101
falesia 51
falesia costiera 51
Falkland, Isole 31
falli 789
Falloppio, tuba di 170
Falloppio, tube di 171
falsa partenza, fune di 830
falsa zampa 97
falsa zampa anale 97
falsabraca 408
falso puntone 252
falso quartiere 855
famiglia 784
famiglia degli archi 437, 439
famiglia degli ottoni 437
famiglia dei legni 437
familiari, sala d'attesa dei 778
fanale 333, 586
fanale anteriore 579, 585
fanale di testa 585
fanale di testa dell'albero 605
fanale posteriore 571, 575, 576, 578
fango, colata di 47
fante 914
fantino 856
faraglione 51
faraona 120, 212

fard in polvere 378
fard, pennello da 378
faretra 859
faretto a pinza 286
faretto da binario 287
faretto orientabile 287
farfalla 96, 832
farfalla femmina,anatomia di una 97
farfalla, morfologia di una 96
farina 204
farina di avena 204
farina di mais 204
farina integrale 204
farina non trattata 204
farina semplice 204
faringe 99, 163, 164
farmacia 714, 725, 778, 781
faro 596, 614
faro di atterraggio 631
faro fendinebbia 554, 570
faro subacqueo 246
faro, lanterna del 614
farro 203
farsetto 338
fascetta 377
fascetta del sigaro 390
fascetta di fissaggio 59
fascia 390, 404, 439, 440, 566
fascia blu 871
fascia catarifrangente 611
fascia degli asteroidi 5
fascia di chiusura 889
fascia di cuoio 350
fascia di gravità 610
fascia di regolazione 502
fascia di sospensione 772
fascia elastica 353
fascia lata, tensore della 150
fascia laterale 551
fascia protettiva della fronte 773
fascia reggibraccio 777
fascia sopracigliare 115
fascia stringitesta 772
fasciatoio 281
fasciatura in gomma 838
fascio blu 494
fascio di conduttori 663
fascio elettronico 494, 694
fascio radar 40
fascio rosso 494
fascio verde 494
fascio, riduzione del diametro del 694
fascione anteriore 550
fase di scivolamento 892
fase di spinta 892
fase, conduttore di 273
fasi 401
fasi della Luna 7
fasi della produzione di elettricità 662
fasi lunari, quadrante a 697
fast food 715
fattore Rh negativo 702
fattore Rh positivo 702
fattoria 182
fattoriale 703
fauce di un lagomorfo: coniglio 123
fauce di un roditore: ratto 123
fauci di lagomorfi 123
fauci di roditori 123
fauci, istmo delle 174
fave 190
favo 100
favo, sezione del 100
fazzoletto da taschino 348
fede nuziale 376
federa 280
Federazione Russa 744
fegato 109, 110, 112, 113, 116, 125, 161, 164, 212
feijoa 197
felce 76
felce arborea 76
felce, struttura di una 76
felci 92
felci, esempi di 76
felpa 370
felpa con cappuccio 370
feltro del martelletto 443
feltro, cappello di 340, 341
feluca 600
femmina 453
femminella 86
femminile 702
femore 96, 98, 111, 116, 122, 126, 131, 138, 141, 142, 152
femore, collo del 153
femore, condilo laterale del 153
femore, condilo mediale del 153
femore, testa del 153
fendinebbia, faro 554, 570
Fenice 10
fenicottero 119
feritoia 238
feritoia di espulsione 755
ferma ago, vite 398
fermacampioni 534
fermacapelli 380

fermacolletto 376
fermacorda 285
fermacravatta 376
fermacravatta, spillo 376
fermagli 534
fermaglio 350, 470
fermaglio a molla 534
fermaglio ad aste 854
fermaglio equilibratore 285
fermapiedi 578, 580, 851
fermaporta 291
fermarsi e dare precedenza 544, 546
fermata dell'autobus 712
fermio 684
fermo 284
fermo a molla 391
fermo del braccio d'attacco dell'occhione 756
fermo del nastro 313
fermo della lama 382
fermo di testa 835
fermo girevole 572
ferodo 559
ferretto 367
ferri per il camino 257
ferro 309, 683, 867, 868
ferro 3 868
ferro 4 868
ferro 5 868
ferro 6 868
ferro 7 868
ferro 8 868
ferro 9 868
ferro circolare 457
ferro da maglia 457
ferro da stiro a vapore 288
ferro di cavallo 127, 376
ferrovia 39
fertilizzante, distribuzione del 69
fertilizzazione del suolo 69
ferzo 834
fessura 147, 149, 227, 386, 424, 444, 463
fessura di aggiornamento dell'estratto conto 730
fessura di alimentazione della carta 511
fessura di alimentazione manuale 519
fessura di registrazione della transazione 730
fessura di sollevamento 535
fessura oculare 749
fessura per gettoni 507
fessura per il deposito 730
fessura per l'introduzione delle monete 920
fessura per la restituzione delle 920
fessura per la scheda PC 526
fessure branchiali 108
fessure, bocchetta per 289
festone drappeggiato 283
fettone 127
fettucce, esempi di 283
fettuccia arricciata 283
fettuccia plissettata 283
fettuccine 206
fez 339
fiala 783
fiamma 681, 739
fiamma, regolatore della 391
fiammiferi, bustina di 391
fiammiferi, scatola di 391
fiammifero minerva 391
fiammifero svedese 391
fiancale 749
fiancata 783
fiancata, muro di 597
fianco 115, 124, 147, 149, 409, 413, 425, 560, 561, 602
fianco destro 740
fianco esterno 255
fianco interno 255
fianco panoramica 713
fianco sinistro 740
fiasca da polvere 752
fiato, strumenti a 446
fibbia 350, 352, 388, 555, 611
fibbia del sottopancia 855
fibbia di regolazione 906
fibra 908
fibra muscolare 168
fibra nervosa 172
fibula 122, 126, 131, 138, 141, 142, 336
fico 197
fico d'India 197
fidanzamento, anello di 376
fienile 182
fieno greco 198
fieno, balle di 875
Figi 747
Figi, Isole 29
figli 785
figlia 784, 785
figlio 784, 785
figura 855
figure, esempi di 741
fila 384, 431
filamento 80, 274
filamento di tungsteno 274
filamento, supporto del 274
Filchner, Banchisa di 29
file 524
file server 523

file, formato del 524
filettatura 268, 439, 440
filetto 302, 471, 854
filetto 214
filetto a D in gomma 854
filetto a oliva 854
filetto ad aste 854
filetto con anello e giocattolo 854
fili dell'ordito 463
filiera per tubi 314
filiere 103
filigrana 729
Filippine 33, 747
Filippine, Fossa delle 50
filmpack 481
filo 227, 229, 300, 313, 689, 908
filo conduttore 274, 275
filo d'appoggio 103
filo da giardino 324
filo da taglio 331
filo della lama 382, 454
filo della trama 463
filo di guardia 663
filo di nylon 332
filo di sicurezza 729
filo di terra 272
filo di tracciamento 313
filo elastico 867
filo interdentale 384
filo interdentale, contenitore per 384
filo metallico 793, 848
filo neutro 272
filo neutro di alimentazione 272
filo per saldatura 318
filo radiale 103
filo spirale 103
filone francese 204
filone strato 44
filtri dello specchio grande 612
filtri dello specchio piccolo 612
filtro 175, 238, 246, 258, 290, 390, 675, 773
filtro colorato 478
filtro dell'aria 261, 331, 552, 586, 636
filtro dello scarico 270
filtro di sicurezza rosso 485
filtro per il tè 233
filtro per lanugine 292, 293
filtro polarizzatore 478
filtro, cassetta 241
filtro, macchina da caffè a 241
filum terminale esterno 167
filum terminale interno 167
finale 789
finale, quarti di 789
finalista 789
finanza 728
fine 515
fine chiamata, tasto di 506
fine corsa, interruttore di 417
fine, tasto di ricerca della 496
finecorsa 303
finestra 249, 251, 485, 663, 797, 836
finestra a battenti 415
finestra a battenti con apertura all'interno 415
finestra a bilico orizzontale 415
finestra a bilico verticale 415
finestra a gelosia 415
finestra a ghigliottina 415
finestra a libro 415
finestra con sbarre 727
finestra del seminterrato 245
finestra di accesso 521
finestra di controllo 238, 239, 290
finestra di lettura 499
finestra panoramica 713
finestra scorrevole 415
finestra zanzariera 902
finestra, tenda per 282
finestra, traversa inferiore di 252
finestra, traversa superiore di 252
finestre, accessori per 282
finestre, esempi di 415
finestrella per la restituzione dei gettoni 507
finestrino 551, 554, 567, 594, 624
finestrino di atterraggio 631
finestrino di osservazione 23
finestrino panoramico 584
finitura 401
finitura, chiodo di 301
finlandese 469
Finlandia 744
finocchio 185
finta 355, 369
fiocco 340, 603, 834
fiocco di dentro 603
fioraio 715
fiordi 51
fiore 77, 80
fiore del pinnacolo 412
fiore, struttura di un 80
fiorettista 848
fioretto 648, 649, 849
fioretto elettrico 848
fiori 914, 917
fiori, esempi di 80

fiori, macchia di 322
fioritura 86
fiosso 342
firewall 523
firma del titolare 729
firma ufficiale 729
fisarmonica 432
fischio 240
fish-eye 478
fisica: elettricità e magnetismo 687
fisica: meccanica 686
fisica: ottica 690
fissaggio a muro, piastra di 284
fissaggio del tubo, dispositivo di 275
fissaggio, bagno di 485
fissaggio, dispositivo di 284, 649
fissativo 400
fissione dell'uranio 665
fissione nucleare 681
fiume 38, 39, 48
Fiume Congo 34
Fiume Danubio 32
Fiume Dnepr 32
Fiume Mackenzie 30
Fiume Mississippi 30
Fiume Niger 34
Fiume Orinoco 31
Fiume Paranà 31
Fiume San Lorenzo 30
Fiume Senegal 34
Fiume Vistola 32
Fiume Volga 32
flacone 783
flagello 104
flap 624
flap, leva dei 626
flash elettronico 482
flash, tubo a 692
flauti 437
flauto 446
flauto di Pan 433
flessibile 482
flessibile pneumatico 482
flessometro 313
flessore ulnare del carpo 150, 151
flettente 913
flip 881
floema 87
floppy disk 521
fluido refrigerante 670, 671, 674
fluido termovettore, pompa del 669
fluido vettore caldo 665, 674
fluido vettore freddo 665, 674
fluido vettore, ingresso del 672
fluido vettore, uscita del 672
fluido, vite di regolazione del 320
fluoro 683
flusso d'acqua 95
flusso d'aria 398
flusso sotterraneo 67
flûte 225
Fobos 4
foca 137
focale, moltiplicatore di 478
focena 137
focolare 256, 259
focone 753
fodera 342, 348, 349, 370, 386, 455, 881
fodera del guanciale 280
fodero 391, 841, 905, 907
fodero di pelle 907
foglia 75, 77, 78, 79, 185
foglia carnosa 78
foglia di acanto 276, 405
foglia nasale 140
foglia, struttura di una 79
fogliame 87
foglie composte 79
foglie semplici 79
foglie squamiformi del cipresso 89
foglie, esempi di 89
foglio 426
foglio di risguardo 426
fogliolina arrotolata 76
foie-gras 216
follicolo 84
follicolo pilifero 172
follicolo, sezione di un 84
fondale 430
fondale oceanico 49
fondazione 538, 660
fondazione del pilone 540
fondazione naturale 538
fondazione, corrente di 252, 253
fondazione, muro di 252, 253
fondazione, rinforzo della 660
fondazioni 253
fondello 494, 816, 822, 860, 912
fondello del caricatore 754
fondello metallico 912
fondina 770
fondista 892
fondo 902, 903
fondo abissale 42
fondo dell'onda 49
fondo protettivo 918
fondo refrattario 256

fondo, pista da 886
fondocampo 821
fondotinta fluido 378
fonduta, forchetta da 228
fonduta, servizio da 231
fonduta, tegame per 234
fonendoscopio 776
fonoteca 733
font, caratteri di un 472
fontana per le abluzioni 738
fontanella anteriore 158
fontanella mastoidea 158
fontanella posteriore 158
fontanella sfenoidale 158
fonte alimentare primaria 67
fonte battesimale 737
fonte del servizio 471
fonte di energia 41
football americano 806
football canadese 809
forame cieco 176
forame intervertebrale 157
forame otturatorio 122
forbice sfoltitrice a doppia lama dentellata 382
forbice sfoltitrice a lama singola dentellata 382
forbice, taglio a 375
forbici 454, 777, 905
forbici da cucina 233
forbici da parrucchiere 382
forbici di sicurezza 377
forbici per dentellare 454
forbici per unghie dei piedi 377
forbici tagliasiepi 330
forbicine per cuticole 377
forbicine per unghie 377
forca di sollevamento, incastro per la 635
forca, braccio della 632
forcella 14, 579, 870, 875
forcella anteriore 870
forcella inferiore 578
forcella superiore 578
forcella telescopica anteriore 574, 577
forche 632, 633
forchetta 227, 697, 905
forchetta da dessert 228
forchetta da fonduta 228
forchetta da insalata 228
forchetta da ostriche 228
forchetta da pesce 228
forchetta da tavola 228
forchette, esempi di 228
forchettone 229
forcina 380
forcone 326
foresta 45
foresta boreale 66
foresta di caducifoglie 66
foresta di conifere 66
foresta mista 66
foresta pluviale tropicale 66
foresta temperata 66
foresta tropicale 66
foreste, incendio delle 69
forma 345
forma dei caratteri 472
formaggi a pasta dura 211
formaggi a pasta molle 211
formaggi di capra 210
formaggi erborinati 211
formaggi freschi 210
formaggio 722
formaggio cremoso 210
formaggio fresco di capra 210
formaggio, coltello da 228
formato del file 524
formazione professionale, ufficio di 730
forme geometriche 704
formica 101
formina da forno 226
formula 1, auto da 873
formula 3000, auto da 873
formula Indy, auto da 873
Fornace 10
fornellino 234
fornello 390
fornello da campo a due fuochi 903
fornello da campo con un bruciatore 903
fornello di accesso 650
fornello di getto 650
forni a microonde 723
fornice, corpo del 167
fornitore del servizio Internet 525
forno 224, 290, 614, 721, 722
forno a microonde 224, 238
forno elettrico 465
forno solare 674
forno tubolare 656
forno, manopola del 290
forno, teglia da 232
foro 342, 346, 350, 371, 423
foro apicale 159
foro centrale 500
foro del piede 444
foro di riempimento 757
foro di risonanza 439

foro di tiraggio 259
foro per l'aria 390
forte 849
forti precipitazioni 63
fortificazione alla Vauban 409
forza del vento 55
forza, linea di 687
forza, unità di misura della 702
forze che agiscono su un aeroplano 630
foschia 57, 65
fosforo 683
fossa biologica 263
Fossa del Giappone 50
Fossa delle Aleutine 50
Fossa delle Curili 50
Fossa delle Filippine 50
Fossa delle Marianne 50
Fossa delle Ryukyu 50
Fossa di Giava 50
Fossa di Kermadec-Tonga 50
Fossa di Puerto Rico 50
fossa di recupero 865
fossa di tiro 860
fossa oceanica 49
Fossa Perù-Cile 50
fossa settica 70
fossa triangolare 173
fossato 408, 409, 538, 864
fosse nasali 175
fosse oceaniche 50
fossetta 112, 867
foto in prima pagina 471
fotocamera 35 mm 20
fotocopiatrice 512, 730, 733
fotografia 476
fotografia, direttore della 429
fotografo 714
fotografo di scena 429
fotone 692
fotorecettori 177
frontoparietale 111
fotosfera 6
fotosintesi 78
fototessere, macchina per 715
fovea 177
foyer 431
fragola 192
fragola, sezione di una 83
frana 47
francese 469
francese, taglio 375
francesina 343
Francia 743
francio 682
francobollo 474
Francoforte, salsiccia di 216
frangente 49
frangia 337
frangia, scopa a 295
frangiflutti 660
frangizolle 333
frantumatore 641, 646
frantumatrice 71
fratelli 785
fratello 785
frattazzo 315
frazione 703
freccetta 918
freccette 918
freccia 739, 750, 859
freccia del vento 56
freccia di orientamento 907
freestyle 890
freestyle, snowboard per 887
fregata 762
fregio 403, 404
frenaggio, cavo di 761
frenata, zona di 891
frenatore 884
freni 559
freno 783, 851, 870, 889
freno a disco 552, 559, 874
freno a disco idraulico 870
freno a disco, pinza del 574
freno a mano 552
freno a mano, leva del 556
freno a mano, leva di azionamento del 587
freno a mano, ruota del 587
freno a tamburo 559
freno a tampone 895
freno aerodinamico 676, 898
freno aerodinamico, comando del 898
freno americano 857
freno anteriore 579
freno anteriore, leva del 576
freno della catena 331
freno di emergenza 594
freno dinamico 586
freno posteriore 578
freno posteriore, pedale del 576
freno, cavo del 579
freno, comando del 896
freno, disco del 574
freno, leva del 579, 876
freno, pedale del 333, 552, 556, 559
freno, tubazione del 559
frequenza, bande di 498
frequenza, cursore di regolazione della 498

frequenza, indicatore digitale di 498
frequenza, unità di misura della 702
frequenze, display delle 503
fresa a coda di rondine 308
fresa a corona 308
fresa a quarto di anello 308
fresa di raccordo 308
fresa per scanalare 308
fresa per smussare 308
fresatrice verticale 308
frese, esempi di 308
friggitrice 238, 721
frigo portatile 906
frigoriferi 720
frigorifero 224, 291, 720, 722
frigorifero, carro 588
frigorifero, scomparto del 291
fringuello 118
frizione 552, 909
frizione a stella 910
frizione, leva d'innesto della 327
frizione, leva della 574, 576
frizione, pedale della 556
frizione, regolazione della 910
frizione, scatola della 576
fronda 76
fronda arrotolata 185
frontale 112, 150, 255, 749, 854
fronte 115, 146, 650
fronte caldo al suolo 56
fronte caldo in quota 56
fronte dello scavo 647
fronte di abbattimento 647
fronte freddo al suolo 56
fronte freddo in quota 56
fronte occluso al suolo 56
fronte stazionario 56
fronti 56
frontone 403, 405, 697
frontura 456
frontura, scanalatura della 456
frullatore 236
frullatore a immersione 236
frullatore elettrico a mano 236
frullino 232
frumento 203
frusta 232, 236
frusta a quattro bracci 236
frusta a spirale 236
frusta ad anello 236
fruste 236
frustino 853, 856
frutta 180, 723
frutteto 182
frutti 81, 192
frutti secchi 84, 193
frutti tropicali 196
fruttificazione 86
frutto carnoso 82, 83
frutto del jack 196
frutto, albero da 182
fucile 860
fucile a canna liscia 912
fucile a canna rigata 912
fucile automatico 755
fucile subacqueo 841
fuco 99
fuga, via di 872
fulani 468
fulcro 686, 828
full 914
fulmine 57, 65
fumaiolo 599, 604, 608
fumarola 44
fumatori, accessori per 390
fumo 57
fumo, deflettore del 256
fumo, rilevatore di 767
fune 686, 824
fune di corsia 831
fune di falsa partenza 830
fune di sollevamento 321, 417
funghi 183
fungicida 69
fungo 76, 591
fungo coltivato 183
fungo velenoso 76
fungo velenoso e mortale 76
fungo, struttura di un 76
funicella 823
funicella di sparo 756
funicolo 83, 84
funivia 886
funivia, partenza della 886
funzionamento automatico, indicatore del 508
funzionamento, pannello di 417
funzione, selettori di 506
funzione, tasti 508, 699, 730
funzione, tasti 507
funzioni, display delle 450
fuoco 43, 691
fuoco Cassegrain 17
fuoco coudé 17
fuoco primario 17

fuoco primario, cabina del 16
fuoco primario, cabina di osservazione del 17
fuoco secondario, cabina del 16
fuoco, bocca da 753, 756
fuoco, profondità del 43
Fuoco, Terra del 31
fuorisicalmo 839
fuoristrada 549
fuoriuscita di idrocarburi 70
furcula 116
furgone 573
furgone postale 474, 475
fuseaux 358
fusello 458
fusibile 273, 663, 673
fusibile a cartuccia 272
fusibile a cartuccia con terminali a coltello 272
fusibile a tappo 272
fusibili, esempi di 272
fusibili, pinza per 317
fusilli 206
fusione 680
fusoliera 625, 898
fusto 77, 185, 391, 405, 793, 815, 816, 822
fusto del bulbo 78
futon 280

G

gabbia 407, 448, 853
gabbia del palcoscenico 430
gabbia di partenza 856
gabbia di protezione 316, 791
gabbia fissa 603
gabbia volante 603
gabbia, lampada portatile a 316
gabbia, vela di straglio di 603
Gabon 745
gadolinio 684
gaffa 611
gagliardetto 739
Gai-lohn 187
galassia 9
galassia a spirale barrata 9
galassia a spirale normale 9
galassia ellittica 9
galassia irregolare di tipo I 9
galassia irregolare di tipo II 9
galassia lenticolare 9
galea 598
galeone 599
Galileo 19
galleggiante 263, 265, 611, 615, 628, 652, 827, 911
galleggiante dell'indicatore di livello 655
galleggiante, asta di 263
galleggiante, valvola del 265
galleria 411, 543, 592
galleria di collegamento 543
galleria di fondo 650
galleria di ispezione 658
galleria di testa 650
galleria in direzione 650
galleria secca 47
galleria, prima 431
galleria, seconda 431
gallese 469
galletta di segale 205
galletta scandinava 205
gallette di riso 207
galletto 311
gallina 120
gallina, uovo di 213
gallio 682
gallo 120
galloccia 834, 835
galloccia di ormeggio 597
galoppo 125, 856
galoscia 342
gamba 124, 139, 147, 149, 156, 278, 280, 281, 351, 815, 823
gamba a capriolo 276
gamba anteriore 277
gamba posteriore 277
gamba telescopica 482, 776
gambale 798, 800, 889, 895
gambaletto 365
gamberetto 218
gambero di acqua dolce 218
Gambia 745
gambo 75, 76, 241, 301, 302, 453, 454, 456, 457, 591, 910, 911
gambo a innesto dello spazzolino 384
gambo filettato 311
gambo, bottone a 453
ganascia 312, 913
ganascia 312, 317, 377, 559, 590
ganascia curva 310
ganascia dentata 310
ganascia diritta 310
ganascia fissa 311, 312
ganascia mobile 311, 312
ganci del pettine 461

ganci di fissaggio 851
ganci, scala con 767
gancio 249, 284, 313, 316, 453, 456, 483, 573, 634, 699, 776, 862, 881, 889
gancio del barbazzale 854
gancio del manganello 770
gancio del piatto 698
gancio della cintura 505
gancio di chiusura 389
gancio di sollevamento 651
gancio di traino 567, 640
gancio di trazione 587
gancio per l'impasto 236
ganglio cerebropleurale 105
ganglio simpatico 167
ganglio spinale 167, 168
ganglio viscerale 105
Ganimede 4
gara 831
gara di ciclismo su strada 870
gara, area di 845, 846, 847
gara, campo di 855
gara, commissario di 875
gara, numero di 875
gara, ufficiali di 801, 846
garage 244, 726, 769
garage, porta basculante del 416
garage, porta sezionale del 416
garam masala 199
garitta 408, 409
garofano 80
garofano, chiodo di 198
garrese 124, 130
garretto 124, 130
garza sterile 777
gas 275, 651, 656, 680
gas combusti 564
gas combusti, cappa di raccolta dei 267
gas di scarico delle automobili, inquinamento da 69
gas di scarico, immissione dei 564
gas inerte 274
gas inquinanti, emissione di 69
gas nobili 684
gas serra 68
gas serra, concentrazione di 68
gas, accendino a 391
gas, manopola di regolazione del 903
gas, rubinetto del 267
gas, scaldabagno a 267
gas, serbatoio del 391
gasolio 656
gassa d'amante 908
gassa d'amante doppia 908
gastrocnemio 150, 151
gastronomia 216
gateway 523
gatti, razze di 132
gatto 132
gatto americano a pelo corto 132
gatto del Maine 132
gatto dell'isola di Man 133
gatto delle nevi 876, 886
gatto, morfologia di un 133
gatto, testa di 132
gattone 411
gattuccio 303
gattuccio stellato 218
gazza 118
gelatiera 240
gelato, porzionatore per 233
gelone 183
Gemelli 13
gemello 361
gemma 78
gemma apicale 77
gemma ascellare 77
gemma fiorale 77
gemma terminale 77
generatore 563, 659, 665, 668
generatore termoelettrico a radioisotopi 18
generatore d'aria calda 258
generatore d'aria calda elettrico 258
generatore di audiofrequenze 488
generatore di energia, modulo del 40
generatore di vapore 646, 669, 670, 671, 674, 763
generatore semovente 622
generatore, gruppo del 658
generatore, produzione di elettricità dal 662
generatori 688
generatori elettrici, locale dei 763
generi alimentari 180
genero 784
gengiva 159, 174
genitali femminili, organi 170
genitali maschili, organi 169
genitori 784, 785
Genova, salame di 216
geografia 28
geologia 42
geometria 704
Georgia 746
gerboa 123
Germania 744
germanio 682
germe 85

germinazione 77
germogli di soia 191
germoglio 77
germoglio di bambù 185
gessetto 863
gesso, pannello di 299
gesso, piastrella di 299
Gesù Cristo 736
getti d'acqua 828
gettoni, fessura per 507
gettoni, finestrella per la restituzione dei 507
geyser 44
Ghana 745
ghepardo 135
gheriglio 84
ghetta 339, 901
ghettina con ruches 368
ghi 210
ghiacciaio 46, 48, 66
ghiaccio 67
ghiaccio, macchina del 721
ghiaia 253
ghiandaia 118
ghiandola albuminogena 104
ghiandola coxale 103
ghiandola del veleno 99, 106
ghiandola di Cowper 169
ghiandola digestiva 104, 105, 106, 107
ghiandola lacrimale 177
ghiandola mammaria 171
ghiandola pedale 104
ghiandola salivare 97, 99, 104, 176
ghiandola sebacea 172
ghiandola sudoripara apocrina 172
ghiandola sudoripara eccrina 172
ghiandola surrenale 165
ghiandola velenifera 103
ghiandola velenigena 112
ghiandole digestive 103
ghiandole salivari 164
ghiandole serigene 103
ghiera 269, 320
ghiera di bloccaggio 302, 700, 756, 900
ghiera di calcolo 479
ghiera di messa a fuoco 478
ghiera di tenuta 270
ghiera femmina 909, 910
ghiera maschio 909, 910
gi 846
giacca 355, 844, 855
giacca a doppiopetto 348
giacca a un petto 348
giacca a vento 353, 901
giacca alla marinara 355
giacca attillata 337
giacca da cavallo 853
giacca tradizionale 846
giacche 348
giacche e pullover, esempi di 358
giacche, esempi di 355
giaccone 355
giacconi, esempi di 352
giacimento minerale 647
giaguaro 135
giallo 400, 690
giallo-arancio 400
giallo-verde 400
Giamaica 742
Giapeto 5
Giappone 33, 747
Giappone, Fossa del 50
Giappone, Mar del 33
giapponese 469
giardinaggio 298, 322
giardinaggio, guanti da 325
giardiniere, sega da 330
giardino 322, 406
giardino pubblico 713
giardino roccioso 322
giardino, filo da 324
giarrettiera 367
Giava, Fossa di 50
giavellotto 748, 793
gibbone 139
Gibilterra, Stretto di 32
Gibuti 745
gigante rossa 8
giglio 80, 741
gilè 348, 354, 359
ginco, noce di 193
ginepro, bacca di 198
ginglimo 156
ginnasta, nome del 825
ginnastica 823, 824
ginnastica ritmica 823
ginnastica, abbigliamento da 371
ginnastica, completo da 369
ginocchielli, cinghia dei 857
ginocchiello 857
ginocchiera 749, 796, 808, 850, 858, 880, 882, 894, 895
ginocchio 124, 130, 146, 148
giocatore 801, 805, 808, 810, 827, 877, 878, 920
giocatore numero 1 858
giocatore numero 2 858
giocatore numero 3 858
giocatore numero 4 858
giocatore, bastone del 880
giocatore, handicap del 858
giocatore, numero del 808, 810, 878
giocatore: battitore 798
giocatori 822
giocatori espulsi, area di rientro dei 827
giocatori, panchina dei 794, 801, 807, 809, 814
giocatori, posizioni dei 794, 803, 804, 811, 814
giocatori, sedie dei 813
giocattoli 717
giocattoli, negozio di 714
giocattolo 854
giochi 788, 914
giochi con la racchetta 815
giochi da tavola 915
giochi di carte 914
gioco 822
gioco del volano 816
gioco di liccioli 460
gioco online 525
gioco, area di 608
giogo 698
giogo anteriore 698
giogo di supporto 14, 15
giogo posteriore 698
gioielleria 714
gioielli 374, 717
Giordania 746
giornale 471
giornale, nome del 471
Giovanni Calvino 736
Giove 4
girabecchino 307
giradischi 488, 500
Giraffa 12
giraffa 129, 490, 492
giraffa, treppiede della 492
giraffista 429
girante 659
girante della turbina 664
giranti 659
girasole 80
giratubi 315
girella 911, 913
girello 863
girino 111
giro 104
giro della spira 105
giro embrionale 105
giro, manica a 361
girocollo 363, 368, 374
girocollo drappeggiato 363
girocollo, maglia 359
girocollo, maglione 354
girorizzonte di riserva 626
giroscopio 759
giubba 338
giubbetto equilibratore 841
giubbotto 848
giubbotto da pescatore 911
giubbotto di salvataggio 611
giudaismo 736
giudice 842, 843, 844, 848, 855
giudice arbitro 858
giudice d'angolo 845
giudice del fallo di piede 821
giudice di arrivo 830, 839, 883
giudice di campo 807
giudice di controllo 823
giudice di linea 805, 807, 812, 813, 816, 818, 820, 824, 877, 879
giudice di linea centrale 820
giudice di partenza 837, 883
giudice di pista 883
giudice di porta 827, 878
giudice di rete 821
giudice di sedia 820
giudice di servizio 816, 820
giudice di stile 830
giudice laterale 807
giudice principale 837
giudici 824, 825, 828, 881
giudici assistenti 883
giudici d'angolo 846
giudici di arrivo 883
giudici di corsa, postazione dei 856
giudici di gara, postazione dei 887
giudici di partenza 882
giudici di virata 831
giudici per la valutazione dell'esecuzione 823
giudici per la valutazione della composizione 823
giudici per la valutazione della difficoltà 823
giudici, banco dei 728
giudici, tribuna dei 890, 891
giudici, ufficio dei 728
giudizio, dente del 159
giuggiola 197
giunca 600
giunto 863, 909
giunto a compressione 270
giunto angolare 635
giunto di rotaia 590
giunto di sollevamento 640
giunto perimetrale 661
giunto scorrevole 310
giunto scorrevole, pinza a 310
giuntura 390
giunzione a linguetta del telaio 249
giunzione positivo-negativa 672
giunzione scanalata del telaio 249
Giurassico 93
giurati, stanza dei 728
giuria 853
giuria, banco della 728
giuria, piattaforma della 871
giuria, presidente di 855, 900
giustacuore 338
giustizia 726
giustizia, palazzo di 710
Glaciale Artico, Mar 28
gladio 748
glande 169
globo di vetro 903
globo oculare 110, 177
globulo bianco 162
globulo rosso 162
glomo 127
glottide 112
glucosio 78
gnocchi 206
gnomone 696
go 916
gobba 890
Gobi, Deserto dei 33
gocce oftalmiche lubrificanti 384
goccia 404
goccia di cristallo 287
gocciolatoio 247, 249, 551
gola 47, 48, 115, 444
goletta 601, 749
golf 866
golf, campo da 708, 788
golf, vettura da 869
golfo 38
Golfo del Bengala 33
Golfo del Messico 30
Golfo dell'Alaska 30
Golfo di Aden 33, 34
Golfo di Botnia 32
Golfo di California 30
Golfo di Carpentaria 29
Golfo di Guinea 34
Golfo di Oman 33
Golfo di Panama 31
golfo mistico 430
Golfo Persico 33
Golgi, apparato del 74, 94
gombo 188
gomiti 206
gomitiera 800, 894, 895
gomito 124, 130, 140, 147, 149, 156, 258
gomitolo 462
gomma 534
gomma da asciutto 872
gomma da bagnato 872
gomma di tenuta del grembiule 605
gomma espansa, isolante di 299
gomma piena 633
gomma, fasciatura in 838
gomma, guarnizione di 270
gomma, piedino di 321
gomma, tubo flessibile di 271
gommino 776
gonade 95, 105, 106
gondola 600
gonfalone 739
gonfiaggio, dispositivo di 611
gonfiatore 904
gonfiatore a soffietto 904
gong 437, 449
goniometro 701
gonna 355
gonna a balze 357
gonna a portafoglio 357
gonna a teli 357
gonna ad anfora 357
gonna arricciata 357
gonna con baschina 357
gonna diritta 357
gonna pantalone 357
gonne, esempi di 357
gonnellino 822
gorgiera 339, 848
gorgonzola 211
gorilla 138
gorilla, morfologia di un 139
gorilla, scheletro di un 138
gracile 151
gradi 770
gradini, taglio a 375
gradino 255, 321, 417, 570, 587, 647, 847
gradino di accesso 631
gradino posteriore 766, 775
gradino rientrabile 567
gradino, altezza del 647
gradino, larghezza del 255
gradino, lunghezza del 255
grado 704
grado Celsius 702
grafite 670
gramigna crestata 186
Gran Deserto Sabbioso 29
Gran Deserto Vittoria 29
gran dorsale 151
granaio 182
granato 375
grancassa 437, 448
granchio 218, 301
Grand Canyon 30
grande adduttore 151
Grande Baia Australiana 29
Grande Barriera Corallina 29
Grande Catena Divisoria 29
grande complesso 151
grande copritrice secondaria 115
grande falciata esterna 844
grande falciata interna 844
grande galleria 402
grande gluteo 151
grande intestino 110
grande labbro 170, 171
grande pettorale 150
grande rotondo 151
grande safena 160
grande trocantere 153
grandi elettrodomestici 716
Grandi Laghi 30
grandi magazzini 715, 716
grandine 64
grandine, rovesci di 57
granella, elevatore della 643
granella, serbatoio della 643
grano 85
grano saraceno 85, 203
grano, chicco di 85
grano: spiga 85
granturismo 549
granulazione 6
granulo d'amido 74
granulo lipidico 74
grappino 610
grappolo d'uva 86
grassella 124
grassetto 472
grassi 209
grassi lubrificanti 656
grasso alimentare 209
grattugia 230
grattugia per noce moscata 230
grattugiaformaggio 230
gravità, fascia di 610
grecaggio 424
Grecia 744
greco 469
green 866, 867
greggio, area di lavorazione del 652
grembiule 605
grembiule, gomma di tenuta del 605
Grenada 743
griffa 302, 306, 307
griffa, rotore a 688
griglia 234, 261, 290, 383, 494, 502, 561, 562, 658, 727, 903
griglia anteriore 261
griglia dei ripiani 291
griglia del radiatore 570
griglia del riscaldamento 594
griglia di aerazione 244, 594
griglia di contatto metallica 672
griglia di illuminazione 429, 492
griglia di illuminazione, accesso alla 490
griglia di partenza 872, 875
griglia di rivestimento 259
griglia di sicurezza 730
griglia di uscita dell'aria 260, 382
griglia di vaporizzazione 261
griglia di ventilazione 289
griglia elettrica 238
griglia elettrica per interni 239
griglia per casco 796
griglia per raclette 239
griglia terminale 667
grill pieghevole 907
grilletto 320, 331, 516, 752, 754, 755, 757, 767, 860, 861, 912
grilletto di accelerazione 331
grilletto di sicurezza 331
grillo 835
Groenlandia 30
Groenlandia, Mar di 28
gronda 412
grondaia 244
groppa 124, 425, 826
groppo 57
grotta 47, 51
groviera 211
Gru 10
gru 602, 606, 634, 652, 761
gru a ponte 658
gru a portale 596, 635, 657, 658
gru a torre 634
gru mobile a braccio 596
gru su pontone 596
gruccia 782
gruista, cabina del 634
gruppetto 435
gruppi strumentali, esempi di 438
gruppo 870, 916
gruppo del generatore 658
gruppo del turbo-alternatore 646
gruppo dell'elettropompa 559
gruppo delle sospensioni 553
gruppo dello sterzo 553
gruppo di continuità 520, 523
gruppo di punti a cappio 459
gruppo di testa 870
gruppo frigorifero 571
gruppo generatore 659
guadino 911
guaiava 197
guaina 79
guaina della lingua 112
guaina di protezione 908
guaina di Schwann 168
guaina isolante 663
guaina mielinica 168
gualdrappa 856
guancia 124, 130, 148, 301, 860, 861, 909
guanciale 280
guanciale, fodera del 280
guanti 346, 872
guanti da donna 346
guanti da giardinaggio 325
guanti da uomo 346
guanti del portiere 802
guanti di lattice, astuccio per i 770
guanti di protezione 318
guanto 20, 796, 797, 798, 800, 841, 848, 853, 855, 869, 870, 871, 874, 875, 878, 882, 884, 887, 888, 891, 892
guanto alla scudiera 346
guanto corto 346
guanto da guida 346
guanto da presa 879
guanto da respinta 879
guanto da sera 346
guanto del difensore 797
guanto di crine 379
guanto di lattice 776
guanto lungo 346
guanto, dito del 346
guanto, dorso del 346
guanto, palmo del 346
guantone 800, 842
guantoni 843
guaranì 469
guardalinee 803, 807
guardamano 754, 860, 861
guardaroba 250, 279, 394, 719, 723, 726, 731
guardaroba dei clienti 720
guardaroba del personale 720
guardia 229, 811, 849, 854
guardia bassa 843
guardia destra 807
guardia giurata, stanzino della 731
guardia in piedi 843
guardia sinistra 807
guardolo 342
guardrail 894
guarnizione 268, 269, 294, 368, 655
guarnizione ad anello 268
guarnizione conica 265
guarnizione della coppa dell'olio 566
guarnizione di gomma 270
guarnizione magnetica 291
guarnizione, anello di tenuta della 268
Guatemala 742
guazzo 397
guazzo, pittura a 396
guepière 367
guerriero gallico 748
gufo reale 119
guglia 52, 410, 411
guida 294, 424, 456, 632, 633
guida circolare 16
guida del contrappeso 417
guida del filo 910
guida del nastro 499, 534
guida della cabina 417
guida della carta 508, 519
guida della catena 331, 580
guida della pellicola 476
guida di appoggio 303, 304
guida di onda 489
guida di scorrimento 587, 835
guida di taglio 424
guida fine, sistema di 17
guida graduata 305
guida graduata, scanalatura della 305
guida metallica 533
guida metallica di protezione 571
guida parallela 304, 305
guida parallela, arresto della 305
guida parallela, carrello della 305
guida parallela, riga della 305
guida parallela, scanalatura della 305
guida per il pane 238
guida, cabina di 585
guida, guanto da 346
guida, leva di manovra della 632, 633
guida, rullo di 499
guida, ruota di 594, 595
guidafilo 452, 453, 457

INDICE DELLE VOCI ITALIANE

1090

ASTRONOMIA > 2-25; **TERRA** > 26-71; **REGNO VEGETALE** >72-89; **REGNO ANIMALE** > 90-143; **ESSERE UMANO** > 144-177; **GENERI ALIMENTARI E CUCINA** > 178-241; **CASA** > 242-295; **FAI DA TE E GIARDINAGGIO** > 296-333; **ABBIGLIAMENTO** > 334-371; **ACCESSORI E ARTICOLI PERSONALI** > 372-391; **ARTE E ARCHITETTURA** > 392-465; **COMUNICAZIONI E BUROTICA** > 466-535; **TRASPORTI E VEICOLI** > 536-643; **ENERGIA** > 644-677; **SCIENZA** > 678-705; **SOCIETÀ** > 706-785; **SPORT E GIOCHI** > 786-920

guidatore 857
guidone 739
Guinea 745
Guinea Bissau 745
Guinea Equatoriale 745
Guinea, Golfo di 34
guscio 84, 117, 389
gusto 174
Gutenberg, discontinuità di 42
Guyana 742
guyot 49
gyoji 847

H

Haiti 742
hakama 846, 847
half-pipe 887
hall 719, 724
handicap del giocatore 858
handicap della squadra 858
handicap, punto di 916
handicap, tabellone degli 858
hangar per elicotteri 762
hard disk estraibile 521
harissa 201
hassio 683
hat switch 516
hausa 468
Havers, canale di 154
hawaiano 469
hertz 702
hijiki 183
Himalaya 33
hindi 469
hockey su ghiaccio 878
hockey su prato 800
hockey su prato, campo da 788
home 515
home theatre 493
homo sapiens 93
Honduras 742
Horn, Capo 31
hovercraft 605
hub 522, 523
Hubble, classificazione di 9
Hubble, telescopio spaziale 17
Hudson, Baia di 30
Huitzilopochtli, tempio di 412
hummus 200
humus 78
Huygens 19
hyracotherium 93

I

identificazione tecnica, banda di 501
identificazione, cartellino di 770
identità, piastrina d' 376
Idra Femmina 11, 13
Idra Maschio 10
idrante a colonna 767
idrante antincendio 712
idrante, chiave per 767
idrante, presa dell' 766
idraulica 262, 270
idrocarburi, fuoriuscita di 70
idroelettricità 657
idrogeno 682
idrogeno liquido, serbatoio dell' 24, 25
idrosfera 66
idrovolante a due galleggianti 628
iena 134
ifa 76
igiene orale 384
igloo 418
igrografo 59
igrometro 261
igrostato 261
iguana 114
ileo 99, 111, 116, 122, 152, 164
illuminazione 274
illuminazione, griglia di 429
illuminazione, lente di 701
ilo renale 165
imballaggio 71
imballatrice 642
imbarcazione, parti di una 838
imbarcazioni a vela, andature delle 833
imbarcazioni antiche 598
imbarcazioni di coppia 839
imbarcazioni di punta 839
imbarcazioni tradizionali 599
imbarco, passerella di 619
imbarco, scaletta di 611
imbardata 630
imboccatura 858
imboccatura, canna di 447
imbottitura 899
imbottitura dell'angolo 842
imbottitura di sicurezza 823
imbottitura per il petto 800
imbracatura 841, 893, 896, 897
imbracatura cosciale 900
imbracatura da scalata 901
imbuto 231, 494
imbuto collettore 59
immagine 917
immagine fotografica 483
immagine stampata 420
immagine, raddrizzatori di 692
immagine, tasti di regolazione dell' 496
immagini, pulsante di visualizzazione delle 477
immagini, pulsante per il salto di 477
immersione, frullatore a 236
immissione dei gas di scarico 564
immissione di energia nella rete di trasmissione 662
impalcato 540
impalmatura normale 908
imparipennata 79
impastatrice 236, 239
impasto, gancio per l' 236
impennaggi, esempi di 629
impennaggio 859
impennaggio a T 629
impennaggio con tre derive 629
impennaggio orizzontale basso con una deriva 629
impennaggio orizzontale rialzato con una deriva 629
impennaggio verticale 625
impermeabile 352
impiallacciatura 300
impianto di climatizzazione 608
impianto di deasfaltizzazione 656
impianto di estrazione con solventi 656
impianto di lavorazione 649
impianto di produzione dei lubrificanti 656
impianto di raffreddamento 553
impianto di reforming catalitico 656
impianto di riscaldamento ad acqua calda 259
impianto di riscaldamento ad aria calda 258
impianto di smistamento 71
impianto di trivellazione 651
impianto elettrico 553
impianto elettrico impermeabilizzato 263
impianto esterno 260
impianto frenante 553
impianto hi-fi di riproduzione del suono 497
impianto idraulico 262
impianto idroelettrico 657
impianto interno 260
impieghi di Internet 525
impiombatura corta 908
impluvio 406
importo da pagare 548
imposta 249, 540
imposta, concio d' 413
impostazione del tempo di esposizione 479
impostazioni, pulsante di visualizzazione delle 477
imposte ripiegabili 282
impugnatura 230, 236, 237, 238, 240, 288, 302, 303, 304, 305, 307, 308, 309, 316, 319, 320, 323, 331, 332, 381, 383, 384, 439, 750, 754, 782, 783, 793, 797, 798, 800, 838, 850, 851, 859, 867, 877, 888, 891, 892, 909, 910, 913
impugnatura a anello 390
impugnatura a penna 815
impugnatura a pistola 306, 318, 754, 755, 860, 912
impugnatura a stretta di mano 815
impugnatura anteriore 757
impugnatura con sistema antivibrazione 331
impugnatura della cassa battente 460
impugnatura della pistola 320
impugnatura di sicurezza 332
impugnatura doppia 840
impugnatura laterale 306, 307, 308
impugnatura per le figure 840
impugnatura principale 307
impugnatura rotante 516
impugnatura sagomata 381
impugnatura, schermo a 318
impugnature, esempi di 840
impulsi, irrigatore a 329
impulso sensoriale 168
impuntura 342, 346, 350, 368, 370
imputato, banco dell' 728
in avanti 828
in poppa 833
in prigione 919
inalatore dosimetrico 783
incamiciatura 912
incamiciatura degli elementi di combustibile difettosi 666
incandescenza, lampadina a 274
incasso, scatola da 274
incastellatura 460
incastonatura 376
incastro per la forca di sollevamento 635
incastro per montante 571
incavo 227
incendi, prevenzione degli 764
incendio delle foreste 69
incenerimento 71
incernieramento, perno di 638
inchiostro 397, 421, 470
inchiostro a colori cangianti 729
inchiostro litografico 423
inchiostro, disegno a 396
incisione 424
incisivi 159
incisivo 121, 123
incisivo centrale 159
incisivo laterale 159
incisura anteriore 173
incisura intertragica 173
inclinazione 13
inclinazione, comando di 898
inclinazione, indicatore di 898
incocco, punto di 913
incordatura 816, 822
incremento dell'effetto serra 68
incrocio 463
incudine 174
India 747
Indiano 10
Indiano, Oceano 28, 29, 33, 34
indicatore del funzionamento automatico 508
indicatore del livello d'acqua 239
indicatore del livello dell'acqua 288
indicatore del livello di carburante 557
indicatore del livello di picco a istogramma 488
indicatore del piano 417
indicatore dell'alimentazione di ossigeno 898
indicatore della pressione dell'acqua 766
indicatore della regolazione 889
indicatore della temperatura del liquido di raffreddamento 557
indicatore delle telefonate 508
indicatore di carica 383
indicatore di destinazione 593
indicatore di direzione 554, 571
indicatore di direzione, comando dell' 556
indicatore di linea 568, 569, 595
indicatore di livello automatico 655
indicatore di livello, galleggiante dell' 655
indicatore di temperatura 381
indicatore digitale di frequenza 498
indicatore generale degli orari 582
indicatori 501
indicatori, tasto di visualizzazione degli 496
indicazione del valore 729
indicazioni di tempo 434
indice 173, 261, 471, 479, 695, 698, 699
indice di esposizione 479
indice di profondità 307
indice di regolazione dell'altezza 304
indice, pulsante per l' 477
Indie Occidentali 30
indio 682
indivia riccia 187
Indonesia 33, 747
indonesiano 469
indorsatura 425
indorsatura, pressa per 425
indorsatura, rotaia di 425
indotto 688
indotto, avvolgimento dell' 688
indotto, nucleo dell' 688
induismo 736
industria 525
industria petrolchimica 656
infermeria 726
infermiera 780
infermiere, sedile dell' 775
infermieri, postazione degli 778, 779
infermieri, sala degli 781
inferriata 403
infila ago 454
infiltrazione 67, 69
infilzacarte 534
infinito 703
infiorescenze, tipi di 81
inflesso 413
inforcamento, tasca di 632
informatica, aula di 734
informazioni 725
informazioni, banco delle 620, 715, 719, 730, 733, 769, 779
informazioni, diffusione di 525
infradito 344
infraspinato 151
infundibolo della tuba di Falloppio 171
infusi 208
ingaggio, cerchio di 878
ingaggio, punto di 878
ingegnere del suono 429
inghiottitoio 47
inglese 469
ingluvie 97, 104, 106, 116
ingranaggi, scatola degli 423
ingranaggio a pignone e cremagliera 686
ingranaggio cilindrico a ruote dentate 686
ingranaggio conico 686
ingranaggio di trascinamento 240
ingranaggio per il moto orario 17
ingranaggio, dente di 686
ingranaggio, sistemi di 686
ingrandimento, pulsante per l' 477
ingrandimento, tasto di 512
ingranditore 485
ingranditore, temporizzatore dell' 485
ingressi uscite audio/video 497
ingresso 250, 394, 509
ingresso al marciapiede 582
ingresso alla piramide 402
ingresso degli attori 402
ingresso dei clienti 720
ingresso dei detenuti 726
ingresso dei veicoli 769
ingresso dei visitatori 726
ingresso del fluido vettore 672
ingresso del personale 720, 726, 735, 768
ingresso del pubblico 402
ingresso del riflusso del condensatore 669
ingresso del vapore a bassa pressione 668
ingresso del vapore ad alta pressione 668
ingresso dell'acqua di raffreddamento del condensatore 669
ingresso dell'acqua fredda 267
ingresso dell'alimentazione dell'utente 273
ingresso della stazione 592
ingresso delle merci 713
ingresso per il computer 518
ingresso principale 713, 733, 735, 768, 781
ingresso, porte d' 427
ingresso, selettore di 497
inguine 146, 148
iniettore 565, 566
iniezione 565
iniziali della banca di emissione 729
inizio lettura 501
inizio, colpo d' 866
innesco 912
innestatoio 330
innesto della sonda 238
innesto marcia avanti/marcia indietro 327
inquartato 740
inquinamento agricolo 69
inquinamento da gas di scarico delle automobili 69
inquinamento del suolo 69
inquinamento dell'acqua 70
inquinamento dell'aria 69
inquinamento domestico 69
inquinamento industriale 69
inquinamento petrolifero 70
inquinanti atmosferici 69
inquinanti non biodegradabili 69
insalata belga 187
insalata riccia 186
insalata, coppetta per l' 226
insalata, forchetta da 228
insalate 722
insalatiera 226
insegna esterna 592
insegnante 734
insegnanti, stanza degli 735
inserimento 515
inserimento dei documenti da trasmettere, punto di 508
inserto 471
inserzione pubblicitaria 471
insetti 96
insetti, esempi di 101
insieme vuoto 703
insilatrice 643
insolazione, lastra di 58
inspirazione 832
installazione 395
intaglio 401
integrale 703
integrazione di energia alla rete di trasmissione 677
intelaiatura 256, 902
intelaiatura di sostegno 485
intelaiatura, base dell' 249
intelaiatura, parte superiore dell' 249
Intelsat 487
intensità luminosa, unità di misura dell' 702
intera 472
interbase 794
intercapedine d'aria 675
interfodera 455
interfono 491
interiora 212
interlinea 472
interlinea 1,5 472
interlinea doppia 472
interlinea singola 472
Internet 523, 524
Internet, impieghi di 525
interno destro 801
interno gamba con abbottonatura a pressione 368, 369
interno sinistro 801
internodo 77
interosseo plantare 150
interpretazione simultanea, cabina per l' 718
interpunzione, segni di 473
interramento 71
interrogatori, stanza per gli 768
interruttore 236, 237, 240, 241, 263, 274, 286, 288, 289, 291, 305, 307, 308, 318, 320, 381, 382, 383, 384, 451, 506, 613, 687
interruttore a grilletto 304, 305, 306, 308
interruttore automatico 260, 658, 663
interruttore bipolare 272
interruttore del portello 293
interruttore dell'autofocus 483
interruttore di accensione 476, 477, 483, 488, 494, 496, 497, 498, 501, 504, 505, 513, 518, 519, 520, 526
interruttore di accensione del VCR 495
interruttore di accensione della TV 495
interruttore di accensione e del volume 504
interruttore di avviamento 576
interruttore di blocco 479
interruttore di emergenza 576
interruttore di fine corsa 417
interruttore di trasmissione 505
interruttore differenziale 272
interruttore generale 495
interruttore motore/luce 452
interruttore principale 272, 273
interruttore unipolare 272
interruttore, dispositivo di blocco dell' 306
interruttore, placca dell' 274
interruzione 515
intersezione 703
intersuola 370
intervalli 434
intervallo 617
intervista 471
intestino 95, 97, 103, 104, 105, 107, 109, 112, 161
intestino crasso 164
intestino tenue 125, 164
intonazione, rotella di 450
intradosso 413
inuktitut 469
invergatura, barra d' 461
inverno 54
inverno, solstizio d' 54
invertitore 302, 306
invio 515
invito, scalino d' 255
involucro 256, 259, 313, 521, 700, 899
involucro di copertura 260, 261
involucro di zinco (anodo) 689
involucro esterno di bachelite 757
Io 4
iodio 683
ipermetropia 691
ipersostentatore 23
ipersostentatore sul bordo di attacco 625
ipofisi 167
iporachide 115
iposcopio 758
ippodromo 856
ippoglosso 221
ippopotamo 129
Iran 746
Iraq 746
iride 177
iridio 683
Irlanda 743
Irlanda, Mar d' 32
irlandese 469
irrigatore a impulsi 329
irrigatore oscillante 329
irrigatore rotativo a pioggia 329
isba 418
ischio 111, 116, 122, 153
islamismo 736
Islanda 32, 744
islandese 469
isobara 55
isola 38, 224, 539, 761
Isola di Baffin 30
isola di Man, gatto dell' 133
Isola di Terranova 30
isola vulcanica 49
isolamento, cella di 727
isolamento, stanza di 778
isolamento, tappo di 689
isolante 672
isolante a lamina metallica elastica 299
isolante di gomma espansa 299
isolante in plastica 272
isolante in rotolo 299
isolante preformato 299
isolante sfuso granulare 299
isolante termico 22, 259
isolante vinilico 299
isolatore 663
isolatori sospesi, catena di 663
Isole Aleutine 30
Isole delle Antille 742
Isole Falkland 31
Isole Figi 29
Isole Marshall 747
Isole Salomone 747
isolotto roccioso 51
isolotto sabbioso 51
ispezione, tappo di 270
Israele 746
issopo 202
istituzioni educative 525
istmo 38
istmo della tuba di Falloppio 171
istmo delle fauci 174
Istmo di Panama 30
istruzione 732

INDICE DELLE VOCI ITALIANE

ASTRONOMIA > 2-25; **TERRA** > 26-71; **REGNO VEGETALE** >72-89; **REGNO ANIMALE** > 90-143; **ESSERE UMANO** > 144-177; **GENERI ALIMENTARI E CUCINA** > 178-241; **CASA** > 242-295; **FAI DA TE E GIARDINAGGIO** > 296-333; **ABBIGLIAMENTO** > 334-371; **ACCESSORI E ARTICOLI PERSONALI** > 372-391; **ARTE E ARCHITETTURA** > 392-465; **COMUNICAZIONI E BUROTICA** > 466-535; **TRASPORTI E VEICOLI** > 536-643; **ENERGIA** > 644-677; **SCIENZA** > 678-705; **SOCIETÀ** > 706-785; **SPORT E GIOCHI** > 786-920

1091

istruzioni per l'uso 548
istruzioni sui tessuti, simboli delle 347
Italia 744
italiano 469
itterbio 684
ittiosauro 93
ittiostegidi 92
ittrio 683
Iugoslavia 744
iurta 418

J

jabot 362
jaboticaba 197
jack 488
jack, area dei 488
jarlsberg 211
jazz-band 438
jeans 358
jet supersonico 53, 629
jicama 184
jolly 914
joule 702
joystick 516, 918
judo 844
judogi 844
jujutsu 846

K

k-way 371
Kalahari, Deserto del 34
karatè 845
karategi 845
karateka 845
karateka, linea dei 845
kayak 837
kayak monoposto (K1) 839
Kazakistan 746
kelvin 702
kendo 847
kendoka 847
kendoka, linea dei 847
Kenya 745
Kermadec-Tonga, Fossa di 50
kerosene, serbatoio del 25
ketch 601
ketch Marconi 601
ketchup 201
kilogrammo 702
kilt 357
kimono 364
kimono, manica a 361
Kinyarwanda 468
Kirghizistan 746
Kiribati 747
kirundi 468
kit con cuffia dotata di microfono 506
kit di attrezzi 580
kiwano 196
kiwi 196
koala 143
Kola, Penisola di 32
kombu 183
kora 433
kote 847
Kuiper, cintura di 4
kumquat 194
kung fu 846
Kuwait 746

L

la 434
la centrale 436
labbra, pennellino per 378
labbra, trucco per le 378
labbro 124, 132
labbro esterno 105
labbro inferiore 174, 444
labbro interno 105
labbro superiore 99, 174, 444
labirinto 885
laboratorio 16, 17, 726
laboratorio americano 21
laboratorio di anatomia patologica 781
laboratorio di conservazione 395
laboratorio spaziale 23
laboratorio superiore 16
laboratorio, strumenti di 685
lacca 400
laccio 370, 913
laccio di pelle 350
laccolite 44
Ladoga, Lago 32
laghetto 322
laghi 48
laghi, acidificazione dei 70
lago 7, 38, 45, 48
lago artificiale 48
Lago Baikal 33
Lago Ciad 34
Lago di Aral 33
lago di meandro abbandonato 48
Lago Eyre 29
lago glaciale 48
Lago Ladoga 32
Lago Malawi 34
lago salato 52
Lago Tanganica 34
lago tettonico 48
Lago Titicaca 31
Lago Vittoria 34
lago vulcanico 48
lagomorfi 122
lagomorfi, esempi di 123
lagomorfo: coniglio, fauce di un 123
laguna 51
lama 128, 227, 229, 237, 240, 302, 303, 304, 305, 315, 320, 331, 332, 382, 383, 390, 453, 454, 534, 636, 639, 849, 878, 880, 881, 884, 900
lama a cucchiaio 401
lama dentellata 382
lama di sega circolare 304
lama di taglio 424
lama diritta 401
lama dritta 382
lama fissa 424
lama grande 905
lama isolata 316
lama per danza 881
lama per pattinaggio libero 881
lama piccola 905
lama ricurva 401
lama smussata 401
lama, cilindro di rotazione della 639
lama, cilindro di sollevamento della 636, 639
lama, dispositivo di blocco dell'inclinazione della 304
lama, fermo della 382
lama, filo della 382
lama, meccanismo di spostamento della 639
lama, regolatore dell'altezza della 305
lama, regolatore dell'inclinazione della 304, 305
lama, vite di blocco della 304
lame, tipi principali di 401
lamella 76, 285
lamelle concentriche 154
lametta a due tagli 383
lamette, caricatore di 383
lamina 75, 76, 79, 881, 888
lamina assorbente 672
lamina bimetallica, termometro a 695
lamina cribrosa dell'etmoide 175
lamina metallica elastica, isolante a 299
lampada 693
lampada a braccio regolabile 286
lampada a petrolio 906
lampada a sospensione 286
lampada a stelo 286
lampada a tubo per flash 482
lampada ad incandescenza 614
lampada al neon 316
lampada alogena al tungsteno 274, 275
lampada alogena da tavolo 286
lampada da comodino 724
lampada da lettura 286
lampada da notte 780
lampada da parete 287
lampada da parete con braccio estensibile 287
lampada da tavolo 286
lampada del presbiterio 737
lampada frontale 901
lampada orientabile 399
lampada per flash 482
lampada per saldare 319
lampada portatile 765
lampada portatile a gabbia 316
lampada provacircuiti 316
lampada, base della 614
lampadario 287
lampade in serie 287
lampadina 316, 687
lampadina a incandescenza 274, 673
lampadina a risparmio di energia 275
lampeggiante 766, 771
lampeggiante, sistema di controllo del 771
lampeggiatore anteriore 574, 576
lampeggiatore posteriore 575, 576
lampione 287, 322, 712
lampione da parete 287
lampone 192
lampone, sezione di un 83
lampreda 219
lanceolata 79
lanceolato 413
lancetta dei decimi di secondo 696
lancetta dei minuti 696, 697
lancetta dei secondi 696
lancetta delle ore 697
lancia 319, 328, 748
lancia antincendio 766
lancia antincendio schiumogena 607
lancia di salvataggio 652
lanciafumogeni 758
lanciamissili 761
lanciarazzi civetta 762
lanciasiluri 763
lanciatore 760, 794, 795, 799, 865
lanciatrice 865
lancio 795, 799, 864
lancio del disco 791
lancio del giavellotto 791
lancio del martello 791
lancio del peso 790
lancio, area di 788
lancio, camera 763
lancio, rampa di 891
lancio, struttura doppia di 24
lancio, tubo di 756, 757
lancio, zona di 865
lantanidi 684
lantanio 684
lanterna 614, 903
lanterna del faro 614
lanugine, filtro per 292, 293
Laos 747
lapide commemorativa 738
lapislazzuli 375
lardatoio 233
lardo 209
larghezza del gradino 255
larice 89
laringe 163
larva 100
lasagne 206
lasco, al 833
lasco, al gran 833
laser a rubino pulsato 692
lastra di insolazione 58
lastra di rame 422
lastra di vetro 291
lastra inchiostratrice 421
lastrico, pietra da 298, 322
latifoglie, esempi di 88
latitudine 36
lato 227, 431, 632, 842
lato bacino 664
lato del re 916
lato della regina 916
lato destro 384
lato di destra 431
lato di sinistra 431
lato mare 664
lato sinistro 384
lato, mezzo 632
latrine 406
latta per alimenti 223
latte 210
latte di capra 210
latte evaporato 210
latte in polvere 210
latte omogeneizzato 210
latte, bricco del 226
latteria 182
latticello 210
latticini 180
latticini, scomparto per i 291
lattina 223
lattuga asparago 186
lattuga cappuccina 186
lattuga iceberg 186
lattuga marina 186
lattuga romana 186
laurenzio 684
lava, strato di 44
lavabo 262
lavaggio 347
lavaggio delle stampe, vasca di 485
lavaggio, torre di 294
lavagna 734
lavallière 349
lavanderia 250, 724, 726
lavanderia a secco 715
lavanderia per le divise 764
lavandino 264, 722, 724, 780
lavandino del chirurgo 781
lavandino per il prelavaggio 721
lavandino per le pentole 721
lavaparabrezza, ugello del 550
lavapiatti 721
lavare a mano in acqua tiepida 347
lavare in lavatrice in acqua calda e velocità normale 347
lavare in lavatrice in acqua calda e velocità ridotta 347
lavare in lavatrice in acqua molto calda e velocità normale 347
lavare in lavatrice in acqua tiepida e velocità ridotta 347
lavastoviglie 224, 271, 294, 721, 723
lavatrice 262, 271, 292
lavello 224, 270
lavello con tritarifiuti 270
lavello, doppio 262
lavori 545, 547
lavoro a maglia 457
lavoro meccanico 662
lavoro, piano di 224, 305, 312
lavoro, tavola di 452
leccarda 234, 239
LED indicatore del livello di picco 499
legabagagli elastico 389
legame chimico 680
legamento 105
legamento elastico 133
legamento largo dell'utero 171
legamento periodontale 159
legamento sospensore 177
legatore 642
legatura 435, 446
legatura, pelle da 425
leggio 436, 444, 451, 737
leggio da orchestra 436
legionario romano 748
legna da ardere, cassone per 256
legni, famiglia dei 437
legno 300, 867, 868
legno 1 868
legno 3 868
legno 5 868
legno, materiali derivati dal 300
legno, scultura in 371
legume, sezione di un 84
legumi 190
legumiera 226
lembo 359, 453, 535
lembo anteriore 349
lembo della camicia 349
lembo graduato 612
lembo posteriore 349
lemure 139
lente 385, 477, 478, 501, 905
lente a contatto monouso 384
lente a contatto morbida 384
lente a contatto rigida 384
lente addizionale per macrofotografie 478
lente biconcava 691
lente biconvessa 691
lente bifocale 385
lente concava 691
lente convessa 691
lente da distanza 385
lente da lettura 385
lente del pendolo 697
lente di campo 692
lente di illuminazione 701
lente di ingrandimento 693
lente di ingrandimento per la messa a fuoco 485
lente obiettivo 692
lente piano-concava 691
lente piano-convessa 691
lente torica 691
lenti 535, 691
lenti a contatto 384
lenti convergenti 691
lenti di focalizzazione 694
lenti divergenti 691
lenti, sistema di 692
lenticchie 190
lenza 909
lenzuolo 280
lenzuolo con angoli 280
Leoncino 13
Leone 13
leone 135
leone marino 137
leone passante 741
leopardo 135
Lepre 11
lepre 123, 212
lepre fischiante 123
lesena corinzia 407
lesena dorica 407
lesena ionica 407
Lesotho 746
lettera 471
lettera al direttore 471
lettera di riferimento 855
lettere 472
lettere al direttore 471
lettere, cassetta delle 474
lettiga 776
lettino 776
lettino a sponde 281
lettino pieghevole con fasciatoio 281
letto 280, 567, 823
letto d'ospedale 780
letto matrimoniale 724
letto singolo 724
letto ungueale 172
letto, biancheria da 280
letto, scompartimento 584
letto, vagone 584
Lettonia 744
lettore audio digitale portatile 503
lettore CD 513, 526
lettore CD portatile 503
lettore CD/DVD 918
lettore CD/DVD-ROM 513
lettore dei codici a barre 517
lettore di carte 548, 730, 731
lettore di compact disc 488, 501, 503, 504, 517
lettore di compact disc, tasti del 504
lettore di microfilm 732
lettore di schede 493, 507
lettore DVD 494
lettore DVD-ROM 513, 526
lettore ottico di caratteri 474
lettura di compact disc 501
lettura, inizio 501
lettura, luce di 771
lettura, specchio di 20
lettura, tasto di 505
leucoplasto 74
leva 238, 268, 270, 310, 377, 423, 686, 912, 920
leva a linguetta 452
leva d'armamento 757
leva d'innesto della frizione 327
leva degli aerofreni 626
leva dei flap 626
leva del cambio 552, 556, 579, 580, 870
leva del carrello 626
leva del freno 579, 870, 876
leva del freno a mano 556
leva del freno anteriore 576
leva del pedale 442
leva del pistone 315
leva della chiave 446
leva della frizione 574, 576
leva della pinza 381
leva dello smorzatore 443
leva di apertura dell'attacco 889
leva di avanzamento 307
leva di azionamento 649
leva di azionamento del freno a mano 587
leva di bloccaggio 312
leva di bloccaggio dell'altezza 14, 15
leva di bloccaggio dell'asse orizzontale 14, 15
leva di chiusura 587
leva di comando manuale 590
leva di contatto 287
leva di fissaggio del venturi 757
leva di manovra dell'otturatore 756
leva di manovra della guida 632, 633
leva di regolazione 436
leva di regolazione dell'ossigeno 319
leva di regolazione della velocità 333
leva di regolazione laterale 309
leva di sbloccaggio 310
leva di scatto 265, 398
leva di scorrimento 555
leva di serraggio 309, 312
leva di sollevamento della piastra di taglio 333
leva di svincolo del premicarta 528
leva direzionale 633
leva liberacarta 528
leva per togliere il paralama inferiore 304
leva spaziatrice dei dischi 643
leva tirafilo 452
leva, cappuccio della 268
levapunti 534
levetta 230
levetta dello sciacquone 265
levetta dello spazzolino 456
levetta di erogazione della vincita 920
levetta per il sollevamento del braccio 500
levigatrice 423
Levrieri 13
levriero 131
Libano 746
libellula 102
liberacarta, leva 528
Liberia 745
libero 803, 812
Libia 745
libreria 714, 734
libretto degli assegni 386
libretto, scala a 321
libri di consultazione 732
libri per bambini 732
libri, banco per il prestito dei 733
libri, banco per la restituzione dei 733
libri, carrello per i 733
libro contabile 535
libro delle firme 531
libro elettronico 527
libro rilegato 426
libro, dorso del 425
licci 460, 461
licciolo 460
lichene 74
lichene crostoso 74
lichene fogliaceo 74
lichene fruticoso 74
lichene, struttura di un 74
licheni, esempi di 74
Liechtenstein 744
lima 309, 905
lima curva 401
limetta 194, 377
limetta di cartoncino vetrato 377
limetta pieghevole 377
limite del campo 795
limone 194
limousine 549
Lince 12
lince 134
linea 434, 813
linea aerea di alimentazione 585, 595
linea attiva, connettore della 663
linea bianca 127
linea blu di zona 879

linea cablata 525
linea centrale 815, 816, 848
linea centrale di servizio 821
linea continua 538
linea corta 819
linea d'acchito 862
linea dedicata 523, 524
linea degli sprinter 871
linea dei 10 metri 804
linea dei 15 metri 805
linea dei 2 metri 827
linea dei 200 metri 871
linea dei 22 metri 800, 804
linea dei 27 metri 858
linea dei 30 metri 859
linea dei 36 metri 858
linea dei 4 metri 827
linea dei 5 metri 800, 805
linea dei 50 metri 859
linea dei 54 metri 858
linea dei 60 metri 859
linea dei 7 metri 814, 827
linea dei 70 metri 859
linea dei 90 metri 859
linea dei karateka 845
linea dei kendoka 847
linea del battitore 799
linea del bersaglio 877
linea del quadrato di servizio 818
linea del traguardo 791
linea dell'acqua 615
linea dell'arbitro 845
linea dell'area di porta 814
linea dell'area di rigore 802
linea della chiusura lampo 455
linea della corsia 791
linea della fila di attesa 731
linea delle yards 806
linea dello scatto finale 871
linea di accrescimento 104, 105
linea di arrivo 833, 839, 856, 871, 890
linea di arrivo dei 500 metri 883
linea di attacco 812
linea di avvertimento per il fioretto 848
linea di avvertimento per la sciabola e la spada 848
linea di battuta 793
linea di battuta del salto in lungo 793
linea di battuta del salto triplo 793
linea di centro 877
linea di centrocampo 801, 806, 809, 810, 879
linea di cucitura 455
linea di demarcazione 799
linea di direzione 907
linea di distribuzione a bassa tensione 273, 663
linea di distribuzione a media tensione 273, 663
linea di fallo 865, 877
linea di fondo 800, 806, 809, 811, 812, 815, 816, 821, 831, 877
linea di forza 687
linea di fuoricampo 794, 819
linea di fuoricampo, palo della 795
linea di lancio 918
linea di limite posteriore 848
linea di messa in gioco 806
linea di messa in guardia 848
linea di meta 804, 806, 809
linea di metà campo 803, 805, 818, 819, 827
linea di mira, regolazione della 692
linea di mischia 807
linea di modifica 455
linea di pallone morto 804
linea di partenza 791, 833, 872
linea di partenza degli 800 metri piani 791
linea di partenza dei 100 metri ostacoli 790
linea di partenza dei 100 metri piani 790
linea di partenza dei 10000 metri piani 791
linea di partenza dei 110 metri ostacoli 790
linea di partenza dei 1500 metri piani 791
linea di partenza dei 200 metri piani 790
linea di partenza dei 400 metri piani, dei 400 metri ostacoli 791
linea di partenza dei 500 metri 882
linea di partenza dei 5000 metri piani 790
linea di partenza della staffetta 4 x 100 metri 791
linea di partenza della staffetta 4 x 400 metri 791
linea di piegatura 455
linea di porta 814, 827, 878
linea di punizione 814
linea di puntamento 907
linea di ricezione 818
linea di rimando 799
linea di rullaggio 619
linea di servizio 818, 819, 821
linea di servizio corto 817
linea di servizio lungo 816
linea di sicurezza 593
linea di spezzatura 362
linea di taglio 455
linea di tiro 859, 865, 893
linea di tiro libero 811
linea di uscita laterale 805
linea ferroviaria locale 583
linea ferroviaria principale 583
linea isosismica 43
linea laterale 108, 800, 803, 806, 809, 810, 812, 814, 815, 819, 858, 864, 877
linea laterale del doppio 817, 820
linea laterale del singolo 817, 821
linea mediana 814
linea meridiana 907
linea neutra 687
linea sottomarina 524
linea telefonica 524
linea telefonica/cablata/satellitare 523
linea tratteggiata 538, 539
linea, aereo di 53
linea, giudice di 813, 816, 818, 820, 824
linea, indicatore di 595
lineare 79
linebacker centrale 806
linebacker esterno 806
linebacker interno 806
linee di costa, esempi di 51
lingala 468
lingua 99, 109, 110, 164, 174, 175, 212
lingua biforcuta 112
lingua di cervo 76
lingua di terra 51
lingua glaciale 46
lingua, dorso della 176
lingua, guaina della 112
lingue aborigene dell'Australia 469
lingue afroasiatiche 468
lingue amerindie 469
lingue bantu 468
lingue celtiche 469
lingue centrafricane 468
lingue del mondo 468
lingue dell'Oceania 469
lingue germaniche 469
lingue indoeuropee 469
lingue indoiraniche 469
lingue isolate 469
lingue maleopolinesiane 469
lingue papuane 469
lingue romanze 469
lingue sinotibetane 468
lingue slave 469
lingue uralo-altaiche 469
linguella 346
linguetta 342, 352, 370, 386, 433, 456, 532, 881
linguetta a strappo 390
linguetta con finestra 532
linguetta di protezione 521
linguetta, ago a 456
linguettone 889
liquidi utilizzabili 400
liquido 680, 681
liquido cefalorachidiano 168
liquido dei freni, serbatoio del 559
liquore, bicchierino da 225
Lira 13
lira 433
liscio 79
lisciviazione 70
lisosoma 94
lista dei vini 721
lista di controllo delle procedure 20
lista serratura 442
listarella 291
listello 404, 405, 676
listello d'ingresso scorrevole 100
listello di cartonfeltro bitumato 299
listello rompitratta 249
listino, collo a 363
litchi 197
litio 682
litografia 420, 423
litosfera 42, 66
litri erogati 548
littorina 217
Lituania 744
livella a bolla 313
livella del basamento 701
livella fissata all'alidada 701
livellatrice 639
livello 650
livello base del moto ondoso 49
livello del mare 42, 49, 53
livello del suolo 647
livello dell'acqua 241, 261
livello dell'acqua, indicatore del 288
livello dell'acqua, selettore del 292
livello di carburante, indicatore del 557
livello di mare calmo 49
livello di picco a istogramma, indicatore del 488
livello di registrazione, selettore del 499
livello inferiore 597
livello superiore 597
livello superiore, dominio di 524
livello, vite di 699, 701
lizza 408
lob wedge 868
lobato 79
lobo 117
lobo inferiore 163
lobo laterale inferiore 86
lobo laterale superiore 86
lobo medio 163
lobo superiore 163
lobo terminale 86
lobulo 173
locale dei generatori elettrici 763
locale del reattore nucleare 763
locale delle pompe 606
locale macchine 763
locale per la biancheria 724
locale tecnico 543
locali per manutenzione 666
locomotiva diesel-elettrica 586
loculo 82
lombo 124, 147, 149
longan 196
longherone 624
longherone laterale 571
longherone laterale inferiore 635
longitudine 36
lontra comune 134
lonza 215
loop di punta 881
lorgnette 385
lorica 748
lotta 843
lotta greco-romana 843
lotta libera 843
lottatore 843, 844, 846
lubrificanti, impianto di produzione dei 656
lubrificazione, sistema di 586
lucchetto 580
luccio 220
luce 14, 15, 17, 381, 594, 615, 617, 626
luce alogena 775
luce anticollisione 624
luce bianca 616
luce della sbarra 591
luce della targa 554
luce di arresto 554
luce di aspirazione 565
luce di ingombro laterale 554, 570, 571
luce di lettura 771
luce di navigazione 605, 625, 631
luce di posizione 554, 585, 775
luce di posizione posteriore 554
luce di retromarcia 554
luce di scarico 565
luce di sicurezza 771
luce gialla 712
luce inattinica 484
luce intermittente 775
luce perpetua 738
luce rossa 712
luce rotante 766
luce segnapunti 848
luce solare, misurazione della 58
luce verde 712
luce visibile 690
lucernario 245
lucernario del bagno 251
lucernario della tromba delle scale 251
Lucertola 12
lucertola 114
luci 286
luci abbaglianti, spia delle 576
luci anteriori 554
luci dei goal 879
luci delle sorgenti 497
luci intermittenti 568
luci pedonali 712
luci posteriori 554, 775
luci, commutatore delle 576
luci, pannello delle 490
luci, regolazione sulle alte 479
luci, regolazione sulle basse 479
luci, regolazione sulle medie 479
luci, sala di regolazione delle 490
luci, tecnico delle 429
luci/video, area di controllo 490
lucidascarpe a batteria 345
lucidaunghie 377
lucido 345
lucioperca 220
Luer-Lock, punta 776
luminosità, regolatore di 518
luminosità, scala della 479
luminosità, tasto di 505
Luna 4, 6, 7
Luna calante 7
Luna crescente 7
Luna gibbosa calante 7
Luna gibbosa crescente 7
Luna nuova 7
Luna piena 7
Luna, caratteristiche della 7
Luna, eclissi di 7
Luna, fasi della 7
Luna, orbita della 6, 7
lunetta 342, 409, 802, 810
lunghezza d'onda 690
lunghezza dei punti, regolatore della 452
lunghezza del gradino 255
lunghezza dell'onda 49
lunghezza della punta 911
lunghezza, misura della 700
lunghezza, unità di misura della 702
lunotto laterale 551
lunula 105, 172, 173
lupino 190
Lupo 11
lupo 134
Lussemburgo 743
luteranesimo 736
lutezio 684
lutz 881

M

macaco 139
macadamia, noce di 193
macao 118
macchia 66
macchia di fiori 322
macchia oculare 95
macchia solare 6
macchina da caffè a filtro 241
macchina da cucire 452
macchina da maglieria 456
macchina da scrivere elettronica 528
macchina del ghiaccio 721
macchina della polizia 769, 771
macchina di carico 666
macchina di carico-scarico 669, 670
macchina di lancio dei piattelli 860
macchina di scarico 666
macchina di smistamento 475
macchina di smistamento-posizionamento-annullamento 474
macchina fotografica a disco 481
macchina fotografica a lastre 480
macchina fotografica autofocus 480
macchina fotografica digitale 481, 517
macchina fotografica reflex 480
macchina fotografica reflex (6x6) 481
macchina fotografica reflex biottica 480
macchina fotografica reflex digitale: dorso 477
macchina fotografica reflex monoculare, sezione di una 477
macchina fotografica reflex monoculare: dorso 476
macchina fotografica reflex monoculare: sezione 477
macchina fotografica reflex monoculare: vista frontale 476
macchina fotografica stereoscopica 481
macchina fotografica subacquea 480
macchina fotografica tascabile 480
macchina fotografica usa e getta 480
macchina fotografica, corpo della 476
macchina fotografica, piattaforma per 482
macchina fotografica, vite di fissaggio della 482
macchina per espresso 241
macchina per fare la pasta 230
macchina per fototessere 715
macchina per lavare i bicchieri 723
Macchina Pneumatica 11
macchine agricole 641
macchine da caffè 241
macchine fotografiche 480
macchine per il caffè 723
macchine pesanti 636
macchine, locale 763
macchine, sala 606, 608
macchinetta 381
macchinista 428
Macedonia 744
machete 751
macinacaffè 240
macinato 214, 215
Mackenzie, Fiume di 30
macrofotografie, lente addizionale per 478
macronucleo 94
macula 177
Madagascar 34, 746
madre 784, 785
maestra, albero di 600, 602
maestra, vela di 603
magazzino 708, 716, 720, 722, 734, 769
magazzino dei surgelati 181
magazzino frigorifero 596
magazzino per l'attrezzatura 764
mage 847
Magellan 19
magenta 690
maggese 182
maggiolino 101
maggiore di 703
maggiore o uguale a 703
maglia 805, 810, 815, 870
maglia a coste 458
maglia del cingolo 758
maglia della squadra 796, 801, 802, 808
maglia dentata 331
maglia diritta 458
maglia girocollo 359
maglia rovescia 458
maglia, ferro da 457
maglia, lavoro a 457
maglie da donna 716
maglie esagonali, reticella metallica a 299
maglieria, macchina da 456
maglietta 791
maglietta alla marinara 359
maglietta intima 368
maglione dolcevita 354
maglione girocollo 354
maglioni 354
maglioni da uomo 717
magma 44, 49
magnesia, polvere di 825
magnesio 682
magnete 488, 687
magnete fermacoperchio 240
magnetismo 687
magnetometro 60
mah-jongg 917
maiale 128
maiale, tagli di 215
mais 85, 203
mais foraggero 182
mais, farina di 204
mais, olio di 209
mais, pane americano di 205
mais, sciroppo di 209
mais: pannocchia 85
maitre 720
maiuscola 514
maiuscoletto 472
maiuscolo 472
malanga 189
Malawi 746
Malawi, Lago 34
Malaysia 747
Maldive 747
malgascio 469
Mali, Repubblica del 745
mallo 84
Malta 744
malta 298
malto, aceto di 201
mammella 127
mammiferi carnivori 130
mammiferi carnivori, esempi di 134
mammiferi insettivori 121
mammiferi insettivori, esempi di 121
mammiferi marini 136
mammiferi marini, esempi di 137
mammiferi marsupiali 142
mammiferi ungulati 124
mammiferi ungulati, esempi di 128
mammiferi volanti 140
mammiferi volanti, esempi di 141
mammut 93
mancorrente 542
mandarino 194
mandibola 97, 99, 108, 111, 112, 116, 121, 122, 123, 126, 131, 136, 138, 141, 142, 152, 158
mandibola inferiore 115
mandibola superiore 115
mandolino 433
mandorla 81, 193
mandrino 306, 307
mandrino autoserrante 306
mandrino, chiave del 306
manetta 750
manetta di caricamento 755
manette di accelerazione dei motori 626
manette, astuccio delle 770
manganello, gancio del 770
manganese 683
mango 197
mangostano 196
mangusta 134
manica 337, 348, 848
manica a giro 349, 361
manica a kimono 361
manica a pagoda 361
manica a palloncino 360
manica a pipistrello 361
manica a prosciutto 361
manica a tre quarti 360
manica a vento 739
manica ad aletta 360
manica alla raglan 352, 355, 361, 369
manica con spallina 360
manica corta 337
manica da vescovo 361
manica di camicia 361
manica di rifornimento 760
manica pendente 338
manica svolazzante 337
Manica, Canale della 32
maniche, esempi di 360
manichetta antincendio 767
manichette, asciugatoio per le 764
manichette, supporto per le 764
manichino da sarta 454
manichino snodabile 398
manico 227, 295, 301, 309, 311, 315, 320, 328, 382, 383, 384, 386, 387, 388, 389, 391, 425, 433, 439, 440, 441, 454, 458, 534, 611, 815, 816, 822, 849, 901, 905

INDICE DELLE VOCI ITALIANE

ASTRONOMIA > 2-25; TERRA > 26-71; REGNO VEGETALE >72-89; REGNO ANIMALE > 90-143; ESSERE UMANO > 144-177; GENERI ALIMENTARI E CUCINA > 178-241; CASA > 242-295; FAI DA TE E GIARDINAGGIO > 296-333; ABBIGLIAMENTO > 334-371; ACCESSORI E ARTICOLI PERSONALI > 372-391; ARTE E ARCHITETTURA > 392-465; COMUNICAZIONI E BUROTICA > 466-535; TRASPORTI E VEICOLI > 536-643; ENERGIA > 644-677; SCIENZA > 678-705; SOCIETÀ > 706-785; SPORT E GIOCHI > 786-920

1093

manico a scomparsa 386
manico della lama 424
manico della manovella 423
manico isolato 316, 317
manicotto 269, 270, 360
manicotto cavo 307
manicotto del cavo 306
manicotto del cordone 308, 318
manicotto di attacco dello scalpello 651
manicotto di bloccaggio 482
manicotto di raffreddamento 755
manicotto di riduzione 269
manicotto inferiore del radiatore 561
manicotto isolante 275
manicotto, borsa a 388
manicure 377
manicure, set per 377
manifesto 427
manifesto della mostra in corso 394
manifesto della mostra successiva 394
maniglia 238, 239, 247, 248, 280, 289, 290, 291, 313, 389, 503, 504, 551, 567, 584, 766, 775, 826, 884
maniglia a crociera 421
maniglia del carrello 456
maniglia della navicella 899
maniglia di salita 570
maniglia di sollevamento 756
maniglia di spinta 416
maniglia di traino 389
maniglia fissa 554
maniglia interna 554
maniglia isolata 239
maniglia laterale 594
maniglia per il trasporto 755
maniglie, cavallo con 824
manioca 184
manipolazione a distanza, sistema di 21
manipolazione del combustibile 666
mannaia 229
mano 139, 147, 149, 173
mano aperta 901
mano, ossa della 154
mano, scudo di protezione della 331
manometro 654, 655, 775, 777, 841
manometro della pressione della bombola 319
manometro della pressione di esercizio 319
manopola 256, 268, 290, 346, 379, 574, 577, 749, 901, 920
manopola alzacristalli 554
manopola del forno 290
manopola del manubrio 871
manopola del volume 503, 504, 505
manopola dell'acceleratore 576
manopola della messa a fuoco 14, 15, 485
manopola della sintonia 504
manopola di bloccaggio 304
manopola di bloccaggio del basamento 701
manopola di controllo 918
manopola di messa a fuoco manuale 483
manopola di posizionamento del campione 694
manopola di regolazione del condensatore 693
manopola di regolazione del gas 903
manopola di regolazione del micrometro 701
manopola di regolazione dell'aggetto 309
manopola di regolazione dell'altezza 289
manopola di regolazione della temperatura 465
manopola di regolazione dello schienale 555
manopola di ricerca delle stazioni 498
manopola di scorrimento 506
manopola di sgancio del cavo di traino 898
manopola di sintonizzazione 503
manopola distanziatrice 528
manopola per l'aerazione della cabina 898
manopola per l'apertura della calotta 898
manopole 318
manopole di comando dei bruciatori 290
manovella 307, 312, 328, 460, 558, 750, 910
manovella d'avvolgimento 313
manovella del supporto 571
manovella della colonna 482
manovella di avviamento 331
manovella, manico della 423
manovra, camera di 763
manovra, motore di 23
manque (da 1 a 18) 919
mansardato, piano 251
mantella 355
mantello 105, 106
mantello d'elica 605
mantello del pistone 566
mantello inferiore 42
mantello superiore 42
mantello, muscoli del 106
mantice 445
mantice a soffietto 432
mantide religiosa 102
manto di usura 538
mantovana 282
manuale 445
manuale del grand'organo 444
manuale dell'organo espressivo 444
manuale dell'organo positivo 444
manuale di pronto soccorso 777
manuale, pistoncino del 444
manuali 444
manubrio 327, 579, 649, 850, 851, 871, 876
manubrio rialzato 870
manubrio, attacco del 579
manubrio, manopola del 871
manzo, tagli di 214
Maometto 736
maori 469
mappamondo 734
Mar Adriatico 32
Mar Baltico 32
Mar Caribico 28, 30
Mar Caspio 28, 33
Mar Cinese Meridionale 28, 33
Mar Cinese Orientale 33
Mar d'Irlanda 32
Mar dei Coralli 29
Mar del Giappone 33
Mar di Barents 32
Mar di Beaufort 30
Mar di Bering 28
Mar di Groenlandia 28
Mar di Norvegia 32
Mar Glaciale Artico 28
Mar Mediterraneo 28, 32, 34
Mar Nero 28, 32, 33
Mar Rosso 28, 33, 34
maracuja 196
marca 390
marcatore per orli 454
marcatura, punto di 455
marchio registrato 473
marcia avanti, pedale della 333
marciapiede 245, 583, 593, 602, 620, 712
marciapiede dei viaggiatori 582
marciapiede, ingresso al 582
marciapiede, margine del 593
Marconi, ketch 601
Marconi, vela 601
mare 7, 38, 48
mare aperto 664
Mare Arabico 33
mare calmo, livello di 49
Mare del Nord 28, 32
Mare di Tasmania 29
Mare di Weddell 29
Mare Egeo 32
mare, beccaccia di 118
mare, livello del 42, 49, 53
mare, orecchia di 217
mare, passera di 221
mare, pressione a livello del 55
mare, riccio di 95
mare, rondine di 118
mare, tartufo di 217
mare-mare, missile 762
margarina 209
marginatore 484
margine 79
margine anteriore 105
margine continentale 49
margine del marciapiede 593
margine fogliare 79
margine libero 172
margine per la cucitura 455
margine posteriore 105
Marianne, Fossa delle 50
Marie Byrd, Terra di 29
marinaio, sacca da 388
marinara, collo alla 362
marinara, giacca alla 355
marinara, maglietta alla 359
Mariner 19
marino 61
marito 785
marmitta 45, 553
marmotta 123
Marocco 745
marquise, taglio a 375
marra 610
Mars Odyssey 19
marsina 338
marsupiali, esempi di 143
marsupio 143
Marte 4, 5
martelletti, barra dei 442
martelletto 442, 443
martelletto, asta del 443
martelletto, barra del 443
martelletto, feltro del 443
martello 174, 317, 793
martello a penna tonda 301
martello da carpentiere 301
martello da falegname 301
martello da muratore 315
martello da rilegatore 425
martello perforatore 648
martello perforatore con servosostegno 648
martello piccozza 901
martello, testa del 901
Martin Lutero 736
martin pescatore 118
martinetto 873
martinetto azionatore dell'ipersostentatore 760
martinetto idraulico 567, 640
martingala 858
martora 134
mascara compatto 378
mascara liquido 378
mascara, spazzolino per 378
mascella 99, 108, 111, 112, 116, 122, 123, 131, 136, 138, 152, 158, 175
mascellare 121
mascellare mobile 112
maschera 765, 796, 798, 800, 808, 841, 848, 879
maschera a pieno facciale bifiltro 773
maschera da saldatore 318
maschera forata 494
maschera per l'ossigeno 775
mascherina 432, 550, 773
mascherina perforata 342
maschile 702
maschio 408, 453
maschio della messa a terra 274
massa 43
massa d'aria, tipo di 55
massa pendolare 436
massa, morsetto di collegamento a 272
massa, unità di misura della 702
massaggiatore 811
massetere 150
massetto 252, 253
massicciata 591
massiccio montuoso 38
mastice di tenuta 265
matafione di terzarolo 603
matematica 703
materassi 716, 824
materassino 281, 776, 904
materassino autogonfiante 904
materassino isolante 904
materassino pneumatico 904
materasso 280, 281
materasso di protezione 883
materia 680
materia inorganica 67
materia, stati della 680
materiale antincendio 767
materiale audiovisivo 716
materiale corrosivo 774
materiale esplosivo 774
materiale infiammabile 774
materiale isolante 253, 254, 266, 267, 294, 689
materiale medico, deposito del 781
materiale pulito, ripostiglio del 778
materiale radarassorbente 629
materiale radioattivo 774
materiale sporco, deposito del 780
materiale sporco, ripostiglio del 778
materiale sterile, deposito del 780
materiale tossico 774
materiale vario 313
materiali da costruzione di base 298
materiali derivati dal legno 300
materiali di rivestimento 299
materiali isolanti 299
materiali metallici, smistamento dei 71
materiali pericolosi 774
materiali, movimentazione dei 632
matita 470
matita correttrice di pomice 423
matita di ematite 423
matita litografica 423
matita per sopracciglia 378
matita sbiancante per unghie 377
matite colorate 396
matite colorate, disegno a 396
matite per il contorno delle labbra 378
matrice in rilievo 420
matrice incisa 420
matrice piana 420
matrice ungueale 172
matterello 232
mattone 298
mattone forato 298
mattone forato per tramezzo 298
mattone perforato 298
mattone pieno 298
mattone refrattario 256, 298, 465
maturazione 86
maturazione, stadi di 86
maturità 86
Mauritania 745
Maurizio 746
mawashi 847
maya 469
mazza 448, 796, 797, 798
mazze 449
mazze, tipi di 867
mazzo 185
mazzuolo 301, 401, 421, 433, 858
meandro 48
meandro abbandonato 48
meandro abbandonato, lago di 48
meato auditivo 173, 174
meato uditivo esterno 158
meato urinario 169
Mecca, direzione della 738
meccanica del pianoforte verticale 443
meccanico 873
meccanico dello start 873
meccanismo a scatto 470
meccanismo antiritorno 909
meccanismo dell'organo 445
meccanismo dell'orologio a peso 697
meccanismo dell'ottava 446
meccanismo di apertura dell'archetto 910
meccanismo di avvolgimento 285
meccanismo di carica 697
meccanismo di chiusura, caricamento e sparo 755
meccanismo di rilascio della bobina 910
meccanismo di scappamento 436
meccanismo di spostamento della lama 639
mecchia 306
mecchia a doppia elica 306
mecchia a lancia 306
mecchia a tortiglione 306
mecchia elicoidale 306
mecchie e punte da trapano, esempi di 306
meda 615
medaglione 374
mede (regione B) 617
media 849
media tensione, linea di distribuzione a 273
mediano destro 801
mediano di apertura 804
mediano di mischia 804
mediano sinistro 801
medici 846
medicinali, confezioni farmaceutiche di 783
medicinali, scomparto dei 775
medico 780, 842
medico di guardia, ufficio del 778
medico interno 780
medie frequenze, pick-up per 441
medio 173, 472
Mediterraneo, Mar 28, 32, 34
meganeura 92
megazostrodon 93
Meissner, corpuscolo di 172
meitnerio 683
mela 82, 193
mela cotogna 193
mela, sezione di una 82
Melanesia 29
melanesiano 469
melanzana 188
melario 100
melassa 209
mele, aceto di 201
melissa 202
melodia, canna della 432
melodia, corde per la 432
melograno 196
melone amaro 188
melone giallo canario 195
melone invernale 189, 195
melone mieloso 195
melone Ogen 195
melone retato 195
meloni 195
membrana 449
membrana alare 140
membrana cellulare 74, 94
membrana del timpano 174
membrana interdigitale 110, 117
membrana interfemorale 140
membrana nittitante 132
membrana nucleare 74, 94
membrana plasmatica 94
membrana testacea 117
membrana vitellina 117
memoria dati 316
memoria dei motivi 456
memoria, tasto di 479
memoria, tasto di cancellazione della 479
memoria, tasto di richiamo della 479
memorizzazione dei dati, dispositivi di 521
memorizzazione, tasto di 497, 498, 501, 506
men 847
mendelevio 684
meningi 167
menisco convergente 691
menisco divergente 691
menorah 738
Mensa 10
mensa 763
mensola 256, 412, 440, 661
mensola portaccessori 14
mensola portautensili 321
mensolone 256
menta 202
mento 115, 148
mento, protezione del 575
mento, protezione per il 765
mentoniera 439
menu 721
menu, pulsante del 477
menu, tasto del 505
merci, area di ricevimento delle 716
merci, banchina di scarico delle 715, 716, 724
merci, ingresso delle 713
merci, scalo 583, 708
Mercurio 4, 5
mercurio 275, 683
mercurio, bulbo di 695
mercurio, colonna di 695
merguez 216
meridiana 696
meridiano celeste 13
meridiano fondamentale 36
meridiano occidentale 36
meridiano orientale 36
méridienne 276
merlano 221
merlano nero 221
merluzzo dell'Atlantico 221
mesa 52
mesenchima 95
mesocarpo 81, 82, 83
mesopausa 53
mesosauro 92
mesosfera 53
mesotorace 97
messa a fuoco manuale, manopola di 483
messa a fuoco, ghiera di 478
messa a fuoco, lente di ingrandimento per la 485
messa a fuoco, manopola della 14, 15, 485
messa a fuoco, schermo per la 477
messa a fuoco, selettore della 476, 496
messa a terra, cavo di 318
messa a terra, maschio della 274
messa a terra, morsetto di 318
messa a terra, terminale della 497
messa in onda, spia luminosa di 488
Messico 742
Messico, Golfo del 30
mestichino 397
mestieri 452
mestolo 233
meta, area di 806, 809
meta, linea di 806, 809
metacarpale 154, 156
metacarpale, 2° 140
metacarpale, 3° 140
metacarpale, 4° 140
metacarpale, 5° 140
metacarpo 111, 116, 122, 126, 131, 133, 136, 138, 142, 154
metafisi 155
metal detector a porta 726
metalli alcalini 682
metalli alcalino-terrosi 682
metalli di transizione 683
metalli, esempi di 741
metallo, bacchetta di 449
metalloidi 682
metatarsale 155
metatarso 98, 111, 122, 126, 131, 138, 141, 142, 155
metatorace 97
meteore 57
meteorite 8
meteorite ferro-rocciosa 8
meteorite ferrosa 8
meteoriti rocciose 8
meteorologia 53
meteorologia, simboli internazionali 56
meteorologia, strumenti di misurazione 58
metodi di pagamento 729
metodo di stampa in cavo 422
metodo di stampa in rilievo 421
metopa 404
metro 702
metro a nastro 454
metronomo 436
metronomo al quarzo 436
metropolitana 592, 594, 713
metropolitana, stazione della 592, 710
metropolitana, treno della 592
mezza barbetta 56
mezza sfera di sughero 817
mezzana, albero di 600, 602
mezzana, tronco di 602
mezzana, vela di 603
mezzana, vela di straglio di 603
mezzanino 592
mezzi integrativi di riscaldamento 260
mezzi occhiali 385
mezzo di pronto intervento 543
mezzo lato 632
mezzo manico 229
mezzoguanto 346
mi 434
micelio 76
Michel Keroularios 736
microfilamento 94
microfilm, lettore di 732
microfilm, registratore di 520
microfilm, stanza dei 732
microfoni 771
microfono 488, 492, 496, 505, 506, 508, 516, 517, 527, 770, 898
microfono dell'interfono 491
microfono dinamico 488
microfono, presa del 505
micrometro a vite 700

INDICE DELLE VOCI ITALIANE

1094

ASTRONOMIA > 2-25; **TERRA** > 26-71; **REGNO VEGETALE** >72-89; **REGNO ANIMALE** > 90-143; **ESSERE UMANO** > 144-177; **GENERI ALIMENTARI E CUCINA** > 178-241; **CASA** > 242-295; **FAI DA TE E GIARDINAGGIO** > 296-333; **ABBIGLIAMENTO** > 334-371; **ACCESSORI E ARTICOLI PERSONALI** > 372-391; **ARTE E ARCHITETTURA** > 392-465; **COMUNICAZIONI E BUROTICA** > 466-535; **TRASPORTI E VEICOLI** > 536-643; **ENERGIA** > 644-677; **SCIENZA** > 678-705; **SOCIETÀ** > 706-785; **SPORT E GIOCHI** > 786-920

micrometro, manopola di regolazione del 701
Micronesia 747
micronucleo 94
microonde 690
microonde, forni a 723
microonde, forno a 238
microscopi 693
Microscopio 10
microscopio 693
microscopio binoculare 693
microscopio elettronico, elementi del 694
microscopio elettronico, sezione di un 694
microtelefono 506, 507
microtelefono, cordone del 506
microtubulo 94
microvettura compatta 549
MIDI (cavo di interfaccia digitale per strumenti musicali) 451
midollo 87, 212
midollo allungato 167
midollo osseo 154
midollo spinale 109, 110, 167, 168
midollo spinale, struttura del 167
midrange 502
miele 209
miele, cella da 100
mietitrebbiatrice 643
migale del Messico 102
miglio 85, 203
miglio: spiga 85
mignolo 173
mihrab 738
mihrab, cupola sul 738
mille 703
milza 109, 110, 113, 125, 161
Mimas 5
mina antiuomo 758
minareto 738
minbar 738
minestra 722
mini impianto hi-fi 503
miniaspiratutto 288
minibus 569
miniera a cielo aperto 647
miniera coltivata con sbancamento 647
miniera di carbone 647
miniera sotterranea 650
miniera, esterno della 648
minima 435
minima, pausa di 435
minore di 703
minore o uguale a 703
minuscolo 472
minuti, lancetta dei 696, 697
miocardio 162
miopia 691
mira, cannocchiale di 692
mira, cuneo di 753
mira, tacca di 754, 755, 757, 861
miraglio 615, 616
Miranda 5
miretta 464
mirino 476, 477, 492, 754, 755, 757, 859, 861, 893, 912, 913
mirino a cannocchiale 912
mirino elettronico 496
mirtillo 192
mirtillo palustre 192
mirtillo rosso 192
miscela aria/carburante 564
miscela di cinque spezie 199
miscela di manganese (catodo) 689
miscela di sostanze depolarizzanti 689
miscela di zinco ed elettroliti (anodo) 689
miscela, condotto di passaggio della 565
miscelatore 270
miscelatore a cartuccia 268
miscelatore a disco 268
miscelatore a sfera 268
miscelatore per dolci 232
miscelatore vasca/doccia 262
miscelatori 268
miscelazione, camera di 319
mischia 806, 807
mischia spontanea 805
mischia, linea di 807
missile antiaereo 762
missile anticarro 759
missile antinave 759
missile antiradar 759
missile antisommergibile 759, 762
missile aria-aria 759, 760
missile aria-terra 759
missile mare-mare 762
missile terra-aria 759
missile, struttura di un 759
missili 759
missili, deposito dei 762
missili, principali tipi di 759
Mississippi, Fiume 30
misura degli angoli 701
misura del peso 698
misura del tempo 696
misura della distanza 700
misura della lunghezza 700
misura della temperatura 695
misura dello spessore 700
misuratore di cucitura 454
misuratore per ferri 457
misurazione dell'altezza delle nubi 59
misurazione dell'umidità 59
misurazione della direzione del vento 59
misurazione della forza del vento 59
misurazione della luce solare 58
misurazione della pressione dell'aria 59
misurazione della temperatura 59
misurazione delle precipitazioni 59
misurazione delle precipitazioni nevose 59
misurazione delle radiazioni solari 58
misurazione, pulsante di avvio della 479
misure di protezione obbligatorie 774
misurini 231
mitilo 217
mitocondrio 74, 94
mitra 257
mitraglia 752
mitragliatrice 758
mitragliatrice leggera 755
mixer audio 489
mixer video ausiliario 491
mobile 494
mobile bar 279
mobile contenitore 510
mobile portaccessori 264
mobili contenitori 278, 510
mobili da lavoro 511
mobili di archivio 510
mobili per bambini 281
mobili per ufficio 510
mocassino 344
mocassino classico 344
modalità FM, tasto di selezione della 497
modanatura 550
modellatore aperto 366
modellatore sgambato 366
modello 455
modello di stazione 55
modem 522, 523, 524
modem cablato 525
moderatore 665, 670, 671
modifica, linea di 455
modiglione 405
modo della sintonia 498
modo di esposizione, tasto per il 476
modo di uscita della copia 512
modo manuale/automatico 465
modo TV 495
modo VCR 495
modo, selettori di 504
modulatore della pressione dei freni 559
modulazione, rotella di 450
moduli fotovoltaici 21
modulo di atterraggio (Viking) 18
modulo abitativo americano 21
modulo centrifugo 21
modulo del carico utile 40
modulo del generatore di energia 40
modulo di affrancamento 531
modulo di comando 19, 25
modulo di comando del motore 563
modulo di comunicazione 486
modulo di controllo della potenza 563
modulo di propulsione 486
modulo di servizio 19, 25, 486
modulo di sollevamento a mezzo gas 652
modulo di sperimentazione europeo 21
modulo di sperimentazione giapponese 21
modulo lunare 19, 25
modulo orbitante (Viking) 18
modulo per la regolazione della carica delle batterie 563
modulo RAM 513
modulo russo 21
moffetta 134
moglie 785
Mohorovicic, discontinuità di 42
mola 308
molare 121, 123
molare, sezione trasversale di un 159
molari 159
molatrice angolare 308
Moldavia 744
mole 702
molecola 680
molibdeno 683
molla 43, 249, 268, 286, 292, 310, 470, 757, 776, 823, 913
molla a spirale 285, 696
molla del ventilabro 445
molla dell'acciarino 752
molla della valvola 566
molla dello scappamento 443
molla di richiamo 559
molla di sospensione 586, 697
molla di tensione 453, 457, 557, 850
molla sturatrice per scarichi 314
molla, aletta a 302
molle 233, 257
molle a forbice 850
molle per chiocciole 233
molle per spaghetti 233
molle, rete a 280
molletta 380
molletta del filo 457
molletta fermavetrino 693
molluschi 104, 217
molo 653, 708
moltiplica, ruota della 870
moltiplicatore 677
moltiplicatore di focale 478
moltiplicazione 703
molto sottile 472
monaco 253
Monaco, Principato di 744
monarca 101
mondo, climi del 61
mondo, lingue del 468
moneta: diritto 729
moneta: rovescio 729
monete, fessura per l'introduzione delle 920
monete, fessura per la restituzione delle 920
monete, slitta delle 920
mongolfiera 899
Mongolia 747
mongolo 469
monitor 507, 518
monitor a schermo piatto 518
monitor audio 488, 489, 490, 491
monitor degli effetti video digitali 491
monitor del direttore tecnico 491
monitor della pressione sanguigna 777
monitor di anteprima 489
monitor di anteprima, serie dei 491
monitor di controllo del regista 428
monitor di fase stereo 491
monitor di ingresso, serie dei 491
monitor di uscita 489, 491
monitor per il controllo della forma d'onda 491
monitor principale di anteprima 491
monitor, parete dei 489, 490, 491
monoblocco 566
monocolo 385
monografie, sezione delle 732
Monopoli® 915
monoscafi 835
monosci da slalom 840
monosci per figure 840
monoscopio 492
monovolume 549
montaggio, tasto di 496
montagna 45
montagna sottomarina 49
montagna, climi di 61
montagnais 469
Montagne Rocciose 30
montante 246, 249, 252, 253, 321, 362, 407, 413, 424, 425, 460, 551, 629, 663, 826
montante angolare 635
montante centrale 247, 278
montante d'angolo 252
montante del filetto 854
montante del morso 854
montante del telaio 278
montante del timpano 252
montante dell'ala 628
montante della ferratura 247
montante della serratura 247
montante imbottito 811
montante scorrevole 824, 825
montante verticale 277, 278
montatura 376, 385
montatura a ferro di cavallo 17
monte di lancio 795
monte di Venere 170
Monte Everest 53
montgomery 353
Monti Appalachi 30
Monti Carpazi 32
Monti dell'Atlante 34
Monti Transantartici 29
Monti Urali 32
montone 353
monumento 39
moquette 254
mora 192
mordente 435
morena di fondo 46
morena frontale 46
morena laterale 46
morena mediana 46
morena terminale 46
morfologia di un astice 107
morfologia di un cane 130
morfologia di un canguro 143
morfologia di un cavallo 124
morfologia di un delfino 136
morfologia di un gatto 133
morfologia di un gorilla 139
morfologia di un persico 108
morfologia di un pipistrello 140
morfologia di un polpo 106
morfologia di un ragno 103
morfologia di un ratto 122
morfologia di un serpente velenoso: testa 112
morfologia di un uccello 115
morfologia di un'ape: operaia 98
morfologia di una chiocciola 104
morfologia di una conchiglia bivalve 105
morfologia di una conchiglia univalve 105
morfologia di una farfalla 96
morfologia di una rana 110
morfologia di una stella marina 95
morfologia di una talpa 121
morfologia di una tartaruga 113
morfologia di uno squalo 108
morsa 312, 901
morsa serratubi 312
morsettiera 673
morsettiera di terra 272
morsetto 274, 284, 302, 303, 462
morsetto a C 312
morsetto a mano 422
morsetto anteriore 892
morsetto dei movimenti azimutali 701
morsetto dell'ago 453
morsetto di bloccaggio della tavola 307
morsetto di collegamento a massa 272
morsetto di messa a terra 318
morsetto inferiore della sfera 58
morsetto nero 558
morsetto regolabile 286
morsetto rosso 558
morsetto terminale a spina 562
morso 426, 854
morso a pompa 854
morso inglese 854
morso Pelham con cannone snodato 854
mortadella 216
mortaio 230, 612, 753
mortaio del XVII° secolo 752
mortaio moderno 756
mortasa 390
morte 702
mosaico 406
Mosca 11
mosca 101
mosca artificiale 909
mosca tse-tse 101
moschea 738
moschettiera, stivale alla 343
moschettone 835, 901, 911
moschettone a D 900
moschettone a ghiera 900
Mosè 736
mosse principali 916
mostra in corso, manifesto della 394
mostra permanente, stanze della 395
mostra successiva, manifesto della 394
mostra temporanea, stanze della 395
mostre, tabellone d'affissione delle 394
motivi 458
motivi, memoria dei 456
motivo 401, 458
moto da Gran premio 874
moto ondoso, livello base del 49
motocicletta 574
motocicletta con telecamera 870
motocicletta da cross 577
motocicletta da motocross 875
motocicletta da rally 875
motocicletta da supercross 875
motocicletta da trial 875
motocicletta da turismo 577
motocicletta di testa 870
motocicletta: vista dall'alto 576
motociclette e ciclomotore, esempi di 577
motociclismo 874
motociclista 874
motocoltivatore 327
motocompressore, turbina del 564
motofalciatrice 332
motore 18, 261, 292, 293, 294, 304, 307, 308, 320, 323, 327, 332, 574, 640, 643, 651, 758
motore a benzina 553, 563, 566
motore a due tempi, ciclo del 565
motore a quattro tempi 564
motore a razzo 24, 759
motore del braccio 521
motore del disco 521
motore del ventilatore 258, 261
motore della pompa 263
motore di atterraggio 18
motore di manovra 23
motore di traino, vano del 638
motore diesel 586
motore diesel del ventilatore di sostentamento 605
motore diesel di propulsione 605
motore diesel, ciclo del 565
motore diesel, vano del 636, 637, 638, 639
motore diesel, ventilatore del 586
motore elettrico 259, 331, 332, 561, 563
motore elettrico d'emergenza 763
motore elettrico principale 763
motore F-1 25
motore fuoribordo 607
motore J-2 25
motore principale 23
motore rotativo, ciclo del 565
motore turbocompresso 564
motore, asse di trasmissione del 237
motore, blocco 236, 237, 240, 288
motore, rivestimento del 331
motore, vano 632
motore, vano del 639
motore, yacht a 607
motori a getto, zona di prova dei 761
motori diesel 762
motori diesel marini, combustibile per 656
motori diesel, combustibile per 656
motori, tipi di 564
motorino d'avviamento 327, 332
motoscafo da diporto 607
motosega 331
motrice 570, 594
motto 729
mountain bike 581, 870
mountain bike da cross 581, 871
mouse a rotella 516
mouse meccanico 516
mouse ottico 516
mouse senza fili 516
mouse, tappetino del 516
movimentazione 632
movimentazione dei materiali 632
movimenti azimutali, morsetto dei 701
movimenti del terreno 47
movimenti di un aeroplano 630
movimento a L 916
movimento diagonale 916
movimento orizzontale 916
movimento orizzontale del suolo 43
movimento verticale 916
movimento verticale del suolo 43
movimento, rilevatore di 416
Mozambico 746
Mozambico, Canale di 34
mozzarella 210
mozzicone 391
mozzo 534, 579, 659, 677, 783
mozzo del rotore 631
mucca 128
mucosa olfattiva 175
muffola 346
muflone 128
mughetto 80
mulinello 909
mulinello a bobina fissa 910
mulinello a bobina rotante 910
mulinello, alloggiamento del 909, 910
mulino a pilastro 676
mulino a torre 676
mulino a vento 676
mulo 128
multimetro 316
multiscafi 835
mummia 904
municipio 710
munizioni, castello per 758
munster 211
mura fortificate 738
muraglia 917
murata 602, 607
muro 813, 852, 917
muro con barriere 852
muro di fiancata 597
muro di fondazione 252, 253
muro di fondo 430, 431
muro di mattoni 298
muro di pietra 298
muro di sponda 657
muro di testata 597
muro in mattoni 253
muschi, esempi di 75
muschio 75
muschio d'Irlanda 183
muschio, struttura di un 75
muscoli 150
muscoli del mantello 106
muscolo adduttore anteriore 105
muscolo adduttore posteriore 105
muscolo bulbocavernoso 169
muscolo erettore del pelo 172
muscolo papillare 162
muscolo retto inferiore 177
muscolo retto superiore 177
museo 394, 711
museo, negozio del 394
museruola 854, 856, 858
musica 432
musica, aula di 734
muso 110, 121, 124, 130, 132, 139, 143, 624, 897, 898
muso abbassabile 629
mussolina 231
muta 841
mutande 351
mutandina 367
mutandina con ruches 368
mutandina elastica 367
mutandina impermeabile 368
mutandoni 351
muting 499
mutulo 404
Myanmar 747

INDICE DELLE VOCI ITALIANE

ASTRONOMIA > 2-25; TERRA > 26-71; REGNO VEGETALE >72-89; REGNO ANIMALE > 90-143; ESSERE UMANO > 144-177; GENERI ALIMENTARI E CUCINA > 178-241; CASA > 242-295; FAI DA TE E GIARDINAGGIO > 296-333; ABBIGLIAMENTO > 334-371; ACCESSORI E ARTICOLI PERSONALI > 372-391; ARTE E ARCHITETTURA > 392-465; COMUNICAZIONI E BUROTICA > 466-535; TRASPORTI E VEICOLI > 536-643; ENERGIA > 644-677; SCIENZA > 678-705; SOCIETÀ > 706-785; SPORT E GIOCHI > 786-920

1095

N

n. 8 avanti 804
nacchere 437, 449
nahuatl 469
Namib, Deserto del 34
Namibia 746
nana bianca 8
nana bruna 8
nana nera 8
naos 403
nappa 282
narice 108, 110, 112, 115, 124, 175
narvalo 137
nasale 749
nascita 702
nasello 385
nasello del paramartello 443
nashi 197
naso 122, 124, 148
naso esterno 175
naso, dorso del 175
naso, punta del 175
naso, radice del 175
nasofaringe 175
nastratrice 534
nastro 313, 340, 459, 757, 800, 821, 823
nastro adesivo, chiocciola per 534
nastro bianco 812, 815, 817
nastro centrale 821
nastro di delimitazione 771
nastro di registrazione 499
nastro di teflon 314
nastro magnetico 495
nastro per correzioni 534
nastro trasportatore 71, 620, 647, 649
nastro trasportatore dei bagagli 623
nastro verticale laterale 812
nastro, chiave a 315
nastro, fermo del 313
nastro, guida del 499
nastro, selettore del 499
natica 147, 149, 169, 170
Nauru 747
navajo 469
navata centrale 411, 738
navata laterale 411
nave 41
nave appoggio 653
nave cisterna 606
nave da perforazione 604
nave da ricognizione meteorologica 54
nave di perforazione 653
nave per il trasporto delle merci 604
nave portacontainer 596, 604
nave traghetto 608
nave, ancora della 610
navetta 461
navetta per arazzi 461
navetta per il trasbordo dei passeggeri 621, 623
navetta piana 461
navetta spaziale 22, 53
navetta spaziale al decollo 22
navi, esempi di 604
navicella 677, 899
navicella in vimini 899
navicella, cavi di sospensione della 899
navicella, maniglia della 899
navicella, sezione trasversale di una 677
navicolare 155, 156
navigazione satellitare, sistema di 613
navigazione, display di 626
navigazione, luce di 605, 625
navigazione, strumenti per la 612
navone 189
Nazca, placca di 43
nazionalità 825
nazionalità del nuotatore 831
NEAR 19
nebbia 57, 65
nebbia, segnalatore di 611
nebulizzatore 329
nebulosa planetaria 8
necroforo 101
necrologia 471
nefridio 107
negativo 485
negozio 710
negozio del museo 394
negozio di abbigliamento 714
negozio di animali 714
negozio di articoli da regalo 714
negozio di articoli sportivi 715
negozio di biancheria intima 714
negozio di bricolage 714
negozio di dischi 714
negozio di elettronica 714
negozio di giocattoli 714
negozio di oggettistica 715
negozio di scarpe 715
negozio per la riproduzione delle chiavi 715
nembostrato 56, 62
neo 684
neodimio 684
neon, lampada al 316

neonati, vestiti per 368
Nepal 747
neri 916
nero 472, 690, 741, 919
Nero, Mar 28, 32, 33
nervatura 79, 426, 639, 772
nervatura alare 96
nervatura centrale 75, 79, 84
nervi cranici 166
nervo 172
nervo ascellare 166
nervo cocleare 174
nervo cutaneo laterale della coscia 166
nervo cutaneo posteriore della coscia 166
nervo digitale 166
nervo femorale 166
nervo gluteo 166
nervo ileoinguinale 166
nervo ileoipogastrico 166
nervo intercostale 166
nervo ischiatico 166
nervo mediano 166
nervo olfattivo 175
nervo olfattorio 109
nervo ottico 177
nervo otturatorio 166
nervo peroniero comune 166
nervo peroniero profondo 166
nervo peroniero superficiale 166
nervo radiale 166
nervo safeno esterno 166
nervo safeno interno 166
nervo spinale 167, 168
nervo tibiale 166
nervo ulnare 166
nervo vestibolare 174
nervoso centrale, sistema 167
nervoso periferico, sistema 166
nervoso, sistema 166
nespola del Giappone 193
netball 809
nettarina 192
nettunio 684
Nettuno 4, 5
neurone motorio 168
neurone sensoriale 168
neuroni, catena di 168
neutrone 680
neutrone incidente 681
neutroni, stella di 8
nevato 46
neve 64
neve acida 70
neve forte continua 57
neve forte intermittente 57
neve leggera continua 57
neve leggera intermittente 57
neve moderata continua 57
neve moderata intermittente 57
neve, cristalli di 64
neve, misurazione delle precipitazioni 59
neve, rovesci di 57
nevi perenni 45
nevischio 57, 64
newton 702
Nicaragua 742
nicchia di sicurezza 543
nicchia per la saracinesca 597
nichel 683
nido 100
Niger 745
Niger, Fiume 34
Nigeria 745
Nilo 34
niobio 683
nipote 784, 785
nipoti 784
nipplo 269
nivometro 58, 59
nobelio 684
nocciola 193
nocciola, sezione di una 84
nocciolo 81
nocciolo del reattore 670, 671
noce 88, 193, 456, 750
noce del Brasile 193
noce di acagiù 193
noce di cocco 193
noce di cola 193
noce di ginco 193
noce di macadamia 193
noce di pecan 193
noce moscata 198
noce, sezione di una 84
nodello 124
nodi 908
nodo 77, 227, 229, 663, 687
nodo a margherita 908
nodo bocca di lupo 908
nodo del pescatore 908
nodo di Ranvier 168
nodo di scotta doppio 908
nodo di scotta semplice 908
nodo parlato doppio 908
nodo parlato semplice 908
nodo piano 908
nodo Savoia 908

nodo scorsoio 908
nodo semplice 908
nodo vaccaio 908
nome del dominio 524
nome del ginnasta 825
nome del giornale 471
nome del nuotatore 831
nome del titolare 729
nome della squadra 858
nome della stazione 592
nome della valuta 729
non appartiene a 703
non candeggiare 347
non centrifugare 347
non coincide con 703
non lavare 347
non metalli 683
non parallelo a 704
non stirare 347
nonio 612, 698, 700
nonio, scala graduata del 700
nonna 784
nonni 784
nonno 784
Nord 37
nord 616, 917
Nord Nord-Est 37
Nord Nord-Ovest 37
Nord, Mare del 28, 32
Nord-Est 37
nord-est 616
Nord-Ovest 37
nord-ovest 616
nori 183
normale 472
norvegese 469
Norvegia 744
Norvegia, Mar di 32
notazione degli scacchi 916
notazione musicale 434
note, valori di durata delle 435
notizie 471
notizie in breve 471
notosauro 93
notte, camicia da 364
nottolino 307
nottolino a scatto 700
nova 8
novità, scaffale delle 733
nube 65
nube a proboscide 63
nube alta, tipo di 55
nube bassa, tipo di 55
nube di ceneri vulcaniche 44
nube di Oort 4
nube media, tipo di 55
nubi 62
nubi a sviluppo verticale 62
nubi alte 62
nubi basse 62
nubi medie 62
nubi, misurazione dell'altezza delle 59
nuca 115, 147, 149
nuclei radioattivi 681
nucleo 6, 8, 9, 74, 94, 168, 170, 680, 867, 912
nucleo centrale di argilla 660
nucleo dell'indotto 688
nucleo esterno 42
nucleo fissile 681
nucleo interno 42
nucleo, membrana del 74
nucleo, scissione del 681
nucleolo 74, 94, 170
numeratore 273, 531
numeri romani 703
numero 791, 919
numero atomico 682
numero del binario 582
numero del brano 501
numero del giocatore 808, 810, 878
numero dell'utente 273
numero della camera 724
numero della carta 729, 731
numero della pompa 548
numero delle copie 512
numero delle righe, display del 456
numero di autostrada 39
numero di corsa 857
numero di corsia 893
numero di gara 875
numero di serie 729
numero di strada 39
nuora 784
nuotatore, nazionalità del 831
nuotatore, nome del 831
nuoto 830
nuoto, stadio per il 788
nuoto, stili di 832
Nuova Caledonia 29
Nuova Zelanda 29, 747
nuovo shekel 728
Nuovo Testamento 736
nuvola 53
nuvole 56
nuvole, assorbimento attraverso le 68
nuvole, parete di 63
nuvolosità 56

O

oasi 48, 52
Oberon 5
obi 845, 846
obice moderno 756
obiettivi 478
obiettivo 14, 476, 478, 479, 483, 517, 518, 693
obiettivo di ingrandimento 485
obiettivo grandangolare 478
obiettivo macro 478
obiettivo normale 478
obiettivo supergrandangolare 478
obiettivo zoom 478
obiettivo, accessori dell' 478
obiettivo, attacco dell' 477
obiettivo, coperchio di protezione dell' 478
obiettivo, lente 692
obiettivo, pulsante di sblocco dell' 476
obliquo esterno dell'addome 150, 151
oblò 608
oboe 446
oboi 437
oca 120, 213
oca, uovo di 213
occhi, trucco per gli 378
occhiali 385, 870, 887, 888, 896
occhiali a forbice 385
occhiali da sole 385
occhiali di protezione 318, 818, 819
occhiali di protezione con ripari laterali 772
occhiali di protezione panoramici 772
occhiali protettivi 861, 870, 875
occhiali, astuccio per 387
occhiali, esempi di 385
occhiali, parti degli 385
occhialini da nuoto 830
occhielli 453
occhiello 342, 352, 371, 387, 457, 461, 471, 881, 900, 911
occhiello diritto 453
occhiello per la cinghia 476
occhiello per la tracolla 477
occhiello rotondo 453
occhio 63, 103, 104, 106, 107, 112, 113, 121, 136, 148, 177, 301, 470, 854, 855
occhio composto 96, 98, 99
occhio di controllo 591
occhio semplice 97, 99
occhio, orbicolare dell' 150
occhio, parete dell' 63
occhiolo 284
occhione 756
occhione di traino 558
occhione, braccio d'attacco dell' 756
occhione, fermo del braccio d'attacco dell' 756
occipitale 151
Oceania 28, 29, 747
Oceania, lingue dell' 469
oceano 7, 38, 67
Oceano Atlantico 28, 29, 32, 34
Oceano Indiano 28, 29, 33, 34
Oceano Pacifico 28, 29, 33
oculare 14, 15, 477, 479, 496, 692, 693
offerta, prodotti in 181
officina di manutenzione dei vagoni 589
officina di riparazione dei locomotori diesel 583
officina meccanica 548
officina riparazioni 648
Ofiuco 11, 13
oftalmologia, sala di 779
oggetti smarriti 725
oggettistica 716
oggettistica, negozio di 715
oggetto 691
ogiva 627, 659
ogivale 413
ohm 702
okapi 128
olandese 469
olecrano 126, 153
oleodotti, rete di 654
oleodotto 654
oleodotto di spedizione 652
oleodotto di superficie 654
oleodotto sottomarino 654
olfatto 174
oli 209
oliatore 648, 649
olii lubrificanti 656
olio combustibile leggero 656
olio combustibile per stufe 656
olio combustibile pesante 656
olio d'oliva 209
olio di arachidi 209
olio di mais 209
olio di semi di girasole 209
olio di semi di lino 400
olio di sesamo 209
olio, colore a 397
olio, pastelli a 396

olio, pittura a 396
olio, tappo di scarico dell' 566
oliva 188
oliva auricolare 776
oliva, olio d' 209
olivetta 353
olmio 684
Oman 746
Oman, Golfo di 33
ombelico 46, 146, 148
ombelico inferiore 115
ombelico superiore 115
ombra 696
ombreggiatura 463
ombrella 81
ombrello 391
ombrello a bastone 391
ombrello pieghevole 391
ombretto 378
omero 111, 116, 121, 122, 126, 131, 136, 138, 141, 142, 152, 156
omero, testa dell' 153
onda 49, 690
onda d'urto 651, 653
onda sismica 43
onda, altezza dell' 49
onda, fondo dell' 49
onda, lunghezza d' 690
onda, lunghezza dell' 49
onde hertziane, trasmissione a 486
onde radio 690
onde ultrasonore, emissione di 41
onori supremi 917
Oort, nube di 4
opale 375
Opera 710
opera morta 835
operatore pannello luci 490
operazioni di base 529
operazioni specifiche 529
operazioni, accesso al secondo livello di 529
operazioni, primo livello di 529
operazioni, secondo livello di 529
opercolo 108, 111
opilione 102
opistodomo 403
opossum 143
ora, tasto di visualizzazione dell' 496
orangotango 139
orari 582
orari dei film 427
orari, tabellone degli 582
orata 219
orbicolare 79
orbicolare dell'occhio 150
orbita 112, 116, 131, 136, 138, 142
orbita dei satelliti 60
orbita della Luna 6, 7
orbita della Terra 6, 7
orbita geostazionaria 60
orbita polare 60
orbiter 22, 23
orca 137
orchestra 402
orchestra sinfonica 437
orchidea 80
ordinata rinforzata 607
ordine corinzio 405
ordine di arrivo 831
ordine dorico 404
ordine ionico 404
ordito 455, 460, 461
ordito alto, telaio a 461
ordito basso, telaio a 460
ordito, fili dell' 463
ordito, subbio dell' 460
orditoio 462
Ordoviciano 92
ore, lancetta delle 697
orecchia di mare 217
orecchie di cane, collo a 362
orecchie, tappi per le 772
orecchini 374
orecchini a clip 374
orecchini a perno 374
orecchini a vite 374
orecchini ad anello 374
orecchini pendenti 374
orecchio 133, 140, 146, 610
orecchio di Giuda 183
orecchio esterno 174
orecchio interno 174
orecchio medio 174
orecchio, struttura dell' 174
orecchione 753
organi di senso 172, 173, 177
organi di trasmissione 580
organi genitali femminili 170
organi genitali maschili 169
organismi autotrofi 67
organismi decompositori 67
organismi eterotrofi 67
organismi semplici 94
organizer 530
organizzatori, uffici degli 719
organizzazione culturale 525
organizzazione governativa 525

ASTRONOMIA > 2-25;   TERRA > 26-71;   REGNO VEGETALE >72-89;   REGNO ANIMALE > 90-143;   ESSERE UMANO > 144-177;   GENERI ALIMENTARI E CUCINA > 178-241;   CASA > 242-295;
FAI DA TE E GIARDINAGGIO > 296-333;   ABBIGLIAMENTO > 334-371;   ACCESSORI E ARTICOLI PERSONALI > 372-391;   ARTE E ARCHITETTURA > 392-465;   COMUNICAZIONI E BUROTICA > 466-535;
TRASPORTI E VEICOLI > 536-643;   ENERGIA > 644-677;   SCIENZA > 678-705;   SOCIETÀ > 706-785;   SPORT E GIOCHI > 786-920

organo 444
organo di raccordo 570
organo, meccanismo dell' 445
Oriente, scisma d' 736
orifiamma 739
orifizio della sacca copulatoria 97
orifizio escretore 104
orifizio genitale 104
origano 202
origine delle specie 92
Orinoco, Fiume 31
Orione 11, 12
orlatura a stella 912
orlo 340, 455
orlo della vasca 292
orlo esterno 127
orlo interno 127
ormeggio, catena di 615
ormeggio, verricello di 607
ornamento di prua 600
oro 683, 741
orologi 717
Orologio 10
orologio 488, 489, 491, 734, 858
orologio a pendolo 697
orologio a peso, meccanismo dell' 697
orologio analogico 696
orologio contaminuti 238
orologio digitale 696
orologio meccanico 696
orologio per la timbratura dei cartellini 530
Orsa Maggiore 13
Orsa Minore 12
orso bruno 135
orso polare 135
ortaggi 184
ortaggi da bulbo 184
ortaggi da foglia 186
ortaggi da frutto 188
ortaggi da fusto 185
ortaggi da infiorescenza 187
ortaggi da radice 189
ortaggi da tubero 184
ortica 187
orto 182, 244
ortocera 92
orzo 85, 203
orzo: spiga 85
osculo 95
oscurità 617
osmio 683
ospedale 711, 725, 778
ospite 379
ossa del piede 155
ossa della mano 154
ossa, tipi di 157
osservatorio 17
osservatorio astronomico 17
osservatorio astronomico, sezione trasversale di un 17
osservazione astronomica 10
osservazione psichiatrica, stanza per 778
osservazione, finestrino di 23
osservazione, punto di 17
osservazione, stanza di 778, 781
oscicini dell'udito 174
ossido d'azoto, emissione di 70
ossigeno 683
ossigeno liquido, serbatoio dell' 24, 25
ossigeno, bombola d' 319
ossigeno, leva di regolazione dell' 319
ossigeno, presa dell' 780
ossigeno, produzione di 78
ossigeno, regolazione della pressione dell' 20
ossigeno, valvola dell' 319
osso alveolare 159
osso compatto 154
osso corto 157
osso frontale 131, 152, 158
osso irregolare 157
osso lungo 157
osso lungo, parti di un 155
osso lungo, struttura di un 154
osso mascellare 159
osso nasale 158, 175
osso occipitale 131, 153, 158
osso parietale 131, 153, 158
osso piatto 157
osso sesamoide falciforme 121
osso sfenoide 158
osso spugnoso 154
osso temporale 152, 158
osso zigomatico 152, 158
ossobuco 214
ostacoli 852, 875
ostacolo 790
ostacolo d'acqua 866, 867
ostacolo per corsa a siepi 790
osteone 154
ostrica 217
ostriche, coltello da 229
ostriche, forchetta da 228
otolito 109
otorinolaringoiatria, sala di 779
ottaedro regolare 705
ottagonale, taglio 375
ottagono regolare 705

Ottante 10
ottava 434, 849
ottava, meccanismo dell' 446
ottavino 437, 446
ottico 715
otto con 839
ottoni, famiglia degli 437
otturatore 513
otturatore a tendina 476, 477
otturatore, leva di manovra dell' 756
ovaia 170, 171
ovale, taglio 375
ovario 80, 97, 103
ovata 79
Ovest 37
ovest 616, 917
Ovest Nord-Ovest 37
Ovest Sud-Ovest 37
ovidotto 97, 103, 113
ovile 182
ovolo 253
ovolo buono 183
ovotestis 104
ovulo 80, 170
oxer 852, 853
oxford, scarpa 342
ozono, strato di 53

P

pacchetto 223
pacchetto di sigarette 390
pacchetto, tenda a 285
pacco postale 475
Pacifico, Oceano 28, 29, 33
Pacifico, placca del 43
Pacifico, salmone del 221
Pacini, corpuscolo di 172
paddock 856
padella 905
padella doppia 235
padella per crêpe 235
padella per friggere 235
padella per rosolare 235
padiglione 174, 374, 444, 710
padiglione auricolare 122, 143, 173
padre 784, 785
paese 37, 708
Paesi Bassi 743
pagaia a doppia pala 837, 839
pagaia a pala singola 837, 838
pagamento elettronico, terminale di 731
pagamento elettronico, terminale per il 181
pagina precedente 515
pagina successiva 515
paglia, spargitore di 643
pagliaccetto 366, 369
paglietta 340
pagnottella inglese 205
pagoda 412
pagoda, manica a 361
pak-choi 186
Pakistan 746
pala 261, 293, 659, 676, 677, 798, 838, 841, 880
pala ausiliaria 676
pala caricatrice 638
pala caricatrice anteriore 637
pala caricatrice posteriore 637
pala caricatrice, braccio della 637
pala caricatrice, cilindro della 637
pala da neve 901
pala del rotore 631
pala del timone 606
pala dell'altare 737
pala della girante 659, 664
pala direttrice 659
pala meccanica 647
palafitta 418
palanchino 301
palatino 112, 123
palato duro 174, 175
palato molle 174, 175
Palau 747
palazzetto dello sport 788
palazzo dei congressi 711, 718
palazzo di giustizia 710
palazzo in condominio 419
palazzo residenziale 408
palchetto 431
palcoscenico 402, 430, 431
palcoscenico, gabbia del 430
palestra 608, 727, 734, 764, 788
palestra, ufficio della 734
paletta 227, 233, 257, 295, 440, 441, 855, 901, 911
paletta del compressore assiale 627
paletta di carico 632
paletta di carico a cassa 632
paletta di carico a due piani 632
paletta di carico a un piano 632
paletta di carico ad alette 632
paletta riempigiunti 315
palettatura dello statore esterno 627
palettatura dello statore interno 627
palette di carico 632

palette di carico, carrello a forca per 633
palette di carico, carrello a piattaforma per 633
palette di carico, carrello idraulico per 633
paletto 842
paliotto 737
palizzata 322, 408
palla 336, 752, 753, 796, 797, 798, 800, 818, 822, 823, 858, 867
palla cava 752
palla da allenamento 819
palla da gara 819
palla di filo 797
palla di protezione 839
palla di sughero 797
palla ovale 805, 808
palla ramata 752
palla, sezione di una 797, 867
pallacanestro 810
palladio 683
pallamano 814
pallanuoto 827
pallavolo 812
palle 819
palleggio 813
pallina 815, 920
pallina d'avorio 919
pallini 912
pallino 864
palloncino, calzoni a 338
palloncino, manica a 360
pallone 685, 802, 809, 810, 812, 813, 814, 827, 899
pallone aerostatico 899
pallone sonda 54
pallone-sonda 59
pallonetto 821
pallottola 752, 912
pallottoline di neve 64
palma 88
palmare breve 150
palmare lungo 150
palmata 79
palmeto 52
palmetta 276
palmo 121, 173, 346
palmo del guanto 346
palo 493, 591, 740, 807, 812, 817, 820, 827, 858
palo con canestro 809
palo della linea di fuoricampo 795
palo di distanza 856
palo frontale 903
palombo liscio 218
palpebra 113
palpebra inferiore 110, 132, 177
palpebra superiore 110, 132, 177
palpo 105
palpo labiale 96, 99
pampino 86, 186
Panama 742
panama 340
Panama, Golfo di 31
Panama, Istmo di 30
panca 737, 851, 855
panca degli ufficiali di gara 879
panca dei puniti 879
panca dei puniti, addetto alla 879
pancetta 216
panchina 277, 593, 715, 775, 803, 827
panchina dei giocatori 794, 801, 807, 809, 812, 814, 878
panciera 367
panciotto 338
panciotto lungo 338
pancreas 110, 116, 164
pane 204, 722
pane azzimo 205
pane bianco 205
pane chapati indiano 205
pane d'argilla 464
pane di mais americano 205
pane di segale danese 205
pane di segale tedesco 205
pane e burro, piattino per 226
pane ebraico 205
pane greco 204
pane integrale 205
pane irlandese 205
pane multicereali 205
pane naan indiano 205
pane nero di segale 204
pane pita 205
pane, coltello da 229
pane, guida per il 238
pane, stampo per 239
panetteria 181, 715
panieri, abito con 337
panna 210
panna acida 210
panna da montare 210
pannelli di vetro 614
pannelli isolanti 299
pannello 247, 367, 400, 554
pannello dei collegamenti elettrici 489
pannello dei collegamenti video 489
pannello dei comandi 261

pannello del display 496
pannello dell'anta 278
pannello delle luci 490
pannello di accesso 258, 266
pannello di assorbimento dei bassi 490
pannello di celle solari 673
pannello di comando 261, 512, 586, 694, 766
pannello di compensato impiallacciato 300
pannello di compensato multistrato 300
pannello di connessione 518
pannello di controllo 518
pannello di copertura 550
pannello di distribuzione 272
pannello di funzionamento 417
pannello di gesso 299
pannello di masonite 300
pannello di mezzo 247
pannello di protezione 577
pannello di truciolato 300
pannello di truciolato forato 300
pannello di truciolato grezzo 300
pannello di truciolato laminato in plastica 300
pannello divisorio 386, 389
pannello fotovoltaico 615
pannello frontale 511
pannello laminato in legno 300
pannello mobile 509, 510, 719
pannello solare 17, 18, 40, 60, 486
pannello solare, comando del 60
pannello superiore degli interruttori 626
panno 862
pannocchia 85
pannolino 368
pannolino usa e getta 368
pantacollant 371
pantaloncini 369, 791, 801, 802, 805, 810, 842, 850, 870
pantaloncini da corsa 371
pantaloni 350, 371, 716, 796, 808, 844, 875, 878, 901
pantaloni a zampa di elefante 358
pantaloni alla pescatora 358
pantaloni alla zuava 358
pantaloni da cavallo 853
pantaloni felpati 370
pantaloni, esempi di 358
pantografo 585, 595
papaia 197
papalina 340
papavero 80, 84
papavero, semi di 199
papilla 172
papilla circonvallata 176
papilla filiforme 176
papilla foliata 176
papilla fungiforme 176
papilla linguale 176
papilla ottica 177
papilla renale 165
papillon 349
paprika 199
Papua Nuova Guinea 747
Papuasia-Nuova Guinea 29
parabraccia 808, 880
parabrezza 550, 570, 574, 577, 607, 624, 626, 628, 876
paracadute 417, 760, 896
paracadute del booster 22
paracadute di riserva 896
paracadute principale 896
paracadute, valvola del 899
paracadutismo in caduta libera 896
paracadutista 896
paracoccige 808
paracollo 808, 880, 882
paracolpi 818
paracolpi di gomma 920
paracosce 808
paracostole 808
paradenti 808, 843
paradita 859
parafango 550, 551, 570, 578, 640
parafango anteriore 574
paraffine 656
parafianchi 808
parafulmine 245, 658, 663, 677
parafuoco 257
paragambe 879, 880
paragomito 857
paragola 796, 880
paragomiti 880
paragomito 808
paragrilletto 912
Paraguay 742
paralama 304, 305
paralama inferiore 304
paralama inferiore, leva per togliere il 304
paralama superiore 304
parallele 825
parallele asimmetriche 824
parallelepipedo 705
parallelo 36
parallelo a 704
parallelogramma 705
paraluce 14, 478, 612

paralume 286
paramano 875
paramartello 443
paramartello, nasello del 443
paramecio 94
paramento a monte 661
paramento a valle 661
paramezzale centrale 607
Paranà, Fiume 31
paraneve 876
paranocca 858
paranocche 853
paraocchi 857
paraorecchi 340
paraorecchie 861
parapendio 897
parapetto 255, 408, 409, 540, 586
parapetto, pilastro del 255
parapunta 796
parasole 558
parasole, aletta 556
paraspalle 808, 880
paraspruzzi 655, 837
parastinchi 796, 801, 802, 882, 887
paratia longitudinale 606
paratia trasversale 606
paratoia 658, 664
paratoia dello sfioratore 657
paratrucioli 305
paraurti 570, 571, 577
paraurti anteriore 885
paraurti posteriore 577, 876, 885
paravento del bruciatore 899
parcheggio 583, 596, 620, 708, 713, 735, 866, 886
parcheggio per le biciclette 735
parco 39, 711
parco nazionale 39
parentela, vincoli di 784
parentesi 473
parentesi quadre 473
pareo 339
parete 7, 82, 127, 246, 902
parete anteriore 571, 818
parete artificiale di arrampicata 900
parete cellulare 74
parete dei monitor 489, 490, 491
parete dell'occhio 63
parete della qibla 738
parete di arrivo 830
parete di calcestruzzo 675
parete di nuvole 63
parete di virata 831, 832
parete frontale 819
parete inferiore 655
parete laterale 571, 635, 655, 818, 819, 831
parete posteriore 818, 819
parete superiore 655
parete Trombe 675
parete, lampada da 287
parete, lampione da 287
pareti di vetro, custodia a 699
pari 919
parietale 112, 122
parigina 589
parigina, cabina di controllo della 589
paripennata 79
parka 353
parlatorio 726
parmigiano 211
parquet 253, 254, 819
parquet a listelli 254
parquet a listoni 254
parquet a mosaico 254
parquet a spina di pesce 254
parquet a tessitura di vimini 254
parquet Arenberg 254
parquet Chantilly 254
parquet su sottofondo di cemento 254
parquet su struttura lignea 254
parquet Versailles 254
parquet, tipi di 254
parrocchetto fisso 603
parrocchetto volante 603
parrocchetto, albero di 602
parrucchiere 428, 714
parrucchiere, forbici da 382
parte anteriore del quartiere 342, 370
parte cellulare 74
parte inferiore del tronco 87
parte intermedia 169
parte piatta 457
parte superiore del collo 362
parte superiore dell'intelaiatura 249
parte terminale 169
partenza 852, 885, 887
partenza a dorso 832
partenza con vento contrario 833
partenza della funivia 886
partenza della seggiovia 886
partenza, area di 875
partenza, boe di 838
partenza, gabbia di 856
partenza, giudice di 837
partenza, griglia di 872, 875
partenza, piazzola di 866, 867
partenza, pontile di 838

partenza, posizioni di 843
partenza, pulsante di 696
partenza, rampa di 891
partenza, zona di 838
parti 276, 277, 280
parti boccali 98
parti degli occhiali 385
parti dell'arma 849
parti della bandiera 739
parti di un cerchio 704
parti di un osso lungo 155
parti di una imbarcazione 838
parti di una scarpa 342
partita, zona di inizio 862
partito 740
partizioni, esempi di 740
pascal 702
pascolo 182
passacavo 835
passacinghia 906
passaggio a livello 547, 583, 591
passaggio a livello con barriere 545
passaggio a livello, segnale di 591
passaggio a soffietto 569
passaggio pedonale 712, 714
passamontagna 341, 901
passante 349, 350, 354
passante del cinturino 352
passante della cintura 352
passascotte 835
passata di pomodoro 200
passavanti 607
passaverdure 230
passe (da 19 a 36) 919
passeggeri, carrozza 594
passeggeri, sala 605, 608, 609
passeggeri, terminal satellite dei 619
passeggeri, treno 582
passeggiata, ponte di 608
passera di mare 221
passerella 408, 430, 593, 606
passerella di imbarco 619
passerotto 118
passività, zona di 843
passo 45, 124
passo alternato 892
passo d'ordito, bacchetta per il 461
passo d'uomo 655
passo pattinato 892
pasta 206
pasta di tamarindo 200
pasta sfoglia 205
pasta won ton 207
pasta, macchina per fare la 230
pastelli a cera 396
pastelli a cera, disegno a 396
pastelli a olio 396
pastelli a olio, disegno a 396
pastelli morbidi 396
pastelli secchi, disegno a 396
pastello litografico 423
pasticceria 715
pastiglia 559, 783
pastiglia di combustibile 667
pastiglie d'acquerello 397
pastinaca 189
pastoia 124, 857
pastoia, cinghia della 857
pastore tedesco 130
Patagonia 31
patata 184
patata americana 184
patella 126, 217
patera 276
paterazzo 602
Pathfinder 19
patio 244, 322
patio, porta del 250
patta 350, 368
patta di chiusura 906
pattinaggio artistico 881
pattinaggio di velocità 882
pattinaggio in linea 895
pattinaggio libero, lama per 881
pattinatore 882, 895
pattini per velocità 883
pattino 631, 878, 880, 884
pattino a rotelle 895
pattino acrobatico 895
pattino ad incastro 883
pattino anteriore 884
pattino da hockey 895
pattino da short track 883
pattino da velocità 895
pattino del portiere 880
pattino di coda 631
pattino distanziatore 667
pattino mobile 885
pattino per pattinaggio artistico 881
pattino posteriore 884
pattino, colpo di 892
pausa 515
pausa di biscroma 435
pausa di croma 435
pausa di minima 435
pausa di semibiscroma 435
pausa di semibreve 435
pausa di semicroma 435
pausa di semiminima 435
pausa, tasto di 499
pause, valori di durata delle 435
pavese 739
pavimenti, piastrella per 299
pavimenti, spazzola per 289
pavimento 257, 818
pavimento della cabina 417
pavimento, rivestimenti in tessuto per 254
pavoncella 118
Pavone 10
pavone 119
paziente 780
pe-tsai 186
pecan, noce di 193
pecari 128
pecora 128
pecorino romano 211
pedale 440, 444, 448, 578, 580, 791, 851, 870
pedale ad ampio appoggio 870
pedale del cambio 575, 576, 577
pedale del crescendo 444
pedale del freno 333, 552, 556, 559, 889
pedale del freno posteriore 576
pedale del piano 442, 451
pedale del timone 898
pedale dell'acceleratore 556
pedale della frizione 556
pedale della marcia avanti 333
pedale della retromarcia 333
pedale della sordina 442
pedale di regolazione 399
pedale di risonanza 442, 451
pedale di sollevamento 783
pedale senza fermapiedi 870
pedale, comando a 452
pedale, leva del 442
pedale, pistoncino del 444
pedali d'espressione 444
pedaliera 444
pedana 699, 824, 848, 876
pedana di lancio 790, 791
pedana di tiro 860
pedana elastica 826
pedana per il corpo libero 824
pedane 871
pedane di rincorsa 824
pedata 255
pedice 472
pedicello ambulacrale 95
pediera 280
pedine 915
pedipalpo 103
pedivella 580
pedivelle albero delle 580
pedometro 700
pedone 916
pedula 344
peduncolo 76, 80, 81, 82, 83, 86
Pegaso 12
pelame 133
pelanda 338
peli radicali 77
pelle armonica 433
pelle da legatura 425
pelle di camoscio 345, 377
pelle, laccio di 350
pellegrina 355
pelletteria 714
pelletteria, articoli di 386
pellicano 119
pellicce, esempi di 741
pelliccia 121, 122, 139, 143
pellicola 477
pellicola a disco 481
pellicola d'alluminio 222
pellicola in rotolo 481
pellicola piana 481
pellicola plastica, condensatore a 689
pellicola sigillata a caldo 223
pellicola trasparente 222
pellicola, guida della 476
pellicola, pulsante di riavvolgimento della 476
pellicola, rocchetto di trascinamento della 476
pellicola, rullo di guida della 476
pellicola, sensibilità della 479
pellicola, sistema di riavvolgimento della 476
pellicola, spia della coda della 476
pellicola, tasto per l'avanzamento della 476
pellicola, tasto per la sensibilità della 476, 479
pellicole e supporti digitali 481
pelo 172
pelo, muscolo erettore del 172
peltata 79
pelvi 126
pelvi renale 165
pelvi vestigiale 136
penalità 789
pendenti 374
pendolo 697
pendolo, asta del 436, 697
pendolo, lente del 697
pendolo, orologio a 697
pene 104, 146, 169
penisola 38
Penisola Antartica 29
Penisola Arabica 33
Penisola Balcanica 32
Penisola Coreana 33
Penisola dello Yucatan 30
Penisola di Camciatca 33
Penisola di Kola 32
Penisola Iberica 32
Penisola Scandinava 32
penna 425
penna a sfera 470
penna con pennino metallico 470
penna copritrice 115
penna copritrice inferiore della coda 115
penna copritrice superiore della coda 115
penna d'oca 470
penna del contorno 115
penna stilografica 470
penna sumi 397
penna timoniera 115
penna tonda 301
pennarelli, disegno a 396
pennarello 397
pennatifida 79
penne 206, 909
pennellino per labbra 378
pennello 320, 397, 422, 739
pennello a ventaglio 378, 397
pennello da barba 383
pennello da cipria in polvere 378
pennello da fard 378
pennello per dolci 232
pennello per scrivere 470
pennello piatto 397
pennello, spazzola a 289
pennino 43, 397, 470
pennone 602
pennone di controbelvedere, braccio del 603
pensile 224
pensilina 583, 712
pentagono regolare 705
pentagramma 434
pentaprisma 477
pentola 235
pentola a pressione 234
pentola a vapore 235
pentola a vapore elettrica 239
pentola per cucinare a bagnomaria 235
pentola per cuscus 235
pentole, lavandino per le 721
pepaiola 226
pepe bianco 198
pepe della Giamaica 198
pepe di Cayenna 199
pepe macinato 199
pepe nero 198
pepe rosa 198
pepe verde 198
peperoncini secchi 199
peperoncino 188, 199
peperoncino in polvere 199
peperoncino rosso 199
peperoncino tritato 199
peperoncino, spray al 770
peperone giallo 188
peperone rosso 188
peperone verde 188
pepino 197
peplo 336
per aprire 230
pera 193
pera, taglio a 375
percento 703
percorso 833, 866
percorso di evacuazione 543
percorso, arbitro di 838
percorso, boe di 838
percussione, barra di 767
percussione, strumenti a 437, 448
percussore 757
peretta per ingrassare 233
perforatore 533
perforazione off-shore 653
pergola 322
pericardio 163
pericarpo 82, 84
pericolo 616
pericolo, area di 846
pericolo, zona di 847
periodici, sala dei 733
periodici, scaffale dei 733
periodo 617
periostio 154
periscopio 758
periscopio di attacco 763
periscopio di esplorazione 763
peristilio 403, 406
peristoma 94
peritoneo 169, 170
perlina di cristallo 287
Permiano 92
pernice 118
perno 317, 382, 383, 390, 398, 436, 443, 454, 612, 686, 907, 913
perno centrale 500
perno centrale a quattro manubri 919
perno d'unione del treppiede 755
perno della cartuccia 268
perno di agganciamento 571
perno di ancoraggio 559
perno di incernieramento 638
perno di incernieramento del gancio di trazione 587
perno di incernieramento della pala caricatrice 637
perno oscillante 557
perno, orecchini a 374
perone 152, 155, 156
peroneo breve 151
peroneo lungo 150
perossisoma 94
perpendicolare 704
Perseo 12
persiana 249
persiana di ventilazione 261
persiano 132, 469
persico 220
persico trota 220
persico, anatomia di un 109
Persico, Golfo 33
persico, morfologia di un 108
personal computer 513
personale ausiliario di produzione 490
personale viaggiante, stanza del 584
personale, bagno del 768
personale, ingresso del 726, 735, 768
personale, sala del 768
personale, spogliatoio del 768
personale, stanza del 779
Perù 742
Perù-Cile, Fossa 50
pesalettere 531
pesca 192, 909
pesca a mosca 909
pesca al lancio 910
pesca subacquea 841
pesca, sezione di una 81
pescatora, pantaloni alla 358
pesce 181
Pesce Australe 10
pesce cappone 219
pesce cartilagineo 108
pesce osseo 108
pesce rospo 220
pesce San Pietro 221
pesce spada 219
Pesce Volante 11
pesce, coltello da 228
pesce, forchetta da 228
pesce, piatto per il 226
pescereccio 606
Pesci 12
pesci 108
pesci cartilaginei 218
pesci ossei 219
pesciera 234
pesi 851
peso 630, 697, 698, 699, 728, 793, 850
peso, misura del 698
pestello 230
pesticida 69, 70
petalo 80
petanque 864
Peter Pan, collo alla 362
Petri, capsula di 685
petroliera 596
petrolio 651
petrolio greggio 656
pettine 217, 460, 461, 643
pettine a coda 380
pettine a forchetta 380
pettine afro 380
pettine da barbiere 380
pettine del polline 98
pettine per cotonare 380
pettine rado 380
pettine, ganci del 461
pettini 380
pettinino per ciglia e spazzolino per sopracciglia 378
pettirosso 118
petto 115, 124, 749
petto, imbottitura per il 800
petto, protezione del 859
pettorale 460, 853
pettorali, barra per i 851
pettorali, piastra per i 851
pettorina 337, 368, 369
pettorina del portiere 880
pettorina di protezione 796
pezze onorevoli, esempi di 740
pezzi 916
pi greco 704
pia madre 167
pialla 309
pialla lunga 309
piana da dilavamento glaciale 46
piana inondabile 48
pianella 344
pianerottolo 251, 255
pianeti 4
pianeti esterni 4
pianeti interni 5
piano 278, 421, 423, 676, 894
piano a scomparti 313
piano aggiuntivo 305
piano da disegno 399
piano della reception 724
piano di alimentazione 531
piano di appoggio 304, 632
piano di caricamento 713
piano di carico 571, 632
piano di cottura 224, 239, 290
piano di cottura, bordo del 290
piano di lavoro 224, 305, 312, 721, 722
piano di lavoro a morsa 312
piano di pressione 425
piano di proiezione 535
piano di servizio 664
piano di stampa 485
piano elettronico 451
piano mansardato 250, 251
piano reggifoglio 528
piano stradale 538
piano superiore 569
piano, indicatore del 417
piano, pedale del 442, 451
piano, primo 250, 251
pianoforte 437
pianoforte a coda da concerto 443
pianoforte a mezza coda 443
pianoforte a un quarto di coda 443
pianoforte verticale 442
pianoforte verticale, meccanica del 443
pianta 77, 245
pianta del tempio greco 403
pianta della cattedrale 411
pianta di città 39
pianta ornamentale 244
pianta rampicante 322
pianta, struttura di una 77
piantabulbi 324
piantana 460, 461
piantana per fleboclisi 780
piantatoio 324
piante a fiori 93
piante aromatiche 202
pianterreno 250
piantone del volante 552
pianura 38, 48
pianura abissale 49
piastra 238, 288, 381, 425, 449, 482
piastra a pietra focaia 752
piastra costale 113
piastra d'appoggio 309
piastra del rullo 920
piastra della valvola 268
piastra di appoggio 590, 756
piastra di base 43, 58, 304, 500, 701, 889, 907
piastra di cottura 239, 721, 722
piastra di fissaggio a muro 284
piastra di fissaggio a soffitto 284
piastra di pressione 476, 758
piastra di protezione 875
piastra di protezione del cingolo 758
piastra di registrazione 488, 499
piastra di scorrimento 590
piastra di supporto 275
piastra di taglio 333
piastra di taglio, leva di sollevamento della 333
piastra elettrica 239, 290
piastra madreporica 95
piastra marginale 113
piastra negativa 562
piastra neurale 113
piastra per i pettorali 851
piastra portaforche 632
piastra positiva 562
piastra riscaldante 241
piastra sopracaudale 113
piastra stiracapelli 381
piastrella 22
piastrella di gesso 299
piastrella per pavimenti 299
piastrina 162, 248
piastrina d'identità 376
piastrina dei dati 273
piastrina, bracciale con 376
piastrone 113
piattaforma 321, 542, 569, 830, 893, 894
piattaforma autoelevatrice 653
piattaforma continentale 49
piattaforma della giuria 871
piattaforma della vasca 264
piattaforma di 10 metri 828
piattaforma di 3 metri 828
piattaforma di 5 metri 828
piattaforma di 7,5 metri 828
piattaforma di appontaggio per elicotteri 762
piattaforma di carico 699
piattaforma di ingresso 584
piattaforma di produzione 652, 654
piattaforma di strumentazione 60
piattaforma di taglio 643
piattaforma fissa 653
piattaforma girevole 236, 766

INDICE DELLE VOCI ITALIANE

piattaforma inferiore 417
piattaforma per macchina fotografica 482
piattaforma semisommergibile 653
piattaforma superiore 417
piattaforma, carrello a 633
piattaforma, scala con 321
piattelli, macchina di lancio dei 860
piattello 464, 860
piatti 437, 449
piatti caldi 722
piatti caldi, tavolo per i 721
piatti di cottura 239
piatti freddi 722
piatti puliti, tavolo per i 721
piatti sporchi, tavolo per i 721
piattino per pane e burro 226
piatto 239, 448, 500, 698, 699, 905
piatto anteriore 426
piatto da portata 226
piatto del lanciatore 795
piatto della casa-base 795
piatto fondo 226
piatto frutta / insalata 226
piatto girevole 464
piatto inferiore 448
piatto per il pesce 226
piatto piano 226
piatto portaceppi 559
piatto posteriore 426
piatto superiore 448
piatto, gancio del 698
piazza d'armi 409
piazzale 618
piazzola di partenza 866, 867
picche 914
picchetti di sicurezza 875
picchetto 883, 902, 903
picchetto, asola per il 902, 903
picchio 118
picciolo 79, 81, 82, 83
piccione 120, 212
picco 45, 602, 663
piccola 472
piccola copritrice secondaria 115
piccola forca a mano 325
piccoli annunci 471
piccoli elettrodomestici 717
piccolo intestino 110, 113, 116
piccolo labbro 170, 171
piccolo quartiere 855
piccolo rotondo 151
piccolo tegame 235
piccone 327
piccone pneumatico 649
piccozza 767, 901
picea 89
pick-up 441
pick-up per alte frequenze 441
pick-up per basse frequenze 441
pick-up per medie frequenze 441
pick-up, selettore dei 441
pickup 549
pidocchio 101
piede 104, 105, 139, 140, 143, 146, 147, 148, 149, 278, 323, 351, 368, 390, 440, 444, 663, 909, 910
piede a monte 660
piede a valle 660
piede a voluta 276
piede antisdrucciolo 826
piede d'albero 836
piede d'appoggio 461
piede di appoggio 571, 641
piede palmato 110
piede, dito del 146, 148
piede, foro del 444
piede, ossa del 155
piedino 215, 448
piedino di gomma 321
piedino di montaggio 482
piedino di regolazione dell'altezza 483
piedino premistoffa 452, 453
piedino regolabile 292, 293, 294
piedino snodato antiscivolo 321
piedistallo 697
piedistallo della telecamera 492
piedritto 411, 413
piega 336, 350
piega a coltello 357
piega della columella 105
piega impunturata 357
piega invertita 357
piega piatta 350
piega sovrapposta 357
piegaciglia 378
piegatura, linea di 455
pieghe, esempi di 357
pieghetta 426
pieno carico, vite di regolazione a 273
pietra 298, 376
pietra affilacoltelli 229
pietra bianca 916
pietra da costruzione 298
pietra da cote 422
pietra da curling 877
pietra da lastrico 298, 322
pietra da taglio 298
pietra di Coyolxauhqui 412
pietra focaia 318, 752
pietra focaia, piastra a 752
pietra litografica 423
pietra nera 916
pietra sacrificale 412
pietre preziose 375
pietre preziose, tagli di 375
pietre semipreziose 375
pietrina, rotella della 391
pietrisco 263
pigiama 364, 369
pigiamino 369
pigiamino a due pezzi 368
pigiatore 230
pignone 307, 697
pignone semplice 871
pigostilo 116
pila 513, 540, 563, 765
pila a carbone-zinco 689
pila alcalina a manganese-zinco 689
pilastro 43, 410, 412, 540, 650, 676
pilastro corinzio 407
pilastro del parapetto 255
pile 687
pile a secco 689
pilone 540, 583
pilone del rotore 631
pilone destro 804
pilone sinistro 804
piloriza 77
pilota 872, 897
pilota automatico, comandi del 626
pilotaggio, cabina di 22, 607, 624, 626, 631
pilotaggio, display di 626
pinacocita 95
pince 455
pince, arricciatura a 283
pince-nez 385
pinguino 119
pinna 836, 840, 841
pinna anale 108
pinna caudale 108, 136
pinna dorsale 136
pinna dorsale, prima 109
pinna dorsale, seconda 109
pinna pelvica 108
pinna pettorale 108, 136
pinna stabilizzatrice 25, 608
pinnacolo 408, 410
pinnacolo, fiore del 412
pinnula 76
pino domestico 89
pino, aghi di 89
pinolo 89, 193
pinza 284, 381, 559
pinza a becchi lunghi 317
pinza a giunto scorrevole 310
pinza a scatto 310
pinza del freno a disco 574
pinza del polline 98
pinza multiuso 317
pinza per capelli 380
pinza per fusibili 317
pinza regolabile 310
pinza spelafili 317
pinza universale 317
pinza, faretto a 286
pinze 310
pinze di serraggio 685
pinzette 777
pinzette per sopracciglia 377
piogge acide 69, 70
pioggia 64, 65
pioggia congelantesi 57, 64
pioggia forte continua 57
pioggia forte intermittente 57
pioggia leggera 64
pioggia leggera continua 57
pioggia leggera intermittente 57
pioggia moderata 64
pioggia moderata continua 57
pioggia moderata intermittente 57
pioggia, irrigatore rotativo a 329
pioggia, rovesci di 57
pioggia, tipologie di 64
piolo 321, 459, 462, 799
piombo 682, 911
piombo, sfera di 757
Pioneer 19
pioppo 88
pioviggine 64
pioviggine leggera continua 57
pioviggine leggera intermittente 57
pioviggine moderata continua 57
pioviggine moderata intermittente 57
pioviggine spessa continua 57
pioviggine spessa intermittente 57
pipa 390
pipa, sezione di una 390
pipetta sierologica 685
pipistrello 140
pipistrello vampiro 141
pipistrello, manica a 361
pipistrello, morfologia di un 140
pipistrello, scheletro di un 141
piramidale 154
piramide 402, 705
piramide, ingresso alla 402
piranometro 58
Pirenei 32
piroga a un bilanciere 599
piroga monoxila 599
piscina 246, 608, 675, 788, 827
piscina fuori terra 246
piscina interrata 246
piscina olimpionica 831
piselli 190
piselli mangiatutto 190
piselli secchi spaccati 190
pisello 84
pisiforme 154
pista 620, 790, 872, 874, 883, 885, 890, 891
pista a difficoltà elevata 886
pista a difficoltà intermedia 886
pista ciclistica 871
pista da bowling 865
pista da fondo 886
pista di accesso 618
pista di appontaggio 761
pista di atletica 788
pista di atterraggio 890, 891
pista di chilometro lanciato 891
pista di gara 887
pista di lancio 891
pista di pattinaggio 881, 886
pista di rincorsa 791, 792, 793
pista di rullaggio 618
pista lunga 882
pista per esperti 886
pista per principianti 886
pista per sci alpino 886
pistacchio 193
piste da sci 886
pistillo 80
pistola 315, 770
pistola 8 mm 861
pistola a tamburo 754
pistola ad aria compressa 861
pistola dello starter 790
pistola di erogazione 548
pistola mitragliatrice 754
pistola per sverniciatura 320
pistola per verniciatura a spruzzo 320
pistola semiautomatica 754
pistola turapori 315
pistola, impugnatura a 306, 318, 754, 755
pistola, impugnatura della 320
pistola, polverizzatore a 329
pistola, saldatore a 318
pistoncino 559
pistoncino del manuale 444
pistoncino del pedale 444
pistone 447, 564, 566
pistone, disinnesto del 315
pistone, leva del 315
pit 501
pitching wedge 868
pitone 114
Pitot, tubo di 873
pittogrammi 514
pittura 396
pittura a guazzo 396
pittura a olio 396
più o meno 703
piumino da cipria 378
pivot 811
pizzo al tombolo 458
placca africana 43
placca antartica 43
placca antifrizione 889
placca caribica 43
placca del Pacifico 43
placca dell'ago 452
placca dell'interruttore 274
placca delle Cocos 43
placca di Nazca 43
placca di Scozia 43
placca euroasiatica 43
placca filippina 43
placca indoaustraliana 43
placca motrice 168
placca nordamericana 43
placca scorrevole 452, 453
placca sudamericana 43
placcatore destro 806
placcatore sinistro 806
placche convergenti 43
placche divergenti 43
placche tettoniche 43
placche trasformi 43
placchetta a bilanciere 444
placchetta del portanasello 385
plafoniera 286
plancia 556, 761
planetario 10
planetario, proiettore per 10
planisfero 28
plantare 151
plasma 162
plasmodesma 74
plastica, smistamento della 71
plastica-acciaio 269
platea 431, 655
platea del bacino 597
platea di fondazione 660
plateosauro 93
platino 683
playmaker 811
plesso brachiale 166
plesso dentale 159
plesso lombare 166
plesso sacrale 166
plettro 433
pleura parietale 163
pleura viscerale 163
plinto di culatta 753
plissé 357
plotter 520
Plutone 4, 5
plutonio 684
pluviale 244
pluviografo 58, 59
pluviometro a lettura diretta 58, 59
pneumatici, barriera di 872
pneumatici, esempi di 560
pneumatico 551, 560, 570, 579, 870, 874
pneumatico a carcassa radiale cinturata 561
pneumatico chiodato 560
pneumatico con carcassa a struttura diagonale 561
pneumatico con carcassa a struttura radiale 561
pneumatico granturismo 560
pneumatico invernale 560
pneumatico per tutte le stagioni 560
pneumatico scolpito 577, 875
pneumatico sportivo 560
podio 412, 734
podio del direttore d'orchestra 437
poggiafreccia 859, 913
poggiamano 304, 433, 516
poggiamano amovibile 514
poggiapiedi 281, 464
poggiatesta 555
poker 914
poker, combinazioni del 914
polacchina 343
polacco 469
Polaroid 480
pole position 872
poliambulatorio 781
poligoni 705
poligono di tiro 769
Polinesia 747
polipodio comune 76
politica 739
politrico comune 75
polizia 725
polizia, agente di 770
polizia, macchina della 769, 771
polizia, stazione di 711, 768
pollaio 182
pollice 140, 141, 156, 173, 346, 797
pollice opponibile 139
pollice, appoggio del 447
polline, cella da 100
polline, pettine del 98
polline, pinza del 98
polline, spazzola del 98
pollo 213
pollone 87
polmone 103, 104, 110, 112, 116, 125
polmone destro 161, 163
polmone sinistro 161, 163
polmoni 163
polo 354, 359, 822, 858
polo negativo 562, 687, 689
Polo Nord 35
polo nord 687
Polo Nord celeste 13
polo positivo 562, 687, 689
Polo Sud 29, 35
polo sud 687
Polo Sud celeste 13
polo, abito a 356
polo, cavallo da 858
polo, collo a 363
Polonia 744
polonio 682
polpa 81, 82, 83, 159
polpaccio 147, 149
polpastrello 172
polpo 106, 217
polpo, anatomia di un 106
polpo, morfologia di un 106
polsiera 850, 895
polsino 349, 808, 822, 850
polsino doppio 361
polsino rivoltato 338
polso 130, 140, 147, 149, 156, 173
poltrona 276
poltrona da salotto 276
poltrona girevole reclinabile 511
poltrona sacco 277
poltrona Wassily 276
poltroncina del paziente 780
poltroncina per bambini 281
poltrone 276
polvere di magnesia 825
polvere, fiasca da 752
polverizzatore 646
polverizzatore a pistola 329
pomello 278, 285, 909, 910
pomello della sicura 554
pomello in gomma 909
pomelo 194
pomi 193
pomice, matita correttrice di 423
pomo 277, 797, 849, 855, 861
pomo d'Adamo 146
pomodorini a grappolo 188
pomodoro 188
pomodoro, concentrato di 200
pomodoro, passata di 200
pomolo 307, 309
pomolo del bastone 880
pomolo di chiusura 284
pomolo esterno 248
pomolo interno 248
pomolo, serratura a 249
pompa 246, 292, 294, 320, 578, 670, 671, 674, 841, 903
pompa del combustibile 259
pompa del fluido termovettore 669
pompa della benzina 548
pompa di calore 260
pompa di circolazione 259, 675
pompa di circolazione del fango 651
pompa di spurgo 263
pompa per gli pneumatici 548
pompa, motore della 263
pompa, numero della 548
pompa, tubo della 548
pompe, locale delle 606
pompelmo 194
pompelmo, coltello da 229
pompetta ad aria 777
pompieri, carri dei 766
poncho 355
pont-l'évêque 211
ponte 39, 542, 692, 750, 854, 875
ponte a cantilever 540
ponte a portale 541
ponte a travata 540
ponte a trave continua 541
ponte a travi semplici indipendenti 541
ponte a via inferiore 541
ponte a via intermedia 541
ponte a via superiore 541
ponte ad arco 540
ponte di caricamento per containers 596
ponte di comando 604, 605, 608, 609
ponte di coperta 607
ponte di passeggiata 608
ponte di raccordo 284
ponte di Varolio 167
ponte di volo 761
ponte galleggiante 542
ponte girevole 542
ponte levatoio 408
ponte luce 431
ponte pedonale 583
ponte per le autovetture 608
ponte principale 761
ponte ribaltabile a due ali 542
ponte ribaltabile a un'ala 542
ponte segnali 583
ponte sollevabile 542
ponte sospeso 540
ponte superiore 624
ponte trasportatore 542
ponti a travata, esempi di 541
ponti ad arco, esempi di 541
ponti fissi 540
ponti mobili 542
ponti strallati 541
ponticello 385, 433, 439, 440, 441
ponticello degli acuti 442
ponticello dei bassi 442
ponticello, blocco del 441
pontile di partenza 838
pontile galleggiante 839
pontone 542
pool 862
Poppa 11
poppa 598, 602, 608, 836
poppa, in 833
porcellana 187
porcile 182
porcino 183
porcospino 123
poro 74, 84
poro genitale 95
poro inalante 95
poro sudoriparo 172
porpora 741
porpora, bordo di 336
porro 184
Porro, prisma di 692
porta 278, 417, 567, 594, 724, 738, 799, 800, 802, 804, 807, 809, 814, 818, 827, 837, 879, 902, 903, 920
porta a bande verticali 416
porta a due battenti 568
porta a fisarmonica 416
porta a infrarossi 526, 527

INDICE DELLE VOCI ITALIANE

porta a libro 416
porta a un battente 416
porta a zanzariera 567
porta antincendio 416
porta automatica 620
porta basculante del garage 416
porta del bacino 596
porta del congelatore 291
porta del laboratorio a tenuta stagna 23
porta del modem interno 513, 526
porta del mouse 513, 518
porta del patio 250
porta dell'elevatore 569
porta della tastiera 513
porta di controllo 890
porta di entrata 568, 569
porta di interfaccia del computer 520
porta di prua 605
porta di rete 513
porta di rete telefonica 487
porta esterna 247
porta Ethernet 526
porta FireWire 526
porta giochi 513
porta girevole manuale 416
porta in discesa 837
porta in risalita 837
porta MIDI 513
porta parallela 513
porta per l'alimentatore 526
porta scorrevole 264, 416
porta scorrevole automatica 416
porta seriale 513
porta sezionale del garage 416
porta terminale 635
porta USB 513, 526
porta video 513, 526
porta, area di 879
porta-finestra 224, 251
portaaccessori, vaschette 399
portabagagli 567, 876
portabatteria, cassa 571
portabici 558
portabiti 389
portablocco 387, 533
portablocco, tavoletta 533
portabombole, carrello 319
portabottiglia 579
portabracciale 282
portacalcolatrice 386
portacarte a soffietto 386
portacenere 391
portaceppi 257
portachiavi 387
portachiodi 901
portacipria 378
portacoltello 423
portaelettrodo 318
portaerei 761
portaetichetta 533
portafermagli 534
portafili 460
portafiltro 241
portafioretto 649
portafoglio 387
portafoglio per carte di credito 386
portafusibili 663
portaindirizzo, etichetta 389
portalampada 275
portalampada, componenti del 275
portalampada, testa 485
portale 411
portalenti 384
portamartello 313
portamine 470
portamonete 387
portanasello 385
portanasello, placchetta del 385
portanegativi 485
portanza 630
portaobiettivi a revolver 693
portaoculare 14
portaoggetti 693, 694
portaombrelli 391
portapacchi 577, 578
portapacchi posteriore 577
portapassaporto 387
portapenne 386
portapipe 390
portarocchetto 452
portarotolo 264
portasacca 869
portasapone 264
portasci 558
portasciugamano 264
portassegni 386, 387
portastanghe 857
portastilo 517
portastrumenti 841
portata, piatto da 226
portatabulati 532
portatimbri 531
portatrucchi 389
portautensili 308
porte d'ingresso 427
porte di controllo 918
porte girevoli manuali 719
porte per le memory card 918
porte, esempi di 416
portello 293, 624, 758
portello di accesso 607
portello di apertura 17
portello di carico del combustibile nuovo 666
portello di scarico del combustibile esaurito 666
portello, interruttore del 293
portellone della cupola 17
portellone dello scomparto di carico 23
portellone laterale 22
portellone posteriore 775
portellone prodiero di carico 608
porticato 738
porticciolo 788
portico 245, 411
portico coperto 738
portiera 551, 554
portiera, telaio interno della 554
portiere 799, 800, 801, 803, 809, 814, 827, 878, 879
portiere, bastone del 880
portiere, pattino del 880
portiere, pettorina del 880
portiere, stanzino del 724
porto 709
porto marittimo 596
porto, bicchiere da 225
Portogallo 743
portoghese 469
porzionatore per gelato 233
posate 722, 905
posate, cestello per le 294
posateria 227
posizionamento del fascio rispetto all'asse 694
posizionamento, braccio di 638
posizionamento, tubo di 638
posizione a terra 861
posizione carpiata 828
posizione d'equilibrio 690
posizione della statua 403
posizione delle braccia 829
posizione delle gambe 829
posizione di un carattere 472
posizione in ginocchio 861
posizione in piedi 861, 893
posizione prona 893
posizione raggruppata 828
posizione tesa 828
posizione, luce di 585
posizione, tasto di 440, 441
posizioni 849
posizioni dei giocatori 794, 803, 804, 811, 814
posizioni di partenza 828, 843
posizioni di tiro 861, 893
posta 474
posta a tariffa ridotta 475
posta aerea 475
posta annullata 474
posta elettronica 525
posta elettronica, software di 524
posta internazionale 475
posta locale 475
posta non annullata 474
posta regionale 475
postazione degli infermieri (pronto soccorso ambulatoriale) 779
postazione degli infermieri (pronto soccorso principale) 778
postazione dei giudici di corsa 856
postazione dei giudici di gara 887
postazione dell'agente di sicurezza 779
postazione di lavoro 509
postazione di sorveglianza 394
postazioni di ascolto 733
posti a sedere 431
posti, divano a due 276
postierla 408, 409
postino 475
postino, borsa da 388
posto a sedere 427
posto del comandante 758
posto del conducente 758
posto di controllo 727, 768
posto di sorveglianza 764
potassio 682
potatoio 330
potenza elettrica, unità di misura della 702
potenza, cavo di 272
potenza, presa di 640, 641, 642
potenziale elettrico, unità di misura della differenza di 702
pouf 277
pozzetto 263, 834, 839
pozzetto d'ispezione 712
pozzo 47
pozzo del minerale 650
pozzo di accesso 664
pozzo di drenaggio 650
pozzo di estrazione 650
pozzo di iniezione 646
pozzo di produzione 646
pozzo off-shore 654
pozzo verticale 650
pozzo, entrata del 649
pranzo, sala da 764
praseodimio 684
prateria 38, 66
praticante 846
prato 182, 245, 322
prato, cura del 332
preavviso di direzione obbligatoria a sinistra 544
Precambriano 92
precipitazione 67
precipitazione, area di 55
precipitazioni 64
precipitazioni invernali 64
precipitazioni, forti 63
precipitazioni, misurazione delle 59
predellino 100, 640
predisposizione sbocco cavi 272
prelavaggio, lavandino per il 721
prelievi, sala dei 781
premascellare 108, 122, 123
premi-apri, serratura 248
premicarta 528
premicarta, leva di svincolo del 528
premio, alimentazione del 920
premio, scatola del 920
premistoffa, barra del 453
premistoppa 268
premistoppa, dado del 268
premitabacco 390
premolare 121, 123
premolari 159
prendisole 356
preparazione chirurgica, stanza per la 780
prepuzio 169
presa a croce 844
presa a terra 844
presa antisovratensione 520
presa audio 513
presa con i piedi 901
presa d'acqua 658
presa d'aria 568, 571, 575, 605, 631, 876
presa d'aria del motore 568, 760
presa d'aria del ventilatore di sostentamento 605
presa d'aria laterale 567
presa d'aria per il raffreddamento del motore 874
presa d'aria posteriore 382
presa d'aria sul tetto 567
presa d'uscita 441
presa del microfono 505
presa dell'idrante 766
presa dell'ossigeno 780
presa di alimentazione 504, 513
presa di carica 563
presa di connessione 452
presa di corrente 316, 567
presa di corrente a strisciamento 595
presa di corrente commutata 497
presa di corrente temporizzata 290
presa di ingresso 520
presa di potenza 640
presa di potenza, albero della 641, 642
presa di ricarica 383
presa di strangolamento 844
presa di terra 272
presa europea 274
presa per cuffia 450, 451, 497, 504
presa per cuffie 513
presa per il comando a distanza 476, 477
presa per ricarica 288
presa per spina americana 274
presa, alveolo della 274
presa, tester di 316
presbiterio, lampada del 737
prese antisovratensione di alimentazione della batteria 520
prese con le mani 901
prese digitali 477
prese telefoniche antisovratensione 520
prese video 477
prese, esempi di 844
preside, ufficio del 735
presidente 848
presidente di giuria 855, 881, 900
presidente di giuria, assistente del 881
presidente di tappeto 843
pressa per indorsatura 425
pressa verticale 425
pressacaffè 241
pressatore 237, 240
pressatura 425
pressione a livello del mare 55
pressione alta, centro di 55
pressione atmosferica 55
pressione bassa, centro di 55
pressione dei freni, modulatore della 559
pressione della bombola, manometro della 319
pressione di esercizio, manometro della 319
pressione sanguigna, monitor della 777
pressione, bottone a 353
pressione, pentola a 234
pressione, piastra di 758
pressione, regolatore della 384
pressione, regolatore di 234, 452
pressione, unità di misura della 702
pressione, variazione di 55
pressione, vasca di abbattimento della 671
pressione, vite di 421, 423
pressore 533
pressurizzatore 670, 671
prevenzione degli incendi 764
prevenzione del crimine 768
previsioni meteorologiche 54
preziose, pietre 375
prezzemolo 202
prezzo per litro/gallone 548
prezzo unitario 699
prigione 915
prima 849
prima base 794
prima base (posizione) 794
prima falange 126
prima galleria 431
prima linea 804
prima maglia 796
prima pagina 471
prima pagina, foto in 471
prima pinna dorsale 108, 109
primati 138
primati, esempi di 139
primavera 54
primavera, equinozio di 13, 54
prime foglie 77
primi violini 437
primo 704
primo arbitro 807, 812, 813
primo assistente cameraman 428
primo aumento di tensione 677
primo cuneiforme 155, 156
primo giocatore al lancio 877
primo livello di operazioni 529
primo molare 159
primo piano 250, 251
primo premolare 159
primo quarto 7
primo spazio 811
primo stadio 25
primo stadio dell'erogatore 841
princesse 356
princesse, cucitura a 366
principali famiglie linguistiche 468
principali segnali stradali internazionali 544
principali segnali stradali nordamericani 546
principali tipi di missili 759
Principato di Monaco 744
prisma astronomico 14
prisma di Porro 692
prisma otturatore 756
proboscide 96
processo mastoideo 158
processo spinoso 168
processo stiloideo 158
processo trasverso 157, 168
processore 513
procione 134
proconsul 93
prodotti caseari 210
prodotti cerealicoli 204
prodotti di bellezza 717
prodotti di fissione 681
prodotti di raffinazione 656
prodotti in offerta 181
prodotti per confezionamento 180
prodotti per la pulizia 721
prodotti petrolchimici 656
prodotto, codice del 699
produttore 429
produzione del suono 445
produzione di calore 665
produzione di elettricità 676
produzione di elettricità da alternatore 665
produzione di elettricità da energia eolica 677
produzione di elettricità da energia geotermica 646
produzione di elettricità da energia nucleare 665
produzione di elettricità da energia solare 674
produzione di elettricità da energia termica 646
produzione di elettricità dal generatore 662
produzione di elettricità, fasi della 662
produzione di ossigeno 78
produzione, designer di 428
produzione, personale ausiliario di 490
produzione, segretaria di 429
profilo del suolo 78
profilo dell'atmosfera terrestre 53
profilo dello spacco 349, 361
profilo di sostegno 417
profilo sbieco 368
profondimetro 841
profondità del fuoco 43
profondità di campo, pulsante di controllo della 476
profondità di campo, scala delle 478
profondità, indice di 307
profondità, regolatore di 308
profondità, scala di 613
profumeria 714, 717
profumeria e igiene personale 181
profumo 379
programma, selettore di 450
programmatore 292, 293, 294
programmazione, tasti di 495
programmi del computer 771
programmi televisivi 471
proietti 752
proiettile anticarro 757
proiettore 427, 428, 518, 535, 550, 570, 574, 576, 640, 758, 876
proiettore abbagliante e anabbagliante 554
proiettore ausiliario 10
proiettore orientabile 766
proiettore per determinare l'altezza delle nubi 59
proiettore per diapositive 483
proiettore per planetario 10
proiettore posteriore 640
proiettori 431
proiettori, comando dei 556
proiezione cilindrica 36
proiezione conica 36
proiezione di spalla e braccio 844
proiezione interrotta 36
proiezione piana 36
proiezione, cabina di 427
proiezione, piano di 535
proiezione, sala di 395, 427
proiezione, schermo di 427
proiezioni cartografiche 36
prolunga 278
prolunga, tubo rigido di 289
promezio 684
promontorio 51
pronao 403
pronatore rotondo 150
pronipote 784
pronipoti 784
pronto intervento, équipe di 853
pronto intervento, mezzo di 543
pronto soccorso 725, 778, 886
pronto soccorso, attrezzature per il 775
pronto soccorso, cassetta di 771, 777
pronto soccorso, manuale di 777
pronto soccorso, stazione di 543
pronto soccorso, strumenti per il 775
propellente, serbatoio del 18
proprietà, confine di 244
propulsione, modulo di 486
propulsore 18, 20, 40
propulsore a reazione 60
propulsore di prua 609
propulsori per il controllo direzionale 22
proscenio 430
prosciutto 216
prosciutto affumicato 215
prosciutto cotto 216
prosciutto, coltello da 229
prosciutto, manica a 361
prospetto 250
prospezione off-shore 653
prospezione terrestre 651
prossimità, spoletta di 759
prostata 169
proteggicavo 317
proteggitendine 880
protestantesimo 736
protezione antisfregamento 874
protezione antiurto 289
protezione del dente 636
protezione del mento 575
protezione del petto 859
protezione delle chiavi 446
protezione esterna 275
protezione per gli occhi 772, 774
protezione per i piedi 773, 774
protezione per il collo 765
protezione per il mento 765
protezione per l'avambraccio 808
protezione per la testa 772, 774
protezione per le mani 774
protezione per le orecchie 772, 774
protezione per le vie respiratorie 773, 774
protezione posteriore 17
protezione, gabbia di 316
protezione, guanti di 318
protezione, occhiali di 318, 818, 819
protezione, palla di 839
protezione, piastra di 875
protezione, schermo di 318, 794
protoattinio 684
protocollo di comunicazione 524
protone 680
protoneurone 168
protorace 97
protuberanza 6
prova in corso, tabellone della 825
prova, pulsante di 767
provacircuiti, lampada 316
proventricolo 116
provetta 685
provincia 37
prua 602, 606, 609, 834, 836
prua affusolata 839
prua al vento 833
prua scolpita 598

INDICE DELLE VOCI ITALIANE

1100

ASTRONOMIA > 2-25; TERRA > 26-71; REGNO VEGETALE >72-89; REGNO ANIMALE > 90-143; ESSERE UMANO > 144-177; GENERI ALIMENTARI E CUCINA > 178-241; CASA > 242-295; FAI DA TE E GIARDINAGGIO > 296-333; ABBIGLIAMENTO > 334-371; ACCESSORI E ARTICOLI PERSONALI > 372-391; ARTE E ARCHITETTURA > 392-465; COMUNICAZIONI E BUROTICA > 466-535; TRASPORTI E VEICOLI > 536-643; ENERGIA > 644-677; SCIENZA > 678-705; SOCIETÀ > 706-785; SPORT E GIOCHI > 786-920

prua, castello di 609
prua, diritto di 838
prua, elica di 606
prua, ornamento di 600
prua, porta di 605
prua, propulsore di 609
prugna 192
prugne, salsa di 201
pseudopodio 94
psicrometro 59
pterigoideo 112
pubblico 728
pubblico, ingresso del 402
pube 116, 122, 146, 148
Puerto Rico, Fossa di 50
pugilato 842
pugile 842
pugnale 751
pugnale d'assalto 751
pulce 101
pulcino 120
puleggia 321, 566, 686, 859, 913
puleggia conduttrice 688
puleggia di tensione del regolatore 417
puleggia, sistema a doppia 686
pulisci unghie 377
pulitura, accessori di 289
pulizia, prodotti per la 721
pullman 568
pulpito 737, 738
pulsante 248, 294, 391, 470
pulsante blocca-mandrino 308
pulsante del menu 477
pulsante del registratore vocale 527
pulsante del touch pad 526
pulsante del vaporizzatore 288
pulsante di accensione 267, 293, 508
pulsante di aggancio 305
pulsante di alimentazione 494, 527
pulsante di alimentazione della carta 519
pulsante di annullamento 519
pulsante di apertura del display 526
pulsante di arresto 308, 331, 696
pulsante di avvio della misurazione 479
pulsante di azzeramento 696, 700
pulsante di bloccaggio 288
pulsante di cancellazione 477
pulsante di chiamata 417
pulsante di chiamata pedonale 712
pulsante di compensazione dell'esposizione 476
pulsante di controllo 516
pulsante di controllo della profondità di campo 476
pulsante di controluce 527
pulsante di espulsione 477, 918
pulsante di espulsione del CD 513
pulsante di espulsione del disco 521
pulsante di espulsione del DVD-ROM 513
pulsante di espulsione del floppy disk 513
pulsante di illuminazione del display dei dati 479
pulsante di inizio del motivo 456
pulsante di partenza 696
pulsante di preselezione della sintonia 498
pulsante di prova 767
pulsante di reset 513, 918
pulsante di riavvolgimento della pellicola 476
pulsante di sblocco dell'obiettivo 476
pulsante di scatto 476
pulsante di uscita 527
pulsante di visualizzazione delle immagini 477
pulsante di visualizzazione delle impostazioni 477
pulsante per il salto di immagini 477
pulsante per la visualizzazione della soglia di allarme 613
pulsanti di avvio delle applicazioni 527
pulsanti di azione 918
pulsanti direzionali 918
pulsanti programmabili 516
pulsar 8
puma 134
Pumpernickel russo 205
punching ball 842
pungiglione 98
punta 127, 185, 227, 229, 288, 301, 302, 303, 304, 307, 309, 315, 318, 350, 439, 453, 457, 470, 740, 776, 792, 793, 840, 859, 868, 880, 887, 888, 893, 894, 901, 909, 911, 912, 915, 918
punta a croce 302
punta a testa quadra 302
punta anteriore del rampone 901
punta articolata 749
punta centrale 740
punta da muro 306
punta del colletto 349
punta del collo 362
punta del naso 175
punta dell'ala 897, 898
punta della trivella 323
punta dello sci 892
punta dentellata 881
punta di centratura 306
punta di diamante 278
punta di freccia in selce 748
punta elicoidale 306
punta fredda 381
punta Luer-Lock 776
punta per piastra 442
punta piana 302
punta, imbarcazioni di 839
punta, lunghezza della 911
punta, remo di 838
puntale 302, 316, 342, 370, 391, 483, 782, 889, 897, 901
puntale di protezione 773
puntale rinforzato 773
puntalino 909, 910
puntapiedi 838
puntasecca 422, 423
puntaspilli 454
puntate, schema americano delle 919
puntate, schema francese delle 919
punte, tipi di 302
punteggio 789, 825
punterie, coperchio delle 552, 566
punteruolo 458, 905
punti 459, 822
punti annodati 459
punti avviati 457
punti cardinali, segnalamento dei 616
punti incrociati 459
punti metallici 534
punti piatti 459
punti stuoia 459
punti, selettore dei 452
punti, tasti di impostazione dei 456
puntine da disegno 534
puntine, distanza tra le 562
puntini di sospensione 473
punto 473, 914
punto catenella 459
punto coronato 435
punto d'appoggio 103
punto d'Oriente 459
punto del cuore 740
punto di alimentazione 273, 663
punto di allacciamento 273
punto di attacco 627
punto di handicap 916
punto di incocco 859, 913
punto di ingaggio 878
punto di inserimento dei documenti da trasmettere 508
punto di interesse 39
punto di marcatura 455
punto di mura 836
punto di osservazione 17
punto di ristoro 725
punto di sospensione 897
punto e virgola 473
punto esclamativo 473
punto gallone 459
punto interrogativo 473
punto K 891
punto nodi 459
punto piatto intercalato 459
punto riso 458
punto rumeno 459
punto spina 459
punto spina di pesce 459
punto strega 459
punto teorico 891
punto vapore 459
puntone 253, 640, 676
punzone 301, 401
pupilla 132, 177
pupilla verticale 112
putter 867, 868
puzzle 917

Q

Qatar 746
qibla, parete della 738
quadrante 273, 695, 696, 697, 698, 704
quadrante a cristalli liquidi 696
quadrante a fasi lunari 697
quadrante graduato 907
quadrante indicatore 613
quadrata, scollatura 363
quadrato 112, 705, 842, 919
quadrato di servizio 818, 819
quadri 914
quadricipiti, rullo per i 851
quadrilatero 705
quadripode 782
quadro 395
quadro degli strumenti di controllo 557
quadro delle temperature 288
quadro di comando 10, 238, 239, 290, 292, 293, 294
quadro di distribuzione 273
quaglia 120, 212
quaglia, uovo di 213
quantità di sostanza, unità di misura della 702
quarantottore 389
quark d 680
quark u 680
quarta 434, 849
quarterback 807
quartetto 438
quartiere 39, 342, 370, 855
quartiere degli affari 708, 710
quartiere fieristico 708
quartiere residenziale 709
quartiere, parte anteriore del 342, 370
quarto 127
quarzo, metronomo al 436
Quaternario 93
quattro alberi, veliero a 602
quattro con 839
quattro quarti, tempo di 434
quattro senza 839
quechua 469
quercia 88
quinoa 203
quinta 434, 849
quinte 430
quintetto 438

R

rabarbaro 185
rabbino, seggio di 738
raccattapalle 820
racchetta 815, 816, 818, 819, 822, 888, 891, 892
racchetta da neve 893
racchetta da neve ellittica 893
racchetta Michigan 893
racchetta, giochi con la 815
raccoglierba 332
raccogligocce, bacinella 290
raccoglipolvere 308
raccoglitore a molla 532
raccoglitore ad anelli 532
raccoglitrice di foraggio 642
raccolta 426
raccolta del vetro, campana per la 71
raccolta della carta, campana per la 71
raccolta differenziata 71
raccolta differenziata, contenitori per la 71
raccolta, vaschetta di 241
raccordi 269
raccordi meccanici 269
raccordi, esempi di 269
raccordo 470, 766
raccordo a collarino pressato 269
raccordo a compressione 269
raccordo a due vie 767
raccordo a gomito 269
raccordo a gomito di 45° 269
raccordo a losanga 538
raccordo a quadrifoglio 538, 539
raccordo a rotatoria 538
raccordo a T 257, 269, 271
raccordo a T del tubo di scarico 271
raccordo a tromba 538
raccordo a U 269
raccordo a Y 269, 776
raccordo del tubo flessibile 649
raccordo femmina 269
raccordo maschio 269
raccordo per unione meccanica 269
raccordo, esempi di 538
raccordo, fresa di 308
racemo 81, 276
rachide 86, 115
rack apparecchiature 489, 490
raclette 211
raclette, griglia per 239
racquetball 818
radar 40, 604, 605, 608, 609, 760
radar di acquisizione del bersaglio 762
radar di appontaggio 761
radar di bordo 40
radar di controllo aereo 761
radar di quota 761
radar di ricerca aerea 761, 762
radar meteorologico 54, 624
radar nautico 761, 762
radar, aeroplano 629
radar, albero del 606
radar, antenna 760, 763
radar, display dei 771
raddrizzatori di immagine 692
radiatore 23, 259, 552, 561, 586
radiatore a colonne 259
radiatore elettrico a olio 260
radiatore, griglia del 570
radiatore, manicotto inferiore del 561
radiatori 21
radiazione 681
radiazione artificiale 41
radiazione infrarossa 68, 690
radiazione naturale 41
radiazione solare 67, 68, 672, 673, 674, 675
radiazione solare assorbita 68
radiazione solare riflessa 68
radiazione ultravioletta 690
radiazioni solari, misurazione delle 58
radiazioni terrestri, scanner delle 60
radiazioni terrestri, sensore delle 60
radicchio 186
radice 78, 159, 176, 227
radice a fittone 87
radice anteriore 168
radice del naso 175
radice dell'elice 173
radice dell'unghia 172
radice filettata 562
radice laterale 77
radice motoria 167, 168
radice posteriore 168
radice principale 77
radice quadrata di 703
radice secondaria 77
radice sensoriale 167, 168
radice superficiale 87
radichetta 77, 87
radici avventizie 76
radio 116, 121, 122, 126, 131, 136, 138, 140, 141, 142, 152, 154, 156, 682, 771, 898
radio CB 505
radio portatile 503
radio, antenna 606, 763, 873
radio, comandi 626
radio-ulna 111
radio: cabina di regia 488
radio: studio 488
radioattività, unità di misura della 702
radiometro 60
radioonda 16
radioregistratore con compact disc 504
radiosonda 59
radiosveglia 503
radiotelefono portatile 770
radiotelescopio 16
radome 760
radon 684
radula 104
rafano giapponese 189
raffinazione, prodotti di 656
raffineria 654, 709
raffreddamento 656
raffreddamento del motore, presa d'aria per il 874
raffreddamento, cilindro di 692
raffreddamento, manicotto di 755
raffreddatore d'aria 564
raganella 111
raggi gamma 690
raggi infrarossi, testa cercante a 759
raggi X 690
raggio 579, 704
raggio laser 501, 692
raggio luminoso 691
raggio midollare 87
raggio molle 108
raggio solare riflesso 674
raggio spinoso 108
raglan, manica alla 352, 355, 361, 369
ragnatela 103
ragnatela, centro della 103
ragno 103
ragno acquatico 102
ragno femmina, anatomia di un 103
ragno, morfologia di un 103
ragno-granchio 102
ralla di rotazione 638, 639
rallentamento, zona di 890, 891
rallentatore, riproduzione al 495
rally, auto da 873
rally, motocicletta da 875
rambutan 197
rame 683
rame, lastra di 422
rame-acciaio 269
rame-plastica 269
rami 87
ramificazione collaterale 168
ramo 86, 87, 89, 127, 687
ramo comunicante 168
ramo con frutti 86
ramo primario 87
ramo secondario 87
ramoscello 77
rampa 403, 407, 539, 540, 647, 871, 894
rampa ad anello 539
rampa di accesso 608
rampa di lancio 890, 891
rampa di partenza 891
rampa di scale 255
rampa per sedie a rotelle 394
ramparo 409
rampicante, pianta 322
rampone 345, 767, 893
rampone, punta anteriore del 901
rana 110, 832
rana comune 111
rana dei boschi 111
rana leopardo 111
rana maschio, anatomia di una 110
rana, ciclo biologico della 111
rana, morfologia di una 110
rana, scheletro di una 111
randa 603, 834
Ranvier, nodo di 168
rapa 189
rapide 837
ras el hanout 199
rasatura 383
raschiatoio 98
raschietto 320, 422, 464
raschietto metallico 892
raso 463
rasoio a mano libera 383
rasoio di sicurezza 383
rasoio elettrico 383
rasoio sfoltitore 381
rasoio usa e getta 383
raspa 309, 401
rastrelliera 485
rastrelliera dei rocchetti 462
rastrelliera di stoccaggio 666
rastrello 327
rastrello meccanico 642
rastrello scopa 333
ratto 123
ratto, morfologia di un 122
ratto, scheletro di un 122
ravanello 189
ravanello nero 189
ravioli 206
razza 218
razze canine 130
razze di gatti 132
razzi spaziali, esempi di 24
razzo a propellente solido 22, 24
razzo illuminante 771
razzo spaziale 24
razzo spaziale (Ariane V), sezione trasversale di un 24
razzo spaziale (Saturn V), sezione trasversale di un 25
razzo, motore a 759
re 434, 914, 916
re, camera del 402
re, lato del 916
Rea 5
reattore 665, 666, 669
reattore ad acqua bollente 671
reattore ad acqua pesante 670
reattore ad acqua pressurizzata 671
reattore ad anidride carbonica 670
reattore nucleare 667, 763
reattore nucleare, locale del 763
reattore, edificio del 669
reattore, nocciolo del 670, 671
reattore, recipiente del 667, 669, 671
reazione a catena 681
reazione reversibile 684
reazione, direzione della 684
rebbio 227, 327, 641
recensione gastronomica 471
reception 509, 724
reception, banco della 730
reception, piano della 724
recettore sensoriale 168
recettori gustativi 176
recinto 182
recinzione 182, 795
recinzione di sicurezza 890
recipiente del moderatore 670
recipiente del reattore 667, 669, 671
recipiente di raccolta 59
recipiente graduato 231
redine 115, 856
redingote 355
redini 857
redini del filetto 854
redini del morso 854
redini, anello per le 854
referenti tecnici 881
refill 470
reforming catalitico, impianto di 656
refrattario, fondo 256
refrattario, mattone 256
refrigerante 665
refrigerante, tubo del 260
refrigeratore della sala del generatore di vapore 669
refrigerazione, cestello di 240
reggicalze 367
reggicoperchio 386, 389
reggilibri 535
reggipiccozza 901
reggiseno 367
reggiseno a balconcino 367
reggiseno a bustino 367
reggiseno décolleté 367
reggiseno, coppa del 367
reggiseno, sottoveste con 366
regia, cabina di 431, 488, 489, 490, 491, 718
regina 916
Regina Maud, Terra della 29
regina, camera della 402
regina, lato della 916
regione auricolare 115
regione malare 115
regione pilifera 87
regioni con segnalamento mediante boe 616
regista 429, 490
regista, monitor di controllo del 428

INDICE DELLE VOCI ITALIANE

ASTRONOMIA > 2-25; TERRA > 26-71; REGNO VEGETALE >72-89; REGNO ANIMALE > 90-143; ESSERE UMANO > 144-177; GENERI ALIMENTARI E CUCINA > 178-241; CASA > 242-295; FAI DA TE E GIARDINAGGIO > 296-333; ABBIGLIAMENTO > 334-371; ACCESSORI E ARTICOLI PERSONALI > 372-391; ARTE E ARCHITETTURA > 392-465; COMUNICAZIONI E BUROTICA > 466-535; TRASPORTI E VEICOLI > 536-643; ENERGIA > 644-677; SCIENZA > 678-705; SOCIETÀ > 706-785; SPORT E GIOCHI > 786-920

1101

regista, sedia da 276
regista, sedia del 429
registratore 59
registratore a bobine 488
registratore di cassa 181
registratore di compact disc 503
registratore di compact disc riscrivibili 521
registratore di dati 58
registratore di microfilm 520
registratore digitale 534
registratore digitale a cassette 488
registratore DVD 521
registratore, tasto di selezione del 497
registrazione dei dati 41
registrazione notturna, selettore di 496
registrazione sismografica 651, 653
registrazione, banco di 620
registrazione, nastro di 499
registrazione, tasto di 495, 499
registrazione, tasto di avvio/arresto 496
registro degli acuti 432
registro dei bassi 432
registro di regolazione 258
registro, asta del 445
registro, tasto di 444, 445
regno animale 92
Regno Unito di Gran Bretagna e Irlanda del Nord 743
regno vegetale 74
regolatore 782
regolatore degli alti 497
regolatore dei bassi 497
regolatore dei toni alti 503
regolatore dei toni bassi 503
regolatore del display 506
regolatore del getto di vapore 288
regolatore del tirante 902
regolatore del volume 507, 508
regolatore del volume di ricezione 506
regolatore dell'alimentazione di ossigeno 898
regolatore dell'altezza 851
regolatore dell'altezza della lama 305
regolatore dell'altezza della testa 485
regolatore dell'inclinazione della lama 304, 305
regolatore della fiamma 391
regolatore della lunghezza dei punti 452
regolatore della pressione 319, 384
regolatore della temperatura 259
regolatore della tensione 460
regolatore della velocità 332, 452
regolatore delle testine 383
regolatore dello sforzo 851
regolatore di alimentazione 627
regolatore di amplificazione 613
regolatore di centratura 518
regolatore di comando del carrello 456
regolatore di contrasto 518
regolatore di corrente 275
regolatore di luminosità 518, 903
regolatore di pressione 234, 452
regolatore di profondità 308
regolatore di tensione 453, 456, 457
regolatore di velocità 236, 417
regolatore di volume 497
regolatore staccabile 239
regolatore, puleggia di tensione del 417
regolazione dei toni 441
regolazione dei toni alti 441
regolazione dei toni bassi 441
regolazione del diaframma 693
regolazione del livello sonoro delle comunicazioni 20
regolazione del passo 700
regolazione del sistema di sopravvivenza 20
regolazione del vapore 241
regolazione del volume 441
regolazione dell'altezza 641, 642
regolazione dell'altezza, manopola di 289
regolazione dell'angolo di elevazione 692
regolazione dell'immagine del cerchio azimutale 701
regolazione dell'immagine del cerchio zenitale 701
regolazione della frizione 910
regolazione della linea di mira 692
regolazione della luminosità dello schermo del computer 20
regolazione della pressione dell'ossigeno 20
regolazione della soglia di allarme 613
regolazione della temperatura 261, 267
regolazione della temperatura corporea 20
regolazione dello specchietto retrovisore esterno 554
regolazione in altezza del condensatore 693
regolazione laterale, leva di 309
regolazione micrometrica dell'altezza 14, 15
regolazione micrometrica dell'asse orizzontale 14, 15
regolazione orizzontale 518
regolazione sulle alte luci 479
regolazione sulle basse luci 479
regolazione sulle medie luci 479
regolazione verticale 518
regolazione, anello di 329
regolazione, bottone di 443
regolazione, dispositivo di 889
regolazione, indicatore della 889
regolazione, leva di 436
regolazione, pedale di 399
regolazione, vite di 309, 310, 317, 319
religione 736
religioni, cronologia delle 736
remi, tipi di 838
remigante primaria 115
remigante secondaria 115
remigante terziaria 115
remo 598, 600, 851
remo di coppia 838
remo di punta 838
remo-timone 598
rene 104, 105, 106, 109, 110, 112, 116, 125, 161
rene destro 165
rene sinistro 165
reniforme 79
renio 683
renna 128
reostato 274
replay 789
replo 84
reptazione 47
Repubblica Ceca 744
Repubblica Centrafricana 745
Repubblica del Mali 745
Repubblica Democratica del Congo 745
Repubblica Democratica Popolare di Corea 747
Repubblica di Corea 747
Repubblica di San Marino 744
Repubblica Dominicana 743
Repubblica Sudafricana 746
repulsione 687
reset, tasto di 508
residuo lungo 656
resina, superficie trasparente in 501
resistenza 630
resistenza elettrica, unità di misura della 702
resistenza idraulica 851
resistenze 689
respingente 583
respiratore 841
respiratorio, apparato 163
responsabile della sicurezza 837
responsabile di regia 489
responsabile per il conteggio dei giri 883
rete 812, 813, 814, 815, 817, 821, 827
rete a bus 522
rete a molle 280
rete a stella 522
rete ad anello 522
rete di distribuzione dell'acqua calda 262
rete di distribuzione dell'acqua fredda 262
rete di oleodotti 654
rete di scarico 262
rete di trasmissione 662
rete di trasmissione dell'elettricità 674
rete di trasmissione, integrazione di energia alla 677
rete di ventilazione 262
rete dorsale 523
rete estesa 523
rete informatica 523
rete per alimenti 222
rete pubblica postale 474
rete stabilizzante 254
rete telefonica 487
rete trasmittente nazionale 486
rete trasmittente privata 486
rete, supporto della 815
reti 716
reti, esempi di 522
reticella metallica a maglie esagonali 299
reticolato geografico 36
Reticolo 10
reticolo 692
reticolo endoplasmatico 74, 94
retina 177, 281, 691, 811
retino di protezione 488
retro 300
retroescavatore 637
retroescavatore, comandi del 637
retromarcia, pedale della 333
rettangolare 904
rettangolo 705
rettangolo destro di servizio 821
rettangolo di battuta 862
rettangolo sinistro di servizio 821
rettili 112
rettili, esempi di 114
rettilinei 871
rettilineo delle tribune 856
rettilineo opposto alle tribune 856
retto 97, 99, 113, 116, 125, 164, 169, 170
retto dell'addome 150
retto della coscia 150
revers 348, 352, 362
revers a punta 348
revolver, portaobiettivi a 693
rialzato 413
rialzo continentale 49
rianimazione, apparecchiatura di 775
rianimazione, sala di 778
riavvolgimento, tasto di 495, 499, 504, 508
ribalta 278, 279
ribaltabile 572, 573
ribassato policentrico 413
ribes 192
ribes nero 192
ribosoma 74, 94
ricalco, rotella da 454
ricamo 459
ricarica, presa di 383
ricarica, presa per 288
riccio 121, 439
riccio di mare 95
ricerca 525
ricerca automatica 498
ricerca rapida, tasti di 501
ricetrasmettitore radar 771
ricetrasmittente di accesso alla rete 522
ricettacolo 75, 80, 83
ricettacolo seminale 97, 103
ricevimento merci 621
ricevimento, area di 395
ricevitore 16, 493, 506, 794, 795, 796, 817, 819, 820
ricevitore auricolare 502
ricevitore esterno 807
ricevuta della transazione 731
ricezione dei dati 41
ricezione privata diretta 486
ricezione, linea di 818
richiamo 913
riciclaggio 71
riciclaggio del vetro, bidone carrellato per il 71
riciclaggio dell'alluminio, bidone carrellato per il 71
riciclaggio della carta, bidone carrellato per il 71
riciclaggio, contenitore per il 71
ricognizione meteorologica, aereo da 54
ricognizione meteorologica, boa di 54
ricognizione meteorologica, nave da 54
riconcentrazione dell'acqua pesante 669
riconoscimento, sezione di 768
ricotta 210
ridotta 472
riduttore 382
riduzione del diametro del fascio 694
riduzione esagonale 269
riduzione maschio/femmina 269
riduzione, manicotto di 269
riduzione, tasto di 512
riempimento, foro di 757
riempimento, tubo di 265
rifilatura 424
rifiuti domestici 69, 70
rifiuti industriali 69, 70
rifiuti non riciclabili 71
rifiuti nucleari 70
rifiuti, bidone dei 295
rifiuti, smistamento selettivo dei 71
rifiuti, strati di 69
riflessione 41
riflessione parziale, specchio a 692
riflessione totale, specchio a 692
riflessione, cilindro di 692
riflettore 316, 492, 765
riflettore con presa a pantografo 492
riflettore orientabile 492
riflettore parabolico 16
riflettore parabolico a microonde 489
riflettore parabolico orientabile 16
riflettore radar passivo 615
riflettore secondario 16
riflettori solari 486
Riforma 736
rifornimento di contanti 731
rifornimento in volo 760
rifornimento, addetto al 873
rifornimento, serbatoio per il 873
rifugio 543
rifugio in vetta 886
rifugio principale 886
riga 399, 424
riga dei dati immessi 529
riga dei risultati 529
riga della guida parallela 305
rigatoni 206
righello 700, 905
righello, scala graduata del 700
rigonfiamento 9
rilascio di energia 681
rilegatore, martello da 425
rilegatura a mano 424
rilegatura con spirale 533
rilevatore agli infrarossi 60
rilevatore di fumo 767
rilevatore di movimento 416
rilievo, matrice in 420
riloga estensibile 284
riloga sagomata 282
rimessa 182, 244, 322
rimorchi 567
rimorchi, carro pianale per il trasporto di 588
rimorchiatore 606
rimorchio 570, 594
rimorchio, dispositivo di 573
rinario 132
rincorsa, pedane di 824
rincorsa, pista di 793
rinculo, slitta di 756
rinfianco 413
rinforzo a crociera 783
rinforzo del calcagno 370
rinforzo della curva 446
rinforzo della fondazione 660
rinforzo di culatta 753
rinforzo di cuoio 880
rinforzo di plastica 868
rinforzo esterno del calcagno 342
rinforzo interno del calcagno 342
rinforzo per serratura 247
rinforzo posteriore 881
rinforzo, bandella di 389
rinforzo, secondo 753
rinfuse, deposito delle 596
ringhiera 251
rinoceronte 129
rinvio 900
Rio delle Amazzoni 31
ripetitore 487
ripetizione, tasti di 501
ripiani, griglia dei 291
ripiano 279, 291, 321
ripiano regolabile 511
ripieno 390
riposizionatore automatico 865
ripostiglio 509, 584
ripostiglio per il materiale pulito 778
ripostiglio per il materiale sporco 778
ripostiglio per l'attrezzatura 734
ripostiglio per la barella spinale 775
ripostiglio per la biancheria 584
ripresa 352
riprese, set delle 428
ripristino, tasto di 519
riproduttore a cassette 504
riproduttore a cassette, tasti del 504
riproduttori portatili 503
riproduzione al rallentatore 495
riproduzione, tasto di 495, 499, 504
riproduzione/pausa, tasto di 501
riquadro 386, 899
risaia 69
riscaldamento 256
riscaldamento a legna 256
riscaldamento ad acqua calda, impianto di 259
riscaldamento ad aria calda, impianto di 258
riscaldamento, comando del 556
riscaldamento, condotto di 293
riscaldamento, griglia del 594
riscaldamento, mezzi integrativi di 260
riscaldatore 465
riscontro 855
risguardo, foglio di 426
riso 85, 203, 207
riso basmati 207
riso bianco 207
riso integrale 207
riso nero selvatico 203
riso parboiled 207
riso, aceto di 201
riso, gallette di 207
riso, spaghetti di 207
riso, vermicelli di 207
riso: spiga 85
risonanza, cassa di 433, 440
risonatore 449, 502
risorgiva 47
risparmio di energia, lampadina a 275
ristorante 584, 608, 710, 713, 714, 719, 720, 725
ristorante, vagone 584
ristoro per sciatori 886
risultati, tabella dei 828
risvolto 285, 350, 362
ritegno, valvola di 319
ritmo dei segnalamenti notturni 617
ritmo, selettore del 451
ritornabocce 865
ritornata 828
ritornello 434
ritorno, tubazione di 259
ritto 792, 825
riunioni, sala 764
riva 664
rivestimenti in tessuto per pavimento 254
rivestimento 252, 253, 425, 660, 689, 815
rivestimento antiriflettente 672
rivestimento del motore 331
rivestimento esterno 267, 797
rivestimento fluorescente 275
rivestimento interno 561
rivestimento isolante 655
rivestimento isolante per tubi 299
rivestimento, griglia di 259
rivestimento, materiali di 299
rivetto 229, 310
riviera 852, 853
rivista 471
rizoide 75
rizoma 76
robe-manteau 356
robot da cucina 237
roccatrice 462
rocce ignee 42
rocce intrusive 42
rocce metamorfiche 42
rocce sedimentarie 42
rocchetti, rastrelliera dei 462
rocchetto 458
rocchetto di avvolgimento 476
rocchetto di trascinamento della pellicola 476
rocchio 404
roccia 900
roccia impermeabile 651
roccia in posto 78
rocker 422
rodio 683
roditore 122
roditore: ratto, fauce di un 123
roditori 122
roditori, esempi di 123
rognone 212
rollio 630
Romania 744
romano 698
rombo 221, 705
rompigetto, vite 329
rompighiaccio 606
roncola 330
rondella 268, 689
rondella di tenuta 562
rondine 118
rondine di mare 118
rondone 118
roquefort 211
rosa 80, 440
rosa dei venti 37, 612, 907
rosetta 248
rosetta a dentatura esterna 310
rosetta a dentatura interna 310
rosetta elastica 310
rosetta piatta 310
rosetta, taglio a 375
rosette 310
rosmarino 202
rosone 411
rospo comune 111
Ross, Banchisa di 29
rossetto 378
rosso 400, 690, 741, 915, 919
Rosso, Mar 28, 33, 34
rosso-arancio 400
rosso-viola 400
rostro 108, 598
rotaia 591
rotaia del carrello di scotta 834, 835
rotaia di guida e di alimentazione di corrente 595
rotaia di indorsatura 425
rotaia di rotolamento 595
rotaia di scorrimento 555, 634, 635
rotaia di sicurezza 595
rotaia, giunto di 590
rotatoria 39
rotazione della turbina 662
rotazione, sistema a 651
rotella 454, 633, 888, 895
rotella centrale di messa a fuoco 692
rotella da ricalco 454
rotella del volume 513
rotella della pietrina 391
rotella di comando 527
rotella di intonazione 450
rotella di modulazione 450
rotella di regolazione 700
rotella di selezione degli effetti speciali 496
rotella orientabile 448
rotella regolatrice vicino/lontano 496
rotella tagliapasta 232
rotellina di scorrimento 516
rotodome 629
rotolamento, superficie di 590
rotoli della Torah 738
rotolo di benda garzata 777
rotonda 713
rotore 249, 565, 659, 662, 676
rotore a griffa 688
rotore anticoppia 631
rotore, mozzo del 631
rotore, pala del 631
rotore, pilone del 631
rotore, testa del 631
rotula 122, 131, 138, 152
rough 866, 867
roulette 422
roulette americana 919
roulette francese 919
roulette, tavolo da 919
roulotte 567
router 523, 524
rovesci di grandine 57
rovesci di neve 57
rovesci di pioggia 57
rovesciata 828
rovesciata all'indietro 844
Ruanda 745
rubidio 682
rubinetti 268

INDICE DELLE VOCI ITALIANE

1102

ASTRONOMIA > 2-25; TERRA > 26-71; REGNO VEGETALE >72-89; REGNO ANIMALE > 90-143; ESSERE UMANO > 144-177; GENERI ALIMENTARI E CUCINA > 178-241; CASA > 242-295; FAI DA TE E GIARDINAGGIO > 296-333; ABBIGLIAMENTO > 334-371; ACCESSORI E ARTICOLI PERSONALI > 372-391; ARTE E ARCHITETTURA > 392-465; COMUNICAZIONI E BUROTICA > 466-535; TRASPORTI E VEICOLI > 536-643; ENERGIA > 644-677; SCIENZA > 678-705; SOCIETÀ > 706-785; SPORT E GIOCHI > 786-920

rubinetto 264
rubinetto a valvola 268
rubinetto del gas 267
rubinetto di arresto 270, 271
rubinetto di regolazione della pressione 765
rubinetto di scarico 266
rubinetto generale 262
rubino 375, 696
rubino pulsato, laser a 692
rubino, cilindro di 692
rubrica telefonica 506, 531
ruches 368
ruches, ghettina con 368
rucola 187
Ruffini, corpuscolo di 172
rugby 804
rugiada 65
rugiada, temperatura di 55
rullaggio, linea di 619
rullaggio, pista di 618
rulli dei cingoli, telaio dei 636
rullini tenditori 580
rullino 311, 516
rullo 284, 285, 320, 333, 380, 381, 423, 528, 920
rullo di compressione 643
rullo di guida 499
rullo di guida della pellicola 476
rullo inchiostratore 421
rullo per i bicipiti femorali 851
rullo per i quadricipiti 851
rullo per verniciare 422
rullo schiacciaforaggi 642
rullo, cuscino a 280
rullo, piastra del 920
rullo, supporto del 320
rumeno 469
runner 915
ruota 320, 323, 389, 423, 560, 570, 753, 870, 874, 894, 895
ruota a denti di sega 697
ruota a pale 599
ruota a raggi 857
ruota ad una sola moltiplica 871
ruota anteriore 333, 639, 640
ruota dei cucchiai 659
ruota dei secondi 696
ruota del freno a mano 587
ruota dell'ingranaggio 307
ruota della moltiplica 870
ruota dentata 462, 686
ruota dentata A 580
ruota dentata B 580
ruota dentata d'arresto 460
ruota dentata motrice 758, 876
ruota di calibratura 333
ruota di carica 696
ruota di centro 696, 697
ruota di guida 594, 595
ruota di scappamento 696, 697
ruota di scorta 567
ruota di sicurezza 595
ruota di spinta 783
ruota elicoidale 686
ruota folle 876
ruota girevole 281, 919
ruota intermedia 696, 697
ruota lenticolare 871
ruota libera 580
ruota motrice 462, 636, 640, 697
ruota orientabile 289
ruota piena o gonfiabile 783
ruota pivotante 783
ruota portante 594, 595, 758
ruota posteriore 333
ruota tendicingolo 636
ruote motrici 639
rupe 45
rupia 728
ruscello 48
ruspa 638
russo 469
rutenio 683
rutherfordio 683
Ryukyu, Fossa delle 50

S

sabbia 660, 813
sabbia, banco di 49
sabbiera 586
sacca 869
sacca a tracolla 388
sacca copulatoria 97, 104
sacca copulatoria, orifizio della 97
sacca da marinaio 388
sacca dell'inchiostro 106
saccatura 55
sacchetti 181
sacchetto 222
sacchetto per freezer 222
sacchetto, scomparto del 289
sacchi a pelo, esempi di 904
sacco 432, 797, 842
sacco del dardo 104
sacco imbottito 897
sacco, poltrona 277
sacrestia 737
sacro 138, 141, 152, 153, 157
Saetta 12
sagari 847
Sagittario 10
sagoma 424
Sahara, Deserto del 34
sahariana 359
saia 463
Saint Kitts e Nevis 743
Saint Lucia 743
Saint Vincent e Grenadine 743
sala 431, 608
sala audiovisiva 733
sala congressi 718
sala d'attesa 768, 779
sala d'attesa dei familiari 778
sala d'attesa dei visitatori 726
sala d'attesa del centro prelievi 781
sala d'attesa principale 781
sala d'attesa secondaria 781
sala da bagno 780
sala da ballo 609
sala da pranzo 250, 608, 720, 723, 724, 727, 764
sala da pranzo del personale 509
sala degli argani 649
sala degli infermieri 781
sala dei computer 763
sala dei periodici 733
sala dei prelievi 781
sala del generatore di vapore, refrigeratore della 669
sala del personale 731, 768
sala della preghiera 738
sala delle esposizioni 719
sala delle strutture ausiliarie 490
sala di attesa 509
sala di comando 10
sala di comando dell'apparato propulsore 763
sala di consultazione 733
sala di controllo 657, 669
sala di imbarco 621
sala di ingresso 250, 738
sala di lettura 732
sala di proiezione 395, 427
sala di regolazione delle luci 490
sala di rianimazione 778
sala di ricreazione 727
sala di servizio 738
sala di sterilizzazione 781
sala di stoccaggio del combustibile nuovo 666
sala gessi 779
sala macchine 606, 608, 657, 658
sala nautica 604
sala operatoria 780, 781
sala passeggeri 605, 608, 609
sala per comunicati 718
sala per conferenze 718, 730
sala per i cocktail 724
sala per il pubblico 10
sala per operazioni di chirurgia minore 778
sala per riunioni 724, 730, 735
sala polivalente 727
sala riunioni 394, 509, 764
sala vip 718
salamandra 111
salame di Genova 216
salame di Tolosa 216
salame tedesco 216
salchow 881
saldatore 314
saldatore a pistola 318
saldatore elettrico 318
saldatore, maschera da 318
saldatrice ad arco 318
saldatura ad arco 318
saldatura ossiacetilenica 319
saldatura, filo per 318
sale 847
sale di colloquio 728
sale fino 201
sale grosso 201
sale marino 201
sale per riunioni 718
salice piangente 88
saliente 409
saliera 226
salita, corridoio di 402
salmerino di fontana 221
salmone del Pacifico 221
salmone dell'Atlantico 221
salmone rosso 221
salone 608, 620
salopette 358, 368
salopette a tutina 368
salopette con bretelle incrociate 369
salotto 250, 724
salotto, poltrona da 276
salsa di prugne 201
salsa di soia 200
salsa hoisin 200
salsa tabasco 200
salsa Worcestershire 200
salsefica 189
salsiccia alle cipolle 216
salsiccia di Francoforte 216
salsiccia di trippa 216
salsiccia kielbasa 216
salsiccia piccante 216
salsiera 226
saltatore 891
salterello 443
salti 792
salti multipli 875
salti, esempi di 881
salto con gli sci 891
salto con l'asta 790, 792
salto in alto 791, 792
salto in lungo 790, 793
salto ostacoli 852
salto triplo 790, 793
salto, area del 890
salto, tecnica di 891
salute 775
salvagente 609, 611, 771
salvatacchi 342
salvataggio, boa di 611
salvataggio, equipaggiamento di 611
salvataggio, giubbotto di 611
salvataggio, scialuppa di 602, 604, 608
salvataggio, zattera di 605, 611
salvia 202
samario 684
sambal oelek 201
Samoa 747
samoano 469
San Lorenzo, Fiume 30
San Marino, Repubblica di 744
san Pietro 736
sanbernardo 131
sand wedge 868
sandalo 343, 344, 748
sandalo indiano 344
sangue deossigenato 162
sangue ossigenato 162
sangue, circolazione del 160
sangue, composizione del 162
sanguinaccio 216
santoreggia 202
São Tomé e Príncipe 745
sapone da barba, tazza per 383
saponetta 379
sapotiglia 197
saracco 303
saracinesca a monte 597
saracinesca a valle 597
saracinesca, nicchia per la 597
sarchiello 326
sarchiello a mano 325
sarchio 326
sardina 219
sarong 357
sartia 602, 834
sartorio 150
sash 846
sassofono 446
satellite 24, 486
satellite artificiale 53
satellite geostazionario 60
satellite in orbita polare 60
satellite meteorologico 54
satellite per le telecomunicazioni 525
satellite radarsat 40
satelliti 4
satelliti meteorologici 60
satelliti per telecomunicazioni 486
satelliti, orbita dei 60
Saturn V 24
Saturno 4, 5
savana 61, 66
saxhorn 447
sbarra 281, 591, 686, 851
sbarra di acciaio 825
sbarra orizzontale 824, 825
sbarra pieghevole 850
sbarra, luce della 591
sbarra, scatola di comando della 591
sbarra, sostegno della 591
sbieco 455
sblocco istantaneo 482
sbuccialimoni 229
sbucciatore 229
scacchi 458, 916
scacchi, notazione degli 916
scacchiera 916
scaccianeve alto 57
scaccianeve basso 57
scacciapensieri 433
scadenza, data di 729
scaffale 181, 723
scaffale dei periodici 733
scaffale delle novità 733
scafo 599, 834, 876, 889
scafoide 154, 156
scaglia 108
scaglione 740
scala 250, 313, 418, 427, 431, 434, 567, 597, 615, 676, 914
scala a chiocciola 655
scala a libretto 321
scala a palchetto con ruote 321
scala a pioli 321
scala a pioli con ganci 321
scala aerea 766
scala Celsius 695
scala cine 479
scala con ganci 767
scala con piattaforma 321
scala dei passi di scrittura 528
scala dei tempi 436
scala dei tempi di esposizione 479
scala dell'altezza 485
scala dell'apertura del diaframma 479
scala dell'apertura di diaframma 478
scala della luminosità 479
scala delle altitudini 53
scala delle distanze 478
scala delle profondità di campo 478
scala delle temperature 53
scala di accesso al piano mansardato 251
scala di conversione 479
scala di profondità in metri 613
scala estensibile 321
scala esterna 245
scala Fahrenheit 695
scala graduata 303, 304, 695, 698, 699, 700, 776, 907
scala graduata del nonio 700
scala graduata del righello 700
scala mobile 417, 427, 592, 713
scala multiuso 321
scala per agricoltura 321
scala reale 914
scala reale massima 914
scala retrattile 321
scala sgabello 321
scalata, imbracatura da 901
scalatore 900
scaldabagno 262, 266, 675
scaldabagno a gas 267
scaldabagno elettrico 266
scaldamuscoli 371
scale 255, 321, 412, 543, 592, 655, 724
scale a libretto 321
scale antincendio 509
scale, rampa di 255
scale, tromba delle 251
scaletta 246, 623, 639, 842
scaletta di imbarco 611
scaletta laterale 586, 587
scaletta posteriore 587
scaletta semovente 623
scalfo 351
scalinata 412
scalini 246
scalino d'invito 255
scalmo 839
scalo ferroviario 596
scalo merci 583, 708
scalogno 184
scalpello 421, 651
scalpello da falegname 309
scalpello dello scarificatore 636
scambiatore di calore 259, 670, 675
scambio 583
scambio automatico 590
scambio manuale 590
scambio, segnale di 590
scamiciato 356
scampo 218
scanalatura 229, 306, 404, 405, 453, 562, 750, 868, 888
scanalatura della frontura 456
scanalatura della guida graduata 305
scanalatura della guida parallela 305
scandagliamento ad alta quota 59
scandio 683
scandola 299
scanner 517
scanner a microonde 60
scanner all'infrarosso 18
scanner delle radiazioni terrestri 60
scanner ottico 181
scapo 172
scapola 111, 116, 121, 122, 126, 131, 136, 138, 141, 142, 147, 149, 152, 153, 156
scapola, spina della 153
scapolare 115
scappamento 443, 553
scappamento, meccanismo di 436
scappamento, molla dello 443
scappamento, ruota di 696, 697
scappamento, tubo di 575, 576, 577, 640
scaricatore 246
scarichi, molla sturatrice per 314
scarico 246, 262, 564, 565, 627, 649
scarico del vapore dai separatori 668
scarico dell'acqua 662
scarico della polvere, bocchetta dello 304
scarico, banchina di 395
scarico, camera di 402
scarico, colonna principale di 262
scarico, rete di 262
scarico, rubinetto di 266
scarico, tappo di 262
scarico, tubatura di 263
scarico, tubazione di 271
scarico, tubo di 262, 265, 271, 292, 631, 636, 639, 643
scarico, ugello di 760
scarico, valvola di 267
scarificatore 636
scarificatore, cilindro dello 636
scarificatore, dente dello 636
scarificatore, scalpello dello 636
scarola 186
scarpa 409, 791, 798, 801, 802, 805, 810, 843, 850, 865, 870, 872, 880, 881, 895, 900
scarpa a collo alto 342
scarpa a lame 749
scarpa alla polacca 339
scarpa chanel 343
scarpa con cinturino 343
scarpa con cinturino a T 343
scarpa con tacchetti 796, 808
scarpa con tacco 339
scarpa da corsa 370
scarpa da tennis 344, 822
scarpa décolleté 343
scarpa oxford 342
scarpa stringata 342
scarpa, parti di una 342
scarpata 7, 244, 538
scarpata continentale 49
scarpe 342, 869
scarpe con chiodi 885
scarpe da donna 343, 716
scarpe da ginnastica 716
scarpe da uomo 342, 716
scarpe per bambini 717
scarpe unisex 344
scarpe, kit per la pulizia delle 345
scarpe, negozio di 715
scarpetta 841, 848
scarpetta interna 889, 895
scarpetta, bordo della 889
scarpiera 345
scarponcino 342
scarponcino di sicurezza 773
scarpone 342, 888, 889, 891, 892, 896, 901
scarpone morbido 887
scarpone rigido 887
scassa di deriva 836
scatola a doppia linea di connessione 689
scatola americana 535
scatola da incasso 274
scatola degli accessori 456
scatola degli ingranaggi 423
scatola degli ingranaggi del freno a mano 587
scatola degli ingranaggi del moltiplicatore 677
scatola dei collegamenti 490
scatola dei comandi ausiliari 627
scatola dei relais 563
scatola del cambio 552
scatola del premio 920
scatola dell'asse 586
scatola della frizione 576
scatola dello scambio 590
scatola di accensione 627
scatola di collegamento 591
scatola di comando 267
scatola di comando della sbarra 591
scatola di culatta 754, 755
scatola di fiammiferi 391
scatola di interconnessione 563
scatola di servizio 273
scatola elettronica di comando 563
scatola per archivio 533
scatola per formaggio 223
scatola portaesche 911
scatola portaprisma 693
scatolame 181
scatto, ancora a 302
scatto, chiavistello a 248
scatto, chiavistello senza 248, 249
scatto, chiusura a 238, 294
scatto, pulsante di 476
scavamelone 233
scavo 647
scavo, braccio di 638
scena 402
scena, fotografo di 429
scheda del circuito stampato 689
scheda di espansione PCI 513
scheda di memoria 477
scheda di memoria compact flash 481
scheda di rete 522
scheda di rete senza fili 522
scheda madre 513
scheda PC, fessura per la 526
schedario 533
schedario a visibilità laterale 510
schedario mobile 510
schedario rotativo 531
schedario, cassetto di 533
schedario, divisori alfabetici per 532
schede 532
scheletro 152
scheletro di un cane 131

scheletro di un canguro 142
scheletro di un cavallo 126
scheletro di un delfino 136
scheletro di un gorilla 138
scheletro di un pipistrello 141
scheletro di un ratto 122
scheletro di un serpente velenoso 112
scheletro di un uccello 116
scheletro di una rana 111
scheletro di una talpa 121
schema americano delle puntate 919
schema della circolazione 161
schema della tessitura 463
schema francese delle puntate 919
scherma 848
scherma, armi della 849
schermatura in calcestruzzo 670, 671
schermidore 848
schermo 17, 483, 494, 507, 724, 799
schermo a impugnatura 318
schermo di aiuto della visibilità 591
schermo di proiezione 427, 483
schermo di protezione 318, 794
schermo per la messa a fuoco 477
schermo, anello di 58
schermo, custodia dello 483
schiaccianoci 230
schiacciapatate 233
schiacciata 813, 821
schiena 147, 149
schienale 277, 281, 555, 577, 783, 876
schienale reclinabile 776
schienale, manopola di regolazione dello 555
schiniere 749, 796
schiuma 49
schiuma da barba 383
schiuma isolante 299
schiumaiola 233
schizzetto 776
schnauzer 130
Schwann, guaina di 168
Schwenkel, bandiera con 739
sci 876, 888
sci alpino 888
sci alpino, pista per 886
sci alpino, snowboard per 887
sci da chilometro lanciato 891
sci da discesa libera 888
sci da fondo 892
sci da salto 840, 891
sci da slalom 888
sci da slalom gigante 888
sci da supergigante 888
sci doppio 840
sci nautici, esempi di 840
sci nautico 840
sci, esempi di 888
sci, piste da 886
sci, scuola di 886
sci, tuta da 369
scia luminosa del cratere 7
scia, punta dello 892
sciabola 751, 849
sciabolatore 848
sciacquone 264
sciacquone, levetta dello 265
scialle 337
scialle, collo a 362
scialuppa 762
scialuppa di salvataggio 602, 604, 608
sciarpa, collo con 362
sciatore 888
sciatore di chilometro lanciato 891
sciavero 300
scienze, aula di 734
sciismo 736
scimpanzé 139
scintilla 564
scintoismo 736
sciolina 892
sciolinatura, accessori per la 892
sciovia 886
sciovia, arrivo della 886
sciroppo d'acero 209
sciroppo di mais 209
scisma d'Oriente 736
scissione del nucleo 681
scissura obliqua 163
scivolamento 891
scivolamento, fase di 892
scivolo della banchina 596
scivolo dello sfioratore 657
scivolo per tronchi d'albero 657
sclera 177
scocca 332, 567
scodella 226
scodellino 752
scoglio 51
scoiattolo 123
scolainsalata, centrifuga 231
scollatura a barchetta 363
scollatura a cuore 363
scollatura a V 363
scollatura drappeggiata 363
scollatura profonda a V 363
scollatura quadrata 363
scollature 363
scollo 351
scollo a V 348, 354
scolpitura del battistrada 560, 561, 640
scompartimento bagagli 585
scompartimento letto 584
scomparto degli accessori 289
scomparto dei medicinali 775
scomparto del congelatore 291
scomparto del frigorifero 291
scomparto del sacchetto 289
scomparto della controporta 291
scomparto della strumentazione 585
scomparto delle attrezzature tecniche 489
scomparto delle bobine dei cavi 489
scomparto di carico 22
scomparto di carico, portellone dello 23
scomparto per banconote 386
scomparto per carte di credito 386
scomparto per i documenti 527
scomparto per i guanti 780
scomparto per i latticini 291
scomparto per il burro 291
scomparto per il computer 527
scomparto per le uova 291
scomparto portadocumenti 386
scontrino 699
scooter 577
scopa 257, 295
scopa a frangia 295
scopa da curling 877
scopa, rastrello 333
scoppio 564, 565
scoppio, carica di 757
Scorpione 10
scorpione 102
scorrimento 515
scorrimento, manopola di 506
scorrimento, piastra di 590
scorrimento, tasto di 505
scorza 82
scorzetta 82
scorzonera 189
scossalina 257
scotta 603
scotta del fiocco 834
scotta della randa 834
scotta, rotaia del carrello di 834, 835
scovolini 390
scovolo 752
scozia 404, 405
Scozia, placca di 43
scozzese 469
scrivania 724
scrivania dei cancellieri 728
scrivania direzionale 511
scrivania operativa 511
scroto 146, 169
scuderie 856
Scudo 10
scudo 748
scudo di protezione della mano 331
scudo termico 22
scudo, divisioni dello 740
scultura 395
scultura in legno 401
scuola 734
scuola di sci 886
scuolabus 568
scutello 105
seaborgio 683
secchiello con cordoncino 387
secchiello piccolo con cordoncino 388
secchio 295
seconda 434, 849
seconda base 794
seconda base (posizione) 794
seconda falange 126, 172
seconda galleria 431
seconda linea 804
seconda linea destra 804
seconda linea sinistra 804
seconda pinna dorsale 108, 109
secondi violini 437
secondi, lancetta dei 696
secondi, ruota dei 696
secondo 702, 704, 842
secondo allenatore 879
secondo arbitro 807, 812, 813
secondo assistente cameraman 428
secondo aumento di tensione 677
secondo cuneiforme 155, 156
secondo giocatore al lancio 877
secondo giro al largo 833
secondo livello di operazioni 529
secondo livello, dominio di 524
secondo molare 159
secondo premolare 159
secondo rinforzo 753
secondo spazio 811
secondo stadio 25
secondo stadio dell'erogatore 841
secrétaire 279
sedano 185
sedano di monte 202
sedano rapa 189
sede della valvola 268
sede della valvola di tenuta 265
sedia 277, 723
sedia a dondolo 276, 277
sedia a rotelle 584, 783
sedia a sdraio 277
sedia con braccioli 734
sedia da regista 276
sedia dattilo 511
sedia del regista 429
sedia impilabili 277
sedia pieghevole 277
sedia scala 277
sedia senza braccioli 734
sedie a rotelle, rampa per 394
sedie degli attori 428
sedie dei giocatori 813
sedie impilabili 277
sedie, esempi di 277
sedile 264, 265, 276, 277, 281, 333, 464, 885, 898
sedile del comandante 626
sedile del copilota 626
sedile del timoniere 838
sedile dell'infermiere 775
sedile doppio 594
sedile eiettabile 760
sedile mobile 838
sedile regolabile 584
sedile scorrevole 851
sedile singolo 594
sedile: vista anteriore 555
sedile: vista laterale 555
sedili 277
seduta 555, 783
seduta del divano posteriore 555
sega a mano 907
sega circolare 304
sega circolare, lama di 304
sega da banco 305
sega da giardiniere 330
sega per augnatura elettrica 304
sega per augnatura manuale 303
segale 85, 203
segale, galletta di 205
segale, pane danese di 205
segale, pane nero di 204
segale, pane tedesco di 205
segale: spiga 85
seggio 855
seggio del rabbino 738
seggiolino 857
seggiolino per bambini 558, 580
seggiolone 281
seggiovia 886
seggiovia, partenza della 886
seghetto 303, 314
seghetto alternativo 305
seghetto da traforo 303
seghetto per dorsi 424
segmento addominale 97
segmento muscolare 109
segmento orientato 56
segnalamenti notturni, ritmo dei 617
segnalamento dei punti cardinali 616
segnalatore di nebbia 611
segnale acustico 436
segnale cardinale: passare a est 617
segnale cardinale: passare a ovest 617
segnale cardinale: passare a sud 617
segnale dell'area di attesa 620
segnale di acque sicure 617
segnale di distanza fissa 621
segnale di identificazione della pista 620
segnale di passaggio a livello 591
segnale di pericolo isolato 617
segnale di scambio 590
segnale di zona di contatto 621
segnale emesso 40
segnale laterale 617
segnale laterale: boa a palo 617
segnale laterale: boa a pilastro cilindrico 617
segnale laterale: boa conica 617
segnale luminoso 436
segnale speciale 617
segnali dell'asse della pista 620
segnali della soglia della pista 621
segnali laterali 620
segnali marittimi 614
segnali stradali 544
segnali stradali internazionali 544
segnali stradali nordamericani 546
segnali visivi 859
segnalino 915
segnapunti 810, 812, 813, 814, 819, 844, 845, 846, 847, 848, 859, 860, 864, 920
segnatura 426
segnavento 834
segni di interpunzione 473
segno centrale 820
segretari 827
segretaria di produzione 429
segretaria, ufficio della 731
segretario 814
segretario di edizione 490
segreteria scolastica, ufficio della 735
segreteria telefonica 508
selce, coltello di 748
selce, punta di freccia in 748
selenio 682
selettore automatico/manuale 316
selettore dei canali 505
selettore dei pick-up 441
selettore dei programmi 476
selettore dei punti 452
selettore del livello dell'acqua 292
selettore del livello di registrazione 499
selettore del movimento orbitale 305
selettore del nastro 499
selettore del numero dei decimali 529
selettore del ritmo 451
selettore del timbro 451
selettore dell'ampiezza dei punti 452
selettore della messa a fuoco 476, 496
selettore della modalità audio 497
selettore della posizione dell'ago 452
selettore della temperatura 238, 382
selettore della velocità 382
selettore di banda 498
selettore di controllo audio 491
selettore di controllo video 491
selettore di funzione 261
selettore di ingresso 497
selettore di programma 450
selettore di registrazione notturna 496
selettore di velocità 236, 237, 305, 306, 500
selettore quadridirezionale 477
selettore stereo/mono 504
selettori di funzione 506
selettori di modo 504
selezione della lingua del display, tasto di 507
selezione manuale, comando di 483
selezione, tasto di 261, 496, 505, 506
self-service 722
self-service, banco del 722
sella 577, 578, 826, 851, 853, 855, 856, 858, 876
sella biposto 575
sella del guidatore 577
sella del passeggero 577
selletta 897
sellino 337, 857
sellino, abito con 337
selvaggina 212
semaforo 545, 547, 583, 712
semaforo a luce intermittente 591
seme 77, 81, 82, 83, 84
semi di girasole, olio di 209
semi di lino, olio di 400
semi di papavero 199
semi di soia 191
semi-grassetto 472
semi-mummia 904
semiasse 553
semibiscroma 435
semibiscroma, pausa di 435
semibreve 435
semibreve, pausa di 435
semicerchio 704
semicroma 435
semicroma, pausa di 435
semifinale 789
semilunare 154, 156
semimembranoso 151
semimetalli 682
semiminima 435
semiminima, pausa di 435
seminatoio a mano 324
seminatrice 643
seminterrato 250
seminterrato, finestra del 245
semipreziose, pietre 375
semirimorchio 570, 571
semirimorchio furgonato 572
semirimorchio portacontainer 572
semirimorchio ribassato per il trasporto del bestiame 572
semirimorchio ribassato per il trasporto di mezzi corazzati 572
semisfera 705
semitendinoso 151
semolino 204
senape americana 200
senape bianca 198
senape di Digione 200
senape in granuli 200
senape in polvere 200
senape inglese 200
senape nera 84, 198
senape tedesca 200
Senegal 745
Senegal, Fiume 34
seno 146, 148, 171, 336
seno frontale 175
seno laterale inferiore 86
seno laterale superiore 86
seno peziolato 86
seno sfenoidale 175
seno urogenitale 109
sensibilità della pellicola 479
senso vietato 544, 546
sensore 58
sensore attivo 41
sensore del telecomando 494, 501
sensore delle radiazioni terrestri 60
sensore di collisione principale 556
sensore di sicurezza 556
sensore di temperatura 18, 561
sensore di velocità delle ruote 559
sensore esposimetrico 477
sensore ottico 516
sensore passivo 41
sensore solare 40, 60
sensore terrestre 40, 60
sepalo 80, 82, 83
separatore 562, 606, 643, 646, 668, 689
separatore dell'acqua 648
separatore elettrolitico 689
separatore gas / petrolio 652
separatore liquido/gas 562
separazione del cartone 71
separazione della carta 71
separazione magnetica 71
séparé 720
seppia 217
sequencer 450
sequencer, controllo del 450
sequenza principale, stella della 8
seracco 46
serbatoi 655
serbatoi di stoccaggio 654
serbatoio 23, 241, 261, 266, 320, 398, 445, 563
serbatoio a espansione 675
serbatoio a tetto fisso 655
serbatoio a tetto galleggiante 655
serbatoio ausiliario 571
serbatoio d'aria 320
serbatoio d'aria compressa 586
serbatoio del carburante 331, 553, 574, 577, 586, 631, 758, 760
serbatoio del carburante riscaldante 563
serbatoio del gas 391
serbatoio del kerosene 25
serbatoio del liquido dei freni 559
serbatoio del propellente 18
serbatoio dell'acqua 241, 261, 384, 586, 589
serbatoio dell'acqua di raffreddamento 665
serbatoio dell'acqua, vano del 628
serbatoio dell'elio 25
serbatoio dell'idrogeno liquido 24, 25
serbatoio dell'impianto di allagamento 669
serbatoio dell'ossigeno liquido 24, 25
serbatoio dell'ossigeno liquido, diaframma del 25
serbatoio della granella 643
serbatoio di accumulo 675
serbatoio di azoto liquido 694
serbatoio di sicurezza 670
serbatoio di stoccaggio 656
serbatoio di stoccaggio temporaneo 654
serbatoio esterno del combustibile 22
serbatoio per il brillantante 294
serbatoio per il carburante 570
serbatoio per il rifornimento 873
serbatoio ventrale 631
serbatoio vetrificato 267
serbatoio, bocchetta del 332
serbatoio, sportello del 551
serbatoio, tappo del 570, 576
serbo-croato 469
serie dei monitor di anteprima 491
serie dei monitor di ingresso 491
serie, lampade in 287
serie, numero di 729
Serpente 11, 13
serpente 112
serpente a sonagli 114
serpente corallo 114
serpente giarrettiera 114
serpente velenoso, anatomia di un 112
serpente velenoso, scheletro di un 112
serpente velenoso: testa, morfologia di un 112
serpentina 290
serpentina del condensatore 261
serpentina del vaporizzatore 261
serpentina di riscaldamento 899
serra 182
serraggio, dispositivo di 685
serraggio, leva di 309, 312
serraggio, pinze di 685
serraggio, vite di 312
serratura 247, 248, 278, 291, 387, 389, 551, 554
serratura a chiave 386
serratura a combinazione 386
serratura a pomolo 249
serratura premi-apri 248
server 522, 523, 524, 525
server d'accesso 525
servizi assicurativi 730
servizi di credito 730
servizi finanziari 730
servizi sociali 781
servizi tecnici 732
servizio 812, 820
servizio corto, linea di 817
servizio da fonduta 234
servizio da wok 234

servizio del doppio, campo di 817
servizio del singolo, campo di 817
servizio destro, area di 819
servizio di assistenza ai clienti 731
servizio di babysitteraggio 715
servizio di navetta 620
servizio di sicurezza 719
servizio Internet, fornitore del 525
servizio lungo, linea di 816
servizio manutenzione 548
servizio mobile a distanza, unità di 21
servizio pacchi 582
servizio per scarpe 345
servizio sinistro, area di 819
servizio, cintura di 770
servizio, entrata di 732
servizio, fonte del 471
servizio, giudice di 816, 820
servizio, linea centrale di 821
servizio, linea di 818, 819, 821
servizio, modulo di 25, 486
servizio, quadrato di 818, 819
servizio, stazione di 711
servizio, tavolo di 720
servizio, zona di 818, 821
servizio, zone di 817
servofreno 552, 559
servomotore 759
servosostegno 648
servosostegno, martello perforatore con 648
sesamo, olio di 209
sesamoide distale 126
sesamoide prossimale 126
sesta 434, 849
Sestante 11
sestante 612
sestante automatico 18
sestetto 438
sestina 919
set 429, 822
set delle riprese 428
set di bussole 311
set di utensili 233
set per cucinare 905
set per manicure 377
set precedenti 822
setaccio 231, 232
setale 911
setola 383, 384
setole 295, 320
settima 434, 849
setto 84, 175
setto interventricolare 162
setto nasale, cartilagine del 175
setto pellucido 167
settore 704
Seychelles 746
sezione 650
sezione del favo 100
sezione della crosta terrestre 42
sezione delle carte geografiche 732
sezione delle monografie 732
sezione di copertura 100
sezione di riconoscimento 768
sezione di rotaia 591
sezione di un acino 83
sezione di un bulbo 78
sezione di un cannocchiale 14
sezione di un cannone ad avancarica 753
sezione di un lampone 83
sezione di un microscopio elettronico 694
sezione di un telescopio 15
sezione di un tronco 300
sezione di un'arancia 82
sezione di una fragola 83
sezione di una mela 82
sezione di una nocciola 84
sezione di una noce 84
sezione di una palla 797, 867
sezione di una pesca 81
sezione di una pipa 390
sezione inferiore 24
sezione per i bambini 732
sezione principale 919
sezione rigida anteriore 569
sezione rigida posteriore 569
sezione sagittale 169, 170
sezione superiore 24
sezione trasversale 920
sezione trasversale di un aerografo 398
sezione trasversale di un molare 159
sezione trasversale di un osservatorio astronomico 17
sezione trasversale di un razzo spaziale (Ariane V) 24
sezione trasversale di un razzo spaziale (Saturn V) 25
sezione trasversale di un tronco 87
sezione trasversale di una centrale elettrica 664
sezione trasversale di una centrale idroelettrica 658
sezione trasversale di una diga a contrafforti 660
sezione trasversale di una diga a gravità 661
sezione trasversale di una diga a volta 661
sezione trasversale di una diga in terra 660
sezione trasversale di una navicella 677
sezione trasversale di una strada 538, 712
sezione variabile, ugello a 629
sfaccettatura inferiore 374
sfaccettatura superiore 374
sfaccettature del taglio a brillante 374
sfagno pungente 75
sfera 268, 470, 516, 705
sfera celeste 13
sfera di piombo 757
sfera di vetro 58
sfera terrestre 13
sfera, penna a 470
sfera, supporto della 558
sfiatatoio 136, 294, 320
sfiato 262
sfiato, tubo di 267
sfiato, valvola di 607
sfintere anale 164
sfioratore 657
sfioratore, paratoia dello 657
sfioratore, scivolo dello 657
sfioratore, soglia dello 657
sfondo piega 283
sforzo 686
sgabello 224, 277, 722, 842
sgabello alto 277
sgabello da bar 720
sgambatura elasticizzata 351
sgarzino 464
sgombro 219
sgorbia 401
sgorbia a U 421
sgorbia a V 421
sgorbia diritta 401
sgorbia incurvata 401
sgrossatura 401
shampoo 379
shekel, nuovo 728
shiitake 183
shinai 847
short track 882, 883
shorts 358
si 434
siamese 133
sicura 755
sicurezza 764
sicurezza, area di 843
sicurezza, cassetta di 731
sicurezza, cintura di 873
sicurezza, corridoio di 728
sicurezza, griglia di 730
sicurezza, grilletto di 331
sicurezza, impugnatura di 332
sicurezza, linea di 593
sicurezza, luce di 771
sicurezza, picchetti di 875
sicurezza, responsabile della 837
sicurezza, ruota di 595
sicurezza, servizio di 719
sicurezza, simboli di 774
sicurezza, spilla di 453
sicurezza, termostato di 293
sicurezza, valvola di 234, 266, 267
sicurezza, zona di 846
siepe 245, 322, 790
siepe con barriere 852
Sierra Leone 745
sifone 106, 262, 265, 269, 270
sigaretta 390
sigarette, cartine per 390
sigarette, pacchetto di 390
sigaro 390
silenziatore 649
silicio 682
siliqua, sezione di una 84
silo del minerale 648
silo orizzontale 182
silo verticale 182
silos 596
Siluriano 92
siluro 763
sima 404
simboli 914
simboli chimici 684
simboli comuni 725
simboli delle istruzioni sui tessuti 347
simboli di sicurezza 774
simboli diacritici 473
simboli meteorologici internazionali 56
simboli scientifici 702
simbolo 682, 920
simbolo della squadra 878
sinagoga 738
sinapsi 168
sinfisi pubica 169, 170
Singapore 747
singolo 839
sinistra 609, 616, 617, 740
sinsacro 116
sintesi additiva 690
sintesi dei colori 690
sintesi sottrattiva 690
sintetizzatore 450
sintetizzatore a fiato 451
sintoamplificatore 503
sintoamplificatore: dorso 497
sintoamplificatore: vista frontale 497
sintonia, comandi di 494
sintonia, manopola della 504
sintonia, modo della 498
sintonia, pulsante di preselezione della 498
sintonia, tasti di selezione della 497
sintonia, tasto di preselezione della 497
sintonizzatore 498, 504
sintonizzazione, manopola di 503
sipario 430, 431, 492
sipario tagliafuoco 430
Siria 746
siringa 776
siringa per decorazioni 232
siringhe usate, contenitore delle 771
sismografi 43
sismografo orizzontale 43
sismografo verticale 43
sismogramma 43
sistema a celle solari 673
sistema a doppia puleggia 686
sistema a rotazione 651
sistema di alimentazione 553
sistema di ancoraggio 595
sistema di autoguida 759
sistema di climatizzazione 68, 489
sistema di condizionamento dell'aria 775
sistema di controllo del lampeggiante 771
sistema di coordinate celesti 13
sistema di coordinate terrestri 35
sistema di cronometraggio elettrico 883
sistema di guida fine 17
sistema di lenti 692
sistema di lubrificazione 586
sistema di manipolazione a distanza 21
sistema di navigazione satellitare 613
sistema di registrazione audio 429
sistema di registrazione dei dati 694
sistema di regolazione dell'altezza 826
sistema di riavvolgimento della pellicola 476
sistema di riempimento e di svuotamento della chiusa 597
sistema di ritenuta degli air bag 556
sistema di segnalamento marittimo per mezzo di boe 616
sistema di sollevamento 635
sistema di sopravvivenza 20
sistema di svuotamento della chiusa 597
sistema di trasmissione 553
sistema di uscita d'emergenza 25
sistema idraulico 632
sistema internazionale di unità di misura 702
sistema nervoso 166
sistema nervoso centrale 167
sistema nervoso periferico 166
sistema solare 4
sistema stradale 538
sistema, tasti di 450
sistemi dell'automobile 553
sistemi dell'automobile: componenti principali 552
sistemi di ingranaggio 686
sistro 449
skateboard 894
skater 894
skeleton 885
skeletonista 885
skimmer 246
slalom gigante 889
slalom speciale 889
slalom supergigante 889
slancio 850
slancio in avanti 864
slider 896
slip 351, 367
slip da bagno 371
slitta 329, 885
slitta delle monete 920
slitta di fissaggio 692
slitta di rinculo 756
slitta per accessori 476
slittino 884
slittino doppio 884
slittino doppio femminile 885
slittino singolo 884
slittino singolo maschile 885
slot-machine 920
Slovacchia 744
slovacco 469
Slovenia 744
sloveno 469
smalto 159
smalto per unghie 377
smeraldo 375
smeraldo, taglio a 375
smerigliatrice eccentrica 308
smilodonte 93
sminuzzamento 71
smistamento dei materiali metallici 71
smistamento del cartone 71
smistamento del vetro 71
smistamento della carta 71
smistamento della plastica 71
smistamento manuale 71
smistamento ottico 71
smistamento primario 474
smistamento regionale, centro di 475
smistamento selettivo dei rifiuti 71
smistamento, centro di 474
smistamento, macchina di 475
smistamento-posizionamento-annullamento, macchina di 474
smog 69
smorzamento magnetico, dispositivo di 698
smorzata 821
smorzatore 443
smorzatore, barra dello 443
smorzatore, leva dello 443
smottamento 47
snack bar 427
snocciolatore 233
snodo 889
snodo per l'attacco degli attrezzi 640
snooker 863
snowboard 887
snowboard per freestyle 887
snowboard per sci alpino 887
snowboardista 887
sobborghi 39
società 708
sodio 682
soffiante 627, 670
soffietto 386, 388, 485
soffietto, borsa a 386
soffietto, mantice a 432
soffietto, portacarte a 386
soffietto, tasca applicata a 359, 360
soffitto 818, 819
soffitto a due spioventi 251
soffitto acustico 431
soffitto della cabina 417
soffitto, travetto del 252
soffitto, ventilatore da 261
softball 797
software di posta elettronica 524
soggiorno 250
soglia 247
soglia dello sfioratore 657
soglia di allarme, pulsante per la visualizzazione della 613
soglia di allarme, regolazione della 613
soglia glaciale 46
sogliola 221
soia, germogli di 191
soia, salsa di 200
soia, semi di 191
sol 434
solaio 257
solaio, collare del 257
solaio, travetto di 253
solarium 607, 609
solco 176
solco concentrico 500
solco di separazione 500
solco finale 500
solco iniziale 500
solco laterale 127
solco mediano 127, 176
solco terminale 176
Sole 4, 6, 7, 54
Sole, eclissi di 6
sole, occhiali da 385
Sole, struttura del 6
soleo 150
soletta 345, 351
soletta antiscivolo 369
solidi 705
solidificazione 680
solido 680, 681
solido amorfo 680
solitario 376
sollevacuticole 377
sollevamento pesi 850
sollevamento, braccio di 637, 638
sollevamento, catena di 632
sollevamento, cavo di 634
sollevamento, cilindro di 634, 766
sollevamento, corda di 285
sollevamento, fessura di 535
sollevamento, fune di 417
sollevamento, giunto di 640
sollevamento, sistema di 635
solstizio d'estate 54
solstizio d'inverno 54
soluzione multiuso 384
solventi, impianto di estrazione con 656
Somalia 745
somiere 445
somiere, tavola del 445
sommatoria 703
sommelier 720
sonagli 449
sonaglio 112
sonar 41
sonar a scafo 762
sonda dell'ecoscandaglio 613
sonda radiometrica 60
sonda spaziale 18, 53
sonda, innesto della 238
sonde spaziali, esempi di 19
soprabiti da donna 716
soprabiti da uomo 717
sopraccapo 854
sopracciglia, matita per 378
sopracciglia, pinzette per 377
soprafusione 680
soprascarpa 800
soprasponda 862
soprastruttura 538
soprattenda 282
sopravveste 337
sopravveste a grembiule 359
sopravvivenza, regolazione del sistema di 20
sopravvivenza, sistema di 20
sordina 442, 447
sordina, pedale della 442
sorella 785
sorgente 48
sorgente di corrente 687
sorgenti, luci delle 497
sorgenti, tasto di selezione delle 497
sorgo 85
sorgo: pannocchia 85
sormonto totale, tende con 283
soro 76
sorvegliante, banco del 732
sorveglianza, postazione di 394
sorveglianza, posto di 764
sorveglianza, telecamera di 395
sospensione 553, 594
sospensione posteriore 870
sospensione, braccio di 292
sospensione, lampada a 286
sospensione, molla di 697
sospensioni, gruppo delle 553
sosta ai box 873
sostanza bianca 167, 168
sostanza corticale 165
sostanza grigia 167, 168
sostanza midollare 165
sostegno 59, 277, 881
sostegno del bracciolo 276
sostegno del coperchio 465
sostegno dell'ala 609
sostegno della sbarra 591
sostegno per il collo 874
sostegno, base di 278
sostegno, profilo di 417
sotterraneo 407, 713
sottile 472
sottocanestro, zona di 809
sottocasco 872
sottofondo 252, 253, 254
sottofondo di cemento 254
sottofondo di cemento, parquet su 254
sottogola 765, 808, 854, 870, 885
sottogonna 337, 366
sottomano 511
sottomarino nucleare 763
sottopalco 430
sottopancia 853, 855, 856, 857
sottopassaggio 583
sottopunto, cucitura a 349
sottostruttura 651
sottosuolo 78
sottotitolo 471
sottotuta 872
sottoveste 366
sottoveste con reggiseno 366
sottovia 540
sottrazione 703
sovrapposizione automatica degli originali 512
sovrastruttura 615
sovratemperatura, dispositivo di sicurezza per 266
spacco centrale 348
spacco laterale 348
spada 849
spada da lato 751
spadice 81
spadista 848
spadone a due mani 751
spaghetti 206
spaghetti all'uovo 207
spaghetti asiatici 207
spaghetti di fagioli mungo 207
spaghetti di riso 207
spaghetti soba 207
spaghetti somen 207
spaghetti udon 207
spaghetti, molle per 233
spaghettini 206
Spagna 743
spagnolo 469
spago 424
spalla 124, 130, 146, 148, 156, 410, 440, 540, 822, 909
spalla a monte 660
spalla a valle 660
spallaccio 749, 906
spallamento 311
spalliera 322
spalliera ad arco 322
spallina 352, 367, 770
spallina, manica con 360
spalto 409
spandiconcime 324
spandiletame 641
spargitore di paglia 643
sparo, funicella di 756

INDICE DELLE VOCI ITALIANE

spartitraffico 539, 712
sparviero 315
spatola 233, 397, 421, 888, 892
spatola metallica 557
spatolata 79
spaziatore 667
spaziatura 472
spaziatura, espansa 472
spaziatura, intera 472
spaziatura, normale 472
spaziatura, piccola 472
spaziatura, ridotta 472
spazio 434, 514, 865
spazio epidurale 168
spazio per la dilatazione 590
spazio unificatore 514
spazzaneve a turbina 573
spazzata d'anca 844
spazzatrice 573
spazzola 233, 289, 295, 345, 384, 688
spazzola a dorso piatto 380
spazzola a pennello 289
spazzola antistatica 380
spazzola da bagno 379
spazzola da neve con raschietto 558
spazzola del polline 98
spazzola di gomma 557
spazzola metallica 449
spazzola per la schiena 379
spazzola per pavimenti 289
spazzola per tappeti e pavimenti 289
spazzola ragno 380
spazzola rotante centrale 573
spazzola rotante laterale 573
spazzola rotonda 380
spazzole 688
spazzole per capelli 380
spazzolino da denti 384
spazzolino da denti elettrico 384
spazzolino di pulizia 383
spazzolino di tessitura 456
spazzolino per mascara 378
spazzolino, gambo a innesto dello 384
spazzolino, levetta dello 456
speaker 828
specchietto 876
specchietto anteriore di accostamento 568
specchietto di cortesia 556
specchietto per il punto cieco 568, 569
specchietto retrovisore 556, 569, 574, 576, 577
specchietto retrovisore esterno 550, 568, 570
specchietto retrovisore esterno, regolazione dello 554
specchio 264, 389, 535, 693, 724
specchio a riflessione parziale 692
specchio a riflessione totale 692
specchio di lettura 20
specchio di puntamento 907
specchio doppio girevole 381
specchio grande 612
specchio laterale 381
specchio luminoso 381
specchio parabolico 674
specchio piano 17
specchio piccolo 612
specchio primario 17
specchio primario concavo 15
specchio riflettore principale 477
specchio secondario 15, 17, 477
specialità 889
specialità gastronomiche 180
spedizione merci 621
spegnifiamma 755
spelafili 317
spelafili, pinza 317
spelucchino 229
spencer 358
sperlano 219
spermateca 104
spermatozoo 169
sperone 45, 98, 130, 861
sperone tarsale 98
spesa, borsa della 388
spessore 312, 472
spessore, misura dello 700
spettro elettromagnetico 690
spettrometro 694
spettrometro agli ultravioletti 60
spettroradiometro 60
spezie 198
spezie cajun, condimento alle 199
spezie marinate 199
spezzatino 214, 215
spezzatura, linea di 362
spia 381
spia cinture di sicurezza non allacciate 557
spia dei proiettori abbaglianti 557
spia dell'indicatore di direzione 557, 576
spia della batteria 557
spia della cartuccia 519
spia della coda della pellicola 476
spia della posizione di folle 576
spia della pressione dell'olio 557, 576
spia della riserva di carburante 557
spia delle luci abbaglianti 576
spia di accensione 731
spia di alimentazione 518, 519
spia di alimentazione della carta 519
spia di allarme 527
spia di messa in carica 527
spia di rilevamento della carta 731
spia luminosa 238, 239, 240, 241, 288, 290, 294, 465, 767
spia luminosa dell'autoscatto 476
spia luminosa di accensione/spegnimento 506
spia luminosa di alimentazione 508
spia luminosa di carica 383
spia luminosa di messa in onda 488
spia porte aperte 557
spiaggia 51
spicchio 82
spicole 6
spider 549
spie 557
spie della modalità audio 497
spie di controllo 519, 520
spie luminose 494, 515
spiga 81, 204
spigolo 404
spigone 602
spilla 376
spilla di sicurezza 453
spille 376
spillo 454
spillo fermacravatta 376
spillone 376, 380
spina 95, 306
spina americana, presa per 274
spina americana 274
spina della scapola 153
spina di alimentazione 527
spina europea 274
spina nasale anteriore 158
spina neurale 109
spinacio 187
spingicuticole 377
spingistantuffo 776
spinnaker, alzare lo 833
spinnaker, ammainare lo 833
spinotto 274, 275, 502, 613
spinotto della cuffia 504
spinotto di connessione 689
spinotto di messa a terra 274
spinta 630
spinta, fase di 892
spinta, maniglia di 416
spinta, telaio di 636
spinterogeno 552, 566
spirale 302, 484
spirale bimetallica 695
spirale, braccio della 9
spirulina 183
splenio 151
spogliatoio 509, 734, 764, 781
spogliatoio dei minatori 649
spogliatoio del personale 768, 781
spoiler 570, 574, 624
spola 461
spoletta di prossimità 759
spoletta, corpo della 757
spolverino 232
sponda 864
sponda frontale 571
sponda inferiore 862
sponda protettiva 281
sponda superiore 862
spongocele 95
spore 76
sporgenza 255
sport 788
sport a motore 872
sport acquatici 827
sport aerei 896
sport alpini 900
sport con la palla 794
sport di combattimento 842
sport di forza 850
sport di precisione 859
sport equestri 852
sport equestri, campo per 788
sport invernali 877
sport nautici 827
sport su rotelle 894
sport, palazzetto dello 788
sporta 388
sportello 238, 290, 699, 731
sportello automatico 730, 731
sportello bancomat 715, 730
sportello commerciale 731
sportello del serbatoio 551
sportello di accesso 584
sportello di carico 256
sportello notturno 731
spostamento 690
spray al peperoncino 770
spremiaglio 230
spremiagrumi 230
spremiagrumi elettrico 237
spremitura, cono di 237
sprinter, linea degli 871
sprone 349
spruzzatore 329
spruzzatore d'acqua 655
spruzzatori 665
spruzzetta 685
spruzzo di vernice 398
spruzzo, vite di regolazione dello 320
spugna 95
spugna abrasiva 295
spugna calcarea 95
spugna naturale 379
spugna sintetica 378
spugna vegetale 379
spugna, anatomia di una 95
spugnetta 531
spugnetta, applicatore a 378
spugnola 183
spumante, coppa da 225
spurgo, pompa di 263
Squadra 10
squadra 313
squadra falsa 313, 701
squadra, handicap della 858
squadra, nome della 858
squadra, simbolo della 878
squalo, morfologia di uno 108
squama 112, 113, 117
squama ventrale 112
squash 819
Sri Lanka 747
stabilimento industriale 708
stabilizzatore 625, 634, 638, 760, 766, 859, 876, 896, 897
stabilizzatore orizzontale 898
stabilizzatore verticale 898
stabilizzazione, barra di 633
staccionata 244
stacco 891
stacco, tavola di 891
stadera 698
stadi di maturazione 86
stadio 709, 788, 790
stadio a propellente solido 24
stadio criogenico principale 24
stadio di baseball 788
stadio per il nuoto 788
stadio superiore a propellente di riserva 24
staff medico 844
staffa 174, 350, 358, 750, 853, 855, 892
staffa di blocco finale 284
staffa di lancio 877
staffile 855
staggio 321, 825
staggio inferiore 824
staggio superiore 824
stagioni 917
stagioni dell'anno 54
stagno 682, 866
stalagmite 47
stalattite 47
stalla 182
stame 80, 82
stampa 127, 420, 515
stampa in cavo 420
stampa in rilievo 420
stampa in rilievo, metodo di 421
stampa, torchio di 421
stampante 523, 529
stampante a getto di inchiostro 519
stampante ad aghi 520
stampante laser 519
stampella canadese 782
stampini per dolci 232
stampo per charlotte 232
stampo per crostata 232
stampo per pane 239
stand espositivo 719
stanga 323, 857
stanghetta 385, 434, 854
stanti, carro pianale con 588
stantuffo 776
stanza da bagno 250, 251, 264, 724
stanza degli insegnanti 735
stanza degli studenti 735
stanza dei giurati 728
stanza dei microfilm 732
stanza del personale 779
stanza del personale viaggiante 584
stanza del triage 779
stanza della fotocopiatrice 509
stanza della gestione della posta 509
stanza della segreteria dell'amministratore delegato 509
stanza della segreteria di direzione 509
stanza di coordinamento 769
stanza di degenza 780
stanza di degenza postoperatoria 780
stanza di isolamento 778
stanza di osservazione 778, 781
stanza di sterilizzazione 780
stanza per esame psichiatrico 778
stanza per gli interrogatori 768
stanza per l'anestesia 780
stanza per l'esame audiometrico 781
stanza per la preparazione chirurgica 780
stanza per le terapie 781
stanza per le visite mediche 781
stanza per osservazione psichiatrica 778
stanza per stilare i rapporti 768
stanza per visite ginecologiche 779
stanze del supporto informatico 509
stanze della mostra permanente 395
stanze della mostra temporanea 395
stanze principali 250
stanzino del portiere 724
stanzino della guardia giurata 731
Stardust 19
start, meccanico dello 873
starter 830, 838
starter, pistola dello 790
stati della materia 680
Stati Uniti d'America 742
station wagon 549
stativo 685
stato 37
stato presente del tempo 55
statore 249, 659
statua 737
statua, posizione della 403
stazione degli autobus 710
stazione dei viaggiatori 582, 583, 596
stazione della metropolitana 592, 710
stazione di caricamento 650
stazione di pattugliamento 886
stazione di polizia 711, 768
stazione di pompaggio 654
stazione di pompaggio intermedia 654
stazione di pompaggio principale 654
stazione di pronto soccorso 543
stazione di rifornimento 725
stazione di servizio 548, 711
stazione di smistamento 589
stazione di superficie 54
stazione di trasformazione 657, 658, 664
stazione ferroviaria 39, 583, 708, 710
stazione locale 486
stazione meteorologica 58
stazione ripetitrice 486
stazione ripetitrice a microonde 524
stazione sciistica 886
stazione spaziale internazionale 21
stazione terminale 654
stazione terrestre per le telecomunicazioni 525
stazione, cerchio di 55
stazione, ingresso della 592
stazione, modello di 55
stazione, nome della 592
stazioni, manopola di ricerca delle 498
stealth 629
stecca 367, 390, 391, 834, 836, 858, 863, 897
stecca scorrevole 445
stecche 464, 777
stecche per modellare 464
stella 8, 741
stella cadente 53
stella della sequenza principale 8
stella di David 738
stella di neutroni 8
stella marina, anatomia di una 95
stella marina, morfologia di una 95
Stella Polare 13
stelle di massa maggiore 8
stelle di massa minore 8
stelo 75, 78, 261, 302, 436
stelo, lampada a 286
stemma 797
stepper 851
steppico 61
stereo/mono, selettore 504
sterilizzazione, sala di 781
sterilizzazione, stanza di 780
sterlina 728
sterno 111, 116, 121, 122, 126, 131, 141, 142, 152
sterno, carena dello 116
sternocleidomastoideo 150
sterzo, gruppo dello 553
stigma 80, 84, 96, 97
stile libero o crawl 832
stiletto 751
stili architettonici 404
stili di nuoto 832
stilo 80, 81, 82, 83, 84, 390, 470, 517, 527
stilo di canna 470
stilo di piombo 470
stilo metallico romano 470
stilobate 403, 404
stilton 211
stimolatore gengivale 384
stinco 215
stipite 247, 256
stipola 79
stirare a bassa temperatura 347
stirare a media temperatura 347
stirare ad alta temperatura 347
stiratura 347
stiva per i containers 605
stivale 343, 444, 855, 874, 875
stivale alla moschettiera 343
stivale di gomma 765
stivaletto 840, 853, 857, 858
stivaloni impermeabili 911
stoccaggio temporaneo, serbatoio di 654
stoccaggio, serbatoi di 654
stoccaggio, serbatoio di 656
stola 336
stomaco 95, 103, 104, 105, 106, 109, 110, 112, 113, 125, 161, 164
stomaco cardiaco 107
stomaco pilorico 107
stop 130
stoppaccio 753
stopper 803
storione 218
stornello 118
strada 39, 543, 708, 713
strada a senso unico 544, 546
strada coperta 409
strada deformata 545, 547
strada di accesso 618
strada di servizio 618
strada ferrata 590, 591
strada panoramica 39
strada sdrucciolevole 545, 547
strada secondaria 39
strada, numero di 39
strada, sezione trasversale di una 538
stradina 866
stralli 541
stralli a ventaglio 541
stralli ad arpa 541
stralli, ancoraggio degli 541
strallo 598, 602, 676
strallo di prua 834
strambata 833
strappo 850
strappo, tenda a 283
strati di rifiuti 69
strato 56, 62, 300
strato basale 172
strato basaltico 42
strato corneo 172
strato di base 538
strato di ceneri 44
strato di collegamento 538
strato di lava 44
strato di ozono 53
strato di sabbia a monte 660
strato di sabbia drenante 660
strato di tetto 650
strato drenante 660
strato granitico 42
strato granulare 172
strato impermeabile 254
strato inferiore confinante 646
strato lucido 172
strato protettivo 20
strato riflettente in alluminio 501
strato spinoso 172
strato sterile 647
strato superficiale del suolo 78
strato superiore confinante 646
stratocumulo 56, 62
stratopausa 53
stratosfera 53
strega 863
stregghia per le antenne 98
stretto 38
Stretto di Bass 29
Stretto di Bering 30
Stretto di Cook 29
Stretto di Gibilterra 32
Stretto di Torres 29
strettoia simmetrica 544, 547
stringa 342, 797, 843, 881
stringhe 893
striscia antiabrasiva 560, 561
striscia catarifrangente 765
striscia di gioco 799
striscia di sfregamento 318, 391
striscia di sicurezza 582
striscia esplorata 40
stroboscopio 611
strofinaccio da cucina 295
stromatolite 92
strombatura 411
stronzio 682
strozzascotte 835
strozzatura 439, 695
strumentazione scientifica 23
strumentazione, alloggiamento della 24
strumentazione, piattaforma di 60
strumenti a corde 439
strumenti a fiato 446
strumenti a percussione 437, 448
strumenti a tastiera 442
strumenti a tastiera, esempi di 443
Strumenti dello Scultore 10
strumenti di laboratorio 685
strumenti di misura 695
strumenti di misurazione e tracciamento 313
strumenti di misurazione meteorologica 58
strumenti di volo 899
strumenti elettronici 450
strumenti musicali tradizionali 432
strumenti per il pronto soccorso 775
strumenti per la navigazione 612
strumenti scientifici 17
strumenti scrittori 470

1106

ASTRONOMIA > 2-25; **TERRA** > 26-71; **REGNO VEGETALE** >72-89; **REGNO ANIMALE** > 90-143; **ESSERE UMANO** > 144-177; **GENERI ALIMENTARI E CUCINA** > 178-241; **CASA** > 242-295; **FAI DA TE E GIARDINAGGIO** > 296-333; **ABBIGLIAMENTO** > 334-371; **ACCESSORI E ARTICOLI PERSONALI** > 372-391; **ARTE E ARCHITETTURA** > 392-465; **COMUNICAZIONI E BUROTICA** > 466-535; **TRASPORTI E VEICOLI** > 536-643; **ENERGIA** > 644-677; **SCIENZA** > 678-705; **SOCIETÀ** > 706-785; **SPORT E GIOCHI** > 786-920

struttura 249, 252
struttura a K 663
struttura del midollo spinale 167
struttura del Sole 6
struttura del tessuto 455
struttura dell'orecchio 174
struttura della biosfera 66
struttura della Terra 42
struttura di lancio doppia 24
struttura di sostegno 16, 40
struttura di un albero 87
struttura di un fiore 80
struttura di un fungo 76
struttura di un lichene 74
struttura di un missile 759
struttura di un muschio 75
struttura di un osso lungo 154
struttura di un'alga 75
struttura di una casa 250
struttura di una felce 76
struttura di una foglia 79
struttura di una pianta 77
struttura esterna 291, 292
struttura in alluminio 893
struttura lignea, parquet su 254
struttura metallica 582
struttura protettiva 873
struttura tubolare 615
strutture ausiliarie, sala delle 490
strutture per i tuffi 828
struzzo 119
struzzo, uovo di 213
studente 734
studenti, armadietti degli 735
studenti, stanza degli 735
studio 251, 488, 490
studio televisivo 490, 492
stufa a combustione lenta 256
stufa a gas 903
stufa radiante 260
stufe, olio combustibile per 656
sturalavandini 314
sub 841
sub woofer 493
sub, coltello da 841
subartico 61
subbio del tessuto 460
subbio dell'ordito 460
subbio superiore 460
subduzione 43
sublimazione 680
subtropicale mediterraneo 61
subtropicale umido 61
suburbio 709
Sud 37
sud 616, 917
Sud Sud-Est 37
Sud Sud-Ovest 37
Sud-Est 37
sud-est 616
Sud-Ovest 37
sud-ovest 616
Sudafricana, Repubblica 746
Sudan 745
sufflè, tegamino per 232
sughero 892
sulky 857
sumac 199
sumi, penna 397
sumo 847
sumotori 847
sunnismo 736
suocera 784
suoceri 784
suocero 784
suola 127, 342, 371, 591, 840, 868, 881, 888, 889
suolo 70, 661
suolo, fertilizzazione del 69
suolo, inquinamento del 69
suolo, movimento orizzontale del 43
suolo, movimento verticale del 43
suolo, profilo del 78
suolo, strato superficiale del 78
suoneria, regolatore della 506
suono, ingegnere del 429
suono, produzione del 445
supercross, circuito di 875
superfici 704
superfici di gioco 822
superficie antiscivolo 894
superficie assorbente 675
superficie centrale di lotta 843
superficie dell'acqua 828
superficie della cute 172
superficie di affissione 535
superficie di gioco 815
superficie di rotolamento 590
superficie dura (cemento) 822
superficie freatica 47
superficie inchiostrata 420
superficie inumidita 420
superficie plantare dello zoccolo 127
superficie riflettente 674
superficie sintetica 822
superficie terrestre, assorbimento attaverso la 68
superficie trasparente in resina 501
superficie verticale 894
superficie, stazione di 54
supergigante 8
supermercato 180, 711, 715
supernova 8
superstrada 539
supplemento a colori 471
supplemento letterario 471
supporti 400
supporti per camminare 782
supporto 15, 274, 284, 285, 381, 445, 448
supporto a tre braccia 464
supporto anteriore retrattile 567
supporto del braccio 500
supporto del cordone 288
supporto del disco abrasivo 308
supporto del filamento 274
supporto del rullo 320
supporto del tabellone 811
supporto dell'albero 307
supporto della lastra 58
supporto della rete 815
supporto della sfera 58, 558
supporto della tavola forata 445
supporto elastico 502, 504, 772
supporto per il braccio 782
supporto per il tallone 783
supporto per la bombola di ossigeno portatile 775
supporto per la coda 623
supporto per le manichette 764
supporto retrattile 571
supporto sottoascellare 782
supporto stabilizzatore 567
supporto, base di 613
supporto, piastra di 275
supporto, telaio di 639
surf 840
surf, tavola da 840
surfista 840
surgelati 181
surgelati, magazzino dei 181
Suriname 742
surriscaldamento globale 68
surriscaldatore 668
sutura 84, 105
sutura coronale 158
sutura coronaria 158
sutura di rinforzo 899
sutura lambdoidea 158
sutura squamosa 158
svedese 469
sverniciatura, pistola per 320
svettatoio 330
Svezia 744
sviluppatrice 484
sviluppo, bagni di 485
sviluppo, bagno di 485
svincolo 709
Svizzera 744
swahili 468
Swaziland 746

T

T centrale 858
tabaccheria 714
tabacco 390
tabacco, borsa del 390
tabasco, salsa 200
tabella dei colori 398
tabella dei risultati 828
tabellone 811
tabellone d'affissione delle mostre 394
tabellone degli arrivi e delle partenze 621
tabellone degli handicap 858
tabellone degli orari 582
tabellone dei salti 793
tabellone del totalizzatore 856
tabellone della classifica generale 824
tabellone della prova in corso 825
tabellone segnapunti 789, 790, 822, 825, 831, 839, 844, 846, 918
tabellone, supporto del 811
tabernacolo 737
tablino 406
tabloid 471
tabulazione a destra 514
tabulazione a sinistra 514
tacca 455, 698, 791
tacca di mira 754, 755, 757, 861, 893, 912
tacchetti intercambiabili 802
tacchetto 371, 798
tacchino 120, 213
tacco 342, 622, 868, 881, 909
tachimetro 557, 576, 851
tafano 101
tagalog 469
Tagikistan 746
tagli di agnello 215
tagli di maiale 215
tagli di manzo 214
tagli di pietre preziose 375
tagli di vitello 214
taglia fissa 651
taglia mobile 651
tagliabasette 383
tagliabiscotti 232
tagliabordi 326, 332
tagliacarte 531
tagliacuticole 377
tagliafili 317
tagliafilo 453
tagliafuoco 252
tagliasiepi 331
tagliasiepi, forbici 330
tagliasigari 390
tagliatelle verdi 206
tagliatubi 314
tagliente 240, 306, 636, 637, 638, 648
tagliere 229
taglierina 424, 484, 535
taglio 302
taglio a baguette 375
taglio a brillante 375
taglio a briolette 375
taglio a cabochon 375
taglio a forbice 375
taglio a gradini 375
taglio a marquise 375
taglio a pera 375
taglio a rosetta 375
taglio a smeraldo 375
taglio a tavola 375
taglio addizionale 434
taglio anteriore 426
taglio francese 375
taglio inferiore 426
taglio ottagonale 375
taglio ovale 375
taglio superiore 426
taglio, filo da 464
taglio, lama di 424
taglio, linea di 455
taglio, piastra di 333
taglio, pietra da 298
tagliola 913
taglione 660, 661
tahini 200
tahitiano 469
tailandese 468
Tailandia 747
tailback 807
tailleur 355
tajina 234
tallio 682
tallo 74, 75
tallonatore 804
tallone 127, 147, 149, 229, 303, 309, 370, 439, 440, 456, 560, 641, 797, 880
tallone d'appoggio 236
tallone di appoggio 288
talloniera 840, 889, 892
Talmud 736
talpa 121
talpa, morfologia di una 121
talpa, scheletro di una 121
tamarillo 196
tamarindo , pasta di 200
tamarino 139
tamburello 449
tamburo 230, 285, 293, 559, 612, 697, 700, 754
tamburo parlante 433
tamburo raccoglitore 642
tamburo rotante 43
tamburo tenore 448
tamburo, pistola a 754
tamia 123
tampone 421, 422, 531
tandem 581
Tanganica, Lago 34
tangenziale 39, 709
tantalio 683
Tanzania 745
tappeti e pavimenti, spazzola per 289
tappetino 558
tappetino del mouse 516
tappetino di gomma 500
tappetino in gomma 864
tappeto 254, 842, 844
tappeto di sicurezza 893
tappeto, presidente di 843
tappezzeria, bocchetta per 289
tappi per le orecchie 772, 872
tappo 236, 379, 484, 561, 906
tappo a vite 223
tappo del fondello 757
tappo del serbatoio 570, 576
tappo di isolamento 689
tappo di ispezione 270
tappo di scarico 262
tappo di scarico dell'olio 566
tappo femmina 269
tappo femmina a vite 269
tappo maschio a testa quadra 269
tappo, fusibile a 272
tarchia, vela a 601
tare 847
targhetta del costruttore 306
targhetta delle avvertenze 306
tarlatana 422
tarlo 101
taro 184
tarso 96, 98, 111, 115, 122, 126, 131, 138, 141, 142, 155, 156
tarso-metatarso 116
tartaruga 113
tartaruga, anatomia di una 113
tartaruga, morfologia di una 113
tartufo 183
tartufo di mare 217
tasca 232, 313, 386, 869
tasca anteriore 350
tasca applicata 348, 353, 360, 368
tasca applicata a soffietto 359, 360
tasca applicata con aletta 349, 360
tasca della stecca 836
tasca di Douglas 170
tasca di inforcamento 632
tasca esterna 386, 388
tasca finta 355
tasca frontale 387
tasca inserita nella cucitura 355, 360
tasca interna 389
tasca interna con aletta 348, 352, 353, 355, 360
tasca nascosta 386
tasca per la stecca 834
tasca portaoggetti 554
tasca posteriore 350
tasca profilata 354, 360
tasca profilata con aletta 348, 352
tasca sagomata 360
tasca tagliata in verticale 355
tasca verticale 337
tasca vescicouterina 170
tasche, esempi di 360
taschino 352
taschino con aletta 348
taschino tagliato con aletta 348
taschino, fazzoletto da 348
Tasmania 29
Tasmania, Mare di 29
tassello 278
tasso 134
tasti degli effetti speciali 496
tasti del cursore 515
tasti del lettore di compact disc 504
tasti del riproduttore a cassette 504
tasti di chiamata automatica 506
tasti di comando 507, 508
tasti di identificazione del conto 731
tasti di impostazione dei punti 456
tasti di posizionamento del cursore 529
tasti di programmazione 495
tasti di regolazione del volume 495
tasti di regolazione dell'immagine 496
tasti di ricerca del brano 501
tasti di ricerca delle emittenti 495
tasti di ricerca emittenti 495
tasti di ricerca rapida 501
tasti di ripetizione 501
tasti di selezione dei canali 495
tasti di selezione della sintonia 497
tasti di selezione delle casse acustiche 497
tasti di sistema 450
tasti di variazione 456
tasti funzione 507, 508, 514, 699, 730, 731
tasti funzione programmabili 731
tasti Internet 514
tasti per l'editing del suono 450
tastiera 432, 439, 441, 442, 450, 506, 507, 514, 526, 865
tastiera alfanumerica 507, 514, 548, 730, 731
tastiera degli acuti 432
tastiera numerica 507, 508
tastiera, strumenti a 442
tastierina per il codice di identificazione personale (PIN) 731
tastierino alfabetico 530
tastierino alfanumerico 506
tastierino numerico 515, 530, 699
tasto 432, 442, 443, 445, 446
tasto Alt 514
tasto Avvio 514
tasto backspace 515
tasto colore 512
tasto Control 514
tasto del blocco delle maiuscole 528
tasto del menu 505
tasto del paragrafo rientrato 528
tasto dell'auto-reverse 504
tasto delle maiuscole 514, 528
tasto di addizione 529
tasto di alimentazione della carta 529
tasto di arresto 495, 499, 508, 512
tasto di arresto e di scorrimento 515
tasto di arresto/cancellazione 501
tasto di ascolto diretto 508
tasto di avanzamento della carta 731
tasto di avanzamento rapido 495, 499, 504, 508
tasto di avvio 508, 512
tasto di avvio registrazione 496
tasto di azzeramento 495, 512, 529
tasto di azzeramento del contatore 499
tasto di azzeramento ultimo dato 529
tasto di blocco 505
tasto di blocco delle maiuscole 514
tasto di blocco numerico 515
tasto di cambio segno 529
tasto di cancellazione 508, 515
tasto di cancellazione della memoria 479, 529
tasto di centratura 528
tasto di chiamata 505, 506
tasto di chiamata successiva 507
tasto di conferma 731
tasto di conferma della tabulazione 528
tasto di controllo 505
tasto di correzione 456
tasto di correzione del carattere 528
tasto di correzione della parola 528
tasto di correzione ortografica 528
tasto di direzione 261
tasto di divisione 529
tasto di doppio zero 529
tasto di espulsione 495, 499, 501
tasto di fine chiamata 506
tasto di impostazione degli arresti di tabulazione 528
tasto di lettura 505
tasto di luminosità 505
tasto di memoria 479
tasto di memorizzazione 497, 498, 501, 506
tasto di memorizzazione del testo 528
tasto di moltiplicazione 529
tasto di movimento di mezza interlinea 528
tasto di pagina giù 515
tasto di pagina precedente 527
tasto di pagina su 515
tasto di pagina successiva 527
tasto di pausa 499
tasto di pausa/fermo immagine 495
tasto di percentuale 529
tasto di più-uguale 529
tasto di posizione 440, 441
tasto di preselezione della sintonia 497
tasto di punto decimale 529
tasto di radice quadrata 529
tasto di registrazione 495, 499
tasto di registrazione del messaggio 508
tasto di registrazione e di visualizzazione dell'ora 496
tasto di registrazione e di visualizzazione della data 496
tasto di registro 444, 445
tasto di reset 508
tasto di riascolto dei messaggi 508
tasto di riavvolgimento 495, 499, 504, 508
tasto di ricerca della fine 496
tasto di richiamo della memoria 479, 529
tasto di riposizionamento 528
tasto di ripristino 519
tasto di riproduzione 495, 499, 504
tasto di riproduzione/pausa 501
tasto di ritorno del carrello 528
tasto di scorrimento 505
tasto di selezione 261, 505, 506
tasto di selezione del registratore 497
tasto di selezione della banda 497
tasto di selezione della lingua del display 507
tasto di selezione della modalità FM 497
tasto di selezione delle sorgenti 497
tasto di selezione dello stato di stampa 528
tasto di somma in memoria 529
tasto di sottrazione 529
tasto di sottrazione in memoria 529
tasto di subtotale/non-addizione 529
tasto di tabulazione 514
tasto di tabulazione decimale 528
tasto di uguale 529
tasto di visualizzazione degli indicatori 496
tasto di visualizzazione dei titoli 496
tasto email 514
tasto Esc 514
tasto Fine 515
tasto Home 515
tasto Ins 515
tasto Invio 515
tasto liberamargine 528
tasto marginatore 528
tasto multifunzionale 529
tasto numerico 529
tasto pausa 515
tasto per il modo di esposizione 476
tasto per l'avanzamento della pellicola 476
tasto per la sensibilità della pellicola 476, 479
tasto per le esposizioni multiple 476
tasto regolatore di contrasto 512
tasto selezionatore di comandi 528
tasto stampa 515
tasto tabulatore 528
tasto TV/video 495
tatami 846
tavola 307, 374, 424, 445, 836, 915, 917
tavola armonica 432, 433, 439, 440, 442
tavola da surf 840

INDICE DELLE VOCI ITALIANE

tavola del somiere 445
tavola di arresto 864
tavola di lavoro 452
tavola di rotazione 651
tavola di stacco 891
tavola esterna 915
tavola forata 445
tavola forata, supporto della 445
tavola inferiore 445
tavola interna 915
tavola periodica degli elementi 682
tavola superiore 445
tavola, coltello da 228
tavola, cucchiaio da 228
tavola, forchetta da 228
tavola, morsetto di bloccaggio della 307
tavola, taglio a 375
tavola, vasellame da 226
tavole 852
tavoletta 254
tavoletta grafica 517
tavoletta portablocco 533
tavoli, esempi di 278
tavolini sovrapponibili 278
tavolino da letto 780
tavolino traslatore 693
tavolino traslatore, comando del 693
tavolo 278, 723, 815, 862
tavolo a cancello 278
tavolo allungabile 278
tavolo da disegno 399
tavolo da roulette 919
tavolo di servizio 584, 720
tavolo operatorio 780
tavolo per i piatti caldi 721
tavolo per i piatti puliti 721
tavolo per i piatti sporchi 721
tavolo portacomputer 511
tavolo portastampante 511
tavolo, lampada da 286
tavolozza con vaschette 398
tavolozza con vasetto 398
taxi 725
tazza 905
tazza alta da caffè 226
tazza da tè 226
tazza graduata 231
tazza per sapone da barba 383
tazzina da caffè 226
tè 208
tè nero 208
tè oolong 208
tè verde 208
tè, bustina di 208
tè, cucchiaino da 228
tè, filtro per il 233
tè, tazza da 226
teatro 430, 710, 711
teatro greco 402
teatro, binocolo da 385
tecnezio 683
tecnica a colombino 465
tecnica a nastro 465
tecnica di salto 891
tecniche 812
tecnico audio 489, 490
tecnico delle luci 429
tecnico di commutazione video 489, 490
tecnico di controllo delle immagini 489
tecnico luci 490
tecnico video 490
tecnigrafo 399
tedesco 469
tee 867
tegame 235, 905
tegame per fonduta 234
tegame per uova in camicia 235
tegamino per chiocciole 233
tegamino per sufflè 232
teglia con fondo staccabile 232
teglia da forno 232
teglia per torta 232
teglie da forno 234
tegola 299, 403, 406, 412
tegole bonus 917
tegole di testa 917
tegumento del seme 81
tegumento seminale 85
teiera 226
tela 400, 463, 676
tela radiale 561
telaietto per diapositive 483
telaio 100, 249, 276, 277, 278, 280, 303, 312, 327, 386, 389, 423, 433, 449, 459, 483, 575, 632, 633, 638, 639, 641, 642, 672, 673, 676, 688, 782, 816, 822, 823, 824, 870, 893, 895
telaio a ordito alto 461
telaio a ordito basso 460
telaio circolare 459
telaio dei rulli dei cingoli 636
telaio del bruciatore 903
telaio del carrello 586
telaio di cucitura 424
telaio di spinta 636
telaio di supporto 639
telaio interno della portiera 554
telaio metallico 442
telaio per tenda esterna 567
telaio regolabile 303
telaio rigido, borsa a 388
telaio verticale 461
telaio, giunzione a linguetta del 249
telaio, giunzione scanalata del 249
telaio, montante del 278
telaio, traverso superiore del 249
telecamera 18, 428, 490, 492, 775, 873
telecamera a colori 20
telecamera di sorveglianza 395
telecamera, piedistallo della 492
telecamere, area di controllo delle 489
telecamere, unità di controllo delle 489
telecomando 483, 493, 495
telecomando, sensore del 494, 501
telecomunicazione, antenna di 762
telecomunicazioni via satellite 487
telecomunicazioni, satelliti per 486
telefax 508
telefoni, esempi di 507
telefono 491, 724, 725
telefono a tastiera 507
telefono cellulare 506
telefono pubblico 427, 715, 720, 723, 779
telefono senza fili 507
teleobiettivo 478
teleprompter 492
telerilevamento 40
telerilevamento mediante satellite 41
Telescopio 10
telescopio 15, 17, 859
telescopio spaziale Hubble 17, 53
telescopio, basamento del 17
telescopio, sezione di un 15
telesensore 518
teletta 455
televisione 489, 724, 734
televisore 494
televisore a grande schermo 493
teli, gonna a 357
tellurio 682
telo di spugna con cappuccio 368
telo esterno 902, 903
telone proteggiauto 558
telson 107
temperamatite 534
temperatura 261
temperatura ambiente 261
temperatura Celsius, unità di misura della 702
temperatura corporea, regolazione della 20
temperatura del liquido di raffreddamento, indicatore della 557
temperatura dell'aria 55
temperatura desiderata 261
temperatura di rugiada 55
temperatura termodinamica, unità di misura della 702
temperatura, indicatore di 381
temperatura, manopola di regolazione della 465
temperatura, misura della 695
temperatura, misurazione della 59
temperatura, regolatore della 259
temperatura, regolazione della 261, 267
temperatura, selettore della 238
temperatura, sensore di 18
temperature, scala delle 53
temperino multiuso 905
tempesta di sabbia o di polvere 57
tempesta tropicale 57
tempi realizzati 831
tempia 146
tempiale 461
tempio azteco 412
tempio di Huitzilopochtli 412
tempio di Tlaloc 412
tempio greco 403
tempio greco, pianta del 403
tempo 789
tempo dei Romani, armi al 748
tempo di due metà 434
tempo di quattro quarti 434
tempo di tre quarti 434
tempo libero all'aria aperta 902
tempo, carta del 54, 55
tempo, controllo del 451
tempo, indicazioni di 434
tempo, misura del 696
tempo, stato presente del 55
tempo, unità di misura del 702
temporale 57
temporale forte 57
temporizzatore 465, 484
temporizzatore dell'ingranditore 485
tenaglia 409
tenda 282, 611
tenda a cupola 903
tenda a due posti 902
tenda a igloo 903
tenda a pacchetto 285
tenda a palloncino 283
tenda a rullo 285
tenda a strappo 283
tenda a un posto 903
tenda a vetro 283
tenda avvolgibile 285
tenda canadese 903
tenda coprifinestra 902
tenda da campo 902
tenda da cucina 902
tenda di tipo familiare 902
tenda interna 902, 903
tenda per finestra 282
tenda trasparente 282
tenda, bastoni da 284
tende avvolgibili 285
tende con sormonto totale 283
tende, esempi di 283, 902
tendenza barometrica 55
tendicollo 349
tendina a mezzovetro 282
tendina arricciata 282
tendina divisoria 780
tendina parasole avvolgibile 558
tendine 133
tenditore rapido 826
tendone oscurante 282
teniere 750
tennis 820
tennis da tavolo 815
tennis, campi da 788
tennis, scarpa da 344
tennista 822
tenone 900
tensione di produzione 662
tensione, aumento di 646, 662, 665
tensione, blocco di 452, 453, 457
tensione, chiavi di 448
tensione, corda di 433
tensione, diminuzione di 646, 662, 677
tensione, disco di 453
tensione, molla di 453, 457
tensione, primo aumento di 677
tensione, regolatore della 460
tensione, regolatore di 453, 456, 457
tensione, secondo aumento di 677
tensore della fascia lata 150
tentacolo 104, 106
tentacolo oculare 104
tenuta, anello di 268
tenuta, mastice di 265
tenuta, valvola di 265
teodolite 59, 701
tepee 418
terapie, stanza per le 779, 781
terbio 684
tergale 276
tergale, base del 276
tergicristallo 550, 557
tergicristallo, comando del 556
terminal dei passeggeri 619, 620
terminal satellite dei passeggeri 619
terminale 272, 274, 290, 385, 663
terminale della messa a terra 497
terminale di ingresso 316
terminale di messa a terra 274
terminale di pagamento elettronico 731
terminale di scarico 553
terminale per il pagamento elettronico 181
terminali di collegamento delle antenne 497
terminali di collegamento delle casse acustiche 497
terminali interattivi 395
terminalia coltello, fusibile a cartuccia con 272
terminatore 522
terminazione nervosa 172
termini comuni 82, 83
termite 101
termoconvettore 260
termometri clinici 777
termometro 655, 695, 841, 899
termometro a lamina bimetallica 695
termometro a lettura istantanea 231
termometro a massima 59
termometro a mercurio 777
termometro a minima 59
termometro clinico 695
termometro del forno 231
termometro digitale 777
termometro per carne 231
termometro per zucchero 231
termopausa 53
termosfera 53
termosonda 238
termostato 238, 260, 261, 267, 288, 291, 292, 293
termostato ambiente 261
termostato dell'acqua 259
termostato di sicurezza 293
termostato inferiore 266
termostato programmabile 261
termostato regolabile 239
termostato superiore 266
termoventilatore 260
terna 637
Terra 0, 4, 5, 6, 7, 28
terra 272
terra battuta 822
Terra del Fuoco 31
Terra della Regina Maud 29
Terra di Marie Byrd 29
Terra di Wilkes 29
terra, attrezzature di 622
terra, conduttore di 272
terra, filo di 272
terra, lingua di 51
Terra, orbita della 6, 7
terra, spinotto di messa a 274
Terra, struttura della 42
terra, terminale di messa a 274
terra-aria, missile 759
Terranova, Isola di 30
terrapieno 409, 538
terrazza 621
terrazza scoperta 609
terre rare 684
terremoto 43
terreno di scarico 647, 648
terreno, trivella a motore per 323
terrina 234
terza 434, 849
terza base 794
terza base (posizione) 794
terza falange 126, 172
terza linea 804
terza linea destra 804
terza linea sinistra 804
terzarolo 603
terzarolo, benda di 603
terzarolo, matafione di 603
Terziario 93
terzina 919
terzino 803, 807
terzino destro 801
terzino di destra 806
terzino di sinistra 806
terzino sinistro 801
terzo stadio 25
tesa 340, 341
tessera 917
tessitura 460
tessitura, schema della 463
tessitura, spazzolino di 456
tessuti di rinforzo 455
tessuto adiposo 171, 172
tessuto connettivo 172
tessuto elastico 350
tessuto gommato 421
tessuto per abiti 455
tessuto ricamato 459
tessuto sottocutaneo 172
tessuto, struttura del 455
tessuto, subbio del 460
testa 8, 140, 147, 149, 161, 169, 300, 301, 302, 308, 311, 384, 390, 425, 452, 457, 458, 516, 757, 793, 800, 816, 822, 826, 863, 867, 901, 909
testa a croce 302
testa bombata 302
testa cercante a raggi infrarossi 759
testa concava 302
testa d'albero 602, 836
testa d'angolo 587
testa del cilindro ricuperatore 756
testa del collettore 18
testa del femore 153
testa del martello 901
testa del martinetto elevatore 632
testa del rotore 631
testa dell'omero 153
testa della condotta di produzione 654
testa di attacco 642
testa di gatto 132
testa di iniezione del fango 651
testa di proiezione 535
testa di taglio 535
testa metallica 793
testa non svitabile 302
testa orientabile 312
testa panoramica 482
testa piatta 302
testa portalampada 485
testa quadra, punta a 302
testa ribaltabile 236
testa tonda 302
testa, regolatore dell'altezza della 485
testata 471, 663
testata di collegamento 641
testata, muro di 597
testatina 471
teste, tipi di 302
tester dell'alta tensione 316
tester di continuità 316
tester di presa 316
testicoli 107, 110
testicolo 169
testiera 280, 281
testimone 52, 790
testimone, zona del passaggio del 790
testimoni, banco dei 728
testina 383, 439, 500
testina di lettura/scrittura 521
testina di stampa 528
testina rotante 383
Teti 5
tetti 414
tetto 100, 245, 257, 412, 551, 567, 635, 639
tetto a bracci 415
tetto a capanna 414
tetto a carena 414
tetto a cono 415
tetto a due spioventi 251
tetto a falda unica 414
tetto a ghimberga 414
tetto a mansarda 414
tetto a ombrello 415
tetto a padiglione 414
tetto a padiglione da torre 415
tetto a piramide 415
tetto a schifo 414
tetto a shed 414
tetto a vetro 250
tetto con lucernario 414
tetto di vetro 713
tetto galleggiante 655
tetto piano 414
tetto, strato di 650
tettoia 902
tettoia vetrata 582
tettuccio 567, 760
tettuccio apribile 551
tettuccio di protezione 632
thermos 906
tibetano 468
tibia 96, 98, 115, 122, 126, 131, 138, 140, 141, 142, 152, 155, 156
tibia-tarso 116
tibiale anteriore 150
tibiofibula 111
tifone 63
tight end 807
tiglio 208
tigre 135
tilde 473
timbro di gomma 531
timbro, selettore del 451
timer 851
timo 202
timone 23, 600, 605, 606, 608, 676, 759, 834, 838, 839
timone di direzione 625, 760, 763, 898
timone di profondità 625, 763, 898
timone di traino 642
timone orizzontale 763
timone, barra del 834
timone, cavo del 838
timone, pala del 606
timone, pedale del 898
timoneria 606
timoniere, sedile del 838
timpani 437
timpano 110, 244, 403, 404, 411, 448
timpano, montante del 252
tin 819
tinello 250
tintura per capelli 379
tipi di ali 630
tipi di articolazioni sinoviali 156
tipi di bandiera 739
tipi di bocchette 258
tipi di eclissi 6, 7
tipi di infiorescenze 81
tipi di mazze 867
tipi di motori 564
tipi di movimenti 916
tipi di ossa 157
tipi di parquet 254
tipi di punte 302
tipi di remi 838
tipi di teste 302
tipi di vagoni passeggeri 584
tipi principali di lame 401
tipo di carburante 548
tipo di nube alta 55
tipo di nube bassa 55
tipo di nube media 55
tipografia 472
tipologie di pioggia 64
tirafilo, leva 452
tirannosauro 93
tirante 265, 443, 448, 453, 540, 590, 824, 825, 902
tirante a vite 448, 842
tirante comandato 590
tirante d'unione 590
tirante del braccio 634
tirante della cordiera 448
tirante, regolatore del 902
tiratore 809, 860
tirella 857
tiri, direttore dei 859
tiro a segno, campo di 788
tiro con carabina 861
tiro con fucile 860
tiro con l'arco 859
tiro con l'arco, campo di 788
tiro con pistola 861
tiro, accessori per il 752

INDICE DELLE VOCI ITALIANE

1108

ASTRONOMIA > 2-25; **TERRA** > 26-71; **REGNO VEGETALE** >72-89; **REGNO ANIMALE** > 90-143; **ESSERE UMANO** > 144-177; **GENERI ALIMENTARI E CUCINA** > 178-241; **CASA** > 242-295; **FAI DA TE E GIARDINAGGIO** > 296-333; **ABBIGLIAMENTO** > 334-371; **ACCESSORI E ARTICOLI PERSONALI** > 372-391; **ARTE E ARCHITETTURA** > 392-465; **COMUNICAZIONI E BUROTICA** > 466-535; **TRASPORTI E VEICOLI** > 536-643; **ENERGIA** > 644-677; **SCIENZA** > 678-705; **SOCIETÀ** > 706-785; **SPORT E GIOCHI** > 786-920

tiro, campo di 859, 860
tiro, direttore di 860
tiro, fossa di 860
tiro, linea di 859
tiro, pedana di 860
tiro, posizioni di 861, 893
tisane 208
Titan IV 24
Titania 5
titanio 683
Titano 5
Titicaca, Lago 31
titolare, firma del 729
titolare, nome del 729
titoli dei film 427
titoli, tasto di visualizzazione dei 496
titolo 471
titolo a caratteri cubitali 471
Tlaloc, tempio di 412
tocco 341
toga 336
Togo 745
toilette 395, 584, 715, 719, 723, 728, 731, 733, 735, 779, 781
toilette (donne) 725
toilette (uomini) 725
toilette degli uomini 724
toilette delle donne 724
toilette per i clienti 720
Tolosa, salame di 216
tom tom 448
tomaia 342, 371
tomatillo 188
tombolo 51, 458
toner, cartuccia del 519
Tonga 747
toni alti, regolatore dei 503
toni alti, regolazione dei 441
toni bassi, regolatore dei 503
toni bassi, regolazione dei 441
toni, regolazione dei 441
tonno 220
tonsilla 174
tonsilla linguale 176
tonsilla palatina 176
top 366
topazio 375
topinambur 184
topo campagnolo 123
toporagno 121
toppa 249
toque 341
torace 96, 97, 98, 146, 148
Torah, rotoli della 738
torchio di stampa a due cilindri 421
torchio litografico 423
torcia 652, 770
torio 684
tormalina 375
tornado 57, 63
tornelli di entrata 592
tornelli di uscita 592
tornietto da tavolo 464
tornio 464
tornitura 464
Toro 12
toro 404, 405, 705
toro centrale 405
torre 410, 614, 635, 674, 676, 677, 916
torre a traliccio 634
torre angolare 408
torre campanaria 411
torre di controllo 618, 761
torre di controllo, cabina della 618
torre di estrazione 649, 650
torre di fiancheggiamento 408
torre di guida 542
torre di lavaggio 294
torre di perforazione 651, 652, 654
torre di raffreddamento 646
torre per i tuffi 828
torre per uffici 713
torre trasmittente 486
torrente montano 45
Torres, Strettodi 29
torretta 408, 410, 411, 638, 758, 762, 763, 858
torretta spiovente 415
torretta, calotta della 692
torsolo 82
torta, teglia per 232
tortellini 206
tortiera 232
tortilla 205
tostapane 238
totale 699
touch pad 526
touch pad, pulsante del 526
touch screen 527
tovaglioli 722
trabattello 321
trabeazione 247, 403, 405
tracciamento, filo di 313
tracciatore 900
tracciatura 401
trachea 116, 125, 163
trackball 517
tracolla 388, 391, 527, 869
tracolla, borsa a 388
tracolla, bottone della 441
traforo 411
traghetto 596
trago 140, 173
traguardo 907
traino, barra di 622
traino, timone di 642
traino, trattore di 622, 623
tralcio 86
traliccio per alta tensione 663
traliccio, torre a 634
tram 595
trama 455, 460, 461
trama, filo della 463
tramezzo, mattone forato per 298
tramoggia 643
tramoggia di caricamento 573
tramoggia, carro a 588
trampoliere, uccello 117
trampolini 890
trampolini, zona dei 890
trampolino 246, 823, 890, 891
trampolino di 1 metro 828
trampolino di 3 metri 828
trampolino per i salti diritti 890
transatlantico 608
transazione, fessura di registrazione della 730
transazione, ricevuta della 731
transazioni commerciali 525
transetto 411
transito vietato agli autocarri 545, 546
transito vietato ai motocicli 545, 546
transito vietato ai pedoni 545, 546
transito vietato ai veicoli con altezza superiore a 545, 547
transito vietato alle biciclette 545, 546
transizione, metalli di 683
trapano a colonna 307
trapano a mano 307
trapano elettrico 306
trapano senza fili 306
trapezio 150, 151, 154, 156, 705, 840, 897
trapezio, abito a 356
trapezoide 154
trapiantatoio 325
trappola petrolifera 651, 653
trapunta 280
trascinamento, ingranaggio di 240
trasduttore 613
trasferimento di calore 681
trasformatore 287, 658, 663, 668, 674
trasformatore di accensione 259
trasformatore principale 585
trasmettitore a microonde 489
trasmissione 292, 563
trasmissione a catena 641, 643
trasmissione a cinghia 605
trasmissione a onde hertziane 486
trasmissione agli utenti 646, 662, 677
trasmissione dei dati 41
trasmissione del movimento rotatorio al rotore 662
trasmissione dell'elettricità 665
trasmissione dell'immagine 694
trasmissione di elettricità 663
trasmissione di elettricità ad alta tensione 646, 662, 677
trasmissione di energia alla tensione di produzione 662
trasmissione via cavo aereo 486
trasmissione via cavo sotterraneo 487
trasmissione via cavo sottomarino 487
trasmissione via satellite 486
trasmissione, albero di 605
trasmissione, cavo di 613
trasmissione, cinghia di 292
trasmissione, organi di 580
trasmissione, sistema di 553
traspirazione 67
trasportatore 453
trasporti 538
trasporto aereo 618
trasporto marittimo 596, 649
trasporto su rotaia 582
trasporto su strada 538, 596
trasporto tattico, elicottero da 631
trattamento chimico 656
trattino 473
tratto olfattivo 175
trattore 640
trattore cingolato 636
trattore di traino 622, 623
trattore gommato 637
trattore tosaerba 333
trattore: vista anteriore 640
trattore: vista posteriore 640
travata a cantilever 540
travata a portale 540
travata appoggiata 540
travata continua 540
travata sollevabile 542
travatura reticolare 21
trave 252, 412, 418, 826
trave di coda 631
trave di colmo 252
trave di equilibrio 824, 826
trave di sicurezza 900
trave in legno 403, 406
traveller's cheque 729
traversa 247, 277, 278, 409, 424, 433, 461, 591, 650, 663, 799, 827
traversa anteriore 460, 893
traversa del cancello 278
traversa della cassa battente 460
traversa inferiore 278
traversa inferiore di finestra 252
traversa laterale 460
traversa mediana 277
traversa orizzontale 632
traversa portadenti 642
traversa posteriore 893
traversa superiore 277, 278
traversa superiore di finestra 252
traversa terminale inferiore 635
traversa terminale superiore 635
traversina 440, 441
traverso superiore del telaio 249
traverso, al 833
travetto 254
travetto del soffitto 252
travetto del solaio 252, 253
travetto di testata 252, 253
trazione integrale 4x4, veicolo a 577
trazione, braccio di 640
tre braccia, supporto a 464
tre quarti, manica a 360
tre quarti, tempo di 434
treccia 458
trefolo 908
tremolo, braccio del 441
trench 352
treno ad alta velocità 585
treno della metropolitana 592
treno locale 583
treno passeggeri 582
treppiede 14, 436, 448, 482, 489
treppiede della giraffa 492
trequarti 352
trequarti ala destra 804
trequarti ala sinistra 804
trequarti centrodestro 804
trequarti centrosinistro 804
trespolo 401
triage, stanza del 779
trial, motocicletta da 875
triangolo 437, 449, 705, 863
Triangolo Australe 10
Triangolo Boreale 12
triangolo divisorio 367
Triassico 93
tribuna coperta 856
tribuna degli allenatori 891
tribuna dei giudici 890, 891
tribunale 728
tribunale, aula di 728
tribune 788, 874
tribune mobili 734
triceratopo 93
tricheco 137
triciclo 581
tricipite brachiale 151
tricipiti, barra per i 851
triclinio 406
tricorno 339
trifogliata 79
triglia 219
triglifo 404
trillo 435
trilobato 413
trilobite 92
trimarano 835
trinchettina 603
trinchetto, albero di 600, 602
trinchetto, vela di 603
trinciante 229
trinciapollo 233
trinciato 740
Trinidad e Tobago 743
trio 438
triplice 852
triplo salto 875
triplo salto mortale e mezzo in avanti raggruppato 829
trippa 212
trippa, salsiccia di 216
trireme 598
tris 914
tritacarne 230
tritarifiuti 270
triticale 203
Tritone 5
tritone 111
trivella a motore per terreno 323
trivella, punta della 323
trivellazione, impianto di 651
trocantere 96, 98
tromba 447, 611, 766
tromba delle scale 251
tromba marina 63
tromba militare 447
trombe 437
trombone 80, 447
tromboni 437
troncato 740
tronchesina per cuticole 377
tronchesina per unghie 377
tronco 76, 86, 87, 110, 147, 149, 300
tronco celiaco 161, 165
tronco di mezzana 602
tronco di testa della scala 766
tronco, armatura protettiva del 808
tronco, parte inferiore del 87
tronco, sezione di un 300
tronco, sezione trasversale di un 87
tropicale della foresta pluviale 61
tropicale umido e secco (savana) 61
Tropico del Cancro 34, 35, 36
Tropico del Capricorno 34, 35, 36
tropopausa 53, 68
troposfera 53
troppopieno 262, 264
troppopieno, tubo del 265, 266, 267
troppopieno, tubo di 485
trota 221
trottatore 857
trotto 124
trotto e ambio 857
trousse 388
truccatore 428
trucco 378
trucco per gli occhi 378
trucco per il viso 378
trucco per le labbra 378
trumeau 411
tuba 437, 447
tuba di Eustachio 174, 175
tuba di Falloppio 170
tuba di Falloppio, ampolla della 171
tuba di Falloppio, infundibolo della 171
tuba di Falloppio, istmo della 171
tubatura di scarico 263
tubazione del freno 559
tubazione di allacciamento 262
tubazione di andata 259
tubazione di immissione principale 655
tubazione di immissione secondaria 655
tubazione di produzione e di spedizione 652
tubazione di riempimento 655
tubazione di ritorno 259
tubazione di scarico 271
tubazione di superficie 652
tubazioni del vapore primario 669
tubazioni di scarico del vapore 669
tube di Falloppio 171
tubetto 223
tubi del carburante 899
tubi malpighiani 97
tubi, filiera per 314
tubi, rivestimento isolante per 299
tubino 356
tubo 275, 312, 777
tubo a flash 692
tubo annaffiatore 573
tubo anodico 266
tubo aspirante 658, 659
tubo capillare 695
tubo d'acquerello 397
tubo del bordo di attacco 897
tubo del drenaggio 253
tubo del refrigerante 260
tubo del troppopieno 265, 266, 267
tubo dell'acqua calda 266
tubo dell'acqua fredda 265, 266
tubo dell'aria 841
tubo della pompa 548
tubo della prima valvola 447
tubo della scala, erogatore del 766
tubo della seconda valvola 447
tubo della terza valvola 447
tubo di accordo 447
tubo di alimentazione 270
tubo di alimentazione dell'acqua 294
tubo di alimentazione dell'aria 765
tubo di aspirazione 766
tubo di caduta del seme 643
tubo di carico 265
tubo di circolazione 672
tubo di drenaggio 292, 294
tubo di entrata 485
tubo di estrazione dell'aria 274, 275
tubo di getto laterale 573
tubo di iniezione del fango 651
tubo di lancio 756, 757
tubo di Pitot 873
tubo di posizionamento 638
tubo di riempimento 265
tubo di scappamento 553, 570, 575, 576, 577, 640
tubo di scarico 262, 265, 271, 292, 552, 564, 631, 636, 639, 643
tubo di scarico, attacco del 256
tubo di sfiato 267, 271
tubo di sterzo 579
tubo di trasferimento del carburante 25
tubo di troppopieno 485
tubo di uscita 485
tubo di uscita dell'acqua calda 267
tubo flessibile 264, 270, 289, 319, 328, 649, 767, 776
tubo flessibile di gomma 271
tubo flessibile per l'acqua 648
tubo flessibile per l'aria 398
tubo flessibile per l'aria compressa 648
tubo flessibile, raccordo del 649
tubo fluorescente 275
tubo graduato 59
tubo idraulico flessibile 641, 642
tubo in pressione 667
tubo malpighiano 99
tubo metallico 894
tubo obliquo 579
tubo per irrigazione 328
tubo per l'orientamento delle lamelle 285
tubo perdente 263
tubo piantone 871
tubo portaoculare 693
tubo principale 14, 15
tubo rigido 289
tubo rigido di prolunga 289
tubo telescopico principale 692
tubo trasversale 897
tubo verticale 271, 578
tubolatura di carico trasversale 607
Tucano 10
tucano 119
Tudor 413
tuffi 828
tuffi, esempi di 829
tuffi, strutture per i 828
tuffi, torre per i 828
tuffi, vasca per 788
tuffo 812
tuffo di partenza 832
tuffo in avanti con avvitamento 829
tuffo rovesciato con avvitamento 829
tuffo sincronizzato 829
tuffo, altezza del 829
tulio 684
tulipano 80
tumbler 225
tundra 66
tundra polare, della 61
tungsteno 683
tungsteno, filamento di 274
tungsteno, lampada alogena al 274, 275
tunica 78, 748
tunica, abito a 356
Tunisia 745
tunnel di comunicazione 23
tuorlo 117
turapori, pistola 315
turbante 339, 341
turbina 646, 659, 665, 668
turbina ad asse verticale 676
turbina del compressore 627
turbina del motocompressore 564
turbina di alimentazione 564
turbina eolica ad asse orizzontale 677
turbina Francis 659
turbina Kaplan 659
turbina motrice 627
turbina Pelton 659
turbina, albero della 665
turbina, coperchio della 659
turbina, girante della 664
turbina, rotazione della 662
turbina, valvola di arresto della 668
turbine eoliche 676
turbine, edificio delle 668
turbo-alternatore, gruppo del 646
turboalternatore 674, 763
turbocompressore, albero del 627
turboreattore 625, 760
turboreattore a doppio flusso 627
turchese 375
Turchia 746
turco 469
turibolo 737
turione 185
turismo, bicicletta da 581
Turkmenistan 746
turno 789
tuta 358, 369, 882, 887, 888, 891, 892
tuta da competizione 874
tuta da sci 369
tuta ignifuga 872
tuta ignifuga e idrofuga 765
tuta monopezzo 884
tuta protettiva 875
tuta spaziale 20
tuta sportiva 370
tutina a sacco 368
tutore 322, 324
Tuvalu 747
TV/video, tasto 495
tweeter 502
twin-set 359

INDICE DELLE VOCI ITALIANE

INDICE DELLE VOCI ITALIANE

U

uadi 52
uccelli 115
uccelli, esempi di 118
uccello 115
uccello acquatico 117
Uccello del Paradiso 10
uccello granivoro 117
uccello insettivoro 117
uccello passeriforme 117
uccello predatore 117
uccello trampoliere 117
uccello, anatomia di un 116
uccello, morfologia di un 115
uccello, scheletro di un 116
Ucraina 744
ucraino 469
uffici 548, 582, 596
uffici amministrativi 718
uffici degli organizzatori 719
uffici, edificio per 710, 713
uffici, torre per 713
ufficiali di gara 801, 846
ufficiali, alloggio degli 762, 763
ufficiali, camera degli 764
ufficio 509, 720, 724, 726
ufficio amministrativo 764, 769
ufficio d'ammissione dei detenuti 726
ufficio dei cancellieri 728
ufficio dei giudici 728
ufficio del bibliotecario 732
ufficio del bidello 735
ufficio del caposala 779
ufficio del comandante 764, 768
ufficio del conservatore 394
ufficio del contabile 509
ufficio del direttore 394, 726, 731, 732
ufficio del direttore della produzione 509
ufficio del direttore generale 509
ufficio del medico di guardia 778
ufficio del preside 735
ufficio del vicecomandante 768
ufficio del vicedirettore 726
ufficio dell'agente di sicurezza 733
ufficio dell'amministratore delegato 509
ufficio dell'assistente sociale 779
ufficio dell'ufficiale addetto alla formazione dei vigili del fuoco 764
ufficio della direzione 718
ufficio della palestra 734
ufficio della segretaria 731
ufficio della segreteria scolastica 735
ufficio delle informazioni 886
ufficio di accettazione dei visitatori 726
ufficio di formazione professionale 730
ufficio per le denunce 768
ufficio postale 474, 475, 711, 715
ufficio, mobili per 510
Uganda 745
ugello 22, 24, 25, 259, 314, 315, 319, 320, 329, 398
ugello a sezione variabile 629
ugello del lavaparabrezza 550
ugello di scarico 627, 760
ugello di taglio 319
ugello orientabile 628
ugello vaporizzatore 241
ugola 174, 175
uguale a 703
uistiti 139
Ulisse 19
ulna 116, 121, 122, 126, 131, 136, 138, 141, 142, 152, 154, 156
ultimo quarto 7
umbone 105
Umbriel 5
umidificatore 261
umidità 261
umidità contenuta nelle nuvole 70
umidità, misurazione dell' 59
umor acqueo 177
uncinato 154
uncinetto 457
uncino 457, 611
ungherese 469
Ungheria 744
unghia 96, 98, 107, 113, 115, 130, 133, 140, 173, 401, 426, 610
unghia per apertura 905
unghia protratta 133
unghia retratta 133
unghia, corpo dell' 172
unghie dei piedi, forbici per 377
unghie, forbicine per 377
unghie, matita sbiancante per 377
unghie, tronchesina per 377
unicellulari 94
Unicorno 11
uniforme 770
uniformi 764
unione 703
Unione Europea, bandiera dell' 729
unipolare, interruttore 272
unisono 434
unità a disco 450
unità astronomica 5
unità astronomiche 4
unità di backup 523
unità di controllo delle telecamere 489
unità di controllo elettronico 559
unità di controllo video 490
unità di cura intensiva 780
unità di misura del tempo 702
unità di misura dell'energia 702
unità di misura dell'intensità luminosa 702
unità di misura della carica elettrica 702
unità di misura della corrente elettrica 702
unità di misura della differenza di potenziale elettrico 702
unità di misura della forza 702
unità di misura della frequenza 702
unità di misura della lunghezza 702
unità di misura della massa 702
unità di misura della potenza elettrica 702
unità di misura della pressione 702
unità di misura della quantità di sostanza 702
unità di misura della radioattività 702
unità di misura della resistenza elettrica 702
unità di misura della temperatura Celsius 702
unità di misura della temperatura termodinamica 702
unità di misura, sistema internazionale di 702
unità di servizio mobile a distanza 21
unità di tensione del filo 457
unità floppy disk 513
unità floppy disk esterna 521
unità hard disk 521
unità hard disk estraibile 521
unità hard disk principale 513
unità hard disk secondaria 513
unità individuale di propulsione e manovra 20
unità mobile 486, 489
unità motrice 585
unità radiologica mobile 778
unità video da tavolo 520
università 710
uno 703
ununbio 683
ununnilio 683
unununio 683
uomo 146
uomo, collo a 355, 362
uomo, scarpe da 342
uova 109, 111, 213
uova alla coque, clessidra per 231
uova in camicia, tegame per 235
uova, confezione in cartone per 222
uova, scomparto per le 291
uovo 100, 117
uovo di anatra 213
uovo di fagiano 213
uovo di gallina 213
uovo di oca 213
uovo di quaglia 213
uovo di struzzo 213
uragano 57, 63
uranio 684
uranio arricchito 671
uranio naturale 670
Urano 4, 5
urdu 469
uretere 104, 116, 165
uretra 165, 169, 170
urinario, apparato 165
URL 524
URL (localizzatore universale di risorse) 524
uropodio 107
urostilo 111
Uruguay 742
usare il candeggiante secondo le istruzioni 347
uscita d'emergenza, sistema di 25
uscita del fluido vettore 672
uscita del flusso di scarico 627
uscita del riflusso del condensatore 669
uscita del vapore 670, 671
uscita dell'acqua calda 259
uscita dell'acqua di raffreddamento del condensatore 669
uscita dell'aria calda 256
uscita S-Video 526
uscita, bordo di 624
usignolo 118
utensili 464
utensili da cucina 229
utensili per avvitare 302
utensili per cucinare 234
utensili per segare 303
utensili, esempi di 401
utensili, set di 233
utente 487
utente di Internet 524
utente privato 525
utente, ingresso dell'alimentazione dell' 273
utero 170, 171
utero, collo dell' 170
utero, legamento largo dell' 171
uva 192
uva, grappolo d' 86
uvaspina 192
Uzbekistan 746

V

V, scollatura a 363
V, scollatura profonda a 363
vacuolo 74, 94
vacuolo digerente 94
vacuolo digerente in formazione 94
vacuolo pulsante 94
vagina 103, 104, 170, 171
vaglia postale 475
vagone di coda del personale viaggiante 588
vagone letto 584
vagone ristorante 584
vagone viaggiatori 584, 585
vagoni passeggeri, tipi di 584
vagoni, officina di manutenzione dei 589
vaio 741
valerianella 187
valigetta per il computer portatile 527
valigia 389
valigie 717
valle 45, 48
valore del segmento 918
valore, indicazione del 729
valori di durata delle note 435
valori di durata delle pause 435
valuta, nome della 729
valute, esempi di simboli di 728
valva 84, 105
valvola 447, 465, 579, 675
valvola a saracinesca principale 654
valvola aortica 162
valvola del bruciatore 899
valvola del galleggiante 265
valvola del paracadute 899
valvola dell'acetilene 319
valvola dell'aria 320, 398
valvola dell'impianto di allagamento 669
valvola dell'ossigeno 319
valvola della pompa 841
valvola di arresto della turbina 668
valvola di aspirazione 564, 566
valvola di chiusura 265
valvola di distribuzione 649
valvola di drenaggio 291
valvola di espirazione 773
valvola di inspirazione 773
valvola di produzione 654
valvola di regolazione 259, 654
valvola di regolazione della pressione 777
valvola di ritegno 319
valvola di ritenuta 263
valvola di scarico 267, 564, 566
valvola di sfiato 607, 655
valvola di sfogo dell'aria 259
valvola di sicurezza 234, 259, 266, 267, 665
valvola di spurgo 655, 841
valvola di tenuta 265
valvola di tenuta, sede della 265
valvola mitrale 162
valvola polmonare 162
valvola tricuspide 162
valvola, corpo della 447
valvola, molla della 566
valvola, piastra della 268
valvola, sede della 268
valvole di controllo del flusso di carburante 626
vampiro dalla lancia 141
vanadio 683
Vanessa atalanta 102
vanga 326
vaniglia, estratto di 200
vano 416
vano accessori 483
vano cassetta 495
vano del disco 501
vano del motore 639
vano del motore di traino 638
vano del motore diesel 636, 637, 638, 639
vano del serbatoio dell'acqua 628
vano della cassetta 499
vano della videocassetta 496
vano motore 568, 632
vano portabagagli 584
vano portamateriale 766
vano portaoggetti 556, 570
vano portaspazzolini 384
vano portattrezzi 567
vano raccoglipolvere 288
Vanuatu 747
vapore 646, 665, 668, 681
vapore a bassa pressione, ingresso del 668
vapore ad alta pressione, ingresso del 668
vapore primario, collettore del 669
vapore primario, tubazioni del 669
vapore, ferro da stiro a 288
vapore, generatore di 646, 670, 671, 674, 763
vapore, pentola a 235
vapore, regolatore del getto di 288
vapore, regolazione del 241
vapore, tubazioni di scarico del 669
vapore, uscita del 670, 671
vaporizzatore 261, 288
vaporizzatore, serpentina del 261
vaporizzazione, griglia di 261
varano 114
variante 872
variazione di pressione 55
variazione, tasti di 456
varie 473
variometro 899
variometro elettrico 898
variometro meccanico 898
Varolio, ponte di 167
vasca 263, 292, 294, 831
vasca da bagno 251, 262, 264, 724
vasca degli elementi di combustibile difettosi 666
vasca del fango 651
vasca di abbattimento della pressione 671
vasca di deposito del combustibile esaurito 666, 667, 669
vasca di lavaggio stampe 485
vasca di raccolta 666
vasca di scarico del combustibile esaurito 666, 668
vasca per immersione 246
vasca per tuffi 788
vasca, orlo della 292
vasca, piattaforma della 264
vasca/doccia, miscelatore 262
vaschetta 320, 484, 485, 919
vaschetta con beccuccio 237
vaschetta di distribuzione 263
vaschetta di raccolta 241
vaschetta filtrante 237, 240
vaschetta per alimenti 222
vaschetta per burro 223
vaschetta per cubetti di ghiaccio 291
vaschetta per il detersivo 294
vaschetta portacorrispondenza 531
vaschette portaccessori 399
vaschette, tavolozza con 398
vasellame da tavola 226
vasellame, cristalleria e argenteria 717
vasetto 223, 398
vasetto, tavolozza con 398
vasi sanguigni 140
vaso 265, 322
vaso capillare 172
vaso di espansione 259
vaso sanguigno 154, 162, 172
vaso sanguigno dorsale 97
vaso sospeso 322
vassoi 722
vassoio 281, 389
vassoio dei documenti ricevuti 508
vassoio dei documenti trasmessi 508
vassoio delle vincite 920
vassoio di alimentazione 519
vassoio di uscita 519
vassoio di uscita della carta 512
vassoio portadischi 494, 521
vasto laterale 150, 151
vasto mediale 150
Vaticano, Città del 744
Vauban, fortificazione alla 409
VCR, comandi del 495
Vecchio Testamento 736
vedretta 46
vegetazione 66
vegetazione, distribuzione della 66
veicoli 538
veicoli, ingresso dei 769
veicolo a trazione integrale 4x4 577
veicolo d'emergenza per l'equipaggio 21
Vela 11
vela 833, 836, 896, 897
vela a tarchia 601
vela al terzo 601
vela aurica 601
vela di maestra 603
vela di mezzana 603
vela di straglio di belvedere 603
vela di straglio di controvelaccio 603
vela di straglio di gabbia 603
vela di straglio di mezzana 603
vela di straglio di velaccio 603
vela di trinchetto 603
vela latina 601
vela Marconi 601
vela quadra 601
velaccino fisso 603
velaccino volante 603
velaccino, albero di 602
velaccio fisso 603
velaccio volante 603
velaccio, vela di straglio di 603
velario 407
velatura 602, 897
velcro® 368
vele 603
vele, esempi di 601
veliero a quattro alberi 602
velluto 254
velluto, collarino di 374
velo 909
velocità di crociera, controllo della 556
velocità, regolatore della 452
velocità, regolatore di 236, 417
velocità, selettore di 236, 237, 305, 306, 500
velodromo 788
vena ascellare 160
vena basilica 160
vena cava inferiore 160, 161, 162, 165
vena cava superiore 160, 161, 162
vena cefalica 160
vena epatica 161
vena femorale 160
vena giugulare esterna 160
vena giugulare interna 160
vena iliaca comune 165
vena iliaca interna 161
vena mesenterica superiore 160
vena polmonare 160
vena polmonare destra 162
vena polmonare sinistra 162
vena porta 161
vena renale 160, 165
vena succlavia 160
venatura 300
vendita dei biglietti 592
vene 160
Venera 19
Venere 4, 5
Venere, monte di 170
veneziana 285
Venezuela 742
ventaglia 749
ventaglio, pennello a 397
venti 917
venti, rosa dei 37
ventilabro 445
ventilabro, molla del 445
ventilatore 258, 259, 260, 293, 445, 561, 566, 643
ventilatore da soffitto 261
ventilatore del condensatore 261
ventilatore del motore diesel 586
ventilatore del vaporizzatore 261
ventilatore di sostentamento 605
ventilatore principale 648
ventilatore, alloggiamento del 382
ventilatore, comando del 261
ventilatore, condotto del 643
ventilatore, motore del 258, 261
ventilazione 675
ventilazione, cappa di 614
ventilazione, colonna principale di 262
ventilazione, elica di 688
ventilazione, griglia di 289
ventilazione, rete di 262
ventiquattrore 386
vento 56, 69, 70, 833
vento contrario, partenza con 833
vento predominante 63
vento, azione del 67
vento, direzione del 55
vento, direzione e forza del 55
vento, forza del 55
vento, freccia del 56
vento, giacca a 353
vento, misurazione della direzione del 59
vento, misurazione della forza del 59
ventola 497
ventola dell'alimentatore 513
ventola dello châssis 513
ventola di raffreddamento 526, 552, 563
ventola di raffreddamento dei radiatori 586
ventola, cinghia della 552
ventosa 106
ventre 124
ventricolo destro 161, 162
ventricolo sinistro 161, 162
ventriglio 116
venturi 757
venturi, leva di fissaggio del 757
verbena 208
verde 400, 690, 741
verdone 183
verdura 180, 233
verdura, cassetto per la 291
Vergine 11, 13
vermicelli di riso 207
vernice, spruzzo di 398
verniciatura a spruzzo, pistola per 320
verniciatura: manutenzione 320
verricello 573
verricello di ormeggio 607
verricello, comandi del 573
versante 45
versoio 641
vertebra 112, 136
vertebra lombare 168
vertebra sacrale 111
vertebre 111
vertebre cervicali 116, 122, 126, 131, 138, 141, 142, 153, 157
vertebre coccigee 122, 126, 131, 138, 141, 142
vertebre dorsali 153, 157
vertebre lombari 122, 126, 131, 138, 141, 142, 153, 157

vertebre sacrali 122, 126, 131, 142
vertebre toraciche 122, 126, 131, 138, 142
verticale sulle braccia 828
vertice 115
vescica 113, 169, 170
vescica natatoria 109
vescica urinaria 109, 110, 165
vescichetta seminale 169
vescovo, manica da 361
vespa 101
vessillo 115
vestaglia 364
vestaglia, abito a 356
vestibolo 174, 406
vestiti per bambini 369
vestiti per neonati 368
veterinari 852
vetrata 737
vetrina 279
vetrinette refrigerate apribili 180
vetrino 693
vetro 249, 672, 673
vetro colorato 411
vetro di controllo 727
vetro di protezione 878
vetro doppio 675
vetro, cupola di 612
vetro, lastra di 291
vetro, smistamento del 71
vetro, tenda a 283
vetro, tetto a 250
vetrone 65
vetta 886
vettura a tre porte 549
vettura da golf 869
VHF, antenna 762
via 39, 711, 915
via commerciale 710
via di carreggio 647
via di fuga 872
Via Lattea 9, 13
Via Lattea (vista dall'alto) 9
Via Lattea (vista laterale) 9
viadotto 541
viaggi, agenzia di 714
viaggiatori, marciapiede dei 582
viaggiatori, stazione dei 582, 583, 596
viaggiatori, vagone 584, 585
viaggio, borsa da 388
viaggio, borsone da 388
vialetto 322
vialetto del giardino 244
vialetto di accesso 245
vibrissa 122
vibrisse 132
vibrovaglio per la depurazione del fango 651
vicecapitano 877
vicecomandante, ufficio del 768
vicedirettore, ufficio del 726
vicolo 711
video 918
video di controllo 694
video, effetti speciali digitali 491
video, selettore di controllo 491
video, unità di controllo 490
videocamera digitale 517
videocamera portatile: dorso 496
videocamera portatile: vista frontale 496
videocassetta 495
videocassetta, comandi della 496
videocassetta, vano della 496
videocassette compatte, adattatore per 496
videogioco 918
videoregistratore 495
videoteca 733
videoterminale 507
vietato fare campeggio 725

vietato fare pic-nic 725
Vietnam 747
vietnamita 468
vigile del fuoco 765
vigile del fuoco, elmo da 765
vigili del fuoco, carro dei 764
vigili del fuoco, caserma dei 711, 764
vigili del fuoco, dormitorio dei 764
vignetta 471
villaggio 886
villetta bifamiliare 419
vinacciolo 83
vincita, comando elettrico di erogazione della 920
vincita, levetta di erogazione della 920
vincite, vassoio delle 920
vincitore 789
vincoli di parentela 784
vincolo del caricatore 754
vini, cantina dei 720
vini, lista dei 721
vino 180
vino alsaziano, bicchiere da 225
vino bianco, bicchiere da 225
vino, aceto di 201
viola 80, 400, 439
viole 437
violino 439
violino, chiave di 434
violoncelli 437
violoncello 439
vipera 114
virata a capriola 832
virata a dorso, contrassegno per la 831
virata a farfalla 832
virata a rana 832
virata, comando di 898
virata, giudici di 831
virata, indicatore di 898
virata, parete di 831, 832
virgola 473
virgolette doppie 473
virgolette semplici 473
visiera 340, 341, 575, 591, 749, 765, 772, 874, 878, 884
visiera antisolare 20
visiera parasole 567
visitatori, ingresso dei 726
visitatori, ufficio di accettazione dei 726
visite ginecologiche, stanza per 779
visite mediche, stanza per le 779, 781
viso, trucco per il 378
visone 134
visore 484, 535, 773
vista 691
vista anteriore 146, 148, 150
vista frontale 798
vista laterale 798
vista laterale del cranio 158
vista normale 691
vista posteriore 147, 149, 151
vista, difetti della 691
Vistola, Fiume 32
visualizzatore digitale 316
vita 147, 149
vita bassa, abito a 356
vita, evoluzione della 92
vite 86, 248, 302, 439
vite centrale 425
vite da ghiaccio 901
vite del morsetto dell'ago 453
vite del supporto inferiore 58
vite di banco da scultore 401
vite di bloccaggio 909, 910
vite di blocco della lama 304
vite di fissaggio 859, 913
vite di fissaggio della macchina fotografica 482

vite di livello 58, 699, 701
vite di pressione 421, 423
vite di regolazione 309, 310, 317, 319
vite di regolazione a basso carico 273
vite di regolazione a pieno carico 273
vite di regolazione del fluido 320
vite di regolazione della tensione 534
vite di regolazione dello spruzzo 320
vite di serraggio 312
vite ferma ago 398
vite macrometrica 693
vite micrometrica 612, 693, 700
vite rompigetto 329
vite senza fine 462, 573
vite, albero della 86
vite, attacco a 275
vite, orecchini a 374
vitello 128
vitello, tagli di 214
viti di bloccaggio 700
viticcio 86
Vittoria, Lago 34
vogatore 851
volano 464, 566, 851
volano a penne naturali 817
volano sintetico 817
volano, gioco del 816
volant 280, 282
volante 333, 425, 552, 556, 607, 640, 873
volante di direzione 766
volante, piantone del 552
volantino 452, 626
volantino di puntamento in direzione 756
volantino di puntamento in elevazione 756
volata 753
volatili 213
volée 820
Volga, Fiume 32
voli 828
volo 829, 891
volo, ponte di 761
volo, rifornimento in 760
volpe 134
volpe del deserto 134
volpe volante nera 141
Volpetta 13
volt 702
volta 410
volta a botte 407
volta esterna della cupola 17
volta interna della cupola 17
volteggi, cavallo per 824, 825, 826
volume di ricezione, regolatore del 506
volume, controllo del 450, 451
volume, manopola del 503, 504, 505
volume, regolatore del 506, 507, 508
volume, regolatore di 497
volume, regolazione del 441
volume, rotella del 513
volume, tasti di regolazione del 495
voluta 276, 404, 405
voluta, piede a 276
volva 76
vomere 641, 756
vongola 217
vongola molle 217
Voyager 19
vulcani, esempi di 44
vulcano 42, 44
vulcano effusivo 44
vulcano esplosivo 44
vulcano in eruzione 44
vulva 148, 171
vumetri 488, 491
vuoto, camera a 694
vuoto, collettore a 694
vuoto, console per il 694

W

wakame 183
walkie-talkie 505
walkman 504
wallaby 143
wapiti 128
wasabi 201
Wassily, poltrona 276
water 251, 262, 264, 265, 724, 780
watt 702
webcam 517
Weddell, Mare di 29
wigwam 418
Wilkes, Terra di 29
winch 835
windsurf 836
wok 234
wok, servizio da 234
wolof 468
woofer 502

X

xeno 684
xilofono 437, 449
xilografia di filo 421
xilografia di testa 421

Y

yacht a motore 607
yak 129
yards, linea delle 806
Yemen 746
yen 728
yiddish 469
yogurt 210
yoruba 468
Yucatan, Penisola dello 30

Z

zafferano 198
zaffiro 375
zaino 580, 901, 906
Zambia 746
zampa 113, 425
zampa anteriore 96, 98, 111, 121
zampa anteriore (superficie esterna) 98
zampa anteriore di un cane 130
zampa di elefante, pantaloni a 358
zampa mediana 96, 98
zampa mediana (superficie esterna) 98
zampa posteriore 96, 98, 111, 121
zampa posteriore (superficie interna) 98
zampe, esempi di 117
zanzara 101
zappa 327
zappa a quattro denti 327
zappa rotante 641
zappetta tridente 326
zattera di salvataggio 605, 611
zavorra 634
zebra 128
zecca 102
zenit 10
zenzero 199
zero 914, 919
zia materna acquisita 785
zia paterna acquisita 785
zigrinatura 417
Zimbabwe 746
zinco 683
zio materno 785

zio paterno 785
zirconio 683
zither 432
zoccoli, esempi di 127
zoccolo 124, 127, 247, 255, 275, 344, 417, 440
zoccolo bidattilo 127
zoccolo monodattilo 127
zoccolo tetradattilo 127
zoccolo tridattilo 127
zoccolo, superficie plantare dello 127
zolfo 683
zona di ricevimento delle merci 180
zona abitabile 902
zona centrale 809, 818
zona commerciale 709
zona convettiva 6
zona cottura 722
zona d'attacco 818
zona dei trampolini 890
zona del passaggio del testimone 790
zona dell'allenatore 794
zona di appontaggio a poppa 761
zona di arrivo 891
zona di attacco 812
zona di atterraggio 891
zona di battuta 797
zona di canestro 809
zona di caduta 792, 793
zona di decelerazione 885
zona di difesa 812, 818
zona di frenata 891
zona di inizio partita 862
zona di lancio 865
zona di partenza 838
zona di passività 843
zona di pericolo 844, 847
zona di preparazione dei prodotti 180
zona di prova dei motori a getto 761
zona di rallentamento 890, 891
zona di ricevimento dei latticini 180
zona di servizio 818, 821
zona di sicurezza 846
zona di sottocanestro 809
zona focale 674
zona industriale 709
zona libera 812, 813
zona negativa 672
zona neutra 806, 879
zona pellucida 170
zona positiva 672
zona pranzo 224
zona protetta 877
zona radiativa 6
zone di servizio 817
zoom 492, 496
zoom, comando elettrico dello 496
zuava, pantaloni alla 358
zucca 189
zucca a collo allungato 189
zucca bianca 188
zucca di Napoli 188
zucca pasticcina 189
zucca spaghetti 189
zucca torta 189
zuccheriera 226
zucchero 209
zucchero a velo 209
zucchero candito 209
zucchero di canna 209
zucchero in grani 209
zucchetta 189
zucchina 188
zulu 468
zuppiera 226